Dictionary

German – English
English – German

Edited by the
Langenscheidt Editorial Staff

Langenscheidt

New York · Berlin · Munich · Vienna · Zurich

*Revised by
Heinz Messinger,
Gisela Türck
and Helmut Willmann*

―――――――――――

*This dictionary is also available in a larger type size
in the Langenscheidt Standard Dictionary Series.*

―――――――――――

Preface

All Langenscheidt dictionaries are regularly revised. The present Compact German Dictionary has been specifically prepared for the English-speaking user; it provides the pronunciation and stress of the German entry, states the genitive and plural of nouns and, in the case of verbs, indicates whether they are conjugated with "haben" or "sein". All irregular forms are also given.

The introduction of new typefaces has made the dictionary even clearer and thus more user-friendly. The headwords now appear in sans serif letters, which makes them easier to find. Phrases – example sentences, idioms, collocations – are emphasized by a new boldface type, which, as it is an italic face, cannot be confused with the boldface of the headwords.

Another feature that adds to the clarity of presentation is the restructuring of the individual entries making more use of Roman and Arabic numerals to separate the main meanings from subsidiary meanings, and more economical use of the tilde to represent the headword.

As part of the updating process, every entry of the previous edition has been carefully examined and any obsolescent vocabulary "rooted out", thus guaranteeing that the present revised edition truly reflects the language of today.

One of the Compact German Dictionary's strengths has always been its large number of new words. Great care has therefore again been taken to ensure that alongside general vocabulary and modern technical terms, a particularly large number of new colloquialisms and young people's jargon should be taken up.

The editors responsible for the present German-English/English-German Compact Dictionary, Helmut Willmann, Heinz Messinger and Gisela Türck, also compiled "Langenscheidts Kleiner Muret-Sanders" (1982, 1985). Thus we have been able to draw on their long experience as lexicographers.

The result is a dictionary ultimately suitable for today's user.

Langenscheidt Publishers

Herausgegeben von der Langenscheidt-Redaktion

Table of Contents

First Part

Second Part

First Part

German – English

Guide for the User

1. Alphabetical order has been maintained throughout the dictionary. Note that the umlaut forms ä, ö and ü are treated as a, o and u. Thus "Müll" will be found directly after "Mull" and before "Müsli". ß is treated as ss.

2. The **tilde** or **swung dash** (~, ~) is used for economy of space. The boldface tilde (~) stands for the entire headword or, in the case of compounds, for the part of the word preceding the vertical bar (|). In the example phrases and the explanations in *italics*, the tilde (~, ~) stands for the boldfaced word immediately preceding, which itself may have been formed with the aid of the boldfaced tilde.

When the initial letter of a headword changes from a capital to a small letter, or vice versa, this is indicated by a circle placed above the tilde: ♀ or ♀, e.g.

Abflug *m* ... takeoff, ... **♀bereit** *adj* ready for takeoff. **~halle** *f* ...

3. Arrangement of the entries. Entries are generally divided up by means of

a) Roman numerals to distinguish parts of speech (noun, adjective, adverb; transitive, intransitive or reflexive verb, etc).

b) Arabic numerals (running consecutively within the article and independent of Roman numerals) to differentiate between meanings,

c) small letters for further differentiation of meaning.

Examples:

a) **gehen** ['geːən] (ging, gegangen, sn) **I** *v/i* **1.** (**zu Fuß ~**) walk, ... **II** *v/impers* **17.** *fig.* **es geht** a) it works, ... **III** *v/t* **20.** walk (*distance etc*), ...

b) **böse** ['bøːzə] **I** *adj* **1.** bad, evil, ... **II** *adv* **6.** badly ...

c) **machen** ... **13.** do: *laß ihn nur ~!* a) let him (do as he pleases)!, b) just leave it to him!

4. Semantic differences are indicated by symbols and abbreviations preceding the translation (see list on page 8).

5. Untranslatable German words are defined in *italics*:

Assessor ... *civil servant* (*lawyer, teacher, etc*) *who has completed his/her second state examination.*

6. Spelling. Differences in British and American spelling are indicated as follows:

colo(u)r
defen/ce (*Am.* -se)
program(me *Br.*)
sulphonamide (*Am.* -f-)

The abbreviations *esp. Am.* and *esp. Br.* indicate that the spelling or translation referred to also occurs in British and American English respectively, though far less frequently.

7. Pronunciation. As a general rule either full or partial pronunciation is given for every simple entry word. The symbols used are those laid down by the International Phonetic Association. All the phonetic symbols used in the dictionary are explained in the Key to Pronunciation on page 10ff.

Every headword that does not consist of words listed and phonetically transcribed elsewhere in the dictionary is followed by its pronunciation in square brackets: **Blüte** ['bly:tə] ...

Compound and derivative entries formed with elements listed and phonetically transcribed elsewhere in the dictionary are provided with a stress mark ['] in front of the stressed syllable: **'Blütenhonig** ...

Derivatives after a simple entry are often only provided with accents and part of the pronunciation. That part of the word which is not transcribed phonetically has, except for differences in stress, a pronunciation identical with that of the corresponding part of the preceding entry:

Kondensat [kɔndɛn'za:t] *n* ... **Kondensation** [-za'tsĭo:n] *f* ... **Kondensator** [-'za:tɔr] *m* ... **kondensieren** [-'zi:rən] ...

A number of the more common initial and final elements occurring in derivatives and compounds have not been transcribed phonetically after every derivative entry. They have been collected, together with their phonetic transcription, in a comprehensive list on page 12.

8. Symbols

~ ⍩ }	see Guide for the User, paragraph 2, on page 7 and paragraph 1.4 on page 722	🚂	railway
		✈	aviation
		✉	postal affairs
F	familiar, colloquial language	♪	musical term
V	vulgar	△	architecture
†	obsolete	⚡	electrical engineering, electronics
⊞	technical term		
♣	botany	⚖	legal term
⊙	technology	A̶	mathematics
⚒	mining	✍	agriculture
✕	military term	🐒	chemistry
⚓	nautical term	✻	medicine
✝	economic term	→	see

9. Abbreviations

a.	also	antiq.	antiquity, Antike
abbr.	abbreviation	art	article
acc	accusative (case)	astr.	astronomy
adj	adjective	attr	attributively
adm.	administrative	bibl.	biblical
adv	adverb	biol.	biology
allg.	allgemein, generally	Br.	in British usage only
Am.	(originally or chiefly) American English	b.s.	bad sense
		coll	collective noun
amer.	American, amerikanisch	comp	comparative
anat.	anatomy		

conj	conjunction	j-n, *j-n*	jemanden, *somebody*
contp.	contemptuously	j-s, *j-s*	jemandes, *of somebody*
cpds.	compound words	k-e, *k-e*	keine
dat	dative (case)	k-m, *k-m*	keinem
dem	demonstrative	k-n, *k-n*	keinen
dial.	dialectal	k-r, *k-r*	keiner
d-m, *d-m*	deinem, to your	k-s, *k-s*	keines
d-n, *d-n*	deinen, your	*ling.*	linguistics
d-r, *d-r*	deiner, of your, to your	*lit.*	literary
d-s, *d-s*	deines, of your	*m*	masculine
eccl.	ecclesiastical	m-e, *m-e*	meine, my
e-e, *e-e*	eine, a, an	*metall.*	metallurgy
e-m, *e-m*	einem, to a(n)	*meteor.*	meteorology
e-n, *e-n*	einen, a, an	*min.*	mineralogy
engS.	in engerem Sinne, *more strictly taken*	m-m, *m-m*	meinem, to my
		m-n, *m-n*	meinen, my
e-r, *e-r*	einer, of a(n), to a(n)	*mot.*	motoring
e-s, *e-s*	eines, of a(n)	*mount.*	mountaineering
esp.	especially	m-r, *m-r*	meiner, of my, to my
et., *et.*	etwas, something	m-s, *m-s*	meines, of my
etc	et cetera, and others, and so forth	*mst*	mostly
euphem.	euphemistic	*myth.*	mythology
f	feminine	*n*	neuter
fenc.	fencing	*neg*	negative
fig.	figurative	*nom*	nominative (case)
fr.	French	*npr*	proper name
gastr.	gastronomical	*n.s.*	in the narrower sense
GB	Great Britain	*nucl.*	nuclear physics
gen	genitive (case)	*obs.*	obsolete
geogr.	geography	*od.*	oder, or
geol.	geology	*opt.*	optics
ger	gerund	*orn.*	ornithology
Ggs.	Gegensatz, antonym	*o.s.*	oneself
gym.	gymnastics	*paint.*	painting
hist.	history	*parl.*	parliamentary term
humor.	humorously	*part*	particle
hunt.	hunting	*ped.*	pedagogics
ichth.	ichthyology	*pers*	personal
imp	imperative (mood)	*pharm.*	pharmacy
impers	impersonal	*philos.*	philosophy
ind	indicative (mood)	*phot.*	photography
indef	indefinite	*phys.*	physics
inf	infinitive (mood)	*physiol.*	physiology
insep	inseparable	*pl*	plural
int	interjection	*poet.*	poetry
interrog	interrogative	*pol.*	politics
invar	invariable	*pos*	possessive
ir.	Irish	*pp*	past participle
iro.	ironically	*pred*	predicative
irr.	irregular	*prep*	preposition
Jh.	Jahrhundert, century	*pres*	present
j-d	jemand, someone	*pres p*	present participle
j-m, *j-m*	jemandem, to somebody	*pret*	preterite
		print.	printing

10

pron	pronoun	*surv.*	surveying
psych.	psychology	*tel.*	telegraphy
reflex	reflexive	*teleph.*	telephone
rel	relative	*textil.*	textiles
rhet.	rhetoric	*thea.*	theatre
s	substantive	*(TM)*	Trademark
s-e, s-e	seine, *his, one's*	*TV*	television
schott.	schottisch, *Scottish*	*univ.*	university
sep	separable	*USA*	United States
sg	singular	*usu.*	usually
sl.	slang	*v/aux*	auxiliary verb
s-m, s-m	seinem, *to his, to one's*	*vet.*	veterinary medicine
s-n, s-n	seinen, *his, one's*	*v/i*	intransitive verb
s.o., s.o.	someone	*v/impers*	impersonal verb
sociol.	sociology	*v/t*	transitive verb
s-r, s-r	seiner, *of his*	*w.s./weitS.*	more widely taken
s-s, s-s	seines, *of his, of one's*	*z. B.*	zum Beispiel, *for instance*
s.th., s.th.	something	*zo.*	zoology
su	substantive	*zs.-, Zs.-*	zusammen, *together*
subj	subjunctive *(mood)*	*Zssg(n)*	Zusammensetzung(en),
sup	superlative		compound word(s)

10. Key to Pronunciation. The phonetic alphabet used in this German-English dictionary is that of the Association Phonétique Internationale (A.P.I. or I.P.A. = International Phonetic Association). A long vowel is indicated by [:] following the vowel symbol, the stress by ['] preceding the stressed syllable. [̃] placed over a vowel indicates that the vowel in question is nonsyllabic. A glottal stop ['] is the forced stop between one word or syllable and the following one beginning with a stressed vowel, as in "beobachten" [bə'ʔoːbaxtən].

Sym-bol	Examples	Nearest English Equivalents	Remarks
		A. Vowels	
a	Mann [man]		short a as in French "carte" or in British English "cast" said quickly
aː	Wagen ['vaːgən]	father	long a
e	egal [e'gaːl]	bed	
eː	Weg [veːk]		unlike any English sound, though it has a resemblance to the sound in "day"
ə	Bitte ['bɪtə]	ago	a short sound, that of unaccented e
ɛ	Männer ['mɛnər]	fair	There is no *-er* sound at the end. It
	Geld [gɛlt]		is one pure short vowel-sound.
ɛː	prägen ['prɛːgən]		same sound, but long
ɪ	Wind [vɪnt]	it	
iː	hier [hiːr]	meet	
ɔ	Ort [ɔrt]	long	
o	Modell [mo'dɛl]	molest	
oː	Boot [boːt]		[oː] resembles the English sound in go [gəʊ] but without the [ʊ]

Symbol	Examples	Nearest English Equivalents	Remarks
øː	schön [ʃøːn]		as in French "**feu**". The sound may be acquired by saying [e] through closely rounded lips.
ø	Ödem [øˈdeːm]		same sound, but short
œ	öffnen [ˈœfnən]		as in French "**neuf**". The sound has a resemblance to the English vowel in "h**er**". Lips, however, must be well rounded as for ɔ.
ʊ	Mutter [ˈmʊtər]	b**oo**k	
uː	Uhr [uːr]	b**oo**t	
ʏ	Glück [glʏk]		almost like the French u as in s**ur**. It may be acquired by saying [i] through fairly closely rounded lips.
yː	führen [ˈfyːrən]		same sound, but long

B. Diphthongs

aɪ	Mai [maɪ]	l**i**ke	
aʊ	Maus [maʊs]	m**ou**se	
ɔʏ	Beute [ˈbɔʏtə]	b**oy**	
	Läufer [ˈlɔʏfər]		

C. Consonants

b	besser [ˈbɛsər]	**b**etter	
d	du [duː]	**d**ance	
f	finden [ˈfɪndən]	**f**ind	
	Vater [ˈfaːtər]		
	Photo [ˈfoːto]		
g	Gold [gɔlt]	**g**old	
	Geld [gɛlt]		
ʒ	Genie [ʒeˈniː]	mea**s**ure	
h	Haus [haʊs]	**h**ouse	
ç	Licht [lɪçt]		An approximation to this sound may be produced by assuming the mouth configuration for [i] and emitting a strong current of breath.
	manch [manç]		
	traurig [ˈtraʊrɪç]		
x	Loch [lɔx]	Scotch: lo**ch**	Whereas [ç] is pronounced at the front of the mouth, x is pronounced in the throat.
j	ja [jaː]	**y**ear	
k	keck [kɛk]	**k**ick	
	Tag [taːk]		
	Chronist [kroˈnɪst]		
	Café [kaˈfeː]		
l	lassen [ˈlasən]	**l**ump	pronounced like English initial "clear l"
m	Maus [maʊs]	**m**ouse	

Sym-bol	Examples	Nearest English Equivalents	Remarks
n	nein [naɪn]	**n**ot	
ŋ	klingen ['klɪŋən] sinken ['zɪŋkən]	si**ng** dri**nk**	
p	Paß [pas] Weib [vaɪp] obgleich [ɔp'glaɪç]	**p**ass	
r	rot [ro:t]	**r**ot	There are two pronunciations: the frontal or lingual r and the uvular r (the latter unknown in England).
s	Glas [gla:s] Masse ['masə] Mast [mast] naß [nas]	mi**ss**	unvoiced when final, doubled, or next to a voiceless consonant
z	Sohn [zo:n] Rose ['ro:zə]	**z**e-ro	voiced when at the beginning of a word or a syllable
ʃ	Schiff [ʃɪf] Charme [ʃarm] Spiel [ʃpi:l] Stein [ʃtaɪn]	**sh**op	
t	Tee [te:] Thron [tro:n] Stadt [ʃtat] Bad [ba:t] Findling ['fɪntlɪŋ] Wind [vɪnt]	**t**ea	
v	Vase ['va:zə] Winter ['vɪntər]	**v**ast	

ã, ɛ̃, ɔ̃ are nasalized vowels. Examples: Engagement [ãgaʒə'mã:], Terrain [tɛ'rɛ̃:], Feuilleton [fœjə'tɔ̃:].

11. List of Initial and Final Elements normally given without Phonetic Transcription

Initial elements

be- [bə]	ent- [ɛnt]	miß- [mɪs]	ver- [fɛr]
er- [ɛr]	ge- [gə]	un- [ʊn]	zer- [tsɛr]

Final elements

-bar [ba:r]	-fach [fax]	-kunft [kʊnft]	-schaft [ʃaft]
-chen [çən]	-haft [haft]	-lein [laɪn]	-st [st]
-d [t]	-halber [halbər]	-lich [lɪç]	-ste [stə]
-e [ə]	-haltig [haltɪç]	-los [lo:s]	-stel [stəl]
-ei [aɪ]	-heit [haɪt]	-n [n]	-t [t]
-el [əl]	-ig [ɪç]	-nis [nɪs]	-te [tə]
-en [ən]	-in [ɪn]	-s [s]	-tät [tɛ:t]
-end [ənt]	-isch [ɪʃ]	-sal [za:l]	-tum [tu:m]
-er [ər]	-keit [kaɪt]	-sam [za:m]	-ung [ʊŋ]
			-wärts [vɛrts]

12. Grammatical References. Parts of speech (adjective, verb, etc.) have been indicated throughout. Entries have been subdivided by Roman numerals to distinguish the various parts of speech.

Nouns. The inflectional forms (genitive singular/nominative plural) follow immediately after the indication of gender. No forms are given for compounds if the parts appear as separate headwords. The horizontal stroke replaces that part of the word which remains unchanged in the inflexion:

Affe *m* (-n; -n): des Affen, die Affen   **Affäre** *f* (-; -n): der Affäre, die Affären

The sign ˮ indicates that an umlaut appears in the inflected form in question:

Blatt *n* (-[e]s; ˮer): des Blatt(e)s, die Blätter

Verbs

a) The past participle is generally formed by prefixing ge- and adding -(e)t to the stem of the verb: **bändigen** – gebändigt, **heiraten** – geheiratet.

  Verbs ending with -ieren or -eien do not use the prefix ge-: **reagieren** – reagiert, **prophezeien** – prophezeit.

  Verbs with the inseparable prefixes be-, em-, ent-, er-, ge-, ver- and zer- simply add -(e)t to the stem: **begrüßen** – begrüßt, **entbehren** – entbehrt, etc.

  In all the above cases the entries indicate only whether the perfect tense is formed with "haben" or "sein": **bändigen** ... *v/t* (h) ..., **klettern** ... *v/i* (sn) ...

b) The preterite and past participle of an irregular verb are given under the headword: **gehen ...** (ging, gegangen, sn) **I** *v/i* **1.** ...: the perfect tense of this verb is formed by means of the auxiliary verb "sein": er ging, er ist gegangen.

c) Separable verbs form the past participle by placing -ge- between the prefix and the stem: **hinausgehen** *v/i* (*irr, sep*, -ge-, sn, → **gehen**): The reference *irr* indicates that the compound verb "hinausgehen" is conjugated like the root verb "gehen", the → refers the user to the entry "gehen" for the preterite and past participle. *sep* indicates that the verb is separated: er geht/ging hinaus, er ist hinausgegangen.

d) Homographic verbs like "über'treten", "'übertreten" are differentiated as follows:

  'übertreten (*irr, sep*, -ge-, sn, → **treten**): er trat über, er ist übergetreten
  über'treten (*irr, insep, no* -ge-, h, → **treten**): er übertrat, er hat übertreten

Prepositions. Prepositions governing a headword are given in both languages. The grammatical construction following a German preposition is indicated only if the preposition governs two different cases. If a German preposition applies to all translations, it is given only with the first, whereas its English equivalents are given after each translation:

  schützen ... (**gegen, vor** *dat*) protect (from, against), defend (against), shelter (from) ...

A

A, a [aː] *n* (-; -) A, a (*a.* ♪): *fig. das A und O* the be-all and end-all, the essence; *von A bis Z* from beginning to end; *wer A sagt, muß auch B sagen* in for a penny, in for a pound.

à [a] *prep* ✝ (at) ... each.

Aal [aːl] *m* (-[e]s, -e) eel: *fig. sich winden wie ein ~* wriggle like an eel.

aalen ['aːlən] *sich ~* (h) F laze; *sich in der Sonne ~* bask in the sun.

'aal'glatt *adj fig.* (as) slippery as an eel.

Aas [aːs] *n* (-[e]s) **1.** *no pl* carrion. **2.** V *pl Äser* beast, (*woman*) *a.* bitch: *kein ~* not a blessed soul.

'Aasgeier *m* (-s; -) F *fig.* vulture.

ab [ap] **I** *adv* **1.** off, away, *thea.* exit, *pl* (*beide* or *alle* ~) exeunt: *links ~* (to the) left; *weit ~* far off; F ~ *(durch die Mitte)!* off with you! **2.** F *der Knopf etc ist ~* the button *etc* is (or has come) off; → *Hut!* 1. **3.** from: ☎ *Berlin ~ 16:30* dep. (= departure from) Berlin 16:30; F *von ... ~* → 6. **4.** *~ und zu* now and then. **II** *prep* **5.** from: *~ Seite 17* from page 17; ✝ *~ Berlin (Fabrik)* ex Berlin (factory). **6.** from ... (on): *~ heute* from (*adm.* as of) today. **7.** *~ 18 Jahren persons* from (the age of) 18 up(wards); *~ 30 DM shoes etc* from DM 30 up. **8.** ✝ less, deducting. **III** *adj pred* **9.** F *sie war ganz ~* she was dead beat (or bushed).

'abändern *v/t* (*sep*, -ge-, h) alter, change, modify, *parl.* amend, ⚖ commute.

'Abänderung *f* (-; -en) alteration, modification, *parl.* amendment, ⚖ commutation. **'Abänderungsantrag** *m parl. e-n ~ einbringen* move an amendment.

'abarbeiten: *sich ~* (*sep*, -ge-, h) slave (away): → *abgearbeitet*.

Abart ['ap'aːrt] *f* (-; -en) *biol.* variety.

abartig ['ap'aːrtɪç] *adj* abnormal, *sexually: a.* perverse.

'Abbau *m* (-[e]s; *no pl*) **1.** ⚙ dismantling. **2.** ⚒ working, exploitation (*of a mine*), mining (*of coal*): *~ unter Tage* underground working. **3.** 🜨 decomposition, disintegration, *physiol.* breakdown (*of* blood alcohol *etc*). **4.** *fig.* decline (*of physical or mental powers*). **5.** *fig.* a) reduction, cutback (*of expenditures etc*), b) dismissal (*of employee*), retrenchment (*of personnel*). **6.** *fig.* (gradual) overcoming (*of prejudices etc*).

'abbauen (*sep*, -ge-, h) **I** *v/t* **1.** ⚙ dismantle, take down. **2.** ⚒ work (*a mine*), mine (*coal etc*). **3.** 🜨 (*a. sich ~*) decompose, *a. physiol.* break down: *sich ~* be broken down. **4.** *fig.* reduce, cut back (*expenditures etc*), dismiss (*employee*). **5.** *fig.* (gradually) overcome (*prejudices etc*). **II** *v/i* **6.** → *nachlassen* 2.

'abbeißen *v/t* (*irr*, *sep*, -ge-, h, → *beißen*) bite off.

'abbeizen *v/t* (*sep*, -ge-, h) remove with corrosives. **'Abbeizmittel** *n* remover.

'abbekommen *v/t* (*irr*, *sep*, h, → *bekommen*) **1.** get *s.th.* off. **2.** get: *et. ~* a) *a. sein Teil ~* get one's share, b) get hurt, c) be damaged.

'abberufen *v/t* (*irr*, *sep*, h, → *berufen*) recall (*ambassador etc*): *j-n von e-m Amt ~* relieve s.o. from office.

'abbestellen *v/t* (*sep*, h) cancel (one's order for), discontinue (*newspaper*).

'Abbestellung *f* (-; -en) cancel(l)ation.

'abbetteln *v/t* (*sep*, -ge-, h) *j-m et. ~* wheedle s.th. out of s.o.

'abbiegen (*irr*, *sep*, -ge-, → *biegen*) **I** *v/i* (sn) turn (off): (*nach*) *links ~* turn off left. **II** *v/t* (h) F *fig.* head off, avoid.

'Abbiegespur *f* (-; -en) turning lane.

'Abbild *n* (-[e]s; -er) **1.** copy. **2.** a) picture, b) image, likeness. **3.** *fig.* reflection. **'abbilden** *v/t* (*sep*, -ge-, h) **1.** copy. **2.** portray, depict: *wie oben abgebildet* as shown above. **'Abbildung** *f* (-; -en) picture, illustration.

'abbinden (*irr*, *sep*, -ge-, h, → *binden*) **I** *v/t* **1.** untie, undo, take off (*necktie etc*). **2.** tie off, 🩺 ligate. **II** *v/i* **3.** *cement:* set.

'Abbitte *f* (-; -n) apology: *j-m ~ leisten* apologize to s.o. (*wegen* for).

'abbitten v/t (irr, sep, -ge-, h, → **bitten**) **j-m et.** ~ ask so.'s pardon for s.th.

'abblasen v/t (irr, sep, -ge-, h, → **blasen**) **1.** ⚙ blow off (steam etc). **2.** F fig. call off, cancel (meeting etc).

'abblättern v/i (sep, -ge-, sn) **1.** shed its leaves (or petals). **2.** paint etc: flake off.

'abblenden (sep, -ge-, h) **I** v/t **1.** dim (light etc), mot. dip (Am. dim) (the headlights). **II** v/i **2.** mot. dip (Am. dim) the headlights. **3.** phot. stop down.

'Abblendlicht n mot. dipped (Am. dimmed) headlights, low beam.

'abblitzen v/i (sep, -ge-, sn) F (**bei j-m**) ~ meet with a rebuff (from s.o.); **j-n** ~ **lassen** send s.o. packing.

abblocken ['apblɔkən] v/t (sep, -ge-, h) a. fig. block.

'abbrechen (irr, sep, -ge-, → **brechen**) **I** v/t (h) **1.** break off: F **sich e-n** ~ nearly kill o.s. (doing s.th.). **2.** demolish, pull down (house etc), take down (scaffolding etc), strike (tent): **das Lager** ~ break camp. **3.** fig. stop (fight, match, etc), break off (relations), call off (a strike), abandon (studies, test, etc), raise (a siege). **II** v/i **4.** (sn) break off. **5.** (h) fig. break off, stop.

'abbremsen v/t, v/i (sep, -ge-, h) slow down, brake.

'abbrennen (irr, sep, -ge-, → **brennen**) **I** v/t (h) burn down, let off (fireworks). **II** v/i (sn) burn down: → **abgebrannt**.

'abbringen v/t (irr, sep, -ge-, h, → **bringen**) **j-n** ~ **von** dissuade s.o. from; **j-n davon** ~, **et. zu tun** stop s.o. doing s.th., talk s.o. out of doing s.th.

'abbröckeln v/i (sep, -ge-, sn) crumble (away), fig. prices etc: crumble.

'Abbruch m (-[e]s; no pl) **1.** demolition. **2.** fig. breaking off (of diplomatic relations etc), esp. sports: break-off, stop(ping). **3.** ~ **tun** (dat) detract from, be detrimental to; **das tut der Sache k-n** ~**!** that makes no difference!

'abbruchreif adj due for demolition, adm. condemned.

'abbuchen v/t (sep, -ge-, h) **1.** **e-e Summe von j-s Konto** ~ debit a sum to s.o.'s account. **2.** → **abschreiben** 2.

'Abbuchung f (-; -en) **1.** debit entry. **2.** payment by standing order.

'Abbuchungsauftrag m debit order.

ABC-Waffen [a:be:'tse:-] pl NBC-weapons.

'Abdampf m (-[e]s; ⁓e) ⚙ exhaust steam.

'abdampfen v/i (sep, -ge-, sn) **1.** F clear (or push) off. **2.** ⚙ (a. v/t) evaporate.

'abdanken v/i (sep, -ge-, h) resign, ruler: abdicate. **'Abdankung** f (-; -en) resignation, abdication.

'abdecken v/t (sep, -ge-, h) **1.** take off, uncover; untile (roof), unroof (house), clear (the table), turn down (the bed). **2.** cover (up), phot. blank out. **3.** ✝ cover, meet (debts).

'abdichten v/t (sep, -ge-, h) ⚙ seal, pack, ca(u)lk, make s.th. watertight.

'abdrängen v/t (sep, -ge-, h) push (or force) s.o., s.th. aside.

'abdrehen (sep, -ge-, h) **I** v/t **1.** ⚙ twist off. **2.** turn off (gas, water), ⚡ a. switch off. **3.** finish (shooting) (a film). **II** v/i **4.** a. (sn) ✈, ⚓ turn away, sheer off.

'abdriften v/i (sep, -ge-, sn) drift off.

'Abdruck¹ m (-[e]s; ⁓e) **1.** (im)print, mark. **2.** in wax etc: impression.

'Abdruck² m (-[e]s) **1.** no pl printing. **2.** (pl -e) copy.

'abdrucken v/t (sep, -ge-, h) print.

'abdrücken (sep, -ge-, h) **I** v/t **1.** fire (off) (gun) (**auf** acc at). **2.** make an impression of s.th.: **sich** ~ leave an imprint. **3.** F **j-n** ~ hug s.o., squeeze s.o. **II** v/i **4.** pull the trigger: **auf** j-n ~ fire at s.o.

'abdüsen v/i (sep, -ge-, sn) F zoom off.

'abebben v/i (sep, -ge-, sn) ebb away, anger, noise, etc: a. die down, subside.

Abend ['a:bənt] m (-s; -e) evening, night (both a. performance): **am** (**spät**en) ~ (late) in the evening, (late) at night; **heute** ⚲ this evening, tonight; **morgen** (**gestern**) ⚲ tomorrow (last) night; **Sonntag** ⚲ Sunday evening; **guten** ~**!** good evening!; **zu** ~ **essen** have supper (or dinner); **es wird** ~ it's getting dark; **man soll den Tag nicht vor dem** ~ **loben** don't count your chickens before they are hatched; **es ist noch nicht aller Tage** ~ things may take a turn yet.

'Abend|andacht f evening prayer(s). **~blatt** n evening paper. **~dämmerung** f dusk. **~essen** n evening meal, dinner, supper. **⚲füllend** adj full-length (film). **~kasse** f box office. **~kleid** n evening dress (Am. gown). **~kurs** m, **~kursus** m evening class(es).

'**Abendland** n (-[e]s; no pl) the Occident.
abendländisch ['a:bəntlɛndiʃ] adj occidental, Western.
'**abendlich** adj of (or in) the evening.
'**Abendmahl** n (-[e]s; no pl) eccl. the Holy Communion, the Lord's (paint. the Last) Supper: **das ~ nehmen** take Communion.
abends ['a:bənts] adv in the evening(s): **bis ~** till evening; **um 7 Uhr ~** at 7 p.m.
'**Abend|schule** f night school. **~sonne** f setting sun. **~stern** m evening star. **~vorstellung** f thea. evening performance. **~zeitung** f → **Abendblatt**.
Abenteuer ['a:bəntɔyər] n (-s; -) adventure (a. in cpds film, novel, playground, etc). '**Abenteuerleben** n adventurous life. '**abenteuerlich** adj adventurous, fig. risky, wild (idea, plan, etc), eccentric, odd (getup etc). '**Abenteuerlust** f (-; no pl) love of adventure.
'**Abenteurer** n (-s; -) adventurer.
'**Abenteurerin** f (-; -nen) adventuress.
aber ['a:bər] I conj but: **~ dennoch** yet, (but) still; **oder ~** otherwise, or else. II interj **~, ~!** come, come!; **~ ja!, ~ sicher!** (but) of course!; **~ nein!** oh no!, of course not!; **das ist ~ nett von dir** that's really nice of you. III adv **hundert und ~ hundert** hundreds and hundreds.
'**Aber** n (-s; -) but: **die Sache hat ein ~** there's just one catch to it; → **Wenn**.
'**Aberglaube** m (-ns; no pl) superstition.
abergläubisch ['a:bərglɔybiʃ] adj superstitious.
'**aberkennen** v/t (irr, sep, h, → **erkennen**) esp. ⚖ j-m et. ~ deprive s.o. of.
'**Aberkennung** f (-; -en) deprivation.
'**abermalig** ['a:bərma:liç] adj renewed, repeated. **abermals** ['a:bərma:ls] adv again, once more.
'**aberwitzig** adj crazy, mad.
'**abfackeln** v/t (h) burn off (gas).
'**abfahren** (irr, sep, -ge-, → **fahren**) I v/i (sn) **1.** (nach for) leave, depart, start, ⚓ sail: F **j-n ~ lassen** send s.o. packing. **2.** skiing: run (n.s. start) downhill. **3.** F **auf j-n (et.) (voll) ~** be wild about s.o. (s.th.), dig s.o. (s.th.) (the big way). II v/t (h) **4.** cart off, remove. **5.** a) cover, travel (a distance), b) patrol. **6.** wear down (a tyre). **7.** start, run (film, tape). **8.** use up (a ticket). **9.** **ihm wurde ein Bein etc abgefahren** he was run over and lost a leg etc.
'**Abfahrt** f (-; -en) **1.** (nach for) start, departure. **2.** exit (of a motorway). **3.** skiing: a) downhill (run), b) slope.
'**abfahrtbereit** adj ready to leave.
'**Abfahrtslauf** m skiing: downhill (run). '**Abfahrtsläufer(in** f) m downhiller.
'**Abfahrtszeit** f time of departure.
'**Abfall**¹ m (-[e]s; ⸗e) **1.** waste (a. ⚙), refuse, rubbish, Am. garbage, b) offal, c) litter.
'**Abfall**² m (-[e]s; no pl) **1.** decrease (a. ⚡, a. fig.), drop. **2.** pol. defection: **~ von e-r Partei** desertion from a party. **3.** eccl. apostasy.
'**Abfallbeseitigung** f waste disposal.
'**Abfalleimer** m rubbish (or litter) bin, Am. garbage can.
'**abfallen** v/i (irr, sep, -ge-, sn, → **fallen**) **1.** fall off, drop off: fig. **von j-m ~** fear etc: fall away from s.o., leave s.o. **2.** terrain: fall away, slope: **steil ~** drop steeply. **3.** fig. fall (off), drop, decrease, runner etc: drop back: **~ gegen** compare badly with. **4.** be left (over). **5.** F be gained (bei by): **was fällt für mich dabei ab?** what's in it for me? **6.** **von e-r Partei ~** break away (or defect) from a party. **7.** eccl. apostatize (**von** from).
'**abfallend** adj sloping (terrain etc): **steil ~** steep, precipitous.
'**abfällig** adj disparaging (remark), adverse (criticism), unfavo(u)rable (opinion etc): **~ sprechen über** (acc) speak disparagingly of.
'**Abfallpro,dukt** n **1.** waste product. **2.** spin-off, by-product. '**Abfallverwertung** f waste recovery, recycling.
'**abfangen** v/t (irr, sep, -ge-, h, → **fangen**) **1.** catch. **2.** intercept (message, letter, etc). **3.** check (attack). **4.** sports: parry (blow), catch up with (a runner). **5.** get a car etc under control, ✈ pull out. **6.** ⚠ prop up. **7.** ⚙ absorb, cushion (shocks).
'**Abfangjäger** m interceptor (plane).
'**abfärben** v/i (sep, -ge-, h) run: **~ auf** (acc) a) run into, b) fig. rub off on.
'**abfassen** v/t (sep, -ge-, h) write, draft, esp. adm. draw up, formulate, word.
'**Abfassung** f (-; -en) composition, drafting, wording.
'**abfaulen** v/i (sep, -ge-, sn) rot off.

'**abfedern** v/t (sep, -ge-, h) ⊕ absorb (shocks), cushion (a. fig.), spring.

'**abfeilen** v/t (sep, -ge-, h) ⊕ file off.

'**abfertigen** v/t (sep, -ge-, h) **1.** a. ✈, 🚋, ⚓ dispatch, clear, b) check in (passengers): **e-n Zug ~** start a train. **2.** attend to, serve, deal with (customers): F **j-n kurz ~** give s.o. short shrift. **3.** F sports: dispose of, beat.

'**Abfertigung** f (-; -en) **1.** dispatch (a. ✈, 🚋), (customs) clearance. **2.** ⚓ attendance (gen to customers, an order). **3.** → '**Abfertigungsschalter** m dispatch counter, ✈ check-in counter.

'**abfeuern** v/t (sep, -ge-, h) fire (off) (gun etc), sports: let go with (a. fig.).

'**abfinden** (irr, sep, -ge-, h) **I** v/t a) pay (off), satisfy (creditors), buy out (a partner), b) pay s.o. compensation. **II** **sich ~ mit** come to terms with, resign o.s. to, put up with, accept; **damit kann ich mich nicht ~!** I just can't accept it!

'**Abfindung** f (-; -en) a) satisfaction, paying off, b) of employees: severance pay, c) compensation.

'**abflachen** v/t (sep, -ge-, h) (a. **sich ~**) flatten (out).

'**abflauen** v/i (sep, -ge-, h) wind etc: drop, a. fig. die down, abate, crisis, traffic, etc: ease off, ⚓ business etc: slacken (off), interest etc: flag.

'**abfliegen** (irr, sep, -ge-, → **fliegen**) **I** v/i (sn) ✈ start, take off, passenger: fly. **II** v/t (h) patrol (by plane).

'**abfließen** v/i (irr, sep, -ge-, sn, → **fließen**) flow off (a. capital).

'**Abflug** m (-[e]s; ⁻e) takeoff, departure. **2bereit** adj ready for takeoff. **~halle** f departure lounge. **~zeit** f (time of) departure.

'**Abfluß** m (-sses; ⁻sse) **1.** flowing off, discharge, outflow (of capital). **2.** ⊕ outlet. '**Abflußrohr** n ⊕ drainpipe.

'**abfordern** v/t (sep, -ge-, h) **j-m et. ~** a. fig. demand s.th. of s.o.

'**abfragen** v/t (sep, -ge-, h) **1.** **j-n (et.) ~** test (Am. quiz) s.o. (on s.th.). **2.** computer: interrogate.

'**abfressen** v/t (irr, sep, -ge-, h, → **fressen**) crop, eat bare.

'**abfrieren** v/i (irr, sep, -ge-, sn, → **frieren**) **ihm sind drei Zehen etc abgefroren** he lost three toes etc through frostbite; F **sich e-n ~** be freezing to death.

Abfuhr ['apfuːr] f (-; -en) **1.** removal. **2.** a) fig. rebuff, F brush-off, b) sports: defeat, beating: **sich e-e ~ holen** get a beating, fig. meet with a rebuff.

'**abführen** (sep, -ge-, h) **I** v/t **1.** lead s.o. away, forcibly: march s.o. off, take prisoner into custody: **j-n ~ lassen** have s.o. taken away. **2.** fig. **von** lead away from (a subject). **3.** **~ an** (acc) pay money, taxes (over) to. **4.** ⊕ drain off (water), carry off (heat). **II** v/i **5.** ⚕ a) act as a laxative, b) move the bowels.

'**abführend** adj, '**Abführmittel** n (-s; -) ⚕ laxative.

'**Abfüllanlage** f bottling plant.

'**abfüllen** v/t (sep, -ge-, h) draw off, fill, rack (off) (wine etc): **in Beutel ~** bag; **in** (or **auf**) **Flaschen ~** bottle.

'**abfüttern** v/t (sep, -ge-, h) a. F fig. feed.

'**Abgabe** f (-; -n) **1.** no pl a) delivery, handing over, b) depositing (luggage), Am. checking (baggage), c) making (an offer, a comment, etc), giving (an opinion etc), d) emission (of heat, steam, etc), release (of energy), ⊕ output, e) ⚓ sale, f) firing (of a shot). **2.** a) tax, duty, b) rate, Am. local tax, c) (social) contribution. **3.** sports: pass.

'**abgabenfrei** adj a) tax-free, b) duty-free. '**abgabenpflichtig** adj person: liable to payment of taxes (etc), goods: dutiable, income: taxable.

'**Abgang** m (-[e]s; ⁻e) **1.** no pl leaving, departure, a. thea. exit, retirement (aus from an office): **nach dem ~ von der Schule** after leaving school; fig. **sich e-n guten ~ verschaffen** make a graceful exit. **2.** no pl a) ⚓ dispatch, b) 🚋 etc departure, ⚓ sailing, c) ⚕ discharge (of blood, pus), passage (of stones). **3.** gym. dismount. **4.** ⚓ a) → **Absatz** 3, b) loss, c) banking: items disposed of.

'**Abgangszeugnis** n (school-)leaving certificate, Am. diploma.

'**Abgas** n (-es; -e) usu. Am. mot. exhaust fumes. **2arm** adj low-emission. **~entgiftung** f waste gas detoxification. **2frei** adj emission-free. **~test** m mot. fume emission test.

'**abgearbeitet** **I** pp of **abarbeiten**. **II** adj worn(-)out.

'**abgeben** (irr, sep, -ge-, h, → **geben**) **I** v/t **1.** (**bei**) a) hand in (or over) (to), deliver (to), b) deposit (luggage etc) (at), *Am.* check (*baggage etc*) (at). **2.** (**an** *acc* to) a) give away, b) transfer (*employee*): **j-m et. ~ von** *a.* share s.th. with s.o. **3.** ✝ sell (**an** *acc* to). **4.** *sports:* (**an** *acc* to) pass (*the ball*), lose (*game, set*), concede (*a point*). **5.** make (*a statement*), give (*one's opinion*), cast (*one's vote*). **6.** give off, emit (*heat, steam, etc*), release (*energy*). **7. e-n Schuß ~** fire (*sports: a.* deliver) a shot, shoot. **8.** ✝ be, act as (*referee etc*), provide, serve as (*background etc*): **er würde e-n guten Lehrer** *etc* ~ he would make a good teacher *etc*. **II** *v/i sports:* pass (the ball). **III** *sich ~ mit* concern o.s. with; F *sich mit j-m ~* have dealings with s.o., associate with s.o.: **damit kann ich mich nicht ~!** I can't be bothered with that!

'abgebrannt I *pp of* **abbrennen.** II *adj* F *fig.* broke.

'abgebrüht *adj* F *fig.* hardened.

'abgedroschen *adj* F trite, hackneyed.

'abgefahren I *pp of* **abfahren.** II *adj* bald (*tyre*).

'abgegriffen *adj* **1.** a) (well-)worn, b) well-thumbed (*book*). **2.** → **abgedroschen.**

'abgehackt I *pp of* **abhacken.** II *adj* chopped (*speech*), disjointed (*sentences*).

'abgehangen I *pp of* **abhängen².** II *adj* hung (*meat*).

'abgehärtet I *pp of* **abhärten.** II *adj* tough, (**gegen**) inured (to), *a. fig.* hardened (against).

'abgehen (*irr, sep,* -ge-, sn, → **gehen**) I *v/i* **1.** leave, ✓, 🚢 *a.* depart, 🚢 *a.* sail (*all: nach* for), *letter, parcel, etc:* go off, be dispatched: **von der Schule ~** leave school. **2.** *thea., a. fig.* make one's exit: **... geht (gehen) ab** exit (*exeunt*) ~ **3.** *button, paint, etc:* come off. **4.** 🩸 *fetus:* be aborted, *stones etc:* be discharged, pass. **5.** *road etc:* branch off. **6.** → **weggehen 2. 7.** *amount etc:* be deducted (**von** from): **hiervon gehen 7% ab** 7 per cent to be deducted (from this amount). **8.** *fig.* **von e-r Regel** *etc* ~ deviate (*totally:* depart) from a rule *etc*; **davon gehe ich nicht ab!** nothing can change my mind about that!; **davon kann ich nicht ~!** I must insist on that! **9.** F *fig.* **was ihm abgeht, ist Mut** what he lacks is courage; **ihm geht jeder**

Humor ab he has no sense of humo(u)r at all; **ihr geht nichts ab** she doesn't go short of anything. **10. gut** (*glatt etc*) ~ go well (smoothly *etc*); **schlecht ~** turn out badly; **es kann nicht gut ~** there's sure to be trouble; **es ging nicht ohne Streit ab** there was a quarrel after all. **II** *v/t* **11.** a) go (*or* walk) along, b) patrol.

'abgehend *adj* 🚌, ☎ outgoing.

'abgehetzt I *pp of* **abhetzen.** II *adj* **1.** breathless, *pred* out of breath. **2.** worn(-)out, exhausted.

'abgekämpft *adj* exhausted, spent.

'abgekartet *adj* F **~es Spiel** put-up job.

'abgeklärt I *pp of* **abklären.** II *adj* balanced (*opinion etc*), mellow (*person*).

'abgelagert I *pp of* **ablagern.** II *adj* seasoned (*wood etc*), matured (*wine*).

'abgelegen *adj* remote, secluded.

'abgelten *v/t* (*irr, sep,* -ge-, h, → **gelten**) satisfy (*claims*).

'abgemagert I *pp of* **abmagern.** II *adj* emaciated.

'abgeneigt *adj* **nicht ~ sein, et. zu tun** be quite prepared to do s.th.

'abgenutzt I *pp of* **abnutzen.** II *adj a. fig.* worn(-)out.

Abgeordnete ['apgə'ɔrdnətə] *m, f* (-n; -n) a) delegate, representative, b) Member of Parliament, *Am.* Congressman (Congresswoman).

'Abgeordnetenhaus *n* chamber of deputies, *Am.* House of Representatives.

'abgepackt I *pp of* **abpacken.** II *adj* ✝ prepacked, packaged.

'abgerissen I *pp of* **abreißen.** II *adj* **1.** ragged, *person: a.* seedy. **2.** incoherent, disjointed (*sentences etc*).

'abgerundet I *pp of* **abrunden.** II *adj* round(ed) (*sum etc*), *fig.* (well-)rounded. **III** *adv* in round figures.

'Abgesandte *m, f* (-n; -n) envoy, *pol. a.* emissary.

'abgeschieden *adj* secluded.

'Abgeschiedenheit *f* (-; *no pl*) seclusion.

'abgeschlafft *adj* F whacked, dead beat.

'abgeschlossen I *pp of* **abschließen.** II *adj* **1.** completed. **2.** ⊙ self-contained.

'abgeschmackt *adj fig.* a) tasteless, *pred* in bad taste, b) fatuous.

'abgesehen *adv* ~ **von** apart (*esp. Am.* aside) from, except for; **vom Wetter ganz ~** to say nothing of the weather.

'abgespannt *adj* worn(-)out, exhausted.

'**Abgespanntheit** f (-; no pl) exhaustion.
'**abgestanden** adj a. fig. stale.
'**abgestorben** I pp of **absterben**. II adj dead, numb.
'**abgestumpft** I pp of **abstumpfen**. II adj fig. deadened, dull(ed), person: insensitive (**gegen** to).
'**abgetakelt** adj F down(-)at(-)heel.
'**abgetragen** I pp of **abtragen**. II adj worn, shabby, worn-down (shoes).
'**abgewinnen** v/t (irr, sep, h, → **gewinnen**) **j-m et. ~** win s.th. from s.o.; **e-r Sache Geschmack ~** acquire a taste for s.th.
'**abgewirtschaftet** adj run(-)down.
'**abgewöhnen** v/t (sep, h) **j-m et. ~** cure (or break) s.o. of s.th.; **j-m das Rauchen ~** make s.o. stop smoking; **sich das Rauchen ~** give up smoking.
'**abgezehrt** adj emaciated.
'**abgießen** v/t (irr, sep, -ge-, h, → **gießen**) **1.** a.) pour off, b) strain (vegetables etc). **2.** ⊙ cast.
'**Abglanz** m (fig. schwacher ~ pale) reflection.
'**abgleichen** v/t (irr, sep, -ge-, h, → **gleichen**) ⊙ equalize, ⚡ align.
'**abgleiten** v/i (irr, sep, -ge-, sn, → **gleiten**) slip (off): fig. **Kritik etc gleitet von ihm ab** he is deaf to criticism etc.
abgöttisch [ˈapgœtɪʃ] adj idolatrous: **~ lieben** idolize, adore.
'**abgrasen** v/t (sep, -ge-, h) **1.** graze. **2.** F fig. (nach for) scour, comb.
'**abgrenzen** v/t (sep, -ge-, h) **1.** a. fig. mark off, demarcate (**gegen** from). **2.** fig. a) differentiate, b) define.
'**Abgrenzung** f (-; -en) **1.** demarcation. **2.** fig. a) differentiation, b) definition.
'**Abgrund** m (-[e]s; ⁺e) abyss (a. fig.), chasm, precipice: fig. **die Abgründe der Seele etc** the depths of the soul etc; **am Rande des ~s** on the brink of ruin (or disaster). **abgründig** [ˈapgryndɪç] adj **1.** cryptic. **2.** → '**abgrundtief** adj abysmal (a. fig.), fig. deadly (hate etc).
'**abgucken** v/t (sep, -ge-, h) F **j-m et. ~** learn (or copy) s.th. from s.o.
'**Abguß** m (-sses; ⁺sse) ⊙ cast.
'**abhaben** v/t (irr, sep, -ge-, h, → **haben**) F **er kann et. ~** he can have some (of it).
'**abhacken** v/t (sep, -ge-, h) chop off, cut off: → **abgehackt**.
'**abhaken** v/t (sep, -ge-, h) **1.** unhook. **2.**

tick (Am. check) off: fig. **et. ~** cross s.th. off one's list.
'**abhalftern** v/t (sep, -ge-, h) F fig. sack.
'**abhalten** v/t (irr, sep, -ge-, h, → **halten**) **1.** hold s.th. away (**von sich** from o.s.). **2.** keep away (or off), ward off. **3.** deter, discourage: **j-n ~ von** stop (or keep, prevent) s.o. from doing; **lassen Sie sich (durch mich) nicht ~!** don't let me disturb you! **4.** hold (conference, exam, election, etc), give (lesson, lecture): **abgehalten werden** be held, take place. **5.** **ein Kind ~** hold a child over the pot. **6.** ⚓ (a. v/i) bear off.
'**abhandeln** v/t (sep, -ge-, h) **1.** **j-m et. ~** buy s.th. from s.o.; **j-m 10 Mark (vom Preis) ~** beat s.o. down by ten marks. **2.** deal with, treat (a subject etc).
abhanden [apˈhandən] adv **~ kommen** get lost; **mir ist mein Bleistift ~ gekommen** I have lost my pencil.
'**Abhandlung** f (-; -en) (**über** acc on) treatise, paper.
'**Abhang** m (-[e]s; ⁺e) slope, precipice.
'**abhängen¹** v/t (h) **1.** take down, unhook, 🚃 etc uncouple. **2.** fig. shake off, give s.o. the slip. II v/i teleph. hang up.
'**abhängen²** v/i (irr, sep, -ge-, h, → **hängen¹**) **1.** hang: → **abgehangen** II. **2.** ~ **von** depend on, financially: be dependent on; **letztlich ~ von** hinge on; **es hängt von ihm ab** it's for him to decide.
'**abhängig** [ˈaphɛŋɪç] adj (**von**) dependent (on), ⚕, psych. addicted (to): ling. **~e Rede** indirect speech; **~er Satz** subordinate clause; **~ sein von → abhängen²** 2; **~ machen von** make s.th. conditional on. '**Abhängigkeit** f (-; -en) (**von**) dependence (on), ⚕, psych. dependency (on), addiction (to): **gegenseitige ~** interdependence.
'**abhärmen: sich ~** (sep, -ge-, h) pine away; **sich ~ um** grieve over.
'**abhärten** v/t (sep, -ge-, h) (**gegen** to, against) toughen, a. fig. harden (**sich** o.s.). '**Abhärtung** f (-; no pl) hardening.
'**abhauen** (irr, sep, -ge-, → **hauen**) I v/t (h) cut off, chop off. II v/i (sn) F beat it: **hau ab!** beat it!, get lost!
'**abheben** (irr, sep, -ge-, h, → **heben**) I v/t **1.** lift off, take off, teleph. lift off. **2.** cut (cards). **3.** slip (meshes). **4.** withdraw (money). II v/i **5.** ✈ take off. **6.** F fig. flip. **7.** answer the (tele)phone. **8.**

cards: cut. **9.** *esp. adm.* **~ auf** (*acc*) refer to. **III sich ~ (gegen, von)** contrast (with), stand out (against).

'**abheften** *v/t* (*sep*, -ge-, h) file (away).

'**abheilen** *v/i* (*sep*, -ge-, sn) heal (up).

'**abhelfen** *v/i* (*irr*, *sep*, -ge-, h, → **helfen**) **e-r Sache ~** remedy s.th.

'**abhetzen: sich ~** (*sep*, -ge-, h) rush, *w.s.* wear (*or* tire) o.s. out.

'**Abhilfe** *f* (-; *no pl*) remedy: **~ schaffen** remedy things.

'**abhobeln** *v/t* (*sep*, -ge-, h) ⚙ plane off.

'**abholen** *v/t* (*sep*, -ge-, h) call for, come for, pick up, collect: **~ lassen** send for; **j-n von der Bahn ~** go to meet s.o. at the station.

'**abholzen** *v/t* (*sep*, -ge-, h) cut down (*trees*), deforest (*area*).

'**Abhöranlage** *f* bugging system.

'**abhorchen** *v/t* (*sep*, -ge-, h) 🖤 sound, auscultate.

'**abhören** *v/t* (*sep*, -ge-, h) **1.** → *abfragen* 1. **2.** → *abhorchen*. **3.** intercept (*radio message etc*), listen in on, monitor, F bug (*phone calls*), tap (*telephone*). **4.** play back (*tape recording*).

Abi ['abi] *n* (-s; *no pl*) F → *Abitur*.

'**abirren** *v/i* (*sep*, -ge-, sn) *a. fig.* stray (**von**) from.

Abitur [abi'tuːr] *n* (-s; *no pl*) school-leaving (*Am.* final) examination.

Abiturient [abitu'riɛnt] *m* (-en; -en) a) candidate for the school-leaving examination, b) school-leaver with the Abitur.

Abi'turzeugnis *n* Abitur certificate, *Br.* GCE A-levels, *Am.* (Senior High School) graduation diploma.

'**abjagen** *v/t* (*sep*, -ge-, h) **j-m et. ~** snatch s.th. away from s.o.

'**abkanzeln** *v/t* (*sep*, -ge-, h) F **j-n ~** give s.o. a dressing-down.

'**abkapseln: sich ~** (*sep*, -ge-, h) shut (*or* cut) o.s. off.

'**abkarten** *v/t* (*sep*, -ge-, h) F fix, rig: → *abgekartet*.

'**abkas,sieren** *v/i* (*sep*, -ge-, h) F *fig.* cash in.

'**abkaufen** *v/t* (*sep*, -ge-, h) buy (*dat* from): F *fig.* **das kaufe ich dir** *etc* **nicht ab!** I won't buy that!

Abkehr ['apkeːr] *f* (-; *no pl*) break (**von** with). '**abkehren** *v/t* (*sep*, -ge-, h) (*a.* **sich ~**) turn away (**von** from): *fig.* **sich**

~ von *a.* turn one's back on (*a person*), abandon (*a policy etc*).

'**abklappern** *v/t* (*sep*, -ge-, h) F scour (*shops*) (**nach** for), do (*museums etc*).

'**abklären** *v/t* (*sep*, -ge-, h) clear: → *abgeklärt*.

'**Abklatsch** *m* (-[e]s; -e) *fig.* imitation.

'**abklemmen** *v/t* (*sep*, -ge-, h) pinch off, 🗲 clamp, ⚡ disconnect.

'**abklingen** *v/i* (*sep*, -ge-, sn, → *klingen*) *noise etc*: abate, *pain*: ease, *fever*, *swelling*: go down, *effect*: wear off, *excitement*, *storm*, *etc*: subside, die down.

'**abklopfen** (*sep*, -ge-, h) **I** *v/t* **1.** brush off (*dust etc*). **2.** *esp.* 🖤 tap, percuss. **3.** F *fig.* scrutinize (**auf** *acc* for). **II** *v/i* **4.** ♩ stop the orchestra.

'**abknallen** *v/t* (*sep*, -ge-, h) F bump *s.o.* off.

'**abknicken** *v/t* (*sep*, -ge-, h), *v/i* (sn) snap (off): **~de Vorfahrt** left-hand (*or* right-hand) turn of a main road at a road junction.

'**abknöpfen** *v/t* (*sep*, -ge-, h) **1.** unbutton. **2.** F *j-m et.* **~** wangle s.th. out of s.o.

'**abknutschen** *v/t* (*sep*, -ge-, h) F kiss and cuddle: **sich ~** snog, smooch.

'**abkochen** *v/t* (*sep*, -ge-, h) boil, scald.

'**abkomman,dieren** *v/t* (*sep*, h) a) detail, b) second (*officer*) (**nach, zu** to).

'**abkommen** *v/i* (*irr*, *sep*, -ge-, sn, → *kommen*) **1.** get away (*a. sports*): **vom Kurs ~** deviate (from one's course); *mot.* **von der Straße ~** get (*or* skid) off the road; **vom Thema ~** stray from the point; **vom Wege ~** lose one's way, *fig.* go astray. **2.** ~ give up, drop (*idea*, *plan*, *etc*); **von e-r Ansicht ~** change one's views about s.th.

'**Abkommen** *n* (-s; -) *esp. pol.* agreement.

abkömmlich ['apkœmlɪç] *adj* available: **er ist nicht ~** he cannot get away.

'**Abkömmling** *m* (-s; -e) 🌱 derivative.

'**abkoppeln** *v/t* (*sep*, -ge-, h) uncouple.

'**abkratzen** (*sep*, -ge-) **I** *v/t* (h) scrape off. **II** *v/i* (sn) F kick the bucket.

'**abkühlen** *v/t, v/i* *and* **sich ~** (*sep*, -ge-, h) *a. fig.* cool off.

'**Abkühlung** *f* (-; *no pl*) cooling.

'**abkürzen** (*sep*, -ge-, h) **I** *v/t* shorten, abridge, abbreviate (*word*): (**den Weg**) **~** take a short cut. **II** *v/i* take (*road etc*: be) a short cut. '**Abkürzung** *f* (-; -en) **1.** abbreviation, abridg(e)ment. **2.** *a. fig.*

short cut. **'Abkürzungsverzeichnis** *n* list of abbreviations.

'abküssen *v/t* (*sep*, -ge-, h) *j-n* ~ smother s.o. with kisses.

'abladen *v/t* (*irr, sep*, -ge-, h, → **laden**) **1.** a) unload, b) dump. **2.** *fig.* off-load: *s-n Ärger* ~ *bei* vent one's anger on.

'Abladeplatz *m* a) unloading point, b) dump.

'Ablage *f* (-; -n) **1.** *no pl* filing. **2.** a) place to put s.th., b) file.

'ablagern *v/t* (*sep*, -ge-, h) **1.** (*a. sich* ~) 🐾, *geol.*, 🌿 deposit. **2.** (*a. v/i*) season (*wood etc*), mature (*wine*).

'Ablagerung *f* (-; -en) 🐾, *geol.*, 🌿 a) deposition, b) deposit, sediment.

Ablaß ['aplas] *m* (-sses; ⸚sse) *eccl.* indulgence.

'ablassen (*irr, sep*, -ge-, h, → **lassen**) **I** *v/t* **1.** let s.th. off (*or* out), drain off (*water etc*), drain (*tank etc*), blow off (*steam*): *die Luft* ~ *aus* deflate. **2.** 🌿 a) sell (*dat* to), b) et. (*vom Preis*) ~ knock s.th. off the price. **II** *v/i* **3.** ~ *von* a) stop doing, give s.th. up, b) leave *s.o.* alone.

Ablativ ['ablati:f; -ap-] *m* (-s; -e) *ling.* ablative.

Ablauf *m* (-[e]s; ⸚e) **1.** 🏺 a) discharge, b) outlet, drain. **2.** course, run, *of program(me)*: order of events: *der* ~ *der Ereignisse* the course of events. **3.** *no pl* end, 🏛, 🌾 expiration (*of contract etc*), maturity (*of bill of exchange*): *nach* ~ upon expiration (*gen* of): *nach* ~ *von zwei Wochen* after two weeks.

'ablaufen (*irr, sep*, -ge-, → **laufen**) **I** *v/i* (sn) **1.**·(*a.* ~ **lassen**) *water etc*: run off, drain off: *fig.* **an ihm läuft alles ab** everything runs off him like water off a duck's back. **2.** *fig.* go: *alles ist gut abgelaufen* everything went off well. **3.** end, run out, expire. **4.** unwind, *film, tape*: run, *watch*: run down: *fig.* **s-e Uhr ist abgelaufen** his hour is come. **II** *v/t* (h) **5.** walk the length of. **6.** (*nach* for) scour, comb (*shops*). **7.** wear out, wear down (*heels*): → **Rang** 1.

'Ableben *n* (-s; *no pl*) death, decease.

'ablecken *v/t* (*sep*, -ge-, h) lick off.

'ablegen (*sep*, -ge-, h) **I** *v/t* **1.** a) take off (*one's coat etc*), b) discard (*old clothes*): *abgelegte Kleider* cast-offs. **2.** put down (*load*). **3.** file (*papers*), discard (*playing cards*). **4.** *zo.* deposit (*eggs*). **5.**

give up, drop (*habit*). **6.** take (*oath etc*): *e-e Prüfung* ~ take (*or* pass) an examination; → **Gelübde, Geständnis, Rechenschaft etc. II** *v/i* **7.** take off one's things (*or* coat, hat, *etc*): *bitte, legen Sie ab!* take off your coat, please! **8.** ⚓ cast off, *space shuttle*: separate.

'Ableger *m* (-s; -) 🌱 layer, scion.

'ablehnen (*sep*, -ge-, h) **I** *v/t* **1.** refuse, turn down, reject (*a. parl.*), decline, 🏛 challenge (*witness*). **2.** disapprove of, condemn. **II** *v/i* **3.** refuse, decline.

'ablehnend *adj* negative, disapproving.

'Ablehnung *f* (-; -en) refusal, rejection (*a. parl.*), disapproval (*gen* of).

'ableisten *v/t* (*sep*, -ge-, h) serve: → **Wehrdienst**.

'ableiten *v/t* (*sep*, -ge-, h) **1.** 🏺 divert, drain off (*water*), carry off (*steam*). **2.** 🐾, 🅰, *ling.*, *a. fig.* derive (*aus* from): *sich* ~ *a.* be derived; *s-e Herkunft* ~ *von* trace one's origin back to.

'Ableitung *f* (-; -en) **1.** 🏺 diversion, draining off (*etc*, → **ableiten** 1). **2.** 🅰, *ling. etc* a) derivation, b) derivative.

'ablenken (*sep*, -ge-, h) **I** *v/t* **1.** a) divert, b) deflect (*ball, light rays, etc*). **2.** *fig.* divert, distract: *den Verdacht von sich* ~ divert suspicion from o.s.; *j-n* (*von s-n Sorgen*) ~ take s.o.'s mind off his worries. **II** *v/i* **3.** change the subject. **4.** be a diversion: *das lenkt ab* that takes one's mind off things. **'Ablenkung** *f* (-; -en) **1.** deviation, deflection. **2.** diversion, distraction. **'Ablenkungsmanöver** *n* diversion, *fig. a.* red herring.

'ablesen[1] *v/t* (*irr, sep*, -ge-, h, → **lesen**) pick off. **'ablesen**[2] *v/t* (*irr, sep*, -ge-, h, → **lesen**) **1.** read *a speech* (from notes). **2.** 🏺 read: *Strom* (*Gas*) ~ read the gas (electricity) meter. **3.** *fig.* see (*an dat* from): *j-m et. vom Gesicht* ~ read s.th. in s.o.'s face; *j-m e-n Wunsch von den Augen* ~ anticipate s.o.'s wish.

'Ablesung *f* (-; -en) 🏺 reading.

'abliefern *v/t* (*sep*, -ge-, h) deliver (*bei* to, at).

'ablösbar *adj* 🌾 redeemable.

Ablöse ['aplø:zə] *f* (-; -n) F *sports:* transfer fee.

'ablösen *v/t* (*sep*, -ge-, h) **1.** remove, detach. **2.** relieve (*guards etc*), take over from, replace (*a colleague*): *j-n* ~ *a.* relieve s.o. of his duties; *sich* (*or einan-*

'der) ~ take turns (**bei** at). **3.** *fig.* follow. **4.** redeem (*mortgage*), pay off (*debt*).
'Ablösesumme *f sports:* transfer fee.
'Ablösung *f* (-; -en) **1.** removal. **2.** relief. **3.** ✝ redemption, repayment.
'Abluft *f* (-; *no pl*) ⚙ waste air.
'ablutschen *v/t* (*sep*, -ge-, h) lick (off).
'abmachen *v/t* (*sep*, -ge-, h) **1.** remove, take off. **2.** arrange, agree on, settle on: **abgemacht!** agreed!, it's a deal!, o.k.!
'Abmachung *f* (-; -en) arrangement, agreement.
'abmagern *v/i* (*sep*, -ge-, sn) grow thin, lose weight: → **abgemagert**.
'Abmagerungskur *f* (-; -en) (**e-e** ~ **machen** go [*or* be] on a) slimming diet.
'abmalen *v/t* (*sep*, -ge-, h) paint, copy.
'Abmarsch *m* (-[e]s, ⸚e) marching off.
'abmar,schieren *v/i* (*sep*, sn) march off.
'abmelden (*sep*, -ge-, h) **I** *v/t* cancel: **sein Auto** ~ take one's car off the road; **sein Telefon** ~ have one's telephone disconnected; **j-n** ~ a) give notice of s.o.'s change of address (*to the police*), b) cancel s.o.'s membership (*of a club etc*); F **bei mir ist er abgemeldet!** I'm through with him! **II sich** ~ a) give notice of one's change of address (*to the police*), b) cancel one's membership (*of a club etc*); **sich bei j-m** (**vom Dienst** *etc*) ~ report to s.o. that one is leaving.
'Abmeldung *f* (-; -en) **1.** cancel(l)ation. **2.** notice of change of address.
'abmessen *v/t* (*irr*, *sep*, -ge-, h, → **messen**) measure. **'Abmessung** *f* (-; -en) measurement: ~**en** a. dimensions.
'abmon,tieren *v/t* (*sep*, h) ⚙ take off, dismount, remove.
'abmühen: sich ~ (*sep*, -ge-, h) try hard (*to do s.th.*); **sich** ~ **mit** struggle with.
'abmurksen *v/t* (*sep*, -ge-, h) F do s.o. in.
'abmustern *v/t* (*sep*, -ge-, h) ⚓ pay off.
'abnabeln *v/t* (*sep*, -ge-, h) cut a baby's umbilical cord; *fig.* **sich** ~ cut the cord.
'abnagen *v/t* (*sep*, -ge-, h) gnaw off: **e-n Knochen** ~ gnaw (*person:* pick) a bone.
'abnähen *v/t* (*sep*, -ge-, h) take in, tuck.
'Abnäher *m* (-s; -) tuck.
'Abnahme *f* (-; *no pl*) **1.** taking off (*or* down), removal, ✂ amputation. **2.** ✝ (**bei** ~ on) purchase (**von** of). **3.** ⚙ a) acceptance, b) inspection (test). **4.** ~ **e-r Parade** review (of the troops). **5.** *fig.*

decrease, decline, drop (*all: gen* in), loss (*gen* in, *of speed, weight*), flagging (*of interest*), waning (*of the moon*).
'abnehmbar *adj* removable.
'abnehmen (*irr*, *sep*, -ge-, h, → **nehmen**) **I** *v/t* **1.** take off, ⚙ *a.* remove, ✂ *a.* amputate, take down (*picture etc*), shave off (*beard*), gather (*fruit*), pick up (*the receiver*): **j-m Blut** ~ take a blood sample from s.o.; **j-m Fingerabdrücke** ~ take s.o.'s fingerprints. **2. j-m et.** ~ a) relieve s.o. of s.th., save s.o. (*trouble, an errand, etc*), b) take s.th. (away) from s.o., c) charge s.o. s.th.; **j-m zuviel** ~ overcharge s.o. **3.** (*dat* from) buy, purchase: F *fig.* **das nimmt ihm keiner ab!** nobody will buy that! **4.** ⚙ a) accept, b) inspect, test. **5. die Parade** ~ review the troops. **6.** hold (*an examination*): → **Beichte, Eid** etc. **7.** decrease (*meshes*). **8.** lose, get rid of (*pounds, weight*). **II** *v/i* **9.** decrease, diminish, drop (*off*), *strength etc:* decline, *vision etc:* fail, *interest:* flag, *speed:* slacken (off), slow down, *storm:* abate, *moon:* be on the wane, *days:* grow shorter. **10.** a) lose weight, b) be slimming. **'Abnehmer** *m* (-s; -) ✝ a) buyer, b) customer, c) consumer: **keine** ~ **finden** find no market.
'Abneigung *f* (-; -en) (**gegen**) dislike (of, for), aversion (to).
abnorm [ap'nɔrm] *adj* abnormal, *w.s.* exceptional, unusual.
Abnormität [apnɔrmi'tɛːt] *f* (-; -en) **1.** abnormality. **2.** monstrosity.
'abnötigen *v/t* (*sep*, -ge-, h) **j-m Respekt** ~ command s.o.'s respect.
'abnutzen *v/t* (*sep*, -ge-, h) (*a.* **sich** ~) wear out. **'Abnutzung** *f* (-; *no pl*) wear and tear. **'Abnutzungserscheinung** *f* sign of wear, ✝ sign of degeneration.
Abonnement [abɔnə'mãː] *n* (-s; -s) subscription (**auf** *acc* to), *thea. a.* season ticket (**bei** for). **Abonnent** [abɔ'nɛnt] *m* (-en; -en) subscriber (*gen* to), *thea.* season-ticket holder.
abonnieren [abɔ'niːrən] *v/t* (h) subscribe to: **abonniert sein auf** (*acc*) have a subscription to, take (*a paper*).
'abordnen *v/t* (*sep*, -ge-, h) delegate.
'Abordnung *f* (-; -en) delegation.
'abpacken *v/t* (*sep*, -ge-, h) ✝ pack(age).
'abpassen *v/t* (*sep*, -ge-, h) wait for.
'abpausen *v/t* (*sep*, -ge-, h) trace.

'**abpfeifen** v/t, v/i (irr, sep, -ge-, h, → pfeifen) (das Spiel) ~ stop the game.

'**Abpfiff** m (-[e]s; -e) sports: final whistle.

'**abprallen** v/i (sep, -ge-, sn) rebound, bounce off, bullet: ricochet: fig. an j-m ~ make no impression on s.o.

'**Abpraller** m (-s; -) sports: rebound.

'**abputzen** v/t (sep, -ge-, h) clean, wipe: sich die Schuhe ~ wipe one's feet.

'**abquälen: sich ~** (sep, -ge-, h) 1. worry (o.s.), fret. 2. slave (away). 3. → abmühen.

'**abqualifi,zieren** v/t (sep, h) dismiss.

'**abrackern: sich ~** (sep, -ge-, h) F slave (away).

'**abraten** v/i (irr, sep, -ge-, h, → raten) j-m ~ von advise (or warn) s.o. against (doing).

'**abräumen** v/t (sep, -ge-, h) clear away, remove: den Tisch ~ clear the table.

'**abrea,gieren** (sep, h) I v/t (an dat on) abreact, work off. II sich ~ get rid of one's aggressions, F let off steam.

'**abrechnen** (sep, -ge-, h) I v/t deduct, account for (expenses etc). II v/i settle accounts: mit j-m ~ settle up with s.o., fig. a. get even with s.o.

'**Abrechnung** f (-; -en) 1. a) settlement (of accounts), b) statement. 2. fig. requital: Tag der ~ day of reckoning.

'**abreiben** v/t (irr, sep, -ge-, h, → reiben) 1. a) rub off, b) rub down (body). 2. wipe s.th. clean, polish. 3. grate (lemon etc). '**Abreibung** f (-; -en) 1. ≠ rub-down, sponge-down. 2. F beating.

'**Abreise** f (-; -n) (bei m-r etc ~ on my etc) departure (nach for).

'**abreisen** v/i (sep, -ge-, sn) (nach for) depart, leave.

'**Abreiß...** tear-off (pad, calendar, etc).

'**abreißen** (irr, sep, -ge-, → reißen) I v/t (h) a) tear (or pull, rip) off, b) pull down, demolish (building). II v/i (sn) come off, thread etc: snap, fig. break off: die Arbeit reißt nicht ab there's no end of work.

'**abrichten** v/t (sep, -ge-, h) train (animal), break in (horse).

'**abriegeln** v/t (sep, -ge-, h) 1. bolt, bar. 2. block (off), cordon off, ✕ seal off.

'**abringen** v/t (irr, sep, -ge-, h, → ringen) j-m et. ~ wrest s.th. from s.o.; sich ein Lächeln ~ force a smile.

'**Abriß** m (-sses, -sse) 1. a) summary,

outline, b) survey, c) compendium. 2. demolition.

'**abrollen** (sep, -ge-) I v/t (h) unroll, unwind, unreel. II v/i (sn) fig. unfold.

'**abrücken** (sep, -ge-) I v/t (h) move away. II v/i (sn) march off, move off: fig. von j-m disassociate o.s. from s.o.

'**Abruf** m (-[e]s; no pl) 1. recall: sich auf ~ bereithalten stand by. 2. ✝ auf ~ on call. '**abrufbereit** adj on call.

'**abrufen** v/t (irr, sep, -ge-, h, → rufen) 1. call s.o. away, recall. 2. ✝ call (for) (goods). 3. computer: call in (data).

'**abrunden** v/t (sep, -ge-, h) round off: nach oben (unten) ~ round up (down); → abgerundet.

abrupt [ap'rupt] adj abrupt, sudden.

'**abrüsten** v/i (sep, -ge-, h) disarm.

'**Abrüstung** f (-; no pl) disarmament.

'**abrutschen** v/i (sep, -ge-, sn) 1. slip off, slip down, knife: slip. 2. fig. go down.

'**absacken** v/i (sep, -ge-, sn) F 1. sag, a. ✈ sink, ✈ pancake. 2. fig. go down.

'**Absage** f (-; -n) 1. cancel(l)ation. 2. refusal, fig. rejection (an acc of).

'**absagen** (sep, -ge-, h) I v/t cancel, call off. II v/i beg off, cry off: j-m ~ tell s.o. that one can't come.

'**absägen** v/t (sep, -ge-, h) 1. saw off. 2. F fig. ax(e), fire.

'**absahnen** v/t (sep, -ge-, h) F cream off.

'**absatteln** v/t (sep, -ge-, h) unsaddle.

'**Absatz** m (-[e]s; -e) 1. heel: Schuhe mit hohen Absätzen high-heeled shoes. 2. ⌸, print. paragraph: neuer ~ new line. 3. ✝ sale(s): guten (reißenden) ~ finden find a ready market (F sell like hot cakes). 4. (staircase) landing.

'**Absatz,gebiet** n ✝ market(ing area). ~**markt** m, ~**möglichkeit** f ✝ market, outlet. ~**steigerung** f ✝ sales increase. ~**stockung** f ✝ stagnation of trade.

'**Absatztrick** m soccer: backheel trick.

'**absaufen** v/i (irr, sep, -ge-, sn, → saufen) F ✕, mot. be flooded, ✈ go down, person: drown.

'**absaugen** v/t (sep, -ge-, h) 1. suck off, a. ≠ aspirate. 2. vacuum (carpet).

'**abschaben** v/t (sep, -ge-, h) scrape off.

'**abschaffen** v/t (sep, -ge-, h) 1. abolish. 2. get rid of, give up.

'**Abschaffung** f (-; no pl) abolition.

'**abschalten** (sep, -ge-, h) I v/t switch off,

turn off, ⚡ cut off, disconnect. **II** v/i F fig. switch off, relax.

'**abschätzen** v/t (sep, -ge-, h) estimate, a. fig. assess, F fig. size s.o., s.th. up.

'**abschätzend** adj assessing, speculative.
abschätzig ['apʃɛtsɪç] adj contemptuous, disparaging.

'**Abschaum** m (-[e]s; no pl) scum: fig. ~ **der Menschheit** scum of the earth.

'**Abscheu** m (-s; no pl) (**vor** dat, **gegen**) disgust (at, for), loathing (for): **e-n ~ haben vor** (dat) detest, loathe.

'**abscheuern** v/t (sep, -ge-, h) **1.** scrub (off). **2.** rub off, scrape. **3.** (a. **sich ~**) wear thin.

ab'**scheulich** adj dreadful, abominable, heinous, atrocious (a. crime etc).

'**abschicken** v/t (sep, -ge-, h) → **absenden.**

'**abschieben** (irr, sep, -ge-, → **schieben**) **I** v/t (h) **1.** push away (**von** from). **2.** deport. **3.** F get rid of. **II** v/i (sn) **4.** F push off. '**Abschiebung** f (-; -en) 🏛 deportation. '**Abschiebungshaft** f (j-n **in ~ nehmen** put s.o. on) remand pending deportation.

Abschied ['apʃiːt] m (-[e]s; no pl) **1.** farewell, parting, departure: ~ **nehmen** (**von**) take leave (of), say goodby(e) (to); **beim ~, zum ~** on parting. **2.** dismissal, ⚔ discharge, resignation.

'**Abschieds...** farewell (letter, visit, etc).
~kuß m goodby(e) kiss: **j-m e-n ~ geben** kiss s.o. goodby(e). **~schmerz** m (-es; no pl) wrench. **~stunde** f hour of parting. **~worte** pl words of farewell.

'**abschießen** v/t (irr, sep, -ge-, h, → **schießen**) **1.** fire (gun), shoot (bullet, arrow, etc), launch (rocket). **2.** shoot, kill, shoot (or bring) down (plane): F fig. **j-n ~** put the skids under s.o.; → **Vogel** 1.

'**abschirmen** v/t (sep, -ge-, h) (**gegen**) shield (from), protect (against).

'**Abschirmung** f (-; -en) protection.

'**abschlachten** v/t (sep, -ge-, h) a. fig. slaughter.

'**abschlaffen** v/i (sep, -ge-, sn) F wilt: → **abgeschlafft.**

'**Abschlag** m (-[e]s; ⁻e) **1.** soccer: goal kick, golf: tee(-off). **2.** ✝ a) drop (in prices), b) reduction, c) part payment: **auf ~** on account. '**abschlagen** v/t (irr, sep, -ge-, h, → **schlagen**) **1.** knock off

(or down), cut off. **2.** (a. v/i) soccer: kick off, golf: tee off. **3.** beat off (attack). **4.** fig. refuse, turn down.

abschlägig ['apʃlɛːgɪç] adj negative: adm. j-n (j-s Bitte) ~ **bescheiden** reject s.o. (s.o.'s request).

'**Abschlagszahlung** f part payment.

'**abschleifen** v/t (irr, sep, -ge-, h, → **schleifen**) ⚙ grind off, a. fig. polish: **sich ~** a. fig. wear off.

'**Abschleppdienst** m breakdown (Am. wrecking) service. '**abschleppen** v/t (sep, -ge-, h) ⚙, mot. tow off.

'**Abschleppwagen** m breakdown lorry, Am. wrecker (truck).

'**abschließbar** adj lockable.

'**abschließen** (irr, sep, -ge-, h, → **schließen**) **I** v/t **1.** lock (up). **2.** shut off, ⚙ a. seal (off): → **abgeschlossen** 2. **3.** a) end, close, finish, b) complete; → **abgeschlossen** 1. **4.** ✝ conclude, sign (contract), settle (accounts), close, balance (books), effect (sale): **e-n Handel ~** strike a bargain, close a deal; **e-e Versicherung ~** take out a policy; → **Wette.** **II** v/i **5.** end, close (a. ✝), finish: **mit dem Leben abgeschlossen haben** have done with life.

'**abschließend** **I** adj concluding, closing, final. **II** adv in conclusion, finally.

'**Abschluß** m (-sses; ⁻sse) **1.** no pl conclusion, ✝ closing (of books etc), settlement (of accounts): **zum ~** → **abschließend** II; **et. zum ~ bringen** bring s.th. to a close. **2.** ✝ deal, sale. **3.** F ped., univ. final examination. **~prüfung** f **1.** final examination, finals, Am. a. graduation: **s-e ~ machen** (**an** dat) graduate (at, Am. from). **2.** ✝ audit (of books). **~zeugnis** n (school-)leaving certificate, Am. (high-school) diploma.

'**abschmecken** v/t (sep, -ge-, h) season.

'**abschmieren** v/t (sep, -ge-, h) ⚙ grease.

'**abschminken** v/t (sep, -ge-, h) (a. **sich ~**) take off (or remove) s.o.'s (one's) make-up: F fig. **das kannst du dir ~!** forget it!

'**abschnallen** v/t (sep, -ge-, h) undo, take off: **sich ~** unfasten one's seat belt.

'**abschneiden** (irr, sep, -ge-, h, → **schneiden**) **I** v/t **1.** cut off (a. fig. supplies etc): **j-m den Weg ~** bar s.o.'s way; **j-m das Wort ~** cut s.o. short. **II** v/i **2.** (**den Weg**) ~ take a short cut. **3.** **gut** (*schlecht*) ~ do (*or* come off) well (badly). '**Abschneiden** *n* (-s) performance.

'**Abschnitt** *m* (-[e]s, -e) **1.** section, paragraph (*of a book etc*) **2.** *biol.*, ⚕ segment. **3.** *a.* ✗ sector. **4.** period, phase, stage (*a. of a trip*). **5.** 🛉 counterfoil, stub (*of ticket etc*), coupon.

'**abschnüren** *v/t* (*sep*, -ge-, h) **1.** → *abbinden* 2. **2.** *esp.* ✗ cut off. **3.** *j-m die Luft* ~ choke s.o.

'**abschöpfen** *v/t* (*sep*, -ge-, h) skim off (*a.* 🛉 *profits*), 🛉 absorb (*excessive buying power*): *a. fig. den Rahm* ~ take the cream off.

'**abschotten: sich** ~ (*sep*, -ge-, h) *fig.* batten down the hatches, seal o.s. off.

'**abschrägen** *v/t* (*sep*, -ge-, h) bevel.

'**abschrauben** *v/t* (*sep*, -ge-, h) screw off.

'**abschrecken** *v/t* (*sep*, -ge-, h) **1.** deter, put *s.o.* off. **2.** ⚙ quench. **3.** *gastr.* rinse with cold water. '**abschreckend** *adj* deterrent: *~es Beispiel* warning; *~e Strafe* exemplary punishment; *~ wirken* act as a deterrent.

'**Abschreckung** *f* (-; -en) deterrence: *zur* ~ *dienen* act as a deterrent.

'**Abschreckungs**|**poli,tik** *f* policy of deterrence. *~waffe f* deterrent (weapon).

'**abschreiben** (*irr*, *sep*, -ge-, h, → *schreiben*) **I** *v/t* **1.** copy (out), *ped.* crib. **2.** 🛉 depreciate, write down (*equipment*), *totally*: write off (*a.* F *fig. s.o.*, *s.th.*), deduct (*amount*). **II** *v/i* **3.** *ped.* crib. '**Abschreibung** *f* (-; -en) 🛉 depreciation, write-off.

'**Abschrift** *f* (-; -en) copy: → *beglaubigt.*

'**abschürfen** *v/t* (*sep*, -ge-, h) 🛉 graze. '**Abschürfung** *f* (-; -en) 🛉 graze.

'**Abschuß** *m* (-sses; ⸚sse) **1.** discharge (*of gun*). **2.** launching (*of rocket*).

abschüssig ['apʃYsɪç] *adj* steep.

'**Abschußliste** *f* F hit list: *j-n auf die* ~ *setzen* put the skids under s.o.; *auf der* ~ *stehen* be a marked man.

'**Abschußrampe** *f* launching pad.

'**abschütteln** *v/t* (*sep*, -ge-, h) *a. fig.* shake off.

'**abschwächen** (*sep*, -ge-, h) **I** *v/t* weaken, soften (*a. impact*), tone down (*a. remark etc*). **II** *sich* ~ weaken, noise, storm, *etc*: subside.

'**abschweifen** *v/i* (*sep*, -ge-, sn) *fig.* deviate, stray, *thoughts etc*: wander: *vom Thema* ~ digress (from one's subject).

'**abschwellen** *v/i* (*irr*, *sep*, -ge-, sn, → *schwellen*) **1.** 🛉 go down. **2.** *noise*: die down.

'**abschwirren** *v/i* (*sep*, -ge-, sn) F buzz off.

'**abschwören** *v/i* (*irr*, *sep*, -ge-, h, → *schwören*) *s-m Glauben* ~ renounce one's faith.

'**absegnen** *v/t* (*sep*, -ge-, h) F *humor.* give one's blessing to.

'**absehbar** *adj in ~er Zeit* in the foreseeable future. '**absehen** (*irr*, *sep*, -ge-, h, → *sehen*) **I** *v/t* **1.** foresee: *es ist kein Ende abzusehen* there's no end in sight. **2.** *es abgesehen haben auf* (*acc*) a) be out to get, have an eye on, b) *j-n* F have it in for s.o. **3.** → *abgucken.* **II** *v/i* **4.** ~ *von* a) refrain from, b) disregard: → *abgesehen.*

'**abseifen** *v/t* (*sep*, -ge-, h) soap down.

'**abseilen** (*sep*, -ge-, h) *v/t* (*a. sich* ~) rope down: F *fig. sich* ~ make off.

'**absein** *v/i* (*irr*, *sep*, -ge-, sn) → *ab* 2, 9.

abseits ['apzaɪts] **I** *prep* (*gen*) off *the road etc.* **II** *adv* ~ *stehen* stand aside, *sports*: be offside: ~ *liegen* be out of the way; *fig. sich* ~ *halten* keep aloof.

'**Abseits** *n* (-; -) *sports*: (*im* ~ *stehen* be) offside; *fig. sich ins* ~ *manövrieren, ins* ~ *geraten* get (o.s.) isolated. *~falle f sports*: offside trap. *~tor n sports*: goal scored from an offside position.

'**absenden** *v/t* (*irr*, *sep*, -ge-, h, → *senden*) send (off), dispatch, forward, post, *Am.* mail. '**Absender** *m* (-s; -) **1.** sender. **2.** sender's address.

'**absetzbar** *adj* **1.** 🛉 sal(e)able. **2.** (*steuerlich* ~) deductible (for taxation). **3.** *official etc*: removable.

'**absetzen** (*sep*, -ge-, h) **I** *v/t* **1.** set down (*load*), take off (*hat, glasses, etc*), lift (*violin bow*). **2.** set down (*passengers*), drop (*a. parachutist*). **3.** remove (*official* from office), depose (*ruler*). **4.** cancel (*meeting etc*), remove (*item on the agenda*), take off (*film etc*). **5.** 🛉 a) deduct, b) sell: *steuerlich* ~ deduct from tax. **6.** 🛉 stop taking (*a medicament*), go off (*a drug*), break off (*treatment*). **7.** *print.* set (up) in type: *e-e Zeile* ~ begin a new paragraph. **8.** 🛉 *etc* deposit. **II** *v/i* **9.** stop, break off: *ohne abzusetzen* in one go, *drink* in one gulp. **III** *sich* ~ **10.** ✗ retreat, *sports*: *runner etc*: break

away, F *fig.* make off. **'Absetzung** *f* (-; -en) **1.** removal (from office), deposition (*of a ruler*). **2.** cancel(l)ation (*of a meeting etc*), withdrawal (*of a film etc*).
absichern (*sep*, -ge-, h) **I** *v/t* → **sichern.** **II** *sich* ~ cover o.s.
'Absicht *f* (-; -en) intention, *a.* 🏛 intent, aim, object: **in der ~ zu** *inf* with the intention of *ger*; **ich habe die ~ zu kommen** I intend (*or* I'm planning) to come; **mit e-r bestimmten ~** for a purpose; **mit ~** on purpose. **'absichtlich** **I** *adj* intentional, deliberate, *esp.* 🏛 wil(l)ful. **II** *adv* intentionally *etc*, on purpose. **'Absichtserklärung** *f* (-; -en) declaration of intent.
'absitzen (*irr*, *sep*, -ge-, → **sitzen**) **I** *v/i* (sn) *rider*: dismount. **II** *v/t* (h) F sit out (*time*), serve (*a sentence*).
absolut [apzo'lu:t] *adj* absolute, total, complete: ~ **nicht** by no means.
Absolution [apzolu'tsjo:n] *f* (-; -en) *eccl.* absolution.
Absolutismus [apzolu'tismʊs] *m* (-; *no pl*) *pol.* absolutism.
Absolvent [apzɔl'vɛnt] *m* (-en; -en), **Absol'ventin** *f* (-; -nen) school-leaver, *Am.* graduate. **absol'vieren** [apzɔl'vi:rən] *v/t* (h) **1.** *ped.* finish, *Am.* graduate from. **2.** attend, complete (*a course*). **3.** pass (*an exam*). **4.** F do, get through.
ab'sonderlich *adj* odd, peculiar.
'absondern (*sep*, -ge-, h) **I** *v/t* **1.** separate, 🐾 isolate. **2.** *biol.* secrete. **II** *sich* ~ *fig.* cut o.s. off (**von** from).
'Absonderung *f* (-; -en) **1.** separation, 🐾 isolation. **2.** *biol.* secretion.
absorbieren [apzɔr'bi:rən] *v/t* (h) *a. fig.* absorb.
'abspalten *v/t* (*irr*, *sep*, -ge-, h, → **spalten**) (*a. sich* ~) split off.
'Abspann *m* (-[e]s, -e) *film*, *TV* end titles (and credits).
'Abspannung *f* (-; *no pl*) exhaustion.
'absparen *v/t* (*sep*, -ge-, h) **sich et. (vom Munde)** ~ pinch and scrape for s.th.
'abspecken (*sep*, -ge-, h) F → **abnehmen** 8, 10.
'abspeisen *v/t* (*sep*, -ge-, h) F feed: *fig.* **j-n ~ mit** fob s.o. off with.
abspenstig ['apʃpɛnstɪç] ~ **machen** lure away (*dat* from), **j-m die Freundin ~ machen** steal s.o.'s girl(friend).
'absperren *v/t* (*sep*, -ge-, h) **1.** block off

(*road*), *police*: cordon off. **2.** turn (*adm.* cut) off (*gas etc*). **3.** *dial.* lock (up).
'Absperrhahn *m* ⚙ stopcock. **'Absperrung** *f* (-; -en) **1.** barrier, cordon. **2.** blocking off (*etc*, → **absperren**).
'abspielen (*sep*, -ge-, h) **I** *v/t* **1.** play (*record*, *tape*, *etc*). **2.** pass (*the ball*). **II** *sich* ~ a) happen, take place, b) be going on: F **da spielt sich nichts ab!** nothing doing!
'absplittern *v/i* (*sep*, -ge-, sn) *and* *v/t* (h) (*a. sich* ~ *fig.* group) splinter off.
'Absprache *f* (-; -en) arrangement: **laut ~** → **'absprachegemäß** *adv* as agreed.
'absprechen (*irr*, *sep*, -ge-, h, → **sprechen**) **I** *v/t* **1.** *j-m et.* ~ dispute (*or* deny) s.o.'s *talent etc*; 🏛 **j-m ein Recht ~** deprive s.o. of a right. **2.** agree (up)on, arrange. **II** *sich mit j-m* ~ agree with s.o. (**über** *acc* about).
'abspringen *v/i* (*irr*, *sep*, -ge-, sn, → **springen**) **1.** jump off, *sports*: **a.** take off, ✈ jump, bail out, *varnish etc*: come off, *ball etc*: bounce off. **2.** F *fig.* quit, get (*or* back) out (**von** of).
'abspritzen *v/t* (*sep*, -ge-, h) hose down.
'Absprung *m* (-[e]s; ⁔e) jump, *sports*: take-off. **~balken** *m* take-off board.
'abspulen *v/t* (*sep*, -ge-, h) unreel.
'abspülen *v/t* (*sep*, -ge-, h) rinse (off).
'abstammen *v/i* (*sep*, *no pp*) (**von** from) be descended, *ling.* be derived.
'Abstammung *f* (-; *no pl*) **1.** descent, origin: **deutscher ~** of German extraction. **2.** *ling.* derivation. **'Abstammungslehre** *f* theory of evolution.
'Abstand *m* (-[e]s; ⁔e) **1.** distance (*a. fig.*), space, *a. time*: interval, *fig.* gap, difference: **mit ~** a) **besser** far better, b) **gewinnen** win by a wide margin; **in regelmäßigen Abständen** at regular intervals; *fig.* **~ halten** (*or* **wahren**) keep one's distance; **von et. ~ nehmen** refrain from (doing) s.th. **2.** → **'Abstandssumme** *f* indemnity.
abstatten ['apʃtatən] *v/t* (*sep*, -ge-, h) *j-m* **e-n Besuch ~** pay s.o. a visit; → **Dank.**
'abstauben (*sep*, -ge-, h) **I** *v/t* **1.** dust. **2.** F swipe. **II** *v/i* **3.** *soccer*: tap the ball in.
'abstechen (*irr*, *sep*, -ge-, h, → **stechen**) **I** *v/t* stick (*pigs*). **II** *v/i* ~ **von** stand out against (*fig.* from).
'Abstecher *m* (-s; -) *a. fig.* excursion.
'abstecken *v/t* (*sep*, -ge-, h) **1.** fit (*dress*

etc). **2.** mark out (*area, course, etc*), stake out, mark (*borders etc*). **3.** *fig.* define (*positions*).

'abstehen *v/i* (*irr, sep,* -ge-, h, → **stehen**) stick out.

Absteige ['apʃtaigə] *f* (-; -n) F *contp.* dosshouse, *Am.* flophouse. **'absteigen** *v/i* (*irr, sep,* -ge-, sn, → **steigen**) **1.** climb down, get off (*a bike, horse*). **2.** (*in dat* at) stay, put up. **3.** *sports:* go down, be relegated. **'Absteiger** *m* (-s; -) *sports:* relegated team (*or* club).

'abstellen *v/t* (*sep,* -ge-, h) **1.** put down. **2.** leave (*bei* with), *mot.* park. **3.** turn (*adm.* cut) off (*gas etc*), stop (*machine*), switch off (*radio, engine, etc*). **4.** *fig.* remedy, stop (*grievances*). **5.** *fig.* (*auf acc*) gear (to), aim (at). **6.** → **abkommandieren.**

'Abstell│fläche *f mot.* parking space. **~gleis** *n* 🚂 siding: *fig. j-n aufs* ~ **schieben** shelve s.o. **~raum** *m* storeroom.

'abstempeln *v/t* (*sep,* -ge-, h) stamp (*a. fig.*), postmark.

'absterben *v/i* (*irr, sep,* -ge-, sn, → **sterben**)**1.** die (*a. fig.*), *toes etc:* go numb. **2.** F *mot.* stall.

Abstieg ['apʃtiːk] *m* (-[e]s; -e) **1.** descent, way down. **2.** *fig.* decline, comedown. **3.** *sports:* relegation.

'abstillen *v/t* (*sep,* -ge-, h) wean (*baby*).

'abstimmen (*sep,* -ge-, h) **I** *v/i* **1.** vote (*über acc* on): *über et.* ~ *lassen* put s.th. to the vote. **II** *v/t* **2.** (*auf acc*) tune (to), *a.* match colo(u)rs (with), tune (to), *a.* match colo(u)rs (with): *aufeinander* ~ synchronize. **3.** ⚖ balance (*accounts*). **III** *sich* ~ come to an agreement (*mit* with). **'Abstimmung** *f* (-; -en) **1.** voting, vote (*über acc* on), poll: *die* ~ *ist geheim* voting is by ballot; *e-e* ~ *vornehmen* take a vote. **2.** tuning (*etc*, → **abstimmen** II).

abstinent [apstiˈnɛnt] *adj* abstinent, abstemious. **Abstinenz** [apstiˈnɛnts] *f* (-; *no pl*) (total) abstinence.

Absti'nenzler *m* (-s; -) teetotal(l)er.

'Abstoß *m* (-[e]s; ⸚e) *soccer:* goal kick.

'abstoßen (*irr, sep,* -ge-, h, → **stoßen**) **I** *v/t* **1.** (*a. v/i*) push off (*boat etc*). **2.** knock, batter (*furniture*), scuff (*shoes*). **3.** shed (*skin, antlers*): → **Horn** 1. **4.** 🏷 reject (*tissue etc*). **5.** *phys.* repel. **6.** *fig.* get rid of. **7.** ⚖ a) sell off, b) get out of

(debt). **8.** *fig.* repel, disgust. **II** *v/i* **9.** *soccer:* take a goal kick. **'abstoßend** *adj fig.* repulsive (*a. phys.*), repellent, revolting. **'Abstoßung** *f* (-; *no pl*) **1.** *phys., a. fig.* repulsion. **2.** 🏷 rejection.

'abstottern *v/t* (*sep,* -ge-, h) F *et.* ~ pay for s.th. in install(l)ments.

abstrahieren [apstraˈhiːrən] *v/t, v/i* (h) abstract. **abstrakt** [apˈstrakt] *adj* abstract. **Abstraktion** [apstrakˈtsi̯oːn] *f* (-; -en) abstraction. **Abstraktum** [apˈstraktʊm] *n* (-s; -ta) abstract noun.

'abstreifen *v/t* (*sep,* -ge-, h) **1.** slip off. **2.** wipe (*shoes*). **3.** search, scour.

'abstreiten *v/t* (*irr, sep,* -ge-, h, → **streiten**) **1.** deny. **2.** → **absprechen** 1.

'Abstrich *m* (-[e]s; -e) **1.** (*an dat* in) cut, curtailment: *fig.* ~*e machen müssen* have to lower one's sights. **2.** 🏷 (*e-n* ~ *machen*) take a) smear (*from tonsils:* swab). **3.** downstroke, ♪ down-bow.

abstrus [apˈstruːs] *adj* abstruse.

'abstufen *v/t* (*sep,* -ge-, h) **1.** terrace. **2.** shade off. **3.** *fig.* grade, graduate. **'Abstufung** *f* (-; -en) **1.** shade. **2.** *fig.* gradation.

'abstumpfen (*sep,* -ge-) **I** *v/t* (h) *a. fig.* blunt, dull: *j-n* ~ make s.o. insensible. **II** *v/i* (sn) become blunt (*fig.* dulled, *person:* insensible); → **abgestumpft.**

'Absturz *m* (-[e]s; ⸚e) **1.** plunge, ✈ crash. **2.** downfall. **'abstürzen** *v/i* (*sep,* -ge-, sn) plunge (down), ✈ crash.

'abstützen *v/t* (*sep,* -ge-, h) △ prop.

'absuchen *v/t* (*sep,* -ge-, h) (*nach* for) search all over, scour, comb (*area*), sweep, scan (*horizon, sky*).

absurd [apˈzʊrt] *adj* absurd. **Absurdität** [apzʊrdiˈtɛːt] *f* (-; -en) absurdity.

Abszeß [apsˈtsɛs] *m* (-sses; -sse) abscess. **Abszisse** [apsˈtsɪsə] *f* (-; -n) ⚖ abscissa.

Abt [apt] *m* (-[e]s; ⸚e) *eccl.* abbot.

'abtasten *v/t* (*sep,* -ge-, h) **1.** feel (*nach* for), 🏷 palpate: *fig. j-n* ~ feel s.o. out, size s.o. up. **2.** ⚡, *TV* scan.

'abtauchen *v/i* (*sep,* -ge-, sn) **1.** dive under. **2.** F *fig.* go to earth.

'abtauen (*sep,* -ge-) **I** *v/t* (h) thaw (*ice*), defrost (*refrigerator*). **II** *v/i* (sn) thaw.

Abtei [apˈtai] *f* (-; -en) *eccl.* abbey.

Abteil [apˈtail] *n* (-[e]s; -e) compartment.

'abteilen *v/t* (*sep,* -ge-, h) divide, partition off. **'Abteilung** *f* (-; -en) division, partitioning.

Ab'teilung² f (-; -en) **1.** department, ✗ ward. **2.** ✗ detachment. **3.** sports: section, squad.

Ab'teilungsleiter(in f) m a) head of a department, b) floor manager(ess).

'**abtippen** v/t (sep, -ge-, h) F type (out).

Äbtissin ['εp'tɪsɪn] f (-; -nen) abbess.

'**abtöten** v/t (sep, -ge-, h) kill, deaden.

'**abtragen** v/t (irr, sep, -ge-, h, → tragen) **1.** clear away, pull down (house), level (hill). **2.** (a. sich ~) wear out. **3.** pay off.

abträglich ['aptrε:klɪç] adj detrimental (dat to).

'**abtrai,nieren** v/t (sep, h) work off.

'**Abtrans,port** m (-[e]s; -e) transportation. '**abtranspor,tieren** v/t (sep, h) take away.

'**abtreiben** (irr, sep, -ge-, → treiben) I v/t (h) **1.** ✗ abort. II v/i **2.** (h) ✗ have an abortion. **3.** (sn) drift off (course).

'**Abtreibung** f (-; -en) ✗ (e-e ~ vornehmen lassen have) an abortion.

'**abtrennen** v/t (sep, -ge-, h) **1.** separate. **2.** detach. **3.** take off (sleeve etc). **4.** sever (limb).

'**abtreten** (irr, sep, -ge-, → treten) I v/t (h) **1.** (dat, an acc to) give up, ⚖ cede: j-m et. ~ a. let s.o. have s.th. **2.** wear (out) (carpet etc), wear down (heels etc). **3.** wipe off (mud, snow): F (sich) die Füße ~ wipe one's shoes. II v/i (sn) **4.** go off, thea. (make one's exit (a. F fig.), government etc: resign. **5.** ✗ ~! dismiss! '**Abtretung** f (-; -en) (an acc to) ⚖ transfer, cession.

'**abtrocknen** v/t, v/i (sep, -ge-, h) dry: (Geschirr) ~ dry up.

abtrünnig ['aptrynɪç] adj unfaithful, disloyal: ~ werden (dat) → abfallen 6, 7. **Abtrünnige** ['aptrynɪgə] m, f (-n; -n) deserter, eccl. apostate.

'**abtun** v/t (irr, sep, -ge-, h, → tun) fig. dismiss (als as).

'**abtupfen** v/t (sep, -ge-, h) dab.

'**abverlangen** v/t (sep, h) → abfordern.

'**abwägen** v/t (irr, sep, -ge-, h, → wägen) fig. weigh.

'**abwählen** v/t (sep, -ge-, h) **1.** j-n ~ vote s.o. out of office. **2.** ped. drop (subject).

'**abwälzen** v/t (sep, -ge-, h) **1.** (auf acc on[to]) shuffle off, offload: die Verantwortung auf j-n ~ shift the responsibility (F pass the buck) to s.o.

'**abwandeln** v/t (sep, -ge-, h) modify.

'**abwandern** v/i (sep, -ge-, sn) **1.** move (away), migrate, sports: leave (the club). **2.** † capital: be drained off.

'**Abwanderung** f (-; -en) migration, a. † exodus, of scientists: brain drain.

'**Abwandlung** f (-; -en) modification.

'**Abwärme** f (-; no pl) waste heat.

'**abwarten** (sep, -ge-, h) I v/t wait for: das bleibt abzuwarten that remains to be seen. II v/i wait (and see): F ~ (und Tee trinken)! (let's) wait and see!

abwärts ['apvεrts] adv down, downward(s). '**abwärtsgehen** v/impers (irr, sep, -ge-, sn, → gehen) es geht abwärts mit s.o., s.th. is going downhill.

'**Abwärtstrend** m downward trend.

'**Abwasch** m (-[e]s; no pl) **1.** washing-up: F das ist ein ~! that can be done in one go! **2.** dirty dishes. '**abwaschbar** adj washable. '**abwaschen** (irr, sep, -ge-, h, → waschen) I v/t wash off, wash up. II v/i do the dishes, do the washing-up.

'**Abwaschwasser** n dishwater.

'**Abwasser** n (-s; ⁀) waste water, sewage.

'**Abwasserleitung** f sewerage.

'**abwechseln** v/i (sep, -ge-, h) alternate, persons: (a. sich ~) a. take turns (bei in), rotate. '**abwechselnd** I adj alternating. II adv alternately, by turns.

'**Abwechslung** f (-; -en) change, diversion: ~ brauchen need a change; ~ bringen in (acc) vary, liven up; zur ~ for a change. '**abwechslungsreich** adj varied, life: eventful.

'**Abweg** m (-[e]s; -e) fig. auf ~e geraten go astray. **abwegig** ['apve:gɪç] adj **1.** wrong. **2.** absurd.

'**Abwehr** f (-; no pl) **1.** warding off, repulse (of attack etc). **2.** sports: a) defen/ce (Am. -se), b) by goalkeeper: save. **3.** fig. refusal. **4.** (auf ~ stoßen meet with) resistance. **5.** F ✗ counterintelligence. '**abwehren** (sep, -ge-, h) I v/t **1.** a) beat back, repulse (attack), b) sports: block (shot, punch), c) fig. ward off (danger etc). **2.** fig. refuse (thanks). II v/i **3.** fig. refuse. **4.** sports: block, goalkeeper: save, soccer: clear.

'**Abwehr|haltung** f psych. defensiveness. **~kräfte** pl ✗ resistance. **~mecha,nismus** m defen/ce (Am. -se) mechanism. **~reakti,on** f defensive reaction (gegen to). **~spieler(in** f) m sports: defender, *pl* defen/ce (*Am.* -se). **~stoffe** *pl* ✻ antibodies.

'abweichen *v/i* (*irr, sep,* -ge-, sn, → **wei-chen**) deviate (**vom Kurs** from the course), depart (**von der Regel** from the rule): (**voneinander**) ~ differ, vary; **vom Thema** ~ digress from the subject.

'abweichend *adj* divergent: (**voneinan-der**) ~ differing, varying.

'Abweichler *m* (-s; -) *pol.* deviationist.

'Abweichung *f* (-; -en) **1.** difference. **2.** (**von** from) deviation, digression, departure.

'abweiden *v/t* (*sep,* -ge-, h) crop.

'abweisen *v/t* (*irr, sep,* -ge-, h, → **wei-sen**) **1.** turn *s.o.* away, refuse to see: **schroff** ~ rebuff. **2.** reject, refuse, ⚖️ dismiss. **3.** ✗ repulse. **'abweisend** *adj* unfriendly, cool. **'Abweisung** *f* (-; -en) rejection, refusal, ⚖️ *etc* dismissal.

'abwenden *v/t* (*irr, sep,* -ge-, h, → **wen-den**) turn away (*a.* **sich ~**), *a. fig.* avert, ward off: **sich** (**innerlich**) ~ **von** turn one's back on.

'abwerben *v/t* (*irr, sep,* -ge-, h, → **wer-ben**) entice away.

'abwerfen *v/t* (*irr, sep,* -ge-, h, → **wer-fen**) **1.** throw off (*coat etc*). **2.** drop (*bombs*). **3.** throw (*rider*). **4.** shed (*skin, leaves, etc*). **5.** discard (*playing card*). **6.** *fig.* yield (*profit*), bear (*interest*).

'abwerten *v/t* (*sep,* -ge-, h) ✝ devalue.

'abwertend *adj fig.* depreciative.

'Abwertung *f* (-; -en) **1.** ✝ devaluation. **2.** *fig.* depreciation.

'abwesend *adj* **1.** absent, *pred* away, out, not in. **2.** *fig.* absent-minded, faraway (*look*). **'Abwesende** *m, f* (-n; -n) absentee: **die ~n** those absent.

'Abwesenheit *f* (-; *no pl*) **1.** (**durch ~ glänzen** be conspicuous by one's) absence. **2.** *fig.* absent-mindedness.

'abwetzen *v/t* (*sep,* -ge-, h) wear out.

'abwickeln *v/t* (*sep,* -ge-, h) **1.** unwind. **2.** ✝ deal with, handle (*orders*), transact, settle (*business*), carry out (*or* through), conduct, ⚖️ wind up.

'Abwicklung *f* (-; -en) ✝ handling, settlement, ⚖️ winding-up, *Am.* wind-up.

'abwiegen *v/t* (*irr, sep,* -ge-, h, → **wie-gen**) weigh out.

'abwimmeln *v/t* (*sep,* -ge-, h) F brush *s.o.* off.

'abwinkeln *v/t* (*sep,* -ge-, h) bend.

'abwinken (*sep,* -ge-, h) **I** *v/t mot. racing:* flag down. **II** *v/i* give a sign of refusal.

'abwischen *v/t* (*sep,* -ge-, h) a) wipe *s.th.* (clean), b) wipe *s.th.* off.

abwracken ['apvrakən] *v/t* (*sep,* -ge-, h) break up, scrap.

'abwürgen *v/t* (*sep,* -ge-, h) **1.** stall, kill (*engine*). **2.** *fig.* choke off (*discussion*).

'abzahlen *v/t* (*sep,* -ge-, h) a) pay off, b) pay by instal(l)ments.

'abzählen *v/t* (*sep,* -ge-, h) a) count, b) count out: F **das kann man sich an den Fingern ~** that's not hard to guess.

'Abzahlung *f* (-; -en) a) payment by (*Am.* on) instal(l)ments, b) payment (in full), c) instal(l)ment: **auf ~** on hire purchase, on the instal(l)ment plan.

'abzapfen *v/t* (*sep,* -ge-, h) tap, draw.

abzäunen ['aptsɔynən] *v/t* (*sep,* -ge-, h) fence off (*or* in).

'Abzeichen *n* (-s; -) badge, ✗ *a.* insignia, ✈ marking.

'abzeichnen (*sep,* -ge-, h) **I** *v/t* **1.** (**von** from) copy, draw. **2.** initial, sign. **II sich ~ 3.** stand out (**gegen** against), show. **4.** *fig.* be emerging, be in the offing, *danger etc*: loom.

'abziehen (*irr, sep,* -ge-, → **ziehen**) **I** *v/t* (h) **1.** take off, pull off (*ring etc*). **2.** strip off (*skin, bedsheets*), strip (*bed*), skin (*rabbit, tomato, etc*). **3.** take out (*key*). **4.** (**von** from) ⅋ subtract, ✝ deduct. **5.** make a copy (*or* copies) of, *phot.* print. **6.** whet, sharpen (*knife*), surface (*parquet*). **7.** ✗ withdraw. **8.** draw off, tap. **9.** F give, throw (*a party*): → **Schau** 2. **II** *v/i*(sn) **10.** move off, F *a.* go off, clear out (*or* off), *esp.* ✗ *a.* withdraw. **11.** *smoke:* escape. **12.** *storm:* pass.

'abzielen *v/i* (*sep,* -ge-, h) **~ auf** (*acc*) aim at, be aimed at.

'Abzug *m* (-[e]s; ⁓e) **1.** *no pl esp.* ✗ withdrawal. **2.** ☯ outlet, escape. **3.** copy, *phot.* print, *print.* proof. **4.** ✝ a) deduction, b) discount: **nach ~ aller Kosten** all charges deducted; **vor** (**nach**) **~ der Steuern** before (after) taxation. **5.** trigger (*of gun*). **abzüglich** ['aptsy:klɪç] *prep* (*gen*) less, deducting.

'abzugsfähig *adj* deductible.

'Abzugshaube *f* cooker hood.

'Abzugsrohr *n* ☯ offlet.

'Abzweigdose *f* ⚡ conduit box.

'abzweigen (*sep*, -ge-) **I** *v/i* (sn) branch off. **II** *v/t* (h) set aside.

'Abzweigung *f* (-; -en) turn-off.

Accessoires [aksɛ'sõa:r(s)] *pl* accessories.

Acetat [atse'ta:t] *n* (-s; -e) 🜊 acetate.

ach [ax] *int* oh!: ~ **je!** oh dear!; ~ **komm!** come on!; ~ **nein?** you don't say so?; ~ **so!** oh, I see!; ~ **was!**, ~ **wo!** of course not!; ~ **und weh schreien** wail. **Ach:** F **mit ~ und Krach** by the skin of one's teeth; **mit ~ und Krach durch e-e Prüfung kommen** scrape through an exam.

Achat [a'xa:t] *m* (-[e]s; -e) *min.* agate.

Achillesferse [a'xɪləs-] *f* (-; *no pl*) *fig.* Achilles' heel. **A'chillessehne** *f anat.* Achilles' tendon.

Achse ['aksə] *f* (-; -n) axis, *pl* axes, ⚙ axle: F **auf** (**der**) ~ **sein** be on the move.

Achsel ['aksəl] *f* (-; -n) shoulder: **die ~** (*or* **mit den ~n**) **zucken** shrug one's shoulders. **~höhle** *f* armpit. **~zucken** *n* (-s) shrug (of one's shoulders).

'Achsschenkel *m* (-s; -) *mot.* stub axle, *Am.* steering knuckle.

'Achsschenkelbolzen *m mot.* kingpin.

acht [axt] *adj* eight: **in ~ Tagen** in a week('s time); **heute in ~ Tagen** today week; **vor ~ Tagen** a week ago; **alle ~ Tage** once a week.

Acht[1] *f* (-; -en) eight.

Acht[2] *f* (-; *no pl*) *hist.* outlawry.

Acht[3]: **außer ~ lassen** disregard; **et. in ~ nehmen** take care of s.th., watch s.th; **sich in ~ nehmen vor** (*dat*) beware of.

'achte *adj* eighth: **am ~n Mai** on the eighth of May, on May the eighth.

'Achteck *n* (-[e]s; -e) ◮ octagon.

Achtel ['axtəl] *n* (-s; -) eighth (part). **~note** *f* ♪ quaver. **~takt** *m* ♪ quaver time.

achten ['axtən] (h) **I** *v/t* **1.** respect. **2.** observe (*laws*). **II** *v/i* ~ **auf** (*acc*) a) pay attention to, b) keep an eye on, c) be careful with, d) attach importance to; ~ **Sie darauf, daß** ... see to it that ...

ächten ['ɛçtən] *v/t* (h) *hist.* outlaw, *fig.* ostracize.

achtens ['axtəns] *adv* eighthly.

'Achter *m* (-s; -) *rowing:* eight. **~bahn** *f* roller coaster. **~deck** *n* ⚓ quarterdeck.

'achtfach *adj* and *adv* eightfold.

'achtgeben *v/i* (*irr*, *sep*, -ge-, h, → **geben**) ~ **auf** (*acc*) → **achten** **II** a-c; **gib acht!** look out!, be careful!

'acht'hundert *adj* eight hundred.

achtjährig ['axtjɛ:rɪç] *adj* **1.** eight-year-old. **2.** *period etc* of eight years.

'achtlos *adj* careless, thoughtless.

'Achtlosigkeit *f* (-; *no pl*) carelessness.

'achtmal *adv* eight times.

'achtsam *adj* attentive, careful.

Acht'stundentag *m* eight-hour day.

'achtstündig [-ʃtʏndɪç] *adj* eight-hour.

'achttägig [-tɛ:gɪç] *adj* lasting a week, a week's *trip etc.*

'Achtung *f* (-; *no pl*) **1.** (**vor** for) respect, esteem: **große ~ genießen** be highly regarded; **in j-s ~ steigen** rise in s.o.'s esteem; **sich ~ verschaffen** make o.s. respected; F **alle ~!** hats off! **2.** ~! look out!, *esp. adm. and* ✗ attention!, *on signboards:* danger!, caution!

'Ächtung *f* (-; -en) *hist.* outlawing, *fig.* ostracism.

'Achtungserfolg *m* succès d'estime.

'achtungsvoll *adj* respectful.

'achtzehn *adj* eighteen.

achtzig ['axtsɪç] *adj* eighty: F **auf ~ sein** be hopping mad. **'Achtzig** *f* (-; *no pl*) eighty: **er ist Mitte** (**der**) ~ he is in his mid-eighties. **achtziger** ['axttsɪgər] *adj* **die ~ Jahre** the eighties. **'Achtziger** *m* (-s; -), **'Achtzigerin** *f* (-; -nen) octogenarian, man (woman) in his (her) eighties. **'achtzigst** *adj* eightieth.

ächzen ['ɛçtsən] *v/i* (h) groan (**vor** with).

Acker ['akər] *m* (-s; ⸚) field, farmland. **~bau** *m* (-[e]s; *no pl*) agriculture, farming. **~land** *n* (-[e]s; *no pl*) farmland.

ackern ['akərn] *v/i* (h) **1.** plough, *Am.* plow. **2.** F slog (away).

Acrylfarbe [a'kry:l-] *f* acrylic paint.

ad absurdum [at ap'zʊrdʊm] **et.** ~ **führen** reduce s.th. to absurdity.

ad acta [at 'akta] *fig.* **et.** ~ **legen** consider s.th. closed.

Adam ['a:dam] *m* (-s; *no pl*) *Bibl. and fig.* Adam: F **seit ~s Zeiten** from the beginning of time. **'Adam 'Riese:** F *humor.* **nach** ~ according to Cocker.

'Adamsapfel *m anat.* Adam's apple.

'Adamsko,stüm *n* F *humor.* **im** ~ in one's birthday suit.

Adapter [a'daptər] *m* (-s; -) ⚡ adapter.

adäquat [adɛ'kva:t] *adj* adequate.

addieren [a'di:rən] *v/t* (h) add (up).

Ad'dierma,schine *f* adding machine.

Addition [adi'tsĩo:n] *f* (-; -en) addition.

ade [a'de:] *int* goodbye(e) (*a. fig.*).

Adel ['a:dəl] *m* (-s; *no pl*) a) aristocracy, b) title: *von ~ sein* be of noble birth. **ad(e)lig** ['a:d(ə)liç] *adj* noble (*a. fig.*), titled. **Ad(e)lige** ['a:d(ə)ligə] *m, f* (-n; -n) aristocrat, nobleman (noblewoman): *die ~n* the nobility. **adeln** ['a:dəln] *v/t* (h) make *s.o.* a peer, *a. fig.* ennoble.

'**Adelskrone** *f* coronet.

'**Adelsstand** *m* (-[e]s; *no pl*) nobility: *in den ~ erheben* raise to the peerage.

Ader ['a:dər] *f* (-; -n) vein, *fig. a.* bent: *er hat e-e humoristische ~* he has a streak of humo(u)r.

'**Aderlaß** *m* (-sses; ⸗sse) ⚕, *a. fig.* bloodletting, bleeding.

ädern ['ɛ:dərn] *v/t* (h) vein.

Adjektiv ['atjɛkti:f] *n* (-s; -e) adjective. **adjektivisch** ['atjɛkti:viʃ] *adj* adjectival.

Adjutant [atju'tant *m* (-en; -en) ✕ adjutant.

Adler ['a:dlər] *m* (-s; -) eagle. '**Adlerauge** *n* eagle eye: *fig. ~n haben* be eagle-eyed. '**Adlernase** *f* aquiline nose.

Admiral [atmi'ra:l] *m* (-s; ⸗e) admiral. **Admiralität** [atmirali'tɛ:t] *f* (-; -en) admiralty. **Ad'miralstab** *m* naval staff.

adoptieren [adɔp'ti:rən] *v/t* (h) adopt. **Adoption** [adɔp'tsĭo:n] *f* (-; -en) adoption. **Adop'tiveltern** *pl* adoptive parents. **Adop'tivkind** *n* adopted child.

Adrenalin [adrena'li:n] *n* (-s; *no pl*) ⚗, ⚕ adrenalin(e).

Adreßbuch [a'drɛsbu:x] *n* directory.

Adresse [a'drɛsə] *f* (-; -n) address: † *erste ~* first-class borrower; F *fig. bei j-m an die falsche ~ geraten* come to the wrong person.

A'dressenverzeichnis *n* mailing list.

adressieren [adrɛ'si:rən] *v/t* (h) (*an acc* to) address, direct: *falsch ~* misdirect.

adrett [a'drɛt] *adj* neat.

adsorbieren [atzɔr'bi:rən] *v/t* (h) ⚗ adsorb. **Adsorption** [atzɔrp'tsĭo:n] *f* (-; -en) ⚗ adsorption.

Advent [at'vɛnt] *m* (-[e]s; *no pl*) Advent. **Ad'vents...** Advent (*wreath, season, etc*).

Adverb [at'vɛrp] *n* (-s; -bien [-bĭən]) adverb. **adverbial** [-'bĭa:l] *adj* adverbial.

Aerobic [ɛ'ro:bɪk] *n* (-s; *no pl*) aerobics.

aerodynamisch [aerody'na:mɪʃ] *adj* aerodynamic.

Affäre [a'fɛ:rə] *f* (-; -n) affair: F *sich aus der ~ ziehen* get out of it.

Affe ['afə] *m* (-n; -n) monkey, ape: F (*blöder*) ~ twit; *eingebildeter* ~ conceited ass.

Affekt [a'fɛkt] *m* (-[e]s; -e) emotion: *im ~* in the heat of passion. *~handlung* f ⚖ act committed in the heat of passion. **affektiert** [afɛk'ti:rt] *adj* affected.

Affek'tiertheit *f* (-; *no pl*) affectation.

'**affenartig** *adj* apelike, simian.

'**Affen|brotbaum** *m* baobab. *~liebe* f F doting love. *~schande* f F crying shame. *~the,ater* n F hell of a fuss. *~zahn* m F (*e-n ~ draufhaben* go at) breakneck speed.

affig ['afɪç] *adj* F silly, affected.

Äffin ['ɛfɪn] *f* (-; -nen) she-ape, she-monkey.

Afghane [af'ga:nə] *m* (-n; -n), **Af'ghanin** *f* (-; -nen), **af'ghanisch** *adj* Afghan. **Afghanistan** [af'ga:nısta:n] *n* (-s) Afghanistan.

Afrika ['a:frika] *n* (-s) Africa. **Afrikaner** [afri'ka:nər] *m* (-s; -), **Afri'kanerin** *f* (-; -nen), **afri'kanisch** *adj* African.

Afro-Look ['afrolʊk] *m* (-s; *no pl*) (*im ~* with an) Afro hairstyle.

After ['aftər] *m* (-s; -) *anat.* anus.

Agent [a'gɛnt] *m* (-en; -en), **A'gentin** *f* (-; -nen) agent.

Agentur [agɛn'tu:r] *f* (-; -en) agency.

Aggregat [agre'ga:t] *n* (-[e]s; -e) aggregate, ⚙ unit. **Aggre'gatzustand** *m* *phys.* aggregate (state).

Aggression [agrɛ'sĭo:n] *f* (-; -en) aggression. **aggressiv** [agrɛ'si:f] *adj* aggressive. **Aggressivität** [agrɛsivi'tɛ:t] *f* (-; *no pl*) aggressiveness. **Aggressor** [a'grɛsɔr] *m* (-s; -en [agrɛ'so:rən]) aggressor.

agieren [a'gi:rən] *v/i* (h) act.

Agitation [agita'tsĭo:n] *f* (-; -en) political agitation. **Agitator** [agi'ta:tɔr] *m* (-s; -en [-'ta'to:rən]) (political) agitator. **agitatorisch** [agita'to:rɪʃ] *adj* rabble-rousing. **agitieren** [agi'ti:rən] *v/i* (h) agitate.

Agonie [ago'ni:] *f* (-; -n) death throes.

Agrar... [a'gra:r-] agrarian, agricultural. *~erzeugnisse* pl agricultural produce. *~markt* m agricultural commodities market. *~poli,tik* f agricultural policy.

Ägypten [ɛ'ɡʏptən] *n* (-s) Egypt.

Ägypter [ɛ'ɡʏptər] *m* (-s; -), **Ä'gypterin** *f* (-; -nen), **ä'gyptisch** *adj* Egyptian.

ah [a:] *int* oh!, ah! **äh** [ɛ:] *int* **1.** ugh! **2.** er!

aha [a'ha:] *int* aha!, I see!

A'ha-Erlebnis *n* aha-experience.

Ahle ['a:lə] *f* (-; -n) awl, pricker.

Ahn [a:n] *m* (-[e]s, -en; -en) ancestor.

ahnden ['a:ndən] *v/t* (h) punish.

ähneln ['ɛ:nəln] *v/i* (h) (*dat*) be (*or* look) like, resemble, take after *one's father*: **sich** (*or* **einander**) ~ be (*or* look) alike.

ahnen ['a:nən] *v/t* (h) **1.** foresee, have a presentiment (*or* foreboding) of. **2.** suspect, guess: **ohne zu ~, daß ...** without dreaming that ...; **wie konnte ich ~, daß ...** how was I to know that ...; **ich habe es geahnt!** I knew it!

'Ahnentafel *f* genealogical table.

ähnlich ['ɛ:nlɪç] *adj* similar (*dat* to): ~ **sein** → **ähneln**; F **das sieht ihm ~!** that's just like him!; **so et. Ähnliches** s.th. like that. **'Ähnlichkeit** *f* (-; -en) (**mit** to) likeness, resemblance, similarity: ~ **haben mit** → **ähneln**.

'Ahnung *f* (-; -en) presentiment, foreboding, misgiving, suspicion, F hunch: F **k-e ~!** no idea!; **er hat k-e** (**blasse**) ~ **davon** he doesn't know the first thing about it, he hasn't got a clue.

'ahnungslos *adj* **1.** unsuspecting. **2.** ignorant.

'ahnungsvoll *adj* full of misgivings.

Ahorn ['a:hɔrn] *m* (-s; -e) maple.

Ähre ['ɛ:rə] *f* (-; -n) ear: ~**n lesen** glean.

A-is ['a:ɪs] *n* (-; -) ♪ A sharp.

Akademie [akade'mi:] *f* (-; -n) academy.

Akademiker [aka'de:mikər] *m* (-s; -), **Aka'demikerin** *f* (-; -nen) university man (woman).

akademisch [aka'de:mɪʃ] *adj* academic: ~**e Bildung** university education.

Akazie [a'ka:tsiə] *f* (-; -n) acacia.

akklimatisieren [aklimati'zi:rən] *v/t* (h) (*a.* **sich** ~) *a. fig.* acclimatize. **Akklimati'sierung** *f* (-; -en) acclimatization.

Akkord¹ [a'kɔrt] *m* (-[e]s; -e) ♪ chord.

Ak'kord² ✝ *V* (**im** ~ **arbeiten** do) piecework. ~**arbeit** *f* → **Akkord²**. ~**arbeiter**(**in** *f*) *m* pieceworker.

Akkordeon [a'kɔrdeɔn] *n* (-s; -s) ♪ accordion.

Ak'kordlohn *m* piece wages.

akkreditieren [akredi'ti:rən] *v/t* (h) **1.** *pol.* accredit (**bei** to). **2.** ✝ open a credit for. **Akkreditiv** [akredi'ti:f] *n* (-s; -e) **1.**

pol. credentials. **2.** ✝ letter of credit (*abbr. L/C*): **j-m ein ~ eröffnen** open a credit in favo(u)r of s.o.

Akku ['aku] *m* (-s; -s) F, **Akkumulator** [akumu'la:tɔr] *m* (-s; -en [-la'to:rən]) accumulator.

Akkusativ ['akuzati:f] *m* (-s; -e) accusative (case). ~**ob,jekt** *n* direct object.

Akne ['aknə] *f* (-; -n) ✿ acne.

Akquisiteur [akvizi'tø:r] *m* (-s; -e) ✝ canvasser, agent.

Akribie [akri'bi:] *f* (-; *no pl*) meticulousness.

Akrobat [akro'ba:t] *m* (-en; -en), **Akro'batin** *f* (-; -nen) acrobat.

akro'batisch *adj* acrobatic.

Akt [akt] *m* (-[e]s; -e) **1.** *a. thea.* act. **2.** (sexual) act. **3.** *paint.*, *phot.* nude.

Akte ['aktə] *f* (-; -n) *usu. pl* file, record: **e-e ~ anlegen** open a file (**über** *acc* on); **zu den ~n legen** file, *fig.* shelve.

'Akten|deckel *m* folder. ~**koffer** *m* attaché case. **2kundig** *adj* on record. ~**mappe** *f* **1.** folder. **2.** → **Aktentasche**. ~**no,tiz** *f* note, memorandum, F memo. ~**ordner** *m* file. ~**schrank** *m* filing cabinet. ~**tasche** *f* briefcase. ~**wolf** *m* (paper) shredder. ~**zeichen** *n* file (*letter*: reference) number.

Akteur [ak'tø:r] *m* (-s; -e) *a. fig.* actor.

'Aktfoto *n* nude (photograph).

Aktie ['aktsiə] *f* (-; -n) share, *Am.* stock: ~**n besitzen** hold shares (*Am.* stock) (*gen* in, of); F **wie stehen die ~n?** how are things?

'Aktien|gesellschaft *f* joint-stock company, *Am.* (stock) corporation. ~**kapi,tal** *n* share capital, (joint) stock. ~**mehrheit** *f* majority of stock: **die ~ besitzen** hold the controlling interest. ~**pa,ket** *n* block of shares.

Aktion [ak'tsio:n] *f* (-; -en) action, measure(s), ✝ campaign, drive: ~**en** activities; **in ~ treten** act.

Aktionär [aktsio'nɛ:r] *m* (-s; -e), **Aktio'närin** *f* (-; -nen) ✝ shareholder, *Am.* stockholder.

Akti'onsradius *m* range (of action).

aktiv [ak'ti:f] *adj* active, ✝ favo(u)rable (*balance*), ✕ regular: ~**es Wahlrecht** right to vote; ~**er Wortschatz** *a.* using vocabulary. **'Aktiv** *n* (-s; *rare* -e) *ling.* active voice. **Aktiva** [ak'ti:va] *pl* ✝ assets: ~ **und Passiva** assets and liabili-

ties. **aktivieren** [akti'vi:rən] *v/t* (h) *a.*
fig. activate.

Ak'tivposten *m* ✝, *a. fig.* asset.

Ak'tivurlaub *m* activity holiday.

'Aktmo‚dell *n* nude model.

aktualisieren [aktŏali'zi:rən] *v/t* (h)
make topical. **aktuell** [ak'tŏɛl] *adj* a)
topical, current, present-day, b) modern, up(-)to(-)date: **~es Problem** acute
(*or* immediate) problem; **~e Sendung**
current-affairs program(me *Br.*).

Akupunkteur [akupʊŋk'tø:r] *m* (-s; -e)
acupuncturist. **Akupunktur** [aku-
pʊŋk'tu:r] *f* (-; -en) acupuncture.

Akustik [a'kʊstık] *f* (-; *no pl*) acoustics.
a'**kustisch** *adj* acoustic.

akut [a'ku:t] *adj* 🕮 acute, *fig. a.* urgent.

Akzent [ak'tsɛnt] *m* (-[e]s; -e) accent: *fig.*
besonderen ~ legen auf (*acc*) stress.
ak'zentfrei *adj and adv* without an accent. **akzentuieren** [aktsɛntu'i:rən] *v/t*
(h) accent, *esp. fig.* accentuate, stress.

Akzept [ak'tsɛpt] *n* (-[e]s; -e) acceptance.

akzeptabel [aktsɛp'ta:bəl] *adj* acceptable (**für** to). **Akzeptanz** [-'tants] *f* (-;
no pl) *fig.* acceptance. **akzeptieren**
[-'ti:rən] *v/t* (h) accept (*a.* ✝), agree to.

Alarm [a'larm] *m* (-[e]s; -e) (*blinder ~*
false) alarm: *a. fig.* **~ schlagen** sound
the alarm. **~anlage** *f* alarm (system).

A'larmbereitschaft *f* (*in ~* on the) alert.

alarmieren [alar'mi:rən] *v/t* (h) alarm
(*a. fig.*), alert, call (*police*).

A'larm‚si‚gnal *n* alarm signal. **~stufe** *f*
alert phase. **~zustand** *m* (-[e]s; *no pl*)
(*in den ~ versetzen* put on the) alert.

Albanien [al'ba:nĭən] *n* (-s) Albania.
Al'baner *m* (-s; -), **Al'banerin** *f* (-;
-nen), **al'banisch** *adj* Albanian.

albern ['albərn] **I** *adj* silly. **II** *v/i* (h) fool
around. **'Albernheit** *f* (-; -en) **1.** *no pl*
silliness. **2.** silly remark.

Album ['albʊm] *n* (-s; Alben) album.

Alchimie [alçi'mi:] *f* (-; *no pl*) alchemy.

Alge ['algə] *f* (-; -n) alga, *pl* algae.

Algebra ['algəbra] *f* (-; *no pl*) algebra.
alge'braisch [-'bra:ıʃ] *adj* algebraic(al).

Algerien [al'ge:rĭən] *n* (-s) Algeria.
Al'gerier *m* (-s; -), **Al'gerierin** *f* (-;
-nen), **al'gerisch** *adj* Algerian.

Alibi [a'li:bi] *n* (-s; -s) alibi.

'Alibifrau *f* token woman.

'Alibifunkti‚on *f* cover-up function.

Alimente [ali'mɛntə] *pl* maintenance.

alkalisch [al'ka:lıʃ] *adj* 🜹 alkaline.

Alkohol ['alkoho:l] *m* (-[e]s; -e) alcohol,
liquor, drink. **~einfluß** *m unter ~* under
the influence of alcohol. 🜹**frei** *adj* non-
alcoholic, soft *drink*. **~gehalt** *m* alcoholic content. **~genuß** *m* consumption
of alcohol.

Alkoholiker [alko'ho:likər] *m* (-s; -),
Alko'holikerin *f* (-; -nen), **alko'ho-
lisch** *adj* alcoholic. **alkoholisieren** [al-
koholi'zi:rən] *v/t* (h) alcoholize: **alkoholisiert** drunk. **Alkoholismus** [alko-
ho'lısmʊs] *m* (-; *no pl*) alcoholism.

'Alkohol‚mißbrauch *m* excessive drinking. **~nachweis** *m mot.* alcohol test.
~schmuggel *m* bootlegging. **~spiegel**
m blood alcohol concentration. **~süch-
tig** *adj* addicted to alcohol. **~sünder(in**
f) *m* F *mot.* drunken driver. **~vergif-
tung** *f* alcoholic poisoning.

all [al] *indef pron* a) all, b) every: **~e**
beide both (of them); **wir ~e** all of us;
fast ~e almost everyone; **~(e) und jeder**
all and sundry; **~e Welt** all the world;
ohne ~en Zweifel without any doubt;
→ **alle, alles, Fall** 2.

All *n* (-s; *no pl*) **1.** universe. **2.** (outer)
space.

alle ['alə] *adj pred* F **1.** all gone, finished,
money: all spent: **~ machen** finish. **2.**
dead beat, bushed.

Allee [a'le:] *f* (-; -n) avenue.

Allegorie [alego'ri:] *f* (-; -n) allegory.

allein [a'laın] **I** *adj pred and adv* a) alone,
a. by oneself, on one's own, *a.* in private, b) only: **ganz ~** all alone; **~ stehen**
be unattached, be single; **einzig und ~**
(simply and) solely; **du ~ bist schuld!**
it's all your fault!; (**schon**) **~ der Gedanke** the very (*or* mere) thought. **II**
conj but, however.

Al'lein‚erbe *m* sole heir. **~erbin** *f* sole
heiress. **~erziehende** *m, f* (-n; -n) single parent (*or* father, mother). **~gang** *m*
solo: **im ~** sports: solo, *fig. a.* single-
-handed. **~herrschaft** *f* autocracy.
~herrscher(in *f*) *m* autocrat.

al'leinig *adj* only, sole, exclusive.

Al'lein‚inhaber(in *f*) *m* sole owner. 🜹**reisend** *adj* **~e Kinder** unaccompanied
minors. **~schuld** *f* (-; *no pl*) sole responsibility. **~sein** *n* (-s; *no pl*) loneliness:
Angst vor dem ~ fear of being alone.
🜹**stehend** *adj* single, *w.s.* unattached.

~**stehende** m, f (-n; -n) single. ~**unterhalter(in** f) m thea. solo entertainer. ~**verdiener(in** f) m sole earner. ~**vertretung** f (-; no pl) sole agency. ~**vertrieb** m (-s; no pl) **den ~ haben für** be the sole distributors of.

'**alle'mal** adv 1. always, every time: **ein für ~** once and for all. 2. F easily.

'**allen'falls** adv 1. if need be. 2. possibly, perhaps. 3. at (the) most, at best.

'**allent'halben** adv everywhere.

aller... ['alər-] with sup very best, highest, etc, best, highest, etc of all.

'**aller'dings** [-'diŋs] adv 1. but, though, however. 2. F indeed, certainly.

'**aller'erst** adv zu ~ first of all.

Allergen [alɛr'ge:n] n (-s; -e) allergenic.

Allergie [alɛr'gi:] f (-; -n) allergy.

al'lergisch adj [-gɪʃ] allergic (**gegen** to).

'**aller'hand** adj F quite a lot, a good deal: **das ist ja ~!** a) not bad!, b) that's a bit thick!

'**Aller'heiligen** n (-) All Saints' Day.

'**aller'höchstens** adv at the very most.

allerlei ['alər'laɪ] adj all kinds of.

'**Aller'lei** n (-s; no pl) medley.

'**aller'letzt** adj very latest.

'**aller'liebst** adj (very) lovely, sweet.

'**Aller'seelen** n (-) All Souls' Day.

'**aller'seits** adv F **guten Morgen ~!** good morning everybody!

'**Aller'welts...** ordinary, common.

'**Aller'werteste** m (-n; -n) F posterior.

'**alles** indef pron 1. all, everything, the lot: ~ **in allem** (taken) in all; **vor allem** above all; **er kann ~** he can do anything; **auf ~ gefaßt sein** be prepared for the worst; **j-n über ~ lieben** love s.o. more than anything; F **um ~ in der Welt!** for heaven's sake!; → **Mädchen** 2. 2. F everybody: ~ **aussteigen!** get out everybody, please!

'**alle'samt** adv F all (of them or us etc).

all'gegenwärtig adj omnipresent.

'**allge'mein** I adj general: **von ~em Interesse** of general interest; **auf ~en Wunsch** by popular request; **unter ~er Zustimmung** by common consent; ~**es Wahlrecht** universal suffrage; ~**e Wehrpflicht** compulsory military service; **im ~en** → II adv generally, in general, on the whole: **es ist ~ bekannt, daß** it is a well-known fact that; ~ **beliebt** popular with everyone; ~ **gespro-**

chen generally speaking; **es ist ~ üblich** it is common usage.

'**Allge'mein|befinden** n general state of health. ~**bildung** f general education.

'**allge'meingültig** adj universally valid.

'**Allge'meinheit** f (-; no pl) (general) public.

'**Allge'meinmedi,zin** f general medicine: **Arzt für ~** general practitioner.

'**allge'meinverständlich** adj (easily) intelligible.

'**Allge'mein|wissen** n general knowledge. ~**wohl** n public welfare.

All'heilmittel n a. fig. cure-all.

Allianz [a'liants] f (-; -en) alliance.

Alligator [ali'ga:tor] m (-s; -en [-ga'to:rən]) alligator.

alliiert [ali'i:rt] adj allied: hist. **die Alliierten** the Allies.

'**all'jährlich** adj annual(ly adv), yearly, adv a. every year.

'**Allmacht** f (-; no pl) omnipotence. ~**wohl** n public welfare.

all'mächtig adj omnipotent, almighty.

allmählich [al'mɛ:lɪç] adj gradual(ly adv), adv a. by degrees, slowly.

Allopathie [alopa'ti:] f (-; no pl) allopathy.

'**Allpar'teien...** all-party ...

'**Allrad...** all-wheel (drive etc).

allseitig ['alzaitiç] adj general, universal, allround: **zur ~en Zufriedenheit** to the satisfaction of everybody.

'**allseits** adv on (or from) all sides.

'**Alltag** m (-[e]s; no pl) everyday life: (grauer) ~ daily routine. **all'täglich** adj everyday, usual, ordinary, banal.

'**alltags** adv on workdays.

'**Alltags...** everyday (clothes etc).

Allüren [a'ly:rən] pl contp. affectation, airs (and graces).

'**all'wissend** adj omniscient.

'**all'wöchentlich** adj and adv weekly.

'**allzu** adv far too: **nicht ~ spät** not too late. ~**'gut** adv only too well. ~**'sehr** adv all too much. ~**'viel** adv too much: ~ **ist ungesund** enough is as good as a feast.

'**Allzweck...** all-purpose ...

Alm [alm] f (-; -en) alpine pasture, alp.

Almosen ['almo:zən] n (-s; -) alms, fig. contp. pittance, Am. handout.

'**Almosenempfänger(in** f) m pauper.

Alpen ['alpən] pl Alps. ~**rose** f Alpine rose. ~**veilchen** n cyclamen. ~**vorland** n (-[e]s; no pl) foothills of the Alps.

Alphabet [alfa'be:t] *n* (-[e]s; -e) alphabet.
 alpha'betisch *adj* alphabetical: ~ *ord-nen* → **alphabetisieren** [-beti'zi:rən] *v/t* (h) arrange in alphabetical order.
alphanu'merisch *adj* alphanumeric.
alpin [al'pi:n] *adj* Alpine: → *Kombination* 5. **Alpinismus** [alpi'nısmʊs] *m* (-; *no pl*) alpinism. **Alpinist** [-'nıst] *m* (-en; -en), **Alpi'nistin** *f* (-; -nen) alpinist.
'Alptraum *m a. fig.* nightmare.
als [als] *conj* **1.** a) as, *after comp*: than: *sobald ~ möglich* as soon as possible; *mehr ~ genug* more than enough, b) *negation*: but: *alles andere ~ hübsch* anything but pretty. **2.** as, in one's capacity of: ~ *Entschuldigung as* (or by way of) excuse; *er starb ~ Bettler* he died (as) a beggar; ~ *Mädchen hatte sie k-e Chance* being a girl she had no chance. **3.** ~ *ob* as if, as though. **4.** a) when, as, b) while: *damals, ~ at* the time when; *gerade ~* just as.
also ['alzo] *conj* **1.** so, therefore. **2.** F then: ~ *gut!* very well (then)!; *na ~!* there you are!; *du kommst ~ nicht?* you're not coming then?
alt [alt] *adj* **1.** old, aged: ~ *werden* → *altern; wie ~ bist du?* how old are you?; *er ist zehn Jahre ~* he is ten (years old); *ein zehn Jahre ~er Junge* a ten-year-old boy; *er ist (doppelt) so ~ wie ich* he is (twice) my age; *auf m-e ~en Tage* in my old age; *fig. das ~e Lied* the same old story; *humor. hier werde ich nicht ~* I won't be here much longer; → *älter, Hase.* **2.** old, ancient: *das ~e Rom* ancient Rome; *die ~en Sprachen* the classical languages. **3.** old, long-standing (*friendship etc*). **4.** old, former (*pupil etc*): *in ~en Zeiten* in former times; *es bleibt alles beim ~en* everything remains as it was (before). **5.** old, stale (*bread etc*), used, second-hand: → *Eisen.*
Alt *m* (-s; -e) ♪ alto.
Altar [al'ta:r] *m* (-[e]s; *÷*e) altar. **~bild** *n*, **~blatt** *n*, **~gemälde** *n* altarpiece.
'altbacken *adj* **1.** stale. **2.** F *fig.* antiquated.
'Altbau *m* (-[e]s; -ten) old building.
'Altbausa nierung *f* rehabilitation of old housing. **'Altbauwohnung** *f* flat (*Am.* apartment) in an old building.
'altbe kannt *adj* well-known.

'altbe währt *adj* well-tried.
'altdeutsch *adj* old German.
Alte¹ ['altə] *m* (-n; -n) old man: *die ~n* old people; F *der ~* a) (*father, husband*) the old man, b) the boss; *er ist wieder ganz der* ♀ he is quite himself again.
'Alte² *f* (-n; -n) **1.** old woman: F *die ~* a) (*mother, wife*) the old lady, b) the boss. **2.** *zo.* mother.
'alt ehrwürdig *adj* time-hono(u)red.
'alt eingesessen *adj* old-established.
'Alteisen *n* scrap iron.
'Altenheim *n* old people's home. **'Altenpfleger(in** *f*) *m* geriatric nurse. **'Altenteil** *n sich aufs ~ zurückziehen* retire.
Alter ['altər] *n* (-s; *no pl*) **1.** a) age, b) (old) age: *im ~ von 20 Jahren* at the age of 20; *er ist in m-m ~* he is my age; *mittleren ~s* middle-aged. **2.** old people.
älter ['ɛltər] *adj* **1.** older, elder: *mein ~er Bruder* my elder brother; *er ist (3 Jahre) ~ als ich* he is my senior (by three years); *er sieht (10 Jahre) ~ aus als er ist* he looks (10 years) more than his age. **2.** elderly. **3.** *‡‡* prior.
altern ['altərn] *v/i* (sn) grow old, age.
alternativ [altɛrna'ti:f] *adj*, **Alternative** [-'ti:və] *f* (-; -n) alternative.
'Alters|erscheinung *f* sign of old age. **~genosse** *m*, **~genossin** *f* contemporary. **~grenze** *f* age-limit: *flexible ~* flexible retirement age. **~gründe** *pl aus ~n* for reasons of age. **~gruppe** *f* age group. **~heim** *n* old people's home. **~klasse** *f esp. sports*.: age group. **~pyra mide** *f sociol.* age pyramid. **~rente** *f* old-age pension. **♀schwach** *adj* infirm, *a.* F *fig.* decrepit, rickety. **~schwäche** *f* (-; *no pl*) infirmity (of old age): *an ~ sterben* die of old age. **~unterschied** *m* age difference. **~versorgung** *f* old-age pension (scheme).
'Altertum *n* (-[e]s; *no pl*) antiquity.
altertümlich ['altərty:mlıç] *adj* **1.** ancient. **2.** antiquated.
ältest ['ɛltəst] *adj* **1.** oldest. **2.** eldest (*son etc*). **'Älteste** *m*, *f* (-n; -n) oldest, eldest: *mein ~r* my eldest son.
'Altglas *n* ⊛ used glass.
'Altgriechisch *n* Old Greek.
'alt hergebracht *adj* traditional.
'Althochdeutsch *n* Old High German.
Altist [al'tıst] *m* (-en; -en), **Al'tistin** *f* (-; -nen) ♪ alto(-singer).

'**altjüngferlich** *adj* old-maidish.

'**altklug** *adj* precocious.

'**Altlasten** *pl* old neglected deposits of toxic waste.

ältlich ['ɛltlɪç] *adj* elderly, oldish.

'**Altmateri,al** *n* ☉ salvage.

'**Altmeister** *m* 1. *sports*: ex-champion. 2. *fig.* past master.

'**Altme,tall** *n* scrap metal.

'**altmodisch** *adj* old-fashioned.

'**Altöl** *n* ☉ waste oil, used oil.

'**Altpa,pier** *n* ☉ waste (*or* used) paper.

'**Altphilo,loge** *m* classical philologist.

altruistisch [altru'ɪstɪʃ] *adj* altruistic.

'**altsprachlich** *adj* classical.

'**Altstadt** *f* old town.

'**Altstimme** *f* ♩ alto (voice).

'**Altwarenhändler(in** *f*) *m* second-hand dealer.

Alt'weibersommer *m* Indian summer.

Alufolie ['a:lu-] *f* alumin(i)um foil.

Aluminium [alu'mi:niʊm] *n* (-s; *no pl*) aluminium, *Am.* aluminum.

am [am] (= *an dem*) *prep* 1. at the, on the, *time*: *a.* in the: ~ **Fenster** at the window; ~ **Ufer** on the shore; ~ **1. Mai** (on) May 1st, (on) the first of May; ~ **Anfang** at the beginning; ~ **Himmel** in the sky; ~ **Leben** alive; ~ **Morgen** in the morning; ~ **Wege** by the wayside. 2. *before sup* **er war** ~ **tapfersten** he was (the) bravest; ~ **besten** best.

Amalgam [amal'ga:m] *n* (-s; -e) 🧪 amalgam. **amalgamieren** [amalga'mi:rən] *v/t* (h) *a. fig.* amalgamate.

Amateur [ama'tø:r] *m* (-s; -e) amateur (*a.* in cpds. boxer, sport, etc).

Amazone [ama'tso:nə] *f* (-; -n) Amazon.

Ambiente [am'biɛntə] *n* (-s; *no pl*) ambience.

Ambition [ambi'tsio:n] *f* (-; -en) ambition.

ambivalent [ambiva'lɛnt] *adj* ambivalent.

Amboß ['ambɔs] *m* (-sses; -sse) anvil.

ambulant [ambu'lant] *adj* 1. ambulant, (*a.* ~ **behandelter Patient**) outpatient; ~ **behandelt werden** receive outpatient treatment. 2. itinerant (*trade etc*).

Ambulanz [ambu'lants] *f* (-; -en) *a*) *mot.* ambulance, *b*) outpatients' department, *c*) first-aid room.

Ameise ['a:maizə] *f* (-; -n) ant.

'**Ameisen|bär** *m* anteater. ~**haufen** *m* anthill. ~**säure** *f* 🧪 formic acid.

amen ['a:mɛn] *int* amen: *zu allem ja und* ~ *sagen* agree (meekly) to everything.

Amerika [a'me:rika] *n* (-s) America. **Amerikaner** [ameri'ka:nər] *m* (-s; -), **Ameri'kanerin** *f* (-; -nen), **ameri'kanisch** *adj* American. **amerikanisieren** [amerikani'zi:rən] *v/t* (h) Americanize. **Amerikanismus** [amerika'nɪsmʊs] *m* (-; -men) *ling.* Americanism.

Amethyst [ame'tʏst] *m* (-en; -en) *min.* amethyst.

Ami ['ami] *m* (-[s]; -[s]) F Yank.

Aminosäure [a'mi:no-] *f* 🧪 amino acid.

Amme ['amə] *f* (-; -n) (wet) nurse. '**Ammenmärchen** *n contp.* old wives' tale.

Ammer ['amər] *f* (-; -n) *zo.* bunting.

Ammoniak [amo'niak] *n* (-s; *no pl*) 🧪 ammonia.

Amnesie [amne'zi:] *f* (-; -n) 🩺 amnesia.

Amnestie [amnɛs'ti:] *f* (-; -n), **amne-'stieren** [-'ti:rən] *v/t* (h) 🩺 amnesty.

Amöbe [a'mø:bə] *f* (-; -n) *zo.* am(o)eba.

Amok ['a:mɔk]: ~ *laufen* (*fahren*) run (drive) amok. '**Amokfahrer** *m* mad driver. '**Amokläufer** *m* person running amok. '**Amokschütze** *m* mad gunman.

Amor ['a:mɔr] *m* (-s; *no pl*) Cupid.

amorph [a'mɔrf] *adj* amorphous.

Amortisation [amɔrtiza'tsio:n] *f* (-; -en) 🕈 amortization. **amortisieren** [amɔrti'zi:rən] *v/t* (h) amortize.

Ampel ['ampəl] *f* (-; -n) 1. hanging lamp. 2. traffic light(s).

Amperemeter [ampɛr'me:tər] *n* (-s; -) ⚡ ammeter. **Amperestunde** [am'pɛ:r-] *f* ⚡ ampere-hour.

Amphibien [am'fi:biən] *pl* amphibian.

Amphitheater [am'fi:teatər] *n* (-s; -) amphitheat/re (*Am.* -er).

Ampulle [am'pʊlə] *f* (-; -n) ampoule.

Amputation [amputa'tsio:n] *f* (-; -en) 🗡 amputation. **amputieren** [ampu'ti:rən] *v/t* (h) 🗡 amputate.

Ampu'tierte *m, f* (-n; -n) 🗡 amputee.

Amsel ['amzəl] *f* (-; -n) *zo.* blackbird.

Amt [amt] *n* (-[e]s, ⸚er) 1. *a*) post, office, *b*) (official) duty, function, *c*) task: *von* ~*s wegen* ex officio, officially; → *antreten* 1 *etc*. 2. office, agency, department. 3. *teleph.* exchange. **amtieren** [am'ti:rən] *v/i* (h) hold office: ~ *als* act (*or* officiate) as. **am'tierend** *adj a*) acting (*mayor etc*), *b*) reigning (*champion etc*). '**amtlich** *adj* official.

'**Amts|antritt** m bei s-m etc ~ upon his etc assuming office. **~arzt** m public-health officer. **~bereich** m competence. **~blatt** n official gazette. **~eid** m den ~ ablegen take the oath of office, be sworn in. **~enthebung** f removal from office, dismissal. **~führung** f administration of [an] office. **~geheimnis** n a) official secret, b) official secrecy. **~gericht** n lower district court. **~geschäfte** pl official duties. **~gewalt** f (official) authority. **~handlung** f official act. **~mißbrauch** m abuse of (official) authority. **2müde** adj weary of one's office. **~peri,ode** f term (of office). **~schimmel** m humor. red tape. **~stunden** pl office hours. **~träger(in** f) m office holder. **~vorgänger(in** f) m predecessor (in office). **~vormund** m public guardian. **~zeichen** n teleph. dial(ling) tone. **~zeit** f term (of office).
Amulett [amu'let] n (-[e]s; -e) charm.
amüsant [amy'zant] adj amusing.
amüsieren [amy'zi:rən] (h) **I** v/t amuse, entertain. **II** sich ~ a) amuse o.s., have a good time, b) (über acc) laugh (at), make fun (of).
an [an] **I** prep (dat) **1.** time: on: ~ e-m kalten Tag on a cold day. **2.** place: on, at, by, near, next to: ~ der Themse on the Thames; ~ der Wand on the wall; ~ der Kreuzung at the crossing; alles ist ~ s-m Platz everything is in its place; Tür ~ Tür wohnen live door to door; fig. Kopf ~ Kopf neck and neck; er hat so et. ~ sich there is s.th. about him; es ist ~ ihm zu reden it is up to him to speak; ~ s-r Stelle in his place. **3.** by: j-n ~ der Hand führen lead s.o. by the hand; j-n ~ der Stimme erkennen recognize s.o. from (or by) his voice. **4.** ~ (und für) sich in itself, as such. **II** prep (acc) **5.** to, for: ein Brief ~ mich a letter for me. **6.** at, against: ~ die Tür klopfen knock at the door. **III** adv **7.** von ... ~ from ... (on or onward); von heute ~ from today (on); von nun ~ from now on, henceforth. **8.** F ~ - aus on - off; das Licht ist ~ the light is on; er hatte noch s-n Mantel ~ he still had his coat on. **9.** F ~ die 100 Mark about 100 marks.
Anabolikum [ana'bo:likʊm] n (-s; -ka) ♣ anabolic drug.

Anachronismus [anakro'nɪzmʊs] m (-; -men) anachronism.
anal [a'na:l] adj ♣, psych. anal.
Analgetikum [anal'ge:tikʊm] n ♣ analgesic.
analog [ana'lo:k] adj analogous (zu to).
Ana'logrechner m analogue computer.
Analpabet [analfa'be:t] m (-en; -en), **Analpha'betin** f (-; -nen) illiterate (person). **Analpha'betentum** n (-s; no pl) illiteracy.
Analyse [ana'ly:zə] f (-; -n) analysis. **analysieren** [analy'zi:rən] v/t (h) analy/se (Am. -ze). **Analysis** [a'na:lyzɪs] f (-; no pl) analysis. **Analytiker** [ana'ly:tikər] m (-s; -) f, **Ana'lytikerin** f (-; -nen) psych. analyst. **ana'lytisch** adj analytic(al).
Anämie [anɛ'mi:] f (-; -n) ♣ an(a)emia.
Ananas ['ananas] f (-; -[se]) pineapple.
Anarchie [anar'çi:] f (-; -n) anarchy.
Anarchismus [anar'çɪsmʊs] m (-; no pl) anarchism. **Anarchist** [-'çɪst] m (-en; -en), **Anar'chistin** f (-; -nen) anarchist. **anar'chistisch** adj anarchic(al).
Anästhesie [anɛste'zi:] f (-; -n) ♣ an(a)esthesia. **anästhesieren** [anɛste'zi:rən] v/t (h) ♣ an(a)esthetize. **Anäs-the'sist** [-'zɪst] m (-en; -en), **Anäs-the'sistin** f (-; -nen) ♣ an(a)esthetist.
Anatomie [anato'mi:] f (-; -n) **1.** anatomy. **2.** institute of anatomy. **anatomisch** [ana'to:mɪʃ] adj anatomical.
'**anbahnen** (sep, -ge-, h) **I** v/t a) pave the way for, b) open, begin (talks etc). **II** sich ~ be developing.
anbändeln ['anbɛndəln] v/i (sep, -ge-, h) F mit j-m ~ a) make up to s.o., b) pick a quarrel with s.o.
'**Anbau¹** m (-[e]s; no pl) ✒cultivation.
'**Anbau²** m (-[e]s; -ten) △ annex, extension. '**anbauen** v/t (sep, -ge-, h) **1.** cultivate, grow. **2.** (an acc) build, add.
'**Anbau|fläche** f ✒ a) arable land, b) area under cultivation. **~küche** f unit kitchen. **~möbel** pl sectional (or unit) furniture. **~schrank** m cupboard unit. **~wand** f wall unit.
'**anbehalten** v/t (irr, sep, h, → behalten) keep on (coat etc).
an'bei adv ✝ enclosed: ~ schicke ich Ihnen ... I am enclosing ...
'**anbeißen** (irr, sep, -ge-, h, → beißen) **I**

v/t bite into. **II** *v/i* bite, *a. fig.* take the bait.

'**anbellen** *v/t* (*sep*, -ge-, h) *a. fig.* bark at.
anberaumen ['anbəraʊmən] *v/t* (*sep*, h) fix, appoint.
'**anbeten** *v/t* (*sep*, -ge-, h) *a. fig.* worship, adore. '**Anbeter** *m* (-s; -) **1.** worship(p)er. **2.** admirer (*of a woman*).
'**Anbetracht:** *in* ~ (*gen*) considering.
'**anbetteln** *v/t* (*sep*, -ge-, h) *j-n* ~ beg s.o. (*um* for).
'**Anbetung** *f* (-; *no pl*) *a. fig.* worship, adoration.
anbiedern ['anbi:dərn] *sich* ~ (*sep*, -ge-, h) *contp.* ingratiate o.s. (*bei* with).
'**anbieten** (*irr*, *sep*, -ge-, h, → **bieten**) **I** *v/t* offer. **II** *sich* ~ *person:* offer one's services, *opportunity:* present itself.
'**Anbieter** *m* (-s; -) ✝ (potential) seller.
'**anbinden** (*irr*, *sep*, -ge-, h, → **binden**) (*an dat or acc* to) tie (up), bind, ⚓ moor, *fig.* link: → **angebunden**.
'**Anblick** *m* (-[e]s; -e) sight.
'**anblicken** *v/t* (*sep*, -ge-, h) look at, glance at: *j-n finster* ~ scowl at s.o.
'**anblinken** *v/t* (*sep*, -ge-, h) flash one's headlights at.
'**anbrechen** (*irr*, *sep*, -ge-, → **brechen**) **I** *v/t* (h) break into (*supplies*), start (on) (*can*, *pack*), open (*bottle*). **II** *v/i* (sn) begin, *a. fig.* dawn.
'**anbrennen** *v/i* (*irr*, *sep*, -ge-, sn, → **brennen**) (*a.* ~ **lassen**) burn: F *fig. er läßt nichts* ~ he doesn't miss a trick.
'**anbringen** *v/t* (*irr*, *sep*, -ge-, h, → **bringen**) **1.** a) put up (*curtain*, *sign*, *etc*, b) (*an dat* to) fix, fasten. **2.** F bring (along). **3.** make (*a request*, *improvements*, *etc*), get in (*a remark etc*), display (*knowledge*), land (*a blow*): *Kritik* ~ criticize; → **angebracht**.
'**Anbruch** *m* (-[e]s; *no pl*) beginning.
'**anbrüllen** *v/t* (*sep*, -ge-, h) bawl at.
Andacht ['andaxt] *f* (-; -en) *eccl.* a) devotion, b) prayers, c) (short) service.
andächtig ['andɛçtɪç] *adj* **1.** devout, pious. **2.** a) rapt, attentive, b) solemn: ~ *zuhören* listen with rapt attention.
'**andauern** *v/i* (*sep*, -ge-, h) continue, last, go on. '**andauernd** *adj* constant, continual, incessant: *er störte uns* ~ he kept interrupting us.
'**Andenken** *n* (-s; -) **1.** *no pl* memory: *zum* ~ *an* (*acc*) in memory of. **2.** a)

keepsake, b) souvenir (*an acc* of).
ander ['andər] **I** *adj* **1.** a) other, b) different: *ein* ~*es Buch* another book; *am* ~*en Tag* (on) the next day; *das* ~*e Geschlecht* the opposite sex; *er ist ein ganz* ~*er Mensch* he is a changed man; → *Ansicht* 1. **II** *indef pron* **2.** *ein* ~*er*, *e-e* ~*e* someone else; *die* ~*en* the others; *der eine oder* ~*e* someone or other; *kein* ~*er als* a) no one else (or none) but, b) no less than. **3.** ~*es*, *an-dres* other things; *alles* ~*e* everything else; *alles* ~*e als* anything but, far from; *unter* ~*em* among other things; *eins nach dem* ~*en* one thing after the other; *das ist et. ganz* ~*es* that's a different thing altogether.
'**anderen'falls** *adv* otherwise.
'**anderer'seits** *adv* on the other hand.
'**andermal** *adv ein* ~ some other time.
ändern ['ɛndərn] **I** *v/t* (h) change, alter, vary: *sein Testament* ~ alter one's will; *es läßt sich nicht* ~ it can't be helped; *ich kann es nicht* ~ I cannot help it; *das ändert nichts an der Tatsache, daß ...* that doesn't alter the fact that ... **II** *sich* ~ alter, change; *die Zeiten* ~ *sich* times are changing.
'**anders** *adv* **1.** differently (*als* from): ~ *werden* change; ~ *als s-e Freunde* unlike his friends; ~ *gesagt* in other words. **2.** *with pron* else: *jemand* ~ somebody (*or* anybody) else; *niemand* ~ *als er* nobody but he; *wer* ~? who else? '**andersartig** *adj* different.
'**andersdenkend** *adj* thinking differently, *pol. a.* dissident. '**andersgläubig** *adj* of a different faith, heterodox.
'**andersher,um** *I adv* the other way round. **II** *adj* F gay, queer.
'**anderswo** *adv*, '**anderswo,hin** *adv* F elsewhere, somewhere else.
'**andert'halb** ['andərt-] *adj* one and a half: ~ *Pfund* a pound and a half.
'**Änderung** *f* (-; -en) change, alteration.
'**Änderungsantrag** *m pol.* amendment.
'**ander'weitig** [-'vaɪtɪç] **I** *adj* **1.** other, further. **II** *adv* **2.** otherwise: ~ *verge-ben* give s.th. to s.o. else. **3.** elsewhere.
'**andeuten** (*sep*, -ge-, h) **I** *v/t* **1.** a) hint at, suggest, intimate, b) indicate, mention *s.th.* briefly. **2.** *a. fig.* outline. **II** *sich* ~ be in the offing. '**Andeutung** *f* (-; -en) hint, suggestion, insinuation.

'**andeutungsweise** *adv* ~ **zu verstehen geben** → **andeuten** I a.

'**Andrang** *m* (-[e]s; *no pl*) a) crush, press, b) rush, ✝ run (**auf** *acc* on).

'**andrehen** *v/t* (*sep*, -ge-, h) **1.** turn on, switch on (*light etc*). **2.** F *fig. j-m et.* ~ fob s.th. off on s.o.

'**androhen** *v/t* (*sep*, -ge-, h) *j-m et.* ~ threaten s.o. with s.th.

'**Androhung** *f* (-; -en) threat.

'**anecken** *v/i* (*sep*, -ge-, sn) F *bei j-m* ~ give offen/ce (*Am.* -se) to s.o.

'**aneignen** *v/t* (*sep*, -ge-, h) *sich* ~ **1.** a) appropriate *s.th.* to o.s., take possession of, b) misappropriate, usurp. **2.** acquire (*knowledge*), adopt (*view etc*).

'**Aneignung** *f* (-; *no pl*) **1.** appropriation. **2.** acquisition.

anein'ander *adv* (to, of, *etc*) each other: ~ **denken** think of each other. **~geraten** *v/i* (*irr*, *sep*, sn, → **geraten**) (*mit* with) a) clash, b) come to blows. **~grenzen** *v/i* (*sep*, -ge-, h) border on each other. **~reihen** *v/t* (*sep*, -ge-, h) line up, *fig.* string *words etc* together.

Anekdote [anɛk'do:tə] *f* (-; -n) anecdote.

'**anekeln** *v/t* (*sep*, -ge-, h) disgust, sicken: *es ekelt mich an* it makes me sick.

Anemone [ane'mo:nə] *f* (-; -n) anemone.

'**Anerbieten** *n* (-s; -) offer.

'**anerkannt** *adj* recognized, accepted.

'**anerkennen** *v/t* (*irr*, *sep*, h, → **erkennen**) a) acknowledge, recognize, b) appreciate, c) approve: *sports:* (**nicht**) ~ (dis)allow; **~de Worte** appreciative words. '**anerkennenswert** *adj* commendable. '**Anerkennung** *f* (-; *no pl*) a) acknowledgement, recognition (*a. pol.*), b) appreciation, c) approval, ✝ acceptance (*of bill*): *in* ~ (*gen*) in recognition of; ~ *verdienen* deserve credit.

'**anerziehen** *v/t* (*irr*, *sep*, h, → **erziehen**) *j-m et.* ~ instil(l) s.th. into s.o.

'**anerzogen** *adj* acquired.

'**anfachen** *v/t* (*sep*, -ge-, h) **1.** fan. **2.** *fig.* kindle, stir up.

'**anfahren** (*irr*, *sep*, -ge-, → **fahren**) I *v/i* (sn) **1.** start (up). II *v/t* (h) **2.** deliver. **3.** ram, run into, hit. **4.** stop (♧ call) at. **5.** ⚙ start. **6.** F *j-n* ~ snap at s.o.

'**Anfahrt** *f* (-; -en) **1.** journey, ride. **2.** approach, drive(way). **3.** delivery.

'**Anfall** *m* (-[e]s; ⁓e) **1.** ✚ attack, fit (*a. fig.*): *humor. in e-m* ~ *von Großzügig-* **keit** in a fit (*or* burst) of generosity. **2.** ✝, ⚖ accrual (*of a dividend etc*).

'**anfallen** (*irr*, *sep*, -ge-, → **fallen**) I *v/t* (h) attack. II *v/i* (sn) result, *work etc*: come up, *costs etc*: arise, *profit etc*: accrue. '**anfällig** *adj* ~ *für a. fig.* susceptible (*or* prone) to. '**Anfälligkeit** *f* (-; *no pl*) proneness (**für** to), *w.s.* delicacy.

'**Anfang** *m* (-[e]s; ⁓e) beginning, start: *am* ~, *im* ~, *zu* ~ → **anfangs**; *von* ~ *an* (right) from the beginning (*or* start); ~ *Mai* early in May; *den* ~ *machen* begin, lead off; *ein* ~ *ist gemacht* a start has been made; *noch in den Anfängen stecken* be still in its infancy.

'**anfangen** (*irr*, *sep*, -ge-, h, → **fangen**) I *v/t* a) begin, start, b) do: *ein neues Leben* ~ turn over a new leaf; *was soll ich bloß* ~? what on earth am I to do?; *er hat wieder angefangen zu rudern* he has taken up rowing again; *et. schlau* ~ set about s.th. cleverly; *mit ihm ist nichts anzufangen* he's hopeless. II *v/i* start: *mit der Arbeit* ~ begin (*or* start) (to) work; *bei e-r Firma* ~ start work(ing) with a firm; *ich weiß nichts damit anzufangen* I don't know what to do with (*fig.* make of) it; *das fängt ja gut an!* that's a fine start; *du hast angefangen!* you started it!; *fängst du schon wieder an?* are you at it again? '**Anfänger** *m* (-s; -), '**Anfängerin** *f* (-; -nen) beginner.

'**Anfängerkurs(us)** *m* beginners' course.

anfänglich ['anfɛŋlɪç] I *adj* initial, original. II *adv* → '**anfangs** *adv* at first, at (*or* in) the beginning.

'**Anfangs|buchstabe** *m* initial letter: *großer* (*kleiner*) ~ capital (small) letter. **~gehalt** *n* starting (*or* initial) salary. **~gründe** *pl* rudiments. **~kapi̱tal** *n* opening capital. **~stadium** *n* initial stage. **~zeit** *f* starting time.

'**anfassen** (*sep*, -ge-, h) I *v/t* **1.** seize, grab (*an dat* by), touch: *j-n* ~ take s.o. by the hand; *fig.* **zum** ♀ politician *etc* of the people, popular. **2.** *fig.* treat, handle, tackle (*problem etc*). II *v/i* (*mit*) ~ lend a hand, help.

'**anfauchen** *v/t* (*sep*, -ge-, h) *cat:* spit at: *fig. j-n* ~ snap at s.o.

anfechtbar ['anfɛçtbaːr] *adj a.* ⚖ contestable. '**anfechten** *v/t* (*irr*, *sep*, -ge-, h, → **fechten**) contest (*a.* ⚖), appeal

from (*sentence*). '**Anfechtung** f (-; -en)
1. contesting, ⚖ appeal (*gen* from). **2.**
temptation.

anfeinden ['anfaɪndən] v/t (*sep*, -ge-, h)
be hostile to: **angefeindet werden**
meet with hostility. '**Anfeindung** f (-;
-en) hostility (*gen* to).

'**anfertigen** v/t (*sep*, -ge-, h) make, do,
⚙, ⚗ manufacture, *pharm.* prepare:
ein Gutachten ~ deliver an expert
opinion (*über acc* on). '**Anfertigung** f
(-; -en) making *etc*, manufacture.

'**anfeuern** v/t (*sep*, -ge-, h) a) encourage,
b) cheer (on), *Am.* F root for.

anflehen v/t (*sep*, -ge-, h) implore.

'**anfliegen** (*irr, sep*, -ge-, → **fliegen**) **I** v/t
(h) a) fly to, b) land at. **II** v/i (sn)
approach: **angeflogen kommen** come
flying (along). '**Anflug** m (-[e]s; ⸚e) **1.** ✈
approach: **im ~ sein auf** (*acc*) be approaching. **2.** *fig.* touch, trace, hint.
'**Anflugschneise** f ✈ approach lane.

'**anfordern** v/t (*sep*, -ge-, h) ask for, demand, request. '**Anforderung** f (-; -en)
1. (*gen* for) demand, request: **auf ~** on
request. **2.** *pl* demands, standard: **allen
~en genügen** meet all requirements,
fill the bill; **den ~en nicht genügen** not
to be up to standard; **hohe ~en stellen**
make high demands (**an** *acc* on), *task
etc*: a. be very exacting.

'**Anfrage** f (-; -n) inquiry, *a. parl.* question. '**anfragen** v/i (*sep*, -ge-, h) inquire
(**bei** *j-m* **wegen** *et.* of s.o. about s.th.).

anfreunden ['anfrɔyndən] **sich ~** (*sep*,
-ge-, h) become friends: **sich mit** *j-m* **~**
make friends with s.o.; **sich mit e-m
Gedanken** *etc* **~** get to like the idea *etc*.

'**anfügen** v/t (*sep*, -ge-, h) **1.** add. **2.** enclose. **3.** ⚙ join, attach.

'**anfühlen** v/t (*sep*, -ge-, h) (*a. sich ~*) feel.

'**anführen** v/t (*sep*, -ge-, h) **1.** lead, be at
the head of, ✕ command. **2.** state,
mention, specify, give (*facts, reasons*),
produce (*evidence*), quote (*example,
book*): **zur Entschuldigung ~** plead (*as
an excuse*). **3.** F dupe. '**Anführer** m (-s;
-), '**Anführerin** f (-; -nen) leader.

'**Anführungs**|**striche**, **~zeichen** *pl* quo-
tation marks, inverted commas.

'**Angabe** f (-; -n) **1.** statement, declaration, specification: **~n** information; **~n
zur Person** personal data; **nähere ~n
machen** give (further) details; **ohne ~**

von Gründen without giving reasons.
2. F showing-off. **3.** *tennis etc*: service.

'**angeben** (*irr, sep*, -ge-, h, → **geben**) **I**
v/t **1.** give, state, specify, fix (*deadline*),
name (*witness etc*). **2.** declare (*value
etc*), quote (*prices*). **3.** indicate (*direction etc*), set (*the pace*). **II** v/i **4.** F (**mit**)
show off ([with] *s.o., s.th.*), brag (about,
of). **5.** *cards*: deal first. **6.** *tennis etc*:
serve. '**Angeber** m (-s; -), '**Angeberin** f
(-; -nen) F show-off. **Angebe'rei** f (-;
-en) F showing-off. '**angeberisch** *adj* F
bragging.

angeblich ['angeˌplɪç] *adj* alleged, *contp.*
would-be: **~ ist er ...** he is said to be ...

'**angeboren** *adj* innate, inborn (*both*:
dat in), ✚ congenital, hereditary.

'**Angebot** n (-[e]s; -e) offer, *auction*: bid,
supply (*of goods*), ✚ tender, *Am.* bid: **~
und Nachfrage** supply and demand.

'**angebracht I** *pp of* **anbringen. II** *adj* a)
advisable, b) proper, appropriate: **es
für ~ halten zu gehen** *etc* see fit to go
etc; **nicht ~** inappropriate.

'**angebunden I** *pp of* **anbinden. II** *adj*
fig. kurz ~ curt, short.

'**angegossen** *adj* F **wie ~ passen** (*or
sitzen*) fit like a glove.

'**angegriffen I** *pp of* **angreifen. II** *adj*
exhausted, weakened, poor (*health*),
affected (*organ*), strained (*nerves*).

'**angehaucht I** *pp of* **anhauchen. II** *adj* F
fig. **er ist kommunistisch ~** he has
Communist leanings.

'**angeheiratet** *adj* (related) by marriage:
~er Vetter cousin by marriage.

'**angeheitert** *adj* (a bit) tipsy, merry.

'**angehen** (*irr, sep*, -ge-, → **gehen**) **I** v/i
(sn) **1.** F begin, start. **2.** *light etc*: go on,
fire etc: (begin to) burn. **3.** *plant etc*:
take root. **4. ~ gegen** fight against. **II**
v/t **5.** (h) attack, *fig.* tackle (*problem*). **6.**
(sn) *fig.* concern: **das geht dich nichts
an!** that's none of your business!; **was
geht mich das an?** what's that got to
do with me? **7.** (sn) F *j-n* **um** *et.* **~** ask
s.o. for s.th. **III** v/*impers* (sn) **8. es geht
an** it's passable; **es kann nicht ~, daß ...**
it can't be true that ...

'**angehend** *adj* future, budding.

'**angehören** v/i (*sep*, h) (*dat*) belong (to)
(*a. fig.*), be a member (of).

'**Angehörige** m, f (-n; -n) **1.** relative,

dependant: **die nächsten ~n** the next of kin; **m-e ~n** my family. **2.** member.

Angeklagte ['angəkla:ktə] *m, f* (-n; -n) ⚖ defendant.

Angel[1] ['aŋəl] *f* (-; -n) hinge: *a. fig.* **aus den ~n heben** unhinge; **zwischen Tür und ~ a)** in passing, **b)** in a hurry.

'Angel[2] *f* (-; -n) fishing rod.

'Angelegenheit *f* (-; -en) affair, matter: **das ist m-e ~** that's my business; **kümmere dich um d-e ~en!** mind your own business!

angelehnt ['angəle:nt] *adj* ajar.

'angelernt I *pp of* **anlernen.** II *adj* semi-skilled (*worker*).

'Angelgerät *n* fishing tackle.

'Angelhaken *m* fish(ing) hook.

angeln ['aŋəln] I *v/i* (h) (*nach* for) fish, angle. II *v/t* (h) (*a. F fig.* **sich ~**) hook.

'Angelpunkt *m fig.* pivot, central issue.

'Angelrute *f* fishing rod.

'Angelsachse *m,* **'Angelsächsin** *f,* **'angelsächsisch** *adj* Anglo-Saxon.

'Angelschein *m* fishing permit.

'Angelschnur *f* fishing line.

'angemessen *adj* suitable, adequate (*both*: *dat* to), reasonable, fair (*price*).

'angenehm *adj* (*dat* to) pleasant, agreeable: → **verbinden** 2.

'angenommen I *pp of* **annehmen.** II *adj* adopted, *a.* assumed (*name*). III *conj* suppose, supposing.

'angepaßt I *pp of* **anpassen.** II *adj* *psych.* adjusted.

'angeregt I *pp of* **anregen.** II *adj* lively.

'angeschlagen I *pp of* **anschlagen.** II *adj* **1.** chipped. **2.** *boxing*: groggy. **3.** shaken, shaky, weakened (*health etc*).

'angeschlossen I *pp of* **anschließen.** II *adj* ⚡ linked-up, connected.

'angeschmutzt *adj* soiled.

'angesehen I *pp of* **ansehen.** II *adj* respected, reputable.

'Angesicht *n* (-[e]s; -er) face: **von ~** by sight; **von ~ zu ~** face to face; **im ~** (*gen*) → **angesichts** 2. **'angesichts** *prep* (*gen*) **1.** at the sight of. **2.** *fig.* in view of.

'angespannt I *pp of* **anspannen.** II *adj* *fig.* tense, strained (*nerves etc*).

Angestellte ['angəʃtɛltə] *m, f* (-n; -n) (salaried) employee: ✝ **die ~n** *a.* the staff. **'Angestelltenversicherung** *f* employees' insurance.

angestrengt ['angəʃtrɛŋt] I *pp of* **an-**

strengen. II *adj* **1.** strained. **2.** close (*attention etc*): **~ nachdenken** think hard.

'angetan I *pp of* **antun.** II *adj* **~ sein von** be taken with.

'angetrunken I *pp of* **antrinken.** II *adj* slightly drunk.

'angewandt I *pp of* **anwenden.** II *adj* applied (*arts etc*).

'angewiesen I *pp of* **anweisen.** II *adj* **~ sein auf** (*acc*) depend on.

'angewöhnen *v/t* (*sep*, h) **j-m et. ~** get s.o. used to s.th.; **sich et. ~** get into the habit of, take to *smoking etc*.

'Angewohnheit *f* (-; -en) habit.

'angewurzelt *adj* **wie ~ dastehen** stand rooted to the spot.

Angina [aŋ'gi:na] *f* (-; -nen) 🦠 tonsil(l)itis: **~ pectoris** angina (pectoris).

'angleichen *v/t* (*irr, sep*, -ge-, h, → **gleichen**) (*a.* **sich ~**) (*dat, an acc* to) adapt, adjust. **'Angleichung** *f* (-; -en) (*an acc* to) adaptation, adjustment.

Angler ['aŋlər] *m* (-s; -) angler.

'angliedern *v/t* (*sep*, -ge-, h) (*an acc* to) affiliate, *pol.* annex. **'Angliederung** *f* (-; -en) affiliation, *pol.* annexation.

Anglikaner [aŋli'ka:nər] *m* (-s; -), **Angli'kanerin** *f* (-; -nen), **angli'kanisch** *adj* Anglican.

Anglist [aŋ'glɪst] *m* (-en; -en), **An'glistin** *f* (-; -nen) professor (*or* student) of English. **Anglistik** [aŋ'glɪstɪk] *f* (-; *no pl*) English language and literature, *Am.* English philology. **Anglizismus** [aŋli'tsɪsmʊs] *m* (-; -men) Anglicism.

Anglo... [aŋlo-] Anglo-...

'anglotzen *v/t* (*sep*, -ge-, h) F stare at.

Angorawolle [aŋgo:ra-] *f* angora wool.

'angreifbar *adj* open to attack, *fig. a.* vulnerable. **'angreifen** (*irr, sep*, -ge-, h, → **greifen**) I *v/t* **1.** attack, 🦠 corrode: → **angegriffen** II. **3.** break into (*supplies*). **4.** → **anpacken** 2. II *v/i* attack. **'Angreifer** *m* (-s; -) attacker, *pol.* aggressor.

'angrenzen *v/i* (*sep*, -ge-, h) **~ an** (*acc*) border on. **'angrenzend** *adj* adjacent, adjoining, *fig.* related (*subjects etc*).

'Angriff *m* (-[e]s; -e) attack: ⚖ **tätlicher ~** assault (and battery); **zum ~ übergehen** take the offensive; *fig.* **et. in ~ nehmen** tackle s.th.

'Angriffs|**fläche** f fig. point of attack: **e-e ~ bieten** be vulnerable to attack; **j-m e-e ~ bieten** give s.o. a handle. **~krieg** m war of aggression. **~lustig** adj aggressive. **~spiel** n sports: attacking play. **~waffe** f offensive weapon.

'**angrinsen** v/t (sep, -ge-, h) grin at.

Angst [aŋst] f (-; ⁻e) fear, dread, terror (all: **vor** dat of), a. psych. anxiety (**um** about): (**nur**) **k-e ~.!** don't be afraid!; **aus ~ lügen** lie out of fear; **aus ~, bestraft zu werden** for fear of being punished; **~ haben** be afraid (**vor** dat of); **um j-n ~ haben** be worried about s.o.; **j-n in ~ (und Schrecken) versetzen** frighten s.o. (to death); **es tät der ~ (zu tun) bekommen** get the wind up; **mir ist ℒ und bange** I'm scared stiff.

'**Angstgegner** m sports: bogy team.

'**Angsthase** m F scaredy-cat.

ängstigen ['ɛŋstɪɡən] v/t (h) a) frighten, alarm, b) worry: **sich ~** be afraid (**vor** dat of), be worried (**um** about).

'**Angstkäufe** [-kɔʏfə] pl panic buying.

ängstlich ['ɛŋstlɪç] adj timid, nervous, anxious: **~ gehütet** jealously guarded; **~ bemüht** anxious (**zu** to). '**Ängstlichkeit** f (-; no pl) nervousness, anxiety.

'**Angstneu|rose** f anxiety neurosis.

'**Angstschrei** m cry of fear.

'**Angstschweiß** m cold sweat.

'**angstvoll** adj anxious, fearful.

'**angucken** v/t (sep, -ge-, h) F look at.

'**anhaben** v/t (irr, sep, -ge-, h, → **haben**) **1.** F wear, have on. **2.** **j-m nichts ~ können** be unable to get at s.o.

'**anhaften** v/i (sep, -ge-, h) **1.** (dat to) stick, cling. **2.** fig. be inherent (dat in).

'**anhalten** (irr, sep, -ge-, h, → **halten**) **I** v/t **1.** stop: **den Atem ~** hold one's breath; **mit angehaltenem Atem** with bated breath. **2.** **j-n zu Fleiß** etc ~ urge s.o. to be diligent etc. **II** v/i **3.** stop, pull up. **4.** last, continue, go on, weather: hold. '**anhaltend** adj constant, persistent, sustained. '**Anhalter** m (-s; -), '**Anhalterin** f (-; -nen) F hitchhiker: **per Anhalter fahren** hitchhike.

'**Anhaltspunkt** m clue: **k-e ~e haben** have nothing to go by.

Anhang ['anhaŋ] m (-[e]s; ⁻e) **1.** a) appendix, b) supplement, c) annex. **2.** dependants, family. **3.** followers.

'**anhängen**¹ (sep, -ge-, h) **I** v/t **1.** hang

up. **2.** (an acc to) mot., 🖷 couple, fig. add. **3.** F **j-m et. ~ → andrehen** 2; **j-m e-n Mord** etc **~** pin a murder etc on s.o. **II sich ~** (an acc to) hold on, cling; F fig. **sich ~ an** (acc) in a race etc: follow.

'**anhängen²** v/i (irr, sep, -ge-, h, → **hängen**¹) follow (a fashion etc), believe in (an idea etc): **j-m ~ reputation** etc: cling to s.o. **Anhänger** ['anhɛŋər] m (-s; -) **1.** follower, supporter, disciple, fan. **2.** pendant. **3.** mot. trailer. **4.** tag, label. '**Anhängerin** f (-; -nen) → **Anhänger** 1. '**Anhängerschaft** f (-; no pl) followers, following, fans. **anhängig** ['anhɛŋɪç] adj esp. 🕮 pending: **e-e Klage ~ machen** institute legal proceedings (**gegen** against). **anhänglich** ['anhɛŋlɪç] adj **1.** devoted. **2.** affectionate. **Anhängsel** ['anhɛŋzəl] n (-s; -) a. fig. appendage.

'**anhauchen** v/t (sep, -ge-, h) **1.** breathe on. **2.** → **angehaucht** II.

'**anhauen** v/t (sep, -ge-, h) F **j-n ~** touch s.o. (um for).

'**anhäufen** v/t (sep, -ge-, h) (a. **sich ~**) accumulate, pile up. '**Anhäufung** f (-; -en) accumulation.

'**anheben** v/t (irr, sep, -ge-, h, → **heben**) lift (up), a. fig. raise.

'**anheften** v/t (sep, -ge-, h) (an acc to) a) fasten, b) tack, baste, c) pin.

anheimelnd ['anhaiməlnd] adj hom(e)y, cosy, familiar.

anheimstellen [an'haim-] v/t (sep, -ge-, h) **es j-m ~** leave it to s.o.('s discretion).

'**anheizen** v/t (sep, -ge-, h) **1.** fire. **2.** F fig. fuel (strife), heat up (🕯 boom): **die Stimmung ~** whip up emotions.

'**anheuern** v/t, v/i (sep, -ge-, h) sign on.

'**Anhieb:** F **auf ~** a) at the first go, b) right off, off the cuff.

'**anhimmeln** v/t (sep, -ge-, h) F idolize.

'**Anhöhe** f (-; -n) rise, hill, elevation.

'**anhören** (sep, -ge-, h) **I** v/t listen to (a. **sich ~**), hear (witness etc): **mit ~** overhear; **j-n bis zu Ende ~** hear s.o. out; **das hört man ihm an!** you can tell by the way he talks! **II sich ~** sound; F **das hört sich gut an!** that sounds good!

'**Anhörung** f (-; -en) 🕮, parl. hearing.

Anilinfarbe [ani'li:n-] f anilin(e) dye.

animalisch [ani'ma:lɪʃ] adj animal.

Animateur [anima'tøːr] m (-s; -e) animator, entertainer.

Animierdame [ani'miːr-] f hostess.
animieren [ani'miːrən] v/t (h) **1.** encourage. **2.** film: animate.
Animosität [animozi'tɛːt] f (-; -en) animosity.
Anis [a'niːs] m (-[es]; -e) **1.** ⚘ anise. **2.** aniseed. **3.** aniseed brandy.
'ankämpfen v/i (sep, -ge-, h) ~ **gegen** fight (or struggle) against.
'Ankauf m (-[e]s; ⁓e) buying, purchase.
'ankaufen v/t (sep, -ge-, h) purchase, buy.
Anker ['aŋkər] m (-s; -) **1.** ⚓ anchor: **vor ~ gehen** drop anchor; **den ~ lichten** weigh anchor; **vor ~ liegen** ride at anchor. **2.** ⚡ armature. **⁓kette** f cable.
ankern ['aŋkərn] v/i (h) a) (cast) anchor, b) ride at anchor.
'Ankerplatz m anchorage.
'Ankerwinde f windlass.
'anketten v/t (sep, -ge-, h) chain (**an** acc to).
'Anklage f (-; -n) accusation, charge, ⚖ a. indictment (**wegen** for): ~ **erheben** bring (or prefer) a charge (**wegen** of); **unter ~ stehen** (**wegen**) a) be accused (of), b) be on trial (for). **'Anklagebank** f (-; ⁓e) ⚖ (**auf der ~** in the) dock.
'anklagen v/t (sep, -ge-, h) (gen or **wegen**) accuse (of), charge (with). **'anklagend** adj accusing. **'Ankläger** m (-s; -) ⚖ accuser: **öffentlicher ~** Public Prosecutor. **'Anklageschrift** f (bill of) indictment. **'Anklagevertreter** m counsel for the prosecution.
'anklammern (sep, -ge-, h) (**an** acc to) **I** v/t peg (on), ⚙ cramp. **II sich ~** cling.
'Anklang m (-[e]s; ⁓e) **1.** reminiscence (**an** acc of). **2.** ~ **finden** (**bei**) be well received (by), go down well (with); **k-n ~ finden** fall flat.
'ankleben v/t (sep, -ge-, h) stick on (**an** acc to).
'Ankleideka,bine f cubicle. **'ankleiden** v/t (sep, -ge-, h) (a. **sich ~**) dress.
'Ankleideraum m dressing room.
'anklopfen v/i (sep, -ge-, h) knock (**an** acc or dat at).
'anknabbern v/t (sep, -ge-, h) nibble at.
'anknipsen v/t (sep, -ge-, h) F switch on.
'anknüpfen (sep, -ge-, h) **I** v/t **1.** (**an** acc to) tie, knot. **2.** fig. begin, start (conversation etc), establish (contacts). **II** v/i **3.** fig. ~ **an** (acc or dat) a) go on from, b)

go back to (s.o.'s words etc), c) pick up the thread of (a story etc), d) continue (a tradition). **'Anknüpfungspunkt** m fig. starting point.
'ankommen (irr, sep, -ge-, sn, → **kommen**) **I** v/i **1.** arrive (**in** dat at, in): ~ **in** (dat) a. reach; ~ **um** train etc: arrive at, be due at. **2.** F ~ (**bei**) with) a) get a job, b) go down well, a. person: be a success; **nicht ~** a. be a flop; **damit kommt er bei mir nicht an** that cuts no ice with me. **3.** ~ **gegen** cope (or deal) with, j-n a. get the better of s.o.; **nicht ~ gegen** a. be powerless against. **II** v/impers **4.** ~ **auf** (acc) depend on; **es kommt (ganz) darauf an** it (all) depends. **5.** ~ **auf** (acc) matter; **worauf es (ihm) ankommt, ist zu gewinnen** the important thing (to him) is to win; **darauf kommt es an** that's the point. **6. es auf et. ~ lassen** risk s.th.; **ich lasse es darauf ~** I'll take a chance. **7. es kommt mich hart an** I find it hard.
Ankömmling ['ankœmlɪŋ] m (-s; -e) arrival.
'ankoppeln v/t (sep, -ge-, h) (**an** acc) couple (to), dock spacecraft (with).
'ankotzen v/t (sep, -ge-, h) V **es kotzt e-n an** it makes you sick.
'ankreiden v/t (sep, -ge-, h) F **j-m et. ~** blame s.o. for s.th.
'ankreuzen v/t (sep, -ge-, h) mark s.th. with a cross.
'ankündigen (sep, -ge-, h) **I** v/t announce, bill, advertise, fig. herald. **II sich ~** announce one's visit (fig. itself).
'Ankündigung f (-; -en) announcement (a. fig.), advertisement.
Ankunft ['ankʊnft] f (-; no pl) arrival.
'Ankunfts... arrival (airport, lounge, etc).
'Ankunftszeit f time of arrival.
'ankurbeln v/t (sep, -ge-, h) fig. step up, boost.
'anlächeln v/t (sep, -ge-, h) smile at.
'anlachen v/t (sep, -ge-, h) smile (or laugh) at: F **sich j-n ~** pick s.o. up.
'Anlage f (-; -n) **1.** no pl a) laying out, b) construction, c) arrangement, layout. **2.** installation, facility, (manufacturing) plant, work(s): **sanitäre ~n** sanitary facilities. **3.** a) (public) garden(s) (or park), grounds, b) sports facilities. **4.** F (hi-fi) set. **5.** draft, structure, design. **6.** (**zu** for) talent, gift. **7.** (**zu**)

(natural) tendency (of), *a.* ⚕ disposition (to). **8.** ⚓ investment: **~n** assets. **9.** enclosure: *in der* (*or* als) **~** *sende ich Ihnen* enclosed please find.

'**anlagebedingt** *adj* inherent.

'**Anlage|berater(in** *f*) *m* investment consultant. **~kapi.tal** *n* invested capital. **~pa,piere** *pl* investment securities. **~vermögen** *n* fixed assets.

Anlaß ['anlas] *m* (-sses; ⸚sse) **1.** occasion: *aus* **~** (*gen*) → *anläßlich*. **2.** cause, reason: **~** *geben zu* give rise to; *j-m* **~** *zur Klage geben* give s.o. cause to complain; *beim geringsten* **~** at the slightest provocation; *ohne jeden* **~** for no reason at all; *ich sehe k-n* **~** *zu gehen* I see no reason to go; *et. zum* **~** *nehmen* take occasion (*zu* to).

'**anlassen** (*irr, sep,* -ge-, h, → *lassen*) I *v/t* **1.** F → *anbehalten*. **2.** leave *the light, radio, etc* on. **3.** start (up) (*engine etc*). II *sich gut* **~** shape up well, *business etc*: promise well; *wie läßt er sich an?* how is he making out?

Anlasser ['anlasər] *m* (-s; -) *mot.* starter.

anläßlich ['anleslıç] *prep* (*gen*) on the occasion of.

'**anlasten** *v/t* (*sep,* -ge-, h) *j-m et.* **~** blame s.o. for s.th.

'**Anlauf** *m* (-[e]s; ⸚e) **1.** *sports*: run-up, *ski jumping*: approach: (*e-n*) **~** *nehmen* take a run. **2.** *fig.* (*beim ersten* **~** at the first) attempt: *e-n neuen* **~** *nehmen* have another go. **3.** *a.* ⚙ start.

'**anlaufen** (*irr, sep,* -ge-, → *laufen*) I *v/i* (sn) **1.** *sports*: run up (for the jump). **2.** *angelaufen kommen* come running along. **3.** **~** *gegen* → *anrennen* I. **4.** (*a.* **~** *lassen*) start (up). **5.** *fig.* start, get under way, *film*: be shown. **6.** *costs etc*: mount up, *interest etc*: accrue. **7.** *glass*: fog, *metal*: tarnish: *blau* **~** go blue. II *v/t* (h) **8.** call at (*a port etc*).

'**Anlauf|schwierigkeiten** *pl* initial problems. **~stelle** *f* address (*or* office) to turn to. **~zeit** *f* initial period.

'**Anlaut** *m* (-[e]s; -e) *ling.* initial sound.

'**anlauten** *v/i* (*sep,* -ge-, h) *ling.* begin.

'**Anlegebrücke** *f* landing stage.

'**anlegen** (*sep,* -ge-, h) I *v/t* **1.** put on (*jewellery etc*). **2.** (*an acc*) put up a *ladder etc* (against), line up *a ruler etc* (against), lay down *a card etc* (next to): *e-n strengen Maßstab* **~** apply a strict

standard; → *Hand*. **3.** lay out (*garden*), plan, design, construct, set up, instal(l). **4.** start (*a file*). **5.** get in (*supplies*). **6.** invest (*capital*), spend *a sum* (*für* on). *e-n Säugling* **~** give a baby the breast. **8.** *die Ohren* **~** *dog etc*: set back its ears. **9.** put on (*coals etc*). **10.** apply (*bandage*). **11.** *es* **~** *auf* (*acc*) be out for (*or* to *inf*); *darauf angelegt sein zu inf* be designed to *inf*. II *v/i* **12.** land: *im Hafen* (*or am Kai*) **~** dock. **13.** (take) aim (*auf acc* at). III *sich mit j-m* **~** tangle with s.o.

Anleger ['anle:gər] *m* (-s; -) ⚓ investor.

'**Anlegestelle** *f* ⚓ landing place.

'**anlehnen** (*sep,* -ge-, h) I *v/t* **1.** lean (*an acc* against). **2.** leave ajar. II *sich* **~** *an* (*acc*) **3.** lean against. **4.** *fig.* be model(l)ed on.

'**Anlehnung** *f* (-; -en) dependence (*an acc* on): *in* **~** *an* (*acc*) following.

Anleihe ['anlaɪə] *f* (-; -n) ⚓ loan: *e-e* **~** *bei j-m machen* borrow money from s.o., *fig.* borrow from s.o.

'**anleiten** *v/t* (*sep,* -ge-, h) **1.** guide, instruct. **2.** → *anhalten* 2.

'**Anleitung** *f* (-; -en) **1.** guidance, direction. **2.** directions, instructions.

'**anlernen** *v/t* (*sep,* -ge-, h) teach, train: → *angelernt* II.

Anlernling ['anlɛrnlɪŋ] *m* (-s; -e) trainee.

'**anliegen** *v/i* (*irr, sep,* -ge-, h, → *liegen*) **1.** *eng* **~** fit tightly, cling (*an dat* to). **2.** F *was liegt an?* what's on the agenda?

'**Anliegen** *n* (-s; -) **1.** request. **2.** matter, concern: *ein nationales* **~** a matter of national concern.

'**anliegend** *adj* **1.** *eng* **~** tight(-fitting), clinging. **2.** adjacent. **3.** ⚓ enclosed (*senden wir Ihnen* please find).

Anlieger ['anli:gər] *m* (-s; -) *mot.* resident: **~** *frei!* residents only! **~staat** *m* neighbo(u)ring (*on waters*: riparian) state. **~verkehr** *m* resident traffic.

'**anlocken** *v/t* (*sep,* -ge-, h) *fig.* attract.

'**anlügen** *v/t* (*irr, sep,* -ge-, h, → *lügen*) *j-n* **~** lie to s.o.

'**anmachen** *v/t* (*sep,* -ge-, h) F **1.** fasten (*an dat* to). **2.** switch on (*light*), light (*fire*). **3.** *gastr.* prepare, dress. **4.** *j-n* **~** a) give s.o. the come-on, b) snap at s.o., c) turn s.o. on.

'**anmalen** *v/t* (*sep,* -ge-, h) paint: F *sich* **~** paint one's face.

'**Anmarsch** *m* (-[e]s; *no pl*) ✕ *im* ~ *sein* be advancing (**auf** *acc* towards).
anmaßen ['anma:sən] *v/t* (*sep*, -ge-, h) *sich et.* ~ arrogate s.th. to o.s., usurp s.th.; *sich* ~ *zu inf* presume to *inf*.
'**anmaßend** *adj* arrogant, overbearing.
'**Anmaßung** *f* (-; -en) arrogance.
'**Anmeldeformu‚lar** *n* application form.
'**anmelden** (*sep*, -ge-, h) **I** *v/t* **1.** announce (*visitor etc*). **2.** *j-n in derSchule* (**zu e-m Kursus** *etc*) ~ enrol(l) s.o. at school (for a course *etc*); *j-n beim Arzt* ~ make an appointment for s.o. with the doctor; *j-n polizeilich* ~ register s.o. (with the police). **3.** *teleph.* book, *Am.* place: **den Fernseher** (**das Radio**) ~ get a television (radio) licen/ce (*Am.* -se). **4.** put forward (*claims etc*), raise (*doubts etc*): → *Patent* 1. **II** *sich* ~ **5.** announce o.s. **6.** enrol(l) (**zu** for, **in** *dat* at): *sich beim Arzt etc* ~ make an appointment with the doctor *etc*; *sich polizeilich* ~ register (with the police).
'**Anmeldung** *f* (-; -en) **1.** announcement. **2.** enrol(l)ment: (*polizeiliche*) ~ registration (with the police); *nur nach vorheriger* ~ by appointment only. **3.** reception (desk).
'**anmerken** *v/t* (*sep*, -ge-, h) **1.** a) mark, b) make a note of. **2.** remark, observe. **3.** *j-m s-e Verlegenheit etc* ~ notice s.o.'s embarrassment *etc*; *sich nichts* ~ *lassen* not to show one's feelings; *man merkte ihr sofort an, daß ...* you only had to look at her to see that ...; *laß dir nichts* ~*!* don't let on!
'**Anmerkung** *f* (-; -en) (*über acc* on) remark, comment, (foot)note, annotation: *mit* ~ *en versehen* annotate.
Anmut ['anmu:t] *f* (-; *no pl*) grace(fulness), charm, sweetness.
'**anmuten** *v/t* (*sep*, -ge-, h) *j-n seltsam etc* ~ strike s.o. as (being) odd *etc*.
'**anmutig** *adj* graceful, charming.
'**annageln** *v/t* (*sep*, -ge-, h) nail on (**an** *acc* to).
'**annähen** *v/t* (*sep*, -ge-, h) sew on (**an** *acc* to).
'**annähernd** **I** *adj* approximate. **II** *adv* (*nicht* ~ not) nearly. '**Annäherung** *f* (-; -en) approximation (*a. fig.*), *pol.* rapprochement. '**Annäherungsversuche** *pl* approaches, (*amorous*) advances.
Annahme ['ana:mə] *f* (-; -n) **1.** accept-

ance. **2.** adoption (*of a child, motion, etc*), passing (*of a law*). **3.** (*in der* ~ on the) assumption (*daß* that): *ich habe Grund zu der* ~, *daß ...* I have reasons to believe that ...; *gehe ich recht in der* ~, *daß ...?* am I right in thinking that ...? **4.** ~*stelle* *f* receiving office. ~*verweigerung* *f* nonacceptance.
Annalen [a'na:lən] *pl* annals.
annehmbar ['ane:mba:r] *adj* a) acceptable (*für* to), *a.* reasonable, fair (*price etc*), b) passable. '**annehmen** (*irr*, *sep*, -ge-, h, → *nehmen*) **I** *v/t* **1.** accept (*gift, letter, etc*). **2.** adopt (*child, name, title*). **3.** *parl.* carry (*a motion*), pass (*a bill*). **4.** admit (*students*). **5.** assume (*shape etc*), take (on) (*colo[u]r, smell, etc*), acquire (*habit etc*). **6.** assume, suppose, guess: *das ist nicht anzunehmen* that's unlikely; *ich nehme es an* I suppose so; *nehmen wir an* (*or angenommen*), *er stirbt* suppose he dies. **II** *sich j-s* (*e-r Sache*) ~ take care of s.o. (s.th.).
'**Annehmlichkeit** *f* (-; -en) amenity: ~*en des Lebens* *a.* comforts of life.
annektieren [anɛk'ti:rən] *v/t* *pol.* annex.
Annonce [a'nõ:sə] *f* (-; -n) advertisement, F ad. **annoncieren** [anõ'si:rən] *v/t*, *v/i* (h) advertise.
annullieren [anʊ'li:rən] *v/t* (h) annul, ✝ cancel (*order*), *sports:* disallow (*goal*).
Anode [a'no:də] *f* (-; -n) ⚡ anode, plate.
anöden ['anø:dən] *v/t* (*sep*, -ge-, h) F *j-n* ~ bore s.o. stiff.
anomal [ano'ma:l] *adj* anomalous.
Anomalie [anoma'li:] *f* (-; -n) anomaly.
anonym [ano'ny:m] *adj* anonymous.
Anonymität [anonymi'tɛ:t] *f* (-; *no pl*) anonymity.
Anorak ['anorak] *m* (-s; -s) anorak.
'**anordnen** *v/t* (*sep*, -ge-, h) **1.** arrange. **2.** order, direct.
'**Anordnung** *f* (-; -en) **1.** arrangement. **2.** order, direction: *auf* ~ *von* (*or gen*) by order of; ~*en treffen* give orders.
Anorexie [anorɛ'ksi:] *f* (-; *no pl*) ⚤ anorexia (nervosa).
'**anor‚ganisch** *adj* inorganic.
'**anormal** *adj* abnormal.
'**anpacken** (*sep*, -ge-, h) **I** *v/t* **1.** → *pakken* 2. **2.** F *fig.* treat, tackle. **II** *v/i* → *anfassen* II.
'**anpassen** (*sep*, -ge-, h) **I** *v/t* **1.** fit (on). **2.** (*dat or an acc*) adapt (to), *a.* ✝, ⊙

adjust (to), *in colo[u]r*: match (with). **II sich ~** (*dat or an acc* to) adapt (o.s.), adjust (o.s.): → **angepaßt**.

'**Anpassung** *f* (-; -en) (*an acc* to) adaptation, adjustment. '**anpassungsfähig** *adj* adaptable (*an acc* to). '**Anpassungsfähigkeit** *f* (-; *no pl*) adaptability. '**Anpassungsschwierigkeiten** *pl* difficulties in adapting.

'**anpeilen** *v/t* (*sep*, -ge-, h) **1.** ✍, ⚓ take a bearing of. **2.** *fig.* aim at.

'**anpfeifen** *v/t* (*irr*, *sep*, -ge-, h, → **pfeifen**) **1.** *sports*: **ein Spiel ~** give the starting whistle. **2.** F **j-n ~** blow s.o. up.

'**Anpfiff** *m* (-[e]s; -e) **1.** *sports*: (starting) whistle. **2.** F **e-n ~ kriegen** get ticked off.

'**anpflanzen** *v/t* (*sep*, -ge-, h) **1.** plant. **2.** cultivate, grow.

'**anpöbeln** *v/t* (*sep*, -ge-, h) molest, mob.

'**Anprall** *m* (-[e]s; *no pl*) impact (**gegen** [up]on).

anprangern ['anpraŋərn] *v/t* (*sep*, -ge-, h) denounce.

'**anpreisen** *v/t* (*irr*, *sep*, -ge-, h, → **preisen**) praise, F plug.

'**Anprobe** *f* (-; -n) (**zur ~** for a) fitting.

'**anpro,bieren** *v/t*, *v/i* (h) try on, fit on.

'**anpumpen** *v/t* (*sep*, -ge-, h) F **j-n ~** touch s.o. (**um** for).

'**Anraten** *n*: **auf ~ des Arztes** *etc* on the doctor's *etc* advice.

'**anrechnen** *v/t* (*sep*, -ge-, h) a) charge, b) credit, allow, c) take into account, d) deduct: *ped.* **et. als Fehler ~** count s.th. as a mistake; *fig.* **j-m et. als Fehler ~** give s.o. credit for s.th.; **j-m et. hoch ~** think highly of s.o. for s.th.

'**Anrecht** *n* (-[e]s; -e) (**auf** *acc* to) right, claim.

'**Anrede** *f* (-; -n) address. '**anreden** *v/t* (*sep*, -ge-, h) **j-n ~** address s.o.

'**anregen** *v/t* (*sep*, -ge-, h) **1.** stimulate (a. *v/i*), whet (*appetite*), *fig. a.* encourage: **j-n zum Nachdenken ~** give s.o. food for thought. **2.** suggest. '**anregend** *adj* stimulating: **~ wirken** have a stimulating effect. '**Anregung** *f* (-; -en) **1.** *no pl* stimulation, *fig. a.* encouragement. **2.** suggestion: **auf ~ von** (or *gen*) at the suggestion of.

'**anreichern** (*sep*, -ge-, h) **I** *v/t* 🜂, ⚗ enrich. **II sich ~** accumulate.

'**Anreise** *f* (-; -n) **1.** journey there (or

here). **2.** arrival. '**anreisen** *v/i* (*sep*, -ge-, sn) **1.** travel. **2.** arrive.

'**anreißen** *v/t* (*irr*, *sep*, -ge-, h, → **reißen**) **1.** F → **anbrechen** I. **2.** *fig.* raise.

'**Anreiz** *m* (-es; -e) incentive.

'**anrennen** *v/i* (*irr*, *sep*, -ge-, sn, → **rennen**) **1.** **~ gegen** run against, ✗ attack. **2.** **angerannt kommen** come running (up).

Anrichte ['anrıçtə] *f* (-; -n) sideboard.

'**anrichten** *v/t* (*sep*, -ge-, h) **1.** *gastr.* prepare, dress: **es ist angerichtet!** dinner *etc* is served! **2.** *fig.* cause (*disaster etc*), do (*damage*).

anrüchig ['anrγçıç] *adj* disreputable, dubious, F shady.

'**anrücken** *v/i* (*sep*, -ge-, sn) approach, ✗ advance, F turn up, come.

'**Anruf** *m* (-[e]s; -e) call. **Anrufbeantworter** *m* (telephone) answering machine. '**anrufen** (*irr*, *sep*, -ge-, h, → **rufen**) **I** *v/t* **j-n ~** a) call s.o., b) *teleph.* call (or ring) s.o. (up), c) *fig.* appeal to s.o. (**um Hilfe** *etc* for help); **ein Gericht ~** appeal to a court. **II** *v/i* make a (phone)call: **bei j-m ~** → I b.

'**anrühren** *v/t* (*sep*, -ge-, h) **1.** touch (*a. fig.*). **2.** mix.

ans = **an das**: → **Herz, Licht** *etc*.

Ansage ['anza·gə] *f* **1.** *radio*, *TV* announcement. **2.** *cards*: bid(ding).

'**ansagen** *v/t*, *v/i* (*sep*, -ge-, h) announce, *cards*: bid: **Trumpf ~** declare trumps; F **Sparen ist angesagt!** saving is the word!; → **Kampf** 1. '**Ansager** *m* (-s; -), '**Ansagerin** *f* (-; -nen) announcer.

'**ansammeln** *v/t* (*sep*, -ge-, h) a) (*a. sich ~*) collect, gather, assemble, b) accumulate, amass. '**Ansammlung** *f* (-; -en) **1.** accumulation. **2.** gathering, crowd.

ansässig ['anzɛsıç] *adj* resident (**in** *dat* at, in): **~ werden** take up (one's) residence, settle.

'**Ansatz** *m* (-es; �ə) **1.** ⚙ deposit, crust. **2.** *anat.* base: → **Haaransatz. 3.** *fig.* a) first sign(s), b) attempt, c) approach: **im ~ richtig** basically right; **gute (gewisse) Ansätze zeigen** show good (some) promise; **in den Ansätzen stekkenbleiben** get stuck at the beginning. **4.** 🜨 statement. **5.** ♈ estimate.

'**Ansatzpunkt** *m fig.* point of departure.

'**ansaugen** *v/t* (*sep*, -ge-, h) suck in.

'**anschaffen** *v/t* (*sep*, -ge-, h) buy: F **sich**

Kinder ~ have children. **'Anschaffung** f (-; -en) **1.** buying, purchase. **2.** acquisition. **'Anschaffungskosten** pl purchase cost.

'anschalten v/t (sep, -ge-, h) switch on.

'anschauen v/t (sep, -ge-, h) → *ansehen*. **anschaulich** ['anʃaʊlɪç] adj clear, vivid, graphic. **'Anschauung** f (-; -en) view, opinion, idea.

'Anschauungs|materi_al n illustrative material, n.s. audiovisual aids. **~unterricht** m **1.** object-teaching, visual instruction. **2.** fig. object-lesson.

'Anschein m (-[e]s; no pl) appearance: *allem* ~ *nach* to all appearances; *den* ~ *erwecken* give the impression; *sich den* ~ *geben* pretend, make believe; *es hat den* ~, *als ob* it looks as if.

'anscheinend adj apparent: *er ist* ~ *krank* he seems to be ill.

'anschicken: *sich* ~ (sep, -ge-, h) get ready (or be going) (*zu* to).

'anschieben v/t (irr, sep, -ge-, h, → *schieben*) mot. push-start.

'anschirren v/t (sep, -ge-, h) harness.

'Anschlag m (-[e]s; =e) **1.** a) poster, bill, b) notice. **2.** attack (*auf* acc on): ~ *auf j-n (j-s Leben)* attempt on s.o.'s life; *e-m* ~ *zum Opfer fallen* be assassinated. **3.** a) ♩ touch, b) on *typewriter*: stroke: *sie schreibt 400 Anschläge in der Minute* she types 400 strokes per minute. **4.** ♣ estimate. **5.** ◎ (limit) stop. **6.** *das Gewehr im* ~ *halten* point the gun (*auf* acc at). **7.** impact, swimming: touch. **'Anschlagbrett** n notice (Am. bulletin) board.

'anschlagen (irr, sep, -ge-, → *schlagen*) **I** v/t (h) **1.** a) fasten (*an* acc to), b) stick up, put up (*notice* etc). **2.** strike, hit (*key*, *note*), ring (*bell*): fig. *e-n anderen Ton* ~ change one's tune; *ein schnelleres Tempo* ~ quicken one's pace. **3.** a) strike, hit, knock, b) chip. **II** v/i **3.** **4.** (sn) hit (*waves*: break) (*an* acc against): *mit dem Kopf an die Wand* ~ hit one's head against the wall. **5.** (h) (begin to) ring, *dog*: bark. **6.** (h) *swimming*: touch. **7.** (h) (*bei* on) take effect, F *food*: show.

'anschleppen v/t (sep, -ge-, h) (a. *angeschleppt bringen*) drag along.

'anschließen (irr, sep, -ge-, h, → *schließen*) **I** v/t **1.** (*an* acc to) lock, chain. **2.** (*an* acc) ♣, ◎ connect (to, with), link

up (with), ⚡ a. plug in: → *angeschlossen*. **3.** add (*dat* to). **II** *sich* ~ **4.** (*an* acc) adjoin (*s.th.*), border (on). **5.** fig. follow: *an den Vortrag schloß sich e-e Diskussion an* the lecture was followed by a discussion. **6.** *sich j-m* ~ follow s.o., join s.o., fig. take s.o.'s side; *sich j-s Meinung* ~ agree with s.o.; *ich schließe mich an!* a) I agree, b) I'll join you! **7.** *sich an j-n* ~ befriend s.o.; *er schließt sich leicht an* he makes friends easily. **III** v/i **8.** fit closely.

'anschließend I adj **1.** adjacent, next. **2.** following. **3.** close-fitting. **II** adv **1.** afterward(s): ~ *an die Vorstellung* following the performance.

'Anschluß m (-sses; ⸗sse) **1.** ♣, 🕿, ◎ etc a) connection, telephone (connection), b) line: teleph. *k-n* ~ *bekommen* not to get through; 🕿 ~ *haben* have a connection (*nach* to): *s-n* ~ *verpassen* miss one's connection; fig. *den* ~ *verpassen* miss the boat; *den* ~ *finden an* (acc) catch up with. **2.** affiliation (*an* acc with a *party* etc), pol. union. **3.** *im* ~ *an* (acc) after, following. **4.** F contact, acquaintance: ~ *finden* make contact (or friends) (*bei* with); ~ *suchen* look for company. **~dose** f ⚡ wall socket. **~flug** m connecting flight. **~schnur** f ⚡ flex. **~treffer** m goal that leaves one more to level the score. **~zug** m connecting train.

'anschmiegen: *sich* ~ (sep, -ge-, h) (*an* acc) nestle (against), dress (*dr:* snuggle (to). **'anschmiegsam** adj affectionate.

'anschmieren v/t (sep, -ge-, h) F cheat.

'anschnallen (sep, -ge-, h) **I** v/t a) buckle on, b) put on (*skis*). **II** *sich* ~ ✈, mot. fasten one's seat belt.

'Anschnallgurt m seat belt.

'anschnauzen v/t (sep, -ge-, h) F *j-n* ~ blow s.o. up.

'anschneiden v/t (irr, sep, -ge-, h, → *schneiden*) **1.** cut into (*bread* etc). **2.** cut (*ball* etc). **3.** fig. broach: *ein anderes Thema* ~ change the subject.

'Anschnitt m (-[e]s; -e) first slice.

'anschreiben (irr, sep, -ge-, h, → *schreiben*) **I** v/t **1.** write down: *j-m et.* ~ charge s.o. with s.th.; *et.* ~ *lassen* buy s.th. on credit; *bei j-m gut (schlecht) angeschrieben sein* be in s.o.'s good (bad) books. **2.** *j-n* ~ write to s.o.

'Anschreiben n (-s; -) covering letter.

'anschreien v/t (irr, sep, -ge-, h, → **schreien**) shout at, scream at.

'Anschrift f (-; -en) address.

Anschuldigung ['anʃʊldɪɡʊŋ] f (-; -en) accusation.

'anschwärzen v/t (sep, -ge-, h) F a) run s.o. down, b) denounce (**bei** to).

'anschwellen v/i (irr, sep, -ge-, sn, → **schwellen**) swell, fig. increase, rise.

'anschwemmen v/t (sep, -ge-, h) a) wash ashore, b) geol. deposit.

'ansehen (irr, sep, -ge-, h, → **sehen**) v/t look at: **sich et.** ~ take a look at, examine, watch; **sich e-n Film** (or **e-e Fernsehsendung**) ~ go and see a film (watch a program[me]); **sich et. genau** ~ have a close look at s.th.; **man sieht es ihr an, daß** ... you can tell by her face that ...; **man sieht ihm sein Alter nicht an** he doesn't look his age; **ich sehe es für** (or **als**) **m-e Pflicht an zu** inf I consider it my duty to inf; **et. mit** ~ watch (or witness) s.th.; **ich kann es nicht länger mit** ~! I can't stand it any longer; F **sieh mal einer an!** fancy that!; → **finster** 2, **schief** 3.

'Ansehen n (-s) **1.** reputation, prestige: **von hohem** ~ of high standing; **großes** ~ **genießen** be highly esteemed; **an** ~ **verlieren** lose credit. **2.** fig. **ohne** ~ **der Person** without respect of persons.

ansehnlich ['anseːnlɪç] adj handsome, considerable.

'anseilen v/t (sep, -ge-, h) (a. **sich** ~) rope (up).

'ansetzen (sep, -ge-, h) **I** v/t **1.** (**an** acc) put (on, to), apply drill etc (to), put flute, glass, etc to one's lips. **2.** (**an** acc to) a) add, join, b) sew on. **3.** fix, set (date etc), assess (costs), quote (price). **4.** ♈ set up (equation). **5.** develop, ♉ a. put forth (buds), put on (rust): **Fett** ~ put on weight. **6.** gastr. prepare (a. ♉), make, mix. **7.** bring in: **j-n auf** (acc) put s.o. onto; **e-n Hund** (**auf e-e Spur**) ~ set a dog on the trail. **II** v/i **8.** begin, (make a) start: a. fig. **zum Endspurt** ~ set o.s. for the final spurt; **zur Landung** ~ come in (to land), aer. make the approach; **zum Sprechen** ~ start to speak; **zum Sprung** ~ get ready for the jump. **9.** fig. criticism, reform, etc: set in. **III sich** ~ accumulate.

'Ansicht f (-; -en) **1.** (**über** acc) opinion

(on), view (of): **m-r** ~ **nach** in my opinion, as I see it; **der** ~ **sein** (or **die** ~ **vertreten**), **daß ...** take the view that ...; **anderer** ~ **sein** take a different view, w.s. disagree; **die** ~**en sind geteilt** opinion differs; **zu der** ~ **gelangen** (or **kommen**), **daß ...** decide that ... **2.** view (a. ⊚). **3.** ✝ **zur** ~ on approval.

'Ansichts(post)karte f picture postcard.

'Ansichtssache: **das ist** ~ that's a matter of opinion.

'ansiedeln v/t (sep, -ge-, h) **1.** settle (a. **sich** ~), ✝ base, site: **in London angesiedelt** London-based. **2.** fig. place.

'Ansiedler(in f) m settler.

'Ansiedlung f (-; -en) settlement.

'Ansinnen n (-s; -) request, demand.

'anspannen v/t (sep, -ge-, h) **1.** harness (**an** acc to). **2.** tighten, stretch (rope etc). **3.** flex (muscles). **4.** fig. strain: **alle Kräfte** ~ strain every nerve.

'Anspannung f (-; -en) fig. strain.

'anspielen (sep, -ge-, h) **I** v/i **1.** cards: (have the) lead. **2.** sports: lead off, soccer: kick off. **3.** fig. ~ **auf** (acc) allude to, insinuate (s.th.). **II** v/t **4.** lead (card). **5.** sports: **j-n** ~ pass to s.o.

'Anspielung f (-; -en) (**auf** acc) allusion (to), insinuation (about).

'anspinnen: **sich** ~ (irr, sep, -ge-, h, → **spinnen**) fig. develop.

'anspitzen v/t (sep, -ge-, h) point.

'Ansporn m (-[e]s; no pl) incentive (**für** to). **'anspornen** v/t (sep, -ge-, h) a. fig. spur (on).

'Ansprache f (-; -n) **1.** (**e-e** ~ **halten** deliver an) address (**an** acc to). **2.** F **k-e** ~ **haben** have no one to talk to.

ansprechbar ['anʃprɛçbaːr] adj **1.** 🕮 responsive. **2.** F **er war nicht** ~ you couldn't talk to him. **'ansprechen** (irr, sep, -ge-, h, → **sprechen**) **I** v/t **1.** speak to, address, appeal to s.o. (**wegen** for). **2.** please, appeal to. **3.** touch (up)on (problem etc). **II** v/i **4.** a. ⊙ respond (**auf** acc to). **5.** appeal (to the public).

'ansprechend adj pleasing, attractive.

'Ansprechpartner m person to turn to.

'anspringen (irr, sep, -ge-, → **springen**) **I** v/i (sn) start up. **II** v/t (h) jump at.

'Anspruch m (-[e]s; ⸱e) (**auf** acc to) a. 🕮 claim, right, contp. pretension: **hohe Ansprüche stellen** be very demanding, **an j-n** make heavy demands on s.o.; ~

haben auf (*acc*) be entitled to; **in ~ nehmen** a) *a.* **~ erheben auf** (*acc*) lay claim to, b) call on (*s.o.*, *s.o.'s help*), take up (*s.o.'s time etc*); **j-n in ~ nehmen** keep s.o. busy; **j-n ganz in ~ nehmen** claim s.o.'s full attention.

'**anspruchslos** *adj* **1.** a) undemanding (*a. fig. book*, *music*, *etc*), b) easily satisfied. **2.** plain, simple. '**Anspruchslosigkeit** *f* (-; *no pl*) undemandingness, modesty. '**anspruchsvoll** *adj* demanding (*a. fig.*), particular.

'**anspucken** *v/t* (*sep*, -ge-, h) spit at.

'**anstacheln** *v/t* (*sep*, -ge-, h) goad on.

Anstalt ['anʃtalt] *f* (-; -en) **1.** establishment, institution, *ped.* institute, school. **2.** a) sanatorium, *Am.* sanitarium, b) F mental home: **j-n in e-e ~ einweisen** institutionalize s.o. **3.** **~en treffen zu** make arrangements for; **~en machen zu gehen** *etc* get ready to go *etc*.

Anstand ['anʃtant] *m* (-[e]s; *no pl*) **1.** (sense of) decency. **2.** (good) manners. **anständig** ['anʃtɛndɪç] *adj* **1.** proper, decent, respectable: **benimm dich ~!** behave yourself! **2.** F fair (*price etc*): **ein ~es Essen** a decent meal; **e-e ~e Arbeit** a good job. '**Anstandsbesuch** *m* formal call. '**Anstandsdame** *f* chaperon. '**anstandshalber** *adv* for decency's sake. '**anstandslos** *adv* **1.** unhesitatingly. **2.** freely.

'**anstarren** *v/t* (*sep*, -ge-, h) stare at.

an'statt I *prep* (*gen*) instead of. II *conj* **~ zu arbeiten** *etc* instead of working *etc*.

'**anstauen** (*sep*, -ge-, h) I *v/t* dam up. II **sich ~** accumulate, *fig. rage etc*: build up; **angestaute Wut** pent-up rage.

'**anstechen** *v/t* (*irr*, *sep*, -ge-, h, → **stechen**) prick, tap (*barrel*).

'**anstecken** (*sep*, -ge-, h) I *v/t* **1.** pin on, put on, slip on. **2.** set *house* on fire, light (*cigar*, *candle*). **3.** 🩺, *a. fig.* infect (**mit** with): **er hat mich (mit s-m Schnupfen) angesteckt** he has given me his cold. II *v/i* **4.** 🩺, *a. fig.* be infectious. III **sich ~ 5.** *ich habe mich bei ihm (mit Grippe) angesteckt** I have caught the flu from him. '**ansteckend** *adj* 🩺, *a. fig.* infectious. '**Anstecknadel** *f* a) pin, b) badge. **Ansteckung** ['anʃtɛkʊŋ] *f* (-; -en) 🩺 infection. '**Ansteckungsgefahr** *f* danger of infection.

'**anstehen** *v/i* (*irr*, *sep*, -ge-, h, → **ste-**

hen) **1.** queue (*Am.* line) up (**nach** for). **2.** ✝, 🎼 be up (**zur Entscheidung** for decision), be on the agenda.

'**ansteigen** *v/i* (*irr*, *sep*, -ge-, sn, → **steigen**) rise.

an'stelle *prep* **~ von** (*or gen*) instead of.

'**anstellen** (*sep*, -ge-, h) I *v/t* **1.** (**an** *acc* against) put, lean. **2.** start (*machine*), turn on (*heating etc*), switch on (*radio etc*). **3.** employ, *Am.* hire: **angestellt sein bei** work for; F **j-n zu et. ~** have s.o. do s.th. **4.** a) make, carry out, b) F do, manage: **Nachforschungen ~** make inquiries; F **was haben sie mit dir angestellt?** what have they done to you?; **Dummheiten ~, et. (Dummes) ~** get up to mischief; **was hast du (da) wieder angestellt?** what have you been up to (again)?; **wie hast du das angestellt?** how did you manage that?; → **Überlegung.** II **sich ~ 5.** queue (*Am.* line) up (**nach** for). **6.** F act, make (**als ob** as if): **sich bei et. ungeschickt ~** go about s.th. clumsily; **stell dich nicht so an!** don't make such a fuss!; **stell dich nicht so dumm an!** don't act stupid!

'**anstellig** ['anʃtɛlɪç] *adj* handy, clever.

'**Anstellung** *f* (-; -en) place, employment, job.

'**ansteuern** *v/t* (*sep*, -ge-, h) head for.

Anstieg ['anʃtiːk] *m* (-[e]s; -e) **1.** ascent. **2.** *fig.* (gen) rise (in), increase (of).

'**anstiften** *v/t* (*sep*, -ge-, h) (**zu** to) incite, instigate: **j-n ~ zu** *a.* put s.o. up to. '**Anstifter** *m* (-s; -), '**Anstifterin** *f* (-; -nen) instigator. '**Anstiftung** *f* (-; -en) (**auf ~** *gen* at the) instigation (of).

'**anstimmen** *v/t* (*sep*, -ge-, h) ♪ strike up: **ein Lied ~** break into a song.

Anstoß *m* (-es; ⸚e) **1.** *soccer*: kickoff. **2.** impulse: **den ~ geben zu** start off, initiate. **3.** F **bei j-m ~ erregen** scandalize s.o., give offen/ce (*Am.* -se) to s.o.; **~ nehmen an** (*dat*) take offense (at). '**anstoßen** (*irr*, *sep*, -ge-, → **stoßen**) I *v/t* (h) **1.** knock (*or* bump) against: **sich den Kopf ~** bump one's head (**an** *dat* against); **j-n (mit dem Ellbogen) ~** nudge s.o. (with the elbow). II *v/i* **2.** (h) clink glasses: **~ auf** (*acc*) drink to. **3.** (sn) (**an** *dat*) knock (against), bump (into): **mit dem Kopf ~** → 1. **4.** (h) **mit der Zunge ~** lisp. **5.** (h) *soccer*: kick off.

anstößig ['anʃtøːsɪç] *adj* a) offensive, scandalous, b) indecent.

'**anstrahlen** *v/t* (*sep*, -ge-, h) illuminate: *mit Scheinwerfern* ~ floodlight; F *fig. j-n* ~ beam at s.o.

'**anstreben** *v/t* (*sep*, -ge-, h) aim at, strive for.

'**anstreichen** *v/t* (*irr, sep*, -ge-, h, → *streichen*) **1.** paint. **2.** mark (*rot etc* in red *etc*). '**Anstreicher** *m* (-s; -) painter.

anstrengen ['anʃtrɛŋən] (*sep*, -ge-, h) **I** *v/t* **1.** strain, be a strain on, exhaust: → *angestrengt* 1. **2.** → *Prozeß* 2. **II** *v/i* **3.** be exhausting, be a strain. **III** *sich* ~ make an effort, try (hard), exert o.s.; *streng dich mal an!* you could try a bit harder! '**anstrengend** *adj* strenuous, trying (*für* to). '**Anstrengung** *f* (-; -en) **1.** (*mit äußerster* ~ with a supreme) effort. **2.** strain, exertion.

'**Anstrich** *m* (-[e]s; -e) **1.** a) painting, b) paint, c) coat. **2.** *no pl* air, semblance.

'**Ansturm** *m* (-[e]s; ⁺e) onrush (*a. fig.*), ✕ assault, *a. sports:* attack, ⚓ *auf acc*) run (on), rush (for). '**anstürmen** *v/i* (*sep*, -ge-, sn) ~ *gegen a. fig.* attack.

Antagonismus [antago'nɪsmʊs] *m* (-; -men) antagonism.

antarktisch [ant'arktɪʃ] *adj* Antarctic.

'**antasten** *v/t* (*sep*, -ge-, h) infringe on (*rights etc*), touch (*capital*), break into (*supplies*).

'**Anteil** *m* (-[e]s; -e) **1.** (*an dat*) share (of, in), ⚓ *a.* interest (in), participation (of): *fig. er hatte k-n* ~ *am Erfolg* he had no part in the success. **2.** a) interest, b) sympathy: ~ *nehmen an* (*dat*) take an interest (in), *j-s Unglück* sympathize with s.o. in his misfortune, *j-s Freude* share in s.o.'s joy. **anteilig** ['antaɪlɪç], '**anteilmäßig** *adj and adv* proportionate(ly). '**Anteilnahme** *f* (-; *no pl*) sympathy (*an dat* with).

'**Anteilschein** *m* (-[e]s; -e) → *Aktie.*

'**Anteilseigner(in** *f*) *m* → *Aktionär(in).*

Antenne [an'tɛnə] *f* (-; -n) aerial, *Am.* antenna (*a. fig.*).

Anthologie [antolo'giː] *f* (-; -n) anthology.

Anthrazit [antra'tsiːt] *m* (-s; -e) *min.* anthracite.

Anti..., anti... [anti-] anti...

Antialko'holiker(in *f*) *m* teetotal(l)er.

Anti'babypille *f* F *the* pill.

Antibiotikum [antibi'oːtɪkʊm] *n* (-s; -ka), **antibi'otisch** [-tɪʃ] *adj* antibiotic.

Antibloc'kiersystem *n* *mot.* (*abbr.* **ABS**) antilocking system.

Antidepressivum [antideprɛ'siːvʊm] *n* (-s; -va) antidepressant.

Antifa'schismus *m* antifascism.

Antifa'schist(in *f*) *m*, **antifa'schistisch** *adj* antifascist.

Antigen [anti'geːn] *n* (-s; -e) ⚕ antigen.

Anti'haftbeschichtung: *mit* ~ nonstick.

antik [an'tiːk] *adj* **1.** classical, ancient. **2.** antique, period (*furniture etc*).

An'tike¹ *f* (-; *no pl*) (classical) antiquity.

An'tike² *f* (-; -n) *usu. pl* antique.

'**Antikörper** *m* ⚕ antibody.

Antilope [anti'loːpə] *f* (-; -n) antelope.

Antipathie [antipa'tiː] *f* (-; -n) (*gegen*) antipathy (to, against), dislike (of, for).

Antipode [anti'poːdə] *m* (-n; -n) antipode.

Antiqua [an'tiːkva] *f* (-; *no pl*) *print.* Roman (type).

Antiquar [anti'kvaːr] *m* (-s; -e), **Anti'quarin** *f* (-; -nen) **1.** second-hand bookseller. **2.** antique dealer.

Antiquariat [antikva'riaːt] *n* (-[e]s; -e) second-hand bookshop. **antiquarisch** [-'kvaːrɪʃ] *adj and adv* second-hand.

antiquiert [anti'kviːrt] *adj* antiquated.

Antiquität [antikvi'tɛːt] *f* (-; -en) antique. **Antiqui'täten|händler(in** *f*) *m* antique dealer. **~laden** *m* antique shop.

Antise'mit(in *f*) *m* anti-Semite.

antise'mitisch *adj* anti-Semitic.

Antisemi'tismus *m* anti-Semitism.

anti'septisch *adj* antiseptic.

anti'statisch *adj* antistatic.

Antrag ['antraːk] *m* (-[e]s; ⁺e) **1.** application (*auf acc* for), ⚖ petition, *parl.* motion, bill: *e-n* ~ *stellen auf* (*acc*) apply (⚖ petition, *parl.* move) for; *auf* ~ *von* (*or gen*) on the application *etc* of. **2.** *er machte ihr e-n* ~ he proposed to her. **3.** → '**Antragsformu|lar** *n* application form. '**Antragsteller** [-ʃtɛlər] *m* (-s; -), '**Antragstellerin** *f* (-; -nen) applicant, *parl.* mover.

'**antreffen** *v/t* (*irr, sep*, -ge-, h, → *treffen*) find, come across.

'**antreiben** *v/t* (*irr, sep*, -ge-, h, → *treiben*) **1.** *a. fig.* drive (on), urge (on). **2.** ⚙ drive. **3.** *a. v/i* drift ashore.

'**antreten** (*irr, sep*, -ge-, → *treten*) **I** *v/t*

(h) **1.** *ein Amt* ~ take up an office; *die Arbeit* (*den Dienst*) ~ report for work (duty); *e-e Reise* ~ start off on a journey; *e-e Strafe* ~ begin to serve a sentence; → *Erbschaft*. **2.** kick (*bike*). **II** *v/i* (sn) **3.** line up. **4.** report (*bei* to). **5.** *sports*: enter (*bei, zu* for): ~ *gegen* compete against.

'**Antrieb** *m* (-[e]s; -e) **1.** *fig*. a) impulse, urge, b) motive, c) incentive: *aus eigenem* ~ of one's own accord; *neuen* ~ *geben* a) give a fresh impetus to s.th., b) *j-m* give s.o. a new interest. **2.** ☉ drive.

'**Antriebs**|**aggre**,**gat** *n* ☉ drive assembly. ~**kraft** *f* driving power. ~**schwäche** *f* (-; *no pl*) *psych*. lack of drive.

'**antriebsstark** *adj psych*. full of drive.

'**Antriebswelle** *f mot*. axle-drive shaft.

'**antrinken** *v/t* (*irr, sep, -ge-, h,* → *trinken*) F *sich e-n* ~ get drunk; *sich Mut* ~ give o.s. Dutch courage.

'**Antritt** *m* (-[e]s; *no pl*) *bei* ~ a) *s-r Reise* upon setting out on his journey, b) *s-s Amtes* on entering upon his office, c) *der Macht* on coming into power, d) *e-r Erbschaft* upon accession to an inheritance. '**Antrittsbesuch** *m* first call. '**Antrittsrede** *f* inaugural speech, *parl*. maiden speech.

'**antun** *v/t* (*irr, sep, -ge-, h,* → *tun*) **1.** *j-m et.* ~ do s.th. to s.o; *j-m et. Gutes* ~ do s.o. a good turn; *sich et.* ~ lay hands upon o.s. **2.** *es j-m* ~ take s.o.'s fancy; → *angetan*.

Antwort ['antvɔrt] *f* (-; -en) (*auf acc* to) answer, *fig. a.* response. '**antworten** *v/i, v/t* (h) answer, reply, *fig.* respond: *auf e-e Frage* ~ answer a question; *j-m* ~ answer s.o., reply to s.o.

'**Antwortschein** *m* (international) reply coupon.

'**anvertrauen** (*sep*, h) **I** *v/t j-m et.* ~ a) entrust s.o. with s.th., b) confide s.th. to s.o. **II** *sich j-m* ~ a) confide in s.o., b) entrust o.s. to s.o.

'**anwachsen** *v/i* (*irr, sep, -ge-, sn,* → *wachsen*[1]) **1.** grow on (*an acc* to), take root. **2.** *fig.* increase (*auf acc* to). '**Anwachsen** *n* (-s) *fig.* increase, growth.

Anwalt ['anvalt] *m* (-[e]s; ⁓e), **Anwältin** ['anvɛltɪn] *f* (-; -nen) **1.** ⚖ a) lawyer, *Am.* attorney(-at-law), b) solicitor, barrister, *Am.* counselor-at-law, coun-

sel (*des Angeklagten* for the defence). **2.** *fig.* advocate.

'**Anwalts**|**hono**,**rar** *n* lawyer's fee. ~**kammer** *f* Bar Council (*Am.* Association). ~**kosten** *pl* lawyer's fees.

'**Anwaltschaft** *f* (-; -en) the Bar.

'**Anwandlung** *f* (-; -en) (*aus e-r* ~ *heraus* on an) impulse.

'**anwärmen** *v/t* (*sep, -ge-,* h) warm (up).

'**Anwärter**(**in** *f*) *m* (*auf acc*) candidate (for), aspirant (to).

Anwartschaft ['anvart∫aft] *f* (-; -en) (*auf acc*) candidacy (for), qualification (for), ⚖ expectancy (of).

'**anweisen** *v/t* (*irr, sep, -ge-,* h, → *weisen*) **1.** a) instruct, direct, b) guide, train. **2.** assign (*dat* to): *j-m e-n Platz* ~ show s.o. to his seat. **3.** (*dat* to) remit (*sum*), order the payment of (*fee etc*).

'**Anweisung** *f* (-; -en) **1.** instruction, direction. **2.** assignment. **3.** remittance.

anwendbar ['anvɛntbaːr] *adj* applicable (*auf acc* to). '**anwenden** *v/t* (*irr, sep, -ge-,* h, → *wenden*) use, make use of, *a.* ⚖, ⚗ apply (*auf acc* to): *falsch* ~ misapply; *nutzbringend* ~ make good use of; → *äußerlich, Gewalt* 1.

'**Anwender** *m* (-s; -) *computer*: user.

'**Anwendung** *f* (-; -en) **1.** use, application (*auf acc* to): *unter* ~ *von Zwang* by (using) force. **2.** ⚗ (hydrotherapeutic) treatment.

'**Anwendungs**|**beispiel** *n* example of use. ~**pro**,**gramm** *n computer*: application program. ~**vorschrift** *f* directions for use.

'**anwerben** *v/t* (*irr, sep, -ge-,* h, → *werben*) recruit, ⚔ *a.* enlist. '**Anwerbung** *f* (-; -en) recruitment.

'**Anwesen** *n* (-s; -) property, estate.

anwesend ['anve:zənt] *adj* present (*bei* at): *nicht* ~ *sein* be absent. '**Anwesende** *m, f* (-n; -n) person present: ~ *ausgenommen* present company excepted. '**Anwesenheit** *f* (-; *no pl*) presence: *in* ~ *von* (*or gen*) in the presence of. '**Anwesenheitsliste** *f* attendance list.

'**anwidern** *v/t* (*sep, -ge-,* h) → *anekeln*.

Anwohner ['anvo:nər] *m* (-s; -), '**Anwohnerin** *f* (-; -nen) resident.

'**Anzahl** *f* (-; *no pl*) number.

'**anzahlen** *v/t* (*sep, -ge-,* h) (pay *a sum* as a) deposit, make a down payment (on).

'**Anzahlung** *f* (-; -en) deposit, down payment.

'**anzapfen** *v/t* (*sep*, -ge-, h) tap (*a.* F *fig.*).

'**Anzeichen** *n* (-s; -) (*für* of) sign, *a.* ✚ symptom: *alle ~ sprechen dafür, daß ...* there is every indication that ...

Anzeige ['antsaɪɡə] *f* (-; -n) **1.** announcement, notice, *esp.* ✚ advice. **2.** advertisement, F ad(vert): *e-e ~ aufgeben a.* advertise. **3.** notification, 𝄞 information: (*bei der Polizei*) *~ erstatten* → *anzeigen*) '**anzeigen** *v/t* (*sep*, -ge-, h) **1.** *j-m et. ~* notify s.o. of s.th. **2.** indicate, ⊙ *a.* register. **3.** denounce: *j-n* (*bei der Polizei*) *~* report s.o. to the police. **4.** *fig.* indicate: *es erscheint angezeigt zu inf* it seems advisable to *inf.*

'**Anzeigen|blatt** *n* advertising paper. *~teil m* newspaper: advertisements.

'**Anzeiger** *m* (-s; -) **1.** gazette. **2.** ⊙ indicator.

'**Anzeigetafel** *f* sports: scoreboard.

'**anzetteln** *v/t* (*sep*, -ge-, h) instigate.

'**anziehen** (*irr*, *sep*, -ge-, h, → *ziehen*) **I** *v/t* **1.** put on (*clothes*): *j-n ~* dress s.o. **2.** *phys.* attract (*a.* *fig.*), absorb (*humidity etc*). **3.** *fig.* draw (*people*). **4.** tighten (*screw*, *rope*), apply (*brake*), draw in (*reins*). **5.** draw up (*legs*). **II** *v/i* **6.** *horse etc*: pull away. **7.** *fig. prices etc*: go up. **III** *sich ~* dress (o.s.), get dressed.

'**anziehend** *adj* fig. attractive, charming: *~ wirken auf* (*acc*) attract.

'**Anziehung** *f* (-; *no pl*) *a. fig.* attraction.

'**Anziehungskraft** *f* **1.** *phys. a.* attraction, b) gravitational pull. **2.** *no pl* (*auf acc*) attraction (for), appeal (to).

'**Anziehungspunkt** *m* fig. cent/re (*Am.* -er) of attraction.

'**Anzug** *m* (-[e]s; ⸚e) **1.** suit. **2.** *im ~ sein* be approaching, *storm*: be coming up.

anzüglich ['antsy:klɪç] *adj* personal (*remark*), suggestive (*joke*): *~ werden* get personal. '**Anzüglichkeit** *f* (-; -en) *usu. pl* personal remark.

'**anzünden** *v/t* (*sep*, -ge-, h) light (*cigar etc*), strike (*match*), set *house* on fire.

'**Anzünder** *m* (-s; -) lighter.

'**anzweifeln** *v/t* (*sep*, -ge-, h) question, doubt.

Aorta [a'ɔrta] *f* (-; -ten) *anat.* aorta.

apart [a'part] *adj* striking, unusual.

Apartheid [a'parthaɪt] *f* (-; *no pl*) apartheid. *~poli,tik f* apartheid policy.

Apartment [a'partmənt] *n* (-s; -s) flatlet, *Am.* apartment. *~haus n* block of flatlets, *Am.* apartment building.

Apathie [apa'ti:] *f* (-; -n) apathy.

apathisch [a'pa:tɪʃ] *adj* apathetic.

Aperitif [aperi'ti:f] *m* (-s; -s, -e) aperitif.

Apfel ['apfəl] *m* (-s; ⸚) apple: → *sauer* 1.

'**Apfel|baum** *m* apple tree. *~kuchen m gedeckter ~* apple pie. *~mus n* apple sauce. *~saft m* apple juice.

Apfelsine [apfəl'zi:nə] *f* (-; -n) orange.

'**Apfelstrudel** *m gastr.* apfelstrudel.

'**Apfelwein** *m* cider.

Aphorismus [afo'rɪsmʊs] *m* (-; -men) aphorism.

Apokalypse [apoka'lypsə] *f* (-; -n) apocalypse.

Apostel [a'pɔstəl] *m* (-s; -) *a. fig.* apostle. **A'postelgeschichte** *f bibl. the* Acts (of the Apostles). **apostolisch** [apɔs'to:lɪʃ] *adj* apostolic.

Apostroph [apɔs'tro:f] *m* (-s; -e) apostrophe.

Apotheke [apo'te:kə] *f* (-; -n) chemist's shop, pharmacy. **apo'thekenpflichtig** *adj* obtainable in a pharmacy only.

Apotheker [apo'te:kər] *m* (-s; -), **Apo'thekerin** *f* (-; -nen) pharmacist, (dispensing) chemist.

Apparat [apa'ra:t] *m* (-[e]s; -e) **1.** a) apparatus (*a. fig.*), *fig. a.* machinery, b) instrument, c) device. **2.** camera. **3.** a) radio, b) (TV) set. **4.** F phone: *am ~!* speaking!; *am ~ bleiben* hold the line.

Apparatur [apara'tu:r] *f* (-; -en) equipment.

Appartement [apartə'mã:] *n* (-s; -s) **1.** → **Apartment. 2.** (hotel) suite.

Appell [a'pɛl] *m* (-s; -e) ✕ roll call: *fig. e-n ~ richten an* (*acc*) → **appellieren** [apɛ'li:rən] *v/i* (h) *~ an* (*acc*) (make an) appeal to.

Appetit [ape'ti:t] *m* (-[e]s; -e) (*j-m ~ machen* give s.o. an) appetite (*auf acc* for); *ich habe ~ auf ...* I feel like ... **appe'titanregend** *adj*, **appe'titlich** *adj a. fig.* appetizing. **Appe'titlosigkeit** *f* (-; *no pl*) loss of appetite. **Appe'titzügler** *m* (-s; -) appetite suppressant.

applaudieren [aplaʊ'di:rən] *v/i* (h) (*dat*) applaud, cheer. **Applaus** [a'plaʊs] *m* (-es; *no pl*) applause.

apportieren [apɔr'ti:rən] *v/t* (h) retrieve.

appretieren [apreˈtiːrən] v/t (h), **Appretur** [apreˈtuːr] f (-; -en) ⊙ finish.

approbiert [aproˈbiːrt] adj qualified.

Aprikose [apriˈkoːzə] f (-; -n) apricot.

April [aˈprɪl] m (-[s]; -e) April: **j-n in den ~ schicken** make an April fool of s.o.; **~, ~!** April fool! **~scherz** m April-fool joke. **~wetter** n April weather.

Aquaplaning [akvaˈplaːnɪŋ] n (-[s]; no pl) mot. aquaplaning.

Aquarell [akvaˈrɛl] n (-s; -e), **Aqua'rellfarbe** f water colo(u)r. **Aqua'rellmaler(in** f) m water colo(u)rist.

Aquarium [aˈkvaːriʊm] n (-s; -rien) aquarium.

Äquator [ɛˈkvaːtɔr] m (-s; no pl) equator. **~taufe** f crossing-the-line ceremony.

äquivalent [ɛkvivaˈlɛnt] adj equivalent. **Äquiva'lent** n (-[e]s; -e) equivalent.

Ära [ˈɛːra] f (-; rare Ären) era.

Araber [ˈarabər] m (-s; -) Arab (a. horse). **'Araberin** f (-; -nen) Arab (woman).

Arabien [aˈraːbiən] n (-s) Arabia.

a'rabisch [-bɪʃ] adj Arab states etc, Arabian nights etc, Arabic language etc.

Arbeit [ˈarbaɪt] f (-; -en) **1.** a) work (a. phys.), b) hard work, labo(u)r, c) task, job: **Tag der ~** May Day, Am. Labor Day; **geistige ~** brainwork; **an** (or **bei**) **der ~** at work; **an die ~ gehen** start work; **zur** (F **auf**) **~ gehen** go to work; **et. in ~ haben** be working on s.th. **2.** (**j-m viel ~ machen** give s.o. a lot of) trouble. **3.** work, employment, job: **~ suchen** look for a job; **~ haben** be in work, have a job; **k-e ~ haben** be out of work, be without a job. **4.** a) (piece of) work, b) workmanship: **künstlerische ~** work of art. **5.** ped., univ. paper: **wissenschaftliche ~** treatise.

'arbeiten (h) **I** v/i work, ⊙ function, run, a. ⚓ operate: **~ an** (dat) be working on; **~ bei** work for; (**geschäftlich**) **~ mit** deal with, do business with; **mit Verlust ~** operate at a loss; **sein Geld ~ lassen** invest one's money. **II** v/t make. **III sich ~ durch** work one's way through.

'Arbeiter m (-s; -) a) worker, workman, b) labo(u)rer: **die ~ → Arbeiterschaft; ~ und Unternehmer** labo(u)r and management.

'Arbeiter... workers' ..., working-class (family, area, etc). **~gewerkschaft** f trade (Am. labor) union.

'Arbeiterin f (-; -nen) **1.** (female) worker. **2.** zo. worker (bee or ant).

'Arbeiterklasse f working class(es).

'Arbeiterpar,tei f workers' party.

'Arbeiterschaft f (-; no pl) working class(es), a. pol. Labo(u)r.

'Arbeitgeber m (-s; -) employer. **~anteil** m employer's contribution. **~verband** m employers' association.

'Arbeitnehmer m (-s; -) employee. **~anteil** m employee's contribution.

'Arbeitsablauf m work routine.

'arbeitsam adj industrious, diligent.

'Arbeits|amt n employment exchange, Br. job centre. **~bedingungen** pl working (⊙ operating) conditions. **~be,schaffungspro,gramm** n job creation scheme. **~bescheinigung** f certificate of employment. **~bogen** m ped. work folder. **~eifer** m zeal. **~einkommen** n earned income. **~einstellung** f a) stoppage of work, b) shutdown, c) strike. **~erlaubnis** f work permit. **~essen** n working lunch (or dinner). **≈fähig** adj fit for work: pol. **~e Mehrheit** working majority. **~fläche** f in kitchen: worktop. **~frieden** m industrial peace. **~gang** m ⊙ working cycle: **in einem ~** in a single pass. **~gebiet** n sphere of work. **~gemeinschaft** f working pool, ped. etc study group. **~gericht** n industrial tribunal. **~grundlage** f work(ing) basis. **≈inten,siv** adj labo(u)r-intensive. **~kampf** m labo(u)r dispute. **~kleidung** f work clothes. **~klima** n work climate. **~kraft f 1.** capacity for work. **2.** worker, pl manpower. **~kräftemangel** m manpower shortage. **~leistung** f efficiency, ⊙ a. output. **~lohn** m wages, pay.

'arbeitslos adj unemployed, jobless: **~ sein** a. be out of work. **'Arbeitslose** m, f (-n; -n) unemployed person: **die ~n** the unemployed, the jobless.

'Arbeitslosen|geld n unemployment benefit: **~ beziehen** F be on the dole. **~hilfe** f unemployment relief. **~zahl** f unemployment figures.

'Arbeitslosigkeit f (-; no pl) unemployment.

'Arbeits|markt m labo(u)r (or job) market: **die Lage auf dem ~** the job situation. **~mi,nister** m employment (Am. labor) minister. **~mo,ral** f (working) morale. **~nachweis** *m* employment agency. **~niederlegung** *f* (-; -en) walkout, strike.

'**arbeitsparend** *adj* labo(u)r-saving.

'**Arbeitspensum** *n* workload.

'**Arbeitsplatz** *m* **1.** job: *freie Arbeitsplätze* vacancies; *Schaffung von Arbeitsplätzen* job creation. **2.** working place. **~beschreibung** *f* job description. **~sicherung** *f* job security. **~vernichter** *m* job killer.

'**Arbeits|pro,zeß** *m* j-n wieder in den ~ *eingliedern* put s.o. back to work. **~raum** *m* workroom. **~recht** *n* industrial law. ²**reich** *adj* busy. ²**scheu** *adj* work-shy. **~schluß** *m* end of work: *~ ist um ...* work finishes at ...; *nach ~* after work. **~schutz** *m* industrial safety. **~speicher** *m* *computer*: main memory. **~stunde** *f* manhour, *pl* working hours. ²**süchtig** *adj* ~ *sein* be a workaholic. **~tag** *m* working day, workday. **~teilung** *f* division of labo(u)r. **~tier** *n* F demon for work.

'**Arbeitsuche** *f* (-; *no pl*) (*auf ~ sein*) be) job-hunting. '**Arbeitsuchende** *m, f* (-n; -n) job seeker, job hunter.

'**arbeitsunfähig** *adj* a) unfit for work, b) permanently disabled.

'**Arbeits|unfall** *m* industrial accident. **~vermittlung** *f* employment agency. **~vertrag** *m* employment contract. **~vorbereitung** *f* ☉ operations scheduling. **~weise** *f* (working) method, ☉ *a.* procedure. **~willige** *m, f* (-n; -n) person willing to work, *n.s.* nonstriker. **~zeit** *f* (*gleitende ~* flexible) working hours. **~zeitverkürzung** *f* reduction in working hours. **~zimmer** *n* study.

Archäologe [arçɛo'lo:gə] *m* (-n; -n) arch(a)eologist. **Archäologie** [-'lo:gi:] *f* (-; *no pl*) arch(a)eology. **archäologisch** [-'lo:gɪʃ] *adj* arch(a)eological.

Arche ['arçə] *f* (-; -n) ark: *die ~ Noah* Noah's ark.

Archipel [arçi'pe:l] *m* (-s; -e) *geogr.* archipelago.

Architekt [arçi'tɛkt] *m* (-en; -en), **Archi'tektin** *f* (-; -nen) architect. **architektonisch** [arçitɛk'to:nɪʃ] *adj* architectural. **Architektur** [arçitɛk'tu:r] *f* (-; -en) architecture.

Archiv [ar'çi:f] *n* (-s; -e) archives. **Ar'chivbild** *n* library picture.

Areal [are'a:l] *n* (-s; -e) area.

Arena [a're:na] *f* (-; -nen) arena.

arg [ark] I *adj* bad: *mein ärgster Feind* my worst enemy; *im ~en liegen* be in a bad way. II *adv* badly, F *a.* awfully.

Argentinien [argɛn'ti:niən] *n* (-s) Argentina, *the* Argentine. **Argen'tinier** *m* (-s; -), **Argen'tinierin** *f* (-; -nen), **argen'tinisch** *adj* Argentine.

Ärger ['ɛrgər] *m* (-s; *no pl*) **1.** (*über acc* at, about *s.th.*, with *s.o.*) annoyance, irritation, anger: *zu m~* to my annoyance. **2.** (*j-m ~ machen* cause s.o.) trouble: *das gibt ~* there will be trouble. '**ärgerlich** *adj* **1.** (*über acc* at, about *s.th.*, with *s.o.*) annoyed, angry, F cross. **2.** annoying: *wie ~!* a. what a nuisance! '**ärgern** (h) I *v/t* annoy, make *s.o.* angry. II *sich ~* (*über acc* at, about *s.th.*, with *s.o.*) be angry, be (*or* get) annoyed: *ärgere dich nicht!* take it easy! '**Ärgernis** *n* (-ses; -se) annoyance: *~ erregen* give offen/ce (*Am.* -se). *²* *öffentliches ~* public nuisance.

'**arglistig** *adj* malicious, *²* fraudulent: *~e Täuschung* wilful deceit.

'**arglos** *adj* a) innocent, b) unsuspecting. '**Arglosigkeit** *f* (-; *no pl*) innocence.

Argument [argu'mɛnt] *n* (-[e]s; -e) argument. **Argumentation** [argumɛnta-'tsi̯o:n] *f* (-; -en) argumentation.

argumen'tieren *v/i* (h) ~ argue, reason.

Argwohn ['arkvo:n] *m* (-[e]s; *no pl*) suspicion (*gegen* of). **argwöhnisch** ['arkvø:nɪʃ] *adj* suspicious (*gegen* of).

Arie ['a:ri̯ə] *f* (-; -n) ♪ aria.

Arier ['a:ri̯ər] *m* (-s; -), '**Arierin** *f* (-; -nen), '**arisch** *adj* Aryan.

Aristokrat [arɪsto'kra:t] *m* (-en; -en), **Aristo'kratin** *f* (-; -nen) aristocrat. **Aristokratie** [arɪstokra'ti:] *f* (-; -n) aristocracy. **aristokratisch** [arɪsto'kra:tɪʃ] *adj* aristocratic.

Arithmetik [arɪt'me:tɪk] *f* (-; *no pl*) arithmetic.

Arktis ['arktɪs] *f* (-; *no pl*) *the* Arctic (regions). '**arktisch** *adj a. fig.* arctic.

arm [arm] *adj* poor (*an dat* in).

Arm *m* (-[e]s; -e) arm: *in die ~e nehmen* embrace, hug; *j-n auf den ~ nehmen* a) pick s.o. up, b) F *fig.* pull s.o.'s leg; *j-m in die ~e laufen* bump into s.o.; *j-m unter die ~e greifen* (*mit*) help s.o. (out with).

Armatur [arma'tu:r] f (-; -en) armature, pl fittings.

Arma'turenbrett n dashboard.

'Armband n (-[e]s; ⸚er) bracelet.

'Armbanduhr f wrist watch.

'Armbinde f 1. armlet. 2. ✶ sling.

'Arme m, f (-n; -n) poor man (woman): **die ⸚n** the poor; **ich ⸚(r)!** poor me!

Armee [ar'me:] f (-; -n) army.

Ar'meekorps n army corps.

Ärmel ['ɛrməl] m (-s; -) sleeve: **ohne ⸚** sleeveless; F **et. aus dem ⸚ schütteln** a) pull s.th. out of a hat, b) do s.th. off the cuff. **'Ärmelaufschlag** m cuff.

'ärmellos adj sleeveless.

armieren [ar'mi:rən] v/t (h) 1. armo(u)r (cable). 2. reinforce (concrete).

...armig [...armıç] ...-armed, ...-branched.

'Armlehne f arm. **'Armleuchter** m (-s; -) 1. chandelier. 2. F contp. idiot, twerp.

ärmlich ['ɛrmlıç] adj poor, w.s. a. shabby: **in ⸚en Verhältnissen leben** be poorly off; **aus ⸚en Verhältnissen stammen** come from a poor family.

'Armreif(en) m bangle.

armselig ['armze:lıç] adj wretched, a. fig. miserable.

'Armsessel m, **'Armstuhl** m armchair.

Armut ['armu:t] f (-; no pl) poverty (a. fig. an dat in, of).

'Armuts|grenze f **an (unter) der ⸚ liegen** be on (under) the poverty line. **⸚zeugnis** n j-m (sich) ein ⸚ ausstellen show s.o.'s (one's) incompetence.

Aroma [a'ro:ma] n (-s; -men a) aroma, b) flavo(u)r. **aromatisch** [aro'ma:tıʃ] adj aromatic. **aromatisieren** [aroma-ti'zi:rən] v/t (h) flavo(u)r.

arrangieren [arã'ʒi:rən] (h) I v/t arrange. II **sich ⸚** come to an arrangement (or agreement) (**mit** with).

Arrest [a'rɛst] m (-[e]s; -e) detention.

arretieren [arɛ'ti:rən] v/t (h) ⊕ arrest, stop.

arriviert [ari'vi:rt] adj successful.

arrogant [aro'gant] adj arrogant.

Arsch [arʃ] m (-[e]s; ⸚e) ∨ 1. arse, Am. a. ass: **leck mich am ⸚!** fuck you!; **er (es) ist im ⸚** he (it) has had it; **j-m in den ⸚ kriechen** suck up to s.o. 2. → **Arschloch.** **'Arschkriecher** m ∨ arse licker.

'Arschloch n ∨ arsehole, Am. a. asshole, (person) a. (stupid) bastard, shit.

Arsen [ar'ze:n] n (-s; no pl) ⚛ arsenic.

Arsenal [arze'na:l] n (-s; -e) arsenal.

Art [art] f (-; -en) 1. nature, kind: **sie hat e-e nette ⸚ mit Kindern** she has a way with children; **es ist nicht s-e ⸚ zu** inf he's not the sort to inf; **das entspricht nicht ihrer ⸚** it's not like her; **Fragen allgemeiner ⸚** questions of general interest. 2. a. **und Weise** way, manner, method; **auf diese ⸚** in this way; **s-e ⸚ zu sprechen** the way he talks; gastr. **nach ⸚ des Hauses** à la maison. 3. F behavio(u)r, manners. 4. kind, sort, type, biol. species: **... aller ⸚** all sorts of ...; iro. **e-e ⸚ Dichter** a poet of sorts; fig. **aus der ⸚ schlagen** go one's own way.

Arterie [ar'te:rĭə] f (-; -n) artery.

Arteriosklerose [arterĭoskle'ro:zə] f (-; -n) ✶ arteriosclerosis.

'artfremd adj biol., ✶ alien, foreign.

artig ['artıç] adj well-behaved: **sei ⸚!** be good!, be a good boy (girl)!

Artikel [ar'ti:kəl] m (-s; -) article.

artikulieren [artiku'li:rən] (h) I v/t articulate. II **sich ⸚** express o.s.

Artillerie [artılə'ri:] f (-; -n) artillery.

Artischocke [arti'ʃɔkə] f (-; -n) ⚘ artichoke. **Arti'schockenboden** m gastr. artichoke heart.

Artist [ar'tıst] m (-en; -en), **Ar'tistin** f (-; -nen) (variety) artist.

ar'tistisch adj artistic, acrobatic.

Arznei [arts'nai] f (-; -en) (**gegen** for) medicine, medicament, drug.

Arz'neikunde f (-; no pl) pharmaceutics.

Arz'neimittel n → **Arznei.** **⸚abhängigkeit** f drug dependence. **⸚mißbrauch** m drug abuse.

Arz'neipflanze f medicinal plant.

Arz'neischrank m medicine cabinet.

Arzt [a:rtst] m (-es; ⸚e) doctor, physician: **zum ⸚ gehen** (go to) see the doctor.

'Arztberuf m medical profession.

Ärztekammer ['ɛrtstə-] f medical association. **'Ärztemuster** n drug sample. **'Ärzteschaft** f (-; no pl) medical profession. **'Arzthelferin** f doctor's receptionist (or assistant). **Ärztin** ['ɛrtstın] f (-; -nen) lady doctor (or physician). **ärztlich** ['ɛrtstlıç] adj medical: **⸚es Attest** medical (or doctor's) certificate; **⸚ behandeln** attend; **⸚ verordnet** prescribed by a doctor.

as [as], **As**[1] n (-; -) ♪ A flat.

As[2] [as] n (-ses; -se) ace (a. F person).

Asbest [as'bɛst] m (-[e]s; -e) asbestos.

Asche ['aʃə] f (-; ◎ -n) ashes (a. fig.), (cigarette etc) ash: **glühende ~** embers.

'Aschen|bahn f sports: cinder (mot. dirt) track. **~becher** m ashtray. **~brödel** [-brø:dəl] n (-s; -), **~puttel** [-pʊtəl] n (-s; -) fig. Cinderella.

Ascher'mittwoch m Ash Wednesday.

'aschfahl adj ashen.

'aschgrau adj ash-grey, Am. ash-gray.

Ascorbinsäure [askɔr'bi:n-] f ascorbic acid.

äsen ['ɛ:zən] v/i (h) graze, browse.

aseptisch [a'zɛptɪʃ] adj aseptic.

Asiat [a'zia:t] m (-en; -en), **Asi'atin** f (-; -nen), **asi'atisch** adj Asian. **Asien** ['a:zĭən] n (-s) Asia.

Askese [as'ke:zə] f (-; no pl) asceticism. **Asket** [as'ke:t] m (-en; -en), **As'ketin** f (-; -nen), **as'ketisch** adj ascetic.

asozial ['azotsĭa:l] adj antisocial.

Aspekt [as'pɛkt] m (-[e]s; -e) aspect.

Asphalt [as'falt] m (-s; ◎ -e), **asphaltieren** [asfal'ti:rən] v/t (h) asphalt.

aß [a:s] pret of **essen**.

Assessor [a'sɛsɔr] m (-s; -en), **Assessorin** [asɛ'so:rɪn] f (-; -nen) civil servant (lawyer, teacher, etc) who has completed his/her second state examination.

Assistent [asɪs'tɛnt] m (-en; -en), **Assi'stentin** f (-; -nen) assistant.

Assi'stenzarzt m assistant doctor.

assistieren [asɪs'ti:rən] v/i (h) assist (**bei** in).

Assoziation [asotsĭa'tsĭo:n] f (-; -en) association. **assoziieren** [asotsi'i:rən] v/t (h) associate.

Ast [ast] m (-[e]s; ⁓e) branch, in wood: knot: **fig. auf dem absteigenden ~ sein** be going downhill.

Aster ['astər] f (-; -n) ❀ aster.

Ästhet [ɛs'te:t] m (-en; -en), **Äs'thetin** f (-; -nen) (a)esthete.

äs'thetisch adj (a)esthetical.

Asthma ['astma] n (-s; no pl) ✽ asthma.

Asthmatiker [ast'ma:tɪkər] m (-s; -), **asth'matisch** [-tɪʃ] adj asthmatic.

Astrologe [astro'lo:gə] m (-n; -n) astrologer. **Astrologie** [-lo'gi:] f (-; no pl) astrology. **Astronaut** [-'naʊt] m (-en; -en) astronaut. **Astronomie** [-no'mi:] f (-; no pl) astronomy. **astronomisch** [-'no:mɪʃ] adj a. F fig. astronomic(al).

Astrophy'sik f astrophysics.

Asyl [a'zy:l] n (-s; no pl) (**um politisches ~ bitten** ask for political) asylum.

Asylant [azy'lant] m (-en; -en), **Asy'lantin** f (-; -nen) person seeking (or having been granted) (political) asylum.

A'sylrecht n right of asylum.

'asymmetrisch adj asymmetric(al).

'asynchron adj asynchronous.

Atelier [ate'lie:] n (-s; -s) studio.

Atem ['a:təm] m (-s; no pl) breath: **außer ~ (kommen** get) out of breath; **~ holen** take a breath; fig. **mir stockte der ~** my heart stood still; **das verschlug mir den ~** that took my breath away; **j-n in ~ halten** keep s.o. on the jump (or in suspense); → **anhalten** 1. **'atemberaubend** adj fig. breathtaking. **'Atembeschwerden** pl difficulty in breathing. **'Atemgerät** n breathing apparatus, ✽ respirator. **'atemlos** adj a. fig. breathless. **'Atempause** f F breather. **'Atemwege** pl respiratory tract. **'Atemzug** m breath: **im gleichen ~** in one breath.

Atheismus [ate'ɪsmʊs] m (-; no pl) atheism. **Atheist** [ate'ɪst] m (-en; -en) atheist. **athe'istisch** adj atheistic(al).

Äther ['ɛ:tər] m (-s; no pl) ⚛ ether.

ätherisch [ɛ'te:rɪʃ] adj ethereal, etheric: **~es Öl** essential (or volatile) oil.

Äthiopien [ɛ'tĭo:pĭən] n (-s) Ethiopia. **Äthi'opier** m (-s; -), **Äthi'opierin** f (-; -nen), **äthi'opisch** adj Ethiopian.

Athlet [at'le:t] m (-en; -en), **Ath'letin** f (-; -nen) athlete. **ath'letisch** adj athletic.

Äthyl [ɛ'ty:l] n (-s; no pl) ethyl.

Äthylen [ɛty'le:n] n (-s; no pl) ethylene.

atlantisch [at'lantɪʃ] adj Atlantic: **der ~e Ozean** the Atlantic (Ocean).

Atlas ['atlas] m (-[ses]; -se) atlas.

atmen ['a:tmən] v/i, v/t (h) breathe: **tief ~** breathe deep. **'Atmen** n (-s) breathing.

Atmosphäre [atmo'sfɛ:rə] f (-; -n) a. fig. atmosphere. **atmo'sphärisch** adj atmospheric: ⚡ **~e Störungen** statics, atmospherics.

'Atmung f (-; no pl) breathing, respiration: **künstliche ~** artificial respiration.

Atom [a'to:m] n (-s; -e) atom.

atomar [ato'ma:r] adj atomic, nuclear.

A'tom|bombe f atom(ic) (or nuclear) bomb, A-bomb. **~bunker** m nuclear shelter. **~ener‚gie** f atomic energy. **~explosi‚on** f atomic explosion. **~forschung** f atomic research. **⚡getrieben**

adj nuclear-powered. **~gewicht** *n* atomic weight. **~hülle** *f* atomic shell.
atomisieren [atomiˈziːrən] *v/t* (h) *a. fig.* atomize.
A'tom|kern *m* atomic nucleus. **~kraft** *f* (-; *no pl*) nuclear power. **~kraftwerk** *n* nuclear power station. **~krieg** *m* atomic (*or* nuclear) war(fare). **~macht** *f pol.* nuclear power. **~mo,dell** *n* atomic model. **~müll** *m* radioactive waste. **~phy,sik** *f* atomic physics. **~pilz** *m fig.* mushroom cloud. **~re,aktor** *m* atom reactor. **~spaltung** *f* atom splitting. **~sperrvertrag** *m pol.* nonproliferation treaty. **~sprengkopf** *m* nuclear warhead. **~test** *m* nuclear test. **~teststopp(abkommen** *n*) *m* test ban (treaty). **~tod** *m* nuclear death. **~-U-Boot** *n* nuclear(-powered) submarine.
A'tomwaffen *pl* atomic (*or* nuclear) weapons. **2frei** *adj* nuclear-free *zone*. **~gegner(in** *f*) *m* anti-nuclear protester.
A'tomzahl *f* atomic number.
A'tomzeitalter *n* atomic age.
atonal [ˈatonaːl] *adj* ♩ atonal.
Atrophie [atroˈfiː] *f* (-; -n) 🞐 atrophy.
ätsch [ɛːtʃ] *int* there!, serves you right!
Attaché [ataˈʃeː] *m* (-s; -s) attaché.
Attacke [aˈtakə] *f* (-; -n), **attackieren** [ataˈkiːrən] *v/t*, *v/i* (h) attack.
Attentat [atɛnˈtaːt] *n* (-[e]s; -e) a) (*ein ~ auf j-n verüben* make an) attempt on s.o.'s life, b) assassination.
Atten'täter(in *f*) *m* assassin.
Attest [aˈtɛst] *n* (-[e]s; -e) certificate.
Attraktion [atrakˈtsjoːn] *f* (-; -en) attraction. **attraktiv** [-ˈtiːf] *adj* attractive.
Attrappe [aˈtrapə] *f* (-; -n) dummy.
Attribut [atriˈbuːt] *n* (-[e]s; -e) attribute. **attributiv** [atribuˈtiːf] *adj* attributive.
ätzen [ˈɛtsən] *v/t* (h) 1. 🜍 corrode, eat into. 2. 🜍 cauterize. 3. *arts:* etch.
'ätzend *adj* corrosive, *a. fig.* caustic.
au [aʊ] *int* 1. ouch! 2. **~ ja!** oh yes!
Aubergine [obɛrˈʒiːnə] *f* (-; -n) 🍆 aubergine, eggplant.
auch [aʊx] *adv* 1. also, too, as well: *ich habe Hunger - ich ~* I am hungry - so am I (F me too); *ich glaube es - ich ~* I believe it - so do I; *ich kann es nicht - ich ~ nicht* I can't do it - nor (*or* neither) can I. 2. even: *ohne ~ nur zu fragen* without so much as asking. 3. *wenn ~* even if, although; *so sehr ich es ~*

bedauere however much I regret it. 4. *wann ~* (*immer*) whenever; *wer es ~* (*immer*) *sei* whoever it may be; *was er ~* (*immer*) *sagt* whatever he may say; *so schwierig es ~ sein mag* difficult as it may be. 5. *wirst du es ~ tun?* are you really going to do it?; *so schlimm ist es ~ wieder nicht!* it's not all that bad!
Audienz [aʊˈdiɛns] *f* (-; -en) audience (*bei* with).
audiovisu'ell [aʊdɪo-] *adj* audiovisual.
Auditorium [aʊdiˈtoːriʊm] *n* (-s; -rien) 1. *univ.* (*~ maximum* main) lecture hall. 2. audience.
auf [aʊf] I *prep* (*dat*) 1. *space:* on, in, at: *~ dem Tisch* on the table; *~ der Straße* in (*Am.* on) the street, on the road; *~ See* at sea; *~ der Post* at the post office; *~ der Welt* in the world; *~ dem Land* in the country; *er ist ~ s-m Zimmer* he is in his room. 2. *at, during, on:* *~ dem Ball* at the ball; *~ s-r Reise* during (*or* on) his journey; *~ Urlaub* on vacation, *esp. Br.* on holiday. II *prep* (*acc*) 3. *place:* a) (down) on, onto, into, b) up, c) to, toward(s): *er setzte sich ~ e-n Stuhl* he sat down on a chair; *~ die Erde fallen* fall (on)to the ground; *er ging ~ die Straße* he went (out) into the street; *ich ging ~ die Post* I went to the post office; *geh ~ dein Zimmer!* go to your room!; *sie zogen ~ das Land* they moved (in)to the country; *fig. ~ Besuch kommen* come for a visit; *~ Reisen gehen* go on a journey. 4. *time:* a) *for:* *~ ein paar Tage* for a few days; *~ Jahre hinaus* for years to come; *es geht ~ 9 (Uhr)* it's getting on for nine (o'clock); F *~ e-e Tasse Kaffee* for a cup of coffee; b) *after:* *Stunde ~ Stunde verging* hour after hour went by, c) *until:* *~ morgen verschieben* postpone until tomorrow; F *~ bald!* see you soon! 5. *~ diese Weise* (in) this way; *~ deutsch* in German; *~ s-n Befehl* by (*or* at) his order; *~ m-e Bitte* (*hin*) on my request. 6. *quantities:* *von 80 Tonnen ~ 100 erhöhen* increase from 80 tons to 100; *~ jeden entfallen ...* there is/are ... (for) each; *~ die Sekunde* to the second; *~ 100 m see, hear, etc* at (*or* from) a hundred metres, *come etc* as close as 100 metres. III *adv* 7. F a) *open:* *Augen ~!* watch out!, b) *awake,*

c) up (and going): **ich war die ganze Nacht ~** I was up all night. **8. ~ und ab gehen** walk up and down (*or* to and fro); F **~ und davon gehen** run away. **IV** *int* **~!** a) (get) up!, b) F *a.* **~ geht's!** let's go!, c) come on!

Auf: *das* **~ und Ab des Lebens** the ups and downs of life; *das* **~ und Ab der Preise** the rise and fall of prices.

aufarbeiten *v/t* (*sep*, -ge-, h) **1.** work (*or* clear) off, catch up on. **2.** furbish up, do up. **3.** *fig.* a) work *s.th.* up, b) digest.

aufatmen *v/i* (*sep*, -ge-, h) draw a deep breath, *fig.* breathe again (*or* freely).

aufbahren *v/t* (*sep*, -ge-, h) put *coffin* on the bier, lay *body* out (in state).

Aufbau *m* (-[e]s; -ten) **1.** *no pl* building, erection, construction, ⚙ assembly: *fig.* **im ~ (begriffen) sein** be in its initial stages. **2.** *no pl fig.* structure. **3.** *mot.* car body. **4.** *no pl* computer: format.

aufbauen (*sep*, -ge-, h) **I** *v/t* **1.** build, erect, construct: **wieder ~** rebuild, reconstruct. **2.** *fig.* a) build up (*business, attack,* F *politician etc*), b) organize, set up: **sich e-e Existenz ~** build o.s. an existence; **e-e Theorie** *etc* **~ auf** (*dat*) base (*or* found) a theory *etc on.* **3.** ⚙ *a.* assemble, b) set up, c) arrange. **II** *v/i* **4.** (*a.* **sich**) **~ auf** (*dat*) be based (*or* founded) on. **III** *sich* **~ 5.** be composed (*aus* of). **6.** F *sich* **~ vor** (*dat*) plant o.s. (*or* line up) in front of.

aufbäumen: sich ~ (*sep*, -ge-, h) *horse:* rear; *fig. sich* **~ gegen** rebel against.

aufbauschen *v/t* (*sep*, -ge-, h) *fig.* exaggerate.

Aufbauten *pl* of **Aufbau** ⚓ superstructure.

aufbegehren *v/i* (*sep*, h) rebel.

aufbehalten *v/t* (*irr, sep*, h, → **behalten**) F **den Hut ~** keep one's hat on.

aufbekommen *v/t* (*irr, sep*, h, → **bekommen**) F **1.** get *the door* open, get *a knot* undone. **2.** be given *a task* (to do).

aufbereiten *v/t* (*sep*, h) prepare, process, ⚙ *a.* treat, *computer:* edit, *fig.* work *s.th.* up.

aufbessern *v/t* (*sep*, -ge-, h) **1.** improve. **2.** raise (*salary*).

aufbewahren *v/t* (*sep*, h) preserve, keep, store (up). **Aufbewahrung** *f* (-; *no pl*) (**sichere ~**) safekeeping: **j-m et. zur ~ geben** leave s.th. with s.o.

aufbieten *v/t* (*irr, sep*, -ge-, h, → **bieten**) **1.** muster, summon (up) (*courage*), use (*one's influence*). **2.** ✕ mobilize.

Aufbietung *f* (-; *no pl*) **unter ~ aller Kräfte** by (a) supreme effort.

aufbinden *v/t* (*irr, sep*, -ge-, h, → **binden**) undo, untie: → **Bär.**

aufblähen (*sep*, -ge-, h) **I** *v/t* **1.** (*a. sich ~*) blow out, swell. **2.** ✝, 🜨 inflate. **II** *sich* **~** F *contp.* puff o.s. up.

aufblasbar *adj* inflatable. **aufblasen** (*irr, sep*, -ge-, h, → **blasen**) **I** *v/t* blow up, inflate. **II** *sich* **~** F puff o.s. up.

aufbleiben *v/i* (*irr, sep*, -ge-, sn, → **bleiben**) **1.** sit up, stay up. **2.** remain open.

aufblenden *v/i* (*sep*, -ge-, h) **1.** *mot.* turn on the headlights full beam. **2.** *phot.* open the diaphragm.

aufblicken *v/i* (*sep*, -ge-, h) look up: **zu j-m ~** look up at s.o. (*esp. fig.* to s.o.).

aufblitzen *v/i* (*sep*, -ge-, sn) flash (up).

aufblühen *v/i* (*sep*, -ge-, sn) **1.** (begin to) bloom. **2.** *fig. girl:* blossom (out), *town, economy, etc:* (begin to) flourish.

aufbocken *v/t* (*sep*, -ge-, h) jack up.

aufbohren *v/t* (*sep*, -ge-, h) a) bore open, b) rebore (*engine*), c) drill (*tooth*).

aufbrauchen *v/t* (*sep*, -ge-, h) use up.

aufbrausen *v/i* (*sep*, -ge-, sn) flare up.

aufbrausend *adj fig.* quick-tempered.

aufbrechen (*irr, sep*, -ge-, → **brechen**) **I** *v/t* (h) **1.** a) break (*or* prize) open, b) break up. **II** *v/i* (sn) **2.** *bud, boil, etc:* (burst) open, *ice:* break up. **3.** (*nach* for) start, set out.

aufbringen *v/t* (*irr, sep*, -ge-, h, → **bringen**) **1.** → **aufbekommen** 1. **2.** muster, summon (up) (*courage etc*). **3.** raise (*money*). **4.** start (*rumo*[*u*]*r, fashion*). **5.** anger: **j-n gegen sich ~** get s.o.'s back up; → **aufgebracht.** **6.** ⚓ capture.

Aufbruch *m* (-[e]s; -e) (*nach, zu* for) departure, start: **das Zeichen zum ~ geben** give the sign to leave.

aufbrühen *v/t* (*sep*, -ge-, h) make (*coffee, tea*).

aufbügeln *v/t* (*sep*, -ge-, h) **1.** transfer *pattern* (**auf** *acc on*). **2.** iron, press.

aufbürden *v/t* (*sep*, -ge-, h) *fig.* **j-m et. ~** saddle s.o. with s.th.

aufdecken (*sep*, -ge-, h) **I** *v/t* **1.** uncover, *fig. a.* reveal, expose. **2.** **das Bett ~** turn down the bed. **II** *v/i* **3.** lay the table.

aufdrängen (*sep*, -ge-, h) **I** *v/t* **j-m et. ~**

force s.th. on s.o. **II sich ~ a)** (dat on) intrude, impose o.s., b) suggest itself.

'**aufdrehen** (sep, -ge-, h) **I** v/t **1.** turn on (gas etc). **2.** untwist (rope). **3.** F turn up (radio). **4.** put up one's hair in curlers. **II** v/i **5.** F mot. step on the gas. **6.** F fig. person: get going: → **aufgedreht.**

'**aufdringlich** adj obtrusive, a. importunate, pushing (person), a. loud (colo[u]r), noisy (music), overpowering (smell). '**Aufdringlichkeit** f (-; no pl) obtrusiveness.

'**Aufdruck** m (-[e]s; -e) imprint, philat. overprint. '**aufdrucken** v/t (sep, -ge-, h) print (**auf** acc on).

'**aufdrücken** v/t (sep, -ge-, h) **1.** push (or press) open. **2.** F squeeze boil open. **3.** impress stamp etc (dat or **auf** acc on).

aufein'ander adv **1.** one on top of another (or the other). **2.** one another, each other: ~ **angewiesen sein** depend on each other; ~ **abgestimmte Farben** matching colo(u)rs. **3.** one after the other. ~**folgen** v/i (sep, -ge-, sn) succeed (one another). ~**folgend** adj successive, consecutive: **an drei ~en Tagen** on three days running. ~**prallen** v/i (sep, -ge-, sn). ~**stoßen** v/i (irr, sep, -ge-, sn, → **stoßen**) collide, fig. a. clash. ~**treffen** v/i (irr, sep, -ge-, sn, → **treffen**) meet (one another).

Aufenthalt ['aʊfɛnthalt] m (-[e]s; -e) **1.** stay. **2.** 🚉 etc (**fünf Minuten** ~ five minutes') stop: **ohne ~** nonstop; **wir hatten zwei Stunden ~ in ...** we stopped in ... for two hours. '**Aufenthalts|erlaubnis** f residence permit. ~**ort** m a) whereabouts, b) residence. ~**raum** m a) hotel etc: lounge, b) school etc: common room.

'**auferlegen** v/t (sep, h) impose (dat on): **sich k-n Zwang ~** be free and easy.

'**auferstehen** v/i (irr, sep, sn, → **erstehen**) eccl. rise (from the dead).

'**Auferstehung** f (-; no pl) resurrection.

'**aufessen** v/t (irr, sep, -ge-, h, → **essen**) eat up, finish.

auffädeln ['aʊfɛːdəln] v/t (sep, -ge-, h) thread, string.

'**auffahren** (irr, sep, -ge-, → **fahren**) **I** v/i (sn) **1.** ~ **auf** (acc) mot. crash into, 🚗 run on; mot. **zu dicht ~** tailgate. **2.** fig. a) (give a) start, b) flare up. **II** v/t (h) **3.** F bring on (food etc). '**Auffahrt** f (-; -en)

1. driving up. **2.** a) approach, b) slip road, c) drive(way Am.).

'**Auffahrunfall** m rear-end collision.

'**auffallen** v/i (irr, sep, -ge-, sn, → **fallen**) be conspicuous, attract attention: **j-m ~** strike s.o.; **das fällt nicht auf** nobody will notice; **unangenehm ~** make a bad impression. '**auffallend** adj a) noticeable, b) striking (beauty, resemblance, etc). '**auffällig** adj **1.** → **auffallend. 2.** a) conspicuous, b) odd, strange, c) loud, F flashy (clothes etc).

'**auffangen** v/t (irr, sep, -ge-, h, → **fangen**) **1.** catch (a. fig. words etc). **2.** pick up, intercept (message). **3.** cushion (fall etc), parry, block (blow), stop (attack), absorb (price increases etc). **4.** collect. **5.** receive (refugees).

'**Auffanglager** n reception camp.

'**auffassen** v/t (sep, -ge-, h) **1.** understand, grasp. **2.** interpret: **et. als Scherz ~** take s.th. as a joke; **falsch ~** misunderstand, misinterpret.

'**Auffassung** f (-; -en) **1.** view, opinion: **nach m-r ~** in my view, as I see it. **2.** interpretation. **3.** no pl → '**Auffassungsgabe** f (-; no pl) intellectual grasp, intelligence.

auffindbar ['aʊffɪntbaːr] adj **nicht ~** not to be found. '**auffinden** v/t (irr, sep, -ge-, h, → **finden**) find, discover.

'**auffischen** v/t (sep, -ge-, h) F **1.** fish out (of the water). **2.** → **aufgabeln.**

'**aufflackern** v/i (sep, -ge-, sn) flicker up.

'**aufflammen** v/i (sep, -ge-, sn) a. fig. flare up.

'**auffliegen** v/i (irr, sep, -ge-, sn, → **fliegen**) **1.** fly up. **2.** door etc: fly open. **3.** F plan etc: blow up: ~ **lassen** expose (s.o.), bust (gang), break up (meeting).

'**auffordern** v/t (sep, -ge-, h) **1.** **j-n ~ (, et. zu tun)** ask (or order, 🚓 summon) s.o. (to do s.th.); **j-n dringend ~** urge s.o. **2.** invite: **e-e Dame (zum Tanz) ~** ask a lady to dance.

'**Aufforderung** f (-; -en) **1.** request, call. **2.** order, 🚓 summons. **3.** invitation.

'**aufforsten** v/t (sep, -ge-, h) reafforest.

'**auffressen** v/t (irr, sep, -ge-, h, → **fressen**) eat up, devour: F fig. **die Arbeit frißt mich auf** I'm drowning in work.

'**auffrischen** (sep, -ge-, h) **I** v/t **1.** freshen up, refresh (a. fig. memory). **2.** replenish (supplies). **3.** fig. brush up (knowl-

edge), revive (*friendship etc*). **II** *v/i* **4.** *wind*: freshen.

'Auffrischungskurs *m* refresher course.

'aufführen (*sep*, -ge-, h) **I** *v/t* **1.** *♪*, *thea. etc* perform, present, *a.* show (*film*). **2.** state, show, list: *namentlich ~* name; *einzeln ~* specify, itemize. **II** *sich ~* behave: *sich schlecht ~ a.* misbehave.

'Aufführung *f* (-; -en) *thea. etc* performance, showing, show. **'Aufführungsrechte** *pl* performing rights.

'auffüllen *v/t* (*sep*, -ge-, h) fill up, top up (*glass etc*), replenish (*stocks*).

'Aufgabe *f* (-; -n) **1.** *no pl* posting, *Am.* mailing (*of letter*), sending (*of telegram[me]*). **2.** *no pl* registering, *Am.* checking (*of luggage*). **3.** *no pl* insertion (*of an ad*), giving, placing (*of orders*). **4.** *no pl* giving up (*a. sports*), *♟* closing down (*of business etc*), resignation (*gen* from *an office*). **5.** a) task, assignment, job, b) duty, c) purpose, function: *es ist nicht m-e ~ zu inf* it's not my job to *inf*; *es sich zur ~ machen zu inf* make it one's business to *inf*. **6.** *♞ etc* problem, *ped.* homework, lesson, exercise. **7.** *sports*: service.

'aufgabeln *v/t* (*sep*, -ge-, h) F pick up.

'Aufgabenbereich *m* (*nicht in j-s ~ fallen* be outside s.o.'s) scope of duties.

'Aufgang *m* (-[e]s; *~e*) **1.** *no pl* rising (*of the sun etc*). **2.** stairway.

'aufgeben (*irr, sep*, -ge-, h, → **geben**) **I** *v/t* **1.** post, *Am.* mail (*letter*), send (*telegram[me]*). **2.** register, *Am.* check (*luggage*). **3.** insert (*ad*), give, place (*orders*). **4.** give up (*job, business, hope, patient, etc*), retire from (*office etc*), abandon (*plan etc*), stop (*contest*): *das Rauchen ~* give up (*or stop*) smoking; **er gib's auf!** give (it) up! **5.** ask (*riddle*), *ped.* set, give (*task*). **6.** *sports*: serve. **II** *v/i* **7.** give up.

'aufgeblasen I *pp of* **aufblasen.** **II** *adj* F *fig.* arrogant, bumptious.

'Aufgebot *n* (-[e]s; -e) **1.** *das ~ bestellen* give notice of an intended marriage, ask the banns. **2.** *no pl* array, crowd, (*police*) force, *sports*: a) team, b) squad, pool of players: *mit starkem ~ erscheinen* turn out (*or* up) in full force.

'aufgebracht I *pp of* **aufbringen.** **II** *adj* (*gegen* with, *über acc* at, about) angry, furious.

'aufgedonnert *adj* F dolled-up.

'aufgedreht I *pp of* **aufdrehen.** **II** *adj* F *fig.* in high spirits.

'aufgehen *v/i* (*irr, sep*, -ge-, sn, → **gehen**) **1.** *sun etc, a.* dough: rise, *curtain*: *a.* go up. **2.** *seed etc*: come up. **3.** open, *knot etc*: *a.* come undone, *seam*: come open, *boil etc*: burst. **4.** *♟* come out even: *die Aufgabe geht nicht auf* the sum doesn't work out; → **Rechnung** 1. **5.** *~ in* (*dat*) be (all) wrapped up in *one's work etc.* **6.** *j-m ~* dawn on s.o.; *jetzt geht mir die Bedeutung s-r Worte auf* now I realize what he meant; → **Licht** 2. **7.** *in Flammen ~* go up in flames.

'aufgehoben I *pp of* **aufheben.** **II** *adj gut ~ sein* be in good hands (*bei* with).

'aufgeilen (*sep*, -ge-, h) V **I** *v/t* turn *s.o.* on. **II** *sich ~ an* (*dat*) get turned on by.

'aufgeklärt I *pp of* **aufklären.** **II** *adj* enlightened: **~ sein** know the facts of life.

'aufgeknöpft I *pp of* **aufknöpfen.** **II** *adj* F *fig.* chatty.

'aufgekratzt I *pp of* **aufkratzen.** **II** *adj* F *fig.* chirpy.

'aufgelegt I *pp of* **auflegen.** **II** *adj zu et. ~ sein* be in the mood for s.th., feel like (doing) s.th.; *gut* (*schlecht*) *~ sein* be in a good (bad) mood.

'aufgelöst I *pp of* **auflösen.** **II** *adj fig.* **1.** distraught. **2.** all in.

'aufgeräumt I *pp of* **aufräumen.** **II** *adj fig.* cheerful.

'aufgeregt I *pp of* **aufregen.** **II** *adj* upset, excited, nervous.

'aufgeschlossen I *pp of* **aufschließen.** **II** *adj fig.* open (*für* to), open-minded.

'Aufgeschlossenheit *f* (-; *no pl*) open-mindedness.

'aufgeschmissen *adj* F **~ sein** be stuck.

'aufgeschossen *adj hoch ~* lanky.

'aufgesetzt I *pp of* **aufsetzen.** **II** *adj fig.* artificial.

'aufgesprungen I *pp of* **aufspringen.** **II** *adj* chapped (*lips etc*).

'aufgestaut I *pp of* **aufstauen.** **II** *adj* pent-up (*rage etc*).

'aufgeweckt I *pp of* **aufwecken.** **II** *adj fig.* bright, clever.

'aufgießen *v/t* (*irr, sep*, -ge-, h, → **gießen**) **1.** make (*tea etc*). **2.** add, pour on.

'aufgliedern *v/t* (*sep*, -ge-, h) a) (sub)divide, b) classify, c) break down (*nach* by), d) analyze (*sentence*).

'**aufgraben** v/t (irr, sep, -ge-, h, → **graben**) dig up.

'**aufgreifen** v/t (irr, sep, -ge-, h, → **greifen**) **1.** seize. **2.** take up (idea).

auf'grund → **Grund** 3.

'**Aufguß** m (-sses; =sse) **1.** infusion. **2.** fig. rehash.

'**aufhaben** (irr, sep, -ge-, h, → **haben**) F **I** v/t **1.** have a hat etc on. **2.** have door etc open. **3.** ped. have to do: **wir haben heute nichts auf** we have no homework today. **II** v/i **4.** shop etc: be open.

'**aufhacken** v/t (sep, -ge-, h) pick up.

'**aufhaken** v/t (sep, -ge-, h) unhook.

aufhalsen ['aufhalzən] v/t (sep, -ge-, h) F **j-m et.** ~ land s.o. with s.th.

'**aufhalten** (irr, sep, -ge-, h, → **halten**) **I** v/t **1.** keep open. **2.** stop, hold up, check, stay, delay: **ich wurde durch den Regen aufgehalten** I was delayed by the rain; **ich will Sie nicht länger** ~ don't let me keep you. **II** sich ~ **3.** stay (**im Ausland** abroad, **bei Freunden** with friends). **4.** sich ~ **mit** spend (contp. waste) one's time on.

'**aufhängen** (irr, sep, -ge-, h, → **hängen**) **I** v/t **1.** (an dat) hang (up) (on), ⊙ suspend (from): **j-n** ~ hang s.o. **2.** F → **aufbürden. II** sich ~ hang o.s.

'**Aufhänger** m (-s; -) **1.** tab. **2.** F fig. ~ (**für e-n Artikel** etc) peg (on which to hang a story etc).

'**Aufhängung** f (-; -en) ⊙ suspension.

'**aufhäufen** v/t (sep, -ge-, h) (a. **sich** ~) pile up, heap up, accumulate.

'**aufheben** v/t (irr, sep, -ge-, h, → **heben**) **1.** pick up, lift (up), raise: **j-n** ~ help s.o. up. **2.** keep (**für später** for later): → **aufgehoben. 3.** close (meeting), raise (siege), call off (boycott etc). **4.** abolish (law), cancel (contract), annul (marriage etc), quash (sentence): **ein Verbot** ~ lift a ban. **5.** compensate, cancel, neutralize: **sich** (or **einander**) ~ cancel each other out (a. Ⓐ), neutralize each other. '**Aufheben** n (-s; no pl) fuss, ado: **viel** ~(**s**) **machen** make a big fuss (**von** about). '**Aufhebung** f (-; -en) **1.** abolition (**der Todesstrafe** of capital punishment), abrogation (of a law), cancel(l)ation (of contract), annulment (of marriage etc). **2.** a) termination, b) calling-off (of strike etc). **3.** neutralization.

aufheitern ['aufhaitərn] (sep, -ge-, h) **I**

v/t **j-n** ~ cheer s.o. up. **II** sich ~ weather: clear (up), a. fig. brighten (up). '**Aufheiterungen** pl meteor. sunny spells.

aufhellen ['aufhɛlən] (sep, -ge-, h) **I** v/t **1.** lighten (a. phot.). **2.** fig. shed light on. **II** sich ~ → **aufheitern II**.

'**aufhetzen** v/t (sep, -ge-, h) **j-n** ~ incite s.o. (**zu et.** to [do] s.th.); **j-n** ~ **gegen** set s.o. against. '**Aufhetzung** f (-; -en) instigation, pol. agitation.

'**aufheulen** v/i (sep, -ge-, h) (give a) howl, mot. roar.

'**aufholen** (sep, -ge-, h) **I** v/t catch up on: **e-n Rückstand** (or **Zeitverlust**) ~ make up leeway. **II** v/i (**gegenüber**) catch up (with, on), gain (on).

'**aufhorchen** v/i (sep, -ge-, h) prick (up) one's ears, fig. sit up (and take notice).

'**aufhören** v/i (sep, -ge-, h) stop (a. ~ **mit**), (come to an) end: **sie hörte nicht auf zu reden** she didn't stop talking; **wo haben wir aufgehört?** where did we leave off?; **hör auf (damit)!** stop it!; ~ **zu arbeiten** F knock off (work); **ohne aufzuhören** without letup.

'**aufkaufen** v/t (sep, -ge-, h) buy up.

'**Aufkäufer** m (-s; -) (wholesale) buyer.

'**aufklappen** (sep, -ge-, h) v/t (h), v/i (sn) open.

'**aufklaren** v/i (sep, -ge-, h) meteor. clear.

'**aufklären** (sep, -ge-, h) **I** v/t **1.** clear up (mystery etc), solve (crime), correct (mistake). **2.** enlighten, inform (**über** acc of): **j-n** ~ explain the facts of life to s.o. **3.** ✕ reconnoit/re (Am. -er). **II** sich ~ **4.** be cleared up, be solved: → **aufklaren. 'Aufklärung** f (-; -en) **1.** clearing up, solution: ~ **verlangen** demand an explanation. **2.** enlightenment, education, information. **3.** no pl (**sexuelle**) ~ sex education. **4.** ✕ reconnaissance. **5.** no pl philos. hist. Enlightenment.

'**Aufklärungs|film** m sex education film. **~flugzeug** n reconnaissance (or scout) plane. **~quote** f clear-up rate.

'**aufkleben** v/t (sep, -ge-, h) stick on (**auf** acc to), phot. mount.

'**Aufkleber** m (-s; -) sticker.

'**aufknöpfen** v/t (sep, -ge-, h) unbutton, undo.

'**aufkochen** v/t (sep, -ge-, h) (a. ~ **lassen**) bring s.th. to the boil.

'**aufkommen** v/i (irr, sep, -ge-, sn, →

kommen) **1.** arise (*a. suspicion etc*): **Zweifel ~ lassen** give rise to doubt; **nicht ~ lassen** suppress. **2.** *wind*: spring up, *fog etc*: come up. **3.** *rumo(u)r etc*: start. **4.** *miniskirts etc*: come into fashion. **5. ~ für** a) answer for, be responsible for, b) pay; **für den Schaden ~** compensate for the damage. **6. ~ gegen** prevail against; **er kommt gegen sie nicht auf** he is no match for her; **niemanden neben sich ~lassen** suffer no rival. **7. → aufholen** II.

'**Aufkommen** *n* (-s) **1.** rise. **2.** ✝ yield.

'**aufkratzen** *v/t* (*sep*, -ge-, h) scratch open: **sich ~** scratch o.s. sore.

'**aufkreuzen** *v/i* (*sep*, -ge-, sn) F turn up.

'**aufladen** (*irr, sep*, -ge-, h, → **laden**) I *v/t* **1.** load (*auf acc* onto): F *fig. j-m* (*sich*) *et.* ~ saddle s.o. (o.s.) with s.th. **2.** supercharge, boost (*engine*), charge (*battery*). II *sich* ~ ⚡ become charged.

'**Auflader** *m* (-s; -) *mot.* supercharger.

'**Auflage** *f* (-; -n) **1.** edition (*of book*), circulation (*of newspaper*). **2.** ([*j-m*] *et.* **zur ~ machen** make s.th. a) condition (for s.o.). **3.** ⊙ a) rest, support, b) layer, c) coating, lining. '**Auflagenhöhe** *f* a) number of copies, b) circulation.

'**auflassen** *v/t* (*irr, sep*, -ge-, h, → **lassen**) **1.** F leave door open. **2.** F keep hat *etc* on. **3.** ⚖ convey (*property*).

'**auflauern** *v/i* (*sep*, -ge-, h) *j-m* ~ waylay s.o., lie in wait for s.o.

'**Auflauf** *m* (-[e]s; ⁀e) **1.** crowd. **2.** riot. **3.** *gastr.* soufflé. '**auflaufen** *v/i* (*irr, sep*, -ge-, sn, → *laufen*) **1.** ⚓ run aground: **auf e-e Mine ~** hit a mine. **2.** run (*or* bump) (*auf acc* into): *j-n ~ lassen* a) *sports*: obstruct s.o. unfairly, b) *fig.* give s.o. what for. **3.** *money etc*: accumulate, run up, *interest*: a. accrue. '**Auflaufform** *f* ovenproof dish.

'**aufleben** *v/i* (*sep*, -ge-, sn) (*wieder*) *~ a.* *fig.* revive; **er lebte förmlich auf** he really livened up.

'**auflegen** (*sep*, -ge-, h) I *v/t* **1.** put on (*coal, disc, make-up, etc*), lay (*tablecloth etc*): **den** (*Telefon*)*Hörer* ~ → 4; → *Gedeck* 1. **2.** publish, print. **3.** ✝ issue (*shares*). II *v/i* **4.** *teleph.* replace the receiver, hang up.

'**auflehnen: sich ~** (*gegen*) oppose (*s.o., s.th.*), rebel (against). '**Auflehnung** *f* (-; -en) rebellion (*gegen* against).

'**auflesen** *v/t* (*irr, sep*, -ge-, h, → *lesen*) pick up (*a.* F *fig. s.o.*).

'**aufleuchten** *v/i* (*sep*, -ge-, h) light up.

'**aufliegen** (*irr, sep*, -ge-, h, → *liegen*) I *v/i* lie (*or* rest, lean) (*auf dat* on). II *sich* ~ F ⚕ get bedsore(s).

'**auflisten** *v/t* (*sep*, -ge-, h) list, make a list of.

'**auflockern** *v/t* (*sep*, -ge-, h) **1.** loosen (*the soil*). **2.** *fig.* a) liven up, b) relax.

'**auflodern** *v/i* (*sep*, -ge-, sn) flare up.

'**auflösen** (*sep*, -ge-, h) I *v/t* **1.** a) dissolve, b) break off (*engagement*), c) ✗ disband (*unit*): ([*sich*] *in s-e Bestandteile*) ~ disintegrate. **2.** ⚕ resolve (*equation, a. riddle*), remove (*brackets*). **3.** a) cancel, annul, b) ✝ liquidate, wind up. II *sich* ~ **4.** dissolve, *meeting etc*: a. break up, ✗ *unit*: disband: **sich in nichts ~** vanish (into thin air), *hope etc*: go up in smoke. '**Auflösung** *f* (-; -en) **1.** disintegration (*a. fig.*), dissolution, *a.* breakup (*of meeting*). **2.** ✝ a) liquidation, b) annulment. **3.** ✗ disbandment. **4.** ⚕, ♩, *phot.* resolution.

'**Auflösungszeichen** *n* ♩ natural.

'**aufmachen** (*sep*, -ge-, h) I *v/t* F **1.** open: **mach d-e Augen auf!** watch out! **2.** make up, get up, design: *et. in der Presse groß ~* splash s.th.; *e-e Rechnung ~* write out (*fig.* present) a bill. II *v/i* F open, answer the door: *j-m* ~ let s.o. in. III *sich* ~ set out (*nach* for). '**Aufmacher** *m* (-s; -) F lead, *n.s.* feature story (*or* photo). '**Aufmachung** *f* (-; -en) **1.** presentation, getup, *print.* layout: **et. in großer ~ herausbringen** feature s.th. prominently. **2.** F outfit, getup.

'**Aufmarsch** *m* (-[e]s; ⁀e) marching up, ✗ *a.* deployment. '**aufmar‚schieren** *v/i* (sn) *a. fig.* march up.

aufmerksam ['aʊfmɛrkzaːm] *adj* a) attentive, b) watchful, c) obliging: *j-n ~ machen auf* (*acc*) call (*or* draw) s.o.'s attention to; *~ werden auf* (*acc*) notice, become aware of; *~ zuhören* listen attentively; *et. ~ verfolgen* follow s.th. closely. '**Aufmerksamkeit** *f* (-; -en) **1.** *no pl* attention, attentiveness: *~ erregen* attract attention; (*dat*) *~ schenken* pay attention (to). **2.** small gift.

'**aufmöbeln** *v/t* (*sep*, -ge-, h) F jazz up.

'**aufmuntern** *v/t* (*sep*, -ge-, h) **1.** → *er-*

muntern 1. 2. *j-n* ~ cheer (F pep) s.o. up: **~de Worte** pep talk.

'**Aufmunterung** *f* (-; -en) cheering up.

aufmüpfig ['aʊfmʏpfɪç] *adj* F rebellious.

'**aufnähen** *v/t* (*sep*, -ge-, h) sew on (**auf** *acc* to).

Aufnahme ['aʊfna:mə] *f* (-; -n) **1.** *no pl a* taking up (*of activity etc*), establishing (*relations*), b) intake (*of food*), c) fig. absorption (*of knowledge, a. phys.*), taking in (*impressions*). **2.** *no pl* (**in** *acc*) a) integration (within), b) inclusion (into), c) admission (in[to]), d) registration: ~ **finden** be admitted (**bei** [in]to). **3.** *no pl* (*a. fig.* **e-e kühle** *etc* ~ **finden** meet with a cool *etc* reception (**bei** from). **4.** *no pl* a) accommodation, *⚕* admission (**in** *acc* to), b) reception (office). **5.** *no pl* **⚕** a) raising (*funds*), b) assessment (*of damage*). **6.** a) *film etc*: taking, shooting, b) photo(graph), shot, c) (sound) recording, pickup: **e-e** ~ **machen** (**von** of) take a picture, make a (tape-)recording; *Achtung ...* Action!, Camera! '**aufnahmefähig** *adj* receptive (**für** to). '**Aufnahmefähigkeit** *f* (-; *no pl*) receptivity.

'**Aufnahme|gebühr** *f* admission fee. **~leiter** *m film*: production (*radio*: recording) manager. **~prüfung** *f* entrance examination. **~raum** *m film etc*: studio. **~wagen** *m* recording van (*Am.* truck).

'**aufnehmen** *v/t* (*irr, sep*, -ge-, h, → **nehmen**) **1.** pick up (*load, fig. trail etc*), take up (*meshes*). **2.** receive (*a. fig. news*), accommodate, admit (**in** *acc* to a *club, hospital, etc*), enter (**in** *acc* to a *list etc*), include (**in** *acc* into): *j-n bei sich* ~ put s.o. up; *fig. et. übel* ~ take s.th. amiss. **3.** hold (*audience, cargo*), seat (*passengers etc*). **4.** take in (*impressions*), (*a.* **in sich** ~) grasp, absorb (*knowledge*). **5.** a) *⚕, phys.* absorb, b) take in (*food*). **6.** take up (*activity etc*), enter into (*relations etc*), open (*traffic*): *wieder* ~ resume; *fig. den Kampf mit j-m* ~ take s.o. on; *ich kann es mit ihm nicht* ~ I'm no match for him; → **Kontakt**. **7.** a) record, draw up, b) make an inventory of, c) assess (*damage*). **8.** record, tape(-record). **9.** take (down) (*dictation etc*), take (*order, picture, telegram[me]*), shoot (*film*): *j-n* ~ take s.o.'s

picture. **10.** **⚕** borrow (*money*), raise mortgage (**auf** *acc* on).

'**aufopfern** *v/t* (*sep*, -ge-, h) sacrifice (**sich** o.s.): **~d** self-sacrificing.

'**aufpäppeln** *v/t* (*sep*, -ge-, h) F feed *s.o.* up.

'**aufpassen** *v/i* (*sep*, -ge-, h) **1.** pay attention: *paß(t) auf!* watch out!; F *paß(t) mal auf!* listen! **2.** ~ **auf** (*acc*) a) look after, take care of, b) watch (over); F *paß gut auf dich auf!* take care (of yourself)! '**Aufpasser** *m* (-s; -), '**Aufpasserin** *f* (-; -nen) *contp.* watchdog.

'**aufpeitschen** *v/t* (*sep*, -ge-, h) *a. fig.* whip up: *sich* ~ whip o.s. up.

'**aufpflanzen** *v/t* (*sep*, -ge-, h) plant: *fig. sich* ~ plant o.s. (**vor** *dat* before).

'**aufplustern:** *sich* ~ (*sep*, -ge-, h) *a bird*: ruffle its feathers, b) F *fig.* puff o.s. up.

'**aufpo,lieren** *v/t* (*sep*, h) polish up.

'**Aufprall** *m* (-[e]s; *no pl*) impact.

'**aufprallen** *v/i* (*sep*, -ge-, sn) ~ **auf** (*acc*) hit, *car etc*: *a.* crash into.

'**Aufpreis** *m* (-es; -e) **⚕** extra charge.

'**aufpumpen** *v/t* (*sep*, -ge-, h) pump up.

'**aufputschen** *v/t* (*sep*, -ge-, h) **1.** → **aufhetzen. 2.** a) *with drugs etc*: F pep up (*sich* o.s.), b) *fig.* hype up, psych up. '**Aufputschmittel** *n* stimulant, F pep pill, *sl.* upper.

'**aufraffen** (*sep*, -ge-, h) **I** *v/t* snatch up. **II** *sich* ~ *fig.* pull o.s. together; *sich* ~, **et. zu tun** bring o.s. to do s.th.

'**aufragen** *v/i* (*sep*, -ge-, h) loom (up).

'**aufräumen** *v/t, v/i* (*sep*, -ge-, h) tidy (up): ~ **mit** do away with (*abuses etc*).

'**aufrechnen** *v/t* (*sep*, -ge-, h) *et.* ~ set s.th. off (**gegen** against).

'**aufrecht** *adj* upright (*a. fig.*), erect: ~ *sitzen* sit up. **~erhalten** *v/t* (*irr, sep*, h, → **erhalten**) **1.** maintain. **2.** adhere to. **Erhaltung** *f* (-; *no pl*) maintenance.

'**aufregen** (*sep*, -ge-, h) **I** *v/t* a) excite, b) worry, upset, c) annoy. **II** *sich* ~ (*über acc* about) get excited, be upset. '**aufregend** *adj* a) exciting, b) upsetting.

'**Aufregung** *f* (-; -en) excitement: *nur k-e ~!* don't panic!

'**aufreiben** (*irr, sep*, -ge-, h, → **reiben**) **I** *v/t* **1.** *fig.* wear down. **2.** ✕ wipe out. **II** *sich* ~ *fig.* wear o.s. out. '**aufreibend** *adj* exhausting, trying, stressful.

'**aufreihen** *v/t* (*sep*, -ge-, h) (*a. sich* ~) line up, put *books etc* in a row.

'**aufreißen** (*irr, sep,* -ge-, → *reißen*) **I** *v/t* (h) **1.** tear open (*package etc*), tear up (*road*). **2.** fling *door etc* open, F open *eyes, mouth* wide. **3.** F a) *j-n* ~ pick s.o. up, b) land (*a job etc*). **II** *v/i* (sn) burst, split, break up.

'**aufreizend** *adj* provocative.

'**aufrichten** (*sep,* -ge-, h) **I** *v/t* **1.** → **er-richten**. **2.** a) set *s.th.* upright, b) straighten up, c) raise (*s.o. in bed*), d) help *s.o.* up. **3.** *fig.* a) comfort, b) encourage. **II** *sich* ~ **4.** a) straighten o.s. (up), b) sit up (*in bed*). **5.** *fig.* take heart (*an dat* from).

'**aufrichtig** *adj* sincere, heartfelt, honest: *es tut mir ~ leid* I really am sorry.

'**Aufrichtigkeit** *f* (-; *no pl*) sincerity.

'**aufriegeln** *v/t* (*sep,* -ge-, h) unbolt.

'**Aufriß** *m* (-sses; -sse) △, A̷ elevation.

'**aufrollen** *v/t* (*sep,* -ge-, h) **1.** roll up, furl. **2.** untroll, unfurl. **3.** *fig.* (*wieder*) ~ bring *a subject etc* up (again), reopen (*a case etc*).

'**aufrücken** *v/i* (*sep,* -ge-, sn) **1.** move up (*zu* to, with). **2.** be promoted, rise. **3.** ✕ close the ranks.

'**Aufruf** *m* (-[e]s; -e) call, appeal (*an acc* to). '**aufrufen** *v/t* (*irr, sep,* -ge-, h, → *rufen*) *j-n* ~ call (out) s.o.'s name; *j-n* ~, *et. zu tun* call (up)on s.o. to do s.th.; *zum Streik* ~ call a strike.

Aufruhr ['aʊfruːr] *m* (-[e]s; -e) a) turmoil (*a. fig.*), b) uprising, revolt, c) riot (*a. ꜰꝛ*). '**aufführen** *v/t* (*sep,* -ge-, h) *fig.* **1.** a) rouse (*feelings etc*), b) rake up (*old scandals etc*). **2.** → **aufwühlen** 2.

Aufrührer ['aʊfryːrɐr] *m* (-s; -), '**Aufrührerin** *f* (-; -nen) rebel, *pol.* agitator.

'**aufrührerisch** *adj* rebellious, seditious.

'**aufrunden** *v/t* (*sep,* -ge-, h) round up (*auf acc* to).

'**aufrüsten** *v/t, v/i* (*sep,* -ge-, h) ✕ arm: *wieder* ~ rearm.

'**Aufrüstung** *f* (-; -en) armament.

aufs [aʊfs] = *auf das*.

'**aufsagen** *v/t* (*sep,* -ge-, h) recite.

'**aufsässig** ['aʊfzɛsɪç] *adj* rebellious.

'**Aufsatz** *m* (-es; ⁻e) **1.** essay, *ped.* a. composition, *univ.* paper, (*newspaper*) article. **2.** ⊙ top, cap.

'**aufsaugen** *v/t* (*sep,* -ge-, h) absorb.

'**aufscheuchen** *v/t* (*sep,* -ge-, h) a. *fig.* startle.

'**aufschichten** *v/t* (*sep,* -ge-, h) stack up.

'**aufschieben** *v/t* (*irr, sep,* -ge-, h, → *schieben*) **1.** push open. **2.** *fig.* (*auf acc, bis* till) put off, postpone.

'**Aufschlag** *m* (-[e]s; ⁻e) **1.** impact (*auf acc or dat* on): *dumpfer* ~ thud. **2.** a) cuff, b) turnup, c) lapel. **3.** † extra charge. **4.** *tennis:* service: *j-m den* ~ *abnehmen* break s.o.'s serve; ~ *haben* serve. **~ball** *m tennis:* service (ball).

'**aufschlagen** (*irr, sep,* -ge-, → *schlagen*) **I** *v/i* **1.** (sn) hit: *auf den* (or *dem*) *Boden* ~ hit the ground; *dumpf* ~ thud. **2.** (h) *tennis:* serve. **II** *v/t* (h) **3.** break (open), crack (*an egg*). **4.** open (*a book, one's eyes*), turn down (*the bed*): *Seite 10* ~ open at page 10. **5.** roll up (*sleeve*). **6.** *sich das Knie etc* ~ bruise one's knee *etc*. F knock up. **7.** pitch (*tent*): *s-n Wohnsitz in X* ~ take up residence in X. **8.** add 5% *etc* (*auf acc* to).

'**Aufschläger** *m* (-s; -) *tennis etc:* server.

'**aufschließen** (*irr, sep,* -ge-, h, → *schließen*) **I** *v/t* **1.** unlock, open. **2.** *biol.,* 🜍 break down (*or up*). **3.** develop (*land, resources*). **II** *v/i* **4.** open the door *etc* (*j-m* for s.o.). **5.** ✕ close (the) ranks, *sports:* move up: ~ *zu* catch up with.

'**aufschlitzen** *v/t* (*sep,* -ge-, h) slit open, slash.

'**Aufschluß** *m* (-sses; ⁻sse) ~ *geben* (*über acc*) give information (on), explain (*s.th.*), *j-m* inform s.o. (about): '**aufschlüsseln** *v/t* (*sep,* -ge-, h) analyze, statistically: break down. '**aufschluß-reich** *adj* informative, *w.s.* revealing.

'**aufschnallen** *v/t* (*sep,* -ge-, h) **1.** unbuckle. **2.** strap *s.th.* on (*auf acc* to).

'**aufschnappen** *v/t* (*sep,* -ge-, h) F *fig.* pick up.

'**aufschneiden** (*irr, sep,* -ge-, h, → *schneiden*) **I** *v/t* cut open, slice (*bread etc*), carve (*meat*), 🝚 open, lance (*boil*). **II** *v/i* F brag, boast, show off.

'**Aufschneider** *m* (-s; -) F show-off.

'**Aufschnitt** *m* (-[e]s; *no pl*) cold cuts.

'**aufschnüren** *v/t* (*sep,* -ge-, h) untie, undo, unlace.

'**aufschrauben** *v/t* (*sep,* -ge-, h) **1.** unscrew. **2.** screw *s.th.* on (*auf acc* to).

'**aufschrecken** (*sep,* -ge-) **I** *v/t* (h) startle: *j-n* ~ *aus* rouse s.o. from. **II** *v/i* (sn) (give a) start: *aus dem Schlaf* ~ wake with a start.

'**Aufschrei** *m* (-[e]s; -e) cry, *fig.* outcry.

'aufschreiben v/t (irr, sep, -ge-, h, → **schreiben**) write down, take a note of: F **j-n ~** book s.o.

'aufschreien v/i (irr, sep, -ge-, h, → **schreien**) cry out (**vor** with).

'Aufschrift f (-; -en) inscription.

'Aufschub m (-[e]s; ¨e) postponement, delay, ✝ respite, ⚖ a. fig. reprieve: **k-n ~ dulden** brook no delay.

'aufschürfen v/t (sep, -ge-, h) graze: **sich das Knie ~** bark one's knee.

'aufschütteln v/t (sep, -ge-, h) plump up.

'aufschütten v/t (sep, -ge-, h) heap up.

'aufschwatzen v/t (sep, -ge-, h) F **j-m et. ~** talk s.o. into buying s.th.

'aufschweißen v/t (sep, -ge-, h) weld open.

'aufschwemmen v/t (sep, -ge-, h) bloat.

'aufschwingen: sich ~ (irr, sep, -ge-, h, → **schwingen**) soar (up).

'Aufschwung m (-[e]s; ¨e) **1.** gym. swing-up. **2.** no pl fig. (fresh) impetus, ✝ upswing, recovery, boom,

'aufsehen v/i (irr, sep, -ge-, h, → **sehen**) → **aufblicken**. **'Aufsehen** n (-s) **~ erregen** attract attention, w.s. cause a stir (or sensation); **um ~ zu vermeiden** to avoid notice. **'aufsehenerregend** adj sensational. **'Aufseher** m (-s; -), **'Aufseherin** f (-; -nen) **1.** attendant. **2.** (prison) warder, Am. guard.

'aufsein v/i (irr, sep, -ge-, sn, → **sein**) F **1.** door etc: be open. **2.** person: be up.

'aufsetzen (sep, -ge-, h) **I** v/t **1.** a. fig. put on: **aufgesetzte Tasche** patch pocket. **2.** draft (speech etc). **3.** a. v/i ✈ land: **weich ~** make a soft landing. **II sich ~** sit up (im Bett in bed). **'Aufsetzer** m (-s; -) soccer etc: bounce shot.

'Aufsicht f (-; -en) **1.** no pl supervision, ⚖ custody: **die ~ haben** (or **führen**) be in charge (**über** acc of), invigilate (an exam); **unter ärztlicher ~** under medical supervision; **ohne ~** unattended (children). **2.** supervisor, person in charge. **'aufsichtführend** adj supervisory, teacher etc in charge.

'Aufsichts|beamte m **1.** supervisor. **2.** (prison) warder, Am. guard. **~behörde** f supervisory board. **~rat** m ✝ supervisory board.

'aufsitzen v/i (irr, sep, -ge-, sn, → **sitzen**) **1.** get on, mount (horse etc). **2.** fig. be

taken in (dat by). **3.** F **j-n ~ lassen** let s.o. down.

'aufspannen v/t (sep, -ge-, h) spread out, put up (umbrella etc).

'aufsparen v/t (sep, -ge-, h) save (up).

'aufsperren v/t (sep, -ge-, h) open wide: F **Mund und Nase ~** gape.

'aufspielen (sep, -ge-, h) **I** v/t, v/i play. **II sich ~** F give o.s. airs; **sich als Held** etc **~** play the hero etc.

'aufspießen v/t (sep, -ge-, h) a) spear, impale, b) a. fig. skewer.

'aufspringen v/i (irr, sep, -ge-, sn, → **springen**) **1.** jump up, leap up, ball: bounce: **~ auf** (acc) jump on to (a train etc). **2.** buds, door: burst open. **3.** skin: chap, lips: crack.

'aufspulen v/t (sep, -ge-, h) wind (up).

'aufspüren v/t (sep, -ge-, h) track down.

'aufstampfen v/i (sep, -ge-, h) (mit dem **Fuß**) ~ stamp one's foot.

'Aufstand m (-[e]s; ¨e) **1.** rebellion, revolt. **2.** F fig. (big) fuss. **'Aufständische** m, f (-n; -n) rebel, insurgent.

'aufstauen v/t (sep, -ge-, h) dam up.

'aufstechen v/t (irr, sep, -ge-, h, → **stechen**) puncture, 🩺 lance.

'aufstecken v/t (sep, -ge-, h) **1.** put up, pin up (one's hair). **2.** put on (candles): → **Licht** 2. **3.** a. v/i F give up.

'aufstehen v/i (irr, sep, -ge-, sn, → **stehen**) **1.** rise, get up (**vom Tisch** from the table): **~ dürfen** patient: be allowed (to get) up. **2.** fig. rise (in arms), rebel.

'aufsteigen v/i (irr, sep, -ge-, sn, → **steigen**) **1.** rise, bird: a. soar (up), ✈ take off, mount. go up. **2.** fig. be promoted (a. sports), rise. **3.** ~ **auf** (acc) get on, mount (vehicle, horse). **4.** fig. feeling etc: rise, well up: **ein Verdacht stieg in mir auf** I had a suspicion (**daß** that).

'Aufsteiger m (-s; -) **1.** F a) social climber, b) (professional) success, F whiz kid. **2.** sports: (newly-)promoted team.

'aufstellen (sep, -ge-, h) **I** v/t **1.** a) set up, put up, raise (ladder), pitch (tent), b) arrange, c) line up, place, post (guard etc), d) erect (monument), e) install (machine), f) set (trap): **die Ohren ~** animal: prick its ears. **2.** nominate (candidate, player), compose (team), ✗ activate (troops): pol. **sich** (**als Kandidaten**) ~ **lassen** stand (Am. run) for election etc. **3.** make (up), prepare (list). **4.** advance (*theory*), lay down, state (*rules etc*), &c form (*equation*): **e-n Rekord ~** set (up) (*or* establish) a record. **II sich ~** place o.s. (**vor** *dat* before), ✗ form up; **sich hintereinander ~** line up.

'Aufstellung *f* (-; -en) **1.** *no pl* setting up (*etc*, → **aufstellen** I), installation. **2.** *no pl* nomination (*of candidate, player*), line-up (*of team*). **3.** list, table, survey, † statement: **~ e-r Bilanz** preparation of a balance sheet.

'aufstemmen *v/t* (*sep*, -ge-, h) prize open.

Aufstieg ['aʊfʃtiːk] *m* (-[e]s; -e) **1.** ascent (*a.* ✈), way up. **2.** *fig.* rise, promotion (*a. sports*): **im ~ begriffen sein** be on the rise, be rising; *sports:* **den ~ schaffen** be promoted.

'Aufstiegs|chancen *pl* promotion prospects. **~spiel** *n sports:* promotion tie.

'aufstöbern *v/t* (*sep*, -ge-, h) track down.

'aufstocken *v/t* (*sep*, -ge-, h) **1.** ⌂ raise. **2.** increase (*one's capital*).

'aufstöhnen *v/i* (*sep*, -ge-, h) (give a loud) groan.

'aufstoßen (*irr, sep*, -ge-, h, → **stoßen**) **I** *v/t* push open. **II** *v/i* burp, belch: **j-m ~** repeat on s.o., F *fig.* strike s.o.

'aufstrebend *adj fig.* a) up-and-coming, rising, b) emergent (*nation*).

'Aufstrich *m* (-[e]s; -e) spread.

'aufstützen (*sep*, -ge-, h) **I** *v/t* prop up (**auf** *dat*, *acc* on). **II sich ~ auf** (*dat*, *acc*) lean (up)on.

'aufsuchen *v/t* (*sep*, -ge-, h) a) visit, (go and) see (*a doctor etc*), b) go to.

'auftakeln (*sep*, -ge-, h) **I** *v/t* ⚓ rig out. **II sich ~** F get dolled up.

'Auftakt *m* (-[e]s; -e) **1.** ♪ upbeat. **2.** *fig.* (**den ~ bilden** be) prelude (**zu** to).

'auftanken *v/t, v/i* (*sep*, -ge-, h) fill up, refuel.

'auftauchen *v/i* (*sep*, -ge-, sn) come up (*a. fig. problem etc*), emerge, *submarine:* surface, *fig.* turn up, *doubts etc:* arise.

'auftauen (*sep*, -ge-) **I** *v/t* (h) a) thaw, b) defrost. **II** *v/i* (sn) *a. fig.* thaw.

'aufteilen *v/t* (*sep*, -ge-, h) **1.** distribute, share (out). **2.** divide (**in** *acc* into).

auftischen ['aʊftɪʃən] *v/t* (*sep*, -ge-, h) *a. fig.* dish up.

Auftrag ['aʊftraːk] *m* (-[e]s; ⸚e) **1.** † order, commission: **et. in ~ geben** order

(*or* commission) s.th. (**bei j-m** from s.o.); **im ~ und auf Rechnung von** by order and for account of. **2.** order(s) (*a.* ✗), instructions, (*a.* ✗ combat) mission: **im ~ von** (*or gen*) by order of, **handeln** act on behalf of.

'auftragen (*irr, sep*, -ge-, h, → **tragen**) **I** *v/t* **1.** serve (up) (*food*). **2.** apply, put on (*make-up, paint, etc*). **3. j-m et. ~, j-m ~, et. zu tun** instruct (*or* tell) s.o. to do s.th. **4.** wear out (*clothes*). **II** *v/i* **5.** pullover *etc*: make s.o. look fat(ter); F *fig.* **dick ~** lay it on thick.

'Auftraggeber(in *f*) *m* client, customer.

'Auftrags|bestätigung *f* † confirmation (*by supplier:* acknowledge[e]ment) of (an) order. **~buch** *n* † order book. **~dienst** *m* telephone answering service. **♀gemäß** *adv* according to instructions, † as per order. **~lage** *f* † orders situation. **~polster** *n* † filled order books. **~werk** *n* commissioned work.

'auftreffen *v/i* (*irr, sep*, -ge-, sn, → **treffen**) hit (**auf** *dat*, *acc* on).

'auftreiben *v/t* (*irr, sep*, -ge-, h, → **treiben**) F get hold of, find.

'auftrennen *v/t* (*sep*, -ge-, h) undo (*a seam*), unravel (*knitting*).

'auftreten *v/i* (*irr, sep*, -ge-, sn, → **treten**) **1. leise ~** tread softly; **er kann mit dem verletzten Fuß nicht ~** he can't walk on his injured foot. **2.** *thea.* a) make one's entrance, b) appear (on stage) (**als** as), *a. musician:* perform: **Hamlet tritt ~** enter Hamlet; **zum ersten Mal ~** make one's debut. **3.** a) appear (**öffentlich** in public, **als Zeuge** as a witness, **vor Gericht** in court), b) present o.s. (**als** as), c) behave: **als Vermittler ~** act as go-between. **4.** *fig.* problem, doubts, *etc:* arise, *epidemic etc:* occur. **'Auftreten** *n* (-s) **1.** appearance, *thea.* performance. **2.** occurrence, arising. **3.** behavio(u)r.

'Auftrieb *m* (-[e]s; *no pl*) **1.** *phys.* buoyancy, ✈ *a.* lift. **2.** *fig.* (fresh) impetus, † upswing: (**neuen) ~ verleihen** give (a fresh) impetus (*dat* to).

'Auftritt *m* (-[e]s; -e) **1.** *thea.* a) entrance, b) scene. **2.** *fig.* scene, F row.

'auftrumpfen *v/i* (*sep*, -ge-, h) *fig.* come it strong; **gegen** make a strong showing against; **mit e-m Rekord** *etc* **~** come up with a record *etc*.

'**auftun: sich ~** (*irr, sep*, -ge-, h, → *tun*) *a. fig.* open.

'**auftürmen** (*sep*, -ge-, h) *v/t* pile up.

'**aufwachen** *v/i* (*sep*, -ge-, sn) wake up: **aus der Narkose ~** come round.

'**aufwachsen** *v/i* (*irr, sep*, -ge-, sn, → *wachsen*) grow up.

'**aufwallen** *v/i* (*sep*, -ge-, sn) **1.** boil (up). **2.** *fig.* surge, well up.

Aufwand ['aʊfvant] *m* (-[e]s; *no pl*) **1.** expenditure (**an** *dat* of), cost, expense: **e-n großen ~ an Energie** *etc* **erfordern** require a great deal of energy *etc*; **der ganze ~ war umsonst** it was a waste of time (energy, money, *etc*). **2.** luxury, extravagance: **e-n großen ~ treiben** be very extravagant. '**Aufwandsentschädigung** *f* expense allowance.

'**aufwärmen** (*sep*, -ge-, h) **I** *v/t* **1.** warm up, heat up. **2.** *fig.* rehash. **II sich ~** warm o.s., *sports*: limber up.

aufwärts ['aʊfvɛrts] *adv* up, upward(s). '**Aufwärtsentwicklung** *f* upward trend. '**aufwärtsgehen** *v/impers* (*irr, sep*, -ge-, sn, → *gehen*) **es geht aufwärts** (**mit ihm**) things are looking up (with him); **mit dem Geschäft geht es aufwärts** business is improving. '**Aufwärtshaken** *m* *boxing*: uppercut.

'**Aufwasch** *m* (-[e]s; *no pl*) → **Abwasch.**

'**aufwaschen** *v/t* (*irr, sep*, -ge-, h) → **abwaschen.**

'**aufwecken** *v/t* (*sep*, -ge-, h) wake (up).

'**aufweichen** (*sep*, -ge-) **I** *v/t* (h) **1.** a) soak, b) make soggy. **2.** *fig.* undermine. **II** *v/i* (sn) become soggy, *a. fig.* soften.

'**aufweisen** *v/t* (*irr, sep*, -ge-, h, → *weisen*) **et. ~, et. aufzuweisen haben** have (or show) s.th.; **große Mängel ~** have many defects.

'**aufwenden** *v/t* (*irr, sep*, -ge-, h, → *wenden*) a) use, apply, b) spend (**für** on): (**viel**) **Mühe ~** take (great) pains.

'**aufwendig** *adj* **1.** large-scale. **2.** expensive. '**Aufwendungen** *pl* expenditure.

'**aufwerfen** (*irr, sep*, -ge-, h, → *werfen*) **I** *v/t* **1.** throw up (*dam etc*). **2.** *fig.* raise (*question etc*). **II sich ~** set o.s. up (**zum Richter** *etc* as judge *etc*).

'**aufwerten** *v/t* (*sep*, -ge-, h) ⚊ revalue (upward), *a. fig.* raise. '**Aufwertung** *f* (-; -en) ⚊ revaluation (upward), *fig.* upgrading.

'**aufwickeln** *v/t* (*sep*, -ge-, h) **1.** (*a.* **sich ~**)

roll (*or* coil) up. **2.** F put *one's hair* up in curlers. **3.** → **auswickeln.**

aufwiegeln ['aʊfviːɡəln] *v/t* (*sep*, -ge-, h) → **aufhetzen.**

'**aufwiegen** *v/t* (*irr, sep*, -ge-, h, → *wiegen*) *fig.* offset, make up for.

'**Aufwind** *m* (-[e]s; -e) **1.** ✈ upwind. **2.** → **Auftrieb** 2. **3.** ✈ **im ~** on the upswing.

'**aufwirbeln** *v/t* (*sep*, -ge-, h) whirl up (*a. v/i*, sn), raise (*dust*): *fig.* (**viel**) **Staub ~** cause quite a stir.

'**aufwischen** *v/t* (*sep*, -ge-, h) a) mop up, b) wipe, mop.

'**aufwühlen** *v/t* (*sep*, -ge-, h) **1.** turn up (*ground*), churn up (*sea*). **2.** *fig.* **j-n ~** stir s.o. deeply; **~d** stirring.

'**aufzählen** *v/t* (*sep*, -ge-, h) enumerate. '**Aufzählung** *f* (-; -en) enumeration.

'**aufzäumen** *v/t* (*sep*, -ge-, h) bridle: → **Pferd** 1.

'**aufzehren** *v/t* (*sep*, -ge-, h) *fig.* use up.

'**aufzeichnen** *v/t* (*sep*, -ge-, h) **1.** a) record, write down, b) tape(-record), *TV* (video-)tape. **2.** draw (**auf** *acc* on), sketch, ⚙ trace. '**Aufzeichnung** *f* (-; -en) **1.** *a.* ⚙, *TV* recording. **2.** *pl* notes, record, *w.s.* papers: **sich ~en machen** make notes (**über** *acc* of).

'**aufzeigen** *v/t* (*sep*, -ge-, h) show, demonstrate, point out.

'**aufziehen** (*irr, sep*, -ge-, → *ziehen*) **I** *v/t* (h) **1.** wind up: **Spielzeug zum ♀** clockwork toys. **2.** draw up, pull up, hoist (*flag etc*), *thea.* raise (*the curtain*). **3.** (pull) open (*drawer*), open, draw (*curtains*), undo (*knot*). **4.** mount (*tyre*), put on (*strings*), mount *picture* (on cardboard): *fig.* **andere Saiten ~** change one's tune. **5.** raise, bring up, rear. **6.** F organize, mount, set up (*business etc*). **7.** F **j-n ~** tease s.o., pull s.o.'s leg. **8.** ⚕ fill (*syringe*). **II** *v/i* (sn) **9.** *clouds*: gather, *storm*: *a.* be brewing (*a. fig.*). **10.** ✕ march up.

'**Aufzucht** *f* (-; -en) breeding, raising.

'**Aufzug** *m* (-[e]s; -̈e) **1.** procession, parade. **2.** lift, *Am.* elevator. **3.** F *contp.* getup. **4.** *thea.* act. **5.** *gym.* pull-up.

'**aufzwingen** *v/t* (*irr, sep*, -ge-, h, → *zwingen*) **j-m et. ~** force *s.th.* (up)on s.o., impose *one's will* on s.o.

'**Augapfel** *m* *anat.* eyeball: *fig.* **et. wie s-n ~ hüten** guard s.th. like gold.

Auge ['aʊɡə] *n* (-s; -n) **1.** *anat.* eye: **gute**

(*schlechte*) ~*n haben* have good (bad) eyesight (*or* eyes); *vor aller* ~*n* openly, in full view; *unter vier* ~*n* in private; *nur fürs* ~ just for show; ~ *um* ~! an eye for an eye!; F *fig. blaues* ~ black eye; *mit e-m blauen* ~ *davonkommen* get off cheaply; *mit bloßem* ~ with the naked eye; *vor m-m geistigen* ~ in my mind's eye; *a. fig. mit verbundenen* ~ blindfold; *das* ~ *des Gesetzes* the law; *im* ~ *behalten* keep an eye on, *fig.* keep *s.th.* in mind; *ins* ~ *fallen* catch the eye; *ins* ~ *fallend* a) striking, b) obvious; *ins* ~ *fassen* consider; *j-m et. vor* ~*n führen* make s.th. clear to s.o.; F *das kann leicht ins* ~ *gehen* that can easily go wrong; *das hätte leicht ins* ~ *gehen können!* that was close!; *et. im* ~ *haben* have s.th. in mind; *ein* ~ *haben auf* (*acc*) have an eye on s.o., s.th.; *s-e* ~*n überall haben* see everything; *sich et. vor* ~*n halten* bear s.th. in mind; *nicht aus den* ~*n lassen* keep one's eyes on; *große* ~*n machen* gape; F *er wird* ~*n machen!* he's in for a surprise!; *sie hat (vielleicht)* ~*n gemacht!* you should have seen her face!; *j-m (schöne)* ~*n machen* make eyes at s.o.; *fig. j-m die* ~*n öffnen* open s.o.'s eyes; *soweit das* ~ *reicht* as far as the eye can see; F *ein* ~ *riskieren* risk a glance; *dem Tod etc ins* ~ *sehen* look death *etc* in the eye, face death *etc*; *j-m in die* ~*n sehen* look s.o. full in the face; *fig. in die* ~*n springen* leap to the eye, be obvious; *das stach mir ins* ~ it caught my fancy; *ich traute m-n* ~*n kaum* I could hardly believe my eyes; *aus den* ~*n verlieren* lose sight of; *die* ~*n verschließen vor* close one's eyes to; F *ein* ~ *zudrücken* turn a blind eye; *ich habe kein* ~ *zugetan* I didn't sleep a wink. **2.** *on dice, card:* pip. **3.** ♀ eye. **4.** globule of fat.

äugen ['ɔygən] *v/i* (h) *esp. hunt.* look.

'**Augen|arzt** *m* eye specialist, ophthalmologist. ~**bank** *f* (-; -en) ♣ eye bank.

'**Augenblick** *m* (-[e]s; -e) moment: *e-n* ~ *bitte!* just a moment, please!; *im* ~ at the moment; *im ersten* ~ for a moment; *im letzten* ~ at the (very) last moment; *alle* ~*e* every (*or* any) moment. '**augenblicklich I** *adj* **1.** immediate. **2.** present, current. **3.** momentary. **II** *adv* **4.** immediately. **5.** at the moment, (just) now.

'**Augen|braue** *f* eyebrow. ~**brauenstift** *m* eyebrow pencil. ~**fältchen** *pl* crow's-feet. ~**farbe** *f* colo(u)r of eyes. ~**heilkunde** *f* ophthalmology. ~**höhe** *f* (*in* ~ at) eye level. ~**höhle** *f anat.* eye socket, orbit. ~**innendruck** *m* ♣ intra-ocular pressure. ~**klappe** *f* eye patch. ~**klinik** *f* eye clinic. ~**leiden** *n* eye disease. ~**licht** *n* (-[e]s; *no pl*) (eye)sight. ~**lid** *n* eyelid. ~**maß** *n* (-es; *no pl*) **1.** *ein gutes* ~ *haben* have a sure eye. **2.** *fig.* (good) *political etc* judg(e)ment.

'**Augenmerk** *n sein* ~ *richten auf* (*acc*) direct one's attention to.

'**Augen|muskel** *m* eye muscle. ~**nerv** *m* optic nerve. ~**operati,on** *f* eye operation. ~**salbe** *f* eye ointment.

'**Augenschein** *m* (-[e]s; *no pl*) appearance(s): *dem* ~ *nach* to all appearances; *in* ~ *nehmen* inspect closely.

'**augenscheinlich** *adj* evident, apparent, obvious.

'**Augen|spiegel** *m* ♣ ophthalmoscope. ~**tropfen** *pl* ♣ eyedrops. ~**weide** *f fig.* feast for the eyes. ~**wimper** *f* eyelash. ~**wischerei** [-vɪʃə'raɪ] *f* (-; -en) F eyewash. ~**zahn** *m* eyetooth. ~**zeuge** *m* eyewitness. ~**zeugenbericht** *m* eyewitness report. ~**zwinkern** *n* (-s) (*mit e-m* ~ with a) wink.

August [aʊ'gʊst] *m* (-[e]s, -; -e) (*im* ~ in) August.

Auktion [aʊk'tsĭo:n] *f* (-; -en) ♣ auction (sale), public sale. **Auktionator** [aʊktsĭo'na:tɔr] *m* (-s; -en [-na'to:rən]) auctioneer. **Aukti'onshaus** *n* auctioneers.

Aula ['aʊla] *f* (-; -s, Aulen) *ped., univ.* assembly hall.

Au-pair-Mädchen [o'pɛ:r-] *n* au pair (girl).

aus [aʊs] **I** *prep* (*dat*) **1.** out of, from: ~ *dem Fenster sehen* look out of (*Am.* out) the window; ~ *dem Haus gehen* leave the house; 🚌 ~ *Berlin* from Berlin; ~ *unserer Mitte* from among us; ~ *der Flasche trinken* drink from the bottle. **2.** (*origin*) from, (*time*) *a.* of: *er ist* ~ *Berlin* he comes from Berlin; ~ *ganz Spanien* from all over Spain; ~ *dem 19. Jh.* of the 19th century; *er liest* ~ *s-m Roman* he reads from his novel; ~ *dem Deutschen translated* from (the) German. **3.** (made) of, from: *fig.* ~ *ihm wurde ein guter Arzt* he became a good doctor. **4.** ~ *Mitleid* (*Neugier etc*) out of pity (curiosity *etc*); ~ *Liebe* from love; ~ *Liebe zu* for the love of; ~ *Prinzip* on principle; ~ *Spaß* for fun; ~ *Versehen* by mistake. **II** *adv* **5.** *von* ... ~ from; *von hier* ~ from here; *fig. von Natur* ~ by nature; *von mir* ~ *kann er gehen* he may go, for all I care; F *von mir* ~! I don't care!; *von sich* ~ of one's own accord. **6.** F a) (*switched*) off, out: *ein - aus* on - off, b) over, out; *die Schule ist* ~ school is over; *damit ist es (jetzt)* ~! that's all over now!; *mit ihm ist es* ~ he has had it; ~ *der Mode* out of fashion. **7.** ~ *und ein* in and out; *fig. bei j-m ein und* ~ *gehen* be a frequent visitor at s.o.'s house; *ich weiß nicht mehr ein noch* ~ I'm at my wits' end.

Aus *n* (-; *no pl*) *sports*: **im** (*ins*) ~ out; *a. fig.* **das bedeutete das** ~ **für ihn** with that he was out (of the game).

'**ausarbeiten** *v/t* (*sep*, -ge-, h) work out, elaborate, develop, draw up.

'**Ausarbeitung** *f* (-; -en) **1.** working out, elaboration, development. **2.** draft.

'**ausarten** *v/i* (*sep*, -ge-, sn) degenerate (*in acc, zu* into), *game, party, etc*: get out of hand.

'**ausatmen** *v/i, v/t* (*sep*, -ge-, h) breathe out, exhale.

'**ausbaden** *v/t* (*sep*, -ge-, h) F *et.* ~ *müssen* have to carry the can.

'**ausbaggern** *v/t* (*sep*, -ge-, h) excavate, dredge.

'**ausbalan,cieren** *v/t* (*sep*, -ge-, h) *a. fig.* balance out.

'**Ausbau** *m* (-[e]s; *no pl*) **1.** ⊙ disassembly, removal. **2.** △ a) extension, b) interior works. **3.** *a. fig.* expansion, development. **4.** *fig.* consolidation.

'**ausbauen** *v/t* (*sep*, -ge-, h) **1.** ⊙ dismantle, remove. **2.** △ extend: *das Dach* ~ build rooms into the attic. **3.** *a. fig.* extend, expand, develop: *sports:* *s-n Vorsprung* ~ increase one's lead. **4.** strengthen, consolidate. '**ausbaufähig** *adj* capable of development: ~*e Stellung* position with good prospects.

'**ausbedingen** *v/t* (*irr, sep*, h, → *bedingen*) *sich et.* ~ reserve (o.s.) s.th.; *sich* ~, *daß* ... make it a condition that ...

'**ausbessern** *v/t* (*sep*, -ge-, h) mend, re-

pair. '**Ausbesserung** *f* (-; -en) repair(s).

'**ausbeulen** *v/t* (*sep*, -ge-, h) **1.** ⊙ beat out. **2.** make *trousers etc* baggy.

'**Ausbeute** *f* (-; *no pl*) profit, *a.* ⚒, ⊙ yield, output, *fig.* result(s). '**ausbeuten** *v/t* (*sep*, -ge-, h) exploit (*a. b.s.*), ⚒ *a.* work. '**Ausbeuter** *m* (-s; -) *b.s.* exploiter. '**ausbeuterisch** *adj b.s.* exploitative. '**Ausbeutung** *f* (-; *no pl*) *a. b.s.* exploitation.

'**ausbilden** (*sep*, -ge-, h) **I** *v/t* **1.** a) train, instruct, educate, b) develop: *j-n zum Sänger* ~ train s.o. to be a singer. **2.** *biol.* form, develop. **II** *sich* ~ (*lassen*) *zu* train (*or* be trained, study) to be: → *ausgebildet*. '**Ausbilder** *m* (-s; -) *a.* ✗ instructor. '**Ausbildung** *f* (-; -en) training, *ped., univ.* education: *in der* ~ *stehen* be undergoing training.

'**Ausbildungs|beihilfe** *f* grant. ~**gang** *m* training. ~**platz** *m* training post. ~**zeit** *f* period of training.

'**ausbitten** *v/t* (*irr, sep*, -ge-, h, → *bitten*) *sich et.* ~ ask for s.th.

'**ausblasen** *v/t* (*irr, sep*, -ge-, h, → *blasen*) blow out.

'**ausbleiben** *v/i* (*irr, sep*, -ge-, sn, → *bleiben*) a) fail to come, b) stay away, c) stop: ♀ *ihre Periode blieb aus* she missed her period; *fig.* *es konnte nicht* ~, *daß* it was inevitable that; (*nicht*) *lange* ~ (not to) be long in coming. '**Ausbleiben** *n* (-s) absence.

'**ausbleichen** *v/i* (*sep*, -ge-, sn) bleach (*a. v/t*, h), fade.

'**ausblenden** *v/t* (*sep*, -ge-, h) *film, radio:* fade out.

'**Ausblick** *m* (-[e]s; -e) view (*auf acc* of): *Zimmer mit* ~ *auf den See* room(s) overlooking the lake.

'**ausbomben** *v/t* (*sep*, -ge-, h) bomb out.

'**ausbooten** *v/t* (*sep*, -ge-, h) **1.** ♣ disembark. **2.** F *fig.* oust, get rid of *s.o.*

'**ausbrechen** (*irr, sep*, -ge-, → *brechen*) **I** *v/t* (h) **1.** break out (*or* off). **2.** → *erbrechen* 2. **II** *v/i* (sn) **3.** ~ *aus* (*dat*) break out of, escape from, *fig.* break away from (*a. sports*): F *aus der Gesellschaft* ~ drop out of society. **4.** *fire, war, epidemic, etc:* break out, *volcano:* erupt. **5.** *in Tränen* ~ burst into tears; *ihm brach der Schweiß aus* he broke into a sweat; *in Gelächter* ~ burst out laughing; *in Beifall* ~ break into applause. **6.** *mot.* swerve out of line.

'**Ausbrecher** *m* (-s; -) escaped prisoner.

'**ausbreiten** (*sep*, -ge-, h) **I** *v/t* **1.** spread (out). **2.** *fig.* extend, expand (*power etc*), display (*knowledge*). **II** *sich* ~ **3.** *fire, epidemic, etc:* spread. **4.** *terrain:* spread (out), stretch (out), *panorama:* open up (*vor j-m* before s.o.). **5.** F spread (o.s.) out. '**Ausbreitung** *f* (-; *no pl*) spread(ing), extension, expansion.

'**ausbrennen** (*irr, sep, -ge-, → brennen*) **I** *v/t* (h) burn out, *🗲 cauterize: → ausgebrannt.* **II** *v/i* (sn) burn out.

'**Ausbruch** *m* (-[e]s; ⸚e) **1.** escape: ~ *aus dem Gefängnis* jailbreak, breakout. **2.** *fig.* outbreak (*of war, epidemic, etc*), eruption (*of volcano*): *zum* ~ *kommen* break out. **3.** *fig.* outburst.

'**ausbrüten** *v/t* (*sep*, -ge-, h) *a. fig.* hatch, F be sickening for (*a disease*).

'**ausbuchen** *v/t* (*sep*, -ge-, h) **1.** *✞* cancel. **2.** → *ausgebucht.*

'**ausbuchten:** *sich* ~ (*sep*, -ge-, h) bulge (*or curve*) out(wards).

'**ausbuddeln** *v/t* (*sep*, -ge-, h) F dig up.

'**ausbügeln** *v/t* (*sep*, -ge-, h) *a.* F *fig.* iron out.

'**ausbürgern** *v/t* (*sep*, -ge-, h) denaturalize.

'**ausbürsten** *v/t* (*sep*, -ge-, h) brush down.

'**Ausdauer** *f* (-; *no pl*) perseverance, *a.* ⚙ endurance, tenacity, *esp. sports:* staying power, stamina. '**ausdauernd** *adj* **1.** persevering, tireless. **2.** *⚘* perennial.

'**ausdehnen** *v/t* (*sep*, -ge-, h) (*a. sich* ~) *a. phys.,* ⚙ stretch, expand, extend (*auf acc* to): → *ausgedehnt.* '**Ausdehnung** *f* (-; en) **1.** *no pl* extension (*auf acc* to), expansion, spread(ing). **2.** extent, size.

'**ausdenken** *v/t* (*irr, sep, -ge-, h, → denken*) *sich et.* ~ a) think s.th. up, F come up with, b) imagine, c) invent, devise; *nicht auszudenken sein* be inconceivable; *die Folgen sind nicht auszudenken* the consequences could be disastrous.

'**ausdiskuˌtieren** *v/t* (*sep*, h) thresh out.

'**ausdörren** *v/t* (*sep*, -ge-, h) dry up, parch: → *ausgedörrt.*

'**ausdrehen** *v/t* (*sep*, -ge-, h) F turn off.

'**Ausdruck** *m* (-[e]s; ⸚e) expression (*a. A etc*), word, term, phrase: *idiomati-*

scher ~ idiom; *juristischer* ~ legal term; *zum* ~ *bringen* express; *zum* ~ *kommen* be expressed; F *das ist gar kein* ~! that's putting it mildly!

'**Ausdruck²** *m* (-[e]s; -e) *computer:* printout. '**ausdrucken** *v/t* (*sep*, -ge-, h) print *s.th.* in full, *computer:* print out.

'**ausdrücken** (*sep*, -ge-, h) **I** *v/t* **1.** stub out (*cigarette*). **2.** squeeze (out). **3.** *fig.* a) express, put into words, b) show, reveal: *ich weiß nicht, wie ich es* ~ *soll* I don't know how to put it; *anders ausgedrückt* in other words. **II** *sich* ~ **4.** express o.s. **5.** be revealed.

'**ausdrücklich I** *adj* express: ~*er Befehl* strict order. **II** *adv* expressly, specially.

'**Ausdruckskraft** *f* (-; *no pl*) expressiveness. '**ausdruckslos** *adj* blank, expressionless. '**ausdrucksvoll** *adj* expressive. '**Ausdrucksweise** *f* style, diction.

'**ausdünsten** *v/t* (*sep*, -ge-, h) give off. '**Ausdünstung** *f* (-; -en) odo(u)r.

ausein'ander *adv* apart, separated, F *marriage:* on the rocks: *... schreibt man* ~ *...* is written in two words; *die Kinder sind zwei Jahre* ~ the children are two years apart in age. ~**brechen** *v/t* (*irr, sep, -ge-, h, → brechen*) *and v/i* (sn) break asunder. ~**bringen** *v/t* (*irr, sep, -ge-, h, → bringen*) separate. ~**fallen** *v/i* (*irr, sep, -ge-, sn, → fallen*) fall apart, *fig. a.* break up. ~**gehen** *v/i* (*irr, sep, -ge-, sn, → gehen*) **1.** separate, part, *crowd:* disperse. **2.** *fig.* opinions *etc:* be divided (*über acc* on): ~*d* differing, divergent. **3.** F come apart, *fig. relationship etc:* break off, *engagement:* be broken off, *marriage:* go on the rocks. **4.** F grow fat. ~**halten** *v/t* (*irr, sep, -ge-, h, → halten*) tell apart, distinguish between. ~**leben:** *sich* ~ (*sep*, -ge-, h) drift apart. ~**nehmen** *v/t* (*sep*, -ge-, h, → *nehmen*) **1.** take apart, ⚙ *a.* dismantle. **2.** F *sports:* clobber. ~**reißen** *v/t* (*irr, sep, -ge-, h, → reißen*) tear apart, *fig. a.* separate.

ausein'andersetzen (*sep*, -ge-, h) **I** *v/t j-m et.* ~ explain s.th. to s.o. **II** *sich* ~ *mit* deal with, tackle (*a problem etc*). **Ausein'andersetzung** *f* (-; -en) **1.** dealing (*mit* with). **2.** argument: *esp. pol. kriegerische* ~ armed conflict.

'**ausfahren** (*irr, sep, -ge-, → fahren*) **I** *v/t* (h) **1.** a) ⚙ extend, b) lower (*landing* *gear*). **2.** *mot.* run *the engine* at top speed, round (*curve*). **3.** take *s.o.* out for a drive. **4.** deliver (*goods*). **5.** wear out, rut: → **ausgefahren** II. **II** *v/i* (sn) **6.** go for a drive. '**Ausfahrt** f (-; -en) **1.** drive. **2.** a) gateway, b) exit (*of motorway*), c) mouth (*of port*): *mot.* ~ *freihalten!* keep exit clear!

'**Ausfall** *m* (-[e]s; ⸚e) **1.** ⊙ failure, breakdown. **2.** *no pl* a) loss, b) absence, c) cancel(l)ation (*of lesson etc*). **3.** *sports:* *ein glatter* ~ (*player*) F a dead loss. **4.** *fenc.* lunge. **5.** *fig.* attack (*gegen* on). '**ausfallen** *v/i* (*irr, sep,* -ge-, sn, → *fallen*) **1.** ⊙ fail, break down. **2.** *hair etc:* fall out. **3.** not to take place: ~ *lassen* call off, cancel (*lecture etc*); *morgen fällt die Schule aus* there is no school tomorrow. **4.** *person:* be absent, be unavailable. **5.** *gut* (*schlecht*) ~ turn out well (badly); *der Sieg fiel knapp aus* it was a close victory.

'**ausfällen** *v/t* (*sep,* -ge-, h) precipitate. '**ausfallend →** '**ausfällig** *adj* (*er wurde* ~ he became) abusive.

'**Ausfall|muster** *n* ⸗ production (*or* proof) sample. ~*s*(**s**)**erscheinung** *f* ⚕ deficiency (*in addicts:* withdrawal) symptom. ~*straße* f arterial road.

'**ausfasern** *v/i* (*sep,* -ge-, sn) fray (out). '**ausfechten** *v/t* (*irr, sep,* -ge-, h, → *fechten*) *fig.* fight out.

'**ausfertigen** *v/t* (*sep,* -ge-, h) draw up, execute (*document*), *adm.* issue (*passport etc*). '**Ausfertigung** f (-; -en) **1.** drawing up, ⚖ execution. **2.** (⚖ certified) copy: → *doppelt* II, *dreifach.*

'**ausfindig** *adv* ~ *machen* find, discover. '**ausfliegen** *v/i* (*irr, sep,* -ge-, sn, → *fliegen*) fly out (*a. v/t* ✕, h), *birds:* leave the nest.

'**ausfließen** *v/i* (*irr, sep,* -ge-, sn, → *fließen*) flow out.

'**ausflippen** *v/i* (*sep,* -ge-, sn) F a) freak out, b) flip one's lid.

'**Ausflucht** f (-; ⸚e) *usu. pl* excuse. '**Ausflug** *m* (-[e]s; ⸚e) (*e-n* ~ *machen*) (make an) excursion, (go on a) trip, (go for an) outing. '**Ausflügler** [-fly:glɔr] *m* (-s; -) day tripper, excursionist.

'**Ausfluß** *m* (-sses; ⸚sse) **1.** ⊙ a) outflow, b) outlet. **2.** ⚕ discharge.

'**ausfragen** *v/t* (*sep,* -ge-, h) (*über acc* about) question, quiz, *contp.* pump.

'**ausfransen** *v/i* (*sep,* -ge-, h) fray (out). '**ausfressen** *v/t* (*irr, sep,* -ge-, h, → *fressen*) F *fig. was hat er etc ausgefressen?* what has he *etc* been up to?

'**Ausfuhr** f (-; -en) **1.** *no pl* export. **2.** exports. '**ausführbar** *adj* **1.** practicable. **2.** ⸗ exportable. '**ausführen** *v/t* (*sep,* -ge, h) **1.** ⸗ export. **2.** carry out, execute: *Reparaturen* ~ make repairs. **3.** explain, argue. **4.** take *s.o.* out, take *a dog* for a walk.

'**Ausführende** *m, f* (-n; -n) ♪ performer. '**Ausfuhr|genehmigung** f ⸗ export licen/ce (*Am.* -se). ~*handel* *m* export trade. ~*land* *n* exporting country.

ausführlich ['aosfy:rlıç] **I** *adj* detailed, full. **II** *adv* in detail: *sehr* ~ at great length; ~ *beschreiben* give a detailed description (*or* account) of.

'**Ausfuhrprämie** f export bounty. '**Ausfuhrquote** f export quota. '**Ausfuhrsperre** f embargo on exports. '**Ausführung** f (-; -en) **1.** *no pl* carrying out, execution, *w.s.* completion. **2.** a) quality, b) type, model, c) design. **3.** *pl* remarks, comments.

'**Ausfuhrzoll** *m* export duty.

'**ausfüllen** *v/t* (*sep,* -ge-, h) **1.** fill, *fig. a.* occupy: *ihre Arbeit füllt sie nicht aus* she is not satisfied by her work. **2.** fill in, *Am.* fill out, complete (*form*).

'**Ausgabe** f (-; -n) **1.** *no pl* a) handing out, distribution, b) issue (*of order, material, etc,* ⸗ *of shares*), emission (*of banknotes*). **2.** a) edition, copy (*of a book*), b) issue, number (*of a periodical*). **3.** *pl* expenditure, expense(s). **4.** *computer:* output. ~*kurs* *m* ⸗ issue price. ~*stelle* f issuing office.

'**Ausgang** *m* (-[e]s; ⸚e) **1.** way out, exit: *am* ~ *des Dorfes* at the end of the village. **2.** *no pl* a) end, close, b) result, outcome: *Unfall mit tödlichem* ~ fatal accident. **3.** *no pl* beginning: *s-n* ~ *nehmen von* start from. **4.** outing: ~ *haben* have the day *etc* off, ✕ have a pass.

'**Ausgangspunkt** *m a. fig.* starting point. '**Ausgangssperre** f → *Ausgehverbot.* '**Ausgangssprache** f source language. '**ausgeben** (*irr, sep,* -ge-, h, → *geben*) **I** *v/t* **1.** hand out, distribute, deal (*cards*), ⸗ issue (*shares etc*), spend (*money*), *computer:* output: F *e-n* (*or e-e Runde*) ~ stand a round (of drinks). **2.** ~ *für,* ~

als pass *s.o., s.th.* off as. **II** *sich* ~ **3.** pose (*für, als* as). **4.** → *verausgaben* 2.

'**ausgebeult** I *pp of* **ausbeulen. II** *adj* baggy (*pants etc*).

'**ausgebildet** I *pp of* **ausbilden. II** *adj* trained.

'**ausgebombt** I *pp of* **ausbomben. II** *adj* bombed(-)out.

'**ausgebrannt** I *pp of* **ausbrennen. II** *adj* gutted (by fire), *a. fig.* burnt(-)out.

'**ausgebucht** I *pp of* **ausbuchen. II** *adj* booked(-)up.

'**ausgedehnt** I *pp of* **ausdehnen. II** *adj* a) *a. fig.* extensive, b) long (*period etc*).

'**ausgedient** *adj* useless, discarded.

'**ausgefahren** I *pp of* **ausfahren. II** *adj* worn(-)out, rutty: → *Gleis*.

'**ausgefallen** I *pp of* **ausfallen. II** *adj fig.* unusual, F off-beat.

'**ausgefeilt** *adj fig.* polished.

'**ausgeglichen** I *pp of* **ausgleichen. II** *adj fig.* (well-)balanced.

'**ausgehen** *v/i* (*irr, sep*, -ge-, sn, → *gehen*) **1.** go out: *er ist ausgegangen a.* he is not in. **2.** end: *gut* ~ *a.* turn out well; *ling. auf e-n Vokal* ~ end in a vowel; *sports:* *unentschieden* ~ end in a draw. **3.** *light, cigar, etc*: go out. **4.** *fig. money, supplies, etc*: run out: *mir ging das Geld aus* I ran out of money; *ihr ging die Geduld aus* she lost all patience; F *ihm ging die Puste aus* he ran out of steam. **5.** → *ausfallen* 2. **6.** ~ *von fig.* a) *idea etc*: come from, b) proceed from, assume; *wenn wir davon* ~*, daß* proceeding on the assumption that; *man kann (ruhig) davon* ~*, daß ...* it is safe to assume that ...; *ich gehe davon aus, daß ...* I would think (that) ... **7.** ~ *auf* (*acc*) be bent on; *auf Abenteuer* ~ seek adventure; *auf Betrug* ~ be out to cheat. **8.** *leer* ~ come away empty(-)handed, *w.s. a.* be left out in the cold; (*straf*)*frei* ~ get off scot-free.

'**ausgehend** *adj das* ~*e Mittelalter* the late Middle Ages; *im* ~*en* 19. *Jh.* toward(s) the end of the 19th century.

'**ausgehungert** I *pp of* **aushungern. II** *adj* starved (*fig. nach* for).

'**Ausgehverbot** *n* curfew: ⚔ ~ *bekommen* (*haben*) be confined to barracks.

'**ausgeklügelt** [-kly:gəlt] *adj* ingenious.

'**ausgekocht** I *pp of* **auskochen. II** *adj* F *fig.* shrewd, crafty.

'**ausgelassen** I *pp of* **auslassen. II** *adj* gay, exuberant, boisterous: ~ *sein a.* be in high spirits.

'**ausgelastet** I *pp of* **auslasten. II** *adj a.* *voll* ~ ✝, ☉ working to capacity, *person:* fully stretched.

'**ausgelaugt** *adj* F ~ *sein* be washed out.

'**ausgemacht** I *pp of* **ausmachen. II** *adj* **1.** settled: *e-e* ~*e Sache* a foregone conclusion. **2.** utter, perfect (*fool etc*).

'**ausgemergelt** [-mɛrgəlt] *adj* emaciated.

'**ausgenommen** I *pp of* **ausnehmen. II** *conj* (*a.* ~*, wenn*) unless it rains etc: ~*, daß* except that. **III** *prep* except(ing), with the exception of: → *Anwesende*.

'**ausgeprägt** *adj* marked, pronounced: ~*es Pflichtgefühl* strongly developed sense of duty.

'**ausgepumpt** I *pp of* **auspumpen. II** *adj* F *fig.* bushed, *Am.* pooped.

'**ausgerechnet** I *pp of* **ausrechnen. II** *adv* F *fig.* ~ *er* he of all people; ~ *Bananen* bananas of all things; ~ *heute* today of all days; ~ *jetzt* just now.

'**ausgereift** *adj* a) mature(d) (*a. fig.*), b) perfected (*design etc*).

'**ausgeschlossen** I *pp of* **ausschließen. II** *adj* **1.** *sich* ~ *fühlen* feel left out of things. **2.** impossible: *das ist* ~*!* that's out of the question!; *jeder Zweifel ist* ~ there is no doubt about it.

'**ausgeschnitten** I *pp of* **ausschneiden. II** *adj* (*tief*) ~ low-necked.

'**ausgesprochen** I *pp of* **aussprechen. II** *adj fig.* pronounced, marked: *das war* ~*es Pech* that really was bad luck; *es ist* ~ *falsch* it is positively wrong.

'**ausgestorben** I *pp of* **aussterben. II** *adj* extinct: *wie* ~ completely deserted.

'**ausgesucht** I *pp of* **aussuchen. II** *adj fig.* select, exquisite: ~*e Qualität* choice quality.

'**ausgewachsen** I *pp of* **auswachsen. II** *adj* **1.** full(y-)grown. **2.** F *fig.* full-blown (*scandal etc*).

'**Ausgewiesene** ['aʊsgəvi:zənə] *m, f* (-n; -n) expellee.

'**ausgewogen** I *pp of* **auswiegen. II** *adj fig.* (well-)balanced.

'**ausgezeichnet** I *pp of* **auszeichnen. II** *adj* excellent: *das paßt mir* ~ that suits me fine.

'**ausgiebig** [-gi:biç] I *adj* ~*en Gebrauch*

machen von make full use of. **II** adv ~ **duschen** have a good long shower.

'**ausgießen** v/t (irr, sep, -ge-, h, → **gießen**) pour out, empty.

'**Ausgleich** m (-[e]s; -e) **1.** a) balance (**für** to), b) settlement (of account, bill), c) compensation: **als** ~ **für** by way of compensation for; **zum** ~ (gen) in settlement of. **2.** sports: equalizer: **den** ~ **erzielen** → **ausgleichen 3.** '**ausgleichen** (irr, sep, -ge-, h, → **gleichen**) **I** v/t **1.** compensate (for), offset: ~**de Gerechtigkeit** poetic justice. **2.** ✝ a) balance, settle (accounts etc), b) cover (loss etc). **II** v/i **3.** sports: equalize.

'**Ausgleichs|getriebe** n mot. differential (gear). ~**sport** m **ich jogge als** ~ I do jogging to keep fit. ~**tor** n, ~**treffer** m equalizer.

'**ausgleiten** v/i (irr, sep, -ge-, sn, → **gleiten**) a. fig. slip.

'**ausgraben** v/t (irr, sep, -ge-, h, → **graben**) a. fig. dig up. '**Ausgrabung** f (-; -en) excavation, F dig.

'**ausgrenzen** v/t (sep, -ge-, h) exclude.

'**Ausguck** m (-[e]s; -e) ⚓, ✕ lookout.

'**Ausguß** m (-sses; ~sse) sink, ⊙ outlet.

'**aushaken** (sep, -ge-, h) **I** v/t unhook. **II** v/impers F **es hakte bei ihm aus** a) he lost the thread, b) he lost his cool, c) he flipped; **da hakt's bei mir aus!** I just don't get it!

'**aushalten** (irr, sep, -ge-, h, → **halten**) **I** v/t **1.** a) bear, stand (pain etc), b) sustain: **es ist nicht auszuhalten** (or **zum** 2) it is unbearable. F keep (a woman). **3.** ♪ hold. **II** v/i **4.** hold out: **er hält (es) nirgends lange aus** he never lasts long in any place (or job).

'**aushandeln** v/t (sep, -ge-, h) negotiate.

aushändigen ['aushɛndigən] v/t (sep, -ge-, h) hand over.

'**Aushang** m (-[e]s; ~e) notice, bulletin.

'**aushängen 1.** v/t (sep, -ge-, h) **1.** take door etc off its hinges. **2.** put up (notice etc), show (paintings). '**Aushängeschild** n **1.** sign. **2.** fig. figurehead.

'**ausharren** v/i (sep, -ge-, h) hold out.

'**ausheben** v/t (irr, sep, -ge-, h, → **heben**) **1.** dig. **2.** → **aushängen 1. 3.** fig. round up (gang).

'**aushecken** v/t (sep, -ge-, h) F cook up.

'**ausheilen** v/i (sep, -ge-, sn) be (completely) cured, wound: heal up.

'**aushelfen** v/i (irr, sep, -ge-, h, → **helfen**) **j-m** ~ help s.o. out (**mit** with).

'**Aushilfe** f (-; -n) **1.** temporary help: **zur** ~ **bei j-m arbeiten** help s.o. out. **2.** → '**Aushilfskraft** f temporary worker.

'**aushilfsweise** adv temporarily.

'**aushöhlen** v/t (sep, -ge-, h) hollow out, geol., a. fig. erode, undermine.

'**ausholen** v/i (sep, -ge-, h) (**weit**) ~ a) swing back (to strike), b) fig. narrator: go far back; **mit der Axt** (**zum Schlag**) ~ raise the axe (to strike).

'**aushorchen** v/t (sep, -ge-, h) **j-n** ~ sound s.o. out (**über** acc on).

'**aushungern** v/t (sep, -ge-, h) starve (out): → **ausgehungert**.

'**auskennen: sich** ~ (irr, sep, -ge-, h, → **kennen**) **1. sich** ~ **in** (dat) know (one's way around) a place. **2.** fig. **sich** ~ **in** (dat), **sich** ~ **mit** know all about s.th.

'**ausklammern** v/t (sep, -ge-, h) fig. leave s.th. out of consideration, ignore.

'**Ausklang** m (-[e]s; no pl) a. fig. finale.

'**auskleiden** v/t (sep, -ge-, h) ⊙ line.

'**ausklingen** v/i (irr, sep, -ge-, sn, → **klingen**) fig. end (**in** dat with).

'**ausklinken** v/t (sep, -ge-, h) ⊙ release.

'**ausknipsen** v/t (sep, -ge-, h) F switch off.

'**ausknobeln** v/t (sep, -ge-, h) F fig. **et.** ~ figure s.th. out.

'**auskochen** v/t (sep, -ge-, h) boil, 🏥 sterilize (by boiling); → **ausgekocht II**.

'**auskommen** v/i (sep, -ge-, sn, → **kommen**) **1.** ~ **mit** make do (or manage) with; **mit s-m Geld** ~ make both ends meet; ~ **ohne** manage (or do) without. **2.** **mit j-m** ~ get on (or along) with s.o. '**Auskommen** n (-s) **1.** livelihood: **sein** ~ **haben** make a (decent) living. **2. mit ihr ist kein** ~ you can't get on with her.

'**auskosten** v/t (sep, -ge-, h) fig. enjoy to the full.

'**auskratzen** v/t (sep, -ge-, h) **1.** scrape out. **2.** 🏥 curette.

'**auskühlen** (sep, -ge-) **I** v/t (h) chill body through. **II** v/i (sn) cool (off).

'**auskundschaften** v/t (sep, -ge-, h) spy out.

Auskunft ['auskunft] f (-; ~e) **1.** information (**über** acc on, about): **nähere** ~ further particulars; **Auskünfte einholen** make inquiries. **2.** information office (or desk), a. teleph. Inquiries.

Auskunftei [aʊskʊnftaɪ] f (-; -en) ☨ inquiry office.

'**Auskunftsbeamte** m inquiry clerk.

'**Auskunftsbü,ro** n inquiry office.

'**auskuppeln** v/i (sep, -ge-, h) mot. declutch.

'**auslachen** v/t (sep, -ge-, h) laugh at.

'**ausladen** v/t (irr, sep, -ge-, h, → **laden**) **1.** unload, ⚓ disembark. **2.** F disinvite: **j-n ~** ask s.o. not to come.

'**ausladend** adj **1.** projecting, jutting out. **2.** fig. sweeping (gesture).

'**Auslage** f (-; -n) **1.** a) (window) display, b) shop-window. **2.** pl (j-m s-e ~n ersetzen refund s.o.'s) expenses.

'**Ausland** n (-[e]s; no pl) foreign countries: **im (ins) ~** abroad; **aus dem ~** from abroad; **die Reaktion des ~s** reactions abroad. **Ausländer** ['aʊslɛndər] m (-s; -), '**Ausländerin** f (-; -nen) foreigner. '**ausländerfeindlich** adj hostile to foreigners. '**Ausländerfeindlichkeit** f anti-alien feeling.

'**ausländisch** adj foreign: **~e Besucher** a. visitors from abroad.

'**Auslands...** foreign (department etc). **~aufenthalt** m stay abroad. **~flug** m international flight. **~gespräch** n teleph. international call. **~reise** f journey (or trip) abroad. **~schutzbrief** m mot. (certificate of) international travel cover. **~tour,nee** f tour abroad. **~verschuldung** f ☨ foreign debts.

'**auslassen** (irr, sep, -ge-, h, → **lassen**) I v/t **1.** leave out, omit (word etc), skip (page etc), miss (opportunity). **2.** vent one's anger etc (**an** dat on): **s-n Ärger an j-m ~** a. take it out on s.o. **3.** melt (butter etc). **4.** let out (seam). II **sich ~** talk (at length) (**über** acc about).

'**Auslassung** f (-; -en) omission.

'**auslasten** v/t (sep, -ge-, h) ☉ use to capacity: → **ausgelastet**.

'**Auslauf** m (-[e]s; **~e**) **1.** sports: run-out. **2.** (chicken etc) run: **die Kinder haben k-n ~** the children have nowhere to play. '**auslaufen** v/i (irr, sep, -ge-, sn, → **laufen**) **1.** liquid, tank etc: run out. **2.** ⚓ sail. **3.** end, contract etc: run out: ☨ ~ **lassen** phase out, discontinue (model). **4.** colo(u)r: run, bleed.

'**Ausläufer** pl **1.** foothills. **2.** outskirts.

'**Auslaufmo,dell** n ☨ phase-out model.

'**Auslaut** m (-[e]s; -e) ling. final sound.

'**ausleben: sich ~** (sep, -ge-, h) live it up.

'**auslecken** v/t (sep, -ge-, h) lick out.

'**auslegen** v/t (sep, -ge-, h) **1.** lay out, display (goods). **2.** a) cover, b) inlay: **mit Teppich ~** a. carpet; **mit Papier ~** line with paper. **3.** advance (sum). **4.** interpret: **falsch ~** misinterpret. **5.** ☉ design (**auf** acc for).

'**Ausleger** m (-s; -) **1.** jib, boom. **2.** a. '**Auslegerboot** n outrigger.

'**Auslegeware** f (-; no pl) floor coverings, a. wall-to-wall carpeting.

'**Auslegung** f (-; -en) interpretation.

'**ausleiern** v/t (sep, -ge-, h) (a. **sich ~**) wear out.

'**ausleihen** v/t (irr, sep, -ge-, h, → **leihen**) **1.** lend (out), loan. **2.** **sich et. ~ von** borrow s.th. from.

'**auslernen** v/i (sep, -ge-, h) complete one's training: **man lernt nie aus** (we) live and learn.

'**Auslese** f (-; -n) **1.** choice, selection: **biol. natürliche ~** natural selection. **2.** fig. élite, flower. **3.** wine made from selected grapes.

'**auslesen**[1] v/t (irr, sep, -ge-, h, → **lesen**) select, ☉ sort. '**auslesen**[2] v/t (irr, sep, -ge-, h, → **lesen**) finish (reading).

'**ausleuchten** v/t (sep, -ge-, h) a. fig. illuminate.

'**ausliefern** v/t (sep, -ge-, h) **1.** hand over (dat to), ☨ deliver: fig. **j-m ausgeliefert sein** be at s.o.'s mercy. **2.** pol. extradite. '**Auslieferung** f (-; -en) **1.** ☨ delivery. **2.** pol. extradition. '**Auslieferungsvertrag** m ⚖, pol. extradition treaty.

'**ausliegen** v/i (irr, sep, -ge-, h, → **liegen**) be on display, newspapers: be available.

'**auslöffeln** v/t (sep, -ge-, h) spoon up: → **Suppe**.

'**auslöschen** v/t (sep, -ge-, h) **1.** → **löschen** 1. **2.** fig. wipe out.

'**auslosen** v/t (sep, -ge-, h) draw (lots) for.

'**auslösen** v/t (sep, -ge-, h) **1.** phot., ☉ release, a. fig. trigger (off). **2.** fig. produce (effect), cause (panic etc), arouse (enthusiasm etc). **3.** redeem (pawned object). '**Auslöser** m (-s; -) release, a. fig. trigger. '**Auslösung** f (-; -en) **1.** releasing, triggering (etc, → **auslösen**). **2.** ☨ compensation.

'**Auslosung** f (-; -en) draw.

'ausloten v/t (sep, -ge-, h) a. fig. sound.
'ausmachen v/t (sep, -ge-, h) **1.** F → a) löschen 1, b) ausschalten 1. **2.** make out, spot, locate. **3.** → abmachen 2. **4.** amount to. **5.** fig. make up, form (part of): das macht den Reiz s-r Bilder aus this is what makes his pictures so attractive. **6.** das macht nichts (viel) aus that doesn't matter (it matters a great deal); wenn es Ihnen nichts ausmacht if you don't mind; macht es Ihnen et. aus, wenn ich rauche? do you mind my smoking?; die Kälte macht mir nichts aus I don't mind the cold.
'ausmalen v/t (sep, -ge-, h) **1.** a) paint, b) colo(u)r (picture). **2.** fig. depict (dat to): sich et. ~ picture s.th. (to o.s.).
'Ausmaß n (-es; -e) dimensions, a. fig. extent: das ~ des Schadens the extent of the damage; gewaltige ~e annehmen assume horrendous proportions.
'ausmerzen v/t (sep, -ge-, h) eliminate.
'ausmessen v/t (irr, sep, -ge-, h, → messen) measure.
'ausmisten v/t (sep, -ge-, h) muck out.
'ausmustern v/t (sep, -ge-, h) **1.** sort out, discard. **2.** ✗ reject (as unfit).
Ausnahme f ('aʊsna:mə] f (-; -n) exception: mit ~ von (or gen) with the exception of, except (for); e-e ~ bilden a. be exceptional; bei j-m e-e ~ machen make an exception in s.o.'s case.
'Ausnahme... exceptional (athlete, case, etc). **'Ausnahmezustand** m (den ~ verhängen declare a) state of emergency (über acc in).
'ausnahmslos adv and adj without exception. **'ausnahmsweise** adv a) by way of exception, b) for once.
'ausnehmen v/t (irr, sep, -ge-, h, → nehmen) **1.** gut (fish etc), draw (goose etc). **2.** F j-n ~ fleece s.o. **3.** exclude, except.
'ausnüchtern v/i (sep, -ge-, h) sober up.
'ausnutzen v/t (sep, -ge-, h) a. b.s. use, exploit, F b.s. take advantage of. **'Ausnutzung** f (-; no pl) a. b.s. exploitation.
'auspacken (sep, -ge-, h) **I** v/t unpack, unwrap. **II** v/i F fig. spill the beans.
'auspfeifen v/t (irr, sep, -ge-, h, → pfeifen) boo.
'ausplaudern v/t (sep, -ge-, h) blab out.
'auspo,saunen v/t (sep, h) F broadcast.
'auspressen v/t (sep, -ge-, h) squeeze (out).

'auspro,bieren v/t (sep, h) try (out).
'Auspuff m (-[e]s; -e) mot. exhaust.
'Auspufftopf m silencer, Am. muffler.
'auspumpen v/t (sep, -ge-, h) pump out.
'ausquar,tieren v/t (sep, -ge-, h) lodge s.o. elsewhere.
'ausquetschen v/t (sep, -ge-, h) F fig. j-n ~ grill s.o.
'ausra,dieren v/t (sep, -ge-, h) **1.** erase. **2.** fig. wipe out, wipe town etc off the map.
'ausran,gieren v/t (sep, -ge-, h) throw out.
'ausrasten v/i (sep, -ge-, sn) **1.** ⊙ be released. **2.** F fig. flip.
'ausrauben v/t (sep, -ge-, h) rob.
'ausräuchern v/t (sep, -ge-, h) fumigate, hunt., a. fig. smoke out.
'ausräumen v/t (sep, -ge-, h) **1.** clear (room etc), remove furniture (aus dat from). **2.** fig. clear up (misunderstanding etc), dispel (doubts).
'ausrechnen v/t (sep, -ge-, h) (fig. sich) et. ~ work s.th. out (for o.s.); F er ist leicht auszurechnen he is quite predictable; → ausgerechnet.
'Ausrede f (-; -n) (faule ~ lame) excuse.
'ausreden (sep, -ge-, h) **I** v/i finish (speaking): j-n ~ lassen hear s.o. out; j-n nicht ~ lassen cut s.o. short. **II** v/t j-m et. ~ talk s.o. out of s.th.
'ausreichen v/i (sep, -ge-, h) be enough: ~ für last (a week etc). **'ausreichend** adj **1.** sufficient, enough. **2.** ped. D.
'Ausreise f (-; -n) departure: bei der ~ on leaving the country; j-m die ~ verweigern refuse s.o. permission to leave the country. **~visum** n exit visa.
'ausreißen (irr, sep, -ge-, → reißen) **I** v/t (h) pull out, tear out. **II** v/i (sn) F run away (vor j-m before s.o., von zu Hause from home). **'Ausreißer** m (-s; -), **'Ausreißerin** f (-; -nen) F runaway.
'ausreiten v/i (irr, sep, -ge-, sn, → reiten) ride out.
'ausrenken v/t (sep, -ge-, h) sich den Arm etc ~ dislocate one's arm etc.
'ausrichten v/t (sep, -ge-, h) **1.** a) straighten, b) align, c) adjust (a. fig., nach to): sich ~ line up. fig. sich (or sein Verhalten) ~ nach orientate o.s. to; ausgerichtet auf (acc) aimed at. **2.** achieve: er wird (bei ihr) nichts ~ (können) he won't get anywhere (with her). **3.** tell: kann ich et. ~? can I take a message?; bitte richten Sie ihm Grüße

von mir aus please give him my (kind) regards. **4.** organize, arrange.

'**Ausrichter** *m* (-s; -) organizer.

'**ausrollen** (*sep*, -ge-, h) **I** *v/t* roll (out) (*dough*). **II** *v/i mot.* coast (✓ *taxi*) to a standstill.

'**ausrotten** *v/t* (*sep*, -ge-, h) exterminate.

'**Ausrottung** *f* (-; -en) extermination.

'**ausrücken** (*sep*, -ge-) **I** *v/i* (sn) **1.** *fire brigade etc*: turn out, ✕ march out. **2.** F → *ausreißen* **II. II** *v/t* (h) **3.** *print.* move out.

'**Ausruf** *m* (-[e]s; -e) cry, exclamation.

'**ausrufen** *v/t* (*irr, sep*, -ge-, h, → *rufen*) **1.** call out (*name etc*): *j-n ~ lassen* page s.o. **2.** call (*strike*), *pol.* proclaim: *j-n zum König ~* proclaim s.o. king. '**Ausrufungszeichen** *n* exclamation mark.

'**ausruhen** *v/i* (*sep*, -ge-, h) (*a. sich ~*) rest.

'**ausrüsten** *v/t* (*sep*, -ge-, h) *a. fig.* equip (*mit* with). '**Ausrüstung** *f* (-; -en) **1.** equipment, gear. **2.** accessories.

'**ausrutschen** *v/i* (*sep*, -ge-, sn) slip (*auf dat* on). '**Ausrutscher** *m* (-s; -) F *fig.* slip, gaffe.

'**Aussaat** *f* (-; -en) a) sowing, b) seed.

'**Aussage** *f* (-; -en) statement, *a. author's etc* message, ♦ *a.* testimony: *nach Ihrer ~* according to what you said; ♦ *die ~ verweigern* refuse to give evidence; *hier steht ~ gegen ~* it's his word against hers *etc*. '**aussagen** (*sep*, -ge-, h) **I** *v/i* ♦ testify, give evidence. **II** *v/t* state, say, *esp. fig.* express.

'**Aussagesatz** *m* clause of statement.

'**Aussatz** *m* (-es; *no pl*) ♦ leprosy.

'**Aussätzige** *m, f* (-n; -n) *a. fig.* leper.

'**aussaugen** *v/t* (*sep*, -ge-, h) suck: *fig. j-n* (*bis aufs Blut*) *~* bleed s.o. (white).

'**ausschaben** *v/t* (*sep*, -ge-, h) ♦ curette.

'**Ausschabung** *f* (-; -en) ♦ curettage.

'**ausschachten** *v/t* (*sep*, -ge-, h) dig.

'**ausschalten** *v/t* (*sep*, -ge-, h) **1.** switch off (*light, radio, etc*), cut out (*current*), stop, cut (*engine*). **2.** *fig.* eliminate, *esp. sports*: neutralize.

'**Ausschaltung** *f* (-; -en) *fig.* elimination.

'**Ausschau** *f*: *~ halten* → '**ausschauen** *v/i* (*sep*, -ge-, h) look out (*nach* for).

'**ausscheiden** (*irr, sep*, -ge-, → *scheiden*) **I** *v/t* (h) **1.** eliminate, exclude, sort out, remove. **2.** *physiol.* excrete. **II** *v/i* (sn) **3.** be ruled out, *person*: be not

eligible. **4.** *~ aus* (*dat*) a) retire from (*an office*), leave (*a firm*), b) *sports*: be eliminated from (*contest*), drop out of (*a race*). '**Ausscheidung** *f* (-; -en) **1.** elimination. **2.** *physiol.* excretion, excrements. **3.** → '**Ausscheidungskampf** *m sports*: qualifying contest.

'**ausschenken** *v/t* (*sep*, -ge-, h) **1.** pour (out). **2.** sell.

'**ausscheren** *v/i* (*sep*, -ge-, sn) **1.** *mot.* swing out. **2.** *fig.* deviate (*aus* from).

'**ausschiffen** *v/t* (*sep*, -ge-, h) (*a. sich ~*) disembark.

'**ausschlachten** *v/t* (*sep*, -ge-, h) **1.** cut up. **2.** F *fig.* a) cannibalize (*car etc*), b) *contp.* exploit, capitalize on.

'**ausschlafen** (*irr, sep*, -ge-, h, → *schlafen*) **I** *v/t* sleep off. **II** *v/i* (*a. sich ~*) a) get a good night's sleep, b) sleep late.

'**Ausschlag** *m* (-[e]s; ⸗e) **1.** ♦ (*e-n ~ bekommen* break out into a) rash. **2.** *fig. den ~ geben für* be decisive of; *das gab den ~* that decided (*or* settled) it. **3.** *phys.* a) swing (*of pendulum*), deflection (*of pointer*), b) amplitude. '**ausschlagen** (*irr, sep*, -ge-, h, → *schlagen*) **I** *v/i* **1.** *horse*: kick out. **2.** *pendulum etc*: swing, *pointer etc*: deflect. **3.** ❀ sprout, *tree*: come into leaf. **II** *v/t* **4.** knock out (*tooth*): → *Faß*. **5.** line. **6.** refuse, turn s.th. down. '**ausschlaggebend** *adj* (*a. von ~er Bedeutung*) decisive (*für* of).

'**ausschließen** (*irr, sep*, -ge-, h, → *schließen*) **I** *v/t* **1.** → *aussperren*. **2.** (*aus* from) exclude, expel (*from the party etc*), bar, *sports*: disqualify: *zeitweilig ~* suspend; ♦ *die Öffentlichkeit ~* exclude the public. **3.** a) rule out (*mistake etc*), b) exclude, → *ausgeschlossen*. **II** *sich ~* exclude o.s. (*von* from).

'**ausschließlich** *adj* exclusive.

'**Ausschluß** *m* (-sses; ⸗sse) (*aus* from) a) exclusion, expulsion, b) *sports*: disqualification: *zeitweiliger ~* suspension; ♦ *unter ~ der Öffentlichkeit* in closed session.

'**ausschmücken** *v/t* (*sep*, -ge-, h) **1.** decorate. **2.** *fig.* embroider (*story etc*).

'**ausschneiden** *v/t* (*irr, sep*, -ge-, h, → *schneiden*) **1.** cut out: → *ausgeschnitten*. **2.** ✗ prune (*trees etc*).

'**Ausschnitt** *m* (-[e]s; -e) **1.** neck(line): *mit tiefem ~* décolleté, low-necked. **2.** (*newspaper*) cutting, *Am.* clipping. **3.**

phot. etc detail, *sports, TV* scene. **4.** *fig.* (*aus*) part (of), extract (from).

'**ausschöpfen** *v/t* (*sep*, -ge-, h) **1.** bail out. **2.** *fig.* exhaust (*subject*).

'**ausschreiben** *v/t* (*irr, sep*, -ge-, h, → **schreiben**) **1.** a) write out, b) write *figure* out (in words). **2.** → **ausstellen** 2. **3.** a) announce, b) advertise (*post*), c) ✝ invite tenders (for): *e-n Wettbewerb* ~ invite entries (✝ tenders) for a competition; *Wahlen* ~ go to the country.

'**Ausschreibung** *f* (-; -en) ✝ invitation to bid (*sports:* to a competition).

'**Ausschreitung** *f* (-; -en) *usu. pl* riot.

'**Ausschuß** *m* (-sses; ⸚sse) **1.** (*in e-m* ~ *sein* be or sit on a) committee. **2.** ✝ rejects, ⊙ waste, scrap. '**Ausschuß-mitglied** *n* committee member. '**Ausschußsitzung** *f* committee meeting.

'**ausschütteln** *v/t* (*sep*, -ge-, h) shake out.

'**ausschütten** (*sep*, -ge-, h) **I** *v/t* **1.** a) pour out, empty (*bucket etc*), b) spill: *fig. j-m sein Herz* ~ unburden o.s. to s.o. **2.** ✝ pay (*dividend*). **II** *sich* (*vor Lachen*) ~ split one's sides laughing.

'**ausschweifend** *adj* unbridled (*imagination*), dissolute (*life*).

'**Ausschweifungen** *pl* excesses.

'**ausschweigen:** *sich* ~ (*irr, sep*, -ge-, h, → **schweigen**) remain silent (*über acc* about).

'**ausschwitzen** *v/t* (*sep*, -ge-, h) exude.

'**aussehen** (*irr, sep*, -ge-, h, → **sehen**) **I** *v/i* look: *gut* ~ a) be good-looking, b) look well; *schlecht* ~ look bad (*or* ill); *wie sieht er aus?* what does he look like?; F *sie sah vielleicht aus!* she did look a sight!; *so siehst du aus!* nothing doing! **II** *v/impers* F *es sieht nach Regen aus* it looks like rain; *damit es nach et. aussieht* to make it look impressive.

'**Aussehen** *n* (-s) looks, appearance.

'**aussein** *v/i* (*irr, sep*, -ge-, sn, → *sein*) F **1.** be over: *fig. mit ihm ist es aus* he is finished. **2.** light, radio, *etc*: be off, *fire etc*: be out. **3.** *wir waren gestern abend aus* we were out last night. **4.** *sports:* be out. **5.** ~ *auf* (*acc*) be out for (*or* to get); *sie ist auf sein Geld aus* she is after his money.

außen ['aʊsən] *adv* outside: *von* ~ from (the) outside; *nach* ~ outward(s), *fig.*

outwardly (*calm etc*); F *er bleibt* ~ *vor* he's (left) out of it.

'**Außen|aufnahmen** *pl* film: location shooting. **~bezirke** *pl* outskirts.

'**Außenbordmotor** *m* outboard motor.

'**aussenden** *v/t* (*irr, sep*, -ge-, h, → *sen-den*) send out.

'**Außendienst** *m* field work: *im* ~ in the field. **~mitarbeiter(in** *f*) *m* field work-er, ✝ *a.* sales representative.

'**Außen|handel** *m* foreign trade. **~kante** *f* outer edge. **~mi̱nister** *m* Foreign Minister (*Br.* Secretary), *Am.* Secretary of State. **~mini̱sterium** *n* Foreign Ministry (*Br.* Office), *Am.* State Department. **~poli̱tik** *f* foreign politics (*or* policy). ♀**po̱litisch** *adj* foreign: **~e** *De-batte* debate on foreign affairs.

'**Außenseite** *f* outside. **Außenseiter** ['aʊsənzaɪtər] *m* (-s; -) outsider.

'**Außenspiegel** *m* mot. outside rear-view mirror.

Außenstände ['aʊsənʃtɛndə] *pl* ✝ out-standing debts.

'**Außen|stelle** *f* branch (office). **~stür-mer** *m sports:* winger, outside. **~wand** *f* outer wall. **~welt** *f* outside world.

außer ['aʊsər] **I** *prep* (*dat*) **1.** out of: → *Atem, Betrieb* 2, *Dienst* 2, *Reichwei-te*; *fig.* ~ *sich sein* be beside o.s. (*vor* with); ~ *sich geraten* lose control of o.s. **2.** apart from, except (for): *alle* ~ *dir* all except (*or* but) you. **3.** besides, in addition to. **II** *conj* **4.** ~ (*wenn*) unless; ~ *daß* except that.

'**außerberuflich** *adj* private.

'**außerbetrieblich** *adj* external.

'**außerdem** *adv* besides.

äußere ['ɔysərə] *adj* outer, outside, ex-ternal, ✝, *pol.* foreign: *k-e* ~*n Verlet-zungen* no external injuries; *pol.* ~ *An-gelegenheiten* foreign affairs.

'**Äußere** *n* (-n) outside, (outward) ap-pearance, *s.o.'s* looks: *von angeneh-mem* ~*n* personable; *auf sein* ~*s ach-ten* be particular about one's appear-ance.

'**außerehelich** *adj* illegitimate (*child*), extramarital (*relationship*).

'**außergerichtlich** *adj* extrajudicial; **~er** *Vergleich* settlement out of court.

'**außergewöhnlich** *adj* exceptional, un-common, ✝ extraordinary.

'**außerhalb I** *prep* (*gen*) out of: ~ *des*

Hauses outdoors, outside. **II** *adv* a) outside, b) out of town.

'**außerirdisch** *adj* (a. **~es Wesen**) extraterrestrial.

äußerlich ['ɔysərlıç] *adj* a. *fig.* a) outward, external, b) superficial: **⚡ nur zur ~en Anwendung** for external use only; **~ betrachtet** on the face of it.

'**Äußerlichkeit** *f* (-; -en) *fig.* superficiality: **bloße ~en** mere formalities.

äußern ['ɔysərn] (h) **I** *v/t* a. utter, express, b) voice (*criticism etc*). **II sich ~** a) (*über acc* on) express o.s., give one's opinion, b) (*in dat* in) be shown, *disease etc:* manifest itself.

'**außerordentlich I** *adj* extraordinary, unusual, remarkable, outstanding: **~er Professor** senior lecturer, *Am.* associate professor. **II** *adv* extremely.

'**außerparlamen,tarisch** *adj* extraparliamentary. '**außerplanmäßig** *adj* a) extraordinary, b) supernumerary (*official*). '**außersinnlich** *adj* **~e Wahrnehmung** extrasensory perception.

äußerst ['ɔysərst] **I** *adj* **1.** outermost, remotest: *pol.* **die ~e Linke** the extreme left. **2.** latest, final: **~er Termin** *a.* deadline. **3.** *fig.* extreme, utmost: **von ~er Wichtigkeit** of utmost importance; **im ~en Fall** at worst; **mit ~er Kraft** by a supreme effort. **II** *adv* **4.** extremely.

'**Äußerste** *n* (-n) *fig.* a) the limit, the most, b) the worst: **sein ~s tun** do one's utmost; **zum ~n entschlossen sein** be desperate; **bis zum ~n gehen** go to the last extreme; **auf das ~ gefaßt sein** be prepared for the worst.

'**außerstande** *adj* **~ sein** be unable.

Äußerung ['ɔysərʊŋ] *f* (-; -en) **1.** statement, remark. **2.** *fig.* expression, sign.

'**aussetzen** (*sep*, -ge-, h) **I** *v/t* **1.** expose (*dat* to, *a. fig.* to danger, *criticism, etc*), abandon (*child*), release (*pet*). **2.** **⚓** lower (*boat*), disembark, *b.s.* maroon (*passengers*). **3.** offer *award etc* (*dat* to): **e-n Preis auf j-s Kopf ~** put a price on s.o.'s head. **4.** interrupt, **✝**, **⚖** suspend: → **Bewährung 2. 5. et. ~** (*or* **auszusetzen haben**) **an** (*dat*) object to, criticize; **was ist daran auszusetzen?** what's wrong with it?; **er hat an allem et. auszusetzen** he finds fault with everything. **II** *v/i* **6.** fail, *mot.* misfire, *heart:* miss a beat. **7.** a) stop, break off, b)

take a rest, c) *in a game:* sit out: **~ mit** interrupt (*treatment etc*); **ohne auszusetzen** without interruption; *at games:* (**e-e Runde**) **~** miss a turn.

'**Aussicht** *f* (-; -en) (**auf** *acc* of) **1.** *no pl* view: **ein Zimmer mit ~ auf das Meer** a room overlooking the sea. **2.** chance, prospect, *pl a.* outlook: **er hat ~en zu gewinnen** he stands a chance to win; **gute ~en auf Erfolg haben** stand a good chance of success. '**aussichtslos** *adj* hopeless: **~e Sache** lost cause; **e-n ~en Kampf führen** fight a losing battle. '**Aussichtslosigkeit** *f* (-; *no pl*) hopelessness.

'**aussichtsreich** *adj* promising.

'**Aussichtsturm** *m* observation tower.

'**aussiedeln** *v/t* (*sep*, -ge-, h) resettle.

'**Aussiedler(in** *f*) *m* → **Umsiedler(in)**.

aussöhnen ['aʊsːøːnən] *v/t* (*sep*, -ge-, h) reconcile (**sich** o.s.) (**mit** with, to).

'**Aussöhnung** *f* (-; -en) reconciliation.

'**aussondern** *v/t* (*sep*, -ge-, h), '**aussor,tieren** *v/t* (*sep*, h) sort out.

'**ausspannen** (*sep*, -ge-, h) **I** *v/t* **1.** unharness: F *fig. j-m* **die Freundin ~** steal s.o.'s girl. **2.** spread out, stretch out. **II** *v/i* **3.** relax, (take a) rest.

'**aussparen** *v/t* (*sep*, -ge-, h) **1.** ⚙ leave open. **2.** leave out, avoid (*subject etc*).

'**aussperren** *v/t* (*sep*, -ge-, h) *j-n* **~** *a.* **✝** lock s.o. out (**aus** of).

'**Aussperrung** *f* (-; -en) **✝** lockout.

'**ausspielen** (*sep*, -ge-, h) **I** *v/t* play (*card*), *fig.* bring *one's skill etc* to bear: *j-n* **gegen** *j-n* **~** play s.o. off against s.o. **II** *v/i cards:* lead: *fig.* **er hat ausgespielt** he's finished.

'**ausspinnen** *v/t* (*irr, sep*, -ge-, h, → **spinnen**) *fig.* spin out.

'**ausspio,nieren** *v/t* (*sep*, h) spy out, spy on s.o.

'**Aussprache** *f* (-; -n) **1.** *no pl* pronunciation. **2.** discussion, *a. parl.* debate.

'**aussprechen** (*irr, sep*, -ge-, h, → **sprechen**) **I** *v/t* **1.** pronounce: → **ausgesprochen**. **2.** express (*one's sympathy, views, etc*): → **Vertrauen. 3.** grant (*divorce*). **II** *v/i* **4.** → **ausreden I. III sich ~ 5.** express one's views (**über** *acc* on, about), speak (**für** for, **gegen** against). **6.** a) **bei** *j-m* unburden o.s. to s.o., b) **mit** *j-m* F have it out with s.o.

'**Ausspruch** *m* (-[e]s; **~e**) remark, saying.

'ausspucken v/t, v/i (sep, -ge-, h) spit out. **'ausspülen** v/t (sep, -ge-, h) rinse. **aus'staf|fieren** v/t (sep, h) F rig out.

'Ausstand m (-[e]s; ⸚e) strike, F walkout: **in den ~ treten** go on strike, walk out.

'ausstatten ['aʊsʃtatan] v/t (sep, -ge-, h) (**mit** with) **1.** fit out, equip, a. furnish (flat), get up (book). **2.** † endow (with capital, a. fig. with talent etc), 🔩 vest (with power etc). **'Ausstattung** f (-; -en) a) outfit, equipment, b) furnishing, décor, c) thea. etc sets and costumes, d) design, e) get-up. **'Ausstattungsstück** n thea. spectacular (show).

'ausstechen v/t (irr, sep, -ge-, h, → **stechen**) **1.** gastr. cut out. **2.** fig. outdo (s.o.), cut out (rival).

'ausstehen (irr, sep, -ge-, h, → **stehen**) **I** v/t stand, bear, suffer: **es ist noch nicht ausgestanden** it's not over yet; F **ich kann ihn nicht ~** I can't stand him. **II** v/i decision: be pending, payment: be outstanding: **s-e Antwort steht noch aus ~** he hasn't answered yet.

'aussteigen v/i (irr, sep, -ge-, sn, → **steigen**) (**aus**) get out (of, a. fig. an enterprise etc), get off (a train, bus, etc), ✈, ⚓ disembark, F ✈ bail out (of), fig. opt out (of business venture, nuclear power, etc), drop out (of society etc). **'Aussteiger** m (-s; -) F dropout.

'ausstellen (sep, -ge-, h) **I** v/t **1.** display, show, exhibit. **2.** make bill, cheque, etc out (**auf j-s Namen** in s.o.'s name), issue (passport), draw bill of exchange (**auf** acc on). **II** v/i **3.** exhibit. **Aussteller** ['aʊsʃtɛlər] m (-s; -) **1.** exhibitor. **2.** † drawer.

'Ausstellfenster n mot. ventipane. **'Ausstellung** f (-; -en) **1.** exhibition, show, fair. **2.** issue (of document etc). **'Ausstellungs|datum** n date of issue. **~gelände** n exhibition grounds. **~halle** f exhibition hall. **~raum** m show-room. **~stück** n exhibit.

'ausstempeln v/i (sep, -ge-, h) clock out. **'aussterben** v/i (irr, sep, -ge-, sn, → **sterben**) die out: → **ausgestorben**. **'Aussteuer** f (-; -n) trousseau. **'aussteuern** v/t (sep, -ge-, h) modulate. **'Ausstieg** m (-[e]s; -e) **1.** exit (door). **2.** (**aus**) exit (from), getting out (of), fig. a. opting out (of nuclear energy, a business, etc). **~luke** f (escape) hatch.

'ausstopfen v/t (sep, -ge-, h) stuff. **'Ausstoß** m (-es; rare ⸚e) † output, production. **'ausstoßen** v/t (irr, sep, -ge-, h, → **stoßen**) **1.** ⚙ eject, blow off, exhaust. **2.** † turn out, produce. **3.** utter (words), give (yell etc), heave (a sigh). **4.** j-n ~ expel s.o. (**aus** from); j-n aus der Gesellschaft ~ ostracize s.o.

'ausstrahlen v/t (sep, -ge-, h) **1.** a. fig. radiate. **2.** broadcast, TV a. televise. **'Ausstrahlung** f (-; -en) **1.** fig. radiation, of person: charisma. **2.** broadcast(ing).

'ausstrecken v/t (sep, -ge-, h) (a. **sich** ~) stretch out: **die Hand ~ nach** reach (out) for; → **Fühler** 1.

'ausstreichen v/t (irr, sep, -ge-, h, → **streichen**) cross out.

'ausströmen (sep, -ge-) **I** v/i (sn) (**aus** from) a. fig. radiate, smell: emanate, gas etc: escape. **II** v/t (h) radiate (a. fig.), pour off (smell).

'aussuchen v/t (sep, -ge-, h) choose, select: → **ausgesucht**.

'Austausch m (-[e]s; no pl) (**im ~** in) exchange (**für** for). **'Austausch...** ped., univ. exchange (teacher, student, etc). **'austauschbar** adj interchangeable. **'austauschen** v/t (sep, -ge-, h) (**gegen**) a) exchange (for), b) replace (by). **'Austauschmotor** m replacement engine.

'austeilen v/t (sep, -ge-, h) distribute (**an** acc to, **unter** acc among), deal (out) (cards, blows).

Auster ['aʊstər] f (-; -n) oyster. **'Austernbank** f (-; ⸚e) oyster bed.

'austoben: sich ~ (sep, -ge-, h) have one's fling, children: have a good romp.

'austragen (irr, sep, -ge-, h, → **tragen**) **I** v/t **1.** deliver (letters etc). **2.** ✿ carry baby to (full) term, w.s. have. **3.** settle (dispute): **die Sache ~** F have it out. **4.** hold (tournament etc), play (match). **5.** cancel (data etc). **II sich ~** sign out. **'Austragungsort** m sports: venue.

Australien [aʊs'traːliən] n (-s) Australia. **Au'stralier** m (-s; -), **Au'stralierin** f (-; -nen), **au'stralisch** adj Australian.

'austreiben (irr, sep, -ge-, h, → **treiben**) **I** v/t exorcize: fig. **j-m et. ~** cure s.o. of s.th. **II** v/i 🌱 sprout.

'austreten (irr, sep, -ge-, → **treten**) **I** v/t (h) **1.** stamp out (fire etc). **2.** tread (path). **3.** wear out (shoes), wear down (steps). **II** v/i (sn) **4.** (**aus**) come out (of, *gas etc*: escape (from). **5.** ~ *aus* leave (*club etc*). **6.** F (go and) spend a penny.

'**austricksen** *v/t* (*sep*, -ge-, h) F trick.

'**austrinken** *v/t, v/i* (*irr, sep*, -ge-, h, → *trinken*) drink up, finish (one's drink).

'**Austritt** *m* (-[e]s; -e) (*aus dat*) leaving (*a club etc*).

'**austrocknen** *v/t* (*sep*, -ge-, h) *and v/i* (sn) dry up.

'**austüfteln** *v/t* (*sep*, -ge-, h) F work out.

'**ausüben** *v/t* (*sep*, -ge-, h) **1.** carry on (*trade etc*), practise (*profession etc*), perform (*function*), hold (*office*). **2.** exercise (*power, right, etc*). **3.** (*auf acc* on) exert (*influence etc*), have (*effect*), use (*coercion*): → *Druck*[1]. '**Ausübung** *f* (-; *no pl*) carrying on (*etc*), exercise: *in ~ s-r Pflicht* in the execution of his duty.

'**ausufern** *v/i* (*sep*, -ge-, sn) get out of hand.

'**Ausverkauf** *m* (-[e]s; ⁓e) ✝ a) selling off, b) (*im ~ kaufen* buy at a) sale, c) *fig.* sellout. '**ausverkaufen** *v/t* (*sep*, h) sell off: *ausverkauft* sold out, *thea. etc a.* full (*house etc*).

'**auswachsen** (*irr, sep*, -ge-, → *wachsen*) I *v/t* (h) grow out of. II sich ~ ₰ go to seed: F *es ist zum ₰!* a) it's enough to drive you crazy, b) it's dreadfully boring. III *sich ~* (h) *fig.* develop (*zu* into): → *ausgewachsen*.

'**Auswahl** *f* (-; *no pl*) **1.** selection, ✝ *a.* choice, range: ... *in großer ~* a large assortment of ...; ... *zur ~* ... to choose from; *e-e ~ treffen* select (*aus* from). **2.** → *Auswahlmannschaft*. '**auswählen** *v/t* (*sep*, -ge-, h) choose, select.

'**Auswahlmannschaft** *f* representative team.

'**Auswanderer** *m* (-s; -) emigrant.

'**auswandern** *v/i* (*sep*, -ge-, sn) emigrate. '**Auswanderung** *f* (-; -en) emigration.

auswärtig ['ausvɛrtɪç] *adj* **1.** nonlocal, *a.* ✝ out-of-town. **2.** *pol.* foreign (*affairs, office, etc*).

auswärts ['ausvɛrts] *adv* **1.** out, away (from home), out of town: ~ *essen* eat out; *sports:* ~ *spielen* play away from home; ~ *wohnen* live out of town. **2.** outward(s). ₰**spiel** *n* away match.

'**auswaschen** *v/t* (*irr, sep*, -ge-, h, → *waschen*) wash out.

auswechselbar ['ausvɛksəlbaːr] *adj* (*gegen*) exchangeable (for), replace-

able (by). '**auswechseln** *v/t* (*sep*, -ge-, h) (*gegen*) exchange (for), replace (by), change (*tyre*), substitute (*player*). '**Auswechselspieler(in** *f*) *m* substitute.

'**Auswechs(e)lung** *f* (-; -en) exchange, replacement, *sports:* substitution.

'**Ausweg** *m* (-[e]s; -e) *fig.* way out (*aus* of): *als letzter ~* as a last resort.

'**ausweglos** *adj* hopeless. '**Ausweglosigkeit** *f* (-; *no pl*) hopelessness.

'**ausweichen** *v/i* (*irr, sep*, -ge-. sn, → *weichen*) **1.** (*dat*) make way (for), get out of the way (of), dodge: *j-s Blicken ~* avoid s.o.'s eyes; *e-r Frage ~* evade a question. **2.** be evasive. **3.** ~ *auf* (*acc*) switch to. '**ausweichend** *adj* evasive. '**Ausweich|ma,növer** *n* *fig.* evasive action. **~möglichkeit** *f* alternative.

'**ausweinen:** *sich ~* (*sep*, -ge-, h) have a good cry (*bei j-m* on s.o.'s shoulder).

'**Ausweis** *m* (-es; -e) identity (*abbr.* ID) card, (*membership*) card, pass.

'**ausweisen** (*irr, sep*, -ge-, h, → *weisen*) I *v/t* **1.** (*aus* from) a) expel, b) deport (*alien*). **2.** *fig. j-n als* show s.o. to be (*an expert etc*). II *sich ~* prove one's identity: *sich als Experte etc ~* prove o.s. an expert *etc*.

'**Ausweis|kon,trolle** *f* ID check. **~pa,piere** *pl* (identification *or* ID) papers.

'**Ausweisung** *f* (-; -en) (*aus* from) a) expulsion, b) deportation (*of aliens*).

'**ausweiten** *v/t* (*sep*, -ge-, h) (*a. sich ~*) expand (*a. fig. zu* into).

'**Ausweitung** *f* (-; -en) expansion.

'**auswendig** *adv* by heart: ♪ ~ *spielen* play from memory; *et. in- und ~ kennen* know s.th. inside out.

'**auswerfen** *v/t* (*irr, sep*, -ge-, h, → *werfen*) cast (*anchor etc*).

'**auswerten** *v/t* (*sep*, -ge-, h) **1.** evaluate. **2.** utilize, ✝ *a.* exploit. '**Auswertung** *f* (-; -en) **1.** evaluation. **2.** utilization.

'**auswickeln** *v/t* (*sep*, -ge-, h) unwrap.

'**auswirken:** *sich ~* (*sep*, -ge-, h) a) have consequences, b) *auf* (*acc*) affect, c) *in* (*dat*) result in; *sich positiv* (*negativ*) ~ have a favo(u)rable (negative) effect. '**Auswirkung** *f* (-; -en) **1.** effect (*auf acc* on). **2.** → *Rückwirkung*.

'**auswischen** *v/t* (*sep*, -ge-, h) wipe out: F *j-m eins ~* play a nasty trick on s.o.

'**auswringen** *v/t* (*irr, sep*, -ge-, h, → *wringen*) wring out.

ˈ**Auswuchs** *m* (-es; ⁓e) **1.** ✿ outgrowth. **2.** *fig.* a) *pl* excesses, b) product (*of the imagination*).

ˈ**Auswurf** *m* (-[e]s; *no pl*) **1.** ✿ sputum. **2.** → **Abschaum.**

ˈ**auszahlen** (*sep*, -ge-, h) **I** *v/t* pay (out) (*sum*), pay *s.o.* off, buy out (*partner*). **II** *sich* ⁓ *fig.* pay.

ˈ**auszählen** *v/t* (*sep*, -ge-, h) count out.

ˈ**Auszahlung** *f* (-; -en) payment.

ˈ**auszeichnen** (*sep*, -ge-, h) **I** *v/t* **1.** distinguish, hono(u)r: **mit e-m Preis** ⁓ award a prize to; (**mit e-m Orden**) ⁓ decorate. **2.** ✝ price (*goods*). **II** *sich* ⁓ distinguish o.s. ˈ**Auszeichnung** *f* (-; -en) **1.** a) (mark of) distinction, b) decoration, c) award: **mit** ⁓ **bestehen** pass *an exam* with distinction. **2.** ✝ pricing.

ˈ**ausziehbar** *adj* pull-out, telescopic.

ˈ**ausziehen** (*irr*, *sep*, -ge-, → *ziehen*) **I** *v/t* (h) **1.** take off (*clothes*): **j-n** ⁓ undress s.o. **2.** pull out (*table etc*). **3.** 🝆, ⚗ extract. **II** *v/i* (sn) **4.** set out. **5.** (*aus e-r Wohnung*) ⁓ move out (of a flat). **III** *sich* ⁓ (h) undress.

ˈ**Auszieh**|**feder** *f* drawing pen. ⁓**platte** *f* (*table*) leaf. ⁓**tisch** *m* pull-out table. ⁓**tusche** *f* drawing ink.

ˈ**Auszubildende** *m*, *f* (-n; -n) trainee.

ˈ**Auszug** *m* (-[e]s; ⁓e) **1.** departure, *demonstrative:* walkout: ⁓ (**aus e-r Wohnung**) move (from a flat). **2.** a) 🝆 extraction, b) *a. fig.* extract (**aus** from), c) ♪ arrangement. **3.** ✝ statement (of account). ˈ**auszugsweise** *adv* in parts: **et.** ⁓ **vorlesen** read extracts from s.th.

ˈ**auszupfen** *v/t* (*sep*, -ge-, h) pluck out.

autark [aʊˈtark] *adj* ✝ autarkic.

Autarkie [aʊtarˈkiː] *f* (-; -n) autarky.

authentisch [aʊˈtɛntɪʃ] *adj* authentic.

Auto [ˈaʊto] *n* (-s; -s) (motor)car, *esp. Am.* auto(mobile): ⁓ **fahren** drive (a car); **mit dem** ⁓ **fahren** go by car; **können Sie** ⁓ **fahren?, fahren Sie** ⁓? do you drive?; → **mitnehmen** 1.

ˈ**Autoapo**ˌ**theke** *f* (driver's) first-aid kit.

ˈ**Autoatlas** *m* road atlas.

ˈ**Autobahn** *f* (-; -en) motorway, *Am.* expressway, freeway. ⁓**auffahrt** *f* motorway *etc* approach, slip road. ⁓**ausfahrt** *f* exit. ⁓**gebühr** *f* toll. ⁓**kreuz** *n* motorway *etc* intersection.

ˈ**Autobahnmeisterei** [-maɪstəraɪ] *f* (-; -en) motorway maintenance area.

ˈ**Autobahn**|**raststätte** *f* motorway service area. ⁓**zubringer** *m* slip road.

Autobiographie [aʊtobiograˈfiː] *f* (-; -n) autobiography.

ˈ**Autobus** *m* bus, *Br. a.* coach.

Autodidakt [aʊtodiˈdakt] *m* (-en; -en), **Autodiˈdaktin** *f* (-; -nen) autodidact.

ˈ**Auto**|**dieb** *m* car thief. ⁓**diebstahl** *m* car theft. ⁓**fähre** *f* car ferry. ⁓**fahrer(in** *f*) *m* motorist, (car) driver. ⁓**fahrt** *f* drive.

ˈ**autofrei** *adj* traffic-free.

ˈ**Autofriedhof** *m* F *fig.* car dump.

autogen [aʊtoˈgeːn] *adj* ✿, ⚙ autogenous: ⁓**es Training** autogenic training.

Autogramm [aʊtoˈgram] *n* (-[e]s; -e) autograph. **Auto**ˈ**grammjäger(in** *f*) *m* F autograph hunter. **Auto**ˈ**grammstunde** *f* autograph(ing) session.

ˈ**Auto**|**händler** *m* car dealer. ⁓**indu**ˌ**strie** *f* car industry. ⁓**kino** *n* drive-in (cinema). ⁓**knacker** *m* (-s; -) F car burglar. ⁓**ko**ˌ**lonne** *f* line of cars, convoy.

Automat [aʊtoˈmaːt] *m* (-en; -en) **1.** a) vending machine, b) slot machine, c) juke box, d) ⚙ automatic machine. **2.** *fig.* (*person*) robot.

Autoˈ**matenrestau**ˌ**rant** *n* automat.

Automatik [aʊtoˈmaːtɪk] *f* (-; ⚙ -en) automatism, ⚙ automatic system, *mot.* automatic transmission. **Auto**ˈ**matik**-**gurt** *m* reel seat belt. **Automation** [aʊtomaˈtsi̯oːn] *f* (-; *no pl*) automation. **automatisch** [aʊtoˈmaːtɪʃ] *adj* automatic. **automatisieren** [aʊtomatiˈziːrən] *v/t* (h) automate.

Automeˌchaniker *m* car mechanic.

Automobil [aʊtomoˈbiːl] *n* (-s; -e) automobile. ⁓**ausstellung** *f* motor show. ⁓**klub** *m* automobile association.

autonom [aʊtoˈnoːm] *adj* autonomous.

Autonomie [aʊtonoˈmiː] *f* (-; -n) autonomy.

ˈ**Autonummer** *f* (car) number.

ˈ**Autopi**ˌ**lot** *m* (-en; -en) ✈ autopilot.

Autopsie [aʊtoˈpsiː] *f* (-; -n) ✿ autopsy, post-mortem.

Autor [ˈaʊtor] *m* (-s; -en), **Autorin** [aʊˈtoːrɪn] *f* (-; -nen) author, writer.

ˈ**Auto**|**radio** *n* car radio. ⁓**reifen** *m* tyre, *Am.* tire. ⁓**reisezug** *m* motorail train. ⁓**rennen** *n* car (or motor) race. ⁓**rennsport** *m* motor racing.

autorisieren [aʊtoriˈziːrən] *v/t* (h) authorize.

autoritär [aʊtoriˈtɛːr] *adj* authoritarian.
Autorität [aʊtoriˈtɛːt] *f* (-; -en) **1.** *no pl* authority. **2.** (*auf dem Gebiet gen*) authority (on), expert (of).
'**Auto|schalter** *m* of a bank: drive-up counter. ~**schlosser** *m* car mechanic. ~**schlüssel** *m* car key. ~**skooter** [-skuː-tər] *m* (-s; -) dodgem. ~**stop(p)** *m* ~ **machen** hitchhike. ~**straße** *f* motor road, *Am.* highway.
Autosuggesti̇on *f* autosuggestion.
'**Auto|tele̦fon** *n* car telephone. ~**unfall** *m* car accident: *er kam bei e-m ~ ums Leben* he died in a car crash. ~**verleih** *m* car hire service, *esp. Am.* rent-a-car

(service). ~**waschanlage** *f* carwash. ~**werkstatt** *f* garage, repair shop.
Avantgarde [avãˈgardə] *f* (-; -n), **avantgardistisch** [-ˈdɪstɪʃ] *adj* avant-garde.
Aversion [averˈzi̯oːn] *f* (-; -en) aversion (*gegen* to).
Avitaminose [avitamiˈnoːzə] *f* (-; -n) 𝔰 avitaminosis.
Avocato [avoˈkaːto] *f* (-; -s) 𝄞 avocado.
Axt [akst] *f* (-; ᵚe) axe, *Am.* ax.
Azalee [atsaˈleːə] *f* (-; -n) 𝄞 azalea.
Azteke [atsˈteːkə] *m* (-n; -n) *hist.* Aztec.
Azubi [aˈtsuːbi] *m* (-s; -s), *f* (-; -s) F → *Auszubildende.*
azurblau [aˈtsuːr-] *adj* azure (blue).

B

B, b [beː] *n* (-; -) B, b, ♪ B flat.
babbeln [ˈbabəln] *v/t, v/i* (h) F babble.
Baby [ˈbeːbi] *n* (-s; -s) baby. ~**ausstattung** *f* layette. ~**nahrung** *f* baby food. ~**sitter** *m* (-s; -) babysitter. ~**speck** *m* F puppy fat. ~**sprache** *f* babytalk. ~**tragetasche** *f* carrycot.
Bach [bax] *m* (-[e]s; ᵚe) stream, brook.
Bache [ˈbaxə] *f* (-; -n) *zo.* (wild) sow.
'**Bachfo̦relle** *f* river trout.
'**Bachstelze** *f zo.* (water) wagtail.
'**Backblech** [ˈbak-] *n* baking tray.
'**backbord** *adv* ⚓ to port.
'**Backbord** *n, m* (-s; *no pl*) ⚓ port (side).
Backe [ˈbakə] *f* (-; -n) **1.** cheek. **2.** ⊙ a) jaw, b) die. **3.** *on ski:* toe piece.
backen [ˈbakən] (backte, † buk, gebakken, h) **I** *v/t, a. v/i* a) bake, b) *dial.* fry. **II** *v/i* snow *etc:* cake, stick.
'**Backen|bart** *m* sideburns. ~**knochen** *m* cheekbone. ~**zahn** *m* molar.
Bäcker [ˈbɛkər] *m* (-s; -) baker: *beim ~* at the baker's. **Bäckerei** [bɛkəˈraɪ] *f* (-; -en) **1.** baker's (shop). **2.** *no pl* a) baking, b) baker's trade. '**Bäckerladen** *m* → *Bäckerei* 1. '**Bäckermeister** *m* master baker.
'**Back|fett** *n gastr.* shortening. ~**form** *f* baking tin. ~**hefe** *f* baker's yeast. ~**obst** *n* dried fruit. ~**ofen** *m* oven. ~**pflaume** *f*

prune. ~**pulver** *n* baking powder. ~**röhre** *f* oven. ~**stein** *m* brick. ~**waren** *pl* bread, cakes and pastries.
Bad [baːt] *n* (-[e]s; ᵚer) **1.** a) bath (*a.* 🐑 *and* 𝔰), b) swim: *ein ~ nehmen* → *baden* 1. **2.** → a) *Badeanstalt,* b) *Badeort,* c) *Badezimmer.*
'**Bade|anstalt** *f* swimming pool, public baths. ~**anzug** *m* swimsuit. ~**gast** *m* **1.** seaside resort. **2.** health resort, spa. **2.** → *Kurgast.* ~**hose** *f* swimming trunks. ~**kappe** *f* bathing cap. ~**mantel** *m* bathrobe. ~**matte** *f* bath mat. ~**meister** *m* **1.** pool attendant. **2.** *at beaches:* lifeguard.
baden [ˈbaːdən] (h) **I** *v/t /i* **1.** have (*or* take) a bath. **2.** swim: *~ gehen* a) go swimming, b) F *fig.* come a cropper, *thing:* go phut. **II** *v/t* **3.** bath, *Am.* bathe. **III** *sich ~* **4.** → 1. **5.** *fig.* bask (*in dat* in).
'**Bade|ofen** *m* bathroom boiler. ~**ort** *m* **1.** seaside resort. **2.** health resort, spa. ~**salz** *n* bath salts. ~**schuhe** *pl* beach shoes. ~**strand** *m* beach. ~**tuch** *n* (-[e]s; ᵚer) bath towel. ~**wanne** *f* bath(tub). ~**zeug** *n* swimming things. ~**zimmer** *n* bathroom.
baff [baf] *adj* F ~ *sein* be flabbergasted.
Bagage [baˈgaːʒə] *f* (-; *no pl*) *contp.* bunch, lot.
Bagatelle [bagaˈtɛlə] *f* (-; -n) trifle.

bagatellisieren [bagatɛli'zi:rən] v/t (h) play down.

Baga'tellschaden m petty damage(s).

Bagger ['bagər] m (-s; -) ☉ excavator. **baggern** ['bagərn] v/i, v/t (h) excavate, dredge. **'Baggersee** m flooded quarry.

Bahn [ba:n] f (-; -en) **1.** path, course: *fig.* **sich ~ brechen** forge ahead; **auf die schiefe ~ geraten** go astray; **~ frei!** make way! **2.** a) road, b) lane, c) (*racing*) track, d) *skiing:* course, piste. **3.** a) trajectory, b) *astr.* course, c) orbit. **4.** a) (*skating*) rink, b) (*bowling*) alley. **5.** a) railway, *Am.* railroad, b) train, c) tram, *Am.* streetcar: **mit der ~** by train, ✈ by rail; **j-n zur ~ bringen** see s.o. off (at the station). **6.** web (*of paper*), width (*of cloth*). **'Bahn...** railway (*Am.* railroad) (*official etc*). **'bahnbrechend** adj pioneer(ing), revolutionary. **'Bahndamm** m railway embankment. **bahnen** ['ba:nən] v/t (h) clear (*path*): **sich e-n Weg ~** force one's way (**durch** through).

'Bahnfahrt f train journey. **~fracht** f ✈ rail carriage (*Am.* freight). **2frei** grid and adv ✈ free on rail (*or* board) (*abbr.* f.o.r., f.o.b.). **~hof** m railway (*Am.* railroad) station: **auf dem ~** at the station; F *fig.* **großer ~** red-carpet treatment.

'Bahnhofs|halle f concourse. **~restaurant** n station restaurant. **~vorsteher** m stationmaster.

'Bahn|körper m permanent way. **2lagernd** adv ✈ to be called for at the station. **~linie** f railway line. **~poli,zei** f railway police. **~reise** f train journey. **~steig** [-ʃtaik] m (-[e]s; -e) platform. **~strecke** f line, *Am.* track. **~übergang** m level (*Am.* grade) crossing. **~wärter** m level crossing attendant.

Bahre ['ba:rə] f **1.** stretcher. **2.** bier.

Baiser [bɛ'ze:] n (-s; -s) *gastr.* meringue.

Baisse ['bɛ:sə] f (-; -n) ✈ slump.

Baissier [bɛ'sie:] m (-s; -s) ✈ bear.

Bajonett [bajo'nɛt] n (-[e]s; -e) bayonet. **Bajo'nettverschluß** m ☉ bayonet joint (*phot.* mount).

Bake ['ba:kə] f (-; -n) beacon.

Bakterie [bak'te:riə] f (-; -n) bacterium, germ. **bakteriell** [bakte'riɛl] adj bacterial. **Bakteriologe** [bakterio'lo:gə] m (-n; -n) bacteriologist.

Balance [ba'laŋsə] f (-; -n) balance. **Ba'lanceakt** m balancing act. **balancie-ren** [balaŋ'si:rən] v/t, v/i (h) balance.

bald [balt] adv **1.** soon: **~ darauf** shortly afterwards; **so ~ als möglich** as soon as possible; **bis ~!** see you soon! **2.** F almost, nearly.

Baldachin ['baldaxi:n] m (-s; -e) canopy.

baldig ['baldiç] adj speedy, early.

Baldrian ['baldria:n] m (-s; -e) valerian.

Balg[1] [balk] m (-[e]s; �ᵁe) **1.** skin. **2.** (*organ*) bellows.

Balg[2] m, n (-[e]s; ⁻er) F brat.

balgen ['balgən] **sich ~** (h), **Balgerei** [-'rai] f (-; -en) (*um* for) scuffle, tussle.

Balken ['balkən] m (-s; -) **1.** beam: F **lügen, daß sich die ~ biegen** lie in one's teeth. **2.** crossbar. **3.** → **Schwebebalken**. **~decke** f timbered ceiling. **~überschrift** f banner headline.

Balkon [bal'koŋ] m (-s; -s) balcony, *thea.* a. dress circle. **~tür** f French window(s).

Ball[1] [bal] m (-[e]s; ⁻e) ball: F *fig.* **am ~ bleiben** keep at it. **Ball[2]** m (-[e]s; ⁻e) (**auf e-m ~** at a) ball (*or* dance).

Ballade [ba'la:də] f (-; -n) ballad.

Ballast [ba'last] m (-[e]s; -e) a. *fig.* ballast. **Bal'laststoffe** pl 𝆕 roughage.

ballen ['balən] (h) **I** v/t **1.** press into a ball. **2.** **die Faust ~** clench one's fist. **II sich ~** form into a ball, *clouds:* gather.

'Ballen m (-s; -) **1.** *anat.* ball (of one's foot *or* hand). **2.** ✶ bale.

Ballerina [balə'ri:na] f (-; -rinen) ballerina, ballet dancer.

Ballermann ['balərman] m (-s; ⁻er) F shooter, *Am. sl.* rod.

ballern ['balərn] v/i (h) F bang (away).

Ballett [ba'lɛt] n (-[e]s; -e) a) ballet, b) ballet company.

Bal'lettänzer(in f) m ballet dancer.

Bal'lettschule f ballet school.

Ballistik [ba'lɪstik] f (-; *no pl*) ballistics. **ballistisch** [ba'lɪstiʃ] adj ballistic.

'Balljunge m ball boy.

'Ballkleid n ball dress.

Ballon [ba'lɔŋ] m (-s; -s) **1.** balloon. **2.** a) carboy, b) demijohn.

Bal'lonreifen m balloon tyre (*Am.* tire).

'Ballsaal m ballroom.

'Ballspiel n ball game.

'Ballung f (-; -en) concentration.

'Ballungs|gebiet n, **~raum** m, **~zentrum** n conurbation, ✈ area of industrial concentration.

'Ballwechsel m *tennis:* exchange.

Balsam ['balza:m] m (-s; -e) a. fig. balm.
balsamieren [balza'mi:rən] v/t (h) embalm.
baltisch ['baltɪʃ] adj Baltic.
Balz [balts] f (-; -en) zo. a) courting, b) mating season.
'**balzen** v/i (h) zo. a) court, b) mate.
Bambus ['bambʊs] m (-[ses]; -se] bamboo. **~sprossen** pl bamboo sprouts.
Bammel ['baməl] m (-s; no pl) F **~ haben** (**vor** dat) be in a blue funk (of).
banal [ba'na:l] adj trite, banal.
Banalität [banali'tɛ:t] f (-; -en) banality.
Banane [ba'na:nə] f (-; -n) banana.
Ba'nanenstecker m ⚡ banana plug.
Banause [ba'naʊzə] m (-n; -n) contp. Philistine, lowbrow.
band [bant] pret of **binden**.
Band¹ m (-[e]s; ⸱e) volume: fig. **das spricht Bände** that speaks volumes.
Band² n (-[e]s; ⸱er) **1.** a) ribbon, b) (apron) string, c) (hat) band. **2.** ⊙, video etc, a. sports: tape: **auf ~ aufnehmen** tape(-record). **3.** ⊙ a) (conveyor) belt, b) assembly line: fig. **am laufenden ~** one after the other, w.s. nonstop. **4.** anat. ligament. **5.** radio: wave band. **6.** (pl -e) fig. bond (of love etc).
Band³ [bɛnt] f (-; -s) ♪ band, group.
Bandage [ban'da:ʒə] f (-; -n) bandage: fig. **mit harten ~n** with the gloves off.
bandagieren [banda'ʒi:rən] v/t (h) bandage.
'**Bandaufnahme** f tape recording.
'**Bandbreite** f **1.** ⚡ band width. **2.** statistics etc: spread. **3.** fig. spectrum.
Bande¹ ['bandə] f (-; -n) gang, F contp. a. bunch: **die ganze ~** the whole lot.
'**Bande²** f billiard, bowling: cushion, ice hockey etc: boards.
Bänderriß ['bɛndər-] m ♣ torn ligament.
'**Bänderzerrung** f ♣ pulled ligament.
'**Bandfilter** n, m radio: band(-pass) filter.
'**Bandförderer** m ⊙ belt conveyor.
bändigen ['bɛndɪgən] v/t (h) tame, fig. a. subdue, restrain, control.
'**Bändigung** f (-; no pl) taming (etc).
'**Bandit** [ban'di:t] m (-en; -en) bandit.
'**Bandmaß** n measuring tape.
'**Bandnudeln** pl ribbon noodles.
'**Bandscheibe** f anat. (intervertebral) disc. '**Bandscheibenschaden** m ♣ **1.** damaged disc. **2.** → '**Bandscheibenvorfall** m slipped disc.

'**Bandwurm** m tapeworm. '**Bandwurmsatz** m humor. endless sentence.
bange ['baŋə] adj (**um** about) anxious, worried: **j-m** (or **j-n**) **~ machen** frighten s.o. '**Bange** f (**nur**) **k-e ~!** don't worry!
bangen ['baŋən] v/i (h) be worried (**um** about): **um j-s Leben ~** fear for s.o.'s life; **es bangt ihr vor** she is afraid of.
Bank¹ [baŋk] f (-; ⸱e) a) bench, b) ped. desk, c) eccl. bank: fig. **et. auf die lange ~ schieben** put s.th. off; F **durch die ~** without exception, down the line.
Bank² f (-; -en) **1.** ✝ bank: **Geld auf der ~ haben** have money in the bank. **2.** bank: **die ~ halten** (**sprengen**) hold (break) the bank. **~angestellte** m, f bank clerk. **~anweisung** f banker's order. **~ausweis** m bank return (Am. statement). **~beamte** m bank clerk. **~di,rektor** m bank manager. **~dis,kont** m bank discount. **~einlage** f deposit.
Bankett [baŋ'kɛt] n (-[e]s; -e] **1.** banquet. **2.** ⊙ shoulder (of road).
'**Bank|fach** n (-[e]s; ⸱er) **1.** no pl banking. **2.** safe(-deposit) box. **2fähig** adj bankable. **~geheimnis** n banker's secrecy. **~geschäft** n **1.** banking transaction. **2.** banking (business). **~guthaben** n **1.** bank balance. **2.** bank account. **~halter** m (-s; -) banker.
Bankier [baŋ'kie:] m (-s; -s) banker.
'**Bank|kaufmann** m bank clerk. **~konto** n bank account. **~leitzahl** f bank code (number). **~note** f (bank)note, Am. bill. **~raub** m bank robbery. **~räuber** m bank robber.
bankrott [baŋ'krɔt] adj a. fig. bankrupt.
Bank'rott m (-[e]s; -e] (a. fig. **den ~ erklären** declare) bankruptcy; **~ machen** go bankrupt. **Bank'rotterklärung** f a. fig. declaration of bankruptcy.
'**Bank|überfall** m bank holdup. **~überweisung** f bank transfer. **~verbindung** f **1.** bank account. **2.** correspondent. **~wesen** n (-s; no pl) banking.
Bann [ban] m (-[e]s; no pl) **1.** ban, eccl. excommunication: **in den ~ tun** outlaw, eccl. excommunicate. **2.** spell: **in s-n ~ schlagen** (or **ziehen**) → **bannen** 3; **unter dem ~ stehen von** (or gen) be under the spell of. '**bannen** v/t (h) **1.** exorcize. **2.** ward off (danger). **3.** a) transfix, b) captivate, spellbind: → **gebannt**. **4.** fig. et. **~ auf** (acc) capture

s.th. on *paper etc.* '**Banner** *n* (-s; -) banner (*a. fig.*), standard.
'**Bannkreis** *m fig.* sphere (of influence).
'**Bannmeile** *f* neutral zone.
Bantamgewicht ['bantam-] *n* (-[e]s; *no pl*) *sports*: bantamweight.
bar [ba:r] *adj* **1.** *~es Geld* (ready) cash; (*in*) *~ bezahlen* pay cash; *gegen ~* for cash; *~ ohne Abzug* net cash. **2.** pure (*gold etc.*), *contp. a.* downright: *~er Unsinn* sheer nonsense; → *Münze* 1. **3.** *~ jeglicher Vernunft* devoid of any sense.
Bar [(-; -s) bar, nightclub: *an der ~* at the bar.
Bär [bɛ:r] *m* (-en; -en) bear (*a.* ♀): *astr. der Große (Kleine) ~* the Great (Little) Bear; *F fig. j-m e-n ~en aufbinden* tell s.o. a whopping lie.
Baracke [ba'rakə] *f* (-; -n) hut, *contp.* shack.
'**Barauszahlung** *f* cash payment.
Barbar [bar'ba:r] *m* (-[e]s; -en) barbarian. **Barbarei** [barba'raɪ] *f* (-; -en) a) barbarism, b) barbarity. **barbarisch** [bar-'ba:rɪʃ] *adj* barbarian, barbarous (*a. fig. contp.*), atrocious, F awful.
bärbeißig ['bɛ:rbaɪsɪç] *adj* gruff.
'**Barbestand** *m* cash in hand, *of bank*: cash reserve.
'**Bardame** *f* barmaid.
'**Bareinnahmen** *pl* cash receipts.
'**Bärendienst** *m j-m e-n ~ erweisen* do s.o. a disservice. '**Bärenhunger** *m* F *e-n ~ haben* be ravenous.
Barett [ba'rɛt] *n* (-[e]s; -e) beret.
'**barfuß**, **barfüßig** ['ba:rfy:sɪç] *adj and adv* barefoot(ed).
barg [bark] *pret of* **bergen.**
'**Bargeld** *n* cash.
'**bargeldlos** *adj and adv* cashless.
'**barhäuptig** [-hɔyptɪç] *adj* bareheaded.
'**Barhocker** *m* barstool.
Bärin ['bɛ:rɪn] *f* (-; -nen) she-bear.
Bariton ['ba:riton] *m* (-s; -e) baritone.
Barkasse [bar'kasə] *f* (-; -n) (motor) launch.
'**Barkauf** *m* cash purchase.
'**Barkeeper** *m* (-s; -) barman.
'**Barkre,dit** *m* cash loan.
barmherzig [barm'hɛrtsɪç] *adj* (*gegen* to) a) merciful, b) charitable; → *Samariter.* **Barm'herzigkeit** *f* (-; *no pl*) a) mercy, b) charity.
'**Barmittel** *pl* cash.

'**Barmixer** *m* (-s; -) barman, bartender.
barock [ba'rɔk] *adj* baroque, *fig. a.* bizarre. **Ba'rock** *n, m* (-s; *no pl*) a) baroque period, b) baroque style.
Barometer [baro'me:tər] *n* (-s; -) *a. fig.* barometer.
Baron [ba'ro:n] *m* (-s; -e) baron.
Ba'ronin *f* (-; -nen) baroness.
Barren ['barən] *m* (-s; -) **1.** bullion, ingot. **2.** *gym.* parallel bars.
Barriere [ba'riɛ:rə] *f* (-; -n) barrier.
Barrikade [bari'ka:də] *f* (-; -n) barricade: *auf die ~n gehen* mount the barricades (*für* for).
barsch [barʃ] *adj* gruff, brusque.
Barsch *m* (-[e]s; -e) *zo.* perch.
'**Barschaft** *f* (-; *no pl*) (ready) money, F cash.
'**Barscheck** *m* uncrossed cheque (*Am.* check).
barst [barst] *pret of* **bersten.**
Bart [ba:rt] *m* (-[e]s; ⸚e) **1.** beard: *sich e-n ~ wachsen lassen* (*or stehenlassen*) grow a beard; *F so ein ~!* that's an old one! **2.** bit (*of key*). **bärtig** ['bɛ:rtɪç] *adj* bearded. '**Bartstoppeln** *pl* stubble.
'**Barvermögen** *n* liquid funds.
'**Barzahlung** *f* cash payment: *gegen ~* cash down.
Basar [ba'za:r] *m* (-s; -e) bazaar.
Base[1] ['ba:zə] *f* (-; -n) female cousin.
'**Base**[2] *f* (-; -n) 🧪 base.
basieren [ba'zi:rən] *v/i* (h) *~ auf* (*dat*) be based on.
Basilika [ba'zi:lika] *f* (-; -ken) basilica.
Basilikum [ba'zi:likom] *n* (-s; *no pl*) 🌿 basil.
Basis ['ba:zɪs] *f* (-; Basen) **1.** △, ⚓, ✗ *etc* base. **2.** *fig.* basis, foundation: *pol.* (*an der*) *~* (at the) grassroots.
basisch ['ba:zɪʃ] *adj* 🧪 basic.
'**Basisdemokra,tie** *f* grassroots democracy. '**Basislager** *n mount.* base camp.
Baskenmütze ['baskən-] *f* beret.
Baß [bas] *m* (-sses; ⸚sse) bass. **~geige** *f* (double) bass. **~gi,tarre** *f* bass guitar.
Bassin [ba'sɛ̃:] *n* (-s; -s) tank, basin.
Bassist [ba'sɪst] *m* (-en; -en) ♩ **1.** bass (singer). **2.** bass player.
'**Baßregler** *m radio etc*: bass control.
'**Baßschlüssel** *m* ♩ bass clef.
'**Baßstimme** *f* bass (voice, ♩ *a.* part).
Bast [bast] *m* (-[e]s; -e) bast, raffia.

basta ['basta] *int* F (**und damit**) ~! and that's that!

Bastard ['bastart] *m* (-[e]s; -e) ♀, *zo.* hybrid, cross(breed), (*dog*) mongrel.

'**Bastelarbeit** *f* 1. handicraft (work). 2. → *Basteln.* **basteln** ['bastəln] (h) I *v/t* make, rig up, build. II *v/i* do handicrafts: ~ *an* (*dat*) *a. fig.* tinker at. '**Basteln** *n* (-s) handicrafts, home mechanics, *a. fig.* tinkering.

Bastion [bas'tio:n] *f* (-; -en) bastion.

'**Bastler** *m* (-s; -) home mechanic, hobbyist.

bat [ba:t] *pret of* **bitten.**

Bataillon [batal'jo:n] *n* (-s; -e) ✕ battalion.

Batik ['ba:tik] *f* (-; -en) batik.

batiken ['ba:tikən] *v/t, v/i* (h) batik.

Batist [ba'tist] *m* (-[e]s; -e) batiste, cambric.

Batterie [batə'ri:] *f* (-; -n) ⚡, ✕, ⊙, *a. fig.* battery. ⚡**betrieben** *adj* battery-operated. ~**ladegerät** *n* battery charger.

Bau [bau] *m* (-[e]s; Bauten) 1. *no pl* construction: *im* ~ under construction, being built. 2. building: → *Bauten.* 3. *no pl* ⊙ design, structure. 4. *no pl* building trade: F *fig.* **er ist vom** ~ he is an expert. 5. (*pl* Baue) earth (*of fox*), burrow (*of rabbits*). 6. *no pl* F ✕ detention: *3 Tage* ~ 3 days in the guardhouse.

'**Bau|amt** *n* Building Authorities. ~**arbeiten** *pl* construction work, roadworks. ~**arbeiter** *m* construction worker. ~**art** *f* a) style, b) design. ~**aufsichtsbehörde** *f* building supervisory board.

Bauch [baux] *m* (-[e]s; ꞏe) belly (*a. fig.*), stomach, *anat.* abdomen, *contp.* paunch: *sich den* ~ *halten vor Lachen* split one's sides laughing; *fig. aus dem* ~ from the guts, guts (*reaction etc*).

'**Bauch|ansatz** *m* beginnings of a paunch. ~**fell** *n anat.* peritoneum. ~**fellentzündung** *f* ⚕ peritonitis.

bauchig ['bauxiç] *adj* bulbous.

'**Bauch|klatscher** *m* (-s; -) F belly flop. ~**landung** *f* ✈ belly landing: *e-e* ~ *machen* bellyland. ~**muskel** *m* stomach muscle. ~**nabel** *m* navel, F belly button. ⚡**reden** *v/i* (*only inf*) ventriloquize. ~**redner** *m* ventriloquist. ~**schmerzen** *pl* stomach-ache. ~**speicheldrüse** *f*

pancreas. ~**tanz** *m* belly dance. ~**tänzerin** *f* belly dancer.

'**Bauchweh** *n* (-s; *no pl*) F stomach-ache.

'**Baudenkmal** *n* historical monument.

bauen ['bauən] (h) I *v/t* 1. build, construct, ⊙ *a.* make. 2. ✗ cultivate, grow. 3. F *fig.* a) make, b) take, pass (*exam*), c) cause: *e-n Unfall* ~ have an accident. II *v/i* 4. build (a house). 5. *fig.* ~ *auf* (*acc*) rely on, count on.

Bauer¹ ['bauər] *n* (-s; -) (bird)cage.

'**Bauer²** *m* (-n; -n) 1. farmer, *fig. contp.* peasant, boor. 2. *chess:* pawn, *cards:* jack. **Bäuerin** ['bɔʏərɪn] *f* (-; -nen) farmer's wife. '**bäuerlich** *adj* rustic.

'**Bauernbrot** *n* (coarse) brown bread.

'**Bauernfänger** *m* con man. **Bauernfängerei** [-fɛŋə'raɪ] *f* (-; *no pl*) con game.

'**Bauern|haus** *n* farmhouse. ~**hof** *n* farm. ~**möbel** *pl* rustic furniture. ~**regel** *f* F peasants' weather maxim.

'**bauernschlau** *adj* crafty.

'**Bauerwartungsland** *n* development area. '**Baufach** *n* (-[e]s; *no pl*) 1. architecture. 2. building trade.

'**baufällig** *adj* dilapidated.

'**Bau|firma** *f* builders and contractors. ~**gelände** *n* 1. building area. 2. → *Baustelle* 1. ~**genehmigung** *f* planning (and building) permission. ~**genossenschaft** *f* cooperative building association. ~**gerüst** *n* scaffolding. ~**gewerbe** *n* building trade. ~**grund**(**stück** *n*) *m* (building) site. ~**handwerker** *m* workman in the building trade. ~**herr** *m* client, building owner. ~**ingenieur** *m* civic engineer. ~**jahr** *n* construction year: *mot.* ~ *1991* (a) 1991 model. ~**kasten** *m* 1. box of bricks. 2. construction set. ~**kastensy**|**stem** *n* ⊙ unit construction system. ~**klotz** *m* building block: F *da staunt man Bauklötze!* it's mind-boggling! ~**kunst** *f* (-; *no pl*) architecture. ~**land** *n* (-[e]s; *no pl*) building land. ~**leiter** *m* site manager.

'**baulich** *adj* architectural, structural: *in gutem* ~**en Zustand** in good repair.

Baum [baum] *m* (-[e]s; ꞏe) tree.

'**Bauma**|**schinen** *pl* construction (*or* building) machines.

'**Baumblüte** *f* **während der** ~ while the trees are in blossom.

'**Baumeister** *m* master builder, *w.s.* architect.

baumeln ['baʊməln] v/i (h) **1.** (*an dat* from) dangle, swing: *mit den Beinen ~* dangle one's legs. **2.** F swing.

'**Baum|grenze** f timberline. **~krone** f tree-top. **~kuchen** m pyramid cake.

'**baumlos** adj treeless.

'**Baum|schere** f pruning shears. **~schule** f (tree) nursery. **~stamm** m a) trunk, b) log. **⚡stark** adj fig. (as) strong as an ox. **~sterben** n (-s) death of trees.

'**Baumwolle** f, '**baumwollen** adj cotton.

'**Bau|plan** m architect's plan, ☉ blueprint. **~platz** m (building) site. **~projekt** n building project.

'**baureif** adj a. ☉ developed.

Bausch [baʊʃ] m (-[e]s; ~e) wad (a. 🖉): fig. in ~ und Bogen lock, stock and barrel. '**bauschen** (h) I v/i (a. sich ~) billow. II v/t puff out.

'**bauschig** adj puffed out.

'**Bau|schlosser** m building fitter. **~sparkasse** f building society. **~sparvertrag** m building savings agreement. **~stahl** m structural steel. **~stein** m **1.** brick, stone (for building). **2.** fig. element, component, contribution. **3.** 🔋 module. **~stelle** f **1.** building site. **2.** roadworks. **~stil** m (architectural) style. **~stoff** m building material. **~stopp** m e-n ~ verhängen impose a halt on building. **~substanz** f fabric (of a building). **~techniker** m constructional engineer. **~teil** n structural member, component part.

Bauten ['baʊtən] pl **1.** buildings, structures. **2.** thea. etc setting.

'**Bau|träger** m **1.** builder. **2.** institution etc responsible for the building project. **~unternehmer** m building contractor. **~vorhaben** n building project. **~weise** f (method of) construction, style of architecture). **~werk** n building. **~zeichnung** f construction drawing.

Bayer ['baɪər] m (-n; -n), '**Bayerin** f (-; -nen), '**bay(e)risch** adj Bavarian.

Bazillenträger(in f) m [ba'tsɪlən-] germ carrier. **Bazillus** [ba'tsɪlʊs] m (-; -len) bacillus (pl -cilli), germ, F bug.

beabsichtigen [bəˈʔapzɪçtɪgən] v/t intend (**zu tun** to do, doing): *das war beabsichtigt* that was intentional.

be'achten v/t (h) a) pay attention to, note, b) take into account, consider, c) notice, d) observe (*rules etc*): *bitte*

zu ~ please note; *nicht ~* ignore, disregard.

be'achtenswert adj noteworthy.

be'achtlich adj considerable.

Be'achtung f (-; no pl) (gen) a) attention (to), b) observing (of), c) consideration (of): *~ schenken* (dat) → **beachten**.

Beamte [bəˈʔamtə] m (-n; -n) (government) official, Br. civil (Am. public) servant, (*police or customs*) officer.

Be'amtenlaufbahn f civil service career.

Be'amtin f (-; -nen) → **Beamte**.

be'ängstigend adj worrying, alarming.

be'anspruchen v/t (h) **1.** claim (*a right etc*). **2.** a) demand, require, b) take up (*room, time*): *j-n ganz ~* keep s.o. busy. **3.** avail o.s. of (*s.o.'s help etc*). **4.** ☉ stress. **Be'anspruchung** f (-; -en) (gen on) **1.** claim. **2.** demand (*on s.o.'s time etc*). **3.** a. ☉ strain, stress.

beanstanden [bəˈʔanʃtandən] v/t (h) object to, criticize, a. † complain about, reject (*goods*).

Be'anstandung f (-; -en) (gen) objection (to), complaint (about).

beantragen [bəˈʔantraːgən] v/t (h) **1.** apply for (*bei j-m* to s.o.). **2.** propose, 🏛 parl. move (for).

be'arbeiten v/t (h) **1.** work, 🔧 a. cultivate, till, ☉ a. machine, process, treat. **2.** fig. a) work on, deal with, adm. a process, b) be in charge of. **3.** edit, revise (*book*), adapt (*a play etc for the stage etc*). **4.** ♪ arrange. **5.** j-n ~ a) work on s.o., b) F give s.o. a working over.

Be'arbeitung f (-; -en) **1.** working (*etc*, → **bearbeiten**), treatment, 🔧 cultivation, adm. processing. **2.** a) revision, b) revised edition, thea. etc adaptation. **3.** ♪ arrangement.

Be'atmung f (-; no pl) (künstliche) ~ artificial respiration.

beaufsichtigen [bəˈʔaʊfzɪçtɪgən] v/t (h) supervise, look after. **Be'aufsichtigung** f (-; -en) supervision.

be'auftragen v/t (h) a) instruct, b) commission (*artist etc*), c) appoint: *j-n mit e-m Fall ~* put s.o. in charge of a case.

Be'auftragte m, f (-n; -n) representative, adm. commissioner.

be'bauen v/t (h) **1.** build on. **2.** 🔧 cultivate. **Be'bauung** f (-; -en) **1.** development. **2.** 🔧 cultivation.

beben ['beːbən] v/i (h) shake, tremble (a.

fig. **vor** *dat* with). **'Beben** *n* (-s; -) trembling, *geol.* tremor, earthquake.

bebildern [bə'bɪldərn] *v/t* (h) illustrate.

bebrillt [bə'brɪlt] *adj* spectacled.

Becher ['bɛçər] *m* (-s; -) **1.** tumbler, mug, beaker. **2.** tub (*of ice cream etc*). **3.** ♀ cup, calix. **'bechern** *v/i* (h) F booze.

Becken ['bɛkən] *n* (-s; -) **1.** bowl, basin (*a.* ☉), (*kitchen*) sink. **2.** (swimming) pool. **3.** *anat.* pelvis. **4.** ♪ cymbal.

'Becken... pelvic (*bone etc*).

'Beckenbruch *m* ⚕ fractured pelvis.

Becquerel [bɛkə'rɛl] *n* (-s; -) Becquerel.

bedacht [bə'daxt] **I** *pp of* **bedenken.** **II** *adj* ~ **sein auf** (*acc*) be intent on; **darauf** ~ **sein zu** *inf* be anxious to *inf*.

be'dachte *pret of* **bedenken.**

bedächtig [bə'dɛçtɪç] *adj* a) careful, b) circumspect, c) slow.

be'danken: sich ~ (h) say thank you, express one's thanks (**bei j-m** to s.o.); **ich bedanke mich!** thank you!; *iro.* **dafür bedanke ich mich!** no, thank you very much!

Bedarf [bə'darf] *m* (-[e]s; *no pl*) (**an** *dat*) need (of), *esp.* ♥ a) demand (for), b) consumption (of), c) requirements (of): **bei** (**nach**) ~ if (as) required; ~ **haben an** (*dat*) need; **den** ~ **decken** meet the demand; **s-n** ~ **decken** get everything one needs.

Be'darfs|ar,tikel *m* commodity, *pl a.* consumer goods. **~fall** *m* **im** ~ in case of need, if required. **~güter** *pl* consumer goods. **~haltestelle** *f* request stop.

bedauerlich [bə'dauərlɪç] *adj* regrettable, unfortunate. **be'dauerlicherweise** *adv* unfortunately. **be'dauern** *v/t* (h) regret (*s.th.*), feel sorry for (*s.o.*): **ich bedaure sehr, daß ...** I am very sorry that ...; *bedaure!* sorry! **Be'dauern** *n* (-s) regret (**über** *acc* for): **zu m-m** ~ to my regret. **be'dauernswert** *adj* **1.** pitiable. **2.** → **bedauerlich.**

be'decken (h) **I** *v/t* cover (up). **II** *sich* ~ cover o.s., *sky:* cloud over. **be'deckt** *adj* **1.** overcast (*sky*). **2.** *fig.* **sich** ~ **halten** keep a low profile. **Be'deckung** *f* (-; -en) **1.** covering. **2.** escort, convoy.

be'denken *v/t* (bedachte, bedacht, h) **1.** a) consider, think *s.th.* over, b) bear *s.th.* in mind. **2.** *j-n* **mit et.** ~ give s.o. s.th.; *j-n* **in s-m Testament** ~ remember s.o. in one's will. **Be'denken** *n* (-s; -)

usu. pl a) objection, b) doubt: **k-e** ~ **haben** have no reservations (**wegen** about). **be'denkenlos I** *adj* unscrupulous. **II** *adv* without hesitation (*or* scruple). **be'denklich** *adj* **1.** dubious. **2.** alarming, critical, serious, dangerous. **3.** worried, sceptical. **Be'denkzeit** *f* time to think it over: **ich gebe dir bis morgen** ~ I'll give you till tomorrow.

be'deuten *v/t* (h) **1.** mean, *symbol, word, etc: a.* stand for: **was soll das** (**denn**) ~? what's the meaning of this?, *picture etc:* what's that supposed to be?, *contp.* what's the idea?; **das hat nichts zu** ~ a) it doesn't mean a thing, b) it doesn't matter; **das bedeutet nichts Gutes** that's a bad thing; **das bedeutet mir viel** that's very important to me. **2.** *j-m* **et.** ~ point s.th. out to s.o.; *j-m* ~, **daß ...** give s.o. to understand that ... **be'deutend I** *adj* important, considerable, great, outstanding. **II** *adv* considerably, a great deal *better etc*.

be'deutsam → **bedeutungsvoll.**

Be'deutung *f* (-; -en) **1.** meaning. **2.** *no pl* importance, *w.s.* import: **von** ~ important (**für** to); **nichts von** ~ nothing important; → **beimessen** b. **be'deutungsvoll** *adj* **1.** important, significant. **2.** meaningful.

be'dienen (h) **I** *v/t* **1.** serve: *iro.* **ich bin bedient!** I've had enough! **2.** operate. **3.** F *sports:* pass (the ball) to. **II** *sich* ~ **4.** help o.s.; ~ **Sie sich!** help yourself! **5.** **sich e-r Sache** ~ use s.th. **III** *v/i* **6.** serve, wait at (*Am.* on) table.

Be'dienung *f* (-; -en) **1.** *no pl* a) service, b) operation. **2.** waiter, waitress.

Be'dienungs|anleitung *f* instructions for use, operating instructions. **~knopf** *m* control knob. **~kom,fort** *m* easy operation.

bedingen [bə'dɪŋən] *v/t* (h) **1.** require. **2.** imply. **3.** entail. **4.** determine. **5.** cause.

be'dingt I *adj* **1.** ~ **durch**, ~ **von** conditional on, dependent on; ~ **sein durch** a. be determined by. **2.** qualified (*approval, success, etc*). **II** *adv* **3.** conditionally. **4.** up to a point, partly.

Be'dingung *f* (-; -en) condition: ~**en** a) terms, b) conditions; ~**en stellen** make stipulations; (**es**) **zur** ~ **machen, daß ...** make it a condition that ...; **unter der** ~**,** **daß ...** provided (that) ...; **unter diesen**

~en under these circumstances; *unter k-r ~* on no account; *† zu günstigen ~en* on easy terms. **be'dingungslos** *adj* **1.** unconditional. **2.** unquestioning.

Be'dingungssatz *m* conditional clause.

be'drängen *v/t* (h) **1.** press *s.o.* hard: *(schwer) bedrängt sein* be in (bad) trouble, be hard-pressed. **2.** pester *(mit Fragen etc* with questions *etc)*: *bedrängt von* beset by *doubts etc*:

be'drohen *v/t* (h) threaten: *zo. bedrohte Arten* endangered species. **be'drohlich** *adj* a) threatening, menacing, b) alarming, c) ominous. **Be'drohung** *f* (-; -en) *(gen* to) *a. fig.* threat, menace.

be'drucken *v/t* (h) print.

be'drücken *v/t* (h) **1.** oppress. **2.** depress. **be'drückend** *adj* depressing. **Be'drückung** *f* (-; -en) **1.** oppression. **2.** depression.

be'dürfen *v/i* (bedurfte, bedurft, h) *(gen)* need, require, take: *es bedarf k-r weiteren Beweise* no further evidence is required. **Bedürfnis** *n* [bə'dүrfnɪs] *n* (-sses; -sse) a) need *(nach* for), requirement, b) urge. **Be'dürfnisanstalt** *f* public convenience. **be'dürfnislos** *adj er ist ~* he doesn't need much.

be'dürftig *adj* needy, poor. **Be'dürftigkeit** *f* (-; *no pl)* neediness, poverty.

Beefsteak *n* ['bi:fste:k] *n* (-s; -s) steak: *deutsches ~* beefburger.

be'ehren *v/t* (h) hono(u)r.

beeid(ig)en [bə'ʔaɪd(ɪg)ən] *v/t* (h) swear to. **be'eidigt** *adj* ⚖ sworn. **Be'eidigung** *f* (-; -en) confirmation by oath.

be'eilen: *sich ~* (h) hurry; *beeil dich!* hurry up!, F get a move on!

beeindrucken [bə'ʔaɪndrʊkən] *v/t* (h) impress.

beeinflussen [bə'ʔaɪnflʊsən] *v/t* (h) influence. **Be'einflussung** *f* (-; -en) influence *(gen* on).

beeinträchtigen [bə'ʔaɪntrɛçtɪgən] *v/t* a) impair, affect, b) detract from *(beauty etc)*, c) impede, d) reduce. **Be'einträchtigung** *f* (-; -en) *(gen)* a) impairment (of), b) detraction (from), c) impeding (of), d) reduction (in).

beend(ig)en [bə'ʔɛnd(ɪg)ən] *v/t* (h) (bring *s.th.* to an) end, conclude, close. **Be'endigung** *f* (-; *no pl)* conclusion.

beengen [bə'ʔɛŋən] *v/t* (h) cramp.

be'erben *v/t* (h) *j-n ~* be *s.o.*'s heir.

beerdigen [bə'ʔɛːrdɪgən] *v/t* (h) bury. **Be'erdigung** *f* (-; -en) burial, funeral. **Be'erdigungsinsti,tut** *n* undertaker's, funeral directors.

Beere ['be:rə] *f* (-; -n) a) berry, b) grape. **'Beerenauslese** *f* quality wine made from selected grapes.

Beet [be:t] *n* (-[e]s; -e) bed.

Beete → **Bete**.

befähigen [bə'fɛ:ɪgən] *v/t* (h) enable, qualify *(für, zu* for): *j-n (dazu) ~, et. zu tun* enable *s.o.* to do *s.th.* **be'fähigt** *adj (zu)* **1.** capable (of). **2.** qualified (for). **Be'fähigung** *f* (-; -en) **1.** qualification *(zu* for). **2.** ability, competence. **Be'fähigungsnachweis** *m* certificate of qualification.

befahl [bə'fa:l] *pret of* **befehlen.**

be'fahrbar *adj* passable, ⚓ navigable. **be'fahren¹** *v/t* (befuhr, befahren, h) drive on, use *(a road)*, cover *(distance)*. **be'fahren²** **I** *pp of* befahren¹. **II** *adj sehr (or stark) ~e Straße* busy road.

be'fallen *v/t* (befiel, befallen, h) attack *(a. 🐛), fig.* seize: *~ werden von* a) be infested by *(insects etc)*, b) be seized by *(fear etc)*.

be'fand *pret of* **befinden.**

be'fangen *adj* **1.** inhibited, shy, self-conscious. **2.** *a.* ⚖ bias(s)ed: *in e-m Irrtum ~ sein* be labo(u)ring under a delusion. **Be'fangenheit** *f* (-; *no pl)* **1.** shyness, self-consciousness. **2.** ⚖ *etc* bias.

be'fassen: *sich ~ mit* (h) concern *o.s.* with, deal with *(a problem etc)*.

Befehl [bə'fe:l] *m* (-[e]s; -e) order, command: *auf ~ von (or gen)* by order of; *(den) ~ haben zu inf* be under orders to *inf*; *den ~ haben (übernehmen)* be in (take) command *(über acc* of).

be'fehlen (befahl, befohlen, h) **I** *v/t j-m et. ~* order *s.o.* to do *s.th.* **II** *v/i* give the orders. **befehligen** [bə'fe:lɪgən] *v/t* (h) be in command of.

Be'fehlsbereich *m* ✕ (area of) command. **Be'fehlsform** *f ling.* imperative. **Befehlshaber** [bə'fe:lsha:bər] *m* (-s; -) commander. **Be'fehlsverweigerung** *f* refusal to obey an order.

be'festigen *v/t* (h) **1.** *(an dat)* fasten, fix. **2.** pave. **3.** ✕ fortify. **Be'festigung** *f* (-; -en) **1.** fastening, fixing. **2.** ✕ fortification.

befeuchten [bə'fɔʏçtən] *v/t* (h) moisten.

be'finden (befand, befunden, h) **I** v/t et. **für gut** etc ~ think s.th. is good etc. **II** **sich ~** a) be, house etc: a. be located, b) be, feel. **III** v/i decide.

Be'finden n (-s) (state) of health.

befindlich [bə'fɪntlɪç] adj **alle im Haus ~en Möbel** all furniture in the house.

befingern [bə'fɪŋərn] v/t (h) finger.

be'flaggen v/t (h) flag.

be'flecken v/t (h) stain, soil, fig. sully.

be'fliegen v/t (beflog, beflogen, h) fly.

beflügeln [bə'fly:gəln] v/t (h) inspire, spur s.o. on, fire (s.o.'s imagination).

befohlen [bə'fo:lən] pp of **befehlen**.

be'folgen v/t (h) a) follow, take (advice), b) observe (rule). **Be'folgung** f (-; no pl) following (etc), observance (gen of).

be'fördern v/t (h) **1.** convey, transport, ✈ forward, ship. **2.** promote: **er wurde zum Major befördert** he was promoted (to the rank of) major. **Be'förderung** f (-; -en) **1.** no pl conveyance, transport(ation), ✈ forwarding, shipment. **2.** promotion. **Be'förderungsmittel** n (means of) transport(ation).

befrachten [bə'fraxtən] v/t (h) load, ⚓, a. fig. freight.

be'fragen v/t (h) (nach, über acc about) **1.** question, ask. **2.** poll, interview. **3.** consult. **Be'fragung** f (-; -en) **1.** interview. **2.** (public opinion) poll.

befreien [bə'fraɪən] (h) (von from) **I** v/t **1.** a) free, liberate, b) rescue. **2.** excuse, exempt (from taxes etc), release (from obligations), relieve (from burden, pain, etc). **II** sich ~ free o.s., liberate o.s.: **sich von et. ~** get rid of s.th. **Be'freier** m (-s; -) liberator. **Be'freiung** f (-; no pl) (von from) **1.** a) freeing, liberation, b) rescue. **2.** exemption, release.

Be'freiungs|bewegung f liberation movement. **~kampf** m fight for independence. **~krieg** m war of liberation.

befremden [bə'frɛmdən] v/t (h) **j-n ~** take s.o. aback. **Be'fremden** n (-s) astonishment (über acc at).

befreunden [bə'frɔʏndən] **sich ~** (h) become friends; **sich ~ mit** make friends with, fig. get used to s.th.

be'freundet adj friendly (a. pol.): **~ sein** be friends (mit with).

be'frieden v/t (h) pol. pacify.

befriedigen [bə'fri:dɪɡən] v/t (h) satisfy (s.o., s.o.'s curiosity etc), please (s.o.),

meet (demand etc), come up to (expectations): **schwer zu ~** hard to please. **be'friedigend** adj satisfactory (a. ped. mark). **be'friedigt** adj and adv satisfied, pleased. **Be'friedigung** f (-; no pl) satisfaction (über acc at, with).

be'fristen v/t (h) et. (auf e-n Monat) ~ set a time limit (of one month) on s.th. **be'fristet** adj limited (in time) (auf acc to). **Be'fristung** f (-; -en) **1.** setting of a time limit. **2.** time limit.

be'fruchten v/t (h) biol. fertilize (a. fig.), ♣ pollinate, fig. stimulate: (künstlich) ~ inseminate (artificially).

Be'fruchtung f (-; -en) biol. fertilization (a. fig.), ♣ pollination: **künstliche ~** artificial insemination.

Befugnis [bə'fu:knɪs] f (-; -se) a. pl authority, power(s): **j-m (die) ~ erteilen** (zu inf) authorize s.o. (to inf).

befugt [bə'fu:kt] adj authorized.

be'fühlen v/t (h) feel, touch.

befuhr [bə'fu:r] pret of **befahren**¹.

Be'fund m (-[e]s; -e) findings: **✗ ohne ~** negative. **be'funden** pp of **befinden**.

be'fürchten v/t (h) fear: **es ist zu ~, daß ...** it is feared that ...; **wir müssen das Schlimmste ~** we must be prepared for the worst. **Be'fürchtung** f (-; -en) fear, pl a. misgivings.

befürworten [bə'fy:rvɔrtən] v/t (h) **1.** advocate, recommend. **2.** support. **Be'fürworter** m (-s; -) supporter, advocate. **Be'fürwortung** f (-; -en) recommendation, support.

begab [bə'ga:p] pret of **begeben**.

begabt [bə'ga:pt] adj gifted, talented.

Begabung [bə'ga:bʊŋ] f (-; -en) gift, (a. person) talent.

begangen [bə'gaŋən] pp of **begehen**.

begann [bə'gan] pret of **beginnen**.

begatten [bə'gatən] v/t (h) copulate with, zo. mate with. **Be'gattung** f (-; -en) copulation, zo. mating.

be'geben (begab, begeben, h) **I** sich ~ **1.** happen, occur. **2.** sich ~ nach (or zu) go to; **sich in ärztliche Behandlung ~** have medical treatment; **sich an die Arbeit ~** set to work; **sich auf die Reise ~** set out (on one's journey); **~ auf Gefahr.** **II** v/t **3.** ✈ negotiate (bill). **Be'gebenheit** f (-; -en) occurrence, incident.

begegnen [bə'ge:gnən] v/i (sn) (dat) **1.** meet, F bump into, come across: **sich ~**

meet. **2.** meet with (*difficulties*), face (*s.o., situation, etc*), obviate (*danger etc*). **3.** be found (*bei* in). **4.** *j-m freundlich etc ~* treat s.o. kindly *etc*.

Be'gegnung *f* (-; -en) **1.** meeting, encounter. **2.** *sports:* bout, match.

begehbar [bə'ge:ba:r] *adj* passable.

be'gehen *v/t* (beging, begangen, h) **1.** walk on. **2.** inspect. **3.** make (*mistake*), commit (*crime*). **4.** celebrate (*birthday etc*), observe (*holiday*).

begehren [bə'ge:rən] *v/t* (h) desire, crave for, demand: (*sehr*) *begehrt* (much) sought after, (very) much in demand. **be'gehren** *n* (-s) desire (*nach* for). **be'gehrenswert** *adj* desirable.

be'gehrlich *adj* covetous, greedy.

Be'gehung *f* (-; -en) **1.** inspection. **2.** commission (*of crime*). **3.** celebration.

begeistern [bə'gaɪstərn] **I** *v/t* (h) fill *s.o.* with enthusiasm (*für* about), inspire. **II** *sich ~ für* be (*or* get) enthusiastic about. **III** *v/i* arouse enthusiasm (*durch* by). **be'geisternd** *adj* rousing, inspiring, marvel(l)ous. **be'geistert I** *adj* (*von*) enthusiastic (about), keen (on): *~er Anhänger* (*gen or von*) fan (of); *...begeistert* ...-minded, F ...-mad. **II** *adv* enthusiastic(ally): *~ sprechen von* a. rave about. **Be'geisterung** *f* (-; *no pl*) enthusiasm (*für* for, about): *mit ~* a. enthusiastically.

Begierde [bə'gi:rdə] *f* (-; -n) (*nach* for) a) appetite, b) desire, lust. **be'gierig** *adj* eager (*nach, auf acc* for): *ich bin ~ zu erfahren* I am anxious to know.

be'gießen *v/t* (begoß, begossen, h) **1.** pour water *etc* over (*or* on), water. **2.** F *fig.* celebrate (with a drink): *das müssen wir ~!* that calls for a drink!

beging [bə'gɪŋ] *pret of begehen.*

Beginn [bə'gɪn] *m* (-[e]s; *no pl*) (*zu ~* at the) beginning. **be'ginnen** *v/t, v/i* (begann, begonnen, h) begin, start.

beglaubigen [bə'glaʊbɪgən] *v/t* (h) **1.** certify (*document*). **2.** accredit *diplomat* (*bei* to). **be'glaubigt** *adj* (*öffentlich*) ~ certified (by a notary public); *~e Abschrift* certified copy, *as a note:* a true copy. **Be'glaubigung** *f* (-; -en) **1.** certification. **2.** accreditation. **Be'glaubigungsschreiben** *n* credentials.

be'gleichen *v/t* (beglich, beglichen, h) ✝

pay, settle. **Be'gleichung** *f* (-; *no pl*) settlement, payment.

be'gleiten *v/t* (h) accompany (a. ♪ *or* fig.), a. ⚓, ✕, mot. escort.

Be'gleiter *m* (-s; -) **1.** companion. **2.** attendant. **3.** ♪ accompanist. **4.** escort.

Be'gleiterin *f* (-; -nen) → *Begleiter* 1-3.

Be'gleiterscheinung *f* concomitant, ✶ attendant symptom. **~flugzeug** *n* escort plane. **~mu,sik** *f* incidental music, *fig.* accompaniment. **~per,son** *f* escort. **~schein** *m* ✝ ✝ waybill. **2.** (custom's) permit. **~schiff** *n* escort vessel. **~schreiben** *n* covering letter. **~umstände** *pl* attendant circumstances. **Be'gleitung** *f* (-; -en) **1.** a) company, a. ⚓, ✕ escort, b) entourage: *ohne ~* unaccompanied; *in ~ von* (*or gen*) accompanied by. **2.** ♪ accompaniment.

beglich [bə'glɪç] *pret of begleichen.*

be'glichen *pp of begleichen.*

be'glücken *v/t* (h) *j-n ~* make s.o. happy.

be'glückwünschen *v/t* (h) *j-n* (*zu et.*) *~* congratulate s.o. (on s.th.).

begnadet [bə'gna:dət] *adj* inspired, highly gifted: *~ mit* blessed with.

begnadigen [bə'gna:dɪgən] *v/t* (h), **Be'gnadigung** *f* (-; -en) pardon, *pol.* amnesty.

begnügen [bə'gny:gən] *sich ~* (h) (*mit* with) be content, make do.

Begonie [be'go:niə] *f* (-; -n) ⚘ begonia.

begonnen [bə'gɔnən] *pp of beginnen.*

begoß [bə'gɔs] *pret of begießen.*

be'gossen *pp of begießen.*

be'graben *v/t* (begrub, begraben, h) a. *fig.* bury. **Begräbnis** [bə'grɛ:pnɪs] *n* (-ses; -se) burial, funeral.

begradigen [bə'gra:dɪgən] *v/t* (h) straighten.

be'greifen *v/t* (begriff, begriffen, h) understand (*a. v/i*), grasp: *das begreife ich nicht!* that's beyond me!; *schnell ~* F catch on quickly, be quick on the uptake. **be'greiflich** *adj* understandable: *j-m et. ~ machen* make s.th. clear to s.o. **be'greiflicherweise** *adv* understandably (enough).

be'grenzen *v/t* (h) **1.** mark off. **2.** form the boundary of. **3.** *fig.* (*auf acc* to) limit, restrict. **Be'grenztheit** *f* (-; *no pl*) limitations. **Be'grenzung** *f* (-; -en) **1.** (*auf acc* to) limiting, restriction. **2.** bounds, limit.

Be'grenzungslicht n mot. sidelight.
begriff [bə'grɪf] pret of **begreifen**.
Be'griff m (-[e]s; -e) **1.** a) idea, notion, philos. concept, b) term: **sich e-n ~ ma-chen von** get an idea of, imagine; **du machst dir k-n ~!** you have no idea!; **ist dir das ein ~?** does that mean anything to you?; **nach m-n ~en** as I see it. **2.** F **schwer von ~** slow (in the uptake). **3.** **im ~ sein, et. zu tun** be about to do s.th.
be'griffen I pp of **begreifen**. **II** adj **im Aufbruch ~ sein** be about to leave.
be'grifflich adj conceptual, abstract.
Be'griffsbestimmung f definition.
be'griffstutzig adj dense, slow.
begrub [bə'gru:p] pret of **begraben**.
be'gründen v/t (h) **1.** give reasons for, explain, justify. **2.** found, establish, set up, fig. lay the foundations of.
be'gründet adj well-founded, justified: **~er Verdacht** reasonable suspicion.
Be'gründung f (-; -en) **1.** reason(s), argument(s), explanation: **mit der ~, daß ...** on the grounds that ...; **ohne jede ~** without giving any reasons. **2.** establishment, foundation, setting up.
be'grüßen v/t (h) greet, welcome: **es ist zu ~, daß** we welcome the fact that.
be'grüßenswert adj welcome.
Be'grüßung f (-; -en) greeting, welcome.
Be'grüßungs|ansprache f welcoming speech. **~worte** pl words of welcome.
begünstigen [bə'gʏnstɪgən] v/t (h) a) favo(u)r, b) promote. **Be'günstigte** m, f (-n; -n) ✝, ⚖ beneficiary. **Be'günstigung** f (-; -en) **1.** a) favo(u)ring, b) promotion. **2.** preferential treatment. **3.** (financial) benefit. **4.** ⚖ acting as accessory after the fact.
be'gutachten v/t (h) **1.** give an (expert's) opinion on: **et. ~ lassen** obtain an expert's opinion on s.th. **2.** examine.
begütert [bə'gy:tərt] adj rich, wealthy, well-off, well-to-do.
begütigen [bə'gy:tɪgən] v/t (h) appease.
behaart [bə'ha:rt] adj hairy, hirsute.
behäbig [bə'hɛ:bɪç] adj **1.** sedate. **2.** portly.
behaftet [bə'haftət] adj **~ mit** full of (mistakes), afflicted with (disease), tainted with (flaw).
behagen [bə'ha:gən] v/i (h) **j-m ~** a) suit s.o., b) please s.o.; **das behagt mir (ganz und gar) nicht** I don't like that

(at all). **Be'hagen** n (-s) a) ease, comfort, b) pleasure. **be'haglich** adj comfortable, cosy. **Be'haglichkeit** f (-; no pl) comfort, cosiness.
be'halten v/t (behielt, behalten, h) **1.** keep: **recht ~** be right (in the end); **für sich ~** keep secret to o.s.; **behalte das für dich!** keep it under your hat! **2.** remember.
Behälter [bə'hɛltər] m (-s; -) container, tank.
be'handeln v/t (h) treat (a. ✂, ⚙), fig. a. deal with, handle. **Be'handlung** f (-; -en) treatment, handling: **in (ärztlicher) ~** under medical treatment.
be'hängen v/t (h) hang, drape, decorate: F contp. **mit Schmuck behängt** decked (out) with jewels.
be'harren v/i (h) (**auf** dat) persist (in), F stick (to): **darauf, daß ...** insist that ...
be'harrlich adj persistent, steadfast, stubborn. **Be'harrlichkeit** f (-; no pl) perseverance, stubbornness.
be'hauen v/t (h) hew.
behaupten [bə'haʊptən] (h) **I** v/t **1.** maintain, claim, say (**daß** that): F **steif und fest ~, daß ...** insist that ... **2.** maintain, assert. **II sich ~ 3.** hold one's own. **4.** ✝ prices etc: remain firm. **Be'hauptung** f (-; -en) **1.** claim, assertion. **2.** no pl maintenance, assertion.
Behausung [bə'haʊzʊŋ] f (-; -en) dwelling.
be'heben v/t (behob, behoben, h) remove, repair (damage), remedy (grievance). **Be'hebung** f (-; no pl) removal.
beheimatet [bə'haɪma:tət] adj **~ in** (dat) resident in, living in, coming from.
be'heizbar adj heatable.
be'heizen v/t (h) heat.
Behelf [bə'hɛlf] m (-[e]s; -e) makeshift.
be'helfen: sich ~ (behalf, beholfen, h) (**mit** with) make do, manage.
Be'helfs..., be'helfsmäßig adj makeshift, temporary.
behelligen [bə'hɛlɪgən] v/t (h) bother.
beherbergen [bə'hɛrbɛrgən] v/t (h) put up, accommodate, a. fig. house.
be'herrschen (h) **I** v/t **1.** rule (over), govern. **2.** fig. control (situation, market, one's feelings, etc): **j-n ~** dominate s.o. **3.** have a good command of, speak (German etc), know: **sein Handwerk ~** know one's trade. **II sich ~** control o.s.

be'herrschend *adj* dominating.
Be'herrscher *m* ruler (*gen* over, of).
Be'herrschung *f* (-; *no pl*) **1.** rule, domination. **2.** *fig.* (*gen* of) a) control, b) mastery, command. **3.** self-control.
beherzigen [bə'hɛrtsɪgən] *v/t* (h) *et.* ~ bear s.th. in mind.
beherzt [bə'hɛrtst] *adj* courageous.
behielt [bə'hi:lt] *pret of* behalten.
behilflich [bə'hɪlflɪç] *adj j-m* ~ *sein* help (*or* assist) s.o. (*bei* in).
be'hindern *v/t* (h) (*bei* in) hinder, hamper, *a. sports:* obstruct.
be'hindert *adj* (*körperlich or geistig*) ~ (physically *or* mentally) handicapped.
Be'hinderte *m, f* (-n; -n) handicapped person. Be'hinderung *f* (-; -en) **1.** hindrance, impediment, *a. sports:* obstruction. **2.** *⚕* handicap.
behob [bə'ho:p] *pret of* beheben.
behoben [bə'ho:bən] *pp of* beheben.
beholfen [bə'hɔlfən] *pp of* behelfen.
Behörde [bə'hø:rdə] *f* (-; -n) (public) authority: *die* ~ the authorities.
behördlich [bə'hø:rtlɪç] *adj* official.
be'hüten *v/t* (h) protect (*vor dat* from).
behutsam [bə'hu:tza:m] *adj* cautious, careful, gentle. Be'hutsamkeit *f* (-; *no pl*) caution, gentleness.
bei [baɪ] *prep* (*dat*) **1.** ~ *Berlin* near Berlin; *die Schlacht* ~ *Waterloo* the Battle of Waterloo; *~m Bäcker* at the baker's; ~ *Familie Braun*, ~ *Brauns* at Braun's; ~ *Braun* c/o (= care of) Braun; ~ *Hofe* at court; ~ *j-m sitzen* sit with s.o.; *arbeiten* ~ work for; *e-e Stellung* ~ a job with; *~m Heer* (~ *der Marine*) in the army (navy); ~ *uns* a) with us, b) (*zu Hause*) at home, c) (*in Deutschland*) in Germany, at home; *ich habe kein Geld* ~ *mir* I have no money one me; *er hatte s-n Hund* ~ *sich* he had his dog with him. **2.** ~ *s-r Geburt* (*Hochzeit*) at his birth (wedding); ~ *Tag* (*Nacht*) by night (day), during the night (day); ~ *Licht* by light; ~ *70 Grad* at 70 degrees; ~ *schönem Wetter* when the weather is fine; *~m Arbeiten* while working; ~ *offenem Fenster* with the window open; ~ *Regen* (*Gefahr*) in case of rain (danger); F *er ist nicht ganz* ~ *sich* he's not all there. **3.** ~ *so vielen Problemen* with (*or* considering) all the problems; ~ *solcher Hitze* in such heat; ~ *all s-n Be-*

mühungen for all his efforts; → *a. corresponding headwords.*
'beibehalten *v/t* (*irr, sep,* h, → *behalten*) retain, maintain, keep.
'Beiblatt *n* supplement (*gen* to).
'Beiboot *n* dinghy.
'beibringen *v/t* (*irr, sep,* -ge-, h, → *bringen*) *j-m et.* ~ a) teach s.o. s.th., b) get s.th. across to s.o.; *j-m et. schonend* ~ break s.th. gently to s.o.
Beichte ['baɪçtə] *f* (-; -n) confession: *j-m die* ~ *abnehmen* hear s.o.'s confession.
beichten ['baɪçtən] *v/t, v/i* (h) confess.
'Beicht|geheimnis *n* confessional secret. *~kind n* confessant. *~stuhl m* confessional. *~vater m* (father) confessor.
beide ['baɪdə] *adj* a) both, b) the two, c) either: *m-e ~n Brüder* both my brothers, my two brothers; *wir* ~ both of us, we two; *alle* ~ both of them; *in ~n Fällen* in either case; *kein(e)s von ~n* neither (of the two).
'beidemal *adv* both times.
beiderlei ['baɪdərlaɪ] *adj* (of) both kinds: ~ *Geschlechts* of either sex. 'beiderseitig [-zaɪtɪç] *adj and adv* a) on both sides, b) mutual(ly *adv*). 'beiderseits [-zaɪts] **I** *adv* on both sides, *fig. a.* mutually. **II** *prep* (*gen*) on both sides (of).
beidhändig ['baɪthɛndɪç] *adj* ambidextrous, *sports:* two-handed.
'beidrehen *v/i* (*sep,* -ge-, h) *⚓* heave to.
beiein'ander *adv* together: (*dicht*) ~ next to each other. *~haben v/t* (*irr, sep,* -ge-, h, → *haben*) F have got s.th. together: *du hast wohl nicht alle beieinander!* you must be out of your mind! *~halten v/t* (*irr, sep,* -ge-, h, → *halten*) F keep s.th. together. *~sein v/i* (*irr, sep,* -ge-, sn, → *sein*) F *gut* ~ be in good shape; *er ist nicht ganz beieinander* he's not all there.
'Beifahrer *m in car:* front passenger, *in truck:* driver's mate, *in races:* co-driver.
'Beifahrersitz *m* front-passenger seat.
'Beifall *m* (-[e]s; *no pl*) applause, (loud) cheers, *fig.* approval: ~ *ernten*, ~ *finden* draw applause, *fig.* meet with approval, be acclaimed; ~ *klatschen*, ~ *spenden* applaud (*j-m* s.o.).
'beifällig *adj* approving.
'Beifallsruf *m* cheer(s).
'Beifallssturm *m* thunderous applause.
'Beifilm *m* supporting film.

'bei|fügen *v/t* (*sep*, -ge-, h) (*dat*) a) add (to), b) enclose (with *a letter*).
'Beifügung *f* (-; -en) *ling*. apposition.
'Beigabe *f* (-; -n) **1.** addition, extra: *als ~ a*. into the bargain. **2.** → *Beilage* 2.
beige [be:ʃ] *adj*, Beige *n* (-; *no pl*) beige.
'beigeben (*irr*, *sep*, -ge-, h, → *geben*) **I** *v/t* add (*dat* to). **II** *v/i* F **klein ~** knuckle under, climb down.
'Beigeordnete *m*, *f* (-n; -n) assistant, *pol*. town council(l)or.
'Beigeschmack *m* (-[e]s; *no pl*) (unpleasant) taste, *fig*. smack (**von** of).
'Beihilfe *f* **1.** a) aid, b) grant, c) subsidy. **2.** ⚖ aiding and abetting: (*j-m*) ~ **leisten** aid and abet (s.o.).
'beikommen *v/i* (*irr*, *sep*, -ge-, sn, → *kommen*) get at (*s.o.'s*), cope with.
Beil [baɪl] *n* (-[e]s; -e) a) ax(e), hatchet, b) (meat) chopper.
'Beilage *f* (-; -n) **1.** supplement, insertion, inset. **2.** *gastr*. side dish: **Fleisch mit ~** meat and vegetables.
'beiläufig **I** *adj* casual. **II** *adv* casually, by the way: **et. ~ erwähnen** mention s.th. in passing.
'beilegen *v/t* (*sep*, -ge-, h) **1.** (*dat*) add (to), enclose (with). **2.** give (*a name*). **3.** settle (*quarrel*).
beileibe [baɪ'laɪbə] *adv* **~ nicht(!)** certainly not(!), by no means(!).
'Beileid *n* (-[e]s; *no pl*) (*j-m sein ~ aussprechen* offer s.o. one's condolences: **(mein) herzliches ~!** *a. iro*. my heartfelt sympathy!
'Beileidsbesuch *m* visit of condolence.
'Beileidsbrief *m* letter of condolence.
'Beileidskarte *f* condolence card.
'beiliegen *v/i* (*irr*, *sep*, -ge-, h, → *liegen*) be enclosed (*dat* with). 'beiliegend *adj and adv* enclosed: **~ übersenden wir Ihnen ...** enclosed please find ...
beim [baɪm] = *bei dem*.
'beimessen *v/t* (*irr*, *sep*, -ge-, h, → *messen*) (*dat*) a) **Glauben ~** give credence to, b) **Bedeutung** *etc* ~ attach importance *etc* to.
'beimischen *v/t* (*sep*, -ge-, h) (*dat*) **et. ~** mix s.th. with, add s.th. to.
'Beimischung *f* (-; -en) admixture.
Bein [baɪn] *n* (-[e]s; -e) leg (*a*. *of pants*, *table*, *etc*): (*früh*) **auf den ~en sein** be up and about (early); **dauernd auf den ~en sein** be always on the go; **wieder**

auf den ~en sein be back on one's feet (again); F **j-m ~e machen** make s.o. get a move on; **ich muß mich auf die ~e machen!** I must be off!; F **die ~e in die Hand nehmen** take to one's heels, run; *fig*. **auf eigenen ~en stehen** stand on one's own two feet; *fig*. **j-n (et.) auf die ~e stellen** set s.o. (s.th.) up; **j-m ein ~ stellen** a. *fig*. trip s.o. up; **sich die ~e vertreten** stretch one's legs; → *Grab*.
beinah(e) ['baɪna:(ə)] *adv* almost, nearly: **~ et. tun** come near doing s.th.
'Beinahezusammenstoß *m* near miss.
'Beiname *m* epithet.
'Bein|arbeit *f* boxing: footwork, swimming: legwork. **~bruch** *m* 🞏 fractured leg: F *fig*. **das ist kein ~!** that's no tragedy! **~freiheit** *f mot*. legroom.
beinhalten [bə'ʔɪnhaltən] *v/t* (h) contain, say, imply.
'Beinpro these *f* artificial leg.
'beiordnen *v/t* (*sep*, -ge-, h) **1.** *j-m j-n ~* assign s.o. to s.o. **2.** *ling*. coordinate.
'Beipackzettel *m* instructions.
beipflichten ['baɪpflɪçtən] *v/i* (*sep*, -ge-, h) agree (*dat* to).
'Beipro gramm *n film*: supporting program(me *Br*.).
'Beirat *m* (-[e]s; -e) advisory board.
beirren [bə'ʔɪrən] *v/t* (h) disconcert: **er läßt sich nicht ~** he stands firm.
beisammen [baɪ'zamən] *adv* together.
Bei'sammensein *n* (-s) being together: **geselliges ~** get-together.
'Beischlaf *m* ⚖ sexual intercourse.
'Beisein: **im ~ von** (*or gen*) in the presence of.
bei'seite *adv* aside: **~ lassen** disregard; **~ legen** set aside; **~ schaffen** remove, get rid of; **~ schieben** push (*argument*: brush) aside; **~ treten** step aside.
'beisetzen *v/t* (*sep*, -ge-, h) bury.
'Beisetzung *f* (-; -en) burial, funeral.
'Beispiel *n* (-[e]s; -e) a) example, b) model: **(wie) zum ~** for instance, for example (*abbr*. e.g.); **ein ~ geben, mit gutem ~ vorangehen** set an example; **sich ein ~ an j-m (et.) nehmen** take s.o. (s.th.) as an example. **'beispielhaft** *adj* exemplary, model. **'beispiellos** *adj* unprecedented, unheard-of. **'beispielsweise** *adv* for example, (as) for instance.
beißen ['baɪsən] *v/t*, *v/i* (biß, gebissen, h) bite (**auf** *acc*, **in** *acc* s.th.), smoke, pep-

per, etc: *a.* burn: **nach j-m ~** snap at s.o.; F **die Farben ~ sich** the colo(u)rs clash; F **er wird dich schon nicht ~!** he won't eat you! **'beißend** *adj* biting (*wind*, *a. criticism etc*), acrid (*smell*).

'Beißring *m* teething ring.

'Beistand *m* (-[e]s; ⁺e) **1.** *no pl* help, aid, support: **j-m ~ leisten** → **beistehen**. **2.** → **Rechtsbeistand**. **'Beistandspakt** *m pol*. mutual assistance pact.

'beistehen *v/i* (*irr, sep*, -ge-, h, → **stehen**) **j-m ~** help (*or* assist, stand by) s.o., come to s.o.'s aid, ⚔ attend s.o.

'beisteuern *v/t*, *v/i* (*sep*, -ge-, h) contribute (**zu** to).

'Beistrich *m* comma.

Beitrag ['baitra:k] *m* (-[e]s; ⁺e) a) contribution (*a. fig*.), b) subscription (fee), fee: **e-n ~ leisten** make a contribution (**zu** to). **'beitragen** *v/t*, *v/i* (*irr, sep*, -ge-, h, → **tragen**) contribute (**zu** to).

'beitragsfrei *adj* noncontributary.

'beitragspflichtig *adj* liable to contributions.

'beitreiben *v/t* (*irr, sep*, -ge-, h, → **treiben**) collect (*taxes etc*), recover (*debts*).

'beitreten *v/i* (*irr, sep*, -ge-, sn, → **treten**) (*dat*) join (*club etc*), accede to (*treaty*).

'Beitritt *m* (-[e]s; -e) (**zu**) joining (*a club etc*). **'Beitrittserklärung** *f* application for membership.

'Beiwagen *m mot*. sidecar. **~ma₁schine** *f* (motorcycle) combination.

'beiwohnen *v/i* (*sep*, -ge-, h) (*dat*) **1.** a) be present at, attend, b) witness. **2.** ⚰ have sexual intercourse with.

'Beiwort *n* (-[e]s; ⁺er) epithet.

Beize¹ ['baitsə] *f* (-; -n) **1.** corrosive, *for wood*: stain, *for dies*: mordant, *metall*. pickle. **2.** (*tobacco*) sauce. **3.** *gastr*. marinade. **Beize²** *f* (-; -n) hawking.

beizeiten [bai'tsaitən] *adv* in good time.

beizen ['baitsən] *v/t* (h) **1.** corrode, stain (*wood*), bate (*hides*), *metall*. pickle. **2.** sauce (*tobacco*). **3.** *gastr*. marinade.

bejahen [bə'ja:ən] *v/t* (h) answer in the affirmative (*a. v/i*), *a. fig*. say yes to.

be'jahend *adj* affirmative.

Be'jahung *f* (-; -en) affirmation, *fig*. positive attitude (*gegen* towards).

bejahrt [bə'ja:rt] *adj* advanced in years.

be'jammern *v/t* (h) lament.

bekam [bə'ka:m] *pret of* **bekommen**.

be'kämpfen *v/t* (h) fight (against), com-

bat. **Be'kämpfung** *f* (-; *no pl*) fight (*gegen* against).

bekannt [bə'kant] **I** *pp of* **bekennen**. **II** *adj* (well-)known (*wegen* for): **~ mit** acquainted with; **j-n ~ machen mit** introduce s.o. to; **sich mit et. ~ machen** familiarize o.s. with s.th.; **das ist mir ~** I know (that); **dafür ~ sein, daß ...** have a reputation for *ger*. **be'kannte** *pret of* **bekennen**. **Be'kannte** *m*, *f* (-n; -n) friend, acquaintance.

Be'kanntenkreis *m* (circle of) friends.

Be'kanntgabe *f* (-; *no pl*) announcement. **be'kanntgeben** *v/t* (*irr, sep*, -ge-, h, → **geben**) announce.

Be'kanntheitsgrad *m* (-[e]s; *no pl*) name recognition (rating).

be'kanntlich *adv* as everybody knows.

be'kanntmachen *v/t* (*sep*, -ge-, h) announce, make *s.th.* known.

Be'kanntmachung *f* (-; -en) announcement, publication, bulletin.

Be'kanntschaft *f* (-; -en) **1.** *no pl* (*bei näherer ~* on closer) acquaintance: **j-s ~ machen** become acquainted with s.o. **2.** (circle of) friends.

be'kanntwerden *v/i* (*irr, sep*, -ge-, sn, → **werden**) become known, come out.

be'kehren *v/t* (h) *a. fig*. convert (**zu** to): **sich ~** (**zu** to) become a convert, *fig. a.* come round.

Be'kehrte *m*, *f* (-n; -n) convert.

Be'kehrung *f* (-; -en) conversion.

be'kennen (bekannte, bekennt, bekennt) **I** *v/t* confess (to). **II** *sich ~* **zu** a) profess (*deed*), b) profess (*faith etc*); **sich zu j-m ~** stand by s.o., stand up for s.o.; → **Farbe 2**, **schuldig 1**.

Be'kenntnis *n* (-ses; -se) **1.** confession. **2.** *eccl*. a) creed, b) denomination. **~schule** *f* denominational school.

be'klagen (h) **I** *v/t* lament, deplore **II** **sich ~** complain (*über acc* of). **be'klagenswert** *adj* deplorable, sorry, *person*: pitiable. **Beklagte** [bə'kla:ktə] *m*, *f* (-n; -n) ⚖ defendant.

be'klauen *v/t* (h) F **j-n ~** steal from s.o.

be'kleben *v/t* (h) **1.** paste *s.th.* over. **2.** **et. ~ mit** stick (*or* paste) *s.th.* on s.th.

be'kleckern (h) **I** *v/t* stain, mess up. **II** **sich ~ mit ...** spill ... over o.s.

be'kleiden *v/t* (h) **1.** dress: *fig.* **~ mit** (in)vest with. **2.** hold (*an office*).

Be'kleidung *f* (-; -en) clothing, clothes.

Be'kleidungsindu,strie *f* clothing industry.

be'klemmen *v/t* (h) oppress. **be'klemmend** *adj* oppressive, *fig. a.* eerie.

Beklemmung *f* (-; -en) oppression, *fig. a.* anxiety. **beklommen** [bə'klɔmən] *adj* uneasy, anxious. **Be'klommenheit** *f* (-; *no pl*) uneasiness, anxiety.

bekloppt [bə'klɔpt], **beknackt** [-'knakt] *adj* F nutty, batty, crazy, *pred* nuts.

be'kommen (bekam, bekommen) **I** *v/t* (h) get, *✗ a.* catch (*a.* F *bus etc*), have (*child, young*): **Hunger** (**Durst**) *~* get hungry (thirsty); **sie bekommt ein Kind** she's going to have a baby; **Zähne** *~* cut one's teeth; *et.* **geschenkt** *~* be given s.th. (as a present); **wieviel** *~* **Sie** (**von mir**)? how much do I owe you? **II** *v/i* (sn) *j-m* (**gut**) *~* agree with s.o.; *j-m* **nicht** (*or* **schlecht**) *~* disagree with s.o.; **wohl bekomm's!** cheers!; *fig.* **es wird ihm schlecht** *~* he will regret it.

bekömmlich [bə'kœmlɪç] *adj* wholesome, *a.* easily digestible, light (*food*), salubrious (*air, climate*).

beköstigen [bə'kœstɪgən] *v/t* (h) feed: **sich selbst** *~* cook for o.s. **Be'köstigung** *f* (-; *no pl*) a) feeding, b) food.

be'kräftigen *v/t* (h) confirm.

Be'kräftigung *f* (-; -en) confirmation.

be'kreuzigen: sich *~* (h) cross o.s.

be'kriegen *v/t* (h) make war on: **sich** *~* be at war with one another.

be'kritteln *v/t* (h) *contp.* criticize.

be'kritzeln *v/t* (h) scribble on.

be'kümmern *v/t* (h) grieve, worry.

bekunden [bə'kʊndən] *v/t* (h) **1.** show, demonstrate. **2.** state, *tt a.* testify.

be'lächeln *v/t* (h) smile (condescendingly) at.

be'laden *v/t* (belud, beladen, h) load, *fig. a.* burden.

Belag [bə'la:k] *m* (-[e]s; ⸚e) **1.** a) covering, ◎ *a.* coating, b) surface (*of road*), c) (*brake*) lining. **2.** (sandwich) filling. **3.** *✗ a.* coating (*of tongue*), b) plaque.

be'lagern *v/t* (h) *a. fig.* besiege.

Be'lagerung *f* (-; -en) siege.

Belang [bə'laŋ] *m* (-[e]s; -e) **1.** *no pl* **von** *~* of importance (**für** to); **ohne** *~* a) unimportant, b) irrelevant. **2.** *pl* interests.

be'langen *v/t* (h) *tt a.* sue, b) prosecute.

be'langlos *adj* a) unimportant, b) irrelevant (**für** to), c) negligible. **Be'langlos-**

sigkeit *f* (-; -en) **1.** *no pl* a) insignificance, b) irrelevance. **2.** *pl* trivialities.

be'lassen *v/t* (beließ, belassen, h) *et.* **an s-m Platz** *~* leave s.th. in its place; **es dabei** *~* leave it at that; **alles beim alten** *~* leave things as they are.

belastbar [bə'lastba:r] *adj* **1.** ◎ having a load capacity (*bis zu* of). **2.** *fig.* strong, resilient. **Be'lastbarkeit** *f* (-; *no pl*) **1.** ◎ load(ing) capacity. **2.** ability to cope with pressure (*or* strain): **bis zur Grenze der** *~* to breaking point. **be'lasten** *v/t* (h) **1.** *✗*, ◎ load. **2.** *fig.* burden (**mit** with, **sich** o.s.), put (*or* be) a strain on, weigh on, worry: **das belastet mich sehr** that's a great burden (*or* worry) to me; **damit kann ich mich jetzt nicht** *~* I can't be bothered with that now; → **erblich. 3.** *✝* a) charge, b) encumber (*house etc*): *j-n* (*or* *j-s* **Konto**) (**mit e-m Betrag**) *~* charge a sum to s.o.'s account. **4.** *tt, pol.* incriminate.

be'lästigen [bə'lɛstɪgən] *v/t* (h) a) molest, b) (**mit**) pester, bother.

Be'lästigung *f* (-; -en) **1.** molestation, pestering: **sexuelle** *~* sexual harassment. **2.** nuisance.

Be'lastung *f* (-; -en) **1.** loading (*etc*, → **belasten**). **2.** *✗*, ◎ load: **zulässige** *~* safe load. **3.** *fig.* (*gen or* **für**) a) (*financial etc*) burden (to, on), b) worry (to), c) trouble (to), d) (*mental*) strain (on), stress (on): **er ist zu e-r** *~* **geworden** he has become a liability. **4.** *✝* (*gen*) a) charge (to *an account*), b) encumbrance (of *property*). **5.** *tt, pol.* incrimination.

Be'lastungs|materi,al *n* *tt* incriminating evidence. *~***probe** *f* **1.** ◎ load test. **2.** *fig.* (severe) test. *~***zeuge** *m*, *~***zeugin** *f* witness for the prosecution.

belaubt [bə'laʊpt] *adj* leafy, in leaf.

be'laufen: sich *~* (belief, belaufen, h) (**auf** *acc*) amount (to), run up (to), total.

be'lauschen *v/t* (h) eavesdrop on.

be'leben *v/t* (h) a) liven up, stimulate, *drink etc*: *a.* revive, b) brighten (*room*): **neu** *~* put new life into. **II sich** *~* *street etc*: come to life. **be'lebt** *adj* animated, lively, busy (*street etc*).

Beleg [bə'le:k] *m* (-[e]s; -e) **1.** *esp. ✝* a) record, b) proof, c) voucher, d) receipt. **2.** *ling.* a) example, b) reference.

be'legen *v/t* (h) **1.** a) cover, b) line (*a.*

brakes): **mit Teppichboden** ~ carpet; **mit Schinken** *etc* ~ put ham *etc* on; → **belegt** 4. **2.** a) occupy (*room etc*), b) reserve (*seat etc*). **3.** *univ.* enrol(l) for (*a subject*). **4.** *sports:* **den ersten (zweiten** *etc*) **Platz** ~ be placed (*or* come in) first (second *etc*). **5. mit e-r Strafe (Steuer** *etc*) ~ impose a penalty (tax *etc*) on. **6.** a) supply evidence for, verify, b) give a reference for (*text, word*); → **belegt** 5.

Be'legexem,plar *n* author's copy.

Be'legschaft *f* (-; -en) personnel, staff, employees, workers, work force.

Be'legschein *m* (-[e]s; -e) voucher.

be'legt *adj* **1.** a) taken, occupied, b) full (up). **2.** *✿* husky (*voice*), coated (*tongue*). **3.** *teleph.* engaged, *Am.* busy. **4.** *gastr.* **es Brot** sandwich; **es Brötchen** filled roll. **5.** documented: **das ist nirgends** ~ there is no evidence for it.

be'lehren *v/t* (h) a) instruct, b) inform (*über acc* of): **er ist nicht zu** ~ he won't listen to reason; **j-n e-s Besseren** ~ set s.o. right, *w.s.* open s.o.'s eyes. **be'lehrend** *adj* instructive. **Be'lehrung** *f* (-; -en) a) instruction, b) advice.

beleibt [bə'laɪpt] *adj* corpulent, stout.

beleidigen [bə'laɪdɪɡən] *v/t* (h) offend (*a. fig.*), insult: **nicht böse gemeint!** no offen/ce (*Am.* -se) meant! **be'leidigend** *adj* insulting. **Be'leidigung** *f* (-; -en) insult, b) slander, b) libel.

be'lesen *adj* well-read.

Be'lesenheit *f* (-; *no pl*) wide reading.

be'leuchten *v/t* (h) light (up), illuminate, *fig.* throw light on.

Be'leuchter *m* (-s; -) *thea. etc* lighting technician.

Be'leuchtung *f* (-; -en) lighting, illumination (*a. fig.*), light(s). **Be'leuchtungskörper** *m* lighting fixture, lamp.

Belgien ['bɛlɡiən] *n* (-s) Belgium. **'Belgier** *m* (-s; -), **'Belgierin** *f* (-; -nen), **'belgisch** *adj* Belgian.

belichten [bə'lɪçtən] *v/t* (h) *phot.* expose. **Be'lichtung** *f* (-; -en) *phot.* exposure. **Be'lichtungs,auto,matik** *f* automatic exposure. **messer** *m* light meter. **zeit** *f* exposure (time).

be'lieben (h) **I** *v/t esp. iro.* deign. **II** *v/i* please: **wie es Ihnen beliebt** as you wish. **Be'lieben** *n* (-s) **nach** ~ at will; **ganz nach** ~ as you like. **be'liebig I** *adj* any ... (you like): **jeder ~e** anyone; **in**

~er Reihenfolge in any order (you *etc* like). **II** *adv* at will: ~ **viele** as many as you *etc* like. **be'liebt** *adj* popular (*bei* with), **✝** very much in demand: **sich ~ machen bei** ingratiate o.s. with.

Be'liebtheit *f* (-; *no pl*) popularity (*bei* with). **Be'liebtheitsgrad** *m* (-[e]s; *no pl*) popularity (rating).

belief [bə'li:f] *pret of* **belaufen**.

be'liefern *v/t* (h) supply (*mit* with).

Be'lieferung *f* (-; -en) supply.

beließ [bə'li:s] *pret of* **belassen**.

bellen ['bɛlən] *v/i, v/t* (h) *a. fig.* bark.

Belletristik [bɛlə'trɪstɪk] *f* (-; *no pl*) fiction. **belle'tristisch** *adj* belletristic.

belobigen [bə'lo:bɪɡən] *v/t* (h) praise. **Be'lobigung** *f* (-; -en) praise.

belog [bə'lo:k] *pret of* **belügen**.

belogen [bə'lo:ɡən] *pp of* **belügen**.

be'lohnen *v/t* (h) reward (*für* for). **Be'lohnung** *f* (-; -en) (*zur* ~ as a) reward.

belud [bə'lu:t] *pret of* **beladen**.

be'lüften *v/t* (h) ventilate.

Be'lüftung *f* (-; *no pl*) ventilation.

Be'lüftungsanlage *f* ventilation system.

be'lügen *v/t* (lestig, belogen, h) *j-n* ~ lie to s.o.; **sich selbst** ~ deceive o.s.

belustigen [bə'lʊstɪɡən] *v/t* (h) amuse. **Be'lustigung** *f* (-; -en) amusement.

bemächtigen [bə'mɛçtɪɡən] **sich** *j-s* (**e-r Sache**) ~ seize s.o. (s.th.).

be'malen *v/t* (h) paint.

bemängeln [bə'mɛŋəln] *v/t* (h) criticize, fault: **daran ist nichts zu** ~ it can't be faulted.

bemannen [bə'manən] *v/t* (h) man: **bemannter Raumflug** manned space flight.

bemänteln [bə'mɛntəln] *v/t* (h) **1.** cover up. **2.** palliate.

bemaß [bə'ma:s] *pret of* **bemessen**.

bemerkbar [bə'mɛrkba:r] *adj* noticeable: **sich ~ machen** draw attention to o.s., show, make itself felt. **be'merken** *v/t* **1.** notice. **2.** remark. **be'merkenswert** *adj* remarkable (*wegen* for).

Be'merkung *f* (-; -en) a) remark, comment, b) note, annotation.

be'messen (bemaß, bemessen, h) **I** *v/t* **1.** (*nach*) a) proportion (to), b) *fig.* measure (by). **2.** a) calculate, b) time. **3.** *◎* a) dimension, b) rate (*performance*). **4.** fix (*penalty etc*). **II sich** ~ be proportioned (*etc*, → I). **III** *adj* (*knapp* ~

limited; *ihre Zeit ist knapp* ~ she is pressed for time.

bemitleiden [bəˈmɪtlaɪdən] *v/t* (h) pity.

be'mitleidenswert *adj* pitiable.

be'mogeln *v/t* (h) F cheat.

be'mühen (h) I *v/t* trouble (*mit* with, *um* for), call in (*doctor etc*). II *sich* ~ take trouble (*or* pains) (*mit* over), make an effort, try (hard); *sich* ~ *um* a) try to get (*a job etc*), apply for (*a post etc*), b) try to help *s.o.*; *sich um j-n* (*or j-s Gunst*) ~ court *s.o.'s* favo(u)r; *bemüht sein zu inf* endeavo(u)r to *inf*, be anxious to *inf*; ~ *Sie sich nicht!* don't trouble (*or* bother)! **Be'mühung** *f* (-; -en) effort(s), endeavo(u)r(s), trouble.

bemüßigt [bəˈmyːsɪçt] *adj sich* ~ *fühlen zu inf* feel bound (*or* obliged) to *inf*.

bemuttern [bəˈmʊtərn] *v/t* (h) mother.

be'nachbart *adj* neighbo(u)ring.

benachrichtigen [bəˈnaːxrɪçtɪɡən] *v/t* (h) (*von* of) inform, notify, ✝ advise. **Be'nachrichtigung** *f* (-; -en) notification, ✝ advice.

benachteiligen [bəˈnaːxtaɪlɪɡən] *v/t* (h) a) put *s.o.* at a disadvantage, b) discriminate against (*sozial*) *benachteiligt* underprivileged. **Be'nachteiligung** *f* (-; -en) **1.** discrimination (*gen* against). **2.** disadvantage, handicap.

benannt [bəˈnant] *pp of* **benennen.**

be'nannte *pret of* **benennen.**

benebelt [bəˈneːbəlt] *adj* F *fig.* fuddled.

Benefiz... [beneˈfiːts-] charity (*concert, match, etc*).

be'nehmen: *sich* ~ (benahm, benommen, h) behave (*gegenüber* towards): *sich gut* ~ behave well, behave o.s.; *sich schlecht* ~ behave badly, misbehave; *benimm dich!* behave yourself! **Be'nehmen** *n* (-s) **1.** behavio(u)r, conduct, manners. **2.** *adm. im* ~ *mit* in agreement with; *sich mit j-m ins* ~ *setzen* get in touch with s.o.

be'neiden *v/t* (h) *j-n* (*um et.*) ~ envy s.o. (s.th.). **be'neidenswert** *adj* enviable.

be'nennen *v/t* (benannte, benannt, h) **1.** name, call. **2.** fix (*date etc*), nominate (*candidate*): *j-n als Zeugen* ~ call s.o. as a witness. **Be'nennung** *f* (-; -en) a) naming, b) name.

be'netzen *v/t* (h) moisten, sprinkle.

Bengel [ˈbɛŋəl] *m* (-s; -) rascal.

benommen [bəˈnɔmən] *adj* dazed.

Be'nommenheit *f* (-; *no pl*) daze.

benoten [bəˈnoːtən] *v/t* (h) *ped.* mark, *Am.* grade.

benötigen [bəˈnøːtɪɡən] *v/t* (h) need: *dringend* ~ be in urgent need of.

Be'notung *f* (-; -en) a) marking, *Am.* grading, b) marks, *Am.* grades.

be'nutzen *v/t* (h) a) use, make use of, b) profit by. **Be'nutzer** *m* (-s; -) user.

be'nutzerfreundlich *adj* user-friendly.

Be'nutzung *f* (-; *no pl*) use.

Be'nutzungsgebühr *f* fee, charge.

Benzin [bɛnˈtsiːn] *n* (-s; -e) **1.** *mot.* petrol, *Am.* gasoline, F gas. **2.** 🔬 benzine. **~feuerzeug** *n* fuel lighter. **~fresser** *m* F *mot.* fuel guzzler. **~gutschein** *m* petrol (*Am.* gas) coupon. **~hahn** *m* fuel cock. **~ka,nister** *m* petrol can, F jerry can. **~leitung** *f* fuel line. **~motor** *m* petrol (*Am.* gasoline) engine. **~pumpe** *f* fuel pump. **~tank** *m* fuel tank. **~uhr** *f* fuel ga(u)ge. **~verbrauch** *m* petrol (*Am.* gasoline) consumption.

Benzol [bɛnˈtsoːl] *n* (-s; -e) 🔬, ⚙ benzene, benzol.

beobachten [bəˈʔoːbaxtən] *v/t* (h) **1.** watch, observe. **2.** notice. **3.** observe (*rule etc*). **Be'obachter** *m* (-s; -) a) observer (*a.* ✕, *pol. etc*), b) onlooker. **Be'obachtung** *f* (-; -en) observation. **2.** observance (*gen* of).

Be'obachtungsgabe *f* powers of observation. **Be'obachtungsstati,on** *f* observation station (⚕ ward).

beordern [bəˈʔɔrdərn] *v/t* (h) a) order (*nach* [to go] to), b) summon.

be'packen *v/t* (h) load (*mit* with).

be'pflanzen *v/t* (h) plant (*mit* with).

be'quatschen *v/t* (h) F **1.** thrash *s.th.* out. **2.** *j-n* ~ *zu* talk s.o. into doing *s.th.*

bequem [bəˈkveːm] I *adj* **1.** comfortable, easy (*a.* ✝ *terms etc*), convenient: *es sich* ~ *machen* make o.s. comfortable (*or* at home), *fig.* take the easy way out. **2.** a) comfort-loving, b) lazy. II *adv* **3.** easily. **be'quemen:** *sich* ~ (h) deign (*or* bring o.s.) (*et. zu tun* to do s.th.): *sich zu e-r Antwort etc* ~ deign to give an answer *etc*. **Be'quemlichkeit** *f* (-; -en) **1.** *no pl* comfort, ease. **2.** *no pl* indolence. **3.** convenience, *pl a.* amenities.

berappen [bəˈrapən] *v/t, v/i* (h) F pay.

be'raten (beriet, beraten, h) I *v/t* **1.** a) advise *s.o.* (*bei* on), b) discuss: *sich* ~

lassen von consult; *gut* (*schlecht*) ~ *sein* be well-(ill-)advised. **II** *sich mit j-m über et.* ~ discuss s.th. with s.o.
be'ratend *adj* advisory. **Be'rater** *m* (-s; -), **Be'raterin** *f* (-; -nen) adviser: *fachmännischer* (or *fachärztlicher*) *Berater* consultant. **Be'ratung** *f* (-; -en) **1.** a) discussion (*über* acc of), b) consultation. **2.** → **Be'ratungsstelle** *f* information cent/re (*Am.* -er).
be'rauben *v/t* (h) (*gen* of) rob, *fig. a.* deprive.
be'rauschen *v/t* (h) intoxicate: *fig. sich* ~ get intoxicated (*an* dat with).
be'rauschend *adj a. fig.* intoxicating: *iro. nicht gerade* ~ not so hot.
berechenbar [bə'rɛçənbaːr] *adj* calculable, *fig.* predictable. **be'rechnen** *v/t* (h) a) calculate (*a. fig.*), b) estimate (*auf* acc at), c) ✝ charge (*j-m et.* s.o. s.th.).
be'rechnend *adj fig.* calculating.
Be'rechnung *f* (-; -en) calculation: *fig. mit* ~ with deliberation.
berechtigen [bə'rɛçtɪgən] (h) **I** *v/t j-n* (*zu e-r Sache*) ~ entitle s.o. (to [do] s.th.), authorize s.o. (to do s.th.). **II** *v/i zu e-r Sache* ~ entitle to s.th.; *zu der Annahme* (*Hoffnung*) ~, *daß* ... warrant the assumption (hope) that ... **be'rechtigt** *adj* (*zu* to) a) entitled, authorized, b) justified, c) legitimate (*claim etc*).
Be'rechtigung *f* (-; -en) right (*zu* to), authorization, authority, legitimacy.
be'reden *v/t* (h) **1.** discuss. **2.** → *überreden.* **Beredsamkeit** [bə're:tza:mkaɪt] *f* (-; *no pl*) eloquence. **beredt** [bə're:t] *adj a. fig.* eloquent.
Be'reich *m* (-[e]s; -e) **1.** area. **2.** *fig.* field, sphere, sector: *im* ~ *des Möglichen liegen* be possible, be within the bounds of possibility; *im sozialen* ~ in the social sector, socially; *im persönlichen* ~ on the personal side, personally.
bereichern [bə'raɪçərn] *v/t* (h) *a. fig.* enrich (*sich* o.s.). **Be'reicherung** *f* (-; -en) *a. fig.* enrichment.
bereifen [bə'raɪfən] *v/t* (h) put tyres (*Am.* tires) on. **Be'reifung** *f* (-; -en) tyres, *Am.* tires.
be'reinigen *v/t* (h) settle (*quarrel*, ✝ *account*), iron out (*mistake etc*), *statistics*: adjust. **Be'reinigung** *f* (-; *no pl*) settlement, adjustment.
be'reisen *v/t* (h) travel around, tour.

bereit [bə'raɪt] *adj pred* ready, prepared, willing: *sich* ~ *erklären* (or *finden*) *zu inf* agree (or volunteer) to *inf*; *bist du* ~? (are you) ready?
be'reiten *v/t* (h) **1.** prepare, make (*tea etc*). **2.** cause (*trouble etc*): *j-m Vergnügen* ~ give s.o. pleasure.
be'reithalten (*irr, sep*, -ge-, h, → *halten*) **I** *v/t et.* ~ have s.th. ready. **II** *sich* ~ be ready (*für* for).
be'reitliegen *v/i* (*irr, sep*, -ge-, h, → *liegen*) be ready.
be'reitmachen *v/t* (*sep*, -ge-, h) (*a. sich* ~) (*zu* for) get ready, prepare (o.s.).
bereits [bə'raɪts] *adv* already.
Be'reitschaft *f* (-; -en) **1.** *no pl* readiness: *in* ~ *sein* → *bereitstehen*; (*sich*) *in* ~ *halten* → *bereithalten.* **2.** (police) squad.
Be'reitschafts|arzt *m* duty doctor. ~*dienst* *m* standby duty. ~*poli,zei* *f* riot police. ~*tasche* *f* carrying (*phot.* camera) case.
be'reitstehen *v/i* (*irr, sep*, -ge-, h, → *stehen*) **1.** be ready, ⨯ stand by. **2.** be available.
be'reitstellen *v/t* (*sep*, -ge-, h) provide, make *s.th.* available.
Be'reitstellung *f* (-; *no pl*) provision.
be'reitwillig *adj* willing, eager.
Be'reitwilligkeit *f* (-; *no pl*) willingness.
bereuen [bə'rɔʏən] *v/t* (h) regret.
Berg [bɛrk] *m* (-[e]s; -e) mountain (*a. fig.*), hill: *fig.* ~*e von* piles of; ~*e versetzen* move mountains; *j-m goldene* ~*e versprechen* promise s.o. the moon; *über den* ~ *sein* be over the worst; *über alle* ~*e* off and away; *die Haare standen ihm zu* ~*e* his hair stood on end; *er hielt damit nicht hinterm* ~ he made no bones about it.
berg'ab *adv a. fig.* downhill.
'Bergarbeiter *m* miner.
berg'auf *adv* uphill: *fig. es geht wieder* ~ things are looking up.
'Berg|bahn *f* mountain railway. ~*bau* *m* (-[e]s; *no pl*) mining (industry).
bergen ['bɛrgən] *v/t* (barg, geborgen, h) **1.** a) rescue, b) recover, salvage, c) ⚓ take in (*sails*). **2.** contain, hold, *a.* involve (*danger*).
'Bergführer *m* mountain guide.
bergig ['bɛrgɪç] *adj* mountainous.
'Berg|kette *f* mountain range. ~*kri,stall*

m crystallized quartz. **~land** *n* mountainous country. **~mas,siv** *n* massif. **~predigt** *f bibl.* Sermon on the Mount. **~rücken** *m* (mountain) ridge. **~schuh** *m* mountaineering boot. **~spitze** *f* mountain peak. **~steigen** *n* (-s) mountaineering. **~steiger** *m* (-s; -) mountaineer. **~straße** *f* mountain road. **~tour** *f* mountain tour.

'**Berg-und-'Tal-Bahn** *f* switchback (railway), *Am.* roller coaster.

'**Bergung** *f* (-; -en) a) rescue, b) recovery, salvage.

'**Bergungs|arbeiten** *pl* rescue work, salvage operations. **~dienst** *m* recovery (*or* salvage) service. **~fahrzeug** *n* recovery (✓ crash) vehicle. **~mannschaft** *f* rescue party, ⚓ salvage crew.

'**Berg|wacht** *f* (-; *no pl*) mountain rescue service. **~wanderung** *f* mountain hike. **~werk** *n* (-[e]s; -e) mine.

Bericht [bəˈrɪçt] *m* (-[e]s; -e) (*über acc*) report (on), account (of): (*j-m* ~) **er-statten** report (to s.o.). **be'richten** *v/t, v/i* (h) report (*über acc* on, *j-m* to s.o.), relate (*j-m etc.* ~ inform s.o. of s.th.

Be'richterstatter *m* (-s; -) reporter, *abroad*: correspondent, *radio, TV a.* commentator.

Be'richterstattung *f* (-; -en) a) reporting, *a.* coverage (*by the press*), b) report, *radio, TV a.* commentary.

berichtigen [bəˈrɪçtɪɡən] *v/t* (h) correct (*sich o.s.*), rectify (*s.th.*), ⚙ *a.* adjust.

Be'richtigung *f* (-; -en) correction, ⚙ *a.* adjustment.

Be'richtsjahr *n* ✝ year under review.

be'riechen *v/t* (beroch, berochen, h) sniff at.

berief [bəˈriːf] *pret of* **berufen**.

be'rieseln *v/t* (h) irrigate, sprinkle.

Be'rieselung *f* (-; *no pl*) **1.** irrigation, sprinkling. **2.** F *fig.* constant exposure (*mit Musik etc.*) to music *etc*).

beriet [bəˈriːt] *pret of* **beraten**.

beritten [bəˈrɪtən] *adj* mounted.

Berliner [bɛrˈliːnər] **I** *m* (-s; -) Berliner. **II** *adj* (of) Berlin.

Ber'liner² *m* (-s; -) *gastr.* doughnut.

Bernhardiner [bɛrnhɑrˈdiːnər] *m* (-s; -) St. Bernard (dog).

Bernstein [ˈbɛrn-] *m* (-[e]s; *no pl*) amber.

beroch [bəˈrɔx] *pret of* **beriechen**.

berochen [bəˈrɔxən] *pp of* **beriechen**.

bersten [ˈbɛrstən] *v/i* (barst, geborsten, sn) burst (*fig. vor dat* with).

berüchtigt [bəˈrʏçtɪçt] *adj* notorious (*wegen* for).

berücksichtigen [bəˈrʏkzɪçtɪɡən] *v/t* (h) consider, take *s.th.* into consideration, bear *s.th.* in mind, allow for. **Be'rück-sichtigung** *f* (-; *no pl*) consideration: *unter ~ s-s Alters* considering his age.

Beruf [bəˈruːf] *m* (-[e]s; -e) a) occupation, *f* job, b) profession, c) trade, d) business, e) line: *von ~* by profession, by trade. **be'rufen** (berief, berufen, h) **I** *v/t j-n ~* appoint s.o. (*zu e-m Amt* to an office, *zum Vorsitzenden* chairman). **II** *sich ~ auf* (*acc*) cite; *sich auf et. ~* a) rely on, b) plead (*ignorance etc*); *sich darauf ~, daß ...* plead that ...; *darf ich mich auf Sie ~?* may I mention your name? **III** *adj adj*: *sich ~ fühlen zu inf* feel called upon to *inf*: *aus ~em Munde* from a competent authority.

be'ruflich *adj* professional, vocational.

Be'rufs|ausbildung *f* vocational training. **~aussichten** *pl* career prospects. **~berater(in)** *f) m* vocational adviser. **~beratung** *f* vocational guidance. **~bild** *n* job description. **~erfahrung** *f* (vocational) experience. **~fachschule** *f* vocational college. **~geheimnis** *n* professional secret (*as duty*: secrecy). **~krankheit** *f* occupational disease. **~leben** *n* professional (*or* active) life. **~risiko** *n* occupational hazard. **~schule** *f* vocational school. **~sol,dat** *m* regular (soldier). **~spieler** *m sports*: professional (player). **~sportler(in** *f) m* professional. **~stand** *m* profession. **⚸tätig** *adj* a) working, b) employed. **~tätige** *m, f* (-n; -n) working person. **~verbot** *n* disqualification from a profession. **~verkehr** *m* rush-hour traffic.

Be'rufung *f* (-; -en) **1.** calling. **2.** appointment (*zu* to). **3.** *unter ~ auf* (*acc*) with reference to. **4.** ⚖ (*~ einlegen* file an) appeal (*bei* with, *gegen* from).

Be'rufungsgericht *n,* **Be'rufungs-in,stanz** *f* ⚖ court of appeal.

Be'rufungsverfahren *n* ⚖ **1.** appeal proceedings. **2.** appellate procedure.

be'ruhen *v/i* (h) **1.** *~ auf* (*dat*) rest on, be based on, b depend on. **2.** *et. auf sich ~ lassen* let s.th. rest; *lassen wir die Sache auf sich ~!* let's leave it at that!

beruhigen [bə'ru:ɪgən] **I** v/t (h) a) reassure, b) calm (down): ~ *Sie sich doch!* calm down!; *seien Sie beruhigt, ich werde ...* rest assured I'll ...; *wenn Sie das beruhigt* if that puts your mind at rest. **II** *sich* ~ calm down, *situation:* quieten down. **be'ruhigend** *adj* **1.** reassuring. **2.** 𝕏 sedative.

Be'ruhigung *f* (-; -en) **1.** *no pl* calming (down), *of situation:* a. stabilization: *sie braucht es. zur* ~ she needs s.th. to calm her down. **2.** reassurance: *zu d-r* ~ to put your mind at rest.

Be'ruhigungs|mittel *n*, **~pille** *f* 𝕏 sedative, *fig.* soporific. **~spritze** *f* sedative injection.

berühmt [bə'ry:mt] *adj* famous (*wegen* for): F *fig.* **das ist nicht gerade ~!** that's nothing to write home about!

Be'rühmtheit *f* (-; -en) **1.** *no pl* fame: ~ *erlangen* become famous. **2.** celebrity.

be'rühren (h) **I** v/t **1.** touch, *fig.* a. affect: *j-n (un)angenehm* ~ (dis)please s.o.; → *peinlich* 3. **2.** *fig.* touch (up)on (*subject*), concern (*s.o.'s interests*). **II** *sich* ~ touch, *fig.* a. meet. **Be'rührung** *f* (-; -en) **1.** touch. **2.** contact: *in* ~ *kommen mit* come into contact with.

Be'rührungspunkt *m* point of contact.

be'sagen v/t (h) say, mean: *das besagt (noch) gar nichts!* that doesn't mean anything! **be'sagt** *adj adm.* aforesaid.

besah [bə'za:] *pret of* **besehen**.

besamen [bə'za:mən] v/t (h) inseminate, 🌿 pollinate.

Besan [be'za:n] *m* (-s; -e) ⚓ miz(z)en.

besänftigen [bə'zɛnftɪgən] v/t (h) (*a. sich* ~) calm down: *j-n* ~ placate s.o.

besang [bə'zaŋ] *pret of* **besingen**.

besann [bə'zan] *pret of* **besinnen**.

besaß [bə'za:s] *pret of* **besitzen**.

besät [bə'zɛ:t] *adj fig.* covered (*mit* with).

Besatz [bə'zats] *m* (-es; ~e) trimming(s).

Be'satzung *f* (-; -en) **1.** 𝕏 a) occupying forces, b) garrison. **2.** ✈, ⚓ crew.

Be'satzungs|macht *f* occupying power. **~streitkräfte** *pl* occupying forces.

be'saufen: *sich* ~ (besoff, besoffen, h) F get sloshed. **Be'säufnis** [bə'zɔyfnɪs] *n* (-ses; -se) F booze-up.

be'schädigen v/t (h) damage.

Be'schädigung *f* (-; -en) **1.** damaging. **2.** *a. pl* damage (*gen* to).

be'schaffen v/t (h) *j-m et.* ~ get (*or* procure) s.o. s.th.; (*sich*) *et.* ~ get s.th.

Be'schaffenheit *f* (-; *no pl*) condition, state, quality, nature.

Be'schaffung *f* (-; *no pl*) procurement.

beschäftigen [bə'ʃɛftɪgən] (h) **I** v/t **1.** *j-n* ~ occupy s.o., keep s.o. busy. **2.** employ. **3.** occupy, *problem:* preoccupy, be on *s.o.'s* mind. **II** *sich* ~ (*mit*) be busy (with), work (at); *sich mit e-m Problem etc* ~ deal with a problem *etc*. **be'schäftigt** *adj* **1.** busy. **2.** employed (*bei* with). **Be'schäftigte** *m, f* (-n; -n) employee. **Be'schäftigung** *f* (-; -en) **1.** occupation, work, activity: *sie muß* ~ *haben* she must have s.th. to do. **2.** employment, job: *ohne* ~ unemployed, out of work. **Be'schäftigungstherapie** *f* occupational therapy.

be'schälen v/t (h) cover (*mare*).

be'schämen v/t (h) *j-n* ~ a) shame s.o., b) put s.o. to shame. **be'schämend** *adj* shameful. **be'schämt** *adj* ashamed (*über acc* of). **Be'schämung** *f* (-; *no pl*) shame: *zu m-r* ~ to my shame.

be'schatten v/t (h) *fig.* shadow.

be'schauen v/t (h) (*a. sich et.* ~) (have a) look at. **be'schaulich** *adj* contemplative, tranquil.

Bescheid [bə'ʃaɪt] *m* (-[e]s; -e) answer, *adm.* notice, information (*über acc* about): ~ *bekommen* be informed; *j-m* ~ *geben* let s.o. know (*über acc* about); F *j-m* ~ *stoßen*, *j-m gehörig* ~ *sagen* give s.o. a piece of one's mind; ~ *wissen* a) be informed (*über acc* of), b) *mit, in* (*dat*) know all about, c) be in the know, *iro.* know the score.

bescheiden¹ [bə'ʃaɪdən] (beschied, beschieden, h) **I** v/t **1.** *adm.* notify: → *abschlägig.* **2.** *es war ihm nicht beschieden zu inf* it was not granted to him to *inf.* **II** *sich* ~ be content (*mit* with).

be'scheiden² *adj* a. *fig.* modest.

Be'scheidenheit *f* (-; *no pl*) modesty.

be'scheinen v/t (beschien, beschienen, h) shine on.

bescheinigen [bə'ʃaɪnɪgən] v/t (h) certify: *j-m et.* ~ a. *iro.* attest s.o. s.th.; *den Empfang* ~ (*gen or von*) a) acknowledge receipt of, b) give a receipt for; *hiermit wird bescheinigt, daß ...* this is to certify that ...

Be'scheinigung f (-; -en) **1.** no pl attestation, certification. **2.** certificate.

be'scheißen v/t (beschiß, beschissen, h) V **j-n ~** cheat (or do) s.o. (**um** out of).

be'schenken v/t (h) **j-n ~** give s.o. a present; **j-n mit et. ~** give s.o. s.th.

be'scheren v/t (h) **j-m et. ~** give (fig. bring) s.o. s.th. **Be'scherung** f (-; -en) distribution of (Christmas) presents: fig. **e-e schöne ~!** a fine mess!; **da haben wir die ~!** there you are!; F **die ganze ~** the whole bag of tricks.

bescheuert [bə'ʃɔʏərt] → **bekloppt**.

be'schichten v/t (h) ⊙ coat.

be'schicken v/t (h) **1.** exhibit at (a fair). **2.** send delegates to. **3.** ⊙ charge.

beschied [bə'ʃiːt] pret, **beschieden** [bə'ʃiːdən] pp of **bescheiden¹**.

beschien [bə'ʃiːn] pret, **be'schienen** pp of **bescheinen**.

be'schießen v/t (beschoß, beschossen, h) a) fire at, b) bombard (a. phys.).

be'schildern v/t (h) ⊙ signpost.

Be'schilderung f (-; -en) **1.** signposting. **2.** signposts.

be'schimpfen v/t (h) call s.o. names. **Be'schimpfung** f (-; -en) abuse.

beschiß [bə'ʃɪs] V pret of **bescheißen**. **Be'schiß** m (-sses; no pl) V **1.** swindle, rip-off. **2.** frost. **be'schissen** V pp of **bescheißen**. **II** adj lousy, rotten.

Be'schlag m (-[e]s; ⸱e) **1.** usu. pl metal fitting(s). **2.** a) condensation, b) film. **3.** **in ~ nehmen, mit ~ belegen** F grab, monopolize. **be'schlagen** v/t (beschlug, beschlagen, h) **I** v/t **1.** put metal fittings on. **2.** shoe (a horse). **3.** steam up. **II** **sich ~** a) mirror etc: steam up, b) metal: oxidize, c) go mo(u)ldy. **III** adj **gut ~ sein in** (dat) be well up in.

Be'schlagenheit f (-; no pl) sound knowledge (**in** dat of).

Beschlagnahme [bə'ʃlaːknaːmə] f (-; -n) seizure, confiscation.

be'schlagnahmen v/t (h) **1.** seize, confiscate. **2.** → **Beschlag** 3.

beschleunigen [bə'ʃlɔʏnɪɡən] v/t, v/i (h) (a. **sich**) accelerate (a. mot., phys.), speed up: **s-e Schritte ~** quicken one's steps; **das Tempo ~** speed up. **Be'schleuniger** m (-s; -) ⊙, phys. accelerator. **Be'schleunigung** f (-; -en) acceleration (a. mot., phys.), speeding up. **be'schleunigungs'spur** f mot. accele-

ration lane. **~vermögen** n (-s; no pl) mot. acceleration.

be'schließen v/t (beschloß, beschlossen, h) **1.** (**zu** inf to inf) decide, make up one's mind. **2.** close, end, settle.

be'schlossen adj agreed, settled.

beschlug [bə'ʃluːk] pret of **beschlagen**.

be'schluß m (-sses; ⸱sse) decision, resolution: **e-n ~ fassen** parl. pass a resolution. **be'schlußfähig** adj **~ sein** constitute a quorum; **die Versammlung** etc **ist** (**nicht**) **~** there is a (no) quorum.

be'schmieren v/t (h) smear.

be'schmutzen v/t (h) dirty, soil, fig. sully; → **Nest** 1.

be'schneiden v/t (beschnitt, beschnitten, h) **1.** trim, prune, curl. **2.** ✶ circumcise. **3.** fig. cut (down), curtail.

Be'schneidung f (-; -en) **1.** trimming (etc). **2.** ✶ circumcision. **3.** fig. curtailment, cut, reduction.

be'schnüffeln v/t (h), **be'schnuppern** v/t (h) sniff at: F fig. sich (gegenseitig) **~** take stock of each other.

beschönigen [bə'ʃøːnɪɡən] v/t (h) palliate, gloss over: **~d** palliative.

Be'schönigung f (-; -en) palliation.

be'schränken [bə'ʃrɛŋkən] (h) **I** v/t (**auf** acc to) limit, restrict. **II** **sich ~ auf** (acc) confine o.s. to, matter: be confined to. **be'schränkt** adj **1.** limited, restricted. **2.** contp. a) dense, b) narrow-minded. **Be'schränktheit** f (-; no pl) **1.** limitedness. **2.** contp. stupidity, narrow-mindedness. **Be'schränkung** f (-; -en) (**auf** acc to) limitation, restriction.

be'schreiben v/t (beschrieb, beschrieben, h) **1.** write on. **2.** describe (a. ⅋): **nicht zu ~** indescribable.

Be'schreibung f (-; -en) **1.** (**das spottet jeder ~** that beggars description. **2.** ⊙ specification.

be'schreiten v/t (beschritt, beschritten, h) walk on: fig. **neue Wege ~** tread new paths.

beschrieb [bə'ʃriːp] pret, **beschrieben** [bə'ʃriːbən] pp of **beschreiben**.

beschriften [bə'ʃrɪftən] v/t (h) a) inscribe, b) mark (boxes), label (goods).

Be'schriftung f (-; -en) inscription.

beschritt [bə'ʃrɪt] pret, **be'schritten** pp of **beschreiten**.

beschuldigen [bə'ʃʊldɪɡən] *v/t* (h) *j-n ~*
accuse s.o. (*gen* of). **Be'schuldigte** *m, f*
(-n; -n) accused. **Be'schuldigung** *f* (-;
-en) accusation, charge.

be'schummeln *v/t* (h) F *j-n (um et.) ~*
cheat s.o. (out of s.th.).

Be'schuß *m* (-sses; *no pl*) fire, bombard-
ment (*a. phys.*): *unter ~ geraten a. fig.*
come under fire; *unter ~ nehmen* a) →
beschießen, b) *fig.* attack.

be'schützen *v/t* (h) protect (*vor dat,
gegen* from). **Be'schützer** *m* (-s; -)
protector. **Be'schützerin** *f* (-; -nen)
protectress.

be'schwatzen *v/t* (h) *j-n ~, et. zu tun*
coax s.o. to do (*or* into doing) s.th.

Beschwerde [bə'ʃveːrdə] *f* (-; -en) **1.**
trouble, *☞ usu. pl* complaint: *sein Herz
macht ihm ~n* his heart is giving him
trouble. **2.** complaint (*über acc* about),
☞ appeal (*gegen* from). *~buch* n complaints book. *☞frei adj ☞* free of pain.
~führer(in f) *m ☞* complainant.

beschweren [bə'ʃveːrən] (h) **I** *v/t* **1.**
weight. **2.** *fig.* weigh down. **II** *sich ~*
complain (*über acc* about, of, *bei* to).

be'schwerlich *adj* onerous, tiring.

beschwichtigen [bə'ʃvɪçtɪɡən] *v/t* (h)
appease (*a. pol.*), calm down, placate.
Be'schwichtigungspoli,tik *f* policy of
appeasement.

be'schwindeln *v/t* (h) *j-n ~* lie to s.o.

beschwingt [bə'ʃvɪŋt] *adj* elated, buoyant, lively, lilting (*melody*).

be'schwipst *adj* F tipsy, merry.

be'schwören *v/t* (beschwor, beschwo-
ren, h) **1.** *esp.* *☞* swear to. **2.** a) conjure
up (*ghosts, a. fig.*), b) exorcize. **3.** *j-n ~*
implore s.o. **Be'schwörung** *f* (-; -en) **1.**
entreaty. **2.** a) invocation, b) exorcism.

beseelt [bə'zeːlt] *adj* (*von* with) inspired,
filled.

be'sehen *v/t* (besah, besehen, h) (*a. sich
et. ~*) have a look at, examine.

beseitigen [bə'zaɪtɪɡən] *v/t* (h) remove,
dispose of, *fig. a.* eliminate: *j-n ~* do
away with s.o. **Be'seitigung** *f* (-; *no pl*)
removal, disposal, *fig. a.* elimination.

Besen ['beːzən] *m* (-s; -) **1.** broom,
brush: *fig. neue ~ kehren gut* a new
broom sweeps clean; F *ich fresse e-n ~,
wenn ...* I'll eat my hat if ... **2.** *contp.*
(old) hag. **'Besenstiel** *m* broomstick.

besessen [bə'zɛsən] **I** *pp of* **besitzen.** **II**

adj **1.** (*von*) possessed (by), *fig. a.* obsessed (with). **2.** frantic: *wie ~* like mad.
Be'sessenheit *f* (-; *no pl*) *fig.* obsession.

be'setzen *v/t* (h) **1.** take (*a seat*), occupy
(*country, house, etc*). **2.** fill (*a post*): *wir
wollen diesen Posten mit e-r Frau ~*
we want to put a woman in this posi-
tion. **3.** *thea.* cast: *neu ~* recast. **4.** trim
dress (*mit* with). **be'setzt** *adj* **1.** occupied (*a. ✕, pol.*), seat: *a.* taken, *bus etc*:
full (up). **2.** *thea. das Stück ist gut
besetzt* the play is well cast. **3.** *teleph.*
engaged, *Am.* busy. **4.** *☞ ~ mit* court *etc*
composed of. **Be'setztzeichen** *n*
teleph. engaged (*Am.* busy) signal.

Be'setzung *f* (-; -en) **1.** occupation. **2.** a)
filling (*of post*), b) staff, c) composition
(*of court, team*), d) entrants. **3.** *thea.* a)
casting, b) cast.

besichtigen [bə'zɪçtɪɡən] *v/t* (h) view,
inspect, visit, see: *zu ~ sein* be on view.
Be'sichtigung *f* (-; -en) inspection (*a.
✕*), visit (*gen* to): *~ von Sehenswürdigkeiten* sight-seeing.

be'siedeln *v/t* (h) settle, colonize: *dicht
(dünn) besiedelt* densely (sparsely)
populated. **Be'sied(e)lung** *f* (-; -en)
settlement, colonization.

be'siegeln *v/t* (h) *a. fig.* seal.

be'siegen *v/t* (h) defeat, beat, *fig.* overcome, conquer. **Be'siegte** *m, f* (-n; -n)
the defeated, loser.

be'singen *v/t* (besang, besungen, h) **1.**
sing (of). **2.** *e-e Platte etc ~* make a
record *etc*.

be'sinnen: *sich ~* (besann, besonnen, h)
1. reflect, think: *ohne sich zu ~* without thinking twice; *sich anders ~*
change one's mind; *sich e-s Besseren
~* think better of it. **2.** *sich auf j-n (et.) ~*
remember s.o. (s.th.).

be'sinnlich *adj* contemplative.

Be'sinnung *f* (-; *no pl*) **1.** (*die ~ verlieren* lose) consciousness; *wieder zur ~
kommen* regain consciousness, *fig.*
come to one's senses; *fig. j-n zur ~ bringen* bring s.o. to his senses. **2.** (*auf acc*)
contemplation (of), reflection (on).

be'sinnungslos *adj* unconscious.

Be'sinnungslosigkeit *f* (-; *no pl*) unconsciousness.

Besitz [bə'zɪts] *m* (-es; *no pl*) **1.** possession (*gen, an dat, von* of): *~ ergreifen
von* a) *a. in ~ nehmen* take possession

of, b) *fig.* take hold of *s.o.*; **im ~ sein von** (*or gen*) be in possession of; → **gelangen** l. **2.** possession(s), property, estate. **be'sitzanzeigend** *adj* **~es Fürwort** possessive pronoun. **besitzen** *v/t* (besaß, besessen, h) possess, own, have. **Be'sitzer** *m* (-s; -), **Be'sitzerin** *f* (-; -nen) possessor, owner, holder (*of passport etc*): **den Besitzer wechseln** change hands. **Be'sitzergreifung** *f* (-; *no pl*) (von) taking possession, seizure. **be'sitzlos** *adj* unpropertied.

Be'sitztum *n* (-s; ⸚er), **Be'sitzung** *f* (-; -en) possession(s), property, estate.

besoff [bə'zɔf] *pret of* **besaufen**.

be'soffen I *pp of* **besaufen. II** *adj* F sloshed, plastered.

besohlen [bə'zo:lən] *v/t* (h) sole.

besolden [bə'zɔldən] *v/t* (h) pay.

be'soldet *adj* salaried.

Be'soldung *f* (-; -en) pay, salary.

besonder [bə'zɔndər] *adj* **1.** a) special, particular, specific, b) exceptional, great (*joy, hono[u]r*): **nichts Besonderes** nothing unusual; **in diesem ~en Fall** in this particular case. **2.** separate. **Be'sonderheit** *f* (-; -en) special quality (*or* feature). **be'sonders** *adv* **1.** especially, particularly, above all. **2.** exceptionally. **3.** very much.

besonnen [bə'zɔnən] **I** *pp of* **besinnen. II** *adj* sensible, level-headed, calm. **Be'sonnenheit** *f* (-; *no pl*) level-headedness, calmness.

be'sorgen *v/t* (h) **1.** **j-m et. ~** get s.o. s.th., provide s.o. with s.th.; **sich et. ~** get (*or* buy) s.th.; F **dem werde ich's ~!** I'll give him what for! **2.** see to, deal with, manage (*household*): F **wird besorgt!** will do! **Besorgnis** [bə'zɔrknıs] *f* (-; -se) anxiety. **be'sorgniserregend** *adj* alarming, worrying. **be'sorgt I** *pp of* **besorgen. II** *adj* (**um** about) worried, concerned. **Be'sorgtheit** *f* (-; *no pl*) **1.** anxiety. **2.** (**um** for) solicitude. **Be'sorgung** *f* (-; -en) **1.** *no pl* procurement. **2.** a) purchase, b) errand: **~en machen** go shopping. **3.** *no pl* (*gen*) dealing (with), management (of).

be'spannen *v/t* (h) **1.** cover (*with silk etc*). **2.** string (*violin etc*). **Be'spannung** *f* (-; -en) **1.** cover. **2.** strings.

be'spielen *v/t* (h) **ein Tonband** *etc* (**mit et.**) **~** record (s.th.) on tape *etc*.

be'spielt *adj* prerecorded (*cassette etc*).

be'spitzeln *v/t* (h) **j-n ~** spy on s.o.

be'sprechen *v/t* (besprach, besprochen, h) **1.** discuss, talk *s.th.* over: **sich mit j-m ~** discuss the matter (*or* talk things over) with s.o. **2.** review. **3.** record *s.th.* on tape *etc*. **4.** ✝ cure by magic formulas. **Be'sprechung** *f* (-; -en) **1.** discussion. **2.** meeting, conference: **er ist in e-r ~** he is in conference. **3.** review. **Be'sprechungsexem,plar** *n* review copy.

be'sprengen *v/t* (h) sprinkle, spray.

be'spritzen *v/t* (h) spatter, splash.

besprochen [bə'ʃprɔxən] *pp of* **besprechen.**

be'spucken *v/t* (h) spit at, spit on.

besser ['bɛsər] *adj and adv* better (**als** than): *contp.* **e-e ~e Scheune** a glorified barn; **immer ~** better and better; **um so ~** so much the better; (**oder**) **~ gesagt** or rather; **~ ist ~** let's keep on the safe side; **~ werden** improve, get better; **es geht ihm heute ~** he is better today; **es geht (wirtschaftlich) ~** things are looking up; **er ist ~ dran als ich** he is better off than me; **ich weiß es ~** I know better; **er täte ~ (daran) zu gehen** he had better go; **Besseres zu tun haben** have more important things to do; **j-n e-s Besseren belehren** set s.o. right, *w.s.* open s.o.'s eyes; → **besinnen** 1, **Hälfte.**

'bessergestellt *adj* better-off.

'bessern (h) **I** *v/t* **1.** improve. **2.** reform (*s.o.*). **II sich ~ 3.** improve. **4.** mend one's ways.

'Besserung *f* (-; *no pl*) improvement: ✝ **auf dem Wege der ~** on the way to recovery; **gute ~!** I hope you feel better soon!

'Besserwisser *m* (-s; -) know-(it-)all.

bestach [bə'ʃta:x] *pret of* **bestechen.**

bestahl [bə'ʃta:l] *pret of* **bestehlen.**

Bestallung [bə'ʃtalʊŋ] *f* (-; -en) appointment.

bestand [bə'ʃtant] *pret of* **bestehen.**

Be'stand *m* (-[e]s; ⸚e) **1.** *no pl* a) (continued) existence, b) duration: **von ~ sein, ~ haben** be lasting, last; **k-n ~ haben** be short-lived, ⚖ not to be valid (in law). **2.** (**an** *dat of*) stock, supplies, ✚, *zo.* population; → **eisern. 3.** ✝ a) assets, b) (stock) holdings, c) cash in hand, d) stock on hand, e) inventory. **4.** rolling stock, fleet. **5.** ✗ (effective) strength.

bestanden [bə'ʃtandən] *pp of* **bestehen.**

be'ständig *adj* **1.** constant, lasting. **2.** steady (*a.* ✝ *demand etc*), stable, settled (*weather*). **3.** resistant (*gegen* to).

Be'ständigkeit *f* (-; *no pl*) **1.** constancy, lastingness. **2.** steadiness, stability. **3.** resistance (*gegen* to).

Be'standsaufnahme *f* (-; -n) ✝ stock-taking, *Am.* inventory: *e-e ~ machen a. fig.* take stock.

Be'standteil *m* (-[e]s; -e) a) part, component, constituent (part), b) element, c) ingredient: → **auflösen** 1.

be'stärken *v/t* (h) (*in dat* in) a) confirm, strengthen, b) encourage.

bestätigen [bə'ʃtɛːtɪgən] (h) **I** *v/t* a) confirm (*a.* ✝ *an order*), b) acknowledge (receipt of), c) certify. **II** *sich ~* be confirmed, prove true.

Be'stätigung *f* (-; -en) **1.** confirmation, acknowledgement. **2.** a) letter of confirmation, b) certificate.

bestatten [bə'ʃtatən] *v/t* (h) bury.

Be'stattung *f* (-; -en) funeral, burial.

Be'stattungsinsti,tut *n* undertakers, *Am.* funeral home.

be'stäuben *v/t* (h) **1.** dust, spray. **2.** ❀ pollinate. **Be'stäubung** *f* (-; -en) **1.** spraying, dusting. **2.** ❀ pollination.

be'staunen *v/t* (h) marvel at.

beste ['bɛstə] *adj and adv* best: *mein ~r Freund* my best friend; *der (die) erste ~* the first comer; *das erste ~* the first thing; *am ~n wissen etc* know *etc* best; *am ~n, wir besuchen ihn* the best thing to do would be to call on him; *im ~n Fall* at best; *im ~n Alter, in den ~n Jahren* in the prime of life; *in ~m Zustand* in perfect condition; *mit ~m Dank* with many thanks; *(von) ~r Qualität* of first-class quality; *e-e Geschichte (ein Lied) zum ~n geben* tell a story (oblige with a song); *j-n zum ~n haben* pull s.o.'s leg; *sein Bestes tun (or geben)* do one's best; *das Beste daraus machen* make the best of it; *... sind nicht die ~n* ... are not of the best; → *bestens, Kraft* 1.

be'stechen *v/t* (bestach, bestochen, h) **1.** bribe: *sich ~ lassen* take bribes. **2.** *fig. a. v/i* impress (*durch* by). **be'stechend** *adj fig.* impressive, brilliant.

be'stechlich *adj* corrupt(ible).

Be'stechlichkeit *f* (-; *no pl*) corruptibility. **Be'stechung** *f* (-; -en) bribery: *passive ~* taking of bribes.

Be'stechungs|af,färe *f* corruption scandal. *~geld n* bribe money. *~versuch m* attempted bribery.

Besteck *n* (-[e]s; -e) **1.** knife, fork and spoon, *coll. or ~e* cutlery. **2.** ✂ (set of) instruments.

be'stehen (bestand, bestanden, h) **I** *v/t* **1.** go (*or* come) through, win (*fight*), pass (*exam*): *nicht ~* fail; *fig. die Probe ~* stand the test. **II** *v/i* **2.** a) exist, be, b) continue, last, c) remain, survive, have survived. **3.** *~ aus* be made of, consist of (*a. fig.*). **4.** *~ auf* (*dat*) insist on; *ich bestehe darauf(, daß du kommst)* I insist (on your coming). **5.** pass.

Be'stehen *n* (-s) **1.** existence: *seit ~ der Firma* ever since the firm was founded; *das 50jährige ~ feiern* celebrate the fiftieth anniversary. **2.** passing. **3.** insistence (*auf* on).

be'stehenbleiben *v/i* (*irr, sep*, -ge-, sn, → *bleiben*) continue (to exist), survive.

be'stehend *adj* existing, present.

be'stehlen *v/t* (bestahl, bestohlen, h) rob, steal from.

be'steigen *v/t* (bestieg, bestiegen, h) climb (up), ascend (*mountain etc*), mount (*horse etc*), board (*train etc*).

Be'steigung *f* (-; -en) ascent.

Bestellbuch [bə'ʃtɛl-] *n* ✝ order book.

be'stellen *v/t* (h) **1.** order (*a.* ✝), book (*room*), call (*taxi*). **2.** *j-n* (*zu sich*) *~* ask s.o. to come, send for s.o. **3.** *j-m e-e Nachricht etc ~* give (*or* send) s.o. a message *etc*; *kann ich et. ~?* can I take a message? **4.** ✒ cultivate. **5.** → *ernennen.* **6.** *es ist schlecht um ihn etc bestellt* things are looking bad for him *etc.* **7.** F *fig. er hat nicht viel zu ~* he doesn't rate high (*bei* with).

Be'steller *m* (-s; -) ✝ orderer, buyer.

Be'stell|karte *f*, *~schein m* order form. **Be'stellung** *f* (-; -en) **1.** order: *auf ~ gemacht* made to order, *Am.* custom-made. **2.** message. **3.** ✒ cultivation. **4.** → *Ernennung.*

'besten'falls *adv* at best.

'bestens *adv* extremely well: *(ich) danke ~!* thank you very much!; F *ist ja ~!* that's just great!

be'steuern v/t (h) tax.
Be'steuerung f (-; -en) taxation.
bestialisch [bɛs'tĭaːlɪʃ] adj atrocious, F fig. a. awful.
Bestie ['bɛstĭə] f (-; -n) beast, fig. brute.
bestieg [bəˈʃtiːk] pret, bestiegen [bəˈʃtiːɡən] pp of besteigen.
be'stimmen (h) I v/t 1. a) determine, b) decide, c) fix (date, price, etc). 2. order, decide: er hat (dabei) nichts zu ~ he has no say (in this matter). 3. contract, law: provide. 4. determine (a policy etc): bestimmt werden durch (or von) be determined by, depend on. 5. intend (für, zu for): j-n zu s-m Nachfolger ~ name s.o. as one's successor; → bestimmt 3. 6. a) a. ℞, phys etc: determine, b) define. II v/i 7. give orders: hier bestimme ich! F I'm the boss here! 8. ~ über (acc) dispose over.
be'stimmend adj determinant (factor etc), ling. determinative.
be'stimmt I pp of bestimmen. II adj 1. a) certain (day, number, etc), b) special (plan etc), c) definite: et. Bestimmtes something (or anything) special (or definite). 2. determined, firm. 3. ~ sein a) für be meant for, b) zu et. be destined for (or to be). 4. (nach for) ✈ destined, ✈, ⚓ bound. II adv 5. certainly, for certain: (ganz) ~ definitely; ~ wissen, daß know for sure that; er kommt ~ he is sure to come; ich kann es nicht ~ sagen I can't say with certainty. 6. firmly, categorically.
Be'stimmtheit f (-; no pl) a) certainty, b) firmness: mit ~ → bestimmt II.
Be'stimmung f (-; -en) 1. no pl (gen) decision (on), fixing (of date etc). 2. regulation, rule, provision. 3. a) a. ℞, phys., etc: determination, b) definition. 4. no pl intended purpose: et. s-r ~ übergeben inaugurate s.th., open s.th. to the public. 5. ling. qualification: adverbiale ~ adverbial element. 6. no pl fate, destiny.
Be'stimmungs|bahnhof m station of destination. ꝰgemäß adj and adv as directed. ~flughafen m airport of destination. ~ort m (place of) destination.
'Bestleistung f sports: best performance: persönliche ~ personal best.
'Bestmarke f sports: record.
best'möglich adj best possible.

bestochen [bəˈʃtɔxən] pp of bestechen.
bestohlen [bəˈʃtoːlən] pp of bestehlen.
be'strafen v/t (h) punish (wegen, für for), a. sports: penalize, 🏛 a. sentence (mit to). Be'strafung f (-; -en) punishment, a. sports: penalty.
be'strahlen v/t (h) 1. shine on, illuminate. 2. phys. irradiate, ✚ a. give s.o. ray treatment. Be'strahlung f (-; -en) phys. irradiation, ✚ a. ray treatment.
bestrebt [bəˈʃtreːpt] adj ~ sein zu inf endeavo(u)r (or strive, be anxious) to inf. Be'strebung f (-; -en) effort, endeavo(u)r.
be'streichen v/t (bestrich, bestrichen, h) ~ mit spread s.th. on; mit Butter ~ butter.
be'streiken v/t (h) go out (or be) on strike against. be'streikt I pp of bestreiken. II adj strike-bound.
be'streiten v/t (bestritt, bestritten, h) 1. a) dispute, contest, b) deny. 2. bear, meet, pay (for) (expenses etc). 3. fill (program[me]): sie bestritt die Unterhaltung allein she did all the talking.
be'streuen v/t (h) strew: mit Salz etc ~ sprinkle with salt etc.
bestrich [bəˈʃtrɪç] pret, be'strichen pp of bestreichen.
be'stritt [bəˈʃtrɪt] pret, be'stritten pp of bestreiten.
'Bestseller m (-s; -) best seller.
be'stücken [bəˈʃtʏkən] v/t (h) ⚓, ✕ arm (with guns), w.s. equip (mit with).
Be'stuhlung f (-; -en) seating.
be'stürmen v/t (h) 1. storm. ✈ fig. a) urge, b) implore, c) bombard (mit with questions etc).
be'stürzen v/t (h) dismay. be'stürzend adj dismaying. be'stürzt adj dismayed (über acc at). Be'stürzung f (-; no pl) (zu s-r etc ~ to his etc) dismay.
Besuch [bəˈzuːx] m (-[e]s; -e) 1. a) visit (gen, bei, in dat to), call (bei j-m on s.o., at s.o.'s house etc), b) stay (bei at): auf ~, zu ~ on a visit; bei j-m zu ~ sein be staying with s.o.; e-n ~ machen bei → besuchen 1. 2. (gen) attendance (at school etc). 3. visitor(s), guest(s), company. be'suchen v/t (h) 1. go and see, visit, pay a visit to, call on. 2. a) visit (place), go to, a. frequent (restaurant etc), b) go to, attend (school, meeting, etc): gut besucht well attended.

Be'sucher *m* (-s; -), **Be'sucherin** *f* (-; -nen) a) visitor (*gen* to), caller, b) guest, c) spectator.

Be'suchszeit *f* visiting hours.

be'sudeln *v/t* (h) soil, *fig.* sully.

besungen [bə'zʊŋən] *pp of* **besingen.**

Betablocker ['be:tablɔkər] *m* (-s; -) 🦴 beta blocker.

betagt [bə'ta:kt] *adj* aged, old.

be'tasten *v/t* (h) feel, touch.

betätigen [bə'tɛ:tɪgən] (h) **I** *v/t* ⚙ operate (*machine*), actuate (*button, lever, etc*), apply (*brake*). **II sich ~** (*in dat* in) be active, work, busy o.s.; *sich ~ als* act (*or* work) as; *sich politisch* (*sportlich*) ~ be active in politics (do sports).

Be'tätigung *f* (-; -en) **1.** activity, work, job: *körperliche* ~ (physical) exercise. **2.** ⚙ actuation, operation.

Be'tätigungsfeld *n* field (of activity), *w.s.* outlet.

betäuben [bə'tɔybən] (h) **I** *v/t* a) *fig.* stun, daze, b) make *s.o.* unconscious, F knock *s.o.* out, c) deafen, d) intoxicate, e) 🦴 an(a)esthetize, deaden: *fig. wie betäubt* stunned. **II sich ~** *fig.* seek consolation (*mit, durch* in). **Be'täubung** *f* (-; -en) **1.** stunning (*etc*). **2.** daze. **3.** a) an(a)esthetization, b) (*örtliche*) ~ (local) an(a)esthesia. **Be'täubungsmittel** *n* narcotic, 🦴 *a.* an(a)esthetic.

Bete ['be:tə] *f* (-; -n) 🌿 beet: *rote* ~ beetroot.

beteiligen [bə'taɪlɪgən] (h) **I** *v/t j-n ~* (*an dat* in) a) *a.* 🟰 give s.o. a share, b) let s.o. take part; *beteiligt sein* (*an dat*) participate (in), 🟰 have a share (in), share (in *the profit*), be involved (in *an accident etc*), 🟰🟰 be a party (to). **II sich ~** (*an dat*) a) participate (in), b) contribute (to), help (in); *sich an den Kosten ~* share (in) the expenses.

Be'teiligte *m, f* (-n, -n) person concerned (*or* involved). **Be'teiligung** *f* (-; -en) **1.** participation. **2.** (*an dat* in) interest, share. **3.** 🟰 a) investment, b) holding(s), c) partnership. **4.** (*an dat* at) attendance, turnout (*at election etc*).

beten ['be:tən] *v/i* (h) pray (*um* for), say a prayer.

beteuern [bə'tɔyərn] *v/t* (h) protest (*s-e Unschuld* one's innocence), swear to, *a.* 🟰🟰 affirm (solemnly).

Be'teuerung *f* (-; -en) protestation, *a.* 🟰🟰 solemn affirmation.

betiteln [bə'ti:təln] *v/t* (h) **1.** entitle (*book etc*). **2.** F *contp. j-n ... ~* call s.o. ...

Beton [be'tɔŋ] *m* (-s; -s, -e) concrete.

betonen [bə'to:nən] *v/t* (h) *a. fig.* stress, emphasize.

betonieren [beto'ni:rən] *v/t* (h) concrete. **Be'tonklotz** *m* **1.** concrete block. **2.** *contp.* concrete pile. **Be'tonmischma,schine** *f* cement mixer.

be'tont I *pp of* **betonen. II** *adj fig.* emphatic, marked: *mit ~er Gleichgültigkeit* with studied (*or* marked) indifference. **III** *adv* markedly. **Be'tonung** *f* (-; -en) *a. fig.* stress, emphasis.

betören [bə'tø:rən] *v/t* (h) bewitch, turn *s.o.'s* head.

Betracht [bə'traxt] *in ~ ziehen* take into consideration; *außer ~ lassen* disregard; (*nicht*) *in ~ kommen* be a possibility (be out of the question).

be'trachten *v/t* (h) look at, *fig. a.* view: *j-n als Freund ~* look upon s.o. as (*or* consider s.o.) a friend; *genau betrachtet* strictly speaking. **Be'trachter** *m* (-s; -), **Be'trachterin** *f* (-; -nen) viewer, observer. **beträchtlich** [bə'trɛçtlɪç] *adj* considerable. **Be'trachtung** *f* (-; -en) **1.** *no pl* view (*gen* of). **2.** reflection: *~en anstellen über* (*acc*) reflect on; *bei näherer ~* on closer inspection.

betraf [bə'tra:f] *pret of* **betreffen.**

Betrag [bə'tra:k] *m* (-[e]s; *~*e) amount, sum: *im ~e von* to the amount of.

be'tragen (betrug, betragen, h) **I** *v/i* amount to, total. **II sich ~** behave.

Be'tragen *n* (-s) behavio(u)r, conduct.

betrank [bə'traŋk] *pret of* **betrinken.**

betrat [bə'tra:t] *pret of* **betreten².**

be'trauen *v/t* (h) entrust (*mit* with).

be'trauern *v/t* (h) mourn.

Betreff [bə'trɛf] *m* (-[e]s; -e) 🟰 reference, *in letters:* (*abbr. Betr.*) re: ... **be'treffen** *v/t* (betraf, betroffen, h) **1.** a) concern, b) refer to: *was mich betrifft* as for me, as far as I am concerned; *was das betrifft* as to that. **2.** affect: → **betroffen** 2. **be'treffend** *adj* **1.** concerning. **2.** concerned: *die ~e Person* the person concerned (*or* in question); *das ~e Buch* the book referred to.

be'treiben *v/t* (betrieb, betrieben, h) **1.** pursue, manage, run (*enterprise etc*), go in for, do (*sports*). **2.** ⚙ operate, run. **Be'treiben** n (-s) *auf* ~ *von* (*or gen*) at the instigation of. **Be'treiber** m (-s; -) person (*pl* body) running an enterprise.

be'treten¹ adj embarrassed, awkward.

be'treten² v/t (betrat, betreten, h) **1.** step on (to). **2.** enter. **Be'treten** n (-s) ~ *verboten!* keep off!, no entrance!

betreuen [bə'trɔʏən] v/t (h) look after, attend to, *sports*: coach, ✝ serve (*area*). **Be'treuer** m (-s; -), **Be'treuerin** f (-; -nen) s.o. who looks after s.o. (*or* s.th.), *sports*: coach. **Be'treuung** f (-; *no pl*) care (*von or gen* of, for).

betrieb [bə'triːp] *pret of* **betreiben**.

Be'trieb m (-[e]s; -e) **1.** enterprise, company, business, firm, factory, works, plant: *öffentliche* ~*e* public utilities. **2.** *no pl* a) management, running, b) ⚙ operation: *in* ~ working, in operation; *außer* ~ a) not working, b) out of order; *in* ~ *setzen* put into operation, start; *außer* ~ *setzen* put out of action. **3.** *no pl* F a) activity, bustle, b) (heavy) traffic: *wir hatten heute viel* ~ we were very busy today.

betrieben [bə'triːbən] *pp of* **betreiben**.

be'trieblich adj internal, company.

be'triebsam adj active, busy. **Be'triebsamkeit** f (-; *no pl*) activity, bustle.

Be'triebs|angehörige m, f employee. **~anleitung** f operating instructions. **~ausflug** m (annual) work outing. **2blind** adj routine-blinded. **2eigen** adj company(-owned). **2fähig** adj in (good) working condition. **~ferien** pl works holidays. **~fest** n company fête. **2fremd** adj outside ...: ~*e Person* outsider. **~geheimnis** n trade secret. **2in,tern** adj internal. **~kapi,tal** n working capital. **~klima** n work climate. **~kosten** pl running costs. **~leiter** m works (*or* production) manager. **~ob**- **mann** m works steward. **~rat** m (member of the) works council. **2sicher** adj fail-safe, reliable (in service). **~sicherheit** f safety (in operation); reliability. **~stillegung** f closure, shutdown. **~störung** f ⚙ stoppage, breakdown. **~sy,stem** n computer: operating system. **~unfall** m industrial accident. **~verfassung** f industrial-relations scheme. **~versammlung** f works meeting. **~wirt** m graduate in business man-

agement. **~wirtschaft** f (-; *no pl*) business management. **~zugehörigkeit** f (period of) employment: *nach zehn-jähriger* ~ after ten years(' employment) with the company.

be'trinken: *sich* ~ (betrank, betrunken, h) get drunk.

betroffen [bə'trɔfən] **I** *pp of* **betreffen**. **II** adj **1.** shocked, dismayed, *pred* taken aback. **2.** affected (*von* by): *die* ~*en Personen* the persons concerned. **Be'troffenheit** f (-; *no pl*) (*über acc* at) dismay, shock.

betrog [bə'troːk] *pret*, **betrogen** [bə'troːgən] *pp of* **betrügen**.

be'trüben v/t (h) sadden.

betrüblich [bə'tryːplɪç] adj sad.

be'trübt adj sad (*über acc* at, about).

betrug [bə'truːk] *pret of* **betragen**.

Be'trug m (-[e]s; *no pl*) cheat, swindle, 𝖟𝖟 fraud, deception. **be'trügen** v/t, v/i (betrog, betrogen, h) cheat, swindle, 𝖟𝖟 defraud, deceive (*wife etc*): *j-n um et.* ~ cheat (*or* do) s.o. out of s.th.; *sich* (*selbst*) ~ deceive o.s. **Be'trüger** m (-s; -), **Be'trügerin** f (-; -nen) swindler, fraud. **Betrüge'rei** f (-; -en) **1.** cheating. **2.** deceit, a. 𝖟𝖟 fraud. **be'trügerisch** adj deceitful, fraudulent.

betrunken [bə'trʊŋkən] **I** *pp of* **betrinken**. **II** adj drunken, *pred* drunk.

Be'trunkene m, f (-n; -n) drunk.

Be'trunkenheit f (-; *no pl*) drunkenness.

Bett [bɛt] n (-[e]s; -en) bed (*a. geol.*, ⚙): *im* ~ in bed; *j-n zu* ~ *bringen* put s.o. to bed; *ins* ~ *gehen* go to bed (F *mit j-m* with s.o.), F turn in; *das* ~ *hüten* (*müssen*) be laid up (*wegen* with).

'Bettbezug m duvet cover. **'Bettcouch** f bed settee. **'Bettdecke** f a) blanket, b) quilt, c) bedspread.

Bettel ['bɛtəl] m (-s; *no pl*) *der ganze* ~ the whole (wretched) business.

bettel'arm adj desperately poor. **'Bettelbrief** m begging letter. **betteln** ['bɛtəln] v/i (h) beg (*um* for): ~ *gehen* go begging. **'Bettelstab** m *j-n an den* ~ *bringen* reduce s.o. to poverty.

betten ['bɛtən] v/t (h) bed (*a.* ⚙): *wie man sich bettet, so liegt man* as you make your bed, so you must lie on it.

'Bettjacke f bed jacket. **bettlägerig** ['bɛtlɛːgərɪç] adj laid up. **'Bettlaken** n sheet. **'Bettlek,türe** f bedtime reading.

Bettler ['bɛtlər] *m* (-s; -), '**Bettlerin** *f* (-; -nen) beggar.

Bettnässer ['bɛtnɛsər] *m* (-s, -), '**Bettnässerin** *f* (-; -nen) bed-wetter.

'**Bettruhe** *f* (period of) bed rest: *j-m ~ verordnen* order s.o. to stay in bed.

'**Bettung** *f* (-; -en) ⚙ bed(ding).

'**Bettvorleger** *m* bedside rug.

'**Bettwäsche** *f* bed linen.

'**Bettzeug** *n* bed linen.

betucht [bə'tu:xt] *adj* F well-heeled.

be'tupfen *v/t* (h) dab, 🖌 swab.

beugen ['bɔʏɡən] (h) **I** *v/t* **1.** bend (*a. fig. the law*), bow: *vom Alter gebeugt* bowed with age. **2.** *ling.* inflect, decline (*noun*), conjugate (*verb*). **II** *sich* ~ **3.** bend. **4.** *fig.* (*dat* to) bow, submit.

Beule ['bɔʏlə] *f* (-; -n) **1.** bump, swelling. **2.** dent.

beunruhigen [bə'ʔʊnru:ɪɡən] (h) **I** *v/t* worry, alarm. **II** *sich* ~ be worried (*über acc*, *wegen* about). **Be'unruhigung** *f* (-; -en) anxiety, worry.

beurkunden [bə'ʔu:rkʊndən] *v/t* (h) a) record, b) certify, c) register (*birth etc*). **Be'urkundung** *f* (-; -en) a) recording, b) certification, c) registration.

beurlauben [bə'ʔu:rlaʊbən] *v/t* (h) give s.o. leave (*or* time off), *w.s.* suspend *s.o.* (from office): *beurlaubt* a) on leave, b) temporarily suspended.

Be'urlaubung *f* (-; -en) (granting of a) leave, *w.s.* suspension (from office).

be'urteilen *v/t* (h) judge (*nach* by): *das kann ich nicht ~!* I am no judge (of this)!; *falsch ~* misjudge. **Be'urteilung** *f* (-; -en) judg(e)ment, assessment, *in personal file*: confidential report.

Beute ['bɔʏtə] *f* (-; *no pl*) **1.** booty, loot. **2.** *zo.* prey (*a. fig. gen* to), *hunt.* bag: (*dat*) *zur ~ fallen a. fig.* fall a prey to.

Beutel ['bɔʏtəl] *m* (-s; -) bag, F purse, *zo.* pouch, sac. '**beuteln** *v/t* (h) F *fig.* shake (up). '**Beuteltier** *n* marsupial.

bevölkern [bə'fœlkərn] *v/t* (h) **1.** populate. **2.** inhabit.

Be'völkerung *f* (-; -en) population.

Be'völkerungs|dichte *f* population density. **~explosi,on** *f* population explosion. **~poli,tik** *f* population policy. **~rückgang** *m* decline in population. **~schicht** *f* social stratum (*or* class).

bevollmächtigen [bə'fɔlmɛçtɪɡən] *v/t* (h) *j-n ~* authorize s.o. (*et. zu tun* to do s.th.), ⚖ give s.o. power of attorney.

Be'vollmächtigte *m*, *f* (-n; -n) authorized person (✝, 🚺 representative), *pol.* plenipotentiary. **Be'vollmächtigung** *f* (-; -en) **1.** authorization. **2.** authority, power, ⚖ power of attorney.

be'vor *adv* before: *nicht ~* not until.

bevormunden [bə'fo:rmʊndən] *v/t* (h) *j-n ~* keep s.o. in leading strings.

bevorrechtigt [bə'fo:rrɛçtɪçt] *adj* privileged.

be'vorstehen *v/i* (*irr, sep*, -ge-, h, → **stehen**) be approaching, *problems etc*: lie ahead, *crisis etc*: be imminent: *j-m ~* be in store for s.o., await s.o. **be'vorstehend** *adj* approaching, forthcoming, *pleasures etc* to come, imminent.

bevorzugen [bə'fo:rtsu:ɡən] *v/t* (h) (*vor dat*) prefer (to), favo(u)r (above), give *s.o.* preferential treatment. **be'vorzugt** *adj* **1.** privileged: *~e Behandlung* preferential treatment. **2.** favo(u)rite. **3.** (most) popular. **Be'vorzugung** *f* (-; -en) preference (*gen* given to).

be'wachen *v/t* (h) guard, watch, *sports*: mark. **Be'wacher** *m* (-s; -) guard, *sports*: marker.

be'wachsen *adj* ~ *mit* overgrown with. **Be'wachung** *f* (-; -en) **1.** *no pl* guarding (*etc*). **2.** guard(s).

bewaffnen [bə'vafnən] *v/t* (h) arm (*sich* o.s., *a. fig.*). **be'waffnet** *adj* armed (*mit* with). **Be'waffnung** *f* (-; -en) **1.** *no pl* arming. **2.** arms, weapons.

be'wahren *v/t* (h) **1.** keep: *die Fassung ~* keep one's head, keep cool. **2.** (*vor dat* from) keep, preserve; → **Gott**.

bewähren [bə'vɛ:rən] *sich* ~ (h) prove one's (*or* its) worth, stand the test, *principle*: hold good; *sich ~ als ...* prove to be ...; *sich nicht ~* prove a failure.

bewahrheiten [bə'va:rhaɪtən] *sich* ~ (h) **1.** prove (to be) true. **2.** come true.

bewährt [bə'vɛ:rt] *adj* **1.** well-tried, reliable. **2.** experienced.

Be'wahrung *f* (-; *no pl*) (*vor dat* from) preservation, keeping.

Be'währung *f* (-; -en) **1.** trial, (crucial) test. **2.** ⚖ (release on) probation: *drei Monate Gefängnis auf ~* a suspended sentence of three months; *die Strafe wurde zur ~ ausgesetzt* the defendant was placed on probation.

Be'währungs|frist *f* ⚖ (period of)

probation. **~helfer(in** f) m probation officer. **~probe** f fig. (acid) test.

bewaldet [bə'valdət] adj wooded.

bewältigen [bə'vɛltɪgən] v/t (h) cope with, master, manage. **Be'wältigung** f (-; no pl) coping (gen with), mastering.

bewandert [bə'vandərt] adj (**gut**) ~ **in** (dat) well versed (or well up) in.

Bewandtnis [bə'vantnɪs] f (-; -se) **damit hat es folgende** ~ the case is this; **das hat s-e eigene** ~ thereby hangs a tale.

bewarb [bə'varp] pret of **bewerben**.

bewarf [bə'varf] pret of **bewerfen**.

be'wässern v/t (h) irrigate.

Be'wässerung f (-; -en) irrigation.

bewegen[1] [bə've:gən] (h) **I** v/t **1.** move, ⚙ a. work, set s.th. going: fig. **et.** ~ move s.th., get things moving. **2.** fig. move, touch: **sage mir, was dich bewegt!** tell me what's on your mind! **II sich** ~ a. fig. move; **sich nicht von der Stelle** ~ (**lassen**) not to budge; **~ sich zwischen ... und ...** prices etc range between ... and ...

be'wegen[2] v/t (bewog, bewogen, h) **j-n** ~ **zu** inf prompt (or get) s.o. to inf; **was hat ihn** (**nur**) **dazu bewogen?** what(ever) made him do it?

be'wegend adj fig. moving.

Be'weggrund m (**tieferer** ~ real) motive.

beweglich [bə've:klɪç] adj **1.** movable (a. holiday), mobile, ⚙ a. fig. flexible: **~e Teile** (**~es Ziel**) moving parts (target); ⚖ **~e Sachen** movables. **2.** agile.

Be'weglichkeit f (-; no pl) **1.** mobility, flexibility. **2.** agility.

be'wegt adj **1.** rough. **2.** fig. turbulent. **3.** fig. moved, touched. **Be'wegung** f (-; -en) **1.** a) movement, motion (a. phys.), b) move: **k-e ~!** don't move!; **in ~** ⚙ in motion, fig. astir; **in ~ setzen** a. fig. start; **sich in ~ setzen** start to move; fig. **in e-e Sache ~ bringen** get s.th. moving. **2.** (physical) exercise. **3.** pol. etc movement. **4.** emotion.

Be'wegungsfreiheit f (-; no pl) freedom of movement (⚙ motion, fig. action), fig. elbowroom.

be'wegungslos adj and adv motionless.

Be'wegungs|studie f motion study. **~thera,pie** f therapeutic exercises. **ⵣunfähig** adj unable to move.

be'weinen v/t (h) mourn, lament.

Beweis [bə'vaɪs] m (-es; -e) (**für** of) proof, ⚖ a. pl evidence: **zum ~** (gen) in proof of, to prove s.th.; **bis zum ~ des Gegenteils** pending proof to the contrary; **den ~ erbringen** (or **liefern**) **für et., et. unter ~ stellen** prove s.th.; **als ~ s-r Zuneigung** as a token of his affection. **Be'weisaufnahme** f (-; no pl) ⚖ hearing of evidence. **be'weisbar** adj provable: **ist es ~?** can it be proved?

be'weisen v/t (bewies, bewiesen, h) **1.** prove (**j-m et.** s.th. to s.o.). **2.** show.

Be'weis|führung f (-; no pl) argumentation, ⚖ presentation of (the) evidence. **~kraft** f (-; no pl) conclusiveness. **ⵣkräftig** adj conclusive. **~lage** f nach der ~ on the evidence. **~last** f **die** ~ **obliegt dem Kläger** the onus (of proof) is on the plaintiff. **~materi,al** n evidence. **~mittel** n (piece of) evidence: **die** ~ the evidence (**für** of). **~stück** n (piece of) evidence, in court: exhibit.

be'wenden v/i **es dabei ~ lassen** leave it at that.

be'werben: sich ~ (bewarb, beworben, h) (**um** for) a) apply (**bei** to), b) pol. stand, Am. a. run, c) compete.

Be'werber m (-s; -) **1.** applicant, candidate. **2.** competitor, sports: a. entrant. **Be'werberin** f (-; -nen) **1.** applicant, candidate. **2.** competitor, sports: a. entrant.

Be'werbung f (-; -en) application (**um** for). **Be'werbungsschreiben** n (letter of) application.

be'werfen v/t (bewarf, beworfen, h) **j-n** ~ **mit** pelt s.o. with.

bewerkstelligen [bə'vɛrkʃtɛlɪgən] v/t (h) manage.

be'werten v/t (h) **1.** assess, judge, rate: **wird mit 7 Punkten bewertet** the jump etc rates (or scores) 7 points. **2.** ✝ (**mit** at) value, assess: **zu hoch** (**niedrig**) ~ overrate (underrate).

Be'wertung f (-; -en) assessment, ✝ a. valuation, ped. mark(s), Am. grade(s), sports: point(s), score(s).

bewies [bə'vi:s] pret, **bewiesen** [bə'vi:zən] pp of **beweisen**.

bewilligen [bə'vɪlɪgən] v/t (h) **1.** allow (**j-m et.** s.o. s.th.). **2.** grant (funds etc), parl. appropriate. **Be'willigung** f (-; -en) **1.** grant(ing), parl. appropriation. **2.** permission.

be'wirken v/t (h) cause, bring s.th. about, give rise to, result in: **das Gegenteil** ~ produce the opposite effect.

bewirten [bə'vɪrtən] v/t (h) entertain.
be'wirtschaften v/t (h) **1.** run (*estate etc*): **bewirtschaftet** *hotel etc*: open (to the public). **2.** ✓ cultivate. **3.** ✝ ration.
Be'wirtschaftung f (-; -en) **1.** running. **2.** ✓ cultivation. **3.** ✝ rationing.
Bewirtung [bə'vɪrtʊŋ] f (-; -en) **1.** entertainment. **2.** food and service.
bewog [bə'vo:k] *pret*, **bewogen** [bə'vo:-gən] *pp of* **bewegen**.
bewohnbar [bə'vo:nba:r] *adj* (in)habitable. **be'wohnen** v/t (h) inhabit, live in. **Be'wohner** m (-s; -), **Be'wohnerin** f (-; -nen) a) occupant, b) tenant, c) inhabitant.
bewölken [bə'vœlkən] **sich ~** (h) cloud over, get cloudy. **be'wölkt** *adj* cloudy. **Be'wölkung** f (-; *no pl*) **1.** clouding over. **2.** clouds. **Be'wölkungsauflockerung** f cloud dispersal. **Be'wölkungszunahme** f increasing cloudiness.
beworben [bə'vɔrbən] *pp of* **bewerben**.
beworfen [bə'vɔrfən] *pp of* **bewerfen**.
Bewunderer [bə'vʊndərər] m (-s; -), **Be'wunderin** f (-; -nen) admirer.
be'wundern v/t (h) admire (**wegen** for).
be'wundernswert, **be'wundernswürdig** *adj* admirable.
Be'wunderung f (-; *no pl*) admiration.
bewußt [bə'vʊst] *adj* **1.** conscious (*gen* of): **sich e-r Sache ~ sein** (**werden**) be aware of (realize) s.th. **2.** deliberate. **3.** said. **be'wußtlos** *adj* unconscious: **~ werden** lose consciousness. **Be'wußtlosigkeit** f (-; *no pl*) unconsciousness.
Be'wußtsein n (-s) consciousness, *fig. a.* awareness: **bei** (**vollem**) **~** (fully) conscious; **das ~ verlieren** lose consciousness; **j-n zum ~ bringen** bring s.o. round; **j-m et. zum ~ bringen** bring s.th. home to s.o.; **wieder zu**(**m**) **~ kommen** come round, regain consciousness; **j-m zum ~ kommen** dawn on s.o.; **im ~ zu inf** (*or* **daß**) conscious of *per.*. **be'wußtseinserweiternd** *adj* mind-expanding (*drug*).
be'zahlen v/t, v/i (h) pay (for): *fig. et.* **teuer ~** pay dearly for s.th.; **sich bezahlt machen** pay (off). **Be'zahlung** f (-; *no pl*) (**gegen ~** for) payment, pay.
be'zähmen v/t (h) restrain (**sich** o.s.).
be'zaubern v/t (h) bewitch, enchant, *fig. a.* charm: **~d** charming, delightful.
be'zeichnen v/t (h) **1.** mark. **2.** a) describe (**als** as), call, b) indicate, c) stand for. **be'zeichnend** *adj* (**für** of) typical, characteristic. **be'zeichnenderweise** *adv* typically (enough). **Be'zeichnung** f (-; -en) **1.** *no pl* marking. **2.** designation, name, term.
be'zeugen v/t (h) ⚖, *a. fig.* testify (to).
bezichtigen [bə'tsɪçtɪgən] v/t (h) accuse (*gen* of).
beziehbar [bə'tsi:ba:r] *adj* **1.** ready for occupation. **2.** ✝ obtainable.
be'ziehen (bezog, bezogen, h) **I** v/t **1.** put clean sheets on (*bed*), (**neu ~** re-)cover (*settee etc*). **2.** move into (*a flat etc*). **3. Posten ~** take up one's post. **4.** a) get, obtain, b) draw (*salary etc*), c) take (*newspaper*). **5. et. ~ auf** (*acc*) relate (*or* apply) s.th. to; **er bezog es auf sich** he took it personally. **II sich ~ 6.** *sky*: cloud over. **7. sich ~ auf** (*acc*) refer to, *matter*: relate to; **sich auf j-n ~** use s.o.'s name (as a reference). **Be'zieher** m (-s; -) **1.** ✝ buyer, customer. **2.** subscriber (*gen* to *a newspaper*).
Be'ziehung f (-; -en) (**zu**) relation (to), relationship (with), connection (with): **diplomatische ~en** diplomatic relations; **gute ~en haben** a) have good connections, b) **zu j-m** be on good terms with s.o.; **in dieser** (**jeder**) **~** in this (every) respect; **in gewisser ~** in a way; **in politischer ~** politically.
Be'ziehungskiste f F *fig.* relationship.
Be'ziehungssatz m *ling.* relative clause.
be'ziehungsvoll *adj* suggestive.
be'ziehungsweise *conj* **1.** or rather. **2.** or ... respectively: **mit dem Auto ~ mit der Bahn** by car or train respectively.
Be'ziehungswort n *ling.* antecedent.
beziffern [bə'tsɪfərn] v/t (h) **1.** number. **2.** estimate (**auf** *acc* at): **sich ~ auf** (*acc*) amount to.
Bezirk [bə'tsɪrk] m (-[e]s; -e) district.
bezog [bə'tso:k] *pret*, **bezogen** [bə'tso:gən] *pp of* **beziehen**.
Bezug [bə'tsu:k] m (-[e]s; ·e) **1.** cover, (pillow) slip. **2.** *no pl* moving in(to *a flat etc*). **3.** *no pl* a) purchase, b) subscription (*gen* to): **bei ~ von ...** on orders of *10 pieces*. **4.** *fig.* reference (**zu** to): **in ♀ auf** (*acc*) → **bezüglich** II; **~ nehmen auf** (*acc*) refer to. **5.** *pl* income, salary. **bezüglich** [bə'tsy:klɪç] **I** *adj* ~ **auf** (*acc*) relating to; *ling.* **~es Fürwort**

relative pronoun. **II** *prep* (*gen*) concerning, with reference to.

Be'zugnahme *f adm.* **unter ~ auf** (*acc*) with reference to.

Be'zugs|bedingungen *pl* terms of sale. **~per,son** *f j-s* ~ person to whom s.o. relates most closely, parent person. **~preis** *m* purchase (*or* subscription) price. **~punkt** *m* reference point. **~quelle** *f* source (of supply).

bezwang [bə'tsvaŋ] *pret of bezwingen*.

bezwecken [bə'tsvɛkən] *v/t* (h) **et. ~** be aiming at s.th.

be'zweifeln *v/t* (h) doubt, question.

be'zwingen *v/t* (bezwang, bezwungen, h) overcome, conquer, *a. sports*: defeat: **sich ~** restrain o.s. **Be'zwinger** *m* (-s; -) conqueror, *sports*: winner (*gen* over). **Be'zwingung** *f* (-; *no pl*) overcoming, defeat(ing), conquest.

Bibel ['bi:bəl] *f* (-; -n) Bible. **'bibelfest** *adj* well versed in the Scriptures.

'Bibelspruch *m* verse from the Bible.

Biber ['bi:bər] *m* (-s; -) *zo.* beaver.

Bibliographie [bibliogra'fi:] *f* (-; -n) bibliography. **Bibliothek** [biblio'te:k] *f* (-; -en) library. **Bibliothekar** [bibliote'ka:r] *m* (-s; -e), **Bibliothe'karin** *f* (-; -nen) librarian. **Biblio'thekswissenschaft** *f* library science.

bieder ['bi:dər] *adj* honest, *iro.* simple.

biegen ['bi:gən] (bog, gebogen) **I** *v/t* (h) bend. **II sich ~** (h) bend; → *Lachen.* **III** *v/i* (sn) **nach links** (**rechts**) ~ turn left (right); **um e-e Ecke ~** turn (round) a corner. **'Biegen** *n* (-s) bending: **auf ~ oder Brechen** by hook or by crook.

biegsam ['bi:kza:m] *adj* pliable, flexible, supple. **'Biegsamkeit** *f* (-; *no pl*) pliability, flexibility, suppleness.

'Biegung *f* (-; -en) bend.

Biene ['bi:nə] *f* (-; -n) **1.** *zo.* bee. **2.** *F* chick.

'Bienen|fleiß *m* assiduity. **~haus** *n* beehouse, apiary. **~königin** *f* queen bee. **~korb** *m* beehive. **~schwarm** *m* swarm of bees. **~staat** *m* colony of bees. **~stich** *m* bee-sting. **~stock** *m* beehive. **~wabe** *f* honeycomb. **~wachs** *n* beeswax. **~zucht** *f* beekeeping. **~züchter** *m* beekeeper.

Bier [bi:r] *n* (-[e]s; -e) beer: **helles ~** lager, *Am.* light beer; **dunkles ~** *etwa* brown ale, *Am.* dark beer; **~ vom Faß**

beer on draught; *F das ist dein ~!* that's your problem!

'Bier|brauerei *f* brewery. **~deckel** *m* beer mat. **~dose** *f* beer can. **~faß** *n* beer barrel. **~flasche** *f* beer bottle. **~garten** *m* beer garden. **~glas** *n* beer glass. **~hefe** *f* brewer's yeast. **~keller** *m* tavern. **~krug** *m* beer mug, *Am.* stein. **~stube** *f* beer tavern. **~zelt** *n* beer tent.

Biest [bi:st] *n* (-[e]s; -er) *a.* F *fig.* beast.

bieten ['bi:tən] (bot, geboten, h) **I** *v/t* **1.** offer (*j-m et.* s.o. s.th.), present (*sight, difficulties, etc*): **das läßt sie sich nicht ~** she won't stand for that; → *Stirn.* **2.** ✝ bid. **II sich ~** present itself. **'Bieter** *m* (-s; -), **'Bieterin** *f* (-; -nen) ✝ bidder.

Bigamie [biga'mi:] *f* (-; -n) bigamy.

bigott [bi'gɔt] *adj contp.* bigoted.

Bikini [bi'ki:ni] *m* (-s; -s) bikini.

Bilanz [bi'lants] *f* (-; -en) *a.)* balance, b) balance sheet: **die ~ ziehen** (*gen of*) strike the balance, *fig. a.* take stock; *fig.* **~ negative** negative record. **Bi'lanzjahr** *n* financial year.

Bi'lanzposten *m* balance-sheet item.

Bild [bɪlt] *n* (-[e]s; -er) *a)* picture (*a.* TV *or fig.*), photo, illustration, image (*a. opt.,* TV), painting, portrait, b) *fig.* sight, c) *fig.* idea, *rhet.* image, metaphor: **~ der Zerstörung** *etc* scene of destruction *etc*; **im ~e sein** be in the picture, **über** (*acc*) know about; **sich ein ~ machen von** an idea of, visualize; *du machst dir kein ~!* you have no idea!; *j-n ins ~ setzen* inform s.o., put s.o. in the picture; *ein falsches ~ bekommen* get a wrong impression.

'Bildar,chiv *n* photographic archives.

'Bildausfall *m* TV picture loss, blackout. **'Bildband** *m* (-[e]s; **~e**) illustrated book. **'Bildbericht** *m* photo-report.

'bilden (h) **I** *v/t* **1.** form, shape (*a. fig.*), make up (*sentence*). **2.** create, establish, set up (*committee etc*), form (*government*). **3.** form, develop (*buds*). **4.** *fig.* form, be; → *Ausnahme.* **5.** educate, cultivate; → *gebildet.* **II** *v/i* **6.** broaden the mind. **III sich ~ 7.** form, develop. **8.** educate o.s., improve one's mind.

'bildend *adj* educational, informative: **~e Künste** fine arts.

'Bilder|buch *n* picture book. **~buch...** *F fig.* storybook (*career, landing, etc*). **~gale,rie** *f* picture gallery. **~rätsel** *n* picture puzzle. **⋄reich** *adj* richly illustrated (*book*), *fig.* language rich in images. **⋄schrift** *f* pictographic script. **⋄sprache** *f* imagery.

'**Bildfläche** *f TV* image area: F *fig.* **auf der ⋄ erscheinen** turn up; **von der ⋄ verschwinden** disappear.

'**Bildfunk** *m* radio picture transmission. '**bildhaft** *adj fig.* graphic.

'**Bildhauer** *m* (-s; -) sculptor.

Bildhaue'**rei** *f* (-; *no pl*) sculpture. '**Bildhauerin** *f* (-; -nen) sculptress. '**bildhauern** [-haʊərn] *v/i*, *v/t* (h) F sculpt. **bild**'**hübsch** *adj* (very) lovely.

'**bildlich** *adj* **1.** pictorial, graphic. **2.** *ling.* figurative (*expression etc*).

'**Bildnis** *n* (-ses; -se) portrait.

'**Bild**|**platte** *f* video disc. **⋄plattenspieler** *m* video disc player. **⋄quali**|**tät** *f* *phot.*, *TV* picture quality. **⋄redak**|**teur** *m* picture editor. **⋄re**|**gie** *f* camera-work. **⋄röhre** *f* picture tube. **⋄schärfe** *f* definition, sharpness.

'**Bildschirm** *m* screen. **⋄gerät** *n* visual display unit. **⋄text** *m* view data.

bild'**schön** *adj* (very) beautiful. '**Bildstörung** *f TV* image interference. '**Bildtele**|**fon** *n* videophone.

'**Bildtonkamera** *f* sound-film camera. '**Bildung** *f* (-; -en) **1.** a) forming, formation, b) development, c) creation, d) establishment, setting-up (*of committee etc*): **⋄ des Perfekts** forming (of) the perfect. **2.** *no pl* a) education, culture, b) *ped.*, *univ.* formal education: **et. für s-e ⋄ tun** improve one's mind. **3.** *no pl* (good) breeding.

'**Bildungs...** educational (*reform etc*). **⋄fähig** *adj* educable. **⋄gang** *m* (course of) education. **⋄grad** *m* educational level. **⋄lücke** *f* gap in one's education. **⋄po**|**litisch** *adj* politico-educational. **⋄urlaub** *m* educational leave. **⋄weg** *m* education: **der zweite ⋄** evening classes (*with a view to obtaining university qualification*); **auf dem zweiten ⋄** through evening classes. **⋄wesen** *n* (-s; *no pl*) education.

Billard ['bɪljart] *n* (-s; -e) billiards. **⋄kugel** *f* billiard ball. **⋄stock** *m* cue.

Billiarde [bɪ'liardə] *f* (-; -n) trillion, *Am.* quadrillion.

billig ['bɪlɪç] *adj* **1.** a) cheap, inexpensive, b) low (*price*). **2.** *fig.* cheap, poor (*ad-*

vice etc), lame (*excuse etc*). **3.** fair. '**Billig...** cut-price, *Am.* cut-rate.

billigen ['bɪlɪgən] *v/t* (h) approve of, sanction, *adm.* approve.

'**Billigkeit** *f* (-; *no pl*) cheapness.

'**Billigung** *f* (-; *no pl*) (*gen* of) approval, sanction.

Billion [bɪ'lĭoːn] *f* (-; -en) trillion, *esp. Br.* million million.

bimmeln ['bɪməln] *v/i* (h) ring, tinkle.

Bimsstein ['bɪms-] *m* pumice (stone).

binär [bi'nɛːr] *adj*, **Bi'när...** binary.

Binde ['bɪndə] *f* (-; -n) **1.** a) armband, bandage, b) sling, c) blindfold, d) F sanitary towel (*Am.* napkin). **2.** F *fig.* **e-n hinter die ⋄ gießen** hoist one.

'**Binde**|**gewebe** *n* *anat.* connective tissue. **⋄glied** *n* (connecting) link. **⋄haut** *f* *anat.* conjunctiva. **⋄hautentzündung** *f* 🦋 conjunctivitis. **⋄mittel** *n* **1.** 🔧 bonding agent. **2.** *gastr.* thickening.

'**binden** (band, gebunden, h) **I** *v/t* **1.** tie (**an** *acc* to), make (*bouquet*), tie (*knot etc*). **2.** bind (*book*). **3.** *gastr.* bind, thicken. **4.** ♪ a) tie, b) slur. **5.** 🌱 tie up (*funds*), fix (*prices*). **6.** *fenc.*, *a.* ✗ bind. **7.** *fig.* bind, commit (*s.o.*); → **gebunden** 4. **II** *v/i* **8.** bind. **9.** *gastr.* bind, thicken. **10.** 🔧 cement (*etc*): harden, set, *plastic*: bond. **III** *sich ⋄ fig.* commit o.s., tie o.s. down. '**bindend** *adj fig.* binding (**für** upon).

'**Bindestrich** *m* hyphen: **mit ⋄ schreiben** hyphen(ate).

'**Bindewort** *n* (-[e]s; **⋄er**) conjunction.

'**Bindfaden** *m* string.

'**Bindung** *f* (-; -en) **1.** a) (**an** *acc*) ties (to, with), bond (with), attachment (to), b) (lasting) relationship. **2.** *ski:* binding. **3.** 🎿, *phys.* bond(ing). **4.** ♪ ligature.

binnen ['bɪnən] *prep* (*dat or gen*) within: **⋄ kurzem** before long.

'**Binnen**|**gewässer** *n* inland water. **⋄hafen** *m* inland port. **⋄handel** *m* domestic trade. **⋄land** *n* interior.

'**binnenländisch** [-lɛndɪʃ] *adj* inland.

'**Binnen**|**markt** *m* home (*EC:* single) market. **⋄meer** *n* inland sea. **⋄schifffahrt** *f* inland navigation. **⋄verkehr** *m* inland traffic.

Binse ['bɪnzə] *f* (-; -n) 🌾 rush: F **in die ⋄n gehen** go to pot.

'**Binsenweisheit** *f* truism.

Biochemie [bɪoçe'miː] *f* biochemistry.

Bio'chemiker(in f) m biochemist.
bio'chemisch adj biochemical.
'Biogas n biogas.
Bioge'netik f biogenetics.
Biograph [bio'graːf] m (-en; -en),
Bio'graphin f (-; -nen) biographer.
Biographie [biogra'fiː] f (-; -n) biography. **bio'graphisch** adj biographical.
'Bioladen m F whole food shop.
Biologe [bio'loːgə] m (-n; -n), **Bio'login**
f (-; -nen) biologist. **Biologie** [biolo'giː]
f (-; no pl) biology. **bio'logisch** adj biological.
'Biomasse f (-; no pl) biomass.
Biophy'sik f biophysics.
Biopsie [biɔp'siː] f (-; -n) 🟥 biopsy.
'Biorhythmus m biorhythm.
'Biotechnik f bioengineering.
Biotop [bio'toːp] n (-s; -e) biotope.
Birke ['bɪrkə] f (-; -n) birch(-tree).
'Birnbaum m pear-tree. **Birne** ['bɪrnə] f
1. 🝙 pear. 2. 🔌 bulb. 3. F noodle.
'birnenförmig adj pear-shaped.
bis [bɪs] **I** prep **1.** a) till, until, b) by: ~
heute so far, to date; ~ **jetzt** up to now;
~ **jetzt (noch) nicht** not as yet; ~ **auf**
weiteres for the present, until further
notice; ~ **in die Nacht** into the night; ~
vor einigen Jahren until a few years
ago; ~ **zum Ende** (right) to the end; (**in**
der Zeit) vom ... ~ between ... and; F ~
dann (morgen)! see you later (tomorrow)! **2.** (up) to, as far as: ~ **hierher** up
to here; ~ **wohin?** how far?; (**von hier**)
~ **London** (from here) to London. **3. 7 -**
10 Tage from 7 to 10 days, between 7
and 10 days; ~ **zu 10 Meter hoch** as
high as ten metres; ~ **zu 100 Personen**
as many as 100 persons; ~ **drei zählen**
count up to three. **4.** ~ **auf das letzte**
Stück down to the last bit. **5.** ~ **auf** (acc)
except, but. **II** conj till, until.
Bisam ['biːzam] m (-s; -e) **1.** zo. musk. **2.**
musquash. **'Bisamratte** f zo. muskrat.
Bischof ['bɪʃɔf] m (-s; ⸚e) bishop.
bischöflich ['bɪʃœflɪç] adj episcopal.
'Bischofssitz m episcopal see.
bisexuell [bisɛˈksu̯ɛl] adj bisexual.
bis'her adv up to now, so far: ~ **(noch)**
nicht not (as) yet; **wie** ~ as before; **die** ~
beste Leistung the best performance
so far. **bisherig** [bɪs'heːrɪç] adj a) past,
previous, b) present: **die** ~**en Ergebnis-**
se results so far.

Biskuit [bɪs'kviːt] m (-[s]; -s, -e) gastr.
sponge. **Bis'kuitrolle** f Swiss roll.
bis'lang → **bisher.**
biß [bɪs] pret of **beißen.**
Biß m (Bisses; Bisse) bite.
'bißchen adj and adv **ein (kleines)** ~ a
(little) bit, a little; **kein** ~ not a bit.
'Bissen m (-s; -) **1.** bite, morsel, mouthful. **2.** bite, snack.
'bissig adj **1.** vicious: **ein** ~**er Hund** a. a
dog that bites. **2.** fig. cutting (remark),
snappish (person). **'Bißwunde** f bite.
Bistum ['bɪstuːm] n (-s; ⸚er) bishopric.
Bit [bɪt] n (-[s]; -[s]) computer: bit.
bitte ['bɪtə] adv **1.** please: ~, **gib mir die**
Zeitung! hand me the paper, please!; ~
nicht! please don't!; (**aber**) ~! certainly!, go ahead! **2.** ~ (**sehr** or **schön**)! a)
after "danke": that's all right!, esp. Am.
(you are) welcome!, b) after excuses:
it's all right!, c) when offering s.th.:
there you are!, d) come in, please! **3.**
wie ~? (I beg your) pardon?, sorry? **4.**
(**na**) ~! there!, I told you so!
'Bitte f (-; -n) a) request, b) entreaty: **auf**
j-s ~ at s.o.'s request; **ich habe e-e** ~ **an**
Sie I have a favo(u)r to ask of you.
bitten ['bɪtən] v/t, v/i (bat, gebeten, h) a)
ask (**j-n um et.** s.o. for s.th.), request,
beg, b) implore: **um j-s Namen** (**Er-**
laubnis) ~ ask s.o.'s name (permission); **j-n zu sich** ~ ask s.o. to come; **für**
j-n ~ intercede for s.o.; **es wird gebe-**
ten, daß ... it is requested that ...; **darf**
ich ~? a) come in, please!, b) may I have
this dance?, c) dinner is served!
bitter ['bɪtər] adj and adv bitter: fig. **es ist**
mein ~**er Ernst** I mean it!; **er hat es** ~
nötig he badly needs it; **das ist** ~! that's
hard! **bitter'böse** adj a) wicked, b) furious. **'Bitterkeit** f (-; no pl) a. fig. bitterness. **'bitterlich** adv ~ **weinen** weep
bitterly. **'bittersüß** adj bitter-sweet.
'Bittgesuch n, **'Bittschrift** f petition.
Bittsteller ['bɪtʃtɛlər] m (-s; -), **'Bittstel-**
lerin f (-; -nen) petitioner.
Biwak ['biːvak] n (-s; -s, -e), **biwakieren**
[biva'kiːrən] v/i (h) bivouac.
bizarr [bi'tsar] adj bizarre.
Bizeps ['biːtsɛps] m (-[es]; -e) biceps.
blähen ['blɛːən] (h) **I** v/i cause flatulence,
give you wind. **II** v/t (**a. sich** ~) fill out.
'Blähungen pl wind, flatulence.
blamabel [bla'maːbəl] adj embarrass-

ing, disgraceful. **Blamage** [bla'ma:ʒə] *f* (-; -n) disgrace, fiasco.

blamieren [bla'mi:rən] (h) **I** *v/t j-n* ~ make s.o. look like a fool, *w.s.* compromise s.o. **II** *sich* ~ make a fool of o.s., *w.s.* compromise o.s.

blank [blaŋk] *adj* **1.** shining, polished, shiny. **2.** naked, bare (*a.* ⊛). **3.** F broke. **4.** F ~*er Unsinn etc* sheer nonsense *etc.*

blanko ['blaŋko] *adj* ✝ (*adv* in) blank.
'**Blankoscheck** *m* blank cheque (*Am.* check). '**Blankovollmacht** *f* full discretionary power, *fig.* carte blanche.

Bläschen ['blɛ:sçən] *n* (-s; -) **1.** small bubble. **2.** ✻ a) small blister, b) pustule.

Blase ['bla:zə] *f* (-; -n) **1.** (air) bubble, *in glass etc*: flaw. **2.** *comics*: balloon. **3.** *anat.* bladder, b) ✻ blister. **4.** F *contp.* bunch, lot. '**Blasebalg** *m* bellows.

blasen ['bla:zən] *v/i, v/t* (blies, geblasen, h) blow, ♪ *a.* play.
'**Blasen|entzündung** *f*, ~**ka͵tarrh** *m* cystitis. ~**leiden** *n* bladder trouble.

Bläser ['blɛ:zər] *m* (-s; -) ♪ wind player: *die* ~ the wind (section).

blasiert [bla'zi:rt] *adj* conceited.
'**Blasinstru͵ment** *n* ♪ wind instrument.
'**Blaska͵pelle** *f* brass band.
'**Blasmu͵sik** *f* **1.** music for brass instruments. **2.** (playing of a) brass band.

Blasphemie [blasfe'mi:] *f* (-; -n) blasphemy.

blaß [blas] *adj* pale (*vor* with), *fig.* colo(u)rless: ~ *werden* (turn) pale; ~ *vor Neid* green with envy; → *Ahnung*.

Blässe ['blɛsə] *f* (-; *no pl*) paleness, pallor.

Blatt [blat] *n* (-[e]s; ⁓er) **1.** ✾ leaf: *fig. kein* ~ *vor den Mund nehmen* not to mince matters. **2.** a) leaf, sheet, b) page: ~ *vom* ~ *spielen* sight-read; *fig. das steht auf e-m anderen* ~ that's a different matter altogether; *das* ~ *hat sich gewendet* the tide has turned. **3.** (news)paper. **4.** *art:* a) print, b) drawing, c) engraving. **5.** (playing) card, *w.s. a good etc* hand. **6.** blade (*of saw etc*).

Blättchen ['blɛtçən] *n* (-s; -) **1.** small leaf (*etc*, → *Blatt*). **2.** *anat.*, ✻, 🎕 membrane. **3.** slip (of paper). **4.** local paper.

Blatter ['blatər] *f* (-; -n) ✻ pock.
'**Blattern** *pl* ✻ smallpox.

blättern ['blɛtərn] *v/i* (h) *in e-m Buch etc* ~ leaf through a book *etc.*

'**Blätterteig** *m* flaky pastry.
'**Blatt|feder** *f* ⊛ leaf spring. ~**gold** *n* gold leaf. ~**grün** *n* (-s; *no pl*) chlorophyll. ~**laus** *f* greenfly. ~**pflanze** *f* green plant. ~**sa͵lat** *m* green salad.

blau [blau] *adj* **1.** blue: ~*er Fleck* bruise; F ~*er Brief* a) (letter of) dismissal, b) *ped.* letter of warning; → *Auge, Blut*. **2.** F tight, sloshed. **Blau** *n* (-s; -) blue.

'**blauäugig** [-ɔygɪç] *adj a. fig.* blue-eyed.
'**Blaubeere** *f* ✿ bilberry, *Am.* blueberry.
'**blaublütig** [-bly:tɪç] *adj* blue-blooded.
'**Blaue in Fahrt ins** ~ mystery tour.

Bläue ['blɔyə] *f* (-; *no pl*) blue(ness).

bläuen ['blɔyən] *v/t* (h) blue.
'**Blaufuchs** *m zo.* arctic (✝ blue) fox.
'**blaugrau** *adj* bluish grey (*Am.* gray).
'**Blaukraut** *n gastr.* red cabbage.
'**bläulich** ['blɔylɪç] *adj* bluish.

'**Blaulicht** *n* flashing light(s): *mit* ~ *ambulance etc* with its lights flashing.
'**blaumachen** *v/i* (*sep*, -ge-, h) F stay away (from work), *sl.* scive.
'**Blaumeise** *f zo.* blue tit. '**Blaupause** *f* blueprint. '**Blausäure** *f* 🎕 prussic acid. '**Blaustrumpf** *m* bluestocking.

Blech [blɛç] *n* (-[e]s; -e) **1.** a) sheet metal, b) metal sheet. **2.** baking tray. **3.** F rubbish. '**Blechbüchse** *f*, '**Blechdose** *f* tin, (tin) can.

blechen ['blɛçən] *v/t, v/i* (h) F cough up.
'**blechern** *adj* **1.** (of) tin. **2.** tinny (*sound*).
'**Blech|instru͵ment** *n* ♪ brass instrument. ~**schaden** *m mot.* bodywork damage. ~**schere** *f* plate shears.

blecken ['blɛkən] *v/t* (h) *die Zähne* ~ *animal:* bare its fangs.

Blei [blaɪ] *n* (-[e]s; *no pl*) **1.** lead: *aus* ~ (made of) lead; *fig.* (*schwer*) *wie* ~ leaden. **2.** *hunt.* shot.

Bleibe ['blaɪbə] *f* (-; -n) F place to stay.

bleiben ['blaɪbən] *v/i* (h) (blieb, geblieben, sn) **1.** stay (*im Bett* in bed, *zu Hause* at home, *zum Essen* for dinner); *wo bleibt er denn nur?* what has taken him?; F *fig. und wo bleibe ich?* and where do I come in?; → *Ball*[1]. **2.** ~ *bei* stick to (*der Wahrheit* the truth); → *Sache* 2. **3.** remain, keep: *geschlossen* (*gesund etc*) ~ stay closed (healthy *etc*); *für sich* ~ keep to o.s.; *das bleibt unter uns!* F keep it under your hat!; ~

Sie (*doch*) *sitzen!* don't get up!; *es bleibt dabei!* that's final!; *und dabei bleibt es!* and that's that! **4.** be left (*dat* to), remain. **'bleibend** *adj* lasting, permanent. **'bleibenlassen** *v/t* (*irr, sep, no -ge-, h,* → *lassen*) **et.** ~ a) not to do s.th., b) stop (doing) s.th.; *laß das bleiben!* stop it!; *das werde ich schön* ~*!* I'll do nothing of the kind!

bleich [blaɪç] *adj* pale (*vor* with): ~ *werden* (turn) pale.

bleichen ['blaɪçən] *v/t, v/i* (h) bleach.
'Bleichgesicht *n* paleface.
'Bleichmittel *n* bleach(ing agent).

bleiern ['blaɪərn] *adj a. fig.* leaden.
'Bleifarbe *f* lead paint. **'bleifrei** *adj* unleaded. **'bleihaltig** [-haltɪç] *adj* containing lead, leaded (*petrol*). **'Bleikri,stall** *n* lead crystal. **'Bleistift** *m* (lead) pencil. **'Bleistiftspitzer** *m* pencil sharpener. **'Bleivergiftung** *f* lead poisoning.

'Blendauto,matik ['blɛnt-] *f phot.* automatic aperture control.

Blende ['blɛndə] *f* (-; -n) **1.** screen. **2.** *phot.* a) diaphragm, b) aperture, c) f-stop: (*bei*) ~ *8* at f-8. **3.** facing.
'blenden (h) **I** *v/t a. fig.* dazzle. **2.** blind. **II** *v/i* **3.** dazzle, be dazzling (*a. fig.*). **4.** *fig.* deceive. **'Blenden** *n* (-s) *mot.* glare. **'blendend** *adj* dazzling, *fig. a.* brilliant: ~ *aussehen* look great; *sich* ~ *amüsieren* have a great time. **'Blenden|einstellung** *f phot.* aperture setting. ~*skala* *f* aperture ring. ~*zahl* *f phot.* f-stop.
'Blender *m* (-s; -) *fig.* fake.
'blendfrei *adj* antiglare.
'Blendschutz|scheibe *f mot.* antiglare screen. ~*zaun* *m mot.* antiglare barrier. **'Blendung** *f* (-; -en) **1.** blinding, *mot. etc* dazzle, glare. **2.** *fig.* deception.

Blick [blɪk] *m* (-[e]s; -e) **1.** (*auf acc* at) look, glance. *auf den ersten* ~ at first sight; *mit einem* ~ at a glance; *e-n* ~ *werfen auf* (*acc*) have a look at. **2.** view (*auf acc* of): *mit* ~ *auf* (*acc*) with a view of, overlooking *the lake etc.*
'blicken *v/i* (h) look (*auf acc* at): *um sich* ~ look around; *sich* ~ *lassen* show o.s.; *das läßt tief* ~*!* that's very revealing!
'Blick|fang *m* eyecatcher. ~*feld* *n fig.* field of vision. ~*kon,takt* *m* eye contact. ~*punkt* *m* **1.** *opt.* visual focus: *fig. im* ~ *stehen* be in the centre of interest. **2.**

fig. point of view. ~*richtung* *f* **1.** line of vision. **2.** *fig.* direction. ~*winkel* *m* **1.** angle of view. **2.** *fig.* point of view.

blieb [bli:p] *pret of* **bleiben**.
blies [bli:s] *pret of* **blasen**.
blind [blɪnt] **I** *adj* **1.** blind (*a.* △, ⊙, *a. fig. gegen, für* to, *vor dat* with): *auf einem Auge* ~ blind in one eye; *j-n* ~ *machen gegen* blind s.o. to; → *Passagier.* **2.** cloudy (*mirror*), tarnished (*metal*). **II** *adv fly etc* blind, *fig. trust etc* blindly.
'Blinddarm *m* appendix. ~*entzündung* *f* appendicitis. ~*operati,on* *f* appendectomy.

'Blinde *m, f* (-n; -n) blind man (woman): *die* ~*n* the blind; *das sieht doch ein* ~*r!* you can see that with half an eye!

'Blinden|heim *n* home for the blind. ~*hund* *m* guide dog, *Am.* seeing-eye dog. ~*schrift* *f* braille. ~*stock* *m* white stick, (blind person's) cane.

'Blindflug *m* instrument flying.
Blindgänger ['blɪntgɛŋər] *m* (-s; -) **1.** ✗ dud. **2.** F *fig.* dud, washout.
'Blindheit *f* (-; *no pl*) blindness.
blindlings ['blɪntlɪŋs] *adv* blindly.
'Blindschleiche *f zo.* blindworm.
'blindschreiben *v/i* (*irr, sep, -ge-, h,* → *schreiben*) touch-type.
blinken ['blɪŋkən] *v/i* (h) **1.** sparkle. **2.** *a. v/t* (flash a) signal, flash. **'Blinker** *m* (-s; -) **1.** *mot.* indicator. **2.** spoon bait.
'Blinklicht *n* (-[e]s; -er) *mot.* a) flashing light, b) → *Blinker* 1. **'Blinkzeichen** *n* flashing (*mot.* indicator) signal.
blinzeln ['blɪntsəln] *v/i* (h) blink.
Blitz [blɪts] *m* (-es; -e) **1.** a) lightning, b) flash (of lightning): *vom* ~ *getroffen* struck by lightning; *fig. ein* ~ *aus heiterem Himmel* a bolt from the blue; *wie vom* ~ *getroffen* thunderstruck; *wie der* ~ → *blitzschnell.* **2.** *phot.* flash. **'Blitzableiter** *m* lightning conductor. **'blitzartig** → *blitzschnell.*
'Blitzaufnahme *f phot.* flash shot.
'Blitzbesuch *m* lightning visit.
'Blitzbirne *f phot.* flashbulb.
'blitzblank *adj and adv* sparkling clean.
blitzen ['blɪtsən] **I** *v/i* (h) **1.** *es hat geblitzt* there was (a flash of) lightning. **2.** flash, *fig. a.* sparkle. **II** *v/t* **3.** *phot.* F flash. **'Blitzgerät** *n* (electronic) flash (gun). **'Blitzlampe** *f phot.* flashbulb. **'Blitzlicht** *n phot.* flashlight: *mit* ~ *foto-*

grafieren (use a) flash. **'blitzsauber** adj F (as) clean as a whistle. **'Blitzschlag** m lightning. **'blitzschnell I** adj lightning ... **II** adv with lightning speed, like a flash. **'Blitzstart** m lightning start. **'Blitzwürfel** m phot. flashcube.

Block [blɔk] m (-[e]s, ⸚e) **1.** block (a. of stamps, houses, etc), (writing) pad, book (of tickets). **2.** boulder. **3.** ✝, parl., pol. bloc.

Blockade [blɔ'ka:də] f (-; -n) **1.** blockade. **2.** ✶ block(ing).

'Blockbuchstabe m block letter.

'Blockflöte f recorder.

'blockfrei adj pol. nonaligned.

'Blockhaus n log cabin.

blockieren [blɔ'ki:rən] v/t (h) block, (a. v/i wheels) lock, ⚙ jam.

Blockschoko,lade f cooking chocolate.

'Blockschrift f block letters.

'Blockstaat m pol. aligned state.

blöd [blø:t] adj **1.** ✶ imbecile. **2.** F stupid, silly. **Blödel...** ['blø:dəl] slapstick (show etc). **'blödeln** v/i (h) fool around. **'Blödheit** f (-; -en) **1.** no pl ✶ imbecility. **2.** F stupidity, silliness. **'Blödmann** m (-[e]s; ⸚er) F idiot, silly ass. **'Blödsinn** m (-s; no pl) **1.** ✶ imbecility. **2.** F nonsense, rubbish. **'blödsinnig** adj idiotic.

blöken ['blø:kən] v/i (h) sheep: bleat, cow: low.

blond [blɔnt] adj blond(e), fair(-haired). **blondieren** [blɔn'di:rən] v/t (h) dye one's hair blond. **Blon'dine** f (-; -n) blonde.

bloß [blo:s] **I** adj **1.** bare, naked: mit ⸚en Füßen barefoot(ed); mit ⸚en Händen with one's bare hands; mit dem ⸚en Auge with the naked eye. **2.** mere: der ⸚e Gedanke the mere thought. **II** adv **3.** only, simply, merely: komm ⸚ nicht rein! don't you dare come in!

Blöße ['blø:sə] f (-; -n) **1.** bareness, nakedness. **2.** sports or fig. opening: sich e-e ⸚ geben leave o.s. wide open.

'bloßlegen v/t (sep, -ge-, h) lay bare, expose (a. fig.). **'bloßstellen** v/t (sep, -ge-, h) expose, show s.o. up.

'Bloßstellung f (-; -en) exposure.

Blouson [blu'zõ:] m, n (-s; -s) blouson.

Bluff [blœf] m (-s; -s), **'bluffen** v/i, v/t (h) contp. bluff.

blühen ['bly:ən] v/i (h) blossom (a. fig.), be in bloom, fig. thrive: F wer weiß, was uns noch blüht! who knows

what's in store for us!

'blühend adj **1.** flowering, blooming. **2.** fig. flourishing, glowing (health), lively (imagination): ~ aussehen look the picture of health.

Blume ['blu:mə] f (-; -n) **1.** flower: j-m et. durch die ~ sagen hint to s.o. that. **2.** bouquet (of wine), head, froth (on beer).

'Blumen|beet n flower bed. **⸚erde** f garden mo(u)ld. **⸚händler(in** f) m florist. **⸚kohl** m cauliflower. **⸚laden** m flower shop. **⸚muster** n floral design. **⸚strauß** m bunch of flowers, bouquet. **⸚topf** m flowerpot. **⸚zwiebel** f flower bulb.

blumig adj **1.** fig. flowery. **2.** wine: with a fine bouquet.

Bluse ['blu:zə] f (-; -n) blouse.

Blut [blu:t] n (-[e]s; no pl) blood: sie kann kein ~ sehen she can't stand the sight of blood; ~ spenden donate (or give) blood; fig. blaues (junges) ~ blue (young) blood; ruhig ~! take it easy!; j-n bis aufs ~ reizen drive s.o. wild; F ~ (und Wasser) schwitzen sweat blood; ~ vergießen shed blood; böses ~ machen breed bad blood; die Musik liegt ihm im ~ music is in his blood.

'Blut|alko,hol(gehalt) m blood alcohol. **⚤arm** adj a(n)emic. **⸚armut** f an(a)emia. **⸚bad** n fig. massacre. **⸚bank** f (-; -en) ✶ blood bank. **⸚bild** n ✶ blood count. **⸚blase** f blood blister.

'Blutdruck m (-[e]s; no pl) (j-s ~ messen take s.o.'s) blood pressure.

'blutdrucksenkend adj hypotensive.

'blutdürstig [-dyrstɪç] adj bloodthirsty.

Blüte ['bly:tə] f (-; -n) **1.** blossom, flower. **2.** no pl flowering time, blossom: in voller ~ in (full) bloom. **3.** no pl fig. heyday, ✝ time of prosperity: in höchster ~ stehen be flourishing; in der ~ s-r Jahre in his prime. **4.** fig. flower, élite. **5.** F fud, counterfeit money.

'Blutegel m zo. leech.

bluten ['blu:tən] v/i (h) bleed (aus from): F fig. schwer ~ müssen have to pay through the nose.

'Blüten|honig m honey made from blossoms and flowers. **⸚knospe** f (flower) bud. **⸚lese** f fig. anthology. **⸚staub** m pollen. **⚤weiß** adj snow-white.

'Bluter m (-s; -) ✶ h(a)emophiliac.

'Blut|erguß m ✶ h(a)ematoma, bruise.

~farbstoff *m* h(a)emoglobin. **~fleck** *m* bloodstain. **~gefäß** *n* ♂ blood vessel. **~gerinnsel** *n* ♂ blood clot. **~gruppe** *f* blood group. **~hochdruck** *m* ♂ high blood pressure. **~hund** *m* bloodhound.

'blutig *adj* **1.** a) bloody (*a. fig.*), b) blood-stained: *fig.* **~er Anfänger** rank beginner. **2.** *gastr.* rare (*steak*).

'blutjung *adj* very young.

'Blut|kon,serve *f* unit of stored blood. **~körperchen** *n* blood corpuscle. **~kreislauf** *m* (blood) circulation. **~lache** *f* pool of blood. **♀leer** *adj* a. fig. bloodless. **~o,range** *f* blood orange. **~plasma** *n* blood plasma. **~probe** *f* **1.** blood (⚖ alcohol) test. **2.** ♂ blood sample. **~rache** *f* vendetta.

'blutrot *adj* (dark) crimson.

blutrünstig ['blu:trynstɪç] *adj fig.* gory: **~er Film** *etc* blood-curdling film *etc.*

'Blutsauger *m* a. fig. bloodsucker.

'Blutschande *f* incest. **blutschände-risch** ['blu:tʃɛndərɪʃ] *adj* incestuous.

'Blutsenkung *f* ♂ blood sedimentation.

'Blutspender(in *f)* *m* blood donor.

'blutstillend *adj* (*a.* **~es Mittel**) styptic.

'Blutstropfen *m* drop of blood.

'Blutsturz *m* ♂ h(a)emorrhage.

'blutsverwandt *adj* related by blood (**mit** to). **Blutsverwandte** *m, f* (-n; -n) blood relation. **'Blutsverwandtschaft** *f* consanguinity.

'Bluttransfusi,on *f* blood transfusion.

'bluttriefend *adj* dripping with blood.

'blutüberströmt *adj* covered with blood.

'Blutübertragung *f* blood transfusion.

'Blutung *f* (-; -en) bleeding, h(a)emorrhage.

'blutunterlaufen *adj* bloodshot.

'Blut|vergießen *n* (-s; *no pl*) bloodshed. **~vergiftung** *f* blood poisoning. **~ver-lust** *m* loss of blood. **~wäsche** *f* (h(a)emo)dialysis. **~wurst** *f gastr.* black pudding. **~zucker(spiegel)** *m* ♂ blood sugar (level). **~zufuhr** *f* blood supply.

Bö [bøː] *f* (-; -en) gust, squall.

Bob [bɔp] *m* (-s; -s) *sports:* bob(sleigh).

'Bobbahn *f* bob(sleigh) run.

Bock [bɔk] *m* (-[e]s; ⸚e) **1.** *zo.* a) buck, b) ram, c) he-goat: *fig.* **e-n ~ schießen** make a blunder; **den ~ zum Gärtner machen** set the fox to keep the geese; → **null**. **2.** ◎ a) stand, b) jack. **3.** *gym.* buck. **4.** bock (beer).

'bockbeinig [-baɪnɪç] *adj* F stubborn.

'Bockbier *n* bock (beer).

'bocken *v/i* (h) **1.** *a. mot.* buck. **2.** be stubborn, sulk. **'bockig** *adj* stubborn.

'Bockshorn *n j-n ins ~ jagen* scare s.o.

'Bockspringen *n* (-s) leapfrog.

Boden ['boːdən] *m* (-s; ⸚) **1.** ground, ✓ soil, bottom (*of a vessel, the sea*), floor: **am ~, auf den ~** on the ground (*or* floor); *sports:* **am ~ sein** be down; **zu ~ fallen** fall to the ground; F *fig.* **er war (völlig) am ~ zerstört** he was abysmally shattered; **auf britischem ~** on British soil; **den ~ unter den Füßen verlieren** *a. fig.* get out of one's depth; **(an) ~ gewinnen (verlieren)** gain (lose) ground; **aus dem ~ schießen** mushroom (up); **et. aus dem ~ stampfen** conjure s.th. up. **2.** attic.

'Boden|abstand *m mot.* ground clearance. **~belag** *m* floor covering. **~fläche** *f* **1.** ✓ acreage. **2.** △ floor space. **~frost** *m* ground frost. **~haftung** *f mot.* road holding.

'bodenlos *adj* **1.** bottomless. **2.** F *fig.* incredible, shocking.

'Boden|nebel *m* ground fog. **~per-so,nal** *n* ✈ ground crew. **~radar** *n* ground-based radar. **~re,form** *f* land reform. **~satz** *m* **1.** sediment. **2.** *fig. contp.* dregs. **~schätze** *pl* mineral resources.

'bodenständig *adj* native, local.

'Boden|stati,on *f* earth (*or* tracking) station. **~stewardeß** *f* ground hostess. **~streitkräfte** *pl* ground forces. **~tur-nen** *n* floor exercises.

bog [boːk] *pret of* **biegen**.

Bogen ['boːgən] *m* (-s; -) **1.** bow: *fig.* **den ~ überspannen** overdo it. **2.** curve, bend: *fig.* **e-n großen ~ um j-n machen** give s.o. a wide berth. **3.** ✏, ✂ arc, △ arch, vault, ◎ bend. **4.** *skating:* curve, *skiing:* turn. **5.** sheet (*of paper*).

'Bogenfenster *n* arched window.

'bogenförmig *adj* arched.

'Bogen|gang *m* arcade. **~lampe** *f* arc lamp. **~schießen** *n* archery. **~schütze** *m* archer.

Bohemien [boe'miɛ̃ː] *m* (-s; -s) bohemian.

Bohle ['boːlə] *f* (-; -n) plank.

Böhme ['bøːmə] *m* (-n; -n), **'Böhmin** *f* (-; -nen) Bohemian. **'böhmisch** *adj* Bohe-

mian: *das sind für mich ~e Dörfer*
that's (all) Greek to me.

Bohne ['bo:nə] *f* (-; -n) **⚥** a) bean, b)
broad bean: *grüne ~n* French (*or*
string) beans; *weiße ~n* haricot beans;
F *nicht die ~!* not a bit!

'**Bohnenkaffee** *m* (F real) coffee.
'**Bohnenstange** *f* beanpole (*a.* F *person*).
'**Bohnenstroh** *n* F *dumm wie ~* as thick
as two short planks.
Bohner ['bo:nər] *m* (-s; -) floor polisher.
'**bohnern** *v/t* (h) polish.
'**Bohnerwachs** *n* floor polish.
bohren ['bo:rən] (h) **I** *v/t* **1.** ⚙ a) drill, b)
bore. **II** *v/i* **2.** drill (*nach* for), bore: →
Nase. **3.** *fig.* pain *etc*: gnaw (*in dat* at).
4. *fig.* a) probe, b) keep at it (*bis* until).
III *sich ~ in* (*acc*) bore into.
'**bohrend** *adj fig.* gnawing (*pain etc*),
piercing (*look*), probing (*questions*).
'**Bohrer** *m* (-s; -) drill.
'**Bohrinsel** *f* oil rig. '**Bohrloch** *n* drill
hole. '**Bohrma,schine** *f* drill(ing machine). '**Bohrmeißel** *m*, '**Bohrstahl** *m*
boring tool. '**Bohrturm** *m* derrick.
'**Bohrung** *f* (-; -en) **1.** drilling. **2.** (drill)
hole. **3.** *mot.* bore.
'**Bohrversuch** *m* trial drilling.
böig ['bø:ıç] *adj* gusty, ✈ bumpy.
Boiler ['bɔylər] *m* (-s; -) water heater, ⚙
boiler.
Boje ['bo:jə] *f* (-; -n) buoy.
Bollwerk ['bɔlvɛrk] *n a. fig.* bulwark.
Bolschewismus [bɔlʃə'vɪsmʊs] *m* (-; *no
pl*) Bolshevism. **Bolschewist** [-'vɪst] *m*
(-en; -en), **Bolsche'wistin** *f* (-; -nen),
bolsche'wistisch *adj* Bolshevist.
Bolzen ['bɔltsən] *m* (-s; -) ⚙ bolt.
bombardieren [bɔmbar'di:rən] *v/t* (h)
bomb, *a. phys. or fig.* bombard.
bombastisch [bɔm'bastɪʃ] *adj* bombastic.
Bombe ['bɔmbə] *f* (-; -n) **1.** bomb: →
einschlagen 6. **2.** F *soccer:* rocket.
'**Bomben|a,larm** *m* bomb alert. **~an-
griff** *m* bomb attack. **~anschlag** *m* **1.**
bomb attack. **2.** → **~atten,tat** *n* bomb
attempt (*auf j-n* on s.o.'s life). **~beset-
zung** *f* F *thea. etc* star cast. **~drohung** *f*
bomb threat. **~erfolg** *m* F huge success,
smash hit. 2**fest** *adj* bombproof: F *~
überzeugt* dead sure. **~gehalt** *n* F fantastic salary. **~geschäft** *n* F roaring
business. **~sache** *f* F knockout. 2**si-**

cher *adj* **1.** bombproof. **2.** F sure-fire:
es ist e-e ~e Sache it's a dead cert.
~stimmung *f* F *es herrschte e-e ~* eve-
rybody was in roaring high spirits.
'**Bomber** *m* (-s; -) bomber (*a.* F *fig.
soccer*). '**bombig** *adj* F great, terrific.
Bon [bɔŋ] *m* (-s; -s) **1.** voucher. **2.** receipt.
Bonbon [bɔŋ'bɔŋ] *m, n* (-s; -s) **1.** sweet,
Am. candy. **2.** *F fig.* bonbon.
Bonmot [bõ'mo:] *n* (-s; -s) bon mot.
Bonus ['bo:nʊs] *m* (-[ses]; -se) **1.** bonus,
premium. **2.** special dividend.
Bonze ['bɔntsə] *m* (-n; -n) *contp.* bigwig.
Boot [bo:t] *n* (-[e]s; -e) boat: *~ fahren* go
boating; *fig. wir sitzen alle im gleichen ~* we are all in the same boat.
'**Bootsfahrt** *f* boat trip. '**Bootshaus** *n*
boathouse. '**Bootsmann** *m* (-[e]s; -leu-
te) ⚓ boatswain, ✕ petty officer.
'**Bootsverleih** *m* boat hire.
Bord[1] [bɔrt] *n* (-[e]s; -e) shelf.
Bord[2] *m* (-[e]s; -e) **1.** ✈, ⚓ *an ~* on
board, aboard; *an ~ gehen* go aboard,
✈ board the plane; *an ~ nehmen* take
aboard; *über ~ gehen a. fig.* go by the
board; *über ~ werfen a. fig.* throw
overboard. **2.** edge. '**Bordbuch** *n* ⚓
logbook. '**Bordcom,puter** *m* on-board
(*mot. a.* dashboard) computer.
Bordell [bɔr'dɛl] *n* (-s; -e) brothel.
'**Bord|funk** *m* a) ship's radio, b) aircraft
radio (equipment). **~karte** *f* ✈ boarding pass. **~me,chaniker** *m* ✈ flight mechanic. **~radar** *n* airborne radar.
~stein *m* kerb(stone), *Am.* curb(stone).
~verpflegung *f* in-flight meals.
Borg [bɔrk] *m auf ~* on credit. **borgen**
['bɔrgən] *v/t* (h) **1.** borrow: *sich et. ~*
borrow s.th. **2.** lend, *Am.* loan.
Borke ['bɔrkə] *f* (-; -n) bark, *a.* ⚘ crust.
borniert [bɔr'ni:rt] *adj* narrow-minded.
Börse ['bœrzə] *f* (-; -n) **1.** purse. **2.** ✝ (*an
[auf] der ~* on the) stock exchange: *an
die ~ gehen* firm: go public.
'**Börsen|bericht** *m* market report.
~blatt *n* financial (news)paper. 2**fähig**
adj marketable, listed: *~e Wertpapiere*
listed securities. **~geschäft** *n* stock-
-market transaction. **~krach** *m* F
(stock-exchange) crash. **~kurs** *m* market price, quotation. **~makler** *m* stockbroker. **~no,tierung** *f* quotation.
~speku,lant *m* stock-exchange speculator. **~zettel** *m* stock list.

Borste ['bɔrstə] f (-; -n) bristle.
'**borstig** adj **1.** bristly. **2.** F fig. gruff.
Borte ['bɔrtə] f (-; -n) border, braid.
bösartig ['bøːz-] adj **1.** vicious. **2.** ♣ malignant. '**Bösartigkeit** f (-; no pl) **1.** viciousness. **2.** ♣ malignancy.
Böschung ['bœʃʊŋ] f (-; -en) slope, embankment.
böse ['bøːzə] **I** adj **1.** bad, evil, wicked: **e-e ~ Sache** a bad business. **2.** vicious, nasty. **3.** naughty, bad. **4.** angry: **j-m** (or **auf j-n**) **~ sein** be angry (F mad) at s.o., be cross with s.o.; **~ werden** get angry; **bist du mir ~, wenn ...?** would you mind terribly if ...? **5.** F ♣ bad, sore: **~ Erkältung** bad cold; **~r Finger** sore finger. **II** adv **6.** badly (etc): **es sieht ~ aus** things look bad; **ich habe es nicht ~ gemeint** I meant no harm.
'**Böse I** m, f (-n; -n) bad person. **II** n (-n) evil, harm: **~s im Sinn haben** be up to no good.
'**Bösewicht** m (-[e]s; -er) a. iro. villain.
boshaft ['boːshaft] adj malicious.
'**Bosheit** f (-; -en) **1.** no pl malice: **aus ~** out of spite. **2.** snide remark. **3.** nasty trick.
Boß [bɔs] m (Bosses; Bosse) F boss.
'**böswillig** adj malicious, 🙰 a. wilful.
'**Böswilligkeit** f (-; no pl) malevolence, 🙰 wilfulness.
bot [boːt] pret of **bieten.**
Botanik [boˈtaːnɪk] f (-; no pl) botany.
Bo'taniker m (-s; -) botanist.
bo'tanisch adj botanic(al).
Bote ['boːtə] m (-n; -n) messenger.
'**Botengang** m (**e-n ~ machen** run an) errand.
Botschaft ['boːtʃaft] f (-; -en) **1.** message (a. fig.), news. **2.** pol. embassy.
'**Botschafter** m (-s; -) ambassador.
'**Botschafterin** f (-; -nen) ambassadress.
Böttcher ['bœtçɐr] m (-s; -) cooper.
Bottich ['bɔtɪç] m (-s; -e) vat, tub.
Bouillon [bʊlˈjɔŋ] f (-; -s) clear soup.
Boulevard [buləˈvaːr] m (-s; -s) boulevard. **~presse** f (-; no pl) gutter press. **~zeitung** f tabloid.
Boutique [buˈtiːk] f (-; -s) boutique.
Bowle ['boːlə] f (-; -n) **1.** punch bowl. **2.** gastr. (cold) punch.
Box [bɔks] f (-; -en) **1.** box (for horses). **2.** motor racing: pit. **3.** parking space. **4.** box camera. **5.** → **Lautsprecherbox.**

'**boxen** v/i (h) box, fight. '**Boxen** n (-s) boxing. '**Boxer** m (-s; -) boxer (a. dog).
'**Boxhandschuh** m boxing glove. '**Boxkampf** m fight, boxing match. '**Boxring** m ring. '**Boxsport** m boxing.
Boykott [bɔyˈkɔt] m (-[e]s; -s, -e), **boykottieren** [-ˈtiːrən] v/t (h) boycott.
brach [braːx] pret of **brechen.**
Brachialgewalt [braˈxiaː-l-] f (**mit ~** by) brute force.
Brachland ['braːx-] n fallow (land).
'**brachliegen** v/i (irr, sep, -ge-, h, → **liegen**) **1.** lie fallow. **2.** fig. go to waste.
brachte ['braxtə] pret of **bringen.**
Brahmane [braˈmaːnə] m (-n; -n), **brah'manisch** adj Brahman.
Branche ['brãːʃə] f (-; -n) **1.** industrial sector, trade. **2.** line (of business).
'**Branchen|kenntnis** f knowledge of the trade. **~üblich** adj usual in the trade. **~verzeichnis** n classified directory.
Brand [brant] m (-[e]s; ⁀e) **1.** (**in ~** on) fire: **in ~ geraten** catch fire; **in ~ stecken** set fire to; F **e-n ~ haben** be dying of thirst. **2.** ♣ blight, mildew. **3.** ♣ gangrene. **~blase** f blister. **~bombe** f incendiary bomb.
branden ['brandən] v/i (sn) a. fig. surge.
'**Brand|gefahr** f fire hazard. **~geruch** m burnt smell. **~herd** m **1.** source of (the) fire. **2.** fig. trouble spot. **~kata,strophe** f fire disaster. **~mal** n (-[e]s; -e) **1.** brand. **2.** fig. stigma.
brandmarken ['brantmarkən] v/t (insep, ge-, h) a. fig. brand.
'**Brand|mauer** f fire wall. **~schaden** m fire damage. **~sohle** f insole. **~stelle** f scene of the fire. **~stifter(in** f) m arsonist, incendiary. **~stiftung** f arson.
'**Brandung** f (-; no pl) surf, breakers.
'**Brand|ursache** f cause of the fire. **~wunde** f burn. **~zeichen** n brand.
brannte ['brantə] pret of **brennen.**
'**Branntwein** m spirits.
Brasilianer [braziˈliaːnɐr] m (-s; -), **Brasili'anerin** f (-; -nen), **brasili'anisch** adj Brazilian. **Brasilien** [braˈziːliən] n (-s) Brazil.
brassen ['brasən] v/t ♣ brace.
'**Bratapfel** m baked apple.
braten ['braːtən] v/t, v/i (briet, gebraten, h) roast, fry: **auf dem Rost ~** grill, broil; **am Spieß ~** barbecue; F (**in der Sonne**) **~** roast (in the sun).

'**Braten** m (-s; -) roast, joint: F fig. **den ~ riechen** smell a rat; **fetter ~** fine catch. '**Bratenfett** n dripping. '**Bratensoße** f gravy. '**bratfertig** adj oven-ready. '**Bratfett** n cooking fat. '**Bratfisch** m fried fish. '**Brathering** m grilled (and pickled) herring. '**Brathuhn** n roaster, broiler. '**Bratkar,toffeln** pl fried potatoes. '**Bratofen** m oven. '**Bratpfanne** f frying-pan. '**Bratröhre** f oven.

Bratsche ['bra:tʃə] f (-; -n) ♪ viola. '**Bratscher** m (-s; -), '**Bratscherin** f (-; -nen) viola player.

'**Bratspieß** m spit.

'**Bratwurst** f fried (or grilled) sausage.

Brauch [braʊx] m (-[e]s; ⁀e) custom, tradition, practice, ⁘ usage. '**brauchbar** adj useful, serviceable. '**Brauchbarkeit** f (-; no pl) usefulness. '**brauchen** (h) I v/t 1. need, require, take: **wie lange wird er ~?** how long will it take him? 2. → a) **gebrauchen**, b) **verbrauchen**. II v/aux need, have to: **du brauchst es nicht zu tun** you needn't (or you don't have to) do it; **du brauchst es nur zu sagen!** just say so! '**Brauchtum** n (-s; no pl) custom(s), tradition.

Braue ['braʊə] f (-; -n) (eye)brow.

'**brauen** v/t (h) brew. '**Brauer** m (-s; -) brewer. **Braue'rei** f (-; -en) brewery.

braun [braʊn] adj brown, a. (sun)-tanned: **~ werden** tan, get a tan.

Bräune ['brɔʏnə] f (-; no pl) 1. brownness. 2. (sun)tan. '**bräunen** (h) I v/t 1. brown. 2. tan (skin, person). II v/i (a. **sich ~**) a) get brown, b) tan, get a tan.

'**braungebrannt** adj tanned.

'**Braunkohle** f brown coal, lignite.

bräunlich ['brɔʏnlɪç] adj brownish.

'**Bräunungs|creme** f liquid tan (make-up). **~studio** n solarium.

Brause ['braʊzə] f (-; -n) 1. sprinkler, rose. 2. → **Dusche**. 3. F pop. '**Brause-bad** n shower. '**Brauselimo,nade** f (fizzy) lemonade, Am. lemon soda.

'**brausen** v/i 1. (h) wind etc: roar, organ etc: surge. 2. (sn) F zoom. 3. (h) (have a) shower.

'**Brausepulver** n sherbet powder.

Braut [braʊt] f (-; ⁀e) a) bride, b) fiancée, c) F (my etc) girl. **Bräutigam** ['brɔʏ-tɪgam] m (-s; -e) a) (bride)groom, b) fiancé. '**Brautjungfer** f bridesmaid. '**Brautkleid** n wedding dress. **Braut-**

paar n a) engaged couple, b) bride and bridegroom. '**Brautschleier** m bridal veil.

brav [bra:f] adj 1. good, well-behaved: **sei ~!** be good!; **sei (schön) ~ und geh zu Bett!** go to bed like a good boy (or girl)! 2. honest, good, a. iro. worthy.

bravo ['bra:vo] int well done!, bravo! '**Bravo** n (-s; -s), **~ruf** m bravo, F cheers.

Bravour [bra'vu:r] f (-; no pl) 1. dash: **mit ~** brilliantly. 2. bravery.

bravourös [bravu'rø:s] adj brilliant. **Bra'vourstück** n 1. brilliant feat. 2. ♪ bravura.

'**Brech|durchfall** m ♨ diarrh(o)ea with vomiting. **~eisen** n ⚙ crowbar.

brechen ['brɛçən] (brach, gebrochen) I v/t (h) 1. break (a. fig. oath, record, resistance, etc), fig. a. violate (contract, law): **(sich) den Arm ~** break one's arm; **die Ehe ~** commit adultery. 2. phys. break, refract (rays). 3. F ♨ vomit. II v/i 4. (sn) break (a. fig. voice etc). 5. (sn) **~ aus** (dat) burst out of. 6. (h) fig. **~ mit** (dat) break with (s.o., a habit, etc). 7. (h) F ♨ be sick, vomit. III **sich ~** (h) 8. waves: break, phys. light etc: be refracted. '**Brecher** m (-s; -) breaker.

'**Brech|mittel** n ♨ emetic. 2. F fig. **er (es) ist ein ~** sl. he (it's) enough to make you want to puke. **~reiz** m ♨ nausea. **~stange** f ⚙ crowbar.

'**Brechung** f (-; -en) phys. refraction.

Brei [braɪ] m (-[e]s; -e) a) mush (a. fig.), b) porridge, c) mash, d) ⚙ pulp: F **j-n zu ~ schlagen** beat s.o. to a pulp; **~ Katze, Koch.** '**breiig** adj mushy.

breit [braɪt] adj broad (a. fig. accent etc), a. ⚙ wide, fig. widespread: **die ~e Öf-fentlichkeit** the public at large; **ein ~es Publikum** a wide public; **~ Masse** 4.

'**Breitband...** radio: wide-band ...

'**breitbeinig** [-baɪnɪç] adj and adv with legs apart.

'**Breite** f (-; -n) width, breadth (a. fig.), astr., geogr. latitude: F **in die ~ gehen** put on weight.

'**Breiten|grad** m (degree of) latitude: **der 30. ~** the 30th parallel. **~kreis** m parallel. **~sport** m mass sport(s).

'**breitgefächert** adj wide-ranging.

'**breitmachen: sich ~** (sep, -ge-, h) F a) spread o.s. out, b) fig. fear etc: spread.

'**breitschlagen** v/t (irr, sep, -ge-, h, → **»**

schlagen F *j-n* ~ talk s.o. round, *zu et.* talk s.o. into (doing) s.th.; *sich* ~ *lassen* give in.

breitschult(e)rig ['braɪtʃʊlt(ə)rɪç] *adj* broad-shouldered.

'**Breitseite** *f* **1.** long side (*of table etc*). **2.** ♣, ✕, *a. fig.* broadside.

'**breitspurig** *adj* 🚂 broad-ga(u)ge.

'**breittreten** *v/t* (*irr, sep, -ge-, h*, → *treten*) F *fig.* enlarge (up)on (*a subject*): *et. überall* ~ talk about s.th. too much.

'**Breitwandfilm** *m* wide-screen film.

Bremsbelag ['brɛms-] *m* brake lining.

Bremse[1] ['brɛmzə] *f* (-; -n) *mot.* brake.

'**Bremse**[2] *f* (-; -n) *zo.* horsefly.

'**bremsen** (h) **I** *v/t* **1.** brake. **2.** cushion (*fall*). **3.** F *fig.* check, slow down. **II** *v/i* **4.** brake, apply the brakes. **III** *sich* ~ F restrain o.s., *mit et.* cut down on s.th.

'**Brems**|**flüssigkeit** *f* brake fluid. ~**kraftverstärker** *m* brake booster. ~**leuchte** *f*, ~**licht** *n* stop light. ~**pe**|**dal** *n* brake pedal. ~**scheibe** *f* brake disc. ~**spur** *f* skid mark(s). ~**trommel** *f* brake drum.

'**Bremsung** *f* (-; -en) **1.** braking. **2.** *nucl.* retardation.

'**Bremsvorrichtung** *f* brake mechanism.

'**Bremsweg** *m* braking distance.

brennbar ['brɛnba:r] *adj* combustible.

brennen ['brɛnən] (brannte, gebrannt, h) **I** *v/t* **1.** burn. **2.** distil(l) (*spirits*), roast (*coffee*). **3.** have *the light etc* on. **II** *v/i* **4.** burn, *house etc: a.* be on fire: *es brennt!* fire!; F *fig. wo brennt's denn?* what's wrong?; *vor Ungeduld* ~ be burning with impatience; F *darauf* ~ *zu inf* be dying to *inf*. **5.** *wound, nettle*: sting, *pepper etc*: be hot, *light, lamp*: be on. '**brennend** *adj* burning (*a. fig. question etc*): *es interessiert mich* ~ a) I'm terribly interested in it, b) *ob* I'm dying to know if.

'**Brenner** *m* (-s; -) **1.** distiller. **2.** ☼ burner. **Brenne'rei** *f* (-; -en) distillery.

'**Brennessel** *f* 🌿 (stinging) nettle.

'**Brenn**|**holz** *n* firewood. ~**materi**|**al** *n* fuel. ~**ofen** *m* kiln, *metall.* furnace. ~**punkt** *m a. fig.* focal point, focus: *fig. in den* ~ *rücken* focus attention on; *im* ~ *des Interesses stehen* be in the focus of attention. ~**spiegel** *m* burning mirror. ~**spiritus** *m* methylated spirit. ~**stab** *m nucl.* fuel rod. ~**stoff** *m* fuel. ~**weite** *f opt.* focal distance.

brenzlig ['brɛntslɪç] *adj* F *fig.* ticklish.

Bresche ['brɛʃə] *f* (-; -n) breach: *e-e* ~ *schlagen a. fig.* clear the way (*für* for); *in die* ~ *springen* step into the breach.

Brett [brɛt] *n* (-[e]s; -er) a) board, b) shelf, c) tray, d) *sports*: springboard: *Schwarzes* ~ notice (*Am.* bulletin) board; F ~*er* skis; F *fig. ein* ~ *vor dem Kopf haben* be very dense.

'**Brettspiel** *n* board game.

Brevier [bre'vi:r] *n* (-s; -e) breviary.

Brezel ['bre:tsəl] *f* (-; -n) pretzel.

Brief [bri:f] *m* (-[e]s; -e) letter (*an acc* to). ~**beschwerer** *m* paperweight. ~**bogen** *m* sheet of writing paper. ~**bombe** *f* letter bomb. ~**freund(in** *f*) *m* penfriend. ~**geheimnis** *n* privacy of correspondence. ~**kasten** *m* **1.** letterbox, *Am.* mailbox: *toter* ~ letter drop. **2.** suggestion box, *newspaper*: Question and Answer Column. ~**kastenfirma** *f* letter-box company. ~**kopf** *m* letterhead.

'**brieflich** *adj and adv* in writing, by letter(s).

'**Briefmarke** *f* (postage) stamp.

'**Briefmarken**|**album** *n* stamp album. ~**auto**|**mat** *m* stamp machine. ~**sammler(in** *f*) *m* stamp collector, philatelist. ~**sammlung** *f* stamp collection.

'**Brief**|**öffner** *m* letter opener. ~**pa**|**pier** *n* notepaper. ~**post** *f* mail, post, *Am.* first-class mail. ~**tasche** *f* wallet, *Am. a.* billfold. ~**taube** *f zo.* carrier pigeon. ~**tele**|**gramm** *n* letter telegram, *Am.* lettergram. ~**träger(in** *f*) *m* mailman, postman (postwoman). ~**umschlag** *m* envelope. ~**waage** *f* letter balance. ~**wahl** *f* postal vote, absentee voting. ~**wechsel** *m* correspondence.

Bries [bri:s] *n* (-es; -e) *gastr.* sweetbread.

briet [bri:t] *pret of* **braten.**

Brigade [bri'ga:də] *f* (-; -n) brigade.

Brikett [bri'kɛt] *n* (-s; -s) briquette.

brillant [brɪl'jant] *adj* brilliant.

Bril'lant *m* (-en; -en) diamond.

Brille ['brɪlə] *f* (-; -n) **1.** (*e-e* ~ a pair of) glasses (*or* spectacles), F specs. **2.** goggles. **3.** toilet seat.

'**Brillen**|**e**|**tui** *n* spectacle case. ~**fassung** *f*, ~**gestell** *n* spectacle frame. ~**glas** *n* lens, glass. ~**schlange** *f* **1.** *zo.* spectacled cobra. **2.** F foureyes. ~**träger(in** *f*) *m* ~ *sein* wear glasses.

bringen ['brɪŋən] *v/t* (brachte, gebracht,

h) **1.** bring, get, fetch (*all: j-m et.* s.o. s.th.). **2.** take (*[zu]* *j-m* to s.o.): *j-n ins Krankenhaus* ~ take s.o. to the hospital; *j-n nach Hause* ~ take (*or* see) s.o. home. **3.** cause, bring (*luck, relief, etc*), bear (*interest*). **4.** *j-n dazu* ~, *daß er et. tut* make s.o. do s.th. **5.** show, present (*film etc*), *thea. a.* bring, ♪ play, sing, *newspaper etc:* bring, have, carry (*an article etc*). **6.** do, manage: *es zu et.* ~ make one's mark (in life); F *das bringt's!* that's the stuff!; *das bringt's* (*auch*) *nicht!* that's no use!; *er bringt es nicht!* a) he just can't do it!, b) he's no good!; → *Leistung* 1, *weit* 6. **7.** *with prep an sich* ~ get hold of; *er brachte es auf 7 Punkte* he managed seven points; *es bis zum Major etc* ~ make it to major *etc*; *mit sich* ~ a) involve, b) require, make it necessary; *ich kann es nicht über mich* (*or übers Herz*) ~, *das zu tun* I can't bring myself to do it; *j-n um et.* ~ rob s.o. of s.th.; *j-n wieder zu sich* ~ bring s.o. round (*or* to); *j-n zum Lachen etc* ~ make s.o. laugh *etc*; → *hinter* I.

brisant [bri'zant] *adj* high-explosive, *fig.* explosive. **Brisanz** [bri'zants] *f* (-; *no pl*) explosive effect, *fig.* explosiveness.

Brise ['bri:zə] *f* (-; -n) breeze.

Brite ['brɪtə] *m* (-n; -n) British man, Briton, F Brit: *die* ~*n* the British. **Britin** *f* (-; -nen) British woman. **'britisch** *adj* British: *die* **Ωen Inseln** the British Isles.

bröck(e)lig ['brœk(ə)lɪç] *adj* crumbly. **bröckeln** ['brœkəln] *v/t, v/i* (h) crumble.

Brocken ['brɔkən] *m* (-s; -) **1.** piece, hunk, lump: F *ein* ~ (*von Mann*) a hulk of a man; *fig. ein harter* ~ a toughie. **2.** *pl* scraps (*of German etc*), snatches (*of conversation*).

brodeln ['bro:dəln] *v/i* (h) bubble, simmer, *fig.* seethe (*vor dat* with).

Brokat [bro'ka:t] *m* (-[e]s; -e) brocade.

Brom [bro:m] *n* (-s; *no pl*) bromine.

Brombeere ['brɔmbe:rə] *f* blackberry.

Bromid [bro'mi:t] *n* (-[e]s; -e) bromide.

'Bromsilber *n* bromide of silver.

Bronchial... [brɔn'çia:l-] bronchial (*asthma etc*). **Bronchien** ['brɔnçiən] *pl* bronchi. **Bronchitis** [brɔn'çi:tɪs] *f* (-; -tiden) [-çi'ti:dən]) bronchitis.

Bronze ['brõ:sə] *f* (-; -n) bronze.

'Bronzeme,daille *f* bronze medal.

'Bronzezeit *f archeol.* Bronze Age.

Brosame ['bro:za:mə] (-; -n) *fig.* crumb.

Brosche ['brɔʃə] *f* (-; -n) brooch.

broschiert [brɔ'ʃi:rt] *adj* paperback.

Broschüre [brɔ'ʃy:rə] *f* (-; -n) pamphlet.

Brot [bro:t] *n* (-[e]s; -e) bread, loaf: (*be-legtes*) ~ sandwich; *fig. das tägliche* ~ one's daily bread; *sein* ~ *verdienen* earn a living. **'Brotaufstrich** *m* spread.

Brötchen ['brø:tçən] *n* (-s; -) roll.

'Brötchengeber(in *f*) *m* F boss.

'Brot|getreide *n* breadgrain. ~*kasten* *m* bread bin, *Am.* breadbox. ~*korb* *m* bread basket: *j-m den* ~ *höher hängen* put s.o. on short commons. ~*krume* *f*, ~*krümel* *m* (bread)crumb.

'brotlos *adj* **1.** jobless. **2.** unprofitable: *das ist e-e* ~*e Kunst!* there is no money in it!

'Brot|messer *n* bread knife. ~*neid* *m* professional jealousy. ~*röster* *m* (-s; -) toaster. ~*schneidema,schine* *f* bread slicer. ~*zeit* *f* (-; -en) *dial.* snack.

brr [br] *int* **1.** whoa! **2.** ugh!

Bruch [brʊx] *m* (-[e]s; ⸚e) **1.** a) breaking, b) breakage: *zu* ~ *gehen* break, be smashed; ~ *machen* crash; *zu* ~ *fahren* smash up (*a car*). **2.** *fig.* breaking-off, rupture, breach (*of oath, peace*), violation (*of a law*): ~ *mit der Vergangenheit* (clean) break with the past; *in die Brüche gehen* break up, *marriage: a.* go on the rocks. **3.** ♪ fracture, b) rupture, hernia: *sich e-n* ~ *heben* rupture o.s. **4.** F *contp.* junk. **5.** ♪ fraction.

'Bruchband *n* (-[e]s; ⸚er) ♪ truss.

'Bruchbude *f* F *contp.* hovel, dump (*sl.*).

brüchig ['brʏçɪç] *adj* **1.** fragile, brittle. **2.** *fig.* cracked (*voice*), shaky (*marriage*).

'Bruch|landung *f* crash landing. ~*rechnung* *f* fractions. ~*schaden* *m* breakage. **Ωsicher** *adj* breakproof. ~*stelle* *f* crack, ♪ point of fracture.

'Bruchstrich *m* ♪ fraction stroke.

'Bruchstück *n* fragment (*a. fig.*), *pl fig. a.* snatches. **'bruchstückhaft I** *adj* fragmentary. **II** *adv* in fragments.

'Bruch|teil *m* fraction: *im* ~ *e-r Sekunde* in a split second. ~*zahl* *f* fraction.

Brücke ['brʏkə] *f* (-; -n) **1.** bridge (*a. ♪, ♪, ♪, gym.*): *e-e* ~ *bauen* (*or schlagen*) *über* (*acc*) build a bridge across; *fig. alle* ~*n hinter sich abbrechen* burn one's boats. **2.** rug.

'**Brückenkopf** m bridgehead.
'**Brückenpfeiler** m bridge pier.
Bruder ['bruːdər] m (-s; ⸚) brother (a. eccl., pl brethren), eccl. monk, F guy! **unter Brüdern** among friends.
'**Bruderkrieg** m fratricidal war. **brüderlich** ['bryːdərliç] adj brotherly. **Brüderlichkeit** f (-; no pl) brotherliness. '**Brudermord** m, '**Brudermörder(in** f) m fratricide. '**Brüderschaft** f (-; -en) 1. brotherhood. 2. (**mit** j-m) ~ **trinken** drink the pledge of close friendship.
Brühe ['bryːə] f (-; -n) 1. gastr. stock, broth. 2. F contp. a) dirty water, b) slop, swill, dishwater. 3. F sweat.
brühen ['bryːən] v/t (h) scald.
'**brüh|heiß** adj scalding (hot). ~**warm** adj fig. hot (news etc): **j-m et. ~ wiedererzählen** tell s.th. straightaway to s.o.
'**Brühwürfel** m stock cube.
brüllen ['brylən] v/i, v/t (h) roar (a. fig. gun, engine, etc), cow: bellow, low, children: shout, bawl: **vor Lachen ~** roar with laughter etc; F **er (es) ist zum ~!** he's (it's) a scream!
Brummbär ['brum-] m fig. grumbler.
brummen ['brumən] v/i (h) 1. bear etc: growl. 2. a. ♭ hum: **mir brummt der Kopf** my head is throbbing. 3. fig. (**über** acc about) growl, grumble. 4. F in prison: do time. '**Brummer** m (-s; -) 1. a) bluebottle, b) bumblebee. 2. F (**dicker**) ~ → '**Brummi** m (-s; -s) F juggernaut. '**brummig** adj grumpy.
'**Brummkreisel** m humming top.
'**Brummschädel** m F 1. headache. 2. hangover.
brünett [bry'nɛt] adj, **Brü'nette** f (-n; -n) brunette.
Brunft [brunft] f (-; ⸚e), '**brunften** v/i (h) hunt. rut. '**Brunftzeit** f rutting season.
Brunnen ['brunən] m (-s; -) well, spring, fountain (a. fig.), ♯ (mineral) waters.
'**Brunnenkresse** f ♀ watercress.
'**Brunnenkur** f mineral-water cure.
'**Brunnenvergiftung** f fig. calumny.
Brunst [brunst] f (-; ⸚e) zo. a) rut, b) heat, c) rutting season. **brünstig** ['brynstiç] adj zo. a) rutting, b) in heat.
brüsk [brysk] adj brusque.
brüskieren [brys'kiːrən] v/t (h) snub.
Brust [brust] f (-; ⸚e) 1. no pl breast, chest: swimming: **100 m ~** 100 metres breaststroke; F fig. **e-n zur ~ nehmen**

have a quick one; **sich j-n zur ~ nehmen** give s.o. hell. 2. bosom, breasts: (dat) **die ~ geben** breastfeed. 3. → **Bruststück. ~bein** n 1. anat. breastbone. 2. wishbone. ~**beutel** m money bag. ~**bild** n head-and-shoulder portrait. ~**drüse** f anat. mammary gland.
brüsten ['brystən] **sich ~** (h) boast (**mit** acc about).
'**Brust|fell** n anat. pleura. ~**fellentzündung** f ♯ pleurisy. ~**kasten** m, ~**korb** m rib cage, chest. ~**krebs** m ♯ breast cancer. ~**schwimmen** n breaststroke. ~**stimme** f ♪ chest voice. ~**stück** n gastr. a) brisket, b) breast. ~**tasche** f breast pocket. ~**ton** m fig. **im ~ der Überzeugung** with deep conviction.
'**Brüstung** f (-; -en) 1. parapet. 2. balustrade.
'**Brustwarze** f nipple.
'**Brustweite** f chest measurement, bust.
Brut [bruːt] f (-; -en) 1. no pl brooding. 2. a) brood, b) spawn. 3. no pl F fig. a) (children) brood, b) scum.
brutal [bru'taːl] adj brutal. **Brutalität** [brutaliˈtɛːt] f (-; -en) brutality.
'**Brutapparat** m incubator.
brüten ['bryːtən] (h) **I** v/i brood (fig. **über** dat over), hatch, hen: sit: ~**de Hitze** sweltering heat. **II** v/t → **Rache**.
'**Brüter** m (-s; -) → **Brutreaktor**: phys. **schneller ~** fast breeder (reactor).
'**Bruthenne** f sitting hen. '**Brutkasten** m incubator. '**Brutplatz** m zo. breeding ground. '**Brutre aktor** m phys. breeder reactor. '**Brutstätte** f fig. hotbed.
brutto ['bruto] adj, '**Brutto...** gross (income, weight, register ton, etc).
'**Bruttosozi alpro dukt** n gross national product.
Bub [buːp] m (-en; -en) dial. boy. **Bube** ['buːbə] m (-n; -n) cards: jack. **Bubi** ['buːbi] m (-s; -s) F contp. pipsqueak.
Buch [buːx] n (-[e]s; ⸚er) 1. book (a. ✝): ~ **führen** keep accounts, do the bookkeeping; ~ **führen über** (acc) keep a record of; fig. **wie er (es) im ~e steht** typical. 2. film: script. '**Buchbesprechung** f book review. '**Buchbinder** m (-s; -) bookbinder. '**Buchdruck** m (-[e]s; no pl) printing. '**Buchdrucker** m printer. '**Buchdruckerei** f (-; -en) 1. printing plant, press. 2. no pl printing.
Buche ['buːxə] f (-; -n) beech (tree).

buchen ['buːxən] v/t (h) **1.** book, reserve (*room, flight, etc*). **2.** ♱ book: *fig. et. als Erfolg ~* put s.th. down as a success.
Bücherei [byːçə'raɪ] f (-; -en) library.
'**Bücher|freund(in** f) m book lover. **~gutschein** m book token. **~narr** m bibliomaniac. **~re,gal** n bookshelf. **~revisi,on** f ♱ audit. **~schrank** m bookcase. **~ständer** m bookstand. **~stütze** f bookend. **~wand** f wall of bookshelves. **~weisheit** f book knowledge. **~wurm** m humor. bookworm.
'**Buchfink** m zo. chaffinch.
'**Buchforderungen** pl ♱ book claims.
'**Buchführung** f (-; no pl) ♱ bookkeeping, accountancy: *doppelte ~* double-entry bookkeeping. '**Buchgemeinschaft** f book club. '**Buchhaltung** f (-; -en) **1.** accounts department. **2.** no pl → **Buchführung.** '**Buchhandel** m book trade. '**Buchhändler(in** f) m bookseller. '**Buchhandlung** f bookshop, Am. bookstore. '**Buchhülle** f jacket, wrapper. '**Buchmacher** m (-s; -) bookmaker. '**buchmäßig** adj and adv ♱ according to the books. '**Buchmesse** f book fair. '**Buchprüfer** m auditor, accountant. '**Buchprüfung** f audit.
Buchsbaum ['buksbaʊm] m (-s; no pl) ♀ box (tree).
Buchse ['buksə] f (-; -n) ⊙ bush(ing), liner, ⚡ socket.
Büchse ['byksə] f (-; -n) **1.** tin, can, box. **2.** gun, rifle.
'**Büchsen|bier** n canned beer. **~fleisch** n tinned (*or* canned) meat. **~milch** f tinned (*or* canned) milk. **~öffner** m (-s; -) tin (*or* can) opener.
Buchstabe ['buːxʃtaːbə] m (-n; -n) letter: *großer (kleiner) ~* capital (small) letter. '**buchstabengetreu** adj literal.
buchstabieren [buːxʃta'biːrən] v/t (h) a) spell, b) spell out: *falsch ~* misspell.
'**Buchsta'bieren** n (-s) spelling.
buchstäblich ['buːxʃtɛːplɪç] adj literal.
Bucht [buxt] f (-; -en) bay, inlet.
'**Buchumschlag** m dustjacket.
'**Buchung** f (-; -en) **1.** booking, reservation. **2.** ♱ a) booking, b) entry.
'**Buchweizen** m ♀ buckwheat.
Buckel ['bukəl] m (-s; -) **1.** a) hump (*a. fig.*), hunchback, b) stoop: *e-n ~ machen* stoop, *cat:* arch its back. **2.** F back. **3.** F hillock. '**buck(e)lig** adj

hunchbacked. '**Buck(e)lige** m, f (-n; -n) hunchback.
bücken ['bykən] *sich ~* (h) bend (down) (*nach et.* to pick up s.th.).
Bückling ['byklɪŋ] m (-s; -e) **1.** gastr. smoked herring. **2.** F bow.
buddeln ['budəln] v/i, v/t (h) F dig.
Buddhismus [bʊ'dɪsmʊs] m (-; no pl) Buddhism. **Buddhist** [bʊ'dɪst] m (-en; -en), **bud'dhistisch** adj Buddhist.
Bude ['buːdə] f (-; -n) **1.** kiosk, stall. **2.** F a) *contp.* hovel, hut, dump, b) place, digs, Am. pad, c) *contp.* joint (*sl.*): *Leben in die ~ bringen* liven things up.
Budget [by'dʒeː] n (-s; -s) budget: *et. im ~ vorsehen* budget for s.th.
Büfett [by'feː] n (-s; -s) **1.** sideboard. **2.** counter, bar. **3.** gastr. buffet.
Büffel ['byfəl] m (-s; -) zo. buffalo.
büffeln ['byfəln] v/t, v/i (h) F swot, cram.
Büffler ['byflər] m (-s; -), **Büfflerin** f (-; -nen) F swot.
Bug [buːk] m (-[e]s; -e) **1.** ⚓ bow, ✈ nose: *fig. Schuß vor den ~* warning shot. **2.** zo. shoulder (*a. gastr.*).
Bügel ['byːgəl] m (-s; -) **1.** hanger. **2.** stirrup. **3.** ear piece (*of spectacles*). **4.** ⊙ bow, shackle. **~brett** n ironing board. **~eisen** n iron. **~falte** f crease.
'**bügelfrei** adj noniron, drip-dry.
bügeln ['byːgəln] v/t, v/i (h) iron, press. '**Bügelpresse** f (laundry) press.
Buggy ['bagi] m (-s; -s) (*car:* beach) buggy.
Bügler ['byːglər] m (-s; -), '**Büglerin** f (-; -nen) ironer, presser.
bugsieren [bʊ'ksiːrən] v/t **1.** ⚓ tow. **2.** F fig. steer.
buh [buː] int boo! **Buh** n (-s; -s) F boo.
buhen ['buːən] v/i (h) F boo.
buhlen ['buːlən] v/i (h) **~ um** strive after; *um j-s Gunst ~* court s.o.'s favo(u)r.
'**Buhmann** m (-[e]s; -er) fig. bogey man.
Buhne ['buːnə] f (-; -n) groyne.
Bühne ['byːnə] f (-; -n) **1.** thea. stage, w.s. theat/re (Am. -er): *hinter der ~ a. fig.* backstage; F fig. *et. über die ~ bringen* bring s.th. off; *glatt über die ~ gehen* go off smoothly; *von der politischen etc ~ abtreten* quit the political etc scene. **2.** a. ⊙ platform.
'**Bühnen|anweisung** f stage direction. **~arbeiter** m stage hand. **~bearbeitung** f stage adaptation. **~beleuchtung**

f stage lighting. **~bild** *n* (stage) set. **~bildner(in** *f*) *m* stage designer. **~fassung** *f* stage version. **~künstler(in** *f*) *m* stage artist. **~laufbahn** *f* stage career. **~meister** *m* stage manager. **~rechte** *pl* stage rights. **2reif** *adj* ready for the stage. **~stück** *n* (stage) play. **~werk** *n* drama. **2wirksam** *adj* stageworthy.

'Buhrufe *pl* boos.

Bukett [bu'kɛt] *n* (-s; -s, -e) bouquet.

Bulette [bu'lɛtə] *f* (-; -n) *gastr.* meatball.

Bulgare [bʊl'ga:rə] *m* (-n; -n) Bulgarian.

Bulgarien [bʊl'ga:riən] *n* (-s) Bulgaria.

Bul'garin *f* (-; -nen), **bul'garisch** *adj* Bulgarian.

'Bullauge *n* ⊕ porthole.

'Bulldogge *f zo.* bulldog.

Bulle¹ ['bʊlə] *m* (-n; -n) **1.** *zo.* bull (*a.* F *contp. man*). **2.** F *contp.* cop, bull: *die ~n a.* the fuzz.

'Bulle² *f* (-; -n) *eccl.* (papal) bull.

Bullenhitze *f* F scorching heat.

Bulletin [bʏl'tɛ̃:] *n* (-s; -s) bulletin.

'bullig *adj* **1.** bull-like, hefty. **2.** F scorching (*heat*).

Bully ['bʊli] *n* (-s; -s) **1.** *hockey:* bully. **2.** *icehockey:* face-off.

bum [bʊm] *int* bang!

Bumerang ['bu:məraŋ] *m* (-s; -e, -s) boomerang.

Bummel ['bʊməl] *m* (-s; -) F stroll. **Bummelant** [bʊmə'lant] *m* (-en; -en), **Bumme'lantin** *f* (-; -nen) → **Bummler(in)** 2. **Bumme'lei** *f* (-; *no pl*) F a) dawdling, b) loafing. **'bumm(e)lig** *adj* F dawdling, slow. **'bummeln** *v/i* (h) F **1.** (go for a) stroll: **~ gehen** go for a stroll, *w.s.* go on a binge. **2.** a) dawdle, b) loaf. **'Bummelstreik** *m* go-slow. **'Bummelzug** *m* F slow train. **'Bummler** *m* (-s; -), **'Bummlerin** *f* (-; -nen) F **1.** stroller. **2.** a) dawdler, b) loafer.

bums [bʊms] *int* bang! **Bums** *m* (-es; -e) bang, crash. **bumsen** ['bʊmzən] *v/i* (h) **1.** bang, crash. **2.** V *mit j-m* (*v/t j-n*) *~* bang s.o., screw s.o., have it off with s.o. **'Bumslo,kal** *n* F low dive.

Bund¹ [bʊnt] *n* (-[e]s; -e) bundle, bunch.

Bund² *m* (-[e]s; *~e*) **1.** union, bond: *~ der Ehe* union, bond of marriage. **2.** pact: *im ~e mit* together with, *b.s.* in league with. **3.** *pol.* alliance, *n.s.* federation: *der ~* a) the Federal Government, b) →

Bundesrepublik, c) F → **Bundeswehr. 4.** association, union.

Bund³ *m* (-[e]s; *~e*) waistband.

Bündel ['bʏndəl] *n* (-s; -) bundle. **'bündeln** *v/t* (h) bundle up, bunch, *phys.* focus.

'bündelweise *adv* in bundles.

'Bundes... *pol.* (German) Federal ... **~bahn** *f* Federal Railway(s). **~bank** *f* (-; *no pl*) German Central Bank. **~behörde** *f* federal authority. **~bürger(in** *f*) *m* German citizen. **2deutsch** *adj* (German) Federal. **~ebene** *f auf ~* on a national level. **~gebiet** *n* Federal territory. **~genosse** *m* ally. **~gerichtshof** *m* Federal Supreme Court. **~kabi,nett** *n* (German) federal cabinet. **~kanzler** *m* German (*or* Federal) Chancellor. **~kar,tellamt** *n* Federal Cartel Office. **~krimi,nalamt** *n* Federal Bureau of Criminal Investigation. **~land** *n* (federal) state, land, Land: *die neuen Bundesländer* the newly-reunified German states. **~liga** *f sports:* **erste** (**zweite**) *~* First (Second) Division. **~mi,nister(in** *f*) *m* minister (*für* of). **~post** *f* Federal Post Office. **~präsi,dent** *m* German (*or* Federal) President. **~presseamt** *n* Federal Information Agency. **~rat** *m* Bundesrat, Upper House (of the Federal parliament). **~re,gierung** *f* Federal Government. **~repu,blik** *f ~ Deutschland* Federal Republic of Germany. **~staat** *m* a) federal state, b) (con)federation. **~straße** *f* major road. **~tag** *m* Bundestag, Lower House (of the German parliament). **~tagsprä-si,dent(in** *f*) *m* speaker of the Bundestag. **~tagswahl** *f* parliamentary elections. **~trainer(in** *f*) *m* coach of the national team. **~verfassungsgericht** *n* Federal Constitutional Court. **~wehr** *f* (-; *no pl*) (German) armed forces.

'bundesweit *adj* and *adv* nation-wide.

bündig ['bʏndɪç] *adj* a) concise, b) precise, c) curt: → *kurz* 4.

Bündnis ['bʏntnɪs] *n* (-ses; -se) alliance. **'bündnisfrei** *adj pol.* nonaligned.

'Bündnispartner *m* ally.

'Bundweite *f* waist (size).

Bungalow ['bʊŋgalo] *m* (-s; -s) bungalow.

Bunker ['bʊŋkər] *m* (-s; -) ✕ a) bunker (*a. for coal, a. golf*), b) air-raid shelter.

Bunsenbrenner ['bʊnzən-] *m* 🜂 Bunsen burner.

bunt [bʊnt] *adj* **1.** colo(u)rful (*a. fig.*), (multi)colo(u)red, stained (*glass*); → **Hund. 2.** *fig.* chequered, *Am.* checkered, motley, mixed, varied: **~er Abend** variety show; F **er treibt es zu ~** he goes too far.

'**Buntdruck** *m* (-[e]s; -e) **1.** colo(u)r printing. **2.** colo(u)r print. '**Buntstift** *m* crayon. '**Buntwäsche** *f* colo(u)reds.

Bürde ['bʏrdə] *f* (-; -n) *a. fig.* burden.

Burg [bʊrk] *f* (-; -en) castle.

Bürge ['bʏrgə] *m* (-n; -n) 🜨 guarantor (*a. fig.*), surety. **2.** reference.

'**bürgen** *v/i* (h) **~ für** 🜨 stand surety for, *w.s.* guarantee, vouch for.

'**Bürger** *m* (-s; -), '**Bürgerin** *f* (-; -nen) a) citizen, b) inhabitant, resident.

'**Bürgerinitia,tive** *f* civic action group. '**Bürgerkrieg** *m* civil war.

'**bürgerlich** *adj* **1.** middle-class, *contp.* bourgeois: **~e Küche** home cooking. **2.** untitled. **3.** civil, civic: **~es Gesetzbuch** Civil Code; **~es Recht** civil law; **~rechtlich** civil-law, under civil law.

'**Bürgerliche** *m*, *f* (-n; -n) commoner.

'**Bürgermeister** *m* mayor. '**bürgernah** *adj* people-oriented, grassroots (*politician, politics, etc*). '**Bürgerpflicht** *f* civic duty. '**Bürgerrecht** *n usu. pl* civil rights. '**Bürgerrechtler** [-rɛçtlər] *m* (-s; -), '**Bürgerrechtlerin** *f* (-; -nen) civil rights activist. '**Bürgerrechtsbewegung** *f* civil rights movement.

'**Bürgerschaft** *f* (-; -) citizens.

'**Bürgersteig** *m* pavement, *Am.* sidewalk.

'**Bürgertum** *n* (-s; *no pl*) the middle classes.

'**Burgfriede** *m fig.* truce. '**Burggraben** *m* moat. '**Burggraf** *m* burgrave.

'**Bürgschaft** *f* (-; -en) 🜨 surety, guarantee (*a. fig.*), bail: **~ leisten, die ~ übernehmen** a) stand surety, b) go (*or* give) bail, c) **für e-n Wechsel** *etc* guarantee a bill *etc.*

Burgunder [bʊr'gʊndər] *m* (-s; -), **Bur'gunderwein** *m* burgundy.

burlesk [bʊr'lɛsk] *adj* burlesque, farcical. **Bur'leske** *f* (-; -n) burlesque, farce.

Büro [by'ro:] *n* (-s; -s) (*im ~ at the*) office. **~angestellte** *m*, *f* office employee (*or* worker, clerk). **~arbeit** *f* office work.

~bedarf *m* office supplies. **~chef** *m* head clerk. **~gebäude** *n* office building. **~klammer** *f* paper clip.

Bürokrat [byro'kra:t] *m* (-en; -en) bureaucrat. **Bürokratie** [byrokra'ti:] *f* (-; -n) **1.** bureaucracy. **2.** → **Bürokratismus. büro'kratisch** *adj* bureaucratic. **Bürokratismus** [byrokra'tɪsmʊs] *m* (-; *no pl*) red tape.

Bü'ro|ma,schine *f* office machine. **~möbel** *pl* office furniture. **~perso,nal** *n* office staff. **~schluß** *m* (-sses; *no pl*) (office) closing time: **nach ~** after hours. **~stunden** *pl* office hours.

Bursche ['bʊrʃə] *m* (-n; -n) **1.** boy, lad. **2.** fellow, F guy: **ein übler ~** a bad egg. '**Burschenschaft** *f* (-; -en) (students') fraternity.

burschikos [bʊrʃi'ko:s] *adj* pert.

Bürste ['bʏrstə] *f* (-; -n) brush (*a. ✄, ⊙*).

'**bürsten** *v/t* (h) brush.

'**Bürstenschnitt** *m* crew cut.

Bürzel ['bʏrtsəl] *m* (-s; -) **1.** *zo.* rump. **2.** *hunt.* tail. **3.** F *gastr.* parson's nose.

Bus [bʊs] *m* (-ses; -se) F bus, coach: **mit dem ~ fahren** go by bus.

'**Busbahnhof** *m* bus terminal.

Busch [bʊʃ] *m* (-es; -e) **1.** a) bush (*a. primeval forest*), shrub, b) copse, thicket: F **bei j-m auf den ~ klopfen** sound s.o.; **hinterm ~ halten mit** be quiet about; **er ist im ~!** there's s.th. going on! **2.** bunch.

'**Büschel** *n* (-s; -) **1.** bunch. **2.** tuft, wisp (*of hair etc*). **3.** cluster (*of flowers etc*). **4.** *phys.* pencil, brush.

'**Buschhemd** *n* jacket shirt.

'**buschig** *adj* bushy.

'**Buschwindröschen** *n* wood anemone.

Busen ['bu:zən] *m* (-s; -) breast(s), bust, bosom (*a. fig.*).

'**Busenfreund(in** *f*) *m* bosom friend.

'**Busfahrer(in** *f*) *m* bus driver.

'**Busfahrt** *f* bus ride, *w.s.* coach tour.

'**Bushaltestelle** *f* bus stop. '**Buslinie** *f* bus route: **die ~ 8** (bus) number 8.

Bussard ['bʊsart] *m* (-s; -e) *zo.* buzzard.

Buße ['bu:sə] *f* (-; -n) **1.** 🜨 penalty, fine. **2.** penance, atonement: **~ tun → büßen** ['by:sən] *v/t, v/i* (h) do penance: **~ für** atone for, *fig.* pay (*or* suffer) for; **das sollst du mir ~!** you'll pay for that!

'**Büßer** *m* (-s; -), '**Büßerin** *f* (-; -nen) penitent. '**bußfertig** *adj* penitent.

'**Bußgeld** n fine. **bescheid** m notice of fine due. **kata,log** m list of fines.
'**Buß- und 'Bettag** m Day of Prayer and Repentance.
Büste ['by:stə] f (-; -n) bust.
'**Büstenhalter** m brassière, F bra.
Butan [bu'ta:n] n (-s; no pl) 🝫 butane.
Butt [but] m (-[e]s; -e) flounder.
Bütte ['bytə] f (-; -n) tub, vat.
'**Büttenpa,pier** n handmade paper.
'**Büttenrede** f carnival speech.
Butter ['butər] f (-; no pl) butter: F **alles in ~!** everything's okay! **berg** m F fig. butter mountain. **blume** f buttercup.

brot n (slice of) bread and butter: F **für ein ~** a) get s.th. for a song, b) work for peanuts. **brotpa,pier** n grease-proof paper. **creme** f gastr. butter cream. **dose** f butter dish. **messer** n butter knife. **milch** f buttermilk.
buttern ['butərn] (h) **I** v/t **1.** (spread with) butter. **2.** F **Geld in et. ~** sink money into s.th. **II** v/i **3.** make butter.
'**butterweich** adj a. F fig. very soft.
Butzenscheibe ['butsən-] f bull's-eye (pane).
Byte [bait] n (-[s]; -[s]) computer: byte.

C

C, c [tse:] n (-; -) a. ♪ C, c.
Café [ka'fe:] n (-s; -s) café. **Cafeteria** [kafete'ri:a] f (-; -s) cafeteria.
campen ['kɛmpən] v/i (h) camp.
'**Camper** m (-s; -) camper (a. mot.).
Camping|ausrüstung ['kɛmpiŋ-] f camping gear. **bus** m camper. **führer** m camping guide. **platz** m camping site, campsite. **tisch** m folding table.
Cape [ke:p] n (-s; -s) cape.
Caravan ['ka(:)ravan] m (-s; -s) a) estate car, Am. station wagon, b) caravan, Am. trailer.
Cäsium ['tsɛ:ziʊm] n (-s; no pl) 🝫 c(a)esium.
Catcher ['kɛtʃər] m (-s; -) all-in wrestler.
CB-Funk ['tse:'be:-] m CB (= citizens' band) radio.
C-Dur ['tse:-] n (-; no pl) ♪ C major.
Cellist [tʃɛ'list] m (-en; -en), **Cel'listin** f (-; -nen) cellist.
Cello ['tʃɛlo] n (-s; -s) cello.
Cellophan [tsɛlo'fa:n] n (-s; no pl) (TM) cellophane.
Celsius ['tsɛlziʊs] n undeclined celsius: **20 Grad ~** a. 20 degrees centigrade.
Cembalist [tʃɛmba'list] m (-en; -en), **Cemba'listin** f (-; -nen) harpsichord-ist. **Cembalo** ['tʃɛmbalo] n (-s; -s, -li) harpsichord.
Ces [tsɛs] n (-; -) ♪ C flat.

Chalet [ʃa'le:] n (-s; -s) chalet.
Chamäleon [ka'mɛ:leɔn] n (-s; -s) zo. or fig. chameleon.
Champagner [ʃam'panjər] m (-s; -) champagne.
Champignon ['ʃampinjɔn] m (-s; -s) (button) mushroom.
Chance ['ʃã:sə] f (-; -n) chance, pl a. prospects: **k-e ~, nicht die geringste ~** not a chance; **bei j-m ~n haben** stand a chance with s.o. '**Chancengleichheit** f equal opportunities.
Chanson [ʃã'sõ:] n (-s; -s) chanson.
Chaos ['ka:ɔs] n (-; no pl) chaos.
Chaote [ka'o:tə] m (-n; -n) F chaotic person, pol. violent anarchist, w.s. yob.
cha'otisch adj chaotic.
Charakter [ka'raktər] m (-s; -e [-'te:rə]) character, nature: **vertraulichen ~s** talks etc of a confidential nature. **Cha'rakter|darsteller(in** f) m character actor (actress). **eigenschaft** f trait. **fehler** m weakness, flaw.
cha'rakterfest adj of strong character.
charakterisieren [karakteri'zi:rən] v/t (h) **1.** characterize, mark. **2.** describe (**als** as). **Charakteri'sierung** f (-; -en) **1.** characterization. **2.** description.
Charakteristik [karakte'ristik] f (-; -en) **1.** characterization. **2.** 🜨, ✪ character-istic. **charakte'ristisch** adj (**für** of)

characteristic, typical. **cha'rakterlich I** adj of (one's) character, moral. **II** adv in character.

cha'rakterlos adj **1.** unprincipled, weak. **2.** colo(u)rless. **Cha'rakterlosigkeit** f (-; no pl) lack of character.

Cha'rakter|rolle f thea. character part. **~schwäche** f weakness (of character). **~stärke** f strength (of character). **♀voll** adj full of character. **~zug** m trait.

Charge ['ʃarʒə] f (-; -n) **1.** thea. supporting part. **2.** metall. charge.

Charisma ['ça:rısma] n (-s; -men, -mata) charisma. **charismatisch** [çarıs'ma:-tıʃ] adj charismatic.

charmant [ʃar'mant] adj charming.

Charme [ʃarm] m (-s; no pl) (**s-n ~ spielen lassen** turn on the old) charm.

Charta ['karta] f (-; -s) pol. charter.

Charter ['ʃ(t)ʃartər] m (-s; -s) charter. **'Charterflug** m charter flight.

'Charterma,schine f charter plane.

chartern ['(t)ʃartərn] v/t (h) charter.

Chassis [ʃa'si:] n (-; -) chassis.

Chauffeur [ʃɔ'føːr] m (-s; -e) driver, chauffeur.

Chauvi ['ʃoːvi] m (-s; -s) F male chauvinist (pig). **Chauvinismus** [ʃovi'nıs-mʊs] m (-; no pl) (**männlicher ~** male) chauvinism. **Chauvi'nist** m (-en; -en) **1.** chauvinist. **2.** → Chauvi. **chauvi'nistisch** adj chauvinistic.

checken ['tʃɛkən] v/t (h) check.

'Checkliste f check list.

Chef [ʃɛf] m (-s; -s) **1.** head, F boss. **2.** gastr. chef. **'Chefarzt** m medical superintendent. **'Chefe,tage** f executive floor. **'Chefideo,loge** m chief ideologue. **'Chefin** f (-; -nen) **1.** → Chef. **2.** F the boss's wife. **'Chefkonstruk,teur** m chief designer. **'Chefpi,lot** m chief pilot. **'Chefredak,teur(in** f) m editor in chief. **'Chefsekre,tär(in** f) m executive (or personal) assistant, Am. executive (or private) secretary.

Chemie [çe'mi:] f (-; no pl) chemistry. **Che'miefaser** f synthetic fibre (Am. fiber). **Che'mieindu,strie** f chemicals industry. **Chemikalien** [çemi'ka:liən] pl chemicals. **Chemiker** ['çe:mikər] m (-s; -), **'Chemikerin** f (-; -nen) (analytical) chemist. **chemisch** ['çe:mıʃ] adj chemical: **~e Reinigung** dry cleaning; **et. ~ reinigen lassen** have s.th. dry-cleaned.

Chemo'techniker(in f) m [çe:mo-] laboratory technician.

Chicorée ['ʃikore] m (-s; no pl) chicory.

Chiffre ['ʃıfrə] f (-; -n) **1.** cipher, code. **2.** box number. **'Chiffreanzeige** f box-number advertisement.

chiffrieren [ʃı'fri:rən] v/t (h) (en)code.

Chile ['tʃi:le] n (-s) Chile. **Chilene** [tʃi'le:nə] m (-n; -n), **Chi'lenin** f (-; -nen), **chi'lenisch** adj Chilean.

China ['çi:na] (-s) China. **Chinese** [çi'ne:zə] m (-n; -n), **Chi'nesin** f (-; -nen), **chi'nesisch** adj Chinese.

Chinin [çi'ni:n] n (-s; no pl) quinine.

Chip [tʃıp] m (-s; -s) **1.** a. computer: chip. **2.** pl gastr. (potato) crisps (Am. chips).

Chirurg [çi'rʊrk] m (-en; -en) surgeon. **Chirurgie** [çirʊr'gi:] f (-; no pl) surgery. **Chir'urgin** [-gın] f (-; -nen) surgeon. **chir'urgisch** [-gıʃ] adj surgical.

Chlor [klo:r] n (-s; no pl) ♈ chlorine. **'Chlorgas** n ♈ chloric gas.

Chlorid [klo'ri:t] n (-s; -e) ♈ chloride. **chlorieren** [klo'ri:rən] v/t (h) chlorinate. **Chlorophyll** [kloro'fyl] n (-s; no pl) ♣ chlorophyll.

Cholera ['ko:lera] f (-; no pl) ♣ cholera. **cholerisch** [ko'le:rıʃ] adj choleric. **Cholesterin** [çoleste'ri:n] n (-s; no pl) ♣ cholesterol. **Choleste'rinspiegel** m ♣ cholesterol level.

Chor [ko:r] m (-[e]s; ʊe) choir (a. △), chorus (a. thea.): fig. **im ~** in chorus.

Choral [ko'ra:l] m (-s; Choräle) hymn, chorale.

Choreograph [koreo'gra:f] m (-en; -en), **Choreo'graphin** f (-; -nen) choreographer. **Choreographie** [koreogra'fi:] f (-; -n) choreography.

'Chor|gesang m choral singing (or music). **~gestühl** n (choir) stalls. **~knabe** m choirboy. **~sänger(in** f) m chorister.

Christ... [krıst-] → **Weihnachts...**

Christ m (-en; -en), **'Christin** f (-; -nen) Christian. **'Christenheit** f (-; no pl) Christendom. **'Christentum** n (-s; no pl) Christianity. **'Christkind** n (-[e]s; no pl) **1.** infant Jesus. **2.** F Father Christmas, Santa Claus. **'christlich** adj (adv like a) Christian.

Chrom [kro:m] n (-s; no pl) chromium. **chromatisch** [kro'ma:tıʃ] adj ♪ chromatic. **Chromosom** [kromo'zo:m] n (-s; -en) chromosome.

Chronik ['kroːnɪk] *f* (-; -en) chronicle.
chronisch ['kroːnɪʃ] *adj* 🏥 chronic.
Chronist [kroˈnɪst] *m* (-en; -en), **Chroˈnistin** *f* (-; -nen) chronicler.
Chronologie [kronoloˈgiː] *f* (-; -n) chronology. **chronologisch** [kronoˈloːgɪʃ] *adj* chronological.
circa ['tsɪrka] *adv* about, approximately.
Cis [tsɪs] *n* (-; -) ♪ C sharp.
City ['sɪti] *f* (-; -s) (town) centre, *Am.* downtown.
Clique ['klɪkə] *f* (-; -n) clique, F crowd.
Clou [kluː] *m* (-s; -s) **1.** high spot, climax. **2.** point.
Cockpit ['kɔkpɪt] *n* ✈, ⚓, *mot.* cockpit.
Code [koːt] *m* (-s; -s) code.
codieren [koˈdiːrən] *v/t* (h) (en)code.
Coˈdierung *f* (-; -en) (en)coding.
Collage [kɔˈlaːʒə] *f* (-; -n) collage.
Computer [kɔmˈpjuːtər] *m* (-s; -) computer. **comˈputergesteuert** *adj* computer-controlled. **comˈputergestützt** *adj* computer-aided. **computerisieren** [kɔmpjuːtəriˈziːrən] *v/t* (h) computerize. **Comˈputerspiel** *n* computer game.
Conférencier [kõferãˈsiːeː] *m* (-s; -s) compère, *Am.* emcee.

Container [kɔnˈteːnər] *m* (-s; -) container. **~schiff** *n* container ship.
Contergankind [kɔntɛrˈgaːn-] *n* F thalidomide child.
Couch [kaʊtʃ] *f* (-; -es) couch.
'Couchgarniˌtur *f* three-piece suite.
'Couchtisch *m* coffee table.
Coup [kuː] *m* (-s; -s) coup.
Coupé [kuˈpeː] *n* (-s; -s) **1.** railway compartment. **2.** coupé (*a. mot.*).
Coupon [kuˈpõː] *m* (-s; -s) coupon, counterfoil.
Courage [kuˈraːʒə] *f* (-; *no pl*) F courage, pluck. **couragiert** [kuraˈʒiːrt] *adj* F courageous, plucky.
Cousin [kuˈzɛ̃ː] *m* (-s; -s) (male) cousin.
Cousine [kuˈziːnə] *f* (-; -n) (female) cousin; → *a.* **Kusine.**
Creme [kreːm] *f* (-; -s) **1.** cream. **2.** *gastr.* crème. **'cremefarben** *adj* cream-colo(u)red. **'Cremetorte** *f* cream gateau. **'cremig** *adj* creamy.
Cup [kap] *m* (-s; -s) *sports:* Cup.
'Cupfiˌnale *n sports:* Cup Final.
Curry ['kœri; 'kari] *n* (-s; -s) **1.** curry. **2.** curry powder.
Cutter ['katər] *m* (-s; -), **'Cutterin** *f* (-; -nen) *film etc:* cutter.

D

D, d [deː] *n* (-; -) D, d, ♪ D.
da [daː] **I** *adv* **1.** a) there, b) here; *der* (*die, das*) ... ~ that ... (there); ~ *und dort* here and there; *er ist* ~ he's here, he has arrived; ~ *kommt sie* here she comes; ~ *liegt die Schwierigkeit* that's the difficulty; ~ (*hast du*)*!* there you are!; *sieh* ~*!* look at that!; ~ *haben wir's!* there (you are)!; *nichts* ~*!* nothing doing!; → *dasein.* **2.** then, at that time: ~ *erst* only then; *hier und* ~ now and then. **3.** (*in that case*) there, here: ~ *bin ich Ihrer Meinung* I do agree with you there; *was kann man* ~ *machen?* what's to be done?; *was gibt's denn* ~ *zu lachen?* what's so funny about it?; *und* ~ *zögerst du noch?* and you still

hesitate. **II** *conj* as, since, because.
dabei [daˈbaɪ] **I** *adv* **1.** near, near by, close by: *ein Brief war nicht* ~ there was no letter (with it). **2.** ~ *sein, et. zu tun* be about to do, be on the point of doing. **3.** at the same time: *sie strickte und hörte Radio* ~ while knitting she listened to the radio. **4.** as well, into the bargain. **5.** yet, nevertheless. **6.** on the occasion, as a result: ~ *gab es Streit* this led to a quarrel; *alle* ~ *entstehenden Kosten* all costs incurred; *es kommt nichts* ~ *heraus* nothing will come of it. **7.** present, there: → *bleiben* 3, **dabeisein. 8.** *ich dachte mir nichts* ~ a) I meant no harm, b) I paid no particular attention to it; *es ist nichts* ~*!* a)

there's nothing to it!, b) there's no harm in it!; **was ist schon ~?** what of it?; **lassen wir es ~!** let's leave it at that! II *conj* but, (and) yet.

da'beibleiben *v/i* (*irr, sep,* -ge-, sn, → **bleiben**) stay (*or* remain) with it, them *etc*; → *a.* **bleiben** 3.

da'beihaben *v/t* (*irr, sep,* -ge-, h, → **haben**) F have *s.o., s.th.* there: **kein Geld ~** have no money on one.

da'beisein *v/i* (*irr, sep,* -ge-, sn, → **sein**) a) be present, be there, take part, b) be a witness: **ich bin dabei!** count me in!

da'beistehen *v/i* (*irr, sep,* -ge-, h, → **stehen**) stand by (*or* there).

'dableiben *v/i* (*irr, sep,* -ge-, sn, → **bleiben**) remain, stay.

Dach [dax] *n* (-[e]s, ⁀er) roof, *mot.* a. top, *fig.* a. shelter: **unter ~ und Fach bringen** a) shelter, b) *fig.* complete; F *fig.* **eins aufs ~ kriegen** get it in the neck.

'Dach|an,tenne *f* roof (*mot.* over-car) aerial (*Am.* antenna). **~balken** *m* rooftree. **~boden** *m* loft. **~decker** [-dɛkər] *m* (-s; -) roofer. **~fenster** *n* dormer (window). **~first** *m* ridge (of a roof). **~garten** *m* roof garden. **~gepäckhalter** *m* roof rack. **~geschoß** *n* attic stor(e)y, loft. **~gesellschaft** *f* ✝ holding company. **~kammer** *f* attic, garret. **~luke** *f* skylight. **~pappe** *f* roofing (felt). **~rinne** *f* gutter, eaves.

Dachs [daks] *m* (-es; -e) *zo.* badger.

'Dachstuhl *m* roof truss, timbering.

dachte ['daxtə] *pret of* **denken**.

'Dach|ter,rasse *f* roof terrace. **~verband** *m* ✝ umbrella organization. **~wohnung** *f* attic flat. **~ziegel** *m* (roofing) tile.

Dackel ['dakəl] *m* (-s; -) *zo.* dachshund.

dadurch [da'durç] I *adv* **1.** through it (*or* there), that way. **2.** a) by it, b) because of that: **alle ~ verursachten Schäden** all damages caused thereby; **sie verschlief und kam ~ zu spät** she overslept, and so she was late. II *conj* **3. ~, daß es regnete** because of the rain. **4. ~, daß er weniger ißt** by eating less.

dafür [da'fy:r] I *adv* **1.** for it (them, this, *etc*). **2.** in return (for it), instead of (it). **3. ~ sein** be for it, be in favo(u)r of it; **ich bin ~ zu bleiben** I'm for staying; **ich bin sehr ~!** I'm all for it!; *parl.* **die**

Mehrheit ist ~ the ayes have it; → **sprechen** I. **4. ~ wirst du ja bezahlt** that's what you are paid for. II *conj* **5. er wurde ~ bestraft, daß er gelogen hatte** he was punished for lying. **6. ~ sorgen, daß** see to it that. **7.** but (then): **sie arbeiten langsam, ~ aber sorgfältig** they are slow but diligent.

Da'fürhalten *n* (-s) **nach m-m** *etc* ~ in my *etc* opinion, as I *etc* see it.

da'fürkönnen *v/i* (*irr, sep,* -ge-, h, → **können**) F **ich kann nicht dafür** it's not my fault, I cannot help it.

dagegen [da'ge:gən] I *adv* **1.** against it (*or* that): **~ hilft Wärme** warmth is good for it; **~ hilft nichts** there is no remedy (for it), *w.s.* it can't be helped; **~ sein** be against it; **ich bin ~, daß du allein gehst** I'm against you(r) going alone; **haben Sie et. ~, wenn ich rauche?** do you mind if I smoke?; **ich habe nichts ~** I don't mind. **2.** by (*or* in) comparison, compared with. **3.** in exchange (for it). II *conj* a) but, however, on the other hand, b) whereas, while.

da'gegenhalten *v/i* (*irr, sep,* -ge-, h, → **halten**) argue (against it). **da'gegensprechen** *v/i* (*irr, sep,* -ge-, h, → **sprechen**) speak against it. **da'gegenstellen: sich ~** (*sep,* -ge-, h) *fig.* oppose it.

daheim [da'haɪm] *adv dial.* a) at home, b) back home. **Da'heim** *n* (-s) home.

daher [da'he:r] I *adv* **1.** from there. **2. ~ von ~** therefore; **~ kommt es, daß** that's why (*or* how); **~ ihr Mißtrauen** hence her suspicion. II *conj* a. **von ~** that's why, (and) so.

da'hergelaufen *adj* F *contp.* **jeder ~e Kerl** any guy who happens along.

dahin [da'hɪn] I *adv* **1.** there: **auf dem Weg ~** on the way there; **ist es noch weit bis ~?** is it much farther? **2. bis ~** a) until then, till then, b) by then; **bis ~ bin ich fertig** I'll be finished by then. **3.** to the effect: **sich ~ (gehend) einigen, daß** agree that. **4. es ~ bringen, daß** bring matters to the stage where; **j-n ~ bringen, daß** bring s.o. to the point of ger. II *adj* gone, lost.

da'hingestellt *adj* et. **~ sein lassen** leave it open as to whether; **das bleibt ~** that remains to be seen.

da'hinreden, da'hinsagen *v/t* (*sep,* -ge-, h) say *s.th.* without thinking.

da'hinschleppen: *sich* ~ (*sep*, -ge-, h) **1.** drag o.s. along. **2.** *fig.* drag on.

da'hinsiechen *v/i* (*sep*, -ge-, sn) waste away.

dahinten [da'hıntən] *adv* back there.

dahinter [da'hıntər] *adv* behind it *etc*, at the back (of him *etc*): *fig.* **es ist nichts ~** there's nothing behind it.

da'hinterklemmen: *sich* ~ (*sep*, -ge-, h) F buckle down (to it).

da'hinterkommen *v/i* (*irr*, *sep*, -ge-, sn, → kommen) F find out (about it).

da'hinterstecken *v/i* (*sep*, -ge-, h) *fig.* be behind it, be at the bottom of it: *es steckt mehr dahinter* there's more to it than meets the eye.

da'hinvege,tieren *v/i* (*sep*, h) vegetate.

da'hinziehen *v/i* (*irr*, *sep*, -ge-, sn, → ziehen) move (*clouds*: drift) along.

Dahlie ['da:liə] *f* (-; -n) ♀ dahlia.

'dalassen *v/t* (*irr*, *sep*, -ge-, h, → lassen) F leave. 'daliegen *v/i* (*irr*, *sep*, -ge-, h, → liegen) lie (there).

dalli ['dali] *adv* F ~, ~!, *ein bißchen* ~!, *mach* ~! get a move on!

damalig ['da:ma:lıç] *adj* then, at that time: *in der* ~*en Zeit* → damals ['da:ma:ls] *adv* then, in those days.

Damast ['da'mast] *m* (-[e]s; -e) damask.

Dame ['da:mə] *f* (-; -n) **1.** a) lady, b) (dancing) partner: ~ *des Hauses* hostess; *m-e* ~*n und Herren!* ladies and gentlemen! **2.** a) draughts, *Am.* checkers, b) king, c) *chess etc*: queen. ~brett *n* draughtboard, *Am.* checkerboard.

'Damen|binde *f* sanitary towel (*Am.* napkin). ~doppel *n* tennis: the women's doubles. ~einzel *n* tennis: the women's singles. ~fahrrad *n* lady's bicycle. ~fri,seur *m* ladies' hairdresser.

'damenhaft *adj* ladylike.

'Damen|konfekti,on *f* ladies' ready-made (*Am.* ready-to-wear) clothing. ~mannschaft *f* women's team. ~schneider(in *f*) *m* dressmaker. ~toi,lette *f* ladies' toilet (*Am.* restroom). ~unterwäsche *f* ladies' underwear, lingerie. ~wahl *f* ladies' choice.

'Damespiel *n* → Dame 2 a.

damit [da'mıt] **I** *adv* with it (*or* them, *emphatic*: that, those), by it: *ich bin* ~ *fertig* I've finished with it; *was willst du* ~? what do you want it for?; *was soll ich* ~? what am I supposed to do

with it?; *was willst du* ~ *sagen?* what are you trying to say?; ~ *ist der Fall erledigt* so much for that. **II** *conj* so that: ~ *nichts passiert* lest anything should happen.

dämlich ['dɛ:mlıç] *adj* F stupid, silly.

Damm [dam] *m* (-[e]s; ~e) **1.** a) bank, b) dike, c) dam, d) embankment, e) roadway: F *fig.* *ich bin nicht auf dem* ~ I don't feel well; *sie ist wieder auf dem* ~ she's fit again. **2.** *anat.* perineum.

'Dammbruch *m* bursting of a dam.

dämm(e)rig ['dɛm(ə)rıç] *adj* **1.** *es ist* ~ → dämmern I a. **2.** faint, dim (*light*).

'Dämmerlicht *n* (-[e]s; *no pl*) twilight.

dämmern ['dɛmərn] (h) **I** *v/impers es dämmert* a) it is getting light (*or* dark), b) F *fig.* (*bei*) *j-m* it's beginning to dawn on s.o. **II** *v/i vor sich hin* ~ doze, be half asleep. 'Dämmerung *f* (-; -en) a) dawn, b) dusk, twilight: *in der* ~ at dawn, at dusk, at nightfall.

Dämmung ['dɛmʊŋ] *f* (-; -en) insulation.

Dämon ['dɛ:mɔn] *m* (-s; -en) demon.

dämonisch [dɛ'mo:nıʃ] *adj* demoniac(al).

Dampf [dampf] *m* (-[e]s; ~e) a) steam, b) vapo(u)r, fume: F *fig.* ~ *ablassen* let off steam; ~ *dahinter machen* put on steam; *j-m* ~ *machen* make s.o. get a move on. 'Dampfbad *n* steam bath. 'Dampfbügeleisen *n* steam iron.

dampfen ['dampfən] *v/i* (h *or* sn) steam.

dämpfen ['dɛmpfən] *v/t* (h) **1.** *gastr.*, ⊕ steam. **2.** deaden, silence, muffle (*sounds*), lower (*one's voice*), mute (*trumpet etc*). **3.** cushion, absorb (*shock*). **4.** soften (*colo[u]r, light*): → *gedämpft*. **5.** *fig.* restrain, subdue (*feelings*), put a damper on (*mood*).

Dampfer ['dampfər] *m* (-s; -) steamer.

Dämpfer ['dɛmpfər] *m* (-s; -) damper, ♪ *a.* mute: F *fig.* *e-n* ~ *bekommen* be damp(en)ed; (*dat*) *e-n* ~ *aufsetzen* put a damper on.

'Dampf|heizung *f* steam heating. ~kessel *m* steam boiler. ~kochtopf *m* pressure cooker. ~ma,schine *f* steam engine. ~schiff *n* steamship. ~walze *f a.* *fig.* steamroller.

Damwild ['dam-] *n* zo. fallow deer.

danach [da'na:x] *adv* **1.** a) after (that), afterward(s), b) later on: *bald* ~ soon after. **2.** then, next, behind (*or* after) him *etc.* **3.** according to it, accordingly: F *aber es war auch ~* the meal etc was cheap but it tasted like it, too; *mir ist nicht ~* I don't feel like it. **4.** *~ fragen* ask for it; *sich ~ sehnen zu inf* long to *inf*; *sich ~ erkundigen* inquire about it.

Däne ['dɛːnə] *m* (-n; -n) Dane.

daneben [da'neːbən] *adv* **1.** beside (or next to) it (or them); *im Haus ~* next door. **2.** *a. conj* a) besides, b) at the same time. **3.** beside it (or them *etc*), in comparison. **4.** off the mark: *~!* missed! *~benehmen: sich ~* (*irr, sep, h, → benehmen*) F behave badly. *~gehen v/i* (*irr, sep, -ge-, sn, → gehen*) **1.** *shot etc*: miss. **2.** F misfire, go wrong. *~greifen v/i* (*irr, sep, -ge-, h, → greifen*) **1.** ♪ strike a wrong (*fig.* false) note. **2.** miss. **3.** F *fig.* be wide of the mark. *~schießen v/i* (*irr, sep, -ge-, h, → schießen*) **1.** miss. **2.** F *fig.* be wide of the mark.

Dänemark ['dɛːnəmark] *n* (-s) Denmark. **Dänin** ['dɛːnɪn] *f* (-; -nen) Dane. '**dänisch** *adj* Danish.

dank [daŋk] *prep* (*gen, dat*) *a. iro.* thanks to. **Dank** *m* (-[e]s; *no pl*) thanks, gratitude, reward: *vielen* (or *herzlichen, besten, schönen*) *~!* many thanks!, thank you very much!; *als ~, zum ~* by way of thanks; *j-m s-n ~ abstatten* express one's thanks to s.o.; *j-m ~ schulden* owe s.o. a debt of gratitude; *das ist der* (*ganze*) *~!* that's gratitude for you!; → *Gott.* '**dankbar** *adj* **1.** grateful (*j-m für et.* to s.o. for s.th.), appreciative: *ich wäre Ihnen ~, wenn Sie kämen* I'd be much obliged if you came. **2.** rewarding (*task etc*). **3.** F hard-wearing (*material etc*). '**Dankbarkeit** *f* (-; *no pl*) (*aus ~* out of) gratitude (*für* for).

danken ['daŋkən] (h) **I** *v/i* **1.** thank (*j-m für et.* s.o. for s.th.): *danke* (*schön*)*!* (many) thanks!, thank you (very much)!; (*nein*) *danke!* no, thank you!, no, thanks!; *nichts zu ~* you are welcome; *wie kann ich Ihnen nur ~?* how can I begin to thank you?; F *na, ich danke!* thank you for nothing! **2.** decline. **II** *v/t* **3.** *j-m et. ~* reward s.o. for s.th. **4.** → *verdanken*.

'**dankenswerter**'**weise** *adv* **1.** kindly. **2.** *fig.* commendably.

'**Dankesbrief** *m* thank-you letter.

'**Dankeschön** *n* (-s; *no pl*) thank-you.

'**Dankesschuld** *f* debt of gratitude.

'**Dankesworte** *pl* words of thanks.

'**Dankgebet** *n* thanksgiving (prayer).

'**Dankschreiben** *n* letter of thanks.

dann [dan] *adv* **1.** then, after that: *~ und wann* every now and then; *was passierte ~?* what happened next?; F *bis ~!* see you (later)! **2.** then, in that case. **II** *conj* F (well) then, so: *~ eben nicht!* all right, forget it!

daran [da'ran] *adv* **1.** at (or on, in, to) it (or that): *halt dich ~ fest!* hold on to it!; *nahe ~* close to it; → *nahe* II. **2.** *~ anschließend, im Anschluß ~* afterward(s). **3.** *es ist et.* (*nichts*) *~* there's s.th. (nothing) in it; *~ ist kein wahres Wort* there's not a word of truth in it; *~ stirbt man nicht* you don't die of it; *du tust gut ~ zu gehen* you are wise to go; *das Schönste ~ war* the best thing about it was; → *denken* 3, *liegen* 4 *etc*.

dar'angehen *v/i* (*irr, sep, -ge-, sn, → gehen*) get down to it: *~, et. zu tun* get down to doing s.th. **dar'anmachen:** *sich ~* (*sep, -ge-, h*) F → *darangehen*. **dar'ansetzen** *v/t* (*sep, -ge-, h*) *alles ~, um zu inf* spare no effort to *inf*.

darauf [da'raʊf] *adv* **1.** on it *etc*, on top of it. **2.** after (that), then: *bald ~* soon after; *e-e Woche ~* a week later. **3.** *fig.* *ich freue mich ~* I'm looking forward to it; *~ wollen wir trinken!* let's drink to that!; *sie ging direkt ~ zu* she went straight for it; *~ steht Gefängnis* there is a prison penalty for that; *~ bin ich stolz* I'm proud of it; *wie kommt er nur ~?* whatever makes him think of that?; *ich komme nicht ~* (F *drauf*) I can't think of it!

daraufhin [daraʊf'hɪn] *adv* **1.** as a result, consequently. **2.** after that. **3.** *et. ~ prüfen, ob* examine s.th. to see if.

daraus [da'raʊs] *adv* **1.** from it *etc*: *~ lernen* (*vorlesen*) learn (read) from it. **2.** of it *etc*: *was ist ~ geworden?* what has become of it?; *~ wird nichts!* F nothing doing! **3.** for it *etc*: *ich mache mir nichts ~* a) I don't care for it, b) that doesn't worry me (a bit).

darben ['darbən] *v/i* (h) suffer want.

darbieten ['daːr-] *v/t* (*irr, sep, -ge-, h, → bieten*) **1.** present (*sich itself*). **2.** perform. '**Darbietung** *f* (-; -en) **1.** presentation. **2.** *thea. etc* performance.

'**darbringen** v/t (irr, sep, -ge-, h, → **bringen**) (dat to) present, give.

darin [da'rɪn] adv **1.** in it etc: **was ist ~?** what's in it (or inside)? **2.** there, in this (respect): **~ irren Sie sich!** there you are mistaken!; **~ liegt der Unterschied** that's the difference. **3.** at it, at that: **~ ist er sehr gut** he is very good at that.

'**darlegen** v/t (sep, -ge-, h) show, state: **j-m et. ~** explain s.th. to s.o.

'**Darlegung** f (-; -en) **1.** explanation. **2.** statement.

Darlehen ['da:rle:ən] n (-s; -) loan: **ein ~ aufnehmen** raise (or take up) a loan.

'**Darlehens...** loan (bank, contract, etc).

Darm [darm] m (-[e]s; ⸚e) **1.** anat. intestine(s), bowel(s), gut(s): **den ~ entleeren** evacuate the bowels, defecate. **2.** (sausage) skin.

'**Darm|entleerung** f defecation. **~flora** f intestinal flora. **~geschwür** n intestinal ulcer. **~grippe** f gastroenteric influenza. **~krebs** m 🎗 cancer of the intestine. **~saite** f ♩ catgut (string). **~spiegelung** f enteroscopy. **~trägheit** f constipation. **~verschluß** m 🎗 ileus.

Darre ['darə] f ⚙ drying kiln.

'**darstellen** v/t (sep, -ge-, h) **1.** represent, describe (a. A.), portray, show, express, constitute, mean: **falsch ~** misrepresent; **was soll das ~?** what's that supposed to be?; **e-e Belastung ~** be a burden. **2.** thea. etc act, play, w.s. interpret. **3.** 🎗 prepare. **4.** computer: display. '**darstellend** adj **1.** ~**e Geometrie** descriptive geometry. **2.** → **Kunst** 1.

'**Darsteller** m (-s; -) player, actor: **der ~ des Faust** the actor playing Faust.

'**Darstellerin** f (-; -nen) actress, player.

'**darstellerisch** adj acting: **s-e ~e Leistung** his performance, his acting.

'**Darstellung** f (-; -en) **1.** representation, description, account: **graphische ~** graph, diagram. **2.** thea. etc acting, per-formance, w.s. interpretation. **3.** 🎗 preparation. **4.** computer: display.

darüber [da'ry:bər] adv **1.** over it (or that) (a. time), above it etc: **das Zimmer ~** the room above; **ich bin ~ eingeschlafen** I fell asleep over it. **2.** more. **3.** **~ hinaus** a) beyond it etc, b) fig. over and above that, moreover; fig. **er ist ~ hinaus** he is past (all) that. **4.** fig. about it (or that), (on a subject) on that, on it:

ich freue mich ~ I'm glad about it; **~ vergißt er alle s-e Sorgen** that takes his mind off his problems; **~ kam sie nicht hinweg** she didn't get over it.

dar'überstehen v/i (irr, sep, -ge-, h, → **stehen**) fig. be above it.

darum [da'rʊm] adv **1.** (a)round it etc. **2.** **ich bat ihn ~** I asked him: a) for it, b) to do it; **~ geht es nicht!** that's not the point! **3.** → **deshalb**.

darunter [da'rʊntər] adv **1.** under it etc, underneath: **das Zimmer ~** the room below; **~ trug sie ...** underneath she was wearing ... **2.** less, under: F **~ tut er es nicht** he won't do it for less. **3.** a) among them, b) including. **4.** **~ leiden, daß** suffer from ger; **was versteht man ~?** what do you understand by it?; **~ kann ich mir nichts vorstellen** that doesn't mean anything to me.

dar'unterfallen v/i (irr, sep, -ge-, sn, → **fallen**) fig. come under (a law etc).

dar'unterliegen v/i (irr, sep, -ge-, h, → **liegen**) fig. be below (standard).

dar'untersetzen v/t (sep, -ge-, h) put signature etc to it.

Darwinismus [darvi'nɪsmʊs] m (-; no pl) Darwinism.

das [das] **I** def art the: **~ Buch des Monats** the book of the month. **II** dem pron this (one), that (one): **~ war sie!** that was her!; **~ sind s-e Bücher** those are his books; **~ ist es ja (gerade)?** that's the point!; **nur ~ nicht!** anything but that! **III** rel pron which: **~ Geschäft, ~ ich meine** the shop (which) I'm talking of. **IV** pers pron F for **es**.

'**dasein** v/i (irr, sep, -ge-, sn, → **sein**) **1.** a) be there, be present, b) exist: **bist du noch da?** are you still here?; **ist noch Brot da?** is there any bread left?; **ich bin gleich wieder da!** I'll be right back!; **ist j-d dagewesen?** has anyone been?; fig. **noch nie dagewesen** unprecedented, unheard-of. **2.** F (voll) **~** a) be all there, b) be in great shape, c) be conscious.

'**Dasein** n (-s; no pl) existence.

'**dasitzen** v/i (irr, sep, -ge-, h, → **sitzen**) sit there: fig. **~ ohne** be left without.

daß [das] conj that: **so ~** so that; **es sei denn, ~** unless; **ohne ~** without ger; **ich weiß, ~ ich recht habe** I know I'm right; **er entschuldigte sich, ~ er zu**

spät kam he apologized for being late; **nicht, ~ ich wüßte** not that I know of; **es ist lange her, ~ ich sie gesehen habe** it's a long time since I saw her; F ~ **du ja hingehst!** be sure to go!

'dastehen v/i (irr, sep, -ge-, h, → **stehen**) stand there: fig. **gut ~** be in a good position, firm: be flourishing; **mittellos ~** be penniless; F **wie stehe ich jetzt da!** what a fool I look now!

Datei [da'tai] f (-; -en) data file.

Daten ['da:tən] pl data, facts, particulars. **~ausgabe** f data output. **~austausch** m data exchange. **~bank** f (-; -en) data bank. **~eingabe** f data input. **~erfassung** f data collection. **~mißbrauch** m data abuse. **~netz** n data network. **~schutz** m data protection. **~schutzbeauftragte** m, f data protection commissioner. **~sichtgerät** n (visual) display unit, (video) terminal. **~speicher** m data memory. **~speicherung** f data storage. **~technik** f data systems engineering. **~träger** m data medium. **~typist** [-ty‚pist] m (-en; -en), **~ty‚pistin** f (-; -nen) data typist. **~übermittlung**, **~übertragung** f data transfer (or communication). **~umsetzung** f data conversion. **2verarbeitend** adj data-processing. **~verarbeitung** f data processing. **~verarbeitungsanlage** f data-processing equipment.

datieren [da'ti:rən] v/t, v/i (h) date.

Dativ ['da:ti:f] m (-s; -e) dative (case). **~ob‚jekt** n dative (or indirect) object.

Dattel ['datəl] f (-; -n) ❀ date.

Datum ['da:tʊm] n (-s; Daten) date: **ohne ~** undated; **welches ~ haben wir heute?** what's the date today?; **neueren ~s** of recent date. **'Datumsgrenze** f geogr. date line. **'Datumsstempel** m a) date stamp, b) dater.

Dauer ['dauər] f (-; no pl) duration (a. ling., ♪), period (of time), esp. ⚖ term, length: **von ~** lasting; **von kurzer** (or **nicht von**) **~ sein** be short-lived, not to last long; **auf die ~** in the long run; **der Lärm ist auf die ~ unerträglich** you can't stand the noise for long; **das kann auf die ~ nicht so weitergehen** that can't go on indefinitely; **für die ~ von** (or gen) for the duration (or a period) of a. **'Dauer|arbeitslosigkeit** f chronic un-

employment. **~auftrag** m ✝ periodical payment order. **~belastung** f 1. ❂ continuous load. 2. fig. permanent stress. **~brenner** m F long-running success (or hit). **~gast** m permanent guest.

'dauerhaft adj permanent, lasting, durable, hard-wearing (goods): **~ sein** a. wear well. **'Dauerhaftigkeit** f (-; no pl) durability, permanence.

'Dauer|karte f season ticket. **~lauf** m jogging: **im ~** at a jog (trot). **~lutscher** m (-s; -) F lollipop.

dauern ['dauərn] v/i (h) last, go on, take: **zwei Stunden ~** take two hours; **wie lange dauert es denn noch?** how much longer will it take?; **es wird lange ~, bis** it will be a long time before; **das dauert mir zu lange!** that's too long for me! **'dauernd I** adj constant: **~er Wohnsitz** permanent residence. **II** adv constantly: **~ et. tun** keep doing; **er kommt ~ zu spät** he is always late; **das passiert ~** that happens all the time.

'Dauer|parker m long-term parker. **~regen** m continuous rain. **~stellung** f permanent post. **~welle** f (~n haben F have a) perm. **~zustand** m zum ~ **werden** become permanent (b.s. chronic).

Daumen ['daumən] m (-s; -) thumb: **~lutschen** suck one's thumb; F **j-m die ~ drücken** keep one's fingers crossed for s.o.; (**die**) **~ drehen** twiddle one's thumbs; **über den ~ gepeilt** at a rough estimate. **~nagel** m thumbnail.

Daunen ['daunən] pl down. **'Daunendecke** f eiderdown.

davon [da'fɔn] adv 1. **das Dorf liegt nicht weit ~** (**entfernt**) the village is not far away (or from it); **~ zweigt ein Weg ab** a path branches off it. 2. **ich wachte ~ auf** I was awakened by it; **~ wird man dick** that makes you fat; F **das kommt ~!** that'll teach you!; **was habe ich ~?** what do I get out of it? 3. **hast du schon ~ gehört?** have you heard about it yet?; **genug ~!** enough of that! 4. **auf und ~** up and away.

da'vonfliegen v/i (irr, sep, -ge-, sn, → **fliegen**) fly off, fly away. **da'vonjagen** v/t (sep, -ge-, h) chase away.

da'vonkommen v/i (irr, sep, -ge-, sn, → **kommen**) get away, get off, escape: **mit dem Leben ~** survive; → **Schreck**.

da'vonlaufen v/i (irr, sep, -ge-, sn, →

laufen) run away. **da'vonmachen:**
sich ~ (*sep*, -ge-, h) F make off, beat it.
da'vonstehlen: *sich* ~ (*irr*, *sep*, -ge-, h,
→ *stehlen*) steal away. **da'vontragen**
v/t (*irr*, *sep*, -ge-, h, → *tragen*) **1.** *a. fig.*
carry off. **2.** sustain (*injury*), get, catch
(*disease*). **da'vonziehen** *v/i* (*irr*, *sep*,
-ge-, sn, → *ziehen*) move away (*or* off):
sports: *j-m* ~ pull away from s.o.

davor [da'fo:r] *adv* **1.** before (*or* in front
of) it *etc*: *mit e-m Garten* ~ with a
garden in front. **2.** *time*: before that. **3.**
~ *habe ich Angst* I'm afraid of that; *ich
habe ihn* ~ *gewarnt* I warned him of it.

dazu [da'tsu:] *adv* **1.** in addition to it,
besides: *sie sang und spielte* ~ *Gitarre*
she sang and accompanied herself on
the guitar; *möchten Sie Reis* ~? would
you like rice with it?; *und sie ist noch* ~
hübsch and she is pretty into the bargain. **2.** for it, for that purpose: ~ *ist er
ja da!* that's what he is there for! **3.** *wie
ist es* ~ *gekommen?* how did that
come about?; ~ *darf es nicht kommen*
that must not happen; *ich kam nie* ~ I
never got (a)round to it; F *wie komme
ich* ~? why on earth should I?

da'zugehören *v/i* (*sep*, -ge-, h) belong to
it *etc*; → *a. gehören*. **da'zugehörig** *adj*
belonging to it (*or* them).

da'zukommen *v/i* (*irr*, *sep*, -ge-, sn, →
kommen) **1.** (*gerade* ~ happen to)
come along (*als* when). **2.** a) join *s.o.*,
b) be added. **da'zulernen** *v/t*, *v/i* (*sep*,
-ge-, h) learn (*s.th.* new). **da'zutun** *v/t*
(*irr*, *sep*, -ge-, h, → *tun*) F add: *ohne
sein etc* ♀ without his *etc* help.

dazwischen [da'tsvɪʃən] *adv* between
(them), in between (*a. time*), among
them. ~**fahren** *v/i* (*irr*, *sep*, -ge-, sn, →
fahren) a) step in, interfere, b) interrupt. ~**kommen** *v/i* (*irr*, *sep*, -ge-, sn, →
kommen) intervene: *wenn nichts da-
zwischenkommt* if all goes well.
~**liegen** *v/i* (*irr*, *sep*, -ge-, h, → *liegen*)
intervene. ~**reden** *v/i* (*sep*, -ge-, h) *j-m* ~
interrupt s.o. ~**treten** *v/i* (*irr*, *sep*, -ge-,
sn, → *treten*) intervene.

Dealer ['di:lər] *m* (-s; -) dealer.
Debakel [de'ba:kəl] *n* (-s; -) débâcle.
Debatte [de'batə] *f* (-; -n) *a. parl.* debate:
zur ~ *stehen* be under discussion; *das
steht nicht zur* ~ that's not the issue.
debattieren [deba'ti:rən] *v/t*, *v/i* (h)

(*über e-e Sache* s.th.) debate, discuss.
Debet [de:bɛt] *n* (-s; -s) ✝ debit. ~**saldo**
m debit balance. ~**seite** *f* debit side.
debil [de'bi:l] *adj* ✝ feebleminded.
Debüt [de'by:] *n* (-s; -s) debut: *sein* ~
geben → **debütieren** [deby'ti:rən] *v/i*
(h) make one's debut.
dechiffrieren [deʃɪ'fri:rən] *v/t* (h) decipher, decode.
Deck [dɛk] *n* (-[e]s; -s) ♣ deck: *an* (*or*
auf) ~ on deck.
'**Decka,dresse** *f* cover (address).
'**Deckanstrich** *m* top (*or* finishing) coat.
'**Deckbett** *n* feather quilt.
'**Deckblatt** *n* wrapper (*of cigar*).
Deckchen ['dɛkçən] *n* (-s; -) doily.
Decke ['dɛkə] *f* (-; -n) **1.** a) blanket, b)
(bed)cover, c) (table)cloth: F *mit j-m*
unter einer ~ *stecken* be in league with
s.o.; *fig. sich nach der* ~ *strecken* cut
one's coat according to one's cloth. **2.**
ceiling: F *fig.* (*vor Freude*) *an die* ~
springen jump with joy; (*vor Wut*) *an
die* ~ *gehen* go through the roof; *mir
fiel die* ~ *auf den Kopf* I felt shut in. **3.**
⊛ cover(ing). **4.** *civ.eng.* surface, sur-
facing. **5.** tyre cover (*of car, bicycle*).
Deckel ['dɛkəl] *m* (-s; -) lid (*a. humor.
hat*), cover, (screw) cap: F *j-m eins auf
den* ~ *geben* tick s.o. off (properly).
decken ['dɛkən] (h) **I** *v/t* **1.** ~ *über* (*acc*)
cover *s.th.* with. **2.** *roof*: *mit Stroh* (*Ziegeln, Schiefer*) ~ thatch (tile, slate) a
roof. **3.** *den Tisch* ~ lay (*or* set) the table
(*für drei Personen* for three). **4.** *a. fig.
or contp.* shield, protect: *j-n* ~ cover up
for s.o., *sports*: mark s.o.; *den Rückzug* ~ cover the retreat. **5.** cover (*costs*),
meet (*demand*). **6.** *zo.* cover, serve. **II** *v/i*
7. *paint etc*: cover (*well etc*). **8.** *sports*:
cover, mark, *boxer*: cover (up). **III** *sich*
~ **9.** cover o.s., *boxer*: cover up. **10.** (*mit*
with) ⚭ coincide, *fig. a.* tally.
'**Decken|balken** *m* ceiling beam. ~**be-
leuchtung** *f* ceiling lighting. ~**gemälde** *n* ceiling fresco. ~**leuchte** *f* ceiling
lamp, *mot.* dome lamp.
'**Deck|farbe** *f* ⊛ body colo(u)r. ~**fe-
der** *f* deck feather. ~**mantel** *m* fig.
cloak. ~**name** *m* pseudonym, ✕ code
name.
'**Deckung** *f* (-; *no pl*) **1.** (*in* ~ *gehen* take)
cover. **2.** ✝ a) cover, security, b) sup-
ply: *k-e* ~ no funds. **3.** *sports*: covering,

marking, *boxing etc*: guard. **4.** Å *or fig.* coincidence.

'**deckungsgleich** *adj* Å congruent.

'**Deckweiß** *n* opaque white.

Defätismus [defɛ'tɪsmʊs] *m* (-; *no pl*) defeatism. **defä'tistisch** *adj* defeatist.

defekt [de'fɛkt] *adj* defective, faulty.

De'fekt *m* (-[e]s; -e) defect (**an** *dat* in).

defensiv [defɛn'ziːf] *adj* defensive.

Defensive [defɛn'ziːvə] *f* (-; -n) (**in der ~** on the) defensive.

defilieren [defi'liːrən] *v/i* (sn) march past.

defi'nierbar *adj* definable: *schwer ~* difficult to define. **definieren** [defi'niːrən] *v/t* (h) define. **Definition** [definɪ'tsioːn] *f* (-; -en) definition. **definitiv** [-'tiːf] *adj* definite (*answer*), positive (*offer*): *es steht ~ fest, daß ...* it is definite that ...

Defizit [de'fitsɪt] *n* (-s; -e) *a.* deficit.

Deflation [defla'tsioːn] *f* (-; -en) ✝ deflation. **deflationär** [-tsioː'nɛːr], **deflatorisch** [-'toːrɪʃ] *adj* ✝ deflationary.

deflorieren [deflo'riːrən] *v/t* (h) deflower.

deformieren [defɔr'miːrən] *v/t* (h) deform, ☉ *a.* distort.

deftig ['dɛftɪç] *adj* F solid (*meal*), earthy (*joke*), steep (*prices*), sound (*blow etc*).

Degen [de'ɡən] *m* (-s; -) sword, *fenc.* épée.

Degeneration [degenera'tsioːn] *f* (-; -en) degeneration. **degenerativ** [degenera'tiːf] *adj* degenerative.

degenerieren [degene'riːrən] *v/i* (sn), **degene'riert** *adj* degenerate.

'**Degenfechten** *n sports*: épée fencing.

degradieren [degra'diːrən] *v/t* (h) ✗ demote, *esp. fig.* degrade.

'**dehnbar** *adj a. fig.* elastic. '**Dehnbarkeit** *f* (-; *no pl*) elasticity. **dehnen** ['deːnən] (h) **I** *v/t* **1.** stretch (*a. fig.*). **2.** lengthen (*vowels*), drawl (*words*). **II** *sich ~* stretch (o.s.). '**Dehnung** *f* (-; -en) **1.** stretch(ing). **2.** *ling.* lengthening.

dehydrieren [dehy'driːrən] *v/t* (h) 🜛 dehydrate.

Deich [daɪç] *m* (-[e]s; -e) dike, dam, *of river*: embankment, *Am.* levee.

Deichsel ['daɪksəl] *f* (-; -n) a) pole, b) shaft. '**deichseln** *v/t* F (h) wangle.

dein [daɪn] *adj* **1.** your: *eccl. ~ Wille geschehe* Thy will be done. **2.** *pred ~er, ~e, ~(e)s, der (die, das) ~e* yours;

e-r ~er Freunde a friend of yours. **3.** *der (die, das) ~(ig)e* your own, yours; *die ♀(ig)en* your family, your people.

'**deiner** *pers pron* (of) you: *wir werden ~ gedenken* we shall remember you.

'**deinerseits** *adv* on your part.

'**deines'gleichen** *indef pron* people like you, *contp.* the likes of you.

deinetwegen ['daɪnətveːɡən] *adv* a) for your sake, b) because of you.

deinig ['daɪnɪç] → *dein* 3.

Dekade [de'kaːdə] *f* (-; -n) decade.

dekadent [deka'dɛnt] *adj* decadent.

Dekadenz [deka'dɛnts] *f* (-; *no pl*) decadence.

Dekan [de'kaːn] *m* (-s; -e) dean. **Dekanat** [deka'naːt] *n* (-s; -e) dean's office.

deklamieren [dekla'miːrən] *v/t*, *v/i* (h) declaim.

deklarieren [dekla'riːrən] *v/t* (h) ✝ declare.

deklassieren [dekla'siːrən] *v/t* (h) declass, *sports*: outclass.

Deklination [deklina'tsioːn] *f* (-; -en) **1.** *ling.* declension. **2.** *phys.* declination.

dekli'nierbar *adj* declinable.

deklinieren [dekli'niːrən] *v/t* (h) decline.

Dékolleté [dekɔl'teː] *n* (-s; -s) (*tiefes ~* plunging) neckline.

dékolletiert [dekɔl'tiːrt] *adj* décolleté.

dekontaminieren [dekɔntami'niːrən] *v/t* (h) decontaminate.

Dekor [de'koːr] *m, n* (-s; -s) **1.** a) decoration, b) décor, c) pattern. **2.** *thea.* décor, set(s). **Dekorateur** [dekora'tøːr] *m* (-s; -e), **Dekora'teurin** *f* (-; -nen) **1.** window-dresser. **2.** interior designer. **3.** *thea. etc* scene painter. **Dekoration** [dekora'tsioːn] *f* (-; -en) decoration, *a.* window display, furnishings, *thea. etc* set(s). **dekorativ** [-'tiːf] *adj* decorative.

dekorieren [deko'riːrən] *v/t* (h) decorate (*a. with an order*), dress (*shop window*).

Dekret [de'kreːt] *n* (-[e]s; -e) decree.

Delegation [delega'tsioːn] *f* (-; -en) delegation. **delegieren** [dele'ɡiːrən] *v/t* (h) delegate.

Dele'gierte *m, f* (-n; -n) delegate.

delikat [deli'kaːt] *adj* delicious, *a. fig.* delicate. **Delikatesse** [delika'tɛsə] *f* (-; -n) delicacy, *fig. a.* discretion.

Delika'teßgeschäft *n* delicatessen.

Delikt [de'lɪkt] *n* (-[e]s; -e) ⚖ offen/ce

(*Am.* -se). **Delinquent** [delɪŋˈkvɛnt] *m* (-en; -en) offender.

Delirium [deˈliːri̯ʊm] *n a. fig.* delirium.

Delle [ˈdɛlə] *f* (-; -n) F dent.

Delphin [dɛlˈfiːn] *m* (-s; -e) *zo.* dolphin. **Del'phin(schwimmen** *n* (-s) butterfly.

Delta [ˈdɛlta] *n* (-s; -s) *geogr.* delta.

'**Deltamuskel** *m* deltoid (muscle).

dem [de:m] **I** *def art* **gib es ~ Jungen** give it to the boy. **II** *dem pron* **wie ~ auch sei** however that may be; **nach ~, was ich gehört habe** from what I've heard. **III** *rel pron* **der, ~ ich es gab** the one (*or* the person) I gave it to.

Demagoge [demaˈgoːgə] *m* (-n; -n) demagogue. **Demagogie** [demagoˈgiː] *f* (-; -n) demagogy. **demagogisch** [demaˈgoːgɪʃ] *adj* demagogic.

Demarkationslinie [demarkaˈtsi̯oːns-] *f* demarcation line.

demaskieren [demasˈkiːrən] *v/t* (h) *a. fig.* unmask.

Dementi [deˈmɛnti] *n* (-s; -s) *pol.* (official) denial. **dementieren** [demɛnˈtiːrən] *v/t* (h) deny (officially).

'**dementsprechend** *adv* accordingly.

'**demgegen'über** *adv* in contrast to this.

'**demge'mäß** *adv* accordingly.

'**demnach** *adv* **1.** therefore. **2.** → *dem gemäß.*

'**dem'nächst** *adv* shortly, soon: **~ er scheinend** *etc* forthcoming.

Demo [ˈdeːmo] *f* (-; -s) F demo.

Demograph [demoˈgraːf] *m* (-en; -en) demographer. **Demographie** [demograˈfiː] *f* (-; -n) demography. **demographisch** [-ˈgraːfɪʃ] *adj* demographic.

'**Demokas̱sette** *f* F demo (tape).

Demokrat [demoˈkraːt] *m* (-en; -en), **Demo'kratin** *f* (-; -nen) *pol.* democrat. **Demokratie** [demokraˈtiː] *f* (-; -n) democracy. **demokratisch** [-ˈkraːtɪʃ] *adj* democratic. **demokratisieren** [demokratiˈziːrən] *v/t* (h) democratize.

demolieren [demoˈliːrən] *v/t* (h) demolish, wreck.

Demo'lierung *f* (-; -en) demolition.

Demonstrant [demɔnˈstrant] *m* (-en; -en), **Demon'strantin** *f* (-; -nen) demonstrator, protester. **Demonstration** [-straˈtsi̯oːn] *f* (-; -en) (*pol.* **e-e ~ veranstalten** hold a) demonstration: *fig.* **e-e ~ der Macht** a show of force. **Demonstrati'ons|recht** *n* right to demonstrate. **~verbot** *n* ban on demonstrations. **~zug** *m* protest march.

demonstrativ [demɔnstraˈtiːf] *adj* demonstrative. **Demonstra'tivpro̱nomen** *n* demonstrative (pronoun).

demonstrieren [demɔnˈstriːrən] *v/t, v/i* (h) demonstrate.

Demontage [demɔnˈtaːʒə] *f* (-; -n) ⚙ *or fig.* dismantling.

demontieren [demɔnˈtiːrən] *v/t* (h) dismantle (*a. fig.*), take down, take apart.

demoralisieren [demoraliˈziːrən] *v/t* (h) demoralize.

Demoskopie [demoskoˈpiː] *f* (-; -n) (public) opinion research. **demoskopisch** [demoˈskoːpɪʃ] *adj* **~e Umfrage** (public) opinion poll.

Demut [ˈdeːmuːt] *f* (-; *no pl*) humility.

demütig [ˈdeːmyːtɪç] *adj* humble.

demütigen [ˈdeːmyːtɪgən] *v/t* (h) humiliate: **sich ~** humble o.s.

'**Demütigung** *f* (-; -en) humiliation.

denaturieren [denatuˈriːrən] *v/t* (h) 🐟, *phys.* denature.

'**Denkanstoß** *m* impulse: **j-m e-n ~ geben, (bei j-m) als ~ wirken** set s.o. thinking. '**Denkart** *f* way of thinking.

'**Denkaufgabe** *f* problem, brain teaser.

'**denkbar** *adj* thinkable, conceivable: **es ist durchaus ~, daß** it's quite possible that; **die ~ beste Methode** the best method imaginable.

denken [ˈdɛŋkən] *v/t, v/i* (dachte, gedacht, h) **1.** think, *a.* imagine, suppose, *Am.* F guess: **das gibt e-m zu ~** that makes you think; **ich denke schon** I (should) think so; **das habe ich mir gedacht** I thought as much; **das hättest du dir ~ können!** you should have known that!; **ich dachte mir nichts dabei** I thought nothing of it; **solange ich ~ kann** as long as I remember; F **denkste!** that's what you think! **2.** think of, consider: **er denkt daran zu kommen** he thinks of coming; **ich denke nicht daran!** I wouldn't dream of it! **3. ~ an** (*acc*) a) think of (*or* about), b) remember; **daran ist nicht zu ~** it's out of the question; **an Schlaf war nicht zu ~** sleep was out of the question; **wenn ich nur daran denke!** the mere thought of it! **4. ~ über** (*acc*) think about (*or* of).

'**Denken** *n* (-s) thinking, thought.

'**Denker** *m* (-s; -) thinker. '**Denkfa̱brik** *f*

F think-tank. **'denkfähig** *adj* intelligent. **'denkfaul** *adj* mentally lazy. **'Denkfehler** *m* flaw in one's reasoning.

'Denkmal *n* (-[e]s; ≃er) monument: *j-m ein ~ setzen* put up a monument to s.o.

'Denkmalpflege *f* preservation of historic buildings and monuments.

'Denkmalschutz *m unter ~ stehen* be listed (as a historic monument).

'Denk|muster *n* thought pattern. **~pause** *f* pause for reflection. **~pro‚zeß** *m* thought process. **~schrift** *f* memorandum. **~vermögen** *n* (-s; *no pl*) intellectual capacity, intelligence. **~weise** *f* way of thinking. **2würdig** *adj* memorable. **~zettel** *m* (*j-m e-n ~ verpassen* teach s.o. a) lesson.

denn [dɛn] **I** *conj* **1.** because, since. **2.** than: *mehr ~ je* more than ever. **3.** *es sei ~* unless. **II** *adv* **4.** then: *war es ~ so schlimm?* was it really that bad?; *was ist ~?* what is it now?; *wieso ~?* (but) why?; *wo warst du ~ nur?* where on earth have you been?

dennoch ['dɛnɔx] *conj* (but) still, yet.

Dental [dɛn'ta:l] *m* (-[e]s; -e) *ling.* dental.

Denunziant [denʊn'tsi̯ant] *m* (-en; -en), **Denunzi'antin** *f* (-; -nen) informer.

denunzieren [denʊn'tsi:rən] *v/t* (h) *j-n ~* denounce s.o. (*bei* to).

Deodorant [deˀodo'rant] *n* (-s; -e, -s) deodorant.

deplaziert [depla'tsi:rt] *adj* out of place, *a.* misplaced (*remark etc*).

Deponie [depo'ni:] *f* (-; -n) dump, tip.

deponieren [depo'ni:rən] *v/t* (h) (*bei* with) deposit, leave.

Deportation [deporta'tsi̯o:n] *f* (-; -en) deportation. **deportieren** [depor'ti:-rən] *v/t* (h) deport. **Depor'tierte** *m, f* (-n; -n) deportee.

Depot [de'po:] *n* (-s; -s) depot, ⚓ (*a. account*) deposit. **De'potwirkung** *f* 🕱 controlled sustained release.

Depression [depre'sʲo:n] *f* (-; -en) depression. **depressiv** [-'si:f] *adj psych.* depressive. **deprimieren** [depri'mi:-rən] *v/t* (h) depress. **~d** depressing.

der [de:r] **I** *art* the: *~ arme Peter* poor Peter. **II** *dem pron* that (one), this (one): *~ mit ~ Brille* the one with the glasses; *contp. ~ und sein Wort halten?* him keep his word? **III** *rel pron* who, which. **IV** *pers pron* F *for* **er.**

derart ['de:rˀ'a:rt] *adv* so, in such a way. **'der'artig I** *adj such*: *nichts Derartiges* nothing of the kind. **II** *adv →* **derart.**

derb [dɛrp] *adj* **1.** strong, sturdy, coarse (*food etc*). **2.** *fig.* coarse, crude (*joke etc*). **'Derbheit** *f* (-; -en) **1.** *no pl* coarseness. **2.** *pl* crude jokes (*or remarks*).

derentwegen ['de:rəntve:gən] **I** *adv* because of her (*or that etc*). **II** *rel pron* because of whom (*or which*).

'der'gleichen *dem pron* **1.** such. **2.** such a thing, the like: *nichts ~* no such thing; *und ~ mehr* and so on, and the like.

Derivat [deri'va:t] *n* (-[e]s; -e) 🜨, *ling.* derivative.

derjenige ['de:rje:nɪgə] *dem pron* that: *~, der* he (*or* the one) who.

dermaßen ['de:rma:sən] *→* **derart.**

Dermatologe [dɛrmato'lo:gə] *m* (-n; -n) 🕱 dermatologist. **Dermatose** [-'to:zə] *f* (-; -n) dermatosis, skin disease.

derselbe [de:r'zɛlbə] *dem pron* the same. **'der'zeit** *adv* at present. **'der'zeitig** *adj* **1.** present. **2.** then, of (*or* at) the time.

Des [dɛs] *n* (-; -) ♪ D flat.

desensibilisieren [dezɛnzibili'zi:rən] *v/t* (h) 🕱, *phot.* desensitize.

Deserteur [dezɛr'tø:r] *m* (-s; -e) deserter. **desertieren** [-'ti:rən] *v/i* (sn) desert.

'des'gleichen *adv* and *conj* likewise.

'deshalb *adv* and *conj* therefore, that's why: *gerade ~!* that's just why!; *sie ist ~ nicht glücklicher* she isn't any happier for it.

designiert [dezɪˀgni:rt] *adj der ~e Präsident* the president designate.

desillusionieren [dɛsˀɪluˑzi̯o'ni:rən] *v/t* (h) disillusion.

Desinfektion [dɛsˀɪnfɛk'tsʲo:n] *f* (-; -en) disinfection. **Desinfekti'onsmittel** *n* disinfectant, 🕱 *a.* antiseptic. **desinfizieren** [-fi'tsi:rən] *v/t* (h) disinfect.

Desinformati'on *f* (-; -en) disinformation.

'Desinter‚esse *n* (-s; *no pl*) lack of interest, indifference (*an dat* to). **'desinteres‚siert** *adj* uninterested, indifferent.

desolat [dezo'la:t] *adj* desolate.

Desorganisati'on *f* disorganization.

desorien'tiert *adj psych.* confused.

Despot [dɛs'po:t] *m* (-en; -en) despot. **des'potisch** *adj* despotic(al).

Despotismus [dɛspo'tɪsmʊs] *m* (-; *no pl*) despotism.

dessen ['dɛsən] **I** *rel pron* whose, of which. **II** *dem pron* **sich ~ bewußt sein, daß ...** be aware (of the fact) that ...; ~ **bin ich sicher** I'm quite sure of that. **III** *poss pron* **mein Bruder und ~ Frau** my brother and his wife.

'dessenunge'achtet *adv* nevertheless.

Dessert [dɛ'sɛːr] *n* (-s; -s) *gastr.* dessert.

Destillat [dɛstɪ'laːt] *n* (-[e]s; -e) distillate.

destillieren [-'liːrən] *v/t, v/i* (h) distil(l).

desto ['dɛsto] **I** *adv* (all) the: ~ **besser** all (*or* so much) the better!; ~ **schlimmer** so much the worse. **II** *conj* the ... the: **je mehr** (*eher etc*), ~ **besser** the more (sooner *etc*) the better.

destruktiv [dɛstrʊk'tiːf] *adj* destructive.

deswegen ['dɛs've:gən] → **deshalb.**

Detail [de'taɪ] *n* (-s; -s) detail.

detaillieren [deta'jiːrən] *v/t* (h) specify. **detail'liert I** *adj* detailed. **II** *adv* in detail.

Detektiv [detɛk'tiːf] *m* (-s; -e) detective.

Detek'tivbü,ro *n* detective agency.

Detek'tivro,man *m* detective story.

Detonation [detona'tsioːn] *f* (-; -en) detonation, blast. **detonieren** [deto-'niːrən] *v/i* (sn) detonate.

deuten ['dɔʏtən] (h) **I** *v/t* interpret, read: **falsch ~** misinterpret, *fig.* misconstrue. **II** *v/i* ~ **auf** (*acc*) point at (*esp. fig.* to); **alles deutet darauf hin, daß** there is every indication that.

deutlich ['dɔʏtlɪç] *adj* clear, distinct, legible, plain: ~**er Wink** broad hint; ~**er Fortschritt** visible progress; F *fig.* ~ **werden** speak in very plain terms; **muß ich noch ~er werden?** do I have to spell it out (for you)?

'Deutlichkeit *f* (-; *no pl*) clarity, clearness: **in aller ~** in plain terms.

deutsch [dɔʏtʃ] *adj* (**auf ~, in ~** in) German: ~ **reden** talk (in) German; F *fig.* **mit j-m ~ reden** speak plainly with s.o.

Deutsch, das ~e German: **er kann gut ~** he speaks German well.

'Deutsch|ameri,kaner(in *f*) *m*, **2ameri,kanisch** *adj* German-American.

'deutsch-'deutsch *adj pol. hist.* inter--German, German-German.

Deutsche *m, f* (-n; -n) German.

'deutsch-'englisch *adj pol.* Anglo--German, *ling.* German-English.

'deutschfeindlich *adj* anti-German.

'deutsch-fran'zösisch *adj pol.* Franco-German, *ling.* German-French.

'deutschfreundlich *adj* pro-German.

'Deutschland *n* (-s) Germany.

'Deutschlehrer *m* German teacher.

'deutschsprachig [-'ʃpraːxɪç] *adj* German-language (*text*), German-speaking (*area*).

'Deutschunterricht *m* German lessons.

'Deutung *f* (-; -en) interpretation.

Devise [de'viːzə] *f* (-; -n) **1.** motto. **2.** *pl* ✝ foreign exchange (*or* currency).

De'visen|abkommen *n* foreign exchange agreement. **~bestimmungen** *pl* currency regulations. **~börse** *f* foreign exchange market. **~geschäft** *n* foreign exchange transaction. **~händler** *m* foreign exchange dealer. **~knappheit** *f* (foreign) currency stringency. **~vergehen** *n* currency offen/ce (*Am.* -se).

devot [de'voːt] *adj contp.* servile.

Devotionalien [devotsio'naːliən] *pl eccl.* devotional objects.

Dezember [de'tsɛmbər] *m* (-[s]; -) (**im ~** in) December.

dezent [de'tsɛnt] *adj* discreet, unobtrusive, soft (*colo[u]r, music, etc*).

dezentralisieren [detsɛntrali'ziːrən] *v/t* (h) decentralize.

Dezernat [detsɛr'naːt] *n* (-[e]s; -e) department (*Am.* -ent). **Dezernent** [detsɛr'nɛnt] *m* (-en; -en) head of (a) department.

Dezibel ['deːtsibɛl] *n* (-s; -) decibel.

Dezimal|bruch [detsi'maːl-] *m* ✝ decimal (fraction). **~stelle** *f* decimal (place). **~sy,stem** *n* decimal system. **~zahl** *f* decimal.

Dezimeter ['deːtsiːmeːtər] *m, n* (-s; -) decimet/re (*Am.* -er). **dezimieren** [detsi'miːrən] *v/t* (h) decimate.

Dia ['diːa] *n* (-s; -s) F slide.

Diabetes [dia'beːtɛs] *m* (-; *no pl*) diabetes. **Diabetiker** [dia'beːtikər] *m* (-s; -), **Dia'betikerin** *f* (-; -nen) diabetic.

'Diabetrachter *m* slide viewer.

diabolisch [dia'boːlɪʃ] *adj* diabolic(al).

'Diafilm *m* dia film.

Diagnose [dia'gnoːzə] *f* (-; -n) (**e-e ~ stellen** make a) diagnosis.

diagnostizieren [diagnɔsti'tsiːrən] *v/t, v/i* (h) diagnose.

diagonal [diago'naːl] *adj,* **Diago'nale** *f* (-; -n) diagonal. **Diago'nalreifen** *m mot.* cross-ply tyre (*Am.* tire).

Diagramm [dia'gram] *n* (-s; -e) diagram, graph.

Diakon [dia'ko:n] *m* (-s, -en; -e[n]) *eccl.* deacon. **Diakonisse** [diako'nɪsə] *f* (-; -n) Protestant (nursing) sister.

Dialekt [dia'lɛkt] *m* (-[e]s; -e) dialect. **Dialektik** [dia'lɛktik] *f* (-; *no pl*) dialectics.

Dialog [dia'lo:k] *m* (-[e]s; -e) (**e-n ~ führen** carry on a) dialog(ue *Br.*).

Dialyse [dia'ly:zə] *f* (-; -n) ✍ dialysis.

Diamant [dia'mant] *m* (-en; -en), **dia'manten** *adj* diamond.

diametral [diame'tra:l] *adj* diametric(al): **~ entgegengesetzt** diametrically opposed (*dat* to).

Diapositiv ['di:apoziti:f] *n* (-s; -e) slide. **'Dia pro,jektor** *m* slide projector. **'Diarahmen** *m* slide frame.

Diät [di'ɛ:t] *f* (-; -en) (special) diet: **~ halten**, ⚥ **leben** (keep to a) diet; **j-n auf ~ setzen** put s.o. on a diet.

Di'ätassi,stent(in *f*) *m* dietician. **Di'äten** *pl parl.* attendance allowance. **Di'ätfahrplan** *m* F dietary schedule. **Di'ätkost** *f* dietary food. **Di'ätvorschrift** *f* dietary.

dich [dɪç] I *pers pron* you. II *reflex pron* yourself: **schau ~ an!** look at yourself!

dicht [dɪçt] I *adj* **1.** dense (*wood, crowd, fog, etc*), *a.* heavy (*traffic*), thick (*hair, hedge*), close(ly-woven) (*fabric*). **2.** watertight, leakproof: F *fig.* **er ist nicht ganz ~** he's got a screw loose. **3.** compact, *fig.* tight (*plot*). II *adv* **4.** densely, thickly: **~ schließen** shut tightly; **~ gedrängt stehen** stand closely packed. **5. ~ an** (*dat*), **~ bei** close to; **~ aufeinanderfolgen** follow closely (*or* in rapid succession); **~ hinter j-m** close (*or* hard) on s.o.'s heels.

'dichtbehaart *adj* (very) hairy. **'dichtbevölkert** *adj* densely populated. **'Dichte** *f* (-; *no pl*) density (*a. phys.*), denseness, thickness, tightness.

dichten¹ ['dɪçtən] *v/t* (h) ⚙ seal, pack. **'dichten²** (h) I *v/t* write. II *v/i* write poetry (*or* plays *etc*).

'Dichter *m* (-s; -) poet, *w.s.* author, writer. **'Dichterin** *f* (-; -nen) poetess, *w.s.* authoress, writer.

'dichterisch *adj* poetic(al); → **Freiheit**. **'dichthalten** *v/i* (*irr, sep,* -ge-, h, → **halten**) F keep one's mouth shut. **'Dichtkunst** *f* (-; *no pl*) poetry.

'dichtmachen (*sep*, -ge-, h) F I *v/t* shut (up). II *v/i* (**den Laden**) ~ shut up shop.

'Dichtung¹ *f* (-; -en) ⚙ seal, packing. **'Dichtung²** *f* (-; -en) a) literature, b) poetry, c) poem, d) (literary *or* poetic) work(s): *fig.* **~ und Wahrheit** fact and fiction.

'Dichtungs|masse *f* ⚙ sealing compound. **~ring** *m*, **~scheibe** *f* washer.

dick [dɪk] I *adj* **1.** thick, *w.s. a.* a) dense, b) big, large, c) stout, fat: F **~er Verkehr** heavy traffic; **~ machen** be fattening; **~ werden** grow fat; **durch ~ und dünn** through thick and thin. **2.** F a) close, intimate, b) big: **sie sind ~e Freunde** they are (as) thick as thieves; **~es Lob ernten** reap lavish praise; **~er Auftrag** fat order; → **Ende** 1, **Luft** 1. II *adv* **3.** thick(ly). **4.** F very: **~ befreundet sein** be great pals (**mit j-m** with s.o.); **ich habe ihn** (es) **~** I'm sick of him (it); → **auftragen** 5.

'dickbäuchig [-bɔyçiç] *adj* fat-bellied. **'Dickdarm** *m anat.* colon. **'Dicke¹** *f* (-; *no pl*) thickness, ⚙ *a.* diameter, *w.s. a.* a) denseness, b) bigness, c) stoutness, fatness. **'Dicke²** *m, f* (-n; -n) F fat person. **'Dickerchen** *n* (-s; -) F fatso. **'dickfellig** [-fɛliç] *adj* F thick-skinned. **'Dickfelligkeit** *f* (-; *no pl*) F callousness. **'dickflüssig** *adj* thick(-flowing). **'Dickhäuter** ['dɪkhɔytər] *m* (-s; -) *zo.* pachyderm. **'Dickicht** ['dɪkiçt] *n* (-s; -e) **1.** thicket. **2.** *fig.* labyrinth. **'Dickkopf** *m* F *fig.* pigheaded fellow: **e-n ~ haben** → **'dickköpfig** [-kœpfiç] *adj* **~ sein** be pigheaded. **'Dickköpfigkeit** *f* (-; *no pl*) pigheadedness, stubbornness. **'dicklich** *adj* **1.** plump. **2.** → **dickflüssig**. **'Dickmilch** *f* soured milk. **'dickschalig** [-ʃa:lɪç] *adj* thick-skinned. **'Dickwanst** *m* F fat slob.

Didaktik [di'daktik] *f* (-; *no pl*) didactics. **di'daktisch** *adj* didactic.

die [di:] I *def art* the. II *dem pron* this (one), that (one): **~ nicht!** not she! III *rel pron* who, which. IV *pers pron* F *for* **sie** 1.

Dieb [di:p] *m* (-[e]s; -e) thief. **'Diebes|bande** ['di:bəs-] *f* gang of thieves. **~beute** *f*, **~gut** *n* stolen goods. **Diebin** ['di:bɪn] *f* (-; -nen) thief. **diebisch** ['di:bɪʃ] *adj* **1.** thievish. **2.** malicious (*joy*): **sich ~ freuen (über** *acc*) F be tickled pink (at), gloat (at, over).

Diebstahl ['di:pʃta:l] *m* (-[e]s; ⁓e) theft, ⚖ larceny: **einfacher (schwerer) ~** petty (grand) larceny; **geistiger ~** plagiarism. **⚖sicher** *adj* theftproof. **~sicherung** *f* mot. theft protection. **~versicherung** *f* insurance against theft.

Diele ['di:lə] *f* (-; -n) **1.** floorboard. **2.** (entrance) hall, *Am.* hallway.

dienen ['di:nən] *v/i* (h) serve (**[bei**] *j*-m s.o., ⚔ **bei** in, **zu** for, **als** as): **dazu ~ zu** *inf* serve to *inf*; **womit kann ich ~?** what can I do for you?; **damit ist mir nicht gedient** that's of no use to me; **wozu soll das ~?** what's the use of that?

'Diener *m* (-s; -) *a. fig.* servant. **'Dienerin** *f* (-; -nen) maid(servant), *fig.* handmaid. **'Dienerschaft** *f* (-; *no pl*) servants. **'dienlich** *adj* useful (*dat* to), expedient: **~ sein** a) *j*-m be of help (*or* use) to s.o., b) **e-r Sache** further s.th.

Dienst [di:nst] *m* (-es; -e) **1.** service (**an** *dat* to), ⚔ *a.* duty: **öffentlicher ~** civil service; **im (außer) ~** on (off) duty; **~ haben** be on duty, *pharmacy:* be open; **j-m e-n guten (schlechten) ~ erweisen** do s.o. a good (bad) turn; **j-m gute ~e leisten** serve s.o. well; **in ~ stellen** put *ship etc* into service; **(j-m) den ~ versagen** fail (s.o.); **~ nach Vorschrift** work-to-rule (campaign). **2.** post, employment, work: **im ~e** (*gen*) **stehen** be employed by, work for, *contp.* be on *s.o.'s* payroll; **außer ~ retired; den ~ quittieren** resign; → **antreten** 1.

Dienstag ['di:nsta:k] *m* (-[e]s; -e) (**am ~** on) Tuesday. **'dienstags** *adv* on Tuesdays: **~ abends** (on) Tuesday evenings.

'Dienst|alter *n* (*nach dem ~* by) seniority. **~älteste** *m, f* (-n; -n) senior. **~antritt** *m* (*bei ~* on) taking up duty (*or* one's job). **~auffassung** *f* work ethic.

'dienstbar *adj* subservient (*dat* to): **sich et. ~ machen** utilize (*or* exploit) s.th.

'dienstbereit *adj* **1.** a) on duty, b) open. **2.** helpful.

'Dienst|eid *m* oath of office. **~eifer** *m* zeal, *b.s.* officiousness. **⚖eifrig** *adj* zealous, *b.s.* officious. **⚖frei** *adj* **~er Tag** day off; **~ haben** be off duty. **~gebrauch** *m* **nur für den ~** for official use only. **~geheimnis** *n* official secret (*or* secrecy). **~gespräch** *n* teleph. official

call. **~grad** *m* ⚔ rank, *Am.* grade, ⚓ rating. **⚖habend** *adj* on duty. **~herr** *m* employer. **~jahre** *pl* years of service. **~leistung** *f* service (rendered): **~en** services.

'Dienstleistungs|betrieb *m* (*öffentlicher ~* public) services enterprise. **~gewerbe** *n* service industries.

'dienstlich *adj* official: **~ verhindert** prevented by official duties.

'Dienst|mädchen *n* maid(servant), help. **~marke** *f* identity disc. **~pi stole** *f* service pistol. **~plan** *m* duty roster. **~reise** *f* official trip. **~schluß** *m* **nach ~** after (office) hours. **~stelle** *f* office, department. **~stunden** *pl* office hours. **⚖tauglich** *adj* fit for (⚔ active) service. **⚖untauglich** *adj* unfit for (military) service. **~verhältnis** *n* (contract of) employment. **~vorschrift** *f* regulations. **~wagen** *m* official car. **~weg** *m* (**auf dem ~** through) official channels. **~wohnung** *f* company, army *etc* flat (*or* house). **~zeit** *f* **1.** office (*or* working) hours. **2.** (period of) service.

diesbezüglich ['di:s-] *adj* and *adv* concerning this, in this connection.

Dieselmotor ['di:zəl-] *m* Diesel engine.

dieser ['di:zər], **diese, dieses,** *a.* **dies** [di:s], *pl* **diese** *dem pron* **I** this, *pl* these: **dieser Tage** a) the other day, b) one of these days. **II** a) this one, *pl* these, b) he, she, it, *pl* they: **dieses und jenes, dies und das** this and that, various things.

diesig ['di:zɪç] *adj* hazy.

diesjährig ['di:sjɛ:rɪç] *adj* this year's.

'diesmal *adv* this time.

'diesseitig ['di:szaɪtɪç] *adj* near, on this side. **diesseits** ['di:szaɪts] *adv* on this side (*gen* of).

Dietrich ['di:trɪç] *m* (-s; -e) a) picklock, b) skeleton key.

diffamieren [dɪfa'mi:rən] *v/t* (h) slander, defame.

Differential|getriebe [dɪfərən'tsĭa:l-] *n* mot. differential (gear). **~rechnung** *f* ℞ differential calculus.

Differenz [dɪfə'rɛnts] *f* (-; -en) difference.

differenzieren [dɪfərən'tsi:rən] *v/t* (h) differentiate. **differieren** [dɪfə'ri:rən] *v/i* (h) differ (**um** by).

diffus [dɪ'fu:s] *adj* **1.** *phys.* diffuse(d). **2.** *fig.* vague.

digital [digi'ta:l] *adj* digital.

Digi'talanzeige f digital display.
digitalisieren [digitali'zi:rən] v/t (h) digitize.
Digi'talrechner m digital computer.
Digi'taluhr f digital watch (or clock).
Diktat [dɪk'ta:t] n (-[e]s; -e) **1.** (ped. ~ schreiben write or do) dictation; das ~ aufnehmen take the dictation. **2.** fig. dictate. **Diktator** [dɪk'ta:tɔr] m (-s; -en [-'ta:to:rən]) dictator. **diktatorisch** [dɪkta'to:rɪʃ] adj dictatorial. **Diktatur** [dɪkta'tu:r] f (-; -en) dictatorship.
diktieren [dɪk'ti:rən] v/t, v/i (h) a. fig. dictate (j-m to s.o.).
Dik'tiergerät n dictating machine.
Dilemma [di'lɛma] n (-s; -s, -ta) dilemma, f fix.
Dilettant [dile'tant] m (-en; -en), **dilet-'tantisch** adj dilettante.
Dill [dɪl] m (-[e]s; -e) ♣ dill.
Dimension [dimɛn'zio:n] f (-; -en) **1.** A, phys. dimension. **2.** pl dimensions, fig. a. extent.
Ding [dɪŋ] n (-[e]s; -e, F -er) **1.** thing, a. object: vor allen ~en above all; F die armen ~er! the poor (little) things!; fig. guter ~e sein be cheerful. **2.** pl things, matters: (der Stand der ~e the state of affairs; (so,) wie die ~e liegen as matters stand; das geht nicht mit rechten ~en zu F there's s.th. fishy about it. **3.** F ein tolles ~ a wow; ein ~ drehen pull a job; → verpassen 2.
'dingfest adj j-n ~ machen arrest s.o.
Dings [dɪŋs] m, f, n (-; no pl), **'Dings-bums** m, f, n (-; no pl), **'Dingsda** m, f, n (-; no pl) F what's-his(-her, -its)-name, thingumajig.
Dinosaurier [dino'zaʊriər] m (-s; -) dinosaur.
Diode [di'o:də] f (-; -n) ♭ diode.
Dioxyd ['di:'ɔksy:t] n (-s; -e) ♠ dioxide.
Diözese [diø'tse:zə] f (-; -n) diocese.
Diphtherie [dɪfte'ri:] f (-; -n) diphtheria.
Diphthong [dɪf'tɔŋ] m (-s; -e) diphthong.
Diplom [di'plo:m] n (-[e]s; -e) diploma.
Di'plom... diplomaed, graduate (engineer etc), qualified (interpreter etc).
Di'plomarbeit f dissertation.
Diplomat [diplo'ma:t] m (-en; -en) diplomat. **Diplo'matenkoffer** m attaché case. **Diplomatie** [diploma'ti:] f (-; no pl) a. fig. diplomacy. **Diplo'matin** f (-;

-nen) diplomat. **diplo'matisch** adj a. fig. diplomatic.
dir [di:r] **I** pers pron you, to you. **II** reflex pron yourself: wasch ~ die Hände! wash your hands!
direkt [di'rɛkt] **I** adj **1.** a) direct (a. ling.), b) immediate, c) plain: ~e Informationen a. firsthand information. **II** adv **2.** direct, a. fig. straight. **3.** directly, immediately: ~ vor dir right in front of you. **4.** directly, exactly: ~ nach Süden liegen face due south. **5.** F das ist ~ lächerlich etc that's downright ridiculous etc. **6.** radio, TV live.
Di'rektflug m direct flight.
Direktion [dirɛk'tsio:n] f (-; -en) **1.** management. **2.** manager's office. **3.** direction. **Direkti'onsassi,stent(in** f) m junior executive, assistant manager.
Direktive [dirɛk'ti:və] f (-; -n) instruction(s).
Direktor [di'rɛktɔr] m (-s; -en [-'to:rən]) **1.** ♣ director, manager. **2.** ped. headmaster, principal. **Direktorat** [dirɛkto-'ra:t] n (-[e]s; -e) **1.** directorship. **2.** headmaster's office. **Direktorin** [dirɛk-'to:rɪn] f (-; -nen) **1.** directress, manageress. **2.** ped. headmistress, principal. **Direktorium** [dirɛk'to:riʊm] n (-s; -rien) board of directors.
Direktrice [dirɛk'tri:sə] f (-; -n) textil. directress.
Di'rektsendung f live broadcast.
Di'rektwahl f teleph. direct dial(l)ing.
Dirigent [diri'gɛnt] m (-en; -en) ♪ conductor. **Diri'gentin** f (-; -nen) conductress. **dirigieren** [diri'gi:rən] v/t, v/i (h) direct, ♪ a. control, ♪ conduct.
Dirigismus [diri'gɪsmʊs] m (-; no pl) ♣ planned economy.
Dirndl ['dɪrndəl] n (-s; -), ~kleid n dirndl.
Dirne ['dɪrnə] f (-; -n) prostitute, whore.
Dis [dɪs] n (-; -) ♪ D sharp.
Disharmonie [dɪsharmo'ni:] f (-; -n) a. fig. discord.
dishar'monisch adj a. fig. discordant.
Diskant [dɪs'kant] m (-s; -e) ♪ treble.
Diskette [dɪs'kɛtə] f computer: disk(ette).
Diskjockey ['dɪsk-] m disc jockey.
Disko ['dɪsko] f (-s; -s) F disco.
Diskont [dɪs'kɔnt] m (-s; -e) discount. **diskontieren** [-'ti:rən] v/t (h) ♣ discount. **Dis'kontsatz** m discount rate.
Diskothek [dɪsko'te:k] f (-; -en) discotheque.

Diskrepanz [dɪskre'pants] f (-; -en) discrepancy.

diskret [dɪs'kre:t] adj discreet.

Diskretion [dɪskre'tsĭo:n] f (-; no pl) discretion.

diskriminieren [dɪskrimi'ni:rən] v/t (h) discriminate against.

Diskrimi'nierung f (-; -en) discrimination (gen against).

Diskus ['dɪskʊs] m (-[ses]; -se, Disken) sports: discus.

Diskussion [dɪskʊ'sĭo:n] f (-; -en) discussion (**über** acc on).

Diskussi'ons|leiter m (panel) chairman. **~teilnehmer(in** f) m panel(l)ist. **~veranstaltung** f forum.

'Diskuswerfen n (-s) discus throwing.

'Diskuswerfer(in f) m discus thrower.

diskutabel [dɪsku'ta:bəl] adj debatable.

diskutieren [dɪsku'ti:rən] v/t, v/i (h) discuss, debate.

dispensieren [dɪspɛn'zi:rən] v/t (h) **j-n ~** exempt s.o. (**von** from [doing]).

disponieren [dɪspo'ni:rən] v/i (h) make (one's) arrangements, plan ahead: **~ über** (acc) dispose of. **dispo'niert** adj **gut** etc **~ sein** be in good etc form. **Disposition** [dɪspozi'tsĭo:n] f (-; -en) **1.** a. ♂ disposition. **2.** (s-e **~en treffen** make one's) arrangements. **Disposi-ti'onskre,dit** m ✝ overdraft facilities.

Disqualifikation [dɪskvalifika'tsĭo:n] f (-; -en) disqualification (**wegen** for).

disqualifizieren [dɪskvalifi'tsi:rən] v/t (h) a. fig. disqualify (**wegen** for).

Dissertation [dɪsɛrta'tsĭo:n] f (-; -en) dissertation, thesis.

Dissident [dɪsi'dɛnt] m (-en; -en), **Dis-si'dentin** f (-; -nen) pol. dissident.

Dissonanz [dɪso'nants] f (-; -en) ♪ dissonance, fig. a. pl discord.

Distanz [dɪs'tants] f (-; no pl) distance, fig. a. detachment: **~ wahren** keep one's distance (**gegenüber** from).

distanzieren [dɪstan'tsi:rən] **sich ~** (h) keep one's distance; **sich ~ von** dis(as)sociate o.s. from. **distan'ziert** adj fig. distanced, reserved.

Distel ['dɪstəl] f (-; -n) ♀ thistle.

'Distelfink m zo. goldfinch.

Distrikt [dɪs'trɪkt] m (-[e]s; -e) district.

Disziplin [dɪstsi'pli:n] f (-; -en) **1.** no pl discipline. **2.** branch, discipline. **3.** sports: event. **disziplinarisch** [dɪstsi-pli'na:rɪʃ] adj disciplinary. **Diszi-pli'narstrafe** f disciplinary punishment. **Diszipli'narverfahren** n disciplinary proceedings. **diszipli'niert** adj disciplined. **diszi'plinlos** adj undisciplined, unruly. **Diszi'plinlosigkeit** f (-; no pl) lack of discipline.

Diva ['di:va] f (-; -s, Diven) star.

divergieren [dɪvɛr'gi:rən] v/i (h) a. fig. diverge.

divers [di'vɛrs] adj various, sundry.

diversifizieren [dɪvɛrzifi'tsi:rən] v/t, v/i (h) ✝ diversify.

Dividend [divi'dɛnt] m (-en; -en) ⅍ dividend. **Dividende** [divi'dɛndə] f (-; -n) ✝ dividend. **dividieren** [divi'di:rən] v/t, v/i (h) ⅍ divide (**durch** by). **Division** [divi'zĭo:n] f (-; -en) ⅍, ⚔ division.

Divisor [di'vi:zɔr] m (-s; -en [divi'zo:rən]) ⅍ divisor.

doch [dɔx] **I** conj **1.** but. **II** adv **2.** yet, however, nevertheless: **höflich, ~ be-stimmt** polite yet firm; **also ~!** I knew it!; **er hat also ~ recht!** so he's right after all! **3.** **du kommst nicht mit? - ~!** you won't come along? - Oh yes, I will!; **er kommt ~?** he will come, won't he?; **ja ~!** of course!; **nicht ~!** a) don't!, b) certainly not!; **setzen Sie sich ~!** do sit down, please!; **frag ihn ~!** just ask him!; **sei(d) ~ mal still!** be quiet, will you!; **das ist ~ Peter!** why, that's Peter!

Docht [dɔxt] m (-[e]s; -e) wick.

Dock [dɔk] n (-s; -s) dock. **Dockarbeiter** m docker. **'docken** v/i (h) dock.

Dogge ['dɔɡə] f (-; -n) zo. **deutsche ~** Great Dane; **englische ~** mastiff.

Dogma ['dɔɡma] n (-s; -men) dogma.

dogmatisch [dɔɡ'ma:tɪʃ] adj dogmatic.

Dohle ['do:lə] f (-; -n) zo. (jack)daw.

Doktor ['dɔktor] m (-s; -en [-'to:rən]) doctor (a. F ♂): **s-n ~ machen** take (or work for) one's doctor's degree.

Doktorand [dɔkto'rant] m (-en; -en) doctoral candidate.

'Doktor|arbeit f (doctoral) thesis. **~va-ter** m supervisor. **~würde** f doctorate.

Doktrin [dɔk'tri:n] f (-; -en) doctrine.

Dokument [doku'mɛnt] n (-[e]s; -e) document (a. fig.), ⚖ a. deed: **~e gegen Zahlung** documents against payment.

Dokumentar... [dokumɛn'ta:r-] documentary (report, play, etc). **Doku-men'tarfilm** m documentary (film).

dokumen'tarisch *adj* documentary.
Dokumentation [dokumɛnta'tsĭoːn] *f* (-; -en) documentation.
dokumentieren [dokumɛn'tiːrən] *v/t* (h) document, *fig. a.* demonstrate, show.
Dolch [dɔlç] *m* (-[e]s; -e) dagger. **~stoß** *m* dagger thrust, *fig.* stab in the back.
Dolde ['dɔldə] *f* (-; -n) ♀ umbel.
Dollar ['dɔlar] *m* (-[s]; -s) dollar.
Dolle ['dɔlə] *f* (-; -n) ⚓ thole(pin).
dolmetschen ['dɔlmɛtʃən] *v/i* (h) interpret (*a. v/t*), act as interpreter.
'Dolmetscher *m* (-s; -), **'Dolmetscherin** *f* (-; -nen) interpreter.
'Dolmetscherinsti,tut *n* school (*univ.* institute) for interpreters.
Dom [doːm] *m* (-[e]s; -e) cathedral.
Domäne [do'mɛːnə] *f* (-; -n) domain.
domestizieren [domɛsti'tsiːrən] *v/t* domesticate.
dominant [domi'nant] *adj* dominant.
Domi'nante *f* (-; -n) ♪, *biol.* dominant.
dominieren [domi'niːrən] *v/t*, *v/i* (h) dominate; **~d** dominant, dominating.
Dominikaner [domini'kaːnər] *m* (-s; -), **Domini'kanerin** *f* (-; -nen), **domini'kanisch** *adj* Dominican.
Domini'kaner(mönch) *m* Dominican.
Domino ['doːmino] *n* (-s; -s), **~spiel** *n* (game of) dominoes. **~stein** *m* domino.
Domizil [domi'tsiːl] *n* (-s; -e) domicile.
Dompteur [dɔmp'tøːr] *m* (-s; -e), **Dompteuse** [-'tøːzə] *f* (-; -n) animal trainer.
Donner ['dɔnər] *m* (-s; -) thunder, *fig. a.* roar: **wie vom ~ gerührt** thunderstruck. **'donnern I** *v/impers* (h) **1. es donnert** it is thundering. **II** *v/i* (sn) *fig.* **2.** thunder, roar. **3.** F **~ gegen** crash against (*or* into). **III** *v/t* (h) *fig.* **4.** roar (*commands etc*). **5.** F slam. **'donnernd** *adj fig.* thunderous (*applause etc*).
'Donnerschlag *m a. fig.* thunderclap.
'Donnerstag *m* (**am ~** on) Thursday.
'donnerstags *adv* (on) Thursdays.
'Donnerwetter F I *n* (-s; -) row. **II** *int* **~!** wow!; **warum** (**wo** *etc*) **zum ~?** why (where *etc*) the hell?
doof [doːf] *adj* F dopey, dumb.
dopen ['dɔpən, 'doːpən] *v/t* (h) dope: **sich ~** take dope. **Doping** ['dɔpɪŋ, 'doːpɪŋ] *n* (-s; -s) doping.
'Dopingkon,trolle *f* dope test.
Doppel ['dɔpəl] *n* (-s; -) **1.** duplicate. **2.**

tennis: doubles. **~a,gent(in** *f*) *m* double agent. **~bett** *n* double bed.
Doppeldecker ['dɔpəldɛkər] *m* (-s; -) **1.** biplane. **2.** F (*bus*) double-decker.
'Doppelfehler *m tennis*: double fault.
'Doppelfenster *n* double window.
Doppelgänger ['dɔpəlgɛŋər] *m* (-s; -), **'Doppelgängerin** *f* (-; -nen) double.
'Doppel|haushälfte *f* semi-detached (house). **~kinn** *n* double chin. **~name** *m* hyphenated name. **~punkt** *m* colon. **~rolle** *f a. fig.* double role.
'doppelseitig [-zaɪtıç] **I** *adj* reversible (*cloth*). **II** *adv* on both sides.
'Doppelsieg *m sports*: double win.
'Doppelsinn *m* double meaning, ambiguity.
'doppelsinnig *adj* ambiguous.
'Doppelspiel *n* **1.** *contp.* (**ein ~ treiben** play a) double game. **2. →** **Doppel** 2.
'Doppelstecker *m* ⚡ two-way adapter.
'doppelt I *adj* double, *esp.* ⊙ dual, twin, *esp.* ⚡ duplex: **den ~en Preis (or das 2e) zahlen** pay double the price; **in ~er Ausfertigung** in duplicate. **II** *adv* doubly (*painful etc*), double, twice: **~ so groß (viel)** twice as big (much).
'Doppel|tür *f* double doors. **~verdiener** *pl* dual-income family. **~vierer** *m* (-s; -) *rowing*: sculling four.
'doppelwandig [-vandıç] *adj* double-walled.
'Doppel|zentner *m* quintal. **~zimmer** *n* double room. **~zweier** *m* (-s; -) *rowing*: double sculls.
Dorf [dɔrf] *n* (-[e]s; ⁀er) village.
'Dorfbewohner(in *f*) *m* villager.
dörflich ['dœrflıç] *adj* village (*life etc*).
Dorn [dɔrn] *m* (-[e]s; -en) **1.** ♀ thorn, spine (*a. zo.*): **j-m ein ~ im Auge sein** be a thorn in s.o.'s side. **2.** ⊙ spike.
'Dornenkrone *f* crown of thorns.
'dornenlos *adj* thornless.
'dornenreich *adj fig.* thorny.
'Dornenstrauch *m* bramble.
Dorn'röschen *n* (-s) Sleeping Beauty.
dörren ['dœrən] *v/t* (h) dry.
'Dörrobst *n* dried fruit.
Dorsch [dɔrʃ] *m* (-es; -e) *zo.* cod.
dort [dɔrt] *adv* there; **~ drüben** over there; **von ~ →** **'dorther** *adv* from there. **'dorthin** *adv* there.
Dose ['doːzə] *f* (-; -n) **1.** box. **2.** tin, can. **3.** ⚡ outlet.

dösen ['dø:zən] *v/i* (h) F **1.** doze. **2.** daydream.

'Dosen... → **Büchsen...**

dosieren [do'zi:rən] *v/t* (h) dose, *fig.* give *s.th.* in small *etc* doses.

Do'sierung *f* (-; -en) *a. fig.* dosage.

Dosis ['do:zɪs] *f* (-; Dosen) *a. fig.* dose: **zu geringe** ~ underdose.

dotieren [do'ti:rən] *v/t* (h) endow (**mit** with): **ein mit 100 000 DM dotiertes Turnier** a tournament carrying a 100,000 mark prize; **e-e gut dotierte Stellung** a well-paid position.

Do'tierung *f* (-; -en) **1.** endowment. **2.** payment, remuneration.

Dotter ['dɔtər] *n* (-s; -) yolk.

doubeln ['du:bəln] *v/t, v/i* (h) *film etc:* double. **Double** ['du:bəl] *n* (-s; -s) double, stand-in.

Dozent [do'tsɛnt] *m* (-en; -en), **Do'zentin** *f* (-; -nen) (university) lecturer, *Am.* assistant professor. **dozieren** [do'tsi:rən] *v/t, v/i* (h) lecture (**über** *acc* on).

Drache ['draxə] *m* (-n; -n) dragon.

Drachen ['draxən] *m* (-s; -) **1.** (**e-n** ~ **steigen lassen** fly a) kite. **2.** *sports:* hang glider. **3.** F *contp.* battle-ax(e).

'Drachen|fliegen *n* (-s) hang gliding. **~flieger(in)** *f) m* hang glider (pilot).

Dragée [dra'ʒe:] *n* (-s; -s) dragée, coated tablet.

Draht [dra:t] *m* (-[e]s; ⁓e) wire: *pol.* **heißer** ~ hot line; F **auf** ~ **sein** a) be in good form, b) be on the ball. **~bürste** *f* wire brush. **~esel** *m* humor. bike. **~funk** *m* wired radio. **~glas** *n* wire(d) glass.

'Drahthaar... *zo.* wirehaired (*terrier etc*).

'drahtig *adj fig.* person: wiry.

'drahtlos *adj* wireless, radio-...

'Drahtsaite *f* ♪ wire.

'Drahtseil *n* wire rope, *circus:* tightrope. **'Drahtseilakt** *m* tightrope act (*fig.* walk). **'Drahtseilbahn** *f* cable railway.

'Drahtzaun *m* wire fence.

'Drahtzieher *m* (-s; -) *fig.* wirepuller.

drakonisch [dra'ko:nɪʃ] *adj* Draconian.

drall [dral] *adj* buxom, strapping.

Drall *m* (-[e]s; -e) ✪ twist, *a. sports:* spin.

Drama ['dra:ma] *n* (-s; -men) drama.

Dramatik [dra'ma:tɪk] *f* (-; *no pl*) drama. **Dramatiker** [dra'ma:tikər] *m* (-s; -) dramatist. **dra'matisch** *adj* dramatic. **dramatisieren** [dramati'zi:rən] *v/t* (h) dramatize.

Dramaturg [drama'tʊrk] *m* (-en; -en), **Drama'turgin** *f* (-; -nen) dramaturge. **Dramaturgie** [dramatʊr'gi:] *f* (-; -n) dramaturgy.

dran [dran] *adv* F **1.** → **daran. 2. ich bin** ~ it's my turn; **jetzt bin ich** ~! now he's (in) for it! **3. du bist gut** ~! you are lucky!; **er ist übel** ~ he's in a bad way; **spät** ~ **sein** be late; **an der Sache ist was** ~ there is s.th. in it; **man weiß nie, wie man mit ihr** ~ **ist** you never know what to make of her; **jetzt weiß ich, wie ich** ~ **bin** now I know where I stand; ~ **drauf** 2, **Drum, glauben** II.

'dranbleiben *v/i* (*irr, sep, -ge-, sn,* → **bleiben**) F *fig.* **~ an** (*dat*) stick to; **bleib dran!** a) keep at it!, b) hold the line!

drang [draŋ] *pret of* **dringen.**

Drang *m* (-[e]s; *no pl*) a) urge, impulse, b) desire (**nach** for).

Drängelei [drɛŋə'laɪ] *f* (-; -en) F pushing and shoving.

drängeln ['drɛŋəln] *v/t, v/i* (h) F **1.** push, shove. **2.** *fig.* pester. **3.** *mot.* tailgate.

drängen ['drɛŋən] (h) **I** *v/t* **1.** push: *fig.* **j-n** ~, **et. zu tun** urge s.o. to do s.th., pressure s.o. into doing s.th.; **ich lasse mich nicht** ~! I won't be rushed. **II** *v/i* **2.** push, throng. **3.** *fig.* be urgent, be pressing: **die Zeit drängt** time is running short. **4. auf Zahlung** ~ press for payment; **auf e-e Entscheidung** ~ urge a decision. **III sich** ~ crowd (**um** round); **sich nach vorne** (**zur Tür** *etc*) ~ force one's way to the front (towards the door *etc*); *fig.* **sich nach et.** ~ be keen on (doing) s.th. **'Drängen** *n* (-s) **auf sein** ~ at his *etc* insistence. **'drängend** *adj* urgent.

'Drängler *m* (-s; -) F **1.** pusher. **2.** *mot.* tailgater.

drangsalieren [draŋza'li:rən] *v/t* (h) torment.

'dranhalten: sich ~ (*irr, sep, -ge-, h,* → **halten**) F a) hurry up, b) keep at it.

'drankommen *v/i* (*irr, sep, -ge-, sn,* → **kommen**) F **1. jetzt komme ich dran** now it's my turn; **als nächster** ~ be next. **2.** *ped.* be asked (a question).

'drankriegen *v/t* (*sep, -ge-, h*) F get.

'drannehmen *v/t* (*irr, sep, -ge-, h,* → **nehmen**) F take (*patient*), ask (*pupil*).

drapieren [dra'pi:rən] *v/t* (h) drape.

drastisch ['drastɪʃ] *adj* drastic.

drauf [draʊf] F *adv* **1.** → **darauf. 2. ~ und dran sein, et. zu tun** be on the point of doing s.th.; **gut ~ sein** a) be in great form, b) *a.* (**schwer**) **was ~ haben** be (just) great (**in** *dat* at); **er hatte 150 Sachen ~** he was doing 100 miles.

Draufgänger ['draʊfgɛŋər] *m* (-s; -) a) daredevil, b) go-getter, c) casanova, wolf. '**draufgängerisch** *adj* reckless.

'**draufgehen** *v/i* (*irr, sep,* -ge-, sn, → **gehen**) F **1.** be killed. **2.** a) be lost, *money:* go down the drain, b) go to pot.

'**draufkommen** *v/i* (*irr, sep,* -ge-, sn, → **kommen**) F *j-m ~* find s.o. out.

'**draufkriegen** *v/t* (*sep,* -ge-, h) F **eins ~** a) get it in the neck, b) *sports:* get a thrashing.

'**drauflegen** *v/t* (*sep,* -ge-, h) F pay an extra *100 marks etc.*

drauf'los F **I** *adv* straight ahead. **II** *int* (**feste**) **~!** come on! **drauf'losgehen** *v/i* (*irr, sep,* -ge-, sn, → **gehen**) F make straight for it. **drauf'losgehen** *v/i* (*sep,* -ge-, h) F start rattling away.

'**draufmachen** *v/t* (*sep,* -ge-, h) F **e-n ~** have a ball (*or* a booze-up) go to town.

'**draufstoßen** *v/t* (*irr, sep,* -ge-, h, → **stoßen**) F *fig. j-n ~* spell it out to s.o.

'**draufzahlen** (*sep,* -ge-, h) F **I** *v/t* pay an extra *100 marks etc.* **II** *v/i* lose money.

draus [draʊs] F *for* **daraus.**

draußen ['draʊsən] *adv* outside, in the open (air), ⚓ at sea: **im Garten** out in the garden; **bleib(t) ~!** keep out!

drechseln ['drɛksəln] *v/t* (h) turn: → **gedrechselt. Drechsler** ['drɛkslər] *m* (-s; -) wood turner.

Dreck [drɛk] *m* (-[e]s; *no pl*) **1.** dirt, filth, mud: *fig.* **im ~ sitzen** be in a mess; *j-n* (**et.**) **in den ~ ziehen** drag s.o.'s name (s.th.) in the mud; *j-n wie* (**den letzten**) **~ behandeln** treat s.o. like dirt; **er hat** (**viel**) **~ am Stecken** he has a lot to answer for. **2.** *fig.* rubbish, crap: **er kümmert sich e-n ~ darum** he doesn't care a damn; **das geht dich e-n ~ an!** that's none of your business!

'**Dreckding** *n* (-[e]s; -er) F damn thing.

'**dreckig** *adj* F dirty, filthy, *fig. a.* nasty, mean: **~e Witze** dirty jokes; **es geht ihm ~** he's having a bad time.

'**Drecknest** *n* F *contp.* dump, hole.

'**Drecksau** *f,* '**Dreckschwein** *n* V **1.** (dirty) pig. **2.** swine.

'**Dreckskerl** *m* F swine, bastard.
'**Dreckwetter** *n* F filthy weather.

Dreh [dre:] *m* (-[e]s; -e) F trick: **den richtigen ~ heraushaben** have got the hang of it.

'**Dreharbeiten** *pl film:* shooting.
'**Drehbank** *f* ⚙ lathe.
'**drehbar** *adj* rotatable.
'**Drehbleistift** *m* propelling pencil.
'**Drehbuch** *n* script, *a. fig.* scenario.
'**Drehbuchautor**(**in** *f*) *m* scriptwriter.
'**Drehbühne** *f* revolving stage.

drehen ['dre:ən] (h) **I** *v/t* **1.** a) turn, b) twist (*a. fig.*): *fig.* **man kann es ~ und wenden** (**wie man will**) whichever way you look at it. **2.** roll (*cigarette etc*). **3.** shoot (*film*). **4.** F *fig.* wangle: → **Ding 3.** **5.** ⚙ turn. **II** *v/i* **6.** turn (round): **~ an** (*dat*) turn, *a. fig.* fiddle with; F **daran ist nichts zu ~ und zu deuteln** that's a fact. **III** *sich ~* turn, go (*or* spin) round; **die Erde dreht sich um die Sonne** the earth revolves around the sun; *mir* **dreht sich alles** my head is spinning; *fig.* **sich ~ um** revolve round, *talk:* be about; **es dreht sich darum, ob** it's a question of whether.

'**Dreher** *m* (-s; -) ⚙ lathe operator.
'**Dreh|kraft** *f* rotatory force. **~kran** *m* slewing crane. **~kreuz** *n* turnstile. **~mo,ment** *n* ⚙ torque. **~orgel** *f* barrel organ. **~pause** *f film:* shooting break. **~punkt** *m* ⚙ *or fig.* pivot. **~schalter** *m* rotary switch. **~scheibe** *f* 🚂 turntable.

'**Drehstrom** *m* ⚡ threephase current.
'**~motor** *m* threephase A.C. motor.
'**Drehstuhl** *m* swivel chair.
'**Drehtür** *f* revolving door.
'**Drehung** *f* (-; -en) turn(ing), rotation: **schnelle ~** spin.
'**Drehzahl** *f* revolutions per minute (*abbr.* r.p.m.). **~messer** *m* revolution counter. **~regelung** *f* speed control.

drei [draɪ] *adj* three: **sie kann nicht bis ~ zählen** she is pretty dim(witted).
Drei *f* (-; -en) a) (number) three, b) *ped.* satisfactory.
'**dreibeinig** [-baɪnɪç] *adj* three-legged.
'**dreidimensio,nal** *adj* three-dimensional.
'**Dreieck** *n* (-[e]s; -e) triangle.
'**dreieckig** *adj* triangular.
'**Dreiecksverhältnis** *n* (love) triangle.
Drei'einigkeit *f* (-; *no pl*) *eccl.* Trinity.

'**dreifach** *adj* threefold, triple: *die ~e Menge* three times the amount; *in ~er Ausfertigung* in triplicate; *das Dreifache* three times as much, triple.

'**dreifarbig** *adj* tricolo(u)r.

'**Dreiganggetriebe** *n* three-speed gear.

'**dreihundert** *adj* three hundred.

'**dreijährig** [-jɛːrɪç] *adj* **1.** three-year-old. **2.** lasting (*or* of) three years.

'**Dreijährige** [-jɛːrɪgə] *m, f* (-n; -n) three--year-old (child).

'**Dreiklang** *m* ♪ triad.

Drei'könige *pl eccl.* (**zu ~** on) Epiphany.

'**dreimal** *adv* three times.

Drei'meilenzone *f* three-mile limit.

'**Dreimeterbrett** *n* three-metre (diving) board.

drein·blicken ['draɪn-] *v/i* (*sep*, -ge-, h) F look *sad etc*.

'**dreinschlagen** *v/i* (*irr, sep*, -ge-, h, → *schlagen*) F lay about one.

'**Dreirad** *n* tricycle.

'**Dreisatz** *m* (-es; *no pl*) ₳ rule of three.

'**dreisilbig** [-zɪlbɪç] *adj* trisyllabic.

'**Dreisprung** *m sports*: triple jump.

'**dreispurig** [-ʃpuːrɪç] *adj* three-lane(d).

dreißig ['draɪsɪç] *adj* thirty. '**Dreißig** *f* (-) thirty: *sie ist Ende* (*der*) *~* she is in her late thirties. **dreißiger** ['draɪsɪgər] *adj* **die *~ Jahre*** the thirties (*of a century*). '**Dreißiger** *m* (-s; -), '**Dreißigerin** *f* (-; -nen) man (woman) in (*or* in his [her] thirties). '**dreißigst** *adj* thirtieth.

dreist [draɪst] *adj* impudent, impertinent, F cheeky, brazen (*lie etc*).

'**dreistellig** [-ʃtɛlɪç] *adj* ₳ three-digit.

'**Dreistigkeit** *f* (-; *no pl*) impudence, impertinence, F cheek.

'**dreistufig** [-ʃtuːfɪç] *adj* ⚙ three-stage.

'**dreitägig** [-tɛːgɪç] *adj* three-day.

'**dreiteilig** [-taɪlɪç] *adj* three-piece.

'**dreiviertel** *adj* three-quarter: *es war ~ zwei* it was a quarter to two; *~ voll* three-quarters full.

'**dreiwertig** [-veːrtɪç] *adj* ❁ trivalent.

'**dreiwöchig** [-vœçɪç] *adj* three-week.

'**Dreizack** *m* (-s; -e) trident.

'**dreizehn** *adj* thirteen: F *jetzt schlägt's aber ~!* that's the limit!

'**dreizehnt** *adj* thirteenth.

Dresche ['drɛʃə] *f* (-; *no pl*) F hiding.

'**dreschen** *v/t, v/i* (drosch, gedroschen, h) ✈ thresh; → *Phrase*.

'**Dreschma·schine** *f* threshing machine.

Dresseur [drɛˈsøːr] *m* (-s; -e) animal trainer. **dressieren** [drɛˈsiːrən] *v/t* (h) train (*animal*), drill (*child*).

Dressman ['drɛsmən] *m* (-s; -men) male model.

Dressur [drɛˈsuːr] *f* (-; -en) **1.** (animal) training. **2.** → **Dres'surreiten** *n* dressage.

Drift [drɪft] *f* (-; -en) ⚓ drift (current).

driften ['drɪftən] *v/i* (sn) ⚓ *or fig.* drift.

Drill [drɪl] *m* (-[e]s; *no pl*) ✕ *or fig.* drill.

drillen ['drɪlən] *v/t* (h) ✕ *a. fig.* drill.

Drilling ['drɪlɪŋ] *m* (-s; -e) triplet.

drin [drɪn] *adv* F **1.** → *darin: er ist ~* he's inside. **2.** *es ist noch alles ~* anything is still possible; *das ist* (*bei mir*) *nicht ~!* that's not on!, that's out!; *mehr war nicht ~* that was the best I *etc* could do.

dringen ['drɪŋən] (drang, gedrungen) *v/i* **1.** (sn) *~ durch* force one's way through, *light etc*: penetrate, *water etc*: seep through. **2.** (sn) *~ aus* (*dat*) *sounds etc*: come from. **3.** (sn) *~ in* (*acc*) penetrate (into), *water*: *a.* seep into, *a. fig.* invade; *in die Öffentlichkeit ~* leak out. **4.** (sn) *~ bis zu* reach, get as far as. **5.** (h) *~ auf* (*acc*) insist on, press for. **6.** (sn) (*mit Fragen etc*) *in j-n ~* press s.o. (with questions *etc*). '**dringend** *adj* urgent, pressing, strong (*suspicion etc*), compelling (*reasons*): *~ brauchen* need urgently (*or* badly); *~ empfehlen* recommend strongly; *~ notwendig* imperative; *~ verdächtig* highly suspect.

'**dringlich** *adj* urgent.

'**Dringlichkeit** *f* (-; *no pl*) urgency: *von größter ~* of top (*or* first) priority.

'**Dringlichkeitsantrag** *m parl.* emergency motion. '**Dringlichkeitsstufe** *f* priority (class): *höchste ~* top priority.

drinnen ['drɪnən] *adv* inside, indoors.

'**drinstecken** *v/i* (sep, -ge-, h) F *da steckt viel Arbeit drin* a lot of work has gone into it.

dritt [drɪt] *adj* third: *~er Klasse* third--class; *wir gingen zu ~ hin* three of us went; *pol. die ₂e Welt* the Third World. '**Dritte** *m, f* (-n; -n) third, ⚖ third party: *~(r) werden sports*: finish third.

Drittel ['drɪtəl] *n* (-s; -) third.

'**drittens** ['drɪtəns] *adv* third(ly).

'**drittklassig** [-klasɪç] *adj fig.* third-rate.

'**drittletzt** *adj* last but two.

Droge ['droːgə] *f* (-; -n) drug.

'**drogenabhängig** *adj* addicted to drugs. '**Drogenabhängige** *m, f* (-n; -n) drug addict. '**Drogenabhängigkeit** *f* (-; *no pl*) drug addiction.

'**Drogen|handel** *m* drug trafficking. **~händler** *m* drug dealer. **~kon͵sum** *m* use of drugs. **~mißbrauch** *m* drug abuse. **~rausch** *m* F (*im* ~ on a) trip. **~sucht** *f* drug addiction. **͛süchtig** *adj* addicted to drugs. **~süchtige** *m, f* (-n; -n) drug addict. **~szene** *f* drug scene.

Drogerie [droɡəˈriː] *f* (-; -n) chemist's (shop), *Am.* drugstore, pharmacy.

Drogist [droˈɡɪst] *m* (-en; -en), **Dro'gistin** *f* (-; -nen) chemist, *Am.* druggist.

'**Drohbrief** *m* threatening letter.

drohen [ˈdroːən] *v/i* (h) threaten (*j-m* s.o.): *j-m* ~ a) *mit der Faust* shake one's fist at s.o., b) *fig.* be in store for s.o.; *mit der Polizei* ~ threaten to call the police; *er drohte zu ertrinken* he was in danger of drowning.

'**drohend** *adj* threatening, *fig. a.* imminent: **~e Gefahr** threat, menace.

Drohne [ˈdroːnə] *f* (-; -n) *a. fig.* drone.

dröhnen [ˈdrøːnən] *v/i* (h) a) boom, roar, b) resound (*von* with): *fig. mein Kopf dröhnt* my head is ringing.

'**Drohung** *f* (-; -en) threat, menace.

drollig [ˈdrɔlɪç] *adj* droll, funny.

Dromedar [ˈdroːmedaːr] *n* (-s; -e) *zo.* dromedary.

Drops [drɔps] *m, n* (-; -) fruit drop.

drosch [drɔʃ] *pret of* **dreschen**.

Drossel¹ [ˈdrɔsəl] *f* (-; -n) *zo.* thrush.

'**Drossel²** *f* (-; -n) ☉ choke.

'**Drosselklappe** *f mot.* throttle (valve).

drosseln [ˈdrɔsəln] *v/t* (h) ☉ throttle (*a. fig.*), turn down (*heating*).

drüben [ˈdryːbən] *adv* (*da*) ~ over there.

Druck¹ [drʊk] *m* (-[e]s; *no pl*) pressure, *fig. a.* stress, 🕱 sensation of pressure: *auf j-n* ~ *ausüben, j-n unter* ~ *setzen* put s.o. under pressure; F *im* ~ *sein* be pressed for time.

Druck² *m* (-[e]s; -e) **1.** *no pl* printing: *in* ~ *gehen* go to press; *im* ~ *sein* be printing. **2.** *paint., print., textil.* print.

'**Druck|abfall** *m* drop in pressure. **~anstieg** *m* increase in pressure. **~ausgleich** *m* pressure compensation.

'**Druckbuchstabe** *m* block letter: *in* ~*n* *schreiben* a. print.

Drückeberger [ˈdrʏkəbɛrɡər] *m* (-s; -) F shirker.

'**druckempfindlich** *adj* sensitive to pressure, *fruit:* easily bruised.

drucken [ˈdrʊkən] *v/t* (h) print.

drücken [ˈdrʏkən] (h) **I** *v/t* **1.** press, squeeze, push (*button, key*): *j-m die Hand* ~ shake hands with s.o.; *j-m et. in die Hand* ~ put (*or* slip) s.th. into s.o.'s hand; *j-n* (*an sich*) ~ hug s.o.; → *Daumen.* **2.** *j-n* ~ *shoe:* pinch s.o., *fig.* worries *etc:* weigh heavily on s.o. **3.** bring (*or* force) down (*performance, prices*), better *a record* (*um* by). **4.** *sl.* shoot up (*drug*). **II** *v/i* **5.** *shoe:* pinch, *backpack etc: a.* hurt, *fig. heat etc:* be oppressive: ~ *auf* (*acc*) press on, press, push (*button etc*); *auf die Stimmung* ~ cast a gloom (on everything). **III** *sich* ~ *vor* (*dat*) F shirk.

'**drückend** *adj fig.* heavy (*debts*), oppressive (*heat etc*).

'**Drucker** *m* (-s; -) *a. computer:* printer.

'**Drücker** *m* (-s; -) a) latch, b) *on gun:* trigger: F *auf den letzten* ~ at the last minute; *am* ~ *sitzen* be at the controls.

Drucke'rei *f* (-; -en) printing office.

'**Druckerzeugnis** *n* publication.

'**Druckfehler** *m* misprint.

'**Druckfehlerverzeichnis** *n* errata.

'**druckfertig** *adj* ready for (the) press: **~es Manuskript** fair copy.

'**Druck|ka͵bine** *f* ✈ pressurized cabin. **~knopf** *m* press-stud, F popper, *Am.* snap fastener, ☉ push button. **~luft** *f* compressed air. **~luftbremse** *f* air brake. **~ma͵schine** *f* printing machine. **~messer** *m* ☉ pressure ga(u)ge. **~mittel** *n fig.* lever. **~posten** *m* F cushy job. **͛reif** → *druckfertig.* **~sache** *f* **1.** 🕾 printed (*Am. a.* second-class) matter. **2.** *parl.* Document. **~schrift** *f* **1.** block letters: *in* ~ *schreiben* a. print. **2.** printing type. **3.** publication. **~stelle** *f* tender spot, *on fruit:* bruise. **~verband** *m* 🕱 compression bandage. **~welle** *f* blast, shock wave. **~zeile** *f* printline.

drum [drʊm] *adv* F → *darum.*

Drum: *das ganze* ~ *und Dran* everything that goes with it; *mit allem* ~ *und Dran* with all the trimmings.

drunter [ˈdrʊntər] *adv* F **1.** → *darunter.* **2.** *es ging alles* ~ *und drüber* it was absolutely chaotic.

Drüse ['dry:zə] f (-; -n) gland.

Dschungel ['dʒʊŋəl] m (-s; -) jungle.

Dschunke ['dʒʊŋkə] f (-; -n) junk.

du [du:] pers pron you: **bist ~ es?** is that you?; **~ Glückliche(r)!** lucky you!; **mit j-m per ~ sein → duzen** b.

Dübel ['dy:bəl] m (-s; -), **'dübeln** v/t (h) dowel, peg.

Dublee... [du'ble:-] gold-plated.

ducken ['dʊkən] (h) **I** v/t **den Kopf ~** duck one's head. **II sich ~** a) crouch (down), b) duck, c) fig. cringe (**vor** before). **Duckmäuser** ['dʊkmɔyzər] m (-s; -) F contp. **1.** cringer. **2.** hypocrite.

dudeln ['du:dəln] v/t, v/i (h) F tootle.

'Dudelsack m bagpipe(s).

Duell [du'ɛl] n (-s; -e) duel (**auf Pistolen** with pistols), fig. a. fight. **duellieren** [duɛ'li:rən] **sich ~** (h) fight a duel.

Duett [du'ɛt] n (-[e]s; -e) ♪ duet.

Duft [dʊft] m (-[e]s; ⁻e) smell, scent, fragrance, aroma. **'dufte** adj F great, super. **'duften** v/i (h) smell (**nach** of): **süß ~** smell sweet. **'duftend** adj fragrant.

duftig ['dʊftiç] adj gossamer, filmy.

'Duftnote f special scent.

'Duftstoff m scent, aroma.

dulden ['dʊldən] v/t (h) **1.** tolerate: **ich dulde es nicht** I won't have it (**daß** that); **→ Aufschub. 2.** endure, suffer. **'Dulder** m (-s; -), **'Dulderin** f (-; -nen) (patient) sufferer. **'Duldermiene** f iro. **mit ~** with a martyred expression.

'duldsam adj (**gegen**) tolerant (of), patient (with). **'Duldsamkeit** f (-; no pl) tolerance (**gegen** of), forbearance. **'Duldung** f (-; no pl) toleration.

dumm [dʊm] adj stupid, F dumb, a. silly, fig. a. awkward: **zu ~!, so et. ♀es!** how stupid!, what a nuisance!; F **~es Zeug** rubbish; **sich ~ stellen** act the fool; **ich lasse mich nicht für ~ verkaufen** I'm not that stupid; **die Sache wird mir zu ~** I'm sick and tired of it; **j-m ~ kommen** get fresh with s.o. **'Dumme** m, f (-n; -n) fool: **der ~ sein** be left holding the baby. **'dummerweise** adv F **1. ~ habe ich es vergessen** like a fool I forgot it. **2.** unfortunately. **'Dummheit** f (-; -en) **1.** no pl stupidity. **2.** stupid thing: **was für e-e ~!** what a stupid thing to do!; **(mach) k-e ~en!** don't do anything stupid!, none of your tricks! **'Dummkopf** m fool, idiot.

dumpf [dʊmpf] adj **1.** dull, muffled: **~er Aufprall** thud. **2.** stuffy, musty. **3.** fig. dark (feeling etc), dull (pain), gloomy (silence etc).

Düne ['dy:nə] f (-; -n) dune.

Dung [dʊŋ] m (-[e]s; no pl) manure, dung. **'Düngemittel** n → **Dünger.**

düngen ['dyŋən] v/t, v/i (h) fertilize.

'Dünger m (-s; -) a) fertilizer, b) manure, dung. **'Dunggrube** f manure pit.

dunkel ['dʊŋkəl] adj **1.** dark, a. fig. gloomy: **es wird ~** it is getting dark. **2.** deep (voice etc). **3.** fig. dark, vague, dim, mysterious, b.s. shady, dubious: **j-n im ~n lassen** leave s.o. in the dark (**über** acc about); F **im ~n tappen** grope in the dark; **sich ~ erinnern** remember dimly. **Dunkel** n (-s) the dark.

Dünkel ['dyŋkəl] m (-s; no pl) conceit.

'dunkelblau adj dark blue. **'dunkelblond** adj dark blond. **'dunkelhaarig** adj dark(-haired). **'dunkelhäutig** [-hɔytɪç] adj dark(-skinned), swarthy.

'Dunkelheit f (-; no pl) darkness, fig. a. obscurity: → **Einbruch** 2.

'Dunkelkammer f phot. darkroom.

'dunkelrot adj dark red.

'Dunkelziffer f estimated number of unknown cases.

dünn [dyn] adj **1.** thin, a. flimsy (dress etc), phys. rare (air), weak (tea etc). **2.** fig. poor. **'dünnbesiedelt** adj sparsely populated. **'Dünndarm** m anat. small intestine. **'Dünndruck(ausgabe** f) m India-paper edition. **'dünnemachen: sich ~** (sep, -ge-, h) F make o.s. scarce. **'dünnflüssig** adj thin, liquid, thin-bodied (oil). **'dünngesät** adj F fig. scarce, rare. **'dünnhäutig** [-hɔytɪç] adj a. fig. thin-skinned. **'Dünnheit** f (-; no pl) thinness, weakness.

Dunst [dʊnst] m (-[e]s; ⁻e) a) haze, mist, b) vapo(u)r, fumes, steam: F fig. **er hat k-n (blassen) ~ davon** he hasn't the foggiest (idea) about it.

dünsten ['dynstən] v/t, v/i (h) stew.

'Dunstglocke f blanket of smog.

'dunstig adj hazy, misty.

'Dunstschleier m (veil of) haze.

Dünung ['dy:nʊŋ] f (-; -en) ♫ swell.

Duo ['du:o] n (-s; -s) ♪ duo.

Duplikat [dupli'ka:t] n (-[e]s; -e) duplicate, copy.

Dur [du:r] n (-; no pl) ♪ (**in ~** in) major.

durch [dʊrç] **I** *prep* **1.** through: *quer ~* across; *~ ganz Amerika travel etc* all over America. **2.** by, by means of, through: *~ Zufall* by chance. **3.** *&* *10 ~ 2* 10 divided by 2. **4.** due to, through. **II** *adv* **5.** during, through(out): *das ganze Jahr ~* throughout the year; *die ganze Nacht ~* all night long; F *es ist 5 Uhr ~* it is past five. **6.** F *~ und ~* through and through, completely.

'**durchackern** *v/t* (*sep*, -ge-, h) F *fig.* plough (*Am.* plow) through.

'**durcharbeiten** (*sep*, -ge-, h) **I** *v/t* work (*or* go) through. **II** *v/i* work through (without a break). **III** *sich ~ a. fig.* work one's way through.

'**durchatmen** *v/i* (*sep*, -ge-, h) (*tief*) *~* breathe deeply.

durch'aus *adv* **1.** thoroughly, quite: *~!* absolutely!; *~ möglich!* quite possible!; *wenn er ~ kommen will* if he insists on coming. **2.** *~ nicht* by no means; *~ nicht!* absolutely not!; *er wollte ~ nicht gehen* he absolutely refused to go.

'**durchbeißen** (*irr*, *sep*, -ge-, h, → *beißen*) **I** *v/t* bite through. **II** *sich ~* F *fig.* struggle through.

'**durchbiegen: sich ~** (*irr*, *sep*, -ge-, h, → *biegen*) sag.

'**durchblättern** *v/t* (*sep*, -ge-, h) leaf through.

'**Durchblick** *m* **1.** view (*auf acc* of). **2.** F *fig.* grasp: *~ haben* → **durchblicken** 3; *sich den* (*nötigen*) *~ verschaffen* find out what's what. '**durchblicken** *v/i* (*sep*, -ge-, h) **1.** look through. **2.** *fig. ~ lassen* intimate (*daß* that). **3.** F a) get it, b) know the score: *da blicke ich nicht durch!* I don't get it!

durch'bluten *v/t* (h) supply with blood. **Durch'blutung** *f* (-; *no pl*) (blood) circulation. **durch'blutungsfördernd** *adj* ✠ stimulating (blood) circulation. **Durch'blutungsstörung** *f* ✠ circulatory disturbance.

durch'bohren *v/t* (*insep*, *no* -ge-, h) stab, pierce: *j-n mit Blicken ~* look daggers at s.o.; *~der Blick* piercing look.

'**durchbrechen¹** (*irr*, *sep*, -ge-, → *brechen*) **I** *v/t* (h) **1.** break *s.th.* in two. **II** *v/i* (sn) **2.** break (in two), break through (*a.* ✗ *or sports*). **3.** ✠ burst, *teeth*: erupt. **4.** *fig.* reveal itself.

durch'brechen² *v/t* (*irr*, *insep*, *no* -ge-, h,

→ *brechen*) **1.** break through *s.th.* **2.** break (*rule etc*).

'**durchbrennen** *v/i* (*irr*, *sep*, -ge-, sn, → *brennen*) **1.** *⚡* fuse: blow, *bulb*: burn out. **2.** F *fig.* run away, make off.

'**durchbringen** (*irr*, *sep*, -ge-, h, → *bringen*) **I** *v/t* **1.** get *s.o.*, *s.th.* through, pull *a patient* through, support (*family etc*). **2.** squander, blue. **II** *sich ~* get by.

'**Durchbruch** *m* (-[e]s; ✠e) **1.** breakthrough (*a. fig.*), ✠ perforation, *of teeth*: eruption: *fig.* **zum ~ kommen** show, become manifest. **2.** opening.

durchdacht [-'daxt] *adj* reasoned.

durch'denken *v/t* (*irr*, *insep*, *no* -ge-, h, → *denken*) reason *s.th.* (out).

'**durchdrängen: sich** (*sep*, -ge-, h) force one's way through.

'**durchdrehen** (*sep*, -ge-, h) **I** *v/t* **1.** *gastr.* mince. **II** *v/i* **2.** *wheels*: spin. **3.** (*a.* sn) F *fig.* a) flip, b) panic.

durch'dringen¹ *v/t* (*irr*, *insep*, *no* -ge-, h, → *dringen*) **1.** go through, penetrate. **2.** *fig.* fill, pervade. '**durchdringen²** *v/i* (*irr*, *sep*, -ge-, sn, → *dringen*) **1.** penetrate, get through, *voice etc*: be heard: *fig. bis zu j-m ~* reach s.o. **2.** *fig. ~ mit* succeed with, get *s.th.* accepted.

'**durchdringend** *adj* penetrating, piercing, loud, shrill (*voice etc*), pungent (*smell*), biting (*cold etc*).

'**durchdrücken** *v/t* (*sep*, -ge-, h) **1.** straighten. **2.** F → **durchsetzen¹**.

durch'drungen I *pp of* **durchdringen¹**. **II** *adj fig.* filled (*von* with).

durchein'ander *adv ~ sein* be at sixes and sevens, be in a mess; *ganz ~ sein* *person*: a) be all mixed up, b) be in a flap. **Durchein'ander** *n* (-s) *a. fig.* confusion, mess.

durchein'ander|bringen *v/t* (*irr*, *sep*, -ge-, h, → *bringen*) jumble up, *a. fig.* mix up (*notions etc*), confuse, get *s.o.* all flustered: *alles ~* get everything mixed up. *~geraten* *v/i* (*irr*, *sep*, -ge-, sn, → *geraten*) get mixed up. *~reden* *v/i* (*sep*, -ge-, h) talk all at once.

'**durchfahren¹** *v/i* (*irr*, *sep*, -ge-, sn, → *fahren*) pass (*or* go, drive) through, 🚆 *a.* go nonstop (*bis* to): *die Nacht ~* travel all night. **durch'fahren²** *v/t* (*irr*, *insep*, *no* -ge-, h, → *fahren*) pass (*or* go, drive, *fig.* flash) through.

'**Durchfahrt** *f* a) passage, b) gate(way): ~ *verboten!* no thoroughfare!

'**Durchfahrtsstraße** *f* through road.

'**Durchfall** *m* **1.** ✻ diarrh(o)ea. **2.** *F thea.* flop. '**durchfallen** *v/i (irr, sep,* -ge-, sn, → *fallen)* **1.** fall through. **2.** F *a) parl., univ. (a. ~ lassen)* fail, *Am.* flunk, b) *in elections:* be defeated, c) *proposal etc:* be turned down, d) *thea. etc* be a flop.

'**Durchfallquote** *f ped. etc* failure rate.

'**durchfeiern** *v/i (sep,* -ge-, h) F make a night of it.

'**durchfinden** *v/i (irr, sep,* -ge-, h, → *finden) (a. sich ~)* find one's way through: *fig. (sich) nicht mehr ~* be lost.

'**durchfliegen** *v/i (irr, sep,* -ge-, sn, → *fliegen)* **1.** fly through, *a.* fly nonstop. **2.** → **durchfallen** 2 a. **durch'fliegen²** *v/t (irr, insep, no* -ge-, h, → *fliegen)* **1.** a) fly through, b) fly, cover *(distance)*. **2.** *fig.* skim *(or* glance) through.

'**durchfließen** *v/t (irr, sep,* -ge-, sn, → *fließen)* flow *(or* run) through.

'**durchfragen:** *sich ~ (sep,* -ge-, h) ask one's way *(zu* to).

durchfroren [-'fro:rən] *adj* frozen stiff.

'**Durchfuhr** *f* (-; -en) ✝ transit.

'**durchführbar** *adj* practicable, feasible: *schwer ~* difficult to carry out.

'**durchführen** *(sep,* -ge-, h) **I** *v/t* **1.** lead *(or* take) s.o., s.th. through. **2.** carry out *(or* through) *(work, plan, etc)*, realize *(project)*, organize *(event)*. **3.** enforce *(a law)*. **II** *v/i* **3.** ~ *durch* lead through. '**Durchführung** *f* (-; -en) carrying out, realization, ⚖ enforcement.

'**Durchfuhrzoll** *m* ✝ transit duty.

'**durchfüttern** *v/t (sep,* -ge-, h) F feed.

'**Durchgang** *m* (-[e]s; ⸚e) **1.** passage, alley: ~ *verboten!, kein ~!* no thoroughfare!; *den ~ versperren* block the passage. **2.** *astr.,* ✝ transit. **3.** stage, *of vote, a. sports:* round, *of race:* heat.

'**durchgängig** *adj* general.

'**Durchgangs|lager** *n* transit camp. **~straße** *f* through road. **~verkehr** *m* **1.** through traffic. **2.** ✝ transit.

'**durchgeben** *v/t (irr, sep,* -ge-, h, → *geben)* pass on: *telefonisch ~* phone; *(im Radio) ~* announce (on the radio).

'**durchgebraten** *adj gastr.* well done.

'**durchgefroren** → **durchfroren.**

'**durchgehen** *(irr, sep,* -ge-, sn, → *gehen)* **I** *v/i* **1.** go through, *motion, bill,*

etc: a. be passed: *et. ~ lassen* let s.th. pass, tolerate s.th.; F *j-m et. ~ lassen* let s.o. get away with s.th. **2.** F run away, make off, *horse:* bolt: *fig. mit j-m ~ imagination etc:* run away with s.o.; *ihm gingen die Nerven durch* he lost his head. **II** *v/t* **3.** go over, go through.

'**durchgehend I** *adj* through *(train etc)*, continuous *(operation etc, a.* ☺). **II** *adv* throughout: ~ *geöffnet* open all day.

durch'geistigt *adj* spiritual.

'**durchgreifen** *v/i (irr, sep,* -ge-, h, → *greifen) (gegen)* take steps (against), F crack down (on). '**Durchgreifen** *n* (-s) *(hartes etc)* ~ *(gegen)* (rigorous *etc)* action (against), F crackdown (on). '**durchgreifend** *adj* drastic *(measures)*, radical, sweeping *(changes etc)*.

'**durchhalten** *(irr, sep,* -ge-, h, → *halten)* **I** *v/i* hold out (to the end), F stick it out. **II** *v/t* keep s.th. up, stand *(the pace)*.

'**Durchhaltevermögen** *n* (-s; *no pl)* staying power, stamina.

'**durchhängen** *v/i (irr, sep,* -ge-, h, → *hängen)* **1.** sag. **2.** F *fig. a)* feel low, b) *show etc:* be dull. '**Durchhänger** *m* (-s; -) F *e-n ~ haben* feel low.

'**durchhecheln** *v/t (sep,* -ge-, h) F *fig.* gossip about, run *s.o., s.th.* down.

'**durchkämmen¹** *v/t (sep,* -ge-, h) **1.** comb out *(hair)*. **2.** → **durch'kämmen²** *v/t (insep, no* -ge-, h) comb *(nach* for).

'**durchkämpfen** *(sep,* -ge-, h) **I** *sich ~ a. fig.* fight one's way through. **II** *v/t* fight *s.th.* through.

'**durchkauen** *v/t (sep,* -ge-, h) chew *s.th.* well: F *fig. et. ~* go over s.th. again and again.

'**durchkommen** *v/i (irr, sep,* -ge-, sn, → *kommen)* **1.** come through, *patient: a.* pull through, *teleph.* get through, *ped.* pass. **2.** *(mit* on) manage, get by: *mit dieser Ausrede kommt er nicht durch* he won't get away with this excuse.

durch'kreuzen *v/t (insep, no* -ge-, h) *fig.* thwart.

'**durchkriechen** *v/i (irr, sep,* -ge-, sn, → *kriechen)* creep *(or* crawl) through.

Durchlaß ['dʊrçlas] *m* (-sses; ⸚sse) passage. '**durchlassen** *v/t (irr, sep,* -ge-, h, → *lassen)* let *s.o., s.th.* through *(or* pass), transmit *(light)*: *Wasser ~* leak; F *fig. et. ~* let s.th. pass, overlook s.th.

'**durchlässig** *adj* pervious *(für* to).

'**Durchlauf** *m* (-[e]s; ⁓e) **1.** ⚙, *computer*: pass. **2.** *sports*: heat. '**durchlaufen¹** (*irr, sep, -ge-,* ⁓ *laufen*) **I** *v/i* (sn) run through, *computer*: (*a.* ⁓ *lassen*) pass (through). **II** *v/t* (h) wear *s.th.* through. **durch'laufen²** *v/t* (*irr, insep, no -ge-,* → *laufen*) run (*fig. a.* pass) through, cover (*distance*). '**durchlaufend** *adj a.* ⚙ continuous. '**Durchlauferhitzer** *m* instantaneous water heater.

durch'leben *v/t* (*insep, no -ge-,* h) go (or live) through: (*im Geiste*) *noch einmal* ⁓ relive.

'**durchlesen** *v/t* (*irr, sep, -ge-,* h, → *lesen*) read *s.th.* through, peruse.

durch'leuchten¹ *v/t* (*insep, no -ge-,* h) **1.** 🔬 screen, x-ray. **2.** investigate, probe into *s.o.'s past etc*. '**durchleuchten²** *v/i* (*sep, -ge-,* h) shine through.

Durch'leuchtung *f* (-; -en) x-ray examination, screening.

durch'löchern *v/t* (*insep, no -ge-,* h) **1.** make holes in, perforate: *von Kugeln durchlöchert* riddled with bullets. **2.** F *fig.* shoot holes in (*argument etc*).

'**durchmachen** (*sep, -ge-,* h) **I** *v/t* go through, undergo: *er hat viel durchgemacht* he has been through a lot. **II** *v/i* F (*die Nacht*) ⁓ make a night of it.

'**Durchmesser** *m* (-s; -) diameter.

'**durchmogeln**: *sich* ⁓ F wangle one's way through.

durch'nässen *v/t* (*insep, no -ge-,* h) soak, drench.

'**durchnehmen** *v/t* (*irr, sep, -ge-,* h, → *nehmen*) *ped.* do, go through.

'**durchpausen** *v/t* (*sep, -ge-,* h) trace.

'**durchpeitschen** *v/t* (*sep, -ge-,* h) *parl.* rush *s.th.* through, F railroad.

durch'queren *v/t* (*insep, no -ge-,* h) cross, traverse.

'**durchrasen** *v/i* (*sep, -ge-,* sn) race (or tear) through.

'**durchrechnen** *v/t* (*sep, -ge-,* h) check.

'**Durchreiche** *f* (-; -n) (service) hatch.

'**Durchreise** *f* (*auf der* ⁓ on one's way through. ⁓*visum* *n* transit visa.

'**durchringen**: *sich* ⁓ (*irr, sep, -ge-,* h, → *ringen*) make up one's mind: *sich* ⁓*, et. zu tun* finally bring o.s. to do s.th.

'**durchrosten** *v/i* (*sep, -ge-,* sn) rust through.

'**durchrutschen** *v/i* (*sep, -ge-,* sn) F slip through (*a. fig.*).

'**durchrütteln** *v/t* (*sep, -ge-,* h) shake (up), jolt.

'**durchsacken** *v/i* (*sep, -ge-,* sn) ✈ pancake.

'**Durchsage** *f* (-; -n) announcement.

'**durchsagen** *v/t* (*sep, -ge-,* h) pass on, *radio*: announce.

'**durchsägen** *v/t* (*sep, -ge-,* h) saw through.

durch'schaubar *adj* obvious, transparent (*motives etc*): *schwer* ⁓ puzzling.

durch'schauen *v/t* (*insep, no -ge-,* h) see through: *du bist durchschaut!* F I've got your number!

'**durchscheinen** *v/i* (*irr, sep, -ge-,* h, → *scheinen*) shine through: ⁓*d* transparent, translucent.

'**durchscheuern** *v/t* (*sep, -ge-,* h) wear through.

'**durchschlafen** *v/i* (*irr, sep, -ge-,* h, → *schlafen*) sleep through.

'**Durchschlag** *m* (-[e]s; ⁓e) **1.** strainer. **2.** (carbon) copy, F carbon. **3.** 🔩 blowout.

'**durchschlagen¹** (*irr, sep, -ge-,* ⁓ *schlagen*) **I** *v/t* (h) **1.** cut in two. **2.** *gastr.* pass *s.th.* through a strainer. **II** *v/i* **3.** (sn) *wetness*: come through, *colo(u)r*: show through. **4.** (sn) 🔩 *fuse*: blow. **5.** (h) *law etc*: have its effect: ⁓ *auf* (*acc*) affect. **III** *sich* ⁓ (h) fight one's way through: *sich mühsam* ⁓ scrape through; *sich allein* ⁓ fend for o.s. **durch'schlagen²** *v/t* (*irr, insep, no -ge-,* h, → *schlagen*) penetrate.

'**durchschlagend** *adj fig.* sweeping (*success*), conclusive (*evidence*): *mit* ⁓*em Erfolg* very effectively.

'**Durchschlagpa,pier** *n* copy paper.

'**Durchschlagskraft** *f* (-; *no pl*) penetration, *fig.* force (*of an argument etc*).

'**durchschlängeln**: *sich* ⁓ (*sep, -ge-,* h) thread one's way (*fig.* wriggle) through.

'**durchschleusen** *v/t* (*sep, -ge-,* h) **1.** ⚓ lock. **2.** *fig.* get *s.o., s.th.* through.

'**durchschlüpfen** *v/i* (*sep, -ge-,* sn) slip through.

'**durchschmoren** *v/i* (*sep, -ge-,* sn) F 🔩 char, scorch.

'**durchschneiden¹** *v/t* (*irr, sep, -ge-,* h, → *schneiden*) cut (in two).

durch'schneiden² *v/t* (*irr, insep, no -ge-,* h, → *schneiden*) **1.** cut. **2.** intersect, cut through (*road*), cleave (*air, waves*).

'**Durchschnitt** m (-[e]s; -e) average: **im ~** → **durchschnittlich** II; **über** (**unter**) ~ above (below) (the) average; (**guter**) ~ **sein** be a (good) average.

'**durchschnittlich I** adj a) average, b) ordinary, c) contp. mediocre. **II** adv on (an or the) average: ~ **verdienen** etc a. average.

'**Durchschnitts...** average (age, income, speed, temperature, etc).

'**Durchschreibeblock** m carbon-copy pad. '**durchschreiben** v/t (irr, sep, -ge-, h, → **schreiben**) make a (carbon) copy of. '**Durchschrift** f (carbon) copy.

durch'schwimmen v/t (irr, insep, no -ge-, h, → **schwimmen**) swim (through or across).

'**durchschwitzen** v/t (sep, -ge-, h) soak with sweat.

'**durchsehen** (irr, sep, -ge-, h, → **sehen**) **I** v/i see (or look) through. **II** v/t look s.th. over, go through, check.

'**durchsetzen¹** (sep, -ge-, h) **I** v/t et. ~ get s.th. through (or accepted): ~, **daß et. geschieht** succeed in getting s.th. done; **s-n Kopf** (or **Willen**) ~ have one's way. **II** sich ~ a) assert o.s., have one's way, b) idea etc: be accepted, catch on, party, candidate: be successful; **sich ~ gegen** prevail against, F win out over (a. sports); **er kann sich nicht ~** he has no authority. **durch'setzen²** v/t (insep, no -ge-, h) intersperse (**mit** with).

'**Durchsetzungsvermögen** n (-s; no pl) self-assertion, authority: ~ **haben** a. be able to assert o.s.

'**Durchsicht** f (-; no pl) examination, inspection: **bei ~ der Akten** on looking through (or on checking) the papers.

durchsichtig ['dʊrçsɪçtɪç] adj transparent, fig. a. obvious. '**Durchsichtigkeit** f (-; no pl) a. fig. transparency.

'**durchsickern** v/i (sep, -ge-, sn) seep out, fig. a. leak out.

'**durchspielen** v/t (sep, -ge-, h) **1.** thea. etc play s.th. right through. **2.** fig. rehearse, go through.

'**durchsprechen** v/t (irr, sep, -ge-, h, → **sprechen**) talk s.th. over, discuss.

'**durchstarten** v/i (sep, -ge-, sn) ✈ climb and reaccelerate, F go round again.

'**durchstecken** v/t (sep, -ge-, h) put (or pass) s.th. through.

'**durchstehen** v/t (irr, sep, -ge-, h, →

stehen) **1.** fig. get through. **2.** → **durchhalten** II.

'**durchstellen** v/t (sep, -ge-, h) teleph. **ein Gespräch ~** put a call through.

'**durchstoßen¹** v/i (irr, sep, -ge-, sn, → **stoßen**) break (or push) through.

durch'stoßen² v/t (irr, insep, no -ge-, h, → **stoßen**) pierce, break through.

'**durchstreichen** v/t (irr, sep, -ge-, h, → **streichen**) cross out, cancel.

durch'strömen v/t (insep, no -ge-, h) a. fig. flow through.

durch'suchen v/t (insep, no -ge-, h) a) search, b) comb. **Durch'suchung** f (-; -en) search. **Durch'suchungsbefehl** m search warrant.

'**durchtrai,niert** adj top fit.

'**durchtreten** v/t (irr, sep, -ge-, h, → **treten**) mot. step on, Am. floor (pedal), kick (starter).

durchtrieben [dʊrç'tri:bən] adj sly.

durch'wachsen adj **1.** streaky (bacon). **2.** pred F fig. so-so, mixed.

'**Durchwahl** f (-; no pl) direct dial(l)ing.

'**durchwählen** v/i (sep, -ge-, h) ~ **nach** dial through to, dial ... direct.

durchweg ['dʊrçvɛk] adv all of it (or them), without exception.

durch'weicht adj drenched, soaked.

durch'wühlen v/t (insep, no -ge-, h) rummage through.

'**durchwursteln: sich ~** (sep, -ge-, h) F muddle through.

'**durchzählen** v/t (sep, -ge-, h) count off.

'**durchziehen¹** (irr, sep, -ge-, h) **I** v/t (h) **1.** pull s.th. through. **2.** F push (or see) project etc through. **II** v/i (sn) **3.** pass (or march) through. **4.** gastr. **gut ~ lassen** soak well. **III sich ~** (h) motif etc: run through.

durch'ziehen² v/t (irr, insep, no -ge-, h, → **ziehen**) pass through, river etc, a. motif etc: run through, smell: fill, pain etc: shoot through.

'**durchzucken** v/t (insep, no -ge-, h) a. fig. flash through.

'**Durchzug** m (-[e]s; ⁻e) **1.** passage, march through. **2.** no pl draught, Am. draft: ~ **machen** air room thoroughly.

dürfen ['dʏrfən] **I** v/aux (durfte, dürfen, h) et. **tun** ~ be allowed to do s.th.; **darf ich es behalten?** may I keep it?; **ja, Sie ~** yes, you may; **nein, Sie ~ es nicht** no, you can't; **wir ~ stolz auf ihn sein** we can be proud of him; *was darf es sein?* *shop assistant*: what can I do for you?, *hostess*: what would you like?; *das dürfte genügen* that should be enough. **II** *v/i* (durfte, gedurft, h) *er darf (es)* he is allowed to; *wenn ich nur dürfte* if only I were allowed to.

dürftig ['dʏrftiç] *adj* poor, meag/re (*Am.* -er), scanty: **∼e Kenntnisse** scanty knowledge. '**Dürftigkeit** *f* (-; *no pl*) poorness, meag/reness (*Am.* -er-).

dürr [dʏr] *adj* **1.** a) dry, b) barren (*soil*). **2.** thin, skinny, scrawny (*neck*), spindly (*legs*); *fig. in ∼en Worten* in plain terms. '**Dürre** *f* (-; -n) drought (*soil*). '**Dürre**|**kata,strophe** *f* disastrous drought. '**Dürreschäden** *pl* drought damage.

Durst [dʊrst] *m* (-; *no pl*) thirst (*fig. nach* for): *∼ haben (bekommen)* be (get) thirsty; F *er hat e-n über den ∼ getrunken* he has had one too many. **dürsten** ['dʏrstən] *v/i* (h) thirst (*nach* for). '**durstig** *adj* thirsty (*fig. nach* for). '**durstlöschend** *adj* thirst-quenching. '**Durststrecke** *f* hard slog, hard times. '**Duschbad** *n* shower bath. **Dusche** ['dʊʃə; 'du:ʃə] *f* (-; -n) shower, douche (*a. ✵*): *wie e-e kalte ∼ auf j-n wirken* bring s.o. down to earth with a bump. '**duschen** *v/i* (h) (*a. sich ∼*) (have a) shower. '**Duschgel** *n* shower foam. '**Duschka,bine** *f* shower cubicle. '**Duschraum** *m* shower room. '**Duschvorhang** *m* shower curtain. **Düse** ['dy:zə] *f* (-; -n) nozzle.

Dusel ['du:zəl] *m* (-s; *no pl*) F fluke, luck: *∼ haben* be lucky; *mit ∼* by a fluke. **düsen** ['dy:zən] *v/i* (sn) F zoom. '**Düsen**|**antrieb** *m* jet propulsion: *mit ∼* jet-propelled. *∼***flugzeug** *n* jet plane. *∼***jäger** *m* ✕ jet fighter. *∼***pi,lot** *m* jet pilot. *∼***triebwerk** *n* jet engine. *∼***ver- kehrsflugzeug** *n* jetliner.

Dussel! ['dʊsəl] *m* (-s; -) F dope. **düster** ['dy:stər] *adj a. fig.* dark, gloomy, dismal: *∼e Aussichten* bleak pros- pects; *∼e Stimmung* black mood.

Dutzend ['dʊtsənt] *n* (-s; -e) dozen: *∼e von Leuten* dozens of people; *zu ∼en* in dozens. '**dutzendmal** *adv* dozens of times. '**dutzendweise** *adv* in dozens. **duzen** ['du:tsən] *v/t* (h) *j-n ∼* a) address s.o. with "du", b) *a. sich mit j-m ∼* be on first-name terms with s.o. '**Duzfreund(in** *f*) *m* intimate friend. **Dynamik** [dy'na:mɪk] *f* (-; *no pl*) dynam- ics, *fig. a.* dynamism. **dy'namisch** *adj a. fig.* dynamic: *∼e Rente* index-linked pension. **dynamisieren** [dynami'zi:- rən] *v/t* (h) **1.** speed *s.th.* up. **2.** in- dex-link (*pensions etc*). **Dynamit** [dyna'mi:t] *n* (-s; *no pl*) dyna- mite. **Dynamo** [dy'na:mo] *m* (-s; -s) dyna- mo. **Dynastie** [dynas'ti:] *f* (-; -n) dynasty. **Dystonie** [dysto'ni:] *f* (-; -n) ✵ dystonia: *vegetative ∼* neurodystonia. '**D-Zug** *m* fast train.

E

E, e [e:] *n* (-; -) E, e (*a. ♪*). **Ebbe** ['ɛbə] *f* (-; -n) low tide: *es ist ∼* the tide is out. **eben** ['e:bən] **I** *adj* **1.** even, level, flat, smooth. **II** *adv* **2.** just (now): *∼ erst* only just; *ich wollte ∼ gehen* I was just going to leave. **3.** just, exactly: (*das ist es ja*) *∼!* that's it!; *∼ nicht!* on the con- trary! **4.** *∼ noch* only just. **5.** just: *es taugt ∼ nichts* it's just no good; *er ist ∼*

der Bessere he's better, that's all; *so ist es ∼!* that's the way it is!; *dann ∼ nicht!* all right, forget it! '**Ebenbild** *n* image: *das ∼ s-s Vaters* the spit and image of his father. **ebenbürtig** ['e:bənbʏrtıç] *adj* equal: *j-m ∼ sein* be s.o.'s equal, match s.o. '**ebender**('**selbe**), '**ebendie**('**selbe**), '**ebendas**('**selbe**) **I** *dem pron* the very same. **II** *adj* that very *man, woman,* *thing.* '**eben'deswegen** *adv* for that very reason.

Ebene ['e:bənə] *f* (-; -n) **1.** *geogr.* plain. **2.** ⚐ plane. **3.** *fig.* level: *auf staatlicher (höchster)* ~ at government (top) level.

'**ebenerdig** *adj* at ground level.

'**ebenfalls** *adv* likewise, too, as well: *er hat* ~ *kein Geld* he has no money either.

'**Ebenheit** *f* (-; *no pl*) evenness, flatness.

'**Ebenholz** *n* ebony.

'**Ebenmaß** *n* (-es; *no pl*) harmony, symmetry. '**ebenmäßig** *adj* well-proportioned, regular (*face, features*).

'**ebenso** *adv* **1.** just as *good etc.* **2.** (in) the same way. **3.** likewise. '**ebensoviel** *adv* (just) as well. '**ebensoviel** *indef pron* just as much (*or* many).

Eber ['e:bər] *m* (-s; -) *zo.* boar.

'**Eberesche** *f* ⚐ mountain ash.

ebnen ['e:bnən] *v/t* (h) level: → *Weg.*

Echo ['εço] *n* (-s; -s) echo: *fig.* ein lebhaftes ~ *finden* meet with a lively response. '**Echolot** *n* echo sounder.

echt [εçt] **I** *adj* genuine (*a. fig.*), authentic (*document*), fast (*colo[u]r*), natural (*hair*), pure, real (*gold, leather, etc*): ~*er Engländer* true Englishman (*friend*). **II** *adv* really: F ~ *gut!* real good!; *das ist* ~ *Paul!* that's Paul all over! '**Echtheit** *f* (-; *no pl*) genuineness (*etc*), authenticity.

'**Eckball** *m* *sports:* corner.

Ecke ['εkə] *f* (-; -n) **1.** corner (*a. sports*): *an der* ~ at (*house:* on) the corner; *fig.* *an allen* ~*n und Enden* everywhere; *es fehlte an allen* ~*n und Enden* we were short on everything; F *j-n um die* ~ *bringen* bump s.o. off. **2.** F a) piece, b) stretch, c) part, region.

'**Eckfahne** *f* *sports:* corner flag.

'**Eckhaus** *n* corner house.

eckig ['εkıç] *adj* square, angular, *fig.* awkward. ...**eckig** ...-cornered.

'**Ecklohn** *m* basic wage. '**Eckpfeiler** *m* **1.** △ corner pillar. **2.** *fig.* cornerstone. '**Eckplatz** *m* corner seat. '**Eckstoß** *m* *sports:* corner kick. '**Eckzahn** *m* eyetooth. '**Eckzins** *m* basic interest rate.

edel ['e:dəl] *adj* **1.** *a. fig.* noble. **2.** exquisite (*wine etc.*), precious (*stone, metal*).

'**Edel|gas** *n* inert gas. ~**holz** *n* rare wood. ~**kitsch** *m* glorified trash. ~**mann** *m* (-[e]s; -leute) nobleman. ~**me₁tall** *n* precious metal. ~**pilzkäse** *m* blue cheese.

~**stahl** *m* high-grade steel. ~**stein** *m* precious stone, gem. ~**tanne** *f* silver fir.

'**Edelweiß** *n* (-[e]s; -e) ⚐ edelweiss.

EDV-Anlage [e:de:'vau-] *f* electronic data-processing equipment.

Efeu ['e:fɔy] *m* (-s; *no pl*) ⚐ ivy.

Eff-eff [εf''εf] *n* F *et. aus dem* ~ *können* be a real wizard at s.th.

Effekten [ε'fεktən] *pl* ✝ a) securities, b) stocks and bonds. ~**börse** *f* stock exchange. ~**händler** *m* stock dealer. ~**makler** *m* stockbroker.

Ef'fekthascherei [-haʃərai] *f* (-; *no pl*) sensationalism, (cheap) showmanship.

effektiv [εfεk'ti:f] *adj* actual.

ef'fektvoll *adj* effective, striking.

Effet [ε'fe:] *m* *sports:* spin.

Effizienz [εfi'tsiεnts] *f* (-; -en) efficiency.

egal [e'ga:l] *adj pred* **1.** F *das ist (ganz)* ~ it doesn't matter; *das ist mir (ganz)* ~ I don't care; *das ist mir nicht* ~ I do care; *ganz* ~, *wer (warum etc)* no matter who (why *etc*). **2.** the same.

Egel ['e:gəl] *m* (-s; -) *zo.* leech.

Egge ['εgə] *f* (-; -n) harrow.

eggen ['εgən] *v/t* (h) harrow.

Egoismus [ego'ısmʊs] *m* (-; *no pl*) egoism. **Egoist** [ego'ıst] *m* (-en; -en), **Ego'istin** *f* (-; -nen) ego(t)ist. **ego'istisch** *adj* egotistic(al), selfish. **ego'zentrisch** *adj* self-centred.

eh [e:] *adv* **1.** *dial.* → *ohnehin.* **2.** *seit* ~ *und je* always; *wie* ~ *und je* as ever.

ehe ['e:ə] *conj* before: *nicht* ~ not until; → *eher, ehest.*

'**Ehe** *f* (-; -n) marriage: *sie hat e-e Tochter aus erster* ~ she has a daughter by her first marriage; *die* ~ *brechen* commit adultery; *sie führen e-e glückliche* ~ they are happily married.

'**Eheberater(in** *f)* *m* marriage guidance counsel(l)or. '**Eheberatung(sstelle)** *f* marriage guidance (bureau). '**Ehebett** *n* marriage bed. '**Ehebrecher(in** *f)* *m* adulterer(-ess). '**ehebrecherisch** *adj* adulterous. '**Ehebruch** *m* adultery. '**Ehefrau** *f* wife, *w.s.* married woman. '**Eheleben** *n* married life. '**Eheleute** *pl* husband and wife. '**ehelich** *adj* **1.** marital. **2.** ⚖ legitimate (*child*).

ehelichen ['e:əlıçən] *v/t* (h) marry.

'**Ehelichkeit** *f* (-; *no pl*) ⚖ legitimacy.

'**Ehelosigkeit** *f* (-; *no pl*) unmarried state, *eccl.* celibacy.

'ehemalig ['eːəmaːlɪç] *adj* **1.** former, ex-... **2.** late.

ehemals ['eːəmaːls] *adv* formerly.

'Ehemann *m* (-[e]s, ⸚er) husband, *w.s.* married man. **'ehemündig** *adj* 🏛 marriageable. **'Ehepaar** *n* married couple: *das ~ Brown* Mr. and Mrs. Brown. **'Ehepartner(in** *f)* *m* (marriage) partner.

eher ['eːər] *adv* **1.** earlier, sooner: *je ~, desto besser* the sooner the better. **2.** a) rather, b) more easily, c) more, d) more likely.

'Eherecht *n* (-[e]s; *no pl*) matrimonial law. **'Ehering** *m* wedding ring.

ehern ['eːərn] *adj* **1.** (of) brass. **2.** *fig.* iron (*law, rule, will*).

'Ehescheidung *f* divorce.

'Eheschließung *f* marriage.

ehest ['eːəst] **I** *adj* earliest. **II** *adv* *am ~en* a) (the) earliest, (the) first, b) best; *er kann uns am ~en helfen* if anyone can help us, it's him.

'Ehestand *m* (-[e]s; *no pl*) matrimony. **'Ehestreit** *m* marital row. **'Ehevermittlungsinsti,tut** *n* marriage bureau.

'ehrbar *adj* hono(u)rable, respectable.

Ehre ['eːrə] *f* (-; -n) hono(u)r: *zu ~n* (*gen or von*) in hono(u)r of; *ihm zu ~n* in his hono(u)r; *die letzte ~ erweisen* pay one's last respects to s.o.; *j-m (k-e) ~ machen* be a (be no) credit to s.o.; *in ~n halten* hold in hono(u)r.

'ehren *v/t* (h) a) hono(u)r, b) respect: *das ehrt ihn* that does him credit.

'Ehren|amt *n* honorary post. **2amtlich I** *adj* honorary. **II** *adv* in an honorary capacity. **~bürger(in** *f)* *m* honorary citizen. **~doktor** *m* honorary doctor. **~gast** *m* guest of hono(u)r. **~gericht** *n* disciplinary court.

'ehrenhaft *adj* hono(u)rable, upright.

'ehrenhalber [-halbər] *adv* for hono(u)r's sake: *Doktor ~* doctor honoris causa.

'Ehren|kodex *m* code of hono(u)r. **~legi,on** *f* Legion of Hono(u)r. **2mann** *m* (-[e]s; ⸚er) man of hono(u)r. **~mitglied** *n* honorary member. **~platz** *m* place of hono(u)r. **~rechte** *pl* 🏛 *bürgerliche ~* civil rights. **~runde** *f* sports: (*e-e ~ laufen or drehen* do a) lap of hono(u)r. **~sache** *f* matter of hono(u)r. **~tag** *m* great day. **~titel** *m* hono-

rary title. **~treffer** *m* sports: consolation goal. **~tri,büne** *f* VIP lounge. **2voll** *adj* hono(u)rable. **2wert** *adj* respectable. **~wort** *n* word of hono(u)r: *sein ~ geben* give one's word; **~!** I promise (you)! **~zeichen** *n* decoration.

ehrerbietig ['eːr'ɔerbiːtɪç] *adj* (*gegen* towards) respectful, deferential.

'Ehrfurcht *f* (-; *no pl*) respect (for), awe (of). **'ehrfurchtgebietend** *adj* awe-inspiring. **ehrfürchtig** ['eːrfvrçtɪç] *adj* respectful, reverential.

'Ehrgefühl *n* (-[e]s; *no pl*) sense of hono(u)r.

'Ehrgeiz *m* (-es; *no pl*) ambition.

'ehrgeizig *adj* ambitious.

'ehrlich I *adj* honest, sincere, frank: *~ währt am längsten* honesty is the best policy; *seien wir (doch) ~!* let's face it! **II** *adv* honestly (*etc*): *~ gesagt* truth to tell; F *~?* really?

'Ehrlichkeit *f* (-; *no pl*) honesty.

'ehrlos *adj* disgraceful.

'Ehrung *f* (-; -en) hono(u)r (*gen* conferred on).

'Ehrwürden *eccl.* *Seine ~* the Reverend.

'ehrwürdig *adj* venerable, *eccl.* Reverend.

ei [aɪ] *int* oh.

Ei *n* (-[e]s; -er) **1.** egg, *physiol.* ovum: *fig. wie ein ~ dem anderen gleichen* be as like as two peas; F *wie aus dem ~ gepellt* spick and span; *j-n wie ein rohes ~ behandeln* handle s.o. with kid gloves. **2.** *pl* F quid, *Am.* bucks. **3.** *pl* V (*testicles*) nuts, balls.

Eibe ['aɪbə] *f* (-; -n) 🌳 yew (tree).

Eiche ['aɪçə] *f* (-; -n) a) oak (tree), b) oak.

Eichel ['aɪçəl] *f* (-; -n) **1.** 🌳 acorn. **2.** *anat.* glans.

'eichen *v/t* (h) ⚙ adjust, calibrate.

'Eichhörnchen *n* (-s; -) *zo.* squirrel.

Eid [aɪt] *m* (-[e]s; -e) oath: *e-n ~ ablegen* (*or leisten, schwören*) take an oath, swear (*auf die Bibel* by the Bible); *j-m e-n ~ abnehmen* administer an oath to s.o.; *unter ~ aussagen* testify on oath; 🏛 *an ~es Statt → eidesstattlich.*

Eidechse ['aɪdɛksə] *f* (-; -n) *zo.* lizard.

'eidesstattlich *adj* in lieu of (an) oath: *~e Erklärung* affidavit.

'Eidgenosse *m* Swiss (citizen). **eidgenössisch** ['aɪtgənœsɪʃ] *adj* Swiss.

'eidlich I *adj* *~e Aussage, ~e Erklärung*

a) sworn statement, b) affidavit. **II** *adv* on (*or* under) oath.

'Eidotter *n* (egg) yolk.

'Eier|becher *m* eggcup. **~kocher** *m* egg boiler. **~kopf** *m* F egghead. **~kuchen** *m* pancake. **~löffel** *m* egg spoon. **~schale** *f* eggshell. **~speise** *f* egg dish. **~stock** *m* anat. ovary. **~wärmer** *m* egg cosy.

Eifer ['aɪfər] *m* (-s; *no pl*) zeal, eagerness, enthusiasm, fervo(u)r: *blinder* **~** rashness; *blinder* **~** *schadet nur* haste is waste; *im* **~** *des Gefechts* in the heat of the moment. **'Eiferer** *m* (-s; -) fanatic.

'eifern *v/i* (h) **1. ~** *nach* strive for. **2. ~** *gegen* rail against. **3. →** *wetteifern*.

'Eifersucht *f* (-; *no pl*) jealousy (*auf acc* of).

'eifersüchtig *adj* jealous (*auf acc* of).

eifrig ['aɪfrɪç] *adj* a) keen, ardent, b) busy: **~** *bemüht zu inf* anxious to *inf*.

eigen ['aɪgən] *adj* **1.** own, of one's own: *sich zu* **~** *machen* make *s.th.* one's own, adopt; *ein* **~es** *Zimmer* a room of one's own. **2.** own, personal, private: *für den* **~en** *Gebrauch* for one's own use; **~e** *Ansichten* personal views. **3.** characteristic, typical: *mit dem ihr* **~en** *Charme* with her characteristic charm. **4.** particular, fussy.

...eigen ...-owned: *staats~* state-owned.

'Eigenart *f* (-; -en) peculiarity.

'eigenartig *adj* peculiar. **'eigenartigerweise** *adv* strangely enough.

'Eigenbedarf *m* a) one's personal needs, b) domestic requirements.

Eigenbrötler *m* ['aɪgənbrøːtlər] *m* (-s; -) **1.** eccentric. **2.** solitary (person).

'Eigenfinan‚zierung *f* self-financing.

'Eigengewicht *n* dead (© net) weight.

'eigenhändig [-hɛndɪç] **I** *adj* personal: **~e** *Unterschrift* one's own signature. **II** *adv* personally, oneself.

'Eigenheim *n* house of one's own.

'Eigenheit *f* (-; -en) peculiarity.

'Eigen|initia‚tive *f* one's own initiative. **~kapi‚tal** *n* capital resources. **~leben** *n* (-s; *no pl*) one's own (*or* private) life: *ein* **~** *entwickeln* take on a life of its own. **~liebe** *f* self-love, narcissism. **~lob** *n* self-praise. **⌂mächtig** *adj* **1.** high-handed. **2.** unauthorized. **~mächtigkeit** *f* (-; -en) **1.** *no pl* high-handedness. **2.** arbitrary act. **~name** *m* proper name (*or* noun).

'Eigennutz *m* (-es; *no pl*) self-interest.

'eigennützig [-nʏtsɪç] *adj* selfish.

eigens ['aɪgəns] *adv* (e)specially.

'Eigenschaft *f* (-; -en) quality, characteristic, feature, ⌂, phys., © property: *in s-r* **~** *als* in his capacity of (*or* as).

'Eigenschaftswort *n* (-[e]s; ⸚er) *ling.* adjective.

'Eigensinn *m* (-[e]s; *no pl*) stubbornness.

'eigensinnig *adj* stubborn.

'eigenständig *adj* independent.

eigentlich ['aɪgəntlɪç] **I** *adj* real, actual: *im* **~en** *Sinne* in the true sense of the word. **II** *adv* a) actually, really, b) by rights.

'Eigentor *n* a. fig. own goal.

'Eigentum *n* (-s; *no pl*) property, ownership. **Eigentümer** ['aɪgəntyːmər] *m* (-s; -), **'Eigentümerin** *f* (-; -nen) owner, proprietor (proprietress).

'eigentümlich [-tyːmlɪç] *adj* **1.** characteristic (*dat* of). **2.** peculiar, strange. **'Eigentümlichkeit** *f* (-; -en) peculiarity.

'Eigentums|recht *n* (right of) ownership, title (*an dat* of). **~wohnung** *f* freehold flat, *Am.* condominium.

'Eigenwille *m* self-will. **'eigenwillig** *adj* **1.** self-willed, headstrong. **2.** *fig.* very individual. **'Eigenwilligkeit** *f* (-; *no pl*) *fig.* (strong) individualism.

eignen ['aɪgnən] *sich* **~** (h) (*als* as, *zu* as, for) be suitable, *person:* be suited; *sich als* (*or zum*) *Lehrer* **~** *a.* make a good teacher. **'Eigner** *m* (-s; -) owner.

'Eignung *f* (-; *no pl*) (*zu, für*) suitability (for), *of a person:* a. qualification (for, to be). **'Eignungstest** *m* aptitude test.

'Eilauftrag *m* ⸚ rush order. **'Eilbote** *m* *durch* **~n** express, *Am.* (by) special delivery. **'Eilbrief** *m* express letter, *Am.* special delivery (letter).

Eile ['aɪlə] *f* (-; *no pl*) hurry, rush: *in* **~** in a hurry; *es hat k-e* **~** there's no hurry.

'Eileiter *m* anat. Fallopian tube.

eilen ['aɪlən] *v/i* **1.** (sn) hurry. **2.** (h) be urgent: *Eilt!* urgent!; *es eilt nicht* there's no hurry. **eilends** ['aɪlənts] *adv* in a hurry, hurriedly, hastily.

'Eilfracht *f* express goods, *Am.* fast freight.

eilig ['aɪlɪç] *adj* a) hurried, b) urgent: *es* **~** *haben* be in a hurry.

'eiligst *adv* in a hurry, hurriedly.

'Eiltempo *n im* **~** in double quick time.

'Eilzug m fast train.

'Eilzustellung f ✆ special delivery.

Eimer ['aımər] m (-s; -) bucket (a. ⊛), pail: F *die Uhr ist im ~* the watch has had it. **'eimerweise** adv in bucketfuls.

ein¹ [aın] **I** adj one: *~ für allemal* once and for all; *~ und derselbe (Mann)* one and the same person. **II** indef art a, an: *~ (gewisser) Herr Brown* a (or one) Mr. Brown; *~es Tages* one day. **III** indef pron a) one (*Mr. X etc*), b) one thing: *~er von beiden* one of them.

ein² adv **1.** switch: on: *~ - aus* on - off. **2.** *~ und aus gehen* come and go (*bei j-m* at s.o.'s place); *ich weiß nicht mehr ~ noch aus* I'm at my wits' end.

Einakter ['aın'aktər] m (-s; -) thea. one-act play.

einander [aı'nandər] adv each other, one another.

'einarbeiten (sep, -ge-, h) **I** v/t **1.** *j-n ~* acquaint s.o. with his (new) work, F break s.o. in. **2.** et. *~ in* (acc) work s.th. into. **II** sich *~* get into the (new) job (or subject etc).

einarmig ['aın'armıç] adj one-armed.

einäschern ['aın'ɛʃərn] v/t (sep, -ge-, h) **1.** burn to ashes. **2.** cremate. **'Einäscherung** f (-; -en) cremation.

'einatmen v/t, v/i (sep, -ge-, h) breathe in, inhale: *tief ~* take a deep breath.

einäugig ['aın'ɔygıç] adj one-eyed.

'Einbahn... one-way (street, traffic).

'einbalsamieren v/t (sep, h) embalm.

'Einband m (-[e]s; *~e) binding, cover.

'einbändig [-bɛndıç] adj in one volume.

'Einbau m (-[e]s; -ten) installation, fitting. **'Einbau...** built-in, fitted (kitchen, cupboard, etc). **'einbauen** v/t (sep, -ge-, h) build in, install, fit: *fig. ein Zitat etc ~* work in a quotation etc.

'einbegriffen adj (*mit*) *~* included.

'einbehalten v/t (irr, sep, h, → behalten) keep back, withhold, deduct.

'einberufen v/t (irr, sep, h, → berufen) **1.** call (assembly), parl. convoke. **2.** ✕ (zu) call up (for), Am. draft (to). **'Einberufung** f (-; -en) **1.** calling, parl. convocation. **2.** ✕ conscription, Am. draft. **'Einberufungsbescheid** m ✕ call-up order, Am. draft papers.

'einbetten v/t (sep, -ge-, h) embed.

'Einbettkabine f ⚓ single-berth cabin.

'Einbettzimmer n single room.

'einbeziehen v/t (irr, sep, h, → beziehen) include (*in* acc in).

'einbiegen v/i (irr, sep, -ge-, sn, → biegen) turn (*in* acc into a street etc): *links ~* turn left.

'einbilden: sich ~ (sep, -ge-, h) **1.** imagine, think: *bilde dir ja nicht ein, daß ...* don't think that ...; *das bildest du dir nur ein* you're imagining things; *was bildest du dir eigentlich ein?* who do you think you are? **2.** sich et. *~* (auf acc) be (very) conceited (about). **'Einbildung** f (-; no pl) **1.** illusion: *das ist reine ~* you're (he is etc) imagining things. **2.** conceit. **'Einbildungskraft** f (-; no pl) imagination.

'einbinden v/t (irr, sep, -ge-, h, → binden) **1.** bind (book). **2.** fig. integrate.

'einblenden (sep, -ge-, h) **I** v/t film, radio, TV fade in. **II** sich *~* (acc) tune in to. **'Einblendung** f (-; -en) fade-in.

'einbleuen ['aınblɔyən] v/t (sep, -ge-, h) *j-m et. ~* drum s.th. into s.o.'s head.

'Einblick m (-[e]s; -e) fig. insight (*in* acc into): *~ nehmen in* (acc) inspect.

'einbrechen (irr, sep, -ge-, → brechen) **I** v/i (sn) **1.** *in ein Haus etc ~* break into a house etc; *bei ihm wurde eingebrochen* his house was burgled. **2.** *~ in* (acc) invade (a country etc). **3.** collapse, fig. break down, sports: a. wilt. **4.** (*ins Eis*) *~* break through the ice. **5.** frost etc: set in, night: fall. **6.** ✝ suffer heavy losses, prices: slump. **II** v/t (h) **7.** break down (door etc).

'Einbrecher m (-s; -) burglar.

'einbringen v/t (irr, sep, -ge-, h, → bringen) **1.** bring in (harvest etc). **2.** invest (capital), a. fig. contribute (acc to). **3.** bring (in), yield (profit etc): *es bringt mir ... ein* it gets me ...; *das bringt nichts ein!* it doesn't pay! **4.** make up (for time etc). **5.** e-e Gesetzesvorlage *~* introduce a bill. **6.** ⚖ bring in, file (action). **7.** print. take in (line).

'einbrocken v/t (sep, -ge-, h) F *sich et. ~* let o.s. in for s.th.; *das hat er sich selbst eingebrockt!* it's his own fault!

'Einbruch m (-[e]s; *~e) **1.** break-in, burglary. **2.** *bei ~ der Dunkelheit* at nightfall; *bei ~ der Kälte* when the cold (weather) sets in; *~ von Kaltluft* influx of cold air. **3.** invasion (*in* acc of a country). **4.** collapse, fig. setback. **5.** ✝

slump. **'Einbruchdiebstahl** m burglary. **'einbruchsicher** adj burglar-proof.

einbürgern ['aınbʏrgərn] v/t (sep, -ge-, h) 🐾, ⚡, zo. naturalize: fig. **sich ~** word: be adopted; **es hat sich (bei uns) so eingebürgert** it has become a custom (with us).

'Einbürgerung f (-; -en) naturalization.

'Einbuße f (-; -en) loss (**an** dat of).

'einbüßen (sep, -ge-, h) **I** v/t lose. **II** v/i **~ an** (dat) lose some of.

'einchecken v/t, v/i (sep, -ge-, h) ✈ check in.

'eincremen v/t (sep, -ge-, h) cream.

'eindämmen v/t (sep, -ge-, h) dam up, fig. a. check, get fire etc under control, pol. contain. **'Eindämmungspoli,tik** f policy of containment.

'eindecken (sep, -ge-, h) **I** v/t j-n ~ mit supply s.o. with; **gut eingedeckt** well stocked; F **mit Arbeit eingedeckt sein** be swamped with work. **II sich ~** stock up (**mit** on).

eindeutig ['aındɔʏtıç] adj clear, plain. **'Eindeutigkeit** f (-; no pl) clearness.

eindeutschen ['aındɔʏtʃən] v/t (sep, -ge-, h) Germanize.

'eindimensio,nal adj one-dimensional.

'eindrängen: sich ~ (sep, -ge-, h) (**in** acc) a) push one's way in(to), b) intrude (into).

'eindringen v/i (irr, sep, -ge-, sn, → **dringen**) (**in** acc) get in(to), force one's way in(to), bullet etc: penetrate (s.th.), ✗ a. invade (a country): **auf j-n ~** a) attack s.o., b) press s.o. (**mit** with questions etc). **'eindringlich** adj urgent (warning etc), forceful (speech etc). **'Eindringlichkeit** f (-; no pl) urgency.

'Eindruck m (-[e]s, ⸗e) **1.** impression: ~ **machen** be impressive; ~ **auf j-n machen** impress s.o.; **e-n schlechten ~ machen** make a bad impression (**auf** acc on); **den ~ erwecken, daß ...** give the impression that ...; **ich habe den ~, daß ...** I have a feeling that ...; ~ **schinden** 2. **2.** imprint.

'eindrücken v/t (sep, -ge-, h) break (window), force (door), dent (car body).

'eindrucksvoll adj impressive.

'einebnen v/t (sep, -ge-, h) flatten, level (out fig.).

'Einehe f monogamy.

eineiig ['aın?aıɪç] adj ~**e Zwillinge** identical twins.

'einengen v/t (sep, -ge-, h) narrow down, restrict: **sich eingeengt fühlen** feel cramped.

'einer pron someone, somebody; → a. **ein¹** III. **'Einer** m (-s; -) **1.** ✚ digit. **2.** ⚓ single (sculler). **'einerlei** adj pred all the same, all one: **das ist mir ~!** I don't care!; ~ **wer** (**wo** etc) no matter who (where etc). **'Einerlei** n (-s; no pl) monotony: **(ewiges)** ~ routine.

'einerseits adv on the one hand.

einfach ['aınfax] **I** adj **1.** simple, a. easy (task), a. plain (food). **2.** single: ~**e Fahrkarte** single (ticket), Am. one-way ticket. **II** adv **3.** simply, just: **ich mußte ~ lachen** I couldn't help laughing. **'Einfachheit** f (-; no pl) simplicity, plainness: **der ~ halber** to simplify matters.

'einfädeln (sep, -ge-, h) **I** v/t **1.** thread. **2.** fig. arrange, contrive. **II sich ~** mot. filter (**in** acc into): **sich links ~** filter to the left.

'einfahren (irr, sep, -ge-, → **fahren**) **I** v/i (sn) **1.** come in, arrive. **2.** ⚒ descend into a mine. **II** v/t (h) **3.** bring in (harvest). **4.** run in (car). **5.** retract (landing gear etc). **6.** crash into.

'Einfahrt f (-; -en) **1.** drive(way), entrance, to motorway: approach: ~ **freihalten!** keep clear of the gate(s)! **2.** no pl entry (**in** acc into): **der Zug aus ... hat ~ auf Gleis 1** the train from ... is now coming in on track 1; **Vorsicht bei der ~!** please stand back! **3.** ⚒ descent.

'Einfall m (-[e]s, ⸗e) **1.** idea. **2.** ✗ invasion (**in** acc of). **3.** no pl phys. incidence (of light).

'einfallen v/i (irr, sep, -ge-, sn, → **fallen**) **1.** j-m ~ occur to s.o.; **mir fällt eben ein, daß ...** a. I've just remembered that...; **es fällt mir (jetzt) nicht ein** I can't think of it now; **was fällt dir ein?** a) how dare you!, b) you must be joking!; **sich et. ~ lassen** come up with s.th.; **das fällt mir nicht im Traum ein!** I wouldn't dream of (doing) it! **2.** ✗ **in ein Land ~** invade a country; F fig. **bei j-m ~** descend on s.o. **3.** light: enter. **4.** ♪ enter, join in.

'einfallslos adj unimaginative, dull. **'Einfallslosigkeit** f (-; no pl) lack of ideas. '**einfallsreich** adj imaginative, inventive. '**Einfallsreichtum** m (-s; no pl) wealth of ideas.

'**Einfallswinkel** m angle of incidence.

einfältig ['aɪnfɛltɪç] adj naive, simple.

'**Einfa͵milienhaus** n detached house.

'**einfangen** v/t (irr, sep, -ge-, h, → **fangen**) a. fig. catch, capture.

'**einfarbig** adj unicolo(u)r(ed), plain.

'**einfassen** v/t (sep, -ge-, h) **1.** a) surround, b) edge, border (dress etc). **2.** set (diamond etc), frame (lens etc).

'**Einfassung** f (-; -en) **1.** a) enclosure, b) border, edge. **2**͵ setting.

'**einfetten** v/t (sep, -ge-, h) grease.

'**einfinden: sich** ~ (irr, sep, -ge-, h, → **finden**) assemble, arrive, F turn up.

'**einflechten** v/t (irr, sep, -ge-, h, → **flechten**) fig. et. ~ mention s.th. in passing; et. ~ **in** (acc) work s.th. into.

'**einfliegen** (irr, sep, -ge-, → **fliegen**) **I** v/t (h) fly in, test(-fly). **II** v/i (sn) approach: ~ **in** (acc) fly into, enter.

'**einfließen** (irr, sep, -ge-, sn, → **fließen**) flow in(to **in** acc): fig. et. ~ **lassen** slip s.th. in, give s.th. to understand.

'**einflößen** v/t sep, -ge-, h) **j-m et.** ~ a) give s.o. s.th. (to drink), b) fill (or inspire) s.o. with admiration, courage, etc; **j-m Angst** ~ fill s.o. with fear.

'**Einflugschneise** f approach corridor.

'**Einfluß** m (-sses; ⸚sse) influence (**auf** acc on): ~ **haben auf** (acc) a) have an influence on, influence, b) have an effect on, affect; → **geltend**. '**Einflußbereich** m sphere of influence. '**Einflußnahme** f (-; no pl) intervention (**auf** acc in).

'**einflußreich** adj influential.

'**einförmig** ['aɪnfœrmɪç] adj uniform, monotonous. '**Einförmigkeit** f (-; no pl) uniformity, monotony.

'**einfrieren** (irr, sep, -ge-, → **frieren**) **I** v/i (sn) **1.** water: freeze over, pipe etc: freeze (up), ship: become icebound. **2.** fig. freeze. **II** v/t (h) **3.** (deep-)freeze (food). **4.** fig. freeze (wages, assets, etc).

'**einfügen** (sep, -ge-, h) **I** v/t (**in** acc) fit in(to), insert (into). **II sich** ~ (**in** acc) fig. fit in (with), person: adjust (to).

'**Einfügung** f (-; -en) insertion, addition.

'**einfühlen: sich** ~ (sep, -ge-, h) empathize (**in** acc with). '**einfühlsam** adj sensitive. '**Einfühlungsvermögen** n (-s; no pl) empathy.

Einfuhr ['aɪnfuːr] f (-; -en) ✝ **1.** no pl import. **2.** imports. **~ar͵tikel** m imported article, pl imports. **~bestimmungen** pl import regulations.

'**einführen** v/t (sep, -ge-, h) **1.** introduce, a. adopt (method etc). **2.** j-n ~ introduce s.o. (**in** acc into, **bei** to); j-n (**in ein Amt**) ~ inaugurate s.o. **3.** (**in** acc into) insert, introduce. **4.** ✝ import.

'**Einfuhr|genehmigung** f import licence (Am. license). **~hafen** m port of entry. **~handel** m import trade. **~land** n importing country. **~stopp** m import ban.

'**Einführung** f (-; -en) (**in** acc) introduction (to), inauguration (into).

'**Einführungs...** introductory (course, price, offer, etc).

'**Einfuhrverbot** n import ban (**für** on).

'**Einfuhrzoll** m import duty.

'**einfüllen** v/t (sep, -ge-, h) pour in(to **in** acc).

'**Eingabe** f (-; -n) **1.** application (**bei** to, um, **für** for). **2.** computer: input. '**Eingabedaten** pl computer: input data.

'**Eingang** m (-[e]s; ⸚e) **1.** entrance, way in, entry. **2.** (**zu** to) access, entry, admission. **3.** no pl arrival (of goods), receipt (of mail): **bei** ~ **nach** ~ on receipt. **4.** pl ✝ a) arrivals, b) incoming mail, c) receipts. **5.** no pl (**zu** ~ at the) beginning (gen of). **6.** ⚡ input.

'**eingängig** adj catchy (tune, slogan).

'**eingangs** ['aɪŋaŋs] **I** adv at the beginning. **II** prep (gen) at the beginning of.

'**Eingangs|datum** n date of receipt. **~halle** f entrance hall. **~stempel** m date stamp. **~worte** pl opening words.

'**eingebaut** adj built-in, ⊙ a. integrated.

'**eingeben** v/t (irr, sep, -ge-, h, → **geben**) (dat) **1.** (to) give, administer (drug): fig. **j-m e-n Gedanken** ~ give s.o. an idea. **2.** feed data (into).

'**eingebildet** adj **1.** imaginary. **2.** conceited (**auf** acc about), arrogant.

'**Eingeborene** m, f (-n; -n) native.

'**Eingebung** f (-; -en) inspiration.

eingedenk ['aɪŋɡədɛŋk] adj pred mindful (gen of).

'**eingefallen** adj fig. hollow (cheeks).

eingefleischt ['aɪŋɡəflaɪʃt] adj inveterate, confirmed (bachelor etc).

'**eingehen** (irr, sep, -ge-, sn, → **gehen**) **I** v/i **1.** goods, mail, etc: come in, arrive: **~d** incoming. **2.** ~ **in** (acc) enter (a lan-

guage etc): → **Geschichte** 2. **3. bei j-m ein- und ausgehen** be a frequent visitor at s.o.'s place. **4. ~ auf** (*acc*) a) accept, agree to, b) deal with (*details etc*), go into (*a question etc*), go along with (*a joke*): **auf j-n ~** listen (*or* respond) to s.o., humo(u)r s.o. **5.** *animal, plant*: die (*a.* F *person*: **vor** *dat* with), F *athlete etc*: go under, *business etc*: fold up. **6.** *fabric*: shrink. **7.** *das geht ihm nicht ein* he can't grasp it. **II** *v/t* enter into (*contract, marriage, etc*); → **Risiko, Wette.**

'**eingehend I** *adj fig.* thorough, detailed. **II** *adv* thoroughly, in detail.

'**eingeklemmt I** *pp of* **einklemmen. II** *adj 🪤* strangulated (*hernia*), trapped (*nerve*).

'**eingemacht I** *pp of* **einmachen. II** *adj* preserved (*fruit*), pickled (*gherkins etc*).

eingemeinden ['aɪŋɡəmaɪndən] *v/t* (*sep*, -ge-, h) incorporate (*in acc* into).

'**eingenommen I** *pp of* **einnehmen. II** *adj ~ sein von* be taken with; *contp.* **von sich ~ sein** be full of o.s.

'**eingerostet** *adj a. fig.* rusty.

'**eingeschnappt I** *pp of* **einschnappen. II** *adj* F cross: **~ sein** be in a huff.

'**eingespielt I** *pp of* **einspielen. II** *adj* (*gut*) *aufeinander ~ sein a. fig.* make a good team.

'**Eingeständnis** *n* (-ses; -se) admission.

'**eingestehen** *v/t* (*irr, sep,* h, → *gestehen*) admit.

'**eingestellt I** *pp of* **einstellen. II** *adj* **1. ~ gegen** opposed to. **2. ~ auf** (*acc*) geared to, prepared for. **3.** *sozial etc ~* socially *etc* minded.

'**eingetragen I** *pp of* **eintragen. II** *adj ✝* registered.

Eingeweide ['aɪŋɡəvaɪdə] *pl* a) insides, F innards, b) intestines, guts.

'**Eingeweihte** *m, f* (-n; -n) initiate, insider.

'**eingewöhnen: sich ~** (*sep,* h) (*in dat*) get accustomed (to), settle (into).

'**eingießen** *v/t* (*irr, sep,* -ge-, h, → *gießen*) pour (out).

'**eingipsen** *v/t* (*sep,* -ge-, h) 🪤 put in plaster.

eingleisig ['aɪŋɡlaɪzɪç] *adj* single-track.

'**eingliedern** (*sep,* -ge-, h) **I** *v/t* (*in acc* into) integrate, incorporate: *j-n wieder*

~ rehabilitate s.o. **II sich ~** (*in acc*) fit in (with), *person*: adjust (to).

'**Eingliederung** *f* (-; -en) integration.

'**eingraben** (*irr, sep,* -ge-, h, → *graben*) **I** *v/t* **1.** bury, dig in. **2.** engrave (*in acc* on). **II sich ~** dig (o.s.) in, entrench o.s., *zo.* burrow itself (*in acc* into).

'**eingra,vieren** *v/t* (*sep,* h) engrave (*in acc* on).

'**eingreifen** *v/i* (*irr, sep,* -ge-, h, → *greifen*) **1.** step in, intervene, *a.* ⚖️ interfere (*in acc* with *rights*), ✗ go into action: *in ein Gespräch ~* cut in on a conversation; *in die Debatte ~* interfere in the debate; *in j-s Leben ~* affect s.o.'s life. **2.** ⚙ mesh (*in acc* with). '**Eingreifen** *n* (-s) intervention, interference, action.

'**eingreifend** *adj fig.* drastic, far-reaching. '**Eingriff** *m* (-[e]s; -e) **1.** 🪤 operation. **2.** (*in acc* into) intervention, interference (*a.* with).

'**einhacken** *v/t* (*sep,* -ge-, h) **~ auf** (*acc*) hack at; *fig. auf j-n ~* keep on at s.o.

'**einhaken** (*sep,* -ge-, h) **I** *v/t* hook s.th. in. **II sich ~** link arms (*bei j-m* with s.o.). **III** *v/i fig.* cut in (*bei* on): *bei e-r Sache ~* take s.th. up.

'**Einhalt:** (*dat*) **~ gebieten** put a stop to.

'**einhalten** *v/t* (*irr, sep,* -ge-, h, → *halten*) keep (*promise*), keep to, observe (*contract, deadline, rule, etc*), meet (*obligation*). '**Einhaltung** *f* (-; *no pl*) (*gen*) adherence (to), observance (of).

'**einhämmern** → *einbleuen.*

'**Einhand...** ⚓ single-handed.

'**einhandeln** *v/t* (*sep,* -ge-, h) *et. für* (*or gegen*) *et. ~* exchange s.th. for s.th.; F *fig. sich et. ~* land o.s. with s.th.

einhändig ['aɪnhɛndɪç] *adj and adv* single-handed.

'**einhängen** (*sep,* -ge-, h) **I** *v/t* **1.** put *door* on its hinges. **2.** *den Hörer ~* hang up, replace the receiver. **II sich bei j-m ~** take s.o.'s arm. **III** *v/i* → 2.

'**einheimisch** *adj* local, native, *a.* 🌾, *zo.* indigenous, ✝ domestic: *~e Mannschaft* home team. '**Einheimische** *m, f* (-n; -n) a) native, b) resident, local.

einheimsen ['aɪnhaɪmzən] *v/t* (*sep,* -ge-, h) F rake in (*money*), win (*praise*).

'**einheiraten** *v/i* (*sep,* -ge-, h) **~ in** (*acc*) marry into.

Einheit ['aɪnhaɪt] *f* (-; -en) **1.** unit: *e-e*

geschlossene **~** *bilden* form an integrated whole. **2.** *a. pol.* unity.

'**einheitlich** *adj* a) uniform, homogeneous, b) standard(ized), c) united.

'**Einheitlichkeit** *f* (-; *no pl*) **1.** uniformity. **2.** unity.

'**Einheits∣front** *f pol.* united front. **~liste** *f pol.* single list (*Am.* ticket). **~preis** *m* a) standard price, b) flat-rate price. **~staat** *m* centralized state. **~wert** *m taxation:* rateable value.

'**einheizen** *v/i* (*sep*, -ge-, h) F *fig.* **j-m ~** give s.o. hell.

einhellig ['aɪnhɛlɪç] *adj* unanimous.

ein'her... *walk etc.* along.

'**einholen** (*sep*, -ge-, h) **I** *v/t* **1.** catch up with (*a. fig.*), make up for (*lost time etc.*). **2.** get, obtain: *Auskünfte* **~** make inquiries (*über acc* about); *Rat* **~** seek advice (*bei* from). **3.** ⚓ strike (*sails*), tow in (*ship*). **II** *v/i* **4.** F **~** *gehen* go shopping.

'**Einhorn** *n* (-[e]s; ·er) unicorn.

'**einhüllen** *v/t* (*sep*, -ge-, h) (*in acc*) wrap up (in), cover (with): *fig.* *eingehüllt in Nebel etc* enveloped in fog *etc.*

'**einhundert** *adj* a (*or* one) hundred.

einig ['aɪnɪç] *adj* **1.** united. **2.** in agreement (*with*): (*sich*) **~** *werden* come to an agreement (*über acc* about); *sich* **~** *sein, daß* ... be agreed that ...; *sich nicht* **~** *sein* (*über acc*) disagree (on).

einige ['aɪnɪgə] *indef pron* **I** *adjectival* **1.** a few, some, several. **2.** a) quite a (bit of), b) some, c) quite a few: *es besteht* **~** *Hoffnung, daß* ... there is some hope that ...; **~s** *Aufsehen erregen* cause quite a stir. **3.** some *hundred marks etc.* **II** *substantival* **4.** *pl* a few, some, several. **5.** → *einiges.*

'**einigemal** *adv* several times.

'**einigen** (h) **I** *v/t* unite. **II** *sich* **~** (*über acc*, *auf acc*) agree (on), reach an agreement (about).

'**einiger'maßen** *adv* a) to some extent, somewhat, b) quite, fairly, c) fairly well, F so-so.

'**einiges** *indef pron* a) something, some things, b) quite a bit: **~** *davon* some of it; *er hat* **~** *gelernt* he has learned a thing or two; *sein Plan hat* **~** *für sich* there is s.th. to be said for his plan.

'**Einigkeit** *f* (-; *no pl*) **1.** unity, harmony. **2.** agreement, consensus: *es herrschte*

~ *darüber, daß* ... we (*or* they) all agreed that ...

'**Einigung** *f* (-; -en) **1.** unification. **2.** agreement: *es wurde k-e* **~** *erzielt* no agreement was reached (*über acc* on).

'**einimpfen** *v/t* (*sep*, -ge-, h) *fig.* **j-m et. ~** a) indoctrinate s.o. with s.th., b) → *einbleuen.*

'**einjagen** *v/t* (*sep*, -ge-, h) **j-m e-n** *Schreck* **~** give s.o. a fright.

einjährig ['aɪnjɛːrɪç] *adj* **1.** one-year-old. **2.** one-year (*course etc*). **3.** ♀ annual.

'**einkalku,lieren** *v/t* (*sep*, h) take *s.th.* into account, allow for.

'**Einkauf** *m* (-[e]s; ·e) **1.** purchase: *Einkäufe machen* → *einkaufen* **II**. **2.** purchasing, buying. **3.** *no pl* ♣ purchasing department. '**einkaufen** (*sep*, -ge-, h) **I** *v/t* buy, purchase. **II** *v/i* **~** (*gehen*) go (*or* do one's) shopping. '**Einkäufer(in** *f*) *m* ♣ buyer.

'**Einkaufs∣bummel** *m e-n* **~** *machen* go on a shopping spree. **~liste** *f* shopping list. **~preis** *m* (*zum* **~** at the) purchase price. **~tasche** *f* shopping bag. **~zentrum** *n* shopping cent/re (*Am.* -er).

'**einkehren** *v/i* (*sep*, -ge-, sn) stop off (*in dat* at).

'**einkeilen** *v/t* (*sep*, -ge-, h) wedge in.

'**einkellern** *v/t* (*sep*, -ge-, h) put down.

'**einkerben** *v/t* (*sep*, -ge-, h), '**Einker-bung** *f* (-; -en) notch.

'**einklagen** *v/t* (*sep*, -ge-, h) *et.* (*gegen j-n*) **~** sue (s.o.) for s.th.

'**einklammern** *v/t* (*sep*, -ge-, h) put *s.th.* in brackets.

'**Einklang** *m* (-[e]s; *no pl*) ♪ unison, *fig. a.* harmony: *fig.* **in** **~** *bringen* reconcile (*mit* with); *nicht im* **~** *stehen* be at variance (*mit* with).

'**einkleben** *v/t* (*sep*, -ge-, h) stick *s.th.* in(to *in acc*).

'**einkleiden** (*sep*, -ge-, h) **I** *v/t* **j-n** **~** *a.* ✗ fit s.o. out. **II** *sich* (*neu*) **~** fit o.s. out with a new set of clothes.

'**einklemmen** *v/t* (*sep*, -ge-, h) (*sich*) **den** *Finger* **~** get one's finger caught (*in dat* in); → *eingeklemmt.*

'**einkochen** *v/t* (*sep*, -ge-, h) **1.** boil down. **2.** preserve.

'**Einkommen** *n* (-s; -) **1.** income, earnings. **2.** revenue. '**Einkommensgruppe** *f* income bracket. '**einkommensschwach** *adj* low-income.

'**Einkommenssteuer** f income tax. **~erklärung** f income-tax return.

'**einköpfen** v/t (sep, -ge-, h) soccer: head in.

'**einkreisen** v/t (sep, -ge-, h) **1.** surround, encircle. **2.** narrow down (problem etc).

Einkünfte ['aɪnkʏnftə] pl **1.** income, earnings. **2.** revenue.

'**einkuppeln** v/i (sep, -ge-, h) mot. let in the clutch.

'**einladen** (irr, sep, -ge-, h, → **laden**) **I** v/t **1.** load (in). **2.** j-n ~ invite s.o. (zum Essen to lunch etc), ask s.o. (round); ich lade dich (dazu) ein! that's my treat!, this is on me! **II** v/i **3.** a. fig. invite. '**einladend** adj fig. a) inviting, b) tempting, c) delicious(-looking).

'**Einladung** f (-; -en) invitation: auf ~ von (or gen) at the invitation of.

'**Einlage** f (-; -n) **1.** in letter: enclosure, in newspaper etc: insert. **2.** a) (arch) support, b) insole. **3.** in panties etc: liner. **4.** padding. **5.** in tooth: temporary filling. **6.** in soups: garnish. **7.** ✝ a) in bank: deposit, b) (capital) contribution. **8.** thea. etc interlude, extra.

Einlaß m ['aɪnlas] m (-sses; no pl) admittance (zu to): sich ~ verschaffen get in; ~ ab 18 Uhr opening at 18:00 hours.

'**einlassen** (irr, sep, -ge-, h, → **lassen**) **I** v/t **1.** let s.o., s.th. in, admit: Wasser (in die Wanne) ~ run a bath. **2.** (in acc in) set (diamond etc), ⚙ embed. **II** sich ~ auf (acc) a) get involved in, b.s. let o.s. in for, b) agree to (a proposal), c) go into (a question); laß dich nicht darauf ein! leave it alone!; sich mit j-m ~ get involved with s.o. (a. amorously); sich mit j-m auf e-n Kampf (ein Wortgefecht) ~ F tangle with s.o.

'**Einlauf** m (-[e]s, ⸚e) **1.** ⚕ (e-n ~ machen give s.o. an) enema. **2.** sports: finish.

'**einlaufen** (irr, sep, -ge-, → **laufen**) **I** v/i (sn) **1.** come in (a. sports), ⚓ put in. **2.** water: run in: Badewasser ~ lassen run a bath. **3.** fabric: shrink: nicht ~d nonshrink. **II** v/t (h) break in (shoes). **III** sich ~ (h) sports: warm up.

'**einläuten** v/t (sep, -ge-, h) ring in.

'**einleben** → **eingewöhnen**.

'**Einlegearbeit** f inlaid work.

'**einlegen** v/t (sep, -ge-, h) **1.** put in, insert (film etc): et. ~ in (acc) a. enclose s.th. in (or with); fig. e-e Pause ~ have

a break; e-n Spurt ~ put in a spurt; → Wort 2. **2.** deposit (money in bank). **3.** gastr. (in Essig) ~ pickle. **4.** ⚙ inlay (mit with). **5.** lodge, file (appeal etc): → Berufung 4, Protest, Veto. **6.** j-m (sich) die Haare ~ set s.o.'s (one's) hair.

'**Einleger** m (-s; -) ✝ depositor.

'**Einlegesohle** f insole.

'**einleiten** v/t (sep, -ge-, h) **1.** start, begin, a. open (negotiations), initiate (reforms etc), introduce (a. ling. clause). **2.** ⚕ induce. ⚖ institute: e-n Prozeß ~ gegen bring an action against. '**einleitend** **I** adj introductory, opening, preliminary. **II** adv by way of introduction. '**Einleitung** f (-; -en) **1.** opening, start, introduction (a. ling.). **2.** preface. **3.** ⚕ induction. **4.** ⚖ institution.

'**einlenken** v/i (sep, -ge-, h) fig. relent.

'**einlesen** v/t (irr, sep, -ge-, h, → **lesen**) computer: read in.

'**einleuchten** v/i (sep, -ge-, h) make sense (j-m to s.o.). '**einleuchtend** adj clear, convincing.

'**einliefern** v/t (sep, -ge-, h) **1.** j-n ins Krankenhaus (Gefängnis) ~ take s.o. to (the) hospital (to prison). **2.** post, mail. '**Einlieferung** f (-; -en) **1.** (in acc) admission (to hospital), committal (to prison etc). **2.** posting, mailing.

'**Einlieferungsschein** m postal receipt.

'**einlochen** v/t (sep, -ge-, h) **1.** golf: put(t). **2.** F j-n ~ put s.o. in clink.

'**einlösen** v/t (sep, -ge-, h) **1.** redeem (pawn, securities), cash (cheque). **2.** fig. keep (promise etc).

'**einlullen** v/t (sep, -ge-, h) F fig. lull.

'**einmachen** v/t (sep, -ge-, h) preserve.

'**einmal** adv **1.** once: ~ im Jahr once a year; ~ und nie wieder never again; noch ~ once more; erst ~ first; auf ~ a) at one go, b) at the same time, c) suddenly. **2.** once, before: das war ~ that's all in the past; es war ~ once upon a time there was; ich war schon ~ da a) I've been there before, b) I was there once; haben Sie schon ~ ...? have you ever ...? **3.** one day, some day (or other), later on: wenn du ~ groß bist when you grow up. **4.** nicht ~ not even, not so much as. **5.** ich bin ~ so! I can't help it!; es ist nun ~ so that's the way it is; laßt ihn doch ~ reden! let him talk, will you!; stell dir ~ vor! just imagine!

Einmal'eins *n* (-; *no pl*) **1.** (multiplication) table. **2.** *fig.* basics.

'**einmalig** *adj* **1.** single, nonrecurring: ~*e* **Abfindung** single payment. **2.** unique, singular, unparallel(l)ed, F fantastic: *e-e ~e Chance* the chance of a lifetime; ~ **schön** absolutely beautiful.

'**Einmannbetrieb** *m* one-man business.

'**Einmarsch** *m* marching in, *a.* invasion.

'**einmar,schieren** *v/i* (*sep*, sn) march in: *in ein Land* ~ invade a country.

'**einmieten:** *sich* ~ (*sep*, -ge-, h) take a room (*or* rooms) (*in dat* at, *bei* with).

'**einmischen:** *sich* ~ (*in acc* in, with) meddle, interfere; *sich in ein Gespräch* ~ join in (*or* F butt in on) a conversation; *misch dich da nicht ein!* just keep out of it!

'**Einmischung** *f* (-; -en) interference.

'**einmo,torig** *adj* single-engined.

einmotten ['aɪnmɔtən] *v/t* (*sep*, -ge-, h) put *s.th.* in mothballs, *fig. a.* mothball.

'**einmünden** *v/i* (*sep*, -ge-, sn) a) flow into, b) *road*: lead into, c) *fig.* lead to.

'**Einmündung** *f* (-; -en) a) estuary, mouth, b) (*road*) junction.

einmütig ['aɪnmyːtɪç] *adj* unanimous.

'**Einmütigkeit** *f* (-; *no pl*) unanimity.

'**Einnahme** ['aɪnnaːmə] *f* (-; -n) **1.** taking, ✕ *a.* capture, occupation. **2.** *pl a*) receipts, b) proceeds, c) income, earnings, d) revenue.

'**Einnahmequelle** *f* source of income.

'**einnehmen** *v/t* (*irr*, *sep*, -ge-, h, → *nehmen*) **1.** have (*lunch etc*), take (*medicament*). **2.** take in, earn (*money*). **3.** ✕ capture, occupy. **4.** take up (*space*): *s-n Platz* ~ take one's seat. **5.** hold (*position etc*). **6.** *fig.* j-*n (für sich)* ~ win s.o. over, charm s.o.; *j-n gegen sich* ~ set s.o. against o.s. '**einnehmend** *adj fig.* winning, engaging.

'**einnicken** *v/i* (*sep*, -ge-, sn) F nod off.

'**einnisten:** *sich* ~ (*sep*, -ge-, h) nest, *fig. person*: install o.s.

'**Einöde** *f* (-; -n) wilderness.

'**einölen** *v/t* (*sep*, -ge-, h) a) oil, b) rub oil into.

'**einordnen** (*sep*, -ge-, h) I *v/t* **1.** arrange (*nach* according to), file (*medicament*). **2.** a) classify, b) integrate (*in acc* into *a system etc*), c) place, date (*work of art*), d) class (*unter acc* with). II *sich* ~ **3.** → *einfügen* II. **4.**

mot. get in lane: *sich links* ~ get into the left lane, *Br.* filter to the left.

'**einpacken** (*sep*, -ge-, h) I *v/t* pack (up), wrap up, do up. II *v/i* pack: F *fig.* **da können wir** ~*!* we might as well pack up and leave!

'**einparken** *v/t*, *v/i* (*sep*, -ge-, h) park (between two cars).

'**einpendeln:** *sich* ~ (*sep*, -ge-, h) *fig.* find its (own) level.

'**einpferchen** *v/t* (*sep*, -ge-, h) coop up.

'**einpflanzen** *v/t* **1.** �($plant. **2.** 🩺 implant (*organ*).

Ein'phasen..., einphasig ['aɪnfaːzɪç] *adj* ⚡ single-phase.

'**einplanen** *v/t* (*sep*, -ge-, h) **1.** include (in the plan), plan. **2.** allow for.

einpolig ['aɪnpoːlɪç] *adj* ⚡ single-pole.

'**einprägen** (*sep*, -ge-, h) I *v/t* imprint (*in acc* on): *j-n et.* ~ impress s.th. on s.o.; *sich et.* ~ a) remember, b) memorize. II *sich j-m* ~ stick in s.o.'s mind.

'**einprägsam** *adj* easily remembered, catchy (*tune*).

'**einquar,tieren** (*sep*, h) I *v/t* ✕ billet (*bei* on). II *sich* ~ *bei* move in with.

'**Einquar,tierung** *f* (-; -en) ✕ billeting.

'**einrahmen** *v/t* (*sep*, -ge-, h) frame.

'**einrammen** *v/t* (*sep*, -ge-, h) ram *s.th.* in(to *in acc*).

'**einrasten** *v/i* (*sep*, -ge-, sn) **1.** ⊙ click into place, engage. **2.** F go into a huff.

'**einräumen** *v/t* (*sep*, -ge-, h) **1.** a) put away, b) put the furniture in *a room*: *e-n Schrank* ~ put (the) things into a cupboard. **2.** *fig.* j-*m et.* ~ grant s.th. to s.o. '**einräumend** *adj* concessive.

'**Einrede** *f* (-; -n) ⚖ plea, demurrer.

'**einreden** (*sep*, -ge-, h) I *v/t* j-*m* (*sich*) *et.* ~ talk s.o. (o.s.) into (believing) s.th.; *j-m* (*sich*) ~*, daß ...* persuade s.o. (o.s.) that ...; *das redest du dir* (*doch*) *nur ein!* you're imagining it! II *v/i auf j-n* ~ a) talk insistently to s.o., b) urge s.o.

'**einregnen** (*sep*, -ge-, h) I *v/i* (sn) **eingeregnet sein** be caught by the rain; *fig. auf j-n* ~ rain on s.o. II *v/impers* (h) *es regnet sich ein* the rain is settling in.

'**einreiben** *v/t* (*irr*, *sep*, -ge-, h, → *reiben*) rub *s.th.* in: ~ *mit* rub with.

'**Einreibemittel** *n* liniment.

'**einreichen** *v/t* (*sep*, -ge-, h) (*bei* to) send in, hand in, submit: ⚖ *e-e Klage* ~ file (*or* bring) an action.

'**einreihen** (*sep*, -ge-, h) **I** *sich ~* (*in acc*) take one's place (in), join (*s.th.*). **II** *v/t* class (*in acc* with): *j-n ~ unter* (*acc*) rank s.o. with.

'**Einreiher** *m* (-s; -) single-breasted suit.

'**Einreise** *f* (-; -n) entry. **~genehmigung** *f* entry permit. **~visum** *n* entry visa.

'**einreißen** (*irr, sep*, -ge-, → *reißen*) **I** *v/t* (h) **1.** tear. **2.** demolish, pull *house etc* down. **II** *v/i* (sn) **3.** tear. **4.** F *nuisance etc*: spread.

einrenken ['aınrɛŋkən] (*sep*, -ge-, h) **I** *v/t* **1.** � set. **2.** F *fig.* straighten *s.th.* out. **II** *sich ~* F *fig.* sort itself out.

'**einrichten** (*sep*, -ge-, h) **I** *v/t* **1.** furnish (*room etc*), fit *kitchen, shop, etc* out, equip, install. **2.** set up, found, establish. **3.** arrange: *es ~, daß ... a.* see (to it) that ...; *wenn du es ~ kannst* if you can (manage to). **4.** ✱ set (*broken bone*). **II** *sich ~* **5.** *sich* (*neu*) ~ (re)furnish one's flat (*or* house); → *häuslich*. **6.** make ends meet. **7.** *sich ~ auf* (*acc*) prepare for; *auf so et. sind wir nicht eingerichtet* we're not prepared for that sort of thing.

'**Einrichtung** *f* (-; -en) **1.** furniture, fittings, equipment. **2.** installation: *die sanitären ~en a.* sanitation. **3.** *no pl* setting up, foundation. **4.** (*öffentliche ~* public) institution, *w.s.* facility: *zu e-r ständigen ~ werden* become a permanent institution. **5.** → *Vorrichtung*.

'**Einrichtungsgegenstände** *pl* equipment, fixtures.

'**einrosten** *v/i* (*sep*, -ge-, sn) get rusty.

'**einrücken** (*sep*, -ge-) **I** *v/t* (h) **1.** indent (*line*). **2.** put *an advertisement* in *a newspaper etc*. **II** *v/i* **3.** ✗ a) be called up, b) march in: *~ in* (*acc*) march into.

eins [aıns] **I** *adj* **1.** one: *um ~ a.* one (o'clock); *sports*: *~ zu zwei* one two; F *fig. ~ zu null für dich!* score one for you! **2.** *es ist mir alles ~* I couldn't care less; *das ist doch alles ~* it all amounts to the same thing. **II** *indef pron* one thing: *~ nach dem andern!* one thing at a time!; *noch ~!* another thing!

Eins *f* (-; -en) (number) one, *ped.* A: *e-e ~ schreiben* get an A; F *wie e-e ~* just super.

'**einsacken** (*sep*, -ge-, h) **I** *v/t* (h) bag, F *fig. a.* pocket. **II** *v/i* (sn) sag.

einsam ['aınza:m] *adj* lonely, isolated,

secluded. '**Einsamkeit** *f* (-; *no pl*) loneliness, seclusion, isolation.

'**einsammeln** *v/t* (*sep*, -ge-, h) gather, collect.

'**Einsatz** *m* (-es; ⸚e) **1.** insert, *on dress*: inset, (*filter*) element. **2.** stake (*a. fig.*): *den ~ verdoppeln* double the stake(s). **3.** risk: *unter ~ s-s Lebens* at the risk of one's life. **4.** ♪ entry: *den ~ geben* give the cue. **5.** effort(s), hard work, zeal, dedication: *harter ~ sports*: hard tackling; *mit vollem ~* all out. **6.** use, employment, ✗ deployment: *im ~ ⊙* in operation. **7.** ✗, *police etc*: action, (*combat*) mission: *im ~ stehen* be on duty, ✗ be in action; *zum ~ kommen* be brought in(to action).

'**Einsatz|befehl** *m* ✗ combat order. **♀bereit** *adj* ready for duty (✗ action, ⊙ use): *sich ~ halten* stand by; *et. ~ halten* have s.th. ready. **~besprechung** *f before a mission*: briefing, *after a mission*: debriefing. **♀fähig** *adj* a) available, usable, ⊙ operational, b) fit to work (*or* play *etc*). **♀freudig** *adj* keen, zealous. **~gruppe** *f*, **~kom⸍mando** *n* task force. **~wagen** *m* police car (*or* van).

'**einsaugen** *v/t* (*sep*, -ge-, h) suck in.

'**einschalten** (*sep*, -ge-, h) **I** *v/t* **1.** switch on, turn on, ⊙ *a.* connect: ✗ *e-n Sender ~* tune in to; *den Motor ~* start the engine; *den dritten Gang ~* shift into third gear. **2.** *fig.* put in, insert: *e-e Pause ~* have a break. **3.** *fig.* call in: *in e-n* (*or bei e-m*) *Fall Sachverständige ~* call (*or* bring) in experts on a case. **II** *sich ~* **4.** *fig.* step in, intervene: *sich in ein Gespräch ~* join in a conversation. **5.** *TV* tune in (*in acc* to). **6.** ⊙ switch itself on (automatically).

'**Einschaltquote** *f radio, TV* viewing figures, ratings.

'**einschärfen** *v/t* (*sep*, -ge-, h) *j-m ~ zu inf* urge (*or* warn) s.o. to *inf*.

'**einschätzen** *v/t* (*sep*, -ge-, h) **1.** judge, assess: *falsch ~* misjudge; *zu hoch* (*niedrig*) *~* overrate (underrate). **2.** assess, estimate. '**Einschätzung** *f* (-; -en) **1.** assessment. **2.** estimation, judg(e)-ment: *nach m-r ~* in my estimation.

'**einschenken** *v/t* (*sep*, -ge-, h) pour (out).

'**einschicken** *v/t* (*sep*, -ge-, h) send in.

'**einschieben** *v/t* (*irr, sep*, -ge-, h, →

schieben) **1.** put in, insert. **2.** *fig.* fit in.

'**Einschiebung** *f* (-; -en) insertion.

'**einschießen: sich ~** (*irr, sep*, -ge-, h, → **schießen**) *a. fig.* zero in (**auf** *acc* on).

'**einschiffen: sich ~** (*sep*, -ge-, h) embark (**nach** for), board a (*or* the) ship.

'**einschlafen** *v/i* (*irr, sep*, -ge-, sn, → **schlafen**) **1.** fall asleep, *a. leg etc*: go to sleep. **2.** *fig. correspondence etc*: peter out. **3.** *fig.* die peacefully, pass away.

'**einschläfern** *v/t* (*sep*, -ge-, h, → **schlafen**) etc), striking (*of lightning*). **2.** *fig.* touch: **ein südländischer ~** an element a) lull s.o. (into a false sense of security). **2.** put down (*dog etc*). '**einschläfernd** *adj* soporific.

'**Einschlag** *m* (-[e]s; ⸚e) **1.** impact (*of bomb etc*), **2.** fig. touch: **ein südländischer ~** an element of the Mediterranean. **3.** *mot.* lock.

'**einschlagen** (*irr, sep*, -ge-, h, → **schla-gen**) **I** *v/t* **1.** drive *nail* in(to **in** *acc*). **2.** break, smash (in): **j-m den Schädel ~** F bash s.o.'s head in; **sich die Zähne ~** knock one's teeth out. **3.** wrap up. **4.** take (*direction, road*). **5.** *fig.* enter (*a career*), adopt (*a policy etc*): **e-n ande-ren Weg ~** adopt a different method. **II** *v/i* **6.** (**in** *acc*) bomb etc: hit (*lightning*: strike) (*the house etc*): *fig.* **wie e-e Bombe ~** fall like a bombshell, cause a sensation. **7.** *fig.* (**gut**) ~ be a (great) success, be a (big) hit. **8. ~ auf** (*acc*) beat. **III** *sich ~* (h) *tennis*: warm up.

'**einschlägig** ['aɪnʃlɛ:gɪç] *adj* relevant: **ein ~er Fall** a case in point; **~ vorbe-straft** previously convicted for the same offence.

'**einschleichen: sich ~** (*irr, sep*, -ge-, h, → **schleichen**) creep in(to **in** *acc*); **sich in j-s Vertrauen ~** worm one's way into s.o.'s confidence.

'**einschleppen** *v/t* (*sep*, -ge-, h) bring *a disease etc* in(to **in** *acc*).

'**einschleusen** *v/t* (*sep*, -ge-, h) (**in** *acc*) infiltrate *s.o.* (into), smuggle *s.o.*, *s.th.* in(to).

'**einschließen** *v/t* (*irr, sep*, -ge-, h, → **schließen**) **1.** lock (*or* shut) *s.o.*, *s.th.* (**sich** o.s.) up (**in** *acc*). **2.** enclose, *a.* ✗ surround, encircle. **3.** *fig.* include (**in** *acc* in). '**einschließlich I** *prep* (*gen*) including, inclusive of: **~ Porto** postage included. **II** *adv* **bis Seite 7 ~** up to and

including page 7; **von Montag bis ~ Freitag** from Monday to Friday inclu-sive, *Am.* Monday through Friday.

'**einschmeicheln: sich ~** (*sep*, -ge-, h) ingratiate o.s. (**bei j-m** with s.o.).

'**einschmeichelnd** *adj* ingratiating.

'**einschmelzen** *v/t* (*irr, sep*, -ge-, h, → **schmelzen**) melt *s.th.* (down).

'**einschnappen** *v/i* (*sep*, -ge-, sn) **1.** catch, click. **2.** F *fig.* go into a huff: → **eingeschnappt**.

'**einschneiden** (*irr, sep*, -ge-, h, → **schneiden**) **I** *v/t* (**in** *acc* into) cut, carve. **II** *v/i* cut into. '**einschneidend** *adj fig.* incisive, drastic, crucial, decisive.

'**einschneien** *v/t* (*sep*, -ge-, sn) **einge-schneit sein** be snowed in (*or* up).

'**Einschnitt** *m* **1.** cut, incision, notch. **2.** *fig.* a) crucial event, b) turning point.

'**einschränken** [-ʃrɛŋkən] (*sep*, -ge-, h) **I** *v/t* **1.** (**auf** *acc* to) restrict, reduce (*pro-duction etc*), cut down (*expenditure*): **das Rauchen ~** cut down on smoking. **2.** qualify (*statement etc*). **II** *sich ~* economize (**in** *dat* in), cut down ex-penses. '**einschränkend** *adj* restrictive (*a. ling.*), qualifying (*remark*).

'**Einschränkung** *f* (-; -en) **1.** restriction, reduction, cut. **2.** qualification: **ohne ~** without reservation.

'**einschrauben** *v/t* (*sep*, -ge-, h) screw in(to **in** *acc*).

'**Einschreibe|brief** *m* registered letter. **~gebühr** *f* registration fee.

'**einschreiben** (*irr, sep*, -ge-, h, → **schreiben**) **I** *v/t* **1. e-n Brief ~ lassen** have a letter registered; **⚲! registered! 2.** enter, *as a member*: enrol(l): **sich ~ las-sen** → **II** **sich ~** sign up, *univ.* register, enrol(l). '**Einschreibung** *f* (-; -en) signing up, *univ.* enrol(l)ment.

'**einschreiten** *v/i* (*irr, sep*, -ge-, sn, → **schreiten**) intervene, step in: **~ gegen** take action against.

'**Einschub** *m* (-[e]s; ⸚e) insertion, ⚙ in-sert, ⚡ slide-in module.

'**einschüchtern** *v/t* (*sep*, -ge-, h) intimi-date. '**Einschüchterung** *f* (-; -en) intimidation.

'**einschulen** *v/t* (*sep*, -ge-, h) **ein Kind ~** put a child to school.

'**Einschuß** *m* (-sses; ⸚sse) bullet hole, ✗ entry wound.

'**einschweißen** v/t (sep, -ge-, h) shrink-wrap.

'**einschwenken** v/i (sep, -ge-, sn) turn (*in* acc into): *nach links* ~ turn (to the) left; fig. ~ (*auf* acc) come round (to).

'**Einsegnung** f (-; -en) eccl. 1. consecration. 2. confirmation.

'**einsehen** v/t (irr, sep, -ge-, h, → *sehen*) 1. have a look at, inspect. 2. see, ✕ observe (*terrain*). 3. fig. understand, see, realize: *ich sehe nicht ein, weshalb* I don't see why. '**Einsehen** n (-s) *ein* ~ *haben* a) show some consideration (*mit* for), b) be reasonable.

'**einseifen** v/t (sep, -ge-, h) 1. lather, soap. 2. F fig. *j-n* ~ take s.o. in.

einseitig ['aɪnzaɪtɪç] adj 1. one-sided (*a.* fig.), pol. unilateral, ✍ a. on one side: *~e Ernährung* unbalanced diet; ~ *beschrieben* written on one side (only). 2. bias(s)ed: *et. sehr* ~ *darstellen* give a one-sided description of s.th. '**Einseitigkeit** f (-; *no pl*) one-sidedness, fig. a. bias, partiality.

'**einsenden** v/t (irr, sep, -ge-, h, → *senden*) send in. '**Einsender(in** f) m 1. sender. 2. contributor. '**Einsendeschluß** m closing date (for entries). '**Einsendung** f (-; -en) a) sending in, b) *at competition:* entry.

Einser ['aɪnzɐ] m (-s; -) F → *Eins.*

'**einsetzen** (sep, -ge-, h) I v/t 1. put in, insert. 2. set up (*committee*). 3. use, employ, apply, bring *influence etc* into play. 4. put into action, call in (*the police*), employ (*work force etc*): *j-n als* (*dat*) (*or bei*) assign s.o. to; *j-n als Erben* ~ appoint s.o. one's heir. 5. stake, bet: fig. *sein Leben* ~ risk one's life. II 6. *sich* ~ exert o.s.; *sich voll* ~ go all out; *sich* ~ *für* support, speak up for, champion; *sich bei j-m für j-n* ~ intercede with s.o. for s.o. III v/i 7. start (off), *rain etc:* set in. 8. ♪ come in.

'**Einsetzung** f (-; -en) 1. insertion. 2. appointment.

'**Einsicht** f (-; -en) 1. *no pl* examination (*in Akten* of records): ~ *nehmen in* (*acc*) examine. 2. insight, understanding: *zur* ~ *kommen* listen to reason. '**einsichtig** adj reasonable. '**Einsichtnahme** f (-; *no pl*) inspection. '**einsickern** v/i (sep, -ge-, sn) seep in: ~ *in* (*acc*) seep into, a. fig. infiltrate into.

'**Einsiedler** m (-s; -) hermit.

einsilbig ['aɪnzɪlbɪç] adj monosyllabic, fig. a. taciturn. '**Einsilbigkeit** f (-; *no pl*) fig. taciturnity.

'**einsinken** v/i (irr, sep, -ge-, sn, → *sinken*) a) sink in(to *in* acc), b) cave in.

'**einsitzen** v/i (irr, sep, -ge-, h, → *sitzen*) ⚖ serve a sentence.

Einsitzer ['aɪnzɪtsɐ] m (-s; -) ✈, mot. single-seater.

'**einsor,tieren** v/t (sep, h) sort in(to *in* acc).

'**einspannen** v/t (sep, -ge-, h) 1. harness. 2. ⚙ clamp, fix: *e-n Bogen* (*in die Schreibmaschine*) ~ insert a sheet of paper into the typewriter. 3. F fig. *j-n* ~ rope s.o. in.

'**einsparen** v/t (sep, -ge-, h) 1. save. 2. eliminate (*jobs*). '**Einsparung** f (-; -en) 1. saving. 2. (job) elimination.

'**einspeichern** v/t (sep, -ge-, h) *computer:* read in.

'**einspeisen** v/t (sep, -ge-, h) ⚙ feed (*in* acc into).

'**einsperren** v/t (sep, -ge-, h) lock up.

'**einspielen** (sep, -ge-, h) I v/t 1. bring in (*money*). 2. *TV* a) show, b) fade in. 3. ♪ play in. 4. record. II *sich* ~ get into practice, *sports:* warm up, fig. get going (properly): *sich aufeinander* ~ get used to one another; → *eingespielt.*

'**Einspielergebnisse** pl box-office returns.

einsprachig ['aɪnʃpraːxɪç] adj monolingual.

'**einspringen** v/i (irr, sep, -ge-, sn, → *springen*) fig. help out, step in(to the breach): *für j-n* ~ fill in for s.o.

'**Einspritz...** mot. (fuel) injection (*engine, pump, etc*). '**einspritzen** v/t (sep, -ge-, h) inject (*in* acc into): *j-m et.* ~ inject s.o. with, give s.o. an injection of.

'**Einspruch** m (-[e]s; ⸚e) (*gegen*) objection (to) (*a.* ⚖), protest (against), *esp. pol.* veto (against), ⚖ appeal (against): ~ *erheben* (*gegen*) object (to), ⚖ (file an) appeal (against), *pol.* veto (s.*th.*). '**Einspruchsfrist** f appeal period. '**Einspruchsrecht** n 1. ⚖ right to appeal. 2. *pol.* (power of) veto.

einspurig ['aɪnʃpuːrɪç] adj a) single-track, b) single-lane.

einst [aɪnst] adv 1. once. 2. one day.

'**einstampfen** v/t (sep, -ge-, h) pulp.

'**Einstand** *m* (-[e]s; *no pl*) **1.** (**s-n ~ geben** celebrate the) start of one's new job. **2.** *fig.* debut. **3.** *tennis:* deuce.

'**einstecken** *v/t* (*sep*, -ge-, h) **1.** put in. **2.** put *s.th.* in one's pocket (*or* bag *etc*), take. **3.** F *fig.* pocket (*profit etc*), swallow (*reprimand etc*), take (*a blow*): **er kann viel ~** he can take a lot.

'**einstehen** *v/i* (*irr*, *sep*, -ge-, h, → **stehen**) **~ für** a) answer for, take reponsibility for, b) vouch for.

'**einsteigen** *v/i* (*irr*, *sep*, -ge-, sn, → **steigen**) get in(to **in** *acc*): **alle(s) ~!** all aboard!; **~ in** (*acc*) a) get on (*a bus, train, plane*), b) F *fig.* get in on (*a project etc*), start on (*or* in): **er ist in die Politik eingestiegen** he went into politics; **hart ~** *sports:* play rough.

'**einstellbar** *adj* adjustable.

'**einstellen** (*sep*, -ge-, h) **I** *v/t* **1.** put *s.th.* in(to **in** *acc*), store (*furniture*), put *car* in the garage. **2.** take on (*workers etc*). **3.** (**auf** *acc*) ⊙ set (to), adjust (to) (*a. fig.*), tune *radio etc* in (to), *opt.* focus (on). **4.** stop, discontinue: (**vorübergehend**) ~ suspend; ⚖ **die Klage ~** drop the action; *thea.* **das Verfahren ~** dismiss the case; **die Arbeit ~** a) stop work, b) (go on) strike, walk out; **den Betrieb ~** shut down; ✕ **das Feuer ~** cease fire. **5.** tie, equal (*a record*). **II** *sich* **~ 6.** appear, turn up, *fig. fever etc:* set in, *problems etc:* arise. **7.** *sich* **~ auf** (*acc*) a) adjust (to), b) prepare (o.s.) for; **sich ganz auf j-n ~** give s.o. one's undivided attention.

'**einstellig** ['aɪnʃtɛlɪç] *adj* ⅍ one-digit.

'**Einstellknopf** *m* control knob.

'**Einstellung** *f* (-; -en) **1.** employment (*of personnel*). **2.** ⊙ adjustment, setting, *opt., phot.* focus(s)ing, focus. **3.** *film:* a) (camera) angle, b) take. **4.** discontinuance, cessation (*a.* ✕ *of hostilities*), stoppage (*of work, operation*), suspension (*of payments*): ⚖ **~ des Verfahrens** dismissal of a case; **~ e-r Klage** withdrawal of an action. **5.** *fig.* adjustment (**auf** *acc* to). **6.** (**zu**) attitude (towards), opinion (of): **s-e politische ~** his political views, F his politics.

'**Einstieg** ['aɪnʃtiːk] *m* (-[e]s; -e) **1.** way in, entrance. **2.** *fig.* (**in** *acc*) entry (into), start (in *or* on), getting (on): **~ in die Kernenergie** opting for nuclear ener-

gy. '**Einstiegluke** *f* (access) hatch.

'**Einstiegsdroge** *f* gateway drug.

einstig ['aɪnstɪç] *adj* former.

'**einstimmen** (*sep*, -ge-, h) **I** *v/i* **1.** *in ein Lied* (**das Gelächter**) **~** join in a song (the laughter). **II** *v/t* **2.** ♪ tune (up). **3.** *fig. j-n* (**sich**) **~** (**auf** *acc*) get s.o. (o.s.) in the proper mood (for).

'**einstimmig** ['aɪnʃtɪmɪç] *adj* **1.** ♪ for one voice. **2.** unanimous (*decision etc*).

'**Einstimmigkeit** *f* (-; *no pl*) unanimity, consensus.

einstöckig ['aɪnʃtœkɪç] *adj* one-stor(e)y.

'**einstöpseln** (*sep*, -ge-, h) plug in.

'**einstreuen** *v/t* (*sep*, -ge-, h) *fig.* insert: **Zitate** *etc* **in s-e Rede ~** intersperse one's speech with quotations *etc*.

'**einströmen** *v/i* (*sep*, -ge-, sn) flow in(to **in** *acc*).

'**einstu,dieren** *v/t* (*sep*, h) learn *s.th.* (by heart), *thea.* rehearse. '**Einstu,dierung** *f* (-; -en) *thea.* production.

'**einstufen** *v/t* (*sep*, -ge-, h) class, grade, rate: **hoch ~** rate high. '**einstufig** *adj* single-stage. '**Einstufung** *f* (-; -en) classification, rating.

einstündig ['aɪnʃtʏndɪç] *adj* one-hour.

'**einstürmen** *v/i* (*sep*, -ge-, sn) **~ auf** (*acc*) rush at, ✕ attack; *fig. auf j-n* **~** assail s.o. (**mit Fragen** with questions).

'**Einsturz** *m* (-es; ⤷e) collapse. '**einstürzen** *v/i* (*sep*, -ge-, sn) collapse, cave in.

einst'weilen *adv* **1.** meanwhile, in the meantime. **2.** for the time being.

einst'weilig *adj* temporary: ⚖ **~e Verfügung** a) interim order, b) injunction.

eintägig ['aɪntɛːgɪç] *adj* one-day.

'**Eintagsfliege** *f* **1.** *zo.* day fly, ephemera. **2.** *fig.* nine days' wonder.

'**eintasten** *v/t* (*sep*, -ge-, h) *computer:* key in.

'**eintauchen** (*sep*, -ge-, h) **I** *v/t* dip in(to **in** *acc*). **II** *v/i* dive in(to **in** *acc*).

'**eintauschen** *v/t* (*sep*, -ge-, h) (**gegen** for) **1.** exchange. **2.** trade *s.th.* in.

'**einteilen** *v/t* (*sep*, -ge-, h) **1.** a) divide (up) (**in** *acc* into), b) rate (**nach** according to). **2.** organize (*one's time*), budget (*money*), use *material etc* sparingly. **3.** *j-n* **~ zu** assign s.o. to, ✕ detail s.o. for.

'**Einteiler** *m* (-s; -), **einteilig** ['aɪntaɪlɪç] *adj* one-piece. '**Einteilung** *f* (-; -en) **1.** (**in** *acc* into) a) division, b) classification. **2.** planning, organization (of work, time, etc), budgeting (of money).

'**eintippen** v/t (sep, -ge-, h) type in(to **in** acc), computer: key in.

eintönig ['aɪntøːnɪç] adj monotonous.

'**Eintönigkeit** f (-; no pl) monotony.

'**Eintopf** m (-[e]s; ⁓e) gastr. stew.

'**Eintracht** f (-; no pl) harmony.

'**einträchtig** adj harmonious, peaceful.

Eintrag ['aɪntraːk] m (-[e]s; ⁓e) entry.

'**eintragen** (irr, sep, -ge-, h, → **tragen**) **I** v/t **1.** enter (a. ✝), adm. register, enrol(l) (**als Mitglied** as a member): **sich ⁓ lassen** (**bei**) register (with), enrol(l) (in); → **eingetragen. 2.** j-m et. ⁓ earn s.o. praise, sympathy, etc. **II** sich ⁓ a) register, b) put one's name down: **sich in e-e Anwesenheitsliste ⁓** sign in.

einträglich ['aɪntrɛːklɪç] adj profitable.

'**Eintragung** f (-; -en) **1.** registration, enrol(l)ment. **2.** → **Eintrag.**

'**eintreffen** v/i (irr, sep, -ge-, sn, → **treffen**) **1.** arrive (**in** dat, **auf** dat at). **2.** fig. a) happen, b) prove (or come) true.

'**Eintreffen** n (-s) arrival.

'**eintreiben** v/t (irr, sep, -ge-, h, → **treiben**) collect.

'**eintreten** (irr, sep, -ge-, → **treten**) **I** v/i **1.** (sn) go in, come in: **er trat ins Haus ein** he went into (or entered) the house; **bitte, treten Sie ein!** do come in, please! **2.** (sn) **⁓ in** (acc) join, enter (club, firm, etc); **in den Krieg ⁓** enter the war; **in Verhandlungen ⁓** enter into negotiations. **3.** (sn) take place, happen, a. death: occur, case etc: arise: **es trat Stille ein** silence fell; **es ist e-e Besserung eingetreten** there has been an improvement. **4.** (sn) **⁓ für** stand up for s.o., support s.th. **5.** (h) **⁓ auf** (acc) kick. **II** v/t (h) **6.** kick in (or down). **7.** break in (shoes). **8. ich habe mir e-n Dorn** (**in den Fuß**) **eingetreten** I've run a thorn into my foot.

'**eintrichtern** → **einbleuen.**

'**Eintritt** m (-[e]s; -e) **1.** (**in** acc into) entry, entrance: **bei s-m ⁓ in den Klub** on his joining the club. **2.** beginning, onset (of winter etc): **nach ⁓ der Dunkelheit** after dark. **3.** occurrence. **4.** admission: **⁓ frei!** admission free!; **⁓ verboten!** no entry! **5.** → '**Eintrittsgebühr**f, '**Eintrittsgeld** n admission (fee).

'**Eintrittskarte** f (admission) ticket.

'**eintrocknen** v/i (sep, -ge-, sn) dry up.

'**eintrudeln** v/i (sep, -ge-, sn) F turn up.

'**einüben** v/t (sep, -ge-, h) practi/se (Am. -ce), learn.

einverleiben ['aɪnfɛrlaɪbən] v/t (sep, no -ge-, h) **1.** (dat, **in** acc to) add, annex (territory). **2.** F **sich et. ⁓** put away (food, drink).

'**Einvernehmen** n (-s; no pl) agreement, (good) understanding: **in gutem ⁓** on good terms; **im ⁓ mit** in agreement with.

'**einverstanden** adj **⁓ sein** agree; **mit et. ⁓ sein** agree to (or approve of) s.th.; **⁓!** all right!, okay! '**Einverständnis** n (-ses; no pl) **1.** (**zu**) approval (of), consent (to): **sein ⁓ erklären** (give one's) consent. **2.** → **Einvernehmen.**

'**einwachsen** v/i (irr, sep, -ge-, sn, → **wachsen**) grow in(to **in** acc).

Einwand ['aɪnvant] m (-[e]s; ⁓e) objection (**gegen** to).

'**Einwanderer** m (-s; -), '**Einwanderin** f (-; -nen) immigrant. '**einwandern** v/i (sep, -ge-, sn) immigrate (**in** acc to). '**Einwanderung** f (-; -en) immigration. '**Einwanderungs...** immigration (quota, country, etc).

'**einwandfrei** adj impeccable, flawless, perfect: **⁓ der Beste** undoubtedly the best; **es steht ⁓ fest** it is beyond question.

einwärts ['aɪnvɛrts] adv inward(s).

'**einwechseln** v/t (sep, -ge-, h) **1.** change money (**in** acc, **gegen** into). **2.** sports: j-n **⁓** send s.o. on the field.

'**einwecken** → **einmachen.**

'**Einwegflasche** f nonreturnable bottle.

'**Einwegspritze** f ✂ disposable syringe.

'**einweichen** v/t (sep, -ge-, h) soak.

'**einweihen** v/t (sep, -ge-, h) **1.** open, inaugurate, eccl. consecrate. **2.** F fig. christen (a. dress etc). **3.** j-n **⁓ in** (acc) initiate s.o. into; **j-n in ein Geheimnis ⁓** let s.o. into a secret; **eingeweiht sein** be in the know; → **Eingeweihte.**

'**Einweihung** f (-; -en) (formal) opening, eccl. consecration.

'**Einweihungsfeier** f opening ceremony.

'**einweisen** v/t (irr, sep, -ge-, h, → **weisen**) **1.** j-n **⁓ in** (acc) a) assign s.o. to a flat etc, b) ✝ commit s.o. to (a mental institution); **j-n in ein Krankenhaus ⁓** hospitalize s.o. **2.** j-n **⁓ in** (acc) brief s.o. in, introduce s.o. to (*a task etc*), inaugurate s.o. into (*an office*). **3.** direct *car, driver* (**in** *acc* into). '**Einweisung** *f* (-; -en) **1.** 🏛 committal (**in** *acc* to *an institution*); **~ ins Krankenhaus** hospitalization. **2.** (**in** *acc*) briefing (in), introduction (to).

'**einwenden** *v/t* (*irr, sep, -ge-*, h, → **wenden**) *et.* **~** (**gegen**) object (to); **~, daß ...** argue that ...; **ich habe nichts dagegen einzuwenden** I have no objections; **es läßt sich nichts dagegen ~** there is nothing to be said against it.

'**Einwendung** *f* (-; -en) → *Einwand*.

'**einwerfen** *v/t* (*irr, sep, -ge-*, h, → **werfen**) **1.** throw in (*a. fig. remark*). **2.** smash (*window etc*). **3.** post, *Am.* mail (*letter etc*). **4.** insert, put in (*coin*).

einwertig ['aɪnveːɐtɪç] *adj* monovalent.

'**einwickeln** *v/t* (*sep, -ge-*, h) **1.** wrap up. **2.** F *j-n* **~** a) take s.o. in, b) softsoap s.o.

einwilligen ['aɪnvɪlɪɡən] *v/i* (*sep, -ge-*, h) (**in** *acc* to) agree, consent. '**Einwilligung** *f* (-; -en) approval, consent.

'**einwirken** *v/i* (*sep, -ge-*, h) **~ auf** (*acc*) a) have an effect on, b) affect (*a.* 🜛), c) influence; **auf j-n ~** work on s.o.; **et. ~ lassen** let s.th. take effect.

'**Einwirkung** *f* (-; -en) (**auf** *acc* on) a) effect, b) influence.

Einwohner ['aɪnvoːnɐ] *m* (-s; -), '**Einwohnerin** *f* (-; -nen) inhabitant, resident. '**Einwohnermeldeamt** *n* residents' registration office. '**Einwohnerschaft** *f* (-; *no pl*) inhabitants, population.

'**Einwurf** *m* **1.** *sports*: throw-in. **2.** a) insertion (*of coins*), b) *for letters etc*: slit, opening, *for coins*: slot. **3.** *fig.* remark.

'**Einzahl** *f* (-; *no pl*) *ling.* singular.

'**einzahlen** *v/t* (*sep, -ge-*, h) pay in: **Geld bei der Bank ~** deposit money at the bank; **Geld (auf ein Konto) ~** pay money into an account. '**Einzahlung** *f* (-; -en) payment, *at bank*: deposit.

'**Einzahlungsschein** *m* paying-in (*or* deposit) slip.

einzäunen ['aɪntsɔʏnən] *v/t* (*sep, -ge-*, h) fence in. '**Einzäunung** *f* (-; -en) fence.

'**einzeichnen** *v/t* (*sep, -ge-*, h) a) sketch in, b) mark (**in, auf** *dat* on): **... ist nicht eingezeichnet** ... isn't on the map.

Einzel ['aɪntsəl] (-s; -) *n* tennis: singles. '**Einzelanfertigung** *f* special design: **es ist e-e ~** it was custom-built. **~antrieb**

m 🜛 separate drive. **~aufstellung** *f* 🕂 itemized list. **~beispiel** *n* isolated case. **~betrag** *m* (single) item. **~bett** *n* single bed. **~disziplin** *f* *sports*: individual event. **~exemplar** *n* unique specimen (*book*: copy). **~fall** *m* isolated case.

Einzelgänger ['aɪntsəlɡɛŋɐ] *m* (-s; -), '**Einzelgängerin** *f* (-; -nen) loner.

'**Einzelhaft** *f* solitary confinement. **~handel** *m* retail trade. **~handelspreis** *m* retail price. **~händler(in** *f*) *m* retailer. **~haus** *n* detached house.

'**Einzelheit** *f* (-; -en) detail: **bis in alle ~en** down to the last detail; **auf ~en eingehen** go into detail.

'**Einzelkind** *n* only child.

einzellig ['aɪntsɛlɪç] *adj* monocellular.

'**einzeln** I *adj* **1.** a) single, individual, b) separate, isolated: **ein ~er Schuh** an odd shoe. **2. ~e** several, some, a few; *meteor.* **~e Schauer** scattered showers. II *adv* **3.** a) singly, individually, b) separately: **~ eintreten** enter one by one (*or* one at a time); **~ aufführen** specify, itemize. '**einzelne** I *m, f* (-n; -n) individual: **~ pl** some, a few; **jeder ~ (von uns)** every (single) one (of us). II **das ~** (-n; *no pl*) the detail(s): **im ~n** a) in detail, b) in particular; **ins ~ gehen** go into detail; **~s gefällt mir nicht** I don't like some things (*or* points).

'**Einzelspiel** *n* tennis: singles (match). **~stück** *n* **1.** odd piece. **2.** unique specimen. **~teil** *n* 🜛 (component) part. **~unterricht** *m* private lessons. **~wesen** *n* individual (being). **~zelle** *f* 🏛 solitary cell. **~zimmer** *n* single room.

'**einziehbar** *adj* **1.** 🜛 retractable. **2.** 🕂 collectible. '**einziehen** (*irr, sep, -ge-*, → **ziehen**) I *v/t* (h) **1.** draw *s.th.* in, 🜛 retract, haul *flag* down: **den Kopf ~** duck; **die Segel ~** take in sail; **die Riemen ~** ship the oars. **2.** draw in, inhale, breathe. **3.** put in. **4.** ✕ call up, draft. **5.** 🏛 seize, confiscate, withdraw *banknotes* (from circulation). **6.** collect (*taxes etc*). **7.** → *Erkundigung*. II *v/i* (sn) **8.** enter, march in(to (**in** *acc*), *lodger*: move in(to (**in** *acc*, **bei** with): **er zog ins Parlament ein** he took his seat in Parliament. **9.** *liquid*: soak in.

einzig ['aɪntsɪç] I *adj* **1.** only, single, sole: **kein ~es Auto** not a single car; **sein ~er Halt** his sole support; **nicht ein ~es Mal**

not once. **2.** *der* (*die*) ～e the only one; *nicht ein* ～er not (a single) one; *das* ～e the only thing. **3.** → *einzigartig* I. **II** *adv* **4.** only, (*a.* ～ *und allein*) solely, entirely: *das ist das* ～ *Richtige* that's the only thing to do.

'einzigartig *adj* unique, singular, unequal(l)ed, fantastic, marvel(l)ous.

Ein'zimmerwohnung *f* one-room flat (*Am.* apartment).

'Einzug *m* (-[e]s; ⁻e) **1.** a) entry, b) moving in(to *in a house etc*), c) *fig.* coming. **2.** *print.* indent.

'Einzugsermächtigung *f* standing order for a direct debit.

'Einzugsgebiet *n geol.* catchment area.

'Eipulver *n* dried egg.

E-is ['eːɪs] *n* (-; -) ♪ E sharp.

Eis [aɪs] *n* (-es; *no pl*) a) ice, b) ice cream: F *fig. et. auf* ～ *legen* put s.th. on ice; *das* ～ *brechen* break the ice. ～**bahn** *f* (ice-)skating rink. ～**bär** *m* polar bear. ～**becher** *m gastr.* sundae. ～**bein** *n gastr.* pickled knuckle of pork. ～**berg** *m* iceberg: → *Spitze*¹ 1. ～**beutel** *m* ♣ ice bag. ～**blumen** *pl* frostwork. ～**bombe** *f* glace bombe. bombe glacée.

'Eischnee *m gastr.* beaten egg white.

'Eisdiele *f* ice-cream parlo(u)r.

Eisen ['aɪzən] *n* (-s; *no pl*) iron: *fig. ein heißes* ～ *anfassen* tackle a hot issue; *j-n zum alten* ～ *werfen* throw s.o. on the scrap heap, shelve s.o.; *er gehört zum alten* ～ he's past it; *zwei* ～ *im Feuer haben* have more than one string to one's bow; (*man muß*) *das* ～ *schmieden, solange es heiß ist* strike while the iron is hot.

'Eisenbahn *f* a) railway, *Am.* railroad, b) train: *mit der* ～ by rail, by train.

Eisenbahner ['aɪzənbaːnər] *m* (-s; -) F railwayman, *Am.* railroadman.

'Eisenbahn|knotenpunkt *m* (railway, *Am.* railroad) junction. ～**netz** *n* railway (*Am.* railroad) network. ～**schaffner** *m* guard, conductor, *Am.* railroad car. ～**wagen** *m* railway carriage, coach, *Am.* railroad car.

'Eisen|erz *n* iron ore. ～**gehalt** *m* iron content. ～**gießerei** *f* iron foundry. ～**guß** *m* (-sses; *no pl*) **1.** iron casting. **2.** cast iron.

'eisenhaltig *adj* **1.** ～ *sein* contain iron. **2.** *min.* ferruginous.

'Eisen|hut *m* (-[e]s; *no pl*) ♣ monkshood.

～**hütte** *f*, ～**hüttenwerk** *n* ironworks. ～**mangel** *m* ♣ iron deficiency. ～**o,xyd** *n* ♣ ferric oxide.

'Eisenwaren *pl* ironware, hardware. ～**geschäft** *n* hardware store.

'Eisenzeit *f* (-; *no pl*) *hist.* the Iron age.

eisern ['aɪzərn] *adj* a) *fig.* iron, of iron, *nerves* of steel, b) adamant, firm: ～**e** *Sparsamkeit* rigorous economy; ～**e** *Gesundheit* cast-iron constitution; ～**er** *Bestand* permanent stock; ～**e** *Regel* hard and fast rule; *s-e* ～**e** *Ruhe* his imperturbability; ～ *festhalten an* (*dat*) adhere rigidly to; ～ *sparen* save rigorously; → *Lunge* 1.

'Eiseskälte *f* icy cold.

'eisfrei *adj* free of ice. **'eisgekühlt** *adj* chilled. **'Eisglätte** *f* icy roads.

'Eishockey *n* ice hockey. ～**schläger** *m* ice-hockey stick. ～**spieler** *m* ice-hockey player.

eisig ['aɪzɪç] *adj a. fig.* icy.

'Eiskaffee *m gastr.* iced coffee.

'eiskalt *adj* **1.** ice-cold. **2.** *gastr.* chilled. **3.** *fig.* a) icy (*look etc*), b) cold (*as ice*), c) cool, d) brazen.

'Eiskübel *m* ice bucket.

'Eiskunstlauf *m* (-[e]s; *no pl*) figure skating. **'Eiskunstläufer(in** *f*) *m* figure skater. **'Eislauf** *m* (-[e]s; *no pl*) ice-skating. **'eislaufen** *v/i* (*sep*, -ge-, *sn*) ice-skate. **'Eisläufer(in** *f*) *m* ice-skater.

'Eismeer *n* polar sea: *Nördliches* (*Südliches*) ～ Arctic (Antarctic) Ocean.

'Eispickel *m* ice pick.

'Eisprung *m physiol.* ovulation.

'Eis|re,vue *f* ice show. ～**sa,lat** *m* iceberg lettuce. ～**schnellauf** *m* (-[e]s; *no pl*) speed skating. ～**schnelläufer(in** *f*) *m* speed skater. ～**scholle** *f* ice floe. ～**schrank** *m* refrigerator, F fridge, *Am.* icebox. ～**stadion** *n* ice stadium. ～**tanz** *m* ice dancing. ～**torte** *f* ice-cream gateau. ～**waffel** *f* ice-cream wafer. ～**wasser** *n* ice water. ～**würfel** *m* ice cube. ～**zapfen** *m* icicle.

'Eiszeit *f* (-; *no pl*) ice age, glacial period. **'Eiszeitmensch** *m* glacial man.

eitel ['aɪtəl] *adj* **1.** vain, conceited. **2.** vain, futile: *eitle Hoffnung* idle hope. **'Eitelkeit** *f* (-; *no pl*) vanity, *a.* futility.

Eiter ['aɪtər] *m* (-s; *no pl*) ♣ pus. **'Eiterbeule** *f* abscess, boil, *fig.* festering sore. **'Eiterbläschen** *n* pustule. **'eit(e)rig**

adj suppurative, festering. **'eitern** *v/i* (h) fester, suppurate. **'Eiterpfropf** *m* core. **'Eiterung** *f* (-; -en) suppuration.
'Eiweiß *n* (-es; -e) white of egg, (egg) white, *biol.* albumen, protein. **2arm** *adj* low in protein, low-protein (*diet*). **~bedarf** *m* protein requirement. **~mangel** *m* protein deficiency. **2reich** *adj* rich in protein, high-protein (*diet*).
'Eizelle *f biol.* egg cell, ovum.
Ejakulation [ejakula'tsĭo:n] *f* (-; -en) *physiol.* ejaculation.
Ekel¹ ['e:kəl] *m* (-s; *no pl*) (*vor dat*) disgust (at), revulsion (against): ~ *empfinden* → *ekeln*; F ... *ist* (*sind*) *mir ein* ~ I can't stand ..., I loathe ...
'Ekel² *n* (-s; -) F nasty person, beast.
'ekelerregend *adj* repulsive. **'Ekelgefühl** *n* revulsion. **'ekelhaft**, **'ek(e)lig** *adj* revolting, disgusting. **'ekeln: sich ~** (h) *ich ekle mich davor* (*vor ihm*) it (he) makes me sick.
Eklat [e'kla:] *m* (-s; -s) a) stir, sensation, b) scandal, c) row.
eklatant [ekla'tant] *adj* a) striking, b) *contp.* flagrant, blatant.
Eklipse [e'klɪpsə] *f* (-; -n) *astr.* eclipse.
Ekstase [ɛk'sta:zə] *f* (-; -n) ecstasy: *in ~ geraten* go into ecstasies (*über acc* over). **ek'statisch** [-tɪʃ] *adj* ecstatic.
Ekzem [ɛk'tse:m] *n* (-s; -e) *med.* eczema.
Elan [e'la:n] *m* (-s; *no pl*) verve, zest.
Elastik [e'lastɪk] *n* (-s; -s) elastic.
elastisch [e'lastɪʃ] *adj* elastic (*a. fig.*), springy, *mot.*, ⊗ flexible (*a. fig.*).
Elastizität [elastitsi'tɛ:t] *f* (-; *no pl*) *a. fig.* elasticity, flexibility.
Elch [ɛlç] *m* (-[e]s; -e) *zo.* elk, moose.
Elefant [ele'fant] *m* (-en; -en) elephant: *wie ein ~ im Porzellanladen* like a bull in a china shop.
Ele'fanten|bulle *m zo.* bull elephant. **~hochzeit** *f* ✝ giant merger. **~kuh** *f zo.* cow elephant. **~rüssel** *m* trunk.
elegant [ele'gant] *adj* elegant (*a. fig.*), smart: *e-e ~e Lösung* a neat (*or* clever) solution. **Eleganz** [ele'gants] *f* (-; *no pl*) *a. fig.* elegance.
Elegie [ele'gi:] *f* (-; -n) elegy. **elegisch** [e'le:gɪʃ] *adj* elegiac, *fig. a.* melancholy.
elektrifizieren [elɛktrifi'tsi:rən] *v/t* (h) electrify. **Elektrifi'zierung** *f* (-; -en) electrification. **Elektrik** [e'lɛktrɪk] *f* (-; *no pl*) **1.** electricity. **2.** electrical system.

Elektriker [e'lɛktrɪkɐ] *m* (-s; -) electrician. **elektrisch** [e'lɛktrɪʃ] **I** *adj* electric(al): **~er Schlag** (*Strom, Stuhl*) electric shock (current, chair). **II** *adv* electrically, by electricity. **elektrisieren** [elɛktri'zi:rən] *v/t* (h) *a. fig.* electrify. **Elektrizität** [elɛktritsi'tɛ:t] *f* (-; *no pl*) electricity, (electric) current.
Elektrizi'tätsversorgung *f* electricity (*or* power) supply. **Elektrizi'tätswerk** *n* (electric) power station.
Elektroauto [e'lɛktro-] *n* electric car.
E'lektrobohrer *m* electric drill.
E'lektroche,mie *f* electrochemistry.
Elektrode [elɛk'tro:də] *f* (-; -n) electrode: *negative ~* cathode; *positive ~* anode.
E'lektro|enzephalo,gramm *n* ∦ (*abbr.* EEG) electroencephalogram. **~fahrzeug** *n* electric vehicle. **~gerät** *n* electrical appliance. **~geschäft** *n* electrical shop. **~herd** *m* electric cooker. **~inge-ni,eur** *m* electrical engineer. **~kardio,gramm** *n* ∦ (*abbr.* EKG) electrocardiogram.
Elektrolyse [elɛktro'ly:zə] *f* (-; -n) electrolysis.
E'lektromotor *m* (electric) motor.
Elektron [e'lɛktrɔn] *n* (-s; -en [elɛk-'tro:nən]) *phys.* electron.
Elek'tronen|blitz(gerät *n*) *m phot.* electronic flash (gun). **~gehirn** *n* electronic brain. **~mikro,skop** *n* electron microscope. **~rechner** *m* computer. **~röhre** *f* electronic valve (*Am.* tube).
Elektronik [elɛk'tro:nɪk] *f* (-; *no pl*) **1.** electronics. **2.** electronic system.
elek'tronisch [-nɪʃ] *adj* electronic.
E'lektro|ofen *m* electric stove. **~ra,sierer** *m* electric razor. **~schock** *m* ∦ electroshock.
Elektro|'technik *f* electrical engineering. **~'techniker** *m* electrical engineer. **2'technisch** *adj* electrotechnical, electrical (*component, industry, etc*).
Elektrothera'pie *f* ∦ electrotherapy.
Element [ele'mɛnt] *n* (-[e]s; -e) element, ⚡ *a.* battery, cell: *fig. in s-m ~ sein* be in one's element; *contp.* *asoziale ~e* antisocial elements.
elementar [elemɛn'ta:r] *adj* **1.** elemental. **2.** elementary (*duty, mistake, etc*).
Elemen'tar|begriff *m* fundamental idea. **~gewalt** *f* elemental force. **~teil-**

chen *n phys.* elementary particle. **~unterricht** *m* elementary instruction.
elend ['e:lɛnt] I *adj* **1.** *a. fig. contp.* miserable, wretched: **~ aussehen** look ill; **sich ~ fühlen** feel wretched (*or* terrible). **2.** poverty-stricken, pitiable. **3.** F *fig.* terrible, awful. II *adv* **4.** miserably. **5.** F *fig.* terribly, awfully. **'Elend** *n* (*-s; no pl*) misery, poverty: → **stürzen** 3.
'Elendsquar,tier *n* hovel.
'Elendsviertel *n* slum(s).
elf [ɛlf] *adj* eleven. **Elf** f (*-; -en*) **1.** (number) eleven. **2.** *soccer:* team.
Elf *m* (*-en; -en*), **Elfe** ['ɛlfə] f (*-; -n*) elf.
'Elfenbein *n* (*-[e]s; no pl*), **'elfenbeinern** *adj*, **'elfenbeinfarbig** *adj* ivory.
'Elfenbeinturm *m fig.* ivory tower.
Elf'meter *m soccer:* penalty (kick). **~schießen** *n* (penalty) shoot-out.
elft [ɛlft] *adj*, **Elfte** ['ɛlftə] *m, f* (*-n; -n*) eleventh. **elftens** ['ɛlftəns] *adv* in the eleventh place.
eliminieren [elimi'ni:rən] *v/t* (h) eliminate.
elitär [eli'tɛ:r] *adj* elitist. **Elite** [e'li:tə] f (*-; -n*) élite. **E'litedenken** *n* elitism.
Elixier [elɪ'ksi:r] *n* (*-s; -e*) elixir.
'Ellbogen *m* (*-s; -*) elbow. **~freiheit** f elbow room. **~gelenk** *n* elbow joint. **~gesellschaft** f dog-eat-dog society. **~mensch** *m* ruthless go-getter.
ellenlang ['ɛlən-] *adj* F *fig.* endless.
Ellipse [ɛ'lɪpsə] f (*-; -n*) A ellipse.
elliptisch [ɛ'lɪptɪʃ] *adj* A elliptic(al).
Elsässer ['ɛlzɛsər] *m* (*-s; -*), **'Elsässerin** f (*-; -nen*), **'elsässisch** *adj* Alsatian.
Elster ['ɛlstər] f (*-; -n*) *zo.* magpie.
elterlich ['ɛltərlɪç] *adj* parental (*duty, love, etc*), parents' (*bedroom etc*).
Eltern ['ɛltərn] *pl* parents: F *fig.* **nicht von schlechten ~** terrific.
'Elternabend *m* parent-teacher meeting. **'Elternbeirat** *m ped.* parents' council. **'Elternhaus** *n* (one's parents') home. **'elternlos** *adj* orphan(ed).
'Elternschaft f (*-; no pl*) **1.** parenthood. **2.** parents. **'Elternsprechtag** *m ped.* open day. **'Elternteil** *m* parent.
Email [e'mai(l)] *n* (*-s; -s*), **Emaille** [e'maljə] f (*-; -n*), **emaillieren** [ema(l)'ji:rən] *v/t* (h) enamel.
Emanze [e'mantsə] f (*-; -n*) F *contp.* women's libber. **Emanzipation** [emantsipa'tsio:n] f (*-; -en*) emancipation: **die**

~ der Frau *a.* women's liberation.
emanzipatorisch [emantsipa'to:rɪʃ] *adj* emancipatory. **emanzipieren** [emantsi'pi:rən] (h) I *v/t* emancipate. II **sich ~** become emancipated.
Embargo [ɛm'bargo] *n* (*-s; -s*) embargo.
Emblem [ɛm'ble:m] *n* (*-s; -e*) emblem.
Embolie [ɛmbo'li:] f (*-; -n*) ✚ embolism.
Embryo ['ɛmbryo] *m* (*-s; -s, -nen* [ɛmbry'o:nən]) embryo. **embryonal** [ɛmbryo'na:l] *adj* embryonic, embryo.
emeritieren [emeri'ti:rən] *v/t* (h) retire.
Emigrant [emi'grant] *m* (*-en; -en*), **Emi'grantin** f (*-; -en*) emigrant.
Emigration [emigra'tsio:n] f (*-; -en*) emigration: **in der (die) ~** in(to) exile.
emigrieren [emi'gri:rən] *v/i* (sn) emigrate.
Emission [emɪ'sio:n] f (*-; -en*) **1.** *phys.* emission. **2.** ✝ issue.
Emotion [emo'tsio:n] f (*-; -en*) emotion.
emotional [emotsio'na:l] *adj* emotional.
emotionalisieren [emotsionali'zi:rən] *v/t* (h) emotionalize.
emotionell [emotsio'nɛl] *adj* emotional.
empfahl [ɛm'pfa:l] *pret* of **empfehlen**.
empfand [ɛm'pfant] *pret* of **empfinden**.
Empfang [ɛm'pfaŋ] *m* (*-[e]s; ⁓e*) **1.** *no pl* receipt: **nach ~, bei ~** on receipt; **in ~ nehmen** a) receive, b) meet (*s.o.*). **2.** *no pl* reception (*a. radio etc*), welcome: **j-m e-n begeisterten ~ bereiten** give s.o. an enthusiastic reception. **3.** *hotel etc:* reception (desk). **4.** reception.
emp'fangen (empfing, empfangen, h) I *v/t* receive (*a. radio etc*), welcome: **sie empfängt niemanden** she refuses to see anybody; **wir wurden sehr freundlich ~** we met with a friendly reception. II *v/i biol.* conceive.
Empfänger [ɛm'pfɛŋər] *m* (*-s; -*) receiver (*a. radio etc*), recipient, ☏ addressee.
empfänglich [ɛm'pfɛŋlɪç] *adj* (**für** to) receptive, susceptible (*a.* ✿), ✚ prone.
Emp'fänglichkeit f (*-; no pl*) (**für** to) receptivity, *a.* ✿ susceptibility.
Empfängnis [ɛm'pfɛŋnɪs] f (*-; no pl*) biol. conception. **⍥verhütend** *adj* (**a. ~es Mittel**) contraceptive. **~verhütung** f contraception.
Emp'fangs|an,tenne f reception aerial (*Am.* antenna). **~bereich** *m radio etc:* **1.** range of reception. **2.** frequency range. **~bescheinigung** f receipt. **~be-**

stätigung *f* acknowledg(e)ment of receipt. **~chef(in** *f*) *m* reception (*Am.* room) clerk. **~dame** *f* receptionist.

empfehlen [ɛm'pfeːlən] (empfahl, empfohlen, h) **I** *v/t* **1.** recommend (*j-m et.* s.th. to s.o.): *nicht zu* ~ not to be recommended; *es empfiehlt sich zu inf* it is advisable to *inf*. **II** *sich* ~ **2.** recommend itself. **3.** take one's leave.

emp'fehlenswert *adj* a) recommendable, b) advisable. **Emp'fehlung** *f* (-; -en) (*auf* ~ on) recommendation: *gute ~en haben* have good references.

Emp'fehlungsschreiben *n* letter of recommendation.

empfinden [ɛm'pfɪndən] *v/t* (empfand, empfunden, h) feel (*a. v/i*): *et. als lästig* ~ find s.th. a nuisance. **Emp'finden** *n* (-s) a) feeling, b) opinion, c) sense: *nach m-m* ~ the way I see it.

empfindlich [ɛm'pfɪntlɪç] *adj* **1.** sensitive (*gegen* to) (*a. ✍, phot., ☉*), delicate: *fig. ~e Stelle* tender spot. **2.** touchy, irritable (*a. stomach*): ~ *reagieren* overreact. **3.** severe (*cold, penalty, etc*), bad (*loss*): ~ *kalt* bitterly cold; *fig. er war* ~ *getroffen* he was badly hit. **Emp'findlichkeit** *f* (-; *no pl*) **1.** a) sensitivity (*gegen* to), *phot. a.* speed, b) delicacy. **2.** touchiness, irritability.

emp'findsam *adj* **1.** sensitive. **2.** sentimental. **Emp'findsamkeit** *f* (-; *no pl*) sensitivity, sentimentality.

Emp'findung *f* (-; -en) a) sensation, perception, b) feeling, emotion.

emp'findungslos *adj* insensitive (*für, gegen* to), numb (*limb*).

empfing [ɛm'pfɪŋ] *pret of* **empfangen.**

empfohlen [ɛm'pfoːlən] **I** *pp of* **empfehlen. II** *adj* recommended.

empfunden [ɛm'pfʊndən] *pp of* **empfinden.**

empirisch [ɛm'piːrɪʃ] *adj* empirical.

empor [ɛm'poːr] *adv lit.* up, upward(s).

Empore [ɛm'poːrə] *f* (-; -n) △ gallery.

empören [ɛm'pøːrən] (h) **I** *v/t* **1.** shock, outrage. **II** *sich* ~ **2.** be outraged (*über acc* at). **3.** rebel (*gegen* against).

em'pörend *adj* outrageous, shocking.

Emporkömmling [ɛm'poːrkœmlɪŋ] *m* (-s; -e) upstart, parvenu.

em'pört I *pp of* **empören. II** *adj* indignant (*über acc* at).

Em'pörung *f* (-; -en) **1.** *no pl* indignation

(*über acc* at). **2.** revolt, rebellion.

emsig ['ɛmzɪç] *adj* busy, industrious, hard-working. **'Emsigkeit** *f* (-; *no pl*) **1.** bustle. **2.** industry, zeal.

Emulsion [emʊl'zɪoːn] *f* (-; -en) emulsion.

'E-Mu₁sik *f* (-; *no pl*) serious music.

'Endabrechnung *f* final account.

'Endbahnhof *m* terminus.

'Endbetrag *m* (sum) total.

Ende ['ɛndə] *n* (-s; -n) **1.** *no pl* end, *a.* ending (*of film etc*): ~ (*der Durchsage*)! end of the message!, *radio:* over (and out)!; ~ *Mai* at the end of May; ~ *der dreißiger Jahre* in the late thirties; *am* ~ a) in the end, after all, b) eventually, c) maybe; *letzten ~s* when all is said and done; *ich bin am* ~ I'm finished; *bis zum bitteren* ~ to the bitter end; *e-r Sache ein ~ machen* (*or bereiten*) put an end to s.th.; *et. zu ~ führen* finish s.th., see s.th. through; *zu ~ gehen* a) → **enden,** b) run short; *zu ~ sein* be over, *time:* be up; *ein böses ~ nehmen* come to a bad end; *~ gut, alles gut* all's well that ends well; F *das dicke ~ kommt nach* there will be hell to pay; *die Arbeit geht ihrem ~ entgegen* the work is nearing completion; *es geht mit ihm zu ~* he's going fast; → **Latein, Lied, Weisheit. 2.** F a) (small) piece, b) *no pl* (long) distance (*or way*).

'Endef,fekt *m* final result: *im* ~ in the final analysis, in the end.

endemisch [ɛn'deːmɪʃ] *adj* ✍ endemic.

enden ['ɛndən] *v/i* (h) (come to an) end, draw to a close, finish, stop, *contract etc:* expire: *mit e-r Prügelei* ~ end in a brawl; *ling.* ~ *auf* (*acc*) end with; *nicht ~ wollend* unending; *das Stück endet tragisch* the play has a tragic ending.

'Endergebnis *n* final result.

'Endgeschwindigkeit *f* final velocity.

'endgültig I *adj* final: *e-e* ~ *Antwort* a definite answer. **II** *adv* a) finally, b) for good: *das steht* ~ *fest* that's final.

'Endgültigkeit *f* (-; *no pl*) finality.

Endivie [ɛn'diːvjə] *f* (-; -n) ✿ endive.

'Endkampf *m sports:* (*in den* ~ *kommen* reach the) final(s). **'Endlagerung** *f* ultimate disposal (*of nuclear waste*).

endlich ['ɛntlɪç] **I** *adj* final, ultimate, A, *philos.* finite. **II** *adv* finally, at last.

'endlos *adj* endless.

'**Endlosigkeit** f (-; no pl) endlessness.
'**Endlösung** f pol. hist. Final Solution.
endogen [ɛndo'geːn] adj endogenous.
Endoskop [ɛndo'skoːp] n (-s; -e) ☞ endoscope.
'**End|phase** f final stage. **~preis** m retail price. **~pro,dukt** n end product. **~reim** m end rhyme. **~resul,tat** n final result. **~runde** f sports: final(s). **~silbe** f final syllable. **~spiel** n sports: final(s): **ins ~ einziehen** go to the finals. **~spurt** m a. fig. final sprint. **~stati,on** f 1. terminus. 2. fig. end of the road. **~summe** f (sum) total.
'**Endung** f (-; -en) ling. ending.
'**End|verbraucher** m end user. **~verstärker** m ⚡ output amplifier. **~ziel** n final objective, ultimate goal. **~ziffer** f last number. **~zweck** m final purpose.
Energie [ɛnɛr'giː] f (-; -n) energy (a. fig.), ⚡ a. power. **Ener'giebedarf** m energy demand. **ener'giegeladen** adj fig. bursting with energy. **Ener'giekrise** f energy crisis. **ener'gielos** adj lacking energy, weak. **Ener'gielosigkeit** f (-; no pl) lack of energy. **Ener'gie|poli,tik** f energy policy. **~quelle** f source of energy. ⚡**sparend** adj energy-saving. **~verbrauch** m energy consumption. **~verschwendung** f waste of energy (fig. of effort). **~versorgung** f power supply. **~wirtschaft** f (-; no pl) energy industry.
energisch [e'nɛrgɪʃ] adj energetic, firm (words etc), strong (protest etc): **~ werden** put one's foot down.
eng [ɛŋ] adj 1. narrow (a. fig.), crowded, cramped, tight (skirt etc): **~er werden** narrow; **ein Kleid ~er machen** take a dress in; **auf ~em Raum zs.-leben** live crowded together; fig. **in ~en Grenzen** within narrow bounds; F **das wird zeitlich sehr ~ für mich** I've got a tight schedule already; F **das darf man nicht so ~ sehen!** let's be (more) broadminded!; → **Sinn** 5, **Wahl** 2. **2.** fig. close (cooperation etc): **~ befreundet sein** be close friends; → **Kreis** 1.
Engagement [ãɡaʒə'mãː] n (-s; -s) **1.** thea. etc engagement. **2.** pol. or fig. commitment. **engagieren** [ãɡa'ʒiːrən] (h) **I** v/t engage, employ, take s.o. on. **II sich ~** pol. or fig. get (or be) involved (**in**

dat **in**). **enga'giert** adj fig. dedicated, pol. committed.
'**enganliegend** adj tight(-fitting).
Enge ['ɛŋə] f (-; -n) **1.** no pl narrowness (a. fig.), tightness: **in großer ~ leben** live in very cramped conditions; fig. **j-n in die ~ treiben** drive s.o. into a corner. **2.** narrow passage, (of sea) strait.
Engel ['ɛŋəl] m (-s; -) angel: F **die ~ im Himmel singen hören** see stars.
'**engelhaft** adj angelic.
'**Engelsgeduld** f endless patience.
'**engherzig** adj small-minded. '**Engherzigkeit** f (-; no pl) small-mindedness.
Engländer ['ɛŋlɛndər] m (-s; -) **1.** Englishman: **er ist ~** he is English; **die ~** the English. **2.** ⚙ monkey wrench.
'**Engländerin** f (-; -nen) Englishwoman.
englisch ['ɛŋlɪʃ] adj English: **die ~e Staatskirche** the Anglican Church; (**gut**) **~ sprechen** speak English (well); **~ geschrieben** (written) in English.
'**Englisch** n (-[s]) English, the English language: **aus dem ~en übersetzt** translated from (the) English; **im ~en** in English; **er spricht gut(es) ~** he speaks good English.
'**englisch-'deutsch** adj **1.** pol. Anglo--German. **2.** ling. English-German.
'**Englischhorn** n ♪ cor anglais.
'**englischsprachig** adj English-language. '**englischsprechend** adj English-speaking. '**Englischunterricht** m English lesson(s).
'**engmaschig** [-maʃɪç] adj fine-meshed, fig. close-meshed.
'**Engpaß** m (-sses; -sse) fig. a) bottleneck, b) supply shortfall.
en gros [ã'gro] adv ☞ wholesale.
engstirnig [-ʃtɪrnɪç] adj narrow-minded. '**Engstirnigkeit** f (-; no pl) narrow-mindedness.
Enkel ['ɛŋkəl] m (-s; -) a) grandchild, b) grandson.
'**Enkelin** f (-; -nen) granddaughter.
Enklave [ɛn'klaːvə] f (-; -n) enclave.
enorm [e'nɔrm] adj enormous, huge, F terrific: **~ schnell** incredibly fast.
en passant [ãpa'sã] adv in passing.
Ensemble [ã'sãːbl] n (-s; -s) **1.** ♪, fashion: ensemble. **2.** thea. a) company, b) cast.
entarten [ɛnt'ʔartən] v/i (sn) degenerate.

ent'artet I *pp of* **entarten. II** *adj* degenerate, *fig. a.* decadent.

Ent'artung *f* (-; -en) degeneration.

entband [ɛnt'bant] *pret of* **entbinden.**

entbehren [ɛnt'be:rən] *v/t* (h) **1.** do without: **kannst du ... ~?** can you spare ...? **2.** miss. **ent'behrlich** *adj* dispensable, expendable.

Ent'behrung *f* (-; -en) privation, want.

ent'binden (entband, entbunden, h) **I** *v/t* **1.** *♣* deliver woman (**von** of): **entbunden werden von ... ** *a.* give birth to ... **2.** *fig.* (**von** from) release, excuse. **II** *v/i* **3.** *♣* give birth to a child.

Ent'bindung *f* (-; -en) **1.** *♣* delivery. **2.** *fig.* release (**von** from).

Ent'bindungsklinik *f* maternity clinic.

Ent'bindungsstati,on *f* maternity ward.

ent'blättern (h) **I** *v/t* **1.** strip *s.th.* of leaves. **II** *sich ~* **2.** shed (its) leaves. **3.** *humor.* shed one's clothes, strip.

entblöden [ɛnt'blø:dən] (h) *sich nicht ~ zu inf* have the nerve to *inf.*

entblößen [ɛnt'blø:sən] *v/t* (h) bare.

ent'blößt I *pp of* **entblößen. II** *adj* bare.

ent'brennen *v/i* (entbrannte, entbrannt, sn) *fight etc*: break out, *a. rage etc*: flare up.

ent'decken *v/t* (h) a) discover, find out, b) see, spot: **zufällig ~** stumble (up)on.

Ent'decker *m* (-s; -) discoverer.

Ent'deckung *f* (-; -en) discovery.

Ent'deckungsreise *f a. fig.* expedition.

Ente ['ɛntə] *f* (-; -n) **1.** *zo.* duck: **junge ~** duckling; *F fig.* **lahme ~** slowpoke. **2.** *gastr.* a) roast duck, b) **kalte ~** white wine cup with champagne. **3.** canard, hoax. **4.** *♣* (bed) urinal.

ent'ehren *v/t* (h) dishono(u)r, disgrace, degrade. **Ent'ehrung** *f* (-; -en) dishono(u)r(ing), degradation.

ent'eignen *v/t* (h) expropriate.

Ent'eignung *f* (-; -en) expropriation.

ent'eisen *v/t* (h) clear of ice, *©* defrost, de-ice. **Ent'eisung** *f* (-; *no pl*) *©* defrosting, de-icing.

'Enten|braten *m* roast duck. **~ei** *n* duck's egg. **~jagd** *f* duck shooting.

ent'erben *v/t* (h) disinherit.

Enterich ['ɛntərɪç] *m* (-s; -e) *zo.* drake.

entern ['ɛntərn] *v/t* (h) board.

entfachen [ɛnt'faxən] *v/t* (h) **1.** kindle (*fire*). **2.** *fig.* a) rouse, b) provoke.

ent'fallen *v/i* (entfiel, entfallen, sn) **1.** *es*

ist mir ~ it has slipped my memory; *der Name ist mir ~* the name escapes me. **2.** be cancel(l)ed: *entfällt* not applicable. **3.** *auf j-n ~* fall to s.o.

ent'falten (h) **I** *v/t* **1.** unfold (*a. fig.*), open, spread out. **2.** *fig.* develop (*talents etc*), launch into (*activity etc*), display (*pomp etc*). **II** *sich ~* **3.** *blossom etc*: open, unfold. **4.** *fig.* develop (*zu* into). **Ent'faltung** *f* (-; -en) **1.** unfolding. **2.** *fig.* a) development, b) display.

ent'färben *v/t* (h) remove the colo(u)r from, *🐾, ©* decolo(u)rize, bleach.

entfernen [ɛnt'fɛrnən] (h) **I** *v/t a.* fig. remove: *j-n von der Schule ~* expel s.o. from school. **II** *sich ~* leave, go away.

ent'fernt *adj a. fig.* remote, distant, *a.* faint (*similarity etc*): *e-e Meile ~ von* a mile away from; *zwei Meilen voneinander ~* two miles apart; (*weit*) *~* far away; *fig. weit davon ~ zu inf* far from ger; *~ verwandt* distantly related; *nicht im ~esten* not in the least.

Ent'fernung *f* (-; -en) **1.** a) distance, b) range: *in e-r ~ von* at a distance of; *aus der* (*einiger*) *~* from the (a) distance; *aus kurzer ~* at close range. **2.** removal.

Ent'fernungs|messer *m phot.* range finder. **~skala** *f phot.* focus(s)ing scale.

ent'fesseln *v/t* (h) unleash, provoke: *e-n Krieg ~* start a war.

ent'fesselt *adj* raging (*elements etc*).

ent'fetten *v/t* (h) remove the grease (*or* fat) from, *©* degrease.

entfiel [ɛnt'fi:l] *pret of* **entfallen.**

ent'flammbar *adj* inflammable.

ent'flammen I *v/t* (h) **1.** *©* ignite. **2.** *fig.* inflame, rouse, kindle. **II** *v/i* (sn) → 1.

ent'flechten *v/t* (entflocht, entflochten, h) *♣* decartelize.

ent'fliegen *v/i* (entflog, entflogen, sn) fly away (*dat* from).

entfliehen *v/i* (entfloh, entflohen, sn) ([*aus*] *dat* from) flee, escape.

entfremden [ɛnt'frɛmdən] (h) **I** *v/t* alienate (*dat* from). **II** *sich* (*j-m*) *~* become estranged (from s.o.).

Ent'fremdung *f* (-; -en) estrangement, *a. sociol.* alienation.

ent'frosten *v/t* (h) *©* defrost.

Ent'froster *m* (-s; -) *©* defroster.

ent'führen *v/t* (h) kidnap, abduct, *✈* hijack. **Ent'führer** *m* (-s; -) kidnap-

(p)er, ✈ hijacker. **Ent'führung** f (-; -en) kidnap(p)ing, ✈ hijacking.

entgalt [ɛntˈɡalt] pret of **entgelten**.

entgangen [ɛntˈɡaŋən] pp of **entgehen**.

ent'gegen I prep (dat) contrary to, against: ~ **allen Erwartungen** contrary to all expectations. **II** adv towards.

ent'gegenbringen v/t (irr, sep, -ge-, h, → **bringen**) j-m **Vertrauen** (**Zuneigung**) ~ show trust in (affection for) s.o.; **e-r Sache Interesse** ~ show an interest in s.th.

ent'gegengehen v/i (irr, sep, -ge-, sn, → **gehen**) (dat) **1.** walk towards, go to meet. **2.** fig. face (danger, the future, etc), be heading for (disaster etc): **dem Ende** ~ be drawing to a close.

ent'gegengesetzt adj **1.** opposite. **2.** fig. contrary, opposed (dat to), opposing.

ent'gegenhalten v/t (irr, sep, -ge-, h, → **halten**) fig. object (dat to): **dem ist nichts entgegenzuhalten** there is no objection to that.

ent'gegenkommen v/i (irr, sep, -ge-, sn, → **kommen**) j-m ~ come towards s.o., fig. oblige s.o., make s.o. concessions; **j-m auf halbem Wege** ~ esp. fig. meet s.o. halfways; **j-s Wünschen** ~ comply with s.o.'s wishes. **Ent'gegenkommen** n (-s) obligingness: ~ **zeigen** be willing to make concessions. **ent'gegenkommend** adj oncoming, fig. obliging.

ent'gegenlaufen v/i (irr, sep, -ge-, sn, → **laufen**) j-m ~ run towards s.o.

Ent'gegennahme [-na:mə] f (-; no pl) acceptance.

ent'gegennehmen v/t (irr, sep, -ge-, h, → **nehmen**) accept, take.

ent'gegensehen v/i (irr, sep, -ge-, h, → **sehen**) (dat) a) await, b) look forward (to), c) face.

ent'gegensetzen v/t (sep, -ge-, h) **Widerstand** ~ offer resistance (dat to).

ent'gegenstehen v/i (irr, sep, -ge-, h, → **stehen**) fig. stand in the way (dat of): **dem steht nichts entgegen** there's nothing to be said against that.

ent'gegenstellen: **sich** ~ (sep, -ge-, h) fig. (dat) resist, oppose.

ent'gegentreten v/i (irr, sep, -ge-, sn, → **treten**) **1.** j-m ~ step (or walk) up to s.o., fig. oppose s.o. **2.** take steps against (abuses etc), contradict (rumo[u]r).

ent'gegenwirken v/i (sep, -ge-, h) (dat)

work against, counteract, fight.

entgegnen [ɛntˈɡe:ɡnən] v/i (h) a) reply (**auf** acc to), b) retort.

ent'gehen v/i (entging, entgangen, sn) escape (a. death etc): fig. j-m ~ escape s.o.('s notice); **sich et.** ~ **lassen** let s.th. slip; **er ließ sich die Gelegenheit nicht** ~ he seized the opportunity.

entgeistert [ɛntˈɡaɪstərt] adj and adv dum(b)founded, aghast.

Entgelt [ɛntˈɡɛlt] n (-[e]s; -e) a) remuneration, payment, b) pay, c) fee, ⚖ consideration, d) reward: **gegen** ~ against payment; **als** ~ **für** in consideration of.

ent'gelten v/t (entgalt, entgolten, h) j-m **et.** ~ pay s.o. for s.th.

entgiften [ɛntˈɡɪftən] v/t (h) a) detoxicate, b) decontaminate (toxic waste etc), c) fig. clear (the atmosphere).

entging [ɛntˈɡɪŋ] pret of **entgehen**.

entgleisen [ɛntˈɡlaɪzən] v/i (sn) **1.** 🚂 run off the rails, be derailed. **2.** fig. go too far, make a faux pas.

Ent'gleisung f (-; -en) **1.** 🚂 derailment. **2.** fig. faux pas, gaffe.

ent'gleiten v/i (entglitt, entglitten, sn) j-m ~ slip out of s.o.'s hand(s), fig. slip away from s.o.

entgolten [ɛntˈɡɔltən] pp of **entgelten**.

entgräten [ɛntˈɡre:tən] v/t (h) bone.

ent'haaren v/t (h) depilate. **Ent'haarungscreme** f depilatory cream.

ent'halten (enthielt, enthalten, h) **I** v/t a) contain, hold, b) comprise: **mit** ~ **sein** be included (**in** dat in). **II sich** ~ abstain (gen from); **sich der Stimme** ~ abstain.

ent'haltsam adj abstinent, abstemious, sexually: continent.

Ent'haltsamkeit f (-; no pl) abstinence.

Ent'haltung f (-; parl. -en) abstention.

ent'härten v/t (h) soften (water).

enthaupten [ɛntˈhaʊptən] v/t (h) behead, decapitate. **Ent'hauptung** f (-; -en) beheading, decapitation.

ent'häuten v/t (h) skin.

ent'heben v/t (enthob, enthoben, h) (gen) relieve (of), release (or exempt) (from), remove (from office).

enthielt [ɛntˈhi:lt] pret of **enthalten**.

enthüllen [ɛntˈhʏlən] (h) **I** v/t **1.** unveil, bare, show. **2.** fig. reveal, bring s.th. to light, expose. **II sich** ~ fig. reveal o.s., matter: be revealed (dat to). **Ent'hüllung** f (-; -en) **1.** unveiling. **2.** fig. disclosure, exposure. **Ent'hüllungsjourna,lismus** m investigative journalism.

Enthusiasmus [εntu'ziasmʊs] m (-; no pl) enthusiasm. **Enthusiast** [εntu'ziast] m (-en; -en), **Enthusi'astin** f (-; -nen) enthusiast, F fan. **enthusi'astisch** adj enthusiastic.

entjungfern [εnt'jʊŋfərn] v/t (h) deflower.

ent'kalken v/t (h) descale.

ent'kernen v/t (h) stone, core.

ent'kleiden v/t (h) 1. (a. sich ~) undress. 2. fig. (gen of) divest, strip.

ent'kommen v/i (entkam, entkommen, sn) ([aus] dat from) get away, escape. **Ent'kommen** n (-s) escape, F getaway.

ent'korken v/t (h) uncork.

entkräften [εnt'krεftən] v/t (h) 1. weaken, exhaust. 2. fig. invalidate (a. ⚖), refute. **Ent'kräftung** f (-; -en) 1. a) weakening, b) weakness, exhaustion. 2. fig. invalidation (a. ⚖), refutation.

ent'laden (entlud, entladen, h) **I** v/t 1. unload, a. ⚡ discharge. 2. fig. give vent to, vent (one's rage). **II** sich ~ 3. storm: break. 4. ⚡ discharge. 5. rifle etc: go off. 6. fig. suspense: be released, rage: erupt. **Ent'ladung** f (-; -en) 1. unloading, a. ⚡ discharge. 2. fig. explosion.

ent'lang adv and prep along: die Straße ~ along (or down) the street; hier ~, bitte! this way, please! **ent'langgehen** v/t (irr, sep, -ge-, sn, → gehen) (v/i ~ an dat) go (or walk) along.

entlarven [εnt'larfən] v/t (h) unmask, expose. **Ent'larvung** f (-; -en) unmasking, exposure.

ent'lassen (entließ, entlassen, h) v/t 1. a) dismiss, b) pension off: j-n fristlos ~ dismiss s.o. without notice. 2. (aus dat from) discharge (patient etc), release (prisoner). **Ent'lassung** f (-; -en) 1. dismissal. 2. (aus dat from) discharge, release. **Ent'lassungspa,piere** pl discharge papers.

ent'lasten v/t (h) relieve (fig. von of), ⚖ exonerate, clear s.o. of a charge, ✝ give s.o. a release. **ent'lastend** adj ⚖ exonerating. **Ent'lastung** f (-; -en) relief, ⚖ exoneration, ✝ release. **Ent'lastungs|materi,al** n ⚖ exonerating evidence. **~straße** f bypass. **~zeuge** m ⚖ witness for the defen|ce (Am. -se). **~zug** m 🚂 relief train.

entlaubt [εnt'laʊpt] adj leafless, bare.

ent'laufen v/i (entlief, entlaufen, sn) run away (dat from).

entlausen [εnt'laʊzən] v/t (h) delouse.

entledigen [εnt'le:dɪgən] sich ~ (h) (gen) 1. get rid of, take off (clothing). 2. carry out, discharge (a task), fulfil(l), meet (an obligation).

ent'leeren v/t (h) empty: den Darm ~ evacuate (the bowels).

ent'legen adj remote, out-of-the-way.

ent'lehnen v/t (h) borrow word etc (dat, aus, von from).

ent'leihen v/t (entlieh, entliehen, h) borrow (aus, von from).

entlief [εnt'li:f] pret of **entlaufen**.

entließ [εnt'li:s] pret of **entlassen**.

ent'loben: sich ~ (h) break off one's engagement.

ent'locken v/t (h) (dat from) elicit, draw.

ent'lohnen v/t (h) pay. **Ent'lohnung** f (-; -en) pay, payment, remuneration.

entlud [εnt'lu:t] pret of **entladen**.

ent'lüften v/t (h) deaerate, bleed (brake). **Ent'lüfter** m (-s; -) deaerator. **Ent'lüftung** f (-; -en) aeration, airing. **Ent'lüftungsschraube** f vent screw.

entmachten [εnt'maxtən] v/t (h) j-n (et.) ~ deprive s.o. (s.th.) of his (its) power.

entmenscht [εnt'mεnʃt] adj inhuman, brutish.

entmilitarisieren [εntmilitari'zi:rən] v/t (h) demilitarize. **Entmilitari'sierung** f (-; -en) demilitarization.

entmündigen [εnt'myndɪgən] v/t (h) (legally) incapacitate. **Ent'mündigung** f (-; -en) (legal) incapacitation.

entmutigen [εnt'mu:tɪgən] v/t (h) discourage, dishearten. **Ent'mutigung** f (-; -en) discouragement, disheartening.

entnahm [εnt'na:m] pret of **entnehmen**.

Ent'nahme f (-; -n) taking (of samples), withdrawal (of money).

entnazifizieren [εntnatsifi'tsi:rən] v/t (h) hist. denazify. **Entnazifi'zierung** f (-; -en) denazification.

ent'nehmen v/t (entnahm, entnommen, h) (dat) take (from, out of), borrow (from a book etc), quote (from): fig. et. ~ aus (or dat) learn (or gather) s.th. from.

ent'nerven v/t (h) enervate.

ent'ölen v/t (h) remove the oil from.

entper'sönlichen v/t (h) depersonalize.

entpoliti'sieren *v/t* (h) depoliticize.

entprivati'sieren *v/t* (h) deprivatize.

entpuppen [ɛnt'pɔpən] (h) *sich ~ als fig.* turn out to be.

ent'rahmen *v/t* (h) skim (*milk*).

entrann [ɛnt'ran] *pret of* **entrinnen.**

ent'rätseln *v/t* (h a) solve, unravel, b) decipher.

entrechten [ɛnt'rɛçtn] *v/t* (h) *j-n ~* deprive s.o. of his rights.

ent'reißen *v/t* (entriß, entrissen, h) *j-m et. ~ a. fig.* snatch s.th. from s.o.

ent'richten *v/t* (h) pay.

entriegeln [ɛnt'ri:gəln] *v/t* (h) unlock.

ent'rinnen *v/i* (entrann, entronnen, sn) (*dat* from) escape, get away. **Ent'rinnen** *n* (-s) escape.

entriß [ɛnt'rɪs] *pret,* **ent'rissen** *pp of* **entreißen.**

ent'rollen *v/t* (h) unroll, unfurl.

ent'rosten *v/t* (h) remove the rust from.

ent'rücken *v/t* (h) (*dat* from) carry away. **ent'rückt** *adj* enraptured.

entrümpeln [ɛnt'rʏmpəln] *v/t* (h) clear out.

ent'rüsten (h) **I** *v/t* fill *s.o.* with indignation, shock, scandalize. **II** *sich ~* (*über acc*) get indignant (at *s.th.*, with *s.o.*), be shocked (at). **ent'rüstet** *adj* indignant, shocked. **Ent'rüstung** *f* (-; -en) indignation: *Schrei der ~* outcry.

entsaften [ɛnt'zaftn] *v/t* (h) extract the juice from. **Ent'safter** *m* (-s; -) juice extractor, juicer.

ent'sagen *v/i* (h) *e-r Sache ~* renounce s.th. **Ent'sagung** *f* (-; -en) renunciation. **ent'sagungsreich** *adj ein ~es Leben* a life full of privations.

entsann [ɛnt'zan] *pret of* **entsinnen.**

ent'schädigen *v/t* (h) (*für* for) compensate (*a. fig.*), reimburse: *die Aussicht entschädigte uns für den langen Aufstieg* the view made up for the long climb. **Ent'schädigung** *f* (-; -en) compensation (*a. fig.*), reimbursement.

ent'schärfen *v/t* (h) defuse (*a. fig. crisis etc*), deactivate (*ammunition*), *fig.* take the edge off (*a speech etc*).

Entscheid [ɛnt'ʃaɪt] *m* (-[e]s; -e) decree, decision. **ent'scheiden** (entschied, entschieden, h) **I** *v/t* decide, settle, ⚖ rule (*über acc* on): *damit war die Sache entschieden* that settled it; *das mußt du ~* that's up to you. **II** *v/i* (*über*

acc) a) decide (on), b) be decisive (for). **III** *sich ~* be decided, *person:* decide, make up one's mind; *sich ~ für* decide on, settle on; *er entschied sich dagegen* he decided against it. **ent'scheidend** *adj* a) decisive, b) crucial (*moment etc*): *~e Stimme* casting vote.

Ent'scheidung *f* (-; -en) (*über acc* on) decision, ⚖ a. ruling: *e-e ~ treffen* (*or fällen*) make (*or* come to) a decision.

Ent'scheidungs|bedarf *m es besteht ~* this calls for a decision. **~freiheit** *f* freedom of choice. **~kampf** *m* 1. ✗ decisive battle. 2. *fig.* showdown. **~spiel** *n sports:* a) deciding match, decider, b) final. **~träger** *m* decision-maker.

entschied [ɛnt'ʃi:t] *pret of* **entscheiden.**

entschieden [ɛnt'ʃi:dən] **I** *pp of* **entscheiden.** **II** *adj* **1.** a) determined, firm, b) sta(u)nch (*supporter*), declared, decided (*enemy etc*). **2.** decided, definite. **II** *adv* **3.** firmly, decidedly, definitely: *ich bin* (*ganz*) *~ dafür* I'm strongly in favo(u)r of it, I'm all for it. **Ent'schiedenheit** *f* (-; *no pl*) determination, firmness: *mit* (*aller*) *~* categorically.

entschlacken [ɛnt'ʃlakn] *v/t* (h) **1.** ⚙ remove the slag from. **2.** ✹ a) purify, b) purge. **Ent'schlackung** *f* (-; -en) ✹ a) purification, b) purge.

ent'schlafen *v/i* (sn) *fig.* pass away.

ent'schließen: *sich ~* (entschloß, entschlossen, h) (*zu, für* on, *zu tun* to do) decide, make up one's mind; *sich anders ~* change one's mind. **Ent'schließung** *f* (-; -en) *pol.* resolution.

entschloß [ɛnt'ʃlɔs] *pret of* **entschließen.** **ent'schlossen I** *pp of* **entschließen.** **II** *adj* determined, firm, resolute: *zu allem ~ sein* be ready for anything; *kurz ~* without a moment's hesitation. **Ent'schlossenheit** *f* (-; *no pl*) determination, resolution, firmness.

Ent'schluß *m* (-sses; «sse) decision: *e-n ~ fassen, zu e-m ~ kommen* make (*or* reach) a decision, make up one's mind.

entschlüsseln [ɛnt'ʃlʏsəln] *v/t* (h) decipher, decode.

entschuldbar [ɛnt'ʃʊltba:r] *adj* excusable. **entschuldigen** [ɛnt'ʃʊldɪgən] (h) **I** *v/t* excuse: *das ist nicht zu ~* that is impardonable; *bitte, ~ Sie mich* (*für heute abend*) I beg to be excused (for tonight). **II** *v/i ~ Sie!* a) excuse me!, b) sorry! **III** *sich* ~ a) apologize (*bei j-m für et.* to s.o. for s.th.), b) excuse o.s. **ent'schuldigend** *adj* apologetic. **Ent'schuldigung** *f* (-; -en) a) excuse, b) apology: *j-n um ~ bitten* apologize to s.o. (*wegen* for); *als ~, zur ~* as an excuse (*für* for); *~! → entschuldigen* **II**. **Ent'schuldigungsgrund** *m* (*et. als ~ anführen* offer s.th. as an) excuse.

Entschwefelungsanlage [ɛnt'ʃveːfəluŋs-] *f* ⊙ desulphurization plant.

ent'setzen (h) **I** *v/t* horrify, shock, appal(l). **II** *sich* ~ (*über acc* at) be horrified, be shocked. **Ent'setzen** *n* (-s) horror, terror. **entsetzlich** [ɛnt'zɛtslɪç] **I** *adj* horrible, terrible, atrocious. **II** *adv* terribly, F a. awfully (*cold, boring, etc*). **Ent'setzlichkeit** *f* (-; -en) a) terribleness, horribleness, b) atrocity.

entseuchen [ɛnt'zɔyçən] *v/t* (h) decontaminate. **Ent'seuchung** *f* (-; -en) decontamination.

ent'sichern *v/t* (h) release the safety catch of (*a gun*), cock.

ent'sinnen: *sich* ~ (entsann, entsonnen, h) (*gen*) recall, recollect; *wenn ich mich recht entsinne* if I remember rightly.

ent'sorgen *v/t* (h) dispose of the nuclear (*or toxic etc*) waste (of *a plant etc*). **Ent'sorgung** *f* (-; -en) disposal of nuclear (*or toxic etc*) waste.

entspann [ɛnt'ʃpan] *pret of* **entspinnen**. **ent'spannen** (h) **I** *sich* ~ relax, *person*: a. take it easy, *fig. situation etc*: ease off. **II** *v/t* relax. **III** *v/i* be relaxing. **Ent'spannung** *f* (-; -en) relaxation (*a. fig.*), *pol.* détente, ⚓ easing.

Ent'spannungs|poli,tik *f* policy of détente, **~übung** *f* relaxation exercise.

ent'spiegelt *adj* opt. antireflection.

ent'spinnen: *sich* ~ (entspann, entsponnen, h) (*aus* from) arise, develop.

ent'sprechen *v/i* (entsprach, entsprochen, h) (*dat*) **1.** a) correspond (to, with), agree (with), b) be equivalent (to): *er entspricht nicht der Beschreibung* he doesn't answer the description. **2.** a) meet, come up (to *expectations etc*), b) comply (with *a request*): *den Anforderungen nicht ~* fail to meet the requirements. **ent'sprechend I** *adj* (*dat* to) a) corresponding, b) appropriate, c) adequate, d) equivalent, e) respective. **II** *adv* correspondingly,

accordingly. **III** *prep* (*dat*) according to: *den Umständen ~* as can be expected under the circumstances.

ent'springen *v/i* (entsprang, entsprungen, sn) **1.** have its source (*in dat* in). **2.** (*dat, aus* from) spring, arise, come.

entstaatlichen [ɛnt'ʃtaːtlɪçən] *v/t* (h) denationalize. **Ent'staatlichung** *f* (-; -en) denationalization.

ent'stammen *v/i* (sn) (*dat* from) descend, *fig.* come, derive.

ent'stehen *v/i* (entstand, entstanden, sn) **1.** come into being, develop (*aus* from). **2.** arise, come about, *costs, emotions, etc*: (*aus, durch*) arise (*or* result) (from), be caused (by). **3.** be created (*or* built, produced, written, composed, painted). **Ent'stehen** *n* (-s) → **Entstehung**: *im ~ begriffen* in the making. **Ent'stehung** *f* (-; -en) a) coming into being, development, emergence, b) origin, beginning, c) creation.

Ent'stehungsgeschichte *f* genesis.

ent'steigen *v/i* (entstieg, entstiegen, sn) (*dat*) get out of.

entsteinen [ɛnt'ʃtaɪnən] *v/t* (h) stone.

ent'stellen *v/t* (h) disfigure, *fig.* distort (*facts*), garble (*report*). **Ent'stellung** *f* (-; -en) disfigurement, *fig.* distortion.

ent'stören *v/t* (h) ∮ radioshield, screen. **Ent'störung** *f* (-; -en) screening, *radio*: interference suppression.

ent'tarnen *v/t* (h) unmask, expose (*spy*).

ent'täuschen (h) **I** *v/t* disappoint, let s.o. down. **II** *v/i* be disappointing. **Ent'täuschung** *f* (-; -en) disappointment.

ent'thronen *v/t* (h) *a. fig.* dethrone.

entvölkert [-'fœlkɐt] *adj* depopulated.

ent'wachsen *v/i* (entwuchs, entwachsen, sn) *e-r Sache* ~ grow out of s.th., outgrow s.th.

entwaffnen [ɛnt'vafnən] *v/t* (h) disarm: *fig. ~des Lächeln* disarming smile.

entwand [ɛnt'vant] *pret of* **entwinden**.

entwarf [ɛnt'varf] *pret of* **entwerfen**.

ent'warnen *v/i* (h) give the all-clear. **Ent'warnung** *f* (-; -en) all-clear (signal).

ent'wässern *v/t* (h) **1.** drain. **2.** ✱ dehydrate. **Ent'wässerung** *f* (-; -en) **1.** draining. **2.** ✱ dehydration. **Ent'wässerungsanlage** *f* drainage system.

entweder ['ɛntveːdɐ] *conj* ~ ... *oder* either ... or; ~ *oder!* take it or leave it! **'Entweder-'Oder** *n* hier gibt es nur *ein* ~ you've got to decide one way or the other.

ent'weichen *v/i* (entwich, entwichen, sn) escape (*dat, aus* from).

ent'weihen *v/t* (h) desecrate.

Ent'weihung *f* (-; -en) desecration.

ent'wenden *v/t* (h) *j-m et.* ~ steal (*or* purloin) s.th. from s.o.

ent'werfen *v/t* (entwarf, entworfen, h) **1.** sketch, outline (*a. fig. a plan etc*), design. **2.** plan (*program[me] etc*), work out, devise (*plan*). **3.** draw up, draft (*contract*). **Ent'werfer(in** *f) m* designer.

ent'werten *v/t* (h) **1.** cancel (*ticket, stamp, etc*). **2.** ✝ a) demonetize, b) → *abwerten*. **3.** *fig.* devalue: (*völlig*) ~ invalidate. **Ent'wertung** *f* (-; -en) **1.** cancel(l)ation. **2.** *fig.* devaluation.

entwich [ɛnt'vɪç] *pret*, **ent'wichen** *pp of* **entweichen**.

ent'wickeln (h) *v/t* **1.** develop (*a. phot.*, ✪), *phys. a.* generate, evolve, work out (*plan, method, etc*): *er entwickelte mir s-e Theorie* he expounded his theory to me. **2.** display, show (*energy, an interest, etc*). **II sich** ~ (*aus, zu*) develop (from, into), grow (out of, into); *sich gut* ~ be shaping well.

Ent'wickler *m* (-s; -) *phot.* developer.

Ent'wicklung *f* (-; -en) development (*a. fig.*), *a.* trend, *a. biol.* evolution.

Ent'wicklungs|abteilung *f* planning department, Development. **~alter** *n* formative years, *n.s.* age of puberty. **⸰fähig** *adj* capable of development, progressive (*spot etc*). **~geschichte** *f* history, *biol.* genesis. **~helfer(in** *f) m* development aid worker, *Br.* member of the Voluntary Service Overseas, *Am.* Peace Corps Worker. **~hilfe** *f* development aid. **~jahre** *pl* → *Entwicklungsalter*. **~land** *n* developing country. **~poli̱tik** *f* third world policy. **~pro,zeß** *m* (process of) development. **~stufe** *f* stage of development, phase. **~zeit** *f* **1.** period of development. **2.** → *Entwicklungsalter*. **3.** *phot.* developing time.

ent'winden *v/t* (entwand, entwunden, h) *j-m et.* ~ wrest s.th. from s.o.

ent'wirren *v/t* (h) disentangle, unravel.

ent'wischen *v/i* (sn) F (*dat* from) escape, slip away: *j-m* ~ *a.* give s.o. the slip.

entwöhnen [ɛnt'vøːnən] *v/t* (h) **1.** wean (*a baby*). **2.** *j-n* ~ cure s.o. (*gen of an*

addiction etc). **Ent'wöhnung** *f* (-; -en) **1.** weaning. **2.** curing, cure.

entworfen [ɛnt'vɔrfən] *pp of* **entwerfen**.

ent'würdigen *v/t* (h) degrade (*sich* o.s.).

ent'würdigend *adj* degrading.

Ent'würdigung *f* (-; -en) degradation.

Ent'wurf *m* (-[e]s; ⸗e) **1.** a) (first) draft, sketch, b) plan, blueprint, c) design, d) model. **2.** ✝, ☷ draft, parl. bill.

Ent'wurfsstadium *n* planning stage.

ent'wurzeln *v/t* (h) *a. fig.* uproot.

ent'ziehen (entzog, entzogen, h) **I** *v/t* **1.** *j-m et.* ~ withdraw s.th. from s.o. (*a. ✻*), withhold s.th. from s.o., deprive (*or* strip) s.o. of *rights etc*; *j-m den Führerschein (die Lizenz etc)* ~ revoke s.o.'s licen/ce (*Am.* -se); *et. j-s Zugriff (Einfluß)* ~ remove s.th. from s.o.'s reach (influence); *parl. etc j-m das Wort* ~ rule s.o. out of order. **2.** 🌡 extract (*dat* from). **II sich** ~ (*dat*) evade, avoid; → *Kenntnis*. **Ent'ziehung** *f* (-; -en) withdrawal (*a. ✻*), deprivation.

Ent'ziehungs|anstalt *f* drying-out cent/re (*Am.* -er). **~erscheinung** *f* ✻ withdrawal symptom. **~kur** *f* withdrawal treatment.

entziffern [ɛnt'tsɪfərn] *v/t* (h) **1.** decipher, *w.s.* make out. **2.** decode.

Ent'zifferung *f* (-; -en) **1.** deciphering. **2.** decoding.

entzücken [ɛnt'tsʏkən] *v/t* (h) charm, delight. **Ent'zücken** *n* (-s) delight (*über acc* at). **ent'zückend** *adj* charming, delightful, lovely, F sweet. **ent'zückt** *adj* delighted (*über acc* at, *von* with).

Ent'zug *m* (-[e]s; *no pl*) → *Entziehung*.

entzündbar [ɛnt'tsʏndbaːr] *adj* inflammable. **ent'zünden** (h) **I** *v/t* **1.** light. **II sich** ~ **2.** catch fire (*an dat* from). **3.** 🌡, ✪ ignite. **4.** ✻ become inflamed. **5.** *fig.* (*an dat* by) *passion etc*: be roused, *argument*: be sparked off. **ent'zündet** *adj* ✻ inflamed, red (*eyes*). **ent'zündlich** *adj* ✻ inflammatory. **Ent'zündung** *f* (-; -en) ✻ inflammation. **ent'zündungshemmend** *adj* ✻ antiphlogistic.

ent'zwei *adj pred* **1.** in two, in half. **2.** in pieces, broken. **ent'zweibrechen** (*irr, sep,* -ge-, → **brechen**) *v/t* (h), *v/i* (sn) break in two. **entzweien** [ɛnt'tsvaɪən] (h) **I** *v/t* divide: *Freunde* ~ turn friends against each other. **II sich** ~ fall out (*mit* with). **ent'zweigehen** *v/i* (*irr, sep,*

-ge-, sn, → **gehen**) break, go to pieces.
Ent'zweiung f (-; -en) split, rupture.
Enzephalitis [entsefa'li:ts] f (-; -litiden [-li'ti:dən]) ✣ encephalitis.
Enzian ['ɛntsiaːn] m (-s; -e) ✤ gentian.
Enzyklopädie [ɛntsyklopɛ'di:] f encyclop(a)edia. **enzyklopädisch** [ɛntsyklo'pɛ:dɪʃ] adj encyclop(a)edic.
Enzym [ɛn'tsy:m] n (-s; -e) biol. enzyme.
Epen ['e:pən] pl of **Epos**.
ephemer [efe'me:r] adj ephemeral.
Epidemie [epide'mi:] f (-; -n) epidemic.
epidemisch [epi'de:mɪʃ] adj epidemic.
Epidermis [epi'dɛrmɪs] f (-; -men) ✤ epidermis.
Epigone [epi'go:nə] m (-n; -n) epigone.
Epigramm [epi'gram] n (-s; -e) epigram.
Epik ['e:pɪk] f (-; no pl) 1. epic poetry. 2. narrative literature. **Epiker** m (-s; -) 1. epic poet. 2. narrative author.
Epilepsie [epilɛp'si:] f (-; -n) ✤ epilepsy.
Epileptiker [epi'lɛptɪkər] m (-s; -), **Epi'leptikerin** f (-; -nen), **epileptisch** [epi'lɛptɪʃ] adj epileptic.
Epilog [epi'lo:k] m (-s; -e) epilog(ue Br.).
episch ['e:pɪʃ] adj epic.
Episode [epi'zo:də] f (-; -n) episode. **epi'sodenhaft** adj episodic.
Epoche [e'pɔxə] f (-; -n) epoch. **e'pochemachend** adj epoch-making.
Epos ['e:pɔs] n (-; Epen) epic (poem).
er [e:r] pers pron he, it: ~ **ist es!** it's him!
Er m (-; -s) f **es ist ein** ~ it's a he.
Er'achten [ɛr-] n **m-s** ~**s** in my opinion.
er'arbeiten v/t (h) **1.** (a. **sich** ~) work (hard) for, acquire. **2.** a) compile, b) develop.
Erbadel ['ɛrp-] m hereditary nobility.
'Erbanlage f genetic make-up, ✤ hereditary disposition.
'Erbanspruch m hereditary title.
erbarmen [ɛr'barmən] (h) **I** v/t j-n ~ move s.o. to pity. **II sich** ~ (gen) take pity (on). **Er'barmen** n (-s) pity, compassion: **kein** ~ **kennen** be merciless.
erbärmlich [ɛr'bɛrmlɪç] **I** adj **1.** pitiful, a. miserable, wretched, a. paltry. **2.** mean, vile. **3.** F terrible, awful. **II** adv **4.** pitifully (etc). **5.** F awfully: ~ **wenig** precious little. **Er'bärmlichkeit** f (-; no pl) pitifulness, miserableness (etc).
er'barmungslos adj merciless.
er'bauen (h) **I** v/t **1.** build, erect. **2.** fig. edify: F **er ist nicht besonders erbaut**

davon he's not exactly enthusiastic about it. **II sich** ~ (**an** dat by) be delighted, be uplifted. **Er'bauer** m (-s; -) a) builder, b) founder. **er'baulich** adj edifying (a. iro.), eccl. devotional.
Er'bauung f (-; no pl) **1.** building, construction, erection. **2.** fig. edification.
Erbe¹ ['ɛrbə] m (-n; -n) heir, successor (j-s of or to s.o., a. fig.): ~ **es Vermögens** heir (or successor) to an estate; **j-n zum** ~**n einsetzen** make s.o. one's heir. **'Erbe²** n (-s; no pl) inheritance, fig. heritage. **'erben** v/t (h) inherit (a. fig.), a. come into (money). **'Erbengemeinschaft** f 🏛️ community of heirs.
er'betteln v/t (h) (**sich**) **et.** ~ get s.th. by begging, b.s. scrounge s.th. (**von** off).
erbeuten [ɛr'bɔytən] v/t (h) ✕ capture.
'Erbfaktor m gene. **'Erbfehler** m hereditary defect. **'Erbfeind** m sworn enemy. **'Erbfolge** f (**gesetzliche** ~ intestate) succession. **'Erbgut** n biol. genotype.
Erbin ['ɛrbɪn] f (-; -nen) heiress.
erbittern [ɛr'bɪtərn] v/t (h) anger. **er'bittert** adj **1.** fierce (enemy, fight, etc). **2.** embittered (**über** acc at, by). **Er'bitterung** f (-; no pl) **1.** bitterness. **2.** anger.
'Erbkrankheit f hereditary disease.
'Erblasser ['ɛrblasər] m (-s; -), **'Erblasserin** f (-; -nen) 🏛️ a) the deceased, b) testator (testatrix). **'Erblast** f fig. (evil) legacy. **erblich** ['ɛrplɪç] adj hereditary, inheritable (title etc): ~ **belastet** ✤ subject to a(n) hereditary taint.
er'blicken v/t (h) see, catch sight of.
erblinden [ɛr'blɪndən] v/i (sn) go blind. **Er'blindung** f (-; -en) going blind, loss of (one's) sight.
er'blühen v/i (sn) blossom (fig. **zu** into).
'Erbmasse f **1.** 🏛️ estate. **2.** biol. genetic make-up. **'Erbonkel** m F rich uncle.
er'brechen (erbrach, erbrochen, h) v/t **1.** break open, force (door), open (letter). **2.** ✤ vomit, bring up. **II** v/i (a. **sich** ~) ✤ vomit, be sick. **Er'brechen** n (-s) ✤ vomiting: fig. **bis zum** ~ ad nauseam.
'Erbrecht n 🏛️ **1.** law of succession. **2.** hereditary title.
'Erbschaft f (-; -en) inheritance: **e-e** ~ **machen** inherit; **e-e** ~ **antreten** succeed to an estate.
'Erbschaftssteuer f death duties.
'Erbschein m certificate of heirship.

Erbschleicher [ˈɛrpʃlaɪçər] *m* (-s; -) *contp.* legacy-hunter.

Erbse [ˈɛrpsə] *f* (-; -n) pea.

'**Erbsensuppe** *f* pea soup.

'**Erbstück** *n* heirloom. '**Erbsünde** *f eccl.* original sin. '**Erbtante** *f* F rich aunt. '**Erbteil** *n* share of the inheritance.

Erd|achse [ˈɛːrt-] *f* earth's axis. **~anziehungskraft** *f* gravity. **~arbeiten** *pl* excavations. **~atmo|sphäre** *f* (earth's) atmosphere. **~bahn** *f* earth's orbit. **~ball** *m* (-[e]s; *no pl*) globe, *w.s.* earth.

'**Erdbeben** *n* (-s; -) earthquake. **~gebiet** *n* 1. earthquake area. 2. area hit by an earthquake. **~herd** *m* seismic focus.

'**Erdbeere** *f* (-; -n) strawberry.

'**Erd|bevölkerung** *f* population of the earth. **~bewohner** *m* inhabitant of the earth. **~boden** *m* ground, earth: *dem ~ gleichmachen* raze *s.th.* to the ground; *es (er) war wie vom ~ verschluckt* it (he) had vanished (into thin air).

Erde [ˈɛːrdə] *f* (-; -n) 1. earth, soil, ground: *über der ~* above ground. 2. *no pl* (planet) earth: *auf ~n* on earth; *auf der ganzen ~* all over the world. 3. ⚡ (*a.* **an ~ legen**) earth, *Am.* ground.

'**erden** *v/t* (h) ⚡ earth, *Am.* ground.

erdenklich [ɛrˈdɛŋklɪç] *adj* imaginable, conceivable: *sich alle ~e Mühe geben* do one's utmost.

'**Erdgas** *n* natural gas.

'**Erdgeschichte** *f* history of the earth.

'**Erdgeschoß** *n* ground (*Am.* first) floor.

er'dichten *v/t* (h) make up, invent.

erdig [ˈɛːrdɪç] *adj* earthy.

'**Erdinnere** *n* interior of the earth.

'**Erdkabel** *n* underground cable.

'**Erdkruste** *f* crust of the earth.

'**Erdkugel** *f* globe, *w.s.* earth.

'**Erdkunde** *f* (-; *no pl*) geography.

'**erdkundlich** *adj* geographic(al).

'**Erdnuß(butter)** *f* peanut (butter).

'**Erdoberfläche** *f* surface of the earth.

'**Erdöl** *n* (mineral) oil, petroleum.

erdolchen [ɛrˈdɔlçən] *v/t* (h) *j-n ~* stab s.o. to death.

'**Erdreich** *n* (-[e]s; *no pl*) earth, soil.

erdreisten [ɛrˈdraɪstən] *sich ~* (h) dare (*or* have the cheek) (*zu inf* to *inf*).

erdrosseln [ɛrˈdrɔsəln] *v/t* (h) strangle.

er'drücken *v/t* (h) crush *s.o.* overwhelm: *von Arbeit erdrückt werden* be swamped with work.

er'drückend *adj fig.* overwhelming (*majority etc*), damning (*evidence*).

'**Erdrutsch** *m* landslide.

'**Erdschicht** *f* layer of the earth, stratum.

'**Erdstoß** *m* seismic shock.

'**Erdteil** *m* continent.

er'dulden *v/t* (h) endure, suffer.

'**Erdumdrehung** *f* rotation of the earth.

'**Erdumkreisung** *f* orbit around the earth.

'**Erdung** *f* (-; -en) ⚡ earth(ing), *Am.* ground(ing).

'**Erdwärme** *f* geothermal energy.

er'eifern: sich ~ (h) get excited (*or* worked up) (*über acc* about).

ereignen [ɛrˈʔaɪɡnən] **sich ~** (h) happen, occur, take place. **Ereignis** [ɛrˈʔaɪɡnɪs] *n* (-ses; -se) *a.* event, b) incident, c) great event, sensation. **er'eignislos** *adj* uneventful. **er'eignisreich** *adj* very eventful, exciting.

er'eilen *v/t* (h) *j-n ~* catch up with s.o.

Erektion [erɛkˈtsi̯oːn] *f* (-; -en) erection.

Eremit [ereˈmiːt] *m* (-en; -en) hermit.

er'erbt *adj* inherited, *biol. a.* hereditary.

er'fahren (erfuhr, erfahren, h) **I** *v/t* **1.** hear, be told, find out. **2.** a) experience, b) suffer, c) receive. **II** *v/i* **3. ~ von** get to know about, hear about (*or* that). **III** *adj* **4.** experienced, seasoned: **~ sein in** (*dat*) be well versed in, be an old hand at. **Er'fahrenheit** *f* (-; *no pl*) experience.

Er'fahrung *f* (-; -en) experience: *technische ~ a.* know-how; *aus (eigener) ~* from experience; *durch ~ klug werden* learn the hard way; *in ~ bringen* learn, find out; *die ~ machen, daß ...* find that ...; *die ~ hat gezeigt, daß ...* past experience has shown that ...

Er'fahrungs|austausch *m* exchange of experience. **2gemäß** *adv* as experience shows, we know from experience.

erfand [ɛrˈfant] *pret of* **erfinden**.

er'fassen *v/t* (h) **1.** seize, grasp, take: *er wurde vom Auto erfaßt* he was hit by the car; *Furcht erfaßte sie* she was seized with fear. **2.** grasp, understand: *er hat's erfaßt!* he's got it! **3.** a) register, record, b) include, cover: *zahlenmäßig ~* count; *steuerlich ~* tax.

Er'fassung *f* (-; -en) a) registration, b) inclusion, coverage.

er'finden *v/t* (erfand, erfunden, h) a) invent, b) make *s.th.* up. **Er'finder** *m* inventor. **Er'findergeist** *m* (-[e]s; *no pl*) inventiveness. **er'finderisch** *adj* inventive, imaginative, resourceful: → **Not** 2. **Er'findung** *f* (-; -en) invention, *fig. contp. a.* fabrication. **Er'findungsgabe** *f* inventive talent, imagination.

Erfolg [ɛr'fɔlk] *m* (-[e]s; -e) a) success, achievement, b) result, outcome, effect: *guter ~* good result; *es war ein großer ~* it was a great success; *~ haben* succeed, be successful; *k-n ~ haben* be unsuccessful, fail; *es zu e-m ~ gestalten* make a success of it; *mit dem ~, daß ...* with the result that ...
er'folgen *v/i* (sn) **1.** follow. **2.** take place, happen, *payment:* be made.
er'folglos *adj* unsuccessful, fruitless.
Erfolglosigkeit *f* (-; *no pl*) failure.
er'folgreich *adj* successful.
Er'folgs|aussichten *pl* chances of success. **~autor** *m* best-selling author. **~beteiligung** *f* profit-sharing. **~chance** *f* chance (of success). **~erlebnis** *n* **1.** success experience. **2.** → **~gefühl** *n* sense of achievement. **~kurs** *m auf ~* on the road to success (*or* victory). **~mensch** *m* go-getter. **~quote** *f* success rate. **~ro,man** *m* best-selling novel. **~typ** *m* born winner, achiever. **~zwang** *m unter ~ stehen* be under pressure to succeed (*or* do well).
er'folgversprechend *adj* promising.
erforderlich [ɛr'fɔrdərlɪç] *adj* necessary, required: *unbedingt ~* essential.
er'fordern *v/t* (h) require, call for, *a.* take (*time, courage, etc*).
Erfordernis [ɛr'fɔrdərnɪs] *n* (-ses; -se) requirement, demand, prerequisite.
er'forschen *v/t* (h) investigate, study, research, explore. **Er'forscher** *m* explorer. **Er'forschung** *f* (-; -en) (*gen*) investigation (of, into), research (into), exploration (of).
er'fragen *v/t* (h) ask (for).
er'freuen (h) **I** *v/t* please. **II** *sich ~ an* (*dat*), *sich ~* (*gen*) enjoy. **erfreulich** [ɛr'frɔylɪç] *adj* a) pleasant, pleasing, welcome (*news etc*), b) encouraging.
er'freulicherweise *adv* fortunately.
er'frieren (erfror, erfroren) **I** *v/i* (sn) freeze to death, *plants:* be killed by frost: *ihm sind zwei Finger erfroren* he lost two fingers through frostbite. **II**

v/t (h) *sich die Ohren erfroren haben* have frostbitten ears.
Er'frierung *f* (-; -en) 𝕊 frostbite.
erfrischen [ɛr'frɪʃən] *v/t* (h) refresh (*sich* o.s.). **er'frischend** *adj* refreshing.
Er'frischung *f* (-; -en) refreshment.
Er'frischungs|getränk *n* **1.** soft drink. **2.** cool drink. **~raum** *m* refreshment room. **~tuch** *n* moistened tissue.
erfuhr [ɛr'fu:r] *pret of* **erfahren**.
er'füllen (h) **I** *v/t* **1.** *a. fig.* fill (*mit* with): *ein erfülltes Leben* a full life; *s-e Arbeit erfüllt ihn* he finds his work very satisfying. **2.** fulfil(l) (*duty, contract, etc*), grant (*a wish*), meet (*conditions, expectations, etc*), keep (*promise*): *s-n Zweck ~* serve its purpose. **II** *sich ~* come true. **Er'füllung** *f* (-; -en) fulfil(l)ment: *in ~ gehen* come true.
Er'füllungsort *m* 𝕋, 𝕊 place of fulfil(l)ment.
erfunden I *pp of* **erfinden**. **II** *adj* imaginary, *contp.* fictitious, (all) made up.
ergangen [ɛr'gaŋən] *pp of* **ergehen**.
ergänzen [ɛr'gɛntsən] *v/t* (h) **1.** complement (*sich or einander* one another). **2.** a) complete, b) supplement, add: *et. laufend ~* keep s.th. up to date. **3.** replenish (*supplies etc*). **er'gänzend I** *adj* a) complementary, b) supplementary, c) additional. **II** *adv* in addition.
Er'gänzung *f* (-; -en) **1.** a) completion, b) supplementation, c) addition. **2.** complement (*a. ling.*, 𝕂), supplement, addition, *parl.* amendment. **Er'gänzungsband** *m* (-[e]s; -e) supplement.
ergattern [ɛr'gatərn] *v/t* (h) F (manage to) get hold of.
er'geben (ergab, ergeben, h) **I** *v/t* **1.** a) result in, b) come to, c) yield. **2.** show, prove. **II** *sich ~* **3.** a) (*dat* to) *esp.* 𝕏 surrender, capitulate, b) (*in acc*) resign o.s. (to), c) (*dat*) take to (drink[ing] *etc*). **4.** *problems etc:* arise, *discussion etc:* ensue: *sich ~ aus* result (*or* arise) from; *daraus ergibt sich, daß ...* it follows that ...; *es hat sich so ~* it just happened that way. **III** *adj* **5.** (*dat* to) a) loyal, devoted, b) (*dat* to) c) addicted. **Er'gebenheit** *f* (-; *no pl*) a) devotion, loyalty, b) resignation.
Ergebnis [ɛr'ge:pnɪs] *n* (-ses; -se) result, outcome, *a.* findings (*of investigation*), *sports: a.* score.

er'gebnislos adj without result: ~ bleiben (or verlaufen) come to nothing.
Er'gebung f (-; no pl) **1.** esp. ✗ surrender. **2.** resignation (in acc to).
er'gehen (erging, ergangen) I v/i (sn) **1.**
(an acc to) order etc: be issued, invitation etc: be sent. **2.** ⚖ law: come out,
decision, judg(e)ment: be passed. **3.** et.
über sich ~ lassen endure s.th. II sich
~ (h) a) hold forth (über acc on a subject), b) indulge (in dat in conjectures
etc). III v/impers es ist ihm schlecht
ergangen he had a bad time of it; wie
ist es dir ergangen? how did you
fare?; mir ist es genauso ergangen it
was the same with me.
ergiebig [ɛr'giːbɪç] adj **1.** productive (a.
fig.), rich (deposits etc), lucrative (business etc), fruitful (subject etc). **2.** economical.
er'gießen: sich ~ (ergoß, ergossen, h)
(in, über acc) pour (into, over).
er'götzen [ɛr'gœtsən] sich ~ (h) (an dat)
a) be amused (by), b) gloat (over).
er'grauen v/i (sn) (turn) grey (Am.
gray): im Dienst ergraut grown old in
service.
er'greifen v/t (ergriff, ergriffen, h) **1.**
seize, a. arrest (criminal). **2.** take
(measures etc): → Besitz **1,** Flucht[1],
Wort **1. 3.** a) overcome, seize, b) move:
Angst ergriff sie she was seized with
fear. **er'greifend** adj moving.
ergriffen [ɛr'grɪfən] I pp of ergreifen. II
adj moved.
Er'griffenheit f (-; no pl) emotion.
er'gründen v/t (h) get to the bottom of.
Er'guß m (-sses; -sse) **1.** 🎇 a) effusion (of
blood), b) ejaculation. **2.** fig. effusion,
a. iro. outpouring.
Er'gußgestein n geol. effusive rock.
er'haben adj **1.** ⊙ raised, embossed. **2.**
fig. lofty, sublime, grand. **3.** fig. ~ über
(acc) above, beyond (reproach etc).
Er'habenheit f (-; no pl) grandeur.
er'halten (erhielt, erhalten, h) I v/t **1.**
get, receive, obtain: e-n Preis ~ be
awarded (or given) a prize. **2.** keep,
maintain, preserve: j-n am Leben ~
keep s.o. alive; das erhält (e-n) jung
that keeps you young; j-m das Augenlicht ~ save s.o.'s eyesight. **3.** keep, support (family etc). II sich ~ a) survive, b)
subsist (von on). III adj gut ~ sein be in

good condition; ~ bleiben survive;
noch ~ sein remain, be left.
erhältlich [ɛr'hɛltlɪç] adj obtainable,
available: schwer ~ hard to get hold of.
Er'haltung f (-; no pl) preservation,
maintenance, upkeep.
er'hängen v/t (h) hang (sich o.s.).
er'härten v/t (h) corroborate, confirm.
er'haschen v/t (h) catch.
er'heben (erhob, erhoben, h) I v/t **1.**
raise (a. fig. one's voice, objections, etc),
lift (up): j-n in den Adelsstand ~ raise
s.o. to the peerage; → Anklage, Anspruch. **2.** levy, impose (duties, taxes),
charge (a fee). II sich ~ **3.** rise (to one's
feet), get up. **4.** hill, house, etc: rise
(über dat above). **5.** wind, fig. doubts,
shouting, etc: arise. **6.** rise (in arms),
revolt. **er'hebend** adj edifying.
erheblich [ɛr'heːplɪç] I adj a) considerable, b) important. II adv considerably:
~ besser much better.
Er'hebung f (-; -en) **1.** elevation, rise (in
the ground). **2.** elevation (in den
Adelsstand to a peerage). **3.** levy (of
duties, taxes), charge (of fees). **4.** statistics: survey: ~en anstellen (über acc)
make investigations (about), investigate (into). **5.** uprising, revolt.
erheitern [ɛr'haɪtərn] v/t (h) amuse.
Er'heiterung f (-; no pl) amusement.
erhellen [ɛr'hɛlən] (h) I v/t light up, illuminate, fig. shed light (up)on. II sich ~
brighten.
erhielt [ɛr'hiːlt] pret of erhalten.
erhitzen [ɛr'hɪtsən] (h) I v/t heat (up):
die Gemüter ~ make feelings run high.
II sich ~ get hot, fig. get heated (person:
excited). **er'hitzt** adj hot, person: a.
flushed, fig. heated (debate etc).
erhob [ɛr'hoːp] pret of erheben.
erhoben [ɛr'hoːbən] pp of erheben.
er'hoffen v/t (h) (a. sich ~) hope for.
er'hofft adj hoped-for.
erhöhen [ɛr'høːən] (h) I v/t raise (a. fig.
auf acc to, um by), fig. a. increase,
intensify, enhance, heighten. II sich ~
increase, price etc: rise, go up.
Er'höhung f (-; -en) **1.** raising. **2.** rise,
increase (gen in), fig. a. intensification,
enhancement, heightening; → Ge-
halts-, Lohnerhöhung.
er'holen: sich ~ (h) a) recover (von
from, a. 🩺), b) take a rest, relax: du

siehst sehr erholt aus you look very rested (*or* fit). **er'holsam** *adj* restful, relaxing. **Er'holung** *f* (-; *no pl*) **1.** a) recovery (*von* from, *a.* ✝), b) rest, relaxation. **2.** holiday, *Am.* vacation. **Er'holungs|aufenthalt** *m* holiday, *Am.* vacation. **⁀bedürftig** *adj* in need of a rest (*or* holiday). **⁀gebiet** *n* recreation area. **⁀heim** *n* rest home. **⁀ort** *m* (health *or* holiday) resort. **⁀pause** *f* rest, breather. **⁀reise** *f* holiday (*Am.* vacation) trip. **⁀urlaub** *m* holiday, *Am.* vacation, ✕ convalescent leave. **⁀wert** *m* recreational value. **⁀zentrum** *n* recreation park.

er'hören *v/t* (h) hear, answer (*prayer*).

erigieren [eri'giːrən] (sn) become erect.

Erika ['eːrika] *f* (-; -s, -ken) ♀ heather.

erinnern [ɛr'ʔɪnərn] (h) **I** *v/t j-n* ⁀ remind s.o. (**an** *acc* of); *j-n daran* ⁀ remind s.o. that. **II** *sich* ⁀ (**an** *acc*) remember, recall; *wenn ich mich recht erinnere* if I remember rightly; *soviel ich mich* ⁀ *kann* as far as I remember. **III** *v/i* ⁀ **an** (*acc*) remind one of, *fig. a.* be suggestive of. **Er'innerung** *f* (-; -en) a) memory, recollection, reminiscence (*all:* **an** *acc* of), b) memento, souvenir, keepsake, c) reminder: *⁀en* reminiscences, memoirs; *zur* ⁀ **an** (*acc*) in memory of; *in guter* ⁀ *behalten* have fond memories of.

Er'innerungstafel *f* memorial tablet.

Er'innerungsvermögen *n* memory.

Er'innerungswert *m* sentimental value.

erkalten [ɛr'kaltən] *v/i* (sn) **1.** get cold. **2.** *fig.* cool (off).

erkälten [ɛr'kɛltən] *sich* ⁀ (h) catch a cold; (*stark*) *erkältet sein* have a (bad) cold. **Er'kältung** *f* (-; -en) cold.

er'kämpfen *v/t* (h) gain (*or* win) (after a hard struggle): *sich et. hart* ⁀ *müssen* have to struggle hard for s.th.

er'kaufen *v/t* (h) buy: *et. teuer* ⁀ *müssen* (have to) pay a high price for s.th.; *j-s Schweigen* ⁀ bribe s.o. into silence.

er'kennbar *adj* **1.** recognizable. **2.** discernible, to be seen.

er'kennen (erkannte, erkannt, h) **I** *v/t* **1.** a) recognize (**an** *dat* by), b) make out, see, c) detect, F spot, d) identify, ✝ diagnose: ⁀ **an** (*dat*) *a.* know by; ⁀ *lassen* show, reveal; *zu* ⁀ *geben* indicate, give to understand; *sich zu* ⁀ *geben*

disclose one's identity; ⚖ *j-n für schuldig* ⁀ find s.o. guilty. **2.** realize, see. **II** *v/i* **3.** ⚖ ⁀ *über* (*acc*) decide on; ⁀ *auf* (*acc*) pass a sentence of.

er'kenntlich *adj sich* (*j-m*) ⁀ *zeigen* show (s.o.) one's gratitude.

Er'kenntnis *f* (-; -se) a) knowledge, b) realization, c) idea, d) discovery: *neueste* *the* latest findings; *zu der* ⁀ *gelangen, daß* (come to) realize that.

Er'kennung *f* (-; *no pl*) a) recognition, b) identification.

Er'kennungs|dienst *m* criminal identification department. **⁀marke** *f* identity disc, *Am.* identification tag. **⁀melo,die** *f* signature tune. **⁀wort** *n* password. **⁀zeichen** *n* **1.** sign to be recognized by. **2.** ✓ identification sign.

Erker ['ɛrkər] *m* (-s; -) △ oriel.

'Erkerfenster *n* bay window.

erklärbar [ɛr'klɛːrbaːr] *adj* explainable.

er'klären (h) **I** *v/t* **1.** explain (*j-m et.* s.th. to s.o.): *kannst du mir* ⁀, *warum?* can you tell me why?; *ich kann es mir nicht* ⁀ I don't understand it. **2.** a) interpret, b) illustrate (*an e-m Beispiel* by an example). **3.** declare, pronounce: *j-n für gesund* ⁀ pronounce s.o. healthy; ⚖ *er wurde für tot erklärt* he was declared dead; → *Einverständnis* 1, *Rücktritt* 1. **II** *sich* ⁀ a) declare o.s., explain o.s., b) be explained; *sich* ⁀ *für* (*gegen*) declare for (against); *sich einverstanden* ⁀ consent (*mit* to); *sich solidarisch* ⁀ declare one's solidarity (*mit* with). **er'klärend** *adj* explanatory.

er'klärlich *adj* **1.** explainable. **2.** understandable. **er'klärlicherweise** *adv* understandably (enough).

er'klärt *adj* declared (*enemy etc*).

Er'klärung *f* (-; -en) **1.** a) explanation (*für* of), b) interpretation. **2.** *a. pol.* declaration, statement: *e-e* ⁀ *abgeben* make a statement (*zu* on).

er'klettern *v/t* (h) climb (up).

er'klingen *v/i* (erklang, erklungen, sn) be heard, sound, ring out.

er'kranken *v/i* (sn) fall ill (*or* sick) (**an** *dat* with), *organ:* be diseased: ⁀ **an** (*dat*) *a.* get, come down with; *erkrankt sein* **an** (*dat*) *a.* have. **Er'krankung** *f* (-; -en) illness, sickness, disease (*of an organ*).

erkunden [ɛr'kʊndən] *v/t* (h) explore, ✕ reconnoit/re (*Am.* -er), find out.

erkundigen [ɛr'kʊndɪgən] *sich ~* (h) (*über acc* about) ask, inquire, make inquiries; *sich nach dem Weg ~* ask the way; *sich nach j-m* (*or j-s Befinden*) *~* inquire after s.o. **Er'kundigung** *f* (-; -en) inquiry: *~en einziehen* make inquiries (*über acc* about).

Er'kundung *f* (-; -en) ✕ reconnaissance.

erlag [ɛr'laːk] *pret of* **erliegen**.

er'lahmen *v/i* (sn) **1.** grow weary, tire. **2.** *fig.* interest, zeal, *etc*: flag, wane.

er'langen *v/t* (h) a) get, obtain, b) attain, reach, c) gain, acquire.

Erlaß [ɛr'las] *m* (-sses; -sse) **1.** (*gen*) release (from *debts etc*), remission (of *penalty etc*). **2.** a) issuing, enactment (of *a law*), b) decree.

er'lassen *v/t* (erließ, erlassen, h) **1.** issue, publish (*ordinance*), enact (*a law*). **2.** remit (*penalty*), waive (*fees*): *j-m et. ~* release s.o. from s.th.

er'lauben [ɛr'laʊbən] *v/t* (h) allow, permit (*j-m et.* s.o. to do s.th.): *j-m ~, zu tun a.* give s.o. permission to do s.th.; *~ Sie, daß ich rauche?* may I smoke?; *wenn Sie ~* if you don't mind; *sich ~ zu inf* take the liberty of *ger, b.s. a.* dare (to) *inf*; *~ Sie mal!, was ~ Sie sich?* who do you think you are?; *er kann sich das ~ w.s.* he can get away with it.

Erlaubnis [ɛr'laʊpnɪs] *f* (-; *no pl*) permission: *j-n um ~ bitten* ask s.o.'s (*or* s.o. for) permission (*et. zu tun* to do s.th.); *die ~ erhalten* be given permission.

er'läutern *v/t* (h) explain, comment (up)on: *durch Beispiele ~* illustrate. **er'läuternd** *adj* explanatory, illustrative. **Er'läuterung** *f* (-; -en) a) explanation, b) illustration, c) note.

Erle ['ɛrlə] *f* (-; -n) ♀ alder.

er'leben *v/t* (h) a) experience, b) have (*adventures etc*), c) go through (*bad times etc*), d) live to see, e) see: *ich habe* (*es*) *selbst erlebt, was es heißt, arm zu sein* I know from experience what it means to be poor; *ich habe es oft erlebt*(*daß*) I've often seen it happen (that); *wir werden es ja ~!* we'll see!

Erlebnis [ɛr'leːpnɪs] *n* (-ses; -se) a) experience, b) event, c) adventure.

er'lebnisreich *adj* eventful.

erledigen [ɛr'leːdɪgən] (h) **I** *v/t* **1.** a) finish (off), b) deal with, take care of, c) settle (*problem, deal, etc*), d) carry out

(*order, task*): *würden Sie das für mich ~?* would you do that for me? **2.** dismiss. **3.** F *j-n ~* finish s.o. (*a. sports*), *a.* do s.o. in. **II** *sich selbst ~* take care of itself, F sort itself out. **er'ledigt** *adj* **1.** settled, finished: *das wäre ~!* that's that!; *das ist für mich ~* the matter's closed as far as I'm concerned; F *du bist für mich ~!* I'm through with you! **2.** F *person*: a) finished, b) done in, whacked: *der ist ~!* he's done for!

Er'ledigung *f* (-; -en) *no pl* settlement: *zur umgehenden ~* for immediate attention. **2.** *pl* errands, shopping.

er'legen *II pp of* **erliegen**. **II** *v/t* (h) *hunt.* shoot, kill.

erleichtern [ɛr'laɪçtərn] *v/t* (h) a) make a task easier, facilitate, b) lighten (*a burden*), c) relieve (*need, pain, etc*), ease (*one's conscience*): *sich das Herz ~* unburden one's heart; *das erleichterte mich sehr* that was a great relief to me; F *j-n ~ um ...* relieve s.o. of *wallet etc*.

er'leichtert *adj* relieved: *ich war ~, als ...* it was a relief to me when ...; *~ aufatmen* breathe a sigh of relief.

Er'leichterung *f* (-; -en) **1.** *no pl* facilitation, lightening, easing. **2.** *no pl* relief (*über acc* at): *zu m-r ~* to my relief. **3.** *pl* ✝, *pol.* relief, facilities.

er'leiden *v/t* (erlitt, erlitten, h) a) suffer, go through, b) sustain: *den Tod ~* die.

erlernbar [ɛr'lɛrnbaːr] *adj* learnable.

er'lernen *v/t* (h) learn.

er'lesen *v/t* (h) select, choice, exquisite.

er'leuchten *v/t* (h) **1.** light (up), illuminate. **2.** *fig.* enlighten. **Er'leuchtung** *f* (-; -en) **1.** illumination. **2.** *fig.* a) enlightenment, b) idea, inspiration.

er'liegen *v/i* (erlag, erlegen, sn) (*dat*) succumb (to *temptation etc*), be the victim (of *a mistake etc*). **Er'liegen** *n* (-s) *zum ~ kommen* break down; *et. zum ~ bringen* bring s.th. to a standstill.

erließ [ɛr'liːs] *pret of* **erlassen**.

erlitt [ɛr'lɪt] *pret of* **erleiden**.

erlogen [ɛr'loːgən] *adj* made(-)up: *das ist ~* that's a lie.

Erlös [ɛr'løːs] *m* (-es; -e) proceeds.

erloschen [ɛr'lɔʃən] **I** *pp of* **erlöschen**. **II** *adj* **1.** extinct. **2.** *fig.* dead. **3.** *contract etc*: expired.

er'löschen *v/i* (erlosch, erloschen, sn)

go out, *a. fig. life:* be extinguished, *contract etc:* expire.

Er'löschen *n* (-s) a) extinction, b) expiry.

er'lösen *v/t* (h) (**von** from) a) release, free, b) rescue: *j-n ~ iro.* put s.o. out of his (her) misery, *eccl.* save (*or* redeem) s.o.; *er ist erlöst* his sufferings are over. **er'lösend** *adj das ~e Wort sprechen* break the tension; *ein ~es Gefühl* a great relief. **Er'lösung** *f* (-; -en) 1. release. 2. *eccl.* salvation. 3. relief.

ermächtigen [ɛr'mɛçtɪɡən] *v/t* (h) authorize (*j-n zu et.* s.o. to do s.th.). **Er'mächtigung** *f* (-; -en) 1. authorization. 2. authority.

er'mahnen *v/t* (h) admonish (*j-n zur Vorsicht etc* s.o. to be careful *etc*), caution, warn (*a. sports*). **Er'mahnung** *f* (-; -en) admonition, warning, *esp. sports:* caution.

Er'mangelung: *in ~* (*gen*) for want of.

er'mäßigen (h) **I** *v/t* reduce, cut: *zu ermäßigten Preisen* at reduced prices. **II sich ~** be reduced (*auf acc* to).

er'messen *v/t* (ermaß, ermessen, h) a) estimate, assess, b) judge, c) appreciate, realize. **Er'messen** *n* (-s) judg(e)ment, discretion: *ich stelle es in Ihr ~* I leave it to you(r discretion); *das liegt ganz in Ihrem ~ a.* it's entirely up to you.

Er'messensfrage *f* matter of opinion.

Er'messensspielraum *m* latitude.

ermitteln [ɛr'mɪtəln] (h) **I** *v/t* a) find out, establish, locate (*place etc*), b) determine. **II** *v/i police:* investigate, carry out investigations (**gegen** concerning). **Er'mittlung** *f* (-; -en) 1. a) finding out *s.th.*, b) determination. 2. *a.* investigation, inquiry: *~en anstellen* a) make inquiries (**über** *acc* about), b) → **ermitteln** II. 3. *pl* findings.

Er'mittlungs|ausschuß *m* fact-finding committee. *~beamte* *m* investigating officer. *~verfahren* *n* ⚖ preliminary proceedings.

ermöglichen [ɛr'møː'klɪçən] *v/t* (h) a) make *s.th.* possible, b) allow: *j-m ~, et. zu tun* make it possible for (*or* enable) s.o. to do s.th.

er'morden *v/t* (h) murder. **Er'mordete** *m, f* (-n; -n) (murder) victim.

Er'mordung *f* (-; -en) murder.

ermüden [ɛr'myːdən] *v/t* (h), *v/i* (sn) tire. **er'müdend** *adj* tiring. **er'müdet** *adj*

tired. **Er'müdung** *f* (-; *no pl*) tiredness, *a.* ⚙ fatigue. **Er'müdungserscheinung** *f a.* ⚙ sign of fatigue.

ermuntern [ɛr'mʊntərn] *v/t* (h) **1.** encourage s.o. (*zu et., et. zu tun* to do s.th.). **2.** stimulate. **er'munternd** *adj* encouraging. **Er'munterung** *f* (-; -en) **1.** encouragement. **2.** stimulation.

ermutigen [ɛr'muːtɪɡən] *v/t* (h) encourage s.o. (*zu et., et. zu tun* to do s.th.). **er'mutigend** *adj* encouraging, reassuring. **Er'mutigung** *f* (-; -en) (*zur ~* as an) encouragement.

er'nähren (h) **I** *v/t* a) feed, nourish, b) support: *schlecht ernährt* malnourished. **II sich ~** (**von**) live (on), *fig.* make a living (by). **Er'nährer** *m* (-s; -), **Er'nährerin** *f* (-; -nen) supporter, breadwinner. **Er'nährung** *f* (-; *no pl*) **1.** a) feeding, 🍴 nutrition, b) food: *schlechte ~* malnutrition. **2.** support.

Er'nährungs|weise *f* eating habits. *~wissenschaft* *f* (-; *no pl*) dietetics. *~wissenschaftler(in* *f*) *m* dietician.

er'nennen *v/t* (ernannte, ernannt, h) appoint (*j-n zu et.* s.o. s.th.). **Er'nennung** *f* (-; -en) appointment (*zum* as *or* to the post of).

erneuern [ɛr'nɔyərn] (h) **I** *v/t* renew (*contract, offer, etc*), ⚙ *a.* replace, *fig. a.* revive. **II sich ~** be renewed, revive. **Er'neuerung** *f* (-; -en) renewal, ⚙ *a.* replacement, *fig. a.* revival.

erneut [ɛr'nɔyt] **I** *adj* renewed, new, repeated, fresh. **II** *adv* again, once more.

erniedrigen [ɛr'niːdrɪɡən] (h) **I** *v/t* **1.** degrade, humiliate. **2.** → **herabsetzen** 2. **II sich ~** degrade o.s.; *sich (so weit) ~, et. zu tun* lower o.s. to do s.th. **er'niedrigend** *adj* degrading, humiliating. **Er'niedrigung** *f* (-; -en) a) degradation, b) humiliation.

ernst [ɛrnst] **I** *adj* serious, a) earnest, b) *a.* grave, solemn, c) *a.* severe, d) *a.* weighty: *~e Musik* serious music. **II** *adv* seriously (*etc*), in earnest: *ich meine es ~* I'm serious about it, I mean it; *j-n* (*et.*) *~ nehmen* take s.o. (s.th.) seriously; *das war nicht ~ gemeint!* I (*etc*) didn't mean it!

Ernst *m* (-es; *no pl*) seriousness, *a.* earnestness, gravity, severity: *allen ~es* in all seriousness; *~ machen mit* go ahead with; *ich meine es im ~, es ist mein voller ~* I'm dead serious.

'**Ernstfall** *m* emergency: *im ~* a) in case of emergency, b) if things come to the worst, c) ✕ in the event of a war.

'**ernstgemeint** *adj* serious, sincere.

'**ernsthaft** *adj* serious: *sich ~e Sorgen machen um* be seriously worried about.

'**Ernsthaftigkeit** *f* (-; *no pl*) seriousness.

'**ernstlich I** *adj* serious. **II** *adv ~ krank* seriously ill; *~ böse* really angry.

'**ernstzunehmend** *adj* serious.

Ernte ['ɛrntə] *f* (-; -en) **1.** *a. fig.* harvest. **2.** crop. '**Ernteausfall** *m* crop failure. '**Erntedankfest** *n* harvest festival. **ernten** ['ɛrntən] *v/t, v/i* (h) harvest, reap (*a. fig.*). '**Ernteschäden** *pl* crop damage. '**Erntezeit** *f* harvest time.

er'**nüchtern** *v/t* (h) sober: *fig. j-n ~ a.* bring s.o. down to earth again.

Er'nüchterung *f* (-; -en) **1.** sobering-up. **2.** *fig.* disillusionment.

Er'oberer *m* (-s; -) conqueror. **erobern** [ɛr'ʔoːbərn] *v/t* (h) *a. fig.* conquer: → *Sturm* 2. **Er'oberung** *f* (-; -en) (*fig. e-e ~ machen*) make a) conquest.

er'**öffnen** (h) **I** *v/t* **1.** open, inaugurate: ✕ *das Feuer ~* open fire. **2.** *fig.* open (up), offer (*prospects etc*). **3.** *j-m et. ~* disclose s.th. to s.o., inform s.o. of s.th. **II** *v/i* open (*a. at chess*). **III** *sich ~ opportunity etc*: present itself.

Er'öffnung *f* (-; -en) **1.** opening (*a. at chess*), inauguration. **2.** disclosure.

Er'öffnungs|ansprache *f* inaugural address. *~***beschluß** *m* ⚖ **1.** order to proceed. **2.** bankruptcy order. *~***feier** *f* opening ceremony. *~***kurs** *m* ✝ opening quotation.

erogen [ero'geːn] *adj* erogenous.

erörtern [ɛr'ʔœrtərn] *v/t* (h) discuss.

Er'örterung *f* (-; -en) discussion (*gen* of).

Erosion [ero'zioːn] *f* (-; -en) erosion.

Erotik [e'roːtɪk] *f* (-; *no pl*) eroticism.

erotisch [e'roːtɪʃ] *adj* erotic.

erpicht [ɛr'pɪçt] *adj ~ sein auf* (*acc*) be very (F dead) keen on, be bent on.

er'**preßbar** *adj* open to blackmail.

er'**pressen** *v/t* (h) *j-n ~* blackmail s.o. (*et. zu tun* into doing s.th.); *et. ~* extort s.th. (*von* from). **Er'presser** *m* (-s; -), **Er'presserin** *f* (-; -nen) blackmailer. **Er'presserbrief** *m* blackmail letter.

Er'pressung *f* (-; -en) blackmail.

Er'pressungsversuch *m* blackmail attempt.

er'**proben** *v/t* (h) try (out), test. **er'probt** *adj* **1.** well-tried. **2.** experienced.

Er'probung *f* (-; -en) trial, test.

errang [ɛr'raŋ] *pret of* **erringen**.

er'**raten** *v/t* (erriet, erraten, h) guess.

er'**rechnen** *v/t* (h) work out, calculate: *sich ~ aus* be calculated from.

erregbar [ɛr're:kbaːr] *adj* a) excitable, b) irritable. **Er'regbarkeit** *f* (-; *no pl*) a) excitability, b) irritability. er'**regen** (h) **I** *v/t* **1.** excite (*a. ⚡, a. sexually*), *b.s.* irritate, infuriate. **2.** *fig.* cause: *j-s Zorn ~* provoke s.o.'s anger; *Bewunderung ~* excite admiration; → *Ärgernis, Aufsehen.* **II** *sich ~* (*über acc* about) a) get excited, get all worked up, b) get angry.

er'**regend** *adj* exciting. **Er'reger** *m* (-s; -) **1.** ⚡ exciter. **2.** 🔬 pathogen, germ.

er'**regt** *adj* excited (*a. sexually*), heated (*debate etc*). **Er'regung** *f* (-; -en) **1.** creation, excitation (*a. ⚡*), causing. **2.** excitement, *sexually: a.* (state of) arousal. **3.** anger.

erreichbar [ɛr'raiçbaːr] *adj* a) within reach, *fig.* attainable, b) available: *leicht ~* within easy reach; *zu Fuß* (*mit dem Wagen*) *leicht ~* within easy walking (driving) distance; *er ist nie ~* you just can't get hold of him. er'**reichen** *v/t* (h) **1.** a) reach, catch (*bus, train, etc*), b) catch up with: *j-n telefonisch ~* get s.o. on the phone; *ein hohes Alter ~* live to an old age; *leicht zu ~* within easy reach. **2.** *fig.* a) achieve, b) obtain, get: *et. ~* get somewhere; (*es*) *~, daß ...* succeed in *ger*; *haben Sie* (*bei ihm*) *et. erreicht?* did you get anywhere (with him)? **Er'reichung** *f* (-; *no pl*) attainment: *nach ~ der Altersgrenze* on reaching the retirement age.

er'**richten** *v/t* (h) **1.** build, erect, put up. **2.** *fig.* found, *esp.* ✝ set up.

Er'richtung *f* (-; *no pl*) **1.** building, erection. **2.** *fig.* foundation.

erriet [ɛr'riːt] *pret of* **erraten**.

er'**ringen** *v/t* (errang, errungen, h) gain, *a.* win (*prize*), *a.* achieve (*success*).

er'**röten** *v/i* (sn) blush (*vor* with, *über acc* at).

Errungenschaft [ɛr'rʊŋənʃaft] *f* (-; -en) **1.** acquisition. **2.** *fig.* achievement.

ersah [ɛrˈzaː] *pret of* **ersehen**.

Ersatz [ɛrˈzats] *m* (-es; *no pl*) **1.** substitute, replacement(s ✕): *als* ~ *für j-n* to replace s.o.; *er (das) ist kein* ~ *für ...* he (that) can't replace ... **2.** ✝, ⚕ a) compensation, b) damages: *als* ~ *für* by way of compensation, in exchange (*or* return) for. **~anspruch** *m* claim for compensation. **~bank** *f sports*: substitutes' bench. **~batterie** *f* spare battery. **~befriedigung** *f psych.* compensation. **~handlung** *f psych.* displacement activity, *w.s.* compensation. **~kasse** *f* health insurance society. **~leistung** *f* compensation. **~mann** *m* substitute (*a.* ✕), replacement (*a.* ✕). **~mine** *f* refill. **~mittel** *n* substitute, ersatz. **~mutter** *f* mother-substitute.

er'satzpflichtig *adj* liable for damages.

Er'satzreifen *m* spare tyre (*Am.* tire).

Er'satzspieler(in *f*) *m sports*: substitute.

Er'satzteil *m*, *n* ⚙ replacement part, spare (part). **~chirurgie** *f* spare parts surgery. **~lager** *n* spare parts store.

er'satzweise *adv* alternatively.

er'saufen *v/i* (ersoff, ersoffen, sn) F drown.

ersäufen [ɛrˈzɔyfən] *v/t* (h) drown.

er'schaffen *v/t* (erschuf, erschaffen, h) create, make.

Er'schaffung *f* (-; *no pl*) creation.

er'scheinen *v/i* (erschien, erschienen, sn) **1.** appear (*a. ghost*: *j-m* to s.o.), come, F turn up: *vor Gericht* ~ appear in court. **2.** appear, come out, be published: *soeben erschienen* just published. **3.** (*j-m* to s.o.) seem, appear: *es erscheint ratsam* it would seem advisable. **Er'scheinen** *n* (-s) **1.** appearance, *a.* publication. **2.** attendance (*bei* at).

Er'scheinung *f* (-; -en) **1.** a) appearance, b) apparition, c) vision: *in* ~ *treten* appear, *fig. a.* make itself felt; *stark (kaum) in* ~ *treten* be very (not) much in evidence; *er tritt kaum in* ~ he keeps very much in the background. **2.** *fig.* sign, symptom (*a.* ☀). **3.** a) (outward) appearance, b) figure. **Er'scheinungsjahr** *n* year of publication.

er'schießen (erschoß, erschossen, h) I *v/t* shoot (dead): *j-n* ~ *lassen* have s.o. shot. II *sich* ~ shoot o.s.

Er'schießung *f* (-; -en) shooting, ✕ execution (by a firing squad).

erschlaffen [ɛrˈʃlafən] *v/i* (sn) *muscles etc*: grow tired, *skin*: (begin to) sag.

er'schlagen (erschlug, erschlagen, h) I *v/t* kill. II *adj* F *wie* ~ a) dum(b)founded, b) dead-beat, whacked.

er'schleichen *v/t* (erschlich, erschlichen, h) *sich et.* ~ obtain s.th. by trickery; *sich j-s Vertrauen* ~ worm o.s. into s.o.'s confidence.

er'schließen (erschloß, erschlossen, h) I *v/t* open (up) (*a. market etc*), develop (*area, building estates*). II *sich j-m* ~ *mystery etc*: be revealed to s.o., *opportunities etc*: open up before s.o.

Er'schließung *f* (-; -en) opening (up), development.

er'schöpfen (h) I *v/t a. fig.* exhaust. II *sich* ~ exhaust o.s., *fig.* be exhausted: *sich* ~ *in* (*dat*) activity *etc*: be limited to. **er'schöpfend** *adj* **1.** exhaustive. **2.** exhaustive. **er'schöpft** *adj* a) exhausted (*von* by), b) spent. **Er'schöpfung** *f* (-; *no pl*) (*bis zur* ~ to the point of) exhaustion. **Er'schöpfungszustand** *m* (state of) exhaustion.

erschoß [ɛrˈʃɔs] *pret*, **er'schossen** *pp of* **er'schießen**.

er'schrecken[1] *v/t* (h) frighten, scare, startle: → *Tod.* **er'schrecken**[2] *v/i* (erschrak, erschrocken, sn) be frightened (*über acc* at). **Er'schrecken** *n* (-s) fright. **er'schreckend** *adj* frightening, appalling: ~ *wenige* alarmingly few.

erschrocken [ɛrˈʃrɔkən] I *pp of* **er'schrecken**[2]. II *adj and adv* frightened.

erschuf [ɛrˈʃuːf] *pret of* **erschaffen**.

er'schüttern [ɛrˈʃytərn] *v/t* (h) **1.** *a. fig.* shake. **2.** *fig.* a) shock, b) move *s.o.* deeply. **er'schütternd** *adj* a) shocking, b) deeply moving. **Er'schütterung** *f* (-; -en) a) shock (*a. fig.*), b) *fig.* emotion.

erschweren [ɛrˈʃveːrən] *v/t* (h) a) make *s.th.* (more) difficult, complicate, impede, b) *a.* ⚖ aggravate.

er'schwerend *adj* ⚖ aggravating.

er'schwindeln *v/t* (h) *sich et. von j-m* ~ cheat s.th. out of s.o.

erschwinglich [ɛrˈʃvɪŋlɪç] *adj* within s.o.'s means: *zu* ~*en Preisen* at reasonable prices.

er'sehen *v/t* (ersah, ersehen, h) (*aus* from) see, gather.

er'sehnen *v/t* (h) long for.

ersetzbar [ɛrˈzɛtsbaːr] *adj* replaceable

(*a.* ⊙), reparable (*damage*), recoverable (*loss*). **er'setzen** *v/t* (h) a) replace (**durch** by), *a.* take the place of *s.o.*, b) compensate for, make up for: *j-m den Schaden* (*die Auslagen*) ~ compensate s.o. for the damage (reimburse s.o. for expenses). **Er'setzung** *f* (-; -en) a) replacement, b) compensation, reimbursement (*of expenses*).

er'sichtlich *adj* apparent, evident, clear: *ohne* ~*en Grund* for no apparent reason; *daraus wird* ~ hence it appears.

ersoff [ɛr'zɔf] *pret of* **ersaufen**.

ersoffen [ɛr'zɔfən] *pp of* **ersaufen**.

er'spähen *v/t* (h) F spot.

er'sparen *v/t* (h) **1.** (*a. sich* ~) save. **2.** *fig. sich et.* ~ spare o.s. s.th.; *j-m Arbeit* (*Kosten etc*) ~ save s.o. work (money *etc*); *ihr bleibt nichts erspart* she gets all the bad breaks.

Ersparnis [ɛr'ʃpaːrnɪs] *f* (-; -se) **1.** saving (*an dat* in). **2.** *pl* savings.

ersprießlich [ɛr'ʃpriːslɪç] *adj* fruitful, profitable.

erst [eːrst] *adv* a) (at) first, b) first, c) only, just, d) only, not till, not until: (*eben*) ~ just (now); ~ *als* (*dann, jetzt*) only when (then, now); ~ *nächste Woche* not before next week; ~ *nach* only (*or* not until) after; *es ist* ~ *fünf Uhr* it's only five o'clock; *ich muß* ~ *telefonieren* I've got to make a phone call first.

erstach [ɛr'ʃtaːx] *pret of* **erstechen**.

erstand [ɛr'ʃtant] *pret of* **erstehen**.

erstanden [ɛr'ʃtandən] *pp of* **erstehen**.

erstarken [ɛr'ʃtarkən] *v/i* (sn) grow strong(er).

er'starren *v/i* (sn) a) grow stiff, stiffen, go numb (*with cold*), b) 🜋 *etc* solidify, *blood:* coagulate, c) freeze (*a. fig. vor dat* with), *fig.* run cold: *vor Schrecken* ~ *a.* be paralysed with fear. **er'starrt** *adj* stiff, numb, *fig.* paralysed. **Er'starrung** *f* (-; *no pl*) a) stiffness, numbness, b) 🜋 solidification, c) *fig.* paralysis, rigidity.

erstatten [ɛr'ʃtatən] *v/t* (h) **1.** refund (*j-m* s.o.s.). **2.** *Anzeige* ~ *gegen* report s.o. to the police; → *Bericht*. **Er'stattung** *f* (-; -en) refund(ing).

'Erstaufführung *f thea. etc* première, *film: a.* first run.

er'staunen I *v/t* (h) astonish, amaze. **II** *v/i* → **staunen** I. **Er'staunen** *n* (-s) astonishment, amazement: *in* ~ *setzen*

astonish, amaze; (*sehr*) *zu* m-m ~ (much) to my surprise. **er'staunlich** *adj* astonishing, amazing. **er'staunlicherweise** *adv* astonishingly, to my *etc* surprise (*or* amazement). **er'staunt** *adj* (*über acc* at) astonished, amazed.

'Erstausgabe *f* first edition.

'erst'beste I *adj the* first, F any (old). **II** *der* (*die*) ~ the first person one happens to see; just anyone; *das* ~ the next best (F any old) thing *etc*.

erste [eːrstə] *adj* first: *Karl der* 2 (*Karl I.*) Charles the First (Charles I); ~ *Qualität* prime quality; *der* 2 *des Monats* the first (day) of the month; *der* ~ *beste* → *erstbeste*; *als* ~(*r*), *als* ~*s* first; *er war der* ~ he was first; *er war der* ~, *der ...* he was the first to *inf*; *fürs* ~ for the moment; → *Blick* 1, *Geige, Hand, Hilfe* 1 *etc*.

er'stechen *v/t* (erstach, erstochen, h) stab *s.o.* (to death).

er'stehen (erstand, erstanden) **I** *v/i* (sn) rise, be built. **II** *v/t* (h) buy, get.

er'steigen *v/t* (erstieg, erstiegen, h) climb (up to), ascend.

er'steigern *v/t* (h) buy at an auction. **Er'steigung** *f* (-; -en) ascent, climbing.

er'stellen *v/t* (h) **1.** erect, build. **2.** prepare, draw up (*report etc*).

erstemal [eːrstəmaːl] *adv das* ~ the first time; *beim erstemal* the first time; *zum erstenmal* for the first time.

erstens [eːrstəns] *adv* first(ly), first of all.

'erster → *erste*.

erstere [eːrstərə] *adj the* former.

'erstgeboren *adj* first-born.

'Erstgeburtsrecht *n* birthright.

'erstgenannt *adj* first-mentioned.

ersticken [ɛr'ʃtɪkən] **I** *v/t* (h) suffocate, choke, *a. fig.* smother, stifle: → *Keim* 1. **II** *v/i* (sn) suffocate (**durch, an** *dat* from): *an e-r Gräte* ~ choke (to death) on a bone; *fig. in Arbeit* ~ be swamped with work. **Er'sticken** *n* (-s) suffocation: *zum* ~ (*heiß*) stifling(ly) hot. **er'stickend** *adj a. fig.* stifling. **Er'stickung** *f* (-; *no pl*) suffocation. **Er'stickungs|anfall** *m* choking fit. ~*tod m* death from suffocation.

erstieg [ɛr'ʃtiːk] *pret of* **ersteigen**.

erstiegen [ɛr'ʃtiːgən] *pp of* **ersteigen**.

'erstklassig *adj* first-class, first-rate, top-quality (*goods etc*).

Erstling ['e:rstlɪŋ] *m* (-s; -e) **1.** first-born child. **2.** *fig.* first work.

erstmalig ['e:rstma:lɪç] **I** *adj* first. **II** *adv*, *a.* **'erstmals** for the first time.

'Erstmeldung *f* exclusive report, F scoop.

erstochen [ɛr'ʃtɔxən] *pp of* **erstechen.**

er'strahlen *v/i* (sn) shine.

erstrangig [ɛr'rstraŋɪç] *adj* first-rate.

er'streben *v/t* (h) strive after, aim for.

er'strebenswert *adj* desirable.

er'strecken: sich ~ a) (*bis zu* to) extend, stretch, b) *fig.* (*über acc*) cover (*area etc*), c) *fig.* (*auf acc*) concern, apply to.

'Erstschlag *m* ✗ first strike.

er'stürmen *v/t* (h) (take by storm.

Er'stürmung *f* (-; -en) storming.

'Erstwähler(in *f*) *m* first-time voter.

er'suchen *v/t* (h) **j-n ~ zu** *inf* ask (*or* request) s.o. to *inf*; **j-n um et. ~** request s.th. from s.o. **Er'suchen** *n* (-s; -) (*auf sein ~ hin* at his) request.

er'tappen *v/t* (h) catch (*bei* at): **j-n beim Stehlen ~** catch s.o. stealing.

er'teilen *v/t* **1.** give (*lessons, advice, etc*): ✝ **j-m e-n Auftrag ~** place an order with s.o.; **j-m das Wort ~** ask s.o. to speak. **2.** (*dat*) grant (*s.o. a patent etc*), confer (*a right etc* on s.o.)

Ertrag [ɛr'tra:k] *m* (-[e]s; ⸚e) **1.** yield, ✗ *etc* output. **2.** (*aus* from) proceeds, returns.

er'tragen *v/t* (ertrug, ertragen, h) a) endure, bear, stand, b) put up with: **das ist kaum noch zu ~** that is hardly bearable; **ich kann den Gedanken nicht ~, daß ...** I can't bear to think that ...

er'tragfähig *adj* **1.** ✔ productive. **2.** ✝ profit-yielding.

er'träglich [ɛr'trɛ:klɪç] **I** *adj* bearable, tolerable. **II** *adv* tolerably well.

er'tragreich *adj* productive, profitable.

Er'tragslage *f* ✝ profit situation.

er'tränken *v/t* (h) drown (*sich* o.s.).

er'träumen *v/t* (h) **sich et. ~** dream of.

er'trinken *v/i* (ertrank, ertrunken, sn) drown, be drowned.

ertrug [ɛr'tru:k] *pret of* **ertragen.**

Ertüchtigung [ɛr'tʏçtɪɡʊŋ] *f* (-; -en) physical training.

erübrigen [ɛr'ˀy:brɪɡən] (h) **I** *v/t* save (*money*), spare (*time*). **II** *sich ~* be unnecessary, be superfluous.

eruieren [eru'i:rən] *v/t* (h) find out.

Eruption [erʊp'tsĭo:n] *f* (-; -en) eruption.

er'wachen *v/i* (sn) wake up (*a. fig.*), awake, *fig. feelings etc*: be awakened, *suspicion etc*: be aroused. **Er'wachen** *n* (-s) (*fig. unsanftes ~* rude) awakening.

er'wachsen[1] *v/i* (erwuchs, erwachsen, sn) arise (*aus* from).

er'wachsen[2] *adj*, **Er'wachsene** *m*, *f* (-n; -n) grown-up, adult. **Er'wachsenenbildung** *f* adult education.

erwägen [ɛr'vɛ:ɡən] *v/t* (erwog, erwogen, h) consider, think s.th. over: **den Kauf e-s Autos ~** consider buying a car. **Er'wägung** *f* (-; -en) (*et. in ~ ziehen* take s.th. into) consideration.

er'wähnen *v/t* (h) mention.

er'wähnenswert *adj* worth mentioning.

Er'wähnung *f* (-; -en) mention.

erwarb [ɛr'varp] *pret of* **erwerben.**

er'wärmen (h) **I** *v/t* warm (up): *fig.* **j-n für et. ~** get s.o. interested in s.th. **II** *sich ~* get warm(er); *fig.* **sich für et. ~** warm to s.th.

er'warten *v/t* (h) a) expect, b) wait for: *fig.* **j-n ~ surprise etc:** be in store for s.o.; **ein Kind ~** be expecting (a baby); **ich kann es kaum ~** (*zu* inf) I can hardly wait (to *inf*); **das war zu ~** that was to be expected. **Er'warten** *n* (-s) **über alles ~** beyond all expectation; **wider ~** contrary to all expectations.

Er'wartung *f* (-; -en) a) expectation, b) expectancy, anticipation: **in ~** (*gen*) awaiting; **den (j-s) ~en entsprechen** come up to (s.o.'s) expectations; **hinter den (j-s) ~en zurückbleiben** fall short of (s.o.'s) expectations.

er'wartungsgemäß *adv* as expected.

Er'wartungs|haltung *f* expectancy, expectations. **~hori,zont** *m* (-[e]s; *no pl*) horizon of expectations.

er'wartungsvoll *adj* expectant.

er'wecken *v/t* **1.** *a. fig.* **wieder zum Leben ~** revive. **2.** *fig.* arouse (*interest, suspicion, etc*), bring back (*memories*), raise (*hopes*), inspire (*trust*): → **Anschein, Eindruck 1** *etc.*

er'wehren: sich ~ (h) (*gen*) ward off, resist; **sich nicht ~ können** (*gen*) be helpless against; **man konnte sich des Eindrucks nicht ~, daß ...** you couldn't help feeling that ...

er'weichen *v/t* (h) soften, *fig. a.* move: **sich ~ lassen** give in.

er'weisen (erwies, erwiesen, h) **I** *v/t*
1. prove, show. **2.** do (*a good turn
etc*), grant (*a favo[u]r*), show (*respect*):
→ **Ehre. II** *sich ~ als* prove (*or* turn
out) to be; *sich (j-m gegenüber) dankbar ~* show one's gratitude (towards
s.o.).

erweitern [ɛr'vaɪtərn] (h) **I** *v/t* widen
(*road etc*), extend (*building, business,
etc, a. fig. powers etc*), enlarge (*book*),
broaden (*knowledge*), ✷ dilate. **II** *sich
~ a.* fig. widen, expand, b) ✷ dilate.

Er'weiterung *f* (-; -en) widening (*etc*),
extension, enlargement, ✷ dilatation.

Erwerb [ɛr'vɛrp] *m* (-[e]s; -e) acquisition,
purchase. **er'werben** *v/t* (erwarb, erworben, h) a) acquire (*a. fig. rights,
knowledge, etc*), purchase, b) earn, fig.
gain, win (*fame, wealth, etc*): *sich Verdienste ~ um* render great service(s) to.

er'werbsfähig *adj* fit for work: *im ~en
Alter* of employable age. **Er'werbs-
fähigkeit** *f* (-; *no pl*) ability to work.

Er'werbsleben *n* working life.

er'werbslos → *arbeitslos.* **Er'werbs-
minderung** *f* (-; *no pl*) reduction in
earning capacity. **Er'werbsquelle** *f*
source of income. **Er'werbstätig** *adj*
(gainfully) employed. **Er'werbstätige**
m, f (-n; -n) (*employed*) person.

Er'werbstätigkeit *f* gainful employment. **er'werbsunfähig** *adj* unfit for
work. **Er'werbsunfähigkeit** *f* inca-
pacity to work. **Er'werbszweig** *m* a)
branch of industry, b) line (of business).

Er'werbung *f* (-; -en) acquisition.

erwidern [ɛr'vi:dərn] *v/t* (h) **1.** (*auf acc
to*) reply, answer: *auf m-e Frage erwi-
derte er ...* in reply to my question he
said ... **2.** return (*greeting, visit, etc*, ✗
fire). **Er'widerung** *f* (-; -en) **1.** (*auf acc
to*) reply, answer. **2.** *fig.* return.

erwies [ɛr'vi:s] *pret,* **erwiesen** [ɛr'vi:-
zən] *pp of* **erweisen.** **Er'wiesenerma-
ßen** *adv* as has been proved.

er'wirken *v/t* (h) obtain, secure.

er'wirtschaften *v/t* (h) make (*profit*).

er'wischen *v/t* (h) catch (*a. fig.*): *sich ~
lassen* get caught; F *ihn hat's bös er-
wischt!* he's got it bad!

erwog [ɛr'vo:k] *pret of* **erwägen.**

erwogen [ɛr'vo:gən] *pp of* **erwägen.**

erworben [ɛr'vɔrbən] *pp of* **erwerben.**

erwuchs [ɛr'vu:ks] *pret of* **erwachsen¹.**

erwünscht [ɛr'vʏnʃt] *adj* a) desired, b)
welcome, c) desirable.

er'würgen *v/t* (h) strangle.

Erz [e:rts] *n* (-es; -e) ore.

er'zählen (h) **I** *v/t* tell, narrate: *man hat
mir erzählt* I've been told; *man erzählt
sich* they say; F *das kannst du mir
nicht ~!* pull another one! **II** *v/i* tell a
story (*or* stories): *~ von, ~ über* (*acc*)
tell (s.o.) of (*or* about); *erzähl mal!* do
tell! **er'zählenswert** *adj* worth telling.
Er'zähler *m* (-s; -), **Er'zählerin** *f* (-;
-nen) **1.** narrator, storyteller. **2.** narrative writer. **Er'zählung** *f* (-; -en) a) nar-
ration, story, tale, b) account, c) *literature:* (short) story.

Erzbischof ['e:rts-] *m* archbishop.
'erzbischöflich *adj* archiepiscopal.
'Erzbistum *n,* **'Erzdiö.zese** *f* archbish-
opric. **'Erzengel** *m* archangel.

er'zeugen *v/t* (h) produce, ☉ *a.* make,
🌱 *a.* grow, 🔩, *phys.* generate, fig. *a.*
cause, create. **Er'zeuger** *m* (-s; -) **1.**
father. **2.** producer, *a.* ☉ manufacturer,
🌱 *a.* grower. **Er'zeugerland** *n* country
of origin. **Er'zeugnis** *n* (-ses; -se) product (*a. fig.*), 🌱 *a.* produce, (*novel
etc*) production: *eigenes ~* my *etc* own
make. **Er'zeugung** *f* (-; *no pl*) production, ☉ *a.* manufacture, 🔩, *phys.* generation, fig. creation. **Er'zeugungs-
kosten** *pl* production costs.

'Erzfeind *m* archenemy. **'Erzfeind-
schaft** *f* archrivalry, deadly feud.

'Erzherzog *m* archduke.

'Erzherzogin *f* archduchess.

'Erzhütte *f* smelting works.

er'ziehbar *adj* educable: *schwer ~es
Kind* problem child. **er'ziehen** *v/t* (erzog, erzogen, h) a) bring *s.o.* up, raise,
b) educate: *j-n zu et. ~* train (*or* teach)
s.o. to be (*or* do) s.th.; → *erzogen.*
Er'zieher *m* (-s; -) a) educator, b)
teacher, c) tutor. **Er'zieherin** *f* (-; -nen)
a) (lady) teacher, b) nursery-school
teacher, c) governess. **er'zieherisch**
adj educational. **Er'ziehung** *f* (-; *no pl*)
1. a) upbringing, b) education, c) training. **2.** a) breeding, b) manners.

Er'ziehungs.anstalt *f* approved (*Am.*
reform) school. **~berater(in** *f*) *m* educational adviser. **~beratung** *f* child
guidance. **~berechtigte** *m, f* (-n; -n) a)
parent, b) (legal) guardian. **~wis-**

senschaft f (-; no pl) educational science.

er'zielen v/t (h) a) obtain, get, achieve (success etc), b) reach (an agreement etc), c) make (a profit), fetch (a prize), d) sports: score (goals, points).

er'zittern v/i (sn) tremble.

'erzkonserva,tiv adj ultra-conservative.

erzog [ɛr'tso:k] pret of **erziehen.**

erzogen [ɛr'tso:gən] I pp of **erziehen.** II adj **gut ~** well-bred; **schlecht ~** ill-bred.

er'zürnen (h) I v/t anger, infuriate. II **sich ~** get angry (**über** acc at).

er'zürnt adj angry, furious.

erzwungen [ɛr'tsvʊŋən] pp of **erzwingen.**

es [ɛs] pers pron a) it, b) he, she: **ich bin ~!** it's me!; **bist du ~?** is it you?; **~ gibt** there is, there are; **ich hoffe ~** I hope so; **ich weiß ~ (nicht)** I (don't) know; **er kann nicht schwimmen, aber ich kann ~** he can't swim, but I can; **du bist müde, ich bin ~ auch** you are tired, so am I; **ich will ~** I want to; **ich will ~ versuchen** I'll try; **~ wurde getanzt** there was dancing, we (they) danced.

Es n (-; -) ♩ E flat.

Esche ['ɛʃə] f (-; -n) ♣ ash (tree).

Esel ['e:zəl] m (-s; -) **1.** donkey, jackass. **2.** F fig. (silly) ass: **alter ~** old fool.

Eselin f (-; -nen) she-ass.

'Eselsbrücke f F mnemonic (aid): **j-m e-e ~ bauen** give s.o. a hint.

Eskalation [ɛskala'tsio:n] f (-; -en) escalation. **eskalieren** [ɛska'li:rən] v/i, v/t (h) escalate.

Eskapade [ɛska'pa:də] f (-; -n) escapade.

Eskimo ['ɛskimo] m (-s; -s) Eskimo.

Eskorte [ɛs'kɔrtə] f (-; -n) escort. **eskortieren** [ɛskɔr'ti:rən] v/t (h) escort.

Espe ['ɛspə] f (-; -n) ♣ asp. **'Espenlaub** n **zittern wie ~** tremble like an aspen leaf.

Espresso [ɛs'prɛso] m (-[s]; -[s]) espresso.

Esprit [ɛs'pri:] m (-s; no pl) wit.

Essay ['ɛsɛ] m (-s; -s) essay (**über** acc on). **Essayist** [ɛsɛ'ɪst] m (-en; -en), **Essay'istin** f (-; -nen) essayist.

'eßbar adj a) eatable, b) edible: **~er Pilz** (edible) mushroom.

'Eßbesteck n cutlery (set).

Esse ['ɛsə] f (-; -n) **1.** chimney. **2.** forge.

essen ['ɛsən] v/t, v/i (aß, gegessen, h) eat: et. **gern ~** like; **man ißt dort ganz**

gut the food is quite good there; → **Abend, Mittag** etc.

'Essen n (-s; -) **1.** no pl eating. **2.** a) food, b) dish, c) meal, d) dinner (party): **~ und Trinken** food and drink. **~marke** f meal ticket, Br. a. luncheon voucher.

'Essenszeit f mealtime, n.s. lunchtime, dinnertime.

Essenz [ɛ'sɛnts] f (-; -en) a. fig. essence.

'Esser m (-s; -) eater: → **stark** 1.

'Eßgeschirr n crockery, dinner service.

'Eßgewohnheiten pl eating habits.

Essig ['ɛsɪç] m (-s; -e) vinegar: F **damit ist es ~!** it's all off! **'Essiggurke** f gherkin. **'Essigsäure** f acetic acid.

'Essig- und 'Ölständer m cruet stand.

'Eßka,stanie f (sweet) chestnut. **'Eßlöffel** m tablespoon: **zwei ~** two tablespoonfuls. **'Eßlo,kal** n restaurant. **'Eßstäbchen** pl chopsticks. **'Eßtisch** m dining table. **'Eßwaren** pl food. **'Eßzimmer** n dining room.

Estragon ['ɛstragɔn] m (-s; no pl) ♣ tarragon.

etablieren [eta'bli:rən] **sich ~** (h) a) fig. establish o.s., become established, b) set (o.s.) up (**als** as), start a business.

Etablissement [etablɪs(ə)'mã:] n (-s; -s) establishment.

Etage [e'ta:ʒə] f (-; -n) floor, stor(e)y. **E'tagen|bett** n bunk bed. **~heizung** f single-stor(e)y heating (system). **~wohnung** f flat, Am. apartment.

Etappe [e'tapə] f (-; -n) a. sports: stage, leg: **in ~n** in stages.

Etat [e'ta:] m (-s; -s) budget. **E'tatansatz** m budgetary estimate. **E'tatentwurf** m draft budget. **E'tatjahr** n fiscal year.

e'tatmäßig adj a) budgetary (expenditure), b) permanent (civil servant).

etepetete [e:təpe'te:tə] adj F **1.** la-di-da. **2.** fussy, finicky.

Ethik ['e:tɪk] f (-; -en) ethics.

ethisch ['e:tɪʃ] adj ethical.

ethnisch ['ɛtnɪʃ] adj ethnic.

Ethnographie [ɛtnogra'fi:] f (-; -n) ethnography. **ethnographisch** [ɛtno'gra:fɪʃ] adj ethnographic.

Ethnologe [ɛtno'lo:gə] m (-n; -n) ethnologist. **Ethnologie** [ɛtnolo'gi:] f (-; -n) ethnology.

Ethos ['e:tɔs] n (-; no pl) ethos, w.s. ethics.

Etikett [eti'kɛt] n (-[e]s; -e) **1.** label. **2.**

price tag. **Etikette** [eti'kɛtə] f (-; -n) (**Verstoß gegen die ~** breach of) etiquette. **etikettieren** [etike'tiːrən] v/t (h) put a label on, fig. label.

etliche ['ɛtlɪçə] indef pron pl several: **~s** a number of things.

'**etlichemal** adv several times.

Etmal ['ɛtmaːl] n (-[e]s; -e) ♣ run.

Etüde [e'tyːdə] f (-; -n) ♪ étude.

Etui [ɛt'viː] n (-s; -s) case.

etwa ['ɛtva] adv **1.** a. **in ~** about, approximately, F around; **in ~ dasselbe** more or less the same; **wann ~?** approximately when?, a. F around what time? **2.** a) by any chance, b) for instance, (let's) say: **nicht ~, daß ...** not that it mattered etc; **ist das ~ besser?** is that any better?; **du glaubst doch nicht ~ ...?** surely you don't think ...?

etwaig ['ɛtvaːɪç] adj any.

etwas ['ɛtvas] **I** indef pron something, anything; **~ anderes** something (anything) else. **II** adj some, any, a little: **ich brauche ~ Geld** I need some money. **III** adv a little: **es erscheint ~ merkwürdig** it seems a bit funny.

'**Etwas** n (-; -) something: F **das gewisse ~** the certain something.

Etymologie [etymolo'giː] f (-; -n) etymology. **etymologisch** [etymo'loːgɪʃ] adj etymological.

euch [ɔʏç] pers pron (to) you, reflexive: yourselves, after prep: you: **setzt ~!** sit down!

Eucharistie [ɔʏçarɪs'tiː] f (-; -n) the Eucharist.

euer ['ɔʏər] **I** adj **1.** your: **eu(e)re Mutter** your mother; **unser und ~ Haus** our house and yours. **2.** der (die, das) **eu(e)re** yours. **II** pers pron (gen of **ihr**) of you.

Eugenik [ɔʏ'geːnɪk] f (-; no pl) eugenics.

Eule ['ɔʏlə] f (-; -n) owl: fig. **~n nach Athen tragen** carry coals to Newcastle.

Eunuch [ɔʏ'nuːx] m (-en; -en) eunuch.

Euphemismus [ɔʏfe'mɪsmʊs] m (-; -men) euphemism. **euphemistisch** [ɔʏfe'mɪstɪʃ] adj euphemistic.

Euphorie [ɔʏfo'riː] f (-; -n) euphoria.

eure ['ɔʏrə] → **euer.** '**eurerseits** adv for (or on) your part. '**euresgleichen** pron people like yourselves, contp. the likes of you. '**eurethalben, euretwe-**

gen, (um) '**euretwillen** adv a) because of you, b) for your sake.

Eurhythmie [ɔʏryt'miː] f (-; no pl) eurhythmics.

eurig ['ɔʏrɪç] → **euer** 2.

Europa [ɔʏ'roːpa] n (-s) Europe. **Europäer** [ɔʏro'pɛːər] m (-s; -), **Euro'päerin** f (-; -nen) European. **euro'päisch** adj European: **Europäische Gemeinschaft** (abbr. **EG**) European (Economic) Community (abbr. E[E]C).

Eu'ropa|meister(in f) m sports: European champion. **~meisterschaft** f European championships. **~po,kal** m European cup. **~poli,tik** f Euro-politics. **~rat** m (-[e]s; no pl) Council of Europe.

Euroscheck ['ɔʏro-] m Eurocheque.

Eurovisi'on f TV Eurovision.

Euter ['ɔʏtər] n (-s; -) udder.

Euthanasie [ɔʏtana'ziː] f (-; no pl) euthanasia.

evakuieren [evaku'iːrən] v/t (h) a. ✕ and phys. evacuate.

Evaku'ierung f (-; -en) evacuation.

evangelisch [evaŋ'geːlɪʃ] adj Protestant. **Evangelist** [evaŋge'lɪst] m (-en; -en) evangelist. **Evangelium** [evaŋ'geːliʊm] n (-s; -lien) gospel (a. fig.): **das ~ des Matthäus** the Gospel according to St. Matthew.

'**Evasko,stüm** ['eːfa-s-] n F **im ~** in the nude.

Eventualität [evɛntuali'tɛːt] f (-; -en) eventuality. **eventuell** [evɛn'tŏɛl] **I** adj possible. **II** adv a) possibly, b) if necessary, c) should the occasion arise.

evident [evi'dɛnt] adj obvious.

Evolution [evolu'tsioːn] f (-; -en) evolution.

ewig ['eːvɪç] **I** adj **1.** eternal, everlasting: **~er Schnee** perpetual snow; **die ♀e Stadt** (Rome) the Eternal City; **seit ~en Zeiten** from time immemorial, F for ages. **2.** F eternal, constant, endless. **II** adv **3.** eternally, forever: **auf immer und ~** for ever and ever; F **es ist ~ schade** it's just too bad; **~** (lange) for ages; **es dauert ~** it's taking ages.

'**Ewigkeit** f (-; -en) eternity: **bis in alle ~** to the end of time; F **es ist e-e ~, seit ...** it's ages since ...; **ich habe e-e ~ gewartet** I've waited for ages.

Ex... [ɛks...] ex-...

exakt [ɛˈksakt] *adj* precise, exact: **~e Wissenschaften** exact sciences.

Ex'aktheit *f* (-; *no pl*) precision.

Examen [ɛˈksaːmən] *n* (-s; -) examination, F exam: **(s)ein ~ machen** take one's exams.

exekutieren [ɛkseku'tiːrən] *v/t* (h) execute. **Exekution** [ɛkseku'tsɪoːn] *f* (-; -en) execution.

exekutiv [ɛkseku'tiːf] *adj*, **Exekutive** [ɛkseku'tiːvə] *f* (-; -n) executive.

Exeku'tivgewalt *f* executive power.

Exempel [ɛˈksɛmpəl] *n* (-s; -) **ein ~ statuieren** set a warning example.

Exemplar [ɛksɛm'plaːr] *n* (-s; -e) **1.** specimen, sample. **2.** a) copy (*of book*), b) number, issue (*of magazine etc*).

exem'plarisch I *adj* exemplary. **II** *adv* **j-n ~ bestrafen** make an example of s.o.

exerzieren [ɛksɛr'tsiːrən] *v/t, v/i* (h) ✕ drill.

Exhibitionismus [ɛkshibitsɪo'nɪsmʊs] *m* (-; *no pl*) exhibitionism, ஐ indecent exposure. **Exhibitionist** [-'nɪst] *m* (-en; -en) exhibitionist.

exhumieren [ɛkshu'miːrən] *v/t* (h) exhume.

Exil [ɛˈksiːl] *n* (-s; -e) (*im ~* in) exile: **ins ~ gehen** go into exile.

E'xilre,gierung *f* government in exile.

Existentialismus [ɛksistɛntsɪa'lɪsmʊs] *m* (-; *no pl*) existentialism. **Existentialist** [-'lɪst] *m* (-en; -en), **existentialistisch** [-'lɪstɪʃ] *adj* existentialist.

existentiell [ɛksistɛn'tsɪɛl] *adj* **1.** existential. **2.** *von* **~er Bedeutung** vitally important.

Existenz [ɛksis'tɛnts] *f* (-; -en) **1.** a) existence, b) livelihood: **gesicherte ~** secure position. **2.** *contp.* character: **~ verkracht 2. ~angst** *f psych.* existential anxiety, *w.s.* economic fears. **~berechtigung** *f* **1.** right to exist. **2.** raison d'être. **~kampf** *m* struggle for existence. **~minimum** *n* subsistence level.

existieren [ɛksis'tiːrən] *v/i* (h) **1.** exist, be: *nur wenige ~ noch* there are only a few left. **2.** (*von* on) exist, live.

Exitus [ˈɛksitʊs] *m* (-; *no pl*) ✚ exitus, death.

exklusiv [ɛksklu'ziːf] *adj* exclusive.

Exklu'sivbericht *m* exclusive (story).

Exklu'sivrechte *pl* exclusive rights.

exkommunizieren [ɛkskɔmuni'tsiːrən] *v/t* (h) excommunicate.

Exkrement [ɛkskre'mɛnt] *n* (-[e]s; -e) excrement.

Exkursion [ɛkskʊr'zɪoːn] *f* (-; -en) excursion, field trip.

exmatrikulieren [ɛksmatriku'liːrən] *v/t* (h) *j-n* (*sich*) **~** take s.o.'s (one's) name off the (university) register.

Exodus [ˈɛksodʊs] *m* (-; *no pl*) exodus.

Exot [ɛˈksoːt] *m* (-en; -en), **E'xotin** *f* (-; -nen) exotic. **e'xotisch** *adj* exotic.

Expander [ɛks'pandər] *m* (-s; -) *sports*: expander.

Expansion [ɛkspan'zɪoːn] *f* (-; -en) expansion.

Expansi'onspoli,tik *f* expansionism.

expedieren [ɛkspe'diːrən] *v/t* (h) dispatch. **Expedition** [ɛkspedi'tsɪoːn] *f* (-; -en) **1.** expedition. **2.** ✝ forwarding (department).

Experiment [ɛksperi'mɛnt] *n* (-[e]s; -e) experiment. **Experimental...** [ɛksperimɛn'taːl-], **experimentell** [-'tɛl] *adj* experimental. **experimentieren** [-'tiːrən] *v/i* (h) experiment (*an dat* on, *mit* with).

Experte [ɛks'pɛrtə] *m* (-n; -n) expert.

Expertise [ɛksper'tiːzə] *f* (-; -n) **1.** expertise. **2.** expert's opinion.

explodieren [ɛksplo'diːrən] *v/i* (sn) explode. **Explosion** [ɛksplo'zɪoːn] *f* (-; -en) explosion, blast.

explosi'onsartig *adj a. fig.* explosive.

Explosi'ons,gefahr *f* danger of explosion. **~kraft** *f* explosive force.

explosiv [ɛksplo'ziːf] *adj* explosive.

Exponat [ɛkspo'naːt] *n* (-[e]s; -e) exhibit.

Exponent [ɛkspo'nɛnt] *m* (-en; -en) ℝ, *a. fig.* exponent.

exponieren [ɛkspo'niːrən] *v/t* (h) expose (*sich* o.s.). **expo'niert** *adj* exposed.

Export [ɛks'pɔrt] *m* (-[e]s; -e) **1.** *no pl* exportation, exporting. **2.** exports. **Ex'port,abteilung** *f* export department. **~ar,tikel** *m* export article (*or* item), *pl a.* exports. **~ausführung** *f* export model.

Exporteur [ɛkspɔr'tøːr] *m* (-s; -e) exporter. **Ex'portgeschäft** *n*, **Ex'porthandel** *m* export trade. **exportieren** [ɛkspɔr'tiːrən] *v/t* (h) export (*nach* to).

Ex'portland *n* exporting country.

Ex'portleiter *m* export manager.

Exposé [ɛkspo'zeː] *n* (-s; -s) exposé.

expreß [ɛks'prɛs] *adv* ~ *schicken* send express (*Am.* by special delivery).

Expressionismus [ɛksprɛsǐo'nɪsmʊs] *m* (-; *no pl*) expressionism. **Expressionist** [-'nɪst] *m* (-en; -en), **expressionistisch** [-'nɪstɪʃ] *adj* expressionist.

extern [ɛks'tɛrn] *adj* external.

extra ['ɛkstra] I *adj* extra. II *adv* a) extra, *a.* separately, b) specially, c) F on purpose: ~ *für dich* just for you.

'Extra *n* (-s; -s) extra. ~**blatt** *n* extra.

extrahieren [ɛkstra'hi:rən] *v/t* (h), **Extrakt** [ɛks'trakt] *m* (-[e]s; -e) extract.

extravagant [ɛkstrava'gant] *adj* flamboyant.

extravertiert [ɛkstraver'ti:rt] *adj* (*a.* ~**er Mensch**) extrovert.

extrem [ɛks'tre:m] *adj* extreme.

Ex'trem *n* (-s; -e) extreme. **Extremismus** [ɛkstre'mɪsmʊs] *m* (-; *no pl*) extremism. **Extremist** [-'mɪst] *m* (-en; -en), **extre'mistisch** *adj* extremist.

Extremitäten [ɛkstremi'tɛːtən] *pl* extremities.

extrover'tiert [ɛkstro-] → **extravertiert**.

Exzellenz [ɛktsɛ'lɛnts] *f* (-; -en) (*Eure, Seine* ~ your, his) Excellency.

Exzentriker [ɛks'tsɛntrikər] *m* (-s; -), **Ex'zentrikerin** *f* (-; -nen) eccentric.

ex'zentrisch [-trɪʃ] *adj a.* Ⓐ, Ⓞ eccentric.

Exzeß [ɛks'tsɛs] *m* (-sses; -sse) excess.

F

F, f [ɛf] *n* (-; -) F, f (*a.* ♪).

Fabel ['faːbəl] *f* (-; -n) a) fable, *fig. a.* story, b) plot (*of drama etc*).

'fabelhaft *adj* fantastic.

Fabrik [fa'briːk] *f* (-; -en) factory, works, mill. **Fa'brikanlage** *f* (manufacturing) plant. **Fabrikant** [fabri'kant] *m* (-en; -en) **1.** factory owner. **2.** manufacturer. **Fa'brikarbeit** *f* **1.** factory work. **2.** → *Fabrikware*. **Fa'brikarbeiter(in** *f*) *m* factory worker. **Fabrikat** [fabri'kaːt] *n* (-[e]s; -e) product, make. **Fabrikation** [fabrika'tsǐoːn] *f* (-; -en) production.

Fabrikati'ons\|nummer *f* serial number. **~pro,gramm** *n* production schedule.

Fa'brik\|besitzer(in *f*) *m* factory owner. **~gebäude** *n* factory building. **~gelände** *n* factory site. Ⓠ**neu** *adj* brand-new. **~schiff** *n* factory ship. **~ware** *f* manufactured product(s).

fabrizieren [fabri'tsiːrən] *v/t* (h) **1.** manufacture, make, *fig.* concoct. **2.** *fig.* get up to.

Facette [fa'sɛtə] *f* (-; -n) facet. **Fa'cettenauge** *n zo.* compound eye.

Fach [fax] *n* (-[e]s; ~er) **1.** a) compartment, partition, b) shelf. **2.** field, line: *er ist vom* ~ he is an expert; *das*

schlägt nicht in mein ~ that's not in my line. **3.** *ped., univ.* subject.

...fach *in cpds.* ...fold, times.

'Fach\|arbeit *f* skilled work. **~arbeiter(in** *f*) *m* skilled worker, *pl* skilled labo(u)r. **~arzt** *m*, **~ärztin** *f* specialist (*für* in). **Ⓠärztlich** *adj* (*adv* by a) specialist. **~ausbildung** *f* special(ized) training. **~ausdruck** *m* technical term. **~bereich** *m* **1.** → *Fachgebiet*. **2.** *univ.* department. **~buch** *n* specialist book.

Fächer ['fɛçər] *m* (-s; -) **1.** fan. **2.** *fig.* range, spectrum. **'fächerförmig** *adj* fan-like: *sich* ~ *ausbreiten* fan out. **'fächern** *v/t* (h) (*a. sich* ~) fan out.

'Fach\|frau *f* (woman) expert. **~gebiet** *n* (special) field. **Ⓠgerecht** *adj* expert, professional. **~geschäft** *n* specialist shop (*Am.* store). **~handel** *m* specialized trade (*or* dealers). **~hochschule** *f* college. **~idi,ot** *m* F *contp.* specialist borné. **~jar,gon** *m* technical jargon. **~kenntnis(se** *pl*) *f* specialized knowledge, know-how. **~kräfte** *pl* qualified personnel. **~kreis** *m in* ~**en** among the experts. **Ⓠkundig** *adj* competent, expert. **~lehrer(in** *f*) *m* subject teacher. **~leute** *pl* experts.

'fachlich *adj* technical, professional.

'**Fachlitera,tur** *f* specialized literature.

'**Fachmann** *m* (-[e]s; -leute) (*in dat* in, at, *für* on) expert, specialist.

fachmännisch ['faxmɛnɪʃ] *adj* expert, specialist, professional (*work*): **~es Urteil** expert opinion.

'**Fach|perso,nal** *n* qualified personnel. **~presse** *f* trade press. **~richtung** *f* field. **~schule** *f* technical college.

Fachsimpelei [faxzɪmpə'laɪ] *f* (-; -en) F shoptalk. '**fachsimpeln** *v/i* (*insep, pp* gefachsimpelt, h) talk shop.

'**Fach|sprache** *f* technical language (*or* terminology). **~studium** *n* special(ized) studies. **~übersetzer(in** *f*) *m* technical translator. **~verband** *m* professional (*or* trade) association. **~werk** *n* (-[e]s; *no pl*) half-timbering. **~werkhaus** *n* half-timbered house. **~wissen** *n* → **Fachkenntnis(se)**. **~wörterbuch** *n* specialized dictionary. **~zeitschrift** *f* (professional *or* trade) journal.

Fackel ['fakəl] *f* (-; -n) *a.* fig. torch.

'**fackeln** *v/i* (h) F *nicht lange* **~** waste no time.

fade ['fa:də] *adj* **1.** tasteless, stale, flat (*beer*). **2.** fig. boring, dull.

Faden ['fa:dən] *m* (-s; ⸚) thread (*a.* fig.), ⚓, ⚙ filament, ⚕ stitch, string (*of puppets etc*): ⚕ *die Fäden ziehen* remove the stitches; *der rote* **~** the thread (running through the story *etc*); *den* **~** *verlieren* lose the thread (of one's speech *etc*); *es hing an e-m* **~** it hang by a thread; *er hält alle Fäden in der Hand* he pulls the strings. '**Fadenkreuz** *n opt.* reticule. '**Fadennudeln** *pl* vermicelli.

fadenscheinig ['fa:dənʃaɪnɪç] *adj* threadbare, fig. *a.* flimsy (*excuse etc*).

Fagott [fa'gɔt] *n* (-[e]s; -e) ♪ bassoon.

Fagottist [fago'tɪst] *m* (-en; -en), **Fagot'tistin** *f* (-; -nen) bassoonist.

fähig ['fɛ:ɪç] *adj* a) able, capable, b) gifted, talented, c) qualified: **~ sein zu** be capable of; *b.s.* *zu allem* **~** capable of anything, desperate; (*dazu*) **~ sein, et. zu tun** be capable of doing s.th., be able (*or* qualified) to do s.th.

'**Fähigkeit** *f* (-; -en) a) ability, capability, b) talent.

fahl [fa:l] *adj* pale, ashen (*face*).

Fähnchen ['fɛ:nçən] *n* (-s; -) **1.** pennant, *sports*: marker. **2.** F cheap, flimsy dress.

fahnden ['fa:ndən] *v/i* (h) **~ nach** search

for. '**Fahnder** *m* (-s; -) investigator. '**Fahndung** *f* (-; -en) search.

'**Fahndungs|akti,on** *f* (police) search. **~dienst** *m* tracing and search department. **~liste** *f* wanted list.

Fahne ['fa:nə] *f* (-; -n) **1.** flag, fig. banner, ⚓, ✗ colo(u)rs: fig. *mit fliegenden* **~n** with flying colo(u)rs. **2.** F *e-e* **~** *haben* reek of the bottle. **3.** *print.* galley (proof).

'**Fahneneid** *m* ✗ oath of allegiance.

'**Fahnenflucht** *f* (-; *no pl*) desertion.

'**fahnenflüchtig** *adj* **~ sein** be a deserter; **~ werden** desert.

'**Fahnen|mast** *m*, **~stange** *f* flagpole.

Fähnrich ['fɛ:nrɪç] *m* (-s; -e) ✗ cadet: ⚓ **~ zur See** midshipman.

'**Fahrausweis** *m* ticket. '**Fahrbahn** *f* road, carriageway, lane. '**fahrbar** *adj* mobile. '**Fahrbereitschaft** *f* car pool.

Fähre ['fɛ:rə] *f* (-; -n) ferry.

'**Fahreigenschaften** *pl mot.* road performance.

fahren ['fa:rən] (fuhr, gefahren) **I** *v/i* (sn) **1.** a) go (*mit* by *bus, train, etc*), ride (on *bicycle, etc*), *mot.* drive, ⚓ sail, b) run, c) leave, depart, go, d) be moving: *der Zug fährt zweimal am Tag* the train runs (*or* goes) twice a day; *über e-e Brücke* **~** cross a bridge; *rechts* **~**! keep to the right!; *mit Diesel* **~** run on diesel, be diesel-driven; fig. *mit der Hand* **~** *über* (*acc*) run one's hand over; *in et.* **~** *bullet, knife, etc*: go into; *gut (schlecht)* **~** *bei* fare well (ill) with, do well (badly) by; *es (der Gedanke) fuhr mir durch den Kopf* it flashed through my mind; *was ist in ihn gefahren?* what has got into him?; F *e-n* **~** *lassen* fart, let go; → *Haut.* **II** *v/t* **2.** (h) a) drive, b) take (*s.o.* or *s.th. somewhere*), transport, ⚓ sail. **3.** (sn) drive, cover (*distance etc*), do: *das Auto fährt 150 km/h* the car does 150 km/h. **4.** (h *or* sn) *sports*: make, clock (*ten minutes etc*): *ein Rennen* **~** participate in a race. **5.** (h) ⚙ ⚙ work (*a shift*), run (*a line*), operate (*plant, unit*). **6.** (h) *TV* run.

'**fahrend** *adj* travel(l)ing, itinerant.

'**Fahrer** *m* (-s; -), '**Fahrerin** *f* (-; -nen) a) driver, b) chauffeur (chauffeuse).

'**Fahrerflucht** *f* **~ begehen** commit a hit-and-run offen/ce (*Am.* -se).

'**Fahrersitz** *m* driver's seat.

'**Fahr|gast** *m* passenger, *of taxi*: fare. **~geld** *n* fare. **~gelegenheit** *f* (means of) transport(ation). **~gemeinschaft** *f* car pool. **~gestell** *n* **1.** *mot.* chassis, ✈ undercarriage. **2.** F (*legs*) pins.

fahrig ['faːrɪç] *adj* a) nervous, jumpy, b) inattentive.

'**Fahrkarte** *f* ticket (**nach** to).

'**Fahrkarten|auto,mat** *m* ticket machine. **~kon,trolle** *f* ticket inspection. **~kontrol,leur** *m* ticket inspector. **~schalter** *m* ticket office.

'**Fahrkom,fort** *m* *mot.* driving comfort.

'**fahrlässig** *adj* careless, *a.* ⚖ negligent: **~e Tötung** manslaughter (*Am.* in the second degree). '**Fahrlässigkeit** *f* (-; -en) carelessness, *a.* ⚖ negligence.

'**Fahrlehrer(in** *f*) *m* driving instructor.

'**Fährmann** *m* ferryman.

'**Fahrplan** *m* timetable (*a. fig.*), schedule. **~änderung** *f* change in the timetable. '**fahrplanmäßig I** *adj* scheduled. **II** *adv* according to schedule, on time.

'**Fahr|praxis** *f* driving experience. **~preis** *m* fare. **~prüfung** *f* driving test. **~rad** *n* bicycle, F bike. **~rinne** *f* ⚓ lane. **~schein** *m* ticket. **~schule** *f* driving school. **~schüler(in** *f*) *m* learner (driver). **~spur** *f* lane. **~stuhl** *m* lift, *Am.* elevator. **~stunde** *f* driving lesson.

Fahrt [faːrt] *f* (-; -en) **1.** a) drive, ride, b) journey, trip, ⚓ a. voyage, cruise: **auf ~ gehen** go on a trip; **auf der ~ nach X** on the way to X; **gute ~!** have a good trip! **2.** speed (*a.* ⚓): **in voller ~** at full speed; **in ~ kommen** a) get under way, b) F *fig.* get going; F **j-n in ~ bringen** a) get s.o. going, b) make s.o. wild; F **in ~ sein** *person*: a) be going it strong, b) be wild.

'**Fahrtdauer** *f* length of the trip: **die ~ beträgt 3 Stunden** it will take 3 hours (to get there).

Fährte ['fɛːrtə] *f* (-; -n) *a. fig.* trail, track: *fig.* **auf der falschen ~ sein** be on the wrong track.

'**Fahrtenbuch** *n* *mot.* logbook.

'**Fahrtenschreiber** *m* *mot.* tachograph.

'**Fahrtrichtungsanzeiger** *m* *mot.* direction indicator.

'**fahrtüchtig** *adj car*: roadworthy, *driver*: fit to drive.

'**Fahrtunterbrechung** *f* stop.

'**Fahrtwind** *m* airstream.

'**Fahr|verbot** *n* **j-n mit ~ belegen** suspend s.o.'s driving licence (*Am.* driver's license). **~verhalten** *n* *mot.* road behavio(u)r. **~wasser** *n* (-s; *no pl*) **1.** → **Fahrrinne. 2.** F *fig.* track: **im richtigen ~ sein** be in one's element. **~weise** *f* (way of) driving. **~werk** *n* *mot.* chassis, ✈ undercarriage. **~zeit** *f* → **Fahrtdauer**.

'**Fahrzeug** *n* (-[e]s; -e) vehicle, ⚓ vessel. **~brief** *m* *mot.* (vehicle) registration document. **~halter(in** *f*) *m* car owner. **~pa,piere** *pl* documents.

Faible ['fɛːbəl] *n* (-s; -s) → **Schwäche** 3.

fair [fɛːr] *adj* fair.

Fairneß ['fɛːrnɛs] *f* (-; *no pl*) fairness.

Fäkalien [fɛ'kaːliən] *pl* f(a)eces.

Fakir ['faːkɪr] *m* (-s; -e) fakir.

Faksimile [fak'ziːmile] *n* (-s; -s) facsimile.

faktisch ['faktɪʃ] *adj* actual(ly *adv*), *adv a.* in fact. **Faktor** ['faktɔr] *m* (-s; -ren [-'toːrən]) *a. biol.*, ♀ factor. '**Faktum** *n* (-s; -ten) a) fact, b) *pl* facts, data.

fakturieren [faktu'riːrən] *v/t* (h) invoice.

Fakultät [fakʊl'tɛːt] *f* (-; -en) *univ.* faculty, *esp. Am.* department.

fakultativ [fakʊlta'tiːf] *adj* optional.

Falke ['falkə] *m* (-n; -n) *zo.* falcon, *hunt. and pol. a.* hawk.

Fall [fal] *m* (-[e]s; ⁓e) **1.** fall (*a.* ✗), ♥ a. drop, *fig.* downfall: **zu ~ bringen** a) **j-n** cause s.o. to fall, *in a fight or fig.* bring s.o. down, trip s.o. up, b) thwart (*plans etc*), defeat (*bill, motion, etc*); *fig.* **zu ~ kommen** fall, be ruined. **2.** case (*a.* ⚖, *ling.*, ♠), matter, affair: **auf alle Fälle** a) in any case, b) definitely, c) *a.* **für alle Fälle** just in case, to be on the safe side; **für den** (*or* **im**) **~, daß er kommt** in case he should come; **im ~e** (*gen*) in the event of; **gesetzt den ~** suppose, supposing; **in diesem ~** in that case; F **klarer ~!** sure (thing)!; **das ist** (*nicht*) **ganz mein ~** that's right up my street (not my cup of tea); **das ist auch bei ihr der ~** it's the same with her.

Falle ['falə] *f* (-; -n) trap (*a. fig.*), snare: *fig.* **j-m in die ~ gehen** walk into the trap set by s.o.; **j-m e-e ~ stellen** set a trap for s.o.

fallen ['falən] *v/i* (fiel, gefallen, sn) **1.** fall (**von** from, off), fall down, drop: **~ lassen** *a. fig.* let fall, drop; **von der Leiter ~** fall off a ladder; **ich bin gefallen** I had a fall; *er ließ sich in e-n Sessel ~* he dropped into a chair. **2.** ✗ fall, *soldier: a.* be killed (in action). **3.** *temperature, prices, etc:* fall, drop, go down. **4.** *name, remark, etc:* fall, *decision etc: a.* be made: *sein Name fiel auch* his name was mentioned too; *es fielen harte Worte* there were harsh words; *die Entscheidung ist noch nicht gefallen* the matter is still undecided. **5.** *sports: goal etc:* be scored: *die Entscheidung fiel in der letzten Minute* the decider came in the last minute. **6.** *Schüsse fielen* shots were fired. **7.** *obstacle etc:* be removed, go. **8.** *an j-n ~ inheritance etc:* fall (*or* go) to s.o. **9.** *~ auf* (*acc*) *a. fig.* fall on; *die Wahl fiel auf sie* she was chosen. **10.** *~ unter* come under. **11.** *~ in* (*acc*) fall into; *in Schlaf ~* fall asleep; *fig. j-m in den Arm ~* restrain s.o.; → *Ohnmacht* 2.

fällen ['fɛlən] *v/t* (h) **1.** cut down (*tree etc*). **2.** ⚖ *ein Urteil ~* (*über acc* on) pass sentence, *a. fig.* pass judg(e)ment; → *Entscheidung*.

'fallenlassen *v/t* (*irr, sep,* h, → *lassen*) drop (*plan, friend, hint, etc*).

'Fallgeschwindigkeit *f phys.* rate of fall.

'Fallgrube *f* pit, *a. fig.* trap.

fällig ['fɛlɪç] *adj* ✝ due, payable: *längst ~* (long) overdue; *~ werden* a) become due (*or* payable), b) expire.

'Fälligkeit *f* (-; *no pl*) (*bei ~* at) maturity.

'Fallobst *n* windfall.

Fallout ['fɔːlaʊt] *m* (-s; -s) *nucl.* fallout.

'Fallrückzieher *m soccer:* falling overhead kick.

falls [fals] *conj* if, in case: *~ nicht* unless.

'Fallschirm *m* parachute. *~absprung m* parachute jump (*or* descent). *~abwurf m* airdrop. *~jäger m* ✗ paratrooper. *~springen n* parachute jumping, *sports:* skydiving. *~springer(in f) m* parachutist, *sports:* skydiver.

'Fallstrick *m fig.* trap. **'Fallstudie** *f* case study. **'Falltreppe** *f* foldaway stairs. **'Falltür** *f* trapdoor.

falsch [falʃ] **I** *adj* **1.** a) wrong, b) untrue, *pred* not true: *~e Darstellung* misrepresentation. **2.** a) false, artificial, b) forged, fake(d), counterfeit: *~er Name* fictitious name. **3.** false, insincere. **II** *adv* **4.** wrongly, falsely (*etc*): *~ aussprechen* mispronounce; *~ gehen watch:*

be wrong; *~ geraten!* wrong guess!; *~ schreiben* misspell; *~ singen* sing out of tune; *~ spielen* cheat; *~ verbunden!* sorry, wrong number!; *~ verstehen* misunderstand.

'Falschaussage *f* ⚖ false testimony.

'Falscheid *m* ⚖ false oath.

fälschen ['fɛlʃən] *v/t* (h) fake, forge, counterfeit, ✝ tamper with (*books etc*).

'Fälscher *m* (-s; -) forger, counterfeiter.

'Falschgeld *n* counterfeit money.

'Falschheit *f* (-; *no pl*) falseness.

'fälschlich ['fɛlʃlɪç] **I** *adj* wrong, false. **II** *adv* → **'fälschlicherweise** *adv* a) wrongly, falsely, b) by mistake.

'Falschmeldung *f* false report, hoax.

'Falschmünzer [-mʏntsər] *m* (-s; -) counterfeiter.

'Falschspieler *m* cardsharper, cheat.

'Fälschung *f* (-; -en) **1.** forging, counterfeiting. **2.** fake, forgery.

'Faltbett *n* folding bed. **'Faltblatt** *n* leaflet. **'Faltboot** *n* folding canoe.

Fältchen ['fɛltçən] *n* (-s; -) wrinkle, *pl* crow's-feet.

Falte ['faltə] *f* (-; -n) a) fold, b) crease, c) pleat (*in skirt etc*), d) wrinkle, line (*in face*): *~n werfen* pucker.

fälteln ['fɛltəln] *v/t* (h) pleat.

falten ['faltən] *v/t* a) fold, b) pleat.

'Faltenrock *m* pleated skirt.

Falter ['faltər] *m* (-s; -) *zo.* butterfly.

faltig ['faltɪç] *adj* creased, *a.* wrinkled (*skin*), *a.* lined (*face*).

'Faltkarte *f* folding (*or* pull-out) map.

'Faltkarton *m* collapsible cardboard box. **'Falttür** *f* folding door.

Falz [falts] *m* (-es; -e), **'falzen** *v/t* (h) **1.** fold. **2.** ⚙ rabbet.

familiär [famiˈlɛːr] *adj* **1.** family (*affairs etc*). **2.** a) familiar, b) informal. **3.** *ling.* familiar, colloquial.

Familie [faˈmiːliə] *f* (-; -n) family: (*die*) *Miller* the Miller family; *e-e ~ gründen* start a family; *~ haben* have children; *es liegt in der ~* it runs in the family.

Fa'milien|angehörige *m, f* member of the family. *~angelegenheit f* family affair. *~anschluß m ~ haben* live (there) as one of the family. *~betrieb m* family business (*or* farm). *~fest n* family celebration. *~gericht n* ⚖ family court. *~kreis m* family circle: *im engsten ~ celebrate etc* with the immediate family. **~leben** n family life. **~mitglied** n member of the family. **~name** m surname, last name. **~oberhaupt** n head of the family. **~packung** f family pack. **~planung** f family planning. **~ro‚man** m roman fleuve. **~sinn** m (-[e]s; *no pl*) sense of family. **~stand** m (-[e]s; *no pl*) marital status. **~unterhalt** m upkeep of the family. **~vater** m **1.** head of the family. **2.** family man. **~verhältnisse** pl family background. **~zuwachs** m addition to the family.

Fan [fɛn] m (-s; -s) fan.

Fanatiker [fa'na:tikər] m (-s; -), **Fa'natikerin** f (-; -nen) fanatic. **fanatisch** [fa'na:tɪʃ] adj fanatic(al). **Fanatismus** [fana'tɪsmʊs] m (-; *no pl*) fanaticism.

fand [fant] pret of **finden**.

Fanfare [fan'fa:rə] f (-; -n) **1.** fanfare. **2.** mot. multitone horn.

Fang [faŋ] m (-[e]s; **~e**) **1.** a. fig. catch, haul. **2.** zo. usu. pl a) claw, b) fang, tusk (of boar). **'Fangarm** m zo. tentacle.

fangen ['faŋən] (fing, gefangen, h) **I** v/t **1.** catch, fig. a. trap: **sich ~ lassen** get caught; → **Feuer** 1. **II sich ~ 2.** be caught. **3.** catch o.s. stumbling etc. **4.** fig. sich (wieder) ~ recover, w.s. get a grip on o.s. (again).

'Fangen n (-s) catch, Am. tag.

Fänger ['fɛŋər] m (-s; -) catcher.

'Fangfrage f trick question.

Fangopackung ['faŋgo-]f 🌿 mud pack.

'Fangzahn m zo. fang.

'Fanklub m fan club.

'Farbabzug m phot. colo(u)r print.

'Farbaufnahme f colo(u)r photo.

'Farbband n typewriter ribbon.

Farbe ['farbə] f (-; -n) **1.** a) colo(u)r, b) shade, c) paint, d) dye: **in ~** TV in colo(u)r; → **leuchtend. 2.** complexion, colo(u)r. **3.** cards: suit: **~ bekennen** follow suit, fig. show one's true colo(u)rs. **4.** pl colo(u)rs (of club etc).

'farbecht adj colo(u)rfast, nonfading.

'Färbemittel n dye.

färben ['fɛrbən] (h) **I** v/t **1.** a) dye (hair, cloth), stain (glass, paper), b) tint, colo(u)r (a. fig.): **gefärbter Bericht** colo(u)red report. **2.** lose colo(u)r, stain. **II sich ~** (leaves: change) colo(u)r: **sich rot** etc **~** turn red etc.

'farbenblind adj colo(u)r-blind.

'farben|freudig, ~froh adj colo(u)rful.

'Farben(kunst)druck m colo(u)r plate.

'Farbenlehre f theory of colo(u)rs.

farbenprächtig adj colo(u)rful.

'Farbenskala f colo(u)r chart.

'Farbenspiel n play of colo(u)rs.

Färber ['fɛrbər] m (-s; -) dyer.

Färberei [fɛrbə'raɪ] f (-; -en) dyeworks.

'Farb|fernsehen n colo(u)r television (or TV). **~fernseher** m, **~fernsehgerät** n colo(u)r television (or TV) set. **~film** m colo(u)r film. **~filter** n, m phot. colo(u)r filter. **~foto** n colo(u)r photo. **~fotogra‚fie** f **1.** colo(u)r photography. **2.** colo(u)r photo.

farbig ['farbɪç] adj colo(u)red (a. race), fig. colo(u)rful. **Farbige** m, f (-n; -n) colo(u)red person (or man, woman), nonwhite: **die ~n** the colo(u)reds, the colo(u)red people, the nonwhites.

'Farbko‚pierer m colo(u)r copier.

'farblich adj colo(u)r, a. adv in colo(u)r.

'farblos adj a. fig. colo(u)rless.

'Farb|skala f colo(u)r chart. **~stift** m colo(u)red pencil, crayon. **~stoff** m ✪ dye, in foods: colo(u)ring. **~ton** m hue, tint, shade, paint., phot. tone.

Färbung f (-; -en) colo(u)ring, hue.

'Farbwiedergabe f colo(u)r fidelity.

'Farbzusammenstellung f colo(u)r scheme.

Farce ['farsə] f (-; -n) thea. burlesque, a. fig. farce.

Farm [farm] f (-; -en) farm.

'Farmer m (-s; -) farmer.

Farn [farn] m (-[e]s; -e), **~kraut** n 🌿 fern.

Färse ['fɛrzə] f (-; -n) zo. heifer.

Fasan [fa'za:n] m (-[e]s; -e) zo. pheasant.

Fasching ['faʃɪŋ] m (-s; -e, -s) carnival **'Faschings...** carnival ...

Faschismus [fa'ʃɪsmʊs] m (-; *no pl*) fascism. **Faschist** [fa'ʃɪst] m (-en; -en), **Fa'schistin** f (-; -nen), **faschistisch** adj [fa'ʃɪstɪʃ] fascist.

faseln ['fa:zəln] v/i (h) F drivel.

Faser ['fa:zər] f (-; -n) fibre, Am. fiber. **'faserig** adj fibrous, stringy (meat etc). **fasern** ['fa:zərn] v/i (h) fray.

'Faserplatte f fib/reboard (Am. -er-).

Faß [fas] n (Fasses; Fässer) a) barrel, b) vat, tub: **Bier vom ~** → **Faßbier;** **(frisch) vom ~ beer** on tap (or draught), wine from the wood; fig. **das ist ein ~ ohne Boden** there is no end to it; **das**

schlägt dem ~ den Boden aus! that's the last straw!

Fassade [fa'sa:də] *f* (-; -n) façade, front.
Fas'sadenkletterer *m* cat burglar.
Fas'sadenreiniger *m* exterior cleaner.
'**faßbar** *adj* comprehensible: *schwer ~* difficult (to understand).
'**Faßbier** *n* draught beer.
Fäßchen ['fɛsçən] *n* (-s; -) keg.
fassen ['fasən] (h) **I** *v/t* **1.** take hold of, grasp, seize, *a.* ⊙ grip: F *zu ~ kriegen* get hold of; *j-n an (or bei) der Hand ~* take s.o. by the hand. **2.** apprehend, catch (*criminal etc*). **3.** mount (*in silver etc*), set (*jewel*). **4.** a) *room etc*: hold, *a.* accommodate, seat (*persons*), b) contain. **5.** *fig.* a) grasp, understand, b) believe: *nicht zu ~* unbelievable, incredible. **6.** put, formulate: *et. in Worte ~* put s.th. into words. **7.** *e-n Gedanken ~* form an idea; → *Beschluß, Entschluß, Fuß* 1, *Plan* 1. **II** *v/i* **8.** ~ *an* (*acc*) touch; ~ *nach* grasp at. **III** *sich ~* **9.** regain one's composure, compose o.s.: → *gefaßt* 1. **10.** *sich kurz ~* be brief; *fasse dich kurz!* make it brief!; → *Geduld*.
'**faßlich** *adj* comprehensible: *leicht (schwer) ~* easy (hard) to understand.
'**Fasson** [fa'sõ:] *f* (-; -s) **1.** a) shape, b) cut: *fig. nach s-r (eigenen) ~* after one's own fashion. **2.** → *Fas'sonschnitt m* trim, short back and sides.
'**Fassung** *f* (-; -en) **1.** frame (*of spectacles*), socket (*of lamp*), setting (*of diamond etc*). **2.** a) formulation, b) text, wording, c) version (*of book, film, etc*). **3.** *no pl* composure: *j-n aus der ~ bringen* put s.o. out; *die ~ bewahren* keep one's head; *die ~ verlieren* lose one's composure (*or* temper); *s-e ~ wiedergewinnen* → *fassen* 9; *er war ganz außer ~* he was completely beside himself; → *ringen* I.
'**Fassungskraft** *f* (-; *no pl*) (powers of) comprehension, mental capacity.
'**fassungslos** *adj* stunned, speechless: ~ *vor Glück* beside o.s. with joy *etc*.
'**Fassungslosigkeit** *f* (-; *no pl*) shock.
'**Fassungsvermögen** *n* **1.** capacity. **2.** → *Fassungskraft*.
fast [fast] *adv* a) almost, nearly, b) hardly: ~ *nie* hardly ever.
fasten ['fastən] *v/i* (h) fast. '**Fasten** *n* (-s

fast(ing). '**Fastenkur** *f* starvation cure.
'**Fastentag** *m* day of fasting.
'**Fastenzeit** *f* Lent.
'**Fastnacht** *f* (-; *no pl*) **1.** Shrove Tuesday, Mardi gras. **2.** → *Fasching(s...).*
Faszination [fastsina'tsĭo:n] *f* (-; *no pl*) fascination. **faszinieren** [fastsi'ni:rən] *v/t* (h) fascinate.
fatal [fa'ta:l] *adj* **1.** fatal, disastrous. **2.** (very) awkward.
Fatalismus [fata'lısmʊs] *m* (-; *no pl*) fatalism. **Fatalist** [fata'lıst] *m* (-en; -en) fatalist. **fata'listisch** *adj* fatalist(ic).
fauchen ['faʊxən] *v/i* (h) snarl, *cat*: hiss.
faul [faʊl] *adj* **1.** a) rotten, bad (*egg, tooth, etc*), b) putrid: F *fig. ~er Kompromiß* hollow compromise; *~er Kunde* shady customer; *~e Sache* fishy business; *~er Witz* bad joke; *an der Sache ist et. ~* there is s.th. fishy about it; → *Ausrede*. **2.** lazy, idle.
Fäule ['fɔylə] *f* (-; *no pl*) **1.** ✍ rot. **2.** → *Fäulnis*. '**faulen** *v/i* (sn, h) go bad, rot.
faulenzen ['faʊlɛntsən] *v/i* (h) loaf, laze around, *contp.* be lazy.
'**Faulenzer** *m* (-s; -) idler, lazybones.
'**Faulheit** *f* (-; *no pl*) laziness.
faulig ['faʊlıç] *adj* a) rotten, b) mo(u)ldy, c) rotting. **Fäulnis** ['fɔylnıs] *f* (-; *no pl*) a) rottenness, decay (*a.* ✿), b) putrefaction: *in ~ übergehen* (begin to) rot.
'**Faulpelz** *m* (-es; -e) F *contp.* lazybones.
'**Faultier** *n* **1.** *zo.* sloth. **2.** → *Faulpelz*.
Faun [faʊn] *m* (-[e]s; -e) faun.
Fauna ['faʊna] *f* (-; Faunen) fauna.
Faust [faʊst] *f* (-; ⸚e) fist: *fig. auf eigene ~* F off one's own bat; *mit eiserner ~* with an iron hand; *mit der ~ auf den Tisch schlagen* put one's foot down; *das paßt wie die ~ aufs Auge* a) it goes together like chalk and cheese, b) *iro.* it fits (perfectly); → *ballen* 2.
Fäustchen ['fɔystçən] *n* (-s; -) *fig. sich ins ~ lachen* laugh up one's sleeve.
'**faust'dick** *adj* as big as your fist: F *fig. ~e Lüge* whopping great lie; *er hat es ~ hinter den Ohren* he's a sly one.
'**fausten** *v/t* (*v/i*) (h) *sports*: fist (the ball).
'**faustgroß** *adj* as big as your fist.
'**Faust|handschuh** *m* mitt(en). *~regel* *f* rule of thumb, general rule. *~schlag m* punch. *~skizze* *f* rough sketch.
favorisieren [favori'zi:rən] *v/t* (h)

favo(u)r. **Favorit** [favoˈriːt] *m* (-en; -en), **Favoˈritin** *f* (-; -nen) favo(u)rite.

Fax [faks] *n* (-; -[e]), **'faxen** *v/t* (h) fax.

Faxen ['faksən] *pl* nonsense: ~ **machen** a) pull faces, b) clown about.

Fazit ['faːtsɪt] *n* (-s; -s) a) result, upshot, b) conclusion: *das ~ ziehen aus* sum *s.th.* up, draw one's conclusion from.

Februar [ˈfeːbruaːr] *m* (-[s]; *rare* -e) (*im ~* in) February.

Fecht... fencing (*glove, mask, etc*).

fechten ['fɛçtən] *v/i* (focht, gefochten, h) **1.** fence, *a. fig.* fight. **2.** *F* beg: ~ **gehen** go begging. **'Fechten** *n* (-s) fencing. **'Fechter** *m* (-s; -), **'Fechterin** *f* (-; -nen) fencer. **'Fechtsport** *m* fencing.

Feder ['feːdər] *f* (-; -n) **1.** a) feather, b) plume: *sich mit fremden ~n schmük-ken* adorn o.s. with borrowed plumes; *F noch in den ~n liegen* be still in bed; *~n lassen müssen* not to escape unscathed. **2.** a) nib, b) pen. **3.** ⚙ spring. **'Federball** *m* (-[e]s; -e) **1.** shuttlecock. **2.** *no pl* badminton. **'Federbett** *n* duvet, featherbed. **'federführend** *adj* responsible. **'Federgewicht** *n sports*: featherweight. **'Federhalter** *m* fountain pen. **'federleicht** *adj* (as) light as a feather. **'Federlesen** *n nicht viel ~s machen mit* make short work of.

federn ['feːdərn] (h) **I** *v/i* **1.** be springy, be elastic, bounce. **2.** *gym.* flex. **II** *v/t* **3.** *a.* ⚙ spring, cushion: *gut gefedert sein* be well sprung. **'federnd** *adj* springy, elastic, resilient. **'Federschmuck** *m zo.* plumage. **'Federstrich** *m* stroke of the pen. **'Federung** *f* (-; -en) springs, *mot.* suspension. **'Federwolke** *f* cirrus (cloud). **'Federzeichnung** *f* pen-and-ink drawing.

Fee [feː] *f* (-; -n) fairy.

Fegefeuer *n* (-s; *no pl*) purgatory.

fegen ['feːgən] **I** *v/t* (h) sweep: *Schnee ~* clear away the snow; → *Platz* 5. **II** *v/i* (sn) *fig.* sweep, *F a.* flit, rush.

Feh [feː] *n* (-[e]s; -e) *zo.* squirrel.

Fehde ['feːdə] *f* (-; -n) feud.

fehl [feːl] *adv* → *Platz* 2.

'Fehlanzeige *f* ✗, ⚙ nil return: *F ~!* negative!

'fehlbar *adj* fallible.

'Fehlbarkeit *f* (-; *no pl*) fallibility.

'Fehlbesetzung *f* **1.** *thea.* miscast. **2.** *sports etc*: wrong choice.

'Fehlbetrag *m* deficit.

'Fehlbezeichnung *f* misnomer.

'Fehldiaˌgnose *f* 🩺 wrong diagnosis.

'Fehleinschätzung *f* misjudg(e)ment.

fehlen ['feːlən] *v/i* (h) **1.** be absent (*in der Schule, bei e-r Sitzung etc* from school, a meeting, *etc*). **2.** be missing: *ihm ~ zwei Zähne* he has two teeth missing; *du hast uns sehr gefehlt!* we really missed you! **3.** be lacking: *ihm fehlt (es an) Mut* he is lacking (in) courage; *uns fehlt es am nötigen Geld* we haven't got the money; *es ~ uns immer noch einige Helfer* we still need some helpers; *es fehlt uns an nichts* we have got everything we want; *es fehlte an jeder Zs.-arbeit* there was no cooperation whatsoever; *das fehlte gerade noch!* that's all we needed!; *wo fehlt's denn?* what's the trouble?; *fehlt Ihnen etwas?* is anything wrong with you?; *es fehlte nicht viel und er ...* he very nearly ... **4.** *weit gefehlt!* far from it!

'Fehlen *n* (-s) **1.** absence (*bei, in dat* from), b) absenteeism. **2.** lack, absence.

'fehlend *adj* **1.** absent. **2.** missing. **3.** outstanding.

'Fehlentscheidung *f* wrong decision.

'Fehlentwicklung *f* undesirable development.

Fehler ['feːlər] *m* (-s; -) **1.** mistake, error, *sports*: fault: *grober ~* blunder; *e-n ~ machen* make a mistake; *dein (eigener) ~!* (that's) your (own) fault! **2.** fault, defect, flaw.

'fehlerfrei *adj* faultless, perfect, flawless.

'fehlerhaft *adj* faulty (*a.* ⚙), incorrect, full of mistakes: ⚙ *~e Stelle* flaw.

'fehlerlos → **fehlerfrei**.

'Fehlerˌquelle *f* source of error (⚙ trouble). **~quote** *f* error rate. **~verzeichnis** *n* errata.

'Fehlgeburt *f* 🩺 miscarriage.

'fehlgeleitet *adj fig.* misguided.

'Fehlgriff *m* mistake, *a.* wrong choice.

'Fehlinvestiˌtion *f* bad investment.

'Fehlkalkulaˌtion *f* miscalculation.

'Fehlkonstrukti̱on *f e-e ~ sein* be badly designed.

'Fehlleistung *f* (*Freudsche ~* Freudian) slip.

'**Fehlpaß** *m sports*: bad pass.
'**Fehlplanung** *f* bad planning.
'**Fehlschlag** *m fig*. failure, F washout.
'**fehlschlagen** *v/i* (*irr, sep, -ge-, sn,* → **schlagen**) fail, go wrong.
'**Fehlschluß** *m* fallacy.
'**Fehlstart** *m* false start: *e-n ~ verursachen sports*: jump the gun.
'**Fehlurteil** *n* misjudg(e)ment.
'**Fehlverhalten** *n* lapse.
'**Fehlversuch** *m* unsuccessful attempt.
'**Fehlzeit** *f* time debit.
'**Fehlzündung** *f mot*. misfire, backfire.
Feier ['faiɔr] *f* (*-; -n*) a) celebration, party, fête, b) ceremony: *zur ~ des Tages* to mark the occasion.
'**Feierabend** *m ~ machen* finish (work), F knock off, *shop*: close; *nach ~* after work.
'**feierlich** *adj* a) solemn, b) ceremonious.
'**Feierlichkeit** *f* (*-; -en*) 1. *no pl* solemnity, ceremoniousness. 2. ceremony.
feiern ['faiɔrn] (h) **I** *v/t* celebrate, *a.* keep, observe (*holiday*), *a.* commemorate (*anniversary*). **II** *v/i* celebrate, have a party.
'**Feiertag** *m* (*gesetzlicher ~* public) holiday; *kirchlicher ~* religious holiday.
feige ['faigɔ] *adj* cowardly.
'**Feige** *f* (*-; -n*) 𝄞 fig.
'**Feigenbaum** *m* fig tree.
'**Feigenblatt** *n a. fig.* fig leaf.
'**Feigheit** *f* (*-; no pl*) cowardice.
Feigling ['faiklIŋ] *m* (*-s; -e*) coward.
Feile ['failɔ] *f* (*-; -n*) file. '**feilen** *v/t, v/i* (h) file: *fig.: ~ an* (*dat*) polish.
feilschen ['failʃɔn] *v/i* (h) haggle (*um* about).
fein [fain] **I** *adj* 1. fine, *a.* delicate: *~es Gebäck* fancy cakes; *~er Regen* (light) drizzle. 2. a) fine, *a.* choice, excellent (*quality*), b) elegant, c) refined: *~e Art, ~er Ton* good form; *nur vom Feinsten* only of the best. 3. keen, sharp (*ear etc*), fine, sensitive: *~er Humor* subtle humo(u)r; *~er Unterschied* subtle (*or* fine) distinction. 4. *a. iro.* nice, fine: *~!* fine!, good! **II** *adv* 5. finely (*etc*): *er ist ~ heraus* he's sitting pretty.
'**Feinabstimmung** *f* 𝄞, ⚙ fine tuning.
'**Feinarbeit** *f* precision work.
Feind [faint] *m* (*-[e]s; -e*) enemy, adversary: *Feund und ~* friend and foe; *sich ~e*

machen make enemies; *sich j-n zum ~ machen* antagonize s.o.
Feindin ['faindin] *f* (*-; -nen*) enemy.
'**feindlich** *adj* ✗ enemy (*troops etc*), *a.* hostile (*attitude etc* **gegen** to[wards]).
'**Feindlichkeit** *f* (*-; -en*) hostility.
'**Feindschaft** *f* (*-; -en*) enmity, hostility.
'**feindselig** *adj* hostile (**gegen** to).
'**Feindseligkeit** *f* (*-; -en*) 1. *no pl* hostility (**gegen** to). 2. *pl* ✗ hostilities.
'**Feindstaat** *m* enemy state.
'**feinfühlig** [-fy:liç] *adj* sensitive, delicate, tactful. '**Feingefühl** *n* (*-[e]s; no pl*) sensitiveness, *a.* tact.
'**Feingehalt** *m* standard.
'**Feingold** *n* fine gold.
'**Feinheit** *f* (*-; -en*) 1. *no pl* a) fineness, *a.* delicacy, *a.* exquisiteness, b) refinement, c) elegance. 2. subtlety: *die ~en* the finer points, the niceties; *die letzten ~en* the finishing touches.
'**Feinkostladen** *m* delicatessen (shop).
'**feinmachen**: *sich ~* (*sep, -ge-, h*) F dress up.
'**feinmaschig** *adj* fine-meshed.
'**Feinme,chanik** *f* precision mechanics.
'**Feinschmecker** *m* (*-s; -*) gourmet. *~lo,kal n* gourmet restaurant.
'**Feinschnitt** *m* (*-[e]s; no pl*) fine cut.
'**feinsinnig** *adj* sensitive, subtle.
'**Feinwäsche** *f* delicate fabrics.
'**Feinwaschmittel** *n* washing powder for delicate fabrics.
feist [faist] *adj* fat, stout.
feixen ['faiksɔn] *v/i* (h) F smirk.
Feld [fɛlt] *n* (*-[e]s; -er*) field (*a. fig.*), ♟ *a.* panel, *chess*: square: *auf dem ~* in the field; *das ~ anführen sports*: lead the field; *das ~ behaupten* stand one's ground; *das ~ räumen* beat a retreat; *zu ~e ziehen gegen* fight against.
'**Feld|arbeit** *f* 1. 🖈 work in the fields. 2. *research etc*: fieldwork. *~bett n* camp-bed. *~flasche f* ✗ water bottle. *~forschung f* field research, fieldwork. *~küche f* field kitchen. *~lager n* bivouac, camp. *~laza,rett n* casualty clearing station, *Am.* evacuation hospital. *~marschall m* field marshal. *~sa,lat m* 𝄞 lamb's lettuce. *~spieler(in f) m sports*: outfield player.
'**Feldstecher** *m* (*-s; -*) field glasses.
Feld-Wald-und-'Wiesen... F common-or-garden ..., run-of-the-mill ...

'**Feldwebel** [-ve:bəl] m (-s; -) sergeant.
'**Feldweg** m country lane.
'**Feldzug** m ✕ campaign.
Felge ['fɛlgə] f (-; -n) **1.** ⊕ rim. **2.** gym. circle. '**Felgenbremse** f rim brake.
Fell [fɛl] n (-[e]s; -e) **1.** zo. coat. **2.** a) hide, skin, b) pelt, c) fur: **das ~ abziehen** (dat) skin; fig. **ein dickes ~ haben** have a thick skin; F **j-m das ~ über die Ohren ziehen** fleece s.o.; **s-e ~ davonschwimmen sehen** see one's hopes dashed.
Fels [fɛls] m (-en; -en) rock.
'**Felsblock** m boulder.
Felsen ['fɛlzən] m (-s; -) rock, cliff.
'**felsenfest** adj unshakable: **~ davon überzeugt** absolutely convinced of it.
'**Felsenküste** f rocky coast.
felsig ['fɛlzɪç] adj rocky.
'**Felsklettern** n (-s) rock climbing.
'**Felsspalte** f crevice. '**Felswand** f wall of rock, rock face. '**Felszacke** f crag.
feminin [femi'ni:n] adj feminine (a. ling.), contp. effeminate. **Feminismus** [femi'nɪsmʊs] m (-; no pl) feminism. **Femi'nist** m (-en; -en), **Femi'nistin** f (-; -nen), **femi'nistisch** adj feminist.
Fenchel ['fɛnçəl] m (-s; no pl) ♣ fennel.
Fenster ['fɛnstər] n (-s; -) window: **das Geld zum ~ hinauswerfen** throw one's money away; F **er ist weg vom ~** he has had his chips.
'**Fenster|bank** f (-; ⸗e), **~brett** n windowsill. **~briefumschlag** m window envelope. **~glas** n window glass. **~laden** m shutter. **~leder** n chamois (leather). **~platz** m window seat. **~rahmen** m window frame. **~scheibe** f windowpane. **~tür** f French window.
Ferien ['fe:riən] pl holidays, ⚖️, univ. or Am. vacation, parl. recess: **die großen ~** the long vacation; **~ machen** go on holiday (Am. vacation).
'**Ferien...** holiday (camp, flat, etc). **~ort** m holiday resort. **~reise** f holiday (Am. vacation) trip. **~reisende** m, f (-n; -n) holidaymaker. **~zeit** f holiday period.
Ferkel ['fɛrkəl] n (-s; -) zo. young pig, piglet; fig. contp. **du ~!** you (dirty) pig!
'**Ferke'lei** f (-; -en) F contp. obscenity, dirty joke. '**ferkeln** v/i (h) zo. farrow.
Fermate [fɛr'ma:tə] f (-; -n) ♪ pause, fermata.

Ferment [fɛr'mɛnt] n (-s; -e) enzyme, ferment.
fern [fɛrn] I adj a) far (a. adv), b) far-off, a. fig. distant, remote: **der ⚬e Osten** the Far East; **von ~** from (or at) a distance, from afar; **in nicht allzu ~er Zukunft** in the not too distant future; **nichts liegt mir ~er (als)** nothing is further from my mind (than). II prep (dat) far (away) from. **fern'ab** adv far away.
'**Fernauslöser** m phot. cable release.
'**Fernbedienung** f remote control.
'**fernbleiben** v/i (irr, sep, -ge-, sn, → **bleiben**) (dat from) stay away, be absent. '**Fernbleiben** n (-s) a) absence, b) absenteeism.
'**Fernbrille** f distance glasses.
Ferne ['fɛrnə] f (-; no pl) distance: **aus der ~** from (or at) a distance, from afar; **in der ~** far away, far off; fig. **(noch) in weiter ~** (still) a long way off.
ferner ['fɛrnər] I adj further: → a. **fernliegen**. II adv further(more), besides: F fig. **er erschien unter ~ liefen** he was among the also rans.
'**fernerhin** adv for the (or in) future: **auch ~ tun** continue to do.
'**Fern|fahrer** m mot. long-distance lorry driver, Am. long-haul truck driver, F trucker. **~fahrt** f long-distance trip. **~flug** m long-distance flight. **⚬gelenkt** adj remote-controlled, ✕ guided (missile etc). **~gespräch** n long-distance call. **~glas** n binoculars.
'**fernhalten** v/t (irr, sep, -ge-, h, → **halten**) keep away (a. **sich ~, von** from): **j-n von sich ~** keep s.o. at a distance; **et. von j-m ~** keep s.th. from s.o.
'**Fernheizung** f district heating.
fern'her adv (von) ~ from afar.
'**Fern|ko,pierer** m telecopier. **~kursus** m correspondence course. **~laster** [-lastər] m (-s; -) F, **~lastwagen** m long-distance lorry, Am. long-haul truck. **~leitung** f teleph. long-distance line, ⚡ transmission line, ⊕ pipeline. **~lenkung** f remote control. **~lenkwaffe** f guided weapon (or missile). **~licht** n mot. full (or high) beam.
'**fernliegen** v/i (irr, sep, -ge-, h, → **liegen**) **es liegt mir fern zu** inf far be it from me to (or inf; **nichts lag mir ferner** nothing was farther from my mind.
'**Fernmelde|amt** n telephone exchange.

~satel¦lit *m* (tele)communication satellite. ~technik *f* (-; *no pl*) (tele)communications. ~turm *m* radio and TV tower. ~wesen *n* (-s; *no pl*) (tele)communications.

'fernmündlich → *telefonisch.*

'Fern¦ost..., 'fern¦östlich *adj* Far Eastern.

'Fernrohr *n* (-[e]s; -e) telescope.

'Fernschreiben *n* (-s; -) (*per ~* by) telex.

'Fernschreiber *m* telex machine.

'Fernseh... television (*or* TV) (*aerial, camera, interview, studio, network, etc*).

'Fernseh¦ansager(in *f*) *m* television (*or* TV) announcer. ~ansprache *f* television (*or* televised) address. ~anstalt *f* television company. ~appa¦rat *m* → *Fernsehgerät.* ~diskussi¦on *f* (TV) panel discussion. ~empfänger *m* → *Fernsehgerät.*

'fernsehen *v/i* (*irr, sep, -ge-, h,* → *sehen*) watch television. '**Fernsehen** *n* (-s) (*im ~* on) television (*or* TV): *im ~ bringen* (*or* **übertragen**) telecast, televise. '**Fernseher** *m* (-s; -) F 1. → *Fernsehgerät.* 2. → *Fernsehzuschauer.*

'Fernseh¦fassung *f* television (*or* TV) adaptation. ~gerät *n* television (set), TV (set). ~pro,gramm *n* 1. television (*or* TV) program(me *Br.*). 2. TV guide. ~publikum *n* television audience. ~röhre *f* television tube. ~satel¦lit *m* TV (*or* television) satellite. ~schirm *m* (television) screen. ~sender *m* 1. television transmitter. 2. television (broadcasting) station. 3. television channel. ~sendung *f* (television *or* TV) program(me *Br.*), telecast. ~spiel *n* television (*or* TV) play. ~teilnehmer *m* 1. TV licen/ce (*Am.* -se) holder. 2. → *Fernsehzuschauer.* ~turm *m* television (*or* TV) tower. ~übertragung *f* television (*or* TV) broadcast. ~zeit-schrift *f* TV guide. ~zuschauer *m* a) (television *or* TV) viewer, b) *pl* → *Fern-sehpublikum.*

'Fernsicht *f* view.

'Fernsprech¦amt *n* telephone exchange. ~auftragsdienst *m* answering service. ~auto,mat *m* pay phone. ~buch *n* telephone directory, F phone book.

'Fernsprecher *m* (-s; -) (*öffentlicher ~* public) telephone, F phone.

'Fernsprech¦gebühren *pl* telephone

charges. ~teilnehmer *m* telephone subscriber.

'fernstehen *v/i* (*irr, sep, -ge-, h,* → *stehen*) *j-m ~* have no contact with s.o.

'fernsteuern *v/t* (*sep, -ge-, h*) operate *s.th.* by remote control.

'Fern¦steuerung *f* remote control. ~straße *f* 1. major road. 2. motorway, *Am.* freeway. ~trans,port *m* long-distance (*Am.* long-haul) transport. ~unterricht *m* correspondence course. ~verkehr *m* long-distance traffic. ~wärmenetz *n* long-distance heating system. ~ziel *n* long-term objective. ~zug *m* long-distance train.

'Ferse ['fɛrzə] *f* (-; -n) heel: *j-m auf den ~n* a) *sein* be hard on s.o.'s heels, b) *folgen* dog s.o.'s footsteps.

'fertig ['fɛrtɪç] *adj* 1. ready: (*Achtung,*) ~, *los!* ready, steady, go! 2. finished, completed: *~ sein mit* have finished (with); *fig. ~ werden mit* a) cope (*or* deal) with, b) get over (*grief etc*); (*gut*) *ohne ... ~ werden* manage (*or* get along) (quite well) without ... 3. a) ⊕ finished, prefabricated, b) ready-to-eat, precooked, instant (*food*), c) ready-made (*clothes*). 4. *fig.* accomplished, mature. 5. F *fig.* a) *a. fix und ~* bushed, b) done for, c) flabbergasted: *der ist ~!* he has had it!; → *fertigmachen.*

'Fertigbauweise *f* ⊕ prefabricated construction.

'fertigbringen *v/t* (*irr, sep, -ge-, h,* → *bringen*) *et. ~* get s.th. done, manage s.th., bring s.th. off; *es ~ zu inf* manage to *inf*; *ich brachte es nicht fertig* I couldn't (*w.s.* bring myself to) do it.

'fertigen ['fɛrtɪɡən] *v/t* (h) produce, make.

'Fertig¦erzeugnis *n* finished product. ~gericht *n gastr.* instant meal. ~haus *n* prefabricated house, F prefab.

'Fertigkeit *f* (-; -en) a) skill, b) talent, c) proficiency (*in dat* in).

'fertigmachen *v/t* (*sep, -ge-, h*) 1. get *s.o., s.th.* ready. 2. finish. 3. F *j-n* ~ a) finish s.o. (off), b) get s.o. down, c) slam s.o., d) *sl.* clobber s.o. (*a. sports*).

'Fertigmon¦tage *f* final assembly.

'Fertigpro,dukt *n* finished product.

'fertigstellen *v/t* (*sep, -ge-, h*) finish, complete.

'Fertigstellung *f* (-; *no pl*) completion.

'**Fertigteil** *n* prefabricated part, *pl* assembly units.

'**Fertigung** *f* (-; *no pl*) manufacture, production.

'**Fertigungsstraße** *f* ✪ production line.

'**Fertigwaren** *pl* finished products.

Fes [fɛs] *m* -[-es]; -[e]) fez.

fesch [feʃ] *adj* F smart, chic.

Fessel¹ ['fɛsəl] *f* (-; -n) *a. fig.* shackle, fetter: **j-m ~n anlegen → fesseln** 1.

'**Fessel²** *f* (-; -n) **1.** ankle. **2.** *zo.* pastern.

'**fesseln** ['fɛsəln] *v/t* (h) **1. j-n ~** tie s.o. up (**an** *acc* to): *fig.* **ans Bett gefesselt** confined to one's bed, bedridden. **2.** *fig.* a) fascinate, captivate, b) catch (*s.o.'s eye, attention, etc*). '**fesselnd** *adj fig.* fascinating, riveting, gripping.

fest [fɛst] **I** *adj* **1.** a) firm (*a. fig.* decision, prices, *etc*), solid (*a. phys.*), ✪ *a.* tight, (firmly) fixed, b) strong, sturdy: **~ werden** harden, solidify, cement *etc*: set. **2.** *fig.* fixed (*costs, date, income, prices, etc*), *a.* binding (*agreement etc*), regular (*customer*), permanent (*domicile, position, etc*), F steady (*girlfriend etc*): **~er Wohnsitz** 🏛 *a.* fixed abode; **~er Schlaf** sound sleep; **~e Freundschaft** lasting friendship. **II** *adv* **3.** firmly (*etc*): **~ schlafen** sleep soundly; *et.* **~ abmachen** settle s.th. definitely; *Kapital* **~ anlegen** tie up capital; *j-n* **~ anstellen** employ s.o. on a permanent basis; *ich bin* **~ davon überzeugt, daß ...** I'm absolutely convinced that ...; *das habe ich ihr* **~ versprochen** I gave her my word for it. **4.** F *a.* **~e** properly; *immer* **~e!** go at it!

Fest *n* (-[e]s; -e) **1.** a) celebration, festivities, b) party, fête: **ein ~ feiern** celebrate. **2.** holiday, *eccl.* feast.

'**Festakt** *m* ceremony.

'**festangelegt** *adj* tied-up (*funds*). '**fest-angestellt** *adj* permanently employed.

'**Festaufführung** *f* gala performance.

'**festbinden** *v/t* (*irr, sep, -ge-, h, → binden*) tie (**an** *dat* to), tie *s.o., s.th.* up.

'**festbleiben** *v/i* (*irr, sep, -ge-, sn, → bleiben*) remain firm.

'**Festessen** *n* dinner, banquet.

'**festfahren: sich ~** (*irr, sep, -ge-, h, → fahren*) *a. fig.* get stuck, *talks:* reach a deadlock.

'**festfressen: sich ~** (*irr, sep, -ge-, h, → fressen*) ✪ seize, jam.

'**Festgeldkonto** *n* fixed-term deposit account.

'**festgelegt, 'festgesetzt** *adj* fixed.

'**festhalten** (*irr, sep, -ge-, h, → halten*) **I** *v/t* **1.** hold on to, grip. **2.** hold, keep, *a.* detain. **3.** *fig.* a) record, b) photograph, film, capture: *with* **~ Gedanken** make a (mental) note of an idea; *et. schriftlich* **~** put s.th. down in writing. **II** *sich* **~** a) hold tight, b) *a. fig.* hold on (**an** *dat* to).

'**festigen** ['fɛstɪɡən] (h) **I** *v/t* strengthen, consolidate, *a.* stabilize (*currency*). **II** *sich* **~** strengthen, grow stronger, *currency etc:* a. stabilize, *knowledge:* improve.

'**Festiger** *m* (-s; -) setting lotion.

'**Festigkeit** *f* (-; *no pl*) firmness, strength, steadiness, stability.

'**Festigung** *f* (-; -en) strengthening, consolidation, stabilization.

'**festklammern: sich ~** (*sep, -ge-, h*) cling (**an** *dat* to).

'**festkleben** *v/t, v/i* (*sep, -ge-, h*) stick (**an** *dat* to).

'**festklemmen** (*sep, -ge-, h*) **I** *v/t* clamp (fast), wedge. **II** *v/i* stick (fast), get stuck, jam, be jammed.

'**Festkon,zert** *n* gala concert.

'**Festkörper** *m phys.* solid.

'**Festkurs** *m* ✝ fixed rate.

'**Festland** *n* a) mainland, b) land, c) continent. '**Festland(s)...** continental.

'**festlegen** (*sep, -ge-, h*) **I** *v/t* **1. →** *festsetzen* 1. **2.** lay down, define (*principles etc*). **3.** ⚓ plot (*course*). **4.** ✝ tie up (*capital*). **5. j-n auf e-e Sache ~** pin s.o. down to s.th. **II** *sich* **~ auf** (*acc*) a) commit o.s. to, b) decide on.

'**festlich** **I** *adj* festive, splendid. **II** *adv* festively (*etc*): **~ begehen** celebrate; **~ gestimmt** in a festive mood.

'**Festlichkeit** *f* (-; -en) **1.** festivity. **2.** *no pl* festive atmosphere.

'**festliegen** *v/i* (*irr, sep, -ge-, h, → liegen*) **1.** be fixed, *capital:* be tied up. **2.** *mot.* be stuck, ⚓ be grounded.

'**festmachen** (*sep, -ge-, h*) **I** *v/t* **1.** (**an** *dat* to) fix, fasten, ⚓ moor. **2.** *fig.* fix, settle, *a.* clinch (*a deal*): *et.* **~ an** (*dat*) fix s.th. on. **II** *v/i* **3.** ⚓ moor.

'**Festmeter** *m, n* cubic met/re (*Am.* -er).

'**festnageln** *v/t* (*sep, -ge-, h*) nail down (*a. fig.* **auf** *acc* to).

Festnahme ['fɛstnaːmə] *f* (-; -n) arrest.

'festnehmen v/t (irr, sep, -ge-, h, → **neh-men**) arrest.
'Festplatte f computer: hard disc.
'Festpreis m fixed price.
'Festrede f (ceremonial) address.
'Festredner(in f) m official speaker.
'Festsaal m (banqueting) hall.
'Festschrift f commemorative publication.
'festsetzen (sep, -ge-, h) **I** v/t **1.** a) (auf acc for) fix, arrange (place, time, etc), b) (auf acc at) fix (price, penalty, salary, etc), c) assess (damage, tax), d) lay down, agree on (conditions). **2.** arrest. **II** sich ~ settle (in dat in).
'festsitzen v/i (irr, sep, -ge-, h, → **sitzen**) mot. be stuck (a. F fig.), ⚓ be stranded.
'Festspeicher m computer: read-only memory (abbr. ROM).
'Festspiel n festival performance: ~e pl → **Festspielwoche** f festival.
'feststehen v/i (irr, sep, -ge-, h, → **stehen**) a) be fixed, b) be certain, be a fact.
'feststehend adj **1.** ⊙ stationary. **2.** fig. established (fact etc).
'feststellbar adj **1.** ascertainable. **2.** noticeable. **3.** ⊙ lock-type.
'Feststellbremse f parking brake.
'feststellen v/t (sep, -ge-, h) **1.** a) find out, discover, establish, b) locate (fault, place, etc), c) ⊗ diagnose. **2.** realize, see, notice. **3.** state, say. **4.** ⊙ lock.
'Feststellung f (-; -en) **1.** establishing (etc, → **feststellen**), discovery. **2.** observation: er machte die ~, daß ... he found (or realized) that ... **3.** a) remark, b) statement.
'Feststoffra,kete f solid-fuel rocket.
'Festtag m (eccl. religious) holiday.
'festtäglich adj festive.
'Festung f (-; -en) fortress, fort.
'festverzinslich adj ✝ fixed interest (bearing): ~e Anlagepapiere investment bonds.
'Festwoche f, a. pl festival.
'Festzelt n marquee.
'festziehen v/t (irr, sep, -ge-, h, → **ziehen**) tighten.
'Festzug m procession.
Fetisch ['fe:tɪʃ] m (-s; -e) fetish.
Fetischismus [feti'ʃɪsmʊs] m (-; no pl) fetishism.
Fetischist [-'ʃɪst] m (-en; -en) fetishist.
fett [fɛt] adj **1.** fat, a. obese (person), fatty

(food): ~ machen fatten; ~ essen eat fatty food. **2.** F fig. fat, rich, big: ~e Beute big haul. **3.** print. bold.
Fett n (-[e]s; -e) **1.** fat: F sein ~ wegha-ben have caught it. **2.** of body: fat, F flab: ~ ansetzen put on (a lot of) weight. **3.** ⊙ grease.
'fettarm adj low-fat ..., pred low in fat.
'Fettauge n blob of fat.
'Fettcreme f rich oil-based cream.
'Fettdruck m print. bold(-faced) type.
fetten ['fɛtən] (h) **I** v/t grease. **II** v/i be greasy.
'Fettfleck m grease spot.
'fettgedruckt adj in bold type.
'Fettgehalt m (-[e]s; -e) fat content.
'Fettgewebe n fatty tissue.
'fetthaltig adj containing fat, fatty, oil-based (lotion).
fettig ['fɛtɪç] adj fat, fatty, oily, greasy (hair, skin, etc).
'Fettleber f ♣ fatty liver.
fettleibig ['fɛtlaɪbɪç] adj obese.
'Fettleibigkeit f (-; no pl) obesity.
'Fettnäpfchen n F (bei j-m) ins ~ treten put one's foot in it. **'Fettsack** m F contp. fatso. **'Fettsalbe** f greasy ointment. **'Fettschicht** f layer of fat. **'Fett-sucht** f (-; no pl) ♣ obesity. **'Fettwanst** m F contp. **1.** paunch. **2.** fatso.
Fetus ['fe:tʊs] m (-[ses]; -se) f(o)etus.
Fetzen ['fɛtsən] m (-s; -) **1.** rag (a. humor. dress), scrap (of paper), shred (of cloth): in ~ in shreds and tatters; F daß die ~ fliegen like crazy. **2.** pl F fig. snatches (of conversation etc).
fetzig ['fɛtsɪç] adj F wild.
feucht [fɔʏçt] adj damp, moist (a. eyes, lips, skin, etc), wet (climate), humid (air): ~e Hände sweaty palms.
'feucht'fröhlich adj F (very) merry.
'Feuchtigkeit f (-; no pl) damp(ness), moisture, humidity: vor ~ schützen! keep in a dry place!
'Feuchtigkeits|creme f moisturizing cream, moisturizer. **~gehalt** m moisture content, of air: a. humidity.
feudal [fɔʏ'da:l] adj **1.** hist. feudal. **2.** F fig. a) sumptuous, b) posh.
Feudalismus [fɔʏda'lɪsmʊs] m (-; no pl) hist. feudalism.
Feuer ['fɔʏər] n (-s; -) **1.** fire: ✗ ~! fire!; haben Sie ~? have you got a light?; ~ fangen catch fire; j-m ~ geben give s.o.

a light; *das Olympische* ~ the Olympic flame; *fig. durchs ~ gehen für* go through fire and water for; *mit dem ~ spielen* play with fire; *zwischen zwei ~ geraten* be caught between the devil and the deep blue sea; → *eröffnen* 1. **2.** ♣ beacon. **3.** *fig.* fire, *a.* fervo(u)r, spirit: *~ und Flamme sein* be all for it.

'**Feuer|alarm** *m* fire alarm. **~anzünder** *m* fire lighter. **~bestattung** *f* cremation. **~eifer** *m* zeal. **~einstellung** *f* ✕ cessation of fire. **2fest** *adj* **1.** fireproof. **2.** incombustible. **~gefahr** *f* danger of fire. **2gefährlich** *adj* flammable. **~gefecht** *n* ✕ gun battle. **~haken** *m* poker. **~kraft** *f* (*-; no pl*) ✕ fire power. **~leiter** *f* **1.** fire ladder. **2.** fire escape. **~löscher** *m* fire extinguisher. **~melder** *m* (*-s; -*) fire alarm.

feuern ['fɔyərn] *v/t* (h) **1.** fire (*stove*, ✕ *salute*), *a.* burn (*wood, coal*). **2.** F hurl, *sports:* slam (*the ball*): *j-m e-e* ~ land s.o. one. **3.** F fire, sack.

'**Feuer|probe** *f fig.* acid test. **2rot** *adj* fiery (red), flaming red. **~schaden** *m* damage caused by fire. **~schiff** *n* lightship. **~schlucker** *m* fire-eater. **~schutz** *m* **1.** fire prevention. **2.** ✕ covering fire. **~stein** *m* flint. **~stelle** *f* fireplace, hearth. **~taufe** *f fig.* baptism of fire. **~teufel** *m* F fire bug. **~treppe** *f* fire escape.

'**Feuerung** *f* (*-; -en*) **1.** heating. **2.** *no pl* fuel.

'**Feuer|versicherung** *f* fire insurance. **~wache** *f* fire station. **~waffe** *f* firearm.

'**Feuerwehr** *f* (*-; -en*) fire brigade: F *wie die* ~ like a flash. **~mann** *m* fireman.

'**Feuerwerk** *n* (*-s; -e*) fireworks (*a. fig.*).

'**Feuerwerkskörper** *m* firework.

'**Feuerzangenbowle** *f* burnt punch.

'**Feuerzeug** *n* (*-[e]s; -e*) (cigarette) lighter. '**Feuerzeug|ben,zin** *n* lighter fluid.

Feuilleton ['fœjə'tõ:] *n* (*-s; -s*) feature pages. **Feuilletonist** [fœjəto'nɪst] *m* (*-en; -en*) feature writer.

feurig ['fɔyrɪç] *adj fig.* **1.** fiery, ardent, passionate. **2.** rich, heady (*wine*).

Fiasko ['fiasko] *n* (*-s; -s*) fiasco.

Fibel ['fiːbəl] *f* (*-; -n*) *ped.* primer.

Fiber ['fiːbər] *f* (*-; -n*) *Am.* fiber. '**Fiberglas** *n* fibre (*Am.* fiber) glass.

Fichte ['fɪçtə] *f* (*-; -n*) ♣ spruce, F pine (tree). '**Fichtenholz** *n* deal.

ficken ['fɪkən] *v/t, v/i* (h) V fuck.

fidel [fi'deːl] *adj* cheerful.

Fieber ['fiːbər] *n* (*-s; no pl*) fever (*a. fig.*), (high) temperature: *~ haben* → *fiebern* 1; *j-m* (*or j-s*) ~ *messen* take s.o.'s temperature.

'**Fieberanfall** *m* attack of fever.

'**fieberfrei** *adj sie ist* ~ her temperature is back to normal again.

'**fieberhaft** *adj a. fig.* feverish.

'**Fieberkranke** *m, f* (*-n; -n*) fever case.

'**Fieberkurve** *f* temperature curve.

'**Fiebermittel** *n* antipyretic.

fiebern ['fiːbərn] *v/i* (h) **1.** a) have (*or* be running) a temperature, b) be delirious. **2.** *fig.* be feverish (*vor* with): ~ *nach* yearn for.

'**Fieber|ta,belle** *f* temperature chart. **~thermo,meter** *n* (clinical) thermometer. **~traum** *m* feverish dream.

fiebrig ['fiːbrɪç] → *fieberhaft*.

Fiedel ['fiːdəl] *f* (*-; -n*) fiddle.

fiedeln ['fiːdəln] *v/t, v/i* (h) F fiddle.

fiel [fiːl] *pret of* **fallen**.

fies [fiːs] *adj* nasty, mean.

Fiesling ['fiːslɪŋ] *m* (*-s; -e*) F meanie.

Figur [fi'guːr] *f* (*-; -en*) **1.** figure (*a.* ✾, ♪), *a.* build: *e-e gute* (*schlechte*) ~ *machen* cut a fine (poor) figure. **2.** *in film, novel, etc:* figure, character: *komische* ~ a) figure of fun, b) strange character. **3.** *chess:* piece, *pl a.* chessmen. **4.** *arts:* a) figure, statue, b) figurine.

figurativ [figura'tiːf] *adj ling.* figurative.

figurieren [figu'riːrən] *v/i* (h) figure (*als* as). **figürlich** [fi'gyːrlɪç] *adj* **1.** *paint. etc* figured. **2.** *ling.* figurative.

Fiktion [fɪk'tsioːn] *f* (*-; -en*) fiction.

fiktiv [fɪk'tiːf] *adj* fictitious.

Filet [fi'leː] *n* (*-s; -s*) *gastr.* fillet. **~steak** *n* fillet steak. **~stück** *n* piece of sirloin.

Filiale [fi'liaːlə] *f* (*-; -n*) **1.** branch (office), subsidiary. **2.** chain store.

Fili'alleiter(in *f*) *m* branch manager.

Filigran [fili'graːn] *n* (*-s; -e*), **Fili'granarbeit** *f* filigree.

Film [fɪlm] *m* (*-s; -e*) **1.** *phot.* film. **2.** film, *esp. Am. a.* movie: *e-n* ~ *drehen* (*über acc*) shoot (*or* make) a film (of), film *s.th.*; F *fig. mir ist der* ~ *gerissen* I had a blackout. **3.** *the cinema, esp. Am. the* movies: *beim* ~ *sein* a) be in the film (*esp. Am. a.* movie) business, b) be a film (*esp. Am. a.* movie) actor (*or* actress). **4.** film, coat(ing). **~ar‚chiv** n film library. **~ateli‚er** n film studio. **~aufnahme** f **1.** shooting (of a film). **2.** shot, take. **~bericht** m film report.

'**Filmemacher(in** f) m film (esp. Am. a. movie) maker.

filmen ['filmən] (h) **I** v/t film, shoot. **II** v/i be filming, make a film, a. be on location.

'**Film|festspiele** pl film festival. **~gelände** n studio lot. **~gesellschaft** f film (Am. motion-picture) company. **~indu‚strie** f film (Am. motion-picture) industry.

filmisch ['filmɪʃ] adj cinematic.

'**Film|kamera** f film (or movie) camera. **2.** cinecamera. **~kri‚tik** f film review. **~kritiker(in** f) m film critic. **~kunst** f (-; no pl) cinematography. **~materi‚al** n footage. **~mu‚sik** f **1.** film music. **2.** the music to the film. **~pack** m film pack. **~preis** m film (esp. Am. a. movie) award. **~produ‚zent(in** f) m (film) producer. **~pro‚jektor** m film (esp. Am. a. movie) projector. **~regis‚seur(in** f) m film (esp. Am. a. movie) director. **~re‚klame** f screen advertising. **~schauspieler(in** f) m film (or screen, esp. Am. a. movie) actor (actress). **~star** m film (esp. Am. a. movie) star. **~streifen** m reel, w.s. strip. **~studio** n film studio. **~the‚ater** n cinema, Am. movie theater. **~verleih** m **1.** film distribution. **2.** film distributors. **~vorführer** m projectionist. **~vorführung** f film (esp. Am. a. movie) show. **~vorschau** f a) preview, b) trailer, c) in newspaper: forthcoming films. **~welt** f film world, Am. a. movieland.

Filter ['filtər] m, n (-s; -) filter. **~anlage** f filtration plant. **~einsatz** m filter element. **~kaffee** m filtered coffee.

filtern ['filtərn] v/t (h) filter, a. percolate. '**Filter|pa‚pier** n filter paper. **~ziga‚rette** f filter(-tipped) cigarette.

Filtrat [fil'tra:t] n (-[e]s; -e) filtrate.

filtrieren [fil'tri:rən] v/t (h) filter.

Filz [fɪlts] m (-es; -e) **1.** felt. **2.** F felt hat. **3.** F contp. a) skinflint, b) pol. corruption. **filzen** ['fɪltsən] (h) **I** v/t F fig. frisk. **II** v/i wool: felt. '**Filzhut** m felt hat.

filzig ['fɪltsɪç] adj **1.** a) felted, b) matted (hair). **2.** F fig. mean, stingy.

'**Filzlaus** f zo. crab louse.

'**Filzpan‚toffel** m felt slipper.

'**Filzstift** m felt(-tipped) pen.

Fimmel ['fɪməl] m (-s; -) F craze: **e-n ~ haben für** be mad about.

Finale [fi'na:lə] n (-s; -) **1.** finale. **2.** sports: final (round), finals.

Finalist [fina'lɪst] m (-en; -en), **Fina'listin** f (-; -nen) sports: finalist.

Fi'nalsatz m ling. final clause.

Finanz... [fi'nants-] financial (adviser, paper, etc). **~amt** n inland (Am. internal) revenue (office), fig. contp. the Tax Man. **~ausschuß** m finance committee. **~beamte** m revenue officer.

Fi'nanzen pl finances.

Fi'nanzgericht n tax tribunal. **Fi'nanzgeschäft** n financial transaction.

finanziell [finan'tsiɛl] adj financial.

finanzieren [finan'tsi:rən] v/t (h) finance: → **frei** 12. **Finan'zierung** f (-; -en) financing. **Finan'zierungsgesellschaft** f finance company.

Fi'nanzjahr n fiscal (or financial) year. **2kräftig** adj financially strong, potent. **~lage** f financial situation. **~mann** m financier. **~mi‚nister** m minister of finance, Br. Chancellor of the Exchequer, Am. Secretary of the Treasury. **~mini‚sterium** n ministry of finance, Br. Treasury, Am. Treasury Department. **~poli‚tik** f financial (or fiscal) policy. **2schwach** adj financially weak. **~spritze** f F shot in the arm. **~welt** f financial world. **~wesen** n (-s; no pl) (public) finance.

finden ['fɪndən] (fand, gefunden, h) **I** v/t find, fig. a. think: **nirgends zu ~** nowhere to be found; fig. **ein Ende ~** come to an end; **ich fand k-e Worte** I was at a loss for words; **ich finde es gut (, daß ...)** I think it's good (that ...); **wie ~ Sie das Buch?** how do you like (or what do you think of) the book?; **~ Sie (nicht)?** do (don't) you think so?; **ich weiß nicht, was sie an ihm findet** I don't know what she sees in him. **II sich ~** a) be found, b) find o.s.; **das wird sich ~** we'll see. **III** v/i **nach Hause ~** find one's way home; **zu sich selbst ~** sort o.s out.

'**Finder** m (-s; -), '**Finderin** f (-; -nen) finder. '**Finderlohn** m finder's reward.

Findling ['fɪntlɪŋ] m (-s; -e) geol. erratic block.

Finesse [fiˈnɛsə] f (-; -n) finesse, pl tricks: *mit allen ~n* car etc with all the refinements.

fing [fɪŋ] pret of **fangen**.

Finger [ˈfɪŋər] m (-s; -) finger: *sich die ~ verbrennen* a. fig. burn one's fingers; *sich in den ~ schneiden* a) cut one's finger, b) fig. make a big mistake; *j-m auf die ~ klopfen* a. fig. rap s.o.'s knuckles; *laß die ~ davon!* a) hands off!, b) fig. leave well alone!; fig. *sich et. aus den ~n saugen* make s.th. up; *j-m auf die ~ sehen* keep a sharp eye on s.o.; *j-n um den kleinen ~ wickeln* twist s.o. round one's little finger; *k-n ~ rühren* not to lift a finger; *er hat überall s-e ~ im Spiel* he's got a finger in every pie; → *abzählen*.

'**Finger|abdruck** m fingerprint: → *abnehmen*. **~alpha‚bet** n finger alphabet.

'**fingerfertig** adj nimble-fingered.

'**Fingerfertigkeit** f (-; no pl) dexterity.

'**Fingerhut** m 1. ♀ foxglove. 2. thimble.

fingern [ˈfɪŋərn] (h) **I** v/i *~ an* (dat) finger. **II** v/t F wangle.

'**Finger|nagel** m fingernail. **~ring** m ring. **~schale** f finger bowl. **~spitze** f fingertip. **~spitzengefühl** n a) sure instinct, b) tact. **~sprache** f finger language. **~übung** f finger exercise.

'**Fingerzeig** m (-[e]s; -e) hint, pointer.

fingieren [fɪŋˈgiːrən] v/t (h) 1. fake: *fingiert* fake(d), fictitious. 2. fabricate.

Finish [ˈfɪnɪʃ] n (-s; -s) sports, ◉ finish.

Fink [fɪŋk] m (-en; -en) zo. finch.

'**Finne¹** [ˈfɪnə] f (-; -n) fin.

'**Finne²** m (-n; -n), '**Finnin** f (-; -nen) Finn. **finnisch** [ˈfɪnɪʃ] adj Finnish.

'**Finnland** n (-s) Finland.

finster [ˈfɪnstər] adj 1. a. fig. dark, black, gloomy. 2. a) grim, b) evil, sinister: *~er Blick* black look; *j-n ~ ansehen* glower at s.o. 3. F fig. a) shady, b) bad: *es sieht ~ aus!* things are looking bad!

'**Finsternis** f (-; -se) a. fig. darkness, gloom(iness).

Finte [ˈfɪntə] f sports: feint, fig. a. trick.

Firlefanz [ˈfɪrləfants] m (-es; no pl) F contp. a) frippery, junk, b) nonsense.

Firma [ˈfɪrma] f (-; -men) firm, company: *die ~ Bosch* (the) Bosch (Company).

Firmament [fɪrmaˈmɛnt] n (-[e]s; -e) firmament, sky.

firmen [ˈfɪrmən] v/t (h) eccl. confirm.

'**Firmen|inhaber(in** f) m owner of a (or the) firm. **~name** m company name. **~schild** n company name, facia, on machine etc: nameplate. **~sitz** m (company) headquarters. **~stempel** m firm('s) stamp. **~verzeichnis** n trade directory. **~wagen** m company car. **~wert** m (-[e]s; no pl) goodwill. **~zeichen** n F logo.

firmieren [fɪrˈmiːrən] v/i (h) **~ als** have the company name of.

'**Firmling** m (-s; -e) eccl. confirmand.

'**Firmung** f (-; -en) eccl. confirmation.

Firn [fɪrn] m (-[e]s; -e) corn snow.

Firnis [ˈfɪrnɪs] m (-ses; -se) varnish.

firnissen [ˈfɪrnɪsən] v/t varnish.

First [fɪrst] m (-[e]s; -e) ridge.

Fis [fɪs] n (-; -) ♪ F sharp.

Fisch [fɪʃ] m (-[e]s; -e) 1. fish: F fig. *ein großer* (or *dicker*) *~* a big fish; *kleine ~e* peanuts, small beer. 2. pl astr. Pisces. '**Fischauge** n phot. fish-eye (lens).

fischen [ˈfɪʃən] v/t, v/i (h) fish (nach for): → *trübe* 1. '**Fischen** n (-s) fishing.

'**Fischer** m (-s; -) fisherman. **~boot** n fishing boat. **~dorf** n fishing village.

Fische'rei f (-; no pl) 1. fishing. 2. fishing industry. **~flotte** f fishing fleet. **~grenze** f fishing limit. **~hafen** m fishing port. **~recht** n fishing right(s).

'**Fisch|fang** m fishing. **~fi‚let** n gastr. fish fillet. **~gabel** f fish fork. **~gericht** n gastr. fish dish. **~geruch** m fishy smell. **~geschäft** n fishmonger's. **~gräten-muster** n herringbone (pattern). **~gründe** pl fishing grounds, fishery. **~händler(in** f) m fishmonger, Am. fish dealer. **~indu‚strie** f fish-processing industry. **~kon‚serven** pl tinned (or canned) fish. **~kunde** f (-; no pl) ichthyology. **~kutter** m (fishing) trawler. **~laich** m (fish) spawn. **~markt** m fish market. **~mehl** n fishmeal. **~messer** n fish knife. **~otter** m zo. otter. **~reiher** m zo. heron. **~restau‚rant** n fish (or seafood) restaurant. **~schuppe** f scale. **~stäbchen** n gastr. fish finger, Am. fish stick. **~sterben** n fish kill. **~vergiftung** f fish poisoning. **~zucht** f fish farming. **~zug** m catch, fig. a. haul.

Fiskus [ˈfɪskʊs] m (-; no pl) 1. Treasury. 2. government.

Fistel [ˈfɪstəl] f (-; -n) ♣ fistula.

'**Fistelstimme** f **1.** ♪ falsetto. **2.** contp. squeaky voice.

fit [fɪt] adj (**sich ~ halten** keep) fit.

Fitneß f ['fɪtnɛs] f (-; no pl) fitness.

'**Fitneßcenter** n health club, gym.

'**Fitneßraum** m exercise room.

Fittich ['fɪtɪç] m (fig. **j-n unter s-e ~e nehmen** take s.o. under one's) wing.

fix [fɪks] **I** adj **1.** fixed (salary, costs, etc): **~e Idee** fixed idea, obsession. **2.** F a) quick (in dat at), b) smart, sharp. **3. ~ und fertig** a) all ready, b) → **fertig** 5 a. **II** adv **4.** F quickly, in a flash.

fixen ['fɪksən] v/i (h) sl. fix, shoot, mainline. **Fixer** ['fɪksər] m (-s; -), '**Fixerin** f (-; -nen) sl. junkie.

Fi'xierbad n phot. fixer.

fixieren [fɪ'ksiːrən] v/t (h) **1.** a. phot, 𝄞 fix, fig. a. determine: **schriftlich ~** formulate, record. **2.** psych. **fixiert sein auf** (acc) be fixated on. **3.** stare at.

Fi'xiermittel n phot. fixative.

Fi'xierung f (-; -en) **1.** fixing (a. phot. etc). **2.** psych. fixation.

'**Fixstern** m fixed star.

Fixum ['fɪksəm] n (-s; Fixa) 🕇 fixed sum (or salary).

Fjord [fjɔrt] m (-[e]s; -e) fjord, fiord.

FKK [ɛfka:'ka:] → **Freikörperkultur**. **FK'K-Strand** m nudist beach.

flach [flax] adj **1.** flat, a. level, even: **~ machen** (**klopfen** etc) flatten; **~ werden** flatten (out); **mit der ~en Hand** with the flat of one's hand. **2.** a. fig. shallow: **~er Teller** shallow (w.s. dinner) plate. **3.** low (a. sports: shot).

'**Flachboot** n flat-bottomed boat.

'**Flachdach** n flat roof.

Fläche ['flɛçə] f (-; -n) a) surface (a. ℀), b) area, space: (**weite**) ~ expanse.

'**Flächen|ausdehnung** f area. **~brand** m extensive fire. **℔deckend** adj overall, global. **~inhalt** m ℀ area. **~maß** n ℀ surface measurement.

'**flachfallen** v/i (irr, sep, -ge-, sn, → **fallen**) F fall through.

'**Flachheit** f (-; no pl) flatness, fig. shallowness.

'**Flachmann** m (-[e]s; ⸚er) F hip flask. '**Flachland** n flat country. '**Flachpaß** m soccer: low pass. '**Flachreli,ef** n bas-relief. '**Flachrennen** n flat race.

Flachs [flaks] m (-es; no pl) **1.** ♀ flax. **2.** F kidding: **ohne ~!** no kidding!

'**Flachschuß** m soccer: low ball.

flachsen ['flaksən] v/i (h) F kid.

flackern ['flakərn] v/i (h) flicker.

Fladen ['fla:dən] m (-s; -) flat cake.

'**Fladenbrot** n round flat loaf.

Flagge ['flagə] f (-; -n) flag: fig. **unter falscher ~ segeln** sail under false colo(u)rs; **~ zeigen** make a stand.

flaggen ['flagən] (h) **I** v/i fly (or hoist) a flag (or flags). **II** v/t flag, signal.

'**Flaggschiff** n a. fig. flagship.

Flair [flɛːr] n (-s; no pl) **1.** aura. **2.** flair.

Flak [flak] f (-; -, -s) **1.** → **Flakgeschütz**. **2.** → '**Flakartille,rie** f antiaircraft artillery. '**Flakfeuer** n antiaircraft fire, F flak. '**Flakgeschütz** n antiaircraft gun.

Flakon [fla'kõː] n, m (-s; -s) small bottle.

flambieren [flam'biːrən] v/t (h) flame.

Flamingo [fla'mɪŋɡo] m (-s; -s) zo. flamingo.

flämisch ['flɛːmɪʃ] adj Flemish.

Flamme ['flamə] f (-; -n) a. fig. flame: **in** (**hellen**) **~n stehen** be ablaze; **auf kleiner ~ cook** on a low heat. '**flammend** adj fig. fiery, stirring (speech etc).

'**Flammenmeer** n sea of flames.

Flanell [fla'nɛl] m (-s; -e) flannel.

Flanke ['flaŋkə] f (-; -n) **1.** flank, side. **2.** a) soccer: cent/re (Am. -er), b) gym. (flank) vault.

'**flanken** v/i (h) soccer: cent/re (Am. -er).

flankieren [flaŋ'kiːrən] v/t (h) flank: fig. **~de Maßnahme** supporting measure.

Flansch [flanʃ] m (-[e]s; -e) ☉ flange.

flapsig ['flapsɪç] adj loutish.

Fläschchen ['flɛʃçən] n (-s; -) **1.** small bottle, pharm. phial. **2.** (baby) bottle.

Flasche ['flaʃə] f (-; -n) **1.** bottle: **e-e ~ Wein** a bottle of wine; **e-m Baby die ~ geben** give a baby its bottle; **mit der ~ aufziehen** bottle-feed. **2.** F dud, flop.

'**Flaschen|bier** n bottled beer. **~gas** n bottled gas. **℔grün** adj bottle-green. **~kind** n bottle-fed baby. **~milch** f bottled milk. **~öffner** m bottle opener. **~pfand** n deposit (on a bottle). **~post** f bottle post. **~wein** n bottled wine.

'**flaschenweise** adv by the bottle.

'**Flaschenzug** m ☉ block and pulley.

flatterhaft adj flighty, fickle.

flattern ['flatərn] v/i **1.** (sn) flutter. **2.** (h) flutter (a. 𝄞, ☉), flap, wheels: wobble.

flau [flaʊ] adj **1.** a) queasy, b) faint,· c)

listless. **2.** stale (*taste*). **3.** *phot.* flat, fuzzy, weak. **4.** ✝ slack.

Flaum [flaʊm] m (-[e]s; *no pl*) down.
'**flaumig** *adj* downy.

Flausch [flaʊʃ] m (-es; -e) *textil.* coating.
'**flauschig** *adj* fluffy.

Flausen ['flaʊzən] *pl* F silly ideas.

Flaute ['flaʊtə] f (-; -n) **1.** ⊕ lull. **2.** ✝ slack period.

Flechte ['flɛçtə] f (-; -n) **1.** ♀ lichen. **2.** ☞ eczema. **3.** braid.

'**flechten** v/t (flocht, geflochten, h) plait (*hair*), bind (*wreath*), weave (*basket*).

Fleck [flɛk] m (-[e]s; -e) **1.** spot, stain: *blauer* ~ bruise. **2.** *fig.* blemish. **3.** F a) spot, place, b) patch: *am falschen* ~ *a. fig.* in the wrong place; *fig. nicht vom* ~ *kommen* not to make any headway; *sich nicht vom* ~ *rühren* not to budge.

'**Fleckchen** n (-s; -) **1.** speck. **2.** *fig.* (*ein schönes* ~ *Erde*) a lovely spot.

flecken ['flɛkən] v/i (h) stain.

'**Flecken** m (-s; -) → *Fleck.*

'**Fleckenentferner** m stain remover.

'**fleckenlos** *adj a. fig.* spotless.

'**fleckig** *adj* a) spotted, b) stained.

'**Flecktyphus** m ☞ (epidemic) typhus.

Fledermaus ['fleːdər-] f zo. bat.

Flegel ['fleːgəl] m (-s; -) lout. **Flege'lei** f (-; -en) loutish behavio(u)r. '**flegelhaft** *adj* loutish. '**Flegeljahre** *pl* (*in den* ~n *sein* be at an) awkward age.

flehen ['fleːən] v/i (h) ~ *um* beg for, implore. '**Flehen** n (-s) entreaty.

'**flehend**, '**flehentlich** *adj* imploring, urgent (*request*): ~ *bitten um* → *flehen.*

Fleisch [flaɪʃ] n (-es; *no pl*) **1.** *a. fig.* flesh: *das eigene* ~ *und Blut* one's own flesh and blood; *j-m in* ~ *und Blut übergehen* become second nature to s.o.; F *sich ins eigene* ~ *schneiden* cut off one's nose to spite one's face; *vom* ~ *fallen* grow thin. **2.** *gastr.* a) meat, b) flesh (*of fruit*). ~**brühe** f a) consommé, beef tea, b) (beef) stock.

'**Fleischer** m (-s; -) butcher.

Fleische'rei f (-; -en), '**Fleischerladen** m butcher's shop.

'**fleischfarben** *adj* flesh-colo(u)red.

'**fleischfressend** *adj* ♞, zo. carnivorous.

'**Fleischfresser** m zo. carnivore.

'**Fleischgericht** n ☞ meat dish.

'**fleischig** *adj* **1.** fleshy. **2.** meaty.

'**Fleisch|kloß** m **1.** *gastr.* meatball. **2.** F *fig.* mound of flesh. ~**kon**₁**serven** *pl* tinned (*or* canned) meat.

'**fleischlich** *adj* carnal.

'**fleischlos** *adj* meatless (*diet*).

'**Fleisch|to₁mate** f beef tomato. ~**vergiftung** f ☞ meat poisoning. ~**waren** *pl* meat products. ~**wolf** m mincer, *Am.* meat grinder. ~**wunde** f ☞ flesh wound. ~**wurst** f pork sausage.

Fleiß [flaɪs] m (-es; *no pl*) diligence, industry, hard work: *viel* ~ *verwenden auf* (*acc*) take great pains over; *ohne* ~ *kein Preis* no sweet without sweat.

'**fleißig I** *adj* diligent, hard-working, busy. **II** *adv* diligently, F a lot.

flektieren [flɛk'tiːrən] v/t (h) *ling.* inflect.

fletschen ['flɛtʃən] v/t (h) *die Zähne* ~ snarl.

flexibel [flɛ'ksiːbəl] *adj a. fig.* flexible.

Flexibilität [flɛksibili'tɛːt] f (-; *no pl*) *a. fig.* flexibility.

Flexion [flɛ'ksi̯oːn] f (-; -en) inflection.

flicken ['flɪkən] v/t (h) a) mend, b) *a.* F *fig.* patch up. '**Flicken** m (-s; -) patch. '**Flickwerk** n (-[e]s; *no pl*) patch-up job(s). '**Flickzeug** n **1.** sewing kit. **2.** *mot. etc* repair kit.

Flieder ['fliːdər] m (-s; -) ♀ lilac.

Fliege ['fliːgə] f (-; -n) **1.** zo. fly: *er tut k-r* ~ *was zuleide* he wouldn't hurt a fly; *sterben wie die* ~n die like flies; *zwei* ~n *mit einer Klappe schlagen* kill two birds with one stone. **2.** bow tie.

fliegen ['fliːgən] (flog, geflogen) **I** v/i (sn) **1.** fly, *a.* go by air: ~ *lassen* fly; → *Luft* **3.** *fig.* fly, rush. **3.** F *fig.* be fired, get the sack: *aus der Schule etc* ~ be kicked out of school *etc.* **4.** F *fig.* ~ *auf* (*acc*) really go for; *auf j-n* ~ *a.* fall for s.o. **II** v/t (h) **5.** fly (*persons, plane, etc*).

'**Fliegen** n (-s) a) flying, b) aviation.

'**fliegend** *adj* flying (*a. sports*): ~*er Händler* hawker.

'**Fliegen|fänger** m flypaper. ~**gewicht** n (-s; *no pl*) *sports:* flyweight. ~**klatsche** f fly swatter. ~**pilz** m toadstool.

'**Flieger** m (-s; -) **1.** zo., *horse racing:* flier, flyer. **2.** airman (*a.* ✈), pilot. **3.** ✖ *Br.* aircraftman 2nd class, *Am.* airman basic. **4.** F plane. **5.** *cycling:* sprinter. ~**a₁larm** m air-raid warning. ~**angriff** m air raid. ~**horst** m air base.

'**Fliegerin** f (-; -nen) airwoman, woman pilot. '**fliegerisch** *adj* flying.

'**Fliegerjacke** *f* bomber jacket.
fliehen ['fliːən] (floh, geflohen) **I** *v/i* (sn) (*vor dat* from, *nach*, *zu* to) flee, run away, escape. **II** *v/t* (h) avoid, shun.
'**fliehend** *adj fig.* receding (*chin etc*).
'**Fliehkraft** *f phys.* centrifugal force.
'**Fliese** ['fliːzə] *f* (-; -n) tile.
'**Fliesenboden** *m* tiled floor.
'**Fliesenleger** *m* (-s; -) tiler.
'**Fließarbeit** *f* (-; *no pl*) assembly-line work.
'**Fließband** *n* (-[e]s; ꙮer) **1.** assembly line. **2.** conveyor belt. **~arbeiter** *m* assembly-line worker. **~fertigung** *f* assembly-line production.
fließen ['fliːsən] *v/i* (floß, geflossen, sn) flow (*a. fig.*), river, water, *etc: a.* run.
'**fließend** *adj* **1.** flowing: **~es Wasser** running water. **2.** fast-moving (*traffic*). **3.** *fig.* fluid, fluent: **er spricht ~ Englisch** he speaks fluent English.
'**Fließ|heck** *n mot.* fastback. **~komma** *n computer:* floating decimal point.
flimmern ['flɪmərn] *v/i* (h) shimmer, *TV* flicker.
flink [flɪŋk] *adj* quick, nimble.
Flinte ['flɪntə] *f* (-; -n) gun: F *fig.* **die ~ ins Korn werfen** throw in the towel.
Flipper ['flɪpər] *m* (-s; -) pinball machine.
flippern ['flɪpərn] *v/i* (h) F play pinball.
Flirt [flœrt] *m* (-s; -s) **1.** flirtation. **2.** flirt.
flirten ['flœrtən] *v/i* (h) flirt.
Flittchen ['flɪtçən] *n* (-s; -) F hussie.
Flitter ['flɪtər] *m* (-s; *no pl*) **1.** *coll.* sequins. **2.** *fig.* a) *a.* '**Flitterglanz** *m* glitter, b) *a.* '**Flitterkram** *m* tinsel.
'**Flitterwochen** *pl* honeymoon.
flitzen ['flɪtsən] *v/i* (sn) F **1.** flit. **2.** streak.
Flitzer ['flɪtsər] *m* (-s; -) F **1.** nippy little car. **2.** streaker.
floaten ['floʊtən] *v/t*, *v/i* (h) 🟊 float.
flocht [flɔxt] *pret of* **flechten.**
Flocke ['flɔkə] *f* (-; -n) **1.** flake. **2.** fluff.
flocken ['flɔkən] *v/i* (h) flake. '**flockig** *adj* **1.** flaky. **2.** fluffy. **3.** 🟊 flocculent.
flog [floːk] *pret of* **fliegen.**
floh [floː] *pret of* **fliehen.**
Floh [floː] *m* (-[e]s; ꙮe) *zo.* flea: F *fig. j-m e-n ~ ins Ohr setzen* put ideas into s.o.'s head. '**Flohmarkt** *m* flea market.
Flor[1] [floːr] *m* (-s; *no pl*) **1.** bloom. **2.** mass of flowers (*or* blossoms).
Flor[2] *m* (-s; -e) *textil.* **1.** gauze. **2.** pile.
Flora ['floːra] *f* (-; Floren) flora.

floral [floˈraːl] *adj* floral.
Florett [floˈrɛt] *n* (-[e]s; -e) foil.
Flo'rettfechten *n* foil fencing.
florieren [floˈriːrən] *v/i* (h) flourish.
Floskel ['flɔskəl] *f* (-; -n) empty phrase.
'**floskelhaft** *adj* meaningless, empty.
Floß [floːs] *n* (-es; ꙮe) raft.
Flosse ['flɔsə] *f* (-; -n) **1.** *zo.* a) fin, b) flipper (*a. sports*). **2.** 🟊 stabilizer fin. **3.** F a) paw, mitt, b) trotter.
flößen ['fløːsən] *v/t*, *v/i* (h) float.
Flöte ['fløːtə] *f* (-; -n) **1.** ♪ flute. **2.** flute glass. **3.** *cards:* flush. '**flöten** *v/t*, *v/i* ♪ play the flute, *a. fig.* flute, *bird:* sing.
'**flötengehen** *v/i* (*irr, sep*, -ge-, sn, → *gehen*) F go down the drain.
Flötist [fløˈtɪst] *m* (-en; -en), **Flö'tistin** *f* (-; -nen) flautist, flute-player.
flott [flɔt] *adj* F **1.** brisk, lively, zippy. **2.** F a) smart, snazzy, b) dashing, c) gay: *ein ~es Leben führen* live it up. **3.** 🟊 **~ sein** be afloat; → *flottmachen* 1.
Flotte ['flɔtə] *f* (-; -n) ✈, 🟊 fleet.
'**Flottenstützpunkt** *m* 🟊 naval base.
Flottille [flɔˈtɪl(j)ə] *f* (-; -n) 🟊 flotilla.
'**flottmachen** *v/t* (*sep*, -ge-, h) **1.** 🟊 float, set *s.th.* afloat. **2.** get car going again.
Flöz [fløːts] *n* (-es; -e) 🟊, *geol.* seam.
Fluch [fluːx] *m* (-[e]s; ꙮe) **1.** curse. **2.** curse, oath, swearword.
fluchen ['fluːxən] *v/i* (h) curse, swear: *auf* (*or über*) *j-n* (*et.*) **~** curse s.o. (s.th.).
Flucht[1] [fluːxt] *f* (-; -en) a) flight (*vor dat* from, *a. fig.*), b) escape: *auf der ~ erschossen etc* shot *etc* while fleeing (*or* attempting to escape); *auf der ~ sein* be on the run (*vor dat* from); *die ~ ergreifen* → *flüchten* 1; *in die ~ schlagen* put *s.o.* to flight; *fig. die ~ nach vorn antreten* seek refuge in attack.
Flucht[2] *f* (-; -en) △, ⬡ alignment, row.
'**fluchtartig** **I** *adj* hasty. **II** *adv* hastily, in a hurry.
flüchten ['flʏçtən] *v/i* (sn) **1.** flee (*nach*, *zu* to), run away, *prisoner:* escape (*aus* from), ⚖ abscond (*vor dat* from). **2.** (*a. sich ~*) take shelter (*or* refuge) (*in acc* in): *fig. sich in Ausreden ~* resort to excuses.
'**Fluchthelfer(in** *f*) *m* escape agent.
'**flüchtig I** *adj* **1.** a) hasty, b) brief, flying, c) cursory, superficial, d) careless, slapdash: **~e Bekanntschaft** passing acquaintance. **2.** fleeting (*glance etc*). **3.**

fugitive, escaped, 🚗 absconding: **~er Fahrer** hit-and-run driver. **4.** 🜍 volatile. **II** adv **5.** hastily (etc): **~ durchlesen** skim over; **~ kennen** know s.o., s.th. vaguely; **~ sehen** catch a glimpse of.

'Flüchtige m, f (-n; -n) fugitive.

'Flüchtigkeitsfehler m slip.

Flüchtling ['flʏçtliŋ] m (-s; -e) fugitive, pol. refugee.

'Flüchtlingslager n refugee camp.

'Fluchtversuch m attempt to escape.

'Fluchtwagen m getaway car.

'Fluchtweg m escape route.

Flug [fluːk] m (-[e]s; ⸚e) flight: fig. (wie) **im ~(e)** very quickly. **~bahn** f trajectory, ✈ flight path. **~ball** m tennis: volley. **~begleiter(in** f) m flight attendant. **2bereit** adj ready for take-off. **~betrieb** m (-[e]s; no pl) air traffic. **~blatt** n leaflet. **~boot** n flying boat, seaplane.

Flügel ['flyːgəl] m (-s; -) wing (a. pol. or sports), ✕ a. flank, blade (of propeller etc), panel (of altar etc): fig. **j-m die ~ stutzen** clip s.o.'s wings; (dat) **~ verleihen** lend wings to; → **link.** ♩ grand (piano): **am ~ ...** accompanied by ...

'Flügelfenster n casement (window).

'flügellos adj wingless.

'Flügel|mutter f ⊙ wing nut. **~schlag** m flapping of wings. **~schraube** f ⊙ thumbscrew. **~stürmer(in** f) m sports: wing, winger. **~tür** f folding door(s).

'flugfähig adj airworthy.

'Fluggast m (air) passenger.

'Fluggastabfertigung f **1.** passenger clearance. **2.** check-in desk.

flügge ['flʏgə] adj fully fledged: **~ werden** a) fledge, b) fig. begin to stand on one's own two feet.

'Flug|geschwindigkeit f flying speed. **~gesellschaft** f airline. **~hafen** m airport. **~höhe** f (flying) altitude. **~kapitän** m (flight) captain. **~karte** f **1.** (air) ticket. **2.** aeronautical map. **~körper** m flying object, ✕ missile. **~lehrer(in** f) m flying instructor. **~leitung** f air traffic control. **~linie** f **1.** (air) route. **2.** F airline (company). **~lotse** m air traffic controller. **~nummer** f flight number. **~ob,jekt** n **unbekanntes ~** unidentified flying object. **~passa,gier** m (air) passenger. **~perso,nal** n aircrew, coll. flying personnel. **~plan** m timetable. **~platz** m a) airfield, b) airport. **~preis**

m (air) fare. **~reise** f journey by air. **~schalter** m flight desk. **~schein** m **1.** (air) ticket. **2.** pilot's licen/ce (Am. -se). **~schneise** f approach corridor. **~schreiber** m flight recorder, black box. **~sicherung** f air traffic control. **~steig** m gate. **~strecke** f **1.** (air) route. **2.** distance flown. **3.** leg. **~stunde** f **1.** flying hour. **2. nach zwei ~n** after a two-hour flight; **sechs ~n entfernt** six flight-hours away. **2tauglich** adj fit to fly, airworthy. **~ticket** n (air) ticket. **~überwachung** f air traffic control. **~verbindung** f air connection. **~verkehr** m **1.** air traffic. **2.** air services. **~wetter** n flying weather. **~zeit** f flying time.

'Flugzeug n (-[e]s; -e) (aero)plane, Am. (air)plane, aircraft: **mit dem ~** by air, by plane. **~absturz** m air (or plane) crash. **~bau** m (-[e]s; no pl) aircraft construction. **~besatzung** f aircrew. **~entführer(in** f) m hijacker, skyjacker. **~entführung** f hijacking, skyjacking. **~fa,brik** f aircraft factory. **~führer** m pilot. **~halle** f hangar. **~indu,strie** f aircraft industry. **~konstruk,teur** m aircraft designer. **~träger** m ⚓, ✕ aircraft carrier. **~unglück** n air disaster, air (or plane) crash.

'Flugziel n destination.

Fluidum ['fluːidɔm] n (-s; -da) aura, air, atmosphere.

fluktuieren [flɔktuˈiːrən] v/i (h) fluctuate.

Flunder ['flʊndər] f (-; -n) zo. flounder.

flunkern ['flʊŋkərn] v/i (h) fib.

Fluor ['fluːɔr] n (-s; no pl) fluorine: **mit ~ anreichern** fluoridate.

fluoreszieren [fluɔrɛsˈtsiːrən] v/i (h) fluoresce: **~d** fluorescent.

Flur¹ [fluːr] m (-[e]s; -e) **1.** hall. **2.** corridor.

Flur² f (-; -en) open fields: fig. **allein auf weiter ~** all alone. **~bereinigung** f consolidation (of farmland). **~schaden** m crop damage.

Fluse ['fluːzə] f (-; -n) fluff, Am. lint.

Fluß [flʊs] m (-sses; ⸚sse) **1.** river. **2.** no pl flow(ing): **in ~ kommen** get going.

fluß'ab(wärts) adv down the river, downstream.

'Flußarm m arm of a river.

fluß'auf(wärts) adv up the river, upstream.

'**Flußbett** n riverbed.
Flüßchen ['flʏsçən] n (-s; -) small river.
'**Flußdia,gramm** n flowchart.
flüssig ['flʏsɪç] **I** adj **1.** a) liquid, b) molten: ~ **werden** liquefy, melt. **2.** fig. flowing, fluent: → a. **fließend 3. 3.** ✝ liquid, available. **II** adv **4.** in liquid form. **5.** write, speak fluently, traffic etc go smoothly. '**Flüssiggas** n liquid gas. '**Flüssigkeit** f (-; -en) **1.** no pl liquidity (a. ✝), a. fig. fluidity. **2.** liquid, fluid. '**Flüssigkeits**|**bremse** f mot. hydraulic brake. ~**getriebe** n mot. fluid drive. ~**maß** n liquid measure.
'**Flüssigkri,stall-Sichtanzeige** f computer: liquid crystal display (LCD).
'**flüssigmachen** v/t (sep, -ge-, h) ✝ realize, convert into cash.
'**Fluß|krebs** m zo. freshwater crayfish. ~**lauf** m course of a river. ~**mündung** f mouth (of a river), estuary. ~**pferd** n hippopotamus, F hippo. ~**ufer** n riverbank, riverside.
flüstern ['flʏstərn] v/t, v/i (h) (speak in a) whisper: F **dem werde ich was ~!** I'll tell him a thing or two! '**Flüstern** n (-s) whisper(ing). '**Flüsterpropa,ganda** f whispering campaign. '**Flüsterton** n im ~ in a whisper.
Flut [fluːt] f (-; -en) **1.** high tide: **es ist ~** the tide is in. **2.** often pl waters, waves. **3.** fig. flood (of tears, letters, etc), a. torrent (of words etc).
fluten ['fluːtən] **I** v/i (sn) a. fig. flood, stream, pour. **II** v/t (h) flood.
'**Flut|kata,strophe** f flood disaster. ~**licht** n (-[e]s; no pl) floodlights: **bei ~** under floodlight. ~**welle** f tidal wave.
focht [fɔxt] pret of **fechten**.
Fock [fɔk] f (-; -en) ⚓ **1.** foremast. **2.** a. **Focksegel** n foresail.
Föderalismus [fœdera'lɪsmʊs] m (-; no pl) federalism. **föderalistisch** [fœdera'lɪstɪʃ] adj a) federal, b) federalistic (efforts etc). **Föderation** [fœdera-'tsjoːn] f (-; -en) (con)federation.
fohlen ['foːlən] v/i (h) zo. foal.
'**Fohlen** n (-s; -) a) foal, b) colt, c) filly.
Föhn ['føːn] m (-[e]s; -e), ~**wind** m föhn.
Föhre ['føːrə] f (-; -n) ✿ pine (tree).
Fokus ['foːkʊs] m (-; -se) focus.
fokussieren [foku'siːrən] v/t (h) focus.
Folge ['fɔlgə] f (-; -n) **1.** succession, sequence: **in der ~** subsequently; **dreimal**

etc **in ~** three times etc running (or in a row); **in rascher ~** in rapid succession. **2.** a) instal(l)ment, TV part, sequel, serial, b) number, issue. **3.** a) consequence, b) aftermath, aftereffect: **als ~ davon** as a consequence; **zur ~ haben** result in, lead to; (üble) ~**n haben** have (dire) consequences; **die ~n tragen** bear the consequences. **4.** (dat) ~ **leisten** → **folgen** 2.
'**Folgeerscheinung** f → **Folge** 3.
'**Folgekosten** pl follow-up costs.
folgen ['fɔlgən] v/i (sn) **1.** (dat) follow (s.o., s.th.): ~ **auf** (acc) a. succeed (s.o.), a. come after (s.o., s.th.); **Brief folgt!** letter will follow!; **wie folgt** as follows; **daraus folgt, daß** (from this) it follows that; **j-s Beispiel ~** follow s.o.'s example; **können Sie mir ~?** do you follow me?; **ich kann Ihnen da(rin) nicht ~** I can't agree with you there. **2.** (dat) obey (an order), comply with a request etc, accept (an invitation). **3.** F obey (j-m s.o.). '**folgend** adj following, next, subsequent: **am ~en Tage** the following (or next) day; **im ~en** in the following; **es handelt sich um ~es** the matter is as follows.
'**folgendermaßen** adv as follows.
'**folgenschwer** adj momentous, grave.
'**folgerichtig** adj logical, consistent.
folgern ['fɔlgərn] v/t (h) (aus from) conclude, deduce. '**Folgerung** f (-; -en) (e-e ~ ziehen draw a) conclusion.
'**Folgesatz** m **1.** ling. consecutive clause. **2.** ⅍, philos. corollary. '**Folgeschäden** pl ✿ secondary (✿ consequential) damage. '**Folgezeit** f (in der ~ in the) period following.
'**folglich** ['fɔlklɪç] conj a) thus, b) consequently, therefore.
folgsam ['fɔlkzaːm] adj obedient, good.
Folie ['foːljə] f (-; -n) foil (a. fig.), film.
'**Folienkar,toffeln** pl baked potatoes.
Folklore [fɔlk'loːrə] f (-;) folklore.
folkloristisch [fɔlklo'rɪstɪʃ] adj folkloristic.
Follikel [fɔ'liːkəl] m (-s; -) follicle.
Fol'likelsprung m physiol. ovulation.
Folter ['fɔltər] f (-; -n) torture, fig. a. torment: **j-n auf die ~ spannen** keep s.o. on tenterhooks. '**foltern** v/t (h) torture. '**Folterung** f (-; -en) torture.
Fön [føːn] m (-[e]s; -e) TM hair drier.

Fond [fõ:] *m* (-s; -s) **1.** background. **2.** *mot.* back (of the car).

Fonds [fõ:] *m* (-; - [fõ:s]) ✝ **1.** fund. **2.** funds. **3.** government stocks.

Fondue [fõ'dy:] *n* (-s; -s) *gastr.* fondue.

fönen [fø:nən] *v/t* (h) (blow-)dry.

Fontäne [fɔn'tɛ:nə] *f* (-; -n) **1.** fountain. **2.** jet of water.

forcieren [fɔr'si:rən] *v/t* (h) force.

'Förderanlage *f* conveyor (system).

'Förderband *n* conveyor belt.

'Förderer *m* (-s; -), **'Förderin** *f* (-; -nen) a) promoter, supporter, b) patron(ess), sponsor. **'förderlich** *adj* (*dat* to) conducive, useful, beneficial.

'Fördermenge *f* ⚒ output.

fordern ['fɔrdərn] *v/t* (h) **1.** demand (**von j-m** of s.o.), a call for, ✝ a. claim, ask (for *a price*): **zuviel ~** a) ask (*or* expect) too much, b) overcharge (**von j-m** s.o.). **2.** challenge, *sports*: a. push *s.o.* to the limit: **er war voll gefordert** he was fully stretched; **nun ist der Minister gefordert** now it's for the minister to act. **3.** claim (*human lives etc*).

fördern ['fœrdərn] *v/t* (h) **1.** a) promote, support, b) patronize, sponsor, c) encourage, d) help, be good for: **~des Mitglied** supporting member. **2.** ⚒ produce; → **zutage**.

'Förderpreis *m* (literary *etc*) award.

'Forderung *f* (-; -en) **1.** demand (**nach** for, **an** *acc* on), ✝ a. claim: **~en stellen** make demands, enter claims. **2.** ✝ a) call, b) charge.

'Förderung *f* (-; -en) **1.** a) promotion, b) patronage, sponsorship, c) encouragement. **2.** production, output (*of oil etc*).

Forelle [fo'rɛlə] *f* (-; -n) *zo.* trout.

Forke ['fɔrkə] *f* (-; -n) ✔ pitchfork.

Form [fɔrm] *f* (-; -en) **1.** form (a. *ling., phys., a. fig.*), shape (a. *fig.*): **aktive (passive) ~** active (passive) voice; **in aller ~** formally; **in ~ von** (*or* gen) in the form of; **in höflicher** (**netter**) **~** politely (in a nice way); **der ~ halber** a) pro forma, b) to keep up appearances; **die ~ wahren** observe the proprieties; *fig.* (**greifbare**) **~(en) annehmen** take shape. **2.** ⚙ a) model, b) mo(u)ld, c) die. **3.** a) cake tin, b) pastry cutter. **4.** *esp. sports*: form, condition: **in (guter) ~** in good form (*or* shape); **in bester ~, groß in ~** in top form; **nicht in ~** off

form; **in ~ bleiben, sich in ~ halten** keep in trim, keep fit; **in ~ kommen** a) get into shape, b) *fig.* get going.

formal [fɔr'ma:l] *adj* formal.

Formaldehyd ['fɔrm?alde'hy:t] *m* (-s; *no pl*) 🜍 formaldehyde.

Formalien [fɔr'ma:liən] *pl* formalities.

Formalität [fɔrmali'tɛ:t] *f* (-; -en) formality.

Format [fɔr'ma:t] *n* (-[e]s; -e) **1.** format, size. **2.** *fig.* stature, calib/re (*Am.* -er).

Formation [fɔrma'tsi̯o:n] *f* (-; -en) formation. **Formati'ons...** formation (*flying, dancing, etc*).

'formbar *adj* metall. malleable.

'Formblatt *n* form.

Formel ['fɔrməl] *f* (-; -n) **1.** 🜍, ♠, *a.* formula. **2.** a) (set) formula, b) (set) phrase. **Formel-l-Rennen** *n mot.* formula-one race.

formell [fɔr'mɛl] *adj* formal.

'Formelwagen *m mot.* formula car.

formen ['fɔrmən] *v/t* (h) form, shape (*both a. sich ~*), ⚙ mo(u)ld (*a. fig. s.o.*).

'Formenlehre *f* **1.** *ling.* morphology. **2.** ♩ theory of musical forms.

'Formfehler *m* a) irregularity, 🜍 formal defect, b) faux pas.

'Formgebung *f* (-; -en), **'Formgestaltung** *f* ⚙ styling, design.

formieren [fɔr'mi:rən] *v/t* (*a.* **sich ~**) form up.

'Formkrise *f sports*: **in e-r ~ stecken** be off form.

förmlich ['fœrmlɪç] **I** *adj* **1.** formal, ceremonious. **2.** F regular. **II** *adv* **3.** F literally. **'Förmlichkeit** *f* (-; -en) formality.

'formlos *adj* **1.** shapeless. **2.** informal.

'Formsache *f* matter of form, (**reine ~**) mere) formality.

'formschön *adj* ⚙ very stylish.

Formular [fɔrmu'la:r] *n* (-s; -e) form.

formulieren [fɔrmu'li:rən] *v/t* (h) formulate, phrase, word: **wie soll ich es ~?** how shall I put it?

Formu'lierung *f* (-; -en) **1.** formulation, wording, phrasing. **2.** phrase.

'Formung *f* (-; -en) forming, shaping.

'formvollendet *adj* a) perfect (*manners etc*), b) perfectly shaped, finished.

forsch [fɔrʃ] *adj* spirited, brisk, F peppy.

forschen ['fɔrʃən] *v/i* (h) **1.** do research (work). **2. ~ nach** search for.

'forschend *adj* inquiring, searching.

'Forscher m (-s; -) **1.** researcher, a. (re-search) scientist. **2.** explorer. **~drang** m, **~geist** m inquiring mind.

'Forscherin f (-; -nen) → *Forscher.*

'Forschheit f (-; no pl) spirit(edness), dash, F pep.

'Forschung f (-; -en) research (*auf dem Gebiet* gen on).

'Forschungs... research (*work, institute, etc*). **~auftrag** m research assignment. **~reise** f **1.** expedition. **2.** research trip. **~reisende** m, f (-n; -n) explorer.

Forst [fɔrst] m (-[e]s; -e[n]) forest.

Förster ['fœrstər] m (-s; -) forester.

'Forsthaus n forester's house.

'Forstre,vier n forest district.

'Forstwirtschaft f (-; no pl) forestry.

fort [fɔrt] adv **1.** away, off, gone: *sie sind schon ~* they have already gone (or left); *ich muß ~* I must be going. **2.** gone, lost. **3.** *und so ~* and so on.

Fort [fo:r] n (-s; -s) ✕ fort.

Fort..., fort... → a. *Weg..., weg..., Weiter..., weiter...*

'Fortbestand m (-[e]s; no pl) continued existence. **'fortbestehen** v/i (irr, sep, h, → *bestehen*) continue (to exist).

'fortbewegen (sep, h) **I** v/t move. **II** *sich ~* move, walk. **'Fortbewegung** f movement, (loco)motion.

'fortbilden: *sich ~* (sep, h) a) continue one's education (or training), b) do a course, c) improve one's knowledge. **'Fortbildung** f further education (or training). **'Fortbildungskurs** m (continuation) course.

'fortbleiben v/i (irr, sep, -ge-, sn, → *bleiben*) stay away.

'fortdauern v/i (sep, -ge-, h) continue, last: **~d** continuous, lasting.

forte ['fɔrtə] adv, **'Forte** n (-s; -s) ♪ forte.

'fortfahren v/i (sep, -ge-, sn, → *fahren*) **1.** leave, mot. a. drive away. **2.** a. (h) continue: *~ zu reden* continue (or go on) talking; *~ mit* continue (with) (one's story etc); *fahren Sie fort!* go on!

'fortfliegen v/i (irr, sep, -ge-, sn, → *fliegen*) fly away, fly off.

'fortführen v/t (sep, -ge-, h) **1.** lead s.o. away. **2.** continue, carry on. **'Fortführung** f (-; no pl) continuation.

'Fortgang m (-[e]s; no pl) **1.** departure. **2.** progress. **'fortgehen** v/i (irr, sep, -ge-,

sn, → *gehen*) **1.** go (away), leave. **2.** go on, continue.

'fortgeschritten adj advanced: *Kurs für Fortgeschrittene* advanced course.

'fortgesetzt I adj continued, constant. **II** adv continually, constantly.

'fortlaufen v/i (irr, sep, -ge-, sn, → *laufen*) **1.** run away ([*vor*] *j-m* from s.o.). **2.** continue. **'fortlaufend** adj a) continuous, b) consecutive (*numbers*): *~ numeriert* numbered consecutively.

'fortpflanzen (sep, -ge-, h) v/t propagate, biol. a. reproduce, phys. a. transmit, fig. a. spread. **II** *sich ~* biol. reproduce, phys. be propagated, travel, fig. spread. **'Fortpflanzung** f (-; no pl) propagation, biol. a. reproduction, phys. a. transmission, fig. a. spread(ing). **'Fortpflanzungsor,gan** n reproductive organ.

'Fortsatz m anat. process, appendix.

'fortschreiben v/t (irr, sep, -ge-, h, → *schreiben*) **1.** update (*statistics etc*), reassess (*value*). **2.** fig. perpetuate.

'fortschreiten v/i (irr, sep, -ge-, sn, → *schreiten*) fig. advance, progress. **'fortschreitend** adj progressive.

'Fortschritt m progress, improvement: *~e machen* make progress (or headway); *große ~e machen* make great strides. **'fortschrittlich** adj progressive, advanced, (very) modern, up-to-date. **'Fortschrittsglaube** m belief in progress.

'fortsetzen v/t (sep, -ge-, h) continue (a. *sich ~*), resume. **'Fortsetzung** f (-; -en) continuation, sequel: *~ folgt* to be continued; *~ auf (von) Seite 2* continued on (from) page 2.

'Fortsetzungsro,man m serial.

Fortuna [fɔr'tu:na] f (-; no pl) fortune.

'fortwährend adj ständig.

'Fortzahlung f continued payment.

Forum ['fo:rʊm] n (-s; Foren, Fora) forum, fig. a. platform.

fossil [fɔ'si:l] adj fossil.

Fossil [fɔ'si:l] n (-s; -ien [-liən]) fossil.

Foto ['fo:to] n (-s; -s) F photo. **~album** n photo album. **~appa,rat** m camera. **~ausrüstung** f photographic equipment. **~finish** n sports: photo finish.

fotogen [foto'ge:n] adj photogenic.

Fotograf [foto'gra:f] m (-en; -en) photographer. **Fotografie** [fotogra'fi:] f (-; -i-

1. *no pl* photography. **2.** photograph, picture. **fotografieren** [fotogra'fiːrən] *v/i, v/t* (h) photograph, take a picture (*or* pictures) (of). **Foto'grafin** *f* (-; -nen) photographer. **fotografisch** [foto'graːfɪʃ] *adj* photographic.

Foto|ko'pie *f*, **ko'pieren** *v/t* (h) photocopy. **ko'piergerät** *n* photocopier. **la,bor** *n* photographic laboratory. **mo,dell** *n* (photographer's) model. **mon,tage** *f* photomontage. **repor,tage** *f* photographic reportage. **satz** *m* print. photocomposition: **im ~ herstellen** photocompose.

Fotothek [foto'teːk] *f* (-; -en) photographic library.

'**Fotozelle** *f* ⚡ photocell.

Fötus ['føːtʊs] *m* (-ses; -se) f(o)etus.

Foul [faʊl] *n* (-s; -s) *sports:* foul.

foulen ['faʊlən] *v/i, v/t* (h) *sports:* foul.

Foxtrott ['fɔkstrɔt] *m* (-s; -e, -s) (*a.* ~ *tanzen*) foxtrot.

Foyer [fŏa'jeː] *n* (-s; -s) foyer, lounge, *Am.* lobby.

Fracht [fraxt] *f* (-; -en) **1.** load, freight, cargo. **2.** carriage, *Am.* freight(age), ⚓ freightage. '**Frachtbrief** *m* consignment note, *Am.* waybill.

'**Frachter** *m* (-s; -) freighter, cargo ship.

'**Fracht|flugzeug** *n* (air) freighter. **⚓frei** *adj* carriage paid, *Am.* freight prepaid. **führer** *m* carrier. **gebühr** *f*, **geld** *n* → **Fracht** 2. **gut** *n* freight, cargo: **als** ~ **by goods** (*Am.* freight) train. **kosten** *pl* freight charges (*or* costs). **raum** *m* **1.** cargo hold. **2.** freight capacity. **sätze** *pl* freight rates. **schiff** *n* cargo ship, freighter. **verkehr** *m* freight traffic.

Frack [frak] *m* (-[e]s; ⸚e) tailcoat, tails: **im ~** in evening dress, in tails.

'**Frackhemd** *n* dress shirt.

Frage ['fraːgə] *f* (-; -n) **1.** a) question, b) query, c) inquiry: **e-e ~ an j-n haben** have a question to ask s.o.; (*j-m*) **e-e ~ stellen** ask (s.o.) a question; **die ~ stellt sich nicht** the question does not arise; **ohne ~** undoubtedly; **das ist eben die ~** that's just the point; **in ~ stellen** a) question, doubt, b) jeopardize; F **gar k-e ~!** of course! **2.** matter, question: **e-e ~ der Zeit** a matter of time; **das ist e-e andere ~** that's a different matter. **3.** **in ~ kommen** be a possibility, *person:*

a. be eligible; **das kommt gar nicht in ~** that's out of the question.

'**Frage|bogen** *m* form, questionnaire. **form** *f ling.* interrogative form. **für,wort** *n ling.* interrogative (pronoun).

fragen ['fraːgən] *v/t, v/i* (h) ask, question: **nach et.** (*j-m*) ~ inquire about s.th. (after s.o.) a question; (*j-n*) **et.** ~ ask (s.o.) a question; (*j-n*) ~ **nach** ask (s.o.) for; *j-n* **nach s-m Namen** (**dem Weg**) ~ ask s.o. his name (the way); **es fragt sich, ob ...** it's a question of whether ...; **ich frage mich, warum** I (just) wonder why; **niemand fragte danach** nobody bothered about it; ✝ (**sehr**) **gefragt** in (great) demand; **da fragst du mich zuviel** I'm afraid I can't tell you that. '**Fragen** (-s) ~ **kostet nichts** there's no harm in asking. '**fragend** *adj* questioning, inquiring, *ling.* interrogative.

Frager ['fraːgər] *m* (-s; -), '**Fragerin** *f* (-; -nen) questioner.

'**Frage|satz** *m ling.* interrogative clause (*or* sentence). **stellung** *f a. fig.* question. **stunde** *f parl.* question time.

'**Frage-und-'Antwort-Spiel** *n* quiz, *a. fig.* question and answer game.

'**Frage|wort** *n ling.* interrogative. **zei,chen** *n* question mark, *a. fig.* query.

fraglich ['fraːklɪç] *adj* **1.** doubtful. **2.** in question. '**fraglos** *adv* undoubtedly.

Fragment [fra'gmɛnt] *n* (-[e]s; -e) fragment. **fragmentarisch** [fragmɛn'taːrɪʃ] **I** *adj* fragmentary. **II** *adv* fragmentarily, in fragmentary form.

fragwürdig ['fraːkvʏrdɪç] *adj* questionable, dubious, F shady.

Fraktion [frak'tsioːn] *f* (-; -en) **1.** *parl.* a) parliamentary party, b) faction. **2.** 🧪 fraction. **frakti'onslos** *adj* independent. **Frakti'onsvorsitzende** *m*, *f* (-n; -n) *parl.* (*Am.* floor) leader. **Frakti'onszwang** *m* obligation to vote according to party policy.

Fraktur [frak'tuːr] *f* (-; -en) 🩹 fracture.

Franke ['fraŋkə] *m* (-n; -n) Franconian.

'**Franken** *m* (-s; -) (Swiss) franc.

frankieren [fraŋ'kiːrən] *v/t* (h) 🖂 prepay, stamp, frank. **fran'kiert** *adj* prepaid, post paid: **der Brief ist nicht ausreichend ~** they didn't put enough stamps on this letter.

franko ['fraŋko] *adv* prepaid.

Franse ['franzə] *f* (-; -n) fringe.

'**fransen** (h) **I** v/i fray. **II** v/t fringe.

'**fransig** adj **1.** fringed. **2.** frayed.

Franziskaner [frantsıs'kaːnər] m (-s; -) Franciscan (friar).

Franzose [fran'tsoːzə] m (-n; -n) Frenchman: *die ~n* the French; *er ist ~* he is a Frenchman, he is French.

Französin [fran'tsoːzın] f (-; -nen) Frenchwoman: *sie ist ~* she is French.

fran'zösisch I adj French: **~es Bett** (double) divan. **II** ⚥ n ling. French: *aus dem ℒen (ins ℒe)* from (into) French.

frappieren [fra'piːrən] v/t (h) amaze: **~d** striking, amazing, remarkable.

Fräse ['frɛːzə] f (-; -n) **1.** ✏ rotary hoe. **2.** milling machine. '**fräsen** v/t, v/i ⚙ mill.

fraß [fraːs] pret of **fressen**.

Fraß m (-es; no pl) **1.** F contp. muck. **2.** feed (for animals). **3.** 🐀 corrosion.

Fratze ['fratsə] f (-; -n) **1.** grimace: **~n schneiden** pull faces. **2.** F mug (sl.).

Frau [frao] f (-; -en) **1.** a) woman, adm. female, b) Mrs, Ms Brown etc: *die ~ von heute* modern woman. **2.** wife: *wie geht es Ihrer ~?* how is Mrs X? **3.** lady: **gnädige ~!** madam!

'**Frauen|arzt** m, **~ärztin** f gyn(a)ecologist. **~beauftragte** f women's representative. **~beruf** m female profession. **~bewegung** f (-; no pl) women's movement. **ℒfeindlich** adj anti-women. **~frage** f question of women's rights. **~fußball** m women's soccer. **~haus** n women's refuge (Am. shelter). **~heilkunde** f gyn(a)ecology. **~held** m ladykiller. **~leiden** n gyn(a)ecological disorder. **~rechte** pl women's rights.

Frauenrechtler ['fraoənrɛçtlər] m (-s; -), '**Frauenrechtlerin** f (-; -nen) feminist.

'**Frauen|sport** m women's sport(s). **~stimmrecht** n votes for women. **~zeitschrift** f women's magazine.

Fräulein ['frɔʏlaɪn] n (-s; -) **1.** a) (young) lady, girl, b) Miss Brown etc. **2.** F a) salesgirl, b) waitress.

'**fraulich** adj womanly, feminine.

'**Fraulichkeit** f (-; no pl) womanliness.

frech [frɛç] adj a) impudent, F cheeky, saucy, Am. fresh, b) bold, brazen.

'**Frechheit** f (-; -en) impudence, F cheek: **so e-e ~!** what (a) cheek!

Fregatte [fre'gatə] f (-; -n) frigate.

frei [fraɪ] **I** adj **1.** free (von from, of), a. clear (road etc): *ist dieser Platz noch*

~? is this seat taken?; *Zimmer ~!* room(s) to let (Am. rent)!; *ein ~er Tag* a) a free day, b) a day off; *den Oberkörper ~ machen* strip to the waist; **~e Fahrt** mot. clear road, 🚩 green light; **~e Fahrt haben** a. fig. have the green light; → **Fuß** 1, **Hand**, **Stück** 1. **2.** a) free, independent, unattached, b) free and easy, c) liberal: **~er Beruf** independent profession; **~e Künste** liberal arts; *die* **~e Wirtschaft** free enterprise; *ein ~er Mensch* a free agent. **3.** free, frank, open. **4.** blank: **e-n ~en Platz lassen** leave a blank. **5.** open, vacant: **~e Stelle** vacancy. **6.** open: **in der ~en Natur, im ℒen** in the open (country); → **Himmel.** **7.** a) free (of charge), b) prepaid: **Eintritt ~** admission free. **8.** freelance (journalist etc). **9.** phys. free, 🐀 a. uncombined: **Wärme wird ~** heat is released. **10.** teleph. vacant, Am. not busy. **11.** sports: unmarked. **II** adv **12.** freely (etc): **~ sprechen** a) speak openly, b) speak without notes; **~ erfunden** entirely fictitious, made(-)up; 🕆 **an Bord** free on board (f.o.b.); **Lieferung ~ Haus** no delivery charge; **~ finanziert** privately financed.

'**Freiaktie** f bonus share.

'**Freibad** n open-air swimming pool.

'**freibekommen** v/t (irr, sep, h, → **bekommen**) **1.** F **e-n Tag** etc ~ get a day etc off. **2.** **j-n** ~ get s.o. released; et. ~ free s.th.

'**Freiberufler** m (-s; -), '**Freiberuflerin** f (-; -nen) freelance. '**freiberuflich** adj self-employed, freelance, lawyer, doctor, etc in private practice: **~ tätig sein** a. work (as a) freelance.

'**Freibetrag** m tax allowance.

'**Freibier** n (-[e]s; no pl) free beer.

'**freibleibend** adj and adv 🕆 without engagement.

'**Freibrief** m fig. excuse (für for).

'**Freidenker(in** f) m freethinker.

Freier ['fraɪər] m (-s; -) **1.** suitor. **2.** customer (of a prostitute).

'**Freiexem,plar** n free copy.

'**Freifahrschein** m free ticket.

'**Freiflug** m free flight.

'**Freifrau** f, '**Freifräulein** n baroness.

'**Freigabe** f (-; no pl) release, 🕆 floating (of exchange rate), ✈ clearance.

'**freigeben** v/t (irr, sep, -ge-, h, → **ge-**

***ben*) 1. *j-m e-n Tag etc* ~ give s.o. a day *etc* off. **2.** release, ✝ float (*exchange rate*), ✓ *etc* clear: **et. für den Verkehr** ~ open s.th. to traffic; **et. zur Veröffentlichung** ~ release s.th. for publication.

freigebig ['fraɪɡeːbɪç] *adj* generous.

Freigebigkeit *f* (-; *no pl*) generosity.

Freigehege *n* open-air enclosure.

Freigepäck *n* baggage allowance.

Freigrenze *f* tax exemption limit.

freihaben *v/i* (*irr, sep*, -ge-, h) F have the day off: **Freitag habe ich frei** Friday is my day off.

Freihafen *m* free port.

freihalten *v/t* (*irr, sep*, -ge-, h, → **halten**) **1.** keep (*seat*). **2.** keep *entrance etc* clear. **3.** keep *a post etc* open. **4.** *j-n* ~ treat s.o., pay for s.o.

Freihandel *m* free trade.

Freihandelszone *f* free trade area.

freihändig ['fraɪhɛndɪç] *adj and adv shooting* without support, *cycling etc* with no hands. **Freihandzeichnung** *f* freehand drawing.

Freiheit *f* (-; -en) freedom, liberty: **dichterische** ~ poetic licen/ce (*Am*. -se); **in** ~ **sein** be free; **sich die** ~ **nehmen zu** *inf* take the liberty of *ger*; **sich ~en erlauben** take liberties (**gegenüber** with).

freiheitlich *adj* free, liberal.

Freiheits|beraubung *f* deprivation of liberty, ⚖ illegal detention. **~bewegung** *f pol.* freedom movement. **~entzug** *m* imprisonment. **~kampf** *m* struggle for freedom, revolt. **~kämpfer**(*in* *f*) *m* freedom fighter. **~krieg** *m* war of liberation. **~liebe** *f* love of freedom. **~strafe** *f* ⚖ prison sentence: **zu e-r** ~ **von 5 Jahren verurteilt werden** be sentenced to 5 years' imprisonment.

freiher'aus *adv* frankly, point-blank.

Freiherr *m* baron.

Freikarte *f* free ticket.

freikaufen (*sep*, -ge-, h) **I** *v/t* pay for s.o.'s release. **II sich** ~ pay to be set free, *fig.* buy a clear conscience.

freikommen *v/i* (*irr, sep*, -ge-, sn, → **kommen**) **1.** get free, get away. **2.** ⚖ a) be released, b) be acquitted.

Freikörperkul,tur *f* (-; *no pl*) nudism: **Anhänger**(*in* *f*) **der** ~ nudist.

Freilandgemüse *n* outdoor vegetables.

freilassen *v/t* (*irr, sep*, -ge-, h, → **lassen**), **Freilassung** *f* (-; -en) release.

Freilauf *m* (*a.* **im** ~ **fahren**) freewheel.

freilaufend *adj* **~e Hühner** free-running chicken.

freilegen *v/t* (*sep*, -ge-, h) lay open, expose, uncover.

freilich *adv* of course.

Freilicht|bühne *f*, **~the,ater** *n* open-air theat/re (*Am*. -er). **~kino** → **Autokino**.

freiliegen *v/i* (*irr, sep*, -ge-, h, → **liegen**) lie exposed, lie open.

Freilos *n* **1.** free (lottery) ticket. **2.** *sports*: (**ein** ~ **ziehen** draw a) bye.

Freiluft... open-air ..., outdoor ...

freimachen (*sep*, -ge-, h) **I** *v/t* ✉ stamp, prepay. **II sich** ~ free o.s. (**von** from), F arrange to be free.

Freimaurer *m* freemason. **~loge** *f* freemason's (*or* Masonic) lodge.

Freimut *m* cando(u)r, openness.

freimütig ['fraɪmyːtɪç] *adj* candid, open.

freinehmen *v/t* (*irr, sep*, -ge-, h, → **nehmen**) (**sich**) **e-n Tag** ~ take a day off.

Freiplastik *f* free-standing sculpture.

freischaffend *adj* freelance.

freischwimmen: sich ~ (*irr, sep*, -ge-, h, → **schwimmen**) a) pass one's 15-minute swimming test, b) *fig.* learn to stand on one's own two feet.

freisetzen *v/t* (*sep*, -ge-, h) 🐅, *phys.* release (*a. fig.*): *j-n* ~ make s.o. redundant; **freigesetzte Arbeitskräfte** redundant workers. **Freisetzung** *f* (-; -en) a) release (*a. fig.*), b) redundancy.

freispielen: sich ~ (*sep*, -ge-, h) *sports*: break clear.

freisprechen *v/t* (*irr, sep*, -ge-, h, → **sprechen**) **1.** (**von**) ⚖ acquit (of), exonerate (from), clear (of *a suspicion*), *eccl.* absolve (from). **2.** release *apprentice* from his (*or* her) articles.

Freispruch *m* (-[e]s; ~e) ⚖ acquittal.

Freistaat *m* free state, republic.

Freistatt *f*, **Freistätte** *f* sanctuary.

freistehen *v/i* (*irr, sep*, -ge-, h, → **stehen**) **1.** *sports*: be unmarked. **2.** *j-m* ~ be up to s.o.; **es steht Ihnen frei zu** *inf* you are at liberty (*or* free) to *inf*.

freistellen *v/t* (*sep*, -ge-, h) **1.** *j-n* ~ *a*. ✗ exempt s.o. (**von** from). **2.** *j-m et.* ~ leave s.th. (up) to s.o. **Freistellung** *f* (-; -en) exemption (**von** from).

Freistil *m* (-[e]s; *no pl*), **Freistil...** *sports*: freestyle.

Freistoß *m* *soccer*: free kick.

'**Freistunde** f ped. free period.
'**Freitag** m (-[e]s; -e) (**am** ~ **on**) Friday.
'**freitags** adv on Friday(s).
'**freitragend** adj △, ⚙ cantilever, self-supporting.
'**Freitreppe** f (outdoor) steps.
'**Freiübungen** pl exercises.
'**Freiumschlag** m stamped addressed envelope.
'**Freiverkehr** m ✝ **im** ~ in the open market, Am. over the counter.
'**Freiverkehrsbörse** f ✝ kerb market.
frei'weg adv F straight out.
'**Freiwild** n fig. fair game.
'**freiwillig I** adj a) voluntary, b) spontaneous. **II** adv voluntarily, of one's own free will: **sich** ~ **melden** volunteer (**zu** for).
'**Freiwillige** m, f (-n; -n) volunteer.
'**Freiwilligkeit** f (-; no pl) voluntariness.
'**Freiwurf** m sports: free throw.
'**Freizeichen** n teleph. dial(l)ing tone.
'**Freizeit** f (-; -en) **1.** no pl free (or leisure, spare) time. **2.** ped. holiday (or weekend) course.
'**Freizeit|beschäftigung** f leisure-time activity (or activities), n.s. hobby. ~**gestaltung** f leisure-time activities. ~**kleidung** f casual (or leisure) wear. ~**zentrum** n leisure cent/re (Am. -er).
'**Freizone** f free zone.
'**freizügig** adj **1.** ✝ unrestricted. **2.** generous, liberal. **3.** permissive, free.
'**Freizügigkeit** f (-; no pl) **1.** ✝ free(dom of) movement. **2.** generosity. **3.** permissiveness.

fremd [frɛmt] adj **1.** strange, a) unfamiliar, unknown, b) odd: ~**e Leute** strangers; ~**e Hilfe** outside help; ~**es Eigentum** other people's property; **ich bin hier** ~ I'm a stranger here. **2.** a. fig. foreign, alien.
'**Fremdarbeiter(in** f) m foreign worker.
'**fremdartig** adj a. fig. foreign, strange, exotic.
'**Fremdartigkeit** f (-; no pl) strangeness.
'**Fremde¹** m, f (-n; -n) a) stranger, b) foreigner, c) tourist.
'**Fremde²** f (-; no pl) foreign parts: **in die** (**der**) ~ away from home, abroad.
'**Fremden|führer(in** f) m (tourist) guide. ~**haß** m xenophobia. ~**heim** n guesthouse. ~**indu,strie** f tourist industry. ~**legi,on** f Foreign Legion. ~**verkehr**

m tourism. ~**verkehrsbü,ro** n tourist office. ~**zimmer** n room (to let).
'**fremdgehen** v/i (irr, sep, -ge-, sn, → **gehen**) be unfaithful (to one's husband or wife).
'**Fremd|herrschaft** f foreign rule. ~**kapi,tal** n loan capital. ~**körper** m **1.** ✻ foreign body. **2.** fig. alien element.
'**fremdländisch** [-lɛndɪʃ] adj foreign, exotic.
'**Fremdling** m (-s; -e) stranger.
'**Fremdsprache** f foreign language.
'**Fremdsprachen|korrespon,dent(in** f) m foreign correspondence clerk. ~**sekre,tär(in** f) m linguist-secretary. ~**unterricht** m foreign-language teaching (or lessons).
'**fremdsprachig** adj **1.** speaking a foreign language. **2.** → '**fremdsprachlich** adj foreign-language.
'**Fremdwort** n (-[e]s; ⁓er) foreign word.
frequentieren [frekvɛn'tiːrən] v/t (h) frequent. **Frequenz** [fre'kvɛnts] f (-; -en) **1.** ♪, phys. frequency. **2.** ✻ (pulse) rate. **3.** number of visitors. **4.** density of traffic. **Fre'quenzbereich** m ♪ frequency range.
Fresko ['frɛsko] n (-s; -ken) fresco.
Fressalien [frɛ'saːliən] pl F grub.
Fresse ['frɛsə] f (-; -n) V mug, kisser.
fressen ['frɛsən] (fraß, gefressen, h) **I** v/t **1.** eat, a. a) devour, F person: a. stuff o.s. with, b) feed on: **e-m Tier (...) zu** ~ **geben** feed an animal (on ...); F **er wird dich schon nicht** ~ he won't bite you; → **Besen** 1, **Narr. 2.** F fig. gobble up (money), guzzle (fuel etc). **II** v/i **3.** eat, F person: guzzle, eat like a pig. **4.** fig. ~ **an** (dat) eat away, corrode. **III sich** ~ **in** (acc) fig. eat into.
'**Fressen** n (-s) food, feed, F grub: F fig. **das war ein gefundenes** ~ **für ihn** that was just what he was waiting for.
'**Fresser** m (-s; -) F guzzler, glutton.
'**Freßgier** f voraciousness.
'**Freßsack** m F glutton.
Frettchen ['frɛtçən] n (-s; -) zo. ferret.
Freude ['frɔydə] f (-; -n) joy (**über** acc at), pleasure, delight: ~ **haben** (or **finden**) **an** (dat) enjoy; **j-m** ~ **bereiten** make s.o. happy; **ich hoffe, es macht dir** ~! I hope it will give you pleasure; **es macht mir k-e** ~ I don't enjoy it; **zu m-r großen** ~ much to my delight.

'**Freuden\fest** n celebration. **~feuer** n bonfire. **~geschrei** n cheers, cheering. **~schrei** m cry of joy. **~tag** m red-letter day. **~taumel** m in e-n ~ geraten go into ecstasies. **~tränen** pl tears of joy.

'**freudestrahlend** adj radiant (with joy).

'**freudig** adj joyful, cheerful, happy (event): **j-n ~ begrüßen** be happy to see s.o.; **~ überrascht** pleasantly surprised.

freudlos ['frɔytloːs] adj cheerless, bleak.

Freudsch [frɔytʃ] adj → **Fehlleistung**.

freuen ['frɔyən] (h) **I** sich ~ be glad (or happy, pleased) (über acc about); sich ~ an (dat) enjoy; sich ~ auf (acc) be looking forward to. **II** v/t please: das freut mich sehr I'm glad to hear that; ich hoffe, es freut dich I hope it will give you pleasure. **III** v/impers es freut mich, Sie zu sehen nice to see you; es würde mich ~, wenn ... I'd be very pleased if ...

Freund [frɔynt] m (-[e]s, -e) friend (a. fig.), boyfriend: ~ und Feind friend and foe; fig. ein ~ sein von be fond of; ein ~ der Musik a music lover; → **dick 3**.

'**Freundchen** n (-s; -) iro. laddie, Am. buddy.

'**Freundeskreis** m (circle of) friends.

Freundin ['frɔyndɪn] f (-; -nen) friend (a. fig.), girlfriend.

'**freundlich** adj **1.** friendly (gegen to), kind, nice: **~e Grüße** kind regards (an acc to); **bitte seien Sie so ~ und ...** (will you) be so kind as to ...; **sehr ~!** very kind of you! **2.** fig. mild, pleasant (climate etc), cheerful (room etc).

'**freundlicherweise** adv kindly.

'**Freundlichkeit** f (-; no pl) friendliness, kindness.

'**Freundschaft** f (-; -en) friendship: **~ schließen mit** make friends with; **aus ~** because we are friends.

'**freundschaftlich** adj amicable, friendly: **~ verbunden** on friendly terms.

'**Freundschafts\besuch** m pol. goodwill visit. **~dienst** m (j-m e-n ~ erweisen do s.o. a) good turn. **~spiel** n sports: friendly (game).

Frevel ['freːfəl] m (-s; -) **1.** sacrilege. **2.** (an dat, gegen against) crime, outrage.

'**frevelhaft** adj sacrilegious, w.s. outrageous. '**Freveltat** f outrage, crime. **Frevler** ['freːflər] m (-s; -), '**Frevlerin** f (-; -nen) offender, esp. eccl. sinner.

Frieden ['friːdən] m (-s; no pl) a) peace, b) tranquil(l)ity: **innerer ~** peace of mind; **im ~** in peacetime; **~ schließen** make peace, **mit j-m** make it up with s.o.; **laß mich in ~!** leave me alone!

'**Friedens\bedingungen** pl peace terms. **~bewegung** f pol. peace movement. **~bruch** m ⚖ breach (pol. violation) of the peace. **~forschung** f peace research. **~gespräche** pl peace talks. **~initia₁tive** f peace initiative. **~konfe₁renz** f peace conference. **~kundgebung** f peace rally. **~no₁belpreis** m Nobel Peace Prize. **~poli₁tik** f policy of peace. **~schluß** m conclusion of the peace treaty. **~taube** f fig. dove of peace. **~truppe** f peacekeeping force. **~verhandlungen** pl peace negotiations. **~vertrag** m peace treaty. **~zeit** f often pl peacetime, time of peace.

friedfertig ['friːt-] adj peaceable.

Friedhof ['friːthoːf] m cemetery.

friedlich ['friːtlɪç] adj peaceful.

'**Friedlichkeit** f (-; no pl) peacefulness.

friedliebend ['friːt-] adj peace-loving.

frieren ['friːrən] v/i and v/impers (fror, gefroren, h) freeze: **ich friere, mich friert, es friert mich** I am cold; **es friert** it is freezing.

frigide [friˈgiːdə] adj frigid. **Frigidität** [frigidiˈtɛːt] f (-; no pl) frigidity.

Frikadelle [frikaˈdɛlə] f (-; -n) meatball.

Frikassee [frikaˈseː] n (-s; -s) fricassee.

Friktion [frɪkˈtsioːn] f (-; -en) friction.

frisch [frɪʃ] **I** adj **1.** fresh, a. freshly-laid (egg), a. new (bread): **~e Farbe** fresh (or wet) paint; **~e Luft schöpfen** get some fresh air; **noch in ~er Erinnerung** fresh in my etc mind. **2.** a) clean (linen etc), b) fresh, new (page etc): **sich ~ machen** freshen up; fig. **mit ~en Kräften** with renewed strength. **3.** fresh, cool, chilly. **4.** fresh, brisk, lively: **~ und munter** F alive and kicking. **5.** fresh (complexion etc), bright (colo[u]r). **II** adv freshly (etc): **~ gestrichen!** wet paint!; **~ gebacken** fresh from the oven.

'**Frische** f (-; no pl) **1.** freshness, fig. a. vigo(u)r, briskness, liveliness: fig. **in alter ~** as alive and well as ever. **2.** coolness, chilliness.

'**Frischei** n fresh(ly laid) egg.

'**Frischfleisch** n fresh meat.

'**Frischhalte|beutel** *m* polythene bag. **~packung** *f* keep-fresh package.
'**Frischmilch** *f* fresh milk.
'**Frischzellenthera,pie** *f* ✱ living-cell therapy.
Friseur [fri'zø:r] *m* (-s; -e) hairdresser: **beim ~** at the hairdresser's. **Fri'seur-sa,lon** *m* hairdresser's shop.
Friseuse [fri'zø:zə] *f* (-; -n) hairdresser.
frisieren [fri'zi:rən] (h) I *v/t* **1. j-n ~** do s.o.'s hair. **2.** F doctor (*accounts etc*), soup up (*engine*). II *sich ~* do one's hair. **Fri'siersa,lon** *m* hairdresser's salon. **Fri'siertisch** *m* dresser.
Frist [frɪst] *f* (-; -en) a) (fixed) period of time, time limit, b) deadline, c) ✝ respite: **e-e ~ setzen** (**einhalten**) fix (meet) a deadline; **innerhalb e-r ~ von 10 Tagen** within a ten-day period; **in kürzester ~** at very short notice.
fristen ['frɪstən] *v/t* (h) **sein Leben** (or **Dasein**) **~** scrape a (bare) living.
'**fristgemäß**, '**fristgerecht** *adj and adv* in time, within the prescribed time limit.
'**fristlos** *adj and adv* without notice.
'**Fristverlängerung** *f* extension (of the deadline).
Frisur [fri'zu:r] *f* (-; -en) a) hairstyle, b) haircut.
Friteuse [fri'tø:zə] *f* (-; -n) deep fryer.
fritieren [fri'ti:rən] *v/t* (h) deep-fry.
frivol [fri'vo:l] *adj* **1.** frivolous. **2.** risqué.
Frivolität [frivoli'tε:t] *f* (-; -en) **1.** *no pl* frivolity. **2.** frivolous remark.
froh [fro:] *adj* glad (**über** *acc* of, about), cheerful: **sei ~, daß du nicht dabei warst** be thankful you weren't there.
fröhlich ['frø:lɪç] *adj* cheerful, merry.
'**Fröhlichkeit** *f* (-; *no pl*) cheerfulness.
froh'locken *v/i* (h) (**über** *acc*) a) rejoice (in, at), b) gloat (over). **Froh'locken** *n* (-s) a) jubilation, b) gloating.
'**Frohna,tur** *f* (-; -en) cheerful person.
'**Frohsinn** *m* (-[e]s; *no pl*) cheerfulness.
fromm [frɔm] *adj* **1.** pious, devout: *fig.* **~er Betrug** pious fraud; **~e Lüge** white lie; **~er Wunsch** wishful thinking. **2.** gentle, steady (*horse*). **Frömmelei** [frœmə'laɪ] *f* (-; -en) sanctimoniousness. **Frömmigkeit** ['frœmɪçkaɪt] *f* (-; *no pl*) piety.
Fron [fro:n] *f* (-; -en) *fig.* drudgery.
frönen ['frø:nən] *v/i* (h) (*dat*) indulge in.
Fron'leichnam *m* (-[e]s) Corpus Christi.

Front [frɔnt] *f* (-; -en) front, ✗ *a.* front line: **an der ~** at the front; **hinter der ~** behind the lines; *fig.* **~ machen gegen** turn against, resist; *sports:* **in ~ gehen** (**liegen**) take (be in) the lead.
Frontal... [frɔn'ta:l-] head-on, frontal. **~angriff** *m* frontal attack. **~zusam-menstoß** *m* head-on collision.
'**Frontantrieb** *m mot.* front-wheel drive.
'**Frontkämpfer** *m* **1.** front-line soldier. **2.** ex-serviceman, *Am.* veteran.
'**Frontlader** *m* (-s; -) a) ⚙ loading shovel, b) ⤢ front loader.
'**Frontwechsel** *m fig.* about-face.
fror [fro:r] *pret of* **frieren**.
Frosch [frɔʃ] *m* (-[e]s; ⸚e) **1.** *zo.* frog: F **sei kein ~!** don't be a spoilsport! **2.** squib. **~laich** *m* frog spawn. **~mann** *m* (-[e]s; ⸚er) frogman. **~perspek,tive** *f* (**aus der ~ sehen** have a) worm's-eye view. **~schenkel** *m gastr.* frog's leg.
Frost [frɔst] *m* (-[e]s; ⸚e) frost.
'**frostbeständig** *adj* frost-resistant.
'**Frostbeule** *f* chilblain.
'**Frosteinbruch** *m* sudden frost.
frösteln ['frœstəln] *v/i* (h) shiver (with cold): **mich fröstelt** I feel shivery. '**Frösteln** *n* (-s) shivering.
frosten ['frɔstən] *v/t* (h) freeze.
'**frostfrei** *adj* free of frost, frost-free.
'**Frostgrenze** *f* frost line.
frostig ['frɔstɪç] *adj* frosty, *fig. a.* icy.
'**Frostsalbe** *f* chilblain ointment.
'**Frostschaden** *m* frost damage.
'**Frostschutz** *m* frost protection. **~mittel** *n* antifreeze. **~scheibe** *f mot.* defrosting screen.
'**Frostwetter** *n* frosty weather.
Frottee [frɔ'te:] *m, n* (-[s]; -s) towel(l)ing, terry(cloth).
frottieren [frɔ'ti:rən] *v/t* (h) rub down. **Frot'tier(hand)tuch** *m* terry towel.
Frucht [frʊxt] *f* (-; ⸚e) **1.** ♀ fruit: *Früchte* **tragen** *a. fig.* bear fruit. **2.** *pl fig.* fruit(s). '**fruchtbar** *adj a. fig.* fertile, fruitful, prolific: **auf ~en Boden fallen** fall on fertile ground. '**Fruchtbarkeit** *f* (-; *no pl*) *a. fig.* fertility, fruitfulness.
'**Fruchtbon,bon** *m, n* fruit drop.
'**Fruchteis** *n* fruit-flavo(u)red ice cream.
fruchten ['frʊxtən] *v/i* (h) be of use, have an effect: **nichts ~** be no use, be in vain.
'**Fruchtfleisch** *n* (fruit) flesh.
'**fruchtlos** *adj* fruitless, *fig. a.* futile.

'**Frucht|presse** f juicer. **~saft** m fruit juice. **~wasser** n physiol. amniotic fluid. **~zucker** m fructose.

frugal [fru'ga:l] adj frugal.

früh [fry:] **I** adj early: **ein ~er van Gogh** an early (work by) van Gogh; → **früher, frühest, frühestens. II** adv early: **heute ~** this morning; (**schon**) ~ early on; **~ genug** soon enough; **von ~ bis spät** from morning till night; **zu ~ kommen** be early.

'**Frühaufsteher** m (-s; -), '**Frühaufste-herin** f (-; -nen) early riser (F bird).

'**Frühe** f (-; no pl) (early) morning: **in aller ~** early in the morning.

'**früher I** adj a) earlier, b) former, c) past: **der ~e Besitzer** the previous owner. **II** adv a) earlier, a. sooner, b) in the past: **~ oder später** sooner or later; **~ habe ich geraucht** I used to smoke; **ich kenne sie von ~** I know her from way back.

'**Früherkennung** f ✻ early diagnosis.

'**frühest** adj earliest: **in ~er Kindheit** at a very early age.

'**frühestens** adv at the earliest.

'**Früh|geburt** f premature birth. **~ge-schichte** f (-; no pl) early history.

'**Frühjahr** n (-s; -e) (**im ~** in [the]) spring.

'**Frühjahrs|mode** f spring fashions. **~müdigkeit** f spring tiredness.

'**Frühkar,toffeln** pl new potatoes.

Frühling ['fry:lɪŋ] m (-s; -e) a. fig. spring(time): **im ~** in (the) spring.

'**frühlingshaft** adj springlike, spring.

'**Frühlingsrolle** f gastr. spring roll.

'**Frühmesse** f eccl. matins.

früh'morgens adv early in the morning.

'**Früh|nebel** m early morning fog. ℜ**reif** adj a. fig. precocious. ℜ**reife** f precociousness, fig. a. precocity. **~schicht** f early shift. **~schoppen** m pre-lunch drink(s). **~sommer** m early summer. **~sport** m early morning exercises. **~stadium** n early stage.

'**Frühstück** n (-s; -e) breakfast: **zweites ~** mid-morning snack, Br. elevenses.

'**frühstücken** (h) **I** v/i (have) breakfast. **II** v/t have s.th. for breakfast.

'**Frühstückspause** f morning break.

'**Früh|warnsy,stem** n early warning system. **~zeit** f **1.** early period. **2.** prehistoric times. ℜ**zeitig I** adj a) early, b) untimely, premature. **II** adv early, in good time. **~zug** m early train. **~zün-dung** f mot. advanced ignition.

Frust [frust] m (-[e]s; no pl) F, **Frustra-tion** [frʊstra'tsĭo:n] f (-; -en) psych. frustration. **frustrieren** [frʊs'tri:rən] v/t (h) frustrate.

Fuchs [fʊks] m (-es; ~e) **1.** zo. a) fox, b) sorrel. **2.** → **Fuchspelz. 3.** fig. alter ~ cunning old devil; **schlauer ~** sly fox.

'**Fuchsbau** m (-[e]s; -e) fox's den.

Fuchsie ['fʊksĭə] f (-; -n) ♣ fuchsia.

Füchsin ['fʏksɪn] f (-; -nen) zo. vixen.

'**Fuchs|jagd** f fox hunt(ing). **~pelz** m fox (fur). ℜ**rot** adj ginger. **~schwanz** m **1.** zo. foxtail. **2.** ⊛ pad saw.

'**fuchs'teufels'wild** adj F hopping mad.

Fuchtel ['fʊxtəl] f (-; no pl) F **unter j-s ~ stehen** be under s.o.'s thumb.

fuchteln ['fʊxtəln] v/i (h) **~ mit** wave s.th. around, brandish; **mit den Händen ~** gesticulate wildly.

Fug [fu:k] **mit ~ und Recht** rightly.

Fuge¹ ['fu:gə] f (-; -n) ♪ fugue.

'**Fuge**² f (-; -n) ⊛ a) joint, b) seam, c) groove: **aus den ~n gehen** fall apart, fig. be thrown out of joint.

fugen ['fu:gən] v/t (h) joint.

fügen ['fy:gən] **I** v/t (h) ⊛ joint. **II** sich ~ (dat or in acc to) a) submit, give in, b) resign o.s.; **sich e-m Befehl ~** comply with an order; → **unabänderlich. III** v/impers **es fügt sich, daß ...** it so happens that ... **fügsam** ['fy:kza:m] adj obedient. '**Fügung** f (-; -en) (act of) providence, (stroke of) fate: **durch e-e glückliche ~** by a lucky coincidence.

'**fühlbar** adj fig. noticeable, considerable: **sich ~ machen** make itself felt.

fühlen ['fy:lən] (h) **I** v/t feel, sense. **II** v/i feel: **~ nach** feel for; **mit j-m ~** feel with s.o. **III** sich glücklich etc **~** feel happy etc; **sich ~ als** see o.s. as.

'**Fühler** m (-s; -) **1.** zo. feeler, antenna, tentacle: fig. **die ~ ausstrecken** put out one's feelers. **2.** ⊛ sensor.

'**Fühlung** f (-; no pl) contact: **~ haben mit** be in touch with; **~ nehmen mit** contact, get in touch with; **die ~ verlieren** lose touch (mit with). '**Fühlungnahme** [-na:mə] f (-; -n) contact.

fuhr [fu:r] pret of **fahren.**

Fuhre ['fu:rə] f (-; -n) a) loaded cart, b) (cart)load.

führen ['fy:rən] (h) **I** v/t **1.** lead (**nach, zu** to), take, guide: **j-n in ein Zimmer**

(**durchs Haus**) ~ show s.o. into a room (over the house); → **Leine**. **2.** a) lead, head, ✗ *a.* command, b) be in charge of, manage, run, c) hold (*an office*), d) keep (*books etc*), e) conduct (*business, lawsuit, etc*), carry on (*negotiations etc*): → **Gespräch, Klage** 2. **3.** bear (*a name*), go by (*the name of*), hold (*a title*), bear (*coat of arms*): → **Schild**[1] 1. **4.** ✝ a) carry (in stock), b) sell, deal in. **5.** use, wield (*brush etc*). **6.** have *s.th.* with (*or* on) one, carry (*weapon etc*): ✦ **Strom** ~ a) be live, b) conduct current. **7. e-n Schlag** ~ strike a blow. **8.** ~ **durch** (**um** *etc*) pass *line, tool, etc* through (around *etc*). **II** *v/i* lead, *sports:* a. be in the lead: ~ **nach**, a. *fig.* ~ **zu** lead to; **das führt zu nichts** that won't get us anywhere; *sports:* **mit zwei Toren** ~ be two goals ahead. **III sich gut** ~ conduct o.s. well *etc*.

'**führend** *adj* leading, prominent: ~ **sein** lead, rank in first place.

'**Führer** *m* (-s; -) **1.** leader, head. **2.** guide. **3.** *mot.* driver, ✈ pilot, ⊙ operator. **4.** guide(book). '**Führerin** *f* (-; -nen) → **Führer** 1-3. '**führerlos** *adj* **1.** without a leader (*or* guide *etc*). **2.** *mot.* driverless, ✈ pilotless.

'**Führerna,tur** *f* born leader. '**Führerschaft** *f* (-; *no pl*) **1.** leadership. **2.** *coll.* the leaders.

'**Führerschein** *m mot.* driving licence, *Am.* driver's license: **s-n** ~ **machen** take one's driving test. ~**entzug** *m* revocation of s.o.'s driving licence (*etc*).

'**Fuhrpark** *m* car pool, fleet (of vehicles).

'**Führung** (-; -en) *f* **1.** *no pl* guidance, *pol. etc* leadership, ✗ command, ✝ management, *coll.* the leaders: **unter der** ~ **von** led by; **die** ~ **übernehmen** take charge (→ *a.* 5). **2.** (guided) tour. **3.** *no pl* conduct (*of negotiations etc*). **4.** *no pl sports:* lead: **in** ~ **gehen, die** ~ **übernehmen** take the lead; **in** ~ **liegen** be in the lead. **6.** *no pl* use (*of title*).

'**Führungs|aufgabe** *f* executive function. ~**e,tage** *f* executive floor. ~**gremium** *n* executive committee. ~**kraft** ✝ executive, *pl* executive personnel, *pol.* leaders. ~**schicht** *f* ruling class(es). ~**schwäche** *f* weak leadership. ~**spitze** *f* top echelons. ~**stil** *m* style of leader-

ship. ~**tor** *n*, ~**treffer** *m* goal that puts a team into the lead. ~**zeugnis** *n* certificate of (good) conduct.

'**Fuhrunternehmen** *n* haulage company. '**Fuhrunternehmer** *m* haulage contractor. '**Fuhrwerk** *n* wag(g)on.

Fülle ['fʏlə] *f* (-; *no pl*) **1.** fullness, *fig. a.* richness: → **Hülle** 4. **2.** wealth, abundance. **3.** corpulence.

füllen ['fʏlən] *v/t* (h) **1.** (*a.* **sich** ~) fill: **in Flaschen** ~ bottle; **der Aufsatz füllte drei Seiten** the essay took up three pages. **2.** *gastr.* stuff.

Füller ['fʏlər] *m* (-s; -) F, **Füll-(feder)halter** *m* fountain pen.

füllig ['fʏlɪç] *adj* full, plump.

Füllsel ['fʏlzəl] *n* (-s; -) filler.

'**Füllung** *f* (-; -en) **1.** filling (*a.* of tooth), *gastr.* a. stuffing, cent/re (*Am.* -er) (*of chocolates*). **2.** padding.

'**Füllwort** *n* (-[e]s; ⸚er) filler.

fummeln ['fʊməln] *v/i* (h) F **1.** fiddle around (**an** *dat* with). **2.** pet.

Fund [fʊnt] *m* (-[e]s; -e) a) discovery, finding, b) (**e-n** ~ **machen**) make a) find.

Fundament [fʊnda'mɛnt] *n* (-[e]s; -e) △ foundations. **fundamental** [fʊnda-mɛn'taːl] *adj* fundamental, basic.

Fundamentalismus [fʊndamɛnta'lɪs-mʊs] *m* (-; *no pl*) fundamentalism.

'**Fundbü,ro** *n* lost property office.

'**Fundgrube** *f fig.* (gold)mine.

fundieren [fʊn'diːrən] *v/t* (h) **1.** substantiate. **2.** ✝ fund. **fun'diert** *adj* **1.** sound (*knowledge etc*). **2.** ✝ founded.

fündig ['fʏndɪç] *adj* ~ **werden** a. *fig.* strike gold.

'**Fundort** *m* (-[e]s; -e) site (of discovery).

'**Fundsache** *f* lost article, *pl* a. lost property.

Fundus ['fʊndʊs] *m* (-; -) **1.** *thea.* general equipment. **2.** store (**von, an** *dat* of).

fünf [fʏnf] *adj* five: *fig.* (**alle**) ~**e gerade sein lassen** stretch a point.

Fünf *f* (-; -en) five, *ped.* poor, *Br.* E, *Am.* F. '**Fünfeck** *n* (-[e]s; -e) pentagon.

'**fünfeckig** *adj* pentagonal.

'**Fünfer** *m* (-s; -) F **1.** five-pfennig (*or* five-mark) piece. **2.** → **Fünf**.

'**fünffach** *adj und adv* fivefold.

'**fünfhundert** *adj* five hundred.

fünfjährig ['fʏnfjɛːrɪç] *adj* **1.** five-year-old: **ein** ~**es Kind** a. a child of five. **2.** five-year, *period etc* of five years.

229 **Fürsorge**

'**Fünfkampf** *m sports:* pentathlon.
'**Fünfkämpfer(in** *f) m* pentathlete.
'**Fünflinge** *pl* quintuplets, F quins.
'**fünfmal** *adv* five times.
Fünfpro'zentklausel *f parl.* five per cent hurdle.
fünfstellig ['fʏnfʃtɛlɪç] *adj* five-digit.
'**Fünf'tagewoche** *f* five-day working week.
fünfte ['fʏnftə] *adj* fifth: → **Kolonne, Rad** 1. '**Fünftel** *n* (-s; -) fifth.
'**fünfzehn** *adj* fifteen.
'**fünfzig** ['fʏnftsɪç] *adj* fifty. '**Fünfzig** *f* (-; *no pl*) fifty: **sie ist Mitte (der)** ~ she is in her mid-fifties. '**fünfziger** *adj* **die ~ Jahre** the fifties (*of a century*).
'**Fünfziger** *m* (-s; -) **1.** man of fifty: **er ist in den** ~ he is in his fifties. **2.** F a) fifty-pfennig piece, b) fifty-mark note (*Am.* bill). '**Fünfzigerin** *f* (-; -nen) woman of fifty (*or* in her fifties).
fungieren [fʊŋ'giːrən] *v/i* (h) ~ **als** *act* (*thing:* serve) as.
Funk [fʊŋk] *m* (-s; *no pl*) radio; → a. **Rundfunk, Radio.** ~**ama,teur** *m* radio ham. ~**ausstellung** *f* radio and TV exhibition. ~**bild** *n* photo-radiogram.
'**Fünkchen** ['fʏŋkçən] *n* (-s; -) → **Funke** ['fʊŋkə] *m* (-n; -n) *a. fig.* spark: **ein** ~ **(von) Verstand** a modicum of sense; **kein** ~ **Hoffnung** not a flicker of hope.
funkeln ['fʊŋkəln] *v/i* (h) sparkle (*a. fig.*).
'**funkel'nagel'neu** *adj* F brand-new.
funken ['fʊŋkən] *v/t* (h) radio. *v/i* send out: F **zwischen uns hat es so-fort gefunkt** we clicked the moment we met.
'**Funken** *m* (-s; -) → **Funke.**
'**funkentstört** *adj* radio-screened.
Funker ['fʊŋkər] *m* (-s; -) radio operator.
'**Funk|gerät** *n* transmitter. ~**haus** *n* broadcasting cent/re (*Am.* -er). ~**meldung** *f* radio message. ~**peilgerät** *n* radio direction finder. ~**rufempfänger** *m* bleep(er). ~**si,gnal** *n* radio signal.
'**Funksprech|gerät** *n* walkie-talkie. ~**verkehr** *m* radio telephony.
'**Funk|spruch** *m* radio message. ~**sta-ti,on** *f*, ~**stelle** *f* radio station. ~**stille** *f* radio silence. ~**streife** *f* **1.** radio patrol. **2.** → ~**streifenwagen** *m* radio patrol car. ~**taxi** *n* radio cab. ~**technik** *f* radio engineering. ~**tele,gramm** *n* radiotele-gram, radiogram.

Funktion [fʊŋk'tsi̯oːn] *f* (-; -en) function, *a.* position: **in** ~ **treten** go into action.
Funktionär [fʊŋktsi̯oˈnɛːr] *m* (-s; -e), **Funktio'närin** *f* (-; -nen) official.
funktionell [fʊŋktsi̯oˈnɛl] *adj* functional.
funktionieren [fʊŋktsi̯oˈniːrən] *v/i* (h) function, work (*a. fig.*).
funkti'onsfähig *adj* functioning.
Funkti'onsstörung *f* ⚕ malfunction.
'**Funk|turm** *m* radio tower. ~**verbindung** *f* radio contact. ~**verkehr** *m* radio communication(s). ~**wagen** *m* **1.** radio van. **2.** → **Funkstreifenwagen.**
für [fyːr] *prep for, a.* a) in exchange (*or* return) for, b) in favo(u)r of, c) instead of: **Jahr** ~ **Jahr** year after year; ~ **mich** for me, to me, in my opinion; **ich** ~ **m-e Person** I myself; ~**s erste** for the moment; ~ **sich leben** live by o.s.; **an und** ~ **sich** actually; **e-e Sache** ~ **sich** another matter entirely; **das hat viel** ~ **sich** there's a lot to be said for it; **was** ~ **(ein) ...?** what (kind of) ...?
Für *n* **das** ~ **und Wider** the pros and cons.
'**Fürbitte** *f a. eccl.* intercession.
Furche ['fʊrçə] *f* (-; -n) **1.** ⚘, *anat.* furrow, *geol.,* ⚙ *a.* groove. **2.** rut.
Furcht [fʊrçt] *f* (-; *no pl*) (**vor** *dat* of) fear, dread: **aus** ~ **vor** for fear of; **j-m** ~ **einflößen** (*or* **einjagen**) frighten s.o.
'**furchtbar I** *adj* terrible, dreadful. **II** *adv* terribly, F *a.* awfully.
'**furchteinflößend** *adj* frightening.
fürchten ['fʏrçtən] (h) **I** *v/t* be afraid of, dread: **ich fürchte, wir schaffen es nicht** I fear we're not going to make it. **II** *v/i* **für j-n** ~ fear for s.o. **III sich** ~ (**vor** *dat* of) be afraid, be scared, be frightened; **sich** ~ **vor** (*dat*) *a.* dread; **sich** (**davor**) ~ **zu** *inf* be afraid of *ger.*
fürchterlich ['fʏrçtərlɪç] → **furchtbar.**
'**furchterregend** *adj* frightening.
'**furchtlos** *adj* fearless, intrepid.
'**Furchtlosigkeit** *f* (-; *no pl*) fearlessness.
'**furchtsam** *adj* timorous.
'**Furchtsamkeit** *f* (-; *no pl*) timorousness.
fürein'ander *adv* for each other, for one another.
Furie ['fuːri̯ə] *f* (-; -n) *fig.* hellcat, virago.
Furnier [fʊrˈniːr] *n* (-s; -e) veneer.
furnieren [fʊrˈniːrən] *v/t* (h) veneer.
Furore [fuˈroːrə] ~ **machen** cause a sensation.
'**Fürsorge** *f* (-; *no pl*) **1.** a) care (**für** for),

b) solicitude: *ärztliche* ~ medical care.
2. *öffentliche* ~ public welfare.

'**fürsorglich** *adj* considerate, solicitous.

'**Fürsprache** *f* (-; *no pl*) **1.** intercession (**für** for, **bei** with). **2.** recommendation.

'**Fürsprecher(in** *f*) *m* a) intercessor, b) advocate.

Fürst [fʏrst] *m* (-en; -en) a) prince, b) ruler: *F leben wie ein* ~ live like a king.

'**Fürstenhaus** *n* dynasty. '**Fürstentum** *n* (-s; ⁻er) principality. '**Fürstin** *f* (-; -nen) princess. '**fürstlich** *adj* princely (*a. fig.*), prince's, *fig.* sumptuous, generous (*tip etc*): *j-n bewirten* (*belohnen*) entertain (reward) s.o. royally.

Furt [fʊrt] *f* (-; -en) fjord.

Furunkel [fu'rʊŋkəl] *m* (-s; -) ♣ boil.

'**Fürwort** *n* (-[e]s; ⁻er) *ling.* pronoun.

Furz [fʊrts] *m* (-es; ⁻e) V fart.

furzen ['fʊrtsən] *v/i* (h) V fart.

Fusel ['fu:zəl] *m* (-s; -) F rotgut.

Fusion [fu'zio:n] *f* (-; -en) **1.** ♣ fusion. **2.** ✝ merger. **fusionieren** [fuzio'ni:rən] *v/t, v/i* (h) ✝ merge.

Fuß [fu:s] *m* (-es; ⁻e) **1.** foot: *zu* ~ on foot; *zu* ~ *gehen* walk; *zu* ~ *erreichbar* within walking distance; *gut zu* ~ *sein* be a good walker; *fig.* (*festen*) ~ *fassen* gain a foothold; (*dat*) *auf dem* ~*e folgen* follow on the heels of; *fig. auf die Füße fallen* fall on one's feet; *auf freiem* ~ at large; *j-n auf freien* ~ *setzen* release s.o.; *auf eigenen Füßen stehen* stand on one's own two feet; *auf großem* ~*e leben* live in grand style; *auf gutem* ~*e stehen mit* be on good terms with; *auf schwachen Füßen stehen* be shaky; *mit beiden Füßen auf der Erde stehen* have both feet firmly on the ground; *kalte Füße bekommen* a. *F fig.* get cold feet; → *link.* **2.** foot, bottom (*of list, page, etc*), leg (*of chair etc*), stem (*of wineglass etc*), stand (*of lamp*): *am* ~*e des Berges* at the foot of the mountain. **3.** foot (= 30,48 cm): *10* ~ ten feet.

'**Fußabdruck** *m* footprint.

'**Fußangel** *f* mantrap, *fig.* trap.

'**Fußbad** *n* footbath.

'**Fußball** *m* (-[e]s; ⁻e) **1.** football, *Am.* soccer ball. **2.** *no pl* football, *esp. Am.* soccer. '**Fußball...** football (*club etc*).

'**Fußballen** *m anat.* ball of the foot.

'**Fußballer** [-balər] *m* (-s; -) F footballer.

'**Fußballländerspiel** *n* (*getr.* -ll,l-) international (football) match.

'**Fußball|platz** *m* football pitch. ~**spieler** *m* football player. ~**toto** *m, n* football pools, F the pools. ~**verband** *m* football association. ~**weltmeister** *m* World Cup holders. ~**weltmeisterschaft** *f* World Cup.

'**Fußbank** *f* footstool.

'**Fußboden** *m* **1.** floor. **2.** → ~**belag** *m* floor covering, flooring. ~**heizung** *f* underfloor heating.

'**Fußbreit** *m k-n* ~ *weichen* not to budge an inch.

'**Fußbremse** *f mot.* footbrake.

Fussel ['fʊsəl] *f* (-; -n) F fluff, *Am.* lint.

'**fusselig** *adj* F covered in fluff: *fig. sich den Mund* ~ *reden* talk one's head off.

fußen ['fu:sən] *v/i* (h) ~ *auf* (*dat*) be based (up)on.

'**Fußende** *n* (*am* ~ at the) foot.

'**Fußgänger** ['fu:sgɛŋər] *m* (-s; -) pedestrian. ~**brücke** *f* footbridge.

'**Fußgängerin** *f* (-; -nen) pedestrian.

'**Fußgänger|übergang** *m*, ~**überweg** *m* pedestrian crossing. ~**unterführung** *f* (pedestrian) underpass, *Br. a.* subway. ~**zone** *f* pedestrian precinct.

'**Fuß|gelenk** *n anat.* ankle. ²**hoch** *adj* ankle-deep. ~**matte** *f* doormat, *mot.* floor mat. ~**note** *f* footnote. ~**pfad** *m* footpath. ~**pflege** *f* pedicure. ~**pfleger(in** *f*) *m* pedicurist, chiropodist. ~**pilz** *m* ♣ athlete's foot. ~**puder** *m* foot powder. ~**sohle** *f* sole (of the foot). ~**spur** *f* footprint. ~**stapfe** *f* (-; -n) footstep: *fig. in j-s* ~*n treten* follow s.o.'s footsteps. ~**tritt** *m* **1.** footstep. **2.** footprint. **3.** kick: *j-m e-n* ~ *geben a.* kick s.o. ~**volk** *n fig.* rank and file. ~**weg** *m* **1.** footpath. **2.** *e-e Stunde etc* ~ an hour's *etc* walk.

futsch [fʊtʃ] *adj pred* F a) gone, b) broken, *sl.* bust: *es ist* ~ *a.* it has had it.

Futter¹ ['fʊtər] *n* (-s; *no pl*) ✓ fodder, feed, food. **2.** F grub (*sl.*), chow (*sl.*).

'**Futter²** *n* (-s; -) lining, ◬ casing.

'**Futteral** [fʊtə'ra:l] *n* (-s; -e) case, cover.

'**Futtermittel** *n* feed, fodder.

futtern ['fʊtərn] *v/i* (h) F tuck in(to *v/t*).

'**füttern¹** ['fʏtərn] *v/t* (h) feed.

'**füttern²** *v/t* (h) line.

'**Futternapf** *m* feeding bowl.

'Futterneid *m fig.* envy, jealousy.
'Futterstoff *m* lining (material).
'Fütterung *f* (-; -en) feeding.
Futur [fu'tu:r] *n* (-s; *no pl*) *ling.* (a. erstes ~) future (tense); zweites ~ future perfect (tense).

Futurismus [futu'rɪsmʊs] *m* (-; *no pl*) futurism. Futurist [futu'rɪst] *m* (-en; -en), futu'ristisch *adj* futurist.
Futurologe [futuro'lo:gə] *m* (-n; -n) futurologist. Futurologie [futurolo'gi:] *f* (-; *no pl*) futurology.

G

G, g [ge:] *n* (-; -) *a.* ♪ G, g.
gab [ga:p] *pret of* geben.
Gabardine ['gabardi:n] *m* (-s; *no pl*), *a. f* (-; *no pl*) gabardine.
Gabe ['ga:bə] *f* (-; -n) 1. (an *acc* to) a) gift, present, b) contribution: milde ~ charity. 2. gift, talent.
Gabel ['ga:bəl] *f* (-; -n) 1. a) fork (*a. on bike*), b) ♪ (pitch)fork. 2. *teleph.* rest, cradle. 3. *zo.* spire. gabeln ['ga:bəln] (h) I sich ~ fork (off *or* out). II *v/t* fork.
'Gabelstapler *m* (-s; -) forklift (truck).
'Gabelung *f* (-; -en) fork.
'Gabentisch *m* table with (the) presents.
gackern ['gakərn] *v/i* (h) cluck.
gaffen ['gafən] *v/i* (h) gape, stare.
Gag [gɛk] *m* (-s; -s) gag.
Gage ['ga:ʒə] *f* (-; -n) fee.
gähnen ['gɛ:nən] *v/i* (h) *a. fig.* yawn: ~d leer completely empty.
'Gähnen *n* (-s) yawn(ing).
Gala ['ga:la] *f* (-; *no pl*) gala dress.
'Gala... gala (*concert, performance, etc*).
galant [ga'lant] *adj* gallant. Galanterie [galantə'ri:] *f* (-; -n) gallantry.
Galeere [ga'le:rə] *f* (-; -n) galley.
Galerie [galə'ri:] *f* (-; -n) gallery.
Galerist [galə'rɪst] *m* (-en; -en), Gale'ristin *f* (-; -nen) gallery owner.
Galgen ['galgən] *m* (-s; -) gallows.
'Galgenhu‚mor *m* gallows humo(u)r.
Gali'onsfi‚gur [ga'lio:ns-] *f* figurehead.
gälisch ['gɛ:lɪʃ] *adj* Gaelic.
'Gallapfel *m* oakapple.
Galle ['galə] *f* (-; -n) 1. *anat.* gall bladder. 2. *physiol., a. fig.* bile, *a. ♀, zo.* gall: mir kam die ~ hoch my blood was up.
'Gallen|blase *f anat.* gall bladder. ~gang *m* bile (*or* gall) duct. ~kolik *f*

bilious attack. ~leiden *n* bilious complaint. ~stein *m* ♣ gallstone.
Gallert ['galərt] *n* (-[e]s; -e) jelly.
'gallertartig *adj* jelly-like, gelatinous.
Gallier ['galiər] *m* (-s; -) *hist.* Gaul.
gallig ['galɪç] *adj a. fig.* bilious.
Galopp [ga'lɔp] *m* (-s; -s, -e) gallop: im ~ at a gallop, *fig. a.* in a hurry.
galoppieren [galɔ'pi:rən] *v/i* (sn) gallop.
galt [galt] *pret of* gelten.
galvanisch [gal'va:nɪʃ] *adj* galvanic.
galvanisieren [galvani'zi:rən] *v/t* (h) galvanize (*a.* ♪), ⊚ *a.* electroplate.
Galvanotechnik [galva'no-] *f* electroplating.
Gamasche [ga'maʃə] *f* (-; -n) a) gaiter, b) puttee.
Gamet [ga'me:t] *m* (-en; -en) gamete.
Gammaglobulin [gamaglobu'li:n] *n* (-s; *no pl*) ♣ gamma globulin.
'Gammastrahl *m phys.* gamma ray.
'Gammastrahlung *f* gamma radiation.
Gamme'lei *f* (-; *no pl*) F loafing around.
'gammelig *adj* F 1. old (*meat etc*), rotten (*fruit etc*). 2. scruffy. gammeln ['ga-məln] *v/i* (h) F loaf (*or* bum) around.
Gammler ['gamlər] *m* (-s; -), 'Gammlerin *f* (-; -nen) F layabout, loafer, bum.
gang [gaŋ] *adj* ~ und gäbe sein be quite common (*or* usual).
Gang *m* (-[e]s; ⸚e) 1. → Gangart. 2. a) walk, b) errand, c) way, d) visit. 3. course: s-n ~ gehen take its course. 4. ⊚ a) running, working, action, b) operation: in ~ setzen (*or* bringen) *a. fig.* start, set s.th. going; in ~ kommen *a. fig.* get going (*or* started); im ~(e) sein ⊚ be running, be working, *fig.* be under way, be in progress; es ist et. im ~e

s.th. is going on; **in vollem ~e sein** be in full swing. **5.** *mot.* gear, *a.* ⊙ speed: **erster ~** first (*or* bottom) gear; **in den dritten ~ schalten** change (*Am.* shift) into third (gear); **den ~ herausnehmen** put the car in neutral. **6.** a) corridor (*a.* 🚆), hall(way), b) passage(way), c) aisle, d) walkway, e) tunnel. **7.** *anat.* duct. **8.** *gastr.* course: **ein Essen mit fünf Gängen** a five-course meal.

'**Gangart** *f* gait, walk, pace (*of horse*).

'**gangbar** *adj* passable (*road etc*), practicable (*a. fig.*).

gängeln ['gɛŋəln] *v/t* (h) F **j-n ~** keep s.o. in leading strings.

gängig ['gɛnɪç] *adj* **1.** current (*expression*), (very) common (*method etc*). **2.** ✝ saleable, fast-selling.

'**Gangschaltung** *f mot.* gear change, *Am.* gearshift.

Gangster ['gɛŋstər] *m* (-s; -) gangster.

'**Gangsterbande** *f* gang of criminals.

'**Gangsterbraut** *f* moll.

'**Gangstertum** *n* (-s; *no pl*) gangsterism.

Gangway ['gɛŋweɪ] *f* (-; -s) **1.** ✈ steps. **2.** ⚓ gangway.

Ganove [ga'no:və] *m* (-n; -n) F crook.

Gans [gans] *f* (-; ⸚e) goose: **junge ~** gosling; **dumme ~** stupid thing (*or* girl).

Gänschen ['gɛnsçən] *n* (-s; -) gosling.

Gänse|blümchen ['gɛnzə-] *n* daisy. **~braten** *m* roast goose. **~füßchen** *pl* F quotation marks, inverted commas. **~haut** *f* gooseflesh, goose pimples: **ich kriege e-e ~** it gives me the creeps. **~leberpastete** *f* pâté de foie gras. **~marsch** *m* **im ~** in single file.

Gänserich ['gɛnzərɪç] *m* (-s; -e) gander.

'**Gänseschmalz** *n* goose dripping.

ganz [gants] **I** *adj* **1.** whole, complete: **~ Deutschland** all (*or* the whole of) Germany; **die ~e Stadt** the whole town; **in der ~en Welt** all over the world; **~e Länge** total (*or* overall) length; **~e Zahl** whole number; **~e zwei Stunden** a) for two solid hours, b) for just two hours; **von ~em Herzen** with all my *etc* heart; **den ~en Tag** all day; **die ~e Nacht** (*hindurch*) all night long; **die ~e Zeit** all the time; **für ihr ~es Geld** all her money. **2.** F intact, in one piece: **~ machen** mend. **II** *adv* **3.** (*a.* **~ und gar**) completely, totally: **~ aus Holz** *etc* all wood *etc*; **das ist et. ~ anderes** that's a

different matter altogether; **nicht ~** not quite; **nicht ~ zehn Minuten** just under ten minutes; **~ und gar nicht** not at all; **~ gewiß** certainly; **~ naß** wet through; **~ wie du willst** just as you like; (**ich bin**) **~ Ihrer Meinung** I quite agree; **er ist ~ der Vater** he's just like his father; → **Ohr. 4.** a) quite, F pretty, b) very, really: **~ gut** quite good, not bad; **~ wenig** a tiny bit; **~ besonders, weil** (e)specially since. **5. im ~en** altogether, in all, ✝ **groß** 6, 7.

Ganze ['gantsə] *n* (-n; *no pl*) whole: **einheitliches ~s** integral whole; **als ~s** as a whole, in its entirety; **das ~** the whole thing; **aufs ~ gehen** go all out; **jetzt geht es ums ~** it's all or nothing now.

'**Ganzheit** *f* (-; *no pl*) (*in s-r ~* as a) whole.

'**Ganzheitsme|thode** *f ped.* **1.** whole-word method. **2.** *a.* '**Ganzheitsunterricht** *m* integrated curriculum.

ganzjährig ['gantsjɛ:rɪç] *adj* all-year: **~ geöffnet** open all year round.

gänzlich ['gɛntslɪç] *adj and adv* total(ly), complete(ly), entire(ly).

'**Ganzme|tall...** ⊙ all-metal.

ganzseitig ['gantszaɪtɪç] *adj* full-page.

ganztägig ['gantstɛ:gɪç] *adj* all-day: **~ geöffnet** open all day.

'**Ganztags|beschäftigung** *f* full-time job. **~schule** *f* all-day school(ing).

gar¹ [ga:r] *adj gastr.* done, cooked.

gar² *adv* **1. ~ nicht** not at all; **~ nichts** not a thing, nothing at all, absolutely nothing; **~ nicht so schlecht** (*viel*) not all that bad (much); **~ keiner** nobody at all; **es besteht ~ kein Zweifel** there's no doubt whatsoever. **2.** a) perhaps, b) even: **oder ~ ...** let alone ...

Garage [ga'ra:ʒə] *f* (-; -n) garage.

Garant [ga'rant] *m* (-en; -en) guarantor.

Garantie [garan'ti:] *f* (-; -n) guarantee: **die Uhr hat ein Jahr ~** the watch has got a year's guarantee; **die Reparatur geht noch auf ~** the repair is covered by the guarantee; **dafür kann ich k-e ~ übernehmen** I can't guarantee that; F **er fällt unter ~ durch** he's bound to fail.

garantieren [garan'ti:rən] *v/t* (h) (*v/i für*) guarantee (*a. fig.*).

Garan'tieschein *m* guarantee.

Garan'tiezeit *f* guarantee.

Garbe ['garbə] *f* (-; -n) ↗ sheaf.

Garde ['gardə] *f* ✗ *the* Guards: *fig.* **die alte ~** the Old Guard.

Garderobe [gardə'ro:bə] *f* (-; -n) **1.** cloakroom, *Am.* checkroom. **2.** *thea.* dressing room. **3.** coat rack. **4.** *no pl* a) coat (and hat), b) clothes, wardrobe.

Garde'roben|frau *f* cloakroom (*Am.* checkroom) attendant. **~marke** *f* cloakroom ticket, *Am.* check. **~ständer** *m* coat rack.

Garderobier [gardə'ro:bĭe:] *m* (-s; -s), **Garderobiere** [gardə'ro:bĭe:rə] *f* (-; -n) *thea.* dresser.

Gardine [gar'di:nə] *f* (-; -n) curtain.

gären ['gɛ:rən] *v/i* (*a.* **lassen**) ferment. **2.** seethe: *im Volk gärte es* there was unrest among the people.

Garn [garn] *n* (-[e]s; -e) thread, cotton: *fig.* **j-m ins ~ gehen** fall into the (*or* s.o.'s) trap; *ein ~ spinnen* spin a yarn.

Garnele [gar'ne:lə] *f* (-; -n) shrimp, prawn.

garnieren [gar'ni:rən] *v/t* (h) decorate, *a.* trim (*hat etc*), *gastr. a.* garnish.

Garnison [garni'zo:n] *f* (-; -en) garrison.

Garnitur [garni'tu:r] *f* (-; -en) **1.** set. **2.** trimmings. **3.** *fig.* **zur ersten (zweiten) ~** gehören be first-rate (second-rate).

Garten ['gartən] *m* (-s; ⸚) garden: *botanischer ~* botanical gardens. **~arbeit** *f* gardening. **~archi,tekt(in** *f*) *m* landscape gardener. **~bau** *m* (-[e]s; *no pl*) horticulture. **~bau...** horticultural (*show etc*). **~fest** *n* garden party. **~geräte** *pl* gardening tools. **~haus** *n* summerhouse. **~lo,kal** *n* beer garden. **~möbel** *pl* garden furniture. **~schere** *f* pruning shears, *esp. Br.* secateurs. **~stadt** *f* garden city. **~zaun** *m* garden fence. **~zwerg** *m* **1.** (garden) gnome. **2.** F *fig.* little squirt.

Gärtner ['gɛrtnər] *m* (-s; -), **'Gärtnerin** *f* (-; -nen) gardener.

Gärtne'rei *f* (-; -en) **1.** *no pl* F gardening. **2.** market garden, *Am.* truck farm.

'Gärung *f* (-; -en) **1.** fermentation. **2.** *fig.* (state of) unrest. **'Gärungspro,zeß** *m* (process of) fermentation.

Gas [ga:s] *n* (-es; -e) gas: *mot.* **~ geben** step on the gas (*a.* F *fig.*); **~ wegnehmen** throttle back (*or* down); *mit ~ vergiften* gas. **'Gasableser** *m* (-s; -) gasman. **'Gasanzünder** *m* gaslighter.

'Gasbehälter *m* gasholder, gas tank.

'gasbeheizt *adj* gas-fired. **'Gasflasche** *f* gas cylinder. **'gasförmig** *adj* gaseous. **'Gashahn** *m* gas tap. **'Gasheizung** *f* gas heating. **'Gasherd** *m* gas stove. **'Gaskammer** *f* gas chamber. **'Gasleitung** *f* gas mains. **'Gasmaske** *f* gas mask. **'Gaspe,dal** *n* *mot.* accelerator, *Am.* gas pedal.

Gasse ['gasə] *f* (-; -n) alley, *a. fig.* lane.

Gast [gast] *m* (-[e]s; ⸚e) **1.** a) guest, b) customer, c) visitor: *Gäste haben a.* have company. **2.** *thea.* guest (artist *or* performer). **~arbeiter(in** *f*) *m* foreign worker. **~diri,gent** *m* guest conductor. **~do,zent(in** *f*) *m* guest lecturer.

Gästebuch ['gɛstə-] *n* visitors' book.

'Gästehaus *n* guesthouse.

'Gästezimmer *n* guestroom.

'gastfreundlich *adj* hospitable. **'Gastfreundschaft** *f* (-; *no pl*) hospitality.

'Gast|geber *m* **1.** host. **2.** *pl sports*: home team. **~geberin** *f* hostess. **~haus** *n*, **~hof** *m* restaurant, inn. **~hörer(in** *f*) *m* *univ.* guest student, *Am.* auditor.

gastieren [gas'ti:rən] *v/i* (h) *thea.* give a guest performance, *esp. Am.* guest.

'Gastland *n* host country.

'gastlich *adj* hospitable.

'Gastlichkeit *f* (-; *no pl*) hospitality.

'Gast|mannschaft *f* visiting team. **~pro,fessor** *m* visiting professor. **~recht** *n* (**~ genießen** enjoy) hospitality.

Gastritis [gas'tri:tıs] *f* (-; -tiden [-tri'ti:-dən]) ♫ gastritis.

'Gastrolle *f* *thea.* guest part.

Gastronom [gastro'no:m] *m* (-en; -en) restaurant proprietor (*cook*: chef).

Gastronomie [gastrono'mi:] *f* (-; *no pl*) **1.** catering trade. **2.** gastronomy.

gastronomisch [gastro'no:mıʃ] *adj* **1.** catering. **2.** gastronomic(al).

'Gastspiel *n* *thea.* guest performance.

'Gaststätte *f* restaurant.

'Gaststättengewerbe *n* catering trade.

'Gaststube *f* lounge, taproom.

'Gastur,bine *f* gas turbine.

'Gastvorlesung *f*, **'Gastvortrag** *m* guest lecture. **'Gastvorstellung** *f* *thea.* guest performance.

'Gastwirt *m* landlord, proprietor.

'Gastwirtin *f* landlady, proprietress.

'Gastwirtschaft *f* restaurant.

'Gasvergiftung *f* gas poisoning.

'**Gaswerk** n gasworks.
'**Gaszähler** m gasmeter.
Gatte ['gatə] m (-n; -n) husband, ⚭ spouse.
Gatter ['gatər] n **1.** gate. **2.** fence.
'**Gattersäge** f ⚙ gate (or frame) saw.
Gattin ['gatın] f (-; -nen) wife, ⚭ spouse.
Gattung ['gatʊŋ] f (-; -en) **1.** biol. genus. **2.** species, kind, type. **3.** a) (art) form, b) literature: genre.
'**Gattungsbegriff** m generic term.
'**Gattungsname** m **1.** biol. generic name. **2.** ling. collective (or common) noun.
gaukeln ['gaʊkəln] v/i (sn) flutter around. **Gaukler** ['gaʊklər] m (-s; -) **1.** tumbler. **2.** clown.
Gaul [gaʊl] m (-[e]s; ⁓e) horse, contp. nag: **alter ∼** (old) jade; fig. **e-m geschenkten ∼ sieht man nicht ins Maul** never look a gift horse in the mouth.
Gaumen ['gaʊmən] m (-s; -) palate.
'**Gaumenlaut** m ling. palatal.
'**Gaumenzäpfchen** n anat. uvula.
Gauner ['gaʊnər] m (-s; -) **1.** swindler, crook, sl. con man. **2.** rascal.
'**Gaunersprache** f thieves' Latin.
'**Gaunerstück** n swindle.
Gaze ['ga:zə] f (-; -n) gauze (a. ⚙).
Gazelle [ga'tsɛlə] f (-; -n) zo. gazelle.
geachtet [gə'ʔaxtət] adj esteemed.
Geächtete [gə'ʔɛçtətə] m, f (-n; -n) outlaw.
Geäder [gə'ʔɛ:dər] n (-s; -) veins.
geädert [gə'ʔɛ:dərt] adj veined.
geartet [gə'ʔartət] adj disposed: **er ist so ∼, daß ...** he is the kind of person that ...; **anders ∼ sein** to be different.
Gebäck [gə'bɛk] n (-[e]s; -e) a) (fancy) cakes, b) biscuits, Am. cookies.
ge'backen pp of **backen**.
Gebälk [gə'bɛlk] n (-[e]s; -e) beams.
geballt [gə'balt] adj **1.** clenched. **2.** fig. concentrated.
gebannt [gə'bant] adj and adv spellbound.
gebar [gə'ba:r] pret of **gebären**.
Gebärde [gə'bɛ:rdə] f (-; -n) gesture.
ge'bärden: sich ∼ (h) behave, act.
Ge'bärden|spiel n gestures, gesticulation, pantomime (a. fig.). **∼sprache** f **1.** sign language. **2.** thea. mimicry.
Gebaren [gə'ba:rən] n (-s; no pl) behavio(u)r, † conduct.
gebären [gə'bɛ:rən] (gebar, geboren, h)

I v/t give birth to: **geboren werden** be born; → **geboren**. **II** v/i give birth.
Ge'bärmutter f (-; ⁓) anat. womb.
Ge'bärmutter|krebs m ⚕ cancer of the womb. **∼vorfall** m (uterine) prolapse.
Gebäude [gə'bɔydə] n (-s; -) building, edifice (a. fig.), fig. structure. **∼komplex** m complex (of buildings).
'**gebefreudig** adj open-handed.
Gebein [gə'baɪn] n (-[e]s; -e) **1.** bones. **2.** pl (mortal) remains.
Gebell [gə'bɛl] n (-[e]s; no pl) barking.
geben ['ge:bən] (gab, gegeben, h) **I** v/t **1.** (j-m et. s.o. s.th., s.th. to s.o.) give, a. hand, b) grant: **laß dir e-e Quittung ∼!** ask for a receipt!; **∼ Sie mir bitte Frau X** teleph. can I speak to Mrs X, please; F fig. **es j-m ∼** let s.o. have it; → **Anlaß 2, Bescheid, gegeben. 2.** give (lessons etc), teach. **3.** give (a concert etc), a. have (a party etc), perform (play etc), show (a film): **was wird heute abend gegeben?** what's on tonight? **4.** yield, produce: **Milch ∼** give milk; **zweimal fünf gibt zehn** two times five makes ten; **das gibt e-e gute Suppe** that will make a good soup; **Flecken ∼** make (or leave) stains; **das gibt k-n Sinn** that doesn't make sense; **ein Wort gab das andere** one word led to another. **5. von sich ∼** a) 🍴 give off, emit, b) make (remark etc), give, let out (shout etc), c) bring up, vomit; **sie gab k-n Ton von sich** she didn't utter a sound. **6. viel ∼ auf** (acc) set great store by s.th., think highly (or a lot) of s.o.; **ich gebe nicht viel auf** (acc) I don't think much of. **II** v/i **7.** give (**mit vollen Händen** freely). **8.** cards: deal: **wer gibt?** whose deal is it? **9.** tennis: serve. **III sich ∼ 10.** act, behave: **sich gelassen ∼** pretend to be calm; **er gibt sich gern als Experte** he likes to act the expert. **11.** a) pass, F blow over, b) come right: **das wird sich alles ∼** everything will be all right. **IV** v/impers **es gibt** there is, there are; **der beste Spieler, den es je gab** the best player of all time; **es gab viel zu tun** there was a lot to do; F **was gibt's?** what's up?; **was gibt's Neues?** what's new?; **was gibt es zum Mittagessen?** what's for lunch?; **was gibt's heute abend im Fernsehen?** what's on in television tonight?; **das gibt es (bei**

mir) nicht! that's out!; *das gibt's doch nicht!* you're joking!; *heute wird's noch was ~* I think we're in for s.th.; *er hat recht, da gibt's nichts!* he's right, and no mistake about it!

'**Geben** *n* (-s) **1.** giving: *~ ist seliger denn Nehmen* it is more blessed to give than to receive. **2.** *cards:* **am ~ sein** be dealing; *er ist am ~* it's his deal.

Geber ['ge:bər] *m* (-s; -) **1.** giver, *cards:* dealer. **2.** *tel.* transmitter. '**Geberin** *f* (-; -nen) → **Geber** 1. '**Geberlaune** *f in ~ sein* be in a generous mood.

Gebet [gə'be:t] *n* (-[e]s; -e) prayer: F *fig. j-n ins ~ nehmen* give s.o. a good talking-to. **Ge'betbuch** *n* prayerbook.

ge'beten *pp of* **bitten**.

Gebiet [gə'bi:t] *n* (-[e]s; -e) **1.** a) region, area, b) district, zone, c) territory. **2.** *fig.* field, *a.* sphere: *er ist Fachmann auf dem ~ (gen)* he is an authority on.

ge'bieten (gebot, geboten, h) **I** *v/t* **1.** *j-m ~ et. zu tun* order s.o. to do s.th. **2.** command (*respect etc*). **3.** require, call for: *die Vernunft gebietet uns zu inf* reason demands of us to *inf*. **II** *v/i* **4.** *~ über (acc)* a) control, rule over, b) have at one's disposal; → **geboten**.

Ge'bieter *m* (-s; -) **1.** master, lord. **2.** ruler. **Ge'bieterin** *f* (-; -nen) mistress.

ge'bieterisch *adj* domineering, peremptory (*tone*).

Ge'biets|anspruch *m* territorial claim. **~hoheit** *f* (-; *no pl*) territorial sovereignty. **~leiter** *m* ✝ regional manager.

Gebilde [gə'bɪldə] *n* (-s; -) a) thing, object, b) work, creation, c) structure.

gebildet [gə'bɪldət] *adj* a) educated, (well-)informed, b) cultured, refined.

Gebinde [gə'bɪndə] *n* (-s; -) arrangement.

Gebirge [gə'bɪrgə] *n* (-s; -) mountains.

gebirgig [gə'bɪrgɪç] *adj* mountainous.

Ge'birgskette *f* mountain range.

Gebiß [gə'bɪs] *n* (-sses; -sse) **1.** a) (set of) teeth, b) dentures. **2.** bit.

Ge'bißabdruck *m* (dental) impression.

gebissen [gə'bɪsən] *pp of* **beißen**.

Gebläse [gə'blɛ:zə] *n* (-s; -) ⚙ a) fan, b) blower. **Ge'bläsemotor** *m mot.* supercharger engine.

ge'blasen *pp of* **blasen**.

geblieben [gə'bli:bən] *pp of* **bleiben**.

geblümt [gə'bly:mt] *adj* floral, flowered.

Geblüt [gə'bly:t] *n* (-[e]s; *no pl*) blood.

gebogen [gə'bo:gən] *pp of* **biegen**.

gebongt [gə'bɔŋt] *adj* F *ist ~!* will do!

geboren [gə'bo:rən] **I** *pp of* **gebären**. **II** *adj* born: *~er Deutscher* (*Berliner*) *sein* be German (a Berliner) by birth; *Frau X, ~e Braun* Mrs X, née Braun; *sie ist e-e ~e Braun* her maiden name is Braun; *fig. ~ sein zu* be born to be (*or* to do), be cut out for (*a job*); *er ist der ~e Geschäftsmann* he is a born businessman; → *a.* **gebären**.

geborgen [gə'bɔrgən] **I** *pp of* **bergen**. **II** *adj* safe, secure. **Ge'borgenheit** *f* (-; *no pl*) safety, security.

geborsten [gə'bɔrstən] *pp of* **bersten**.

gebot [gə'bo:t] *pret of* **gebieten**.

Ge'bot *n* (-[e]s; -e) **1.** *bibl.* commandment. **2.** rule. **3.** requirement, necessity: *das ~ der Vernunft (des Herzens, der Stunde)* the dictates of reason (of one's heart, of the moment). **4.** ✝ bid. **5.** *j-m zu ~e stehen* be at s.o.'s disposal.

ge'boten I *pp of* **bieten** and **gebieten**. **II** *adj* a) necessary, b) imperative, c) due.

Ge'botsschild *n* mandatory sign.

gebracht [gə'braxt] *pp of* **bringen**.

gebrannt [gə'brant] **I** *pp of* **brennen**. **II** *adj* burnt, roasted, fired; → **Kind**.

ge'braten *pp of* **braten**.

Gebräu [gə'brɔy] *n* (-[e]s; -e) *contp.* brew, *fig. a.* concoction.

Ge'brauch *m* (-[e]s; ~e) **1.** *no pl* use, ⚒ application, *ling.* usage: *~ machen von* use, make use of; *guten ~ machen von* put *s.th.* to good use; *außer ~ kommen* pass out of use; *im ~ sein* be in use, be used; *et. in ~ nehmen* put s.th. into use; *der ~ s-s linken Arms* the use of his left arm; *zum persönlichen ~* for personal use; *vor ~ schütteln!* shake before use! **2.** *usu. pl* practice, custom.

ge'brauchen *v/t* (h) **1.** use: *kannst du das ~?* can you make use of that?; *das kann ich gut ~* I can make good use of that; F *er ist zu nichts zu ~* he is hopeless. **2.** F use, do with (*a drink etc*).

gebräuchlich [gə'brɔyçlɪç] *adj* common (*a.* ling.), normal: *allgemein ~* in common use; *nicht mehr ~* no longer used.

Ge'brauchs|anleitung *f*, **~anweisung** *f* directions for use, instructions (for use). **~artikel** *m* article of daily use. **⚸fähig** *adj* usable. **~fahrzeug** *n* utility vehicle. ⚇**fertig** *adj* ready for use. **~graphik** *f* commercial art. **~güter** *pl* (consumer) durables. **~muster** *n* registered design. **~wert** *m* practical value.

ge'braucht **I** *pp of* brauchen. **II** *adj* used, ✝ *a.* second-hand.

Ge'brauchtwagen *m* used (*or* second-hand) car. **~händler** *m* used car dealer.

gebräunt [gə'brɔʏnt] *adj* tanned.

Ge'brechen *n* (-s; -) disability, (physical) handicap, infirmity. **gebrechlich** [gə'brɛçlɪç] *adj* frail, infirm. Ge'brechlichkeit *f* (-; *no pl*) frailty, infirmity.

gebrochen [gə'brɔxən] **I** *pp of* brechen. **II** *adj* broken (*a. ling.*), *fig. a.* broken-hearted: sie spricht nur **~** Englisch she speaks only broken English.

Gebrüder [gə'bry:dər] *pl* **~** (*abbr.* Gebr.) Wolf Wolf Brothers (*abbr.* Bros.).

Gebrüll [gə'brʏl] *n* (-[e]s; *no pl*) roar(ing), bellow(ing) (*a. zo.*).

gebückt [gə'bʏkt] *adj* stooping.

Gebühr [gə'by:r] *f* (-; -en) **1.** a) charge, fee, b) rate, c) postage, d) *mot.* toll: ermäßigte **~** reduced rate. **2.** nach **~** duly; über **~** unduly, excessively.

ge'bühren *v/i* (h) j-m **~** be due to s.o.

ge'bührend **I** *adj* due (*dat* to), proper. **II** *adv* duly, properly.

Ge'bühren|einheit *f* unit. **~erlaß** *m* remission of fees. ⚇**frei** *adj* free of charge. **~ordnung** *f* scale of fees (*or* charges).

ge'bührenpflichtig *adj* subject to charges: **~e** Straße toll road; **~e** Verwarnung summary fine.

gebündelt [gə'bʏndəlt] *adj* bundled.

gebunden [gə'bʊndən] **I** *pp of* binden. **II** *adj* **1.** *print.* bound. **2.** ⚛ bound (*a. phys.*), fixed: **~e** Wärme latent heat. **3.** ♩ legato. **4.** *fig.* bound, tied, engaged: vertraglich **~** bound by contract; sich **~** fühlen an (*acc*) feel committed to. **5.** tied (up) (*capital*). **6.** *gastr.* thickened.

Geburt [gə'bu:rt] *f* (-; -en) **1.** birth (*a. fig.*), descent: er ist von **~** Deutscher he is German by birth. **2.** ✻ a) (child)birth, b) delivery: von **~** an from birth; F *fig.* e-e schwere **~** a tough job.

Ge'burten|kon,trolle *f*, **~regelung** *f* birth control. **~rückgang** *m* decline in the birthrate. ⚇**schwach** *adj* low-birth-rate (*year etc*). ⚇**stark** *adj* high-birth-rate (*year etc*). **~überschuß** *m* excess of births. **~ziffer** *f* birthrate.

gebürtig [gə'bʏrtɪç] *adj* er ist **~er** Engländer he was born in England.

Ge'burts|anzeige *f* birth announcement. **~datum** *n* date of birth. **~haus** *n* mein *etc* **~** the house where I *etc* was born. **~helfer** *m* obstetrician. **~helferin** *f* midwife. **~hilfe** *f* a) obstetrics, b) midwifery. **~jahr** *n* year of birth. **~jahrgang** *m* cohort. **~land** *n* native country. **~ort** *m* birthplace: **~** und Geburtstag place and date of birth. ⚇**stadt** *f* native town. **~stunde** *f* **1.** hour of birth. **2.** *fig.* birth.

Ge'burtstag *m* birthday, *adm.* date of birth: sie hat heute **~** it's her birthday today; (ich) gratuliere zum **~** many happy returns of the day.

Ge'burtstags... birthday (*present etc*).

Ge'burtstagskind *n* birthday boy (girl).

Ge'burtsurkunde *f* birth certificate.

Gebüsch [gə'bʏʃ] *n* (-[e]s; -e) bushes, shrubbery.

gedacht [gə'daxt] **I** *pp of* denken *and* gedenken. **II** *adj* assumed: **~** als intended as (*or* to be).

ge'dachte *pret of* gedenken.

Gedächtnis [gə'dɛçtnɪs] *n* (-ses; -se) **1.** memory: aus dem **~** a) from memory, b) by heart; sich et. ins **~** zurückrufen recall s.th. **2.** *no pl* commemoration: zum **~** an (*acc*) *a.* in memory of. **~hilfe** *f* mnemonic (aid). **~lücke** *f* lapse of memory. **~schwund** *m* amnesia, loss of memory. **~störung** *f* partial amnesia. **~training** *n* memory training.

gedämpft [gə'dɛmpft] *adj* **1.** muffled (*sound*), subdued (*colo[u]r, light, voice, etc, fig. mood etc*): **~er** Optimismus guarded optimism. **2.** *gastr.* steamed.

Gedanke [gə'daŋkə] *m* (-n; -n) thought (an *acc* of, über *acc* on), idea: kein schlechter **~**! not a bad idea!; in **~n** absent-mindedly; in **~n** versunken lost in thought; s-e **~n** beisammen halten keep one's wits about one; j-n auf andere **~n** bringen get s.o.'s mind on to other things; j-n auf den **~n** bringen zu *inf* give s.o. the idea of *ger*; j-n auf dumme **~n** bringen give s.o. silly ideas; j-s **~n** lesen read s.o.'s mind; sich **~n** machen über (*acc*) a) think about, b) be worried about; wie kommst du auf den **~n**? what makes you think of that?; → spielen 1, tragen 9.

Ge'danken|austausch m exchange of ideas. **~blitz** m sudden inspiration, F brainwave. **~freiheit** f (-; no pl) freedom of thought. **~gang** m train of thought. **~leser(in** f) m mind-reader.

ge'dankenlos adj a) thoughtless, inconsiderate, b) careless. **Ge'dankenlosigkeit** f (-; no pl) thoughtlessness.

ge'dankenreich adj full of ideas.

Ge'danken|sprung m jump (from one idea to the other). **~strich** m dash. **~übertragung** f telepathy.

ge'dankenvoll adj pensive.

ge'danklich adj intellectual.

Gedärm [gə'dɛrm] n (-[e]s, -e) usu. pl intestines, zo. entrails.

Gedeck [gə'dɛk] n (-[e]s; -e) **1.** cover: **ein ~ mehr auflegen** set another place. **2.** set meal. **3.** cover charge.

Gedeih [gə'daɪ]: **auf ~ und Verderb** come what may. **ge'deihen** v/i (gedieh, gediehen, sn) thrive, prosper, develop well, fig. a. progress: **so weit gediehen sein, daß** have reached a point where.

Ge'deihen n (-s) thriving, prosperity.

ge'denken (gedachte, gedacht, h) **I** v/i (gen) a) think of, remember, b) mention, c) commemorate. **II** v/t **zu tun ~** think of doing, intend to do.

Ge'denken n (-s) (**zum ~ an** acc in) memory (of); → a. **Andenken**.

Ge'denk|feier f commemoration (ceremony). **~gottesdienst** m memorial service. **~mi‚nute** f a minute's silence (**für** in memory of). **~münze** f commemorative coin. **~rede** f commemorative address. **~stätte** f memorial (place). **~stein** m memorial (stone). **~stunde** f hour of remembrance. **~tafel** f commemorative plaque. **~tag** m day of remembrance.

Gedicht [gə'dɪçt] n (-[e]s; -e) poem: **das Kleid ist ein ~** the dress is a (perfect) dream. **Ge'dichtsammlung** f a) collection of poems, b) anthology.

gediegen [gə'di:gən] adj **1.** metall. solid (a. fig. character etc), pure. **2. ✝** a) good-quality, b) tasteful.

Ge'diegenheit f (-; no pl) solidity.

gedieh [gə'di:] pret of **gedeihen**.

ge'diehen pp of **gedeihen**.

Gedränge [gə'drɛŋə] n (-s; no pl) **1.** crowd, F crush: F fig. **damit wir nicht ins ~ kommen** so that we don't get

pushed for time. **2.** rush (**nach, um** for). **3.** rugby: scrummage.

Ge'drängel n (-s; no pl) F pushing.

ge'drängt adj **1.** (a. ~ **voll**) crowded, F (jam-)packed. **2.** concise (style etc).

gedrechselt [gə'drɛksəlt] adj fig. stilted.

gedroschen [gə'drɔʃən] pp of **dreschen**.

gedruckt [gə'drʊkt] adj printed: F **lügen wie ~** lie through one's teeth.

gedrückt [gə'drʏkt] adj a. **✝** depressed: **~er Stimmung sein** a. be in low spirits; **die Stimmung war ~** spirits were low.

gedrungen [gə'drʊŋən] **I** pp of **dringen**. **II** adj stocky.

Geduld [gə'dʊlt] f (-; no pl) patience: **~ haben mit** be patient with; **jetzt reißt mir aber die ~!** that's done it!; **sich in ~ fassen** have patience.

ge'dulden [gə'dʊldən] **sich ~** (h) have patience, be patient; **~ Sie sich bitte e-n Augenblick!** wait a minute, please!

geduldig [gə'dʊldɪç] adj patient.

Ge'dulds|probe f e-e ~ **für j-n sein** be a test of s.o.'s patience. **~spiel** n puzzle.

gedungen [gə'dʊŋən] adj hired (killer).

gedunsen [gə'dʊnzən] adj bloated.

gedurft [gə'dʊrft] pp of **dürfen**.

geehrt [gə'e:rt] adj hono(u)red: in letter: **Sehr ~er Herr X!** Dear Mr X; **Sehr ~e Herren!** Dear Sirs, Gentlemen.

geeignet [gə'aɪgnət] adj (**für** for) suited, suitable, right, qualified: **er ist nicht dafür ~** he's not the right man for it; **im ~en Augenblick** at the right moment; **~e Maßnahmen** appropriate measures.

Gefahr [gə'fa:r] f (-; -en) danger, threat (both: **für** for, to), risk: **auf eigene ~** at one's own risk; **außer ~** out of danger; **auf die ~ hin zu** inf at the risk of ger; **sich e-r ~ aussetzen, sich in ~ begeben** expose o.s. to danger, take risks; **~ laufen zu** inf run the risk of ger; **in ~ bringen** → **gefährden**; **es besteht k-e ~** it's perfectly safe; → **schweben** I.

gefährden [gə'fɛ:rdən] v/t (h) endanger, threaten, (put at) risk, jeopardize.

ge'fährdet adj endangered: **~ sein** a. be in danger, be at risk. **Ge'fährdung** f (-; -en) **1.** endangering (etc, → **gefährden**). **2.** (gen to) danger, threat.

ge'fahren pp of **fahren**.

Ge'fahren|herd m (constant) source of danger, pol. trouble spot. **~stelle** f danger spot. **~zone** f danger zone. **~zu-lage** f danger money.

gefährlich [gə'fɛːrlɪç] adj dangerous (dat, **für** to), risky, grave, critical: **~e Krankheit** serious illness.

Ge'fährlichkeit f (-; no pl) danger(ous-ness), risk, gravity, seriousness.

ge'fahrlos adj not dangerous, safe.

Gefährte [gə'fɛːrtə] m (-n; -n), **Ge'fährtin** f (-; -nen) companion.

ge'fahrvoll adj dangerous, risky.

Gefälle [gə'fɛlə] n (-s; -) 1. fall, slope, incline, gradient, esp. Am. grade. 2. ⚡, ⚕, phys. gradient. 3. a) difference(s), b) (wage etc) differential.

ge'fallen[1] v/i (gefiel, gefallen, h) 1. please: **es gefällt mir** (**nicht**) I (don't) like it; F **er gefällt mir nicht** he doesn't look too well; **solche Filme ~ der Masse** films like that appeal to the masses; **hat dir das Konzert ~?** did you enjoy the concert?; **wie gefällt es Ihnen in Berlin?** how do you like Berlin? 2. **sich et. ~ lassen** put up with s.th.; **das lasse ich mir nicht ~!** I'm not going to put up with it!; **sie läßt sich von ihm nichts ~** she won't stand any nonsense from him; **das lasse ich mir ~!** now you're talking! 3. **sich ~ in** (dat) indulge in; **sich in der Rolle des Fachmanns ~** fancy o.s. as an expert.

ge'fallen[2] I pp of **fallen** and **gefallen**[1]. II adj fallen, ✗ a. killed in action: **die Gefallenen** the dead.

Ge'fallen[1] m (-s; -) (**j-m e-n ~ tun** do s.o. a) favo(u)r: **j-n um e-n ~ bitten** ask a favo(u)r of s.o.

Ge'fallen[2] n (-s; no pl) pleasure: **~ finden an** a) enjoy, take pleasure in (s.th.), b) like, take (a fancy) to (s.o.).

Ge'fallenendenkmal n war memorial.

ge'fällig adj 1. agreeable, pleasant. 2. obliging, kind: **j-m ~ sein** oblige s.o., help s.o.; F **et. zu trinken ~?** would you like s.th. to drink?; → **gefälligst.**

Ge'fälligkeit f (-; -en) 1. no pl obliging-ness: **et. aus ~ tun** do s.th. out of sheer kindness. 2. → **Gefallen**[1].

ge'fälligst adv iro. if you don't mind: **sei ~ still!** be quiet, will you!

ge'fangen I pp of **fangen.** II adj a) caught, ✗ captive, b) imprisoned, in prison, c) fig. captivated. **Ge'fangene** m, f (-n; -n) prisoner, convict.

Ge'fangenenlager n prison camp, ✗ prisoner-of-war camp.

ge'fangenhalten v/t (irr, sep, -ge-, h, → **halten**) **j-n** keep (or hold) s.o. prisoner, fig. have s.o. spellbound.

Ge'fangennahme f (-; no pl) arrest, ✗ capture. **ge'fangennehmen** v/t (irr, sep, -ge-, h, → **nehmen**) arrest, ✗ capture, take s.o. prisoner, fig. captivate.

Ge'fangenschaft f (-; no pl) (**in ~** in) captivity (a. zo.), imprisonment: **in ~ geraten** be taken prisoner.

Gefängnis [gə'fɛŋnɪs] n (-ses; -se) prison, jail, Br. a. gaol: **ins ~ kommen** be sent (or go) to prison. **~direktor** m governor, Am. warden. **~strafe** f → **Freiheitsstrafe. ~zelle** f prison cell.

Gefasel [gə'faːzəl] n (-s; no pl) F drivel.

Gefäß [gə'fɛːs] n (-es; -e) a vessel (a. anat., biol.), receptacle, b) bowl, c) jar. **ge'fäßerweiternd** adj 💊 vasodilating.

Ge'fäßkrankheit f vascular disease.

gefaßt [gə'fast] adj 1. calm, composed. 2. **~ sein auf** (acc) be prepared for; **sich ~ machen auf** (acc) prepare for; F **er kann sich auf et. ~ machen** he's in for it now. **Ge'faßtheit** f (-; no pl) calm-ness, composure.

Gefecht n (-[e]s; -e) 1. fight, battle: **au-ßer ~ setzen** a. fig. fust s.o., s.th. out of action; → **Eifer, Hitze.** 2. fencing bout.

Ge'fechtskopf m ✗ warhead.

gefeit [gə'faɪt] adj immune (**gegen** to).

Gefieder [gə'fiːdər] n (-s; -) plumage, feathers. **ge'fiedert** adj feathered.

gefiel [gə'fiːl] pret of **gefallen.**

Geflecht [gə'flɛçt] n (-[e]s; -e) 1. a. fig. network, mesh. 2. anat. plexus.

gefleckt [gə'flɛkt] adj spotted.

geflochten [gə'flɔxtən] pp of **flechten.**

geflogen [gə'floːgən] pp of **fliegen.**

geflohen [gə'floːən] pp of **fliehen.**

geflossen [gə'flɔsən] pp of **fließen.**

Ge'flügel n (-s; no pl) poultry (a. in cpds. disease, farm, farming, etc).

Ge'flügelhändler(in) f(m) poulterer.

Ge'flügelsalat m gastr. chicken salad.

Ge'flügelschere f poultry shears.

ge'flügelt adj winged: **~es Wort** saying.

Geflunker [gə'flʊŋkər] n (-s; no pl) fib-bing, fibs.

Geflüster [gə'flʏstər] n (-s; no pl) whis-pering, whispers.

gefochten [gə'fɔxtən] pp of **fechten.**

Gefolge [gə'fɔlgə] *n* (-s; -) **1.** entourage, attendants. **2.** cortège, mourners. **3.** *fig.* **im ~ von** (*or* gen) in the wake of.

Ge'folgschaft *f* (-; -en) followers, adherents. **Ge'folgsmann** *m* **1.** *hist.* vassal. **2.** *esp. pol.* follower, supporter.

gefräßig [gə'frɛːsɪç] *adj* greedy, *zo.* voracious. **Ge'fräßigkeit** *f* (-; *no pl*) greediness, *zo.* voracity.

Gefreite [gə'fraɪtə] *m* (-n; -n) ✕ lance corporal, *Am.* private first class, ✈ aircraftman first class, *Am.* airman third class.

ge'fressen *pp* of **fressen**.

Ge'frieranlage *f* refrigeration plant.

Ge'frierbeutel *m* freezer bag.

ge'frieren *v/i* (gefror, gefroren, sn) freeze.

Ge'frier|fach *n* freezer, freezing compartment. **~punkt** *m* (*auf dem ~* at) freezing point. **~schrank** *m* freezer. **~schutzmittel** *n* ⊙ antifreeze.

ge'friertrocknen *v/t* (h) freeze-dry.

Ge'friertruhe *f* deep freeze, freezer.

gefror [gə'froːr] *pret* of **gefrieren**.

ge'froren *pp* of **frieren** and **gefrieren**.

Gefüge [gə'fyːgə] *n* (-s; -) structure.

gefügig [gə'fyːgɪç] *adj* docile, compliant: **j-n ~ machen** bring s.o. to heel.

Gefühl [gə'fyːl] *n* (-[e]s; -e) **1.** feeling, sentiment: **für mein ~, m-m ~ nach** my feeling is that, I think that; **ich habe das ~, daß ...** I have a feeling that ...; **mit ~ ~ gefühlvoll** II. **2.** *no pl* sensation, touch, feel: **ein ~ der Kälte** a cold sensation. **3.** *no pl* (**für**) a) sense (of), b) flair (*for languages etc*): **sich auf sein ~ verlassen** rely on one's instinct. **4.** *usu. pl* feeling, emotion: **j-s ~e verletzen** hurt s.o.'s feelings.

ge'fühllos *adj* **1.** numb. **2.** *fig.* insensitive (**gegen** to), unfeeling, heartless.

Ge'fühllosigkeit *f* (-; *no pl*) **1.** numbness. **2.** *fig.* heartlessness, cruelty.

ge'fühlsarm *adj* (emotionally) cold.

Ge'fühlsausbruch *m* outburst.

ge'fühlsbetont *adj* emotional.

Gefühlsduse'lei *f* (-; -en) F sentimentality.

Ge'fühlsleben *n* emotional life.

ge'fühlsmäßig *adj* emotional, *w.s.* intuitive, instinctive.

ge'fühlvoll I *adj* full of feeling, emotion-

al, *a. contp.* sentimental. II *adv* feelingly (*etc*), **sing etc** with feeling.

ge'füllt *adj* filled, *gastr. a.* stuffed.

gefunden [gə'fʊndən] *pp* of **finden**.

gegangen [gə'gaŋən] *pp* of **gehen**.

ge'geben I *pp* of **geben**. II *adj* given: **als ~ voraussetzen** take s.th. for granted; **unter den ~en Umständen** under the circumstances; **zu ~er Zeit** a) when the occasion arises, b) at some future time.

ge'gebenenfalls *adv* **1.** should the occasion arise. **2.** if necessary.

Ge'gebenheit *f* (-; -en) given fact: **~en** a) circumstances, b) reality.

gegen [ge:gən] I *prep* **1.** toward(s), *time: a.* at about: **~ Osten** toward(s) the east, eastward(s); **~ zehn (Uhr)** (at) about ten o'clock. **2.** against (*a. fig.*): **die Wand lehnen** lean against the wall; **ein Mittel ~** a remedy for; **~ die Vernunft** contrary to reason. **3.** toward(s), to: **freundlich ~** kind to. **4.** compared with. **5.** in return for: **♥ ~ Bezahlung** against payment; **~ bar** for cash. **6.** ⚖, *sports*: versus. II *adv* **7.** about, around.

'Gegen|angebot *n* counteroffer. **~angriff** *m* *a. fig.* counterattack. **~argu,ment** *n* counterargument. **~beispiel** *n* counterexample. **~besuch** *m* return visit: **j-m e-n ~ machen** return s.o.'s visit. **~bewegung** *f* *esp. fig.* countermovement. **~beweis** *m* (**den ~ antreten** furnish) proof to the contrary.

Gegend ['ge:gənt] *f* (-; -en) a) region (*a. anat.*), area, b) countryside, c) neighbo(u)rhood: **in der ~ von** (*or* gen) near, around, in the *Munich etc* area; **in unserer ~** where we live.

'Gegendarstellung *f* correction, reply.

'Gegendemonstrati,on *f* counterdemonstration.

gegenein'ander *adv* **1.** against (*or* toward[s]) each other (*or* one another). **2.** mutually.

'Gegen|einladung *f* return invitation. **~erklärung** *f* counterstatement. **~fahrbahn** *f* opposite lane. **~frage** *f* counterquestion. **~gerade** *f* *sports*: back straight, *Am.* backstretch. **~gewicht** *n* counterweight: *fig.* **das ~ bilden zu** counterbalance. **~gift** *n* antidote. **~kandi,dat(in** *f*) *m* rival (candidate). **~klage** *f* ⚖ cross action. **~leistung** *f* return (service): **als ~ in** return (**für** for).

'**Gegenlicht** *n* back light(ing): *bei ~* against the light. **~aufnahme** *f* contre-jour shot. **~blende** *f* lens hood.

'**Gegen|liebe** *f* **er stieß mit s-m Vorschlag auf wenig ~** his suggestion didn't go down particularly well. **~maßnahme** *f* countermeasure: **~n ergreifen** take steps (*gegen* against). **~mittel** *n a. fig.* antidote. **~offen,sive** *f* counteroffensive. **~par,tei** *f* opposite (*or* other) side, *pol.* opposition, *sports:* opponents. **~pol** *m fig.* counterpart. **~probe** *f* (*a.* **die ~ machen**) crosscheck. **~revoluti,on** *f* counterrevolution. **~richtung** *f* the opposite direction: *aus der ~* oncoming (*traffic etc*).

'**Gegensatz** *m* (-es; ¨e) **1.** contrast: *im ~ zu* in contrast to (*or* with), as opposed to, unlike *the British etc; im ~ dazu* by way of contrast. **2.** the opposite. **3.** *pl* differences. '**gegensätzlich** [-zɛtslıç] *adj* contrary, opposite, different.

'**Gegenschlag** *m a. fig.* counterblow: *zum ~ ausholen* get ready to hit back.

'**Gegenseite** *f* opposite (*or* other) side. '**gegenseitig** [-zaıtıç] *adj* mutual, reciprocal: **~e Abhängigkeit** interdependence; **~es Interesse** mutual interest; *sich ~ helfen* help one another (*or* each other). '**Gegenseitigkeit** *f* (-; *no pl*) reciprocity, mutuality: *auf ~ beruhen* be mutual; *iro.* *das beruht auf ~!* the feeling is mutual!

'**Gegen|sinn** *m im ~* in the opposite direction. **~spieler** *m* antagonist, *a. sports:* opponent, *a. pol.* opposite number. **~spio,nage** *f* counterespionage. **~sprechanlage** *f* intercom (system).

'**Gegenstand** *m* (-[e]s; ¨e) **1.** object (*a. fig.*), thing, *esp.* ✝ item, article: *~ des Mitleids* object of pity; *~ des Spottes* figure of fun. **2.** a) subject, b) subject-matter, c) matter, affair, d) issue: *zum ~ haben* deal with. '**gegenständlich** [-ʃtɛntlıç] *adj* **1.** *a. ling.* concrete. **2.** graphic. **3.** *paint. etc:* representational.

'**gegenstandslos** *adj* **1.** abstract, *paint. etc: a.* nonrepresentational, *paint. a. fig.* a) invalid, b) unfounded.

'**Gegen|stimme** *f* **1.** *parl.* vote against. **2.** *fig.* objection. **~strömung** *f* **1.** countercurrent. **2.** *fig.* countermovement. **~stück** *n* (*zu*) counterpart (of), *paint. etc* pendant (to). **~teil** *n* opposite (*von*

of): (*ganz*) *im ~* on the contrary.

'**gegenteilig** *adj* contrary, opposite: **~er Meinung sein** disagree; ⚖ **~ entscheiden** come to a different decision.

Gegen|tor *n*, **~treffer** *m* goal against.

gegen'über I *adv* **1.** opposite, across the way (*or* street), *person: a.* face to face: *sie saßen einander ~* they sat facing one another. **II** *prep* (*dat*) **2.** opposite, facing. **3.** *fig.* to, toward(s): *er war mir ~ sehr höflich* he was very polite to me. **4.** compared with, as against. **5.** in contrast to. **6.** in view of, in the face of.

Gegen'über *n* (-s; -) **1.** person opposite, vis-à-vis, *sports:* opponent, *pol. etc* opposite number. **2.** house opposite.

gegen'überliegen *v/i* (*irr, sep,* -ge-, h, → *liegen*) (*dat*) be opposite, face.

gegen'übersehen: *sich ~* (*irr, sep,* -ge-, h, → *sehen*) (*dat*) be faced with.

gegen'überstehen *v/i* (*irr, sep,* -ge-, h, → *stehen*) **1.** *j-m ~* face s.o.; *sich* (*or einander*) *~* be facing each other, *feindlich* be enemies. **2.** (*dat*) be faced (*or* confronted) with, F be up against.

gegen'überstellen *v/t* (*sep,* -ge-, h) *fig.* (*dat* with) confront (*s.o.*), compare (*s.th.*). **Gegen'überstellung** *f* (-; -en) **1.** *a.* ⚖ confrontation. **2.** comparison.

gegen'übertreten *v/i* (*irr, sep,* -ge-, sn, → *treten*) *j-m ~* face s.o.

'**Gegenverkehr** *m* oncoming traffic.

'**Gegenvorschlag** *m* counterproposal.

Gegenwart ['ge:gənvart] *f* (-; *no pl*) **1.** *the* present (time): *... der ~* present-day, contemporary. **2.** (*in ihrer etc ~* in her *etc*) presence. **3.** *ling.* present (tense).

gegenwärtig ['ge:gənvɛrtıç] **I** *adj* present, current, present-day, contemporary, today's. **II** *adv* a) at the moment, at present, b) nowadays, these days.

'**Gegenwarts|litera,tur** *f* contemporary literature. **ℒnah(e)** *adj* topical. **~pro,bleme** *pl* present-day problems.

'**Gegenwehr** *f* (-; *no pl*) resistance.

'**Gegenwert** *m* equivalent (value).

'**Gegenwind** *m* headwind.

'**Gegenwirkung** *f* countereffect.

'**gegenzeichnen** *v/i, v/t* (*sep,* -ge-, h) countersign.

'**Gegenzug** *m* **1.** *chess:* countermove: *fig. im ~ zu* as a countermove. **2.** train coming from the other direction.

gegessen [gə'gɛsən] *pp of* **essen**.

gehen

geglichen [gəˈgliçən] *pp of* **gleichen**.
ge'gliedert *adj* **1.** jointed. **2.** *fig.* a) organized, structured, b) subdivided.
geglitten [gəˈglɪtən] *pp of* **gleiten**.
Gegner [ˈgeːgnər] *m* (-s; -) **1.** opponent (*a. sports*), adversary, enemy, rival: *im ~ sein von* be against. **2.** 🏛 opposing party. **'Gegnerin** *f* (-; -nen) → **Gegner**.
'gegnerisch *adj* opposing (*a.* 🏛 *or sports*), antagonistic, *a.* ✕ enemy, hostile: *die ~e Partei a.* the other side.
'Gegnerschaft *f* (-; -en) **1.** opposition, opponents. **2.** *no pl* opposition (*gegen* to).

gegolten [gəˈgɔltən] *pp of* **gelten**.
gegoren [gəˈgoːrən] *pp of* **gären**.
gegossen [gəˈgɔsən] *pp of* **gießen**.
ge'graben *pp of* **graben**.
gegriffen [gəˈgrɪfən] *pp of* **greifen**.
Ge'habe *n* (-s; *no pl*) affectation, airs.
gehabt [gəˈhaːpt] *pr of* **haben**.
Ge'hackte *n* (-n; *no pl*) → **Hackfleisch**.
Ge'halt¹ *m* (-[e]s; -e) **1.** *fig.* a) content, b) substance. **2.** (*an dat* of) content, 🔬 *a.* concentration: *~ an Öl* oil content.
Gehalt² *n* (-[e]s; ⁺er) salary, pay: *bei vollem ~* on full pay.
ge'halten *pp of* **halten**.
ge'haltlos *adj* **1.** unsubstantial (*food*). **2.** *fig.* empty, lacking substance.
Ge'halts|abzug *m* deduction from salary. **~ansprüche** *pl* salary expectations. **~empfänger** *m* salaried employee. **~erhöhung** *f* salary increase, (pay) rise, *esp. Am.* raise. **~forderung** *f* salary claim. **~gruppe** *f*, **~klasse** *f* salary bracket. **~kürzung** *f* salary cut. **~liste** *f* payroll. **~streifen** *m* pay slip. **~stufe** *f* salary bracket. **~zahlung** *f* payment of salary. **~zulage** *f* **1.** bonus. **2.** → **Gehaltserhöhung.**
ge'haltvoll *adj* **1.** substantial (*food*). **2.** *fig.* rich in content, profound.
gehangen [gəˈhaŋən] *pp of* **hängen¹**.
ge'harnischt *adj fig.* sharp, withering.
gehässig [gəˈhɛsɪç] *adj* spiteful, venomous. **Ge'hässigkeit** *f* (-; -en) **1.** *no pl* spite(fulness), venom, venomousness. **2.** spiteful words (*or* act).
ge'hauen *pp of* **hauen**.
Gehäuse [gəˈhɔyzə] *n* (-s; -) **1.** ⚙ case, casing, cabinet, *phot.* body. **2.** *zo.* shell.
'gehbehindert *adj* **sie ist ~** she can't walk properly.

Gehege [gəˈheːgə] *n* (-s; -) enclosure, pen, *hunt.* preserve: *fig. j-m ins ~ kommen* get in s.o.'s way, cross s.o.
geheim [gəˈhaɪm] *adj* **1.** secret, *a.* a) confidential, b) hidden: *im ~en* secretly; *in ~er Wahl* by closed ballot; *streng ~!* top-secret! **2.** occult.
Ge'heim... a) secret (*agent, agreement, order, etc*), b) occult. **~akte** *f* classified document, *pl* secret files. **~dienst** *m* secret service. **~fach** *n* secret drawer.
ge'heimhalten *v/t* (*irr, sep, -ge-, h,* → **halten**) keep *s.th.* secret (*vor dat* from).
Ge'heimhaltung *f* (-; *no pl*) secrecy.
Ge'heimkonto *n* secret account.
Ge'heimnis *n* (-ses; -se) secret (*vor dat* from), *a.* mystery: *kein ~ machen aus* make no secret out of. **Ge'heimniskrämer** [-krɛːmər] *m* (-s; -) mystery-monger. **Ge'heimnisträger** *m* bearer of official secrets. **ge'heimnisumwittert** *adj* shrouded in mystery, mysterious. **Ge'heimnisverrat** *m* betrayal of a state (*or* trade) secret. **ge'heimnisvoll** *adj* mysterious.
Ge'heim|nummer *f* secret (*teleph.* ex-directory) number. **~poli,zei** *f* secret police. **~poli,zist** *m* member of the secret police. **~sache** *f* secret (✕, *pol.* security) matter. **~tip** *m* F hot tip.
ge'heißen *pp of* **heißen**.
ge'hemmt *adj* inhibited.
gehen [ˈgeːən] (ging, gegangen, sn) **I** *v/i* **1.** (*zu Fuß ~*) walk, go (on foot): *schwimmen ~* go swimming; *auf die* (*or zur*) *Bank* (*Post*) *~* go to the bank (post office); *auf die Straße ~* a) go out into the street, b) *fig.* take to the streets; *über die Brücke ~* cross the bridge; *fig. an die Arbeit ~* get down to work; *das geht zu weit* that is going too far; *wie ich ging und stand* a) as I was, b) at once. **2.** go, leave, *adm. a.* resign: *er ist gegangen* he's gone, he has left; *j-n ~ lassen* let s.o. go. **3.** 🚂 *etc* (*nach, bis* to, as far as) go, run: *über München ~* go via Munich. **4.** (*nach* to) go, lead: *~ um* go round. **5.** ⚙ go, work, *machine*: *a.* run, *bell*: go, ring, *radio etc*: be on: *fig. das Gedicht geht so ...* the poem goes like this ... **6.** ♀ (*gut*) *~* sell (well); *wie ~ die Geschäfte?* how's business? **7.** *dough*: rise. **8.** *wind*: blow. **9.** *~ an* (*acc*) *fig.* a) go as far as, reach to, b)

inheritance etc: fall to, go to. **10. das Fenster geht auf die Straße** the window looks out on(to) the street. **11. das geht gegen dich** this is meant for you. **12. in die Industrie (Politik** *etc*) ~ go into industry (politics *etc*); **in den Saal ~ 100 Personen** the hall holds (*or* seats) 100 persons; **der Schaden geht in die Millionen** the damage runs into millions; **wie oft geht 2 in 10?** how many times goes 2 into 10?; **in sich ~** do a bit of soul-searching. **13.** F ~ **mit** go out with (*a boy or girl*); **fest ~** go steady. **14. die Fenster ~ nach Westen** the windows face (*or* look) west; **nach s-n Worten zu ~** to go by his words; **wenn es nach ihr ginge** if she had her way. **15.** ~ **über** (*acc*) go beyond; **es geht nichts über ~** there's nothing like ...; **ihre Familie geht ihr über alles** her family means everything to her. **16. vor sich ~** happen; **wie geht das vor sich?** how does it go (*or* work)? **II** *v/impers* **17.** *fig.* **es geht** a) it works, b) I can manage; **es geht nicht** a) it doesn't work, b) it can't be done, it's impossible; **es wird schon ~** it'll be all right; **es geht (eben) nicht anders** it can't be helped. **18.** be, feel: **wie geht es Ihnen?,** F **wie geht's?** a) how are you?, b) how are you feeling?; **es geht mir gut** a) I'm fine, b) ✝ I'm doing fine; **es geht mir schlecht** a) I'm not feeling too good, b) ✝ things aren't going too well; **mir geht es genauso** F same here; **ihm ist es genauso gegangen** it was the same with him; **so geht es, wenn man lügt** that's what comes of lying; **es sich gut ~ lassen** have a good time, enjoy o.s. **19. es geht auf 10 (Uhr)** it is getting on for ten. **20. es geht über m-e Kraft** it's too much for me. **21. es geht um den Frieden (sein Leben)** peace (his life) is at stake; **ihr geht es nur ums Geld** she's just interested in the money; **worum geht es?** what's it all about?, what's the problem?; **es geht darum zu** *inf* it's a question of *ger*; **darum geht es (ja)!** that's the (whole) point!; **darum geht es hier gar nicht** that's not the point. **III** *v/t* **22.** walk (*distance etc*), go (on foot): *humor.* **er ist gegangen worden** he was sacked.

'Gehen *n* (-s) walking: **50 km ~** *sports*: 50 kilomet/res (*Am.* -ers) walk.

'gehenlassen: **sich ~** (*irr, sep, no* -ge-, h, → **lassen**) **1.** let o.s. go, lose one's temper. **2.** relax.

Geher ['ge:ər] *m* (-s; -) *sports*: walker.

geheuer [gə'hɔyər] *adj nicht (ganz) ~* a) creepy, b) fishy, c) a bit risky; **er (die Sache) ist mir nicht ~** I've got a funny feeling about him (it).

Geheul [gə'hɔyl] *n* (-[e]s; *no pl*) F howling, howls.

Gehilfe [gə'hɪlfə] *m* (-n; -n) **1.** helper, assistant. **2.** clerk. **3.** ⚖ accessory before the fact. **Ge'hilfin** *f* (-; -nen)

Gehirn [gə'hɪrn] *n* (-[e]s; -e) **1.** *a. fig.* brain. **2.** F brain(s), mind.

Ge'hirn... cerebral; **~blutung** *f* cerebral h(a)emorrhage. **~chirur,gie** *f* brain surgery. **~erschütterung** *f* concussion. **~hautentzündung** *f* meningitis. **~tumor** *m* cerebral tumo(u)r. **~wäsche** *f* *pol.* brainwashing: **j-n e-r ~ unterziehen** brainwash s.o.

gehoben [gə'ho:bən] **I** *pp of* **heben. II** *adj* high, senior, elevated, ✝ up-market (*article, shop, etc*): **~e Ansprüche** expensive tastes; **in ~er Stimmung** in high spirits.

Gehöft [gə'hœft] *n* (-[e]s; -e) farm(stead).

geholfen [gə'hɔlfən] *pp of* **helfen.**

Gehölz [gə'hœlts] *n* (-es; -e) copse, coppice, small wood.

Gehör [gə'hø:r] *n* (-[e]s; *no pl*) **1.** (sense of) hearing, ear(s): **feines ~** sensitive ear; ♪ **absolutes ~** perfect pitch; **nach dem ~** by ear. **2.** (~ **finden** get a) hearing: **e-r Bitte kein ~ schenken** turn a deaf ear to a request; **sich ~ verschaffen** make o.s. heard.

ge'horchen *v/i* (h) **j-m** (**j-m Befehl** *etc*) **(nicht) ~** (dis)obey s.o. (an order *etc*).

gehören [gə'hø:rən] (h) **I** *v/i* **1.** belong (*dat* to): **wem gehört das Buch?** whose book is this?; **gehört es dir?** is it yours?; **es gehört mir** it belongs to me, it is mine; *fig.* **das gehört nicht hierher** that's beside the point; **der Raumfahrt gehört die Zukunft** the future belongs to space travel. **2.** ~ **zu** a) belong to, be part of, b) rank (*or* be) among; **er gehört zu den besten Spielern** he is one of the best players; **es gehört zu s-r Arbeit** it is part of his job; **dazu gehört**

a) *Geld* you need money for that, b) *Zeit* that kind of thing takes time, c) (*viel*) *Mut* it takes (a lot of) courage; *dazu gehört schon einiges!* that takes a lot of doing!; *es gehört nicht viel dazu!* there's nothing to it! 3. ~ *unter* (*acc*) come under. 4. ~ *in* (*acc*) belong in; F *du gehörst ins Bett!* you should be in bed! II *sich* ~ be proper; *wie es sich gehört* properly; *er weiß, was sich gehört* he knows how to behave; *das gehört sich nicht!* it's not done!

Ge'hörfehler *m* hearing defect.

Ge'hörgang *m* auditory canal.

gehörig [gə'høːrɪç] I *adj* 1. ~ *zu* belonging to; (*nicht*) *zur Sache* ~ (ir)relevant. 2. right, due, proper. 3. F good, sound: *j-m e-n ~en Schrecken einjagen* put the fear of God into s.o. II *adv* 4. duly, properly: → *Meinung.*

ge'hörlos *adj* deaf. **Ge'hörlosenschule** *f* school for the deaf.

Ge'hörnerv *m* auditory nerve.

gehörnt [gə'hœrnt] *adj* horned: *~er Ehemann* cuckolded husband.

gehorsam [gə'hoːrzaːm] *adj* obedient (*gegen* to). **Ge'horsam** *m* (-s; *no pl*) obedience (*gegen*[*über*] to): *j-m den ~ verweigern* disobey s.o.

Ge'hörsinn *m* (-[e]s; *no pl*) → *Gehör.*

'**Gehsteig** *m* pavement, *Am.* sidewalk.

Ge'hupe *n* (-s; *no pl*) F blaring horns.

'**Gehversuch** *m* attempt to walk.

Geier ['gaɪɐ] *m* (-s; -) *a. fig.* vulture.

Geifer ['gaɪfɐ] *m* (-s; *no pl*) 1. slaver, foam. 2. *fig.* venom. **geifern** *v/i* (h) 1. dribble, slaver. 2. *fig.* ~ *gegen* rail at.

Geige ['gaɪgə] *f* (-; -n) violin: (*auf der*) ~ *spielen* play (on) the violin; (*die*) *erste* (*zweite*) ~ *spielen* play first (second) violin (*fig.* fiddle).

geigen ['gaɪgən] *v/i* (h) play the violin.

'**Geigen|bauer** *m* (-s; -) violin-maker. *~harz* *n* resin. *~kasten* *m* violin case. *~strich* *m* stroke (of the bow).

Geiger ['gaɪgɐ] *m* (-s; -), **'Geigerin** *f* (-; -nen) violinist.

'**Geigerzähler** *m* Geiger counter.

geil [gaɪl] *adj* 1. F *contp.* a) randy, V horny, b) lecherous: *fig.* ~ *sein auf* (*acc*) be hot for, be dead keen on. 2. rank (*plant*). 3. F (*echt*) ~ hot, terrific.

Geisel ['gaɪzəl] *f* (-; -n) (*j-n als* ~ *nehmen* take s.o.) hostage. '**Geiseldrama**

n hostage drama. '**Geiselnahme** *f* (-; -n) taking of hostages. '**Geiselnehmer** *m* (-s; -) hostage-taker.

Geiß [gaɪs] *f* (-; -en) *zo.* 1. (nanny) goat. 2. doe.

Geißel ['gaɪsəl] *f* (-; -n) 1. whip. 2. *biol.* flagellum. 3. *fig.* scourge. '**geißeln** *v/t* (h) whip, *eccl.* flagellate, *fig.* castigate. '**Geißeltierchen** *n* flagellate. '**Geißelung** *f* (-; -en) 1. flagellation. 2. *fig.* castigation.

Geist [gaɪst] *m* (-[e]s; -er) 1. *no pl* a) mind, intellect, b) spirit, c) wit: ~ *und Körper* mind and body; *ein Mann von* ~ a (man of) wit; *im* ~ a. in one's mind's eye, b) *be with s.o.* in one's thoughts; *humor.* *den* ~ *aufgeben* give up the ghost, *engine etc: a.* conk out; F *j-m auf den* ~ *gehen* get on s.o.'s nerves; → *scheiden* III. 2. *no pl* spirit, morale: *der* ~ *der Zeit* the spirit of the times; *wes* ~*es Kind er ist* what sort of person he is. 3. spirit, ghost: *böser* ~ evil spirit, demon; *der Heilige* ~ the Holy Ghost. 4. mind: *ein großer* ~ a great mind (*or* thinker).

'**Geister|bahn** *f* ghost train. *~beschwörung* *f* exorcism. *~bild* *n* TV double image. *~erscheinung* *f* apparition. *~fahrer* *m* wrong-way driver, *Am.* ghost driver.

'**geisterhaft** *adj* ghostly.

'**Geisterhand** *f wie von* ~ as if by magic.

'**Geisterstadt** *f* ghost town.

'**Geisterstunde** *f* witching hour.

'**geistesabwesend** *adj* absent-minded.

'**Geistesabwesenheit** *f* (-; *no pl*) absent-mindedness.

'**Geistes|arbeit** *f* brainwork. *~blitz* *m* (flash of) inspiration, brainwave.

'**Geistesgegenwart** *f* presence of mind.

'**geistesgegenwärtig** *adv* ~ *sprang er zur Seite* he had the presence of mind to jump aside.

'**Geistesgeschichte** *f* (-; *no pl*) history of thought (*or* ideas): *die deutsche* ~ the history of German thought.

'**geistesgestört** *adj* mentally disturbed.

'**geisteskrank** *adj* mentally ill, *a. contp.* insane. '**Geisteskranke** *m*, *f* (-n; -n) insane person, mental case (*or* patient), *pl the* mentally ill. '**Geisteskrankheit** *f* insanity, mental disease (*or* illness).

'**Geistes|leben** *n* (-s; *no pl*) intellectual

life. **~schwach** *adj* feeble-minded. **~schwäche** *f* (-; *no pl*) feeble-mindedness. **~störung** *f* mental disorder. **~verfassung** *f* frame of mind. **~verwandt** *adj* congenial. **~verwirrung** *f* confused state of mind. **~wissenschaft** *f* arts subject, *pl the* arts, the humanities. **~wissenschaftler** *m* 1. scholar. 2. arts student. **~wissenschaftlich** *adj* arts ... **~zerrüttung** *f* mental derangement, dementia. **~zustand** *m* (-[e]s; *no pl*) mental state.

'geistig¹ *adj* a) mental (*a. psych.*), b) intellectual, c) spiritual: **~es Eigentum** intellectual property; **~ anspruchsvoll** demanding, highbrow; **~ behindert** mentally handicapped; → *Diebstahl*.

'geistig² *adj* **~e Getränke** spirits, alcoholic drinks.

'geistlich *adj* 1. religious, spiritual, sacred (*music etc*): **~er Orden** religious order. 2. clerical, ecclesiastical: **der ~e Stand** the clergy; **~es Amt** ministry.

'Geistliche *m* (-n; -n) clergyman, (*Protestant*) minister, (*Catholic*) priest, ✗ chaplain, padre.

'Geistlichkeit *f* (-; *no pl*) the clergy.

'geistlos *adj* trivial, dull, insipid, stupid.

'Geistlosigkeit *f* (-; -en) 1. *no pl* lack of wit, dullness, insipidity. 2. platitude.

'geistreich *adj* witty, clever, brilliant.

'geisttötend *adj* soul-destroying.

'geistvoll *adj* 1. witty. 2. profound.

Geiz [gaɪts] *m* (-es; *no pl*) stinginess, meanness. **'geizen** *v/i* (*h*) be stingy (*mit* with); **mit Lob ~** be sparing with one's praise. **'Geizhals** *m* miser, F meanie. **'geizig** *adj* miserly, stingy, mean.

Ge'jammer *n* (-s; *no pl*) F *contp.* moaning, (endless) lamentation.

Gejohle [gə'joːlə] *n* (-s; *no pl*) F howling.

gekannt [gə'kant] *pp of* **kennen**.

Gekicher [gə'kɪçər] *n* (-s; *no pl*) F *contp.* giggling, (happy) tittering.

Gekläff [gə'klɛf] *n* (-[e]s; *no pl*) F *contp.* yapping.

Ge'klapper *n* (-s; *no pl*) F rattling.

Geklimper [gə'klɪmpər] *n* (-s; *no pl*) F *contp.* tinkling.

geklungen [gə'klʊŋən] *pp of* **klingen**.

geknickt [gə'knɪkt] *adj* F *fig.* crestfallen.

gekniffen [gə'knɪfən] *pp of* **kneifen**.

Geknister [gə'knɪstər] *n* (-s; *no pl*) F *contp.* rustling.

ge'kommen *pp of* **kommen**.

gekonnt [gə'kɔnt] **I** *pp of* **können**. **II** *adj* competent, masterly.

gekränkt [gə'krɛŋkt] *adj* offended, hurt.

Gekreisch [gə'kraɪʃ] *n* (-[e]s; *no pl*) screaming, shrieking.

Gekritzel [gə'krɪtsəl] *n* (-s; *no pl*) *contp.* scrawl(ing), scribbling, scribble.

gekrochen [gə'krɔxən] *pp of* **kriechen**.

gekünstelt [gə'kʏnstəlt] *adj* affected.

gekürzt [gə'kʏrtst] *adj* abridged.

Gel [geːl] *n* (-s; -e) ⚗, *cosmetics*: gel.

Gelächter [gə'lɛçtər] *n* (-s; -) laughter.

ge'laden I *pp of* **laden¹** and **laden²**. **II** *adj* 1. loaded, ✗ *a.* charged. 2. F *auf j-n* **~ sein** be furious (*or* mad) at s.o.

Ge'lage *n* (-s; -) feast, banquet.

ge'lagert *adj fig. anders ~* different; *in besonders ~en Fällen* in special cases.

Gelände [gə'lɛndə] *n* (-s; -) country, ground, terrain, site. **Gelände...** cross-country (*car, race, etc*).

ge'ländegängig *adj mot.* all-terrain.

Geländer [gə'lɛndər] *n* (-s; -) a) railing, b) banisters, c) balustrade.

gelang [gə'laŋ] *pret of* **gelingen**.

ge'langen *v/i* (sn) 1. **~ an** (*acc*) (*or nach, zu, auf acc*) reach, arrive at, get (*or come*) to; **ans Ziel ~** a) reach one's destination, b) *fig.* achieve one's end, F make it; **in den Besitz ~ von** (*or gen*) get hold of, acquire; **in j-s Hände ~** get into (*or reach*) s.o.'s hands. 2. **zu et. ~** win (*or gain, achieve*) s.th.; **zu Reichtum ~** become rich; → *Ansicht* 1, *Erkenntnis, Macht* 1. 3. **zur Aufführung ~** be performed.

ge'langweilt *adj and adv* bored.

ge'lassen I *pp of* **lassen**. **II** *adj* calm, composed. **Ge'lassenheit** *f* (-; *no pl*) calmness, composure: **mit ~** calmly.

Gelatine [ʒela'tiːnə] *f* (-; -n) gelatine.

ge'laufen *pp of* **laufen**.

ge'läufig *adj* 1. a) common, current (*expression etc*), b) familiar: **das ist mir ~** I'm familiar with that. 2. fluent.

Ge'läufigkeit *f* (-; *no pl*) 1. familiarity. 2. fluency.

gelaunt [gə'laʊnt] *adj* **gut** (**schlecht**) **~ sein** be in a good (bad) mood.

Geläut [gə'lɔʏt] *n* (-[e]s; *no pl*) ringing.

gelb [gɛlp] *adj*, **Gelb** *n* (-s; -, F -s) yellow, *traffic lights*: amber: **bei Gelb** at amber; **Gelbe Seiten** Yellow Pages.

Gelbe ['gɛlbə] n (-n; no pl) yolk: F **auch nicht das ~ vom Ei!** not all that good!
'**Gelbfilter** n, m phot. yellow filter.
'**gelblich** adj yellowish.
'**Gelbsucht** f (-; no pl) ✽ jaundice.
Geld [gɛlt] n (-[e]s; -er) money: **~er** funds, money; **bares ~** cash; **großes ~** notes, Am. bills; **kleines ~** change; F **das große ~ machen** make big money, make a packet; **et. zu ~ machen** turn s.th. into cash, sell s.th. off; **um ~ spielen** play for money; F **im ~ schwimmen** be rolling in money; **das geht ins ~** that costs a packet; **~ spielt k-e Rolle** money is no object; → **Heu.**
'**Geld|abwertung** f (currency) devaluation. **~angelegenheiten** pl money (or financial) matters. **~anlage** f investment. **~anweisung** f money order, remittance. **~aufwertung** f (currency) revaluation. **~ausgabe** f (financial) expenditure. **~auto,mat** m cash dispenser. **~betrag** m amount (or sum) of money. **~beutel** m purse. **~buße** f fine. **~einwurf** m 1. insertion of coins. 2. (coin) slot. **~entwertung** f currency depreciation, inflation. **~geber** m financial backer, investor. **~geschäfte** pl money transactions. **~geschenk** n gift of money. **~gier** f greed for money, avarice. ℒ**gierig** adj greedy for money, avaricious. **~knappheit** f lack of money, (financial) stringency.
'**geldlich** adj financial, pecuniary.
'**Geld|mangel** m lack of money. **~mann** m (-[e]s; -leute) financier. **~markt** m money market. **~mittel** pl funds. **~prämie** f a) bonus, b) reward, c) award, (cash) prize. **~quelle** f source of money (or income). **~schein** m (bank)note, Am. bill. **~schrank** m safe. **~sendung** f (cash) remittance. **~sorgen** pl (financial) worries. **~spende** f donation, contribution. **~strafe** f (a. j-n mit e-r ~ belegen) fine. **~stück** n coin. **~umtausch** m exchange of money, conversion. **~verdienen** n (-s) moneymaking. **~verdiener(in** f) m moneymaker, breadwinner. **~verlegenheit** f financial embarrassment: **in ~ sein** be short of money, F be hard up. **~verschwendung** f waste of money. **~wäsche** f money laundering. **~wechsel** m 1. → **Geldumtausch.** 2. (office) Change. **~wechsler** m change

machine. **~wert** m cash (or currency) value.
Gelee [ʒe'leː] n (-s; -s) jelly.
ge'legen I pp of **liegen.** II adj 1. situated, located. 2. convenient, suitable: **es kommt mir sehr ~** it suits me fine.
Ge'legenheit f (-; -en) 1. opportunity, chance: **die ~ nutzen** (or **beim Schopf packen**) seize the opportunity; **die ~ verpassen** miss the chance; **bei der ersten besten ~** at the first opportunity; → **passend** 2. occasion: **bei ~** sometime; **bei dieser ~** on this occasion. 3. ✝ bargain.
Ge'legenheits|arbeit f casual work (or job). **~arbeiter** m casual labo(u)rer.
gelegentlich [gə'leːgəntlɪç] I adj occasional. II adv a) occasionally, a. sometimes, b) sometime.
gelehrig [gə'leːrɪç] adj clever, quick to learn. **gelehrt** [gə'leːrt] adj learned.
Ge'lehrte m, f (-n; -n) learned man (woman), scholar, scientist.
Geleit [gə'laɪt] n (-[e]s; -e) a. ✕ escort, ⚓ a. convoy: **freies ~** 🚊 safe-conduct.
ge'leiten v/t (h) escort (a. ⚓, ✕).
Ge'leit|schiff n escort ship. **~schutz** m escort, ⚓ a. convoy. **~zug** m ⚓ convoy.
Gelenk [gə'lɛŋk] n (-[e]s; -e) joint, ⚙ a. link. **ℒgelenk...** ⚙ articulated.
Ge'lenkentzündung f ✽ arthritis.
ge'lenkig adj flexible (a. ⚙), supple, lithe. **Ge'lenkigkeit** f (-; no pl) flexibility, suppleness, litheness.
Ge'lenkrheuma,tismus m ✽ articular rheumatism.
gelernt [gə'lɛrnt] adj trained.
ge'lesen pp of **lesen.**
geliebt [gə'liːpt] adj dear, beloved.
Ge'liebte¹ m (-n; -n) lover. **Ge'liebte²** f (-n; -n) a) love(r), sweetheart, b) mistress.
geliehen [gə'liːən] pp of **leihen.**
gelieren [ʒe'liːrən] v/i (h) jell.
gelinde [gə'lɪndə] adv ~ **gesagt** to put it mildly.
gelingen [gə'lɪŋən] v/i and v/impers (gelang, gelungen, sn) succeed, be successful, be a success, turn out well: **nicht ~** not to succeed (etc), fail; **ihm gelang die Flucht, es gelang ihm zu fliehen** he succeeded in escaping, he managed to escape; **es gelang ihm nicht(, das zu tun)** he failed (to bring it

off); *endlich ist es mir gelungen* at last I managed (*or* made) it.

Ge'lingen *n* (-s) success: *gutes ~!* good luck!; *auf gutes ~!* to success!

gelitten [gə'lɪtən] *pp of* **leiden.**

gellend ['gɛlənt] *adj* piercing, shrill: *~er Schrei* scream; *~ aufschreien* shriek (*vor dat* with).

ge'loben *v/t* (h) promise, vow, swear.

Gelöbnis [gə'løːpnɪs] *n* (-ses; -se) vow.

gelobt [gə'loːpt] *adj das Gelobte Land* Bibl. the Land of Promise.

gelogen [gə'loːgən] *pp of* **lügen.**

gelöst [gə'løːst] *adj fig.* relaxed.

gelten ['gɛltən] (galt, gegolten, h) I *v/t* **1.** be worth (*10 dollars etc*): *fig. wenig ~* count for little (*bei* with); *was er sagt, gilt* what he says goes; → **Wette.** II *v/i* **2.** be valid, be good, *contract etc:* be effective: (*weiterhin*) *~* hold (good); *~ für* apply to (F goes for) all of you; *~ lassen* allow (*a. sports*), (*als*) accept (as), let *s.o., s.th.* pass (for); *das lasse ich ~!* I'll agree to that!; *es gilt!* done!, it's a deal!; *das gilt nicht!* a) that's not allowed (*or* fair), b) *sports etc:* that doesn't count!; *mein Angebot gilt noch!* my offer still stands! **3.** *~ als* be regarded as, be considered to be: *4. j-m ~ remark etc:* be meant for (*or* aimed at) s.o. III *v/impers es gilt zu inf* it is necessary (for us *etc*) to *inf*; *es gilt als sicher, daß ...* it seems certain that ...

'**geltend** *adj* a) current(ly valid), *a.* effective (*law etc*), b) accepted, prevailing: *~ machen* assert, enforce (*claims, rights*), plead (*illness etc*); *~ machen, daß ...* maintain that ...; (*bei j-m*) *s-n Einfluß ~ machen* bring one's influence to bear (on s.o.).

'**Geltung** *f* (-; *no pl*) **1.** validity: *~ haben* → **gelten** 2. **2.** a) value, b) prestige: *an ~ verlieren* lose prestige. **3.** weight, influence, *of person:* authority: (*dat*) *~ verschaffen* enforce; *sich ~ verschaffen* make o.s. respected; *et. zur ~ bringen* show s.th. (off) to advantage; *zur ~ kommen* show to advantage.

'**Geltungsbedürfnis** *n,* '**geltungsbedürftig** *adj* craving for admiration.

Gelübde [gə'lʏpdə] *n* (-s; -) vow: *ein ~ ablegen* take (*or* make a) vow.

gelungen [gə'lʊŋən] I *pp of* **gelingen.** II *adj* successful: *die Party war ~* the party was a success.

Gelüst [gə'lʏst] *n* (-[e]s; -e) craving (*nach* for). **ge'lüsten** *v/impers* (h) *es gelüstet mich nach* I am craving for, I feel like.

gemächlich [gə'mɛːçlɪç] *adj* leisurely, unhurried.

gemacht [gə'maxt] *adj ein ~er Mann* a made man; *sie waren ~e Leute* they had got it made.

ge'mahlen *pp of* **mahlen.**

Gemälde [gə'mɛːldə] *n* (-s; -) painting, picture. *~ausstellung f* exhibition of paintings. *~gale,rie f* picture gallery.

gemäß [gə'mɛːs] (*dat*) I *adj* appropriate (to). II *prep* according to, in accordance with, pursuant to, under (*a law*).

gemäßigt [gə'mɛːsɪçt] *adj* **1.** moderate (*a. pol.*). **2.** *geogr.* temperate.

Gemecker [gə'mɛkər] *n* (-s) F *contp.* grouch, *sl.* bellyaching.

ge'mein *adj* **1.** *contp.* a) low, mean, nasty, F awful (*job etc*), b) vulgar, dirty, filthy (*joke etc*): *~er Trick* dirty trick. **2.** *et. ~ haben* have s.th. in common (*mit* with). **3.** common (*a. ♀, ♃, zo.*), general: *das ~e Volk* the common people.

Gemeinde [gə'maɪndə] *f* (-; -n) **1.** *pol.* a) municipality, b) local government (*or* authority), c) community. **2.** *eccl.* a) parish, b) parishioners, c) congregation. **3.** *fig.* following, audience.

Ge'meinde|amt *n* **1.** local authority. **2.** municipal office. *~bezirk m* district. *~haus n* **1.** parish hall. **2.** → **Gemeindezentrum.** *~rat m* municipal council (*person:* council[l]or). *~schwester f* district nurse. *~steuern pl* (local) rates, *Am.* local taxes. *~verwaltung f* → **Gemeinde** 1 b. *~vorstand m* local board. *~wahl f* local election. *~zentrum n* community cent/re (*Am.* -er).

ge'meingefährlich *adj* dangerous: *~ sein a.* be a public danger.

Ge'meingut *n* (-[e]s; *no pl*) *a. fig.* common property.

Ge'meinheit *f* (-; -en) **1.** *no pl* meanness, nastiness. **2.** mean thing (to do *or* say): *so e-e ~!* a) what a dirty trick!, b) what rotten luck!

ge'meinhin *adv* generally.

Ge'meinkosten *pl* overhead (cost).

gemeinnützig [gə'maɪnnʏtsɪç] *adj* for

the public benefit, public welfare ..., nonprofit(-making) (*organization etc*).

Ge'meinplatz *m* commonplace.

ge'meinsam I *adj* common (*a.* ♈), joint (*account, ownership, etc*), mutual: **~e Sache machen** make common cause (*mit* with); *vieles ~ haben* have a great deal in common; → *Nenner.* **II** *adv* jointly, together; **~ tun** do s.th. together; **~ vorgehen** take joint action.

Ge'meinsamkeit *f* (-; -en) **1.** common ground: **~en entdecken** discover things in common. **2.** *no pl* a) mutuality, b) solidarity.

Ge'meinschaft *f* (-; -en) a) community (*a. pol.*), b) team, c) association: *eheliche ~* ⚖ matrimony; *in enger ~ leben* live close together (*mit* with).

ge'meinschaftlich → *gemeinsam.*

Ge'meinschafts|anschluß *m teleph.* party line. **~antenne** *f* communal aerial (*Am.* antenna). **~arbeit** *f* teamwork. **~erziehung** *f* **1.** *ped.* coeducation. **2.** social education. **~geist** *m* community spirit. **~produkti,on** *f* coproduction. **~raum** *m* communal room. **~sendung** *f* simultaneous broadcast, hookup.

Ge'mein|schuldner *m* bankrupt. **~sinn** *m* (-[e]s; *no pl*) public spirit. **2verständlich** *adj* intelligible to all, popular. **~wesen** *n* **1.** community. **2.** polity.

ge'messen I *pp of* **messen. II** *adj fig.* **1.** measured. **2.** formal. **3.** solemn, grave.

Gemetzel [gə'mɛtsəl] *n* (-s; -) slaughter.

gemieden [gə'miːdən] *pp of* **meiden.**

Gemisch [gə'mɪʃ] *n* (-[e]s; -e) mixture.

ge'mischt *adj a. fig.* mixed. **ge'mischtwirtschaftlich** *adj* ⚓ mixed-type.

Gemme ['gɛmə] *f* (-; -n) gem.

gemocht [gə'mɔxt] *pp of* **mögen.**

gemolken [gə'mɔlkən] *pp of* **melken.**

'Gemsbock *m zo.* chamois buck.

Gemse ['gɛmzə] *f* (-; -n) *zo.* chamois.

Gemüse [gə'myːzə] *n* (-s; -) vegetable, *coll.* vegetables, greens. **~(an)bau** *m* (-[e]s; *no pl*) vegetable gardening, *Am.* truck farming. **~garten** *m* kitchen garden. **~händler** *m* greengrocer. **~konserven** *pl* tinned (*or* canned) vegetables. **~laden** *m* greengrocer's shop.

gemußt [gə'mʊst] *pp of* **müssen** II.

ge'mustert *adj* (*a. in sich ~*) patterned.

Gemüt [gə'myːt] *n* (-[e]s; -er) **1.** *no pl* mind, soul, heart, feeling, disposition,

nature: F *sich e-e Flasche Wein zu ~e führen* get outside a bottle of wine. **2.** soul: *die ~er bewegen* cause quite a stir; → *erhitzen* I.

ge'mütlich *adj* **1.** comfortable, snug, cosy, pleasant: *mach es dir ~!* a) make yourself at home!, b) *a. sei ~!* relax! **2.** good-natured, pleasant (*person*). **3.** leisurely, unhurried. **Ge'mütlichkeit** *f* (-; *no pl*) **1.** cosiness (*etc*). **2.** cosy (*or* relaxed) atmosphere. **3.** leisure(liness).

Ge'müts|art *f* disposition, nature. **~bewegung** *f* emotion. **2krank** *adj* emotionally disturbed. **~krankheit** *f* emotional disturbance, mental disorder. **~mensch** *m* F a) warm-hearted person, b) *iro.* callous beast. **~ruhe** *f* peace of mind: *in aller ~* calmly, *iro.* as cool as you please. **~verfassung** *f*, **~zustand** *m* frame of mind, (mental) state.

ge'mütvoll *adj* a) soulful, sentimental, b) warm(-hearted) (*person*).

Gen [geːn] *n* (-s; -e) *biol.* gene.

genannt [gə'nant] *pp of* **nennen.**

genas [gə'naːs] *pret of* **genesen.**

genau [gə'naʊ] **I** *adj* a) exact, accurate, precise, b) detailed (*report etc*), c) careful, d) strict: *Genaueres* particulars, further details; *man weiß nichts Genaues* we don't know anything definite. **II** *adv* exactly (*etc*): *~ das Gegenteil* exactly (*or* just) the opposite; *~ das, was ich brauche* just what I need; *~ in der Mitte* right in the middle; *~ (um) 10 Uhr* (at) ten o'clock sharp; *~ zuhören* listen closely; *ich weiß es ~* I know it for sure; *sich ~ an die Regeln halten* keep strictly to the rules; *es nicht sehr ~ nehmen* not to be particular (*mit* about); (*stimmt*) *~!* exactly!

ge'naugenommen *adv* strictly speaking, to be exact.

Ge'nauigkeit *f* (-; *no pl*) exactness, accuracy, precision, thoroughness.

ge'nauso → *ebenso.*

ge'nausogut → *ebensogut.*

Genealogie [genealo'giː] *f* (-; *no pl*) genealogy.

genehm [gə'neːm] *adj j-m ~ sein* suit s.o.

genehmigen [gə'neːmɪgən] *v/t* (h) approve (*a. adm.*, ⚖), permit, *adm.* authorize: F *sich e-n ~* have a drink.

Ge'nehmigung *f* (-; -en) **1.** approval, permission, authorization. **2.** permit.

geneigt [gə'naıkt] *adj* inclined (**zu** to).
General [gene'ra:l] *m* (-s; -e, ∗e) general.
Gene'ral... general (*agency, amnesty, etc*). **∼baß** *m* ♪ basso continuo. **∼bevollmächtigte** *m, f* (-n; -n) **1.** *pol.* plenipotentiary. **2.** ✝ general representative. **∼di,rektor** *m* general manager. **∼konsul** *m* consul general. **∼konsu,lat** *n* consulate general. **∼leutnant** *m* lieutenant general. **∼ma,jor** *m* major general. **∼probe** *f a. fig.* dress rehearsal. **∼sekre,tär(in** *f*) *m* secretary-general. **∼staatsanwalt** *m* Chief State Prosecutor. **∼stab** *m* ✕ General Staff. **∼stabskarte** *f* (*1:100 000*) ordnance survey map, *Am.* strategic map. **∼streik** *m* general strike. **∼überholung** *f* ⊙ complete overhaul. **∼versammlung** *f* **1.** ✝ general meeting. **2.** *pol.* General Assembly (of the UN). **∼vertreter** *m* general agent. **∼vollmacht** *f* general power of attorney.
Generation [genera'tsĭo:n] *f* (-; -en) generation. **Generati'onskon,flikt** *m* generation gap.
Generator [gene'ra:tor] *m* (-s; -en [-ra'to:rən]) ⚡ generator.
generell [gene'rɛl] *adj* general.
genesen [gə'ne:zən] *v/i* (genas, genesen, sn) recover (**von** from), get well.
Ge'nesung *f* (-; *no pl*) a) convalescence, b) recovery. **Ge'nesungs...** convalescent (*home, leave, etc*).
Genetik [ge'ne:tık] *f* (-; *no pl*) genetics.
Genetiker [ge'ne:tıkər] *m* (-s; -) genetic scientist. **ge'netisch** *adj* genetic.
genial [ge'nĭa:l] *adj* of genius, inspired, brilliant, ingenious: *e-e ∼e Idee* a. iro. a brilliant idea. **Genialität** [genĭali'tɛ:t] *f* (-; *no pl*) genius, brilliancy, ingenuity.
Genick [gə'nık] *n* (-[e]s; -e) (back of the) neck: (*sich*) *das ∼ brechen* break one's neck; *fig. das brach ihm das ∼* that was his undoing.
Ge'nickschuß *m* shot in the neck.
Genie [ʒe'ni:] *n* (-s; -s) genius.
genieren [ʒe'ni:rən] (h) **I** *v/t* **j-n ∼** a) embarrass s.o., b) bother s.o. **II** *sich ∼* be embarrassed, be shy; **∼** *Sie sich nicht!* don't be shy!
ge'nießbar *adj* edible, eatable, drinkable. **genießen** [gə'ni:sən] *v/t* (genoß, genossen, h) **1.** enjoy. **2.** have, eat, drink. **3.** *fig.* enjoy, have (*reputation*

etc), receive, get (*education etc*): *j-s Vertrauen ∼* be in s.o.'s confidence.
Ge'nießer *m* (-s; -) bon vivant.
Genitalien [geni'ta:lĭən] *pl* genitals.
Genitiv ['ge:niti:f] *m* (-s; -e) *ling.* genitive (case), possessive (case).
Genius ['ge:nĭus] *m* (-; *no pl*) genius.
genommen [gə'nɔmən] *pp of* **nehmen.**
genormt [gə'nɔrmt] *adj* standardized.
genoß [gə'nɔs] *pret of* **genießen.**
Genosse [gə'nɔsə] *m* (-n; -n), **Ge'nossin** *f* (-; -nen) **1.** *pol.* comrade. **2.** F pal.
genossen [gə'nɔsən] *pp of* **genießen.**
Ge'nossenschaft *f* (-; -en), **ge'nossenschaftlich** *adj* ✝ cooperative.
Genre [ʒã:r] *n* (-s; -s) genre.
'Gentechnolo,gie *f* genetic engineering.
genug [gə'nu:k] *adj and adv* enough, sufficient(ly): *mehr als ∼* more than enough; *ich habe nicht ∼ Zeit* I haven't enough time (*or* time enough) *to do it*; *∼* (*davon*)*!* enough (of that)!; *ich habe ∼ davon!* I've had enough of that!
Genüge [gə'ny:gə] **1.** *zur ∼* a) enough, sufficiently, b) only too well, c) often enough. **2. ∼ tun** (*dat*) → **genügen 2.**
ge'nügen *v/i* (h) **1.** be enough, be sufficient: *das genügt* (*mir*)*!* that's enough (for me)!, that'll do (for me)!; *j-m* a. that's good enough (for me)! **2.** satisfy, meet (*requirements etc*). **ge'nügend** *adj* **1.** *a. adv* → **genug. 2.** satisfactory.
genügsam [gə'ny:kza:m] *adj* content with little, modest, frugal. **Ge'nügsamkeit** *f* (-; *no pl*) modesty, frugality.
Ge'nugtuung *f* (-; *no pl*) (*über acc* at) satisfaction, gratification: *mit ∼ hören, daß ...* be gratified to hear that ...
Genuß [gə'nʊs] *m* (-sses; ∗sse) **1.** *no pl* a) consumption, eating, drinking, b) taking (*of drugs*). **2.** pleasure: *mit ∼* with relish; *ein wahrer ∼* a real treat. **3.** *a.* ⚖ enjoyment: *in den ∼ e-r Sache kommen* get (the benefit of) s.th.
Ge'nußmittel *n* **1.** semiluxury food, drink, and tobacco. **2.** stimulant.
ge'nußsüchtig *adj* hedonistic.
Geodäsie [geodɛ'zi:] *f* (-; *no pl*) geodesy.
Geograph [geo'gra:f] *m* (-en; -en) geographer. **Geographie** [geogra'fi:] *f* (-; *no pl*) geography. **geographisch** [geo-'gra:fıʃ] *adj* geographic(al).
Geologe [geo'lo:gə] *m* (-n; -n) geologist.

Geologie [geolo'giː] f (-; no pl) geology.
geologisch [geo'loːɡɪʃ] adj geological.
Geometer [geo'meːtər] m (-s; -) surveyor. **Geometrie** [geome'triː] f (-; -n) geometry. **geometrisch** [geo'meːtrɪʃ] adj geometric(al).
Geophy'sik f geophysics.
Geopoli'tik f geopolitics.
geopo'litisch adj geopolitical.
Gepäck [ɡə'pɛk] n (-[e]s; no pl) luggage, esp. Am. baggage. **~abfertigung** f 1. ✈ luggage (esp. Am. baggage) processing, ✈ checking-in of luggage (esp. Am. baggage). 2. luggage (esp. Am. baggage) office, ✈ check-in counter. **~ablage** f luggage rack (esp. Am. baggage) rack. **~aufbewahrung** f left-luggage office, Am. baggage room. **~kon,trolle** f luggage (esp. Am. baggage) check. **~schein** m luggage ticket, Am. baggage check. **~stück** n piece of luggage (esp. Am. baggage). **~träger** m 1. porter. 2. on bike: carrier, mot. roof rack. **~wagen** m 🚃 luggage van, Am. baggage car.
ge'panzert adj armo(u)red.
Gepard [ɡe'part] m (-s; -e) zo. cheetah.
ge'pfeffert adj steep (prices etc), tough (test etc), sharp (letter etc), juicy (joke).
gepfiffen [ɡə'pfɪfən] pp of pfeifen.
ge'pflegt adj 1. well-groomed. 2. select, excellent (wine). 3. cultured, refined.
Gepflogenheit [ɡə'pfloːɡənhaɪt] f (-; -en) habit, custom, ✝ etc practice.
Geplänkel [ɡə'plɛŋkəl] n (-s; -) a. fig. skirmish.
Ge'plapper n (-s; no pl) F babbling, contp. a. chatter(ing).
Ge'plauder n (-s; no pl) chatting, chat.
Ge'polter n (-s; no pl) rumbling.
Gepräge [ɡə'prɛːɡə] n (-s; no pl) fig. stamp, character.
gepriesen [ɡə'priːzən] pp of preisen.
ge'quält adj pained, forced (smile).
Ge'quassel n (-s; no pl), **Ge'quatsche** n (-s; no pl) F blather.
gequollen [ɡə'kvɔlən] pp of quellen.
gerade [ɡə'raːdə] I adj 1. a) straight, b) upright, erect, c) even (a. number). 2. fig. straight, sincere, upright. II adv 3. just: **~ erst** only just; **nicht ~ schön** not exactly beautiful etc; **er wollte ~ gehen** he was just about to leave; **ich war ~ dort als ...** I happened to be there

when ...; **nun ~!** now more than ever!; **~ du!** especially you!; **warum ~ ich?** why me of all people?; **~ an diesem Tag** on that very day.
Ge'rade f (-n; -n) 1. ✏ straight line. 2. sports: straight: **linke (rechte) ~** boxing: straight left (right).
gerade'aus adv straight ahead (or on).
ge'radebiegen v/t (irr, sep, -ge-, h, → biegen) F fig. straighten out.
geradeher'aus adv openly, bluntly.
gerädert [ɡə'rɛːdərt] adj F fig. (**wie ~**) whacked.
ge'radeso etc → ebenso etc.
ge'radestehen v/i (irr, sep, -ge-, h, → stehen) fig. answer (**für** for).
ge'radewegs adv a) straight, directly, b) straightaway.
ge'radezu¹ adv almost, next to, really.
gerade'zu² adv openly, bluntly.
Geradheit [ɡə'raːthaɪt] f (-; no pl) straightness, fig. a. uprightness.
geradlinig [ɡə'raːtliːnɪç] adj 1. straight (a. adv), lineal, direct (descent etc), linear (motion). 2. fig. straight(forward).
gerammelt [ɡə'raməlt] adj F **~ voll (von)** chock-full (of), jam-packed (with).
Gerangel [ɡə'raŋəl] n (-s; no pl) (**um** over) F tussle, fig. a. wrangling.
gerann [ɡə'ran] pret of gerinnen.
gerannt [ɡə'rant] pp of rennen.
Gerät [ɡə'rɛːt] n (-[e]s; -e) 1. ⚙ device, instrument, appliance, apparatus (a. gym.), F gadget. 2. (radio or TV) set. 3. coll. a) equipment, gear, b) tools, c) utensils. 4. (motorbike etc) machine.
ge'raten v/i (geriet, geraten, sn) 1. turn out (**zu kurz** too short etc). 2. **~ an** (acc) come across s.o., come by (or get) s.th.; **an e-n Betrüger ~** fall into the hands of a swindler; **in Schwierigkeiten ~** get into difficulties; **in e-n Sturm ~** be caught in a storm; → Abweg, Adresse, außer 1, Bahn 1, Brand 1 etc. 3. **~ nach** take after (one's father etc).
ge'raten² II pp of raten and geraten¹. II adj advisable.
Ge'räteschuppen m toolshed.
Ge'räteturnen n apparatus gymnastics.
Gerate'wohl n F **aufs ~** at random.
Ge'rätschaften pl → Gerät 3.
Ge'ratter n (-s; no pl) rattling, rattle.
geräumig [ɡə'rɔʏmɪç] adj roomy, spa-

cious. **Ge'räumigkeit** f (-; no pl) roominess, spaciousness.

Geräusch [gə'rɔʏʃ] n (-[e]s; -e) sound, a. ☺ noise. **ge'räuscharm** adj noiseless, silent. **Ge'räuschdämpfung** f (-; -en) silencing. **Ge'räuschku,lisse** f background noise. **ge'räuschlos** adj ☺ noiseless, silent, quiet. **Ge'räuschlosigkeit** f (-; no pl) noiselessness. **Ge'räuschpegel** m decibel (or noise) level. **ge'räuschvoll** adj noisy, loud.

gerben ['gɛrbən] v/t (h) tan. '**Gerber** m (-s; -) tanner. **Gerbe'rei** f (-; -en) tannery. **Gerbsäure** ['gɛrp-] f tannic acid.

ge'recht adj 1. just, fair. 2. (dat) ~ **werden** do justice to (s.o., s.th.), meet, fulfil(l) (requirements etc), come up to (expectations). **ge'rechterweise** adv 1. justly. 2. to be fair.

ge'rechtfertigt adj justified.

Ge'rechtigkeit f (-; no pl) justice, fairness: → **widerfahren**.

Ge'rechtigkeitssinn m sense of justice.

Ge'rede n (-s; no pl) F 1. (leeres ~ idle) talk. 2. gossip: **ins ~ kommen** get o.s. talked about, set tongues wagging.

ge'regelt adj regular.

ge'reizt adj irritable, irritated (a. ✶).

Ge'reiztheit f (-; no pl) irritation.

Geriatrie [geria'tri:] f (-; no pl) geriatrics.

Gericht¹ [gə'rɪçt] n (-[e]s; -e) gastr. 1. dish. 2. course.

Ge'richt² n (-[e]s; -e) a) (law) court, fig. tribunal, b) the court, c) courthouse: **das Jüngste ~** eccl. the Last Judgement; **vor ~ bringen** take s.o., s.th. to court; **vor ~ gehen** go to court; **vor ~ aussagen** testify in court; **j-n vor ~ stellen** bring s.o. to trial; fig. **mit j-m ins ~ gehen** take s.o. to task; **zu ~ sitzen über** (acc) sit in judg(e)ment on.

ge'richtlich adj judicial, legal.

Ge'richtsbarkeit f (-; no pl) jurisdiction.

Ge'richts|beschluß m court order: **durch ~** by order of the court. **~gebäude** n law court, courthouse. **~hof** m court of justice, law court. **~kosten** pl costs (of an action). **~medi,zin** f forensic medicine. **~medi,ziner** m medical expert (Am. examiner). **~referen,dar(in** f) m junior lawyer (who has passed his/her first State Examination). **~saal** m courtroom. **~stand** m venue,

legal domicile, place of jurisdiction. **~urteil** n a) sentence, b) judg(e)ment. **~verfahren** n 1. a) (legal) proceedings, lawsuit, b) trial. 2. court procedure. **~verhandlung** f a) (judicial) hearing, b) trial. **~vollzieher** m bailiff, Am. marshal. **~weg** m auf dem ~ by legal proceedings; **den ~ einschlagen** take legal action.

gerieben [gə'ri:bən] pp of reiben.

geriet [gə'ri:t] pret of geraten¹.

gering [gə'rɪŋ] adj a) little, small, slight, b) low (price etc), a. poor (opinion etc), slim (chance, hope, etc), minor (importance etc): **in ~erem Maße** to a less degree; **kein ~erer als** no less a person than; **nicht im ~sten** not in the least; **das soll m-e ~ste Sorge sein!** that's the least of my worries!; → **Chance.**

ge'ringachten v/t (sep, -ge-, h) 1. think little of. 2. disregard (danger etc).

ge'ringfügig [-fy:gɪç] adj insignificant, negligible, slight, minor, small, petty.

Ge'ringfügigkeit f (-; no pl) insignificance, slightness, smallness.

ge'ringschätzig [-ʃɛtsɪç] adj contemptuous, disparaging.

Ge'ringschätzung f (-; no pl) (für, gen) disdain (of), low regard (for).

ge'rinnen v/i (gerann, geronnen, sn) coagulate, clot, milk: curdle.

Gerinnsel [gə'rɪnzəl] n (-s; -) ✶ clot.

Ge'rinnung f (-; no pl) coagulation, clotting, curdling.

Gerippe [gə'rɪpə] n (-s; -) a. fig. skeleton.

ge'rippt adj ribbed.

gerissen [gə'rɪsən] I pp of reißen. II adj F fig. cunning, crafty.

geritten [gə'rɪtən] pp of reiten.

Germane [gɛr'ma:nə] m (-n; -n), **Ger'manin** f (-; -nen) Teuton.

ger'manisch adj Germanic (a. ling.), Teutonic. **Germanist** [gɛrma'nɪst] m (-en; -en), **Germa'nistin** f (-; -nen) Germanist, a. student of German.

Germanistik [gɛrma'nɪstɪk] f (-; no pl) German (studies or philology).

gern [gɛrn], '**gerne** adv gladly, with pleasure: (ja,) ~! a) yes, certainly!, b) I'd love to!; (aber) ~! of course!, gladly!; **herzlich** (or **liebend**) ~! with great pleasure!; ~ **geschehen!** not at all!, (you're) welcome!; ~ **haben** like, be fond of; (sehr) ~ **tun** a) like (love) to do (*or* doing), b) tend to do; **~ essen (trinken)** like; **~ lesen** like reading; **ich hätte ~ e-e Tasse Tee** I'd like a cup of tea; **ich möchte ~ wissen, ob ...** a) I'd like to know if ..., b) I wonder if ...; **er kann ~ kommen!** a) he's welcome!, b) I don't mind if he comes!; **das kannst du ~ haben!** you're welcome to it!; **er sieht es nicht ~** he doesn't like it; F **du kannst mich ~ haben!** go to blazes!

'Gernegroß *m* (-; -e) F show-off.

gerochen [gə'rɔxən] *pp of* **riechen**.

Geröll [gə'rœl] *n* (-[e]s; -e) scree, rubble.

geronnen [gə'rɔnən] *pp of* **gerinnen** *and* **rinnen**.

Gerste ['gɛrstə] *f* (-; -n) ♆ barley.

'Gerstenkorn *n* **1.** barleycorn. **2.** ♂ sty.

Gerte ['gɛrtə] *f* (-; -n) switch, twig.

'gertenschlank *adj* (slim and) willowy.

Geruch [gə'rʊx] *m* (-[e]s; ⸚e) smell, scent, *b.s.* odo(u)r (*a. fig.*).

ge'ruchlos *adj* odo(u)rless.

Ge'ruchs|nerv *m* olfactory nerve. **~sinn** *m* (-[e]s; *no pl*) (sense of) smell.

Gerücht [gə'rʏçt] *n* (-[e]s; -e) rumo(u)r: **es geht das ~** it is rumo(u)red.

gerufen [gə'ru:fən] *pp of* **rufen**.

ge'ruhen *v/t* (h) **~, et. zu tun** deign to do s.th.

ge'rührt *adj fig.* touched, moved.

Gerümpel [gə'rʏmpəl] *n* (-s; *no pl*) junk.

Gerundium [ge'rʊndiʊm] *n* (-s; -dien) *ling.* gerund.

gerungen [gə'rʊŋən] *pp of* **ringen**.

Gerüst [gə'rʏst] *n* (-[e]s; -e) **1.** a) scaffold(ing), b) stage, c) frame. **2.** *fig.* frame(work).

ge'rüttelt *adj fig.* **ein ~ Maß an** (*dat*) a fair amount of.

ges, Ges [gɛs] *n* (-; -) ♩ G flat.

ge'salzen I *pp of* **salzen**. **II** *adj* **1.** salted. **2.** → **gepfeffert**.

ge'sammelt *adj* **1. ~e Werke** collected works. **2.** *fig.* concentrated.

gesamt [gə'zamt] *adj* **1.** whole, entire, all. **2.** total (*amount etc*).

Ge'samt|ansicht *f* general view. **~auflage** *f* a) total circulation, b) total number of copies published. **~ausgabe** *f* **1.** complete edition. **2.** *pl* ♱ total expenditure. **~betrag** *m* total (amount). **~bevölkerung** *f* total population. **~bild** *n* overall picture. ⚥**deutsch** *adj* all-German. **~eindruck** *m* general impression.

Ge'samtheit *f* (-; *no pl*) totality, *the* whole: **die ~ der Arbeiter** all the workers; **in s-r ~** in its entirety, as a whole.

Ge'samt|hochschule *f* comprehensive university. **~kosten** *pl* overall (*or* total) cost. **~länge** *f* overall length. **~note** *f ped.* aggregate mark. **~schule** *f* comprehensive school. **~sieger(in** *f*) *m* overall winner. **~summe** *f* (sum) total, total amount. **~werk** *n* complete works. **~zahl** *f* total (number).

gesandt [gə'zant] *pp of* **senden²**.

Gesandte [gə'zantə] *m,f* (-n; -n) envoy.

Ge'sandtschaft *f* (-; -en) legation.

Gesang [gə'zaŋ] *m* (-[e]s; ⸚e) **1.** *no pl* singing: **~ studieren** study voice. **2.** song. **Ge'sangbuch** *n eccl.* hymnbook. **Ge'sanglehrer(in** *f*) *m* singing teacher. **ge'sanglich** *adj* vocal. **Ge'sangunterricht** *m* singing lessons. **Ge'sangverein** *m* choral society.

Gesäß [gə'zɛ:s] *n* (-es; -e) buttocks, F bottom. **Ge'säßtasche** *f* back pocket.

ge'schaffen *pp of* **schaffen**.

Geschäft [gə'ʃɛft] *n* (-[e]s; -e) **1.** a) business, b) trade, c) (business) deal, transaction: **ein gutes (schlechtes) ~** a good (bad) deal; **ein gutes ~ machen** make a good profit (F a packet) (**mit** out of); **~e machen mit** deal in, *w.s.* make money out of; **mit j-m ~e machen, mit j-m ins ~ kommen** do business with s.o.; **gut im ~ sein** be doing well; **~ ist ~!** business is business!; **er versteht sein ~!** he knows his business (*or* stuff)! **2.** a) enterprise, firm, b) office, c) shop, store. **3.** *fig.* business, affair.

ge'schäftehalber *adv* on business.

Ge'schäftemacher *m contp.* profiteer.

ge'schäftig *adj* busy, active.

Ge'schäftigkeit *f* (-; *no pl*) activity.

ge'schäftlich *adj* business, commercial: **~ verreist** away on business; **~ zu tun haben** have (some) business (**mit** with); **~ verhindert** prevented by business.

Ge'schäfts|abschluß *m* (business) transaction (*or* deal). **~bedingungen** *pl* terms of business. **~bereich** *m* sphere of activity, scope, *pol.* portfolio, ⚖ jurisdiction. **~bericht** *m* (business) report. **~beziehungen** *pl* business connections. **~brief** *m* business letter. ⚥**fähig** *adj* competent, having legal capacity. **~fähigkeit** *f* (-; *no pl*) legal capacity.

~frau *f* businesswoman. ~freund *m* business friend. 2führend *adj* managing, executive, acting. ~führer(in *f*) *m* manager(ess), secretary (*of a club etc*). ~führung *f* management. ~gebaren *n* business methods. ~geheimnis *n* business secret. ~haus *n* 1. office building. 2. commercial firm, company. ~inhaber(in *f*) *m* owner (of a business), proprietor (proprietress). ~jahr *n* financial year. ~kosten *pl* business expenses: *auf* ~ on expense account. ~lage *f* business situation. ~leben *n* (*im* ~ in) business (life). ~leitung *f* management. ~mann *m* (-[e]s; -leute) businessman.

ge'schäftsmäßig *adj* businesslike.

Ge'schäfts|ordnung *f* rules of procedure, *parl.* standing orders: *zur* ~ on a point of order. ~partner(in *f*) *m* (business) partner. ~räume *pl* business premises, offices. ~reise *f* (*auf* ~ on a) business trip. 2schädigend *adj* damaging to business. ~schädigung *f* 🏛 injurious malpractice, *w.s.* trade libel (*gen* on). ~schluß *m* closing time: *nach* ~ *a.* after business hours. ~sinn *m* (-[e]s; *no pl*) business sense. ~sitz *m* place of business. ~stelle *f* office(s). ~straße *f* shopping street. ~träger *m pol.* chargé d'affaires. 2tüchtig *adj* smart, efficient (in business). ~tüchtigkeit *f* (-; *no pl*) business efficiency, smartness. 2unfähig *adj* 🏛 legally incapacitated. ~unfähigkeit *f* (-; *no pl*) 🏛 legal incapacity. ~verbindung *f* business connection. ~verkehr *m* business (dealings). ~viertel *n* commercial district, *Am. a.* downtown. ~wert *m* goodwill. ~zweig *m* branch of business.

geschehen [gə'ʃeːən] *v/i* (geschah, geschehen, sn) happen, occur, take place: *ihm wird nichts* ~ nothing will happen to him; *was soll damit* ~? what's to be done with it?; *es muß et.* ~ s.th. must be done!; *da war es um ihn* ~ he was done for; → *recht* 5.

Ge'schehen *n* (-s) happenings, events.

gescheit [gə'ʃaɪt] *adj* 1. clever, intelligent, bright. 2. wise, sensible.

Geschenk [gə'ʃɛŋk] *n* (-[e]s; -e) present, gift: *j-m et. zum* ~ *machen* give s.o. s.th. (as a present); *als* ~ *verpacken* gift-wrap; *als* ~ *verpacken* gift-wrap. ~ar,tikel *m* gift. ~packung *f* gift box.

Geschichte [gə'ʃɪçtə] *f* (-; -n) 1. story, *a.* narrative. 2. *no pl* history: *die* ~ *der Neuzeit* modern history; ~ *machen* make history; *in die* ~ *eingehen* go down in history. 3. F business, thing: *die ganze* (*iro. e-e schöne*) ~ the whole (a nice) business.

ge'schichtlich *adj* historical, historic.

Ge'schichts|buch *n* history book. ~forscher(in *f*) *m* historian. ~forschung *f* historical research. ~lehrer(in *f*) *m* history teacher. ~unterricht *m* history lessons.

Geschick¹ [gə'ʃɪk] *n* (-[e]s; -e) fate, lot.

Ge'schick² *n* (-[e]s; *no pl*) skill.

Ge'schicklichkeit *f* (-; *no pl*) 1. skill, dexterity. 2. cleverness.

ge'schickt *adj* skil(l)ful (*zu* at, in *dat* in), *a.* clever.

geschieden [gə'ʃiːdən] I *pp of* **scheiden.** II *adj person:* divorced, *marriage:* dissolved: *m-e* ~*e Frau* my ex-wife.

Ge'schiedene¹ *m* (-n; -n) divorcé, divorced man. **Ge'schiedene²** *f* (-n; -n) divorcée, divorced woman.

geschienen [gə'ʃiːnən] *pp of* **scheinen.**

Geschirr [gə'ʃɪr] *n* (-[e]s; -e) 1. *no pl a)* dishes, tableware, *b)* kitchenware, pots and pans: *das* ~ *abräumen* clear the table; ~ *spülen* do the dishes, wash up. 2. *china.* 3. harness.

Ge'schirr|schrank *m* (china) cupboard. ~spüler *m* (-s; -) F, ~spülma,schine *f* dishwasher. ~tuch *n* tea towel.

geschissen [gə'ʃɪsən] *pp of* **scheißen.**

ge'schlafen *pp of* **schlafen.**

ge'schlagen I *pp of* **schlagen.** II *adj* 1. beaten, defeated: *sich* ~ *geben* admit defeat. 2. F full: *zwei* ~*e Stunden* (*lang* for) two solid hours.

Geschlecht [gə'ʃlɛçt] *n* (-[e]s; -er) 1. *biol.* sex: *beiderlei* ~*s* of both sexes; *das andere* (*schwache, schöne*) ~ the opposite (weaker, fair) sex. 2. *ling.* gender. 3. *a)* race, *b)* lineage, *c)* family: *das menschliche* ~ the human race.

ge'schlechtlich *adj* sexual.

Ge'schlechts|akt *m* sexual act. ~hor,mon *n* sex hormone. 2krank *adj* suffering from a venereal disease, having VD. ~krankheit *f* venereal disease (*abbr.* V.D.). ~leben *n* sex life. **ge'schlechtslos** *adj* sexless, asexual. **Ge'schlechts|merkmal** *n* sex characteristic. ~or,gan *n* sex(ual) organ. ~reife *f*

~teile *pl* genitals. ~trieb *m* sexual urge. ~umwandlung *f* sex change. ~verkehr *m* sexual intercourse. ~wort *n ling.* article.

geschlichen [gə'ʃlɪçən] *pp of schleichen.*

geschliffen [gə'ʃlɪfən] I *pp of schleifen¹.* II *adj* 1. cut (*glass*). 2. *fig.* polished.

geschlossen [gə'ʃlɔsən] I *pp of schlie-ßen.* II *adj* 1. closed, *ling.*, ✗ close: (*in sich*) ~ *a.* ⊙ self-contained, *fig.* compact; ~e *Gesellschaft* a) closed society, b) private party; ~e *Veranstaltung* private meeting; ~e *Ortschaft* built-up area. 2. united: ~ *stimmen für* vote unanimously for, be solid for; ~ *hinter j-m stehen* be solidly behind s.o.

geschlungen [gə'ʃlʊŋən] *pp of schlin-gen.*

Geschmack [gə'ʃmak] *m* (-[e]s; ⁓e, F ⁓er) taste (*a. fig. an dat* for), flavo(u)r: ~ *finden an* (*dat*) develop a taste for; *e-n guten* ~ *haben* a) taste good, b) *fig.* have good taste; *für m-n* ~ for my taste; *das ist nicht nach m-m* ~ that's not to my taste; *über* ~ *läßt sich nicht strei-ten* there's no accounting for tastes. **ge'schmacklich** *adj* in taste. **ge'schmacklos** *adj* tasteless: ~ *sein fig. a.* be in bad taste. **Ge'schmacklosig-keit** *f* (-; *no pl*) *a. fig.* tastelessness: *das war e-e* ~ that was in bad taste. **Ge'schmacks|richtung** *f* taste. ~sache *f* (*es ist* ~) it's a) matter of taste. ~sinn *m* (-[e]s; *no pl*) (sense of) taste. ~verir-rung *f* lapse of taste.

ge'schmackvoll *adj* tasteful: ~ *sein fig. a.* be in good taste.

Geschmeide [gə'ʃmaɪdə] *n* (-s; -) jewels, jewel(le)ry.

geschmeidig [gə'ʃmaɪdɪç] *adj* 1. supple, pliant, slick, soft. 2. *fig.* flexible.

geschmissen [gə'ʃmɪsən] *pp of schmeißen.*

geschmolzen [gə'ʃmɔltsən] *pp of schmelzen.*

Geschmuse [gə'ʃmuːzə] *n* (-s; *no pl*) F smooching.

Ge'schnatter *n* (-s; *no pl*) 1. cackling. 2. F *fig.* chatter(ing).

geschnitten [gə'ʃnɪtən] *pp of schnei-den.*

geschoben [gə'ʃoːbən] *pp of schieben.*

gescholten [gə'ʃɔltən] *pp of schelten.*

Geschöpf [gə'ʃœpf] *n* (-[e]s; -e) 1. crea-ture. 2. *fig.* creation.

geschoren [gə'ʃoːrən] *pp of scheren.*

Geschoß¹ [gə'ʃɔs] *n* (-sses; -sse) projec-tile, bullet, missile.

Ge'schoß² *n* (-sses; -sse) stor(e)y, floor.

geschossen [gə'ʃɔsən] *pp of schießen.*

geschraubt [gə'ʃraʊpt] *adj fig.* stilted.

Ge'schrei *n* (-[e]s; *no pl*) 1. a) shouting, yelling, bawling, b) shouts, screams. 2. F *fig.* (*um*) fuss, noise.

geschrieben [gə'ʃriːbən] *pp of schrei-ben.*

geschrie(e)n [gə'ʃriː(ə)n] *pp of schreien.*

geschritten [gə'ʃrɪtən] *pp of schreiten.*

ge'schult *adj* trained (*a. eye*).

geschunden [gə'ʃʊndən] *pp of schin-den.*

Geschütz [gə'ʃʏts] *n* (-es; -e) gun: *fig. schweres* ~ *auffahren* bring up one's heavy guns. ~feuer *n* gunfire, shelling.

ge'schützt *adj* protected.

Ge'schützturm *m* turret.

Geschwader [gə'ʃvaːdər] *n* (-s; -) ⚓ squadron, ✈ group, *Am.* wing.

Ge'schwafel *n* (-s; *no pl*) F contp. waffle.

Geschwätz [gə'ʃvɛts] *n* (-es; *no pl*) F contp. 1. twaddle. 2. gossip. **ge'schwätzig** *adj* contp. 1. talkative, F gabby. 2. gossipy. **Ge'schwätzigkeit** *f* (-; *no pl*) contp. talkativeness.

ge'schweige *conj* (~ *denn*) not to men-tion, let alone, much less.

geschwiegen [gə'ʃviːgən] *pp of schweigen.*

Geschwindigkeit [gə'ʃvɪndɪçkaɪt] *f* (-; -en) speed, pace, rate, *phys.* velocity: *mit e-r* ~ *von* at a speed (*or* rate) of. **Ge'schwindigkeits|beschränkung** *f* speed limit. ~messer *m* tachometer, *mot. a.* speedometer. ~re,kord *m* speed record. ~überschreitung *f* speeding.

Geschwister [gə'ʃvɪstər] *pl* brother(s) and sister(s), siblings.

ge'schwisterlich *adj* a) brotherly, b) sisterly.

Ge'schwisterpaar *n* a) brother and sis-ter, b) two brothers (*or* sisters).

geschwollen [gə'ʃvɔlən] I *pp of schwel-len.* II *adj* 1. swollen. 2. *fig.* pompous, bombastic.

geschwommen [gə'ʃvɔmən] *pp of schwimmen.*

geschworen [gə'ʃvoːrən] **II** *pp of* *schwören*. **II** *adj* sworn (*enemy*).

Ge'schworene *m, f* (-{n; -n) ⚖ juror: *die ~n* the (members of the) jury.

Ge'schworenenbank *f* **1.** jury box. **2.** *the* jury.

Ge'schwulst *f* (-; ⸚e) ✝ tumo(u)r.

geschwunden [gə'ʃvʊndən] *pp of* *schwinden*.

geschwungen [gə'ʃvʊŋən] **I** *pp of* *schwingen*. **II** *adj* curved.

Geschwür [gə'ʃvyːr] *n* (-[e]s; -e) ✝ ulcer, abscess, boil.

ge'sehen *pp of* **sehen**.

Geselle [gə'zɛlə] *m* (-n; -n) journeyman.

ge'sellen: (h) *sich zu j-m ~* join s.o.

ge'sellig *adj* social, gregarious (*a. fig.*), sociable (*person*): *~es Leben* social life.

Ge'selligkeit *f* (-; *no pl*) **1.** sociability. **2.** social life: *die ~ lieben* be fond of company.

Gesellschaft [gə'zɛlʃaft] *f* (-; -en) **1.** *no pl* society: *die vornehme ~* high society; *Dame der ~* society lady. **2.** *no pl* company: *in s-r ~* in his company; *j-m ~ leisten* a) keep s.o. company, b) join s.o. (*bei* in). **3.** a) party, b) guests: *e-e ~ geben* give a party. **4.** society, ✝ company; → *Haftung*². **5.** *no pl* F bunch.

Ge'sellschafter *m* (-s; -), **Ge'sellschafterin** *f* (-; -nen) **1.** companion. **2.** ✝ partner. **ge'sellschaftlich** *adj* social.

Gesellschafts|anzug *m* formal dress. **⸚fähig** *adj* **1.** socially acceptable. **2.** presentable. **⸚kri¸tik** *f* social criticism. **⸚kritisch** *adj* socio-critical. **⸚ordnung** *f* social order. **⸚recht** *n* (-[e]s; *no pl*) company law. **⸚reise** *f* package (*or* conducted) tour. **⸚schicht** *f* (social) class, social stratum. **⸚spiel** *n* parlo(u)r game. **⸚sy¸stem** *n* social system. **⸚tanz** *m* ballroom dance. **⸚wissenschaft** *f* **1.** sociology. **2.** *pl* social sciences.

Gesenk [gə'zɛŋk] *n* (-[e]s; -e) ⚙ swage.

gesessen [gə'zɛsən] *pp of* **sitzen**.

Gesetz [gə'zɛts] *n* (-es; -e) law, *parl.* act: *nach dem ~* under the law (*über acc* on); *vor dem ~* in the eyes of the law.

Ge'setz|blatt *n* law gazette. **⸚buch** *n* code (of law). **⸚entwurf** *m* (draft) bill.

Ge'setzeskraft *f* legal force: *~ erhalten* pass into law; (*dat*) *~ verleihen* enact.

Ge'setzeslücke *f* loophole in the law.

Ge'setzesvorlage *f* (draft) bill.

ge'setzgebend *adj* legislative.

Ge'setzgeber *m* (-s; -) legislator.

Ge'setzgebung *f* (-; *no pl*) legislation.

ge'setzlich *adj* legal, statutory, lawful, legitimate: *~ geschützt* protected (by law), patented (*invention etc*), registered (*trademark etc*), copyright (*book etc*). **Ge'setzlichkeit** *f* (-; *no pl*) legality, lawfulness.

Ge'setzlosigkeit *f* (-; *no pl*) lawlessness.

ge'setzmäßig *adj* **1.** ⚖ legal, lawful, legitimate. **2.** regular. **Ge'setzmäßigkeit** *f* (-; *no pl*) **1.** ⚖ legality, lawfulness, legitimacy. **2.** regularity.

ge'setzt I *adj* **1.** sedate: *~en Alters, in ~em Alter* of mature age. **2.** *sports:* seeded: *~er Spieler* seed. **II** *conj* → *Fall* 2. **Ge'setztheit** *f* (-; *no pl*) sedateness.

ge'setzwidrig *adj* unlawful, illegal.

Ge'setzwidrigkeit *f* (-; -en) **1.** *no pl* lawlessness, illegality. **2.** offen/ce (*Am.* -se), illegal act.

Gesicht [gə'zɪçt] *n* (-[e]s; -er) **1.** face, *a.* look: *ein trauriges ~ machen* look sad; *ein langes ~ machen* pull a long face; *das ~ verziehen* make a face; *j-m et. ins ~ sagen* tell s.o. s.th. to his (her) face; *j-m wie aus dem ~ geschnitten sein* be the spit and image of s.o.; *fig. sein wahres ~ zeigen* show one's true face; *das ~ verlieren* (*wahren*) lose (save one's) face; *das gibt der Sache ein ganz anderes ~* that puts a different complexion on the matter. **2.** (eye)-sight: *das zweite ~* second sight; *zu ~ bekommen* catch sight of, see; *aus dem ~ verlieren* lose sight of.

Ge'sichts|ausdruck *m* (facial) expression, face. **⸚creme** *f* face cream. **⸚farbe** *f* complexion. **⸚feld** *n* opt. field of vision. **⸚kreis** *m* horizon.

ge'sichtslos *adj fig.* featureless.

Ge'sichts|maske *f* face mask. **⸚mas¸sage** *f* facial massage, F facial. **⸚muskel** *m* facial muscle. **⸚packung** *f* face pack. **⸚pflege** *f* care of one's face. **⸚punkt** *m* **1.** point of view, viewpoint, angle: *von diesem ~ aus* (*gesehen*) (looked at) from this point of view. **2.** point, aspect. **⸚wasser** *n* face lotion. **⸚winkel** *m* opt. visual angle. **⸚züge** *pl* features.

Gesindel [gə'zɪndəl] *n* (-s; *no pl*) riffraff.

gesinnt [gəˈzɪnt] *adj* **1.** disposed (*dat* toward). **2.** *in cpds.* ...-minded.

Gesinnung [gəˈzɪnʊŋ] *f* (-; -en) **1.** mind, character. **2.** convictions, views.

ge'sinnungslos *adj* unprincipled.

Ge'sinnungswandel *m* change of heart.

gesittet [gəˈzɪtət] *adj* civilized.

Gesöff [gəˈzœf] *n* [-[e]s; -e] F *contp.* awful stuff.

gesoffen [gəˈzɔfən] *pp of* **saufen.**

gesondert [gəˈzɔndərt] *adj* separate.

gesonnen [gəˈzɔnən] *pp of* **sinnen.**

ge'spalten I *pp of* **spalten. II** *adj* split.

Gespann [gəˈʃpan] *n* [-[e]s; -e] **1.** team. **2.** *mot.* combination. **3.** *fig.* pair.

ge'spannt *adj* **1.** tight, taut. **2.** *fig.* tense (*nerves, situation*), strained (*relations*), close (*attention*). **3.** a) eager, anxious, b) curious, c) excited: **~ sein auf** (*acc*) be anxious to see (*or know*); **ich bin ~, ob** (*wie*) **...** I wonder if (how) ...; **da bin ich aber ~!** I can't wait to see that!

Ge'spanntheit *f* (-; *no pl*) **1.** tension (*a. fig.*), tenseness. **2.** a) eagerness, intentness, b) (anxious) anticipation.

Gespenst [gəˈʃpɛnst] *n* [-[e]s; -er] ghost, *a. fig.* spectre/re (*Am.* -er).

ge'spenstisch *adj* **1.** ghostly, F spooky. **2.** *fig.* eerie, nightmarish.

Gespinst [gəˈʃpɪnst] *n* [-[e]s; -e] tissue.

gesponnen [gəˈʃpɔnən] *pp of* **spinnen.**

Gespött [gəˈʃpœt] *n* [-[e]s; *no pl*] derision, mockery: **j-n zum ~ machen** make a laughingstock of s.o.

Gespräch [gəˈʃprɛːç] *n* [-[e]s; -e] talk (*a. pol.*), conversation, discussion, *teleph.* call: **ein ~ führen mit** have a talk *etc* with; **das ~ bringen auf** (*acc*) steer the conversation round to; **im ~ sein** be under discussion; **ins ~ kommen** get talking (**mit** to); **mit j-m im ~ bleiben** stay in contact (*or* touch) with s.o.

ge'sprächig *adj* **1.** talkative. **2.** communicative. **Ge'sprächigkeit** *f* (-; *no pl*) talkativeness.

Ge'sprächs|partner(in *f*) *m* interlocutor, *w.s interesting etc* person to talk to. **~pause** *f* lull in the conversation. **~runde** *f pol.* round of talks. **~stoff** *m* topic(s) (of conversation).

ge'spreizt *adj fig.* affected.

gesprochen [gəˈʃprɔxən] *pp of* **sprechen.**

gesprossen [gəˈʃprɔsən] *pp of* **sprießen.**

gesprungen [gəˈʃprʊŋən] *pp of* **springen.**

Gespür [gəˈʃpyːr] *n* (-s; *no pl*) (**für** for) flair, nose.

ge'staffelt *adj* staggered, graduated.

Gestalt [gəˈʃtalt] *f* (-; -en) **1.** form, shape: **in ~ von** in the form (*or* shape) of; **(feste) ~ annehmen** take shape. **2.** (*literary etc*) figure, character. **3.** build.

ge'stalten (h) **I** *v/t* **1.** a) shape, fashion, design, b) decorate (*room etc*), c) create: **et. interessant ~** make s.th. interesting. **2.** arrange, organize. **II sich ~** develop; **sich ~ zu** become, turn into, (turn out to) be (*a success etc*); **sich anders ~** turn out differently.

Ge'stalter *m* (-s; -), **Ge'stalterin** *f* (-; -nen) **1.** a) designer, stylist, b) creator. **2.** organizer. **ge'stalterisch** *adj* a) designing, stylistic, b) creative, artistic.

Ge'staltung *f* (-; *no pl*) **1.** a) shaping (*a. fig.*), forming, design, b) creation. **2.** arrangement, organization.

Ge'stammel *n* (-s; *no pl*) stammering.

gestand [gəˈʃtant] *pret of* **gestehen.**

gestanden [gəˈʃtandən] **I** *pp of* **stehen** *and* **gestehen. II** *adj* **ein ~er Mann** a man who has made his mark in (life).

geständig [gəˈʃtɛndɪç] *adj* confessing (one's guilt): **~ sein** confess.

Geständnis [gəˈʃtɛntnɪs] *n* (-ses; -se) *a.* ⚖ confession: **ein ~ ablegen** confess; **j-m ein ~ machen** confess s.th. to s.o.

Gestank [gəˈʃtaŋk] *m* [-[e]s; *no pl*] stench, F stink.

gestatten [gəˈʃtatən] *v/t* (h) allow, permit: **~ Sie, daß ich ...?** may I ...?, do you mind if I ...?; **~ Sie e-e Frage** may I ask you s.th.; **wenn Sie ~** with your permission.

Geste [ˈɡɛstə] *f* (-; -n) *a. fig.* gesture.

ge'stehen *v/t, v/i* (gestand, gestanden, h) confess: → **offen.**

Ge'stehungskosten *pl* ✝ production costs, prime cost.

Ge'stein *n* [-[e]s; -e] rock.

Gestell [gəˈʃtɛl] *n* [-[e]s; -e] a) stand, rack, shelve, b) trestle, c) frame.

gestellt [gəˈʃtɛlt] *adj* **1.** *phot.* posed, unnatural. **2.** → **stellen** 5.

Ge'stellungsbefehl *m* ✕ call-up (*Am.* induction) order.

gestern [ˈɡɛstərn] *adv* yesterday: **~ abend** yesterday evening, last night;

von ~ yesterday's (*paper etc*); F **er ist nicht von ~** he wasn't born yesterday.

gestiegen [gə'ʃtiːgən] *pp of* **steigen**.

gestielt [gə'ʃtiːlt] *adj* stemmed.

Gestik ['gɛstɪk] *f* (-; *no pl*) gestures.

gestikulieren [gɛstiku'liːrən] *v/i* (h) gesticulate.

Gestirn [gə'ʃtɪrn] *n* (-[e]s; -e) star.

Gestöber [gə'ʃtøːbər] *n* (-s; -) drift(ing).

gestochen [gə'ʃtɔxən] **I** *pp of* **stechen**. **II** *adj* **wie ~** very neat (*hand*); *phot*. **~ scharf** very sharp.

gestohlen [gə'ʃtoːlən] *pp of* **stehlen**.

gestorben [gə'ʃtɔrbən] *pp of* **sterben**.

gestört [gə'ʃtøːrt] *adj* disturbed, disordered, *psych*. unbalanced, ⊗ faulty.

ge'stoßen *pp of* **stoßen**.

Gestotter [gə'ʃtɔtər] *n* (-s; *no pl*) stuttering, stammering.

gesträhnt [gə'ʃtrɛːnt] *adj* streaked-in.

Gesträuch [gə'ʃtrɔʏç] *n* (-[e]s; -e) shrubbery, bushes.

gestreift [gə'ʃtraɪft] *adj* striped.

gestrichen [gə'ʃtrɪçən] **I** *pp of* **streichen**. **II** *adj* **1.** painted. **2.** deleted. **3.** **~ voll** a) level, b) brimful(l); *drei* **~e Teelöffel** (**voll**) three level teaspoons (full).

gestrig ['gɛstrɪç] *adj* of yesterday: *die* **~e Zeitung** yesterday's paper.

gestritten [gə'ʃtrɪtən] *pp of* **streiten**.

Gestrüpp [gə'ʃtrʏp] *n* (-[e]s; -e) **1.** undergrowth, brushwood. **2.** *fig*. jungle.

Gestühl [gə'ʃtyːl] *n* (-[e]s; -e) seats, *eccl*. pews.

gestunken [gə'ʃtʊŋkən] *pp of* **stinken**.

Gestüt [gə'ʃtyːt] *n* (-[e]s; -e) a) stud farm, b) stud.

Gesuch [gə'zuːx] *n* (-[e]s; -e) application, request, petition. **ge'sucht** *adj* **1.** wanted (*a*. ⚠), much sought-after, in (great) demand. **2.** *fig*. studied.

gesund [gə'zʊnt] *adj* healthy, *fig. a.* sound (*firm, sleep, views, etc*): **~ sein** a. be in good health, be well; *geistig* **~** sane; **~ und munter** (as) fit as a fiddle; (**wieder**) **~ werden** get well (again), recover; *Gemüse ist* **~** vegetables are good for you(r health); *iro. das ist* (*ganz*) **~ für ihn!** that's good for him!; → **Menschenverstand**.

Ge'sundbeter(in *f*) *m* faith healer.

gesunden [gə'zʊndən] *v/i* (sn) recover (*a. fig.*), get well (again).

Ge'sundheit *f* (-; *no pl*) a) health, b) healthiness: *geistige* **~** sanity; *bei guter* **~** *sein* be in good health; *auf j-s* **~** *trinken* drink to s.o.'s health; **~!** *at a sneeze*: bless you!

ge'sundheitlich *adj* physical: *aus* **~en Gründen** for health reasons; **~ geht es ihm gut** he is in good health; *ich bin* **~ nicht auf der Höhe** I don't feel too well.

Ge'sundheits|amt *n* public health office. **~a,postel** *m* *iro.* health freak. **⚠fördernd** *adj* healthy. **~pflege** *f* (personal) hygiene, health care. **~schädlich** *adj* injurious to health, unhealthy. **~wesen** *n* (-s; *no pl*) Public Health (Service). **~zeugnis** *n* health certificate. **~zustand** *m* (state of) health.

ge'sundschrumpfen *v/t, a. sich* **~** (*sep, -ge-*, h) F slim down.

ge'sundstoßen: sich **~** (*irr, sep, -ge-*, h, → **stoßen**) F make a pile.

Ge'sundung *f* (-; *no pl*) *a. fig.* recovery.

gesungen [gə'zʊŋən] *pp of* **singen**.

gesunken [gə'zʊŋkən] *pp of* **sinken**.

getan [gə'taːn] *pp of* **tun**.

geteilt [gə'taɪlt] *adj* **1.** divided: **~er Meinung sein** disagree; *darüber kann man* **~er Meinung sein** that's a matter of opinion. **2.** shared.

Getöse [gə'tøːzə] *n* (-s; *no pl*) din.

ge'tragen **I** *pp of* **tragen**. **II** *adj* **1.** second-hand, old (*clothes*). **2.** *fig*. solemn, measured, slow.

Ge'trampel *n* (-s; *no pl*) F trampling.

Getränk [gə'trɛŋk] *n* (-[e]s; -e) drink, beverage.

Ge'tränkeauto,mat *m* drinks dispenser.

Ge'tränkekarte *f* list of beverages.

Ge'tränkesteuer *f* alcohol tax.

Getrappel [gə'trapəl] *n* (-s; *no pl*) patter.

Getreide [gə'traɪdə] *n* (-s; -) cereal(s), grain. **~(an)bau** *m* (-[e]s; *no pl*) cultivation of cereals. **~arten** *pl* cereals. **~ernte** *f* a) grain harvest, b) grain crop. **~feld** *n* grain field. **~land** *n* **1.** grain-growing country (or land). **2.** *no pl* grain fields. **~pflanze** *f* cereal plant. **~silo** *m* (grain) silo.

ge'treten *pp of* **treten**.

getreu [gə'trɔʏ] *adj* true, faithful.

Getriebe [gə'triːbə] *n* (-s; -) **1.** ⊗ gear(ing), mechanism, *mot*. transmission, gearbox. **2.** *fig*. wheels. **3.** *fig*. bustle, rush.

getrieben [gə'triːbən] *pp of* **treiben**.

Ge'triebeschaden m mot. gearbox trouble.

getroffen [gə'trɔfən] pp of **treffen.**

getrogen [gə'tro:gən] pp of **trügen.**

ge'trost adj confidently, safely.

getrunken [gə'trʊŋkən] pp of **trinken.**

Getto ['gɛto] n (-s; -s) ghetto.

Getue [gə'tu:ə] n (-s; no pl) F fuss (um about).

Getümmel [gə'tʏml] n (-s; -) turmoil.

geübt [gə'y:pt] adj practised, trained (eye etc), experienced.

Gewächs [gə'vɛks] n (-es; -e) 1. plant. 2. ♣ produce, growth. 3. a) wine, b) vintage. 4. ♣ growth.

ge'wachsen I pp of **wachsen¹. II** adj j-m ~ **sein** be a match for s.o.; e-r Sache ~ **sein** be up (or equal) to s.th.; sich der Lage ~ zeigen rise to the occasion.

Ge'wächshaus n greenhouse, hothouse.

gewagt [gə'va:kt] adj a) daring (a. fig.), risky, b) risqué (joke etc).

gewählt [gə've:lt] adj fig. refined.

Gewähr [gə'vɛ:r] f (-; no pl) guarantee: ohne ~ a) without guarantee, b) subject to change; für et. ~ bieten (or leisten) guarantee s.th. **ge'währen** v/t (h) a) grant (j-m e-e Bitte s.o. a request), b) give, afford (an insight, protection, etc): j-n ~ lassen let s.o. have his way.

ge'währleisten v/t (h) guarantee.

Ge'wahrsam m (-s; no pl) in ~ nehmen a) take s.th. in safe keeping, b) take s.o. into custody.

Ge'währsmann m informant, source.

Gewalt [gə'valt] f (-; -en) 1. no pl force, violence: mit ~ by force; mit aller ~ a) with all one's strength, b) fig. at all costs; ~ anwenden use force; → roh 3. 2. a) power, adm., ⚖ authority, b) control (über acc of): höhere ~ act of God; die gesetzgebende ~ the legislature; et. in s-e ~ bringen gain control of s.th.; et. (sich) in der ~ haben have s.th. (o.s.) under control; in j-s ~ sein be in s.o.'s power (or hands); die ~ verlieren über (acc) lose control over.

Ge'waltakt m act of violence.

Ge'waltanwendung f (use of) force.

Ge'waltenteilung f pol. separation of powers.

Ge'waltherrschaft f tyranny. **Ge'waltherrscher(in** f) m despot, tyrant.

ge'waltig adj 1. powerful, mighty. 2. enormous, huge.

ge'waltlos I adj nonviolent. **II** adv without violence. **Ge'waltlosigkeit** f (-; no pl) nonviolence.

Ge'waltmaßnahme f drastic measure.

ge'waltsam I adj forcible, violent: ~er Tod violent death. **II** adv forcibly, by force: et. ~ öffnen force s.th. (open). **Ge'waltsamkeit** f (-; no pl) violence.

Ge'walttat f act of violence, outrage.

ge'walttätig adj violent, brutal.

Ge'walttätigkeit f (-; -en) 1. no pl violence, brutality. 2. act of violence.

Ge'waltverbrechen n crime of violence.

Ge'waltverbrecher m violent criminal.

Ge'waltverzichtsabkommen n pol. nonaggression treaty.

Gewand [gə'vant] n (-[e]s; "er) robe.

gewandt [gə'vant] **I** pp of **wenden². II** adj a) agile, nimble, b) elegant, c) clever. **Ge'wandtheit** f (-; no pl) a) agility, nimbleness, b) elegance, c) cleverness.

gewann [gə'van] pret of **gewinnen.**

gewappnet [gə'vapnət] adj fig. prepared (für for).

gewärtig [gə'vɛrtıç] adj ~ sein (gen) → **ge'wärtigen** [-tıgən] v/t (h) expect, reckon with: zu ~ haben be in for s.th.

Gewäsch [gə'vɛʃ] n (-[e]s; no pl) F contp. blather.

ge'waschen pp of **waschen.**

Gewässer [gə'vɛsər] n (-s; -) (stretch of) water, pl waters, rivers and lakes.

Ge'wässerschutz m prevention of water pollution.

Gewebe [gə've:bə] n (-s; -) a) (woven) fabric, b) tissue (a. anat. or fig.), c) weave. ~probe f ♣ tissue sample.

Gewehr [gə've:r] n (-[e]s; -e) gun, rifle. ~kolben m (rifle) butt. ~kugel f (rifle) bullet. ~lauf m (rifle) barrel.

Geweih [gə'vaı] n (-[e]s; -e) antlers, horns.

Gewerbe [gə'vɛrbə] n (-s; -) trade, business, occupation: Handel und ~ trade and industry. ~freiheit f freedom of trade. ~lehrer(in f) m teacher at a trade school. ~ordnung f industrial code. ~schein m trade licen/ce (Am. -se). ~schule f trade school. ~steuer f trade tax. 2treibend adj carrying on a trade, industrial. ~treibende m, f (-n; -n) person carrying on a trade, trader. ~zweig m (branch of) trade (or industry).

gewerblich [gə'vɛrplıç] *adj* commercial, industrial, trade. **ge'werbsmäßig** *adj* professional, gainful, *adv a.* for gain.

Gewerkschaft [gə'vɛrkʃaft] *f* (-; -en) trade (*Am.* labor) union.

Ge'werkschaftler *m* (-s; -) (trade, *Am.* labor) unionist. **ge'werkschaftlich** *adj* trade (*Am.* labor) union: **~ organisiert** unionized, organized.

Ge'werkschafts... (trade, *Am.* labor) union (*boss, member, etc.*). **~bund** *m* federation of trade (*Am.* labor) unions.

ge'wesen *pp of* **sein**[1].

gewichen [gə'vıçən] *pp of* **weichen**.

Gewicht [gə'vıçt] *n* (-[e]s; -e) *a. fig.* weight: **ein ~ von ... haben** weigh ...; **nach ~ verkaufen** sell by weight; *fig.* **~ haben** carry weight (**bei** with); (**nicht**) **ins ~ fallen** be of (no) importance; **~ legen auf** (*acc*) stress, emphasize; (*dat*) **~ beimessen** attach importance to; (*dat*) **~ verleihen** lend weight to; → **spezifisch. ge'wichten** *v/t* (h) *statistics:* weigh: *fig.* **(neu) ~** (re)assess.

Ge'wichtheben *n* (-s) weight lifting. **Ge'wichtheber** *m* (-s; -) weight lifter. **gewichtig** [gə'vıçtıç] *adj a. fig.* weighty. **Ge'wichts|klasse** *f sports:* weight (class). **~verlust** *m* loss of weight. **~zunahme** *f* increase in weight.

gewiesen [gə'vi:zən] *pp of* **weisen**.

gewillt [gə'vılt] *adj* **~ sein, et. zu tun** be willing (*or* ready) to do s.th.

Gewimmel [gə'vıməl] *n* (-s; *no pl*) a) swarm(ing), swarming mass (*of insects etc*), b) milling crowd.

Gewinde [gə'vındə] *n* (-s; -) ⊕ thread. **Ge'windebohrer** *m* (screw) tap.

Gewinn [gə'vın] *m* (-[e]s; -e) **1.** ✝ profit, gain(s): **mit ~** at a profit; **~ ziehen aus** profit by. **2.** *fig.* a) profit, gain, advantage, b) asset (**für** to). **3.** a) prize, b) winnings. **4.** → **Gewinnlos. ~anteil** *m* share in (the) profits, dividend. **~beteiligung** *f* profit sharing. **2bringend** *adj* profitable. **~chance** *f* chance (of winning).

gewinnen [gə'vınən] (gewann, gewonnen, h) **I** *v/t* **1.** win, *fig. a.* get, gain: **Höhe ~** ✈ gain height; **j-n für sich ~** win s.o. over (**für** to); **j-n für et. ~** win s.o. to s.th.; → **Spiel** 2. **2.** produce, ✗ mine, win, recover (**aus** from *scrap etc*). **II** *v/i* **3.** (**bei, in** *dat* at) win, be the winner,

number, ticket, etc: come up a winner. **4.** gain: *fig.* **an Bedeutung ~** gain in importance; **sie hat sehr gewonnen** she has greatly improved.

ge'winnend *adj a. fig.* winning, engaging. **Ge'winner** *m* (-s; -), **Ge'winnerin** *f* (-; -nen) winner.

Ge'winn|los *n* winning ticket, winner. **~maxi,mierung** *f* ✝ maximization of profits. **~spanne** *f* profit margin. **~sucht** *f* (-; *no pl*) (**aus ~** from) greed.

Ge'winn-und-Ver'lust-Rechnung *f* profit and loss account.

Ge'winnung *f* (-; *no pl*) winning, production.

Ge'winnzahl *f* winning number.

Gewinsel [gə'vınzəl] *n* (-s; *no pl*) *contp.* whining.

Gewirr [gə'vır] *n* (-[e]s; -e) tangle (*a. fig.*).

gewiß [gə'vıs] **I** *adj* certain: **in gewissem Sinne** in a sense; **ich bin mir m-r Sache ~** I am sure of my ground; → **Etwas. II** *adv* certainly, for certain: **~!** certainly!, sure!; **aber ~!** but of course!

Ge'wissen *n* (-s; -) conscience: **j-m ins ~ reden** reason with s.o.

ge'wissenhaft *adj* conscientious.

Ge'wissenhaftigkeit *f* (-; *no pl*) conscientiousness.

ge'wissenlos *adj* unscrupulous.

Ge'wissenlosigkeit *f* (-; *no pl*) unscrupulousness.

Ge'wissens|bisse *pl* twinges of remorse. **~frage** *f* matter of conscience. **~freiheit** *f* (-; *no pl*) freedom of conscience. **~gründe** *pl aus ~n* for reasons of conscience. **~kon,flikt** *m*, **~not** *f* moral dilemma.

gewissermaßen [gə'vısər'ma:sən] *adv* in a way, so to speak.

Ge'wißheit *f* (-; *no pl*) certainty: **mit ~** for certain; **sich ~ verschaffen** make sure (**über** *acc* of); (**zur**) **~ werden** become a certainty.

Gewitter [gə'vıtər] *n* (-s; -) thunderstorm, *fig.* storm. **ge'wittern** *v/impers* (h) **es gewittert** there is a thunderstorm. **Ge'witterwolke** *f* thundercloud. **ge'wittrig** [-trıç] *adj* thundery.

gewitzt [gə'vıtst] *adj* F smart, clever.

gewogen [gə'vo:gən] **I** *pp of* **wiegen**[2]. **II** *adj fig.* **j-m ~ sein** be well disposed to (*or* toward[s]) s.o.

gewöhnen [gə'vø:nən] *v/t, a.* **sich ~** (h)

get used (**an** *acc* to); **man gewöhnt sich an alles** you get used to anything.

Gewohnheit [gə'vo:nhait] *f* (-; -en) (**aus** ~ from) habit: **die ~ haben, et. zu tun** be in the habit of doing s.th.; **sich et. zur ~ machen** make a habit of s.th.

Ge'wohnheits... habitual (*drinker etc*).

ge'wohnheitsmäßig *adj and adv* habitual(ly), *adv a.* out of habit.

Ge'wohnheitssache *f* matter of habit.

Ge'wohnheitstier *n* F creature of habit.

gewöhnlich [gə'vø:nlıç] **I** *adj* **1.** a) common, ordinary, b) usual. **2.** common, vulgar. **II** *adv* **3.** commonly (*etc*): (**für**) ~ usually, normally; **wie ~** as usual.

gewohnt [gə'vo:nt] *adj* usual: **et.** (**zu tun**) ~ **sein** be used to (doing) s.th.

Ge'wöhnung *f* (-; *no pl*) (**an** *acc* to) **1.** habituation. **2.** addiction.

Gewölbe [gə'vœlbə] *n* (-s; -) vault.

gewölbt [gə'vœlpt] *adj* **1.** △ arched, vaulted. **2.** domed.

gewollt [gə'vɔlt] *pp of* **wollen²**.

gewonnen [gə'vɔnən] *pp of* **gewinnen**.

geworben [gə'vɔrbən] *pp of* **werben**.

geworden [gə'vɔrdən] *pp of* **werden**.

geworfen [gə'vɔrfən] *pp of* **werfen**.

gewrungen [gə'vrʊŋən] *pp of* **wringen**.

Gewühl [gə'vy:l] *n* (-[e]s; *no pl*) milling crowd.

gewunden [gə'vʊndən] **I** *pp of* **winden**. **II** *adj* winding, *a. fig.* tortuous.

Gewürz [gə'vyrts] *n* (-es; -e) spice, condiment, seasoning.

Ge'würz|gurke *f* pickled gherkin. **~mischung** *f* mixed herbs (*or* spices). **~nelke** *f* clove. **~ständer** *m* spice rack.

gewußt [gə'vʊst] *pp of* **wissen**.

ge'zackt, ge'zähnt *adj* toothed, serrated (*a.* ⚭), perforated (*stamp*).

Ge'zeiten *pl* tide(s).

Ge'zeiten... tidal (*power plant etc*). **~wechsel** *m* turn of the tide.

Ge'zeter *n* (-s; *no pl*) *contp.* nagging.

ge'zielt *adj fig.* specific (*measure etc*), calculated (*indiscretion etc*).

ge'ziert *adj* affected.

gezogen [gə'tso:gən] *pp of* **ziehen**.

Ge'zwitscher *n* (-s; *no pl*) chirping, twitter(ing).

gezwungen [gə'tsvʊŋən] **I** *pp of* **zwingen. II** *adj fig.* forced (*smile etc*), stiff, constrained (*manner etc*): ~ **lachen** force a laugh.

ge'zwungenermaßen *adv* of necessity: ~ **et. tun** be forced to do s.th.

Gicht [gıçt] *f* (-; *no pl*) ⚕ gout. **'Gichtknoten** *m* gouty node. **'Gichtkranke** *m, f* (-n; -n) gout case, gouty person.

Giebel ['gi:bəl] *m* (-s; -) gable. **'Giebelseite** *f*, **'Giebelwand** *f* gable end.

Gier [gi:r] *f* (-; *no pl*) greed(iness) (**nach** for). **'gierig** *adj* greedy (**nach** for).

gießen ['gi:sən] (goß, gegossen, h) **I** *v/t* **1.** pour. **2.** water. **3.** ⚙ found, *art:* cast. **II** *v/i* **4.** pour: **es gießt** (**in Strömen**) it is pouring (with rain). **'Gießer** *m* (-s; -) ⚙ founder. **Gießerei** [gi:sə'rai] *f* (-; -en) ⚙ **1.** *no pl* casting. **2.** foundry.

'Gießkanne *f* watering can.

Gift [gıft] *n* (-[e]s; -e) *a. fig.* poison, *zo.* venom: F **darauf kannst du ~ nehmen!** you bet your life on it! **'Giftgas** *n* poison gas. **'giftig** *adj* a) poisonous, *fig. a.* venomous, ⚘, ⚭ toxic, b) poisoned. **'Giftmischer** *m* (-s; -), **'Giftmischerin** *f* (-; -nen) F poisoner. **'Giftmüll** *m* toxic waste. **'Giftpilz** *m* poisonous mushroom, toadstool. **'Giftschlange** *f* venomous (*or* poisonous) snake, *fig.* snake. **'Giftstoff** *m* poisonous (*or* toxic) substance. **'Giftzahn** *m* (poison) fang.

Gigant [gi'gant] *m* (-en; -en) *fig.* giant. **gi'gantisch** *adj* gigantic.

Gilde ['gıldə] *f* (-; -n) guild.

ging [gıŋ] *pret of* **gehen**.

Ginster ['gınstər] *m* (-s; -) ⚘ broom.

Gipfel ['gıpfəl] *m* (-s; -) summit (*a. fig. pol.*), top, peak: *fig.* **auf dem ~ der Macht** at the height (*or* peak) of power; F **das ist** (**doch**) **der ~!** that's the limit. **~konfe,renz** *f pol.* summit conference. **'gipfeln** *v/i* (h) ~ **in** (*dat*) culminate in. **'Gipfeltreffen** *n pol.* summit (meeting).

Gips [gıps] *m* (-es; -e) ⚙ plaster, *art*, ⚕ *a.* plaster of Paris, ⚭ gypsum. **~abdruck** *m* plaster cast. **~bein** *n* F leg in plaster. **'gipsen** *v/t* (h) (⚕ put in) plaster. **'Gipsverband** *m* ⚕ plaster cast.

Giraffe [gi'rafə] *f* (-; -n) *zo.* giraffe.

girieren [ʒi'ri:rən] *v/t* (h) ✝ endorse.

Girlande [gır'landə] *f* (-; -n) garland.

Giro|bank ['ʒi:ro-] *f* (-; -en) ✝ clearing bank. **~konto** *n* current (*Am.* checking) account. **~zen,trale** *f* clearing house.

Gis, gis [gıs] *n* (-; -) ♪ G sharp.

Gischt [gıʃt] *m* (-[e]s; *no pl*) (sea) spray.

Gitarre [gi'tarə] *f* (-; -n) guitar.

Gitarrist [gita'rɪst] *m* (-en; -en), **Gitar'ri-stin** *f* (-; -nen) guitarist.

Gitter ['gɪtər] *n* (-s; -) **1.** a) lattice, grille, b) bars, c) (wire) screen, d) grate: *hinter ~n* behind bars. **2.** *opt.* grating. **3.** *⚡, a. maps:* grid. **~bett** *n* cot, *Am.* crib. **~fenster** *n* lattice (*or* barred) window. **~mast** *m* ⚡ pylon. **~netz** *n maps:* grid.

Glacéhandschuhe [gla'se:-] *pl* (*fig. j-n mit ~n anfassen*) handle s.o. with) kid gloves.

Gladiole [gla'dɪo:lə] *f* (-; -n) ⚘ gladiolus.

Glanz [glants] *m* (-es; *no pl*) **1.** lust/re (*Am.* -er) (*a. fig.*), shine, gloss, glitter, brilliance (*a. fig.*). **2.** *fig.* glamo(u)r, splendo(u)r.

glänzen ['glɛntsən] *v/i* (h) shine (*a. fig.*), gleam, *fabric, nose, etc:* be shiny.

'glänzend *adj* **1.** lustrous, glossy, shining, shiny. **2.** *fig.* brilliant, splendid: *sich ~ amüsieren* have a great time.

'Glanzleistung *f* brilliant performance (*or* feat). **'glanzlos** *adj* dull. **'Glanznummer** *f* star turn. **'Glanzpa,pier** *n* glazed paper. **'Glanzpunkt** *m* highlight, high spot. **'Glanzstück** *n* pièce de résistance. **'glanzvoll** *adj* splendid, magnificent. **'Glanzzeit** *f* heyday.

Glas [gla:s] *n* (-es; ⸗er) **1.** *no pl* glass. **2.** a) glass, b) jar: *drei ~ Wein* three glasses of wine. **3.** *opt.* a) lens, glass, b) glasses.

'Glasbläser *m* glass blower.

Glaser ['gla:zər] *m* (-s; -) glazier.

Glase'rei *f* (-; -en) glazier's (work)shop.

gläsern ['glɛ:zərn] *adj* **1.** (of) glass. **2.** *fig.* glassy.

'Glas|faser *f*, **~fiber** *f* glass fib/re (*Am.* -er). **~haus** *n wer im ~ sitzt, soll nicht mit Steinen werfen* people who live in glass houses should not throw stones. **~hütte** *f* ⚙ glassworks.

glasieren [gla'zi:rən] *v/t* (h) **1.** ⚙ glaze. **2.** *gastr.* ice, *Am.* frost.

glasig ['gla:zɪç] *adj* glassy (*a. fig.*), vitreous.

'Glas|kasten *m* glass case. **⸗klar** *adj a. fig.* crystal-clear. **~körper** *m anat.* vitreous body. **~malerei** *f* glass painting. **~scheibe** *f* (glass) pane. **~scherben** *pl* (pieces of) broken glass. **~schneider** *m* glass cutter. **~schrank** *m* glass-fronted cupboard.

Glasur [gla'zu:r] *f* (-; -en) **1.** ⚙ glaze, enamel. **2.** *gastr.* icing, *Am.* frosting.

'Glaswaren *pl* glassware.

'glasweise *adv* by the glass.

'Glaswolle *f* glass wool.

glatt [glat] **I** *adj* **1.** a) smooth (*a. fig.*), even, c) polished: *~es Haar* straight hair. **2.** slippery. **3.** F *fig.* plain, clear: *~e Absage* flat refusal; *~e Lüge* downright (*or* outright) lie; *das ist ~er Wahnsinn* that's sheer madness. **II** *adv* **4.** a) smoothly (*etc*), b) clean: *~ (anliegend)* ⊙ flush; *~ durchschneiden* cut clean through; *~ gestrickt* plainly knit; *fig. ~ gewinnen* win clearly, win hands down. **5.** F *fig. ~ ablehnen (leugnen)* refuse (deny) flatly; *das bringt er ~ fertig* I wouldn't put it past him; *et. ~ vergessen* clean forget (about) s.th.

Glätte ['glɛtə] *f* (-; *no pl a. fig.*) a) smoothness, b) slipperiness (*a. contp.*).

'Glatteis *n* a) (black, *Am.* glare) ice, b) icy ground, icy roads: *fig. j-n aufs ~ führen* trip s.o. up.

glätten ['glɛtən] (h) **I** *v/t* a) smooth, b) polish (*a. fig.*). **II** *sich ~* smooth down.

'glattgehen *v/i* (*irr, sep*, -ge-, sn, → *gehen*) go smoothly.

'glattra,siert *adj* clean-shaven.

'glattstellen *v/t* (*sep*, -ge-, h) ✝ square, even up.

'glattweg *adv* F → *glatt* 5.

Glatze ['glatsə] *f* (-; -n) bald head: *e-e ~ haben (bekommen)* be (go) bald.

'Glatzkopf *m* **1.** → *Glatze.* **2.** F bald-head, baldy. **glatzköpfig** ['glatskœpfɪç] *adj* bald(headed).

Glaube ['glaʊbə] *m* (-ns; *no pl*) (*an acc in*) belief, faith: *~n schenken (dat)* believe, give credence to; *in gutem ~n* in good faith; *den ~n verlieren* lose faith.

'glauben (h) **I** *v/t* believe, *a.* think, suppose: *das glaube ich dir nicht!* I don't believe you!; *es ist nicht zu ~!* it's incredible! **II** *v/i* believe (*an acc* in): *an j-n ~ a.* have faith in s.o., trust s.o.; *ich glaube, ja!* I think so!; F *er (es) hat dran ~ müssen* he (it) has had it; *er wird dran ~ müssen* he's for it.

'Glaubens|bekenntnis *n* creed (*a. fig.*), confession. **~freiheit** *f* (-; *no pl*) religious freedom. **~gemeinschaft** *f* denomination, church. **~genosse** *m* fellow believer. **~krieg** *m* religious war. **~lehre** *f*, **~satz** *m* dogma.

glaubhaft ['glaʊphaft] *adj* a) credible,

plausible, b) convincing: *et. ~ machen a.* ⚖ substantiate s.th.

gläubig ['glɔʏbɪç] *adj* believing, *eccl. a.* religious, devout. **Gläubige** ['glɔʏbɪgə] *m, f* (-n; -n) believer: *die ~n* the faithful.

Gläubiger ['glɔʏbɪgər] *m* (-s; -) creditor.

glaublich ['glaʊplɪç] *adj das ist kaum ~* that's hard to believe.

glaubwürdig ['glaʊpvʏrdɪç] *adj* credible, reliable. **Glaubwürdigkeit** *f* (-; no pl) credibility, reliability.

gleich [glaɪç] **I** *adj* **1.** same, equal (*a.* &). identical: *3 mal 3 ist ~ 9* three times three equals (*or* is) nine; *in ~er Höhe mit* level with; *auf ~e Weise* (in) the same way; *zur ~en Zeit* at the same time; *das ist mir ~!* it's all the same to me!, *contp.* I don't care!; *ganz ~, wann (wer etc)* no matter when (who *etc*); *das* &e the same (thing). **II** *adv* **2.** equally, alike: *~ alt (groß)* of the same age (size); *~ schnell* just as fast; *~ aussehen* look alike; *alle ~ behandeln* treat everybody the same way. **3.** at once, right away, in a moment: *~ darauf* immediately afterwards; *~ nach ...* right after ...; *es ist ~ 11 (Uhr)* it's almost eleven (o'clock); *ich komme ~!* (I'm) coming!, just a minute!; *ich bin ~ wieder da!* I'll be right back!; F *bis ~!* see you soon (*or* later)! **4.** immediately, directly: *~ neben ...* right next to ...; *~ gegenüber* just (*or* directly) opposite.

'gleichaltrig [-ʔaltrɪç] *adj* (of) the same age. **'gleichartig** *adj* **1.** of the same kind, homogeneous. **2.** like, similar. **'gleichbedeutend** *adj* (*mit*) synonymous (with) (*a. ling.*), equivalent (to).

'Gleichbehandlung *f* equal treatment.

'gleichberechtigt *adj* having equal rights. **'Gleichberechtigung** *f* (-; no pl) equal rights, equality.

'gleichbleiben *v/i* (*irr, sep, -ge-, sn, →* **bleiben**) (*a.* **sich** *~*) stay the same (*or* unchanged): F *das bleibt sich gleich!* that makes no difference!

gleichen ['glaɪçən] *v/i* (glich, geglichen, h) (*dat*) be (*or* look): *sich (or einander) ~* be (*or* look) alike, be similar; *j-m ~ an* (*dat*) equal s.o. in.

'gleicher'maßen *adv* **1.** equally. **2.** → *~'weise adv* in like manner, likewise.

'gleichfalls *adv* also, likewise: *danke, ~!* (thanks,) the same to you!

'gleichförmig *adj* **1.** uniform, monotonous. **2.** regular.

'Gleichförmigkeit *f* (-; no pl) **1.** uniformity, monotony. **2.** regularity.

'gleichgesinnt *adj* like-minded.

'Gleichgewicht *n* (-[e]s; no pl) *a. fig* balance, equilibrium: *das ~ verlieren (halten)* lose (keep) one's balance; *j-n aus dem ~ bringen a. fig.* throw s.o. off balance; *seelisches ~* (mental) equilibrium; *das ~ der Kräfte pol.* the balance of power.

'gleichgültig *adj* **1.** indifferent (*gegen* to): *er ist mir ~* I don't care for him. **2.** unimportant, trivial: *es ist mir ~* I don't care; *es ist ~, ob ...* it doesn't matter whether ...; *~, wann* no matter when. **'Gleichgültigkeit** *f* (-; no pl) **1.** indifference (*gegen* to). **2.** apathy.

'Gleichheit *f* (-; no pl) **1.** equality, identity. **2.** uniformity.

'Gleichheitszeichen *n* & equality sign.

'gleichkommen *v/i* (*irr, sep, -ge-, sn, →* **kommen**) (*dat*) **1.** equal (*an dat* in). **2.** amount to.

'gleichlautend *adj* identical: *~es Wort* homonym.

gleichmachen *v/t* (*sep, -ge-, h*) make equal (*dat* to): → **Erdboden. Gleichmache'rei** *f* (-; no pl) egalitarianism.

'gleichmäßig *adj* a) regular, even, b) constant: *et. ~ verteilen* distribute s.th. evenly. **'Gleichmäßigkeit** *f* (-; no pl) a) regularity, evenness, b) constancy.

'Gleichmut *m* (-[e]s; no pl) equanimity, calmness. **gleichmütig** ['glaɪçmy:tɪç] *adj* calm, imperturbable.

gleichnamig ['glaɪçna:mɪç] *adj* **1.** of the same name. **2.** & with a common denominator.

'Gleichnis *n* (-ses; -se) parable.

gleichrangig ['glaɪçraŋɪç] *adj* **1.** of the same rank. **2.** *fig* of equal importance.

'Gleichrichter *m* (-s; -) ⚡ rectifier.

'gleichschalten *v/t* (*sep, -ge-, h*) *fig.* coordinate, *pol.* bring into line.

'gleichseitig *adj* equilateral.

'gleichsetzen *v/t* (*sep, -ge-, h*) **1.** equate (*dat, mit* with). **2.** → **gleichstellen 2.**

'Gleichstand *m* (-[e]s; no pl) level score.

'gleichstellen *v/t* (*sep, -ge-, h*) **1.** → **gleichsetzen 1.** *j-n ~* put s.o. on an equal footing (*dat* with).

'Gleichstellung *f* (-; no pl) equalization.

'**Gleichstrom** *m* ⚡ direct current (DC).

'**gleichtun** *v/t* (*irr, sep,* -ge-, h, → *tun*) *es j-m ~* equal s.o. (*an or in dat* in).

'**Gleichung** *f* (-; -en) equation.

'**gleichwertig** *adj* **1.** of the same value, equivalent. **2.** equally good: *~e Gegner* evenly matched opponents.

'**gleichzeitig** *adj and adv* simultaneous(ly), *adv a.* at the same time.

'**gleichziehen** *v/i* (*irr, sep,* -ge-, h, → *ziehen*) a) *a. fig.* (*mit* with) catch up, draw level, b) equalize, level the score.

Gleis [glaɪs] *n* (-es; -e) rail(s), track(s), line: *fig. auf ein totes ~ schieben* put s.o., s.th. on ice; *das ausgefahrene ~* a) the beaten track, b) *a. das alte ~* the same old rut.

'**Gleiskörper** *m* permanent way.

'**Gleitboot** *n* hydroglider, hydroplane.

gleiten ['glaɪtən] *v/i* (glitt, geglitten, sn) **1.** glide, slide, slip, *hand etc*: pass. **2.** F *employee*: make use of flex(i)time.

'**gleitend** *adj fig.* sliding (*scale*): *~e Arbeitszeit → Gleitzeit.*

'**Gleit|fläche** *f* sliding surface. *~***flug** *m* glide. *~***flugzeug** *n* glider. *~***klausel** *f* ✈ escalator clause. *~***komma** *n* floating point. *~***mittel** *n* lubricant. *~***schirm** *m* paraglider. *~***schutz** *m* *mot.* antiskid device. *~***sichtgläser** *pl* multifocal lenses. *~***wachs** *n* skiing: gliding wax.

'**Gleitzeit** *f* (-; *no pl*) flexible working hours, flex(i)time. *~***karte** *f* time card.

Gletscher ['glɛtʃər] *m* (-s; -) glacier.

'**Gletscherbrand** *m* glacial sunburn.

'**Gletscherspalte** *f* crevasse.

glich [glɪç] *pret of* **gleichen.**

Glied [gliːt] *n* (-[e]s; -er) **1.** limb, member (*a. fig.*): *der Schreck fuhr ihr in die ~er* she had a bad shock. **2.** penis, (male) member. **3.** *a. fig.* link. **4.** ✕ rank.

gliedern ['gliːdərn] (h) **I** *v/t a*) arrange, organize, b) (sub)divide (*in acc* into). **II** *sich ~ in* (*acc*) be (sub)divided into.

'**Glieder|puppe** *f* jointed doll, *art*: lay figure. *~***schmerz** *m* rheumatism.

Gliederung ['gliːdərʊŋ] *f* (-; -en) a) arrangement, organization, structure, b) (sub)division.

'**Gliedmaßen** *pl* limbs.

'**Glimmer** *m* (-s; -) *min.* mica.

'**Glimmstengel** *m* F fag.

glimpflich ['glɪmpflɪç] *adj* mild, light: *~ mit j-m verfahren* be lenient with s.o.;

~ davonkommen get off lightly.

glitschig ['glɪtʃɪç] *adj* F slippery.

glitt [glɪt] *pret of* **gleiten.**

glitzern ['glɪtsərn] *v/i* (h) glitter.

global [glo'baːl] *adj* global.

Globus ['gloːbʊs] *m* (-/-[es]; -ben) globe.

Glöckchen ['glœkçən] *n* (-s; -) little bell.

Glocke ['glɔkə] *f* (-; -n) **1.** bell: F *et. an die große ~ hängen* shout s.th. from the housetops. **2.** (*cheese etc*) cover.

'**Glocken|blume** *f* bellflower. *~***geläut** *n* bell ringing. *~***gießer** *m* bell founder. *~***rock** *m* flared skirt. *~***schlag** *m* stroke (of the clock). *~***spiel** *n* chime(s), carillon. *~***stuhl** *m,* *~***turm** *m* belfry.

Glorie ['gloːriə] *f* (-; -n) **1.** glory. **2.** → '**Glorienschein** *m fig.* halo.

glorreich ['gloːraɪç] *adj* glorious.

Glossar [glɔ'saːr] *n* (-s; -e) glossary.

Glosse ['glɔsə] *f* (-; -n) **1.** gloss. **2.** commentary. **3.** *pl* snide remarks: *~en machen über* (*acc*) remark on, jeer at.

'**Glotzaugen** *pl* F goggle-eyes.

Glotze ['glɔtsə] *f* (-; -n) F gogglebox, *Am.* tube. '**glotzen** *v/i* (h) F goggle, gawp.

Glück *n* **1.** fortune, (good) luck: *auf gut ~* a) on the off-chance, b) at random; *zum ~* fortunately; *zu m-m* luckily for me; *~ haben* be lucky; *er hatte kein ~* he had no luck; *das ~ haben zu inf* have the good fortune to *inf*; *~ gehabt!* that was luck!; *nochmal ~ gehabt!* that was close!; *viel ~!* good luck!; *j-m ~ wünschen* a) wish s.o. luck, b) congratulate s.o. (*zu et.* on s.th.), *zum Geburtstag* wish s.o. (a) happy birthday; (*es ist*) *ein ~, daß ...* (it's a) good thing that ...; *er kann von ~ sagen, daß ...* he may thank his lucky stars that ... **2.** happiness, bliss.

'**glückbringend** *adj* lucky.

Glucke ['glʊkə] *f* (-; -n) **1.** *zo.* sitting hen. **2.** *fig.* (mother-)hen.

'**glucken** *v/i* (h) a) sit, b) cluck.

'**glücken** *v/i, v/impers* (sn) → **gelingen** I.

'**gluckern** *v/i* (h) glug, gurgle.

'**glücklich** **I** *adj* a) happy, b) lucky, fortunate: *sich ~ preisen* (*or schätzen*) count o.s. lucky; *ein ~er Einfall* a happy thought. **II** *adv* a) happily, b) luckily, c) safely, d) F finally, at (long) last.

'**glücklicherweise** *adv* luckily, fortunately, as luck would have it.

'**Glücksache** f *es ist* ~ it is a matter of luck.

'**Glücksbringer** m mascot, lucky charm.

glück'selig adj blissful, very happy.

Glück'seligkeit f (-; no pl) bliss.

glucksen ['glʊksən] v/i (h) **1.** gurgle. **2.** chuckle.

'**Glücks|fall** m lucky chance (F break), stroke of luck. ~**göttin** f Fortune. ~**kind** n child of Fortune. ~**klee** m four--leaf clover. ~**pfennig** m lucky penny. ~**pilz** m F fig. lucky dog. ~**ritter** m soldier of fortune. ~**spiel** n **1.** game of chance, coll. gambling. **2.** fig. gamble. ~**spieler(in** f) m gambler. ~**stern** m lucky star. ~**strähne** f streak of luck. ~**tag** m lucky (or happy) day.

'**glückstrahlend** adj radiant (with happiness).

'**Glückstreffer** m **1.** sports: fluke (hit or shot). **2.** fig. stroke of luck.

'**Glückwunsch** m congratulations (**zu** on), good wishes (**für** for): **m-n** (or **herzlichen**) ~! congratulations!, **zum Geburtstag** happy birthday!

'**Glückwunsch|karte** f greetings card. ~**tele,gramm** n greetings telegram.

'**Glühbirne** f (incandescent) bulb.

glühen ['gly:ən] (h) **I** v/i (**vor** dat with) glow, fig. a. burn. **II** v/t ⊙ anneal.

'**glühend** adj **1.** glowing (a. fig.), red-hot (metal), live (coals): ~ **heiß** scorching. **2.** fig. burning, ardent.

'**Glühkerze** f mot. heater plug.

'**Glühlampe** f incandescent lamp.

'**Glühwein** m mulled claret.

'**Glühwürmchen** n (-s; -) glow-worm.

Glut [glu:t] f (-; -en) **1.** (blazing) heat. **2.** (glowing) fire. **3.** a) embers, b) live coals. **4.** fig. ardo(u)r, glow.

Glutaminsäure [gluta'mi:n-] f glutamic acid.

Glyzerin [glytse'ri:n] n (-s; no pl) glycerin(e).

Gnade ['gna:də] f (-; no pl) **1.** mercy: **j-m auf** ~ **und Ungnade ausgeliefert sein** be at s.o.'s mercy; ~ **vor Recht ergehen lassen** show mercy. **2.** favo(u)r. **3.** eccl. grace. '**gnaden** v/i **dann gnade dir Gott!** (then) God help you!

'**Gnaden|akt** m ⚖ act of grace. ~**frist** f reprieve: **e-e** ~ **von drei Tagen** three days' grace. ~**gesuch** n ⚖ petition for mercy.

'**gnadenlos** adj merciless.

'**Gnadenstoß** m coup de grâce.

gnädig ['gnɛːdɪç] adj a) gracious, b) merciful: ~**e Frau** madam.

Gnom [gno:m] m (-en; -en) gnome.

Gobelin [gobə'lɛ̃:] m (-s; -s) Gobelin (tapestry).

Gold [gɔlt] n (-[e]s; no pl) gold: ~ **waschen** pan for gold; ~ **gewinnen** sports: win gold; **treu wie** ~ good as gold; **das ist nicht mit** ~ **aufzuwiegen** that is priceless; **es ist nicht alles** ~, **was glänzt** all that glitters is not gold.

'**Goldader** f vein of gold.

'**Goldbarren** m ingot of gold.

golden ['gɔldən] adj **1.** a) (of) gold, b) gilt. **2.** fig. golden (wedding, disc, etc)

'**Gold|fisch** m goldfish. ⚲**gelb** adj golden(-yellow). ~**gräber** [-grɛbər] m gold digger. ~**grube** f F fig. goldmine. ~**hamster** m zo. golden hamster.

goldig ['gɔldɪç] adj F sweet, Am. a. cute.

'**Gold|krone** f ⚕ gold cap. ~**me,daille** f gold medal. ~**me,daillengewinner(in** f) m gold medal(l)ist. ~**mine** f ⚒ goldmine. ~**münze** f gold coin. ~**plombe** f gold filling. ~**rahmen** m gilt frame. ⚲'**richtig** adj and adv F dead right: **er ist** ~ he is okay. ~**schmied** m goldsmith. ~**schnitt** m gilt edge(s): **Buch mit** ~ gilt-edged book. ~**stück** n **1.** gold coin. **2.** F fig. jewel. ~**waage** f **jedes Wort auf die** ~ **legen** weigh every word. ~**währung** f gold standard. ~**waren** pl gold articles.

Golf¹ [gɔlf] m (-[e]s; -e) geogr. gulf.

Golf² n (-s; no pl) sports: golf.

'**Golfplatz** m golf course, (golf) links.

'**Golfschläger** m golf club.

'**Golfspiel** n **1.** golf. **2.** game of golf.

'**Golfspieler(in** f) m golfer.

'**Golfstrom** m geogr. Gulf Stream.

Gondel ['gɔndəl] f (-; -n) gondola.

Gong [gɔŋ] m (-s; -e) gong.

gönnen ['gœnən] v/t (h) **1.** j-m et. ~ not to (be)grudge s.o. s.th.; j-m et. nicht ~ → mißgönnen. **2.** j-m (sich) et. ~ allow s.o. (o.s.) s.th.

'**Gönner** m (-s; -) patron.

'**gönnerhaft** adj patronizing.

'**Gönnerin** f (-; -nen) patroness.

Gonokokken [gono'kɔkən] pl ⚕ gonococci.

gor [go:r] pret of **gären.**

Gör [gøːr] *n* (-[e]s; -en) F *contp.* brat.

Gorilla [go'rɪla] *m* (-s; -s) gorilla (*a. sl. bodyguard*).

goß [gɔs] *pret of* **gießen**.

Gosse ['gɔsə] *f* (-; -n) *a. fig.* gutter.

Gotik ['goːtɪk] *f a*) Gothic (style), *b*) Gothic period. **'gotisch** *adj* Gothic.

Gott [gɔt] *m* (-es; ⁀er) *a*) *no pl* God, *b*) god, deity: *der liebe ~* the good Lord; *~ sei Dank!* thank God!; *leider ~es* unfortunately; *~ bewahre!*, *~ behüte!* God forbid!; *weiß ~(, was etc*) God knows (what *etc*); *um ~es Willen!* for God's sake!; *großer ~!*, *lieber ~!* good Lord!; → *gnaden, wahr*.

'gottähnlich *adj* godlike.

'gottbegnadet *adj* god-gifted, inspired.

Götterbild ['gœtər-] *n* idol.

'Götterspeise *f gastr.* jelly.

Gottesdienst ['gɔtəs-] *m* (divine) service.

'gottesfürchtig [-fʏrçtıç] *adj* godfearing.

'Gottes|haus *n* house of God, church. **~lästerer** *m* (-s; -) blasphemer. **~läste-rung** *f* (-; -en) blasphemy. **~mutter** *f* (-; *no pl*) Mother of God. **~sohn** *m* (-[e]s; *no pl*) Son of God.

Gottheit *f* (-; -en) deity, god, goddess.

Göttin ['gœtɪn] *f* (-; -nen) goddess.

'göttlich *adj* divine, godlike.

'gottlos *adj* godless, ungodly, wicked.

gotter'bärmlich *adj* F awful.

'gottverdammt *adj* V (god)damned.

'gottverlassen *adj* F godforsaken.

'Gottvertrauen *n* trust in God.

'gottvoll *adj* F *fig.* capital, very funny.

Götze ['gœtsə] *m* (-n; -n) idol.

Gouverneur [guvɛr'nøːr] *m* (-s; -e) governor.

Grab [graːp] *n* (-[e]s; ⁀er) grave, tomb: *mit einem Bein im ~e stehen* have one foot in the grave; *sich im ~e umdrehen* turn in one's grave; *verschwiegen wie das ~* (as) silent as the grave.

graben ['graːbən] (grub, gegraben, h) I *v/t* dig, burrow (*hole etc*), sink (*shaft etc*). II *v/i* dig (*nach* for). III *sich ~* (*in acc* into) dig, *zo.* burrow itself, *fig.* bury itself; *sich in j-s Gedächtnis ~* engrave itself on s.o.'s memory.

'Graben *m* (-s; ⁀) ditch, ✕ trench, *hist.* moat, *geol.* graben, rift.

Grabesstille ['graːbəs-] *f* deathly silence. **'Grabesstimme** *f* (*mit ~* in a) sepulchral voice.

'Grab|fund *m* grave find. **~gewölbe** *n* (burial) vault, tomb. **~inschrift** *f* epitaph. **~kammer** *f* burial chamber. **~mal** *n* (-[e]s; ⁀er) *a*) tomb, *b*) monument. **~rede** *f* funeral oration. **~stätte** *f* burial place, tomb. **~stein** *m* tombstone, gravestone.

Grad [graːt] *m* (-[e]s; -e) degree (*a. univ. or fig.*), ✕ *etc* rank, grade: *10 ~ Wärme* (*Kälte*) ten degrees above (below) zero (*or* freezing point); *Verbrennungen dritten ~es* third-degree burns; *Verwandte(r) zweiten* (*dritten*) *~es* relative once (twice) removed; *bis zu e-m gewissen ~* to a certain degree, up to a point; *im höchsten ~e* in the highest degree, extremely.

'Gradeinteilung *f* graduation.

gradieren [gra'diːrən] *v/t* (h) graduate.

'Gradmesser *m fig.* ga(u)ge, barometer.

'Gradnetz *n* (map) grid.

graduell [gra'dŭel] *adj* gradual.

graduieren [gradu'iːrən] (h) I *v/t* 1. ✪ graduate. 2. *univ.* confer a degree upon. II *v/i* 3. *univ.* graduate.

Gradu'ierte *m, f* (-n; -n) graduate.

Graf [graːf] *m* (-en; -en) count, *Br.* earl.

Graffito [gra'fiːto] *m, n* (-[s]; -ti) graffito.

Gräfin ['grɛfɪn] *f* (-; -nen) countess.

'Grafschaft *f* (-; -en) county.

gram [graːm] *adj j-m ~ sein* bear s.o. a grudge (*wegen gen* because of *s.th.*).

Gram *m* (-[e]s; *no pl*) grief, sorrow.

grämen ['grɛːmən] (h) I *v/t* grieve. II *sich ~* (*über acc, wegen*) *a*) grieve (over), *b*) worry (about).

Gramm [gram] *n* (-s; -e) gram, *Br. a.* gramme: *100 ~* 100 grams.

Grammatik [gra'matɪk] *f* (-; -en) 1. *no pl* grammar. 2. grammar book. **grammatikalisch** [gramati'kaːlɪʃ], **grammatisch** [gra'matɪʃ] *adj* grammatical.

Grammophon [gramo'foːn] *n* (-s; -e) TM gramophone, *Am.* phonograph.

Granat [gra'naːt] *m* (-[e]s; -e) *min.* garnet. **Gra'natapfel** *m* ❦ pomegranate.

Granate [gra'naːtə] *f* (-; -n) 1. ✕ *a*) shell, *b*) grenade. 2. F *sports:* cannonball.

Gra'nat|feuer *n* shellfire. **~splitter** *m* shell splinter. **~werfer** *m* mortar.

grandios [gran'diŏːs] *adj* grandiose, F terrific.

Granit [gra'niːt] *m* (-s; -e) granite.

Granne ['granə] f (-; -n) **1.** ⚘ beard, awn. **2.** zo. kemp.

Graphik ['graːfɪk] f (-; -en) **1.** no pl a) graphic arts, b) art(work). **2.** a) graphic (a. computer), print, b) ⚙ graph, diagram, c) illustration(s). ~**dia‚gramm** n computer: graphic drawing.

Graphiker ['graːfɪkər] m (-s; -), **'Graphikerin** f (-; -nen) **1.** (graphic) artist. **2.** commercial artist, (graphic) designer.

'**graphisch** adj **1.** graphic, art ... **2.** ⚙ graphic, diagrammatic: ~e Darstellung → Graphik 2.

Graphit [gra'fiːt] m (-s; -e) graphite.

Graphologe [grafo'loːgə] m (-n; -n), graphologist. **Graphologie** [grafolo'giː] f (-; no pl) graphology. **graphologisch** [grafo'loːgɪʃ] adj graphological.

Gras [graːs] n (-es; ⁻er ['grɛːzər]) grass: F **ins ~ beißen** bite the dust; **das ~ wachsen hören** hear the grass grow; **über et. ~ wachsen lassen** let the grass grow over s.th. '**grasbedeckt** adj grassy.

grasen ['graːzən] v/i (h) graze.

'**grasfressend** adj zo. graminivorous. '**grasgrün** adj grass-green. '**Grashalm** m blade of grass. '**Grashüpfer** m zo. grasshopper. '**Grasnarbe** f turf.

grassieren [gra'siːrən] v/i (h) be rife, disease: a. rage: **es ~ Gerüchte, daß ...** there are rumo(u)rs that ...

gräßlich ['grɛslɪç] adj horrible, ghastly, dreadful, monstrous, atrocious.

Grat [graːt] m (-[e]s; -e) **1.** ⚙ bur(r). **2.** ridge.

Gräte ['grɛːtə] f (-; -n) (fish)bone.

Gratifikation [gratifika'tsioːn] f (-; -en) gratuity, bonus.

gratis ['graːtɪs] adv free (of charge).

'**Gratisaktie** f bonus share, pl scrip issues. '**Gratisprobe** f free sample.

Grätsche ['grɛːtʃə] f (-; -n) gym. a) straddle, b) straddle vault.

'**grätschen** v/i, v/i (h) gym. straddle.

Gratulant [gratu'lant] m (-en; -en) congratulator, well-wisher. **Gratulation** [gratula'tsioːn] f (-; -en) congratulations (zu on). **gratulieren** [gratu'liːrən] v/i (h) congratulate (j-m zu et. s.o. on s.th.): **j-m zum Geburtstag ~** wish s.o. many happy returns (of the day); (**ich) gratuliere!** congratulations!

'**Gratwanderung** f fig. tightrope walk.

grau [grau] adj grey, Am. gray, fig. a. bleak: **der ~e Alltag** the drab monotony of everyday life; → Haar, Vorzeit.

'**Graubrot** n rye bread.

grauen ['grauən] v/i, v/impers (h) **mir graut (or es graut mir) vor** (dat) I dread (the thought of), I am terrified of. '**Grauen** n (-s; -) horror (**vor** dat of).

'**grauenhaft**, '**grauenvoll** adj horrible.

'**grauhaarig** adj grey-(Am. gray-)haired.

graulen ['graulən] (h) F **I sich ~** be afraid (**vor** dat of). **II** v/t **j-n aus dem Haus ~** freeze s.o. out.

gräulich ['grɔylɪç] adj greyish, Am. grayish.

'**graume‚liert** adj greying, Am. graying.

Graupe ['graupə] f (-; -n) pearl barley.

Graupel ['graupəl] f (-; -n) soft hail.

'**graupeln** v/impers (h) **es graupelt** a soft hail is falling.

grausam adj **1.** cruel. **2.** F fig. awful.

'**Grausamkeit** f (-; -en) cruelty.

grausen ['grauzən] → grauen.

'**Grausen** n (-s; no pl) horror.

'**grausig** ['grauzɪç] → grauenhaft.

'**Grauzone** f fig. grey (Am. gray) area.

Graveur [gra'vøːr] m (-s; -e) engraver.

gravieren [gra'viːrən] v/t (h) engrave.

gra'vierend adj fig. serious.

Gra'vierung f (-; -en) engraving.

Gravitation [gravita'tsioːn] f (-; no pl) phys. gravitation. **gravitieren** [gravi'tiːrən] v/i (h) a. fig. (**zu, auf** acc towards) gravitate, tend.

Grazie ['graːtsiə] f (-; no pl) grace.

graziös [gra'tsiøːs] adj graceful.

'**greifbar** adj **1.** handy, available: **in ~er Nähe, ~ nahe** a. fig. within reach, near at hand. **2.** fig. tangible, concrete: ~**e Formen annehmen** be taking shape.

greifen ['graifən] (griff, gegriffen, h) **I** v/t **1.** seize, take hold of, grab: **zum ♀ nah** within reach; **fig. zu hoch gegriffen** figure etc: too high. **2.** ♪ stop (string), strike (note etc). **II** v/i **3.** ~ **an** (acc) touch; ~ **nach** reach for, grasp at, grab for; ~ **in** (acc) reach into; ~ **zu** reach for, fig. resort to; fig. **um sich ~** spread; → Arm, Tasche **4.** ⚙ grip, grab. **5.** fig. be effective, F bite.

'**Greifer** m (-s; -) ⚙ grab, gripper.

'**Greifvogel** m bird of prey.

'**Greifzange** f gripping tongs.

'**Greifzirkel** m cal(l)ipers.

greis [grais] adj (very) old. **Greis** m (-es;

-e) (very) old man. '**Greisenalter** n old age. '**greisenhaft** adj senile. '**Greisenhaftigkeit** f (-; no pl) senility. **Greisin** ['graɪzɪn] f (-; -nen) (very) old woman.

grell [grɛl] adj glaring (a. fig.), a. loud (colo[u]r), shrill, strident (sound).

Gremium ['greːmiʊm] n (-s; -mien) body (of experts etc), group.

'**Grenzbereich** m **1.** border area. **2.** fig. borderland. '**Grenzbewohner(in** f) m inhabitant of the border area.

Grenze ['grɛntsə] f (-; -n) **1.** border, frontier, boundary (a. fig.): **an der** ~ **on** the border, at the frontier; fig. **die** ~ **ziehen bei** draw the line at. **2.** fig. a) borderline, b) limit (gen to), bounds (gen of): **in** ~**n** within limits, up to a point; **ohne** ~ = **grenzenlos**; **sich in** ~**n halten** keep within (reasonable) limits, iro. success etc: be rather limited; ~**n setzen** set limits (dat to); **alles hat s-e** ~**n** there is a limit to everything. '**grenzen** v/i (h) border (**an** acc on). '**grenzenlos** adj boundless, immense, infinite (misery, patience, etc), unlimited (power): ~ **dumm** incredibly stupid. '**Grenzfall** m fig. borderline case.

Grenzgänger ['grɛntsgɛŋər] m (-s; -) frontier commuter.

'**Grenz|gebiet** n **1.** border area. **2.** fig. borderland. ~**kon,flikt** m border dispute. ~**kon,trolle** f border control. ~**kosten** pl † marginal cost. ~**linie** f boundary (line), borderline (a. fig.), pol. demarcation line, sports: line. ~**pfahl** m boundary post. ~**posten** m border guard. ~**schutz** m **1.** frontier protection. **2.** border police. ~**stadt** f frontier town. ~**stein** m boundary stone. ~**übergang** m checkpoint, border crossing(-point). ⚲**überschreitend** adj border-crossing, across the border(s). ~**verkehr** m (**kleiner** ~ local) border traffic. ~**wert** m limit(ing value), threshold value. ~**zwischenfall** m border incident.

Greuel ['grɔyəl] m (-s; -) **1.** horror: **er (es) ist mir ein** ~ I loathe him (it). **2.** atrocity. '**Greuelmärchen** n atrocity story. '**Greueltat** f atrocity.

greulich ['grɔylɪç] → **gräßlich**.

Grieben ['griːbən] pl gastr. greaves.

Grieche ['griːçə] m (-n; -n) Greek. '**Griechenland** n (-s) Greece.

'**Griechin** f (-; -nen) Greek (woman).

'**griechisch** adj Greek, art: a. Grecian: ~**römisch** Gr(a)eco-Roman; ~**orthodox** Greek (Orthodox).

'**Griechisch** n (-[s]) ling. Greek.

griesgrämig ['griːsgrɛːmɪç] adj F sullen, grumpy, grouchy.

Grieß [griːs] m (-es; -e) **1.** gastr. semolina. **2.** ☉ grit. **3.** 🜨 gravel.

'**Grießbrei** m semolina pudding.

griff [grɪf] pret of **greifen**.

Griff m (-[e]s; -e) **1.** no pl (**nach**) grasp (at), grab (for), reaching (for): ~ **nach der Macht** bid for power; **e-n guten** ~ **tun** make a good choice (**mit** with); **im** ~ **haben** (**in den** ~ **bekommen**) have (get) s.th. under control, have (get) a (good) grip on; **mit sicherem** ~ right away, fig. with a sure touch. **2.** grip (a. gym.), wrestling etc: hold, ♪ stop. **3.** a) handle, b) grip, c) in bus etc: strap. **4.** textil. feel.

'**griffbereit** adj (ready) to hand, handy. '**Griffbrett** n ♪ fingerboard.

Griffel ['grɪfəl] m (-s; -) style.

griffig ['grɪfɪç] adj **1.** handy. **2.** road: having a good grip, nonskid (wheels).

Grill [grɪl] m (-s; -s) gastr. grill.

Grille ['grɪlə] f (-; -n) **1.** zo. cricket. **2.** F fig. silly idea, whim.

grillen ['grɪlən] v/t (h) grill, barbecue.

'**Grillparty** f barbecue.

Grimasse [gri'masə] f (-; -n) grimace: ~**n schneiden** pull faces, grimace.

grimmig ['grɪmɪç] adj a. fig. grim, fierce.

Grind [grɪnt] m (-[e]s; -e) 🜨 scab.

grinsen ['grɪnzən] v/i (h), **Grinsen** n (-s) (**über** acc at) a) grin, b) sneer.

grippal [grɪ'paːl] adj ~**er Infekt** influenza(l) infection. **Grippe** ['grɪpə] f (-; -n) influenza, F 'flu. '**Grippe...** influenza (epidemic, virus, etc). '**grippekrank** adj down with influenza, F having the 'flu. '**Grippewelle** f wave of influenza.

grob [groːp] adj **1.** coarse (a. ☉), rough (a. fig. sketch, work, etc): ~ **behauen** rough-hewn; **in** ~**en Zügen** roughly; F **wir sind aus dem Gröbsten heraus** we are over the worst; → **schätzen** 1. **2.** fig. gross (lie, mistake, etc). **3.** fig. rude, coarse: ~ **werden gegen** be rude to. '**grobgemahlen** adj coarse-ground.

'**Grobheit** f (-; -en) **1.** no pl coarseness, roughness, fig. a. rudeness. **2.** pl rude words: *j-m ~en an den Kopf werfen* be rude to s.o., insult s.o.

Grobian ['gro:biːaːn] *m* (-s; -e) rude fellow.

'grobkörnig *adj* coarse-grained.

'grobmaschig *adj* wide-meshed.

'Grobschnitt *m* (*tobacco*) coarse cut.

grölen ['grøːlən] *v/i, v/t* (h) bawl, roar.

Groll [grɔl] *m* (-[e]s; *no pl*) ranco(u)r, resentment, anger. **'grollen** *v/i* (h) **1.** be angry: *j-m ~* have a grudge against s.o. (*wegen* because of). **2.** *fig.* rumble.

Gros [groː] *n* (- [groː(s)]; - [groːs]) main body.

Groschen ['grɔʃən] *m* (-s; -) ten-pfennig piece, *fig.* penny, *Am.* cent: F *der ~ ist gefallen!* the penny has dropped!

'Groschenro‚man *m* F penny dreadful, *Am.* dime novel.

groß [groːs] **I** *adj* **1.** big, large, *a.* capital (*letter*): *wie ~ ist es?* what size is it? **2.** tall, high: *wie ~ sind Sie?* what is your height?; *sie sind gleich ~* they are of equal height. **3.** great (*distance*), long (*trip etc*). **4.** a) elder, F big (*brother, sister*), b) grown-up: *die Großen* the grown-ups. **5.** *fig.* great, big, bad (*mistake etc*), severe (*loss etc*): *Friedrich der Große* Frederick the Great; *e-e größere Sache* a major affair; *~e Worte* big words; *Großes leisten* achieve great things; → *Ferien, Geld, Los* 1, *Rede* 1, *Welt.* **6.** great, grand: F *ganz ~* super, terrific; *in et. ~ sein* be great at (doing) s.th.; *er ist kein ~er Tänzer* he's no great dancer. **7.** *im ~en* on a large scale, ✝ wholesale, in bulk; *im ~en (und) ganzen* on the whole, by and large. **II** *adv* **8.** ~ *schreiben* capitalize; F *et. ~ feiern* celebrate s.th. in great style; *~ in Mode sein* be all the rage; *~ ankommen* be a big success (*bei* with); *er kümmert sich nicht ~ darum* he doesn't bother much about it; → *herausbringen, herauskommen* 1.

'Großabnehmer *m* ✝ bulk purchaser.

'Großaktio‚när *m* major shareholder.

'großangelegt *adj* large-scale.

'Großangriff *m* ✕ large-scale attack.

'großartig *adj* grand, great, marvel-(l)ous, fantastic.

'Großaufnahme *f film:* close-up.

'Großauftrag *m* ✝ large (*or* big) order.

'Großbank *f* (-; -en) big (*or* major) bank.

'Großbetrieb *m* large-scale enterprise.

'Großbuchstabe *m* capital (letter).

Größe ['grøːsə] *f* (-; -n) **1.** a) size, b) height, c) dimensions, area: *welche ~ haben Sie?* what size do you take? **2.** A, *phys.* quantity, *astr.* magnitude. **3.** *no pl fig.* a) extent, b) greatness. **4.** F *fig.* great figure, celebrity, *film, sports, etc:* star: *e-e ~ auf dem Gebiet* (*gen*) an authority on.

'Großeinkauf *m* ✝ bulk purchase.

'Großeinsatz *m* large-scale operation.

'Großeltern *pl* grandparents.

'Großenkel *m etc* → *Urenkel etc.*

'Größenordnung *f* **1.** *astr. etc* order (of magnitude). **2.** *fig.* scale: *dieser ~* of this order.

'großenteils *adv* mostly, largely.

'Größenverhältnisse *pl* proportions.

'Größenwahn *m* megalomania.

'größenwahnsinnig *adj* megalomaniac.

'Großfahndung *f* dragnet operation.

'Großfa‚milie *f* extended family.

'Großfeuer *n* big blaze, four-alarm fire.

'Großflughafen *m* major airport.

'Großfor‚mat *n* large size.

'Großgrundbesitz *m* large land holdings, large estates. **'Großgrundbesitzer(in** *f)* *m* big landowner.

'Großhandel *m* wholesale trade: *im ~* wholesale. **'Großhandels...** wholesale.

'Großhändler(in *f)* *m* wholesaler.

'Großhandlung *f* wholesale firm.

'Großherzog(in *f)* *m* grand duke (duchess).

'Großhirn *n* *anat.* cerebrum.

'Großindu‚strie *f* big industry.

'Großindustri‚elle *m* big industrialist.

Grossist [grɔ'sɪst] *m* (-en; -en) wholesaler.

'großjährig → *volljährig.*

'Großkapi‚tal *n* big business.

'Großkaufmann *m* big merchant.

'Großkon‚zern *m* big concern.

großkotzig ['groːskɔtsɪç] *adj* F a) flash, b) show-off(ish), arrogant.

'Großkraftwerk *n* super power station.

'Großküche *f* canteen kitchen.

'Großkundgebung *f* mass rally.

'Großmacht *f* super power.

'Großmama *f* F grandma.

'Großmaul *n* F bigmouth.

'Großmut *f* (-; *no pl*) magnanimity, generosity. **großmütig** ['groːsmyːtɪç] *adj* magnanimous, generous.

'**Großmutter** f grandmother.
'**Großneffe** m grandnephew.
'**Großnichte** f grandniece.
'**Großonkel** m great-uncle.
'**Großpapa** m F grandpa.
'**Großpro,jekt** n large-scale project.
'**Großraum** m der **~ München** Greater Munich. **~bü,ro** n open-plan office.
'**Großrechner** m large(-scale) computer.
'**Großschreibung** f capitalization.
'**großsprecherisch** adj boastful.
großspurig ['gro:sʃpu:rɪç] adj arrogant.
'**Großstadt** f big city.
'**Großstädter(in** f) m city-dweller.
'**großstädtisch** adj of a big city, urban.
'**Großtante** f great-aunt.
'**Großtat** f great feat.
'**Großteil** m large part. '**größtenteils** adv for the most part, mostly.
'**großtun** v/i (irr, sep, -ge-, h, → **tun**) talk big: **~ mit** brag about, show off with.
'**Großunternehmen** n ✝ large-scale (or big) enterprise.
'**Großvater** m grandfather.
'**Großveranstaltung** f big event.
'**Großverdiener(in** f) m big earner.
'**Großwildjagd** f big game hunt(ing).
'**großziehen** v/t (irr, sep, -ge-, h, → **ziehen**) raise, rear, bring up (child).
'**großzügig** adj **1.** generous. **2.** broad-minded. **3.** spacious. **4.** large-scale.
'**Großzügigkeit** f (-; no pl) **1.** generosity. **2.** broad-mindedness. **3.** large scale.
grotesk [gro'tɛsk] adj grotesque.
Grotte ['grɔtə] f (-; -n) grotto.
grub [gru:p] pret of **graben**.
Grübchen ['gry:pçən] n (-s; -) dimple.
Grube ['gru:bə] f (-; -n) pit, ⚒ a. mine.
Grübelei [gry:bə'laɪ] f (-; -en) brooding.
grübeln ['gry:bəln] v/i (h) (**über** acc over, on) brood, muse.
'**Grubenarbeiter** m miner.
'**Grubenunglück** n mine disaster.
Grübler ['gry:blər] m (-s; -) brooder.
Gruft [grʊft] f (-; ⸚e) tomb, vault, crypt.
grün [gry:n] adj green (a. fig.): **~er Hering** fresh herring; **~er Salat** lettuce; F **~er Junge** greenhorn; **die Grünen** pol. the Green (Party); fig. **~es Licht geben (bekommen)** give s.o. (get) the green light (**für** for); **e-e Entscheidung vom ~en Tisch** an armchair decision; **~ vor Neid** green with envy; **j-n ~ und blau schlagen** beat s.o. black and blue; **auf**

k-n ~en Zweig kommen get nowhere; F **er ist dir nicht ~** he has it in for you.
Grün n (-s; -) green (a. golf): **bei ~, auf ~** mot. at green; F **das ist dasselbe in ~** it's practically the same thing.
Grund [grʊnt] m (-[e]s; ⸚e) **1.** no pl a) ground, b) bottom (a. fig.): **am ~, auf dem ~** at the bottom; **auf ~ laufen** ⚓ run aground; **e-r Sache auf den ~ gehen (kommen)** go (get) to the bottom of s.th. **2.** no pl **~ (und Boden)** land, property; **sich in ~ und Boden schämen** be terribly ashamed; **in ~ und Boden verdammen** condemn s.o., s.th. outright. **3.** no pl fig. basis, foundation(s): **auf ~ von** (or gen) a) on the basis (or strength) of, b) because of; **von ~ auf** change etc entirely (or radically); **im ~e (genommen)** actually, basically. **4.** reason, cause: **aus diesem ~** for this reason; **aus persönlichen Gründen** for personal reasons; **aus gutem ~** for good reason, justly; **allen ~ haben zu** inf have every reason to inf; **ich frage aus e-m bestimmten ~** I ask for a reason; **(k-n) ~ zur Klage haben** have (no) cause for complaint.
'**Grund|anstrich** m priming coat. **~ausbildung** f ✕ basic training. **~bedeutung** f primary meaning. **~bedingung** f basic condition, prerequisite. **~begriff** m basic concept, pl fundamentals.
'**Grund|besitz** m landed property, real estate. **~besitzer(in** f) m landowner.
'**Grundbestandteil** m basic component.
'**Grundbuch** n land register. **~amt** n land registry. **~auszug** m extract from the land register.
'**grundehrlich** adj thoroughly honest.
gründen ['grʏndən] (h) **I** v/t found, establish, set up: fig. **et. ~ auf** (acc) base (or found) s.th. on. **II** sich **~ auf** (acc) fig. be based on. **III** v/i **~ auf** (dat) a) rest (or be based) on, b) be due to.
Gründer ['grʏndər] m (-s; -), '**Gründerin** f (-; -nen) founder.
'**grundfalsch** adj absolutely wrong.
'**Grund|farbe** f phys. primary colo(u)r. **~fläche** f area, ♣ base, △ floor space. **~gebühr** f basic rate. **~gedanke** m basic idea. **~gehalt** n (-[e]s; ⸚er) basic salary. **~gesetz** n basic (constitutional) law.
grundieren [grʊn'di:rən] v/t (h) ground,

◎ prime. **Grun'dierfarbe** f primer. **Grun'dierung** f (-; -en) priming coat.
'**Grund|kapi,tal** n initial capital, stock. **~kenntnisse** pl basic knowledge. **~la-ge** f foundation, fig. a. basis: jeder ~ entbehren be completely unfounded. **~lagenforschung** f basic research.

'**grundlegend** adj basic, fundamental, definitive (book etc).

gründlich ['grʏntlɪç] adj thorough, careful: F sich ~ irren be jolly well mistaken.

'**Gründlichkeit** f (-; no pl) thoroughness.
'**Grundlinie** f ℛ, sports: base line.
'**Grundlohn** m basic wage(s).
'**grundlos** I adj fig. groundless, unfounded. II adv for no reason (at all).
'**Grund|mauer** f foundation wall. **~nah-rungsmittel** pl basic food(stuff).

Grün'donnerstag m Maundy Thursday.
'**Grund|pfeiler** m 1. △ supporting pillar. 2. fig. cornerstone. **~prin,zip** n basic principle. **~rechnungsart** f die vier **~en** the four fundamental operations of arithmetics. **~rechte** pl pol. basic rights. **~regel** f ground rule. **~riß** m 1. △ ground plan. 2. fig. outline(s).

'**Grundsatz** m principle: es sich zum ~ machen zu inf make it a rule to inf.
'**grundsätzlich** [-zetslɪç] I adj fundamental. II adv in principle: ich bin ~ dagegen I am absolutely against it.
'**Grund|schule** f primary (Am. a. grade) school. **~schüler(in** f) m primary pupil. **~stein** m △ foundation stone: fig. den ~ legen zu lay the foundations of. **~steinlegung** f (-; -en) laying (of) the foundation stone. **~stock** m 1. -[e]s; no pl) basis. **~stoff** m 1. 🜍 element. 2. raw material. **~stoffindu,strie** f basic industry. **~stein** m 1. plot of land), †, ✝ property, real estate. 2. (building) site.
'**Grundstücks|makler(in** f) m (real) estate agent, Am. realtor. **~markt** m property market. **~preis** m land price.
'**Grund|studium** n basic study. **~stufe** f ped. elementary classes. **~ton** m 1. ♩ keynote. 2. paint. ground shade. **~um-satz** m 🜨 basal metabolic rate.
'**Gründung** f (-; -en) foundation.
'**grund|ver'kehrt** adj utterly wrong. **~ver'schieden** adj entirely different.
'**Grundwasser** n (-s; no pl) ground wa-

ter. **~spiegel** m ground-water level.
'**Grund|wehrdienst** m basic military service. **~wortschatz** m basic vocabulary. **~zahl** f cardinal number. **~zug** m characteristic (feature), pl outline(s), basics: in s-n Grundzügen schildern outline.
'**Grün|fläche** f a) green space, lawn, b) park area. **~futter** n ✿ green fodder. **~gürtel** m green belt. **~kohl** m kale.
'**grünlich** adj greenish.
'**Grünschnabel** m F whippersnapper.
'**Grünspan** m (-[e]s; no pl) verdigris.
'**Grünspecht** m zo. green woodpecker.
'**Grünstreifen** m → **Mittelstreifen**.

grunzen ['grʊntsən] v/i, v/t (h) grunt.
'**Grünzeug** n F a) greens, b) herbs.
Gruppe ['grʊpə] f (-; -n) 1. group (a. ✝). 2. team. 3. ✕ squad.
'**Gruppen|arbeit** f teamwork. **~dy,na-mik** f group dynamics. **~reise** f group travel. **~sex** m group sex. **~thera,pie** f group therapy.
'**gruppenweise** adv in groups.
gruppieren [grʊ'pi:rən] (h) I v/t group: neu ~ regroup. II sich ~ form a group (or groups) (um [a]round).
Grup'pierung f (-; -en) 1. grouping, formation. 2. group(s).
Grusel... ['gru:zəl...] horror (film, story, etc). '**gruselig** adj creepy, spooky. '**gruseln** v/t, v/i, v/impers es gruselt mir (or mich), mich gruselt it gives me the creeps; es war zum Gruseln it was enough to give you the creeps.
Gruß [gru:s] m (-es; ⸚e) greeting(s) (aus from), ✕ salute: viele Grüße (or e-n schönen ~) an ... give my regards (or my love) to ...; in letter: mit besten (or freundlichen) Grüßen Yours sincerely; herzliche Grüße love, best wishes.
grüßen ['gry:sən] (h) I v/t greet, esp. ✕ salute, F say hello: F grüß dich! hello (there)!, hi!; ~ Sie ihn von mir! give my regards (or my love) to him! II v/i say good morning (etc), say hello, esp. ✕ salute.
'**Grußwort** n (-[e]s; -e) greeting.
gucken ['gʊkən] v/i (h) look, peep.
'**Guckloch** n peephole.
Guerillakrieg [ge'rɪlja-] m guer(r)illa war(fare).
Gulasch ['gʊlaʃ] n (-[e]s; -e, -s) goulash.
'**Gulaschsuppe** f goulash soup.

Gulden ['gʊldən] m (-s; -) guilder.

gültig ['gʏltɪç] adj valid (a. fig.), good (a. sports), effective (**ab, vom** as from), in force, legal: **~ werden** become valid, contract etc: become effective.

'**Gültigkeit** f (-; no pl) validity, ⚖, pol. legal force.

'**Gültigkeitsdauer** f (period of) validity, a. term (of contract).

Gummi ['gʊmi] **1.** m, n (-s; -[s]) ⚙ a) rubber, b) gum. **2.** m (-s; -s) F rubber. **3.** n (-s; -s) → **Gummiband. 4.** m (-s; -s) → **Radiergummi.**

'**gummiartig** adj rubbery.

'**Gummiband** n rubber band, elastic. **~bärchen** n gastr. jelly baby. **~baum** m **1.** rubber tree. **2.** rubber plant.

gummieren [gʊˈmiːrən] v/t (h) gum, ⚙ rubberize.

'**Gummihandschuh** m rubber glove. **~linse** f phot. zoom lens. **~para,graph** m F elastic clause. **~stiefel** m wellington (boot), Am. rubber boot. **~strumpf** m elastic stocking. **~waren** pl rubber goods. **~zug** m elastic.

Gunst [gʊnst] f (-; no pl) favo(u)r.

günstig ['gʏnstɪç] adj **1.** favo(u)rable (**für** to): **~e Gelegenheit** opportunity; **im ~sten Fall** at best; **zu ~en Bedingungen** on easy terms; **~es Angebot, ~er Kauf** bargain. **2.** convenient.

'**Günstling** m (-s; -e) favo(u)rite. '**Günstlingswirtschaft** f (-; no pl) favo(u)ritism.

Gurgel ['gʊrgəl] f (-; -n) a) throat, b) gullet. '**Gurgelmittel** n gargle.

'**gurgeln** v/i (h) **1.** gargle. **2.** gurgle.

Gurke ['gʊrkə] f (-; -n) **1.** a) cucumber, b) gherkin. **2.** F contp. lemon.

'**Gurkenhobel** m cucumber slicer. '**Gurkensa,lat** m cucumber salad.

gurren ['gʊrən] v/i (h) coo.

Gurt [gʊrt] m (-[e]s; -e) **1.** belt, ✈, mot. seat belt. **2.** strap.

'**Gurtband** n (-[e]s; =er) waistband.

Gürtel ['gʏrtəl] m (-s; -) belt: **den ~ enger schnallen** a. fig. tighten one's belt. **~linie** f waist(line): **unter der (or die) ~** a. fig. below the belt. **~reifen** m mot. radial(-ply) tyre (Am. tire). **~rose** f (-; no pl) ✻ shingles. **~schnalle** f belt buckle. **~tier** n armadillo.

Guß [gʊs] m (-sses; =sse) **1.** ⚙ a) casting, founding, b) cast iron: fig. (**wie**) **aus einem ~** of a piece. **2.** a) gush, jet, b) downpour. **3.** gastr. icing.

'**Gußbe,ton** m cast concrete. '**Gußeisen** n cast iron. '**gußeisern** adj cast-iron. '**Gußform** f casting mo(u)ld. '**Gußstahl** m cast steel. '**Gußstück** n casting.

gut [guːt] **I** adj good, fine: **ganz ~** quite good, not bad; **also ~!** all right (then); **schon ~!** never mind!; (**es ist**) **~, daß ...**, **nur ~, daß ...** (it's a) good thing that ...; **auch ~!, es ist ganz ~ so!** it's just as well!; (**wieder**) **~ werden** come right (again), be all right; **sei** (**bitte**) **so ~ und ...** would you be good enough to ...; **~ sein in** (dat) be good at (doing s.th.); **das ist ~ gegen** (or **für**) **Erkältungen** that's good for colds; **mir ist nicht ~!** I don't feel (so) well!; **wozu soll das ~ sein?** what's that in aid of?; **laß** (**mal** or **es**) **~ sein!** that'll do!; **Gut und Böse** good and evil; **im ~en** in a friendly way, amicably. **II** adv well, look, taste, etc good: **er spricht ~ Englisch** he speaks good English; **es ~ haben** have it good, have a good time; **du hast es ~!** you are lucky!; **es ~ möglich, es kann ~ sein** it may well be; **es gefällt mir ~** I (do) like it; **~ gemacht!** well done!; **so ~ wie gewonnen** as good as won; **so ~ wie nichts** hardly anything; **so ~ wie unmöglich** practically impossible; **~ zwei Stunden** a good two hours; **~** (**und gern**) easily; **ich kann ihn doch nicht ~ fragen** I can't very well ask him; F **mach's ~!** a) good luck, b) so long!, take care (of yourself!); → **Gute, gutgehen** etc, **Reise.**

Gut n (-[e]s; Güter) **1.** good(s), property, possession(s): fig. **das höchste ~** the greatest good. **2.** usu. pl a) ✝ goods, b) 🚂 goods, Am. freight. **3.** estate. **4.** ⚙ material, stock.

'**Gutachten** n (-s; -) (expert) opinion.

'**Gutachter** m (-s; -) expert, '**Gutachterin** f (-; -nen) expert, ⚖ expert witness.

'**gutartig** adj **1.** good-natured. **2.** ✻ benign. '**Gutartigkeit** f (-; no pl) **1.** good nature. **2.** ✻ benignity.

'**gutaussehend** adj good-looking.

'**gutbezahlt** adj well-paid.

'**gut'bürgerlich** adj solid middle-class: **~e Küche** good plain cooking.

Gutdünken ['guːtdʏŋkən] n (-s; no pl)

discretion: *handle nach (eigenem)* ~ use your own discretion.

'**Gute** *n* (-n) the good: *das ~ an der Sache* the good thing about it; *~s tun* do good; *des ~n zuviel tun* overdo it; *das ist des ~n zuviel* that's too much of a good thing; *alles ~!* all the best!

Güte ['gy:tə] *f* (-; *no pl*) **1.** goodness, kindness: *würden Sie die ~ haben zu inf* would you be so kind as to *inf*; F (*du*) *m-e ~!* good gracious! **2.** quality: *erster ~* a) first-class, b) *iro.* of the first water. '**Güteklasse** *f* ✝ grade, quality.

Gute'nachtgeschichte *f* bedtime story.

Gute'nachtkuß *m* goodnight kiss.

Güter|bahnhof ['gy:tər-] *m* goods station, *Am.* freight depot. **~gemeinschaft** *f* ⚖ community of property. **~trennung** *f* ⚖ separation of property. **~verkehr** *m* goods (*Am.* freight) traffic. **~wagen** *m* 🚃 (goods) waggon, *Am.* freight car. **~zug** *m* goods (*Am.* freight) train.

'**Gütezeichen** *n* mark of quality.

'**gutgebaut** *adj* well-built.

'**gutgehen** *v/i* (*irr, sep,* -ge-, sn, → **gehen**) **1.** go (off) well, work out well: *das kann nicht ~!* that's bound to go wrong!; *wenn alles gutgeht* if nothing goes wrong. **2.** *mir geht es gut* a) I'm fine, b) I'm doing fine.

'**gutgelaunt** *adj* in a good mood.

'**gutgemeint** *adj* well-meant.

'**gutgläubig** *adj* **1.** credulous. **2.** acting (*or* done) in good faith, bona fide. '**Gutgläubigkeit** *f* (-; *no pl*) credulity, gullibility.

'**Guthaben** *n* (-s; -) **1.** credit (balance). **2.** account.

'**gutheißen** *v/t* (*irr, sep,* -ge-, h, → **heißen**) *et.* ~ approve (of) s.th.

'**gutherzig** *adj* kind(-hearted).

gütig ['gy:tɪç] *adj* kind (*zu* to).

gütlich ['gy:tlɪç] **I** *adj* **1.** amicable. **II** *adv* **2.** amicably. **3.** *sich ~ tun an* (*dat*) help o.s. to, take (*or* eat, drink) one's fill of.

'**gutmachen** *v/t* (*sep,* -ge-, h) make good, make up for.

'**gutmütig** [-my:tɪç] *adj* good-natured. '**Gutmütigkeit** *f* (-; *no pl*) good nature.

'**Gutschein** *m* coupon, voucher.

'**gutschreiben** *v/t* (*irr, sep,* -ge-, h, → **schreiben**) *j-m et.* ~ credit s.o. with s.th., pass s.th. to s.o.'s credit.

'**Gutschrift** *f* **1.** credit (entry). **2.** credit voucher. **~anzeige** *f* credit note.

'**Gutshaus** *n* manor (house).

'**Gutsherr**(**in**) *f* *m* lord (lady) of the manor. '**Gutshof** *m* estate.

'**gutsituiert** *adj* well-to-do, well-off.

'**guttun** *v/i* (*irr, sep,* -ge-, h, → **tun**) *j-m ~* do s.o. good.

guttural [gʊtuˈraːl] *adj* guttural.

'**gutunterrichtet** *adj* well-informed.

'**gutwillig** *adj* willing (to oblige).

'**Gutwilligkeit** *f* (-; *no pl*) willingness.

Gymnasialbildung [gymnaˈzi̯aːl-] *f* secondary school education. **Gymnasiast** [gymnaˈzi̯ast] *m* (-en; -en) grammar-school (*Am.* high-school) student.

Gymnasium [gymˈnaːzi̯ʊm] *n* (-s; -ien) (*humanistisches ~* classical) secondary school, *Br. a.* grammar school.

Gymnastik [gymˈnastɪk] *f* (-; *no pl*) gymnastics, (physical) exercises, callisthenics. **Gym'nastikanzug** *m* leotard. **gym'nastisch** *adj* gymnastic.

Gynäkologe [gynɛkoˈloːgə] *m* (-n; -n) gyn(a)ecologist. **Gynäkologie** [gynɛkoloˈgiː] *f* (-; *no pl*) gyn(a)ecology. **gynäko'logisch** *adj* gyn(a)ecological.

H

H, h [haː] *n* (-; -) **1.** H, h. **2.** ♪ B. **ha** [haˈ(ː)] *int* ha, ah.

Haar [haːr] *n* (-[e]s; -e) hair: *sich die ~e kämmen* (F *machen*) comb (do) one's hair; *sich die ~e schneiden lassen* get a haircut; *sich die ~e raufen* tear one's hair; *fig. aufs ~* to a T; *sich aufs ~ gleichen* be absolutely identical; *um ein ~* by a hair's breadth; *um ein ~ wäre er überfahren worden* he just missed being run over, he had a narrow escape; *er (es) ist um kein ~ besser* he (it) is not a bit better; *~e spalten* split hairs; *ein ~ in der Suppe finden* find a fly in the ointment; *sich in die ~e geraten* quarrel, clash; *sich in den ~en liegen* be at loggerheads, be quarrel-(l)ing; *sie hat ~e auf den Zähnen* she's a tough customer; *das ist bei den ~en herbeigezogen* that's (pretty) far-fetched; *ihr wurde kein ~ gekrümmt* they did not touch a hair on her head; *~e lassen müssen* not to escape unscathed; *kein gutes ~ an j-m lassen* pull s.o. to pieces; *ihm standen die ~e zu Berge, ihm sträubten sich die ~e* it made his hair stand on end; *laß dir deshalb k-e grauen ~e wachsen!* don't lose any sleep over it!

'**Haar|ansatz** *m* hairline. **~ausfall** *m* loss of hair. **~bürste** *f* hairbrush.

'**haaren** *v/i* (h) **1.** *a. sich ~ zo.* lose its hair. **2.** *fur etc:* shed (hairs).

'**Haarentferner** *m* (-s; -) hair remover.

'**Haaresbreite** *f se entging um ~ e-m Unfall* he escaped an accident by a hair's breadth; *sie ging nicht um ~ von ihrer Meinung ab* she didn't budge from her opinion one little bit.

'**Haar|farbe** *f* hair colo(u)r. **~färbemittel** *n* hair dye. **~festiger** *m* setting lotion. **~gefäß** *n anat.* capillary (vessel).

'**haarge'nau** *adj* F precise: (*stimmt*) *~!* dead right!

haarig ['haːrɪç] *adj* hairy (*a.* F *fig.*).

...haarig *...-*haired.

'**haar'klein** *adj* (down) to the last detail.

'**Haarklemme** *f* hair clip.

'**haarlos** *adj* **1.** hairless. **2.** bald.

'**Haar|mittel** *n* hair restorer. **~nadel** *f* hairpin. **~nadelkurve** *f mot.* hairpin bend. **~netz** *n* **1.** hairnet. **2.** hair lacquer. **~öl** *n* hair oil. **~pflege** *f* hair care. **~riß** *m* hairline crack. **²scharf** I *adj* very precise, exact. **II** *adv* by a hair's breadth. **~schleife** *f* (hair) ribbon, bow. **~schnitt** *m* a) haircut, b) hairstyle. **~schuppen** *pl* dandruff.

Haarspalte'rei *f* (-; -en) (*das ist ~* that's just) splitting hairs.

'**Haar|spange** *f* (hair) slide, *Am.* barrette. **~spitzen** *pl* hair tips. **~spray** *m*, *n* hairspray. **~strähne** *f* strand of hair.

'**haarsträubend** *adj* hair-raising.

'**Haar|teil** *n* hairpiece. **~trockner** *m* hair-drier. **~wäsche** *f* shampoo. **~waschmittel** *n* shampoo. **~wasser** *n* hair tonic. **~wuchs** *m* **1.** growth of (the) hair. **2.** hair. **~wuchsmittel** *n* hair restorer. **~wurzeln** *pl* roots of one's hair.

Hab [haːp] (*all sein*) *~ und Gut* all one's possessions.

Habe ['haːbə] *f* (-; *no pl*) possessions.

haben ['haːbən] (hatte, gehabt, h) **I** *v/t* have (got), own, possess: *et. ~ wollen* want (to have) s.th.; *er will es so ~* that's the way he wants it; (*noch*) *zu ~ sein* be (still) available; F *sie ist noch zu ~* she's still to be had; *was hast du?* what's wrong?; F *er hat es im Hals* he has a bad throat; *wir ~ schönes Wetter* the weather is fine (here); *wir ~ Winter!* it's winter!; *dial.* *es hat viel Schnee* there's a lot of snow; *welche Farbe hat das Kleid?* what colo(u)r is the dress?; *da hast du's!* there you are!, *fig. a.* I told you so!; *das hätten wir!* well, that's that!; F *er hat's ja!* he can (well) afford it!; *woher hast du das?* a) where did you get that from?, b) who told you?; *was hast du gegen ihn?* what have you got against him?; *was habe ich davon?* a) what do I get out of it?, b) *wenn ...?* what's the good of ...?; *ich habe nicht viel davon gehabt* I didn't get much out of it; *das hast du nun davon!* there (you are)!; F *ich hab's!* (I've) got it!; *das werden wir gleich ~!* (that's) no problem!; *wie gehabt* as had, same as ever; F *sie ~ et. miteinander* they are lovers; *die Prüfung hatte es in sich* the exam was pretty tough; *er hat et. Überspanntes* there's s.th. eccentric about him; *das hat er so an sich* that's the way he is; *ich habe viel zu erzählen* I have a lot to tell; *dafür bin ich nicht zu ~!* count me out!; *hab dich nicht so!* a) don't make a fuss!, b) don't take on so! **II** *v/aux* have: *hast du ihn gesehen?* have you seen him?; *du hättest es mir sagen sollen!* you should (*or* might) have told me!; *er hätte es tun können* he could have done it.

'**Haben** *n* (-s; -) ✝ credit: → **Soll.**

'**Habenichts** *m* (-[e]s; -e) have-not.

'**Habenseite** *f* ✝ credit side.

Habgier ['haːpgiːr] *f* (-; *no pl*) greed.

'habgierig *adj* greedy.
habhaft ['ha:phaft] *adj* ~ **werden** (*gen*) get hold of, *a.* catch (*criminal etc*).
Habicht ['ha:bıçt] *m* (-[e]s; -e) *zo.* hawk.
Habilitation [habilita'tsĭo:n] *f* (-; -en) university lecturing qualification.
habilitieren [habili'ti:rən] **sich** ~ (h) qualify to give lectures at a university.
Habitat ['habi'ta:t] *n* (-s; -e) *zo.* habitat.
Habseligkeiten ['ha:p-] *pl* belongings.
Habsucht ['ha:p-] *f* (-; *no pl*) greed.
'habsüchtig *adj* greedy.
Hachse [haksə] *f* (-; -n) **1.** *zo.* hock. **2.** *gastr.* knuckles. **3.** F leg, *pl* pins.
'Hackbeil *n* chopper. 'Hackbraten *m* meat loaf. 'Hackbrett *n* **1.** chopping board. **2.** ♪ dulcimer.
Hacke¹ ['hakə] *f* (-; -n) **1.** ✗ hoe. **2.** pickax(e). 'Hacke² *f* (-; -n) *dial.* heel.
'hacken (h) **I** *v/t* **1.** hack, ✗ a. hoe. **2.** chop. **II** *v/i* **3.** (*nach* at) pick, peck.
'Hackepeter *m* (-s; *no pl*) *raw minced meat mixed with onions and spices.*
'Hacker *m* (-s; -) F *computer:* hacker.
'Hackfleisch *n* minced (*Am.* ground) meat: F *aus dir mache ich* ~*!* I'll make mincemeat of you!
'Hackmesser *n* chopper.
'Hackordnung *f a.* fig. pecking order.
'Häcksel ['hɛksəl] *m, n* (-s; *no pl*) ✗ chaff.
'Hacksteak *n* gastr. beefburger.
Hader ['ha:dər] *m* (-s; *no pl*) quarrel.
'hadern *v/i* (h) quarrel (*mit* with).
Hafen *m* **1.** a) harbo(u)r, b) port, c) dock(s): *in den* ~ *einlaufen* put into port. **2.** *fig.* (*ruhiger*) ~ haven.
'Hafen|anlagen *f* docks. ~**arbeiter** *m* docker. ~**becken** *n* harbo(u)r basin, (wet) dock. ~**einfahrt** *f* harbo(u)r entrance. ~**gebühren** *pl* harbo(u)r dues. ~**meister** *m* harbo(u)r master. ~**rundfahrt** *f* boat tour of a harbo(u)r. ~**stadt** *f* (sea)port. ~**viertel** *n* dockland(s).
Hafer ['ha:fər] *m* (-s; *no pl*) oats: F *ihn sticht der* ~ he's getting cocky. 'Haferbrei *m* porridge. 'Haferflocken *pl* rolled oats. 'Hafergrütze *f* groats. 'Hafermehl *n* oatmeal. 'Haferschleim *m* gruel.
Haff [haf] *n* (-[e]s; -s) lagoon.
Haft [haft] *f* (-; *no pl*) **1.** custody: *in* ~ under arrest, in custody; *j-n in* ~ *nehmen* take s.o. into custody. **2.** imprisonment. 'Haftanstalt *f* prison.
'haftbar *adj* (*für* for) responsible, ⚖

liable: *j-n* ~ *machen* make s.o. liable.
'Haftbefehl *m* arrest warrant: ~ *gegen j-n* warrant for s.o.'s arrest.
'haften¹ *v/i* (h) (*an dat* to) cling, stick: *im Gedächtnis* ~ stick (in one's mind).
'haften² *v/i* (h) (*für* for) be (held) responsible, ⚖ be liable: ~ *für* guarantee.
'Haftfähigkeit *f* (-; *no pl*) **1.** → *Haftvermögen*. **2.** ⚖ fitness to undergo detention.
Häftling ['hɛftlıŋ] *m* (-s; -e) prisoner.
'Haftpflicht *f* (legal) liability.
'haftpflichtig *adj* liable (*für* for).
'Haftpflichtversicherung *f* third party (liability) insurance.
'Haftrichter(in *f*) *m* magistrate.
'Haftschale *f* opt. contact lens.
'Haftstrafe *f* imprisonment.
'Haftung¹ *f* (-; *no pl*) ⊕ adhesion.
'Haftung² *f* (-; -en) a) (legal) liability, b) guarantee: *beschränkte* ~ limited liability; *Gesellschaft mit beschränkter* ~ private limited (liability) company; ~ *übernehmen* accept liability (*für* for).
'Haftvermögen *n* (-s; *no pl*) adhesive power(s).
Hagebutte ['ha:gəbutə] *f* (-; -n) rose hip.
Hagel ['ha:gəl] *m* (-s; *no pl*) **1.** hail. **2.** fig. hail, shower (*of blows etc*), torrent (*of invective etc*). 'Hagelkorn *n* hailstone.
hager ['ha:gər] *adj* gaunt.
haha [ha'ha(:)] *int* ha ha.
Häher ['hɛ:ər] *m* (-s; -) *zo.* jay.
Hahn [ha:n] *m* (-[e]s; ⁓e) **1.** *zo.* cock, rooster: F ~ *im Korbe sein* be cock of the walk; *es kräht kein* ~ *danach* nobody cares (two hoots) about it. **2.** ⊕ a) tap, *Am.* faucet, b) spigot. **3.** *of gun:* hammer.
Hähnchen ['hɛ:nçən] *n* (-s; -) chicken.
'Hahnenkamm *m a.* ✿ cockscomb.
'Hahnenkampf *m* cockfight.
Hahnrei ['ha:nraı] *m* (-[e]s; -e) cuckold.
Hai [haı] *m* (-[e]s; -e), 'Haifisch *m* shark.
'Haifischflosse *f* shark fin.
Häkchen ['hɛ:kçən] *n* (-s; -) **1.** small hook. **2.** *on list etc:* tick, *Am.* check. **3.** *ling.* apostrophe.
'Häkelarbeit *f*, Häke'lei *f* (-; -en) crochet work. häkeln ['hɛ:kəln] *v/t, v/i* (h) crochet. 'Häkelnadel *f* crochet needle.
haken ['ha:kən] *v/t* (h) hook (*an acc* onto).
'Haken *m* (-s; -) **1.** hook, peg: ~ *und Öse*

hook and eye; *boxing*: *rechter* (*linker*) ~ right (left) hook. **2.** → *Häkchen* 2. **3.** F *fig. der* ~ *an der Sache* the snag; *die Sache hat e-n* ~ there is a catch to it.

'**Hakenkreuz** *n* swastika.

'**Hakennase** *f* hooked nose.

Halali [hala'li:] *n* (-s; -[s]) *hunt.* mort.

halb [halp] **I** *adj* half: *e-e* ~*e Stunde* half an hour; ~ *drei* half past two; ~ *Europa* half of Europe; ~*e Note* ♩ half note; ~*er Ton* ♩ semitone; *auf* ~*er Höhe* halfway (up); *die* ~*e Summe* half the sum; *zum* ~*en Preis* for half the price, (at) half-price; *nur die* ~*e Wahrheit* only half the truth; *fig.* *e-e* ~*e Sache* a half-measure; *er macht k-e* ~*en Sachen* he doesn't do things by halves; *nichts Halbes und nichts Ganzes* neither one thing nor the other; *j-m auf* ~*em Wege entgegenkommen* meet s.o. halfway; *sich auf* ~*em Wege einigen* split the difference. **II** *adv* half: ~ *soviel* half as much; ~ *und* ~ a) half and half, b) partly; F *(mit j-m) halbe-halbe machen* go halves (*or* fifty-fifty) (with s.o.); *es ist* ~ *so schlimm* it's not as bad as all that; *das ist ja* ~ *geschenkt* that's a giveaway; *damit war die Sache* ~ *gewonnen* that was half the battle.

'**halbamtlich** *adj* semiofficial.

'**Halbärmel** *m* half-sleeve.

'**halbauto,matisch** *adj* semiautomatic.

'**Halbbildung** *f* superficial knowledge.

'**halbbitter** *adj* plain (*chocolate*).

'**Halbblut** *n* **1.** half-caste. **2.** half-breed.

'**Halbblut...**, '**Halbblüter** [-bly:tər] *m* (-s; -), '**halbblütig** *adj zo.* half-breed.

'**Halbbruder** *m* half brother.

'**halbdunkel** *adj* dusky, dimly-lit (*room*).

'**Halbdunkel** *n* semidarkness, twilight.

Halbe ['halbə] *m, f, n* (-n; -n) pint (of beer).

'**Halbedelstein** *m* semiprecious stone.

...halben, ...halber *in cpds.* on account of, due to, b) for the sake of, c) for.

'**Halbfabri,kat** *n* semifinished product.

'**halbfertig** *adj* half-finished, ✝ semifinished.

'**halbfett** *adj* **1.** semibold. **2.** medium-fat.

'**Halbfi,nale** *n sports*: semifinal.

'**halbgar** *adj gastr.* underdone, rare.

'**halbgebildet** *adj* semiliterate.

'**Halbgott** *m* (~**göttin** *f*) demigod(dess).

'**Halbheit** *f* (-; -en) half measure.

'**halbherzig** *adj* half-hearted.

'**halbhoch** *adj* medium-high, *sports etc*: shoulder-high.

halbieren [hal'bi:rən] *v/t* (h) halve, cut (*or* divide) in half, ⅍ bisect. **Hal'bie- rung** *f* (-; -en) halving, ⅍ bisection.

'**Halbinsel** *f* peninsula.

'**Halbjahr** *n* half-year, (period of) six months. '**Halbjahr(e)s...** half-yearly, six-month ... '**halbjährig** [-jɛːrɪç] *adj* a) half-yearly, six-month ..., of six months, b) six-month-old. '**halbjähr- lich** *adj and adv* half-yearly, semian- nual(ly), *adv a.* every six months.

'**Halbkreis** *m* semicircle.

'**Halbkugel** *f a.* geogr. hemisphere.

'**halblang** *adj* a) medium-length, b) knee-length (*skirt etc*), c) *ling.* half-long (*vowel*): F *mach mal* ~*!* draw it mild!

'**halblaut I** *adj* low. **II** *adv* in an under- tone.

'**Halbleder** *n print.* half-leather: *in* ~ *ge- bunden* half-bound.

'**Halbleinen** *n* half-linen (cloth): *in* ~ *ge- bunden print.* half-cloth.

'**Halbleiter** *m* ⚡ semiconductor.

Halb'linke *m, f* (-n; -n), **halb'links** *adv sports*: inside left.

'**halbmast** *adv* (*auf* ~ at) half-mast.

'**Halbmesser** *m* (-s; -) radius.

'**Halbmittelgewicht** *n sports*: light mid- dleweight.

'**Halbmond** *m* half moon, crescent: *wir haben* ~ there's a half moon.

'**halbmondförmig** *adj* crescent-shaped.

'**halbnackt** *adj* half-naked.

'**halboffen** *adj a. ling.* half-open.

'**halboffizi,ell** *adj* semiofficial.

'**halbpart** [-part] *adv* F (*mit j-m*) ~ *machen* go halves (*or* fifty-fifty) with s.o.

'**Halbpensi,on** *f* half-board.

'**Halbpro,fil** *n* semiprofile.

Halb'rechte *m, f* (-n; -n), **halb'rechts** *adv sports*: inside right.

'**Halbreli,ef** *n* half relief, mezzo-relievo.

'**halbrund** *adj* semicircular.

'**Halbrund** *n* (-[e]s; *no pl*) semicircle.

'**Halbschlaf** *m* doze: *im* ~ half asleep.

'**Halbschuh** *m* (low) shoe.

'**Halbschwergewicht** *n sports*: light heavyweight.

'**Halbschwester** *f* half sister.

'**halbseiden** adj **1.** half-silk. **2.** contp. (a. ~es Milieu) demimonde.

'**halbseitig** adj **1.** print. half-page. **2.** ✻ unilateral: ~e Lähmung hemiplegia.

'**Halbstarke** m, f (-n; -n) F yob(bo).

'**Halbstiefel** m ankle boot.

'**halbstündig** [-ʃtʏndıç] adj half-hour.

'**halbstündlich** adj and adv half-hourly, adv a. every half-hour.

'**halbtägig** [-tɛːɡıç] adj half a day's, half-day. '**halbtags** adv ~ arbeiten work part-time. '**Halbtags...** half-time, part-time (job etc). '**Halbtagskraft** f part-time worker, part-timer.

'**Halbton** m **1.** ♪ semitone. **2.** phot., print. half-tone.

'**halbtot** adj half-dead.

'**halbverhungert** adj starving.

'**Halbvo̱kal** m ling. semivowel.

'**halbvoll** adj half-full.

'**halbwach** adj half-awake, dozing.

'**Halbwahrheit** f (-; -en) half-truth.

'**Halbwaise** f half-orphan.

'**Halbwelt** f (-; no pl) demimonde.

'**Halbwertszeit** f nucl. half-life.

'**Halbwissen** n superficial knowledge.

'**Halbwüchsige** ['halpvyːksıɡə] m, f (-n; -n) adolescent, teenager.

'**Halbzeit** f **1.** half(-time): erste (zweite) ~ first (second) half. **2.** → ~pause f half-time. '~**stand** m half-time score.

Halde ['haldə] f (-; -n) **1.** a) dump, b) slag heap, c) coal stocks. **2.** ✝ (surplus) stocks: auf ~ legen stockpile; auf ~ liegen be (excessively) stockpiled.

half [half] pret of helfen.

Hälfte ['hɛlftə] f (-; -n) half: die ~ der Leute (Zeit) half the people (time); um die ~ teurer sein cost half as much again; Kinder zahlen die ~ children pay half(-price); zur ~ half (of it or them); F me-e bessere ~ my better half.

Halfter ['halftər] n (-s; -) **1.** a. m halter. **2.** a. f (-; -n) (pistol) holster.

Halle ['halə] f (-; -n) **1.** a) hall, b) foyer, lounge, c) entrance hall. **2.** ⚙ shop, ✈ hangar. **3.** a) gymnasium, F gym, b) covered (court), c) indoor (swimming) pool: in der ~ indoors. **4.** ⚙ concourse.

Halleluja [hale'luːja] n (-s; -s) hallelujah.

hallen ['halən] v/i (h) (von with) reverberate, echo.

'**Hallen...** indoor (handball, tennis, etc).

'**Hallenfußball** m five-a-side football.

'**Hallen(schwimm)bad** n indoor (swimming) pool.

hallo ['halo] int a) hello, F hi, b) hey: ~ (, Sie)! excuse me!, F hey, you! **Hallo** [ha'loː] n (-s; -s) fig. hullabaloo. **Hallodri** [ha'loːdri] m (-s; -[s]) F scallywag.

Halluzination [halutsina'tsɪ̯oːn] f (-; -en) hallucination. **halluzinatorisch** [-'toːrıʃ] adj hallucinatory. **halluzinieren** [-'niːrən] v/i (h) hallucinate. **Halluzinogen** [-no'ɡeːn] n (-s; -e) hallucinogenic.

Halm [halm] m (-[e]s; -e) blade, stalk.

Halogenscheinwerfer [halo'ɡeːn-] m mot. halogen headlight.

Hals [hals] m (-es; ⸚e) a) neck, b) throat: ✻ steifer ~ stiff neck; aus vollem ~(e) a) yell etc at the top of one's voice, b) lachen roar with laughter; ~ über Kopf headlong, helter-skelter; sich ~ über Kopf verlieben fall in love head over heels; bis an den ~ up to one's neck (fig. a. ears); F auf dem (or am) ~ haben have s.o., s.th. on one's back; be stuck with; j-m die Polizei etc auf den ~ hetzen get the police etc onto s.o.; sich j-n (et.) vom ~(e) schaffen get rid of s.o. (s.th.); j-m um den ~ fallen fling one's arms round s.o.'s neck; sich j-m an den ~ werfen throw o.s. at s.o.; sich den ~ brechen break one's neck; fig. das bricht ihm den ~ that'll be his undoing; F e-r Flasche den ~ brechen crack a bottle; F er hat es in den falschen ~ bekommen he took it the wrong way; F es hängt mir zum ~(e) heraus! I'm fed up (to the teeth) with it!; bleib mir damit vom ~(e)! don't bother me with that!; → umdrehen, Wasser. '**Halsabschneider** m (-s; -) F fig. cutthroat. '**Halsband** n (-[e]s; ⸚er) **1.** necklace. **2.** (dog) collar.

'**halsbrecherisch** adj breakneck.

'**Halsentzündung** f ✻ sore throat.

'**Halskette** f necklace.

'**Hals-'Nasen-'Ohren[-]Arzt** m, ~Ärztin f ear, nose and throat specialist.

'**Halsschlagader** f carotid (artery).

'**Halsschmerzen** pl ~ haben have a sore throat.

halsstarrig ['halsʃtarıç] adj stubborn.

'**Halstuch** n a) neckerchief, b) scarf.

'**Hals- und 'Beinbruch** F break a leg!

'**Halsweite** f collar size.

'**Halswirbel** m anat. cervical vertebra.

halt[1] [halt] *int* a) stop, *esp.* ✗ halt, b) wait (a minute), c) that'll do.

halt[2] *adv dial.* → **eben** 5.

Halt *m* (-[e]s; -e, -s) **1.** *no pl* hold, *a.* foothold, *a. fig.* support, *fig.* (moral) stability. **2.** stop: **ohne ~** nonstop; *fig.* **~ gebieten** (*dat*) call a halt to, stop; → **haltmachen**.

'**haltbar** *adj* **1.** durable, hard-wearing, ⊚ *a.* wear-resistant. **2.** not perishable: **begrenzt ~** perishable; **~ sein** keep (well); **~ machen** preserve; **~ bis ...** best before ... **3.** *fig.* tenable. '**Haltbarkeit** *f* (-; *no pl*) **1.** durability, ⊚ *a.* (long *etc*) service life, ▼ shelf life. **2.** keeping quality: **von geringer ~** perishable. **3.** *fig.* tenability. '**Haltbarkeitsdatum** *n* best-by (or best-before, *Am.* pull) date.

'**Haltebucht** *f mot.* lay-by, *Am.* rest stop.

'**Haltegriff** *m* strap.

'**Haltelinie** *f mot.* stop line.

halten ['haltən] (hielt, gehalten, h) **I** *v/t* **1.** a) hold, b) hold (up) support: **er hielt ihr den Mantel** he held her coat for her; **et. gegen das Licht ~** hold s.th. to the light; → **Stellung** 1. **2.** hold back, stop, keep: **er war nicht zu ~** there was no holding him; **mich hält hier nichts mehr** there is nothing holding me here any more; **haltet den Dieb!** stop thief! **3.** a) keep (*sauber, trocken etc* clean, dry, *etc*), b) keep (up), maintain, hold: **der Raum war ganz in Weiß gehalten** everything in the room was done in white; **der Film hielt nicht, was er versprach** the film did not live up to its promise; → **Diät, Ordnung, Schritt** 1, **Takt**[1] 1, **Wort** 3. **4.** *sports:* a) stop, block, save, b) hold (*a record*): **s-n Vorsprung ~** stay in the lead. **5.** hold, contain. **6.** make, deliver (*speech etc*), give (*lecture*): → **Predigt, Rede** 1, **Vorlesung. 7. sich ~** keep (*car, dog, personnel, etc*), take (*newspaper*). **8.** treat: **er hielt s-e Kinder sehr streng** he was very strict with his children. **9. ~ für** (mis)take *s.o., s.th.* for, consider *s.o., s.th.* (to be); **ich halte es für ratsam** I think it advisable; **man sollte es nicht für möglich ~, aber ...** you wouldn't believe it but ...; **wofür ~ Sie mich (eigentlich)?** who do you think I am?; **für wie alt hältst du ihn?** how old do you think he is? **10. viel ~ von** think highly (*or* the world) of; **nicht viel ~ von** not to think much of; **er hält nichts vom Sparen** he doesn't believe in saving; **was ~ Sie von ...?** a) what do you think of ...?, b) **e-r Tasse Tee** *etc?* how about a cup of tea *etc?* **11.** do, handle: **wie hältst du es mit ...?** what do you usually do about ...?; **das kannst du ~, wie du willst!** please yourself! **12. et. auf sich ~** → **19. II** *v/i* **13.** hold (*a. fig.* weather), last, *flowers, food, etc:* keep. **14.** stop, *mot. a.* draw up, pull up. **15.** *sports:* save. **16. an sich ~** restrain o.s., control o.s. **17. ~ auf** (*acc*) a) pay attention to, b) set great store by, c) insist on. **18. ~ auf** (*acc*) a) ⚓ *a.* → **nach** head for, b) aim at; **nach Süden ~** be heading south; **mehr nach links ~** keep (aim) more to the left. **19. auf sich ~** a) be particular about one's appearance, b) be self-respecting. **20. zu j-m ~** a) stand by s.o., F stick to s.o., b) side with s.o. **III sich ~ 21.** hold on (*an dat* to): *fig.* **sich ~ an** (*acc*) keep to, F stick to (*facts, rules, etc*); **sich an j-n ~** a) rely on s.o., b) hold s.o. liable. **22.** wear well, last long, *food, flowers, etc:* keep, *weather:* hold: F **sie hat sich gut gehalten** she is well-preserved. **23. sich ~** for think (*or* consider) o.s. (to be); **sie hält sich für et. Besonderes** she thinks she's s.th. special. **24. sich aufrecht ~** hold (*or* carry) o.s. upright; **ich kann mich kaum noch auf den Beinen ~** I'm ready to drop. **25.** keep, stay: **sich warm ~** keep warm; **halte dich mehr links** keep more to the left; **er hat sich bei der Firma nicht lange gehalten** he didn't last long with the firm.

'**Halten** *n* (-s) **1.** *mot.* **zum ~ bringen** stop, bring *s.th.* to a standstill; *fig.* **da gab es kein ~ mehr** there was no holding them (*etc*). **2.** → **Haltung** 4.

'**Haltepunkt** *m.*

'**Halter** *m* (-s; -) **1.** ⊚ a) holder, b) handle, c) rest. **2.** ⚶ owner.

'**Halterung** *f* (-; -en) ⊚ holding device.

'**Halteschild** *n* stop sign. '**Haltesignal** *n* stop signal. '**Haltestelle** *f* stop. '**Halteverbot** *n* no stopping (zone). '**Halteverbotsschild** *n* no stopping sign.

'**haltlos** *adj* **1.** unstable, weak. **2.** untenable, unfounded. '**Haltlosigkeit** *f* (-; *no* *pl* **1.** weakness, instability. **2.** untenableness, unfoundedness.

'**haltmachen** *v/i* (*sep*, -ge-, h) (make a) stop: *fig.* **vor nichts ~** stop at nothing.

'**Haltung** *f* (-; -en) **1.** a) posture, b) *a. sports:* position, c) pose: **~ annehmen** ✕ stand to attention. **2.** *no pl* a) deportment, behavio(u)r, b) attitude (**gegenüber** towards): **politische ~** political outlook (*or* views). **3.** *no pl* composure: **~ bewahren** a) control o.s., b) *a.* **~ zeigen** bear up well. **4.** *no pl* keeping (*animals etc*).

Halunke [ha'luŋkə] *m* (-n; -n) scoundrel.

Hamburger ['hambʊrgər] **I** *m* (-s; -) **1.** *a.* '**Hamburgerin** *f* (-; -nen) Hamburgian. **2.** *gastr.* hamburger. **II** *adj* **3.** (of) Hamburg.

Häme ['hɛːmə] *f* (-; *no pl*) F sneers, snide remarks: **voller ~** sneeringly.

'**hämisch** *adj* malicious, sneering.

Hammel ['haməl] *m* (-s; -) **1.** *zo.* wether. **2.** *gastr.* mutton. **3.** F *fig.* idiot.

'**Hammelbraten** *m* roast mutton.

'**Hammelfleisch** *n* mutton.

'**Hammelkeule** *f* leg of mutton.

'**Hammelsprung** *m parl.* division.

Hammer ['hamər] *m* (-s; ⸚) **1.** hammer (*a.* ♪, *sports or at auctions*), mallet, *parl. etc:* gavel: **unter den ~ kommen** come under the hammer. **2.** F *fig.* whammy: **das ist ein ~!** that beats everything!

'**Hammerkla̱vier** *n* piano(forte).

hämmern ['hɛmərn] (h) **I** *v/i* **1.** hammer, *fig. heart etc: a.* pound. **2. ~ auf** (*acc*), **~ gegen** hammer away at, pound (at). **II** *v/t* **3.** ⚙ a) hammer, beat, b) forge.

'**Hammer|werfen** *n* (-s) *sports:* hammer throwing. **~werfer** *m* hammer thrower.

Hämoglobin [hɛmoglo'biːn] *n* (-s; *no pl*) h(a)emoglobin.

Hämophile [hɛmo'fiːlə] *m* (-n; -n) ♯ h(a)emophiliac.

Hämorrhoiden [hɛmoro'iːdən] *pl* ♯ h(a)emorrhoids, F piles.

Hampelmann ['hampəlman] *m* (-[e]s; ⸚er) **1.** jumping Jack. **2.** F *contp.* clown.

Hamster ['hamstər] *m* (-s; -) *zo.* hamster.

'**Hamsterer** *m* (-s; -) hoarder.

'**Hamsterkäufe** *pl* panic buying.

hamstern ['hamstərn] *v/t, v/i* (h) hoard.

Hand [hant] *f* (-; ⸚e) hand (*a. cards*): *j-m* **die ~ geben** (*or* **reichen, schütteln**)

shake hands with s.o.; **~ in ~ gehen** walk (*fig.* go) hand in hand (**mit** with); **Hände hoch** (**weg**)**!** hands up (off)!; **~!** *soccer:* hands!; *fig.* **die öffentliche ~** the public authorities, the State; *j-s* **rechte ~** s.o.'s right-hand man; **an ~ von** (*or* **gen**) by means of, on the basis of; **aus erster** (**zweiter**) **~** *buy, know, etc* firsthand (secondhand); **bei der ~, zur ~** at hand, handy; **mit der ~, von ~** *make etc* by hand; **unter der ~** on the quiet; **zu Händen** (*z. H.* = care of), *adm.* Attention *Mr Smith etc*; **mit leeren Händen abziehen** go away empty-handed; (**mit**) **~ anlegen** lend a hand; **et. in die Hände bekommen** get hold of s.th.; *j-m* **in die Hände fallen** fall into s.o.'s hands; *j-m* **et. an die ~ geben** furnish s.o. with s.th.; **aus der ~ geben** part with; *j-n* **in der ~ haben** have s.o. in one's grip (F over a barrel); **~ und Fuß haben** make sense; *j-m* **freie ~ lassen** give s.o. a free hand; **von der ~ in den Mund leben** live from hand to mouth; **letzte ~ an et. legen** put the finishing touches to s.th.; *fig.* **die Hände in den Schoß legen** twiddle one's thumbs; **aus der ~ legen** lay aside; *s-e* **~ ins Feuer legen für** put one's hand into the fire for; **es liegt in s-r ~** it's up to him; **es liegt klar auf der ~** it's obvious; *fig.* **et. in die ~ nehmen** take charge of s.th.; *j-m* (**et.**) **in die Hände spielen** play (s.th.) into s.o.'s hands; **alle Hände voll zu tun haben** have one's hands full; **in andere Hände übergehen** change hands; **das war lange ~ vorbereitet** that was carefully planned long beforehand; *e-e* **~ wäscht die andere** you scratch my back and I'll scratch yours; **sich mit Händen und Füßen** (**gegen et.**) **wehren** fight (s.th.) tooth and nail; **von der ~ weisen** dismiss; **es läßt sich nicht von der ~ weisen, daß ...** it can't be denied that ...; **mit beiden Händen zugreifen** jump at the chance; → **Spiel** 2.

'**Handarbeit** *f* **1.** *no pl* manual work. **2.** a) *no pl* handiwork, handicraft, b) handmade article: **diese Vase ist ~** this vase is handmade. **3.** needlework.

'**Handarbeiter**(**in** *f*) *m* manual worker.

'**Handaufheben** *n* (-s) *parl.* **durch ~** by a show of hands.

'**Handball** m (-[e]s; no pl) handball.
'**Handballen** m anat. ball of the thumb.
'**Handballer** [-balər] m (-s; -), '**Handballerin** f (-; -nen) F, '**Handballspieler(in** f) m handball player.
'**handbetätigt** adj ⚙ hand-operated, manual.
'**Handbetrieb** m (-[e]s; no pl) manual operation: mit ~ → handbetätigt.
'**Handbewegung** f gesture.
'**Handbiblio,thek** f reference library.
'**Handbohrma,schine** f hand drill.
'**handbreit** adj a few inches wide.
'**Handbreit** f (-; -) hand's breadth.
'**Handbremse** f handbrake.
'**Handbuch** n manual, handbook, guide.
Händchen ['hɛntçən] n (-s; -) little hand: F ~ halten hold hands.
'**Handcreme** f hand cream.
Hände|druck ['hɛndə-] m handshake. ~**klatschen** n (-s) clapping, applause.
Handel ['handəl] m (-s; no pl) **1.** commerce, business, trade (mit in s.th., with s.o.), a. contp. traffic: ~ und Gewerbe trade and industry; ~ mit Waffen (Drogen etc) trade (or traffic) in arms (drugs etc); im ~ on the market; nicht mehr im ~ off the market; in den ~ bringen (kommen) put (be) on the market; ~ treiben mit a) s.th. deal in s.th., b) j-m trade (or do business) with s.o. **2.** (business) transaction, F deal, fig. a. bargain.
Händel ['hɛndəl] pl quarrel, fight.
handeln ['handəln] (h) **I** v/i **1.** act, take action. **2.** ⚓ trade, do business (mit j-m with s.o.): ~ mit trade (or deal, contp. traffic) in. **3.** (um) bargain (for), haggle (over): er läßt mit sich ~ he is open to an offer (w.s. a suggestion). **4.** ~ von book, film, etc: be about, deal with. **II** v/t gehandelt werden a) ⚓ be sold, on the stock exchange: be traded, be listed, b) name etc: be mentioned. **III** v/impers es handelt sich um it concerns, it is a question of, it is about; worum handelt es sich? what is it (all) about?, what's the problem?; es handelt sich darum, ob (wer etc) the question is whether (who etc); darum handelt es sich (nicht)! that's just (not) the point!; bei dem Opfer handelt es sich um e-n Ausländer the victim is a foreigner.
'**Handeln** n (-s) acting (etc): gemeinsa-

mes (rasches) ~ joint (quick) action.
'**Handels|abkommen** n trade agreement. ~**atta,ché** m commercial attaché. ~**bank** f (-; -en) merchant bank. ~**beschränkungen** pl trade restrictions. ~**betrieb** m commercial enterprise. ~**bezeichnung** f trade name. ~**beziehungen** pl trade relations. ~**bi,lanz** f (aktive ~ surplus, passive ~ adverse) balance of trade. ~**defizit** n trading deficit. ²**einig** adj ~ werden come to terms (mit with). ~**em,bargo** n (trade) embargo. ~**flotte** f merchant fleet. ~**genossenschaft** f traders' cooperative. ~**gericht** n commercial court. ~**gesellschaft** f (trading) company, Am. (business) corporation: offene ~ general partnership. ~**gesetzbuch** n Commercial Code. ~**hafen** m trading port. ~**kammer** f Chamber of Commerce. ~**klasse** f Äpfel der A grade one apples. ~**korrespon,denz** f commercial correspondence. ~**lehrer** m teacher at a commercial school. ~**macht** f (great) trading nation. ~**ma,rine** f merchant navy. ~**marke** f brand. ~**mi,nister** m minister of commerce, Br. Secretary of State for Trade and Industry, Am. Secretary of Commerce. ~**mini,sterium** n ministry of commerce, Br. Board of Trade, Am. Department of Commerce. ~**name** m trade name. ~**nati,on** f trading nation. ~**niederlassung** f **1.** business establishment. **2.** registered seat. **3.** branch. ~**partner** m trading partner. ~**platz** m trading cent/re (Am. -er). ~**poli,tik** f trade policy. ~**recht** n (-[e]s; no pl) commercial law. ~**re,gister** n trade register: ins ~ eintragen (lassen) register, Am. incorporate. ~**reisende** m, f (-n; -n) commercial travel(l)er. ~**schiff** n trading vessel. ~**schiffahrt** f merchant shipping. ~**schranke** f trade barrier. ~**schule** f commercial school. ~**spanne** f trade margin. ²**üblich** adj usual in the trade: ~**e Qualität** commercial quality. ~**verkehr** m trade, trading. ~**vertrag** m trade agreement. ~**vertreter(in** f) m commercial representative. ~**vertretung** f commercial agency, pol. trade mission. ~**vo,lumen** n volume of trade. ~**ware** f commodity: ~**n** merchandise. ~**weg** m trade

route. **~wert** m market value. **~zweig** m line of business.

'**handeltreibend** adj trading.

'**händeringend** adv a) imploringly, b) despairingly.

'**Händeschütteln** n (-s) shaking of hands, handshake.

'**Handfertigkeit** f manual skill.

'**handfest** adj **1.** sturdy, strong. **2.** fig. huge (scandal etc), solid (proof etc), whopping (lie).

'**Hand|feuerlöscher** m fire extinguisher. **~feuerwaffe** f hand gun, pl small arms. **~fläche** f palm. **♀gearbeitet, ♀gefertigt** adj handmade. **~gelenk** n wrist: F **aus dem ~** off the cuff, just like that. **♀gemalt** adj handpainted. **~gemenge** n (-s; -) fray, brawl. **~gepäck** n hand luggage (Am. baggage). **♀geschrieben** adj handwritten. **♀gestrickt** adj **1.** handknitted. **2.** F contp. home-made. **♀gewebt** adj handwoven. **~gra͵nate** f hand grenade.

handgreiflich ['hantgraɪflɪç] adj **1.** **er wurde ~** a) he got violent, b) he started to paw. **2.** fig. obvious, plain.

'**Handgreiflichkeiten** pl violence.

'**Handgriff** m **1.** handle, grip. **2.** fig. a) movement of the hand, b) manipulation: **mit wenigen ~en** do s.th. in no time (or deftly).

'**Handhabe** f (-; -n) a) proof, b) lever: **er hat keinerlei ~** he hasn't got a leg to stand on. '**handhaben** v/t (handhabte, gehandhabt, h) **1.** use, handle, operate. **2.** fig. a) handle, deal with, b) apply.

'**Handhabung** f (-; -en) handling (a. fig.), use, operation.

Handicap ['hɛndikɛp] n (-s; -s) a. fig. handicap (**für** to).

'**Hand|kante** f side of the hand: **Schlag mit der ~ → ~kantenschlag** m (karate) chop. **~karren** m handcart. **~koffer** m small suitcase. **~kuß** m **j-m e-n ~ geben** kiss s.o.'s hand; F fig. **mit ~** gladly.

'**Handlanger** m (-s; -) odd-job man, contp. handyman, pol. etc henchman.

Händler ['hɛndlər] m (-s; -), '**Händlerin** f (-; -nen) trader, merchant, dealer.

'**Handlesekunst** f (-; no pl) palmistry.

'**handlich** adj handy.

'**Handlichkeit** f (-; no pl) handiness.

'**Handlung** f (-; -en) **1.** act, action. **2.** of film etc: action, story, plot: **Ort der ~** scene (of action). **3.** ♱ shop.

'**Handlungs|bedarf** m **es besteht (kein) ~** this calls (there is no need) for action. **~bevollmächtigte** m, f (authorized) agent, proxy. **♀fähig** adj **1.** ⚖ having disposing capacity. **2.** functioning, working (government etc). **~fähigkeit** f (-; no pl) **1.** ⚖ legal capacity. **2.** capacity to act. **~freiheit** f freedom of action: **j-m ~ geben** give s.o. a free hand. **~gehilfe** m, **~gehilfin** f **1.** (commercial) clerk. **2.** shop assistant. **♀reich** adj full of action, action-packed. **~reisende** m, f commercial travel(l)er. **~spielraum** m room for manoeuvre (Am. maneuver). **~vollmacht** f limited authority to act and sign. **~weise** f **1.** way of acting, conduct. **2.** procedure.

Hand|pflege f manicure. **~puppe** f glove puppet. **~rücken** m back of the hand. **~schelle** f handcuff: **j-m ~n anlegen** handcuff s.o. **~schlag** m (-[e]s; no pl) handshake: **durch ~ bekräftigen** shake hands on; F **er tut k-n ~** he doesn't lift a finger. **~schrift** f **1.** handwriting, hand. **2.** manuscript. **♀schriftlich I** adj handwritten. **II** adv in writing, correct etc by hand. **~schuh** m glove. **~schuhfach** n mot. glove compartment. **~spiegel** m hand mirror. **~spiel** n soccer: hands. **~stand** m gym. handstand. **~standüberschlag** m handspring. **~steuerung** f manual control. **~streich** m coup (de main). **~tasche** f handbag, Am. purse.

'**Handtuch** n (das ~ **werfen** a. F fig. throw in the) towel. **~auto͵mat** m towel dispenser. **~halter** m towel rack.

'**Handumdrehen** n **im ~** in no time.

'**handverlesen** adj a. fig. handpicked.

'**Handvoll** f (-; -) a. fig. handful.

'**handwarm** adj lukewarm.

'**Handwaschbecken** n hand basin.

'**Handwerk** n (-[e]s; -e) trade, craft: **das ~** the trade; **ein ~ lernen** learn a trade; fig. **j-m das ~ legen** put a stop to s.o.('s game); **j-m ins ~ pfuschen** botch at s.o.'s trade; **er versteht sein ~** he knows his stuff. '**Handwerker** m (-s; -) (skilled) workman, craftsman.

'**handwerklich** adj craftsman's, craft: **~er Beruf** skilled trade; **~es Können** craftsmanship, craft skills.

'**Handwerks|kammer** *f* chamber of handicrafts. **~meister** *m* master craftsman. **~zeug** *n* tools (*a. fig.*).
'**Hand|wörterbuch** *n* concise dictionary. **~wurzel** *f anat.* wrist, carpus. **~zeichen** *n* **1.** sign. **2.** *parl.* show of hands. **~zettel** *m* leaflet.
Hanf [hanf] *m* (-[e]s; *no pl*) hemp.
Hang [haŋ] *m* (-[e]s; ⸚e) **1.** slope. **2.** *gym.* hang. **3.** *fig.* (**zu**) a) bent (for), tendency (to), b) proneness (to).
Hangar ['haŋgar] *m* (-s; -s) hangar.
'**Hängebacken** *pl* flabby cheeks.
'**Hängebrücke** *f* suspension bridge.
'**Hängebusen** *m* sagging breasts.
'**Hängelampe** *f* hanging lamp.
hangeln ['haŋəln] *v/i* (h) *gym.* climb (*or* travel) hand over hand.
'**Hängematte** *f* hammock.
'**Hangen: mit ~ und Bangen** in anxious anticipation.
hängen¹ ['hɛŋən] *v/i* (hing, gehangen, h) **1.** hang (**an** *dat* from *or* on): **voller Äpfel** *etc* ~ be full of apples *etc*; **über j-m** ~ *a. fig.* hang over s.o.; *fig.* **die ganze Arbeit hängt an mir** I am stuck with all the work; → **Tropf. 2.** (**an** *dat* to) *mud etc*: cling, stick. **3.** be stuck, be caught: F *fig.* **woran hängt's?** what's the problem?; **er hängt in Latein** he's bad at Latin. **4.** ~ **an** (*dat*) love (*life, money, etc*), cling to (*a custom etc*); **an j-m** ~ be fond of (*or* devoted to) s.o. **5.** be lopsided.
'**hängen²** (h) **I** *v/t* **1.** *j-n* ~ hang s.o.; **gehängt werden** be hanged. **2. et. ~ an** (*acc*) hang s.th. from (*or* on); *fig.* **sein Herz ~ an** (*acc*) set one's heart on. **II sich ~ an** (*acc*) hang on to; F **sich ans Telefon ~** get on the phone; **sich an j-n ~** a) cling to s.o., b) trail s.o., c) *runner:* drop in behind s.o.
'**Hängen** *n* (-s) F **mit ~ und Würgen** only just, barely.
'**hängenbleiben** *v/i* (*irr, sep,* -ge-, sn, → **bleiben**) F **1.** (**an** *dat*) get (*or* be) caught (by), catch (on, in), get (*or* be) stuck (in): *fig.* **im Gedächtnis ~** stick in one's mind. **2.** *fig.* be held up, *sports:* be stopped (**an** *dat* by).
'**hängenlassen** (*irr, sep, no* -ge-, h, → **lassen**) **I** *v/t* **1.** *et. s.th.* hang, (let *s.th.*) dangle. **2.** F *j-n* ~ leave s.o. in the lurch. **II sich ~** let o.s. go.

'**Hängeohren** *pl* floppy ears.
'**Hängepar,tie** *f chess:* adjourned game.
'**Hängepflanze** *f* hanging plant.
'**Hänger** *m* (-s; -) loose dress (*or* coat).
'**Hängeschrank** *m* wall cabinet.
Hans'dampf *m* (-[e]s; -e) F **~ in allen Gassen** jack-of-all-trades.
hanseatisch [hanze'a:tɪʃ] *adj* Hanseatic.
Hänse'lei *f* (-; -en) teasing, F kidding.
hänseln ['hɛnzəln] *v/t* (h) tease, F kid.
Hansestadt ['hanzə-] *f* Hanse town.
'**Hanswurst** *m* (-[e]s; -e) *a. contp.* clown.
Hantel ['hantəl] *f* (-; -n) dumbbell.
hantieren [han'ti:rən] *v/i* (h) **1.** potter around. **2. ~ mit** work with, handle; **~ an** (*dat*) work on, *contp.* fiddle with.
hapern ['ha:pərn] *v/impers* (h) F **es hapert mit** (*or* **bei**) there are problems with; **es hapert an** (*dat*) there isn't (*or* aren't) enough; **im Englischen hapert es bei ihm** English is his weak point.
Häppchen ['hɛpçən] *n* (-s; -) a) morsel, b) titbit, c) canapé.
Happen ['hapən] *m* (-s; -) **1.** bite (to eat): **e-n ~ essen** have a bite. **2.** *fig.* (**ein fetter ~** a fine) catch.
happig ['hapıç] *adj* F steep (*prices etc*).
Härchen ['hɛːrçən] *n* (-s; -) little hair.
Harem ['ha:rɛm] *m* (-s; -s) harem.
Harfe ['harfə] *f* (-; -n) ♪ harp. **Harfenist** [harfə'nɪst] *m* (-en; -en), **Harfe'nistin** *f* (-; -nen) harpist.
Harke ['harkə] *f* (-; -n) rake: F *j-m zeigen, was e-e ~ ist* show (*or* tell) s.o. what's what.
harmlos ['harmlo:s] *adj* harmless.
'**Harmlosigkeit** *f* (-; *no pl*) harmlessness.
Harmonie [harmo'ni:] *f* (-; -n) harmony. **Harmo'nielehre** *f* (-; *no pl*) ♪ harmony. **harmonieren** [harmo'ni:rən] *v/i* (h) harmonize (**mit** with). **harmonisch** [har'mo:nıʃ] *adj* ♪, ♪ harmonic(al), *a. fig.* harmonious. **harmonisieren** [harmoni'zi:rən] *v/t* (h) *a. fig.* harmonize.
Harn [harn] *m* (-[e]s; -e) ♥ urine.
'**Harnblase** *f anat.* bladder.
'**harnen** *v/i* (h) pass water, urinate.
'**Harnflasche** *f* urinal.
'**Harngrieß** *m* ♥ gravel.
Harnisch ['harnıʃ] *m* (-s; -e) a) (suit of) armo(u)r, b) cuirass: F *j-n in ~ bringen* get s.o.'s back up; **in ~ geraten** get (really) furious; **in ~ sein** be up in arms.
'**Harn|leiter** *m anat.* ureter. **~probe** *f* ♥

urine sample. **~röhre** f anat. urethra.
~säure f 🜍 uric acid. **2treibend** adj
diuretic. **~untersuchung** f urinalysis.
~wege pl anat. urinary tract.
Harpune [har'puːnə] f (-; -n) harpoon.
harren ['harən] v/i (h) (gen or auf acc)
wait (for), await (s.o., s.th.).
Harsch [harʃ] m (-es; no pl) crusted
snow. **'harschig** adj crusted.
hart [hart] **I** adj **1.** hard: ~ werden harden (a. fig.); **~es Ei** hard-boiled egg;
fig. **~e Währung (Droge)** hard currency
(drug). **2.** fig. a) hard, b) hardened,
tough, sports: rough: **er ist ~ im Nehmen** he can take a lot of punishment;
er blieb ~ he stood firm. **3.** fig. hard
(work, life, winter, etc), severe (criticism, punishment, etc), harsh (words
etc), heavy (blow, loss, etc), tough (policy etc): **~e Tatsachen** hard facts; **das
war ~!** that was tough!; **das war ~ für
ihn** that was hard on him; → **Nuß,
Schule. II** adv **4.** hard, severely: ~ arbeiten work hard; **es ging ~ auf ~** it
was either do or die; **wenn es ~ auf ~
geht** when it comes to the crunch. **5.** ~
an (dat) close to; ⚓ ~ **am Wind** close-
hauled.
Härte ['hɛrtə] f (-; -n) **1.** hardness. **2.** fig.
toughness, sports: roughness, rough
play. **3.** fig. hardness, harshness, severity: 🜪 (unbillige) ~ undue(d) hardship. **4.**
phot. contrast. **~fall** m hardship case.
härten ['hɛrtən] (h) **I** v/t a) harden, b)
temper (steel). **II** v/i harden, grow hard.
'Hartfaserplatte f hardboard, Am.
fiberboard.
'hartgefroren adj frozen hard.
'hartgekocht adj hard-boiled.
'Hartgeld n (-es; no pl) coins.
'hartgesotten [-gəzɔtən] adj fig. hard-
-boiled.
'Hartgummi n, m hard rubber.
'hartherzig adj hard-hearted.
'Hartkäse m hard cheese.
'hartnäckig [-nɛkıç] adj stubborn, persistent, 🜪 refractory. **'Hartnäckigkeit** f
(-; no pl) stubbornness, persistence.
'Hartplatz m hard pitch (tennis: court).
'Härtung f (-; -en) hardening, tempering.
'Hartwurst f hard sausage.
Harz [harts] n (-es; -e) resin, rosin.
harzig adj resinous.
Hasardspiel [ha'zart-] n fig. gamble.

Hasch [haʃ] n (-s; no pl) F hash.
Haschee [ha'ʃeː] n (-s; -s) gastr. hash.
haschen¹ ['haʃən] (h) **I** v/t (sich ~ play)
catch. **II** v/i **nach** snatch at, fig. seek;
nach Komplimenten ~ fish for compliments.
'haschen² v/i (h) F smoke hash.
Häschen ['hɛːsçən] n (-s; -) **1.** young
hare. **2.** F bunny.
Hascherl ['haʃərl] n (-s; -[n]) dial. (ar-
mes) ~ poor little thing, poor creature.
Haschisch ['haʃıʃ] n (-; no pl) hashish.
Hase ['haːzə] m (-n; -n) hare: fig. alter ~
old hand; **sehen, wie der ~ läuft** see
how things develop; **da liegt der ~ im
Pfeffer** that's the real problem; **mein
Name ist ~(, ich weiß von nichts)**!
search me!
Haselnuß ['haːzəl-] f **1.** hazelnut. **2.** →
'Haselnußstrauch m hazelnut (tree).
'Hasenbraten m roast hare.
'Hasenfuß m F fig. coward.
'Hasenpfeffer m gastr. jugged hare.
'Hasenscharte f 🜪 hare lip.
Häsin ['hɛːzın] f (-; -nen) female hare,
doe.
Haspel ['haspəl] f (-; -n) ⚙ hasp, reel.
haspeln ['haspəln] v/t (h) **1.** ⚙ reel,
wind. **2.** a. v/i splutter.
Haß [has] m (-sses; no pl) (auf acc, gegen
of, for) hatred, hate: **aus** ~ out of hatred; **e-n** ~ **haben auf** (acc) → **hassen**
['hasən] v/t (h) hate: → **Pest.**
'hassenswert adj hateful. **'haßerfüllt**
adj full of hate, venomous (look etc).
häßlich ['hɛslıç] adj ugly, fig. a. nasty.
'Haßliebe f love-hate relationship.
Hast [hast] f (-; no pl) hurry, rush.
hasten ['hastən] v/i (sn) hurry.
'hastig I adj **1.** hasty, hurried: nicht so ~!
just a minute! **2.** slapdash. **3.** nervous.
II adv **4.** hastily, in a hurry.
hätscheln ['hɛːtʃəln] v/t (h) **1.** cuddle. **2.**
fig. pamper.
hatte ['hatə] pret of **haben.**
Haube ['haʊbə] f (-; -n) **1.** a) bonnet, b)
hood (a. ⚙), c) cap, d) eccl. cornet: fig.
unter die ~ bringen find a husband for.
2. (hair-)drier. **3.** zo. crest. **4.** mot. bonnet, Am. hood.
Hauch [haʊx] m (-[e]s; no pl) **1.** a) breath,
b) breath (of wind), c) whiff. **2.** ling.
aspiration. **3.** fig. touch. **'hauch'dünn**
adj **1.** a) wafer-thin, b) flimsy. **2.** fig.

very slim (chance etc), bare (majority etc): **~er Sieg** knife-edge victory.

hauchen ['haʊxən] v/i, v/t (h) breathe, ling. aspirate.

'**Hauchlaut** m ling. aspirate.

'**Haudegen** m (-s; -) **alter ~** F warhorse.

Haue[1] ['haʊə] f (-; -n) dial. hoe.

'**Haue**[2] f (-; no pl) F (**~ kriegen** get a) spanking.

hauen ['haʊən] (haute or hieb, gehauen, h) **I** v/t **1.** F hit, slap, thrash, spank: **sich ~** fight, scrap; → **Ohr, Pauke. 2.** F bang, slam. **3.** dial. a) hew, cut, b) chop (wood), c) chop down (tree). **II** v/i **4.** hit (out) (**nach** at). **'Hauer** m (-s; -) **1.** zo. tusk. **2.** ⚒ face worker.

Häufchen ['hɔʏfçən] n (-s; -) small heap (or pile): **wie ein ~ Unglück** (looking) the picture of misery.

Haufen ['haʊfən] m (-s; -) **1.** heap, pile: F **über den ~ rennen (fahren)** knock s.o., s.th. down; **j-n über den ~ schießen** shoot s.o. down; **über den ~ werfen** a) upset (plan etc), b) explode (theory etc). **2.** F loads of, a lot (or lots) of (friends, money, etc): **e-n ~ Geld kosten (verdienen)** cost (make) a packet. **3.** F crowd, bunch, ✕ outfit. **4.** V turd.

häufen ['hɔʏfən] (h) **I** v/t heap up, fig. a. accumulate: → **gehäuft. II sich ~** fig. a) accumulate, pile up, debts: a. mount, b) increase (in number).

'**haufenweise** adv F a) in piles, b) in crowds, c) a lot or lots, of, loads of.

'**Haufenwolke** f cumulus (cloud).

häufig ['hɔʏfɪç] **I** adj frequent, a. widespread. **II** adv frequently, often: **~ besuchen** a. frequent. '**Häufigkeit** f (-; no pl) frequency, (high) incidence.

'**Häufung** f (-; -en) accumulation, increase, spreading, frequent occurrence.

Haupt [haʊpt] n (-[e]s; ⁔er) a. fig. head: **et. an ~ und Gliedern reformieren** reform s.th. root and branch.

'**Haupt...** main, chief, principal. **~abteilungsleiter** m senior head of department. **~aktio,när** m principal shareholder (Am. stockholder). **~ak,zent** m ling. primary stress. **~al,tar** m high altar. ⒉**amtlich** adj and adv full-time. **~angeklagte** m, f principal defendant. **~anschluß** m teleph. main line. **~anteil** m principal (fig. lion's) share. **~attrakti,on** f main attraction, highlight. **~auf**-

gabe f main duty (or work). **~augenmerk** n **sein ~ richten auf** (acc) give one's special attention to. **~bahnhof** m main station. ⒉**beruflich** adj and adv full-time, adv a. as one's main job. **~beschäftigung** f main job. **~bestandteil** m main constituent. **~betrieb** m ✝ a) head office, b) central works. **~buch** n ✝ main ledger. **~darsteller(in** f) m leading actor (actress), lead. **~einfahrt** f, **~eingang** m main entrance. **~erbe** m chief (or principal) heir. **~fach** n ped., univ. main subject, Am. major: **als** (or **im**) **~ studieren** study s.th. as a main subject, Am. major in. **~feldwebel** m ✕ sergeant major, Am. first sergeant. **~fi,gur** f central figure, thea. etc main character. **~film** m feature film. **~gang** m gastr. main course. **~gebäude** n main building. **~gericht** n gastr. main course. **~geschäft** n **1.** main business. **2.** → **~geschäftsstelle** f a) head office, b) main store. **~geschäftszeit** f peak business hours. **~gewicht** n fig. main emphasis. **~gewinn** m first prize. **~grund** m main reason. **~hahn** m ⚙ main tap. **~kasse** f main cash desk, thea. box office. **~last** f main burden: **die ~ tragen** bear the brunt (gen of).

Häuptling ['hɔʏptlɪŋ] m (-s; -e) **1.** chieftain. **2.** F boss.

'**Haupt|mahlzeit** f main meal. **~mangel** m main fault (or weakness). **~mann** m (-[e]s; -leute) ✕ captain. **~merkmal** n chief characteristic. **~nahrung** f staple (food). **~nenner** m A⊢ common denominator. **~niederlassung** f ✝ head office, headquarters. **~per,son** f most important person, central figure (thea. a. character). **~postamt** n main post office. **~probe** f thea. dress (♩ general) rehearsal. **~quar,tier** n headquarters. **~reisezeit** f peak tourist season. **~rolle** f thea. etc leading role, main part, lead: fig. **die ~ spielen** a) be all-important, b) be the central figure. **~sache** f (-; no pl) main (or most important) thing: **~, du bist da!** (the) main thing (is), you're here! ⒉**sächlich** adj and adv main(ly), chief(ly), adv a. above all. **~sai,son** f peak season. **~satz** m ling. main clause. **~schalter** m ⚡ master switch. **~schlagader** f anat. aorta. **~schlüssel** m master key. **~schuld** f **er trägt die ~ daran** it's mainly his fault. **~schuldige** m, f chief culprit, ⚹ principal. **~schule** f secondary modern school. **~sendezeit** f TV prime time. **~sitz** m head office, headquarters. **~sorge** f main concern. **~speicher** m computer: main memory. **~stadt** f capital (city). **~straße** f main street. **~stütze** f fig. mainstay. **~täter** m ⚹ principal (in the first degree). **~teil** m main part, most of it. **~thema** n main subject. **~ton** m **1.** ling. main stress. **2.** ♩ keynote. **~tor** n main gate. **~treffer** m first prize, F jackpot. **~tri,büne** f grandstand. **~unterschied** m main difference. **~verfahren** n, **~verhandlung** f ⚹ trial. **~verkehrsstraße** f main road. **~verkehrszeit** f rush hour. **~versammlung** f general meeting. **~vertreter** m general agent. **~verwaltung** f head office. **~wort** n (-[e]s; ⸚er) noun. **~zeuge** m, **~zeugin** f chief witness. **~ziel** n main objective. **~zweck** m main object, chief purpose.

hau ruck ['haʊ 'rʊk] int heave-ho.

Haus [haʊs] n (-es; ⸚er) a) house (a. astr., ✝, thea.), building, b) family, c) dynasty: parl. das (Hohe) **~** the House; aus gutem (e) sein come from a good family; außer **~** out, not in; im **~** inside, ✝ on the premises; ins **~** in(doors); ins **~** stehen be forthcoming; das steht uns noch ins **~** we are yet in for that; j-n nach **~**(e) bringen take (or see) s.o. home; nach **~**(e) kommen come (or get) home; zu **~**(e) a. sports: at home; er ist nicht zu **~** a. he is not in; bei uns zu **~**(e) where I come from, at home; fig. in e-r Sache zu **~**e sein be at home in s.th.; sich wie zu **~**(e) fühlen feel at home; fühl dich (ganz) wie zu **~**e! make yourself at home!; fig. von **~**(e) aus originally, actually; thea. vor vollem **~**(e) spielen play to a full house.

'Haus|al,tar m family altar. **~angestellte** f domestic (servant). **~an,tenne** f roof aerial (Am. antenna). **~apo,theke** f medicine cabinet. **~arbeit** f **1.** housework. **2.** a. pl ped. homework. **~ar,rest** m (j-n unter **~** stellen place s.o. under) house arrest. **~arzt** m, **~ärztin** f family doctor, at spa etc: resident doctor. **~aufgabe(n** pl) f (s-e **~** machen a. fig. do one's) homework. **~aufsatz** m ped. essay to be written at home. **~ball** m

private dance, house party. **~bar** f a) cocktail cabinet, b) bar. **~bau** m (-[e]s; no pl) house building. **~besetzer** m squatter. **~besetzung** f (-; -en) squatting. **~besitzer(in** f) m **1.** house owner. **2.** landlord (landlady). **~besuch** m home visit. **~bewohner** m a) occupant, b) tenant. **~boot** n houseboat. **~brand** m (-[e]s; no pl) domestic fuel.

Häuschen ['hɔʏsçən] n (-s; -) **1.** small house, cottage: F (ganz) aus dem **~** geraten get into a flap (wegen about, vor dat with); ganz aus dem **~** sein F be wild (vor with). **2.** F loo, Am. john.

'Hausdetek,tiv(in f) m store detective.

hausen ['haʊzən] v/i (h) F **1.** live. **2.** (übel) **~** wreak havoc (unter dat among).

Häuserblock ['hɔʏzərblɔk] m block (of houses).

'Haus|flur m hall(way). **~frau** f housewife. **~freund** m iro. (secret) lover. **~friedensbruch** m ⚹ illegal entry of s.o.'s house, w.s. violation of s.o.'s privacy. **~gebrauch** m für den **~** for use in the home; F fig. für den **~** reichen be enough to get by on. **2gemacht** adj a. fig. home-made. **~gemeinschaft** f **1.** house community. **2.** household.

'Haushalt m (-[e]s; -e) **1.** household: (j-m) den **~** führen run the household (for s.o.); im **~** helfen help in the house. **2.** pol. budget. **3.** biol. balance. **'haushalten** v/i (irr, sep, -ge-, h, → halten) economize: **~** mit be economical with; mit s-n Kräften **~** husband one's energies. **'Haushälterin** f (-; -nen) housekeeper. **'haushälterisch** adj economical.

'Haushalts... a) household (article etc), b) ✝, pol. budget (committee, debate, etc), budgetary (deficit, policy, etc). **~führung** f (-; no pl) housekeeping. **~geld** n housekeeping money. **~gerät** n household appliance. **~jahr** n fiscal year. **~mittel** pl budgetary means: (gebilligte) **~** appropriations. **~packung** f economy pack. **~plan** m parl. budget: im **~** vorsehen budget for.

'Hausherr m **1.** head of (the) household. **2.** landlord. **3.** host.

'Hausherrin f **1.** lady of the house. **2.** landlady. **3.** hostess.

'haushoch adj huge: haushoher Sieg

smashing victory; **haushohe Niederlage** crushing defeat; **~ gewinnen** win hands down; **~ schlagen** trounce; **~ verlieren** get an awful drubbing; **j-m ~ überlegen sein** be streets ahead of s.o.

hausieren [hau'zi:rən] *v/i* (h) mit et. ~ (**gehen**) hawk s.th., *a. fig.* peddle s.th.

Hausierer *m* (-s; -) hawker, peddler.

'Hauslehrer(in *f*) *m* private tutor(ess).

häuslich ['hɔyslıç] *adj* a) household, domestic, b) family, c) homekeeping, domesticated; 🏛 **~e Gemeinschaft** joint household; **im ~en Kreis** in the family circle; **er ist sehr ~** he's a real housebody; **sich ~ einrichten** (*or niederlassen*) settle down, *iro.* **bei j-m** come to stay with s.o.

'Häuslichkeit *f* (-; *no pl*) domesticity.

'Hausmacherart *f gastr.* **nach ~** home-made, traditional-style ...

'Haus|mädchen *n* maid. **~mann** *m* (-[e]s; ⸚er) house husband. **~mannskost** *f* good plain cooking. **~marke** *f* a) own brand, b) house wine, c) F *one's* favo(u)rite brand. **~meister** *m* caretaker. **~mittel** *n* household remedy. **~müll** *m* household waste. **~mu̇,sik** *f* music-making in the home. **~nummer** *f* house number. **~ordnung** *f* house rules. **~pflege** *f* home nursing (*or* care).

'Hausrat *m* (-[e]s; *no pl*) household effects. **'Hausratversicherung** *f* household contents insurance.

'Haus|sammlung *f* door-to-door collection. **~schlüssel** *m* front-door key. **~schuh** *m* slipper.

Hausse ['ho:s(ə)] *f* (-; -n) bull market, boom: **auf ~ spekulieren** bull the market. **'Haussespeku,lant** *m* bull.

'Haussuchung *f* (-; -en) house search.

'Haus|tele,fon *n* intercom. **~tier** *n* domestic animal, pet. **~tür** *f* front door. **~verwalter** *m* **1.** → *Hausmeister*. **2.** property manager. **~verwaltung** *f* property management. **~wirt** *m* landlord. **~wirtin** *f* landlady. **~wirtschaft** *f* (-; *no pl*) **1.** housekeeping. **2.** → **~wirtschaftslehre** *f* domestic science, *Am.* home economics. **~zelt** *n* frame tent.

Haut [haut] *f* (-; ⸚e) skin (*a.* hide, *anat.*, 🐟 *a.* membrane, 🐟 *a.* peel, *on milk etc*: *a.* film: **bis auf die ~ durchnäßt** soaked to the skin; F **mit ~ und Haar** completely; F **auf der faulen ~ liegen,**

sich auf die faule ~ legen loaf; **e-e dicke ~ haben** *a. fig.* have a thick skin; **mit heiler ~ davonkommen** come out of it unscathed; F **aus der ~ fahren** go through the roof; **s-e (eigene) ~ retten** save one's skin; **sich s-r ~ wehren** defend o.s.; **ich möchte nicht in s-r ~ stecken** I wouldn't like to be in his shoes; **er ist nur noch ~ und Knochen** he's just skin and bones; **es kann eben k-r aus s-r ~** a leopard can't change his spots; **das geht e-m unter die ~** it gets under your skin.

'Hautabschürfung *f* abrasion, graze.

'Hautarzt *m* dermatologist.

'Hautausschlag *m* (skin) rash: **e-n ~ bekommen** come out in a rash.

Häutchen ['hɔytçən] *n* (-s; -) *anat.*, 🐟 membrane, cuticle, *on milk etc*: skin.

'Hautcreme *f* skin cream.

haute ['hautə] *pret of* **hauen**.

häuten ['hɔytən] (h) **I** *v/t* skin, flay. **II** **sich ~** *zo.* shed its skin, slough off.

'hauteng *adj* skin-tight.

Hautevolee [(h)o:tvo'le:] *f* (-; *no pl*) *a.* *iro.* upper crust (F).

'Hautfarbe *f* colo(u)r (of one's skin), complexion. **'hautfarben** *adj* flesh-colo(u)red, skin-colo(u)red.

'Hautkrankheit *f* skin disease.

'Hautkrebs *m* 🟥 skin cancer.

'hautnah *adj* **1.** *a. sports:* (very) close. **2.** F *fig.* vivid, realistic.

'Hautpflege *f* skin care.

'Hautpflegemittel *n* skin-care product.

'Hautpilz *m* 🟥 fungal infection.

'Hautschere *f* cuticle scissors.

'Hauttransplantati,on *f* skin graft(ing).

'Häutung *f* (-; -en) *zo.* sloughing.

'Hautunreinheit *f* (skin) blemish.

'Hautwunde *f* (skin) wound.

Havarie [hava'ri:] *f* (-; -n) a) accident, b) damage: ⚓ **(große) ~** (general) average; **(kleine) ~** (petty) average.

he [he:] *int* F hey.

Hebamme ['he:p'amə] *f* (-; -n) midwife.

'Hebebaum *m* ⊙ heaver. **'Hebebühne** *f* ⊙ lifting platform, *mot.* car lift.

Hebel ['he:bəl] *m* (-s; -) lever: **den ~ ansetzen** apply the lever, *fig.* tackle it; *fig.* **alle ~ in Bewegung setzen** move heaven and earth; **am längeren ~ sitzen** be in the stronger position; **an den ~n der Macht sitzen** be at the controls.

~arm *m* lever arm. **~griff** *m* lever hold. **~kraft** *f*, **~mo̱,ment** *n phys.* leverage.

heben ['he:bən] (hob, gehoben, h) **I** *v/t* **1.** lift, raise, ☉ *a.* hoist: *ein Wrack* (*e-n Schatz*) **~** raise a wreck (treasure); F *fig.* **e-n ~** have a drink, hoist one. **2.** *fig.* raise (*eyes, voice, morale, etc*), improve, enhance. **3.** *dial.* hold. **II** *sich* **~ 4.** *curtain etc*: rise, go up, *fog*: lift: *sich* **~ *und senken*** rise and fall. **5.** *fig.* rise. ¹**Heben** *n* (-s) lifting (*etc*). ¹**Heber** *m* (-s; -) **1.** ♈ siphon. **2.** → *Gewichtheber*.

¹**Hebezeug** *n* (-[e]s; -e) ☉ hoist.

hebräisch [he'brɛ:ɪʃ] *adj* Hebrew.

¹**Hebung** *f* (-; -en) **1.** lifting, *a.* raising (*of treasure, wreck*). **2.** *no pl fig.* improvement, rise, increase, promotion. **3.** *metr.* stress(ed syllable).

hecheln ['hɛçəln] *v/i* (h) pant.

Hecht [hɛçt] *m* (-[e]s; -e) **1.** *zo.* pike: F *fig. toller* **~** some guy; *er ist* (*wie*) *der* **~ *im Karpfenteich*** he really stirs things up. **2.** F *fug.* ¹**hechten** *v/i* (h) do a pike-dive, *gym.* do a long-fly, *soccer etc*: dive full-length.

¹**Hechtsprung** *m* pike-dive, *gym.* long-fly, *soccer etc*: dive (flying) dive.

Heck [hɛk] *n* (-[e]s; -e, -s) ⚓ stern, *mot.* rear, back, ✈ tail. ¹**Heckantrieb** *m mot.* rear-wheel drive.

Hecke ['hɛkə] *f* (-; -n) hedge.

¹**Hecken|rose** *f* dogrose. **~schere** *f* hedge clippers. **~schütze** *m* sniper.

¹**Heckfenster** *n mot.* rear window. ¹**Heckklappe** *f mot.* tailgate. ¹**hecklastig** *adj* ✈, *mot.* tailheavy. ¹**Hecklicht** *n* ✈, *mot.* taillight. ¹**Heckmotor** *m* rear engine. ¹**Heckscheibe** *f mot.* rear window. ¹**Heckscheibenheizung** *f* rear-window defroster. ¹**Heckscheibenwischer** *m* rear wiper. **Heckspoiler** *m mot.* back spoiler.

heda ['he:da] *int* hey (there).

Hedonismus [hedo'nɪsmʊs] *m* (-; *no pl*) hedonism. **Hedonist** [hedo'nɪst] *m* (-en; -en) hedonist. **hedo'nistisch** *adj* hedonistic.

Heer [he:r] *n* (-[e]s; -e) army, *fig.* host. ¹**Heeres...** army (*command, group, etc*). ¹**Heerschar** *f fig.* host.

Hefe ['he:fə] *f* (-; -n) **1.** yeast. **2.** *fig.* dregs. ¹**Hefeteig** *m* yeast dough.

Heft¹ [hɛft] *n* (-[e]s; -e) **1.** *ped.* exercise book. **2.** number, issue. **3.** booklet.

Heft² *n* (-[e]s; -e) handle, *of dagger etc*: hilt: *fig. das* **~ *in der Hand haben*** (*behalten*) hold the rein (stay in control).

Heftchen ['hɛftçən] *n* (-s; -) book.

heften ['hɛftən] (h) **I** *v/t* **1.** (*an acc* to) fix, pin. **2.** baste, tack. **3.** *print.* stitch: *geheftet* in sheets. **II** *sich an j-s Fersen* **~** stick hard on s.o.'s heels; *sich* **~ *auf*** (*acc*) *eyes etc*: be fixed (*or* riveted) on.

Hefter ['hɛftər] *m* (-s; -) file.

¹**Heft|faden** *m*, **~garn** *n* tacking thread.

heftig ['hɛftɪç] *adj* **1.** violent, severe, fierce (*argument*), heavy (*rain*), acute (*pain*), splitting (*headache*), heated (*debate etc*): *et.* **~ *verteidigen*** defend s.th. vehemently. **2.** irascible, vehement: *er wird schnell* **~** he flares up quickly. ¹**Heftigkeit** *f* (-; *no pl*) **1.** violence, fierceness, vehemence. **2.** hot temper.

¹**Heft|klammer** *f* paper clip, ☉ staple. **~ma̱schine** *f* ☉ stapler. **~pflaster** *n* ⚕ (sticking) plaster. **~zwecke** *f* drawing pin, *Am.* thumbtack.

Hegemonie [hegemo'ni:] *f* (-; -n) hegemony.

hegen ['he:gən] *v/t* (h) **1.** preserve (*wildlife etc*), tend (*plants*), protect: **~ *und pflegen*** *a. fig.* take loving care of. **2.** *fig.* have (*doubts, a suspicion, etc*), cherish (*hope, love, etc*).

Hehl [he:l] *kein*(*en*) **~** *machen aus* make no secret of.

Hehler ['he:lər] *m* (-s; -) ⚖ receiver, *sl.* fence. **Hehle'rei** *f* (-; -en) ⚖ receiving, *sl.* fencing.

hehr [he:r] *adj* sublime, noble.

Heide¹ ['haɪdə] *m* (-n; -n) heathen, pagan.

¹**Heide²** *f* (-; -n) **1.** heath(land). **2.** → ¹**Heidekraut** *n* (-[e]s; *no pl*) ♣ heather.

Heidelbeere ['haɪdəlbe:rə] ♣ bilberry, *Am.* blueberry.

¹**Heiden...** F → *Mords...* ¹**Heidengeld** *n* F **ein ~** a fortune, a packet.

¹**Heidentum** *n* (-s; *no pl*) heathenism, paganism.

Heidin ['haɪdɪn] *f* (-; -nen) → *Heide¹*.

heidnisch ['haɪdnɪʃ] *adj* heathen, pagan.

Heidschnucke ['haɪtʃnʊkə] *f* (-; -n) *zo.* moorland sheep.

heikel ['haɪkəl] *adj* **1.** delicate, tricky: *ein heikler Punkt* a sore point. **2.** *dial.* a) fussy, b) squeamish.

heil [haɪl] *adj person:* unharmed, safe

and sound, *thing*: undamaged, whole, intact: *wieder ~* a) healed(-up), mended, b) repaired; *fig. e-e ~e Welt* an intact world. **Heil** *n* (-s; *no pl*) well-being, good, *eccl.* salvation: *sein ~ versuchen* try one's luck; *sein ~ in der Flucht suchen* take flight, run for it.

Heiland ['haɪlant] *m* (-[e]s; *no pl*) *eccl.* Savio(u)r.

'**Heilanstalt** *f* **1.** sanatorium. **2.** (mental) home.

'**heilbar** *adj* curable.

'**Heilbarkeit** *f* (-; *no pl*) curability.

Heilbutt ['haɪlbʊt] *m* (-[e]s; -e) halibut.

heilen ['haɪlən] I *v/t* (h) cure, heal: *j-n ~ von* a. *fig.* cure s.o. of. II *v/i* (sn) heal (up). '**heilend** *adj* healing, curative.

'**Heilerde** *f* healing earth.

'**heilfroh** *adj* F *~ sein* be really glad.

heilig ['haɪlɪç] *adj* a) holy, b) sacred (*a. fig.*), c) sacrosanct, d) saintly, pious: *der ~e* (*abbr. hl.*) *Paulus* Saint (*abbr.* St.) Paul; *der ~e Abend* Christmas Eve; *die ~e Jungfrau* the Blessed Virgin; *die ~e Nacht* Holy Night; *der ~e Vater* the Holy Father; *das ~e Land* the Holy Land; *die ~e Kuh* sacred cow; *ihm ist nichts ~* nothing is sacred to him; → *Geist* 3, *Schrift* 2, *Stuhl* 1.

'**Heilige** *m*, *f* (-n; -n) *a. fig.* saint.

heiligen ['haɪlɪgən] *v/t* (h) **1.** hallow, sanctify; → *Zweck.* **2.** → *heilighalten.*

'**Heiligenschein** *m* halo, gloriole.

'**heilighalten** *v/t* (*irr, sep, -ge-, h, → halten*) a) hold s.th. sacred, b) keep *s.th.* (holy), observe (*Sunday etc*).

'**Heiligkeit** *f* (-; *no pl*) a) holiness, *a. fig.* sacredness, sanctity, b) saintliness: *Seine ~* (*the Pope*) His Holiness.

'**heiligsprechen** *v/t* (*irr, sep, -ge-, h, → sprechen*) canonize. '**Heiligsprechung** *f* (-; -en) canonization.

'**Heiligtum** *n* (-s; -̈er) **1.** shrine. **2.** (sacred) relic, F s.th. sacred: *das ist sein ~!* that's sacred to him!

'**Heiligung** *f* (-; *no pl*) **1.** *a. fig.* sanctification. **2.** observance (*of Sunday etc*).

'**Heilklima** *n* healthy climate.

'**Heilkraft** *f* healing power(s).

'**heilkräftig** *adj* curative.

'**Heilkunde** *f* (-; *no pl*) medicine.

'**heillos** *adj* F hopeless, unholy (*mess etc*), *a.* frightful (*scare etc*).

'**Heil|me,thode** *f* cure, treatment. **~mit-**

tel *n* (*gegen* for) a) *a. fig.* cure, remedy, b) medicine. **~päda,gogik** *f* therapeutic pedagogy. **~pflanze** *f* medicinal herb. **~praktiker(in** *f*) *m* nonmedical practitioner. **~quelle** *f* mineral spring.

'**heilsam** *adj a. fig.* salutary, healthy: *~ sein (für)* a. be good (for).

'**Heilsar,mee** *f* Salvation Army.

'**Heilschlaf** *m* ⚕ hypnotherapy.

'**Heilserum** *n* ⚕ antiserum.

'**Heilung** *f* (-; -en) a) (*von* of) curing, cure (*a. fig.*), b) healing, c) recovery.

'**Heilungs|aussichten** *pl* chances of recovery. **~pro,zeß** *m* healing process.

'**Heilverfahren** *n* treatment, therapy.

'**Heilwirkung** *f* therapeutic effect.

heim [haɪm] *adv* home.

Heim *n* (-[e]s; -e) **1.** *no pl* home. **2.** home, hostel. '**Heimarbeit** *f* homework. '**Heimarbeiter(in** *f*) *m* homeworker.

Heimat ['haɪmaːt] *f* (-; *no pl*) home (*a. fig.*), ⚕, *zo.* habitat: *zweite ~* second home, F home from home; *in der ~* at home; *in m-r ~* a. where I come from. **~dichtung** *f* regional literature. **~film** *m* (sentimental) film with a regional background. **~hafen** *m* ⚓ home port. **~kunde** *f* (-; *no pl*) *ped.* local studies. **~land** *n* home country.

'**heimatlich** *adj* a) home, native, b) homelike, *pred* like home, *Am.* hom(e)y. '**heimatlos** *adj* homeless.

'**Heimat|mu,seum** *n* museum of local history. **~ort** *m* home town (*or village*). **~stadt** *f* home town. **~vertriebene** *m*, *f* (-n; -n) expellee.

'**heimbegleiten** *v/t* (*sep*, h) *j-n ~* see s.o. home.

Heimchen ['haɪmçən] *n* (-s; -) *zo.* (house) cricket.

'**Heimcom,puter** *m* home computer.

heimelig ['haɪməlɪç] *adj* cosy, F hom(e)y.

'**heimfahren** *v/i* (*irr, sep, -ge-, sn*, → *fahren*) go home, (*a. v/t*) drive home.

'**Heimfahrt** *f* journey home.

'**heimfinden** *v/i* (*irr, sep, -ge-, h*, → *finden*) find one's way home.

'**heimgehen** *v/i* (*irr, sep, -ge-, sn*, → *gehen*) **1.** go home. **2.** pass away, die.

'**Heimindu,strie** *f* cottage industry.

'**heimisch** *adj* a) domestic, home, b) ⚕, *zo.* native, indigenous, c) inland: **~e** *Gewässer* home waters; *~ sein in* (*dat*) *a. fig.* be at home in; **~ werden** settle (down), become acclimatized (*in dat* to); **sich ~ fühlen** feel at home.

Heimkehr ['haimke:r] *f* (-; *no pl*) return (home). '**heimkehren** *v/i* (*sep*, -ge-, sn) return home, come back. '**Heimkehrer** *m* (-s; -) homecomer, *pol.* repatriate.

'**Heimkind** *n* institution child.

'**Heimkino** *n* home movies.

'**heimkommen** *v/i* (*irr, sep*, -ge-, sn, → **kommen**) return (*or* come, get) home.

'**Heimleiter(in** *f*) *m* head of a home (*or* hostel).

'**heimleuchten** *v/t* (*sep*, -ge-, h) F *j-m ~* send s.o. packing.

'**heimlich I** *adj* secret, b) clandestine, c) furtive. **II** *adv* secretly (*etc*), in secret, (*a. ~, still und leise*) F on the quiet. '**Heimlichkeit** *f* (-; -en) **1.** *no pl* secrecy, furtiveness. **2.** *pl* secrets.

Heimlichtue'rei *f* (-; *no pl*) secretiveness.

'**heimlichtun** *v/i* (*irr, sep*, -ge-, h, → **tun**) F be secretive (**mit** about).

'**Heimmannschaft** *f sports*: home team.

'**Heimniederlage** *f sports*: home defeat.

'**Heimorgel** *f* ♪ electric organ.

'**Heimreise** *f* journey home: **auf der ~** on the way home. '**heimreisen** *v/i* (*sep*, -ge-, sn) go (*or* travel) home.

'**Heimsieg** *m sports*: home victory.

'**Heimspiel** *n sports*: home game.

'**Heimstärke** *f sports*: home strength.

'**Heimstätte** *f a. fig.* home.

'**heimsuchen** *v/t* (*sep*, -ge-, h) **1.** strike, visit (*a. bibl.*), plague, afflict, *premonitions etc*, *a.* ghost: haunt: *heimgesucht von* struck (*etc*) by; *von Dürre (Krieg) heimgesucht* drought-ridden (war-torn). **2.** F descend on. '**Heimsuchung** *f* (-; -en) visitation, affliction, trial.

'**Heimtrainer** *m* home exerciser.

'**Heimtücke** *f* (-; *no pl*) perfidy, treachery. '**heimtückisch** *adj* insidious (*a.* ♫), treacherous.

'**Heimvorteil** *m sports*: home advantage.

heimwärts ['haimverts] *adv* homeward(s), home.

'**Heimweg** *m* way home.

'**Heimweh** *n* (-[e]s; *no pl*) homesickness: **~ haben** be homesick (**nach** for).

Heimwerker ['haimverkər] *m* (-s; -) do-it-yourselfer, home mechanic. '**Heimwerker...** do-it-yourself (*kit etc*).

'**heimzahlen** *v/t* (*sep*, -ge-, h) *j-m et. ~* repay s.o. for s.th.

'**heimzu** *adv* F on the way home.

Heini ['haini] *m* (-s; -s) F *contp.* twerp.

Heinzelmännchen ['haintsəlmɛnçən] *n* (-s; -) brownie.

Heirat ['haira:t] *f* (-; -en) marriage.

heiraten ['haira:tən] *v/t*, *v/i* (h) (*j-n*) ~ marry (s.o.), get married (*to* s.o.).

'**Heirats|an,nonce** *f* marriage ad. **~antrag** *m* (marriage) proposal: *e-n ~ machen* propose (*dat* to). **~anzeige** *f* **1.** marriage announcement. **2.** marriage ad. ℒ**fähig** *adj* marriageable: *im ~en Alter* of marriageable age. **~markt** *m* marriage market. **~schwindler** *m* marriage impostor. **~urkunde** *f* marriage certificate. **~vermittlung** *f* **1.** marriage brokerage. **2.** marriage bureau.

heiser ['haizər] *adj* hoarse.

'**Heiserkeit** *f* (-; *no pl*) hoarseness.

heiß [hais] **I** *adj* **1.** hot, *fig. a.* a) ardent, passionate, b) fierce (*battle etc*), heated (*discussion etc*): **~e Zone** torrid zone; *et. ~ machen* heat s.th. up; *mir ist* (*wird*) **~** I'm (getting) hot; → **Draht, Eisen, Hölle, Ofen** 2. F *fig.* hot: **~e Ware** hot goods; **~er Tip** hot tip. **II** *adv* **3.** hotly (*etc*): *et. ~ ersehnen* long for s.th. (fervently); *sich ~ und innig lieben* adore each other; → **hergehen.**

'**heißblütig** [-bly:tıç] *adj* hot-blooded, passionate.

heißen ['haisən] (hieß, geheißen, h) **I** *v/i* **1.** be called (*nach* after): *wie ~ Sie?* what's your name?; *wie heißt das?* a) what's that called?, b) *auf Englisch?* what's that (called) in English. **2.** *text*: read, be. **3.** *mean*: *was heißt das?*, *was soll das ~?* a) what does it mean?, b) what do you mean (by this)?, c) what's the (big) idea?; *das hieße, das würde~* that would mean; *das will (et)was ~!* that's saying something!; *das will nichts ~!* that doesn't mean a thing!; *soll das ~, daß ...?* do you mean to say that ...?; *das soll nicht ~, daß* that doesn't mean that; *das heißt* that is (*abbr.* i.e.). **II** *v/impers* **4.** *es heißt, daß* they say that; *in dem Brief heißt es, daß* the letter says that. **5.** *jetzt heißt es handeln!* now it's time to act! **III** *v/t* **6.** call. **7.** *j-n et. tun ~* tell s.o. to do s.th.; → **willkommen.**

'**heißersehnt** adj longed-for.
'**heißgeliebt** adj dearly loved.
'**Heißhunger** m ♂ b(o)ulimia, a. fig. (sudden) craving (**nach** for).
'**heißlaufen** v/i (irr, sep, -ge-, sn, → **laufen**) (a. **sich** ~ [h]) ⚙ overheat, F telephone lines: be buzzing.
'**Heißluft**... hot-air ...
'**heißumkämpft** adj fiercely embattled.
'**heißumstritten** adj **1.** highly controversial. **2.** hotly debated.
heiter ['haɪtər] adj **1.** a) cheerful, gay, b) serene, c) funny, amusing: F iro. (**das**) **kann ja ~ werden!** nice prospects! **2.** bright, sunny: → **Himmel. 3.** ♪ scherzando. '**Heiterkeit** f (-; no pl) **1.** a) cheerfulness, b) serenity: ~ **erregen** cause amusement. **2.** brightness.
'**Heizanlage** f heating system.
'**heizbar** adj heatable, with heating.
'**Heizdecke** f electric blanket.
'**Heizele,ment** n heating element.
heizen ['haɪtsən] (h) **I** v/t heat (room etc), fire (stove). **II** v/i put (or have) the heating on.
Heizer m (-s; -) boilerman, ♨, ⚓ stoker.
'**Heizgas** n fuel gas. '**Heizgerät** n heater. '**Heizkessel** m boiler. '**Heizkissen** n electric pad. '**Heizkörper** m radiator, ⚡ heater. '**Heizkosten** pl heating costs. '**Heizlüfter** m fan heater. '**Heizmateri,al** n fuel. '**Heizöl** n (fuel) oil.
'**Heizung** f (-; -en) **1.** (central) heating. **2.** → **Heizkörper.**
'**Heizungsanlage** f heating system.
'**Heizungsmon,teur** m heating engineer.
Hektar ['hɛktaːr] n, m (-s; -e) hectare.
Hektik ['hɛktɪk] f (-; no pl) a) hectic atmosphere, mad rush, b) nervy state: F **nur k-e ~!** take it easy!
'**hektisch** adj hectic.
Hektoliter ['hɛktoliːtər] m, n hectolit/re (Am. -er).
Held [hɛlt] m (-en; -en) hero.
heldenhaft ['hɛldən-] adj heroic.
'**Heldensage** f saga. '**Heldentat** f heroic deed. '**Heldente,nor** m ♪ heroic tenor.
'**Heldentum** n (-s; no pl) heroism.
'**Heldenverehrung** f hero worship.
Heldin ['hɛldɪn] f (-; -nen) heroine.
helfen ['hɛlfən] v/i (half, geholfen, h) **1.** (dat) help, assist, aid, lend s.o. a hand: **j-m bei et.~** help s.o. with s.th.; **j-m aus dem (in den) Mantel ~** help s.o. off (on)

with his etc coat; fig. **j-m aus e-r Verlegenheit ~** help s.o. out of a difficulty; **ihm ist nicht zu ~** there is no help for him, iro. he's hopeless; **er weiß sich zu ~** a) he can look after himself, b) he is resourceful; **sich nicht mehr zu ~ wissen** be at one's wits' end; **ich kann mir nicht ~** a) I can't help it, b) ..., **ich muß einfach lachen** I can't help laughing. **2.** help: **das half** that worked; **das hilft gegen Schnupfen** that's good for colds; **das hilft mir wenig!** that's not much help!, F a fat lot it helps!; **es hilft nichts** it's no use; **da hilft kein Jammern!** it's no use complaining!; **da hilft nur eines** there's only one thing for it.
'**Helfer** m (-s; -), '**Helferin** f (-; -nen) helper, assistant: **ein Helfer in der Not** a friend in need.
'**Helfershelfer(in** f) m accomplice.
Helium ['heːliʊm] n (-s; no pl) ⚗ helium.
hell [hɛl] adj **1.** light, bright (sunshine etc), fair (hair, complexion, etc), light-colo(u)red (clothes), clear (voice etc): **~es Bier** lager; **~es Blau** light blue; fig. **~es Gelächter** loud laughter; **es wird schon ~** it is getting light already. **2.** fig. bright, intelligent. **3.** F great, utter (nonsense etc), pure (envy etc): **~er Wahnsinn** sheer madness; **~ begeistert** (absolutely) enthusiastic.
'**hellblond** adj very fair.
helle ['hɛlə] adj pred F bright, intelligent.
'**Helle**[1] f, n (-; no pl) brightness, (bright) light. '**Helle**[2] n (-n; -n) F (glass of) beer (Br. lager): **zwei ~!** two beers!
Heller ['hɛlər] m (-s; -) F **k-n (roten) ~ wert** not worth a cent; **auf ~ und Pfennig** to the last penny.
'**hellgrün** adj light-green.
'**hellhörig** adj **1.** fig. **das machte ihn ~** that made him prick up his ears. **2.** poorly soundproofed.
hellicht ['hɛlɪçt] adj **am ~en Tage** in broad daylight.
Helligkeit ['hɛlɪçkaɪt] f (-; no pl) brightness (a. TV), light, phys. luminosity.
Helling ['hɛlɪŋ] f (-; -en) ⚓ slip(way), (building) cradle.
'**hellrot** adj light-red.
'**hellsehen** v/i (only inf) have second sight, be clairvoyant. '**Hellsehen** n (-s) clairvoyance. '**Hellseher(in** f) m, '**hellseherisch** adj clairvoyant.

'hell'wach adj a. fig. wide-awake.
Helm [hɛlm] m (-[e]s; -e) helmet.
Hemd [hɛmt] n (-[e]s; -en) a) shirt, b) vest, Am. undershirt: fig. j-n bis aufs ~ ausziehen fleece s.o.
'Hemdbluse f shirt.
'Hemdblusenkleid n shirtwaister.
'Hemdsärmel m shirtsleeve: in ~n in (one's) shirtsleeves. 'hemdsärm(e)lig [-ɛrm(ə)lıç] adj a. fig. shirtsleeve.
Hemisphäre [hemi'sfɛːrə] f (-; -n) hemisphere.
hemmen ['hɛmən] v/t (h) 1. a. fig. a) stop, check, b) hinder, impede. 2. psych. inhibit: → gehemmt.
Hemmnis ['hɛmnıs] n (-ses; -se) obstacle.
'Hemmschuh m fig. drag (für on).
'Hemmung f (-; -en) 1. hindrance, check. 2. psych. inhibition, w.s. scruple: ~en haben be inhibited; nur k-e ~en! don't be shy! 3. ⚙ stop, escapement (of watch). 'hemmungslos adj 1. unrestrained, uncontrollable (weeping etc). 2. unscrupulous. 'Hemmungslosigkeit f (-; no pl) 1. lack of restraint, recklessness. 2. unscrupulousness.
Hengst [hɛŋst] m (-[e]s; -e) a) stallion, b) stud. 'Hengstfohlen n colt.
Henkel ['hɛŋkəl] m (-s; -) handle.
henken ['hɛŋkən] v/t (h) hang.
'Henker m (-s; -) executioner: F wer (wo etc) zum ~? who (where etc) the hell?
Henna ['hɛna] n (-; no pl) henna.
Henne ['hɛnə] f (-; -n) zo. hen.
Hepatitis [hepa'tiːtıs] f (-; -titiden [-ti'tiːdən]) 🩺 hepatitis.
her [heːr] adv 1. ago: wie lange ist es ~? how long ago was it?; das ist lange ~ that was a long time ago; es ist ein Jahr ~, daß ... it's a year since ... 2. von ... ~ from; von oben ~ from above; von weit ~ from afar; um mich ~ around me; ~ damit! give (it to me)!; → her- haben etc, hinter I. 3. fig. von ... ~ from the point of view of; vom Technischen ~ from a technical point of view, technically (speaking).
herab [hɛ'rap] adv down: fig. von oben ~ condescendingly.
her'ab... down; → a. herunter.
her'abgehen, her'abhängen, her'ab- kommen → heruntergehen etc.
her'ablassen (irr, sep, -ge-, h, → las- sen) I v/t let down, lower. II fig. sich ~

zu antworten etc deign to answer etc. her'ablassend adj condescending (zu towards). Her'ablassung f (-; no pl) condescension.
her'absehen v/i (irr, sep, -ge-, h, → sehen) ~ auf (acc) a. fig. look down on.
her'absetzen v/t (sep, -ge-, h) 1. reduce, lower, cut (back): (im Preis) ~ reduce (in price); zu herabgesetzten Preisen at reduced prices, cut-price ... 2. fig. disparage, belittle.
her'absetzend adj fig. disparaging.
Her'absetzung f (-; -en) 1. reduction, cut. 2. fig. disparagement.
her'absteigen v/i (irr, sep, -ge-, sn, → steigen) 1. descend, climb (or come) down. 2. dismount.
her'abwürdigen v/t (h) degrade (sich o.s.).
Heraldik [he'raldık] f (-; no pl) heraldry.
heran [hɛ'ran] adv near, close: ~ an (acc) up to; nur ~! come closer!
her'anbilden v/t (sep, -ge-, h) (a. sich ~) train (zu to be).
her'anbringen v/t (irr, sep, -ge-, h, → bringen) bring up (an acc to).
her'anführen v/t (sep, -ge-, h) lead (or bring) up (an acc to): fig. j-n an et. ~ introduce s.o. to s.th.
her'angehen v/i (irr, sep, -ge-, sn, → gehen) ~ an (acc) a) go up to, b) fig. approach, tackle (a task etc).
her'anholen v/t (sep, -ge-, h) 1. fetch, get. 2. phot. zoom in on.
her'ankämpfen: sich ~ (sep, -ge-, h) (an acc) sports: close in (on), pull up (to).
her'ankommen v/i (irr, sep, -ge-, sn, → kommen) 1. draw near, approach. 2. ~ an (acc) a) come up to (a. fig.), approach, come near (a standard etc), b) get at, get hold of; er (es) kommt nicht an ... heran a. he (it) can't touch ...; fig. an j-n ~ get through to s.o.; die Sache (or es) an sich ~ lassen wait and see.
her'anmachen: sich ~ (sep, -ge-, h) (an acc) F a) set to work (on s.th.), b) sidle up (to s.o.): fig. sich an j-n ~ a) approach s.o., b) make up to s.o., c) start working on s.o.
her'anreichen v/i (sep, -ge-, h) ~ an (acc) come up to, fig. a. touch.
her'anreifen v/i (sep, -ge-, sn) (zu into) ripen, fig. plan etc: a. mature, person: a. grow up.

her'anrücken *v/i* (*sep*, -ge-, sn) **1.** come close(r) (**an** *acc* to): **an j-n ~** move up (close) to s.o. **2.** draw near, approach.

her'antreten *v/i* (*irr*, *sep*, -ge-, sn, → **treten**) **an j-n ~** go up to s.o., *a. fig.* approach s.o., *fig.* confront s.o.

her'anwachsen *v/i* (*irr*, *sep*, -ge-, sn, → **wachsen**) grow up: **~ zu** grow into.

Her'anwachsende *m, f* (-n; -n) young person, adolescent.

her'anwagen: sich ~ (*sep*, -ge-, h) (**an** *acc*) venture near, draw near to approach (*s.o.*), *fig.* dare to tackle (*a task etc*).

her'anziehen (*irr*, *sep*, -ge-, → **ziehen**) **I** *v/t* (h) **1.** pull *s.th.* up (**an** *acc* to). **2.** a) raise, b) train. **3.** **j-n ~** (**zu**) call on s.o. (to do *s.th.*), enlist s.o.('s services) (for *s.th.*); **e-n Fachmann ~** call in an expert. **4.** cite, invoke. **II** *v/i* (sn) **5.** draw near, approach.

herauf [hɛ'raʊf] *adv* up, upwards: (**hier**) **~** up here; **den Berg ~** up the hill, uphill; **den Fluß ~** up the river, upstream; **die Treppe ~** up the stairs, upstairs; *in cpds.* → *a.* **empor...**

her'aufbeschwören *v/t* (*irr*, *sep*, h, → **beschwören**) **1.** conjure up (*memories etc*). **2.** bring on (*disaster etc*).

her'aufkommen *v/i* (*irr*, *sep*, -ge-, sn, → **kommen**) come up (**zu** to).

her'aufsetzen *v/t* (*sep*, -ge-, h) raise.

her'aufsteigen *v/t* (*irr*, *sep*, -ge-, sn, → **steigen**) climb, mount (*stairs etc*).

her'aufziehen (*irr*, *sep*, -ge-, → **ziehen**) **I** *v/t* (h) pull *s.o.*, *s.th.* up. **II** *v/i* (sn) draw near, approach.

heraus [hɛ'raʊs] *adv* out (**aus** of): **zum Fenster ~** out of the window; *fig.* **aus e-m Gefühl der Verlassenheit** *etc* **~** from (*or* out of) a sense of loneliness *etc;* **~ damit!** out with it!; **~ mit der Sprache!** F spit it out!; F **jetzt ist es ~!** now the secret's out!

her'ausarbeiten (*sep*, -ge-, h) **I** *v/t a. fig.* work out. **II** **sich ~ aus** work one's way out of, *fig. a.* manage to get out of.

her'ausbekommen *v/t* (*irr*, *sep*, h, → **bekommen**) **1.** get *stain etc* out (**aus** of). **2.** *fig.* a) F work out, solve, figure out, get, b) find *s.th.* out: **et. aus j-m ~** get s.th. out of s.o. **3.** **Sie bekommen noch 10 Mark heraus** you get ten marks change.

her'ausbringen *v/t* (*irr*, *sep*, -ge-, h, →

bringen) **1.** bring out (*a. fig.*), *print. a.* publish, *thea.* produce: **sie brachte kein Wort heraus** she couldn't say a word; **j-n** (*et.*) **groß ~** give s.o. (s.th.) a big buildup.

her'ausfahren (*irr*, *sep*, -ge-, → **fahren**) **I** *v/i* (sn) **1.** come (*or* drive) out (**aus** of). **2.** *remark etc:* slip out. **II** *v/t* (h) **3.** drive out (**aus** of): *sports:* **er hat e-e gute Zeit** (**den Sieg**) **herausgefahren** he made good time (won the race).

her'ausfallen *v/i* (*irr*, *sep*, -ge-, sn, → **fallen**) (**aus** of) fall out, drop out.

her'ausfiltern *v/t* (*sep*, -ge-, h) *a. fig.* filter out.

her'ausfinden (*irr*, *sep*, -ge-, h, → **finden**) **I** *v/t* a) find, b) find out, discover. **II** *v/i* find one's way out (**aus** of).

Her'ausforderer *m* (-s; -) challenger, *pol.* rival (candidate). **her'ausfordern** (*sep*, -ge-, h) **I** *v/t* challenge, defy, provoke: **das Schicksal ~** court disaster, F ask for it; **Kritik** (**Protest**) **~** → **II. II** *v/i* **zur Kritik** (**zum Protest**) **~** invite (*or* provoke) criticism (protest). **her'ausfordernd** *adj* challenging, defiant, provocative. **Her'ausforderung** *f* (-; -en) challenge (*a. fig.*), provocation.

Her'ausgabe *f* (-; *no pl*) **1.** surrender, delivery. **2.** *print.* editing, publication.

her'ausgeben *v/t* (*irr*, *sep*, -ge-, h, → **geben**) **I** *v/t* **1.** (*dat* to) hand *s.th.* over, give *s.th.* back, return. **2.** a) publish, b) edit, c) issue (*stamps, a. rules etc*). **3.** **j-m zehn Mark ~** give ten marks change. **II** *v/i* **4.** (**j-m**) **~** give (s.o.) change (**auf** *acc* for). **Her'ausgeber(in** *f*) *m* a) publisher, b) editor.

her'ausgehen *v/i* (*irr*, *sep*, -ge-, sn, → **gehen**) **1.** → **hinausgehen** 1; *fig.* **aus sich ~** come out of one's shell. **2.** *stain etc:* come out (**aus** of).

her'ausgreifen *v/t* (*irr*, *sep*, -ge-, h, → **greifen**) a) pick out, b) cite (*examples*).

her'aushaben *v/t* (*irr*, *sep*, -ge-, h, → **haben**) F *fig.* have found *s.th.* out, have got, have solved (*problem etc*): **er hat es heraus** he has got the hang of it.

her'aushalten *v/t* (*irr*, *sep*, -ge-, h, → **halten**) F **j-n** (**sich**) **aus der Sache ~** keep s.o. (o.s.) out of it.

her'ausheben *v/t* (*irr*, *sep*, -ge-, h, → **heben**) **1.** lift (*or* take) *s.o.*, *s.th.* out (**aus** of). **2.** → **hervorheben**.

her'aushelfen v/i (irr, sep, -ge-, h, → **helfen**) j-m ~ help s.o. out (**aus** of).

her'ausholen v/t (sep, -ge-, h) a. fig. get s.o., s.th. out (**aus** of): **das Letzte aus sich ~** make a supreme effort.

her'aushören v/t (sep, -ge-, h) hear, fig. detect (**aus** in s.o.'s words etc).

her'auskehren v/t (sep, -ge-, h) fig. act, play the expert etc, show, display.

her'auskommen v/i (irr, sep, -ge-, sn, → **kommen**) **1.** (**aus**) emerge (from), come out (of), a. fig. get out (of): **er kam aus dem Lachen nicht heraus** he couldn't stop laughing; F **groß ~** be a great success. **2.** fig. come out, book: a. be published, appear, stamps etc: be issued: **✝ mit e-m neuen Modell ~** come out with a new model; **~ mit** come out with, admit. **3.** (**aus** of) a) ᴁ be the result, b) fig. come (out): **es kommt nichts dabei heraus** it doesn't pay; **es kommt auf eins** (or **dasselbe**) **heraus** it boils down to the same thing; → a. **herausspringen** 2.

her'auskristalli,sieren v/t (sep, h) (a. **sich ~**) a. fig. crystallize (**aus** out of).

her'auslassen v/t (irr, sep, -ge-, h, → **lassen**) let out (**aus** of).

her'auslaufen (irr, sep, -ge-, → **laufen**) **I** v/i (sn) run out (**aus** of). **II** v/t (h) sports: gain (lead, victory, etc).

her'auslocken v/t (sep, -ge-, h) **1.** j-n ~ lure s.o. out (**aus** of). **2.** et. aus j-m ~ draw (or worm) s.th. out of s.o.

her'ausmachen: sich ~ (sep, -ge-, h) fig. be coming on well.

her'ausnehmen v/t (irr, sep, -ge-, h, → **nehmen**) (**aus**) take s.o., s.th. out (of), remove (from): fig. **sich Freiheiten ~** take liberties (**gegenüber** with).

her'ausplatzen v/i (sep, -ge-, sn) F **1.** burst out laughing. **2. ~ mit** blurt out.

her'ausputzen v/t (sep, -ge-, h) (**sich ~**) dress (o.s.) up, F spruce (o.s.) up.

her'ausragen v/t (sep, -ge-, h) (**aus** from) a) jut out, b) fig. stand out.

her'ausragend adj fig. outstanding.

her'ausreden: sich ~ (sep, -ge-, h) talk one's way out (**aus** of).

her'ausreißen v/t (irr, sep, -ge-, h, → **reißen**) **1.** pull (or tear) s.th. out. **2.** fig. j-n ~ aus tear s.o. away from (surroundings etc), rouse s.o. from (sleep etc),

interrupt s.o. in (one's work etc); F j-n ~ performance etc: save s.o.

her'ausrücken (sep, -ge-) F **I** v/t (h) → II b. **II** v/i (sn) ~ **mit** a) come out with, b) fork out, cough up (money); **mit der Sprache ~** talk, come out with it.

her'ausrutschen v/i (sep, -ge-, sn) F fig. slip out: **das ist mir einfach so herausgerutscht** it just slipped out.

her'ausschinden v/t (irr, sep, -ge-, h, → **schinden**) manage to get (**aus** out of).

her'ausschlagen v/t (irr, sep, -ge-, h, → **schlagen**) (**aus** of) **1.** knock s.th. out. **2.** F get s.th. out: **Geld ~ aus** make money out of it; **möglichst viel ~** make the most of it.

her'ausschneiden v/t (irr, sep, -ge-, h, → **schneiden**) cut s.th. out (**aus** of).

her'aussehen v/i (irr, sep, -ge-, h, → **sehen**) look out (**aus** of).

her'ausspringen v/i (irr, sep, -ge-, sn, → **springen**) **1.** jump out (**aus** of). **2.** F fig. be gained (**bei** by): **was springt für Sie dabei heraus?** what's in it for you?

her'ausstellen (sep, -ge-, h) **I** v/t **1.** put s.th. out(side). **2.** fig. a) point out, b) emphasize, underline: **groß ~** highlight, feature (a. thea.). **3.** → **hinausstellen** 2. **II sich ~** turn out (**als** to be), come to light: **es stellte sich heraus, daß sie recht hatte** she turned out to be right.

her'ausstrecken v/t (sep, -ge-, h) stick out (**aus** of): → **Zunge**.

her'ausstreichen v/t (irr, sep, -ge-, h, → **streichen**) **1.** cross out (**aus** of). **2.** fig. praise s.o., s.th. (to the skies).

her'aussuchen v/t (sep, -ge-, h) (**aus** from) choose (from), pick out (of).

her'auswinden: sich ~ (irr, sep, -ge-, h, → **winden**) fig. wriggle out (**aus** of).

herb [hɛrp] adj **1.** sour, tart, dry (wine), tangy (smell). **2.** fig. harsh (words, criticism, etc), bitter (disappointment, loss, etc), austere (beauty, style, etc).

herbei [hɛr'baɪ] adv here, up, over; → a. **her...**, **heran...** **her'beieilen** v/i (sep, -ge-, sn) come running (up).

her'beiführen v/t (sep, -ge-, h) fig. bring about, cause, lead to, esp. ⚕ induce.

her'beilassen: sich ~ (irr, sep, -ge-, h, → **lassen**) condescend (**zu** to).

her'beischaffen v/t (sep, -ge-, h) bring (up), fetch, get.

her'beisehnen v/t (sep, -ge-, h) long for.

'herbemühen (*sep*, h) **I** *v/t j-n* ~ ask s.o. to come (here). **II sich** ~ take the trouble to come.

Herberge ['hɛrbɛrgə] *f* (-; -n) youth hostel. **'Herbergsmutter** *f*, **'Herbergsvater** *m* (hostel) warden.

'herbeten *v/t* (*sep*, -ge-, h) rattle off.

'Herbheit *f* (-; *no pl*) **1.** sourness, *of wine*: dryness. **2.** *fig.* austerity.

'herbitten *v/t* (*irr*, *sep*, -ge-, h, → **bitten**) *j-n* ~ ask s.o. to come.

'herbringen *v/t* (*irr*, *sep*, -ge-, h, → **bringen**) bring *s.o.*, *s.th.* (along).

Herbst [hɛrpst] *m* (-[e]s; -e) autumn, *Am. a.* fall. **'Herbstfärbung** *f* autumnal tints. **'Herbstferien** *pl* autumn break. **'herbstlich** *adj* autumn(al). **'Herbstzeitlose** *f* (-; -n) 🌺 meadow saffron.

Herd [hɛrt] *m* (-[e]s; -e) **1.** a) (kitchen) stove, cooker, b) oven. **2.** *fig.* hearth. **3.** *fig.* cent/re (*Am.* -er), seat, focus (*a.* 🎯).

Herde ['hɛrdə] *f* (-; -n) **1.** herd, flock. **2.** *fig. contp.* the (common) herd.

'Herdentier *n zo.* gregarious animal: *fig. contp.* **ein** ~ **sein** follow the herd.

'Herdentrieb *m a. fig.* herd instinct.

'Herdplatte *f* hotplate.

herein [hɛ'raɪn] *adv* in: **von draußen** ~ from outside; ~! come in!; → *a.* **ein...**, **hinein...**, **rein...**.

her'einbekommen *v/t* (*irr*, *sep*, h, → **bekommen**) F ❖ get *s.th.* in.

her'einbitten *v/t* (*irr*, *sep*, -ge-, h, → **bitten**) *j-n* ~ ask s.o. (to come) in.

her'einbrechen *v/i* (*irr*, *sep*, -ge-, sn, → **brechen**) *night*: fall, *storm*: break, *winter*: set in: ~ **über** (*acc*) *misfortune etc*: befall.

her'einbringen *v/t* (*irr*, *sep*, -ge-, h, → **bringen**) bring in, get in.

her'einfallen *v/i* (*irr*, *sep*, -ge-, sn, → **fallen**) F *fig.* ~ **auf** (*acc*) be taken in by (*or* fall for) *s.o.*, *s.th.*; ~ **mit** make a (bad) mistake with.

her'einführen *v/t* (*sep*, -ge-, h) *j-n* ~ show s.o. in(to *in acc*).

her'einkommen *v/i* (*irr*, *sep*, -ge-, sn, → **kommen**) a) come in (a. ❖ *orders*), b) get in: ~ **in** (*acc*) come into (*or* inside).

her'einlassen *v/t* (*irr*, *sep*, -ge-, h, → **lassen**) let *s.o.*, *s.th.* in.

her'einlegen *v/t* (*sep*, -ge-, h) F *fig. j-n* ~

take s.o. for a ride, take s.o. in; *man hat uns hereingelegt* we have been had.

her'einplatzen *v/i* (*sep*, -ge-, sn) F burst in(to *in acc*).

her'einschauen *v/i* (*sep*, -ge-, h) F (*bei j-m*) ~ drop by (at s.o.'s place).

her'einschneien *v/i* (*sep*, -ge-, sn) F *fig.* (*bei j-m*) ~ blow in (at s.o.'s place).

'herfahren (*irr*, *sep*, -ge-, → **fahren**) **I** *v/i* (sn) travel (*or* come, drive) here: **hinter j-m** ~ drive behind s.o., follow s.o.'s car. **II** *v/t* (h) *j-n* ~ drive s.o. here.

'Herfahrt *f* (**auf der** ~ on the) journey (*or* way) here.

'herfallen *v/i* (*irr*, *sep*, -ge-, sn, → **fallen**) ~ **über** (*acc*) fall upon, attack.

'herfinden *v/i* (*irr*, *sep*, -ge-, h, → **finden**) find one's way.

'herführen *v/t* (*sep*, -ge-, h) *j-n* ~ bring s.o. here; *was führt Sie her?* what brings you here?

'Hergang *m* (-[e]s; *no pl*) course (of events), *the* way s.th. happened, *the* circumstances: *schildern Sie (mir) den* ~! tell me what (*or* how it) happened!

'hergeben *v/t* (*irr*, *sep*, -ge-, h, → **geben**) *et.* ~ hand s.th. over, give s.th. away; *et. wieder* ~ give s.th. back; *gib (es) her!* give (it to me)!; *sich* (*or* *s-n Namen*) ~ lend one's name (**zu**, **für** to).

'hergehen *v/impers* (*irr*, *sep*, -ge-, sn, → **gehen**) *es ging hoch* (*heiß*) *her* things were pretty lively (the sparks flew).

'herhaben *v/t* (*irr*, *sep*, -ge-, h, → **haben**) F *wo hast du das her?* a) where did you get that (from)?, b) *fig.* who told you that?

'herhalten *v/i* (*irr*, *sep*, -ge-, h, → **halten**) F ~ **müssen** a) have to suffer (for it), b) have to serve (**als** as).

'herholen *v/t* (*sep*, -ge-, h) fetch: *fig. weit hergeholt* far-fetched.

Hering ['he:rɪŋ] *m* (-s; -e) **1.** *zo.* herring: *humor.* **wie die** ~**e** packed like sardines. **2.** tent peg.

'herkommen *v/i* (*irr*, *sep*, -ge-, sn, → **kommen**) come (here): *komm her!* come here!; *fig.* ~ **von** come from; *wo kommen Sie her?* where do you come from?

herkömmlich ['he:rkœmlɪç] *adj* conventional, customary, traditional.

Herkunft ['he:rkʊnft] *f* (-; *no pl*) origin, *of person*: *a.* birth, descent, *w.s.* origins, background: **er ist deutscher ~** he is of German extraction.

'**Herkunftsland** n country of origin.

'**herlaufen** v/i (*irr, sep,* -ge-, sn, → *laufen*) run here: *hinter j-m ~ a. fig.* run after s.o.

'**herleiten** v/t (*sep,* -ge-, h) (*a. sich*) **~ von** derive from.

'**hermachen: sich ~** (*sep,* -ge-, h) F (*über acc*) set about, tackle (*task etc*), attack (*food, fig. s.o.*)

Hermelin [hɛrməˈliːn] (-s; -e) **1.** n zo. ermine. **2.** m ermine (fur).

hermetisch [hɛrˈmeːtɪʃ] adj hermetic.

'**hernehmen** v/t (*irr, sep,* -ge-, h, → *nehmen*) (*von* from) take, get.

hernieder(...) [hɛrˈniːdər] → **herab(...), herunter(...)**

Heroin [heroˈiːn] n (-s; no pl) heroin.

hero'insüchtig adj heroin-addicted.

Hero'insüchtige m, f heroin addict.

heroisch [heˈroːɪʃ] adj heroic.

Heroismus [heroˈɪsmʊs] m (-; no pl) heroism. **Heros** [ˈheːrɔs] m (-; Heroen [heˈroːən]) hero.

Herr [hɛr] m (-en; -en) a) gentleman, b) master, c) ruler (*über acc* over, of): *mein ~!* Sir!; *m-e ~en!* gentlemen!; *~ Miller* Mr Miller; *~ Doktor* (*Professor etc*) Doctor (*Professor etc*); *Ihr ~ Vater* your father; *sports:* **~en** men; (*Gott*) *der ~* the Lord (God); *der ~ Jesus* Our Lord Jesus; *sein eigener ~ sein* be one's own boss; *~ werden* (*gen*) master, (get *s.th.* under) control; *~ der Lage sein* have the situation well in hand; → *Land* 3.

'**Herrchen** n (-s; -) master (*of a dog*).

Herren|ausstatter [ˈhɛrən-] m (-s; -) men's outfitter, *Am.* haberdasher. **~bekleidung** f men's wear. **~doppel** n *tennis:* men's doubles. **~einzel** n *tennis:* men's singles. **~fahrrad** n man's bicycle. **~fri,seur** m barber, men's hairdresser. **~haus** n mansion. **~konfekti,on** f men's ready-to-wear clothes.

'**herrenlos** adj ownerless, stray (*dog*).

'**Herren|mode** f men's fashion. **~schneider** m men's tailor. **~toi,lette** f men's toilet (*Am.* restroom).

'**Herrgott** m (-s; no pl) the Lord (God), God; V **~ (noch mal)!** for God's sake!

'**Herrgottsfrühe** f *in aller* **~** at an unearthly hour.

'**herrichten** v/t (*sep,* -ge-, h) **1.** get *s.th.* ready. **2.** do up. **3.** tidy (*room*).

Herrin [ˈhɛrɪn] f (-; -nen) **1.** mistress, lady. **2.** ruler. '**herrisch** adj **1.** imperious. **2.** peremptory.

herrlich [ˈhɛrlɪç] adj marvel(l)ous, wonderful, magnificent, F fantastic.

'**Herrschaft** f (-; -en) **1.** no pl a) (*über acc* over) a) power, control, b) rule, reign: *fig.* **die ~ verlieren über** (*acc*) lose control of. **2.** *m-e* **~en!** ladies and gentlemen!, F folks! '**herrschaftlich** adj a) nobleman's, *hist.* manorial, b) stately.

herrschen [ˈhɛrʃən] v/i (h) **1.** rule (*über acc* over): *über j-n im Staat etc* **~** rule a state *etc.* **2.** *fig.* prevail, reign: *es herrschte Frieden a.* there was peace; *es herrschte Stille* silence reigned. '**herrschend** adj **1.** ruling (*class etc*). **2.** *fig.* prevailing, current (*opinion etc*).

Herrscher [ˈhɛrʃər] m (-s; -) ruler, sovereign, monarch. '**Herrscherhaus** n a) dynasty, b) ruling house. '**Herrscherin** f (-; -nen) → **Herrscher**.

'**Herrschsucht** f (-; no pl) domineering (F bossy) nature. '**herrschsüchtig** adj domineering, F bossy.

'**herrühren** v/i (*sep,* -ge-, h) **~ von** come (or date) from, be due to.

'**hersehen** v/i (*irr, sep,* -ge-, h, → *sehen*) look (here).

'**herstellen** v/t (*sep,* -ge-, h) **1.** ✝, ⚙ produce (*a. film*), manufacture, make. **2.** *fig.* establish (*order, contact, etc*)

Hersteller [ˈheːrʃtɛlər] m (-s; -) maker, manufacturer, producer (*a. film*).

'**Herstellerfirma** f manufacturers.

'**Herstellerin** f (-; -nen) → **Hersteller**.

'**Herstellung** f (-; no pl) **1.** a) manufacture, production (*a. print. and film*), b) Production (Department). **2.** *fig.* establishment, making (*of contacts etc*).

'**Herstellungs|kosten** pl production cost(s). **~land** n producer country. **~verfahren** n manufacturing process.

Hertz [hɛrts] n (-; -) *phys.* hertz.

herüber [hɛˈryːbər] adv **1.** over (here), across: *hier ~!* over here!, this way! **2.** F → **hinüber.** **her'überkommen** v/i (*irr, sep,* -ge-, sn, → *kommen*) come over (*a. on a visit*), come across.

'**Herübersetzung** f translation from the foreign language.

herum [hɛˈrʊm] adv **1.** around: *immer*

um et. ~ round and round s.th. **2.** about, (a)round (*the room, town, etc*). **3.** around, near(by): **(irgendwo) hier ~** somewhere around here, hereabouts. **4. um die Ecke ~** (a)round the corner; **rechts ~** (to the) right; **anders** (*falsch, so*) **~** the other (the wrong, this) way round. **5.** F **um ... ~** around, about (*two o'clock, ten dollars, etc*); **um Ostern ~** around Easter. **6.** *time etc*: over, up.

her'um... *dance, move, travel, walk, etc* (a)round, about.

her'umärgern: sich ~ (*sep, -ge-, h*) be plagued (*with*).

her'umdrehen (*sep, -ge-, h*) **I** *v/t* a) (**a. sich ~**) turn round, b) F turn over. **II** *v/i* F **~ an** (*dat*) fiddle with.

her'umdrücken: sich ~ (*sep, -ge-, h*) F **1.** hang around. **2. um et.** dodge s.th.

her'umfahren (*irr, sep, -ge-, → fahren*) **I** *v/i* (sn) **1.** drive (*or* go, travel) around: **um et. ~** drive round s.th. **2.** spin round. **II** *v/t* (h) **3.** drive (*or* take) *s.o., s.th.* around.

her'umfragen *v/i* (*sep, -ge-, h*) ask around.

her'umführen (*sep, -ge-, h*) **I** *v/t j-m ~* lead s.o. around; **j-m im Haus etc ~** show s.o. around the house *etc*; **~ Nase. II** *v/i* **um et. ~** *road, fence, etc*: run (a)round s.th.

her'umfuhrwerken *v/i* (*sep, -ge-, h*) F bustle around.

her'umgehen *v/i* (*irr, sep, -ge-, sn, → gehen*) **1.** walk (*or* go) around (**im Park** *etc* the park *etc*): **j-m im Kopf ~** go round and round in s.o.'s head. **2. um et. ~** *a.* F belt *etc*: go round s.th. **3.** be passed around. **4.** *rumo[u]r etc*: make the round. **5.** *time, day, etc*: pass.

her'umhängen *v/i* (*irr, sep, -ge-, h, → hängen*) F *fig.* hang around (**mit** with).

her'umkomman,dieren *v/t* (*sep, h*) *j-n ~* order s.o. around.

her'umkommen *v/i* (*irr, sep, -ge-, sn, → kommen*) **1. um et. ~** come (*fig.* get) round s.th., *fig. a.* avoid s.th.; **um diese Tatsache kommen wir nicht herum** we can't get away from that (fact). **2.** get around: **er ist weit herumgekommen** he has seen a lot of the world.

her'umkriegen *v/t* (*sep, -ge-, h*) F **1.** *j-n ~* get s.o. round; *j-n dazu ~, daß er et. tut*

talk s.o. into doing s.th. **2.** get through (*time, day, etc*).

her'umlaufen *v/i* (*irr, sep, -ge-, sn, → laufen*) (**um et.**) **~** run (*or* go) around (s.th.); **frei ~** *criminal etc*: be at large, *dog etc*: run free.

her'umliegen *v/i* (*irr, sep, -ge-, h, → liegen*) F lie around, lie about.

her'umlungern *v/i* (*sep, -ge-, h*) loiter (*or* hang, loaf) around.

her'umpfuschen *v/i* (*sep, -ge-, h*) **~ an** (*dat*) monkey (about) with.

her'umreichen (*sep, -ge-, h*) **I** *v/t* hand (*or* pass) *s.th.* (a)round: F *j-n ~* introduce s.o. to (all) one's friends. **II** *v/i* (**um et.**) **~ belt** *etc*: go (a)round (s.th.).

her'umreiten *v/i* (*irr, sep, -ge-, sn, → reiten*) (**um et.**) **~** ride (a)round (s.th.); F *fig.* **~ auf** (*dat*) keep harping on.

her'umschlagen: sich ~ (*irr, sep, -ge-, h, → schlagen*) a) *mit j-m* fight with s.o., b) *mit e-r Sache* struggle with s.th.

her'umschnüffeln *v/i* (*sep, -ge-, h*) F *fig.* snoop around.

her'umsein *v/i* (*irr, sep, -ge-, sn, → sein*) *time etc*: be over.

her'umstehen *v/i* (*irr, sep, -ge-, h, → stehen*) **~ um** stand (a)round.

her'umstoßen *v/t* (*irr, sep, -ge-, h, → stoßen*) F *fig. j-n ~* push s.o. around.

her'umtragen *v/t* (*irr, sep, -ge-, h, → tragen*) **1.** carry *s.o., s.th.* around (**mit sich** with one). **2.** *fig.* spread (*news etc*).

her'umtrampeln *v/i* (*sep, -ge-, h*) trample (**auf** *dat* on): *fig.* **auf j-m ~** treat s.o. like a doormat.

her'umtreiben: sich ~ (*irr, sep, -ge-, h, → treiben*) F **1.** knock around. **2.** → **herumlungern. Her'umtreiber** *m* (-s; -) **1.** loiterer, loafer. **2.** tramp.

her'umzeigen *v/t* (*sep, -ge-, h*) **et. ~** show (*or* pass) s.th. round.

herunter [hɛ'rɔntər] *adv* **1.** a) down, b) off: **~ damit!** down (*or* off) with it!; **die Treppe ~** down the stairs, downstairs; → **heruntersein. 2.** F → **hinunter.**

herunter... [hɛ'rɔntər] down; → *a.* **herab..., F hinab..., hinunter....**

her'unterbekommen *v/t* (*irr, sep, h, → bekommen*) F get *s.th.* down (*or* off).

her'unterfallen *v/i* (*irr, sep, -ge-, sn, → fallen*) fall down (*or* off).

her'untergehen *v/i* (*irr, sep, -ge-, sn, → gehen*) go down (a. ✈), *fig. a.* fall, drop: *mit der Geschwindigkeit* (*den Preisen*) ~ slow down (reduce prices).

her'untergekommen I *pp of herunterkommen.* **II** *adj* F a) seedy, shabby, down-at-heel, b) run-down, *pred in* bad shape, c) dissolute, d) dilapidated.

her'unterhandeln *v/t* (*sep, -ge-, h*) beat *price etc* down (*um* by).

her'unterholen *v/t* (*sep, -ge-, h*) **1.** get *s.o., s.th.* down. **2.** F shoot *s.th.* down.

her'unterklappen *v/t* (*sep, -ge-, h*) turn *s.th.* down.

her'unterkommen *v/i* (*irr, sep, -ge-, sn,* → *kommen*) **1.** come (*or* get) down. **2.** F a) go to seed, b) get into bad shape, c) go downhill, go to rack and ruin, d) sink low; → *heruntergekommen.* **3.** ~ *von* F get over, *sl.* kick (*drugs etc*).

her'untermachen *v/t* (*sep, -ge-, h*) F **1.** knock, pull *s.o., s.th.* to pieces. **2.** → **her'unterputzen** *v/t* (*sep, -ge-, h*) F *j-n* ~ blow s.o. up.

her'unterrasseln *v/t* (*sep, -ge-, h*) F rattle off.

her'unterschalten *v/i* (*sep, -ge-, h*) *mot.* (*in den ersten Gang*) ~ change (*or* shift) down (into first [gear]).

her'unterschrauben *v/t* (*sep, -ge-, h*) *fig.* lower.

her'untersein *v/i* (*irr, sep, -ge-, sn,* → *sein*) F *fig.* be run down, be in bad shape: *er ist mit den Nerven ganz herunter* he is a nervous wreck.

her'unterspielen *v/t* (*sep, -ge-, h*) F *fig.* *et.* ~ play s.th. down.

her'unterwirtschaften *v/t* (*sep, h*) F *et.* ~ run s.th. down, mismanage s.th.

hervor [her'fo:r] *adv* out of, (out) from, forth: *hinter ... ~* from behind *a tree etc*; *unter ... ~* from under *the bed etc*.

her'vorbringen *v/t* (*irr, sep, -ge-, h,* → *bringen*) produce.

her'vorgehen *v/i* (*irr, sep, -ge-, sn,* → *gehen*) **1.** (*aus* from) follow, result: *daraus geht hervor, daß* from this follows that; *aus dem Brief geht nicht hervor, ob* the letter doesn't say whether; *als Sieger* ~ emerge victorious; *aus der Ehe gingen drei Kinder hervor* there were three children of this marriage.

her'vorheben *v/t* (*irr, sep, -ge-, h,* → *heben*) **1.** *paint., print.* set *s.th.* off. **2.** *fig.* a) emphasize, stress, b) point out.

her'vorholen *v/t* (*sep, -ge-, h*) *et.* ~ (*aus*) get s.th. out (of), produce s.th. (from).

her'vorragen *v/i* (*sep, -ge-, h*) **1.** project, stick out. **2.** *fig.* stand out (*unter dat* among). **her'vorragend I** *adj* **1.** projecting. **2.** *fig.* outstanding, excellent, superior, prominent. **II** *adv* **1.** excellently, outstandingly (well).

her'vorrufen *v/t* (*irr, sep, -ge-, h,* → *rufen*) **1.** *thea.* call for. **2.** *fig.* cause, give rise to, provoke.

her'vorstechen *v/i* (*irr, sep, -ge-, h,* → *stechen*) stand out (*aus* from).

her'vorstechend *adj* **1.** → *hervorragend* **2.** striking.

her'vortreten *v/i* (*irr, sep, -ge-, sn,* → *treten*) **1.** step forth, (*aus dat*) step out (of), emerge (from). **2.** a) stand out, b) *fig.* emerge, become evident: *et.* ~ *lassen* set s.th. off, *fig.* bring s.th. out, show s.th. **3.** *veins, eyes:* protrude. **4.** → **her'vortun:** *sich* ~ (*irr, sep, -ge-, h,* → *tun*) distinguish o.s. (*als* as, *durch* by).

'herwagen: *sich* ~ (*sep, -ge-, h*) dare to come (here).

'Herweg [her'fo:r] *adv* (*auf dem* ~ on the) way here.

Herz [hɛrts] *n* (*-en; -en*) heart (*a. fig.*), *cards:* hearts: *im Grunde s-s* ~*ens* at heart; *leichten* ~*ens* with a light heart; *schweren* ~*ens* with a heavy heart, very reluctantly; *von* ~*en gern* with (the greatest) pleasure, gladly; *j-m von* (*ganzem*) ~*en danken* thank s.o. with all one's heart; *von* ~*en kommend* heartfelt; *auf* ~ *und Nieren prüfen* put *s.th.* to the acid test, F vet *s.o., s.th.* (thoroughly); *j-m das* ~ *brechen* break s.o.'s heart; *sich ein* ~ *fassen* take heart, pluck up courage; *j-m zu* ~*en gehen* move s.o. deeply; *er ist mir sehr ans* ~ *gewachsen* I have grown very fond of him; *was haben Sie auf dem* ~*en?* a) what's on your mind?, b) what can I do for you?; *j-m et.* ~*en legen* enjoin s.th. on s.o.; *das liegt mir sehr am* ~*en* that's very important to me; *s-m* ~*en Luft machen* give vent to one's feelings; *j-n ins* ~ *schließen* take s.o. to one's heart; *sie sind ein* ~ *und eine Seele* they are very close, F they are as thick as thieves; → *ausschütten* 1, *bringen* 7, *Stoß* 1, *tief* I.

'Herzanfall *m* heart attack.

'Herzas *n cards:* ace of hearts.

'**Herzasthma** *n* ✻ cardiac asthma.
'**Herzbeschwerden** *pl* heart trouble.
'**Herzbeutel** *m anat.* pericardium.
Herzchen ['hɛrtsçən] *n* (-s; -) darling.
'**Herzchir,urg** *m* heart surgeon.
'**Herzdame** *f cards:* queen of hearts.
'**herzeigen** *v/t* (*sep*, -ge-, h) F show: *zeig* (*mal*) *her!* let me see!
herzen ['hɛrtsən] *v/t* (h) hug, cuddle.
'**Herzens|brecher** *m* (-s; -) F ladykiller.
~**lust** *f nach* ~ to one's heart's content.
~**wunsch** *m* dearest wish.
'**herzerfrischend** *adj* (very) refreshing.
'**herzergreifend** *adj* (deeply) moving.
'**Herzfehler** *m* ✻ cardiac defect.
'**Herzflimmern** *n* (-s) ✻ heart flutter.
'**herzförmig** [-fœrmiç] *adj* heart-shaped.
'**herzhaft** *adj* **1.** hearty. **2.** → *beherzt*.
'**herziehen** (*irr*, *sep*, -ge-, → *ziehen*) **I**
v/t (h) **1.** *hinter sich* ~ drag *s.o.*, *s.th.*
along (behind one). **II** *v/i* (sn) **2.** move
here. **3.** F ~ *über* (*acc*) run *s.o.*, *s.th.*
down.
herzig ['hɛrtsiç] *adj* sweet, lovely.
'**Herz|in,farkt** *m* ✻ cardiac infarction, F
heart attack, coronary. ~**kammer** *f*
anat. ventricle. ~**ka,theter** *m* ✻ cardiac
catheter. ~**klappe** *f anat.* cardiac valve.
~**klappenfehler** *m* ✻ valvular (heart)
defect. ~**klopfen** *n* (-s) beating (✻ pal-
pitation) of the heart: *er hatte* ~ his
heart was thumping (*vor* dat with).
♀**krank** *adj* suffering from a heart condition, cardiac. ~**kranke** *m, f* cardiac.
~**kranzgefäß** *n anat.* coronary vessel.
~**leiden** *n* heart disease (*or* condition).
'**herzlich I** *adj* a) cordial, warm, friendly, b) sincere, heartfelt: ~*e Grüße, mit*
~*en Grüßen* kind regards (*an acc* to),
(with) love; → *Beileid, Dank, Gruß.*
'**Herzlichkeit** *f* (-; *no pl*) a) warmth, cor-
diality, b) sincerity.
'**herzlos** *adj* heartless.
'**Herzlosigkeit** *f* (-; *no pl*) heartlessness.
'**Herz-'Lungen-Ma'schine** *f* ✻ heart-
-lung machine.
'**Herzmas,sage** *f* ✻ heart massage.
Herzog ['hɛrtso:k] *m* (-s; ~e) duke.
Herzogin ['hɛrtso:gɪn] *f* (-en; -en)
duchess. '**herzoglich** *adj* ducal.
'**Herzogtum** *n* (-s; ~er) dukedom, duchy.
'**Herz|operati,on** *f* heart operation.
~**rhythmusstörung** *f* arrhythmia.
~**schlag** *m* **1.** heartbeat. **2.** heart attack

(*or* failure). ~**schrittmacher** *m* cardiac
pacemaker. ~**schwäche** *f* cardiac insufficiency. ~**spezia,list** *m* heart specialist. ♀**stärkend** *adj* cardiotonic.
~**stillstand** *m* cardiac arrest. ~**stück** *n*
fig. core. ~**tod** *m* death by heart failure.
herzu(...) [hɛr'tsu:] → *heran(...)*, *her-
bei(...)*, *hinzu(...)*.
'**Herzversagen** *n* ✻ heart failure.
'**Herzverpflanzung** *f* heart transplant.
'**herzzerbrechend** *adj* heartbreaking.
'**herzzerreißend** *adj* heartrending.
Hesse ['hɛsə] *m* (-n; -n), '**Hessin** *f* (-;
-nen), '**hessisch** *adj* Hessian.
heterogen [hetero'ge:n] *adj* heteroge-
neous.
heterosexu'ell *adj*, **Heterosexu'elle** *m,
f* (-n; -n) heterosexual.
Hetze ['hɛtsə] *f* (-; -n) **1.** (*gegen*
against) agitation, smear campaign. **2.**
F (mad) rush. **3.** → *Hetzjagd* 1, 2.
'**hetzen I** *v/t* (h) **1.** *a. fig.* hunt,
hound. **2.** *e-n Hund etc* ~ *auf* (*acc*) set a
dog *etc* on. **3.** (*a. sich* ~) rush. **II** *v/i*
4. (h) (*gegen* against) agitate, stir up
hatred. **5.** (sn) F rush, hurry.
'**Hetzer** *m* (-s; -) agitator.
Hetze'rei *f* (-; *no pl*) → *Hetze* 1, 2.
'**hetzerisch** *adj* inflammatory.
'**Hetzjagd** *f* **1.** hunt(ing) (with hounds).
2. *fig.* chase. **3.** → *Hetze* 1, 2.
'**Hetzrede** *f* inflammatory speech.
Heu [hɔy] *n* (-[e]s; *no pl*) hay: F *er hat
Geld wie* ~ he's rolling in money.
'**Heuboden** *m* hayloft.
Heuche'lei *f* (-; -en) **1.** *no pl* hypocrisy,
dissimulation. **2.** cant. **heucheln** ['hɔy-
çəln] (h) **I** *v/t* simulate, feign. **II** *v/i* a)
play the hypocrite, b) dissemble, c)
cant. '**Heuchler** *m* (-s; -), '**Heuchlerin**
f (-; -nen) hypocrite. '**heuchlerisch** *adj*
hypocritical.
heuen ['hɔyən] *v/i* (h) make hay.
Heuer ['hɔyər] *f* (-; -n) ♪ pay.
heuern ['hɔyərn] *v/t* (h) ♪ hire.
'**Heuernte** *f* hay harvest.
'**Heugabel** *f* hayfork, pitchfork.
heulen ['hɔylən] *v/i* (h) **1.** *zo.* howl. **2.** F
bawl, *a. fig.* siren: wail: *fig.* **es ist zum** ♀
it's a (great) shame.
'**Heuler** *m* (-s; -) **1.** F *das ist (ja) der
letzte* ~*!* a) would you believe it, b) it's
absolutely super. **2.** *zo.* baby seal.
'**Heulsuse** *f* (-; -n) F crybaby.

Heurige ['hɔʏrɪɡə] *m* (-n; *no pl*) *Austrian* new wine.

'**Heuschnupfen** *m* hay fever.

'**Heuschober** *m* haystack.

Heuschrecke ['hɔʏʃrɛkə] *f* (-; -n) *zo.* grasshopper, locust.

heute ['hɔʏtə] **I** *adv* today, this day: ~ **abend** this evening, tonight; ~ **in acht Tagen** a week from now, *Br. a.* today week; ~ **vor acht Tagen** a week ago (today); *von* ~ → *heutig*; *von* ~ **an** from today; *fig.* **von** ~ **auf morgen** overnight. **II** *das Heute* the present, today.

heutig ['hɔʏtɪç] *adj* today's, of today, *a.* present(-day), modern: *bis auf den* ~**en Tag** to this day.

'**heutzutage** *adv* nowadays, today.

Hexe ['hɛksə] *f* (-; -n) witch (*a. fig.*), sorceress, *fig.* hellcat: (*alte*) ~ (old) hag.

hexen ['hɛksən] *v/i* (h) practise witchcraft: F **ich kann doch nicht** ~! I can't work miracles!

'**Hexen|jagd** *f fig.* witch-hunt. ~**kessel** *m fig.* inferno. ~**meister** *m* sorcerer. ~**schuß** *m* (-sses; *no pl*) ✠ F lumbago.

Hexe'rei *f* (-; -en) witchcraft, magic (*a. fig.*): **das ist k-e** ~! there's nothing to it!

hieb [hiːp] *pret of* **hauen**.

Hieb *m* (-[e]s; -e) **1.** stroke, blow, punch: F ~**e bekommen** get a thrashing; *auf einen* ~ at one go. **2.** *fig.* dig (*auf acc* at). '**hieb- und 'stichfest** *adj* watertight (*argument*), cast-iron (*proof etc*).

hielt [hiːlt] *pret of* **halten**.

hier [hiːr] *adv* here (*a. fig. in this case*), *a.* present: ~ **drinnen** (**draußen, oben**) in (out, up) here; ~ **und da** a) here and there, b) now and then; ~ **und heute** here and now; *von* ~ *an* (*or ab*) from here (on); ~, *bitte!* here you are!

hieran ['hiːran] *adv* **1.** ~ **kann man sehen, daß** you can see from this that; ~ **ist kein wahres Wort** there is not a word of truth in this. **2.** ~ **schließt sich ... an** this is followed by ...

Hierarchie [hiːrar'çiː] *f* (-; -n) hierarchy.

hieraus ['hiːraʊs] *adv* from it (*or* this).

'**hier'bei** *adv* a) here, b) on this occasion, c) in this connection.

'**hierbleiben** *v/i* (*irr, sep, -ge-, sn,* → **bleiben**) stay here.

'**hier'durch** *adv* by this, hereby.

'**hier'für** *adv* for this, for it.

'**hier'her** *adv* here, this way, over here:

bis ~ up to here, *a. time*: so far; *bis* ~ **und nicht weiter** this far and no further; (*komm*) ~! come here!

hier'hergehören *v/i* (*sep,* h) belong here: *fig. das gehört nicht hierher* that's irrelevant.

hierherum ['hiːrhɛ'rʊm] *adv* **1.** this way (a)round. **2.** F hereabout(s).

'**hier'hin** *adv* here. **hierhin'auf** *adv* up here. '**hierhin'ein** *adv* in here.

hierin ['hiː'rɪn] *adv a. fig.* in this, here.

'**hier'mit** *adv* with this, herewith.

'**hier'nach** *adv* **1.** after this (*or* it). **2.** according to this.

Hieroglyphe [hiːro'glyːfə] *f* (-; -n) hieroglyph.

'**hiersein** *v/i* (*irr, sep, -ge-, sn,* → **sein**) be here, be present: *während s-s Hierseins* during his stay (here).

hierüber ['hiː'ryːbər] *adv fig.* about this.

hierum ['hiː'rʊm] *adv* **1.** (a)round this. **2.** → **hierherum** 2. **3.** *fig.* about this (*or* it): ~ **geht es nicht** that's not the point.

hierunter ['hiː'rʊntər] *adv* **1.** under this, among these. **2.** *fig. understand etc*: by this, by that: ~ **fällt ...** this includes ...

'**hier'von** *adv* of (*or* from) this.

'**hier'zu** *adv* **1.** for this. **2.** to this (*or* these): *im Gegensatz* ~ in contrast to this.

'**hierzu'lande** *adv* in this country, here.

hiesig ['hiːzɪç] *adj* local, here, of this place (*or* country).

hieß [hiːs] *pret of* **heißen**.

hieven ['hiːfən] *v/t* (h) *a. fig.* heave.

Hi-Fi ['haɪfi] *abbr. of* **High Fidelity**.

'**Hi-Fi-'Anlage** *f* hi-fi set.

Hilfe ['hɪlfə] *f* (-; -n) **1.** help, aid, assistance, relief: *ärztliche* ~ medical assistance; *Erste* ~ first aid; *j-m* ~ **leisten** help s.o., aid s.o.; *j-m zu* ~ **kommen** come to s.o.'s aid; *zu* ~ **nehmen** make use of, use; *um* ~ **rufen** call for help; *mit* ~ **von** (*or gen*) with the help of, *fig. a.* by means of; *ohne* ~ unaided, without help; (*zu*) ~! help! **2.** (*person*) help.

'**hilfeflehend** *adj* imploring.

'**Hilfeleistung** *f* aid, assistance, help.

'**Hilferuf** *m a. fig.* cry for help.

'**Hilfestellung** *f* (-; *no pl*) *a. fig.* support.

'**hilfesuchend** *adj* seeking (for) help.

'**hilflos** *adj* helpless.

'**Hilflosigkeit** *f* (-; *no pl*) helplessness.

'**hilfreich** *adj a. fig.* helpful.

'**Hilfs|akti,on** f relief (or rescue) action. **⏜arbeiter(in** f) m unskilled worker. ⏜**bedürftig** adj a) in need (of help), b) needy. ⏜**bedürftigkeit** f (-; no pl) neediness, need. ⏜**bereit** adj ready to help, helpful. ⏜**bereitschaft** f (-; no pl) readiness to help. ⏜**fonds** m relief fund. ⏜**kraft** f **1.** assistant, help. **2.** temporary worker. ⏜**mittel** n aid. ⏜**motor** m auxiliary engine (⚡ motor). ⏜**organisati,on** f relief organization. ⏜**quelle** f source of help, of resources. ⏜**verb** n auxiliary verb. ⏜**werk** n relief organization. ⏜**wissenschaft** f auxiliary science.

Himbeere ['hɪmbeːrə] f (-; -n) raspberry.
'**Himbeersaft** m raspberry juice.
'**Himbeerstrauch** m raspberry bush.

Himmel ['hɪməl] m (-s; -) sky, eccl. or fig. heaven: **der ⏜ auf Erden** heaven on earth; **am ⏜** in the sky; fig. (**wie) aus heiterem ⏜** out of the blue; **unter freiem ⏜** in the open air; **zum ⏜** (**empor**) skyward(s), heavenward(s); **im ⏜ sein** be in heaven; **in den ⏜ heben** praise s.o., s.th. to the skies; F **weiß der ⏜(, wo)!** God knows (where)!; **das schreit zum ⏜** it's a crying shame; F **das stinkt zum ⏜** that stinks to high heaven; **um ⏜s willen!** a) a. (**ach,) du lieber ⏜!** good heavens!, b) a. ⏜ (**noch mal**)! for Heaven's sake!

'**himmel|angst** adj **mir war (or wurde) ⏜** I was scared to death.
'**Himmelbett** n four-poster.
'**himmelblau** adj sky-blue.
'**Himmelfahrt** f (-; no pl) **Christi ⏜** a) the Ascension of Christ, b) Ascension Day; **Mariä ⏜** a) the Assumption of the Virgin Mary, b) Assumption Day.
'**Himmelfahrtstag** m (**am ⏜** on) Ascension Day.
'**Himmelreich** n kingdom of heaven.
'**Himmelschlüssel** m ⚘ primrose.
'**himmelschreiend** adj outrageous, terrible: **⏜e Schande** crying shame.
'**Himmelskarte** f star map.
'**Himmelskörper** m celestial body.
'**Himmelsrichtung** f direction.
'**himmelweit** adj fig. vast: **es ist ein ⏜er Unterschied zwischen ...** there is a world of difference between ...; **⏜ verschieden sein** differ enormously.
himmlisch ['hɪmlɪʃ] adj heavenly, divine.
hin [hɪn] I adv **1.** there: **nichts wie ⏜!** let's

go!; **⏜ zu** to, towards; **bis ⏜ zu** a) as far as, b) fig. (even) including, c) till; **über** (acc) ⏜ over; **⏜ und her** to and fro, back and forth; **⏜ und zurück** a) there and back, b) return (Am. round-trip) (ticket); **⏜ und her gerissen sein** a) **zwischen** be torn between, b) F **von** be gone over. **2. auf e-e Sache ⏜** a) as a result of, b) on the basis of, c) because of, d) in reply to, on; **auf s-e Bitte ⏜** at his request; **auf s-n Rat ⏜** at his advice. **⏜ und wieder** now and then. **4.** F **⏜ oder her** a) more or less, give or take (ten dollars, years, etc), b) a. ⏜ ...⏜, ...**her** I don't care; **Anstand ⏜, Anstand her** fairness or no. **II** adj pred → **hin-sein.**

Hin n → **Hin und Her.**
hinab(...) [hɪˈnap] → **hinunter(...), herab(...), herunter(...).**
'**hinarbeiten** v/i (sep, -ge-, h) **⏜ auf** (acc) work towards, aim at.

hinauf [hɪˈnaʊf] adv up: **da ⏜** up there; **bis ⏜ zu** up to; **den Berg ⏜** up the hill, uphill; (**die Treppe**) ⏜ upstairs.
hin'auf... climb, drive, look, etc up, → a. **empor..., hoch...**
hin'aufgehen (irr, sep, -ge-, sn, → **gehen**) **I** v/i go up (a. fig.): **mit dem Preis ⏜** raise the price. **II** v/t go up: **die Treppe** ⏜ a. go upstairs.

hinaus [hɪˈnaʊs] adv **1.** out, outside: **aus** out of; **da ⏜!** this way (out)!; **zum Fenster ⏜** out of the window; **nach vorn (hinten) ⏜** wohnen live at the front (back); **⏜ (mit dir or euch)!** out (with you)!, get out!; **⏜ damit!** out with it! **2. über** (acc) ⏜ a. fig. a) beyond, b) above, over; **auf Jahre ⏜** for years (to come); → **darüber** 3, **hinaussein.**
hin'ausbegleiten v/t (sep, h) **j-n ⏜** see s.o. out (**aus** of).
hin'ausekeln v/t (sep, -ge-, h) F **j-n ⏜** freeze s.o. out (**aus** of).
hin'ausfliegen v/i (irr, sep, -ge-, sn, → **fliegen**) **1.** fly out. **2.** F fig. get kicked out, a. get the sack.
hin'ausgehen v/i (irr, sep, -ge-, sn, → **gehen**) **1.** go out (**aus** of). **2.** fig. ⏜ **auf** (acc) window etc: open on(to). **3.** fig. ⏜ **über** (acc) go beyond, a. exceed.
hin'auslaufen v/i (irr, sep, -ge-, sn, → **laufen**) **1.** run out (**aus** of). **2.** fig. ⏜ **auf** (acc) come to, amount to, lead to; **es**

läuft auf dasselbe hinaus it comes (*or* amounts) to the same thing.

hin'ausschieben *v/t* (*irr, sep,* -ge-, h, → *schieben*) *fig.* put *s.th.* off, postpone.

hin'aussein *v/i* (*irr, sep,* -ge-, sn, → *sein*) ~ *über* (*acc*) be beyond, be past; *über das Alter* (*or darüber*) *ist er hinaus* he is past that age.

hin'ausstellen *v/t* (*sep,* -ge-, h) **1.** put *s.th.* out(side). **2.** *sports:* *j-n* ~ send (*or* order) s.o. off the field.

hin'auswachsen *v/i* (*irr, sep,* -ge-, sn, → *wachsen*) *fig.* ~ *über* (*acc*) surpass.

hin'auswagen: sich ~ (*sep,* -ge-, h) venture (*to go*) out (*aus* of).

hin'auswerfen *v/t* (*irr, sep,* -ge-, h, → *werfen*) **1.** throw *s.th.* out (*aus* of): → *Fenster.* **2.** F throw (*or* kick) *s.o.* out (*aus* of), *a.* sack, fire.

hin'auswollen *v/i* (*irr, sep,* -ge-, h, → *wollen*) **1.** want to go (*or* get) out (*aus* of). **2.** *fig. worauf will er hinaus?* what is he driving at?; *hoch* ~ be aiming high.

hin'ausziehen (*irr, sep,* -ge-, → *ziehen*) **I** *v/t* (h) **1.** pull *s.o., s.th.* out (*aus* of). **2.** *fig. et.* ~ drag s.th. out. **II** *v/i* (sn) go out, march out. **III** *sich* ~ (h) *a.*) drag on, b) take longer than expected.

hin'auszögern *v/t* (*sep,* -ge-, h) delay: *sich* ~ be delayed.

'hinbiegen *v/t* (*irr, sep,* -ge-, h, → *biegen*) F *fig. et.* ~ wangle s.th.

'Hinblick *m im* ~ *auf* (*acc*) with regard to.

'hinbringen *v/t* (*irr, sep,* -ge-, h, → *bringen*) **1.** take *s.o., s.th.* there. **2.** pass, spend (*time*). **3.** → *fertigbringen.*

hinderlich ['hɪndərlɪç] *adj* troublesome: ~ *sein* (*dat*) hamper, impede, be a handicap to. **hindern** ['hɪndərn] *v/t* (h) *a.*) hamper, impede, b) interfere (*bei* with): *j-n am Arbeiten* ~ prevent (*or* keep) s.o. from working.

'Hindernis *n* (-ses; -se) obstacle (*für* to): *j-m* ~*se in den Weg legen* put obstacles in s.o.'s way; *auf* ~*se stoßen* run into difficulties. ~*lauf* *m sports:* obstacle race. ~*rennen* *n* steeplechase.

'hindeuten *v/i* (*sep,* -ge-, h) ~ *auf* (*acc*) point at, *fig.* point to, indicate.

Hindu ['hɪndʊ] *m* (-[s]; -[s]) Hindu.

Hinduismus [hɪndʊ'ɪsmʊs] *m* (-; *no pl*) Hinduism.

hin'durch *adv* **1.** through. **2.** through(out): *die Nacht* ~ all night (long); *das*

ganze Jahr ~ throughout the year.

hinein [hɪ'naɪn] *adv* in, inside, *a.* into (*May etc*): *da* ~ in there; *bis tief in die Nacht* ~ far into the night; F ~*!* let's go!

hin'einbekommen *v/t* (*irr, sep,* h, → *bekommen*) get *s.o., s.th.* in(*to in acc*).

hin'eindenken *v/i* (*irr, sep,* -ge-, h, → *denken*) *sich* ~ **in** (*acc*) go into; *sich in j-n* ~ put o.s. into s.o.'s position.

hin'eingehen *v/i* (*irr, sep,* -ge-, sn, → *gehen*) **1.** (*in acc*) go in(to), enter (*the house etc*). **2.** hold (*two litres etc*), seat, accommodate (*500 persons etc*).

hin'einknien: sich ~ (*sep,* -ge-, h) F *fig.* buckle down (*in acc* to).

hin'einkommen *v/i* (*irr, sep,* -ge-, sn, → *kommen*) come (*or* get) in(to *in acc*).

hin'einleben *v/i* (*sep,* -ge-, h) *in den Tag* ~ take it easy.

hin'einlegen *v/t* (*sep,* -ge-, h) **1.** put *s.th.* in(to *in acc*). **2.** → *hereinlegen.*

hin'einpassen *v/i* (*sep,* -ge-, h) **1.** fit in(to *in acc*). **2.** → *hineingehen* 2.

hin'einreden *v/i* (*sep,* -ge-, h) *j-m* ~ interrupt s.o.; *j-m in s-e Angelegenheiten*) ~ interfere with s.o.'s affairs.

hin'einstecken *v/t* (*sep,* -ge-, h) F *a. fig.* put *s.th.* in(to *in acc*): → *Nase.*

hin'einsteigern: sich ~ (*sep,* -ge-, h) get worked up (*in acc* over); *sich in s-e Wut* ~ work o.s. up into a rage.

hin'einziehen (*irr, sep,* -ge-, → *ziehen*) **I** *v/t* (h) pull *s.o., s.th.* in(to *in acc*): *j-n in e-e Sache* ~ involve s.o. in s.th. **II** *v/i* (sn) march (*or* move) in(to *in acc*).

'hinfahren (*irr, sep,* -ge-, → *fahren*) **I** *v/t* (h) take (*or* drive) *s.o., s.th.* there. **II** *v/i* (sn) go (*mot. a.* drive) there.

'Hinfahrt *f* journey there: *auf der* on the (*or our etc*) way there.

'hinfallen *v/i* (*irr, sep,* -ge-, sn, → *fallen*) fall (down). **'hinfällig** *adj* **1.** frail. **2.** *fig.* invalid: *et.* ~ *machen* invalidate s.th.

'hinfinden *v/i* (*irr, sep,* -ge-, h, → *finden*) (*a. sich* ~) find one's way there.

'Hinflug *m* outward flight: *auf dem* ~ *a.* on the flight there.

'hinführen (*sep,* -ge-, h) **I** *v/t j-n* ~ lead (*or* take) s.o. there (*or zu* to). **II** *v/i* lead (*or* go) there: *fig. wo soll das* (*noch*) ~*?* where is this leading to?

hing [hɪŋ] *pret of hängen*[1].

'Hingabe *f* (-; *no pl*) **1.** (*an acc* to) devotion, dedication: *mit* ~ *a.* lovingly. **2.**

sacrifice. **'hingeben** (*irr, sep, -ge-, h, →* **geben**) **I** *v/t* give away, sacrifice, give up. **II** *sich ~* (*dat*) devote (*or* dedicate) o.s. to a task etc, abandon o.s. to *despair etc*; **sich j-m ~** give o.s. to s.o.; **sich Hoffnungen** (**Illusionen**) **~** have hopes (illusions).

'hingebungsvoll *adj and adv* devoted(ly), *adv a.* with dedication.

hin'gegen *conj* however, on the other hand.

'hingehen *v/i* (*irr, sep, -ge-, sn, →* **gehen**) **1.** go (there): **wo gehst du hin?** where are you going? **2.** pass, go by. **3.** *fig.* pass, do: **et. ~ lassen** let s.th. pass.

'hingehören *v/i* (*sep, h*) belong: **wo gehört das hin?** *a.* where does this go?

'hingeraten *v/i* (*irr, sep, sn, →* **geraten**) get (*irgendwo* somewhere): **wo ist es ~?** what has become of it?

'hingerissen **I** *adj* (**von**) enraptured (by), ecstatic (*pred* in raptures, F gone) (over). **II** *adv* in raptures, ecstatically.

'hinhalten *v/t* (*irr, sep, -ge-, h, →* **halten**) **1.** *j-m et. ~* hold s.th. out to s.o.; **~ Kopf** l. **2.** *fig.* **j-n ~** put s.o. off, keep s.o. on a string.

'Hinhaltetaktik *f* delaying tactics.

'hinhauen (*irr, sep, -ge-, h, →* **hauen**) F **I** *v/t* **1.** slam s.th. down. **2.** *fig.* knock off (*essay, sketch, etc*). **II** *v/i fig.* a) work, b) be okay, c) be right, d) do. **III** *sich ~* a) hit the ground, b) hit the sack.

'hinhören *v/i* (*sep, -ge-, h*) listen.

hinken ['hɪŋkən] *v/i* (h) (walk with a) limp: **der Vergleich hinkt** that's a lame comparison.

'hinkommen *v/i* (*irr, sep, -ge-, sn, →* **kommen**) **1.** come (*or* get) there: **wo kämen wir denn hin, wenn ...** where would we be if ... **2.** F go, belong: **wo kommt das hin?** where does that go? **3.** F manage (**mit** with). **4.** F be right: **wieder ~** come right.

'hinkriegen *v/t* (*sep, -ge-, h*) F manage: **das hat er prima hingekriegt** he's made a first-rate job of it; **j-n wieder ~** put s.o. right again.

'hinlangen *v/i* (*sep, -ge-, h*) F (**kräftig**) **~** a) let go with a wallop, b) *fig.* (really) go to town (**bei** on).

'hinlänglich *adj* sufficient.

'hinlegen (*sep, -ge-, h*) **I** *v/t* **1.** put (*or* lay) down. **2.** F fork out (*money*). **3.** F

do *s.th.* brilliantly: **sie haben ein tolles Spiel hingelegt** they played a fantastic game. **II** *sich ~* lie down.

'hinmachen (*sep, -ge-, h*) F **I** *v/t* **1.** fix. **2.** a) kill, b) wreck, break. **II** *v/i* **3.** *dial.* hurry up: **mach(t) hin!** get a move on!

'hinnehmen *v/t* (*irr, sep, -ge-, h, →* **nehmen**) **1.** accept, *fig. a.* take, put up with. **2.** F *mit ~* take *s.o., s.th.* along.

'hinreichend *adj* sufficient.

'Hinreise *f* journey there (*or* out), ⚓ voyage out: **auf der ~** on the way there.

'hinreißen *v/t* (*irr, sep, -ge-, h, →* **reißen**) **1.** enrapture, thrill: **→ hingerissen. 2.** *sich ~ lassen* (let o.s.) be carried away (**von** by, **zu** into doing).

'hinreißend *adj* breathtaking, fantastic.

'hinrichten *v/t* (*sep, -ge-, h*) execute.

'Hinrichtung *f* (*-; -en*) execution.

'hinsehen *v/i* (*irr, sep, -ge-, h, →* **sehen**) look: **ohne hinzusehen** without looking; **bei näherem** ♀ at a closer look.

'hinsein *v/i* (*irr, sep, -ge-, sn, →* **sein**) F **1.** a) be wrecked, *a. fig.* be ruined, b) be gone, c) be dead(-beat), d) be done for: **es** (**er**) **ist hin** *a.* it (he) has had it; **hin ist hin!** gone is gone! **2.** (**ganz**) **~** (**von**) **→ hingerissen** I.

'hinsetzen (*sep, -ge-, h*) **I** *v/t* a) set (*or* put) *s.th.* down, b) seat (*a child*), sit *child* down. **II** *sich ~* sit down, take a seat.

'Hinsicht *f* **in dieser** (**in jeder**) **~** in this (in every) respect; **in mancher** (**vieler**) **~** in some (many) respects (*or* ways); **in politischer ~** politically. **'hinsichtlich** *prep* (*gen*) with regard to, concerning.

'Hinspiel *n sports:* first leg.

'hinstellen (*sep, -ge-, h*) **I** *v/t* **1.** a) put, place, b) put down. **2.** F put up (*a house etc*). **3.** *fig.* **j-n** (**et.**) **~ als** make s.o. (s.th.) out to be. **II** *sich ~* stand (**vor** *j-n* in front of s.o.). **5.** *fig.* **sich ~ als** claim (*or* pretend) to be.

hintan setzen [hɪnt'ʔan-], **hint'anstellen** *v/t* (*sep, -ge-, h*) *fig.* a) put *s.th.* last, b) neglect.

hinten ['hɪntən] *adv* a) at the back (*or* rear), b) in the background: **~ im Garten** at the back of the garden; **~ am Auto** at the rear of the car; **~ im Buch** at the end of the book; **nach ~** a) to the back, b) back, c) backwards; **von ~** from the back, from behind; F **das reicht ~ und vorn nicht** that's not nearly enough; *das stimmt ~ und vorn nicht* that's all wrong.

'**hintenherum** *adv* F **1.** (a)round the back. **2.** *fig.* on the quiet.

'**hinten'über** *adv* backwards.

hinter ['hɪntər] **I** *prep* (*dat or acc*) behind: *~ dem Haus* behind (*or* at the back of) the house; *et. ~ sich bringen* a) get s.th. over (with), b) cover (*distance*); *~ et. kommen* a) find out about s.th., b) get (the hang of) s.th.; *j-n* (*et.*) *~ sich lassen* leave s.o. (s.th.) behind; *et. ~ sich haben* have s.th. behind one; *er hat schon viel ~ sich* he's been through a lot; *fig. ~ j-m stehen* be behind s.o., a. *sich ~ j-n stellen* back s.o. (up); *~ j-m* (*et.*) *her sein* be after s.o. (s.th.). **II** *adj* → *hintere*.

'**Hinterachse** *f mot.* rear axle.

'**Hinterausgang** *m* rear exit.

'**Hinterbacke** *f* F buttock.

Hinterbänkler ['hɪntərbɛŋklər] *m* (-s; -) *parl.* backbencher.

'**Hinterbein** *n* hind leg: F *fig. sich auf die ~e stellen* put up a fight.

Hinterbliebene [hɪntər'bli:bənə] *m, f* (-n; -n) surviving dependant: *die ~n* the bereaved.

hinter'bringen *v/t* (*irr, insep, no* -ge-, h, → *bringen*) *j-m et. ~* inform s.o. of s.th.

'**Hinterdeck** *n* ⚓ afterdeck.

hintere ['hɪntərə] *adj* back, rear: *die ~n Reihen* the back rows, the rows at the back; *am ~n Ende* at the far end.

hinterein'ander *adv* a) one behind the other, b) one after the other: *drei Tage* (*dreimal*) *~* three days (times) running (*or* in a row). **2.** → *nacheinander*. *~gehen* *v/i* (*irr, sep,* -ge-, sn, → *gehen*) walk one behind the other. *~schalten* *v/t* (*sep*, -ge-, h) ⚡ connect in series.

'**Hintereingang** *m* back entrance.

hinter'fragen *v/t* (*insep, no* -ge-, h) scrutinize (closely).

'**Hinterfuß** *m* hind foot.

'**Hintergedanke** *m* ulterior motive.

hinter'gehen *v/t* (*irr, insep, no* -ge-, h, → *gehen*) deceive, cheat.

'**Hintergrund** *m* (*fig. vor dem ~* against the) background (*gen* of); *in den ~ drängen* push *s.o., s.th.* into the background; *sich im ~ halten* keep a low profile; *die Hintergründe* the background (*of a deed etc*). '**Hinter-**

grund... background (*information, music, etc*).

'**hintergründig** [-grʏndɪç] *adj* a) enigmatic, cryptic, b) profound, c) subtle (*humo[u]r etc*).

'**Hinterhalt** *m* (-[e]s; -e) **1.** (*a. aus dem ~ angreifen*) ambush. **2.** *fig. et. im ~ haben* have s.th. in reserve.

'**hinterhältig** [-hɛltɪç] → *hinterlistig*.

'**Hinterhand** *f* (-; *no pl*) **1.** *zo.* hindquarters. **2.** *fig.* (*noch*) *et. in der ~ haben* have s.th. up one's sleeve.

'**Hinterhaus** *n* back building.

hinter'her *adv* **1.** behind, after. **2.** afterwards, after the event.

hinter'hersein *v/i* (*irr, sep,* -ge-, sn, → *sein*) F **1.** *j-m ~* be after s.o. (s.th.). **2.** *~, daß* see (to it) that, make sure that.

'**Hinterhof** *m* backyard. '**Hinterkopf** *m* back of one's head: F *et. im ~ haben* have s.th. at the back of one's mind. '**Hinterland** *n* (-[e]s; *no pl*) hinterland.

hinter'lassen (*irr, insep, no* -ge-, h, → *lassen*) **I** *v/t* leave (behind), *testator: a.* bequeath (*dat* to). **II** *adj* posthumous (*works*). **Hinter'lassenschaft** *f* (-; -en) ⚖ estate, *fig.* legacy.

Hinter'lassung *f unter ~ von* (*or gen*) leaving *s.th.* behind.

hinter'legen *v/t* (*insep, no* -ge-, h) deposit (*bei* with). **Hinter'legung** *f gegen ~ von* (*or gen*) on depositing *s.th.*

'**Hinterlist** *f* (-; *no pl*) **1.** a) cunning, b) underhandedness. **2.** underhand(ed) trick. '**hinterlistig** *adj* a) crafty, cunning, b) underhand(ed).

'**Hintermann** *m* (-[e]s; ⸚er) **1.** *mein etc ~* the man (*or* car) behind me *etc*. **2.** *fig. usu. pl* the man behind it.

'**Hintermannschaft** *f* defen/ce (*Am.* -se).

'**Hintern** *m* (-s; -) F bottom, backside, behind: *j-m in den ~ kriechen* suck up to s.o.

'**Hinterrad** *n* rear wheel. '**Hinterradantrieb** *m mot.* rear-wheel drive.

hinterrücks ['hɪntərrʏks] *adv* **1.** from behind. **2.** *fig.* behind *s.o.'s* back.

'**Hinterseite** *f* back.

'**Hintersitz** *m* back seat.

'**hinterste** *adj* (very) last, hindmost: *am ~n Ende* at the very end.

'**Hinterteil** *n* → *Hintern.*

'**Hintertreffen** *n ins ~ geraten* a) fall behind, b) be losing out.

hinter'treiben v/t (irr, insep, no -ge-, h, → **treiben**) prevent, foil.

'Hintertreppe f back stairs.

'Hintertür f **1.** back door. **2.** a. 'Hintertürchen n fig. loophole.

'Hinterwäldler [-vɛltlər] m (-s; -) backwoodsman, Am. a. hick.

hinter'ziehen v/t (irr, insep, no -ge-, h, → **ziehen**) Steuern ~ evade taxes.

'Hinterzimmer n back room.

'hintun v/t (irr, sep, -ge-, h, → **tun**) F put: fig. **ich weiß nicht, wo ich ihn ~ soll** I can't place him.

hinüber [hɪ'ny:bər] adv over, across: **da ~!** over there! **~fahren** (irr, sep, -ge-, → **fahren**) **I** v/t (h) take (or drive) s.o., s.th. over (or across) (**über** acc a bridge etc). **II** v/i (sn) go (or travel, drive) across (or over) (**nach, zu** to). **~sein** v/i (irr, sep, -ge-, sn, → **sein**) F a) be dead, be gone, b) be dead to the world, c) be ruined, have had it, d) food: have gone bad.

'Hinübersetzung f translation into the foreign language.

Hin und Her: das ~ the coming and going, a. fig. the to-and-fro; **nach langem ~** after endless discussions.

'Hin- und 'Rückfahrkarte f return (Am. round-trip) ticket. **~fahrt** f return journey, Am. round trip. **~flug** m return (Am. round-trip) flight.

hinunter [hɪ'nɔntər] adv down: **die Treppe ~** down the stairs, downstairs; **die Straße ~** down the street.

hin'unterspülen v/t (sep, -ge-, h) a. fig. wash down.

hin'unterstürzen (sep, -ge-) **I** v/t **1.** (h) throw s.o., s.th. down. **2.** (sn) rush down (the stairs etc). **3.** (h) gulp down. **II** v/i **4.** (sn) crash down.

'hinwagen: sich ~ (sep, -ge-, h) venture there.

hinweg [hɪn'vɛk] adv **1.** away, off. **2.** ~ **über** (acc) over, across; fig. **über j-n** (or **j-s Kopf**) ~ over s.o.'s head; **darüber ist er ~** he has got over it.

'Hinweg m (auf dem ~ on the) way there.

hin'weggehen v/i (irr, sep, -ge-, sn, → **gehen**) fig. ~ **über** (acc) pass over, ignore; **lachend** (**achselzuckend**) **über et. ~** laugh (shrug) s.th. off.

hin'weghelfen v/i (irr, sep, -ge-, h, →

helfen) **j-m über et. ~** a. fig. help s.o. to get over s.th.

hin'wegkommen v/i (irr, sep, -ge-, sn, → **kommen**) **über et. ~** a. fig. get over s.th.

hin'wegsehen v/i (irr, sep, -ge-, h, → **sehen**) **über et. ~** a) see (or look) over s.th., b) fig. ignore s.th., overlook s.th.

hin'wegsetzen (sep, -ge-) **I** v/i (h, sn) **über** (acc) jump over. **II sich ~** (h) → hinweggehen.

Hinweis ['hɪnvaɪs] m (-es; -e) (**auf** acc) **1.** a) tip, hint (as to), b) a. pl information (on, about), c) indication (of), clue (as to), d) note (about), comment (on): **sachdienliche ~e** relevant information; **~e zur Benutzung** directions for use. **2.** reference (to). **3.** allusion (to).

'hinweisen (irr, sep, -ge-, h, → **weisen**) **I** v/t **j-n auf et. ~** point s.th. out to s.o. **II** v/i ~ **auf** (acc) a) point to, fig. a. indicate, b) refer to; **darauf ~, daß** point out that. **'hinweisend** adj **~es Fürwort** demonstrative pronoun.

'Hinweisschild n, **~tafel** f sign.

'hinwerfen v/t (irr, sep, -ge-, h, → **werfen**) **1.** throw s.th. down, F drop (a. fig. remark etc): **sich ~** throw o.s. down; **j-m et. ~** throw s.th. to s.o. **2.** F chuck (job). **3.** F dash off (letter etc).

'hinwirken v/i (sep, -ge-, h) ~ **auf** (acc) work towards.

'hinwollen v/i (irr, sep, -ge-, h, → **wollen**) F want to go: **wo willst du hin?** where are you going?

'hinziehen (irr, sep, -ge-, → **ziehen**) **I** v/t (h) **1.** draw s.o., s.th. (**zu** to, towards): fig. **sich hingezogen fühlen zu** feel drawn towards. **2.** fig. drag s.th. out. **II** v/i (sn) **3.** a) move (**über** acc across, **zu** towards), b) move there. **III sich ~** (h) **4.** drag on (**über Wochen** etc for weeks etc). **5.** stretch (**bis zu** to, as far as).

hinzu [hɪn'tsu:] adv in addition, besides.

hin'zufügen v/t (dat to) add, append.

Hin'zufügung f (-; no pl) addition: **unter ~ von** (or gen) (by) adding.

hin'zukommen v/i (irr, sep, -ge-, sn, → **kommen**) **1.** come (along): ~ **zu** join (s.o., s.th.). **2.** a) be added, b) follow: **hinzu kommt, daß ...** add to this ..., besides ...; **es kommt noch hinzu, daß er ...** what is more he ...

hin'zuziehen v/t (irr, sep, -ge-, h, → **ziehen**) **j-n ~** call s.o. in, consult s.o.

Hiobsbotschaft ['hi:ɔps-] f bad news.
Hirn [hɪrn] n (-[e]s; -e) **1.** *anat.* brain. **2.** *gastr.* brains. **3.** *fig.* brain(s), head, mind: **sich das ~ zermartern** rack one's brains.
'**Hirngespinst** n (**ein reines ~** a mere) fantasy, *w.s.* pipe dream.
'**Hirnhaut** f *anat.* meninges. '**Hirnhautentzündung** f ✿ meningitis.
'**hirnlos** *adj* a. F *fig.* brainless.
'**Hirnrinde** f *anat.* cerebral cortex.
'**hirnrissig**, '**hirnverbrannt** *adj* F mad.
Hirsch [hɪrʃ] m (-es; -e) stag. **~braten** m roast venison. **~fänger** m hunting knife. **~kalb** n fawn. **~keule** f *gastr.* haunch of venison. **~kuh** f hind. **~leder** n, **~ledern** *adj* buckskin.
Hirse ['hɪrzə] f (-; -n) ✿ millet.
Hirte ['hɪrtə] m (-n; -n) herdsman, shepherd (a. *eccl.*). '**Hirtenbrief** m *eccl.* pastoral letter. '**Hirtenvolk** n pastoral tribe. '**Hirtin** f (-; -nen) shepherdess.
his, His [hɪs] n (-; -) ♩ B sharp.
hissen ['hɪsən] v/t (h) hoist.
Historiker [hɪs'to:rikər] m (-s; -) historian. **historisch** [hɪs'to:rɪʃ] *adj* a) historical, b) historic (*figure, moment, etc*).
Hit [hɪt] m (-[s]; -s) ♩ or F *fig.* hit.
'**Hitliste** f ♩ the top ten *etc* (of the week *etc*). '**Hitpa,rade** f ♩ ♩ hit parade.
Hitze ['hɪtsə] f (-; *no pl*) (**bei dieser ~** in this) heat: ✿ **fliegende ~** hot flushes; **in der ~ des Gefechts** in the heat of the moment. **2beständig** *adj* heat-resistant. **2empfindlich** *adj* sensitive to heat. **2frei** *adj* **~ haben** have time off from school because of very hot weather. **~grad** m degree of heat. **~schild** m heat shield. **~welle** f heat wave.
'**Hitzkopf** m hothead.
'**hitzköpfig** [-kœpfɪç] *adj* hotheaded.
'**Hitzschlag** m heat stroke.
H-Milch ['ha:mɪlç] f long-life milk.
hob [ho:p] *pret of* **heben**.
Hobby ['hɔbi] n (-s; -s) hobby.
Hobel ['ho:bəl] m (-s; -) plane.
hobeln ['ho:bəln] v/t, v/i (h) plane.
hoch [ho:x] **I** *adj* **1.** high (a. *fig.* costs, income, etc), a. tall (*tree etc*), deep (*snow, water*), a. great (*speed etc, a. hono[u]r, value, etc*), heavy (*penalty*), high(-pitched) (*sound, voice*): **ein hohes Alter erreichen** live to a ripe old age; **hohe Niederlage** *sports*: crushing

defeat; ♩ **das hohe C** top C; *parl.* **das Hohe Haus** the House; **der hohe Norden** the far North; *fig.* **das ist mir zu ~!** that's above me!; → **Maß**[1] 3, **Roß, Tier** *etc.* **II** *adv* **2.** high, *fig.* highly: **~ oben** high up, on high; **~ gewinnen** win high; **~ verlieren** *sports*: get trounced; **~ spielen** play (a. *fig.* gamble) high; **sie kamen drei Mann ~** there were three of them; **j-m et. ~ und heilig versprechen** promise s.o. s.th. solemnly; **wenn es ~ kommt** at (the) most; **Hände ~!** hands up!; **~ lebe ...!** long live ...!; **~ soll er leben!** three cheers for him!; → **hinauswollen** 2. **3.** → a) **hinauf,** b) **herauf. 4.** ⅍ **fünf ~ zwei** five (raised) to the second power; **sechs ~ drei** six cubed.
Hoch n (-s; -s) **1.** *meteor.* high(-pressure area). **2.** cheers. **3.** *fig.* high.
'**Hochachtung** f deep respect: **alle ~!** my compliment!; **mit vorzüglicher ~** → '**hochachtungsvoll** *adv* Yours faithfully, Sincerely yours.
'**Hochadel** m high nobility.
'**hochaktu,ell** *adj* highly topical.
'**hochal,pin** *adj* (high) alpine.
'**Hochal,tar** m high altar.
'**hochangesehen** *adj* highly esteemed.
'**Hochan,tenne** f overhead aerial (*Am.* antenna).
'**hocharbeiten: sich ~** (*sep,* -ge-, h) work one's way up.
'**Hochbahn** f elevated railway (*Am.* railroad).
'**Hochbau** m (-[e]s; -ten) structural engineering.
'**hochbegabt** *adj* highly gifted.
'**hochbetagt** *adj* very old, aged.
'**Hochbetrieb** m (-[e]s; *no pl*) intense activity, rush: **es herrschte ~** they (*or* we) were extremely busy.
'**hochbezahlt** *adj* highly paid.
'**hochbringen** v/t (*irr, sep,* -ge-, h, → **bringen**) **1.** bring s.o., s.th. up. **2.** F get s.th. up. **3.** make a firm a going concern: **e-e Firma wieder ~** put a firm back on its feet.
'**Hochburg** f stronghold.
'**hochdeutsch** *adj,* '**Hochdeutsch** n standard (*or* High) German.
'**hochdo,tiert** *adj* a) highly paid, b) *tournament etc* carrying a high prize.
'**Hochdruck** m (-[e]s; *no pl*) **1.** *meteor., phys.* high pressure: *fig.* **mit ~ arbeiten**

work (at) full blast. **2.** ✍ high blood pressure. '**Hochdruckgebiet** n meteor. high-pressure area.

'**Hochebene** f plateau.

'**hochempfindlich** adj highly sensitive, phot. high-speed (film).

'**hochentwickelt** adj highly developed, ◎ sophisticated.

'**hocherfreut** adj (most) delighted (**über** acc at).

'**Hochfi,nanz** f (-; no pl) high finance.

'**hochfliegen** v/i (irr, sep, -ge-, sn, → **fliegen**) fly up, soar. '**hochfliegend** adj fig. ambitious, high-flown (plans).

'**Hochform** f (-; no pl) (**in** ~ in) top form.

'**Hochfor,mat** n upright format.

'**Hochfre,quenz** f high frequency.

'**Hochga,rage** f multistor(e)y car park.

'**Hochgebirge** n high mountain region.

'**Hochgebirgs...** alpine, mountain.

'**hochgehen** (irr, sep, -ge-, sn, → **gehen**) **I** v/i **1.** go up, curtain, prices: a. rise. **2.** F bomb etc: explode, blow up, fig. person: a. hit the ceiling: **et.** ~ **lassen** blow s.th. up. **3.** F criminal etc: be caught: ~ **lassen** a) expose, b) nab, c) round up, sl. bust (gang). **II** v/t → **hinaufgehen** II.

'**Hochgenuß** m (real) treat.

'**hochgeschlossen** adj high-necked.

'**Hochgeschwindigkeits...** high-speed ...

'**hochgespannt** adj high (expectations etc), ambitious (plans).

'**hochgestellt** adj fig. high-ranking.

'**hochgestochen** adj F **1.** stuck-up. **2.** jumped-up, very highbrow.

'**hochgewachsen** adj tall.

'**Hochglanz** m high polish (or gloss).

'**Hochglanzpa,pier** n high-gloss paper.

'**hochgradig** [-gra:dıç] adj **1.** extreme, ◎ high-grade. **2.** F utter (nonsense etc).

'**hochhackig** [-hakıç] adj high-heeled.

'**hochhalten** v/t (irr, sep, -ge-, h, → **halten**) **1.** hold s.o., s.th. up. **2.** fig. uphold, hono(u)r (s.o.'s memory).

'**Hochhaus** n tower block, high rise.

'**hochheben** v/t (irr, sep, -ge-, h, → **heben**) lift (up), raise.

'**hochinteres,sant** adj most interesting.

'**hochjubeln** v/t (sep, -ge-, h) F glorify.

'**hochkant** adv on end: ~ **stellen** up-end.

'**hochka,rätig** adj **1.** high-carat. **2.** fig. 24-carat, top-flight.

'**hochklappen** v/t (sep, -ge-, h) turn up (collar etc), tip (seat etc).

'**hochkommen** v/i (irr, sep, -ge-, sn, → **kommen**) **1.** come up: (**wieder**) ~ get up (again), fig. get back on one's feet. **2.** fig. get ahead, F make it. **3.** **wenn es hochkommt** at the most, at best.

'**Hochkonjunk,tur** f ↑ boom.

'**hochkrempeln** v/t (sep, -ge-, h) roll up.

'**Hochland** n highland(s).

'**hochleben** v/i (sep, -ge-, h) ~ **lassen** a) give three cheers for, b) toast; **er lebe hoch!** three cheers for him!

'**Hochleistung** f high performance.

'**Hochleistungs...** ◎ high-power(ed), high-speed ..., heavy-duty ... **~sport** m high-performance sport(s). **~sport-ler(in** f) m top athlete.

'**hochmo,dern** adj ultramodern.

'**Hochmut** m arrogance: ~ **kommt vor dem Fall** pride goes before a fall.

'**hochmütig** ['ho:xmy:tıç] adj arrogant.

'**hochnäsig** ['ho:xnε:zıç] adj stuck-up.

'**hochnehmen** v/t (irr, sep, -ge-, h, → **nehmen**) **1.** pick s.o., s.th. up. **2.** F fig. j-n ~ a) pull s.o.'s leg, b) fleece s.o., take s.o. for a ride, c) nab s.o.

'**Hochofen** m ◎ (blast) furnace.

'**hochpro,zentig** adj **1.** ⚗ highly concentrated. **2.** high-proof (spirits).

'**hochqualifi,ziert** adj highly qualified.

'**hochrechnen** v/t (sep, -ge-, h) project.

'**Hochrechnung** f projection, a. (computer) forecast.

'**Hochruf** m cheer.

'**Hochsai,son** f peak season.

'**hochschätzen** v/t (sep, -ge-, h) j-n ~ esteem s.o. highly.

'**hochschaukeln** v/t (sep, -ge-, h) F fig. play up: **sich (gegenseitig)** ~ get each other all worked up.

'**hochschnellen** v/i (sep, -ge-, sn) **1.** bounce up. **2.** fig. prices: rocket.

'**hochschrauben** v/t (sep, -ge-, h) force up (prices), raise (expectations etc).

'**Hochschul|absol,vent** m (university or college) graduate. **~ausbildung** f university (or college) education.

'**Hochschule** f a) university, b) college; → **technisch.** '**Hochschüler(in** f) m university (or college) student.

'**Hochschul|lehrer(in** f) m university (or college) teacher (or lecturer). **~reife** f university entrance qualification(s).

'**hochschwanger** adj far advanced in pregnancy.

'**Hochsee** *f* (-; *no pl*) high sea(s).
'**Hochseefische,rei** *f* deep-sea fishing.
'**Hochseejacht** *f* ocean-going yacht.
'**Hochseilakt** *m* tight-rope act.
'**Hochsitz** *m hunt.* (raised) hide.
'**Hochsommer** *m* (**im** ~ in) midsummer.
'**Hochspannung** *f* (-; -en) **1.** *⚡* high tension (*or* voltage). **2.** *no pl fig.* a) high tension, b) great suspense: *politische* ~ high political tension. '**Hochspannungskabel** *n* high-voltage cable.
'**hochspielen** *v/t* (*sep*, -ge-, h) *fig.* **et.** ~ play s.th. up.
'**Hochsprache** *f* standard language: *die deutsche* ~ Standard German.
'**hochsprachlich** *adj* standard: *nicht* ~ substandard.
'**Hochspringer(in** *f*) *m* high jumper.
'**Hochsprung** *m* (-[e]s; *no pl*) high jump.
höchst [høːçst] *adv* highly, extremely, most: → **höchste**.
'**Höchstalter** *n* maximum age.
Hochstape'lei *f* (-; -en) **1.** *a. fig.* imposture. **2.** (gross) overstatement.
'**hochstapeln** *v/i* (*sep*, -ge-, h) **1.** be an impostor. **2.** exaggerate.
'**Hochstapler** *m* (-s; -), '**Hochstaplerin** *f* (-; -nen) impostor, *fig.* fraud.
'**Höchstbelastung** *f* ⊙ maximum load.
'**Höchstbetrag** *m* maximum (amount).
höchste ['høːçstə] *adj* highest, ✝, ⊙ *a.* maximum, top, *a.* tallest, *a.* uppermost, *a.* extreme, utmost: *am* ~**n** highest; → *Instanz, Zeit.*
'**höchstens** *adv* **1.** at (the) most, at best; *adm. von* ~ not exceeding. **2.** except.
'**Höchstfall** *m im* ~ → **höchstens** 1.
'**Höchstform** *f sports:* top form.
'**Höchstgeschwindigkeit** *f* maximum (*or* top) speed: *mit* ~ at top speed; *zulässige* ~ speed limit.
'**Höchstgrenze** *f* upper limit.
'**Höchstleistung** *f* top performance, *sports:* a. record, ⊙ *a.* maximum output, *research etc:* supreme achievement.
'**Höchstmaß** *n ein* ~ *an Sicherheit etc* a maximum of safety *etc.*
'**Höchstpreis** *m* maximum price: *zum* ~ at the highest price.
'**Höchststand** *m* highest level: *e-n* ~ *erreichen* peak.
'**Höchststrafe** *f* maximum penalty.
'**höchstwahr'scheinlich** *adv* in all probability.

'**Höchstwert** *m* maximum value.
'**höchstzulässig** *adj* maximum (permissible).
'**Hochtouren** *pl auf* ~ *bringen* a) rev *engine* up to full speed, b) *fig.* get *s.o., s.th.* really going; *auf* ~ *laufen* run at full speed, *a. fig.* go at full blast.
'**hochtrabend** *adj* pompous.
'**Hoch- und 'Tiefbau** *m* (-[e]s; *no pl*) structural and civil engineering.
'**hochverdient** *adj* a) well-deserved (*success etc*), b) *person* of great merit.
'**hochverehrt** *adj* a) highly esteemed, b) Dear *Mr Brown etc.*
'**Hochverrat** *m* high treason.
'**hochverräterisch** *adj* treasonable.
'**hochverzinslich** *adj* high-interest-bearing.
'**Hochwald** *m* timber forest.
'**Hochwasser** *n* (-s; -) **1.** high tide (*or* water). **2.** flood: *der Fluß führt* ~ the river is in flood. ~**gefahr** *f* danger of flooding. ~**kata,strophe** *f* flood disaster. ~**stand** *m* high-water level.
'**hochwerfen** *v/t* (*irr, sep*, -ge-, h, → **werfen**) throw *s.o., s.th.* up.
'**hochwertig** *adj* a) high-grade, high--quality, b) highly nutritious.
'**Hochwild** *n* big game.
Hochzeit [ˈhɔxtsaɪt] *f* (-; -en) wedding, marriage: ~ *haben*, ~ *feiern* get married; *zur* ~ *schenken* (*bekommen*) give (get) as a wedding present.
'**Hochzeits...** wedding (*present, dress, etc*). ~**nacht** *f* wedding night. ~**reise** *f* honeymoon (trip): *auf* ~ honeymooning. ~**tag** *m* a) wedding day, b) wedding anniversary.
'**hochziehen** *v/t* (*irr, sep*, -ge-, h, → **ziehen**) draw up, pull up (*a.* ✈), hoist (*flag, sail*): *sich* ~ *an* (*dat*) pull o.s. up by, b) F *fig.* get an ego-boost out of.
Hocke ['hɔkə] *f* (-; -n) **1.** squat, crouch: *in der* ~ in a crouch; *in die* ~ *gehen* squat down. **2.** *diving:* tuck (position).
hocken ['hɔkən] *v/i* (h) **1.** squat, crouch. **2.** *dial.* sit, *bird:* perch: *über s-n Büchern* ~ pore over one's books.
'**Hocker** *m* (-s; -) stool.
Höcker ['hœkər] *m* (-s; -) *zo.* hump.
Hockey ['hɔkɪ] *n* (-s; *no pl*) hockey.
'**Hockeyschläger** *m* hockey stick.
'**Hockeyspieler(in** *f*) *m* hockey player.

'**Hocksprung** *m* a) *gym.* squat jump, squat vault, b) *diving:* tuck(ed) jump.
Hode ['ho:də] *f* (-; -n), **Hoden** *m* (-s; -) *anat.* testicle. '**Hodensack** *m* scrotum.
Hof [ho:f] *m* (-[e]s; ⸚e) **1.** a) yard, b) court(yard), c) backyard, d) schoolyard. **2.** farm. **3.** court: *am ~, bei ~e* at court; *j-m den ~ machen* court s.o. **4.** *astr.*, 🖈, *opt.* halo.
'**Hofdame** *f* lady-in-waiting.
hoffen ['hɔfən] *v/i* (h) (*auf acc*) a) hope (for), b) trust (in): *ich hoffe* I hope so; *ich hoffe nicht* I hope not; *ich hoffe es* I hope so; *das will ich nicht ~* I hope not; *~ wir das Beste!* let's hope for the best!; *verzweifelt ~* hope against hope.
hoffentlich ['hɔfəntlɪç] *adv* I (*or* we) hope so, let's hope so, F hopefully: *~ nicht!* I hope not!
Hoffnung ['hɔfnʊŋ] *f* (-; -en) hope (*auf acc* of): *die ~ aufgeben* abandon hope; *j-m ~en machen* raise s.o.'s hopes; *er machte mir k-e ~en* he didn't hold out any hopes for me; *sich ~en machen* have hopes (*auf acc* of ger): *mach dir k-e (falschen) ~en!* don't be too hopeful!; *s-e ~ setzen auf* (*acc*) pin one's hopes on; *j-n in s-n ~en enttäuschen* dash s.o.'s hopes; (*neue*) *~ schöpfen* have new hopes; *es besteht k-e ~* there is no hope; *in die ~ zu inf* hoping to inf: *er ist m-e einzige ~* he is my only hope; *pol.*, *sports etc* *die große ~* the great white hope.
'**Hoffnungslauf** *m sports:* repechage.
'**hoffnungslos** *adj* hopeless, *pred a.* past (all) hope: *fig.* *er ist ein ~er Fall* he's hopeless. '**Hoffnungslosigkeit** *f* (-; -n) hopelessness, despair.
'**Hoffnungsschimmer** *m* glimmer of hope. '**Hoffnungsträger** *m pol.*, *sports etc:* the great white hope.
'**hoffnungsvoll** *adj* hopeful, *pred* full of hope (*a. adv*), promising (*talent etc*).
höfisch ['hø:fɪʃ] *adj* courtly.
höflich ['hø:flɪç] *adj* (*zu* to) polite, courteous. '**Höflichkeit** *f* (-; -en) **1.** *no pl* (*aus ~* out of) politeness: *in aller ~* very politely. **2.** *usu. pl* compliment.
'**Höflichkeitsbesuch** *m* courtesy visit.
'**Hofnarr** *m hist. or iro.* court jester.
hohe ['ho:ə] → *hoch* I.
Höhe ['hø:ə] *f* (-; -n) **1.** height, *astr.*, 🖈, *geogr.* altitude, level: *in e-r ~ von ... an* a

height (*or* an altitude) of ...; *in die ~* up (→ *a.* cpds. with *hoch*...); *an ~ verlieren* lose height; *auf der ~ von* a) *geogr.* in the latitude of *London etc*, b) 🛥 off *Dover etc*; *auf gleicher ~* (*fig.* on a) level (*mit* with); *fig. auf der ~ s-s Ruhms* (*s-r Macht*) at the height of his fame (power); F *auf der ~ sein* be in good form; *auf der ~ (der Zeit) sein* be up to date; *ich bin nicht ganz auf der ~* I'm not feeling up to the mark; F *das ist doch die ~!* that's the limit!; → *treiben* 1. **2.** amount: *e-e Summe in ~ von* a sum (to the amount of); *bis zu e-r ~ von* up to, not exceeding. **3.** → *Anhöhe.*
Hoheit ['ho:haɪt] *f* (-; -en) **1.** *no pl pol.* sovereignty. **2.** (*Seine*, *Ihre*) ⬥ (His, Her) Highness. **3.** *no pl fig.* grandeur, majesty. '**hoheitlich** *adj* sovereign.
'**Hoheits|abzeichen** *n* national emblem. **~gebiet** *n* territory. **~gewässer** *pl* territorial waters.
'**Höhen|flosse** *f* ✈ tail plane. **~flug** *m* **1.** high-altitude flight. **2.** *fig.* (intellectual *etc*) flight. **~krankheit** *f* altitude sickness. **~kurort** *m* mountain (health) resort. **~lage** *f* altitude. **~leitwerk** *n* ✈ elevator unit. **~sonne** *f* **1.** mountain sun. **2.** 🖈 sunray lamp, sunlamp. **~unterschied** *m* difference in altitude. **~zug** *m* range of hills, mountain range.
'**Höhepunkt** *m* peak, height, climax (*a. orgasm*), highlight (*of event etc*): *auf dem ~* (*gen*) at the height of ([one's] *power, fame, etc*).
höher ['hø:ər] *adj and adv* higher (*a. fig.*), *a.* senior: **~er Dienst** senior service; **~e Bildung** higher education; **~e Schule** secondary school; *in ~em Maße* to a greater extent, more; *nach Höherem streben* strive for higher things.
hohl [ho:l] *adj. fig.* hollow: *in der ~en Hand* in the hollow of one's hand.
'**hohläugig** ['-ɔygɪç] *adj* hollow-eyed.
'**Hohlblock(stein)** *m* cavity block.
Höhle ['hø:lə] *f* (-; -n) **1.** cave. **2.** *zo.* hole: *fig. sich in die ~ des Löwen wagen* beard the lion in his den. **3.** *anat.* cavity, (*eye*) socket. **4.** F hole, hovel.
'**Höhlen|forscher** *m* spel(a)eologist, potholer. **~forschung** *f* spel(a)eology. **~mensch** *m* cave man.
'**Hohlheit** *f* (-; *no pl*) *a. fig.* hollowness.

'**Hohl|kehle** f ☺ groove. **~kopf** m F numskull. **~körper** m Ⓐ hollow body. **~kreuz** n ✞ hollow back. **~kugel** f hollow sphere. **~maß** n measure of capacity, dry measure. **~raum** m cavity, hollow. **~saum** m hemstitch. **~schliff** m hollow grinding; **mit ~** hollow-ground. **~spiegel** m concave mirror.

'**Höhlung** f (-; -en) hollow, cavity.

'**Hohl|weg** m ravine. **~ziegel** m a) cavity brick, b) hollow tile.

Hohn [hoːn] m (-[e]s; no pl) a) scorn, b) derision: **nur ~ und Spott ernten** earn but scorn and derision; **der rein(st)e** (or **blanke**) **~** sheer mockery. **höhnen** ['høːnən] v/i (h) (**über** acc at) sneer, jeer. '**Hohngelächter** n derisive laughter. '**höhnisch** adj sneering: **~e Bemerkung, ~es Lächeln** sneer.

'**hohnlächeln** v/i (sep or insep, -ge-, h), '**Hohnlächeln** n (-s) sneer.

'**hohnsprechen** v/i (irr, sep, -ge-, h, → **sprechen**) make a mockery (dat of).

Hokuspokus [hoːkʊs'poːkʊs] m (-; no pl) hocus-pocus, contp. a. mumbo jumbo: **~!** hey presto!

hold [hɔlt] adj **1.** lovely, sweet. **2. das Glück war ihm ~** he was lucky.

Holdinggesellschaft ['hoːldɪŋ-] f ✝ holding company.

holen ['hoːlən] v/t (h) **1.** get, fetch: **j-m et. ~** get s.th. for s.o.; **et. aus der Tasche ~** take (or draw) s.th. out of one's pocket; F **da ist nichts zu ~!** there's nothing in it (for us)!; **bei ihm ist nichts zu ~!** you won't get anything out of him!; → **Atem, Luft 2. 2.** call: **j-n ~ lassen** send for s.o. **3.** come for, pick s.o., s.th. up. **4. sich et. ~** a) get s.s., fetch, b) F catch, get (a cold etc): **du wirst dir noch et. ~!** you'll catch s.th. yet!; **sich bei j-m e-n Rat ~** ask s.o.'s advice; F **sich e-n Preis ~** win (or get) a prize; → **Abfuhr 2.**

Holland ['hɔlant] n (-s) Holland, the Netherlands. **Holländer** ['hɔlɛndər] m (-s; -) Dutchman: **die ~** the Dutch. '**Holländerin** f (-; -nen) Dutchwoman. '**holländisch** [-dɪʃ] adj, ♀ n (-[s]) Dutch.

Hölle ['hœlə] f (-; -n) hell: **in der ~** in hell; **die ~ auf Erden** hell on earth; F **j-m die ~ heiß machen** give s.o. hell; **j-m das Leben zur ~ machen** make life a perfect hell for s.o.; **zur ~ damit!** to hell

with it!; **die ~ ist los!** all hell has broken loose!

'**Höllen|angst** f F e-e **~ haben** be scared stiff (**vor** dat of). **~lärm** m infernal noise: **e-n ~ machen** make a hell of a noise. **~qual** f F agony: **~en ausstehen** suffer hell. **~tempo** n F (**mit e-m ~** at) breakneck speed.

höllisch ['hœlɪʃ] adj infernal, F hellish: **~ aufpassen** watch out like a hawk, be damn careful; **~ weh tun** hurt like hell.

Holm [hɔlm] m (-[e]s; -e) beam, gym. bar, ✈ spar.

Hologramm [holo'gram] n (-s; -e) opt. holograph.

holp(e)rig ['hɔlp(ə)rɪç] adj **1.** bumpy. **2.** fig. clumsy. **holpern** ['hɔlpərn] v/i **1.** (sn) bump, jolt. **2.** (h) fig. stumble.

Holunder [ho'lʊndər] m (-s; -) ♣ elder.

Ho'lunderbeere f elderberry.

Ho'lundertee m elderflower tea.

Holz [hɔlts] n (-es; ⁓er) **1.** a) no pl wood, b) timber: **aus ~** wooden, (made of) wood; fig. **klopf auf ~!** touch wood!; **aus e-m anderen ~ geschnitzt** of a different stamp; **aus härterem ~ geschnitzt** made of sterner stuff; F **sie hat ~ vor der Hütte** she's well stacked. **2.** (nine)pin: **Gut ~!** good bowling! **3.** no pl ♪ the woodwind. **~bauweise** f timber construction. **~bearbeitung** f woodworking. **~bläser** m ♪ woodwind player, pl the woodwind (section).

holzen ['hɔltsən] v/i (h) F soccer: clog, play rough.

hölzern ['hœltsərn] adj wooden, fig. a. clumsy.

'**Holzfäller** [-fɛlər] m (-s; -) woodcutter, Am. lumberjack.

'**Holzfaser** f wood fibre (Am. fiber). **~platte** f wood fibreboard (Am. fiberboard). **~stoff** m a) wood cellulose, b) wood pulp.

'**holzfrei** adj wood-free (paper).

'**Holz|hacken** n (-s) wood chopping. **~hammer** m mallet: F fig. **mit dem ~** with a sledgehammer. **~handel** m timber (Am. lumber) trade. **~haus** n wooden house.

holzig ['hɔltsɪç] adj a) woody, b) stringy.

'**Holz|kitt** m plastic wood. **~kohle** f charcoal. **~scheit** n log. **~schnitt** m wood engraving. **~stoß** m stack of wood. **~täfelung** f wood(en) panel(l)ing. ♀**verar-**

beitend *adj,* **~verarbeitung** *f* wood processing. **~weg** *m* F *auf dem ~ sein* a) be on the wrong track, b) be very much mistaken. **~wolle** *f* wood wool, excelsior. **~wurm** *m* woodworm.

Homo ['ho:mo] *m* (-s; -s) F homo, queer, gay.

homogen [homo'ge:n] *adj* homogeneous.

Homonym [homo'ny:m] *n* (-s; -e) *ling.* homonym.

Homöopath [homøo'pa:t] *m* (-en; -en) ♂ hom(o)eopath. **Homöopathie** [-pa'ti:] *f* (-; *no pl*) hom(o)eopathy. **homöopathisch** [-'pa:tʃ] *adj* hom(o)eopathic.

Homosexuali'tät [homo-] *f* homosexuality. **homosexu'ell** *adj,* **Homosexu'elle** *m, f* (-n; -n) homosexual, F gay.

Honig ['ho:nɪç] *m* (-s; -e) honey: F *j-m ~ ums Maul schmieren* soft-soap s.o. **~kuchen** *m* gingerbread. **~lecken** *n* F *das war kein ~!* that was no picnic! **~me lone** *f* honeydew melon. **♀süß** *adj* (as) sweet as honey, *fig.* honeyed.

Honorar [hono'ra:r] *n* (-s; -e) fee, *of author:* royalty.

Honoratioren [honora'tsio:rən] *pl* notabilities, local dignitaries.

honorieren [hono'ri:rən] *v/t* (h) **1.** *j-n ~* pay (a fee to) s.o. **2.** *et. ~* pay for s.th. **3.** ♄ hono(u)r, *fig. a.* reward.

honoris causa [ho'no:rɪs 'kauza] *Professor etc* ~ honorary professor *etc.*

Hopfen ['hɔpfən] *m* (-s; *no pl*) ♀ hop: F *an ihm ist ~ und Malz verloren* he's hopeless, he's a dead loss.

hopp [hɔp] *int* a) hop!, b) quick!

hoppeln ['hɔpəln] *v/i* (sn) hop.

hoppla ['hɔpla] *int* a) (wh)oops!, b) hey!

hops [hɔps] *int* jump! **Hops** *m* (-es; -e) hop. **hopsa** ['hɔpsa] *int* (wh)oops!

hopsen ['hɔpsən] *v/i* (sn) F hop.

Hopser ['hɔpsər] *m* (-s; -) F hop.

'hopsgehen *v/i* (*irr, sep,* -ge-, sn, → *gehen*) F a) go down the drain, b) go down the drain, c) get nabbed, d) kick the bucket. **'hopsnehmen** *v/t* (*irr, sep,* -ge-, h, → *nehmen*) F *j-n ~* nab s.o.

'hörbar *adj* audible. **'Hörbehinderte** *m, f* hearing-impaired person. **'Hörbild** *n* radio feature. **'Hörbrille** *f* earglasses. **'Hörbuch** *n* talking book.

horchen ['hɔrçən] *v/i* (h) listen (*auf acc* to), *a.* eavesdrop: *horch!* listen!

'Horcher *m* (-s; -) eavesdropper.

Horde ['hɔrdə] *f* (-; -n) *a. fig.* horde, *contp. a.* mob, gang.

hören ['hø:rən] (h) **I** *v/i* **1.** a) hear, b) listen (*auf acc* to): *univ.* **~** *bei* attend the lectures of; F *mir verging* ♀ *und Sehen* I was stunned; **~** *Sie mal!* listen!, look here!; *na,* **~** *Sie mal!* well, really!; *das lässt sich eher* ~ that sounds more like it; *ich lasse von mir* ~ I'll be in touch; *man hörte nie wieder von ihm* he was never heard of again; → *schwer* 4. **2.** obey, listen. **II** *v/t* **3.** a) hear, b) listen to (*concert etc*): *et.* ~ *von* hear s.th. about (or of); *er ließ nichts von sich* ~ he sent no news; *er wollte nichts davon* ~ he would not hear of it; *wie ich höre, will er kommen* I understand he wants to come; *soviel man hört* from all accounts; → *Radio.* **4.** *univ.* attend (*lectures*), take (*subject*).

'Hörensagen *n* (-s) (*vom* ~ by) hearsay.

'Hörer *m* (-s; -) **1.** listener, *univ.* student. **2.** *teleph.* receiver: *den* ~ *auflegen* hang up. **'Hörerin** *f* (-; -nen) → *Hörer* 1.

'Hörerschaft *f* (-; -en) **1.** *the* listeners, audience. **2.** (number of) students.

'Hörfolge *f* radio series (*or* serial).

'Hörfunk *m* radio.

'Hörgerät *n,* **'Hörhilfe** *f* hearing aid.

hörig ['hø:rɪç] *adj j-m* ~ *sein* be enslaved to s.o. **'Hörigkeit** *f* (-; *no pl*) bondage.

Horizont [hori'tsɔnt] *m* (-[e]s; -e) (*am* ~ on the) horizon (*a. fig.*): *s-n* ~ *erweitern* broaden one's mind; F *das geht über m-n* ~ that's beyond me.

horizontal [horitsɔn'ta:l] *adj* horizontal. **Horizon'tale** *f* (-; -n) horizontal.

Hormon [hɔr'mo:n] *n* (-s; -e) hormone. **Hor'mon...,** **hormonal** [hɔrmo'na:l] *adj* hormonal.

'Hörmuschel *f teleph.* earpiece.

Horn [hɔrn] *n* (-[e]s; ⁻er) **1.** *zo.* horn, *a.* feeler (*of snail*): *aus ~* (made of) horn; *fig. sich die Hörner abstoßen* sow one's wild oats; F *j-m Hörner aufsetzen* cuckold s.o.; → *Stier* 1. **2.** ♪ horn. **3.** ✕ bugle: F *ins gleiche ~ stoßen* chime in with s.o.

'Hornbläser(in *f) m* ♪ horn player.

'Hornbrille *f* horn-rimmed spectacles.

'Hörnerv *m* auditory nerve.

'Hornhaut *f* **1.** callus. **2.** *of eye:* cornea.

Hornisse [hɔr'nɪsə] *f* (-; -n) *zo.* hornet.

Hornist [hɔr'nɪst] m (-en; -en) ♩ hornist.

'**Hornvieh** n (-s; no pl) horned cattle.

Horoskop [horo'sko:p] n (-s; -e) (j-m das ~ stellen cast s.o.'s) horoscope.

Horror ['hɔrɔr] m (-s; no pl) horror (vor dat of). '**Horrorfilm** m horror film.

'**Hörsaal** m lecture hall.

'**Hörspiel** n radio play.

Horst [hɔrst] m (-es; -e) nest, eyrie.

'**Hörsturz** m ⚕ aural attack.

Hort [hɔrt] m (-[e]s; -e) 1. hoard, treasure. 2. (safe) refuge. 3. fig. stronghold. 4. day nursery. '**horten** v/t (h) hoard.

Hortensie [hɔr'tɛnziə] f (-; -n) ⚘ hydrangea.

'**Hörtest** m hearing test: e-n ~ machen lassen have one's ears tested.

'**Hörvermögen** n (-s; no pl) hearing.

'**Hörweite** f (-; no pl) hearing range: in (außer) ~ within (out of) earshot.

Höschen ['hø:sçən] n (-s; -) panties.

Hose ['ho:zə] f (-; -n) (a. ein Paar ~n) (a pair of) trousers (Am. pants): kurze ~(n) shorts; zwei ~n two pairs of trousers (etc); (sich) in die ~(n) machen make a mess in one's pants, F fig. be scared stiff; F die ~n anhaben wear the trousers (Am. pants); das ging in die ~ that was a complete flop; e-e tote ~ sein be a complete washout.

'**Hosen|anzug** m trouser suit, Am. pantsuit. **~bein** n trouser leg. **~boden** m F sich auf den ~ setzen buckle down to work. **~bügel** m trouser hanger. **~bund** m waistband. **~klammer** f trouser clip. **~rock** m culottes. **~schlitz** m fly. **~tasche** f trouser(s) pocket. **~träger** pl (pair of) braces (Am. suspenders).

hospitieren [hɔspi'ti:rən] v/i (h) sit in on classes (or lectures) (bei with).

Hospiz [hɔs'pi:ts] n (-es; -e) hospice.

Hostess [hɔs'tɛs] f (-; -en) hostess.

Hostie ['hɔstiə] f (-; -n) eccl. host.

Hotel [ho'tɛl] n (-s; -s) hotel: ~ garni bed and breakfast hotel.

Ho'telfach n (-[e]s; no pl) hotel business. **Ho'telgewerbe** n hotel industry. **Hotelier** [hotə'lie:] m (-s; -s) hotelier. **Ho'telverzeichnis** n list of hotels. **Ho'telzimmer** n hotel room.

Hub [hu:p] m (-[e]s; ⁻e) mot., ⚙ stroke. **hüben** ['hy:bən] adv over here, on this side: ~ wie drüben on both sides.

'**Hubraum** m mot. cubic capacity.

hübsch [hypʃ] adj a) pretty, good-looking, b) nice, F fig. a. fine: ein ~es Sümmchen a tidy sum; das wirst du ~ bleiben lassen! you're not going to do anything of the sort!

'**Hubschrauber** m (-s; -) helicopter.

'**Hubschrauberlandeplatz** m heliport.

'**Hubstapler** [-ʃta:plər] m (-s; -) stacker truck.

huch [hʊx] int ooh!

'**huckepack** adv F pick-a-back. '**Huckepackverkehr** m pick-a-back traffic.

hudeln ['hu:dəln] v/i (h) F work sloppily.

Huf [hu:f] m (-[e]s; -e) hoof.

'**Hufeisen** n horseshoe. '**Hufeisenform** f (in ~ arranged in) horseshoe.

'**hufeisenförmig** [-fœrmɪç] adj horseshoe-shaped.

'**Huflattich** m ⚘ coltsfoot.

Hüfte ['hyftə] f (-; -n) hip. '**Hüftgelenk** n hip joint. '**Hüft|gürtel** m, '**Hüfthalter** m suspender (Am. garter) belt. '**hüfthoch** adj and adv waist-high, water: waist-deep. '**Hüftweite** f hip measurement.

Hügel ['hy:gəl] m (-s; -) a) hill, a. hillock, b) mound. '**hüg(e)lig** adj hilly.

Huhn [hu:n] n (-[e]s; ⁻er) fowl, chicken (a. gastr.), hen: mit den Hühnern aufstehen (zu Bett gehen) get up with the lark (go to bed early); F da lachen ja die Hühner! that's a laugh!; dummes ~ silly goose; verrücktes ~ crazy thing.

Hühnchen ['hy:nçən] n (-s; -) 1. (young) chicken: F mit j-m ein ~ zu rupfen haben have a score to settle with s.o. 2. gastr. (roast) chicken.

Hühnerauge ['hy:nər-] n corn: F fig. j-m auf die ~n treten tread on s.o.'s corns. '**Hühneraugenpflaster** n corn plaster. '**Hühner|brühe** f chicken broth. **~brust** f 1. gastr. chicken breast. 2. ⚕ pigeon breast. **~ei** n hen's egg. **~farm** f chicken farm. **~futter** n chickenfeed. **~hof** m chicken yard. **~leiter** f chicken ladder. **~pest** f vet. fowl pest. **~stall** m henhouse. **~zucht** f chicken farming.

huldigen ['hʊldɪgən] v/i (h) j-m ~ pay homage to s.o. '**Huldigung** f (-; -en) homage (an acc to).

Hülle ['hylə] f (-; -n) 1. wrap(ping), cover, (record) sleeve, Am. jacket (a. of book), envelope: die sterbliche ~ the mortal remains. **2.** F clothes. **3.** *fig.* veil, cloak. **4. in ~ und Fülle** in abundance, plenty of, *whisky etc* galore.

hüllen ['hʏlən] *v/t* (h) (*in* acc) wrap s.o., s.th. (up) (in), cover (with): **sich in Schweigen ~** remain silent (*über acc* about); **in Dunkel (Nebel) gehüllt** shrouded in darkness (fog).

'hüllenlos *adj* naked.

Hülse ['hʏlzə] *f* (-; -n) **1.** ♠ a) hull, husk, b) pod. **2.** ☉ a) sleeve, socket, b) case.

'Hülsenfrucht *f* legume(n), *pl* pulse.

human [hu'ma:n] *adj* humane, F *a.* decent, ⚚ human. **Hu'mange,netik** *f* human genetics.

Humanismus [huma'nɪsmʊs] *m* (-; *no pl*) humanism: *hist. der ~* Humanism. **Humanist** [-'nɪst] *m* (-en; -en) humanist, *ped.*, *univ.* classicist, *hist.* Humanist. **huma'nistisch** *adj* humanist(ic), *ped.*, *univ.* classical: → *Gymnasium.*

humanitär [humani'tɛ:r] *adj* humanitarian. **Humanität** [humani'tɛ:t] *f* (-; *no pl*) humaneness, humanity.

Hu'manmedi,zin *f* human medicine.

Humbug ['hʊmbʊk] *m* (-s; *no pl*) humbug.

Hummel ['hʊməl] *f* (-; -n) bumblebee.

Hummer ['hʊmər] *m* (-s; -) lobster.

Humor [hu'mo:r] *m* (-s; *no pl*) humo(u)r: *k-n Sinn für ~ haben* have no sense of humo(u)r; *den ~ behalten* keep one's sense of humo(u)r; *et. mit ~ nehmen* take s.th. in good humo(u)r; *du hast (vielleicht) ~!* you've got a nerve!

Humoreske [humo'rɛskə] *f* (-; -n) humoresque, humorous sketch (*or* story).

Humorist [humo'rɪst] *m* (-en; -en) humorist. **humo'ristisch** *adj* humorous.

hu'morlos *adj* humo(u)rless: *er ist völlig ~ a.* he has absolutely no sense of humo(u)r. **hu'morvoll** *adj* humorous.

humpeln ['hʊmpəln] *v/i* (h *or* sn) limp.

Humpen ['hʊmpən] *m* (-s; -) tankard.

Humus ['hu:mʊs] *m* (-; *no pl*) humus.

'Humusschicht *f* humus layer, topsoil.

Hund [hʊnt] *m* (-[e]s; -e) dog, *hunt.* hound: *junger ~* puppy; *fig. schlauer (feiger) ~* sly (yellow) dog; F *(gemeiner) ~* bastard; *der arme ~!* F (the) poor sod!; *das ist ja ein dicker ~!* that takes the cake!; *auf den ~ kommen* go to the dogs; *(ganz) auf dem ~ sein* be down and out, *a.* be a wreck; *vor die ~e*

gehen a) go to the dogs, b) kick the bucket; *wie ~ und Katze leben* lead a cat-and-dog life; *er ist bekannt wie ein bunter ~* he's known all over the place; *da liegt der ~ begraben!* that's it (*or* why)!; *damit kannst man k-n ~ hinterm Ofen hervorlocken!* that won't tempt anybody!; *~e, die bellen, beißen nicht* barking dogs seldom bite.

'Hundeausstellung *f* dog show.

'hunde'elend *adj* F *mir ist ~* I feel lousy.

'Hunde|futter *n* dog food. **~halsband** *n* dog collar. **~hütte** *f* (dog) kennel.

'hunde'kalt *adj* F freezing cold.

'Hunde|kuchen *m* dog biscuit. **~leben** *n* F dog's life. **~leine** *f* dog lead, dog leash. **~marke** *f* dog licence disc, *Am.* dog tag.

'hunde'müde *adj* F dog-tired.

hundert ['hʊndərt] *adj* a (*or* one) hundred: *einige (or ein paar) ~ Leute* a few hundred people. **'Hundert**[1] *n* (-s; -e) hundred: *zu ~en* in hundreds; *zehn von ~* ten in a hundred, ten per cent. **'Hundert**[2] *f* (-; -en) hundred.

Hunderter ['hʊndərtər] *m* (-s; -) **1.** A a) (the) hundred, b) three-figure number. **2.** F one-hundred-mark *etc* note (*Am.* bill). **'hunderter'lei** [-'laɪ] *adj* a hundred and one. **'hundertfach I** *adj* hundredfold. **II** *adv* a hundred times.

Hundert'jahrfeier *f* centenary, *Am.* centennial. **'hundertjährig** [-jɛ:rɪç] *adj* **1.** one-hundred-year-old. **2.** of a hundred years, hundred years' ...

'hundertmal *adv* a hundred times.

Hundert'markschein *m* one-hundred--mark note (*Am.* bill). **Hundert'meterlauf** *m* the 100-metres (*Am.* meters).

'hundertpro,zentig *adj* a hundred per cent (*a. fig.*), pure (*alcohol, wool, etc*), *fig.* out-and-out (*conservative etc*): F *das weiß ich ~* I'm dead sure.

'hundertst *adj* hundredth. **'hundertstel** *adj*, **'Hundertstel** *n* (-s; -) hundredth.

'hundert'tausend *adj* a (*or* one) hundred thousand.

'Hundesa,lon *m* dog parlo(u)r.

'Hundezucht *f* **1.** dog breeding. **2.** (breeding) kennel(s).

'Hundezüchter(in *f*) *m* dog breeder.

Hündin ['hʏndɪn] *f* (-; -nen) bitch.

hündisch ['hʏndɪʃ] *adj fig.* cringing.

'hundsge'mein *adj* F a) dirty, low-down, nasty, b) hellish (*job etc*).
'hundsmise,rabel *adj* F lousy.
'Hundstage *pl* dog days.
Hüne ['hy:nə] *m* (-n; -n) giant.
'Hünengrab *n* megalithic grave.
'hünenhaft *adj* gigantic.
Hunger ['hoŋər] *m* (-s; *no pl*) **1.** hunger (*a. fig.* nach for): ~ haben (bekommen) be (get) hungry; ~ leiden go hungry; vor ~ sterben starve to death; F ich sterbe vor ~ I'm starving; ~ ist der beste Koch hunger is the best sauce. **2.** → Hungersnot.
'Hungerleider [-laɪdər] *m* (-s; -) starveling.
'Hungerlohn *m* starvation wages.
hungern ['hoŋərn] (h) **I** *v/i* a) go hungry, starve, *fig.* hunger (nach for), b) starve o.s., go without food. **II** sich zu Tode ~ starve o.s. to death.
'hungernd *adj* hungry, starving.
'Hungerö,dem *n* ☞ famine (o)edema.
'Hungersnot *f* famine.
'Hungerstreik *m* (in den ~ treten go on a) hunger strike. Hungertod *m* (-[e]s; *no pl*) death from starvation. 'Hungertuch *n* F *fig.* am ~ nagen be starving.
hungrig ['hoŋrɪç] *adj a. fig.* hungry (nach for): ~ sein be (or feel) hungry; das macht ~ that makes you hungry.
Hunne ['hunə] *m* (-n; -n) *hist.* Hun.
Hupe ['hu:pə] *f* (-; -n) horn: auf die ~ drücken → hupen ['hu:pən] *v/i* (h) hoot, honk, sound the horn.
hüpfen ['hypfən] *v/i* (sn) hop, skip, *ball*: bounce.
'Hupsi,gnal *n* honk, hoot.
Hürde ['hʏrdə] *f* (-; -n) **1.** (*a. fig.* e-e ~ nehmen take a) hurdle. **2.** fold.
'Hürdenlauf *m sports*: hurdles.
'Hürdenläufer(in *f*) *m sports*: hurdler.
Hure ['hu:rə] *f* (-; -n) whore.
hurra [ho'ra:] *int* hurray!, hurrah!
Hurrikan ['horikan] *m* (-s; -e) hurricane.
husch [hoʃ] *int* a) whoosh!, b) shoo!
huschen ['hoʃən] *v/i* (sn) flit.
hüsteln ['hy:stəln] *v/i* (h) cough slightly.
husten ['hu:stən] (h) **I** *v/i* cough (*a.* F *engine*): stark ~ have a bad cough; F ~ auf (*acc*) not to give a damn for. **II** *v/t* cough up: F dem werde ich was ~! to hell with him!

'Husten *m* (-s; -) cough. ~anfall *m* coughing fit. ~bon,bon *m*, *n* cough drop. ~reiz *m* tickle in one's throat. ~saft *m* cough syrup. ~tee *m* bronchial tea. ~tropfen *pl* cough drops.
Hut¹ *m* (-[e]s; ⸚e) **1.** hat: F *fig.* ein alter ~ old hat; den ~ abnehmen (*or* ziehen) take off one's hat (*fig.* vor j-m to s.o.); ~ ab (vor dir)! I'll take my hat off to you!; alles unter einen ~ bringen reconcile things; F damit habe ich nichts am ~ I can't be bothered with that!; ihm ging der ~ hoch he blew his top; F *fig.* den ~ nehmen müssen have to go (*or* resign); das kannst du dir an den ~ stecken! (you can) keep it! **2.** ☝ cap.
Hut² *f* (-; *no pl*) **1.** in j-s ~ in s.o.'s care; in guter (*or* sicherer) ~ sein be safe (bei with). **2.** auf der ~ sein be on one's guard (vor *dat* against).
'Hutablage *f* hat rack.
hüten ['hy:tən] (h) **I** *v/t* look after, mind (*children etc*), guard (*a. secret etc*): → Bett. **II** sich ~ (vor *dat*) be on one's guard (against), watch out (for); sich ~, et. zu tun take care not to do s.th.; ich werde mich ~! I'll do nothing of the sort!; hüte dich vor ...! beware of ...!
'Hüter *m* (-s; -), 'Hüterin *f* (-; -nen) guardian, keeper; *humor.* der Hüter des Gesetzes (the arm of) the Law.
'Hutgeschäft *n* hat shop. 'Hutgröße *f* hat size. 'Hutkrempe *f* (hat) brim.
'Hutmacher *m* (-s; -) hatter.
'Hutmacherin *f* (-; -nen) milliner.
'Hutschnur *f* hat string: F *fig.* das geht mir über die ~! that's going too far!
Hütte ['hʏtə] *f* (-; -n) **1.** a) hut, cabin, b) *contp.* shack, shanty, c) refuge. **2.** → Hüttenwerk.
'Hüttenindu,strie *f* iron and steel industry. 'Hüttenwerk *n* metallurgical plant.
Hyäne [hy'ε:nə] *f* (-; -n) *zo.* hyena.
Hyazinthe [hya'tsɪntə] *f* (-; -n) hyacinth.
Hybride [hy'bri:də] *f* (-; -n) hybrid.
Hydrant [hy'drant] *m* (-en; -en) hydrant.
Hydrat [hy'dra:t] *n* (-[e]s; -e) ☝ hydrate.
Hydraulik [hy'draolɪk] *f* (-; *no pl*) hydraulics. hy'draulisch *adj* hydraulic.
hydrieren [hy'dri:rən] *v/t* (h) hydrogenate.
Hy'drierwerk *n* hydrogenation plant.
Hydrody'namik [hydro-] *f* hydrodynamics.

Hydrokul,tur ['hy:dro-] *f* hydroponics.
Hydrolyse [hydro'ly:zə] *f* (-; -n) 🐍 hydrolysis.
Hygiene [hy'gĭe:nə] *f* (-; *no pl*) hygiene.
hygi'enisch *adj* hygienic.
Hygrometer [hygro'me:tər] *n* (-s; -) hygrometer.
Hymne ['hymnə] *f* (-; -n) hymn (*an acc* to).
Hyperbel [hy'pɛrbəl] *f* (-; -n) **1.** 🅐 hyperbola. **2.** *ling.* hyperbole.
hypermo'dern [hypər-] *adj* ultramodern.
Hypertonie [hypərto'ni:] *f* (-; -n) 🔬 hypertension.
Hypnose [hyp'no:zə] *f* (-; -n) (*in ~* under) hypnosis. **hyp'notisch** [-tɪʃ] *adj* hypnotic. **Hypnotiseur** [hypnoti'zø:r] *m* (-s; -e) hypnotist. **hypnotisieren** [hypnoti'zi:rən] *v/t* (h) hypnotize.
Hypochonder [hypo'xɔndər] *m* (-s; -),

hypo'chondrisch *adj* hypochondriac.
Hypotenuse [hypote'nu:zə] *f* (-; -n) 🅐 hypotenuse.
Hypothek [hypo'te:k] *f* (-; -en) 🔨 mortgage: *e-e ~ aufnehmen* raise a mortgage (*auf acc* on); *mit e-r ~ belasten* (encumber *s.th.* with a) mortgage.
hypothekarisch [hypote'ka:rɪʃ] *adj and adv* by (*or* on) mortgage.
Hypo'theken|bank *f* mortgage bank. **~brief** *m* mortgage deed. **2frei** *adj* unmortgaged. **~gläubiger(in** *f)* *m* mortgagee. **~pfandbrief** *m* mortgage bond. **~schuldner(in** *f)* *m* mortgagor.
Hypothese [hypo'te:zə] *f* (-; -n) hypothesis. **hypo'thetisch** *adj* hypothetical.
Hypotonie [hypoto'ni:] *f* (-; -n) 🔬 hypotension.
Hysterie [hyste'ri:] *f* (-; *no pl*) 🔬 hysteria.
hysterisch [hys'te:rɪʃ] *adj* hysterical: *~er Anfall* hysterics.

I

I, i [i:] *n* (-; -) I, i: *i wo!* not a bit of it!
iberisch [i'be:rɪʃ] *adj geogr.* Iberian.
ich [ɪç] *pers pron* I: *~ bin's!* it is I!, F it's me!; *~ selbst* (I) myself; *~ Idiot!* what a fool I am!
Ich *n* (-[s]; -[s]) self, *psych.* ego: *mein besseres ~* my better self; *zweites ~* alter ego. **F** ~ egocentric.
'Ichform *f* (-; *no pl*) (*in der ~ geschrieben* written in) first person.
ideal [ide'a:l] *adj*, **Ide'al** *n* (-s; -e) ideal.
idealisieren [ideali'zi:rən] *v/t* (h) idealize. **Idealismus** [idea'lɪsmʊs] *m* (-; *no pl*) idealism. **Idealist** [idea'lɪst] *m* (-en; -en), **Idea'listin** *f* (-; -nen) idealist. **idea'listisch** *adj* idealistic.
Idee [i'de:] *f* (-; -n) **1.** idea, *a.* thought, concept: *gute ~!* good idea!; *ich kam auf die ~ zu inf* it occurred to me to *inf*; *wie kamst du auf die ~?* what gave you the idea?; *wie kamst du auf die ~ ihn einzuladen?* what made you invite him? **2.** F *e-e ~* (just) a bit.

ideell [ide'ɛl] *adj* a) ideal (*a.* 🅐), b) idealistic: *~er Wert* sentimental value.
i'deenarm, i'deenlos *adj* lacking in ideas, unimaginative. **i'deenreich** *adj* full of ideas, imaginative. **I'deenreichtum** *m* (-s; *no pl*) wealth of ideas.
identifi'zierbar *adj* identifiable.
identifizieren [idɛntifi'tsi:rən] *v/t* (h) identify: *sich ~ mit* identify (o.s.) with. **Identifi'zierung** *f* (-; -en) identification.
identisch [i'dɛntɪʃ] *adj* identical.
Identität [idɛnti'tɛ:t] *f* (-; *no pl*) identity. **Identi'täts|krise** *f* identity crisis. **~nachweis** *m* proof of (one's) identity.
Ideologe [ideo'lo:gə] *m* (-n; -n) ideologue. **Ideologie** [ideolo'gi:] *f* (-; -n) ideology. **ideo'logisch** *adj* ideological.
Idiom [i'dĭo:m] *n* (-s; -e) **1.** idiom. **2.** language.
Idiomatik [idĭo'ma:tɪk] *f* (-; *no pl*) **1.** phraseology. **2.** idioms (and phrases).
idiomatisch [idĭo'ma:tɪʃ] *adj* idiomatic.
Idiot [i'dĭo:t] *m* (-en; -en) idiot.
Idi'otenhügel *m* F nursery slope.

idi'otensicher adj F foolproof.

Idiotie [idĭo'tiː] f (-; -en) **1.** 🗲 idiocy. **2.** F imbecility, idiocy: *pure ~* sheer lunacy.

idiotisch [i'dĭoːtiʃ] adj idiotic.

Idol [i'doːl] n (-s; -e) idol.

Idyll [i'dyl] n (-s; -e) idyll. **Idylle** [i'dylə] f (-; -n) **1.** idyll. **2.** pastoral poem (paint. scene). **idyllisch** [i'dylɪʃ] adj idyllic.

Igel ['iːgəl] m (-s; -) zo. hedgehog.

ignorant [ɪgno'rant] adj ignorant.

Igno'rant m (-en; -en) ignorant person.

Ignoranz [ɪgno'rants] f (-; no pl) ignorance.

ignorieren [ɪgno'riːrən] v/t (h) ignore.

ihm [iːm] pers pron (dat of er and es) (to) him, (to) it: *ich glaube (es) ~ I* believe him; *ein Freund von ~* a friend of his.

ihn [iːn] pers pron (acc of er) him, of things: it.

ihnen ['iːnən] **I** pers pron (dat pl of er, sie, es) (to) them: *ich habe es ~ ge- sagt* I've told them; *ein Freund von ~* a friend of theirs. **II Ihnen** (dat of Sie) (to) you: *ist er ein Freund von Ihnen?* is he a friend of yours?

ihr [iːr] **I** pers pron **1.** (dat of sie sg) (to) her, of things: (to) it: *e-e Tante von ~* an aunt of hers; → a. **ihm. 2.** (nom pl of du, in letters: **Ihr**) you. **II** adj **3.** sg her, of things: its, pl their: *e-r ~er Brüder* one of her (or their) brothers, a brother of hers (or theirs). **4. Ihr** address: your. **III** pos pron **5.** der (die, das) **ihr(ig)e** hers (pl theirs, address: **Ihr(ig)e** yours).

'ihrer'seits [-'zaɪts] adv as far as she's (pl they're, address: **Ihrerseits** you're) concerned.

'ihres'gleichen indef pron **1.** the likes of her (pl them), her (pl their) equals. **2. Ihresgleichen** the likes of you, your equals.

'ihret'wegen adv **1.** for her (pl their) sake. **2. 'Ihret'wegen** for your sake.

'ihrig → ihr III.

Ikone [i'koːnə] f (-; -n) icon.

illegal ['ɪlega:l] adj illegal.

illegitim ['ɪlegiti:m] adj illegitimate.

Illusion [ɪlu'zĭoːn] f (-; -en) illusion: *sich ~en hingeben* delude o.s.; *darüber mache ich mir k-e ~en* I have no illusions about that. **illusi'onslos** adj and adv without (any) illusions.

illusorisch [ɪlu'zoːrɪʃ] adj illusory.

Illustration [ɪlostra'tsĭoːn] f (-; -en) illus-

tration, picture. **illustrieren** [ɪlos'triː- rən] v/t illustrate, fig. a. demonstrate. **Illu'strierte** f (-n; -en) magazine, F mag.

im [ɪm] = *in dem → in*[1].

Image ['ɪmɪtʃ] n (-[s]; -s) image. **'Image- pflege** f (-; no pl) image cultivation.

imaginär [imagi'nɛːr] adj imaginary.

Imbiß ['ɪmbɪs] m (-sses; -sse) snack. **'Imbißhalle** f, **'Imbißstube** f snack bar.

Imitation [imita'tsĭoːn] f (-; -en) imitation, copy.

imitieren [imi'tiːrən] v/t (h) imitate.

Imker ['ɪmkər] m (-s; -) beekeeper.

immanent [ɪma'nɛnt] adj inherent (dat in).

Immatrikulation [ɪmatrikula'tsĭoːn] f (-; -en) univ. enrolment.

immatrikulieren [ɪmatriku'liːrən] v/t (h) (a. sich ~ lassen) enrol (an dat at).

immens [ɪ'mɛns] adj immense.

immer ['ɪmər] adv **1.** always, constantly, all the time, a. every time: *noch ~* still; *noch ~ nicht* not yet; *~ wenn* whenever; *~ wieder* over and over again, time and again; *~ wieder tun* keep doing; *sie redete ~ weiter* F she went on and on. **2.** before comp: *~ besser* better and better; *~ schlimmer* worse and worse; *~ größer werdend* ever increasing. **3.** F *~ zwei* two at a time. **4.** *wann (auch) ~* whenever; *was (auch) ~* whatever; *wer (auch) ~* whoever; *wie (auch) ~* however; *wo (auch) ~* wherever.

'immergrün adj evergreen.

'immer'hin adv **1.** still, after all: *~!* not too bad! **2.** at least.

'immer'während adj everlasting.

Immigrant [ɪmi'grant] m (-en; -en), **Immi'grantin** f (-; -nen) immigrant.

Immigration [ɪmigra'tsĭoːn] f (-; -en) immigration. **immigrieren** [ɪmi'griːrən] v/i (sn) immigrate.

Immobilien [ɪmo'biːlĭən] pl real estate, (real) property. **~händler(in** f) m, **~makler(in** f) m estate agent, Am. realtor. **~markt** m property market.

immun [ɪ'muːn] adj immune (gegen to): *~ machen → immunisieren* [ɪmuni'ziːrən] v/t immunize (gegen against).

Immunität [ɪmuni'tɛːt] f (-; no pl) immunity (gegen to, against, from).

Im'munkörper m 🗲 antibody.

Immunologe [ɪmuno'loːgə] m (-n; -n)

immunologist. **Immunologie** [ɪmuno-lo'giː] f (-; no pl) immunology.
Im'mun|schwäche f ✠ immunodefi-ciency. **~sy,stem** n immune system.
Impedanz [ɪmpe'dants] f (-; -en) ⚡ impedance.
Imperativ ['ɪmperatiːf] m (-s; -e) ling. imperative.
Imperfekt ['ɪmpɛrfɛkt] n (-s; -e) ling. imperfect (tense).
Imperialismus [ɪmperia'lɪsmʊs] m (-; no pl) imperialism.
imperia'listisch adj imperialist(ic).
Imperium [ɪm'peːriʊm] n (-s; -rien) a. fig. empire.
Impf|akti,on f ✠ vaccination pro-gram(me Br.). **~arzt** m vaccinator.
impfen ['ɪmpfən] v/t (h) vaccinate, inoc-ulate: **sich ~ lassen** (**gegen** against) be vaccinated, get a vaccination.
Impf|paß m vaccination card. **~pi,stole** f vaccination gun. **~schein** m vaccina-tion certificate. **~stoff** m vaccine.
'Impfung f (-; -en) vaccination, inocula-tion.
Implantat [ɪmplan'taːt] n (-[e]s; -e), **im-plantieren** [-'tiːrən] v/t (h) ✠ implant.
implizieren [ɪmpli'tsiːrən] v/t (h) imply.
implodieren [ɪmplo'diːrən] v/i (sn) im-plode. **Implosion** [ɪmplo'zioːn] f (-; -en) implosion.
imponieren [ɪmpo'niːrən] v/i (h) **j-m ~** a) impress s.o., b) command s.o.'s re-spect. **impo'nierend** adj impressive.
Impo'niergehabe n 1. zo. display beha-vio(u)r. 2. fig. attempt to impress.
Import [ɪm'pɔrt] m (-[e]s; -e) 1. no pl importing. 2. imports. **Im'port...** im-port (agency, trade, etc). **Importeur** [ɪmpɔr'tøːr] m (-s; -e) importer.
Im'portgeschäft n 1. import trade. 2. import company. **importieren** [ɪmpɔr-'tiːrən] v/t (h) import.
imposant [ɪmpo'zant] adj imposing, im-pressive.
impotent ['ɪmpotɛnt] adj impotent.
'Impotenz [-tɛnts] f (-; no pl) impotence.
imprägnieren [ɪmprɛ'gniːrən] v/t (h) impregnate, a. waterproof.
Imprä'gnierung f (-; -en) impregnation, waterproofing.
Impression [ɪmprɛ'sioːn] f (-; -en) im-pression. **Impressionismus** [ɪmprɛsio-'nɪsmʊs] m (-; no pl) impressionism.

Impressionist [-'nɪst] m (-en; -en) im-pressionist. **impressio'nistisch** adj impressionist(ic).
Impressum [ɪm'prɛsʊm] n (-s; -sen) im-print, of newspaper: a. masthead.
Improvisation [ɪmproviza'tsioːn] f (-; -en) improvisation. **improvisieren** [ɪmprovi'ziːrən] v/t, v/i (h) improvise, speaker etc: a. extemporize, F ad-lib.
Impuls [ɪm'pʊls] m (-es; -e) impulse: **e-m ~ folgend** on (an) impulse; fig. **neue ~e geben** give a fresh impetus (dat to).
impulsiv [ɪmpʊl'ziːf] adj impulsive: **~ handeln** act on impulse.
Im'pulskauf m ♱ impulsive buying.
im'stande adj pred **zu et. ~ sein** be ca-pable of (doing) s.th.; (**nicht**) **~ sein, et. zu tun** be (un)able to do s.th.; **dazu ist er glatt ~** iro. I wouldn't put it past him.
in¹ [ɪn] prep **1.** a) in, at, b) within, c) into, in: **~ England** in England; **waren Sie schon einmal ~ England?** have you ever been to England?; **im Haus** in(side) the house, indoors; **~ der (die) Schule** at (to) school; **er ist Kassierer ~ e-r Bank** he is a cashier in (or at) a bank. **2.** a) in b) during, c) within: **im Mai** in May; **~ diesem Jahr** this year; **~ diesem Alter** at this age. **3. ~ größter Eile** in a great rush; **im Kreis** in a circle; **~ Behandlung sein** be having treat-ment; **ein Mann ~ s-r Stellung** a man in his position; **gut ~ Chemie** good at chemistry.
in² adj **~ sein** F be in.
'inaktiv adj inactive, ♱ a. inert.
Inaktivi'tät f (-; no pl) inactivity.
'inakzep,tabel adj unacceptable.
In'angriffnahme [-naːmə] f (-; -n) adm. (gen) starting (on), tackling (of).
In'anspruchnahme [-naːmə] f (-; -n) (gen, von) **1.** use (of). **2.** demands (on).
'Inbegriff m (-[e]s; -e) epitome.
'inbegriffen adj ~ **sein** be included.
Inbe'sitznahme [-naːmə] f (-; -n) (gen of) taking possession, occupation.
Inbe'triebnahme [-naːmə] f (-; -n) (gen of) opening, starting: **bei ~ der Anlage** when the plant is put into operation.
'Inbrunst f (-; no pl) ardo(u)r, fervo(u)r.
'inbrünstig adj ardent, fervent.
in'dem conj **1.** by: **er entkam, ~ er aus dem Fenster sprang** he escaped by jumping out of the window. **2.** while.

Inder ['ɪndər] m (-s; -), **'Inderin** f (-; -nen) Indian.

in'dessen I adv **1.** meanwhile. **2.** however. **II** conj → **wohingegen**.

Index ['ɪndɛks] m (-es; -e, -dizes [-ditsɛs]) index. **~lohn** m index-linked wages.

Indianer [ɪn'dīa:nər] m (-s; -), **Indi'anerin** f (-; -nen), **indi'anisch** adj (Red) Indian.

Indien ['ɪndīən] n (-s) India.

Indikation [ɪndika'tsīo:n] f (-; -en) 🟐 indication: **soziale ~** social grounds for termination of pregnancy.

Indikativ ['ɪndikati:f] m (-s; -e) ling. indicative (mood).

'indirekt adj indirect: **~e Rede** ling. indirect (or reported) speech.

indisch ['ɪndɪʃ] adj Indian.

'indiskret adj indiscreet.

Indiskreti'on f (-; -en) indiscretion.

indiskutabel ['ɪndɪskuta:bəl] adj impossible: **~ sein** a. be out of the question.

'indisponiert adj indisposed.

individualisieren [ɪndividuali'zi:rən] v/t (h) individualize. **Individualismus** [-'lɪsmʊs] m (-; no pl) individualism. **Individualist** [-'lɪst] m (-en; -en) individualist. **individua'listisch** adj individualist(ic). **Individualität** [-'tɛ:t] f (-; no pl) individuality. **individuell** [ɪndivi'dŭɛl] adj individual: **~ gestalten** individualize; **das ist ~ verschieden** that varies from person to person.

Individuum [ɪndi'vi:dŭɔm] n (-s; -duen [-dŭən]) individual.

Indiz [ɪn'di:ts] n (-es; -zien [-tsīən]) **1.** indication, sign. **2.** usu. pl → **In'dizienbeweis(e** pl) m ⚖ circumstantial evidence.

indoeuro'päisch [ɪndo-], **indoger'manisch** adj Indo-European.

indoktrinieren [ɪndɔktri'ni:rən] v/t (h) indoctrinate.

Indonesien [ɪndo'ne:zĭən] n (-s) Indonesia. **Indonesier** [ɪndo'ne:zĭər] m (-s; -), **Indo'nesierin** f (-; -nen), **indo'nesisch** [-zɪʃ] adj Indonesian.

Indossament [ɪndɔsa'mɛnt] n (-s; -e) ✝ endorsement. **Indossant** [ɪndɔ'sant] m (-en; -en) endorser. **Indossat** [ɪndɔ'sa:t] m (-en; -en) endorsee. **indossieren** [ɪndɔ'si:rən] v/t (h) endorse.

Induktion [ɪndʊk'tsīo:n] f (-; -en) induc-

tion. **Induktivität** [ɪndʊktivi'tɛ:t] f (-; no pl) inductivity.

industrialisieren [ɪndʊstrīali'zi:rən] v/t (h) industrialize. **Industriali'sierung** f (-; no pl) industrialization.

Industrie [ɪndʊs'tri:] f (-; -n) a) industry, b) → **Industriezweig**.

Indu'strie... industrial (nation, diamond, product, etc). **~anlage** f industrial plant. **~arbeiter(in** f) m industrial worker. **~betrieb** m industrial company (or plant). **~gebiet** n industrial area. **~gelände** n industrial estate. **~gesellschaft** f industrial society. **~gewerkschaft** f industry-wide union: **~ Metall** metalworkers' union. **~kaufmann** m officer (or clerk) in an industrial company.

industriell [ɪndʊstri'ɛl] adj industrial. **Industri'elle** m, f (-n; -n) industrialist.

Indu'strie|macht f industrial power. **~messe** f industrial fair. **~müll** m industrial waste. **~park** m industrial park. **~spio₍nage** f industrial espionage. **~stadt** f industrial town. **~- und Handelskammer** f chamber of industry and commerce. **~verband** m federation of industries. **~zweig** m (branch of) industry.

induzieren [ɪndu'tsi:rən] v/t (h) induce.

inein'ander adv in(to) one another (or each other), in cpds. a. inter...: **~ verliebt** in love (with each other).

inein'anderfließen v/i (irr, sep, -ge-, sn, → **fließen**) merge into one another, colo(u)rs: a. run.

inein'andergreifen v/i (irr, sep, -ge-, h, → **greifen**) **1.** 🟐 interlock, gears etc: mesh. **2.** fig. interlock.

inein'anderschieben v/t (irr, sep, -ge-, h, → **schieben**) (a. **sich ~ lassen**) telescope.

infam [ɪn'fa:m] adj infamous, disgraceful. **Infamie** [ɪnfa'mi:] f (-; -n) infamy.

Infanterie [ɪnfantə'ri:] f (-; -n) infantry. **Infanterist** [ɪnfantə'rɪst] m (-en; -en) infantryman.

infantil [ɪnfan'ti:l] adj infantile.

Infarkt [ɪn'farkt] m (-[e]s; -e) 🟐 infarct.

Infekt [ɪn'fɛkt] m (-[e]s; -e), **Infektion** [ɪnfɛk'tsīo:n] f (-; -en) infection.

Infekti'ons|gefahr f risk of infection. **~herd** m focus of infection. **~krankheit** f infectious disease.

infektiös [ɪnfɛk'tsiøːs] *adj* infectious, contagious.
Inferno [ɪn'fɛrno] *n* (-s; *no pl*) inferno.
infiltrieren [ɪnfɪl'triːrən] *v/t* (h), *v/i* (sn) infiltrate.
Infinitesimalrechnung [ɪnfinitezi'maːl-] *f* infinitesimal calculus.
Infinitiv ['ɪnfinitiːf] *m* (-s; -e) infinitive.
infizieren [ɪnfi'tsiːrən] (h) **I** *v/t* infect. **II sich ~** catch an infection, become infected: *er hat sich bei ihr infiziert* he caught the disease from her.
in flagranti [ɪn fla'granti] *adv* **~ertappen** catch *s.o.* in the act (*or* red-handed).
Inflation [ɪnfla'tsioːn] *f* (-; -en) inflation.
inflationär [ɪnflatsio'nɛːr], **inflationistisch** [-'nɪstɪʃ] *adj* inflationary.
Inflati'onspoli,tik *f* inflationary policy.
Inflati'onsrate *f* inflation rate.
Info ['ɪnfo] *n* (-s; -s) F → *Informationsblatt.*
in'folge *prep* (*gen*) as a result of, owing to. **infolge'dessen** *adv* as a result (of this), consequently.
Informant [ɪnfɔr'mant] *m* (-en; -en), **Infor'mantin** *f* (-; -nen) informant.
Informatik [ɪnfɔr'maːtɪk] *f* (-; *no pl*) computer science, informatics. **Infor'matiker** [-tikər] *m* (-s; -) computer specialist.
Information [ɪnfɔrma'tsioːn] *f* (-; -en) (*zu Ihrer ~* for your) information.
Informati'ons|blatt *n* newssheet. **~bü,ro** *n* information office. **~fluß** *m* (-sses; *no pl*) flow of information. **~materi,al** *n* information(al material). **~schalter** *m*, **~stand** *m* information desk.
informativ [ɪnfɔrma'tiːf] *adj* informative.
informieren [ɪnfɔr'miːrən] (h) **I** *v/t* (*über acc*) inform (of, about), *a.* notify (of), let *s.o.* know (about), *a.* instruct (as to), brief (on): *falsch ~* misinform. **II sich ~** (*über acc* about) inform o.s., find out. **infor'miert** *adj* informed: *~e Kreise* well-informed circles.
'Infostand *m* F → *Informationsstand.*
infrarot ['ɪnfra-] *adj*, **'Infrarot...** infrared.
'Infraschall *m* infrasound.
'Infraschall... infrasonic.
'Infrastruk,tur *f* infrastructure.
Infusion [ɪnfu'zioːn] *f* (-; -en) infusion.
Infusorien [ɪnfu'zoːriən] *pl zo.* infusoria.
Inge'brauchnahme [-na:mə] *f* (-; *no pl*)

adm. vor ~ (*gen*) before using *s.th.*
Ingenieur [ɪnʒe'niøːr] *m* (-s; -e) engineer.
Ingeni'eurbü,ro *n* **1.** (firm of) consulting engineers. **2.** engineering office.
Ingwer ['ɪŋvər] *m* (-s; *no pl*) ginger.
Inhaber ['ɪnha:bər] *m* (-s; -), **'Inhaberin** *f* (-; -nen) a) owner, proprietor (-tress), b) occupant (*of flat*), c) holder (*of title, office, patent, record, etc*), ✝ *a.* bearer.
'Inhaber|aktie *f* bearer share. **~scheck** *m* cheque (*Am.* check) to bearer.
inhaftieren [ɪnhaf'tiːrən] *v/t* (h) arrest, take *s.o.* into custody. **Inhaf'tierung** *f* (-; -en) **1.** arrest(ing). **2.** detention.
Inhalation [ɪnhala'tsioːn] *f* (-; -en) inhalation. **Inhalati'onssappa,rat** *m* inhaler. **inhalieren** [-'liːrən] *v/t* (h) inhale.
Inhalt ['ɪnhalt] *m* (-[e]s; -e) **1.** a) contents, b) capacity, volume. **2.** *fig.* a) content(s), subject matter, b) meaning: *des ~s, daß* to the effect that; *wesentlicher ~* essence; *mein Leben hat k-n ~* my life is meaningless (*or* empty).
'inhaltlich *adv* in content.
'Inhaltsangabe *f* summary, synopsis.
'Inhaltserklärung *f* ✝ list of contents.
'inhaltslos *adj* empty, meaningless, lacking in substance. **'inhaltsreich** *adj* rich in substance, full, rich (*life*).
'Inhaltsverzeichnis *n* list (*book:* table) of contents.
'inhuman *adj* inhuman.
Initiale [ini'tsia:lə] *f* (-; -n) initial.
Initiative [initsia'tiːvə] *f* (-; -n) **1.** (*die ~ ergreifen* take the) initiative: *auf s-e ~ hin* on his initiative; *aus eigener ~* on one's own initiative. **2.** action group.
Initiator [ini'tsia:tɔr] *m* (-s; -en [-tsia'to:rən]), **Initia'torin** *f* (-; -nen) initiator.
Injektion [ɪnjɛk'tsioːn] *f* (-; -en) injection, F shot. **Injekti'onsnadel** *f* hypodermic needle. **Injekti'onsspritze** *f* (hypodermic) syringe.
injizieren [ɪnji'tsiːrən] *v/t* (h) inject.
Inkasso [ɪn'kaso] *n* (-s; -s) ✝ collection.
In'kasso... collection (*agency, business, etc*). **~vollmacht** *f* authority to collect.
inklusive [ɪnklu'ziːvə] **I** *prep* (*nom, gen*) including, inclusive of: *~ Verpackung* packing included. **II** *adv* **bis zum 4. Mai ~** up to and including May 4th.
inkognito [ɪn'kɔgnito] *adv* incognito.
In'kognito *n* (-s; -s) incognito.
'inkompetent *adj* incompetent.

in puncto

'inkonsequent *adj* inconsistent.

'Inkonsequenz *f* (-; -en) inconsistency.

In'krafttreten *n* (-s) coming into force: **bei ~** upon taking effect; **Tag des ~s** effective date.

inkriminieren [ɪnkrimi'niːrən] *v/t* (h) incriminate.

Inkubationszeit [ɪnkubaˈtsjoːns-] *f* ✵ incubation period.

Inkubator [ɪnkuˈbaːtɔr] *m* (-s; -en [-baˈtoːrən]) ✵ incubator.

'Inland *n* (-[e]s; *no pl*) **1.** home: **im In- und Ausland** at home and abroad. **2.** inland, interior. **'Inland... → inlän-disch. Inländer** ['ɪnlɛndər] *m* (-s; -), **'Inländerin** *f* (-; -nen) native. **'inlän-disch** *adj* home, domestic, internal.

'Inlands|absatz *m* ✵ domestic sales. **~flug** *m* domestic (*or* internal) flight. **~markt** *m* home (*or* domestic) market. **~post** *f* (*Am.* domestic) mail.

Inlett ['ɪnlɛt] *n* (-[e]s; -e) ticking.

in'mitten *prep* (*gen*) in the middle of.

innehaben ['ɪnə-] *v/t* (*irr, sep,* -ge-, h, → **haben**) hold.

'innehalten *v/i* (*irr, sep,* -ge-, h, → **hal-ten**) stop, pause.

innen ['ɪnən] *adv* inside, *a.* indoors: **~ und außen** inside and out(side); **nach ~ (zu)** inwards; **von ~** from (the) inside.

'Innen|ansicht *f* interior view. **~archi-tekt(in** *f*) *m* interior designer. **~archi-tek,tur** *f* interior design. **~aufnahme** *f* *phot.* indoor (*film:* studio) shot. **~aus-stattung** *f* a) interior decoration, b) décor, furnishings, *mot.* trim. **~bahn** *f* *sports:* inside lane. **~dienst** *m* office work: **im ~ tätig sein** work in the office. **~durchmesser** *m* inside diameter. **~einrichtung** *f* interior decoration. **~hof** *m* (inner) courtyard. **~leben** *n* (-s; *no pl*) inner life. **~leuchte** *f* *mot.* interior light. **~mi,nister** *m* minister of the interior, *Br.* Home Secretary, *Am.* Secretary of the Interior. **~mini,sterium** *n* ministry of the interior, *Br.* Home Office, *Am.* Department of the Interior. **~poli,tik** *f* domestic politics (*or* policy), home affairs. **2po,litisch** *adj* domestic, internal: **~ (gesehen)** concerning domestic policy. **~raum** *m* interior. **~sei-te** *f* inside. **~spiegel** *m* *mot.* inside mir-ror. **~stadt** *f* inner city, (town) cent/re (*Am.* -er), *Am. a.* downtown: **in der ~**

von Chicago in downtown Chicago. **~tasche** *f* inside pocket. **~tempera,tur** *f* internal (*or* indoor) temperature. **~wand** *f* inside wall.

inner ['ɪnər] *adj* a) inside, ✞, *pol.* domes-tic, *a.* ✵ internal, b) *fig.* inner, mental: **~er Halt** moral backbone; **~e Ruhe** peace of mind; **ein ~er Widerspruch** an inconsistency.

'innerbetrieblich *adj* ✞ internal.

'innerdeutsch *adj* **1.** German, (Ger-man) domestic, internal. **2.** *hist.* Ger-man-German (*relations, traffic, etc*).

Innere ['ɪnərə] *n* (-n; *no pl*) **1.** interior (*a. geogr.*), inside, heart, cent/re (*Am.* -er): **im ~n** inside, *geogr.* in the interior. **2.** *fig.* heart, soul, mind, core: **in ihrem tiefsten ~n** deep down; → *a.* **Innere.**

Innereien [ɪnəˈraɪən] *pl* innards, guts.

'innerhalb I *prep* (*gen*) **1.** inside, within: **~ der Familie** within the family. **2.** a) in, within, b) during: **~ der Arbeitszeit** during working hours; **~ weniger Tage** within a few days. **II** *adv* **~ von** within.

'innerlich I *adj* **1.** inner, *a.* ✵ internal. **2.** *fig.* a) inward(-looking), b) emotional, c) thoughtful. **II** *adv* **3.** internally: **~ (anzuwenden)** *pharm.* for internal use (only). **4.** *fig.* inwardly, *a.* secretly.

'Innerlichkeit *f* (-; *no pl*) a) inwardness, b) sensitivity, depth of feeling.

'innerpar,teilich *adj* inner-party ..., in-ternal.

innerst ['ɪnərst] *adj* innermost, inmost.

'innerstaatlich *adj* internal.

'innerstädtisch *adj* urban.

'Innerste *n* (-n; *no pl*) the innermost part, *a.* heart, midst.

'innewohnen *v/i* (*sep,* -ge-, h) be inher-ent (*dat* in).

innig ['ɪnɪç] *adj* a) tender, b) ardent, fer-vent, *a.* devout, c) heartfelt, sincere, d) close, intimate: **j-n ~ lieben** love s.o. dearly, be devoted to s.o.

'Innigkeit *f* (-; *no pl*) a) tenderness, b) ardo(u)r, c) sincerity.

Innovation [ɪnovaˈtsjoːn] *f* (-; -en) inno-vation. **innovati'onsfreudig, innova-tiv** [ɪnovaˈtiːf] *adj* innovative.

Innung ['ɪnʊŋ] *f* (-; -en) guild.

'inoffi,zi,ell *adj* **1.** unofficial. **2.** informal.

in petto [ɪn ˈpɛto] *adv* **et. ~ haben** have s.th. up one's sleeve.

in puncto [ɪn ˈpʊŋkto] *prep* as regards.

Insasse ['ɪnzasə] m (-n; -n), 'I**nsassin** f (-; -nen) **1.** passenger. **2.** inmate.

'I**nsassenversicherung** f mot. passenger insurance (cover).

'I**nschrift** f (-; -en) inscription.

Insekt [ɪn'zɛkt] n (-[e]s; -en) insect, bug. I**n'sekten|bekämpfungsmittel** n insecticide. **~fresser** m zo. insectivore. **~kunde** f (-; no pl) entomology. **~stich** m insect bite.

Insektizid [ɪnzɛkti'tsi:t] n (-s; -e) insecticide.

Insel ['ɪnzəl] f island (a. fig.), poet. or before proper names: isle: **die ~ Wight** the Isle of Wight; **die Britischen ~n** the British Isles. **~bewohner** m islander. **~gruppe** f archipelago. **~staat** m island state. **~volk** n islanders. **~welt** f islands.

Inserat [ɪnze'ra:t] n (-[e]s; -e) advertisement, F ad. **Inserent** [ɪnze'rɛnt] m (-en; -en), **Inse'rentin** [ɪnze'rɛntin] f (-; -nen) advertiser. **inserieren** [ɪnze'ri:rən] (h) **I** v/t advertise. **II** v/i **~ in** (dat) advertise in, put an advertisement (F ad) into.

insge'heim adv secretly.

insge'samt adv a) altogether, in all, b) as a whole: **~ betragen** total.

in'sofern[1] adv as far as that goes.

inso'fern[2] conj **~ (als)** in so far as.

Insolvenz ['ɪnzɔlvɛnts] f (-; -en) † insolvency.

Inspekteur [ɪnspɛk'tø:r] m (-s; -e) inspector. **Inspektion** [ɪnspɛk'tsĭo:n] f (-; -en) **1.** inspection. **2.** (**das Auto zur ~ bringen** put the car in for a) service. **Inspektor** [ɪn'spɛktɔr] m (-s; -en [-'to:rən]), **Inspektorin** [ɪnspɛk'to:rɪn] f (-; -nen) inspector.

Inspiration [ɪnspira'tsĭo:n] f (-; -en) inspiration. **inspirieren** [ɪnspi'ri:rən] v/t (h) **j-n zu et. ~** inspire s.o. to (do) s.th.; **sich ~ lassen** be inspired (**von** by).

Inspizient [ɪnspi'tsĭɛnt] m (-en; -en) thea. etc stage manager. **inspizieren** [ɪnspi'tsi:rən] v/t (h) inspect, examine.

Installateur [ɪnstala'tø:r] m (-s; -e) **1.** plumber. **2.** electrician. **3.** gas fitter. **Installation** [ɪnstala'tsĭo:n] f (-; -en) installation. **installieren** [ɪnsta'li:rən] (h) **I** v/t install. **II sich ~** install o.s.

instand [ɪn'ʃtant] adv **~ halten** keep s.th. in good condition, maintain, service; **~ setzen** a) repair, b) renovate. **In'standhaltung** f (-; -en) maintenance.

'i**nständig** adj urgent: **j-n ~ um et. bitten** implore s.o. for s.th.

In'standsetzung f (-; -en) a) repair, b) renovation. **In'standsetzungsarbeit** f repair work, repairs.

Instanz [ɪn'stants] f (-; -en) authority, ⟪⟫ instance: **höhere ~en** higher authorities (⟪⟫ courts); **in erster ~** ⟪⟫ at first instance; **Gericht erster ~** court of first instance; **in letzter ~** a. fig. in the last instance. **In'stanzenweg** m ⟪⟫ (successive) stages of appeal; **auf dem ~** through the prescribed channels.

Instinkt [ɪn'stɪŋkt] m (-[e]s; -e) instinct, w.s. feeling: **aus ~** from (or by) instinct, instinctively. **instinktiv** [ɪnstɪŋk'ti:f] adj instinctive. **in'stinktlos** adj fig. showing a sad lack of flair.

Institut [ɪnsti'tu:t] n (-s; -e) institute. **Institution** [ɪnstitu'tsĭo:n] f (-; -en) a. fig. institution. **institutionalisieren** [ɪnstitutsĭonali'zi:rən] v/t (h) institutionalize. **institutionell** [ɪnstitutsĭo'nɛl] adj institutional.

instruieren [ɪnstru'i:rən] v/t (h) a) give s.o. instructions, a. ⚔ brief, b) inform. **Instruktion** [ɪnstrʊk'tsĭo:n] f (-; -en) instruction.

instruktiv [ɪnstrʊk'ti:f] adj instructive. **Instrument** [ɪnstru'mɛnt] n (-[e]s; -e) instrument.

Instrumentalmu‚sik [ɪnstrumen'ta:l-] f instrumental music.

Instrumentarium [ɪnstrumen'ta:rĭʊm] n (-s; -rien) instruments.

Instru'menten|bau m (-[e]s; no pl) ♪ instrument making. **~brett** n instrument panel, mot. a. dashboard. **~flug** m instrument flying.

instrumentieren [ɪnstrumen'ti:rən] v/t (h) ♪ orchestrate.

Insuffizienz ['ɪnzʊfitsĭɛnts] f (-; -en) a. ✻ insufficiency.

Insulaner [ɪnzu'la:nər] m (-s; -) islander.

Insulin [ɪnzu'li:n] n (-s; no pl) insulin.

inszenieren [ɪntse'ni:rən] v/t (h) thea. a) stage (a. fig.), a. film, TV produce, b) direct. **Insze'nierung** f (-; -en) production: **in der ~ von X** produced by X.

intakt [ɪn'takt] adj intact.

Intarsien [ɪn'tarzĭən] pl inlaid work.

integer [ɪn'te:gər] adj man of integrity.

integral [ɪnte'gra:l] adj integral.

Inte'gral n (-s; -e) & integral.

Inte'gralrechnung f integral calculus.

Integration [ɪntegraˈtsɪoːn] f (-; -en) integration. **integrieren** [ɪnteˈɡriːrən] v/t (h) (a. **sich ~**) integrate (**in** acc into, within). **inteˈgriert** adj integrated.

Integrität [ɪnteɡriˈtɛːt] f (-; no pl) integrity.

Intellekt [ɪnteˈlɛkt] m (-[e]s; no pl) intellect. **intellektuell** [ɪntɛlɛkˈtŭɛl] adj, **Intellektuˈelle** m, f (-n; -n) intellectual, F highbrow.

intelligent [ɪnteliˈɡɛnt] adj intelligent.

Intelligenz [ɪnteliˈɡɛnts] f (-; no pl) **1.** intelligence. **2.** intelligentsia.

Intelligenzˌquotient m intelligence quotient, I.Q. **~test** m intelligence test.

Intendant [ɪntɛnˈdant] m (-en; -en) thea. etc director.

Intensität [ɪntɛnziˈtɛːt] f (-; no pl) intensity. **intensiv** [ɪntɛnˈziːf] adj **1.** intensive. **2.** intense, strong. **intensivieren** [ɪntɛnziviˈrən] v/t (h) intensify. **Intensiˈvierung** f (-; no pl) intensification. **Intenˈsivkurs** m crash course.

Intenˈsivstatiˌon f ⚕ intensive-care unit: **auf der ~ liegen** be in intensive care.

Intercity-Zug [ɪntərˈsɪti-] m inter-city train.

interessant [ɪntərɛˈsant] adj interesting.

Interesse [ɪntəˈrɛsə] n (-s; -n) interest (**an** dat, **für** in): **~ haben an** (or **für**) → **interessieren** II; **~ zeigen** show an interest (**an** dat, **für** in): **im öffentlichen ~** in the public interest; **ich tat es in d-m ~** I did it for your sake; **es liegt in d-m eigenen ~** it's in your own interest; **j-s ~n vertreten** (or **wahrnehmen**) look after (or represent) s.o.'s interests; **es besteht kein ~ an** (dat) nobody is interested in, ✝ there is no demand for.

interˈessehalber [-halbər] adv out of interest. **interˈesselos** adj uninterested, indifferent. **Interˈesselosigkeit** f (-; no pl) indifference.

Interˈessenˌgebiet n field (or area) of interest. **~gemeinschaft** f community of interests, ✝ combine, pool. **~kollisiˌon** f clash of interests. **~sphäre** f sphere of influence.

Interessent [ɪntərɛˈsɛnt] m (-en; -en) person interested, interested party, ✝ prospective buyer: **~en werden gebeten** those interested are requested.

interessieren [ɪntərɛˈsiːrən] (h) **I** v/t in-

terest (**für** in): **das Buch interessiert mich nicht** the book doesn't interest me, I'm not interested in the book; **das interessiert mich (überhaupt) nicht!** a) I'm not (a bit) interested!, b) I couldn't care less!; **es wird dich ~ (zu hören), daß** you'll be interested to know that; **wen interessiert das schon?** who cares? **II sich ~ für** be interested in, take (or show) an interest in. **III** v/i be of interest: **das interessiert hier nicht!** that's irrelevant!

interesˈsiert I adj interested (**an** dat in). **II** adv with interest, interestedly.

Interimsreˌgierung ['ɪntərɪms-] f interim government.

interkonfessioˈnell [ɪntərkɔnfɛsɪoˈnɛl] adj interdenominational.

Interkontinentalflug [ɪntərkɔntinɛnˈtaːl-] m intercontinental flight.

Interkontinenˈtalraˌkete f intercontinental ballistic missile.

Intermezzo [ɪntərˈmɛtso] n (-s; -s or -zi) ♪ intermezzo, interlude (a. fig.).

intern [ɪnˈtɛrn] adj internal.

Internat [ɪntərˈnaːt] n (-[e]s; -e) boarding school.

international [ɪntərnatsɪoˈnaːl] adj international. **internationalisieren** [-naliˈziːrən] v/t (h) internationalize.

Interˈnatsschüler(in f) m boarder.

internieren [ɪntərˈniːrən] v/t (h) intern. **Interˈnierte** m, f (-n; -n) internee. **Interˈnierung** f (-; -en) internment. **Interˈnierungslager** n internment camp.

Internist [ɪntərˈnɪst] m (-en; -en), **Interˈnistin** f (-; -nen) ⚕ internist.

interparlamenˈtarisch adj interparliamentary.

Interpret [ɪntərˈpreːt] m (-en; -en), **Interˈpretin** f (-; -nen) interpreter, ♪ a. performer, singer. **Interpretation** [ɪntərpretaˈtsɪoːn] f (-; -en) interpretation. **interpretieren** [ɪntərpreˈtiːrən] v/t (h) interpret, a. read, ⚖ construe.

Interpunktion [ɪntərpʊŋkˈtsɪoːn] f (-; no pl) punctuation. **Interpunktiˈonszeichen** n punctuation mark.

Interrogativ... [ɪntəroɡaˈtiːf] interrogative (pronoun, sentence, etc).

Intervall [ɪntərˈval] n (-s; -e) interval. **~training** n sports: interval training.

intervenieren [ɪntərveˈniːrən] v/i (h) intervene. **Intervention** [ɪntərvɛnˈtsi̯oːn] f (-; -en) intervention.

Interview [ɪntərˈvju:] n (-s; -s) interview.

interviewen [-ˈvjuːən] v/t (h) interview.

Inter'viewer m (-s; -) interviewer.

intim [ɪnˈtiːm] adj intimate, a. cosy (*room etc*): **mit j-m ⁓e Beziehungen haben** (*or ⁓ sein*) have intimate relations with s.o.; **ein ⁓er Kenner sein von** (*or gen*) have an intimate knowledge of.

In'tim|bereich m 1. *anat.* genitals. 2. → **Intimsphäre. ⁓feind** m archenemy.

Intimität [ɪntimiˈtɛːt] f (-; -en) intimacy: **es kam zu ⁓en zwischen ihnen** they became intimate.

In'timsphäre f (-; *no pl*) (**in j-s ⁓ eindringen** violate s.o.'s) privacy.

In'timspray m vaginal spray.

'intolerant adj intolerant.

'Intoleranz f intolerance.

Intonation [ɪntonaˈtsi̯oːn] f (-; -en) *ling.*, ♪ intonation.

intonieren [ɪntoˈniːrən] v/t (h) intonate.

'intransitiv adj *ling.* intransitive.

intrave'nös [ɪntra-] adj 💉 intravenous.

Intrigant [ɪntriˈgant] m (-en; -en), **Intri'gantin** f (-; -nen) schemer.

Intrige [ɪnˈtriːgə] f (-; -n) plot, intrigue, scheme. **intrigieren** [ɪntriˈgiːrən] v/i (h) (plot and) scheme.

introvertiert [ɪntrovɛrˈtiːrt] adj introverted: **⁓er Mensch** introvert.

intuitiv [ɪntuiˈtiːf] adj intuitive.

Intuition [ɪntuiˈtsi̯oːn] f (-; -en) intuition.

Invalide [ɪnvaˈliːdə] m (-n; -n) invalid.

Inva'lidenversicherung f disability insurance.

Invalidität [ɪnvalidiˈtɛːt] f (-; *no pl*) disablement, disability.

Invasion [ɪnvaˈzi̯oːn] f (-; -en) invasion.

Inventar [ɪnvɛnˈtaːr] n (-s; -e) a) inventory, b) stock: **festes ⁓** fixture(s); **totes ⁓** dead stock; **lebendes ⁓** livestock; **ein ⁓ aufnehmen** → **inventarisieren** [ɪnvɛntariˈziːrən] (h) **I** v/i take inventory (*or* stock). **II** v/t take an inventory of.

Inventur [ɪnvɛnˈtuːr] f (-; -en) inventory, stocktaking: **⁓ machen** take inventory (*or* stock).

Inversion [ɪnvɛrˈzi̯oːn] f (-; -en) inversion.

investieren [ɪnvɛsˈtiːrən] v/t, v/i (h) invest (**in** *acc or dat* in).

Inve'stierung f (-; -en) investment.

Investition [ɪnvɛstiˈtsi̯oːn] f (-; -en) 1. investment. 2. capital expenditure.

Investiti'ons... investment (*bank, loan, etc*). **⁓anreiz** m investment incentive. **⁓güter** pl capital goods. **⁓pro,gramm** n capital expenditure program(me *Br.*).

In'vestment|fonds m investment fund. **⁓gesellschaft** f investment company.

Investor [ɪnˈvɛstər] m (-s; -en [-ˈtoːrən]) † investor.

'inwendig adj inwardly: F **in- und auswendig kennen** know *s.th.* inside out.

inwie'fern conj in what way, how.

inwie'weit conj to what extent.

In'zahlungnahme [-naːmə] f (-; *no pl*) part exchange, trade-in.

Inzest [ɪnˈtsɛst] m (-[e]s; -e) incest.

inzestuös [ɪntsɛstuˈøːs] adj incestuous.

'Inzucht f (-; *no pl*) intermarriage, a. *zo.* inbreeding.

in'zwischen adv meanwhile.

Ion [iˈoːn] n (-s; -en) *phys.* ion.

ionisieren [ioniˈziːrən] v/t (h) ionize.

Iono'sphäre [iono-] f (-; *no pl*) ionosphere.

'I-Punkt m dot over the i: **bis auf den ⁓** *fig.* down to the last detail.

Irak [iˈraːk] m (-s) Iraq, Irak. **I'raker** m (-s; -), **I'rakerin** f (-; -nen), **i'rakisch** adj Iraqi, Iraki.

Iran [iˈraːn] m (-s) Iran. **I'raner** m (-s; -), **I'ranerin** f (-; -nen), **i'ranisch** adj Iranian.

irdisch [ˈɪrdɪʃ] adj a) earthly, b) worldly, c) mortal.

Ire [ˈiːrə] m (-n; -n) Irishman: **die ⁓n** the Irish.

irgend [ˈɪrgənt] adv 1. **⁓ jemand** someone, anyone, somebody, anybody. 2. **⁓ etwas** something, anything; **wir müssen ⁓ etwas tun** we've got to do something; F **⁓ so ein ...** some sort of ... 3. **wann (wo) es ⁓ geht** whenever (wherever) it might be possible; **wenn ich ⁓ kann** if I possibly can; **so rasch wie ⁓ möglich** as soon as at all possible.

'irgend'ein indef pron some, any: **auf ⁓e Weise** somehow; **besteht noch ⁓e Hoffnung?** is there any hope at all?

'irgend'einer → **irgend** 1.

'irgend'wann adv 1. some time (or other). 2. any time.

'irgend'was F → **irgend** 2.

'irgend'welche *indef pron* any: **ohne ~ Kosten** without any expense at all.
'irgend'wie *adv* somehow, some way (or other).
'irgend'wo *adv* somewhere, anywhere: **~ anders** somewhere else. **~wo'her** *adv* from somewhere, from anywhere. **~wo'hin** *adv* somewhere, anywhere.
Irin ['i:rɪn] *f* (-; -nen) Irishwoman: **sie ist ~** she is Irish.
Iris ['i:rɪs] *f* (-; -) *anat.*, ♀ iris.
irisch ['i:rɪʃ] *adj* Irish: **Qe Republik** Irish Republic, Eire. **'Irisch** *n ling.* Irish.
Irland ['ɪrlant] *n* (-s) Ireland.
Irländer ['ɪrlɛndɐ] *m* (-s; -) Irishman.
'Irländerin *f* (-; -nen) Irishwoman.
Ironie [iro'ni:] *f* (-; -n) irony.
ironisch [i'ro:nɪʃ] *adj* ironic.
ironisieren [ironi'zi:rən] *v/t* (h) *et.* **~** treat s.th. with irony.
irrational ['ɪratsĭona:l] *adj* irrational.
irre ['ɪrə] **I** *adj* **1.** mad, insane, crazy: **~s Zeug reden** be raving. **2.** F *fig.* mind-blowing, crazy, mad: **~ (gut)** fantastic, super, wild; **ein ~r Typ** a super guy; **es war e-e ~e Hitze** it was awfully hot; **wie ~** *work etc* like crazy. **II** *adv* **3.** F a) awfully (*big*, *hot*, *etc*), b) *work etc* like crazy: **~ viel(e)** an awful lot of.
'Irre¹ *m, f* (-n; -n) madman (madwoman), lunatic, F *fig.* nutcase: F **wie ein ~r** *work*, *drive*, *etc* like crazy.
'Irre² *f* j-n *in die* **~** *führen* → **irreführen**.
'irreal *adj* **1.** unreal. **2.** unrealistic.
irreführen *v/t* (*sep*, *-ge-*, *h*) *fig.* mislead, a. deceive: **sich ~ lassen** be deceived (**von** by). **'irreführend** *adj* misleading.
'irregeleitet *adj fig.* misguided.
'irregulär *adj* irregular.
'irrelevant *adj* irrelevant.
irren ['ɪrən] **I** *sich ~* (h) **1.** (*in dat* about *s.o.*, *in s.th.*) be wrong, be mistaken; **ich habe mich im Datum geirrt** I got the date wrong; **er hat sich in der Tür geirrt** he went to the wrong door; **ich kann mich (auch) ~** (of course,) I may be wrong; **da irrst du dich aber (gewaltig)!** you're very much mistaken there!; **wenn ich mich nicht irre** if I'm not mistaken. **II** *v/i* **2.** (sn) *a. fig.* wander, err, stray. **3.** (h) be wrong, be mistaken: **Irren ist menschlich** we all make mistakes.
'Irrenanstalt *m* mental home.

'Irrenhaus *n* F *fig.* madhouse.
'irreparabel *adj* irreparable.
'Irrfahrt *f* odyssey. **'Irrgarten** *m* mace, labyrinth. **'Irrglaube** *m* **1.** heresy. **2.** erroneous belief.
'irrig(er'weise) *adv) adj* wrong(ly).
irritieren [ɪri'ti:rən] *v/t* (h) irritate, a. annoy, a. confuse.
'Irrläufer *m* stray letter *etc*.
'Irrlehre *f* false doctrine, heresy.
'Irrlicht *n* (-[e]s, -er) will-o'-the-wisp.
'Irrsinn *m* (-[e]s; *no pl*) *a. fig.* madness.
irrsinnig ['ɪrzɪnɪç] → **irre. Irrsinnige** ['ɪrzɪnɪgə] *m, f* (-[n; -n) → **Irre¹**.
'Irrtum *m* (-s; ~er) a) mistake, error (a. 🖉⁄ᴢ), b) misunderstanding: **im ~ sein** be mistaken, be wrong; **da muß ein ~ vorliegen!** there must be some mistake!; **da ~! you're wrong there!
irrtümlich ['ɪrty:mlɪç] *adj* wrong(ly *adv*).
'irrtümlicher'weise *adv* by mistake.
Ischias ['ɪʃĭas] *n, m, ♣ f* (-; *no pl*) sciatica.
'Ischiasnerv *m* sciatic nerve.
Islam [ɪs'la:m; 'ɪslam] *m* (-s; *no pl*) Islam.
islamisch [ɪs'la:mɪʃ] *adj* Islamic.
Island ['i:slant] *n* (-s) Iceland. **Isländer** ['i:slɛndɐ] *m* (-s; -), **'Isländerin** *f* (-; -nen) Icelander. **'isländisch** [-dɪʃ] *adj* Icelandic.
Isobare [izo'ba:rə] *f* (-; -n) isobar.
Isolation [izola'tsĭo:n] *f* (-; -en) **1.** isolation. **2.** ⚡, ⚙ insulation.
Iso'lierband *n* (-[e]s; ~er) insulating tape.
isolieren [izo'li:rən] (h) **I** *v/t* **1.** isolate. **2.** ⚡, ⚙ insulate (**gegen** against). **II** *sich ~* isolate o.s., cut o.s. off.
Iso'lier|materi,al *n* insulating material, insulant. **~schicht** *f* insulating layer. **~stati,on** *f* ⚚ isolation ward.
Iso'lierung *f* (-; -en) **1.** isolation. **2.** ⚡, ⚙ insulation.
Isotop [izo'to:p] *n* (-s; -e) isotope.
Israel ['ɪsraɛl] *n* (-s) Israel. **Israeli** [ɪsra'e:li] *m* (-[s]; -[s]), *f* (-; -[s]) Israeli. **isra'elisch** [-lɪʃ] *adj* Israeli.
Israelit [ɪsrae'li:t] *m* (-en; -en), **Israeli'tin** *f* (-; -nen), **israe'litisch** *adj* Israelite.
'Ist-Bestand *m* ♣ a) actual amount , b) actual stock.
Italien [i'ta:lĭən] *n* (-s) Italy. **Italiener** [ita'lĭe:nɐr] *m* (-s; -), **Itali'enerin** *f* (-; -nen) Italian. **itali'enisch** *adj* Italian. **Itali'enisch** *n ling.* Italian.

J

J, j [jɔt] *n* (-; -) J, j.

ja [ja] *adv* **1.** yes, *parl*. aye, *Am*. yea, *at wedding*: I do; **~?** a) really?, b) right?, c) *teleph*. hello; *nun ~* well (yes); **~ doch!, aber ~!** yes, of course!, sure!; **~ sagen (zu** to) say yes, *fig. a.* agree; **ich glaube ~!** I think so! **2.** after all: **du kennst ihn ~** you know what he's like. **3. da bist du ~!** there you are!; **ich hab's dir ~ gesagt** didn't I tell you?; **das ist ~ schrecklich!** but that's just terrible!; **es regnet ~!** oh dear, it's raining! **4. sei ~ vorsichtig!** do be careful!; **bring es ~ mit!** make sure you bring it!; **sag's ihm ~ nicht!** don't tell him! **5. ~, weißt (or wußtest) du denn (das) nicht?** do you mean to say you didn't know? **6. ich würde es ~ gern tun, aber ...** I'd really like to do it, but ...

Ja *n* (-[s]; -[s]) yes, *parl*. aye, *Am*. yea: **mit ~ oder Nein antworten** answer yes or no.

Jacht [jaxt] *f* (-; -en) yacht.

'Jachtklub *m* yacht club.

Jacke ['jakə] *f* (-; -n) jacket, coat, *a.* cardigan: F **das ist ~ wie Hose** it's much of a muchness.

'Jackenkleid *n* two-piece dress.

Jacketkrone ['dʒɛkɪt-] *f* jacket crown.

Jackett [ʒa'kɛt] *n* (-s; -s) jacket, coat.

Jade ['ja:də] *m* (-[s]; *no pl*) *min*. jade.

Jagd [ja:kt] *f* (-; -en) **1.** hunt(ing), shoot(ing): **auf (die) ~ gehen** go hunting. **2.** *fig*. (**nach** after) chase (after), pursuit (of): **~ machen auf** (*acc*) chase (after), pursue; **wilde ~ nach** mad rush for.

'Jagd|beute *f* bag. **~bomber** *m* fighter bomber. **~flieger** *m* fighter pilot. **~flugzeug** *n* fighter (plane). **~hund** *m* **1.** hound. **2.** short-haired pointer. **~hütte** *f* (hunting) lodge. **~rennen** *n* steeplechase. **~re,vier** *n* hunting ground. **~schein** *m* hunting licen/ce (*Am*. -se). **~zeit** *f* hunting season.

jagen ['ja:gən] *I v/t (h)* **1.** hunt, shoot. **2.** *fig. a.* chase (after), b) hunt (for): *ein Ereignis jagte das andere* things happened really fast; F **damit kannst du mich ~!** I just hate that! **3.** F *j-m (sich) e-e Kugel durch den Kopf ~* blow s.o.'s

(one's) brains out; **den Ball ins Netz ~** slam the ball home; **et. in die Luft ~** blow s.th. up. **II** *v/i* **4.** (h) go hunting, go shooting, hunt. **5.** (sn) *fig*. race. **6.** (h) **~ nach** *fig*. chase after, hunt for.

'Jagen *n* (-s) hunt(ing), shoot(ing).

Jäger ['jɛ:gər] *m* (-s; -) **1.** huntsman, hunter. **2. →** *Jagdflieger, -flugzeug*.

Jaguar ['ja:gũa:r] *m* (-s; -e) *zo*. jaguar.

jäh [jɛ:] *I adj* **1.** sudden, abrupt: *fig. ein ~es Erwachen* a rude awakening. **2.** steep: *~er Abhang* precipice. **II** *adv* **3.** all of a sudden, abruptly. **4. ~abfallend** precipitous.

Jahr [ja:r] *n* (-[e]s; -e) year: *ein halbes ~* half a year, six months; *das Kind ist zwei ~e (alt)* the child is two (years old); *mit 20 ~en* at the age of twenty; *alle ~e* every year; *~ für ~* year after year; *im ~e 1989* in the year (of) 1989; *in diesem (im nächsten) ~* this (next) year; *heute vor einem ~* a year ago today; *von ~ zu ~* from year to year; *auf ~e hinaus* for years to come; *seit ~en (nicht)* (not) for years; *im Lauf der ~e* through (or over) the years; *in die ~e kommen* be getting on; *in den besten ~en* in the prime of life; → *jünger* 1.

jahr'aus *adv* **~, jahrein** year in, year out.

'Jahrbuch *n* yearbook, almanac.

'jahrelang I *adj* longstanding, lasting for years: *~e Erfahrung* years of experience. **II** *adv* for years.

jähren ['jɛ:rən] *heute jährt sich ...* it's a year today since (or that) ...

'Jahres... annual (*balance sheet, report, ring, etc*), yearly. **~abrechnung** *f*, **~abschluß** *m* **†** annual accounts. **~beginn** *m* (**zum ~** at the) beginning of the year. **~bestleistung** *f sports*: record of the year. **~einkommen** *n* yearly income. **~ende** *n* (**zum ~, am ~** at the) end of the year. **~gehalt** *n* (-[e]s; ~er) annual salary. **~hälfte** *f* **erste (zweite) ~** first (second) half of the year. **~hauptversammlung** *f* annual general meeting. **~tag** *m* anniversary. **~zahl** *f* year. **~zeit** *f* season: *in dieser ~* at this time of year. **2zeitlich** *adj* seasonal.

'Jahrgang *m* **1.** age group, *ped*. year: *sie*

ist ~ 1900 she was born in 1900; *er ist mein ~* we were born in the same year; *die Jahrgänge 1970-80* the 1970-80 age group. **2.** *gastr.* vintage, year. **3.** volume (*of magazine etc*).

Jahr'hundert *n* (-s; -e) century.

jahr'hunderte|alt *adj* centuries old. **~lang** *adv* (*adj* lasting) for centuries.

Jahr'hundert|feier *f* centenary, centennial. **~wende** *f* turn of the century.

...jährig [-jɛːrɪç] *in cpds.* ...-year-old.

jährlich ['jɛːrlɪç] **I** *adj* yearly, annual. **II** *adv* a) yearly, every year, once a year, b) *1000 marks* a year (*or* per annum).

'Jahrmarkt *m* (*auf dem ~* at the) fair.

Jahr'tausend *n* (-s; -e) millennium.

Jahr'tausendfeier *f* millenary.

Jahr'zehnt *n* (-[e]s; -e) decade, ten years.

jahr'zehntelang I *adj* lasting for decades: **~e Forschungsarbeit** decades of research. **II** *adv* for decades.

'Jähzorn *m* (*im ~* in a fit of) violent temper. **'jähzornig** *adj* irascible: *er ist ~ a.* he has a violent temper.

Jalousie [ʒaluˈziː] *f* (-; -n) (Venetian) blind(s).

Jammer ['jamər] *m* (-s; *no pl*) **1.** misery: **F** *es ist ein ~, daß* it's such a shame (*or* too bad) that. **2.** lamentation, wailing.

jämmerlich ['jɛmərlɪç] **I** *adj* **1.** miserable, wretched, pitiful, *fig. contp. a.* deplorable: *mir war ~ zumute* I felt (just) miserable. **2.** heart-rending, piteous. **II** *adv* **3.** miserably (*etc*): *~ weinen* cry piteously; *~* (*schlecht*) *sing etc* terribly; *~ versagen* fail miserably.

jammern ['jamərn] *v/i* (h) moan, wail: *~ nach* cry for; *~ über* (*acc*) a) moan (about), b) complain (of).

'Jammern *n* (-s) moaning, wailing.

'jammerschade *adj* (*es ist*) *~, daß* ... it's such a shame (*or* too bad) that ...

Januar ['janūaːr] *m* (-[s]; -e) (*im ~* in) January.

Japan ['jaːpan] *n* (-s) Japan. **Japaner** [jaˈpaːnər] *m* (-s; -), **Ja'panerin** *f* (-; -nen) Japanese. **ja'panisch** *adj*, **Ja'panisch** *n ling.* Japanese.

Jargon [ʒarˈgõː] *m* (-s; -s) jargon.

'Jasager *m* (-s; -) *contp.* yes-man.

Jasmin [jasˈmiːn] *m* (-s; -e) ♣ jasmin.

'Ja-Stimme *f parl.* aye, *Am.* yea.

Jauche ['jaʊxə] *f* (-; -n) liquid manure.

'Jauchegrube *f* cesspool.

jauchzen ['jaʊxtsən] *v/i* (h) shout for joy.

jaulen ['jaʊlən] *v/i* (h) *a. fig.* howl.

ja'wohl *adv* a) yes, ✕ yes, Sir, b) that's right.

Jazz [dʒɛs] *m* (-; *no pl*) jazz.

'Jazzband *f*, **'Jazzka,pelle** *f* jazz band.

'Jazzmu,sik *f* jazz (music).

'Jazzsänger(in *f*) *m* jazz singer.

je [jeː] **I** *adv* **1.** ever: *ohne ihn ~ gesehen zu haben* without ever having seen him. **2.** → *eh* **2**, *jeher*. **3.** *sie kosten ~ e-n Dollar* they cost a dollar each; *für ~ 10 Personen* for every ten persons; *es gibt sie in Schachteln mit ~ 10 Stück* they come in boxes of ten. **4.** *~ nach* according to; *~ nachdem* it (all) depends (→ 6). **II** *conj* **5.** *~ eher, desto besser* the sooner the better; *~ länger, ~ lieber* the longer the better. **6.** *~ nachdem* according to *what he says*, depending on *how you do it* (→ 4).

Jeansanzug ['dʒiːns-] *m* denim suit.

'Jeansjacke *f* denim jacket.

jede ['jeːdə], **'jeder**, **'jedes** *indef pron* **1.** a) each, b) any, c) either, d) every: *ich hörte ~s (einzelne) Wort* I heard every (single) word; *~s zweite Auto* every other car; *ohne ~n Zweifel* without any doubt; (*zu*) *~r Zeit* any time; *bei ~m Wetter* in any weather. **2.** each (*or* every) one, everyone: *~(r) von ihnen* each (*or* all) of them.

'jeden'falls *adv* **1.** in any case, at any rate, anyway. **2.** be that as it may. **3.** at least.

'jedermann *indef pron* everyone, everybody: *das ist nicht ~s Sache* it's not everyone's cup of tea.

'jeder'zeit *adv* any time, always.

'jedes'mal *adv* a) every time, b) always.

je'doch *adv* however, still.

je'her *adv von ~* always.

jein [jaɪn] *adv* F yes and no.

jemals ['jeːmaːls] *adv* ever.

jemand ['jeːmant] *indef pron* a) somebody, someone, b) anybody, anyone: *es kommt ~* somebody's coming; *ist ~ hier?* is anybody here?; *~ anders* someone (*or* anyone) else; *sonst noch ~?* anyone else?

jene ['jeːnə], **'jener**, **'jenes** *dem pron* **1.** that, *pl* those: *seit ~m Tag* from that day on. **2.** that one, *pl* those.

jenseitig ['jɛ:nzaɪtɪç] *adj* on the other side: *das ~e Ufer* the opposite bank.

jenseits ['jɛ:nzaɪts] **I** *prep* (*gen*) on the other side of, beyond, across. **II** *adv* on the other side: *~ von* beyond. '**Jenseits** *n* (-; *no pl*) the hereafter: F *j-n ins ~ befördern* send s.o. to kingdom come.

Jesus ['je:zʊs] *m* (Jesu; *no pl*) Jesus: *~ Christus* Jesus Christ.

'**Jesuskind** *n the* infant Jesus.

Jet [dʒɛt] *m* (-[s]; -s) ✈ jet. '**Jet-set** *m* (-s; -s) jet set. '**jetten** *v/i* (sn) F jet.

jetzig ['jɛtsɪç] *adj* a) present(-day), current, b) existing.

jetzt [jɛtst] *adv* now, *a.* nowadays: *erst ~* only now; *noch ~* even now; *bis ~* so far, *negative: a.* (as) yet.

Jetzt *n* (-; *no pl*) *the* present (time).

jeweilig ['je:vaɪlɪç] **I** *adj* a) respective, b) prevailing: *der ~e Präsident* the president then in office; *der ~en Mode entsprechend* according to the fashion (at the time). **II** *adv* → *jeweils* 4.

jeweils ['je:vaɪls] *adv* **1.** *~ zwei* two at a time. **2.** always: *sie kommt ~ am Montag* she comes every Monday; *er trainiert ~ zwei Stunden* he does two hours of training a time. **3.** each: *mit ~ 20 Fragen* exercises *etc* with 20 questions each. **4.** in each case.

jiddisch ['jɪdɪʃ] *adj* Yiddish.

'**Jiddisch** *n ling.* Yiddish.

Job [dʒɔp] *m* (-s; -s) F job.

jobben ['dʒɔbən] *v/i* (h) F job.

Joch [jɔx] *n* (-[e]s; -e) yoke.

'**Jochbein** *n anat.* cheekbone.

Jockei, Jockey ['dʒɔke] *m* (-s; -s) jockey.

Jod [jo:t] *n* (-[e]s; *no pl*) 🝆 iodine.

jodeln ['jo:dəln] *v/t, v/i* (h) yodel.

'**jodhaltig** *adj* containing iodine.

jodieren [jo'di:rən] *v/t* (h) **1.** 🝆 iodinate. **2.** ♣, *phot.* iodize.

'**Jodsalbe** *f* iodine ointment. '**Jodsalz** *n* iodized salt. '**Jodta;blette** *f* iodine tablet. '**Jodtink,tur** *f* tincture of iodine.

Joga → *Yoga.*

joggen ['dʒɔgən] *v/i* (h) jog, go jogging.

Jogger ['dʒɔgər] *m* (-s; -), '**Joggerin** *f* (-; -nen) jogger.

Jogging ['dʒɔgɪŋ] *n* (-s) jogging.

Joghurt ['jo:gʊrt] *m, n* (-[s]; *no pl*) yog(h)urt.

Johannisbeere [jo'hanɪs-] *f rote ~* redcurrant; *schwarze ~* blackcurrant.

johlen ['jo:lən] *v/i* (h) bawl, yell.

Jolle ['jɔlə] *f* (-; -n) ⚓ dinghy.

Jongleur [ʒõ'glø:r] *m* (-s; -e) juggler.

jonglieren [ʒõ'gli:rən] *v/t, v/i* (h) *a. fig.* juggle (*mit* [with] *s.th.*).

Jordanien [jɔr'da:niən] *n* (-s) Jordan. **Jor'danier** [-niər] *m* (-s; -), **Jor'danierin** *f* (-; -nen), **jor'danisch** *adj* Jordanian.

Jota ['jo:ta] *n* (-[s]; -s) iota.

Joule [dʒu:l] *n* (-[s]; -) *phys.* joule.

Journalismus [ʒʊrna'lɪsmʊs] *m* (-; *no pl*) journalism. **Journalist** [ʒʊrna'lɪst] *m* (-en; -en), **Journa'listin** *f* (-; -nen) journalist. **journalistisch** [ʒʊrna'lɪstɪʃ] *adj* journalistic.

jovial [jo'vĭa:l] *adj* affable.

Jubel ['ju:bəl] *m* (-s; *no pl*) jubilation, cheers. '**Jubeljahr** *n eccl.* jubilee: F *alle ~e einmal* once in a blue moon.

jubeln ['ju:bəln] *v/i* (h) cheer: (*vor Freude*) *~* shout for joy, rejoice.

Jubilar [jubi'la:r] *m* (-s; -e), **Jubi'larin** *f* (-; -nen) person celebrating his (her) jubilee. **Jubiläum** [jubi'lɛ:ʊm] *n* (-s; -läen) jubilee, anniversary.

Jubi'läumsausgabe *f* jubilee edition.

jucken ['jʊkən] *v/t, v/i, v/impers* (h) itch: *mich juckt's* I'm itching; *sich ~* scratch o.s.; *es juckt mich am Arm, mein Arm juckt* my arm's itchy; *der Pullover juckt* the pullover's scratchy; F *fig. es juckt mich zu inf* I'm itching to *inf*; *das juckt mich nicht!* what do I care.

'**Jucken** *n* (-s) itch, itching.

'**Juckreiz** *m* itch, itching.

Jude ['ju:də] *m* (-n; -n) Jew. '**Judenhaß** *m* anti-Semitism. '**Judentum** *n* (-s; *no pl*) **1.** Judaism. **2.** *the* Jews, Jewry. **3.** Jewishness. '**Judenverfolgung** *f* persecution of (the) Jews. **Jüdin** ['jy:dɪn] *f* (-; -nen) Jewess. '**jüdisch** *adj* Jewish.

Judo ['ju:do] *n* (-[s]; *no pl*) judo.

Judoka [ju'do:ka] *m* (-s; -s) judoka.

Jugend ['ju:gənt] *f* (-; *no pl*) **1.** youth: *von ~ an* from childhood, from a child; *in m-r ~* when I was young. **2.** youth, youthfulness. **3.** youth, young people: *die ~ von heute* the young people of today; *die deutsche ~* the young Germans (of today). **4.** → *Jugendklasse, Jugendmannschaft.*

'**Jugend|amt** *n* youth welfare department. *~arbeitslosigkeit* *f* youth unemployment. **~ar,rest** m 🔒 short-term detention for young offenders. **~buch** n book for young people. ⚥**frei** adj film: U-certificate, Am. G-rated; **nicht ~** for adults only. **~freund(in** f) m friend from one's youth. ⚥**gefährdend** adj harmful to young persons. **~gericht** n juvenile court. **~herberge** f youth hostel. **~klasse** f sports: youth class. **~kriminali,tät** f juvenile delinquency. **~lager** n youth camp.

'**jugendlich** adj youthful (a. clothes, look), young, 🔒 juvenile.

'**Jugendliche** m, f (-n; -n) young person, m a. youth, 🔒 a. juvenile.

'**Jugendlichkeit** f (-; no pl) youthfulness.

'**Jugend|liebe** f a) puppy love, b) old flame. **~mannschaft** f sports: youth team. **~meister(in** f) m sports: youth champion. **~richter(in** f) m judge of a juvenile court. **~schutz** m legal protection for children and young persons. **~stil** m (-s; no pl) Jugendstil, art nouveau. **~strafanstalt** f remand home. **~zeit** f (-; no pl) youth.

Jugoslawe [jugo'slaːvə] m (-n; -n) Yugoslav. **Jugoslawien** [jugo'slaːviən] n (-s) Yugoslavia. **Jugo'slawin** f (-; -nen), **jugo'slawisch** adj Yugoslav.

Juli ['juːli] m (-[s]; -s) (im ~ in) July.

jung [jʊŋ] adj a) young, b) youthful: **ziemlich ~** youngish; **~es Unternehmen** new company; **~er Wein** new wine; **von ~ auf** from childhood; **~ und alt** young and old; **~ heiraten (sterben)** marry (die) young; → **jünger, jüngst** 1, **Gemüse, Hund.**

Junge¹ ['jʊŋə] m (-n; -n) boy: **dummer ~** silly boy; F **schwerer ~** (criminal) heavy; **~, ~!** boy, oh boy!

'**Junge²** n (-n; -n) zo. young (one), a. puppy, a. kitten, a. cub, of elephant, seal etc: calf: **die ~n** the young; **~ werfen (or bekommen)** → **jungen** ['jʊŋən] v/i (h) zo. have young (or puppies or kittens).

'**jungenhaft** adj boyish.

jünger ['jʏŋər] adj **1.** younger: **sie sieht ~ aus als sie ist** she doesn't look her age; **das macht sie um Jahre ~** that takes years off her age. **2.** more recent, later: **ein Foto ~en Datums** a more recent photograph.

'**Jünger** m (-s; -) disciple, fig. a. follower.

Jungfer ['jʊŋfər] f (-; -n) **alte ~** old maid.

'**Jungfern|fahrt** f maiden voyage. **~flug** m maiden flight. **~häutchen** n anat. hymen. **~rede** f maiden speech.

'**Jungfrau** f **1.** virgin: **die Heilige ~, die ~ Maria** the Holy Virgin, the Virgin Mary. **2.** astr. (**er ist ~** he is [a]) Virgo.

jungfräulich ['jʊŋfrɔʏlɪç] adj virginal, fig. virgin.

'**Jungfräulichkeit** f (-; no pl) virginity.

'**Junggeselle** m (-n; -n) bachelor.

'**Junggesellin** f (-; -nen) bachelor girl.

Jüngling ['jʏŋlɪŋ] m (-s; -e) youth.

jüngst [jʏŋst] adj **1.** youngest. **2.** latest (events etc): **der Jüngste Tag** the Day of Judg(e)ment; **der ~en Vergangenheit** of the recent past.

'**Jüngste** m, f, n (-n; -n) the youngest: **unser ~r, unsere ~** our youngest (child); **sie ist auch nicht mehr die ~** she is no spring chicken any more.

'**Jungsteinzeit** f (-; no pl) Neolithic age.

'**jungverheiratet** adj newly-wed.

'**Jungvieh** n young stock.

Juni ['juːni] m (-[s]; -s) (im ~ in) June.

junior ['juːniɔr] adj **1. Herr X ~** (abbr. jun., jr.) Mr. X, Junior (abbr. jr.).

'**Junior** m (-s; -en [juˈnioːrən]) **1.** F and sports: junior. **2.** ✝ a) son of the owner, b) a. '**Juniorchef** m junior partner.

Juni'oren... sports: junior (team etc).

Junktim ['jʊŋktɪm] n (-s; -s) pol. package deal.

Junta ['xʊnta] f (-; -ten) pol. junta.

Jura¹ ['juːra] m (-; no pl) geol. Jurassic (period).

Jura²: ~ studieren study (Br. a. read) law. '**Jurastu,dent(in** f) m law student. '**Jurastudium** n law studies.

Jurist [juˈrɪst] m (-en; -en) **1.** lawyer. **2.** law student. **Ju'ristensprache** f legalese. **Ju'ristin** f (-; -nen) → **Jurist.**

ju'ristisch adj legal: **~e Fakultät** faculty of law. Am. a. law school; **~e Person** legal entity, juristic person.

Jury [ʒyˈriː] f (-; -s) **1.** a) jury, (panel of) judges, b) selection committee. **2.** 🔒 jury.

ju'stierbar adj adjustable.

justieren [jʊsˈtiːrən] v/t (h) adjust. **Ju'stierung** f (-; -en) adjustment.

Justitiar [jʊstiˈtsiaːr] m (-s; -e), **Justiti'arin** f (-; -nen) legal adviser.

Justiz [jʊsˈtiːts] f (-; no pl) justice, the

law. **~beamte** *m*, **~beamtin** *f* judicial officer. **~behörde** *f* judicial authority. **~gewalt** *f* judiciary (power). **~irrtum** *m* judicial error, miscarriage of justice. **~mi,nister** *m* minister of justice, *Br.* Lord Chancellor, *Am.* Attorney General. **~mini,sterium** *n* ministry of justice, *Am.* Department of Justice. **~mord** *m* judicial murder. **~verwal-**

tung *f* a) administration of justice, b) legal administrative body.
Jute ['ju:tə] *f* (-; *no pl*) jute.
Juwel [ju've:l] *n* (-s; -en) *a. fig.* jewel: **~en** jewel(le)ry, precious stones.
Juwelier [juvə'li:r] *m* (-s; -e) jewel(l)er.
Juwe'liergeschäft *n* jewel(l)er's shop.
Jux [jʊks] *m* (-es; -e) F (practical) joke.

K

K, k [ka:] *n* (-; -) K, k.
Kabarett [kaba'rɛt] *n* (-s; -s, -e) cabaret (show), (satirical) revue.
Kabarettist [kabarɛ'tɪst] *m* (-en; -en), **Kabaret'tistin** *f* (-; -nen) cabaret artist.
kabbelig ['kabəlɪç] *adj* choppy (*sea*).
Kabel ['ka:bəl] *n* (-s; -) cable. **'Kabelfernsehen** *n* cable television (*or* TV).
Kabeljau ['ka:bəljaʊ] *m* (-s; -e, -s) cod(fish).
Kabine [ka'bi:nə] *f* (-; -n) **1.** ✈, ⚓ cabin. **2.** a) cage (*of lift*), b) cable car. **3.** cubicle, *sports:* a. locker room.
Kabinett [kabi'nɛt] *n* (-s; -e) *pol.* cabinet. **Kabi'netts|beschluß** *m* decision of the cabinet. **~bildung** *f* formation of a (*or* the) cabinet. **~krise** *f* cabinet crisis. **~liste** *f* list of cabinet members. **~sitzung** *f* cabinet meeting. **~umbildung** *f* cabinet reshuffle.
Kabrio ['ka:brio] *n* (-s; -s), **Kabriolett** [ka:brio'lɛt] *n* (-s; -s) *mot.* convertible.
Kachel ['kaxəl] *f* (-; -n) tile. **'kacheln** *v/t* (h) tile. **'Kachelofen** *m* tiled stove.
Kacke ['kakə] *f* (-; *no pl*), **'kacken** *v/t*, *v/i* (h) V crap, shit. **'Kacker** *m* (-s; -) V shit.
Kadaver [ka'da:vər] *m* (-s; -) carcass. **~gehorsam** *m contp.* blind obedience.
Kadenz [ka'dɛnts] *f* (-; -en) ♩ cadence, cadenza.
Kader ['ka:dər] *m* (-s; -) ⚔, *pol.* cadre, *sports:* a. pool.
Kadett [ka'dɛt] *m* (-en; -en) ⚓, ⚔ cadet.
Kadi ['ka:di] *m* (-s; -s) F (*j-n vor den ~ schleppen* haul s.o. before the) judge.
Kadmium *n* (-s; *no pl*) ⚗ cadmium.

Käfer ['kɛ:fər] *m* (-s; -) **1.** *zo.* beetle (*a. mot.* F *VW*). **2.** F *fig.* chick, girlie.
Kaff [kaf] (-s; -s, -e) *n* F *contp.* dump, awful hole.
Kaffee ['kafe, ka'fe:] *m* (-s; -s) coffee: **~ kochen** (*or machen*) make coffee; **zwei ~, bitte!** two coffees, please!; **~ mit Milch** white coffee; F *fig.* **das ist doch kalter ~!** that's old hat!
'Kaffee|auto,mat *m* coffee machine. **~bohne** *f* coffee (bean). **~haus** *n* café, coffee house. **~kanne** *f* coffee pot. **~klatsch** *m* F coffee (*or* hen) party, *Am.* coffee klatsch. **~löffel** *m* coffee spoon. **~ma,schine** *f* coffeemaker, percolator, coffee urn. **~mühle** *f* coffee grinder. **~pause** *f* coffee break. **~satz** *m* coffee grounds. **~ser,vice** *n* coffee set. **~strauch** *m* coffee shrub. **~tasse** *f* coffee cup. **~weißer** *m* coffee whitener (*Am.* creamer).
Käfig ['kɛ:fɪç] *m* (-s; -e) cage.
kahl [ka:l] *adj* **1.** (**~ werden** go *or* grow) bald. **2.** *fig.* bare, a. leafless (*tree*), a. barren, bleak (*region etc*).
'kahlgeschoren *adj* shaven.
'Kahlheit *f* (-; *no pl*) **1.** baldness. **2.** *fig.* bareness (*etc*, → *kahl* 2).
'Kahlkopf *m* F baldhead(ed person).
'kahlköpfig [-kœpfɪç] *adj* bald(headed).
'Kahlschlag *m* **1.** a) deforestation, b) clearing. **2.** *fig.* demolition. **~sa,nierung** *f* wholesale redevelopment.
Kahn [ka:n] *m* (-[e]s; ⸚e) **1.** (rowing *or* fishing) boat: **~ fahren** go boating. **2.** barge. **3.** F tub. **'Kahnfahrt** *f* boat trip.

Kai [kaɪ] *m* (-s; -s) quay, wharf.
'**Kaimauer** *f* quay wall.
Kaiser ['kaɪzər] *m* (-s; -) emperor.
'**Kaiserin** *f* (-; -nen) empress.
'**Kaiserkrone** *f* imperial crown.
'**kaiserlich** *adj* imperial.
'**Kaiserreich** *n* empire.
'**Kaiserschnitt** *m* ♯ C(a)esarean section.
Kajak ['ka:jak] *m* (-s; -s) *a. sports:* kayak.
Ka'jütboot *n* cabin boat.
Kajüte [ka'jy:tə] *f* (-; -n) cabin.
Kakadu ['kakadu] *m* (-s; -s) cockatoo.
Kakao [ka'kaʊ, ka'ka:o] *m* (-s; -s) cocoa:
F *fig. durch den ~ ziehen* make fun of,
roast. **Ka'kaobaum** *m* cacao (tree).
Kaktee [kak'te:] *f* (-; -n), **Kaktus**
['kaktʊs] *m* (-; -teen) ♀ cactus.
Kalauer ['ka:laʊər] *m* (-s; -) dreadful
pun, corny joke.
Kalb [kalp] *n* (-[e]s; ⁗er) calf. **kalben**
['kalbən] *v/i* (h) calve. '**Kalbfell** *n* calf-
skin. '**Kalbfleisch** *n* veal.
'**Kalbs|braten** *m* roast veal. **~haxe** *f*
knuckle of veal. **~keule** *f* leg of veal.
~kopf *m* calf's head. **~leder** *n* calf-
(skin). **~schnitzel** *n* escalope of veal.
Kaleidoskop [kalaɪdo'sko:p] *n* (-s; -e) *a.
fig.* kaleidoscope.
Kalender [ka'lɛndər] *m* (-s; -) calendar.
Ka'lenderjahr *n* calendar year.
Kali ['ka:li] *n* (-s; -s) ♣ potash.
Kaliber [ka'li:bər] *n* (-s; -) calib/re (*Am.*
-er), *F fig. a.* sort, type.
Kalium ['ka:liʊm] *n* (-s; *no pl*) ♣ potassium.
Kalk [kalk] *m* (-[e]s; -e) **1.** ♣ a) lime, b)
quicklime. **2.** ♯ calcium. **3.** *min.* limestone. **4.** → **~dünger** *m* lime fertilizer.
'**kalken** *v/t* (h) **1.** whitewash. **2.** ✓ lime.
'**kalkig** *adj* limy.
'**Kalkmangel** *m* (-s; *no pl*) ♯ calcium
deficiency. '**Kalkstein** *m* limestone.
Kalkül [kal'ky:l] *n* (-s; -e) calculation: *et.
ins ~ ziehen* take s.th. into consideration.
Kalkulation [kalkula'tsǐo:n] *f* (-; -en) *a.
fig.* calculation.
kalkulieren [kalku'li:rən] *v/t, v/i* (h) *a.
fig.* calculate: *falsch ~* miscalculate.
Kalorie [kalo'ri:] *f* (-; -n) calorie.
kalo'rienarm *adj* low-calorie: *~ sein* be
low in calories. **Kalo'rienbedarf** *m*
calorie requirement. **Kalo'riengehalt**
m calorie content. **kalo'rienreich** *adj*

high-calorie: *~ sein* be rich in calories.
kalt [kalt] **I** *adj* cold, *fig. a.* frigid: *mir ist
~* I'm cold; *es (mir) wird ~* it's (I'm)
getting cold; *~er Krieg* Cold War;
gastr. ~e Platte cold meats; F *j-m die
~e Schulter zeigen* give s.o. the cold
shoulder. **II** *adv* coldly: *et. ~ stellen* put
s.th. to cool; *~ essen* have a cold meal;
es überlief mich ~ a cold shiver ran
down my spine.
'**kaltbleiben** *v/i* (*irr, sep,* -ge-, sn, → **bleiben**) F *fig.* keep cool, keep one's head.
'**Kaltblüter** [-bly:tər] *m* (-s; -) cold-
-blooded animal. '**kaltblütig** [-bly:tɪç] **I**
adj cold-blooded, *fig. a.* cool. **II** *adv* a)
coolly, b) *kill etc* in cold blood. '**Kaltblütigkeit** *f* (-; *no pl*) a) coolness, sang-
froid, b) cold-bloodedness.
Kälte ['kɛltə] *f* (-; *no pl*) cold, *a. fig.*
coldness, frigidity: *es sind 10 Grad ~*
the temperature is ten degrees below
zero; *bei dieser ~* in this cold.
'**kältebeständig** *adj* cold-resistant.
'**Kälte|einbruch** *m* cold snap. **~grad** *m*
degree of frost. **~peri,ode** *f* cold spell.
~pol *m* cold pole. **~welle** *f* cold wave.
'**kaltlächelnd** *adv* F (as) cool as you
please, without turning a hair.
'**kaltlassen** *v/t* (*irr, sep,* -ge-, h, → **lassen**) F *das läßt mich kalt* that leaves
me cold.
'**Kaltluft** *f* (-; *no pl*) cold air: *polare ~*
polar air.
'**kaltmachen** *v/t* (*sep,* -ge-, h) F *j-n ~*
bump s.o. off, do s.o. in.
'**Kaltmiete** *f* rent exclusive of heating
charges.
'**kaltschnäuzig** [-ʃnɔʏtsɪç] *adj* F cool.
'**Kaltstart** *m mot.* cold start.
'**kaltstellen** *v/t* (*sep,* -ge-, h) F neutralize.
Kalzium ['kaltsǐʊm] *n* (-s; *no pl*) calcium.
kam [ka:m] *pret of* **kommen**.
Kamel [ka'me:l] *n* (-[e]s; -e) **1.** *zo.* camel.
2. F idiot, blockhead.
Ka'melhaar... camel-hair.
Kamelie [ka'me:lǐə] *f* (-; -n) ♀ camellia.
Kamera ['kaməra] *f* (-; -s) camera.
Kamerad [kamə'ra:t] *m* (-en; -en) comrade, companion, fellow, mate, F pal,
buddy. **Kame'radschaft** *f* (-; *no pl*)
comradeship, fellowship. **kame'rad-
schaftlich** *adj and adv* comradely.
'**Kameraführung** *f film:* camerawork.
'**Kameramann** *m* cameraman.

'**Kameratasche** f camera case.
Kamille [ka'mɪlə] f (-; -n) camomile.
Kamin [ka'mi:n] m (-s; -e) **1.** chimney (a. mount.). **2.** (offener) ~ fireside, fireplace; am ~ by the fireside.
Kamm [kam] m (-[e]s; ᵕe) **1.** comb: fig. alle über einen ~ scheren lump them all together. **2.** zo. comb, crest. **3.** crest (of wave). **4.** (mountain) ridge.
kämmen ['kɛmən] (h) **I** v/t comb (a. ⊛): j-n ~, j-m die Haare ~ comb s.o.'s hair; sich die Haare ~ → **II** sich ~ comb (or do) one's hair.
Kammer ['kamər] f (-; -n) **1.** chamber (a. anat., ⊛), small room, closet. **2.** parl. chamber, house. **3.** association.
'**Kammer|diener** m valet. ~**mu‚sik** f chamber music. ~**or‚chester** n chamber orchestra. ~**ton** m ♪ concert pitch.
'**Kammgarn** n, '**Kammgarn...** worsted.
Kampagne [kam'panjə] f (-; -n) campaign.
Kampf [kampf] m (-[e]s; ᵕe) **1.** a) fig. fight, battle, struggle (gegen against, um for), b) conflict, controversy: den ~ ansagen declare war (dat on); j-m den ~ ansagen challenge s.o.; ~ dem Hunger! war on hunger!; sich zum ~ stellen give battle; innere Kämpfe inner conflicts; → **Dasein. 2.** ✗ combat, fight. **3.** sports: contest, fight, bout, match. ~**abstimmung** f **1.** parl. crucial vote. **2.** strike ballot. ~**ansage** f challenge (an acc to). ²**bereit** adj fig. ready for battle (sports: to fight).
kämpfen ['kɛmpfən] (h) **I** v/i (für, um for) a. fig. fight, battle, struggle: mit Schwierigkeiten zu ~ haben have (to struggle against) difficulties; mit j-m ~ sports: fight (with) s.o.; ich habe lange mit mir gekämpft I had a long battle with myself; sie kämpfte mit den Tränen she was fighting back her tears. **II** v/t fight. **III** sich ~ struggle (or fight one's way) (durch through, nach oben a. fig. up). '**kämpfend** adj fighting: ~e Truppen combatant troops.
Kampfer ['kampfər] m (-s; no pl) 🜍 camphor.
Kämpfer ['kɛmpfər] m (-s; -) fighter, ✗ a. combatant. '**kämpferisch** adj fighting, fig. a. aggressive.
Kampf|flugzeug n tactical (or combat) aircraft. ~**geist** m (-[e]s; no pl) fighting

spirit: ~ zeigen show fight. ~**gericht** n sports: the judges. ~**handlung** f ✗ fighting, action. ~**hubschrauber** m (helicopter) gunship.
'**kampflos** adj and adv without a fight: ~ gewinnen sports: win by default.
'**kampflustig** adj belligerent.
'**Kampf|maßnahme** f militant action. ~**platz** m battlefield, sports: arena (a. fig.). ~**richter(in** f) m judge, tennis etc: umpire. ~**schwimmer** m ✗ frogman. ~**sport** m combative sports, (carate etc) martial arts. ~**stoff** m ✗ agent, chemical etc weapon. ~**truppe** f ✗ combat troops. ²**unfähig** adj disabled, out of action: j-n ~ machen put s.o. out of action. ~**verband** m ✗ combat unit.
kampieren [kam'pi:rən] v/i (h) camp.
Kanada ['kanada] n (-s) Canada.
Kanadier¹ [ka'na:diər] m (-s; -) Canadian (canoe).
Ka'nadier² m (-s; -), **Ka'nadierin** f (-; -nen), **ka'nadisch** adj Canadian.
Kanal [ka'na:l] m (-s; ᵕe) **1.** a) channel (a. fig.), canal, duct, c) conduit: fig. dunkle Kanäle secret channels; F den ~ voll haben a) be sloshed, b) be fed up to here. **2.** anat. duct. **3.** radio, TV: channel.
Kanalisation [kanaliza'tsio:n] f (-; -en) **1.** canalization. **2.** drains (in house), sewage system (of town). **kanalisieren** [kanali'zi:rən] v/t (h) **1.** canalize. **2.** provide with sewers. **3.** fig. channel.
Ka'nalküste f the Channel coast.
Ka'nalwähler m radio, TV tuner.
Kanarienvogel [ka'na:riən-] m canary.
kanarisch [ka'na:rɪʃ] adj die ²en Inseln the Canaries, the Canary Islands.
Kandare [kan'da:rə] f (-; -n) curb (bit): j-n an die ~ nehmen take s.o. in hand.
Kandelaber [kandə'la:bər] m (-s; -) candelabrum.
Kandidat [kandi'da:t] m (-en; -en), **Kan-di'datin** f (-; -nen) a. fig. candidate.
Kandi'datenliste f list of candidates, pol. Am. a. ticket. **Kandidatur** [kandida'tu:r] f (-; -en) candidacy.
kandidieren [kandi'di:rən] v/i (h) be a candidate, stand, run: für das Amt des Präsidenten ~ run for president.
kandiert [kan'di:rt] adj candied (fruit).
Kandiszucker ['kandɪs-] m candy.
Känguruh ['kɛŋguru] m (-s; -s) kangaroo.

Kaninchen [ka'ni:nçən] n (-s; -) rabbit.
Ka'ninchenstall m rabbit hutch.
Kanister [ka'nɪstər] m (-s; -) can(ister).
Kännchen ['kɛnçən] n (-s; -) jug: *ein ~ Kaffee* gastr. a pot of coffee.
Kanne ['kanə] f (-; -n) a) can, b) pot.
Kannibale [kani'ba:lə] m (-n; -n) cannibal. **kanni'balisch** adj cannibal.
kannte ['kantə] pret of **kennen**.
Kanon ['ka:nɔn] m (-s; -s) canon.
Kanone [ka'no:nə] f (-; -n) 1. ✗ cannon, gun: *unter aller ~* just lousy. 2. F gun, shooter. 3. F (*in* dat at) wizard, ace.
Kanonier [kano'ni:r] m (-s; -e) gunner.
kanonisch [ka'no:nɪʃ] adj eccl. canonical: *~es Recht* canon law.
Kantate [kan'ta:tə] f (-; -n) ♪ cantata.
Kante ['kantə] f (-; -n) 1. edge, a. border: F *et. auf die hohe ~ legen* save some money; *et. auf der hohen ~ haben* have saved some money. 2. selvage.
kanten ['kantən] v/t (h) 1. cant, tilt, carve (*ski*). 2. ⊚ edge.
¹Kanten m (-s; -) crust (*of bread*).
Kanter ['kantər] m (-s; -) canter.
kantig ['kantɪç] adj squared, angular.
Kantine [kan'ti:nə] f (-; -n) canteen.
Kanton [kan'to:n] m (-s; -e) canton.
Kanu ['ka:nu, ka'nu:] n (-s; -s) canoe.
Kanüle [ka'ny:lə] f (-; -n) ♂ cannula, (drain) tube.
Kanute [ka'nu:tə] m (-n; -n) canoeist.
Kanzel ['kantsəl] f (-; -n) 1. (*auf der ~* in the) pulpit. 2. ✓ cockpit. 3. ✗ turret.
Kanzlei [kants'laɪ] f (-; -en) office.
Kanzler ['kantslər] m (-s; -) 1. pol. chancellor. 2. univ. vice-chancellor. **~amt** n 1. chancellor's office. 2. chancellorship. **~kandi,dat** m candidate for the chancellorship.
Kap [kap] n (-s; -s) geogr. cape.
Kapazität [kapatsi'tɛ:t] f (-; -en) 1. no pl capacity (a. fig.), ∉ capacitance. 2. fig. (leading) authority (*auf dem Gebiet* gen on the subject of).
Kapelle [ka'pɛlə] f (-; -n) 1. eccl. chapel. 2. ♪ band. **Ka'pellmeister** m a) director of music, b) conductor, c) bandmaster (a. ✗), bandleader.
Kaper ['ka:pər] f (-; -) ⚘ caper.
kapern ['ka:pərn] v/t (h) ⚓ capture, seize, F fig. nab.
kapieren [ka'pi:rən] (h) F I v/t get. II v/i

get it, catch on to: *kapiert?* (have you) got it?
Kapillargefäß [kapɪ'la:r-] n anat. capillary (vessel).
kapital [kapi'ta:l] adj F capital (error).
Kapi'tal n (-s; -e, -ien) a) capital, b) capital stock: *~ und Zinsen* principal and interest; *~ schlagen aus* capitalize on.
Kapi'tal,abwanderung f capital outflow. **~anlage** f investment. **~anlagegesellschaft** f investment trust. **~anleger(in** f) m investor. **~bildung** f accumulation of capital. **~einkommen** n investment income. **~erhöhung** f increase of capital. **~ertragssteuer** f capital yields tax. **~flucht** f flight of capital. **~geber(in** f) m financier. **~gesellschaft** f joint-stock company, Am. (stock) corporation.
kapitalisieren [kapitali'zi:rən] v/t (h) capitalize. **Kapitalismus** [-'lɪsmus] m (-; no pl) capitalism. **Kapitalist** [-'lɪst] m (-en; -en) capitalist. **kapita'listisch** adj capitalist(ic).
kapi'talkräftig adj (financially) powerful, potent.
Kapi'talmarkt m capital market.
Kapi'talverbrechen n capital crime.
Kapitän [kapi'tɛ:n] m (-s; -e) captain.
Kapi'tänspa,tent n master's certificate.
Kapitel [ka'pɪtəl] n (-s; -) chapter (a. eccl.): fig. *ein ~ für sich* another story.
Kapitell [kapi'tɛl] n (-s; -e) △ capital.
Kapitulation [kapitula'tsio:n] f (-; -en) a. fig. capitulation, surrender.
kapitulieren [kapitu'li:rən] v/i (h) (*vor* dat to) a. fig. capitulate, surrender.
Kaplan [ka'pla:n] m (-s; Kapläne) chaplain.
Kappe ['kapə] f (-; -n) 1. cap: F *et. auf s-e ~ nehmen* take the responsibility for s.th. 2. ⊚ top, cap. 3. (toe) cap.
kappen ['kapən] v/t (h) 1. cut (*rope etc*). 2. lop (*tree etc*).
Käppi ['kɛpi] n (-s; -s) cap, ✗ a. kepi.
Kapriole [kapri'o:lə] f (-; -n) caper.
kaprizieren [kapri'tsi:rən] *sich ~* (h) *auf* (acc) set one's heart on, insist on.
kapriziös [kapri'tsiø:s] adj capricious.
Kapsel ['kapsəl] f (-; -n) 1. case, container. 2. anat., ♀, pharm. etc: capsule.
kaputt [ka'pʊt] adj F *~ sein* 1. be broken, be bust, be torn, ⊚ be out of order, ♂ heart etc: be ruined, be bad, nerves: be

shattered, *fig. marriage etc*: be broken; **mein Auto ist ~** my car has broken down (*or* has had it). **2.** *person*: a) be ruined, be finished, b) be worn out, be all in: **~er Typ** complete wreck.

ka'puttfahren *v/t (irr, sep, -ge-, h, → fahren)* F smash up, wreck.

ka'puttgehen *v/i (irr, sep, -ge-, sn, → gehen)* F **1.** break, tear, *car etc*: break down, *fig. marriage etc*: break up. **2.** *person*: crack (up), go to pieces.

ka'puttlachen: *sich ~ (sep, -ge-, h)* F kill o.s. laughing.

ka'puttmachen *(sep, -ge-, h)* F **I** *v/t* **1.** break, smash, *fig.* ruin, bust. **2.** *j-n ~* a) ruin s.o., b) get s.o. down, wear s.o. out, c) kill s.o. **II** *sich ~* wear o.s. out, kill o.s. (*mit* over, doing *s.th.*).

Kapuze [ka'pu:tsə] *f (-; -n)* **1.** hood. **2.** cowl.

Karabiner [kara'bi:nər] *m (-s; -)* ✗ carbine. **2.** → **~haken** *m* spring hook.

Karaffe [ka'rafə] *f* carafe, *a.* decanter.

Karambolage [karambo'la:ʒə] *f (-; -n)* **1.** *billiards*: cannon, *Am.* carom. **2.** F crash, collision.

Karamel [kara'mɛl] *n (-s; no pl)* caramel.

Karat [ka'ra:t] *n (-[e]s; -e)* carat.

Karate [ka'ra:tə] *n (-[e]s; no pl)* karate. **Ka'ratekämpfer** *m* karateka. **Ka'rateschlag** *m* karate chop.

...karätig [karɛtɪç] *...*-carat.

Karawane [kara'va:nə] *f (-; -n)* caravan.

Kardangelenk [kar'da:n-] *n* ⚙ cardan (*or* universal) joint.

Kar'danwelle *f* ⚙ cardan shaft.

Kardinal [kardi'na:l] *m (-s; ...le)* cardinal. **Kardi'nal...** cardinal (*fault, question, etc*). **~zahl** *f* cardinal (number).

Kardiologe [kardio'lo:gə] *m (-n; -n)* ✠ cardiologist.

Karenzzeit [ka'rɛnts-] *f insurance*: waiting period, ✠ period of restriction.

Kar'freitag [ka:r-] *m eccl.* Good Friday.

karg [kark] *adj* **1.** meagre, *Am.* meager, scanty, poor, frugal (*meal, life*), barren (*soil*). **2.** austere. **3.** sparing: **~ bemessen** (very) meagre, *fig.* (very) limited.

kargen ['kargən] *v/i (h)* **~ mit** be sparing of *praise etc*, be stingy with *money*.

'Kargheit *f (-; no pl)* meag/reness (*Am.* -er-), poorness.

kärglich ['kɛrklɪç] *adj* → **karg** 1.

kariert [ka'ri:rt] *adj* checked, chequered, *Am.* checkered.

Karies ['ka:riɛs] *f (-; no pl)* ✠ tooth decay, dental caries.

Karikatur [karika'tu:r] *f (-; -en)* cartoon, caricature (*a. fig.*). **Karikaturist** [karikatu'rɪst] *m (-en; -en)* cartoonist, caricaturist. **karikieren** [kari'ki:rən] *v/t (h)* cartoon, caricature.

kariös [ka'riø:s] *adj* ✠ carious, decayed.

karitativ [karita'ti:f] *adj* charitable.

Karmin [kar'mi:n] *n (-s; no pl)* crimson. **kar'minrot** *adj* crimson.

Karneval ['karnəval] *m (-s; -e)* carnival.

Karo ['ka:ro] *n (-s; -s)* **1.** check, square. **2.** *cards*: diamonds.

Karosserie [karɔsə'ri:] *f (-; -n)* *mot.* (car) body.

Karotin [karo'ti:n] *n (-s; no pl)* carotene.

Karotte [ka'rɔtə] *f (-; -n)* carrot.

Karpfen ['karpfən] *m (-s; -)* *zo.* carp.

Karre ['karə] *f (-; -n)* **1.** F (*alte*) ~ bus, crate, banger. **2.** → **Karren**.

Karren ['karən] *m (-s; -)* cart, (wheel)barrow: F *fig. j-m an den ~ fahren* step on s.o.'s toes; *den ~ in den Dreck fahren* mess things up; *den ~ wieder aus dem Dreck ziehen* clear up the mess; *j-n vor s-n ~ spannen* rope s.o. in.

Karriere [ka'riɛ:rə] *f (-; -n)* career: **~ machen** make a career for o.s.

Karri'erefrau *f* career woman (*or* girl). **Karri'eremacher** *m contp.* careerist.

Karte ['kartə] *f (-; -n)* a) card, b) map, ⚓ chart, c) 🍴, *thea. etc*: ticket, d) menu, wine list: *nach der ~ speisen* dine à la carte; *die gelbe (rote) ~ soccer*: the yellow (red) card; **~n spielen** play cards; *gute* **~n haben** have a good hand; *s-e* **~n auf den Tisch legen** *a. fig.* show one's hand, put one's cards on the table; *alles auf eine ~ setzen* put all one's eggs in one basket; → *legen* 6.

Kartei [kar'tai] *f (-; -en)* (**~ führen** keep a) card index (*über acc* on).

Kar'teikarte *f* file (*or* index) card.

Kar'teikasten *m* card-index box.

Kartell [kar'tɛl] *n (-s; -e)* cartel, ✟ *a.* combine, trust.

'Karten|haus *n* **1.** ⚓ chartroom. **2.** house of cards. **~kunststück** *n* card trick. **~leger** *m (-s; -)*, **~legerin** *f (-; -nen)* fortune-teller. **~spiel** *n* **1.** a) card playing, b) card game. **2.** pack (*Am. a.*

deck) of cards. **~verkauf** m sale of tickets. **~vorverkauf** m advance booking. **~zeichen** n conventional sign.

Kartoffel [kar'tɔfəl] f (-; -n) potato.

Kar'toffel|brei m mashed potatoes. **~chips** pl potato crisps (*Am.* chips). **~käfer** m potato beetle (*Am.* bug). **~puffer** m potato fritter. **~sa,lat** m potato salad. **~schäler** m potato peeler.

Kartograph [karto'graːf] m (-en; -en) cartographer. **Kartographie** [kartogra'fiː] f (-; no pl) cartography.

Karton [kar'tɔŋ, kar'toːn] m (-s; -s) **1.** cardboard. **2.** cardboard box, carton.

kartoniert [karto'niːrt] adj print. paperback(ed).

Karussell [karʊ'sɛl] n (-s; -s, -e) roundabout, merry-go-round, whirligig.

'Karwoche f eccl. Holy Week.

karzinogen [kartsino'geːn] adj ☤ carcinogenic. **Karzinom** [kartsi'noːm] n (-s; -e) ☤ carcinoma, cancer.

kaschieren [ka'ʃiːrən] v/t (h) conceal.

Kaschmir ['kaʃmɪr] m (-s; -e) cashmere.

Käse ['kɛːzə] m (-s; -) **1.** cheese. **2.** F a) rubbish, b) stupid business.

'Käse|blatt n F rag. **~gebäck** n cheese biscuits. **~glocke** f cheese cover. **~kuchen** m cheesecake. **~platte** f gastr. cheese platter. **~rinde** f cheese rind.

Kaserne [ka'zɛrnə] f (-; -n) barracks. **Ka'sernenhof** m barrack square.

kasernieren [kazɛr'niːrən] v/t (h) quarter in barracks.

'Käsestange f cheese straw.

käsig ['kɛːzɪç] adj **1.** caseous, cheesy. **2.** F pale, pasty (*face*).

Kasino [ka'ziːno] n (-s; -s) **1.** casino, club. **2.** a) (officers') mess, b) cafeteria, canteen.

Kaskoversicherung ['kasko-] f mot. insurance against damage to one's own vehicle; → **Teilkaskoversicherung**, **Vollkaskoversicherung**.

Kasper ['kaspər] m (-s; -) **1.** Punch. **2.** fig. clown. **'Kasperlethe,ather** n Punch and Judy (show).

Kassageschäft ['kasa-] n ☫ cash transaction. **'Kassara,batt** m cash discount.

Kasse ['kasə] f (-; -n) **1.** a) moneybox, b) till, c) cash register: *der Film hat volle ~n gebracht* the film was a box-office success. **2.** in shop, bank, etc: cash desk, in supermarket: checkout (counter), in

cinema etc: ticket window, thea. etc a. box office: *zahlen Sie bitte an der ~!* pay at the desk, please!; *fig. j-n zur ~ bitten* make s.o. pay up. **3.** ☫ cash (payment): *gegen ~* for cash; *netto ~* net cash. **4.** cash: **~ machen** a) cash up, b) F count one's cash, c) F fig. cash in heavily, make a packet; F *gut bei ~ sein* be flush; *knapp bei ~ sein* be (a bit) hard up; *gemeinsame ~ machen* split the expenses; *getrennte ~ machen* go Dutch. **5.** F (*er ist in k-r ~* he has no) health insurance. **6.** F (savings) bank.

'Kassen|abschluß m balancing of the (cash) accounts. **~anweisung** f cash order. **~arzt** m health-plan doctor. **~bestand** m cash balance. **~bon** m sales check (*Am.* slip), receipt. **~buch** n cashbook. **~erfolg** m thea. etc box-office hit. **~ma,gnet** m F crowd-puller. **~pati,ent(in** f) m health-plan patient. **~prüfung** f cash audit: *e-e ~ vornehmen* audit the cash. **~schlager** m F **1.** crowd-puller. **2.** moneymaker. **~sturz** m ~ machen count one's cash. **~wart** m (-[e]s; -e) treasurer. **~zettel** m sales check (*Am.* slip), receipt.

Kasserolle [kasə'rɔlə] f (-; -n) casserole.

Kassette [ka'sɛtə] f (-; -n) **1.** a) box, b) casket, c) cashbox. **2.** a) slipcase (*for books*), box set (*for records*). **3.** phot., TV etc cassette, cartridge. **4.** △ coffer.

Kas'setten|deck n cassette deck. **~re,corder** m cassette recorder.

kassieren [ka'siːrən] (h) **I** v/t **1.** collect (*rent etc*). **2.** F a) collect, take (*fees etc*), b) seize (*property*), c) nab, catch (*criminal*), d) suffer (*loss etc*), take, get (*beating, etc*). **3.** ☫ quash (*sentence*). **II** v/i **4.** collect (the money): F *fig. kräftig ~ cash in (heavily) (*bei* on); *darf ich bei Ihnen ~?* would you mind paying now?

Kassierer [ka'siːrər] m (-s; -), **Kas'siererin** f (-; -nen) cashier, esp. *Am.* teller.

Kastagnette [kastan'jɛtə] f (-; -n) castanet.

Kastanie [kas'taːniə] f (-; -n) chestnut: fig. *für j-n die ~n aus dem Feuer holen* pull the chestnuts out of the fire for s.o. **Ka'stanienbaum** m chestnut (tree). **ka'stanienbraun** adj chestnut.

Kästchen ['kɛstçən] n (-s; -) **1.** small box (or case), casket. **2.** print. square, box.

Kaste ['kastə] f (-; -n) caste.

kasteien [kas'taɪən] *sich ~* (h) **1.** *eccl.* mortify the flesh. **2.** *fig.* deny o.s.

Kasten ['kastən] *m* (-s; ") **1.** box (*a. print.*), case, chest, (*beer etc*) crate: F *er hat was auf dem ~* he's brainy, he's on the ball. **2.** F (*goal, house, TV set*) box, (*car, plane*) bus, crate, (*ship*) tub.

'**Kastengeist** *m* (-[e]s; *no pl*) caste spirit.

'**Kastenwesen** *n* (-s; *no pl*) caste system.

Kastration [kastra'tsɪoːn] *f* (-; -en) castration.

kastrieren [kas'triːrən] *v/t* (h) castrate.

Kasus ['kaːzʊs] *m* (-; -) *ling.* case.

Kat [kat] *m* (-s; -s) → *Katalysator* 2.

Katakomben [kata'kɔmbən] *pl* catacombs.

Katalog [kata'loːk] *m* (-[e]s; -e) catalog(ue *Br.*). **katalogisieren** [katalogi'ziːrən] *v/t* (h) catalog(ue *Br.*).

Katalysator [kataly'zaːtɔr] *m* (-s; -en [-za'toːrən]) **1.** 🔬 *or fig.* catalyst. **2.** *mot.* catalytic converter.

Katapult [kata'pʊlt] *n, m* (-[e]s; -e), **katapultieren** [-'tiːrən] *v/t* (h) catapult.

Kata'pultstart *m* ✈ catapult takeoff.

Katarrh [ka'tar] *m* (-s; -e) 🦠 catarrh.

Kataster [ka'tastər] *m, n* (-s; -) land register.

katastrophal [kastastroː'faːl] *adj* catastrophic, *a.* F *fig.* disastrous.

Katastrophe [kata'stroːfə] *f* (-; -n) *a.* F *fig.* catastrophe, disaster.

Kata'strophen|a,larm *m* red alert. **~einsatz** *m* (*im ~* on) duty in a disaster area. **~fall** *m* (*im ~* in an) emergency. **~film** *m* disaster film. **~gebiet** *n* disaster area. **~hilfe** *f* disaster relief. **~schutz** *m* disaster control (*or* prevention).

Katechismus [kate'çɪsmʊs] *m* (-; -men) *eccl.* catechism.

Kategorie [katego'riː] *f* (-; -n) category.

kategorisch [kate'goːrɪʃ] *adj* categorical: *~ ablehnen a.* refuse flatly.

Kater ['kaːtər] *m* (-s; -) **1.** *zo.* tom(cat). **2.** F hangover: *e-n ~ haben a.* be hung over.

Katheder [ka'teːdər] *n, a. m* (-s; -) (teacher's *or* lecturer's) desk.

Kathedrale [kate'draːlə] *f* (-; -n) cathedral.

Katheter [ka'teːtər] *m* (-s; -) 🦠 catheter.

Kathode [ka'toːdə] *f* (-; -n) cathode.

Katholik [kato'liːk] *m* (-en; -en), **Katho'likin** *f* (-; -nen), **katholisch** [ka'toːlɪʃ] *adj* (Roman) Catholic.

Katholizismus [katoli'tsɪsmʊs] *m* (-; *no pl*) Catholicism.

Kätzchen ['kɛtsçən] *n* (-s; -) **1.** *zo.* kitten. **2.** 🌿 catkin.

Katze ['katsə] *f* (-; -n) cat: F *fig. das ist für die Katz* that's all for nothing; *Katz und Maus spielen mit* play cat and mouse with; *die ~ im Sack kaufen* buy a pig in a poke; *die ~ aus dem Sack lassen* let the cat out of the bag; *wie die ~ um den heißen Brei gehen* beat about the bush.

'**Katzenauge** *n* **1.** cat's eye (*a. min.*). **2.** F rear reflector.

'**katzenhaft** *adj* catlike, feline.

'**Katzen|jammer** *m* F hangover: (*moralischen*) *~ haben a.* have the blues. **~klo** *n* cat tray. **~sprung** *m fig. ein ~ von hier* a stone's throw from here. **~streu** *f* cat litter. **~wäsche** *f* F *fig.* (*~ machen* have a) cat's lick.

Kauderwelsch ['kaʊdərvɛlʃ] *n* (-[s]; *no pl*) double Dutch, lingo.

kauen ['kaʊən] *v/t, v/i* (h) chew: *an den Nägeln ~* bite one's nails; *fig. an e-r Sache ~* chew s.th. over.

kauern ['kaʊərn] *v/i* (*a. sich ~*) (h) crouch (*or* squat) (down).

Kauf [kaʊf] *m* (-[e]s; "e) **1.** buying, purchase: *zum ~* for sale; *beim ~* when buying; *et. in ~ nehmen* put up with s.th.; *leichten ~es davonkommen* get off cheaply. **2.** purchase, F buy: *ein guter ~* a good bargain (*or* buy).

'**kaufen** *v/t, v/i* (h) buy (*a.* F *fig.*), purchase: *~ bei* go to, buy at; *sich ein Auto ~* buy (o.s.) a car; F *dafür kann ich mir nichts ~!* that's no use to me!; *den kaufe ich mir!* I'll tell him what's what!

Käufer ['kɔyfər] *m* (-s; -), '**Käuferin** *f* (-; -nen) buyer, purchaser.

'**Kauf|frau** *f* businesswoman. **~halle** *f* small department store. **~haus** *n* department store. **~kraft** *f* (-; *no pl*) purchasing power (*of money*), spending power (*of consumers*). **2kräftig** *adj* a) well-to-do, b) hard (*currency*)

käuflich ['kɔyflɪç] *adj* **1.** purchasable: (*nicht*) *~ sein* (not to) be for sale; *~e Liebe* prostitution; *~ erwerben* purchase. **2.** *fig.* venal, corrupt.

'**Käuflichkeit** *f* (-; *no pl*) *fig.* venality.

'**Kaufmann** *m* (-[e]s; -leute) **1.** business-

kein

man, merchant, trader, dealer. **2.** shop-keeper, *Am. a.* storekeeper, *n.s.* grocer.
kaufmännisch ['kaʊfmɛnɪʃ] *adj* commercial, business: **~e(r) Angestellte(r)** (commercial) clerk.

'**Kaufpreis** *m* (purchase) price.

'**Kaufvertrag** *m* contract of sale.

'**Kaufzwang** *m* obligation (to buy).

'**Kaugummi** *m, a. n* (-s; -s) chewing gum.

Kaulquappe ['kaʊlkvapə] *f* (-; -n) *zo.* tadpole.

kaum [kaʊm] *adv* a) hardly, scarcely, b) barely, only just: **~ zu glauben** hard to believe; **~ möglich** hardly possible; **wohl ~(!)** hardly(!); **ich glaube ~, daß I** hardly think that; **~ war sie gegangen, als ...** no sooner had she gone than ...

'**Kaumuskel** *m* masticatory muscle.

kausal [kaʊ'za:l] *adj* causal. **Kausalität** [kaʊzali'tɛ:t] *f* (-; -en) causality.

Kau'sal|satz *m ling.* causal clause. **~zusammenhang** *m* causal connection.

Kaution [kaʊ'tsi̯o:n] *f* (-; -en) ⚥ security, ⚖ bail: **~ stellen** ⚖ furnish security, ⚖ stand bail; **gegen ~** ⚖ on bail.

Kautschuk ['kaʊtʃʊk] *m* (-s; -e) caoutchouc, India rubber.

'**Kauwerkzeuge** *pl* masticatory organs.

Kauz [kaʊts] *m* (-es; ⁓e) **1.** *zo.* screech-owl. **2.** F (**komischer**) **~** odd (*or* queer) fellow, *Am.* oddball.

kauzig ['kaʊtsɪç] *adj* F queer, odd.

Kavalier [kava'li:r] *m* (-s; -e) gentleman.

Kava'liersde,likt *n* peccadillo.

Kavallerie [kavalə'ri:] *f* (-; -n) cavalry.

Kavallerist [kavalə'rɪst] *m* (-en; -en) cavalryman, trooper.

Kaviar ['ka:vi̯ar] *m* (-s; -e) caviar(e).

keck [kɛk] *adj* pert, saucy.

Kegel ['ke:gəl] *m* (-s; -) **1.** ⚥, ◉ cone. **2.** ninepin, skittle(pin): **→ Kind.**

'**Kegelbahn** *f* skittle (*or* bowling) alley.

'**kegelförmig** [-fœrmɪç] *adj* conical.

'**Kegelklub** *m* skittles (*or* bowling) club.

'**Kegelkugel** *f* skittle (*or* bowling) ball.

kegeln ['ke:gəln] *v/i* (h) play (at) skittles (*or* ninepins), bowl, go bowling.

'**Kegelsport** *m* skittles, bowling.

'**Kegelstumpf** *m* ⚥ truncated cone.

Kegler ['ke:glər] *m* (-s; -), '**Keglerin** *f* (-; -nen) skittles player, bowler.

Kehle ['ke:lə] *f* (-; -n) **1.** *anat.* throat: **j-m die ~ durchschneiden** cut s.o.'s throat; *fig.* **et. in die falsche ~ bekommen** take

s.th. the wrong way. **2.** ◉ flute.

'**Kehlkopf** *m anat.* larynx. **~entzündung** *f* ✚ laryngitis. **~krebs** *m* ✚ cancer of the larynx, F throat cancer.

'**Kehllaut** *m* guttural (sound).

Kehre ['ke:rə] *f* (-; -n) **1.** (sharp) bend. **2.** *skating etc:* turn, *gym.* rear vault.

kehren[1] ['ke:rən] (h) **I** *v/t* **1.** *et. nach oben* (*unten, außen etc*) **~** turn s.th. upwards (down, outside, *etc*); **den Rücken ~** *a. fig.* turn one's back (*dat* on); **in sich gekehrt** withdrawn, *psych.* introvert(ed); **→ oberst. II sich ~ 2. →** **wenden 4. 3. sich nicht ~ an** (*dat*) ignore. **III** *v/i* **4. kehrt!** 🗡 about turn!

'**kehren**[2] *v/t, v/i* (h) sweep.

Kehricht ['ke:rɪçt] *m, n* (-s; *no pl*) **1.** sweepings. **2.** rubbish, *Am.* garbage.

'**Kehrma,schine** *f* road sweeper.

'**Kehrreim** *m* burden, refrain.

'**Kehrseite** *f* **1.** reverse. **2.** *humor.* back. **3.** *fig.* a) *the* other side, b) drawback.

kehrtmachen ['ke:rt] *v/i* (*sep*, -ge-, h) **1.** turn round, 🗡 face about. **2.** turn back.

'**Kehrtwendung** *f a. fig.* about-face.

keifen ['kaɪfən] *v/i* (h) nag, bicker.

Keil [kaɪl] *m* (-[e]s; -e) **1.** wedge. **2.** gore, gusset. '**Keilabsatz** *m* wedge heel.

keilen ['kaɪlən] (h) **I** *v/t* **1.** *j-n* **~** rope s.o. in (*für* for). **II sich ~** fight.

Keiler ['kaɪlər] *m* (-s; -) *zo.* wild boar.

'**keilförmig** [-fœrmɪç] *adj* wedge-shaped.

'**Keilriemen** *m* ◉ V-belt.

'**Keilschrift** *f* cuneiform (script).

Keim [kaɪm] *m* (-[e]s; -e) **1.** *biol.* germ, embryo (*both a. fig.*), 🌱 *a.* bud, *fig. a.* seed(s): **im ~** in embryo; **im ~ ersticken** nip *s.th.* in the bud. **2.** ✚ germ, bacillus. **~blatt** *n* **1.** 🌱 cotyledon. **2.** *biol.* germ layer. **~drüse** *f physiol.* gonad.

keimen ['kaɪmən] *v/i* (h) **1.** *biol.* germinate. **2.** *fig.* grow, stir.

'**keimfähig** *adj* germinable.

'**keimfrei** *adj* sterile: **~ machen** sterilize.

'**Keimling** *m* (-s; -e) *biol.* embryo.

'**keimtötend** *adj* germicidal, antiseptic: **~es Mittel** germicide.

'**Keimträger** *m* ✚ (germ) carrier.

'**Keimzelle** *f* **1.** germ cell. **2.** *fig.* nucleus.

kein [kaɪn] *indef pron* no, not any, not a: **ich habe ~ Geld** I haven't (got) any money; **du bist ~ Kind mehr** you are not a child any more; **~ Wort mehr!** not another word!; **~ anderer als X** none other than X; **es kostet ~e 100 Mark** it costs less than 100 marks.

'**keine, 'keiner, 'keines** (*or* **keins**) *indef pron* **1.** no one, nobody, not one, none: **~(r) von uns** a) neither of us, b) none of us. **2.** not any, none, not one: **keins von beiden** neither (of the two).

'**keinerlei** *adj* no ... what(so)ever, no ... at all.

'**keines'falls** *adv* on no account, under no circumstances. '**keines'wegs** *adv* by no means, not at all, not in the least.

'**keinmal** *adv* not once, never.

Keks [ke:ks] *m* (-[es]; -e) biscuit, *Am.* cookie.

Kelch [kɛlç] *m* (-[e]s; -e) **1.** goblet, *eccl.* chalice, cup (*a. fig.*). **2.** ♀ calyx, cup. **~blatt** *n* ♀ sepal. **~hülle** *f* ♀ calycle.

Kelle ['kɛlə] *f* (-; -n) **1.** *gastr.* ladle. **2.** △ trowel. **3.** ⛟ *etc* signal(l)ing disc.

Keller ['kɛlər] *m* (-s; -) cellar.

Kellerei [kɛlə'raɪ] *f* (-; -en) wine cellars.

'**Kellergeschoß** *n* basement.

'**Kellermeister** *m* cellarman.

Kellner ['kɛlnər] *m* (-s; -) waiter. '**Kellnerin** *f* (-; -nen) waitress.

Kelte ['kɛltə] *m* (-n; -n) Celt.

Kelter ['kɛltər] *f* (-; -n) (wine)press. **keltern** ['kɛltərn] *v/t* (h) press.

'**Keltin** *f* (-; -nen) Celt.

keltisch ['kɛltɪʃ] *adj* Celtic.

kennen ['kɛnən] *v/t* (kannte, gekannt, h) know, *a.* be acquainted (*or* familiar) with, *a.* recognize (**an** *dat* by): **wir ~ uns** we know each other, **schon** *a.* we have already met; **ich kenne sie von der Schule** we were at school together; **kennst du mich noch?** do you remember me?; **das ~ wir!** we know all about that!; **er kennt nichts als s-e Arbeit** he lives only for his work; **sie kennt k-e Müdigkeit** she never gets tired; **kein Erbarmen ~** know no mercy.

'**kennenlernen** *v/t* (*sep*, -ge-, h) become acquainted with, get (*or* come) to know: **j-n ~** meet s.o.; **j-n näher ~** (get to) know s.o. better; **wir haben uns in B. kennengelernt** we first met in B.

Kenner ['kɛnər] *m* (-s; -), '**Kennerin** *f* (-; -nen) **1.** connoisseur. **2.** (*gen*) expert (at, in, of), authority (on).

'**Kennerblick** *m* (**mit** ~ with an) expert's eye. '**Kennermiene** *f* (**e-e ~ aufsetzen**) assume (*or*) air of an expert.

'**Kennmelo,die** *f* signature tune.

kenntlich ['kɛntlɪç] *adj* recognizable (**an** *dat* by): ~ **machen** mark.

Kenntnis ['kɛntnɪs] *f* (-; -se) knowledge: **gute ~se haben in** (*dat*) have a good knowledge of, be well grounded in; **das entzieht sich m-r ~** I don't know anything about it; **von et. ~ haben** know (about) s.th., be aware of s.th.; **et. zur ~ nehmen** take note of (*or* note) s.th.; **j-n in ~ setzen von** inform s.o. of.

'**Kenntnisnahme** [-na:mə] *f* **zu Ihrer** *etc* ~ for your *etc* attention.

'**Kennwort** *n* code word, ✕ *a.* password (*a. computer*).

'**Kennzeichen** *n* **1.** a) (distinguishing) mark, characteristic, b) sign, symptom (*a.* 🐾): **besondere ~** distinguishing marks. **2.** *fig.* hallmark. **3.** (*polizeiliches*) ~ *mot.* registration (*Am.* license) number. **4.** *computer:* flag.

'**Kennzeichen|leuchte** *f* *mot.* number-plate (*Am.* license-plate) light. **~schild** *n* number (*Am.* license) plate.

'**kennzeichnen** *v/t* (h) **1.** mark. **2.** *fig.* characterize, (go to) show. '**kennzeichnend** *adj* characteristic (**für** of).

'**Kennziffer** *f* code number, ✝ reference number, *of ad:* box number.

kentern ['kɛntərn] *v/i* (sn) capsize.

Keramik [ke'ra:mɪk] *f* (-; -en) **1.** *no pl* ceramics, pottery. **2.** ceramic (article), piece of pottery. **Ke'ramiker** *m* (-s; -), **Ke'ramikerin** *f* (-; -nen) ceramist.

Kerbe ['kɛrbə] *f* (-; -n) notch.

Kerbel ['kɛrbəl] *m* (-s; *no pl*) ♀ chervil.

kerben ['kɛrbən] *v/t* (h) notch.

'**Kerbholz** ['kɛrp-] *n* F **et. auf dem ~ haben** have done s.th. wrong; **er hat einiges auf dem ~** he has quite a record.

Kerl [kɛrl] *m* (-s; -e) F fellow, bloke, chap, *Am.* guy, *contp.* type: **er ist ein anständiger ~** he is a decent sort; **ein feiner ~** a splendid fellow, *Am.* a great guy; **ein lieber** (*or* **netter**) ~ a dear; **ein** (**ganzer**) ~ a real man; **ein übler ~** a nasty customer.

Kern [kɛrn] *m* (-[e]s; -e) **1.** ♀ a) pip, b) stone, *Am.* pit, c) kernel: *fig.* **sie hat e-n guten ~** she is good at heart. **2.** *fig.* core (*a.* ⚡, *phys.*, ⚙), nucleus (*a. phys.*), essence: **der ~ der Sache** the heart of the matter; *pol.* **harter ~** hard core. **~brennstoff** *m* nuclear fuel. **~ener,gie**

f nuclear energy. **~explosi̱on** *f* nuclear explosion. **~fach** *n ped., univ.* basic subject. **~fa̱milie** *f sociol.* nuclear family. **~forschung** *f* nuclear research. **~frage** *f* crucial question. **~fusi̱on** *f* nuclear fusion. **~gehäuse** *n* ⚛ core.

'**kerngesund** *adj* thoroughly healthy, F (as) sound as a bell.

'**kernig** *adj fig.* a) robust, b) pithy, c) earthy, d) F super, terrific.

'**Kernkraft** *f* nuclear power. **~gegner(in** *f*) *m* antinuclear campaigner. **~werk** *n* nuclear power station.

'**kernlos** *adj* ⚛ seedless.

'**Kern|obst** *n* pome. **~phy̱sik** *f* nuclear physics. **~physiker** *m* nuclear physicist. **~punkt** *m* central point (*or* issue). **~re̱aktor** *m* nuclear reactor. **~schmelze** *f* (-; *no pl*) (nuclear core) meltdown. **~seife** *f* curd soap. **~spaltung** *f* nuclear fission. **~stück** *n fig.* essential part, main item. **~waffe** *f* nuclear weapon. **~waffenverbot** *n* ban on nuclear weapons. **~waffenversuch** *m* nuclear weapons test. **~zeit** *f* core time. **~zerfall** *m* nuclear disintegration.

Kerosin [kero'zi:n] *n* (-s; *no pl*) kerosene.

Kerze ['kɛrtsə] *f* (-; -n) **1.** candle (*a.* ⚡, *phys.*). **2.** *mot.* spark(ing) plug.

'**kerzengerade** *adv* bolt upright.

'**Kerzenhalter** *m* candlestick.

'**Kerzenlicht** *n* (*bei ~* by) candlelight.

'**Kerzenschlüssel** *m mot.* plug wrench.

keß [kɛs] *adj* F pert, saucy.

Kessel ['kɛsəl] *m* (-s; -) **1.** kettle, cauldron, ⚙ vat, boiler. **2.** *geol.* basin, hollow. **3.** ✗ pocket.

'**Kesselstein** *m* (-[e]s; *no pl*) scale, fur.

'**Kesseltreiben** *n* (-s) *fig.* (**gegen**) hunt (for), *pol.* witch hunt (against).

Kette ['kɛtə] *f* (-; -n) **1.** chain (*a.* ⚓, ⚒, ⚛), *a.* necklace: **j-n an die ~ legen** put s.o. on a short leash. **2.** *fig.* a) chain, series (*of accidents, events, etc*), b) string, line: **e-e ~ bilden** form a cordon (*or* line). **3.** *hunt.* covey. **4.** *mot.* track. **5.** *textil.* warp: **~ und Schuß** warp and weft.

ketten ['kɛtən] *v/t* (h) chain (**an** *acc* to).

'**Ketten|brief** *m* chain letter. **~fahrzeug** *n* tracked vehicle. **~glied** *n* chain link. **~karus̱sell** *n* chairoplane. **~laden** *m* chain store. **~raucher(in** *f*) *m* chain-smoker. **~reakti̱on** *f* chain reaction.

Ketzer ['kɛtsər] *m* (-s; -) heretic.

Ketzerei [kɛtsə'raɪ] *f* (-; -en) heresy.

'**Ketzerin** *f* (-; -nen) heretic.

'**ketzerisch** *adj* heretical.

keuchen ['kɔʏçən] *v/i* (h) pant, puff (*a.* 🚂), *a. v/t* gasp.

'**Keuchhusten** *m* 🩺 whooping cough.

Keule ['kɔʏlə] *f* (-; -n) **1.** club. **2.** *chemische ~* Mace (*TM*). **3.** *gastr.* leg.

'**Keulenschlag** *m* **1.** blow with a club. **2.** *fig.* crushing blow.

keusch [kɔʏʃ] *adj* chaste.

'**Keuschheit** *f* (-; *no pl*) chastity.

Kibbuz [kɪ'bu:ts] *m* (-; -e) kibbutz.

kichern ['kɪçərn] *v/i* (h) (**über** *acc* at) giggle, snigger.

kicken ['kɪkən] *v/t, v/i* (h) kick.

Kiebitz ['ki:bɪts] *m* (-es; -e) **1.** *zo.* peewit, lapwing. **2.** F *fig.* kibitzer.

Kiefer[1] ['ki:fər] *f* (-; -n) ⚘ pine.

'**Kiefer**[2] *m* (-s; -) *anat.* jaw.

'**Kieferhöhle** *f anat.* maxillary sinus.

'**Kiefernzapfen** *m* ⚘ pine cone.

'**Kieferortho̱päde** *m* ⚕ orthodontist.

Kiel [ki:l] *m* (-[e]s; -e) ⚓ keel. **kiel'oben** *adv* ⚓ bottom up. '**Kielraum** *m* ⚓ bilge. '**Kielwasser** *n* (-s) (*fig. in j-s ~ segeln* sail in s.o.'s) wake.

Kieme ['ki:mə] *f* (-; -n) gill.

Kies [ki:s] *m* (-es; -e) **1.** (*a. mit ~ bestreuen*) gravel. **2.** F *fig.* lolly, *Am.* bread.

Kiesel ['ki:zəl] *m* (-s; -) flint, pebble.

'**Kieselerde** *f* 🧪 silica, siliceous earth.

'**Kieselsäure** *f* 🧪 silicic acid.

'**Kieselstein** *m* → **Kiesel**.

'**Kies|grube** *f* gravel pit. **~strand** *m* shingle (beach). **~weg** *m* gravel path.

Kiez [ki:ts] *m* (-es; -e) F district, area.

kiffen ['kɪfən] *v/i* (h) F smoke pot (*or* hash).

killen ['kɪlən] *v/t* (h) F kill.

Killer ['kɪlər] *m* (-s; -) F killer.

Kilo ['ki:lo] *n* (-s; -[s]), **Kilogramm** [kilo'gram] *n* kilogram(me).

Kilo'hertz [kilo-] *n* ⚡, *phys.* kilohertz.

Kilo'joule *n phys.* kilojoule.

Kilo'meter *m* kilomet/re (*Am.* -er). **~geld** *n* mileage allowance. **~pau̱schale** *f* flat mileage allowance. **~stand** *m* mileage (reading). **~stein** *m* milestone. **⟨weit** *adv* for miles (and miles). **~zähler** *m* mileage indicator.

Kilo'volt *n* kilovolt.

Kilo'watt(stunde) *f*) *n* kilowatt (hour).

Kimm [kɪm] *f* (-; *no pl*) ♆ visual horizon.
Kimme ['kɪmə] *f* (-; -n) ✕ notch.
Kind [kɪnt] *n* (-[e]s; -er) child (*a. fig.*), F kid, *a.* baby: **ein ~ erwarten** (**bekommen**) be expecting (going to have) a baby; **von ~ auf** from childhood; F **mit ~ und Kegel** (with) bag and baggage; *fig.* **das ~ mit dem Bade ausschütten** throw the baby out with the bathwater; **das ~ beim rechten Namen nennen** call a spade a spade; (**ein**) **gebranntes ~ scheut das Feuer** once bitten, twice shy; → **Geist** 2, **lieb.**
'**Kindbettfieber** *n* ♀ puerperal fever.
'**Kinder|arbeit** *f* child labo(u)r. **~arzt** *m*, **~ärztin** *f* p(a)ediatrician. **~bett(chen)** *n* cot, *Am.* crib. **~buch** *n* children's book. **~dorf** *n* children's village. **~ermäßigung** *f* reduction for children. **~erziehung** *f* bringing up children. **~fahrrad** *n* child's bicycle. ♀**feindlich** *adj* hostile to children, antichildren. ♀**freundlich** *adj* **1.** fond of children. **2.** suitable for children. **~garten** *m* kindergarten. **~gärtner(in** *f) m* kindergarten teacher. **~geld** *n* children's allowance. **~heim** *n* children's home. **~hort** *m* day nursery. **~kleidung** *f* children's wear. **~krankheit** *f* children's disease, *fig.* teething troubles. **~krippe** *f* crèche, day nursery. **~lähmung** *f* ♀ (**spinale**) **~** polio(myelitis). ♀**leicht** *adj* dead easy. ♀**lieb** *adj* very fond of children. **~lied** *n* children's song.
'**kinderlos** *adj* childless.
'**Kinder|mädchen** *n* nurse(maid), nanny. **~pflege** *f* child care. **~psychologie** *f* child psychology. ♀**reich** *adj* with many children: **~e Familie** large family. **~schuhe** *pl* children's shoes: *fig.* **noch in den ~n stecken** be still in its infancy. **~sendung** *f* children's program(me *Br.*). ♀**sicher** *adj* childproof. **~sicherung** *f* mot. childproof lock. **~spiel** *n fig.* **das ist ein ~ (für ihn)** that's child's play (for him). **~spielplatz** *m* children's playground. **~stube** *f* fig. upbringing. **~tagesstätte** *f* day nursery, day-care cent/re (*Am.* -er). **~wagen** *m* pram, *Am.* baby carriage. **~zimmer** *n* children's room, nursery. **~zulage** *f* children's allowance.
'**Kindes|alter** *n* a) infancy, b) childhood. **~liebe** *f* filial love. **~mißhandlung** *f*

child abuse. **~tötung** *f* ♣♣ infanticide.
'**Kindheit** *f* (-; *no pl*) childhood: **von ~ an** from a child.
'**kindisch** *adj* childish.
'**kindlich** *adj* **1.** childlike, childish. **2.** filial (*love etc*).
'**Kindlichkeit** *f* (-; *no pl*) childishness.
'**Kindskopf** *m* F fig. (big) child, silly.
'**Kindtaufe** *f* christening.
Kinetik [ki'ne:tɪk] *f* (-; *no pl*) kinetics.
ki'netisch *adj* kinetic.
Kinkerlitzchen ['kɪŋkɐlɪtsçən] *pl* F **1.** gimcrackery, frills. **2.** trivia.
Kinn [kɪn] *n* (-[e]s; -e) chin.
'**Kinnlade** [-la:də] *f* (-; -n) jaw(bone).
'**Kinnhaken** *m boxing*: hook to the chin.
Kino ['ki:no] *n* (-s; -s) **1.** cinema, *Am.* motion-picture (F movie) theater. **2.** cinema, *esp. Am. the* movies: **ins ~ gehen** go to the pictures (or movies).
'**Kinogänger** [-gɛŋɐ] *m* (-s; -) cinemagoer, *esp. Am.* moviegoer.
Kiosk [kiɔsk] *m* (-[e]s; -e) kiosk.
Kippe¹ ['kɪpə] *f* (-; -n) F stub, fag end, butt.
'**Kippe²** *f* (-; -n) **1.** ✕ tip, (*a. rubbish*) dump. **2.** *gym.* upstart, *Am.* kip. **3.** F *fig.* **es (er) steht auf der ~** it is touch and go (with him).
kippen ['kɪpən] **I** *v/t* (h) **1.** a) tilt, tip over, b) tip out: F **e-n ~** have a quick one. **2.** F *fig.* overturn (*government, project, etc*), drop (*program[me]*), sack (*s.o.*), *sports:* turn (*the match*). **II** *v/i* (sn) **3.** a) tip (over), b) overturn, capsize.
'**Kipper** *m* (-s; -) *mot.* tipper, *Am.* dump truck.
'**Kippfenster** *n* tilting window.
'**Kippfre,quenz** *f* ⚡ sweep frequency.
'**Kippschalter** *m* ⚡ toggle switch.
'**kippsicher** *adj* stable.
Kirche ['kɪrçə] *f* (-; -n) (**in der ~** at) church: **zur ~ gehen** go to church; F **wir wollen doch die ~ im Dorf lassen!** let's not exaggerate things!
'**Kirchen|buch** *n* parish register. **~chor** *m* church choir. **~diener** *m* sexton. **~gemeinde** *f* parish. **~geschichte** *f* church history. **~jahr** *n* ecclesiastical year. **~lied** *n* hymn. **~mu,sik** *f* sacred music. **~rat** *m* (member of the) consistory. **~recht** *n* (-[e]s; *no pl*) canon law. **~schiff** *n* △ nave. **~steuer** *f* church tax. **~stuhl** *m* pew. **~tag** *m* Church congress.

'**Kirchgang** *m* churchgoing. '**Kirch-gänger** [-gɛŋər] *m* (-s; -) churchgoer.

'**Kirchhof** *m* churchyard, graveyard.

'**kirchlich** *adj* church ..., ecclesiastical: *sich ~ trauen lassen*, *~ heiraten* have a church wedding; *~ bestattet werden* be given a Christian burial.

'**Kirchturm** *m* church tower, steeple.

'**Kirschbaum** *m* cherry tree.

'**Kirschblüte** *f* a) cherry blossom, b) (*zur Zeit der ~* at) cherry-blossom time.

Kirsche ['kɪrʃə] *f* (-; -n) cherry: *fig. mit ihm ist nicht gut ~n essen* it's best not to tangle with him.

'**Kirsch|kern** *m* cherry stone. **~kuchen** *m* cherry cake. **~li̱,kör** *m* cherry brandy. **2rot** *adj.* cherry(-red). **~saft** *m* cherry juice. **~torte** *f* cherry gateau. **~was-ser** *n* (-s; ») kirsch.

Kissen ['kɪsən] *n* (-s; -) a) cushion, b) pillow. '**Kissenbezug** *m* a) cushion slip, b) pillowcase.

Kiste ['kɪstə] *f* (-; -n) 1. box, ✝ case, chest, crate. 2. *~* → **Kasten**.

Kitsch [kɪtʃ] *m* (-es; *no pl*) kitsch, trash.

'**kitschig** *adj* kitschy, trashy.

Kitt [kɪt] *m* (-[e]s; -e) 1. cement. 2. putty.

'**Kittchen** ['kɪtçən] *n* (-s; -) → **Knast.**

Kittel ['kɪtəl] *m* (-s; -) a) smock, b) overall, c) (*doctor's*) (white) coat.

kitten ['kɪtən] *v/t* (h) cement, putty, *fig.* patch up (*marriage etc*).

Kitz [kɪts] *n* (-es; -e) *zo.* a) kid, b) fawn.

Kitzel ['kɪtsəl] *m* (-s; *no pl*) 1. tickle, itch. 2. *fig.* thrill, kick. '**kitzeln** *v/t*, *v/i* (h) tickle. **Kitzler** ['kɪtslər] *m* (-s; -) *anat.* clitoris, F clit. '**kitzlig** *adj a.fig.* ticklish.

Kiwi¹ ['kiːvi] *m* (-s; -s) *zo.* kiwi.

'**Kiwi²** *f* (-; -s) ❀ kiwi.

Klacks [klaks] *m* (-es; -e) F dollop, blob: *fig. das ist ein ~* that's nothing.

Kladde ['kladə] *f* (-; -n) 1. scribbling pad. 2. ✝ waste book. 3. rough copy.

klaffen ['klafən] *v/i* (h) gape, *fig. a.* yawn: *~de Wunde* gaping wound.

kläffen ['klɛfən] *v/i* (h) *a.* F *fig.* yap.

Klage ['klaːgə] *f* (-; -n) 1. lament(ation) (*um*, *über acc* for, over). 2. complaint (*über acc* about): *~ führen über* (*acc*) make complaints (*or* complain) about; *es sind ~n laut geworden* there have been complaints. 3. ⚖ a) action (*auf acc* for), lawsuit, b) statement of claim: *~ erheben* institute proceedings (*ge-*

gen against, *wegen* for) (→ *a.* **klagen** 3); *e-e ~ abweisen* dismiss an action.

'**Klagegrund** *m* ⚖ cause of action.

'**Klagelied** *n* lamentation.

klagen ['klaːgən] (h) **I** *v/i* 1. lament (*um*, *über acc* over, about). 2. *~ über* (*acc*) complain of (*a.* ✲) (*or* about); *ohne zu ~* without complaining; *ich kann nicht ~* I have no cause for complaint. 3. ⚖ go to court: *gegen j-n ~* (*wegen* for) sue s.o., bring an action against s.o. **II** *v/t* → **Leid** 1.

Kläger ['klɛːgər] *m* (-s; -), '**Klägerin** *f* (-; -nen) ⚖ plaintiff.

'**Klageschrift** *f* ⚖ statement of claim.

'**Klageweg** *m* ⚖ *auf dem* (*or im*) *~* by entering legal action.

'**klaglos** *adv* without complaining.

Klamauk [klaˈmaʊk] *m* (-s; *no pl*) F 1. racket. 2. to-do. 3. *thea. etc* slapstick.

klamm [klam] *adj* 1. clammy. 2. *~* numb (with cold). 3. F *fig. ~ sein* be hard up.

Klamm *f* (-; -en) *geol.* narrow gorge.

Klammer ['klamər] *f* (-; -n) 1. a) clip, ⊙ *a.* clamp, cramp, b) clothes peg, *Am.* clothespin. 2. ✲ brace(s). 3. A, *print.* parenthesis, bracket, brace: *in ~n set-zen* put *s.th.* in parentheses, bracket; *~ auf* (*zu*) open (close) brackets; *die ~(n) auflösen* A remove the brackets.

klammern ['klamərn] (h) **I** *v/t* (*an acc* to) a) clip, ⊙ *a.* clamp, b) peg, pin. **II** *sich ~ an* (*acc*) *a.* fig. cling to.

'**klamm'heimlich** *adv* F on the quiet.

Klamotte [klaˈmɔtə] *f* (-; -n) F 1. (*alte*) *~* (*film etc*) oldie. 2. *pl* a) rags, togs, b) things, junk.

klang [klaŋ] *pret* of **klingen.**

Klang *m* (-[e]s; »e) a) sound, ring, b) tone, c) timbre: *unter den Klängen von* (*or gen*) to the strains of.

'**Klangfarbe** *f* timbre.

'**Klangfülle** *f* sonority.

'**klanglich** *adj* tonal.

'**klanglos** *adj* toneless.

'**Klangregler** *m* radio *etc*: tone control.

'**klangrein** *adj* *~ sein* have a pure sound.

'**Klangtreue** *f* fidelity.

'**klangvoll** *adj* 1. sonorous, melodious. 2. *fig.* illustrious (*name etc*).

'**Klangwiedergabe** *f* sound reproduction.

'**klappbar** *adj* 1. collapsible, folding. 2.

hinged. '**Klappbett** n folding bed. '**Klappdeckel** m snap lid.

Klappe ['klapə] f (-; -n) **1.** flap (a. ☉), leaf (of table). **2.** anat. valve. **3.** (eye) patch. **4.** ♪ key. **5.** F fig. mouth, trap: *e-e große ~ haben* have a big mouth; *halt die ~!* shut up!

klappen ['klapən] (h) **I** v/t **1.** *nach oben ~ → hochklappen; nach unten ~ → herunterklappen; der Sitz läßt sich nach hinten ~* the seat folds back. **II** v/i **2.** a) clack, bang, b) click shut. **3.** F fig. work, go off well: *~ wie am Schnürchen* go like clockwork; *es klappt nicht* it won't work; *nichts klappte* nothing worked; *wenn alles klappt* if all goes well; *es wird schon ~!* it'll work out all right!; *hat es mit dem Job geklappt?* did you get the job all right?

'**Klappentext** m blurb.
'**Klappenventil** n ☉ flap valve.
Klapper ['klapər] f (-; -n) rattle. **~kasten** m, **~kiste** f F rattletrap, old banger.
klappern ['klapərn] v/i (h) **1.** clatter, rattle, *knitting needles:* clack: *mit dem Geschirr ~* rattle the dishes; *auf der Schreibmaschine ~* clatter away on the typewriter. **2.** shiver: *er klapperte vor Kälte (Angst) mit den Zähnen* his teeth were chattering with cold (fear).
'**Klappern** n (-s) clatter(ing) (etc.).
'**Klapperschlange** f zo. rattlesnake.
'**Klapp(fahr)rad** n folding bicycle.
'**Klappfenster** n top-hung window.
'**Klappmesser** n jackknife.
klapprig ['klapriç] adj F **1.** rattly, rickety. **2.** fig. shaky, doddering.
'**Klappsitz** m folding (or jump) seat.
'**Klappstuhl** m folding (or camp) chair.
'**Klapptisch** m folding table.
'**Klappverdeck** n mot. folding hood (Am. top).
Klaps [klaps] m (-es; -e) **1.** (a. j-m e-n ~ geben) slap, smack. **2.** F e-n ~ haben be nuts, have a screw loose.
'**Klapsmühle** f F funny farm, nut-house.
klar [klaːr] adj clear (a. fig.), a. distinct, fig. a. clear-cut (aim, decision, etc), a. lucid (moments etc), a. plain, obvious: *~er Sieg* clear victory; *~ zum Start* ready for takeoff; *e-n ~en Kopf behalten* keep one's wits about one; *sich ein ~es Bild machen von* get a clear idea of; *~e Verhältnisse schaffen* get things

straight; *es ist ~, daß* it is clear (or evident) that; *es ist mir ~ (or ich bin mir darüber im ~en), daß* I realize (or I'm aware) that; *ist das ~?* is that clear?; *das ist mir (nicht ganz) ~* I (don't quite) understand; *(na) ~!* of course!, sure!; *alles ~?* a) everything o.k.?, b) got it?; *~ und deutlich* a) clearly, distinctly, b) fig. straight; *et. ~ zum Ausdruck bringen* make s.th. plain; → a. *klargehen, klarkommen etc.*

'**Kläranlage** f sewage (purification) plant. '**Klärbecken** n settling basin.
klären ['klɛːrən] (h) **I** v/t **1.** purify, clear. **2.** fig. clear up, clarify, sort s.th. out. **II** sich ~ **3.** weather: clear (up). **4.** fig. issue: be settled, problem: be solved.
'**klargehen** v/i (irr, sep, -ge-, sn, → gehen) F be all right.
'**Klarheit** f (-; no pl) a. fig. clearness, clarity: *sich ~ verschaffen über (acc)* find out about.
Klarinette [klari'nɛtə] f (-; -n) clarinet.
'**klarkommen** v/i (irr, sep, -ge-, sn, → kommen) F manage: *mit j-m ~* get along (fine) with s.o.; *kommst du damit klar?* can you manage?
'**klarmachen** v/t (sep, -ge-, h) **1.** F *j-m et. ~* make s.th. clear (or explain s.th.) to s.o.; *sich ~, daß* realize that. **2.** ⚓ clear, get s.th. ready. **3.** F *alles ~* settle it.
'**Klärschlamm** m sewage sludge.
'**Klarschrift** f computer: (a. in ~) clear. **~leser** m (optical) character reader.
'**klarsehen** v/i (irr, sep, -ge-, h, → sehen) F fig. see (the light).
'**Klarsicht|folie** f cling film, transparent sheet. **~packung** f transparent packing. **~scheibe** f mot. antimist panel.
'**klarstellen** v/t (sep, -ge-, h) **et. ~** a) get s.th. straight, b) state s.th. clearly.
'**Klartext** m clear text: *im ~* a) in clear, b) fig. in plain language.
'**Klärung** f (-; -en) **1.** purification. **2.** fig. clarification, clearing up.
'**klarwerden** v/i (irr, sep, -ge-, sn, → werden) become clear (dat to): *sich ~ über (acc)* a) get s.th. clear in one's mind, b) make up one's mind about; *es wurde mir klar, daß* I realized that.
Klasse ['klasə] f (-; -n) **1.** class, ped. a. form, Am. grade. **2.** ✝ class, quality, grade, (tax, age) bracket: *erster ~ a.* f fig. first-class; *nach ~n ordnen* class,

classify; F ~*!* super!, great!; *große (or einsame)* ~ *sein* be super (*or* fantastic).

'**Klassen|arbeit** f ped. (class) test. **~bewußtsein** n class consciousness. **~buch** n (class) register, Am. classbook. **~gesellschaft** f class society. **~kame,rad(in** f) m classmate. **~kampf** m pol. class struggle. **~lehrer(in** f) m class (*Am. a.* homeroom) teacher.

'**klassenlos** adj classless.

'**Klassen|lotte,rie** f class lottery. **~sprecher(in** f) m ped. class representative, Br. form captain. **~unterschied** m class difference. **~zimmer** n classroom.

klassifizieren [klasifi'tsi:rən] v/t (h) classify. **Klassifi'zierung** f (-; -en) classification.

'**Klassik** ['klasɪk] f (-; *no pl*) **1.** classical period. **2.** classical music. **Klassiker** ['klasɪkər] m (-s; -) **1.** classic(al author). **2. a)** great artist (*etc*), **b)** (*work*) classic.

'**klassisch** adj. classical. **2.** *fig.* classic. **Klassizismus** [klasi'tsɪsmʊs] m (-; *no pl*) classicism. **klassizistisch** [klasi'tsɪstɪʃ] adj classicistic.

Klatsch [klatʃ] m (-es; -e) **1.** splash. **2.** smack, slap. **3.** *no pl* F gossip.

'**Klatschbase** f F gossip(monger).

'**Klatsche** ['klatʃə] f (-; -n) **1.** (fly)swatter. **2.** F ped. crib. **3.** F gossip(monger).

klatschen ['klatʃən] (h) **I** v/i **1.** applaud, clap: *in die Hände* ~ clap one's hands. **2.** (*an acc* against) *rain etc*: splash, *waves*: crash. **3.** F gossip (*über acc* about). **II** v/t **4.** *et.* ~ *auf* (acc) (*or gegen, an acc*) slap (*or* bang) s.th. on (*or* against). **5.** *Beifall* ~ applaud, clap.

Klatsche'rei f (-; -en) F gossip(ing).

'**Klatsch|kolum,nist(in** f) m F gossip columnist. **~maul** n F real gossip.

'**klatschnaß** adj F dripping wet.

'**Klatschspalte** f F gossip column.

Klaue ['klaʊə] f (-; -n) **1.** zo. claw (*a.* ⚙), *a.* talon: *fig. in j-s* ~*n geraten* fall into s.o.'s clutches. **2.** F *fig.* scrawl.

klauen ['klaʊən] v/t, v/i (h) F swipe, pinch, *fig.* steal, borrow (*ideas etc*).

Klause ['klaʊzə] f (-; -n) hermitage.

Klausel ['klaʊzəl] f (-; -n) ⚖ a) clause, stipulation, b) proviso.

Klaustrophobie [klaʊstrofo'bi:] f (-; *no pl*) claustrophobia.

Klausur [klaʊ'zu:r] f (-; -en) **1.** *no pl* seclusion. **2.** ped., univ. test, paper.

Klau'surarbeit f → *Klausur* 2.

Klau'surtagung f closed meeting.

Klaviatur [klavia'tu:r] f (-; -en) ♪ keyboard.

Klavier [kla'vi:r] n (-s; -e) piano(forte): *auf dem (am)* ~ on (at) the piano; ~ *spielen (können)* play the piano.

Kla'vier|abend m piano recital. **~auszug** m piano score. **~begleitung** f piano accompaniment. **~kon,zert** m **1.** piano concert. **2.** → *Klavierabend.* **~lehrer(in** f) m piano teacher. **~schemel** m piano stool. **~schule** f (*book*) piano tutor. **~so,nate** f piano sonata. **~spieler(in** f) m pianist. **~stimmer** m (piano) tuner. **~stunde** f piano lesson. **~unterricht** m piano lessons.

'**Klebeband** n adhesive (*or* sticky) tape.

'**Klebefolie** f adhesive film.

kleben ['kle:bən] (h) **I** v/t **1.** (*an acc* to) glue, paste. **2.** F *j-m* e-e~ paste s.o. one. **II** v/i **3.** be sticky. **4.** (*an dat* to) adhere, stick: *fig. an j-m* ~ remain glued to s.o.; *an s-m Posten* ~ hang on to one's job.

'**klebenbleiben** v/i (*irr, sep,* -ge-, sn, → *bleiben*) **1.** stick (*an dat* to). **2.** F *fig.* get stuck (*in dat* in, at).

'**Klebepresse** f *film:* splicer.

'**Kleber** m (-s; -) **1.** gluten. **2.** F adhesive, glue.

'**Klebe|stelle** f *film:* splice. **~stift** m glue stick. **~streifen** m adhesive (*or* sticky) tape. **~zettel** m gummed label.

klebrig ['kle:brɪç] adj sticky.

'**Klebrigkeit** f (-; *no pl*) stickiness.

Klebstoff m (-s; -e) adhesive, glue.

kleckern ['klɛkərn] (h) F **I** v/i **1.** make a mess. **2.** drip. **II** v/t **3.** *et.* ~ *auf* (acc) spill s.th. on.

'**kleckerweise** adv F in dribs and drabs.

Klecks [klɛks] m (-es; -e) F **1.** stain, blot. **2.** blob. '**klecksen** v/i (h) F **1.** make blots (*or* stains), make a mess. **2.** daub.

Klee [kle:] m (-s; *no pl*) ♣ clover: F *über den grünen* ~ *loben* praise s.o., s.th. to the skies. '**Kleeblatt** n **1.** cloverleaf: *vierblättriges* ~ four-leaf(ed) clover. **2.** *mot.* cloverleaf (intersection).

Kleiber ['klaɪbər] m (-s; -) zo. nut hatch.

Kleid [klaɪt] n (-es; -er) **1.** dress (*a. fig.*), frock, gown. **2.** *pl* clothes, clothing: *~er machen Leute* fine feathers make fine birds. **3.** *hunt.* a) fur, coat, b) plumage.

kleiden ['klaɪdən] (h) **I** v/t **1.** clothe,

Kleiderbügel

dress: *fig. et. in Worte* ~ couch s.th. in words. **2.** *j-n (gut)* ~ suit (*or* become) s.o., look well on s.o. **II** *sich* ~ dress; *sich* ~ *in* (*acc*) wear.

Kleider|bügel ['klaɪdər-] *m* coat hanger. **~bürste** *f* clothes brush. **~haken** *m* coat hook. **~puppe** *f* dummy, mannequin. **~schrank** *m* wardrobe. **~ständer** *m* clothes tree (*or* rack). **~stoff** *m* dress material.

'**kleidsam** *adj* becoming.

Kleidung ['klaɪdʊŋ] *f* (-; *no pl*) clothing, clothes, garments. '**Kleidungsstück** *n* article of clothing, garment.

Kleie ['klaɪə] *f* (-; -n) bran.

klein [klaɪn] **I** *adj* **1.** small, little (*finger, toe, house, etc*): *sehr* ~, *winzig* ~ very small, tiny, *F* teeny; *ziemlich* ~ rather small, smallish; *von* ~ *auf* from a child; *im* ~*en* in miniature; *mein* ~*er Bruder* my little (*or* young) brother; *die Welt ist (doch)* ~*!* it's a small world! **2.** *fig.* small, little, *a.* ♟ minor, petty: *aus* ~*en Verhältnissen kommen* have a humble background; ~*e Geister* small minds; *der* ~*e Mann* the man in (*Am.* on) the street; *das* ~*ere Übel* the lesser evil; *bis ins* ~*ste* (down) to the last detail; *das ist m-e* ~*ste Sorge* that's the least of my worries. **II** *adv* small: *ein Wort* ~ *schreiben* write a word with a small (initial) letter; *F ein (ganz)* ~ *wenig* a little (*or* tiny) bit; ~ *anfangen* start in a small way; → *beigeben* II.

'**Klein|aktie** *f* baby share (*Am.* stock). **~aktio,när(in** *f) m* small shareholder (*Am.* stockholder). **~anzeige** *f* classified advertisement (*F* ad). **~arbeit** *f a.* mühevolle ~ painstaking and detailed work. **~auto** *n* small car. **~bauer** *m* small farmer. **~betrieb** *m* small enterprise. **~bildkamera** *f* 35 mm camera. **~buchstabe** *m* small letter. **~bürger(in** *f) m,* ⚭**bürgerlich** *adj* petty bourgeois. **~bus** *m* minibus.

'**Kleine**[1] *m, f* (-n; -n) little one.

'**Kleine**[2] *n* (-n; -n) *F* baby.

'**Klein|fa,milie** *f sociol.* nuclear family. **~for,mat** *n* small size: *im* ~ small-format. **~garten** *m* allotment (garden). **~gärtner(in** *f) m* allotment gardener.

'**Kleingedruckte** *n das* ~ *lesen* read the small print.

'**Kleingeld** *n* (small) change: *fig. das nö-*

tige ~ *haben* have the wherewithal.

'**kleingläubig** *adj* of little faith.

'**Kleinhandel** *m* → *Einzelhandel.*

'**Kleinheit** *f* (-; *no pl*) smallness (*a. fig.*).

'**Kleinhirn** *n anat.* cerebellum.

'**Kleinholz** *n* (-es; *no pl*) firewood: *F fig.* ~ *machen aus* a) *j-n* make mincemeat of s.o., b) *e-r Sache* smash s.th. to pieces.

'**Kleinigkeit** *f* (-; -en) a) trifle, small thing, b) (*gift*) little something, c) minor detail: *e-e* ~ *essen* have a bite; *das war e-e (k-e)* ~ that was (not) easy.

'**Kleinindu,strie** *f* small industry.

'**kleinka,riert** *adj* **1.** small-check(ed). **2.** *F fig.* small-minded.

'**Klein|kind** *n* infant. **~kram** *m* trifles. **~kre,dit** *m* small-(scale) credit. **~krieg** *m* guer(r)illa warfare: *fig. e-n* ~ *führen mit* keep up a running battle with.

'**kleinkriegen** *v/t* (*sep,* -ge-, h) *F* (manage to) break: *fig. j-n* ~ a) wear s.o. out, b) get s.o. down; *nicht kleinzukriegen a. person:* indestructible.

'**kleinlich** *adj* **1.** pedantic. **2.** narrow-minded. **3.** mean.

'**Kleinlichkeit** *f* (-; *no pl*) **1.** pedantry. **2.** narrow-mindedness. **3.** meanness.

Kleinod ['klaɪnoːt] *n* (-[e]s; -e) jewel.

'**Kleinrentner(in** *f) m* person receiving a small pension.

'**kleinschneiden** *v/t* (*irr, sep,* -ge-, h, → *schneiden*) cut up, chop (up).

'**kleinschreiben** *v/t* (*irr, sep,* -ge-, h, → *schreiben*) *F Ordnung etc wird bei ihm kleingeschrieben* he isn't a great one for order *etc.*

'**Kleinstaat** *m* minor state.

'**Klein|stadt** *f* small town. **~städter(in** *f) m,* ⚭**städtisch** *adj* provincial.

'**Kleinst|bildkamera** *f* subminiature camera. **~lebewesen** *n biol.* microorganism. ⚭**möglich** *adj* smallest possible. **~wagen** *m* minicar, midget car.

'**Klein|tier** *n* small (domestic) animal. **~vieh** *n* small domestic animals: *F fig.* ~ *macht auch Mist* many a little makes a mickle. **~wagen** *m* small car.

kleinwüchsig ['klaɪnvyːksɪç] *adj* small, short.

Kleister ['klaɪstər] *m* (-s; -) paste.

'**kleistern** *v/t* (h) paste (*an, auf acc* on).

Klematis [kle'maːtɪs] *f* (-; -) ⚘ clematis.

Klemme ['klɛmə] *f* (-; -n) **1.** clamp (*a.* ⚡, ☉), clip, ⚡ terminal. **2.** *F fig. in der* ~

sein (*or* **sitzen**) be in a fix (*or* tight spot); *j-m aus der* ~ *helfen* help s.o. out of a fix.

klemmen ['klɛmən] (h) **I** *v/t* **1.** a) jam (a. ⚙), b) squeeze, pinch, c) stick: *ich habe mir den Finger geklemmt* → 3. **II** *v/i* **2.** be jammed, be stuck: F *wo klemmt's?* what's wrong?, where's the snag? **III** *sich* ~ **3.** jam one's finger (*etc*), get one's finger (*etc*) caught. **4.** squeeze o.s. (*in acc* into, *hinter acc* behind): F *sich* ~ *hinter* a) e-e *Sache* get down to s.th., b) *j-n* get to work on s.o.

Klempner ['klɛmpnər] *m* (-s; -) **1.** tin-smith. **2.** plumber. **Klempnerei** [klɛmpnə'raɪ] *f* (-; -en) tinsmith's (*or* plumber's) workshop. '**Klempnermeister** *m* master tinsmith (*or* plumber).

Kleptomane [klɛpto'maːnə] *m* (-n; -n) kleptomaniac. **Kleptomanie** [-ma'niː] *f* (-; *no pl*) kleptomania. **Klepto'manin** *f* (-; -nen) kleptomaniac.

klerikal [kleri'kaːl] *adj* clerical.
Kleriker ['kleːrikər] *m* (-s; -) cleric.
Klerus ['kleːrʊs] *m* (-; *no pl*) clergy.
Klette ['klɛtə] *f* (-; -n) ⚘ bur(r) (a. *fig.*): *sich wie e-e* ~ *an j-n hängen* cling to s.o. like a leech.

'**Kletterer** *m* (-s; -) climber.
'**Klettergerüst** *n* climbing frame.
klettern ['klɛtərn] *v/i* (sn) climb, ⚘ *a.* creep, *fig. a.* go up (*auf acc* to): *auf e-n Baum* ~ climb a tree.
'**Kletterpflanze** *f* climber. **~rose** *f* rambler. **~stange** *f* climbing pole.
'**Kletterverschluß** *m* Velcro (*TM*).
klicken ['klɪkən] *v/i* (h) click.
Klient [kli'ɛnt] *m* (-en; -en) ⚖ client.
Kliff [klɪf] *n* (-[e]s; -e) *geol.* cliff.
Klima ['kliːma] *n* (-s; -s) climate, *fig. a.* atmosphere: *soziales* ~ social climate.
'**Klimaanlage** *f* air-conditioning: *mit e-r* ~ *ausrüsten* air-condition.
Klimakterium [klimak'teːriʊm] *n* (-s; *no pl*) menopause, climacteric.
klimatisch [kli'maːtɪʃ] *adj* climatic.
klimatisieren [klimati'ziːrən] *v/t* (h) air-condition.
Klimatologie [klimatolo'giː] *f* (-; *no pl*) climatology.
'**Klimaveränderung** *f*, '**Klimawechsel** *m* change in climate.
'**Klimmzug** ['klɪm-] *m gym.* chin-up: *e-n* ~ *machen* do a chin-up, chin o.s. up.

klimpern ['klɪmpərn] *v/i* (h) **1.** (a. ~ *mit*) jingle. **2.** ~ *auf* (*dat*) strum on *the guitar*, tinkle on *the piano*.
Klinge ['klɪŋə] *f* (-; -n) blade.
Klingel ['klɪŋəl] *f* (-; -n) bell.
'**Klingelknopf** *m* bell push, call button.
klingeln ['klɪŋəln] (h) **I** *v/i* **1.** ring ([*nach*] *j-m* for s.o., *bei j-m* s.o.'s doorbell): *es klingelt* a) the doorbell is ringing, b) there's the bell. **2.** *engine*: ping. **II** *v/t* **3.** *j-n aus dem Bett* ~ get s.o. out of bed.
'**Klingelzeichen** *n* ring, bell (signal).
klingen ['klɪŋən] *v/i* (klang, geklungen, h) sound (a. *fig.*), ring, *glasses*: clink, *metal*: clank: *fig. das klingt schon besser* that sounds better; *das klingt nach Neid* that sounds like envy.
'**klingend** *adj* melodious.
Klinik ['kliːnɪk] *f* (-; -en) clinic, nursing home. **Klinikum** ['kliːnikʊm] *n* (-s; -ka, -ken) clinical cent/re (*Am.* -er).
klinisch ['kliːnɪʃ] *adj* clinical: ~ *tot* clinically dead.
Klinke ['klɪŋkə] *f* (-; -n) (door) handle.
Klinker ['klɪŋkər] *m* (-s; -) △ clinker.
klipp [klɪp] *adv* ~ *und klar* clearly, plainly; *ich habe ihm* ~ *und klar gesagt, daß* ... I told him straight out that ...
Klippe ['klɪpə] *f* (-; -n) *geol.* reef, rock: *fig.* e-e ~ *umschiffen* get around an obstacle.
klirren ['klɪrən] *v/i* (h) **1.** a) rattle, clatter, b) clink, chink, jingle: ~ *mit* rattle (*one's chains, keys, etc*). **2.** *radio*: produce harmonic distortion.
'**Klirrfaktor** *m radio*: distortion factor.
Klischee [kli'ʃeː] *n* (-s; -s) *fig.* cliché. **~vorstellung** *f* stereotyped idea.
Klistier [klɪs'tiːr] *n* (-s; -e) ⚕ enema.
Kli'stierspritze *f* enema syringe.
Klitoris ['kliːtorɪs] *f* (-; -) *anat.* clitoris.
klitschig ['klɪtʃɪç] *adj* doughy (*bread etc*).
klitzeklein ['klɪtsə-] *adj* F teeny(-weeny).
Klo [kloː] *n* (-s; -s) F loo, *Am.* john.
Kloake [klo'aːkə] *f* (-; -n) sewer.
Kloben ['kloːbən] *m* (-s; -) **1.** ⚙ block. **2.** log.
'**klobig** *adj* bulky, a. *fig.* clumsy.
klönen ['kløːnən] *v/i* (h) F have a natter.
'**Klopa,pier** *n* F toilet (*Br. a.* loo) paper.
klopfen ['klɔpfən] (h) **I** *v/i* **1.** (*an acc* at, on) knock, tap: *es klopft* there's somebody (knocking) at the door; → *Busch* 1, *Finger*, *Schulter*. **2.** *heart etc*: beat, throb: *fig. mit* ~*dem Herzen* with (a)

beating heart. **3.** *engine:* knock. **II** *v/t* **4.** beat (*carpet etc*): **den Takt ~** beat time.

'**Klopfer** *m* (-s; -) **1.** doorknocker. **2.** carpet-beater.

'**klopffest** *adj* mot. knockproof.

Klöppel ['klœpəl] *m* (-s; -) **1.** clapper (*of bell*). **2.** textil. (lace) bobbin. '**Klöppel- kissen** *n* lace pillow. '**klöppeln** *v/i* (h) make lace. '**Klöppelspitze** *f* bone lace.

Klosett [klo'zɛt] *n* (-s; -s) lavatory, toilet. **~deckel** *m* toilet lid. **~pa¦pier** *n* toilet paper. **~sitz** *m* toilet seat.

Kloß [klo:s] *m* (-es; ¨e) dumpling: *fig.* **ich hatte e-n ~ im Hals** I had a lump in my throat.

Kloster ['klo:stər] *n* (-s; ¨) a) monastery, b) convent, nunnery: **ins ~ gehen** enter a monastery (*etc*), become a monk (*or* nun). **~bruder** *m* friar. **~frau** *f* nun. **~leben** *n* monastic life.

klösterlich ['klø:stərlıç] *adj* monastic.

Klotz [klɔts] *m* (-es; ¨e) **1.** block (*of* wood), log: **F er ist mir nur ein ~ am Bein** he is just a millstone round my neck. **2.** F *contp.* oaf, *Am. sl.* klutz.

'**klotzig** *adj* bulky, heavy.

Kluft¹ [kluft] *f* (-; ¨e) *fig.* gap.

Kluft² *f* (-; -en) F togs, gear.

klug [klu:k] **I** *adj* **1.** a) intelligent, clever, smart, bright, shrewd, b) sensible, wise, judicious, c) prudent: **ein ~er Rat** a sound advice; **so ~ wie zuvor** none the wiser; **der Klügere gibt nach** the wiser head gives in. **2.** F **ich werde aus ihr** (**der Sache**) **nicht ~** I can't make her (it) out; **wirst du daraus ~?** does it make sense to you? **II** *adv* intelligently (*etc*): **du hättest klüger daran getan zu** *inf* you would have been wise to *inf*.

klugerweise ['klu:gər-] *adv* wisely, sensibly: **~ hat sie geschwiegen** a. she had the good sense to keep quiet.

'**Klugheit** *f* (-; *no pl*) a) intelligence, brightness, b) good sense, c) prudence.

'**Klugscheißer** *m* F smart aleck, smarty.

klumpen ['klʊmpən] *v/i* (h) clot, become lumpy. '**Klumpen** *m* (-s; -) lump, clot, clod. '**Klumpfuß** *m* clubfoot. **klumpig** ['klʊmpıç] *adj* lumpy, clotted.

Klüngel ['klʏŋəl] *m* (-s; -) *contp.* clique.

Klunkern ['klʊŋkərn] *pl* F rocks, ice.

Klüver ['kly:vər] *m* (-s; -) ⚓ jib.

knabbern ['knabərn] *v/i, v/t* (h) (**an** *dat* at) nibble, gnaw: F *fig.* **ich hatte lange**

daran zu ~ a) I didn't get over it easily, b) it took me some time to figure it out.

Knabe ['kna:bə] *m* (-n; -n) boy, lad. '**Knabenalter** *n* boyhood. '**Knabenchor** *m* boys' choir. '**knabenhaft** *adj* boyish.

'**Knäckebrot** ['knɛkə-] *n* crispbread.

knacken ['knakən] (h) **I** *v/t a. fig.* crack: **F ein Auto ~** break into a car. **II** *v/i* a) crack, b) snap. '**Knacker** *m* (-s; -) **F alter ~** old fog(e)y. **Knacki** ['knaki] *m* (-s; -s) F jailbird. '**knackig** *adj* **1.** crisp, crunchy. **2.** F *fig.* dishy.

'**Knacklaut** *m* ling. glottal stop.

'**Knackpunkt** *m* F *fig.* crunch (point).

Knacks [knaks] *m* (-es; -e) **1.** crack. **2.** *fig.* defect: **er hat e-n ~ (weg)** a) his health is shaken, b) his nerves are all shot, c) he is badly hit; **ihre Ehe hat e-n ~** their marriage is cracking up.

Knall [knal] *m* (-[e]s; -e) **1.** bang, pop (*of a cork*). **2.** *fig.* quarrel, row. **3.** F **e-n ~ haben** be nuts. **4.** F **~ und Fall** (all) of a sudden; **j-n ~ und Fall entlassen** dismiss s.o. on the spot.

'**Knallbon¦bon** *m, n* (party) cracker.

'**Knallef¦fekt** *m* F clou, sensation.

knallen ['knalən] (h) **I** *v/i* **1.** (*a.* **~ mit**) *door etc:* bang, slam, *whip:* crack, *cork:* pop: **es knallte zweimal** there were to loud bangs. **2.** F bang, fire. **3.** F crash (**gegen** into): **mit dem Kopf an die Windschutzscheibe ~** hit one's head on the windscreen; **F sonst knallt's!** or else! **4.** F *sun:* beat down. **II** *v/t* **5.** bang, slam: **den Ball ins Tor ~** slam the ball home; **F j-m e-e ~** paste s.o. one.

'**Knaller** *m* (-s; -) F **1.** → **Knallkörper**. **2.** → **Knüller**.

'**Knallerbse** *f* (toy) torpedo.

'**Knallfrosch** *m* jumping cracker.

'**Knallgas** *n* 🔬 oxyhydrogen (gas).

'**knall'hart** *adj* F **1.** smashing, powerful (*blow etc*). **2.** *fig.* tough, brutal: **~ fragen** *etc* ask *etc* with brutal frankness.

'**knallig** F **I** *adj* **1.** loud, glaring (*colo[u]r*). **2.** skintight. **II** *adv* **~ bunt** gaudy; **~ heiß** scorching.

'**Knallkopf** *m* F idiot.

'**Knallkörper** *m* banger.

'**knall'rot** *adj* bright red, crimson.

'**knall'voll** *adj* F **1.** jam-packed. **2.** dead drunk, paralytic.

knapp [knap] **I** *adj* **1.** scanty, meag/re

(*Am.* -er): ~ *sein* be scarce, be in short supply; ~ *werden* run short; → *Kasse* 4. **2.** *fig.* narrow: ~*e Mehrheit* bare majority. **3.** *fig.* concise, terse (*style etc*), brief, short (*answer etc*): *in ~en Worten* in a few words. **4.** ~(*e*) *zwei Stunden* just under two hours; *in e-m ~en Jahr* in less than a year; ~ *10 Minuten* barely (*or* just) ten minutes. **5.** tight (*skirt etc*). **II** *adv* **6.** only just: ~ *gewinnen* win by a narrow margin; *e-e Prüfung ~ bestehen* scrape through an examination; F (*aber*) *nicht zu ~!* a) you bet!, b) plenty of it!, c) and how! **7.** ~ *sitzen* fit tightly; *fig. m-e Zeit ist ~ bemessen* I'm pushed for time.

'**knapphalten** *v/t* (*irr, sep, -ge-, h,* → *halten*) F keep s.o. short.

'**Knappheit** *f* (-; *no pl*) **1.** a) scantiness, b) scarcity, shortage. **2.** *fig.* narrowness. **3.** *fig.* terseness, conciseness, shortness. **4.** tightness.

'**Knappschaft** *f* (-; -en) miners' association.

'**Knarre** ['knarə] *f* (-; -n) F gun.

knarren ['knarən] *v/i* (h) creak.

Knast [knast] *m* (-[e]s; -e, ⸚e) F (*im ~* in) clink: ~ *schieben* do time.

'**Knastbruder** *m* F jailbird.

knattern ['knatərn] *v/i* (h) rattle, *motorbike etc*: roar, *flag, sail*: flap.

Knäuel ['knɔɐəl] *m, n* (-s; -) **1.** ball (*of wool*). **2.** tangle. **3.** cluster (*of people*).

Knauf [knaʊf] *m* (-[e]s; ⸚e) **1.** knob. **2.** △ capital. **3.** pommel.

Knauser ['knaʊzər] *m* (-s; -) F miser.

Knause'rei *f* (-; -en) F stinginess.

'**knauserig** *adj* F stingy.

knausern ['knaʊzərn] *v/i* (h) F be stingy.

knautschen ['knaʊtʃən] *v/i* (h) F crease, crumple.

'**Knautschzone** *f mot.* crumple zone.

Knebel ['kneːbəl] *m* (-s; -) gag.

knebeln ['kneːbəln] *v/t* (h) *a. fig.* gag.

Knecht [knɛçt] *m* (-[e]s; -e) **1.** farmhand. **2.** *fig.* slave. **knechten** ['knɛçtən] *v/t* (h) enslave. '**Knechtschaft** *f* (-; *no pl*) slavery. '**Knechtung** *f* (-; -en) enslavement.

kneifen ['knaɪfən] (kniff, gekniffen, h) I *v/t* **1.** pinch: *j-n* (*or j-m*) *in den Arm ~* pinch s.o.'s arm. **II** *v/i* **2.** pinch. **3.** F (*vor dat*) dodge (*s.th.*), back out (of), chicken out (of, on).

'**Kneifzange** *f* (-e-e ~ a pair of) pincers.

Kneipe ['knaɪpə] *f* (-; -n) F pub, *Am.* bar. '**Kneipenbummel** *m* (*a.* **e-n ~ machen**) pub-crawl.

Kneippkur ['knaɪp-] *f* ⚕ Kneipp('s) cure.

Knete ['kneːtə] *f* (-; *no pl*) F **1.** → **Knetmasse. 2.** lolly, *Am.* bread. '**kneten** *v/t* (h) a) knead, *a.* massage, b) mo(u)ld. '**Knetmasse** *f* plasticine.

Knick [knɪk] *m* (-[e]s; -e) **1.** (sharp) bend: *die Straße macht e-n ~ a.* the road bends sharply. **2.** a) crease, fold, b) kink. **3.** *fig.* (sharp) drop, falling off.

knicken ['knɪkən] *v/t* (h) **1.** (*a. v/i*) break, snap: → *geknickt.* **2.** crease, fold: *nicht ~!* do not bend! **3.** (*a. v/i*) buckle, bend.

knickerig ['knɪkərɪç] *adj* F stingy, mean.

Knicks [knɪks] *m* (-es; -e) curtsy: **e-n ~ machen** → **knicksen** ['knɪksən] *v/i* (h) (drop a) curtsy (*vor j-m* to s.o.).

Knie [kniː] *n* (-s; - ['kniː(ə)]) **1.** → **Kniescheibe:** *bis an die ~* up to one's knees, knee-deep; *j-n auf den ~n bitten* beg s.o. on bended knees; *in die ~ brechen* collapse; *in die ~ gehen* a) sag at the knees, b) *fig.* go to the wall; *j-n in die ~ zwingen a. fig.* force s.o. on his knees; *fig. et. übers ~ brechen* rush s.th.; F *weiche ~ bekommen* go weak at the knees, become scared; *j-n übers ~ legen* give s.o. a spanking. **2.** ⊕ elbow, bend.

'**Kniebeuge** *f gym.* knee bend. '**Kniefall** *m eccl.* genuflection. '**kniefrei** *adj* above-the-knee. '**Kniegelenk** *n a.* ⊕ knee joint. '**Kniekehle** *f anat.* hollow of the knee. '**knielang** *adj* knee-length.

knien [kniːn, 'kniːən] (h) I *v/i* (*vor dat* before) kneel, be on one's knees. **II** *sich ~* kneel down; F *fig. sich ~ in* (*acc*) get down to.

'**Kniescheibe** *f anat.* kneecap.

'**Knieschützer** *m sports:* kneepad.

'**Kniestrumpf** *m* knee-length sock.

'**knietief** *adj* knee-deep.

kniff [knɪf] *pret of* **kneifen.**

Kniff [knɪf] *m* (-[e]s; -e) **1.** crease, fold. **2.** *fig.* trick. **kniffelig** [knɪfəlɪç] *adj* tricky.

kniffen ['knɪfən] *v/t* (h) fold, crease.

knipsen ['knɪpsən] (h) I *v/t* **1.** punch (*ticket*). **2.** F *j-n ~* take s.o.'s picture, snap s.o. **II** *v/i* **3.** F take photos, snap.

Knirps [knɪrps] *m* (-es; -e) little chap (*Am.* guy), *contp.* squirt.

knirschen ['knɪrʃən] *v/i* (h) grate, *snow,*

sand, etc: crunch: **mit den Zähnen ~** grind (*or* gnash) one's teeth.

knistern ['knɪstərn] *v/i* (h) crackle, *silk, paper, etc*: rustle: *fig. der Saal knisterte vor Spannung* the atmosphere in the hall was electric.

'Knitterfalte *f* crease. **'knitterfrei** *adj* creaseproof, noncrease. **knittern** ['knɪtərn] *v/i, v/t* (h) crease, wrinkle.

knobeln ['knoːbəln] *v/i* (h) **1.** (**um** for) throw dice, toss. **2.** F puzzle (**an** *dat* over).

Knoblauch ['knoːp-] *m* 🌿 garlic. **~kapsel** *f* garlic pill. **~zehe** *f* clove of garlic.

Knöchel ['knœçəl] *m* (-s; -) **1.** knuckle, b) ankle. **'Knöchelbruch** *m* 🦴 ankle fracture. **'knöchellang** *adj* ankle-length.

Knochen ['knɔxən] *m* (-s; -) bone: *Fleisch mit* (*ohne*) **~** meat on (off) the bone; *bis auf die* **~** a) *abgemagert* just skin and bones, b) *naß* soaked to the skin; F *der Schreck fuhr mir in die* **~** I was shaken to the core; *das ist ihm in die* **~***gefahren* it really got to him; *sich bis auf die* **~** *blamieren* make an absolute fool of o.s.

'Knochen|arbeit *f* hard slog, gruel(l)ing work. **~bau** *m* (-[e]s; *no pl*) bone structure. **~bruch** *m* fracture. **~gerüst** *n* skeleton. **~mark** *n* a) (bone) marrow, b) *naß* soaked to the skin. **~haut** *f* periosteum. **~krebs** *m* 🦴 bone cancer. **~mark** *n* (bone) marrow. **~mehl** *n* 🌾 bone meal. **~mühle** *f* F sweatshop. **~splitter** *m* bone splinter. **'knochentrocken** *adj* F bone-dry. **knöchern** ['knœçərn] *adj* bone ..., bony. **knochig** ['knɔxɪç] *adj* bony.

Knödel ['knøːdəl] *m* (-s; -) dumpling.

Knolle ['knɔlə] *f* (-; -n) 🌿 tuber, bulb. **Knollen** ['knɔlən] *m* (-s; -) lump. **'Knollenblätterpilz** *m* death cap. **'Knollennase** *f* F bulbous nose. **knollig** ['knɔlɪç] *adj* 🌿 tuberous, bulbous.

Knopf [knɔpf] *m* (-[e]s; ⁓e) **1.** button: *auf e-n* **~** *drücken* push a button. **2.** → *Knauf* 1, 3. **'Knopfdruck** *m auf* (*or per*) **~** at the touch of a button.

knöpfen ['knœpfən] *v/t* (h) button: *zum* 🔲 buttoned.

'Knopfloch *n* buttonhole.

Knorpel ['knɔrpəl] *m* (-s; -) **1.** *anat.* cartilage. **2.** *gastr.* gristle. **'knorpelig** *adj* **1.** *anat.* cartilaginous. **2.** *gastr.* gristly.

Knorren ['knɔrən] *m* (-s; -) knot, snag.

'knorrig *adj* **1.** gnarled, knotty. **2.** *fig.* gruff.

Knospe ['knɔspə] *f* (-; -n) bud.

knospen ['knɔspən] *v/i* (h) bud.

knospig ['knɔspɪç] *adj* full of buds.

knoten ['knoːtən] *v/t* (h) knot, tie a knot.

'Knoten *m* (-s; -) **1.** knot: *e-n* **~** *machen* tie a knot (*in* *acc* into); F *bei ihm ist endlich der* **~** *geplatzt* he has caught on at last. **2.** bun, knot. **3.** ⚓ knot: *10* **~** *machen* do ten knots. **4.** 🔬, 🌿 knot, *a. astr., phys.* node. **'Knotenpunkt** *m* 🏛️ *etc* junction. **2.** *fig.* cent/re (*Am.* -er).

knotig ['knoːtɪç] *adj a. fig.* knotty.

Knuff [knʊf] *m* (-[e]s; ⁓e) poke, nudge: *j-m e-n* **~** *geben* → **knuffen** ['knʊfən] *v/t* (h) *j-n* **~** punch (*or* nudge) s.o.

Knülch [knʏlç] *m* (-[e]s; -e) F bloke, *Am.* guy, *sl.* creep.

knüllen ['knʏlən] *v/t, v/i* (h) crumple.

Knüller ['knʏlər] *m* (-s; -) F sensation, (big) hit, scoop.

knüpfen ['knʏpfən] (h) **I** *v/t* tie, make, knot (*carpet*): **~** *an* (*acc*) attach (*fig.* attach *conditions, hopes, etc*) to. **II** *sich* **~** *an* (*acc*) *fig.* condition *etc*: be attached to, *memories etc*: be connected with.

Knüppel ['knʏpəl] *m* (-s; -) **1.** a) (heavy) stick, club, b) truncheon, *Am.* billy: *fig. j-m e-n* **~** *zwischen die Beine werfen* put a spoke in s.o.'s wheels. **2.** ✈ stick. **'Knüppeldamm** *m* corduroy road.

knüppeln ['knʏpəln] *v/t* (h) beat, club.

'Knüppelschaltung *f mot.* floor shift, floor-mounted gear change

knurren ['knʊrən] *v/i* (h) **1.** (*a. v/t*) growl, snarl. **2.** *fig.* grumble (*über* *acc* at). **3.** *stomach*: rumble: *mir knurrt der Magen* I'm famished.

knurrig ['knʊrɪç] *adj* F *fig.* grumpy.

knusp(e)rig ['knʊsp(ə)rɪç] *adj* crisp.

Knute ['knuːtə] *f* (-; -n) knout: *fig. unter j-s* **~** *stehen* be under s.o.'s thumb.

knutschen ['knuːtʃən] *v/i* (h) F (*a. sich* **~**) neck, smooch, snog.

'Knutschfleck *m* F love bite.

k.o. [kaːˈʔoː] *adj pred boxing*: knocked out: *j-n* **~** *schlagen* knock s.o. out; F *fig. ich bin* **~** I'm all in, I'm bushed.

K.O. *m* (-; -) *boxing*: knockout.

Koalition [koʔaliˈtsioːn] *f* (-; -en) *pol.* coalition.

Kobalt ['koːbalt] *m* (-[e]s; *no pl*) cobalt.

'Kobaltblau *n* cobalt blue.

Kobold ['koːbɔlt] *m* (-[e]s; -e) goblin.
Koch [kɔx] *m* (-[e]s; ⸚e) cook: *viele Köche verderben den Brei* too many cooks spoil the broth.
'**Kochbuch** *n* cookery book, cookbook.
'**kochecht** *adj* (boil)fast.
kochen ['kɔxən] (h) **I** *v/t* **1.** a) cook, b) boil, c) make (*tea etc*). **II** *v/i* **2.** cook, do the cooking: *sie kocht gut* she is a good cook. **3.** *food*: be cooking, *water*: be boiling: *leicht ~, auf kleiner Flamme ~* simmer; *fig. er kochte innerlich (or vor Wut)* he was seething with rage.
'**Kochen** *n* (-s) cooking: *et. zum ~ bringen* bring s.th. to the boil; *fig. j-n zum ~ bringen* make s.o.'s blood boil.
'**kochendheiß** *adj* boiling hot, scalding.
Kocher ['kɔxər] *m* (-s; -) cooker.
Köcher ['kœçər] *m* (-s; -) **1.** quiver. **2.** *phot.* lens case.
'**kochfertig** *adj* ready-to-cook, instant.
'**Kochgelegenheit** *f* cooking facilities.
'**Kochgeschirr** *n* ✗ mess tin (*Am.* kit).
'**Köchin** ['kœçɪn] *f* (-; -nen) cook.
'**Kochkunst** *f* **1.** *no pl* gastronomy. **2.** *ihre Kochkünste* her cooking (ability).
~**kurs(us)** *m* cookery course. ~**löffel** *m* spoon. ~**nische** *f* kitchenette. ~**platte** *f* hot plate. ~**re,zept** *n* recipe.
'**Kochsalz** *n* **1.** table salt. **2.** 🜨 sodium chloride. ~**lösung** *f* 🜨 saline (solution).
'**Kochtopf** *m* cooking pot, saucepan.
'**Kochwäsche** *f* boil wash.
Köder ['køːdər] *m* (-s; -) bait.
ködern ['køːdərn] *v/t* (h) *a. fig.* bait: *er läßt sich mit Geld nicht ~* he is not tempted by money.
Koeffizient [koˀɛfiˈtsiɛnt] *m* (-en; -en) 𝔸 coefficient.
Koexistenz ['koːˀɛksɪstɛnts] *f* (-; *no pl*) coexistence.
Koffein [kɔfeˈiːn] *n* (-s; *no pl*) caffeine.
koffe'infrei *adj* decaffeinated.
Koffer ['kɔfər] *m* (-s; -) a) bag, case, suitcase, b) trunk: ~ *packen* pack one's bags; F *fig.* **die** ~ *packen* leave; *aus dem* ~ *leben* live out of a suitcase. ~**anhänger** *m* luggage tag. ~**gerät** *n*, ~**radio** *n* portable. ~**raum** *m mot.* boot, *Am.* trunk: *viel* ~ *haben* have much luggage space.
Kognak ['kɔnjak] *m* (-s; -s) cognac, brandy.
Kohl [koːl] *m* (-[e]s; -e) **1.** 🌢 cabbage. **2.** F

fig. (**red** *k-n* ~ don't talk) rubbish.
'**Kohldampf** *m* F ~ *haben* be starving.
Kohle ['koːlə] *f* (-; -n) **1.** a) coal, b) charcoal (*a. paint.*): *ausgeglühte* ~ cinders; *glühende* ~ ember; *fig. weiße* ~ white coal, waterpower; *ich saß (wie) auf (glühenden)* ~*n* I was on tenterhooks. **2.** F *fig.* lolly, *Am.* bread: *Hauptsache, die* ~*n stimmen!* it's all right as long as the money is right!
'**kohlehaltig** *adj* carboniferous.
'**Kohlehy,drat** *n* carbohydrate.
'**Kohlekraftwerk** *n* coal power plant.
'**Kohlenbergbau** *m* coal mining.
'**Kohlenbergwerk** *n* coal mine.
Kohlen'di,oxyd *n* 🜨 carbon dioxide.
'**Kohlen|eimer** *m* coal scuttle. ~**flöz** *n* coal seam. ~**grube** *f* coal mine. ~**händler(in** *f*) *m* coal merchant.
Kohlen'mono,xyd *n* 🜨 carbon monoxide.
'**Kohlen|re,vier** *n* coalfield. ~**säure** *f* 🜨 carbonic acid. ~**staub** *m* coal dust. ~**stoff** *m* 🜨 carbon. ~**wasserstoff** *m* 🜨 hydrocarbon.
'**Kohle|pa,pier** *n* carbon (paper). ~**stift** *m* charcoal. ~**ta,blette** *f* charcoal tablet. ~**vorkommen** *n* coal deposit(s). ~**zeichnung** *f* charcoal (drawing).
'**Kohlkopf** *m* 🌢 cabbage.
'**Kohlmeise** *f zo.* great titmouse.
'**kohl'raben'schwarz** *adj* coal-black.
Kohlrabi [koːlˈraːbi] *m* (-[s]; -[s]) 🌢 kohlrabi.
'**Kohlrübe** *f* 🌢 swede.
Kohlweißling ['koːlvaɪslɪŋ] *m* (-s; -e) *zo.* cabbage butterfly.
Koitus ['koːitʊs] *m* (-; -) coitus, coition.
Koje ['koːjə] *f* (-; -n) ⚓ berth, bunk.
Kokain [kokaˈiːn] *n* (-s; *no pl*) cocaine.
Kokarde [koˈkardə] *f* (-; -n) ✗ cockade.
kokett [koˈket] *adj* coquettish, flirtatious. **Koketterie** [kokɛtəˈriː] *f* (-; -n) coquetry. **kokettieren** [kokɛˈtiːrən] *v/i* (h) *a. fig.* flirt (*mit* with).
Kokken ['kɔkən] *pl* 🜨 cocci.
Kokolores [kokoˈloːrəs] *m* (-; *no pl*) F rubbish.
Kokon [koˈkõː] *m* (-s; -s) cocoon.
Kokos|faser ['koːkɔs-] *f* coconut fibre (*Am.* fiber), coir. ~**fett** *n* coconut fat. ~**milch** *f* coconut milk. ~**nuß** *f* coconut. ~**palme** *f* coconut palm.

Koks¹ [ko:ks] *m* (-es; -e) **1.** ⊙ coke. **2.** F *fig.* lolly, *Am.* bread.

Koks² *m* (-es; *no pl*) *sl.* coke.

koksen [ko'ksən] *v/i* (h) *sl.* take coke.

Kolben ['kɔlbən] *m* (-s; -) **1.** ⊙ a) piston, b) plunger (*a.* ✸). **2.** ⚗ flask. **3.** (*rifle*) butt. **4.** ⚘ spike. **5.** F conk.

'**Kolben|fresser** *m mot.* F jamming of the piston. **~hub** *m* piston stroke. **~ring** *m* piston ring. **~stange** *f* piston rod.

Kolchos [kɔlçɔs] *m* (-; -e [kɔl'ço:zə]), **Kolchose** [kɔl'ço:zə] *f* (-; -n) kolkhoz, collective farm.

Kolibak,terie [ko:li-] *f* ✸ colibacillus.

Kolibri [ko:libri] *m* (-s; -s) *zo.* humming-bird.

Kolik ['ko:lık] *f* (-; -en) ✸ colic.

Kollaborateur [kɔlabora'tø:r] *m* (-s; -e) *pol.* collaborator.

Kollaps [kɔ'laps] *m* (-es; -e) ✸ (*a.* **e-n ~ erleiden**) collapse.

Kolleg [kɔ'le:k] *n* (-s; -s, -ien [-gĭən]) *univ.* a) (single) lecture, b) course of lectures, c) → *Kollegstufe:* **ein ~ halten über** (*acc*) lecture on.

Kollege [kɔ'le:gə] *m* (-n; -n) colleague.

kollegial [kɔle'gĭa:l] *adj* cooperative, helpful: **sich ~ verhalten** be loyal (**gegenüber** to[wards]).

Kollegin [kɔ'le:gın] *f* (-; -nen).

Kollegium [kɔ'le:gĭɔm] *n* (-s; -ien) *ped.* (teaching) staff, *Am. a.* faculty.

Kol'legmappe *f* (underarm) briefcase.

Kol'legstufe *f ped.* sixth-form college.

Kollekte [kɔ'lɛktə] *f* (-; -n) collection.

Kollektion [kɔlɛk'tsĭo:n] *f* (-; -en) a) collection, ✝ *a.* range, b) samples, c) selection.

kollektiv [kɔlɛk'ti:f] *adj*, **Kollek'tiv** *n* (-s; -e) collective. **kollektivieren** [kɔlɛkti-'vi:rən] *v/t* (h) collectivize.

Kollek'tivschuld *f* collective guilt.

Kollektivum [kɔlɛk'ti:vɔm] *n ling.* (-s; -va) collective (noun).

Kollektor [kɔ'lɛktɔr] *m* (-s; -en [-'to:rən]) ✎ commutator, collector.

Koller ['kɔlər] *m* (-s; -) F (**e-n ~ kriegen** fly into a) tantrum.

kollern ['kɔlərn] *v/i* **1.** (sn) roll. **2.** (h) *turkey:* gobble.

kollidieren [kɔli'di:rən] *v/i* **1.** (sn) collide. **2.** (h) *fig.* collide, clash.

Kollier [kɔ'lĭe:] *n* (-s; -s) necklace.

Kollision [kɔli'zĭo:n] *f* (-; -en) collision,

fig. a. clash, conflict. **Kollisi'onskurs** *m a. fig.* (**auf ~** on a) collision course.

Kolloquium [kɔ'lo:kvĭɔm] *n* (-s; -ien) colloquium.

Kölner ['kœlnər] **I** *m* (-s; -) inhabitant of Cologne. **II** *adj* (of) Cologne: **der ~ Dom** Cologne Cathedral.

'**Kölnerin** *f* (-; -nen) → *Kölner* I.

Kölnischwasser ['kœlnıʃ-] *n* (-s; *no pl*) eau-de-Cologne.

Kolonial... [kolo'nĭa:l] colonial (*empire, power, etc*). **Kolonialismus** [kolonĭa-'lısmʊs] *m* (-; *no pl*) colonialism.

Kolonie [kolo'ni:] *f* (-; -n) colony.

Kolonisation [kolonĭza'tsĭo:n] *f* (-; -en) colonization. **kolonisieren** [koloni-'zi:rən] *v/t* (h) colonize. **Kolonist** [kolo'nıst] *m* (-en; -en) colonist, settler.

Kolonnade [kolɔ'na:də] *f* (-; -n) △ colonnade.

Kolonne [ko'lɔnə] *f* (-; -n) column (*a.* Ⓧ, *print.*), *a. mot.* line, ✕ convoy: **~ fahren** drive in line (*or* convoy); *pol.* **die Fünfte ~** the Fifth Column.

Ko'lonnenspringer *m mot.* F queue jumper.

Kolophonium [kolo'fo:nĭɔm] *n* (-s; *no pl*) colophony, rosin.

Koloratur [kolora'tu:r] *f* (-; -en) coloratura. **~so,pran** *m* coloratura soprano.

kolorieren [kolo'ri:rən] *v/t* (h) colo(u)r.

Kolorit [kolo'ri:t, -'rıt] *n* (-[e]s; -e) **1.** ♪ colo(u)r. **2.** *paint.* colo(u)ring. **3.** *fig.* (local) colo(u)r, atmosphere.

Koloß [ko'lɔs] *m* (-sses; -sse) colossus.

kolossal [kolɔ'sa:l] *adj* colossal, huge, gigantic, F *fig. a.* enormous: **~ viel** an enormous amount (of).

Kolportage [kɔlpɔr'ta:ʒə] *f* (-; -n) **1.** sensationalism. **2.** → **Kolpor'tageliteratur** *f* trashy (*or* sensational) literature. **kolportieren** [kɔlpɔr'ti:rən] *v/t* (h) spread.

Kolumne [ko'lʊmnə] *f* (-; -n) *print.* column. **Ko'lumnentitel** *m* (**lebender ~** running) head(line). **Kolumnist** [ko-lʊm'nıst] *m* (-en; -en) columnist.

Kombi ['kɔmbi] *m* (-[s]; -s) → **Kombiwagen.** '**Kombikarte** *f* combi-ticket.

Kombinat [kɔmbi'na:t] *n* (-[e]s; -e) ✝ combined enterprise.

Kombination [kɔmbina'tsĭo:n] *f* (-; -en) **1.** combination (*a. chess, of lock etc*), *soccer etc:* (combined) move. **2.** *fig. a)* deduction, b) conjecture. **3.** *fashion:* set, ensemble. **4.** a) overalls, b) flying suit. **5.** *skiing:* **Alpine (Nordische)** ~ Alpine (Nordic) Combined.

Kombinati'ons|gabe f power(s) of deduction. **~schloß** n combination lock.

kombinieren [kɔmbi'ni:rən] (h) **I** v/t **1.** combine (**mit** with). **II** v/i **2.** *sports:* combine: **gut** ~ show excellent teamwork. **3.** *fig.* a) deduct, b) conjecture.

'**Kombiwagen** m estate car, *Am.* station wagon.

Kombüse [kɔm'by:zə] f (-; -n) ♺ galley.

Komet [ko'me:t] m (-en; -en) comet.

ko'metenhaft adj comet-like, meteoric.

Komfort [kɔm'fo:r] m (-s; *no pl*) a) comfort, b) luxury, c) conveniences: **mit allem** ~ *flat etc* with all modern conveniences, *car etc* with all the extras.

komfortabel [kɔmfɔr'ta:bəl] adj a) comfortable, b) luxurious.

Kom'fortwohnung f luxury flat.

Komik ['ko:mɪk] f (-; *no pl*) a) *the* comic, b) comic effect (*or* touch): **e-r gewissen** ~ **nicht entbehren** have a comic side. '**Komiker** m (-s; -) comedian (a. f fig.), comic actor. '**Komikerin** f (-; -nen) comedienne, comic actress.

komisch ['ko:mɪʃ] adj **1.** comic(al), funny: **~e Oper** comic opera; **was ist daran so ~?** what's so funny about it? **2.** f fig. funny, queer: **ich habe so ein ~es Gefühl** I feel funny; **das kam mir sehr ~ vor** I found that very strange; **das Komische daran ist** the funny thing about it is; **~, daß ...** (it's) funny that ...

'**komischerweise** adv funnily enough.

Komitee [komi'te:] n (-s; -s) committee.

Komma ['kɔma] n (-s; -s, -ta) a) comma, b) ₳ (decimal) point: **vier ~ fünf** (4,5) four point five; **null ~ drei** point three.

Kommandant [kɔman'dant] m (-en; -en) commander. **Kommandantur** [kɔmandan'tu:r] f (-; -en) (garrison, *Am.* post) headquarters. **Kommandeur** [kɔman'dø:r] m (-s; -e) commanding officer.

kommandieren [kɔman'di:rən] (h) **I** v/t **1.** command, be in command of: **j-n** ~ **zu** detach (*or* detail) s.o. to. **II** v/i **2.** (be in) command: **~der General** commanding general. **3.** f give the orders.

Kommanditgesellschaft [kɔman'di:t-] f ♱ limited partnership.

Kommanditist [kɔmandi'tɪst] m (-en; -en) ♱ limited partner.

Kommando [kɔ'mando] n (-s; -s) a) command, order, b) command (unit), c) detachment: (**wie**) **auf** ~ (as if) by command. **~brücke** f ♺ bridge. **~kapsel** f command module. **~raum** m control room. **~sprache** f *computer:* command language. **~zen,trale** f control cen tre (*Am.* -er).

kommen ['kɔmən] (kam, gekommen, sn) **I** v/i **1.** come (a. F *orgasmically*), a. arrive, a. approach, a. get (**bis** to): **angelaufen** ~ come running; **j-n** ~ **sehen** see s.o. coming (*or* come); **ich habe es ~ sehen** I saw it coming; **a) lassen** a) send for, call (*s.o.*), b) order (*s.th.*); **weit** ~ a. fig. get far; **er wird bald** ~ he won't be long; **wann kommt der nächste Zug?** when is the next train due (to arrive)?; **zur Schule** ~ start school; **komme, was wolle** come what may; **mir kam der Gedanke** it occurred to me; **ihr kamen die Tränen** her eyes filled with tears; **später kamen mir Zweifel** afterwards I started to have doubts; **(na,) kommen Sie!** come on!; **ich komme (schon)!** (I'm) coming!; F ~ **Sie mir nicht so!** don't (you) try that on me!; → **Gefängnis, spät II. 2.** ~ **auf** (acc) a) hit on, b) think of, c) amount to, come to: **ich komme nicht darauf!** I just can't think of it!; **darauf komme ich gleich (zu sprechen)** I'll be coming to that!; **wie kommst du darauf?** what makes you think (*or* say) that?; **auf jeden von uns** ~ **zwei Äpfel** each of us will get two apples; **er kommt auf 3000 Mark im Monat** he makes 3,000 marks a month; → **Schliche, Sprache** 2 *etc.* **3.** **hinter** *et.* ~ find out. **4.** F **er kommt nach s-r Mutter** he takes after his mother. **5.** **was ist über dich gekommen?** what has come over (*or* got into) you? **6.** ~ **um** (acc) a) lose, b) miss. **7.** ~ **von** come from, *fig.* a. be due to. **8.** ~ **zu** come by, get; **zu Geld** ~ come into money; (**wieder**) **zu sich** ~ come round (*or* to), *w.s.* recover; **sie ist nicht dazu gekommen, den Brief zu schreiben** she didn't get round to writing the letter; **wie** ~ **Sie dazu?** how dare you? **II** v/impers **9.** **es kommt j-d** s.o. is coming. **10.** happen, come (about): **so mußte**

es ja ~! it was bound to happen that way!; *wie kommt es, daß ...?* why is it that ...?, F how come ...?; *daher kommt es, daß ...* that's why ...; *es kam zum Krieg* there was a war; *es ist so weit gekommen, daß ...* things have got to a stage where ...

'**Kommen** *n* (-s) a) coming, b) arrival: *fig. ... sind wieder im ~* ... are coming (*or* are on the way in) again.

'**kommend** *adj* coming, *a.* future: *~e Woche* next week; *in den ~en Jahren* in the years to come; *die ~e Generation* the rising generation; *er ist der ~e Mann* he is the coming man.

Kommentar [kɔmɛn'taːr] *m* (-s; -e) (*zu* on) a) commentary, b) (*kein ~!* no) comment(!). **kommen'tarlos** *adv* without comment. **Kommentator** [-'taːtɔr] *m* (-s; -en [-'taːtoːrən]) commentator. **kommentieren** [kɔmɛn'tiːrən] *v/t* (h) comment (on).

kommerzialisieren [kɔmɛrtsĭali'tsiːrən] *v/t* (h) commercialize. **kommerziell** [kɔmɛr'tsĭɛl] *adj* commercial.

Kommilitone [kɔmili'toːnə] *m* (-n; -n), **Kommili'tonin** *f* (-; -nen) *univ.* fellow student.

Kommiß [kɔ'mɪs] *m* (-sses; *no pl*) F (*beim ~* in the) army.

Kommissar [kɔmɪ'saːr] *m* (-s; -e) **1.** commissioner. **2.** → *Kriminalkommissar.*

kommissarisch [kɔmɪ'saːrɪʃ] *adj* **1.** temporary. **2.** deputy.

Kommission [kɔmɪ'sĭoːn] *f* (-; -en) (*a.* ✝ *in ~* on) commission, committee.

Kommissionär [kɔmɪsĭoˈnɛːr] *m* (-s; -e) ✝ commission agent.

Kommissi'onsbuchhändler(in *f)* *m* wholesale bookseller.

Kommode [kɔ'moːdə] *f* (-; -n) chest of drawers.

Kommodore [kɔmo'doːrə] *m* (-s; -n, -s) ⚓ commodore.

kommunal [kɔmu'naːl] *adj* local, municipal.

Kommu'nal|abgaben *pl* local rates (*Am.* taxes). **~beamte** *m* municipal officer. **~poli,tik** *f* local politics. **~verwaltung** *f* local government. **~wahlen** *pl* local elections.

Kommune [kɔ'muːnə] *f* (-; -n) **1.** community. **2.** commune.

Kommunikation [kɔmunikaˈtsĭoːn] *f* (-; -en) communication.

Kommunikati'ons|mittel *n* means of communication, *pl a.* (mass) media. **~schwierigkeiten** *pl* **~haben** have difficulty communicating. **~technik** *f* communications technology. **~wissenschaft** *f* communication(s) science.

kommunikativ [kɔmunika'tiːf] *adj* communicative.

Kommunion [kɔmu'nĭoːn] *f* (-; -en) *eccl.* (Holy) Communion.

Kommuniqué [kɔmyni'keː] *n* (-s; -s) communiqué.

Kommunismus [kɔmu'nɪsmʊs] *m* (-; *no pl*) communism.

Kommunist [kɔmu'nɪst] *m* (-en; -en), **Kommu'nistin** *f* (-; -nen) communist. **kommu'nistisch** *adj* communist(ic).

kommunizieren [kɔmuni'tsiːrən] *v/i* (h) communicate.

kommutieren [kɔmu'tiːrən] *v/t* (h) ⚡ commutate.

Komödiant [kɔmøˈdĭant] *m* (-en; -en), **Komödi'antin** *f* (-; -nen) actor (actress), *fig. contp.* play-actor. **Komödie** [ko'møːdĭə] *f* (-; -n) comedy, *fig.* farce.

Kompagnon [kɔmpanˈjõː] *m* (-s; -s) ✝ partner.

kompakt [kɔm'pakt] *adj* compact.

Kompanie [kɔmpa'niː] *f* (-; -n) ✕ company. **~chef** *m* company commander.

Komparativ ['kɔmparatiːf] *m* (-s; -e) *ling.* comparative (degree).

Komparse [kɔm'parzə] *m* (-n; -n), **Kom'parsin** *f* (-; -nen) *film etc:* extra.

Kompaß ['kɔmpas] *m* (-sses; -sse) compass. **~haus** *n* ⚓ binnacle. **~nadel** *f* compass needle. **~rose** *f* compass card.

kompatibel [kɔmpa'tiːbəl] *adj* compatible.

Kompensation [kɔmpɛnza'tsĭoːn] *f* (-; -en) compensation.

kompensieren [kɔmpɛn'ziːrən] *v/t* (h) compensate (for) (*a. psych.*).

kompetent [kɔmpe'tɛnt] *adj* competent, *a.* responsible (*für* for), *a.* authorized. **Kompetenz** [kɔmpe'tɛnts] *f* (-; -en) competence, *a.* responsibility (*für* for), *a.* authority: *s-e ~en überschreiten* exceed one's authority. **~bereich** *m* sphere of authority. **~streit** *m*, **~streitigkeit** *f* *usu. pl* demarcation dispute.

kompilieren [kɔmpi'li:rən] v/t (h) compile.

Komplementärfarbe [kɔmplemɛn'tɛ:r-] f complementary colo(u)r.

komplett [kɔm'plɛt] adj complete.

komplex [kɔm'plɛks] adj complex.

Kom'plex m (-es; -e) psych. (wegen about) complex, F hangup.

Komplikation [kɔmplika'tsi̯o:n] f (-; -en) complication.

Kompliment [kɔmpli'mɛnt] n (-[e]s; -e) (j-m ein ~ machen pay s.o. a) compliment; ~! congratulations!

Komplize [kɔm'pli:tsə] m (-n; -n), **Kom'plizin** f (-; -nen) accomplice.

komplizieren [kɔmpli'tsi:rən] v/t (h) complicate. **kompli'ziert** adj complicated, complex (character etc), intricate (problem etc): ✽ ~er Bruch compound fracture. **Kompli'ziertheit** f (-; no pl) complexity.

Komplott [kɔm'plɔt] n (-[e]s; -e) (a. ein ~ schmieden) plot (gegen against).

Komponente [kɔmpo'nɛntə] f (-; -n) component.

komponieren [kɔmpo'ni:rən] v/t, v/i (h) a. fig. compose. **Komponist** [-'nɪst] m (-en; -en) composer. **Komposition** [kɔmpozi'tsi̯o:n] f (-; -en) composition. **Kompositum** [kɔm'po:zitʊm] n (-s; -ta) ling. compound (word).

Kompost [kɔm'pɔst] m (-[e]s; -e), **kompostieren** [-'ti:rən] v/t (h) compost.

Kompott [kɔm'pɔt] n (-[e]s; -e) stewed fruit.

Kompresse [kɔm'prɛsə] f (-; -n) ✽ compress. **Kompressor** [kɔm'prɛsɔr] m (-s; -en [-'so:rən] ☼ compressor, mot. supercharger. **komprimieren** [kɔmpri'mi:rən] v/t (h) compress.

Kompromiß [kɔmpro'mɪs] m (-sses; -sse) compromise: e-n ~ schließen (make a) compromise (über acc on). ~bereitschaft f willingness to compromise. **kompro'mißlos** adj uncompromising. **Kompro'miß|lösung** f compromise solution. ~vorschlag m compromise proposal: e-n ~ machen suggest a compromise.

kompromittieren [kɔmprɔmi'ti:rən] v/t (h) compromise (sich o.s.).

Kondensat [kɔndɛn'za:t] n (-[e]s; -e) condensate. **Kondensation** [-za'tsi̯o:n] f (-; -en) condensation. **Kondensator**

[-'za:tɔr] m (-s; -en [-za'to:rən]) 1. ☼ condenser. 2. ⚡ capacitor. **kondensieren** [-'zi:rən] v/t, v/i (h) condense.

Kondens|milch [kɔn'dɛns-] f evaporated milk. ~streifen m ✈ condensation trail. ~wasser n condensation water.

Kondition [kɔndi'tsi̯o:n] f (-; no pl sports: condition, trim, shape: e-e ausgezeichnete ~ haben be very fit. 2. usu. pl ✝ condition.

Konditional [kɔnditsi̯o'na:l] m (-s; -e) ling. conditional (mood).

Konditio'nalsatz m conditional clause.

Konditi'ons|schwäche f sports: lack of stamina, poor shape. ♀**stark** adj very fit. ~training n fitness training.

Konditor [kɔn'di:tɔr] m (-s; -en [-di'to:rən]) pastry cook. **Konditorei** [kɔndito'raɪ] f (-; -en) a) cake shop, b) café.

Kondolenz(...) [kɔndo'lɛnts-] → **Beileid(s...)**. **kondolieren** [kɔndo'li:rən] v/i (h) j-m ~ express one's condolences to s.o. (zu on).

Kondom [kɔn'do:m] n, m (-s; -e) condom, Am. a. prophylactic.

Konfekt [kɔn'fɛkt] n (-[e]s; -e) sweets, Am. (soft) candy, b) chocolates.

Konfektion [kɔnfɛk'tsi̯o:n] f (-; -en) (manufacture of) ready-to-wear (or ready-made) clothing (or clothes).

Konfekti'ons... ready-to-wear (clothes, suit, etc). ~größe f size.

Konferenz [kɔnfe'rɛnts] f (-; -en) meeting, conference. **Konfe'renzschaltung** f radio etc: conference system.

konferieren [kɔnfe'ri:rən] v/i (h) 1. confer (über acc on). 2. a. v/t compère.

Konfession [kɔnfɛ'si̯o:n] f (-; -en) (welcher ~ gehören Sie an? what is your [religious] denomination(?). **konfessionell** [kɔnfɛsi̯o'nɛl] adj denominational. **konfessi'onslos** adj nondenominational. **Konfessi'onsschule** f denominational school.

Konfetti [kɔn'fɛti] n (-[s]; no pl) confetti.

Konfirmand [kɔnfɪr'mant] (-en; -en), **Konfir'mandin** [-dɪn] f (-; -nen) confirmand. **Konfirmation** [kɔnfɪrma'tsi̯o:n] f (-; -en) confirmation. **konfirmieren** [kɔnfɪr'mi:rən] v/t (h) confirm.

konfiszieren [kɔnfɪs'tsi:rən] v/t (h) confiscate, seize.

Konfitüre [kɔnfi'ty:rə] f (-; -en) jam.

Konflikt [kɔn'flɪkt] *m* (-[e]s; -e) (*in ~ geraten* come into) conflict (*mit* with).
Kon'fliktstoff *m* matter for conflict.
Konföderation [kɔnfødera'tsɪoːn] *f* (-; -en) confederation.
konform [kɔn'fɔrm] *adj* conforming, Am conformal: *mit j-m ~ gehen* agree with s.o. (*in dat* about).
Konformist [kɔnfɔr'mɪst] *m* (-en; -en), **komfor'mistisch** *adj* conformist.
Konfrontation [kɔnfrɔnta'tsɪoːn] *f* (-; -en) confrontation. **konfrontieren** [-'tiːrən] *v/t* (h) confront (*mit* with).
konfus [kɔn'fuːs] *adj* confused: *ich bin ganz ~ a.* I'm in a muddle. **Konfusion** [kɔnfu'zɪoːn] *f* (-; -en) confusion.
Konglomerat [kɔnglome'raːt] *n* (-[e]s; -e) *a. fig.* conglomerate.
Kongreß [kɔn'grɛs] *m* (-sses; -sse) congress, convention: *pol. Am. der ~* Congress. **Kon'greßmitglied** *n pol. Am.* Congressman (Congresswoman).
kongruent [kɔngru'ɛnt] *adj* Am congruent (*a. fig.*). **Kongruenz** [-'ɛnts] *f* (-; -en) congruence (*a. fig.*). **kongruieren** [-'iːrən] *v/i* (h) Am be congruent (*a. fig.*).
Konifere [koni'feːrə] *f* (-; -n) Am conifer.
König ['køːnɪç] *m* (-s; -e) king.
Königin ['køːnɪgɪn] *f* (-; -nen) *a. zo.* queen. **'Königinmutter** *f* queen mother. **'Königinwitwe** *f* queen dowager.
königlich ['køːnɪklɪç] *adj* royal, *a.* regal (*insignia, power, etc*), *fig. a.* kingly: F *sich ~ amüsieren* have great fun.
Königreich ['køːnɪk-] *n* kingdom.
'Königshaus *n* royal house (*or* dynasty). **~krone** *f* royal crown. **~sohn** *m* king's son, prince. **~tiger** *m zo.* Bengal tiger. **~tochter** *f* king's daughter, princess. **2treu** *adj* a) loyal (to the king), b) royalist.
'Königtum *n* (-s; *no pl*) monarchy.
konisch ['koːnɪʃ] *adj* conic(al).
Konjugation [kɔnjuga'tsɪoːn] *f* (-; -en) *ling.* conjugation. **konjugieren** [kɔnju'giːrən] *v/t* (h) *ling.* conjugate.
Konjunktion [kɔnjʊŋk'tsɪoːn] *f* (-; -en) *ling.* conjunction.
Konjunktiv ['kɔnjʊŋktiːf] *m* (-s; -e) *ling.* subjunctive (mood).
'Konjunktivsatz *m* subjunctive clause.
Konjunktur [kɔnjʊŋk'tuːr] *f* (-; -en) Am a) business cycle, b) boom, c) economic trend (*or* situation). **~abschwächung** *f*

downswing. **~aufschwung** *m* upswing. **2bedingt** *adj* cyclic(al). **~bericht** *m* economic report. **2dämpfend** *adj* countercyclical.
konjunkturell [kɔnjʊŋktu'rɛl] *adj* cyclical, economic, business (*trend etc*).
Konjunk'tur|poli|tik *f* trade-cycle policy. **~schwankungen** *pl* cyclical fluctuations. **~spritze** *f* F shot in the arm. **~verlauf** *m* economic trend.
konkav [kɔn'kaːf] *adj* concave.
Konkordat [kɔnkɔr'daːt] *n* (-[e]s; -e) concordat.
konkret [kɔn'kreːt] *adj* concrete, *a.* definite, specific, precise.
konkretisieren [kɔnkreti'ziːrən] *v/t* put *s.th.* in concrete form (*or* terms).
Konkurrent [kɔnkʊ'rɛnt] *m* (-en; -en) competitor, (✝ *a.* business) rival.
Konkurrenz [kɔnkʊ'rɛnts] *f* (-; -en) **1.** *no pl* competition, rivalry: *j-m ~ machen* compete with s.o. **2.** *no pl* competitor(s), rival(s), *coll. a.* competition: *die ~ ausschalten* eliminate one's competitors. **3.** competition, contest, *sports: a.* event: *außer ~* hors concours.
Konkur'renz|erzeugnis *n* rival product. **~fähig** *adj* competitive. **~firma** *f*, **~geschäft** *n* rival firm. **~kampf** *m* (*mörderischer ~* cutthroat) competition; *endloser ~* F rat race. **~klausel** *f* restraint clause.
konkur'renzlos *adj* unrival(l)ed.
konkurrieren [kɔnkʊ'riːrən] *v/i* (h) *mit j-m ~* compete with s.o. (*um* for).
Konkurs [kɔn'kʊrs] *m* (-es; -e) bankruptcy: *in ~ gehen,* **~ machen** go bankrupt. **~antrag** *m* petition in bankruptcy. **~erklärung** *f* declaration of insolvency. **~masse** *f* bankrupt's estate. **~verfahren** *n* (*das ~ eröffnen* institute) bankruptcy proceedings. **~verwalter** *m* a) trustee in bankruptcy, b) ✻ receiver.
können ['kœnən] *v/aux*, *v/i*, *v/t* (konnte, gekonnt, h) **1.** be able to: *kannst du es?* can you do it?; *er hätte es tun ~* he could have done it; *ich habe nicht arbeiten ~* I was unable to work; *ich kann nicht mehr!* a) I can't go on!, F I've had it!, b) I can't take any more!; I can't manage (*or* eat) any more!; F *da kann man nichts machen!* there's nothing to be done!; *du kannst mich mal!* go to hell! **2.** know: *~ Sie tanzen*

do you (know how to) dance?, can you dance?; *sie kann kein Spanisch* she doesn't know (*or* speak) Spanish; F *er kann etwas* (*gar nichts*) he is a capable fellow (he's absolutely incapable). **3.** be allowed to: *kann ich jetzt gehen?* can I go now?; *Sie ~* (*es*) *mir glauben!* (you may) believe me!; F *das kann doch nicht wahr sein!* but that's impossible! **4.** *es kann sein, daß er noch kommt* he may (*or* might) come yet; *ich kann mich irren* I may be mistaken; *wann könnte das gewesen sein?* when might that have been?; *du könntest recht haben* you may (*or* could) be right; F *kann sein!* maybe! **5.** *ich kann nichts für ...* I'm not responsible for ...; *ich konnte doch nichts dafür!* it wasn't my fault! **6.** F *mit j-m* (*gut*) *~* get on with s.o. (like a house on fire).

'**Können** *n* (-s) skill, ability.
Könner ['kœnər] *m* (-s; -), '**Könnerin** *f* (-; -nen) expert, *sports:* ace.
Konsekutivsatz [kɔnzeku'ti:f-] *m ling.* consecutive clause.
konsequent [kɔnze'kvɛnt] *adj* a) consistent, logical, b) firm, resolute, c) uncompromising: *~ bleiben* remain firm.
Konsequenz [kɔnze'kvɛnts] *f* (-; -en) **1.** consequence: *die ~en ziehen* draw the conclusions (*aus* from), act accordingly. **2.** consistency.
konservativ [kɔnzɛrva'ti:f] *adj,* **Konservative** [kɔnzɛrva'ti:və] *m, f* (-n; -n) conservative, *pol. Br. a.* Tory.
Konservator [kɔnzɛr'va:tɔr] *m* (-s; -en [-va'to:rən]) curator.
Konservatorium [kɔnzɛrva'to:rĭom] *n* (-s; -rien) conservatory.
Konserve [kɔn'zɛrvə] *f* (-; -n) **1.** a) preserve(d food), b) tin, can: *~n* tinned (*or* canned) food; *von ~n leben* live out of tins (*or* cans); F *fig. Musik aus der ~* canned music. **2.** → **Blutkonserve.**
Kon'serven|büchse *f,* **~dose** *f* tin, can. **~fa,brik** *f* canning factory, cannery.
konservieren [kɔnzɛr'vi:rən] *v/t* (h) preserve. **Konser'vierung** *f* (-; -en) preservation. **Konser'vierungsmittel** *n* preservative.
Konsistenz [kɔnzɪs'tɛnts] *f* (-; -en) consistency.
Konsole [kɔn'zo:lə] *f* (-; -n) console.

konsolidieren [kɔnzoli'di:rən] *v/t* (*a. sich ~*) (h) consolidate.
Konsonant [kɔnzo'nant] *m* (-en; -en) consonant. **konso'nantisch** *adj* consonant(al).
Konsortium [kɔn'zɔrtsĭom] *n* (-s; -tien) † syndicate.
Konspiration [kɔnspira'tsĭo:n] *f* (-; -en) conspiracy, plot. **konspirativ** [-'ti:f] *adj* conspiratorial. **konspirieren** [kɔnspi-'ri:rən] *v/i* (h) conspire, plot.
konstant [kɔn'stant] *adj* constant.
Kon'stante *f* (-; -n) *a. fig.* constant.
Konstellation [kɔnstɛla'tsĭo:n] *f* (-; -en) constellation.
konstituieren [kɔnstitu'i:rən] (h) constitute: *parl. sich ~ als ...* resolve itself into ...; *konstituierende Versammlung* constituent assembly.
Konstitution [kɔnstitu'tsĭo:n] *f* (-; -en) *, pol.* constitution. **konstitutionell** [kɔnstitutsĭo'nɛl] *adj* constitutional.
konstruieren [kɔnstru'i:rən] *v/t* (h) construct (*a. ling.,* Ⓐ), Ⓞ *a.* design, build, *fig. contp.* fabricate. **Konstrukteur** [kɔnstrʊk'tø:r] *m* (-s; -e) design engineer. **Konstruktion** [kɔnstrʊk'tsĭo:n] *f* (-; -en) a) construction (*a. ling.,* Ⓐ), b) design, c) structure. **Konstrukti'onsfehler** *m* constructional fault, faulty design. **konstruktiv** [kɔnstrʊk'ti:f] *adj* **1.** *fig.* constructive. **2.** Ⓞ constructional, structural, design.
Konsul ['kɔnzʊl] *m* (-s; -n) consul.
Konsular... [kɔnzu'la:r-] consular.
Konsulat [-'la:t] *n* (-[e]s; -e) consulate.
Konsultation [kɔnzʊlta'tsĭo:n] *f* (-; -en) consultation. **konsultieren** [kɔnzʊl-'ti:rən] *v/t* (h) consult.
Konsum¹ ['kɔnzu:m] *m* (-s; -s) cooperative (store), F co-op.
Konsum² [kɔn'zu:m] *m* (-s; *no pl*) *a. fig.* consumption. **konsumieren** [kɔnzu-'mɛnt] *m* (-en; -en) *a. fig.* consumer. **Konsument** [kɔnzu-'mɛnt] *m* (-en; -en) *a. fig.* consumer. **Kon'sumdenken** *n* (-s) consumerism. **Konsument** [kɔnzu-'mɛnt] *m* (-en; -en) *a. fig.* consumer. **Kon'sumgesellschaft** *f* consumer society. **Kon'sumgüter** *pl* consumer goods. **konsumieren** [kɔnzu'mi:rən] *v/t* (h) *a. fig.* consume. **Kon'sumterror** *m* F pressure to buy.
Kontakt [kɔn'takt] *m* (-[e]s; -e) contact: *mit j-m in ~ stehen* be in contact (*or* touch) with s.o.; *mit j-m ~ aufnehmen* get in touch with s.o., contact s.o. *~ab-*

zug *m phot.* contact print. **~arm** *adj* unsociable: *er ist ~ a.* F he is a bad mixer. **~freudig** *adj* sociable: *er ist ~ a.* F he is a good mixer. **~gespräche** *pl* initial talks. **~gift** *n* contact poison. **~linse** *f opt.* contact lens. **~mann** *n* contact. **~per¦son** *f a.* ✶ contact. **~schalter** *m* touch sensitive switch.

Kontamination [kɔntamina'tsi̯oːn] *f* (-; -en) contamination. **kontaminieren** [kɔntami'niːrən] *v/t* (h) contaminate.

Konteradmi¦ral ['kɔntər-] *m* ♆ rear admiral.

kontern ['kɔntərn] *v/i, v/t* (h) counter.

'Konterrevoluti¦on *f* counterrevolution.

Kontext ['kɔntɛkst] *m* (-[e]s; -e) context.

Kontinent [kɔnti'nɛnt] *m* (-[e]s; -e) continent. **kontinental** [kɔntinɛn'taːl] *adj* continental.

Kontingent [kɔntɪŋ'gɛnt] *n* (-[e]s; -e) contingent (*a.* ✕), ✦ *a.* quota.

kontingentieren [kɔntɪŋgɛn'tiːrən] *v/t* (h) **1.** fix a quota for. **2.** ration.

kontinuierlich [kɔntinu'iːrlɪç] *adj* continuous. **Kontinuität** [kɔntinui'tɛːt] *f* (-; *no pl*) continuity.

Konto ['kɔnto] *n* (-s; -ten) account: *ein ~ haben bei* have (*or* keep) an account with (*or* at); F *fig. das geht auf sein ~* that's his doing. **~auszug** *m* bank statement. **~führungsgebühr** *f* service charge. **~inhaber(in** *f) m* account holder. **~nummer** *f* account number.

Kontorist [kɔnto'rɪst] *m* (-en; -en), **Konto'ristin** *f* (-; -nen) (office) clerk.

'Kontostand *m* balance: *wie ist der ~?* how does the account stand?; *Ihr ~ beläuft sich auf ...* you have ... to your credit.

kontra ['kɔntra] **I** *prep* contra, ⚖ *or fig.* versus (*abbr.* vs.). **II** *adv sie ist immer ~ (eingestellt)* she's against everything.

'Kontra *n* (-s; -s) *fig.* objection: *~ geben cards:* double; F *j-m ~ geben* hit back at s.o.; → *Pro.*

'Kontrabaß *m* ♩ double bass.

Kontrahent [kɔntra'hɛnt] *m* (-en; -en) ⚖ contracting party, *fig.* opponent, *a. sports:* rival.

'Kontraindikati¦on *f* contraindication.

Kontraktion [kɔntrak'tsi̯oːn] *f* (-; -en) contraction.

'kontraproduk¦tiv *adj* counterproductive.

'Kontrapunkt *m* (-[e]s; *no pl*) ♩ counterpoint.

konträr [kɔn'trɛːr] *adj* contrary.

Kontrast [kɔn'trast] *m* (-[e]s; -e) contrast: *e-n ~ bilden (zu)* → **kontrastieren. kon'trastarm** *adj phot.* flat. **kontrastieren** [-'tiːrən] *v/i* (h) (*mit*) contrast (with), form a contrast (to).

Kon'trast¦mittel *n* ✚ radiopaque material. **¦reich** *adj phot.*, *TV* contrasty.

Kon'trollabschnitt *m* stub.

Kon'trollbehörde *f* control authority.

Kontrolle [kɔn'trɔlə] *f* (-; -n) a) control (*über acc* of), *a.* ✪ inspection, check, b) supervision: *unter (außer) ~* under (out of) control; *unter ärztlicher ~* under medical supervision; *er verlor die ~ über s-n Wagen* he lost control of his car; *... steht unter ständiger ~* a constant check is kept on ...

Kon'trolleuchte *f* pilot lamp.

Kontrolleur [kɔntrɔ'løːr] *m* (-s; -e) inspector, supervisor.

Kon'troll¦funkti¦on *f* controlling function. **¦gang** *m* round.

kontrollieren [kɔntrɔ'liːrən] *v/t* (h) a) control, check, b) supervise.

Kon'trolliste *f* checklist.

Kon'troll¦punkt *m* checkpoint. **¦turm** *m* ✈ control tower. **¦uhr** *f* time clock.

Kontroverse [kɔntro'vɛrzə] *f* (-; -n) controversy, argument.

Kontur [kɔn'tuːr] *f* (-; -en) contour, outline.

Konus ['koːnʊs] *m* (-; -se) ⚙ cone.

Konvention [kɔnvɛn'tsi̯oːn] *f* (-; -en) convention.

Konventionalstrafe [kɔnvɛntsi̯o'naːl-] *f* (contractual) penalty.

konventionell [kɔnvɛntsi̯o'nɛl] *adj* conventional.

konvergieren [kɔnvɛr'giːrən] *v/i* (h) ⚙ converge.

Konversation [kɔnvɛrza'tsi̯oːn] *f* (-; -en) conversation. **Konversati'onslexikon** *n* encyclop(a)edia.

konver'tierbar *adj* convertible.

konvertieren [kɔnvɛr'tiːrən] *v/t* (h), *v/i* (sn) convert (✦ *in acc* into, *eccl. zu* to): *er ist (or hat) konvertiert a.* he was converted.

Konvertit [kɔnvɛr'tiːt] *m* (-en; -en), **Konver'titin** *f* (-; -nen) *eccl.* convert.

konvex [kɔn'vɛks] *adj* ⚙ convex.

Konvoi ['kɔnvoi] *m* (-s; -s) convoy.
Konzentrat [kɔntsɛn'traːt] *n* (-[e]s; -e) 🔬 concentrate. **Konzentration** [kɔntsɛntra'tsioːn] *f* (-; -en) *a.* 🔬 concentration.
Konzentrati'ons|fähigkeit *f* power(s) of concentration. **~lager** *n pol.* concentration camp. **~schwäche** *f* lack of concentration.
konzentrieren [kɔntsɛn'triːrən] *v/t* (*a.* **sich ~**) (h) concentrate (**auf** *acc* on). **konzen'triert** *adj* concentrated: *in ~er Form a.* in tabloid form; **~ arbeiten** *etc a.* work *etc* with concentration.
konzentrisch [kɔn'tsɛntrɪʃ] *adj* concentric.
Konzept [kɔn'tsɛpt] *n* (-[e]s; -e) a) rough draft (*or* copy), *a.* notes, b) plan(s): *fig.* **j-n aus dem ~ bringen** put s.o. off his stroke, F rattle s.o.; **aus dem ~ kommen** lose the thread; F **j-m das ~ verderben** thwart s.o.'s plans; **das paßte ihr nicht ins ~** that didn't suit her at all.
Konzeption [kɔntsɛp'tsioːn] *f* (-; -en) conception.
Konzern [kɔn'tsɛrn] *m* (-s; -e) 💰 group, combine.
Konzert [kɔn'tsɛrt] *n* (-[e]s; -e) **1.** a) concert, b) recital: *ins ~ gehen* go to a concert. **2.** ♪ concerto. **~agen|tur** *f* concert agency. **~besucher** *m* concert-goer. **~flügel** *m* concert grand. **~führer** *m* concert guide.
konzer'tiert *adj* 💰, *pol.* **~e Aktion** concerted action.
Kon'zert|meister *m* leader, *Am.* concertmaster. **~saal** *m* concert hall.
Konzession [kɔntsɛ'sioːn] *f* (-; -en) **1.** concession (*an acc* to). **2.** licen/ce (*Am.* -se). **Konzessivsatz** [kɔntsɛ'siːf-] *m* concessive clause.
Konzil [kɔn'tsiːl] *n* (-s; -e) council.
konzipieren [kɔntsi'piːrən] *v/t* (h) a) conceive, b) draft: *konzipiert für a.* ⚙ designed for.
Kooperation [koʔopera'tsioːn] *f* (-; *no pl*) cooperation. **kooperativ** [koʔopera'tiːf] *adj* cooperative. **kooperieren** [koʔopeˈriːrən] *v/i* (h) cooperate.
Koordinate [koʔɔrdiˈnaːtə] *f* (-; -n) ⬧ coordinate. **Koordination** [-naˈtsioːn] *f* (-; -en) coordination. **koordinieren** [koʔɔrdiˈniːrən] *v/t* (h) coordinate.
Kopf [kɔpf] *m* (-[e]s; ⸚e) **1.** a) head (*a.* 🐎,

♪, ⚙), b) (letter)head, c) (pipe) bowl, d) top: *~ hoch!* cheer up!, chin up!; *an ~ in race, election:* neck to neck; *von ~ bis Fuß* from head to foot, from top to toe; *mit bloßem ~* bare-headed; *über j-s ~ hinweg a. fig.* over s.o.'s head; *fig. pro ~* per person, a head; *sie ist nicht auf den ~ gefallen* she is no fool; *ich war wie vor den ~ geschlagen* I was thunderstruck; *den ~ hängen lassen a. fig.* hang one's head; F *sein Geld auf den ~ hauen* blow one's money; *den ~ hinhalten* take the blame (*für* for); *~ und Kragen riskieren* risk one's neck; *ich weiß nicht, wo mir der ~ steht* I don't know whether I'm coming or going; *j-m zu ~e steigen* go to s.o.'s head; *auf den ~ stellen* turn *s.th.* upside down: F *und wenn du dich auf den ~ stellst!* and if it kills you!; *j-n vor den ~ stoßen* offend s.o.; *j-m über den ~ wachsen* a) outgrow s.o., b) *fig.* be too much for s.o.; *j-m den ~ waschen* a) wash s.o.'s hair, b) *a. fig.* zurechtrücken straighten s.o. out; *sie will immer mit dem ~ durch die Wand* she always wants to have her own way regardless; *j-m et. auf den ~ zusagen* tell s.o. straight out; → *Nagel, schütteln.* **2.** *fig.* head, *a.* mind, brains, *a.* leader, brain: *er war der ~ des Unternehmens* he was the head (*or* brain) of the enterprise; *aus dem ~* by heart; *im ~ rechnen* work s.th. out in one's head; F *das hältst du ja im ~ nicht aus!* it's incredible!; *e-n kühlen (klaren) ~ bewahren* keep a cool (clear) head; *sich et. durch den ~ gehen lassen* think s.th. over; *ich habe die Zahlen nicht im ~* I can't give you the figures off the cuff; *er hat andere Dinge im ~* he has other things on his mind; *er hat nur Fußball im ~* he thinks of nothing but football; *schlag dir das aus dem ~!* forget it!; *sich et. in den ~ setzen* take s.th. into one's head; *j-m den ~ verdrehen* turn s.o.'s head; *den ~ verlieren* lose one's head; *sich den ~ zerbrechen* rack one's brains (*über acc* over); → *herumgehen 1, richtig 1.*
'Kopf|-an-Kopf-Rennen *n sports:* neck--and-neck race. **~arbeit** *f* brainwork. **~arbeiter(in** *f*) *m* brainworker. **~bahnhof** *m* terminal. **~ball** *m* header.

Köpfchen ['kœpfçən] *n* (-s; -) **1.** small head. **2.** F ~ *haben* have brains.

köpfen ['kœpfən] *v/t* (h) **1.** behead. **2.** head (*ball*).

'**Kopf|ende** *n* head. **~haar** *n* hair (on the head). **~haut** *f* scalp. **~hörer** *m* headphone, *pl a.* headset. **~kissen** *n* pillow.

'**kopflastig** [-lastiç] *adj* top-heavy.

'**kopflos** *adj* **1.** headless. **2.** *fig.* panicky: ~ *werden* lose one's head, panic.

'**Kopf|nicken** *n* nod. **~rechnen** *n* mental arithmetic. **~sa,lat** *m* lettuce. **2scheu** *adj* ~ *machen* confuse, intimidate; ~ *werden* become confused. **~schmerzen** *pl* (~ *haben* have a) headache. **~schuß** *m* shot in the head. **2schüttelnd** *adv* with a shake of the head. **~sprung** *m* header. **~stand** *m* headstand.

'**kopfstehen** *v/i* (*irr, sep,* -ge-, h, → *stehen*) F *fig.* be in a flap.

'**Kopf|steinpflaster** *n* cobblestone pavement. **~steuer** *f* poll tax. **~stimme** *f* ♪ head voice, falsetto. **~stütze** *f* headrest. **~tuch** *n* (head)scarf.

kopf'über *adv* head first, headlong.

'**Kopf|verletzung** *f* head injury. **~zerbrechen** *n j-m* ~ *machen* puzzle s.o.

Kopie [ko'pi:] *f* (-; -n) copy, *phot. a.* print, *a.* duplicate. **kopieren** [ko'pi:rən] *v/t* (h) copy (*a. fig.*), *a.* ◉ duplicate, *phot. a.* print, *fig. a.* imitate.

Ko'pier|gerät *n* copier. **~pa,pier** *n* copying paper. **~stift** *m* indelible pencil.

Kopi,lot ['ko:-] *m* copilot.

Koppel¹ ['kɔpəl] *f* (-; -n) **1.** a) enclosure, b) paddock. **2.** *e-e* ~ a leash (*of dogs*), a string (*of horses*).

'**Koppel²** *n* (-s; -) ✕ belt.

koppeln ['kɔpəln] *v/t* (h) (*an acc* to) link, couple: *Raumschiffe* ~ dock spaceships; *fig. et.* ~ *mit* couple (*or* combine) s.th. with.

'**Kopplung** *f* (-; -en) coupling (*a. fig.*), docking (*of spaceships*).

Koralle [ko'ralə] *f* (-; -n) coral.
Ko'rallenbank *f* coral reef.

Koran [ko'ra:n] *m* (-s; *no pl*) Koran.

Korb [kɔrp] *m* (-[e]s; ~e ['kœrbə]) **1.** basket (*a. sports*): *ein* ~ (*voll*) *Äpfel* a basketful of apples; → *Hahn* 1. **2.** *fig.* *j-m* *e-n* ~ *geben* turn s.o. down; *e-n* ~ *bekommen* be turned down.

'**Korbball** *m* (-[e]s; *no pl*) netball.

'**Korbblüter** [-bly:tər] *m* (-s; -) ⚘ composite.

Körbchen ['kœrpçən] *n* (-s; -) **1.** basket. **2.** cup (*of bra*).

'**Korbmöbel** *pl* wicker furniture.

'**Korbwaren** *pl* wickerwork.

Kord [kɔrt] *m* (-[e]s; -e) corduroy.

Kordel ['kɔrdəl] *f* (-; -n) cord.

'**Kordhose** *f* cords, corduroys.

Kordon [kɔr'dõ:] *m* (-s; -s) cordon.

'**Kordsamt** *m* corduroy, cord velvet.

Korea [ko're:a] *n* (-s; -) Korea. **Koreaner** [kore'a:nər] *m* (-s; -), **Kore'anerin** *f* (-; -nen), **kore'anisch** *adj* Korean.

Korinthe [ko'rɪntə] *f* (-; -n) currant.

Kork [kɔrk] *m* (-[e]s; -e) *no pl* cork.

Korken ['kɔrkən] *m* (-s; -) cork.

'**Korkenzieher** *m* (-s; -) corkscrew.

Korn¹ [kɔrn] *n* (-[e]s; ~er) **1.** *no pl* grain, cereals: → *Flinte*. **2.** grain.

Korn² *f* (-[e]s; *no pl*) **1.** ✕ front sight: F *fig. aufs* ~ *nehmen* attack, go for. **2.** *phot.,* ◉ grain.

Korn³ *m* (-[e]s; -) F grain whisky.

'**Kornblume** *f* cornflower.

Körnchen ['kœrnçən] *n* (-s; -) granule: *fig. ein* ~ *Wahrheit* a grain of truth.

'**Kornfeld** *n* cornfield, *Am.* grainfield.

körnig ['kœrnɪç] *adj* grainy, granular, *rice etc*: al dente, *in cpds.* ...-grained.

'**Kornkammer** *f a. fig.* granary.

Koronar... [koro'na:r-] *anat.,* ✿ coronary (*artery, vessel, sclerosis*).

Körper ['kœrpər] *m* (-s; -) body (*a. of wine*), ♠, *phys. a.* solid: ~ *und Geist* body and mind; *am ganzen* ~ all over one's body; *am ganzen* ~ *zittern* tremble all over. **~bau** *m* (-[e]s; *no pl*) build, physique. **~behinderte** *m,* *f* (-n; -n) physically disabled (*or* handicapped) person: *die* ~*n* *a.* the handicapped. **~behinderung** *f* physical handicap.

'**Körperchen** *n* (-s; -) corpuscle, particle.

'**körpereigen** *adj biol.* endogenous.

'**Körper|geruch** *m* body odo(u)r. **~haltung** *f* posture. **~kon,takt** *m* physical contact. **~kraft** *f* physical strength.

'**körperlich** *adj* a) physical, bodily, b) corporeal (*a.* ♦): ~*e Arbeit* manual work; → *Züchtigung.*

'**Körperpflege** *f* care of the body, personal hygiene. **~mittel** *n* cosmetic.

'**Körperschaft** *f* (-; -en) corporation, (corporate) body: *gesetzgebende* ~

legislative (body). **'Körperschafts-steuer** f corporation tax.

'Körper|sprache f body language. **~teil** m part (or member) of the body. **~verletzung** f (**schwere ~** grievous) bodily harm. **~wärme** f body heat.

Korps [koːr] n (-s; -) corps.

korpulent [kɔrpuˈlɛnt] adj corpulent, stout. **Korpulenz** [kɔrpuˈlɛnts] f (-; no pl) corpulence, stoutness.

korrekt [kɔˈrɛkt] adj correct.

Kor'rektheit f (-; no pl) correctness.

Korrektor [kɔˈrɛktɔr] m (-s; -en [-ˈtoː-rən]) (proof)reader.

Korrektur [kɔrɛkˈtuːr] f (-; -en) a) correction, b) print. proofreading: **~ lesen** proofread. **~bogen** m, **~fahne** f proof. **~zeichen** n proofreader's mark.

Korrespondent [kɔrɛspɔnˈdɛnt] m (-en; -en) **1.** correspondent. **2.** ✝ correspondence clerk. **Korrespondenz** [-ˈdɛnts] f (-; -en) correspondence. **korrespondieren** [-ˈdiːrən] v/i (h) correspond.

Korridor [ˈkɔridoːr] m (-s; -e) corridor.

korrigieren [kɔriˈgiːrən] v/t (h) correct, ped. a. mark, a. change, alter.

korrodieren [kɔroˈdiːrən] v/t (h), v/i (sn) corrode. **Korrosion** [kɔroˈzioːn] f (-; -en) corrosion. **korrosi'onsbeständig** adj corrosion-resistant. **Korrosi'onsschutz** m corrosion prevention, in cpds. anticorrosive (agent, paint, etc).

korrumpieren [kɔrʊmˈpiːrən] v/t (h) corrupt. **korrupt** [kɔˈrʊpt] adj corrupt. **Korruption** [kɔrʊpˈtsioːn] f (-; -en) corruption.

Korse [ˈkɔrzə] m (-n; -n) Corsican.

Korsett [kɔrˈzɛt] n (-[e]s; -e) corset.

Korsika [ˈkɔrzika] n (-s) Corsica.

Korsin [ˈkɔrzɪn] f (-; -nen), **'korsisch** adj Corsican.

Kortison [kɔrtiˈzoːn] n (-s; no pl) cortisone.

Koryphäe [koryˈfɛːə] f (-; -n) (eminent) authority.

koscher [ˈkoːʃər] adj a. F fig. kosher.

Kosename [ˈkoːzə-] m pet name.

Kosinus [ˈkoːzinʊs] m (-; -, -se) & cosine.

Kosmetik [kɔsˈmeːtɪk] f (-; no pl) **1.** beauty care. **2.** fig. cosmetics.

Kosmetikerin [kɔsˈmeːtikərɪn] f (-; -nen) cosmetician, beautician.

Kos'metik|koffer m vanity box (or case). **~sa,lon** m beauty parlo(u)r.

Kosmetikum [kɔsˈmeːtikʊm] n (-s; -ka) cosmetic. **kos'metisch** adj cosmetic.

kosmisch [ˈkɔsmɪʃ] adj cosmic.

Kosmonaut [kɔsmoˈnaʊt] m (-en; -en), **Kosmo'nautin** f (-; -nen) cosmonaut.

Kosmopolit [kɔsmopoˈliːt] m (-en; -en), **kosmopo'litisch** adj cosmopolitan.

Kosmos [ˈkɔsmɔs] m (-; no pl) cosmos.

Kost [kɔst] f (-; no pl) a) food, fare (a. fig.), diet, b) cooking, c) board: **fleischlose ~** meatless diet; **(freie) ~ und Logis** (free) board and lodging.

'kostbar adj precious, valuable (a. fig. time etc), a. expensive: **jede Minute ist ~** every minute counts.

'Kostbarkeit f (-; -en) **1.** no pl preciousness, valuableness. **2.** precious object, treasure, pl a. valuables.

kosten¹ [ˈkɔstən] v/t (v/i ~ von) (h) taste (a. fig.), try.

'kosten² v/t (h) cost, fig. a. take (time etc): **was kostet das?** how much is that?; F **er hat es sich et. ~ lassen** he spent a lot of money on it; **es hat mich viel Mühe gekostet** it gave me a lot of trouble; **es kostete ihn das Leben** it cost him his life; **koste es, was es wolle** at all costs; F **das kostet Nerven!** that's hard on the nerves.

'Kosten pl cost(s), expenses, expenditure: **die ~ tragen** bear (or meet) the cost(s); **auf ~ von** (or gen) a. fig. at the expense of; **auf m-e ~** at my expense; **k-e ~ scheuen** spare no expense; ⚖ **j-n zu den ~ verurteilen** award costs against s.o.; fig. **auf s-e ~ kommen** get one's money's worth. **~anstieg** m increase in costs. **~aufwand** m expenditure, cost: **mit e-m ~ von ...** at a cost of ... **~beteiligung** f cost sharing. ⚖**dämpfend** adj cost-cutting. **~dämpfung** f curbing (of) costs. ⚖**deckend** adj cost-covering. **~explosi,on** f runaway costs. **~faktor** m cost factor. **~frage** f **es ist e-e ~** it is a question of cost (or of what it costs). ⚖**günstig** adj cost-effective. **~inten,siv** adj cost-intensive. **~la,wine** f escalating costs.

kostenlos adj and adv free, gratis.

'Kosten-'Nutzen-Ana'lyse f cost-benefit analysis.

'kostenpflichtig adj a) liable to pay the costs, b) tow away etc at the owner's expense: *e-e Klage ~ abweisen* dismiss a case with costs.

'**Kosten|punkt** *m* F costs: *~?* how much? *~rechnung* *f* ⊤ cost accounting. 2**senkend** *adj* cost-cutting. *~senkung* *f* reduction in costs. 2**sparend** *adj* cost-saving. *~steigerung* *f* cost increase. *~voranschlag* *m* estimate, quotation.

'**Kostgeld** *n* board (allowance).

köstlich ['kœstlɪç] *adj* a) delicious (*food etc*), b) *fig.* delightful (*humo[u]r etc*): *sich ~ amüsieren* have great fun.

'**Köstlichkeit** *f* (-; -en) 1. *no pl* deliciousness. 2. *gastr.* titbit, delicacy.

'**Kostprobe** *f a. fig.* sample, taste.

'**kostspielig** ['kɔst∫piːlɪç] *adj* expensive.

Kostüm [kɔs'tyːm] *n* (-s; -e) 1. (woman's) suit. 2. costume (*a. thea.*), dress.

Ko'stümball *m* fancy-dress ball.

kostümieren [kɔsty'miːrən] *v/t* (h) dress *s.o.* up: *sich ~* dress up (*als* as).

Ko'stümprobe *f thea.* dress rehearsal.

Ko'stümverleih *m* costume rental.

Kot [koːt] *m* (-[e]s; *no pl*) excrement, f(a)eces.

Kotelett [kɔt'lɛt] *n* (-s; -s) *gastr.* chop, cutlet. **Kote'letten** *pl* sideboards, *Am.* sideburns.

Köter ['køːtər] *m* (-s; -) *contp.* cur.

'**Kotflügel** *m* mudguard, *Am.* fender.

kotzen ['kɔtsən] *v/i* (h) V throw up, *sl.* puke: *ich finde ihn zum Kotzen!* he makes me sick!; *das ist ja zum Kotzen!* that's enough to make one puke!

Krabbe ['krabə] *f* (-; -n) shrimp, prawn.

krabbeln ['krabəln] I *v/i* (sn) crawl. II *v/t* (h) tickle.

Krach [krax] *m* (-[e]s; *⁀e*) 1. crash, bang. 2. *no pl* (loud) noise, din, F row, racket: *~ machen* make a racket, be noisy. 3. F row, quarrel: *mit j-m ~ haben* have a row with s.o.; *~ schlagen* raise hell.

krachen ['kraxən] I *v/i* 1. (h) crash, crack. 2. (sn) slam, bang: *~ gegen* (*or in acc*) crash into. II *sich ~* (h) F have a row.

krächzen ['krɛçtsən] *v/t, v/i* (h) croak.

kraft [kraft] *prep* (*gen*) ⚖ by virtue of.

Kraft *f* (-; *⁀e*) 1. *a. fig.* strength, *a. phys.* force, energy, 🔌, *phys.*, ⚙ power: *mit aller ~* with all one's might; *mit frischer* (*letzter*) *~* with renewed (one's last ounce of) strength; ⚓ *volle ~ voraus* full speed ahead; *Kräfte sammeln*

build up one's strength; *m-e Kräfte lassen nach* my strength fails; *das geht über m-e ~* that's too much for me; *ich bin am Ende m-r Kräfte* I can't take any more; *nach* (*besten*) *Kräften* to the best of one's ability; *~ schöpfen* gain strength (*aus* from); *er tat, was in s-n Kräften stand* he did everything within his power; → *vereinen*. 2. *pol. etc:* force. 3. 🔧 *in ~ sein* (*setzen*) be in (put into) force; *in ~ treten* come into force, become effective; *außer ~ setzen* a) annul, invalidate, repeal (*law*), cancel (*contract*), b) suspend; *außer ~ treten* expire. 4. worker, employee, *pl a.* personnel, staff.

'**Kraft|akt** *m* stunt. *~anstrengung* *f*, *~aufwand* *m* (strenuous) effort. *~ausdruck* *m* swearword. *~brühe* *f* beef tea.

'**Kräfteverfall** *m* loss of strength.

'**Kräfteverschleiß** *m* waste of energy.

'**Kraftfahrer(in** *f*) *m* driver, motorist.

'**Kraftfahrzeug** *n* motor vehicle. *~brief* *m* vehicle registration document. *~me-,chaniker* *m* car mechanic. *~schein* *m* vehicle registration document. *~steuer* *f* road (*Am.* automobile) tax.

'**Kraftfeld** *n phys.* field of force.

'**Kraftfutter** *n* 🌱 concentrated feed.

kräftig ['krɛftɪç] I *adj* 1. a) a. ⚙ strong, robust, sturdy, b) powerful (*a. blow etc*): F *er nahm e-n ~en Schluck* he took a good swig; *fig. ~e Farbe* deep (*or rich*) colo(u)r; ⊤ *~er Aufschwung* sharp upswing. 2. substantial, nourishing. II *adv* 3. strongly (*etc*), F soundly, heartily: *er ist ~ gebaut* he is powerfully built; *~ zuschlagen* hit hard.

kräftigen ['krɛftɪgən] *v/t* (h) strengthen.

'**Kräftigungsmittel** *n ⚕* tonic.

'**kraftlos** *adj* weak, feeble.

'**Kraft|probe** *f* trial of strength. *~protz* *m* F muscleman. *~rad* *n* motorcycle.

'**Kraftstoff** *m* fuel. *~anzeiger* *m* fuel ga(u)ge. *~leitung* *f* fuel pipe (*or line*). *~'Luft-Gemisch* *n* fuel(-air) mixture. *~pumpe* *f* fuel pump. *~verbrauch* *m* fuel consumption.

'**kraftstrotzend** *adj* bursting with strength, vigorous, powerful.

'**Kraft|übertragung** *f* power transmission. *~verkehr* *m* motor traffic. *~verschwendung* *f* waste of energy.

'**kraftvoll** *adj* powerful, vigorous, strong.

'**Kraftwagen** *m* motor vehicle.
'**Kraftwerk** *n* power station.
Kragen ['kra:gən] *m* (-s; ⸗) collar: F *ihm platzte der ~* he blew his top; *jetzt geht es ihm an den ~* he is in for it now.
'**Kragenweite** *f* collar size: *welche ~ haben Sie?* what size collar do you take?; F *sie (das) ist genau m-e ~!* she's (it's) just my cup of tea!
Krähe ['krɛ:ə] *f* (-; -n) *zo.* crow: *fig.* *e-e ~ hackt der anderen kein Auge aus* dog does not eat dog.
krähen ['krɛ:ən] *v/i* (h) crow.
'**Krähenfüße** *pl fig.* crow's-feet.
Krake ['kra:kə] *m* (-n; -n) *zo.* octopus.
Krakeel [kra'ke:l] *m* (-s; *no pl*) F row.
kra'keelen *v/i* (h) F make a row.
Kra'keeler *m* (-s; -) F roisterer.
Krakel ['kra:kəl] *m* (-s; -) F scrawl.
'**krak(e)lig** *adj* F scrawly.
krakeln ['kra:kəln] *v/t, v/i* (h) F scrawl.
Kral [kra:l] *m* (-s; -e) kraal.
Kralle ['kralə] *f* (-; -n) claw: *fig. j-m die ~n zeigen* show s.o. one's claws.
krallen ['kralən] (h) **I** *v/t* *s-e Finger ~ in* (*acc*) dig one's fingers into. **II** *sich ~* a) *an* (*acc*) cling to, b) *in* (*acc*) dig one's claws (*person*: nails) into.
Kram [kra:m] *m* (-[e]s; *no pl*) F **1.** a) things, stuff, b) junk, rubbish. **2.** *fig.* business: *den ganzen ~ hinschmeißen* chuck the whole thing; *j-m nicht in den ~ passen* not to suit s.o.'s plans.
kramen ['kra:mən] (h) F **I** *v/i* rummage (about) (*nach* for): *in Erinnerungen ~* take a trip down memory lane. **II** *v/t* et. *~ aus* fish s.th. out of *one's* bag etc.
Krampe ['krampə] *f* (-; -n) ⊙ cramp.
Krampf [krampf] *m* (-[e]s; ⸗e) **1.** 🌶 *a)* cramp, b) spasm, convulsion: *e-n ~ bekommen* get a cramp. **2.** *no pl F fig.* (*das ist doch alles ~* that's just a lot of) rubbish. '**Krampfader** *f* varicose vein.
'**krampfartig** *adj* convulsive.
krampfen ['krampfən] *v/t* (*a. sich ~*) (h) clench (*hand* etc).
'**krampfhaft** *adj* **1.** 🌶 convulsive, spasmodic. **2.** *fig.* desperate, frantic, forced (*laughter*): *sich ~ festhalten an* (*dat*) cling desperately to.
'**krampflösend** *adj* spasmolytic.
Kran [kra:n] *m* (-[e]s; ⸗e) ⊙ crane.
'**Kranführer** *m* crane driver.
Kranich ['kra:nɪç] *m* (-s; -e) *zo.* crane.

krank [kraŋk] *adj* a) sick (*a. fig.*), *pred* ill, diseased (*organ*), bad (*tooth*), b) invalid, suffering, ailing (*a. fig.*): *~ werden* fall ill (*or* sick), be taken ill; *sich ~ fühlen* feel ill; *sich ~ melden* report sick; *j-n ~ schreiben* write s.o. off sick, ✗ put s.o. on the sick list; *er macht mich ganz ~!* he's driving me crazy!
'**Kranke** *m, f* (*a. sing.*) sick person, patient.
kränkeln ['krɛŋkəln] *v/i* (h) be in poor health, be sickly, be ailing (*a. fig.*).
kranken ['kraŋkən] *v/i* (h) *a. fig. ~ an* (*dat*) suffer from.
kränken ['krɛŋkən] *v/t* (h) hurt, wound, offend: *j-n ~* hurt s.o.('s feelings).
'**Kranken|anstalt** *f* hospital. **~auto** *n* ambulance. **~besuch** *m* visit (*to a sick person*), *of doctor*: sick call: **~e machen** *a.* visit patients. **~bett** *n* sickbed. **~blatt** *n* medical record. **~geld** *n* sick pay. **~geschichte** *f* case (*or* medical) history. **~gym|nast(in** *f)* *m* physiotherapist. **~gym|nastik** *f* remedial gymnastics.
'**Krankenhaus** *n* hospital. **~aufenthalt** *m* stay in (at) a hospital. **~einweisung** *f* hospitalization. **~kosten** *pl* hospital expenses. **~tagegeld** *n* sum *paid by a private sickness insurance fund for each day in hospital*.
'**Kranken|kasse** *f* a) health insurance scheme, b) health insurance company. **~lager** *n* sickbed: *nach langem ~* after a long illness. **~pflege** *f* nursing. **~pfleger** *m* male nurse. **~pflegerin** *f* nurse. **~schein** *m* health insurance certificate. **~schwester** *f* nurse. **~stand** *m* number of sick persons. **~träger** *m* stretcher-bearer. **~versicherung** *f* health insurance. **~wagen** *m* ambulance. **~zimmer** *n* sickroom.
'**krankfeiern** *v/i* (*sep*, -ge-, h) F go sick, malinger, *Br.* skive off.
'**krankhaft** *adj* **1.** 🌶 pathological. **2.** *fig.* morbid, abnormal.
Krankheit *f* (-; -en) illness, sickness, disease: *nach langer ~* after a long illness.
'**Krankheits|bild** *n* clinical picture. **~erscheinung** *f* symptom.
'**krankheitshalber** [-halbər] *adv* owing to illness.
'**Krankheits|herd** *m* focus of a disease. **~keim** *m* germ. **~überträger** *m* carrier.
'**kranklachen: sich ~** (*sep*, -ge-, h) F nearly die with laughter.

kränklich ['krɛŋkliç] *adj* sickly.
'**Krankmeldung** *f* notification of illness (to one's employer): *zehn ~en* ten persons reported sick.
'**Kränkung** *f* (-; -en) insult.
Kranz [krants] *m* (-es; ⁓e) **1.** garland, (*e-n ~ niederlegen* lay a) wreath. **2.** *fig.* circle, ring. **3.** *gastr.* ring. **4.** *astr.* corona. **Känzchen** ['krɛntsçən] *n* (-s; -) *fig.* (ladies') circle, coffee (F hen) party.
'**Kranzgefäß** *n anat.* coronary artery.
Krapfen ['krapfən] *m* (-s; -) doughnut.
kraß [kras] *adj* crass, gross: *krasser Egoist* (*Außenseiter*) crass egotist (rank outsider); *krasser Widerspruch* (*Unterschied*) flagrant contradiction (huge difference); *krasse Lüge* blatant lie; *sich ~ ausdrücken* be very blunt.
Krater ['kra:tər] *m* (-s; -) crater.
Krätze ['krɛtsə] *f* (-; *no pl*) 𝒮 scabies.
kratzen ['kratsən] *v/t, v/i* (h) a) scratch, b) scrape: *sich ~* scratch o.s.; *sich am Ohr ~* scratch one's ear; *den Rest aus dem Topf ~* scrape the last bit from the pot; *der Pullover kratzt* (*mich am Hals*) the pullover scratches (my neck); *fig. mein Hals kratzt* I've got a sore throat; F *das kratzt mich nicht!* that doesn't worry me!; → *Kurve*. '**Kratzer** *m* (-s; -) F scratch. '**kratzfest** *adj* scratch-resistant. '**kratzig** *adj* scratchy.
'**Kratzwunde** *f* scratch.
Kraul [kraʊl] *n* (-s; *no pl*) crawl.
kraulen[1] ['kraʊlən] *v/t, v/i* (h, sn) crawl.
'**kraulen**[2] *v/t* (h) ruffle (*fur etc*).
'**Kraulschwimmen** *n* crawl.
'**Kraulschwimmer(in** *f*) *m* crawler.
kraus [kraʊs] *adj* **1.** frizzy, curly (*hair*), wrinkled (*brow*): *~ ziehen* → *krausen*. **2.** *fig.* confused, muddled (*ideas*).
Krause ['kraʊzə] *f* (-; -n) frill, ruffle.
kräuseln ['krɔʏzəln] (h) **I** *v/t* **1.** gather (*cloth*). **2.** friz(z), crimp (*hair*). **3.** ruffle, ripple (*water*). **4.** *die Lippen ~* curl one's lips; *~ a. krausen*. **II** *sich ~* **5.** → 2. **6.** *smoke etc:* curl up.
krausen ['kraʊzən] *v/t* (h) wrinkle, pucker: *die Nase ~* wrinkle one's nose.
'**kraushaarig** *adj* curly-haired.
Kraut [kraʊt] *n* (-[e]s; ⁓er) *no pl* (stem and) leaves, tops: *ins ~ schießen* run to leaf, *fig.* run wild; F *wie ~ und Rüben* (*durcheinander*) in a jumble (*or* mess). **2.** herb: *fig. gegen ... ist kein ~ ge-*

wachsen there is no remedy for ... **3.** *no pl dial.* a) cabbage, b) sauerkraut. **4.** F weed, tobacco.
Kräuter|butter ['krɔʏtər-] *f* herb butter. *~essig* *m* aromatic vinegar. *~käse* *m* green cheese. *~li,kör* *m* herb-flavo(u)red liqueur. *~tee* *m* herb tea.
Krawall [kra'val] *m* (-s; -e) **1.** riot. **2.** F (*~ machen or schlagen* kick up a) row.
Kra'wallmacher *m* rioter, rowdy.
Krawatte [kra'vatə] *f* (-; -n) tie, *Am.* necktie.
Kra'watten|muffel *m* (-s; -) *er ist ein ~* he's no tie man. *~nadel* *f* tiepin.
kraxeln ['kraksəln] *v/i* (sn) F *dial.* climb.
Kreation [krea'tsʰo:n] *f* (-; -en) creation.
kreativ [krea'ti:f] *adj* creative. **Kreativität** [kreativi'tɛ:t] *f* (-; *no pl*) creativity.
Kreatur [krea'tu:r] *f* (-; -en) creature.
Krebs [kre:ps] *m* (-es; -e) **1.** a) crayfish, *Am.* crawfish, b) crab. **2.** *astrol.* (*ich bin* [*ein*] *~* I am [a]) Cancer. **3.** 𝒮 cancer.
'**krebsartig** *adj* 𝒮 cancerous.
krebserregend, krebserzeugend *adj* carcinogenic: *~ wirken* cause cancer.
'**Krebs|forschung** *f* 𝒮 cancer research. *~früherkennung* *f* early cancer diagnosis. *~geschwulst* *f* carcinoma, cancerous tumo(u)r. *~geschwür* *n* **1.** cancerous ulcer. **2.** *fig.* canker. *~knoten* *m* cancerous lump. *~kranke* *m*, *f* (-n; -n) person suffering from cancer, cancer patient. *~krankheit* *f*, *~leiden* *n* cancer. *~tiere* *pl* crustaceans.
'**Krebsvorsorge** *f* 𝒮 cancer prevention. *~untersuchung* *f* cancer screening.
'**Krebszelle** *f* 𝒮 cancer(ous) cell.
Kredit[1] ['kre:dɪt] *n* (-s; -s) † credit (side).
Kredit[2] [kre'di:t] *m* (-[e]s; -e) † credit, *a.* loan: *e-n ~ aufnehmen* (*überziehen*) raise (overdraw) a credit; *ich habe bei der Bank ~* my credit with the bank is good; *auf ~ kaufen* buy on credit.
Kre'dit|aufnahme *f* borrowing. *~brief* *m* letter of credit. *~geber* *m* lender. *~hai* *m* F *contp.* loan shark.
kreditieren [kredi'ti:rən] *v/t* (h) *j-m et. ~* credit s.o.('s account) with s.th.
'**Kredit|institu,t** *n* credit bank. *~karte* *f* credit card. *~kauf* *m* purchase on credit. *~markt* *m* credit market. *~nehmer* *m* borrower. *~spritze* *f* credit injection.
kre'ditwürdig *adj* creditworthy.
kregel ['kre:gəl] *adj* F chirpy, chipper.

Kreide ['kraɪdə] *f* (-; -n) chalk, *paint. a.* crayon: F *bei j-m in der ~ stehen* owe s.o. money. ♀'**bleich**, ♀'**weiß** *adj* (as) white as a sheet. ~**zeichnung** *f* chalk drawing. ~**zeit** *f* (-; *no pl*) the Cretaceous period.

kreieren [kre'iːrən] *v/t* (h) create.

Kreis [kraɪs] *m* (-es; -e) **1.** a. circle (*a. fig.* of friends etc), b) cycle, c) ⚡ circuit, d) *fig.* sphere, field: *sich im ~e drehen a. fig.* move in a circle; *der Skandal zog weite ~e* the scandal involved more and more persons; *hier schließt sich der ~* we've come full circle; *im engsten ~ feiern* celebrate within the family circle (*or* with one's close friends); *im ~e der Familie* in the family (circle); *weite ~e der Bevölkerung* wide sections of the population; *aus gutunterrichteten ~en* from well-informed quarters. **2.** *pol.* district, *Am.* county. '**Kreis**|**abschnitt** *m* ⅋ segment. ~**ausschnitt** *m* ⅋ sector. ~**bahn** *f* orbit. ~**bogen** *m* ⅋ arc of a circle.

kreischen ['kraɪʃən] *v/i* (h) shriek. '**Kreischen** *n* (-s) shrieking, shrieks *pl*.

Kreisel ['kraɪzəl] *m* (-s; -) **1.** (peg)top. **2.** *phys.* gyro(scope).

'**Kreiselkompaß** *m* gyrocompass.

kreisen ['kraɪzən] I *v/i* (sn) (move in a) circle, *esp.* ☉ rotate, revolve (*a. fig.* thoughts *etc*), blood, money: circulate, ✈ orbit: *et. ~ lassen* pass s.th. round; *die Erde kreist um die Sonne* the earth revolves (a)round the sun. II *v/t* (h) *gym.* *die Arme etc ~* swing one's arms *etc* around.

'**Kreisfläche** *f* ⅋ area of a circle.

'**kreisförmig** *adj* circular.

'**Kreislauf** *m* cycle (*a.* ☉), *of blood, money*: circulation, ⚡, ☉ *a.* circuit, *astr.* revolution. ~**störung** *f* 💊 circulatory disturbance, *pl* bad circulation. ~**versagen** *n* 💊 circulatory collapse.

'**kreisrund** *adj* circular.

'**Kreissäge** *f* circular saw.

Kreißsaal ['kraɪs-] *m* 💊 delivery room.

'**Kreisstadt** *f* district town, *Am.* county seat.

'**Kreisverkehr** *m* roundabout, *Am.* rotary (traffic).

Krem [kreːm] *f* (-; -s) → *Creme etc.*

Krematorium [krema'toːriʊm] *n* (-s; -rien) crematorium, *Am.* crematory.

Kreml ['kreːməl; 'krɛməl] *m* (-s; *no pl*) the Kremlin.

Krempe ['krɛmpə] *f* (-; -n) brim.

krepieren [kre'piːrən] *v/i* (sn) **1.** F die, perish. **2.** *bomb etc*: burst, explode.

Krepp [krɛp] *m* (-s; -s) crepe.

'**Kreppa**|**pier** *n* crepe paper.

Kresse ['krɛsə] *f* (-; -n) 🌿 cress.

Kreta ['kreːta] *n* (-s) Crete. **Kreter** ['kreːtər] *m* (-s; -), '**Kreterin** *f* (-; -nen), '**kretisch** *adj* Cretan.

kreuz [krɔʏts] *adv* ~ *und quer, a.* ~ *und quer durchziehen* crisscross.

Kreuz *n* (-es; -e) **1.** cross (*a. fig.*), *print.* dagger, obelisk: *astr. das ~ des Südens* the Southern Cross; *über ~* crosswise; *ein ~ schlagen* make the sign of the cross; *es ist ein ~ mit ihm* he is a real problem; F *zu ~e kriechen* knuckle under (*vor j-m* to s.o.). **2.** (small of the) back: *mir tut das ~ weh* my back aches; F *j-n aufs ~ legen* take s.o. for a ride. **3.** ♩ sharp. **4.** *cards*: club(s).

'**Kreuz**|**band** *n* (-[e]s; ⸚er) *anat.* crucial ligament. ~**bein** *n anat.* sacrum.

kreuzen ['krɔʏtsən] (h) I *v/t* **1.** cross, ☉ *a.* intersect, *biol. a.* crossbreed. II *v/i* **2.** ⚓ cruise. III *sich ~* **3.** → **1. 4.** *fig.* cross, *interests etc*: clash: *ihre Blicke kreuzten sich* their eyes met.

'**Kreuzer** *m* (-s; -) ⚓ **1.** ✕ cruiser. **2.** *sports*: (cabin) cruiser.

'**Kreuzfahrer** *m hist.* crusader.

'**Kreuzfahrt** *f* **1.** *hist.* crusade. **2.** ⚓ (*e-e ~ machen* go on a) cruise.

'**Kreuzfeuer** *n a. fig.* crossfire: *ins ~ der öffentlichen Meinung* (*or der Kritik*) *geraten* come under fire from all sides.

'**Kreuzgang** *m* ⛪ cloister.

kreuzigen ['krɔʏtsɪgən] *v/t* (h) crucify. '**Kreuzigung** *f* (-; -en) crucifixion.

'**Kreuzotter** *f zo.* common viper.

'**Kreuzritter** *m hist.* Knight of the Cross.

'**Kreuzstich** *m* cross-stitch.

'**Kreuzung** *f* (-; -en) **1.** crossing, *biol. a.* crossbreeding, (*race*) crossbreed. **2.** crossing, intersection, junction.

'**Kreuzverhör** *n* cross-examination, F grilling: *j-n ins ~ nehmen* cross-examine (F grill) s.o.

'**Kreuzweg** *m eccl.* Way of the Cross.

'**kreuzweise** *adv* crosswise.

'**Kreuzworträtsel** *n* crossword (puzzle).

'**Kreuzzug** m *hist. or fig.* (*a. e-n ~ unter-nehmen*) crusade (*gegen* against).

kribbelig ['krɪbəlɪç] *adj* F a) nervous, jittery, b) edgy: *sie macht mich ganz ~* she gets terribly on my nerves.

kribbeln ['krɪbəln] *v/i* **1.** (h) itch, tickle, tingle: F *es kribbelte mir in den Fingern, et. zu tun* I was itching to do s.th. **2.** (sn) crawl, swarm.

Kricket ['krɪkət] n (-s; *no pl*) cricket.

'**Kricketspieler** m cricketer.

kriechen ['kri:çən] *v/i* (kroch, gekrochen, sn) creep, crawl: *fig. contp. vor j-m ~* toady to s.o. '**Kriecher** m (-s; -) *contp.* crawler, toady. '**kriecherisch** *adj contp.* crawling, toadying.

'**Kriechspur** f **1.** trail. **2.** *mot.* slow (*or* creeper) lane. '**Kriechstrom** m ⚡ leak current. '**Kriechtier** n reptile.

Krieg [kri:k] m (-[e]s; -e) a) war, b) warfare: *kalter ~* cold war; *im ~ mit* at war with; (*dat*) *den ~ erklären* a. *fig.* declare war on; *~ führen gegen* be at war against; *in den ~ ziehen* go to war.

kriegen ['kri:ɡən] *v/t* (h) F get, *a.* catch; → *a. bekommen* I; *es mit j-m zu tun ~* get into trouble with s.o.

Krieger ['kri:ɡər] m (-s; -) warrior.

'**Kriegerdenkmal** n war memorial.

'**kriegerisch** *adj* warlike, martial, *a. fig.* belligerent: *~e Auseinandersetzung* armed conflict.

'**Kriegerwitwe** f war widow.

'**kriegführend** *adj* belligerent.

'**Kriegführung** f (-; *no pl*) warfare.

'**Kriegs|ausbruch** m outbreak of (the) war: *bei ~* when the war broke out. *~berichterstatter* m war correspondent. *~beschädigte* m, f (-n; -n) war-disabled person. *~dienst* m military service. *~dienstverweigerer* m conscientious objector. *~ende* n end of (the) war: *bei ~a.* when the war ended. *~entschädigungen* pl reparations. *~erklärung* f declaration of war. *~fall* m im *~* in case of war. *~film* m war film. *~flotte* f navy, fleet. *~freiwillige* m (war) volunteer. *~fuß* m auf *~ stehen mit a.*) *j-m* be at daggers drawn with s.o., b) *e-r Sache* have (great) trouble with s.th. *~gebiet* n war zone. *~gefahr* f threat of war. *~gefangene* m prisoner of war, P.O.W. *~gefangenenlager* n prisoner-of-war (*or* P.O.W.) camp. *~gefan-*

~genschaft f captivity: *in ~ geraten* be taken prisoner. *~gegner* m **1.** pacifist. **2.** *the* enemy. *~gericht* n (*a. vor ein ~ stellen*) court-martial.

'**Kriegsgewinnler** [-ɡəvɪnlər] m (-s; -) war profiteer.

'**Kriegs|gräberfürsorge** f War Graves Commission. *~hafen* m naval port. *~held* m war hero. *~hetzer* m warmonger. *~hinterbliebenen* pl war widows and orphans. *~kame,rad* m fellow soldier. *~ma,rine* f navy. *~materi,al* n matériel. *~opfer* n war victim. *~pfad* m auf dem *~ sein* a. F *fig.* be on the warpath. *~recht* n (-[e]s; *no pl*) martial law. *~schauplatz* n theat/re (*Am.* -er) of war. *~schiff* n warship. *~schulden* pl war debts. *~schuld(frage)* f (question of) war guilt. *~spielzeug* n war toys. *~tanz* m war dance. *~teilnehmer* m **1.** combatant. **2.** ex-serviceman, *Am.* (war) veteran. *~trauung* f wartime wedding. *~treiber* m warmonger. *~verbrechen* n war crime.

'**Kriegsverbrecher** m war criminal. *~pro,zeß* m war crimes trial.

'**Kriegs|waise** f war orphan. ⚖**wichtig** *adj* essential to the war effort: *~e Ziele* strategic targets. *~zeit* f wartime: *in ~en* in time(s) of war. *~zustand* m (state of) war: *im ~* at war.

Krimi ['kri:mi; 'krɪmi]] m (-[s]; -[s]) F thriller (*a. fig.*), whodun(n)it.

Kriminal|beamte [krimi'na:l-] m detective, C.I.D. officer. *~fall* m criminal case. *~film* m crime film (*or* thriller).

kriminalisieren [kriminali'zi:rən] *v/t* (h) criminalize.

Kriminalist [krimina'lɪst] m (-en; -en) **1.** criminologist. **2.** detective.

Kriminalität [kriminali'tɛ:t] f (-; *no pl*) **1.** criminality. **2.** crime: *ansteigende ~* increasing crime rate.

Krimi'nal|kommis,sar m detective superintendent, *Am.* captain of police. *~poli,zei* f criminal investigation department (C.I.D.), plain-clothes police. *~poli,zist* m → *Kriminalbeamte*. *~ro,man* m detective (*or* crime) novel.

kriminell [krimi'nɛl] *adj* criminal.

Krimi'nelle m, f (-n; -n) criminal.

Krippe ['krɪpə] f (-; -n) **1.** 🐴 manger, crib. **2.** (Christmas) crib, *Am.* crèche. **3.** crèche, day nursery.

'Krippenspiel n Nativity play.
Krise ['kri:zə] f (-; -n) crisis: **in e-e ~ geraten** enter a state of crisis.
kriseln ['kri:zəln] v/impers (h) **es kriselt** a) there is trouble brewing, b) **in ihrer Ehe** they seem to be going through a crisis, c) **in der Regierung** a government crisis is looming.
'krisenanfällig adj crisis-prone.
'krisenfest adj stable.
'Krisengebiet n crisis area.
'krisen|geschüttelt adj crisis-ridden.
~herd m trouble spot. **~management** n crisis management. **~situati,on** f crisis (situation). **~sitzung** f crisis meeting. **~stab** m crisis management group. **~zeit** f time of crisis.
Kristall[1] ['krɪs'tal] m (-[e]s; -e) crystal.
Kri'stall[2] n (-[e]s; no pl) **1.** crystal (glass), cut glass. **2.** crystal (goods).
kri'stallen adj crystalline, a. fig. crystal.
kristallinisch [krɪsta'li:nɪʃ] adj crystalline. **Kristallisation** [krɪstaliza'tsjo:n] f (-; -en) crystallization. **kristallisieren** [krɪstali'zi:rən] v/i (h) crystallize.
kri'stallklar adj crystal-clear.
Kristallographie [krɪstalogra'fi:] f (-; no pl) crystallography.
Kriterium [kri'te:rĭom] n (-s; -rien) **1.** criterion (**für** of). **2.** sports: circuit race.
Kritik [kri'ti:k] f (-; -en) a) criticism (**an** dat of), b) review, c) the critics: **~ hervorrufen** give rise to criticism; **~ üben an** (dat) criticize; **e-e ~ schreiben über** (acc) a. review; **gute ~en haben** get (or have) good reviews, have a good press; F **unter aller ~ sein** be beneath contempt. **Kritiker** ['kri:tikər] m (-s; -), **'Kritikerin** f (-; -nen) a) critic, b) reviewer. **Kri'tikfähigkeit** f critical faculties. **kri'tiklos** adj uncritical. **kritisch** ['kri:tɪʃ] adj a. phys., ⊙ critical (**gegenüber** of), fig. a. crucial. **kritisieren** [kriti'zi:rən] v/t, v/i (h) criticize.
kritteln ['krɪtəln] v/i (h) carp (**an** dat at).
Kritzelei [krɪtsə'laɪ] f (-; -en) scribble.
kritzeln ['krɪtsəln] v/t, v/i (h) scribble.
kroch [krɔx] pret of **kriechen**.
Krocket ['krɔkət] n (-s; no pl) croquet.
Krokant [kro'kant] m (-[e]s; no pl) brittle.
Krokette [kro'kɛtə] f (-; -n) croquette.
Kroko ['kro:ko] n (-[-s]; -s) 🐊 → **Krokodilleder**. **Krokodil** [kroko'di:l] n (-s; -e) crocodile. **Kroko'dilleder** n crocodile

(skin or leather). **Kroko'dilstränen** pl F (**~ vergießen** shed) crocodile tears.
Krokus ['kro:kus] m (-; -[se]) 🌸 crocus.
Krone ['kro:nə] f (-; -n) **1.** crown (a. fig.), coronet: **die ~ der Schöpfung** the pride of creation; F **das setzt allem die ~ auf!** that beats everything!; **e-n in der ~ haben** be tight. **2.** ⊙ a) cap, top, b) crown, crest. **3.** crown (of tooth). **4.** (Swedish coin) krona, (Danish or Norwegian coin) krone. **5.** chandelier.
krönen ['krø:nən] v/t (h) crown (**j-n zum König** s.o. king), fig. a. climax: **von Erfolg gekrönt** crowned with success.
'Kronenkorken m crown cork.
'Kronju,welen pl crown jewels.
'Kronleuchter m chandelier.
'Kronprinz m crown prince (a. fig.), Br. Prince of Wales. **'Kronprin,zessin** f crown princess, Br. Princess Royal.
'Krönung f (-; -en) **1.** coronation. **2.** fig. crowning (event): **die ~ s-r Laufbahn** the climax of his career; **die ~ des Abends** the highlight (F high spot) of the evening.
'Kronzeuge m, **'Kronzeugin** f chief witness: **~ werden** turn Queen's (King's, Am. State's) evidence.
Kropf [krɔpf] m (-[e]s; ⁻e) **1.** zo. crop. **2.** 🌿 goitre, Am. goiter.
kroß [krɔs] adj crisp.
Kröte ['krø:tə] f (-; -n) **1.** zo. toad. **2.** pl F dough, pennies.
Krücke ['krkyə] f (-; -n) **1.** crutch: **an ~n gehen** walk on crutches. **2.** crook (of walking stick etc). **3.** F contp. a) washout, b) alte ~ rattletrap.
Krug [kru:k] m (-[e]s; ⁻e) **1.** jug, pitcher. **2.** → **Maßkrug. 3.** dial. pub, inn.
Krume ['kru:mə] f (-; -n) **1.** 🌱 topsoil. **2.** → **Krümel** ['kry:məl] m (-s; -) crumb.
krümelig ['kry:məlɪç] adj crumbly.
krümeln ['kry:məln] v/t, v/i (h) crumble.
krumm [krɔm] **I** adj crooked (a. F fig. dishonest), hooked, a. bent: **~e Haltung** stoop; **~er Schnabel** curved beak; **~ biegen** bend; **ganz ~ und schief** awry, lopsided; F **sich ~ und schief lachen** laugh one's head off; **~e Sache, ~e Tour** crooked business; **ein ~es Ding drehen** pull a fast one; **et. auf die ~e Tour versuchen** try to wangle s.th. **II** adv **~ gewachsen** crooked; **sich ~ halten, ~ gehen** stoop.

'**krummbeinig** [-baɪnɪç] *adj* bow-legged.

krümmen ['krʏmən] (h) **I** *v/t* bend, crook. **II** *sich* ~ bend, round: *a.* curve, *worm etc*: squirm: *sich* ~ *vor* (*dat*) writhe with *pain etc*, squirm with *embarrassment*; *sich vor Lachen* ~ → **krummlachen**.

Krümmer ['krʏmər] *m* (-s; -) **1.** *mot.* manifold. **2.** ⊙ bend, elbow.

'**krummlachen**: *sich* ~ (*sep*, -ge-, h) F laugh one's head off. '**krummlegen**: *sich* ~ (*sep*, -ge-, h) F pinch and scrape. '**krummnehmen** *v/t* (*irr, sep*, -ge-, h, → **nehmen**) F *et.* ~ take s.th. amiss.

'**Krümmung** *f* (-; -en) bend, curve, turn, A⊱, ✈, *phys.*, ⊙ curvature.

Kruppe ['krʊpə] *f* (-; -n) croup (*of horse*).

Krüppel ['krʏpəl] *m* (-s; -) (*a.* **zum** ~ **machen**) cripple: **zum** ~ **werden** be crippled. '**krüpp(e)lig** *adj* crippled.

Kruste ['krʊstə] *f* (-; -n) crust, *gastr. a.* crackling. '**Krustentier** *n* crustacean.

krustig ['krʊstɪç] *adj* crusty.

Kruzifix ['kru:tsifɪks] *n* (-es; -e) crucifix.

Krypta ['krʏpta] *f* (-; -ten) △ crypt.

Kuba ['ku:ba] *n* (-s) Cuba. **Kubaner** [ku'ba:nər] *m* (-s; -), **Ku'banerin** *f* (-; -nen), **ku'banisch** *adj* Cuban.

Kübel ['ky:bəl] *m* (-s; -) a) bucket (*a.* ⊙), pail, b) tub: *es gießt wie aus ~n* it's coming down in buckets.

Kubik|inhalt [ku'bi:k-] *m* cubic content. ~**maß** *n* cubic measure. ~**meter** *m, n* cubic metre (*Am.* meter). ~**wurzel** *f* A⊱ cube root. ~**zahl** *f* cube.

kubisch ['ku:bɪʃ] *adj* cubic(al).

Kubismus [ku'bɪsmʊs] *m* (-; *no pl*) cubism. **Ku'bist** *m* (-en; -en) cubist. **ku'bistisch** *adj* cubistic.

Kubus ['ku:bʊs] *m* (-; Kuben) A⊱ cube.

Küche ['kʏçə] *f* (-; -n) **1.** kitchen, kitchenette; → *Teufel*. **2.** a) cooking, cookery, cuisine, b) meals, food: *kalte* (*warme*) ~ cold (hot) meals; *die chinesische* ~ Chinese cooking; → *gutbürgerlich*. **3.** F → *Küchenpersonal*.

Kuchen ['ku:xən] *m* (-s; -) cake.

'**Küchenbenutzung** *f mit* ~ with use of kitchen.

'**Kuchenblech** *n* baking sheet (*or* tin).

'**Küchenchef** *m* chef de cuisine).

'**Kücheneinrichtung** *f* kitchen furniture and fittings.

'**Kuchenform** *f* cake tin.

'**Kuchengabel** *f* pastry fork.

'**Küchen|gerät** *n* kitchen utensil (*or* appliance). ~**geschirr** *n* kitchenware. ~**herd** *m* kitchen range. ~**hilfe** *f* kitchenmaid. ~**kraut** *n* potherb. ~**messer** *n* kitchen knife. ~**perso,nal** *n* kitchen staff. ~**schrank** *m* (kitchen) cupboard.

'**Kuchenteig** *m* cake mixture.

'**Kuchenteller** *m* dessert plate.

'**Küchen|tisch** *m* kitchen table. ~**waage** *f* kitchen scales. ~**wecker** *m* (kitchen) timer. ~**zettel** *m* menu.

Kuckuck ['kʊkʊk] *m* (-s; -e) **1.** cuckoo: F *wo* (*wer etc*) *zum* ~*!* where (who *etc*) the devil! **2.** *humor.* bailiff's seal.

'**Kuckucksei** *n* F *fig.* *ein* ~ a cuckoo in the nest. ~**uhr** *f* cuckoo clock.

Kufe ['ku:fə] *f* (-; -n) runner, ✈ skid.

Küfer ['ky:fər] *m* (-s; -) cooper.

Kugel ['ku:gəl] *f* (-; -n) **1.** ball (*a.* ⊙), globe, *astr.*, A⊱ sphere: *die Erde ist e-e* ~ the earth is a sphere. **2.** bullet: → *jagen* 3. **3.** *sports:* a) shot, b) bowl: *er stieß die* ~ *auf 22 m* he put the shot at 22 metres; F *fig. e-e ruhige* ~ *schieben* have a cushy job.

'**Kugelabschnitt** *m* A⊱ spherical segment.

'**Kugelfang** *m* butt.

'**kugelförmig** *adj* globular, spherical.

'**Kugelgelenk** *n* (ball-and-)socket joint.

'**Kugelhagel** *m* hail of bullets.

'**Kugelkopf(schreibma,schine** *f*) *m* golfball (typewriter).

'**Kugellager** *n* ⊙ ball bearing.

kugeln ['ku:gəln] (h) **I** *v/t, v/i* roll. **II** *sich* ~ roll about (*im Schnee* in the snow).

'**kugel'rund** *adj* (as) round as a ball.

'**Kugelschreiber** *m* ballpoint (pen), *Br. a.* Biro (*TM*). ~**mine** *f* refill.

'**kugelsicher** *adj* bulletproof.

'**Kugelstoßen** *n* shot put. '**Kugelstoßer** *m* (-s; -), '**Kugelstoßerin** *f* (-; -nen) shot-putter.

Kuh [ku:] *f* (-; ⸚e) cow: *fig. heilige* ~ sacred cow; F *contp. dumme* ~*!* silly cow! ~**fladen** *m* cowpat. ~**glocke** *f* cowbell. ~**handel** *m* F *fig.* horse trading. ~**haut** *f* cowhide: F *fig. das geht auf k-e* ~*!* it's just incredible!

kühl [ky:l] *adj a. fig.* cool, chilly: *es* (*mir*) *wird* ~ it's getting (I feel) chilly; (*j-m gegenüber*) ~ *bleiben* remain cool (toward[s] s.o.); *et.* ~ *lagern* store s.th.

cool; *j-n ~ empfangen* give s.o. a cool reception; → *Kopf* 2.

'**Kühl|anlage** *f* cooling plant (*mot.* system). **~appa,rat** *m* cooling apparatus. **~con,tainer** *m* (-s; -) cooltainer.

'**Kühle** *f* (-; *no pl*) coolness (*a. fig.*), cool.

'**kühlen** (h) **I** *v/t* cool (*a.* ☻), chill. **II** *v/i* have a cooling effect.

'**Kühler** *m* (-s; -) **1.** ☻ cooler. **2.** *mot.* radiator. **~block** *m mot.* radiator core. **~fi,gur** *f mot.* radiator mascot.

'**Kühl|haus** *n* cold-storage house. **~mittel** *n* coolant. **~raum** *m* cold-storage chamber, ⚓ refrigerating hold. **~schiff** *n* refrigerator ship. **~schlange** *f* ☻ cooling coil. **~schrank** *m* refrigerator, F fridge. **~tasche** *f* cool box (*or* bag). **~truhe** *f* (chest) freezer, deep-freeze. **~turm** *m* cooling tower.

'**Kühlung** *f* (-; -en) **1.** *a.* ☻ cooling. **2.** ☻ cooling system. **3.** *no pl* coolness.

'**Kühlwagen** *m* 🚃 refrigerator wagon (*Am.* car), *mot.* refrigerator truck.

'**Kühlwasser** *n* cooling water.

'**Kuhmilch** *f* cow's milk.

kühn [ky:n] *adj a. fig.* bold, daring: *das übertrifft m-e ~sten Träume* that goes beyond my wildest dreams.

'**Kühnheit** *f* (-; *no pl*) boldness.

'**Kuhpocken** *pl* 🐄 cowpox.

'**Kuhstall** *m* cowshed.

Küken ['ky:kən] *n* (-s; -) *a. fig.* chick.

kulant [ku'lant] *adj* ✝ accommodating, fair (*price etc*).

Kuli ['ku:li] *m* (-s; -s) coolie.

kulinarisch [kuli'na:rɪʃ] *f* culinary.

Kulisse [ku'lɪsə] *f* (-; -n) *usu. pl thea. etc* scenery, set, wing, *a. fig.* background: *hinter den ~n a. fig.* behind the scenes, backstage.

kulminieren [kulmi'ni:rən] *v/i* (h) *astr.* culminate (*fig. in dat in*).

Kult [kult] *m* (-[e]s; -e) cult: *e-n ~ treiben* make a cult (*mit* out of). '**Kultfi,gur** *f* cult figure. '**Kulthandlung** *f* ritual act.

'**kultisch** *adj* ritual, cultic.

kultivieren [kulti'vi:rən] *v/t* (h) cultivate. **kulti'viert** *adj* cultured, cultivated, *a.* civilized (*person*), refined (*taste*).

Kultur [kol'tu:r] *f* (-; -en) **1.** *no pl a.* culture, *a.* refinement, ⚇ civilization: *die abendländische ~* (the) Western civilization; *er hat (k-e)* he is (un)cultured; F *in ~ machen* be into culture. **2.**

no pl ✔ cultivation. **3.** ✔, ✳ culture.

Kul'tur|abkommen *n pol.* cultural agreement. **~austausch** *m* cultural exchange. **~ba,nause** *m* F philistine. **~betrieb** *m* (-[e]s *no pl*) F cultural activities. **~beutel** *m* toilet bag. **~denkmal** *n* cultural monument.

kulturell [kultu'rɛl] *adj* cultural.

Kul'tur|erbe *n* cultural heritage. **~film** *m* documentary. **~geschichte** *f* **1.** history of civilization (*a. book*). **2.** *no pl* a) cultural history of France *etc*, b) history of culture. ♀**geschichtlich** *adj* cultural-historical. **~gut** *n* cultural asset(s). **~landschaft** *f* **1.** land developed and cultivated by man. **2.** *fig.* cultural scene. **~leben** *n* cultural life.

kul'turlos *adj* uncultured, uncivilized.

Kul'tur|mensch *m* civilized man. **~pessi,mismus** *m* cultural pessimism. **~pflanze** *f* cultivated plant. **~poli,tik** *f* cultural and educational policy. ♀**poli,tisch** *adj* politico-cultural. **~revoluti,on** *f* cultural revolution. **~schock** *m* cultural shock. **~sprache** *f* cultural (*or* civilized) language. **~stätte** *f* place of cultural interest. **~stufe** *f* stage (*or* level) of civilization. **~szene** *f* (-; *no pl*) cultural scene. **~volk** *n* civilized people (*or* nation, race).

Kultusmi,nister ['kultos-] *m* Minister of Culture, Education, and Church Affairs.

Kümmel ['kyməl] *m* (-s; -) **1.** ☘ caraway: *Echter ~* cumin. **2.** *gastr.* kümmel.

Kummer ['komər] *m* (-s; *no pl*) grief, sorrow, b) trouble, worry, worries, problems: *~ haben* have problems; *j-m viel ~ machen* cause s.o. a lot of worry (*or* trouble); F *ich bin ~ gewöhnt!* I'm used to this sort of thing!

kümmerlich ['kymərlıç] *adj* miserable, *a.* poor, meagre, *Am.* meager, sparse (*vegetation etc*): *sich ~ durchschlagen* (*mit Stundengeben etc*) eke out a bare existence (by giving lessons *etc*).

kümmern ['kymərn] (h) **I** *sich ~ um* a) look after, take care of, b) care about, c) pay attention to, d) see to; *ich muß mich um das Mittagessen ~* I must see to our lunch; *kümmere dich um d-e eigenen Angelegenheiten!* mind your own business!; *sich nicht ~ um* a) not to bother about, ignore, b) neglect. **II**

v/t was kümmert mich ... what do I care about ...; *was kümmert's mich?* that's not my problem!; *was kümmert dich das?* what concern is that of yours? **III** *v/i* develop poorly.

'kummervoll *adj* woebegone, sad.

Kumpan [kʊm'paːn] *m* (-s; -e) F a) companion, fellow, b) *b.s.* accomplice.

Kumpel ['kʊmpəl] *m* (-s; -) **1.** ⚒ pitman, miner. **2.** F mate, pal, chum, *Am.* buddy. **'kumpelhaft** *adj* chummy.

kündbar ['kʏntbaːr] *adj* terminable (*contract*), *capital* at call, redeemable (*loan*), *lease*, *position*, *etc* subject to notice: *er ist jederzeit ~* he can be given notice at any time.

Kunde ['kʊndə] *m* (-n; -n) customer, client: *fester ~* regular customer.

'Kunden|beratung *f* (customer) advisory service (*or* office). **~dienst** *m* a) service (to the customer), b) after-sales service, c) service department. **~fang** *m* (-[e]s; *no pl*) *contp.* (*auf ~ ausgehen* be) touting. **~kar,tei** *f* list of customers. **~kreis** *m* customers, clientele. **~nummer** *f* client code. **~stamm** *m* regular customers (*or* clientele). **~werbung** *f* canvassing (of customers).

Kundgebung ['kʊntgeːbʊŋ] *f* (-; -en) *pol.* meeting, rally.

kundig ['kʊndɪç] *adj* experienced, expert, *a.* practised (*eye*, *hand*).

kündigen ['kʏndɪgən] (h) **I** *v/t* terminate (*contract etc*), cancel (*subscription etc*), call in (*capital*): *s-e Stellung ~* quit one's job; *die Wohnung ~* give notice of one's intention to leave, *j-m* give s.o. notice to quit; F *j-n ~* dismiss s.o., sack s.o. **II** *v/i j-m* (*zum 1. Mai*) *~* give notice (*landlord:* to quit) (for May 1st), dismiss s.o. (as of May 1st); (*j-m*) *drei Monate im voraus ~* give (s.o.) three months' notice; *bei e-r Firma ~* hand in one's notice to a firm; *mir ist* (*zum 1. Mai*) *gekündigt worden* I'm under notice to leave (on May 1st).

'Kündigung *f* (-; -en) a) notice, notice of withdrawal (*of loan etc*), termination (*of contract*), cancel(l)ation (*of subscription etc*), b) dismissal: *~* (*e-r Wohnung*) by landlord: notice to quit, by tenant: notice of one's intention to leave; *vierteljährliche ~ vereinbaren* agree on three months' notice.

'Kündigungs|frist *f* period of notice: *mit halbjähriger ~* at six months' notice. **~grund** *m* grounds for giving notice (*or* for dismissal). **~schreiben** *n* a) (written) notice, b) letter of dismissal. **~schutz** *m* protection against unlawful dismissal (*or* unwarrranted eviction).

Kundin ['kʊndɪn] *f* (-; -nen) (female) customer (*etc*); → **Kunde.**

Kundschaft ['kʊntʃaft] *f* (-; *no pl*) a) customers, clientele, b) F customer, c) patronage.

'Kundschafter *m* (-s; -) scout, spy.

künftig ['kʏnftɪç] **I** *adj* future, coming: **~e Generationen** *a.* generations to come. **II** *adv* in future, from now on.

Kunst [kʊnst] *f* (-; ⁺e) **1.** art: *die schönen Künste* the fine arts; *die bildende ~* graphic art; *die darstellenden Künste* a) the performing arts, b) the pictorial arts; *die ~ der Gegenwart* contemporary art; F *was macht die ~?* how are things?; → *schön* 1. **2.** a) skill, art, b) trick: *die ~ des Schreibens* the art of writing; *ärztliche ~* medical skill; F *das ist k-e ~!* that's easy!; *das ist e-e brotlose ~* there's no money in it; *die ganze ~ besteht darin zu inf* the whole trick is to *inf*; *sie ließ alle ihre Künste spielen* she used all her wiles.

'Kunst|akade,mie *f* academy of arts. **~auge** *n* artificial eye. **~ausstellung** *f* art exhibition. **~band** *m* (-[e]s; ⁺e) art book. **~betrieb** *m* (-[e]s; *no pl*) *contp.* cultural activities. **~denkmal** *n* monument of art. **~druck** *m* (-[e]s; -e) **1.** *no pl* art printing. **2.** art print. **~dünger** *m* artificial fertilizer. **~eisbahn** *f* artificial ice rink. **~erzieher(in** *f*) *m* art teacher. **~erziehung** *f* art (education). **~faser** *f* synthetic fibre (*Am.* fiber). **~fehler** *m* ⚕ professional blunder.

'kunstfertig *adj* skil(l)ful, skilled.

'Kunst|flieger *m* stunt flyer. **~flug** *m* aerobatics, stunt flying. **~flug...** aerobatic (*figure*, *team*, *etc*). **~freund(in** *f*) *m* art lover. **~gale,rie** *f* art gallery. **~gegenstand** *m* objet d'art.

'kunstgerecht *adj* skil(l)ful, expert.

'Kunst|geschichte *f* (-; *no pl*) art history. **~gewerbe** *n* (-s; *no pl*) arts and crafts, applied art(s). **~glied** *n* artificial limb. **~griff** *m* trick. **~handel** *m* art trade. **~händler** *m* art dealer. **~hand-**

kurieren

lung f art dealer('s shop). **~handwerk** n → **Kunstgewerbe**. **~handwerker(in** f) m artisan. **~herz** n 🌣 artificial heart. **~hi₁storiker** m art historian. **~hoch-schule** f art college. **~honig** m artificial honey. **~kritiker** m art critic. **~leder** n imitation leather.

Künstler ['kynstlər] m (-s; -), **'Künstle-rin** f (-; -nen) artist, ♪, thea. performer, (circus etc) artiste. **'künstlerisch** adj artistic: **~er Leiter** art director; **ein ~ wertvoller Film** a film of artistic merit; **~ begabt sein** have an artistic talent. **'Künstlername** m thea. etc stage name. **'Künstlertum** n (-s; no pl) artistry, coll. the artistic world. **'Künstlerviertel** n artists' quarter.

'künstlich ['kynstlıç] adj artificial (a. fig.), a. false (teeth etc), man-made, synthetic (fibres): **~e Niere** kidney machine; **~ ernähren** feed s.o. artificially. **'Kunstlicht** n phot. artificial light. **'Kunstliebhaber(in** f) m art lover. **'kunstlos** adj simple, plain. **'Kunst|maler(in** f) m artist, painter. **~pause** f iro. **e-e ~ machen** pause for effect. **~reiter(in** f) m trick rider. **~sammler(in** f) m art collector. **~sammlung** f art collection. **~schätze** pl art treasures. **~schule** f art school. **~schwimmen** n water ballet. **~seide** f artificial silk, rayon. **2seiden** adj (of) rayon. **~sprache** f artificial language. **~springen** n (fancy) diving. **~sprin-ger(in** f) m (fancy) diver.

'Kunststoff m synthetic material, plastic (material): **~e** plastics; **aus ~** (of) plastic. **2beschichtet** adj plastic-laminat-ed. **~indu₁strie** f plastics industry. **~rasen** m artificial lawn.

'Kunst|stopfen n (-s) invisible mending. **~stück** n a) trick, b) stunt, fig. a. (great) feat: iro. **~!** small wonder!, big deal!; **das ist doch kein ~!** anyone can do that! **~stu₁dent(in** f) m art student. **~tischler** m cabinetmaker. **~turnen** n gymnastics. **~turner(in** f) m gymnast. **2verständig** adj 1. artistic. 2. expert. **~verständnis** n appreciation (or expert knowledge) of art.

'kunstvoll adj a) (highly) artistic, b) elaborate, c) ingenious. **'Kunst|werk** n work of art. **~wort** n coinage. **~zeitschrift** f art magazine.

kunterbunt ['kʊntər-] adv **~ durcheinan-der** higgledy-piggledy, in a jumble.

Kupfer ['kʊpfər] n (-s; no pl) copper. **'Kupferblech** n sheet copper. **'Kupfer-draht** m copper wire. **'kupferhaltig** adj containing copper. **kupfern** ['kʊpfərn] adj (of) copper. **'Kupferstecher** m (-s; -) copperplate engraver. **'Kupferstich** m (-[e]s; -e) copperplate (engraving).

kupieren [ku'piːrən] v/t (h) dock.

Kupon [ku'põː] m (-s; -s) coupon.

Kuppe ['kʊpə] f (-; -n) 1. (hill)top. 2. (finger)tip.

Kuppel ['kʊpəl] f (-; -n) dome. **'kuppelförmig** adj dome-shaped.

Kuppelei [kʊpə'laɪ] f (-; -en) ⚖ procuration. **kuppeln** ['kʊpəln] (h) **I** v/t 1. ⚙ (an acc) couple (with), connect (to). **II** v/i 2. mot. a) (let in the) clutch, b) declutch. 3. matchmake. **'Kuppler** m (-s; -), **'Kupplerin** f (-; -nen) a) ⚖ procurer (procuress), b) matchmaker.

'Kupplung f (-; -en) 1. 🔗, ⚙ coupling. 2. mot. clutch: **die ~ treten** (**loslassen**) → **kuppeln** 2.

'Kupplungs|belag m mot. clutch facing. **~pe₁dal** n clutch pedal. **~scheibe** f clutch disc. **~stecker** m ⚡ coupler plug.

Kur [kuːr] f (-; -en) cure, (course of) treatment: **e-e ~ machen** take a cure (or a course of treatment); **zur ~ fahren** go to a health resort (or spa).

Kür [kyːr] f (-; -en) a) gym. free (or voluntary) exercise(s), b) free skating (etc).

Kurator [ku'raːtɔr] m (-s; -en [kura-'toːrən]) trustee. **Kuratorium** [kura-'toːrɪʊm] n (-s; -rien) board of trustees.

'Kuraufenthalt m stay at a health resort.

Kurbel ['kʊrbəl] f (-; -n) crank, handle. **kurbeln** ['kʊrbəln] (h) **I** v/i crank, F mot. turn the steering wheel. **II** v/t et. **in die Höhe ~** wind s.th. up.

'Kurbelwelle f mot. crankshaft.

Kürbis ['kyrbɪs] m (-ses; -se) 1. 🌿 pumpkin. 2. F nut.

Kurde ['kʊrdə] m (-n; -n), **'Kurdin** f (-; -nen), **'kurdisch** adj Kurd.

'Kurfürst(in f) m elector (electress).

'Kurgast m visitor (to a health resort).

'Kurhaus n kurhaus, casino.

'Kurho₁tel n health-resort hotel.

Kurie ['kuːriə] f (-; -en) eccl. Curia.

Kurier [ku'riːr] m (-s; -e) courier.

kurieren [ku'riːrən] v/t (h) cure (**von** of).

Ku'riergepäck n diplomatic bag.
kurios [ku'riːoːs] adj curious, odd.
  Kuriosität [kuriozi'tɛːt] f (-; -en) **1.** curiosity. **2.** curio. **Kuriosum** [ku'riːo-zʊm] n (-s; -sa) odd thing, odd fact.
'Kurort m spa, health resort.
'Kurpfuscher(in f) m quack.
  Kurpfusche'rei f (-; no pl) quackery.
Kurs [kʊrs] m (-es; -e) **1.** ✝ a) rate (of exchange), exchange rate, b) price, quotation: **zum ~ von** at a rate of; **au-ßer ~ setzen** withdraw from circulation; **die ~e geben nach (ziehen an)** prices are softening (hardening); **hoch im ~ stehen** a) be high, b) fig. be popular (**bei** with). **2.** ✓, ⚓ course, fig. a. line: **~ nehmen auf** (acc) set course for, a. fig. head for; **e-n falschen ~ ein-schlagen** take the wrong course (fig. a wrong line); pol. **harter (weicher) ~** hard (soft) line; → **abweichen. 3.** class, course: **e-n ~ für Englisch besuchen** attend a course in English.
'Kursänderung f **1.** ✓, ⚓ change of course (a. fig.). **2.** ✝ change in the ex-change rate. **'Kursanstieg** m ✝ rise (in rates or prices). **'Kursbericht** m ✝ (stock) market report. **'Kursbuch** n (railway, Am. railroad) timetable.
Kürschner ['kʏrʃnər] m (-s; -) furrier.
  Kürschnerei [kʏrʃnə'raɪ] f (-; -en) **1.** no pl furrier's trade. **2.** furrier's shop.
'Kurseinbruch m ✝ fall in prices, slump.
'Kursgewinn m ✝ a) (price) gains, b) exchange profits.
kursieren [kʊr'ziːrən] v/i (h) circulate, fig. rumo(u)r etc: a. go round.
'Kursindex m ✝ share price index.
kursiv [kʊr'ziːf] adj italic: **et. ~ drucken** print s.th. in italics.
'Kurskorrek,tur f course correction: **e-e ~ vornehmen** correct the course.
'Kursleiter m instructor, teacher.
'Kursno,tierung f ✝ quotation.
'Kursrückgang m ✝ decline in prices.
'Kursschwankung f ✝ a) exchange rate fluctuation, b) price fluctuation.
'Kursus ['kʊrzʊs] m (-; Kurse) → **Kurs** 3.
'Kursverlust m ✝ a) exchange loss, b) (stock) price) loss.
'Kurswechsel m pol. change of policy.
'Kurswert m ✝ market value.
'Kurszettel m ✝ price list, stock list.
'Kurtaxe f health resort tax.

'Kürübung f sports: free exercise.
Kurve ['kʊrvə] f (-; -n) curve, ♪ a. graph, a. bend, turn (of road etc), pl F curves (of woman): **die Straße macht e-e ~** the road bends; **unübersichtliche ~** blind bend; mot. **die ~ schneiden** cut the curve; **e-e ~ fliegen** bank; F fig. **die ~ kratzen** beat it, push off; **der kriegt die ~ nie!** he'll never make it!
kurven ['kʊrvən] v/i (sn) curve, ✓ bank.
'Kurven|bild n diagram, graph. **~festig-keit** f, **~lage** f mot. cornering stability. **~line,al** n (French) curve. **ℓreich** adj **1.** road: full of bends, winding. **2.** F fig. curvaceous. **~technik** f mot. cornering technique. **~vorgabe** f sports: stagger.
kurz [kʊrts] **I** adj **1.** short (a. fig.), brief: **kürzer werden (machen)** get (make) shorter, shorten; **5 m zu ~ sein** be five metres short; **den kürzeren ziehen** come off worst, lose out; F **et. ~ und klein schlagen** smash s.th. to bits; **~es Gedächtnis** short memory; **mit ein paar ~en Worten** in a few words, briefly; **in kürzester Zeit** in no time; **binnen ~em** shortly; **seit ~em** for some little time (now); **bis vor ~em** until quite recently; F **mach's ~!** be brief! **2.** short, curt (**gegen** j-n with s.o.). **II** adv **3.** short: **~ vor ...** just before ... ; **~ hinter dem Bahnhof** just after the station; **zu ~ werfen** throw (too) short; **er wird ~ Tom genannt** he is called Tom for short; **zu ~ kommen** get a bad deal, matter: be neglected. **4.** a) briefly, b) for a while, c) for a moment; **~ vor ..., ~ zuvor** shortly before (...); **~ nach ..., ~ darauf** shortly after (...); **über ~ oder lang** sooner or later; **j-n ~ abweisen** be short with s.o.; **sich ~ ausruhen** take a short rest; **~ entschlossen** without the slightest hesitation; **~ (gesagt), um es ~ zu machen** to cut a long story short; **~ und gut** in short; **fasse dich ~!** please be brief!; **~ und bündig** brief(ly), concise(ly); **~ angebunden** short, curt (**gegen** with).
'Kurzarbeit f short time, short-time working. **'kurzarbeiten** v/i (sep, -ge-, h) be on (or work) short time. **'Kurzarbeiter(in** f) m short-time worker.
'kurzärm(e)lig [-ɛrm(ə)lɪç] adj short--sleeved.

'**kurzatmig** [-a:tmɪç] *adj* short-winded.
'**kurzbeinig** [-baɪnɪç] *adj* short-legged.
'**Kurzbericht** *m* brief report, summary.
'**Kurzbiogra͵phie** *f* profile.
Kürze ['kʏrtsə] *f* (-; *no pl*) shortness (*a. fig.*), *a.* briefness, brevity, *fig.* conciseness: **in** ~ shortly, before long; **in aller** ~ very briefly. **Kürzel** ['kʏrtsəl] *n* (-s; -) shorthand symbol. '**kürzen** *v/t* (h) shorten (**um** by), *a.* abridge (*book etc*), cut (*wages etc*), ₣ reduce (*fraction*): **drastisch** ~ ₣ slash; **j-s Lohn um 50 Mark** ~ dock 50 marks off s.o.'s wages.
'**kurzerhand** *adv* without further ado: ~ **ablehnen** refuse flatly.
'**kürzertreten** *v/i* (*irr, sep*, -ge-, h, → **treten**) ₣ a) tighten one's belt, b) take things easy, go slow.
'**Kurzfassung** *f* abridged version.
'**Kurzfilm** *m* short (film).
'**Kurzform** *f* short(ened) form.
'**kurzfristig** [-frɪstɪç] **I** *adj* **1.** ♣ short--term. **2.** *fig.* a) short-range (*plans etc*), b) sudden, c) immediate. **II** *adv* **3.** a) at short notice, b) for a short period.
'**Kurzgeschichte** *f* short story.
'**kurzgeschnitten** *adj* cropped.
'**Kurzhaar...** *esp. zo.*, '**kurzhaarig** *adj* short-haired.
'**kurzhalten** *v/t* (*irr, sep*, -ge-, h, → **halten**) ₣ *j-n* ~ keep s.o. very short (**mit Geld** of money).
'**kurzlebig** [-le:bɪç] *adj* short-lived.
'**Kurzlehrgang** *m* short (*or* crash) course.
kürzlich ['kʏrtslɪç] *adv* recently, not long ago: (**erst**) ~ (just) the other day.
'**Kurzmeldung** *f* news flash.
'**Kurznachrichten** *pl* news bulletin.
'**kurzschließen** *v/t* (*irr, sep*, -ge-, h, → **schließen**) ⚡ short(-circuit).
'**Kurzschluß** *m* **1.** ⚡ short circuit: *e-n* ~ **verursachen in** (*dat*) short-circuit. **2.** → ~**handlung** *f* panic action: *e-e* ~ **begehen** a) do s.th. rash, b) panic.
'**Kurzschrift** *f* (**in** ~ in) shorthand.
'**kurzsichtig** *adj* shortsighted (*a. fig.*), nearsighted. '**Kurzsichtige** *m, f* (-n; -n) shortsighted (*or* nearsighted) person. '**Kurzsichtigkeit** *f* (-; *no pl*) shortsightedness (*a. fig.*), nearsightedness.
'**Kurzstrecke** *f* short distance.
'**Kurzstrecken...** short-distance, short-

-range. ~**läufer(in** *f*) *m* sprinter. ~**ra͵kete** *f* short-range missile.
'**kurztreten** → **kürzertreten.**
kurz'um *adv* in short.
Kürzung *f* (-; -en) shortening, *a.* abridg(e)ment (*of book etc*), cut (*gen* in *expenses etc*), ₣ reduction (*of fraction*).
'**Kurzurlaub** *m* short holiday.
'**Kurzwaren** *pl* haberdashery, *Am.* dry goods, notions.
'**Kurzwelle** *f* **1.** *radio*: short wave. **2.** ∦ radiothermy.
'**Kurzwellen...** short-wave (*transmitter, range, etc*). ~**thera͵pie** *f* radiothermy.
'**kurzwellig** *adj* short-wave.
'**Kurzwort** *n* (-[e]s; ~er) contraction.
'**Kurzzeitgedächtnis** *n* short-term memory. '**kurzzeitig** *adj* brief, short.
kuschelig ['kʊʃəlɪç] *adj* ₣ a) (soft and) cuddly, b) cosy.
kuscheln ['kʊʃəln] **sich** ~ (h) snuggle (**an** *acc* up to s.o., **in** *acc* down in **bed** *etc*).
'**Kuscheltier** *n* cuddly toy.
kuschen ['kʊʃən] *v/i* (h) **1.** *dog*: lie down. **2.** ₣ (**vor** *j-m*) ~ knuckle under (to s.o.).
Kusine [ku'zi:nə] *f* (-; -n) (female) cousin.
Kuß [kʊs] *m* (Kusses; Küsse) kiss: **flüchtiger** ~ peck; **sich mit e-m** ~ (**von** *j-m*) **verabschieden** kiss s.o. goodbye.
'**kußecht** *adj* kissproof.
küssen ['kʏsən] *v/t, v/i* (h) kiss: **sie küßten sich** (**zum Abschied**) they kissed (goodbye); *j-m* **die Hand** ~ kiss s.o.'s hand.
'**Kußhand** *f j-m* **e-e** ~ **zuwerfen** blow s.o. a kiss; *fig.* **mit** ~ gladly.
Küste ['kʏstə] *f* (-; -n) coast, shore: **an der** ~ **leben** live at the seaside.
'**Küsten͵bewohner(in** *f*) *m* coastal inhabitant. ~**fischerei** *f* inshore fishing. ~**gebiet** *n* coastal area. ~**gewässer** *pl* coastal waters. ~**linie** *f* coast line. ~**schiffahrt** *f* coastal shipping. ~**schutz** *m* shore protection. ~**straße** *f* coast(al) road. ~**streifen** *m*, ~**strich** *m* coastal strip. ~**wache** *f* coast guard (station).
Küster ['kʏstər] *m* (-s; -) *eccl.* sexton.
Kutsche ['kʊtʃə] *f* (-; -n) carriage, coach: *humor.* **alte** ~ (old) rattletrap.
'**Kutscher** *m* (-s; -) coachman, driver.
Kutte ['kʊtə] *f* (-; -n) cowl.

Kutter ['kʊtər] *m* (-s; -) ♣ cutter.
Kuwait [ku'vaɪt] *n* (-s) Kuwait. **Ku'waiter** *m* (-s; -), **Ku'waiterin** *f* (-; -nen), **ku'waitisch** *adj* Kuwaiti.
Kybernetik [kybɛr'ne:tɪk] *f* (-; *no pl*) cybernetics.

Kyber'netiker *m* (-s; -) cyberneticist.
kyber'netisch *adj* cybernetic.
kyrillisch [ky'rɪlɪʃ] *adj* Cyrillic.
KZ [ka:'tsɛt] *n* (-[s]; -[s]) concentration camp. **K'Z-Häftling** *m* concentration camp prisoner.

L

L, l [ɛl] *n* (-; -) L, l.
labberig ['labərɪç] *adj* F *a. fig.* **1.** a) sloppy, b) insipid, c) stale. **2.** limp.
Labial [la'bia:l] *m* (-s; -e) labial (sound).
labil [la'bi:l] *adj* unstable, labile.
Labilität [labili'tɛ:t] *f* (-; *no pl*) instability, lability.
Labor [la'bo:r] *n* (-s; -s, -e) F lab: *im ~ untersuchen* lab-examine.
Laborant [labo'rant] *m* (-en; -en), **Labo'rantin** *f* (-; -nen) laboratory assistant. **Laboratorium** [labora'to:riʊm] *n* (-s; -rien) laboratory.
La'borbefund *m* test result(s).
laborieren [labo'ri:rən] *v/i* (h) ♣ suffer (*an dat* from).
La'bortechniker(in *f*) *m* laboratory technician.
Labyrinth [laby'rɪnt] *n* (-[e]s; -e) *a. fig.* labyrinth, maze.
'Lachanfall *m* laughing fit.
Lache[1] ['laxə] *f* (-; -n) pool, puddle.
'Lache[2] *f* (-; -n) F laugh.
lächeln ['lɛçəln] *v/i* (h) (*über acc* at) smile, grin: *sie lächelte freundlich* she gave a friendly smile; *immer nur ~!* keep smiling! **'Lächeln** *n* (-s) smile.
lachen ['laxən] *v/i* (h) laugh (*über acc* at): *er lachte schallend* he roared with laughter; *sie lachte verlegen* she gave an embarrassed laugh; F *daß ich nicht lache!* don't make me laugh!; *sie hat nichts zu ~* her life is no bed of roses; *du hast gut ~!* you can laugh!; *da kann ich nur ~!* excuse me while I laugh!; *es wäre ja gelacht, wenn ...* it would be ridiculous if ...; *wer zuletzt lacht, lacht am besten* he who laughs last laughs loudest; → *Fäustchen.*

'Lachen *n* (-s) laughing, laugh(ter): *j-n zum ~ bringen* make s.o. laugh; *sich vor ~ biegen* nearly die laughing; *~ ist gesund* laughter is the best medicine; F *das ist nicht zum ~* that's no joke; → *zumute.*
'lachend *adj* laughing: *~e Erben* joyful heirs; *der ~e Dritte* the real winner.
'Lacher *m* (-s; -) **1.** laugher: *er hatte die ~ auf s-r Seite* he had the laugh on his side. **2.** F laugh.
'Lacherfolg *m* e-n ~ *ernten* (*or haben*) raise a laugh.
lächerlich ['lɛçərlɪç] *adj* **1.** ridiculous, absurd, funny: *~ machen* make fun of, ridicule; *sich ~ machen* make a fool of o.s.; *das ₂e daran* the ridiculous thing about it; *et. ins ₂e ziehen* turn s.th. into a joke; *sich ~ vorkommen* feel ridiculous. **2.** *fig.* trifling, petty: *für e-e ~e Summe* for a ridiculously low sum.
'Lächerlichkeit *f* (-; -en) **1.** *no pl* ridiculousness. **2.** *usu. pl* trifles.
'Lachfältchen *pl* laughter lines.
'Lachgas *n* ♣ laughing gas.
'lachhaft *adj* laughable, ridiculous.
Lachs [laks] *m* (-es; -e) salmon.
'Lachsalve *f* burst of laughter.
'Lachsfang *m* salmon fishing.
'lachs farben, ~rosa *adj* salmon-pink.
'Lachsschinken *m* smoked, rolled fillet of ham.
Lack [lak] *m* (-[e]s; -e) a) varnish, b) lacquer, c) enamel, d) *mot.* paint(work): F *fig. der ~ ist ab!* all the glamo(u)r is gone! **~farbe** *f* varnish (paint).
lackieren [la'ki:rən] *v/t* (h) **1.** varnish, lacquer, *mot.* paint: *sich die Fingernä-*

gel ~ paint one's nails. **2.** F *fig.* dupe: *er war der Lackierte* he was the dupe.

Lac'kierer *m* (-s; -) ⊙ varnisher, painter.

Lac'kierung *f* (-; -en) → **Lack.**

'**Lackleder** *n* patent leather.

'**Lackmuspa,pier** ['lakmʊs-] *n* 🜨 litmus paper.

'**Lackschaden** *m* mot. damage to the paintwork.

'**Lackschuhe** *pl* patent-leather shoes.

'**Lackstift** *m* mot. touch-up applicator.

'**Lade|baum** *m* ⚓ beam. **~fläche** *f* loading area. **~gerät** *n* ⚡ battery charger. **~hemmung** *f* ✕ (*a.* ~ *haben*) jam. **~klappe** *f* mot. tailboard. **~kon,trolleuchte** *f* mot. charge control lamp.

laden¹ ['la:dən] *v/t* (lud, geladen, h) **1.** load. **2.** ⚡, *phys.* charge. **3.** *fig. et. auf sich* ~ burden (*or* saddle) o.s. with.

'**laden²** *v/t* (lud, geladen, h) **1.** invite. **2.** 🏛 summon.

'**Laden** *m* (-s; ") **1.** shop, *Am.* store: → *dichtmachen* II. **2.** F *fig.* shop, outfit: → *schmeißen* **3. 3.** shutter.

'**Laden|dieb(in** *f*) *m* shoplifter. **~diebstahl** *m* shoplifting. **~hüter** *m* shelf warmer, drug in (*Am.* on) the market. **~inhaber** *m* shopkeeper, *Am.* storekeeper. **~kasse** *f* till. **~kette** *f* chain of shops). **~mädchen** *n* F shopgirl. **~preis** *m* retail price. **~schild** *n* shop sign. **~schluß** *m* closing time. **~straße** *f* shopping street. **~tisch** *m* (*fig. unter dem* ~ under the) counter.

'**Laderampe** *f* loading ramp.

'**Laderaum** *m* loading space, (ship's) hold, ✈ cargo bay.

lädieren [lɛ'di:rən] *v/t* (h) a) damage, b) injure, c) *a. fig.* batter, *fig.* dent.

'**Ladung¹** *f* (-; -en) **1.** ⚡ a) load, freight, ✈, ⚓ cargo, b) shipment: F *e-e* ~ *Sand* a load of sand. **2.** ⚡, ✕, *phys.* charge.

'**Ladung²** *f* (-; -en) 🏛 summons.

lag [la:k] *pret of* **liegen.**

Lage ['la:gə] *f* (-; -n) **1.** a) *a. fig.* position, situation, b) site, location: *in zentraler* ~ centrally situated; *die politische* ~ the political situation; *die rechtliche* ~ the legal position; *unangenehme* ~ predicament; *nach* ~ *der Dinge* as matters stand; *in der* ~ *sein, et. zu tun* be in a position to do s.th.; → *Herr, peilen* I, *versetzen* **5, 9. 2.** layer, *geol. a.* stratum, ✕ bed, ⊙ ply. **3.** ♪ register. **4.** F

e-e ~ *Bier ausgeben* buy a round of beer.

'**Lagenstaffel** *f swimming:* medley relay.

'**Lageplan** *m* site plan.

Lager ['la:gər] *n* (-s; -, ✝ *a.* ") **1.** bed, *hunt.* lair. **2.** *a. fig.* camp: *ein* ~ *aufschlagen* pitch camp; *ins gegnerische* ~ *überwechseln* change sides. **3.** ✝ a) stock, store(s), b) storehouse, warehouse: *et. auf* ~ *haben* have s.th. in store (*or* stock, F *fig. a.* up one's sleeve). **4.** ✕ bed, deposit. **5.** ⊙ a) support, b) bearing.

'**Lagerarbeiter** *m* warehouseman.

'**Lagerbier** *n* lager.

'**lagerfähig** *adj* storable.

'**Lagerfähigkeit** *f* (-; *no pl*) shelf life.

'**Lagerfeuer** *n* campfire.

'**Lagergebühr** *f* storage (fee).

'**Lagerhaltung** *f* (-; *no pl*) storekeeping.

'**Lagerhaus** *n* warehouse.

Lagerist [la:gə'rɪst] *m* (-en; -en), **Lage'ristin** *f* (-; -nen) storekeeper.

'**Lagerleben** *n* camp life.

'**Lagerleiter(in** *f*) *m* camp leader.

lagern ['la:gərn] (h) **I** *v/i* **1.** rest, lie down (*both a. geol.* ~), ✕ be stored. **3.** mature. **II** *v/t* **4.** ✝ store, keep. **5.** lay, rest: ✍ *das Bein hoch* ~ put the leg up; → *gelagert*, ⊙ rest.

'**Lager|raum** *m* storeroom. **~stätte** *f* **1.** bed, *hunt.* lair. **2.** ✕, *geol.* deposit.

'**Lagerung** *f* (-; *no pl*) **1.** storage, warehousing. **2.** seasoning. **3.** ⊙ bearing application.

'**Lagerverwalter(in** *f*) *m* storekeeper.

'**Lageskizze** *f* sketch map.

Lagune [la'gu:nə] *f* (-; -n) lagoon.

lahm [la:m] *adj* **1.** lame. **2.** F stiff, tired, limp. **3.** F *fig.* lame (*excuse etc*), tame, dull (*film etc*): → *Ente* 1. '**Lahmarsch** *m* V drip. '**lahmarschig** *adj* V slow, lame, listless. '**lahmen** *v/i* (h) limp.

lähmen ['lɛːmən] *v/t* (h) paralyze: *wie gelähmt vor ...* paralyzed with *fear etc.*

'**Lahmheit** *f* (-; *no pl*) lameness, F *fig. a.* dullness, slowness.

'**lahmlegen** *v/t* (*sep*, -ge-, h) paralyze, *a.* bring *traffic etc* to a standstill, knock out (*machine etc*).

'**Lähmung** *f* (-; -en) **1.** ✍ paralysis. **2.** *fig.* paralyzing.

Laib [laɪp] *m* (-[e]s; -e) loaf.

Laich [laɪç] *m* (-[e]s; -e) spawn.

laichen ['laɪçən] v/i (h) spawn.

Laie ['laɪə] m (-n; -n) layman: *da bin ich absoluter ~* I don't know the first thing about it. **'Laien...** 1. lay (*priest etc*). 2. amateur (*actor etc*).

'laienhaft *adj* amateurish.

Lakai [la'kaɪ] m (-en; -en) *a. fig. contp.* lackey.

Lake ['la:kə] f (-; -n) *gastr.* brine.

Laken ['la:kən] n (-s; -) sheet.

lakonisch [la'ko:nɪʃ] *adj* laconic.

Lakritze [la'krɪtsə] f (-; -n) liquorice.

lallen ['lalən] v/t, v/i (h) speak thickly.

Lama¹ ['la:ma] m (-[s]; -s) *eccl.* Lama.

Lama² ['la:ma] n (-s) *zo.* llama.

Lamelle [la'mɛlə] f (-; -n) 1. ♣, ⊙ lamella. 2. *mot.* a) rib, b) disc.

lamentieren [lamɛn'ti:rən] v/i (h) F (*über acc* about) complain, moan.

Lametta [la'mɛta] n (-s; *no pl*) tinsel.

Lamm [lam] n (-[e]s; ⁓er) lamb.

'Lammbraten m roast lamb.

Lämmchen ['lɛmçən] n (-s; -) lambkin.

lammen ['lamən] v/i (h) lamb.

'Lamm|fell n lambskin. **~fleisch** n lamb. **~keule** f *gastr.* leg of lamb.

Lampe ['lampə] f (-; -n) 1. lamp, light. 2. bulb.

'Lampenfieber n stagefright.

'Lampenschirm m lampshade.

Lampion [lam'piɔ̃] m (-s; -s) Chinese lantern.

lancieren [lã'si:rən] v/t (h) *fig.* launch.

Land [lant] n (-es; ⁓er) 1. land: *zu ~e* by land; *ans ~* ashore; F *e-n Job an ~ ziehen* land a job; *wieder ~ sehen* see daylight again. 2. a) country, b) soil, c) land: *auf dem ~e* in the country; *aufs ~* (in)to the country. 3. *pol.* a) country, b) territory, c) *FRG*: (Federal) Land, d) *Austria*: Province: *außer ~es gehen* go abroad; *aus aller Herren Länder* from all four corners of the earth.

'Landarbeiter(in f) m farm hand.

'Landarzt m country doctor.

'Landbesitz m landed property.

'Landbevölkerung f rural population.

'Lande|anflug m ✈ landing approach. **~bahn** f runway. **~brücke** f ⚓ landing stage. **~deck** n ⚓ flight deck. **~erlaubnis** f landing clearance, permission to land. **~fähre** f landing module.

land'einwärts adv (further) inland.

'Landeklappe f ✈ landing flap.

landen ['landən] v/i (sn), v/t (h) land (*a. fig. blow, success, etc*), ⚓ *a.* disembark, F *fig. a.* end up (*in dat* in): *weich ~* make a soft landing; *sports*: *auf dem 4. Platz ~* come in fourth; F *damit kannst du bei ihr nicht ~* with that you won't get anywhere with her.

'Landenge f *geogr.* isthmus.

'Lande|piste f landing strip. **~platz** m ✈ airstrip. 2. ⚓ quay, wharf.

Ländereien [lɛndə'raɪən] *pl* lands, estates.

'Länderkampf m *sports*: 1. international competition. 2. → **'Länderspiel** n international match.

'Landes... a) national, b) regional, *FRG*: (of the) Land, *in Austria*: Provincial. **~farben** *pl* national colo(u)rs. **~innere** n interior. **~meister(in** f) m *sports*: national champion. **~sprache** f national language. **~tracht** f national costume. **~verrat** m treason. **~verteidigung** f national defen/ce (*Am.* -se). **~währung** f national currency.

'landesweit *adj and adv* nationwide.

'Landeverbot n ✈ *~ erhalten* be refused permission to land.

'Land|fahrzeug n land vehicle. **~flucht** f rural exodus. **~friedensbruch** m breach of the public peace. **~gemeinde** f rural community. **~gericht** n ⚖ district (*or* superior) court.

'landgestützt *adj* ✗ land-based *missile*.

'Land|gewinnung f land reclamation. **~haus** n country house. **~karte** f map. **~kreis** m (administrative) district.

'landläufig *adj* common, general.

'Landleben n country life.

ländlich ['lɛntlɪç] *adj* a) rural, b) rustic.

'Landluft f country air.

'Landma|schine f agricultural machine.

'Landmesser m (-s; -) surveyor.

'Landpfarrer m country parson.

'Landrat m district administrator.

'Landratsamt n district administration (office).

'Landregen m persistent rain.

'Landschaft f (-; -en) 1. landscape (*a. paint.*), scenery, countryside: *die politische ~* the political scene. 2. region, country. **landschaftlich** *adj* 1. *geogr.* regional. 2. scenic (*beauty etc*): *~ schöne Strecke* scenic road.

'Landschafts|gärtner(in f) m landscape

gardener. **~maler(in** f) m landscape painter. **~pflege** f, **~schutz** m conservation. **~schutzgebiet** n (natural) preserve.

'**Landsitz** m country seat.

'**Landsmann** m (-[e]s; -leute) (fellow) countryman, compatriot.

'**Landsmannschaft** f (-; -en) FRG: expellee organization.

'**Landstraße** f country road.

'**Landstreicher(in** f) m tramp.

Landstreiche'rei f (-; no pl) vagrancy.

'**Landstreitkräfte** pl land forces.

'**Landtag** m FRG: Landtag, parliament of a Land.

'**Landung** f (-; -en) landing, ✈ a. touchdown, ⚓ a. disembarkation: ✈ **zur ~ ansetzen** come in to land.

'**Landungsbrücke** f landing stage, jetty.

'**Landurlaub** m ⚓ shore leave.

'**Landvermessung** f (land) surveying.

'**Landweg** m **1.** country road. **2.** overland route: **auf dem ~** by land.

'**Landwirt** m farmer.

'**Landwirtschaft** f (-; -en) **1.** no pl agriculture, farming. **2.** farm.

'**landwirtschaftlich** adj agricultural.

'**Landwirtschafts...** agricultural (show, school, etc.). **~mi,nister** m Minister of Agriculture. **~mini,sterium** n Ministry of Agriculture.

'**Landzunge** f geogr. promontory.

lang [laŋ] I adj **1.** long, a. lengthy, F tall: **über kurz oder ~** sooner or later; **seit ~em** for a long time; → **Bank**[1], **Gesicht** 1, **Hand**, **Sicht** 1 etc. II adv **2.** long: **4 Fuß ~** 4 feet long; **~ entbehrt** long missed; **länger werden** lengthen; **die Zeit wird mir ~** time hangs heavy on my hands; F **~ und breit** at great length; **e-e Woche ~** for a week; **die ganze Woche ~** all week, the whole week long; **mein ganzes Leben ~** all my life. **3.** along: fig. **wissen, wo's ~ geht** know the score; **j-m zeigen, wo's ~ geht** tell s.o. what's what. **4.** → **lange**.

'**langärm(e)lig** [-ɛrm(ə)lıç] adj long-sleeved. '**langatmig** [-a:tmıç] adj fig. lengthy, long-winded. '**langbeinig** [-baınıç] adj long-legged, F leggy.

lange ['laŋə] adv long, a long time: **das ist (schon) ~ her** that was a long time ago (→ a. **her** 1); **das ist noch ~ hin** that's still a long way off; **wie ~ noch?**

how much longer?; **wie ~ lernen Sie schon Englisch?** how long have you been learning English?; **noch ~ nicht** not for a long time (yet); **noch ~ nicht fertig (gut genug** etc) not nearly ready (good enough etc); **bis ~ nach MItternacht** until well past midnight; **ich bleibe nicht ~ (weg)** I won't be long.

Länge ['lɛŋə] f (-; -n) **1.** no pl length: **von 10 Metern ~** ten metres long (or in length); **der ~ nach** lengthwise; **in die ~ ziehen** stretch, fig. drag s.th. out; fig. **sich in die ~ ziehen** drag on. **2.** sports: **er gewann mit zwei ~n Vorsprung** he won by two lengths. **3.** fig., usu. pl dull passage, longueur. **4.** geogr. longitude. **5.** ling., metr. long.

'**längelang** adv (at) full length.

langen ['laŋən] (h) F I v/t **1.** j-m et. ~ hand s.o. s.th.; **j-m e-e ~** land s.o. one. II v/i **2.** ~ **nach** reach for; ~ **in** (acc) reach into. **3.** reach (**bis** to or as far as). **4.** a) be enough (**für** for), b) manage (**mit** with, on): **langt das?** will that do?; **das langt mir** that will do for me; fig. **mir langt's!, jetzt langt's mir!** I've had enough!, I'm sick of it!; → a. **reichen** 3.

'**Längen,grad** m geogr. degree of longitude. **~kreis** m geogr. meridian. **~maß** n linear (or long) measure.

'**längerfristig** [-frıstıç] adj and adv covering (or for) a prolonged period.

'**langersehnt** adj long-awaited.

'**Langeweile** f (-; no pl) boredom: ~ **haben** be (or feel) bored; F **ich sterbe vor ~** I'm bored to death.

'**langfristig** [-frıstıç] I adj long-term. II adv on a long-term basis: ~ (**gesehen**) in the long term.

'**Langhaar...**, '**langhaarig** adj long-haired.

'**langjährig** [-jɛːrıç] adj of many years, long-standing (friendship etc), long: ~**e Erfahrung** many years of experience.

'**Langlauf** m (-[e]s; no pl) cross-country skiing.

'**Langläufer(in** f) m cross-country skier.

'**langlebig** [-le:bıç] adj long-lived, durable, nucl. long-life. '**Langlebigkeit** f (-; no pl) longevity, ✝ durability.

'**länglich** ['lɛŋlıç] adj long(ish), oblong.

'**langmütig** [-my:tıç] adj forbearing.

längs [lɛŋs] I prep along: ~ **der Küste** alongshore. II adv lengthwise.

'**Längsachse** f longitudinal axis.
'**langsam** I adj a. fig. slow: ~er werden (fahren etc) slow down; F fig. ~ treten slow down, a. take it easy. II adv slowly: (immer schön) ~! not so fast!; er wird ~ alt he's getting old; F es wurde ~ Zeit! it was about time!; ~ reicht's mir! I'm getting fed up with this!
'**Langsamkeit** f (-; no pl) slowness.
'**Langschläfer(in)** f) m late riser.
'**Langspielplatte** f long-playing record.
'**Längsschnitt** m longitudinal section.
'**längsseits** adv alongside.
längst [lɛŋst] adv long ago, long since: am ~en longest; ~ nicht so gut not nearly as good; das ist ~ vorbei (vergessen) that's long past (forgotten); ich weiß es ~ I've known it for a long time; er sollte ~ dasein he should have been here long ago; → fällig.
'**längstens** ['lɛŋstəns] adv 1. at the longest (or most). 2. at the latest.
'**langstielig** [-ʃtiːlɪç] adj long-stemmed.
'**Langstrecke** f long range, sports: (long) distance.
'**Langstrecken...** long-range (flight, missile, etc), sports: long-distance. ~lauf m (long-)distance run (or race). ~läufer(in f) m (long-)distance runner.
langweilen ['laŋvailən] v/t (h) bore: sich ~ be (or get) bored; sich zu Tode ~ F be bored stiff. '**Langweiler** m (-s; -) �muⱼ bore. '**langweilig** adj boring, dull: ~ sein a. be a bore.
'**Langwelle** f radio: long wave.
'**Langwellen|bereich** m long-wave band. ~sender m long-wave radio station (or transmitter).
langwierig ['laŋviːrɪç] adj lengthy, protracted (a. ✍).
'**Langwierigkeit** f (-; no pl) lengthiness.
'**Langzeit...** long-term (memory, effect).
Lanze ['lantsə] f (-; -n) lance.
lapidar [lapiˈdaːr] adj terse, succinct.
Lappalie [laˈpaːliə] f (-; -n) (mere) trifle.
Lappe ['lapə] m (-n; -n) Lapp.
Lappen ['lapən] m (-s; -) 1. (piece of) cloth, rag: F j-m durch die ~ gehen a) slip through s.o.'s fingers, b) person: give s.o. the slip. 2. anat., ⚘ lobe. 3. F (bank)note, Am. bill. 4. F (dress) rag.
läppern ['lɛpərn] v/impers (h) F es läppert sich it all adds up.
lappig ['lapɪç] adj F limp, flabby.

Lappin ['lapɪn] f (-; -nen) Lapp.
läppisch ['lɛpɪʃ] adj F silly, childish.
Lapsus ['lapsʊs] m (-; -) slip, lapse.
Lärche ['lɛrçə] f (-; -n) ⚘ larch.
Lärm [lɛrm] m (-[e]s; no pl) 1. noise, din, racket, roar (of engine etc): ~ machen make much noise, be noisy; F ~ schlagen raise a hue and cry (gegen against). 2. fig. fuss (um about).
'**Lärmbekämpfung** f noise abatement.
'**Lärmbelästigung** f noise pollution.
'**lärmempfindlich** adj sensitive to noise.
lärmen ['lɛrmən] v/i (h) make much noise, be noisy. '**lärmend** adj noisy.
'**Lärmpegel** m noise (or decibel) level.
'**Lärmschutzwand** f noise barrier.
Larve ['larfə] f (-; -n) zo. larva.
las [laːs] pret of **lesen**[1] and **lesen**[2].
lasch [laʃ] adj F 1. limp (handshake). 2. fig. lax, slack (discipline etc). 3. insipid.
Lasche ['laʃə] f (-; -n) 1. flap, on shoe: tongue, ⊙ fishplate, flat link.
Laser ['leːzər] m (-s; -) phys. laser.
'**Laserchirur|gie** f laser surgery.
'**Laserstrahl** m laser beam.
'**Lasertechnik** f laser technology.
lassen ['lasən] (ließ, gelassen, h) I v/aux 1. let: laß mich sehen let me see; das Licht brennen ~ leave the light(s) on; j-n warten ~ keep s.o. waiting; er läßt sich nicht zwingen he won't be forced. 2. j-n et. tun ~ have (or make) s.o. do s.th.; den Arzt kommen ~ send for the doctor. 3. machen ~ have s.th. made (or done); sich die Haare schneiden ~ have one's hair cut; ich ließ es mir zuschicken I had it sent to me. 4. ich habe mir sagen ~ I have been told; der Wein läßt sich trinken the wine is drinkable; dies Wort läßt sich nicht übersetzen this word is untranslatable; das läßt sich nicht mehr ändern it's too late now to do anything about it; das läßt sich nicht beweisen it can't be proved; die Tür ließ sich leicht öffnen the door opened easily; → machen 13, sagen etc. II v/t 5. leave: laß alles, wie es ist! leave everything as it is!; wo soll ich mein Gepäck ~? where shall I leave (or put) my luggage? 6. j-m et. ~ leave s.o. s.th., let s.o. have s.th.; laß mir das Buch noch e-e Weile! let me keep the book a while longer!; F fig. das muß man ihm ~! you've got to

hand it to him! **7.** stop: *laß das!* don't!, stop that!; *~ wir das!* enough of that!; *du solltest das Rauchen ~!* you ought to stop smoking! **III** *v/i* **8.** *von j-m (e-r Sache)* ~ part from s.o. (with s.th.).

lässig ['lɛsɪç] **I** *adj* a) casual, nonchalant, F cool, b) careless. **II** *adv* F easily: *er gewann* ~ he won hands down.

'Lässigkeit *f* (-; *no pl*) nonchalance.

Lasso ['laso] *n, m* (-s; -s) lasso.

Last [last] *f* (-; -en) **1.** *a. fig.* a) load, burden, b) weight: ⚖ *der Beweise* weight of the evidence; *j-m zur ~ fallen* be a burden to s.o.; *j-m et. zur ~ legen* charge s.o. with s.th. **2.** ✝ burden, charge: *öffentliche ~en* public charges; *soziale ~en* social burdens; *zu ~en von ... * to the debit of ... **3.** ⚓ load.

'Lastauto *n* lorry, *Am.* truck.

lasten ['lastən] *v/i* (h) *~ auf* (*dat*) *a. fig.* weigh (heavily) on, rest on.

'Lasten|aufzug *m* goods lift, *Am.* freight elevator. **~ausgleich** *m* equalization of burdens.

'lastend *adj fig.* oppressive.

Laster[1] ['lastər] *m* (-s; -) F *mot.* lorry, *Am.* truck.

'Laster[2] *n* (-s; -) vice. **'lasterhaft** *adj* depraved, corrupt, wicked, dissolute.

'Lasterhöhle *f* F *contp.* den of iniquity.

'Lasterleben *n* dissolute life.

lästerlich ['lɛstərlɪç] *adj* a) abusive, b) blasphemous.

lästern ['lɛstərn] *v/i* (h) *~ über* (*acc*) run s.o., s.th. down; *Gott ~* blaspheme.

lästig ['lɛstɪç] *adj* troublesome, annoying: *j-m ~ fallen (or sein)* be a nuisance to s.o., get on s.o.'s nerves.

'Lastkahn *m* barge.

'Lastkraftwagen *m* lorry, *Am.* truck.

'Lastschrift *f* ✝ **1.** debit entry. **2.** → **'Lastschriftanzeige** *f* debit note.

'Lasttier *n* pack animal.

'Lastwagen *m* lorry, *Am.* truck. **~fahrer** *m* lorry (*Am.* truck) driver.

'Lastzug *m mot.* truck trailer.

Lasur [la'zu:r] *f* (-; -en) glaze.

Latein [la'taɪn] *n* (-s; *no pl*) Latin: *fig. ich bin mit m-m ~ am Ende!* I give up!

La'teinameri,kaner(in *f*) *m*, **la'teinameri,kanisch** *adj* Latin-American.

la'teinisch *adj* Latin: *auf ♀* in Latin.

latent [la'tɛnt] *adj* latent.

Latenzzeit [la'tɛnts-] *f biol.*, ⚡ latency

period, *nucl. etc* latency time.

Laterne [la'tɛrnə] *f* (-; -n) lantern, lamp.

La'ternenpfahl *m* lamppost.

Latinum [la'ti:nʊm] *n* (-s; *no pl*) *ped. hist.* *großes* (*kleines*) ~ Latin proficiency (intermediate Latin) certificate.

Latrine [la'tri:nə] *f* (-; -n) latrine.

Latsche ['latʃə] *f* (-; -n) ♣ dwarf pine.

latschen ['la:tʃən] F **I** *v/i* (sn) slouch (along), trudge: *~ auf* (*acc*) step on. **II** *v/t* (h) *j-m e-e ~* paste s.o. one.

'Latschen *m* (-s; -) F a) slipper, b) (old) shoe: *aus den ~ kippen* keel over.

Latte ['latə] *f* (-; -n) **1.** lath, slat, picket. **2.** *sports:* (cross-)bar: *die ~ überqueren* clear the bar. **3.** F *fig.* ~ *e ganze ~ von* a whole string of; *j-n auf der ~ haben* have it in for s.o.

'Lattenkiste *f* crate.

'Lattenzaun *m* paling, picket fence.

Latz [lats] *m* (-es; ⁀e) bib: F *fig. j-m e-e vor den ~ knallen* zap s.o.

Lätzchen ['lɛtsçən] *n* (-s; -) bib.

'Latzhose *f* (pair of) dungarees.

lau [lau] *adj* lukewarm (*a. fig.*), tepid, mild (*air, weather*).

Laub [laup] *n* (-[e]s; *no pl*) foliage, leaves.

'Laubbaum *m* deciduous tree.

Laube ['laubə] *f* (-; -n) a) arbo(u)r, b) summerhouse.

'Laubengang *m* arcade.

'Laubenkolo,nie *f* allotment gardens.

'Laubfrosch *m* tree frog.

'Laubsäge *f* fretsaw. **~arbeit** *f* fretwork.

'Laubwald *m* deciduous forest.

'Laubwerk *n* (-[e]s; *no pl*) foliage.

Lauch [laux] *m* (-[e]s; -e) ♣ leek.

Lauer ['lauər] *f auf der ~ liegen* be lying in wait.

lauern ['lauərn] *v/i* (h) lurk: *~ auf* (*acc*) a) be lying in wait for, b) be watching out for an opportunity etc.

'lauernd *adj* **1.** lurking. **2.** watchful.

Lauf [lauf] *m* (-[e]s; ⁀e) **1.** *no pl* run(ning): *sie ließ ihren Tränen freien ~* she let her tears flow freely; *s-n Gefühlen freien ~ lassen* give vent to one's feelings. **2.** *sports:* run, race: *100-Meter-~* 100 metre run (*or* dash). **3.** *no pl* course: *im ~ der Zeit* (*des Gesprächs*) in the course of time (of the conversation); *im ~e der letzten Jahre* during the last few years; *den Dingen ihren ~ lassen* let things ride. **4.** *no pl* ⚙ movement, run, action, working, operation. **5.** barrel (*of rifle etc*). **6.** *hunt.* leg. **7.** ♪ run, passage. '**Laufbahn** *f* (*e-e ~ einschlagen* take up a) career. '**Laufdiszi‚plin** *f sports:* running event.

laufen ['laʊfən] (lief, gelaufen) **I** *v/i* (sn) **1.** a) run (*a. fig.*), b) walk, go, c) run, flow: *er ließ Wasser in die Wanne ~* he ran water into the tub; F *m-e Nase läuft* my nose is running; *mir lief ein Schauer über den Rücken* a shudder ran down my spine. **2.** ⚙ work, *engine etc:* run: *Kamera läuft!* camera on! **3.** *film, play, etc:* run, show, be on: *läuft der Hauptfilm schon?* has the main film started yet? **4.** *fig.* go: F *wie ist es denn gelaufen?* how did it go?; *die Sache ist gelaufen* a) it's all over, b) it's in the bag; *da läuft nichts!* nothing doing!; *so läuft das!* that's the name of the game!; *was da in Berlin so läuft* what's going on in Berlin. **5.** a) *trial etc:* be in progress, b) *application etc:* be under consideration. **6.** ⚕, ⚗ run, be valid: *der Mietvertrag läuft 5 Jahre* the lease runs for five years; *auf j-s Namen ~* be (made out) in s.o.'s name; *unter dem Namen X ~* go by the name of X. **7.** leak. **II** *v/t* **8.** (sn) walk. **9.** (h or sn) *sports:* run: do: *e-n neuen Rekord ~* run a new record; *e-e Zeit von 20 Sekunden ~* clock a time of 20 seconds. **10.** (h) *sich Blasen ~* get blisters (from walking). **III** *v/impers* (h) *hier läuft es sich schlecht* walking *etc* is bad here. **IV** *sich warm ~* h) warm up.

'**laufend I** *adj* **1.** current: *im ~en Monat* this month; *~e Berichterstattung* running commentary; *~e Kosten* overheads; ⚕ *~er Meter* running metre; *~e Nummern* serial numbers; *~e Kontrolle* regular inspection. **2.** *auf dem ~en sein* be up to date, *a.* be fully informed; *j-n (sich) auf dem ~en halten* keep s.o. (o.s.) informed. **3.** *mit ~em Motor* with the engine running. **II** *adv* **4.** constantly, continually.

'**laufenlassen** *v/t* (*irr, sep, no* -ge-, h, → *lassen*) F *j-n ~* let s.o. go (*or* off); *die Dinge ~* let things ride.

Läufer ['lɔyfər] *m* (-s; -) **1.** a) runner, b) skater, c) skier. **2.** *chess:* bishop. **3.** runner, rug. **4.** ⚙ slide, cursor, ⚡ rotor.

Lauferei [laʊfə'raɪ] *f* (-; -en) F running around, *fig. a.* trouble.

'**Läuferin** *f* (-; -nen) → *Läufer* 1.

'**Lauf|feuer** *n* (*sich verbreiten wie ein ~* spread like) wildfire. *~gitter* *n* playpen.

läufig ['lɔyfɪç] *adj zo.* in heat, on heat.

'**Lauf|junge** *m* errand boy. *~kran* *m* travel(l)ing crane. *~kundschaft* *f* casual customers. *~masche* *f* ladder, *Am.* run. *~paß* *m* F *j-m den ~ geben* send s.o. packing, ditch s.o. *~planke* *f* ⚓ gangway. *~schritt* *m* *im ~* at the double. *~schuhe* *pl* running (*or* track) shoes. *~sport* *m* running. *~steg* *m* catwalk, ⚓ gangway. *~zeit* *f* **1.** life, term (*of contract etc*). **2.** run (*of film etc*). **3.** ⚙, *a.* of tape *etc*: running time. *~zettel* *m* inter-office slip, tracer.

Lauge ['laʊgə] *f* (-; -n) **1.** lye. **2.** suds.

'**Lauheit** *f* (-; *no pl*) *a. fig.* lukewarmness.

Laune ['laʊnə] *f* (-; -n) **1.** mood, temper: *schlechte ~ haben, schlechter ~ sein* be in a bad mood (*or* temper); *bester ~ sein* be in a great mood; *j-m bei (guter) ~ halten a. iro.* keep s.o. happy; *~n haben* be moody. **2.** whim, caprice.

'**launenhaft** *adj* moody, *fig.* capricious, fickle, *weather:* changeable.

launig ['laʊnɪç] *adj* humorous.

launisch ['laʊnɪʃ] *adj* **1.** → **launenhaft.** **2.** ill-tempered, peevish.

Laus [laʊs] *f* (-; *~e*) louse (*pl* lice).

lauschen ['laʊʃən] *v/i* (h) listen (*dat, auf acc* to): (*heimlich*) ~ eavesdrop (*dat* on). '**Lauscher** *m* (-s; -), '**Lauscherin** *f* (-; -nen) listener, eavesdropper.

lauschig *adj* snug, cosy.

lausen ['laʊzən] *v/t* (h) louse: F *mich laust der Affe!* did you ever!

lausig ['laʊzɪç] *adj* **1.** F lousy, bad. **2.** dreadful, awful (*cold etc*): ~ *wehtun* hurt awfully; ~ *kalt* beastly cold.

laut¹ [laʊt] **I** *adj* loud (*a. fig.*), noisy: ~ *werden* a) become audible, b) *fig.* become known, *wishes etc:* be expressed, c) *person:* begin to shout; *es wurde das Gerücht ~, daß ...* it was rumo(u)red that ... **II** *adv* loud: ~ *sagen* say s.th. out loud; ~ (*vor*)*lesen* read aloud; ~ *und deutlich* loud and clear.

laut² *prep* according to, ~ as per.

Laut *m* (-[e]s; -e) sound (*a. ling.*), noise: *hunt.* ~ *geben* give tongue; *sie gab k-n ~ von sich* she didn't utter a sound.

Laute ['laʊtə] f (-; -n) ♪ lute.

lauten ['laʊtən] v/i (h) **1.** run, read, go: *der Text lautet wie folgt* the text reads as follows. **2.** ~ *auf* (acc) 🖂 *sentence etc*: be; *auf* (*den Namen*) *X* ~ *passport etc*: be (made out) in the name of X.

läuten ['lɔytən] v/i, v/t (h) ring, toll: *es läutet* there is a ring at the door, *ped.* the bell is ringing; F *ich habe davon* ~ *hören* I've heard s.th. to that effect.

lauter ['laʊtər] **I** adj **1.** pure (*gold etc*). **2.** fig. sincere, hono(u)rable. **II** adv **3.** nothing but: *aus* ~ *Bosheit* from sheer spite; *vor* ~ *Lärm* for all the noise; *das sind* ~ *Lügen* it's all lies.

'Lauterkeit f (-; *no pl*) fig. integrity.

läutern ['lɔytərn] (h) **I** v/t purify, fig. a. chasten. **II** *sich* ~ fig. reform.

'Läuterung f (-; -en) fig. reformation.

'lauthals adv at the top of one's voice: ~ *lachen* roar with laughter.

'Lautheit f (-; *no pl*) loudness, noisiness.

'Lautlehre f phonetics.

'lautlos adj soundless, noiseless, silent: ~*e Stille* hushed silence.

'Lautschrift f phonetic transcription.

'Lautsprecher m ⚡ (loud)speaker. ~*anlage* f public-address system. ~*box* f loudspeaker (cabinet). ~*wagen* m loudspeaker van, *Am.* sound truck.

'lautstark adj a. fig. loud: ~*e Minderheit* vocal minority.

'Lautstärke f loudness, ⚡ a. (sound) volume: *mit voller* ~ (at) full blast.

'Lautstärkeregler m volume control.

'Lautverschiebung f *ling.* sound shift.

'Lautzeichen n phonetic symbol.

'lauwarm adj lukewarm (a. fig.), tepid.

Lava ['la:va] f (-; Laven) lava.

Lavendel [la'vɛndəl] m (-s; -) 🌿 lavender.

lavieren [la'vi:rən] v/i (h) fig. manoeuvre, *Am.* maneuver.

Lawine [la'vi:nə] f (-; -n) avalanche.

la'winenartig adj and adv avalanche-like: ~ *anwachsen* snowball.

La'winen|gefahr f danger of avalanches. 2*sicher* adj avalanche-proof. ~(*such*)*hund* m avalanche search dog. ~*warnung* f avalanche warning.

lax [laks] adj lax, loose.

Layout [lɛɪ'aʊt] n (-s; -s) layout.

Lay'outer m (-s; -) layout man.

Lazarett [latsa'rɛt] n (-[e]s; -e) (military) hospital. ~*schiff* n hospital ship.

leasen ['li:zən] v/t (h) lease.

Leasing ['li:zɪŋ] n (-s; -s) leasing.

'Lebemann m (-[e]s; ⸚er) playboy.

leben ['le:bən] (h) **I** v/t **1.** live, a. be alive, exist: *hier lebt es sich gut* it's not a bad life here; *lebt er noch?* is he still alive?; *bescheiden* ~ lead a modest life; ~ *von* live on; *er lebt vom Stundengeben* he makes a living by teaching; ~ *für* live for, devote one's life to; ~ *und* ~ *lassen* live and let live; *es lebe ...!* long live ...! **2.** live, reside: *sie lebt bei ihrer Mutter* she lives with her mother. **II** v/t **3.** live.

'Leben[1] n (-s) living (*etc*): *zum* ~ *zuwenig, zum Sterben zuviel* barely enough to keep body and soul together.

'Leben[2] n (-s; -) **1.** life: *das* ~ *in Kanada* life in Canada; *ein Kampf auf* ~ *und Tod* a life-and-death struggle; *aus dem* ~ *gegriffen* taken from life; *am* ~ *sein* live, be alive; *am* ~ *bleiben* (*erhalten*) stay (keep) alive; *sich das* ~ *nehmen* kill o.s., commit suicide; *ums* ~ *kommen* lose one's life, be killed; *mit dem* ~ *davonkommen* escape (alive); *ein neues* ~ *beginnen* turn over a new leaf; *ins* ~ *rufen* call into being, launch; *im öffentlichen* ~ *stehen* be a public figure; *mein* ~ *lang* all my life; *ich tanze für mein* ~ *gern* I just love to dance; *ich würde für mein* ~ *gern ...* I would give anything to *inf*; F *nie im* ~*!*, *im* ~ *nicht!* not on your life!; *so ist das* ~ (*eben*)*!* such is life!; → *Hölle, schwermachen*. **2.** a) life, activity, b) liveliness, vitality: ~ *bringen in* (acc) liven up; → *Bude* 2.

'lebend adj living, *ling.* a. modern (*language*), alive, *biol.* live: ~*es Inventar* livestock; *die Lebenden* the living; *die noch Lebenden* those still alive.

'lebendgebärend adj *biol.* viviparous.

'Lebendgewicht n live weight.

lebendig [le'bɛndɪç] adj **1.** living, *pred* alive: *bei* ~*em Leibe* alive; *wieder* ~ *werden* memories *etc*: come back. **2.** lively, alert. **3.** vivid. **Le'bendigkeit** f (-; *no pl*) **1.** liveliness. **2.** vividness.

'Lebens|abend m old age. ~*abschnitt* m period of (one's) life. ~*ader* f fig. lifeline. ~*alter* n age. ~*angst* f existential dread. ~*anschauung* f view of life, approach to life. ~*arbeitszeit* f working life. ~*art* f **1.** way of life. **2.** manners. ~*auffassung* f philosophy (of life).

~aufgabe *f* life task: **sich et. zur ~ machen** devote one's life to s.th. **~bedingungen** *pl* (living) conditions. **'lebensbedrohlich** *adj* life-threatening. **'Lebens|bedürfnisse** *pl* necessaries of life. **~bejahung** *f* positive approach to life. **~bereich** *m* sphere of life. **~beschreibung** *f* life, biography. **~dauer** *f* duration of life, lifespan. **© life. ~ende** *n bis an mein etc ~* to the end of my *etc* days. **~erfahrung** *f* experience of life. **~erhaltungssy,stem** *n ⚓*. **©** life-support system. **~erinnerungen** *pl* memoirs. **~erwartung** *f* life expectancy. **'lebensfähig** *adj a. fig.* viable. **'Lebens|form** *f* **1.** way of life. **2.** *biol.* form of life. **~frage** *f* vital question. **~freude** *f* joy of life, zest (for life). **'Lebensgefahr** *f* danger to life: **~!** danger!; **in ~ schweben** be in danger of one's life, **außer ~ sein** be out of danger, *⚓* be off the critical list; **unter ~** at the risk of one's life. **'lebensgefährlich** *adj* extremely dangerous, perilous, very serious (*disease, injury*). **'Lebens|gefährte** *m*, **~gefährtin** *f* (life) companion, partner in life. **~gemeinschaft** *f* life partnership. **~geschichte** *f* life story. **'lebensgroß** *adj* life-size(d). **'Lebensgröße** *f in ~* a) life-size(d), in its actual size, b) F *fig.* large as life. **'Lebenshaltung** *f* (-; *no pl*) standard of living. **'Lebenshaltungskosten(index** *m*) *pl* cost of living (index). **'Lebens|inter,essen** *pl* vital interests. **~jahr** *n* year of one's life: **im 20. ~** at the age of 20. **~kampf** *m* struggle for survival. **~kraft** *f* vigo(u)r, vitality. **'lebenslang** I *adj* lifelong. II *adv* all one's life. **'lebenslänglich** *adj* ⚖ (for) life: **~e Freiheitsstrafe** life imprisonment; F **er hat ~ bekommen** he got a life term. **'Lebenslauf** *m* **1.** (course of) life, career. **2.** personal record, curriculum vitae. **'lebenslustig** *adj* fond of life, merry. **'Lebensmittel** *pl* food(stuffs), groceries, provisions. **~ab,teilung** *f* food department. **~geschäft** *n* grocery, food shop (*Am.* store). **~händler(in** *f*) *m* grocer. **~indu,strie** *f* food industry. **~vergiftung** *f* food poisoning.

'lebensmüde *adj* weary of life. **'lebensnotwendig** *adj* vital, essential. **'Lebens|quali,tät** *f* quality of life. **~raum** *m* living space. **~retter(in** *f*) *m* life-saver, rescuer. **~rhythmus** *m* rhythm (of life). **~standard** *m* standard of living. **~stellung** *f* permanent position. **~stil** *m* life style. **'lebensunfähig** *adj* nonviable. **'Lebens|unterhalt** *m* (*s-n ~ verdienen* earn one's) living (*or* livelihood) (*mit* out of). **~versicherung** *f* life insurance. **~wandel** *m* life, conduct. **~weise** *f* **1.** way of life: *gesunde ~* a) healthy living, b) regimen. **2.** habits. **~weisheit** *f* **1.** worldly wisdom. **2.** maxim. **~werk** *n* lifework. **'lebenswert** *adj* worth living. **'lebenswichtig** *adj* vital, essential. **'Lebens|wille** *m* will to live. **~zeichen** *n* sign of life. **~zeit** *f* lifetime: *auf ~* for life. **~ziel** *n*, **~zweck** *m* aim in life.

Leber ['le:bar] *f* (-; -n) liver: *frisch* (*or frei*) *von der ~ weg* frankly. **'Leber|fleck** *m* mole. **~knödel** *m* gastr. liver dumpling. **~krankheit** *f* liver disease. **~krebs** *m ⚓* cancer of the liver. **~pa,stete** *f* gastr. liver pâté. **~tran** *m* cod-liver oil. **~wurst** *f* liver sausage, *Am.* liverwurst. **~zir,rhose** *f ⚓* cirrhosis of the liver.

'Lebewesen *n* (-s; -) living being, creature, *biol.* organism.

lebhaft ['le:phaft] *adj* lively, *fig. a.* vivid (*imagination etc*), *a.* keen (*interest*), busy (*traffic etc*), *a.* gay (*colours*), animated (*discussion etc*), *✝* brisk: *et. ~ bedauern* regret s.th. very much; *das kann ich mir ~ vorstellen* I can just imagine. **'Lebhaftigkeit** *f* (-; *no pl*) liveliness, *fig. a.* vividness.

'Lebkuchen *m* gingerbread (cake). **'leblos** *adj* lifeless (*a. fig.*), inanimate. **'Lebzeiten** *pl zu s-n ~* a) in his (life)time, b) when he was still alive.

leck [lek] *adj* leaky: **~ sein → lecken¹**; **⚓ ~ werden** spring a leak. **Leck** *n* (-[e]s; -s) leak. **lecken¹** ['lekən] *v/i* (h) leak, **⚓** have sprung a leak.

'lecken² *v/t* (h) a) lick, b) lap (up); **→ Arsch 1.**

lecker ['lekər] *adj* delicious, tasty, F yummy. **'Leckerbissen** *m a. fig.* titbit,

Am. tidbit. **Leckerei** [lɛkə'raɪ] *f* (-; -en) dainty, sweet.

Leder ['le:dər] *n* (-s; -) leather: F *vom ~ ziehen* let go (*gegen* against).

'**Leder...** leather (*coat, glove, etc*). **~fett** *n* ⚙ dubbing. **~gebunden** *adj* leather-bound. **~hose** *f* leather trousers.

ledern¹ ['le:dərn] *adj* **1.** leather. **2.** *fig.* leathery. **3.** *fig.* dull.

'**ledern²** *v/t* (h) polish with a chamois.

'**Lederwaren** *pl* leather goods.

ledig ['le:dɪç] *adj* single, unmarried: *~e Mutter* unmarried mother.

lediglich ['le:dɪklɪç] *adv* only, merely.

Lee [le:] *f* (-; *no pl*) ⚓ lee: *nach ~* leeward.

leer [le:r] *adj* empty (*a. fig.*), a. vacant (*house, post, etc*), blank (*cassette, page*): *die Batterie ist ~* the battery has run out (*mot.* is dead); *~es Gerede* idle talk, F hot air; *~ laufen (lassen)* ⚙ idle; *~ stehen house etc*: be empty, be unoccupied; *ins Leere starren* stare into space; *ins Leere gehen blow etc*: miss; → *ausgehen* 8, *Hand, Magen.*

Leere ['le:rə] *f* (-; *no pl*) *fig.* emptiness, void. '**leeren** *v/t* (h) empty (*a. sich ~*), *a.* drain (*glass*).

'**Leer|gewicht** *n* dead weight. **~gut** *n* 🍶 empties. **~kas,sette** *f* blank cassette.

'**Leerlauf** *m* (-[e]s; *no pl*) **1.** *a.* ⚙ idle running, b) *mot.* neutral (gear): *im ~ fahren* coast. **2.** *fig.* a) wastage (of energy), b) running on the spot.

'**leerlaufen** *v/i* (*irr, sep, -ge-, sn,* → *laufen*) **1.** (*a. ~ lassen*) drain, run dry. **2.** *sports: j-n ~ lassen* sell s.o. a dummy.

'**Leerpackung** *f* 🍶 dummy.

'**leerstehend** *adj* unoccupied, vacant.

'**Leertaste** *f typewriter:* space bar.

'**Leerung** *f* (-; -en) emptying (*etc*): 📮 *nächste ~* next collection.

Lefzen ['lɛftsən] *pl* flews.

legal [le'ga:l] *adj* legal, lawful: *auf ~em Wege* by legal means, lawfully.

legalisieren [legali'zi:rən] *v/t* (h) legalize.

Legali'sierung *f* (-; -en) legalization.

Legalität [legali'tɛ:t] *f* (-; *no pl*) legality, lawfulness: *außerhalb der ~* outside the law.

Legasthenie [legaste'ni:] *f* (-; *no pl*) dyslexia. **Legastheniker** [legas'te:nikər] *m* (-s; -) dyslexic.

Legat¹ [le'ga:t] *m* (-en; -en) legate.

Le'gat² *n* (-[e]s; -e) ⚖ legacy.

legen ['le:gən] (h) **I** *v/t* **1.** a) put, place, b) lay *s.o., s.th.* down: *ein Kind ins Bett ~* put a child to bed; *er legte die Entscheidung in m-e Hände* he placed the decision in my hands. **2.** lay (*carpet, cable, mines, etc*), plant (*bomb*). **3.** fold. **4.** set (*hair*): *bitte, waschen und ~* shampoo and set, please. **5.** *zo.* lay (*eggs*). **6. Karten ~** tell fortunes by the cards. **7.** *sports: j-n ~* bring s.o. down. **II** *sich ~* **8.** lie down: *sich ins Bett ~* go to bed. **9.** *wind, rage, noise, etc:* die down, blow over, *pain, enthusiasm, etc:* wear off, *tension:* ease off. **10.** *fig.* *~ auf* (acc) take up, go in for (*activity etc*). **11. sich j-m aufs Gemüt ~** (begin to) depress s.o. **III** *v/i* **12.** *zo.* lay (eggs).

legendär [legɛn'dɛ:r] *adj* legendary.

Legende [le'gɛndə] *f* (-; -n) legend.

leger [le'ʒe:r] *adj* casual, informal.

legieren [le'gi:rən] *v/t* (h) **1.** ⚙ alloy. **2.** *gastr.* thicken.

Le'gierung *f* (-; -en) ⚙ alloy.

Legion [le'gio:n] *f* (-; -en) legion. **Legionär** [legio'nɛ:r] *m* (-s; -e) legionnaire.

Legislative [legisla'ti:və] *f* (-; -n) **1.** legislative body, legislature. **2.** legislative power.

Legisla'turperi,ode *f* legislative period.

legitim [legi'ti:m] *adj* legitimate.

Legitimation [legitima'tsĭo:n] *f* (-; -en) **1.** legitimation, proof of identity, credentials. **2.** authority.

legitimieren [legiti'mi:rən] (h) **I** *v/t* **1.** legitimate. **2.** authorize. **II** *sich ~* prove one's identity.

Legitimität [legitimi'tɛ:t] *f* (-; *no pl*) legitimacy.

Leguan [le'gŭa:n] *m* (-s; -e) *zo.* iguana.

Lehen ['le:ən] *n* (-s; -) *hist.* fief.

Lehm [le:m] *m* (-[e]s; -e) a) loam, b) clay, c) F mud. '**Lehmboden** *m* loamy soil. '**lehmig** *adj* a) loamy, b) F muddy.

Lehne ['le:nə] *f* (-; -n) a) back(rest), b) arm(rest). '**lehnen** *v/t, v/i (a. sich ~)* (h) lean (*an acc, gegen* against): *sich aus dem Fenster ~* lean out of the window.

'**Lehnsherr** *m hist.* feudal lord.

'**Lehnsmann** *m hist.* vassal.

'**Lehnwort** *n* (-[e]s; *~er*) loan (word).

'**Lehramt** *n* a) teaching (profession), b) teaching post. '**Lehranstalt** *f* educational establishment, school. '**Lehrauf-**

trag *m univ.* teaching assignment, lectureship. '**Lehrbeauftragte** *m, f* (-n; -n) *univ.* assistant (*Am.* associate) lecturer. '**Lehrberuf** *m* **1.** *ped.* teaching profession. **2.** ⚔ skilled trade. '**Lehrbrief** *m* a) certificate of apprenticeship, b) indentures. '**Lehrbuch** *n* textbook.

Lehre¹ ['le:rə] *f* (-; -n) **1.** teaching(s), doctrine: *die ~ Hegels* the teachings of Hegel; *die christliche ~* the Christian doctrine. **2.** theory, science: *die ~ vom Schall* acoustics. **3.** a) lesson, b) (piece of) advice, c) moral (*of a tale etc*): *e-e ~ ziehen aus* draw a lesson from. **4.** (*e-e ~ machen* serve one's) apprenticeship (*bei* with).

'**Lehre²** *f* (-; -n) ⊙ **1.** ga(u)ge. **2.** model.

lehren ['le:rən] *v/t, v/i* (h) teach: *j-n lesen ~* teach s.o. (how) to read; *er lehrt Recht univ. a.* he lectures on law; *fig. das wird die Zukunft ~* time will show.

'**Lehrer** *m* (-s; -) a) teacher, *Br. a.* master, b) instructor. **~ausbildung** *f* teacher training. **~beruf** *m* teaching profession. **~fortbildung** *f* in-service training for teachers.

Lehrerin ['le:rərɪn] *f* (-; -nen) (lady) teacher, *Br. a.* mistress.

'**Lehrer|kol,legium** *n* (teaching) staff, *Am. a.* faculty. **~konfe,renz** *f* staff (*Am. a.* faculty) meeting. **~mangel** *m* teacher shortage, *Am. a.* teacher's room. **~zimmer** *n* staff room, *Am. a.* teacher's room.

'**Lehrfach** *n* **1.** subject. **2.** → **Lehramt** *a.*

'**Lehrfilm** *m* educational film. '**Lehrgang** *m* course (*für* in). '**Lehrgeld** *n* ~ *zahlen müssen* learn it the hard way. '**Lehrherr** *m* master. '**Lehrjahre** *pl* (years of) apprenticeship. '**Lehrkörper** *m* teaching (*univ.* academic) staff, *Am. a.* faculty. '**Lehrkraft** *f* teacher.

Lehrling ['le:rlɪŋ] *m* (-s; -e) apprentice, trainee.

'**Lehrmeister** *m* master. '**Lehrme,thode** *f* teaching method. '**Lehrmittel** *pl* teaching aids. '**Lehrplan** *m* syllabus, curriculum. '**lehrreich** *adj* instructive, informative. '**Lehrsatz** *m* ⅋ theorem, *eccl.* dogma. '**Lehrstelle** *f* apprenticeship: *offene ~* vacancy for an apprentice. '**Lehrstoff** *m* **1.** a) subject, b) subject matter. **2.** → **Lehrplan.** '**Lehrstuhl** *m* chair (*für* of *law etc*), professorship. '**Lehrveranstaltung** *f* lecture, sem-

inar. '**Lehrvertrag** *m* articles of apprenticeship. '**Lehrwerkstatt** *f* training workshop. '**Lehrzeit** *f* apprenticeship.

Leib [laɪp] *m* (-[e]s; -er) a) body, b) abdomen, c) womb: *am ganzen ~e zittern* tremble all over; *et. am eigenen ~e erfahren* experience s.th. for o.s.; F *zu ~e rücken* a) *j-m* press s.o. hard, attack s.o., b) *e-m Problem* tackle a problem; *sich j-n vom ~e halten* keep s.o. at arm's length; *~ und Leben riskieren* risk life and limb; *die Rolle war ihr auf den ~ geschrieben* she was made for the part; *mit ~ und Seele* heart and soul; → *lebendig* 1.

'**Leibeigene** *m, f* (-n; -n) serf.

'**Leibes|erben** *pl* ⅋⅋ issue. **~frucht** *f* ⅋⅋, ⚕ f(o)etus. **~kräfte** *pl aus ~n* a) with all one's might, b) *yell etc* at the top of one's voice. **~übungen** *pl* physical exercise (*ped.* education). **~visitati,on** *f* body search.

'**Leibgarde** *f* bodyguard.

'**Leibgericht** *n* favo(u)rite dish.

leib|haftig I *adj* real, true: *~es Ebenbild* living image; *der ~e Teufel* the devil incarnate. **II** *adv* in person, in the flesh.

'**leiblich** *adj* **1.** bodily, physical: *das ~e Wohl* a) physical well-being, b) creature comforts. **2.** natural (*parents etc*), full, own: *~er Bruder* blood brother.

'**Leibrente** *f* life annuity.

'**Leibschmerzen** *pl* stomach-ache.

'**Leib|wache** *f,* **~wächter** *m* bodyguard.

Leiche ['laɪçə] *f* (-; -n) corpse, (dead) body: *über ~n gehen* stop at nothing; F *nur über m-e ~!* over my dead body!

'**Leichen|beschauer** *m* doctor testifying a death. **~bestatter** *m* undertaker, *Am.* mortician. ⅋'**blaß** *adj* deathly pale. **~gift** *n* ptomaine. **~halle** *f* mortuary. **~rede** *f* funeral oration. **~schauhaus** *n* morgue. **~starre** *f* ⚕ rigor mortis. **~tuch** *n a. fig.* shroud. **~verbrennung** *f* cremation. **~wagen** *m* hearse. **~zug** *m* funeral procession.

Leichnam ['laɪçna:m] *m* (-s; -e) (dead) body, corpse.

leicht [laɪçt] **I** *adj* **1.** light (*a. fig. food, music, rain, reading, wine, work, etc*), ⊙ *a.* lightweight: *e-e Erkältung* slight cold; *e-e ~e Bronchitis* a mild case (F a touch) of bronchitis; *~e Steigung* gentle slope; F *~es Mädchen* hussy;

mit ~er Hand effortlessly; *et. auf die ~e Schulter nehmen* make light of s.th. **2.** easy, simple: *~er Sieg* walkover; *das ist ~* that's easy; *nichts ~er als das!* no problem at all!; *sie hat es nicht ~ (mit ihm)* she is having a rough time (with him); *es war ihm ein ~es* it was easy for him. **3.** slight, minor (*a.* ⚖); mild (*penalty*): *~er Fehler* slight (*or* minor) mistake; *~e Verletzung* minor injury. **II** *adv* **4.** lightly (*etc*): *~ berühren* touch s.th. gently (*or* lightly). **5.** easily: *sie lernt ~* she is a good learner; *es ist ~ möglich* it is well possible; *das ist ~ gesagt* it's not as easy as that; *~er gesagt als getan* easier said than done; *nimm's ~!* take it easy! **6.** slightly: *ich bin ~ erkältet* I've (got) a slight cold.

'**Leichtath,let(in** *f*) *m* (track-and-field) athlete. '**Leichtath,letik** *f* (track-and-field) athletics.

'**Leichtbauweise** *f* lightweight construction.

'**leichtbekleidet** *adj* lightly (*or* scantily) dressed.

'**Leichtben,zin** *n* light petrol (*Am.* gasoline).

'**leichtblütig** [-bly:tıç] *adj* lighthearted.

'**leichtentzündlich** *adj* inflammable.

'**Leichter** ['laıçtər] *m* (-s; -) ⚓ lighter.

'**leichtfallen** *v/i* (*irr, sep,* -ge-, sn, → *fallen*) *so et. fällt ihm leicht* he finds that sort of thing easy; *es fällt ihm nicht leicht* it isn't easy for him.

'**leichtfertig** *adj* **1.** light, frivolous. **2.** a) careless, b) irresponsible.

'**Leichtfertigkeit** *f* (-; *no pl*) **1.** frivolity. **2.** carelessness.

'**leichtfüßig** [-fy:sıç] *adj* light-footed.

'**Leichtgewicht** *n* (-[e]s; *no pl*) *sports:* lightweight.

'**leichtgläubig** *adj* gullible.

'**Leichtgläubigkeit** *f* (-; *no pl*) gullibility.

'**leicht'hin** *adv* airily, casually.

'**Leichtigkeit** *f* (-; *no pl*) lightness, *fig. a.* easiness, ease: *mit ~* easily.

'**leichtlebig** [-le:bıç] *adj* easy-going.

'**Leichtlohngruppe** *f* low-wage unskilled labo(u)r.

'**leichtmachen** *v/t* (*sep,* -ge-, h) *j-m et. ~* make s.th. easy for s.o.; *sich das Leben ~* take it easy; *du machst es dir zu leicht!* it's not as easy as that!

'**Leichtma,trose** *m* ordinary seaman.

'**Leichtme,tall** *n* light metal.

'**Leichtsinn** *m* (-[e]s; *no pl*) **1.** carelessness, recklessness: *sträflicher ~* criminal negligence. **2.** frivolity, flightiness.

'**leichtsinnig** *adj* **1.** careless, reckless, rash. **2.** frivolous, flighty. '**leichtsinniger'weise** *adv* carelessly (enough).

'**leichttun:** *sich ~* (*irr, sep,* -ge-, h, → *tun*) F *mit* e-r *Sache ~* find s.th. easy.

'**leicht|verdaulich** *adj* easily digestible, light. *~***verderblich** *adj* perishable: *~e Waren* perishables. *~***verletzt** *adj* slightly injured. *~***verständlich** *adj* easy to understand.

leid [laıt] *adj pred* (**es**) **tut mir ~!** (I'm) sorry!; *es tut mir ~* a) *um* I feel sorry for, b) *daß ...* I am (so) sorry that ...; *das tut mir aber ~!* I'm sorry to hear that!; *es tut mir (ja) ~, aber ich kann nicht kommen etc* I'm afraid I can't come *etc*; *sie tut mir ~* I feel sorry for her; *das wird dir noch ~ tun!* you'll regret it!; *ich bin es ~* I'm tired of it, b) *et. zu tun* I'm tired of doing s.th.

Leid *n* (-[e]s; *no pl*) **1.** a) grief, sorrow, b) misfortune: *j-m sein ~ klagen* pour out one's heart to s.o. **2.** a) harm, b) wrong: *j-m ein ~ zufügen* harm s.o.

leiden ['laıdən] (litt, gelitten, h) **I** *v/t* **1.** suffer, bear, endure: *Hunger ~* a. starve; → *Not* 1. **2.** (*nicht*) *~ können* (dis)like; *ich kann ihn nicht ~* I can't stand him. **II** *v/i* **3.** a) suffer (**an** *or* **unter** *dat* from), b) be suffering, be in pain: *s-e Gesundheit hat darunter gelitten* it told on his health.

'**Leiden** *n* (-s; -) **1.** suffering. **2.** ✚ illness, disease, complaint.

'**leidend** *adj* a) suffering, b) ailing, sickly: *~ aussehen* look ill.

'**Leidenschaft** *f* (-; -en) passion.

'**leidenschaftlich** *adj* passionate, ardent: *ich esse ~ gern Pizza* I just love pizza. '**Leidenschaftlichkeit** *f* (-; *no pl*) passionateness, ardo(u)r.

'**leidenschaftslos** *adj* dispassionate.

'**Leidensgenosse** *m* fellow sufferer.

'**Leidensgeschichte** *f* **1.** *no pl* **die** *~* (**Christi**) Christ's Passion. **2.** *fig.* sad story, *iro.* tale of woe.

'**Leidensmiene** *f iro.* doleful expression.

'**Leidensweg** *m* *ihr Leben war ein einziger ~* hers was a life of suffering.

leider ['laıdər] *adv* unfortunately: *~! a.*

alas!; *ich muß ~ gehen* (I am) sorry, but I must be going; I am afraid I have to go; *ja*, *~!* I'm afraid so; *~ nein*, *~ nicht* unfortunately not, I'm afraid not.

'**leidgeprüft** *adj* sorely tried.

'**leidig** ['laɪdɪç] *adj* tiresome, unpleasant.

'**leidlich** *adj* tolerable, passable: *mir geht es ~* I'm not too bad.

'**Leidtragende** *m, f* (-n; -n) **1.** mourner: *die ~n* the bereaved. **2.** *er ist* (*immer*) *der ~* he is (always) the one to suffer.

'**Leidwesen** *n zu m–m ~* to my regret.

Leier ['laɪər] *f* (-; -n) *♩ hist.* lyre: F *die alte ~* the same old story.

'**Leierkasten** *m* barrel-organ.

leiern ['laɪərn] *v/t, v/i* (h) drone.

'**Leihbiblio,thek** *f*, '**Leihbüche,rei** *f* lending library.

leihen ['laɪən] *v/t* (lieh, geliehen, h) **1.** *j-m et. ~* lend (*Am.* loan) s.o. s.th. **2.** *sich et. ~* borrow s.th. (*bei, von* from).

'**Leihgabe** *f art:* loan. '**Leihgebühr** *f* hire charge, *for books:* lending fee. '**Leihhaus** *n* pawnshop. '**Leihmutter** *f* surrogate mother. '**Leihwagen** *m* hire car. '**leihweise** *adv* on loan.

Leim [laɪm] *m* (-[e]s; -e) glue: F *aus dem ~ gehen* a) come apart, b) grow fat; *j-m auf den ~ gehen* be taken in by s.o.

leimen ['laɪmən] *v/t* (h) **1.** glue. **2.** F *j-n ~* take s.o. for a ride.

'**Leimfarbe** *f* glue colo(u)r.

Lein [laɪn] *m* (-[e]s; -e) ♃ flax.

Leine ['laɪnə] *f* (-; -n) a) string, cord, b) clothesline, c) leash, lead, d) (fishing) line: *den Hund an die ~ nehmen* (*an der ~ führen*) put (keep) the dog on the lead; *j-n an der ~ halten* keep s.o. on a short lead; F *~ ziehen* push off, scram.

leinen ['laɪnən] *adj* linen.

'**Leinen** *n* (-s; -) a) linen, b) canvas, c) *print.* cloth: *in ~ gebunden* cloth-bound. **~kleid** *n* linen dress. **~pa,pier** *n* linen paper. **~schuh** *m* canvas shoe.

'**Leinöl** *n* linseed oil.

'**Leinsamen** *m* ♃ linseed.

'**Leinwand** *f* **1.** *a. paint.* canvas. **2.** *film etc:* screen.

leise ['laɪzə] *adj* quiet, low, soft (*voice etc*): *sei*(*d*) *~!* be quiet!; don't make such a noise!; *das Radio ~*(*r*) *stellen* turn the radio down; *auf ~n Sohlen* treading softly; *ich habe nicht die leiseste Ahnung* I haven't the faintest idea; (*sprich*) *~*(*r*)*!* not so loud!

'**Leisetreter** *m* (-s; -) F pussyfoot(er).

'**Leiste** ['laɪstə] *f* (-; -n) **1.** *anat.* groin. **2.** lath, strip of wood. **3.** △ fillet.

leisten ['laɪstən] *v/t* (h) **1.** a) do, manage, b) achieve, accomplish, c) *a. ☆☆* perform: *gute Arbeit ~* do a good job; *Erstaunliches ~* achieve amazing things. **2.** render: *für geleistete Dienste* for services rendered; *Ersatz ~* provide a replacement; *Zahlungen ~* make payments; → *Beitrag, Eid etc.* **3.** *sich ~* a) afford, b) treat o.s. to, c) *fig.* get up to (do); *ich kann mir kein Auto ~* I can't afford a car; *fig.* ich kann mir das nicht ~ I can't afford to do that; *er darf sich k-n Fehler mehr ~* he can't afford another mistake; *was hat er sich da wieder geleistet?* what has he been up to again?

'**Leisten** *m* (-s; -) last: F *fig.* alles über einen ~ schlagen measure everything by the same yardstick.

'**Leistenbruch** *m* ♫ inguinal hernia.

'**Leistung** *f* (-; -en) **1.** a) *a. ☆, ped., sports,* ☉ *etc* performance, b) achievement, feat, c) work, d) output, e) result(s), *⚡, phys.,* ☉ *a.* power, *⚡* wattage, output, input: *schulische ~en* achievements at school; *nach ~ bezahlt werden* be paid by results; *e-e gute ~ bringen* make a good showing; F *e-e reife ~!* (*iro.* jolly) good show!; *schwache ~!* poor show! **2.** *☆* a) service(s) rendered, b) contribution, c) benefit, d) payment.

'**leistungs|berechtigt** *adj ☆* entitled to claim. **~bezogen** *adj* performance-oriented.

'**Leistungs|bi,lanz** *f* balance of current transactions. **~denken** *n* performance-oriented outlook. **~druck** *m* (-[e]s; *no pl*) pressure (to perform).

'**leistungsfähig** *adj* a) efficient, ☉ *a.* powerful, b) *☆* productive, c) fit.

'**Leistungsfähigkeit** *f* (-; *no pl*) a) efficiency, ☉ *a.* power, capacity, b) *☆* productivity, c) *ped. etc* ability, d) fitness.

'**leistungsgerecht** *adj and adv* according to performance.

'**Leistungs|gesellschaft** *f* achievement-oriented society. **~knick** *m* sudden drop in performance. **~kon,trolle** *f ped.* achievement control. **~kurs** *m ped.* (*ich bin im ~ Geschichte* I am taking history as a) special subject. **~lohn** m 🕀 achievement wage(s). **~ni‚veau** n standard (of performance), ped. a. achievement level. **~prin‚zip** n performance principle. **~prüfung** f performance (ped. achievement) test.

'**leistungsschwach** adj inefficient, low--performance (both a. ⊙), weak.

'**Leistungs|sport** m competitive sport(s). **~sportler(in** f) m competitive athlete. **~stand** m performance level.

'**leistungsstark** adj (highly) efficient, a. ⊙ high-performance, powerful.

'**leistungssteigernd** adj performance--enhancing. '**Leistungssteigerung** f increase in performance (or efficiency).

'**Leistungs|träger(in** f) m top performer. **~wettbewerb** m 🕀 efficiency contest. **~wille** m will to achieve. **~zentrum** n sports: training cent/re (Am. -er). **~zuschlag** m efficiency bonus.

'**Leitar‚tikel** m editorial, esp. Br. leader.

'**Leitbild** n model, example.

'**leiten** ['laɪtən] v/t (h) **1.** a) lead, a. guide (s.o.), b) head, run, be in charge of, manage, c) direct, route traffic (**über** acc over): **ein Sitzung** (**Diskussion**) **~** chair a meeting (discussion); sports: **das Spiel ~** (be the) referee; **ein Orchester ~** conduct an orchestra; **wer leitet die Delegation?** who is the head of the delegation? **2.** pass on (**an** acc to). **3.** (a. v/i) phys. conduct.

'**leitend** adj **1.** a) leading, guiding, b) 🕀 managing, executive: **~e(r) Angestellte(r)** executive; **~e Stellung** managerial (Am. executive) post. **2.** phys. (**nicht**) **~** (non)conductive.

'**Leiter**[1] ['laɪtər] f (-; -n) ladder.

'**Leiter**[2] m (-s; -) **1.** a) leader, b) 🕀 head, managing director, manager, c) ped. headmaster, Am. principal, d) 🎵 conductor. **2.** phys. conductor.

'**Leiterin** f (-; -nen) a) leader, b) 🕀 head, manageress, c) ped. headmistress, Am. principal, d) 🎵 conductress.

'**Leiterwagen** m (hand)cart.

'**Leitfaden** m textbook, manual, guide.

'**leitfähig** adj phys. conductive.

'**Leitfähigkeit** f (-; no pl) conductivity.

'**Leit|gedanke** m central theme. **~hammel** m a. fig. contp. bellwether. **~linie** f **1.** mot. white line. **2.** pl fig. guidelines. **~planke** f mot. crash barrier. **~satz** m

guiding principle. **~stelle** f central office. **~strahl** m 🖅 guide beam. **~studie** f pilot study. **~tier** n leader.

'**Leitung** f (-; -en) **1.** no pl a) leadership, b) 🕀 management, (a. artistic) direction, c) organization, d) administration, e) supervision, control: **die ~ haben von** (or gen) be in charge of, be the head of, head; **unter s-r ~** under his direction; **↑ unter der ~ von X** conducted by X. **2.** the leaders, management. **3.** a) no pl phys. conduction, ⚡ transmission, b) ⚡, ⊙ line, c) (gas, water, etc) main(s), d) ⚡ lead. **4.** teleph. line: **die ~ ist besetzt** the line is busy (or engaged); F **e-e lange ~ haben** be slow in the uptake.

'**Leitungs|mast** m pole, pylon. **~netz** n a) supply network, b) mains system. **~schnur** f ⚡ cord, Br. flex. **~wasser** n tap water.

'**Leitwährung** f 🕀 key currency.

'**Leitwerk** n 🖅 tail unit.

'**Leitzins** m central bank discount rate.

Lektion [lɛk'tsioːn] f (-; -en) ped. unit: F **j-m e-e ~ erteilen** teach s.o. a lesson.

Lektor ['lɛktɔr] m (-s; -toren ['lɛk'toːrən]), **Lektorin** [lɛk'toːrɪn] f (-; -nen) **1.** univ. lecturer. **2.** (publisher's) reader.

Lektüre [lɛk'tyːrə] f (-; -n) **1.** no pl reading. **2.** reading matter.

Lende ['lɛndə] f (-; -n) anat., gastr. loin.

'**Lenden|gegend** f anat. lumbar region. **~schurz** m loincloth. **~stück** n gastr. sirloin. **~wirbel** m lumbar vertebra.

Leninist [leni'nɪst] m (-en; -en) Leninist.

leni'nistisch adj Leninist.

'**lenkbar** adj **1.** ⊙ manoeuvrable, Am. maneuverable, guided (missile). **2.** tractable (child).

lenken ['lɛŋkən] v/t (h) **1.** steer, mot. a. drive, b) fig. direct, guide, govern, control. **3.** j-s **Aufmerksamkeit ~ auf** (acc) direct (or draw) s.o.'s attention to; **die Unterhaltung ~ auf** (acc) steer the conversation round to; **den Verdacht ~ auf** (acc) throw suspicion on.

Lenker ['lɛŋkər] m (-s; -) **1.** driver. **2.** a) steering wheel, b) handlebar.

'**Lenkflugkörper** m ✕ guided missile.

'**Lenkrad** n mot. steering wheel. **~schaltung** f (steering-)column gear change (Am. shift). **~schloß** n steering-column (or steering-wheel) lock.

'**Lenksäule** f mot. steering column.
'**Lenkstange** f handlebar.
'**Lenkung** f (-; -en) **1.** a) steering (etc, → lenken), b) ⊕ guidance, control (a. ✦). **2.** mot. steering mechanism.
lenzen ['lɛntsən] (h) ♨ **I** v/t pump out. **II** v/i scud.
Leopard [leo'part] m (-en; -en) leopard.
Lepra ['le:pra] f (-; no pl) ♣ leprosy.
'**Leprakranke** m, f (-n; -n) leper.
Lerche ['lɛrçə] f (-; -n) zo. lark.
'**lernbar** adj learnable.
'**lernbegierig** adj eager to learn, keen.
'**lernbehindert** adj learning-disabled.
'**Lerneifer** m eagerness to learn.
lernen ['lɛrnən] v/t, v/i (h) learn (aus, bei, von from), study: kochen ~ learn (how) to cook; er lernt gut (schlecht) he is a good (slow) learner; et. auswendig ~ learn s. th. by heart; F er lernt Autoschlosser he's training as a car mechanic (bei at); aus s-n Fehlern ~ learn from one's mistakes; j-n (et.) schätzen ~ come to appreciate s. o. (s.th.); das will gelernt sein! that's not so easy!; F manche ~'s nie! some people never learn; → gelernt.
'**Lernende** m, f (-n; -n) learner.
'**lernfähig** adj able to learn.
'**Lern** | **hilfe** f learning aid. **~mittelfreiheit** f (-; no pl) free learning aids. **~pro,gramm** n computer: educational program(me Br.). **~pro,zeß** m learning process. **~schwester** f ♣ student nurse. **~spiel** n educational game. **~stoff** m subject matter. **~ziel** n educational objective.
'**Lesart** f reading, version (a. fig.).
'**lesbar** adj a) legible, b) readable.
Lesbierin ['lɛsbiər] f (-; -n) F dike (sl.).
Lesbierin ['lɛsbiərɪn] f (-; -nen) lesbian.
lesbisch ['lɛsbɪʃ] adj lesbian.
Lese ['le:zə] f (-; -n) ✦ **1.** gathering. **2.** vintage.
'**Lesebrille** f reading glasses.
'**Lesebuch** n reading-book, reader.
'**Lesekopf** m computer: reading head.
'**Leselampe** f reading lamp.
lesen¹ ['le:zən] (las, gelesen, h) **I** v/t **1.** read: falsch ~ misread; flüchtig ~ skim (through); s-e Schrift ist kaum zu ~ his handwriting is hard to decipher; das Buch liest sich gut the book reads well; da war (or stand) zu ~, daß ... it said

there that ...; et. in j-s Gesicht ~ see s.th. in s.o.'s face; → Messe¹. **2.** univ. lecture on. **II** v/i **3.** read (in dat in, aus from). **4.** univ. lecture (über acc on).
lesen² v/t (las, gelesen, h) a) gather, b) glean, c) vintage.
'**lesenswert** adj worth reading.
Leser ['le:zər] m (-s; -) reader.
'**Leseratte** f F bookworm.
'**Leserbrief** m a) reader's letter, b) letter to the editor.
Leserin f (-; -nen) reader.
'**Leserkreis** m readers: e-n großen ~ haben be widely read.
'**leserlich** adj legible.
'**Leserlichkeit** f (-; no pl) legibility.
'**Lesesaal** m reading room.
'**Lesestift** m computer: scanner.
'**Lesestoff** m reading (matter).
'**Lesestück** n ped. reading (selection).
'**Lesezeichen** n bookmark.
'**Lesung** f (-; -en) reading: parl. in zweiter ~ on second reading.
letal [le'ta:l] adj ♣ lethal.
Lethargie [letar'gi:] f (-; no pl) lethargy.
Lette ['lɛtə] m (-n; -n), '**Lettin** f (-; -nen), '**lettisch** adj Latvian. '**Lettland** n (-s) Latvia.
letzt [lɛtst] adj **1.** last, a. final, a. latter, a. former: ~e Nachrichten late(st) news; m-e ~en Ersparnisse the last of my savings; (am) ~en Sonntag last Sunday; in ~er Zeit lately, recently; ~en Endes after all; ~e(r) sein be last; als ~e(r) gehen go last, be the last to go; er wäre der Letzte, dem ich vertrauen würde he is the last person I would trust; das wäre das Letzte, was ich tun würde that's the last thing I would do; F das (er) ist doch das Letzte! that (he) is the absolute end!; → Augenblick, Hand, Mal², Schrei etc. **2.** last, extreme: bis ins ~e down to the last detail; bis aufs ~e completely, totally; → Ehre, herausholen, Kraft 1, Ölung 2. **3.** F poorest, worst: der ~e Mist! absolute rubbish!; → Dreck 1.
Letzt: zu guter ~ in the end.
'**letztemal** adv das ~ the last time.
'**letztens** adv lately.
'**letztere** adj der (die, das) ~ the latter.
'**letztgenannt** adj the last-mentioned.
'**letzthin** adv lately.

'**letztjährig** [-jɛ:rɪç] adj das ~e Festival etc last year's festival etc.

'**letztlich** adj **1.** ultimately, in the end. **2.** after all.

'**letztmals** adv for the last time.

'**letztwillig** adj 🏛 testamentary, a. adv by will: ~e Verfügung last will (and testament).

'**Leuchtbombe** f flare (bomb).

'**Leuchte** ['lɔʏçtə] f (-; -n) **1.** lamp, light. **2.** F luminary: k-e ~ sein be no genius.

'**leuchten** ['lɔʏçtən] v/i (h) a) shine, b) flash, fig. eyes: light (up), c) gleam, sparkle: mit e-r Lampe ~ shine a light; j-m ~ light the way (or shine the torch) for s.o.; j-m ins Gesicht ~ shine the (or a) lamp (or torch) in s.o.'s face.

'**leuchtend** adj shining (eyes etc), luminous, bright (colour etc): ~es Beispiel shining example; in ~en Farben schildern paint s.th. in glowing colo(u)rs.

'**Leuchter** m (-s; -) a) candlestick, b) sconce, c) chandelier.

'**Leucht|farbe** f luminous paint. ~feuer n beacon. ~gas n → Stadtgas. ~kraft f (-; no pl) luminosity. ~kugel f (signal) flare. ~pistole f flare pistol. ~re¦klame f luminous advertising, neon lights. ~röhre f neon tube (or lamp). ~schirm m fluorescent screen. ~spurgeschoß n tracer bullet. ~stofflampe f, ~stoffröhre f fluorescent lamp (or tube). ~turm m lighthouse. ~zeiger m luminous hand. ~zifferblatt n luminous dial.

leugnen ['lɔʏɡnən] (h) **I** v/t deny (et. getan zu haben having done s.th.): es läßt sich nicht ~, es ist nicht zu ~ it cannot be denied, it is undeniable. **II** v/i deny everything, 🏛 deny the charge.

Leukämie [lɔʏkɛ'mi:] f (-; -n) 🏥 leuk(a)emia.

Leumund ['lɔʏmʊnt] m (-[e]s; no pl) reputation. '**Leumundszeugnis** n certificate of good character.

Leute ['lɔʏtə] pl people, ✕ etc men: die ~ people; m-e ~ my people, F my folks; F hallo, ~! hi, folks!; es waren etwa 20 ~ da there were about 20 persons present; et. unter die ~ bringen make s.th. public, spread s.th.

Leutnant ['lɔʏtnant] m (-s; -s) ✕ second lieutenant (a. ✈ Am.), ✈ pilot officer: ~ zur See acting sublieutenant, Am. ensign.

'**leutselig** adj affable.

'**Leutseligkeit** f (-; no pl) affability.

Leviten [le'vi:tən] pl j-m die ~ lesen read s.o. the riot act.

Levkoje [lɛf'ko:jə] f (-; -n) ♀ stock.

lexikalisch [lɛksi'ka:lɪʃ] adj lexical.

Lexikograph [lɛksiko'gra:f] m (-en; -en) lexicographer. **Lexikographie** [lɛksi-kogra'fi:] f (-; no pl) lexicography.

lexiko'graphisch adj lexicographical.

Lexikon ['lɛksikɔn] n (-s; -ka) **1.** encyclop(a)edia. **2.** → Wörterbuch.

Libanese [liba'ne:zə] m (-n; -n), **Liba'nesin** f (-; -nen), **liba'nesisch** adj Lebanese. **Libanon** ['li:banɔn] m (-s) der ~ the Lebanon.

Libelle [li'bɛlə] f (-; -n) **1.** zo. dragonfly. **2.** ⊙ water level, bubble.

liberal [libe'ra:l] adj, **Libe'rale** m, f (-[n]; -n) liberal, pol. Liberal. **liberalisieren** [liberali'zi:rən] v/t (h) liberalize.

Liberalismus [libera'lɪsmʊs] m (-; no pl) liberalism. **liberalistisch** [libera'lɪstɪʃ] adj liberalistic. **Liberalität** [liberali'tɛ:t] f (-; no pl) liberality.

Libero ['li:bero] m (-s; -s) soccer: libero.

Libido ['li:bido] f (-; no pl) psych. libido.

Libretto [li'brɛto] n (-s; -s, -tti) libretto.

Libyen ['li:byən] n (-s) Libya. '**Libyer** ['li:byər] m (-s; -), '**Libyerin** f (-; -nen), **libysch** ['li:bɪʃ] adj Libyan.

licht [lɪçt] adj **1.** bright: ~er Augenblick lucid interval. **2.** thin, open (woods), a. thinning (hair). **3.** ⊙ ~e Höhe clear height, overhead clearance; ~e Weite inside width.

Licht n (-[e]s; -er) **1.** no pl a) light, b) daylight: fig. bei ~(e) besehen a) on closer inspection, b) strictly speaking; ans ~ bringen (kommen) bring (come) to light; ~ bringen in (acc) throw light on; das ~ der Welt erblicken see the light of day, be born; et. in e-m anderen ~ erscheinen lassen reveal s.th. in a different light; F j-n hinters ~ führen deceive (or dupe) s.o.; et. ins rechte ~ rücken put s.th. in its true light; das ~ scheuen shun the light; ein schlechtes (or schiefes) ~ werfen auf (acc) show s.o., s.th. in a bad light. **2.** a) light, b) lamp, c) candle: ~ machen, das ~ anmachen turn on the light(s); bei ~ arbeiten work by lamplight; die ~er der Großstadt the lights of the city; F er ist *kein großes* ~ he is no genius; *mir geht ein* ~ *auf* I see (daylight); *j-m ein* ~ *aufstecken* open s.o.'s eyes; → *grün*, *Scheffel*. **3.** *paint.* (high)light. **4.** *pl hunt.* eyes.

'**Licht|anlage** f lighting system. ~**bild** n a) photo(graph), b) slide. ~**bildervortrag** m slide lecture. ~**blick** m fig. a) ray of hope, b) comfort: *der einzige* ~ (*in m-m Leben*) the only bright spot in my life). ~**bogen** m ∉ arc. **2brechend** adj opt. refractive. ~**druck** m (-[e]s, no pl) phototype. **2durchlässig** adj permeable to light. **2echt** adj lightproof, nonfading. ~**empfindlich** adj sensitive to light, opt., phot. (photo)sensitive: ~ **machen** phot. sensitize. ~**empfindlichkeit** f sensitivity to light, phot. speed.

lichten¹ ['lıçtən] (h) **I** v/t **1.** thin (out) (*trees* etc). **II** *sich* ~ **2.** fog etc: clear, lift. **3.** trees, ranks, hair, etc: be thinning (out), supplies etc: dwindle.

'**lichten**² v/t (h) *den Anker* ~ weigh anchor.

'**lichterloh** ['lıçtərlo:] adv ~ **brennen** be ablaze.

'**Licht|filter** n, m phot. light filter. ~**geschwindigkeit** f (*mit* ~ at) speed of light. ~**griffel** m computer: light pen. ~**hof** m **1.** △ atrium. **2.** astr., phot., TV halo. ~**hupe** f mot. (headlamp) flasher: *die* ~ *betätigen* flash one's lights. ~**jahr** n light year. ~**kegel** m cone of light. ~**leitung** f ∉ light circuit (*or* mains). ~**maschine** f mot. dynamo. ~**orgel** f colo(u)r organ. ~**quelle** f source of light. ~**schacht** m △ light well. ~**schalter** m ∉ light switch.

'**lichtscheu** adj **1.** shunning the light. **2.** fig. shady.

'**Lichtschranke** f photoelectric barrier.

'**Lichtschutzfaktor** m protection factor.

'**lichtstark** adj fast (*lens*). '**Lichtstärke** f luminous intensity, phot. speed.

'**Lichtstift** m computer: light pen.

'**Lichtstrahl** m ray (*or* beam) of light.

'**lichtundurchlässig** adj opaque.

'**Lichtung** f (-; -en) clearing.

Lid [li:t] n (-[e]s; -er) (eye)lid.

'**Lidschatten** m eye-shadow.

lieb [li:p] adj a) dear, b) sweet, nice, kind, c) good: *Lieber Herr X* in letters: Dear Mr. X; *sei* ~*l* be good!; *sei so* ~*l* be a dear!, do you mind?; *sei so* ~ *und* ... do

me a favo(u)r and ...; *es ist mir* ~, *daß* ... I am glad that ...; *es ist mir nicht* ~, *daß* ... I don't like it that ...; *mehr als mir* ~ *war* more than I really wanted; *das* ~*e Geld* always the money; *sich bei j-m* ~ *Kind machen* ingratiate o.s. with s.o.; → *Gott, lieber, liebst.*

liebäugeln ['li:p?ɔygəln] v/i (insep, ge-, h) ~ *mit* have one's eye on.

'**Liebchen** n (-s; -) love, sweetheart.

Liebe¹ ['li:bə] f (-; -n) **1.** no pl (*zu*) love (of, for), affection (for): *die große* ~ the love of one's life; *aus* ~ *zu* out of love for; *aus* ~ *heiraten* marry for love; *mit* ~ *decorate* etc with loving care; ~ *macht blind* love is blind; *die* ~ *geht durch den Magen* the way to a man's heart is through his stomach. **2.** no pl (*körperliche*) ~ love(making), sex. **3.** F sweetheart, love, flame.

'**Liebe**² m, f(-n; -n) dear (person): *m-e* ~*l* my dear (girl)!; *mein* ~*r*! my dear man!; *m-e* ~*n*! my dears!

'**liebebedürftig** adj ~ *sein* need a lot of affection.

Liebelei [li:bə'laı] f (-; -en) flirtation.

lieben ['li:bən] (h) **I** v/t **1.** love, a. like: *j-n* ~ a) love s.o., b) make love to s.o.; *sich* ~ a) love each other, b) make love; *er liebt es nicht, wenn* ... he doesn't like it if ...; *liebend gern!* gladly!; *ich würde liebend gern* ... I'd love to ... **II** v/i **2.** (be in) love. **3.** make love.

'**Liebende** m, f (-n; -n) lover.

'**liebenswert** adj lovable, amiable.

'**liebenswürdig** adj kind, obliging: *sehr* ~ *von Ihnen!* very kind of you!

'**liebenswürdiger'weise** adv kindly.

'**Liebenswürdigkeit** f (-; -en) **1.** no pl kindness. **2.** pl a) compliments, b) iro. insults.

lieber ['li:bər] adv rather, sooner, better: ~ *haben* (*als*) prefer (to), like s.o., sth. better (than); *du solltest* ~ *gehen* you had better go; *ich wüßte nicht, was ich* ~ *täte!, nichts* ~ *als das!* there's nothing I'd like better; (*ich möchte*) ~ *nicht!* I would (*or* I'd) rather not!

'**Liebes|abenteuer** n, ~**af,färe** f love affair. ~**brief** m love letter. ~**entzug** m psych. deprivation. ~**erklärung** f declaration of love: (*j-m*) *e-e* ~ *machen* declare one's love (to s.o.). ~**erlebnis** n **1.** experience of love. **2.** love (affair).

~gabe f (charitable) gift. **~gedicht** n love poem. **~geschichte** f love story. **~heirat** f love match. **~kummer** m lovesickness: **~ haben** be lovesick. **~leben** n love life. **~lied** n love song. **~mühe** f **das ist verlorene ~!** that's a waste of time! **~paar** n (pair of) lovers, courting couple. **~ro|man** m romance. **~spiel** n loveplay. **~szene** f love scene.

'**liebevoll** adj loving, affectionate: **~ pflegen** take loving care of.

'**liebgewinnen** v/t (irr, sep, -ge-, h, → **gewinnen**) grow (very) fond of.

'**liebhaben** v/t (irr, sep, -ge-, h, → **haben**) love, be fond of.

Liebhaber ['li:pha:bər] m (-s; -) **1.** lover. **2.** a) (art etc) lover, enthusiast, fan, b) collector, c) at auctions etc: taker. **3.** thea. jugendlicher **~** juvenile lead.

'**Liebhaber...** collector's (value etc).

Liebhabe'rei f (-; -en) hobby.

'**Liebhaberin** f (-; -nen) **1.** → Liebhaber **2.** thea. jugendliche **~** jeune première.

liebkosen [li:p'ko:zən] v/t (insep, ge-, h), **Lieb'kosung** f (-; -en) caress.

'**lieblich** adj **1.** a) lovely, charming, sweet, b) delightful, pleasant. **2.** mellow (wine), sweet (bouquet).

'**Lieblichkeit** f (-; no pl) loveliness, charm, sweetness.

'**Liebling** m a) darling, favo(u)rite, b) pet: **~!** (my) love!, darling!

'**Lieblings...** favo(u)rite. **~schüler(in** f) m teacher's pet. **~thema** n pet subject.

'**lieblos** adj loveless, unkind (words etc), uncaring (parents): **~ zubereitet** prepared carelessly (F any old how).

'**Lieblosigkeit** f (-; no pl) unkindness, coldness.

'**Liebschaft** f (-; -en) (love) affair.

liebst I adj a) dearest, b) favo(u)rite: **m-e ~e Sendung** etc a. the program(me) etc I like best. **II** adv **am ~en** best (or most) of all; **am ~en spiele ich Tennis** I like tennis best; **es wäre mir am ~en, wenn ...** it would suit me best if ...

'**Liebste** m, f(-n; -n) (mein ~r, m-e ~) my darling (or love, sweetheart).

Lied [li:t] n (-[e]s; -er) song, air, tune, lied: **geistliches ~** hymn; **es ist immer das alte ~** it's the same old story every time; **das Ende vom ~** the upshot; **ich**

kann ein ~ davon singen I can tell you a thing or two about it.

Liederabend ['li:dər-] m lieder recital.

'**Liederbuch** n songbook.

liederlich ['li:dərlıç] adj **1.** slovenly, sloppy. **2.** dissolute (life etc).

'**Liederlichkeit** f (-; no pl) **1.** slovenliness. **2.** dissoluteness.

'**Liedermacher** m singer-songwriter.

Lieferant [lifə'rant] m (-en; -en) a) supplier, b) contractor: **~ für Speisen und Getränke** caterer.

'**lieferbar** adj available: **die Ware ist sofort ~** the article can be supplied (or delivered) at once.

liefern ['li:fərn] (h) **I** v/t **1.** a. fig. **j-m et.** supply s.o. with s.th. **2.** deliver (dat to). **3.** yield, give, a. fig. provide: **e-n harten Kampf ~** put up a good fight; **ein gutes Spiel ~** play well, make a good showing. **4.** F **er ist geliefert!** he's done for!, he's had it! **II** v/i **5.** supply, deliver.

'**Lieferschein** m delivery note.

'**Liefer|ter,min** m date of delivery. **~ung** f (-; -en) **1.** a) supply, b) delivery: **zahlbar bei ~** cash on delivery (abbr. C.O.D.). **2.** consignment, Am. shipment. **3.** print. instal(l)ment.

'**Liefer|vertrag** m supply contract. **~wagen** m delivery van (Am. truck), pickup. **~werk** n supplier's plant, suppliers. **~zeit** f delivery time.

Liege ['li:gə] f (-; -n) **1.** couch. **2.** campbed. **3.** sunbed.

'**Liegegeld** n ⚓ demurrage.

liegen ['li:gən] v/i (lag, gelegen, h) **1.** lie, be: **laß das Buch ~!** leave the book alone!; **liegst du bequem?** are you comfortable?; **(krank) im Bett ~** be (ill) in bed; F fig. **damit liegst du richtig!** (there) you are on the right track!; **an der Kette ~** be chained up; **es lag Schnee** there was snow; **das Geld liegt auf der Bank** the money is in the bank; sports: **er lag auf dem dritten Platz ~** he was (lying) in third place; **wie die Dinge ~** as matters stand; **die Sache liegt so ...** the matter is as follows ...; **die Preise ~ bei ...** prices are at (or around) ...; **wo ~ s-e Schwächen?** what are his weak points?; **da liegt der Fehler!** that's where the trouble lies! **2.** (an dat) lie (on), be (situated) (at, near): **das Hotel liegt zentral** the hotel is centrally situated; *nach Süden* ~ face south; → *fern* I. 3. *fig. j-m* ~ a) suit s.o., b) appeal to s.o.; *die Rolle liegt ihr* the part suits her; *er* (*es*) *liegt mir nicht* he (it) isn't my cup of tea. **4.** *fig. woran liegt es?* what's the reason (of it)?; *woran liegt es, daß er nie gewinnt?* why is it (that) he never wins?; *daran liegt es* that's (the reason) why; *es liegt daran, daß ...* the reason is that ...; *was liegt daran?* who cares?; *mir liegt viel* (*wenig*) *daran* it means a ton (it doesn't mean much) to me; *es liegt nicht an ihr* (*wenn*) it's not her fault (if); *an mir soll's nicht* ~! a) it's all right by me!, b) I'll do my best!; *es liegt bei* (*or an*) *dir* (*zu entscheiden*) it is up to you (to decide).

'**liegenbleiben** *v/i* (*irr, sep, -ge-, sn,* → *bleiben*) **1.** remain lying: (*im Bett*) ~ stay in bed; *bleib liegen!* don't get up! **2.** *car etc:* break down, *driver etc:* be (*or* get) stranded. **3.** *snow:* settle. **4.** *work etc:* be left unfinished: *das kann* ~! that can wait! **5.** *goods:* be left unsold. **6.** be left behind.

'**liegenlassen** *v/t* (*irr, sep, -ge-, h,* → *lassen*) **1.** leave *s.th.* behind. **2.** leave *task etc* unfinished. **3.** leave *things* lying around: *alles stehen- und* ~ drop everything; → *links* 1.

'**Liegenschaften** *pl* real estate.

'**Liege**|**platz** *m* ♿ berth. ~**sitz** *m mot.* reclining seat. ~**stuhl** *m* deckchair. ~**stütz** [-ʃtʏts] *m* (*-es; -e*) *gym.* (*e-n* ~ *machen* do a) press-up. ~**wagen** *m* ♿ couchette. ~**wiese** *f* lawn.

lieh [liː] *pret of* **leihen.**

ließ [liːs] *pret of* **lassen.**

Lift [lɪft] *m* (*-[e]s; -e, -s*) lift, *Am.* elevator. '**liften** *v/t* (*h*) ✄ lift: *sich* (*das Gesicht*) ~ *lassen* have a facelift.

Liga ['liːɡa] *f* (*-; Ligen*) league, *sports: a.* division.

liieren [li'iːrən] *sich* ~ (*h*) team up (*mit* with); *mit j-m liiert sein* have an affair with s.o.

Likör [li'køːr] *m* (*-s; -e*) liqueur.

lila ['liːla] *adj,* '**Lila** *n* (*-s; -*) lilac, mauve.

Lilie ['liːliə] *f* (*-; -n*) ❀ lily.

Liliputaner [lilipu'taːnər] *m* (*-s; -*), **Liliputanerin** *f* (*-; -nen*) Lilliputian.

Limonade [limo'naːdə] *f* (*-; -n*) fizzy drink, *Am.* soda pop.

Limousine [limu'ziːnə] *f* (*-; -n*) *mot.* limousine, saloon (car), *Am.* sedan.

Linde ['lɪndə] *f* (*-; -n*) ❀ lime (tree).

'**Lindenblütentee** *m* lime-blossom tea.

lindern ['lɪndərn] *v/t* (*h*) relieve, alleviate, ease. '**Linderung** *f* (*-; no pl*) relief, alleviation, easing: (*j-m*) ~ *verschaffen* bring (s.o.) relief.

Lineal [line'aːl] *n* (*-s; -e*) ruler.

linear [line'aːr] *adj* ✦, ✦ linear.

Linguist [lɪŋ'ɡʊɪst] *m* (*-en; -en*) linguist. **Linguistik** [lɪŋ'ɡʊɪstɪk] *f* (*-; no pl*) linguistics.

Linie ['liːniə] *f* (*-; -n*) line (*a. fig.*), ♿ route, *pol. etc* course, policy: *auf* (*die* schlanke) ~ *achten* watch one's figure; *mit der* ~ 2 *fahren* take the number two; *fig. auf der ganzen* ~ all along (*or* down) the line; *auf gleicher* ~ *mit* on a level with; *in erster* ~ in the first place.

'**Linien**|**bus** *m* regular bus. ~**dienst** *m* regular service. ~**flug** *m* scheduled flight. ~**flugzeug** *n,* ~**ma**₁**schine** *f* scheduled plane. ~**netz** *n* (rail *etc*) network: *das* ~ *der U-Bahn* the underground (system). ~**pa**₁**pier** *n* ruled paper. ~**richter** *m sports:* linesman. ₂**treu** *adj pol.* loyal (to the line): ~ *sein* follow the party line. ~**treue** *m, f* (*-n; -n*) party liner. ~**verkehr** *m* regular service (*or* traffic).

linieren [li'niːrən], **liniieren** [lini'iːrən] *v/t* (*h*) rule, line.

link [lɪŋk] *adj* left: *die* ~**e** *Seite* of cloth: the reverse (side); *auf der* ~**en** *Seite,* ~*er Hand* on the left; ~*er Hand sehen Sie ...* on your left you see ...; *pol., sports:* ~*er Flügel* left wing; *pol. dem* ~*en Flügel angehören* be left-wing; *fig. er ist wohl mit dem* ~*en Fuß zuerst aufgestanden!* he must have got out of bed on the wrong side; ~*e Masche* a) purl (stitch), b) *a.* ~*e Tour* F dirty trick; F *ein ganz* ~*er Typ* a real bastard.

'**Linke**¹ *f* (*-n; -n*) **1.** left hand, *boxing:* left. **2.** *pol. the* Left. **3.** left (side): *zu ihrer* ~ on her left.

'**Linke**² *m, f* (*-n; -n*) *pol.* leftist.

'**linken** *v/t* (*h*) F con, take *s.o.* for a ride.

'**linkisch** *adj* awkward, clumsy.

links *adv* **1.** on (*or* to) the left; *nach* ~ (to the) left; *von* ~ from the left; ~ *von* (on *or* to the) left of; ~ *von mir* (on *or* to) my left; ~ *abbiegen* turn left; *sich* ~

halten keep (to the) left; *fig.* **~ liegenlassen** ignore; F **~ sein** a) be left-handed, b) *a.* **~ stehen** *pol.* be left-wing; **~ stricken** purl; F *fig.* **das mache ich mit ~** that's kid's stuff (for me). **2.** on the wrong side, inside out.

'**Linksabbieger** *m* (-s; -) *mot.* vehicle (*pl* traffic) turning left.

'**Linksaußen** *m sports:* outside left.

'**Linksextre,mist(in** *f*) *m pol.* left-wing extremist. '**linksextre,mistisch** *adj pol.* (of the) extreme left.

'**linksgerichtet** *adj pol.* left-wing.

'**Linkshänder** [-hɛndər] *m* (-s; -) left-hander: **~ sein** be left-handed.

'**linksherum** *adv* **1.** ☺ anticlockwise. **2.** inside out.

'**Linkskurve** *f* left turn.

'**linksradi,kal** *adj pol.* (of the) extreme left: *die Linksradikalen* the left-wing radicals.

'**linksrheinisch** *adj and adv* on the left bank of the Rhine.

'**Linksruck** *m pol.* swing to the left.

'**Linkssteuerung** *f mot.* left-hand drive.

'**Linksverkehr** *m* **in Großbritannien ist ~** in Great Britain they drive on the left.

Linoleum [li'no:leʊm] *n* (-s; *no pl*) linoleum, F lino.

Linse ['lɪnzə] *f* (-; -n) **1.** 🌿 lentil. **2.** *opt.* lens.

Lippe ['lɪpə] *f* (-; -n) lip: *von den ~n ablesen* lip-read; *ich bringe es nicht über die ~n* I can't bring myself to say it; *sich auf die ~n beißen* bite one's lip.

'**Lippenbekenntnis** *n* (*ein* **~ ablegen** pay) lip service (**zu** to).

'**Lippenblütler** [-bly:tlər] *m* (-s; -) 🌿 labiate.

'**Lippenlaut** *m ling.* labial (sound).

'**Lippenstift** *m* lipstick.

liquid [li'kvi:t] *adj* ✝ liquid, solvent.

Liquidation [likvida'tsi̯o:n] *f* (-; -en) **1.** ✝ liquidation (*a. pol. murder*), winding up. **2.** fee, charge, bill.

liquidieren [likvi'di:rən] *v/t* (h) **1.** ✝ liquidate (*a. pol. kill*), wind up. **2.** charge.

Liquidität [likvidi'tɛ:t] *f* (-; *no pl*) ✝ liquidity, solvency.

lispeln ['lɪspəln] *v/t, v/i* (h) lisp.

List [lɪst] *f* (-; -en) ruse, trick, cunning: *zu e-r ~ greifen* resort to a ruse.

Liste ['lɪstə] *f* (-; -n) list: *j-n auf die ~ setzen* put s.o.'s name on the list; F

schwarze **~** black list; *j-n auf die schwarze* **~ setzen** blacklist s.o.

'**Listenpreis** *m* ✝ list price.

'**listig** *adj* cunning, sly, crafty.

Litanei [lita'naɪ] *f* (-; -en) litany.

Liter ['li:tər] *n, m* (-s; -) litre, *Am.* liter.

literarisch [lɪtə'ra:rɪʃ] *adj* literary.

Literat [lɪtə'ra:t] *m* (-en; -en) man of letters, literary man. **Literatur** [lɪtəra'tu:r] *f* (-; *no pl*) literature.

Litera'tur... literary. **~angaben** *pl* bibliography. **~gattung** *f* literary genre. **~geschichte** *f* history of literature. **~kritiker(in** *f*) *m* literary critic. **~preis** *m* literary award. **~wissenschaft** *f* literature, literary studies.

'**literweise** *adv fig.* by the gallon.

'**Litfaßsäule** *f* advertising pillar.

Lithographie [litogra'fi:] *f* (-; -n) lithography.

litt [lɪt] *pret of* **leiden**.

Liturgie [litʊr'gi:] *f* (-; -n) liturgy.

Litze ['lɪtsə] *f* (-; -n) **1.** braid, lace. **2.** ⚡ cord, flex, stranded conductor.

live [laɪf] *adj and adv* live.

'**Live-Sendung** *f* live broadcast.

Livree [li'vre:] *f* (-; -n) livery: *in ~ →* **livriert** [li'vri:rt] *adj* liveried.

Lizenz [li'tsɛnts] *f* (-; -en) licen/ce (*Am.* -se): *in* **~ produce** etc under licence.

Li'zenz|ausgabe *f print.* edition printed under licence. **~geber** *m* (-s; -) licenser, licensor. **~gebühr** *f* royalty. **~inhaber** *m*, **~nehmer** *m* (-s; -) licensee. **~vertrag** *m* licensing agreement.

LKW-Fahrer ['ɛlkave-] *m* lorry driver, *Am.* truck driver.

Lob [lo:p] *n* (-[e]s; *no pl*) (*über jedes* **~ erhaben** beyond) praise: *j-s* **~ singen** sing s.o.'s praises.

Lobby ['lɔbi] *f* (-; -bys, -bies) lobby.

Lobbyist [lɔbi'ɪst] *m* (-en; -en) lobbyist.

loben ['lo:bən] *v/t, v/i* (h) (*wegen gen, dat* for) praise, commend: *das lobe ich mir!* that's what I like!; *da lobe ich mir ... give me ...* any time; *j-n ~d hervorheben* single s.o. out for praise.

'**lobenswert** *adj* laudable.

Lobhudelei [lo:phu:də'laɪ] *f* (-; -en) base flattery.

löblich ['lø:plɪç] *adj esp. iro.* laudable.

'**Loblied** *n fig.* *ein* **~ auf j-n singen** sing s.o.'s praises.

'**Lobrede** *f* eulogy.

Loch [lɔx] *n* (-[e]s; ⁓er) **1.** hole, *in tooth*: a. cavity, *in tyre*: puncture, *in fence etc*: gap: *fig.* **ein ⁓ reißen in** (*acc*) make a hole in; **ein ⁓ im Haushalt stopfen** stop a gap in the budget; F **er pfeift auf dem letzten ⁓** he's on his last legs. **2.** F *fig.* a) hole, dump, b) jug (*sl.*).

lochen ['lɔxən] *v/t* (h) a) punch, b) stamp, c) perforate.

'**Locher** *m* (-s; -) ⊕ punch, perforator.

löcherig ['lœçərɪç] *adj* a. *fig.* full of holes.

löchern ['lœçərn] *v/t* (h) F pester.

'**Lochstreifen** *m* punched tape.

'**Lochung** *f* (-; -en) perforation.

'**Lochzange** *f* punch pliers, 🚄 ticket punch.

Locke ['lɔkə] *f* (-; -n) curl: **⁓n haben** have curly hair.

locken[1] ['lɔkən] *v/t* (a. **sich ⁓**) curl.

'**locken**[2] *v/t* (h) **1.** lure, bait, call (*animal*). **2.** *fig.* lure, tempt: **es lockt mich sehr zu inf** I'm very much tempted to *inf*; **⁓des Angebot** tempting offer.

'**Lockenkopf** *m* curly-head.

'**Lockenwickler** *m* curler.

locker ['lɔkər] *adj* **1.** a) loose (*a. fig. morals, etc*), a. slack, b) light (*soil, dough, etc*), → **Schraube** 1. **2.** *fig.* easy, relaxed, *person*: a. cool: F **es geht sehr ⁓ zu** it's all very relaxed; **das schafft er ⁓** he can do that easily. '**Lockerheit** *f* (-; *no pl*) **1.** a) looseness, slackness, b) lightness. **2.** *fig.* easy manner.

'**lockerlassen** *v/i* (*irr, sep,* -ge-, h, ⁓) **lassen**) F **nicht ⁓** not to let up, keep (on) trying.

'**lockermachen** *v/t* (*sep,* -ge-, h) F (**bei j-m**) **Geld ⁓** (make s.o.) fork out (*or* come across with) money.

lockern ['lɔkərn] (h) **I** *v/t* loosen, slacken (*rope etc*), relax (*grip, fig. discipline etc*): **s-e Muskeln ⁓** loosen up one's muscles. **II sich ⁓** become loose (*a. fig. morals etc*), slacken, *sports*: limber up, *fig. mood etc*: relax. '**Lockerung** *f* (-; *no pl*) loosening, slackening, *fig.* relaxation. '**Lockerungsübung** *f sports*: limbering-up exercise.

lockig ['lɔkɪç] *adj* curly.

'**Lockmittel** *n a. fig.* bait. '**Lockruf** *m zo.* (mating) call. '**Lockspitzel** *m pol.* stool pigeon, agent provocateur.

'**Lockung** *f* (-; -en) lure, temptation.

'**Lockvogel** *m a. fig.* decoy. **⁓werbung** *f*

🎯 loss-leader selling.

Lodenmantel ['lo:dən-] *m* loden (coat).

lodern ['lo:dərn] *v/i* (h) a. *fig.* blaze.

Löffel ['lœfəl] *m* (-s; -) **1.** a) spoon, b) spoonful: **zwei ⁓ (voll) Zucker** two spoonfuls of sugar; F *fig.* **den ⁓ weglegen** peg out. **2.** *hunt. or* F ear: **schreib dir das hinter die ⁓!** get that into your thick head once and for all!

'**Löffelbagger** *m* (power) shovel.

'**Löffelbis**|**kuit** *m* spongefinger.

löffeln ['lœfəln] *v/t* (h) spoon.

'**Löffelstiel** *m* spoon handle.

'**löffelweise** *adv* by the spoonful.

log [lo:k] *pret of* **lügen**.

Loga'rithmentafel *f* A✓ log table.

Logarithmus [loga'rɪtmʊs] *m* (-; -men) A✓ logarithm.

Logbuch ['lɔk-] *n* ⚓ log(book).

Loge ['lo:ʒə] *f* (-; -n) **1.** *thea.* box. **2.** (*freemason's*) lodge.

Logik ['lo:gɪk] *f* (-; *no pl*) logic.

logisch ['lo:gɪʃ] *adj* logical: F (**das ist doch**) **⁓!** naturally!, of course!

'**logischerweise** *adv* logically.

Logistik [lo'gɪstɪk] *f* (-; *no pl*) logistics.

logo ['lo:go] *adj pred* F sure (thing).

'**Logo** *m, n* (-s; -s) 🎯 logo.

Logopäde [logo'pɛ:də] *m* (-n; -n), **Logo'pädin** *f* (-; -nen) speech therapist. **Logopädie** [logopɛ'di:] *f* (-; *no pl*) logop(a)edics, speech therapy.

Lohn [lo:n] *m* (-[e]s; ⁓e) **1.** wages, pay. **2.** *fig.* (**zum ⁓** in) reward (**für** for): **s-n wohlverdienten ⁓ erhalten** a. *iro.* get one's just deserts. **⁓abschluß** *m* wage agreement. **⁓anteil** *m* wages. **⁓ausfall** *m* loss of wages. **⁓ausgleich** *m* **bei vollem ⁓** without cuts in pay. **⁓buchhalter(in** *f*) *m* wages clerk. **⁓bü**|**ro** *n* pay office. **⁓empfänger(in** *f*) *m* wage earner.

lohnen ['lo:nən] (h) **I sich ⁓ 1.** be worth(-while), pay; **die Mühe lohnt sich** it's worth the trouble; **es lohnt sich zu inf** it's worth *ger*, it pays to *inf*; **der Film lohnt sich** the film is worth seeing; **Verbrechen lohnt sich nicht** crime doesn't pay. **II** *v/t* **2.** reward: **j-m et. schlecht ⁓** ill repay s.o. **3.** **die Mühe (e-n Besuch) ⁓** be worth the trouble (a visit). '**lohnend** *adj* **1.** paying, profitable. **2.** worthwhile, rewarding, *a.* worth seeing (*etc*).

'**Lohn|erhöhung** f wage increase, (pay) rise, Am. raise. **∼forderung** f wage claim. **∼fortzahlung** f continued pay (to sick workers). **∼gefälle** n pay differential. **∼gruppe** f pay bracket.

'**Lohn∼inten,siv** adj wage-intensive.

'**Lohn|kampf** m wage dispute. **∼kosten** pl wage costs: **sehr hohe ∼ haben** have a huge payroll. **∼kürzung** f wage cut. **∼runde** f round of wage negotiations.

Lohnsteuer f wage(s) tax. **∼jahresausgleich** m annual adjustment of income tax. **∼karte** f wage(s) tax card.

'**Lohn|stopp** m pay freeze. **∼streifen** m pay slip. **∼ta,rif** m wage rate.

Löhnung ['lø:nʊŋ] f (-; -en) ✗ pay.

Loipe ['lɔypə] f (-; -n) cross-country (skiing) trail.

Lok [lɔk] f (-; -s) 🚂 F engine.

lokal [lo'ka:l] adj local.

Lo'kal n (-s; -e) a) restaurant, b) pub, Am. saloon. **Lo'kal...** local (newspaper, reporter, press, etc).

Lo'kalanästhe,sie f local an(a)esthesia.

lokalisieren [lokali'zi:rən] v/t (h) locate, a. 🏥 localize (**auf** acc to).

Lo'kal|kolo,rit n local colo(u)r. **∼ter,min** m ⚖ visit to the scene (of the crime).

Lokomotive [lokomo'ti:və] f (-; -n) engine. **Lokomo'tivführer** m engine driver, Am. engineer.

Lokus ['lo:kʊs] m (-[ses]; -[se]) F loo, Am. john.

Lombardkre,dit ['lɔmbart-] m ⚹ collateral loan. **'Lombardsatz** m rate for (central bank) loans on securities.

Londoner ['lɔndɔnər] **I** m (-s; -) Londoner. **II** adj (of) London.

Lorbeer ['lɔrbe:r] m (-s; -en) **1.** ♀ laurel (tree), bay (tree). **2.** gastr. bay leaf. **3.** pl fig. laurels: **sich auf s-n ∼en ausruhen** rest on one's laurels; **damit kannst du (bei ihr) k-e ∼en ernten** that won't get you anywhere with her).

Lore ['lo:rə] f (-; -n) 🚂 tipper.

los¹ [lo:s] adj pred **1.** off: **der Knopf ist ∼** the button is off; **der Hund ist ∼** the dog is loose. **2.** F **∼ sein** be rid of s.o., s.th.; **den wären wir ∼!** good riddance!; **mein Geld bin ich ∼** my money is gone; → a. **losgehen, loslegen** etc. **3.** F **was ist ∼** a) (**mit dir**)? what's the matter (with you)?, b) (**hier**)? what's going on (here)?, c) **in Berlin** events etc: what's

on in Berlin?, politically etc: what's going on in Berlin?; **da war (schwer) was ∼** a) things were really happening, b) the sparks were flying; **hier ist nichts (or nie was) ∼!** nothing doing (or no action) around here!; **wo ist hier was ∼?** where can you go around here?; **mit ihm ist nicht viel ∼** he isn't up to much. **4.** F **er hat (schwer) was ∼** he's very good (**in** dat at), he's on the ball.

los² int a) let's go!, b) go!: fig. **schieß ∼!** fire away!; sports: **Achtung, fertig, ∼!** ready, steady, go!; **nun aber ∼!** let's get going (or cracking)!; **nun mal ∼!** here goes!; **∼, sag schon!** come on, tell me!

Los n (-es; -e) **1.** a) lot, b) ticket, number: **ein ∼ ziehen** draw a lot (or ticket); **das große ∼ ziehen** win the first prize, fig. hit the jackpot; **mit j-m (et.) das große ∼ ziehen** strike it lucky with s.o. (s.th.); **et. durch das ∼ entscheiden** decide s.th. by drawing lots (or by a toss-up); **das ∼ fiel auf ihn zu** inf it fell upon him to inf. **2.** fig. lot, fate: **ein schweres ∼** a hard lot. **3.** ✝ lot.

'**lösbar** adj soluble (a. 🧪), solvable.

'**losbinden** v/t (irr, sep, -ge-, h, → binden) untie.

'**losbrechen** (irr, sep, -ge-, → brechen) **I** v/t (h) break off. **II** v/i (sn) storm etc: break, laughter etc: break out.

löschen¹ ['lœʃən] v/t (h) **1.** extinguish, put out (fire, light, etc): **den Durst ∼** quench one's thirst. **2.** ⚙ quench, slake (lime). **3.** blot (ink). **4.** strike off, cancel (a. mortgage), a. computer: delete, erase (a. tape recording etc), settle (debt), close (account). **5.** fig. efface.

'**löschen²** v/t (h) 🚢 unload.

'**Lösch|fahrzeug** n fire engine. **∼gerät** n fire extinguisher, coll. fire-fighting equipment. **∼kopf** m erasing head. **∼mannschaft** f fire brigade. **∼pa,pier** n blotting paper. **∼taste** f erase button, computer: cancel key.

lose ['lo:zə] adj a. fig. loose.

'**Lösegeld** n ransom.

'**loseisen: sich** (v/t j-n) ∼ (sep, -ge-, h) F get (s.o.) away (**von** from).

losen ['lo:zən] v/i (h) draw lots (or toss up) (**um** for).

lösen ['lø:zən] (h) **I** v/t **1.** remove, detach. **2.** a) undo (hair, tie, etc), b) a. 🏥 loosen, relax, c) release (brake etc). **3.**

fig. solve (*a.* ✍), answer (*question*), resolve, settle (*conflict etc*). **4.** *fig.* dissolve (*marriage etc*), break off (*engagement*), sever (*relations etc*), terminate (*contract*). **5.** buy, get (*ticket*). **6.** 🧪 dissolve. **II sich ~ 7.** a) come loos (*or* undone), b) come off, c) loosen (*a.* ⚽). **8. sich ~** (*von* from) free o.s., *a. sports:* break away. **9.** *problem etc:* solve itself, *conflict etc:* resolve itself. **10.** *tension etc:* ease; → **gelöst. 11.** 🧪 dissolve.

'losfahren *v/i* (*irr, sep,* -ge-, sn, → **fahren**) a) leave, b) drive off.

'losgehen *v/i* (*irr, sep,* -ge-, sn, → **gehen**). **1.** leave, *a.* rifle, *shot, etc:* go off. **2.** F start, begin: *gleich geht's los!* it's just about to begin!; *jetzt geht's los!* here goes!, here we go!; *es kann ~!* we're (*or* I'm *etc*) ready!; *jetzt geht's schon wieder los!* here we go again! **3.** F come off. **4. ~ auf** (*acc*) head (*or* make) for; *mit dem Messer auf j-n ~* go for s.o. with a knife.

'losheulen *v/i* (*sep,* -ge-, h) F burst into tears.

'losketten *v/t* (*sep,* -ge-, h) unchain.

'loskommen *v/i* (*irr, sep,* -ge-, sn, → **kommen**) *a. fig.* get away (*von* from).

'loslassen (*irr, sep,* -ge-, h, → **lassen**) **I** *v/t* **1.** let go of, let *s.o.* go, release: F *j-n auf die Menschheit ~* let s.o. loose on humanity; *das Buch läßt e-n nicht mehr los* the book is quite unputdownable; *der Gedanke läßt mich nicht (mehr) los* I can't get it out of my mind. **2.** let go with *a blow etc*, let off *fireworks*, launch (*protest etc*), let fly with *a letter etc*, crack (*joke etc*). **II** *v/i* **3.** let go: *nicht ~!* a. hang on!

'loslegen *v/i* (*sep,* -ge-, h) F **1.** get cracking. **2.** let fly (*gegen* at): *dann legte er los!* then he really got going; *leg schon los!* fire away!

'löslich *adj* 🧪 soluble.

'losmachen (*sep,* -ge-, h) **I** *v/t* **1.** untie, undo. **2.** ⚓ cast off. **II sich ~** *a. fig.* free o.s. (*von* from).

'losrasen *v/i* (*sep,* -ge-, sn) zoom off.

'losreißen: sich ~ (*irr, sep,* -ge-, h, → **reißen**) (*von* from) break away, *fig.* tear o.s. away.

'losrennen *v/i* (*irr, sep,* -ge-, sn, → **rennen**) dash off, run off.

'lossagen: sich ~ von (*sep,* -ge-, h) break with.

'losschlagen *v/i* (*irr, sep,* -ge-, h, → **schlagen**) ✕ strike.

'losschnallen *v/t* (*sep,* -ge-, h) unbuckle: ✈, *mot. sich ~* undo one's seat belt.

'lossteuern *v/i* (*sep,* -ge-, sn) **~ auf** (*acc*) *a. fig.* make (*or* head) for.

Losung¹ ['lo:zʊŋ] *f* (-; -en) ✕ password, *fig.* watchword, *pol. a.* slogan.

Losung² *f* (-; *no pl*) *hunt.* droppings.

Lösung *f* (-; -en) 🧪 *or fig.* solution.

Lösungsmittel *n* 🧪 solvent.

Lösungswort *n* answer.

'loswerden *v/t* (*irr, sep,* -ge-, sn, → **werden**) **1.** get rid of: *ich werde das Gefühl nicht los, daß ...* I can't help feeling that ...; *das mußte ich mal ~!* I had to get that off my chest! **2.** F a) lose, b) spend.

'losziehen *v/i* (*irr, sep,* -ge-, sn, → **ziehen**) **1.** set out, march off. **2.** *fig.* **gegen** lay into, let fly at.

Lot [lo:t] *n* (-[e]s; -e) **1.** ✍ (*ein ~ fällen* drop a) perpendicular: *aus dem ~* out of plumb; *fig. im ~ sein* be in good order; *et. wieder ins ~ bringen* set s.th. right again. **2.** ⚙ plumb (bob). **3.** ⚙ solder.

'loten ['lo:tən] *v/t, v/i* (h) plumb, sound.

'löten ['lø:tən] *v/t* (h) ⚙ solder.

Lotion [lo'tsi̯o:n] *f* (-; -en) lotion.

'Lötkolben *m* soldering iron. **'Lötlampe** *f* soldering lamp, *Am.* blowtorch. **'Lötnaht** *f* soldered joint.

'lotrecht *adj* perpendicular, vertical.

Lotse ['lo:tsə] *m* (-n; -n) ⚓ pilot.

lotsen ['lo:tsən] *v/t* (h) **1.** ⚓ pilot. **2.** F *j-n ~* a) guide s.o. (*durch* through), b) drag s.o. off (*in acc* to).

'Lotsendienst *m mot.* driver-guide service. **'Lotsengebühr** *f* ⚓ pilotage.

Lotterie [lɔtə'ri:] *f* (-; -n) lottery. **~gewinn** *m* (lottery) prize. **~los** *n* (lottery) ticket. **~spiel** *n* lottery, *fig.* gamble.

Lotto ['lɔto] *n* (-s; -s) **1.** lotto, bingo. **2.** Lotto, (West German numbers pool) lottery: *im ~ spielen* do Lotto.

'Lottoannahme(stelle) *f* Lotto ticket agency. **'Lottoschein** *m* Lotto ticket.

Löwe ['lø:və] *m* (-n; -n) **1.** *zo.* lion. **2.** *astr.* Leo: *er ist (ein) ~* he's (a) Leo.

'Löwen|anteil *m fig.* lion's share.

~mähne f fig. (thick) mane. **~maul** n (-[e]s; no pl) ⚘ snapdragon. **~zahn** m (-[e]s; no pl) ⚘ dandelion.

Löwin ['lø:vɪn] f (-; -nen) zo. lioness.

loyal [lŏa'jaːl] adj loyal.

Loyalität [lŏajali'tɛːt] f (-; no pl) loyalty.

Luchs [lʊks] m (-es; -e) zo. lynx: fig. **Augen haben** (**aufpassen**) **wie ein ~** have eyes (watch) like a hawk.

Lücke ['lʏkə] f (-; -n) gap, fig. a. loophole: fig. **e-e ~ schließen** fill a gap.

'Lückenbüßer(in f) m stopgap.

'lückenhaft adj 1. full of gaps, gappy. 2. fig. incomplete: **~es Wissen** a. sketchy knowledge.

'lückenlos adj 1. without gaps. 2. fig. complete, full, unbroken (line etc).

lud [luːt] pret of **laden¹** and **laden²**.

Luder ['luːdər] n (-s; -) F 1. (**gemeines**) **~** beast, bitch; (**ordinäres**) **~** hussy. 2. **armes ~** poor creature; **dummes ~** silly fool. 3. (**kleines**) **~** brat, (little) devil.

Luft [lʊft] f (-; ⸚e) 1. no pl air: **die ~ ablassen aus** deflate; F fig. **da war die ~ raus** all the steam was gone; **an die** (**frische**) **~ gehen**, F **~ schnappen** get some (fresh) air; F fig. **j-n an die** (**frische**) **~ setzen** chuck s.o. out, a. fire s.o.; fig. **sich in ~ auflösen** a) vanish into thin air, b) plan etc: go up in smoke; **j-n wie ~ behandeln** cut s.o. dead; (**völlig**) **aus der ~ gegriffen sein** be (totally) unfounded; **es liegt et. in der ~** there is s.th. in the wind; **die ~ ist rein** the coast is clear; F **es ist dicke ~** there is trouble brewing. 2. no pl breath: **die ~ anhalten** hold one's breath; F **halt** (**mal**) **die ~ an!** a) pipe down!, b) come off it!; **tief ~ holen** take a deep breath, fig. swallow hard; **nach ~ ringen** gasp for air; F **mir blieb die ~ weg** I was dumbfounded, vor **Schreck** I was breathless with shock. 3. sky, air: **in die ~ jagen**, **in die ~ fliegen** blow up; F fig. **in die ~ gehen** blow one's top, hit the roof; **das hängt** (**alles**) **noch in der ~** it's all (still) up in the air. 4. breeze. 5. no pl F space, room: **ich muß erst et. ~ schaffen** I must make some room first; fig. **sich** (or **s-m Herzen**, **Zorn** etc) **~ machen** let off steam.

'Luft|abwehr f air defen/ce (Am. -se). **~angriff** m air raid. **~bal,lon** m balloon. **~bild** n aerial view. **~bildkarte** f aerial map. **~blase** f air bubble.

'Luft-'Boden-... ✕ air-to-ground ...

'Luftbrücke f airlift.

'luftdicht adj (a. **~ machen**) airproof: **~ verschließen** airseal.

'Luftdruck m (-[e]s; no pl) meteor. atmospheric pressure, ⚙ air pressure.

'Luftdruck... ⚙ air-pressure.

'luftdurchlässig adj permeable to air.

lüften ['lʏftən] v/t (h) 1. (a. v/i) air, ventilate: **s-e Kleidung ~** give one's clothes an airing. 2. lift, raise. 3. fig. **ein Geheimnis ~** reveal (or disclose) a secret.

Lüfter ['lʏftər] m (-s; -) ⚙ a) ventilator, b) exhaustor, c) blower.

'Luft|fahrt f (-; no pl) aviation. **~fahrtgesellschaft** f airline. **~fahrtindu,strie** f aircraft industry. **~fahrzeug** n aircraft. **~feuchtigkeit** f (atmospheric) humidity. **~filter** n, m air filter. **~flotte** f air fleet. **~fracht** f airfreight. **~frachtbrief** m air waybill. ⚙**gekühlt** adj air-cooled. ⚙**getrocknet** adj air-dried. **~gewehr** n air gun. **~herrschaft** f (-; no pl) air supremacy. **~hoheit** f (-; no pl) air sovereignty. **~hülle** f atmosphere.

'luftig adj 1. airy, breezy: **in ~er Höhe** high up. 2. fig. flimsy, light (clothes).

'Luft|kammer f biol., ⚙ air chamber. **~kampf** m air combat. **~kissenfahrzeug** n air-cushion vehicle, hovercraft. **~korridor** m air corridor. ⚙**krank** adj airsick. **~kühlung** f air cooling. **~kurort** m climatic health resort. **~landetruppen** pl airborne troops. ⚙**leer** adj air-void: **~ machen** evacuate; **der Raum** vacuum. **~linie** f **100 km ~** 100 km as the crow flies. **~loch** n airhole, ✈ a. air pocket. **~mangel** m (-s; no pl) ✈ want of air. **~ma,tratze** f air mattress, air bed. **~pi,rat** m hijacker, skyjacker. **~pi,stole** f air pistol.

'Luftpost f (**mit** or **per ~** by) airmail. **~brief** m air letter. **~pa,ket** n air parcel.

'Luft|pumpe f air pump. **~raum** m air space. **~reinhaltung** f air-pollution control. **~rettungsdienst** m air rescue service. **~röhre** f anat. windpipe. **~sack** m ✈ windsock, mot. airbag. **~schiff** n airship, dirigible. **~schlauch** m air tube, mot. etc inner tube. **~schlösser** pl castles in the air. **~schraube** f ✈ airscrew.

'Luftschutz m air-raid precautions.

~**keller** m, ~**raum** m air-raid shelter.
~**übung** f air-raid drill.

'**Luft|spiegelung** f mirage. ~**sprung** m **vor Freude e-n** ~ **machen** jump for joy.
~**streitkräfte** pl air force. ~**strom** m,
~**strömung** f air current. ~**stützpunkt** m ✕ air base. ~**taxi** n air taxi.
~**trans,port** m air transport, airlift.

'**Lüftung** f (-; -en) ventilation.

'**Luftverkehr** m air traffic.

'**Luftverkehrs|gesellschaft** f airline
(company). ~**linie** f airline, airway.

'**Luft|verschmutzung** f air pollution.
~**verteidigung** f air defen|ce (Am. -se).
~**waffe** f ✕ air force. ~**weg** m 1. air
route: **auf dem** ~ **e** by air route. 2. pl anat.
respiratory tracts. ~**widerstand** m air
resistance, ✈, ⚙ a. drag. ~**zufuhr** f air
supply. ~**zug** m draught, Am. draft.

Lüge ['ly:gə] f (-; -n) lie: ~**n strafen** belie.

lügen ['ly:gən] v/i (log, gelogen, h) lie,
tell a lie (or lies): **das ist gelogen!**
that's a lie!

'**Lügen|de,tektor** m lie detector. ~**ge-
schichte** f cock-and-bull story.

Lügner ['ly:gnər] m (-s; -) liar.

'**lügnerisch** adj a) lying, b) untrue, false.

Luke ['lu:kə] f (-; -n) 1. hatch. 2. skylight.

lukrativ [lukra'ti:f] adj lucrative.

lukullisch [lu'kʊlɪʃ] adj sumptuous.

Lümmel ['lʏməl] m (-s; -) lout.

'**lümmelhaft** adj loutish.

lümmeln ['lʏməln] **sich** ~ (h) F sprawl.

Lump [lʊmp] m (-en; -en) scoundrel.

lumpen ['lʊmpən] v/t (h) F **sich nicht** ~
lassen come down handsomely.

'**Lumpen** m (-s; -) 1. rag. 2. pl rags.

'**lumpig** adj F fig. 1. shabby. 2. paltry,
measly (**ten dollars** etc).

Lunchpa,ket ['lanʃ-] n packed lunch.

Lunge ['lʊŋə] f (-; -n) 1. anat. lungs: ✿
eiserne ~ iron lung; **die grünen** ~**n e-r
Stadt** the lungs of a city. 2. gastr. lights.

'**Lungen...** pulmonary (**artery**, **embolism**, etc). ~**entzündung** f pneumonia.
~**flügel** m anat. lung. ~**heilstätte** f sanatorium, Am. sanitarium.

'**lungenkrank** adj ('**Lungenkranke** m, f
person) suffering from (a) lung disease.

'**Lungen|krankheit** f lung disease.
~**krebs** m ✿ lung cancer. ~**tuberku-
,lose** f pulmonary tuberculosis. ~**zug**
m **e-n** ~ **machen** inhale.

Lunte ['lʊntə] f (-; -n) fuse: F fig. ~ **riechen** smell a rat.

Lupe ['lu:pə] f (-; -n) magnifying glass: F
fig. **unter die** ~ **nehmen** scrutinize s.o.,
s.th. closely.

'**lupenrein** adj 1. flawless (**diamond**). 2. F
clean, perfectly honest.

Lupine [lu'pi:nə] f (-; -n) ⚘ lupine.

Lust [lʊst] f (-; ⸚e) 1. no pl a) inclination,
b) desire, c) interest: **hätten Sie** ~ **zu
kommen?** would you like to come?; **ich
hätte große** ~ **zu kommen** I'd love to
come; **ich habe** ~ **zu tanzen** I feel like
dancing; F **ich hätte** ~ **auf ein Bier** I feel
like a beer; **ich hätte nicht übel** ~ **zu** inf
I have half a mind to inf; **ich habe k-e** ~
(**dazu** or **darauf**) I don't feel like it, I'm
not in the mood (for it); **die** (or **alle**) ~
verlieren (**an** dat) lose all interest (in).
2. psych. a) pleasure, b) (sexual) desire
(or appetite, pleasure), contr. lust.

'**lustbetont** adj psych. hedonistic.

lüstern ['lʏstərn] adj 1. greedy (**nach**
for). 2. lecherous, lewd.

'**Lüsternheit** f (-; no pl) 1. greediness. 2.
lecherousness, lewdness.

'**Lustgefühl** n pleasurable sensation.

'**Lustgewinn** m psych. pleasure gain.

'**lustig** adj a) merry, cheerful, jolly, b)
funny, amusing: **er** (**es**) **ist sehr** ~ he
(it) is great fun; **sich** ~ **machen über**
(acc) make fun of; iro. **das kann ja** ~
werden! nice prospects!; F **sie unter-
hielten sich** ~ **weiter** they blithely went
on talking (regardless).

'**Lustigkeit** f (-; no pl) 1. gaiety, cheerfulness. 2. funniness, fun.

Lüstling ['lʏstlɪŋ] m (-s; -e) lecher.

'**lustlos** adj listless, ✦ a. slack.

'**Lust|molch** m F (old) lecher. ~**mord** m
sex murder. ~**mörder** m sex killer.
~**ob,jekt** n sex object. ~**schloß** n summer residence. ~**spiel** n thea. comedy.

lutschen ['lʊtʃən] v/t, v/i (h) suck (**an** dat
s.th.): → **Daumen**. '**Lutscher** m (-s; -)
1. lollipop. 2. F dummy, Am. pacifier.

Luv [lu:f] n (-s; no pl) ✦, '**Luvseite** f, '**luvwärts** adv ⚓ windward.

luxuriös [lʊksu'riø:s] adj luxurious.

Luxus ['lʊksʊs] m (-; no pl) a. fig. luxury.

'**Luxus...** luxury, de luxe. ~**ar,tikel** m
luxury (article), pl a. luxury goods.
~**ausführung** f de luxe model. ~**leben**
n life of luxury. ~**restau,rant** n first-

-class restaurant. **⁓wagen** m mot. luxury car.

'Lymphdrüse f anat. lymph gland.

Lymphe ['lymfə] f (-; -n) **1.** physiol. lymph. **2.** ⚕ vaccine.

'Lymphgefäß n anat. lymphatic (vessel).

'Lymphknoten m anat. lymph node.

lynchen ['lynçən] v/t (h) lynch.

'Lynchju̱stiz f (⁓ üben resort to) lynch law. **'Lynchmord** m lynching.

Lyrik ['ly:rɪk] f (-; no pl) **1.** poetry. **2.** lyricism. **'Lyriker** m (-s; -), **'Lyrikerin** f (-; -nen) (lyric) poet(ess), lyricist.

'lyrisch adj lyric, a. fig. lyrical.

M

M, m [ɛm] n (-; -) M, m.

Maat [ma:t] m (-[e]s; -e[n]) (ship's) mate.

'Machart f make, style, type.

'machbar adj practicable, possible.

Mache ['maxə] f (-; no pl) F **1.** make-believe, show. **2.** j-n in die ⁓ nehmen work s.o. over.

machen ['maxən] (h) **I** v/t **1.** make, a. prepare (dinner etc), a. do (one's homework etc), take (snapshot, examination, etc): **et. ⁓ aus** (dat) make s.th. of (or from); **aus dem Keller e-e Werkstatt ⁓** turn the cellar into a workshop; **aus j-m e-n Star ⁓** make a star of s.o.; **j-n zum Abteilungsleiter ⁓** make s.o. head of the department; → **gemacht. 2.** put in order, a. fix, repair, make (bed), do, tidy up (room). **3.** do: **was macht er?** a) what is he doing?, b) what does he do for a living?, c) how is he (getting on)?; **was machst du morgen?** what are you doing tomorrow?; **wird gemacht!** okay, I'll do it!, sl. will do!; **gut gemacht!** well done!; **mach's gut!** take care (of yourself)!; **das läßt sich ⁓** that can be done (or arranged); **so et. macht man nicht!** that isn't done!; **da ist nichts zu ⁓** nothing doing; **da(gegen) kann man nichts ⁓** it can't be helped; F **er wird es nicht mehr lange ⁓** he (the engine etc: it) won't last much longer; **der Wagen macht 160 km/h** the car does 100 mph. **4.** give (appetite, pleasure, etc): **das macht Durst** that makes you thirsty. **5.** j-n gesund ⁓ cure s.o.; **j-n glücklich ⁓** make s.o. happy. **6.** matter: **das macht nichts!** that doesn't matter!, never mind!; **das macht mir**

nichts I don't mind (contp. care). **7.** **sich et. (nichts) ⁓ aus** (dat) (not to) care about (gastr. for); **mach dir nichts daraus!** don't worry (about it)!; **ich mache mir nichts aus ihm** I don't care (much) for him. **8.** F be: **4 mal 5 macht 20** four times five is twenty; **was** (or **wieviel**) **macht das?** how much is that?; **das macht 10 Mark** that will be ten marks. **9.** F be, act as: **den Schiedsrichter ⁓** be (the) referee. **II sich ⁓ 10.** F come along (well), be getting on (well): **wie macht sich der Neue?** how is the new man coming along?; **die Sache macht sich** things are shaping up well; **das Bild macht sich gut dort** the picture looks nice there. **11. sich an e-e Sache ⁓** get down to (doing) s.th.; **sich an die Arbeit ⁓** get down to work. **III** v/i **12.** F **mach, daß du fortkommst!** off with you!, get lost!; **mach schnell!, mach schon!** hurry up!, get a move on! **13.** do: **laß ihn nur ⁓!** a) let him (do as he pleases)!, b) just leave it to him!; **das läßt sich ⁓** that can be done. **14.** F **er macht in Radios** he deals in (or sells) radios; **sie macht jetzt in moderner Kunst** she's into modern art now.

'Machenschaften pl machinations.

Macher ['maxər] m (-s; -) fig. doer.

Macho ['matʃo] m (-s; -s) F macho.

Macht [maxt] f (-; ⁓e) **1.** no pl power (über acc of), a. might, force: **mit aller ⁓** with all one's might; **die ⁓ der Gewohnheit** the force of habit; **die ⁓ ergreifen** seize power, take over; **an die ⁓ kommen** (or **gelangen**) come into power; **an der ⁓ sein** be in power; **es**

steht nicht in m-r ~ it is not within my power. **2.** *pol. etc* power.
'Machtbefugnis *f* power, authority.
'Machtbereich *m* sphere of influence.
'Machtergreifung *f* seizure of power.
'machtgierig *adj* power-hungry.
'Machthaber [-ha:bər] *m* (-s; -) ruler.
mächtig ['mɛçtɪç] **I** *adj* powerful, mighty (*both a.* blow, *voice, etc*), *a.* enormous. **II** *adv* F tremendously, awfully: ~ **ge-wachsen sein** have grown a lot.
'Machtkampf *m* power struggle.
'machtlos *adj* powerless, helpless.
'Machtpoli,tik *f* power politics.
'Machtübernahme *f* assumption of power, takeover. **'machtvoll** *adj a. fig.* powerful. **'Machtwechsel** *m* transition of power. **'Machtwort** *n ein* ~ *sprechen* put one's foot down.
'Machwerk *n* concoction, F lousy job.
Macke ['makə] *f* (-; -n) F kink: **e-e** ~ **haben** a) be nuts, b) ⊙ be acting up.
Mädchen ['mɛːtçən] *n* (-s; -) **1.** girl. **2.** maid: *fig.* ~ *für alles* dogsbody. **'mäd-chenhaft** *adj* girlish. **'Mädchenname** *m* **1.** girl's name. **2.** maiden name.
Made ['maːdə] *f* (-; -n) maggot, worm: F *wie die* ~ *im Speck leben* be in clover.
Mädel ['mɛːdəl] *n* (-s; -s) F girl(ie).
madig ['maːdɪç] *adj* maggoty, worm-eat-en: F ~ *machen* knock (*s.o., s.th.*); *j-m et.* ~ *machen* spoil s.th. for s.o.
Madonna [ma'dɔna] *f* (-; -en) Madonna.
Maf(f)ia ['mafia] *f* (-; -s) *a.* F *fig.* mafia.
Mafioso [ma'fio:zo] *m* (-[s]; -si) mafioso.
Magazin [maga'tsi:n] *n* (-s; -e) **1.** depot (*a.* ✕), warehouse. **2.** *phot.*, ⊙ maga-zine (*a. of gun etc*). **3.** *print.* magazine.
Magd [ma:kt] *f* (-; -ᵉe) maid.
Magen ['maːgən] *m* (-s; -ᵉ) stomach: *auf nüchternen* (*or leeren*) ~ on an empty stomach; *j-m schwer im* ~ *liegen* lie heavily on s.o.'s stomach, F *fig.* worry s.o. terribly; *sich den* ~ *verderben* up-set one's stomach. ~*beschwerden* *pl* stomach trouble. ~*bitter* *m* gastr. bit-ters. ~*geschwür* *n* (stomach) ulcer. ~*grube* *f* pit of the stomach. ⊉*krank adj* ~ *sein* suffer from a stomach com-plaint. ~*krebs* *m* ♣ stomach cancer. ~*leiden* *n* gastric complaint. ~*säure* *f* ♣ gastric acid.
'Magenschleimhaut *f* stomach lining. ~*entzündung* *f* gastritis.

'Magenschmerzen *pl* stomach-ache.
'Magenverstimmung *f* indigestion.
mager ['maːgər] *adj* **1.** lean (*a. fig.*), *a.* thin, *a.* low-fat: ~*e Kost a. fig.* slender fare. **2.** *fig.* meag/re (*Am.* -er), poor. **3.** *print.* light-faced.
'Magermilch *f* skimmed milk.
'Magerquark *m* low-fat curd cheese.
'Magersucht *f* (-; *no pl*) ♣ anorexia.
Magie [ma'gi:] *f* (-; *no pl*) magic.
Magier ['maːgiər] *m* (-s; -) magician.
magisch ['maːgɪʃ] *adj* magic(al).
Magister [ma'gɪstər] *m* (-s; -) *univ.* Master (*Artium* of Arts, *abbr.* M.A.).
Magistrat [magɪs'tra:t] *m* (-[e]s; -e) town council.
Magnat [ma'gna:t] *m* (-en; -en) mag-nate, tycoon.
Magnesium [ma'gne:ziʊm] *n* (-s; *no pl*) ♣ magnesium.
Magnet [ma'gne:t] *m* (-en; -e) magnet.
Ma'gnet... magnetic (*field, needle, etc*).
ma'gnetisch *adj* magnetic: *fig. j-n* ~ *an-ziehen* have a magnetic effect on s.o.
magnetisieren [magneti'zi:rən] *v/t* (h) magnetize. **Magnetismus** [magne'tɪs-mʊs] *m* (-; *no pl*) magnetism.
Ma'gnetkarte *f* magnetic card.
Ma'gnetzündung *f* magneto ignition.
mähen[1] ['mɛːən] *v/t*, *v/i* (h) mow, cut.
mähen[2] *v/i* (h) *sheep:* bleat.
mahlen ['maːlən] *v/t*, *v/i* (h) grind.
Mahlzeit ['maːltsait] *f* (-; -en) meal: F (*na dann*) *prost* ~! good night!
'Mähma,schine *f* reaper.
'Mahnbescheid *m* (court) order to pay.
Mähne ['mɛːnə] *f* (-; -n) mane.
mahnen ['maːnən] *v/t* (h) **1.** admonish, urge (*j-n zur Vorsicht etc* s.o. to be careful *etc*). **2.** a) *fig.* remind (*an acc, wegen etc*), b) ✝ send *s.o.* a reminder.
'Mahnmal *n* memorial.
'Mahnschreiben *n* (-s; -) ✝ reminder.
'Mahnung *f* (-; -en) **1.** admonition, warning. **2.** ✝ reminder.
'Mahnwache *f pol.* protest vigil.
Mai [mai] *m* (-[e]s; *no pl*) (*im* ~ in) May: *der Erste* ~ May Day.
'Mai|baum *m* maypole. ~*feier* *f* May Day celebrations. ~*glöckchen* *n* ♣ lily of the valley. ~*käfer* *m* cockchafer.
Mais [mais] *m* (-es; -e) maize, *Am.* corn.

Mais|flocken pl cornflakes. **~kolben** m (corn)cob, gastr. corn on the cob. **~mehl** n Indian (Am. corn) meal.

Maison(n)ette [mɛzɔ'nɛt] f (-; -s) maison(n)ette, Am. duplex.

Majestät [majɛs'tɛːt] f (-; no pl) a. fig. majesty: **Seine ~** His Majesty.

maje'stätisch adj majestic.

Major [ma'joːr] m (-s; -e) ✕ major.

Majoran ['maːjoraːn] m (-s; -e) ♀ marjoram.

makaber [ma'kaːbər] adj macab|re (Am. -er).

Makel ['maːkəl] m (-s; -) a. fig. flaw.

'makellos adj immaculate, perfect.

mäkeln ['mɛːkəln] v/i (h) carp (**an** dat at).

Makkaroni [maka'roːni] pl macaroni.

Makler ['maːklər] m (-s; -) **1.** (stock)broker. **2.** (Am. real) estate agent.

Makrele [ma'kreːlə] f (-; -n) mackerel.

Makro... ['maːkro-], **'makro...** macro...

Makrone [ma'kroːnə] f (-; -n) macaroon.

mal [maːl] adv **1.** times, multiplied by: **der Raum ist 6 ~ 4 Meter** the room is six metres by four. **2.** F → **einmal.**

Mal[1] n (-[e]s; -e) **1.** a) mark, sign, b) spot; → **Muttermal** etc. **2.** baseball etc: base, rugby: in-goal.

Mal[2] n (-[e]s; -e) time: **dieses ~** this time; **dieses eine ~** this once; **ein anderes ~** some other time; **das erste ~, beim ersten ~** the first time; **zum letzten ~** for the last time; **das nächste ~** the next time; **mit einem ~** all of a sudden; **ein für alle ~** once and for all; **von ~ zu ~ besser** better every time.

Malaria [ma'laːria] f (-; no pl) ✚ malaria.

malen ['maːlən] (h) **I** v/t paint (a. fig.), portray: **et. zu schwarz ~** paint too black a picture of s.th. **II** sich **~** fig. be reflected (in s.o.'s face etc).

'Maler m (-s; -) painter, artist. **Male'rei** f (-; -en) painting. **'Malerin** f (-; -nen) (woman) painter, artist. **'malerisch** adj **1.** picturesque. **2.** artistic (talent).

maliziös [mali'tsiøːs] adj malicious.

'malnehmen v/t (irr, sep, -ge-, h, → **nehmen**) ✕ multiply (**mit** by).

Malve ['malvə] f (-; -n) ♀ mallow.

Malz [malts] n (-es; no pl) malt.

'Malzbier n malt beer.

'Malzeichen n ✕ multiplication sign.

Malzkaf|fee m malt coffee.

Mama ['mama] f (-; -s) F mummy, mum, Am. mom.

Mammographie [mamogra'fiː] f (-; -n) ✚ mammography.

Mammon ['mamɔn] m (-s; no pl) contp. mammon: **schnöder ~** filthy lucre.

Mammut ['mamʊt] n (-s; -s) mammoth.

man [man] indef pron **1.** one, you, we: **~ kann nie wissen** you never can tell; **~ muß es tun** it must be done; **~ nehme** take. **2.** they, people: **~ hat mir gesagt** I have been told; **~ sagt** people say; **~ holte ihn** he was fetched.

managen ['mɛnidʒən] v/t (h) F manage.

'Manager m (-s; -) manager.

'Managerkrankheit f stress disease.

manch [manç] indef pron many a: **~ eine(r)** many (people); **in ~em hat er recht** he's right about some things; **so ~er (~es)** a good many people (things).

'manche pl some, quite a few.

'mancherlei adj a) various, many, a number of, b) a number of things.

'manchmal adv sometimes.

Mandant [man'dant] m (-en; -en), **Man'dantin** f (-; -nen) ⚖ client.

Mandarine [manda'riːnə] f (-; -n) ♀ tangerine.

Mandat [man'daːt] n (-[e]s; -e) ⚖, parl., pol. mandate, of lawyer: brief: parl. **sein ~ niederlegen** resign one's seat.

Mandel ['mandəl] f (-; -n) **1.** ♀ almond. **2.** anat. tonsil. **~baum** m almond (tree). **~entzündung** f ✚ tonsillitis.

Mandoline [mando'liːnə] f (-; -n) ♪ mandolin(e).

Manege [ma'neːʒə] f (-; -n) (circus) ring.

Mangan [maŋ'gaːn] n (-s; no pl) 🜍 manganese.

Mangel[1] ['maŋəl] f (-; -n) mangle: F **in die ~ nehmen** put s.o. through the mill.

Mangel[2] m (-s; ⸗) **1.** a) defect, fault, flaw, b) drawback. **2.** (an dat) shortage, lack, scarcity (all: of), deficiency (in): **aus ~ an ~** mangels. **~beruf** m understaffed occupation. **~erscheinung** f ✚ deficiency symptom.

'mangelhaft adj a) faulty, defective, b) insufficient, inadequate, deficient, unsatisfactory (a. ped.), poor.

Mängelhaftung ['mɛŋəl-] f ✚ responsibility for defects.

mangeln[1] ['maŋəln] v/t (h) press.

'mangeln[2] v/i, v/impers (h) be wanting,

be lacking: **es mangelt an** (*dat*) there is a lack (*or* want, shortage) of; **es mangelt mir an Geld** *etc* I am short of money *etc*; **es mangelt ihm an** (*or* **der**) **Mut** he lacks courage; **ihr ~des Selbstvertrauen** her lack of self-confidence.

'Mängelrüge *f* ✝ notice of defects.

'mangels *prep* (*gen*) for lack (*or* want) of: **~ Beweisen** for lack of evidence.

'Mangelware *f* scarce commodity: **~ sein** *a.* F *fig.* be in short supply.

Manie [ma'niː] *f* (-; -n) mania.

Manier [ma'niːr] *f* (-; -en) **1.** *no pl* manner, way (of doing *s.th.*), *art:* style. **2.** *pl* manners. **ma'nierlich** *adj* a) well-mannered, b) good, well-behaved: **sich ~ benehmen** behave o.s., be good.

Manifest [mani'fɛst] *n* (-[e]s; -e) *pol.* manifesto. **manifestieren** [manifɛs-'tiːrən] *v/t* (h) manifest.

Maniküre [mani'kyːrə] *f* (-; -n) **1.** *no pl* manicure. **2.** manicurist.

mani'küren *v/t, v/i* (h) manicure.

Manipulation [manipula'tsjoːn] *f* (-; -en) manipulation. **manipulieren** [manipu'liːrən] *v/t* (h) manipulate.

manisch ['maːnɪʃ] *adj psych.* manic. **~-depres'siv** *adj* manic-depressive.

Manko ['maŋko] *n* (-s; -s) **1.** ✝ a) deficiency, b) deficit. **2.** *fig.* shortcoming.

Mann [man] *m* (-[e]s; "er) a) man, b) husband: **100 ~** a hundred men; F **der kleine ~** the man in the street; **ein ~ von Welt** a man of the world; **ein Gespräch von ~ zu ~** a man-to-man talk; **wie ein ~** as one man; **bis auf den letzten ~** to a man; **ein Kampf ~ gegen ~** a hand-to-hand fight; **s-n ~ stehen** stand one's ground; ⚓ **alle ~ an Deck!** all hands on deck!; **mit ~ und Maus sinken** go down with all hands (on board); F **an den ~ bringen** get rid of (*goods, a joke, etc*); **den starken ~ markieren** throw one's weight about; **ein ~, ein Wort!** a promise is a promise; F **10 Mark pro ~** 10 marks per head; **wir gingen alle ~ (hoch) hin** all of us went; F (**mein lieber**) **~!** (oh) boy!, wow!

Männchen ['mɛnçən] *n* (-s; -) **1.** little man, manikin: **~ malen** doodle. **2.** *zo.* male, cock: F **~ machen** sit up and beg.

Mannequin ['manəkɛ̃] *n* (-s; -s) mannequin, model.

Männer ['mɛnər] *pl of* **Mann**: **~** on WC: Men, Gentlemen. **'Männer...** man's, men's ... **'Männerchor** *m* male(-voice) choir. **'männerfeindlich** *adj* hostile towards men.

'Mannesalter *n* manhood: **im besten ~** in the prime of life.

'mannhaft *adj* manly, *a.* brave.

mannigfach ['manɪçfax], **'mannigfaltig** *adj* diverse, manifold.

'männlich ['mɛnlɪç] *adj* **1.** *biol.*, ⚥, ⚙ male. **2.** manly, masculine (*a. ling.*), mannish. **'Männlichkeit** *f* (-; *no pl*) masculinity, manliness, virility.

'Mannsbild *n* F man, fellow.

'Mannschaft *f* (-; -en) *sports:* team, ✈, ⚓, ✕ crew, ✕ detail, (*rescue etc*) party: ✕ **die ~en** the ranks.

'Mannschafts|aufstellung *f sports:* line-up. **~führer** (*in f*) *m sports:* (team) captain. **~geist** *m* (-[e]s; *no pl*) team spirit. **~kapi,tän** *m sports:* (team) captain. **~sport** *m* team sport. **~wagen** *m* a) ✕ personnel carrier, b) police van. **~wertung** *f sports:* team classification. **~wettbewerb** *m* team event.

'mannshoch *adj and adv* head-high.

'Mannstoll *adj* F *contr.* man-crazy.

'Mannweib *n contp.* mannish woman.

Manometer [mano'meːtər] *n* (-s; -) pressure ga(u)ge.

Manöver [ma'nøːvər] *n* (-s; -) **1.** *a. fig.* manoeuvre, *Am.* maneuver. **2.** ✕ manoeuvres, *Am.* maneuvers, exercise. **Ma'növerkri,tik** *f fig.* post-mortem.

manövrieren [manø'vriːrən] *v/i* (h) *a. fig.* manoeuvre, *Am.* maneuver. **manö'vrierunfähig** *adj* disabled.

Mansarde [man'zardə] *f* (-; -n) attic room.

Mansch [manʃ] *m* (-es; *no pl*) F **1.** slush. **2.** *contp.* mush. **manschen** ['manʃən] *v/i* (h) F mess about.

Manschette [man'ʃɛtə] *f* (-; -n) **1.** cuff: F **~n bekommen** get the wind up; **~n haben vor** be scared stiff of. **2.** ⚙ sleeve. **Man'schettenknopf** *m* cuff-link.

Mantel ['mantəl] *m* (-s; ") **1.** coat, cloak: *fig.* **den ~ nach dem Wind hängen** trim one's sails to the wind. **2.** ⚙ casing.

'Mantelta,rif(vertrag) *m* collective agreement (on working conditions).

manuell [ma'nŭɛl] *adj* manual.

Manuskript [manu'skrɪpt] *n* (-[e]s; -e) manuscript, *film:* script, *print.* copy.

Mappe ['mapə] f (-; -n) a) briefcase, b) schoolbag, c) folder, file, d) portfolio.
Marathon ['ma:raton] m (-s; -s), **'Marathonlauf** m marathon (race).
Märchen ['mɛ:rçən] n (-s; -) fairytale, *fig.* (tall) story, yarn.
'Märchenbuch n book of fairytales.
'märchenhaft adj magical, fairytale ..., F *fig.* fantastic.
'Märchen|land n, **∼welt** f fairyland.
Marder ['mardər] m (-s; -) *zo.* marten.
Margarine [marga'ri:nə] f (-; -n) margarine.
Marienbild [ma'ri:ən-] n Madonna.
Ma'rienkäfer m *zo.* ladybird.
Marihuana [mari'hua:na] n (-s; *no pl*) marijuana, *sl.* pot.
Marinade [mari'na:də] f (-; -n) *gastr.* marinade.
Marine [ma'ri:nə] f (-; -n) a) merchant navy, b) navy.
Ma'rine|blau n, **⚲blau** adj navy blue.
∼offi‚zier m naval officer. **∼sol‚dat** m marine. **∼stützpunkt** m naval base.
marinieren [mari'ni:rən] v/t (h) *gastr.* marinade.
Marionette [mario'nɛtə] f (-; -n) *a. fig.* marionette, puppet.
Mario'netten|re‚gierung f *fig.* puppet government. **∼spiel** n puppet show. **∼the‚ater** n puppet theat/re (*Am.* -er).
Mark¹ [mark] n (-[e]s; *no pl*) marrow, *fig. a.* core: **j-m durch ∼ und Bein gehen** set s.o.'s teeth on edge; **j-n bis ins ∼ treffen** cut s.o. to the quick.
Mark² f (-; -) mark ∼ten marks; F **jede ∼ umdrehen** count every penny.
Mark³ f (-; -en) *hist.* march.
markant [mar'kant] adj striking, prominent: **∼e Persönlichkeit** outstanding personality.
Marke ['markə] f (-; -n) 1. ✝ make, type, brand. 2. mark, sign, *computer:* flag, label. 3. a) voucher, b) coupon, c) stamp; → **Dienstmarke, Essenmarke, Spielmarke** etc. 4. F character.
'Marken|ar‚tikel m ✝ proprietary article. **∼ben‚zin** n brand name petrol (*Am.* gasoline). **∼butter** f best quality butter. **∼fabri‚kat** n proprietary make. **∼name** m trade (*or* brand) name. **∼zeichen** n trademark.
'markerschütternd adj bloodcurdling.
markieren [mar'ki:rən] v/t (h) 1. a)

mark (*a. fig.*), b) accentuate, underline. 2. act, play: → **Mann**. 3. *sports:* mark (*player*), score (*goal*).
Mar'kierung f (-; -en) mark(ing).
'markig adj *fig.* pithy.
Markise [mar'ki:zə] f (-; -n) sunblind, awning.
'Markstein m *fig.* milestone.
Markt [markt] m (-[e]s; ∼e) 1. market: **auf dem ∼** in (*or* on) the market; *et.* **auf den ∼ bringen** market s.th. 2. marketplace.
∼ana‚lyse f market analysis. **∼anteil** m share of the market. **∼bericht** m market report. **∼entwicklung** f market trend. **∼forscher** m market researcher. **∼forschung** f market research. **∼führer** m market leader. **⚲gängig** adj a) marketable, b) current (*price*). **∼halle** f covered market. **∼lücke** f opening: **in e-e ∼ stoßen** fill a gap in the market. **∼platz** m marketplace.
'marktschreierisch adj *fig.* loud.
'Markt|stand m (market) stall. **∼studie** f market analysis. **∼wert** m market value. **∼wirtschaft** f market economy: **freie ∼** a. free enterprise; **soziale ∼** social market economy.
Marmelade [marmə'la:də] f (-; -n) jam.
Marme'ladenglas n jam jar.
Marmor ['marmor] m (-s; -e), **marmorieren** [marmo'ri:rən] v/t (h) marble.
Marokkaner [marɔ'ka:nər] m (-s; -), **Marok'kanerin** f (-; -nen), **marok'kanisch** adj Moroccan. **Marokko** [ma'rɔko] n (-s) Morocco.
Marone [ma'ro:nə] f (-; -n) ⚘ (sweet) chestnut.
Marotte [ma'rɔtə] f (-; -n) quirk.
Mars [mars] m (-; *no pl*) Mars.
'Marsmensch m Martian.
marsch [marʃ] int 1. ✕ (**vorwärts ∼!** forward) march! 2. F **∼!** get a move on!
Marsch¹ m (-[e]s; ∼e) ✕ march (*a.* ♪): **sich in ∼ setzen** move off.
Marsch² f (-; -en) *geol.* marsh.
'Marschbefehl m ✕ marching orders.
'Marschflugkörper m ✕ cruise missile.
'Marschgepäck n ✕ field kit.
marschieren [mar'ʃi:rən] v/i (sn) (*a.* ∼ lassen) march.
'Marsch|mu‚sik f military marches. **∼ordnung** f ✕ march formation. **∼route** f 1. ✕ route. 2. *fig.* strategy. **∼verpflegung** f ✕ marching rations.

Marstall ['mar-] *m* royal stables.
Marter ['martər] *f* (-; -n) torture, *fig. a.* ordeal. **'martern** *v/t* (h) torture, *fig. a.* torment. **'Marterpfahl** *m* stake.
Martinshorn ['marti:ns-] *n* F (police, ambulance *or* fire-engine) siren.
Märtyrer ['mɛrtyrər] *m* (-s; -) martyr: *iro.* **sich zum ~ machen** make a martyr of o.s. **Martyrium** [mar'ty:riʊm] *n* (-s; -rien) martyrdom.
Marxismus [mar'ksɪsmʊs] *m* (-; *no pl*) Marxism. **Marxist** [mar'ksɪst] *m* (-en; -en), **mar'xistisch** *adj* Marxist.
März [mɛrts] *m* (-[es]; *no pl*) (*im* ~ in) March.
Marzipan [martsi'pa:n] *n* (-s; -e) marzipan.
Masche ['maʃə] *f* (-; -n) **1.** a) stitch, b) mesh: *durch die* ~*n des Gesetzes schlüpfen* find a loophole in the law. F a) trick, ploy, b) fad, craze.
'Maschendraht *m* wire netting.
Maschine [ma'ʃi:nə] *f* (-; -n) **1.** a) machine, b) F engine. **2.** plane, jetliner. **3.** F motorcycle. **4.** typewriter: *mit der* ~ *schreiben* type. **5.** sewing machine. **6.** washing machine.
maschinell [maʃi'nɛl] **I** *adj* machine ..., mechanical. **II** *adv* machine-..., by machine: ~ *bearbeiten* machine; ~ *hergestellt* machine-made.
Ma'schinen|bau *m* (-[e]s; *no pl*) mechanical engineering. ~**bauer** *m* (-s; -), ~**bauingeni,eur** *m* mechanical engineer. ~**befehl** *m computer:* machine--code instruction. ~**fa,brik** *f* engineering works. **2geschrieben** *adj* typewritten, typed. ~**gewehr** *n* machine-gun. ~**park** *m* machinery. ~**pi,stole** *f* submachine-gun. ~**raum** *m* engine-room. ~**schaden** *m* mechanical breakdown, ⚓, *mot.* engine trouble. ~**schlosser** *m* engine fitter. ~**schreiben** *n* (-s) typewriting, typing. ~**schrift** *f* typescript. **2waschbar** *adj* machine-washable.
Maschinerie [maʃinə'ri:] *f* (-; -n) a) machinery, b) mechanism.
ma'schineschreiben *v/i* (*schrieb Maschine, hat maschinegeschrieben*) type.
Maschinist [maʃi'nɪst] *m* (-en; -en) machinist, machine operator, ⚓ engine driver, *Am.* engineer.
Maser ['ma:zər] *f* (-; -n) *wood etc:* vein.

Masern ['ma:zərn] *pl* ⚕ measles.
'Maserung *f* (-; -en) *of wood:* grain.
Maske ['maskə] *f* (-; -n) mask (*a.* ⚕, *computer*, *phot., a. person*), *thea.* make--up, *fig. a.* guise: *in der* ~ (*gen*) under the guise of; *fig. die* ~ *fallen lassen* show one's true face.
'Maskenball *m* fancy-dress ball.
'Maskenbildner [-bɪldnər] *m* (-s; -) make-up artist.
'maskenhaft *adj* mask-like.
'Maskenko,stüm *n* fancy dress.
Maskerade [maskə'ra:də] *f* (-; -n) *a. fig.* masquerade.
maskieren [mas'ki:rən] (h) **I** *v/t* **1.** *j-n* ~ a) mask s.o., b) dress s.o. up. **2.** *a.* ⊚ conceal. **II** *sich* ~ a) dress up, disguise o.s., b) put on a mask. **mas'kiert** *adj* masked. **Mas'kierung** *f* (-; -en) a) disguise, b) mask.
Maskottchen [mas'kɔtçən] *n* (-s; -) mascot.
maskulin [masku'li:n] *adj,* **Maskulinum** [-'li:nʊm] *n* (-s; -na) *ling.* masculine.
Masochismus [mazo'xɪsmʊs] *m* (-; *no pl*) masochism. **Masochist** [-'xɪst] *m* (-en; -en) masochist. **maso'chistisch** *adj* masochistic.
maß [ma:s] *pret of* **messen.**
Maß¹ *n* (-es; -e) **1.** measure: ~*e und Gewichte* weights and measures; *mit zweierlei* ~ *messen* apply double standards; *das* ~ *überschreiten* overshoot the mark. **2.** *pl* measurements, *of room etc: a.* dimensions: *bei j-m* ~ *nehmen* take s.o.'s measurements; *nach* ~ (*angefertigt*) made-to-measure (→ *a.* *maßgeschneidert*). **3.** *fig.* degree, extent: *ein gewisses* (*hohes*) ~ *an* (*dat*) a certain degree (a high measure) of; *in hohem* ~*e* to a high degree, highly; *in höchstem* ~*e* extremely; *in gleichem* ~*e* to the same extent, equally; *in zunehmendem* ~*e* increasingly; *in dem* ~*e, wie* ... as ... (accordingly); *über alle* ~*en* exceedingly. **4.** moderation: *in* ~*en* a) *mit* ~ *und Ziel* with moderation, b) to some extent; *ohne* ~ *und Ziel* immoderately; → *maßhalten.*
Maß² *f* (-; -e) a) litre (*Am.* liter) of beer, b) → *Maßkrug.*
Massage [ma'sa:ʒə] *f* (-; -n) massage.
Massaker [ma'sa:kər] *n* (-s; -), **massa-**

krieren [masa'kri:rən] v/t (h) massacre, slaughter.

'**Maßanzug** m tailor-made (Am. custom-made) suit.

'**Maßarbeit** f fig. precision work.

'**Maßband** n (-[e]s, ⁀er) tape measure.

Masse ['masə] f (-; -n) **1.** mass (a. phys.), a. substance, gastr. mixture, ⚒ compound. **2.** F **e-e ~ (von), ~n von** masses (or lots, loads) of; **e-e ~ Geld** loads of money. **3.** bulk, majority. **4.** crowd: **die (breite) ~** a. contp. the masses. **5.** ⚕ estate, assets. **6.** ⚡ (a. **an ~ legen**) earth, Am. ground.

'**Maßeinheit** f unit of measure(ment).

'**Massen...** mass (demonstration, production, tourism, etc). **~abfertigung** f a. contp. mass processing. **~andrang** m huge crowd, F terrible crush. **~arbeitslosigkeit** f mass unemployment. **~ar,tikel** m ⚒ mass-produced article. **~entlassungen** pl mass dismissals. **~erzeugung** f, **~fabrikati,on** f, **~fertigung** f mass production. **~flucht** f mass exodus, stampede. **~grab** n mass grave. **~güter** pl bulk goods.

'**massenhaft** adv F masses (or lots, heaps) of: **sich ~ vermehren** multiply in large numbers.

'**Massen,karambo,lage** f mot. (multiple) pile-up. **~medium** n mass medium (pl media). **~mensch** m mass man. **~mord** m mass murder. **~mörder** m mass murderer. **~psy,chose** f mass hysteria. **~quar,tier** n mass accommodation. **~schläge,rei** f F free-for-all. **~sport** m popular sport. **~sterben** n widespread deaths (zo. dying-off). **~veranstaltung** f mass meeting.

Masseur [ma'sø:r] m (-s; -e) masseur.

Mas'seurin f (-; -nen) masseuse.

Masseuse [ma'sø:zə] f (-; -n) esp. sex: masseuse.

'**Maßgabe** f nach ~ (gen) in accordance with; **mit der ~, daß ...** provided that ...

'**maßgebend** adj **1.** decisive, authoritative (opinion etc), leading, prominent (personality etc): **das ist (für mich) nicht ~** that's no criterion (for me); **s-e Meinung ist nicht ~** his opinion does not count (here). **2.** a) competent, b) standard, definitive (book etc).

maßgeblich ['ma:sge:pliç] adj decisive: **~en Anteil haben** (or **~ beteiligt sein**)

an (dat) play a decisive role in, be instrumental in; **~e Kreise** influential circles.

'**maßgerecht** adj true-to-size.

'**maßgeschneidert** adj tailor-made (a. fig.), made-to-measure, Am. custom-made.

'**maßhalten** v/i (irr, sep, -ge-, h, → **halten**) be moderate.

massieren [ma'si:rən] v/t (h) massage.

mas'sieren² v/t (a. **sich ~**) (h) mass, concentrate.

massig ['masiç] adj massive, bulky.

mäßig ['mɛ:siç] **I** adj **1.** moderate, a. temperate. **2.** mediocre, (rather) poor, F (fair to) middling. **II** adv **3.** moderately, in moderation. **mäßigen** ['mɛ:siɡən] (h) **I** v/t moderate, a. curb, control (one's rage etc); → **gemäßigt**. **II sich ~** restrain (or control) o.s.; **sich beim Trinken** etc ~ cut down on drinks etc.

'**Mäßigung** f (-; no pl) moderation.

massiv [ma'si:f] adj **1.** solid (gold, wood, etc). **2.** fig. massive (threat, attack, etc): F **~ werden** cut up rough.

Mas'siv n (-s, -e) geol. massif. **~bau(weise** f) m △ massive construction.

'**Maßkrug** m beer mug, stein.

'**maßlos I** adj immoderate, excessive (demands etc). **II** adv immoderately (etc): **~ übertrieben** grossly exaggerated; **~ eifersüchtig** extremely jealous.

'**Maßlosigkeit** f (-; no pl) immoderateness, lack of restraint, excess.

'**Maßnahme** [-na:mə] f (-; -n) measure.

'**maßregeln** v/t (insep, ge-, h) (wegen for) a) reprimand, b) punish, discipline, sports: penalize.

'**Maßregelung** f (-; -en) a) reprimand, b) disciplinary action, sports: penalty.

'**Maßschneider** m bespoke (Am. custom) tailor.

'**Maßstab** m **1.** scale: **im ~ 1:10** on a scale of 1:10; **im verkleinerten (vergrößerten) ~** on a reduced (an enlarged) scale; **in großem ~** a. fig. large-scale. **2.** fig. standard, yardstick: **hohe Maßstäbe anlegen** apply strict standards (**an** acc to); **das ist kein ~** that's no criterion.

'**maßstabgerecht** adj (true) to scale.

'**maßvoll** adj a) moderate, reasonable, b) restrained.

Mast¹ [mast] m (-[e]s; -e[n]) a) ⚓ mast, b) ⚡ pylon, c) pole.

Mast² *f* (-; -en) ⚓ **1.** fattening. **2.** mast.
'**Mastdarm** *m* anat. rectum.
mästen ['mɛstən] (h) **I** *v/t* fatten. **II** *sich* ~ gorge o.s. (*an dat* on).
Masturbation [mastʊrba'tsĭoːn] *f* (-; -en) masturbation. **masturbieren** [mastʊr'biːrən] *v/i* (h) masturbate.
'**Mastvieh** *n* fat stock.
Match [mɛtʃ] *n, a. m* -[e]s; -s, -e) match, game. **~ball** *m tennis*: match point.
Material [mate'rĭaːl] *n* (-s; -ien) material (*a. fig.*), ◎ *coll.* materials.
Materi'alfehler *m* material defect.
Materialismus [materĭa'lɪsmʊs] *m* (-; *no pl*) materialism. **Materialist** [materĭa'lɪst] *m* (-en; -en) materialist.
materia'listisch *adj* materialist(ic).
Materi'alkosten *pl* cost of materials.
Materi'alprüfung *f* material test(ing).
Materie [ma'teːrĭə] *f* (-; -n) **1.** *no pl a. phys.* matter. **2.** *fig.* subject (matter).
materiell [mate'rĭɛl] *adj* **1.** material. **2.** → *materialistisch*. **3.** financial.
Mathe ['matə] *f* (-; *no pl*) F maths, *Am.* math. **Mathematik** [matema'tiːk] *f* (-; *no pl*) mathematics. **Mathematiker** [mate'maːtikər] *m* (-s; -) mathematician. **mathematisch** [mate'maːtɪʃ] *adj* mathematical.
Matinee [mati'neː] *f* (-; -n) *thea.* morning performance.
Matjeshering ['matjəs-] *m gastr.* young salted herring.
Matratze [ma'tratsə] *f* (-; -n) mattress.
Mätresse [mɛ'trɛsə] *f* (-; -n) mistress.
Matriarchat [matrĭar'çaːt] *n* (-[e]s; -e) matriarchate.
Matrize [ma'triːtsə] *f* (-; -n) **1.** (*a. auf ~ schreiben*) stencil. **2.** *print.* matrix. **3.** ◎ a) die, b) stencil.
Matrose [ma'troːzə] *m* (-n; -n) sailor, seaman.
Matsch [matʃ] *m* (-[e]s; *no pl*) F a) mush, b) mud, c) slush. '**matschig** *adj* F **1.** muddy, slushy. **2.** *fruit etc*: mushy.
matt [mat] *adj* **1.** dull (*shine, colour, eyes, etc*), *a. phot.* mat(t), frosted (*glass*), opal (*bulb*), dim (*light*). **2.** faint, weak, feeble (*a. fig. voice, applause, etc*), exhausted. **3.** ♟ slack. **4.** (check)mate.
Matte ['matə] *f* (-; -n) mat.
'**Mattglas** *n* frosted glass.
mattieren [ma'tiːrən] *v/t* (h) a) mat(t), b) frost (*glass*).

Mattigkeit ['matɪç-] *f* (-; *no pl*) fatigue.
'**Mattscheibe** *f* **1.** *phot.* focus(s)ing screen. **2.** a) *TV* screen, b) F telly, *Am.* tube. **3.** F ~ *haben* have a blackout.
Mätzchen ['mɛtsçən] *pl* F **1.** nonsense. **2.** tricks: *k-e ~!* none of your tricks!
Mauer ['maʊər] *f* (-; -n) wall: *hist. die (Berliner)* ~ the (Berlin) Wall.
'**Mauerblümchen** *n* F *fig.* wallflower.
mauern ['maʊərn] (h) **I** *v/i* **1.** build a wall *etc*, lay bricks. **2.** F *cards*: stonewall, *sports*: shut up shop. **II** *v/t* build.
'**Mauer|stein** *m* (building) brick. **~werk** *n* (-[e]s; *no pl*) masonry, brickwork.
Maul [maʊl] *n* (-[e]s; ≠er) **1.** zo. mouth, jaws. **2.** V trap (*sl.*): *das ~ aufreißen* brag; *halt's ~!* shut up!
maulen ['maʊlən] *v/i* (h) F grumble.
'**Maulesel** *m* mule. '**Maulheld** *m* F braggart. '**Maulkorb** *m* (*a. dat e-n ~ anlegen*) muzzle (*a. fig.*). '**Maultier** *n* mule.
'**Maul- und 'Klauenseuche** *f vet.* foot-and-mouth disease.
'**Maulwurf** *m* (-[e]s; ≠e) zo. mole.
'**Maulwurfshügel** *m* molehill.
Maurer ['maʊrər] *m* (-s; -) bricklayer.
'**Maurerkelle** *f* trowel.
'**Maurermeister** *m* master mason.
maurisch ['maʊrɪʃ] *adj* Moorish.
Maus [maʊs] *f* (-; ≠e) mouse: *humor. weiße ~* traffic policeman; F *graue ~* nondescript person; → *Katze, Mäuse*.
mäuschenstill ['mɔysçən-] *adj* a) (as) quiet as a mouse, b) stockstill: *es war ~* not a sound was to be heard.
Mäuse ['mɔyzə] *pl* **1.** mice: F *weiße ~ sehen* see pink elephants. **2.** F lolly, *Am.* bread.
'**Mausefalle** *f* **1.** mousetrap. **2.** *fig.* deathtrap. '**Mauseloch** *n* mousehole.
mausern ['maʊzərn] *v/i* (*a. sich ~*) (h) moult: F *fig. sich ~ zu* develop into.
'**mause'tot** *adj* F stone-dead.
Mausoleum [maʊzo'leːʊm] *n* (-s; -leen) mausoleum.
Maut [maʊt] *f* (-; -en) toll. '**Mautstraße** *f* toll road, *Am.* turnpike (road). '**Mautstelle** *f* tollhouse, *Am.* turnpike.
maximal [maksi'maːl] **I** *adj* maximum. **II** *adv* maximally, at (the) most.
Maxime [ma'ksiːmə] *f* (-; -n) maxim.
Maximum ['maksimʊm] *n* (-s; -xima) maximum.

Mayonnaise [majɔˈnɛːzə] f (-; -n) gastr. mayonnaise.

Mäzen [mɛˈtseːn] m (-s; -e) patron, sponsor.

Mechanik [meˈçaːnɪk] f (-; -en) **1.** no pl mechanics. **2.** mechanism. **Mechaniker** [meˈçaːnikər] m (-s; -) mechanic. **mechanisch** [meˈçaːnɪʃ] adj mechanical, fig. a. automatic. **mechanisieren** [meçaniˈziːrən] v/t (h) mechanize. **Mechaniˈsierung** f (-; -en) mechanization. **Mechanismus** [meçaˈnɪsmʊs] m (-; -men) mechanism.

Meckerer [ˈmɛkərər] m (-s; -) F grumbler. **meckern** [ˈmɛkərn] v/i (h) **1.** zo. bleat. **2.** F grumble (über acc about).

Medaille [meˈdaljə] f (-; -n) medal; → **Kehrseite.**

Meˈdaillengewinner(in f) m sports: medal(l)ist.

Medaillon [medalˈjõː] n (-s; -s) **1.** art, gastr. medallion. **2.** locket.

Medien [ˈmeːdi̯ən] pl media.

ˈMedienforschung f media research.

ˈMedienverbund m multimedia system.

Medikament [medikaˈment] n (-[e]s; -e) drug, medicament.

Mediothek [medi̯oˈteːk] f (-; -en) media library.

Meditation [meditaˈtsi̯oːn] f (-; -en) meditation.

meditieren [mediˈtiːrən] v/i (h) meditate (über acc on).

Medium [ˈmeːdi̯ʊm] n (-s; -ien) medium.

Medizin [mediˈtsiːn] f (-; -en) **1.** no pl medicine: **Doktor der** ~ doctor of medicine (abbr. M.D.). **2.** medicine, medicament.

Mediˈziner m (-s; -) **1.** medical student, F medic. **2.** physician, doctor.

mediˈzinisch adj a) medical, b) medicinal. ~**technische Assiˈstentin** (abbr. MTA) medical laboratory assistant.

Mediˈzinmann m (-[e]s; ~er) medicine man.

Meer [meːr] n (-[e]s; -e) sea (a. fig.), ocean: **das offene** ~ the high seas; **am** ~ by the sea, a. holidays etc at the seaside.

ˈMeer|busen m gulf. ~**enge** f strait(s).

ˈMeeres|arm m arm of the sea, inlet. ~**biolo**\gie f marine biology. ~**boden** m → **Meeresgrund.** ~**früchte** pl seafood. ~**grund** m seafloor, bottom of the sea. ~**kunde** f (-; no pl) oceanography.

~**spiegel** m (**über dem** ~ above) sea level.

ˈMeerrettich m (-s; -e) ♀ horseradish.

ˈMeersalz n sea salt.

ˈMeerschweinchen n zo. guinea pig.

ˈMeerwasser n sea water.

Mega... [mega-] mega (ton, volt, etc). **Megaˈhertz** n megahertz, megacycle.

Megaphon [megaˈfoːn] n (-s; -e) megaphone.

Mehl [meːl] n (-[e]s; -e) flour. **ˈmehlig** adj mealy. **ˈMehlspeise** f **1.** farinaceous food. **2.** Austrian sweet dish.

mehr [meːr] **I** indef pron more: ~ **als 50 Autos** more than (or over) 50 cars; **und dergleichen** ~ and the like; (**immer**) ~ **und** ~ more and more; **was willst du noch** ~? what more do you want? **II** adj more: ~ **und** ~ (or **immer** ~) **Leute** more and more people. **III** adv more: **um so** ~, **nur noch** ~ all the more; **um so** ~ (**als**) all the more (as); **nicht** ~ a) no more, b) no longer, not any longer; **nie** ~ never again; **ich habe keins** (or **keine**) ~ I haven't got any more; **ich habe nichts** ~ I've got nothing left; **kein Wort** ~ (**davon**)! not another word (about it)!; **ich kann nicht** ~! a) I'm finished!, b) I couldn't eat another thing!; **er ist** ~ **praktisch veranlagt** he is more of a practical man.

Mehr n (-[s]; no pl) **ein** ~ **an Zeit** (**Erfahrung** etc) more time (experience etc).

ˈMehrarbeit f (-; no pl) **1.** extra work. **2.** overtime. **ˈMehraufwand** m extra (or additional) cost(s), time, etc. **ˈMehrausgaben** pl additional expenditure.

ˈmehrbändig [-bɛndɪç] adj in several volumes.

ˈMehrbedarf m extra (or increased) demand. **ˈMehrbelastung** f additional load (fig. burden). **ˈMehrbetrag** m **1.** surplus. **2.** extra charge.

ˈmehrdeutig [-dɔytɪç] adj ambiguous.

ˈMehreinkommen n additional revenue.

mehren [ˈmeːrən] v/t (a. **sich** ~) (h) increase.

mehrere [ˈmeːrərə] adj or indef pron several.

ˈmehrfach I adj a) several, b) repeated, c) esp. ◎ etc multiple: ~**e Verletzungen** multiple injuries; **in** ~**er Hinsicht** in several respects; ~**er deutscher Mei-**

ster several times German champion. **II** adv a) several times, b) repeatedly: **ein Mehrfaches der Summe** several times the amount; **er ist ~ vorbestraft** he has several previous convictions.

'**Mehrfachstecker** m multiple plug.

'**Mehrfa,milienhaus** n multiple dwelling. '**Mehrgepäck** n excess luggage. '**Mehrgewicht** n excess weight.

'**Mehrheit** f (-; -en) majority: **mit absoluter (einfacher, knapper, großer) ~** by an absolute (a simple, a narrow, a large) majority; **mit zehn Stimmen ~** by a majority of ten; → **schweigend.**

'**mehrheitlich** adj and adv (by the) majority.

'**Mehrheits|beschluß** m majority decision. **~beteiligung** f ✝ controlling interest. **~wahlrecht** n majority vote system.

'**mehrjährig** [-jɛ:rɪç] adj of (or lasting) several years, several years' ...

'**Mehrkosten** pl a) additional (or extra) cost(s), b) extra charge.

'**mehrmalig** [-ma:lɪç] adj repeated.

'**mehrmals** adv several times.

'**Mehrpar,teiensy,stem** n multiparty system.

'**mehrseitig** [-zaıtıç] adj **1.** ✚ polygonal. **2.** pol. multilateral.

'**mehrsilbig** [-zɪlbıç] adj polysyllabic.

'**mehrsprachig** [-ʃpra:xıç] adj polyglot, multilingual.

'**mehrstellig** [-ʃtɛlıç] adj multidigit.

'**mehrstimmig** [-ʃtımıç] adj polyphonic, for several voices: **~er Gesang** part singing.

'**mehrstöckig** [-ʃtœkıç] adj multistor(e)y.

'**mehrstündig** [-ʃtyndıç] adj of (or lasting) several hours.

'**mehrtägig** [-tɛ:gıç] adj of (or lasting) several days.

'**mehrteilig** [-taılıç] adj consisting of several parts, film etc: in several parts.

'**Mehrverbrauch** m increased consumption. '**Mehrwertsteuer** f value-added tax (abbr. VAT). '**Mehrzahl** f (-; no pl) **1.** majority. **2.** ling. plural.

'**Mehrzweck...** multipurpose ...

meiden ['maıdən] v/t (mied, gemieden, h) avoid.

Meile ['maılə] f (-; -n) mile.

'**Meilenstein** m a. fig. milestone.

'**meilenweit** adv for miles (and miles): **~ entfernt von** a. fig. miles (away) from.

mein [maın] pos pron my: **~er, ~e, ~(e)s, der (die, das) Mein(ig)e** mine; **die Mein(ig)en** my family, F my people, my folks; **ich habe das Mein(ig)e getan** I've done my share (or bit).

'**Meineid** m (e-n ~ leisten commit) perjury. '**meineidig** adj perjured: **~ werden** perjure o.s., commit perjury.

meinen ['maınən] v/i (h) **1.** think, believe: **was ~ Sie dazu?** what do you think?; **~ Sie (wirklich)?** do you (really) think so? **2.** mean: **wie ~ Sie das?** a) how do you mean?, b) what do you mean by that?; **~ Sie das ernst?** do you really mean it?; **so war es nicht gemeint** I (he etc) didn't mean it (like that); **sie meint es gut** she means well (**mit dir** by you); **es war gut gemeint** it was well-meant; **er hat es nicht Böse gemeint** he meant no harm. **3.** refer to, mean: **~ Sie ihn?** do you mean him? **4.** mean, signify. **5.** **wenn du meinst** if you say so; **wie Sie ~** as you wish; **ich meine ja nur!** it was just a thought!

meiner ['maınər] pers pron (gen of **ich**) (of) me: **erinnern Sie sich ~?** do you remember me? '**meinerseits** [-zaıts] adv for my part: **ich ~** I for one; **ganz ~** a) the pleasure is (or has been) mine, b) humor. same here!

'**meines|gleichen** indef pron people like me, F the likes of me.

meinet'wegen ['maınət-] adv **1.** a) on my account, because of me, b) for my sake. **2.** **~ kann er gehen** I don't mind if he goes, iro. he can go for all I care. **3.** let's say.

meinige ['maınıgə] → **mein.**

'**Meinung** f (-; -en) opinion (**über** acc of, about, on): **e-e schlechte ~ haben von** have a low opinion of; **m-r ~ nach** in my opinion; **der ~ sein** think, believe, be of the opinion; **derselben (anderer) ~ sein** (dis)agree; **ganz m-r ~!** I quite agree!; F **j-m gehörig die ~ sagen** give s.o. a piece of one's mind; → **geteilt.**

'**Meinungs|äußerung** f expression of one's opinion, statement. **~austausch** m exchange of views (**über** acc on). **♀bildend** adj opinion-forming. **~bildung** f forming of an opinion: **öffentliche ~** forming of public opinion. **~for-**

scher *m* pollster. **~forschung** *f* opinion research. **~freiheit** *f* (-; *no pl*) freedom of opinion (*or* speech). **~führer** *m* opinion-leader. **~umfrage** *f* (public) opinion poll. **~umschwung** *m* swing of opinion. **~verschiedenheit** *f* **1.** difference of opinion. **2.** disagreement, argument (*über acc* about).

Meise ['maɪzə] *f* (-; -n) **1.** tit(mouse). **2.** F *du hast wohl 'ne ~?* you must be nuts!

Meißel ['maɪsəl] *m* (-s; -) chisel.

meißeln ['maɪsəln] *v/t, v/i* (h) chisel.

Meißner ['maɪsnər] **~ Porzellan** Dresden china.

meist [maɪst] **I** *adj* **1.** most, most of: *die ~en Leute* most people; *die ~e Zeit* most of the time. **II** *indef pron* **2.** *das ~e* (*davon*) most of it; *die ~en* **a)** most (of them), **b)** most people. **III** *adv* **3.** → *meistens*. **4.** *am ~en* most.

'meistbietend *adj* **~er Interessent** highest bidder: **~ verkaufen** sell to the highest bidder.

meistens ['maɪstəns], **'meistenteils** *adv* mostly, usually, most of the time.

Meister ['maɪstər] *m* (-s; -) **1.** master (craftsman): *s-n ~ machen* take one's master craftsman's diploma. **2.** foreman. **3.** *a. fig. or iro.* master: → *Übung* **1.** **4.** *sports:* champion(s). **'Meisterbrief** *m* master craftsman's diploma.

'meisterhaft **I** *adj* masterly. **II** *adv* brilliantly: *iro.* *es ~ verstehen zu lügen etc* be an expert liar *etc*.

'Meisterin *f* (-; -nen) **1.** master craftswoman. **2.** forewoman. **3.** master's wife. **4.** → *Meister* 3, 4.

'Meisterleistung *f* masterly performance, great feat.

meistern ['maɪstərn] *v/t* (h) master.

'Meisterprüfung *f* examination for the master craftsman's diploma.

'Meisterschaft *f* (-; -en) **1.** *no pl* mastery. **2.** *sports:* championship, *a.* title.

'Meisterstück *n* fig. masterstroke.

'Meisterwerk *n* masterpiece.

Melancholie [melaŋkoˈliː] *f* (-; -n) melancholy. **melancholisch** [melaŋˈkoːlɪʃ] *adj* melancholy.

Melanom [melaˈnoːm] *n* (-s; -e) ℳ melanoma.

melden ['mɛldən] (h) **I** *v/t* **1.** **a)** report, register (*birth etc*), **b)** announce: *j-m et. ~* notify s.o. of s.th.; F *er hat nichts zu ~*

he has no say (in the matter), *w.s.* he has no chance (*gegen j-n* against s.o.). **2.** *sports:* enter. **II** *sich* **~ 3.** report (*bei* to, *zur Arbeit* for work): *sich polizeilich ~* register with the police; → *krank.* **4.** get in touch (*bei* with): *sich freiwillig ~* volunteer (*zu* for); *ich werde mich* (*wieder*) *~* I'll be in touch; *wenn du et. brauchst, melde dich!* if you need anything, let me know!; *sich auf ein Inserat ~* answer an advertisement. **5.** answer (the phone): *es meldet sich niemand* there is no reply. *~ ped.* put up one's hand. **7.** *sports:* enter (one's name) (*für* for). **8.** *fig.* make itself felt.

'Meldepflicht *f* obligatory registration, ℱ duty of notification.

'meldepflichtig *adj* subject to registration, ℱ notifiable.

'Meldung *f* (-; -en) **1.** report, *a.* news (item), announcement, notification, (*radio etc*) message. **2.** registration (*bei* with). **3.** (*zu* for) application, *for exam etc, a. sports:* entry.

melken ['mɛlkən] *v/t, v/i* (melkte/molk, gemelkt/gemolken, h) *a. fig.* milk.

'Melkmaˌschine *f* milking machine.

Melodie [meloˈdiː] *f* (-; -n) melody, tune.

melodiös [meloˈdiøːs], **melodisch** [meˈloːdɪʃ] *adj* melodic.

Melodrama [meloˈdraːma] *n* (-s; -en) *a.* F *fig.* melodrama. **melodraˈmatisch** *adj a.* F *fig.* melodramatic.

Melone [meˈloːnə] *f* (-; -n) ℛ melon.

Membran [mɛmˈbraːn] *f* (-; -en) *anat.* membrane, *a.* ⚙ diaphragm.

Memoiren [meˈmoaːrən] *pl* memoirs.

Memorandum [memoˈrandʊm] *n* (-s; -den, -da) memorandum.

Menge ['mɛŋə] *f* (-; -n) **1.** quantity, amount, Å set: *e-e* (*große*) *~ von* a lot of, F lots of; *e-e ~ Bücher* a great many books; F *jede ~ Geld, Geld in rauhen ~n* heaps of money. **2.** crowd.

mengen ['mɛŋən] (h) **I** *v/t* mix (*in acc* into). **II** *sich* **~** → *mischen* II.

'Mengenangabe *f* (indication of) quantity. **'Mengenlehre** *f* (-; *no pl*) Å set theory. **'mengenmäßig** *adj* quantitative. **'Mengenˌrabatt** *m* ♰ bulk (*or* quantity) discount.

Meniskus [meˈnɪskʊs] *m* (-; -ken) *anat.* meniscus.

Mensa ['mɛnza] f (-; -s, Mensen) (university) canteen.

Mensch [mɛnʃ] m (-en; -en) **1.** human being: *der ~* man; *ich bin auch nur ein ~!* I'm only human! **2.** → *Menschheit.* **3.** person, man (woman): *kein ~* not a soul, nobody; *(die) ~en* people; *gern unter ~en sein* enjoy human company; F *~!* → *Menschenkind.*

Mensch, ärgere dich nicht! n ludo.

'**Menschen|affe** m ape. **~alter** n **1.** generation. **2.** lifetime. **~feind** m misanthropist. **~fresser** m **1.** cannibal. **2.** zo. man-eater. **~freund** m philanthropist. **~gedenken** n *seit ~* within living memory. **~gestalt** f *in ~* in human form; *ein Teufel in ~* a devil incarnate. **~hand** f *von ~ geschaffen* man-made. **~handel** m slave trade. **~haß** m misanthropy. **~kenner** m good judge of character. **~kenntnis** f (-; *no pl*) knowledge of human nature. **~leben** n **1.** (human) life: *~ sind nicht zu beklagen* there were no fatalities. **2.** lifetime. **2leer** adj deserted. **~menge** f crowd (of people). **2möglich** adj *das ~e* everything that is humanly possible. **~raub** m kidnapping. **~rechte** pl human rights. **2scheu** adj shy, unsociable. **~schlag** m (-[e]s; *no pl*) breed (of people). **~seele** f **1.** human soul. **2.** *k-e ~* not a living soul.

'**Menschenkind** int a) good heavens!, b) for heaven's sake!

'**menschenunwürdig** adj a) degrading, b) *dwelling etc*: unfit for human beings.

'**Menschenverstand** m *gesunder ~* common sense.

'**Menschenwürde** f *the* dignity of man.

'**Menschheit** *die ~* (-; *no pl*) mankind.

'**menschlich** adj **1.** human: *die ~e Natur* human nature; *nach ~em Ermessen* as far as one can possibly judge. **2.** humane. **3.** F tolerable.

'**Menschlichkeit** f (-; *no pl*) humaneness, humanity: *Verbrechen gegen die ~* crime against humanity.

Menstruation [mɛnstruaˈtsɪoːn] f (-; -en) 🌶 menstruation. **menstruieren** [mɛnstruˈiːrən] v/i (h) 🌶 menstruate.

Mentalität [mɛntaliˈtɛːt] f (-; -en) mentality.

Menthol [mɛnˈtoːl] n (-s; *no pl*) 🌿 menthol: *mit ~* mentholated.

Menü [meˈnyː] n (-s; -s) **1.** *gastr.* set meal,

set lunch. **2.** *computer*: menu.

Menuett [meˈnuɛt] n (-[e]s; -e) ♪ minuet.

Meridian [meriˈdiaːn] m (-s; -e) *astr.*, *geogr.* meridian.

'**Merkblatt** n leaflet.

merken ['mɛrkən] v/t (h) **1.** a) notice, b) feel, sense, c) realize, note, d) discover: *et. ~ a.* become aware of s.th.; *man merkte an s-r Stimme, daß* you could tell by his voice that. **2.** *~ lassen* show, let on. **3.** *sich ~* a) remember, b) make a mental note of; *merk dir das!* remember say that.

'**merklich I** adj a) noticeable, b) marked, c) considerable. **II** adv noticeably (*etc*).

'**Merkmal** n (-[e]s; -e) characteristic: *besondere ~e* distinguishing marks.

Merkur [mɛrˈkuːr] m (-s; *no pl*) *astr.* Mercury.

'**merkwürdig** adj strange, odd. '**merkwürdigerweise** adv oddly enough.

'**Meßband** n (-[e]s; ~er) tape measure.

'**meßbar** adj measurable.

'**Meßbecher** m measuring cup.

'**Meßdiener** m *eccl.* server.

Messe¹ ['mɛsə] f (-; -n) *eccl.* mass: *(die) ~ lesen* say Mass.

'**Messe²** f (-; -n) ✕ mess.

'**Messe³** f (-; -n) (trade) fair.

'**Messe|besucher(in** f) m visitor to a (*or* the) fair. **~gelände** n exhibition cent/re (*Am.* -er). **~halle** f exhibition hall.

messen ['mɛsən] (maß, gemessen, h) **I** v/t measure, ⊙ *a.* ga(u)ge: *die Zeit ~* time; *j-n mit Blicken ~* size s.o. up. **II** *sich mit j-m ~* match o.s. against s.o., *sports:* compete with s.o.; *sich nicht ~ können mit* a) *j-m* be no match for s.o., b) *e-r Sache* not to stand comparison with s.th. **III** v/i measure, be ... long (*or* high, wide, *etc*), *person:* be ... (tall).

Messer ['mɛsər] n (-s; -) knife, 🔪 *a.* scalpel, ⊙ *a.* blade: *Kampf bis aufs ~* fight to the death; *auf (des) ~s Schneide stehen* be on a razor's edge; F *j-n ans ~ liefern* betray s.o.

'**messerscharf** adj *a.* fig. razor-sharp.

'**Messerspitze** f knife point: *e-e ~ Salz* a pinch of salt.

Messersteche'rei f (-; -en) knifing.

'**Messerstich** m **1.** stab. **2.** stab wound.

'**Messestand** m exhibition stand.

'**Meßgerät** n measuring instrument.

'**Meßglas** n graduated measuring glass.

Messias [mɛˈsiːas] m (-; no pl) Messiah.

Messing [ˈmɛsɪŋ] n (-s; no pl) brass.

'**Meßinstru,ment** → **Meßgerät.**

'**Meßuhr** f meter, dial ga(u)ge.

'**Meßtischblatt** n ordnance map.

'**Messung** f (-; -en) measurement.

Metall [meˈtal] n (-s; -e) metal.

Me'tall|arbeiter m metalworker. **~in-du,strie** f metalworking industry.

me'tallisch adj metal, a. fig. metallic.

Metallurgie [metalʊrˈgiː] f (-; no pl) metallurgy. **metallurgisch** [metaˈlʊrgɪʃ] adj metallurgic(al).

Me'tall|verarbeitung f metal processing. **~waren** pl metal goods, hardware.

Metamorphose [metamɔrˈfoːzə] f (-; -n) metamorphosis.

Metapher [meˈtafər] f (-; -n) metaphor.

Metaphy'sik [meta-] f metaphysics.

meta'physisch adj metaphysical.

Metastase [metaˈstaːzə] f (-; -n) 🗡 metastasis.

Meteor [meteˈoːr] m (-s; -e) meteor.

Meteorit [meteoˈriːt] m (-s; -e) meteorite.

Meteorologe [meteoroˈloːgə] m (-n; -n) meteorologist. **Meteorologie** [meteoroloˈgiː] f (-; no pl) meteorology.

meteoro'logisch adj meteorological.

Meter [ˈmeːtər] n, m (-s; -) metre, Am. meter. '**meterlang** adj very long.

'**Meterware** f yard goods.

Methode [meˈtoːdə] f (-; -n) method.

Methodik [meˈtoːdɪk] f (-; -en) 1. no pl methodology. 2. method(s).

me'thodisch adj methodical.

Methylalkohol [meˈtyːl-] m (-s; no pl) methyl alcohol.

Metier [meˈtie̯ː] n (-s; -s) profession, job.

Metrik [ˈmeːtrɪk] f (-; -en) metre, Am. meter. **metrisch** [ˈmeːtrɪʃ] adj 1. metric. 2. ♪ etc metrical.

Metropole [metroˈpoːlə] f (-; -n) metropolis.

Metzger [ˈmɛtsgər] m (-s; -) butcher.

Metzge'rei f (-; -en) butcher's shop.

Meute [ˈmɔɪtə] f (-; -n) 1. hunt. pack (of hounds). 2. F mob.

Meute'rei f (-; -en) mutiny. '**Meuterer** m (-s; -) mutineer. **meutern** [ˈmɔɪtərn] v/i (h) a) mutiny, b) F rebel. '**meuternd** adj mutinous.

Mexikaner [mɛksiˈkaːnər] m (-s; -), **Mexi'kanerin** f (-; -nen), **mexi'ka-**

nisch [-nɪʃ] adj Mexican. **Mexiko** [ˈmɛksiko] n (-s) Mexico.

miau [miˈaʊ] int, **mi'auen** v/i (h) miaow.

mich [mɪç] I pers pron me. II reflex pron myself.

mick(e)rig [ˈmɪk(ə)rɪç] adj F 1. measly (pay etc). 2. puny, sickly.

mied [miːt] pret of **meiden.**

Mieder [ˈmiːdər] n (-s; -) bodice. '**Miederhöschen** n panty girdle.

'**Miederwaren** pl foundation garments.

Mief [miːf] m (-[e]s; no pl) F fug, pong.

Miene [ˈmiːnə] f (-; -n) expression, face: überlegene ~ superior air; e-e ernste ~ aufsetzen look serious; gute ~ zum bösen Spiel machen put on a brave face, grin and bear it; ~ machen, et. zu tun make as if to do s.th.; ohne e-e ~ zu verziehen without batting an eyelid. '**Mienenspiel** n facial expressions.

mies [miːs] F I adj bad, lousy: ~e Laune haben be in a foul mood; j-n (et.) ~ machen run s.o. (s.th.) down; ~er Kerl bastard; ~e Sache awful mess. II adv sich ~ fühlen feel lousy; es geht ihm ~ he's in a bad way.

Miesepeter [ˈmiːzəpeːtər] m (-s; -) F sourpuss.

Miesmuschel [ˈmiːs-] f zo. mussel.

Miete [ˈmiːtə] f (-; -n) rent: zur ~ wohnen live in a rented flat.

'**Mieteinnahme** f rental income.

mieten [ˈmiːtən] v/t (h) rent, a. hire (car).

Mieter [ˈmiːtər] m (-s; -), '**Mieterin** f (-; -nen) tenant. '**Mieterschutz** m (legal) protection of tenants.

'**mietfrei** adj rent-free.

'**Miet|gebühr** f rental (charge). **~kauf** m hire purchase. **~preis** m rent.

'**Mietshaus** n block of flats, Am. apartment house.

'**Miet|verhältnis** n tenancy. **~vertrag** m ๅ) lease, b) hire contract. **~wagen** m hʌre(d) car. **~wohnung** f (rented) flat, Am. apartment.

Migräne [miˈgrɛːnə] f (-; -n) 🗡 migraine.

Mikro [ˈmiːkro] n (-s; -s) F mike.

Mikrobe [miˈkroːbə] f (-; -n) microbe.

Mikroche'mie [mikro-] f microchemistry. **Mikrochirur'gie** f microsurgery.

Mikrocom,puter [ˈmiːkro-] m microcomputer. '**Mikroelek,tronik** f microelectronics. '**Mikrofilm** m microfilm.

Mikro'kosmos m microcosm.

Mikroorga'nismus *m* microorganism.

Mikrophon [mikro'fo:n] *n* (-s; -e) microphone.

'**Mikropro,zessor** *m* microprocessor.

Mikroskop [mikro'sko:p] *n* (-s; -e) microscope. **mikro'skopisch** *adj* (*a.* ~ **klein**) microscopic(al).

'**Mikrowelle** *f* microwave.

'**Mikrowellenherd** *m* microwave oven.

Milbe ['milbə] *f* (-; -n) *zo.* mite.

Milch [milç] *f* (-; *no pl*) **1.** (**dicke** *or* **saure** ~ curdled) milk. **2.** *zo.* (soft) roe.

'**Milch|bar** *f* milk bar. ~**brei** *m* milk pudding. ~**flasche** *f* milk bottle. ~**geschäft** *n* dairy. ~**glas** *n* ☉ frosted glass.

'**milchig** *adj* milky.

'**Milch|kaf,fee** *m* white coffee. ~**kännchen** *n* milk jug. ~**kanne** *f* milk can. ~**kuh** *f* milcher. ~**mädchenrechnung** *F* naive reasoning. ~**mixgetränk** *n* milk shake. ~**pro,dukte** *pl* dairy products. ~**pulver** *n* powdered milk. ~**reis** *m* rice pudding. ~**schorf** *m* ☧ milk crust. ~**straße** *f* Milky Way. ~**wirtschaft** *f* dairy farming. ~**zahn** *m* milk tooth.

mild [milt] *adj* mild, *a.* gentle (*climate, reproof, etc*), *a.* lenient (*judge, penalty, etc*), *a.* light (*food*), soft (*light*): **~e gesagt** to put it mildly; **et. ~e beurteilen** take a lenient view of s.th.

Milde ['mildə] *f* (-; *no pl*) **1.** mildness (*etc*, → **mild**). **2.** leniency.

mildern ['mildərn] (h) **I** *v/t* soften (*blow, contrast, etc*), ease (*pain etc*), soothe, alleviate (*a.* grief *etc*), moderate (*one's views etc*), mitigate (*sentence etc*), reduce (*effect*): ☧ **~de Umstände** extenuating circumstances. **II** *sich* ~ grow milder, *pain:* ease, *views etc:* soften.

'**Milderung** *f* (-; *no pl*) alleviation, mitigation, moderation. '**Milderungsgrund** *m* ☧ extenuating circumstance.

Milieu [mi'liø:] *n* (-s; -s) environment (*a. biol.*, 🐟), *a.* (social) background.

mili'eubedingt *adj* due to environmental factors.

mili'eugeschädigt *adj* deprived.

militant [mili'tant] *adj* militant.

Militär [mili'tɛ:r] *n* (-s; *no pl*) **1.** (**beim** ~ in the) armed forces (*or* army). **2.** military personnel, soldiers. ~**arzt** *m* medical officer. ~**atta,ché** *m* military attaché. ~**dikta,tur** *f* military dictatorship.

mili'tärisch *adj* **1.** military. **2.** martial.

Militarismus [milita'rismʊs] *m* (-; *no pl*) militarism. **Militarist** [milita'rist] *m* (-en; -en) militarist. **milita'ristisch** *adj* militaristic.

Mili'tär|ka,pelle *f* military band. ~**mission** *f* military mission. ~**poli,zei** *f* military police. ~**putsch** *m* military putsch. ~**re,gierung** *f* military government.

Military ['militəri] *f* (-; -s) three-day event. ~**reiter** *m* three-day eventer.

Mili'tärzeit *f* time of (military) service.

Miliz [mi'li:ts] *f* (-; -en) militia.

Milliardär [miliar'dɛ:r] *m* (-s; -e) multimillionaire.

Milliarde [mi'liardə] *f* (-; -n) billion.

Milli'meter [mili-] *n*, *m* millimet/re (*Am.* -er). ~**arbeit** *F* F das war ~ that was a precision job. ~**pa,pier** *n* graph paper.

Million [mi'lio:n] *f* (-; -en) million: **5 ~en Dollar** five million dollars. **Millionär** [milio'nɛ:r] *m* (-s; -e) millionaire.

Milli'onengeschäft *n* multimillion dollar *etc* deal. **Milli'onenstadt** *f* city of over a million inhabitants.

milli'onstel *adj* millionth.

Milz [milts] *f* (-; -en) *anat.* spleen.

Mime ['mi:mə] *m* (-n; -n) actor. '**mimen** *v/t* (h) act, play. **Mimik** ['mi:mik] *f* (-; *no pl*) mimic art. '**mimisch** *adj* mimic.

Mimose [mi'mo:zə] *f* (-; -n) **1.** 🌿 mimosa. **2.** *fig.* oversensitive person.

Minarett [mina'rɛt] *n* (-s; -e) minaret.

minder [mindər] **I** *adv* less: **nicht** ~ no less. **II** *adj* a) less(er), b) minor, c) inferior (*quality*). '**minderbegabt** *adj* less gifted. '**minderbemittelt** *adj* less well-off: F **geistig** ~ not very bright.

'**Minderheit** *f* (-; -en) minority; → *a.* **Minderzahl.** '**Minderheitsre,gierung** *f* minority(-party) government.

'**minderjährig** [-jɛ:riç] *adj* ☧ minor, under age. '**Minderjährige** [-jɛ:rigə] *m, f* (-n; -n) minor.

'**Minderjährigkeit** *f* (-; *no pl*) minority.

mindern ['mindərn] (h) **I** *v/t* a) lessen, reduce, lower, b) detract from. **II** *sich* ~ diminish, decrease.

'**Minderung** *f* (-; -en) a) (*gen*) decrease (in), reduction (in, of), b) depreciation.

'**minderwertig** *adj* inferior, ✝ *a.* of inferior quality. '**Minderwertigkeit** *f* (-; *no pl*) inferiority, ✝ inferior quality.

'**Minderwertigkeitskom,plex** *m* inferiority complex.

'**Minderzahl** *f* (-; *no pl*) **in der ~ sein** a) be in the minority, b) be outnumbered.

mindest ['mındəst] *adj* least, slightest: *nicht im ~en* not in the least, not at all; *zum ~en* at least; *das ~e* the least. '**Mindest...** minimum (*age, price, wage, etc*). **~betrag** *m* minimum (amount).

mindestens ['mındəstəns] *adv* at least.

'**Mindestmaß** *n* (*auf das ~ beschränken*) keep *s.th.* down to a minimum.

Mine ['mi:nə] *f* (-; -n) **1.** ⚔, ✕ mine. **2.** *of pencil*: lead, *of ball pen*: refill.

'**Minen|feld** *n* ✕ minefield. **~leger** *m* (-s; -) ⚓, ✕ minelayer. **~räumboot** *n*, **~suchboot** *n* ✕ minesweeper.

Mineral [minə'ra:l] *n* (-s; -e, -ien) mineral. **Mineralogie** [minəralo'gi:] *f* (-; *no pl*) mineralogy.

Mine'ral|öl *n* mineral oil. **~quelle** *f* mineral spring. **~wasser** *n* mineral water.

Miniatur [minia'tu:r] *f* (-; -en) miniature.

miniaturisieren [miniaturi'zi:rən] *v/t* (h) ❂ miniaturize.

Minigolf ['mi:ni-] *n* miniature golf.

'**Miniklei**d *n* minidress.

minimal [mini'ma:l] *adj* minimal, minimum, *fig.* negligible. **Minimum** ['mi:ni-mɔm] *n* (-s; -ma) minimum.

'**Minirock** *m* miniskirt.

Minister [mi'nıstər] *m* (-s; -) minister, *Br.* Secretary (of State), *Am.* Secretary.

Ministerialbeamte [minıste'rĭa:l-] *m* ministry official.

Ministerium [minıs'te:rĭɔm] *n* (-s; -rien) ministry, *Am.* department.

Mi'nisterpräsi,dent *m* Prime Minister.

Mi'nisterrat *m* **1.** cabinet (council). **2.** *EC:* Council of Ministers.

Ministrant [minıs'trant] *m* (-en; -en) *eccl.* altar server.

Minnesänger ['mınə-] *m* minnesinger.

minus ['mi:nʊs] **I** *prep* minus. **II** *adv* **~ 10 Grad** ten degrees below zero.

'**Minus** *n* (-; *no pl*) **1.** deficit. **2.** *fig.* disadvantage. '**Minuspunkt** *m* **1.** *sports:* penalty point. **2.** *fig.* minus, drawback. '**Minuszeichen** *n* A minus sign.

Minute [mi'nu:tə] *f* (-; -n) minute (*a. astr., A*): *auf die ~ pünktlich* on the dot; *in letzter ~* at the last moment; *es klappte auf die ~* it was perfectly timed.

mi'nutenlang I *adj* lasting several minutes, several minutes of ... **II** *adv* for (several) minutes.

Mi'nutenzeiger *m* minute-hand.

minuziös [minu'tsĭø:s] *adj* detailed, meticulous.

Minze ['mıntsə] *f* (-; -n) ⚘ mint.

mir [mi:r] *pers pron* a) me, to me, b) (to) myself: *gib es ~!* give it to me!; *ich wusch ~ die Hände* I washed my hands; *ein Freund von ~* a friend of mine; *von ~ aus ~ meinetwegen;* F *~ nichts, dir nichts* just like that; *wie du ~, so ich dir* tit for tat.

Mirabelle [mira'bɛlə] *f* (-; -n) ⚘ yellow plum.

'**Mischehe** *f* mixed marriage.

mischen ['mıʃən] (h) **I** *v/t* mix (*a. radio, film, etc*), blend (*tea, tobacco, etc*), shuffle (*cards*), *computer:* merge. **II** *sich ~ unter* (*acc*) mix (*or* mingle) with; *sich ~ in* (*acc*) interfere (*or* meddle) in; *sich in ein Gespräch ~* join in (*or* butt in on) the conversation. **III** *v/i* shuffle.

'**Mischer** *m* (-s; -) *a.* TV mixer.

'**Mischling** *m* (-s; -e) **1.** *biol.* hybrid. **2.** half-caste, half-breed.

Mischmasch ['mıʃmaʃ] *m* (-[e]s; -e) F hotchpotch.

'**Mischpult** *n* radio, TV mixer.

'**Mischrasse** *f* mixed race.

'**Mischung** *f* (-; -en) mixture (*a. fig.*), blend (*of tea etc*), assortment (*of chocolates etc*).

'**Mischwald** *m* mixed forest.

'**Mischwort** *n* (-[e]s; ~er) hybrid (word).

miserabel [mize'ra:bəl] *adj* F lousy.

Misere [mi'ze:rə] *f* (-; -n) calamity.

miß'achten [mıs-] *v/t* (*insep, no* -ge-, h) **1.** ignore. **2.** disdain, despise.

'**Mißachtung** *f* **1.** disregard. **2.** disdain: *~ des Gerichts* contempt of court.

'**Mißbehagen** *n* feeling of uneasiness.

'**Mißbildung** *f* (-; -en) deformity.

miß'billigen *v/t* (*insep, no* -ge-, h) disapprove (of).

'**Mißbilligung** *f* (-; *no pl*) disapproval.

'**Mißbrauch** *m* abuse, misuse. **miß'brauchen** *v/t* (*insep, no* -ge-, h) abuse.

miß'deuten *v/t* (*insep, no* -ge-, h) misinterpret.

'**Mißdeutung** *f* misinterpretation.

'**Mißerfolg** *m* failure, F flop.

'**Mißernte** *f* crop failure.

miß'fallen *v/i* (*irr, insep, no* -ge-, h, →

fallen) **er** (**es**) **mißfällt mir** I don't like him (it). '**Mißfallen** *n* (-s) disapproval: *j-s ~ erregen* incur s.o.'s displeasure. '**Mißfallensäußerung** *f* expression of disapproval.

'**mißgebildet** *adj* deformed.
'**Mißgeburt** *f* freak.
'**Mißgeschick** *n* (-[e]s; -e) a) bad luck, misfortune, b) mishap.
miß'gönnen *v/t* (*insep, no* -ge-, h) *j-m et. ~* begrudge s.o. s.th.
'**Mißgriff** *m* mistake.
'**Mißgunst** *f* resentment.
'**mißgünstig** *adj* resentful.
miß'handeln *v/t* (*insep, no* -ge-, h) maltreat. **Miß'handlung** *f* maltreatment, ☰ assault and battery.
Mission [mɪ'sǐoːn] *f* (-; -en) mission.
Missionar [mɪsǐo'naːr] *m* (-s; -e), **missio'narisch** *adj* missionary.
missionieren [mɪsǐo'niːrən] (h) **I** *v/i* do missionary work. **II** *v/t* convert.
'**Mißklang** *m a. fig.* dissonance.
'**Mißkre,dit** *m* **in ~ bringen** (**geraten**) bring discredit upon (get a bad name).
'**mißlich** *adj* awkward, difficult.
mißlingen [mɪs'lɪŋən] (h) **I** *v/i* (*mißlang, mißlungen, sn*) *v/i* fail, be unsuccessful.
'**mißmutig** *adj* disgruntled, morose.
miß'raten **I** *v/i* (*mißriet, mißraten, sn*) fail, turn out a failure: *das ist mir ~* I've bungled it. **II** *adj* wayward (*child*).
'**Mißstand** *m* deplorable state of affairs: *Mißstände abschaffen* remedy abuses.
miß'trauen *v/i* (*insep, no* -ge-, h) (*dat*) distrust, mistrust. '**Mißtrauen** *n* (-s) (*gegen* of) distrust, mistrust: *j-s ~ erregen* arouse s.o.'s suspicion.
'**Mißtrauensantrag** *m parl.* motion of no confidence. '**Mißtrauensvotum** *n parl.* vote of no confidence.
'**mißtrauisch** [-trauɪʃ] *adj* (*gegen* of) a) distrustful, b) suspicious, c) doubtful: *j-n ~ machen* arouse s.o.'s suspicion.
'**Mißverhältnis** *n* disproportion: *in ᴠ-m ~ stehen* be out of proportion (*zu* to).
'**mißverständlich** *adj* misleading.
'**Mißverständnis** *n* (-ses; -se) misunderstanding. '**mißverstehen** *v/t* (*mißverstand, mißverstanden, h*) misunderstand, mistake.
'**Mißwahl** *f* beauty contest.
'**Mißwirtschaft** *f* mismanagement.

Mist [mɪst] *m* (-[e]s; *no pl*) **1.** a) dung, manure, b) droppings. **2.** F rubbish, crap: *~ machen* mess it up; *~ verzapfen* talk rot; (*so ein*) *~!* damn it!
Mistel ['mɪstəl] *f* (-; -n) ⚘ mistletoe.
'**Mistelzweig** *m* sprig of mistletoe.
'**Mistgabel** *f* pitchfork. '**Misthaufen** *m* manure heap. '**Mistkäfer** *m* dungbeetle. '**Mistkerl** *m* V bastard. '**Miststück** *n* V a) bastard, b) bitch.
mit [mɪt] **I** *prep* **1.** with: *ein Haus ~ Garten* a house with a garden; *Zimmer ~ Frühstück* bed and breakfast; *ein Korb ~ Obst* a basket of fruit. **2.** by, with: *~ der Bahn etc* by train etc; *~ Bleistift* in pencil; *~ Gewalt* by force. **3.** *~ Absicht* intentionally; *~ lauter Stimme* in a loud voice; *~ Verlust* at a loss; *~ einem Wort* in a word; *~ 8 zu 11 Stimmen* by 8 votes to 11; *was ist ~ ihm?* what's the matter with him?; *wie steht's ~ dir?* how about you? **4.** *~ 20 Jahren* at the age of) twenty; *~ dem 3. Mai* as of May 3rd; *~ Zeit* **1.** **III** *adv* **5.** also, too: *~ dabeisein* be there too; *das gehört ~ dazu* that's part (and parcel) of it; *er war ~ der beste* he was one of the best.
'**Mitangeklagte** *m, f* co-defendant.
'**Mitarbeit** *f* (-; *no pl*) cooperation, collaboration, *a.* assistance (*bei* in): *unter ~ von* (*or gen*) in collaboration with.
'**mitarbeiten** *v/i* (*sep,* -ge-, h) a) (*an dat, bei*) a) cooperate (in), collaborate (on), b) contribute (to *a paper etc*), c) *ped.* take an active part in the lessons.
'**Mitarbeiter(in** *f*) *m* **1.** a) employee, *pl* staff, b) collaborator (*bei* on), c) contributor (*bei* to *a paper etc*): *freier Mitarbeiter* freelance(r). **2.** colleague.
'**Mitarbeiterstab** *m* staff.
'**mitbekommen** *v/t* (*irr, sep,* h, → *bekommen*) **1.** get. **2.** F a) catch, get (*joke e..*), b) pick up: *hast du das mitbekom.men?* did you get that?
'**mitbenutzen** *v/t* (*sep,* h) share.
'**mitbestimmen** *v/i* (*sep,* h) (*bei e-r Sache*) *~* have a say in the matter.
'**Mitbestimmung** *f* (-; *no pl*) codetermination, *a.* worker participation.
'**Mitbewerber(in** *f*) *m* competitor.
'**Mitbewohner(in** *f*) *m* fellow occupant.
'**mitbringen** *v/t* (*irr, sep,* -ge-, h, → *bringen*) **1.** bring *s.o., s.th.* along (with one). **2.** *fig.* have, possess (*talents etc*).

Mitbringsel ['mɪtbrɪŋzəl] *n* (-s; -) little present.

'**Mitbürger(in** *f*) *m* fellow citizen.

'**Miteigentümer(in** *f*) *m* joint owner.

mitein'ander *adv* a) with each other, b) together: **alle ~** one and all.

Mitein'ander *n* (-[s]; *no pl*) togetherness.

'**Mit|erbe** *m* co-heir. **~erbin** *f* co-heiress.

'**miterleben** *v/t* (*sep*, h) witness.

'**Mitesser** *m* (-s; -) 🐛 blackhead.

'**mitfahren** *v/i* (*irr, sep*, -ge-, sn, → **fahren**) **mit j-m ~** ride (*or* go) with s.o.

'**Mitfahrgelegenheit** *f* **biete ~ nach Köln** lift offered to Cologne.

'**mitfühlen** *v/i* (*sep*, -ge-, h) **mit j-m ~** sympathize with s.o.: **~d** sympathetic.

'**mitführen** *v/t* (*sep*, -ge-, h) carry with one.

'**mitgeben** *v/t* (*irr, sep*, -ge-, h, → **geben**) **j-m et. ~** give s.o. s.th. (to take with him).

'**Mitgefangene** *m, f* fellow-prisoner.

'**Mitgefühl** *n* (-[e]s; *no pl*) sympathy: **j-m sein ~ ausdrücken** offer one's sympathies (*or* condolences) to s.o.

'**mitgehen** *v/i* (*irr, sep*, -ge-, sn, → **gehen**) **1.** go along (**mit j-m** with s.o.): F **et. ~ lassen** pinch (*or* lift) s.th. **2.** *fig.* *audience:* respond (**mit** to).

'**mitgenommen I** *pp* of **mitnehmen**. **II** *adj* worn out, exhausted: **~ aussehen** look the worse for wear.

'**Mitgift** *f* (-; -en) dowry.

'**Mitglied** *n* (-[e]s; -er) member.

'**Mitglieder|versammlung** *f* general meeting. **~zahl** *f* membership.

'**Mitgliedsausweis** *m* membership card.

'**Mitgliedsbeitrag** *m* (membership) fee (*Am.* dues).

'**Mitgliedschaft** *f* (-; -en) membership.

'**Mitgliedstaat** *m* member state.

'**mithalten** *v/i* (*irr, sep*, -ge-, h → **halten**) **1.** *a. fig.* keep up (**mit** with). **2.** *cards:* stay in the bidding.

'**Mitherausgeber(in** *f*) *m* co-editor.

'**Mithilfe** *f* (-; *no pl*) aid, help, assistance.

'**mithören** (*sep*, -ge-, h) **I** *v/t* a) listen (in) to, b) overhear, c) eavesdrop on, d) monitor, e) intercept. **II** *v/i* listen.

'**Mitinhaber(in** *f*) *m* joint owner, copartner.

'**mitkommen** *v/i* (*irr, sep*, -ge-, sn, → **kommen**) **1.** come along. **2.** *ped.* keep up (with the class): **gut ~** get on well;

nicht **~** do badly; F **da komme ich (einfach) nicht mit!** that's beyond me!

'**mitlaufen** *v/i* (*irr, sep*, -ge-, sn, → **laufen**) run (along) with, *sports:* run (in the race). '**Mitläufer(in** *f*) *m pol. contp.* **1.** hanger-on. **2.** fellow-travel(l)er.

'**Mitlaut** *m ling.* consonant.

'**Mitleid** *n* (-[e]s; *no pl*) (**aus ~** out of) pity (**für** for); **mit j-m ~ haben** have pity on s.o., be sorry for s.o.

'**Mitleidenschaft** *f* **in ~ gezogen werden** be (adversely) affected (**durch** by).

'**mitleiderregend** *adj* pitiful, pitiable.

'**mitleidig** [-laɪdɪç] *adj* compassionate, sympathetic: **ein ~es Lächeln** a contemptuous smile.

'**mitleid(s)los** *adj* pitiless.

'**mitmachen** (*sep*, -ge-, h) **I** *v/i* **1.** a) take part, join in, b) cooperate: F **da mache ich nicht mit!** count me out on that! **II** *v/t* **2.** take part in a. attend (*course etc*), go with (*the fashion*), join in (*game etc*). **3.** F **j-s Arbeit ~** do s.o.'s job as well. **4.** F live (*or* go) through, suffer: **das mache ich nicht mehr lange mit!** I won't take that much longer!

'**Mitmensch** *m* fellow (man, being).

'**mitmischen** *v/i* (*sep*, -ge-, h) F be in on the action: **bei et. ~** take part in s.th.

'**mitnehmen** *v/t* (*irr, sep*, -ge-, h, → **nehmen**) **1.** a) take along, take with one, b) borrow: **j-n im Auto ~** give s.o. a lift. **2.** take away. **3.** F take, buy. **4.** F take in (*sights etc*). **5.** *fig.* profit (**aus** from). **6.** F *fig.* **j-n (sehr) ~** take it out of s.o.; → **mitgenommen II.**

'**mitreden** *v/t* (*sep*, -ge-, h) **et. mitzureden haben** have a say (**bei** in).

'**Mitreisende** *m, f* fellow-passenger.

'**mitreißen** *v/t* (*irr, sep*, -ge-, h, → **reißen**) carry along, *fig.* carry away.

'**mitreißend** *adj fig.* thrilling, rousing.

mit'samt *prep* (*dat*) together with.

'**mitschleppen** *v/t* (*sep*, -ge-, h) drag along (with one).

'**mitschneiden** *v/t* (*irr, sep*, -ge-, h, → **schneiden**) tape-record.

'**mitschreiben** (*sep*, -ge-, h, → **schreiben**) **I** *v/t* write down. **II** *v/i* take notes.

'**Mitschuld** *f* (-; *no pl*) joint guilt, complicity (**an** *dat* in). '**mitschuldig** *adj* **an e-r Sache ~ sein** be implicated in s.th.

'**Mitschuldige** *m, f* accessory (**an** *dat* to).

'**Mitschüler(in** f) m classmate.

'**mitschwingen** v/i (irr, sep, -ge-, h, → **schwingen**) 1. phys. resonate. 2. fig. have overtones of.

'**mitsingen** v/t, v/i (irr, sep, -ge-, h, → **singen**) join in the singing (of).

'**mitspielen** v/i (sep, -ge-, h) 1. join in, sports: play, be on the team, thea. appear. 2. F fig. (**bei**) person: go along (with), matter: play a part (in): **ich spiele nicht mehr mit!** count me out! 3. F **j-m übel ~** a) treat s.o. badly, b) play a nasty trick on s.o.

'**Mitspieler(in** f) m player, partner, thea. etc member of the cast.

'**Mitspracherecht** n (-[e]s; no pl) right to a say: **ein ~ haben** have a say (**bei** in).

'**Mitstreiter(in** f) m comrade-in-arms.

'**Mittag** ['mɪtaːk] m (-[e]s; -e) midday, noon: **heute** ⚋ at noon today; **zu ~ essen** have lunch. '**Mittagessen** n (**beim** [**zum**] **~** at [for]) lunch.

'**mittags** adv a) at noon, b) at lunchtime. '**Mittags|pause** f lunch break. **~schlaf** m, **~schläfchen** n siesta, afternoon nap. **~zeit** f (-; no pl) lunchtime.

'**Mittäter(in** f) m ⚖ accomplice.

Mitte ['mɪtə] f (-; -) middle, cent/re (Am. -er): **die goldene ~** the golden mean; pol. **die ~** the centre; **in unserer ~** in our midst; **in der ~ zwischen** halfway between; **~ Juli** in the middle of July, in mid-July; **in der ~ des 18. Jhs.** in the mid-18th-century; **~ Dreißig sein** be in one's mid-thirties; F **ab durch die ~!** a) off you go!, b) let's go!

'**mitteilen** (sep, -ge-, h) I v/t **j-m et. ~** a) inform (or notify) s.o. of s.th., tell s.o. s.th., b) impart knowledge to s.o. II **sich j-m ~** a) confide in s.o., b) fig. joy etc: communicate itself to s.o.

'**mitteilsam** adj communicative.

'**Mitteilung** f (-; -en) information, communication, report, notification, message, news.

mittel ['mɪtəl] I adj → **mittler**. II adv F middling, so-so.

'**Mittel** n (-s; -) 1. a) means, b) method, way, c) expedient: **~ und Wege finden** find ways and means; **~ zum Zweck sein** be a means to an end; **als letztes ~** as a last resort; **ihm ist jedes ~ recht** he stops at nothing. 2. ⚕ remedy (**gegen** for). 3. pl a) resources, b) funds, means:

aus öffentlichen ~n from the public purse. 4. (**im ~** on an) average.

'**Mittelalter** n (-s; no pl) Middle Ages.

'**mittelalterlich** adj medi(a)eval.

'**mittelbar** adj indirect.

'**Mittelding** n cross, s.th. in between.

'**mitteleuro,päisch** adj **~e Zeit** (abbr. MEZ) Central European Time.

'**Mittelfeld** n (-[e]s; no pl) soccer: midfield. **~spieler** m midfield player.

'**Mittelfinger** m middle finger.

'**mittelfristig** adj ✝ medium-term.

'**Mittelgebirge** n highlands.

'**Mittelgewicht** n (-[e]s; no pl) sports: middleweight.

'**mittelgroß** adj medium-sized, person: of medium height.

'**Mittelklasse** f 1. ✝ medium price range. 2. → **Mittelstand** 1. **~wagen** m medium-range car.

'**Mittellinie** f 1. a. sports: cent/re (Am. -er) line, tennis: cent/re (Am. -er) service line. 2. ⚴ median line.

'**mittellos** adj destitute, poor, penniless.

'**Mittelmaß** n (-es; no pl) average, contp. mediocrity.

'**mittelmäßig** adj average, mediocre.

'**Mittelmäßigkeit** f (-; no pl) mediocrity.

'**Mittelmeer...** Mediterranean.

'**Mittelohrentzündung** f inflammation of the middle ear.

'**Mittelpunkt** m cent/re (Am. -er), fig. a. heart, hub: **im ~ des Interesses stehen** be the focus of interest.

'**mittels** prep by (means of), through.

'**Mittelschiff** n ⚛ nave.

'**Mittelstand** m (-[e]s; no pl) 1. middle classes: **gehobener ~** upper middle class. 2. ✝ medium-sized and small enterprises. '**mittelständisch** [-ʃtɛndɪʃ] adj, '**Mittelstands...** middle-class: ✝ **mittelständische Betriebe** → **Mittelstand** 2.

'**Mittelstrecken|flugzeug** n medium-range plane. **~läufer(in** f) m sports: middle-distance runner. **~ra,kete** f ⚔ medium-range missile.

'**Mittel|streifen** m central reservation, Am. median strip. **~stück** n middle. **~stufe** f ped. middle school, Am. junior high. **~stürmer** m sports: cent/re (Am. -er) forward. **~weg** m (e-n ~ **einschlagen** steer a) middle course: **der goldene ~** the golden mean. **~welle** f ⚡ medium wave. **~wert** m ✝, A mean (value). **~wort** n (-[e]s; ⁔er) ling. participle.

mitten ['mɪtən] adv ~ **in** (**an, auf, unter** dat) in the middle of; ~ **in** a. in the thick of; ~ **unter uns** in our midst; ~ **durch** clean through; ~ **hinein** right into it; ~ **ins Herz** right into the heart.

mitten'drin adv F right in the middle (of it). **mitten'durch** adv right through (or across), a. cut etc clean through.

Mitternacht ['mɪtər-] f (-; no pl) midnight.

mittler ['mɪtlər] adj a) middle, central, b) average, medium, c) middling, d) phys., ☉ mean: **~en Alters** middle-aged; **~er Beamter** lower-grade civil servant; **~es Management** middle management; **der ~e Osten** the Middle East; **von ~er Qualität** of medium quality; → **Reife** 2.

'Mittler m (-s; -) mediator.

'mittler'weile adv meanwhile, (in the) meantime, since, by now.

'Mittsommer m midsummer.

Mittwoch ['mɪtvɔx] m (-[e]s; -e) (**am** ~ on) Wednesday.

'mittwochs adv on Wednesday(s).

mit'unter adv now and then.

'mitverantwortlich adj jointly responsible. **'Mitverantwortung** f joint responsibility.

'mitverdienen v/i (sep, h) be earning as well.

'Mitverfasser(in f) m coauthor.

'Mitverschulden n (-s) ⚖ contributory negligence.

'mitwirken v/i (sep, -ge-, h) (**bei**) a) cooperate (in), a. thea. take part (in), ♪ perform, b) matter: contribute (to).

'Mitwirkende m, f (-n; -n) thea. actor, player (a. ♪), pl cast: ~ **sind ...** the cast includes ... **'Mitwirkung** f (-; no pl) a) cooperation, b) participation: **unter ~ von** (or gen) assisted by, thea. starring.

'Mitwisser m (-s; -) person who is in on the secret, ⚖ accessory.

'Mixbecher m shaker. **mixen** ['mɪksən] v/t (h) mix. **'Mixer** m (-s; -) **1.** barman, Am. bartender. **2.** TV etc: mixer. **3.** → **'Mixgerät** n mixer, liquidizer.

'Mixgetränk n mixed drink.

Mixtur [mɪks'tuːr] f (-; -en) mixture.

Mob [mɔp] m (-s; no pl) mob.

Möbel ['møːbəl] n (-s; -) a) → **Möbelstück**, b) pl furniture.

'Möbel|geschäft n furniture shop. **~händler** m furniture dealer. **~poli,tur** f furniture polish. **~spediti,on** f removal firm. **~stoff** m furniture fabric. **~stück** n piece of furniture. **~tischler** m cabinet-maker. **~wagen** m furniture van, Am. moving truck.

mobil [mo'biːl] adj **1.** mobile: ✕ ~ **machen** mobilize. **2.** F active.

Mobile ['moːbilə] n (-s; -s) mobile.

Mobiliar [mobi'liaːr] n (-s; no pl) furniture.

mobilisieren [mobili'ziːrən] v/t (h) mobilize. **Mobili'sierung** f (-; -en) mobilization. **Mo'bilmachung** f (-; -en) ✕ mobilization.

möblieren [mø'bliːrən] v/t (h) furnish: **neu ~** refurnish; **möbliertes Zimmer** furnished room, bed-sitter; F **möbliert wohnen** live in lodgings.

mochte ['mɔxtə] pret of **mögen.**

Möchtegern... ['mœçtə-] iro. would-be.

modal [mo'daːl] adj modal. **Modalität** [modali'tɛːt] f (-; -en) modality.

Mode ['moːdə] f (-; -n) fashion: contp. **neue ~n** new-fangled ideas; (**die) große ~ sein** be (all) the fashion (or rage); **in (aus der) ~ kommen** come into (go out of) fashion; **mit der ~ gehen** follow the latest fashion.

'Modear,tikel m novelty.

'modebewußt adj fashion-conscious.

'Mode|farbe f fashionable colo(u)r. **~geschäft** n fashion shop. **~haus** n **1.** fashion house. **2.** fashion shop.

Modell [mo'dɛl] n (-s; -e) a) model, b) design, type, c) mock-up: **j-m ~ stehen** sit (or pose) for s.o.

Mo'dell|ath,let(in f) m model athlete. **~bauer** m (-s; -) ☉ model(l)er, model builder. **~eisenbahn** f model railway. **~flugzeug** n model airplane.

modellieren [modɛ'liːrən] v/t (h) model.

Mo'dellkleid n model (dress).

Modem [mo'dɛm] n (-s; -s) ≸ modem.

'Modenschau f fashion show.

Moder ['moːdər] m (-s; no pl) mo(u)ld.

Moderation [modera'tsioːn] f (-; no pl) TV presentation, Am. moderation.

Moderator [mode'raːtɔr] m (-s; -en [-ra'toːrən], **Moderatorin** [modera-'toːrɪn] f (-; -nen) TV presenter, Am. moderator. **moderieren** [mode'riːrən] v/t (h) TV present, Am. moderate.

'mod(e)rig adj mo(u)ldy, a. musty.

modern¹ ['mo:dɛrn] v/i (h) mo(u)lder.

modern² [mo'dɛrn] adj a) modern, up-to-date, b) fashionable.

Mo'derne f (-; no pl) **1.** modern age. **2. Kunst** etc **der ~** modernist art etc.

modernisieren [modɛrni'zi:rən] v/t (h) modernize. **Moderni'sierung** f (-; -en) modernization.

'Modesa,lon m fashion house.

'Modeschmuck m costume jewel(le)ry.

'Modeschöpfer m couturier.

'Modeschöpferin f couturière.

'Modewort n vogue word.

'Modezeichner m fashion designer.

'Modezeitschrift f fashion magazine.

modifizieren [modifi'tsi:rən] v/t (h) modify, a. qualify (expression). **Modifi'zierung** f (-; -en) modification, qualification.

'modisch adj fashionable, stylish.

Modul ['mo:dʊl] n (-s; -n) ⊕ module.

modulieren [modu'li:rən] v/t (h) modulate.

'Modultechnik f modular technique.

Modus ['mo:dʊs] m (-; Modi) **1.** way, method, a. ♪ mode. **2.** ling. mood.

Mofa ['mo:fa] n (-s; -s) → **Motorfahrrad**.

mogeln ['mo:gəln] v/i (h) F cheat.

'Mogelpackung f deception package.

mögen ['mø:gən] (mochte, gemocht, h) **I** v/t like, be fond of: **nicht ~** dislike; **ich möchte gern ein Bier** I'd like (to have) a beer; **ich mag k-n Kaffee** I don't like (or care for) coffee; **lieber ~** like better, prefer; **ich möchte lieber ...** I would rather ...; **ich möchte noch nicht nach Hause** I didn't want to go home yet. **II** v/aux (pp mögen) **ich mag nicht essen** I don't want to eat; **ich möchte ihn sehen** I want (or would like) to see him; **ich möchte wissen** I should like to know, I wonder; **mag er sagen, was er will** let him say what he wants; **das mag (wohl) sein** that may be so; **mag sein, daß** perhaps; **wie dem auch sein mag** be that as it may; **wo er auch sein mag** wherever he may be; **was mag das bedeuten?** I wonder what it could mean?

Mogler ['mo:glər] m (-s; -) F cheat.

möglich ['mø:klɪç] adj possible, a. practicable: **~er Käufer** potential buyer; **alle ~en** all sorts of; **alles ~e** all sorts of

things; **sein möglichstes tun** do one's utmost; **es ~ machen** → **ermöglichen**; **nicht ~!** impossible!, F no kidding?; **das ist eher ~!** that's more likely!; **es ist ~, daß er kommt** he may come; **so bald wie ~** as soon as possible.

'möglicherweise adv possibly, perhaps.

'Möglichkeit f (-; -en) possibility, a. opportunity, a. chance: **nach ~** if possible, as far as possible; **es besteht die ~, daß** it is possible that; **ich sehe k-e ~ zu** inf I cannot see any chance of ger; **ist das die ~!** that's not possible!

'möglichst adv **~ bald** etc as soon etc as possible; **~ klein** as small as possible, attr the smallest possible.

Mohammedaner [mohame'da:nər] m (-s; -), **Mohamme'danerin** f (-; -en) Moslem. **mohamme'danisch** adj Moslem.

Mohn [mo:n] m (-[e]s; -e) **1.** ♣ poppy. **2.** → **'Mohnsamen** m poppy-seed.

Möhre ['mø:rə] f (-; -n), **Mohrrübe** ['mo:r-] f ♣ carrot.

Mokka ['mɔka] m (-s; -s) mocha.

Molch [mɔlç] m (-[e]s; -e) zo. newt.

Mole ['mo:lə] f (-; -n) ♣ mole, jetty.

Molekül [mole'ky:l] n (-s; -e) molecule.

molekular adj, **Molekular...** [moleku'la:r-] molecular.

molk [mɔlk] pret of **melken**.

Molke ['mɔlkə] f (-; no pl) whey.

Molkerei [mɔlkə'raɪ] f (-; -en) dairy.

Moll [mɔl] n (-; no pl) ♪ minor (key).

mollig ['mɔlɪç] adj F **1.** cosy. **2.** plump.

Molotowcocktail ['mɔlɔtɔf-] m (-s; -s) Molotov cocktail, petrol bomb.

Moment¹ [mo'mɛnt] m (-[e]s; -e) (**im ~** at the) moment.

Mo'ment² n (-[e]s; -e) **1.** factor, element, aspect. **2.** phys. momentum.

momentan [momɛn'ta:n] **I** adj **1.** momentary. **2.** present. **II** adv **3.** momentarily. **4.** at the moment.

Monarch [mo'narç] m (-en; -en). **Mon'archin** f (-; -nen) monarch, sovereign. **Monarchie** [monar'çi:] f (-; -n) monarchy. **Monarchist** [monar'çɪst] m (-en; -en), **Monar'chistin** f (-; -nen), **monar'chistisch** adj monarchic.

Monat ['mo:nat] m (-[e]s; -e) month: **im ~ Mai** in (the month of) May; **im ~, pro ~** a month, monthly; F **sie ist im dritten ~** she is three months gone. **'monatelang I** adj months of. **II** adv for months.

'**monatlich** *adj* monthly, *adv a.* a month.
'**Monats|gehalt** *n* monthly salary (*or* pay). **~karte** *f* monthly season ticket, *Am.* monthly ticket. **~rate** *f* monthly instal(l)ment. **~schrift** *f* monthly.

Mönch [mœnç] *m* (-[e]s; -e) monk.

'**Mönchskloster** *n* monastery.

'**Mönchsorden** *m* monastic order.

Mond [moːnt] *m* (-[e]s; -e) moon, *a.* satellite: F *auf* (*or* *hinter*) *dem ~ leben* be behind the times.

mondän [mɔnˈdɛːn] *adj* fashionable.

'**Mond|aufgang** *m* moonrise. **~finsternis** *f* lunar eclipse. **~gestein** *n* moon rocks. **~landefähre** *f* lunar module. **~landschaft** *f a. fig.* moonscape. **~landung** *f* moon landing. **~nacht** *f* moonlit night. **~schein** *m* (-[e]s; *no pl*) moonlight. **~sichel** *f* crescent (of the moon). **~stein** *m min.* moonstone.

Moneten [moˈneːtən] *pl* F dough.

Mongole [mɔŋˈgoːlə] *m* (-n; -n), **Mon'golin** *f* (-; -nen), **mon'golisch** *adj* Mongol(ian). **Mongolismus** [mɔŋgoˈlɪsmʊs] *m* (-; *no pl*) 🔬 Down's syndrome. **mongoloid** [mɔŋgoloˈiːt] *adj* 🔬 mongoloid.

Monitor [ˈmoːnitɔr] *m* (-s; -en [moniˈtoːrən]) *TV* monitor.

mono [ˈmoːno] *adj* F (*a.* **~ abspielbar**) mono.

monogam [monoˈgaːm] *adj* monogamous.

Monogramm [monoˈgram] *n* (-s; -e) monogram.

Monographie [monograˈfiː] *f* (-; -n) monograph.

Monolog [monoˈloːk] *m* (-s; -e) monolog(ue *Br.*).

Monopol [monoˈpoːl] *n* (-s; -e) monopoly (*auf acc* on). **monopolisieren** [monopoliˈziːrən] *v/t* (h) monopolize.

monoton [monoˈtoːn] *adj* monotonous. **Monotonie** [monotoˈniː] *f* (-; -n) monotony.

Monster [ˈmɔnstər] *n* (-s; -) monster.

'**Monster...** F mammoth (*enterprise, film, trial, etc*).

Monstranz [mɔnˈstrants] *f* (-; -en) *eccl.* monstrance.

monströs [mɔnˈstrøːs] *adj* monstrous.

Monstrum [ˈmɔnstrʊm] *n* (-s; Monstren) monster.

Monsun [mɔnˈzuːn] *m* (-s; -e) monsoon.

Montag [ˈmoːntaːk] *m* (-[e]s; -e) (*am ~ on*) Monday.

Montage [mɔnˈtaːʒə] *f* (-; -n) **1.** ⚙ a) mounting, fitting, installation, b) assembly: *auf ~ sein* be away on a construction job. **2.** *phot. etc* montage.

Mon'tageband *n* assembly line.

Mon'tagehalle *f* assembly shop.

'**montags** *adv* on Monday(s).

Montanindu,strie [mɔnˈtaːn-] *f* coal, iron, and steel industries.

Monteur [mɔnˈtøːr] *m* (-s; -e) ⚙ fitter, ✈, *mot.* mechanic. **montieren** [mɔnˈtiːrən] *v/t* (h) ⚙ a) mount (*a. phot. etc*), fit, instal(l), b) assemble.

Montur [mɔnˈtuːr] *f* (-; -en) F get-up.

Monument [monuˈmɛnt] *n* (-[e]s; -e) monument (*für* to). **monumental** [monumɛnˈtaːl] *adj* monumental.

Moor [moːr] *n* (-[e]s; -e) fen, bog, moor.

Moos [moːs] *n* (-es; -e) **1.** 🌿 moss. **2.** F dough, *sl.* lolly.

Moped [ˈmoːpɛt] *n* (-s; -s) moped.

Mops [mɔps] *m* (-es; Möpse) *zo.* pug.

Moral [moˈraːl] *f* (-; *no pl*) a) morals, b) ethics, c) (*working etc*) morale: *doppelte ~* double standards; *die ~ heben* raise the morale; *~ predigen* moralize.

moralisch [moˈraːlɪʃ] *adj* moral.

Moralist [moraˈlɪst] *m* (-en; -en) moralist.

Morast [moˈrast] *m* (-[e]s; -e) morass.

morbid [mɔrˈbiːt] *adj* morbid.

Morchel [ˈmɔrçəl] *f* (-; -n) 🌿 morel.

Mord [mɔrt] *m* (-[e]s; -e) murder (*an dat* of): *e-n ~ begehen* commit murder; F *es gibt ~ und Totschlag* there will be a hell of a row.

'**Mordanklage** *f* murder charge: *unter ~ stehen* be charged with murder.

'**Mordanschlag** *m* attempted murder: *e-n ~ auf j-n verüben* make an attempt on s.o.'s life.

morden [ˈmɔrdən] (h) **I** *v/i* commit murder, kill. **II** *v/t* murder, kill.

Mörder [ˈmœrdər] *m* (-s; -) murderer.

'**Mörderin** *f* (-; -nen) murderess.

'**mörderisch** *adj* murderous, *a.* deadly (*fight etc*), *a.* terrible (*heat etc*), *a.* gruel(l)ing (*job etc*), *a.* breakneck (*pace etc*), cutthroat (*competition etc*).

'**Mordfall** *m* murder case.

'**Mordkommissi,on** *f* murder (*Am.* homicide) squad.

'Mords... F a) great, terrific, fantastic, b) terrible. **~angst** f e-e ~ **haben** be in a flat panic, be scared stiff. **~ding** n whopper, humdinger. **~glück** n fantastic stroke of luck. **~kerl** m great guy. **~krach** m F terrific noise, awful racket: **e-n ~ schlagen** raise hell.

'mordsmäßig F **I** adj terrific. **II** adv terribly, awfully.

'Mordverdacht m suspicion of murder.

'Mordversuch m attempted murder.

'Mordwaffe f murder weapon.

morgen ['mɔrgən] adv tomorrow: ~ **früh** tomorrow morning; ~ **mittag** at noon tomorrow; **heute ~** this morning; ~ **in 14 Tagen** a fortnight tomorrow; ~ **in e-r Woche** a week from tomorrow; ~ **um diese Zeit** this time tomorrow.

'Morgen¹ m (-s; -) morning: **am (frühen)** ~ (early) in the morning.

'Morgen² m (-s; -) acre.

'Morgen|andacht f morning prayer. **~dämmerung** f dawn, daybreak. **~grauen** n **beim** ~ at dawn. **~gym,na-stik** f **s-e ~ machen** do one's daily dozen. **~luft** f morning air: fig. ~ **wittern** see a chance. **~muffel** m F **ein** ~ **sein** be grumpy in the morning. **~rock** m dressing gown. **~rot** n (-s; no pl) **1.** red sky. **2.** fig. dawn.

'morgens adv in the morning(s): ~ **um 4 (Uhr)** at four (o'clock) in the morning; **von ~ bis abends** from morning till midnight.

'Morgen|sonne f (~ **haben** get the) morning sun. **~stunde** f morning hour: **in den frühen ~n** in the small hours.

morgig ['mɔrgɪç] adj tomorrow's: **der ~e Tag** tomorrow.

Mormone [mɔr'mo:nə] m (-n; -n), **Mor'monin** f (-; -nen), **mor'monisch** adj Mormon.

Morphium ['mɔrfiʊm] n (-s; no pl) morphine.

morsch [mɔrʃ] adj rotten, fig. a. shaky.

Morsealpha,bet ['mɔrzə-] n (-[e]s; no pl) Morse (code).

morsen ['mɔrzən] v/t, v/i (h) morse.

Mörser ['mœrzər] m (-s; -) mortar.

'Morsezeichen n Morse signal.

Mörtel ['mœrtəl] m (-s; -) mortar.

Mosaik [moza'i:k] n (-s; -en) mosaic.

Mosa'ikfußboden m tessellated floor.

Moschee [mɔ'ʃe:] f (-; -n) mosque.

Moschus ['mɔʃʊs] m (-; no pl) musk.

Mosel ['mo:zəl] m (-s; -) Moselle.

Moskito [mɔs'ki:to] m (-s; -s) (tropical) mosquito. **~netz** n mosquito net.

Moslem ['mɔslɛm] m (-s; -s) Moslem, Muslim.

Most [mɔst] m (-[e]s; -e) must.

Mostrich ['mɔstrɪç] m (-s; no pl) gastr. mustard.

Motel ['mo:tɛl] n (-s; -s) motel.

Motiv [mo'ti:f] n (-s; -e) **1.** motive (**zu** for). **2.** art: motif, film etc: a. theme, phot. subject. **Motivation** [motiva-'tsio:n] f (-; -en) motivation.

motivieren [moti'vi:rən] v/t (h) **1.** motivate. **2.** explain, give reasons for.

Motor ['mo:tɔr] m (-s; -en [mo'to:rən]) engine, ⚡ motor (a. fig.). **~boot** n motorboat. **~fahrrad** n motorized bicycle. **~haube** f a) mot. bonnet, Am. hood, b) ✈ (engine) cowling.

motorisch [mo'to:rɪʃ] adj ♂ motor.

motorisieren [motori'zi:rən] v/t (h) motorize, esp. ✗ mechanize.

'Motorpumpe f power pump.

'Motorrad n (~ **fahren** ride a) motorcycle (F motorbike): ~ **mit Beiwagen** combination. **~fahrer(in** f) m motorcyclist.

'Motor|roller m (motor) scooter. **~säge** f power saw. **~schaden** m engine trouble. **~schlitten** m snowmobile. **~sport** m motor sport.

Motte ['mɔtə] f (-; -n) zo. moth.

'Mottenkugel f mothball.

'mottenzerfressen adj motheaten.

Motto ['mɔto] n (-s; -s) motto.

motzen ['mɔtsən] v/i (h) F beef.

Möwe ['mø:və] f (-; -n) zo. (sea)gull.

Mücke ['mykə] f (-; -n) zo. mosquito, midge: **aus e-r ~ e-n Elefanten machen** make a mountain out of a molehill. **'Mückenstich** m mosquito bite.

Mucks [mʊks] m (-es; -e) F (**k-n ~ sagen** not to a utter a) sound. **'mucksen** v/i (a. **sich ~**) (h) stir, make a sound.

'mucksmäuschen'still adj F person: as quiet as a mouse: **es war ~** you could have heard a pin drop.

müde ['my:də] adj (~ **werden** get) tired: **zum Umfallen ~** ready to drop; fig. **nicht ~ werden zu** inf not to tire of ger.

'Müdigkeit f (-; no pl) tiredness.

Muff [mʊf] m (-[e]s; -e) muff.

Muffe ['mʊfə] f (-; -n) ⊙ sleeve, socket.

Muffel ['mʊfəl] m (-s; -) F sourpuss.
...muffel m → *Krawatten-, Partymuffel.*
muffig ['mʊfɪç] adj **1.** musty (*air etc*). **2.** *fig*. a) stuffy, b) grumpy.
Mühe ['my:ə] f (-; -n) a) trouble, pains, b) effort, c) difficulties (*mit* with, in doing): *vergebliche ~* waste of time (*or* energy); *mit ~ und Not* barely, with (great) difficulty; *(nicht) der ~ wert* (not) worth the trouble; *sich (große) ~ geben* take (great) trouble (*or* pains) (*mit* over), try hard; *sich die ~ machen zu inf* go to the trouble of *ger*; *k-e ~ scheuen* spare no effort (*or* pains); *gib dir k-e ~!, spar dir die ~!* save yourself the trouble!, don't bother!
'**mühelos** adj effortless, easy.
'**mühevoll** adj hard, difficult, laborious.
Mühle ['my:lə] f (-; -n) **1.** mill: → *Wasser.* **2.** F *contp.* ✈, *mot*. crate, bus. **3.** a.
'**Mühlespiel** n (nine men's) morris.
'**Mühlrad** n millwheel.
'**Mühlstein** m millstone.
Mühsal ['my:za:l] f (-; *no pl*) a) toil, trouble(s), b) strain.
'**mühsam I** adj a) troublesome, b) hard, c) tiring. **II** adv with difficulty: *sich et. ~ verdienen* work hard for s.th.; *sich ~ erheben* struggle to one's feet.
Mulatte [mu'latə] m (-n; -n), **Mu'lattin** f (-; -nen) mulatto.
Mulde ['mʊldə] f (-; -n) hollow.
Mull [mʊl] m (-[e]s; -e) muslin, 🩹 gauze.
Müll [mʏl] m (-s; *no pl*) rubbish, refuse, *Am*. garbage. '**Müllabfuhr** f refuse (*Am*. garbage) collection.
'**Mullbinde** f 🩹 gauze bandage.
'**Mülleimer** m rubbish bin, *Am*. garbage can.
Müller ['mʏlɔr] m (-s; -) miller.
'**Müll|fahrer** m dustman, *Am*. garbage man. **~platz** m F dump. **~schlucker** m rubbish chute. **~tonne** f dustbin, *Am*. garbage can. **~verbrennungsanlage** f incinerating plant. **~verwertungsanlage** f waste utilization plant. **~wagen** m dustcart, *Am*. garbage truck.
mulmig ['mʊlmɪç] adj F **1.** ticklish. **2.** *mir ist ganz ~ zumute* a) I feel queasy (*or* funny), b) I've got an uneasy feeling, c) I am scared.
Multi ['mʊlti] m (-s; -s) F multinational (concern).
Multimillio,när m multimillionaire.

Multiplikation [mʊltiplika'tsio:n] f (-; -en) ✚ multiplication. **Multiplikator** [mʊltipli'ka:tɔr] m (-s; -en [-ka'to:rən]) multiplier. **multiplizieren** [mʊltipli'tsi:rən] v/t (h) multiply (*mit* by).
Mumie ['mu:miə] f (-; -n) mummy.
Mumm [mʊm] m (-s; *no pl*) F spunk, guts.
Mumps [mʊmps] m (-; *no pl*) 🩹 mumps.
Mund [mʊnt] m (-[e]s; ⸚er) mouth: *wie aus einem ~e* as one man; *~ und Nase aufsperren* be dum(b)founded; *den ~ halten* keep one's mouth shut; *halt den ~!* shut up!; F *den ~ voll nehmen* talk big; *du nimmst mir das Wort aus dem ~e* you are taking the very words out of my mouth; F *j-m über den ~ fahren* cut s.o. short; *in aller ~e sein* be the talk of the town; *nicht auf den ~ gefallen sein* have a ready (*or* glib) tongue; → *absparen, Blatt* 1, *stopfen* 3, *verbrennen* 1, *wässerig etc*.
'**Mundart** f dialect.
'**Munddusche** f oral spray.
Mündel ['mʏndəl] n (-s; -) 🏛 ward.
'**mündelsicher** adj ✝ *~e Papiere* gilt-edged securities.
münden ['mʏndən] v/i (sn) *~ in* (*acc*) a) *river*: flow into, b) (a. *auf acc*) *road etc*: lead into, c) *fig*. lead to, end in.
'**Mundgeruch** m 🩹 bad breath, halitosis.
'**Mundhar,monika** f mouth organ.
mündig ['mʏndɪç] adj **1.** 🏛 (*~ werden* come) of age. **2.** *fig*. responsible.
mündlich ['mʏntlɪç] adj verbal (*statement etc*), oral (*exam*): *~e Überlieferung* oral tradition; *alles weitere ~* I'll tell you the rest when I see you.
'**Mund|pflege** f oral hygiene. **~schutz** m 🩹 mask, *boxing*: gumshield. **~stück** n **1.** ♪, 🎙 mouthpiece. **2.** (cigarette) tip.
'**mundtot** adj ~ *machen* (reduce to) silence, *pol*. gag, muzzle.
'**Mündung** f (-; -en) **1.** *river*: a) mouth, b) estuary. **2.** *anat*., 🎙 mouth, ✖ muzzle.
'**Mund|wasser** n (-s; ⸚) mouthwash. **~werbung** f word-of-mouth advertising. **~werk** n (-[e]s; *no pl*) F *ein loses (gutes) ~ haben* have a loose tongue (the gift of the gab). **~winkel** m corner of one's mouth.
'**Mund-zu-'Mund-Beatmung** f mouth-to-mouth resuscitation, F kiss of life.

Munition [muni'tsĭo:n] *f* (-; *no pl*) ammunition.

Muniti'onslager *n* ammunition dump.

munkeln ['mʊŋkəln] *v/i, v/t* (h) whisper: *man munkelt, daß ...* it is rumo(u)red that ...

Münster ['mʏnstər] *n* (-s; -) minster, cathedral.

munter ['mʊntər] *adj* **1.** a) awake, b) up (and about). **2.** a) lively, b) cheerful, chirpy, c) vigorous; → *frisch 4, gesund.* '**Munterkeit** *f* (-; *no pl*) liveliness.

'**Muntermacher** *m* (-s; -) F pick-me-up.

'**Münzauto,mat** *m* slot machine.

Münze ['mʏntsə] *f* (-; -n) **1.** coin: *fig. et. für bare ~ nehmen* take s.th. at face value. **2.** medal. **3.** mint.

'**Münzeinwurf** *m* coin slot.

münzen ['mʏntsən] *v/t, v/i* (h) coin, mint: *fig. gemünzt sein auf* (*acc*) be meant for.

'**Münz|fernsprecher** *m* pay phone. **~sammlung** *f* coin collection. **~tank-(auto,mat)** *m* coin-operated petrol (*Am.* gas) pump. **~wechsler** *m* (-s; -) change machine.

mürbe ['mʏrbə] *adj* **1.** a) crumbly (*pastry etc*), mellow, very ripe (*fruit*), tender (*meat*), b) rotten (*wood*). **2.** *fig.* worn out: *j-n ~ machen* wear s.o. down; *~ werden* give in, wilt.

'**Mürbekuchen** *m* shortcake.

'**Mürbeteig** *m* short pastry.

Murks [mʊrks] *m* (-es; *no pl*) F botch-up: *~ machen* → '**murksen** *v/i* (h) F make a hash of things.

Murmel ['mʊrməl] *f* (-; -n) marble.

murmeln ['mʊrməln] *v/i, v/t* (h) murmur, mutter.

'**Murmeltier** *n* marmot: *fig. schlafen wie ein ~* sleep like a top (*or* log).

murren ['mʊrən] *v/i* (h) grumble (*über acc* about).

mürrisch ['mʏrɪʃ] *adj* surly, grumpy.

Mus [mu:s] *n* (-es; -e) puree, mash.

Muschel ['mʊʃəl] *f* (-; -n) **1.** *zo.* a) mussel, b) shell. **2.** *teleph.* a) earpiece, b) mouthpiece.

'**muschelförmig** *adj* shell-shaped.

Muse ['mu:zə] *f* (-; -n) *fig.* muse.

Museum [mu'ze:ʊm] *n* (-s; Museen) museum.

Musik [mu'zi:k] *f* (-; *no pl*) **1.** music. **2.** F band. **musikalisch** [muzi'ka:lɪʃ] *adj*

musical: **~e Untermalung** incidental music. **Musikalität** [muzikali'tɛ:t] *f* (-; *no pl*) musicality.

Mu'sikbegleitung *f* (musical) accompaniment. **Mu'sikbox** *f* jukebox.

Musiker ['mu:zikər] *m* (-s; -), **'Musikerin** *f* (-; -nen) musician.

Mu'sik|festspiele *pl* music festival. **~hochschule** *f* conservatory. **~instru,ment** *n* musical instrument. **~ka,pelle** *f* band. **~lehrer(in** *f)* *m* music teacher. **~stück** *n* piece of music. **~stunde** *f* music lesson. **~unterricht** *m* music lessons. **~wissenschaft** *f* (-; *no pl*) musicology.

musisch ['mu:zɪʃ] *adj* artistic (*talent etc*): *ped.* **~e Fächer** fine arts (subjects).

musizieren [muzi'tsi:rən] (h) **I** *v/i* make music. **II** *v/t* play.

Muskat [mʊs'ka:t] *m* (-[e]s; -e) nutmeg. **~blüte** *f* mace. **~nuß** *f* nutmeg apple.

Muskel ['mʊskəl] *m* (-s; -n) muscle: *die ~n spielen lassen* flex one's muscles. **~faser** *f* muscular fib/re (*Am.* -er). **~kater** *m* (-s; *no pl*) F sore muscles: *~ haben* feel stiff and aching. **~pa,ket** *n*, **~protz** *m* F muscleman. **~riß** *m* torn muscle. **~zerrung** *f* pulled muscle.

Muskulatur [mʊskula'tu:r] *f* (-; -en) muscular system, muscles.

muskulös [mʊsku'lø:s] *adj* muscular.

Müsli ['my:sli] *n* (-s; -) muesli.

Muß [mʊs] *es ist ein ~* it is a must.

Muße ['mu:sə] *f* (-; *no pl*) leisure.

'**Mußehe** *f* shotgun wedding.

müssen ['mʏsən] (mußte, müssen, h) **I** *v/i/aux* have to: *du mußt nicht hingehen* you needn't (*or* don't have to) go; *sie ~ bald kommen* they are bound to come soon; *der Zug müßte längst hier sein* the train is (long) overdue; *ich mußte (einfach) lachen* I couldn't help laughing; *muß das sein?* is that really necessary?, do you have to?; *wenn es unbedingt sein muß* if it can't be helped. **II** *v/i* (*pp* gemußt) *ich muß* I must, I have (got) to; *ich mußte* I had to; *ich müßte (eigentlich)* I ought to.

'**Mußestunde** *f* leisure hour.

müßig ['my:sɪç] *adj* **1.** idle. **2.** pointless.

'**Müßiggang** *m* (-[e]s; *no pl*) idleness.

'**Müßiggänger** [-gɛŋər] *m* (-s; -) idler.

mußte ['mʊstə] *pret of* **müssen.**

Muster ['mʊstər] *n* (-s; -) **1.** pattern, model: *sie ist das ~ e-r guten Haus-*

frau she's a model housewife. **2.** sample, specimen. **3.** *textil.* pattern, design.
'**Muster|beispiel** *n* classic example (*für* of). **~betrieb** *m* model plant. **~exem,plar** *n* **1.** ✝ sample specimen. **2.** *print.* specimen copy. **3.** *a. iro.* perfect example. **~gatte** *m iro.* model husband.
'**mustergültig,** '**musterhaft** *adj* exemplary, model: *sich ~ benehmen* behave perfectly.
'**Muster|haus** *n* show house. **~knabe** *m iro.* paragon, *contp. prig.* **~koffer** *m* ✝ sample case. **~kollekti,on** *f* ✝ sample collection.
mustern ['mʊstərn] *v/t* (h) **1.** a) study, scrutinize, b) eye, look *s.o.* up and down, c) size *s.o.* up. **2.** ✕ inspect (*troops*), examine (*conscripts*): *gemustert werden* F have one's medical. **3.** pattern: → *gemustert.*
'**Musterpro,zeß** *m* ⚖ test case.
'**Musterung** *f* (-; -en) **1.** scrutiny. **2.** ✕ a) review (*of troops*), b) medical examination (for military service).
Mut [muːt] *m* (-[e]s; *no pl*) courage, F pluck: ~ *fassen* pluck up courage; *j-m den ~ nehmen* discourage s.o.; *den ~ sinken lassen* (*or verlieren*) lose heart, despair; *nur ~!* cheer up!
Mutation [muta'tsïoːn] *f* (-; -en) **1.** *biol.* mutation. **2.** → *Stimmbruch.*
mutieren [mu'tiːrən] *v/i* (h) mutate.
'**mutig** *adj* courageous, brave.
'**mutlos** *adj* discouraged, disheartened, despondent. '**Mutlosigkeit** *f* (-; *no pl*) discouragement, despondency.
mutmaßlich ['muːtmaːslɪç] *adj* probable, ⚖ putative.
'**Mutmaßung** *f* (-; -en) (*über acc* about) conjecture, speculation.
'**Mutprobe** *f* test of courage.
Mutter[1] ['mʊtər] *f* (-; ⸚) mother: *werdende ~* expectant mother; *e-e ~ von vier Kindern* a mother of four.
'**Mutter**[2] *f* (-; -n) ⊕ nut.
'**Mütterberatungsstelle** *f* child welfare centre, *Am.* maternity center.
'**Mutter|bindung** *f psych.* mother tie. **~boden** *m*, **~erde** *f* ✎ topsoil. **~gesell-**

schaft *f* ✝ parent company.
Mutter'gottes *f* (-; *no pl*) (Virgin) Mary.
'**Mutter|haus** *n eccl.* mother house. **~herz** *n* mother's heart. **~in,stinkt** *m* maternal instinct. **~kom,plex** *m* mother fixation. **~kuchen** *m* ✿ placenta. **~leib** *m* (-[e]s; *no pl*) womb.
mütterlich ['mʏtərlɪç] *adj* motherly, maternal. '**mütterlicherseits** *adv* on one's mother's side: *Onkel ~* maternal uncle.
'**Mütterlichkeit** *f* (-; *no pl*) motherliness.
'**Mutter|liebe** *f* motherly love. **~mal** *n* ✿ birthmark. **~milch** *f* mother's milk: *mit ~ genährt* breast-fed. **~mund** *m* (-[e]s; *no pl*) *anat.* uterine orifice.
'**Mutterschaft** *f* (-; *no pl*) motherhood, maternity.
'**Mutterschafts|hilfe** *f* maternity benefits. **~urlaub** *m* maternity leave.
'**Mutterschutz** *m* legal (job-)protection for expectant and nursing mothers.
'**mutter'seelenal'lein** *adj pred* all alone.
'**Muttersöhnchen** [-zøːnçən] *n* (-s; -) F mummy's darling.
'**Muttersprache** *f* mother tongue.
'**Muttersprachler** [-ʃpraːxlər] *m* (-s; -) native speaker.
'**Muttertag** *m* (-[e]s; *no pl*) Mother's Day.
'**Muttertier** *n* mother, dam.
'**Mutterwitz** *m* (-es; *no pl*) **1.** common sense. **2.** natural wit.
Mutti ['mʊti] *f* (-; -s) F mum(my), *Am.* mom.
'**mutwillig** *adj* wilful, wanton.
Mütze ['mʏtsə] *f* (-; -n) cap.
Myrrhe ['myrə] *f* (-; -n) myrrh.
mysteriös [mysteˈrïøːs] *adj* mysterious.
Mystik ['mʏstɪk] *f* (-; *no pl*) mysticism.
Mystiker ['mʏstɪkər] *m* (-s; -) mystic.
mystisch ['mʏstɪʃ] *adj* **1.** a) mystic, b) mystical. **2.** mysterious.
Mythe ['myːtə] *f* (-; -n) myth.
'**mythisch** *adj* mythical.
Mythologie [mytoloˈgiː] *f* (-; -n) mythology. **mythologisch** [mytoˈloːgɪʃ] *adj* mythological. **mythologisieren** [mytologiˈziːrən] *v/t* (h) mythologize.
Mythos ['myːtɔs] *m* (-; Mythen) myth.

N

N, n [ɛn] *n* (-; -) N, n.

na [na] *int* F a) well, b) hey: ~, ~! come on (now)!; → **also!** there you are!; ~ **schön!** all right then!; ~, **so (et)was!** just fancy that!; → **warten!, und.**

Nabe ['na:bə] *f* (-; -n) ⊙ hub.

Nabel ['na:bəl] *m* (-s; -) navel.

Nabelschnur *f* umbilical cord.

nach [na:x] **I** *prep (dat)* **1.** to, toward(s), for: ~ *England gehen* (*abreisen*) go to (leave) for England; *der Zug* ~ *Paris* the train for Paris; *das Schiff fährt* ~ *Singapur* the ship is bound for Singapore. **2.** after: *e-r* ~ *dem anderen* one after the other, one by one. **3.** a) after, b) within, in (*three days etc*): *zehn Minuten* ~ *drei* ten minutes past three. **4.** according to, by, from: ~ *deutschem Recht* under German law; ~ *e-m Roman von Balzac* after a novel by Balzac; *wenn es* ~ *mir ginge* if I had my way; → *Ansicht* 1, *Natur, Uhr etc.* **5.** for: ~ *Gold graben* dig for gold; ~ *j-m fragen* ask for s.o. **II** *adv* **6.** after: *mir* ~! after me!, follow me! **7.** ~ *und* ~ little by little, gradually; ~ *wie vor* (now) as ever.

'nachäffen [-ɛfən] *v/t (sep, -ge-, h)* F ape.

'nachahmen [-a:mən] *v/t (sep, -ge-, h)* a) imitate, copy, b) take off, parody.

'nachahmenswert *adj* exemplary.

'Nachahmung *f* (-; -en) imitation.

Nachbar ['naxba:r] *m* (-n; -n) neighbo(u)r: *die* ~*n a.* the neighbo(u)rhood.

'Nachbar... neighbo(u)ring (*district, house, country, etc*).

'Nachbarin *f* (-; -nen) neighbo(u)r.

'nachbarlich *adj* **1.** a. *gut* ~ neighbo(u)rly. **2.** next-door (*garden etc*).

'Nachbarschaft *f* (-; *no pl*) neighbo(u)rhood, a. the neighbo(u)rs.

'nachbauen *v/t (sep, -ge-, h)* ⊙ copy.

'Nachbehandlung *f* ⊙ subsequent treatment, a. ⚕ after-treatment.

'nachbessern *v/t (sep, -ge-, h)* touch up.

'nachbestellen *v/t (sep, h)* order some more, ✝ place a repeat order for.

'Nachbestellung *f* ✝ repeat order (*gen* for).

'nachbeten *v/t (sep, -ge-, h)* F parrot.

'nachbilden *v/t (sep, -ge-, h)* copy, reproduce.

'Nachbildung *f* (-; -en) copy, replica.

'nachda,tieren *v/t (sep, h)* postdate.

nach'dem *conj* **1.** after, when. **2.** → *je* 4. **3.** since.

'nachdenken *v/i (irr, sep, -ge-, h,* → *denken)* think (*über acc* about): *denk mal nach!* think a little!; *Zeit zum* ⚷ *brauchen* need time to think (it over).

'nachdenklich *adj* thoughtful, pensive: *j-n* ~ *machen* set s.o. thinking.

'Nachdruck¹ *m* (-[e]s; *no pl*) stress, emphasis: *mit* ~ a) emphatically, b) energetically; ~ *legen auf (acc), (dat)* ~ *verleihen* stress, emphasize.

'Nachdruck² *m* (-[e]s; -e) reprint: ~ *verboten!* all rights reserved!

'nachdrucken *v/t (sep, -ge-, h)* reprint: *unerlaubt* ~ pirate.

'nachdrücklich [-drʏklɪç] *adj* emphatic (*warning etc*), forceful (*claim etc*): **et.** ~ *empfehlen* recommend s.th. strongly; ~ *verlangen* insist on.

'Nachdrucksrecht *n* right of reproduction.

'nacheifern *v/i (sep, -ge-, h) j-m* ~ emulate s.o.

nachein'ander *adv* **1.** one after another, a. in succession. **2.** by turns.

'Nacherzählung *f ped.* summary.

'nachfahren *v/i (irr, sep, -ge-, sn,* → *fahren) j-m* ~ follow s.o.

'Nachfaß|schreiben *n* follow-up letter. **~werbung** *f* follow-up advertising.

'Nachfolge *f* (-; *no pl*) succession: *j-s* ~ *antreten* → **'nachfolgen** *v/i (sep, -ge-, sn) j-m (im Amt)* ~ succeed s.o. (in office). **'nachfolgend** *adj* following.

'Nachfolger *m* (-s; -) successor.

'Nachforderung *f* additional claim.

'nachforschen *v/i (sep, -ge-, h) (dat)* investigate. **'Nachforschung** *f* (-; -en) investigation: *~en anstellen* (*über acc*) investigate (*s.th.*).

'Nachfrage *f* (-; -n) **1.** ✝ demand (*nach* for). **2.** inquiry. **'nachfragen** *v/i (sep, -ge-, h)* inquire, ask.

'nachfühlen *v/i (sep , -ge-, h) j-m et.*

(**können**) feel with s.o., understand s.o.'s feelings about s.th.

'**nachfüllen** v/t (sep, -ge-, h) **1.** fill up, refill, top up. **2.** add (water etc).

'**nachgeben** v/i (irr, sep, -ge-, h, → **geben**) **1.** ground etc: give (way). **2.** prices etc: drop. **3.** (dat to) give in, yield.

'**Nachgebühr** f ⚹ surcharge.

'**Nachgeburt** f ⚹ afterbirth.

'**nachgehen** v/i (irr, sep, -ge-, sn, → **gehen**) (dat) **1.** follow. **2.** fig. look into (a matter), follow, check up on (rumour, tip, etc), attend to (business etc), pursue (one's studies): **s-r Arbeit** ~ go about one's work. **3.** indulge in, seek, pursue (pleasure etc). **4.** be slow, lose: **m-e Uhr geht (e-e Minute) nach** my watch loses (a minute). **5.** fig. **j-m** ~ haunt s.o.

'**nachgemacht** I pp of **nachmachen**. II adj a) counterfeit, b) imitation.

'**nachgerade** adv **1.** really. **2.** by now.

'**Nachgeschmack** m a. fig. aftertaste.

'**nachgiebig** [-gi:bɪç] adj **1.** compliant, soft. **2.** ⚙ flexible, pliant. '**Nachgiebigkeit** f (-; no pl) compliance, softness.

'**nachhaken** v/i (sep, -ge-, h) F follow (it) up: **bei j-m in e-m Punkt** ~ press s.o. on a point.

'**nachhaltig** adj a) lasting (effect etc), sustained (efforts etc), b) strong, effective: ~ **wirken** have a lasting effect; ~ **beeinflussen** influence strongly.

'**nachhelfen** v/i (irr, sep, -ge-, h, → **helfen**) help: **e-r Sache** ~ help s.th. along.

nach'**her** adv a) afterward(s), b) later (on): **bis** ~**!** see you later!, so long!

'**Nachhilfe** f private lessons. ~**lehrer(in** f) m (private) tutor. ~**stunde** f **1.** private lesson. **2.** pl → ~**unterricht** m private lessons.

'**nachhinein** adv **im** ~ after the event.

'**nachhinken** v/i (sep, -ge-, sn) fig. lag behind.

'**Nachholbedarf** m **1.** ⚹ backlog demand. **2.** fig. deficit.

'**nachholen** v/t (sep, -ge-, h) **1.** make up for lost time etc, catch up on work, sleep, etc. **2.** fetch s.o., s.th. later.

'**Nachhut** f (-; -en) ✕ rearguard: **die** ~ **bilden** a. fig. bring up the rear.

'**nachjagen** v/i (sep, -ge-, sn) (dat) chase after, a. fig. pursue.

'**Nachklang** m fig. echo, reminiscence.

'**Nachkomme** m (-n; -n) descendant, off-

spring: **ohne** ~**n** ⚹ without issue.

'**nachkommen** v/i (irr, sep, -ge-, sn, → **kommen**) **1.** come later, follow. **2.** a. fig. keep up (**mit** with). **3.** (dat) comply with (order, wish, etc), meet (obligation), keep (promise).

'**Nachkommenschaft** f descendants, ⚹ issue. '**Nachkömmling** [-kœmlɪŋ] m (-s; -e) late arrival.

'**Nachkriegs...** post-war ...

'**Nachlaß** [-las] m (-sses; -lässe) **1.** estate: **literarischer** ~ unpublished works. **2.** ⚹ reduction: **e-n** ~ **gewähren** allow a discount (**auf** acc on).

'**nachlassen** (irr, sep, -ge-, h, → **lassen**) I v/i **1.** decrease, weaken, wind: drop, rain, storm etc: let up, noise etc: subside, pain: ease, effect, strength, etc: wear off, performance, demand, etc: drop (off), interest etc: flag, slacken. **2.** a) deteriorate, grow weaker, fail, b) go off, be slowing down, runner etc: wilt, c) mentally: lose one's grip; **nicht** ~**!** hang on! II v/t **3.** leave (behind): **nachgelassene Werke** unpublished works. **4.** et. vom Preis ~ allow a discount.

'**Nachlaßgericht** n ⚹⚹ probate court.

'**nachlässig** adj careless, negligent, sloppy. '**Nachlässigkeit** f (-; no pl) carelessness, negligence, sloppiness.

'**nachlaufen** v/i (irr, sep, -ge-, sn, → **laufen**) **j-m** ~ run after s.o.; **den Mädchen** ~ chase (after) the girls.

'**nachlesen** v/t (irr, sep, -ge-, h, → **lesen**) read up, look s.th. up.

'**nachliefern** v/t (sep, -ge-, h) supply s.th. later (or in addition).

'**nachlösen** v/i, v/t (sep, -ge-, h) (**e-e Fahrkarte**) ~ buy a ticket on the train.

'**nachmachen** v/t (sep, -ge-, h) a) copy, imitate, b) forge: **j-m et.** ~ copy s.th. s.o. does; **das soll ihm erst mal e-r** ~**!** I'd like to see anyone do better!

'**nachmessen** v/t (irr, sep, -ge-, h, → **messen**) check.

'**Nachmittag** m (**am** ~ in the) afternoon; **heute** ~ this afternoon. '**nachmittags** adv in the afternoon. '**Nachmittagsvorstellung** f thea. etc matinée.

'**Nachnahme** [-na:mə] f (-; -n) **et. als** (or **per**) ~ **schicken** send s.th. cash (Am. collect) on delivery (abbr. C.O.D.).

'**Nachnahmesendung** f C.O.D. parcel.

'**Nachname** m surname, last name.

'**nachplappern** v/t (sep, -ge-, h) F parrot.

'**Nachporto** n surcharge.

'**nachprüfbar** adj verifiable.

'**nachprüfen** v/t (sep, -ge-, h) **1.** check. **2.** a) re-examine, b) examine at a later date. '**Nachprüfung** f (-; -en) **1.** check(ing). **2.** examination at a later date.

'**nachrechnen** v/t (sep, -ge-, h) check.

'**Nachrede** f üble ~ defamation.

Nachricht ['naːxrɪçt] f (-; -en) a) (e-e ~ a piece of) news, b) message, c) news (item); ~ *item*; ~ *erhalten von* hear from; *j-m* ~ *geben* let s.o. know; *e-e* ~ *hinterlassen* leave a message.

'**Nachrichten|agen,tur** f, ~**bü,ro** n press agency. ~**dienst** m **1.** radio, TV news service. **2.** ✕ intelligence service. ~**sa-tel,lit** m communications satellite. ~**sendung** f radio, TV newscast, news broadcast. ~**sperre** f pol. news blackout. ~**sprecher(in** f) m news reader, newscaster. ~**technik** f (tele)communication(s) (engineering). ~**wesen** n (-s; no pl) communications.

'**nachrücken** v/i (sep, -ge-, sn) **1.** a. fig. move up. **2.** ✕ follow on.

'**Nachruf** m (-[e]s; -e) obituary.

'**nachrüsten** v/i (sep, -ge-, h) **1.** pol. close the armament gap. **2.** a. v/t ☼ retrofit. '**Nachrüstsatz** m ☼ retrofit kit.

'**nachsagen** v/t (sep, -ge-, h) **1.** repeat. **2.** *j-m et.* ~ say s.th. of s.o.

'**Nachsai,son** f off season.

'**Nachsatz** m **1.** postscript. **2.** ling. final clause.

'**nachschenken** v/t, v/i (sep, -ge-, h) j-m (et.) ~ top s.o. up (with s.th.).

'**nachschlagen** (irr, sep, -ge-, h, → **schlagen**) I v/t **1.** look s.th. up. II v/i **2.** im Lexikon ~ consult a dictionary. **3.** F *j-m* ~ take after s.o.

'**Nachschlagewerk** n reference book.

'**Nachschlüssel** m duplicate key.

'**Nachschrift** f postscript.

'**Nachschub** m (-[e]s; no pl) (an dat of) supply (a. fig.), coll. supplies.

'**Nachschuß** m soccer: follow-up shot.

'**nachsehen** (irr, sep, -ge-, h, → **sehen**) I v/i **1.** gaze after. **2.** mach ... ~ ob ... (go and) see whether ... II v/t **3.** inspect, check, ped. correct. **4.** → **nachschlagen** 1. **5.** j-m et. ~ forgive s.o. s.th.

'**Nachsehen**: das ~ haben be the loser.

'**nachsenden** v/t (irr, sep, -ge-, h, → senden²) forward.

'**Nachsicht** f a) forbearance, b) leniency; ~ **üben** be lenient; mit j-m ~ haben be lenient towards s.o.

'**nachsichtig** adj lenient, forbearing.

'**Nachsilbe** f ling. suffix.

'**nachsitzen** v/i (irr, sep, -ge-, h, → sitzen) ~ müssen be kept in.

'**Nachsommer** m late (or Indian) summer. '**Nachsorge** f (-; no pl) ✚ aftercare. '**Nachspeise** f dessert.

'**Nachspiel** n **1.** ♪ postlude. **2.** thea. epilog(ue Br.). **3.** sex: afterplay. **4.** fig. sequel: die Sache wird ein ~ haben there are bound to be consequences.

'**nachspielen** v/i (sep, -ge-, h) sports: play (~ lassen allow) extra time.

nächst [nɛːçst] I sup of nahe. II adj **1.** nearest (a. fig. relatives etc), a. shortest: die ~e Umgebung the immediate vicinity; aus ~er Entfernung at close range. **2.** next: am ~en Tage the next day; in den ~en Tagen in the next few days; Mittwoch ~er Woche Wednesday week; in ~er Zeit in the near future; bei ~er Gelegenheit at the first opportunity; im ~en Augenblick the next moment. III adv **3.** am ~en (dat to) next, nearest, closest; fig. j-m am ~en stehen be closest to s.o.; (dat) am ~en kommen come closest to. **4.** fürs ~e for the time being. IV prep **5.** (dat) next to.

'**nächst'best** adj **1.** first (comer etc). **2.** second-best, next-best.

'**Nächstbeste 1.** m, f the next best, the first person. **2.** n the next best (thing).

'**Nächste 1.** m, f (-n; -n) a) neighbo(u)r, one's fellow, b) the next (one): jeder ist sich selbst der ~ charity begins at home; der ~, bitte! next (one) please! **2.** n (-n; -n) the next (or first) thing.

'**nachstehen** v/i (irr, sep, -ge-, h, → stehen) j-m ~ in (or an dat) be inferior to s.o. in; j-m in nichts ~ be in no way inferior to s.o. '**nachstehend** I adj following. II adv in the following.

'**nachstellen** (sep, -ge-, h) I v/t **1.** put back (clock etc). **2.** ☼ (re)adjust. II v/i (dat) a) be after, b) persecute. '**Nachstellung** f (-; -en) fig. persecution. '**Nächstenliebe** f (-; no pl) charity.

nächstens ['nɛːçstəns] adv (very) soon.

'**nächstliegend** *adj* nearest: *fig. das Nächstliegende* the obvious thing.

Nacht [naxt] *f* (-; ˙˙e) (*bei ~* at) night: *gute ~! a. iro.* good night!; *heute ~* tonight; *die ~ zum Tage machen* turn night into day; *es wird ~* it is getting dark; *zu ~ essen* have supper; *bis spät* (*or tief*) *in die ~* till late in the night; *über ~ a. fig.* overnight; *die ganze ~* (*hindurch or lang*) all night (long); *im Schutze* (*or Dunkel*) *der ~, bei ~ und Nebel* under the cover of night, *w.s.* secretly.

'**Nacht|arbeit** *f* nightwork. ˷**blind** *adj* night-blind. ˷**creme** *f* night cream. ˷**dienst** *m* night duty: *~ haben* be on night duty, *chemist's shop etc:* be open all night.

'**Nachteil** *m* (-[e]s; -e) disadvantage, *a.* drawback, *sports, a. fig.* handicap: *zum ~ von* to the disadvantage of; *im ~ sein* be at a disadvantage.

'**nachteilig** *adj* disadvantageous, detrimental (*für* to): *nichts Nachteiliges* nothing unfavo(u)rable; *~ beeinflussen* affect adversely.

nächtelang ['nɛçtə-] **I** *adj* ˷**e Diskussionen** *etc* night after night of discussions *etc.* **II** *adv* night after night.

'**Nacht|essen** *n* supper. ˷**frost** *m* night frost. ˷**hemd** *n* a) nightshirt, b) nightdress, F nightie.

Nachtigall ['naxtɪɡal] *f* (-; -en) *zo.* nightingale.

'**Nachtisch** *m* (-[e]s; -e) dessert, sweet, F afters.

'**Nachtklub** *m* nightclub.
'**Nachtleben** *n* nightlife.

nächtlich ['nɛçtlɪç] *adj* nocturnal, nightly: *der ~e Park* the park at night.

'**Nacht|lo̩kal** *n* nightclub. ˷**porti̩er** *m* night porter. ˷**quar̩tier** *n* place for the night, ✕ night quarters.

'**Nachtrag** [-tra:k] *m* (-[e]s; ˙˙e [-trɛːɡə]) supplement. '**nachtragen** *v/t* (*irr, sep, -ge-*, h, → *tragen*) **1.** *j-m et.* → *fig.* bear s.o. a grudge for s.th. **2.** add (*in writing*). '**nachtragend** *adj* unforgiving.

'**nachträglich** [-trɛ:klɪç] **I** *adj* a) additional, b) belated, c) later. **II** *adv* subsequently, later: *~ herzlichen Glückwunsch!* belated best wishes!

'**Nachtragshaushalt** *m* supplementary budget.

'**nachtrauern** *v/i* (*sep, -ge-*, h) *j-m* (*e-r*

Sache) *~* mourn s.o. (s.th.).
'**Nachtruhe** *f* sleep.

nachts *adv* at (*or* during the) night.
'**Nacht|schicht** *f* night shift. ˷**schwärmer** *m* night owl. ˷**schwester** *f* night nurse. ˷**speicherofen** *m* night storage heater. ˷**strom** *m* off-peak electricity. ˷**tisch** *m* bedside table. ˷**topf** *m* chamber pot. ˷**tre̩sor** *m* night safe. ˷**-und-'Nebel-Akti̩on** *f* undercover operation. ˷**wache** *f* night watch. ˷**wächter** *m* **1.** night watchman. **2.** F *contp.* dope. ˷**zug** *m* night train.

'**Nachuntersuchung** *f* checkup.
'**nachvollziehen** *v/t* (*irr, sep,* h, → *vollziehen*) understand, duplicate.
'**nachwachsen** *v/i* (*irr, sep, -ge-*, sn, → *wachsen*) grow again.
'**Nachwahl** *f parl.* by-election, *Am.* special election.

'**Nachwehen** *pl fig.* aftermath.
'**nachweinen** (*sep, -ge-*, h) **I** *v/i* → *nachtrauern.* **II** *v/t* → *Träne.*

Nachweis ['na:xvaɪs] *m* (-es; -e) **1.** a) proof, evidence, b) certificate: *den ~ führen* (*or* *erbringen*) prove, show. **2.** detection. '**nachweisbar** *adj* demonstrable, detectable: *... sind ~ a. ...* can be proved. '**nachweisen** *v/t* (*irr, sep, -ge-*, h, → *weisen*) prove, establish: *man konnte ihm nichts ~* nothing could be proved against him; *j-m e-n Fehler ~* show that s.o. has made a mistake. '**nachweislich I** *adj* demonstrable. **II** *adv* demonstrably: *er war ~ da* there is evidence that he was there.

'**Nachwelt** *f* (-; *no pl*) posterity.
'**nachwirken** *v/i* (*sep, -ge-*, h) have a lasting effect. '**Nachwirkung** *f* after-effect: ˷**en** *fig. a.* aftermath.
'**Nachwort** *n* (-[e]s; -e) epilog(ue *Br.*).
'**Nachwuchs** *m* (-es; *no pl*) **1.** a) the young generation, b) young talent (*a. sports*), F new blood, ✝ junior staff, trainees, ✕ *etc* recruits: *der ärztliche ~* the new generation of doctors. **2.** F a) offspring, b) addition to the family.
'**Nachwuchs...** a) talented, young, up-and-coming (*author, actor, etc*), b) ✝ junior, trainee (*salesman etc*).
'**Nachwuchssorgen** *pl* ˷ **haben** have difficulty in) finding young talent.
'**nachzahlen** *v/t, v/i* (*sep, -ge-*, h) pay extra, pay later.

'**nachzählen** v/t (sep, -ge-, h) check.
'**Nachzahlung** f additional payment.
'**nachziehen** (irr, sep, -ge-, → ziehen) I
v/t (h) **1.** drag (or pull) behind one, drag
(foot etc). **2.** trace (line etc), pencil (eye-
brows): die Lippen ~ touch up one's
lips. **3.** ⊕ tighten (screw etc). II v/i **4.**
(sn) follow. **5.** (h) F fig. follow suit.
'**Nachzügler** [-tsy:glər] m (-s; -) **1.** strag-
gler, latecomer. **2.** F late arrival.
Nacken ['nakən] m (-s; -) (nape of the)
neck: j-m im ~ sitzen a) be hard on
s.o.'s heels, b) fig. be breathing down
s.o.'s neck; fig. den ~ steifhalten keep a
stiff upper lip; → steifen.
'**Nackenschlag** m fig. blow.
'**Nackenwirbel** m cervical vertebra.
nackt [nakt] adj naked, bare (a. fig.), esp.
art: nude: völlig ~ stark naked; ~ baden (malen) swim (paint) in the nude;
sich ~ ausziehen strip; ~e Tatsachen
hard facts; die ~e Wahrheit the plain
truth; das ~e Leben retten escape with
one's bare life.
'**Nacktbadestrand** m nudist beach.
'**Nacktheit** f (-; no pl) nakedness, fig. a.
bareness.
'**Nacktkul,tur** f (-; no pl) nudism.
Nadel ['na:dəl] f (-; -n) a) needle, b) of
record player: stylus, c) pin. ~baum m
conifer(ous tree). ~öhr n **1.** eye of a
needle. **2.** fig. bottleneck. ~stich m (fig.
pin)prick. ~streifen m Anzug etc mit ~
pinstripe(d) suit etc. ~wald m conife-
rous forest.
Nagel ['na:gəl] m (-s; ") nail: fig. et. an
den ~ hängen give s.th. up; Nägel mit
Köpfen machen do things properly;
den ~ auf den Kopf treffen hit the nail
on the head; er ist ein ~ zu m-m Sarg
he is a nail in my coffin. ~bett n anat.
nail bed. ~bürste f nail brush. ~feile f
nail file. ~häutchen n cuticle.
'**Nagellack** m nail varnish (or polish,
Am. enamel). ~entferner m nail-var-
nish (or nail-polish) remover.
nageln ['na:gəln] v/t (h) nail (an acc to).
'**nagel'neu** adj F brand-new.
'**Nagelschere** f (pair of) nail scissors.
nagen ['na:gən] v/t, v/i (h) a. fig. gnaw: ~
an (dat) a. fig. gnaw at. **'nagend** adj
fig. gnawing, nagging (doubt etc).
'**Nager** m (-s; -), '**Nagetier** n rodent.
'**Nahaufnahme** f film etc: close-up.

nahe ['na:ə] I adj a) near, close (both a.
fig.), nearby, b) approaching, imminent (death etc): der Nahe Osten the
Middle East; in ~r Zukunft in the near
future; den Tränen ~ on the verge of
tears. II adv near, close, nearby: ~ bei
near (to), close to; ~ beieinander close
together; ~ verwandt closely related;
von nah und fern from far and near;
von ~m up close, at close range; j-m zu
~ treten offend s.o.; ich war ~ daran,
ihn zu ohrfeigen I very nearly slapped
his face. III prep (dat) near, close to.
Nähe ['nɛ:ə] f (-; no pl) a) nearness (a.
fig.), b) vicinity, neighbo(u)rhood: aus
der ~ at close range; ganz in der ~ quite
near; in der ~ bleiben stay around; in
d-r ~ near you; in greifbare ~ gerückt
near at hand.
'**nahe'bei** adv nearby.
'**nahebringen** v/t (irr, sep, -ge-, h, →
bringen) fig. j-m et. ~ make s.o. appreciate s.th.
'**nahegehen** v/i (irr, sep, -ge-, sn, →
gehen) fig. j-m ~ affect s.o. deeply.
'**nahegelegen** I pp of naheliegen. II adj
nearby.
'**nahekommen** v/i (irr, sep, -ge-, sn, →
kommen) fig. come close (dat to): sich
(or einander) ~ become close.
'**nahelegen** v/t (sep, -ge-, h) fig. j-m et. ~
suggest s.th. to s.o.; j-m ~, et. zu tun
urge s.o. to do s.th.
'**naheliegen** v/i (irr, sep, -ge-, h, → liegen) fig. a) seem (very) likely, b) be the
obvious thing: die Vermutung liegt
nahe, daß ... it is fair to assume that ...
'**naheliegend** adj obvious.
nähen ['nɛ:ən] (h) I v/t sew, a. ✂ stitch:
sich ein Kleid ~ make a dress for o.s. II
v/i sew.
näher ['nɛ:ər] I comp of nahe. II adj **1.**
nearer, closer: die ~e Umgebung the
(immediate) vicinity. **2.** further (data
etc), more detailed: bei ~er Betrachtung on closer inspection. III adv **3.** (an
dat, bei to) nearer, closer: ~ kommen
come (or draw) nearer. **4.** more closely:
ich kenne ihn ~ I know him quite well;
sich mit e-r Sache ~ befassen go into
a matter (more closely); et. ~ erläutern
explain s.th. at greater detail.
'**näherbringen** v/t (irr, sep, -ge-, h, →
bringen) fig. j-m et. ~ make s.th. acces-

sible to s.o.; *Menschen einander ~* bring people closer together.

'**Nähere** n (-n; *no pl*) the details, (further) particulars: *ich weiß nichts ~s* I don't know any details.

Näherei [nɛːəˈraɪ] f (-; -en) sewing.

'**Naherholungsgebiet** n recreation area in the immediate vicinity of a big city.

'**näherkommen** v/i (*irr, sep,* -ge-, sn, → **kommen**) get (*or* be) nearer (*dat* to): *fig. j-m ~* become closer to s.o.; *jetzt kommen wir der Sache schon näher!* now we're getting somewhere!

'**näherliegen** v/i (*irr, sep,* -ge-, h, → **liegen**) *fig.* be more obvious.

nähern [ˈnɛːərn] *sich ~* (h) approach, a. draw near; *sich j-m ~* approach s.o.

'**Näherungs...** Æ approximate (*calculation, value, etc*).

'**nahestehen** v/i (*irr, sep,* -ge-, h, → **stehen**) *fig. j-m ~* be close to s.o.

'**nahezu** adv almost, nearly, next to.

'**Nähgarn** n sewing thread.

'**Nahkampf** m **1.** ✗ close combat. **2.** *boxing:* infighting.

nahm [naːm] *pret of* **nehmen**.

'**Nähma,schine** f sewing machine.

'**Nährboden** m **1.** culture medium (*for bacteria*). **2.** *fig.* breeding ground.

'**Nährcreme** f nutrient cream.

nähren [ˈnɛːrən] (h) **I** v/t feed, *fig.* nourish (*hope etc*), a. harbo(u)r (*hatred etc*): *sich ~ von* live on. **II** v/i be nourishing.

'**nahrhaft** adj nutritious, nourishing.

'**Nährmittel** pl cereal products.

'**Nährstoff** m nutrient.

Nahrung [ˈnaːrʊŋ] f (-; *no pl*) food, diet: *geistige ~* food for the mind.

'**Nahrungsaufnahme** f food intake.

'**Nahrungskette** f *biol.* food chain.

'**Nahrungsmangel** m lack of food.

'**Nahrungsmittel** n food(stuff), pl foodstuffs. **~chemiker** m food chemist.

'**Nährwert** m nutritional value.

'**Nähseide** f sewing silk.

Naht [naːt] f (-; ⸗e) seam, ⚙ a. joint: F *aus den* (*or allen*) *Nähten platzen* a. *fig.* be bursting at the seams.

'**nahtlos** adj **1.** seamless. **2.** *fig.* smooth.

'**Nahverkehr** m local traffic.

'**Nahverkehrszug** m commuter train.

'**Nähzeug** n (-[e]s; *no pl*) sewing kit.

'**Nahziel** n immediate objective.

naiv [naˈiːf] adj naive: *~er Maler* primitive.

Naivität [naiviˈtɛːt] f (-; *no pl*) naivety.

Name [ˈnaːmə] m (-n; -n) name, a. reputation: *wie ist Ihr ~?* what is your name?; *im ~n* (*gen*), *in j-s ~n* → *namens* II; (*nur*) *dem ~n nach* by name (only); *sich e-n ~n machen* make a name for o.s.; *das Kind beim rechten ~n nennen* call a spade a spade.

'**Namenliste** f list of names.

'**namenlos** adj **1.** nameless, a. anonymous. **2.** *fig.* unspeakable.

'**namens I** adv by the name of, called. **II** prep (*gen*) in the name of, on behalf of.

'**Namens|aktie** f registered share (*Am.* stock). **~schild** n name plate. **~tag** m name day. **~vetter** m namesake. **~zug** m signature.

namentlich [ˈnaːməntlɪç] **I** adj **1.** by name: **~e Abstimmung** roll-call vote. **II** adv **2.** by name. **3.** *fig.* (e)specially.

'**namhaft** adj **1.** considerable (*sum etc*). **2.** well-known (*artist etc*). **3.** *~ machen* name.

nämlich [ˈnɛːmlɪç] adv **1.** namely, that is (to say). **2.** for, you see, you know.

nannte [ˈnantə] *pret of* **nennen**.

nanu [naˈnuː] int hey.

Napalm [ˈnaːpalm] n (-s; *no pl*) napalm.

Napf [napf] m (-[e]s; ⸗e) bowl.

'**Napfkuchen** m deep-dish cake.

Nappa [ˈnapa] n (-[s]; -s), '**Nappaleder** n nap(p)a (leather).

Narbe [ˈnarbə] f (-; -n) **1.** ✿ scar: *fig. ~n hinterlassen* leave a scar. **2.** ♀ stigma.

'**narbig** adj scarred.

Narkose [narˈkoːzə] f (-; -n) (*in ~* under) an(a)esthesia: *aus der ~ aufwachen* come round. **Nar'kosefacharzt** m an(a)esthetist. **Narkotikum** [narˈkoːtikʊm] n (-s; -ka), **narkotisch** [narˈkoːtɪʃ] adj narcotic. **narkotisieren** [narkoti'ziːrən] v/t (h) an(a)esthetize.

Narr [nar] m (-en; -en) fool: F *e-n ~en gefressen haben an* (*dat*) be crazy about; *j-n zum ~en halten* → '**narren** v/t *j-n ~* make a fool of s.o., fool s.o. '**Narrenfreiheit** f fool's licen/ce (*Am.* -se). '**narrensicher** adj F foolproof.

Närrin [ˈnɛrɪn] f (-; -nen) fool.

'**närrisch** adj a) foolish, b) mad, c) odd.

Narzisse [narˈtsɪsə] f (-; -n) ♀ narcissus: *Gelbe ~* daffodil.

Narzißmus [nar'tsɪsmʊs] *m* (-; *no pl*) *psych.* narcissism. **nar'zißtisch** [-tɪʃ] *adj* narcissistic.

nasal [na'zaːl] *adj* nasal.

nasalieren [naza'liːrən] *v/t* (h) nasalize.

Na'sallaut *m* nasal (sound).

naschen ['naʃən] *v/i*, *v/t* (h) nibble (*an dat*, *von* at): **gern ~** have a sweet tooth.

Nasche'rei *f* (-; -en) sweets, F goodies.

'naschhaft *adj* sweet-toothed.

Nase ['naːzə] *f* (-; -n) nose: F **pro ~ e-n Dollar** one dollar each; *fig.* **e-e gute** (or **feine**) **~ haben für** have a good nose for; *in der ~ bohren* pick one's nose; F *fig. auf die ~ fallen* come a cropper; *j-m et. auf die ~ binden* tell (s.th. to) s.o.; *j-n an der ~ herumführen* lead s.o. up the garden path; *j-m auf der ~ herumtanzen* do what one likes with s.o.; *auf der ~ liegen* be laid up; *man sieht es dir an der ~ an* it's written all over your face; *es j-m unter die ~ reiben* rub it in; *s-e ~ in alles (hinein)stecken* poke one's nose into everything; *die ~ voll haben* be fed up (*von* with); *die ~ vorn haben* be one step ahead (of one's competitors); *j-m et. vor der ~ wegschnappen* take s.th. away from under s.o.'s nose; *der Zug fuhr mir vor der ~ weg* I missed the train by an inch; → **zuhalten** 2.

näseln ['nɛːzəln] *v/i* (h) speak through one's nose. **'Näseln** *n* (-s) (nasal) twang. **'näselnd** *adj* nasal.

'Nasen|bein *n* nasal bone. **~bluten** *n* nosebleed. **~flügel** *m* nostril. **~länge** *f* um e-e **~ gewinnen** win by a whisker. **~loch** *n* nostril. **~rücken** *m* bridge of the nose. **~scheidewand** *f* nasal septum. **~schleimhaut** *f* nasal mucous membrane. **~spitze** *f* tip of the nose. **~spray** *m*, *n* nose spray. **~tropfen** *pl* nose drops. **~wurzel** *f* root of the nose.

Nashorn ['naːs-] *n* rhinoceros, F rhino.

naß [nas] *adj* wet: **~ machen** wet (*sich* o.s.); **~ werden** get wet; *durch und durch ~*, **~ bis auf die Haut** wet through, wet to the skin; → **triefen**.

Nassauer ['nasaʊər] *m* (-s; -) F sponge.

'nassauern *v/i* (h) F sponge (*bei* on).

Nässe ['nɛsə] *f* (-; *no pl*) wet, wetness: *„vor ~ schützen!"* "keep dry!"

'nässen (h) **I** *v/t* wet. **II** *v/i* wound: weep.

'naßkalt *adj* damp and cold, clammy.

'Naßra,sur *f* wet shave.

'Naßzelle *f* (prefab) bathroom unit.

Nation [na'tsioːn] *f* (-; -en) nation.

national [natsio'naːl] *adj* national.

Natio'nalfeiertag *m* national holiday.

Natio'nalflagge *f* national flag.

Natio'nalheld *m* national hero.

Natio'nalhymne *f* national anthem.

nationalisieren [natsionali'ziːrən] *v/t* (h) nationalize. **Nationali'sierung** *f* (-; -en) nationalization.

Nationalismus [natsiona'lɪsmʊs] *m* (-; *no pl*) nationalism. **Nationalist** [-'lɪst] *m* (-en; -en) nationalist.

nationa'listisch *adj* nationalist(ic).

Nationalität [natsionali'tɛːt] *f* (-; -en) nationality.

Natio'nal|mannschaft *f sports*: national team. **~park** *m* national park. **~sozialismus** *m pol. hist.* National Socialism, *contp.* Nazism. **~sozia,list** *m*, 2**sozia,listisch** *adj pol. hist.* National Socialist, *contp.* Nazi. **~spieler(in** *f*) *m sports*: international. **~stolz** *m* national pride.

Natrium ['naːtriʊm] *n* (-s; *no pl*) sodium.

Natron ['naːtrɔn] *n* (-s; *no pl*) bicarbonate of soda.

Natter ['natər] *f* (-; -n) *zo.* adder.

Natur [na'tuːr] *f* (-; -en) **1.** *no pl* nature: *in der freien ~* in the open country; *nach der ~ zeichnen* draw from nature (or life); *von ~* (*aus*) by nature; *Fragen grundsätzlicher ~* fundamental questions; *die Sache ist ernster ~* it's a serious matter; *er hat e-e gesunde ~* he has a healthy constitution. **2.** character, person.

Naturalien [natu'raːliən] *pl* natural produce: *in ~ zahlen* pay in kind.

naturalisieren [naturali'ziːrən] *v/t* (h) naturalize.

Naturalismus [natura'lɪsmʊs] *m* (-; *no pl*) naturalism.

natura'listisch *adj* naturalist(ic).

Na'turdenkmal *n* natural monument.

Naturell [natu'rɛl] *n* (-s; -e) disposition, temperament.

Na'tur|ereignis *n*, **~erscheinung** *f* natural phenomenon. **~forscher** *m* naturalist. **~forschung** *f* natural science. **~freund(in** *f*) *m* nature lover. 2**gemäß** *adj* natural. **~geschichte** *f* natural history. **~gesetz** *n* law of nature. 2**getreu**

adj true to nature, lifelike. **~gewalt** *f* force of nature. **~heilkunde** *f* naturopathy. **~kata‚strophe** *f* natural disaster. **~kunde** *f* (-; *no pl*) natural history. **~lehrpfad** *m* nature trail.

natürlich [na'ty:rlɪç] **I** *adj* natural: **~e Größe** actual size. **II** *adv* naturally, *int a.* of course.

Na‚türlichkeit *f* (-; *no pl*) naturalness.

Na‚tur|park *m* wildlife park. **~pro‚dukt** *n* natural product. **~schutz** *m* conservation: **unter ~ stehen** be protected. **~schützer** *m* (-s; -) conservationist. **~schutzgebiet** *n* nature reserve. **~ta‚lent** *n* **ein ~ sein** be a natural. **²ver-bunden** *adj* nature-loving. **~volk** *n* primitive race. **~wissenschaft** *f* (natural) science. **~wissenschaftler** *m* (natural) scientist. **²wissenschaftlich** *adj* scientific. **~wunder** *n* natural wonder. **~zustand** *m* (-[e]s; *no pl*) natural state, (*im ~* in) a state of nature.

nautisch ['naʊtɪʃ] *adj* nautical.

Navigation [naviga'tsĭo:n] *f* (-; *no pl*) navigation. **Navigator** [-'ga:tɔr] *m* (-s; -en [-ga'to:rən]) navigator. **navigieren** [-'gi:rən] *v/t, v/i* (h) navigate.

Nazi ['na:tsi] *m* (-s; -s) *pol. hist. contp.* Nazi. **Nazismus** ['na:tsɪsmʊs] *m* (-; *no pl*) *pol. hist. contp.* Nazism. **na'zistisch** [-tʃ] *adj pol. hist. contp.* Nazi.

Nebel ['ne:bəl] *m* (-s; -) **1.** fog (*a. fig.*), mist, haze. **2.** *astr.* nebula.

'nebelhaft *adj fig.* nebulous, hazy.

'Nebelscheinwerfer *m mot.* fog lamp.

'Nebelschlußleuchte *f* rear fog lamp.

neben ['ne:bən] *prep* (*dat*) **1.** (*a. acc*) a) beside, by (*or* at) the side of, by, b) close to, near, next to: **setzen Sie sich ~ mich** sit beside (*or* next to) me. **2.** apart from, besides: **~ anderen Dingen** among other things. **3.** compared with (*or* to). **4.** simultaneously with.

'Neben|absicht *f* secondary objective. **~ak‚zent** *m ling.* secondary stress.

'nebenamtlich *adj* part-time (*job etc*).

neben'an *adv* a) next door, b) in the next room.

'Neben|anschluß *m teleph.* extension. **~arbeit** *f* **1.** extra work. **2.** minor job. **~ausgaben** *pl* incidental expenses, extras. **~ausgang** *m* side exit. **~bedeutung** *f ling.* connotation.

neben'bei *adv* **1.** besides, in addition. **2.**

in passing: **~ bemerkt** incidentally.

'Nebenberuf *m* sideline: **im ~ → nebenberuflich** II. **'nebenberuflich I** *adj* sideline. **II** *adv* as a sideline.

'Nebenbeschäftigung *f* sideline.

'Nebenbuhler [-bu:lər] *m* (-s; -) rival.

nebenein'ander *adv* side by side: **~ bestehen** coexist. **Nebenein'ander** *n* (-s; *no pl*) coexistence.

nebenein'anderstellen *v/t* (*sep*, -ge-, h) **1.** put (*or* place) side by side (*or* next to each other). **2.** compare.

'Neben|eingang *m* side entrance. **~einkommen** *n*, **~einkünfte** *pl*, **~einnahmen** *pl* incidental earnings, extra income. **~erscheinung** *f* side effect (*♣* symptom). **~fach** *n ped.* subsidiary subject, *Am.* minor (subject). **~fluß** *m* tributary. **~gebäude** *n* **1.** adjoining building. **2.** annex(e). **~handlung** *f* subplot.

neben'her *adv* **1.** → **nebenbei** 1. **2.** by his (*or* her) side, beside.

'Neben|höhle *f anat.* sinus. **~kosten** *pl* extras. **~linie** *f* **1.** ♣ branch line. **2.** *descent:* collateral line. **~mann** *m* **mein** *etc* **~** the person next to me *etc*. **~pro‚dukt** *n* (*gen*) by-product (of), spin-off (from). **~rolle** *f thea.* minor part, *fig.* minor role. **~sache** *f* minor matter: **das ist ~!** that's quite unimportant (here)! **²sächlich** *adj* a) minor, unimportant, b) irrelevant. **~satz** *m ling.* subordinate clause. **~sai‚son** *f* low season. **²stehend** *adj* in the margin: **~ (abgebildet)** opposite. **~stelle** *f* a) branch (office), b) *teleph.* extension. **~straße** *f* side street, byroad. **~tisch** *m* (**am ~** at the) next table. **~wirkung** *f* side effect. **~zimmer** *n* next (*or* adjoining) room.

neblig ['ne:blɪç] *adj* foggy, misty.

Necessaire [nesɛ'sɛ:r] *n* (-s; -s) **1.** toilet bag. **2.** manicure set.

necken ['nɛkən] *v/t* (h) tease.

'neckisch *adj* playful.

Neffe ['nɛfə] *m* (-n; -n) nephew.

Negation [nega'tsĭo:n] *f* (-; -en) negation. **negativ**, **Negativ** ['ne:gati:f] *n* (-s; -e) ♣, *phot.*, *phys.* negative.

Neger ['ne:gər] *m* (-s; -) **1.** negro. **2.** F *fig.* a) ghostwriter, b) *TV* idiot board.

'Negerin *f* (-; -nen) negress.

negieren [ne'gi:rən] *v/t* (h) negate, deny.

Negligé [negli'ʒe:] *n* (-s; -s) négligé.

nehmen ['ne:mən] v/t (nahm, genommen, h) **1.** take (a. an sich ~, a. bus, curve, obstacle, etc, at table): help o.s. to, a. accept, a. buy, a. engage, hire (s.o.): **et. zu sich ~** eat s.th.; **ich nehme Wein** I'll have wine; **(sich) e-n Anwalt ~** retain counsel; **er versteht es, die Kunden zu ~** he has a way with the customers; **wie man's nimmt!** that depends!; F **er ist hart im Nehmen** he can take a lot (of punishment); → **Angriff, Anspruch, Beispiel, ernst** II, **Hürde** I etc. **2.** j-m et. ~ take s.th. away from s.o., free s.o. of (pain, inhibitions, etc), deprive s.o. of (hope, rights, etc); **es sich nicht ~ lassen zu** inf insist on ger. **3.** fig. auf sich ~ take upon o.s., assume (office, obstacle, etc). **4.** take, charge (für for).

Nehrung ['ne:rʊŋ] f (-; -en) geogr. spit.

Neid [nait] m (-[e]s; no pl) envy (auf acc of), jealousy; **aus ~** out of envy; **blaß** (or **gelb, grün**) **vor ~** green with envy; F **das muß ihm der ~ lassen** you have to hand it to him.

neiden ['naidən] v/t (h) **j-m et.** ~ envy s.o. s.th.

'**Neider** m (-s; -) **viele ~ haben** be envied by many people.

'**neidisch** I adj (auf acc of) envious, jealous. II adv enviously, with envy.

'**neidlos** adj and adv without envy.

Neige ['naigə] f (-; -n) rest, dregs: fig. **bis zur bitteren ~** to the bitter end.

neigen ['naigən] (h) I v/t a) incline, b) bend, bow, c) tilt. II sich ~ a) incline, terrain: slope, b) bend, bow (**vor** dat to). III v/i ~ zu have a tendency to, be inclined to, esp. ⚕ be prone to; **ich neige zu der Ansicht, daß ...** I am inclined to think that ...

'**Neigung** f (-; -en) **1.** inclination, slope, gradient. **2.** fig. (**zu**) a) inclination, tendency (to, towards), trend (to), esp. ⚕ proneness (to), b) liking (for, of), penchant, predilection (for), c) affection (for), love (of).

'**Neigungswinkel** m angle of inclination.

nein [nain] adv no: ~, **so was!** well, I never!; **aber ...!** of course (or certainly) not!; fig. **er kann nicht ~ sagen** he can't refuse anything.

Nein n (-[s]; -[s]) no: **mit (e-m) ~ antwor-**

ten answer in the negative, say no.

'**Neinstimme** f no (pl noes), Am. nay.

Nektar ['nɛktar] m (-s; -e) nectar.

Nektarine [nɛkta'ri:nə] f (-; -n) ⚘ nectarine.

Nelke ['nɛlkə] f (-; -n) **1.** ⚘ carnation. **2.** gastr. clove.

nennen ['nɛnən] (nannte, genannt, h) I v/t **1.** call, name: **das nenne ich ...** that's what I call ... **2.** name, mention, give (example, one's name, etc), nominate (candidate), sports: enter (für for). II sich ~ call o.s. (a. iro.), be called: **und das nennt sich Fachmann!** and he is supposed to be an expert!

'**nennenswert** adj worth mentioning.

'**Nenner** m (-s; -) ⅍ (a. fig. et. auf e-n gemeinsamen ~ bringen reduce s.th. to a common) denominator; fig. e-n gemeinsamen ~ finden reach an agreement (on the matter).

'**Nennleistung** f ⊗ rated output (⚡ power). '**Nennspannung** f ⚡ rated voltage. '**Nennung** f (-; -en) naming, mention, pol. nomination, sports etc: entry.

'**Nennwert** m ⊤ nominal (or face) value: **zum ~** at par; **unter dem ~** below par.

Neofa'schismus [neo-] m neo-fascism.

Neofa'schist m (-en; -en), **neofa'schistisch** adj neo-fascist.

Neon ['ne:ɔn] n (-s; no pl) neon.

'**Neonleuchte** f neon light.

Nepp [nɛp] m (-s; no pl) F rip-off. '**neppen** v/t (h) F fleece, rip s.o. off. '**Nepplo,kal** n clip joint.

Nerv [nɛrf] m (-s; -en) nerve, ⚘ a. vein: **er hat ~en wie Drahtseile** he's got nerves of steel; **die ~en behalten (verlieren)** keep (lose) one's head; F **j-m auf die ~en gehen** get on s.o.'s nerves; **sie ist mit den ~en am Ende** (F völlig fertig) she's a nervous wreck; **~en zeigen** get nervy; F **du hast vielleicht ~en!** you've got a nerve!

nerven ['nɛrfən] v/t (h) F **j-n ~** get on s.o.'s nerves.

'**Nerven|arzt** m neurologist. ⟨aufreibend adj nerve-racking. **~belastung** f (nervous) strain. **~bündel** n F **sie ist ein ~** she is a bundle of nerves. **~entzündung** f neuritis. **~gas** n ✕ nerve gas. **~kitzel** m fig. thrill. **~klinik** f mental hospital, psychiatric clinic. ⟨krank adj mentally ill. **~krankheit** f nervous disease. **~krieg** m fig. war of nerves. **~probe** f fig. ordeal. **~sache** f F **das ist reine ~!** that's just a question of nerves! **~säge** f F pain in the neck. **~schmerz** m neuralgia. 2**stark** adj strong-nerved. **~stärke** f strong nerves: **~ beweisen** remain cool. **~sy₁stem** n nervous system. **~zentrum** n nerve cent/re (Am. -er). **~zusammenbruch** m nervous breakdown.

'**nervlich** adj nervous.

nervös [nɛr'vøːs] adj nervous: **~ werden** get nervous; **j-n ~ machen** a) make s.o. nervous, b) get on s.o.'s nerves.

Nervosität [nɛrvozi'tɛːt] f (-; no pl) nervousness.

'**nervtötend** adj F nerve-racking (noise etc), soul-destroying (work etc).

Nerz [nɛrts] m (-es; -e) **1.** zo. mink. **2.** → '**Nerzmantel** m mink (coat).

Nessel ['nɛsəl] f (-; -n) **‡** nettle: F **sich in die ~n setzen** get o.s. into trouble. '**Nesselfieber** n **‡** nettle rash.

Nest [nɛst] n (-[e]s; -er) nest: fig. **das eigene ~ beschmutzen** foul one's own nest; F **das ~ war leer** the bird(s) had flown. **2.** F small place, dump. '**Nesthäkchen** n pet of the family. '**Nestwärme** f fig. warmth and security.

nett [nɛt] adj nice (a. iro.): **sei so ~ und hilf mir** be so kind as to help me; F **ein ~es Sümmchen** a nice (or tidy) sum.

netto ['nɛto] adv † net, clear.

'**Netto|einkommen** n net income. **~gewicht** n net weight. **~lohn** m take-home pay. **~preis** m net price.

Netz [nɛts] n (-es; -e) **1.** net: fig. **j-m ins ~ gehen** walk into s.o.'s net. **2.** fig. network, system, **‡** mains: **ans ~ gehen** power station: go into operation.

'**Netz|anschluß** m **‡** mains connection. **~ausfall** m **‡** power failure. **~ball** m tennis: net (ball). **~haut** f anat. retina. **~hemd** n string vest. **~kabel** n **‡** mains cable. **~karte** f turnaround ticket. **~plan** m network. **~plantechnik** f network analysis. **~schalter** m **‡** power switch. **~stecker** m **‡** mains plug. **~strumpf** m net (or mesh) stocking. **~teil** n **‡** power supply unit. **~werk** n network.

neu ['nɔy] I adj a) new, a. fresh (a. fig.), a. novel, b) recent, modern, c) renewed: **ganz ~** brand-new; **wie ~** as good as new; **~er Anfang** fresh start; **neueren**

Datums of recent date; **~e Schwierigkeiten** more problems; **neuere Sprachen** modern languages; **neueste Nachrichten** latest news; **das ist mir ~!** that's new to me! II adv a) newly, b) recently, c) anew, afresh: **~ anfangen** start anew; **~ beleben** revive; **~ eröffnen** reopen; **~ gestalten** reorganize, ◎ remodel; **~ schreiben** rewrite.

'**Neuankömmling** m newcomer.

'**Neuanschaffung** f new acquisition.

'**neuartig** adj novel, new (type of).

'**Neuauflage** f **1.** print. a) new edition, b) reprint. **2.** fig. repeat (performance).

'**Neuausgabe** f new edition.

'**Neubau** m (-[e]s; -ten) new building.

'**Neubaugebiet** n new housing estate.

'**Neubearbeitung** f **1.** a) revised edition, b) revision. **2.** thea. etc adaptation.

'**Neubildung** f **1.** (new) formation, reorganization. **2.** a) physiol. regeneration, b) **‡** tumo(u)r. **3.** ling. neologism.

'**Neudruck** m reprint.

'**Neue¹** n (-n) **1.** s.th. new: **das ~ daran** what's new about it; **das Neueste** the latest thing; **was gibt's Neues?** what's new?; **das ist mir nichts Neues** that's no news to me. **2.** aufs neue, von neuem afresh, anew; **seit neuem** of late.

'**Neue²** m, f (-n; -n) new man (woman).

'**Neueinstellung** f **1.** taking on (new) labo(u)r. **2.** new employee.

'**Neuentdeckung** f **1.** recent discovery. **2.** rediscovery.

'**neuerdings** adv recently, lately, of late.

'**Neuerer** f ['nɔyərər] m (-s; -) innovator.

'**Neuerscheinung** f new publication.

'**Neuerung** f (-; -en) innovation.

'**neuestens** adv recently, lately.

'**Neufassung** f **1.** revision. **2.** revised version.

'**neugebacken** adj F fig. newly-fledged.

'**neugeboren** adj newborn: fig. **ich fühle mich wie ~** I feel a different person.

'**Neugeborene** n (-n; -n) newborn (child).

'**Neugestaltung** f reshaping, reorganization, ◎ remodel(l)ing.

'**Neugier** f (-; no pl) curiosity.

'**neugierig** adj (**auf** acc) curious (about, of), inquisitive (after, about): **ich bin ~, ob ...** I wonder if ...

'**Neugliederung** f reorganization.

'**neugotisch** adj neo-Gothic.

'Neugründung f (new) foundation.

'Neuheit f (-; -en) **1.** no pl newness, novelty. **2.** novelty, ⊙ a. innovation.

'Neuigkeit f (-; -en) (piece of) news.

'Neuinsze,nierung f new production.

'Neujahr n New Year('s Day): Prosit ∼! Happy New Year!

'Neujahrstag m New Year's Day.

'Neuland n (-[e]s; no pl) fig. ∼ erschließen break new ground; das ist ∼ für mich that is new territory to me.

'neulich adv the other day, recently.

'Neuling m (-s; -e) (in dat, auf e-m Gebiet) newcomer (to), novice (at).

'neumodisch adj contp. newfangled.

'Neumond m new moon.

neun [nɔyn] adj nine: alle ∼e! strike!

Neun f (-; -en) (number) nine.

'neunhundert adj nine hundred.

'neunjährig [-jɛːrɪç] adj **1.** nine-year-old. **2.** nine-year, of nine years.

'neunmalklug adj iro. smart-alecky.

neunt adj **1.** ninth. **2.** zu ∼ (the) nine of us (or them etc). **'Neunte** m, f (-n; -n) ninth. **'neuntens** adv ninth(ly).

'neunzehn adj nineteen.

'neunzehnt adj nineteenth.

neunzig ['nɔyntsɪç] adj **1.** ninety. **'Neunzig** f (-; -en) (number) ninety: er ist Anfang ∼ he is in his early nineties.

neunziger ['nɔyntsɪgər] adj die ∼ Jahre the nineties. **'Neunziger** m (-s; -), **'Neunzigerin** f (-; -nen) man (woman) of ninety, nonagenarian.

'Neuordnung f reorganization.

'Neuori,entierung f reorientation.

'Neuphilo,loge m teacher (or student) of modern languages.

'Neuphilolo,gie f modern languages.

Neuralgie [nɔyral'giː] f (-; -n) neuralgia. **neuralgisch** [nɔy'ralgɪʃ] adj ♫ neuralgic: fig. ∼er Punkt critical point, pol. trouble spot.

'Neuregelung f revision.

'Neureiche m, f (-n; -n) parvenue: die ∼n the nouveau riches.

Neurochir'urg m neurosurgeon.

Neurologe [nɔyro'loːgə] m (-n; -n) neurologist.

Neurose [nɔy'roːzə] f (-; -n) ♫ neurosis.

Neurotiker [nɔy'roːtikər] m (-s; -), **neu'rotisch** [-tɪʃ] adj neurotic.

'Neuschnee m fresh-fallen snow.

Neu'seeland n (-s) New Zealand.

Neu'seeländer m (-s; -), **Neu'seeländerin** f (-; -nen) New Zealander.

neu'seeländisch adj New Zealand.

'neusprachlich adj modern-language.

neutral [nɔy'traːl] adj neutral.

neutralisieren [nɔytrali'ziːrən] v/t (h) neutralize. **Neutralität** [nɔytraliˈtɛːt] f (-; no pl) neutrality.

Neutron ['nɔytrɔn] n (-s; -en [nɔy'troːnən]) neutron. **Neu'tronenbombe** f neutron bomb.

Neutrum ['nɔytrʊm] n (-s; -tra) neuter.

'Neuverfilmung f remake.

'Neuwahl f new election.

'neuwertig adj practically new.

'Neuwort n (-[e]s; ∼er) neologism.

'Neuzeit f (-; no pl) modern times.

'neuzeitlich adj modern.

nicht [nɪçt] adv not: ∼ besser no better; ∼ (ein)mal not even; ∼ mehr no longer; (bitte) ∼! (please) don't!; ∼, daß ich wüßte! not that I know of!; er ist krank, ∼ wahr? he is ill, isn't he?; du tust es doch, ∼ wahr? you will do it, won't you?; → auch 1, gar² 1, nur.

Nichte ['nɪçtə] f (-; -n) niece.

'Nicht|achtung f disregard. **∼angriffspakt** m nonaggression treaty. **∼beachtung** f (gen of) a) disregard, b) nonobservance (of rules etc).

'Nicht|einhaltung f noncompliance (gen with). **∼einmischung** f pol. noninterference, nonintervention. **∼erfüllung** f ♫♫ nonperformance. **∼erscheinen** n nonappearance, ♫♫ a. default.

'nichtexi,stent adj nonexisting.

'nichtig adj **1.** trivial, vain: **∼er Vorwand** flimsy excuse. **2.** ♫♫ (null und) ∼ (null and) void.

'Nichtigkeit f (-; -en) **1.** no pl a) triviality, vanity, b) ♫♫ nullity. **2.** pl trifles.

'Nichtmitglied n nonmember.

'Nichtraucher(in f) m nonsmoker.

'nichtrostend adj rustproof, stainless.

nichts indef pron nothing, not ... anything: ∼ als Ärger nothing but trouble; ∼ weniger als das anything but that; ∼ da! nothing doing!; so gut wie ∼ next to nothing; das ist ∼ für mich! that's not my thing!; mir ∼, dir ∼ just like that, quite coolly; weiter ∼? is that all?; wie ∼ in a flash; F ∼ wie hin! let's go (there fast)!; → dergleichen 2, gar² 1, Nähere etc.

Nichts n (-; *no pl*) **1.** nothing(ness), void: *aus dem ~* appear etc from nowhere, *make etc* out of nothing; *vor dem ~ stehen* be left with nothing. **2.** *ein ~* a) a trifle, nothing, b) *contp.* a nobody.

'nichtsahnend adj unsuspecting.

'Nichtschwimmer(in f) m nonswimmer.

nichtsdesto'trotz adv F, **~'weniger** adv nevertheless, none the less.

'Nichtskönner m (-s; -) incompetent person, F washout.

'nichtssagend adj empty (*words etc*), meaningless, vague (*answer*).

'Nichtstuer m (-s; -) idler, loafer.

'Nichtstun n idling, loafing, inactivity.

'Nichtswisser m (-s; -) ignoramus.

'Nichtvorhandensein n nonexistence.

'Nichtzahlung f ✝ *bei* **~** in default of payment.

'Nichtzutreffende n **~s streichen!** delete where inapplicable!

Nickel m (-s; *no pl*) nickel.

'Nickelbrille f steel-rimmed spectacles.

nicken ['nɪkən] v/i (h) nod (one's head).

Nickerchen ['nɪkərçən] n (-s; -) F nap.

nie [niː] adv never: *fast ~* hardly ever; *noch ~* never (before); *~ wieder* never again; *~ und nimmer* never ever.

nieder ['niːdər] **I** adj low (a. fig.), inferior (*rank, value*), lower (*echelon etc*). **II** adv low, down: **~** *mit ...!* down with ...!

'niederbrennen v/t, v/i (irr, sep, -ge-, h, → *brennen*) burn down.

'niederbrüllen v/t (sep, -ge-, h) *j-n ~* shout s.o. down.

'niederdeutsch adj Low German.

'niederdrücken v/t (sep, -ge-, h) **1.** press s.th. down. **2.** fig. depress (*s.o.*).

'Niederfre,quenz f ⚡ low frequency.

'Niedergang m (-[e]s; *no pl*) decline.

'niedergehen v/i (irr, sep, -ge-, sn, → *gehen*) come down (a. ✈), rain: fall, *storm:* burst.

'niedergeschlagen I pp of *niederschlagen*. II adj fig. depressed, dejected. **'Niedergeschlagenheit** f (-; *no pl*) depression, dejection.

'niederknien v/i (sep,-ge-,sn) kneel down.

'Niederlage f (-; -n) **1.** defeat: *e-e ~ erleiden* be defeated. **2.** ✝ a) depot, warehouse, b) → *Niederlassung* 2.

'Niederlande pl the Netherlands.

'Niederländer m (-s; -) Dutchman, Netherlander: *die ~* the Dutch.

'Niederländerin f (-; -nen) Dutch woman, Netherlander.

'niederländisch adj Dutch.

'niederlassen (irr, sep, -ge-, h, → *lassen*) **I** v/t **1.** lower, let s.th. down. **II** sich **~ 2.** sit down. **3.** settle (*in dat* in, at). **4.** set up in business (*or* as a doctor, lawyer, *etc*), establish o.s. (*als* as).

'Niederlassung f (-; -en) **1.** establishment, settling. **2.** ✝ a) place of business, b) branch (office).

'niederlegen (sep, -ge-, h) **I** v/t lay down (*one's arms etc*): *ein Amt ~* resign an office; *die Arbeit ~* (go on) strike, walk out; *et. schriftlich ~* put s.th. down in writing. **II** sich **~** lie down.

'Niederlegung f (-; *no pl*) (*gen*) **1.** laying down (of). **2.** resignation (from).

'niedermachen v/t (sep, -ge-, h) **1.** massacre, slaughter. **2.** → *fertigmachen* 3.

'niederreißen v/t (irr, sep, -ge-, h, → *reißen*) pull down (a. fig.), demolish.

'Niederschlag m **1.** meteor. precipitation, rain(fall). **2.** 🜛 a) precipitate, b) sediment: *radioaktiver ~* (nuclear) fallout; fig. *s-n ~ finden in* (dat) be reflected in. **3.** boxing: a) knockdown, b) knockout. **'niederschlagen** (irr, sep, -ge-, h, → *schlagen*) **I** v/t **1.** *j-n ~* knock s.o. down, boxing: knock s.o. out. **2.** cast down (*one's eyes*). **3.** fig. suppress, put down (*revolt etc*). **4.** 🜨 quash (*proceedings*). **II** sich **~ 5.** 🜛 precipitate. **6.** fig. be reflected (*in* dat in).

'niederschlagsreich adj rainy, wet.

'niederschmettern v/t (sep, -ge-, h) *j-n ~* knock s.o. down, fig. shatter s.o.

'niederschmetternd adj fig. shattering.

'Niederschrift f (-; -en) **1.** writing down. **2.** notes, record, minutes.

'Niederspannung f ⚡ low tension.

'niederstrecken v/t (sep, -ge-, h) fell.

'Niedertracht f (-; *no pl*) **1.** baseness. **2.** perfidy, F dirty trick.

'niederträchtig adj low, perfidious.

'Niederung f (-; -en) lowland(s).

'niederwerfen: sich ~ (irr, sep, -ge-, h, → *werfen*) throw o.s. down; *sich vor j-m ~* throw o.s. at s.o.'s feet.

niedlich ['niːtlɪç] adj sweet, cute.

niedrig ['niːdrɪç] adj low, inferior (*quality etc*), a. lowly, humble (*origin etc*), b.s. a. base: *~ fliegen* fly low; *~ halten* keep *prices etc* down.

'**Niedrigkeit** f (-; no pl) lowness.
'**niemals** → **nie**.
niemand ['ni:mant] indef pron nobody, no one: **ich habe ~(en) gesehen** I didn't see anybody; **~ anders** nobody else; **~ anders als** none other than; **es ist sonst ~ da** nobody else is present.
'**Niemand** m (-s; no pl) contp. nobody.
'**Niemandsland** n a. fig. no man's land.
Niere ['ni:rə] f (-; -n) kidney: **künstliche ~** kidney machine; F **das geht mir an die ~n** that really gets me down.
'**Nierenbeckenentzündung** f pyelitis.
'**nierenförmig** adj kidney-shaped.
'**Nieren|leiden** n kidney disease. **~spender(in** f) m kidney donor. **~stein** m ✴ kidney stone. **~verpflanzung** f kidney transplant.
nieseln ['ni:zəln] v/i (h) drizzle.
'**Nieselregen** m drizzle.
niesen ['ni:zən] v/i (h) sneeze.
Nießbrauch ['ni:s-] m (-[e]s; no pl) ⚖ usufruct.
Niet [ni:t] m (-[e]s; -e) stud, ⚙ rivet.
Niete ['ni:tə] f (-; -n) **1.** (e-e ~ ziehen draw a) blank. **2.** F flop, washout.
nieten ['ni:tən] v/t, v/i (h) ⚙ rivet.
'**Nietenhose** f jeans (with studs).
Nihilismus [nihi'lɪsmʊs] m (-; no pl) nihilism. **Nihilist** [nihi'lɪst] m (-en; -en) nihilist. **nihi'listisch** [-tɪʃ] adj nihilist(ic).
Nikolaustag ['ni:kolaʊs-] m St. Nicholas' Day.
Nikotin [niko'ti:n] n (-s; no pl) nicotine.
niko'tinarm adj low-nicotine.
niko'tinfrei adj nicotine-free.
Niko'tinvergiftung f nicotine poisoning.
Nilpferd ['ni:l-] n zo. hippopotamus.
Nimbus ['nɪmbʊs] m (-; -se) nimbus, halo, fig. no pl a. aura.
'**Nimmerwiedersehen** n auf ~ for good.
Nippel ['nɪpəl] m (-s; -) ⚙ nipple.
nippen ['nɪpən] v/t, v/i (h) sip (an dat at).
'**Nippsachen** ['nɪp-] pl knick-knacks.
nirgends ['nɪrgənts] adv nowhere.
'**nirgendwo,** '**nirgendwohin** adv nowhere, not ... anywhere.
Nische ['ni:ʃə] f (-; -n) niche, recess.
nisten ['nɪstən] v/i (h) nest.
'**Nistplatz** m nesting place.
Nitrat [ni'tra:t] n (-[e]s; -e) 🜋 nitrate.
Nitroglyze'rin [nitro-] n nitroglycerine.
Niveau [ni'vo:] n (-s; -s) level, a. standard: **~ haben** have class; **ein hohes ~**

haben have high standards; **das ist unter m-m ~** that's beneath me; **geistiges ~** level of intelligence (or education).
nivellieren [nive'li:rən] v/t (h) level.
Nixe ['nɪksə] f (-; -n) water-nymph.
nobel ['no:bəl] adj **1.** noble(-minded). **2.** F generous. **3.** high-class, F posh, ritzy.
'**Nobelherberge** f F posh hotel.
Nobelpreis [no'bɛl-] m Nobel prize. **~träger(in** f) m Nobel prize winner.
noch [nɔx] **I** adv **1.** still: **immer ~** still; **~ nicht** not yet; **~ nie** never before; **~ gestern** only yesterday; **~ heute** even today; **~ lange nicht** not by a long chalk; **~ im 18. Jahrhundert** as late as the 18th century; **wie heißt sie ~?** what's her name again?; F **~ und ~** a) oodles (of, piles of, b) awfully. **2.** more: **~ einer** one more, another; **~ more:** **~ einmal** once more; **~ einmal so viel** as much again; **~ etwas!** and another thing!; **~ etwas?** anything else?; **~ besser** even better; **nur ~ 5 Minuten** only five minutes more. **3.** sei es **~ so klein** no matter how small (it is). **II** conj → **weder**.
'**nochmalig** adj repeated, second, new.
nochmals ['nɔxma:ls] adv once more.
Nocke ['nɔkə] f (-; -n) ⚙ cam.
'**Nockenwelle** f mot. camshaft.
Nomade [no'ma:də] m (-n; -n) nomad.
No'maden..., no'madisch adj nomadic.
Nominativ ['no:minati:f] m (-s; -e) ling. nominative (case).
nominell [nomi'nɛl] adj nominal.
nominieren [nomi'ni:rən] v/t (h) nominate, name.
Nonne ['nɔnə] f (-; -n) nun.
'**Nonnenkloster** n nunnery, convent.
Nonsens ['nɔnzɛns] m (-[es]; no pl) nonsense.
Nonstop... [nɔn'stɔp-] nonstop.
Noppe ['nɔpə] f (-; -n) nap.
Nord [nɔrt] inv North.
'**Nord'afrika** n (-s) North Africa. **Nord-afri'kaner(in** f) m, '**nordafri'kanisch** adj North African.
'**Norda'merika** n (-s) North America. '**Nordameri'kaner(in** f) m, '**nordame-ri'kanisch** adj North American.
'**norddeutsch** adj. '**Norddeutsche** m, f (-n; -n) North German.
Norden ['nɔrdən] m (-s; no pl) north, North: **nach ~** to(wards) the north; **im ~ von** (or gen) north of.

nordisch ['nɔrdɪʃ] *adj* a) northern, b) Nordic; → **Kombination** 5.

nördlich ['nœrtlɪç] **I** *adj* a) northern (*hemisphere etc*), b) northerly (*direction etc*), c) arctic (*ocean*). **II** *adv* ~ **von** (*or gen*) (to the) north of.

'**Nordlicht** *n* northern lights.

Nord'ost(en) *m*, **nord'östlich** *adj and adv* northeast.

'**Nordpol** *m* North Pole.

'**Nordsee** *f* North Sea.

'**nordwärts** *adv* north(wards).

Nord'west(en) *m*, **nord'westlich** *adj and adv* northwest.

'**Nordwind** *m* north wind.

Nörge'lei *f* (-; -en) grumbling, niggling. **nörgeln** ['nœrgəln] *v/i* (h) (**an** *dat* about) grumble, niggle. **Nörgler** ['nœrglər] *m* (-s; -) grumbler, niggler.

Norm [nɔrm] *f* (-; -en) norm, standard.

normal [nɔr'ma:l] *adj* normal, ✪ standard. **Nor'malbenzin** *n* regular (grade) petrol (*Am.* gasoline).

nor'malerweise *adv* normally.

Nor'malfall *m im* ~ normally.

normalisieren [nɔrmali'zi:rən] (h) **I** *v/t* normalize. **II** *sich* ~ return to normal.

Nor'malverbraucher *m* average consumer: F *Otto* ~ Mr. Average.

Nor'malzustand *m* normal state.

normen ['nɔrmən], **normieren** [nɔr'mi:-rən] *v/t* (h) standardize.

'**Normung** *f* (-; -en) standardization.

Norwegen ['nɔrve:gən] *n* (-s) Norway. '**Norweger** *m* (-s; -), '**Norwegerin** *f* (-; -nen), '**norwegisch** [-gɪʃ] *adj* Norwegian.

Nostalgie [nɔstal'gi:] *f* (-; *no pl*) nostalgia. **nost'algisch** [-gɪʃ] *adj* nostalgic.

Not [no:t] *f* (-; ✝e) **1.** *no pl* need, misery: ~ **leiden** suffer want; **in** ~ **geraten** become destitute (→ 3). **2.** *no pl* necessity: ~ **macht erfinderisch** necessity is the mother of invention; **zur** ~, F **wenn** ~ **am Mann ist** if need be; **es tut not, daß** it is necessssary that. **3.** distress (*a.* ⚓), difficulty, trouble: **in** ~ (*or* **Nöten**) **sein** be in trouble; **in** ~ **geraten** run into difficulties (→ 1); F **s-e** (**liebe**) ~ **haben mit** really have problems with.

Notar [no'ta:r] *m* (-s; -e), **No'tarin** *f* (-; -nen) notary. **Notariat** [nota'rïa:t] *n* (-[e]s; -e) notary's office. **notariell** [nota'rïel] *adj* notarial: ~ **beglaubigt** attested by a notary.

'**Not|arzt** *m* doctor on call. **~arztwagen** *m* emergency ambulance. **~aufnahme-lager** *n* transit camp. **~ausgang** *m* emergency exit. **~behelf** *m* makeshift. **~beleuchtung** *f* emergency lighting. **~bremse** *f* emergency brake. **~dienst** *m* (~ **haben** be on) emergency duty.

'**notdürftig** *adj* **1.** scanty: ~ **bekleidet** scantily dressed. **2.** makeshift: **et.** ~ **reparieren** patch s.th. up.

Note ['no:tə] *f* (-; -n) **1.** *ped.* mark, *Am.* grade. **2.** ♪ note: **ganze** ~ semibreve, *Am.* whole note; **halbe** ~ minim, *Am.* half note; **nach** ~**n singen** *etc* sing *etc* from music. **3.** *pol.* note, memorandum. **4.** *no pl fig.* touch: **e-r Sache e-e besondere** ~ **verleihen** add a special touch to s.th. **5.** → **Banknote**.

'**Noten|bank** *f* (-; -en) bank of issue. **~blatt** *n* sheet of music. **~heft** *n* music book. **~pult** *n* music stand. **~sy,stem** *n* *ped.* marking (*Am.* grading) system.

'**Notfall** *m* emergency: **für den** ~ (just) in case; **im** ~ → '**notfalls** *adv* if necessary, if need be, in an emergency.

'**notgedrungen** *adv* of necessity.

'**Notgroschen** *m* nest egg.

notieren [no'ti:rən] (h) **I** *v/t* **1.** make a note of. **2.** ✝ quote (**zu** at). **II** *v/i* **3.** ✝ be quoted (**mit** at, with).

No'tierung *f* (-; -en) ✝ quotation.

nötig ['nø:tɪç] *adj* necessary: **et.** (**dringend**) ~ **haben** need s.th. (badly); *iro.* **du hast es** (**gerade**) ~! you of all people!; **mit dem** ~**en Respekt** with due respect; (**nur**) **das Nötigste** (just) what is absolutely necessary.

nötigen ['nø:tɪgən] *v/t* (h) force, compel, urge, press (*guest*): **lassen Sie sich nicht** ~! help yourself!; **er ließ sich nicht lange** ~ he needed no coaxing.

'**Nötigung** *f* (-; -en) coercion.

Notiz [no'ti:ts] *f* (-; -en) **1.** note: **sich** ~**en machen** take notes. **2.** (news) item. **3.** (**k-e**) ~ **nehmen von** take (no) notice of.

No'tizblock *m* notepad, *Am.* memo pad.

No'tizbuch *n* notebook.

'**Notlage** *f* predicament, plight.

'**Notlager** *n* shakedown.

'**notlanden** *v/i* (*insep*, -ge-, sn) make a forced landing.

'**Notlandung** *f* forced landing.

'**Notleidend** *adj* needy.
'**Notlösung** *f* temporary solution.
'**Notlüge** *f* white lie.
'**Notmaßnahme** *f* emergency measure.
notorisch [no'to:rɪʃ] *adj* notorious.
'**Notruf** *m* teleph. emergency call.
'**Notrufsäule** *f* emergency telephone.
'**Notschrei** *m* a. fig. cry for help.
'**Notsi,gnal** *n* distress signal.
'**Notsitz** *m* jump seat.
'**Notstand** *m* **1.** → **Notlage. 2.** pol. state of emergency: **den nationalen ~ ausrufen** declare a state of national emergency. '**Notstandsgebiet** *n* **1.** ✝ depressed area. **2.** disaster area.
'**Notstromaggre,gat** *n* emergency generator.
'**Notunterkunft** *f* provisional accommodation.
'**Notverband** *m* ✱ emergency dressing.
'**Notwehr** *f* (-; *no pl*) (**aus ~, in ~ in**) self-defen/ce (*Am.* -se).
'**notwendig** *adj* necessary (**für** to, for): **unbedingt ~** imperative.
'**notwendiger'weise** *adv* of necessity.
'**Notwendigkeit** *f* (-; -en) necessity.
'**Notzucht** *f* (-; *no pl*) ⚖ rape.
Nougat ['nu:gat] *m*, *n* (-s; -s) chocolate nut cream.
Novelle [no'vɛlə] *f* (-; -n) **1.** novella. **2.** parl. amendment.
November [no'vɛmbər] *m* (-s; -) (**im ~ in**) November.
Novize [no'vi:tsə] *m* (-n; -n) novice.
Novum ['no:vʊm] *n* (-s; -va) s.th. new.
Nu [nu:] F **im ~** in no time, in a jiffy.
Nuance [ny'ã:sə] *f* (-; -n) nuance, shade.
nüchtern ['nʏçtərn] *adj* **1.** with an empty stomach: → **Magen. 2.** sober: **wieder ~ werden** sober up. **3.** bland (*food*). **4.** fig. a) sober, matter-of-fact, a. unemotional, b) austere, functional (*building etc*). '**Nüchternheit** *f* (-; *no pl*) sobriety, fig. a. austerity.
Nudel ['nu:dəl] *f* (-; -n) **1.** noodle. **2.** F **sie ist e-e ulkige ~** she is a funny bird.
nuklear [nukle'a:r] *adj* nuclear.
Nukle'ar... nuclear (*medicine etc*).
null [nʊl] *adj* nought, *esp. Am. or phys.*, ⊙ *etc* zero, teleph. 0, *Am.* zero, sports: nil, *Am.* zero: **~ Grad** zero degrees; **~ Komma drei** (nought) point three; **~ Fehler** no (*Am.* zero) mistakes; **zwei zu ~** two-nil, *Am.* two-zero; tennis: **15:0**

fifteen love; **das Spiel endete 0:0** the match was a scoreless draw; F **er hat ~ Ahnung (davon)** he doesn't know a thing about it; **ich habe ~ Bock darauf** I'm not a bit keen on that; → **nichtig** 2.
Null *f* (-; -en) nought, *esp. Am. or phys.*, ⊙ *etc* zero: F **er ist e-e ~** he's a cipher (*or* nobody); **in ~ Komma nichts** in a jiffy; **gleich ~ sein** be nil.
nullacht'fünfzehn *adj* F run-of-the-mill.
'**Nulldi,ät** *f* no-calorie (*or* crash) diet.
'**Nullmenge** *f* ℵ null set.
'**Nullösung** *f* zero option.
'**Nullpunkt** *m* zero, ⚡, ⊙ neutral point: **auf dem ~** a. fig. at zero.
'**Nulltarif** *m* a) free transport, b) free admission: **zum ~** free.
'**Nullwachstum** *n* ✝ zero growth.
numerieren [nume'ri:rən] *v/t* (h) number. **Nume'rierung** *f* (-; -en) numbering. **Nummer** ['nʊmər] *f* (-; -n) **1.** a) number, a. issue, copy (*of newspaper etc*), b) size (*of shoes etc*): F **auf ~ Sicher gehen** play it safe. **2.** thea. etc act. **3.** V fuck, trick, screw.
'**Nummernkonto** *n* numbered account.
'**Nummernschild** *n* mot. number plate.
nun [nu:n] **I** *adv* **1.** a) now, b) then: **von ~ an** from now on, from that time (onward). **2.** well: **~ ja** well (, you see); **~ gut!** all right!; **was ~?** what now (*or* next)?; **es geht ~ mal nicht!** it's just not on! **II** *conj* **3. ~** (**da**) now that, since.
nur [nu:r] *adv* a) only, just, simply, b) nothing but, c) except: **~ einmal** just once; **~ noch** only; **~ daß** except (that); **~ weil** just because; **wenn ~** if only; **nicht ~ ..., sondern auch ...** not only ..., but also ...; **~ zu!** go on!; **warum hat er das ~ gesagt?** F why on earth did he say that?; **was meint er ~?** whatever does he mean?; **~ das nicht!** anything but that!; **du weißt ~ zu gut, daß** you know very well that; **soviel ich ~ kann** as much as I possibly can; **ohne auch ~ zu lächeln** without so much as a mumble.
nuscheln ['nʊʃəln] *v/i* (h) mumble.
Nuß [nʊs] *f* (-; Nüsse) nut: fig. **e-e harte ~** a hard nut to crack.
'**Nußbaum** *m* **1.** walnut tree. **2.** *no pl* → '**Nußbaumholz** *n* walnut.
'**nußbraun** *adj* hazel.
'**Nußknacker** *m* nutcracker.
'**Nußschale** *f* nutshell.

Nüster ['nʏstər] f (-; -n) zo. nostril.
Nut [nu:t] f (-; -en) ⚙ groove.
Nutte ['nʊtə] f (-; -n) F tart, Am. hooker.
'**Nutzanwendung** f practical use.
'**nutzbar** adj useful: ~ **machen** utilize, ✔ cultivate.
'**Nutzbarkeit** f (-; no pl) usefulness.
'**Nutzbarmachung** f (-; no pl) utilization, ⚒ etc exploitation, ✔ cultivation.
'**nutzbringend** adj profitable, useful: ~ **anwenden** turn s.th. to good account.
nütze ['nʏtsə] adj **zu et.** (**nichts**) ~ **sein** be useful, be of use (be [of] no use).
'**Nutzef,fekt** m ⚙ etc efficiency.
nutzen ['nʊtsən], **nützen** ['nʏtsən] (h) **I** v/i a) be of use, be useful (**zu** for, **j-m** to s.o.), b) **j-m** be of advantage to s.o., benefit s.o.: **was nützt das?** what good is that?; **das nützt nichts!** that's no use! **II** v/t use, make use of. '**Nutzen** m (-s; no pl) a) use, b) profit, c) advantage, a.

🏷 benefit: ~ **ziehen aus** profit (or benefit) from; **von** ~ **sein** → nutzen I.
Nutzer ['nʊtsər] m (-s; -) adm. user.
'**Nutz|fahrzeug** n utility vehicle. ~**fläche** f **1.** usable area. **2.** floor space. ~**holz** n timber. ~**last** f payload. ~**leistung** f effective output (or power).
nützlich ['nʏtslɪç] adj useful, helpful.
'**Nützlichkeit** f (-; no pl) usefulness.
'**nutzlos** adj useless.
'**Nutzlosigkeit** f (-; no pl) uselessness.
Nutznießer ['nʊtsni:sər] m (-s; -), '**Nutz-nießerin** f (-; -nen) beneficiary.
'**Nutzpflanze** f useful plant.
'**Nutzung** f (-; -en) use, utilization.
'**Nutzungsrecht** n usufruct, right to use.
Nylon ['naɪlɔn] TM n (-s; no pl) nylon.
'**Nylonstrümpfe** pl nylons.
Nymphe ['nʏmfə] f (-; -n) nymph.
Nymphomanin [nʏmfoˈmaːnɪn] f (-; -nen) 🗲, psych. nymphomaniac.

O

O, o [o:] n (-; -) O, o.
o int oh: **o ja!** oh yes!
Oase [oˈaːzə] f (-; -n) oasis.
ob [ɔp] conj whether, if: **als** ~ as if; **so tun als** ~ make as if; F (**na**) **und** ~! you bet!; ~ **er wohl geht?** I wonder if he will go.
Obacht ['oːbaxt] f dial. ~ **geben auf** (acc) pay attention to; ~**! look out!
'**Obdach** n (-[e]s; no pl) shelter.
'**obdachlos** adj (~ **werden** be left) homeless. '**Obdachlose** m, f (-n; -n) homeless person. '**Obdachlosena,syl** n shelter for the homeless.
Obduktion [ɔpdʊkˈtsi̯oːn] f (-; -en) postmortem (examination), autopsy.
obduzieren [ɔpduˈtsiːrən] v/t (h) **j-n** carry out an autopsy on s.o.
'**O-Beine** pl F bow legs, bandy legs.
'**O-beinig** [-baɪnɪç] adj F bow-legged.
oben ['oːbən] adv a) at the top, b) upstairs, c) (~ **schwimmen** float) on the surface; **ganz** ~ a. fig. right at the top; **hier** ~ up here; **hoch** ~ high up; **nach** ~ up(wards), a. upstairs; **von** ~ a. fig.

from above; **von** ~ **bis unten** from top to bottom; fig. **von** ~ **herab** condescendingly; F ~ **ohne** topless.
oben'an adv at the top (or head).
oben'auf adv on top: F fig. ~ **sein** be fit and well, be on top of the world.
obendrein [-'draɪn] adv on top of it (all).
'**obenerwähnt** adj above(-mentioned).
oben'hin adv superficially, casually.
'**Oben-'ohne-...** topless (bar etc).
ober ['oːbər] adj upper; → oberst.
'**Ober** m (-s; -) waiter.
'**Ober|arm** m upper arm. ~**arzt** m, ~**ärztin** f assistant medical director. ~**befehl** m supreme command (**über** acc of). ~**befehlshaber** m ✗ commander-in--chief. ~**begriff** m generic term. ~**bekleidung** f outer garments. ~**bürgermeister** m (Br. Lord) Mayor. ~**deck** n ⚓ upper deck. ~**feldwebel** m staff sergeant, Am. sergeant 1st class.
'**Oberfläche** f surface: **an** (or **auf**) **der** ~ on the surface; **an die** ~ **kommen** (come to the) surface.

'oberflächlich [-fleçliç] *adj* superficial, *fig. a.* shallow: **~e Bekanntschaft** casual acquaintance; **~ (betrachtet)** on the face of it. **'Oberflächlichkeit** *f* (-; *no pl*) superficiality.

'Ober|gefreite *m* lance corporal, *Am.* private 1st class. **~geschoß** *n* upper floor. **~grenze** *f* upper limit, ceiling.

'oberhalb *prep* (*gen*) above.

'Oberhand *f* **die ~ gewinnen** get the upper hand (*über acc* of).

'Ober|haupt *n* head, chief. **~haus** *n parl.* upper house, *Br.* House of Lords. **~haut** *f* epidermis. **~hemd** *n* shirt. **~herrschaft** *f* supremacy.

Oberin ['o:bərɪn] *f* (-; -nen) **1.** *eccl.* Mother Superior. **2.** 🎗 matron.

'oberirdisch *adj and adv* overground, 🗲 overhead.

'Ober|kellner *m* head waiter. **~kiefer** *m* upper jaw. **~körper** *m* upper part of the body: **den ~ freimachen** strip to the waist. **~landesgericht** *n* regional court of appeal. **~lauf** *m* upper course (*or* reaches). **~leder** *n* upper. **~leitung** *f* **1.** overall control. **2.** 🗲 overhead cable. **~leutnant** *m* (*Am.* first) lieutenant. **~licht** *n* skylight. **~liga** *f sports:* third division. **~lippe** *f* upper lip. **~priester** *m* high priest. **~schenkel** *m* thigh. **~schicht** *f sociol.* upper class(es). **~schwester** *f* senior nursing officer. **~seite** *f* upper side, top (side).

oberst ['o:bərst] *adj* uppermost, top(most), *a.* highest, *fig. a.* supreme, chief: **das Oberste zuunterst kehren** turn everything upside down.

'Oberst *m* (-en; -en) colonel.

'Oberstaatsanwalt *m* senior public prosecutor.

'Oberstimme *f* 🎵 upper part.

'Oberstleutnant *m* lieutenant colonel.

Ober'studien|di,rektor *m* headmaster, *Am.* principal. **~direk,torin** *f* headmistress, *Am.* principal. **~rat** *m* senior assistant master. **~rätin** [-rɛ:tɪn] *f* (-; -nen) senior assistant mistress.

'Oberstufe *f* (-; *no pl*) *ped.* upper school (*Am.* grades).

'Oberteil *m, n* top.

'Oberwasser *n fig.* (**wieder**) **~ bekommen** (*or* **haben**) be on top (again).

ob'gleich *conj* (al)though, even though.

Obhut ['ɔphu:t] *f* (-; *no pl*) care: **in s-e ~**

nehmen take care (*or* charge) of.

obig ['o:bɪç] *adj* above.

Objekt [ɔp'jɛkt] *n* (-[e]s; -e) object (*a. ling. or art*). **~ (*or* art)**, 🕆 *a.* property.

objektiv [ɔpjɛk'ti:f] *adj* objective, *a.* impartial. **Objek'tiv** *n* (-s; -e) *opt.* (object) lens. **objektivieren** [ɔpjɛkti'vi:rən] *v/t* (h) objectify. **Objektivität** [ɔpjɛktivi-'tɛ:t] *f* (-; *no pl*) objectiveness.

Oblate [o'bla:tə] *f* (-; -n) wafer.

obligat [obli'ga:t] *adj iro.* inevitable.

Obligation [obliga'tsĭo:n] *f* (-; -en) 🕆 bond, debenture.

obligatorisch [obliga'to:rɪʃ] *adj* (*für*) obligatory (on), compulsory (for).

'Obmann *m* **1.** chief. **2.** arbitration: umpire, *of jury:* foreman.

Oboe [o'bo:ə] *f* (-; -n) oboe.

Oboist [obo'ɪst] *m* (-en; -en) oboist.

Observatorium [ɔpzɛrva'to:rĭʊm] *n* (-s; -rien) observatory. **observieren** [-'vi:-rən] *v/t* (h) put under surveillance.

obskur [ɔps'ku:r] *adj* **1.** obscure. **2.** dubious, F shady.

Obst [o:pst] *n* (-[e]s; *no pl*) fruit. **~bau** *m* (-[e]s; *no pl*) fruit-growing. **~baum** *m* fruit tree. **~ernte** *f* a) fruit-gathering, b) fruit crop. **~garten** *m* orchard. **~händler(in** *f*) *m* fruiterer, *Am.* fruit seller. **~kon,serven** *pl* tinned (*or* canned) fruit. **~kuchen** *m* fruit tart. **~messer** *n* fruit knife.

Obstruktion [ɔpstrʊk'tsĭo:n] *f* (-; *no pl*) *pol.* obstruction.

'Obst|saft *m* (fruit) juice. **~sa,lat** *m* fruit salad. **~wasser** *n* fruit brandy.

obszön [ɔps'tsø:n] *adj* obscene, filthy. **Obszönität** [ɔpstsøni'tɛ:t] *f* (-; -en) obscenity.

Obus ['o:bʊs] *m* (-ses; -se) trolley bus.

ob'wohl *conj* (al)though, even though.

Ochse ['ɔksə] *m* (-n; -n) **1.** ox, bullock. **2.** F ass. **'ochsen** *v/t, v/i* (h) F cram, swot.

'Ochsenschwanzsuppe *f* oxtail soup.

Ocker ['ɔkər] *m* (-s; -) ochre, *Am.* ocher.

Ode ['o:də] *f* (-; -n) ode.

öde ['ø:də] *adj* **1.** a) deserted, desolate, b) barren, waste. **2.** *fig.* dreary, dull.

'Öde *f* (-; -n) **1.** desert, waste(land). **2.** *no pl fig.* dreariness, tedium, emptiness.

Ödem [ø'de:m] *n* (-s; -e) 🎗 (o)edema.

oder ['o:dər] *conj* or: **~ (aber)** (or) else, otherwise; **~ ...!** or else!; F **du kommst**

doch, ~? you are coming, aren't you?
→ **entweder, nicht.**

Odysse [odyˈseː] f (-; -n) fig. odyssey.

Ofen [ˈoːfən] m (-s; ¨) **1.** a) stove, b) oven, c) furnace, d) kiln: F **jetzt ist der ~ aus!** it's curtains (for us etc)! **2.** F **heißer ~ a** hot rod, b) (big motor)bike. **~heizung** f stove heating. **~rohr** n stovepipe.

offen [ˈɔfən] adj open (a. fig.), a. frank, outspoken: **~e Rechnung** outstanding account; **~e Stelle** vacant post, vacancy; **~er Wein** wine served by the glass; **die ~e See** the open (sea); **mit ~en Augen** with one's eyes open; **zu j-m ~ sein** be open with s.o.; **für Vorschläge ~ sein** be open to suggestions; **s-e Meinung ~ sagen** speak one's mind freely; **~ gestanden, ~ gesagt** frankly (speaking); → **Handelsgesellschaft, Straße** 1, **Tür.**

'offenbar I adj → **offensichtlich. II** adv evidently, it seems ...

offenbaren [ɔfənˈbaːrən] v/t (offenbarte, offenbart, h) reveal.

Offen'barung f (-; -en) revelation.

Offen'barungseid m ⚖ or fig. declaration of bankruptcy.

'offenbleiben v/i (irr, sep, -ge-, sn, → **bleiben**) a. fig. remain open.

'offenhalten v/t (irr, sep, -ge-, h, → **halten**) a. fig. keep s.th. open.

'Offenheit f (-; no pl) openness, frankness.

'offenherzig adj **1.** open-hearted, candid, frank. **2.** fig. revealing (dress etc).

'offenkundig adj obvious.

'offenlassen v/t (irr, sep, -ge-, h, → **lassen**) a. fig. leave s.th. open.

'offensichtlich adj evident, obvious.

offensiv [ɔfənˈziːf] adj offensive.

Offensive [ɔfənˈziːvə] f (-; -n) (**die ~ ergreifen** take) the offensive.

'offenstehen v/i (irr, sep, -ge-, h, → **stehen**) **1.** be open (fig. j-m to s.o.): **es steht ihm offen zu gehen** he is free to go. **2.** accounts: be outstanding.

öffentlich [ˈœfəntlɪç] adj public: **~er Dienst** a) public sector, b) civil service; **~e Mittel** public funds; **~e Schulen** state (Am. public) schools; **~ in der Sitzung** in open court; **~ auftreten** appear in public; **~ bekanntmachen** make public, publicize; → **Ärgernis, beglaubigt, Persönlichkeit** etc.

'Öffentlichkeit f (-; no pl) a) the (general) public, b) a. ⚖ publicity: **an die ~ treten** appear before the public; **et. an die ~ bringen** bring s.th. before the public; **an (or in) die ~ dringen** leak out; **in die ~ flüchten** resort to publicity; → **Ausschluß.** **'Öffentlichkeitsarbeit** f (-; no pl) public relations.

'öffentlich-'rechtlich adj under public law, public.

Offerte [ɔˈfɛrtə] f (-; -n) ✝ offer.

offiziell [ɔfiˈtsiɛl] adj official.

Offizier [ɔfiˈtsiːr] m (-s; -e) ✗ officer.

Offi'ziersanwärter m officer cadet.

offizinell [ɔfitsiˈnɛl] adj pharm. officinal.

offiziös [ɔfiˈtsiøːs] adj semiofficial.

öffnen [ˈœfnən] v/t (a. **sich ~**) (h) open. **'Öffner** m (-s; -) opener. **'Öffnung** f (-; -en) opening, a. gap, a. aperture.

'Öffnungszeiten pl opening hours.

Offsetdruck [ˈɔfsɛt-] m offset (printing).

oft [ɔft] adv often, frequently.

öfter [ˈœftər] adv a. **des öfteren** often.

oh [oː] int oh.

Ohm [oːm] n (-[s]; -) ⚡ ohm.

ohmsch [oːmʃ] adj ⚡ ohmic: **Ohmsches Gesetz** Ohm's law.

ohne [ˈoːnə] **I** prep (acc) without: **~ s-e Verletzung hätte er gewonnen** but for his injury he would have won; F **~ mich!** count me out!; **nicht ~** not half bad; → **Frage** 1 etc. **II** conj without.

ohne'gleichen adj unparallel(l)ed: **e-e Frechheit ~** (an) incredible impudence.

ohne'hin adv anyhow, anyway.

'Ohnmacht f (-; -en) **1.** no pl fig. powerlessness. **2.** 🩺 unconsciousness, faint: **in ~ fallen** faint.

'ohnmächtig adj **1.** powerless, helpless. **2.** 🩺 unconscious: **~ werden** faint.

Ohr [oːr] n (-[e]s; -en) ear: **ganz ~ sein** be all ears; **nur mit halbem ~ zuhören** listen only with half an ear; F **j-m in den ~en liegen** pester s.o. (**mit** for, with); **viel um die ~en haben** have a lot on one's plate; **sich aufs ~ legen** get some shut-eye; **schreib dir das hinter die ~en!** now don't forget that!; **ich traute m-n ~en nicht!** I couldn't believe my ears!; **j-n übers ~ hauen** cheat s.o.; **j-m zu ~en kommen** come to s.o.'s ears; **halt die ~en steif!** chin up!; **bis über die ~en in Arbeit (Schulden) stecken** be up to one's (or the) ears in work (debt); → **faustdick, spitzen, taub** 1.

Öhr [ør] n (-[e]s; -e) eye.

'Ohren|arzt m, **∼ärztin** f ear specialist. **₂betäubend** adj deafening. **∼leiden** n ear complaint. **∼sausen** n buzzing in one's ears. **∼schmalz** m ⚕ earwax. **∼schmerzen** pl earache. **∼schützer** pl earmuffs. **∼sessel** m wing chair. **∼zeuge** m earwitness.

'Ohrfeige f (-; -n) slap in the face: **j-m e-e ∼ geben** → **'ohrfeigen** v/t (h) **j-n ∼** slap s.o.('s face).

'Ohrläppchen [-lɛpçən] n (-s; -) earlobe. **'Ohrmuschel** f anat. external (or outer) ear, auricle. **'Ohrring** m earring. **'Ohrstecker** m (ear) stud. **'Ohrwurm** m **1.** zo. earwig. **2.** F catchy tune.

okkult [ɔ'kʊlt] adj occult. **Okkultismus** [ɔkʊl'tɪsmʊs] m (-; no pl) occultism.

Ökologe [øko'lo:gə] m (-n; -n) ecologist. **Ökologie** [økolo'gi:] f (-; no pl) ecology. **ökologisch** [øko'lo:gɪʃ] adj ecological. **Ökonomie** [økono'mi:] f (-; -n) **1.** economy. **2.** economics. **ökonomisch** [øko-'no:mɪʃ] adj economical.

Ökosy,stem ['ø:ko-] n ecosystem.

Oktaeder [ɔkta''e:dər] m (-s; -) ⅋ octahedron.

Oktan [ɔk'ta:n] n (-s; no pl) 🔥 octane.

Ok'tanzahl f octane number.

Oktave [ɔk'ta:və] f (-; -n) ♪ octave.

Oktober [ɔk'to:bər] m (-[s]; -) (**im ∼ in**) October.

okulieren [oku'li:rən] v/t (h) 🌳 graft.

Ökumene [øku'me:nə] f (-; no pl) eccl. ecumenical movement. **öku'menisch** [-nɪʃ] adj eccl. ecumenical.

Öl [ø:l] n (-[e]s; -e) oil: **nach ∼ bohren** drill for oil; **auf ∼ stoßen** strike oil; **in ∼ malen** paint in oils; **∼ ins Feuer gießen** add fuel to the flames; **∼ auf die Wogen gießen** pour oil on troubled waters.

'Ölbaum m olive tree. **'Ölberg** m bibl. Mount of Olives. **'Ölbild** n oil painting. **'Ölbohrung** f oil drilling. **'Öldruck** m **1.** paint. oleograph. **2.** ⊙ oil pressure.

Oldtimer ['ɔʊldtaɪmər] m (-s; -) **1.** veteran car (or plane etc). **2.** F old-timer.

Oleander [ole'andər] m (-s; -) oleander.

ölen ['ø:lən] v/t (h) oil, ⊙ a. lubricate.

'Ölfarbe f oil paint: **mit ∼n malen** paint in oils. **'Ölfeld** n oilfield. **'Ölfilter** m, n oil filter. **'Ölförderland** n oil-produc-

ing country. **'Ölgemälde** n oil painting. **'Ölgesellschaft** f petroleum (or oil) company. **'Ölgewinnung** f **1.** oil production. **2.** oil extraction. **'Ölgötze** m F **wie ein ∼** like a stuffed dummy. **'Ölhafen** m oil tanker terminal. **'ölhaltig** adj containing oil, ⚛ oleiferous. **'Ölhaut** f oilskin. **'Ölheizung** f oil heating.

'ölig adj oily, fig. a. unctuous.

oliv [o'li:f] adj olive-colo[u]red).

Olive [o'li:və] f (-; -n) olive. **O'livenbaum** m olive tree. **O'livenöl** n olive oil. **o'livgrün** adj olive-green.

'Ölkanne f oil can. **'Ölkrise** f oil crisis. **'Ölkuchen** m ⊙ oil cake. **'Öllampe** f oil lamp. **'Ölleitung** f a) mot. oil pipe, oil line, b) ⊙ pipeline. **'Ölmale'rei** f oil painting. **'Ölmeßstab** m mot. (oil) dipstick. **'Ölofen** m oil furnace. **'Ölpest** f oil pollution. **'Ölprodu,zent** m oil producer. **'Ölquelle** f oil well, gusher. **'Ölsar,dine** f sardine. **'Ölschiefer** m oil shale. **'Ölstandsanzeiger** m oil-level ga(u)ge. **'Öltank** m oil tank. **'Öltanker** m oil tanker, oiler. **'Ölteppich** m oil slick.

'Ölung f (-; no pl) **1.** oiling, ⊙ a. lubrication. **2.** eccl. **letzte ∼** Extreme Unction.

'Ölvorkommen n oil deposit (coll. resources). **'Ölwanne** f mot. oil sump. **'Ölwechsel** m oil change. **'Ölzeug** n oilskins. **'Ölzweig** m olive branch.

Olymp [o'lʏmp] m (-s; no pl) Olympus. **Olympia(...)** [o'lʏmpɪa-] sports: Olympic. **Olympiade** [olʏm'pɪa:də] f (-; -n) sports: Olympic Games, Olympics.

olympisch [o'lʏmpɪʃ] adj **1.** Olympian. **2.** sports: Olympic.

Oma ['o:ma] f (-; -s) F grandma, granny.

Omelett [ɔm(ə)'lɛt] n (-[e]s; -e, -s), **Ome'lette** f (-; -n) omelet(te).

Omen ['o:mən] n (-s; -) omen. **ominös** [omi'nø:s] adj **1.** ominous. **2.** F dubious.

Omnibus(...) ['ɔmnibus-] → **Bus(...)**.

Onanie [ona'ni:] f (-; no pl) masturbation. **ona'nieren** v/i (h) masturbate.

Onkel ['ɔŋkəl] m (-s; -) uncle.

Onyx ['o:nʏks] m (-[es]; -e) min. onyx.

Opa ['o:pa] m (-s; -s) F grandpa.

Opal [o'pa:l] m (-s; -e) min. opal.

Oper ['o:pər] f (-; -n) opera.

operabel [ope'ra:bəl] adj 🩺 operable.

Operateur [opera'tø:r] *m* (-s; -e) (operating) surgeon. **Operation** [opera'tsĭo:n] *f* (-; -en) operation.
Operati'ons|basis *f* ✗ base of operations. **~narbe** *f* postoperative scar. **~saal** *m* operating theatre (*Am.* operating room). **~schwester** *f* theatre (*Am.* operating-room) nurse. **~tisch** *m* operating table.
operativ [opera'ti:f] *adj* **1.** ✚ surgical, operative: **~er Eingriff** operation; **et. ~ entfernen** remove s.th. surgically (*or* by surgery). **2.** ✗ operational.
Operette [ope'rɛtə] *f* (-; -n) operetta.
operieren [ope'ri:rən] *v/t, v/i* (h) operate: *j-n ~* operate on s.o. (*wegen* for); *sich ~ lassen* have an operation; *ich muß am Magen operiert werden* I have to have a stomach operation.
'Opern|arie *f* operatic aria. **~ball** *m* opera ball. **~führer** *m* opera guidebook. **~glas** *n* opera glass(es). **~haus** *n* opera house. **~kompo,nist** *m* opera composer. **~mu,sik** *f* operatic music. **~sänger(in** *f) m* opera singer.
Opfer ['ɔpfər] *n* (-s; -) **1.** a) sacrifice (*a. fig.*), b) offering: **~ bringen** make sacrifices. **2.** victim: (*dat*) **zum ~ fallen** fall victim to. **'opferbereit** *adj* ready to make sacrifices. **'Opferbereitschaft** *f* readiness to make sacrifices. **'Opfergabe** *f* offering. **'opfern** *v/t, v/i* (h) sacrifice (*a. fig.*), give. **'Opferstock** *m eccl.* offertory. **'Opfertier** *n* sacrificial animal. **'Opferung** *f* (-; -en) sacrifice.
Opiat [o'pĭa:t] *n* (-[e]s; -e) *pharm.* opiate.
Opium ['o:pĭʊm] *n* (-s; *no pl*) opium.
Opossum [o'pɔsʊm] *n* (-s; -s) opossum.
Opponent [ɔpo'nɛnt] *m* (-en; -en), **Oppo'nentin** *f* (-; -nen) opponent.
opponieren [ɔpo'ni:rən] *v/i* (h) (*gegen j-n or et.*) *~* oppose (s.o. *or* s.th.).
Opportunist [ɔpɔrtu'nɪst] *m* (-en; -en), **opportu'nistisch** [-tɪʃ] *adj* opportunist.
Opposition [ɔpozi'tsĭo:n] *f* (-; -en) opposition (*gegen* to). **Oppositi'ons|führer** *m pol.* opposition leader. **~partei** *f* opposition (party).
Optativ ['ɔptati:f] *m* (-s; -e) *ling.* optative (mood).
Optik ['ɔptɪk] *f* (-; -en) **1.** *no pl* optics: *fig.* **nur der ~ wegen** for (optical) effect only. **2.** *phot.* lens system. **'Optiker** *m* (-s; -), **'Optikerin** *f* (-; -nen) optician.
optimal [ɔpti'ma:l] *adj* optimal: **~e Be-**

dingungen optimum conditions.
optimieren [ɔpti'mi:rən] *v/t* (h) optimize.
Optimismus [ɔpti'mɪsmʊs] *m* (-; *no pl*) optimism. **Optimist** [ɔpti'mɪst] *m* (-en; -en), **Opti'mistin** *f* (-; -nen) optimist. **opti'mistisch** [-tɪʃ] *adj* optimistic.
Optimum ['ɔptimʊm] *n* (-s; -ma) optimum.
Option [ɔp'tsĭo:n] *f* (-; -en) option.
optisch ['ɔptɪʃ] *adj* optical.
Opus ['o:pʊs] *n* (-; Opera) work: ♪ *~ 12* opus 12.
Orakel [o'ra:kəl] *n* (-s; -) oracle.
oral [o'ra:l] *adj* oral.
orange [o'rãːʒə] *adj* orange(-colo[u]red).
O'range *f* (-; -n) orange.
Orangeat [orã'ʒa:t] *n* (-s; -e) candied orange peel.
O'rangen|baum *m* orange tree. **~marme,lade** *f* marmalade. **~saft** *m* orange juice. **~schale** *f* orange peel.
Orang-Utan ['o:raŋ'']u:tan] *m* (-s; -s) *zo.* orang-outang.
Oratorium [ora'to:rĭʊm] *n* (-s; -rien) ♪ oratorio.
Orbital... [ɔrbi'ta:l-] orbital (*rocket etc*).
Orchester [ɔr'kɛstər] *n* (-s; -) orchestra, *a.* band. **~graben** *m* (orchestra) pit. **~mu,sik** *f* orchestral music.
orchestrieren [ɔrkɛs'tri:rən] *v/t* (h) orchestrate.
Orchidee [ɔrçi'de:(ə)] *f* (-; -n) ❀ orchid.
Orden ['ɔrdən] *m* (-s; -) **1.** *eccl.* order. **2.** order, decoration, medal.
'Ordens|band *n* (-[e]s; *⸚er*) (medal) ribbon. **~bruder** *m eccl.* monk. **~schwester** *f eccl.* sister, nun.
ordentlich ['ɔrdəntlɪç] **I** *adj* **1.** tidy, orderly, neat. **2.** decent, good, respectable. **3.** F a) good, proper, b) decent: **~e Ausbildung** proper training; **~e Leistung** good job; **ein ~es Frühstück** a decent breakfast. **4.** full (*member, professor*). **II** *adv* **5.** tidily, properly (*etc*): **s-e Sache ~ machen** do a good job. **6.** F properly: **j-m ~ die Meinung sagen** give s.o. a good piece of one's mind; **ich hab's ihm mal ~ gegeben** I really let him have it.
'Ordentlichkeit *f* (-; *no pl*) orderliness.
ordern ['ɔrdərn] *v/t* (h) ✝ order.
Ordinalzahl [ɔrdi'na:l-] *f* ✚ ordinal (number).

ordinär [ɔrdi'nɛ:r] *adj* vulgar, common.
Ordinariat [ɔrdina'rĭa:t] *n* (-[e]s; -e) **1.** *univ.* (full) professorship. **2.** *eccl.* diocesan authorities.
Ordinarius [ɔrdi'na:rĭʊs] *m* (-; -rien) *univ.* (full) professor.
Ordination [ɔrdina'tsĭo:n] *f* (-; -en) **1.** *eccl.* ordination. **2.** *Austrian* ⚕ surgery.
ordnen ['ɔrdnən] *v/t* (h) **1.** a) put *s.th.* in order, b) file (*documents*), c) sort (out), d) arrange: **nach Klassen** ~ classify; **s-e Gedanken** ~ marshal one's thoughts; → **alphabetisch. 2.** settle.
'**Ordner** *m* (-s; -) **1.** steward. **2.** file.
'**Ordnung** *f* (-; -en) order (a. *biol.*, ♄), a. orderliness: **in alphabetischer** ~ in alphabetical order; **Straße erster** ~ primary road; F *fig.* **erster** ~ of the first order; F (**das ist**) **in** ~! all right!, okay!, o.k.!; **es** (**er**) **ist in** ~ it's (he's) all right; **nicht in** ~ **sein** a) be out of order, *fig. a.* be wrong, b) *person*: be out of sorts; **et. ist nicht in** ~ (**damit**) s.th. is wrong (with it); **in** ~ **bringen** a) put *s.th.* right, *fig. a.* straighten *s.th.* out, b) tidy up (*room etc*), c) repair, F fix; ~ **halten** keep order; **et. in** ~ **halten** keep s.th. in order; ~ **schaffen** establish order; *parl.* **j-n zur** ~ **rufen** call s.o. to order.
'**ordnungsgemäß I** *adj* regular, orderly. **II** *adv* duly.
'**ordnungshalber** [-halbər] *adv* (only) as a matter of form.
'**ordnungsliebend** *adj* orderly.
'**Ordnungsruf** *m parl.* call to order.
'**Ordnungsstrafe** *f* fine.
'**Ordnungszahl** *f* ordinal (number).
Organ [ɔr'ga:n] *n* (-s; -e) **1.** *anat.* organ: *fig.* **kein** ~ **haben für** have no feeling for. **2.** *fig.* organ, publication. **3.** *fig.* organ, authority: **ausführendes** ~ executive body. **4.** F voice. ~**bank** *f* (-; -en) ⚕ organ bank. ~**empfänger(in** *f*) *m* ⚕ organ recipient. ~**erkrankung** *f* organic disease. ~**handel** *m* sale of (transplant) organs.
Organisation [ɔrganiza'tsĭo:n] *f* (-; -en) organization.
Organisa'onsta,lent *n* **er hat** (*or* **er ist ein**) ~ he has organizing ability.
Organisator [ɔrgani'za:tɔr] *m* (-s; -en [-za'to:rən]) organizer. **organisatorisch** [-iza'to:rɪʃ] *adj* organizational:

~**e Fähigkeit(en**) organizing ability.
organisch [ɔr'ga:nɪʃ] *adj* organic.
organisieren [ɔrgani'zi:rən] *v/t* (h) **1.** organize: (**nicht**) **organisierter Arbeiter** (non)unionist. **2.** F rustle up.
Organismus [ɔrga'nɪsmʊs] *m* (-; -men) organism.
Organist [ɔrga'nɪst] *m* (-en; -en), **Orga'nistin** *f* (-; -nen) organist.
Or'gan|spende *f* donation of an organ. ~**spender(in** *f*) *m* organ donor. ~**verpflanzung** *f* organ transplant(ation).
Orgasmus [ɔr'gasmʊs] *m* (-; -men) orgasm, climax.
Orgel ['ɔrgəl] *f* (-; -n) organ. ~**bauer** *m* (-s; -) organ builder. ~**kon,zert** *n* organ recital. ~**pfeife** *f* organ pipe: F *fig.* **wie die** ~ **n** in order of size. ~**re,gister** *n* organ stop.
Orgie ['ɔrgĭə] *f* (-; -n) orgy: ~**n feiern** have orgies.
Orient ['o:rĭɛnt] *m* (-s) Orient, East: **der Vordere** ~ the Near East.
Orientale [orĭɛn'ta:lə] *m* (-n; -n), **Orien'talin** *f* (-; -nen) Oriental.
orien'talisch [-lɪʃ] *adj* oriental.
orientieren [orĭɛn'ti:rən] (h) **I** *v/t* **1.** orient(ate) (**nach** according to). **2.** inform (**über** *acc* about, of): **gut orientiert** well informed. **II** *sich* ~ **3.** (**an** *dat* by) orient(ate) o.s., be guided. **4.** inform o.s. (**über** *acc* of, about). **Orien'tierung** *f* (-; *no pl*) **1.** orientation: **die** ~ **verlieren** lose one's bearings. **2.** information: **zu Ihrer** ~ for your guidance.
Orien'tierungs|punkt *m* point of reference. ~**sinn** *m* sense of direction. ~**stufe** *f ped.* orienteering form.
original [origi'na:l] *adj* original: ~ **französisch** genuine French; *et.* ~ **übertragen** broadcast s.th. live.
Origi'nal *n* (-s; -e) original, F (*person*) *a.* character: **im** ~ **read** in the original. ~**fassung** *f* original version: **in der deutschen** ~ in the original German version. ⅔**getreu** *adj* faithful.
Originalität [originali'tɛ:t] *f* (-; *no pl*) *a.* *fig.* originality.
Origi'nal|ko,pie *f* film *etc*: master copy. ~**übertragung** *f* live broadcast. ~**verpackung** *f* original packing.
originell [origi'nɛl] *adj* **1.** original, novel. **2.** F funny, quaint.
Orkan [ɔr'ka:n] *m* (-[e]s; -e) hurricane.

or'kanartig adj of hurricane force.
Ornament [ɔrnaˈmɛnt] n (-[e]s; -e) ornament.
Ornat [ɔrˈnaːt] m (-[e]s; -e) 🏛 robe(s), eccl. vestments.
Ornithologe [ɔrnitoˈloːgə] m (-n; -n) ornithologist.
Ort¹ [ɔrt] m (-[e]s; -e) place (→ a. *Ortschaft*), spot, locality, scene: *(hier) am ~* (here) in this place; *~ und Zeit* place and time; *~ der Handlung* scene (of action); *an ~ und Stelle* on the spot; *höheren ~(e)s* at high quarters.
Ort² n (-[e]s; Örter) *vor ~* ⚒ at the pit face, *fig.* on the scene (of action); *Besichtigung vor ~* on-site inspection.
orten [ˈɔrtən] v/t (h) ⚓ etc locate.
orthodox [ɔrtoˈdɔks] adj orthodox.
Orthographie [ɔrtograˈfiː] f (-; -en) orthography, spelling. **orthographisch** [ɔrtoˈgraˈfɪʃ] adj orthographic(al): *~ richtig schreiben* spell correctly.
Orthopäde [ɔrtoˈpɛːdə] m (-n; -n) orthop(a)edist. **Orthopädie** [-pɛˈdiː] f (-; no pl) orthop(a)edics. **ortho'pädisch** [-dɪʃ] adj orthop(a)edic.
örtlich [ˈœrtlɪç] adj a. ⚕ local: *~ begrenzen* localize (*auf* acc to); *~ verschieden sein* vary from place to place.
Örtlichkeit f (-; -en) locality.
'Ortsangabe f statement of place.
'ortsansässig adj, **'Ortsansässige** m, f (-n; -n) resident, local.
'Ortschaft f (-; -en) place, village, (small) town: *geschlossene ~* built-up area.
'ortsfest adj stationary.
'Ortsgespräch n teleph. local call.
'Ortskenntnis f knowledge of a place: *~ besitzen* → **'ortskundig** adj *~ sein* know (one's way around) the place.
'Orts|name m place name. **~netz** n teleph. local exchange. **~schild** n place-name sign. **~sinn** m sense of direction. **~teil** m district. ⚕**üblich** adj customary, local. **~wechsel** m change of (place). **~zeit** f (-; no pl) local time. **~zuschlag** m ✉ weighting (allowance).
Ortung f (-; -en) ⚓ etc location.
Öse [ˈøːzə] f (-; -n) eye.
Osmose [ɔsˈmoːzə] f (-; -n) osmosis.
Ost [ɔst] invar geogr. east, pol. East.
'Ostblock m pol. Eastern bloc.
'ostdeutsch adj, **'Ostdeutsche** m, f (-n; -n) East German.

Osten [ˈɔstən] m (-s; no pl) east, of town: East End, geogr., pol. the East: *der Ferne (Nahe)* ~ the Far (Middle) East; *im ~* in the east; *nach ~* (to the) east, eastward(s); *von ~, aus ~* from the east, easterly (wind).
ostentativ [ɔstɛntaˈtiːf] adj pointed: *~er Beifall* demonstrative applause.
Osteoporose [ɔsteopoˈroːzə] f (-; -n) 💊 osteoporosis.
Osterei [ˈoːstərʔaɪ] n Easter egg.
'Osterfest n → *Ostern.*
'Osterglocke f ❀ (yellow) daffodil.
'Osterhase m Easter bunny.
österlich [ˈøːstərlɪç] adj (of) Easter.
Oster'montag m Easter Monday.
Ostern [ˈoːstərn] n (-; -) (*zu ~* at) Easter.
Österreich [ˈøːstəraɪç] n (-s) Austria. **'Österreicher** m (-s; -), **'Österreicherin** f (-; -nen), **'österreichisch** adj Austrian.
Oster'sonntag m Easter Sunday.
'Osteu,ropa n Eastern Europe.
östlich [ˈœstlɪç] I adj eastern, easterly. II adv *~ von* (to the) east of.
Östrogen [œstroˈgeːn] n (-s; -e) biol. (o)estrogen.
'Ostsee f Baltic (Sea).
ostwärts [ˈɔstvɛrts] adv east(wards).
Ostwind m east wind.
Oszillograph [ɔstsiloˈgraːf] m (-en; -en) oscilloscope, oscillograph.
Otter¹ [ˈɔtər] m (-s; -) zo. otter.
'Otter² f (-; -n) zo. viper.
Ouvertüre [uverˈtyːrə] f (-; -n) overture.
oval [oˈvaːl] adj, **O'val** n (-s; -e) oval.
Ovation [ovaˈtsɪoːn] f (-; -en) ovation.
Ovulation [ovulaˈtsɪoːn] f (-; -en) biol. ovulation.
Oxyd [ɔˈksyːt] n (-[e]s; -e) 🜍 oxide.
Oxydation [ɔksydaˈtsɪoːn] f (-; -en) oxidation. **oxydieren** [ɔksyˈdiːrən] v/i (h, sn) oxidize.
Ozean [ˈoːtseaːn] m (-s; -e) ocean.
'Ozeandampfer m ocean liner.
ozeanisch [otseˈaːnɪʃ] adj oceanic.
Ozeanographie [otseanograˈfiː] f (-; no pl) oceanography.
Ozelot [ˈoːtselɔt] m (-s; -e) zo. ocelot.
Ozon [oˈtsoːn] n (-s; no pl) ozone.
o'zonhaltig adj ozoniferous.
O'zon|loch n hole in the ozone layer. **~schicht** f ozone layer, ozonosphere. **~werte** pl ozone levels.

P

P, p [pe:] *n* (-; -) P, p.

paar [pa:r] *indef pron* **ein ~** a few, some,
F a couple of. **Paar** *n* (-[e]s; -e) pair,
couple: **ein ~ (neue) Schuhe** a (new)
pair of shoes. **'paaren** *v/t* (h) **1.** (*a. sich
~*) *zo.* pair, couple, mate. **2.** *sports*:
match. **3.** *fig.* (*a. sich ~*) combine.
'Paarlaufen *n* pair skating.
'paarmal *adv* **ein ~** several (*or* a few, F a
couple of) times.
'Paarung *f* (-; -en) **1.** *zo.* pairing, mating.
2. *sports*: a) matching, b) match.
'Paarungszeit *f zo.* mating season.
'paarweise *adv* in pairs, two by two.
Pacht [paxt] *f* (-; -en) a) lease, b) rent.
'pachten *v/t* (h) (take on) lease: F *fig.*
**er meint, er habe es (für sich) ge-
pachtet** he thinks he has got a monopoly on that. **Pächter** ['pɛçtər] *m* (-s; -)
lessee, leaseholder, tenant. **'Pachtung** *f*
(-; -en) leasing. **'Pachtvertrag** *m* lease.
Pack¹ [pak] *m* (-[e]s; -e, ⁻e) a) pack, pile,
b) bundle: → **Sack**.
Pack² *n* (-[e]s; *no pl*) F *contp.* riffraff.
Päckchen ['pɛkçən] *n* (-s; -) small parcel
(*a. ☜*), packet, *esp. Am.* pack (*a. of
cigarettes*).
'Packeis *n* pack ice.
packen ['pakən] (h) **I** *v/t* **1.** pack (*one's
clothes, suitcase, etc*), make up (*parcel
etc*): F **pack dich!** beat it! **2.** (*an dat* by)
grab, seize. **3.** *fig. j-n ~* a) *fear etc*: seize
s.o., b) *novel etc*: grip s.o., thrill s.o.; F
es hat ihn gepackt he's got it bad. **4.** F
fig. lick (*problem etc*): **es ~** a) make it,
manage, b) get it. **II** *v/i* **5.** pack (up).
'Packen *m* (-s; -) pack, pile (*a. fig.*).
'packend *adj fig.* gripping, thrilling.
'Packer *m* (-s; -), **'Packerin** *f* (-; -nen)
packer.
'Packesel *m* pack-mule, *fig.* pack-horse.
'Packpa‚pier *n* wrapping paper.
'Packung *f* (-; -en) **1.** pack, *esp. Am.*
pack (*a. of cigarettes*). **2.** ⚕ pack. **3.** ⚙
packing, gasket. **4.** F *sports*: **e-e ~ bekommen** take a hammering.
Pädagoge [pɛda'go:gə] *m* (-n; -n),
Päda'gogin *f* (-; -nen) a) teacher, b)
education(al)ist, educator. **Pädagogik**
[-'go:gɪk] *f* (-; *no pl*) pedagogy, educa-

tion. **päda'gogisch** [-gɪʃ] *adj* pedagog-
ical, educational.
Paddel ['padəl] *n* (-s; -) paddle.
'Paddelboot *n* canoe.
paddeln ['padəln] *v/t*, *v/i* (h) paddle.
paffen ['pafən] *v/i*, *v/t* (h) F puff (away)
(*at one's pipe etc*), smoke.
Page ['pa:ʒə] *m* (-n; -n) **1.** *hist.* page. **2.**
page, *Am.* bellboy, bellhop.
Pagode [pa'go:də] *f* (-; -n) pagoda.
pah [pa:] *int* bah, pshaw.
Paket [pa'ke:t] *n* (-[e]s; -e) package (*a.
fig. pol. etc*), packet, ☜ parcel: **ein ~
Aktien** a parcel (*or* block) of shares.
Pa'ketkarte *f* (parcel) mailing form.
~post *f* parcel post. **~schalter** *m* par-
cels counter. **~zustellung** *f* parcel de-
livery.
Pakistan ['pa:kɪsta:n] *n* (-s) Pakistan.
Pakistaner [pakɪs'ta:nər] *m* (-s; -),
Paki'stanerin *f* (-; -nen), **paki'sta-
nisch** *adj* Pakistani.
Pakt [pakt] *m* (-[e]s; -e) pact, agreement.
paktieren [pak'ti:rən] *v/i* (h) make a deal
(**mit** with).
Palast [pa'last] *m* (-[e]s; -läste) palace.
Palästina [pale'sti:na] *n* (-s) Palestine.
Palästinenser [palesti'nɛnzər] *m* (-s;
-), **Palästi'nenserin** *f* (-; -nen), **palä-
sti'nensisch** [-zɪʃ] *adj* Palestinian.
Palatschinke [pala'tʃɪŋkə] *f* (-; -n)
Austrian gastr. pancake.
Palaver [pa'la:vər] *n* (-s; -) F palaver.
Palette [pa'lɛtə] *f* (-; -n) **1.** *paint.* palette.
2. *fig.* range. **3.** ⚙ pallet.
Palisade [pali'za:də] *f* (-; -n) palisade.
Palme ['palmə] *f* (-; -n) palm (tree): F *j-n
auf die ~ bringen* drive s.o. up the wall.
Palm'sonntag *m eccl.* Palm Sunday.
'Palm‚wedel *m*, **~zweig** *m* palm branch.
Pampe ['pampə] *f* (-; *no pl*) F mush.
Pampelmuse [pampəl'mu:zə] *f* (-; -n) ☜
grapefruit.
Pamphlet [pam'fle:t] *n* (-[e]s; -e) pam-
phlet, lampoon.
'pampig *adj* F **1.** mushy. **2.** stroppy.
panieren [pa'ni:rən] *v/t* (h) bread.
Pa'niermehl *n* breadcrumbs.
Panik ['pa:nɪk] *f* (-; -en) panic: **in ~** pan-
ic-stricken, F panicky; **in ~ geraten**

(*versetzen*) panic; F *nur k-e* ~*!* don't panic! '**Panikmache** *f* (-; *no pl*) scaremongering. '**panisch** *adj* panic: *von ~er Angst erfaßt* panic-stricken; *e-e ~e Angst haben vor* be terrified of.

Panne ['panə] *f* (-; -n) **1.** a) breakdown, b) puncture: *ich hatte e-e ~* my car broke down, I had a puncture. **2.** *fig.* a) mishap, b) F slip-up: *böse ~* foul-up.

'**Pannendienst** *m* breakdown service.

Panorama [pano'ra:ma] *n* (-s; -men) panorama. ~**fenster** *n* picture window.

panschen ['panʃən] (h) **I** *v/i* F splash (about). **II** *v/t* water down, adulterate.

Pansen ['panzən] *m* (-s; -) *zo.* rumen.

Panther ['pantər] *m* (-s; -) panther.

Pantoffel [pan'tɔfəl] *m* (-s; -n) slipper: F *unter dem ~ stehen* be henpecked.

Pan'toffelheld *m* F henpecked husband.

Pan'toffelkino *n* F telly, *Am.* the tube.

Pantomime[1] [panto'mi:mə] *f* (-; -n) (panto)mime, dumb show.

Panto'mime[2] *m* (-n; -n) mime.

panto'mimisch *adj* pantomimic: *~ darstellen* mime.

Panzer ['pantsər] *m* (-s; -) **1.** *hist.* armo(u)r. **2.** ⚔ tank. **3.** *zo.* shell. ~**abwehr...** ⚔ antitank (*rocket, gun, etc*). ~**divisi̱on** *f* ⚔ armo(u)red division. ~**faust** *f* antitank grenade launcher. ~**glas** *n* bulletproof glass. ~**kreuzer** *f* ⚓ ⚔ armo(u)red cruiser.

panzern ['pantsərn] *v/t* (h) armo(u)r: *fig. sich ~* arm o.s.; → *gepanzert.*

'**Panzer|schrank** *m* safe. ~**sperre** *f* ⚔ antitank obstacle. ~**truppe** *f* ⚔ tank force. ~**tür** *f* armo(u)red door. ~**wagen** *m* ⚔ armo(u)red car.

Papa ['papa] *m* (-s; -s) F daddy, dad, pa.

Papagei [papa'gaɪ] *m* (-en; -e[n]) parrot.

Papa'geienkrankheit *f* psittacosis.

Papier [pa'pi:r] *n* (-s; -e) paper: *~e* a) (identity) papers, b) ✝ securities, papers; (*nur*) *auf dem ~* on paper (only); *zu ~ bringen* commit to paper; *s-e ~e bekommen* get one's cards, be sacked.

pa'pieren *adj* **1.** (of) paper. **2.** *fig.* prosy.

Pa'pier|fa‚brik *f* paper mill. ~**geld** *n* paper money. ~**korb** *m* waste-paper basket. ~**krieg** *m* F red tape, paper warfare. ~**schlange** *f* paper streamer. ~**schnipsel** *m* scrap of paper. ~**servi‚ette** *f* paper napkin. ~**taschentuch** *n* tissue. ~**tiger** *m* *iro.* paper tiger.

Pa'pierwaren *pl* stationery. ~**geschäft** *n* stationer's (shop *or* store).

'**Pappband** *m* **1.** pasteboard (binding). **2.** paperback. '**Pappbecher** *m* paper cup. '**Pappdeckel** *m* pasteboard.

Pappe ['papə] *f* (-; -n) cardboard, pasteboard: F *nicht von ~* quite something, *person:* quite formidable.

Pappel ['papəl] *f* (-; -n) ♣ poplar.

'**Pappenstiel** *m* F *für e-n ~* buy etc s.th. for a song; *k-n ~ wert* not worth a bean.

'**Pappkar‚ton** *m* cardboard box.

Pappmaché [papma'ʃe:] *n* (-s; -s) papier mâché.

'**Pappteller** *m* paper plate.

Paprika ['paprika] *m* (-s; -[s]) **1.** *no pl* paprika. **2.** → '**Paprikaschote** *f* green (*or* sweet) pepper.

Papst [pa:pst] *m* (-[e]s; ⁻e) pope.

päpstlich ['pɛ:pstlɪç] *adj* papal.

'**Papsttum** *n* (-s; *no pl*) papacy.

Parabel [pa'ra:bəl] *f* (-; -n) **1.** parable. **2.** Å parabola.

Parabolan‚tenne [para'bo:l-] *f* TV parabolic aerial (*Am.* antenna), F dish.

Parade [pa'ra:də] *f* (-; -n) **1.** ⚔ parade, review: F *j-m in die ~ fahren* cut s.o. short. **2.** *boxing, fenc.* parry, *soccer:* save. ~**beispiel** *n* classic example.

Paradeiser [para'daɪzər] *m* (-s; -) *Austrian* tomato.

Paradies [para'di:s] *n* (-es; -e) (*im ~ in*) paradise. **paradiesisch** [para'di:zɪʃ] *adj* paradisiac(al), *fig.* heavenly.

paradox [para'dɔks] *adj* **1.** paradoxical. **2.** F strange, absurd.

para'doxerweise *adv* **1.** paradoxically. **2.** F strangely enough.

Paraffin [para'fi:n] *n* (-s; -e) 🜂 paraffin.

Paragraph [para'gra:f] *m* (-en; -en) **1.** section, article. **2.** paragraph. **3.** (*symbol* §) section mark.

parallel [para'le:l] *adj and adv* parallel (*mit, zu* to). **Paral'lele** *f* (-; -n) parallel (line): *fig.* *e-e ~ ziehen* draw a parallel (*zu* to). **Parallelogramm** [paralelo'gram] *n* (-s; -e) Å parallelogram.

paramili‚tärisch ['pa:ra-] *adj* paramilitary.

Paranoia [para'nɔya] *f* (-; *no pl*) 🜁 paranoia. **Paranoiker** [para'nɔikər] *m* (-s; -), **paranoisch** [-'nɔ:ɪʃ] *adj* paranoiac.

Paranuß ['pa:ra-] *f* Brazil nut.

paraphieren [para'fi:rən] *v/t* (h) initial.

Parapsycholo'gie f parapsychology.
Parasit [para'zi:t] m (-en; -en) parasite.
para'sitisch [-tiʃ] adj parasitic(al).
parat [pa'ra:t] adj pred ready.
Pärchen ['pɛːrçən] n (-s; -) (courting) couple, twosome.
pardon [par'dõ:] int sorry.
Parenthese [parɛn'te:zə] f (-; -n) ling. parenthesis.
Parfüm [par'fy:m] n (-s; -e, -s) perfume, scent. **Parfümerie** [parfymə'ri:] f (-; -n) perfumery.
Par'fümfläschchen n scent bottle.
parfümieren [parfy'mi:rən] (h) **I** v/t perfume, scent. **II** sich ~ put on perfume.
parieren [pa'ri:rən] (h) **I** v/t **1.** sports or fig. parry. **2.** pull up (horse). **II** v/i **3.** parry. **4.** F obey.
Pariser [pa'ri:zər] m (-s; -), **Pa'riserin** f (-; -nen) Parisian.
Parität [pari'tɛ:t] f (-; no pl) parity.
pari'tätisch adj proportional, pro rata.
Park [park] m (-s; -s) park. **~anlage** f park. **~bank** f (-; ⁓e) park bench. **~bucht** f mot. lay-by. **~deck** n mot. parking level.
parken ['parkən] v/t, v/i (h) park: **~de Autos** parked cars; **Parken verboten!** no parking!; schräg ~ angle-park; in zweiter Reihe ~ double-park.
Parkett [par'kɛt] n (-[e]s; -e) **1.** parquet. **2.** (dance) floor. **3.** thea. stalls, Am. parquet. **~(fuß)boden** m parquet floor.
'Park|gebühr f parking fee. **~hochhaus** n multistor(e)y car park, Am. parking garage. **~licht** n parking light. **~lücke** f parking space. **~platz** m a) car park, Am. parking lot, b) parking space. **~scheibe** f parking disc. **~sünder(in)** f m F parking offender. **~uhr** f parking meter. **~verbot** n hier ist ~ there's no parking here; im ~ stehen be parked in a towaway zone. **~wächter** m **1.** park keeper. **2.** mot. car park attendant.
Parlament [parla'mɛnt] n (-[e]s; -e) (im ~ sitzen be or sit in) parliament.
Parlamentarier [parlamɛn'ta:riər] m (-s; -) parliamentarian.
parlamen'tarisch adj parliamentary.
Parlamentarismus [parlamɛn'rɪsmʊs] m (-; no pl) parliamentarianism.
Parla'ments|ausschuß m parliamentary committee. **~ferien** pl recess. **~mitglied** n member of parliament.

~sitzung f sitting (of parliament). **~wahlen** pl parliamentary elections.
Parmesan [parme'za:n] m (-s; no pl) Parmesan.
Parodie [paro'di:] f (-; -n) parody, F take-off. **parodieren** [paro'di:rən] v/t (h) parody, F take s.o. off. **Parodist** [paro'dɪst] m (-en; -en) parodist.
Parodontose [parodɔn'to:zə] f (-; -n) ⚕ paradontosis.
Parole [pa'ro:lə] f (-; -n) ✗ password, fig. watchword, pol. a. slogan.
Partei [par'taɪ] f (-; -en) a) a. pol. or ⚖ party, b) sports: side, c) tenant: **j-s ~ ergreifen, für j-n ~ nehmen** side with s.o.; **gegen j-n ~ ergreifen** take sides against s.o.; ~ sein be biassed; die ~ wechseln change sides (pol. parties). **~apparat** m party machine. **~basis** f rank and file (of a party). **~buch** n party membership book. **~freund** m fellow-member (of a party). **~führer** m party leader. **~führung** f **1.** party leadership. **2.** coll. party leaders. **~gänger** [-gɛŋər] m (-s; -) partisan, party man. **~genosse** m party member.
par'teiisch, par'teilich adj partial.
Par'teilinie f party line.
par'teilos adj independent.
Par'teilose m, f (-n; -n) independent.
Par'teimitglied n party member.
Par'teinahme f (-; -n) partisanship.
Par'tei|poli‚tik f party politics. **~po‚litisch** adj party-political. **~pro‚gramm** n (party) platform. **~spende** f party donation. **~tag** m party conference (Am. convention). **~versammlung** f party meeting. **~vorsitzende** m party leader. **~vorstand** m executive committee (of a party). **~zugehörigkeit** f party membership.
Parterre [par'tɛrə] n (-s; -s) ground (Am. first) floor.
Partie [par'ti:] f (-; -n) **1.** part. **2.** ⚘ lot. **3.** ♩ etc part. **4.** game, sports: a. match. **5.** F ich bin mit von der ~! count me in! **6.** F e-e gute ~ sein be a good match (or catch); e-e gute ~ machen marry a fortune.
partiell [par'tsiɛl] adj partial.
Partikel [par'ti:kəl] f (-; -n) particle.
Partisan [parti'za:n] m (-s, -en; -en) partisan, guerilla.
Partitur [parti'tu:r] f (-; -en) ♩ score.

Partizip [parti'tsi:p] *n* (-s; -ien) *ling.* participle.

Partner ['partnər] *m* (-s; -), **'Partnerin** *f* (-; -nen) partner. **'Partnerschaft** *f* (-; -en) partnership. **'partnerschaftlich** *adj and adv* as (equal) partners, joint(ly). **'Partnerstadt** *f* twin town.

Party ['pa:rti] *f* (-; -s, -ties) (*auf e-e* ~ *gehen* go to a) party. ~**muffel** *m* F party pooper. ~**raum** *m* party room.

Parzelle [par'tsɛlə] *f* (-; -n) plot, lot.

parzellieren [partsɛ'li:rən] *v/t* (h) parcel out.

Pascha ['paʃa] *m* (-s; *no pl*) *hist.* pasha.

Paß [pas] *m* (Passes; Pässe) **1.** (mountain) pass. **2.** passport. **3.** *sports:* pass.

passabel [pa'sa:bəl] *adj* passable.

Passage [pa'sa:ʒə] *f* (-; -n) **1.** passage (*a. ♪, in book etc*). **2.** (shopping) arcade.

Passagier [pasa'ʒi:r] *m* (-s; -e) passenger: *blinder* ~ ♇ stowaway. ~**liste** *f* passenger list. ~**schiff** *n* passenger ship.

Passant [pa'sant] *m* (-en; -en), **Pas'santin** *f* (-; -nen) passer-by.

Passat [pa'sa:t] *m* (-[e]s; -e) trade wind.

'Paßbild *n* passport photo(graph).

Passe ['pasə] *f* (-; -n) *dress:* yoke.

passen ['pasən] (h) **I** *v/i* **1.** *a. fig.* match (*j-m , auf j-n* s.o., *für or zu et.* s.th.): ~ *zu in colo(u)r etc*: go well with, match; *fig. sie* ~ (*gut*) *zueinander* they are well suited to each other; *das paßt* (*nicht*) *zu ihm!* that's just like him (not like him!). **2.** *j-m* ~ suit s.o.: *paßt es dir morgen?* would tomorrow suit you (*or* be all right then you])?; *das paßt mir gut* that suits me fine; *das* (*er*) *paßt mir gar nicht!* I don't like it (him) at all!; F *das könnte dir so* ~! nothing doing! **3.** *cards, a. sports:* pass: *ich passe!* pass!; *fig. da muß ich* ~! you've got me there! **II** *v/t* **4.** *den Ball* ~ *zu* pass (the ball) to.

'passend *adj* **1.** fitting (*a. fig.*), in *colo(u)r etc*: matching: *e-e dazu* ~*e Krawatte* a (neck)tie to match. **2.** suitable, right: *die* ~*en Worte* the right words; *bei* ~*er Gelegenheit* at the right moment. **3.** F *haben Sie es* ~? have you got the right money?

Passepartout [paspar'tu:] *n* (-s; -s) mount.

'Paßform *f* (-; *no pl*) fit.

pas'sierbar *adj* passable, practicable.

passieren [pa'si:rən] **I** *v/i* (sn) **1.** take

place, happen: *j-m* ~ happen to s.o.; *was ist passiert?* what's happened?; *mir ist nichts passiert* I'm all right. **II** *v/t* (h) **2.** pass (by *or* through). **3.** *gastr.* pass (through a sieve *etc*), strain.

Pas'sierschein *m* pass, permit.

Pas'sierschlag *m* *tennis:* passing shot.

Passion [pa'sĭo:n] *f* (-; -en) **1.** passion. **2.** *eccl., ♪ etc* Passion. **passioniert** [pasĭo'ni:rt] *adj* enthusiastic, keen.

Passi'onsspiel *n* Passion play.

passiv ['pasi:f] *adj* passive: ~*es Mitglied* nonactive member; ~*er Wortschatz* recognition vocabulary; → *Beste-chung.*

'Passiv *n* (-s; -e) *ling.* passive (voice).

Passiva [pa'si:va] *pl* ✝ liabilities.

Passivität [pasivi'tɛ:t] *f* (-; *no pl*) passivity, passiveness, inaction.

'Passivposten *m* ✝ debit item.

'Passivseite *f* ✝ liability side.

'Paßkon,trolle *f* passport control.

'Paßstelle *f* passport office.

'Paßstraße *f* (mountain) pass.

'Paßstück *n* ⚙ fitting piece, adapter.

Passus ['pasʊs] *m* (-; -) passage.

'Paßwort *n a. computer:* password.

Paste ['pastə] *f* (-; -n) paste.

Pastell [pas'tɛl] *n* (-[e]s; -e) pastel. ~**farben** *pl* pastel shades. ~**stift** *m* crayon.

Pastete [pas'te:tə] *f* (-; -n) pie, pâté.

pasteurisieren [pastøri'zi:rən] *v/t* (h) pasteurize.

Pastille [pas'tılə] *f* (-; -n) lozenge.

Pastor ['pasto:r] *m* (-s; -en) pastor.

Pate ['pa:tə] *m* (-n; -n): **a)** godfather, **b)** → *Patin,* **c)** → *Patenkind:* ~ *stehen bei* be godfather (*or* godmother) to, *fig.* sponsor, *w.s.* be behind.

'Patenkind *n* godchild, godson, goddaughter. **'Patenonkel** *m* godfather.

Patenschaft *f* (-; -en) sponsorship: *fig. die* ~ *übernehmen für* sponsor.

patent [pa'tɛnt] *adj* F ingenious, clever.

Pa'tent *n:* (-[e]s; -e) **1.** patent (*auf acc* for): *ein* ~ *anmelden* apply for a patent; (*zum*) ~ *angemeldet* patent pending. **2.** ⚒ commission. ~**amt** *n* Patent Office. ~**anmeldung** *f* patent application. ~**anspruch** *m* patent claim. ~**anwalt** *m* patent attorney. ~**beschreibung** *f* patent specification.

patentieren [patɛn'ti:rən] *v/t* (h) patent: *et.* ~ *lassen* take out a patent for s.th.

Pa'tent|inhaber *m* patentee. **~lösung** *f*
F *fig.* ready-made solution. **~recht** *n* a)
patent law, b) patent right. **2rechtlich**
adj and adv under patent law: **~ geschützt** patented. **~schrift** *f* patent
specification. **~schutz** *m* protection by
patent.

Pater ['pa:tər] *m* (-s; -, Patres) father.

pathetisch [pa'te:tɪʃ] *adj* lofty, emotional, *contp.* pompous.

Pathologe [pato'lo:gə] *m* (-n; -n) pa-
thologist. **Pathologie** [patolo'gi:] *f* (-;
no pl) pathology. **pathologisch** [pato-
'lo:gɪʃ] *adj* pathological.

Pathos ['pa:tɔs] *n* (-; *no pl*) emotion(al
style or tone).

Patience [pa'sĭã:s] *f* (-; -n) (**e-e ~ legen**
play a) patience (*Am.* solitaire).

Patient [pa'tsĭɛnt] *m* (-en; -en), **Pati'en-
tin** *f* (-; -nen) patient.

Patin ['pa:tɪn] *f* (-; -nen) godmother.

Patina ['pa:tina] *f* (-; *no pl*) (**~ ansetzen**
a. fig. develop a) patina.

Patriarch [patri'arç] *m* (-en; -en) patriarch. **patriarchalisch** [patriar'ça:lɪʃ]
adj patriarchal.

Patriot [patri'o:t] *m* (-en; -en), **Patri'otin**
f (-; -nen) patriot. **patri'otisch** [-tɪʃ] *adj*
patriotic. **Patriotismus** [patrio'tɪsmʊs]
m (-; *no pl*) patriotism.

Patron [pa'tro:n] *m* (-s; -e) **1.** *eccl.* patron saint. **2.** F fellow: *contp.* **übler ~**
nasty customer.

Patrone [pa'tro:nə] *f* (-; -n) cartridge.
Pa'tronenhülse *f* cartridge case.

Pa'tronin *f* (-; -nen) *eccl.* patron
saint.

Patrouille [pa'trʊljə] *f* (-; -n), **patrouil-
lieren** [patrʊl'ji:rən] *v/i* (h) ⚔ patrol.

patsch [patʃ] *int* splat!, smack!

Patsche ['patʃə] *f* F **in der ~ sitzen** be in
a scrape; *j-m aus der ~ helfen* help s.o.
out of a (tight) spot.

'patschen *v/i* (h, sn) a) splash, b) smack.

Patt [pat] *n chess:* stalemate (*a. fig. pol.*).

patzen ['patsən] *v/i* (h), **Patzer** ['patsər]
m (-s; -) F blunder, boob.

patzig ['patsɪç] *adj* F snotty, stroppy.

Pauke ['paʊkə] *f* (-; -n) a) bass drum, b)
kettledrum: F *fig. auf die ~ hauen*
paint the town red; *mit ~n und Trompeten durchfallen iro.* fail gloriously.

'pauken *v/i* (h) **1.** play the kettledrum(s).
2. F *ped.* (*a. v/t*) cram, swot.

'Paukenschlag *m* drumbeat: *fig. wie
ein ~* like a bombshell.

Pauker ['paʊkər] *m* (-s; -) **1.** ♪ drummer.
2. F teacher.

pausbäckig ['paʊsbɛkɪç] *adj* chubby.

pauschal [paʊ'ʃa:l] **I** *adj* **1.** all-in(clu-
sive) (*price etc*). **2.** *fig.* sweeping. **II** *adv*
3. in a lump sum. **4.** *fig.* wholesale.

Pau'schale *f* (-; -n) lump sum.

Pau'schal|gebühr *f* flat rate. **~reise** *f*
package tour. **~urteil** *n fig.* sweeping
judg(e)ment.

Pause¹ ['paʊzə] *f* (-; -n) pause, rest (*a. ♪*),
ped. break, *Am.* recess, *thea. etc* interval, *Am.* intermission: *e-e ~ machen* a)
take a break (*or* rest), b) pause.

'Pause² *f* (-; -n) ⊙ tracing, copy, blueprint. **'pausen** *v/t* (h) trace.

'pausenlos *adj* uninterrupted, nonstop.

'Pausenzeichen *n radio, TV* interval
signal.

pausieren [paʊ'zi:rən] *v/i* (h) a) pause,
b) take a break (*or* rest).

'Pauspa,pier *n* tracing paper.

Pavian ['pa:vĭa:n] *m* (-s; -e) *zo.* baboon.

Pavillon ['pavɪljõ:] *m* (-s; -s) pavilion.

Pazifismus [patsi'fɪsmʊs] *m* (-; *no pl*)
pacifism. **Pazifist** [patsi'fɪst] *m* (-en;
-en), **pazi'fistisch** [-tɪʃ] *adj* pacifist.

Pech [pɛç] *n* (-s; -e) **1.** pitch: *fig. wie ~
und Schwefel zs.-halten* be as thick as
thieves. **2.** *no pl* F bad luck: **~ gehabt!**
tough luck!; **~ haben** be unlucky (*bei*
with). **'pechschwarz** *adj* F jet-black
(*hair etc*), pitch-dark (*night*).

'Pechsträhne *f* run of bad luck.

'Pechvogel *m* F unlucky fellow (*or* girl).

Pedal [pe'da:l] *n* (-s; -e) pedal.

Pedant [pe'dant] *m* (-en; -en) pedant.
Pedanterie [-tə'ri:] *f* (-; *no pl*) pedantry. **pe'dantisch** [-tɪʃ] *adj* pedantic.

Pediküre [pedi'ky:rə] *f* (-; -n) pedicure.

Pegel ['pe:gəl] *m* (-s; -) *a. fig.* level.

'Pegelstand *m* water level.

peilen ['paɪlən] (h) **I** *v/t* take the bearings
of: *fig. die Lage ~* see how the land lies;
→ **Daumen. II** *v/i* take the bearings.

'Peilfunk *m* directional radio.

'Peilgerät *n* radio direction finder.

'Peilung *f* (-; -en) a) locating, b) bearing.

Pein [paɪn] *f* (-; *no pl*) pain, agony.

peinigen ['paɪnɪgən] *v/t* (h) torment.

'Peiniger *m* (-s; -) tormentor.

'peinlich I *adj* **1.** embarrassing, *a.* awkward (silence, situation, etc): **es ist mir sehr ~** I feel awful about it. **2.** meticulous, scrupulous. **II** adv **3.** j-n ~ berühren pain s.o.; ~ berührt embarrassed, pained. **4.** ~ (genau) meticulously; ~ sauber scrupulously clean; et. ~st vermeiden take great care to avoid s.th.

'Peinlichkeit f (-; -en) **1.** no pl awkwardness. **2.** awkward situation (or remark).

Peitsche ['paɪtʃə] f (-; -n) whip.

'peitschen v/i, v/t (h) whip, a. fig. lash.

'Peitschenhieb m (whip)lash.

Pekinese [peki'ne:zə] m (-n; -n) zo. Pekin(g)ese.

Pelargonie [pelar'go:niə] f (-; -n) ♀ pelargonium.

Pelikan ['pe:lika:n] m (-s; -e) zo. pelican.

Pelle ['pɛlə] f (-; -n) dial. skin, peel.

'pellen v/t skin, peel; → Ei 1.

'Pellkartoffeln pl potatoes (boiled) in their skins, jacket potatoes.

Pelz [pɛlts] m (-es; -e) a) fur, b) skin, hide: F j-m auf den ~ rücken press s.o. hard. ♀gefüttert adj fur-lined. ~handel m fur trade. ~händler m furrier.

pelzig ['pɛltsɪç] adj **1.** furry. **2.** ♯ furred, coated (tongue etc).

'Pelz|jacke f fur jacket. ~kragen m fur collar. ~mantel m fur coat. ~mütze f fur hat.

'Pelztier n fur-bearing animal. ~farm f fur farm. ~jäger m trapper. ~zucht f fur farming.

Pendel ['pɛndəl] n (-s; -) pendulum.

'pendeln v/i **1.** (h) swing, oscillate. **2.** (sn) shuttle, person: commute.

'Pendel|tür f swing door. ~uhr f pendulum clock. ~verkehr m **1.** ♛ shuttle service. **2.** commuter traffic.

Pendler ['pɛndlər] m (-s; -) commuter.

penetrant [pene'trant] adj **1.** penetrating (smell etc). **2.** contp. pushy (person).

peng [pɛŋ] int bang!

penibel [pe'ni:bəl] adj fussy.

Penis ['pe:nɪs] m (-; -se) anat. penis.

Penizillin [penɪtsɪ'li:n] n (-s; -e) penicillin.

Penne ['pɛnə] f (-; -n) F **1.** school. **2.** contp. sl. dosshouse, Am. flophouse.

'pennen v/i (h) F contp. a) sl. (have a) kip, b) fig. sleep. 'Penner m (-s; -) F contp. **1.** sl. dosser, bum. **2.** sleepyhead.

Pension [pã'zĭo:n] f (-; -en) **1.** (old-age) pension: in ~ gehen retire; in ~ sein be

retired. **2.** boarding-house, private hotel. **3.** board. **Pensionär** [pãzĭo'nɛ:r] m (-s; -e) pensioner. **pensionieren** [-'ni:rən] v/t pension (off): sich ~ lassen retire. **pensio'niert** adj retired. **Pensi'onsalter** n retirement age. **Pensi'onierung** f (-; -en) retirement.

pensi'ons|berechtigt adj eligible for a pension. ~reif adj F due for retirement.

Pensum ['pɛnzom] n (-s; -sen, Pensen) (allotted) task, w.s. workload.

Peperoni [pepe'ro:ni] pl red peppers.

Pepsin [pɛ'psi:n] n (-s; -e) ♯ pepsin.

per [pɛr] prep per, by: ~ Adresse care of (abbr. c/o); ~ Bahn by train; → du.

Perestroika [pere'strɔyka] f (-; no pl) pol. perestroika.

perfekt [pɛr'fɛkt] adj **1.** perfect. **2.** F settled: et. ~ machen clinch s.th.

'Perfekt n (-s; -e) ling. perfect (tense).

Perfektion [pɛrfɛk'tsĭo:n] f (-; no pl) perfection. **perfektionieren** [-tsĭo'ni:rən] v/t (h) (make) perfect. **Perfektionist** [-tsĭo'nɪst] m (-en; -en) perfectionist.

perforieren [pɛrfo'ri:rən] v/t (h) perforate.

Pergament [pɛrga'mɛnt] n (-[e]s; -e) parchment. **Perga'mentpa,pier** n greaseproof paper.

Periode [pe'rio:də] f (-; -n) period (a. physiol.), ♮ cycle. peri'odisch [-dɪʃ] adj periodic(al), ♭ recurring (decimal).

Peripherie [perife'ri:] f (-; -n) periphery, a. outskirts (of a town).

Periskop [peri'sko:p] n (-s; -e) periscope.

Perle ['pɛrlə] f (-; -n) **1.** a) pearl, b) bead: F ~n vor die Säue werfen cast (one's) pearls before swine. **2.** bead, drop. **3.** fig. jewel, gem.

perlen ['pɛrlən] v/i **1.** (h) drink: sparkle. **2.** (sn) sweat, water: trickle (down).

'Perlen|kette f pearl (or bead) necklace. ~schnur f string of pearls (or beads).

'Perlhuhn n zo. guinea fowl.

'Perlmuschel f pearl oyster.

'Perlmutt [-mot] n (-s; no pl), 'Perlmutter f (-; no pl) mother-of-pearl.

perplex [pɛr'plɛks] adj F bewildered.

Persenning [pɛr'zɛnɪŋ] f (-; -e[n]) ♻ tarpaulin.

Perser ['pɛrzər] m (-s; -), ~teppich m Persian carpet.

Persianer [pɛr'zĭa:nər] m (-s; -) **1.** Per-

sian lamb(skin). **2.** → **Persi'anerman-tel** *m* Persian lamb coat.
persisch ['pɛrzɪʃ] *adj* Persian.
Person [pɛr'zoːn] *f* (-; -en) person, *thea.* character: *ling.* **erste ~** first person; *in eigener ~* personally; *ich für m-e ~* I for my part; *pro ~* each; *ein Tisch für sechs ~en* a table for six; *sie ist die Güte in ~* she is kindness personified; → *juristisch*.
Personal [pɛrzo'naːl] *n* (-s; *no pl*) personnel, staff: *zuwenig ~ haben* be understaffed. **~abbau** *m* personnel reduction. **~ab,teilung** *f* personnel department. **~akte** *f* personal file. **~ausweis** *m* identity card. **~chef** *m* personnel manager. **~com,puter** *m* personal computer.
Personalien [pɛrzo'naːli̯ən] *pl* particulars, personal data.
Perso'nal|poli,tik *f* personnel policy. **~pro,nomen** *n ling.* personal pronoun.
personell [pɛrzo'nɛl] *adj* **1.** personal. **2.** personnel.
Per'sonen|beförderung *f* passenger transport. **~beschreibung** *f* personal description. **~gesellschaft** *f* ✝ partnership. **~kraftwagen** *m* (*abbr.* PKW) motor car, *Am. a.* auto(mobile). **~kreis** *m* circle. **~kult** *m* personality cult. **~schaden** *m* personal injury. **~stand** *m* marital status. **~wagen** *m* **1.** 🚆 passenger coach (*Am.* car). **2.** → *Personen-kraftwagen.* **~zug** *m* slow train.
personifizieren [pɛrzonifi'tsiːrən] *v/t* (h) personify.
persönlich [pɛr'zøːnlɪç] **I** *adj* personal. **II** *adv* personally, *a.* in person.
Per'sönlichkeit *f* (-; -en) personality: *e-e ~ des öffentlichen Lebens* a public figure.
Perspektive [pɛrspɛk'tiːvə] *f* (-; -n) perspective, *fig. a.* a) prospect, b) point of view: *das eröffnet neue ~n* that opens up new vistas. **perspek'tivisch** [-vɪʃ] *adj* perspective, *drawing* in perspective.
Peru [pe'ruː] *n* (-s) Peru. **Peruaner** [pe'ruaːnər] *m* (-s; -), **Peru'anerin** *f* (-; -nen), **peru'anisch** *adj* Peruvian.
Perücke [pe'rʏkə] *f* (-; -n) wig.
pervers [pɛr'vɛrs] *adj* perverse.
Perversität [pɛrvɛrzi'tɛːt] *f* (-; -en) perversity. **pervertieren** [pɛrvɛr'tiːrən] *v/t* (h) pervert.

Peseta [pe'zeːta] *f* (-; Peseten) peseta.
Pessar [pɛ'saːr] *n* (-s; -e) ✝ pessary.
Pessimismus [pɛsi'mɪsmʊs] *m* (-; *no pl*) pessimism. **Pessimist** [-'mɪst] *m* (-en; -en), **Pessi'mistin** *f* (-; -nen) pessimist. **pessi'mistisch** *adj* pessimistic.
Pest [pɛst] *f* (-; *no pl*) plague: *j-n hassen wie die ~* hate s.o.'s guts; F *stinken wie die ~* stink to high heaven.
Petersilie [pe:tər'zi:li̯ə] *f* (-; -en) parsley.
Petition [peti'tsi̯oːn] *f* (-; -en) petition.
Petroche'mie [petro-] *f* petrochemistry. **petro'chemisch** *adj* (*a.* **~es Produkt**) petrochemical.
Petroleum [pe'troːleʊm] *n* (-s; *no pl*) **1.** → *Erdöl.* **2.** paraffin, *Am.* kerosene.
petto ['pɛto] *et. in ~ haben* have s.th. up one's sleeve.
Petze ['pɛtsə] *f* (-; -n) F *ped.* telltale, sneak. **'petzen** *v/i* (h) F *ped.* sneak.
Pfad [pfaːt] *m* (-[e]s; -e) path.
'Pfadfinder *m* boy scout. **'Pfadfinderin** *f* girl guide, *Am.* girl scout.
Pfaffe ['pfafə] *m* (-n; -n) F *contp.* cleric, Holy Joe.
Pfahl [pfaːl] *m* (-[e]s; ⸗e) a) stake, b) post, △ pile, c) pole. **'Pfahlbau** *m* (-[e]s; -ten) pile dwelling. **'Pfahlwurzel** *f* tap root.
Pfand [pfant] *n* (-[e]s; ⸗er ['pfɛndər]) a) security, b) pledge, *in games:* forfeit, c) deposit: *als ~ geben a. fig.* pledge; *~ zahlen* pay a deposit (*für* on).
pfändbar ['pfɛntbaːr] *adj* distrainable.
'Pfandbrief *m* ✝ bond.
pfänden ['pfɛndən] *v/t* (h) distrain (up)on, seize, attach (*claim etc*).
'Pfänderspiel *n* (game of) forfeits.
'Pfandflasche *f* returnable bottle.
'Pfandhaus *n*, **'Pfandleihe** *f* (-; -n) pawnshop. **'Pfandleiher** *m* (-s; -), **'Pfandleiherin** *f* (-; -nen) pawnbroker.
'Pfandschein *m* pawn ticket.
'Pfändung *f* (-; -en) (upon) seizure (of), distraint (upon).
'Pfändungsbefehl *m* distress warrant.
Pfanne ['pfanə] *f* (-; -n) **1.** pan: F *j-n in die ~ hauen* a) clobber s.o., b) give s.o. a roasting. **2.** *anat.* socket. **3.** pantile.
'Pfannkuchen *m* pancake: *Berliner ~* doughnut.
'Pfarramt *n* rectory. **'Pfarrbezirk** *m* parish. **Pfarrei** [pfa'raɪ] *f* (-; -en) rectory, vicarage. **Pfarrer** ['pfarər] *m* (-s; -) a)

pastor, minister, b) (parish) priest.
'**Pfarrerin** f (-; -nen) woman pastor.
'**Pfarr|gemeinde** f parish. **~haus** n rectory, vicarage. **~kirche** f parish church.

Pfau [pfaʊ] m [-[e]s; -e] zo. peacock.
'**Pfauenauge** n zo. peacock (butterfly).

Pfeffer ['pfɛfər] m (-s; -) 1. pepper: → **Hase**. 2. F pep. **~gurke** f gastr. gherkin. **~kuchen** m gingerbread.
'**Pfefferminz** n (-es; -e) peppermint (drop). '**Pfefferminze** f ♀ peppermint.
'**Pfeffermühle** f pepper mill.
pfeffern ['pfɛfərn] v/t (h) 1. a. fig. pepper: → **gepfeffert**. 2. F chuck.
'**Pfefferstreuer** m pepper caster.

Pfeife ['pfaɪfə] f (-; -n) 1. a) whistle, b) (organ) pipe: fig. **nach j-s ~ tanzen** dance to s.o.'s tune. 2. pipe: **~ rauchen** a) smoke a pipe, b) be a pipe smoker. 3. F idiot, dope.
pfeifen ['pfaɪfən] (pfiff, gepfiffen, h) I v/i 1. whistle (**j-m** to s.o.), referee etc: blow the whistle, spectator: boo: F **ich pfeife auf das Geld** I don't give a damn about the money. II v/t 2. whistle: F **ich werd' dir was ~!** to hell with you! 3. sports: **ein Spiel ~** referee a match.
'**Pfeifen|kopf** m bowl. **~raucher** m pipe smoker. **~reiniger** m pipe cleaner. **~stiel** m pipe stem. **~stopfer** m tamper.
'**Pfeifkon,zert** n (hail of) catcalls.

Pfeil [pfaɪl] m [-[e]s; -e] a) arrow, b) dart: **mit ~ und Bogen** with bow and arrow.
Pfeiler ['pfaɪlər] m (-s; -) pillar (a. fig.), pier.
'**pfeilförmig** [-fœrmɪç] adj V-shaped.
'**pfeilgerade** I adj (as) straight as an arrow. II adv straight. '**pfeilschnell** adj and adv (as) quick as lightning.
'**Pfeilspitze** f arrowhead.

Pfennig ['pfɛnɪç] m (-s; -e) pfennig, fig. penny, Am. cent: F **jeden ~ umdrehen** count every penny; **k-n ~ wert** not worth a thing. **~absatz** m stiletto heel.

Pferch [pfɛrç] m [-[e]s; -e] pen, fold.
'**pferchen** v/t pen, cram (**in** acc into).
Pferd [pfe:rt] n [-[e]s; -e] 1. horse: **zu ~** on horseback; F fig. **das beste ~ im Stall** the number one; **aufs falsche ~ setzen** back the wrong horse; **das ~ beim Schwanze aufzäumen** put the cart before the horse; **mit ihr kann man ~e stehlen** she's a good sport. 2. gym. (vaulting-)horse. 3. chess: knight.

Pferde|äpfel ['pfe:rdə-] pl horse droppings. **~fleisch** n horse-meat. **~fuß** m fig. snag. **~koppel** f paddock. **~länge** f sports: **um zwei ~n** by two lengths. **~rennbahn** f racecourse, racetrack. **~rennen** n a) horse racing, b) horse race. **~schwanz** m 1. zo. horse's tail. 2. ponytail. **~stall** m stable. **~stärke** f (abbr. PS) horsepower (abbr. H.P.). **~wagen** m horse-drawn vehicle. **~zucht** f 1. horse breeding. 2. stud farm.

pfiff [pfɪf] pret of **pfeifen**.
Pfiff m (-[e]s; -e) 1. whistle. 2. F pep: **mit ~** film etc with a difference; **der Mantel hat ~** the coat's got real style; **der richtige ~** that something extra.
'**Pfifferling** ['pfɪfərlɪŋ] m (-s; -e) chanterelle: **k-n ~ wert** not worth a damn.
'**pfiffig** adj smart. '**Pfiffigkeit** f (-; no pl) smartness. **Pfiffikus** ['pfɪfikʊs] m (-[ses]; -se) F smart fellow.
Pfingsten ['pfɪŋstən] n (-; -) Whitsun.
'**Pfingst|fest** n → **Pfingsten**. **~montag** m Whit Monday. **~rose** f ♀ peony. **~'sonntag** m Whitsunday.
Pfirsich ['pfɪrzɪç] m (-s; -e) peach.
Pflanze ['pflantsə] f (-; -n) 1. plant. 2. F type, character. '**pflanzen** v/t (h) plant.
'**Pflanzen|faser** f plant fibre (Am. fiber). **~fett** n vegetable fat. **~fresser** m zo. herbivore. **~kost** f vegetable foodstuffs. **~kunde** f botany. **~öl** n vegetable oil. **~reich** n (-[e]s; no pl) vegetable kingdom, flora. **~schutzmittel** n pesticide. **~welt** f (-; no pl) flora.
'**pflanzlich** adj plant, vegetable.
'**Pflanzung** f (-; -en) plantation.
Pflaster ['pflastər] n (-s; -) 1. pavement: fig. **ein heißes (teures) ~** a dangerous (an expensive) place. 2. ♣ (sticking) plaster, Am. band-aid.
'**Pflastermaler(in** f) m pavement artist.
'**pflastern** v/t (h) 1. pave. 2. ♣ plaster.
'**Pflasterstein** m paving stone.
Pflaume ['pflaʊmə] f (-; -n) 1. a) plum, b) prune. 2. F contp. dope, twit.
'**Pflaumen|baum** m plum (tree). **~kuchen** m plum tart. **~mus** n plum jam.
Pflege ['pfle:gə] f (-; no pl) care, ♣ nursing, ⚙ maintenance, servicing, fig. cultivation (of the arts etc): **in ~ geben** put into care; **in ~ nehmen** a) look after, take into care, b) foster (child).

≗bedürftig *adj* in need of care. **~eltern** *pl* foster parents. **~fall** *m* nursing case. **~heim** *n* nursing home. **~kind** *n* foster child. **≗leicht** *adj* easy-care. **~mutter** *f* foster mother.

pflegen ['pfle:gən] (h) **I** *v/t* a) look after, care for, **~** *a.* nurse, b) *fig.* cultivate (*the arts, a friendship, etc*), c) keep *s.th.* in good condition, **☉** *a.* service, groom: → *gepflegt*. **II** *v/i* (et.) *zu tun* **~** be in the habit of doing (s.th.), usually do (s.th.); *sie pflegte zu sagen* she used to say, she would say. **III** *sich* **~** a) take care of one's appearance, b) look after o.s.

'**Pflegeperso,nal** *n* **⚕** nursing staff.
Pfleger ['pfle:gər] *m* (-s; -) **1.** **⚕** (male) nurse. **2.** **🏛** curator.
'**Pflegerin** *f* (-; -nen) **⚕** nurse.
'**Pflege|sohn** *m* foster son. **~stelle** *f* foster home. **~tochter** *f* foster daughter. **~vater** *m* foster father.

pfleglich ['pfle:klıç] *adj* careful: *et.* **~** *behandeln* take good care of s.th.
'**Pflegschaft** *f* (-; -en) **🏛** curatorship.
Pflicht [pflıçt] *f* (-; -en) duty: *die* **~** *ruft!* duty calls! **2.** → *Pflichtübung*.
'**pflichtbewußt** *adj* conscientious, dutiful. '**Pflichtbewußtsein** *n* conscientiousness, sense of duty.
'**Pflicht|eifer** *m* zeal. **~fach** *n ped.* compulsory subject. **~gefühl** *n* sense of duty. **≗gemäß I** *adj* dutiful, due. **II** *adv* duly. **≗getreu** *adj* dutiful. **~lek,türe** *f* required reading, set books. **~teil** *m, n* **🏛** legal portion. **~übung** *f sports:* compulsory (*or* set) exercise: *fig.* **e-e reine** **~** purely a matter of duty. **≗vergessen** *adj* derelict of duty. **~versäumnis** *n* dereliction of duty. **~versicherung** *f* compulsory insurance. **~verteidiger** *m* **🏛** assigned counsel.

Pflock [pflɔk] *m* (-[e]s; ⁓e) **1.** peg. **2.** stake.
pflücken ['pflʏkən] *v/t* (h) pick.
Pflug [pflu:k] *m* (-[e]s; ⁓e), **pflügen** ['pfly:gən] *v/t, v/i* (h) plough, *Am.* plow.
Pforte ['pfɔrtə] *f* (-; -n) gate, door, *fig.* gateway.
Pförtner ['pfœrtnər] *m* (-s; -) gatekeeper, porter, *Am.* doorman. **~haus** *n* lodge. **~loge** *f* porter's office (*or* lodge).
Pfosten ['pfɔstən] *m* (-s; -) **1.** post. **2.** jamb.

Pfote ['pfo:tə] *f* (-; -n) *zo.* paw, F (*hand*) *a. sl.* mitt.
Pfropf [pfrɔpf] *m* (-[e]s; -e) **⚕** clot.
pfropfen ['pfrɔpfən] *v/t* (h) **1.** stopper. **2.** F cram. **3.** **🌱** graft.
'**Pfropfen** *m* (-s; -) stopper, cork, plug.
'**Pfropf|messer** *n* grafter. **~reis** *n* graft.
Pfründe ['pfrʏndə] *f* (-; -n) a) *eccl.* living, b) *fig.* sinecure.
Pfuhl [pfu:l] *m* (-[e]s; -e) murky pool.
pfui [pfɔi] *int* a) (for) shame!, *sports etc:* boo!, b) ugh!, *to child or dog:* no!: **~** *Teufel!* ugh!, how disgusting!
Pfund [pfʊnt] *n* (-[e]s; -e) **1.** pound (*abbr.* lb.): **3 ~** *Mehl* three pounds of flour. **2.** **~** (*Sterling*) pound (sterling) (*abbr.* L).
'**pfundweise** *adj and adv* by the pound.
Pfusch [pfʊʃ] *m* (-[e]s; *no pl*), '**Pfuscharbeit** *f* F bad job, botch-up.
pfuschen ['pfʊʃən] *v/i, v/t* (h) F bungle: → *Handwerk*.
'**Pfuscher** *m* (-s; -) F bungler.
Pfusche'rei *f* (-; -en) F bungling.
Pfütze ['pfʏtsə] *f* (-; -n) puddle.
Phallus ['falʊs] *m* (-; Phalli) phallus.
'**Phallussym,bol** *n* phallic symbol.
Phänomen [fɛnoˈmeːn] *n* (-s; -e) phenomenon. **phänomenal** [fɛnomeˈnaːl] *adj* phenomenal.
Phantasie [fantaˈziː] *f* (-; -n) **1.** a) imagination, b) mind: *schmutzige* **~** dirty mind; *nur in s-r* **~** only in his mind; *ohne* **~** → *phantasielos*. **2.** *usu. pl* fantasy. **3.** **♪** fantasia. **phantasieren** [fantaˈziːrən] *v/i* (h) **1.** fantasize, dream. **2.** **⚕** be delirious, *a. fig.* rave (*von* about). **3.** **♪** improvise. **phanta'sievoll** *adj* imaginative.
Phantast [fanˈtast] *m* (-en; -en) dreamer, visionary. **Phantaste'rei** [fantastəˈrai] *f* (-; -en) fantasy. **phan'tastisch** [-tıʃ] *adj* fantastic, F *a.* terrific, incredible.
Phantom [fanˈtoːm] *n* (-s; -e) phantom. **Phan'tombild** *n* identikit (*or* photofit) picture (*TM*).
'**Pharmaindu,strie** ['farma-] *f* pharmaceutical industry.
Pharmakologe [farmakoˈloːgə] *m* (-n; -n) pharmacologist. **Pharmakologie** [-loˈgiː] *f* (-; *no pl*) pharmacology.
'**Pharmakon,zern** *m* pharmaceutical company.
Pharmazeut [farmaˈtsɔyt] *m* (-en; -en),

Pharma'zeutin f (-; -nen) pharmacist.
pharma'zeutisch adj pharmaceutical.
Pharmazie [farma'tsi:] f (-; no pl) pharmacy.
Phase ['fa:zə] f (-; -n) a. ⚡ phase.
Philanthrop [filan'tro:p] m (-en; -en) philanthropist. **Philanthropie** [filantro'pi:] f (-; no pl) philanthropism.
philan'thropisch adj philanthropic.
Philatelie [filate'li:] f (-; no pl) philately.
Philatelist [-'lıst] m (-en; -en) philatelist.
Philharmonie [filharmo'ni:] f (-; -n) philharmonic orchestra (or society).
Philologe [filo'lo:gə] m (-n; -n) teacher (or scholar) of language and literature, Am. philologist. **Philologie** [-lo'gi:] f (-; -n) study of language and literature, Am. philology. **philo'logisch** [-gɪʃ] adj language and literature ..., Am. philological.
Philosoph [filo'zo:f] m (-en; -en) philosopher. **Philosophie** [-zo'fi:] f (-; -n) philosophy. **philosophieren** [-zo'fi:rən] v/i (h) philosophize. **philo'sophisch** [-fɪʃ] adj philosophic(al).
Phlegma ['flɛgma] n (-s; no pl) phlegm. **Phlegmatiker** [flɛ'gma:tikər] m (-s; -) phlegmatic person. **phleg'matisch** [-tɪʃ] adj phlegmatic.
Phobie [fo'bi:] f (-; -n) psych. phobia.
Phon [fo:n] n (-s; -s) phys. phon: **50 ∼** 50 phons.
Phonem [fo'ne:m] n (-s; -e) phoneme.
Phonetik [fo'ne:tık] f (-; no pl) phonetics. **Pho'netiker** [-tikər] m (-s; -) phonetician. **pho'netisch** [-tɪʃ] adj phonetic.
Phonotypistin [fonoty'pıstın] f (-; -nen) audio typist.
Phosphat [fɔs'fa:t] n (-[e]s; -e) 🝣 phosphate.
Phosphor ['fɔsfɔr] m (-s; no pl) 🝣 phosphorus.
phosphoreszieren [fɔsfɔrɛs'tsi:rən] v/i (h) phosphoresce: **∼d** phosphorescent.
Photo(...) → **Foto(...).**
Photoche'mie [foto-] f photochemistry.
Photosyn'these f photosynthesis.
Phrase ['fra:zə] f (-; -n) phrase (a. ♩), contp. a. cliché, pol. catchphrase: F **∼n dreschen** talk in platitudes.
'Phrasendrescher m F phrasemonger.
'phrasenhaft adj empty, meaningless.
Physik [fy'zi:k] f (-; no pl) physics.
physikalisch [fyzi'ka:lıʃ] adj physical.

Physiker ['fy:zikər] m (-s; -) physicist.
Physikum ['fy:zikʊm] n (-s; -ka) preliminary (medical) examination.
Physiognomie [fyziɔgno'mi:] f (-; -n) physiognomy.
Physiologie [fyziolo'gi:] f (-; no pl) physiology. **physiologisch** [fyzio'lo:gɪʃ] adj physiological.
Physiothera'peut(in f) m [fyzio-] ♨ physiotherapist.
Physiothera'pie f physiotherapy.
physisch ['fy:zıʃ] adj physical.
Pianist [pia'nıst] m (-en; -en), **Pia'nistin** f (-; -nen) pianist.
Pickel¹ ['pıkəl] m (-s; -) a) ⊙ pick(axe), b) ice-pick.
Pickel² m (-s; -) 🝣 pimple, spot.
pick(e)lig ['pık(ə)lıç] adj pimply, spotty.
picken ['pıkən] v/t, v/i (h) peck (**nach** at).
Picknick ['pıknık] n (-s; -s) picnic.
'picknicken v/i (h) (have a) picnic.
pieken ['pi:kən] v/t, v/i (h) F prick.
'piek'fein adj F posh, very smart.
piepen ['pi:pən] v/i (h) bird: cheep, chirp, mouse: squeak, ⚡ bleep: F **bei dir piept's wohl?** are you off your rocker?
piepsen ['pi:psən] → **piepen.**
Pier [pi:r] f (-; -s) ⚓ jetty, pier.
Pietät [pie'tɛ:t] f (-; no pl) reverence: **aus ∼** out of respect (**gegenüber** of).
pie'tätlos adj irreverent.
pie'tätvoll adj reverent.
Pigment [pɪ'gmɛnt] n (-[e]s; -e) pigment.
Pik¹ [pi:k] m F **e-n ∼ auf j-n haben** have it in for s.o.
Pik² n (-s; -s) cards: spade(s).
pikant [pi'kant] adj a. fig. piquant, spicy.
Pike ['pi:kə] f F **et. von der ∼ auf lernen** learn s.th. from the bottom up.
pikiert [pi'ki:rt] adj fig. piqued (**über** acc about).
Pikkolo ['pıkolo] m (-s; -s) **1.** apprentice waiter. **2.** F champagne miniature.
'Pikkoloflöte f ♩ piccolo.
Pilger ['pılgər] m (-s; -) pilgrim. **'Pilgerfahrt** f pilgrimage. **'pilgern** v/i (sn) **1.** go on a pilgrimage. **2.** F wander.
Pille ['pılə] f (-; -n) pill: **die ∼ nehmen** be on the pill; fig. **e-e bittere ∼** a bitter pill (to swallow).
'Pillenknick m F sudden drop in birthrates. **'Pillenschachtel** f pillbox.
Pilot [pi'lo:t] m (-en; -en) **1.** ✈ pilot. **2.** (racing) driver. **∼film** m pilot (film).

~pro.jekt *n* pilot project. **~sendung** *f* pilot broadcast.

Pilz [pɪlts] *m* (-es; -e) a) fungus (*a.* 🌶), b) mushroom, c) toadstool: **~e suchen** (**gehen**) go mushrooming; **wie ~e aus dem Boden schießen** mushroom (up).

'Pilzvergiftung *f* mushroom poisoning.

pingelig ['pɪŋɪlɪç] *adj*, **'Pingeligkeit** *f* (-; *no pl*) F nitpicking.

Pinguin ['pɪŋguiːn] *m* (-s; -e) penguin.

Pinie ['piːniə] *f* (-; -n) 🌲 (stone) pine.

Pinkel ['pɪŋkəl] *m* (-s; -) F *feiner ~* toff.

'pinkeln *v/i* (h) F (**~ gehen** go for a) pee.

Pinne ['pɪnə] *f* (-; -n) ⚓ helm.

'Pinnwand *f* pinboard.

Pinscher ['pɪnʃər] *m* (-s; -) *zo.* pinscher.

Pinsel ['pɪnzəl] *m* (-s; -) brush.

'pinseln *v/i, v/t* (h) paint (*a.* 🌶).

'Pinselstrich *m* stroke of the brush.

Pinzette [pɪn'tsetə] *f* (-; -n) tweezers.

Pionier [pĭo'niːr] *m* (-s; -e) **1.** ✕ engineer. **2.** *fig.* pioneer. **~arbeit** *f* (-; *no pl*) pioneering work: **~ leisten für** *a.* pioneer *s.th.* **~geist** *m* pioneering spirit.

Pipette [pi'petə] *f* (-; -n) 🧪 pipette.

Pipi [pi'piː] *n* (-s; *no pl*) F **~ machen** wee.

Pirat [pi'raːt] *m* (-en; -en) pirate.

Pi'ratensender *m* radio: pirate station.

Pirouette [pi'rŭetə] *f* (-; -n) pirouette.

Pirsch [pɪrʃ] *f* (-; *no pl*) stalk, still hunt: **auf die ~ gehen** go (*or* be on the) (deer-)stalking.

'pirschen *v/i* (h) **~ auf** (*acc*) stalk.

Pisse ['pɪsə] *f* (-; *no pl*) V piss.

'pissen *v/i* (h) V piss.

Pistazie [pɪs'taːtsiə] *f* (-; -n) pistachio.

Piste ['pɪstə] *f* (-; -n) **1.** a) (racing) track, course, b) piste, ski-run. **2.** ✈ runway.

'Pistenrowdy *m* terror of the slopes.

Pistole [pɪs'toːlə] *f* (-; -n) pistol: **mit vorgehaltener ~** at pistol-point; *fig. j-m* **die ~ auf die Brust setzen** hold a pistol to s.o.'s head; **wie aus der ~ geschossen** like a shot.

Pi'stolentasche *f* holster.

Pizza ['pɪtsa] *f* (-; -s) *gastr.* pizza.

Pizzeria [pɪtse'riːa] *f* (-; -s) pizzeria.

Plackerei [plakə'raɪ] *f* (-; -en) F grind.

plädieren [plɛ'diːrən] *v/i* (h) ⚖ plead (**für, auf** *acc* for). **Plädoyer** [plɛdŏa'jeː] *n* (-s; -s) final speech, *fig.* plea.

Plage ['plaːgə] *f* (-; -n) a) trouble, bother, b) nuisance, *a. bibl.* plague.

plagen ['plaːgən] (h) **I** *v/t* a) trouble, worry, b) torment, harass, F plague (*a.*

pester (*mit* with *requests etc*): **geplagt von** troubled by. **II** *sich ~* toil away, take pains (*mit* with).

Plagiat [pla'gĭaːt] *n* (-[e]s; -e) plagiarism.

plagiieren [plagi'iːrən] *v/i, v/t* (h) plagiarize.

Plakat [pla'kaːt] *n* (-[e]s; -e) a) poster, b) placard. **plakatieren** [plaka'tiːrən] *v/t* (h) placard. **plakativ** [plaka'tiːf] *adj fig.* slogan-like, graphic.

Plakette [pla'ketə] *f* (-; -n) badge.

plan [plaːn] *adj* plane, level.

Plan *m* (-[e]s; ⁓e) **1.** plan, *a.* schedule, *a.* project, scheme (*a. b.s.*): **e-n ~ fassen** make a plan; **Pläne schmieden** make plans; **was steht heute auf dem ~?** what's on today? **2.** a) plan, *a.* design, b) diagram. **3.** map.

Plane ['plaːnə] *f* (-; -n) tarpaulin.

planen ['plaːnən] *v/t* (h) plan, *a.* schedule, *a.* design. **'Planer** *m* (-s; -) planner.

Planet [pla'neːt] *m* (-en; -en) planet.

planetarisch [plane'taːrɪʃ] *adj* planetary. **Planetarium** [plane'taːrĭom] *n* (-s; -rien) planetarium.

planieren [pla'niːrən] *v/t* (h) level, grade. **Pla'nierraupe** *f* ⚙ bulldozer.

Planke ['plaŋkə] *f* (-; -n) plank, board.

Plankton ['plaŋktɔn] *n* (-s; *no pl*) plankton.

'planlos *adj* without plan, aimless, unsystematic. **'Planlosigkeit** *f* (-; *no pl*) aimlessness, lack of system.

'planmäßig I *adj* **1.** planned, systematic. **2.** scheduled (*arrival, flight, etc*). **II** *adv* as planned, according to plan (*or* schedule), *arrive etc* on schedule.

'Planschbecken *n* paddle pond.

planschen ['planʃən] *v/i* (h) splash (about).

'Planstelle *f* permanent post.

Plantage [plan'taːʒə] *f* (-; -n) plantation.

'Planung *f* (-; -en) **1.** → *Plan* 2. **2.** planning: *in der ~* → **'Planungsstadium** *n* *im ~* in the planning stage.

'planvoll *adj* methodical, systematic.

'Planwirtschaft *f* planned economy.

'Plappermaul *n* F chatterbox.

plappern ['plapərn] *v/t, v/i* (h) F chatter.

plärren ['plɛrən] *v/i* (h) a) blubber, cry, b) bawl, c) *radio etc.* blare.

Plasma ['plasma] *n* (-s; -men) plasma.

Plastik¹ ['plastɪk] *f* (-; -en) **1.** sculpture. **2.** 🌶 plastic surgery.

'**Plastik²** n (-s; *no pl*) plastic.
'**Plastik|bombe** f plastic bomb. **~folie** f polythene sheet. **~geld** n F plastic money. **~tüte** f plastic bag.
plastisch ['plastiʃ] *adj* **1.** plastic. **2.** *fig.* vivid, graphic. **3.** **~e Chirurgie** plastic surgery; *Facharzt für* **~e Chirurgie** plastic surgeon.
Platane [pla'taːnə] f (-; -n) plane (tree).
Plateau [pla'toː] n (-s; -s) plateau.
Platin ['plaːtiːn] n (-s; *no pl*) platinum.
platonisch [pla'toːniʃ] *adj* a) Platonic, b) platonic.
platsch *int*, **platschen** ['platʃən] v/i (h, sn) F splash.
plätschern ['plɛtʃərn] v/i (h) ripple, *brook etc*: murmur, *waves*: lap.
platt [plat] *adj* **1.** a) flat, b) level: **~ drükken** flatten; F **~ e Platten haben** have a flat tyre (*Am.* tire). **2.** *fig.* trite, banal. **3.** F **~ sein** be flabbergasted.
Platt n (-[e]s; *no pl*) Low German.
'**plattdeutsch** *adj*, '**Plattdeutsch(e)** n Low German.
Platte ['platə] f (-; -n) **1.** a) (stone) slab, b) flag(stone), c) board, d) panel, e) tile, f) sheet (*of glass, metal*). **2.** (rock) ledge. **3.** (table) top. **4.** hotplate. **5.** dish: *kalte* **~** cold cuts. **6.** record, disc, *Am.* disk: F *fig. die* **~** *kenn' ich!* I know that line! **7.** (dental) plate. **8.** F bald pate.
'**Platten|album** n record album. **~hülle** f record sleeve. **~laufwerk** n *computer*: disk drive. **~spieler** m record player. **~teller** m turntable. **~wechsler** m record changer.
'**Plattform** f a. *fig.* platform.
'**Plattfuß** m **1.** flatfoot. **2.** F *mot.* flat.
'**plattfüßig** [-fyːsɪç] *adj* flat-footed.
Plattheit f (-; -en) **1.** *no pl* a) flatness, b) *fig.* triteness. **2.** platitude.
plattieren [pla'tiːrən] v/t (h) ⊕ plate.
Platz [plats] m (-es; *~e*) **1.** *no pl* room, space: **~** *machen* (*für* for) a) make room, b) make way (*a. fig.*); **~** *sparen* save space; *fig.* **~** *greifen* spread, arise. **2.** place, spot, position, (*camp, building, etc*) site: *fig. fehl am* **~** *sein* be out of place. **3.** (public) square. **4.** seat: **~** *nehmen* take a seat, sit down. **5.** (sports) field, (tennis) court, (golf) course: F *j-n vom* **~** *fegen* play s.o. into the ground; *j-n vom* **~** *verweisen* send s.o. off; *auf eigenem* (*gegnerischem*)

~ *spielen* play at home (out of town). **6.** *sports*: place: *auf* **~** *drei* in third place; → *belegen* 4.
'**Platzangst** f **1.** *psych.* agoraphobia. **2.** F claustrophobia.
'**Platzanweiser** m (-s; -) usher. '**Platzanweiserin** f (-; -nen) usherette.
Plätzchen ['plɛtsçən] n (-s; -) **1.** little place, spot. **2.** biscuit, *Am.* cookie.
platzen ['platsən] v/i (sn) **1.** burst, *bomb etc*: a. explode; *fig.* **vor Wut** **~** explode (with rage), blow up; *vor Neid* **~** be bursting with envy; F *ins Zimmer* **~** burst into the room; → *Kragen, Naht*. **2.** F *fig.* come to nothing, *sl.* bust, go phut, *plan etc*: fall through, *engagement*: be broken off, † *cheque etc*: bounce: **~** *lassen* bust up (*gang etc*).
'**Platz|karte** f reservation card. **~mangel** m lack of space. **~pa.trone** f blank cartridge. **ℒraubend** *adj* space-consuming. **~regen** m cloudburst. **ℒsparend** *adj* space-saving. **~verweis** m *sports*: **e-n** **~** *erhalten* be sent off. **~wunde** f laceration.
Plauderei [plaudə'raɪ] f (-; -en) chat.
'**Plauderer** m (-s; -) conversationalist.
plaudern ['plaudərn] v/i (h) a) (have a) chat, b) blab; → *Schule*.
plausibel [plau'ziːbəl] *adj* plausible: *j-m* **et.** **~** *machen* make s.th. clear to s.o.
plazieren [pla'tsiːrən] v/t (h) place: *sich* **~** position o.s.; *sports*: *sich als Dritter* **~** be placed third.
Pla'zierung f (-; -en) *sports*: place.
Plebiszit [plebɪs'tsiːt] n (-[e]s; -e) plebiscite.
pleite ['plaɪtə] *adj* F **~** *sein* be broke.
'**Pleite** f (-; -n) F **1.** bankruptcy: **~** *machen* go bust. **2.** *fig.* flop: *so 'ne* **~!** what a frost!
Plenarsaal [ple'naːr-] m *parl.* (plenary) assembly room.
Ple'narsitzung f plenary session.
Plenum ['pleːnom] n (-s; *no pl*) plenum.
Pleuelstange ['plɔyəl-] f ⊕ connecting rod.
Plissee [plɪ'seː] n (-s; -s) pleats.
Plis'seerock m pleated skirt.
plissieren [plɪ'siːrən] v/t (h) pleat.
Plombe ['plɔmbə] f (-; -n) **1.** ⊕ (lead) seal. **2.** ⚕ filling.
plombieren [plɔm'biːrən] v/t (h) **1.** seal (with lead). **2.** fill (*tooth*).

plötzlich ['plœtslıç] **I** *adj* sudden. **II** *adv* suddenly: *ganz* ~ all of a sudden.

plump [plʊmp] *adj* **1.** a) plump, b) clumsy. **2.** *fig.* clumsy, tactless, gross (*lie etc*), crude (*joke etc*): *plump-vertraulich* chummy.

'**Plumpheit** *f* (-; *no pl*) **1.** plumpness. **2.** *fig.* clumsiness, grossness, *etc.*

plumps [plʊmps] *int,* **Plumps** *m* (-es; -e) F thud. '**plumpsen** *v/i* (sn) F thud.

Plunder ['plʊndər] *m* (-s; *no pl*) F junk, rubbish.

'**Plünderer** *m* (-s; -) looter.

plündern ['plʏndərn] *v/t, v/i* (h) plunder, loot, pillage, F raid (*fridge etc*).

'**Plünderung** *f* (-; -en) plundering, looting, pillage.

Plural ['plu:ra:l] *m* (-s; *no pl*) *ling.* plural (number). **Pluralismus** [plura'lɪsmʊs] *m* (-; *no pl*) pluralism. **pluralistisch** [-tɪʃ] *adj* pluralistic.

plus [plʊs] *prep* plus.

Plus *n* (-; -) **1.** & plus sign. **2.** a) surplus, b) profit. **3.** *fig.* plus, asset, advantage.

Plüsch [ply:ʃ] *m* (-[e]s; -e) plush.

'**Plüschtier** *n* cuddly toy.

'**Pluspunkt** *m* **1.** credit point. **2.** *fig.* plus, asset, advantage.

Plusquamperfekt ['plʊskvampɛrfɛkt] *n* (-s; -e) pluperfect (tense), past perfect.

'**Pluszeichen** *n* & plus sign.

pneumatisch [pnɔy'ma:tɪʃ] *adj* pneumatic.

Po [po:] *m* (-s; -s) F bottom, bum.

Pöbel ['pø:bəl] *m* (-s; *no pl*) rabble.

'**pöbelhaft** *adj* vulgar.

pochen ['pɔxən] *v/i* (h) **1.** (*an dat* at) knock, rap. **2.** *blood etc:* throb, *heart: a.* beat. **3.** *fig.* ~ *auf* (*acc*) insist on.

pochieren [pɔ'ʃi:rən] *v/t* (h) poach.

Pocke ['pɔkə] *f* (-; -n) & **1.** pock. **2.** *pl* smallpox.

'**Pockenimpfung** *f* & (smallpox) vaccination. '**Pockennarbe** *f* pockmark.

'**pockennarbig** *adj* pockmarked, pitted.

Podest [po'dɛst] *n, m* (-[e]s; -e) platform, *fig.* pedestal.

Podium ['po:dĭʊm] *n* (-s; -dien) rostrum, platform.

'**Podiumsdiskussi,on** *f,* '**Podiumsgespräch** *n* panel discussion.

Poesie [poe'zi:] *f* (-; *no pl*) poetry.

Poet [po'e:t] *m* (-en; -en) poet.

Poetin [po'e:tɪn] *f* (-; -nen) poetess.

poetisch [po'e:tɪʃ] *adj* poetic(al).

Pogrom [po'gro:m] *n* (-s; -e) pogrom.

Pointe ['põɛ:tə] *f* (-; -n) point, *a.* punch line. **pointiert** [põɛ̃'ti:rt] *adj* pointed.

Pokal [po'ka:l] *m* (-s; -e) cup (*a. sports*), goblet. ~**endspiel** *n* cup final. ~**sieger** *m* cup winner. ~**spiel** *n* cup tie.

Pökelfleisch ['pø:kəl-] *n* salt meat.

pökeln ['pø:kəln] *v/t* (h) salt.

pokern [po:karn] *v/i* (h) play poker.

'**Pokerspiel** *n* game of poker.

Pol [po:l] *m* (-s; -e) pole, & *a.* terminal: *fig. ruhender* ~ stabilizing element.

polar [po'la:r] *adj,* **Po'lar...** polar.

polarisieren [polari'zi:rən] *v/t* (*a. sich* ~) polarize.

Polarität [polari'tɛ:t] *f* (-; -en) polarity.

Po'larkreis *m* **nördlicher** (**südlicher**) ~ Arctic (Antarctic) Circle.

Po'larlicht *n* **nördliches** (**südliches**) ~ northern (southern) lights.

Po'larstern *m* Pole Star.

Pole ['po:lə] *m* (-n; -n) Pole.

Polemik [po'le:mɪk] *f* (-; -en) polemic(s).

polemisch [po'le:mɪʃ] *adj* polemic.

polemisieren [polemi'zi:rən] *v/i* (h) polemize.

polen ['po:lən] *v/t* (h) & pole.

'**Polen** *n* (-s) Poland.

Police [po'li:sə] *f* (-; -n) policy.

Polier [po'li:r] *m* (-s; -e) foreman.

polieren [po'li:rən] *v/t* (h) polish.

Poliklinik ['po:li-] *f* outpatients' clinic.

Polin ['po:lɪn] *f* (-; -nen) Pole, Polish woman.

Po'litbü,ro [po'li:t-] *n* politburo.

Politesse [poli'tɛsə] *f* (-; -n) (woman) traffic warden, F meter maid.

Politik [poli'ti:k] *f* (-; -en) **1.** politics: *in der* ~ in politics; *in die* ~ *gehen* go into politics; *über* ~ *reden* talk politics. **2.** policy. **Politiker** [po'li:tikər] *m* (-s; -), **Po'litikerin** *f* (-; -nen) politician.

Politikum [po'li:tikʊm] *n* (-s; -ka) political issue.

politisch [po'li:tɪʃ] *adj* **1.** political: ~*er Berater* policy adviser; *er ist* ~ *tätig* he is in politics; ~ *interessiert sein* be politically minded. **2.** politic.

politisieren [politi'zi:rən] **I** *v/i* talk politics. **II** *v/t* politicize. **Politi'sierung** *f* (-; *no pl*) politicization.

Politologe [polito'lo:gə] *m* (-n; -n) political scientist. **Politologie** [politolo'gi:] f (-; no pl) political science.

Politur [poli'tu:r] f (-; -en) polish.

Polizei [poli'tsaɪ] f (-; -en) police: *die ~ rufen* call the police; F *er ist bei der ~* he is in the police force. **~aufgebot** n police detachment. **~aufsicht** f police supervision. **~beamte** m police officer. **~behörde** f police (authorities). **~dienststelle** f police station. **~einsatz** m police operation. **~es,korte** f police motorcade. **~funk** m police radio. **~hund** m police dog. **~knüppel** m truncheon, Am. billy. **~kommis,sar** m police inspector. **~kon,trolle** f police check.

poli'zeilich adj and adv a) (of the) police, b) by the police.

Poli'zei|präsi,dent m chief of police, Br. chief constable. **~prä,sidium** n police headquarters. **~re,vier** n 1. (police) district, Am. precinct. 2. police station, Am. station house. **~schüler** m police cadet. **~schutz** m police protection. **~staat** m police state. **~streife** f a) police patrol, b) patrolman. **~stunde** f closing time. **~wache** f police station, Am. station house.

Polizist [poli'tsɪst] m (-en; -en) policeman, constable.

Poli'zistin f (-; -nen) policewoman.

Pollen ['pɔlən] m (-s; -) ♀ pollen.

polnisch ['pɔlnɪʃ] adj Polish.

Polo ['po:lo] n (-s; -s) sports: polo.

'**Polohemd** n polo (shirt).

Polster ['pɔlstər] n (-s; -) 1. a) upholstery, b) cushion. 2. pad(ding). 3. F flab, layer of fat. 4. fig. bolster, reserves.

'**Polsterer** m (-s; -) upholsterer.

'**Polster|garni,tur** f three-piece suite. **~möbel** pl upholstered furniture.

polstern ['pɔlstərn] v/t (h) a) upholster, b) pad: F *gut gepolstert* well padded.

'**Polsterpflanze** f cushion plant.

'**Polstersessel** m easy chair, armchair.

'**Polsterstuhl** m upholstered chair.

'**Polsterung** f (-; -en) 1. upholstery. 2. padding.

'**Polterabend** m eve-of-the-wedding party. **poltern** ['pɔltərn] v/i (h) 1. make a racket, crash about. 2. bluster.

Polyamid [poly'a'mi:t] n (-[e]s; -e) polyamide.

Polyäthy'len n polythene.

polygam [poly'ga:m] adj polygamous.

polyglott [poly'glɔt] adj polyglott.

Polyp [po'ly:p] m (-en; -en) 1. zo. polyp. 2. ♐ polypus, pl adenoids. 3. F cop (sl.).

polyphon [poly'fo:n] adj ♪ polyphonic.

Polytechnikum [poly'tɛçnikʊm] n (-s; -ka) polytechnic.

Pomade [po'ma:də] f (-; -n) pomade.

Pommes frites [pɔm'frit] pl chips, Am. French fries.

Pomp [pɔmp] m (-[e]s; no pl) pomp.

pompös [pɔm'pø:s] adj pompous.

Pontifikat [pɔntifi'ka:t] n (-[e]s; -e) pontificate.

Pontius ['pɔntsiʊs] *von ~ zu Pilatus laufen* F run from pillar to post.

Ponton [põ'tõ:] m (-s; -s) pontoon.

Pony[1] ['pɔni] n (-s; -s) zo. pony.

'**Pony**[2] m (-s; -s) fringe, Am. bangs.

Popel ['po:pəl] m (-s; -) F bogey.

'**popelig** adj F piffling, miserable.

Popelin [popə'li:n] m (-s; -e) poplin.

popeln ['po:pəln] v/i (h) F pick one's nose.

Popgruppe ['pɔp-] f pop group.

'**Popmu,sik** f pop music.

Popo [po'po:] m (-s; -s) F bottom, bum.

populär [popu'lɛ:r] adj popular.

popularisieren [populari'zi:rən] v/t (h) popularize. **Popularität** [populari'tɛ:t] f (-; no pl) popularity.

Pore ['po:rə] f (-; -n) pore.

Porno ['pɔrno] m (-s; -s), '**Pornofilm** m porn (or blue) movie.

Pornographie [pɔrnogra'fi:] f (-; no pl) pornography. **pornographisch** [pɔrno'gra:fɪʃ] adj pornographic.

'**Pornoheft** n porn (or girlie) magazine.

Porree ['pɔre] m (-s; -s) ♀ leek.

Portal [pɔr'ta:l] n (-s; -e) portal.

Portemonnaie [pɔrtmɔ'nɛ:] n (-s; -s) purse.

Portier [pɔr'tie:] m (-s; -s) 1. porter. 2. → *Pförtner.*

Portion [pɔr'tsio:n] f (-; -en) a) portion, b) helping, c) pot of *tea etc:* F *fig. halbe ~ shrimp; e-e gehörige ~ Frechheit* a good deal of impudence.

Porto ['pɔrto] n (-s; -s, Porti) postage.

'**portofrei** adj postage paid.

'**Portokasse** f ♐ petty cash.

Porträt [pɔr'trɛ:] n (-s; -s) portrait.

porträtieren [pɔrtrɛ'ti:rən] v/t (h) *j-n ~* paint s.o.'s portrait, *fig.* portray s.o.

Por'trätmaler(in f) m portraitist.
Portugal ['pɔrtugal] n (-s) Portugal.
Portugiese [pɔrtu'giːzə] m (-n; -n), **Por-tu'giesin** f (-; -nen), **portu'giesisch** adj Portuguese.
Portwein ['pɔrt-] m port.
Porzellan [pɔrtsɛ'laːn] n (-s; -e) porcelain, china: F fig. ~ **zerschlagen** do a lot of damage. ~**laden** m china shop: → **Elefant**. ~**waren** pl chinaware.
Posaune [po'zaʊnə] f (-; -n) **1.** (~ **blasen** play the) trombone. **2.** fig. trumpet.
Posaunist [pozaʊ'nɪst] m (-en; -en) trombonist.
Pose ['poːzə] f (-; -n) pose, fig. a. air, act.
posieren [po'ziːrən] v/i (h) pose (als als).
Position [pozi'tsioːn] f (-; -en) **1.** position, sports: a. place: fig. ~ **beziehen** take one's stand. **2.** ✝ item.
positiv ['poːzitiːf] **I** adj positive, a. affirmative. **II** adv F for certain.
Positur [pozi'tuːr] f (-; -en) posture: **sich in ~ setzen** strike an attitude.
Posse ['pɔsə] f (-; -n) farce, burlesque.
possessiv ['pɔsɛsiːf] adj ling. possessive.
Posses'sivpro,nomen n possessive pronoun.
possierlich [pɔ'siːrlɪç] adj droll, funny.
Post [pɔst] f (-; no pl) a) post, mail, b) postal service, c) post office: **mit der ~** by post, by mail; **mit gleicher** (or **getrennter**) ~ under separate cover; **mit der ~ schicken** post, Am. mail; **ist ~ für mich da?** are there any letters for me?
postalisch [pɔs'taːlɪʃ] adj postal.
'**Post|amt** n post office. ~**anschrift** f postal (or mailing) address. ~**anweisung** f postal (or money) order. ~**auto** n post-office van, mail van. ~**barscheck** m postal cheque (Am. check). ~**beamte** m post-office (Am. postal) clerk. ~**bote** m postman, Am. mailman. ~**botin** f postwoman. ~**bus** m post bus.
Posten ['pɔstən] m (-s; -) **1.** ✕ post: fig. **auf dem ~ sein** a) be on one's toes, b) be in good shape; **nicht (ganz) auf dem ~ sein** be a bit under the weather; → **beziehen 3, verloren II. 2.** ✕ guard, sentry: ~ **stehen** be on guard, stand sentry. **3.** post, position, job. **4.** ✝ a) lot, b) item, c) entry.
'**Post|fach** n post-office box, PO box. ~**flugzeug** n mail plane. ~**gebühr** f postage, pl a. postal charges. ~**geheim-**

nis n secrecy of the mails. ~**giroamt** n postal giro office. ~**girokonto** n (post-office) giro account, Br. national giro account.
posthum [pɔs'tuːm] adj posthumous.
postieren [pɔs'tiːrən] v/t (h) place.
'**Post|karte** f postcard, Am. postal card. ⚲**lagernd** adj and adv poste restante, Am. (in care of) general delivery. ~**leitzahl** f postcode, Am. zip code. ~**mi,nister** m postmaster general. ~**scheck** m (post-office) giro cheque (Am. check). ~**sparbuch** n post-office savings book. ~**sparkasse** f post-office savings bank. ~**stempel** m postmark. ~**versandhaus** n mail-order house. ~**wagen** m 🚋 mail van, Am. postal car. ⚲**wendend** adv by return (of post), by return mail, F fig. right away. ~**wertzeichen** n (postage) stamp. ~**wurfsendung** f direct mail. ~**zug** m mail train. ~**zustellung** f postal delivery.
potent [po'tɛnt] adj potent.
Potential [poten'tsiaːl] n (-s; -e), **potentiell** [poten'tsiɛl] adj potential.
Potenz [po'tɛnts] f (-; -en) **1.** no pl potency. **2.** ♂ power: **zweite** ~ square; **dritte** ~ cube. **3.** fig. power, strength.
potenzieren [poten'tsiːrən] v/t (h) **1.** ♂ raise to a higher power. **2.** fig. magnify.
Potpourri ['pɔtpuri] n (-s; -s) ♪ potpourri, medley.
Präambel [prɛ'ʔambəl] f (-; -n) preamble.
Pracht [praxt] f (-; no pl) splendo(u)r: F **es war e-e wahre** ~ it was just great.
'**Prachtexem,plar** n F splendid specimen, a. beauty.
prächtig ['prɛçtɪç] adj **1.** a) splendid, magnificent, b) glorious (weather). **2.** F fig. great, super.
'**Prachtkerl** m F great guy.
'**Prachtstraße** f boulevard.
'**prachtvoll** → **prächtig**.
prädestinieren [prɛdɛsti'niːrən] v/t (h) predestine.
Prädikat [prɛdi'kaːt] n (-[e]s; -e) **1.** ling. predicate. **2.** title. **3.** rating, attribute, ped. mark, grade.
Prädi'kats|nomen n ling. predicate complement. ~**wein** m quality-tested wine (with special attributes).
Präfix [prɛ'fɪks] n (-es; -e) ling. prefix.
prägen ['prɛːgən] v/t (h) **1.** a) stamp, b)

mint (*coin*), c) emboss (*leather, metal, etc.*). **2.** *fig.* a) coin (*word etc*), b) form, shape, determine, characterize.

Pragmatiker [pra'gma:tikər] *m* (-s; -) pragmatist. **prag'matisch** [-tɪʃ] *adj* pragmatic(al). **Pragmatismus** [pragma'tɪsmʊs] *m* (-; *no pl*) pragmatism.

prägnant [prɛ'gnant] *adj* terse, pithy. **'Prägung** *f* (-; -en) **1.** stamping, coining. **2.** *fig.* a) stamp, character, b) forming.

prähi'storisch [prɛ-] *adj* prehistoric.

prahlen ['pra:lən] *v/i* (h) talk big: **mit et. ~** brag about s.th., show off (with) s.th. **'Prahler** *m* (-s; -) braggart, F show-off.

Prahlerei [pra:lə'raɪ] *f* (-; -en) a) showing-off, boasting, b) boast(s).

Praktik ['praktɪk] *f* (-; -en) practice, method, *pl b.s.* (sharp) practices.

Praktikant [prakti'kant] *m* (-en; -en), **Prakti'kantin** *f* (-; -nen) trainee. **'Praktiker** *m* (-s; -) practical man.

Praktikum ['praktikʊm] *n* (-s; -ka) (period of) practical training.

praktisch ['praktɪʃ] **I** *adj* practical, *a.* handy: **~er Arzt** general practitioner; **~e Ausbildung** on-the-job training; **~es Beispiel** concrete example; **~er Versuch** field test. **II** *adv* a) practically, as good as (*done etc*), b) in practice.

praktizieren [prakti'tsi:rən] *v/t, v/i* (h) practise.

Prälat [prɛ'la:t] *m* (-en; -en) *eccl.* prelate.

Praline [pra'li:nə] *f* (-; -n), **Praliné** [prali'ne:] *n* (-s; -s) chocolate.

prall [pral] *adj* **1.** bulging (*bag etc*), hard (*ball etc*), full (*sails*), firm, taut (*muscles*). **2.** blazing (*sun*).

prallen ['pralən] *v/i* (sn) **1.** bounce (**auf** *acc* against), crash (**an** *acc*, **gegen** into). **2.** *sun:* blaze down (**auf** *acc* on).

'prallvoll *adj* F (full to) bursting.

Präludium [prɛ'lu:diʊm] *n* (-s; -dien) prelude.

Prämie ['prɛ:mjə] *f* (-; -n) **1.** a) award, prize, b) reward, c) bonus. **2.** premium.

'prämienbegünstigt *adj* bonus-linked: **~es Sparen** → **'Prämiensparen** *n* saving under the (Federal) bonus system.

prämieren [prɛ'mi:rən], **prämiieren** [prɛmi'i:rən] *v/t* (h) **1.** award a prize to. **2.** give a bonus for.

Pranger ['praŋər] *m* (-s; -) *hist.* stocks: *a. fig.* **an den ~ stellen** pillory.

Pranke ['praŋkə] *f* (-; -n) *zo.* paw.

Präparat [prɛpa'ra:t] *n* (-[e]s; -e) **1.** preparation. **2.** *biol.*, *🎗* specimen.

präparieren [prɛpa'ri:rən] *v/t* (h) **1.** prepare (*a.* **sich ~, auf** *acc* for). **2.** dissect. **3.** preserve.

Präposition [prɛpozi'tsjo:n] *f* (-; -en) *ling.* preposition.

Prärie [prɛ'ri:] *f* (-; -n) prairie.

Präsens ['prɛ:zɛns] *n* (-; Präsentia [prɛ'zɛntsia]) *ling.* present (tense).

präsentieren [prɛzɛn'ti:rən] (h) **I** *v/t* present (**j-m et.** s.o. with s.th.) **II** *v/i* ✕ present arms. **III** *sich ~* present o.s.

Präsenz [prɛ'zɛnts] *f* (-; *no pl*) presence. **~biblio,thek** *f* reference library.

Präserva'tiv [prɛzɛrva'ti:f] *n* (-s; -e) condom, sheath, *Am. a.* prophylactic.

Präsident [prɛzi'dɛnt] *m* (-en; -en) president, chairman, *parl.* Speaker, 🚉 presiding judge. **Präsi'dentenwahl** *f* presidential election. **Präsi'dentschaft** *f* (-; -en) presidency. **Präsi'dentschaftskandi,dat** *m* presidential candidate.

präsidieren [-'di:rən] *v/i* (h) preside (over). **Präsidium** [prɛ'zi:diʊm] *n* (-s; -dien) **1.** presidency. **2.** (presiding) committee. **3.** → *Polizeipräsidium.*

prasseln ['prasəln] *v/i* (h) rain, hail: patter, *fire:* crackle.

prassen ['prasən] *v/i* (h) feast.

Präteritum [prɛ'te:ritʊm] *n* (-s; -ta) *ling.* preterite, past tense.

präventiv [prɛvɛn'ti:f] *adj*, **Präven'tiv...** preventive, *🎗* prophylactic.

Praxis ['praksɪs] *f* (-; Praxen) **1.** *no pl* practice, experience: **in der ~** in practice; *et. in die* **~ umsetzen** put s.th. into practice. **2.** 🚉 *🎗* practice.

Präzedenzfall [prɛtse'dɛnts-] *m* (**e-n ~ schaffen** set a) precedent.

präzis [prɛ'tsi:s] *adj* precise, exact.

präzisieren [prɛtsi'zi:rən] *v/t* (h) specify. **Präzision** [prɛtsi'zjo:n] *f* (-; *no pl*) precision.

predigen ['pre:dɪgən] *v/t, v/i* (h) preach. **Prediger** ['pre:dɪgər] *m* (-s; -) preacher. **Predigt** ['pre:dɪçt] *f* (-; -en) sermon: **e-e ~ halten** preach (a sermon); F *fig.* **j-m e-e ~ halten** lecture s.o.

Preis [praɪs] *m* (-es; -e) **1.** a) price, b) fare: **zum ~e von** at a price of; **im ~ steigen (fallen)** go up (drop); *fig.* **um jeden ~** at all costs; **um k-n ~** not at any price. **2.** prize, award: **e-n ~ erringen**

win a prize. **3.** prize, reward. **4.** praise. ~**absprache** f price agreement. ~**änderung** f change in price: ~**en vorbehalten** subject to change. ~**angabe** f quotation (of prices): **ohne ~** not priced, not marked. ~**anstieg** m rise in prices. ~**aufschlag** m extra charge. ~**ausschreiben** n competition. ⎕**bewußt** adj price-conscious. ~**bindung** f price maintenance.

Preiselbeere ['praɪzəl-] f 🌹 cranberry.

preisen ['praɪzən] v/t (pries, gepriesen, h) praise; → **glücklich** I.

'**Preis|entwicklung** f price trend. ~**erhöhung** f price increase. ~**ermäßigung** f price reduction. ~**frage** f price question. ⎕**gekrönt** adj prize-winning. ~**gericht** n jury. ~**gestaltung** f price formation. ~**grenze** f price limit. ⎕**günstig** → **preiswert**. ~**klasse** f price range. ~**lage** f price range: **in mittlerer** (jeder) ~ medium-priced (in all prices).

'**preislich** adj and adv in price.

'**Preis|liste** f price list. ~**nachlaß** m discount. ~**poli,tik** f price policy. ~**rätsel** n competition. ~**richter(in** f) m judge. ~**schild** n price tag. ~**schwankung** f price fluctuation. ~**senkung** f price reduction. ~**steigerung** f rise in prices. ~**stopp** m price freeze. ~**sturz** m sudden drop in price(s). ~**träger(in** f) m prize winner.

Preistreibe'rei f forcing up of prices.

'**Preis|vergleich** m price comparison. ~**verleihung** f presentation (of prizes).

'**preiswert** adj cheap, low-priced: ~ **sein** a. be good value, be a bargain.

prekär [prɛˈkɛːr] adj precarious.

'**Prellbock** m 🚂 buffer stop, fig. buffer.

prellen ['prɛlən] v/t (h) **1.** 🏥 bruise. **2.** fig. cheat (**um** of).

'**Prellung** f (-; -en) 🏥 contusion, bruise.

Premiere [prəˈmɪ̯eːrə] f (-; -n) thea. etc first night.

Premiermi,nister [prəˈmɪ̯eː-] m prime minister.

Presse¹ ['prɛsə] f (-; -n) 🔘 press.

'**Presse²** f (-; no pl) the press: **er hatte e-e gute ~** he got (or had) a good press. ~**agen,tur** f press agency. ~**amt** n press office. ~**ausweis** m press card. ~**bericht** m press report. ~**bü,ro** n press agency. ~**chef** m chief press officer. ~**dienst** m news service. ~**empfang** m

press reception. ~**erklärung** f press release. ~**feldzug** m press campaign. ~**fo-to,graf** m press photographer. ~**freiheit** f freedom of the press. ~**konfe,renz** f press conference. ~**meldung** f a) press report, b) news item.

pressen ['prɛsən] v/t (h) a) press (a. v/i), b) squeeze.

'**Presse|refe,rent** m press officer. ~**schau** f press review. ~**sprecher** m press spokesman. ~**stelle** f public relations department. ~**stimmen** pl press commentaries. ~**tri,büne** f press box (parl. gallery). ~**vertreter** m reporter. ~**zen,sur** f censorship of the press. ~**zentrum** n press cent/re (Am. -er).

'**Preßluft** f compressed air. ~**bohrer** m pneumatic drill. ~**hammer** m pneumatic hammer.

'**Preßwehen** pl 🏥 bearing-down pains.

Prestige [prɛsˈtiːʒə] n (-s; no pl) prestige.

Pre'stigeverlust m loss of prestige.

Preuße ['prɔʏsə] m (-n; -n), '**Preußin** f (-; -nen), '**preußisch** adj Prussian.

prickeln ['prɪkəln] v/i (h) **1.** tingle, prickle. **2.** champagne: sparkle. '**prickelnd** adj **1.** tingling, prickly. **2.** fig. thrilling: ~**er Reiz** thrill.

pries [priːs] pret of **preisen**.

Priester ['priːstər] m (-s; -) priest.

'**Priesteramt** n priesthood.

'**Priesterin** f (-; -nen) priestess.

'**Priesterschaft** f (-; no pl), '**Priestertum** n (-s; no pl) priesthood.

'**Priesterweihe** f ordination.

prima ['priːma] adj **1.** ✝ prime, first--rate. **2.** F (a. int) great, super.

primär [priˈmɛːr] adj primary.

Primaten [priˈmaːtən] pl zo. primates.

Primel ['priːməl] f (-; -n) 🌹 primrose.

primitiv [primiˈtiːf] adj primitive.

Primitivität [primitiviˈtɛːt] f (-; no pl) primitiveness.

Primzahl ['priːm-] f ➗ prime number.

Prinz [prɪnts] m (-en; -en) prince.

Prinzessin [prɪnˈtsɛsɪn] f (-; -nen) princess.

'**Prinzgemahl** m prince consort.

Prinzip [prɪnˈtsiːp] n (-s; -ien) (**aus** ~ on, **im** ~ in) principle. **prinzipiell** [prɪntsiˈpɪ̯ɛl] adj and adv on principle.

Prior ['priːɔr] m (-s; -en [priˈoːrən]) eccl. prior. **Pri'orin** f (-; -nen) prioress.

Priorität [prioriˈtɛːt] f (-; -en) priority

(**über, vor** *dat* over): **~en setzen** establish priorities.

Prise ['pri:zə] *f* (-; -n) **1. e-e ~ Salz** a pinch of salt. **2. ⚓** prize.

Prisma ['prɪsma] *n* (-s; -men) prism.

prismatisch [prɪs'ma:tɪʃ] *adj* prismatic.

'Prismensucher *m phot.* prismatic viewfinder.

Pritsche ['prɪtʃə] *f* (-; -n) **1.** plank bed. **2.** *mot.* platform. **3.** slapstick.

privat [pri'va:t] **I** *adj* private, *a.* personal. **II** *adv* privately, in private.

Pri'vat|a,dresse *f* home address. **~besitz** *m* private (*or* personal) property: **in ~** privately owned. **~do,zent** *m* (unsalaried) lecturer, *Am.* associate professor. **~gespräch** *n teleph.* private call. **~initia,tive** *f* private venture.

privatisieren [privati'zi:rən] (h) **I** *v/t* **✝** privatize. **II** *v/i* live on one's private income.

Pri'vat|klinik *f* private clinic. **~leben** *n* private (*or* personal) life. **~pati,ent(in** *f*) *m* private patient. **~recht** *n* (-[e]s; *no pl*) private (*or* civil) law. **~sache** *f* private matter (*or* affair): **das ist m-e ~!** that's my (own) business! **~schule** *f* private school. **~sekre,tär(in** *f*) *m* private secretary. **~stunden** *pl*, **~unterricht** *m* private lessons. **~wirtschaft** *f* (-; *no pl*) private enterprise.

Privileg [privi'le:k] *n* (-[e]s; -ien [-'gi̯ən]) privilege. **privilegieren** [privile'gi:rən] *v/t* (h) privilege.

pro [pro:] *prep* per: **~ Jahr** per annum, a year; **~ Kopf** per head, each; **~ Stück** a piece; **~ Stunde** per hour.

Pro das ~ und Kontra the pros and cons.

Probe ['pro:bə] *f* (-; -n) **1. ✝, ⚙** *etc* sample, *a.* ⊙ specimen, *iro.* taste: **✶ e-e ~ ablegen** (*gen*) give a sample (*iro.* taste) of *one's courage etc*. **2.** a) test, try-out, b) check: **auf → ~ probeweise; j-n auf die ~ stellen** put s.o. to the test, test s.o.; **er, auf e-e harte ~ stellen** put s.th. to a severe test. **3.** *thea.* rehearsal. **~abzug** *m print.* proof. **~a,larm** *m* practice alarm. **~aufnahme** *f* **1.** *film:* screen test: **~n machen von** screen-test *s.o.* **2.** ♪ test recording. **~auftrag** *m* trial order. **~bohrung** *f* trial drill. **~exem,plar** *n* specimen copy. **⚓fahren** *v/t* (*only inf and pp* probegefahren, h) test-drive. **~fahrt** *f* test (*or* trial) run.

~flug *m* test (*or* trial) flight. **~jahr** *n* year of probation. **~lauf** *m* ⊙ test run.

proben ['pro:bən] *v/t, v/i* (h) rehearse.

'Probenummer *f* specimen copy.

'probeweise *adv* on a trial basis.

'Probezeit *f* trial period: **nach e-r ~ von 3 Monaten** at the end of three months' probation.

probieren [pro'bi:rən] *v/t* (h) **1.** try, *a.* taste, *a.* test: **es ~ mit** try; **F es bei j-m ~** try it on with s.o. **2. →** anprobieren.

Problem [pro'ble:m] *n* (-s; -e) (**vor e-m ~ stehen** be faced with a) problem.

Problematik [proble'ma:tɪk] *f* (-; *no pl*) problematic nature, problems.

proble'matisch *adj* problematic(al).

Pro'blemkind *n* problem child.

Pro'blemkreis *m* complex of problems.

pro'blemlos *adj* unproblematic(ally *adv*), *adv a.* without (any) difficulties.

Pro'blemstellung *f* **1.** formulation of a problem. **2.** problem.

Pro'blemstück *n thea.* thesis play.

Produkt [pro'dʊkt] *n* (-[e]s; -e) *a.* **⚓** a) product, b) produce. **Pro'duktenwerbung** *f* **✝** product advertising.

Produktion [prodʊk'tsi̯o:n] *f* (-; -en) (**in ~ gehen** go into) production.

Produkti'ons|anlage *f* production plant(s). **~ausfall** *m* loss of production. **~güter** *pl* producer goods. **~kapazi,tät** *f* production capacity. **~kosten** *pl* production costs. **~leiter** *m* production manager. **~mittel** *pl* means of production. **~rückgang** *m* fall in production. **~steigerung** *f* increase in production. **~ziel** *n* production target. **~zweig** *m* line of production.

produktiv [prodʊk'ti:f] *adj* productive.

Produktivität [prodʊktivi'tɛ:t] *f* (-; *no pl*) productivity.

Produzent [produ'tsɛnt] *m* (-en; -en) producer, *a.* grower.

produzieren [produ'tsi:rən] (h) **I** *v/t* produce, *a.* grow. **II** *sich ~* F show off.

profan [pro'fa:n] *adj* **1.** profane, secular. **2.** mundane, trivial.

professionell [profɛsi̯o'nɛl] *adj* professional.

Professor [pro'fɛsɔr] *m* (-s; -en [-'so:-rən]) professor. **Professorin** [profɛ-'so:rɪn] *f* (-; -nen) (woman) professor.

Professur [profɛ'su:r] *f* (-; -en) professorship, chair.

Profi ['pro:fi] *m* (-s; -s) F pro.
'**Profi...** professional (*football etc*).
Profil [pro'fi:l] *n* (-s; -e) profile (*a. fig.*),
⊚ *a.* section, *mot.* (tyre) tread: **im ~** in
profile; *fig.* **~ haben** have personality;
an ~ gewinnen improve one's image.
profilieren [profi'li:rən] (h) **I** *v/t* **1.** ⊚
profile, contour. **2.** *fig.* present in clear
outline. **II** *sich* **~** distinguish o.s.
profi'liert *adj fig.* distinguished.
Pro'fil|neu,rose *f* obsession with one's
image. **~sohle** *f* profiled sole. **~stahl** *m*
⊚ section steel.
Profit [pro'fi:t] *m* (-[e]s; -e) profit: **~**
schlagen aus profit from (*or* by).
profitabel [profi'ta:bəl] *adj* profitable.
profitieren [profi'ti:rən] *v/i*, *v/t* (h) profit
(*von* by, from).
Pro'fitjäger *m contp.* profiteer.
pro forma [pro: 'fɔrma] *adv* as a matter
of form.
profund [pro'fʊnt] *adj* profound.
Prognose [pro'gno:zə] *f* (-; -n) forecast,
esp. ⚕ prognosis.
Programm [pro'gram] *n* (-s; -e) **1.** pro-
gram(me *Br.*), *pol. a.* platform, *thea. a.*
bill, *TV a.* channel: **was steht heute**
auf dem ~? what's the program(me)
for today?; F **das paßt mir gar nicht**
ins ~! that doesn't suit me at all! **2.**
computer: program. **3.** ⊚ cycle. **~ände-**
rung *f* change of program(me *Br.*).
programmatisch [progra'ma:tɪʃ] *adj*
programmatic.
pro'grammgemäß *adv* according to
plan.
Pro'gramm|gestaltung *f* program(me
Br.) planning, program(m)ing. **⚕ge-**
steuert *adj computer:* program-con-
trolled. **~heft** *n* program(me *Br.*). **~hin-**
weis *m* program(me *Br.*) note.
program'mierbar *adj* program(m)able.
programmieren [progra'mi:rən] *v/t* (h)
program(me *Br.*): *fig.* **programmiert**
sein auf (*acc*) be conditioned to (*do*)
s.th. **Program'mierer** *m* (-s; -) pro-
gram(m)er. **Program'miersprache** *f*
program(m)ing language. **Program-**
'**mierung** *f* (-; -en) program(m)ing.
Pro'gramm|punkt *m* item, *pol.* plank.
~steuerung *f computer:* program control. **~taste** *f* program key. **~vorschau**
f program(me *Br.*) roundup, *film:*
trailer(s). **~wahl** *f* **1.** *TV* channel selec-

tion. **2.** ⊚ cycle selection. **~zeitschrift** *f*
program(me *Br.*) guide.
Progression [progrɛ'sio:n] *f* (-; -en)
progression. **progressiv** [-'si:f] *adj*
progressive. **Progressive** [-'si:və] *m, f*
(-n; -n) progressive.
Projekt [pro'jɛkt] *n* (-[e]s; -e) project.
Pro'jektgruppe *f* task force.
Projektion [projɛk'tsio:n] *f* (-; -en)
projection. **Projekti'onsappa,rat** *m*,
Projektor [pro'jɛktɔr] *m* (-s; -en
[-'to:rən]) projector. **projizieren**
[proji'tsi:rən] *v/t* (h) project.
Proklamation [proklama'tsio:n] *f* (-;
-en) proclamation. **proklamieren**
[prokla'mi:rən] *v/t* (h) proclaim.
Pro-'Kopf-Einkommen *n* per capita
income.
Prokura [pro'ku:ra] *f* (-; -ren) ✝ (power
of) procuration. **Prokurist** [proku'rɪst]
m (-en; -en), **Proku'ristin** *f* (-; -nen)
authorized representative.
Prolet [pro'le:t] *m* (-en; -en) *contp.* prole.
Proletariat [proleta'ria:t] *n* (-[e]s; -e)
proletariat(e). **Proletarier** [prole'ta:-
riər] *m* (-s; -), **prole'tarisch** [-rɪʃ] *adj*
proletarian.
Prolog [pro'lo:k] *m* (-[e]s; -e) prolog(ue).
prolongieren [prolɔŋ'gi:rən] *v/t* (h) ✝
renew.
Promenade [prome'na:də] *f* (-; -n)
promenade.
Promille [pro'mɪlə] *n* (-[s]; -) per mil, F
mot. blood alcohol. **Pro'millegrenze** *f*
mot. (blood) alcohol limit.
prominent [promi'nɛnt] *adj* prominent.
Promi'nente *m, f* (-n; -n) public figure,
celebrity. **Prominenz** [promi'nɛnts] *f*
(-; -en) public figures, celebrities.
Promotion [promo'tsio:n] *f* (-; -en) *univ.*
doctorate. **promovieren** [promo'vi:-
rən] (h) **I** *v/t* confer a doctorate on. **II**
v/i take one's (doctor's) degree.
prompt [prɔmpt] *adj* prompt, quick.
Pronomen [pro'no:mən] *n* (-s; -, -mina)
ling. pronoun.
Propaganda [propa'ganda] *f* (-; *no pl*) **1.**
pol. propaganda. **2.** ✝ publicity.
Propagandist [propagan'dɪst] *m* (-en;
-en), **Propagan'distin** *f* (-; -nen),
propagan'distisch *adj* propagandist.
propagieren [propa'gi:rən] *v/t* (h)
propagate.
Propan [pro'pa:n] *n* (-s; *no pl*) propane.

Propeller [pro'pɛlər] m (-s; -) propeller.
Prophet [pro'fe:t] m (-en; -en) prophet. **pro'phetisch** [-tɪʃ] adj prophetic.
prophezeien [profe'tsaɪən] v/t (h) prophesy, predict. **Prophe'zeiung** f (-; -en) prophecy, prediction.
prophylaktisch [profy'laktɪʃ] adj 🟥 prophylactic. **Prophylaxe** [profy'laksə] f (-; -n) prophylaxis.
Proportion [propɔr'tsio:n] f (-; -en) proportion. **proportional** [propɔrtsio'na:l] adj proportional (**zu** to).
Proporz [pro'pɔrts] m (-es; -e) proportional representation.
'**Prorektor** m univ. vice-chancellor.
Prosa ['pro:za] f (-; no pl) prose. '**Prosadichtung** f prose writing.
Prosaiker [pro'za:ikər] m (-s; -) **1.** prose writer, prosaist. **2.** fig. prosaic person.
prosaisch [pro'za:ɪʃ] adj fig. prosaic, matter-of-fact, dull.
prosit ['pro:zɪt] int your health!, cheers!
Prospekt [pro'spɛkt] m (-[e]s; -e) **1.** a) brochure, b) leaflet. **2.** thea. backdrop.
prost [pro:st] → **prosit**.
Prostata ['prɔstata] f (-; no pl) prostate (gland).
prostituieren [prostitu'i:rən] **sich ~** (h) prostitute o.s. **Prostitu'ierte** f (-n; -n) prostitute. **Prostitution** [prostitu-'tsio:n] f (-; no pl) prostitution.
protegieren [prote'ʒi:rən] v/t (h) patronize, sponsor: **von j-m protegiert werden** be s.o.'s protégé.
Protein [prote'i:n] n (-s; -e) protein.
Protektion [protɛk'tsio:n] f (-; -en) patronage. **Protektionismus** [protɛktsio'nɪsmʊs] m (-; no pl) 🟥 protectionism. **protektio'nistisch** [-tɪʃ] adj 🟥 protectionist.
Protektorat [protɛkto'ra:t] n (-[e]s; -e) **1.** pol. protectorate. **2.** fig. patronage.
Protest [pro'tɛst] m (-[e]s; -e) protest (a. 🟥): **aus ~** in protest; **~ einlegen** enter a protest (**gegen** against).
Protestant [protɛs'tant] m (-en; -en), **Prote'stantin** f (-; -nen), **prote'stantisch** adj Protestant.
Protestantismus [protɛstan'tɪsmʊs] m (-; no pl) Protestantism.
protestieren [protɛs'ti:rən] v/i (h) protest (**gegen et.** against s.th., Am. s.th.).
Pro'testkundgebung f protest rally.
Pro'testmarsch m protest march.

Prothese [pro'te:zə] f (-; -n) **1.** artificial limb. **2.** denture(s).
Protokoll [proto'kɔl] n (-s; -e) **1.** record, minutes: **~ führen** take the minutes; **zu ~ geben** 🟥 depose, state (in evidence); **zu ~ nehmen** take down. **2.** protocol.
protokollarisch [protokɔ'la:rɪʃ] adj **1.** on record, minuted: **~ festhalten →** **protokollieren**. **2.** (of) protocol.
Proto'kollchef m chief of protocol. **~führer(in** f) m keeper of the minutes, recording clerk, 🟥 clerk of the court.
protokollieren [protokɔ'li:rən] v/t (h) record, enter in the minutes, take s.th. down.
Proton ['pro:tɔn] n (-s; -en [-'to:nən]) phys. proton.
Proto'plasma [proto-] n protoplasm.
Prototyp ['pro:to-] m prototype.
protzen ['prɔtsən] v/i (h) F show off (**mit** [with] s.o., s.th.). '**protzig** adj F showy.
Proviant [pro'vĭant] m (-s; -e) provisions.
Provinz [pro'vɪnts] f (-; -en) **1.** province. **2.** the provinces, fig. contp. backwater: **finsterste ~ sein** be utterly provincial.
provinziell [provɪn'tsĭɛl] adj provincial.
Pro'vinzler m (-s; -) contp. provincial.
Provision [provi'zio:n] f (-; -en) ✝ (**auf ~** on) commission.
provisorisch [provi'zo:rɪʃ] adj provisional, temporary. **Provisorium** [provi'zo:rĭʊm] n (-s; -rien) **1.** provisional agreement. **2.** makeshift.
Provokation [provoka'tsio:n] f (-; -en) provocation. **provozieren** [provo'tsi:rən] v/t (h) provoke: **~d** provocative.
Prozedur [protse'du:r] f (-; -en) procedure, iro. ritual.
Prozent [pro'tsɛnt] n (-[e]s; -e) **1.** per cent, percent: **zu 5 ~** at five per cent (or percent); **zu wieviel ~?** at what percentage? **2.** pl F a) percentage, b) discount. **...pro,zentig** in cpds. per cent, percent. **Pro'zentsatz** m percentage.
prozentual [protsɛn'tŭa:l] adj proportional: **~er Anteil** percentage; **~ am Gewinn beteiligt sein** receive a percentage of the profit.
Prozeß [pro'tsɛs] m (-sses; -sse) **1.** process. **2.** 🟥 a) lawsuit, b) trial: **e-n ~ anstrengen gegen** bring an action against; **gegen j-n e-n ~ führen** be engaged in a lawsuit with s.o.; **e-n ~ ver-**

lieren lose a case; *j-m den ~ machen* put s.o. on trial; *fig. kurzen ~ machen* make short work (*mit* of).

prozessieren [protsɛ'si:rən] *v/i* (h) go to court, litigate: *gegen j-n ~* bring an action against s.o.

Prozession [protsɛ'sĭo:n] *f* (-; -en) procession.

Pro'zeßkosten *pl* (legal) costs.

Pro'zeßkostenhilfe *f* (-; *no pl*) legal aid.

Prozessor [pro'tsɛsɔr] *m* (-s; -en [-'so:rən]) *computer*: processor.

Pro'zeßordnung *f* code of procedure.

Pro'zeßsteuerung *f* ⊙ process control.

prüde ['pry:də] *adj* prudish: (*nicht*) ~ *sein* be a (no) prude.

Prüderie [pryda'ri:] *f* (-; -n) prudery.

prüfen ['pry:fən] *v/t* (h) **1.** a) examine, *a.* ⊙ inspect, test, check, ✝ audit, ⚖ review, b) investigate, look into *a matter etc*, c) consider (*proposal etc*): *~der Blick* searching glance. **2.** *ped., univ.* examine, test: → *geprüft*. **3.** afflict.

'Prüfer *m* (-s; -) *ped., univ.* examiner, ⊙ tester, ✝ auditor.

'Prüfling *m* (-s; -e) examinee, candidate.

'Prüfstand *m* ⊙ test bed: *fig. auf dem ~ being tested.* *~stein m fig.* touchstone.

'Prüfung *f* (-; -en) **1.** *ped.* examination, test, F exam: → *ablegen* 6. **2.** a) examination, inspection, check(ing), ⊙ test, trial, ✝ audit, ⚖ review, b) investigation, c) consideration. **3.** trial, affliction. **4.** *sports*: event.

'Prüfungs|angst *f* F exam nerves. *~arbeit f* **~aufgabe** *f* examination (*or* test) paper. **~ausschuß** *m*, **~kommission,on** *f* board of examiners. **~ordnung** *f* examination regulations.

'Prüfverfahren *n* method of testing.

Prügel ['pry:gəl] *m* (-s; -) **1.** cudgel. **2.** *pl* F **~ beziehen** get a (sound) thrashing, *a. sports*: get clobbered.

Prüge'lei *f* (-; -en) fight, brawl.

'Prügelknabe *m* scapegoat.

prügeln ['pry:gəln] *v/t* (h) thrash, clobber: *sich ~* (have a) fight.

'Prügelstrafe *f* corporal punishment.

Prunk [prʊŋk] *m* (-[e]s; *no pl*) splendo(u)r, *contp.* pomp. **'Prunkgemach** *n* stateroom. **'Prunkstück** *n* F showpiece.

'prunkvoll *adj* splendid, magnificent.

prusten ['pru:stən] *v/i* (h) snort.

Psalm [psalm] *m* (-s; -e) psalm.

Pseudonym [psɔydo'ny:m] *n* (-s; -e) pseudonym, *a.* pen name.

pst [pst] *int* a) shh!, b) psst!

Psyche ['psy:çə] *f* (-; -n) psyche.

Psychiater [psy'çĭa:tər] *m* (-s; -) psychiatrist, F shrink. **Psychiatrie** [psyçĭa'tri:] *f* (-; *no pl*) **1.** psychiatry. **2.** psychiatric ward. **psychi'atrisch** [-trɪʃ] *adj* psychiatric.

psychisch ['psy:çɪʃ] *adj* a) psychic(al), b) psychological, mental: *~e Erkrankung* mental illness.

Psycho|ana'lyse [psyço-] *f* psychoanalysis. **~ana'lytiker** *m* psychoanalyst.

Psychogramm [psyço'gram] *n* (-s; -e) psychograph, *fig. a.* profile.

Psychologe [psyço'lo:gə] *m* (-n; -n) psychologist. **Psychologie** [psyçolo'gi:] *f* (-; *no pl*) psychology. **psycho'logisch** [-gɪʃ] *adj* psychological.

Psychopath [psyço'pa:t] *m* (-en; -en) psychopath. **psycho'pathisch** [-tɪʃ] *adj* psychopathic.

Psychopharmakon [psyço'farmakɔn] *n* (-s; -ka) psychochemical.

Psychose [psy'ço:zə] *f* (-; -n) psychosis.

psychoso'matisch *adj* psychosomatic.

Psychothera'peut *m* psychotherapist. **psychothera'peutisch** *adj* psychotherapeutic. **Psychothera'pie** *f* psychotherapy.

Pubertät [pubɛr'tɛ:t] *f* (-; *no pl*) puberty.

pubertieren [pubɛr'ti:rən] *v/i* (h) go through puberty.

publik [pu'bli:k] *adj* ~ *sein* (*werden*) be (become) common knowledge; *et. ~ machen* make s.th. public.

Publikation [publika'tsĭo:n] *f* (-; -en) publication.

Publikum ['pu:blikʊm] *n* (-s; *no pl*) a) *the* public, audience, *TV a.* viewers, *radio: a.* listeners, b) *sports*: spectators, c) customers, visitors.

'Publikums|erfolg *m* great (popular) success. **~geschmack** *m* public taste. **~liebling** *m* darling of the public.

publizieren [publi'tsi:rən] *v/t* (h) publish. **Publizist** [publi'tsɪst] *m* (-en; -en) publicist, journalist. **Publizistik** [publi'tsɪstɪk] *f* (-; *no pl*) journalism.

Pudding ['pʊdɪŋ] *m* (-s; -e) pudding, blancmange.

Pudel ['pu:dəl] *m* zo. poodle: F *daste-*

hen *wie ein begossener* ~ look crestfallen. '**Pudelmütze** f bobble hat.
'**pudelnaß** *adj* F soaking wet. '**pudelwohl** *adj* F *sich ~ fühlen* feel great.
Puder ['pu:dər] m, F a. n (-s; -) powder.
'**Puderdose** f powder compact.
pudern ['pu:dərn] v/t (h) powder.
'**Puderquaste** f puff.
'**Puderzucker** m icing (*Am.* confectioner's) sugar.
Puff¹ [pʊf] m (-[e]s; ⸚e) **1.** a) thump, b) poke, dig, nudge: F *fig.* *er (es) kann schon e-n ~ vertragen* he (it) can stand a knock. **2.** pop, bang.
Puff² m, a. n (-s; -s) brothel.
'**Puffärmel** m puffed sleeve.
puffen ['pʊfən] v/t (h) thump, nudge.
Puffer ['pʊfər] m (-s; -) **1.** buffer. **2.** potato fritter. '**Pufferstaat** m buffer state.
'**Puffmais** m popcorn.
Pulle ['pʊlə] f (-; -n) F bottle: *fig.* *volle ~* full blast.
Pulli ['pʊli] m (-s; -s) (light) sweater.
Pullover [pʊ'lo:vər] m (-s; -) sweater, pullover.
Puls [pʊls] m (-es; -e) pulse: *j-m den ~ fühlen* feel s.o.'s pulse, *fig.* sound s.o. out. '**Pulsader** f artery. **pulsieren** [pʊl'zi:rən] v/i (h) pulsate. '**Pulsschlag** m pulse beat. '**Pulszahl** f pulse rate.
Pult [pʊlt] n (-[e]s; -e) a) desk, b) lectern: ♩ *am ~ XY* XY conducting.
Pulver ['pʊlvər] n (-s; -) a) powder, b) gunpowder: F *er hat das ~ nicht erfunden* he is no great light; → *Schuß* 1.
'**Pulverfaß** n powder keg: *wie auf e-m ~ sitzen* be sitting on top of a volcano.
pulverisieren [pʊlveri'zi:rən] v/t (h) pulverize.
'**Pulverkaf,fee** m instant coffee.
'**Pulverschnee** m powdery snow.
Puma ['pu:ma] m (-s; -s) zo. puma.
pummelig ['pʊməliç] *adj* F plump.
Pump [pʊmp] F *auf ~* on tick.
Pumpe ['pʊmpə] f (-; -n) **1.** pump. **2.** F ticker. '**pumpen** v/t, v/i (h) **1.** pump. **2.** F lend, *Am.* loan: *sich et. ~ borrow* s.th. (*bei j-m* from s.o.).
Pumps [pœmps] m (-; -) court shoe.
Punker ['pʌŋkər] m (-s; -) punk.
Punkt [pʊŋkt] m (-[e]s; -e) **1.** point (a. ♙, *sports etc*), dot, *ling.*, *print.* full stop, *Am.* period: *nach ~en siegen* win on points; *~ 10 Uhr* at ten o'clock sharp. **2.**

spot: *fig.* *bis zu e-m gewissen ~* up to a point; → *tot, wund.* **3.** *fig.* a) point, item, b) subject: *in vielen ~en* in many respects; F *der springende ~* the crux (of the matter), the whole point; *die Sache auf den ~ bringen* put it in a nutshell; → *strittig.*
punkten ['pʊŋktən] (h) **I** v/t dot. **II** v/i *sports*: score (points).
punktieren [pʊŋk'ti:rən] v/t (h) ⚕ puncture.
pünktlich ['pʏŋktlıç] **I** *adj* punctual: *sei ~!* be on time! **II** *adv* punctually, on time: *~ um 10 Uhr* at ten o'clock sharp.
'**Pünktlichkeit** f (-; *no pl*) punctuality.
'**Punkt|richter(in** f) m *sports*: judge. **~sieg** m win on points. **~sieger(in** f) m winner on points. **~spiel** n league match. **~streik** m strike at selective sites. **~sy,stem** n points system.
punktuell [pʊŋk'tu̯ɛl] *adj* selective(ly *adv*), *adv a.* at certain points.
Punsch [pʊnʃ] m (-[e]s; -e) *gastr.* punch.
Pupille [pu'pılə] f (-; -n) pupil.
Püppchen ['pʏpçən] n (-s; -) dolly.
Puppe ['pʊpə] f (-; -n) **1.** doll (a. F *girl*), b) *a. fig.* puppet, c) dummy: F *bis in die ~n schlafen* sleep till all hours. **2.** *zo.* a) chrysalis, pupa, b) cocoon.
'**Puppen|spiel** n puppet show. **~spieler(in** f) m puppeteer. **~stube** f doll's house. **~the,ater** n puppet theat/re (*Am.* -er). **~wagen** m doll's pram.
pur [pu:r] *adj* pure, *a.* sheer, *whisky*: neat, *Am.* straight.
Püree [py're:] n (-s; -s) purée, mash.
puritanisch [puri'ta:nıʃ] *adj* a) *hist.* Puritan, b) *contp.* puritanical.
purpurrot ['pʊrpʊr-ro:t] *adj* purple.
Purzelbaum ['pʊrtsəl-] m forward roll.
purzeln ['pʊrtsəln] v/t (sn) tumble.
Puste ['pu:stə] f (-; *no pl*) F breath: *außer ~ sein* be puffed.
Pustel ['pʊstəl] f (-; -n) ⚕ pustule.
pusten ['pu:stən] v/i, v/t (h) puff: F *mot. er mußte ~* he was breathalyzed.
Pute ['pu:tə] f (-; -n) *zo.* turkey (hen): F *dumme ~* silly goose.
Puter ['pu:tər] m (-s; -) *zo.* turkey (cock).
'**puterrot** *adj* (*~ werden* turn) scarlet.
Putsch [pʊtʃ] m (-[e]s; -e) *pol.* putsch, coup (d'état), revolt. '**putschen** v/i (h) *pol.* stage a putsch (*or* coup), revolt.
Putte ['pʊtə] f (-; -n) putto.

Putz [pʊts] *m* (-es; *no pl*) **1.** △ plaster: *∡
unter ~* buried, concealed; F *auf den ~
hauen* a) paint the town red, b) show
off. **2.** F row: *~ machen* raise hell.
putzen ['pʊtsən] (h) **I** *v/t* clean, polish,
Am. shine (*shoes*), preen (*one's feathers*): *sich die Nase ~* blow one's nose;
sich die Zähne ~ brush one's teeth. **II**
v/i clean: *~ (gehen)* work as a cleaner.
III *sich ~ a. fig.* preen o.s.
'Putzfrau *f* cleaning lady.
'putzig *adj* F funny.

'Putzlappen *m* cloth.
'Putzmacherin *f* (-; -nen) milliner.
'Putzmittel *n* cleaning agent.
'Putzwaren *pl* millinery.
'Putzzeug *n* cleaning things.
puzzeln ['pazəln] *v/i* (h) do a puzzle.
Puzzle ['pazəl] *n* (-s; -) (jigsaw) puzzle.
Pygmäe [py'gmɛːə] *m* (-n; -n) pygmy.
Pyjama [py'dʒaːma] *m* (-s; -s) (pair of)
pyjamas (*Am.* pajamas).
Pyramide [pyra'miːdə] *f* (-; -n) pyramid.
pyra'midenförmig *adj* pyramidal.

Q

Q, q [kuː] *n* (-; -) Q, q.
Quacksalber ['kvak-] *m* (-s; -) quack.
Quadrat [kva'draːt] *n* (-[e]s; -e) square: *2
Fuß im ~* 2 feet square; *zum ~ erheben*
square; *3 zum* (*or im*) *~* three squared.
Qua'drat... square (*metre, root, etc*).
qua'dratisch *adj* square, ♣ quadratic.
Quadratur [kvadra'tuːr] *f* (-; -en) quad-
rature: *die ~ des Kreises* the squaring
of the circle.
quadrieren [kva'driːrən] *v/t* (h) square.
quadrophon [kvadro'foːn] *adj* quadro-
phonic.
quaken ['kvaːkən] *v/i* (h) quack, croak.
quäken ['kvɛːkən] *v/i* (h) squawk.
Qual [kvaːl] *f* (-; -en) a) *a. pl* agony,
(mental) anguish, b) ordeal: *unter ~en*
in (great) pain, *fig.* with great difficulty; *es war e-e ~* it was hell.
quälen ['kvɛːlən] (h) **I** *v/t a*) torment,
torture, *fig. a.* haunt, b) pester; → *gequält.* **II** *sich ~* (*mit*) a) torment o.s.
(with), b) struggle hard (with), c) suffer
(badly) (from). **'quälend** → *qualvoll.*
Quäle'rei *f* (-; -en) **1.** tormenting (*etc*,
→ *quälen* I). **2.** torment, torture.
'Quälgeist *m* (-es; -er) pest, tormentor.
Qualifikation [kvalifika'tsi̯oːn] *f* (-; -en)
qualification. **Qualifikati'onsrunde** *f
sports:* qualifying round.
qualifizieren [kvalifi'tsiːrən] *v/t* (*a. sich
~*) (h) qualify (*für* for).
Qualität [kvali'tɛːt] *f* (-; -en) quality.

qualitativ [kvalita'tiːf] *adj* qualitative.
Quali'täts|kon,trolle *f* quality control.
~ware *f* high-quality article, *coll.* quality goods. **~wein** *m* quality-tested wine.
Qualle ['kvalə] *f* (-; -n) *zo.* jellyfish.
Qualm [kvalm] *m* (-[e]s; *no pl*) smoke.
qualmen ['kvalmən] *v/i, v/t* (h) smoke.
'qualmig *adj* smoky, full of smoke.
'qualvoll *adj* agonizing, very painful,
excruciating (*pains*).
Quantenphy,sik ['kvantən-] *f* quantum
physics.
Quantität [kvanti'tɛːt] *f* (-; -en) quantity.
quantitativ [kvantita'tiːf] *adj* quantitative.
Quantum ['kvantʊm] *n* (-s; Quanten) **1.**
quantum, amount. **2.** share, quota.
Quarantäne [karan'tɛːnə] *f* (-; -n) (*unter
~ stellen* put in) quarantine.
Quark [kvark] *m* (-s; *no pl*) **1.** *gastr.* curd
cheese. **2.** → *Quatsch.*
Quartal [kvar'taːl] *n* (-s; -e) quarter
(year).
Quartett [kvar'tɛt] *n* (-[e]s; -e) **1.** ♪ quar-
tet(te). **2.** *fig.* foursome. **3.** (*game*) happy families.
Quartier [kvar'tiːr] *n* (-s; -e) accommodation, *esp.* ✕ quarters.
Quarz [kvaːrts] *m* (-es; -e) quartz.
quasi ['kvaːzi] *adv* as it were.
quasseln ['kvasəln] *v/i* (h) blather.
Quaste ['kvastə] *f* (-; -n) tassel.
Quatsch [kvatʃ] *m* (-es; *no pl*) F rubbish,

rot: **~ machen** a) fool around, b) do s.th. stupid; **red k-n ~!** a) don't talk rubbish!, b) you're kidding!

quatschen ['kvatʃən] *v/i* (h) F **1.** talk rubbish. **2.** gossip. **3.** chat, waffle. **4.** blab. '**Quatschkopf** *m* F silly ass.

Quecke ['kvɛkə] *f* (-; -n) ℛ couch grass.

Quecksilber ['kvɛk-] *n* quicksilver, mercury. **~säule** *f* mercury column. **~vergiftung** *f* mercury poisoning.

Quelle ['kvɛlə] *f* (-; -n) a) spring, ℛ source (*of river etc, a. fig.*), c) well: **et. aus sicherer ~ wissen** have s.th. on good authority. '**quellen** *v/i* (quoll, gequollen, sn) **1.** (**aus** from) pour (*a. fig.*), *blood, water*: well, gush. **2.** swell: **~ lassen** soak (*peas etc*).

'**Quellen|angabe** *f* reference, *pl* bibliography. **~material** *n* source material. **~steuer** *f* withholding tax. **~studium** *n* basic research.

'**Quellgebiet** *n* headwaters.

'**Quellwasser** *n* spring water.

quengelig ['kvɛŋəlɪç] *adj* whining.

quengeln ['kvɛŋəln] *v/i* (h) whine.

quer [kve:r] *adv* a) crosswise, across, b) diagonally, c) at right angles (**zu** to): **~ über** (*acc*) across.

'**Querbalken** *m* crossbeam.

Quere ['kve:rə] *f* **j-m in die ~ kommen** get in s.o.'s way.

querfeld'ein *adv* across country. **Querfeld'einlauf** *m* cross-country race.

'**Querflöte** *f* transverse flute.

'**Querfor,mat** *n* horizontal format.

'**quergestreift** *adj* horizontally striped.

'**Querkopf** *m* F pigheaded fellow.

'**querlegen: sich ~** (*sep*, -ge-, h) F *fig.* make trouble.

'**Querpaß** *m sports*: cross pass.

'**querschießen** *v/i* (*irr, sep*, -ge-, h, → **schießen**) F *fig.* make trouble.

'**Querschiff** *n* △ transept.

'**Querschläger** *m* ✗ ricochet.

'**Querschnitt** *m* cross-section (*a. fig.* **durch** of).

'**querschnitt(s)gelähmt** *adj*, '**Querschnitt(s)gelähmte** *m, f* ✚ paraplegic.

'**Querschnittzeichnung** *f* sectional drawing.

'**Querstraße** *f* intersecting road: **zweite ~ rechts** second turning on the right.

'**Querstrich** *m* horizontal line, dash.

'**Quersumme** *f* ℛ sum of the digits.

'**Quertreiber** *m* (-s; -) F obstructionist.

'**Querverbindung** *f* cross connection.

'**Querverweis** *m* cross reference.

quetschen ['kvɛtʃən] *v/t* (h) a) squeeze (*a. fig.* **sich** o.s.), b) ✚ bruise, crush. '**Quetschung** *f* (-; -en) ✚ bruise.

quickle'bendig ['kvɪk-] *adj* F very lively, active.

quieken ['kvi:kən] *v/i* (h) squeak.

quietschen ['kvi:tʃən] *v/i* (h) squeal, squeak.

'**quietschvergnügt** *adj* F chirpy.

Quinte ['kvɪntə] *f* (-; -n) ♪ fifth.

'**Quintes,senz** *f* (-; -en) essence.

Quintett [kvɪn'tɛt] *n* (-[e]s; -e) quintet(te).

Quirl [kvɪrl] *m* (-[e]s; -e) **1.** *gastr.* beater. **2.** ℛ whorl. **3.** *fig.* live wire.

'**quirlen** *v/t* (h) whisk, beat.

'**quirlig** *adj fig.* lively.

quitt [kvɪt] *adj* **mit j-m ~ sein** (**werden**) be (get) quits with s.o.

Quitte ['kvɪtə] *f* (-; -n) ℛ quince.

quittieren [kvɪ'ti:rən] *v/t* (h) give a receipt for: **et. mit e-m Lächeln ~** meet s.th. with a smile.

Quittung ['kvɪtʊŋ] *f* (-; -en) (**gegen ~** on) receipt: **das ist die ~ für d-n Leichtsinn** that's what you get for being so careless. '**Quittungsblock** *m* receipt book.

Quiz [kvɪz] *n* (-; -) quiz.

'**Quizmaster** *m* (-s; -) quizmaster.

'**Quizsendung** *f* quiz program(me Br.).

quoll [kvɔl] *pret of* **quellen**.

Quote ['kvo:tə] *f* (-; -n) quota, share.

Quotient [kvo'tsiɛnt] *m* (-en; -en) ℛ quotient.

R

R, r [ɛr] *n* (-; -) R, r.

Rabatt [ra'bat] *m* (-[e]s; -e) discount.

Rabbi ['rabi] *m* (-[s]; -nen [ra'bi:nən]), **Rabbiner** [ra'bi:nər] *m* (-s; -) rabbi.

Rabe ['ra:bə] *m* (-n; -n) raven.

'Rabenmutter *f* uncaring mother.

'raben'schwarz *adj* jet-black.

'Rabenvater *m* uncaring father.

rabiat [ra'bĭa:t] *adj* a) furious, b) rough, brutal, c) ruthless.

Rache ['raxə] *f* (-; *no pl*) revenge, vengeance: *aus* ~ in revenge (*für* for); ~ *schwören* vow vengeance; ~ *nehmen* (*or üben*) → **rächen** II.

'Rache‚akt *m* act of revenge.

Rachen ['raxən] *m* (-s; -) **1.** *anat.* throat. **2.** *zo.*, *a. fig.* jaws, maw: F *j-m et. in den* ~ *schmeißen* cast s.th. into s.o.'s hungry maw; *er kann den* ~ *nicht voll kriegen* he can't get enough.

rächen ['rɛçən] (h) **I** *v/t* (*an dat* on, upon) avenge, revenge. **II** *sich* ~ take revenge, get one's own back; *sich an j-m* ~ revenge o.s. (*or take revenge) on s.o.; *es rächte sich (bitter), daß er ...* he had to pay dearly for ger.

'Rachenka‚tarrh *m ✻* pharyngitis.

Rächer ['rɛçər] *m* (-s; -) avenger.

Rachitis [ra'xi:tɪs] *f* (-; *no pl*) ✻ rickets. **ra'chitisch** [-tɪʃ] *adj* ✻ rickety.

'Rachsucht *f* (-; *no pl*) vindictiveness. **'rachsüchtig** *adj* vindictive, revengeful.

rackern ['rakərn] *v/i* (h) F slave away.

Rad [ra:t] *n* (-[e]s; ⁓er ['rɛ:dər]) **1.** wheel: *ein* ~ *schlagen* a) peacock: spread the tail, b) → **radschlagen**; *das fünfte* ~ *am Wagen sein* be the fifth wheel; F *unter die Räder kommen* go to the dogs. **2.** bicycle, F bike.

Radar [ra'da:r] *m, n* (-s; *no pl*) radar. ~**falle** *f mot.* F radar (speed) trap. ~**ge‚rät** *n* radar (set). ~**kon‚trolle** *f* radar control. ~**schirm** *m* radar screen.

Radau [ra'dau] *m* (-s; *no pl*) F row.

'Raddampfer *m* paddle steamer.

radeln ['ra:dəln] *v/i* (sn) F cycle, pedal.

Rädelsführer ['rɛ:dəls-] *m* ringleader.

'Räderwerk *n* a) wheels, b) clockwork, c) gear(ing), d) *fig.* machinery.

'radfahren *v/i* (*irr, sep,* -ge-, sn, → *fah-*

---

ren) **1.** cycle, (ride a) bicycle, F bike. **2.** F *contp.* toady. **'Radfahrer(in** *f*) *m* **1.** cyclist. **2.** F *contp.* toady.

'Radfahrweg *m* cycle track.

radieren [ra'di:rən] *v/t*, *v/i* (h) **1.** erase, rub *s.th.* out. **2.** *art:* etch.

Ra'diergummi *m* eraser, rubber, *Br. a.* rubber.

Ra'dierung *f* (-; -en) *art:* etching.

Radieschen [ra'di:sçən] *n* (-s; -) radish.

radikal [radi'ka:l] *adj*, **Radi'kale** *m, f* (-n; -n) radical. **radikalisieren** [-kali-'zi:rən] *v/t* (h) radicalize. **Radikalismus** [-ka'lɪsmʊs] *m* (-; *no pl*) radicalism. **Radi'kalkur** *f* drastic cure.

Radio ['ra:dĭo] *n* (-s; -s) radio, *Br. a.* wireless: *im* ~ on the radio; ~ *hören* listen to the radio, listen in.

radioak'tiv *adj* radioactive; ~*er Niederschlag* fallout.

Radioaktivi'tät *f* (-; *no pl*) radioactivity.

'Radioappa‚rat *m* radio (set).

Radiologe [radĭo'lo:gə] *m* (-n; -n) ✻ radiologist.

'Radiore‚corder *m* radio cassette recorder. **'Radiowecker** *m* clock radio.

Radium ['ra:dĭʊm] *n* (-s; *no pl*) radium.

Radius ['ra:dĭʊs] *m* (-; Radien) radius.

'Radkappe *f* hub cap. **'Radrennbahn** *f* cycling track. **'Radrennen** *n* cycle race. **'radschlagen** *v/i* (*irr, sep,* -ge-, h, → *schlagen*) turn cartwheels. **'Radsport** *m* cycling. **'Radtour** *f* cycle tour. **'Radweg** *m* cycle track.

raffen ['rafən] (h) *v/t* **1.** snatch up, gather up (*skirt etc*). **2.** *fig.* condense, tighten.

Raffinade [rafi'na:də] *f* (-; -en) refined sugar. **Raffinerie** [rafinə'ri:] *f* (-; -n) ◎ refinery. **Raffinesse** [rafi'nɛsə] *f* (-; -en) cleverness, subtlety, sophistication, *a.* refinement (*of taste etc*). **raffinieren** [rafi'ni:rən] *v/t* (h) ◎ refine. **raffi'niert** *fig.* clever, ingenious (*plan etc*), subtle, sophisticated (*taste etc*).

Rage ['ra:ʒə] *f* (-; *no pl*) rage, fury: *j-n in* ~ *bringen* make s.o. furious.

ragen ['ra:gən] *v/i* (h) tower, loom: ~ *aus* (*dat*) rise (*or* project) from.

Raglanärmel ['ragla(:)n-] *pl* raglan sleeves.

Ragout [ra'gu:] *n* (-s; -s) *gastr.* ragout.

Rahe ['ra:ə] *f* (-; -n) ⚓ yard.
Rahm [ra:m] *m* (-[e]s; *no pl*) cream; →
abschöpfen.
rahmen ['ra:mən] *v/t* (h) frame (*picture etc*), mount (*slides*).
'**Rahmen** *m* (-s; -) frame (*a. mot.*, ⚙), *fig. a.* framework, scope, limits, setting: *im ~ von* (*or gen*) within the scope of; *im ~ des Festes* in the course of the festival; *im ~ der Ausstellung finden ... statt* the exhibition will include ...; *im ~ des Möglichen* within the bounds of possibility; *in großem ~* on a large scale; *aus dem ~ fallen* a) be unusual, be off-beat, b) F get out of line, misbehave; *den ~ sprengen* go beyond the scope (*gen* of). **~abkommen** *n* skeleton agreement. **~bedingungen** *pl* general conditions. **~erzählung** *f* framework story. **~gesetz** *n* skeleton law. **~handlung** *f* frame (story). **~kampf** *m boxing:* supporting fight. **~pro₁gramm** *n* fringe events.
rahmig ['ra:mɪç] *adj* creamy.
'**Rahmkäse** *m* cream cheese.
'**Rahsegel** *n* square sail.
Rakete [ra'ke:tə] *f* (-; -n) rocket, ✗ *a.* missile.
Ra'keten|abschußbasis *f* rocket launching site, ✗ missile base. **~antrieb** *m* rocket propulsion: *mit ~* rocket-propelled. **~start** *m* rocket-assisted takeoff. **~stützpunkt** *m* ✗ missile base.
Rallye ['rali] *f* (-; -s) (motor) rally.
Ramme ['ramə] *f* (-; -n) pile-driver.
rammen ['ramən] *v/t* (h) ram.
Rampe ['rampə] *f* (-; -n) **1.** ramp. **2.** *thea.* apron.
'**Rampenlicht** *n thea.* footlights: *fig. im ~ stehen* be in the limelight.
ramponieren [rampo'ni:rən] *v/t* (h) F *a. fig.* batter.
Ramsch [ramʃ] *m* (-es; -e) *a)* ✝ rejects, b) F *contp.* junk, trash.
ran [ran] F let's go!; *in cpds.* → heran.
Rand [rant] *m* (-[e]s; ⍰er) **1.** edge, rim (*of plate etc*), brim (*of hat, glass, etc*), margin (*of page etc*), lip (*of wound*), brink (*of abyss, fig. of ruin etc*): *bis zum ~ voll* brimful; *e-n ~ lassen* leave a margin; *am ~e des Waldes* (*der Stadt*) on the edge of the wood (on the outskirts of the town); *am ~e a)* *note etc* in the margin, b) *mention etc* in passing; (*nur*)

am ~e (only) marginally; *am ~e bemerkt* by the way. **2.** mark, *a.* tidemark. **3.** F *außer ~ und Band* be completely out of hand, b) quite beside o.s. (*vor* with *joy etc*). **4.** F *er kommt (damit) nicht zu ~e* he can't cope (with it).
randalieren [randa'li:rən] *v/i* (h) raise hell, riot. **Randa'lierer** *m* (-s; -) hooligan, rioter.
'**Rand|bemerkung** *f* a) marginal note, b) passing remark. **~erscheinung** *f* side issue. **~gebiet** *n* borderland (*a. fig.*), outskirts (*of town*). **~gruppe** *f* fringe group.
'**randlos** *adj* rimless (*glasses*).
'**Randpro₁blem** *n* side issue.
'**Randstreifen** *m mot.* shoulder.
rang [raŋ] *pret of* ringen.
Rang *m* (-[e]s; ⍰e) **1.** a) rank (*a.* ✗), status, position, b) quality: *fig. ersten ~es* first-class, first-rate; *j-m den ~ ablaufen* outstrip s.o.; *j-m den ~ streitig machen* compete with s.o.; *alles, was ~ und Namen hat* all the notables (F VIPs). **2.** *thea. erster ~* dress circle, *Am.* first balcony; *zweiter ~* upper circle, *Am.* second balcony; *dritter ~* gallery; *sports: die Ränge* the terraces. **3.** *lottery etc:* (dividend) class.
'**Rangabzeichen** *pl* insignia.
'**rangehen** *v/i* (*irr, sep, -ge-, sn,* → gehen) F go it.
'**rangeln** ['raŋəln] *v/i* (h) F scuffle: *fig. um et. ~* wrangle for s.th.
'**Rangfolge** *f* order of precedence.
rangieren [rã'ʒi:rən] (h) **I** *v/t* 🚂 shunt, *Am.* switch. **II** *v/i fig.* rank (*vor* before).
Ran'giergleis *n* siding.
'**Rangliste** *f sports:* ranking list, table.
'**Rangordnung** *f* order of precedence.
'**ranhalten:** *sich ~* (*irr, sep, -ge-, h,* → halten) F a) get on with it, b) dig in.
rank [raŋk] *adj a. ~ und schlank* slim.
Ranke ['raŋkə] *f* (-; -n) tendril. '**ranken** *v/i* (*a. sich ~*) (h) climb, creep.
'**ranlassen** *v/t* (*irr, sep, -ge-, h,* → lassen) F *j-n ~ an* (*acc*) let s.o. (have a go) at; *laß mich mal ran!* let me have a go!
rann [ran] *pret of* rinnen.
'**rannehmen** *v/t* (*irr, sep, -ge-, h,* → nehmen) F *j-n ~* ride s.o. hard.
rannte ['rantə] *pret of* rennen.
Ranzen ['rantsən] *m* (-s; -) a) knapsack, b) satchel.

ranzig ['rantsɪç] *adj* rancid.
rapide [ra'pi:də] *adj* rapid.
Rappe ['rapə] *m* (-n; -n) black horse.
Rappel ['rapəl] *m* (-s; -) F cazy mood: *e-n ~ kriegen* flip (one's lid).
Raps [raps] *m* (-es; -e) ⚥ rape(-seed).
rar [ra:r] *adj* rare (*a. fig.*), scarce: F *sich ~ machen* make o.s. scarce. **Rarität** [rari'tɛ:t] *f* (-; -en) rarity, *a.* curiosity.
rasant [ra'zant] *adj* **1.** flat (*trajectory*). **2.** F a) fast (*car etc*), b) rapid (*development etc*), c) terrific, d) snazzy.
rasch [raʃ] *adj* quick, swift, speedy, fast: *mach ~!* be quick!
rascheln ['raʃəln] *v/i* (h) rustle.
rasen ['ra:zən] *v/i* **1.** (h) rage: *fig.* (*vor Begeisterung*) *~* be wild with enthusiasm. **2.** (sn) F race, tear.
Rasen ['ra:zən] *m* a) grass, b) lawn.
'rasend I *adj* **1.** raging (*fury etc*), agonizing (*pains*): *~e Kopfschmerzen* a splitting headache; *~e Wut* towering rage; *~ werden* (*machen*) go (drive *s.o.*) mad. **2.** breakneck. **II** *adv* **3.** F madly (*in love etc*): *et. ~ gern tun* just love to do s.th.
'Rasenmäher *m* lawn mower.
'Rasensprenger *m* sprinkler.
Raser ['ra:zər] *m* (-s; -) F speeder.
Rase'rei *f* (-; -en) **1.** F *mot.* speeding. **2.** *no pl* a) fury, b) frenzy: *j-n zur ~ bringen* drive s.o. mad.
Ra'sierappa,rat *m* (safety) razor: *elektrischer ~* electric shaver (*or* razor).
Ra'siercreme *f* shaving cream.
rasieren [ra'zi:rən] (h) **I** *v/t* (*sich ~ lassen*) get a) shave. **II** *v/i* (have a) shave: *sich elektrisch ~* use an electric shaver.
Ra'sier|klinge *f* razor blade. **~messer** *n* razor. **~pinsel** *m* shaving brush. **~seife** *f* shaving soap. **~wasser** *n* aftershave (lotion). **~zeug** *n* shaving things.
raspeln ['raspəln] *v/t* (h) grate.
Rasse ['rasə] *f* (-; -n) race, *zo.* breed.
'Rassehund *m* pedigree dog.
Rassel ['rasəl] *f* (-; -n) rattle.
'rasseln *v/i* (sn) rattle: F *durch e-e Prüfung ~* fail (*Am.* flunk) (an exam).
'Rassen... racial (*discrimination, problem, policy, etc*). **~kra,wall** *m* race riot. **~mischung** *f* mixture of races, *zo.* crossbreed. **~schranke** *f* colo(u)r bar. **~trennung** *f* segregation, *South Africa*: apartheid. **~unruhen** *pl* race riots.

'Rassepferd *n* thoroughbred (horse).
'rasserein *adj* purebred, thoroughbred.
rassig ['rasɪç] *adj* thoroughbred.
Rassismus [ra'sɪsmʊs] *m* (-; *no pl*) racism. **Rassist** [ra'sɪst] *m* (-en; -en), **ras'sistisch** *adj* racist.
Rast [rast] *f* (-; *no pl*) rest, *a.* break: (*e-e*) *~ machen* → **rasten.**
Raste ['rastə] *f* (-; -n) ⚙ catch
rasten ['rastən] *v/i* (h) (take a) rest.
Raster ['rastər] *m* (-s; -) *phot., print.* screen, *TV a.* raster, ⚡ grid.
'Rasthaus *n* motorway restaurant.
'rastlos *adj* restless.
'Rastlosigkeit *f* (-; *no pl*) restlessness.
'Rastplatz *m* resting place, *mot.* layby, *Am.* rest stop.
'Raststätte *f mot.* service area.
Rasur [ra'zu:r] *f* (-; -en) shave.
Rat [ra:t] *m* (-[e]s; *~e*) **1.** *no pl* (piece of) advice, suggestion, recommendation: *auf s-n ~ hin* on his advice; *j-n um ~ fragen* (*j-s ~ folgen*) ask (take) s.o.'s advice; *~ schaffen* find a way out; *~ suchen* seek advice; *zu ~e ziehen* consult; *~ wissen* know what to do; *k-n ~ mehr wissen* be at a loss. **2.** a) council, board, b) council(l)or.
Rate ['ra:tə] *f* (-; -n) **1.** instal(l)ment: *in ~n zahlen* pay by (*or* in) instal(l)ments. **2.** (*birth, growth, etc*) rate.
raten ['ra:tən] *v/t, v/i* (riet, geraten, h) **1.** *j-m* (*zu et.*) *~* advise s.o. (to do s.th.); *~ et. zu tun* recommend doing s.th.; *zur Vorsicht ~* recommend caution; *wozu ~ Sie mir?* what do you advise me to do?, what would you recommend? **2.** guess, *a.* solve (*puzzle*): F *rate mal!* just guess!; *falsch geraten!* wrong guess!
'Ratenzahlung *f* payment by instal(l)ments.
'Ratespiel *n* guessing (*TV panel*) game.
'Ratgeber *m* (-s; -) **1.** adviser. **2.** reference book.
'Rathaus *n* townhall, *Am.* city hall.
Ratifikation [ratifika'tsʲo:n] *f* (-; -en), **Ratifi'zierung** *f* (-; -en) ratification.
ratifizieren [ratifi'tsi:rən] *v/t* (h) ratify.
Ration [ra'tsʲo:n] *f* (-; -en) ration.
rational [ratsʲo'na:l] *adj* rational.
rationalisieren [ratsʲonali'zi:rən] *v/t* (h) rationalize. **Rationali'sierung** *f* (-; -en) rationalization. **Rationali'sierungsfachmann** *m* efficiency expert.

Rationalismus [ratsǐona'lɪsmʊs] *m* (-; *no pl*) rationalism.

rationell [ratsǐo'nɛl] *adj* a) rational, b) efficient.

rationieren [ratsǐo'niːrən] *v/t* (h) ration. **Ratio'nierung** *f* (-; -en) rationing.

'ratlos *adj* helpless: ~ **sein** *a.* be at a loss. **'Ratlosigkeit** *f* (-; *no pl*) helplessness.

'ratsam *adj* advisable, wise.

'Ratschlag *m* (piece of) advice: *einige gute Ratschläge* some good advice.

Rätsel ['rɛːtsəl] *n* (-s; -) riddle, puzzle, *fig. a.* mystery: *es ist mir ein (völliges) ~* it's a (complete) mystery to me, F it beats me; *er ist mir ein ~* I can't make him out; *vor e-m ~ stehen* be baffled.

'rätselhaft *adj* a) baffling, puzzling, b) mysterious.

'Rätselraten *n* (-s) *fig.* speculation.

'Ratsherr *m hist.* council(l)or.

Ratte ['ratə] *f* (-; -n) *zo.* rat.

'Rattenfänger *m* ratcatcher, *fig.* Pied Piper. **'Rattengift** *n* rat poison.

rattern ['ratərn] *v/i* (h *and* sn), **'Rattern** *n* (-s) rattle, clatter.

Raub [raʊp] *m* (-[e]s; *no pl*) **1.** a) (armed) robbery, b) kidnap(p)ing. **2.** a) loot, b) prey: *ein ~ der Flammen werden* be destroyed by fire.

'Raubbau *m* (-[e]s; *no pl*) ruinous exploitation: ~ *treiben mit* a) exploit ruthlessly, b) *s-r Gesundheit* ruin one's health.

'Raubdruck *m* (-[e]s; -e) pirate edition.

rauben ['raʊbən] *v/t* (h a) rob, b) kidnap: *j-m et.* ~ *a. fig.* rob s.o. of s.th.

Räuber ['rɔʏbər] *m* (-s; -) robber, highwayman. ~**bande** *f* gang of robbers, holdup gang. ~**geschichte** *f* F cock-and-bull story.

'räuberisch *adj* rapacious, predatory: ~*er Überfall* (armed) robbery, holdup.

'Raub|**fisch** *m* predatory fish. ~**gier** *f* rapacity. **gierig** *adj* rapacious. ~**mord** *m* murder with robbery. ~**mörder** *m* murderer and robber. ~**ritter** *m hist.* robber baron. ~**tier** *n* beast of prey. ~**überfall** *m* (armed) robbery, holdup. ~**vogel** *m* bird of prey. ~**zug** *m* raid.

Rauch [raʊx] *m* (-[e]s; *no pl*) (*fig. sich in* ~ *auflösen* go up in smoke).

rauchen ['raʊxən] *v/i, v/t* (h) smoke, 🔥 fume: F *e-e* ~ have a smoke; *Rauchen verboten!* No smoking!; → *Pfeife* 2.

Raucher ['raʊxər] *m* (-s; -) **1.** (*starker* ~ heavy) smoker. **2.** → *Raucherabteil*.

Räucher... ['rɔʏçər-] *gastr.* smoked.

'Raucher|**ab,teil** *n* smoking compartment. ~**husten** *m* 🔥 smoker's cough.

'Raucherin *f* (-; -nen) → *Raucher* 1.

räuchern ['rɔʏçərn] *v/t* (h) smoke(-dry).

'Räucherstäbchen *n* joss stick.

'Rauchfahne *f* trail of smoke.

'rauchig *adj* smoky (*a. fig. voice*).

'Rauch|**pilz** *m* mushroom cloud. ~**säule** *f* column of smoke. ~**verbot** *n* ban on smoking: ~*!* No smoking! ~**vergiftung** *f* smoke poisoning. ~**waren** *pl* **1.** furs. **2.** tobacco products. ~**wolke** *f* cloud of smoke. ~**zeichen** *n* smoke signal.

Räude ['rɔʏdə] *f* (-; -n) *vet.* mange.

'räudig *adj* mangy.

rauf(...) [raʊf] F → *herauf(...)*, *hinauf(...)*.

'Raufbold [-bɔlt] *m* (-[e]s; -e) brawler.

raufen ['raʊfən] (h) **I** *v/t sich die Haare* ~ tear one's hair. **II** *v/i* (*a. sich* ~) brawl, fight (*um* for).

Raufe'rei *f* (-; -en) brawl, fight.

rauh [raʊ] *adj* rough, *a.* harsh (*climate, treatment, voice, etc*), *a.* raw (*air etc*), sore (*throat*), wild, bleak (*region etc*), coarse (*cloth etc*): ~*e Hände* chapped hands; ~*e See* stormy sea; ~*e Stimme* hoarse (*or* husky) voice; ~*e Sitten* rough practices; ~*, aber herzlich* pretty rough; *die ~e Wirklichkeit* (the) harsh reality; F *in ~en Mengen* lots of.

'Rauheit *f* (-; *no pl*) roughness (*etc*).

'Rauhfaserta,pete *f* woodchip paper.

'Rauhhaar... *zo.* wirehaired.

'Rauhreif *m* hoarfrost.

Raum [raʊm] *m* (-[e]s; ~e) **1.** room. **2.** *no pl* room, space (*a. philos., phys.*), *fig. a.* scope: *auf engstem ~ leben* live in cramped surroundings; *fig. im ~ stehen* *problem etc*: be there; → *luftleer*. **3.** area, region: *im ~ (von) München* in the Munich area. **4.** *no pl* (outer) space. ~**anzug** *m* space suit. ~**ausstatter** *m* (-s; -) interior decorator. ~**deckung** *f* *sports:* zone defen/ce (*Am.* -se).

räumen ['rɔʏmən] *v/t* (h) **1.** leave, *a.* ✕ evacuate, quit, vacate (*house etc*), clear (*hall, street, etc, a.* ♣ *stores*); → *Feld.*2. **2.** remove: *Minen* ~ sweep mines; → *Weg.*

'Raumfähre *f* space shuttle.

'Raumfahrt *f* (-; *no pl*) space travel (*or*

flight), astronautics. **'Raumfahrt...** space (*medicine, programme, etc*).

'Räumfahrzeug n **1.** bulldozer. **2.** snow clearer.

'Raumflug m space flight.

'Rauminhalt m volume, capacity.

'Raumkapsel f space capsule.

räumlich ['rɔʏmlɪç] adj a) (of) space, spatial, three-dimensional, b) stereophonic, c) opt. stereoscopic: **~** (**sehr**) **beengt** cramped (for space).

'Räumlichkeit f (-; -en) **1.** room, pl premises. **2.** no pl three-dimensionality.

'Raummaß n solid measure. **'Raum-meter** n, a. m cubic metre (Am. meter).

'Raumpflegerin f cleaning lady.

'Raumschiff n spacecraft, spaceship.

'Raumsonde f space probe.

'raumsparend adj space-saving.

'Raumstati|on f space station.

'Räumung f (-; -en) clearing, a. ✝ clearance, a. ✗ evacuation, ✝✝ eviction. **'Räumungs|befehl** m ✝✝ eviction order. **~klage** f ✝✝ action for eviction. **~verkauf** m ✝ clearance sale.

raunen ['raʊnən] v/i, v/t (h) whisper.

Raupe ['raʊpə] f (-; -n) zo. caterpillar.

'Raupen|fahrzeug n crawler (truck). **~kette** f crawler. **~schlepper** m tracklaying (or crawler) tractor.

raus [raʊs] int F get out!

raus(...) F → **heraus(...), hinaus(...).**

Rausch [raʊʃ] m (-[e]s; **¨e**) intoxication (a. fig.), drunkenness, F high, fig. ecstasy: **e-n ~ haben** be drunk; **s-n ~ ausschlafen** sleep it off.

'rauscharm adj low-noise.

rauschen ['raʊʃən] v/i **1.** (h) leaves, silk: rustle, water, stream, etc: roar. **2.** (sn) sweep. **'Rauschen** n (-s) rustling (etc), 𝄞 noise. **'rauschend** adj **1.** rustling (etc). **2.** fig. glittering (parties), thunderous (applause).

'Rauschgift n drug(s pl coll). **~bekämpfung** f fight against drugs. **~handel** m drug traffic. **~händler** m drug trafficker, F pusher, sl. dealer. **~sucht** f drug addiction. **𝄞süchtig** adj drug-addicted: **~ sein** a. be a drug addict, be on drugs. **~süchtige** m, f (-n; -n) drug addict.

'rausfliegen F → **hinausfliegen** 2.

'rausgeben F → **herausgeben.**

räuspern ['rɔʏspərn] sich **~** (h) clear one's throat.

'rausreißen F → **herausreißen.**

'rausschmeißen v/t (irr, sep, -ge-, h, → **schmeißen**) F kick s.o. out, a. fire.

'Rausschmeißer m (-s; -) F **1.** bouncer. **2.** get-out dance.

Raute ['raʊtə] f (-; -n) **1.** lozenge, esp. ♣ rhomb. **2.** ♣ rue.

Razzia ['ratsĭa] f (-; -ien) (police) raid.

Reagenzglas [re'ʔa'gɛnts-] n test tube.

reagieren [re'ʔa'giːrən] v/i (h) (auf acc to) react, fig. a. respond.

Reaktion [re'ʔak'tsĭoːn] f (-; -en) (auf acc to) reaction, fig. a. response.

reaktionär [re'ʔaktsĭoˈnɛːr] adj, **Reaktio'när** m (-s; -e) reactionary.

Reakti'ons|fähigkeit f (-; no pl) reactions. **𝄞schnell** adj **~ sein** have fast reactions. **~zeit** f reaction time.

Reaktor [re'ʔaktɔr] m (-s; -en [-'toːrən]) phys. reactor.

real [re'aːl] adj **1.** real. **2.** realistic.

Re'aleinkommen n real income.

realisieren [reali'ziːrən] v/t (h) realize.

Realismus [rea'lɪsmʊs] m (-; no pl) realism. **Realist** [-'lɪst] m (-en; -en) realist. **rea'listisch** [-tɪʃ] adj realistic.

Realität [reali'tɛːt] f (-; -en) reality.

Re'allohn m real wages.

Re'alschule f secondary school (leading to O-levels), Am. junior high school.

Rebe ['reːbə] f (-; -n) a vine, b) tendril.

Rebell [re'bɛl] m (-en; -en) rebel.

rebellieren [rebɛ'liːrən] v/i (h) rebel.

Rebellion [rebɛ'lĭoːn] f (-; -en) rebellion. **re'bellisch** [lɪʃ] adj rebellious.

Rebhuhn ['reːp-] n zo. partridge.

'Rebstock m ♣ vine.

Rechen ['rɛçən] m (-s; -) rake.

'Rechen|anlage f computer. **~aufgabe** f (arithmetical) problem, sum. **~buch** n arithmetic book. **~fehler** m miscalculation, mistake. **~ma,schine** f calculator: **elektronische ~** computer.

'Rechenschaft f **~ ablegen über** (acc) answer for; **j-n zur ~ ziehen** call s.o. to account (wegen for); **j-m ~ schuldig sein** be answerable to s.o. (über acc for). **'Rechenschaftsbericht** m **1.** report. **2.** statement (of accounts).

'Rechen|schieber m slide rule. **~zentrum** n computer cent(re (Am. -er).

Recherche [re'ʃɛrʃə] f (-; -n) investigation. **recherchieren** [reʃɛrˈʃiːrən] v/i (h) investigate.

rechnen ['rɛçnən] (h) **I** v/t **1.** ⊕ calculate, work out. **2.** a) estimate, b) count, allow for: *die Kinder nicht gerechnet* not counting the children. **3.** *j-n ~ zu* count s.o. among. **II** v/i **4.** calculate, *esp. ped.* do sums: *falsch ~* miscalculate; *gut ~ können* be good at figures. **5.** *fig. ~ zu* count among; *~ mit, ~ auf (acc)* a) count on, b) expect, reckon with; *mit mir kannst du nicht ~!* count me out! **6.** economize. **'Rechnen** n (-s) calculation, *ped.* arithmetic.

'Rechner m (-s; -) **1.** calculator: *er ist ein guter ~* he is good at figures. **2.** ⊙ a) calculator, b) computer. **'rechnergesteuert** adj computer-controlled.

'Rechnung f (-; -en) **1.** a) calculation, b) problem, sum: *die ~ ging nicht auf a. fig.* it didn't work out; → *Strich* 1. **2.** ✝ account, bill, invoice, *in restaurant:* bill, *Am.* check: *die ~, bitte!* can I have the bill, please!; *auf ~* on account; *auf ~ kaufen* buy on credit; *das geht auf m-e ~* that's on me!; *fig.* **das geht auf s-e ~** that's his doing; F *auf s-e ~ kommen* get one's money's worth; *laut ~* as per invoice; *e-r Sache ~ tragen* take s.th. into account; *j-m et. in ~ stellen* charge s.th. to s.o.'s account.

'Rechnungs|betrag m invoice total. **~führung** f accountancy. **~hof** m audit division. **~jahr** n financial year. **~prüfer** m accountant. **~prüfung** f audit. **~wesen** n (-s; no pl) accountancy.

recht [rɛçt] **I** adj **1.** right, right-hand, pol. right(-wing), rightist: *~er Hand* on the right; *~er Hand sehen Sie ...* on your right you see ...; *im ~en Winkel (zu)* at right angles (to); → *Hand* 8. **2.** right, a. correct, a. suitable, a. just, fair: *das ist nur ~ und billig* that's only fair; *so ist's ~!* that's it!; *ganz ~!* quite right!, exactly!; *zur ~en Zeit* at the right moment; *mir ist's ~* that's all right with me, I don't mind; *mir ist alles ~* I don't care; *ist es Ihnen ~, wenn ...?* would you mind if ...?; *schon ~!* it's all right!; → *Ding* 2, *Mittel* 1. **3.** real, true, regular: *er hat k-n ~en Erfolg* he is not much of a success. **4.** *~ haben* be right; *~ behalten* be right in the end; *j-m ~ geben* agree with s.o. **II** adv **5.** a) right(ly), well, correctly, b) properly, c) very, d) rather, quite: *~ gut* not bad; *es gefällt*

mir ~ gut I rather like it; *erst ~* all the more; *(nun) erst ~ nicht* (now) less than ever; *wenn ich es ~ überlege* (when I) come to think of it; *ich weiß nicht ~* I wonder; *~ daran tun zu inf* do right to inf; *es geschieht ihm ~* it serves him right; *das kommt mir gerade ~* that comes in handy; *man kann es nicht allen ~ machen* you can't please everybody; *verstehen Sie mich ~* don't get me wrong.

Recht n (-[e]s; -e) **1.** no pl law, justice: *~ und Ordnung* law and order; *nach deutschem ~* under German law; *von ~s wegen* by law, *fig.* by rights; *gleiches ~ für alle* equal rights for all; *~ sprechen* administer justice; *im ~ sein* be in the right; → a. **recht** 4. **2.** a) right, a. claim, title (*all: auf acc* to), b) privilege, c) power, authority: *mit ~, zu ~* justly, rightly; *das ~ haben zu inf* have the right (or be entitled) to inf; *zu s-m ~ kommen* come into one's own; *er hat es mit vollem ~ getan* he had every right to do so; *alle ~e vorbehalten* all rights reserved.

'Rechte¹ f (-n; -n) **1.** right (hand or side): *zur ~n* on the right (hand); *zu s-r ~n* on (or to) his right. **2.** boxing: right. **3.** pol. the Right.

'Rechte² n (-n) the right thing: *nicht das ~, nichts ~s* not the real thing; *nach dem ~n sehen* look after things.

'Rechteck n (-[e]s; -e) rectangle.

'rechteckig adj rectangular.

'rechtfertigen v/t (h) justify (*sich* o.s.).

'Rechtfertigung f (-; -en) justification: *zu m-r ~* in my defen/ce (*Am.* -se).

'rechtgläubig adj orthodox.

'rechthaberisch [-haːbərɪʃ] adj dogmatic, opinionated, pigheaded.

'rechtlich I adj legal, a. lawful. **II** adv legally; *~ verpflichtet* bound by law.

'rechtlos adj without rights.

'rechtmäßig adj lawful, legitimate (*heir, claim, etc*), legal: *das steht ihm ~ zu* he is (legally) entitled to it.

'Rechtmäßigkeit f (-; no pl) lawfulness, legitimacy, legality.

rechts [rɛçts] adv on the right (hand side): *nach ~* to the right; *von ihm ~* on his right; *~ abbiegen* turn off right; *sich ~ halten* keep to the right; *pol. ~ stehen* belong to the Right.

'**Rechtsabbieger** *m mot.* vehicle (*pl* traffic) turning right.
'**Rechts|anspruch** *m* legal claim (*auf acc* to). **~anwalt** *m*, **~anwältin** *f* lawyer, *Br. a.* solicitor, *in court:* counsel, barrister, *Am.* attorney(-at-law).
'**Rechtsaußen** *m* (-; -) outside right.
'**Rechts|behelf** *m* legal remedy. **~beistand** *m* legal adviser, *in court:* counsel. **~beratungsstelle** *f* legal aid office. **~beugung** *f* perversion of justice. **~bruch** *m* breach of law.
'**rechtschaffen** *adj* honest, upright.
'**Rechtschreibfehler** *m* spelling mistake. '**Rechtschreibung** *f* spelling.
'**Rechtsextre,mist(in** *f)* *m* right-wing extremist.
'**rechtsfähig** *adj* having legal capacity.
'**Rechts|fall** *m* (law) case. **~frage** *f* question of law. **~geschäft** *n* legal transaction. **2gültig** *adj* legal(ly valid): **~ machen** validate. **~gutachten** *n* legal opinion.
'**Rechtshänder** [-hɛndər] *m* (-s; -) right-hander: **~ sein** be right-handed.
'**rechtsherum** *adv* to the right.
'**Rechtskraft** *f* legal force, validity: **~ erlangen** become effective.
'**rechtskräftig** *adj* legal(ly binding), final (*judg[e]ment*), effective (*law*).
'**Rechtskurve** *f* right-hand bend.
'**Rechts|lage** *f* legal position. **~mittel** *n* legal remedy: **ein ~ einlegen** lodge an appeal. **~nachfolger(in** *f)* *m* successor in interest. **~norm** *f* legal norm.
'**rechtsorien,tiert** *adj pol.* right-wing.
'**Rechtspar,tei** *f* right-wing party.
'**Rechtspflege** *f* (-; *no pl*) administration of justice. '**Rechtsprechung** *f* (-; -en) jurisdiction, administration of justice.
'**Rechts|radi,kale** *m, f* right-wing extremist. **~ruck** *m pol.* swing to the right. '**Rechtsschutz** *m* legal protection. **~versicherung** *f* legal costs insurance.
'**Rechts|spruch** *m* legal decision, *in civil matters:* judg(e)ment, *in criminal cases:* sentence. **~staat** *m* constitutional state. **2staatlich** *adj* constitutional. **~staatlichkeit** *f* (-; *no pl*) rule of law.
'**Rechtssteuerung** *f* right-hand drive.
'**Rechts|streit** *m* lawsuit, action. **~titel** *m* legal title. **2unfähig** *adj* (legally) disabled. **2unwirksam** *adj* ineffective. **2verbindlich** *adj* (legally) binding (**für**

on). **~verfahren** *n* **1.** legal procedure. **2.** (legal) proceedings.
'**Rechtsverkehr** *m* right-hand traffic: **in ... ist ~** in ... they drive on the right.
'**Rechts|verletzung** *f* infringement. **~vertreter** *m* legal representative, (authorized) agent. **~weg** *m* course of law: **auf dem ~** by legal action; **den ~ beschreiten** go to law. **2widrig** *adj* illegal. **~widrigkeit** *f* (-; -en) **1.** *no pl* illegality. **2.** unlawful act. **~wissenschaft** *f* (-; *no pl*) jurisprudence, law.
'**rechtwink(e)lig** *adj* right-angled, rectangular.
'**rechtzeitig I** *adj* punctual. **II** *adv* a) in time (**zu** for), b) on time: **gerade** (*or* **genau**) **~** in the nick of time.
Reck [rɛk] *n* (-[e]s; -e) horizontal bar.
recken ['rɛkən] *v/t* (h) stretch: **den Hals ~** crane one's neck.
'**Reckturnen** *n* bar exercises.
Redakteur [redak'tø:r] *m* (-s; -e) editor. **Redak'teurin** *f* (-; -nen) (woman) editor. **Redaktion** [-'tsĭo:n] *f* (-; -en) **1.** *no pl* editing. **2.** a) editorial staff, b) editorial office. **redaktionell** [-tsĭo'nɛl] *adj* editorial: **~ bearbeiten** edit.
Rede ['re:də] *f* (-; -n) **1.** speech, address: **e-e ~ halten** make a speech; F **große ~n schwingen** talk big. **2.** a) talk(ing), speech (*a. ling.*), b) conversation, talk, c) words, language: **direkte** (**indirekte**) **~** direct (reported *or* indirect) speech; **es geht die ~, daß** it is rumo(u)red (that); **die ~ kam auf** (*acc*) the conversation (*or* talk) turned to; **(j-m)** (**und Antwort**) **stehen** account (to s.o.) (**über** *acc* for); **j-n zur ~ stellen** take s.o. to task (**wegen** for); **davon kann k-e ~ sein!** that's out of the question!; **(aber) k-e ~!** by no means!; **es ist nicht der ~ wert** a) it is not worth mentioning, b) don't mention it!, c) never mind!; **der langen ~ kurzer Sinn** to cut a long story short; → **verschlagen** 4.
'**Rede|freiheit** *f* (-; *no pl*) freedom of speech. **~gabe** *f* (-; *no pl*) eloquence.
'**redegewandt** *adj* eloquent.
'**Redekunst** *f* rhetoric.
reden ['re:dən] (h) **I** *v/t, v/i* (**mit** to, **über** *acc* about, of) speak, talk: **über Politik ~** talk politics; **von sich ~ machen** cause a stir; **j-m ins Gewissen ~** appeal to s.o.'s conscience; **ich habe mit dir zu**

~ I'd like a word with you; **laß uns vernünftig darüber ~!** let's talk sense!; **sie läßt nicht mit sich ~** she won't listen to reason; **nicht zu ~ von ...** not to mention ...; **~ wir von et. anderem!** let's change the subject!; **du hast gut ~!** you can talk!; **darüber läßt sich ~!** that's a possibility! II **sich heiser (in Wut) ~** talk o.s. hoarse (into a rage).

'**Reden** n (-s) talking: **j-n zum ~ bringen** make s.o. talk.

'**Redensart** f a) phrase, b) saying, c) pl empty talk: **das ist nur so e-e ~** it's just a way of speaking.

'**Rede|schwall** m flood of words. **~verbot** n ban on speaking: **j-m ~ erteilen** ban s.o. from speaking. **~weise** f s-e etc ~ the way s.o. etc talks. **~wendung** f figure of speech, idiom.

redigieren [redi'gi:rən] v/t (h) edit.

redlich ['re:tlıç] adj honest, upright: **sich ~(e) Mühe geben** do one's best.

'**Redlichkeit** f (-; no pl) honesty, probity.

Redner ['re:dnər] m (-s; -) speaker. **~bühne** f rostrum, (speaker's) platform. **~pult** n lectern.

'**redselig** adj talkative.

'**Redseligkeit** f (-; no pl) talkativeness.

reduzieren [redu'tsi:rən] v/t (h) reduce (**auf** acc to): **sich ~** be reduced.

Reede ['re:də] f (-; -n) ⚓ roadstead, road(s): **das Schiff liegt auf der ~** the ship is (lying) in the roads. **Reeder** ['re:dər] m (-s; -) shipowner. **Reede'rei** f (-; -en) shipping company.

reell [re'εl] adj 1. real (chance etc). 2. honest, decent, ✝ good, fair (price etc).

Reep [re:p] n (-[e]s; -e) ⚓ rope.

Reetdach ['re:t-] n thatched roof.

Referat [refe'ra:t] n (-[e]s; -e) 1. report, a. lecture, ped., univ. (seminar) paper: **ein ~ halten → referieren.** 2. department.

Referendar [referen'da:r] m (-s; -e), **Referen'darin** f (-; -nen) → **Gerichts-, Studienreferendar(in)**.

Referendum [refe'rεndʊm] n (-s; -den, -da) referendum.

Referent [refe'rεnt] m (-en; -en) 1. official in charge: **er ist persönlicher Referent** he is personal assistant (gen to). 2. speaker, 🎓, parl. referee.

Referenz [refe'rεnts] f (-; -en) reference.

referieren [refe'ri:rən] v/t, v/i (h) (**über**

acc on) a) report, b) (give a) lecture, univ. give a paper.

reffen ['rεfən] v/t (h) ⚓ reef.

reflektieren [reflεk'ti:rən] (h) I v/t phys. reflect. II v/i F **auf** (acc) have one's eye on. **Reflektor** [re'flεktor] m (-s; -en [-'to:rən]) reflector.

Reflex [re'flεks] m (-es; -e) reflex.

Re'flexbewegung f reflex action.

Reflexion [reflε'ksio:n] f (-; -en) reflection.

reflexiv [reflε'ksi:f] adj ling. reflexive.

Refle'xivpro,nomen n reflexive pronoun.

Reform [re'form] f (-; -en) reform.

Reformation [reforma'tsio:n] f (-; -en) reformation. **Reformator** [refor'ma:tor] m (-s; -en [-ma'to:rən]) reformer.

re'formbedürftig adj in need of reform.

Re'formhaus n health food shop.

reformieren [refor'mi:rən] v/t (h) reform. **Refor'mierte** m, f (-n; -n) member of the Reformed Church.

Re'formkost f health food(s).

Refrain [rə'frɛ̃:] m (-s; -s) refrain.

Regal [re'ga:l] n (-s; -e) shelves. **Re'galwand** f wall lined with shelve units.

Regatta [re'gata] f (-; -ten) regatta.

rege ['re:gə] adj lively, a. active, vivid (imagination), busy (traffic etc): **~n Anteil nehmen an** (dat) show an active interest in; **~ Nachfrage** keen demand.

Regel ['re:gəl] f (-; -n) 1. rule: **in der ~** as a rule; **zur ~ werden** become a rule (or habit); **es sich zur ~ machen zu** inf make it a rule to inf; **nach allen ~n der Kunst** in superior style. 2. 🩺 period.

'**regelbar** adj adjustable.

'**Regelblutung** f 🩺 menstruation.

'**Regelfall** m **im ~** as a rule.

'**regellos** adj 1. irregular. 2. disorderly.

'**Regellosigkeit** f (-; no pl) irregularity.

'**regelmäßig** adj a) regular, b) periodical, a) regulated, orderly.

'**Regelmäßigkeit** f (-; no pl) regularity.

regeln ['re:gəln] v/t (h) regulate, ⚙ a. adjust, a. direct (traffic), settle (matter etc): **das wird sich (schon) alles ~** that will sort itself out.

'**regelrecht** I adj 1. proper. 2. F regular, real. II adv 3. properly. 4. F downright.

'**Regelstudienzeit** f time limit for a course of study.

'**Regelung** f (-; -en) 1. regulation, ⚙ a.

adjustment, settlement. **2.** provision, rule. **'Regelungstechnik** f control engineering.

'Regelverstoß m sports: foul.

'regelwidrig adj irregular, sports: against the rules, foul. **'Regelwidrigkeit** f (-; -en) irregularity, sports: foul.

regen ['re:gən] v/t (a. **sich ~**) (h) move, stir; fig. **sich ~** feelings etc: stir, arise.

'Regen m (-s; -) rain, fig. a. shower: **saurer ~** acid rain; **ich bin in den ~ gekommen** I was caught in the rain; F **vom ~ in die Traufe kommen** jump out of the frying-pan into the fire; F fig. **ein warmer ~** a windfall.

'regenarm adj with low rainfall.

'Regenbogen m rainbow. **~farben** pl colo(u)rs of the rainbow. **~haut** f anat. iris. **~presse** f trashy weeklies.

Regeneration [regenera'tsio:n] f (-; -en) regeneration. **Regenerati'onsfähigkeit** f regenerative power.

regenerieren [regene'ri:rən] v/i (a. **sich ~**) (h) regenerate.

'Regen|fälle pl rain(fall). **~guß** m downpour. **~haut** f plastic mac. **~mantel** m raincoat. **~reich** adj rainy. **~rinne** f gutter, mot. roof rail. **~schauer** m shower. **~schirm** m umbrella.

Regent [re'gɛnt] m (-en; -en) regent.

'Regen|tag m rainy day. **~tonne** f water butt. **~tropfen** m raindrop. **~wald** m rain forest. **~wasser** n rainwater. **~wetter** n rainy weather. **~wolke** f raincloud. **~wurm** m earthworm. **~zeit** f rainy season, the rains.

Regie [re'ʒi:] f (-; no pl) **1.** thea. etc direction: **unter der ~ von** a. directed by; **~ führen (bei)** direct (s.th.). **2.** a) management, b) administration: fig. **in eigener ~** on one's own. **~anweisung** f stage direction. **~assi.stent** m assistant director. **~fehler** m humor. slip-up. **~raum** m TV central control room.

regieren [re'gi:rən] (h) **I** v/t a) govern (a. ling.), rule, b) manage, control. **II** v/i rule, monarch: a. reign (a. fig.).

Re'gierung f (-; -en) **1.** reign: **unter der ~ von** (or gen) under the reign of; **an der ~ sein** be in power; **an die ~ kommen** take over, come into power. **2.** government.

Re'gierungs|beamte m government official. **~bezirk** m administration dis-

trict. **~bildung** f formation of the government. **~chef** m head of government. **~erklärung** f policy statement. **♀fähig** adj in a position to govern the country: **~e Mehrheit** etc working majority etc. **~par.tei** f ruling party. **~sitz** m seat of government. **~sprecher** m government spokesman. **~umbildung** f (government) reshuffle. **~vorlage** f government bill. **~wechsel** m change of government. **~zeit** f a) reign, b) term of office.

Regime [re'ʒi:m] n (-s; - [-mə]) regime.

Re'gimekritiker m pol. dissident.

Regiment [regi'mɛnt] n (-[e]s) **1.** (-e) (a. **das ~ führen**) rule. **2.** (-er) ✗ regiment.

Region [re'gio:n] f (-; -en) region.

regional [regio'na:l] adj, **Regio'nal...** regional.

Regisseur [reʒi'sø:r] m (-s; -e), **Regis'seurin** f (-; -nen) thea., film: director, TV producer.

Register [re'gɪstər] n (-s; -) register (a. ♪), in book: index: F **alle ~ ziehen** pull all the stops.

Registratur [regɪstra'tu.r] f (-; -en) registry. **registrieren** [regɪs'tri:rən] v/t (h) register (a. fig.), record (a. ⊙), fig. note.

Regi'strierkasse f cash register.

Reglement [reglə'mã:] n (-s; -s) regulation(s).

Regler ['re:glər] m (-s; -) ⊙ controller.

'reglos adj motionless.

regnen ['re:gnən] v/impers (h) rain: **es regnete in Strömen** it was pouring (with rain); fig. **es regnete Anfragen** there was a flood of inquiries.

'regnerisch adj rainy.

Regreß [re'grɛs] m (-sses; -sse) ✝, ⚖ recourse.

re'greßpflichtig adj liable to recourse.

'regsam adj active.

'Regsamkeit f (-; no pl) activity.

regulär [regu'lɛ:r] adj regular.

'regulierbar adj ⊙ adjustable.

regulieren [regu'li:rən] v/t (h) **1.** a) regulate, b) adjust. **2.** settle (account etc).

Regung ['re:gʊŋ] f (-; -en) a) movement, b) emotion, c) impulse.

'regungslos adj motionless.

Reh [re:] n (-[e]s; -e) **1.** zo. (roe) deer. **2.** gastr. venison.

Rehabilitation [rehabilita'tsio:n] f (-; -en) rehabilitation.

Rehabilitati'onszentrum n 🏥 rehabilitation cent/re (Am. -er).

rehabilitieren [rehabili'tiːrən] v/t (h) rehabilitate. **Rehabili'tierung** f (-; -en) rehabilitation.

'Reh|bock m roebuck. **~braten** m roast venison. **~geiß** f doe. **~keule** f gastr. leg of venison. **~kitz** n fawn. **~rücken** m gastr. saddle of venison.

Reibach ['raɪbax] m (-s; no pl) F **e-n ~ machen** make one's pile.

'Reibe f (-; -n), **'Reibeisen** n grater.

reiben ['raɪbən] (rieb, gerieben, h) **I** v/t **1.** rub: **sich die Hände ~** rub one's hands; → **Nase. 2.** grate. **II** v/i **3.** chafe.

Reibe'reien pl (constant) friction.

'Reibfläche f striking surface.

'Reibung f (-; -en) a. fig. friction.

'reibungslos adj. a. fig. smooth.

'Reibungspunkt m fig. cause of friction.

'Reibungsverlust m ⚙ friction(al) loss.

'Reibungswärme f ⚙ frictional heat.

reich [raɪç] **I** adj rich (**an** dat in), a. abundant, copious, a. sumptuous: **e-e ~e Auswahl** a wide selection (**an** dat, **von** of). **II** adv richly, copiously: **~ beschenkt** loaded with gifts.

Reich n (-[e]s; -e) empire, kingdom (a. eccl. or fig.), rhet. or fig. realm: hist. **das Dritte ~** the Third Reich; **das ~ der Tiere** animal kingdom.

reichen ['raɪçən] (h) **I** v/t **1.** j-m et. **~** hand (or pass) s.o. s.th.; **sich die Hände ~** shake hands. **2.** offer, serve. **II** v/i **3. ~ bis** (or **an** acc) reach to, extend to, come up (or go down) to; **soweit das Auge reicht** as far as the eye can see. **4.** last (out), do, be enough: **das reicht!** that will do!; **das Brot reicht nicht** there isn't enough bread; **damit ~ wir bis Mai** it will last us till May; **es reicht für alle** there is enough to go round; F **mir reicht's!** I've had enough!

'reichhaltig adj extensive, large: **~e Auswahl** wide selection; **~es Programm** varied program(me Br.).

'reichlich I adj ample, abundant, plentiful, plenty of (time, food, etc), generous (pay etc). **II** adv F rather, pretty: **~ versehen sein mit** have plenty of.

'Reichtum m (-s; ⸚er) (**an** dat of) riches, a. fig. wealth, abundance.

'Reichweite f reach, ✈, ⚔ range: **in** (**außer**) **~** within (out of) reach.

reif [raɪf] adj ripe, a. fig. mature: **~ werden** → **reifen.**

Reif¹ m (-[e]s; no pl) hoarfrost.

Reif² m (-[e]s; -e) ring, bracelet, circlet.

Reife ['raɪfə] f (-; no pl) **1.** ripeness, esp. fig. maturity. **2.** **mittlere ~** intermediate high school certificate, GCE O-levels.

reifen ['raɪfən] v/i (sn) ripen, mature (a. fig.): **~ lassen** mature.

'Reifen m (-s; -) **1.** mot. etc tyre, Am. tire: **die ~ wechseln** change tyres. **2.** hoop. **~panne** f puncture, blowout, Am. flat. **~pro,fil** n tyre (Am. tire) engraving. **~wechsel** m tyre (Am. tire) change.

'Reifeprüfung f → **Abitur.**

'Reifglätte f mot. slippery frost.

'reiflich I adj nach **~er Überlegung** after careful consideration. **II** adv (**sich**) **et. ~ überlegen** consider s.th. carefully.

Reigen ['raɪgən] m (-s; -) round dance: **den ~ eröffnen** a. fig. lead off.

Reihe ['raɪə] f (-; -n) a) row, b) line, c) row (of seats), d) series, number, e) succession: **geometrische ~** geometric progression; **sich in e-r ~ aufstellen** line up; F **e-e ganze ~ von** a whole string of; **aus den ~n** (gen) from among; **Kritiker aus den eigenen ~n** critics from among the own ranks; (**immer**) **der ~ nach** in turn, one after the other; **außer der ~** out of turn; **ich bin an der ~** it's my turn; **warten, bis man an die ~ kommt** wait one's turn; F fig. **aus der ~ sein** be out of sorts; **aus der ~ tanzen** step out of line; **wieder in die ~ bringen** straighten s.o., s.th. out.

'Reihen|folge f order, sequence: **in zeitlicher ~** in chronological order. **~haus** n terrace (Am. row) house. **~untersuchung** f 🏥 mass screening.

'reihenweise adv **1.** in rows. **2.** F fig. by the dozen.

Reiher ['raɪər] m (-s; -) zo. heron.

Reim [raɪm] m (-[e]s; -e) rhyme.

reimen ['raɪmən] v/t, v/i (a. **sich ~**) (h) rhyme (**auf** acc with).

rein [raɪn] **I** adj **1.** pure (a. biol., 🏭, a. fig.), clean, clear (a. skin, conscience, etc), net, clear (profit), fig. mere, sheer: **~e Wolle** pure wool; **e-e ~e Formalität** a mere formality; **~er Wahnsinn** sheer madness; **die ~e Wahrheit** the (plain) truth; **durch ~en Zufall** by pure accident; **et. ins ~e bringen** sort s.th. out;

mit j-m ins ~e kommen get things straightened out with s.o.; **ins ~e schreiben** make a fair copy of; → **Luft** 1, **Tisch, Wein** 2 etc. **II** adv **2.** purely: **aus ~ persönlichen Gründen** for purely personal reasons; → **zufällig. 3.** F absolutely.

rein(...) F → **herein(...), hinein(...).**

Reineclaude [rɛːnəˈkloːdə] f (-; -n) ⚘ greengage.

'**Reinertrag** m net proceeds.

'**Reinfall** m F a) flop, b) letdown, frost.

'**reinfallen** F → **hereinfallen** 2.

'**Reingewicht** n net weight.

'**Reingewinn** m net (or clear) profit.

'**reinhängen** (sep, -ge-, h) F fig. **I** v/t j-n ~ set s.o. up, frame s.o. **II** sich (voll) ~ go flat out.

'**reinhauen** v/i (irr, sep, -ge-, h, → **hauen**) F dig in, tuck in.

'**Reinheit** f (-; no pl) purity (a. fig.), cleanness.

reinigen [ˈraɪnɪɡən] v/t (h) clean, dry--clean (clothes), a. ⚕ cleanse (von of), purify (a. fig.), metall. refine.

'**Reinigung** f (-; -en) **1.** cleaning (etc.) **2.** dry cleaners: et. in die ~ geben send s.th. to the cleaners.

'**Reinigungs,milch** f cosmetics: cleansing milk. ~mittel n detergent.

'**Reinkul,tur** f F Kitsch in ~ pure unadulterated trash.

'**reinlegen** F → **hereinlegen.**

'**reinlich** adj clean, person: cleanly, a. neat, tidy. '**Reinlichkeit** f (-; no pl) cleanliness, neatness, tidiness.

'**reinrassig** adj pedigree (dog etc), thoroughbred (horse).

'**Reinschrift** f fair copy.

'**reinseiden** adj (of) pure silk.

'**reinwaschen** v/t (irr, sep, -ge-, h, → **waschen**) fig. clear (von of).

Reis¹ [raɪs] n (-es; -er) ⚘ **1.** twig. **2.** scion.

Reis² m (-es; no pl) rice.

'**Reisauflauf** m rice pudding.

Reise [ˈraɪzə] f (-; -n) journey, travel, trip, a. tour, ✈, ⚓ voyage: **gute ~!** have a nice trip!, bon voyage!; **e-e ~ mit dem Auto** a journey by car; **ich plane e-e ~ durch Amerika** I'm planning to travel through America; **auf ~n sein** be travel(l)ing; → **antreten** 1.

'**Reise|andenken** n souvenir. ~apo,theke f first-aid kit. ~bekanntschaft f travel(l)ing acquaintance. ~bericht m travelog(ue) Br.). ~beschreibung f book of travels. ~bü,ro n travel agency. ~bus m coach. ~diploma,tie f pol. shuttle-diplomacy. ⚥fertig adj ready to start. ~führer m **1.** guide. **2.** guide-(book). ~gefährte m travel companion. ~geschwindigkeit f cruising speed. ~gesellschaft f **1.** tourist party. **2.** → **Reiseveranstalter.**

'**Reisekosten** pl travel(l)ing expenses. ~zuschuß m travel([l]ing) allowance.

'**Reiseland** n tourist country.

'**Reiseleiter(in** f) m courier.

'**reiselustig** adj fond of travel(l)ing.

'**Reisemo,bil** n (-[e]s; -e) camper, Am. mobile home.

reisen [ˈraɪzən] v/i (sn) (nach to) travel, go, make a trip: **zu s-n Verwandten ~** go to visit one's relatives; **er ist weit gereist** he has travel(l)ed a lot; **ins Ausland ~** go abroad; F fig. ~ **auf** (acc) coast on. '**Reisen** n (-s) travel, travel(l)ing. '**Reisende** m, f (-n; -n) **1.** a) travel(l)er, b) tourist, c) passenger. **2.** → **Handlungsreisende.**

'**Reise|neces,saire** n sponge bag. ~paß m passport. ~pro,spekt m travel brochure. ~provi,ant m provisions for the journey. ~route f route, itinerary. ~scheck m traveller's cheque, Am. traveler's check. ~schreibma,schine f portable typewriter. ~tasche f travel(l)ing (or overnight) bag, holdall. ~unterlagen pl travel documents. ~veranstalter m tour operator. ~verkehr m holiday traffic. ~wecker m travel(l)ing (alarm) clock. ~zeit f holiday season. ~ziel n destination.

'**Reißaus**: ~ nehmen take to one's heels.

'**Reißbrett** n drawing-board.

reißen [ˈraɪsən] (riß, gerissen) **I** v/t (h) **1.** tear (in Stücke to pieces), a. snatch (off), pull (off, out, etc): **mit sich ~** drag, flood: sweep; **an sich ~** snatch; **die Macht an sich ~** seize power; **sich ~** tear o.s. (an dat on); F fig. **sich ~ um** fight over; F **ich reiße mich nicht darum** I can do without; → **Witz** 1. **2.** sports: a) knock down (the bar), b) snatch (the weight). **3.** zo. kill. **II** v/i **4.** (sn) tear, burst, split, ⚕ rupture, rope etc: break, snap; → **Geduld** 5. (h) ~ **an** (dat) tear at. **6.** (h) sports: knock down the bar. **'Reißen** n (-s) F ✚ rheumatism. **'reißend** adj **1.** rapid, torrential (river etc): → **Absatz** 3. **2.** rapacious (animal): ➤ searing (pain).

'Reißer m (-s; -) F **1.** thriller. **2.** hit. **'reißerisch** adj sensational, loud: ➤e **Werbung** a. F ballyhoo.

'Reiß|feder f drawing-pen. **➤leine** f rip cord. **➤nagel** m drawing-pin, Am. thumbtack. **➤verschluß** m zip(per): **den ➤ e-r Jacke zumachen** (aufmachen) zip up (unzip) a jacket. **➤zahn** m zo. fang, canine tooth. **➤zwecke** f drawing-pin, Am. thumbtack.

reiten ['raɪtən] v/i (ritt, geritten, sn) ride (a. v/t), go on horseback. **'Reiten** n (-s) riding. **'Reiter** m (-s; -) **1.** rider, horseman. **2.** tab. **Reite'rei** f (-; -en) cavalry.

'Reiterin f (-; -nen) rider, horsewoman.

'Reit|gerte f riding crop. **➤hose** f (riding) breeches. **➤peitsche** f riding crop. **➤pferd** n saddle horse. **➤schule** f riding school. **➤sport** m riding. **➤stiefel** pl riding boots. **➤tur,nier** n horse show. **➤weg** m bridle path.

Reiz [raɪts] m (-es; -e) **1.** physiol., psych. or fig. stimulus, **2.** fig. a) charm, b) appeal, attraction, c) lure, d) thrill: **der ➤ des Neuen** the novelty; **s-n ➤ (für j-n) verlieren** pall (on s.o.); **s-e ➤e spielen lassen** display one's charms; **das hat k-n ➤ für mich** that does not appeal to me.

'reizbar adj irritable, touchy.

'Reizbarkeit f (-; no pl) irritability.

reizen ['raɪtsən] (h) **I** v/t **1.** irritate (a. ✚), a. annoy, provoke. **2.** a) stimulate, b) (a)rouse (curiosity etc). **3.** a) tempt, b) appeal to: **es reizte ihn zu inf** he was tempted to inf; **es würde mich ➤ zu inf** I wouldn't mind ger; **das reizt mich gar nicht** that doesn't appeal to me at all. **4.** cards: bid. **'reizend** adj charming, delightful, a. lovely, sweet.

'Reizhusten m ✚ dry cough.

'reizlos adj **1.** a) unattractive, a. plain, b) boring. **2.** ✚ bland (food).

'Reizschwelle f stimulus threshold.

'Reizüberflutung f stimulus satiation.

'Reizung f (-; -en) a. ✚ irritation, stimulation.

'reizvoll adj charming, attractive, fascinating, challenging (task etc).

'Reizwäsche f sexy underwear.

'Reizwort n emotive word.

rekapitulieren [rekapitu'liːrən] v/t (h) recapitulate.

rekeln ['rɛːkəln] **sich ➤** (h) loll (about).

Reklamation [reklamaˈtsioːn] f (-; -en) complaint.

Reklame [reˈklaːmə] f (-; -n) a) advertising, b) advertisement, F ad: **für et. ➤ machen** advertise (F plug) s.th. **➤rummel** m F contp. ballyhoo. **➤tafel** f hoarding, esp. Am. billboard.

reklamieren [reklaˈmiːrən] (h) **I** v/i complain (**wegen** about), esp. sports: protest (**gegen** against). **II** v/t complain about.

rekonstruieren [rekonstruˈiːrən] v/t (h) reconstruct.

Rekonvaleszent [rekɔnvalɛsˈtsɛnt] m (-en; -en) convalescent.

Rekonvaleszenz [rekɔnvalɛsˈtsɛnts] f (-; no pl) convalescence.

Rekord [reˈkɔrt] m (-[e]s; -e) (**e-n ➤ aufstellen** set up a) record. **➤besuch** m record attendance. **➤ernte** f bumper crop. **➤halter(in** f) m, **➤inhaber(in** f) m record holder. **➤versuch** m attempt on the record. **➤zeit** f record time.

Rekrut [reˈkruːt] m (-en; -en), **rekrutieren** [rekruˈtiːrən] v/t (h) recruit.

rektal [rɛkˈtaːl] adj ✝ rectal.

Rektion [rɛkˈtsioːn] f (-; -en) ling. government: **die ➤ e-s Verbs** the case governed by a verb.

Rektor ['rɛktɔr] m (-s; -en [-ˈtoːrən]) **1.** ped. headmaster, principal. **2.** univ. rector. **Rektorat** [rɛktoˈraːt] n (-[e]s; -e) **1.** rectorship, rectorate. **2.** headmaster's (or principal's, univ. rector's) office.

Rektorin [rɛkˈtoːrɪn] f (-; -nen) ped. headmistress, principal.

Relais [rəˈlɛː] n (-; - [rəˈlɛːs]) ⚡ relay.

Relation [relaˈtsioːn] f (-; -en) relation(ship): **in k-r ➤ stehen zu** be out of all proportion to.

relativ [relaˈtiːf] adj relative(ly adv), adv a. comparatively. **Relativität** [relativiˈtɛːt] f (-; no pl) relativity. **Relativi'tätstheo,rie** f theory of relativity.

Rela'tivsatz m ling. relative clause.

relevant [releˈvant] adj relevant (**für** to).

Relief [reˈliɛf] n (-s; -s, -e) relief.

Religion [reliˈgioːn] f (-; -en) **1.** religion. **2.** no pl ped. religious instruction.

Religi'ons... → **Glaubens... ➤freiheit** f

freedom of worship. **~gemeinschaft** f
a) confession, b) religious community.
religi'onslos adj irreligious.
Religi'ons|unterricht m → **Religion** 2.
~zugehörigkeit f religious affiliation.
religiös [reli'giøːs] adj religious.
Relikt [re'lɪkt] n (-[e]s; -e) **1.** relic. **2.** biol.
relict.
Reling ['reːlɪŋ] f (-; -s) ♣ rail.
Reliquie [re'liːkviə] f (-; -n) relic.
Re'liquienschrein m reliquary.
Remis [rə'miː] n (-; - [rə'miːs]) draw.
Remittenden [remɪ'tɛndən] pl returns.
Remoulade [remu'laːdə] f (-; -n) gastr.
tartar sauce.
rempeln ['rɛmpəln] v/t (h) F jostle, push.
Ren [rɛn, reːn] n (-s; -s) zo. reindeer.
Renaissance [rənɛ'sãːs] f (-; -n) a) no pl
hist. Renaissance, b) fig. renaissance.
Rendezvous [rãde'vuː] n (-; - [-'vuːs])
rendezvous (a. space travel), date.
Rendite [rɛn'diːtə] f (-; -n) ♦ (net) yield.
'Rennbahn f a) racecourse, racetrack (a.
mot.), b) (cycling) track.
'Rennboot n speedboat.
rennen ['rɛnən] (rannte, gerannt) **I** v/i
(sn) a) run, rush, dash, b) race: **~ gegen**
run into; **schneller ~ als** outrun; **sie
rannten um die Wette** they raced each
other; → **Verderben. II** v/t (h) F **j-m
ein Messer** etc **in die Brust ~** run a
knife etc into s.o.'s chest; **j-n über den
Haufen ~** knock s.o. down. **'Rennen** n
(-s; -) a) running (etc), b) race, c) heat:
totes ~ dead heat; **das ~ machen** come
in first, win, fig. come out on top.
'Renner m (-s; -) F fig. (great) hit.
'Renn|fahrer m a) racing driver, b) rac-
ing cyclist. **~läufer** m ski racer. **~pferd**
n racehorse. **~rad** n racing cycle. **~schi**
m racing ski. **~schuhe** pl spikes. **~sport**
m racing. **~stall** m **1.** (racing) stable. **2.**
F mot. racing team. **~strecke** f mot.
racing course. **~wagen** m racing car.
renommiert [reno'miːrt] adj (**wegen** for)
famous, noted.
renovieren [reno'viːrən] v/t (h) a) renovate (building), b) redecorate (room).
Reno'vierung f (-; -en) a) renovation, b)
redecoration.
rentabel [rɛn'taːbəl] adj profitable.
Rentabilität [rɛntabili'tɛːt] f (-; no pl)
profitability.
Rente ['rɛntə] f (-; -en) **1.** pension: F **auf**

(or **in**) **~ gehen** retire; **auf** (or **in**) **~ sein**
be retired; → **dynamisch. 2.** annuity.
'Renten|alter n retirement age. **~anpas-
sung** f index-linked adjustment of pensions. **~empfänger(in** f) m → **Rent-
ner(in). ~markt** m ♦ bond market.
~pa,piere pl fixed interest bonds.
~versicherung f pension scheme.
rentieren [rɛn'tiːrən] **sich ~** (h) be profitable, a. pay, be worthwhile.
Rentner ['rɛntnər] m (-s; -), **'Rentnerin** f
(-; -nen) pensioner.
reorgani'sieren v/t (h) reorganize.
reparabel [repa'raːbəl] adj repairable.
Reparation [repara'tsjoːn] f (-; -en)
reparation.
Reparatur [repara'tuːr] f (-; -en) re-
pair(s): **in ~** being repaired; **zur ~ geben** have s.th. repaired. **♦bedürftig** adj
in need of repair. **~kosten** pl cost of
repairs. **~werkstatt** f mot. garage.
reparieren [repa'riːrən] v/t (h) repair, F
fix: **nicht mehr zu ~** beyond repair.
repatriieren [repatri'iːrən] v/t (h) repatriate.
Repertoire [repɛr'tŏaːr] n (-s; -s) a. fig.
repertoire.
Reportage [repɔr'taːʒə] f (-; -n) report,
commentary: **s-e ~ über** (acc) a. his
coverage of. **Reporter** [re'pɔrtər] m (-s;
-), **Re'porterin** f (-; -nen) reporter.
Repräsentant [reprɛzɛn'tant] m (-en;
-en) representative.
Repräsen'tantenhaus n parl. Am.
House of Representatives.
Repräsentation [reprɛzɛnta'tsjoːn] f (-;
no pl) representation: **der ~ dienen** be a
status symbol. **repräsentativ** [reprɛ-
zɛnta'tiːf] adj **1.** representative (**für** of).
2. impressive. **repräsentieren** [reprɛ-
zɛn'tiːrən] v/t (h) represent.
Repressalie [reprɛ'saːliə] f (-; -n)
reprisal.
repressiv [reprɛ'siːf] adj repressive.
reprivati'sieren v/t (h) ♦ denationalize.
Reproduktion [reprodʊk'tsjoːn] f (-;
-en) reproduction, a. print. **reproduzieren** [-du'tsiːrən] v/t (h) reproduce.
Reptil [rɛp'tiːl] n (-[e]s; -ien) reptile.
Republik [repu'bliːk] f (-; -en) republic.
Republikaner [republi'kaːnər] m (-s; -),
republi'kanisch [-nɪʃ] adj republican,
pol. Am. Republican.
Requiem ['reːkviɛm] n (-s; -s) requiem.

requirieren [rekvi'ri:rən] v/t (h) ✕ requisition.

Requisiten [rekvi'zi:tən] pl thea. etc properties, F props.

Reservat [rezɛr'va:t] n (-[e]s; -e) **1.** (nature) reserve. **2.** reservation.

Reserve [re'zɛrvə] f (-; -n) **1.** reserve (a. ✕ or fig.): ✝ **stille** ~n hidden reserves; F **j-n aus der ~ (heraus)locken** bring s.o. out of his shell. **2.** sports: reserve team. **~bank** f (-; ~e) sports: (substitutes') bench. **~ka͵nister** m spare can. **~rad** n mot. spare wheel. **~spieler(in** f) m sports: substitute.

reservieren [rezɛr'vi:rən] v/t (h) (a. ~ lassen) reserve, a. book. **reser'viert** adj a. fig. reserved: **sich ~ verhalten** keep one's distance.

Reservist [rezɛr'vɪst] m (-en; -en) ✕ reservist.

Reservoir [rezɛr'voa:r] n (-s; -e) a. fig. reservoir.

Residenz [rezi'dɛnts] f (-; -en) residence.

residieren [rezi'di:rən] v/i (h) reside.

Resignation [rezɪgna'tsi̯o:n] f (-; no pl) resignation.

resignieren [rezɪ'gni:rən] v/i (h) resign, give up. **resi'gniert** adj resigned.

resistent [rezɪs'tɛnt] adj biol., ⚕ resistent (**gegen** to).

resolut [rezo'lu:t] adj resolute, determined, forceful.

Resolution [rezolu'tsi̯o:n] f (-; -en) resolution.

Resonanz [rezo'nants] f (-; -en) a. fig. resonance.

resorbieren [rezɔr'bi:rən] v/t (h) resorb.

Resorption [rezɔrp'tsi̯o:n] f (-; -en) resorption.

resoziali͵sieren v/t (h) rehabilitate.

Resoziali͵sierung f (-; -en) rehabilitation.

Respekt [re'spɛkt] m (-[e]s; no pl) respect (**vor** for): **sich ~ verschaffen** make o.s. respected; **bei allem ~** with all due respect. **respektabel** [respɛk'ta:bəl] adj respectable. **respektieren** [respɛk'ti:rən] v/t (h) respect. **re'spektlos** adj irreverent. **re'spektvoll** adj respectful.

Ressentiment [rɛsãti'mã:] n (-s; -s) resentment.

Ressort [rɛ'so:r] n (-s; -s) (**das fällt nicht in mein ~** that is not my) department.

Rest [rɛst] m (-[e]s; -e) rest, a. ⚕ remain-

der, a. textil. remnant, ⚶, ᨓᨓ, ◎ residue, gastr. leftovers, ✝ balance, fig. vestige, pl remains: **der letzte ~** the last bit(s); **sterbliche ~e** mortal remains; F **das gab ihm den ~** that finished him (off). **~alkohol** m residual alcohol.

Restaurant [rɛsto'rã:] n (-s; -s) restaurant.

Restaurator [rɛstaʊ'ra:tɔr] m (-s; -en [-ra'to:rən] restorer. **restaurieren** [-'ri:rən] v/t (h) restore.

'**Restbestand** m ✝ remaining stock.

'**Restbetrag** m ✝ balance.

'**restlich** adj remaining, a. ⚶, ᨓᨓ, A residual: **die ~e Zeit** a. the rest of his etc time. '**restlos I** adj complete, total. **II** adv completely, perfectly.

'**Restrisiko** n residual risk.

Resultat [rezʊl'ta:t] n (-[e]s; -e) result, sports: score, results. **resultieren** [rezʊl'ti:rən] v/i (h) result (**aus** from).

Resümee [rezy'me:] n (-s; -s) summary.

Retorte [re'tɔrtə] f (-; -n) retort.

Re'tortenbaby n test-tube baby.

Retourkutsche [re'tu:r-] f e-e ~ tit for tat.

Retrospektive [retrospɛk'ti:və] f (-; -n) retrospective.

retten ['rɛtən] (h) **I** v/t (**aus, vor** dat from) save, rescue, a. deliver, a. recover, salvage (a. fig.): **j-m das Leben ~** save s.o.'s life; **sich ~** escape; **sich nicht mehr ~ können vor** (dat) be swamped with; F **der Abend war gerettet** the evening was saved. **II** v/i sports: save.

'**Retter** m (-s; -), '**Retterin** f (-; -nen) rescuer.

Rettich ['rɛtɪç] m (-s; -e) ⚘ radish.

'**Rettung** f (-; -en) a) rescue, b) escape, c) recovery, esp. ⚓ salvage, d) eccl. salvation: **das war s-e ~** that saved him; **es gab k-e ~ für ihn** he was past help; **du bist m-e einzige (or letzte) ~** you are my last hope.

'**Rettungs|akti͵on** f a. fig. rescue operation. **~anker** m sheet anchor. **~boje** f life-buoy. **~boot** n lifeboat. **~dienst** m rescue service. **~gerät** n life-saving equipment. **~hubschrauber** m rescue helicopter.

'**rettungslos** adj hopeless: **~ verloren sein** be beyond all hope.

'**Rettungs|mannschaft** f rescue party. **~ring** m lifebelt. **~schwimmer** m lifeguard. **~wagen** m ambulance.

retuschieren [retu'ʃiːrən] v/t (h) touch up.

Reue ['rɔʏə] f (-; no pl) (**über** acc for) remorse, esp. eccl. repentance. **'reuen** (h) I v/t **s-e Tat (das Geld)** reute ihn he regretted what he had done (the money). II v/impers es reut mich, daß I regret that. **'reuevoll, 'reuig, 'reumü-tig** [-myːtɪç] adj repentant, remorseful.

Revanche [re'vãː(ʃ)ə] f (-; no pl) revenge. **Re'vanchespiel** n sports: return match. **revanchieren** [revã'ʃiːrən] sich ~ (h) **1.** take one's revenge (**an** dat on), F get one's own back. **2.** return the favo(u)r. **Revanchismus** [revã'ʃɪsmʊs] m (-; no pl) pol. revanchism.

Revers [re'vɛːr] m, n (-; -['vɛːrs]) lapel.

revidieren [revi'diːrən] v/t (h) **1.** revise. **2.** check, audit.

Revier [re'viːr] n (-s; -e) a) district, b) police station, c) (policeman's) beat, (postman's) round, d) a. fig. territory.

Revision [revi'zjoːn] f (-; -en) **1.** check(ing), ✝ audit(ing), (custom's) examination. **2.** revision. **3.** ⚖ (~ einlegen lodge an) appeal (**bei** with). **4.** print. final proofreading.

Revolte [re'vɔltə] f (-; -n) revolt. **revoltieren** [revɔl'tiːrən] v/i (h) revolt. **Revolution** [revolu'tsjoːn] f (-; -en) revolution. **revolutionär** [revolutsjo'nɛːr] adj, **Revolutio'när** m (-s; -e) revolutionary. **revolutionieren** [revolutsjo-'niːrən] v/t (h) revolutionize. **Revolver** [re'vɔlvər] m (-s; -) revolver. **Re'volverblatt** n contp. sensational rag. **Re'volverheld** m contp. gunslinger.

Revue [rə'vyː] f (-; -n) **1.** thea. revue. **2.** (publication) review.

Rezensent [retsɛn'zɛnt] m (-en; -en), **Rezen'sentin** f (-; -nen) critic, reviewer. **rezensieren** [retsɛn'ziːrən] v/t (h), **Rezension** [-'zjoːn] f (-; -en) review.

Rezept [re'tsɛpt] n (-[e]s; -e) a) 💊 prescription, b) gastr. or fig. recipe.

Rezeption [retsɛp'tsjoːn] f (-; -en) hotel: reception, Am. check-in desk.

re'zeptpflichtig adj available only on prescription, prescription(-only) ...

Rezession [retsɛ'sjoːn] f (-; -en) ✝ recession.

Rezitativ [retsita'tiːf] n (-s; -e) recitative. **rezitieren** [retsi'tiːrən] v/t, v/i (h) recite.

'R-Gespräch n teleph. reversed-charge call, Am. collect call.

Rhabarber [ra'barbər] m (-s; no pl) 🌰 rhubarb.

Rhapsodie [rapso'diː] f (-; -n) rhapsody.

Rheinwein ['raɪn-] m Rhine wine, hock.

Rhesus|affe ['reːzʊs-] m rhesus (monkey). **~faktor** m (-s; no pl) rhesus factor.

Rhetorik [re'toːrɪk] f (-; no pl) rhetoric. **rhetorisch** [re'toːrɪʃ] adj rhetorical.

Rheuma ['rɔʏma] n (-s; no pl) F ✦ rheumatism. **rheumatisch** [rɔʏ'maːtɪʃ] adj ✦ rheumatic. **Rheumatismus** [rɔʏma-'tɪsmʊs] m (-; -men) ✦ rheumatism.

Rhinozeros [ri'noːtserɔs] n (-[ses]; -[se]) zo. rhinoceros.

Rhombus ['rɔmbʊs] m (-; -ben) 🔶 rhomb(us).

rhythmisch ['rʏtmɪʃ] adj rhythmical.

Rhythmus ['rʏtmʊs] m (-; -men) rhythm.

'Richt|an,tenne f directional aerial (Am. antenna).

richten¹ ['rɪçtən] (h) I v/t **1.** direct (**auf** acc to, **gegen** against): ~ **auf** (acc) a. point (or level, aim) weapon, camera at, a. turn one's eyes on, a. concentrate attention, efforts, etc on; ~ **an** (acc) address letter etc to, put question to. **2.** a) fix, get s.th. ready, prepare, b) bring s.th. in order, tidy s.th. (up), a. do (one's hair, room, etc), c) repair, mend, fix, d) align, adjust, trim (sails), straighten (out fig.): sich die Zähne ~ lassen have one's teeth done. II sich ~ an (acc) address o.s. to; sich ~ auf (acc) attention etc: focus on; sich ~ gegen be directed against, remark etc: be aimed at; sich ~ nach a) orient(ate) o.s. by, comply with s.o.'s wishes, a. keep to rules, go by s.o.'s judgment, follow the fashion, follow s.o.'s example, b) matter: be model(l)ed on, depend on, be determined by, a. ling. agree with; ich richte mich nach dir I leave it to you.

richten² v/t, v/i (h) judge.

'Richter m (-s; -) judge. **'Richteramt** n judicial office. **'Richterin** f (-; -nen) judge. **'richterlich** adj judicial.

'Richtfest n topping-out ceremony.

'Richtfunk m directional radio.

'Richtgeschwindigkeit f mot. recommended speed.

richtig ['rɪçtɪç] I adj **1.** right, correct, true, accurate: (**sehr**) ~! (quite) right!, exactly!; F er ist nicht ganz ~ im Kopf he is not quite right in the head. **2.** a) right, suitable, appropriate, proper, b) fair, just: **es war ~, daß du ihnen geholfen hast** you did right to help them; **so ist's ~!** that's it! **3.** real, true: **ein ~er Engländer** a true Englishman; **s-e ~e Mutter** his real mother; **ein ~er Feigling** a regular coward. **II** *adv* **4.** a) right(ly), correctly (*etc*), b) F thoroughly, properly: **et. ~ machen** do s.th. right; **~ böse** really (F real) angry; **geht d-e Uhr ~?** is your watch right?

'**Richtige**¹ ['rıçtıgə] *m, f* (-n; -n) *the right man* (*woman*), F Mr. (Mrs.) Right: *iro.* **Ihr seid mir die ~n!** a fine lot you are!; F **sechs ~ haben** *Lotto:* have six right.

'**Richtige**² (-n; -n) *the right thing:* **er hat nichts ~s gelernt** he hasn't really learnt anything; **das ist für sie genau das ~** that's just right for her.

'**richtiggehend** *adj* real, regular.

'**Richtigkeit** *f* (-; *no pl*) correctness, rightness: **das hat schon s-e ~** it's all right.

'**richtigstellen** *v/t* (*sep*, -ge-, h) *put s.th.* right, correct.

'**Richtlinien** *pl* guidelines.

'**Richtpreis** *m* ✝ recommended price.

'**Richtschnur** *f fig.* guiding principle.

'**Richtung** *f* (-; -en) **1.** direction, course (*a.* ✈, ⚓), *fig. a.* line, trend: **in ~ auf** (*acc*) in the direction of; **aus allen ~en** from all directions; *fig.* **in dieser ~** s.th. along these lines. **2.** a) line (of thought), views, b) movement, school.

'**richtungweisend** *adj* trendsetting.

'**Richtwert** *m,* '**Richtzahl** *f* index.

Ricke ['rıkə] *f* (-; -n) *zo.* doe.

rieb [ri:p] *pret of* **reiben**.

Riege ['ri:gə] *f* (-; -n) *gym.* squad.

Riegel ['ri:gəl] *m* (-s; -) **1.** a) bolt, bar, b) latch: **e-r Sache e-n ~ vorschieben** put

a stop to s.th. **2.** bar (*of soap*), row, *Am.* strip (*of chocolate*).

Riemen¹ ['ri:mən] *m* (-s; -) strap, sling (*of rifle*), ⚙ belt: **sich am ~ reißen** pull o.s. together.

'**Riemen**² *m* (-s; -) oar.

Riese ['ri:zə] *m* (-n; -n) **1.** giant. **2.** F thousand-mark *etc* note, *sl.* grand.

rieseln ['ri:zəln] *v/i* (sn) *water, sand, etc:* trickle, run, *rain:* drizzle, *snow:* fall softly: **es rieselte mir kalt über den Rücken** a shiver ran down my spine.

'**Riesen...** giant, gigantic, enormous. **~erfolg** *m* huge success, *a. film etc:* smash hit. **~felge** *f gym.* giant swing.

'**riesengroß,** '**riesenhaft → riesig** I.

'**Riesen|rad** *n* Ferris wheel. **~schlange** *f* boa constrictor. **~schritt** *m* giant stride. **~slalom** *m skiing:* giant slalom.

riesig ['ri:zıç] **I** *adj* **1.** *a. fig.* gigantic, colossal, enormous, huge. **2.** F a) tremendous, b) terrific, super. **II** *adv* **3.** tremendously, terribly, enormously.

Riesin ['ri:zın] *f* (-; -nen) giantess.

riet [ri:t] *pret of* **raten**.

Riff [rıf] *n* (-[e]s; -e) reef.

rigoros [rigo'ro:s] *adj* rigorous.

Rigorosum [rigo'ro:zum] *n* (-s; -sa) *univ.* viva (voce).

Rille ['rılə] *f* (-; -n) groove.

Rind [rınt] *n* (-[e]s; -er) **1.** a) cow, b) bull, c) ox: **~er** cattle. **2.** *gastr.* beef.

Rinde ['rındə] *f* (-; -n) **1.** bark. **2.** (*bread*) crust, (*cheese*) rind.

Rinder|braten ['rındər-] *m* roast beef. **~fi_let** *n* fillet of beef. **~lende** *f* beef tenderloin. **~zucht** *f* cattle farming. **~zunge** *f gastr.* ox tongue.

'**Rindfleisch** *n* beef.

'**Rind(s)leder** *n* cowhide.

'**Rindvieh** *n* **1.** cattle. **2.** F *contp.* idiot.

Ring [rıŋ] *m* (-[e]s; -e) ring, circle (*a. fig.*).

'**Ringbuch** *n* ring (*or* loose-leaf) binder. **~einlage** *f* loose-leaf pages.

ringeln ['rıŋəln] **I** *v/t* (h) a) curl, b) coil (**um** around). **II** *sich* ~ a) curl, coil, b) wind, meander.

'**Ringelnatter** *f zo.* grass snake.

ringen ['rıŋən] (rang, gerungen, h) **I** *v/i* wrestle (**mit** with), *fig. a.* struggle (**um, nach** for): **nach Atem ~** gasp for breath; **nach Fassung ~** try to regain one's composure; **nach Worten ~** struggle for words. **II** *v/t* wring.

Riecher *m* (-s; -) F nose: *fig.* **e-n guten ~ haben für** have a good nose for.

Ried [ri:t] *n* (-[e]s; -e) **1.** reed. **2.** marsh.

rief [ri:f] *pret of* **rufen**.

'**Ringen** n (-s) wrestling, *fig.* struggle.
'**Ringer** m (-s; -) *sports:* wrestler.
'**Ringfinger** m ring finger.
'**ringförmig** adj ring-shaped, annular.
'**Ringkampf** m wrestling (match).
'**Ringrichter** m *boxing:* referee.
rings [rɪŋs], '**ringsher'um**, '**rings'um**
  adv all around.
Rinne ['rɪnə] f (-; -n) a) groove (*a. anat.*,
  ⚛), b) gutter, c) conduit, channel.
rinnen ['rɪnən] (rann, geronnen, sn) v/i **1.**
  a) run, flow, b) drip, trickle: *das Geld*
  rinnt ihr durch die Finger money just
  slips through her fingers. **2.** leak.
'**Rinnstein** m gutter.
'**Rippchen** ['rɪpçən] n (-s; -) rib (of pork).
'**Rippe** ['rɪpə] f (-; -n) **1.** *anat.* rib. **2.** ⚙ rib,
  fin. **3.** row, *Am.* strip (*of chocolate*).
'**rippen** ['rɪpən] v/t (h) rib.
'**Rippenfell** n *anat.* pleura.
'**Rippenfellentzündung** f 🕮 pleurisy.
'**Rippenstoß** m dig in the ribs.
Rips [rɪps] m (-es; -e) *textil.* rep.
Risiko ['ri:ziko] n (-s; -s, -ken) risk: *auf*
  eigenes ~ at one's own risk; *mit vol-*
  lem ~ at all risks; *ein* ~ *eingehen* take a
  risk. '**risikofrei** adj safe. '**risikofreudig**
  adj risk-taking, prepared to take a risk
  (*or* risks). '**Risikogruppe** f high-risk
  group. '**risikoreich** adj risky.
riskant [rɪs'kant] adj risky.
riskieren [rɪs'ki:rən] v/t (h) risk.
Rispe ['rɪspə] f (-; -n) 🌿 panicle.
riß [rɪs] *pret of* **reißen.**
Riß m (Risses; Risse) **1.** a) tear, rent, *in*
  dry skin: chap, b) cleft, crevice, *fig.* rift,
  split; *e-n* ~ *bekommen friendship etc:*
  begin to break up. **2.** △, ⊙ draft.
rissig ['rɪsɪç] adj cracked, fissured, chap-
  py, chapped (*skin etc*): ~ *werden* crack,
  skin: chap; ~*e Hände* chapped hands.
'**Rißwunde** f laceration.
Rist [rɪst] m (-es; -e) **1.** instep. **2.** back of
  the hand.
ritt [rɪt] *pret of* **reiten.**
Ritt m (-[e]s; -e) ride.
Ritter ['rɪtər] m (-s; -) (*a. zum* ~ *schla-*
  gen) knight. '**Rittergut** n manor.
'**ritterlich** adj knightly, *fig.* chivalrous.
'**Ritterorden** m order (of knights).
'**Rittersporn** m (-[e]s; -e) 🌿 larkspur.
'**rittlings** ['rɪtlɪŋs] adv astride: ~ *auf e-m*
  Stuhl sitzen sit astride a chair.
Ritual [ri'tuaːl] n (-s; -e, -lien) ritual.

rituell [ri'tʊɛl] adj ritual.
Ritus ['ri:tʊs] m (-; Riten) rite.
Ritz [rɪts] m (-es; -e) scratch.
Ritze ['rɪtsə] f (-; -n) crack, gap, chink.
Ritzel ['rɪtsəl] n (-s; -) ⊙ pinion.
ritzen ['rɪtsən] v/t (h) **1.** scratch. **2.** carve.
Rivale [ri'va:lə] m (-n; -n), **Ri'valin** f (-;
  -nen) rival.
rivalisieren [rivali'zi:rən] v/i (h) rival.
Rivalität [rivali'tɛːt] f (-; -en) rivalry.
Rizinusöl ['ri:tsinʊs-] n castor oil.
Robbe ['rɔbə] f (-; -n) *zo.* seal.
Robe ['ro:bə] f (-; -n) gown, robe.
Roboter ['rɔbɔtər] m (-s; -) robot.
'**Robotertechnik** f robotics.
robust [ro'bʊst] adj *a. fig.* robust.
roch [rɔx] *pret of* **riechen.**
röcheln ['rœçəln] v/i (h) breathe sterto-
  rously, rattle.
Rochen ['rɔxən] m (-s; -) *zo.* ray.
Rock¹ [rɔk] m (-[e]s; ⸚e) **1.** skirt. **2.** jacket,
  coat.
Rock² m (-[s]; *no pl*) rock (music).
Rocker ['rɔkər] m (-s; -) F rocker.
'**Rockmu,sik** f rock (music).
'**Rodelbahn** f toboggan run.
rodeln ['ro:dəln] v/i (h *or* sn) toboggan.
roden ['ro:dən] v/t (h) **1.** root out. **2.**
  clear, stub (*land, woods*).
Rodler ['ro:dlər] m (-s; -) tobogganist.
'**Rodung** f (-; -en) clearing.
Rogen ['ro:gən] m (-s; -) roe.
Roggen ['rɔgən] m (-s; -) rye.
'**Roggenbrot** n rye-bread.
roh [ro:] adj **1.** raw, *a.* crude, *a.* rough
  (*diamond, draft, etc*). **2.** 🌿 gross. **3.** *fig.*
  crude, rough, *a.* brutal: *mit* ~*er Gewalt*
  with brute force.
'**Rohbau** m shell. '**Rohbi,lanz** f 🌿 trial
  balance. '**Rohdia,mant** m rough diamond. '**Roheisen** n pig iron.
'**Roheit** f (-; -en) **1.** *no pl* roughness, *a.*
  brutality. **2.** brutal act.
'**Roherz** n crude ore. '**Rohfaser** f crude
  fibre (*Am.* fiber). '**Rohfassung** f rough
  draft. '**Rohgewinn** m 🌿 gross profit.
'**Rohkost** f raw vegetables and fruit.
'**Rohköstler** [-kœstlər] m (-s; -) vegetarian. '**Rohleder** n rawhide.
Rohling ['ro:lɪŋ] m (-s; -e) **1.** brute. **2.** ⊙
  blank.
'**Rohmateri,al** n raw material. '**Rohöl** n
  crude oil. '**Rohpro,dukt** n raw product.
Rohr [ro:r] n (-[e]s; -e) **1.** 🌿 a) reed, b)

cane. **2.** ☯ a) tube, pipe, b) duct. **3.** (gun) barrel: F *fig.* **volles ~** flat out.
'**Rohrbruch** *m* burst pipe.
Röhrchen ['rø:rçən] *n* (small) tube: **j-n ins ~ blasen lassen** breathalyze s.o.
Röhre ['rø:rə] *f* (-; -n) **1.** a) tube, b) pipe. **2.** ⚡, *radio*, *TV* valve, *Am.* tube: F **in die ~ gucken** a) *TV* sit in front of the box, b) *fig.* be left out in the cold. **3.** oven. **4.** *hunt.* gallery.
röhren ['rø:rən] *v/i* (h) *stag*: bell.
'**Röhrenknochen** *m* long bone.
'**Rohr|kolben** *m* ⚘ reed mace. **~leitung** *f* a) conduit, b) plumbing, c) pipeline. **~netz** *n* (water *etc*) mains. **~post** *f* pneumatic post. **~spatz** *m* F *schimpfen wie ein ~* rant and rave. **~stock** *m* cane. **~zange** *f* ☯ pipe wrench. **~zucker** *m* cane sugar.
'**Rohseide** *f* raw silk. '**Rohstahl** *m* crude steel. '**Rohstoff** *m* raw material. '**Rohzucker** *m* unrefined sugar.
'**Rohzustand** *m* (*im ~* in the) crude state.
'**Rolladen** *m* shutters.
'**Rollbahn** *f* ✈ runway.
Rolle¹ ['rɔlə] *f* (-; -n) a) roll (*a.* ✈, *gym.*), ☯ a. roller, *a.* pulley, b) castor, c) reel, coil: **e-e ~ Garn** a reel of cotton.
'**Rolle²** *f* (-; -n) *thea.* part, role (*a. psych.*): **e-e ~ spielen** play a part (*a. fig. bei,* in *dat* in), *fig. a.* figure (in); **das spielt k-e ~** that doesn't make any difference; **Geld spielt k-e ~** money is no object; **aus der ~ fallen** forget o.s.; *fig.* **die ~n (ver)tauschen** reverse roles.
rollen ['rɔlən] *v/i* (sn), *v/t* (h) roll, wheel, ✈ taxi: **~des Material** 🚃 rolling stock; *fig.* **ins Rollen kommen** get under way.
'**Rollen|besetzung** *f thea.* casting. **~lager** *n* ☯ roller bearing. **~spiel** *n psych.* role-playing. **~tausch** *m fig.* reversal of roles. **~verteilung** *f* **1.** *thea.* casting. **2.** *fig.* respective roles.
'**Roller** *m* (-s; -) **1.** *mot. etc* scooter. **2.** *soccer:* daisy cutter.
'**Roll|feld** *n* ✈ taxiway, runway. **~film** *m* roll film. **~kom|mando** *n* ⚡ heavies. **~kragen(pull,over)** *m* polo neck.
'**Rollschuh** *m* roller skate: **~ laufen** roller-skate. **~bahn** *f* roller-skating rink. **~läufer** *m* roller skater.
'**Roll|stuhl** *m* wheelchair. **~treppe** *f* escalator. **~verdeck** *n* roller roof.
Roman [ro'ma:n] *m* (-[e]s; -e) novel.

~held(in *f*) *m* hero(ine) (of the novel).
Romanik [ro'ma:nɪk] *f* (-; *no pl*) Romanesque (style or period). **ro'manisch** *adj* **1.** *ling.* Romance. **2.** Romanesque.
Romanist [roma'nɪst] *m* (-en; -en) student of (*or* lecturer in) Romance languages and literature.
Ro'manlitera,tur *f* fiction.
Ro'manschriftsteller(in *f*) *m* novelist.
Romantik [ro'mantɪk] *f* (-; *no pl*) romanticism, *art*: Romanticism. **Ro'mantiker** *m* (-s; -) Romantic, *fig.* romantic. **ro'mantisch** *adj* romantic, *art etc*: Romantic. **romantisieren** [-ti'zi:rən] *v/t* (h) romanticize.
Romanze [ro'mantsə] *f* (-; -n) romance.
Römer ['rø:mər] *m* (-s; -) **1.** Roman. **2.** rummer. **römisch** ['rø:mɪʃ] *adj* Roman: **~katholisch** Roman Catholic.
Rommé [rɔ'me:] *n* (-s; -s) rummy.
röntgen ['rœntɡən] *v/t* (h) ✗ x-ray.
'**Röntgen|appa,rat** *m* x-ray unit. **~arzt** *m* radiologist. **~aufnahme** *f* x-ray (picture). **~behandlung** *f*, **~bestrahlung** *f* x-ray treatment, radiotherapy.
Röntgenologe [rœntɡeno'lo:ɡə] *m* (-n; -n) radiologist.
'**Röntgen|schirm** *m* (fluorescent) screen. **~strahlen** *pl* x-rays. **~untersuchung** *f* x-ray examination.
rosa ['ro:za] *adj* pink.
'**rosarot** *adj a. fig.* rose-colo(u)red.
Rose ['ro:zə] *f* (-; -n) **1.** ⚘ rose. **2.** ✗ erysipelas.
Rosé [ro'ze:] *m* (-s; -s) rosé (wine).
'**Rosenkohl** *m* Brussels sprouts.
'**Rosenkranz** *m eccl.* (*den ~ beten* say the) rosary.
Rosen'montag *m* Monday before Lent.
'**Rosenstock** *m* rose-tree.
'**Rosenstrauß** *m* bunch of roses.
rosig ['ro:zɪç] *adj a. fig.* rosy.
Rosine [ro'zi:nə] *f* (-; -n) raisin: F (**große**) **~n im Kopf haben** have big ideas.
Rosmarin ['ro:smari:n] *m* (-s; *no pl*) ⚘ rosemary.
Roß [rɔs] *n* (Rosses; Rösser ['rœsər]) horse: *fig.* **sich aufs hohe ~ setzen** give o.s. airs. **~äpfel** *pl* horse droppings.
'**Roßhaar** *n* horsehair.
Rost¹ [rɔst] *m* (-[e]s; *no pl*) *a. fig.* rust.
Rost² *m* (-[e]s; -e) **1.** grate. **2.** grill.
'**Röstbrot** *n* toast.

rosten ['rɔstən] v/i (sn or h) rust: *nicht ~d*
→ *rostfrei*.

rösten ['rœstən] v/t (h) roast (*coffee*),
toast (*bread*), fry (*potatoes*).

'**rostfrei** adj rustproof, stainless.

rostig ['rɔstiç] adj a. fig. rusty.

'**Röstkar**,**toffeln** pl fried potatoes.

'**Roststelle** f patch of rust.

rot [ro:t] adj red, pol. Red: *das Rote
Kreuz* the Red Cross; *~ werden* a) go
red, flush, b) blush; ✝ *in den ~en Zahlen stehen* be in the red; → *rotsehen,
Faden, Tuch*.

Rot n (-s; -) red: *bei ~* at red; *die Ampel
steht auf ~* the lights are at red.

Rotation [rota'tsio:n] f (-; -en) rotation.

Rotati'onsdruck m rotary printing.

'**rotblond** adj sandy-haired, sandy (*hair*).

'**rotbraun** adj reddish brown.

'**Rotbuche** f copper beech.

'**Rotdorn** m (-[e]s; -e) pink hawthorn.

Rote ['ro:tə] m, f (-n; -n) pol. Red.

Röte ['rø:tə] f (-; -) redness, blush.

Rötel ['rø:təl] m (-s; no pl) red chalk.

'**Röteln** pl ✻ German measles.

röten ['rø:tən] v/t (h) redden: *sich ~* a. go
red, flush.

'**rotglühend** adj red-hot.

'**rothaarig** adj red-haired.

'**Rothaarige** m, f (-n; -n) redhead.

rotieren [ro'ti:rən] v/i (h) a) rotate,
b) F fig. flap: *am Rotieren sein* be in a
flap.

Rotkäppchen ['ro:tkɛpçən] n (Little)
Red Riding Hood.

'**Rotkehlchen** n zo. robin (redbreast).

'**Rotkohl** m, '**Rotkraut** n red cabbage.

rötlich ['rø:tliç] adj reddish.

'**rotsehen** v/i irr, sep, -ge-, h, → *sehen*)
F fig. see red.

'**Rotstift** m red pencil: fig. *den ~ ansetzen* make cuts (*bei* in).

Rotte ['rɔtə] f (-; -n) gang, horde.

'**Rötung** f (-; -en) reddening.

'**Rotwein** m red wine.

'**Rotwild** n red deer.

Rotz [rɔts] m (-es; no pl) V snot. '**Rotzfah-
ne** f V snotrag. '**rotzfrech** adj F snotty.

Rouge [ru:ʒ] n (-s; -s [ru:ʒ]) rouge.

Roulade [ru'la:də] f (-; -n) roulade, roll.

Rouleau [ru'lo:] n (-s; -s) roller blind.

Roulett [ru'lɛt] n (-[e]s; -e) roulette.

Route ['ru:tə] f (-; -n) route, itinerary.

Routine [ru'ti:nə] f (-; no pl) routine, a.
practice, experience.

rou'tinemäßig adj routine.

routiniert [ruti'ni:rt] adj experienced.

Rowdy ['raudi] m (-s; -s) hooligan.

'**Rowdytum** n (-s; no pl) hooliganism.

Rübe ['ry:bə] f (-; -n) **1.** *weiße ~* turnip;
rote ~ beetroot; *gelbe ~* carrot. **2.** F
nut.

Rubel ['ru:bəl] m (-s; -) rouble.

rüber(...) ['ry:bər-] F → *herüber*(...),
hinüber(...). '**rüberkommen** v/i (irr,
sep, -ge-, sn, → *kommen*) F **1.** come
over. **2.** thea. etc come across. **3.** *~ mit*
come across with *money* etc.

Rubin [ru'bi:n] m (-s; -e) min. ruby.

Rubrik [ru'bri:k] f (-; -en) **1.** heading. **2.**
column. **3.** category.

'**ruchbar** adj *~ werden* become
known.

Ruck [rʊk] m (-[e]s; -e) jerk, start, jolt (a.
fig.), F pol. swing: *in einem ~* at one go;
sich e-n ~ geben pull o.s. together.

'**Rückansicht** f back view.

'**ruckartig I** adj jerky. **II** adv a) with a
jerk, b) abruptly.

'**rückbezüglich** adj ling. reflexive.

'**Rückblende** f film: flashback (*auf acc*
to).

'**Rückblick** m review (*auf acc* of): *im ~* in
retrospect, *auf* (*acc*) looking back on.

'**rückda,tieren** v/t (h) backdate.

rücken ['rʏkən] **I** v/t (h) move, a. shift, a.
push (away). **II** v/i (sn) a) move, b)
move over: *näher ~* draw near, approach; *an j-s Stelle ~* take s.o.'s place.

'**Rücken** m (-s; -) a) back, b) (*mountain*)
ridge, c) bridge (*of nose*), d) gastr. saddle: *hinter j-s ~* behind s.o.'s back; *j-m
in den ~ fallen* fig. stab s.o. in the back.

'**Rücken|deckung** f fig. backing, sup-
port. *~lehne* f back(-rest). *~mark* n
anat. spinal cord. *~muskula,tur* f back
muscles. *~schmerzen* pl backache.
~schwimmen n backstroke. *~wind* m
following wind. *~wirbel* m anat. dorsal
vertebra.

'**Rückeroberung** f reconquest.

'**rückerstatten** v/t (only inf and rücker-
stattet, h) return, a. refund.

'**Rückfahrkarte** f return (ticket), Am.
round-trip ticket.

'**Rückfahrt** f return journey (or trip): *auf
der ~* a. on the way back.

'Rückfall *m* relapse (*a. fig.*), ⚖ *a.* recidivism. **'rückfällig** *adj* relapsing, ⚖ *a.* recidivist: **~ werden** (have a) relapse.

'Rückfenster *n* rear window.

'Rückflug *m* return flight.

'Rückfrage *f* checkback.

'rückfragen *v/i* (*only inf and pp* rückgefragt, h) check (**bei** with).

'Rückführung *f* repatriation.

'Rückgabe *f* return, *sports*: pass back.

'Rückgang *m* (*gen* in) decline, drop, fall.

'rückgängig *adj* **1.** → **rückläufig. 2.** **~ machen** a) undo, b) cancel (*order etc*).

'Rückgewinnung *f* recovery.

'Rückgrat *n* spine, backbone (*a. fig.*).

'rückgratlos *adj fig.* spineless.

'Rückhalt *m* support. **'rückhaltlos I** *adj* unreserved, *a.* frank. **II** *adv* without reserve: **j-m ~ vertrauen** have complete confidence in s.o.

'Rückhand *f* (-; *no pl*) *tennis*: backhand.

'Rückkampf *m sports*: return match.

'Rückkaufsrecht *n* right of repurchase (*or* redemption).

'Rückkehr *f* (-; *no pl*) return.

'Rückkopplung *f* ⚡ feedback (*a. fig.*).

'Rücklagen *pl* reserve(s), savings.

'rückläufig *adj* dropping, declining: **~e Tendenz** downward tendency.

'Rücklicht *n* (-[e]s; -er) *mot.* rear light, taillight.

rücklings ['rʏklɪŋs] *adv* a) backwards, b) from behind.

'Rückmarsch *m* march back. **'Rückpaß** *m sports*: back pass. **'Rückporto** *n* return postage. **'Rückprall** *m* rebound. **'Rückreise** *f* → **Rückfahrt. 'Rückruf** *m* **1.** ☎ recall. **2.** *teleph.* ring back.

'Rucksack *m* rucksack, *Am.* backpack. **~tou‚rismus** *m* backpacking. **~tou‚rist** *m* backpacker.

'Rückschlag *m fig.* setback.

'Rückschluß *m* conclusion.

'Rückschritt *m* step back(ward).

'rückschrittlich *adj pol.* reactionary.

'Rückseite *f* back, rear, reverse (*of coin etc*), B-side, F flip side (*of record*): **siehe ~!** see overleaf!

'Rücksendung *f* return.

'Rücksicht *f* (-; *no pl*) consideration: **mit ~ auf** (*acc*) out of consideration for; **ohne ~ auf** (*acc*) regardless of; **(k-e) ~ nehmen auf** (*acc*) show (no) consideration for, make (no) allowances for.

'Rücksichtnahme [-naːˌmə] *f* (-; *no pl*) consideration (**auf** *acc* for).

'rücksichtslos *adj* inconsiderate (**gegen** of), thoughtless, reckless (*driving etc*), *a.* ruthless. **'Rücksichtslosigkeit** *f* (-; *no pl*) lack of consideration, recklessness. **'rücksichtsvoll** *adj* considerate (**gegen** of).

'Rücksitz *m* a) backseat, b) pillion.

'Rückspiegel *m mot.* rearview mirror.

'Rückspiel *n sports*: return match.

'Rücksprache *f* (-; -n) consultation: **mit j-m ~ nehmen** consult (with) s.o.

'Rückstand *m* (-[e]s; ⁻e) **1.** 🜪 residue. **2.** ✝ arrears, *a.* backlog (*of work*): **im ~ sein** mit be behind with *one's payments etc*, *sports*: be down *one goal etc*.

'rückständig *adj* **1.** backward, *a.* underdeveloped. **2. ~e Miete** arrears of rent.

'Rückständigkeit *f* (-; *no pl*) backwardness.

'Rückstau *m mot.* tailback.

'Rückstoß *m* recoil (*of gun*).

'Rückstrahler *m* rear reflector.

'Rücktaste *f of typewriter*: back spacer, *of tape recorder etc*: rewind key.

'Rücktritt *m* **1.** (**von**) resignation (from *office*), withdrawal (from *contract*): **s-n ~ erklären** announce (*or* tender) one's resignation. **2.** F → **'Rücktrittbremse** *f* backpedal brake.

'Rücktritts|gesuch *n* (letter of) resignation. **~recht** *n* right of rescission.

'rückübersetzen *v/t* (*only inf and pp* rückübersetzt, h) translate back (**in** *acc* into *English etc*).

'Rückübersetzung *f* retranslation.

'rückvergüten *v/t* (*only inf and pp* rückvergütet, h), **'Rückvergütung** *f* refund.

'rückversichern *v/t* (*only inf and pp* rückversichert, h) reinsure (**sich** o.s.): *fig.* **sich ~** play safe.

'Rückversicherung *f* reinsurance.

'Rückwand *f* back, back wall.

rückwärtig ['rʏkvɛrtɪç] *adj* back, rear.

rückwärts ['rʏkvɛrts] *adv* backwards: **~ fahren in** (*acc*) (*or* **aus** *dat*) back into (*or* out of). **'Rückwärtsgang** *m mot.* (**im ~** in) reverse (gear).

'Rückweg *m* way back, return: **den ~ antreten** head for home.

'ruckweise I *adj* jerky. **II** *adv* jerkily, in jerks.

'rückwirkend *adj* ⚖ retroactive: **~ ab**

backdated to. '**Rückwirkung** f (*auf acc* upon*) reaction, repercussion.
'**rückzahlbar** *adj* repayable.
'**Rückzahlung** f repayment, refund.
'**Rückzieher** m (-s; -) **1.** *soccer:* overhead kick. **2.** F *e-n ~ machen* back down.
'**Rückzug** m retreat. '**Rückzugsgefecht** n a. fig. rearguard action.
rüde ['ry:də] *adj* rude, coarse.
'**Rüde** m (-n; -n) male dog (*or* wolf, fox).
Rudel ['ru:dəl] n (-s; -) pack (*of wolves etc*), herd (*of deer etc*), fig. swarm.
Ruder ['ru:dər] n (-s; -) a) oar, b) rudder (*a. ✈*), helm: *am ~* at the helm (*a. fig.*); *fig. ans ~ kommen* come into power.
'**Ruderboot** n rowing boat.
'**Ruderer** m (-s; -) rower, oarsman.
'**Ruderin** f (-; -nen) oarswoman.
'**Ruderklub** m rowing club.
rudern ['ru:dərn] v/t (h), v/i (h, sn) row.
'**Rudern** n (-s) rowing.
'**Ruderre|gatta** f boat race, regatta.
'**Rudersport** m rowing.
Ruf [ru:f] m (-[e]s; -e) **1.** call (*a. teleph. or fig.*), cry, shout: *e-n ~ erhalten nach* be offered an appointment (*univ.* a chair) at. **2.** *no pl* reputation: *von ~* artist etc* of high repute, noted *artist etc*.
rufen ['ru:fən] (rief, gerufen, h) **I** v/i a) call, b) cry, shout: *~ nach* call for (*a. fig.*); *um Hilfe ~* cry for help. **II** v/t call, a. summon: *~ lassen* send for; *du kommst mir wie gerufen* you're just the person I need. '**Rufen** n (-s) a) calling, b) calls. '**Rufer** m (-s; -) caller.
Rüffel ['ryfəl] m (-s; -) F dressing-down.
'**Ruf|mord** m character assassination. *~name* m name by which one is called. *~nummer* f telephone number. *~weite* f *in ~* within calling distance.
Rüge ['ry:gə] f (-; -n) reprimand, rebuke.
'**rügen** v/t (h) (*wegen* for) reprimand, rebuke (*s.o.*), criticize, censure (*s.th.*).
Ruhe ['ru:ə] f (-; *no pl*) a) rest (*a. phys.*), b) quiet, silence, c) peace, d) calm(ness), composure: *~ und Ordnung* law and order; *die ~ vor dem Sturm* the calm before the storm; *in aller ~* very calmly, leisurely; *überlege es dir in aller ~* take your time about it; *~ bewahren* keep calm, keep cool; *sich zur ~ setzen* retire; *zur ~ bringen* quieten down; *~, bitte!* quiet, please!; *laß mich in ~!* leave me alone!; *laß mich damit in*

~! I don't want to hear about it!; *er möchte s-e ~ haben* he wants to be left in peace; F *er hat die ~ weg!* he's (as) cool as a cucumber; *immer mit der ~!* take it easy!
'**ruhebedürftig** *adj* in need of (a) rest.
'**Ruhegehalt** n pension.
'**ruhelos** *adj* restless.
'**Ruhelosigkeit** f (-; *no pl*) restlessness.
ruhen ['ru:ən] v/i (h) rest, work, traffic, etc: be at a standstill, negotiations etc: be suspended: *~ auf* (*dat*) fig. rest on; *er ruhte nicht, bis* he didn't rest until; *hier ruht* here lies; *laß die Vergangenheit ~!* let bygones be bygones!
'**Ruhe|pause** f break, rest. *~stand* m (-[e]s; *no pl*) (*vorzeitiger ~* early) retirement: *im ~* retired; *in den ~ treten* (*versetzen*) retire. *~stätte* f resting place. *~stellung* f ⊙ neutral position. *~störer* m disturber of the peace. *~störung* f *öffentliche ~* disturbance of the peace. *~tag* m a) day of rest, b) day off, c) closing day: *Montag ~!* closed on Mondays!
ruhig ['ru:iç] **I** *adj* **1.** a) quiet (*a. fig.*), a. silent, b) still, c) peaceful, restful, d) calm (*sea, a. voice*), steady (*hand*), smooth (*a. ⊙*), e) leisurely: (*sei*) *~!* (be) quiet!; *sei ganz ~!* don't worry!; *~ bleiben* keep calm; *k-e ~e Minute haben* not to have a moment's peace. **II** *adv* **2.** quietly (*etc*): *das Haus liegt ~* the house is in a quiet area; *~ verlaufen* be uneventful. **3.** F easily, very well: *tu das ~!* go right ahead!; *du kannst ~ dableiben!* (you can) stay if you want!
Ruhm [ru:m] m (-[e]s; *no pl*) fame, glory.
rühmen ['ry:mən] v/t (h) praise (*wegen* for): *sich ~* (*gen*) pride o.s. (on), boast (*s.th.*). '**rühmenswert → rühmlich.**
'**Ruhmesblatt** n *das ist kein ~ für ihn* that's not exactly to his credit.
'**rühmlich** *adj* laudable, praiseworthy: *~e Ausnahme* noteworthy exception.
'**ruhmlos** *adj* inglorious.
'**ruhmreich**, '**ruhmvoll** *adj* glorious.
Ruhr [ru:r] f (-; *no pl*) ✿ dysentery.
'**Rührbesen** m *gastr.* whisk.
'**Rühreier** pl scrambled eggs.
rühren ['ry:rən] (h) **I** v/t **1.** stir, a. move: *er hat k-n Finger gerührt* he did not lift a finger; → *Donner, Trommel.* **2.** fig. touch, move (*zu Tränen* to tears): *das*

rührt mich wenig that leaves me cold.
II *v/i* **3.** stir. **4.** ~ *an* (*acc*) a) touch, b) touch (up)on *a subject etc.* **III** *v/t* sich ~ **5.** stir, move: ✕ *rührt euch!* (stand) at ease!; *sich nicht (von der Stelle)* ~ not to budge (an inch) **6.** F *fig.* do (*or* say) s.th. '**rührend** *adj* **1.** touching, moving. **2.** very kind.

'**rührig** *adj* active, busy, enterprising.
'**Rührigkeit** *f* (-; *no pl*) activity.
'**rührselig** *adj* sentimental, mawkish: ~*e Geschichte* F sob story.
'**Rührung** *f* (-; *no pl*) emotion: *er brachte vor* ~ *kein Wort heraus* he was choked with emotion.

Ruin [ru'i:n] *m* (-s; *no pl*) (*vor dem* ~ *stehen* be on the brink of) ruin.
Ruine [ru'i:nə] *f* (-; -n) ruin(s).
ruinieren [rui'ni:rən] *v/t* (h) ruin.
ruinös [rui'nøːs] *adj* ruinous.
rülpsen ['rʏlpsən] *v/i* (h) F belch.
Rum [rʊm] *m* (-s; -s) rum.
rum(...) F → *herum*(...).
Rumäne [ru'mɛːnə] *m* (-n; -n) Romanian. **Ru'mänien** [-ïən] *n* (-s) Romania. **Ru'mänin** *f* (-; -nen), **ru'mänisch** *adj* Romanian.
Rummel ['rʊməl] *m* (-s; *no pl*) F **1.** (hustle and) bustle. **2.** fuss, to-do: *großen* ~ *machen* make a big fuss about. **3.** a) fun fair, b) → **'Rummelplatz** *m* fairground, amusement park.
rumoren [ru'mo:rən] *v/i* (h) F bang around.
'**Rumpelkammer** *f* lumber room.
rumpeln ['rʊmpəln] *v/i* (h, sn) F rumble.
Rumpf [rʊmpf] *m* (-es; ∺e) **1.** *anat.* trunk. **2.** ⚓ hull, ✈ fuselage.
rümpfen ['rʏmpfən] *v/t* (h) *die Nase* ~ turn up one's nose (*über acc* at).
rund [rʊnt] **I** *adj* **1.** round (*a. fig.*): *Gespräche am* ~*en Tisch* round-table talks; ~*e 1000 Mark* 1,000 marks or so; *e-e* ~*e Leistung* a perfect performance. **II** *adv* **2.** about, roughly: ~ *gerechnet* in round figures. **3.** ~ *um* (a)round.
'**Rundbau** *m* (-[e]s; -ten) rotunda.
'**Rundblick** *m* panorama.
Runde ['rʊndə] *f* (-; -n) **1.** circle. **2.** round: *s-e* ~ *machen* make one's rounds, *policeman*: be on one's beat; F *die* ~ *machen* story etc: go the round. **3.** *boxing, golf, etc*: round (*a. fig.* of negotiations), *racing*: lap: F *fig.* **gerade**

so über die ~*n kommen* just about make it, scrape by, *a. financially*: get by. **4.** round (*of beer etc*). '**runden:** *sich* ~ (h) grow round, *fig.* take shape.
'**runderneuern** *v/t* (*only inf and pp* runderneuert, h) retread (*tyres*).
'**Rundfahrt** *f* tour (*durch* of).
'**Rundflug** *m* circuit.
'**Rundfunk** *m* (-s; *no pl*) **1.** broadcasting, radio: *im* ~ on the radio; ~ *hören* listen to the radio; *im* ~ *übertragen* (*or senden, bringen*) broadcast; *beim* ~ *sein* work in broadcasting. **2.** → ~**anstalt** *f* broadcasting company, *Am.* radio corporation. ~**gebühren** *pl* radio licen/ce (*Am.* -se) fees. ~**gerät** *n* radio (set). ~**hörer(in** *f*) *m* listener. ~**pro,gramm** *n* radio program(me *Br.*). ~**sender** *m* → *Rundfunkstation*. ~**sendung** *f* broadcast, radio program(me *Br.*). ~**sprecher** *m* (radio) announcer. ~**stati,on** *f* radio station. ~**zeitung** *f* radio journal.
'**Rundgang** *m* round, tour (*durch* of).
'**rundher'aus** *adv* flatly, straight out.
'**rundher'um** *adv* all (a)round.
'**rundlich** *adj* plump, chubby.
'**Rundreise** *f* tour (*durch* of).
'**Rundschreiben** *n* circular (letter).
'**Rundstrecke** *f* circuit.
'**rund'um** *adv* all (a)round.
'**Rundung** *f* (-; -en) curve.
'**rund'weg** *adv* flatly.
Rune ['ru:nə] *f* (-; -n) rune.
runter(...) ['rʊntər-] F → *herunter*(...), *hinunter*(...). '**runterhauen** *v/t* (*sep*, -ge-, h) F *j-m e-e* ~ slap s.o.('s face).
Runzel ['rʊntsəl] *f* (-; -n) wrinkle, line. '**runz(e)lig** *adj* wrinkled, lined. '**runzeln** *v/t* (h) wrinkle: *die Stirn* ~ frown.
Rüpel ['ry:pəl] *m* (-s; -) lout.
'**rüpelhaft** *adj* rude, loutish, uncouth.
rupfen ['rʊpfən] *v/t* (h) pluck (*chicken etc*): F *j-n* ~ fleece s.o.; → *Hühnchen* 1.
ruppig ['rʊpɪç] *adj* **1.** shaggy. **2.** gruff.
Rüsche ['ry:ʃə] *f* (-; -n) frill.
Ruß [ru:s] *m* (-es; *no pl*) soot.
Russe ['rʊsə] *m* (-n; -n) Russian.
Rüssel ['rʏsəl] *m* (-s; -) proboscis, *a.* (elephant's) trunk, (pig's) snout.
rußen ['ru:sən] *v/i* (h) smoke.
rußig *adj* sooty.
'**Russin** *f* (-; -nen), '**russisch** *adj* Russian. **Rußland** ['rʊs-] *n* (-s) Russia.
rüsten ['rʏstən] (h) (*für, zu* for) **I** *v/i* ✕

arm: *fig.* **gerüstet** armed, ready. **II** *sich*
~ prepare, get ready.
Rüster ['ry:stər] *f* (-; -n) ♀ elm.
rüstig ['rystıç] *adj* vigorous, sprightly.
rustikal [rusti'ka:l] *adj* rustic.
'Rüstung[1] *f* (-; -en) (knight's) armo(u)r.
'Rüstung[2] *f* (-; -en) ✗ armament.
'Rüstungs|ausgaben *pl* defen/ce (*Am.*
-se) expenditure. **~begrenzung** *f* arms
limitation. **~indu,strie** *f* defen/ce (*Am.*
-se) industry. **~kon,trolle** *f* arms control. **~stopp** *m* arms freeze. **~wettlauf**
m arms race.
'Rüstzeug *n fig.* equipment.
Rute ['ru:tə] *f* (-; -n) **1.** a) switch, b) rod.
2. fishing rod. **3.** *hunt.* a) penis, b) tail,
(fox's) brush.

'**Rutengänger** [-gɛŋər] *m* (-s; -) diviner.
Rutsch [rʊtʃ] *m* (-[e]s; -e) **1.** slide, *a.*
landslide: F *in einem* ~ in one go; *guten* ~ (*ins Neue Jahr*)! Happy New
Year! **2.** F (short) trip, jaunt.
'Rutschbahn *f* slide.
'Rutsche *f* (-; -n) slide, ⚙ *a.* chute.
'rutschen *v/i* (sn) slide, glide, slip, *mot.
etc* skid. **'rutschig** *adj* slippery.
'rutschsicher *adj* nonslip, *mot.* nonskid.
rütteln ['rytəln] (h) **I** *v/t* shake, ⚙ vibrate. **II** *v/i mot.* shake, jolt, ⚙ vibrate:
~ *an* (*dat*) a) rattle (at) *the door*, b) *fig.*
shake, *a.* question; *daran ist nicht zu* ~!
that's a fact!

S

S, s [s] *n* (-; -) S, s.
Saal [za:l] *m* (-[e]s; ᵘe) hall.
Saat [za:t] *f* (-; -en) **1.** *no pl* sowing. **2.**
seed (*a. fig.*), *a.* crop(s). **~gut** *n* (-[e]s; *no
pl*) seed(s). **~kar,toffel** *f* seed potato.
Sabbat ['zabat] *m* (-s; -e) Sabbath.
sabbern ['zabərn] *v/i* (h) slaver, drool.
Säbel ['zɛ:bəl] *m* (-s; -) sab/re (*Am.* -er).
Sabotage [zabo'ta:ʒə] *f* (-; -n) sabotage.
Sabo'tageakt *m* act of sabotage.
Saboteur [zabo'tø:r] *m* (-s; -e) saboteur.
sabotieren [-'ti:rən] *v/t* (h) sabotage.
'**Sach|bearbeiter(in** *f*) *m* official (✝
clerk) in charge (*für* of). **~beschädi-
gung** *f* damage to property. ⓶**bezogen**
adj pertinent. **~buch** *n* nonfiction
book, *pl coll.* nonfiction.
'**sachdienlich** *adj* relevant, pertinent.
Sache ['zaxə] *f* (-; -n) **1.** a) thing, object,
b) F things (*a. food etc*), *a.* belongings; F *mot. mit 100* ~*n* at 60 (miles per
hour). **2.** *a.* affair, matter, business, b)
problem, c) subject, d) case, ⚖ *or fig.*
cause: *e-e* ~ *für sich* a matter apart; *in*
~*n Umwelt* concerning the environment; *in eigener* ~ on one's own behalf; *bei der* ~ *bleiben* stick to the
point; *er war nicht bei der* ~ he was

inattentive; *für e-e gute* ~ *kämpfen*
fight for a good cause; *s-e* ~ *gut machen* do a good job; *(sich) s-r* ~ *sicher
sein* be sure of one's ground; *zur* ~
kommen get to the point, *w.s.* get down
to business; *das ist s-e* ~! that's his
problem (*or* affair)!; *es ist s-e* ~ *zu inf*
it's his business to *inf*; *es ist* ~ *des
Vertrauens* it's a matter of trust; *das
tut nichts zur* ~ that makes no difference; *die* ~ *ist die, daß* the point is that;
F *j-m sagen, was* ~ *ist* tell s.o. what's
what; → *gemeinsam* I.
'**Sach|frage** *f* factual issue. ⓶**fremd** *adj*
irrelevant. **~gebiet** *n* subject, field.
⓶**gemäß**, ⓶**gerecht** *adj* proper, appropriate. **~kenner** *m* expert. **~kenntnis** *f*
expertise, know-how. **~kunde** *f* (-; *no
pl*) *ped.* general knowledge. ⓶**kundig**
adj expert: *sich* ~ *machen* inform o.s.
~lage *f* (-; *no pl*) state of affairs. **~lei-
stung** *f* payment in kind.
'**sachlich** *adj* **1.** factual, *a.* technical, *a.*
△, ⚙ functional: *aus* ~*en Gründen* for
technical (*or* practical) reasons; ~ *richtig* factually correct. **2.** a) matter-of-
-fact, realistic, unemotional, b) objective, c) practical(-minded).

sächlich ['zɛçlɪç] *adj ling.* neuter.
'**Sachlichkeit** *f* (-; *no pl*) matter-of-factness, objectivity, △, ❂ functionalism.
'**Sachre|gister** *n* (subject) index.
'**Sachschaden** *m* material damage.
Sachse ['zaksə] *m* (-n; -n), **Sächsin** ['zɛksɪn] *f* (-; -nen), **sächsisch** ['zɛksɪʃ] *adj* Saxon.
'**Sachspende** *f* donation in kind.
sacht [zaxt] **I** *adj* soft, gentle. **II** *adv a.* **~e** a) softly, gently, b) cautiously, c) slowly: F (*immer*) **~e!** take it easy!
'**Sachverhalt** *m* the facts (of the case).
'**Sachvermögen** *n* tangible property.
'**Sachverstand** *m* expertise, know-how.
'**sachverständig** *adj* expert, competent.
'**Sachverständige, m, f** (-n; -n) expert, ⚖ expert witness. '**Sachverständigengutachten** *n* expert opinion.
'**Sachwalter** [-valtər] *m* (-s; -) **1.** ⚖ trustee. **2.** *fig.* advocate, champion.
'**Sachwert** *m* (-[e]s; -e) **1.** *no pl* real value. **2.** *pl* material assets.
Sack [zak] *m* (-[e]s; **~e) 1.** sack, bag, *anat., zo.* sac: *mit ~ und Pack* with bag and baggage. **2.** V balls.
sacken ['zakən] *v/i* (sn) sink, give way, sag, *person:* slump.
'**Sack|gasse** *f* **1.** cul-de-sac. **2.** *fig.* dead end, impasse. **~hüpfen** *n* sack race.
Sadismus [za'dɪsmʊs] *m* (-; *no pl*) sadism. **Sadist** [za'dɪst] *m* (-en; -en) sadist. **sa'distisch** [-tɪʃ] *adj* sadistic.
säen ['zɛːən] *v/t, v/i* (h) sow: *fig. dünn gesät* scarce, few and far between.
Safari [za'faːri] *f* (-; -s) safari.
Sa'faripark *m* wildlife reserve.
Safe [seɪf] *m, n* (-s; -s) safe.
Safran ['zafran] *m* (-s; -e) saffron.
Saft [zaft] *m* (-[e]s; **~e) juice (*a.* F ⚡), ⚘ sap: *fig. ohne ~ und Kraft* → *saftlos* 2; → *schmoren.*
'**saftig** *adj* **1.** juicy, ⚘ lush. **2.** F *fig.* juicy, spicy (*joke etc*), resounding (*slap*), stiff, steep (*prices*), crushing (*defeat etc*).
'**saftlos** *adj* **1.** juiceless, dry. **2.** *fig. a. saft- u. kraftlos* lame, wishy-washy.
'**Saftpresse** *f* squeezer, juice extractor.
Sage ['zaːɡə] *f* (-; -n) **1.** legend. **2.** *fig.* rumo(u)r.
Säge ['zɛːɡə] *f* (-; -n) saw. **~blatt** *n* saw blade. **~bock** *m* sawhorse. **~fisch** *m* sawfish. **~mehl** *n* sawdust.
sagen ['zaːɡən] *v/t, v/i* (h) say: *j-m et. ~*

say s.th. to s.o., tell s.o. s.th.; *ich habe mir ~ lassen, daß* I've been told that; *et. (nichts) zu ~ haben* have a (no) say (*bei* in); *das hat nichts zu ~* that doesn't matter; *~ Sie ihm, er soll kommen* tell him to come; *was sagst du zu ...?* a) what do you say to ...?, b) how about ...?; *was willst du damit ~?* what do you mean (by that)?; *das Buch sagt mir nichts* the book doesn't mean a thing to me; *wie sagt man ... auf Englisch?* what is the English for ...?; *ich hab's dir ja gleich gesagt!* I told you so!; *laß dir das gesagt sein!* put that in your pipe and smoke it!; *man sagt, er sei krank* he is said to be ill; *was Sie nicht ~!* you don't say!; F *wem ~ Sie das!* you're telling me!; (*das*) *sagt dir das?* F says you!!; *sage und schreibe* no less than; *es* (*or damit*) *ist nicht gesagt, daß* that doesn't necessarily mean that; *unter uns gesagt* between you and me; *gesagt, getan* no sooner said than done; → *Meinung etc, schwer* II.
'**Sagen** *n* (-s) F *das ~ haben* be the boss, *bei* (*or in dat*) have the (final) say in.
sägen ['zɛːɡən] *v/t, v/i* (h) saw.
'**sagenhaft** *adj* **1.** legendary, mythical. **2.** F *fig.* fantastic, terrific, incredible.
'**Sägespäne** *pl* wood shavings.
'**Sägewerk** *n* sawmill.
sah [zaː] *pret of* **sehen.**
Sahne ['zaːnə] *f* (-; *no pl*) cream.
'**Sahnebon,bon** *m, n* toffee, *Am.* taffy.
'**Sahnetorte** *f* cream gateau.
sahnig ['zaːnɪç] *adj* creamy.
Saison [zɛ'zõː] *f* (-; -s) season. ♀**abhängig** *adj* seasonal. **~arbeiter** *m* seasonal worker. **~schlußverkauf** *m* ✝ seasonal sale.
Saite ['zaɪtə] *f* (-; -n) ♪ string, chord: → *aufziehen* 4. '**Saiteninstru,ment** *n* stringed instrument.
Sakko ['zako] *m, n* (-s; -s) jacket.
sakral [za'kraːl] *adj eccl.* sacred.
Sakrament [zakra'mɛnt] *n* (-[e]s; -e) *eccl.* sacrament.
Sakrileg [zakri'leːk] *n* (-s; -e) sacrilege.
Sakristei [zakrɪs'taɪ] *f* (-; -en) vestry.
Salamander [zala'mandər] *m* (-s; -) *zo.* salamander.
Salami [za'laːmi] *f* (-; -[s]) salami.
Salat [za'laːt] *m* (-[e]s; -e) **1.** *gastr.* salad: F *da haben wir den ~!* there you are! **2.**

no pl ♀ lettuce. **~besteck** *n* salad servers. **~kopf** *m* (head of) lettuce. **~öl** *n* salad oil. **~soße** *f* salad dressing.

Salbe ['zalbə] *f* (-; -n) ointment.

Salbei ['zalbaɪ] *m* (-s; *no pl*) ♀ sage.

salben ['zalbən] *v/t* (h) anoint.

'**Salbung** *f* (-; -en) anointing, *a.* fig. unction. '**salbungsvoll** *adj* unctuous.

Saldo ['zaldo] *m* (-s; Salden) ✝ balance.

Saline [za'li:nə] *f* (-; -n) saltworks.

Salmiak [zal'mĩak] *m* (-s; *no pl*) 🜨 ammonium chloride.

Salmonellen [zalmo'nɛlən] *pl* salmonellae. **~erkrankung** *f* salmonellosis.

Salon [za'lõ:] *m* (-s; -s) drawing-room, salon (*a.* ✝), *Am.* parlor, ♣ saloon.

sa'lonfähig *adj* a) presentable, b) respectable: **nicht ~** risqué (*joke*).

salopp [za'lɔp] *adj* casual, off-hand.

Salpeter [zal'pe:tər] *m* (-s; *no pl*) 🜨 saltpet/re (*Am.* -er). **~säure** *f* nitric acid.

Salto ['zalto] *m* (-s; -s, -ti) somersault.

Salut [za'lu:t] *m* (-[e]s; -e) salute.

salutieren [zalu'ti:rən] *v/t, v/i* (h) salute.

Salve ['zalvə] *f* (-; -n) ✗ volley, salvo.

Salz [zalts] *n* (-es; -e) salt.

'**salzarm** *adj* **~e Kost** low-salt diet.

'**Salzbergwerk** *m* salt mine.

salzen ['zaltsən] *v/t* (salzte, gesalzen, h) salt, *fig. a.* season; → **gesalzen.**

'**Salzfäßchen** *n* salt cellar.

'**Salzgurke** *f* pickled gherkin.

'**salzhaltig** *adj* saline.

'**Salzhering** *m* salted herring.

salzig ['zaltsɪç] *adj* salty.

'**Salzkartoffeln** *pl* boiled potatoes.

'**salzlos** *adj* salt-free.

'**Salzsäure** *f* 🜨 hydrochloric acid.

'**Salzstange** *f* saltstick. '**Salzstreuer** *m* salt shaker. '**Salzwasser** *n* salt water.

Samariter [zama'ri:tər] *m* (-s; -) (*barmherziger ~* good) Samaritan.

Samen ['za:mən] *m* (-s; -) **1.** ♀ *or fig.* seed. **2.** *physiol.* sperm, semen. **~bank** *f* (-; -en) 🜨, *vet.* sperm bank. **~erguß** *f* ejaculation. **~faden** *m* spermatozoon. **~flüssigkeit** *f* semen. **~kapsel** *f* ♀ seed capsule. **~leiter** *m* anat. vas deferens. **~spender** *m* (sperm) donor. **~strang** *m* anat. spermatic cord.

'**Sammel|akti,on** *f* **1.** fund-raising campaign. **2.** (salvage) collection. **~band** *m* (-[e]s; ⁓e) anthology. **~becken** *n* reservoir (*a.* fig.), geogr. catchment area.

~begriff *m* generic term. **~bestellung** *f* collective order. **~büchse** *f* collecting box. **~fahrschein** *m* group ticket. **~lager** *n* assembly camp. **~mappe** *f* file.

sammeln ['zamələn] (h) **I** *v/t* **1.** collect (*money, stamps, etc*), gather (*wood etc, fig.* experience); → **gesammelt** 1. **2.** assemble, gather: (*wieder*) **~** rally. **3.** *opt.* focus. **II** *v/i* **4.** (*für* for) collect money, pass the hat (around). **III** *sich* **~ 5.** gather, accumulate. **6.** assemble, meet, rally. **7.** *fig. a)* **~ s-e Gedanken ~** collect one's thoughts, *b)* compose o.s.; → **gesammelt** 2. **8.** *opt.* focus.

'**Sammel|name** *m* collective (noun). **~platz** *m*, **~punkt** *m* **1.** assembly point. **2.** *a.* **~stelle** *f* collecting point.

Sammelsurium [zaml'zu:rĩom] *n* (-s; -rien) omnium gatherum.

'**Sammelvisum** *n* group visa.

Sammler¹ ['zamlər] *m* (-s; -) collector. **Sammler²** *m* (-s; -) ≯ accumulator. '**Sammler²** *m* (-s; -), '**Sammlerin** *f* (-; -nen) collector.

'**Sammlerwert** *m* collector's value.

Sammlung *f* (-; -en) **1.** collection. **2.** anthology. **3.** museum. **4.** *fig. a)* concentration, b) composure.

Samstag ['zams-]*m* (*am ~* on) Saturday. '**samstags** *adv* on Saturdays.

samt [zamt] **I** *adv* **~ und sonders** all of them, F the whole lot. **II** *prep* together with, along with.

Samt *m* (-[e]s; -e) a) velvet, b) velveteen. '**samtartig** *adj* velvety.

'**Samthandschuh** *m fig. j-n mit ~en anfassen* handle s.o. with kid gloves.

sämtlich ['zɛmtlɪç] **I** *adj* all: **~e Werke** the complete works. **II** *adv* all of them.

Sanatorium [zana'to:rĩom] *n* (-s; -rien) sanatorium, *Am.* sanitarium.

Sand [zant] *m* (-[e]s; ⁓e) sand: F **wie ~ am Meer** any number of; *im ~e verlaufen* come to nothing; *j-m ~ in die Augen streuen* throw dust in s.o.'s eyes; F *in den ~ setzen* waste (*a project etc*).

Sandale [zan'da:lə] *f* (-; -n) sandal.

Sandalette [zanda'lɛtə] *f* (-; -n) high-heeled sandal.

'**Sand|bahn** *f mot.* dirt track. **~bank** *f* (-; ⁓e) sandbank. **~boden** *m* sandy soil.

'**Sanddorn** *m* (-[e]s; -e) ♀ sea buckthorn.

sandig ['zandɪç] *adj* sandy.

'**Sand|kasten** *m* sandpit, ✗ sandtable. **~männchen** *n* sandman. **~pa,pier** *n* sandpaper. **~sack** *m* sandbag. **~stein** *m* sandstone. **~strand** *m* sandy beach. **~sturm** *m* sandstorm.

sandte ['zantə] *pret of* **senden²**.

'**Sanduhr** *f* hourglass.

sanft [zanft] *adj* soft, gentle, peaceful, easy (*death etc*). '**Sanftheit** *f* (-; *no pl*) softness, gentleness.

'**sanftmütig** [-my:tɪç] *adj* gentle, meek.

sang [zaŋ] *pret of* **singen**.

Sänger ['zɛŋər] *m* (-s; -) **1.** singer. **2.** *zo.* songbird. **~fest** *n* choral festival.

'**Sängerin** *f* (-; -nen) singer.

'**sang- und 'klanglos** *adv* F quietly.

sanieren [za'ni:rən] (h) **I** *v/t* redevelop, *a.* ✝ rehabilitate. **II** *sich* **~** *a*) ✝ get back on one's feet again, *b*) F line one's own pockets. **Sa'nierung** *f* (-; -en) redevelopment, *a.* ✝ rehabilitation.

Sa'nierungsgebiet *n* redevelopment area.

sanitär [zani'tɛːr] *adj* sanitary.

Sanitäter [zani'tɛːtər] *m* (-s; -) **1.** ambulance (*or* first-aid) man. **2.** ✕ medical orderly.

Sani'täts|dienst *m* medical service. **~korps** *n* ✕ medical corps. **~wache** *f* first-aid post. **~wagen** *m* ambulance. **~zelt** *n* hospital tent.

sank [zaŋk] *pret of* **sinken**.

Sankt [zaŋkt] (*abbr.* St.) Saint (*abbr.* St.).

Sanktion [zaŋk'tsi̯o:n] *f* (-; -en) sanction.

sanktionieren [zaŋktsi̯o'ni:rən] *v/t* (h) sanction.

sann [zan] *pret of* **sinnen**.

Saphir ['za:fir] *m* (-s; -e) **1.** sapphire. **2.** *a.* '**Saphirnadel** *f* sapphire (needle).

Sardelle [zar'dɛlə] *f* (-; -n) anchovy.

Sardine [zar'di:nə] *f* (-; -n) sardine.

Sarg [zark] *m* (-[e]s; ⁀e) coffin, *Am. a.* casket.

Sarkasmus [zar'kasmʊs] *m* (-; *no pl*) sarcasm.

sarkastisch [zar'kastɪʃ] *adj* sarcastic.

saß [za:s] *pret of* **sitzen**.

Satan ['za:tan] *m* (-s; -e) Satan.

satanisch [za'ta:nɪʃ] *adj* satanic.

Satellit [zatɛ'li:t] *m* (-en; -en) satellite.

Satel'liten|bild *n*, **~foto** *n* satellite picture. **~staat** *m pol.* satellite (state). **~stadt** *f* satellite town. **~übertragung** *f* TV satellite transmission.

Satin [za'tɛ̃:] *m* (-s; -s) *a*) satin, *b*) sateen.

Satire [za'ti:rə] *f* (-; -n) satire (*auf acc*

on). **Satiriker** [za'ti:rikər] *m* (-s; -) satirist. **satirisch** [za'ti:rɪʃ] *adj* satirical.

satt [zat] *adj* **1.** satisfied, F full up: *ich bin* **~** I've had enough; *sich* **~** *essen* eat one's fill; *das macht* **~** that's very filling; **~** *zu essen haben* have enough to eat; F *et.* (*j-n*) (*gründlich*) **~** *haben* be sick and tired of (*or* be fed up with) s.th. (s.o.). **2.** full (*sound*), deep, rich (*colour*). **3.** *fig.* complacent. **4.** F stiff, steep (*price etc*), powerful (*blow*).

Sattel ['zatəl] *m* saddle: *fig. j-n aus dem* **~** *heben* oust s.o.; *fest im* **~** *sitzen* be firmly in the saddle. '**sattelfest** *adj* well up (*in dat* in). '**satteln** *v/t* (h) saddle.

'**Sattel|schlepper** *m mot.* **1.** road tractor. **2.** articulated lorry, *Am.* semitrailer (truck). **~tasche** *f* saddle-bag. **~zeug** *n* saddle and harness.

sättigen ['zɛtɪgən] (h) **I** *v/t* **1.** satisfy, fill. **2.** 🜊, *a.* ✝ saturate. **II** *v/i* **3.** be filling.

'**Sättigung** *f* (-; *no pl*) *a*) satiation, *b*) satiety, *c*) 🜊 *or fig.* saturation.

Sattler ['zatlər] *m* (-s; -) saddler.

Sattlerei [zatlə'raɪ] *f* (-; -en) saddlery.

saturieren [zatu'ri:rən] *v/t* (h) saturate.

Satyr ['za:tyr] *m* (-s, -n; -n) satyr.

Satz [zats] *m* (-es; ⁀e) **1.** *ling.* sentence, clause. **2.** principle, tenet, A̸ theorem. **3.** *print.* a) (type)setting, composition, b) (set) matter. **4.** ♪ movement. **5.** *tennis:* set. **6.** set (*of tools, stamps, etc*). **7.** sediment, dregs, (coffee) grounds. **8.** rate: *zum* **~** *von* at the rate of. **9.** leap: *e-n* **~** *machen* (take) a leap.

'**Satz|aussage** *f ling.* predicate. **~ball** *m tennis:* set point. **~bau** *m* (-[e]s; *no pl*) *ling.* syntax, construction. **~gefüge** *n ling.* compound sentence. **~gegenstand** *m ling.* subject. **~lehre** *f ling.* syntax. **~spiegel** *m print.* type area. **~teil** *m ling.* part of sentence, clause.

'**Satzung** *f* (-; -en) statute, *a. pl* statutes and articles.

'**satzungsgemäß** *adj* statutory, *a.* in accordance with the statutes.

'**Satzzeichen** *n* punctuation mark.

Sau [zaʊ] *f* (-; ⁀e) **1.** *zo.* sow. **2.** V *fig. a.*) (dirty) pig, b) slut, *a*) *contp.* swine, a) bitch: *unter aller* **~** lousy; *j-n* (*et.*) *zur* **~** *machen* let s.o. have it (tear s.th. to pieces); *die* **~** *rauslassen* let one's hair down.

sauber ['zaʊbər] *adj* **1.** *a. fig.* clean, neat:

~ *sein child*: be potty-trained; *e-e* ~e **Lösung** a neat solution. **2.** F *iro.* nice, (just) great.

säuberlich ['zɔybərlıç] *adj* **1.** clean, neat. **2.** careful.

'**saubermachen** *v/t, v/i* (*sep, -ge-, h*) clean (up), tidy (up).

säubern ['zɔybərn] *v/t* (h) **1.** clean (up), tidy (up). **2.** clear (*von* of). **3.** *fig.* purge.

'**Säuberung** *f* (-; -en) **1.** cleaning (*etc.*). **2.** *fig.* purge.

'**Saubohne** *f* ♀ broad bean.

'**Sauciere** [zo'sǐ:rə] *f* (-; -n) gravy boat.

Saudi ['zaʊdi] *m* (-s; -s) saudi.

Saudi-A'rabien *n* (-s) Saudi Arabia.

'**sau'dumm** *adj* V damned stupid.

sauer ['zaʊər] **I** *adj* **1.** sour, ♠ acid (*a. drops, rain*), *gastr.* pickled: ~ **werden** *milk*: turn (sour), curdle; *in den sauren Apfel beißen müssen* have to swallow the bitter pill. **2.** F sour, cross: ~ **werden** get cross; *j-m das Leben ~ machen* make life miserable for s.o. **II** *adv* **3.** ~ **verdientes Geld** hard-earned money; F ~ **reagieren auf** (*acc*) be annoyed (*or* mad) at.

'**Sauerampfer** *m* (-s; *no pl*) ♀ sorrel.

Saue'rei *f* (-; -en) → **Schweinerei.**

'**Sauerkirsche** *f* ♀ sour cherry.

säuerlich ['zɔybərlıç] *adj* (a bit) sour.

'**Sauermilch** *f* curdled milk.

säuern ['zɔybərn] *v/t* (h) make sour.

'**Sauerstoff** *m* (-[e]s; *no pl*) oxygen. ~**fla-sche** *f* oxygen cylinder. ~**mangel** *m* lack of oxygen. ~**maske** *f* oxygen mask. ~**zelt** *n* ♠ oxygen tent.

'**Sauerteig** *m* leaven.

saufen ['zaʊfən] *v/t, v/i* (soff, gesoffen, h) **1.** *animal*: drink. **2.** F *person*: booze, guzzle. **Säufer** ['zɔyfər] *m* (-s; -) F alcoholic, boozer. **Saufe'rei** *f* (-; -en) F **1.** boozing. **2.** F drinking bout, booze-up. '**Säuferin** *f* (-; -nen) → **Säufer.**

saugen ['zaʊgən] *v/t, v/i* (h) **1.** suck (*an dat* s.th.); → **Finger. 2.** vacuum.

säugen ['zɔygən] *v/t* (h) suckle (*a. zo.*), nurse, breastfeed.

'**Sauger** *m* (-s; -) teat, *Am.* nipple.

'**Säugetier** *n* mammal.

saugfähig ['zaʊk-] *adj* absorbent.

Säugling ['zɔyklıŋ] *m* (-s; -e) baby.

'**Säuglings|alter** *n* (*im* ~ in) infancy. ~**nahrung** *f* baby food. ~**pflege** *f* baby care. ~**schwester** *f* baby nurse.

~**sterblichkeit** *f* infant mortality.

'**Saugwirkung** *f* suction.

'**sau'kalt** *adj* V bloody cold.

Säule ['zɔylə] *f* (-; -n) column, pillar (*a. fig.*). '**Säulengang** *m* colonnade.

Saum [zaʊm] *m* (-[e]s; ~e) hem.

'**saumäßig** *adj* V awful, lousy.

säumen ['zɔymən] *v/t* (h) **1.** hem. **2.** *fig.* line, skirt.

säumig ['zɔymıç] *adj* **1.** late, tardy. **2.** ✝ ~**er Zahler** (*Schuldner*) defaulter.

Sauna ['zaʊna] *f* (-; Saunen) sauna.

Säure ['zɔyrə] *f* (-; -n) **1.** *no pl* sourness, *a.* ♠ acidity. **2.** ♠ acid.

'**säure|beständig,** ~**fest** *adj* acid-proof. **Saure'gurkenzeit** *f* F (-; *no pl*) a) ✝ off-season, b) *in the press*: silly season.

'**säurehaltig** *adj* acid(ic).

'**säurelöslich** *adj* acid-soluble.

Saurier ['zaʊrǐər] *m* (-s; -) saurian.

Saus [zaʊs] *in* ~ **und Braus leben** live on (*or* off) the fat of the land.

säuseln ['zɔyzəln] *v/i, v/t* (h) whisper, *iro. person*: purr.

sausen ['zaʊzən] *v/i* **1.** (sn) F whiz, rush, dash. **2.** (h) *wind*: rush, *a. bullet etc.*: whistle, *ears*: buzz. **sausenlassen** *v/t* (*irr, sep, no -ge-,* h) F a) pass up, give *s.th.* a miss, b) drop (*s.o.*).

'**Saustall** *m* pigsty (*a.* F *fig.*).

'**Sauwetter** *n* F filthy weather.

'**sau'wohl** *adj* F *sich ~ fühlen* feel real good.

Saxophon [zakso'fo:n] *n* (-s; -e) saxophone.

'**S-Bahn** *f* suburban (fast) train(s).

Schabe ['ʃa:bə] *f* (-; -n) *zo.* cockroach.

schaben ['ʃa:bən] *v/t, v/i* (h) scrape.

Schabernack ['ʃa:bərnak] *m* (-[e]s; -e) practical joke, hoax.

schäbig ['ʃɛ:bıç] *adj* shabby, *fig. a.* mean. '**Schäbigkeit** *f* (-; *no pl*) shabbiness, *fig. a.* meanness.

Schablone [ʃa'blo:nə] *f* (-; -n) **1.** stencil, ⊕ template. **2.** *fig.* a) stereotype, cliché, b) (fixed) routine. **Scha'blonenden-ken** *n* stereotyped thinking.

scha'blonenhaft *adj fig.* stereotyped.

Schach [ʃax] *n* (-s; -s) **1.** *no pl* chess: ~ **spielen** play (at) chess. **2.** check: ~ **und matt!** checkmate!; *j-m* ~ **bieten** check s.o., *fig.* stand up to s.o.; *in* ~ **halten** keep in check (*a. fig.*), *with gun*: a. cover. **~brett** *n* chessboard. **~com,puter** *m* chess computer.

Schacher ['ʃaxər] *m* (-s; *no pl*) haggling.

'**schachern** *v/i* (h) haggle (**um** over).

'**Schach|fi,gur** *f* chessman, (chess) piece. ♀'**matt** *adj* **1.** (check)mate: **~ setzen** *a. fig.* checkmate. **2.** F exhausted. **~par,tie** *f* game of chess. **~spiel** *n* **1.** (game of) chess. **2.** chess set. **~spieler(in** *f*) *m* chess player.

Schacht [ʃaxt] *m* (-[e]s; ⁀e) a) shaft (*a.* ⚒), b) manhole.

Schachtel ['ʃaxtəl] *f* (-; -n) **1.** box, *a.* carton, packet. **2.** F *alte ~* old bag.

'**Schachtelsatz** *m* involved sentence.

'**Schachtur,nier** *n* chess tournament.

'**Schachzug** *m a. fig.* move.

schade ['ʃaːdə] *adj pred* (**es ist [sehr]**) **~** it's a (great) pity (**um** about, **daß** that), F it's too bad (*he couldn't come etc*); **wie ~!** what a pity!; **dafür ist es** (*er*) **zu ~** it (he) is too good for that!; **darum ist es nicht ~!** it is no great loss!

Schädel ['ʃɛːdəl] *m* (-s; -) skull, cranium. **~basisbruch** *m* fracture of the skull-base. **~bruch** *m* fracture of the skull. **~dach** *n anat.* skullcap, calvaria.

schaden ['ʃaːdən] *v/i* (h) (*dat*) damage, harm, be detrimental (to): **das schadet der Gesundheit** that's bad for your health; **das schadet nichts** a) it won't do any harm, b) it doesn't matter; *iro.* **das schadet ihr gar nichts!** that serves her right!; **ein Versuch kann nicht ~** there is no harm in trying.

'**Schaden** *m* (-s; ⁀) a) damage (**an** *dat* to), b) injury, harm, c) *a.* ⊙ defect, d) disadvantage, e) loss: **~ nehmen** be damaged, *person:* be harmed; **durch ~ wird man klug** once bitten twice shy.

'**Schadenersatz** *m* a) compensation, indemnification, b) damages: **~ erhalten** (**fordern, leisten**) recover (claim, pay) damages; **auf ~ (ver)klagen** sue for damages. **~klage** *f* action for damages.

'**schadenersatzpflichtig** *adj* liable for damages.

'**Schadenfreiheitsra,batt** *m mot.* no-claims bonus.

'**Schadenfreude** *f* (-; *no pl*) malicious glee, gloating: **voller ~ → 'schadenfroh** *adj* gloating (*ly adv*): **~ sein** gloat.

'**Schadenversicherung** *f* indemnity insurance.

schadhaft ['ʃa:t-] *adj* defective.

schädigen ['ʃɛ:dɪgən] *v/t* (h) damage, *a.* injure, harm, impair (*a. fig.*): **wir sind schwer geschädigt worden** we have suffered heavy losses. '**Schädigung** *f* (-; -en) (*gen* to) damage, harm.

schädlich ['ʃɛ:tlɪç] *adj* (*dat* to) harmful, injurious, *a.* detrimental: **~ für die Gesundheit** bad for your health. '**Schädlichkeit** *f* (-; *no pl*) harmfulness.

Schädling ['ʃɛ:tlɪŋ] *m* (-s; -e) *zo.* pest. '**Schädlings|bekämpfung** *f* pest control. **~bekämpfungsmittel** *n* pesticide.

'**schadlos** *adj* **j-n** (**sich**) **~ halten** indemnify s.o. (recoup o.s.) (**für** for); **sich an j-m ~ halten** recoup one's losses from s.o.

'**Schadstoff** *m* a) harmful substance, b) pollutant.

Schaf [ʃa:f] *n* (-[e]s; -e) **1.** *zo.* sheep: *fig.* **schwarzes ~** black sheep. **2.** F ninny.

'**Schafbock** *m zo.* ram.

Schäfchen ['ʃɛ:fçən] *n* (-s; -) lamb: *fig.* **sein ~ ins trockene bringen** feather one's nest.

Schäfer ['ʃɛ:fər] *m* (-s; -) shepherd.

'**Schäferhund** *m* (**deutscher**) **~** Alsatian, German shepherd (dog).

'**Schäferin** *f* (-; -nen) shepherdess.

schaffen ['ʃafən] (schuf, geschaffen, h) **I** *v/t* **1.** a) create, produce, *fig. a.* make, b) bring about, cause, c) found, set up, establish: **er ist zum Lehrer** (**für den Posten**) **wie geschaffen** he is a born teacher (cut out for the job); **→ Ordnung. 2.** take (**in** *acc*, **nach**, **zu**) to: **→ Hals, Weg, Welt. 3.** a) manage, b) F catch (*bus, train, etc*), c) set up (*record*): **es ~** make it, *a.* succeed; **das hätten wir geschafft!** we've done it!; **~ wir es bis dorthin** (**in 3 Stunden**)**?** can we make it there (in three hours)? **4. ich habe damit nichts zu ~** that's no business of mine, I wash my hands of it; **mit ihm will ich nichts zu ~ haben** I don't want anything to do with him. **5.** F **j-n ~** a) take it out of s.o., b) get s.o. down; **ich bin geschafft!** I've had it! **II** *v/i* **6.** *dial.* work. **7. sich zu ~ machen** potter about, **an** (*dat*) busy o.s. (*b.s.* tamper) with. **8. j-m** (**viel** *or* **schwer**) **zu ~ machen** give (*or* cause) s.o. (no end of) trouble, *illness:* trouble s.o.

'**Schaffen** n (-s) a) work, (creative) activity, b) work(s).
'**schaffend** adj **1.** creative. **2.** working.
'**Schaffensdrang** m **1.** creative urge. **2.** zest for work. **Schaffenskraft** f (-; no pl) **1.** creative power. **2.** vigo(u)r.
Schaffner ['ʃafnər] m (-s; -) conductor, 🚋 guard.
'**Schaffnerin** f (-; -nen) conductress.
'**Schaffung** f (-; no pl) a) creation, b) foundation, setting-up (→ **schaffen** 1).
'**Schafherde** f flock of sheep. '**Schafhirt** m shepherd. '**Schafleder** n sheepskin.
Schafott [ʃaˈfɔt] n (-[e]s; -e) scaffold.
'**Schafpelz** m sheepskin: fig. **Wolf im ~** wolf in sheep's clothing.
'**Schafschur** f sheep shearing.
'**Schafskäse** m sheep's milk cheese.
Schaft [ʃaft] m (-[e]s; ^e) shaft (of axe etc), stock (of rifle), shank (of tool etc), leg (of boot). **~stiefel** m high boot.
'**Schafwolle** f sheep's wool.
'**Schafzucht** f sheep breeding.
Schah [ʃaː] m (-s; -s) Shah.
Schakal [ʃaˈkaːl] m (-s; -e) zo. jackal.
schäkern ['ʃɛːkərn] v/i (h) **1.** joke around. **2.** flirt.
schal [ʃaːl] adj stale, flat, fig. a. empty.
Schal m (-s; -s, -e) scarf.
'**Schale**[1] [ʃaːlə] f (-; -n) a) bowl, b) dish.
'**Schale**[2] f (-; -n) **1.** shell (of eggs, nuts, etc. 🥚 and zo.), skin (of fruit etc), peel(ing) (of potatoes etc), husk. **2.** F **sich in ~ werfen** dress up.
schälen ['ʃɛːlən] (h) **I** v/t peel (orange, potatoes, etc), shell (eggs, nuts, husk (peas etc), skin (tomatoes etc). **II sich ~** skin: peel off.
'**Schalensitz** m mot. bucket seat.
'**Schalheit** f (-; no pl) a. fig. staleness.
Schall [ʃal] m (-[e]s; -e) **1.** sound: **schneller als der ~** supersonic. **2.** echo.
'**schalldämpfend** adj sound-deadening.
'**Schalldämpfer** m sound absorber, mot. silencer (a. on guns), Am. muffler.
'**schalldicht** adj soundproof.
schallen ['ʃalən] v/i (h) resound, ring: **~de Ohrfeige** resounding slap; **~des Gelächter** peals of laughter; **er lachte ~d** he roared with laughter.
'**Schallgeschwindigkeit** f sonic speed.
'**Schallmauer** f sound barrier.
'**Schallplatte** f record, disc, disk.
'**Schallplattenaufnahme** f recording.

'**schallschluckend** adj sound-absorbing.
'**Schallwelle** f sound wave.
schalt [ʃalt] pret of **schelten**.
'**Schaltauto,matik** f mot. automatic gear change.
schalten ['ʃaltən] (h) **I** v/i **1.** ⚡, ⚙ switch (**auf** acc to), shift (the levers), mot. change (or shift) the gears: **in den dritten Gang ~** change (or shift) into third (gear). **2.** F get it, catch on: **schnell ~** a) do some quick thinking, b) catch on quickly, be quick in the uptake. **3.** **~ und walten** be in charge (of things); **j-n ~ und walten lassen** give s.o. a free hand. **II** v/t **4.** ⚙ switch, turn, shift (gear, lever). **5.** ⚡ switch (**auf** acc to).
'**Schalter** m (-s; -) **1.** counter, 🚋 ticket window, ✈ desk. **2.** ⚡ switch. **~beamte** m counter (or booking) clerk. **~dienst** m counter duty. **~halle** f main hall. **~stunden** pl business hours.
'**Schalt|getriebe** n gear box. **~hebel** m mot. (gear)shift lever, ⚡ switch lever, ⚙ control lever: **an den ~n der Macht sitzen** be at the controls. **~jahr** n leap year: F **alle ~e (mal)** once in a blue moon. **~kasten** m ⚡ switchbox. **~knopf** m (control) button. **~kreis** m ⚡ circuit. **~plan** m wiring diagram. **~pult** n control desk. **~tafel** f ⚡ switchboard. **~tag** m intercalary day. **~uhr** f timer.
'**Schaltung** f (-; -en) **1.** mot. a) gearshift assembly, b) gear change (or shift). **2.** ⚡ a) circuit, b) wiring. **3.** ⚙ control(s).
Scham [ʃaːm] f (-; no pl) **1.** shame: **rot vor ~** → **schamrot**. **2.** private parts, genitals. **~bein** n anat. pubic bone.
schämen ['ʃɛːmən] sich ~ (h) be (or feel) ashamed ([wegen] gen, für of): **schäme dich!** shame on you!
'**Schamgefühl** n (-[e]s; no pl) sense of shame. **~haare** pl pubic hair.
'**schamhaft** adj bashful, modest.
'**Schamlippen** pl anat. labia.
'**schamlos** adj a) shameless, b) indecent: **~e Lüge** barefaced lie. '**Schamlosigkeit** f (-; no pl) shamelessness.
Schamottestein [ʃaˈmɔtə-] m firebrick.
'**schamrot** adj red with shame: **~ werden** blush with shame.
Schande ['ʃandə] f (-; no pl) disgrace (**für** to), a. shame: **~ machen** (dat) be a disgrace to.

schänden ['ʃɛndən] v/t (h) a) dishon-o(u)r, b) violate, rape, c) desecrate.
'**Schandfleck** m blot, eyesore.
schändlich ['ʃɛntlɪç] adj disgraceful, scandalous.
Schandtat ['ʃant-] f outrage.
'**Schändung** f (-; -en) a) disgrace (gen to), b) violation, rape, c) desecration.
Schankstube ['ʃaŋk-] f (public) bar.
Schanze ['ʃantsə] f (-; -n) ski-jump.
'**Schanzentisch** m ski-jump platform.
Schar [ʃaːr] f (-; -en) crowd (of people), troop (of children), flock (of birds).
scharen ['ʃaːrən] v/t (h) (a. sich ~) gather (or rally) (um round); e-e Menge etc um sich ~ rally a crowd etc round one.
'**scharenweise** adv in droves.
scharf [ʃarf] I adj 1. sharp (a. fig. eye, criticism, tongue, etc), a. biting (wind etc, fig. words etc), a. piercing (sound), a. keen (mind, glance, etc). 2. live (ammunition), armed (bomb etc). 3. hot (food, pepper, etc), strong (spirits, vinegar, etc), pungent, acrid (smell), 🔥 or fig. caustic. 4. sharp, abrupt. 5. sharp, exact, clear: phot. ein ~es Bild a sharp(ly defined) picture. 6. a) sharp, severe, strict, b) hard, fierce: ~e Konkurrenz stiff competition; ~er Protest fierce protest; ~es Tempo hard pace; ~e Bewachung close guard(ing); ~er Hund savage dog, F fig. tough guy. 7. F randy, hot, a. sexy: ~ sein auf (acc) be very keen on, sexually: be hot for. II adv 8. sharply (etc): ~ aufpassen pay close attention, watch out; ~ bremsen brake hard; phot. ~ einstellen focus; ~ nachdenken think hard; ~ schießen shoot with live ammunition; ~ verurteilen condemn severely.
'**Scharfblick** m (-[e]s; no pl) perspicacity.
Schärfe ['ʃɛrfə] f (-; no pl) 1. sharpness, fig. a. severity, a. keenness (of mind), a. fierceness: in aller ~ very severely. 2. a) gastr. hotness, b) pungency (of smell), c) 🔥 or fig. causticity. 3. acuteness (of sight, hearing), opt., phot. sharpness.
'**Scharfeinstellung** f opt., phot. a) focus(s)ing, b) focus(s)ing control.
schärfen ['ʃɛrfən] v/t (h) a. fig. sharpen.
'**Schärfentiefe** f phot. depth of focus.
'**scharfkantig** adj sharp-edged.
'**scharfmachen** v/t (sep, -ge-, h) F j-n ~ a) gegen set s.o. against, b) auf (acc)

make s.o. keen on, c) turn s.o. on.
'**Scharfmacher** m (-s; -) F agitator.
'**Scharfschießen** n live shooting.
'**Scharfschütze** m sharpshooter, sniper.
'**scharfsichtig** adj fig. perspicacious.
'**Scharfsinn** m (-[e]s; no pl) acumen.
'**scharfsinnig** adj astute, shrewd.
Scharlach ['ʃarlax] m (-s; no pl) 🔬 scarlet fever. '**scharlachrot** adj scarlet.
Scharlatan ['ʃarlatan] m (-s; -e) charlatan, F quack, fraud.
Scharnier [ʃar'niːr] n (-s; -e) hinge.
Schärpe ['ʃɛrpə] f (-; -n) sash.
scharren ['ʃarən] v/i (h) scrape (mit den Füßen one's feet), horse etc: paw.
Scharte ['ʃartə] f (-; -n) nick: fig. die ~ (wieder) auswetzen make up for it.
schartig ['ʃartɪç] adj jagged.
Schaschlik ['ʃaʃlɪk] m, n (-s; -s) shashlik.
Schatten ['ʃatən] m (-s; -) a) a. fig. shadow, b) shade: im ~ in the shade; fig. in den ~ stellen outshine, eclipse; in j-s ~ stehen live in s.o.'s shadow; man kann nicht über s-n (eigenen) ~ springen the leopard can't change its spots.
'**Schattendasein** n ein ~ führen live in the shadow.
'**schattenhaft** adj shadowy.
'**Schatten|kabi,nett** n pol. shadow cabinet. **~riß** m silhouette. **~seite** f shady (fig. seamy) side. **~spiel** n shadow play.
schattieren [ʃa'tiːrən] v/t (h) shade.
Schat'tierung f (-; -en) a) shading, b) a. fig. shade.
'**schattig** ['ʃatɪç] adj shady.
Schatulle [ʃa'tʊlə] f (-; -n) casket.
Schatz [ʃats] m (-es; ~e) 1. a. fig. treasure. 2. F darling, love.
'**Schatzamt** n pol. Treasury.
'**Schatzanweisung** f ♱ treasury bond.
'**schätzbar** adj assessable.
'**Schätzchen** ['ʃɛtsçən] n (-s; -) darling.
schätzen ['ʃɛtsən] v/t (h) 1. estimate, guess, a. assess (damage, value, etc) (auf acc at): wie alt ~ Sie ihn? how old would you say he is?; grob geschätzt at a rough guess. 2. suppose, Am. F guess. 3. a) esteem, think highly of, b) appreciate: → glücklich I.
'**Schätzer** m (-s; -) ♱ valuer, assessor.
'**Schatzgräber** [-grɛːbər] m (-s; -) treasure seeker.
'**Schatz|kammer** f treasury. **~meister** m treasurer. **~suche** f treasure hunt.

'**Schätzung** f (-; -en) estimate, guess, ✝, ⚖ assessment.

'**schätzungsweise** adv approximately.

'**Schau** f [ʃaʊ] f (-; -en) **1.** show, exhibition: **zur ~ stellen** exhibit, display, fig. a. parade; fig. **nur zur ~** only for show. **2.** TV etc show: F **e-e ~ abziehen** put on a show; **j-m die ~ stehlen** steal the show from s.o., upstage s.o.

'**Schaubild** n chart, graph, diagram.

Schauder ['ʃaʊdər] m (-s; -) shudder, shiver. '**schauderhaft** adj horrible, dreadful. '**schaudern** v/i (h) (**vor** dat with, **bei** at) shudder, shiver.

schauen ['ʃaʊən] v/i (h) look (**auf** acc at, fig. upon): F **schau, daß du ...** mind you ...; iro. **schau, schau!** well, well!

Schauer ['ʃaʊər] m (-s; -) **1.** meteor. shower. **2.** shudder, shiver, a. thrill; → **laufen** 1. '**schauerartig** adj **~e Regenfälle** showers.

'**schauerlich** adj **1.** horrible, terrible (a. fig.). **2.** weird, F creepy.

'**Schauermärchen** n F horror story.

Schaufel ['ʃaʊfəl] f (-; -n) **1.** a) shovel, b) scoop, c) ⚙ paddle (of water wheel), blade (of turbine). **2.** hunt. palm.

'**schaufeln** v/t (h) a) shovel, b) dig.

'**Schaufenster** n shop window, fig. showcase. **~bummel** m e-n ~ **machen** go window-shopping. **~dekorati,on** f window dressing.

'**Schau|fliegen** n, **~flug** m air display.

'**Schaugeschäft** n show business.

'**Schaukampf** m exhibition bout.

'**Schaukasten** m showcase.

Schaukel ['ʃaʊkəl] f (-; -n) swing.

schaukeln ['ʃaʊkəln] v/t, v/i (h) swing, cradle, chair, ship: rock: F **die Sache ~** manage (or swing) it.

'**Schaukelpoli,tik** f seesaw politics.

'**Schaukelstuhl** m rocking chair.

'**Schaulaufen** n exhibition skating.

'**Schaulustige**, m, f (-n; -n) curious onlooker, contp. gaper.

Schaum [ʃaʊm] m (-[e]s; **~e**) foam (a. ⚙), froth (a. on beer), lather: gastr. **zu ~ schlagen** beat (to a froth).

'**Schaumbad** n bubble bath.

schäumen ['ʃɔʏmən] v/i (h) foam, froth: (**vor Wut**) ~ foam (with rage).

'**Schaumgummi** m, n foam rubber.

schaumig ['ʃaʊmɪç] adj frothy.

'**Schaum|krone** f white crest. **~löscher**

m foam extinguisher. **~schläger** m contp. hot-air artist. **~schläge'rei** f (-; no pl) contp. hot air. **~stoff** m ⚙ foamed material. **~teppich** m ✈ foam carpet. **~wein** m sparkling wine.

'**Schaupackung** f ✝ dummy.

'**Schauplatz** m (am ~ at the) scene.

'**Schaupro,zeß** m ⚖ show trial.

schaurig ['ʃaʊrɪç] → **schauerlich**.

'**Schauspiel** n **1.** play, drama. **2.** fig. spectacle, sight. '**Schauspieler** m (fig. play-)actor. **Schauspiele'rei** f (-; no pl) (fig. play-)acting. '**Schauspielerin** f actress. '**schauspielerisch** adj theatrical, acting (talent etc). '**schauspielern** v/i (h) fig. play-act, F put on an act.

'**Schauspielhaus** n theat/re (Am. -er).

'**Schauspielschule** f drama school.

'**Schausteller** m (-s; -) exhibitor, at fairs etc: showman.

Scheck [ʃɛk] m (-s; -s) cheque, Am. check (**über** acc for). **~buch** n, **~heft** n chequebook, Am. checkbook. **~karte** f cheque (Am. check) card.

scheel [ʃe:l] ~ **ansehen** look askance at.

Scheffel ['ʃɛfəl] m (-s; -) bushel: fig. **sein Licht unter den ~ stellen** hide one's light under a bushel.

'**scheffeln** v/t (h) rake in money.

Scheibe ['ʃaɪbə] f (-; -n) **1.** disc (a. F record), ⚙ a. wheel, a. washer. **2.** (window etc) pane, mot. windscreen, Am. windshield. **3.** target. **4.** ice hockey: puck. **5.** slice (of bread etc): F **da(von) kannst du dir e-e ~ abschneiden!** you can take a leaf out of his (her etc) book!

'**Scheiben|bremse** f mot. disc brake. **~kupplung** f disc clutch. **~schießen** n target practice. **~waschanlage** f mot. windscreen (Am. windshield) washers. **~wischer** m mot. windscreen (Am. windshield) wiper.

Scheich [ʃaɪç] m (-[e]s; -s, -e) sheik(h).

'**Scheichtum** n (-s; **~er**) sheikhdom.

Scheide ['ʃaɪdə] f (-; -n) **1.** sheath (a. ⚘), a. scabbard. **2.** anat. vagina.

scheiden ['ʃaɪdən] (schied, geschieden) **I** v/t (h) separate, divide, ⚖ divorce (a married couple), dissolve (marriage): **sich ~ lassen**, a. **geschieden werden** get a divorce (**von** from). **II** v/i (sn) part (**von** from): **aus dem Dienst ~** retire from service, resign; **aus e-r Firma ~**

leave a firm. **III sich ~** (h) separate; **hier ~ sich die Geister** here opinions are divided.

'**Scheide|wand** f partition, fig. barrier. **~weg** m fig. **am ~** at a crossroads.

'**Scheidung** f (-; -en) **1.** separation. **2.** divorce (**von** from), dissolution (of marriage): **die ~ einreichen** file a petition for divorce.

'**Scheidungs|grund** m ground for divorce. **~klage** f petition for divorce.

Schein¹ [ʃaın] m (-[e]s; -e) **1.** light, a. glow. **2.** appearance: **et. nur zum ~ tun** pretend to do s.th.; **dem ~ nach** (**zu urteilen**) to all appearances; **den ~ wahren** keep up appearances; **der ~ trügt** appearances are deceptive.

Schein² m (-[e]s; -e) **1.** a) slip, b) a. univ. certificate. **2.** (bank)note, Am. a. bill.

'**scheinbar** adj seeming, apparent: **er ging nur ~ darauf ein** he only pretended to agree.

'**Scheinehe** f fictitious marriage.

scheinen ['ʃaınən] v/i (schien, geschienen, h) **1.** a) shine, b) gleam. **2.** appear, seem: **wie es scheint** as it seems; **es scheint mir** it seems to me; **er scheint nicht zu wollen**; **mir scheint, er will nicht** he doesn't seem to want to.

'**Schein|firma** f dummy firm. **~friede** m hollow peace. **~geschäft** n fictitious transaction.

'**scheinheilig** adj F contp. hypocritical. '**Scheinheiligkeit** f (-; no pl) hypocrisy. '**Scheintod** m suspended animation. '**scheintot** adj seemingly dead.

'**Scheinwerfer** m (-s; -) floodlight, searchlight, mot. headlight, film: klieg light, thea. (a. **~licht** n) spotlight.

Scheiß... [ʃaıs-] V bloody, sl. fucking. '**Scheißdreck** m → **Scheiße** 2.

'**Scheiße** f (-; no pl) V a. fig. shit, crap: fig. **in der ~ sitzen** be in the shit; **~!** shit!; **~ bauen** make a foul-up; **große ~ sein** be a load of crap. '**scheißen** v/i (schiß, geschissen, h) V shit, crap: **scheiß drauf!** to hell with it!, fuck it!

'**Scheißer** m (-s; -) V **1.** kleiner **~** little shit. **2.** a. '**Scheißkerl** m bastard.

Scheit [ʃaıt] n (-[e]s; -e) piece of wood, log.

Scheitel ['ʃaıtəl] m (-s; -) parting: **vom ~ bis zur Sohle** from top to toe.

scheiteln ['ʃaıtəln] v/t (h) (**sich**) **das Haar ~** part one's hair.

'**Scheitelpunkt** m Å vertex, astr. zenith. **Scheiterhaufen** ['ʃaıtər-] m (funeral) pyre, hist. (**auf dem ~** at the) stake.

scheitern ['ʃaıtərn] v/i (sn) (**an dat**) fail (because of), negotiations: a. break down, sports: be stopped (by): **daran ist er gescheitert** that was his undoing. '**Scheitern** n (-s) failure, breakdown.

Schelle ['ʃɛlə] f (-; -n) **1.** (little) bell. **2.** ⚙ clamp, clip.

schellen ['ʃɛlən] dial. → **klingeln** 1.

'**Schellfisch** m haddock.

Schelm [ʃɛlm] m (-[e]s; -e) rogue.

'**schelmisch** adj roguish, impish.

schelten ['ʃɛltən] v/t (schalt, gescholten, h) scold, chide (a. v/i).

Schema ['ʃeːma] n (-s; -s, -ta) **1.** pattern, system: **nach e-m ~** schematically; F **nach ~ F** by rote. **2.** diagram, scheme.

schematisch [ʃeˈmaːtıʃ] adj schematic, systematic, contr. mechanical.

schematisieren [ʃematiˈziːrən] v/t (h) schematize.

Schemel ['ʃeːməl] m (-s; -) (foot)stool.

Schemen ['ʃeːmən] n (-s; -) phantom.

'**schemenhaft** adj shadowy.

Schenke ['ʃɛŋkə] f (-; -n) tavern.

Schenkel ['ʃɛŋkəl] m (-s; -) **1.** anat. a) thigh, b) shank. **2.** Å side, leg.

schenken ['ʃɛŋkən] v/t (h) a) give (as a present), a. 🏛 donate, b) pour: **j-m et. ~** give s.o. s.th. (as a present) (**zum Geburtstag** for his etc birthday); fig. **sich et. ~** skip s.th., give s.th. a miss; F **geschenkt!** forget it!; → **Aufmerksamkeit** 1, **Gehör** 2, **Glaube** etc.

'**Schenkung** f (-; -en) donation.

'**Schenkungsurkunde** f deed of donation.

scheppern ['ʃɛpərn] v/i (h) F rattle.

Scherbe ['ʃɛrbə] f (-; -n) broken piece, fragment.

Schere ['ʃeːrə] f (-; -n) **1.** (e-e **~** a pair of) scissors (✂ shears). **2.** zo. pincer. **3.** sports: scissors.

scheren ['ʃeːrən] **I** v/t (schor, geschoren, h) trim, cut (a. hair), shear (sheep), clip (hedge). **II** F **sich nicht ~ um** not to care about; **sich nach Hause (ins Bett) ~** go home (to bed); **scher dich!** beat it!

'**Scherenschnitt** m silhouette.

Schere'rei f (-; -en) F trouble.

Scherflein ['ʃɛrflaɪn] n (-s; -) **sein ~ beitragen** give one's mite, a. do one's bit.

Scherz [ʃɛrts] m (-es; -e) joke: (**s-n**) ~ **treiben mit** make fun of; **im ~, zum ~** as a joke, for fun; **~ beiseite** joking apart.

scherzen ['ʃɛrtsən] v/i (h) joke: **damit ist nicht zu ~** that's not to be trifled with.

'**scherzhaft** adj joking, humorous.

scheu [ʃɔy] adj shy, timid: **~ machen** frighten (horse etc); **Scheu** f (-; no pl) a) shyness, timidity, b) awe.

scheuchen ['ʃɔyçən] v/t (h) chase.

scheuen ['ʃɔyən] I v/i horse etc: shy, take fright (**vor** dat at). II v/t shun, avoid, shy away from: **~ Licht** 1. spare no expense; → **Licht** 1. III **sich ~, et. zu tun** be afraid of (or shrink from) doing s.th.; **sich nicht ~ zu** inf not to be afraid to inf, b.s. have the nerve to inf.

'**Scheuerbürste** f scrubbing brush.

'**Scheuerlappen** m floor cloth.

scheuern ['ʃɔyərn] (h) I v/t 1. scour, scrub. 2. chafe. 3. F **j-m e-e ~** slap s.o.('s face). II v/i 4. chafe.

'**Scheuklappe** f a. fig. blinker.

Scheune ['ʃɔynə] f (-; -n) barn.

Scheusal ['ʃɔyzaːl] n (-s; -e) monster (a. fig.), F beast: **kleines ~** little horror.

scheußlich ['ʃɔyslɪç] adj horrible (a. F fig.), a. hideous, revolting: F **~es Wetter** filthy weather; **~ kalt** terribly cold.

Schi(...) [ʃiː] → **Ski**(...).

Schicht [ʃɪçt] f (-; -en) **1.** layer, a. coat(ing), geol. stratum, bed, phot. emulsion. **2.** class, pl a. social strata: **breite ~en** large sections (of the population). **3.** shift: **~ arbeiten** do shift work.

'**Schichtarbeit** f shift work.

'**Schichtarbeiter**(in f) m shift worker.

schichten ['ʃɪçtən] v/t (h) pile up, stack.

'**Schichtunterricht** m teaching in shifts.

'**Schichtwechsel** m change of shift.

'**schichtweise** adv **1.** in layers. **2.** work etc in shifts.

schick [ʃɪk] adj **1.** a) smart, chic, stylish, b) posh, c) trendy. **2.** F great, super.

Schick m (-[e]s; no pl) chic, stylishness.

schicken ['ʃɪkən] (h) I v/t **1.** send (**nach, zu** to). II **sich ~ 2.** befit (**für j-n** s.o.): **es schickt sich nicht!** that is not the done thing! **3. sich ~ in** can resign o.s. to.

Schickeria [ʃɪkəˈriːa] f (-; no pl) the chic set, the trendies. **Schickimicki** [ˈʃɪkiˈmɪki] m (-s; -s) F trendy.

'**schicklich** adj proper, fitting.

Schicksal [ˈʃɪksaːl] n (-s; -e) fate, destiny, a. lot: **das ~ herausfordern** tempt fate. '**schicksalhaft** adj fateful.

'**Schicksals|frage** f vital question. **~gefährte** m, **~genosse** m companion in distress. **~schlag** m (bad) blow.

'**Schiebedach** n mot. sliding roof, sunroof. '**Schiebefenster** n sliding (or sash) window.

schieben [ˈʃiːbən] (schob, geschoben, h) I v/t **1.** a) push, b) slip, put (**in** acc into): **sich durch die Menge ~** push one's way through the crowd; → **Bank¹**. II v/i **2.** push. **3.** F **~ mit** traffic in.

'**Schieber** m (-s; -) **1.** ⚙ a) slide, b) gate, c) bar, bolt. **2.** F racketeer.

'**Schiebesitz** m sliding seat.

'**Schiebetür** f sliding door.

'**Schiebung** f (-; -en) F put-up job, fix.

'**schied** [ʃiːt] pret of **scheiden**.

Schiedsgericht [ˈʃiːts-] n court of arbitration, sports etc: jury.

'**Schiedsrichter** m arbitrator, at competitions: judge, pl jury, sports: umpire, referee: **als ~ fungieren** → **schiedsrichtern**.

'**schiedsrichterlich** adj and adv sports: of (or by) the umpire (or referee).

'**schiedsrichtern** v/i (h) referee, umpire.

'**Schiedsspruch** m award, arbitration.

schief [ʃiːf] I adj **1.** oblique, a. slanting, lop-sided: **~e Absätze** worn-down heels; **~e Ebene** inclined plane; **der ~e Turm von Pisa** the Leaning Tower of Pisa; fig. **~es Lächeln** wry smile. **2.** fig. false, wrong, distorted, warped: → **Bahn** 1, **Licht** 1. II adv **3.** obliquely, aslant, at an angle: F fig. **j-n ~ ansehen** look askance at s.o.

Schiefer [ˈʃiːfər] m (-s; -) slate. **~dach** n slate roof. **~platte** f, **~tafel** f slate.

'**schiefgehen** v/i (irr, sep, -ge-, sn) F go wrong.

'**schieflachen: sich ~** (sep, -ge-, h) F laugh one's head off.

schielen [ˈʃiːlən] v/i (h) **1.** (have a) squint, be cross-eyed: **auf dem rechten Auge ~** have a squint in one's right eye. **2.** F peer: **~ auf** (acc) (or **nach**) a) steal a glance at, b) have an eye on.

schien [ʃiːn] pret of **scheinen**.

'**Schienbein** n anat. shin(bone), tibia. **~schützer** m sports: shin-guard.

Schiene ['ʃiːnə] f (-; -n) **1.** 🚆 etc rail, pl a. track. **2.** ⊙ bar. **3.** ⚕ splint.

schienen ['ʃiːnən] v/t (h) ⚕ put in a splint (or in splints).

'**Schienen|bus** m rail bus. **~fahrzeug** n rail vehicle. **~netz** n railway (Am. railroad) system. **~strang** m track, railway line. **~verkehr** m rail traffic.

schier [ʃiːr] **I** adj sheer, pure. **II** adv almost, nearly.

Schierling ['ʃiːrlɪŋ] m (-s; -e) ♣ hemlock.

'**Schießbefehl** m order to fire.

'**Schießbude** f shooting gallery.

schießen ['ʃiːsən] (schoß, geschossen) **I** v/i **1.** (h) (**auf** acc at) shoot (a. sports), fire: **gut ~** be a good shot; **ein Tor ~** score (a goal); F fig. **~ Sie los!** fire away!; → **Pistole. 2.** (sn) shoot (**durch** through): **ein Gedanke schoß durch m-n Kopf** a thought flashed through my mind. **3.** (sn) shoot (or gush) (**aus** from or out of). **4.** (sn) shoot up: → **Kraut** 1, **Pilz. 5.** (h) sl. shoot, mainline. **II** v/t (h) **6.** shoot (a. sports or phot.).

'**Schießen** n (-s) a) shooting, b) shooting match: F **es (er) ist zum ~** it (he) is a scream. **Schieße'rei** f (-; -en) **1.** gunfight. **2.** (incessant) shooting.

'**Schieß|hund** m F **aufpassen wie ein ~** watch like a hawk. **~platz** m (shooting) range. **~pulver** n gunpowder. **~scharte** f embrasure. **~scheibe** f target. **~stand** m shooting range, ⚔ rifle range.

'**schießwütig** [-vy:tɪç] adj trigger-happy.

Schiff [ʃɪf] n (-[e]s; -e) **1.** (**auf dem ~** on board) ship. **2.** △ a) nave, b) aisle.

'**Schiffahrt** f (-; no pl) navigation.

'**Schiffahrtslinie** f shipping line.

'**Schiffahrtsweg** m shipping route.

'**schiffbar** adj navigable.

'**Schiffbau** m (-[e]s; no pl) shipbuilding.

'**Schiffbruch** m shipwreck: **~ erleiden** fig. fail. '**Schiffbrüchige** m, f (-n; -n) shipwrecked person.

'**Schiffchen** n (-s; -) **1.** little ship (or boat). **2.** ⚔ forage cap.

'**Schiffer** m (-s; -) a) bargee, Am. bargeman, b) (ship's) captain, F skipper.

'**Schifferkla,vier** n accordion.

'**Schifferknoten** m sailor's knot.

'**Schiffsarzt** m ship's doctor.

'**Schiffsbesatzung** f (ship's) crew.

'**Schiffschaukel** f swingboat.

'**Schiffs|eigner** m (-s; -) shipowner.

~junge m ship's boy. **~koch** m ship's cook. **~küche** f galley. **~ladung** f a) shipload, b) cargo, freight. **~rumpf** m hull. **~schraube** f screw. **~verkehr** m shipping. **~werft** f shipyard.

Schikane [ʃiˈkaːnə] f (-; -n) harassment, pl a. persecution, mot. racing: chicane: F **mit allen ~n** with all the trimmings.

schikanieren [ʃikaˈniːrən] v/t (h) harass.

schikanös [ʃikaˈnøːs] adj harassing.

Schild[1] [ʃɪlt] m (-[e]s; -e) **1.** ⚔, a. ⊙ shield: fig. et. **im ~e führen** be up to s.th. **2.** peak, visor.

Schild[2] n (-[e]s; -er) a) sign, a. road (or street) sign, b) nameplate, c) label, tag.

'**Schildbürger** m Gothamite, w.s. simpleton. **~streich** m folly.

'**Schilddrüse** f anat. thyroid gland.

schildern ['ʃɪldərn] v/t (h) describe, a. relate, a. outline. '**Schilderung** f (-; -en) description, account.

'**Schilderwald** m F jungle of road signs.

'**Schildkröte** f a) tortoise, b) turtle.

Schildpatt ['ʃɪltpat] n (-[e]s; no pl) tortoiseshell.

Schilf [ʃɪlf] n (-[e]s; -e) ♣ **1.** reed. **2.** reeds. '**schilfig** adj reedy. '**Schilfmatte** f rush mat. '**Schilfrohr** n ♣ reed.

schillern ['ʃɪlərn] v/i (h) shine in various colo(u)rs, shimmer, sparkle. '**schillernd** adj **1.** iridescent, opalescent. **2.** fig. (dazzling but) dubious.

Schimmel[1] ['ʃɪməl] m (-s; -) white horse. **Schimmel**[2] m (-s; no pl) mo(u)ld, mildew. '**schimm(e)lig** adj mo(u)ldy. '**schimmeln** v/i (h) go mo(u)ldy.

'**Schimmelpilz** m mo(u)ld.

Schimmer ['ʃɪmər] m (-s; no pl) gleam, glimmer (a. fig.): F **k-n (blassen) ~ haben** not to have the foggiest (idea). '**schimmern** v/i (h) gleam, glisten.

Schimpanse [ʃɪmˈpanzə] m (-n; -n) zo. chimpanzee.

Schimpf [ʃɪmpf] m **mit ~ und Schande** ignominiously.

schimpfen ['ʃɪmpfən] (h) **I** v/i **1.** scold (**mit** j-m s.o.): **~ auf** (acc) complain about, rail at. **II** v/t **2.** scold. **3.** j-n e-n **Lügner** etc **~** call s.o. a liar etc.

'**Schimpfname** m abusive name.

'**Schimpfwort** n swearword, pl abuse.

Schindel ['ʃɪndəl] f (-; -n) shingle.

schinden ['ʃɪndən] v/t (schindete, geschunden, h) **1.** drive s.o. hard, a. maltreat: **sich ~** slave away. **2.** F wangle: **Eindruck ~ (wollen)** try to impress, show off; **Zeit ~** play for time.

'**Schinder** m (-s; -) slave-driver.

Schinde'rei f (-; -en) (real) grind.

'**Schindluder** n F **~ treiben mit** play fast and loose with.

Schinken ['ʃɪŋkən] m (-s; -) **1.** gastr. ham. **2.** F a) (great) daub, b) fat tome, c) slushy film. **~speck** m bacon.

Schippe ['ʃɪpə] f (-; -n) shovel: F **j-n auf die ~ nehmen** pull s.o.'s leg.

schippen ['ʃɪpən] v/t, v/i (h) shovel.

Schirm [ʃɪrm] m (-[e]s; -e) **1.** a) umbrella, b) parasol, c) (lamp)shade, d) shield, screen, e) peak. **2.** screen. **3.** parachute. **4.** ♀ pileus. **5.** fig. protection.

schirmen ['ʃɪrmən] v/t (h) shield.

'**Schirmherr**(**in** f m) patron(ess).

'**Schirmherrschaft** f patronage: **unter der ~ von ...** under the auspices of ...

'**Schirmmütze** f peaked cap.

'**Schirmständer** m umbrella stand.

schiß [ʃɪs] pret of **scheißen**.

Schiß m F **~ haben** be scared stiff; **~ bekommen** get the jitters (V shits).

schizophren [ʃitso'fre:n] adj, **Schizo'phrene** m, f (-n; -n) schizophrenic. **Schizophrenie** [ʃitsofre'ni:] f (-; -n) schizophrenia.

Schlacht [ʃlaxt] f (-; -en) battle (**bei** of): **e-e ~ liefern** give battle (dat to).

'**schlachten** v/t (h) slaughter, kill.

'**Schlachtenbummler** m sports: fan, supporter.

Schlächter ['ʃlɛçtər] m (-s; -) butcher.

Schlächte'rei f (-; -en) butcher's shop.

'**Schlacht|feld** n battlefield. **~hof** m slaughterhouse, abattoir. **~plan** m a. F fig. plan of action. **~schiff** n battleship.

'**Schlachtung** f (-; -en) slaughter(ing).

'**Schlachtvieh** n meat stock.

Schlacke ['ʃlakə] f (-; -n) **1.** a) metall. dross, slag (a. geol.), b) cinders. **2.** pl ♂ a) waste products, b) roughage.

schlackern ['ʃlakərn] v/i (h) F wobble, dress etc: flap, knees: tremble: fig. **mit den Ohren ~** be flabbergasted.

Schlaf [ʃla:f] m (-[e]s; no pl) sleep: **e-n festen (leichten) ~ haben** be a sound (light) sleeper; F **das kann ich im ~!** I can do that blindfold.

'**Schlafanzug** m pyjamas, Am. pajamas.

Schläfchen ['ʃlɛːfçən] n (-s; -) nap.

'**Schlafcouch** f studio couch, sofa bed.

Schläfe ['ʃlɛːfə] f (-; -n) anat. temple.

schlafen ['ʃla:fən] v/i (schlief, geschlafen, h) a. F fig. a) sleep, b) be asleep: **tief** (or **fest**) **~** be sound asleep; **~ gehen** go to bed; **im Hotel ~** stay at a hotel; **~ Sie darüber!** sleep on it!

'**Schlafenszeit** f bedtime.

Schläfer ['ʃlɛːfər] m (-s; -), '**Schläferin** f (-; -nen) sleeper.

schlaff [ʃlaf] adj a) slack (rope, sail), b) flabby (skin, muscles, etc), c) limp (body etc, a. handshake), d) F listless, lame: **~er Typ** lame fellow.

'**Schlaffheit** f (-; no pl) slackness, flabbiness, limpness, F lameness.

'**Schlaf|gelegenheit** f sleeping accommodation. **~krankheit** f sleeping sickness. **~lied** n lullaby.

'**schlaflos** adj sleepless: **~ liegen** lie awake; **~e Nächte** sleepless nights.

'**Schlaflosigkeit** f (-; no pl) insomnia.

'**Schlafmittel** n soporific (drug).

'**Schlafmütze** f F fig. sleepyhead.

schläfrig ['ʃlɛːfrɪç] adj sleepy, drowsy.

'**Schläfrigkeit** f (-; no pl) sleepiness.

'**Schlaf|rock** m dressing gown. **~saal** m dormitory. **~sack** m sleeping bag. **~stadt** f dormitory town. **~störungen** pl disturbed sleep. **~ta,blette** f sleeping pill. **~trunk** m F nightcap.

'**schlaftrunken** adj drowsy.

'**Schlafwagen** m 🚃 sleeping car, sleeper.

'**schlafwandeln** v/i (insep, ge-, h or sn) sleepwalk. '**Schlafwandler** [-vandlər] m (-s; -) sleepwalker, somnambulist.

'**Schlafzimmer** n bedroom. '**Schlafzimmerblick** m humor. bedroom eyes.

Schlag [ʃla:k] m (-[e]s; e) **1.** a) blow (a. fig.), stroke (a. punch), b) slap, c) thump, thud: **j-m e-n ~ versetzen** deal s.o. a blow, fig. hit s.o. hard; **~ ins Gesicht** a. fig. slap in the face; **das war ein ~ für ihn** that was a blow to him; **ein ~ ins Wasser** a flop; **~ auf ~** in rapid succession; **auf einen ~** at a (or one) stroke, in one go; **mit einem ~** abruptly. **2.** ⚔ strike. **3.** ⚙ impact, a. ⚡ shock. **4.** rowing, swimming: stroke, golf, tennis: shot. **5.** stroke (of lightning). **6.** beat (of heart, pulse, etc), stroke (of clock etc). **7.** F stroke: **ich dachte, mich trifft der ~!** I was floored! **8.** F helping. **9.** door (of carriage etc). **10.**

race, sort, breed: **Leute s-s ~es** men of his stamp (*contp.* his sort).

'**Schlag|abtausch** *m* boxing: exchange of punches, *fig.* crossing of swords. **~ader** *f* artery. **~anfall** *m* 🟰 stroke.

'**schlagartig** *adj* abrupt.

'**Schlagbaum** *m* turnpike.

'**Schlagbohrer** *m* ✪ percussion drill.

'**Schlagbolzen** *m* 🗡 striking pin.

schlagen ['ʃlaːgən] (schlug, geschlagen) **I** *v/t* (h) **1.** strike, hit, beat, punch, slap: **e-n Nagel in die Wand ~** drive a nail into the wall; **die Trommel ~** beat the drum; **j-m et. aus der Hand ~** knock s.th. from s.o.'s hand; **j-n zu Boden ~** knock s.o. down; → **Alarm, Brücke** 1, **Flucht**[1], **geschlagen. 2.** whip (*cream*), beat (*eggs etc*): **Eier in die Pfanne ~** break eggs into the frying pan. **3.** fell (*tree*), cut (*wood*). **4.** *fig.* beat (*in dat* at), *a.* defeat: **sich geschlagen geben** admit defeat, give up. **II** *v/i* **5.** (h) strike, hit: **nach j-m ~** hit out at s.o.; **um sich ~** lash out. **6.** (sn) **~ an** (*acc*) (*or* **gegen**) beat against; **mit dem Kopf ~ an** (*acc*) strike (*or* bump) one's head against; **die Nachricht ist mir auf den Magen geschlagen** the news has affected my stomach; **Flammen schlugen aus dem Dach** flames leapt out of the roof; → **Art** 4, **Fach** 2 *etc.* **7.** (h) heart, pulse: beat, throb, *clock*: strike. **8.** (h) bird: sing. **III** *v/i* **~ sich ~** (h) **9.** (have a) fight: **sich um et. ~** fight over s.th.; **sich gut ~** give a good account of o.s. **10.** **sich auf j-s Seite ~** side with s.o., *a.* go over to s.o.; **die Erkältung hat sich mir auf den Magen geschlagen** the cold has affected my stomach.

'**schlagend** *adj* **1.** *fig.* convincing, conclusive (*evidence*). **2.** → **Wetter** 2.

Schlager ['ʃlaːgər] *m* (-s; -) **1.** *a.* pop-song, b) hit (tune). **2.** *fig.* hit, sensation, ✝ (sales) hit, moneymaker.

Schläger ['ʃlɛːgər] *m* (-s; -) **1.** tough, *boxing etc*: slugger. **2.** *sports*: a) batsman, b) (cricket, baseball, *etc*) bat, (tennis) racket, (golf) club, (hockey) stick. **Schläge'rei** *f* (-; -en) brawl, F punch-up: **allgemeine ~** F free-for-all.

'**Schlagerfestival** *n* pop festival.

'**Schlagermu,sik** *f* pop music.

'**Schlagersänger(in** *f*) *m* pop singer.

'**schlagfertig** *adj* quick-witted: **~ sein** be

quick at repartee. '**Schlagfertigkeit** *f* (-; *no pl*) quick-wittedness, ready wit.

'**Schlag|instru,ment** *n* ♪ percussion instrument. **~kraft** *f* (-; *no pl*) **1.** *boxing or fig.* punch. **2.** 🗡 combat effectiveness. **2kräftig** *adj* **1.** powerful. **2.** convincing, conclusive. **~licht** *n* (-[e]s; -er) paint. (*a. fig.* **ein ~ werfen auf** [*acc*]) highlight. **~loch** *n* pothole. **~mann** *m* (-[e]s; ˝er) rowing: stroke. **~obers** *n* (-; *no pl*) Austrian, **~rahm** *m* → **Schlagsahne. ~ring** *m* **1.** knuckleduster. **2.** ♪ plectrum, F pick. **~sahne** *f* whipped cream. **~seite** *f* ⚓ list: **~ haben** be listing, F *fig.* be halfseas-over. **~stock** *m* **1.** truncheon, riot stick. **2.** ♪ drumstick. **~wechsel** *m* boxing: exchange of blows. **~werk** *n* striking mechanism.

'**Schlagwort** *n* **1.** catchword, slogan, *pl contp.* platitudes. **2.** (*pl* ˝er) catchword. **~kata,log** *m* subject catalog(ue Br.).

'**Schlagzeile** *f* headline: **~n machen, in die ~n geraten** make the headlines.

'**Schlagzeug** *n* ♪ percussion, drums. '**Schlagzeuger** [-tsɔʏɡər] *m* (-s; -) ♪ percussionist, drummer.

schlaksig ['ʃlaːksɪç] *adj* gangling, lanky.

Schlamassel [ʃlaˈmasəl] *m, n* (-s; -) F mess.

Schlamm [ʃlam] *m* (-[e]s; -e, ˝e) mud.

'**Schlammbad** *n* 🟰 mud bath.

'**schlammig** *adj* muddy.

'**Schlammpackung** *f* 🟰 mud pack.

Schlampe ['ʃlampə] *f* (-; -n) F slut.

'**schlampen** *v/i* (h) F do a sloppy job.

'**Schlamper** *m* (-s; -) F sloven, slouch.

Schlampe'rei *f* (-; -en) F a) sloppiness, b) mess, sloppy work.

'**schlampig** *adj* F slovenly, sloppy.

schlang [ʃlaŋ] *pret of* **schlingen**[1] *and* [2].

Schlange ['ʃlaŋə] *f* (-; -n) **1.** *zo.* snake: *fig.* **falsche ~** snake in the grass. **2.** queue, *Am.* line (*of people, cars*): F **~ stehen** (**nach**) für) stand in a queue (*Am.* in line), queue up, *Am.* line up. **3.** ✪ coil.

schlängeln ['ʃlɛŋəln] **sich ~** (h) wriggle, *fig. road etc*: wind, *river*: *a.* meander; **sich ~ durch** worm one's way through.

'**Schlangen|biß** *m* snakebite. **~gift** *n* snake poison. **~haut** *f*, **~leder** *n* snakeskin. **~linie** *f* wavy line: **in ~n fahren** zigzag (along the road).

schlank [ʃlaŋk] *adj* slender, slim: *auf die ~e Linie achten* watch one's weight.

'**Schlankheit** *f* (-; *no pl*) slimness.

'**Schlankheitskur** *f* slimming (diet): *e-e ~ machen* be slimming.

schlapp [ʃlap] *adj* **1.** → *schlaff*. **2.** worn-out, listless.

'**Schlappe** *f* (-; -n) a) setback, b) beating.

'**schlappmachen** *v/i* (*sep*, -ge-, h) F wilt.

'**Schlappschwanz** *m* F softie, sissy.

Schlaraffenland [ʃla'rafən-] *n* (-[e]s; *no pl*) Cockaigne.

schlau [ʃlau] *adj* a) clever, smart, b) sly, cunning, crafty: F *~e Bücher* clever books; *ich werde nicht ~ daraus* I can't make head or tail of it.

Schlauberger ['ʃlauˌbɛrɡər] *m* (-s; -) F smartie.

Schlauch [ʃlaux] *m* (-[e]s; ⁓e) **1.** flexible tube, (water) hose. **2.** *mot. etc* inner tube. **3.** F hard slog. **4.** F (*room*) tunnel.

'**Schlauchboot** *n* rubber dinghy.

schlauchen ['ʃlauxən] (h) F **I** *v/t j-n ~* take it out of s.o., *a.* go hard with s.o. **II** *v/i das schlaucht!* that's tough going!

Schläue ['ʃlɔyə] *f* → *Schlauheit*.

Schlaufe ['ʃlaufə] *f* (-; -n) loop.

'**Schlauheit** *f* (-; *no pl*) a) cleverness, smartness, b) slyness, cunning.

schlecht [ʃlɛçt] **I** *adj* bad, poor (*eyes, health, memory, etc*), *a.* wicked: *nicht ~!* not bad!; *~e Laune* bad mood; *~e Zeiten* bad (*or* hard) times; *~ sein* in (*dat*) be poor at; *~ werden* meat etc: go bad, go off; *~er werden* get worse, deteriorate; *mir ist ~* I feel sick; F *es kann e-m ~ dabei werden!* it's enough to make you sick!; → *Dienst* 1. **II** *adv* bad(ly): *~ aussehen* look bad, *a.* look ill; *~ und recht* after a fashion; *~ beraten sein* be ill-advised; *~ reden von* speak ill of; *es steht ~ um ihn* he's in a bad way; *~ daran sein* be badly off; *es bekam ihm ~* food etc: it didn't agree with him, *fig.* it did him no good; *er kann es sich ~ leisten zu inf* he can ill afford to *inf*; *heute geht es ~* it's awkward today; *ich kann ~ ablehnen* I can't very well refuse; *ich staunte nicht ~* I wasn't half surprised.

'**schlechtgelaunt** *adj* bad-tempered.

'**schlechthin** *adv* **1.** absolutely. **2.** as such.

'**Schlechtigkeit** *f* (-; *no pl*) badness, wickedness, baseness.

'**schlechtmachen** *v/t* (*sep*, -ge-, h) run *s.o.*, *s.th.* down, knock.

Schlecht'wetter|front *f* bad weather front. *~peri,ode* *f* spell of bad weather.

Schlehe ['ʃleːə] *f* (-; -n) ⚘ sloe.

schleichen ['ʃlaiçən] *v/i* (schlich, geschlichen, sn) creep, sneak, crawl (*a. car, time*): *auf den Zehenspitzen ~* tiptoe; *ums Haus ~* prowl around the house; *dial. schleich dich! sl.* beat it! '**schleichend** *adj* lingering (*illness*), slow (*poison etc*), creeping (*inflation*).

'**Schleich|handel** *m* illicit trade. *~weg* *m* secret path: *fig. auf ~en* by secret means, surreptitiously. *~werbung* *f* surreptitious advertising, F plugging.

Schleier ['ʃlaiər] *m* (-s; -) **1.** *a. fig.* veil. **2.** haze, *phot.* fog. *~eule* *f zo.* barn owl.

'**schleierhaft** *adj* mysterious: *das ist mir ~!* that's a mystery to me!

Schleife ['ʃlaifə] *f* (-; -n) **1.** bow, *a.* ribbon. **2.** *a.* ⚡, ⊙ loop.

schleifen¹ ['ʃlaifən] *v/t* (schliff, geschliffen, h) **1.** grind, whet. **2.** ⊙ smooth, sand (*wood*), cut (*glass, diamond*). **3.** ✕ F drill *s.o.* hard.

schleifen² (h) **I** *v/t* drag (along) (*a. fig. s.o.*), trail (*skirt etc*). **II** *v/i ~ lassen* drag; *die Kupplung ~ lassen* let the clutch slip.

'**Schleifer** *m* (-s; -) **1.** ⊙ grinder, *a.* cutter. **2.** ✕ F martinet.

'**Schleif|lackausführung** *f* egg-shell finish. *~ma,schine* *f* grinding machine. *~mittel* *n* abrasive. *~pa,pier* *n* emery paper. *~scheibe* *f* grinding wheel. *~stein* *m* a) whetstone, b) grindstone.

Schleim [ʃlaim] *m* (-[e]s; -e) slime, ⚘, *physiol.* mucus, phlegm. *~beutel* *m anat.* bursa. *~drüse* *f* mucous gland. *~haut* *f* mucous membrane.

'**schleimig** *adj* slimy (*a. fig. contp.*).

'**schleimlösend** *adj* expectorant.

'**Schleimsuppe** *f* gruel.

schlemmen ['ʃlɛmən] *v/i* (h) feast.

'**Schlemmer** *m* (-s; -) gormandizer.

Schlemme'rei *f* (-; *no pl*) feasting.

schlendern ['ʃlɛndərn] *v/i* (sn) stroll.

Schlendrian ['ʃlɛndriaːn] *m* (-[e]s; *no pl*) F *contp.* a) dawdling, b) rut.

Schlenker ['ʃlɛŋkər] *m* (-s; -) (*a. e-n ~ machen*) F swerve. '**schlenkern** *v/t, v/i*

(h) swing, dangle (*mit den Armen* one's arms).

schlenzen ['ʃlɛntsən] *v/t*, *v/i* (h) scoop.

Schlepp [ʃlɛp] *m in ~ nehmen* (*im ~ haben*) *a. fig.* take (have) in tow.

'**Schleppdampfer** *m* tug.

Schleppe ['ʃlɛpə] *f* (-; -n) train, trail. '**schleppen** (h) **I** *v/t a.* drag (*a. fig. s.o.*), ⚓, ✈, *mot.* tow, b) carry, F tote: F (*Kunden*) ~ tout. **II** *sich ~ a*) drag on, b) drag *o.s.* (along), limp (along). '**schleppend** *adj* sluggish, slow (*a.* ♥), labo(u)red, slow, drawling (*speech*). '**Schlepper** *m* (-s; -) **1.** ⚓ tug. **2.** *mot.* tractor. **3.** F tout.

'**Schlepp|flugzeug** *n* towplane. ~**kahn** *m* lighter, barge (in tow). ~**lift** *m* ski tow. ~**netz** *n* dragnet. ~**schiff** *n* tug. ~**tau** *n* tow-rope, tow-line: F *fig. j-n ins ~ nehmen* take s.o. in tow. ~**zug** *m* **1.** ⚓ train of barges. **2.** semitrailer truck.

Schleuder ['ʃlɔydər] *f* (-; -n) **1.** catapult (*a.* ✈), sling, *Am.* slingshot. **2.** ⊙ a) → **Zentrifuge**, b) spin dryer.

'**Schleudergefahr** *f* slippery road.

schleudern ['ʃlɔydərn] (h) **I** *v/t* **1.** fling, hurl, sling, ✈ catapult. **2.** ⊙ centrifuge, strain (*honey*), spin-dry (*laundry*). **II** *v/i* (*a.* sn) *mot.* skid, (*a.* **ins Schleudern geraten**) go into a skid (*a. fig.*).

'**Schleuder|preis** *m* knockdown price. ~**sitz** *m* ✈ ejector seat, F *fig.* hot seat. ~**ware** *f* cut-price article(s).

schleunig ['ʃlɔynɪç] **I** *adj* quick, prompt, *a.* hasty. **II** *adv a.* '**schleunigst** quickly, promptly, *a.* hastily.

Schleuse ['ʃlɔyzə] *f* (-; -n) sluice, floodgate (*a. fig.*), (canal) lock. '**schleusen** *v/t* (h) **1.** ⚓ lock. **2.** *fig.* a) channel, b) steer, *a.* smuggle (*s.o.*).

'**Schleusentor** *n* floodgate.

schlich [ʃlɪç] *pret of* **schleichen**.

Schliche ['ʃlɪçə] *pl* tricks: *j-m auf die ~ kommen* find s.o. out.

schlicht [ʃlɪçt] **I** *adj* simple, plain. **II** *adv ~ (und einfach)* (quite) simply.

schlichten ['ʃlɪçtən] **I** *v/t* settle (*dispute*). **II** *v/i* mediate (*zwischen* between).

'**Schlichter** *m* (-s; -) mediator.

'**Schlichtheit** *f* (-; *no pl*) simplicity, plainness.

'**Schlichtung** *f* (-; -en) a) settlement, b) arbitration.

'**Schlichtungs|ausschuß** *m* arbitration

committee. ~**versuch** *m* attempt at conciliation.

Schlick [ʃlɪk] *m* (-[e]s; -e) sludge, silt.

schlief [ʃliːf] *pret of* **schlafen.**

Schliere ['ʃliːrə] *f* (-; -n) streak.

Schließe ['ʃliːsə] *f* (-; -n) fastening, clasp.

schließen ['ʃliːsən] (schloß, geschlossen, h) **I** *v/t* **1.** close (*a.* ⚡ *circuit*), shut, *a.* shut down (*factory etc*): → **Lücke. 2.** enter into *an alliance etc*, reach, come to *a settlement*: → **Ehe, Freundschaft, Frieden** *etc.* **3.** close, conclude, end (*debate etc*), *a.* wind up (*letter, speech* **mit den Worten** by saying). **II** *v/i* **4.** shut, close, *factory etc*: *a.* shut down. **5.** (come to a) close: *er schloß mit den Worten* he wound up by saying. **6.** conclude (*aus* from): *von sich auf andere ~* judge others by *o.s.*; *auf et. ~ lassen* suggest (*or* point to) s.th. **III** *sich ~* close, shut; → **Kreis 1.**

'**Schließfach** *n* **1.** safe deposit box. **2.** 🏤 (left-luggage) locker. **3.** → **Postfach.**

'**schließlich** *adv* a) finally, b) eventually, c) after all.

'**Schließmuskel** *m anat.* sphincter.

'**Schließung** *f* (-; -en) **1.** closing, shutting, shutdown, closure (*of factory etc*). **2.** contraction (*of marriage etc*).

schliff [ʃlɪf] *pret of* **schleifen¹.**

Schliff *m* (-[e]s; -e) **1.** *no pl* grinding, *a.* sharpening. **2.** cut (*of glass etc*). **3.** *fig.* polish, refinement: *den letzten ~ geben* put the finishing touches (*dat* to).

schlimm [ʃlɪm] *adj* bad, F *a.* nasty (*wound etc*): F ~**er Finger** (*Hals*) sore finger (throat); *das ist e-e ~e Sache* that's a bad business; *es sieht ~ aus* it looks bad; *das ist halb so ~!* a) it's not as bad as all that!, b) it doesn't matter!, never mind!; F *ist es ~, wenn ...?* would you mind terribly if ...?; ~**er machen** (*werden*) → **verschlimmern**; *es wird immer ~er* things are going from bad to worse; *um so ~er* so much the worse; *am ~sten* worst of all; *auf das Schlimmste gefaßt sein* be prepared for the worst; *es gibt Schlimmeres* things could be worse.

'**schlimmstenfalls** *adv* if the worst comes to the worst.

Schlinge ['ʃlɪŋə] *f* (-; -n) loop, noose (*a. fig.*), *a.* ✚ sling, *hunt.* snare (*a. fig.*): *fig. sich aus der ~ ziehen* wriggle out of it.

Schlingel ['ʃlɪŋəl] *m* (-s; -) rascal.
schlingen[1] ['ʃlɪŋən] (schlang, geschlungen, h) (**um** around) **I** *v/t* tie, wrap, wind. **II** *sich* ~ wind, coil.
'schlingen[2] (schlang, geschlungen, h) **I** *v/i* gobble, bolt one's food. **II** *v/t* gobble (up), gulp *s.th.* down.
schlingern ['ʃlɪŋərn] *v/i* (h) ♣ roll.
'Schlingpflanze *f* climbing plant.
Schlips [ʃlɪps] *m* (-es; -e) tie: *fig.* **j-m auf den ~ treten** tread on s.o.'s toes.
Schlitten ['ʃlɪtən] *m* (-s; -) **1.** a) sledge, *Am.* sled, b) sleigh, c) toboggan: ~ **fahren** sledge, toboggan; F *fig.* **mit j-m ~ fahren** give s.o. hell. **2.** F car: **alter** ~ crate, bus, jalopy.
'Schlittenfahrt *f* sledge (*or* sleigh) ride.
schlittern ['ʃlɪtərn] *v/i* (sn) slide (**in** *acc* into, *a. fig.*), *a.* slip, *mot.* skid.
'Schlittschuh *m* (ice-)skate: ~ **laufen** skate. ~**laufen** *n* (ice-)skating. ~**läufer(in** *f*) *m* (ice-)skater.
Schlitz [ʃlɪts] *m* (-es; -e) **1.** slit. **2.** slot.
'Schlitzauge *n* **1.** slit eye: ~**n haben** be slit-eyed. **2.** *contp.* slit-eye.
schlitzen ['ʃlɪtsən] *v/t, v/i* (h) slit, slash.
schloß [ʃlɔs] *pret of* **schließen**.
Schloß [ʃlɔs] *n* (-sses; =sser) **1.** castle, palace. **2.** a) lock, b) clasp: **hinter** ~ **und Riegel** behind bars.
Schloße ['ʃloːsə] *f usu. pl* sleet.
Schlosser ['ʃlɔsər] *m* (-s; -) locksmith.
Schlosse'rei *f* (-; -en) **1.** *no pl* locksmith's trade. **2.** locksmith's shop.
Schlot [ʃloːt] *m* (-[e]s; -e) (F **rauchen wie ein** ~ smoke like a) chimney.
schlottern ['ʃlɔtərn] *v/i* (h) **1.** (**vor** with) shake, tremble: **mit ~den Knien** with shaking knees. **2.** *clothes:* hang loosely.
Schlucht [ʃlʊxt] *f* (-; -en) gorge, ravine, *a.* canyon.
schluchzen ['ʃlʊxtsən] *v/t, v/i* (h) sob.
'Schluchzen *n* (-s) sobbing, sobs.
Schluck [ʃlʊk] *m* (-[e]s; -e) swallow, gulp: **kräftiger** ~ F swig. **'Schluckauf** *m* (-s; *no pl*) (**e-n** ~ **haben** have the) hiccups. **Schlückchen** ['ʃlʏkçən] *n* (-s; -) sip. **'schlucken** (h) **I** *v/t* swallow (*a. fig. insult etc*, *a.* F believe), *fig.* swallow up (*savings etc*), absorb (*light, sound*). **II** *v/i* swallow. **'Schlucker** *m* (-s; -) **armer** ~ poor devil.
'Schluckimpfung *f* 💉 oral vaccination.
schlud(e)rig ['ʃluːd(ə)rɪç] → **schlampig**.

schludern ['ʃluːdərn] → **schlampen**.
schlug [ʃluːk] *pret of* **schlagen**.
schlummern ['ʃlʊmərn] *v/i* (h) slumber, sleep, *fig.* lie dormant.
'schlummernd *adj fig.* dormant, latent.
Schlund [ʃlʊnt] *m* (-es; =e) **1.** *anat.* (back of the) throat, pharynx. **2.** *zo.* maw. **3.** *fig.* abyss.
schlüpfen ['ʃlʏpfən] *v/i* (sn) **1.** slip (**in** *acc* into, **aus** out of). **2.** *zo.* hatch (out).
'Schlüpfer *m* (-s; -) briefs, panties.
Schlupfloch ['ʃlʊpf-] *n* **1.** gap. **2.** *fig.* loophole.
schlüpfrig ['ʃlʏpfrɪç] *adj* slippery, *fig.* lewd, risqué (*joke etc*).
'Schlupfwinkel *m* hideout, haunt.
schlurfen ['ʃlʊrfən] *v/i* (sn) shuffle.
schlürfen ['ʃlʏrfən] *v/t, v/i* (h) a) slurp, b) sip.
Schluß [ʃlʊs] *m* (-sses; =sse) **1.** end, conclusion, ending (*of book, film, etc*): ~ (**damit!**) stop it!; F ~ **machen** a) call it a day, b) put an end to o.s.; ~ **machen mit** a) **et.** stop *s.th.*, b) *j-m* break up with s.o.; **am** ~ at the end; **zum** ~ finally. **2.** conclusion: **voreilige Schlüsse ziehen** jump to conclusions. ~**akkord** *m* ♪ final chord. ~**akt** *m* **1.** *thea.* final act. **2.** closing ceremony. ~**bemerkung** *f* final comment.
Schlüssel ['ʃlʏsəl] *m* (-s; -) **1.** key (**zu, für** of, *fig.* to). **2.** ♪ clef. **3.** ratio. **4.** ⚙ spanner, *Am.* wrench. ~**bein** *n anat.* collarbone. ~**blume** *f* primrose, cowslip. ~**bund** *m*, *n* bunch of keys. ~**erlebnis** *n* crucial experience. ~**figur** *f* key figure. ~**indu**strie *f* key industry. ~**kind** *n* latchkey child. ~**loch** *n* keyhole. ~**ring** *m* key ring. ~**ro**man *m* roman-à-clef. ~**stellung** *f* key position. ~**wort** *n* (-[e]s; =er) code word, keyword, *computer: a.* password.
'Schlußfeier *f* closing ceremony, *ped.* speech day, *Am.* commencement.
'Schlußfolgerung *f* (-; -en) conclusion.
schlüssig ['ʃlʏsɪç] *adj* **1.** logical **2.** conclusive (*evidence*). **3.** *sich* ~ **werden** make up one's mind (**über** *acc* about).
'Schluß|läufer(in *f*) *m* anchor. ~**licht** *n* (-[e]s; -er) **1.** *mot.* taillight. **2.** F *esp. sports:* tailender: **das** ~ **bilden** bring up the rear. ~**pfiff** *m sports:* final whistle. ~**satz** *m* **1.** closing sentence. **2.** ♪ final movement. ~**strich** *m fig.* **e-n** ~ **unter**

et. **ziehen** consider the matter closed.
~verkauf *m* (end-of-season) sale.
~wort *n* (-[e]s; -e) closing words.

Schmach [ʃmaːx] *f* (-; *no pl*) disgrace.
schmächtig ['ʃmɛçtɪç] *adj* slight, thin.
'**schmachvoll** *adj* disgraceful.
schmackhaft ['ʃmakhaft] *adj* savo(u)ry,
tasty: *fig. j-m et.* **~ machen** make s.th.
palatable to s.o.

schmal [ʃmaːl] *adj* narrow, *a.* thin, slender (*a. fig.*), *fig.* meag/re (*Am.* -er).
schmälern ['ʃmɛːlərn] *v/t* (h) **1.** curtail,
impair. **2.** detract from.
'**Schmalfilm** *m* cine-film.
'**Schmalfilmkamera** *f* cine-camera.
'**Schmalspur** *f* (-; *no pl*) narrow ga(u)ge.
'**Schmalspur...** F *fig.* small-time ...
Schmalz[1] [ʃmalts] *n* (-es; -e) lard.
Schmalz[2] *m* (-es; *no pl*) F schmaltz.
'**schmalzig** *adj* F schmaltzy.
schmarotzen [ʃma'rɔtsən] *v/i* (h) sponge
(**bei** on). **Schma'rotzer** *m* (-s; -) parasite, *fig. a.* sponger.
schmatzen ['ʃmatsən] *v/i* (h) eat noisily.
schmecken ['ʃmɛkən] (h) **I** *v/i* taste. **II**
v/i **~ nach** taste of, *fig.* smack of; **es
schmeckt (gut)** it tastes good; **sich et. ~
lassen** tuck in; **schmeckt es (Ihnen)?**
do you like it?; *fig.* **das schmeckte ihm
nicht** he didn't like it one bit.
Schmeichelei [ʃmaɪçə'laɪ] *f* (-; -en) flattery, (flattering) compliment.
'**schmeichelhaft** *adj a. fig.* flattering.
schmeicheln ['ʃmaɪçəln] *v/i* (h) *j-m ~* a)
flatter s.o. (*a. fig.*), b) cajole s.o.; *sich
geschmeichelt fühlen* feel flattered
(**durch** by); *das Bild ist geschmeichelt*
the picture is flattering.
Schmeichler ['ʃmaɪçlər] *m* (-s; -) flat-
terer. '**schmeichlerisch** *adj* a) flattering, b) cajoling.
schmeißen ['ʃmaɪsən] (schmiß, geschmissen, h) F **I** *v/t* **1.** a) throw, chuck,
b) slam, bang (*door etc*). **2.** chuck up
(*job etc*), *thea.* muff (*scene*). **3.** manage:
den Laden ~ run the show. **4.** *e-e Lage
~* stand a round of drinks. **II** *v/i* **5. ~ mit**
throw; *mit Geld um sich ~* throw one's
money around.
'**Schmeißfliege** *f* bluebottle.
Schmelz [ʃmɛlts] *m* (-es; -e) **1.** enamel. **2.**
fig. mellowness, ♩ melodiousness.
'**schmelzbar** *adj* ⊙ fusible.
Schmelze ['ʃmɛltsə] *f* (-; -n) ⊙ melting,

molten mass. '**schmelzen** (schmolz,
geschmolzen) **I** *v/i* (sn) liquefy, melt (*a.
fig. supply etc*). **II** *v/t* (h) liquefy, melt,
metall. smelt. '**schmelzend** *adj fig.*
melting (*look*), sweet (*voice*).
'**Schmelz|käse** *m* soft cheese. **~punkt** *m*
melting point. **~tiegel** *m a. fig.* melting
pot. **~wasser** *n* melted snow and ice.
Schmerbauch ['ʃmeːr-] *m* paunch.
Schmerz [ʃmɛrts] *m* (-es; -en) a) pain,
ache, b) grief, sorrow, c) agony: **~en haben** be in pain. '**schmerzen** (h) **I** *v/i* hurt
(*a. fig.*), ache. **II** *v/t* hurt (*a. fig.*), pain.
'**Schmerzensgeld** *n* compensation for
personal suffering, *Am.* smart-money.
'**Schmerzensschrei** *m* scream of pain.
'**schmerzfrei** *adj* free of pain.
'**Schmerzgrenze** *f* pain threshold.
'**schmerzhaft** *adj fig.* painful.
'**schmerzlich I** *adj* painful, *fig.* sad (*loss,
smile, etc*). **II** *adv* badly, sadly: *j-n ~
berühren* pain s.o.
'**schmerzlindernd** *adj* soothing, (*a. ~es
Mittel*) analgesic.
'**schmerzlos** *adj* painless.
'**schmerzstillend** *adj* painkilling.
'**Schmerzta,blette** *f* painkiller.
Schmetterball *m tennis:* smash.
Schmetterling ['ʃmɛtərlɪŋ] *m* (-s; -e) *zo.*
butterfly. '**Schmetterlingsstil** *m swimming:* butterfly (stroke).
schmettern ['ʃmɛtərn] (h) **I** *v/t* **1.** smash
(*a. tennis*), slam. **2.** belt out (*song*). **II** *v/i*
3. ring (out), *trumpet:* blare, *bird:*
warble.
Schmied [ʃmiːt] *m* (-[e]s; -e) a) smith, b)
blacksmith. **Schmiede** ['ʃmiːdə] *f* (-;
-n) forge, smithy.
'**Schmiedeeisen** *n* wrought iron.
'**schmiedeeisern** *adj* wrought-iron.
schmieden ['ʃmiːdən] *v/t, v/i* (h) *a. fig.*
forge: → **Eisen, Plan 1.**
schmiegen ['ʃmiːgən] *sich ~* (h) cling (*or*
cuddle up) (**an** *acc* to). **schmiegsam**
['ʃmiːk-] *adj* pliant, flexible.
Schmiere[1] ['ʃmiːrə] *f* (-; -n) **1.** ⊙ grease,
lubricant. **2.** F mess, goo.
'**Schmiere**[2] *f* F **~ stehen** keep a lookout.
schmieren ['ʃmiːrən] *v/t* (h) **1.** smear, *a.*
butter (*bread*), spread (*butter etc*): F
wie geschmiert like clockwork; *j-m
e-e ~* slap s.o.('s face). **2.** ⊙ grease, b)
lubricate, oil. **3.** *a. v/i* scrawl. **4.** F *j-n ~*
grease s.o.'s palm.

'**Schmierenkomödi,ant** *m* ham actor.
Schmiere'rei *f* (-; -en) **1.** scribble, scrawl. **2.** daub. **3.** *pl* graffiti.
'**Schmier|fett** *n* ⊕ (lubricating) grease. **~fink** *m* F **1.** a) scrawler, b) messy fellow. **2.** muckraker. **~geld** *n* F bribe (money), payoff, *pol.* slush fund.
schmierig ['ʃmiːrɪç] *adj* **1.** greasy. **2.** messy. **3.** *fig.* a) smutty, b) F smarmy.
'**Schmier|mittel** *n* ⊕ lubricant. **~öl** *n* ⊕ lubricating oil. **~pa,pier** *n* scribbling paper. **~seife** *f* soft soap.
'**Schmierung** *f* (-; -en) ⊕ a) lubrication, b) greasing.
Schminke ['ʃmɪŋkə] *f* (-; -n) make-up.
'**schminken** (h) **I** *v/t* make up: *sich die Lippen ~* put on lipstick. **II** *sich ~* put on make-up, make one's face up.
schmirgeln ['ʃmɪrgəln] *v/t* (h), '**Schmirgelpa,pier** *n* ⊕ sandpaper.
schmiß [ʃmɪs] *pret of* **schmeißen.**
Schmiß *m* (-sses; -sse) **1.** (duelling) scar. **2.** *no pl* F *fig.* pep, zip.
'**schmissig** *adj* F zippy, rousing (*music*).
Schmöker ['ʃmøːkər] *m* (-s; -) F **1.** old book. **2.** light novel. '**schmökern** *v/i* (h) a) do some light reading, b) browse.
schmollen ['ʃmɔlən] *v/i* (h) sulk.
'**Schmollmund** *m* pout.
schmolz [ʃmɔlts] *pret of* **schmelzen.**
'**Schmorbraten** *m* pot roast.
schmoren ['ʃmoːrən] *v/t, v/i* (h) *gastr.* braise: *F j-n (in s-m eigenen Saft) ~ lassen* let s.o. stew (in his own juice); *in der Sonne ~* roast in the sun.
Schmuck [ʃmʊk] *m* (-[e]s; *no pl*) **1.** decoration. **2.** jewel(le)ry, jewels.
schmücken ['ʃmʏkən] (h) **I** *v/t* decorate, *fig.* embellish (*speech etc*). **II** *sich ~* dress up; → **Feder** 1.
'**Schmuckkästchen** *n* **1.** jewel(le)ry box. **2.** *fig.* jewel of a house.
'**schmucklos** *adj* plain, austere.
'**Schmuckstück** *n* **1.** piece of jewel(le)ry. **2.** *fig.* gem.
schmudd(e)lig ['ʃmʊd(ə)lɪç] *adj* F grubby, grimy, scruffy.
Schmuggel ['ʃmʊgəl] *m* (-s; *no pl*) smuggling. '**schmuggeln** *v/t, v/i* (h) smuggle. '**Schmuggelware** *f* smuggled goods, contraband. '**Schmuggler** *m* (-s; -) smuggler.
schmunzeln ['ʃmʊntsəln] *v/i* (h) smile to o.s., grin.

Schmus [ʃmuːs] *m* (-es; *no pl*) F blarney.
schmusen ['ʃmuːzən] *v/i* (h) F cuddle, *lovers: a.* smooch.
Schmutz [ʃmʊts] *m* (-es; *no pl*) dirt, filth, mud, *fig. a.* smut: *fig.* **in den ~ ziehen** drag s.o., s.th. through the mud.
'**schmutzen** *v/i* (h) soil, get dirty.
'**Schmutzfink** *m* F **1.** pig. **2.** *fig.* dirty fellow. '**Schmutzfleck** *m* smudge.
'**schmutzig** *adj* **1.** dirty, filthy, soiled: *~ machen* dirty, soil; *sich ~ machen*, *~ werden* get dirty; *fig. ~e Phantasie* dirty mind; → **Wäsche** 1. **2.** *contp.* a) dirty, shabby, b) smutty (*joke etc*).
Schnabel ['ʃnaːbəl] *m* (-s; -) **1.** *zo.* bill, beak. **2.** spout. **3.** F trap: *halt den ~!* shut up!
schnäbeln ['ʃnɛːbəln] *v/i* (h) *zo.* bill.
Schnake ['ʃnaːkə] *f* (-; -n) *zo.* mosquito.
Schnalle ['ʃnalə] *f* (-; -n) buckle, clasp.
schnallen ['ʃnalən] *v/t* (h) **1.** buckle, strap (*an acc* to): → **Gürtel** 2. **2.** F get: *ich schnalle das nicht!* I don't get it!
schnalzen ['ʃnaltsən] *v/i* (h) *mit der Zunge ~* click one's tongue; *mit den Fingern ~* snap one's fingers.
schnappen ['ʃnapən] (h) **I** *v/t* **1.** F catch, nab: (*sich*) *et. ~* grab s.th.; → **Luft** 1. **II** *v/i* **2.** snap, click. **3.** *~ nach* grab at, *dog:* snap at; *nach Luft ~* gasp for air.
'**Schnappschuß** *m phot.* snapshot: *e-n ~ machen von* take a snap of, snap.
Schnaps [ʃnaps] *m* (-es; -e) spirits, schnapps. **~brenne'rei** *f* distillery.
'**Schnäpschen** ['ʃnɛpsçən] *n* (-s; -) F snifter.
'**Schnapsi,dee** *f* F *fig.* crazy idea.
schnarchen ['ʃnarçən] *v/i* (h) snore.
schnarren ['ʃnarən] *v/i* (h) **1.** rattle. **2.** *bell etc:* buzz. **3.** *a. v/t* rasp, bark.
schnattern ['ʃnatərn] *v/i* (h) **1.** *goose:* cackle, *duck:* quack. **2.** F *fig.* gabble.
schnauben ['ʃnaʊbən] *v/i, v/t* (h) snort: *sich (die Nase) ~* blow one's nose; *vor Wut ~* foam with rage.
schnaufen ['ʃnaʊfən] *v/i* (h) **1.** breathe hard, puff, pant. **2.** *dial.* breathe.
'**Schnauzbart** *m* walrus m(o)ustache.
Schnauze ['ʃnaʊtsə] *f* (-; -n) **1.** *zo.* snout, muzzle, nose. **2.** lip (*of jug etc*), ⊕ nozzle, F *mot.* nose. **3.** F trap: *halt die ~!* shut up!; *die ~ voll haben* be fed up (to the teeth) (*von* with).
'**Schnauzer** *m* (-s; -) *zo.* schnauzer.

Schnecke ['ʃnɛkə] f (-; -n) **1.** zo. a) snail, b) slug: F *j-n zur ~ machen* give s.o. hell. **2.** △ scroll. **3.** gastr. Chelsea bun. **4.** pl earphones. '**Schneckenhaus** n (snail) shell. '**Schneckentempo** n *im ~* at a snail's pace.

Schnee [ʃneː] m (-s; no pl) **1.** snow. **2.** *Eiweiß zu ~ schlagen* beat white of egg until stiff. **3.** sl. snow. **~ball** m snowball. **~ballschlacht** f snowball fight. ⚤**bedeckt** adj snow-covered. **~besen** m egg-beater, whisk. ⚤**blind** adj snow-blind. **~brille** f (e-e ~ a pair of) snow goggles. **~decke** f (blanket of) snow. **~fall** m snowfall. **~flocke** f snowflake. **~gestöber** n snow flurry. **~glätte** f packed snow. **~glöckchen** n ⚤ snowdrop. **~grenze** f snowline. **~kette** f snowchain. **~mann** m (-[e]s; ⬝er) snowman. **~matsch** m slush. **~mo,bil** n snowmobile. **~pflug** m snowplough, Am. snowplow. **~regen** m sleet. **~schleuder** f snowblower. **~schmelze** f thaw. **~schuh** m snowshoe. **~sturm** m snowstorm. **~treiben** n snow flurry. **~verhältnisse** pl snow conditions. **~verwehung** f, **~wehe** f snowdrift. ⚤**weiß** adj snow-white.

Schneid [ʃnaɪt] m (-[e]s; no pl) F guts.

'**Schneidbrenner** m cutting torch.

Schneide ['ʃnaɪdə] f (-; -n) edge.

schneiden ['ʃnaɪdən] (schnitt, geschnitten, h) **I** v/t **1.** a) cut (a. ball, curve), carve (meat), b) cut, mow (lawn), prune (tree), trim (hedge): *in Stücke ~* cut up; F *j-n ~* fig. cut s.o. dead, mot. cut in on s.o.; → *Grimasse, Haar.* **2.** edit (film, tape). **II** sich ~ a) cut o.s., b) lines: intersect; F *da hat er sich aber geschnitten!* he is very much mistaken there! '**schneidend** adj fig. sharp (pain, voice, etc), biting (cold, sarcasm, etc).

'**Schneider** m (-s; -) tailor: F *aus dem ~ sein* be out of the woods.

Schneide'rei f (-; no pl) tailoring, dressmaking.

'**Schneiderin** f (-; -nen) dressmaker.

schneidern ['ʃnaɪdərn] (h) **I** v/i do tailoring (or dressmaking). **II** v/t make.

'**Schneidetisch** m film etc: editing table.

'**Schneidezahn** m incisor.

'**schneidig** adj plucky, snappy, dashing, w.s. brisk (a. pace), rousing (music).

schneien ['ʃnaɪən] **I** v/impers (h) *es*

schneit it's snowing. **II** v/i (sn) F (j-m) *ins Haus ~* drop in (on s.o.) unexpectedly.

Schneise ['ʃnaɪzə] f (-; -n) **1.** (forest) lane, fire-break. **2.** → *Flugschneise.*

schnell [ʃnɛl] **I** adj quick (movement, decision, etc), fast (car, runner, track, etc), a. rapid, a. prompt, speedy: *in ~er Folge* in rapid succession; *~es Handeln* prompt action; *~e Fortschritte machen* make rapid progress; F *e-e ~e Mark machen* make a fast buck; *auf dem ~sten Wege* as quickly as possible; F *auf die Schnelle* quickly, contp. slapdash; → *Brüter.* **II** adv fast, quick(ly), rapidly (etc): *~ fahren (handeln)* drive (act) fast; *das geht ~* that won't take long; *das ist ~ gegangen* that was quick; *~er ging es nicht* I (we etc) couldn't do it any faster; *so ~ wie möglich, schnellstens* as quickly as possible; (mach) ~! hurry up!, F get a move on!; *nicht so ~!* easy!; *sie ist ~ beleidigt* she is quick to take offence; *wie ~ die Zeit vergeht!* how time flies!

'**Schnellboot** n ⚔ speedboat.

schnelllebig [-leːbɪç] adj fast-moving (times), short-lived (fashion etc).

schnellen ['ʃnɛlən] **I** v/i (sn) bounce, pop: *in die Höhe ~ → hochschnellen.* **II** v/t (h) toss, flick.

'**Schnellfeuerwaffe** f automatic weapon. **~gang** m mot. overdrive. **~gaststätte** f cafeteria. **~gericht** n **1.** ⚖ summary court. **2.** gastr. instant meal. **~hefter** m (-s; -) letter file.

'**Schnelligkeit** f (-; no pl) a) quickness, fastness, rapidity, speediness, b) speed.

'**Schnell|imbiß** m **1.** snack. **2.** → *imbißstube* f snack bar. **~kochtopf** m pressure cooker. **~reinigung** f express dry-cleaning. **~straße** f dual carriageway, Am. divided highway. **~verband** m first-aid dressing. **~verfahren** n **1.** ⚖ summary procedure (or proceedings). **2.** ⊚ high-speed process: fig. *im ~* very quickly. ⚤**wirkend** adj pharm. fast-acting. **~zug** m fast train.

Schnepfe ['ʃnɛpfə] f (-; -n) zo. snipe.

schneuzen ['ʃnɔʏtsən] sich ~ (h) blow one's nose.

schniefen ['ʃniːfən] v/i (h) F sniffle.

Schnippchen ['ʃnɪpçən] n *j-m ein ~ schlagen* outwit (or fool) s.o.

schnippeln ['ʃnɪpəln] v/t, v/i (h) snip (away) (**an** dat at).

schnippen ['ʃnɪpən] (h) **I** v/i snip: (**mit den Fingern**) ~ snap one's fingers. **II** v/t flick (off).

schnippisch ['ʃnɪpɪʃ] adj pert, saucy.

Schnipsel ['ʃnɪpsəl] m, n (-s; -) shred.

schnitt [ʃnɪt] pret of **schneiden**.

Schnitt m (-[e]s; -e) **1.** no pl cutting, ⚘ mowing, film etc: editing. **2.** cut, ⚕ incision, gash: film etc: **harter** ~ jump cut. **3.** cut (of hair, dress, etc), shape. **4.** pattern. **5.** ⚵ intersection. **6.** ⚙ section(al view). **7.** (a. **im** ~ **erreichen** etc) average: **im** ~ on average. **8.** F profit.

'**Schnittblumen** pl cut flowers.

Schnitte ['ʃnɪtə] f (-; -n) **1.** slice. **2.** (open) sandwich.

'**schnittfest** adj firm (tomatoes etc).

'**schnittig** adj racy, sleek, streamlined.

'**Schnittlauch** m ⚘ chives.

'**Schnittmuster** n pattern.

'**Schnittpunkt** m (point of) intersection.

'**Schnittwunde** f cut, gash.

'**Schnittzeichnung** f ⚙ section(al view).

Schnitzarbeit ['ʃnɪts-] f (wood-)carving.

Schnitzel¹ ['ʃnɪtsəl] n (-s; -) gastr. a. **Wiener** ~ escalope.

Schnitzel² n, m (-s; -) shred, scrap.

'**Schnitzeljagd** f paper chase.

'**Schnitzelwerk** n shredder.

schnitzen ['ʃnɪtsən] v/t, v/i (h) carve.

Schnitzer m (-s; -) **1.** (wood-)carver. **2.** F blunder.

Schnitze'rei f (-; -en) (wood-)carving.

schnodd(e)rig ['ʃnɔd(ə)rɪç] adj F snotty.

Schnorchel ['ʃnɔrçəl] m (-s; -) snorkel.

Schnörkel ['ʃnœrkəl] m (-s; -) **1.** scroll. **2.** flourish: fig. **ohne** ~ without frills.

schnorren ['ʃnɔrən] v/i, v/t (h) scrounge (**bei j-m** s.th. off s.o.).

'**Schnorrer** m (-s; -) scrounger.

Schnösel ['ʃnøːzəl] m (-s; -) F snot-nose.

schnuck(e)lig ['ʃnʊk(ə)lɪç] adj F cuddly, pretty, cute.

schnüffeln ['ʃnʏfəln] v/i (h) **1.** sniff (**an** dat at). **2.** F snoop (around).

'**Schnüffler** m (-s; -) F snooper, sleuth.

Schnuller ['ʃnʊlər] m (-s; -) comforter, dummy, Am. pacifier.

Schnulze ['ʃnʊltsə] f (-; -n) F **1.** sobstuff, tearjerker. **2.** schmaltzy song.

schnupfen ['ʃnʊpfən] v/i (h) take snuff.

'**Schnupfen** m (-s; -) cold, F the sniffles.

'**Schnupftabak** m snuff.

schnuppe ['ʃnʊpə] → **schnurz**.

'**schnuppern** → **schnüffeln** 1.

Schnur [ʃnuːr] f (-; ⁀e) cord, (piece of) string, ⚡ flex: F **über die** ~ **hauen** overdo it.

Schnürchen ['ʃnyːrçən] n F **das ging wie am** ~ it went like clockwork.

schnüren ['ʃnyːrən] v/t (h) lace up.

'**schnurgerade** adj and adv F (as) straight as an arrow, dead straight.

'**Schnurrbart** m m(o)ustache.

schnurren ['ʃnʊrən] v/i (h) purr.

'**Schnür|riemen** m strap. **~schuh** m lace-up shoe. **~senkel** [-zɛŋkəl] m (-s; -) shoelace, bootlace.

schnurstracks ['ʃnuːrʃtraks] adv F a) straight, b) straightaway.

schnurz [ʃnʊrts] adj F **das ist mir** ~ I couldn't care less.

schob [ʃoːp] pret of **schieben**.

Schober ['ʃoːbər] m (-s; -) **1.** rick. **2.** barn, shed.

Schock [ʃɔk] m (-[e]s; -s) a. ⚕ shock: **e-n** ~ **haben** be in (a state of) shock.

'**schocken** v/t (h) F shock.

schockieren [ʃɔ'kiːrən] v/t (h) shock, scandalize: **~d** shocking, scandalizing.

'**Schockthera,pie** f ⚕ (electro-)shock therapy.

schofel ['ʃoːfəl] adj F shabby, mean.

Schöffe ['ʃœfə] m (-n; -n) lay assessor.

Schokolade [ʃoko'laːdə] f (-; -n) (**e-e Tafel** ~ a bar of) chocolate.

Scholle¹ ['ʃɔlə] f (-; -n) **1.** clod (of earth). **2.** (ice) floe. **3.** fig. (native) soil.

Scholle² f (-; -n) zo. plaice.

schon [ʃoːn] adv **1.** a) already, yet, b) before, c) ever, d) even: ~ **damals** even then; ~ **früher** before; ~ **immer** always, all along; ~ **oft** often (enough); ~ **wieder** again; (**nicht**) ~ **wieder**! not again!; ~ **am nächsten Tage** the very next day; ~ **im 16. Jahrhundert** as early as the 16th century; **ist er** ~ **da?** has he come yet?; **hast du** ~ (**einmal**) ...? have you ever ...?; **ich habe ihn** ~ **einmal gesehen** I have seen him before; **ich komme** (**ja**) ~! (I'm) coming!; **das kennen wir** ~! that's an old story! **2.** **er wird** ~ **kommen** he is sure to come; **don't worry**, he'll come; **er wird es** ~ **machen** leave it to him; **das ist** ~ **möglich** that's quite possible; (**das ist**) ~ **wahr, aber ...**

that's (certainly) true, but ...; **er ist ~ ein guter Spieler** he really is a good player. **3. ~ gar nicht** least of all. **4. ~ der Gedanke** the very sight (idea *etc*); **~ deswegen** if only for that reason; **~ weil** if only because. **5.** F **na, wenn ~!** so what!; **was macht das ~?** what does it matter?; **wenn ~, denn ~!** if we do it at all, let's do it properly!

schön [ʃøːn] **I** *adj* **1.** beautiful: **~e Geschlecht** the fair sex; **die ~en Künste** the fine arts; **~es Wetter** good (*or* fine) weather. **2.** a) good, fine, b) pleasant, nice: **~!** all right!, okay!; **e-s ~en Tages** one of these days; **~es Wochenende!** have a nice weekend!; **~er Tod** easy death; **das ist alles ~ und gut, aber ...** that's all very well, but ...; **es war sehr ~** I (we *etc*) had a good time; **wär's!** some hope!; **das wäre ja noch ~er!** F nothing doing!; *iro*. **du bist mir ein ~er Freund!** a fine friend you are!; → **Dank. 3.** F handsome, nice (*gift etc*). **II** *adv* **4.** beautifully, nicely, pleasantly: **sie war ~ braun** she had a beautiful tan. **5.** F very, really, pretty: **ganz ~ teuer** pretty expensive; *iro*. **da wärst du ~ dumm** you'd be a fool; **sei ~ brav!** be a good boy (*or* girl) now!; **~ warm** nice and warm.

'**Schöne** *n* (-n) *the* beautiful: **das ~ daran** the nice thing about it; **es gibt nichts Schöneres als** there's nothing nicer (*or* better) than.

schonen ['ʃoːnən] (h) **I** *v/t* spare (*s.o., s.o.'s feelings*), save (*one's energy, supplies, etc*), treat *s.th.* with care, *detergent etc*: *a.* be easy on (*the carpet etc*). **II sich ~** take it easy; **sich für et. ~** save one's strength for *s.th.*; **sich nicht ~** drive o.s. (hard). '**schonend** *adj* a) gentle, careful, considerate, b) mild (*detergent etc*): **~ umgehen mit** go easy on; → **beibringen.**

'**Schoner** *m* (-s; -) ♣ schooner.

Schöngeist *m* (-[e]s; -er) (a)esthete. '**schöngeistig** *adj* (a)esthetical. '**Schönheit** *f* (-; -en) beauty. '**Schönheits|fehler** *m* blemish, flaw. **~königin** *f* beauty queen. **~operati,on** *f* cosmetic operation. **~pflege** *f* beauty care. **~sa,lon** *m* beauty parlo(u)r. **~wettbewerb** *m* beauty contest.

'**Schonkost** *f* light food, bland diet.

'**schönmachen** (*sep*, -ge-, h) **I** *v/i dog*: sit up (and beg). **II sich ~** a) dress up, b) make (o.s.) up.

'**Schonung** *f* (-; -en) **1.** *no pl* a) mercy, b) forbearance, c) good care, d) protection, e) rest: **sie braucht ~** she needs a rest; **zur ~** (*gen*) to protect (*one's hands etc*), to save (*one's eyes, strength, etc*). **2.** (young) forest plantation.

'**schonungsbedürftig** *adj* in need of rest. '**schonungslos** *adj* merciless. '**Schonwaschgang** *m* program(me *Br.*) for delicate fabrics.

'**Schön'wetterlage** *f* period of fine weather.

'**Schonzeit** *f hunt*. close season.

Schopf [ʃɔpf] *m* (-[e]s; ~e) mop (of hair), *of birds*: tuft; → **Gelegenheit.**

schöpfen ['ʃœpfən] *v/t* **1.** scoop, ladle; → **Hoffnung, Kraft** 1, **Verdacht** *etc*. '**Schöpfer** *m* (-s; -) creator, *bibl. the* Creator. **~geist** *m* creative genius. '**schöpferisch** *adj* creative.

'**Schöpfkelle** *f*, '**Schöpflöffel** *m* ladle.

'**Schöpfung** *f* (-; -en) **1.** creation, work. **2.** *no pl bibl. the* Creation. '**Schöpfungsgeschichte** *f* Genesis.

schor [ʃoːr] *pret of* **scheren.**

Schorf [ʃɔrf] *m* (-[e]s; -e) ♣ scab.

Schornstein ['ʃɔrn-] *m* chimney, smoke stack, ♣, ♠ funnel. '**Schornsteinfeger** *m* (-s; -) chimney sweep.

schoß [ʃoːs] *pret of* **schießen.**

Schoß [ʃoːs] *m* (-es; ~e) **1.** lap: → **Hand. 2.** a) womb, b) (*woman's*) sex.

Schößling ['ʃœslɪŋ] *m* (-s; -e) ♣ shoot.

Schote ['ʃoːtə] *f* (-; -n) ♣ husk, pod.

Schotte ['ʃɔtə] *m* (-n; -n) Scot, Scotsman: **die ~n** the Scots.

Schotter ['ʃɔtər] *m* (-s; -) gravel, *a.* (road) metal. '**schottern** *v/t* (h) gravel, metal.

Schottin ['ʃɔtɪn] *f* (-; -nen) Scotswoman. '**schottisch** *adj* Scottish: **~er Whisky** Scotch (whisky). '**Schottland** *n* (-s) Scotland.

schraffieren [ʃraˈfiːrən] *v/t* (h) hatch.

schräg [ʃrɛːk] **I** *adj* oblique, slanting, sloping (*ground, roof, etc*), diagonal (*line*). **II** *adv* cut, set, *etc* at an angle: **~ gegenüber** diagonally opposite.

Schräge ['ʃrɛːgə] *f* (-; -n) **1.** slant. **2.** incline, slope.

'**Schrägstrich** *m* slash, oblique.

Schramme ['ʃramə] *f* (-; -n) scratch.

'**schrammen** v/t (h) scratch, graze.
Schrank [ʃraŋk] m (-[e]s, ⸗e) a) cupboard, closet, wardrobe, b) locker: F **er ist ein ~** he's a hulking fellow.
'**Schrankbett** n foldaway bed.
Schranke ['ʃraŋkə] f (-; -n) **1.** barrier, 🚆 a. gate, 🚋 bar. **2.** fig. a) (social etc, a. trade) barrier, b) bounds, limits: **~n setzen** set bounds (dat to); **(sich) in ~n halten** keep within bounds, restrain (o.s.); **j-n in s-e ~n weisen** put s.o. in his place.
'**schrankenlos** adj fig. boundless.
'**Schrankenwärter** m 🚆 gatekeeper.
'**schrankfertig** adj washed and ironed.
'**Schrankwand** f wall-to-wall cupboard.
'**Schraubdeckel** m screw cap.
Schraube ['ʃraʊbə] f (-; -n) **1.** screw (a. ♄), ✈ propeller: **~ und Mutter** bolt and nut; F **bei ihm ist e-e ~ locker** he has a screw loose. **2.** gym. etc twist.
'**schrauben** v/t (h) screw, a. twist: **fester ~** tighten the screw(s) of; fig. **niedriger ~** lower, scale down; **(sich) in die Höhe ~** → **hochschrauben**; → **geschraubt**.
'**Schraubendreher** m screwdriver.
'**schraubenförmig** adj helical, spiral.
'**Schrauben|schlüssel** m wrench, spanner. **~zieher** m (-s; -) screwdriver.
'**Schraubstock** m vice, Am. vise.
Schrebergarten ['ʃre:bər-] m allotment (garden).
Schreck [ʃrɛk] m (-[e]s, -e) fright, shock: F **krieg k-n ~!** don't be alarmed!; **ach du ~!** good God!, dear me! '**schrecken** v/t (h) frighten, startle: **das schreckt mich nicht** that can't scare me.
'**Schrecken** m (-s; -) fright, shock: **in ~en versetzen** frighten, terrify; **mit dem ~en davonkommen** get off with a bad fright; **zu m-m ~en** to my dismay; **die ~ des Krieges** the horrors of war.
'**Schreckens|herrschaft** f reign of terror. **~nachricht** f alarming (or dreadful) news. **~tat** f atrocity.
'**Schreckgespenst** n fig. nightmare.
'**schreckhaft** adj jumpy, nervous.
'**schrecklich** I adj terrible, dreadful, horrible. II adv F awfully, terribly.
'**Schreckschuß** m warning shot. **~pistole** f blank (cartridge) pistol.
'**Schrecke,kunde** f mot. reaction time.
Schrei [ʃraɪ] m (-[e]s, -e) cry, shout, scream, yell: fig. **~ der Entrüstung** outcry; F **der letzte ~** the latest rage.
'**Schreib|arbeit** ['ʃraɪp-] f desk work, paperwork. **~block** m writing pad.
schreiben ['ʃraɪbən] v/t, v/i (schrieb, geschrieben, h) write (**über** acc about, on), write out (bill etc), ⊙ record: **j-m ~** write to s.o., Am. a. **j-m et. ~** write to s.o. about s.th.; **mit Bleistift etc ~** write in pencil etc; **mit der Maschine ~** type; **sich mit j-m ~** correspond with s.o.; **noch einmal ~** rewrite; **gut ~** a) write a good hand, b) be a good writer; **(richtig) ~** spell (correctly); **falsch ~** misspell; **wie schreibt er sich?** how do you spell his name?; **an e-m Roman ~** be working on a novel; ped. etc **e-e Arbeit ~** do a test; → **Ohr, rein** 1 etc.
'**Schreiben** n (-s; -) **1.** no pl writing. **2.** letter. '**Schreiber** m (-s; -) writer.
Schreibe'rei f (-; -en) (endless) writing, paperwork. '**Schreiberin** f (-; -nen) writer. '**Schreiberling** m (-s; -e) contp. hack. '**schreibfaul** adj lazy about writing letters.
'**Schreib|feder** f pen. **~fehler** m a) spelling mistake, b) slip of the pen. **~gerät** n writing utensils, ⊙ recorder. **~heft** n exercise-book. **~kopf** m ⊙ golfball. **~kraft** f (shorthand) typist. **~mappe** f writing case. **~ma,schine** f typewriter: **~ schreiben** type; **mit ~ geschrieben** typewritten, typed. **~ma,schinen-pa,pier** n typing paper. **~pa,pier** n writing paper. **~stube** f ✗ orderly room. **~tisch** m (writing) desk. **~tischlampe** f desk lamp.
'**Schreibung** f (-; -en) spelling.
'**Schreibwaren** pl stationery. **~geschäft** n stationer's (shop).
'**Schreibweise** f **1.** style. **2.** spelling.
schreien ['ʃraɪən] v/i, v/t (schrie, geschrien, h) shout, yell, scream, bawl; howl: **~ nach** cry for; F **es (er) ist zum Schreien!** it (he) is a scream!
'**schreiend** adj fig. loud (colo[u]r), flagrant (injustice), glaring (contrast).
'**Schreihals** m F **1.** loudmouth. **2.** brawler. **3.** (baby) bawler, (child) noisy brat.
Schrein [ʃraɪn] m (-[e]s, -e) shrine.
Schreiner ['ʃraɪnər] m (-s; -) etc → **Tischler** etc.
schreiten ['ʃraɪtən] v/i (schritt, geschritten, sn) **1.** walk, stride. **2.** **zu et. ~** proceed to (do) s.th.; **zur Tat ~** set to work.

schrie [ʃriː] *pret of* **schreien.**

schrieb [ʃriːp] *pret of* **schreiben.**

Schrift [ʃrɪft] *f* (-; -en) **1.** writing, hand(writing), *print.* script, type: *in lateinischer* ~ in Roman characters (*or* letters). **2.** publication, paper, pamphlet: *s.o.'s* writings, works; *die Heilige* ~ the Holy Scripture(s). **~art** *f* script, type. **~bild** *n* typeface. **~deutsch** *n* standard German. **~führer(in** *f*) *m* secretary. **~gelehrte** *m bibl.* scribe. **~grad** *m* type size.

'schriftlich I *adj* written, in writing: **~e Prüfung** written examination. **II** *adv* in writing, *a.* by letter: F *das kann ich dir* ~ *geben!* I can guarantee you that!

'Schrift|probe *f* specimen *of s.o.'s* handwriting. **~satz** *m* 🜪 written statement. **~setzer** *m* (-s; -) typesetter. **~sprache** *f* standard language.

'Schriftsteller *m* (-s; -) writer.

'Schriftstelle'rei *f* (-; *no pl*) writing.

'Schriftstellerin *f* (-; -nen) writer.

'schriftstellerisch I *adj* literary. **II** *adv* as a writer.

'Schriftstück *n* document, paper.

'Schrifttum *n* (-s; *no pl*) literature.

'Schriftwechsel *m* correspondence.

'Schriftzeichen *n* letter, character.

schrill [ʃrɪl] *adj* shrill, piercing.

schritt [ʃrɪt] *pret of* **schreiten.**

Schritt *m* (-[e]s; -e) **1.** a) step, stride, b) footstep, c) pace: ~ *halten mit* keep pace with, *fig. a.* keep abreast of; ~ *für* ~ *a. fig.* step by step; *auf* ~ *und Tritt* at every turn, everywhere; *im* ~ at a walking pace; *mot.* (*im*) ~ *fahren!* dead slow! **3.** *a.* F *anat.* crotch. **4.** *fig.* step, *a.* measure, move: *diplomatischer* ~ démarche; *Politik der kleinen* ~*e* step-by-step policy; *den ersten* ~ *tun* take the first step; *wir sind k-n* ~ *weitergekommen* we haven't made the slightest bit of progress.

'Schrittmacher *m* (-s; -) *sports:* pacemaker, *fig. a.* trendsetter. **~dienste** *pl j-m* ~ *leisten sports:* make the pace for s.o., *fig.* smooth the way for s.o.

'schrittweise I *adj* step-by-step, gradual. **II** *adv* step by step.

schroff [ʃrɔf] *adj* **1.** steep, precipitous. **2.** gruff, curt, abrupt: ~*e Ablehnung* flat refusal; ~*er Gegensatz* sharp contrast.

schröpfen [ˈʃrœpfən] *v/t* (h) **1.** 🜪 bleed.

2. F *j-n* ~ fleece s.o. (*um* for).

Schrot [ʃroːt] *m, n* (-[e]s; -e) **1.** wholemeal. **2.** *hunt.* (small) shot. **3.** *fig. von echtem* ~ *und Korn* true.

schroten [ˈʃroːtən] *v/t* (h) bruise.

'Schrot|flinte *f* shotgun. **~korn** *n,* **~kugel** *f* pellet. **~säge** *f* crosscut saw.

Schrott [ʃrɔt] *m* (-[e]s; -e) **1.** scrap metal: *ein Auto zu* ~ *fahren* smash up a car. **2.** F *a.*) junk, b) rubbish. **~händler** *m* scrap dealer. **~haufen** *m* scrap heap. **~platz** *m* scrap yard. **2reif** *adj* ready for the scrap heap. **~wert** *m* scrap value.

schrubben [ˈʃrʊbən] *v/t* (h) scrub.

'Schrubber *m* (-s; -) scrubbing brush.

Schrulle [ˈʃrʊlə] *f* (-; -n) quirk, (cranky) whim. **'schrullig** *adj* F cranky.

schrump(e)lig [ˈʃrʊmp(ə)lɪç] *adj* shrivel(l)ed.

schrumpfen [ˈʃrʊmpfən] *v/i* (sn) shrink (*a.* ⚙), 🜪 *a.* atrophy, *fig. a.* dwindle.

Schub [ʃuːp] *m* (-[e]s; -e) **1.** push, *phys. a.* thrust. **2.** batch. **3.** 🜪 phase, *a.* attack, rush (*of adrenaline etc*): *in Schüben* intermittent(ly). **~fach** *n* drawer. **~kraft** *f phys.* thrust. **~lade** *f* (-; -n) drawer.

Schubs [ʃʊps] *m* (-es; -e) F (*a. dat e-n* ~ *geben*) push, shove.

'schubsen *v/t* (h) F push, shove.

schubweise *adv* in batches.

schüchtern [ˈʃʏçtərn] *adj* shy, timid, bashful. **'Schüchternheit** *f* (-; *no pl*) shyness, timidity, bashfulness.

Schuft [ʃʊft] *m* (-[e]s; -e) scoundrel.

schuften [ˈʃʊftən] *v/i* (h) F slave away.

Schufte'rei *f* (-; *no pl*) F drudgery, grind.

Schuh [ʃuː] *m* (-[e]s; -e) shoe (*a.* ⚙), *fig. j-m et. in die* ~*e schieben* put the blame for s.th. on s.o.; *wo drückt dich der* ~? what's the trouble? **~bürste** *f* shoe brush. **~creme** *f* shoe polish. **~geschäft** *n* shoe shop. **~größe** *f* shoe size: *welche* ~ *haben Sie?* what size shoe(s) do you take? **~löffel** *m* shoehorn. **~macher** *m* (-s; -) shoemaker. **~putzer** *m* (-s; -) shoeblack. **~sohle** *f* sole. **~spanner** *m* shoe tree. **~werk** *n* (-[e]s; *no pl*) footwear, shoes.

Schukostecker [ˈʃuːko-] *m* (*TM*) ⚡ shockproof plug.

'Schul|abgänger [-gɛŋər] *m* (-s; -) school-leaver. **~alter** *n* school age. **~anfänger** *m* (-s; -) (school) beginner.

~arbeiten *pl*, ~aufgaben *pl* homework. ~ausflug *m* school outing. ~bank *f* (-; ~e) desk: **die ~ drücken** go to school. ~behörde *f* education authority. ~beispiel *n* classic example (**für** of). ~besuch *m* (school) attendance. ~bildung *f* (-; *no pl*) education: **höhere ~** secondary education. ~buch *n* textbook. ~buchverlag *m* educational publishers. ~bus *m* school bus.

Schuld [ʃʊlt] *f* (-; -en) **1.** *no pl* guilt (*a.* 🕮), blame, *eccl.* sin(s): **ihn trifft die ~, er ist schuld** he is to blame for it; **die ~ auf sich nehmen** take the blame; **die ~ geben** (*dat*) blame it on; **ohne m-e ~** through no fault of mine; → **zuschieben 2. 2.** *usu. pl* debt: **~en haben, in ~en stecken** be in debt; **in ~en geraten** run into debt; *fig.* (**tief**) **in j-s ~ stehen** be (greatly) indebted to s.o.

'schuldbewußt *adj* guilty (**look** *etc*).

schulden ['ʃʊldən] *v/t* (h) **j-m et. ~** owe s.o. s.th.; → **Dank.**

'**Schuldenberg** *m* F enormous debt(s).

'**schuldenfrei** *adj* a) free of debt, b) unencumbered (*house etc*).

'**Schuldentilgung** *f* liquidation of debts.

'**Schuldforderung** *f* claim, (active) debt.

'**Schuldfrage** *f* question of guilt.

'**Schuldgefühl(e** *pl*) *n* guilty conscience.

'**schuldhaft** *adj* 🕮 culpable.

'**Schuldienst** *m* (-[e]s; *no pl*) teaching: **im ~ sein** be a teacher.

schuldig ['ʃʊldɪç] *adj* **1.** (*gen*) *a.* 🕮 guilty (of), responsible (for): **j-n für ~ befinden** find s.o. guilty (**e-s Verbrechens** of a crime, **e-r Anklage** on a charge); **j-n ~ sprechen** pronounce s.o. guilty; **sich ~ bekennen** plead guilty. **2.** **j-m et. ~ sein** owe s.o. s.th.; **was bin ich Ihnen ~?** how much do I owe you?; **das ist man ihm ~** that's his due; **j-m die Antwort ~ bleiben** give s.o. no answer.

Schuldige ['ʃʊldɪgə] *m*, *f* (-n, -n) culprit, 🕮 guilty party, offender.

'**Schuldigkeit** *f* (-; *no pl*) duty.

'**Schuldi.rektor** *m* headmaster, *Am.* principal.

'**schuldlos** *adj* innocent (**an** *dat* of).

'**Schuldner** ['ʃʊldnər] *m* (-s; -) debtor.

'**Schuldnerland** *n* debtor nation.

'**Schuld|schein** *m* (-[e]s; -e) promissory note, IOU (= I owe you). ~spruch *m*

🕮 verdict of guilty, conviction. ~verschreibung *f* 🕮 (debenture) bond.

Schule ['ʃuːlə] *f* (-; -n) school: **höhere ~** secondary school, *Am.* senior high school; **auf** (*or* **in**) **der ~** at school; **in die** (*or* **zur**) **~ gehen** go to school; *fig.* **aus der ~ plaudern** tell tales out of school, blab; **~ machen** set a precedent, be imitated, spread; **durch e-e harte ~ gehen** learn the hard way; → **besuchen, schwänzen.**

'**schulen** *v/t* (h) train; → **geschult.**

'**Schulenglisch** *n* school English.

Schüler ['ʃyːlər] *m* (-s; -) a) schoolboy, *a.* pupil, student, b) disciple.

'**Schüleraustausch** *m* school exchange.

'**Schülerin** *f* (-; -nen) schoolgirl (*etc*, → **Schüler**).

'**Schüler|lotse** *m* pupil acting as a school crossing warden. ~zeitung *f* school magazine.

'**Schul|fach** *n* subject. ~ferien *pl* holidays, *Am.* vacation. ~fernsehen *n* educational television. ~flugzeug *n* training aircraft, trainer. 2frei *adj* ~ haben have a holiday; **heute ist ~** there's no school today. ~freund(in *f*) *m* schoolmate. ~funk *m* school broadcasts. ~gelände *n* school grounds, *Am.* campus. ~geld *n* (-[e]s; *no pl*) school fees. ~heft *n* exercise book. ~hof *m* playground, schoolyard.

schulisch ['ʃuːlɪʃ] *adj* school (*affairs etc*): ~e **Leistungen** progress at school.

'**Schul|jahr** *n* school year: **m-e ~e** my school days. ~junge *m* schoolboy. ~kame.rad(in *f*) *m* schoolmate. ~kenntnisse *pl* school knowledge. ~klasse *f* class, *Br. a.* form, *Am.* grade. ~leiter(in *f*) *m* headmaster (-mistress), *Am.* principal. ~mädchen *n* schoolgirl. ~mappe *f* schoolbag. ~medi.zin *f* orthodox medicine. ~meinung *f* received opinion. ~ordnung *f* school regulations. ~pflicht *f* compulsory education.

'**schulpflichtig** *adj* school-age, of school age: ~es **Alter** school(-entering) age.

'**Schul|psycho.loge** *m* educational psychologist. ~ranzen *m* satchel. ~rat *m* school inspector. ~schiff *n* training ship. ~schluß *m* (-sses; *no pl*) a) end of school, b) end of term: **nach ~** after school. ~schwänzer *m* (-s; -) truant. ~speisung *f* school meals. ~spre-

cher(in f) m head boy (girl). **~stunde** f lesson, class. **~tasche** f schoolbag.

Schulter ['ʃʊltər] f (-; -n) shoulder: **~ an ~** shoulder to shoulder; **mit den ~n zukken** shrug one's shoulders; **j-m auf die ~ klopfen** slap s.o.'s back; → **kalt** I, **leicht** 1. **~blatt** n anat. shoulder blade.

'schulter|frei adj off-the-shoulder (dress). **~lang** adj shoulder-length.

schultern ['ʃʊltərn] v/t (h) shoulder.

'Schulung f (-; -en) **1.** training, a. practice. **2.** pol. indoctrination.

'Schulungskurs m course of training.

'Schul|unterricht m lessons, classes. **~weg** m (**auf dem ~** on one's way to school. **~weisheit** f book learning. **~wesen** n (-s; no pl) school system. **~zeit** f school days. **~zeugnis** n (school) report, report card.

schummeln ['ʃʊməln] v/i (h) F cheat.

schumm(e)rig ['ʃʊm(ə)rɪç] adj F dim.

Schund [ʃʊnt] m (-[e]s; no pl) trash, rubbish. **'Schundro,man** m trashy novel.

schunkeln ['ʃʊŋkəln] v/i (h) rock, sway.

Schuppe ['ʃʊpə] f (-; -n) **1.** scale: **es fiel mir wie ~n von den Augen** the scales fell from my eyes. **2.** pl dandruff.

schuppen ['ʃʊpən] (h) **I** v/t scale (fish). **II sich ~** skin: peel.

'Schuppen m (-s; -) **1.** shed, **✗** a. hangar. **2.** F a) contp. hovel, b) joint.

schuppig ['ʃʊpɪç] adj scaly.

Schur [ʃuːr] f (-; -en) a) shearing, b) fleece.

schürfen ['ʃʏrfən] (h) **I** v/i **1.** (**nach** for) prospect, dig. fig. **tiefer ~** dig below the surface. **II** v/t **2.** prospect (or dig) for (ore etc). **3.** scrape, graze (skin).

'Schürfwunde f graze, abrasion.

Schurke ['ʃʊrkə] m (-n; -n) villain.

'Schurwolle f virgin (or new) wool.

Schurz [ʃʊrts] m (-es; -e) apron.

Schürze ['ʃʏrtsə] f (-; -n) apron.

schürzen ['ʃʏrtsən] v/t (h) gather up (skirt), purse (lips).

'Schürzenjäger m F womanizer.

Schuß [ʃʊs] m (-sses; ⸗sse) **1.** shot (a. phot. or sports), round (of ammunition): **ein ~ ins Schwarze** a. fig. a bull's-eye; **e-n ~ abgeben** fire (a shot); **weit vom ~** well out of harm's way; **er (es) ist k-n ~ Pulver wert** he (it) is no good; fig. **der ~ ging nach hinten los** it backfired; → **Bug** 1. **2.** → **Schußverletzung**. **3.** F

shot, sl. fix: **sich e-n ~ setzen** give o.s. a fix. **4.** skiing: (a. **im ~ fahren**) schuss. **5.** dash (a. fig.): **Tee mit e-m ~ Milch** tea with a dash of milk; **e-e Cola mit ~** a spiked coke. **6.** fig. (**gut**) **in** (or **im**) **~ sein** be in good shape; **in ~ bringen** knock s.th. into shape, bring s.o. up to the mark; **in ~ halten** keep s.o., s.th. in good shape. **7.** textil. weft.

'schußbereit adj ready to shoot (a. phot.), gun: at the ready.

Schussel ['ʃʊsəl] m (-s; -) F scatterbrain.

Schüssel ['ʃʏsəl] f (-; -n) bowl, basin, a. F TV dish.

'schusselig adj F scatterbrained.

'Schuß|fahrt f skiing: schuss. **~linie** f line of fire: fig. **in die ~ geraten** come under fire (gen from). **~verletzung** f gunshot wound. **~waffe** f firearm. **~wechsel** m exchange of shots. **~weite** f (firing) range: **außer ~** out of range.

Schuster ['ʃuːstər] m (-s; -) shoemaker.

Schutt [ʃʊt] m (-[e]s; no pl) rubble, geol. a. debris: **in ~ und Asche liegen** be in ruins.

'Schüttelfrost m 🅜 shivering fit.

schütteln ['ʃʏtəln] v/t (h) shake: **den Kopf ~** shake one's head; **j-m die Hand ~** shake hands with s.o., shake s.o. by the hand; → **Ärmel**.

schütten ['ʃʏtən] v/t (h) pour: F **es schüttet** it's pouring (with rain).

schütter ['ʃʏtər] adj thin (hair etc).

'Schutthaufen m heap of rubble.

Schutz [ʃʊts] m (-es; no pl) protection (**gegen, vor** against, from), a. shelter, esp. ✗ cover, escort, (esp. legal) safeguard, a. preservation: **~ suchen** seek refuge (**vor** from, **bei** with); **j-n in ~ nehmen** come to s.o.'s defence, back s.o. up; **im ~e der Dunkelheit** under cover of darkness.

Schütz [ʃʏts] n (-es; -e) ⚡ contactor.

'Schutzanzug m protective suit.

'Schutzbefohlene m, f (-n; -n) charge.

'Schutzblech n mudguard, Am. fender.

'Schutzbrille f (safety) goggles.

Schütze ['ʃʏtsə] m (-n; -n) **1.** shot, marksman. **2.** sports: scorer. **3.** ✗ private. **4.** no pl astr. ([**ein**] **~ sein** be [a]) Sagittarius.

'schützen v/t (h) (**gegen, vor** dat) protect (from, against), defend (against), shelter (from), guard (against), a. fig. shield

(from), *esp.* ⚔ cover (against): **sich ~ (vor)** guard (against), protect o.s. (from): **~des Dach** shelter; → **Nässe**.
'**Schutzengel** *m* guardian angel.
'**Schützen|graben** *m* ⚔ trench. **~hilfe** *f j-m ~ geben* back s.o. up. **~könig** *m* champion shot, *sports:* top scorer. **~panzer** *m* ⚔ armo(u)red personnel carrier.
'**Schutz|gebiet** *n* protectorate. **~geld** *n* protection money. **~haft** *f* protective custody. **~heilige** *m, f* (-n; -n) patron saint. **~helm** *m* helmet. **~herrschaft** *f* protectorate. **~hülle** *f* protective cover, ☉ sheath, *for passport etc:* holder. **~hütte** *f* shelter. **~impfung** *f* inoculation, vaccination. **~kappe** *f* protective cap, *phot.* lens cap. **~kleidung** *f* protective clothing.
Schützling ['ʃʏtslɪŋ] *m* (-s; -e) a) charge, b) protégé(e *f*).
'**schutzlos** *adj* unprotected, defenceless, *Am.* defenseless.
'**Schutz|macht** *f pol.* protecting power. **~marke** *f (eingetragene ~* registered) trademark. **~maske** *f* (protective) mask. **~maßnahme** *f* protective (*or* safety) measure, precaution. **~rechte** *pl* patent (*or* trademark) rights. **~schicht** *f* protective layer. **~schild** *m* shield. **~umschlag** *m* (dust) jacket. **~vorrichtung** *f* safety device. **~zoll** *m* protective duty.
schwabb(e)lig ['ʃvab(ə)lɪç] *adj* flabby.
Schwabe ['ʃvaːbə] *m* (-n; -n) Swabian. '**Schwaben** *n* (-s) Swabia. **Schwäbin** ['ʃvɛːbɪn] *f* (-; -nen) Swabian (girl *or* woman). '**schwäbisch** *adj* Swabian.
schwach [ʃvax] **I** *adj* **1.** weak (*a. ling.*), *a.* faint, *a.* infirm: *humor. das ~ Geschlecht* the weaker sex; **~ werden** weaken; *schwächer werden* weaken, *eyesight:* fail, *sound, light:* fade, ⚕ *demand:* fall off; F *nur nicht ~ werden!* don't weaken!; **~e Erinnerung** faint (*or* vague) recollection; **~e Hoffnung** faint hope; → **Trost. 2.** *fig.* weak, *a.* poor (*hearing, memory, etc*), low (*battery*), low-powered (*engine*), slow (*pulse*), dim (*light*): **~e Leistung** poor performance; **~e Seite** weakness. **3.** ⚗ dilute (*solution*). **II** *adv* **~ bevölkert** sparsely populated; **~ besucht** poorly attended.
Schwäche ['ʃvɛçə] *f* (-; -n) **1.** weakness,

faintness (*a. fig.*). **2.** *fig.* weakness, failing, shortcoming, weak point. **3.** *no pl* weakness (**für** for): *e-e ~ für j-n haben* F have a soft spot for s.o. **~anfall** *m,* **~gefühl** *n* (sudden feeling of) faintness.
schwächen ['ʃvɛçən] *v/t* (h) weaken.
'**Schwachheit** *f* (-; *no pl*) weakness.
'**Schwachkopf** *m* F idiot, twit.
'**schwächlich** ['ʃvɛçlɪç] *adj* weakly, *a.* delicate, sickly.
'**Schwächling** *m* (-s; -e) weakling.
'**schwachsichtig** *adj* ⚕ weak-sighted.
'**Schwachsinn** *m* (-[e]s; *no pl*) **1.** ⚕ mental deficiency. **2.** F *contp.* a) idiocy, b) rubbish. '**schwachsinnig** *adj* **1.** ⚕ mentally deficient. **2.** F *contp.* idiotic. '**Schwachsinnige** *m, f* (-n; -n) *a.* F *contp.* imbecile.
'**Schwachstelle** *f* weak point.
'**Schwachstrom** *m* low-voltage current.
'**Schwachstromtechnik** *f* communications engineering.
'**Schwächung** *f* (-; -en) weakening.
Schwaden ['ʃvaːdən] *m* (-s; -) cloud.
schwafeln ['ʃvaːfəln] *v/i* (h) F blether.
Schwager ['ʃvaːgər] *m* (-s; ·) brother-in-law. **Schwägerin** ['ʃvɛːgərɪn] *f* (-; -nen) sister-in-law.
Schwalbe ['ʃvalbə] *f* (-; -n) *zo.* swallow.
'**Schwalbennest** *n* swallow's nest.
Schwall [ʃval] *m* (-[e]s; -e) *a. fig.* gush, flood, torrent.
schwamm [ʃvam] *pret of* **schwimmen.**
Schwamm *m* (-[e]s; ·e) **1.** sponge: *fig. ~ drüber!* (let's) forget it! **2.** a) fungus, b) → *Pilz,* c) dry rot. '**schwammig** *adj* **1.** spongy, flabby (*body*), puffy (*face*). **2.** *fig.* woolly (*idea, concept, etc*).
Schwan [ʃvaːn] *m* (-[e]s; ·e) *zo.* swan.
schwand [ʃvant] *pret of* **schwinden.**
schwanen ['ʃvaːnən] *v/impers* (h) F *mir schwant* s.th. tells me; *ihr schwante nichts Gutes* she feared the worst.
schwang [ʃvaŋ] *pret of* **schwingen.**
Schwang *m im ~ (e) sein* be in vogue.
schwanger ['ʃvaŋər] *adj (im vierten etc Monat ~* four months *etc*) pregnant.
'**Schwangere** *f* (-n; -n) pregnant woman, expectant mother.
schwängern ['ʃvɛŋərn] *v/t* (h) **1.** make *woman* pregnant. **2.** *fig.* impregnate.
'**Schwangerschaft** *f* (-; -en) pregnancy.
'**Schwangerschafts|abbruch** *m* termination of pregnancy, induced abor-

tion. **~gym,nastik** f antenatal exercises. **~streifen** pl stretchmarks. **~test** m pregnancy test.

Schwank [ʃvaŋk] m (-[e]s; ⁓e) **1.** anecdote. **2.** thea. farce.

schwanken ['ʃvaŋkən] v/i **1.** (h) sway, ground etc: a. shake, rock. **2.** (sn) sway, stagger, totter. **3.** (h) (**zwischen** between) waver, vacillate: **ich schwanke noch** I'm still undecided. **4.** (h) temperature, prices, etc: fluctuate, a. vary, alternate: **die Preise ~ zwischen ... und ...** a. prices range from ... to ...

'**Schwanken** n (-s) **1.** swaying (etc). **2.** vacillation. **3.** → **Schwankung** 2.

'**schwankend** adj **1.** swaying (etc). **2.** a) undecided, wavering, b) unstable.

'**Schwankung** f (-; -en) **1.** → **Schwanken** 2. **2.** variation, a. ♄ fluctuation.

Schwanz [ʃvants] m (-es; ⁓e) **1.** zo. tail (a. ☙ etc): F **kein ~** not a (blessed) soul. **2.** fig. tail end. **3.** V cock, dick.

schwänzen ['ʃvɛntsən] v/i, v/t (h) F (**die Schule**) ⁓ play truant (Am. hooky).

'**Schwanzfeder** f tail feather.

'**Schwanzflosse** f tail fin.

'**schwanzlastig** adj ☙ tail-heavy.

schwappen ['ʃvapən] v/i **1.** (h) slosh around. **2.** (sn) slop, spill.

Schwarm [ʃvarm] m (-[e]s; ⁓e) **1.** swarm, a. crowd, flight (of birds), shoal (of fish). **2.** F a) heartthrob, b) dream.

schwärmen ['ʃvɛrmən] v/i (h) **1.** swarm. **2.** enthuse (or rave) (**von** about): **~ für** be crazy about; **für j-n ~** a. have a crush on s.o.; **ins Schwärmen geraten** go into raptures. '**Schwärmer** m (-s; -) **1.** enthusiast, dreamer. **2.** squib. **3.** zo. hawk moth. **Schwärme'rei** f (-; -en) enthusiasm, passion. '**schwärmerisch** adj enthusiastic, gushing.

Schwarte ['ʃvartə] f (-; -n) **1.** (bacon) rind. **2.** F old book, tome.

schwarz [ʃvarts] adj **1.** black (a. coffee, tea), a. swarthy, dark-skinned, F a. dirty, a. deeply tanned: **Schwarzer Erdteil** Black Continent; **~er Humor** black humo(u)r, thea. Black Comedy; **~ auf weiß** in black and white, in cold print; **mir wurde ~ vor den Augen** everything went black; F **sich ~ ärgern** be terribly annoyed; **da kann er warten, bis er ~ wird** he can wait till he's blue in the face; → **Brett, Liste, Schaf** 1 etc;

schwarzfahren, schwarzsehen. 2. fig. black, gloomy: **~er Tag** black day. **3.** F fig. black, illicit: **der ~e Markt** the black market. **4.** F Catholic(-Conservative).

Schwarz n (-[es]; -) black: **in ~ gehen** be dressed in black (or in mourning). **~arbeit** f illicit work, F moonlighting. **~arbeiter** m illicit worker, F moonlighter. **~brot** n brown bread.

'**Schwarze¹** m (-n; -n) **1.** black: **die ~n** the Blacks. **2.** black-haired man (or boy). **3.** F Catholic(-Conservative).

'**Schwarze²** f (-n; -n) **1.** black (woman or girl). **2.** black-haired woman (or girl).

'**Schwarze³** n (-n; -n) **1.** black dress. **2.** a. fig. **ins ~ treffen** hit the bull's-eye.

Schwärze ['ʃvɛrtsə] f (-; no pl) **1.** blackness. **2.** darkness.

schwärzen ['ʃvɛrtsən] v/t (h) blacken.

'**Schwarzfahren** v/i (irr, sep, -ge-, sn, → **fahren**) **1.** a) go without paying, b) mot. drive without a licen/ce (Am. -se).

'**Schwarzfahrer(in** f) m fare dodger.

'**schwarzhaarig** adj black-haired.

'**Schwarz|handel** m black market(eering): **im ~** on the black market. **~händler** m black marketeer. **~hörer** m (radio) licen/ce (Am. -se) dodger.

'**schwärzlich** adj blackish, swarthy.

'**Schwarz|markt** m black market. **⁓sehen** v/i (irr, sep, -ge-, h, → **sehen**) be pessimistic (**für** about): **ich sehe schwarz (für dich)!** things look bad (for you)! **~seher** m **1.** pessimist. **2.** TV-licen/ce (Am. -se) dodger. **~sender** m pirate (radio) station.

Schwarz'weiß... black-and-white (film, television, etc).

'**Schwarzwild** n hunt. wild boars.

Schwatz [ʃvats] m (-es; -e) chat.

'**schwatzen, dial. schwätzen** ['ʃvɛtsən] (h) **I** v/i a) chat, b) blab. **II** v/t **dummes Zeug ~** talk rubbish.

'**Schwätzer** m (-s; -), '**Schwätzerin** f (-; -nen) chatterbox, blab(ber), F gasbag.

'**schwatzhaft** adj talkative, chatty.

Schwebe ['ʃve:bə] f **in der ~ sein** be undecided, ♄ be pending. **~bahn** f cableway. **~balken** m (balance) beam.

schweben ['ʃve:bən] v/i (sn) **1.** glide, float, sail (all a. fig.), a. hover (a. fig.), a. soar, be suspended, hang: **in Gefahr ~** be in danger; → **Ungewißheit. 2.** be undecided, esp. ♄ be pending.

'**schwebend** *adj* **1.** floating (*etc*, → *schweben* 1). **2.** *esp.* ⚖ pending.
Schwede ['ʃveːdə] *m* (-n; -n) Swede. '**Schweden** *n* (-s) Sweden. '**Schwedin** *f* (-; -nen) Swede. '**schwedisch** *adj* Swedish.
Schwefel ['ʃveːfəl] *m* (-s; *no pl*) sulphur, *Am.* sulfur. '**Schwefeldioxyd** *n* sulphur (*Am.* -f-) dioxide. '**schwefelhaltig** *adj* sulphur(e)ous (*Am.* -f-). '**schwefeln** *v/t* (h) 🜍 sulphurate (*Am.* -f-), *a.* 🜍 sulphurize (*Am.* -f-).
'**Schwefelsäure** *f* sulphuric (*Am.* -f-) acid. **Schwefel'wasserstoff** *m* hydrogen sulphide (*Am.* -f-).
'**schweflig** ['ʃveːflɪç] *adj* sulphur(e)ous (*Am.* -f-).
Schweif [ʃvaɪf] *m* (-[e]s; -e) **1.** tail (*a. astr.*). **2.** *fig.* train.
'**schweifen** *v/i* (sn) *a. fig.* wander, roam.
'**Schweige|geld** *n* hush money. **~marsch** *m* silent protest march. **~mi‚nute** *f* one minute's silence (**zu Ehren** *gen* in memory of).
schweigen ['ʃvaɪgən] (schwieg, geschwiegen, h) *v/i* (**über** *acc*, **zu**) be silent (on), keep mum (on, about), say nothing: **ganz zu ~ von ...** to say nothing of ..., let alone ... '**Schweigen** *n* (-s) (*a.* **zum ~ bringen**) silence: → **hüllen**. '**schweigend** *adj* silent(ly *adv*), *adv a.* in silence: **~e Mehrheit** silent majority.
'**Schweigepflicht** *f* secrecy, professional discretion.
'**schweigsam** *adj* quiet, silent, *a.* taciturn. '**Schweigsamkeit** *f* (-; *no pl*) quietness, silence, taciturnity.
Schwein [ʃvaɪn] *n* (-[e]s; -e) **1.** *zo.* pig, hog, swine, *a.* sow. **2.** *gastr.* pork. **3.** *contp.* a) F (filthy) pig, b) V bastard, swine, c) F soul: **kein ~** not a (blessed) soul; **armes ~!** poor sod! **4.** F luck: **~ haben** be lucky.
'**Schweine|braten** *m* roast pork. **~fi‚let** *n* fillet of pork. **~fleisch** *n* pork. **~hund** *m* V swine, bastard: F **den inneren ~ überwinden** conquer one's weaker self. **~kote‚lett** *n* pork chop.
Schweine'rei *f* (-; -en) F **1.** (awful) mess, filth. **2.** a) dirty trick, b) crying shame. **3.** → **Schweinigelei**.
'**Schweine|stall** *m a. fig.* pigsty. **~zucht** *f* pig-breeding, hog raising.
Schweinigel ['ʃvaɪnʔiːgəl] *m* (-s; -) F fil-

thy pig. **Schweinige'lei** *f* (-; -en) F dirty joke, obscenity. '**schweinigeln** *v/i* (h) F **1.** mess about. **2.** talk smut.
'**schweinisch** *adj* F filthy.
'**Schweins|haxe** *f* (-; -n) *gastr.* knuckle of pork. **~leder** *n* pigskin.
Schweiß [ʃvaɪs] *m* (-es; -e) **1.** sweat, perspiration: **in ~ geraten** get into a sweat; **das hat viel ~ gekostet** that was hard work. **2.** *hunt.* blood. **~band** *n* (-[e]s; ⸚er) sweatband. **~blatt** *n* dress-shield. **~brenner** *m* 🜍 welding torch. **~drüse** *f* *anat.* sweat gland.
schweißen ['ʃvaɪsən] *v/t* (h) 🜍 weld. '**Schweißer** *m* (-s; -) 🜍 welder.
'**Schweißfüße** *pl* sweaty feet.
'**schweißgebadet** *adj* bathed in sweat.
'**Schweißgeruch** *m* smell of sweat.
'**schweißig** ['ʃvaɪsɪç] *adj* sweaty.
'**Schweiß|naht** *f* (welding) seam. **~perle** *f* bead of perspiration. **~stelle** *f* weld. **Ꝗtriefend** *adj* dripping with sweat. **~tropfen** *m* bead of perspiration.
Schweiz [ʃvaɪts] *f* (-) Switzerland.
Schweizer ['ʃvaɪtsər] **I** *m* (-s; -) Swiss: **die ~** the Swiss. **II** *adj* Swiss: **~ Käse** Swiss cheese. '**Schweizerdeutsch** *n* Swiss German. '**Schweizerin** *f* (-; -nen) Swiss (woman *or* girl).
'**schweizerisch** *adj* Swiss.
schwelen ['ʃveːlən] *v/i* (h) smo(u)lder.
schwelgen ['ʃvɛlgən] *v/i* (h) revel (**in** *dat* in).
Schwelle ['ʃvɛlə] *f* (-; -n) **1.** threshold (*a. fig.*). **2.** 🛤 sleeper, *Am.* tie.
schwellen ['ʃvɛlən] *v/i*, *v/t* (schwoll, geschwollen, sn) swell.
'**Schwellenland** *n* emergent nation.
'**Schwellung** *f* (-; -en) swelling.
Schwemme ['ʃvɛmə] *f* (-; -n) **1.** watering place. **2.** pub. **3.** ✝ glut (**an** *dat* of).
schwemmen ['ʃvɛmən] *v/t* (h) wash.
'**Schwemmland** *n* alluvial land.
Schwengel ['ʃvɛŋəl] *m* (-s; -) handle.
Schwenk [ʃvɛŋk] *m* (-[e]s; -s) *film:* pan.
'**Schwenkarm** *m* 🜍 swivel arm.
'**schwenkbar** *adj* swivel(l)ing, slewing.
schwenken ['ʃvɛŋkən] **I** *v/t* (h) **1.** a) swing, 🜍 *a.* turn, slew, b) wave (*hat, flag, etc*), brandish (*stick*), c) *film etc:* pan (*camera*). **2.** rinse. **3.** *gastr.* toss. **II** *v/i* (sn) **4.** turn, swing (round), *camera:* pan, ✗ wheel. '**Schwenkung** *f* (-; -en) **1.** turn, swing, ✗ wheel(ing), *film*

etc: pan. **2.** change of mind (*pol.* of front).

schwer [ʃveːr] **I** *adj* **1.** heavy: **100 Pfund ~ sein** weigh 100 pounds. **2.** *fig.* heavy (*storm, losses, etc*), bad (*mistake etc*), hard, difficult, F tough (*decision, struggle, work, etc*), serious (*illness, accident, etc*), onerous (*duty etc*), grave (*crime etc*): **ein ~er Schock** a bad (or terrible) shock; **~er Diebstahl** aggravated larceny; **~er Gegner** formidable opponent; **~es Schicksal** hard lot; **~er Tag** hard day; **~e Zeit(en)** hard times; **~en Herzens** with a heavy heart, reluctantly; **er hat es ~** he has a hard time; → **Begriff** 2 *etc*. **3.** rich, heavy (*food*), strong (*cigar, scent, etc*): **~er Wein** heady wine. **II** *adv* **4.** heavily (*etc*), F very much, awfully, badly: **~ arbeiten** work hard; F **~ aufpassen** watch (out) like hell; F **~ zu bekommen** hard to get; F **~ beleidigt** deeply offended; **~ büßen müssen** have to pay dearly; **~ hören** be hard of hearing; **~ krank** seriously ill; **~ zu sagen** hard to say; **sie ist ~ gestürzt** she had a nasty fall; **~ zu verstehen** difficult to understand; F **da hat er sich aber ~ getäuscht** he's very much mistaken there.

'**Schwer|arbeit** *f* heavy labo(u)r. **~ath,let** *m* heavy athlete. **~behinderte** *m, f* 🏃 severely handicapped person.

'**schwerbeladen** *adj* heavily laden.

'**schwerbewaffnet** *adj* heavily armed.

'**Schwere** [ʃveːrə] *f* (-; *no pl*) **1.** weight, *phys.* gravity. **2.** *fig.* seriousness, gravity, severity, *a.* weightiness. **3.** heaviness (*of food etc*). '**schwerelos** *adj* weightless. '**Schwerelosigkeit** *f* (-; *no pl*) weightlessness.

Schwerenöter ['ʃveːrənøːtər] *m* (-s; -) *humor.* philanderer.

'**schwererziehbar** *adj* difficult, recalcitrant: **~es Kind** *a.* problem child.

'**schwerfallen** *v/i* (*irr, sep,* -ge-, sn, → **fallen**) be difficult (*dat* for): **es fällt mir schwer** *a.* I find it hard.

'**schwerfällig** *adj* awkward, clumsy, heavy, ponderous (*a. fig.*), slow. '**Schwerfälligkeit** *f* (-; *no pl*) clumsiness, heaviness, ponderousness.

'**Schwergewicht** *n* (-[e]s; *no pl*) **1.** *sports*: heavyweight. **2.** *fig.* emphasis.

'**schwerhalten** *v/impers* (*irr, sep,* -ge-, h, → **halten**) **es hält schwer** it is difficult.

'**schwerhörig** *adj* hard of hearing.

'**Schwerhörigkeit** *f* (-; *no pl*) partial deafness.

'**Schwerindu,strie** *f* heavy industry.

'**Schwerkraft** *f* (-; *no pl*) (force of) gravity.

'**schwerlich** *adv* hardly.

'**schwermachen** *v/t* (*sep,* -ge-, h) **j-m et. ~** make s.th. difficult (or hard) for s.o.; **j-m das Leben ~** make life difficult for s.o; **mach es mir nicht so schwer!** don't make it so hard for me!

'**Schwermut** *f* (-; *no pl*) melancholy.

'**schwermütig** [-myːtɪç] *adj* melancholy.

'**schwernehmen** *v/t* (*irr, sep,* -ge-, h, → **nehmen**) **et. ~** take s.th. hard.

'**Schwerpunkt** *m* **1.** cent/re (*Am.* -er) of gravity. **2.** *fig.* a) focal point, b) emphasis: **~e bilden** set up priorities.

'**Schwerpunktstreik** *m* pinpoint strike.

'**schwerreich** *adj* F exceedingly rich.

Schwert [ʃveɐt] *n* (-[e]s; -er) sword. **~fisch** *m* swordfish. **~lilie** *f* iris.

'**schwertun: sich ~** (*irr, sep,* -ge-, h, → **tun**) have a hard time (**mit** with).

'**Schwerverbrecher** *m* felon, dangerous criminal.

'**schwerverdaulich** *adj* indigestible (*a. fig.*), heavy.

'**Schwerverletzte** *m, f* (-n; -n) seriously injured person. '**Schwerverwundete** *m, f* (-n; -n) seriously wounded person.

'**schwerwiegend** *adj* weighty, grave.

Schwester ['ʃvɛstər] *f* (-; -n) **1.** *a. fig.* sister. **2.** (hospital) nurse, sister. **3.** *eccl.* sister, nun. **4.** → '**Schwesterfirma** *f* sister company.

'**schwesterlich** *adj* sisterly.

schwieg [ʃviːk] *pret of* **schweigen**.

Schwieger|eltern ['ʃviːgər-] *pl* parents-in-law. **~mutter** *f* mother-in-law. **~sohn** *m* son-in-law. **~tochter** *f* daughter-in-law. **~vater** *m* father-in-law.

Schwiele ['ʃviːlə] *f* (-; -n) callus.

'**schwielig** *adj* horny, callused.

schwierig ['ʃviːrɪç] *adj* difficult, hard, F tough. '**Schwierigkeit** *f* (-; -en) difficulty, trouble: (**j-m**) **~en machen** be a problem (to s.o.), *pers:* make things difficult (for s.o.); **in ~en geraten**, **~en bekommen** get into trouble; **~en haben zu** *inf* find it difficult to *inf*.

'**Schwimm|bad** n swimming pool (or bath). **~dock** n floating dock.

schwimmen ['ʃvɪmən] v/i (shwamm, geschwommen, h and sn) **1.** swim (a. v/t distance, record, etc), object: float, F floor etc: be flooded: **~ gehen** go swimming; F **im Geld ~** be rolling in money. **2.** F fig. flounder.

'**Schwimmen** n (-s) swimming: F fig. **ins ~ kommen** (begin to) flounder.

Schwimmer ['ʃvɪmər] m (-s; -) **1.** swimmer. **2.** fishing, ⊙ float.

'**Schwimmerin** f (-; -nen) swimmer.

'**Schwimm|gürtel** m swimming belt. **~halle** f indoor pool. **~haut** f zo. web. **~lehrer(in** f) m swimming instructor. **~sport** m swimming. **~verein** m swimming club. **~weste** f life jacket.

Schwindel ['ʃvɪndəl] m (-s; no pl) **1.** ⚕ dizziness, vertigo. **2.** F a) swindle, b) lie. **3.** F **der ganze ~** the whole lot.

'**Schwindelanfall** m ⚕ dizzy spell.

Schwinde|lei f (-; -en) **1.** → Schwindel 2. **2.** a) cheating, b) lying.

'**schwindelerregend** adj dizzy, giddy (a. fig.), fig. staggering (prices etc).

'**schwindelfrei** adj: **nicht ~ sein** have a good head for heights; **nicht ~ sein** be afraid of heights.

schwind(e)lig ['ʃvɪnd(ə)lɪç] adj giddy, dizzy (a. fig.): **mir ist ~** I feel dizzy.

'**schwindeln** v/i (h) **1. mir schwindelt** I feel dizzy, my head reels. **2.** lie, F tell fibs. **3. in ~der Höhe** at a giddy height.

schwinden ['ʃvɪndən] v/i (schwand, geschwunden, sn) strength, supplies, etc: dwindle, colo(u)r, light, beauty, etc: fade: **~de Hoffnung** dwindling hope.

Schwindler ['ʃvɪndlər] m (-s; -) a) swindler, F con man, b) liar.

Schwinge ['ʃvɪŋə] f (-; -n) wing.

schwingen ['ʃvɪŋən] (schwang, geschwungen, h) **I** v/t **1.** swing, wave, brandish: **er schwang sich auf sein Rad** he swung himself on his bicycle; **~ Rede.** **II** v/i **2.** a. (sn) swing. **3.** phys. oscillate, vibrate.

'**Schwinger** m (-s; -) boxing: swing.

'**Schwingkreis** m ⚡ resonant circuit.

'**Schwingung** f (-; -en) phys. vibration, oscillation: a. fig. et. in **~en versetzen** set s.th. vibrating. '**schwingungsfrei** adj free from vibration.

Schwips [ʃvɪps] m F **e-n ~ haben** be tipsy.

schwirren ['ʃvɪrən] v/i **1.** (sn) whir(r), insects etc: buzz, arrow etc: whizz: **Gerüchte ~ durch die Stadt** the town is buzzing with rumo(u)rs. **2.** (h) **mir schwirrt der Kopf** my head is in a whirl.

schwitzen ['ʃvɪtsən] v/i, v/t (h) sweat (a. ⊙), perspire: fig. **ins Schwitzen kommen** get into a sweat.

Schwof [ʃvoːf] m (-[e]s; -e) F hop.

schwofen ['ʃvoːfən] v/i (h) F shake a leg.

schwoll [ʃvɔl] pret of schwellen.

schwören ['ʃvøːrən] v/i, v/t (schwor, geschworen, h) swear (bei by), ⚖ take the oath: F fig. **ich schwöre auf** (acc) swear by ...; **ich schwöre dir, daß** I swear to you that; → **Eid, Rache.**

schwul [ʃvuːl] adj F gay, contp. queer.

schwül [ʃvyːl] adj a) **1.** sultry, muggy, oppressive. **2.** fig. sultry, sensuous.

'**Schwule** m (-n; -n) F gay, contp. queer.

'**Schwüle** f (-; no pl) a. fig. sultriness.

Schwulst [ʃvʊlst] m (-[e]s; no pl) bombast. **schwülstig** ['ʃvʏlstɪç] adj bombastic.

Schwund [ʃvʊnt] m (-[e]s; no pl) dwindling, decline, ↑, ⊙ shrinkage, ⚕ atrophy, ⚡ fading.

Schwung [ʃvʊŋ] m (-[e]s; ~e) **1.** swing. **2.** no pl swing, impetus (a. fig.), speed: **et. (j-n) in ~ bringen** speed s.th. (s.o.) going; **(richtig) in ~ kommen** get going; **im ~ sein** party etc: be in full swing, person: be in full stride. **3.** no pl verve, zest, drive, F pep. **4.** no pl F batch.

'**Schwungfeder** f zo. pinion.

'**schwunghaft** adj ↑ brisk, roaring.

'**schwunglos** adj spiritless, lifeless.

'**Schwungrad** n ⊙ flywheel.

'**schwungvoll** adj a) full of drive (F go), zestful, b) bold (handwriting), c) swinging (tune). **II** adv with a swing.

Schwur [ʃvuːr] m (-[e]s; ~e) a) oath, b) vow. '**Schwurgericht** n jury court.

sechs [zɛks] adj six. **Sechs** f (-; -en) **1.** six. **2.** ped. very poor (mark). '**Sechseck** n (-[e]s; -e) hexagon. '**sechseckig** adj hexagonal. **Sechs'tagerennen** n six-day (cycling) race. '**sechste** adj sixth. '**Sechstel** n (-s; -) sixth (part). '**sechstens** adv sixthly.

sechzehn(te) ['zɛçtseːn(tə)] adj sixteen(th). '**Sechzehntel** n (-s; -) sixteenth (part).

sechzig ['zɛçtsɪç] adj sixty. '**Sechzig** f (-;

no pl **1.** sixty. **2. sie ist Anfang (der) ~** she is in her early sixties. **sechziger** ['zɛçtsɪɡər] *adj* **die ~ Jahre** the sixties. **'Sechziger** *m* (-s; -) man in his sixties, sexagenarian: **in den ~n sein** be in one's sixties. **'Sechzigerin** *f* (-; -nen) woman in her sixties, sexagenarian. **'sechzigst** *adj* sixtieth.

Sediment [zedi'mɛnt] *n* (-[e]s; -e) sediment.

See¹ [ze:] *m* (-s; -n) lake.

See² *f* (-; -n) **1.** *no pl* sea, ocean: **an der ~** by the seaside; **an die ~ fahren** go to the seaside; **auf ~** at sea; **auf hoher ~** on the high seas; **in ~ gehen** (*or* **stechen**) put to sea; **zur ~ gehen** go to sea; **e-e schwere ~** a heavy sea. **2.** ⚓ big wave, surge, breaker. **~bad** *n* seaside resort. **~bär** *m humor.* **alter ~** old salt. **~beben** *n* (-s; -) seaquake. **~Ele,fant** *m zo.* elephant seal. **~fahrt** *f* (-; -en) **1.** *no pl* seafaring. **2.** voyage, cruise. ⚓**fest** *adj* seaworthy: **(nicht) ~ sein** be a good (bad) sailor. **~fisch** *m* saltwater fish. **~fracht** *f* sea (*or* ocean) freight. **~frachtbrief** *m* bill of lading (B/L). **~gang** *m* (-[e]s; *no pl*) **hoher ~** rough sea; **schwerer ~** heavy sea gang. ⚓**gestützt** *adj* ✕ sea-based. **~gras** *n* seaweed. **~hafen** *m* seaport. **~handel** *m* maritime trade. **~herrschaft** *f* (-; *no pl*) naval supremacy. **~hund** *m* seal. **~igel** *m* sea urchin. **~karte** *f* nautical chart. ⚓**klar** *adj* ⚓ ready to sail. ⚓**krank** *adj* seasick: **leicht ~ werden** be a bad sailor. **~krankheit** *f* (-; *no pl*) seasickness. **~krieg(führung** *f)* *m* naval war(fare). **~lachs** *m zo.* pollack.

Seele ['ze:lə] *f* (-; -n) **1.** soul, mind, *a.* heart: **e-e gute (treue) ~** a good (faithful) soul; **k-e ~** not a (blessed) soul; **zwei ~n und ein Gedanke** two minds and but a single thought; **aus tiefster ~** wish *etc* with all one's heart, *thank etc* from the bottom of one's heart, *hate* like poison; **er ist die ~ des Betriebs** he is the life and soul of the firm; **es liegt mir auf der ~** it weighs heavily on me; **es tat mir in der ~ weh** it hurt me deeply; **du sprichst mir aus der ~** that's exactly how I feel (about it); **sich et. von der ~ reden** F get s.th. off one's chest; → **Leib** *etc.* **2.** core (*of cable*), bore (*of gun*).

'Seelen|arzt *m* F mind doctor, shrink. **~frieden** *m* peace of mind. **~größe** *f* magnanimity. **~heil** *n eccl.* salvation. **~leben** *n* (-s; *no pl*) inner life.

'seelenlos *adj* soulless.

'Seelen|mas,sage *f* F pep talk. **~messe** *f* requiem. **~qual** *f* mental anguish. **~ruhe** *f* a) peace of mind, b) calmness: **in aller ~** → ⚓**ruhig** *adv* (quite) coolly. ⚓**verwandt** *adj* congenial: **~ sein** be kindred souls. ⚓**voll** *adj. a. iro.* soulful. **~wanderung** *f* transmigration of souls. **~zustand** *m* emotional state.

'Seeleute *pl* seamen, sailors.

seelisch *adj* psychological, mental, emotional, *a. eccl.* spiritual: **~e Belastung** (⚖ **Grausamkeit**) mental strain (cruelty); **~ bedingt sein** have psychological causes; → **Gleichgewicht.**

'Seelöwe *m zo.* sea lion.

'Seelsorge *f* (-; *no pl*) pastoral care.

'Seelsorger *m* (-s; -) pastor.

'Seeluft *f* sea air.

'Seemacht *f* naval (*or* sea) power.

'Seemann *m* (-[e]s; -leute) seaman, sailor. **'seemännisch** [-mɛnɪʃ] *adj* a) sailor's ..., b) nautical. **'Seemannsgarn** *n* F **ein ~ spinnen** spin a yarn.

'See|meile *f* nautical mile. **~not** *f* distress at sea: **Schiffe in ~** distressed ships. **~not(rettungs)dienst** *m* sea rescue service. **~pferdchen** *n zo.* seahorse. **~räuber** *m* pirate. **~reise** *f* voyage, cruise. **~rose** *f* ⚘ water lily. **~schiffahrt** *f* **1.** ocean shipping. **2.** ocean navigation. **~schlacht** *f* naval battle. **~stern** *m zo.* starfish. **~streitkräfte** *pl* naval forces. **~tang** *m* ⚘ seaweed. ⚓**tüchtig** *adj* seaworthy. **~salz** *n* salt water. **~weg** *m* sea route: **auf dem ~** by sea. **~wind** *m* sea breeze. **~zunge** *f zo.* sole.

Segel ['ze:ɡəl] *n* (-s; -) sail: **~ setzen** set sail; **~ hissen** make sail; **die ~ streichen** strike sail, *fig. a.* give in; → **Wind.** **~boot** *n* sailing boat, *Am.* sailboat, *sports*: yacht. **~fliegen** *n* gliding. **~flieger** *m* glider pilot. **~flug** *m* **1.** glider flight. **2.** gliding. **~flugplatz** *m* gliding field. **~flugzeug** *n* glider. ⚓**klar** *adj* ready to sail. **~klub** *m* yachting club.

segeln ['ze:ɡəln] I *v/i* **1.** (sn *and* h) sail, 🜉 glide. **2.** (sn) *fig.* sail, *bird: a.* soar. II *v/t* **3.** (h *and* sn) sail.

'Segeln *n* (-s) sailing.

'Segel|schiff *n* sailing ship. **~sport** *m* sailing, yachting. **~tuch** *n* (-[e]s; -e) canvas. **~tuchschuhe** *pl* canvas shoes.

Segen ['ze:gən] *m* (-s; -) **1.** blessing (*a. fig.*), *eccl. a.* benediction: **s-n ~ geben** give one's blessing (**zu** to); **ein wahrer ~** a real blessing, *iro.* (quite) a mercy. **2.** F **der ganze ~** the whole lot.

'segensreich *adj* beneficial: **~ sein** be a blessing.

'Segenswünsche *pl* good wishes.

Segler ['ze:glər] *m* (-s; -) **1.** yachtsman. **2.** → *Segelboot, -schiff, -flugzeug.*

'Seglerin *f* (-; -nen) yachtswoman.

segnen ['ze:gnən] *v/t* (h) bless.

'Segnung *f* (-; -en) blessing (*a. fig.*), *eccl. a.* benediction.

sehen ['ze:ən] (sah, gesehen, h) **I** *v/i* **1.** see, look: **gut** (**schlecht**) **~** have good (bad *or* weak) eyes; **sieh nur!,** ~ **Sie mal!** look!; **siehe da!** lo and behold!; **siehe oben** (**unten**)! see above (below)!; F **sieh mal e-r an!** what do you know!; F **na, siehst du!** there you are!, what did I tell you?; **wir werden** (**schon**) **~** we shall see, let's wait and see; **sich gezwungen ~ zu** *inf* find o.s. compelled to *inf*. **2.** ~ **auf** (*acc*) set great store by. **3.** ~ **nach** look after; **ich muß nach dem Essen ~** I have to see to the dinner. **II** *v/t* **4.** see, *a.* watch (*program etc*), look at, *a.* notice: **gern** ~ like (to see); **zu ~ sein** a) show, b) be on show; **es war nichts zu ~** there was nothing to be seen; **niemand war zu ~** there was nobody in sight; **man sieht's (kaum)!** it (hardly) shows!; **ich habe es kommen ~** I have seen it coming; **sich ~ lassen** show one's face, *a.* turn up; **sie (es) kann sich ~ lassen** she (it) isn't half bad; **ich sehe die Sache anders** I see it differently; **wie ich die Dinge sehe** as I see it; **ich kann ihn (es) nicht mehr ~!** I can't stand (the sight of) him (it) any more! **5.** see, meet: **sich ~ (***or* **einander***) häufig* ~ see a lot of each other.

'Sehen *n* (-s) seeing: **vom ~** by sight.

'sehenswert, 'sehenswürdig *adj* worth seeing, worthwhile.

'Sehenswürdigkeit *f* (-; -en) object of interest, sight, *pl* sights: **die ~en besichtigen** go sightseeing.

'Sehfehler *m* eye defect.

'Sehkraft *f* (-; *no pl*) (eye)sight, vision.

Sehne ['ze:nə] *f* (-; -n) **1.** *anat.* sinew, tendon. **2.** string (*of bow*). **3.** *A* chord.

sehnen ['ze:nən] **sich ~** (h) (*nach* for) long, yearn: **er sehnte sich danach zu** *inf* he was longing to *inf*.

'Sehnenzerrung *f* pulled tendon.

'Sehnerv *m* optic nerve.

sehnig ['ze:nɪç] *adj* sinewy, wiry (*a. person*), stringy (*meat*).

sehnlich ['ze:nlɪç] *adj* ardent.

'Sehnsucht *f* (-; *~e*) (*nach* for) longing, yearning. 'sehnsüchtig *adj* longing, yearning, wistful.

sehr [ze:r] *adv* **1.** *preceding adj and adv* very, most, extremely: ~ **gern** with pleasure, gladly; ~ **viel** much, a lot (*better etc*). **2.** *with verb:* (very) much: ~ **vermissen** miss *s.o.*, *s.th.* badly (or a lot); **ich freue mich ~** I am very glad.

'Sehschärfe *f* visual power, (eye)sight.

'Sehschwäche *f* poor (eye)sight.

'Sehstörung *f* impaired vision.

'Sehtest *m* eye test: **e-n ~ machen lassen** have one's eyes tested.

seicht [zaɪçt] *adj a. fig.* shallow.

Seide ['zaɪdə] *f* (-; -n) (*reine ~* pure) silk.

seiden ['zaɪdən] *adj* (of) silk.

'Seiden|pa‚pier *n* silk tissue paper. **~raupe** *f* zo. silkworm. **~raupenzucht** *f* sericulture. **~strümpfe** *pl* silk stockings.

'seiden'weich *adj* (as) soft as silk, silky.

seidig ['zaɪdɪç] *adj* silky.

Seife ['zaɪfə] *f* (-; -n) soap.

seifen ['zaɪfən] *v/t* (h) soap.

'Seifen|blase *f* **1.** soap bubble. **2.** *fig.* bubble. **~lauge** *f* soapsuds. **~pulver** *n* soap powder. **~schale** *f* soap dish. **~schaum** *m* lather. **~spender** *m* soap dispenser.

seifig ['zaɪfɪç] *adj* soapy.

seihen ['zaɪən] *v/t* (h) strain, filter.

Seil [zaɪl] *n* (-[e]s; -e) rope: ~ **springen** skip. 'Seilbahn *f* cable railway.

'Seilschaft *f* (-; -en) **1.** *mount.* rope (team). **2.** F *fig.* team.

'Seiltänzer(in *f*) *m* tightrope walker.

sein¹ [zaɪn] *v/i* (war, gewesen, sn) be, *as v/aux a.* have: **bist du es?** is that you?; **ich bin's** it's me; **ich bin für e-e Reform** I am for a reform; **mir ist nicht nach Arbeiten** I don't feel like working; **mir ist, als höre ich ihn** I think I can hear him now; **wenn er nicht gewesen wäre** but for him; **er ist aus Mexiko** he comes from Mexico; **ich bin bei m-m Anwalt gewesen** I have been to see my lawyer; **laß das ~!** stop it!; **laß es ~!** don't bother!; **muß das ~?** do I (you *etc*) have to?; **was soll das ~?** what's that supposed to be?; **(das) mag** (or **kann**) ~ that may be; that's possible; **es sei denn, daß** unless; **nun, wie ist's?** w519ell, what about it?; **und das wäre?** and what might that be?

sein² *pos pron* **1.** ~(e) his, her, its, *of countries, ships*: her, *indefinite*: one's: ~ **Glück machen** make one's fortune; **all ~ Geld** what money he had; **es kostet** (**gut**) ~**e 100 Dollar** it will easily cost a hundred dollars. **2.** ~**er**, ~**e**, ~(**e**)**s**, **der**, **die**, **das** ~ his, hers, its. **3. der**, **die**, **das Seine** his (own), hers, her own, its (own); **die Seinen** *pl* his family; **jedem das Seine** to each his own; **das Seine tun** do one's bit.

Sein *n* (-s; *no pl*) being, existence.

seinerseits ['zaɪnərzaɪts] *adv* as far as he is concerned.

'seinerzeit *adv* then, in those days.

'seines'gleichen *indef pron* his (her) equals, F his (her) sort.

'seinet'wegen *adv* **1.** for his sake. **2.** on his behself.

Seismograph [zaɪsmo'graːf] *m* (-en; -en) seismograph. **Seismologe** [zaɪs-mo'loːɡə] *m* (-n; -n) seismologist.

seit [zaɪt] **I** *prep* **1.** since: ~ **wann sind Sie hier?** how long have you been here?; ~ **damals** → **seitdem** I. **2.** for: ~ **drei Wochen** for (the last) three weeks; ~ **langem** for a long time. **II** *conj* **3.** since: **es ist ein Jahr her, ~** it is a year since.

'seit'dem I *adv* since then, ever since. **II** *conj* → **seit** 3.

Seite ['zaɪtə] *f* (-; -n) **1.** side (*a. fig. aspect, descent, etc*). *a.* direction: **rechte** (**linke**) ~ *textil.* right (wrong) side; *fig.* **starke** (**schwache**) ~ weak (strong) point; **an j-s** ~ at (or by) s.o.'s side; **an** ~ side by side; **nach allen** ~**n** in all directions; **von allen** ~**n** on all sides; **auf der e-n** ~ on the one side (*fig.* hand); **auf j-s** ~ **sein** side with s.o.; **j-n auf s-e** ~ **bringen** (or **ziehen**) win s.o. over to one's side; **et. auf die** ~ **legen** put s.th. by; **j-m nicht von der** ~ **gehen** stick to s.o. like a leech; **von dieser** ~ **betrachtet** seen from that angle (or in

that light); **sich von der besten** ~ **zeigen** show o.s. at one's best; **j-m zur** ~ **stehen** stand by s.o. **2.** page. **3.** *auf* (or *von*) **seiten** (*gen*) on the part of.

'Seiten|ansicht *f* side view. **~blick** *m* sidelong glance. **~eingang** *m* side entrance. **~flügel** *m* △ wing. **~hieb** *m* (**gegen** at) cut, F sideswipe. **⊇lang** *adj* pages (and pages) of. **~linie** *f* **1.** *sports:* sideline. **2.** → **Nebenlinie.**

'seitens *prep* (*gen*) on the part of, by.

'Seiten|schiff *n* △ aisle. **~sprung** *m* escapade. **~stechen** *n* (-s) (~ **haben** have a) stitch. **~straße** *f* side street. **~streifen** *m* verge (*of road*). **~tasche** *f* side pocket. **~tür** *f* side door. **⊇verkehrt** *adj* the wrong way round. **~wagen** *m mot.* sidecar. **~wechsel** *m sports:* change of ends. **~wind** *m* crosswind. **~zahl** *f* a) page number, b) number of pages.

'seitlich I *adj* lateral, side. **II** *adv* at the side: **✔ ~ abrutschen** slip.

'seitwärts *adv* **1.** sideways. **2.** at the side.

Sekret [ze'kreːt] *n* (-[e]s; -e) secretion.

Sekretär [zekre'tɛːr] *m* (-s; -e) **1.** secretary. **2.** secretary, bureau. **Sekretariat** [zekreta'rɪaːt] *n* (-[e]s; -e) (secretary's) office. **Sekre'tärin** *f* (-; -nen) secretary.

Sekt [zɛkt] *m* (-[e]s; -e) sparkling wine.

Sekte ['zɛktə] *f* (-; -n) sect.

'Sektglas *n* champagne glass.

Sektierer [zɛk'tiːrər] *m* (-s; -), **sek'tiererisch** *adj* sectarian.

Sektion [zɛk'tsɪoːn] *f* (-; -en) **1.** section, division. **2.** ✚ dissection, autopsy.

Sektor ['zɛktor] *m* (-s; -en [-'toːrən]) sector, *fig. a.* field.

sekundär [zekʊn'dɛːr] *adj*, **Sekun'där...** secondary.

Sekunde [ze'kʊndə] *f* (-; -n) second (*a.* ♪ *or* ♪): **auf die** ~ **pünktlich** on the dot; F (**eine**) ~**!** just a second.

Se'kundenzeiger *m* second hand.

selb [zɛlp] *adj* same: **zur** ~**en Zeit** at the same time.

selber ['zɛlbər] → **selbst** I.

selbst [zɛlbst] **I** *pron* **ich** ~ I myself; **sie will es** ~ **machen** she wants to do it herself (*or* on her own); **er möchte** ~ **kochen** he wants to do his own cooking; **er war die Höflichkeit** ~ he was politeness itself; **von** ~ a) (by) itself, automatically, b) of one's own accord; → **verstehen** 9. **II** *adv* even.

Selbst n (-; *no pl*) (one's own) self.
'**Selbstachtung** f self-respect.
'**selbständig I** adj independent, a. self-employed: **sich ~ machen** set up on one's own. **II** adv independently, on one's own: **~ denken** think for o.s.
'**Selbständigkeit** f (-; *no pl*) independence.
'**Selbst**|**anklage** f self-accusation. **~auslöser** m *phot.* selftimer. **~bedienungsrestau,rant** n self-service restaurant, cafeteria. **~befriedigung** f masturbation. **~behauptung** f self-assertion. **~beherrschung** f self-control: **die ~ verlieren** a. lose one's temper. **~bestätigung** f ego-boost: **zu s-r ~** to prove himself. **~bestimmungsrecht** n right of self-determination. **~beteiligung** f *insurance*: percentage excess. **~betrug** m self-deception. **2bewußt** adj self-confident. **~bewußtsein** n self-confidence. **~bildnis** n self-portrait. **~darstellung** f promotion of one's public image, *contp.* showmanship. **~diszi,plin** f self-discipline. **~einschätzung** f self-assessment. **~erhaltungstrieb** m survival instinct. **~erkenntnis** f self-knowledge. **2ernannt** adj *iro.* self-styled. **~fahrer** m owner-driver.
'**selbstgebacken** adj home-made.
'**selbstgefällig** adj complacent.
'**Selbstgefälligkeit** f (-; *no pl*) complacency.
'**selbstgemacht** adj home-made.
'**selbstgerecht** adj self-righteous.
'**Selbstgespräch** n monologue: **~e führen** talk to o.s.
'**selbstherrlich** adj high-handed.
'**Selbst**|**hilfe** f (-; *no pl*) self-help. **~hilfegruppe** f self-help group. **2klebend** adj (self-)adhesive. **~kon,trolle** f self-control. **~kostenpreis** m cost price. **~kri,tik** f self-criticism. **~laut** m vowel.
'**selbstlos** adj selfless, unselfish.
'**Selbst**|**mitleid** n self-pity. **~mord** m, **~mörder** m suicide. **2mörderisch** adj suicidal. **~mordversuch** m attempted suicide. **~por,trät** n self-portrait. **2sicher** adj self-confident. **~sicherheit** f (-; *no pl*) self-confidence.
'**Selbstsucht** f (-; *no pl*) selfishness.
'**selbstsüchtig** adj selfish.
'**selbsttätig** adj automatic.
'**Selbst**|**täuschung** f self-deception.

~überschätzung f exaggerated opinion of o.s. **~unterricht** m self-instruction. **~verlag** m *im ~* published by the author. **~verleugnung** f self-denial. **2verschuldet** adj brought about by o.s. **~versorger** m self-supplier: **Bungalows für ~** self-catering bungalows.
'**selbstverständlich I** adj self-evident, obvious, natural: **es ist ~(, daß)** it goes without saying (that); **et. als ~ betrachten** take s.th. for granted. **II** adv of course, naturally. '**Selbstverständlichkeit** f (-; -en) matter of course.
'**Selbst**|**verständnis** n self-image: **sein ~** a. the way he sees himself. **~verteidigung** f self-defen/ce (*Am.* -se). **~vertrauen** n self-confidence. **~verwaltung** f self-government. **~verwirklichung** f self-realization. **~wählferndienst** m subscriber trunk dialling, *Am.* direct dialing. **~wertgefühl** n (-[e]s; *no pl*) self-esteem. **2zerstörerisch** adj self-destructive. **2zufrieden** adj complacent. **~zufriedenheit** f complacency. **~zweck** m end in itself.
selektiv [zelɛk'tiːf] adj selective.
Selen [ze'leːn] n (-s; *no pl*) ⚗ selenium.
selig ['zeːlɪç] adj **1.** *eccl.* blessed. **2.** overjoyed, blissful. **3.** late. '**Seligkeit** f (-; -en) **1.** *no pl eccl.* salvation, everlasting life. **2.** bliss, ecstasy. '**Seligsprechung** f (-; -en) *eccl.* beatification.
Sellerie ['zɛləri] m (-s; -[s]) ⚘ a) celeriac, b) celery.
selten ['zɛltən] **I** adj rare (a. *fig. beauty etc*), scarce. **II** adv seldom, rarely: **höchst ~** very rarely.
'**Seltenheit** f (-; -en) **1.** *no pl* rareness, scarcity. **2.** rarity.
'**Selterswasser** ['zɛltərs-] n (-s; ⸚) soda water.
seltsam ['zɛltzaːm] adj strange, odd.
'**seltsamer'weise** adv oddly enough.
'**Seltsamkeit** f (-; -en) **1.** *no pl* oddness. **2.** oddity.
Semantik [ze'mantɪk] f (-; *no pl*) semantics. **se'mantisch** [-tɪʃ] adj semantic.
Semester [ze'mɛstər] n (-s; -) semester.
Se'mesterferien pl vacation.
Semikolon [zemi'koːlɔn] n (-s; -s, -kola) semicolon.
Seminar [zemi'naːr] n (-s; -e) **1.** *univ.* a) seminar, b) department. **2.** *eccl.* seminary.

Semit [zeˈmiːt] *m* (-en; -en), **Seˈmitin** *f* (-; -nen) Semite.

seˈmitisch *adj* Semitic.

Semmel [ˈzɛməl] *f* (-; -n) roll: F **weggehen wie warme ~n** be selling like hot cakes. **ˈSemmelbrösel** [-brøːzəl] *pl* breadcrumbs.

Senat [zeˈnaːt] *m* (-[e]s; -e) **1.** *pol.*, *univ.* senate. **2.** ⚖ division(al court).

Senator [zeˈnaːtɔr] *m* (-s; -en [zenaˈtoːrən]) senator.

Sende|anlage *f* transmitter. **~anstalt** *f* → *Sender* **2.** **~bereich** *m* transmission range. **~folge** *f* program(me *Br.*). **~freˌquenz** *f* transmitting frequency. **~leiter(in** *f*) *m* producer.

senden¹ [ˈzɛndən] *v/t*, *v/i* (h) ⚡ transmit, *radio*: *a.* broadcast, *TV a.* telecast.

ˈsenden² *v/t*, *v/i* (sandte, gesandt, h) send (*dat*, **an** *acc* to).

ˈSender *m* (-s; -) **1.** transmitter. **2.** radio (*or* television) station.

ˈSende|raum *m* studio. **~reihe** *f* series. **~schluß** *m* closedown. **~zeichen** *n* call sign. **~zeit** *f* broadcasting time: **zur besten ~** at prime time.

ˈSendung¹ *f* (-; -en) a) transmission, b) program(me *Br.*), *radio*: *a.* broadcast, *TV a.* telecast: **auf ~ gehen** (*sein*) go (be) on the air.

ˈSendung² *f* (-; -en) **1.** ✝ consignment, shipment. **2.** parcel. **3.** *no pl fig.* mission. **ˈSendungsbewußtsein** *n* sense of mission.

Senf [zɛnf] *m* (-[e]s; -e) mustard. **~gurke** *f* gherkin (pickled with mustard seeds).

sengen [ˈzɛŋən] (h) **I** *v/t* singe. **II** *v/i* scorch: **~de Hitze** scorching heat.

senil [zeˈniːl] *adj* senile.

Senilität [zeniliˈtɛːt] *f* (-; *no pl*) senility.

senior [ˈzeːniɔr] *adj* senior (*abbr.* sen.).

ˈSenior *m* (-s; -en [zeˈniːorən]) a) senior (*a. sports*), b) senior citizen.

ˈSeniorchef *m* ✝ senior partner.

Senioren|heim [zeˈniːorən-] *n* (first-class) home for the aged. **~paß** *m* senior citizen's railcard.

Seniorin [zeˈniːorɪn] (-; -nen) → *Senior*.

ˈSenkblei *n* (-[e]s; -e) △ plumb-line.

Senke [ˈzɛŋkə] *f* (-; -n) *geogr.* depression. **ˈsenken** (h) **I** *v/t* **1.** sink (*a.* ⚙), lower (*a. fig. blood pressure, voice, etc*), *fig. a.* reduce (*costs, prices, etc*): **den Kopf ~** bow one's head. **II sich ~ 2.**

drop (*a. voice*), ground, *building*: subside, *wall*: sag, *road etc*: dip. **3.** *fig.* silence *etc*: descend (**über** *acc* on).

ˈSenkfüße *pl* ⚕ fallen arches.

ˈSenkgrube *f* cesspool.

ˈsenkrecht *adj*, **ˈSenkrechte** *f* (-n; -n) vertical, A perpendicular.

ˈSenkrechtstarter *m* (-s; -) **1.** ✈ vertical takeoff plane. **2.** F whiz(z) kid.

ˈSenkung *f* (-; -en) **1.** *no pl* a) lowering, *fig. a.* reduction, b) sag(ging) (*of wall*). **2.** dip. **3.** ✍ descent (*of organ*), sedimentation (*of blood corpuscles*). **4.** *metr.* thesis.

Sensation [zɛnzaˈtsioːn] *f* (-; -en) sensation. **sensationell** [zɛnzatsioˈnɛl] *adj* sensational.

Sensatiˈons|gier *f* *contp.* sensation-seeking. **~mache** *f contp.* sensationalism. **~meldung** *f* sensational report, scoop. **~presse** *f* yellow press. **~proˌzeß** *m* sensational trial.

Sense [ˈzɛnzə] *f* (-; -n) scythe: F **damit war ~!** that was the end of that!

sensibel [zɛnˈziːbəl] *adj* sensitive (*a. fig. problem etc*). **Sensibilität** [zɛnzibiliˈtɛːt] *f* (-; *no pl*) sensitivity.

Sensor [ˈzɛnzɔr] *m* (-s; -en [-ˈzoːrən]) sensor.

sentimental [zɛntimɛnˈtaːl] *adj* sentimental. **Sentimentalität** [zɛntimɛntaliˈtɛːt] *f* (-; -en) sentimentality.

separat [zepaˈraːt] *adj* separate.

Separatismus [zepараˈtɪsmʊs] *m* (-; *no pl*) separatism.

September [zɛpˈtɛmbər] *m* (-[s]; -) (**im ~** in) September.

septisch [ˈzɛptɪʃ] *adj* septic.

serbokroatisch [zɛrbokroˈaːtɪʃ] *adj ling.* Serbo-Croat(ian).

Serenade [zereˈnaːdə] *f* (-; -n) serenade.

Serie [ˈzeːriə] *f* (-; -n) a) series, *TV etc a.* serial, b) set, line, range: ⚙ **in ~ gehen** go into production; **in ~ bauen** (*or* **herstellen**) produce in series.

seriell [zeˈriɛl] *adj computer*: serial.

ˈSerienausstattung *f* standard fittings.

ˈSerienbau *m* (-[e]s; *no pl*) serial production.

ˈserienmäßig *adj* series(-produced), standard (*fittings etc*): **et. ~ herstellen** produce s.th. in series. **ˈserienreif** *adj* ready to go into production.

ˈSerienwagen *m* standard-type car.

seriös [ze'riø:s] *adj* respectable, *🖝 a.* reliable, serious (*applicant, offer, etc*).

Serpentine [zɛrpɛn'ti:nə] *f* (-; -n) a) serpentine, b) double bend.

Serum ['ze:rʊm] *n* (-s; Seren) *🖝* serum.

Service¹ [zɛr'vi:s] *n* (-; - [-'vi:sə]) service.

Service² ['sœrvɪs] *m* (-; *no pl*) **1.** service. **2.** ⊙ (after-sales) service.

servieren [zɛr'vi:rən] (h) **I** *v/t* serve: **es ist serviert!** dinner is served! **II** *v/i* serve, wait at (*Am.* on) table.

Ser'viererin *f* (-; -nen) waitress.

Ser'viertisch *m* serving table.

Ser'vierwagen *m* trolley.

Serviette [zɛr'vjɛtə] *f* (-; -n) napkin.

servil [zɛr'vi:l] *adj* servile.

Servobremse ['zɛrvo-] *f* servo (*or* power) brake. **'Servolenkung** *f* servo(-assisted) steering.

Sessel ['zɛsəl] *m* (-s; -) easy chair, armchair. **'Sessellift** *m* chairlift.

seßhaft ['zɛshaft] *adj* settled, *a.* resident: **~ werden** settle (down).

'Seßhaftigkeit *f* (-; *no pl*) settledness.

Set [sɛt] *n, m* (-[-s]; -s) **1.** set. **2.** place mat.

'Setzei *n gastr.* fried egg.

setzen ['zɛtsən] (h) **I** *v/t* **1.** put, place, *a.* seat (*s.o.*), put, make (*comma etc*), *✎* set, plant: **an Land ~** put ashore; **das Glas an die Lippen ~** raise (*or* set) the glass to one's lips; **s-e Unterschrift ~ unter** (*acc*) put one's signature to; → **Bild, Denkmal, Druck¹, Frist** *etc.* **2. et. ~** stake (*or* bet) s.th. (**auf** *acc* on). **3.** *sports:* seed (*player, team*): → **gesetzt** 2. **4.** *print.* set. **II sich ~ 5.** sit down, take a seat: **sich aufs Rad ~** mount (*or* get on) one's bicycle; **sich ins Auto ~** get into the car; **sich zu j-m ~** sit down beside s.o. **6.** *fig.* sink, grounds, dust, *etc:* settle, *impression etc:* sink in. **III** *v/i* **7. ~ über** (*acc*) jump (over), clear (*ditch etc*), cross (*river etc*). **8.** place one's bet: **~ auf** (*acc*) bet on, back, *fig. a.* bank on.

'Setzer *m* (-s; -) compositor, typesetter.

Setze'rei *f* (-; -en) composing room.

'Setzling *m* (-s; -e) *✎* seedling.

'Setzma,schine *f* typesetting machine.

Seuche ['zɔʏçə] *f* (-; -n) epidemic.

'Seuchenbekämpfung *f* epidemic control.

seufzen ['zɔʏftsən] *v/i* (h) sigh (**über** *acc* at, **vor** with): **~d** with a sigh.

'Seufzer *m* (-s; -) sigh.

Sex [zɛks, sɛks] *m* (-[es]; *no pl*) sex: **F ~ haben** (*or* **machen**) have sex. **~bombe** *f* F sexpot. **~film** *m* sex film.

Sexismus [zɛ'ksɪsmʊs] *m* (-; *no pl*) sexism. **se'xistisch** [-tʃ] *adj* sexist.

'Sexprotz *m* F sexual athlete, sexpot.

Sextett [zɛks'tɛt] *n* (-[e]s; -e) sextet(te).

sexual [zɛ'ksø:a:l] → **sexuell.**

Sexu'al... sexual, sex (*life etc*).

Sexu'alerziehung *f* sex education.

Sexualität [zɛksøali'tɛ:t] *f* (-; *no pl*) sexuality.

Sexu'alkunde *f* (-; *no pl*) *ped.* sex education. **~täter** *m* sex offender. **~verbrechen** *n* sex crime.

sexuell [zɛ'ksøɛl] *adj* sexual.

sexy ['zɛksi, sɛksi] *adj* F sexy.

sezieren [ze'tsi:rən] *v/t* (h) a) dissect (*a. fig.*), b) perform an autopsy on.

Showmaster ['ʃo:ma:stər] *m* (-s; -) *TV* compère, host.

Sibirien [zi'bi:riən] *n* (-s) Siberia.

Sibirier [zi'bi:riər] *m* (-s; -), **Si'birierin** *f* (-; -nen), **si'birisch** [-rɪʃ] *adj* Siberian.

sich [zɪç] *reflex pron* oneself, *3 sg* himself, herself, itself, *pl* themselves, *after prep* him, her, it, *pl* them, *a.* each other, one another: **~ ansehen** a) look at o.s., b) look at each other; **sie blickte hinter ~** she looked behind her.

Sichel ['zɪçəl] *f* (-; -n) sickle.

sicher ['zɪçər] **I** *adj* **1.** a) (**vor** *dat* from) safe, secure, b) safe (*a.* ⊙), secure (*income etc*): **in ~em Abstand** at a safe distance; **~ ist ~!** better safe than sorry! **2.** reliable, sound, sure (*goalkeeper, marksman, etc*), *a.* safe (*driver, method, etc*). **3.** *fig.* sure (*instinct, judg[e]ment, sign, etc*): **~es Auftreten** self-assurance; **mit ~em Blick** (**Griff**) with a sure eye (hand). **4.** certain, sure: **der ~e Sieg** (**Tod**) certain victory (death); **das ist ~** a) so much is certain, b) that's a fact; **ist das ~?** is that for certain?; **der Erfolg** (**die Stellung**) **ist ihm ~** he is sure to succeed (get the job). **5.** *pred* sure, certain: **sind Sie** (**sich dessen**) **~?** are you sure (about that)?; → **Sache** 2. **II** *adv* **6.** securely, safely (*etc*): **er fährt sehr ~** he is a safe driver. **7.** *a. int* certainly, surely, definitely: (**aber** *or* **ganz**) **~!** (but) of course!, F sure thing!; **du hast ~ kein Geld bei dir** I'm sure you have no money on you.

'**sichergehen** v/i (irr, sep, -ge-, sn, → **gehen**) er wollte ganz ~ he wanted to be quite sure; **um sicherzugehen** to be on the safe side.

'**Sicherheit** f (-; -en) **1.** no pl safety (a. ⊚), security: **öffentliche** (**soziale, innere**) ~ public (social, internal) security; ~ **im Flugverkehr** safety in flying; **in ~ bringen** get s.o., s.th. out of harm's way; **sich in ~ bringen** get out of danger, **durch e-n Sprung** jump to safety; **in ~ sein**; **zur ~ →** **sicherheitshalber**; **~ wiegen**¹ II. **2.** certainty: **mit ~** definitely, certainly; **man kann mit ~ sagen** it is safe to say. **3.** a) self-assurance, b) competence, skill, c) reliability. **4.** †, ⚖ security (**gegen** on, against): ~ **leisten** give security, stand bail; **e-m Gläubiger ~ bieten** secure a creditor.

'**Sicherheits|abstand** m safe distance. **~beamte** m security officer. **~bindung** f skiing: safety binding. **~faktor** m factor of safety. **~glas** n (-es; ⸚er) safety glass. **~gurt** m safety (✈, mot. a. seat) belt.

'**sicherheitshalber** adv as a precaution, to be on the safe side.

'**Sicherheits|kon,trolle** f security check. **~maßnahme** f safety (opt. security) measure, precaution. **~nadel** f safety pin. **~poli,zei** f security police. **~rat** m (-es; no pl) pol. Security Council. **~risi-ko** n security risk. **~schloß** n safety lock. **~ven,til** n safety valve.

'**sicherlich →** **sicher** 7.

sichern ['zıçɐn] v/t (h) **1.** (**gegen, vor** dat) secure (a. ⊚ or †), (safe)guard (both: against), protect (from): **sich ~ vor** (or **gegen**) protect o.s. from, guard against. **2.** put gun etc at safety: **gesichert sein** be at safety. **3.** secure: **sich Karten ~** secure tickets. **4. →** **sicherstellen** 1.

'**sicherstellen** v/t (sep, -ge-, h) **1.** guarantee, a. secure. **2.** seize.

'**Sicherung** f (-; -en) **1.** no pl a) securing (etc, → **sichern**), b) protection. **2.** ⊚ safety device, safety (catch) (on gun etc). **3.** ⚡ fuse.

'**Sicherungskasten** m ⚡ fuse box.

Sicht [zıçt] f (-; no pl) **1.** a) sight, b) view, c) visibility: **in** (**außer**) ~ in (out of) sight (a. fig.); **in ~ kommen** come into view; fig. **auf weite** (or **lange**) ~ on a long-term basis, a. in the long run; **auf kurze** ~ in the short term; **aus s-r** ~ from his point of view, as he sees it. **2.** † (**fällig**) **bei** ~ (due) at sight; **60 Tage nach** ~ payable at sixty days' sight.

'**sichtbar** adj visible, a. noticeable, evident, a. marked: ~ **machen** show; ~ **werden** appear, become visible.

'**Sichtbe,ton** m fair-faced concrete.

sichten ['zıçtən] v/t (h) **1.** sight. **2.** sift, look through, sort out.

'**Sichtflug** m contact flight.

'**Sichtgerät** n visual display unit.

'**sichtlich** adj visible, evident.

'**Sicht|verhältnisse** pl (**gute, schlechte** ~ high, low) visibility. **~vermerk** m **1.** visa. **2.** † endorsement. **~wechsel** m † sight draft. **~weite** f visual range: **in ~** (with)in sight.

sickern ['zıkɐn] v/i (sn) seep, ooze.

sie [zi:] pers pron she, thing: it, pl they, (acc) her, it, pl them.

Sie¹ polite address: you.

Sie² f (-; -s) F she, female.

Sieb [zi:p] n (-[e]s; -e) sieve, strainer, ⊚ screen, ✓ filter: **ein Gedächtnis wie ein** ~ a memory like a sieve.

'**Siebdruck** m (-[e]s; -e) **1.** silk-screen print. **2.** no pl silk-screen printing.

sieben¹ ['zi:bən] v/t (h) **1.** sift, sieve. **2.** → **aussieben.**

sieben² adj, '**Sieben** f (-; -) seven.

'**Sieben'sachen** pl F things, belongings.

'**siebente** adj, '**Siebentel** n (-s; -) seventh. '**siebentens** adv seventh.

siebte ['zi:ptə] → **siebente.**

siebzehn(t) ['zi:p-] adj seventeen(th).

siebzig ['zi:psıç] adj seventy: **er ist Mitte** (**der**) ~ he is in his mid-seventies. **siebzig** f (-; -en) seventy. **siebziger** ['zi:p-tsıgɐ] adj **die ~ Jahre** the seventies. '**Siebziger** m (-s; -) man in his seventies, septuagenarian. '**Siebzigerin** f (-; -nen) woman in her seventies, septuagenarian. '**siebzigst** adj seventieth.

Siechtum ['zi:çtu:m] n (-s; no pl) lingering illness, invalidism.

siedeln ['zi:dəln] v/i (h) settle.

sieden ['zi:dən] (h) **I** v/i boil: **~d heiß** boiling hot. **II** v/t boil gently.

'**Siedepunkt** m (-[e]s; no pl) boiling point.

Siedler ['zi:dlɐ] m (-s; -), '**Siedlerin** f (-;

-nen) settler. 'Siedlung f (-; -en) a) settlement, b) housing estate.

Sieg [zi:k] m (-[e]s; -e) (*über acc* over) victory, *sports etc:* win, *fig.* triumph: **den ~ davontragen** carry the day.

Siegel ['zi:gəl] n (-s; -) a) seal, b) signet: *fig.* **unter dem ~ der Verschwiegenheit** under the seal of secrecy.

'Siegellack m sealing wax.

'siegeln ['zi:gəln] v/t (h) seal.

'Siegelring m signet ring.

siegen ['zi:gən] v/i (h) (*über acc*) be victorious (over), *sports etc:* win (against), *fig.* triumph (over), win (over).

Sieger ['zi:gər] m (-s; -) victor, *sport etc:* winner. 'Siegerehrung f *sports:* presentation ceremony.

'Siegerin f (-; -nen) → Sieger.

'Siegermächte pl victorious powers.

'Siegerpo,dest n (victory) rostrum.

'sieges|bewußt, ~sicher adj confident of victory, *fig.* sure of one's success.

'Siegeszug m *fig.* triumphant advance.

'siegreich adj victorious, triumphant.

siezen ['zi:tsən] v/t (h) *j-n ~* address s.o. as "Sie".

Signal [zi'gna:l] n (-[e]s; -e) signal.

signalisieren [zɪgnali'zi:rən] v/t, v/i (h) signal.

Signatarmacht [zɪgna'ta:r-] f *pol.* signatory power (*e-s Vertrages* to a treaty).

Signatur [zɪgna'tu:r] f (-; -en) 1. signature. 2. shelfmark (*of book*). 3. conventional sign. **signieren** [zɪ'gni:rən] v/t (h) sign, *author:* autograph.

Silbe ['zɪlbə] f (-; -n) syllable: *fig.* **k-e ~** not a word.

'Silbentrennung f syllabification.

Silber ['zɪlbər] n (-s; *no pl*) 1. silver. 2. silver plate.

'Silber|besteck n silver (cutlery). ~blick m F (slight) squint. ~distel f ♣ carline thistle. ~hochzeit f silver wedding. ~me,daille f silver medal. ~me,daillengewinner(in f) m silver medal(l)ist.

'silbern adj (of) silver, *fig.* silvery.

'Silber|pa,pier n tin foil. ~streifen m ~ am Horizont silver lining. ~waren pl silverware.

Silhouette [zi'luɛtə] f (-; -n) silhouette.

Silikat [zili'ka:t] n (-[e]s; -e) silicate.

Silikon [zili'ko:n] n (-s; -e) silicon.

Silo ['zi:lo] m (-s; -s) silo.

Silvester [zɪl'vɛstər] m, n (-s; -), ~abend m New Year's Eve.

simpel ['zɪmpəl] adj simple.

Sims [zɪms] m, n (-es; -e) 1. ledge. 2. sill.

Simulant [zimu'lant] m (-en; -en) malingerer. **Simulator** [zimu'la:tɔr] m (-s; -en [-la'to:rən]) ◎, ✕ simulator.

simulieren [zimu'li:rən] (h) **I** v/t sham, feign, a. ◎ simulate. **II** v/i malinger.

simultan [zimʊl'ta:n] adj simultaneous.

Simul'tan|dolmetschen n (-s) simultaneous translation. ~**dolmetscher** m simultaneous translator.

Sinfonie [zɪnfo'ni:] f (-; -n) symphony. ~or,chester n symphony orchestra.

sinfonisch [zɪn'fo:nɪʃ] adj symphonic.

singen ['zɪŋən] v/t, v/i (sang, gesungen, h) sing.

Single¹ ['sɪŋl] f (-; -[s]) (*record*) single.

Single² m (-[s]; -s) single (person).

Single³ n (-[s]; -[s]) *tennis etc:* singles.

'Singstimme f singing voice.

Singular ['zɪŋgula:r] m (-s; -e) *ling.* (*im ~* in the) singular.

'Singvogel m songbird.

sinken ['zɪŋkən] v/i (sank, gesunken, sn) sink (a. *fig.*), *sun:* a. set, *fig. prices, temperature, etc:* drop (*auf acc* to), fall, go down: *fig.* **er ist tief gesunken** he has sunk very low; ~ **lassen** lower, drop (a. *voice*); → *Mut, Wert* 1 *etc.*

Sinn [zɪn] m (-[e]s; -e) 1. *physiol.* sense: *fig.* **sechster ~** sixth sense; **s-e fünf ~e beisammen haben** have one's wits about one. 2. *pl a)* mind, b) consciousness: *sie war wie von ~en* she was quite beside herself (*vor* with); *bist du von ~en?* are you out of your mind? 3. *no pl* mind: *et. im ~ haben* have s.th. in mind, intend (to do) s.th.; *damit habe ich nichts im ~* I don't want any of that; *j-m in den ~ kommen* occur to s.o. 4. *no pl* (*für*) a) sense (of), appreciation (of), b) taste (of), c) interest (in): ~ *für Musik* an ear for music; ~ *für das Schöne* an eye for beauty; ~ *für Humor* a sense of humo(u)r; *das ist ganz nach s-m ~* that's just what he likes; *das war ganz in m-m ~(e)* that was just what I would have done. 5. *no pl a)* sense, meaning, b) (basic) idea: *im weiteren (engeren) ~(e)* in a wider (narrower) sense; *im wahrsten ~(e) des Wortes* literally; *in gewissem ~* in a sense; *im ~e des Ge-*

setzes as defined by the law; **der ~ des Lebens** the meaning of life; **das ergibt** (F **macht**) **k-n ~** that makes no sense; **dem ~ nach →** **sinngemäß. 6.** *no pl* sense, purpose: **~ und Zweck** (aim and) object; **das hat k-n ~** that's no use, it's pointless; **das ist (nicht) der ~ der Sache!** that's (not) the idea!

'**Sinnbild** *n* symbol.

'**sinnbildlich** *adj* symbolic(al).

sinnen ['zɪnən] *v/i* (sann, gesonnen, h) (*über acc* [up]on) meditate, reflect: **~ auf** (*acc*) contemplate, plan, *b.s.* plot.

'**Sinnen** *n* (-s) thoughts: **all sein ~ und Trachten** his every thought and wish.

'**sinnenfroh** *adj* sensuous.

'**Sinnenlust** *f* (-; *no pl*) sensual pleasure.

'**sinnentstellend** *adj* distorting (the meaning): **~ sein** distort the meaning.

'**Sinnes**|**or,gan** *n* sense organ. **~reiz** *m* sense stimulus. **~täuschung** *f* hallucination. **~wahrnehmung** *f* sensory perception. **~wandel** *m* change of heart.

'**sinnfällig** *adj* obvious, clear.

'**sinngemäß** *adj* giving the gist (*of s.th.*), *esp.* 🏛 analogous: **et. ~ übersetzen** give the general meaning of s.th.

sinnieren [zɪ'niːrən] *v/i* (h) F ruminate (*über acc* on).

'**sinnig** ['zɪnɪç] *adj a. iro.* clever.

'**sinnlich** *adj* sensual (*impression, pleasure, etc*), *a.* sensuous: **~e Wahrnehmung** sensory perception.

'**Sinnlichkeit** *f* (-; *no pl*) sensuality.

'**sinnlos** *adj* a) senseless, meaningless, b) absurd, c) useless: **~ betrunken** blind drunk. '**Sinnlosigkeit** *f* (-; *no pl*) senselessness (*etc*), absurdity.

'**sinnreich** *adj* ingenious, clever.

'**sinnverwandt** *adj* synonymous: **~es Wort** synonym.

'**sinnvoll** *adj* **1.** meaningful. **2.** a) useful, b) wise. **3.** ingenious, clever.

Sintflut ['zɪnt-] *f* (-; *no pl*) *bibl.* the Flood.

Sinus ['ziːnʊs] *m* (-; -, -se) **1.** ⅄ sine. **2.** *anat.* sinus. '**Sinuskurve** *f* sine curve.

Siphon ['ziːfõ:] *m* (-s; -s) siphon.

Sippe ['zɪpə] *f* (-; -n) **1.** family, tribe. **2.** → '**Sippschaft** *f* (-; -en) *contp.* a) clan, b) gang, lot.

Sirene [zi're:nə] *f* (-; -n) siren.

Sirup ['ziːrʊp] *m* (-s; -e) syrup, treacle, *Am.* molasses.

Sitte ['zɪtə] *f* (-; -n) **1.** custom, *a.* practice,

habit: **~n und Gebräuche** manners and customs. **2.** *pl* a) morals, b) manners.

'**Sittenlehre** *f* ethics.

'**sittenlos** *adj* immoral, dissolute.

'**Sittenlosigkeit** *f* (-; *no pl*) immorality.

'**Sittenpoli,zei** *f* vice squad.

'**Sittenrichter** *m* moralizer.

'**sittenstreng** *adj* puritanical.

'**sittenwidrig** *adj* immoral.

Sittich ['zɪtɪç] *m* (-s; -e) *zo.* parakeet.

'**sittlich** *adj* moral, ethical.

'**Sittlichkeit** *f* (-; *no pl*) morality, morals.

'**Sittlichkeits**|**verbrechen** *n* sex crime. **~verbrecher** *m* sex offender.

Situation [zitŭa'tsio:n] *f* (-; -en) situation, position: **sich der ~ gewachsen zeigen** rise to the occasion.

Situati'onskomik *f* situational comedy.

Sitz [zɪts] *m* (-es; -e) **1.** a) seat (*a. fig.*), b) (place of) residence, 🕈 headquarters: **Firma mit ~ in London** London-based firm; **die Zuschauer von den ~en reißen** electrify the audience. **2.** *no pl* fit.

'**Sitzecke** *f* corner unit.

sitzen ['zɪtsən] *v/i* (saß, gesessen, h) **1.** sit, *bird*: perch: **~ bleiben** remain seated; **sie saßen beim Essen** they were having lunch; **im Parlament ~** have a seat in Parliament; **an e-r Arbeit (bei e-m Glas Wein) ~** be sitting over a task (a glass of wine); F **e-n ~ haben** be soused; **~de Lebensweise** sedentary life; **~ Patsche** *etc.* **2.** be, *firm etc*: have one's headquarters (*in dat* in). **3.** sit, fit. **4.** F (*im Gefängnis*) **~** do time, be in jail. **5.** F *blow, remark, etc*: hit home. **6.** F stick (in the mind).

'**sitzenbleiben** *v/i* (*irr, sep*, -ge-, sn, → **bleiben**) F **1.** *ped.* have to repeat the year. **2.** *woman*: be left on the shelf. **3. ~ auf** (*dat*) be left with *goods*.

'**sitzenlassen** *v/t* (*irr, sep, pp* sitzenlassen, h, → **lassen**) *fig.* **1.** *j-n ~* a) leave s.o. in the lurch, b) walk out on s.o., jilt s.o. **2.** **das lasse ich nicht auf mir sitzen!** I won't stand for that!

'**Sitz**|**gelegenheit** *f* seat. **~gruppe** *f* three-piece suite. **~ordnung** *f* seating plan. **~platz** *m* seat. **~streik** *m* sit-down strike.

'**Sitzung** *f* (-; -en) meeting, conference, *parl.* sitting, session, 🏛 hearing.

'**Sitzungs**|**bericht** *m* minutes (of the meeting). **~peri,ode** *f parl.* session.

~**saal** m conference room, *parl.* chamber. ~**zimmer** n conference room.

Sizilianer [zitsiˈliːanɔr] m (-s; -) Sicilian. **Sizili'anerin** f (-; -nen) Sicilian (woman or girl). **sizili'anisch** adj Sicilian.

Sizilien [ziˈtsiːliən] n (-s) Sicily.

Skala [ˈskaːla] f (-; -len, -s) **1.** ♪, ☺ scale. **2.** *fig.* range.

Skalp [skalp] m (-s; -e) scalp.

Skalpell [skalˈpɛl] n (-s; -e) ♯ scalpel.

skalpieren [skalˈpiːrən] v/t (h) scalp.

Skandal [skanˈdaːl] m (-s; -e) **1.** scandal, disgrace, shame. ~**blatt** n scandal sheet.

skandalös [skandaˈløːs] adj scandalous.

Skan'dalpresse f (-; *no pl*) gutter press.

Skandinavien [skandiˈnaːviən] n (-s) Scandinavia. **Skandi'navier** m (-s; -), **Skandi'navierin** f (-; -nen), **skandi'navisch** [-vɪʃ] adj Scandinavian.

Skat [skaːt] m (-[e]s; -e, -s) skat.

Skelett [skeˈlɛt] n (-[e]s; -e) skeleton.

Skepsis [ˈskɛpsɪs] f (-; *no pl*) scepticism, *Am.* skepticism. **Skeptiker** [ˈskɛptikər] m (-s; -) sceptic, *Am.* skeptic.

'skeptisch adj sceptical, *Am.* skeptic.

Ski [ʃiː] m (-s; -er, -) ski: ~ **fahren**, ~ **laufen** ski.

'Ski|anzug m ski suit. ~**ausrüstung** f skiing gear. ~**bob** m skibob. ~**fahren** n skiing. ~**fahrer** m skier. ~**fliegen** n, ~**flug** m ski flying. ~**gebiet** n skiing area. ~**hütte** f ski hut, ski lodge. ~**kurs** m skiing course. ~**langlauf** m cross-country skiing. ~**lauf** m, ~**laufen** n skiing. ~**läufer** m skier. ~**lehrer** m skiing instructor. ~**lift** m ski lift. ~**piste** f ski run, piste. ~**schuh** m ski boot. ~**sport** m skiing. ~**springen** n, ~**sprung** m ski jumping. ~**stiefel** m ski boot. ~**stock** m ski pole. ~**träger** m *mot.* ski rack. ~**wandern** n ski hiking. ~**zirkus** m F ski circus (or circuit).

Skizze [ˈskɪtsə] f (-; -n) sketch.

'Skizzenbuch n sketchbook.

'skizzenhaft adj sketchy.

skizzieren [skɪˈtsiːrən] v/t (h) sketch, *fig. a.* outline.

Sklave [ˈsklaːvə] m (-n; -n) slave. **'Sklavenhandel** m slave trade. **Sklave'rei** f (-; *no pl*) slavery. **'Sklavin** f (-; -nen) slave. **'sklavisch** adj slavish.

Sklerose [skleˈroːzə] f (-; -n) ♯ sclerosis.

Skonto [ˈskɔnto] m, n (-s; -s) ✝ (cash) discount.

Skorbut [skɔrˈbuːt] m (-[e]s; *no pl*) ♯ scurvy.

Skorpion [skɔrˈpioːn] m (-s; -e) **1.** *zo.* scorpion. **2.** *no pl astr.* ([*ein*] ~ **sein** be [a]) Scorpio.

Skrupel [ˈskruːpəl] m (-s; -) scruple.

'skrupellos adj unscrupulous.

Skulptur [skʊlpˈtuːr] f (-; -en) sculpture.

skurril [skʊˈriːl] adj bizarre.

Slalom [ˈslaːlɔm] m (-s; -s) *skiing:* slalom. ~**läufer(in** f) m slalom racer.

Slawe [ˈslaːvə] m (-n; -n), **'Slawin** f (-; -nen), **'slawisch** adj Slav.

Slip [slɪp] m (-s; -s) briefs, panties.

'Slipeinlage f panty liner.

Smaragd [smaˈrakt] m (-[e]s; -e), **sma'ragdgrün** adj emerald.

Smog [smɔk] m (-[s]; -s) smog.

'Smoga,larm m smog alert.

Smoking [ˈsmoːkɪŋ] m (-s; -s) dinner jacket, *Am.* tuxedo.

Snob [snɔp] m (-s; -s) snob. **Snobismus** [snoˈbɪsmʊs] m (-; -men) snobbery. **sno'bistisch** [-tɪʃ] adj snobbish.

so [zoː] I adv **1.** so, so much: *nicht ~ einfach* not so easy; *das hat ihn ~ gefreut, daß* it pleased him so much that. **2.** like this (or that), this (or that) way, thus: ~ *ist es!* that's how it is!; ~ *ist das Leben!* such is life!; ~ *oder ~* one way or another, b) anyway. **3.** such: ~ *etwas* such a thing; ~ *ein Trottel!* what a fool! **4.** about: ~ *alle acht Tage* every week or so. II *conj* ~ *daß* so that, so as to *inf*; ~ *leid es mir tut* however much I regret it. III *int* ~! a) (all) right!, okay!, b) that's that!; ~, ~! well, well!; ~? really?; (*na*) ~ *was!* you don't say!; *ach ~!* oh(, I see!)

so'bald *conj* as soon as.

Söckchen [ˈzœkçən] n (-s; -) ankle sock, *Am.* anklet.

Socke [ˈzɔkə] f (-; -n) sock: F *sich auf die ~n machen* buzz off; *von den ~n sein* be flabbergasted, be dum(b)founded.

Sockel [ˈzɔkəl] m (-s; -e) pedestal, *a.* ♯, ☺ base. ~**betrag** m basic allowance.

Sockenhalter m suspender, *Am.* garter.

Soda [ˈzoːda] f (-; *no pl*), n (-s; *no pl*) soda. **'Sodawasser** n soda water.

Sodbrennen [ˈzoːt-] n (-s; *no pl*) ♯ heartburn.

so'eben *adv* just (now).

Sofa [ˈzoːfa] n (-s; -s) sofa, settee.

so'fern *conj* a) if, so far as, b) provided that: ~ *nicht* unless.

soff [zɔf] *pret of* **saufen.**

so'fort *adv* at once, instantly, immediately, right away: *ab* ~ a) as of now, b) *a.* (*ab*) ~ *gültig* effective immediately; ✝ ~ *zahlbar* spot cash; *er war* ~ *tot* he died instantaneously.

So'fort|bildkamera *f* instant camera. **~hilfe** *f* immediate (*or* emergency) aid.

so'fortig *adj* immediate, prompt.

So'fort|maßnahme *f* immediate action. **~pro,gramm** *n* crash program(me *Br.*).

Software ['sɔftwɛə] *f* (-; -s) software.

Sog *m* (-[e]s; -e) suction, ✈, ⚓ *a.* wake (*a. fig.*).

so'gar *adv* even.

'sogenannt *adj* so-called.

Sohle ['zoːlə] *f* (-; -n) 1. sole. 2. bottom (*of valley etc*), ⚒ floor.

Sohn [zoːn] *m* (-[e]s; ⸚e) son.

Soja|bohne ['zoːja-] *f* soybean. **~mehl** *n* soybean flour. **~soße** *f* soy sauce.

so'lang(e) *adv* as long as.

Solarener,gie [zo'laːr-] *f* solar energy.

Solarium [zo'laːriʊm] *n* (-s; -rien) solarium.

So'larzelle *f* solar cell.

solch [zɔlç] *pron or adj* such.

'solcher'lei *adj* of such kind, such.

Sold [zɔlt] *m* (-[e]s; -e) pay.

Soldat [zɔl'daːt] *m* (-en; -en) soldier, *a.* serviceman.

Sol'datenfriedhof *m* war cemetery.

sol'datisch *adj* soldierlike, military.

'Soldbuch *n* ✕ pay book.

Söldner ['zœltnər] *m* (-s; -) mercenary.

Sole ['zoːlə] *f* (-; -n) brine.

solidarisch [zoli'daːrɪʃ] **I** *adj* solidary, ✝, ⚖ joint (*and several*): *sich* ~ *erklären mit* → **solidarisieren.** **II** *adv* in solidarity, ✝, ⚖ jointly (*and severally*).

solidarisieren [zolidari'ziːrən] *sich* ~ *mit* (h) declare one's solidarity with, be solidly behind. **Solidarität** [zolidari-'tɛːt] *f* (-; *no pl*) solidarity.

solide [zo'liːdə] *adj* solid (*a. fig. person*), *fig. a.* steady (*person etc*), *a.* sound (*knowledge etc*), *a.* reliable (*firm*), reasonable (*price*), good (*profession*).

Solist [zo'lɪst] *m* (-en; -en), **So'listin** *f* (-; -nen) soloist.

Soll [zɔl] *n* (-[s]; -[s]) **1.** debit: ~ *und Haben* debit and credit. **2.** (*production*

etc) target, quota: *sein* ~ *erfüllen* reach the target, *fig.* do one's bit.

sollen ['zɔlən] (sollte, sollen, h) **I** *v/aux* **1.** be to: *ich soll dir ausrichten* I am to tell you; *soll ich kommen?* shall I come?; *er soll nur kommen!* just let him come!; *was soll ich tun?* what should I do? **2.** *moral obligation:* *ich hätte hingehen* ~ I ought to have gone; *ich hätte es wissen* ~ I should have known; *du hättest das nicht tun* ~ you shouldn't have done that! **3.** *intention:* *hier soll ein Schwimmbad entstehen* a swimming pool is to be built here; *es soll nicht wieder vorkommen* it won't happen again; *was soll das sein?* what's that supposed to be?; *es sollte ein Scherz sein* it was meant as (*or* supposed to be) a joke. **4.** *rumo(u)r:* *er soll reich sein* he is said to be rich; *die Rebellen* ~ *die Macht übernommen haben* the rebels are reported to have seized power. **5.** *possibility:* *sollte es wahr sein?* could it be true?; *sollte sie kommen* in case (*or* if) she should come. **6.** *fate:* *er sollte nie mehr zurückkehren* he was never to return again; *es sollte alles ganz anders kommen* things were to turn out quite differently; *ein Jahr sollte vergehen, bis ...* a year was to pass till ...; *es hat nicht* ~ *sein* it was not to be. **II** *v/i* (*pp* gesollt) *was soll ich hier?* what am I here for?; *was soll ich damit?* what am I to do with it?; *soll* (*sollte*) *ich?* shall (should) I?; *weshalb sollte ich* (*auch*)? why should I?; *was soll das?* a) what's the idea?, b) what's the use?, c) F *a. was soll's?* so what?

'Soll-Leistung *f* ⚙ nominal output.

'Soll-Wert *m* ⚙ rated value.

solo ['zoːlo] *adj* solo, F *fig. a.* alone.

'Solo *n* (-s; -s, Soli) solo, *sports:* solo attempt (*or* run).

'Solostimme *f* solo voice (*or* part).

'Solotänzer(in *f*) *m* solo dancer.

solvent [zɔl'vɛnt] *adj* ✝ solvent.

somatisch [zo'maːtɪʃ] *adj* somatic.

so'mit *adv* consequently, thus.

Sommer ['zɔmər] *m* (-s; -) summer: *im* ~ in (the) summer; *im nächsten* ~ next summer. **~ferien** *pl* summer holidays (*Am.* vacation). **~kleidung** *f* summer clothes, ✝ summer wear.

'sommerlich adj summerly, summery.

'Sommer|loch n F fig. silly season. **⁓rei-fen** m mot. normal tyre (Am. tire). **⁓spiele** pl Olympische ⁓ Summer Olympics. **⁓sprosse** f freckle.

'sommersprossig adj freckled.

'Sommerzeit f summer time, a. daylight saving time.

Sonate [zo'na:tə] f (-; -n) ♪ sonata.

Sonde ['zɔndə] f (-; -n) ♪, astronautics: probe, meteor., radar: sonde.

Sonder... ['zɔndər-] special. **⁓anfertigung** f special design, custom-made article (etc). **⁓angebot** n special offer. **⁓ausgabe** f 1. special edition. 2. extra (expenditure).

'sonderbar adj strange, odd, peculiar.

'sonderbarer'weise adv oddly enough.

'Sonder|beauftragte m, f special representative. **⁓beilage** f (special) supplement, inset. **⁓berichterstatter** m special correspondent. **⁓bevollmächtigte** m, f plenipotentiary. **⁓druck** m (-[e]s; -e) offprint. **⁓fall** m special case. **⁓inter,esse** n private interest.

'sonderlich I adj special: ohne ⁓e Mühe without any great effort. II adv nicht ⁓ not particularly, not much, not very.

Sonderling ['zɔndərlɪŋ] m (-s; -e) eccentric, crank.

'Sonder|marke f special issue. **⁓ma,schine** f ✈ special flight. **⁓meldung** f special announcement. **⁓müll** m toxic waste.

sondern ['zɔndərn] conj but: nicht nur ..., ⁓ auch ... not only ..., but also ...

'Sonder|nummer f special edition. **⁓recht** n privilege. **⁓regelung** f special arrangement. **⁓schule** f special school (for handicapped or maladjusted children). **⁓sitzung** f special session. **⁓stempel** m special postmark. **⁓wunsch** m special request. **⁓zug** m special train. **⁓zulage** f special bonus.

sondieren [zɔn'di:rən] (h) I v/t ♪ or fig. probe, sound (out). II v/i fig. put out feelers. **Son'dierungsgespräch** n exploratory talk.

Sonett [zo'nɛt] n (-[e]s; -e) sonnet.

'Sonnabend m (am ⁓ on) Saturday.

'sonnabends adv on Saturday(s).

Sonne ['zɔnə] f (-; no pl) sun: an (or in) der ⁓ in the sun.

sonnen ['zɔnən] sich ⁓ (h) sun o.s., bask

in the sun, fig. bask (in dat in).

'Sonnenaufgang m (bei ⁓ at) sunrise.

'Sonnenbad n sunbath: ein ⁓ nehmen → 'sonnenbaden v/i (only inf and pp sonnengebadet, h) sunbathe.

'Sonnen|bank f sun bed. **⁓blende** f phot. lens hood. **⁓blume** f sunflower. **⁓brand** m sunburn. **⁓brille** f (e-e ⁓ a pair of) sunglasses. **⁓creme** f su(n)tan cream. **⁓dach** n sun blind, mot. sunshine roof. **⁓deck** n ♪ sun deck. **⁓ener,gie** f solar energy. **⁓finsternis** f eclipse of the sun. **⁓fleck** m sunspot. **⁓hut** m sunhat. **⁓kol,lektor** m solar panel. **⁓kraftwerk** n solar power plant. **⁓licht** n (bei ⁓ in) sunlight. **⁓öl** n suntan oil. **⁓schein** m sunshine. **⁓schirm** m sunshade, for ladies: parasol. **⁓schutzcreme** f sun (filter) cream. **⁓seite** f a. fig. sunny side. **⁓stich** m sunstroke. **⁓strahl** m sunbeam. **⁓sy,stem** n solar system. **⁓uhr** f sundial. **⁓untergang** m (bei ⁓ at) sunset. **⁓wende** f solstice. **⁓zelle** f solar cell.

'sonnig adj a. fig. sunny.

'Sonntag m (am ⁓ on) Sunday. **'sonntäglich** adj Sunday. **'sonntags** adv on Sunday(s), on a Sunday.

'Sonntags|anzug m Sunday best. **⁓beilage** f Sunday supplement. **⁓dienst** m ⁓ haben be on Sunday duty, pharmacy: be open on Sunday(s). **⁓fahrer** m contp. Sunday driver. **⁓kind** n er ist ein ⁓ he was born on a Sunday (fig. under a lucky star). **⁓maler** m Sunday painter.

'sonnverbrannt adj (deeply) tanned.

sonor [zo'no:r] adj sonorous.

sonst [zɔnst] adv 1. otherwise, or, or else. 2. usually, normally: wie ⁓ as usual. 3. otherwise, apart from that. 4. else: wer ⁓? who else?; ⁓ noch etwas? anything else?; nirgends ⁓ nowhere else. 5. always: alles war wie ⁓ everything was as it used to be. 6. 'sonstig adj other. 'sonstjemand pron F a) somebody else, b) anybody. 'sonstwas pron F a) something else, b) anything. 'sonstwie adv F some other way. 'sonstwo(hin) adv F somewhere else.

so'oft conj whenever: ⁓ du willst as often as you like.

Sopran [zo'pra:n] m (-s; -e) soprano.

Sopranist [zopra'nist] m (-en; -en), **Sopra'nistin** f (-; -nen) soprano.

Sorge ['zɔrgə] f (-; -n) **1.** a) worry, concern, b) trouble: *finanzielle (berufliche)* ~*n* financial (professional) worries (or problems); *j-m* ~*n machen* worry s.o., cause s.o. trouble; *sich* ~*n machen* a) *um* be worried about, b) *daß* be concerned that; *mach dir k-e* ~*n!*, *k-e* ~*!* don't worry!; *lassen Sie das m-e* ~ *sein!* leave that to me!; → *gering.* **2.** care: ~ *tragen für* → *sorgen* I.

sorgen ['zɔrgən] (h) **I** *v/i* ~ *für* a) see to, take care of, ensure, b) look after, c) provide; *dafür* ~, *daß* see to it that; *dafür werde ich* ~ I'll see to that; *für sich selbst* ~ fend for o.s.; *für ihn ist gesorgt* he's taken care of. **II** *sich* ~ (*um, wegen* about) be worried, worry.

'sorgenfrei *adj* free from care(s), carefree. **'Sorgenkind** *n* problem child. **'sorgenvoll** *adj* life etc full of worries, *a.* worried (*face, look, etc*).

'Sorgerecht *n* (-[e]s; *no pl*) custody (*für* of).

Sorgfalt ['zɔrkfalt] f (-; *no pl*) care: *große* ~ *verwenden auf* (acc) take great pains over. **'sorgfältig** [-fɛltɪç] *adj* careful.

'sorglos *adj* **1.** careless. **2.** carefree. **'Sorglosigkeit** f (-; *no pl*) carelessness.

'sorgsam → *sorgfältig.*

Sorte ['zɔrtə] f (-; -n) sort, kind, type, ✝ brand, *a.* quality; ~*n* foreign exchange; *übelster* ~ of the worst kind.

sortieren [zɔr'ti:rən] *v/t* (h) sort, *a.* grade, *a.* size. **Sortiment** [zɔrti'mɛnt] *n* (-[e]s; -e) **1.** range. **2.** → *Sorti'mentsbuchhandel* *m* retail book trade.

so'sehr *conj* ~ (*auch*) however much.

Soße ['zo:sə] f (-; -n) **1.** a) sauce, b) gravy, c) dressing. **2.** F juice, goo.

'Soßenschüssel f sauceboat.

Souffleur [zu'flø:r] *m* (-s; -e) prompter.

Souf'fleurkasten *m* prompt box.

Souffleuse [zu'flø:zə] f (-; -n) prompter.

soufflieren [zu'fli:rən] *v/t, v/i* (h) *j-m* ~ prompt s.o.

'sound'so *adv* F so and so: ~ *viel* so much; ~ *viele* so and so many; ~ *oft* time and again; *Herr* ⚥ Mr what's-his-name. **~so'vielt** *adj* F **1.** *am* ~*en* on such and such a date. **2.** umpteenth.

Soutane [zu'ta:nə] f (-; -n) cassock.

Souterrain [zutɛ'rɛ̃:] *n* (-s; -s) basement.

Souvenir [zuvə'ni:r] *n* (-s; -s) souvenir.

souverän [zuvə'rɛ:n] *adj* sovereign, *fig.*

superior, *a. adv* in superior style.

Souveränität [zuvərɛni'tɛ:t] f (-; *no pl*) sovereignty.

so'viel **I** *conj* ~ *ich weiß* as far as I know; ~ *ich gehört habe* from what I have heard. **II** *adj and adv* so much: ~ *wie* as much as; *doppelt* ~ twice as much; ~ *steht fest* one thing is certain.

so'weit **I** *conj* as far as (*I know etc*). **II** *adv* ~ *sein* be ready; *es ist* ~ *fertig* it's more or less finished; *es ist* ~*!* a) it's time!, b) here goes!

so'wenig **I** *adv* not more (*als* than): ~ *wie möglich* as little as possible. **II** *conj* however little.

so'wie *conj* **1.** as soon as. **2.** as well as.

sowie'so *adv* **1.** anyway, in any case. **2.** F (*das*) ~*! that goes without saying!

Sowjet [zɔ'vjɛt] *m* (-s; -s) *hist.* Soviet.

sowjetisch [zɔ'vjɛtɪʃ] *adj hist.* Soviet.

So'wjetuni,on f *hist.* Soviet Union.

so'wohl *conj* ~ ... *als* (*auch*) ... ... as well as ..., both ... and ...

sozial [zo'tsia:l] *adj* social: ~ *Stellung* social rank (or status); ~ *denken* be social-minded.

Sozi'al|**abgaben** *pl* social contributions. **~amt** *n* social welfare office. **~arbeit** f (-; *no pl*) social (or welfare) work. **~arbeiter** *m* social (or welfare) worker. **~demo,krat** *m* social democrat. **~demokra,tie** f social democracy. **2demokratisch** *adj* social-democratic. **2denkend** *adj* social-minded. **~einrichtungen** *pl* social services. **~hilfe** f social security, *Am.* welfare: ~ *beziehen* be on social security (*Am.* welfare).

sozialisieren [zotsiali'zi:rən] *v/t* (h) nationalize. **Sozialismus** [zotsia'lɪsmʊs] *m* (-; *no pl*) socialism. **Sozialist** [-'lɪst] *m* (-en; -en), **Sozia'listin** f (-; -nen) socialist. **sozia'listisch** *adj* socialistic.

sozi'alkritisch *adj* sociocritical.

Sozi'al|**kunde** f (-; *no pl*) *ped.* social studies. **~lasten** *pl* social expenditure. **~leistungen** *pl* **1.** social contributions. **2.** *of company:* fringe benefits. **~poli,tik** f social policy. **2politisch** *adj* sociopolitical. **~pre,stige** *n* social prestige. **~pro,dukt** *n* (gross) national product. **~staat** *m* welfare state. **~versicherung** f social security, *Am.* welfare: ~ *wohnung* f council flat.

Soziologe [zotsio'lo:gə] *m* (-n; -n) sociologist. **Soziologie** [zotsĩolo'giː] f (-; no pl) sociology. **sozio'logisch** adj sociological.

Sozius ['zoːtsĩʊs] m (-; -se) **1.** ♥ partner. **2.** a. **~fahrer** m pillion rider. **~sitz** m (auf dem ~ mitfahren ride) pillion.

sozu'sagen adv so to speak, as it were.

Spachtel ['ʃpaxtəl] m (-s; -) **1.** spatula. **2.** → **~masse** f filler. **~messer** n putty knife.

spachteln ['ʃpaxtəln] v/t (h) surface.

Spagat [ʃpa'gaːt] m, n (-[e]s; -e) (~ machen do the) splits.

Spaghetti [ʃpa'gɛti] pl spaghetti.

spähen ['ʃpɛːən] v/i (h) peer, look out (nach for).

'Spähtrupp m ✕ reconnaissance patrol.

'Spalier [ʃpa'liːɐ] n (-s; -e) **1.** ✗ trellis, espalier. **2.** a) guard of hono(u)r, b) lane, c) rows: ein ~ bilden, ~ stehen form a lane. **Spa'lierobst** n wall fruit.

Spalt [ʃpalt] m (-[e]s; -e) crack, gap, slit. **'spaltbar** adj phys. fissionable. **'Spalte** f (-; -n) **1.** crack, gap, split, geol. cleft, crevice, crevasse. **2.** print. column. **'spalten** v/t (spaltete, gespalten, h) split (a. atom), chop (wood), ⚛ decompose, fig. split (up), divide; → **Haar**. **'Spaltung** f (-; -en) splitting, phys. fission, fig. split, division, eccl. schism.

Span [ʃpaːn] m (-[e]s; ⁀e) chip, pl shavings, (metal) filings: wo gehobelt wird, da fallen Späne you can't make an omelette without breaking eggs.

'Spanferkel n sucking pig.

Spange ['ʃpaŋə] f (-; -n) a) clasp, b) buckle, c) bangle, d) (hair) slide, e) (shoe) strap, f) (dental) brace.

Spanien ['ʃpaːniən] n (-s) Spain.

'Spanier m (-s; -), **'Spanierin** f (-; -nen) Spaniard. **'spanisch** adj Spanish: **~e Wand** folding screen; F das kommt mir ~ vor! that's strange! **Spanisch** n (auf ~ in) Spanish.

spann [ʃpan] pret of **spinnen**.

Spann m (-[e]s; -e) instep.

'Spannbe,ton m prestressed concrete.

Spanne ['ʃpanə] f (-; -n) **1.** span: fig. e-e kurze ~ a short space (of time). **2.** ♥ margin. **'spannen** (h) **I** v/t stretch, tighten, put up (clothesline etc), cock (camera, gun), flex, tense (muscles), bend (bow), fig. strain (nerves): e-n Bogen in die Schreibmaschine ~ insert a

sheet of paper into the typewriter; → **gespannt**, **Folter**. **II** sich ~ stretch: sich ~ über (acc) span. **III** v/i dress etc: be (too) tight, skin: be taut. **'spannend** adj exciting, thrilling, gripping, book, film full of suspense, suspense-packed.

'Spanner m (-s; -) **1.** (racket etc) press; → **Schuhspanner**. **2.** F peeping Tom.

'Spannkraft f (-; no pl) energy, vigo(u)r.

'Spannung f (-; -en) **1.** ⚡ tension (a. ⚡, ⚡ a. voltage, stress; ⚡ unter ~ (stehend) live. **2.** fig. a) excitement, suspense (a. of book etc), b) a. pol. tension: mit (or voll) ~ expect, watch, etc with bated breath; j-n in ~ halten keep s.o. in suspense; in ~ versetzen thrill, excite.

'Spannungsgebiet n pol. area of tension, trouble spot.

'spannungsgeladen adj **1.** → **spannend**. **2.** (extremely) tense (atmosphere etc).

'Spannungsmesser m ⚡ voltmeter.

'Spannweite f wingspan, △ span, fig. scope, range.

'Spanplatte f chipboard.

'Spar|buch n savings book. **~büchse** f money box. **~einlage** f savings deposit.

sparen ['ʃpaːrən] (h) **I** v/t save: das hättest du dir ~ können! that was unnecessary. **II** v/i a) save (up) (auf acc for), b) economize (an dat, mit on): mit Lob etc ~ be sparing of praise etc. **'Sparer** m (-s; -), **'Sparerin** f (-; -nen) saver.

Spargel ['ʃpargəl] m (-s; -) asparagus.

'Spar|groschen m F nest egg. **~guthaben** n savings balance. **~kasse** f savings bank. **~konto** n savings account.

spärlich ['ʃpɛːrlɪç] adj scant(y), sparse, thin (a. hair), poor (attendance): ~ bekleidet scantily dressed; ~ besucht poorly attended.

'Spar|maßnahme f economy measure. **~prämie** f savings premium. **~programm** n **1.** pol. cuts (or austerity) program(me pr.) **2.** washing machine: energy-saving cycle.

Sparren ['ʃparən] m (-s; -) rafter.

'sparsam adj (mit) economical (of), thrifty (of, with): ~ im Verbrauch economical; a. fig. ~ umgehen mit be sparing of.

'Sparsamkeit f (-; no pl) economy, thrift, austerity, contp. parsimony.

'Sparschwein n F piggy bank.

spartanisch [ʃparˈtaːnɪʃ] *adj* Spartan, *fig.* spartan: ~ *leben* lead a spartan life.
Sparte [ˈʃpartə] *f* (-; -n) field, line.
'Sparvertrag *m* savings agreement.
Spaß [ʃpaːs] *m* (-es; ⸗e [ˈʃpɛːsə]) a) joke, b) fun: *aus* (*or im, zum*) ~ for fun; *er hat nur ~ gemacht!* he was only joking; *es macht* (*k-n*) ~ it's (no) fun; *es macht ihm viel ~* he really enjoys it; *er versteht k-n ~* he can't take a joke, *w.s.* he doesn't stand for any nonsense; ~ *beiseite!* joking aside; *viel ~!* have fun!; *ein teurer ~* an expensive business.
'spaßen *v/i* (h) joke: *damit ist nicht zu ~!* that's no joking matter!; *er läßt nicht mit sich ~* he doesn't stand for any nonsense. **'spaßeshalber** *adv* (just) for fun. **'spaßig** *adj* funny.
'Spaßverderber *m* (-s; -) spoilsport, killjoy. **'Spaßvogel** *m* joker, wag.
Spastiker [ˈʃpastikar] *m* (-s; -) ✶ spastic. **'spastisch** *adj* (*a.* ~ *gelähmt*) spastic.
spät [ʃpɛːt] **I** *adj* late: *am ~en Nachmittag* late in the afternoon; *wie ~ ist es?* what time is it?; *es ist* (*wird*) ~ it's (getting) late. **II** *adv* late, at a late hour (*a. fig.*): *zu ~ kommen* be late (*zu* for); *er kam 5 Minuten zu ~* he was five minutes late; ~ *zu Abend essen* have a late dinner; *bis ~ in die Nacht* till late at night; *du bist ~ dran!* you are late!
Spatel [ˈʃpaːtəl] *m* (-s; -) ✶ spatula.
Spaten [ˈʃpaːtən] *m* (-s; -) spade.
'Spätentwickler *m* late developer.
'später I *adj* later. **II** *adv* later (*als* than), later on: *bis ~!* see you later!; → *früher* II. **spätestens** [ˈʃpɛːtəstəns] *adv* at the latest.
'Spät|herbst *m* late autumn (*Am.* fall). **~lese** *f* late vintage (wine). **~schäden** *pl* ✶ late sequelae. **~schicht** *f* (~ *haben* be on) late shift. **~vorstellung** *f* late-night performance.
Spatz [ʃpats] *m* (-en, -es; -en) sparrow: F *das pfeifen die ~en von den Dächern* that's everybody's secret.
'Spätzünder *m* F **1.** *ein ~ sein* be slow on the uptake. **2.** → *Spätentwickler.*
'Spätzündung *f mot.* retarded ignition.
spazieren [ʃpaˈtsiːrən] *v/i* (sn) walk (around), stroll. **~fahren** (*irr, sep, -ge-, sn,* → *fahren*) **I** *v/i* take a ride. **II** *v/t* take *s.o.* for a ride. **~gehen** *v/i* (*irr, sep, -ge-, sn,* → *gehen*) go for a walk.

Spa'ziergang *m* **1.** walk, stroll: *e-n ~ machen* go for a walk. **2.** *sports etc:* walkover. **Spa'ziergänger** [-gɛŋər] *m* (-s; -) walker, stroller.
Spa'zierstock *m* walking stick.
Specht [ʃpɛçt] *m* (-[e]s; -e) woodpecker.
Speck [ʃpɛk] *m* (-[e]s; -e) **1.** *gastr.* bacon: → *Made.* **2.** F flab: ~ *ansetzen* get fat.
'speckig *adj* **1.** fat. **2.** *fig.* greasy.
'Speckscheibe *f* bacon rasher.
'Speckschwarte *f* bacon rind.
'Speckseite *f* flitch (of bacon).
Spediteur [ʃpediˈtøːr] *m* (-s; -e) **1.** forwarding (⚓ shipping) agent. **2.** (furniture) remover. **Spedition** [ʃpediˈtsi̯oːn] *f* (-; -en) **1.** forwarding (⚓ shipping) (business). **2.** → **Spediti'onsfirma** / **1.** forwarding (⚓ shipping) agency. **2.** removal firm. **Spediti'onskaufmann** *m* forwarding agent.
Speer [ʃpeːr] *m* (-[e]s; -e) spear, *sports:* javelin. **'Speerwerfen** *n sports:* javelin throw, *the* javelin. **'Speerwerfer(in** *f)* *m sports:* javelin thrower.
Speiche [ˈʃpaɪçə] *f* (-; -n) **1.** spoke. **2.** *anat.* radius.
Speichel [ˈʃpaɪçəl] *m* (-s; *no pl*) spittle, saliva. **~drüse** *f* salivary gland. **~lecker** *m contp.* toady, bootlicker.
Speicher [ˈʃpaɪçər] *m* (-s; -) **1.** a) granary, elevator, b) warehouse, c) reservoir. **2.** loft, attic. **3.** *computer:* store, memory. **~chip** *m computer:* memory chip. **~kapazi,tät** *f* storage (*computer:* memory) capacity.
speichern [ˈʃpaɪçərn] *v/t* (h) store (*a.* ⚡, *computer*), ⚓ *a.* stockpile. **'Speicherung** *f* (-; *no pl*) storage (*a. computer*).
Speise [ˈʃpaɪzə] *f* (-; -n) a) food, b) dish, meal. **~aufzug** *m* dumb waiter. **~eis** *n* ice cream. **~kammer** *f* larder, pantry. **~karte** *f* menu. **~leitung** *f* ⚡ feeder.
speisen [ˈʃpaɪzən] (h) **I** *v/i* eat, dine: *zu Mittag ~* (have) lunch; *zu Abend ~* have dinner, dine. **II** *v/t* feed (*a.* ⚡, ⚙).
'Speisenfolge *f* order of courses.
'Speise|öl *n* cooking oil. **~röhre** *f anat.* gullet, (o)esophagus. **~saal** *m* dining hall (*in hotel:* room, ⚓ saloon). **~wagen** *m* 🚃 dining car, *Am.* diner. **~zettel** *m* menu. **~zimmer** *n* dining room.
'Speisung *f* (-; -en) feeding, ⚙ *a.* supply.
Spektakel [ʃpɛkˈtaːkəl] *m* (-s; *no pl*) row, racket, *fig.* fuss.

Spektrana,lyse [ʃpɛk'traːl-] f spectrum analysis. **Spektrum** ['ʃpɛktrʊm] n (-s; -tren) a. fig. spectrum.

Spekulant [ʃpeku'lant] m (-en; -en) speculator. **Spekulation** [ʃpekula'tsĭoːn] f (-; -en) speculation. **Spekulati'onsge-schäft** n speculative operation.

spekulieren [ʃpeku'liːrən] v/i (h) speculate (**über** acc on, **♥** **mit** in): **~ auf** (acc) a) speculate on, b) F have one's eye on.

Spelunke [ʃpe'lʊŋkə] f (-; -n) F dive.

spendabel [ʃpɛn'daːbəl] adj F generous.

Spende ['ʃpɛndə] f (-; -n) donation, contribution. **'spenden** v/t, v/i (h) 1. donate (a. blood etc), contribute. 2. machine: dispense. 3. fig. give (praise etc). **'Spenden|akti,on** f collection campaign. **~konto** n account for donations. **'Spender** m (-s; -) 1. a. **'Spenderin** f (-; -nen) donator, contributor, a. **♣** donor. 2. (machine) dispenser.

spendieren [ʃpɛn'diːrən] v/t (h) F j-m et. **~** treat s.o. to s.th.; **j-m ein Bier ~** stand s.o. a beer.

Sperber ['ʃpɛrbər] m (-s; -) zo. sparrow hawk.

Sperling ['ʃpɛrlɪŋ] m (-s; -e) zo. sparrow.

Sperma ['ʃpɛrma] n (-s; -men) sperm.

Sperre ['ʃpɛrə] f (-; -n) 1. barrier, a. barricade, road block. 2. **◉** lock, stop, stoppage. 3. psych. mental block. 4. **♥** embargo, blockade: **e-e ~ verhängen über** (acc) impose a ban (**♥** an embargo) on. 5. sports: suspension. **'sperren** (h) I v/t 1. shut, block (road etc), police etc: cordon off: **e-e Straße für den Verkehr ~** close a road to traffic. 2. **◉** a) lock, block, stop, b) cut off (gas etc). 3. **♥** a) embargo, b) freeze (payments etc), block (account), stop (cheque). 4. sports: **j-n ~** a) obstruct s.o. (unfairly), b) suspend s.o. 5. print. space out: **gesperrt gedruckt** spaced out. 6. **j-n ~ in** (acc) lock s.o. up in. II **sich ~** balk (**gegen** at).

'Sperr|feuer n **✕** barrage. **~frist** f blocking period. **~gebiet** n restricted area. **~gürtel** m cordon. **~holz** n plywood.

'sperrig adj bulky.

'Sperr|klausel f restrictive clause. **~konto** n blocked account. **~minori,tät** f blocking minority. **~müll** m bulk rubbish. **~sitz** m thea. orchestra stalls.

~stunde f closing time, **✕** curfew. **~taste** f locking key.

'Sperrung f (-; -en) 1. closing (etc, → sperren I). 2. blockage, obstruction, stoppage, **♥** embargo.

Spesen ['ʃpeːzən] pl expenses. **2frei** adj free of charge(s). **~konto** n expense account. **~rechnung** f bill of expenses.

Spezi ['ʃpeːtsi] m (-s; -[s]) F chum, pal.

Spezial|ausbildung [ʃpe'tsĭaːl-] f special(ized) training. **~einheit** f task force. **~fach** n special subject. **~gebiet** n special field, speciality.

spezialisieren [ʃpetsĭali'ziːrən] **sich ~** (h) specialize (**auf** acc in). **Speziali'sierung** f (-; no pl) specialization. **Spezialist** [ʃpetsĭa'lɪst] m (-en; -en), **Spezia'listin** f (-; -nen) specialist. **Spezialität** [ʃpetsĭali'tɛːt] f (-; -en) speciality.

speziell [ʃpe'tsĭɛl] adj special, specific.

Spezies ['ʃpeːtsĭɛs] f (-; -) species.

spezifisch [ʃpe'tsiːfɪʃ] adj specific: phys. **~es Gewicht** specific gravity.

spezifizieren [ʃpetsifi'tsiːrən] v/t (h) specify, itemize.

Sphäre ['sfɛːrə] f (-; -n) sphere.

'sphärisch adj spheric.

Sphinx [sfɪŋks] f (-; -e) a. fig. sphinx.

spicken ['ʃpɪkən] v/t (h) 1. gastr. lard. 2. F fig. interlard speech etc (**mit** with): **gespickt mit Fehlern** full of mistakes.

Spiegel ['ʃpiːgəl] m (-s; -) 1. mirror (a. fig.), **♣** speculum, opt., **◉** reflector. 2. surface (of water), (a. blood sugar etc) level. **~bild** n 1. mirror image. 2. fig. reflection. **~ei** n gastr. fried egg.

'spiegel|frei adj nonglare. **~glatt** adj water (as) smooth as glass, floor etc like glass, a. icy (road).

spiegeln ['ʃpiːgəln] (h) I v/i shine, a. dazzle. II v/t a. fig. mirror, reflect. III **sich ~** be reflected, fig. a. be mirrored. **'Spiegelre,flexkamera** f reflex camera. **'Spiegelschrift** f mirror writing. **'Spiegelung** f (-; -en) 1. reflection. 2. mirage.

Spiel [ʃpiːl] n (-[e]s; -e) 1. play (a. fig. of colo[u]rs, muscles), **♪** playing, thea. a. acting, performance. 2. game, match, a. gamble: **wie steht das ~?** what's the score?; fig. **das ~ ist aus!** the game is up!; **gewagtes ~** gamble; **et. ins ~ bringen** bring s.th. up; **gewonnenes ~ haben** have made it; **leichtes ~ haben**

have little trouble (*mit* with); *die Hand im ~ haben* have one's (*or* a) finger in the pie; *ins ~ kommen* come into play; *aus dem ~ lassen* leave *s.o.*, *s.th.* out of it; *(mit) im ~ sein* be at work, *bei et.* be involved in *s.th.*; *aufs ~ setzen* risk; *auf dem ~ stehen* be at stake; *mit j-m sein ~ treiben* play games with *s.o.*; *mit j-m ein falsches ~ treiben* doublecross *s.o.*; → *abgekartet*. **3.** *thea.*, *TV* play. **4.** ~ (*Karten*) pack (*Am.* deck) (of cards). **5.** ⊙ *et.* ⊙ a) play, b) clearance.

'**Spiel**|**anzug** *m* playsuit. ~**art** *f biol. or fig.* variety. ~**auto**|**mat** *m* a) gaming machine, b) slot machine, F one-armed bandit. ~**ball** *m* **1.** ball, *tennis*: game ball. **2.** *fig.* plaything. ~**bank** *f* (-; -en) (gambling) casino.

spielen ['ʃpiːlən] (h) **I** *v/i* **1.** a) play (*a. fig.*), b) gamble: ~ *um* play for; *hoch* ~ play for high stakes; *sports*: *A. spielte gegen B.* A. played B.; *mit dem Gedanken ~ zu inf* toy with the idea of *ger*; *s-e Beziehungen ~ lassen* pull a few strings; *ins Rötliche* ~ have a reddish tinge; → *Charme*, *Feuer* 1, *Muskel*. **2.** *thea.* play, act: ~ *in* (*dat*) *film*, *scene*, *etc*: be set in. **II** *v/t* **3.** play: *Klavier* ~ play the piano; *sports*: *den Ball zu j-m* ~ pass (the ball) to *s.o.*; → *Geige*, *Hand*. **4.** *thea. or fig.* play, act: *fig.* *den Beleidigten* ~ act all offended; *mit gespielter Gleichgültigkeit* with studied indifference; F *fig.* *was wird hier gespielt?* what's going on here?; → *Rolle*[2]. **5.** *thea. etc* play, perform: *was wird heute abend gespielt?* what's on tonight?; → *Theater*.

'**spielend** *adv fig.* ~ (*leicht*) easily, effortlessly; *es ist* ~ *leicht* it's child's play; ~ *gewinnen* win hands down.

'**Spieler** *m* (-s; -) a) player, b) gambler. **Spiele'rei** *f* (-; -en) **1.** *no pl* playing around. **2.** pastime. **3.** *pl* a) gewgaws, b) gadgets. '**Spielerin** *f* (-; -nen) → *Spieler*. '**spielerisch** *adj* **1.** *sports*: playing, *thea.* acting. **2.** playful. **3.** *mit* ~ *er Leichtigkeit* effortlessly.

'**Spiel**|**feld** *n sports*: field, pitch, *tennis*: *a.* court. ~**film** *m* feature film. ~**halle** *f* amusement arcade. ~**hölle** *f contp.* gambling den. ~**kame**,**rad**(**in**) *f*) *m* playmate. ~**karte** *f* playing card. ~**ka**,**sino** *n* (gambling) casino. ~**leiter**(**in** *f*) *m* →

Regisseur(**in**). ~**macher** *m sports*: strategist. ~**marke** *f* counter, chip. ~**plan** *n thea. etc* program(me *Br.*). ~**platz** *m* playground. ~**raum** *m fig.* a) elbowroom, scope, b) time, c) margin. ~**regel** *f* rule: *a. fig.* *sich an die* ~*n halten* play the game. ~**sachen** *pl* toys. ~**sa**,**lon** *m* amusement arcade. ~**schuld** *f* gambling debt. ~**stand** *m* score. ~**tisch** *m* **1.** card table. **2.** gambling table. ~**trieb** *m* play instinct. ~**uhr** *f* musical clock. ~**verbot** *n sports*: suspension: ~ *haben* have been suspended. ~**waren** *pl* toys. ~**warengeschäft** *n* toy shop (*or* store). ~**zeit** *f sports*, *thea.* season, *of match*: playing time, *of film etc*: run. ~**zeug** *n* toy(s), *fig.* toy. ~**zeugpi**,**stole** *f* toy pistol.

Spieß [ʃpiːs] *m* (-es; -e) spear, *gastr.* spit, skewer: *am* ~ *braten* barbecue; F *fig.* *den* ~ *umdrehen* turn the tables (*gegen* on); *schreien wie am* ~ scream blue murder. '**Spießbürger**(**in** *f*) *m*, '**spießbürgerlich** *adj* petty bourgeois, F square. '**Spießer** *m* (-s; -), '**Spieße**-**rin** *f* (-; -nen), '**spießig** *adj* petty bourgeois, F square. '**Spieß**|**ruten** *pl* ~ *laufen a. fig.* run the gauntlet.

Spikes [ʃpaɪks] *pl* **1.** *sports*: spikes. **2.** *mot.* a) studs, b) → '**Spikesreifen** *pl* studded tyres (*Am.* tires).

spinal [ʃpiˈnaːl] *adj* spinal: ⚕ ~*e Kinderlähmung* polio(myelitis).

Spinat [ʃpiˈnaːt] *m* (-[e]s; -e) spinach.

Spind [ʃpɪnt] *m*, *n* (-[e]s; -e) locker.

Spindel [ʃpɪndəl] *f* (-; -n) spindle.

Spinett [ʃpiˈnɛt] *n* (-[e]s; -e) spinet.

Spinne ['ʃpɪnə] *f* (-; -n) spider. '**spinnen** (spann, gesponnen, h) **I** *v/t* **1.** spin: *fig.* *Ränke* ~ hatch plots. **II** *v/i* **2.** spin. **3.** F a) be crazy, b) talk (a lot of) rubbish. '**Spinnennetz** *n* cobweb. '**Spinner** *m* (-s; -) **1.** spinner. **2.** F nut, crackpot, *Am.* screwball. **Spinne'rei** *f* (-; -en) **1.** *no pl* spinning. **2.** spinning mill. **3.** F a) crazy idea, b) rubbish. '**Spinnerin** *f* (-; -nen) → *Spinner*.

'**Spinn**|**gewebe** *n* cobweb. ~**rad** *n* spinning wheel. ~**webe** *f* (-; -n) cobweb.

Spion [ʃpiˈoːn] *m* (-s; -e) **1.** spy. **2.** a) spyhole, b) window mirror.

Spionage [ʃpioˈnaːʒə] *f* (-; *no pl*) espionage, spying. ~**abwehr** *f* counterespionage, counterintelligence. **~netz** ' n, **~ring** m spy ring. **~ro|man** m spy story.

spionieren [ʃpio'ni:rən] v/i (h) spy, fig. contp. a. snoop (around).

Spi'onin f (-; -nen) spy.

Spirale [ʃpi'ra:lə] f (-; -n) spiral (a. ✝etc), ☼ coil (a. F pessary). **Spi'ralfeder** f coil spring, of watch: mainspring. **spi'ralförmig** adj spiral.

Spiritismus [ʃpiri'tɪsmʊs] m (-; no pl) spiritualism. **Spiri'tist** m (-en; -en), **spiri'tistisch** adj spiritualist.

Spirituosen [ʃpiri'tǔo:zən] pl spirits, liquor.

Spiritus ['ʃpi:ritʊs] m (-; -se) spirit.

'Spirituskocher m spirit stove.

spitz [ʃpɪts] adj **1.** pointed, sharp: ~ **zulaufend** tapering. **2.** A acute (angle). **3.** F peaky. **4.** fig. pointed (remark etc), sarcastic: **~e Zunge** sharp tongue.

Spitz m (-es; -e) (dog) Pomeranian.

'Spitz|bart m goatee. **~bauch** m paunch.

'Spitze[1] f (-; -n) **1.** point, tip (a. of finger, nose, etc), peak, top, a. spire: fig. die ~ **des Eisbergs** the tip of the iceberg; e-r **Sache die ~ nehmen** take the edge off s.th.; **et. auf die ~ treiben** carry s.th. too far. **2.** head (a. fig.), ✗ (spear)head, sports: lead, a. leading group: F ~ **spielen** soccer: be striker; **an der ~ der Tabelle** at the top of the table; a. fig. **an der ~ liegen** be in front; **sich an die ~ setzen** take the lead. **3.** peak, maximum: F **das Auto macht 220 km ~** the car does a maximum speed of 220 km per hour; F **das ist (einsame) ~!** that's super! **4.** a) top position, b) (top) management, c) pl leading figures, élite: **an der ~ der Firma** at the head of the firm. **5.** A apex. **6.** F dig (**gegen** at).

'Spitze[2] f (-; -n) lace.

Spitzel ['ʃpɪtsəl] m (-s; -) a) informer, sl. nark, b) company spy.

spitzen ['ʃpɪtsən] v/t (h) point, sharpen: **die Ohren ~** prick up one's ears, fig. a. listen carefully.

'Spitzen|fabri,kat n top-quality product (or make). **~gehalt** n top salary. **~geschwindigkeit** f maximum (or top) speed. **~gespräch** n top-level talks. **~kandi,dat(in** f) m leading candidate, front-runner. **~klasse** f top class: **Läufer (Auto) der ~** top-class runner (car).

'Spitzenkleid n lace dress.

'Spitzen|kraft f highly qualified worker, top-level executive, thea. etc star performer. **~leistung** f **1.** ☼ maximum output, ⚡ peak power. **2.** sports: top performance, fig. a. great feat. **~lohn** m top wage(s). **~reiter** m front-runner, sports: leader, leading team, (film, tune, etc) (top) hit. **~sport** m high-performance sports. **~sportler(in** f) m top athlete. **~tanz** m toe-dancing. **~technolo,gie** f high technology. **~verdiener(in** f) m top earner. **~wein** m vintage wine. **~zeit** f **1.** sports: record time. **2.** peak hours (of traffic etc).

'spitzfindig adj over-subtle.

'Spitzfindigkeit f (-; -en) subtlety: **das sind ~en** that's splitting hairs.

'Spitzhacke f pickax(e).

'spitzkriegen v/t (sep, -ge-, h) F **et. ~** cotton on to s.th.

'Spitzname m nickname.

'spitzwink(e)lig adj A acute.

Spleen [ʃpli:n] m (-s; -e, -s) F tic, quirk.

splitten ['ʃplɪtən] v/t (h) ✝, pol. split.

Splitter ['ʃplɪtər] m (-s; -) splinter, fragment. **~bruch** m ✚ chip fracture. **2frei** adj shatterproof. **~gruppe** f pol. splinter group.

splittern ['ʃplɪtərn] v/i **1.** (h) splinter. **2.** (sn) glass: shatter.

'splitternackt adj stark naked.

'Splitterpar,tei f splinter party.

Spoiler ['ʃpɔylər] m (-s; -) mot. spoiler.

sponsern ['ʃpɔnzərn] v/t (h) sponsor.

Sponsor ['ʃpɔnzɔr] m (-s; -s, -en [-'zo:rən]) sponsor.

spontan [ʃpɔn'ta:n] adj spontaneous.

sporadisch [ʃpo'ra:dɪʃ] adj sporadic.

Spore ['ʃpo:rə] f (-; -n) ⚘ spore.

Sporn [ʃpɔrn] m (-[e]s; Sporen ['ʃpo:rən]) spur (a. ⚘), ✈ (tail) skid: **s-m Pferd die Sporen geben** spur one's horse.

Sport [ʃpɔrt] m (-[e]s; no pl) **1.** sport, coll. sports, ped. a. physical education: ~ **treiben** go in for sports; **viel ~ treiben** do a lot of sport. **2.** fig. (**als ~** as a) hobby. **~abzeichen** n sports badge. **~angler** m angler. **~anlage** f sports grounds (or facilities). **~art** f (kind of) sport. **~ar,tikel** m sports article. **~arzt** m sports physician. **2begeistert** adj sporty. **~bericht** m sports report. **~fest** n sports day. **~flieger** m amateur pilot. **~geschäft** n sports shop (or store).

~**halle** f gymnasium. ~**hochschule** f physical education college. ~**kleidung** f sportswear. ~**klub** m sports club. ~**lehrer(in** f) m ped. PE (= physical education) teacher.

'**Sportler** m (-s; -) sportsman, athlete. '**Sportlerin** f (-; -nen) sportswoman.

'**sportlich** adj sporting, sporty, a. fair (behavio[u]r, play), a. sports (meeting etc), athletic (person, figure, etc), casual (wear).

'**Sport|medi,zin** f sports medicine. ~**nachrichten** pl sports news. ~**platz** m sports ground. ~**repor,tage** f sports report, sportscast. ~**re,porter** m sports reporter, sportscaster. ~**sendung** f sports broadcast, sportscast. ~**zeitung** f sporting paper.

'**Sporta|s,none** f F (sports) ace. '**Sportsmann** m sportsman. '**Sport|tauchen** n skin (or scuba) diving. ~**veranstaltung** f sporting event, sports meeting. ~**verein** m sports club. ~**wagen** m 1. sports car. 2. pushchair, Am. stroller. ~**zeitung** f sporting paper.

Spott [ʃpɔt] m (-[e]s; no pl) mockery, ridicule, a. derision, scorn. '**spottbillig** adj F dirt-cheap. **Spötte'lei** f (-; -en) mockery, a. gibe. **spötteln** ['ʃpœtəln] v/i (h) gibe (über acc at). '**spotten** v/t (h) (über acc) mock (at), scoff (at), make fun (of); → **Beschreibung** 1.

Spötter ['ʃpœtər] m (-s; -) 1. mocker. 2. cynic. '**spöttisch** adj a) mocking, b) derisive, c) sarcastic.

'**Spottlied** n satirical song.

'**Spottpreis** m ridiculous(ly low) price.

sprach [ʃpraːx] pret of **sprechen**.

'**sprachbegabt** adj good at languages.

'**Sprachbegabung** f gift for languages.

Sprache ['ʃpraːxə] f (-; -n) 1. no pl speech: → **verschlagen**[1] 4. 2. language (a. fig.), a. vernacular, idiom, a. jargon, a. diction: **heraus mit der ~!** out with it!, **et. zur ~ bringen** bring s.th. up; **ein Thema zur ~ bringen** raise a subject; **zur ~ kommen** come up (for discussion); → **herausrücken** II.

'**Sprach|ebene** f speech level. ~**eigenheit** f idiom(atic expression).

'**Sprachenschule** f language school.

'**Sprach|fehler** m speech defect. ~**führer** m phrasebook. ~**gebiet** n speech area: **deutsches ~** German-speaking area. ~**gebrauch** m (-[e]s; no pl) (linguistic)

usage: **im gewöhnlichen ~** in everyday usage. ~**gefühl** n (-[e]s; no pl) linguistic instinct. 2**gewandt** adj 1. articulate. 2. proficient in languages. ~**kenntnisse** pl knowledge of languages (or of a language): **gute deutsche ~ erwünscht** good command of German desirable. 2**kundig** adj proficient in languages, polyglot. ~**kurs** m language course. ~**la,bor** n language laboratory. ~**lehre** f 1. grammar. 2. grammar book. ~**lehrer** m language teacher.

'**sprachlich** adj a) linguistic, b) grammatical, c) stylistic.

'**sprachlos** adj speechless.

'**Sprach|regelung** f iro. (prescribed) phraseology. ~**rohr** n fig. mouthpiece. ~**störung** f ✚ speech disorder. ~**studium** n language studies. ~**ta,lent** n gift for languages. ~**unterricht** m language teaching: **englischer ~** English lessons. ~**wissenschaft** f philology. ~**wissenschaftler(in** f) m philologist, linguist. 2**wissenschaftlich** adj philological, linguistic.

sprang [ʃpraŋ] pret of **springen**.

Spray [ʃpreː] m, n (-s; -s) spray.

'**Sprech|anlage** f intercom. ~**blase** f in cartoons: balloon. ~**chor** m chorus: **im ~ rufen** chant.

sprechen ['ʃprɛçən] (sprach, gesprochen, h) I v/i speak, a. give a speech, a. talk (mit j-m to s.o., über acc, von about): **~ mit** see (one's doctor etc) about; **über Geschäfte (Politik) ~** talk business (politics); **von et. anderem ~** change the subject; **j-n zum 2 bringen** make s.o. talk; **~ für** a) speak on behalf of s.o., b) put in a good word for s.o., c) plead for; **das spricht für ihn** that says s.th. for him; **das spricht für sich selbst** that speaks for itself; **vieles spricht dafür (dagegen)** there is much to be said for (against) it; **alles spricht dafür, daß** there is every indication that; **auf ihn ist sie nicht gut zu ~** he's in her bad books; **wir kamen (man kam) auf ... zu ~** the subject of ... came up. II v/t speak (language etc), say (prayer etc): **j-n ~** speak to s.o., see s.o.; **j-n zu ~ wünschen** wish to see s.o.; **kann ich Sie kurz ~?** may I have a word with you?; **er ist nicht zu ~** he is busy; → **Recht** 1, **schuldig** 1.

'**sprechend** adj fig. eloquent (gesture etc), striking (resemblance).

'**Sprecher** m (-s; -) **1.** speaker, radio, TV announcer. **2.** spokesman (gen for).

'**Sprecherin** f (-; -nen) **1.** → **Sprecher** 1. **2.** spokeswoman (gen for).

'**Sprecherziehung** f speech training.

'**Sprechfunk** m radiotelephony. ~**gerät** n a) radiotelephone, b) walkie-talkie.

'**Sprechstunde** f a) office hours, b) (doctor's) consulting hours.

'**Sprechstundenhilfe** f receptionist.

'**Sprechzimmer** n a) office, b) (doctor's) consulting room, surgery.

'**spreizen** ['∫praɪtsən] v/t (h) spread, a. straddle (legs).

'**Spreizfuß** m ☙ splayfoot.

'**Sprengbombe** f high-explosive bomb.

'**sprengen¹** ['∫prɛŋən] v/t (h) sprinkle, spray.

'**sprengen²** v/t (h) **1.** burst open, force (door), break (fetters etc). **2.** blast, blow up. **3.** fig. break up (meeting): **die Bank** ~ break the bank; → **Rahmen**.

'**Spreng|kapsel** f detonator. ~**kopf** m warhead. ~**körper** m, ~**ladung** f, ~**satz** m explosive charge.

'**Sprengstoff** m explosive, fig. dynamite. ~**anschlag** m bomb attack.

'**Sprengung** f (-; -en) **1.** blasting, blowing up. **2.** fig. breaking-up (of meeting).

'**sprenkeln** ['∫prɛŋkəln] v/t (h) dot.

'**Spreu** [∫prɔʏ] f (-; no pl) (fig. **die** ~ **vom Weizen trennen** separate the wheat from the) chaff.

'**Sprichwort** n proverb: **wie das** ~ **sagt** as the saying goes.

'**sprichwörtlich** adj a. fig. proverbial.

'**sprießen** ['∫pri:sən] v/i (sproß, gesprossen, sn) shoot up, sprout.

'**Springbrunnen** m fountain.

'**springen** ['∫prɪŋən] v/i (sprang, gesprungen, sn) **1.** a) jump, sports: a. dive, a. (pole)vault, b) leap, hop, skip, a. ball etc: bounce; → **Auge** 1, **Punkt** 2. **2.** F run, nip. **3.** F fig. et. ~ **lassen** fork out, **für j-n** treat s.o. to s.th. **4.** crack, break.

'**Springen** n (-s) jumping, sports: diving. '**Springer** m (-s; -) **1.** sports: a) jumper, b) diver, c) vaulter. **2.** chess: knight. **3.** F ✝ stand-in. '**Springerin** f (-; -nen) → **Springer** 1, 3.

'**Spring|flut** f spring tide. ~**reiter(in** f) m show jumper. ~**seil** n skipping rope.

Sprinkleranlage ['∫prɪŋklər-] f sprinkler system.

Sprint [∫prɪnt] m (-s; -s), '**sprinten** v/i, v/t (sn, h) sprint. '**Sprinter** m (-s; -), '**Sprinterin** f (-; -nen) sprinter.

Sprit [∫prɪt] m (-[e]s; -e) F **1.** spirit(s), alcohol. **2.** petrol, F juice, Am. gas.

Spritze ['∫prɪtsə] f (-; -n) a) syringe, b) injection, F jab, Am. shot, c) → **Finanzspritze**.

spritzen ['∫prɪtsən] **I** v/t (h) **1.** squirt, spray. **2.** → **sprengen¹**. **3.** F a) inject (s.o.), b) sl. shoot, mainline (drugs). **4.** mix drink with (soda) water. **5.** ☙ inject (plastic). **II** v/i **6.** splash, spatter, blood: gush. **7.** spray. **8.** F mainline (sl.). '**Spritzer** m (-s; -) splash, a. dash (of rum etc). '**Spritzguß** m ☙ a) die-casting, b) injection mo(u)lding.

'**spritzig** adj **1.** sparkling (wine etc). **2.** fig. lively, F peppy, nippy, zippy (car).

'**spritzlac,kieren** v/t (h) spray(-paint). '**Spritzmittel** n ✿ spray. '**Spritz,pistole** f ☙ spray gun. '**Spritztour** f F mot. (e-e ~ **machen** go for a) spin.

spröde ['∫prø:də] adj **1.** brittle (a. voice), rough, chapped (skin). **2.** fig. standoffish, demure, prim (girl).

sproß [∫prɔs] pret of **sprießen**.

Sproß m (-sses; -sse) **1.** ✎ shoot. **2.** fig. scion.

Sprosse ['∫prɔsə] f (-; -n) **1.** a. fig. rung. **2.** hunt. tine.

'**Sprossenwand** f gym. wall bars.

Sprößling ['∫prœslɪŋ] m (-s; -e) F a) child, → **Auge** 1, b) son, junior.

Sprotte ['∫prɔtə] f (-; -n) zo. sprat.

Spruch [∫prʊx] m (-[e]s; ∸e) **1.** saying, dictum, a. aphorism, epigram, (bible) quotation, verse: F (**große**) **Sprüche klopfen** talk big. **2.** decision.

'**Spruchband** n banner.

'**spruchreif** adj **die Sache ist noch nicht** ~ nothing has been decided yet.

Sprudel ['∫pru:dəl] m (-s; -) (carbonated) mineral water. '**sprudeln** v/i (sn) **1.** gush (forth). **2.** bubble, drink: a. fizz: fig. ~ **vor** bubble (over) with.

'**Sprühdose** f spray can, aerosole (can).

sprühen ['∫pry:ən] (h) **I** v/t **1.** spray, sprinkle. **II** v/i **2.** (sn) spray. **3.** (a. sn) sparks: fly. **4.** fig. (**vor** dat with) bubble (over), eyes: flash: **vor Geist** ~ sparkle with wit. **'sprühend** adj fig. sparkling (wit etc). **'Sprühregen** m drizzle.

Sprung¹ [ʃprʊŋ] m (-[e]s; ⸚e) jump (a. fig.), leap, gym., sport, pole-vaulting: vault, high-diving: dive: fig. **ein großer ~ nach vorn** a great leap forward; F **auf dem ~ sein zu** inf be about to inf; **j-m auf die Sprünge helfen** help s.o. along; **mit dem Gehalt kann er k-e großen Sprünge machen** he can't go far on that salary.

Sprung² m (-[e]s; ⸚e) crack: **e-n ~ haben** be cracked.

'Sprung|balken m sports: takeoff board. **⸚becken** n diving pool. **⸚brett** n springboard (a. fig.), high-diving: a. diving board. **⸚feder** f spring. **⸚federma|tratze** f spring (coil) mattress. **⸚grube** f sports: (jumping) pit.

'sprunghaft I adj **1.** erratic. **2.** rapid, a. sharp (increase etc). **II** adv rapidly: **~ ansteigen** go up by leaps and bounds, shoot up. **'Sprunghaftigkeit** f (-; no pl) **1.** of person: volatility. **2.** a) instability, b) rapidity.

'Sprung|lauf m ski-jumping. **⸚schanze** f ski jump. **⸚tuch** n jumping sheet. **⸚turm** m high-diving platforms.

'Spucke [ʃpʊkə] f (-; no pl) F spittle: **da blieb mir die ~ weg** I was flabbergasted. **'spucken** (h) **I** v/i **1.** spit, engine: splutter. **2.** F be sick, puke. **II** v/t **3.** spit s.th. out: **Blut ~ spit blood;** → **Ton²** f.

Spuk [ʃpuːk] m (-[e]s; -e) **1.** apparition, ghost, spectre, Am. specter, w.s. eerie happenings. **2.** fig. nightmare. **'spuken** (h) **I** v/i haunt. **II** v/impers **in der Burg spukt es** the castle is haunted.

Spule [ʃpuːlə] f (-; -n) **1.** ⊙ spool, reel. **2.** bobbin coil.

Spüle [ˈʃpyːlə] f (-; -n) sink unit.

spulen [ˈʃpuːlən] v/t (h) a) reel, spool, b) wind (film etc).

spülen [ˈʃpyːlən] (h) **I** v/t **1.** rinse. **2.** wash (up): **Geschirr ~** → **3. et. ans Ufer ~** wash s.th. ashore. **II** v/i **4.** wash up, wash (or do) the dishes. **5.** flush the toilet. **'Spülmittel** n washing-up liquid.

'Spülung f (-; -en) **1.** rinse, ⚕ douche, irrigation. **2.** a) flushing, b) flush. **'Spülwasser** n rinsing water, washing-up water, a. dishwater (a. fig. contp.).

'Spulwurm m ⚕, zo. roundworm.

Spur [ʃpuːr] f (-; -en) **1.** print, track(s),

trace(s), trail (a. fig.), hunt. a. scent: **e-e ~ aufnehmen** pick up a trail; fig. **auf die ~ kommen** (dat) get on to s.o., s.th.; **auf der falschen ~ sein** be on the wrong track; **s-e ~en verwischen** cover up one's tracks; **(bei j-m) s-e ~en hinterlassen** leave its mark (on s.o.). **2.** fig. trace, esp. ⚖ clue: **k-e ~ von ...** not a trace of ...; F **k-e ~!** not a bit! **3.** fig. trace, gastr. dash (of pepper etc). **4.** 🛢 a) ga(u)ge, b) track(s). **5.** computer, tape: track. **6.** mot. a) (**~ halten** keep) track, b) (**die ~ wechseln**) change lane.

'spürbar adj noticeable, marked, considerable: **~ sein** be felt; **~ werden** make itself felt.

spuren [ˈʃpuːrən] v/i (h) **1.** skiing: lay a track. **2.** F toe the line.

spüren [ˈʃpyːrən] v/t (h) feel, a. sense: **am eigenen Leibe zu ~ bekommen** have experience of; **von ... war nichts zu ~** there was no sign of ...

'Spurenele|ment n trace element.

'Spürhund m **1.** tracker dog. **2.** humor. sleuth.

'spurlos adv **~ verschwinden** disappear without a trace; **nicht ~ an j-m vorübergehen** leave its mark on s.o.

'Spürnase f, **'Spürsinn** m (-[e]s; no pl) (good) nose.

Spurt [ʃpʊrt] m (-[e]s; -s), **'spurten** v/i (h, sn) sprint, spurt.

'Spurwechsel m mot. changing lane.

'Spurweite f **1.** 🛢 ga(u)ge. **2.** mot. track.

Staat¹ [ʃtaːt] m (-[e]s; -en) **1.** pol. a) state, a. country, nation, b) government: F **die ~en** (USA) the States. **2.** zo. colony.

Staat² m (-[e]s; no pl) finery: fig. **damit kannst du k-n ~ machen!** that's nothing to write home about!

'Staatenbund m confederation.

'staatenlos adj stateless. **'Staatenlose** m, f (-n; -n) stateless person.

'staatlich adj state(-)...., government ..., national, public, a. state-owned (plant etc): **~e Mittel** government funds; **~ gefördert** state-sponsored; **~ gelenkt** state-run; **~ geprüft** qualified, registered.

'Staats|akt m a) act of state, b) state occasion. **⸚akti|on** f F **e-e ~ machen aus** (dat) make a big affair out of it. **⸚angehörige** m, f national, citizen, Br. a. subject. **⸚angehörigkeit** f (doppelte ~

dual) nationality. **~angestellte** m, f state (or government) employee. **~anleihe** f government loan (or bond). **~anwalt** m 👗 public prosecutor, Am. district attorney. **~anwaltschaft** f 👗 a) the public prosecutor's office, b) the public prosecutors. **~beamte** m civil servant. **~begräbnis** n state funeral. **~besuch** m state visit. **~bürger** m citizen. **2bürgerlich** adj civic: **~e Rechte** civil rights. **~bürgerschaft** f → **Staatsangehörigkeit**. **~chef** m head of state. **~dienst** m civil (Am. public) service. **2eigen** adj state-owned. **~ex,amen** n univ. state examination. **~feiertag** m national holiday. **~feind** m public enemy. **2feindlich** adj subversive. **~form** f form of government. **~gebiet** n German etc territory. **~geheimnis** n state secret: F **das ist kein ~!** that's not top-secret. **~grenze** f border, frontier. **~haushalt** m national budget. **~hoheit** f (-; no pl) sovereignty. **~kasse** f (public) treasury. **~kosten** pl auf **~** at (the) public expense.

'Staatsmann m (-[e]s, ⁻er) statesman. **'staatsmännisch** [-mɛnɪʃ] adj statesmanlike.

'Staats|mi,nister m secretary of state, Am. secretary. **~mini,sterium** n ministry. **~oberhaupt** n head of state. **~präsi,dent** m president. **~rat** m a) council of state, Br. Privy Council, b) council(l)or of state. **~recht** n (-[e]s; no pl) constitutional law. **~religi,on** f state religion. **~schulden** pl national debt. **~sekre,tär** m permanent secretary. **~sicherheitsdienst** m DDR pol. hist. State Security (Service). **~streich** m coup (d'état). **2tragend** adj supportive of the State. **~trauer** f national mourning. **~verbrechen** n political crime. **~vertrag** m (international) treaty. **~wesen** n (-s; no pl) **1.** state, body politic. **2.** political system. **~wissenschaft(en** pl) f political science. **~wohl** n public weal. **~zuschuß** m government grant, subsidy.

Stab¹ [ʃtaːp] m (-[e]s; ⁻e) a) staff, b) stick, c) rod, bar, d) wand, e) ♪, sports: baton, f) sports: pole: fig. **den ~ brechen über** (acc) condemn.

Stab² m (-[e]s; ⁻e) **1.** a) (administrative etc) staff, b) team (of experts etc). **2.** ✕

a) staff, b) staff officers, c) headquarters.

Stäbchen ['ʃtɛːpçən] n (-s; -) chopstick. **'Stabhochspringer** m pole-vaulter. **'Stabhochsprung** m pole-vault(ing).

stabil [ʃtaˈbiːl] adj **1.** stable. **2.** solid, sturdy. **stabilisieren** [ʃtabiliˈziːrən] v/t (h) stabilize: **sich ~** a. become stabilized. **Stabili'sierung** f (-; -en) stabilization. **Stabilität** [ʃtabiliˈtɛːt] f (-; no pl) stability.

'Stabreim m alliteration. **'Stabs|arzt** m captain (medical corps). **~chef** m chief of staff. **~feldwebel** m warrant officer, Am. master sergeant. **'Stabwechsel** m sports: baton change.

stach [ʃtax] pret of **stechen**. **Stachel** ['ʃtaxəl] m (-s; -n) **1.** prickle, zo. a. spine, sting, ✿ a. thorn. **2.** ✿ spike. **'Stachelbeere** f gooseberry. **'Stacheldraht** m barbed wire. **'stach(e)lig** adj **1.** prickly, zo. a. spiny, ✿ a. thorny. **2.** fig. bristly (chin, beard). **'Stachelschwein** n porcupine.

Stadion ['ʃtaːdi̯ɔn] n (-s; -dien) stadium. **Stadium** ['ʃtaːdi̯ʊm] n (-s; -dien) stage, phase.

Stadt [ʃtat] f (-; ⁻e) **1.** town, city: **in die ~ gehen** go to town. **2.** adm. municipality. **~autobahn** f urban motorway (Am. expressway). **~bahn** f city railway. **2bekannt** adj known all over town, notorious. **~bevölkerung** f urban population. **~bewohner** m city dweller. **~bezirk** m municipal district. **~bild** n townscape.

Städtchen ['ʃtɛːtçən] n (-s; -) small town. **Städte|bau** ['ʃtɛːtə-] m (-[e]s; no pl) urban development. **~planung** f town planning.

Städter ['ʃtɛːtər] m (-s; -) city dweller. **'Stadt|gas** n (-es; no pl) town gas. **~gebiet** n municipal area. **~gemeinde** f township. **~gespräch** n fig. **~ sein** be the talk of the town. **~gue,rilla** f urban guer(r)illa. **~halle** f municipal hall.

städtisch ['ʃtɛːtɪʃ] adj town ..., city ..., urban, adm. municipal.

'Stadt|kern m town (or city) cent/re (Am. -er). **~leben** n city life. **~luft** f city air. **~mauer** f city wall. **~mitte** f → **Innenstadt**. **~plan** m city map. **~planung** f town planning.

'Stadtrand m (am **~** at the) outskirts of

the town (or city). **~siedlung** f suburban estate (or housing development).

'**Stadt|rat** m **1.** municipal council. **2.** town (Am. city) council(l)or. **~rundfahrt** f city sightseeing tour. **~sa,nierung** f urban renewal. **~staat** m city state. **~streicher** m (-s; -) city vagrant. **~teil** m district. **~tor** n town gate. **~verkehr** m town (or city) traffic. **~verwaltung** f municipality. **~viertel** n district. **~zentrum** n → **Innenstadt**.

Staffage [ʃtaˈfaːʒə] f (-; -n) mere show.

Staffel ['ʃtafəl] f (-; -n) **1.** sports: relay (race or team). **2.** ✈, ✕ squadron.

Staffelei [ʃtafəˈlaɪ] f (-; -en) easel.

'**Staffellauf** m sports: relay race.

staffeln ['ʃtafəln] v/t (h) a) stagger, b) grade, graduate (taxes, wages, etc); → **gestaffelt**. '**Staffelung** f (-; -en) a) staggering, b) graduation (of taxes etc), progressive rates.

Stagnation [ʃtagnaˈtsi̯oːn] f (-; -en) stagnation.

stagnieren [ʃtaˈgniːrən] v/i (h) stagnate.

stahl [ʃtaːl] pret of **stehlen**.

Stahl m (-[e]s; ⁓e) steel: **Nerven aus ~** nerves of steel. **~arbeiter** m steelworker. **~bau** m steel(-girder) construction. **~be,ton** m reinforced concrete. **2blau** adj steel-blue. **~blech** n sheet steel.

stählen ['ʃtɛːlən] v/t (h) **1.** ⊙ steel-face. **2.** fig. steel (sich o.s.). '**stählern** adj **1.** (of) steel. **2.** fig. of steel, steely.

'**Stahl|gürtelreifen** m mot. steel breaker tyre (Am. tire). **2hart** adj (as) hard as steel, steely. **~helm** m steel helmet. **~(rohr)möbel** pl tubular steel furniture. **~stich** m steel engraving. **~waren** pl steel goods. **~werk** n steelworks. **~wolle** f steel wool.

Stall [ʃtal] m (-[e]s; ⁓e) stable (a. fig.), a. cowshed: F **e-n ganzen ~ voll** a horde of children etc. **~bursche** m groom. **~gefährte** m sports: stable mate. **~meister** m riding master.

'**Stallungen** pl stabling, stables.

Stamm [ʃtam] m (-[e]s; ⁓e) **1.** ♀ stem (a. ling.), (tree) trunk. **2.** a) race, tribe, b) family. **3.** fig. core, nucleus. **4.** permanent staff, ✝ regular customers, sports: regular players. **5.** biol. division. **~aktie** f ordinary share, Am. common stock. **~baum** m family tree, zo. pedigree, biol. phylogenetic tree. **~buch** n family

register. **~burg** f ancestral castle. **~da,tei** f master file.

stammeln ['ʃtaməln] v/t, v/i (h) stammer.

stammen ['ʃtamən] v/i (h) (**von, aus**) a) come (from), b) date (from), go back (to): **der Ausspruch stammt von ihm** the word was coined by him.

'**Stammform** f ling. principal form.

'**Stammgast** m regular (guest).

'**Stammhalter** m humor. son and heir.

'**Stammhaus** n ✝ parent firm.

stämmig ['ʃtɛmɪç] adj stocky, burly.

'**Stamm|kapi,tal** n ordinary share capital, Am. common capital stock. **~kneipe** f F local. **~kunde** m regular customer, F regular. **~lo,kal** n favo(u)rite haunt. **~perso,nal** n permanent (or skeleton) staff. **~platz** m favo(u)rite seat: sports: **sich e-n ~ erobern** make the regular team. **~spieler** m sports: regular player. **~tafel** f genealogical table. **~tisch** m (table reserved for) regular guests. **~tischpo,litiker** m armchair politician. **~wähler** m pol. standing voter.

stampfen ['ʃtampfən] **I** v/i **1.** (sn) stamp, ♣ pitch. **2.** (h) **mit dem Fuß** stamp one's foot. **II** v/t (h) a) pound, crush, mash, b) tamp: → **Boden** 1.

stand [ʃtant] pret of **stehen**.

Stand¹ m (-[e]s; ⁓e) **1.** no pl a) (**aus dem ~** from a standing position, b) footing, foothold: **k-n (festen) ~ haben** be wobbly, person: have no firm foothold; fig. (**bei j-m**) **e-n schweren ~ haben** have a hard time of it (with s.o.). **2.** no pl a) state, condition, b) position (a. astr.), c) (a. water etc) level, standard, d) figure (barometer etc) reading, e) sports: score: **beim ~ von 4:2** at 4:2; **nach dem ~ vom 1. Mai** as of May 1st; **den höchsten ~ erreichen** reach its peak; **et. auf den neuesten ~ bringen** bring s.th. up to date, update s.th.; **der ~ der Dinge** the state of affairs; **nach dem ~ der Dinge** as matters stand; **der neueste ~ der Technik** (or **Wissenschaft**) the state of the art. **3.** no pl social standing, rank, (a. legal, marital) status. **4.** a) class, b) profession.

Stand² m (-[e]s; ⁓e) stall, booth.

Standard ['ʃtandart] m (-s; -s) standard.

standardisieren [ʃtandardiˈziːrən] v/t

(h) standardize. **Standardi'sierung** *f* (-; -en) standardization.

'Standardwerk *n* standard work.

Standarte [ʃtanˈdartə] *f* (-; -n) standard.

'Standbild *n* statue.

Ständchen [ˈʃtɛntçən] *n* (-s; -) serenade: **j-m ein ~ bringen** serenade s.o.

Stander [ˈʃtandər] *m* (-s; -) pennant.

Ständer [ˈʃtɛndər] *m* (-s; -) **1.** stand, (*pipe, rifle, etc*) rack. **2.** V hard-on.

'Standes|amt *n* registry office. **2amtlich** *adj* **~e Trauung** registry office wedding. **~beamte** *m* registrar. **2gemäß** *adj* and *adv* in keeping with one's station. **~unterschied** *m* social difference.

'standfest *adj* steady, ⊚ stable.

'Standfestigkeit *f* (-; *no pl*) **1.** steadiness, ⊚ stability. **2.** → *Standhaftigkeit*.

'Stand|foto *n* film: still. **~gericht** *n* ✗ drumhead court martial.

'standhaft *adj* steadfast, firm.

'Standhaftigkeit *f* (-; *no pl*) steadfastness, firmness.

'standhalten *v/i* (*irr, sep, -ge-, h, →halten*) a) hold one's ground, stand firm, b) withstand, resist (*attack etc*), c) stand up to (*criticism etc*): → *Vergleich* 1.

ständig [ˈʃtɛndiç] **I** *adj* a) constant, continuous, b) permanent (*abode, personnel, etc*), c) fixed, regular (*income*), standing (*committee*): **~er Begleiter** constant companion. **II** *adv* permanently, constantly, always: **et. ~ tun** keep doing s.th.

'Stand|licht *n mot.* (-[e]s; *no pl*) parking light. **~ort** *m* position (*a.* ✪ *or fig.*), location, site (*of firm etc*), ✗ garrison, *Am.* post, *biol.* habitat: **den ~** (*gen*) **bestimmen** locate. **~pauke** *f* F lecture: **j-m e-e ~ halten** lecture s.o. (*über acc* on). **~punkt** *m* **1.** post, point. **2.** *fig.* (*von s-m etc*) **~ aus** from his *etc*) point of view; **den ~ vertreten, auf dem ~ stehen** take the view (**daß** that). **~quar,tier** *n* base. **~recht** *n* (-[e]s; *no pl*) martial law. **2rechtlich** *adj and adv* by order of a court martial. **~spur** *f mot.* hard shoulder. **~uhr** *f* grandfather clock.

Stange [ˈʃtaŋə] *f* (-; -n) **1.** pole (*a. sports*), (flag) staff, (metal) rod, bar, *for birds*: perch, (*sugar, celery, etc*) stick: **e-e ~** (**Zigaretten**) a carton (of cigarettes);

Kleidung von der ~ clothes off the peg; F **e-e ~ Geld** a packet; **bei der ~ bleiben** stick to it, *a.* stick it out; **j-n bei der ~ halten** keep s.o. at it; **j-m die ~ halten** stick up for s.o. **2.** branch (*on antlers*).

'Stangen|bohne *f* runner (*or string*) bean. **~spargel** *m* asparagus spears.

stank [ʃtaŋk] *pret of* **stinken**.

stänkern [ˈʃtɛŋkərn] *v/i* (h) F *contp.* stir up trouble: **~ gegen** rail against.

Stanniol [ʃtaˈnioːl] *n* (-s; -e) tinfoil.

Stanze [ˈʃtantsə] *f* (-; -n) ⊚ stamp(ing machine). **'stanzen** *v/t* (h) a) punch, b) stamp.

Stapel [ˈʃtaːpəl] *m* (-s; -) **1.** pile, stack. **2.** ⚓ stocks: **auf ~ legen** lay down; **vom ~ lassen** launch (*a. fig. project etc*), *fig.* deliver (*speech*), crack (*joke*); **vom ~ laufen** be launched. **'Stapellauf** *m* launching. **'stapeln** *v/t* (h) **1.** stack, (*a. sich ~*) pile up. **2.** store, stockpile.

stapfen [ˈʃtapfən] *v/i* (sn) trudge.

Star¹ [ʃtaːr] *m* (-[e]s; -e) *orn.* starling.

Star² *m* (-[e]s; -e) ⚕ **grauer ~** cataract; **grüner ~** glaucoma.

Star³ [staːr; ʃtaːr] *m* (-s; -s) *film etc*: star.

'Staral,lüren *pl contp.* airs and graces.

starb [ʃtarp] *pret of* **sterben**.

'Stargast *m* star guest.

stark [ʃtark] **I** *adj* **1.** strong (*a. ling. or fig.*), *w.s.* great, intense (*heat, cold, etc*), heavy (*rain, traffic, ✝ demand, etc*): **ein ~es Polizeiaufgebot** a strong force of police; **ein 20 Mann ~er Trupp** a group of 20; **er ist ein ~er Raucher (Esser)** he is a heavy smoker (big eater); *fig.* **~e Seite** strong point; **sich ~ machen für** stand up for; F **das ist ein ~es Stück!** that's a bit thick! **2.** thick: **2 cm ~e Pappe** pasteboard two centimetres thick; **das Buch ist 150 Seiten ~** the book has 150 pages. **3.** *in performance, a. opt.,* ⊚ strong, powerful, high-powered (*engine*): **ein ~es Medikament** a powerful (*or potent*) drug. **4.** stout, corpulent. **5.** bad, severe (*cold, pain, etc*). **6.** F (*echt*) ~ super, great. **II** *adv* strongly, highly, very much: **~ beschädigt** badly damaged; **~ übertrieben** grossly exaggerated; **~ erkälten**.

Stärke¹ [ˈʃtɛrkə] *f* (-; -n) **1.** *no pl* strength, power. **2.** *opt.,* ⊚ power, *a.* 🐾 strength. **3.** thickness, diameter. **4.** intensity, force, *a.* heaviness (*of rain, traffic, etc*), *a.* severity (*of pain etc*). **5.** *fig.* **j-s ~** s.o.'s strong point (*or* forte).

'**Stärke²** *f* (-; -n) 🐾 starch.

stärken¹ ['ʃtɛrkən] *v/t* (h) strengthen (*a. fig.*), invigorate: **sich ~** fortify o.s.

'**stärken²** *v/t* (h) starch.

'**stärkend** *adj* (*a.* **~es Mittel**) tonic.

'**Starkstrom** *m* ⚡ high-voltage (*or* heavy) current. **~leitung** *f* power line. **~technik** *f* heavy-current engineering.

'**Stärkung** *f* (-; -en) **1.** strengthening. **2.** refreshment, F pick-me-up.

'**Stärkungsmittel** *n* tonic.

starr [ʃtar] *adj* rigid (*a. fig.*), stiff, *a.* motionless: **~er Blick** (fixed) stare; **ich war ~** (**vor Staunen**) I was dum(b)-founded.

starren¹ ['ʃtarən] *v/i* (h) stare (**auf** *acc* at).

'**starren²** *v/i* (h) **~ vor** (*or* **von**) be full of; **vor Schmutz ~** be thick with dirt.

'**Starrheit** *f* (-; *no pl*) rigidity (*a. fig.*), stiffness.

'**starrköpfig** [-kœpfɪç] *adj* pigheaded.

'**Starrsinn** *m* (-[e]s; *no pl*) obstinacy, pigheadedness.

Start [ʃtart] *m* (-[e]s; -s) start (*a. fig.*), takeoff, *of rocket etc*: liftoff: ✈ **zum ~ freigeben** clear for takeoff; *sports:* **an den ~ gehen** a) *runner etc*: take up one's starting position, b) take part. **~auto,matik** *f mot.* automatic choke (control). **~bahn** *f* ✈ runway.

'**startbereit** *adj* ready to start, ✈ ready for takeoff.

starten ['ʃtartən] **I** *v/i* (sn) **1.** *sports:* start, *a.* take part (**in** *dat*, **bei**). **2.** ✈ take off, *rocket etc:* lift off. **II** *v/t* (h) start, F *fig.* a. launch. '**Starter** *m* (-s; -), '**Starterin** *f* (-; -nen) *sports:* starter.

'**Starterlaubnis** *f* **1.** *sports:* permission to take part. **2.** ✈ clearance for takeoff.

'**Starthilfe** *f* **1.** *j-m ~ geben* a) *mot.* give s.o. a jump-start, b) *fig.* give s.o. a start (in life). **2.** **Abflug mit ~** assisted takeoff. **~kabel** *n mot.* jump leads.

'**Startkapi,tal** *n* start-up capital.

'**Startschuß** *m sports:* starting shot.

'**Startverbot** *n sports:* suspension, ✈ grounding: **~ erhalten** a) be suspended, b) be grounded.

Stasi ['ʃta:zi] *f* (-; *no pl*) F *DDR pol. hist.* State Security (Service).

Statik ['ʃta:tɪk] *f* (-; *no pl*) △, ⚡, *phys.* statics. **Statiker** ['ʃta:tɪkər] *m* (-s; -) △ stress analyst.

Station [ʃta'tsi̯oːn] *f* (-; -en) **1.** *radio, TV, etc:* station. **2.** 🚉 station, stop: **~ machen** break one's journey. **3.** (*hospital*) ward. **4.** *fig.* stage. **stationär** [ʃtatsi̯o-'nɛːr] *adj a.* ⚕ stationary: 🩺 **~e Behandlung** in-patient treatment; **~er** (*or* **~ behandelter**) *Patient* in-patient.

stationieren [ʃtatsi̯o'niːrən] *v/t* (h) station, deploy (*rockets etc*). **Statio'nierung** *f* (-; -en) stationing, deployment.

Stati'ons|arzt *m* ward doctor. **~schwester** *f* ward sister. **~vorsteher** *m* 🚉 stationmaster.

statisch ['ʃta:tɪʃ] *adj* static.

Statist [ʃta'tɪst] *m* (-en; -en), **Sta'tistin** *f* (-; -nen) *thea., film:* extra.

Statistik [ʃta'tɪstɪk] *f* (-; -en) statistics. **Sta'tistiker** [-tɪkər] *m* (-s; -) statistician. **sta'tistisch** [-tɪʃ] *adj* statistical.

Stativ [ʃta'tiːf] *n* (-s; -e) tripod.

statt [ʃtat] → **anstatt.**

Statt *f an j-s* ~ in s.o.'s place; **an Kindes ~ annehmen** adopt.

Stätte ['ʃtɛtə] *f* (-; -n) place, *a.* scene.

'**statt|finden** *v/i* (*irr, sep, -ge-*, h, → **finden**) take place, be held. **~geben** *v/i* (*irr, sep, -ge-*, h, → **geben**) *adm.* grant.

'**statthaft** *adj* admissible: **nicht ~** not allowed.

'**Statthalter** *m* (-s; -) governor.

'**stattlich** *adj* **1.** stately, impressive. **2.** large (*sum etc*). **3.** portly: **e-e ~e Erscheinung** a fine figure of a man *etc*.

Statue ['ʃta:tu̯ə] *f* (-; -n) statue.

statuieren [ʃtatu'iːrən] *v/t* (h) → **Exempel.**

Statur [ʃta'tuːr] *f* (-; -en) stature (*a. fig.*).

Status ['ʃta:tʊs] *m* (-; -) state, *a.* (legal) status. **~sym,bol** *n* status symbol.

Stau [ʃtaʊ] *m* (-[e]s; -s, -e) **1.** accumulation, pile-up. **2.** ✈ congestion. **3.** a) traffic jam (*or* congestion), b) tailback.

Staub [ʃtaʊp] *m* (-[e]s; *no pl*) dust: **~ wischen** do the dusting; F **sich aus dem ~(e) machen** clear off; → **aufwirbeln.** '**Staubbeutel** *m* **1.** 🌼 anther. **2.** ⚙ dust bag. **Stäubchen** ['ʃtɔʏpçən] *n* (-s; -) speck of dust, dust particle.

'**Staubecken** *n* ⚙ reservoir.

stauben ['ʃtaʊbən] *v/i* (h) make a lot of dust: **es staubt** it's dusty. '**Staubflocke**

f piece of fluff. **'Staubgefäß** *n* ♀ stamen. **'staubig** *adj* dusty. **'staubsaugen** *v/t, v/i* (insep, -ge-, h) vacuum, Br. F hoover (*TM*). **'Staubsauger** *m* (-s; -) vacuum cleaner, Br. F hoover (*TM*). **'Staubwolke** *f* cloud of dust.

stauchen ['ʃtaʊxən] *v/t* (h) ⊕ jolt, upset.

'Staudamm *m* dam.

Staude ['ʃtaʊdə] *f* (-; -n) herbaceous plant.

stauen ['ʃtaʊən] (h) **I** *v/t* dam up (water), stop (the flow of blood). **II sich ~** water: build up (a. fig. anger, traffic, etc), rise, ice, fig. mail etc: accumulate, pile up, ♣ be(come) congested.

'Stauer *m* (-s; -) ♣ stevedore.

staunen ['ʃtaʊnən] *v/i* (h) (über acc at) be astonished, be amazed, marvel. **'Staunen** *n* (-s) astonishment, amazement: **in ~ versetzen** amaze; → **starr. 'staunenswert** *adj* astonishing, amazing.

Staupe ['ʃtaʊpə] *f* (-; -n) vet. distemper.

'Stausee *m* reservoir.

'Stauung *f* (-; -en) **1.** damming up. **2.** → **Stau.**

Steak [steːk] *n* (-s; -s) gastr. steak.

Stearin [ʃteaˈriːn] *n* (-s; -e) stearin.

stechen ['ʃtɛçən] (stach, gestochen, h) **I** *v/t* **1.** prick, wasp etc: sting, gnat: bite: **sich ~** prick o.s.; **sich in den Finger ~** prick one's finger; → **Hafer, gestochen. 2.** cut (asparagus, peat, etc), stick, kill (pig etc). **3.** punch (time clock). **4.** engrave (picture). **II** *v/i* **5.** prick, wasp etc: sting, gnat: bite. **6.** **nach j-m ~** stab at s.o.; **mit et. ~ in** (acc) stick s.th. in(to). **7.** sun: burn. **8.** pain: stab, shoot. **9.** sports: jump (or shoot etc) off. **10.** cards: a) be trump, b) trump. **11.** F fig. **j-m in die Augen ~** catch s.o.'s eye. **'Stechen** *n* (-s) **1.** stabbing (or shooting) pain. **2.** show jumping: jump-off. **'stechend** *adj fig.* piercing (look), pungent (smell), stabbing (pain), burning (sun).

'Stech|karte *f* time-punch card. **~mücke** *f* mosquito. **~palme** *f* holly. **~uhr** *f* time clock. **~zirkel** *m* dividers.

'Steckbrief *m* **1.** "wanted" circular. **2.** fig. description, fact file (gen of). **'steckbrieflich** *adv* **~ gesucht werden** be wanted for arrest.

'Steckdose *f* ∮ (wall) socket.

stecken ['ʃtɛkən] (h) **I** *v/t* a) put, secretly: slip, b) stick (pin etc), c) pin (fabric, paper), d) ⊕ insert (in acc into): fig. **Geld ~ in** (acc) put money into, invest in; **j-n ins Gefängnis (Bett) ~** put s.o. in prison (to bed); F **wer hat ihm das gesteckt?** who told him?; → **Brand** 1, **Nase. II** *v/i* be stuck, bullet, splinter, etc: be lodged, person, thing: be: **der Schlüssel steckt** the key is in the lock; F **wo steckst du denn (so lange)?** where have you been (all this time)?; **da steckt 'er dahinter** he's at the bottom of it; **sie steckt mitten in den Prüfungen** she's in the middle of her exams; → **Decke** 1.

'Stecken *m* (-s; -) stick: → **Dreck** 1.

'stecken|bleiben *v/i* (irr, sep, -ge-, sn, → **bleiben**) a. fig. get stuck. **~lassen** *v/t* (irr, sep, -ge-, h, → **lassen**) **den Schlüssel ~** leave the key in the lock.

'Steckenpferd *n* hobbyhorse, fig. mst hobby.

'Stecker *m* (-s; -) ∮ plug.

'Steckkon,takt *m* ∮ plug (connection).

'Steckling *m* (-s; -e) ♀ cutting.

'Stecknadel *f* pin. **~kopf** *m* pinhead.

'Steckschlüssel *m* ⊕ box spanner.

'Steckschuh *m* phot. accessory shoe.

Steg [ʃteːk] *n* (-[e]s; -e) **1.** footpath. **2.** a) footbridge, b) landing stage, c) gangplank. **3.** bridge (of spectacles, violin).

'Stegreif *m* **aus dem ~** off the cuff; **aus dem ~ spielen** etc improvise; **aus dem ~ sprechen** extemporize, F ad-lib.

stehen ['ʃteːən] (stand, gestanden, h) **I** *v/i* **1.** stand, be: F **wie steht's?** a) how are things?, b) **mit dir?** how about you?, c) a. **wie steht das Spiel?** what's the score?; **wie steht's mit e-m Bier?** how about a beer?; **das Programm steht** the program(me Br.) is complete (or in the bag); **es steht zu befürchten, daß ...** it is to be feared that ...; F **mir steht's bis hier(her)!** I am fed up to here with it); **gut (schlecht) mit j-m ~** (not to) get on well with s.o.; **er steht sich gut (dabei)** he's not doing badly (out of it); **unter Alkohol (Drogen) ~** be under the influence of alcohol (drugs); **~ vor** be faced with (decision, problem, etc); **er steht vor s-r Prüfung** his exam is coming up; **zu j-m ~** stand by s.o.; **zu s-m Versprechen** etc **~** keep one's promise; *wie stehst du dazu?* what do you think (of it)?; *pol.* **er steht links** he belongs to the left; **die Aktie (das Thermometer** *etc*) **steht auf ...** the share (the thermometer *etc*) is at ...; **auf Diebstahl steht e-e Freiheitsstrafe** theft is punishable by imprisonment; → *Debatte, teuer* II. **2.** stand still, *a. clock etc*: have stopped. **3.** be written, say: *in dem Brief steht* the letter says; *wo steht das?* where does it say so? **4.** *fig. j-m* ~ *dress etc*: suit s.o., look well on s.o. **II** *v/t* → *Mann, Modell, Posten* 2, *Wache etc*. '**Stehen** *n* (-s) (*a. im* ~) standing; **zum** ~ **bringen** a) (bring to a) stop, b) staunch (*bleeding*); **zum** ~ **kommen** come to a halt.

'**stehenbleiben** *v/i* (*irr, sep, -ge-, sn,* → *bleiben*) **1.** stop (*a. clock etc*), engine: stall, *heart*: stop (beating): *wo waren wir stehengeblieben?* where did we leave off? **2.** *umbrella etc*: be left (behind): *fig. der Satz kann so nicht* ~ the sentence cannot be left like this.

'**stehend** *adj* standing (*a. army, waters*), stationary: ~*e Redensart* stock phrase.

'**stehenlassen** *v/t* (*irr, sep, -ge-, h,* → *lassen*) **1.** leave (behind): *alles stehen- und liegenlassen* drop everything. **2.** leave *food etc* untouched. **3.** overlook (*mistake*): *fig. das kann man so nicht* ~ that's not quite correct. **4.** *j-n* ~ leave s.o. standing there. **5.** → *Bart* 1.

'**Steher** *m* (-s; -) *cycling:* stayer.

'**Steh|imbiß** *m* stand-up snack bar. ~**kragen** *m* stand-up collar. ~**lampe** *f* standard (*Am.* floor) lamp.

stehlen ['ʃteːlən] *v/t, v/i* (stahl, gestohlen, h) steal: *j-m et.* ~ steal s.th. from s.o.; *j-m die Zeit* ~ waste s.o.'s time; *F* **er kann mir gestohlen bleiben!** to hell with him!

'**Stehplatz** *m* standing room.

'**Stehvermögen** *n* (-s; *no pl*) stamina, staying power.

steif [ʃtaɪf] *adj* stiff (*a. fig.*), *a.* ⊙ rigid: ~ **vor Kälte** numb with cold; ~*e Brise* (~*er Grog*) stiff breeze (grog); *gastr.* ~ **schlagen** beat (until stiff); *F* ~ *und fest behaupten* insist, swear.

steifen ['ʃtaɪfən] *v/t* (h) *fig. j-m den Nacken (or Rücken)* ~ stiffen s.o.'s back.

'**Steifheit** *f* (-; *no pl*) *a. fig.* stiffness.

'**Steigbügel** *m* stirrup. '**Steigeisen** *n* climbing iron, *mount. a.* crampon.

steigen ['ʃtaɪgən] (stieg, gestiegen, sn) **I** *v/i* **1.** go up, climb (up), rise (*into the air*), ✈ climb (*auf acc* to): *auf e-n Baum (Berg)* ~ climb (up) a tree (mountain); *auf ein Pferd* ~ mount a horse; *vom Pferd* ~ dismount; *aus dem Bus etc* ~ get out (*or* off) the bus *etc*; *in den Zug etc* ~ get on (*or* board) a train *etc*; ~ *lassen* fly (*kite*), send up (*balloon*); → *Kopf* 1. **2.** increase, grow, *temperature etc*: rise, *prices: a.* go up: → *Achtung* 1, *Wert* 1. **3.** *F* be on, take place: *e-e Party* ~ *lassen* throw a party. **II** *v/t* **4.** go up: *Treppen* ~ climb stairs. '**Steigen** *n* (-s) **1.** climbing (*etc,* → I). **2.** rise, increase: *das* ~ *und Fallen* the rise and fall; *im* ~ *begriffen sein* be rising. '**steigend** *adj fig.* rising, increasing: ~*e Tendenz* upward tendency.

'**Steiger** *m* (-s; -) ⚒ pit foreman.

steigern ['ʃtaɪgərn] (h) **I** *v/t* **1.** increase, *a.* heighten (*effect, suspense, etc*), step up (*pace, production, etc*), raise (*bet, offer, etc*): *s-e Leistung* ~ improve one's performance; *den Wert* ~ add to the value (*gen* of). **2.** *ling.* compare. **II** *sich* ~ **3.** a) increase, *a.* grow, *interest, suspense, etc*: rise, b) improve (one's performance). **III** *v/i* a) *at auction:* bid, b) rise the amount (*auf acc* to). '**Steigerung** *f* (-; -en) **1.** a) increase, rise, b) improvement. **2.** *ling.* comparison.

'**Steigfähigkeit** *f* ✈ climbing power, *mot.* hill-climbing ability.

'**Steigung** *f* (-; -en) rise, ascent, gradient.

steil [ʃtaɪl] *adj a. fig.* steep: ~*e Karriere* meteoric career; ~ *ansteigen* rise steeply, *prices: a.* soar. '**Steilkurve** *f* steep turn. '**Steilküste** *f* steep coast. '**Steilpaß** *m soccer:* through pass.

Stein [ʃtaɪn] *m* (-[e]s; -e) *a.* stone (*a.* ♞, ♣), ⊙ *a.* brick, b) (precious) stone, gem, jewel, *of watch:* ruby, s) *board games:* piece: *den* ~ *ins Rollen bringen* set the ball rolling; *bei j-m e-n* ~ *im Brett haben* be in s.o.'s good books; *mir fällt ein* ~ *vom Herzen* that takes a load off my mind; → *Tropfen* 1. ~**adler** *m zo.* golden eagle. ʒ**alt** *adj* ancient. ~**bock** *m* **1.** *zo.* ibex. **2.** *no pl astr.* ([*ein*] ~ *sein* be [a]) Capricorn. ~**bruch** *m* quarry. ~**butt** *m zo.* turbot. ~**druck** *m*

(-[e]s; -e) **1.** *no pl* lithography. **2.** lithograph.

'**steinern** *adj* (of) stone, *fig.* stony.

'**Steinfrucht** *f* stone fruit.

'**Steingarten** *m* rock garden.

'**Steingut** *n* (-[e]s; -e) earthenware.

'**steinig** *adj* stony.

'**Steinkohle** *f* hard coal.

'**Steinmetz** [-mɛts] *m* (-en; -en) stonemason.

'**Steinobst** *n* stone fruit.

'**Steinpilz** *m* edible boletus.

'**steinreich** *adj* F filthy rich.

'**Steinschlag** *m* falling rocks.

'**Steinzeit** *f* (-; *no pl*) Stone Age.

Steiß [ʃtaɪs] *m* (-es; -e) buttocks, rump.

'**Steißbein** *n anat.* coccyx.

'**Stelldichein** *n* (-[s]; -[s]) rendezvous.

Stelle ['ʃtɛlə] *f* (-; -n) **1.** place, spot, point, position: *an dieser ~* here; *an anderer ~* elsewhere; *an erster ~* in the first place, first(ly); *an erster ~ stehen* come first; *an ~ von* (*or gen*) in place of, instead of; (*ich*) *an d-r ~* if I were you; *an die ~ treten von* (*or gen*) take the place of, *person*: *a.* take over from, replace; *auf der ~* on the spot; *fig. auf der ~ treten* mark time; *nicht von der ~ kommen* not to make any progress; *er rührte sich nicht von der ~* he didn't budge; *zur ~ sein* be at hand. **2.** passage (*a.* ♪). **3.** ♣ a) digit, b) (decimal) place. **4.** situation, job, post: *freie* (*or offene*) *~* vacancy. **5.** → *Dienststelle.*

stellen ['ʃtɛlən] (h) **I** *v/t* **1.** put, place, set, arrange: → *Antrag* 1, *Bedingung, Bein, Falle, Frage* 1, *gestellt.* **2.** set *clock etc* (*auf acc* at), adjust; *leiser* (*or niedriger*) *~* turn down; *lauter* (*or höher*) *~* turn up. **3.** provide, supply. **4.** hunt down (*game, criminal*). **II** *sich ~* **5.** place o.s.: *stell dich dorthin!* (go and) stand over there; *auf sich selbst gestellt sein* be on one's own; *gut* (*schlecht*) *gestellt sein* be well (badly) off; *sich gegen ... ~* oppose; *sich hinter* (*vor*) *j-n ~* back s.o. up (shield s.o.); *wie stellt er sich dazu?* what does he say (to this)? **6.** *sich* (*der Polizei*) *~* turn o.s. in; *sich* (*zum Wehrdienst*) *~* report for military service. **7.** (*dat*) take on *opponent*, face up to *criticism etc*, take up *challenge*: *sich der Presse ~* be prepared to meet (*or* face) the Press. **8.**

sich krank etc ~ pretend to be ill *etc.*

'**Stellen|angebot** *n* job offer: *~e newspaper*: vacancies. *~gesuch* *n* application (for a job): *~e newspaper*: situations wanted. *~markt* *m* job market. *~suche* *f* (*auf ~ sein* be) job-hunting. *~wechsel* *m* job change.

'**stellenweise** *adv* in places.

'**Stellenwert** *m* rating, (relative) importance: *e-n hohen ~ haben* rate high.

...stellig [-ʃtɛlɪç] *in cpds.* ...-digit.

'**Stellplatz** *m mot.* carport.

'**Stellschraube** *f* ⚙ adjusting screw.

'**Stellung** *f* (-; -en) **1.** *a.* ✕ position: *fig. die ~ halten* hold the fort; *~ nehmen* (*zu*) take a stand (on), give one's view (on); *~ nehmen für* stand up for; *~ nehmen gegen* oppose. **2.** situation, job, post, position: *e-e leitende ~* an executive position. **3.** a) position, rank, b) status, standing.

'**Stellungnahme** *f* (-; -n) (*zu* on) opinion, comment, statement.

'**Stellungskrieg** *m* static warfare.

'**stellungslos** *adj* unemployed, jobless.

'**Stellungs|spiel** *n sports*: positional play. *~suche* *f* search for a post (*or* job): *auf ~ sein* be looking for a job, be job-hunting. *~suchende* *m, f* (-n; -n) person looking for a job, job-hunter. *~wechsel* *m* change of post (*or* job): *häufiger ~* job-hopping.

'**stellvertretend** *adj* acting, deputy: *~er Vorsitzender* vice-chairman; *~ für* a) acting for, b) on behalf of.

'**Stellvertreter**(**in** *f*) *m* representative, substitute, *of doctor etc*: locum (tenens), *adm.* deputy, ♱, ⚖ proxy.

'**Stellvertretung** *f* representation, ♱, ⚖ proxy: *j-s ~ übernehmen* act as representative of s.o.

'**Stellwerk** *n* 🚂 signal box.

Stelze ['ʃtɛltsə] *f* (-; -n) stilt.

stelzen ['ʃtɛltsən] *v/i* (sn) stalk (along).

'**Stemmbogen** *m skiing*: stem turn.

'**Stemmeisen** *n* ⚙ mortise chisel.

stemmen ['ʃtɛmən] *v/t* (h) **1.** press: *sich ~ gegen* press against, *fig.* resist. **2.** heave up, *sports*: lift.

Stempel ['ʃtɛmpəl] *m* (-s; -) **1.** stamp (*a. fig.*), *a.* seal. **2.** postmark. **3.** ⚙ die. **4.** hallmark. **5.** ♀ pistil. *~farbe* *f* stamp(ing) ink. *~kissen* *n* ink pad.

'**stempeln** (h) **I** *v/t* **1.** a) stamp, b) cancel:

fig. **j-n ~ zu** stamp (*or* label, *b.s.* brand) s.o. as. **II** *v/i* **2.** *employee:* clock in (out). **3.** F **~ gehen** be on the dole.

'**Stempeluhr** *f* time clock.

Stengel ['ʃtɛŋəl] *m* (-s; -) stalk, stem.

Stenogramm [ʃteno'gram] *n* (-s; -e) shorthand notes. **Stenograph** ['-gra:f] *m* (-en; -en) stenographer. **Stenographie** [-gra'fi:] *f* (-; -n) stenography, shorthand. **stenographieren** [-gra-'fi:rən] (h) **I** *v/i* write shorthand. **II** *v/t* take down in shorthand. **stenographisch** ['-'gra:fiʃ] *adj* shorthand.

Stenotypistin [ʃtenoty'pistɪn] *f* (-; -nen) shorthand typist.

'**Steppdecke** *f* (continental) quilt.

Steppe ['ʃtɛpə] *f* (-; -n) steppe.

steppen[1] ['ʃtɛpən] *v/t* (h) backstitch.

steppen[2] *v/i* (h) tap-dance.

'**Stepptanz** *m* tap dance.

'**Sterbe|bett** *n* (**auf dem ~** on one's) deathbed. **~fall** *m* (case of) death. **~hilfe** *f* euthanasia. **~klinik** *f* hospice.

sterben ['ʃtɛrbən] *v/i* (starb, gestorben, sn) die (**an** *dat*, *fig.* **vor** *dat* of). '**Sterben** *n* (-s) dying, death: **im ~ liegen** be dying; **zum ~ langweilig** deadly dull.

'**sterbenskrank** *adj* mortally ill.

'**Sterbens|wort** *n*, **~wörtchen** *n* **kein ~ sagen** not to breathe a word.

'**Sterbesakra|mente** *pl* last rites.

'**Sterbeurkunde** *f* death certificate.

sterblich ['ʃtɛrplɪç] *adj* mortal: *iro.* **gewöhnliche 2e** ordinary mortals. '**Sterblichkeit** *f* (-; *no pl*) mortality.

Stereo..., **stereo...** ['ʃte:reo] stereo.

'**Stereo|anlage** *f* stereo system. **~aufnahme** *f* stereo recording. **~bild** *n* stereoscopic picture. **~gerät** *n* stereo set.

stereophon [-'fo:n] *adj* stereophonic.

stereoskopisch [-'sko:pɪʃ] *adj* stereoscopic.

'**Stereoton** *m* stereo sound.

stereotyp [-'ty:p] *adj fig.* stereotyped.

steril [ʃte'ri:l] *adj* sterile. **sterilisieren** [ʃterili'zi:rən] *v/t* (h) sterilize. **Sterilisation** [ʃteriliza'tsio:n] *f* (-; -en) sterilization. **Sterilität** [ʃterili'tɛ:t] *f* (-; *no pl*) sterility.

Stern [ʃtɛrn] *m* (-[e]s; -e) *a. fig.* star: **unter e-m glücklichen (unglücklichen) ~ stehen** have fortune on one's side (be ill-fated); F **~e sehen** see stars.

'**Sternbild** *n* **1.** constellation. **2.** sign of the zodiac.

'**Sternchen** *n* **1.** little star, starlet (*a. fig. actress*). **2.** *print.* asterisk.

'**Sternenbanner: das ~** the Star-Spangled Banner, the Stars and Stripes.

'**Sternenhimmel** *m* starry sky.

'**Sternfahrt** *f mot.* car rally.

'**sternförmig** *adj* star-shaped.

'**sternhagel|voll** *adj* F rolling drunk.

'**sternhell**, '**sternklar** *adj* starlit.

'**Sternmarsch** *m* demonstration march from different starting points.

'**Sternschnuppe** *f* (-; -n) shooting star.

'**Sternstunde** *f fig.* great moment.

'**Sternwarte** *f* (-; -n) observatory.

stet [ʃte:t] → **stetig, Tropfen** 1.

Stethoskop [ʃteto'sko:p] *n* (-s; -e) 🩺 stethoscope.

'**stetig** *adj* continual, constant, steady. '**Stetigkeit** *f* (-; *no pl*) constancy, steadiness. **stets** *adv* always, constantly.

Steuer[1] ['ʃtɔʏər] *n* (-s; -) ⚓ helm, rudder, *mot.* (steering) wheel, ✈ controls: **am ~** at the helm (*a. fig.*), at the wheel.

Steuer[2] *f* (-; -n) (**auf** *acc* on) a) tax, b) duty, c) rate, *Am.* local tax: **vor (nach) Abzug der ~n** before (after) tax.

'**Steuer|abzug** *m* tax deduction. **~aufkommen** *n* tax yield. **~ausgleich** *m* tax equalization. **~befreiung** *f* tax exemption. **2begünstigt** *adj* a) tax-privileged, b) tax-linked (*saving*). **~belastung** *f* tax burden. **~berater(in** *f*) *m* tax adviser. **~bescheid** *m* tax assessment.

'**Steuerbord** *n*, '**steuerbord(s)** *adv* ⚓ starboard.

'**Steuer|de|likt** *n* tax offen/ce (*Am.* -se). **~einnahmen** *pl* → **Steueraufkommen.** **~erklärung** *f* tax return. **~erleichterung** *f* tax relief. **~ermäßigung** *f* tax allowance. **2frei** *adj* tax-free. **~freibetrag** *m* tax-free allowance. **~hinterzieher** *m* tax dodger. **~hinterziehung** *f* tax fraud. **~karte** *f* (wage) tax card. **~klasse** *f* tax bracket.

'**Steuerknüppel** *m* ✈ control stick, F joystick.

'**steuerlich** *adj* tax ...: **aus ~en Gründen** for tax purposes; **~ günstig** with low tax liability; **~ veranlagen** assess for taxation.

'**Steuermann** *m* **1.** ⚓ helmsman (*a. fig.*). **2.** *rowing:* coxswain.

'**Steuermarke** f revenue stamp.
steuern ['ʃtɔʏərn] **I** v/t (h) steer, mot. a. drive, ✈, ⚓ a. navigate, pilot, ⊚ control. **II** v/i (h or sn) steer, mot. a. drive, ⚓ a. head (*nach Süden* southward).
'**Steuero,ase** f tax haven.
'**steuerpflichtig** adj taxable.
'**Steuer|poli,tik** f fiscal policy. **~pro-gressi,on** f progressive taxation.
'**Steuerpult** n ⊚ control desk.
'**Steuerrad** n ⚓, mot. (steering) wheel.
'**steuerrechtlich** adj and adv under the tax laws.
Steuer|rückerstattung f tax refund. **~satz** m tax rate. **~schuld** f tax(es) due. **~senkung** f tax reduction.
'**Steuerung** f (-; -en) **1.** steering, ✈ piloting, ⚙, ⊚ control (a. fig.). **2.** control system, mot. steering, ✈ controls.
'**Steuerveranlagung** f assessment.
'**Steuervorteil** m tax benefit.
'**Steuerzahler(in** f) m taxpayer.
Steward ['stju:ərt] m (-s; -s) steward.
Stewardeß ['stju:ərdɛs] f (-; -dessen) stewardess, air hostess.
Stich [ʃtɪç] m (-es; -e) **1.** with knife: stab, thrust, (needle) prick, (wasp etc) sting, (gnat) bite: fig. **es gibt ihr e-n ~** it cut her to the quick. **2.** sewing: stitch. **3.** (copper etc) engraving. **4.** stitch, stabbing pain. **5.** fig. cut, dig. **6. im ~ lassen** abandon, desert, j-n a. leave s.o. in the lurch, let s.o. down; **sein Gedächtnis ließ ihn im ~** his memory failed him. **7. e-n ~ haben** a) milk etc: be off, b) F person: be a bit touched. **8. ein ~ ins Blaue** a tinge of blue. **9.** cards: **e-n ~ machen** make a trick.
Stiche'lei f (-; -en) needling: **~en** a. gibe(s). **sticheln** ['ʃtɪçəln] v/i (h) fig. (gegen at) gibe, make snide remarks.
'**Stichflamme** f jet of flame, flash.
'**stichhaltig** adj valid, sound: **das Argument ist nicht ~** the argument doesn't hold water. '**Stichhaltigkeit** f (-; no pl) validity, soundness.
'**Stichling** m (-s; -e) zo. stickleback.
'**Stichprobe** f **e-e ~ machen** carry out a spot check, ⚙ take a random sample, customs: make a random search.
'**Stichtag** m a) effective day, b) deadline.
'**Stichwahl** f second ballot.
'**Stichwort** n (-[e]s) **1.** (pl -e) esp. thea. (**auf ~** on) cue: **~ „Umwelt"** à propos

"Environment". **2.** (pl **~er**) headword. **3. ~e** pl notes: **das Wichtigste in ~en** an outline of the main points; '**stichwort-artig** adj and adv in brief outlines. '**Stichwortverzeichnis** n index.
'**Stichwunde** f stab wound.
sticken ['ʃtɪkən] v/t, v/i (h) embroider. **Sticke'rei** f (-; -en) embroidery.
stickig ['ʃtɪkɪç] adj stuffy, close.
'**Sticko,xyd** n ⚗ nitrogen oxide.
'**Stickstoff** m (-[e]s; no pl) ⚗ nitrogen.
'**stickstoffhaltig** adj nitrogenous.
'**Stiefbruder** ['ʃti:f-] m stepbrother.
Stiefel ['ʃti:fəl] m (-s; -) boot. **Stiefelette** [ʃti:fə'lɛtə] f (-; -n) ankle boot, (ladies') bootee. '**stiefeln** v/i (sn) F trudge.
'**Stiefmutter** f a. fig. stepmother. '**Stief-mütterchen** n (-s; -) ♣ pansy. '**stief-mütterlich** adv **~ behandeln** neglect badly. '**Stiefschwester** f stepsister. '**Stiefsohn** m stepson. '**Stieftochter** f stepdaughter. '**Stiefvater** m stepfather.
stieg [ʃti:k] pret of **steigen**.
Stieglitz ['ʃti:glɪts] m (-es; -e) goldfinch.
Stiel [ʃti:l] m (-[e]s; -e) **1.** handle, stem (of glass, pipe), (broom)stick: **Eis am ~** ice lolly. **2.** ♣ stalk, stem.
'**Stielaugen** pl F **~ machen** goggle.
Stier [ʃti:r] m (-[e]s; -e) **1.** zo. bull: fig. **den ~ bei den Hörnern fassen** take the bull by the horns. **2.** no pl astr. ([ein] **~ sein** be [a]) Taurus.
'**stieren** v/i (h) stare (auf acc at).
'**Stierkampf** m bullfight. '**Stierkämpfer** m bullfighter.
'**stiernackig** [-nakɪç] adj bullnecked.
stieß [ʃti:s] pret of **stoßen**.
Stift [ʃtɪft] m (-[e]s; -e) **1.** a) pin, b) peg, c) stud. **2.** a) pencil, b) crayon. **3.** cosmetics: stick. **4.** F apprentice.
Stift n (-[e]s; -e) religious foundation.
stiften ['ʃtɪftən] v/t (h) **1.** found. **2.** give, donate. **3.** cause: → **Unfrieden** etc.
'**Stifter** m (-s; -) **1.** founder. **2.** donor.
'**Stiftung** f (-; -en) **1.** foundation. **2.** donation.
'**Stiftzahn** m pivot tooth.
Stil [ʃti:l] m (-[e]s; -e) style: **im großen ~, großen ~s** on a large scale, large-scale; **das ist schlechter ~** that's bad style. '**Stilblüte** f howler. '**Stilbruch** m break in style. '**Stilebene** f ling. level of style.
'**stilecht** adj in period.
Stilett [ʃti'lɛt] n (-s; -e) stiletto.

'**Stilgefühl** *n* sense of style.

stilisieren [ʃtili'ziːrən] *v/t* (h) stylize.

Stilist [ʃti'lɪst] *m* (-en; -en) stylist (*a. sports etc*). **Sti'listik** [-tɪk] *f* (-; *no pl*) stylistics. **sti'listisch** *adj* stylistic.

'**Stilkunde** *f* → **Stilistik**.

still [ʃtʊl] *adj* a) quiet, silent, still, b) calm, peaceful, c) secret (*a. hope, love, etc*): **~e Jahreszeit** dead season; **~e Reserven** hidden reserves; **~er Teilhaber** sleeping (*Am.* silent) partner; **~e Übereinkunft** tacit understanding; (**sei**) **~!** (be) quiet!; **im ~en** inwardly, secretly; → **Wasser** 1. '**Stille** *f* (-; *no pl*) a) silence, b) quiet, calm, c) hush: **die ~ vor dem Sturm** the calm before the storm; **in aller ~** quietly, a. secretly.

'**Stilleben** *n* (-s; -) *paint.* still life.

'**stillegen** *v/t* (*sep*, -ge-, h) **1.** shut down (*firm*), *by strike*: paralyse. **2.** lay up (*car*), put *machine etc* out of operation. '**Stillegung** *f* (-; -en) **1.** shutdown. **2.** *mot.* laying-up.

stillen ['ʃtɪlən] *v/t* (h) **1.** nurse, breastfeed: **~de Mutter** nursing mother. **2.** stop, sta(u)nch (*bleeding*), quench (*thirst*), satisfy (*desire*), soothe (*pain*).

'**Stillhalteabkommen** *n pol.* standstill agreement. '**stillhalten** *v/i* (*irr, sep*, -ge-, h, → **halten**) **1.** keep still. **2.** *fig.* keep quiet. '**stilliegen** *v/i* (*irr, sep*, -ge-, h, → **liegen**) **1.** lie still. **2.** *fig.* lie dormant, *works*: lie idle.

'**stillos** *adj* in bad style, tasteless.

'**stillschweigen** *v/i* (*irr, sep*, -ge-, h, → **schweigen**) be silent, be quiet, say nothing. '**Stillschweigen** *n* (-s) silence: (**strengstes**) **~ bewahren** maintain (absolute) silence (**über** *acc* on). '**stillschweigend I** *adj* **1.** silent. **2.** *fig.* tacit. **II** *adv* **3.** in silence, without a word. **4.** *fig.* tacitly.

'**Stillstand** *m* (-[e]s; *no pl*) standstill, stoppage, *fig. a.* stagnation, *of negotiations*: deadlock: **zum ~ bringen** stop; **zum ~ kommen** come to a standstill, stop, *negotiations*: reach a deadlock. '**stillstehen** *v/i* (*irr, sep*, -ge-, h, → **stehen**) **1.** stand still, come to a standstill, stop, ⊙ be idle, be out of action: **~d** *a.* stagnant. **2.** ✕ stand to attention: **stillgestanden!** attention!

'**Stillzeit** *f* nursing period.

'**Stilmöbel** *pl* period furniture.

'**stilvoll** *adj* stylish: **~ sein** have style.

'**Stimm|abgabe** *f* voting. **~band** *n anat.* vocal c(h)ord. **2berechtigt** *adj* eligible to vote. **~bildung** *f* ♪ voice training. **~bruch** *m* (-[e]s; *no pl*) change of voice: **er ist im ~** his voice is breaking.

Stimme ['ʃtɪmə] *f* (-; -n) **1.** (**mit lauter** *etc* **~** in a loud *etc*) voice. **2.** ♪ voice, b) part: **gut bei ~ sein** be in good voice. **3.** *fig.* voice, opinion: **die ~n mehren sich, die fordern ...** there is a growing number of people calling for ... **4.** vote: **entscheidende ~** casting vote; **s-e ~ abgeben** (cast one's) vote; **sich der ~ enthalten** abstain (from voting).

stimmen ['ʃtɪmən] (h) **I** *v/t* **1.** ♪ tune (**nach** to). **2.** *j-n* **glücklich** (**traurig** *etc*) **~** make s.o. happy (sad *etc*). **II** *v/i* **3.** be right, be correct, be true: **da stimmt et. nicht** a) there is s.th. wrong here, b) there is s.th. fishy going on. **4. ~ für** (**gegen**) vote for (against).

'**Stimmen|fang** *m* vote catching. **~gleichheit** *f* (**bei ~** in the event of a) tie. **~mehrheit** *f* majority (of votes). '**Stimm|enthaltung** *f* abstention (from voting). **~gabel** *f* ♪ tuning fork.

'**stimmhaft** *adj ling.* voiced.

'**Stimmlage** *f* ♪ register, voice.

'**stimmlos** *adj ling.* voiceless, unvoiced.

'**Stimmrecht** *n* (right to) vote: **allgemeines ~** universal suffrage.

'**Stimmung** *f* (-; -en) **1.** mood (*a.* ♪, *paint.*), spirits, *fig. a.* atmosphere, ✕ *etc*: morale: **in guter** (**gedrückter**) **~ sein** be in high (low) spirits; **festliche ~** festive mood (*or* atmosphere); **nicht in der ~ sein zu** *inf* not to be in the mood to *inf*, not to feel like *ger*; **für ~ sorgen** liven things up. **2.** opinion.

'**Stimmungs|baro,meter** *n* F barometer of opinion. **~mache** *f* (-; *no pl*) F *contp.* propaganda. **~mu,sik** *f* mood music. **~umschwung** *m* change of mood. '**stimmungsvoll** *adj* atmospheric: **~e Musik** mood music.

'**Stimmzettel** *m* ballot paper.

Stimulans ['ʃti:mulans] *n* (-; -lantia [ʃti-mu'lantsĭa]) *♂ or fig.* stimulant. **stimulieren** [ʃtimu'li:rən] *v/t* (h) stimulate.

'**Stinkbombe** *f* stink bomb.

stinken ['ʃtɪŋkən] *v/i* (stank, gestunken, h) stink (**nach** of, *a. fig.*): F **das** (**er**) **stinkt mir!** I'm sick of it (him).

'stink|'faul *adj* F bone-lazy. ~'langwei-lig *adj* F deadly boring. ~'reich *adj* F stinking rich.

'Stink|tier *n* skunk. ~wut *f* F *e-e ~ haben* be hopping mad (*auf acc* with).

Stipendiat [ʃtipɛn'diaːt] *m* (-en; -en) scholarship holder. **Stipendium** [ʃti-'pɛndiʊm] *n* (-s; -dien) scholarship.

'Stippvi,site *f* F flying visit.

Stirn [ʃtɪrn] *f* (-; -en) forehead: *fig. die ~ haben zu inf* have the cheek to *inf; j-m die ~ bieten* face up to s.o. squarely; → *runzeln.* ~band *n* (-[e]s; ⸚er) headband. ~höhle *f anat.* (frontal) sinus. ~höh-lenentzündung *f* frontal sinusitis. ~runzeln *n* (-s) frown(ing). ~seite *f* front (side *or* end). ~wand *f* front (*or* end) wall.

stöbern ['ʃtøːbərn] *v/i* (h) (*nach* for) rummage (around), *dog:* hunt about.

stochern ['ʃtɔxərn] *v/i* (h) *~ in* (*dat*) poke; *in den Zähnen* (*s-m Essen*) *~* pick one's teeth (at one's food).

Stock [ʃtɔk] *m* (-[e]s; ⸚e) **1.** a) stick, b) cane, c) (billiard) cue, d) ♪ baton. **2.** ♪ stock: *über ~ und Stein* up hill and down dale. **3.** (bee)hive. **4.** → *Stock-werk.*

'stockbe'soffen *adj* F paralytic.

'stock'dunkel *adj* F pitch-dark.

Stöckelschuhe ['ʃtœkəl-] *pl* stilettos.

stocken ['ʃtɔkən] *v/i* (h) **1.** a) stop short, *voice:* falter, b) hesitate: *~d sprechen* speak haltingly. **2.** *trade etc:* stagnate, slacken off, *negotiations etc:* reach a deadlock, *traffic:* be at a standstill: *ihr stockte das Herz (der Atem)* her heart missed a beat (she caught her breath).

'**Stocken** *n* (-s) *ins ~ geraten* → *stocken.*

'**Stockfisch** *m* dried cod.

...**stöckig** [-ʃtœkɪç] *in cpds* ...-storied.

'stock|konserva'tiv *adj* F ultra-conser-vative. ~'nüchtern *adj* F stone-cold so-ber. ~'sauer *adj* F furious. ~'steif *adj* F (as) stiff as a poker, starchy. ~'taub *adj* F stone-deaf.

'**Stockung** *f* (-; -en) hold-up, interrup-tion, *in negotiations etc:* a deadlock, *in talks etc:* pause, ♥ stagnation.

'**Stockwerk** *n* stor(e)y, floor: *im ersten ~* on the first (*Am.* second) floor.

Stoff [ʃtɔf] *m* (-[e]s; -e) **1.** 🍖 substance, stuff (*a.* F *alcohol, drug*), agent. **2.** ma-terial, *a.* fabric, cloth. **3.** *fig.* a) subject

matter, b) topic (for discussion): *~ zu e-m Roman* material for a novel. ~mu-ster *n* pattern. ~tier *n* stuffed animal.

'**Stoffwechsel** *m* metabolism. ~krank-heit *f* metabolic disorder.

stöhnen ['ʃtøːnən] *v/i* (h) groan.

'**Stöhnen** *n* (-s) groaning, groan(s).

stoisch ['ʃtoːɪʃ] *adj* stoical.

Stola ['ʃtoːla] *f* (-; Stolen) stole.

Stollen ['ʃtɔlən] *m* (-s; -) **1.** ⚒ tunnel. **2.** stud (*on shoe etc*). **3.** *gastr.* fruit loaf.

stolpern ['ʃtɔlpərn] *v/i* (sn) (*über acc* over) *a. fig.* stumble, trip.

'**Stolperstein** *m fig.* stumbling block.

stolz [ʃtɔlts] *adj* **1.** proud (*auf acc* of). **2.** *fig.* proud, splendid: *iro.* ~*e Preise* (*Summe*) steep prices (tidy sum).

Stolz *m* (-es; *no pl*) pride (*a. fig.*): *voller ~, mit ~* proudly.

stolzieren [ʃtɔl'tsiːrən] *v/i* (sn) strut.

stopfen ['ʃtɔpfən] (h) **I** *v/t* **1.** darn, mend: → *Loch* 1. **2.** cram, stuff: *gestopft voll* crammed (full). **3.** fill (*hole, pipe, saus-age, etc*): *fig. j-m den Mund ~* silence s.o. **4.** stuff (*geese etc*). **II** *v/i* **5.** 💊 cause constipation.

'**Stopfgarn** *n* darning cotton.

stopp [ʃtɔp] *int* stop. **Stopp** *m* (-s; -s) stop, a. (price, wage, *etc*) freeze.

Stoppel ['ʃtɔpəl] *f* (-; -n) stubble. ~bart *m* stubbly beard. ~feld *n* stubble field.

'stopp(e)lig *adj* stubbly.

stoppen ['ʃtɔpən] *v/t* (h) **1.** a. *v/i* stop. **2.** *sports etc:* time, clock.

'**Stopp|schild** *n mot.* stop sign. ~taste *f* stop button. ~uhr *f* stop watch.

Stöpsel ['ʃtœpsəl] *m* (-s; -) stopper, cork, *for bathtub etc,* a. ⚡ plug.

stöpseln ['ʃtœpsəln] *v/t* (h) a. ⚡ plug.

Stör [ʃtøːr] *m* (-[e]s; -e) *zo.* sturgeon.

'**Störakti,on** *f* disruptive action.

'**störanfällig** *adj* ⚙ sensitive, trouble--prone, ⚡ interference-prone.

Storch [ʃtɔrç] *m* (-[e]s; ⸚e) *zo.* stork.

Store [ʃtoːr] *m* (-s; -s) net curtain.

stören ['ʃtøːrən] (h) **I** *v/t* a) disturb, b) bother, c) disrupt (*meeting etc*), d) jam (*radio station*), interfere with (*recep-tion*): *j-s Pläne ~* upset s.o.'s plans; *das (Gesamt)Bild ~* mar the picture; *was mich daran (an ihr) stört* what I don't like about it (her); *lassen Sie sich nicht ~!* don't let me disturb you; *darf ich Sie kurz ~?* may I trouble you for a

minute?; **stört es Sie(, wenn ich rauche)?** do you mind (if I smoke)?; **das stört mich nicht** I don't mind (that); **er stört mich nicht** he doesn't bother me; → **gestört.** II v/i a) interfere, b) be in the way, c) be a nuisance, d) be an eyesore, e) sports: tackle: „**Bitte nicht ~!**" "please do not disturb!" 'störend adj disturbing, troublesome, annoying.
'**Störenfried** [-fri:t] m [-[e]s; -e) troublemaker.
'**Störfaktor** m disruptive element.
'**Störfall** m ⊕ breakdown, accident.
stornieren [ʃtɔrˈniːrən] v/t (h) ✝ reverse (entry), cancel (order). **Stor'nierung** f (-; -en), **Storno** ['ʃtɔrno] n (-s; Storni) reversal, cancellation.
Störrigkeit ['ʃtœrɪçkaɪt] f (-; no pl) stubbornness, obstinacy, restiveness.
störrisch ['ʃtœrɪʃ] adj stubborn, obstinate, restive (horse).
'**Störsender** m jamming station.
'**Störung** f (-; -en) disturbance, ⚖ disorder, ⊕ trouble, defect, breakdown, interruption: **verzeihen Sie die ~!** sorry to disturb you; (**atmosphärische ~**) a) statics, b) interference, c) jamming.
'**störungsfrei** adj undisturbed, ⊕ trouble-free, radio, TV: interference-free.
'**Störungsstelle** f teleph. the engineers.
Stoß [ʃto:s] m (-es; ⁓e) **1.** a) push, b) kick, c) butt, d) dig, e) a. fenc. thrust, swimming, billiards: stroke, shot-put: put, f) jolt, bump, shock, a. phys. impact: fig. **j-m e-n ~ versetzen** shake s.o.; **sich (or s-m Herzen) e-n ~ geben** make an effort; **gib d-m Herzen e-n ~!** be a sport! **2.** ⚖ massive dose (of vitamines etc), rush (of adrenaline). **3.** pile, a. stack (of wood etc), a. batch (of letters).
'**Stoßdämpfer** m mot. shock-absorber.
Stößel ['ʃtøːsəl] m (-s; -) **1.** pestle. **2.** mot. tappet.
stoßen ['ʃtoːsən] (stieß, gestoßen, h) I v/t **1.** push, poke, a. kick, a. butt, a. jostle: **von sich ~** push away, fig. reject; **er stieß ihr das Messer in die Brust** he plunged his knife into her chest. **2.** sports: **die Kugel ~** put the shot. **3.** pound. II **sich ~ 4.** hurt o.s.; **sich ~ an** (dat) a) knock (or bump) against, b) fig. object to, take exception to. III v/i **5.** push (etc, → 1). **6.** (sn) **~ an** (acc) a) a. **~ gegen** knock against, bump into, b)

border on; **er stieß mit dem Kopf an die Wand** he bumped his head against the wall; fig. **~ auf** (acc) a) come across, stumble on, b) meet with (opposition etc); **~ zu** join (up with) (s.o., party, etc); → **Horn** 2, **Kopf** 1.
'**stoßfest** adj shockproof.
'**Stoß|gebet** n quick prayer. **~kraft** f (-; no pl) fig. impetus, force. **~seufzer** m deep sigh. **~stange** f mot. bumper. **~trupp** m ✗ assault party. **~verkehr** m rush-hour traffic.
'**stoßweise** adv intermittently, sporadically, by fits and starts.
'**Stoß|zahn** m zo. tusk. **~zeit** f a) peak hours, b) rush hour.
'**Stotterer** m (-s; -) stutterer, stammerer.
stottern ['ʃtɔtərn] v/i, v/t (h) stutter, stammer: F **auf Stottern kaufen** buy on the never-never.
'**Straf|anstalt** f prison, penal institution. **~antrag** m **1.** private application (by the injured party). **2.** sentence demanded (by the public prosecutor). **~anzeige** f **~ erstatten** bring a charge (gegen against). **~arbeit** f ped. extra work. **~bank** f (-; ⁓e) sports: penalty bank.
'**strafbar** adj a) punishable, b) criminal: **~e Handlung** (criminal) offen/ce (Am. -se); **sich ~ machen** make o.s. liable to prosecution.
'**Strafbefehl** m ⚖ order (of summary punishment).
Strafe ['ʃtraːfə] f (-; -n) punishment (a. fig.), penalty (a. sports), a. fine, a. sentence: **bei ~ von** on pain (or penalty) of; **zur ~** as a punishment; **~ zahlen** pay a fine; → **antreten** 1, **verbüßen.**
strafen ['ʃtraːfən] v/t (h) punish, esp. sports: penalize: **~der Blick** censorious look; → **Lüge, Verachtung.**
'**Straf|entlassene** m, f (-n; -n) ex-convict. **~erlaß** m remission (of sentence).
straff [ʃtraf] adj **1.** tight, taut, a. firm, erect (posture): **~ anziehen** tighten; **~ sitzen** fit tightly. **2.** fig. strict, tight.
'**straffällig** adj **~ werden** commit an offen/ce (Am. -se). '**Straffällige** m, f (-n; -n) offender, delinquent.
straffen ['ʃtrafən] v/t (h) a. fig. tighten (up). '**Straffheit** f (-; no pl) tightness.
'**straffrei** adj: **~ ausgehen** go unpunished. '**Straffreiheit** f (-; no pl) immunity.
'**Straf|gebühr** f fine. **~gefangene** m, f

(-n; -n) prisoner, convict. **~gericht** n **1.** criminal court. **2.** *fig.* punishment. **~gesetz** n penal law. **~gesetzbuch** n penal code.

sträflich ['ʃtrɛːflɪç] **I** *adj* punishable, *a. fig.* criminal. **II** *adv fig.* badly.

Sträfling ['ʃtrɛːflɪŋ] m (-s; -e) prisoner, convict.

'straflos → **straffrei.**

'Straf|mandat n ticket. **~maß** n ⚖ sentence. **⚥mildernd** *adj* mitigating. **⚥mündig** *adj* of responsible age. **~porto** n surcharge. **~predigt** f F lecture. **~pro¸zeß** m trial, criminal case (*or* proceedings). **~pro¸zeßordnung** f code of criminal procedure. **~punkt** m *sports:* penalty point. **~raum** m *soccer:* penalty area. **~recht** n (-[e]s; *no pl*) criminal law. **⚥rechtlich** *adj* criminal, penal: **~verfolgen** prosecute. **~re¸gister** n a) criminal records, b) *s.o.'s* criminal record. **~sache** f criminal case. **~stoß** m *soccer:* penalty kick. **~tat** f (criminal) offen/ce (*Am.* -se), crime. **~täter** m (criminal) offender. **~verfahren** n **1.** → **Strafprozeß. 2.** criminal procedure.

'strafverschärfend *adj* aggravating.

'strafversetzen v/t (*only inf and pp* strafversetzt, h), **'Strafversetzung** f (-; -en) transfer for disciplinary reasons.

'Straf|verteidiger(in f) m trial lawyer; → *a.* **Verteidiger(in) 2. ~vollzug** m **1.** a) execution of the sentence, b) imprisonment. **2.** prison system. **~vollzugsbeamte** m prison officer. **⚥würdig** *adj* ⚖ punishable. **~zettel** m ticket.

Strahl [ʃtraːl] m (-[e]s; -en) **1.** ray (*a. fig. of hope etc*), *a.* beam (*of light*), flash (*of fire etc*). **2.** stream, jet (*of water etc*).

'Strahlantrieb m ✈ jet propulsion.

strahlen ['ʃtraːlən] v/i (h) **1.** *phys.* radiate, emit radiation, be radioactive. **2.** shine, sparkle: *die Sonne strahlte* the sun shone brightly. **3.** *fig.* beam (*vor* with): *sie strahlte* (*vor Glück*) she was radiant (with happiness).

'Strahlen|belastung f ☢ exposure to radiation. **~bündel** n *opt.*, *phys.* pencil of rays. **~dosis** f ☢ radiation dose.

'strahlenförmig *adj* radial.

'Strahlen|krankheit f radiation sickness. **~schutz** m radiation protection. **~thera¸pie** f radiotherapy. **~tod** m death by radiation.

'Strahler m (-s; -) **1.** radiator, *a.* heater. **2.** spotlight.

'Strahltriebwerk n ✈ jet engine.

'Strahlung f (-; -en) radiation.

'Strahlungs|ener¸gie f radiation energy. **~wärme** f radiant heat.

Strähne ['ʃtrɛːnə] f (-; -n) a) strand, b) streak. **'strähnen** v/t (h) streak in (*hair*). **'strähnig** *adj* straggly.

stramm [ʃtram] **I** *adj* **1.** tight. **2.** strapping, sturdy, firm. **3.** strict (*discipline*), brisk (*pace*): F **~er Sozialist** sta(u)nch socialist. **II** *adv* **4.** tight(ly): **~ sitzen** fit tightly; F **~ arbeiten** work hard.

'strammstehen v/i (*irr, sep*, -ge-, h, → **stehen**) ✗ stand to attention.

'Strampelhöschen n rompers.

strampeln ['ʃtrampəln] v/i (h) **1.** a) kick, b) struggle. **2.** F pedal (away).

'Strampelsack m baby's sleeping bag.

Strand [ʃtrant] m (-[e]s; ⸗e) (sea)shore, beach. **~bad** n swimming area.

stranden ['ʃtrandən] v/i (sn) run aground: *gestrandet a. fig.* stranded.

'Strand|gut n (-[e]s; *no pl*) flotsam and jetsam (*a. fig.*). **~ho¸tel** n seaside (*or* beach) hotel. **~kleidung** f beachwear. **~korb** m (canopied) beach chair. **~prome¸nade** f promenade.

Strang [ʃtraŋ] m (-[e]s; ⸗e) **1.** rope: *fig.* **an 'einem ~ ziehen** pull together; **über die Stränge schlagen** kick over the traces; **wenn alle Stränge reißen** if all else fails. **2.** *anat.* cord. **3.** skein, hank.

strangulieren [ʃtraŋguˈliːrən] v/t (h) strangle.

Strapaze [ʃtraˈpaːtsə] f (-; -n) strain.

strapazieren [ʃtrapaˈtsiːrən] v/t (h) wear *s.o.*, *s.th.* out, strain (*a. fig.*): F **j-s Geduld ~** tax *s.o.'s* patience. **strapa¸zierfähig** *adj* hardwearing, tough.

strapaziös [ʃtrapaˈtsiøːs] *adj* strenuous, F tough: **~ sein** be a (great) strain.

Straße ['ʃtraːsə] f (-; -n) **1.** road, street: **auf der ~** on the road, in (*Am.* on) the street; **der Mann auf der ~** the man in the street; **j-n auf die ~ setzen** a) turn *s.o.* out, b) sack *s.o.*; **auf offener ~** in broad daylight. **2.** *geogr.* **die ~ von Dover** the Strait(s) of Dover. **3.** ◎ (production *etc*) line.

'Straßen|anzug m lounge (*Am.* business) suit. **~arbeiten** pl roadworks. **~arbeiter** m roadman.

'**Straßenbahn** f tram, *Am.* streetcar. **~haltestelle** f tram (*Am.* streetcar) stop. **~linie** f tram (*Am.* streetcar) line. **~wagen** m tram(car), *Am.* streetcar.
'**Straßen|bau** m (-[e]s; *no pl*) road construction. **~belag** m road surface. **~beleuchtung** f street lighting. **~ca,fé** n pavement (*Am.* sidewalk) café. **~fest** n street party. **~glätte** f slippery road(s). **~graben** m (road) ditch. **~händler** m street vendor. **~junge** m street urchin. **~kampf** m street fighting. **~karte** f road map. **~kehrer** m, **~kehrma,schine** f street sweeper. **~kreuzung** f crossroads. **~lage** f mot. roadholding. **~lärm** m noise from the street(s). **~la,terne** f street lamp. **~musi,kant** m street musician. **~name** m street name. **~netz** n road network. **~rand** m (*am* ~ *on the*) roadside. **~rennen** n road race. **~sammlung** f street collection. **~schild** n street sign. **~sperre** f road block. **~tunnel** m road tunnel. **~überführung** f flyover. **~unterführung** f underpass. **~verhältnisse** *pl* road conditions. **~verkehr** m (road) traffic. **~verkehrsordnung** f traffic regulations. **~zustand** m road condition(s).
Stratege [ʃtra'te:gə] m (-n; -n) strategist. **Strategie** [ʃtrate'gi:] f (-; -n) strategy. **stra'tegisch** [-gɪʃ] *adj* strategic(al).
Stratosphäre [ʃtrato'sfɛːrə] f (-; *no pl*) stratosphere.
sträuben ['ʃtrɔybən] (h) **I** *v/t* ruffle (up) (*feathers*), bristle (*hair*). **II** *sich* ~ *hair*: stand on end, *fur*: bristle up; *fig. sich* ~ *gegen* struggle against, resist; *sich* ~ *zu inf* refuse to *inf*.
Strauch [ʃtraux] m (-[e]s; ˝er) shrub, bush.
straucheln ['ʃtrauxəln] *v/i* (sn) **1.** stumble, trip. **2.** *fig.* go astray.
Strauß¹ [ʃtraus] m (-es; ˝e) bunch of flowers.
Strauß² m (-es; -e) *zo.* ostrich.
'**Straußenfeder** f ostrich feather.
Strebe ['ʃtre:bə] f (-; -n) strut.
streben ['ʃtre:bən] *v/i* **1.** (sn) ~ *zu*, ~ *nach* move towards, *person*: make for. **2.** (h) *fig.* ~ *nach* strive (for), aim (at).
'**Streben** n (-s) *fig.* efforts, (*nach*) striving (for), aspiration (for, after).
'**Streber** m (-s; -) *contp.* a) careerist, b) social climber, c) *ped.* swot.
'**Strebertum** n (-s; *no pl*) *contp.*

pushiness, *ped.* swotting.
strebsam ['ʃtre:p-] *adj* industrious, ambitious. '**Strebsamkeit** f (-; *no pl*) industriousness, ambition.
Strecke ['ʃtrɛkə] f (-; -n) **1.** stretch, a. leg, a. route (a. ✈, ⚓), a. distance (a. *sports*), *sports*: (racing) course, ☍, ☏, *teleph.* line, ⚒ roadway: ⚑ *auf freier* ~ between stations; *auf e-r* ~ *von 10 km* for a stretch of 10 km; *fig. auf der* ~ *bleiben* fail, come to grief. **2.** *hunt.* bag: *zur* ~ *bringen* kill, shoot down, bag, *fig.* hunt down, catch (*criminal etc*), defeat (*opponent*).
strecken ['ʃtrɛkən] *v/t* (h) **1.** stretch: *sich* (*or* *s-e Glieder*) ~ stretch (o.s.) (*or* one's limbs); → *Decke* 1. **2.** eke out, spin out (*supplies etc*).
'**Streckennetz** n railway network.
'**streckenweise** *adv* a) in parts, in places, b) now and then, at times.
'**Streckmuskel** ✗ extensor (muscle).
'**Streckverband** m ✚ *im* ~ in traction.
Streich [ʃtraiç] m (-[e]s; -e) trick, prank: *j-m e-n* (*bösen*) ~ *spielen* play a (nasty) trick on s.o.
streicheln ['ʃtraiçəln] *v/t*, *v/i* (h) stroke.
streichen ['ʃtraiçən] (strich, gestrichen, h) **I** *v/t* **1.** spread (*butter, bread, etc*), apply, put *ointment etc* (*auf acc* on). **2.** paint: → *gestrichen* 1. **3.** stroke. **4.** a) cross out, delete, b) cancel (*order etc*), cut (*funds*): *j-n von der Liste* ~ strike s.o. off the list. **5.** strike, haul down (*flag, sail*). **II** *v/i* **6.** (*mit der Hand*) ~ *über* (*acc*) stroke, pass one's hand over. **7.** (sn) *durch die Gegend* ~ roam the countryside; *ums Haus* ~ prowl around the house.
'**Streicher** *pl* ♪ *the* strings.
'**Streichholz** n match, matchstick.
'**Streichholzschachtel** f matchbox.
'**Streichinstru,ment** n string(ed) instrument: *die* ~e the strings.
'**Streichor,chester** f string orchestra.
'**Streichquar,tett** n string quartet.
'**Streichung** f (-; -en) cancel(l)ation (a. *fig.*), cut (*of funds etc*), *print.* deletion.
'**Streichwurst** f sausage spread.
'**Streifband** n (-[e]s; ˝er) wrapper.
Streife ['ʃtraifə] f (-; -n) ([*auf*] ~ *gehen* go on) patrol.
streifen ['ʃtraifən] (h) **I** *v/t* **1.** touch, brush against, *car*: scrape against, *bul-*

let: graze: *ein Thema ~* touch (up)on a subject. **2. vom Finger (Leibe)** ~ slip off (*ring, dress*). **3. mit e-m Blick** ~ glance at. **II** *v/i* (sn) **4. durch den Wald** *etc* ~ roam the woods *etc*.

'**Streif|licht** *n* fig. sidelight. **~schuß** *m* grazing shot. **~zug** *m* a. fig. excursion.

Streik [ʃtraik] *m* (-[e]s; -s) strike: *wilder ~* wildcat strike; *e-n ~ ausrufen* (*abbrechen*) call (call off) a strike; *in den ~ treten* go on strike. **~aufruf** *m* strike call. **~brecher** *m* strikebreaker, F blackleg, *contp.* scab.

streiken ['ʃtraikən] *v/i* (h) **1.** (be *or* go on) strike. **2.** F refuse, *a.* stomach: rebel, *machine etc*: refuse to work, pack up. '**Streikende** *m, f* (-n; -n) striker.

'**Streik|geld** *n* strike pay. **~posten** *m* (*a. ~ aufstellen vor, ~ stehen*) picket. **~recht** *n* right to strike. **~welle** *f* series of strikes.

Streit [ʃtrait] *m* (-[e]s; -e) a) quarrel, argument, F row, b) brawl, fight, c) controversy, dispute: *in ~ geraten mit* have an argument (*or* a fight) with; → *suchen, Zaun.* '**streitbar** *adj* belligerent.

'**streiten** *v/i* (stritt, gestritten, h) (*a. miteinander or sich ~*) a) quarrel, have an argument (F a row), b) fight: *darüber läßt sich ~* that's a moot point. '**Streiter** *m* (-s; -) fig. (*für*) fighter (for), champion (of). **Streite'rei** *f* (-; -en) (constant) quarrel(l)ing, fights, F rows.

'**Streitfall** *m* dispute, conflict, ⚖ case. '**Streitfrage** *f* (controversial) issue.

'**Streitgespräch** *n* debate, dispute.

'**streitig** *adj* **1.** ⚖ contentious. **2.** *j-m* (*das Recht auf*) *et.* ~ *machen* dispute s.o.'s right to s.th.; → *Rang* 1. '**Streitigkeit** *f* (-; -en) → *Streit*.

'**Streitkräfte** *pl* armed forces.

'**streitlustig** *adj* belligerent.

'**Streitpunkt** *m* (point at) issue.

'**Streitsache** *f* ⚖ a) case, b) lawsuit. '**Streitsucht** *f* (-; *no pl*) quarrelsomeness. '**streitsüchtig** *adj* quarrelsome.

'**Streitwert** *m* ⚖ value in dispute.

streng [ʃtrɛŋ] **I** *adj* severe (*a. cold, criticism, look, etc*), austere (*a. style*), strict (*discipline, regulation, etc*), harsh (*taste*), acrid (*smell etc*): (*mit j-m*) ~ *sein* be strict (with s.o.); *~es Stillschweigen* strict secrecy. **II** *adv* severely (*etc*): *sich ~ halten an* (*acc*) ad-

here strictly to; *~ geheim* top-secret; *~ vertraulich* strictly confidential.

'**Strenge** *f* (-; *no pl*) severity, austerity, strictness, harshness.

'**strenggläubig** *adj* orthodox.

Streß [ʃtrɛs] *m* (-sses; -sse) (*im ~* under) stress. '**stressen** *v/t* (h) F *j-n* ~ put s.o. under stress. '**stressig** *adj* F stressful. '**Streßkrankheit** *f* stress disease.

streuen ['ʃtrɔyən] **I** *v/t* scatter, strew, spread, sprinkle: *den Gehweg* ~ grit the sidewalk. **II** *v/i* ✕, *phys.* scatter.

streunen ['ʃtrɔynən] *v/i* (sn) stray, roam about: *~de Katze* stray cat.

strich [ʃtrɪç] *pret of* **streichen**.

Strich *m* (-[e]s; -e) a) stroke, b) line, c) dash, d) mark, e) (compass) point, f) stroke (of the brush): *j-m e-n ~ durch die Rechnung machen* thwart s.o.'s plans; *unter dem ~* on balance; *e-n (dicken) ~ unter et. machen* make a clean break with s.th.; *F auf den ~ gehen* walk the streets, be on the game. **2.** *textiles*: nap: *gegen den ~* against the nap; F *das ging mir gegen den ~* it went against the grain with me; F *nach ~ und Faden* good and proper. **3.** F cut. **4.** ♪ a) stroke, b) bowing technique.

stricheln ['ʃtrɪçəln] *v/t* (h) a) sketch b) hatch: *gestrichelte Linie* broken line.

'**Strich|junge** *m* F male prostitute. **~kode** *m* bar code. **~liste** *f* check list. **~mädchen** *n* F streetwalker, *Am. sl.* hooker. **~männchen** *n* matchstick man. **~punkt** *m* semicolon.

'**strichweise** *adv* in parts: *meteor.* ~ *Regen* scattered showers.

Strick [ʃtrɪk] *m* (-[e]s; -e) cord, rope: *fig. wenn alle ~e reißen* if all else fails; *j-m aus e-r Sache e-n ~ drehen* (*wollen*) use s.th. against s.o.

stricken ['ʃtrɪkən] *v/t, v/i* (h) knit. '**Stricker** *m* (-s; -), '**Strickerin** *f* (-; -nen) knitter.

'**Strick|jacke** *f* cardigan. **~leiter** *f* rope ladder. **~maschine** *f* knitting machine. **~nadel** *f* knitting needle. **~waren** *pl* knitwear. **~wolle** *f* knitting wool. **~zeug** *n* knitting (things).

striegeln ['ʃtriːɡəln] *v/t* (h) curry(comb).

Strieme ['ʃtriːmə] *f* (-; -n), '**Striemen** *m* (-s; -) weal.

strikt [ʃtrɪkt] *adj* strict: *et. ~ ablehnen* refuse s.th. flatly.

Strippe ['ʃtrɪpə] f (-; -n) F cord, string: fig. **an der ~ hängen** be on the blower.

stritt [ʃtrɪt] pret of **streiten**.

strittig ['ʃtrɪtɪç] adj controversial: **der ~e Punkt** the point at issue.

Stroh [ʃtro:] n (-[e]s; no pl) **1.** straw. **2.** (a. **mit ~ decken**) thatch. ⚤**blond** adj flaxen(-haired). ~**blume** f immortelle. ~**dach** n thatched roof. ~**feuer** n fig. flash in the pan. ~**halm** m straw: **nach e-m ~ greifen, sich an e-n ~ klammern** clutch at a straw. ~**hut** m straw hat. ~**mann** m (-[e]s; ¨er) front. ~**witwe(r** m) f F grass widow(er).

Strom [ʃtro:m] m (-[e]s; ¨e) **1.** a) (large) river, b) torrent, c) stream, current (a. fig.), fig. flood (of blood, tears, etc), stream (of people, cars, etc): **mit dem (gegen den) ~ schwimmen** swim with (against) the current (fig. a. tide); **es gießt in Strömen** it is pouring with rain. **2.** a) (electrical) current, b) electricity: **unter ~ stehend** live.

strom'ab(wärts) adv downstream.

strom'auf(wärts) adv upstream.

'**Stromausfall** m power failure.

strömen ['ʃtrø:mən] v/i (sn) stream, pour, air, gas, etc: a. flow, people: a. throng, flock.

'**Stromer** m (-s; -) F contp. tramp.

'**Strom|erzeuger** m ⚡ **1.** generator. **2.** power station. ~**erzeugung** f power generation. ⚤**führend** adj live. ~**kreis** m (electric) circuit. ~**leitung** f power line.

'**stromlinienförmig** adj streamlined.

'**Strom|netz** n ⚡ power supply system. ~**schnelle** f (-; -n) rapid. ~**spannung** f ⚡ voltage. ~**sperre** f power cut. ~**stärke** f current intensity, amperage. ~**stoß** m **1.** impulse. **2.** electric shock.

'**Strömung** f (-; -en) current, fig. a. trend.

'**Strom|verbrauch** m power consumption. ~**versorgung** f power supply. ~**zähler** m electric meter.

Strophe ['ʃtro:fə] f (-; -n) stanza, verse.

strotzen ['ʃtrɔtsən] v/i (h) **~ von, ~ vor** (dat) be full of, a. teeming with (mistakes), be bursting with (energy, health, etc); **vor Dreck ~** be caked with dirt.

Strudel ['ʃtru:dəl] m (-s; -) **1.** a. fig. whirlpool, maelstrom. **2.** gastr. strudel.

strudeln ['ʃtru:dəln] v/i (h) swirl, whirl.

Struktur [ʃtrʊk'tu:r] f (-; -en) structure.

Struk'tur... structural (change, policy, etc). **strukturell** [ʃtrʊktu'rɛl] adj (a. **~ bedingt**) structural.

Strumpf [ʃtrʊmpf] m (-[e]s; ¨e) stocking. ~**band** n garter. ~**halter** m suspender, Am. garter. ~**hose** f (**e-e ~** a pair of) tights, pantihose. ~**maske** f stocking mask. ~**waren** pl hosiery.

Strunk [ʃtrʊŋk] m (-[e]s; ¨e) stalk.

struppig ['ʃtrʊpɪç] adj unkempt (hair), bristly (beard), shaggy (dog).

Strychnin [ʃtryç'ni:n] n (-s; no pl) 🜍 strychnine.

Stube ['ʃtu:bə] f (-; -n) room.

'**Stubenhocker** m (-s; -) stay-at-home.

'**Stubenmädchen** n chambermaid.

'**stubenrein** adj house-broken (dog).

'**Stubenwagen** m bassinet.

Stuck [ʃtʊk] m (-s; no pl) stucco.

Stück [ʃtyk] n (-[e]s; -e) **1.** piece, a. slice (of bread etc), a. lump (of sugar), a. bar (of soap), a. head (of cattle): **ein ~ Land** a piece of land, a plot; **im ~, am ~** in one piece, a. unsliced (cheese etc); **50 Cent das ~** fifty cents each; **50 ~ Vieh** 50 head of cattle; **j-n ein ~ (Weges) begleiten** accompany s.o. part of the way; **~ für ~** piece by piece; **in ~e gehen** go to pieces; **in ~e schlagen** smash (to bits); fig. **aus freien ~en** of one's own free will; **große ~e halten auf** (acc) think highly of; **wir sind ein gutes ~ weitergekommen** we have made considerable headway; **das ist ein starkes ~!** that's a bit thick. **2.** piece (of music), thea. play, passage (of book etc).

'**Stückchen** n (-s; -) small piece (etc, → **Stück**).

'**Stückelung** f (-; -en) 🜚 denomination.

'**Stückeschreiber(in** f) m playwright.

'**Stück|gut** n parcel(s). ~**kosten** pl unit cost. ~**liste** f ⚙ parts list. ~**lohn** m piece rate. ~**preis** m unit price.

'**stückweise** adv bit by bit.

'**Stück|werk** n (-[e]s; no pl) contp. patchwork. ~**zahl** f number of pieces.

Student [ʃtu'dɛnt] m (-en; -en) student.

Stu'dentenausweis m student's identity card.

Stu'dentenschaft f (-; -en) the students.

Stu'denten|verbindung f fraternity. ~**wohnheim** n students' hostel.

Stu'dentin f (-; -nen) student.

Studie ['ʃtuːdiə] f (-; -n) study (a. paint. etc) (über acc on), sketch.

'**Studien|aufenthalt** m study visit. **~beratung** f student advisory service. **~bewerber** m university applicant. **~di,rektor** m deputy headmaster. **~fach** n subject. **~gang** m course of studies. **~gebühren** pl tuition fees.

'**studienhalber** adv for study purposes.

'**Studien|jahr** n academic year: **~e →** **Studienzeit. ~platz** m place at a university. **~rat** m, **~rätin** [-rɛːtɪn] f (-; -nen) secondary school teacher. **~referen,dar(in** f) m student teacher at a secondary school. **~reise** f study trip. **~zeit** f university (Am. college) days.

studieren [ʃtuˈdiːrən] (h) **I** v/t study, read: **er studiert Medizin** he studies medicine, he is a medical student. **II** v/i study, go to university: **wo hat er studiert?** which university did he go to?

Studio ['ʃtuːdĭo] n (-s; -s) studio.

Studium ['ʃtuːdĭʊm] n (-s; -dien) studies, study (gen of).

Stufe ['ʃtuːfə] f (-; -n) **1.** step. **2.** ling., ♪ degree. **3.** fig. a) stage, b) level, standard, c) rank: **j-n auf eine ~ stellen mit** place s.o. on a level with. **4.** (income etc) bracket. **5.** stage (of rocket etc).

'**Stufen|barren** m asymmetrical bars. **~heck** n mot. notchback. **~leiter** f stepladder: **~ des Erfolgs** ladder to success.

'**stufenlos** adj ⊙ continuous: **~ regelbar** infinitely variable. '**stufenweise I** adj gradual. **II** adv step by step, by degrees.

Stuhl [ʃtuːl] m (-[e]s; ⁓e) **1.** chair, (piano etc) stool: **der Heilige ~** the Holy See; fig. **sich zwischen zwei Stühle setzen** fall between two stools; → **elektrisch I. 2. ♂** a) stool, b) → **Stuhlgang.**

'**Stuhl|bein** n leg of a chair. **~gang** m (-[e]s; no pl) bowel movement.

stülpen ['ʃtʏlpən] v/t (h) put (auf acc on, über acc over): **et. nach außen ~** turn s.th. inside out.

stumm [ʃtʊm] adj dumb, mute, fig. a. silent (a. ling.), speechless (vor dat with).

Stummel ['ʃtʊməl] m (-s; -) stump, butt, stub (a. of candle etc).

'**Stummfilm** m silent film.

Stumpen ['ʃtʊmpən] m (-s; -) cheroot.

Stümper ['ʃtʏmpər] m (-s; -) bungler.

Stümpe'rei f (-; -en) **1.** no pl bungling.

2. botch. '**stümperhaft** adj bungling. '**stümpern** v/i, v/t (h) bungle, botch.

stumpf [ʃtʊmpf] adj **1.** blunt. **2.** ⩑ obtuse (angle), truncated (cone). **3.** dull. **4.** fig. apathetic, dull, dulled (senses).

Stumpf m (-[e]s; ⁓e) stump: F **mit ~ und Stiel** root and branch.

'**Stumpfheit** f (-; no pl) **1.** bluntness. **2.** a. fig. dullness. '**Stumpfsinn** m (-[e]s; no pl) dullness, a. mindlessness (of work etc). '**stumpfsinnig** adj dull, a. mindless, soul-destroying (work etc).

'**stumpfwink(e)lig** adj ⩑ obtuse.

Stunde ['ʃtʊndə] f (-; -n) **1.** hour: **zur ~** at this hour; **bis zur ~** as yet; mot. **50 Meilen in der ~** 50 miles per hour; **die ~ der Wahrheit** the moment of truth. **2.** ped. lesson, class, period: **bei j-m ~n nehmen** have lessons with s.o.

'**stunden** v/t (h) **(j-m) die Zahlung ~** extend the term of payment (to s.o.).

'**Stunden|geschwindigkeit** f (average) speed per hour: **e-e ~ von 60 Meilen** an average of 60 miles per hour (abbr. mph). **~kilo,meter** f kilomet/res (Am. -ers) per hour. **~lang I** adj lasting (for) hours. **II** adv for hours (and hours). **~lohn** m hourly wage. **~plan** m timetable, Am. schedule.

'**stundenweise** adj and adv by the hour.

'**Stundenzeiger** m hour hand.

...stündig [-ʃtʏndɪç] in cpds. ...-hour.

stündlich ['ʃtʏntlɪç] **I** adj hourly. **II** adv a) every hour, b) any time (now).

Stunk [ʃtʊŋk] m F **~ machen** kick up a stink; **das gibt ~!** there will be trouble.

stupide [ʃtuˈpiːdə] adj dull, mindless.

Stups [ʃtʊps] m (-es; -e), '**stupsen** v/t (h) F prod. '**Stupsnase** f snub nose.

stur [ʃtuːr] adj F **1.** stubborn, pigheaded, stolid. **2.** → **stumpfsinnig.**

'**Sturheit** f (-; no pl) F **1.** stubbornness (etc). **2.** → **Stumpfsinn.**

Sturm [ʃtʊrm] m (-[e]s; ⁓e) **1.** storm (a. fig.), gale: **~ der Entrüstung** outcry; **~ im Wasserglas** storm in a teacup. **2.** ✕ storm, attack: a. fig. **im ~ erobern** take by storm; **~ laufen gegen** attack, assail; **♱ ~ auf** (acc) rush for (goods), run on (a bank). **3.** sports: forwards. **~angriff** m ✕ assault. **~bö** f squall.

stürmen ['ʃtʏrmən] **I** v/t (h) **1.** ✕ storm: fig. **e-e Bank ~ make** a run on a bank. **II** v/i **2.** (h) ✕ or sports: attack. **3.** (sn) *fig.* rush. **III** *v/impers* (h) **es stürmt** there's a gale blowing.

'**Stürmer** *m* (-s; -) *sports*: forward.

'**stürmisch** *adj* stormy (*a. fig. debate, love, etc*), passionate (*lover*), tumultuous (*applause etc*), vehement (*protest*), turbulent (*time*), rapid (*development etc*): **nicht so ~!** easy does it!

'**Sturm**|**lauf** *m* ✗ assault, *fig. a.* run (**auf** *acc* on). **~spitze** *f* soccer: spearhead. **~tief** *n* cyclone. **~warnung** *f* gale warning. **~wolke** *f* storm cloud.

Sturz [ʃtʊrts] *m* (-es; ⁼e) **1.** (sudden) fall, plunge (*a. fig.*), *fig.* (sudden) drop (*in temperature etc*), *a.* slump (*in prices etc*). **2.** (down)fall, overthrow (*of a government*). '**Sturzbach** *m* torrent.

stürzen ['ʃtʏrtsən] **I** *v/i* (sn) **1.** fall, *a. fig.* plunge: **sie ist (mit dem Fahrrad) gestürzt** she had a fall (with her bicycle). **2.** rush, dash: **er kam ins Zimmer gestürzt** he burst into the room. **II** *v/t* (h) **3.** throw: **j-n ins Elend ~** plunge s.o. into misery. **4.** turn *s.th.* upside down, turn *pudding etc* out of the mo(u)ld: **Nicht ~!** this side up! **5.** bring down, overthrow (*government etc*) **III sich ~** (h) **6.** plunge (**ins Wasser** into the water); **sich aus dem Fenster ~** throw o.s. out of the window; *fig.* **sich in die Arbeit ~** throw o.s. into one's work; **sich in Schulden ~** plunge into debt; **sich in Unkosten ~** go to great expense. **7.** *bes.* ✗ **auf** (*acc*) pounce on, *a.* rush at (*s.o.*), *a.* make straight for.

'**Sturz**|**flug** *m* (nose)dive. **~helm** *m* crash helmet. **~regen** *m* (heavy) downpour.

Stute ['ʃtuːtə] *f* (-; -n) mare.

'**Stutenfohlen** *n* filly.

'**Stützbalken** *m* supporting beam.

Stütze ['ʃtʏtsə] *f* (-; -n) *a. fig.* support, prop, (*person*) mainstay.

stutzen[1] ['ʃtʊtsən] *v/t* (h) cut, trim (*hair, beard*), lop (*tree*), clip (*hedge, wings*), crop (*ears*), dock (*tail*).

'**stutzen**[2] *v/i* (h) (**bei**) a) stop short (at), b) be puzzled (by), c) become suspicious (at).

'**Stutzen** *m* (-s; -) **1.** short rifle. **2.** ⚙ connecting piece. **3.** (football) sock.

stützen ['ʃtʏtsən] *v/t* (h) support (*a. fig.*), prop, *fig.* back (up): **die Ellbogen auf den Tisch ~** prop (*or* rest) one's elbows on the table; *fig. et.* **~ auf** (*acc*) base

s.th. on; **sich ~ auf** (*acc*) rely on, *opinion etc*: be based on.

stutzig ['ʃtʊtsɪç] *adj* **j-n ~ machen** a) puzzle s.o., b) make s.o. suspicious; **~ werden** a) be puzzled, b) become suspicious.

'**Stütz**|**mauer** *f* retaining wall. **~pfeiler** *m* buttress. **~punkt** *m* ✗ *or fig.* base.

Styropor [ʃtyroˈpoːr] *n* (-s; *no pl*) (*TM*) polystyrene.

Subjekt [zʊpˈjɛkt] *n* (-[e]s; -e) **1.** *ling.* subject. **2.** F *contp.* fellow.

subjektiv [zʊpjɛkˈtiːf] *adj* subjective.

Subjektivität [zʊpjɛktiviˈtɛːt] *f* (-; *no pl*) subjectivity.

'**Subkonti**,**nent** *m* subcontinent.

'**Subkul**,**tur** *f* (-; -en) subculture.

subkutan [zʊpkuˈtaːn] *adj* ⚕ subcutaneous.

Sublimat [zubliˈmaːt] *n* (-[e]s; -e) 🜍 sublimate. **sublimieren** [zubliˈmiːrən] *v/t* (h) 🜍 *or fig.* sublimate.

Subskription [zʊpskrɪpˈtsĭoːn] *f* (-; -en) subscription. **Subskripti'onspreis** *m* subscription price.

substantiell [zʊpstanˈtsĭɛl] *adj* substantial.

Substantiv ['zʊpstantiːf] *n* (-s; -e) noun, substantive. **substantivieren** [zʊpstantiˈviːrən] *v/t* (h) use as a noun. '**substantivisch** [-tiːvɪʃ] *adj* substantival, *adv a.* as a noun.

Substanz [zʊpˈstants] *f* (-; -en) **1.** substance. **2.** 🜍 (**von der ~ leben** live on one's) capital; F *fig.* **das geht an die ~** that really takes it out of you.

subtil [zʊpˈtiːl] *adj* subtle.

subtropisch *adj* subtropical.

subtrahieren [zʊptraˈhiːrən] *v/t* (h) subtract. **Subtraktion** [zʊptrakˈtsĭoːn] *f* (-; -en) subtraction.

Subvention [zʊpvɛnˈtsĭoːn] *f* (-; -en) subsidy. **subventionieren** [zʊpvɛntsĭoˈniːrən] *v/t* (h) subsidize.

'**Such**|**akti**,**on** *f* search (operation). **~dienst** *m* tracing service.

Suche ['zuːxə] *f* (-; -n) (**nach** for) search, hunt: **auf der ~ nach** in search of; **auf der ~ sein nach** be looking for.

suchen ['zuːxən] (h) **I** *v/t* a) look for, search for, b) seek (*advice, happiness, etc*), c) try to trace (*person, mistake, etc*): (**mit j-m**) **Streit ~** pick a quarrel (with s.o.); **Sie haben hier nichts zu ~!**

you have no business to be here; → **gesucht**, **Rat** 1, **Weite**[2]. **II** v/i look, search: ~ **nach** → I; **nach Worten** ~ be at a loss for words.

'**Sucher** m (-s; -) *phot.* viewfinder.

'**Sucherkamera** f rangefinder camera.

'**Such**|**gerät** n detector. **~hund** m tracker dog. **~lauf** m *video etc:* a) scanning, b) scanner. **~mannschaft** f search party. **~scheinwerfer** m searchlight.

Sucht [zʊxt] f (-; ⁀e) (**nach**) a) craving (for), b) *a.* 🍷 addiction (to).

'**suchterzeugend** *adj* 🍷 addictive.

süchtig ['zʏçtɪç] *adj* addicted (**nach** to): ~ **machen** be addictive; *fig.* ~ **sein nach** a) have a craving for, b) be obsessed with. '**Süchtige** m, f (-n; -n) addict.

'**Suchtmittel** n addictive drug.

'**Suchtrupp** m search party.

Süd|'**afrika** ['zy:t-] n (-s) South Africa. '**Südafri**'**kaner(in** f) m, '**südafri**'**kanisch** *adj* South African.

'**Süda**'**merika** n (-s) South America. '**Südameri**'**kaner(in** f) m, '**südameri**'**kanisch** *adj* South American.

'**süddeutsch** *adj*, '**Süddeutsche** m, f (-n; -n) South German.

Sude'**lei** (-; -en) F *contp.* mess. **sudeln** ['zu:dəln] v/i (h) F *contp.* make a mess.

Süden ['zy:dən] m (-s; *no pl*) south, South: **im** ~ in the south; **im** ~ **von** (*or* **gen**) (to) the south of; **nach** ~ south(ward).

'**Südfrüchte** *pl* tropical fruits.

'**Südküste** f south(ern) coast.

'**Südländer** [-lɛndər] m (-s; -), '**Südländerin** f (-; -nen) Mediterranean type, Latin. '**südländisch** *adj* Mediterranean, Latin (*temper etc*).

'**südlich** I *adj* southern, south, southerly (*wind, direction*). **II** *adv* south(wards). **III** *prep* ~ **von** (*or* **gen**) (to) the south of.

Süd'**osten** m South(east).

süd'**östlich** I *adj* southeast(ern), southeasterly (*wind, direction*). **II** *adv* (to) the southeast. **III** *prep* ~ **von** (*or* **gen**) (to) the southeast of.

'**Südpol** m South Pole.

Südpo'**lar...** Antarctic.

'**Südsee** f (-; *no pl*) South Sea.

'**südwärts** *adv* southward(s).

Süd'**westen** m southwest.

süd'**westlich** I *adj* southwest(ern), southwesterly (*wind, direction*). **II** *adv*

(to the) southwest. **III** *prep* ~ **von** (*or* **gen**) (to the) southwest of.

'**Südwind** m south wind.

Suff [zʊf] m (-[e]s; *no pl*) F boozing.

süffig ['zʏfɪç] *adj* F pleasant (to drink).

süffisant [zʏfi'zant] *adj* smug.

suggerieren [zʊgeˈriːrən] v/t (h) suggest. **Suggestion** [zʊgɛsˈtioːn] f (-; -en) suggestion. **suggestiv** [zʊgɛsˈtiːf] *adj* suggestive. **Sugge**'**stivfrage** f leading question.

Sühne ['zyːnə] f (-; -n) atonement.

sühnen ['zyːnən] v/t (h) atone for.

Suite ['sviːt(ə)] f (-; -n) suite.

Sujet [zyˈʒeː] n (-s; -s) subject.

sukzessiv [zʊktseˈsiːf] *adj* gradual.

Sulfat [zʊlˈfaːt] n (-[e]s; -e) 🧪 sulphate (*Am.* -f-). **Sulfid** [zʊlˈfiːt] n (-[e]s; -e) 🧪 sulphide (*Am.* -f-).

Sulfonamid [zʊlfonaˈmiːd] n (-[e]s; -e) sulphonamide (*Am.* -f-).

Sultan ['zʊltaːn] m (-s; -e) sultan. **Sultanine** [zʊltaˈniːnə] f (-; -n) *gastr.* sultana.

Sülze ['zʏltsə] f (-; -n) jellied meat.

summarisch [zʊˈmaːrɪʃ] *adj* summary.

Summe ['zʊmə] f (-; -n) a) sum, b) (sum) total, c) amount, d) *fig.* sum total.

summen ['zʊmən] v/b (h) **I** v/i buzz, hum, drone. **II** v/t hum (*tune etc*).

'**Summer** m (-s; -) 🔔 buzzer.

summieren [zʊˈmiːrən] v/t (*a.* **sich** ~) (h) add up.

Sumpf [zʊmpf] m (-[e]s; ⁀e) **1.** swamp. **2.** *fig.* (quag)mire. '**sumpfen** v/i (h) F live it up. '**sumpfig** *adj* marshy. '**Sumpfland** n (-[e]s; *no pl*) marshland.

Sund [zʊnt] m (-[e]s; -e) sound, strait(s).

Sünde ['zʏndə] f (-; -n) sin.

'**Sünden**|**erlaß** m absolution. **~fall** m the Fall (of Man). **~re**|**gister** n *humor.* **sein** *etc* ~ the list of his *etc* sins.

'**Sünder** m (-s; -), '**Sünderin** f (-; -nen) sinner. '**sündhaft** *adj* sinful: F ~ **teuer** awfully expensive. '**sündig** *adj* sinful. **sündigen** ['zʏndɪgən] v/i (h) **1.** sin (**gegen** against): **an j-m** ~ wrong s.o. **2.** F indulge, overeat *etc*.

super ['zuːpər] *adj or int* F super.

'**Super** n (-s; *no pl*) F *mot.* super, four-star (petrol), *Am.* premium.

Superlativ ['zuːpərlatiːf] m (-s; -e) *ling. or fig.* superlative.

'**Supermacht** f *pol.* superpower.

'**Supermarkt** *m* supermarket.
'**supermo,dern** *adj* ultramodern.
Suppe ['zʊpə] *f* (-; -n) soup: F *die* ~ *auslöffeln müssen* have to face the music; *j-m* (*sich*) *e-e schöne* ~ *einbrocken* get s.o. (o.s.) into a nice mess. '**Suppen|fleisch** *n* meat for making soup. **~grün** *n* (bunch of) herbs and vegetables. **~huhn** *n* boiling fowl. **~kelle** *f* soup ladle. **~löffel** *m* soup spoon. **~schüssel** *f* soup tureen. **~teller** *m* soup plate. **~würfel** *m* stock cube.
Surfbrett ['sɛ:f-] *n* surfboard. '**surfen** *v/i* (h, sn) do surfing, surf. '**Surfer** *m* (-s; -), '**Surferin** *f* (-; -nen) surfer.
Surrealismus [sʊrea'lɪsmʊs] *m* (-; *no pl*) surrealism.
surrea'listisch *adj* surrealist(ic).
surren ['zʊrən] *v/i* (h) whirr, hum, *insect etc:* buzz.
suspekt [zʊs'pɛkt] *adj* suspect.
suspendieren [zʊspɛn'di:rən] *v/t* (h) suspend.
Suspensorium [zʊspɛn'zo:riʊm] *n* (-s; -rien) 🏥 *surgery, sports:* jockstrap.
süß [zy:s] *adj* sweet. '**Süße¹** *f* (-; *no pl*) sweetness. '**Süße²** *m, f* (-n; -n) F sweetie. '**süßen** *v/t* (h) sweeten.
'**Süßigkeiten** *pl* sweets, *Am.* candy.
'**süßlich** *adj* **1.** sweetish. **2.** *fig.* a) sugary, b) mawkish.
'**süß-'sauer** *adj gastr.* sweet and sour: F ~ *lächeln* smile sourly, force a smile.
'**Süßspeise** *f* sweet, dessert.
'**Süßstoff** *m* sweetener.
'**Süßwaren** *pl* sweets, *Am.* candy. **~geschäft** *n* sweet shop, *Am.* candy store.
'**Süßwasser** *n* fresh water.
Symbiose [zʏm'bĭo:zə] *f* (-; -n) *biol.* or *fig.* symbiosis.
Symbol [zʏm'bo:l] *n* (-s; -e) symbol (*für* of), 🏥, ♈ *etc* a. (conventional) sign.
Symbolik [zʏm'bo:lɪk] *f* (-; *no pl*) symbolism. **sym'bolisch** *adj* symbolic(al).
symbolisieren [zʏmboli'zi:rən] *v/t* (h) symbolize.
Symmetrie [zʏme'tri:] *f* (-; -n) symmetry. **symmetrisch** [zʏ'me:trɪʃ] *adj* symmetric(al).
Sympathie [zʏmpa'ti:] *f* (-; -n) **1.** liking: ~ *empfinden für* have a liking for. **2.** sympathy: *sich j-s* ~*n verscherzen* lose s.o.'s sympathies (*or* support).
Sympa'thiestreik *m* sympathetic strike.

Sympathisant [zʏmpati'zant] *m* (-en; -en) sympathizer. **sympathisch** [zʏm'pa:tɪʃ] *adj* **1.** likeable, F nice: *er ist mir* (*nicht*) ~ I (don't) like him. **2.** *physiol.* sympathetic. **sympathisieren** [zʏmpati'zi:rən] *v/i* (h) sympathize.
Symphonie [zʏmfo'ni:] *f* (-; -n) *etc* → *Sinfonie etc*.
Symposium [zʏm'po:ziʊm] *n* (-s; -sien) symposium.
Symptom [zʏmp'to:m] *n* (-s; -e) symptom. **symptomatisch** [zʏmpto'ma:tɪʃ] *adj* symptomatic (*für* of).
Synagoge [zyna'go:gə] *f* (-; -n) synagogue.
synchron [zʏn'kro:n] *adj* synchronous, *ling.* synchronic: ~ *laufen etc* be synchronized. **Syn'chron...** synchronous.
synchronisieren [zʏnkroni'zi:rən] *v/t* (h) synchronize, *film:* a. dub.
Syndikat [zʏndi'ka:t] *n* (-[e]s; -e) syndicate.
Syndikus ['zʏndikʊs] *m* (-; -se) company lawyer, in-house legal counsel.
Syndrom [zʏn'dro:m] *n* (-s; -e) 🏥 syndrome.
Synkope *f* (-; -n) **1.** ['zʏnkope] *ling.* syncope. **2.** ['zʏnko:pə] ♪ syncopation.
Synode [zy'no:də] *f* (-; -n) *eccl.* synod.
synonym [zyno'ny:m] *adj ling.* synonymous. **Syno'nym** *n* (-s; -e) synonym.
syntaktisch [zʏn'taktɪʃ] *adj ling.* syntactic(al).
Syntax ['zʏntaks] *f* (-; -en) *ling.* syntax.
Synthese [zʏn'te:zə] *f* (-; -n) synthesis.
synthetisch [zʏn'te:tɪʃ] *adj* synthetic.
Syphilis ['zy:filɪs] *f* (-; *no pl*) 🏥 syphilis.
Syrien ['zy:riən] *n* (-s) Syria. **Syrier** ['zy:riər] *m* (-s; -), '**Syrierin** *f* (-; -nen), '**syrisch** *adj* Syrian.
System [zʏs'te:m] *n* (-s; -e) system, *of traffic etc:* a. network. **Systematik** [zʏste'ma:tik] *f* (-; -en) systematics, system. **syste'matisch** *adj* systematic.
Sy'stemkritiker(in *f*) *m* dissident.
sy'stemlos *adj* unmethodical.
Szenario [stse'na:rĭo] *n* (-s; -s) scenario.
Szene ['stse:nə] *f* (-; -n) scene; *fig.* *sich in* ~ *setzen* put on a show; (*j-m*) *e-e* ~ *machen* make (s.o.) a scene.
'**Szenen|ap,plaus** *m* applause during the scene. **~wechsel** *m* scene change.
Szenerie [stsenə'ri:] *f* (-; -n) scenery, *thea.* a. setting.

T

T, t [te:] *n* (-; -) T, t.
Tabak ['ta:bak] *m* (-s; -e) tobacco.
'Tabakpflanze *f* tobacco (plant).
'Tabakwaren *pl* tobacco goods.
'Tabakwarenladen *m* tobacconist's.
tabellarisch [tabɛ'la:rɪʃ] *adj* tabulated,
  tabular. **Tabelle** [ta'bɛlə] *f* (-; -n) table.
Ta'bellen|führer *m* sports: top team,
  leader. **~letzte** *m* bottom team. **~spitze**
  f (*an der ~* at) top of the table.
Tabernakel [tabɛr'na:kəl] *n, m* (-s; -)
  eccl. tabernacle.
Tablett [ta'blɛt] *n* (-[e]s; -s, -e) tray.
Tablette [ta'blɛtə] *f* (-; -n) tablet, pill.
tabu [ta'bu:] *adj* taboo: **für ~ erklären**
  (put under a) taboo. **Ta'bu** *n* (-s; -s)
  taboo. **ta'bufrei** *adj* **~e Gesellschaft**
  permissive society.
Tabulator [tabu'la:tor] *m* (-s; -en [-la'to:-
  rən]) tabulator.
Tacho ['taxo] *m* (-s; -s) F, **Tachometer**
  [taxo'me:tər] *n* (-s; -) *mot.* speedometer.
Tadel ['ta:dəl] *m* (-s; -) reproach, rebuke,
  ped. bad mark: **ohne ~** → **tadellos** *adj*
  faultless, flawless, blameless, perfect,
  impeccable (*a. clothing*). **'tadeln** *v/t* (h)
  (**wegen** for) a) rebuke, reprimand,
  blame, b) criticize, censure. **'tadelnswert** *adj* reprehensible.
Tafel ['ta:fəl] *f* (-; -n) **1.** *ped.* a) black-
  board, b) slate. **2.** notice (*Am.* bulletin)
  board. **3.** plate (*a. in book*). **4.** a) slab, b)
  tablet, plaque, c) panel. **5.** bar (*of chocolate*). **6.** (dinner) table: **die ~ aufheben**
  rise from table. **'tafelfertig** *adj* ready to
  serve. **'Tafelgeschirr** *n* dinner service.
tafeln ['ta:fəln] *v/i* (h) dine.
täfeln ['tɛ:fəln] *v/t* (h) panel.
'Tafelobst *n* dessert fruit.
'Tafelsilber *n* silver(ware).
'Täfelung *f* (-; -en) panel(l)ing.
'Tafelwasser *n* mineral (*or* table) water.
Taft [taft] *m* (-[e]s; -e) taffeta.
Tag [ta:k] *m* (-[e]s; -e) day: **am ~e, bei ~e**
  a) in the daytime, b) by daylight; **~ für ~**
  day after day, *get better etc* day by day;
  am nächsten ~ the day after; **am ~
  zuvor** the day before; **dieser ~e** a) one
  of these days, b) the other day; **e-s ~es**
  one day, *a.* some day; **den ganzen ~** all

day long; **alle paar ~e** every few days;
jeden zweiten ~ every other day; ⚔
unter (über) ~e underground (above
ground); **von e-m ~ auf den anderen**
overnight; **guten ~!** a) good morning!,
good afternoon!, F hello!, b) how do
you do!; **j-m guten ~ sagen** say hello to
s.o.; **an den ~ bringen (kommen)** bring
(come) to light; **an den ~ legen** display,
show; **welchen ~ haben wir heute?**
what's (the date) today?; → *Abend,
heute* I, *heutig.*
tag'aus → *tagein.*
Tage|bau ['ta:gə-] *m* (-[e]s; *no pl*) ⚔
  opencast mining. **~buch** *n* diary. **~dieb**
  m idler. **~geld(er** *pl*) daily allowance.
tag'ein: **~, tagaus** day in, day out.
'tagelang I *adj* lasting for days. **II** *adv*
  for day (and days).
'Tagelöhner [-lø:nər] *m* (-s; -), **'Tage-
  löhnerin** *f* (-; -nen) day labo(u)rer.
tagen ['ta:gən] *v/i* (h) have a meeting, sit
  (in conference), ⚖ be in session.
Tages|anbruch ['ta:gəs-] *m* (**bei ~ at**)
  daybreak. **~ausflug** *m* day trip.
  ~creme *f* day cream. **~decke** *f*
  bedspread. **~einnahme(n** *pl*) *f* day's
  takings. **~gericht** *n gastr.* dish of the
  day. **~gespräch** *n* the talk of the day.
  ~karte *f* **1.** *gastr.* menu for the day. **2.** *gastr.* menu
  for the day. **~kasse** *f* **1.** *thea. etc*
  booking office. **2.** ✈ a) petty cash, b) →
  Tageseinnahme(n). **~kurs** *m* **1.** ✈ *foreign exchange:* current rate, *stock exchange:* current price. **2.** *ped.* day
  course. **~leistung** *f* daily output. **~licht**
  n (-[e]s; *no pl*) daylight: *fig.* **ans ~ bringen (kommen)** bring (come) to light.
  ~mutter *f* child minder. **~ordnung** *f*
  (**auf der ~ stehen** be on the) agenda: *a.
  fig.* **zur ~ übergehen** proceed to the
  order of the day; *fig.* **an der ~ sein** be
  nothing unusual. **~presse** *f* daily
  press. **~raum** *m* dayroom. **~rückfahr-
  karte** *f* day return (ticket). **~satz** *m* **1.**
  daily rate. **2.** daily ration. **~stätte** *f*
  day-care cent/re (*Am.* -er). **~tour** *f* day
  trip. **~zeit** *f* **1.** time of day. **2.** daytime:
  zu jeder ~ at any time of the day.
  ~zeitung *f* daily (newspaper).

'**tageweise** *adv* on a day-to-day basis.
'**taghell** *adj and adv* (as) light as day.
...**tägig** [-tɛːgɪç] *in cpds.* ...-day.
täglich ['tɛːklɪç] **I** *adj* a) daily, b) everyday. **II** *adv* every day, daily: *zweimal ~* twice a day.
tags [taːks] *adv* ~ *darauf* (*zuvor*) the day after (before).
'**Tagschicht** *f* (*~ haben* be on) day shift.
'**tagsüber** *adv* during the day.
'**tag'täglich** *adv* day in, day out.
'**Tagung** *f* (-; -en) conference, convention. '**Tagungsbericht** *m* proceedings.
'**Tagungsort** *m* conference venue.
Taifun [taɪ'fuːn] *m* (-s; -e) typhoon.
Taille ['taljə] *f* (-; -n) waist, *a.* waistline.
tailliert [ta'jiːrt] *adj* waisted.
Takelage [takə'laːʒə] *f* (-; -n) ✤ rigging.
takeln ['taːkəln] *v/t* (h) rig.
Takt[1] [takt] *m* (-[e]s; -e) **1.** ♩ a) bar, b) beat, c) (*waltz etc*) time: *3/4-~* three-four-time; *~ halten* keep time; *den ~ schlagen* beat the time; *aus dem ~ kommen* lose the beat, *fig.* be put off one's stroke. **2.** rhythm, (work *etc*) cycle, *mot.* stroke: *im 15-Minuten-Takt* at 15-minute intervals.
Takt[2] *m* (-[e]s; *no pl*), '**Taktgefühl** *n* (-[e]s; *no pl*) tact.
taktieren [tak'tiːrən] *v/i* (h) *geschickt ~* use clever tactics. **Taktik** ['taktɪk] *f* (-; -en) (*die ~ ändern* change) tactics. '**Taktiker** *m* (-s; -) tactician. '**taktisch** *adj a. fig.* tactical.
'**taktlos** *adj* tactless. '**Taktlosigkeit** *f* (-; *no pl*) tactlessness, indiscretion.
'**Takt|stock** *m* baton. **~strich** *m* ♩ bar.
'**taktvoll** *adj* tactful.
Tal [taːl] *n* (-[e]s; ⁻er) valley.
Talar [ta'laːr] *m* (-s; -e) *univ.* gown, *eccl.* cassock, ⚖ robe.
Talent [ta'lɛnt] *n* (-[e]s; -e) **1.** talent (*für*, *zu* for). **2.** talent(ed person). **talentiert** [talɛn'tiːrt] *adj* talented, gifted. **ta'lentlos** *adj* untalented. **Ta'lentsucher** *m* (-s; -) talent scout. **ta'lentvoll** *adj* talented, gifted.
'**Talfahrt** *f* **1.** descent. **2.** ✝ downswing.
Talg [talk] *m* (-[e]s; -e) **1.** *gastr.* a) suet, b) tallow. **2.** *physiol.* sebum.
'**Talgdrüse** *f* sebaceous gland.
Talisman ['taːlɪsman] *m* (-s; -e) talisman, (lucky) charm, mascot.
Talk [talk] *m* (-[e]s; *no pl*) *min.* talc(um).

Talkmaster ['tɔːkmaːstər] *m* (-s; -) *TV* host. **Talk-Show** *f* (-; -s) *TV* chat (*esp. Am.* talk) show.
'**Talsohle** *f* **1.** bottom of the valley. **2.** ✝ low. '**Talsperre** *f* dam.
Tamburin [tambu'riːn] *n* (-s; -e) tambourine.
Tampon ['tampɔn] *m* (-s; -s), **tamponieren** [tampo'niːrən] *v/t* (h) 🕮 tampon.
Tamtam ['tamtam] *n* (-s; *no pl*) F *contp.* fuss (*um* about).
Tandem ['tandɛm] *n* (-s; -s) tandem.
Tang [taŋ] *m* (-[e]s; -e) 🝆 seaweed.
Tangahöschen ['taŋga-] *n* G-string.
Tangente [taŋ'gɛnta] *f* (-; -n) 🝆 tangent.
tangieren [taŋ'giːrən] *v/t* (h) **1.** 🝆 be tangent to. **2.** *fig.* affect, concern.
Tango ['taŋgo] *m* (-s; -s) tango.
Tank [taŋk] *m* (-[e]s; -s) tank. '**tanken** [-] **I** *v/t* **1.** a) fill up with, b) refill, refuel. **2.** F *fig.* get (*fresh air etc*). **II** *v/i* **3.** tank up (*a.* F *drink*), refuel.
'**Tanker** *m* (-s; -) ✤ (oil) tanker.
'**Tank|schiff** *n* → **Tanker.** **~stelle** *f* filling (*or* petrol, *Am.* gas) station. **~verschluß** *m mot.* fuel cap. **~wagen** *n mot.* tanker. **~wart** *m* (-[e]s; -e) petrol pump (*Am.* gas station) attendant.
Tanne ['tana] *f* (-; -n) fir (tree).
'**Tannen|baum** *m* fir (tree). **~nadel** *f* fir needle. **~zapfen** *m* fir cone.
Tante ['tanta] *f* (-; -n) **1.** aunt: *~ Helene* Aunt Helen. **2.** F woman, bird.
Tante-'Emma-Laden *m* F corner shop, *Am.* mom-and-pop store.
Tantieme [tã'tiɛːmə] *f* (-; -n) royalty.
Tanz [tants] *m* (-es; ⁓e) **1.** dance. **2.** F *fig.* fuss. '**Tanzbein** *n* F *das ~ schwingen* shake a leg. **tänzeln** ['tɛntsəln] *v/i* **1.** (sn) skip. **2.** (h) *horse:* prance. '**tanzen** *v/t, v/i* (h) dance. **Tänzer** ['tɛntsər] *m* (-s; -), '**Tänzerin** *f* (-; -nen) dancer, *thea.* (ballet) dancer.
'**Tanz|fläche** *f* dance floor. **~kurs** *m* dancing course. **~lehrer(in** *f*) *m* dancing instructor. **~lo,kal** *n* dance hall. **~mu,sik** *f* dance music. **~or,chester** *n* dance band. **~partner(in** *f*) *m* dancing partner. **~saal** *m* dance hall, ballroom. **~schule** *f* dancing school. **~stunde** *f in die ~ gehen* go to a dancing class. **~tur,nier** *n* dancing contest.
Tapet [ta'peːt] *n* F *et. aufs ~ bringen* bring s.th. up.

Tapete [ta'pe:tə] f (-; -n) wallpaper. **Ta'petenwechsel** m F fig. change of scenery. **tapezieren** [tape'tsi:rən] v/t, v/i (h) (wall)paper: neu ~ repaper.

tapfer ['tapfər] adj brave, courageous.

'Tapferkeit f (-; no pl) bravery, courage.

tappen ['tapən] v/i 1. (sn) a) pad, b) grope one's way. 2. (h) grope (or fumble) (about) (nach for): a. fig. im dunkeln ~ be groping in the dark.

Tara ['ta:ra] f (-; Taren) † tare.

Tarantel [ta'rantəl] f (-; -n) tarantula.

Tarif [ta'ri:f] m (-s; -e) a) scale of charges, b) rate, c) charge, d) pay scale, e) tariff. **~abschluß** m wage settlement. **~autono‚mie** f free collective bargaining. **~kon‚flikt** m pay dispute.

ta'riflich adj tariff ..., standard ...

Ta'rif‖lohn m standard wage(s). **~part-ner** m party to a wage agreement, pl union(s) and management. **~runde** f pay round. **~satz** m 1. (tariff) rate. 2. (standard) wage rate. **~verhandlungen** pl wage negotiations. **~vertrag** m wage agreement.

tarnen ['tarnən] v/t (h) camouflage.

'Tarn‖farbe f camouflage colo(u)r. **~organisati‚on** f cover organization.

'Tarnung f (-; -en) camouflage, fig. a. cover.

Tasche ['taʃə] f (-; -n) 1. a) (shopping etc) bag, b) (hand)bag, Am. purse. 2. pocket: et. aus der eigenen ~ bezahlen pay for s.th. out of one's own pocket; den Gewinn in die eigene ~ stek-ken pocket the profit; F fig. j-n in die ~ stecken put s.o. in one's pocket; den Auftrag haben wir in der ~! the order is in the bag; F j-m auf der ~ liegen live off s.o.; in die eigene ~ arbeiten line one's (own) pockets; tief in die ~ grei-fen (müssen) have to) dig deep into one's pockets.

'Taschen‖buch n paperback. **~dieb**(in f) m pickpocket. **~feuerzeug** n pocket lighter. **~for‚mat** n pocket size: im ~ pocket-size(d). **~geld** n pocket money. **~ka‚lender** m pocket diary. **~lampe** f torch, Am. flashlight. **~messer** n pen-knife. **~rechner** m pocket calculator. **~spiegel** m pocket mirror. **~tuch** n handkerchief. **~uhr** f fob watch. **~wör-terbuch** n pocket dictionary.

Tasse ['tasə] f (-; -n) cup: e-e ~ Tee a cup of tea; F contp. trübe ~ drip.

Tastatur [tasta'tu:r] f (-; -en) keyboard, keys. **Taste** ['tastə] f (-; -n) key, a. push button.

tasten ['tastən] (h) I v/t touch, feel. II v/i (nach for) a. fig. grope, fumble. III sich ~ grope one's way. **'tastend** adj groping, fig. a. tentative. **'Tasten‖instru‚ment** n ♪ keyboard in-strument. **~tele‚fon** n push-button tele-phone.

'Taster m (-s; -) 1. zo. feeler. 2. ⊕ a) key, b) sensor.

'Tastsinn m (-[e]s; no pl) sense of touch.

tat [ta:t] pret of tun.

Tat f (-; -en) 1. a) deed, act, b) achieve-ment, feat, c) action: er ist ein Mann der ~ he is a man of action; ~ umset-zen 3. 2. (criminal) offen|ce (Am. -se), crime: auf frischer ~ ertappen catch s.o. redhanded. 3. in der ~ indeed.

Tatar [ta'ta:r] n (-[s]; no pl) gastr. spiced raw minced beef.

'Tatbestand m state of affairs, 𝕤𝕥𝕤 facts of the case.

'Tatendrang m thirst for action.

'tatenlos adj inactive.

Täter ['tɛ:tər] m (-s; -), **'Täterin** f (-; -nen) culprit, 𝕤𝕥𝕤 offender.

tätig ['tɛ:tɪç] adj active (a. volcano), busy: ~ sein als a) work as, b) act as; ~ sein bei work for a firm, work at an institute etc; ~ werden act, take action.

tätigen ['tɛ:tɪgən] v/t (h) effect, transact (business), make (purchases).

'Tätigkeit f (-; -en) a) activity, b) occupa-tion, job, c) function, d) physiol., ⊕ etc action: in ~ in action; welche ~ üben Sie aus? what is your job?

'Tätigkeitsfeld n field of activity.

'Tatkraft f (-; no pl) energy, drive, enter-prise. **'tatkräftig** adj energetic, active: ~e Hilfe effective help.

tätlich ['tɛ:tlɪç] adj violent: 𝕤𝕥𝕤 ~e Belei-digung assault and battery; ~ werden become violent; gegen j-n ~ werden assault s.o. **'Tätlichkeit** f (-; -en) (act of) violence, 𝕤𝕥𝕤 assault (and battery).

'Tatort m scene of the crime.

tätowieren [tɛto'vi:rən] v/t (h) tattoo. **Täto'wierung** f (-; -en) tattoo.

'Tatsache f fact: j-n vor vollendete ~n stellen confront s.o. with a fait accompli; **~ ist, daß** the fact is that; **das ändert nichts an der ~, daß** that doesn't alter the fact that; **den ~n ins Auge blicken** face the facts.

'Tatsachenbericht *m* documentary.

'tatsächlich **I** *adj* actual, real. **II** *adv* actually, really, in fact: **~? really?

tätscheln ['tɛːtʃəln] *v/t* (h) pat.

tatterig ['tatərɪç] *adj* F doddery, shaky.

Tatze ['tatsə] *f* (-; -n) paw.

Tau¹ [taʊ] *n* (-[e]s; -e) rope.

Tau² *m* (-[e]s; *no pl*) dew.

taub [taʊp] *adj* **1.** deaf (*fig. gegen, für* to): **auf einem Ohr ~** deaf in one ear. **2.** empty¹ (*nut*), dead (*rock*), numb (*limbs*).

Taube¹ ['taʊbə] *m*, *f* (-n; -n) deaf person: **die ~n** the deaf.

'Taube² *f* (-; -n) *zo.* pigeon, *a. pol.* dove.

'Taubenschlag *m* dovecote.

'Taubheit *f* (-; *no pl*) **1.** deafness. **2.** numbness. **taubstumm** *adj* deaf and dumb. 'Taubstumme *m*, *f* (-n; -n) deaf-mute. 'Taubstummensprache *f* deaf-and-dumb language.

tauchen ['taʊxən] **I** *v/i* (sn) dive (*nach* for), *a.* skin-dive, *submarine: a.* submerge. **II** *v/t* (h) dip, immerse: **j-n ~** duck s.o.

'Taucher *m* (-s; -) (*sports:* skin) diver. **~anzug** *m* diving suit, *a.* wetsuit. **~brille** *f* diving goggles. **~glocke** *f* diving bell. **~maske** *f* diving mask.

'Tauch|sieder *m* (-s; -) ⚡ immersion heater. **~sport** *m* skin diving.

tauen ['taʊən] **I** *v/i* (sn) thaw, melt. **II** *v/impers* (h) **es taut** a) it is thawing, b) dew is falling.

'Taufbecken *n* font. **Taufe** ['taʊfə] *f* (-; -n) baptism, *a.* christening: **aus der ~ heben** stand godfather (*or* godmother) to, *fig.* launch. **'taufen** *v/t* (h) **1.** baptize, christen. **2.** call. **Täufling** ['tɔʏflɪŋ] *m* (-s; -e) child (*or* person) to be baptized. **'Taufname** *m* Christian (*esp. Am.* given) name. **'Taufschein** *m* certificate of baptism. **'Taufstein** *m* font.

taugen ['taʊgən] *v/i* (h) (**zu, für** for) be suited, be of use: **nichts ~** be no good; **taugt es (et)was?** is it any good?

tauglich ['taʊklɪç] *adj* a) suitable (**für, zu** for), b) ✗ fit (for service). **'Tauglichkeit** *f* (-; *no pl*) a) suitability, b) fitness.

Taumel ['taʊməl] *m* (-s; *no pl*) **1.** dizziness. **2.** *fig.* a) whirl, b) rapture, frenzy.

taum(e)lig ['taʊm(ə)lɪç] *adj* dizzy.

taumeln ['taʊməln] *v/i* (sn) reel, stagger.

Tausch [taʊʃ] *m* (-[e]s; -e) exchange, F swap, barter. **'tauschen** *v/t, v/i* (h) exchange (*a. looks etc*), *a.* barter, F swap (**gegen** for): **ich möchte nicht mit ihr ~** I wouldn't like to be in her shoes.

täuschen ['tɔʏʃən] (h) **I** *v/t* a) mislead, deceive, b) cheat, fool: **wenn mich nicht alles täuscht** if I am not very much mistaken; **wenn mich mein Gedächtnis nicht täuscht** if my memory serves me right; **sich ~ lassen** be taken in (**von** by). **II** *v/i* be deceptive, *sports:* feint, fake a blow *etc.* **III** **sich ~** be mistaken, be wrong (*in j-m* about s.o.): **da täuscht er sich aber!** he's very much mistaken there! **'täuschend** *adj* a) deceptive, b) striking: **~ ähnlich sehen** look remarkably like s.o.

'Tausch|geschäft *n*, **~handel** *m* barter, F swap. **~ob,jekt** *n* object of exchange.

'Täuschung *f* (-; -en) a) deception, b) delusion, c) mistake, d) ⚖ deceit: **optische ~** optical illusion.

'Täuschungs|ma,növer *n* feint, diversion. **~versuch** *m* attempt to deceive.

tausend ['taʊzənt] *adj* (a) thousand: **~ und aber ~** thousands and thousands of. **Tausend** *n* (-s; -e) thousand: **zu ~en** by the thousand. **'Tausender** *m* (-s; -) F thousand mark note. **'tausendfach** **I** *adj* thousandfold. **II** *adv* → **tausendmal. 'Tausendfüß(l)er** [-fy:s(l)ər] *m* (-s; -) *zo.* centipede. **'tausendjährig** *adj* of a thousand years, millennial. **'tausendmal** *adv* a thousand times. **'tausendst** *adj*, **'Tausendste** *m*, *f* (-n; -n) thousandth. **'Tausendstel** *n* (-s; -) thousandth (part).

'Tautropfen *m* dewdrop.

'Tauwetter *n a. fig. pol.* thaw.

'Tauziehen *n a. fig.* tug-of-war.

Taxameter [taksa'me:tər] *m* (-s; -) taximeter.

Taxator [ta'ksa:tor] *m* (-s; -en [taksa'to:-rən]) ✝, ⚖ valuer, assessor.

Taxe ['taksə] *f* (-; -n) **1.** a) rate, fee, b) tax. **2.** → **Taxi** ['taksi] *n* (-s; -s) taxi, cab: **~ fahren** a) drive a taxi, b) go by taxi.

taxieren [ta'ksi:rən] *v/t* (h) **1.** estimate, ✝, ⚖ value, assess. **2.** F size up.

'Taxifahrer(in *f*) *m* taxi driver.

'**Taxistand** *m* taxi rank.

Teak [ti:k] *n* (-s; *no pl*), **~holz** *n* teak.

Technik ['tɛçnɪk] *f* (-; -en) **1.** *no pl* a) technology, technics, b) engineering. **2.** *a. art, sports, etc:* technique.

'**Techniker** *m* (-s; -) (technical) engineer, *a. sports etc:* technician.

'**technisch** *adj* engineering (*process etc*), *a. art, sports, etc:* technical, technological (*a. age, progress, etc*): *sports:* **~e Disziplin** field event; **~er K.o.** technical knockout; **~es Personal** technical staff; **~e Hochschule** college (*Am.* institute) of technology; **~ begabt** gifted technically.

technisieren [tɛçni'zi:rən] *v/t* (h) mechanize.

Technokrat [tɛçno'kra:t] *m* (-en; -en) technocrat.

Technologie [tɛçnolo'gi:] *f* (-; -n) technology. **Technolo'gietrans,fer** *m* technology transfer. **technologisch** [tɛçno'lo:gɪʃ] *adj* technological.

Teddybär ['tɛdi-] *m* teddy (bear).

Tee [te:] *m* (-s; -s) **1.** tea: *~en ~ machen* make some tea; *e-n ~ trinken* have a cup of tea; → *abwarten* II. **2.** tea party. **~beutel** *m* tea bag. **~büchse** *f* tea caddy. **~Ei** *n* infuser, tea egg, *esp. Am.* tea ball. **~gebäck** *n* biscuits, *Am.* cookies. **~haus** *n* teahouse. **~kanne** *f* teapot. **~kessel** *m* teakettle. **~löffel** *m* teaspoon. **~ma,schine** *f* tea-urn.

Teer [te:r] *m* (-[e]s; -e) tar.

teeren ['te:rən] *v/t* (h) tar.

'**Tee|sieb** *n* tea strainer. **~stube** *f* tearoom. **~tasse** *f* teacup. **~wagen** *m* tea trolley (*Am.* wagon).

Teich [taɪç] *m* (-[e]s; -e) pond, pool.

Teig [taɪk] *m* (-[e]s; -e) dough. **teigig** ['taɪgɪç] *adj* doughy, pasty (*a. fig.*).

'**Teigwaren** *pl* pasta.

Teil [taɪl] *m*, *n* (-[e]s; -e) part (*a.* ⊙), share, *a.* ⊙ component, element: *esp.* ⚖ **beide ~e** both sides; *ein ~ davon* part of it; *zum ~* partly; *zum großen* (*or größten*) *~* largely, for the most part; *der größte ~* the greater part (*gen* of); *zu gleichen ~en* in equal shares; *sein ~ beitragen* do one's bit; *sich sein ~ denken* have one's own thoughts about it; *ich für mein ~* I for my part.

'**Teilansicht** *f* partial view.

'**teilbar** *adj* divisible.

'**Teilbetrag** *m* partial amount.

'**Teilchen** *n* (-s; -) *a. phys.* particle.

teilen ['taɪlən] (h) **I** *v/t* a) divide, b) distribute, share out, c) share: *die Kosten ~* share expenses; *Freud und Leid mit j-m ~* share s.o.'s joys and troubles. **II** *sich ~* divide, *curtain:* part; *sich in et. ~* share s.th.; → *geteilt*.

'**Teiler** *m* (-s; -) ℞ divisor.

'**Teilerfolg** *m* partial success.

'**teilhaben** *v/i* (*irr, sep, -ge-*, h, → *haben*) (*an dat* in) participate, share.

Teilhaber ['taɪlha:bər] *m* (-s; -) ⚒ partner, associate. '**Teilhaberschaft** *f* (-; *no pl*) partnership.

'**Teilkaskoversicherung** *f mot.* partial coverage insurance.

'**Teillieferung** *f* part delivery.

Teilnahme ['taɪlna:mə] *f* (-; *no pl*) (*an dat*) **1.** a) participation (in), b) attendance (at). **2.** *fig.* a) interest (in), b) sympathy (with), c) condolence(s).

'**teilnahmeberechtigt** *adj* eligible.

'**teilnahmslos** *adj* indifferent, listless, apathetic. '**Teilnahmslosigkeit** *f* (-; *no pl*) indifference, listlessness, apathy.

'**teilnahmsvoll** *adj* sympathetic.

'**teilnehmen** *v/i* (*irr, sep, -ge-*, h, → *nehmen*) (*an dat*) **1.** a) take part (in), b) be present (at), attend (*s.th.*). **2.** *fig.* a) take an interest (in), b) sympathize (with).

'**Teilnehmer** *m* (-s; -), '**Teilnehmerin** *f* (-; -nen) participant, *sports etc:* competitor, entrant, *teleph.* subscriber.

'**Teilpro,these** *f* partial (denture).

'**teils** [taɪls] *adv* partly.

'**Teilstrecke** *f* bus etc: (fare) stage, 🚆 section, *w.s.* stage, *a. sports:* leg.

'**Teilstrich** *m* ⊙ graduation mark.

'**Teilstück** *n* section.

'**Teilung** *f* (-; -en) division (*a. biol.,* ℞).

'**teilweise I** *adj* partial. **II** *adv* partly, partially, in part.

'**Teilzahlung** *f* **1.** part payment. **2.** payment by instal(l)ments: *auf ~ kaufen* buy on instal(l)ment (*or* hire purchase).

'**Teilzahlungsvertrag** *m* hire-purchase contract.

'**Teilzeit|arbeit** *f*, **~beschäftigung** *f* part-time employment (*or* job).

Teint [tɛ̃] *m* (-s; -s) complexion.

Tele ['te:lə] *n* (-[s]; -[s]) F telephoto lens.

Telefax ['te:ləfaks] *n* (-; -[e]), '**telefaxen** *v/t* (h) telefax.

Telefon [tele'foːn] n (-s; -e) (tele)phone: **am ~** on the (tele)phone; **ans ~ gehen** answer the (tele)phone; **~ haben** be on the (tele)phone. **~anschluß** m telephone connection: **~ haben** be on the (tele)phone. **~appa‚rat** m telephone.

Telefonat [telefo'naːt] n (-[e]s; -e) → *Telefongespräch.*

Tele'fon|buch n phone book, telephone directory. **~gebühr** f telephone charge. **~gespräch** n telephone conversation, phone call. **~hörer** m receiver.

telefonieren [telefo'niːrən] v/i (h) (tel-e)phone: **mit j-m ~** talk to s.o. over the (tele)phone; **sie telefoniert gerade** is on the phone; **nach Amerika ~** make a (tele)phone call to America; **darf ich mal ~?** may I use your (tele)phone?

tele'fonisch I adj telephonic. **II** adv by (or over the) (tele)phone: **~ übermitteln** (tele)phone; **sind Sie ~ zu erreichen?** are you on the phone?, can I call you?

Telefonist [telefo'nıst] m (-en; -en), **Telefo'nistin** f (-; -nen) switchboard operator.

Tele'fon|karte f phonecard. **~netz** n telephone network. **~nummer** f (tele)phone number. **~verbindung** f telephone connection. **~zelle** f telephone box (or booth), call box. **~zen‚trale** f (telephone) exchange, of firm: switchboard.

Telegraf [tele'graːf] m (-en; -en) telegraph. **Telegrafie** [telegra'fiː] f (-; no pl) telegraphy: **drahtlose ~** radiotelegraphy. **telegrafieren** [telegra'fiːrən] v/t, v/i (h) telegraph, wire. **tele'grafisch I** adj telegraphic: **~e Überweisung** telegraphic (or cable) transfer. **II** adv by telegram, by wire. **Telegrafist** [telegra'fıst] m (-en; -en), **Telegra'fistin** f (-; -nen) telegraphist.

Telegramm [tele'gram] n (-s; -e) telegram. **~anschrift** f telegraphic address. **~stil** m (im ~ in) telegraphese.

'**Teleko‚pierer** m (-s; -) telecopier.

'**Teleobjek‚tiv** n telephoto lens.

Telepathie [telepa'tiː] f (-; no pl) telepathy.

telepathisch [tele'paːtıʃ] adj telepathic.

Teleskop [tele'skoːp] n (-s; -e) telescope.

tele'skopisch adj telescopic.

Telespiel ['teːlə-] n TV game.

Telex ['teːlɛks] n (-; -[e]), '**telexen** v/t (h) telex.

Teller ['tɛlər] m (-s; -) **1.** plate. **2.** ☉, a. on *ski stick:* disc, disk.

'**Tellervoll** m (-s; -) plateful.

Tempel ['tɛmpəl] m (-s; -) temple.

Temperament [tɛmpera'mɛnt] n (-[e]s; -e) a) temperament, temper, b) verve, vivacity, F pep: **hitziges ~** hot temper.

tempera'mentlos adj lifeless.

tempera'mentvoll adj (high-)spirited.

Temperatur [tɛmpera'tuːr] f (-; -en) (**bei e-r ~ von** at a) temperature (of); ♀ **~ haben** have (or run) a temperature; **~anstieg** m rise in temperature. **~sturz** m sudden drop in temperature.

temperieren [tɛmpə'riːrən] v/t (h) a. ♪ temper.

Tempo ['tɛmpo] n (-s; -s, -pi) tempo (a. ♪), speed, rate, pace: **das ~ bestimmen** (**durchhalten, forcieren** or **steigern**) set (stand, force) the pace; **~!** step on it!, go! '**Tempolimit** n mot. speed limit.

Tempomat [tɛmpo'maːt] m (-en; -en) mot. cruise control, speedhold.

Tendenz [tɛn'dɛnts] f (-; -en) tendency, trend (a. ♥), contp. bias, slant. **tenden-ziös** [tɛndɛn'tsjøːs] adj tendentious.

tendieren [tɛn'diːrən] v/i (h) tend (**nach, zu** to).

Tennis ['tɛnıs] n (-; no pl) tennis. **~ball** m tennis ball. **~halle** f covered court. **~platz** m tennis court. **~schläger** m tennis racket. **~spieler(in** f) m tennis player. **~tur‚nier** n tennis tournament.

Tenor¹ ['teːnɔr] m (-s; no pl) tenor, substance.

Tenor² [te'noːr] m (-s; ⸚e) ♪ **1.** (a. **~stim-me** f, **~par‚tie** f) tenor (voice, part). **2.** tenor (singer or player).

Teppich ['tɛpıç] m (-s; -e) carpet: fig. et. unter den ~ kehren sweep s.th. under the carpet; F bleib auf dem ~! be reasonable. **~boden** m fitted carpet, wall-to-wall carpeting. **~fliese** f carpet tile. **~händler** m carpet dealer.

Termin [tɛr'miːn] m (-s; -e) **1.** a) (set) date, time limit, b) deadline: **e-n ~ fest-setzen** fix a date etc; **bis zu diesem ~** by this date. **2.** (**sich e-n ~ geben las-sen** make an) appointment (**bei** with one's doctor etc). **3.** ⚖ hearing.

Ter'mindruck m time pressure: **unter ~ stehen** be pressed for time.

ter'mingebunden adj scheduled (work).

ter'mingemäß adj and adv on schedule.

Ter'minka‚lender m appointments book, 🔢 cause list, Am. calendar: **e-n vollen ~ haben** have a busy schedule.

Terminologie [tɛrminolo'giː] f (-; -n) terminology.

Ter'minplan m schedule.

Termite [tɛr'miːtə] f (-; -n) zo. termite.

Terpentin [tɛrpɛn'tiːn] n, m (-s; no pl) 🌿 turpentine.

Terrain [tɛ'rɛ̃ː] n (-s; -s) **1.** terrain. **2.** plot of land, (building) site.

Terrasse [tɛ'rasə] f (-; -n) terrace.

ter'rassenförmig adj terraced.

Ter'rassenhaus n stepped building.

Ter'rassentür f French window.

territorial [tɛrito'riaːl] adj territorial.

Territorium [tɛri'toːriʊm] n (-s; -rien) territory.

Terror ['tɛrɔr] m (-s; no pl) terror.

'Terroranschlag m terrorist attack.

terrorisieren [tɛrori'ziːrən] v/t (h) terrorize. **Terrorismus** [tɛro'rɪsmʊs] m (-; no pl) terrorism. **Terrorist** [-'rɪst] m (-en; -en), **Terro'ristin** f (-; -nen) terrorist. **terro'ristisch** adj terrorist.

Terz [tɛrts] f (-; -en) **1.** ♪ third. **2.** fenc. tierce.

Terzett [tɛr'tsɛt] n (-[e]s; -e) ♪ trio.

Tesafilm ['teːza-] m (TM) sellotape (TM), esp. Am. Scotch tape (TM).

Test [tɛst] m (-[e]s; -s, a. -e) test.

Testament [tɛsta'mɛnt] n (-[e]s; -e) **1.** (last) will, 🔢 last will and testament: **sein ~ machen** make a will. **2.** eccl. **Altes (Neues) ~** Old (New) Testament.

testamentarisch [tɛstamɛn'taːrɪʃ] **I** adj testamentary. **II** adv by will.

Testa'ments|eröffnung f opening of the will. **~vollstrecker** m executor.

testen ['tɛstən] v/t (h) test.

'Testper‚son f (test) subject.

'Teststrecke f mot. test track.

Tetanus(schutz)impfung ['teː‚tanʊs-] f 💉 tetanus vaccination.

teuer ['tɔyər] **I** adj expensive, dear: **wie ~ ist es?** how much is it?; **Fleisch ist teurer geworden** meat prices have gone up; fig. **j-m ~ sein** be dear to s.o. **II** adv dear(ly): **das wird ihn ~ zu stehen kommen** he will have to pay dearly for that. **'Teuerung** f (-; -en) high (or rising) prices, high cost of living.

'Teuerungsrate f rate of price increases.

Teufel ['tɔyfəl] m (-s; -) devil: **der ~** the Devil; F **wer (wo, was) zum ~?** who (where, what) the devil (or hell)?; **wie der ~, auf ~ komm raus** like blazes; **in (des) ~s Küche kommen** get into a hell of a mess; **j-n zum ~ jagen** send s.o. packing; **der ~ war los** all hell had broken loose; **das Geld ist zum ~** the money is down the drain; **mal' den ~ nicht an die Wand!** don't tempt fate; **scher dich zum ~!** go to hell!

'Teufelskerl m of a fellow.

'Teufelskreis m fig. vicious circle.

teuflisch ['tɔyflɪʃ] adj devilish, fig. a. hellish.

Text [tɛkst] m (-[e]s; -e) text, words, lyrics. **'Textbuch** n libretto. **'Texter** m (-s; -) **1.** copywriter. **2.** songwriter.

Textilien [tɛks'tiːliən] pl textiles.

Tex'tilindu‚strie f textile industry.

'Text|kri‚tik f textual criticism. **~verarbeitung** f word processing. **~verarbeitungssy‚stem** n word processor.

Theater [te'aːtər] n (-s; -) **1.** theatre, Am. theater: **zum ~ gehen** go on the stage; **ins ~ gehen** go to the theatre. **2.** fig. a) play-acting, b) contr. farce, c) fuss: **~ spielen** put on an act; **mach kein ~!** don't make a fuss! **~abonne‚ment** n theatre subscription. **~besuch** m visit to the theatre. **~besucher** m theat/regoer (Am. -er-). **~karte** f theat/re (Am. -er) ticket. **~kasse** f box office. **~probe** f rehearsal. **~stück** n (stage) play. **~vorstellung** f theatrical performance. **~zettel** m playbill.

theatralisch [tea'traːlɪʃ] adj theatrical.

Theke ['teːkə] f (-; -n) bar, a. counter.

Thema ['teːma] n (-s; -men) subject, a. topic, ♪ etc theme: **beim ~ bleiben** stick to the point; **das ~ wechseln** change the subject. **Thematik** [te'maːtɪk] f (-; -en) subject (matter).

Themenkreis ['teː‚mən-] m subject area.

Theologe [teo'loːgə] m (-n; -n) theologian. **Theologie** [teolo'giː] f (-; -n) theology. **theo'logisch** adj theological.

Theoretiker [teo're'tikər] m (-s; -) theorist. **theo'retisch** adj and adv theoretical(ly), adv a. in theory. **theoretisieren** [teoreti'ziːrən] v/i (h) theorize. **Theorie** [teo'riː] f (-; -n) theory.

Therapeut [tera'pɔyt] *m* (-en; -en), **The-ra'peutin** *f* (-; -nen) therapist.
thera'peutisch *adj* therapeutic.
Therapie [tera'pi:] *f* (-; -n) therapy.
Thermal|bad [tɛr'ma:l-] *n* **1.** thermal spa. **2.** thermal bath. **~quelle** *f* thermal spring.
Thermik ['tɛrmɪk] *f* (-; *no pl*) thermionics. **'thermisch** *adj* thermic.
Thermody'namik [tɛrmo-] *f* thermodynamics.
'Thermoele,ment *n* thermocouple.
Thermometer [tɛrmo'me:tər] *n* (-s; -) thermometer: *das ~ zeigt 5 Grad über (unter) Null* the thermometer is at (or shows) 5 degrees above (below) zero.
thermonukle'ar *adj* thermonuclear.
Thermosflasche ['tɛrmɔs-] *f* (*TM*) Thermos (flask) (*TM*).
Thermostat [tɛrmo'sta:t] *m* (-[e]s, -en; -e[n]) thermostat.
'Thermowäsche *f* thermal underwear.
These ['te:zə] *f* (-; -n) **1.** thesis. **2.** theory.
Thrombose [trɔm'bo:zə] *f* (-; -n) 🩸 thrombosis.
Thron [tro:n] *m* (-[e]s; -e) throne.
thronen ['tro:nən] *v/i* (h) be enthroned.
'Thronerbe *m* heir to the throne.
'Thronfolge *f* succession to the throne.
'Thronfolger *m* (-s; -), **'Thronfolgerin** *f* (-; -nen) successor to the throne.
Thunfisch ['tu:n-] *m* **1.** tunny. **2.** 🐟 tuna.
Thymian ['ty:mia:n] *m* (-s; -e) 🌿 thyme.
Tibet ['ti:bɛt] *n* (-s) Tibet. **Tibeter** [ti'be:tər] *m* (-s; -), **Ti'beterin** *f* (-; -nen), **ti'betisch** *adj* Tibetan.
Tick [tɪk] *m* (-[e]s; -s) quirk, tic.
ticken ['tɪkən] *v/i* (h) tick.
tief [ti:f] **I** *adj* deep (*a. fig.*), low, *fig.* profound (*knowledge etc*): *aus ~stem Herzen* from the bottom of one's heart; *im ~sten Winter* in the dead of winter. **II** *adv* deep, low, *fig. a.* deeply, b) far: *~ in Gedanken* deep in thought; *~ enttäuscht* badly disappointed; *~ schlafen* be fast asleep, sleep soundly; *bis ~ in die Nacht* far into the night.
Tief *n* (-s; -s) *meteor.* low, depression.
'Tiefbau *m* (-[e]s; *no pl*) civil engineering. **~ingeni,eur** *m* construction engineer.
'tiefblau *adj* deep blue.
'Tiefdruck *m* (-[e]s; *no pl*) **1.** *meteor.* low pressure. **2.** intaglio (printing). **~gebiet** *n* cyclone, low-pressure area.

'Tiefe *f* (-; -n) **1.** depth, *fig. a.* profundity. **2.** *pl radio etc:* bass.
'Tiefebene *f* lowland(s).
'tiefempfunden *adj* heartfelt.
'Tiefen|inter,view *n* (in-)depth interview. **~psycho,logie** *f* depth psychology. **~regler** *m* radio etc: bass control. **~schärfe** *f phot.* depth of focus.
'tiefernst *adj* very grave.
'Tief|flug *m* low-level flight. **~gang** *m* (-[e]s; *no pl*) **1.** ⚓ draught. **2.** *fig.* depth. **~ga,rage** *f* underground car park.
'tiefgefroren *adj* deep-frozen.
'tiefgreifend *adj* far-reaching.
'tiefgründig [-ɡryndɪç] *adj* profound.
'Tiefkühlfach *n* freezing compartment.
'Tiefkühlkost *f* frozen foods.
'Tiefkühltruhe *f* freezer, deep-freeze.
'tiefliegend *adj* **1.** deep-(lying). **2.** deep-set (*eyes*). **3.** *fig.* deep(-seated).
'Tiefpunkt *m fig.* low: *e-n seelischen ~ haben* feel very depressed.
'Tiefschlag *m a. fig.* hit below the belt.
'tiefschürfend *adj fig.* profound.
'tiefschwarz *adj* jet-black.
'Tiefsee *f* deep sea.
'tiefsinnig *adj* profound.
'Tiefstand *m* (-[e]s; *no pl*) low: *e-n absoluten ~ erreichen* hit an all-time low.
Tiegel ['ti:ɡəl] *m* (-s; -) saucepan.
Tier [ti:r] *n* (-[e]s; -e) animal (*a. fig.*), beast, *fig. contp.* brute: F *großes (or hohes) ~* bigwig, big shot. **~art** *f* (animal) species. **~arzt** *m* veterinary surgeon, *Am.* veterinarian, F vet. **~freund** *m* animal lover. **~handlung** *f* pet shop. **~heim** *n* home for animals.
'tierisch I *adj* animal ..., *fig. contp. a.* brutish: **~e Fette** animal fats. **II** *adv* F *fig.* awfully, terribly.
'Tier|kreis *m* (-es; *no pl*) *astr.* zodiac. **~kreiszeichen** *n* sign of the zodiac. **2lieb** *adj* fond of animals. **~medi,zin** *f* veterinary medicine. **~nahrung** *f* pet food. **~park** *m* zoological gardens, zoo. **~pfleger** *m* keeper. **~quäle'rei** *f* cruelty to animals. **~reich** *n* animal kingdom. **~schutzverein** *m* society for the prevention of cruelty to animals. **~versuch** *m* animal experiment. **~welt** *f* animal world.
Tiger ['ti:ɡər] *m* (-s; -) tiger. **'Tigerfell** *n* tiger skin. **'Tigerin** *f* (-; -nen) tigress.
tigern ['ti:ɡərn] *v/i* (sn) F traipse, trot.

Tilde ['tɪldə] f (-; -n) ling. tilde.

tilgbar ['tɪlk-] adj ♱ redeemable. **tilgen** ['tɪlɡən] v/t (h) **1.** wipe out (a. fig.), blot out (a. fig. memories etc), print. delete, cancel, a. fig. efface, erase. **2.** ♱ a) pay off, b) redeem (loan). '**Tilgung** f (-; -en) ♱ repayment, redemption.

timen ['taɪmən] v/t (h) time: **gut** (**schlecht**) **getimt** well (badly) timed.

Tinktur [tɪŋk'tuːr] f (-; -en) tincture.

Tinnef ['tɪnɛf] m (-s; no pl) F rubbish.

Tinte ['tɪntə] f (-; -n) ink: F **in der ~ sitzen** be in the soup.

'**Tinten|fisch** m **1.** squid. **2.** octopus. **~klecks** m inkblot. **~kuli** m stylograph. **~stift** m indelible pencil.

Tip [tɪp] m (-s; -s) tip, a. hint: **ein sicherer ~** a sure bet; **j-m e-n ~ geben** a) give s.o. a tip, b) tip s.o. off.

tippen ['tɪpən] (h) **I** v/i **1.** **~ an** (acc) tap. **2.** F a) do the Lotto, b) do the pools. **3.** F **~ auf** (acc) tip: **ich tippe auf ihn** my bet is on him. **4.** F type. **II** v/t **5.** F type. '**Tippfehler** m typing error.

Tippse ['tɪpsə] f (-; -n) F contp. typist.

'**tipp'topp** adj F first-class: **~ gekleidet** immaculately dressed; **~ sauber** spick and span.

'**Tippzettel** m lotto (or pools) coupon.

Tisch [tɪʃ] m (-[e]s; -e) table: **er ist zu ~** he's having his lunch hour; **am ~ sitzen** sit at the table; **bei ~ sitzen** sit at table; **den ~ decken** (**abräumen**) lay (clear) the table; fig. **reinen ~ machen** make a clean sweep (or make tabula rasa) (**mit** of); **unter den ~ fallen** fall flat; **die Sache ist auf dem** (**vom**) **~** the matter is on (off) the table; → **grün. ~dame** f partner at table. **~decke** f tablecloth. **⊘fertig** adj ready(-to-)serve. **~gebet** n **das ~ sprechen** say grace. **~karte** f place card.

Tischler ['tɪʃlər] m (-s; -) **1.** joiner. **2.** cabinetmaker. **Tischle'rei** f (-; -en) **1.** no pl joinery. **2.** joiner's workshop. '**tischlern** (h) **I** v/t make. **II** v/i do joiner's work.

'**Tisch|ordnung** f seating plan. **~platte** f a) tabletop, b) leaf. **~rede** f after-dinner speech. **~rücken** n table turning.

'**Tischtennis** n table tennis. **~ball** m table tennis ball. **~schläger** m table tennis bat (Am. paddle).

'**Tisch|tuch** n tablecloth. **~wein** m table

wine. **~zeit** f lunch hour (or break).

Titan [ti'taːn] n (-s; no pl) ♆ titanium.

Titel ['tiːtəl] m (-s; -) title. **~bild** n frontispiece (of book), cover picture (of magazine). **~blatt** n title page (of book), front page (of magazine). **~geschichte** f cover story. **~halter** m sports: titleholder. **~kampf** m title match (boxing: bout). **~melo,die** f theme tune. **~rolle** f title role. **~seite** f → **Titelblatt**. **~verteidiger** m sports: titleholder.

Titten ['tɪtən] pl V tits, boobs.

Toast [toːst] m (-[e]s; -e, -s) **1.** toast: **e-n ~ ausbringen** → **toasten** II. **2.** gastr. toast. '**toasten** (h) **I** v/t toast (bread). **II** v/i propose (or drink) a toast (**auf** acc to). '**Toaster** m (-s; -) toaster.

toben ['toːbən] v/i (h) **1.** a. fig. rage. **2.** children: romp.

'**tobsüchtig** adj raving mad, frantic.

'**Tobsuchtsanfall** m F fig. **e-n ~ bekommen** fly into a tantrum.

Tochter ['tɔxtər] f (-; ⸚) **1.** daughter. **2.** → **~gesellschaft** f subsidiary (company).

Tod [toːt] m (-es; -e) death: **den ~ finden** be killed; fig. **et. zu ~e reiten** flog s.th. to death; F **j-n zu ~e erschrecken** (**langweilen**) frighten (bore) s.o. to death (or stiff); **auf den ~ nicht ausstehen können** loathe, hate like poison.

'**tod'ernst I** adj deadly serious. **II** adv in dead earnest.

Todes|angst f **1.** fear of death. **2.** fig. mortal fear: **Todesängste ausstehen** be scared to death. **~anzeige** f obituary (notice). **~fall** m (**im ~** in case of) death. **~gefahr** f mortal danger. **~jahr** n year of s.o.'s death. **~kampf** m throes of death. **~kandi,dat** m doomed man, F goner. **~opfer** pl casualties, victims: **Zahl der ~** a. death toll. **~stoß** m death blow. **~strafe** f death penalty, capital punishment: **bei ~** on penalty of death. **~stunde** f hour of death. **~tag** m day (w.s. anniversary) of s.o.'s death. **~ursache** f cause of death. **~urteil** n death sentence (fig. warrant). **~verachtung** f defiance of death: F **mit ~** unflinchingly. **~wunsch** m death wish. **~zelle** f death cell, pl a. death row.

'**Todfeind(in** f) m deadly enemy.

'**todgeweiht** adj doomed.

'**tod'krank** adj fatally ill.

tödlich ['tøːtlɪç] adj a) fatal, a. fig. mortal

(*für* to), lethal (*poison, dose, etc*), b) *fig.* deadly (*accuracy etc*): **~ verunglücken** be killed in an accident; F **sich ~ langweilen** be bored stiff; **~ beleidigt** mortally offended.

'**tod|müde** *adj* dead tired. '**tod'schick** *adj* F snazzy: **~ angezogen** *a.* dressed to kill. '**tod'sicher** F **I** *adj* dead sure, sure-fire (*method, tip, etc*): **e-e ~e Sache** a dead certainty, a cinch. **II** *adv* for sure: **er kommt ~** he is sure to come. '**Todsünde** *f* deadly (*or* mortal) sin.

Tohuwabohu [tohuva'bo:hu] *n* (-[s]; -s) complete chaos.

Toilette [töa'lɛtə] *f* (-; -n) **1.** lavatory, toilet, *Am.* bathroom, restroom: **öffentliche ~n** public conveniences. **2. ~ machen** make one's toilet. **3.** dress. **Toi'letten|ar,tikel** *m* toilet article. **~frau** *f*, **~mann** *m* lavatory attendant. **~pa,pier** *n* toilet paper. **~seife** *f* toilet soap. **~tisch** *m* dressing table.

toi, toi, toi [tɔy'tɔy'tɔy] *int* F **1.** (**unberufen**) **~, ~, ~!** touch wood! **2.** good luck!

tolerant [tole'rant] *adj* tolerant (**gegen** of). **Toleranz** [tole'rants] *f* (-; *no pl*) tolerance (**gegen** of). **Tole'ranzschwelle** *f* tolerance threshold.

tolerieren [tole'ri:rən] *v/t* (h) tolerate.

toll [tɔl] *adj* **1.** *a.* F *fig.* a) crazy, mad, b) wild: **e-e ~e Sache, ein ~es Ding** a wild affair, a wow. F terrific, fantastic: **ein ~er Kerl** a terrific guy; **e-e ~e Frau** a smasher; **er (es) ist nicht so ~** he (it) is not so hot. **II** *adv* **3.** F (**wie**) **~** like mad; **er spielt (ganz) ~** he's a fantastic player, he's terrific; → **treiben** 5.

tollen ['tɔlən] *v/i* (h, sn) romp.

'**Tollkirsche** *f* ♀ deadly nightshade.

'**tollkühn** *adj* foolhardy, daredevil. '**Tollkühnheit** *f* (-; *no pl*) foolhardiness. '**Tollwut** *f vet.* rabies. '**tollwütig** [-vy:tɪç] *adj* rabid.

'**Tolpatsch** ['tɔlpatʃ] *m* (-[e]s; -e), **Tölpel** ['tœlpəl] *m* (-s; -) clumsy oaf.

Tomate [to'ma:tə] *f* (-; -n) tomato.

Tombola ['tɔmbola] *f* (-; -s) raffle.

Ton[1] [to:n] *m* (-[e]s; -e) *geol.* clay.

Ton[2] *m* (-[e]s; **~e**) **1.** tone, sound (*a. film, TV*): F **er hat k-n ~ gesagt** he didn't say a word; **in den höchsten Tönen loben** sing the praises of; **große Töne spucken** talk big; **hat man Töne?** can you believe it? **2.** tone (of voice): **ich verbit-**

te mir diesen ~! don't take that tone with me; **e-n anderen ~ anschlagen** change one's tune; **den ~ angeben** call the tune, *in fashion etc*: set the trend; **es gehört zum guten ~ zu** *inf* it is good form to *inf.* **3.** *ling.* accent, stress: **den ~ legen auf** (*acc*) *a. fig.* emphasize. **4.** tone (*a. phot.*), shade: **~ in ~** in matching colo(u)rs; **rötlicher ~** tinge of red.

'**tonangebend** *adj* leading, *fashion:* trend-setting.

'**Ton|arm** *m* pickup (arm). **~art** *f* ♪ key. **~aufnahme** *f* (sound) recording. **~ausfall** *m* TV loss of sound.

Tonband *n* tape: **auf ~ aufnehmen** tape(-record). **~aufnahme** *f* tape recording. **~gerät** *n* tape recorder.

tönen[1] ['tø:nən] *v/i* (h) **1.** sound. **2.** F *fig.* sound off.

tönen[2] *v/t* (h) a) tint, b) tone down.

'**Tonerde** *f* argillaceous earth: **essigsaure ~** alumin(i)um acetate.

'**tönern** *adj* (of) clay.

'**Ton|fall** *m* (-[e]s; *no pl*) intonation. **~film** *m* sound film. **~fre,quenz** *f* acoustic (*or* audio) frequency.

'**Tongeschirr** *n* earthenware, pottery.

'**Tonhöhe** *f* pitch.

Tonikum ['to:nikʊm] *n* (-s; -ka) ♣ tonic.

'**Ton|ingeni,eur** *m* sound engineer. **~kamera** *f* sound camera. **~kopf** *m* sound (*video:* audio) head. **~lage** *f* pitch. **~leiter** *f* ♪ scale.

'**tonlos** *adj fig.* toneless, flat.

'**Tonmeister** *m* sound engineer.

Tonnage [tɔ'na:ʒə] *f* (-; -n) ♣ tonnage.

Tonne ['tɔnə] *f* (-; -n) **1.** barrel, cask. **2.** (metric) ton. **3.** ♣ a) buoy, b) (register) ton.

'**Ton|regler** *m* tone control. **~spur** *f*, **~streifen** *m film:* sound track. **~studio** *n* recording studio.

Tonsur [tɔn'zu:r] *f* (-; -en) tonsure.

'**Tontaubenschießen** *n* trap shooting.

'**Tontechniker** *m* sound engineer.

'**Tonträger** *m* sound carrier.

'**Tönung** *f* (-; -en) tinge, shade, *a. phot.* tone.

'**Tonwaren** *pl* earthenware, pottery.

Topas [to'pa:s] *m* (-es; -e) *min.* topaz.

Topf [tɔpf] *m* (-[e]s; **~e**) pot: *fig.* **in 'einen ~ werfen** lump together.

'**Töpfchen** ['tœpfçən] *n* (-s; -) pot, potty.

Töpfer ['tœpfər] *m* (-s; -) potter. **Töp-**

fe'rei f (-; -en) **1.** no pl pottery. **2.** potter's workshop. **'Töpferin** f (-; -nen) potter. **'Töpferscheibe** f potter's wheel. **'Töpferwaren** pl pottery.

'top'fit adj in top form.

'Topfpflanze f potted plant.

Topographie [topogra'fi:] f (-; -n) topography.

Topp [tɔp] m (-s; -e[n], -s) ♔ top(mast).

'Toppsegel n topsail.

Tor [to:r] n (-[e]s; -e) **1.** a) gate, b) (garage etc) door, c) gateway (a. fig. **zu** to). **2.** soccer: goal: **im ~ stehen** keep goal; **ein ~ schießen** score (a goal).

'Torbogen m archway.

'Torchance f sports: chance to score.

Torf [tɔrf] m (-[e]s; no pl) peat. **~moor** n peat bog. **~mull** m peat dust.

'Torhüter(in f) m goalkeeper, F goalie.

töricht ['tø:rɪçt] adj foolish.

'Torjäger(in f) m sports: goalgetter.

torkeln ['tɔrkəln] v/i (sn) stagger, reel.

'Torlatte f crossbar.

'Torlinie f sports: goal line.

'torlos adj sports: scoreless.

Tornado [tɔr'na:do] m (-s; -s) tornado, Am. F twister.

Tornister [tɔr'nɪstər] m (-s; -) knapsack.

torpedieren [tɔrpe'di:rən] v/t (h) a. fig. torpedo.

Torpedo [tɔr'pe:do] m (-s; -s) torpedo.

'Torpfosten m sports: goalpost.

'Torraum m soccer: goal area.

'Torschlußpanik f a) last-minute panic, b) fear of being left on the shelf.

'Torschütze m sports: scorer. **'Torschützenkönig** m sports: top scorer.

Torso ['tɔrzo] m (-s; -s, -si) a. fig. torso.

Törtchen ['tœrtçən] n (-s; -) tartlet.

Torte ['tɔrtə] f (-; -n) gateau, layer cake, (fruit) tart. **'Tortenheber** m cake slice.

Tortur [tɔr'tu:r] f (-; -en) torture, fig. a. ordeal.

'Torverhältnis n sports: goal difference.

'Torwart m sports: goalkeeper, F goalie.

tosen ['to:zən] v/i (h) roar, rage: **~der Beifall** thunderous applause.

tot [to:t] adj dead (a. fig. capital, season, language, etc, ⚡ wire): **an e-m ~en Punkt ankommen** a) reach a low point, b) negotiations etc: reach (a) deadlock; **den ~en Punkt überwinden** a) get one's second wind, b) break the deadlock; **~er Winkel** blind spot, mot. blind

angle; **halb ~ vor Angst** scared stiff; **j-n für ~ erklären** declare s.o. dead; **~ umfallen** drop dead; → **Gleis, Rennen.**

total [to'ta:l] adj total, complete.

To'talausfall m dead loss.

To'talausverkauf m clearance sale.

To'tale f (-; -n) film: long shot.

totalitär [totali'tɛ:r] adj pol. totalitarian.

To'talschaden m mot. write-off.

'totarbeiten: F **sich ~** (sep, -ge-, h) work o.s. to death.

'Tote m, f (-n; -n) a) dead man (woman), b) (dead) body: **die ~n** the dead; **bei dem Unfall gab es zwei ~** two persons were killed in the accident.

töten ['tø:tən] v/t (h) kill.

'Toten|bett n deathbed. **♀blaß, ♀bleich** adj deathly pale. **~gräber** [-grɛ:bər] m (-s; -) gravedigger. **~hemd** n shroud. **~kopf** m skull, death's-head (a. symbol), (poison sign) skull and crossbones. **~maske** f death mask. **~messe** f requiem. **~schein** m death certificate. **~starre** f 🕮 rigor mortis. **♀still** adj deathly silent. **~stille** f deathly silence.

'totgeboren adj stillborn, fig. a. abortive. **'Totgeburt** f stillbirth.

'totlachen: **sich ~** (sep, -ge-, h) laugh one's head off: **es** (**er**) **ist zum ♀** it's (he's) a scream.

'totlaufen: **sich ~** (irr, sep, -ge-, h, → **laufen**) fig. peter out.

Toto ['to:to] m (-s; -s) (football) pools: **im ~ spielen** (**gewinnen**) do (win) the pools. **'Totoschein** m pools coupon.

'Totschlag m (-[e]s; no pl) 🕮 manslaughter, Am. second-degree murder. **'totschlagen** v/t (irr, sep, -ge-, h, → **schlagen**) kill, beat s.o. to death: **die Zeit ~** kill time. **'Totschläger** m **1.** killer. **2.** cosh, Am. blackjack.

'totschweigen v/t (irr, sep, -ge-, h, → **schweigen**) hush up, not to mention.

'totstellen: **sich ~** (sep, -ge-, h) play dead, F play possum.

'Tötung f (-; -en) killing, 🕮 homicide.

Toupet [tu'pe:] n (-s; -s) toupee.

toupieren [tu'pi:rən] v/t (h) back-comb.

Tour [tu:r] f (-; -en) **1.** tour (**durch England** of England), trip, excursion, a. hike. **2.** usu. pl ⚙ revolution: **auf ~en bringen** a) mot. rev up, b) fig. get s.o., s.th. going; **auf ~en kommen** a) mot. pick up, rev up, b) fig. get going; **auf**

vollen ~en laufen be going full blast; F **in 'einer ~ reden** talk incessantly. **3.** F *fig.* ploy: **auf die sanfte** (**langsame**) **~** the sweet (slow) way; → *krumm* I.

'Touren... touring (*bicycle, ski, car, etc*).

Tourismus [tu'rɪsmʊs] *m* (-; *no pl*) tourism. **Tou'rist** *m* (-en; -en) tourist.

Tou'risten... tourist ... **~klasse** *f* economy class.

Touristik [tu'rɪstɪk] *f* (-; *no pl*) tourism. **Tou'ristin** *f* (-; -nen) tourist.

tou'ristisch *adj* tourist(ic).

Tournee [tur'ne:] *f* (-; -s, -n) tour.

Trab [tra:p] *m* (-[e]s; -e) (**im ~** at a) trot: **j-n auf ~ bringen** make s.o. get a move on; **j-n in ~ halten** keep s.o. on the trot.

Trabant [tra'bant] *m* (-en; -en) *astr.* satellite. **Tra'bantenstadt** *f* satellite town.

traben ['tra:bən] *v/i* (sn) trot.

'Traber *m* (-s; -) (*horse*) trotter.

'Trabrennen *n* trotting race.

Tracht [traxt] *f* (-; -en) **1.** dress, attire, (*a.* traditional) costume. **2.** (*nurse's etc*) uniform. **3.** yield (*of honey*). **4.** F **e-e** (**gehörige**) **~ Prügel** a sound thrashing.

trachten ['traxtən] *v/i* (h) **j-m nach dem Leben ~** be out to kill s.o.; → *Sinnen*. **'Trachtengruppe** *f* (folklorist) group in traditional costume.

trächtig ['trɛçtiç] *adj zo.* pregnant.

Tradition [tradi'tsio:n] *f* (-; -en) (**nach alter ~** by) tradition. **traditionell** [traditsio'nɛl] *adj* traditional.

traf [tra:f] *pret of* **treffen**.

Trafo ['tra:fo] *m* (-[s]; -s) transformer.

tragbar ['tra:k-] *adj* **1.** ✪ portable. **2.** wearable (*clothes*). **3.** *fig.* a) acceptable (*price etc*), b) bearable, tolerable.

Trage ['tra:gə] *f* (-; -n) stretcher.

träge ['trɛ:gə] *adj* sluggish (*a.* ✝), lethargic, *phys.* inert.

tragen ['tra:gən] (trug, getragen, h) **I** *v/t* **1.** carry, *a.* support (*a. fig.*): *fig.* **zum** ♀ **kommen** take effect; ✝ **sich** (**selbst**) **~** pay its way. **2.** wear (*clothes, one's hair, etc*): → *getragen* 1, *Trauer*. **3.** bear, yield (*fruit etc, a. interest*): → *Zins*. **4.** bear (*name, title, costs, etc*): **er trägt die Schuld** he is to blame; **wer trägt das Risiko?** who takes the risk?; → *Rechnung* 2. **5.** bear, endure: **sie trägt es tapfer** she is bearing up well. **II** *v/i* **6.** carry (*a. sound, voice*), ice *etc*: hold, *water*: be buoyant: **schwer zu ~ haben**

(**an** *dat*) be loaded (*fig.* weighed) down (by). **7.** *zo.* be pregnant. **III sich ~ 8. sich gut ~** *cloth etc*: wear well. **9. sich mit der Absicht** (*or* **dem Gedanken**) **~ zu** *inf* be thinking of *ger*. **'tragend** *adj* supporting (*wall etc*), powerful (*voice*): *thea.* **~e Rolle** lead(ing part).

Träger ['trɛ:gər] *m* (-s; -) **1.** carrier (*a.* 🦗, 🐀), bearer (*a. of name, title*), porter, stretcher-bearer, *fig.* upholder (*of idea etc*), (*organization etc*) body responsible (*gen for*). **2.** (shoulder) strap. **3.** ✪ support, △ beam, girder.

'Trägerkleid *n* pinafore dress.

'trägerlos *adj* strapless (*dress etc*).

'Trägerra̱kete *f* launcher rocket.

'Trage|tasche *f* **1.** carrier (*Am.* tote) bag. **2.** carrycot. **~zeit** *f zo.* gestation.

'tragfähig *adj* **1.** ✪ capable of bearing. **2.** *fig.* sound. **'Tragfähigkeit** *f* (-; *no pl*) ✪ load capacity.

Tragfläche *f* ✈ wing. **'Tragflächenboot** *n*, **'Tragflügelboot** *n* hydrofoil.

Trägheit ['trɛ:k-] *f* (-; *no pl*) sluggishness, lethargy, *a. phys.* inertia.

Tragik ['tra:gɪk] *f* (-; *no pl*) tragedy.

Tragi'komik [tragi-] *f* tragicomedy.

tragi'komisch *adj* tragicomic.

Tragiko'mödie *f* tragicomedy.

tragisch ['tra:gɪʃ] *adj* tragic: **das Tragische daran** the tragic thing about it; F **nimm's nicht so ~!** don't take it to heart! **Tragödie** [tra'gø:diə] *f* (-; -n) *a. fig.* tragedy.

'Tragweite *f* (-; *no pl*) **1.** range. **2.** significance: **von großer ~** of great import.

'Tragwerk *n* ✈ wing unit.

Trainer ['trɛ:nər] *m* (-s; -), **'Trainerin** *f* (-; -nen) trainer, coach. **trainieren** [trɛ'ni:rən] *v/t, v/i* (h) train, coach. **Training** ['trɛ:nɪŋ] *n* (-s; -s) training.

'Trainings... training (*camp, partner, etc*). **~anzug** *m* track suit.

Trakt [trakt] *m* (-[e]s; -e) section, wing.

Traktor ['traktɔr] *m* (-s; -en [-'to:rən]) tractor.

trällern ['trɛlərn] *v/t, v/i* (h) trill, warble.

Tram(bahn) ['tram-] *f* → **Straßenbahn**.

Trampel ['trampəl] *m, n* (-s; -) F *contp.* clod. **'trampeln** *v/i* (h) trample, stamp.

'Trampelpfad *m* beaten path.

trampen ['trɛmpən] *v/i* (sn) F a) hitchhike, thumb a lift (*or* ride), b) backpack it. '**Tramper** m (-s; -), '**Tramperin** f (-; -nen) F hitchhiker.

Trampolin ['trampoli:n] n (-s; -e) trampoline.

Tran [tra:n] m (-[e]s; -e) train oil.

Trance ['trã:s(ə)] f (-; -n [-sən]) trance.

tranchieren [trã'ʃi:rən] v/t (h) carve.

Tran'chiermesser n carving knife.

Träne ['trɛ:nə] f (-; -n) tear: **den ∼n nahe** on the verge of tears; **unter ∼n** in tears; **wir haben ∼n gelacht** we laughed till we cried; **ihr werde ich k-e ∼ nachweinen** I won't shed any tears over her; → **ausbrechen** 5. '**tränen** v/i (h) water.

'**Tränendrüse** f lachrymal gland: F **auf die ∼ drücken** be a real tear-jerker.

'**Tränengas** n tear gas.

'**Tränensack** m anat. lachrymal sac.

trank [traŋk] pret of **trinken**.

Trank m (-[e]s; ⁓e) drink, ♣ potion.

Tränke ['trɛŋkə] f (-; -n) watering place. '**tränken** v/t (h) a) water, b) soak.

Transaktion [transʔak'tsịo:n] f (-; -en) transaction.

Transat'lantik..., transat'lantisch adj transatlantic.

Transfer [trans'fe:r] m (-s; -s), **transferieren** [transfe'ri:rən] v/t (h) transfer.

Transformator [transfɔr'ma:tɔr] m (-s; -en [-ma'to:rən]) ⚡ transformer. **transformieren** [-'mi:rən] v/t (h) transform.

Transfusion [transfu'zịo:n] f (-; -en) transfusion.

Transistor [tran'zɪstɔr] m (-s; -en [-'to:rən]) transistor.

Tran'sistorradio n transistor (radio).

Transit [tran'zi:t] m (-s; -e) transit (a. in cpds. charge, goods, road, traffic, etc).

transitiv [tranzi'ti:f] adj ling. transitive.

Tran'sitraum m ✈ transit lounge.

Transmission [transmɪ'sịo:n] f (-; -en) ⚙ transmission.

transparent [transpa'rɛnt] adj transparent. **Transpa'rent** n (-[e]s; -e) banner.

Transplantat [transplan'ta:t] n (-[e]s; -e) ⚕ transplant, graft. **Transplantation** [transplanta'tsịo:n] f (-; -en) transplantation, graft(ing). **transplantieren** [-'ti:rən] v/t (h) transplant, graft.

Transport [trans'pɔrt] m (-[e]s; -e) transport(ation), conveyance, ♣ shipment, haulage: **während des ∼s** in transit.

transportabel [transpɔr'ta:bəl] adj transportable, ⚙ portable, mov(e)able.

Trans'portband n (-[e]s; ⁓er) ⚙ conveyor belt.

Trans'porter m (-s; -) → Transportfahrzeug, -flugzeug, -schiff.

Transporteur [transpɔr'tø:r] m (-s; -e) carrier.

trans'portfähig adj transportable.

Trans'portfahrzeug n transporter.

Trans'portflugzeug n transport plane.

transportieren [transpɔr'ti:rən] v/t (h) 1. transport. 2. **den Film ∼** advance the film.

Trans'port|kosten pl transport(ation) charges, ♣ freight (charges). **∼mittel** n (means of) transport(ation). **∼schaden** m damage in transit. **∼schiff** n transport ship. **∼unternehmen** n carriers, haulage contractors. **∼versicherung** f transport insurance.

Transvestit [transvɛs'ti:t] m (-en; -en) transvestite.

transzendental [transtsɛndɛn'ta:l] adj transcendental.

Trapez [tra'pe:ts] n (-es; -e) 1. ▲ trapezium, Am. trapezoid. 2. gym. trapeze.

trappeln ['trapəln] v/i (sn) horse etc: clatter, child: patter.

Trara [tra'ra:] n (-s; no pl) F fuss, to-do.

Trasse ['trasə] f (-; -n) ⚙ location line.

trassieren [tra'si:rən] v/t (h) 1. ⚙ trace (out). 2. ♣ draw bill (auf acc on).

trat [tra:t] pret of **treten**.

Tratsch [tra:tʃ] m (-[e]s; no pl), '**tratschen** v/i (h) F contp. gossip.

Tratte ['tratə] f (-; -n) ♣ draft.

Traube ['traubə] f (-; -n) 1. a) bunch of grapes, b) grape. 2. fig. cluster (of people). '**Traubensaft** m grape juice. '**Traubenzucker** m glucose.

trauen¹ ['trauən] v/t (h) marry: **sich ∼ lassen** get married; → **kirchlich**.

'**trauen²** (h) I v/i (dat) trust (s.o., s.th.): **ich traute m-n Ohren nicht** I couldn't believe my ears; → **Weg**. II sich ∼ zu inf dare (to) inf; **du traust dich nur nicht!** you're just scared.

Trauer ['trauər] f (-; no pl) mourning (um for), b) grief (um, wegen, über): **∼ tragen** be in mourning. **∼fall** m death. **∼feier** f funeral obsequies. **∼flor** m mourning band, crape. **∼kleidung** f mourning. **∼marsch** m funeral march.

trauern ['trauərn] v/i (h) a) mourn (for), b) grieve (for, over).

Trauer|rede f funeral oration. **~schleier** m mourning veil, weeper. **~spiel** n F fig. sorry affair. **~weide** f ♀ weeping willow. **~zug** m funeral procession.

Traufe ['traʊfə] f (-; -n) eaves, gutter: → **Regen**.

träufeln ['trɔʏfəln] v/t (h) drip, trickle.

traulich ['traʊlɪç] adj cosy, Am. cozy.

Traum [traʊm] m (-[e]s; **~e**) dream (a. fig.): F **das fällt mir nicht im ~e ein!** I wouldn't dream of (doing) it; → **einfallen** 1, **kühn**.

Trauma ['traʊma] n (-s; -men, -mata) ♣, psych. trauma.

traumatisch [traʊ'ma:tɪʃ] adj traumatic.

'Traumberuf m dream job.

'Traumbild n a) dream vision, b) dream.

träumen ['trɔʏmən] (h) **I** v/t dream: **das hätte ich mir nicht ~ lassen** I never dreamt of such a thing. **II** v/i dream (**von** about, of), a. daydream: **schlecht ~** have a bad dream. **'Träumer** m (-s; -) dreamer. **Träume'rei** f (-; -en) reverie (a. ♪), (day)dream(s). **'träumerisch** adj dreamy.

'Traumfa,brik f dream factory.

'Traumfrau f woman of one's dreams.

'traumhaft adj dreamlike, (a. **~ schön**) absolutely beautiful, a dream.

'Traum|haus n F dream house. **~land** n dreamland. **~mann** m F man of one's dreams. **~welt** f dream world.

traurig ['traʊrɪç] adj sad (**über** acc at, about), a. sorry: **~ stimmen** sadden; **~er Anblick** sorry sight; **~e Reste** sad remains.

'Traurigkeit f (-; no pl) sadness.

'Trauring m wedding ring (or band).

'Trauschein m marriage certificate.

'Trauung f (-; -en) marriage ceremony, wedding.

'Trauzeuge m, **'Trauzeugin** f witness to a marriage.

Travestie [traves'ti:] f (-; -n) travesty.

Treck [trɛk] m (-s; -s) trek. **'trecken** v/i (sn) trek. **'Trecker** m (-s; -) tractor.

Treff [trɛf] m (-s; -s) F a) meeting, b) meeting place.

treffen ['trɛfən] (traf, getroffen, h) **I** v/t **1.** hit (**j-n an** am Arm s.o.'s arm): **nicht ~** miss; F fig. **er ist gut getroffen (auf dem Bild)** that's a good photo (or painting) of him; → **Blitz** 1. **2.** a) concern, b) affect, hit s.o. hard, c) hurt:

das hat ihn hart getroffen he took it very hard, it's been a severe blow to him; → **Schuld** 1. **3.** reach, make (agreement etc); → **Anstalt** 1, **Entscheidung** etc. **4.** j-n ~ meet s.o.; **j-n zufällig ~** come across s.o. **II** v/i **5.** hit: **nicht ~** miss. **6. auf j-n ~** a. sports: meet s.o. **7. ~ auf** (acc) a) meet with, b) strike (or hit) on. **III sich ~ 8.** meet (**mit** j-m s.o.). **9.** F **das trifft sich gut** (schlecht) that suits me (or us etc) fine (that's a bit awkward); **es trifft sich gut, daß** (it's a) good thing that; **das trifft sich großartig!** well, that's lucky. **'Treffen** n (-; -) meeting, sports: meet. **'treffend** adj apt (remark etc): **kurz und ~** short and to the point; **~ gesagt!** well put.

'Treffer m (-s; -) **1.** hit, soccer etc: goal. **2.** win. **3.** fig. lucky strike.

'Treffpunkt m meeting place.

treiben ['traɪbən] (trieb, getrieben) **I** v/t (h) **1.** drive: **die Preise in die Höhe ~** force up prices; **j-n in den Selbstmord ~** drive s.o. to suicide; **was hat sie dazu getrieben?** what made her do that? **2.** sprout (leaves etc), force (plants). **3.** physiol. produce (urine, sweat). **4.** chase (metal). **5.** do, a. go in for (sports etc): **was treibst du (zur Zeit)?** what are you doing (these days)?; **was treibst du da?** what are you up to?; F **es toll ~** carry on like mad, live it up; **es zu weit ~** go too far; → **Aufwand** 2, **Enge** 1, **Spitze**[1] 1 etc. **II** v/i (sn) **6.** float, a. snow, smoke, etc: drift: **sich ~ lassen** a. fig. drift; **die Dinge ~ lassen** let things drift; **~de Kraft** driving force. **7.** ♀ sprout.

'Treiben n (-s) a) activity, F goings-on, b) (hustle and) bustle.

'Treiber m (-s; -) drover, hunt. beater.

'Treib|gas n fuel gas, for sprays: propellent. **~haus** n hothouse. **~hausef,fekt** m meteor. greenhouse effect. **~holz** n (-es; no pl) driftwood. **~jagd** f 1. battue. **2.** fig. hunt (**auf** acc for), pol. witch hunt. **~rad** n ⚙ driving wheel. **~riemen** m ⚙ drive belt. **~satz** m propelling charge. **~stoff** m fuel.

Trend [trɛnt] m (-s; -s) trend (**zu** towards). **~wende** f change in trend.

'trennbar adj separable, detachable.

trennen ['trɛnən] (h) **I** v/t a) separate, b) divide, c) detach, cut off, ⚡, teleph. a. disconnect, d) undo, e) segregate. **II** v/i

~ *zwischen* distinguish between. **III**
sich ~ separate, *a. fig.* part (*von* with);
getrennt leben be separated (*von*
from), live apart; *getrennt schlafen*
have separate bedrooms; → *Kasse* 4.
'**Trennschärfe** *f radio:* selectivity.
'**Trennung** *f* (-; -en) separation (*a.* 🐾,
⚙️), segregation (*of races*), division, ⚡,
teleph. disconnection: ⚖️ *eheliche* ~
judicial separation.
'**Trennungsstrich** *m* hyphen.
Trense ['trɛnzə] *f* (-; -n) snaffle (bit).
trepp'auf: ~, *treppab* up and down the
stairs. '**Treppchen** *n* F *sports:* (victory)
rostrum. **Treppe** ['trɛpə] *f* (-; -n) staircase, (*e-e* ~ a flight of stairs (*or* steps):
zwei ~*n hoch* on the second floor; *die* ~
hinauf (*hinab*) up (down) the stairs.
'**Treppen|absatz** *m* landing. ~**geländer**
n banisters. ~**haus** *n* staircase.
Tresen ['treːzən] *m* (-s; -) bar, *a.* counter.
Tresor [tre'zoːr] *m* (-s; -e) **1.** strong-
room, vault. **2.** safe.
Tre'sorfach *n* safe deposit box.
'**Tret|auto** *n* pedal car. ~**boot** *n* pedal
boat. ~**eimer** *m* pedal bin.
treten ['treːtən] (trat, getreten) **I** *v/i* (sn)
step, *cyclist etc:* pedal: ~ *auf* (*acc*) step
on, tread on; *aufs Gas(pedal)* (*auf die
Bremse*) ~ step on the gas (brake); *ins
Zimmer* ~ enter the room; *nach j-m* ~
(take a) kick at s.o.; *bitte* ~ *Sie näher!*
please come in!; *über die Ufer* ~
overflow its banks; → *Kraft* 3, *nahe* II *etc.*
II *v/t* (h) tread: *j-n* (*in den Bauch*) ~
kick s.o. (in the stomach); *fig. et. mit
Füßen* ~ trample on s.th.
'**Tretmühle** *f a. fig.* treadmill.
treu [trɔy] *adj* (*dat* to) faithful (*a. fig.*),
loyal, devoted: *sich* (*s-n Grundsätzen*)
~ *bleiben* remain true to o.s. (one's
principles). '**Treue** *f* (-; *no pl*) faithful-
ness (*a. fig.*), loyalty, (*a. marital*) fidelity: *j-m die* ~ *halten* remain loyal to s.o.
'**Treueid** *m* oath of allegiance.
'**treuergeben** *adj* loyal, devoted.
'**Treuhänder** [-hɛndər] *m* (-s; -) trustee.
'**treuhänderisch** *adj* fiduciary: *et.* ~ *verwalten* hold s.th. in trust.
'**Treuhand|gesellschaft** *f* trust compa-
ny. ~**verwaltung** *f* trusteeship.
'**treuherzig** *adj* **1.** guileless. **2.** ingen-
uous, naive. **3.** trusting.
'**treulos** *adj* disloyal (*gegen* to).

'**Treulosigkeit** *f* (-; *no pl*) disloyalty.
Tribunal [tribu'naːl] *n* (-s; -e) tribunal.
Tribüne [tri'byːnə] *f* (-; -n) **1.** (*speaker's*)
platform, rostrum. **2.** (grand)stand, *in
stadium: a.* terraces.
Trichine [tri'çiːnə] *f* (-; -n) *vet.* trichina.
Trichter ['trɪçtər] *m* (-s; -) **1.** ⚙️ funnel. **2.**
flare, mouth. **3.** crater.
'**trichterförmig** *adj* funnel-shaped.
Trick [trɪk] *m* (-s; -s) trick. ~**aufnahme** *f*
1. *film:* trick shot, *pl* trick photography. **2.** *on tape:* trick recording. ~**betrüger** *m* trickster. ~**film** *m* a) trick
film, b) animated cartoon.
'**trickreich** *adj* artful.
'**Trickskilaufen** *n* freestyle skiing.
trieb [triːp] *pret of* **treiben.**
Trieb *m* (-[e]s; -e) **1.** ⚘ young shoot. **2.** a)
instinct, b) sexual drive, c) impulse, d)
urge. '**Triebfeder** *f fig.* mainspring.
'**triebhaft** *adj* a) instinctive, b) sexual, *a.*
highly sexed (*person*).
'**Trieb|kraft** *f* **1.** motive force (*or* power).
2. *fig.* driving force. ~**täter** *m*, ~**verbrecher** *m* sex offender. ~**wagen** *m* tram-
car, 🚂 railcar. ~**werk** *n* a) driving gear,
b) ✈ power unit, c) drive, gear.
triefen ['triːfən] *v/i* (h) drip (*von*
with), *eyes, nose:* run: ~*d naß* dripping
wet.
triftig ['trɪftɪç] *adj* **1.** valid, sound. **2.**
weighty, convincing.
Trigonometrie [trigonome'triː] *f* (-; *no
pl*) trigonometry.
Trikot [tri'koː] **1.** *m, n* (-s; -s) *textil.* tri-
cot. **2.** *n* (-s; -s) a) leotard, tights, b)
shirt, *sports: a.* jersey.
Triller ['trɪlər] *m* (-s; -) trill.
trillern ['trɪlərn] *v/t, v/i* (h) trill, warble.
Trillion [trɪ'lioːn] *f* (-; -en) trillion, *Am.*
quintillion.
Trilogie [trilo'giː] *f* (-; -n) trilogy.
Trimester [tri'mɛstər] *n* (-s; -) *ped., univ.*
trimester.
trimmen ['trɪmən] (h) **I** *v/t* **1.** trim (*a.* ✈,
⚡, ⚓), F tune *engine* up (*auf acc* to). **2.**
train. **II** *sich* ~ keep fit, keep in (good)
trim. '**Trimmpfad** *m* fitness trail.
'**trinkbar** *adj* drinkable. **trinken** ['trɪŋ-
kən] *v/t, v/i* (trank, getrunken, h) drink,
have (*tea etc*): ~ *auf* (*acc*) drink to; *was*
~ *Sie?* what are you having?; *er trinkt*
he drinks, he is a drinker. '**Trinker** *m*
(-s; -), '**Trinkerin** *f* (-; -nen) drinker,

alcoholic. '**trinkfest** *adj* **er** *etc* **ist** ~ **he** *etc* holds his liquor well.

'**Trink|geld** *n* tip: **j-m (5 Mark)** ~ **geben** tip s.o. (five marks). ~**halle** *f* pump room. ~**halm** *m* (drinking) straw. ~**kur** *f* mineral water cure. ~**milch** *f* certified milk. ~**spruch** *m* toast. ~**wasser** *n* drinking water.

Trio ['tri:o] *n* (-s; -s) ♪ *or* F *fig.* trio.

trippeln ['trɪpəln] *v/i* (sn) trip.

Tripper ['trɪpər] *m* (-s; -) ♂ gonorrh(o)ea, F clap.

trist [trɪst] *adj* dreary, bleak, dismal.

Tritt [trɪt] *m* (-[e]s; -e) **1.** a) step, b) footstep: ~ **fassen** fall in step; **aus dem** ~ **geraten** (**sein**) fall (be) out of step; → **Schritt** 1. **2.** footprint. **3.** kick: **j-m e-n** ~ **versetzen** give s.o. a kick, kick s.o. **4.** step (*of stairs etc*). ~**brett** *n mot.* running board. ~**leiter** *f* stepladder.

Triumph [tri'ʊmf] *m* (-[e]s; -e) triumph.

triumphal [triʊm'fa:l] *adj* triumphant.

triumphieren [triʊm'fi:rən] *v/i* (h) (**über** *acc* over) triumph, *contp. a.* gloat.

trivial [tri'via:l] *adj* trivial.

Trivi'allitera,tur *f* light fiction.

trocken ['trɔkən] **I** *adj* dry (*a. wine etc*, *fig. remark, humo[u]r, etc*), *fig. a.* dull: F *fig.* **auf dem trocknen sitzen** be in a fix; → **Schäfchen.** **II** *adv fig.* drily, dryly: **sich** ~ **rasieren** dry-shave.

'**Trocken|dock** *n* dry dock. ~**eis** *n* dry ice. ~**ele,ment** *n* ⚡ dry cell. ~**gewicht** *n* dry weight. ~**haube** *f* hairdrier.

Trockenheit *f* (-; *no pl*) **1.** dryness (*a. fig.*). **2.** drought.

'**trockenlegen** *v/t* (*sep*, -ge-, h) **1.** drain (*land etc*). **2.** **ein Baby** ~ change a baby.

'**Trocken|milch** *f* dried milk. ~**obst** *n* dried fruit. ~**ra,sierer** *m* dry shaver. ~**schleuder** *f* spin drier. ~**skikurs** *m* dry skiing (course). ~**zeit** *f* dry season.

trocknen ['trɔknən] *v/t*, *v/i* (h) dry.

'**Trockner** *m* (-s; -) drier.

Troddel ['trɔdəl] *f* (-; -n) tassel.

Trödel ['trø:dəl] *m* (-s; *no pl*) *a. contp.* junk. '**Trödelladen** *m* junk shop. '**Trödelmarkt** *m* flea market. '**trödeln** *v/i* F a) (h) dawdle, b) (sn) saunter. **Trödler** ['trø:dlər] *m* (-s; -), '**Trödlerin** *f* (-; -nen) **1.** junk dealer. **2.** dawdler.

trog [tro:k] *pret of* **trügen.**

Trog *m* (-[e]s; ⁻e) trough.

trollen ['trɔlən] **sich** ~ (h) toddle off.

Trommel ['trɔməl] *f* (-; -n) drum, ⚙ *a.* cylinder: **die** ~ **rühren** beat the drum (**für** for). ~**bremse** *f* drumbrake. ~**fell** *n* **1.** drumskin. **2.** *anat.* eardrum. ~**feuer** *n a. fig.* barrage.

trommeln ['trɔməln] (h) **I** *v/i* (**auf** *acc* at, on) drum, *rain*: beat. **II** *v/t* drum, beat.

'**Trommel|schlegel** *m*, ~**stock** *m* drumstick. ~**wirbel** *m* drum roll.

Trommler ['trɔmlər] *m* (-s; -) drummer.

Trompete [trɔm'pe:tə] *f* (-; -n) trumpet. **trom'peten** *v/t*, *v/i* (h) trumpet.

Tropen ['tro:pən] *pl* the tropics.

'**Tropen...** tropical (*suit, fever, etc*).

'**tropenfest** *adj* ♂ tropicalized.

'**Tropenhelm** *m* pith helmet, topee.

Tropf [trɔpf] *m* (-[e]s; -e) ♂ (**am** ~ **hängen** be on the) drip.

Tröpfchen ['trœpfçən] *n* (-s; -) droplet.

'**tröpfchenweise** *adv* drop by drop.

tröpfeln ['trœpfəln] *v/i* (h) drip (*a. v/t*), trickle: F **es tröpfelt** it's spitting.

tropfen ['trɔpfən] *v/i* (h) drip, drop.

'**Tropfen** *m* (-s; -) **1.** drop, *a.* bead (*of sweat*): **ein edler** (*or* **guter**) ~ a capital wine; **ein** ~ **auf den heißen Stein** a drop in the bucket; **steter** ~ **höhlt den Stein** little strokes fell big oaks. **2.** *pl* ♂ drops. '**tropfenweise** *adv* in drops, drop by drop.

'**Tropfflasche** *f* dropper bottle.

'**Tropfinfusi,on** *f* ♂ intravenous drip.

'**tropfnaß** *adj* dripping wet.

'**Tropfstein** *m* stalactite, stalagmite.

Trophäe [tro'fɛ:ə] *f* (-; -n) trophy.

tropisch ['tro:pɪʃ] *adj* tropical.

Trosse ['trɔsə] *f* (-; -n) cable, ⚓ hawser.

Trost [tro:st] *m* (-[e]s; *no pl*) comfort, consolation: **zum** ~ as a consolation; **ein schwacher** ~ cold comfort. **trösten** ['trø:stən] *v/t* (h) console (**sich** o.s.), comfort. '**tröstlich** *adj* comforting.

'**trostlos** *adj* a) disconsolate, b) hopeless (*state etc*), c) cheerless, dreary, bleak.

'**Trostlosigkeit** *f* (-; *no pl*) a) hopelessness, b) dreariness, bleakness.

'**Trost|pflaster** *n humor.* (small) consolation. ~**preis** *m* consolation prize.

'**trostreich** *adj* comforting.

Trott [trɔt] *m* (-[e]s; -e) trot, *a. fig.* jogtrot: **in e-n** ~ **verfallen** get into a rut.

Trottel ['trɔtəl] *m* (-s; -) F dope, idiot.

trotten ['trɔtən] *v/i* (sn) trot, jog.

trotz [trɔts] *prep* (*gen*) in spite of, despite.

Trotz m (-es; no pl) defiance: **aus ~** out of spite; **mir zum ~** to spite me.

'**trotzdem I** adv nevertheless, all the same, still, anyway. **II** conj although.

trotzen ['trɔtsən] v/i (h) **1.** (dat) defy (s.o., s.th.), a. brave (danger etc). **2.** be obstinate.

'**trotzig** adj defiant, obstinate.

'**Trotzreakti,on** f act of defiance.

trübe ['try:bə] adj **1.** cloudy (liquid, glass, etc), muddy: F fig. **im trüben fischen** fish in troubled waters. **2.** dull, dim, murky. **3.** dreary (day). **4.** gloomy (mood, thoughts, etc), bleak (prospects etc), sad (experience etc).

Trubel ['tru:bəl] m (-s; no pl) (hustle and) bustle.

trüben ['try:bən] (h) **I** v/t **1.** (a. sich ~) cloud (liquid, glass, etc, a. mind, relations, etc). **2.** fig. spoil (joy etc), obscure (s.o.'s view), warp (judgement), blur (sight, mind). **II sich ~ 3.** become clouded, glass etc: cloud over. **4.** fig. relations etc: become strained.

trübselig ['try:p-] adj **1.** gloomy. **2.** dreary. '**Trübseligkeit** f (-; no pl) **1.** gloominess. **2.** dreariness.

'**Trübsinn** m (-[e]s; no pl) gloom, low spirits. '**trübsinnig** adj gloomy.

'**Trübung** f (-; -en) **1.** clouding (etc, → trüben). **2.** cloudiness, dullness.

trudeln ['tru:dəln] v/i (sn) ✈ spin: **ins ≈ geraten** go into a spin.

Trüffel ['tryfəl] f (-; -n) ♣ truffle.

trug [tru:k] pret of **tragen.**

'**Trugbild** n illusion, hallucination.

trügen ['try:gən] (trog, getrogen, h) **I** v/t deceive: **wenn mein Gedächtnis mich nicht trügt** if my memory serves me right. **II** v/i be deceptive: → **Schein¹.**

trügerisch ['try:gərɪʃ] adj deceptive, misleading, illusive (hope etc).

'**Trugschluß** m fallacy.

Truhe ['tru:ə] f (-; -n) chest.

Trümmer ['trymər] pl **1.** ruins, rubble. **2.** debris. **3.** fragments.

'**Trümmerhaufen** m heap of rubble.

Trumpf ['trʊmpf] m (-[e]s; ⸗e) a) trump(s), b) trump card: **was ist ~?** what's trumps?; fig. **~ sein** be the thing; a. fig. **alle Trümpfe in der Hand haben** hold all the trumps; fig. **s-n letzten ~ ausspielen** play one's trump card.

Trunk [trʊŋk] m (-[e]s; no pl) drinking.

'**Trunkenheit** f (-; no pl) drunkenness: **~ am Steuer** drunken driving.

'**Trunksucht** f (-; no pl) alcoholism.

'**trunksüchtig** adj **~ sein** be an alcoholic.

Trupp [trʊp] m (-s; -s) troop, gang, ✕ detachment. '**Truppe** f (-; -n) **1.** ✕ a) troops, pl a. forces, b) unit. **2.** thea. company, troupe. **3.** sports: team.

'**Truppen|abbau** m reduction in forces. **~abzug** m withdrawal of troops, pull-out. **~gattung** f branch (of the service), arm. **~teil** m unit. **~trans,porter** m ⚓ transport, troopship, ✈ troop carrier. **~übungsplatz** m training area.

'**Truppführer** m squad leader.

'**Truthahn** ['tru:t-] m turkey(-cock).

'**Truthenne** f turkey-hen.

Tscheche ['tʃɛçə] m (-n; -n), '**Tschechin** f (-; -nen), '**tschechisch** [-çɪʃ] adj Czech. **Tschechoslowakei** [tʃɛçoslova'kaɪ] f (-) Czechoslovakia.

tschüs [tʃy:s] int F bye!, see you!

Tube ['tu:bə] f (-; -n) tube: F mot. or fig. **auf die ~ drücken** step on it.

tuberkulös [tubɛrku'lø:s] adj tubercular, tuberculous. **Tuberkulose** [tubɛrku'lo:zə] f (-; -n) tuberculosis.

Tuch [tu:x] n (-[e]s; ⸗er) **1.** textil. cloth, fabric. **2.** a) cloth, b) scarf: **das wirkt auf ihn wie ein rotes ~** that's a red rag to him. '**Tuchfühlung** f **~ haben mit** be in close contact with.

tüchtig ['tyçtɪç] **I** adj **1.** good (in dat at), capable, competent, efficient, hard-working. **2.** F good. **II** adv **3.** F tremendously, like hell: **~ arbeiten** work hard; **~ zulangen**, **~ essen** tuck in.

'**Tüchtigkeit** f (-; no pl) ability, competence, efficiency, industry.

Tücke ['tykə] f (-; -n) malice, perfidy, trick: **s-e ~n haben** be tricky, river etc: be treacherous.

tuckern ['tʊkərn] v/i (sn) F chug.

tückisch ['tykɪʃ] adj **1.** malicious, insidious (a. ✿). **2.** treacherous (road etc).

tüfteln ['tyftəln] v/i (h) (an dat) **1.** tinker (with). **2.** puzzle (over).

'**Tüftler** ['tyftlər] m (-s; -) tinkerer.

Tugend ['tu:gənt] f (-; -en) virtue.

'**tugendhaft** adj virtuous.

Tüll [tyl] m (-s; -e) textil. tulle.

Tülle ['tylə] f (-; -n) **1.** spout. **2.** ⚙ socket.

Tulpe ['tʊlpə] f (-; -n) tulip.

tummeln ['tʊməln] **sich ~** (h) disport o.s.

'**Tummelplatz** m **1.** playground. **2.** fig. stomping ground.

Tumor ['tu:mɔr] m (-s; -en [tu'mo:rən]) ✠ tumo(u)r.

Tümpel ['tympəl] m (-s; -) pool.

Tumult [tu'mʊlt] m (-[e]s; -e) tumult, uproar, riot.

tun [tu:n] v/t, v/i (tat, getan, h) a) do (→ a. **machen**), b) make (vow etc), take (step etc), c) put (s.th. somewhere), d) F machine etc: go, work: **höflich** etc ~ act (or do) the polite etc; **so** ~, **als ob** pretend to inf; **er tut nur so** he's only pretending; **was hat er dir getan?** what has he done to you?; **dagegen müssen wir et.** ~! we must do s.th. about it!; **was (ist zu)** ~? what's to be done?; **wir haben zu** ~ we have work to do, we are busy; **das tut nichts!** never mind!, it doesn't matter!; **was tut's!** what does it matter!; **das tut man nicht** that just isn't done!; **mit ihm (damit) habe ich nichts zu** ~ I have nothing to do with him (it); **das hat nichts damit zu** ~ that's nothing to do with it; **du wirst es mit ihm zu** ~ **bekommen** you'll get into trouble with him; F **es tut sich was!** there is s.th. going on.

Tun n (-s) doing, (a. ~ **und Treiben**, ~ **und Lassen**) doings, activities.

Tünche ['tynçə] f (-; -n) **1.** whitewash. **2.** fig. veneer. '**tünchen** v/t (h) whitewash.

Tundra ['tʊndra] f (-; -dren) tundra.

tunen ['tju:nən] v/t (h) mot. tune (up).

Tunesien [tu'ne:zɪən] n (-s) Tunisia. **Tu'nesier** m (-s; -), **Tu'nesierin** f (-; -nen), **tu'nesisch** adj Tunisian.

Tunke ['tʊŋkə] f (-; -n) sauce.

tunken ['tʊŋkən] v/t (h) dip.

Tunnel ['tʊnəl] m (-s; -) tunnel.

tüpfeln ['typfəln] v/t (h) dot.

tupfen ['tʊpfən] v/t (h) **1.** ✠ swab. **2.** dot. '**Tupfen** m (-s; -) dot, spot. '**Tupfer** m (-s; -) ✠ swab. **2.** dot.

Tür ['ty:r] f (-; -en) door: **Tag der offenen** ~ Open Day; **in der** ~ in the doorway; F fig. **offene** ~**en einrennen** force an open door; **mit der** ~ **ins Haus fallen** blurt it out; (dat) ~ **und Tor öffnen** open the door to s.th.; **j-n vor die** ~ **setzen** turn s.o. out.

Turban ['tʊrba:n] m (-s; -e) turban.

Turbine [tʊr'bi:nə] f (-; -n) turbine.

Turbo-Prop-Ma'schine ['tʊrbo'prɔp-] f ✈ turboprop (engine).

turbulent [tʊrbu'lɛnt] adj turbulent.

Turbulenz [tʊrbu'lɛnts] f (-; -en) a. phys. turbulence.

Türke ['tʏrkə] m (-n; -n) **1.** Turk. **2.** F press etc: fake. **Türkei** [tʏr'kaɪ] f (-) Turkey. '**türken** v/t (h) F fake. '**Türkin** f (-; -nen) Turk(ish woman).

Türkis [tʏr'ki:s] m (-es; -e) min. turquoise. '**türkisch** adj Turkish.

'**Türklinke** f doorhandle.

'**Türklopfer** m knocker.

Turm [tʊrm] m (-[e]s; ⸚e) **1.** a) tower (a. fig.), b) steeple. **2.** sports: (diving) platform. **3.** chess: castle.

Türmchen ['tʏrmçən] n (-s; -) turret.

türmen[1] ['tʏrmən] (h) **I** v/t pile (up). **II sich** ~ a. fig. pile up.

'**türmen**[2] v/i (sn) F bolt, make off.

'**Turmspitze** f spire.

'**Turmspringen** n sports: high diving.

'**Turmuhr** f church clock.

'**Turnanzug** m gymsuit. **turnen** ['tʊrnən] (h) **I** v/i do gymnastics. **II** v/t do (an exercise). '**Turnen** n (-s) gymnastics. '**Turner** m (-s; -), '**Turnerin** f (-; -nen) gymnast.

'**Turn|gerät** n gymnastic apparatus. ~**halle** f gymnasium, F gym. ~**hemd** n singlet, gym top. ~**hose** f gym shorts.

Turnier [tʊr'ni:r] n (-s; -e) tournament. ~**tanz** m ballroom dancing.

'**Turnschuhe** pl gym shoes, trainers.

'**Turnübung** f gymnastic exercise.

Turnus ['tʊrnʊs] m (-; -se) rotation: **im** ~ → **turnusmäßig** II. '**turnusmäßig** **I** adj a) rotational, b) regular. **II** adv in turns: ~ **(aus)wechseln** rotate.

'**Turnverein** m gymnastics club.

'**Tür|pfosten** m door post. ~**rahmen** m door frame. ~**schild** n door plate. ~**schließer** m ◎ door closer.

turteln ['tʊrtəln] v/i (h) F bill and coo.

'**Turteltaube** f turtledove.

Tusch [tʊʃ] m (-[e]s; -e) ♪ flourish.

Tusche ['tʊʃə] f (-; -n) **1.** a) Indian ink, b) drawing ink. **2.** mascara.

tuscheln ['tʊʃəln] v/i, v/t (h) whisper.

tuschen ['tʊʃən] v/t (h) draw in Indian ink: **sich die Wimpern** ~ put some mascara on.

'**Tuschkasten** m paintbox.

'**Tuschzeichnung** f Indian drawing.

Tüte ['tyːtə] f (-; -n) **1.** (paper) bag. **2.** cone.

tuten ['tuːtən] v/i (h) F toot, *mot.* honk.

Tutor ['tuːtɔr] m (-s; -en [tuˈtoːrən]), **Tutorin** [tuˈtoːrɪn] f (-; -nen) *univ.* tutor.

Typ [tyːp] m (-s; -en) **1.** type, ⊙ a. model: F *sie ist mein ∼* she is my type. **2.** F fellow, chap.

Type ['tyːpə] f (-; -n) **1.** *print.* type. **2.** F *komische etc ∼* queer *etc* character.

'**Typenrad** n daisywheel.

'**Typenschild** n ⊙ type plate.

Typhus ['tyːfʊs] m (-; *no pl*) ⚕ typhoid (*a. in cpds.* epidemic, patient, *etc*).

typisch ['tyːpɪʃ] *adj* typical (*für* of): F *das ist ∼ John!* that's John all over.

typisieren [typiˈziːrən] v/t (h) typify.

Typographie [typograˈfiː] f (-; -n) typography.

Typus ['tyːpʊs] m (-; Typen) type.

Tyrann [tyˈran] m (-en; -en) tyrant. **Tyrannei** [tyraˈnaɪ] f (-; -en) tyranny. **ty'rannisch** *adj* tyrannical. **tyrannisieren** [tyraniˈziːrən] v/t (h) tyrannize.

U

U, u [uː] n (-; -) U, u.

'**U-Bahn** f → **Untergrundbahn.**

übel ['yːbəl] *adj* bad, a. nasty: F (*gar*) *nicht ∼* not bad (at all); *mir ist* (*wird*) *∼* I'm feeling (getting) sick; F *fig. dabei kann e-m ∼ werden!* it's enough to make you sick; *ein übler Kerl* a bad lot; *e-e üble Sache* a bad business; *∼ riechen* smell (terrible).

'**Übel** n (-s; -) a) evil, b) illness: *das kleinere ∼* the lesser of two evils; *zu allem ∼* to top it all.

'**übelgelaunt** *adj* bad-tempered.

'**Übelkeit** f (-; -en) nausea.

'**übelnehmen** v/t (*irr, sep*, -ge-, h, → **nehmen**) *et. ∼* take s.th. amiss, take offen/ce (*Am.* -se) at s.th.; *j-m et. ∼* hold s.th. against s.o.; *nimm es mir nicht übel, aber ...* don't be offended but ...

'**übelriechend** *adj* foul-smelling, foul.

'**Übeltäter(in** f) m malefactor.

üben ['yːbən] v/t, v/i (h) practi/se (*Am.* -ce) (*a. sich ∼ in dat*), a. train: *Klavier ∼* practise the piano; *fig.* Geduld ∼ have patience; → **Nachsicht, Rache.**

über ['yːbər] I *prep* **1.** over, a. above, a. across (*the river etc*): *∼ die Straße gehen* cross the street; *∼ München nach Rom reisen* go to Rome via Munich. **2.** over (*a period*): *∼ Nacht* overnight; *∼ das Wochenende* over the weekend; *∼ die Ferien* during the holidays; *∼s Jahr* (this time) next year; *∼ der Arbeit* over

one's work. **3.** a) over, more than, b) beyond, *adm.* exceeding (*a sum etc*): *er ist ∼ siebzig (Jahre alt)* he is past (or over) seventy; *es geht nichts ∼ Musik!* there's nothing like music; → **Verstand. 4.** about (*a subject*), *essay, book, etc*: *a.* on: *∼ Geschäfte* (*Politik, den Beruf*) *reden* talk business (politics, shop). **5.** for: *e-e Rechnung ∼ 100 Mark* a bill for 100 marks. **6.** over, by: *e-e Treppe* over (*or* by) a staircase; *∼ die Auskunft* from the information; *∼ e-n Makler* through a broker. **7.** *Fehler ∼ Fehler* one mistake after the other. II *adv ∼ und ∼* all over; *die ganze Zeit ∼* all along; → **überhaben.**

'**überall** *adv* everywhere, all over: *∼ wo* wherever. '**überallher** *adv* from everywhere. '**überallhin** *adv* everywhere.

über'altert *adj* overaged (*population*).

'**Überangebot** n oversupply.

'**überängstlich** *adj* overanxious.

über'anstrengen v/t (*insep, no* -ge-, h) overexert (*sich* o.s.), strain.

Über'anstrengung f (-; *no pl*) overexertion, strain.

über'arbeiten (*insep, no* -ge-, h) I v/t revise (*book etc*). II *sich ∼* overwork. **über'arbeitet** *adj* **1.** revised. **2.** overworked. **Über'arbeitung** f (-; -en) **1.** a) revision, b) revised edition. **2.** *no pl* overwork.

'**überaus** *adv* extremely.

über'backen adj gastr. au gratin.
'**überbeanspruchen** v/t (insep, no -ge-, h) **1.** ⚙ overload, overstress. **2.** strain: **j-n ~** overtax s.o.
'**Überbein** n 🟐 node, exostosis.
'**überbelegt** adj overcrowded.
'**überbelichten** v/t (insep, no -ge-, h) phot. overexpose.
'**überbesetzt** adj overstaffed.
'**überbewerten** v/t (insep, no -ge-, h) overvalue, overrate.
über'bieten v/t (irr, insep, no -ge-, h, → **bieten**) **1.** ✝ outbid (**um** by). **2.** outdo, beat (record): **sich** (**gegenseitig**) ~ **vie** with each other (**in** dat in).
'**Überbleibsel** [-blaɪpsəl] n (-s; -) a. fig. remnant.
über'blenden v/t (insep, no -ge-, h) film etc: fade over.
'**Überblick** m **1.** view (**über** acc of). **2.** fig. overall view: **sich e-n ~ verschaffen** get a general idea (**über** acc of); **den ~ verlieren** lose track of things, be confused.
über'blicken v/t (insep, no -ge-, h) **1.** overlook, survey. **2.** a) grasp, b) assess.
über'bringen v/t (irr, insep, no -ge-, h, → **bringen**) **j-n et. ~** deliver (or bring) s.th. to s.o. **Über'bringer** m (-s; -) bearer. **Über'bringung** f (-; no pl) delivery.
über'brücken v/t (insep, no -ge-, h) span, a. fig. bridge. **Über'brückungskre,dit** m ✝ bridging loan.
über'buchen v/t (insep, no -ge-, h) ✝ overbook.
über'dacht adj roofed, covered.
über'dauern v/t (insep, no -ge-, h) outlast, survive. ~'**dehnen** v/t (insep, no -ge-, h) overstretch, pull (muscle). ~'**denken** v/t (irr, insep, no -ge-, h, → **denken**) think s.th. over, reconsider.
'**überdeutlich** adj all too clear.
über'dies adv besides, moreover.
'**überdimensio,nal** adj outsize(d).
'**Überdosis** f overdose.
über'drehen v/t (insep, no -ge-, h) overspeed (engine).
'**Überdruck** m ⚙ overpressure. ~**ka,bine** f pressurized cabin. ~**ven,til** n pressure relief valve.
'**Überdruß** [-drʊs] m (-sses; no pl) weariness: **bis zum ~** ad nauseam.
'**überdrüssig** [-drʏsɪç] adj ~ **sein** be weary (or tired) (gen of).

über'düngen v/t (insep, no -ge-, h) overfertilize.
'**überdurchschnittlich** adj above average.
'**Übereifer** m overzealousness.
'**übereifrig** adj overzealous, officious.
über'eignen v/t (insep, no -ge-, h) **j-m et. ~** make s.th. over to s.o. **Über'eignung** f (-; -en) transfer (**an** acc to).
über'eilen v/t (h) rush: **et. ~** a. rush things. **über'eilt** adj (over)hasty.
überein'ander adv **1.** one on top of the other. **2.** ~ **sprechen** talk about one another. ~**schlagen** v/t (irr, sep, -ge-, h, → **schlagen**) cross (legs).
über'einkommen v/i (irr, sep, -ge-, sn, → **kommen**) (**über** acc on) agree, reach an agreement. **Über'einkommen** n (-s; -), **Über'einkunft** [-kʊnft] f (-; ⸚e) agreement.
über'einstimmen v/i (sep, -ge-, h) **1.** tally, correspond, colo(u)rs etc: match. **2.** **mit j-m ~** agree with s.o. (**über** acc, in dat on). **über'einstimmend** adj corresponding, a. concurring, matching (colo[u]rs etc). **Über'einstimmung** f (-; -en) agreement, correspondence: **in ~ mit** in accordance (or keeping) with.
'**überempfindlich** adj hypersensitive, 🟐 or fig. allergic (**gegen** to).
'**überernährt** adj overfed.
über'fahren v/t (irr, insep, no -ge-, h, → **fahren**) drive through (signal etc): **j-n ~** run s.o. over, F fig. bulldoze s.o., sports: clobber s.o. '**Überfahrt** f (-; -en) ⚓ crossing, passage.
'**Überfall** m (-[e]s; ⸚e) **1.** (**auf** acc) attack (on), raid (on), invasion (of). **2.** a) holdup, b) mugging. **3.** F surprise visit.
über'fallen v/t (irr, insep, no -ge-, h, → **fallen**) a) attack, assault, b) hold up, raid (bank etc), c) invade (country): F **j-n ~** descend on s.o.; **j-n mit e-r Frage** etc ~ pounce on s.o. with a question etc.
'**überfällig** adj overdue.
'**Überfallkom,mando** n riot squad.
über'fliegen v/t (irr, insep, no -ge-, h, → **fliegen**) **1.** fly over. **2.** skim (letter etc).
'**überfließen** v/i (irr, sep, -ge-, sn, → **fließen**) overflow.
über'flügeln v/t (insep, no -ge-, h) **j-n ~** outstrip s.o.
'**Überfluß** m (-sses; no pl) abundance (**an** dat of): ~ **haben an** (dat) abound in,

have plenty of; **zu allem ~** to top it all.
~gesellschaft f affluent society.

'**überflüssig** adj superfluous.

über'fluten v/t (insep, no -ge-, h) flood.

über'fordern v/t (insep, no -ge-, h) over-tax, a. overstretch (staff etc): **j-n ~** a) expect too much of s.o., b) be too much for s.o.; **damit war sie überfordert** this was more than she could handle.

über'fragt adj F **da bin ich ~!** you've got me there.

Über'fremdung f (-; -en) foreign in-filtration, ✝ control by foreign capi-tal.

über'führen v/t (insep, no -ge-, h) **1.** transport. **2.** find s.o. guilty (gen of).

Über'führung f (-; -en) **1.** transfer. **2.** ⚖ conviction. **3.** flyover, overpass.

'**Überfülle** f (-; no pl) (over)abundance.

über'füllt adj overcrowded, congested (streets), (jam-)packed (room, room, etc).

'**Überfunkti͵on** f ⚕ hyperactivity.

über'füttert adj overfed.

Übergabe f (-; -n) delivery, handing--over (a. of an office), ✕ surrender.

'**Übergang** m (-[e]s; ⸚e) **1.** crossing, pas-sage. **2.** transition. '**übergangslos** adv without transition, directly.

'**Übergangs͵re͵gierung** f caretaker government. **~stadium** n transition(al stage). **~zeit** f transition(al period).

über'geben (irr, insep, no -ge-, h, → **geben**) **I** v/t (j-m et.) ~ hand over (s.th. to s.o.), present (s.o. with s.th.); **dem Verkehr ~** open s.th. to the traffic. **II sich ~** vomit, be sick.

'**übergehen**[1] v/i (irr, sep, -ge-, sn, → **gehen**) pass over (**zu** to): ~ **auf** (acc) devolve upon (successor etc); ~ **in** (acc) pass (or turn) into; **in j-s Besitz ~** pass into s.o.'s possession; **in andere Hän-de ~** change hands; **in Verwesung ~** begin to putrefy; ~ **zu** proceed to (s.th.).

über'gehen[2] v/t (irr, insep, no -ge-, h, → **gehen**) a) ignore, b) omit, skip, c) pass s.o., s.th. over.

'**übergeordnet** adj **1.** higher (office etc). **2.** of overriding importance.

'**Übergepäck** n ✈ excess baggage.

'**übergeschnappt** adj F crazy, mad.

'**Übergewicht** n (-[e]s; no pl) **1.** (~ **haben** be) overweight. **2.** fig. preponderance: **das ~ haben** predominate.

'**überglücklich** adj overjoyed.

'**übergreifen** v/i (irr, sep, -ge-, h, → **grei-fen**) fig. spread (**auf** acc to).

'**Übergriff** m (-[e]s; -e) (**in** acc) encroach-ment ([up]on), infringement (of).

'**übergroß** adj outsize(d).

'**Übergröße** f outsize.

'**überhaben** v/t (irr, sep, -ge-, h, → **ha-ben**) F **1.** have coat etc on. **2.** be fed up with.

über'handnehmen v/i (irr, sep, -ge-, h, → **nehmen**) increase, spread.

'**Überhang** m (-[e]s; ⸚e) **1.** ✓, △, ☉ over-hang. **2.** surplus (of money), backlog (of orders etc). '**überhängen**[1] v/i (irr, sep, -ge-, h, → **hängen**[1]) overhang, △ pro-ject. '**überhängen**[2] v/t (sep, h) throw coat etc over one's shoulders.

über'häufen v/t (insep, no -ge-, h) **j-n ~ mit** swamp s.o. with work etc, shower s.o. with presents etc, heap hono(u)rs etc on s.o.

über'haupt adv at all, actually, really: **was willst du ~?** what really do you want?; ~ **nicht** not at all; ~ **nichts** noth-ing at all; **er versteht davon ~ nichts** he doesn't know the first thing about it; ~ **kein ...** no ... whatever; **wenn ~** if at all.

überheblich [-'he:plɪç] adj arrogant.

Über'heblichkeit f (-; no pl) arrogance.

über'hitzt adj a. fig. overheated.

über'höht adj excessive (prices etc).

über'holen v/t (insep, no -ge-, h) **1.** pass, overtake, fig. outstrip. **2.** ☉ overhaul.

Über'holma͵növer n overtaking ma-noeuvre, Am. passing maneuver.

Über'holspur f mot. passing lane.

Über'holung f (-; -en) ☉ overhaul.

'**Überholverbot** n "No Passing" sign.

über'hören v/t (insep, no -ge-, h) a) not to hear, miss, not to catch, b) ignore.

'**überirdisch** adj supernatural.

'**Überkapazi͵tät** f overcapacity.

über'kleben v/t (insep, no -ge-, h) **et. ~** paste s.th. over.

'**überkochen** v/i (sep, sn) boil over.

über'kommen v/t (irr, insep, no -ge-, h, → **kommen**) **Furcht** etc **überkam ihn** he was overcome by fear etc.

'**überkonfessio͵nell** adj interdenomi-national.

über'kronen v/t (insep, no -ge-, h) crown, cap (tooth).

über'laden (irr, insep, no -ge-, h, → **la-den**) **I** v/t **1.** overload (a. ⚡), overbur-

den, swamp (*mit* with *work etc*). **II** *adj*
2. overloaded. **3.** *fig.* a) cluttered, b)
overladen, florid (*style*).
über'lagern *v/t* (*insep, no* -ge-, h) super-
impose, *partially*: overlap (*a.* **sich ~**),
radio: a) heterodyne, b) jam (*station*).
'Überlandbus *m* long-distance coach.
'Überlänge *f* exceptional length.
über'lassen *v/t* (*irr, insep, no* -ge-, h, →
lassen) *j-m et.* ~ let s.o. have s.th., *a.*
fig. leave s.th. to s.o.; *j-n s-m Schicksal*
~ leave s.o. to his fate; **sich selbst ~**
sein be left to one's own devices; ~ **Sie**
das mir! leave it to me; **das bleibt ihm**
~**!** that's up to him.
über'lasten *v/t* (*insep, no* -ge-, h) **1.** *a.* ⚡,
⊚ overload. **2.** *fig.* a) overtax, overbur-
den, b) overwork, overstretch.
Über'lastung *f* (-; -en) **1.** *a.* ⚡, ⊚
overload. **2.** *fig.* a) overburdening, b)
strain.
'überlaufen[1] *v/i* (*irr, sep,* -ge-, sn, →
laufen) **1.** run over. **2.** (*zu* to) desert, go
over, defect. **über'laufen**[2] (*irr, insep,
no* -ge-, h, → **laufen**) **I** *v/t* seize: *Angst*
überlief mich I was seized with fear. **II**
v/impers **es überlief mich heiß und**
kalt I went hot and cold.
über'laufen[3] *adj* overcrowded.
'Überläufer *m* deserter, defector.
über'leben *v/t, v/i* (*insep, no* -ge-, h)
survive. **Über'leben** *n* (-s) survival.
Über'lebende *m, f* (-n; -n) survivor.
Über'lebenschance *f* chance of survival.
'überlebensgroß *adj* larger than life,
larger-than-life ...
überlebt [-'le:pt] *adj* antiquated.
über'legen[1] *v/t, v/i* (*insep, no* -ge-, h)
think (*s.th.* over): *ich will es mir* ~ I'll
think it over; *es sich anders* ~ change
one's mind; *sich et. genau* ~ think
carefully about it; *ohne zu* ~ a) without
thinking, b) rashly, c) F like a shot; →
reiflich II.
über'legen[2] **I** *adj* superior (*dat* to, *an*
dat in), *contp. a.* supercilious: *j-m weit*
~ **sein** be head and shoulders above s.o.
II *adv* a) in superior style, b) supercili-
ously: ~ **siegen** win in style.
Über'legenheit *f* (-; *no pl*) superiority.
überlegt [-'le:kt] *adj* (well-)considered.
Über'legung *f* (-; -en) consideration, reflection: ~**en anstellen** a) *über* (*acc*)

think about, reflect on, b) *ob* consider
if; → **reiflich** I.
'überleiten *v/i* (*sep,* h) lead over (*zu*
to).
über'liefern *v/t* (*insep, no* -ge-, h) *et.* ~
hand s.th. down (*dat* to). **über'liefert**
adj traditional. **Über'lieferung** *f* (-;
-en) tradition.
über'listen *v/t* (*insep, no* -ge-, h) outwit.
'Übermacht *f* (-; *no pl*) superiority.
'übermächtig *adj* too strong, *fig.* overpowering.
über'malen *v/t* (*insep, no* -ge-, h) *et.* ~
paint s.th. over.
'Übermaß *n* (-es; *no pl*) excess (*an dat*
of). **'übermäßig** *adj* excessive.
'Übermensch *m* superman.
'übermenschlich *adj* superhuman.
über'mitteln *v/t* (*insep, no* -ge-, h) transmit (*dat* to).
Über'mittlung *f* (-; *no pl*) transmission.
'übermorgen *adv* the day after tomorrow.
über'müdet *adj* overtired.
'Übermut *m* (-[e]s; *no pl*) high spirits.
'übermütig [-my:tɪç] *adj* high-spirited,
pred in high spirits.
'übernächst *adj the* next but one: ~**e**
Woche the week after next.
über'nachten *v/i* (*insep, no* -ge-, h)
spend the night.
übernächtigt [-'nɛçtɪçt] *adj* bleary-eyed.
Über'nachtung *f* (-; -en) overnight stay:
~ **und Frühstück** bed and breakfast.
Über'nachtungsmöglichkeit *f* overnight accommodation.
'Übernahme [-na:mə] *f* (-; -n) taking
over, takeover (*of firm, power*), assumption (*of office, responsibility*),
adoption (*of idea*). ~**angebot** *n* ✝ takeover bid.
'übernatio,nal *adj* supranational.
'überna,türlich *adj* supernatural.
über'nehmen (*irr, insep, no* -ge-, h, →
nehmen) **I** *v/t* take over (*firm, power,
etc*), *a.* accept (*goods*), take on (*responsibility, work, etc*), adopt (*ideas etc*): *es*
~ *zu inf* take it upon o.s. to *inf*; *et.* ~
take care of s.th. **II** *sich* ~ take on more
than one can handle, *financially*: over-
reach o.s., *physically*: overdo it; *iro.*
übernimm dich nur nicht! don't kill
yourself!

'**über**ordnen *v/t* (*sep*, h) (*dat*) set *s.o.*, *s.th.* above *s.o.*, *s.th.*

'**überpar,teilich** *adj* nonpartisan.

'**Überprodukti,on** *f* overproduction.

über'prüfen *v/t* (*insep*, *no* -ge-, h) **1.** check, examine. **2.** screen, F vet (*person*). **Über'prüfung** *f* (-; -en) check-(up), examination, *a.* F vetting.

'**überquellen** *v/i* (*irr*, *sep*, -ge-, sn, → **quellen**) overflow (**von** with).

über'queren *v/t* (*insep*, *no* -ge-, h) cross. **Über'querung** *f* (-; -en) crossing.

über'ragen *v/t* (*insep*, *no* -ge-, h) **1.** tower above, be taller than. **2.** *fig.* outclass.

über'ragend *adj fig.* outstanding.

überraschen [-'raʃən] *v/t* (*insep*, *no* -ge-, h) surprise, *a.* take *s.o.* by surprise, catch *s.o.* (**bei** at); **von e-m Gewitter überrascht werden** be caught in a thunderstorm. **über'raschend** *adj* a) surprising, b) unexpected, sudden.

Über'raschung *f* (-; -en) surprise. **Über'raschungs|mo,ment** *n* element of surprise. **~sieg** *m* unexpected win.

'**überrea,gieren** *v/i* (*insep*, h) overreact.

über'reden *v/t* (*insep*, *no* -ge-, h) persuade, talk *s.o.* round; **j-n zu et. ~** *a.* talk *s.o.* into doing *s.th.*

Über'redung *f* (-; *no pl*) persuasion. **Über'redungskunst** *f* powers of persuasion.

'**überregio,nal** *adj* supraregional, national (*paper*), nationwide (*broadcast*).

'**überreich** *adj* **~ sein an** abound in.

über'reichen *v/t* (*insep*, *no* -ge-, h) hand *s.th.* over (*or present s.th.*) (**j-m** to *s.o.*).

Über'reichung *f* (-; *no pl*) presentation.

'**überreif** *adj* overripe.

über'reizt *adj* overwrought: **~ sein** *a.* be on edge.

'**Überrest** *m* remains, *fig. a.* relics.

'**Überrollbügel** *m mot.* rollbar. **über'rollen** *v/t* (*insep*, *no* -ge-, h) overrun.

über'rumpeln *v/t* (*insep*, *no* -ge-, h) **j-n ~** take *s.o.* unawares (*or* by surprise).

über'runden *v/t* (*insep*, *no* -ge-, h) *sports:* lap, *fig.* outstrip.

übersät [-'zɛ:t] *adj* littered, *fig.* studded.

über'sättigen *v/t* (*insep*, *no* -ge-, h) over-saturate, ♥ *a.* glut, 🔥 supersaturate, *fig.* surfeit. **Über'sättigung** *f* (-; *no pl*) surfeit, ♥ glut, 🔥 supersaturation.

über'säuern *v/t* (*insep*, *no* -ge-, h) *a.* ⚕

overacidify. **Über'säuerung** *f* (-; *no pl*) *a.* ⚕ hyperacidity.

'**Überschall...** supersonic (*aircraft etc*).

'**Überschallknall** *m* sonic boom.

über'schatten *v/t* (*insep*, *no* -ge-, h) overshadow, *fig.* cast a cloud over.

über'schätzen *v/t* (*insep*, *no* -ge-, h) overestimate, overrate. **Über'schätzung** *f* (-; *no pl*) overestimation.

über'schaubar *adj fig.* clear, easy to grasp: **~, von ~er Größe** of manageable size. **über'schauen** → **überblicken** 2.

'**überschäumen** *v/i* (*sep*, h) **1.** froth over. **2.** *fig.* bubble over (**vor** *dat* with).

'**Überschlag** *m* (-[e]s; ~e) **1.** *gym.* a) somersault, b) handspring. **2.** (rough) estimate. **3.** ⚡ flashover. **über'schlagen** (*irr*, *insep*, *no* -ge-, h, → **schlagen**) **I** *v/t* **1.** skip. **2.** calculate roughly. **II** *sich* **~ 3.** fall head over heels, *mot.* overturn, ✈ nose over: F *fig.* **sich fast ~** bend over backwards; **die Ereignisse überschlugen sich** things started happening very fast. **4.** *voice:* crack.

'**überschnappen** *v/i* (*sep*, sn) **1.** F go mad, go crazy: → **übergeschnappt. 2.** *voice:* crack.

über'schneiden: sich ~ (*irr*, *insep*, *no* -ge-, h, → **schneiden**) overlap (*a. fig.*), *lines:* intersect; *fig. zeitlich* ~ coincide. **Über'schneidung** *f* (-; -en) 🔀 intersection, *a. fig.* overlap(ping).

über'schreiben *v/t* (*irr*, *insep*, *no* -ge-, h, → **schreiben**) **1.** head, title. **2.** transfer (*dat* to): **j-m et. ~** make over *s.th.* to *s.o.*

über'schreiten *v/t* (*irr*, *insep*, *no* -ge-, h, → **schreiten**) **1.** cross. **2.** *fig.* exceed.

'**Überschrift** *f* (-; -en) heading, title.

'**Überschuß** *m* (-sses; ~sse) surplus (**an** *dat* of).

'**überschüssig** *adj* surplus.

über'schütten *v/t* (*insep*, *no* -ge-, h) **j-n ~ mit** shower *s.o.* with (*gifts etc*).

'**Überschwang** *m* (-[e]s; *no pl*) exuberance.

über'schwemmen *v/t* (*insep*, *no* -ge-, h) flood, *fig. a.* inundate, ♥ *a.* glut. **Über'schwemmung** *f* (-; -en) flooding.

'**überschwenglich** [-'ʃvɛŋlɪç] *adj* effusive, exuberant: **~e Kritik** F rave review.

'**Übersee:** *in* (*nach*) ~ overseas.

'**überseeisch** *adj* overseas.

über'sehbar *adj* **1.** open (*terrain etc*). **2.** foreseeable, clear. **über'sehen** *v/t* (*irr*,

insep, no -ge-, h, → *sehen*) **1.** → **über-blicken 2. 2.** a) overlook, b) ignore.
über'senden *v/t* (*irr, insep, no* -ge-, h, → *senden*) send, forward.
'**übersetzen**[1] (*sep,* h) **I** *v/t* ferry *s.o., s.th.* over. **II** *v/i* (*a.* sn) cross the river *etc.*
über'setzen[2] *v/t* (*insep, no* -ge-, h) **1.** *v/i* translate. **2.** ⊕ transmit. **Über'set-zer** *m* (-s; -), **Über'setzerin** *f* (-; -nen) translator. **Über'setzung** *f* (-; -en) **1.** translation (*aus* from, *in acc* into). **2.** ⊕ gear ratio, transmission.
Über'setzungs|bü₁ro *n* translating agency. **⟋fehler** *m* error in translation.
'**Übersicht** *f* (-; -en) **1.** survey, summary, outline. **2.** → *Überblick*. '**übersicht-lich** *adj* **1.** open (*terrain etc*), clear. **2.** *fig.* clear(ly arranged), lucid. '**Über-sichtlichkeit** *f* (-; *no pl*) clearness.
'**übersiedeln** *v/i* (*sep,* sn) move (*nach* to). '**Übersiedler(in** *f*) *m pol. hist.* migrant (from East to West Germany).
'**Übersiedlung** *f* (-; -en) move (*nach* to).
'**übersinnlich** *adj* supernatural, psychic.
über'spannen *v/t* (*insep, no* -ge-, h) **1.** span, △ vault. **2.** *fig.* exaggerate: → *Bogen* **1. über'spannt** *adj* extravagant, eccentric. **Über'spanntheit** *f* (-; -en) extravagance, eccentricity.
'**überspielen** *v/t* (*insep, no* -ge-, h) **1.** rerecord (*tape etc*): *auf Band* **⟋** tape(-record). **2.** *fig.* cover *s.th.* up.
über'spitzt *adj* **1.** exaggerated. **2.** oversubtle.
'**überspringen**[1] *v/i* (*irr, sep,* -ge-, sn, → *springen*) ⚡ flash over.
über'springen[2] *v/t* (*irr, insep, no* -ge-, h, → *springen*) **1.** jump over (*or* across), clear. **2.** *fig.* skip (*page etc*).
'**überstaatlich** *adj* supranational.
'**überstehen**[1] *v/i* (*irr, sep,* -ge-, h, → *stehen*) jut out, project.
über'stehen[2] *v/t* (*irr, insep, no* -ge-, h, → *stehen*) survive, weather, ride out (*storm, crisis, etc*): *das wäre überstanden!* that's that; *das Schlimmste ist* **⟋** the worst is over now.
über'steigen *v/t* (*irr, insep, no* -ge-, h, → *steigen*) **1.** climb over. **2.** *fig.* exceed.
über'steuern *v/t* (*insep, no* -ge-, h) **1.** *mot.* oversteer. **2.** ⚡ overmodulate.
⟋'stimmen *v/t* (*insep, no* -ge-, h) outvote. **⟋'strahlen** *v/t* (*insep, no* -ge-, h) eclipse. **⟋'streichen** *v/t* (*irr, insep, no*

-ge-, h, → *streichen*) coat (*mit* with).
'**überstreifen** *v/t* (*sep,* h) slip *s.th.* on.
'**Überstunden** *pl* (**⟋ machen** work *or* do) overtime.
über'stürzen *v/t* (*insep, no* -ge-, h) rush: *nur nichts* **⟋***!* don't rush things; *die Ereignisse überstürzten sich* things started happening very fast.
über'stürzt *adj* hasty, rash.
'**übertariflich** *adj* in excess of the (collectively agreed) scale.
über'teuert *adj* overpriced.
über'tönen *v/t* (*insep, no* -ge-, h) drown (out).
'**Übertrag** [-tra:k] *m* (-[e]s; ⟋e) ✝ carryover. **über'tragbar** *adj* **1.** (*auf acc* to) transferable, *fig. a.* applicable. **2.** ✝ negotiable (*bill*). **3.** ✽ infectious, contagious. **über'tragen** (*irr, insep, no* -ge-, h, → *tragen*) **I** *v/t* **1.** (*auf acc* to) transfer, *a.* make over, give (*powers*), assign, delegate (*task etc*): *j-m et.* **⟋** *a.* entrust *s.th. to s.o.* **2.** ⚡, *phys.*, ⊕ a) transmit (*auf acc* to), b) broadcast. **3.** (*in acc* into) a) transcribe, b) translate (*a. computer*). **4.** transmit *disease* (*auf acc* to), transfuse (*blood*). **5.** *fig.* **et. ⟋ auf** (*acc*) apply *s.th. to*; *im* **⟋***en Sinne* in the figurative sense. **II** *sich* **⟋** *auf* (*acc*) *disease*: be passed on (to), *mood, panic, etc*: communicate itself (to).
Über'tragung *f* (-; -en) **1.** (*auf acc* to) transfer (*a.* ✝, ⚖), assignment (*of rights, tasks, etc*), delegation (*of powers*), conferment (*of offices, titles, etc*). **2.** ⚡, ✽, *phys.*, ⊕ transmission (*auf acc* to), *radio, TV*: a. broadcast. **3.** (*in acc* into) a) transcription, b) translation.
Über'tragungswagen *m radio, TV* outside broadcast (*or* OB) van.
über'treffen *v/t* (*irr, insep, no* -ge-, h, → *treffen*) a) (*an or in dat* in) excel (*sich selbst* o.s.), outdo, surpass, b) exceed (*expectations etc*), go beyond, beat.
über'treiben *v/t* (*irr, insep, no* -ge-, h, → *treiben*) **1. et. ⟋** overdo *s.th.*, carry *s.th.* too far. **2.** *a. v/i* exaggerate.
Über'treibung *f* (-; -en) exaggeration.
'**übertreten**[1] *v/i* (*irr, sep,* -ge-, sn, → *treten*) **1.** (*zu* to) *pol.* change over, convert: *zum Katholizismus* **⟋** *a.* F turn (Roman) Catholic. **2.** *sports*: foul (a jump *or* throw).
über'treten[2] *v/t* (*irr, insep, no* -ge-, h, →

treten) 1. violate (*law etc*). **2. sich den Fuß ~** sprain one's ankle.

Über'tretung *f* (-; -en) 🏛 a) violation, b) (petty) offen/ce (*Am.* -se).

übertrieben [-'tri:bən] *adj* exaggerated, excessive (*demands etc*).

'Übertritt *m* (-[e]s; -e) (**zu** to) change, *pol.* defection, *eccl.* conversion.

über'trumpfen *v/t* (h) *fig.* outdo.

über'tünchen *v/t* (*insep, no* -ge-, h) a. *fig.* whitewash.

über'völkert *adj* overpopulated.

über'vorteilen *v/t* (*insep, no* -ge- h) cheat.

über'wachen *v/t* (*insep, no* -ge-, h) supervise, a. 🔬 *etc* observe, *police:* keep under surveillance, ⚙ check, inspect, monitor. **Über'wachung** *f* (-; -en) supervision, observation, surveillance, ⚙ inspection, checking, monitoring.

überwältigen [-'vɛltɪɡən] *v/t* (*insep, no* -ge-, h) a. *fig.* overpower, overwhelm. **über'wältigend** *adj fig.* overwhelming, a. stunning, breathtaking (*beauty*): **mit ~er Mehrheit** with an overwhelming majority; **nicht gerade ~!** nothing to write home about.

über'weisen *v/t* (*irr, insep, no* -ge-, h, → **weisen**) **1.** transfer (**auf ein Konto** to an account, *j-m* to s.o.'s account). **2.** refer *case, patient, etc* (**an** *acc* to).

Über'weisung *f* (-; -en) **1.** transfer, remittance. **2.** referral (**an** *acc* to).

'überwerfen[1] *v/t* (*irr, sep,* -ge-, h, → **werfen**) fling on (*coat etc*).

über'werfen²: sich ~ (*irr, insep, no* -ge-, h, → **werfen**) fall out (**mit** with).

über'wiegen *v/i* (*irr, insep, no* -ge-, h, → **wiegen**) predominate, prevail.

über'wiegend I *adj* predominant, prevailing: **die ~e Mehrheit** the vast majority. **II** *adv* predominantly, mainly.

über'winden (*irr, insep, no* -ge-, h, → **winden**) **I** *v/t* overcome, get over, surmount (*crisis, illness, etc*). **II sich ~ zu** *inf* bring o.s. to *inf.* **Über'windung** *f* (-; *no pl*) **1.** overcoming (*etc*). **2. es kostete mich ~** it cost me quite an effort.

über'wintern *v/i* (*insep, no* -ge-, h) spend the winter, *zo.* hibernate.

über'wuchern *v/t* (*insep, no* -ge-, h) overgrow.

'Überzahl *f* (-; *no pl*) (**in der ~ sein** be in the) majority.

'überzählig [-tsɛ:lɪç] *adj* surplus, spare.

über'zeichnen *v/t* (*insep, no* -ge-, h) **1.** ✝ oversubscribe. **2.** *fig.* overdraw.

über'zeugen (*insep, no* -ge-, h) **I** *v/t* (**von**) convince (of), *esp.* 🏛 satisfy (as to). **II** *v/i* be convincing. **III sich ~** satisfy o.s. (**von** as to): **~ Sie sich selbst!** go and see for yourself. **über'zeugend** *adj* convincing: **wenig ~** (rather) unconvincing. **über'zeugt** *adj* convinced (**von** of), ardent (*socialist etc*): **von sich selbst** (**sehr**) **~ sein** have a high opinion of o.s. **Über'zeugung** *f* (-; -en) conviction, (*political etc*) convictions: **der ~ sein, daß** be convinced that; **zu der ~ gelangen, daß** come to the conclusion that. **Über'zeugungskraft** *f* powers of persuasion.

'überziehen[1] *v/t* (*irr, sep,* -ge-, h, → **ziehen**) put on (*coat etc*).

über'ziehen² (*irr, insep, no* -ge-, h, → **ziehen**) **I** *v/t* **1.** a) cover, b) coat, c) line. **2.** put fresh linen on (*bed*). **3.** overdraw (*account*). **4.** overrun (*air time*). **5.** *fig.* exaggerate. **II** *v/i* exceed the time limit. **III sich ~** become covered (**mit** with), *sky:* become overcast. **Über'ziehung** *f* (-; *no pl*) ✝ overdraft. **Über'ziehungskre,dit** *m* overdraft credit.

'Überzug *m* a) cover, b) coat(ing).

üblich ['y:plɪç] *adj* usual, customary, normal: **wie ~** as usual; **es ist bei uns** (**so**) **~, daß** it is a custom with us that; **das Übliche** the usual (thing).

'U-Boot *n* submarine.

übrig ['y:brɪç] *adj* remaining, left (over), other: **das ~e, alles ~e** the rest; **das ~e Geld** the rest of the money; **die ~en** the others, the rest; **im ~en** a) as for the rest, b) → **übrigens**; **et. ~ haben** have s.th. left (*fig.* **für** have a soft spot for); **nichts ~ haben für** have no time for; **nichts ~ haben für** have no time for.

übrigbleiben *v/i* (*irr, sep,* -ge-, sn, → **bleiben**) be left, remain: **es blieb mir nichts anderes übrig** (**als**) I had no choice (but).

übrigens ['y:brɪɡəns] *adv* by the way, incidentally.

'übriglassen *v/t* (*irr, sep,* -ge-, h, → **lassen**) leave: **viel** (**nichts**) **zu wünschen ~** leave a lot (nothing) to be desired.

'Übung *f* (-; -en) **1.** practice: **aus der ~ sein** (**kommen**) be (get) out of practice; **in der ~ bleiben** keep one's hand in; **~**

macht den Meister practice makes perfect. **2.** *gym.*, ✗, ♪ exercise.

'**Übungs|aufgabe** f exercise. ~**buch** n book of exercises. ~**hang** m skiing: nursery slope. ~**sache** f *das ist reine ~!* it's just a matter of practice.

Ufer ['u:fɐ] n (-s; -) a) shore, b) bank: *am ~, ans ~* ashore; *über die ~ treten* overflow its banks. '**uferlos** *adj fig.* a) boundless, b) endless (*debate etc*): *ins ~e gehen* lead nowhere.

Ufo ['u:fo] n (-s; -s) UFO, unidentified flying object.

Uhr [u:r] f (-; -en) clock, watch: *wieviel ~ ist es?* what time is it?; *es ist zwei ~* it's two o'clock (*or* 2 p.m., 14.00 hours); *nach m-r ~* by my watch; *um wieviel ~?* (at) what time?; *sports: ein Rennen gegen die ~* a race against time; F *rund um die ~* around the clock. ~**armband** n watch strap. ~**macher** m (-s; -) clock-maker, watchmaker. ~**werk** n clock mechanism, works. ~**zeiger** m hand. ~**zeigersinn** m *im ~* clockwise; *entgegen dem ~* anticlockwise. ~**zeit** f time.

Uhu ['u:hu] m (-s; -s) *zo.* eagle-owl.

Ulk [ʊlk] m (-[e]s; -e) joke, lark: *aus ~* for a joke. '**ulkig** *adj* funny.

Ulme ['ʊlmə] f (-; -n) ♀ elm.

Ultimatum [ʊlti'ma:tʊm] n (-s; -ten) (*ein ~ stellen* deliver an) ultimatum.

Ultra ['ʊltra] m (-s; -s) *pol.* extremist.

Ultrakurzwelle f ⚡ very high frequency (*abbr.* VHF), a. 📡 ultrashort wave.

'**ultrarot** *adj* ultrared, infrared.

'**Ultraschall** m *phys.* ultrasound.

'**Ultraschall...** ultrasonic, supersonic. ~**untersuchung** f 📡 ultrasound scan.

'**ultravio,lett** *adj* ultraviolet.

um [ʊm] **I** *prep* **1.** *space*: (a)round, *time*: at, about, around: ~ *Ostern (herum)* some time around Easter. **2.** *denoting difference*: by: ~ *die Hälfte billiger sein* be only half the price; ~ *so besser* so much the better; ~ *so mehr (weniger)* (*als* as, *weil* because) all the more (less), (so much) the more (less). **3.** for, about: *bitten (schreien)* ~ ask (cry) for. **4.** *es steht schlecht* ~ *ihn* he's in a bad way; *schade* ~ ... it's too bad about ... **II** *conj* ~ *zu inf* (in order) to *inf.* **III** *adv* about, around (*100 persons etc*).

'**umadres,sieren** v/t (*sep, h*) redirect.

'**umarbeiten** v/t (*sep, h*) alter, remodel

(*dress etc*), revise (*book etc*), adapt (*for the screen etc*). '**Umarbeitung** f (-; -en) alteration, revision, adaptation.

um'**armen** v/t (*insep, no* -ge-, h) (*a. sich* ~), **Um'armung** f (-; -en) embrace, hug.

'**Umbau** m (-[e]s; -e, -ten) **1.** a) reconstruction, conversion (*in acc, zu* into), b) altered section. **2.** reorganization.

'**umbauen**[1] (*sep, h*) **I** v/t alter, a. redesign, remodel, convert *flat etc* (*in acc, zu* into). **II** v/i *thea.* change the setting.

um'**bauen**[2] v/t (*insep, no* -ge-, h) build round: *umbauter Raum* interior space.

'**umbenennen** v/t (*irr, sep, h,* → *benennen*) rename.

'**umbesetzen** v/t (*sep, h*) *thea.* recast.

'**umbiegen** v/t (*irr, sep,* -ge-, h, → *biegen*) bend.

'**umbilden** v/t (*sep, h*) reorganize, *pol.* reshuffle (*cabinet etc*). '**Umbildung** f (-; -en) reorganization, *pol.* reshuffle.

'**umbinden** v/t (*irr, sep,* -ge-, h, → *binden*) tie round, (*a. sich* ~) put on (*tie, apron, etc*).

'**umblättern** v/t (*sep, h*) turn over (the page v/i).

'**umbrechen**[1] v/t (*irr, sep,* -ge-, h, → *brechen*) break down.

um'**brechen**[2] v/t (*irr, insep, no* -ge-, h, → *brechen*) make up (*into pages*).

'**umbringen** (*irr, sep,* -ge-, h, → *bringen*) **I** v/t kill: F *nicht umzubringen* indestructible. **II** *sich* ~ kill o.s.; F *fig. sich (fast)* ~ bend over backwards.

'**Umbruch** m (-[e]s; ⁻e) **1.** *print.* makeup, on VSU. **2.** *fig.* upheaval.

'**umbuchen** v/t (*sep, h*) **1.** change one's booking for. **2.** 💲 transfer (*auf acc* to).

'**umdenken** v/i (*irr, sep,* -ge-, h, → *denken*) ~ *müssen* have to do some rethinking. '**Umdenken** n (-s) rethink.

'**umdispo,nieren** v/i (*sep, h*) change one's plans.

'**umdrehen** v/t (*sep, h*) turn (round) (*a. sich* ~), twist (*arm*): *j-m den Hals* ~ wring s.o.'s neck; → *Spieß.*

Um'drehung f (-; -en) turn, *phys.,* ⚙ revolution, rotation: ~*en pro Minute* revolutions per minute (*abbr.* rpm).

umein'**ander** *adv sich* ~ *kümmern etc* take care *etc* of each other (*or* of one another).

'**Umerziehung** f (-; *no pl*) reeducation.

'**umfahren**[1] *v/t* (*irr, sep,* -ge-, h, → **fahren**) run (*or* knock) down.

um'fahren[2] *v/t* (*irr, insep, no* -ge-, h, → **fahren**) drive (*or* sail) round.

'**umfallen** *v/i* (*irr, sep,* -ge-, sn, → **fallen**) **1.** fall (down *or* over), collapse: **zum ﬩ müde** ready to drop. **2.** F *fig.* cave in.

'**Umfang** *m* (-[e]s; *no pl*) a) circumference, girth, b) *a. fig.* extent, size, *fig.* scope, volume (*of sales, traffic, etc*): **10 Zoll im ﬩** 10 inches round; *fig.* **in vollem ﬩** fully; **in großem ﬩** on a large scale, large-scale. '**umfangreich** *adj* **1.** extensive. **2.** voluminous.

um'fassen *v/t* (*insep, no* -ge-, h) *fig.* **1.** comprise. **2.** cover (*period*).

um'fassend *adj* extensive, comprehensive (*knowledge etc*), complete, full (*confession*), sweeping (*reforms etc*).

'**Umfeld** *n* (-[e]s; -er) *fig.* surrounding(s).

'**umformen** *v/t* (*sep,* h) reshape (*a. fig.*), ⚡ transform, convert. '**Umformer** *m* (-s; -) ⚡ transformer, converter.

'**Umfrage** *f* (-; -n) a) inquiry, b) (public) opinion poll, survey.

'**umfüllen** *v/t* (*sep,* h) pour *s.th.* into another container (*etc*), decant (*wine*).

'**umfunktio,nieren** *v/t* (*sep,* h) **et. ﬩ in** (*acc*) convert (*or* turn) s.th. into.

'**Umgang** *m* (-[e]s; *no pl*) **1.** a) social intercourse, relations, b) company, friends: **﬩ haben mit** associate with; **guten** (**schlechten**) **﬩ haben** keep good (bad) company. **2. der ﬩ mit Kindern** *etc* dealing with children *etc*; **im ﬩ mit ...** (in) dealing with ...

umgänglich ['ʊmɡɛŋlɪç] *adj* affable, sociable, easy to get along with.

'**Umgangs|formen** *pl* manners. **﬩sprache** *f* colloquial language: **die englische ﬩** colloquial English. '**umgangssprachlich** *adj* colloquial.

um'garnen *v/t* (*insep, no* -ge-, h) *fig.* ensnare.

um'geben *v/t* (*irr, insep, no* -ge-, h, → **geben**) surround (**sich** o.s.) (**mit** with). **Um'gebung** *f* (-; -en) environs, neighbo(u)rhood, vicinity, *a. biol., sociol.* environment, surroundings.

'**Umgegend** *f* (-; -en) environs, vicinity.

'**umgehen**[1] *v/i* (*irr, sep,* -ge-, sn, → **gehen**) **1.** disease, *rumo(u)r, etc*: circulate, go round. **2.** *ghost:* walk. **3. ﬩ mit** associate with (*s.o.*), treat, deal with, handle

(*s.th., problem*); **sie kann** (**gut**) **mit Leuten ﬩** she knows how to handle people; **er weiß mit Pferden umzugehen** he has a way with horses; **kannst du mit der Maschine ﬩?** do you know how to use (*or* handle) the machine?; → **schonend** II, **sparsam** II.

um'gehen[2] *v/t* (*irr, insep, no* -ge-, h, → **gehen**) **1.** bypass. **2.** *fig.* avoid, evade. '**umgehend** *adj* immediate.

Um'gehung *f* (-; *no pl*) **1.** bypassing. **2.** *fig.* avoidance, *a.* ⚖ evasion.

Um'gehungsstraße *f* bypass, perimeter road.

'**umgekehrt I** *adj* a) reverse, b) inverse, opposite: **im ﬩en Falle** in the reverse case; **in ﬩er Reihenfolge** in reverse order; (**genau**) **﬩!** it's exactly the other way round. **II** *adv* the other way round, conversely.

'**umgestalten** *v/t* (*sep,* h) reshape, *fig. a.* reorganize, ⊙ *etc* redesign.

'**umgraben** *v/t* (*irr, sep,* -ge-, h, → **graben**) dig (up), turn (over).

um'grenzen *v/t* (*insep, no* -ge-, h) *fig.* define.

'**umgrup,pieren** *v/t* (*sep,* h) regroup, *pol.* reshuffle. '**Umgrup,pierung** *f* (-; -en) regrouping, *pol.* reshuffle.

'**Umhang** *m* (-[e]s; ⸚e) cape, wrap.

'**umhängen** *v/t* (*sep,* h) **1.** put on (*coat etc*), sling (*rifle*). **2.** rehang (*picture*). '**Umhängetasche** *f* shoulder bag.

'**umhauen** *v/t* (*irr, sep,* -ge-, h, → **hauen**) **1.** fell, cut down. **2.** F *fig. j-n ﬩* drink *etc*: knock s.o. out, *news etc*: bowl s.o. over.

um'her *adv* about, (a)round.

um'hinkönnen *v/i* (*irr, sep,* -ge-, h, → **können**) **ich kann nicht umhin zu** *inf* I cannot help *ger*.

um'hören: sich ﬩ (*sep,* h) keep one's ears open, ask around.

um'hüllen *v/t* (*insep, no* -ge-, h) (**mit**) wrap up (*or* envelop) (in), cover (with). **Um'hüllung** *f* (-; -en) wrapping, cover.

'**Umkehr** *f* (-; *no pl*) *j-n zur ﬩ zwingen* force s.o. (to turn) back. '**umkehren** (*sep*) **I** *v/i* (sn) turn back. **II** *v/t* (h) turn round (*a. sich ﬩*), reverse (*a. fig.*).

'**Umkehrfilm** *m* reversal film.

'**umkippen** (*sep*) **I** *v/t* (h) **1.** tip over, upset. **II** *v/i* (sn) **2.** fall over, *car etc:* overturn, ⚓ *a.* capsize. **3.** F faint, keel over. **4.** F *fig.* turn, change completely, *river etc*: die, *wine*: turn sour.

um'klammern *v/t* (*insep, no* -ge-, h) clutch, clinch.

'umklappen *v/t* (*sep*, h) turn down.

'Umkleideka|bine *f* changing cubicle. **'umkleiden: sich ~** (*sep*, h) change (one's clothes). **'Umkleideraum** *m* changing (*sports:* locker) room.

'umknicken *v/i* (*sep*, sn) (*mit dem Fuß*) **~** sprain one's ankle.

'umkommen *v/i* (*irr, sep*, -ge-, sn, → **kommen**) die (*a*. F *vor* with), be killed.

'Umkreis *m* (-es; *no pl*) vicinity: *im ~ von* within a radius of, for *three miles etc* round. **um'kreisen** *v/t* (*insep, no* -ge-, h) circle (*astr.* revolve) round.

'umkrempeln *v/t* (*sep*, h) **1.** roll up (*sleeve etc*). **2.** F *fig.* change completely.

'umladen *v/t* (*irr, sep*, -ge-, h, → **laden**) reload.

'Umlage *f* (-; -n) distribution of cost: *die ~ betrug ...* each person had to pay ...

'Umland *n* (-[e]s; *no pl*) environs, surrounding countryside.

'Umlauf *m* (-[e]s; ⸚e) **1.** circulation: *in ~ bringen* a) put *s.th.* in circulation, issue, b) start (*rumo*[*u*]*r*); *im ~ sein* circulate, *rumo*(*u*)*r*: *a.* be going round. **2.** *astr., phys.* a) revolution, b) cycle, c) orbit. **3.** circular (letter). **'Umlaufbahn** *f* (*in s-e ~ bringen or gelangen* put *or* get into) orbit. **'umlaufen** *v/i* (*irr, sep*, -ge-, sn, → **laufen**) circulate. **'Umlaufkapi,tal** *n* † floating capital.

'Umlaut *m* (-[e]s; -e) a) umlaut, b) (vowel) mutation.

'umlegen *v/t* (*sep*, h) **1.** lay flat (*wheat etc*), lay down (*tree*), tear down (*fence*). **2.** put on (*coat etc*). **3.** throw (*lever*). **4.** transfer (*a. teleph.*), *a.* move (*patient etc*), shift *appointment etc* (*auf acc* to). **5.** (*auf acc* among) apportion, divide (*costs etc*). **6.** *j-n ~* a) F knock s.o. down, b) bump s.o. off, c) V lay s.o.

'umleiten *v/t* (*sep*, h) divert, detour.

'Umleitung *f* (-; -en) diversion, detour. **'Umleitungsschild** *n* detour sign.

'umlernen *v/i* (*sep*, h) *wir müssen sehr ~* we have a lot of relearning to do.

'umliegend *adj* surrounding.

'ummelden *v/t* (*sep*, h) (*a. sich ~*) register one's change of address (*bei* with).

'ummodeln *v/t* (*sep*, h) *fig.* change.

'umorgani,sieren *v/t* (*sep*, h) reorganize.

'umpacken *v/t* (*sep*, h) repack.

'umpflanzen *v/t* (*sep*, h) replant.

'umquar,tieren *v/t* (*sep*, h) move.

um'randen *v/t* (*insep, no* -ge-, h), **Um'randung** *f* (-; -en) border.

'umräumen *v/t* (*sep*, h) move *s.th.* (to another place), rearrange (*room*).

'umrechnen *v/t* (*sep*, h) convert (*in acc* into). **'Umrechnung** *f* (-; -en) conversion (*in acc* into).

'Umrechnungs|kurs *m* rate of exchange. **~ta,belle** *f* conversion table.

'umreißen[1] *v/t* (*irr, sep*, -ge-, h, → **reißen**) pull (*or* knock) down.

um'reißen[2] *v/t* (*irr, insep, no* -ge-, h, → **reißen**) *fig.* outline.

'umrennen *v/t* (*sep*, -ge-, h, → **rennen**) run (*or* knock) down.

um'ringen *v/t* (*insep, no* -ge-, h) surround.

'Umriß *m* contour, *a. fig.* outline: *feste Umrisse annehmen* take shape.

'umrühren *v/t* (*sep*, h) stir.

'umrüsten *v/t* (*sep*, h) ⚙ change *s.th.* over (*auf acc* to).

'umsatteln *v/i* (*sep*, h) F change one's job (*student:* one's subject): *~* (*von ...*) *auf* (*acc*) switch (from ...) to.

'Umsatz *m* (-es; ⸚e) † turnover, sales. **~beteiligung** *f* sales commission. **~steuer** *f* turnover tax.

'umschalten (*sep*, h) **I** *v/t, a. v/i* ⚡, ⚙ *or fig.* switch (*or* change) (over) (*auf acc* to). **II** *v/i* TV change channels.

'Umschalttaste *f typewriter:* shift key.

'umschichten *v/t* (*sep*, h) **1.** rearrange. **2.** *fig.* regroup.

'Umschichtung *f* (-; -en) *fig.* regrouping: *soziale ~* social upheaval.

um'schiffen *v/t* (*insep, no* -ge-, h) sail round, double: → **Klippe**.

'Umschlag *m* (-[e]s; ⸚e) **1.** a) envelope, b) cover, (*book etc*) dust jacket. **2.** a) cuff, b) turnup. **3.** ✚ (*feuchter*) *~* compress. **4.** *no pl* † a) handling (*of goods*), b) goods handled, c) transshipment.

'umschlagen (*irr, sep*, -ge-, → **schlagen**) **I** *v/i* (sn) **1.** → **umkippen** 2. **2.** *weather, wind, mood, etc:* change (suddenly). **II** *v/t* (h) **3.** turn up (*sleeve etc*). **4.** a) handle (*goods*), b) transship.

'Umschlag|hafen *m* port of transshipment. **~platz** m trading cent/re (*Am.* -er), ♣ place of transshipment.

um'schließen v/t (*irr, insep, no* -ge-, h, → *schließen*) **1.** surround, enclose. **2.** *fig.* encompass.

'**umschnallen** v/t (*sep*, h) buckle on.

'**umschreiben**[1] v/t (*irr, sep,* -ge-, h, → *schreiben*) **1.** rewrite. **2.** transfer *property (auf acc* to). **um'schreiben**[2] v/t (*irr, insep, no* -ge-, h, → *schreiben*) **1.** paraphrase, circumscribe (*a.* Ⓐ). **2.** outline. '**Umschreibung**[1] f (-; -en) **1.** rewriting. **2.** ♱ transfer. **Um'schreibung**[2] f (-; -en) paraphrase, circumscription (*a.* Ⓐ).

'**Umschrift** f (-; -en) transcription.

'**Umschuldung** f (-; -en) ♱ conversion (of a debt).

'**umschulen** v/t (*sep*, h) **1.** retrain. **2.** transfer *student* to another school.

um'schwärmen v/t (*insep, no* -ge-, h) **1.** swarm round. **2.** *fig.* idolize.

'**Umschweife:** *ohne* **~** a) *say etc s.th.* straight out, b) *do s.th.* straightaway.

'**umschwenken** v/i (*sep*, sn) **1.** wheel round. **2.** *fig.* veer round.

'**Umschwung** m (-[e]s; ⸚e) change, reversal, *esp. pol.* swing, about-face.

um'segeln v/t (*insep, no* -ge-, h) sail round, double.

'**umsehen:** *sich* **~** (*irr, sep,* -ge-, h, → *sehen*) **1.** look back. **2.** look (a)round (*nach* for): *sich in der Stadt* **~** (have a) look (a)round the city.

'**umsein** v/i (*irr, sep,* -ge-, sn, → *sein*) F be over: *s-e Zeit ist um* his time is up.

'**umseitig** [-zaɪtɪç] adj and adv overleaf.

'**umsetzen** v/t (*sep*, h) **1.** move, transfer, ✗ transplant. **2.** sell, turn over. **3.** *et.* **~** *in (acc)* a. 🜊, *phys.* convert (*or* transform) s.th. into; (*in die Praxis*) **~** realize; *et. in die Tat* **~** put s.th. into action.

'**Umsicht** f (-; *no pl*) circumspection.

'**umsichtig** adj circumspect.

'**umsiedeln** v/t (*sep*, h) resettle.

'**Umsiedler(in** f) m resettler, *pol.* Ethnic German repatriate (from the East).

'**Umsiedlung** f (-; -en) resettlement.

um'sonst adv **1.** for nothing, free (of charge). **2.** in vain: *nicht* **~** not without (good) reason, not for nothing.

um'spannen v/t (*insep, no* -ge-, h) span.

'**Umspannwerk** n transformer station.

um'spielen v/t (*insep, no* -ge-, h) soccer

etc: dribble round, *fig.* play (a)round.

'**umspringen** v/i (*irr, sep,* -ge-, sn, → *springen*) **1.** → *umschlagen* 2. **2.** *mit j-m grob etc* **~** treat s.o. roughly *etc.*

'**Umstand** m **1.** fact, circumstance. **2.** *pl* circumstances, conditions, situation: *unter Umständen* possibly, perhaps; *unter allen Umständen* at all events; *unter diesen* (*k-n*) *Umständen* under the (no) circumstances; F *in anderen Umständen sein* be in the family way; → *mildern* I. **3.** *ohne viel Umstände* without much fuss; *Umstände machen* a) cause trouble, b) make a fuss; *machen Sie* (*sich*) *k-e Umstände!* don't go to any trouble. '**umstände-halber** adv owing to circumstances.

umständlich ['ʊmʃtɛntlɪç] adj a) complicated, b) long-winded, c) awkward, d) fussy: *das ist* (*mir*) *viel zu* **~** that's far too much trouble (for me).

'**Umstandskleid** n maternity dress.

'**Umstandskrämer** m (-s; -) F fusspot.

'**Umstandswort** n (-[e]s; ⸚er) adverb.

'**umstehend** adj next (*page*), a. adv overleaf: *die Umstehenden* the bystanders.

'**Umsteige(fahr)karte** f transfer ticket.

'**umsteigen** v/i (*irr, sep,* -ge-, sn, → *steigen*) **1.** change (*nach* for). **2.** F *fig.* switch (*auf acc* to).

um'stellen[1] v/t (*insep, no* -ge-, h) surround.

'**umstellen**[2] (*sep*, h) **I** v/t a) change, b) rearrange (*furniture etc*), c) regroup (*team*), d) reset (*watch*), e) 🜊 change over (*auf acc* to), f) reorganize (*firm etc*): **~** *auf* (*acc*) switch to, convert to; *auf Computer* **~** computerize; *s-e Lebensweise* **~** readjust one's way of life. **II** v/i **~** get used to new conditions, adjust (*auf acc* to). '**Umstellung** f (-; -en) change, rearrangement, 🜊 change-over (*or* switch) (*auf acc* to), reorganization, adjustment (*auf acc* to): *e-e große* **~** *sein* be quite a change.

'**umstimmen** v/t (*sep*, h) *j-n* **~** bring s.o. round.

'**umstoßen** v/t (*irr, sep,* -ge-, h, → *stoßen*) **1.** knock over (*or* down). **2.** *fig.* change (*last will, plan, etc*), reverse (*judg[e]ment etc*), upset (*plan*).

umstritten [ʊm'ʃtrɪtən] adj contested.

'**umstrukturieren** v/t (*sep*, h) restructure.

'**umstülpen** v/t (*sep*, h) a) turn *s.th.* upside down, b) turn *s.th.* inside out.

'**Umsturz** *m* (-es; ⸚e) overthrow, revolution. '**umstürzen** (*sep*) **I** *v/t* (h) upset, knock over, *pol.* overthrow. **II** *v/i* (sn) fall down (*or* over), overturn. '**Umstürzler** [-ʃtyrtslər] *m* (-s; -) revolutionary. '**umstürzlerisch** *adj* subversive. '**Umsturzversuch** *m* attempted coup.

'**Umtausch** *m* (-[e]s; -e), '**umtauschen** *v/t* (*sep*, h) exchange (*gegen* for).

'**umtopfen** *v/t* (*sep*, h) ✄ repot.

'**Umtriebe** *pl contp.* activities, intrigues.

'**umtun**: *sich* ~ (*irr, sep*, -ge-, h, → *tun*) look around (*nach* for).

'**U-Mu͵sik** *f* light music.

'**umwälzen** *v/t* (*sep*, h) **1.** ⊙ circulate. **2.** *fig.* revolutionize.

'**umwälzend** *adj fig.* revolutionary.

'**Umwälzpumpe** *f* circulating pump.

'**Umwälzung** *f* (-; -en) **1.** ⊙ circulation. **2.** *fig.* revolution, upheaval.

'**umwandeln** *v/t* (*sep*, h) change (*in acc, zu* into), *phys.* transform, convert (*a.* ✝), 🙼 commute (*sentence*): *sie ist wie umgewandelt* she is a completely different person. '**Umwandler** *m* (-s; -) ⚡, ⊙ converter. '**Umwandlung** *f* (-; -en) change, transformation, conversion, 🙼 commutation.

'**Umweg** *m* detour, roundabout way: *e-n* ~ *machen* make a detour; *das ist ein* ~ *für mich* that takes me out of my way; *fig. auf ~en* indirectly, in a roundabout way; *ohne* ~*e* straight.

'**Umwelt** *f* (-; *no pl*) environment: *unsere* ~ *a.* the world around us.

'**Umwelt...** environmental. ~**belastung** *f* (environmental) pollution. ⥈**bewußt** *adj* environment-conscious. ⥈**feindlich** → *umweltschädlich*. ~**forscher** *m* ecologist. ~**forschung** *f* (-; *no pl*) ecology. ⥈**freundlich** *adj* ecologically friendly, nonpolluting, *a.* biodegradable. ~**kata͵strophe** *f* ecocatastrophe. ~**krimi͵nali͵tät** *f* environmental crime. ~**krise** *f* ecological crisis, ecocrisis. ~**mini͵sterium** *n* Department of the Environment. ~**poli͵tik** *f* ecopolicy. ⥈**po͵li͵tisch** *adj* ecopolitical. ~**schäden** *pl* damage done by pollution. ⥈**schädlich** *adj* harmful (to the environment), polluting. ~**schutz** *m* environmental (*or* pollution) control, conservation. ~**schützer** *m* (-s; -) environmentalist, conservationist. ~**sünder** *m* F polluter.

~**verbrechen** *n* environmental crime. ~**verschmutzung** *f* pollution. ~**zerstörung** *f* ecocide.

'**umwenden**: *sich* ~ (*irr, sep*, -ge-, h, → *wenden*) turn round.

um'werben *v/t* (*irr, insep, no* -ge-, h, → *werben*) court, *a. fig.* woo.

'**umwerfen** *v/t* (*irr, sep*, -ge-, h, → *werfen*) **1.** → *umstoßen.* **2.** → *umhauen* 2. '**umwerfend** *adj* fantastic, mind-blowing: ~ *komisch* too funny for words.

'**Umwertung** *f* (-; -en) revaluation.

um'wickeln *v/t* (*insep, no* -ge-, h) wind *s.th.* round, bandage *s.th.* (*mit* with).

'**umziehen** (*irr, sep*, -ge-, → *ziehen*) **I** *v/i* (sn) move (house). **II** *v/t* (h) *j-n* ~ change s.o.'s clothes; *sich* ~ change.

umzingeln [ʊm'tsiŋəln] *v/t* (*insep, no* -ge-, h) surround, encircle.

'**Umzug** *m* (-[e]s; ⸚e) **1.** move. **2.** procession, *pol.* demonstration march.

unab'änderlich [ʊn'ap'ɛndərlıç] *adj* unalterable, irrevocable: *sich ins* ⥈**e** *fügen* resign o.s. to the inevitable.

'**unabhängig** *adj* independent (*von* of): ~ *von* irrespective of; ~ *davon ob* regardless whether. '**Unabhängige** *m, f* (-n; -n) *pol.* independent. '**Unabhängigkeit** *f* (-; *no pl*) independence.

unab'kömmlich *adj* indispensable: *er ist* ~ he is busy, he can't get away.

unablässig [ʊn'ap'lɛsıç] *adj* incessant.

unab'sehbar *adj* a) unforeseeable, b) incalculable, immense (*damage etc*): *auf* ~**e Zeit** for an indefinite period of time.

'**unabsichtlich** *adj* unintentional.

unab'wendbar *adj* unavoidable.

'**unachtsam** *adj* inattentive, careless. '**Unachtsamkeit** *f* (-; *no pl*) carelessness.

'**unähnlich** *adj* (*dat*) unlike (*s.o., s.th.*).

unan'fechtbar *adj* incontestable.

'**unangebracht** *adj* inappropriate: ~ *sein a.* be out of place.

'**unangefochten** *adj and adv* **1.** undisputed(ly). **2.** unhindered.

'**unangemeldet** *adj* unannounced.

'**unangemessen** *adj* **1.** inappropriate, inadequate. **2.** unreasonable (*price etc*).

'**unangenehm** *adj* unpleasant, *a.* nasty, awkward: *das* ⥈**e dabei ist** the unpleasant thing about it is.

'**unangetastet** *adj* untouched.

unan'greifbar *adj a. fig.* unassailable.

unan'nehmbar *adj* unacceptable.

'Unannehmlichkeiten *pl* (*j-m ~ berei-ten* cause s.o.) trouble: ~ *bekommen* get into trouble.

'unansehnlich *adj* unsightly, plain.

'unanständig *adj* 1. indecent, obscene. 2. unfair.

unan'tastbar *adj* unimpeachable, invio-lable (*rights*), *iro.* sacrosanct.

'unappe,titlich *adj* unappetizing, *a. fig.* unsavo(u)ry.

'Unart *f* (-; -en) bad habit, bad trick.

'unartig *adj* naughty.

'unäs,thetisch *adj* un(a)esthetic, *w.s.* unpleasant, unsavo(u)ry, ugly.

'unaufdringlich *adj* unobtrusive.

'unauffällig *adj* 1. inconspicuous. 2. unobtrusive, discreet.

unauf'findbar *adj* untraceable, *pred* not to be found.

'unaufgefordert *adj and adv* unasked, *adv a.* of one's own accord.

unauf'haltsam [ʊnʔaʊf'haltsaːm] *adj* unstoppable.

unauf'hörlich [ʊnʔaʊf'høːrlɪç] *adj* incessant, continuous.

unauf'lösbar, unauf'löslich *adj* indissoluble, *a.* 🜛, 🜨 insoluble.

'unaufmerksam *adj* 1. inattentive. 2. thoughtless, careless.

'Unaufmerksamkeit *f* (-; *no pl*) 1. inattention. 2. thoughtlessness.

'unaufrichtig *adj* insincere. '**Unaufrich-tigkeit** *f* (-; *no pl*) insincerity.

unauf'schiebbar [ʊnʔaʊf'ʃiːpbaːr] *adj* urgent.

unaus'bleiblich [ʊnʔaʊs'blaɪplɪç] *adj* inevitable.

unaus'führbar *adj* impracticable.

'unausgefüllt *adj* 1. blank (*form*). 2. *fig.* unfulfilled (*life, person*).

'unausgeglichen *adj* unbalanced, unstable. **Unausgeglichenheit** *f* (-; *no pl*) imbalance, instability.

'unausgesprochen *adj* unspoken.

unaus'löschlich [ʊnʔaʊs'lœʃlɪç] *adj fig.* indelible.

unaus'rottbar *adj* ineradicable.

unaus'sprechlich [ʊnʔaʊs'ʃprɛçlɪç] *adj* unpronounceable, *fig.* unspeakable.

unaus'stehlich [ʊnʔaʊs'ʃteːlɪç] *adj* insufferable, intolerable.

unaus'weichlich [ʊnʔaʊs'vaɪçlɪç] *adj* unavoidable, inevitable.

'unbändig ['ʊnbɛndɪç] *adj* 1. unruly. 2. *fig.* tremendous (*rage, hate, etc*).

'unbarmherzig *adj* merciless. '**Unbarm-herzigkeit** *f* (-; *no pl*) mercilessness.

'unbeabsichtigt *adj* unintentional.

'unbeachtet *adj and adv* (~ *bleiben* go) unnoticed: ~ *lassen* disregard.

'unbeanstandet *adj* unobjected: *et. ~ lassen* let s.th. pass.

'unbeantwortet *adj* unanswered.

'unbearbeitet *adj* a) untreated, unfinished, b) undealt with, c) unedited.

'unbebaut *adj* 1. 🌱 untilled. 2. undeveloped (*land*).

'unbedacht *adj* thoughtless, rash.

unbedarft ['ʊnbədarft] *adj* F naive.

'unbedenklich *adj* safe.

'unbedeutend *adj* insignificant, unimportant, *a.* negligible.

'unbedingt I *adj* a) unconditional, b) absolute. II *adv* absolutely, at all costs: *et. ~ brauchen* need s.th. badly; *nicht ~* a) not necessarily, b) not exactly.

unbe'fahrbar *adj* impassable.

'unbefangen *adj* 1. unbias(s)ed, impartial. 2. uninhibited, natural.

'Unbefangenheit *f* (-; *no pl*) 1. impartiality. 2. naturalness.

'unbefleckt *adj fig.* unsullied: *eccl. ~e Empfängnis* Immaculate Conception.

'unbefriedigend *adj* unsatisfactory.

'unbefriedigt *adj* unsatisfied.

'unbefristet I *adj* unlimited. II *adv* for an unlimited period.

'unbefugt *adj* unauthorized.

'Unbefugte *m, f* (-n; -n) unauthorized person: *Zutritt für ~ verboten!* no unauthorized entry!

'unbegabt *adj* untalented.

'unbegreiflich *adj* incomprehensible: *es ist mir völlig ~* it's beyond me.

'unbegrenzt I *adj* unlimited, boundless. II *adv* indefinitely: *ich habe ~ Zeit* I have unlimited time.

'unbegründet *adj* unfounded.

'Unbehagen *n* (-s; *no pl*) unease.

'unbehaglich *adj* uncomfortable, *fig. a.* uneasy: *sich ~ fühlen* a. feel ill at ease.

'unbehelligt *adj and adv* a) unmolested, b) unhindered.

'unbeherrscht *adj* unrestrained: ~ *sein* have no self-control. '**Unbeherrscht-heit** *f* (-; *no pl*) lack of self-control.

unbeholfen ['ʊnbəhɔlfən] *adj* clumsy.

'**Unbeholfenheit** f (-; no pl) clumsiness.
unbe'irrbar adj imperturbable.
unbe'irrt adj unswerving, unperturbed.
'**unbekannt** adj unknown: *das war mir* ~ I didn't know that; ~*e Größe* → '**Unbekannte** f (-n; -n) A or fig. unknown (quantity).
'**unbekleidet** adj and adv undressed.
'**unbekömmlich** adj indigestible.
'**unbekümmert** adj carefree: ~ *um* unconcerned about.
'**unbelastet** adj **1.** carefree: ~ *sein* be free from worries, pol. have a clean record. **2.** ✝ unencumbered (*property*).
unbe'lehrbar adj hopeless.
'**unbeleuchtet** adj mot. without lights.
'**unbeliebt** adj unpopular (*bei* with).
'**Unbeliebtheit** f (-; no pl) unpopularity.
'**unbemannt** adj unmanned, ✈ pilotless.
'**unbemerkt** adj and adv unnoticed.
'**unbemittelt** adj without means, poor.
unbenommen ['ʊnbənɔmən] adj *es ist Ihnen* ~ *zu* inf you are at liberty to inf.
'**unbenutzt** adj unused.
'**unbeobachtet** adj and adv unobserved.
'**unbequem** adj **1.** uncomfortable. **2.** fig. a) inconvenient, b) embarrassing (*question* etc), c) difficult (*person*). '**Unbequemlichkeit** f (-; -en) **1.** no pl uncomfortableness. **2.** fig. inconvenience.
unbe'rechenbar adj incalculable, fig. a. unpredictable (*person*).
'**unberechtigt** adj **1.** unauthorized. **2.** unjustified, unfair.
'**unberechtigter'weise** adv **1.** without permission. **2.** without good reason.
unbe'rücksichtigt adj unconsidered: *et.* ~ *lassen* leave s.th. out of account.
unbe'rufen int touch wood!
'**unberührt** adj untouched (a. fig.), virgin (*girl, nature, etc*): fig. ~ *bleiben von* not to be affected by.
unbeschadet [ʊnbə'ʃaːdət] adj (gen) a) without prejudice to, b) irrespective of.
'**unbeschädigt** adj undamaged, intact.
'**unbeschäftigt** adj unemployed, idle.
'**unbescheiden** adj immodest. '**Unbescheidenheit** f (-; no pl) immodesty.
unbescholten ['ʊnbəʃɔltən] adj blameless: ⚖ ~ *sein* have no police record.
'**unbeschränkt** adj unrestricted, absolute (*power, right, etc*).
unbeschreiblich [ʊnbə'ʃraɪplɪç] adj indescribable.

'**unbeschrieben** adj blank (*paper*): fig. ~*es Blatt* unknown quantity.
'**unbeschwert** adj fig. a) carefree, b) light (*conscience*): ~ *von* free from.
'**unbesehen** adv et. ~ *kaufen* buy s.th. sight unseen; *das glaube ich dir* ~ I well believe you.
'**unbesetzt** adj vacant (*post*), a. unoccupied, free (*seat* etc).
unbe'siegbar adj invincible.
unbe'siegt adj undefeated.
'**unbesonnen** adj imprudent, rash.
'**Unbesonnenheit** f (-; no pl) rashness.
'**unbesorgt** I adj unconcerned (*wegen* about): *seien Sie (deswegen)* ~*!* don't worry! II adj safely.
'**unbespielt** adj blank (*tape, cassette*).
'**unbeständig** adj unstable, changeable, unsettled (*weather* etc). '**Unbeständigkeit** f (-; no pl) unstableness (*etc*).
'**unbestätigt** adj unconfirmed.
'**unbestechlich** adj **1.** incorruptible. **2.** unerring (*judgement* etc). '**Unbestechlichkeit** f (-; no pl) incorruptibility.
'**unbestimmt** adj a) vague (*idea* etc), b) indeterminate, a. ling. indefinite: *auf* ~*e Zeit* for an indefinite period. '**Unbestimmtheit** f (-; no pl) vagueness.
unbe'streitbar adj indisputable.
unbe'stritten I adj undisputed. II adv indisputably, without doubt.
'**unbeteiligt** adj **1.** not involved (*an* dat in). **2.** indifferent.
'**unbetont** adj unstressed.
'**unbeträchtlich** adj negligible, insignificant: *nicht* ~ quite considerable.
unbeugsam [ʊn'bɔykzaːm] adj fig. uncompromising.
'**unbewacht** adj a. fig. unguarded.
'**unbewaffnet** adj unarmed.
'**unbeweglich** adj immobile, a. ⚖ immovable (*possessions, holiday, etc*), motionless, ⚙ fixed, rigid (a. fig.), (*mentally*) inflexible: ~*e Güter* immovables. '**Unbeweglichkeit** f (-; no pl) immobility, (*mental*) inflexibility.
'**unbewegt** adj a) expressionless, b) unmoved (a. adv).
unbe'weisbar adj unprovable.
unbe'wiesen adj unproved.
unbe'wohnbar adj uninhabitable. '**unbewohnt** adj uninhabited, unoccupied.
'**unbewußt** adj unconscious.

unbe'zahlbar *adj* **1.** too expensive. **2.** *fig.* priceless (*a.* F *funny*).

'unbezahlt *adj* unpaid.

unbe'zähmbar *adj fig.* indomitable.

unbe'zwingbar *adj* invincible.

'Unbildung *f* (-; *no pl*) lack of education.

'unblutig **I** *adj* bloodless, ♣ nonoperative. **II** *adv* without bloodshed.

'unbrauchbar *adj* useless, unsuitable, impracticable (*plan etc*), ⊕ unserviceable: *et.* ~ *machen* render s.th. useless.

'Unbrauchbarkeit *f* (-; *no pl*) uselessness, impracticability, unserviceability.

un'brennbar *adj* nonflammable.

'unbüro,kratisch *adj* unbureaucratic.

'unchristlich *adj* unchristian.

und [ʊnt] *conj* and: ~? well?; F ~ *ob!* you bet!; *na* ~? so what?; ~ *so weiter* (*or fort*) and so on; ~ *wenn* (*auch*) even if.

'Undank *m* (-[e]s; *no pl*) ingratitude: F *nur* ~ *ernten* get small thanks for it.

'undankbar *adj* **1.** ungrateful (*gegen* to). **2.** thankless (*task etc*).

'Undankbarkeit *f* (-; *no pl*) **1.** ingratitude. **2.** thanklessness.

'unda,tiert *adj* undated.

,undefi'nierbar *adj* undefinable.

'undemo,kratisch *adj* undemocratic.

un'denkbar *adj* unthinkable.

undenklich *adj seit* ~*en Zeiten* from time immemorial.

'undeutlich *adj* indistinct, *pred* not clear, inarticulate (*speech*), blurred (*picture etc*), vague (*idea etc*).

'undicht *adj* leaking, *pred* not tight: ~*e Stelle* leak (*a. fig. pol.*).

'Unding *n* (-[e]s; *no pl*) absurdity: *es ist ein* ~ it is preposterous (*or* absurd).

'undiszipli,niert *adj* undisciplined.

'unduldsam *adj* intolerant.

'Unduldsamkeit *f* (-; *no pl*) intolerance.

undurch'dringlich *adj* impenetrable, *fig. a.* inscrutable.

undurch'führbar *adj* impracticable.

'undurchlässig *adj* impermeable (*für* to).

'undurchsichtig *adj* **1.** opaque. **2.** *fig.* mysterious, inscrutable.

'uneben *adj* uneven, rough (*road etc*).

'unecht *adj* **1.** a) *a. fig.* false, *pred* not genuine, b) artificial, c) imitation(ed), fake(d), F phon(e)y. **2.** ♣ improper.

'unehelich *adj* illegitimate.

'unehrenhaft *adj* dishono(u)rable.

'unehrlich *adj* dishonest, insincere.

'Unehrlichkeit *f* (-; *no pl*) dishonesty.

'uneigennützig *adj* unselfish.

'uneingeschränkt *adj* unrestricted, unqualified (*praise*), absolute (*trust etc*).

'uneingeweiht *adj* uninitiated.

'uneinheitlich *adj* nonuniform, varied.

'uneinig *adj* divided: (*sich*) ~ *sein* a. be at variance, disagree. 'Uneinigkeit *f* (-; *no pl*) disagreement, discord.

unein'nehmbar *adj* impregnable.

'unempfänglich *adj* (*für* to) insusceptible, unreceptive.

'unempfindlich *adj* **1.** insensitive (*gegen* to). **2.** durable, rugged.

'Unempfindlichkeit *f* (-; *no pl*) **1.** insensitiveness (*gegen* to). **2.** durability.

un'endlich **I** *adj* ♪, ♩, *phys.* infinite (*a. fig.*), endless: *phot. auf* ~ *einstellen* focus at infinity; *fig. bis ins* ~*e* ad infinitum. **II** *adv* infinitely (*etc*), *fig. a.* immensely: ~ *klein* infinitesimal; ~ *lang* endless; ~ *viel* a tremendous amount of; ~ *viele* no end of.

Un'endlichkeit *f* (-; *no pl*) infinity.

unent'behrlich *adj* indispensable (*dat*, *für* to).

unent'geltlich *adj and adv* free (of charge), *adv a.* for nothing.

unent'rinnbar *adj* inescapable.

'unentschieden *adj* undecided (*a. person*), *a.* open (*question*), *sports:* drawn: ~ *enden* end in a draw; ~ *spielen* draw.

'Unentschieden *n* (-s; -) *sports:* draw.

'unentschlossen *adj* undecided, irresolute. 'Unentschlossenheit *f* (-; *no pl*) irresolution, indecision.

unent'schuldbar *adj* inexcusable.

'unentschuldigt *adj* ~*es Fehlen* unexcused absence.

unent'wegt [ʊn'ɛntveːkt] *adj* incessant.

Unent'wegte *m, f* (-n; -n) *pol.* diehard.

unent'wirrbar *adj* inextricable.

unerbittlich [ʊn'ɛr'bɪtlɪç] *adj* merciless.

'unerfahren *adj* inexperienced. 'Unerfahrenheit *f* (-; *no pl*) inexperience.

unerforschlich [ʊn'ɛr'fɔrʃlɪç] *adj fig.* unfathomable.

'unerforscht *adj* unexplored.

'unerfreulich *adj* unpleasant.

uner'füllbar *adj* unrealizable.

'unerfüllt *adj* unfulfilled.

'unergiebig *adj* unproductive.

'uner**gründlich** *adj* unfathomable, *fig. a.* inscrutable.

'uner**heblich** *adj* insignificant, *esp.* ⚖ irrelevant (*für* to).

uner'**hört** *adj* **1.** a) unheard-of, b) outrageous, scandalous: *~!* what a cheek! **2.** F terrific, fantastic.

'uner**kannt** *adj* unrecognized.

'uner**klärlich** *adj* inexplicable.

uner'**läßlich** [ʊnʔɛr'lɛslɪç] *adj* essential.

'uner**laubt I** *adj* a) unauthorized, *pred* not allowed, b) illegal, illicit. **II** *adv* without permission.

'uner**ledigt** *adj* not yet dealt with, unanswered (*mail*), unfulfilled (*orders etc*): *~e Dinge* unfinished business.

uner**meßlich** [ʊnʔɛr'mɛslɪç] *adj* immeasurable, immense, vast.

uner**müdlich** [ʊnʔɛr'my:tlɪç] *adj* indefatigable, untiring.

'uner**quicklich** *adj* unpleasant.

uner'**reichbar** *adj* inaccessible, *fig.* unattainable (*goal etc*): *für j-n ~* out of s.o.'s reach; *er war ~ I* (we *etc*) couldn't get hold of him. **'uner'reicht** *adj fig.* unequal(l)ed, unrival(l)ed, record ...

uner**sättlich** [ʊnʔɛr'zɛtlɪç] *adj a. fig.* insatiable.

'uner**schlossen** *adj* undeveloped.

'uner**schöpflich** [ʊnʔɛr'ʃœpflɪç] *adj* inexhaustible.

'uner**schrocken** *adj* undaunted.

uner**schütterlich** [ʊnʔɛr'ʃʏtɐlɪç] *adj* unshak(e)able, imperturbable.

uner'**schwinglich** *adj* unaffordable (*goods*), exorbitant (*price*): *für j-n ~ sein* be beyond s.o.'s means.

uner'**setzlich** *adj* **1.** irreplaceable. **2.** irreparable (*damage*).

uner'**träglich** *adj* unbearable.

'uner**wähnt** *adj* unmentioned: *et. ~ lassen* make no mention of s.th.

'uner**widert** *adj* unrequited (*love*).

'uner**wünscht** *adj* undesirable.

'un**fähig** *adj* **1.** incapable, incompetent: *~ zu* unqualified for (*a task etc*). **2.** *~ zu inf.* unable to *inf.*, incapable of *ger.*

'**Unfähigkeit** *f* (-; *no pl*) **1.** incompetence. **2.** inability.

'un**fair** *adj* unfair.

'**Unfall** *m* (-[e]s; *~e*) accident. *~arzt m* casualty doctor. *~flucht f → Fahrerflucht*. ⚖**frei** *adj* accident-free. ⚖**gefährdet** *adj* accident-prone. *~krankenhaus*

n casualty hospital. *~opfer n* accident victim. *~quote f*, *~rate f* accident rate. *~stati,on f* a) first-aid station, b) casualty ward. *~stelle f* scene of (the) accident. *~tod m* accidental death. ⚖**trächtig** *adj* hazardous. *~ursache f* cause of the accident. *~verhütung f* prevention of accidents. *~versicherung f* accident insurance. *~wagen m* **1.** car damaged in an accident. **2.** ✈ crash tender.

un'**faßbar**, un'**faßlich** *adj* incomprehensible, inconceivable.

un'**fehlbar I** *adj* infallible (*a. eccl.*), unerring. **II** *adv* infallibly, without fail.

Un'fehlbarkeit *f* (-; *no pl*) infallibility.

'un**fein** *adj* indelicate, unrefined, *pred* not nice, bad form.

'un**fertig** *adj* **1.** unfinished. **2.** *fig.* immature (*person*).

un**flätig** ['ʊnfle:tɪç] *adj* filthy, obscene.

'un**folgsam** *adj* disobedient.

un**förmig** ['ʊnfœrmɪç] *adj* a) shapeless, b) bulky, c) misshapen.

'un**fran,kiert** *adj* unstamped (*letter*).

'un**frei** *adj* **1.** not free. **2.** *fig.* inhibited.

'un**freiwillig** *adj* a) involuntary, unintentional, b) unconscious (*humo[u]r*).

'un**freundlich** *adj* unfriendly, inclement (*climate, weather*), cheerless (*room etc*).

'**Unfreundlichkeit** *f* (-; *no pl*) unfriendliness, inclemency, cheerlessness.

'**Unfriede** *m* (-n; *no pl*) discord.

'un**fruchtbar** *adj* infertile, *a. fig.* barren, sterile, *fig.* fruitless. '**Unfruchtbarkeit** *f* (-; *no pl*) infertility, *fig.* fruitlessness.

Unfug ['ʊnfu:k] *m* (-[e]s; *no pl*) a) (*~ treiben* be up to) mischief, b) nonsense: ⚖ *grober ~* disorderly conduct.

Ungar ['ʊngar] *m* (-n; -n), '**Ungarin** *f* (-; -nen), '**ungarisch** *adj* Hungarian.

'**Ungarn** *n* (-s) Hungary.

'un**gastlich** *adj* inhospitable.

'un**geachtet** *prep* (*gen*) regardless of.

un**geahnt** ['ʊngə'a:nt] *adj* undreamt-of.

'un**gebeten** *adj* unasked, uninvited.

'un**gebildet** *adj* uneducated.

'un**geboren** *adj* unborn.

'un**gebräuchlich** *adj* unusual.

'un**gebraucht** *adj* unused.

'un**gebunden** *adj* **1.** *print.* unbound, in sheets. **2.** *fig.* unattached, independent.

'un**gedeckt** *adj* uncovered (*a. cheque*), unsecured (*credit*), *sports:* unmarked.

'**Ungeduld** *f* (-; *no pl*) impatience.

'ungeduldig *adj* impatient.

'ungeeignet *adj* (**zu** for) unsuitable, *person: a.* unqualified, inopportune (*time*).

ungefähr ['ʊŋgəfɛːr] I *adj* approximate, rough. II *adv* approximately, about, around: **so ~** s.th. like that; **wo ~?** roughly where?

'ungefährlich *adj* harmless, safe.

'ungefällig *adj* unobliging.

'ungehalten *adj* annoyed (**über** *acc* at).

'ungehemmt I *adj* unchecked, *psych.* uninhibited. II *adv* without restraint.

'ungeheuchelt *adj* unfeigned.

'ungeheuer I *adj* 1. immense, enormous. 2. F tremendous, terrific. II *adv* 3. enormously (*etc*). **'Ungeheuer** *n* (-s; -) monster. **'ungeheuerlich** *adj* monstrous, outrageous. **'Ungeheuerlichkeit** *f* (-; -en) monstrosity, outrage.

'ungehindert *adj and adv* unhindered.

'ungehobelt *adj fig.* rude, uncouth.

'ungehörig *adj* improper, impertinent.

'ungehorsam *adj* disobedient. **'Ungehorsam** *m* (-s; *no pl*) disobedience.

'ungeklärt *adj* 1. unsettled (*question etc*), unsolved (*case, problem, etc*). 2. **~e Abwässer** untreated sewage.

'ungekünstelt *adj* unaffected.

'ungekürzt *adj* unabridged (*book*), uncut (*film*).

'ungeladen *adj* 1. uninvited (*guest*). 2. unloaded (*gun*).

'ungelegen *adj* inconvenient: **das kommt mir sehr ~!** that doesn't suit me at all! **'Ungelegenheiten** *pl* **j-m ~ machen** put s.o. out, inconvenience s.o.

'ungelenk *adj* clumsy, stiff.

'ungelernt *adj* unskilled (*worker*).

'ungemein *adv* immensely.

'ungemischt *adj* unmixed.

'ungemütlich *adj* uncomfortable (*a. fig.*), cheerless (*room*): F **~ werden** get unpleasant, turn nasty. **'Ungemütlichkeit** *f* (-; *no pl*) uncomfortableness.

'ungenannt *adj* unnamed, anonymous.

'ungenau *adj* inaccurate, inexact, *fig.* vague, hazy.

'Ungenauigkeit *f* (-; -en) inaccuracy.

'unge‚niert I *adj* uninhibited. II *adv* without inhibition, openly.

'ungenießbar *adj* 1. a) inedible, b) undrinkable. 2. F *person:* unbearable.

'ungenügend *adj* insufficient, *ped.* unsatisfactory, poor.

'ungenutzt *adj* unused: **e-e Gelegenheit ~ lassen** let an opportunity slip.

'ungepflegt *adj* unkempt, neglected.

'ungerade *adj* uneven, odd (*number*).

'ungerecht *adj* unjust. **'ungerechtfertigt** *adj* unjustified. **'Ungerechtigkeit** *f* (-; -en) injustice (**gegen** to).

'ungeregelt *adj* unregulated, irregular (*life, working hours, etc*).

'ungern *adv* unwillingly, reluctantly: **ich tue es ~** I don't like doing it.

'ungerührt *adj fig.* unmoved (**von** by).

'ungesagt *adj* (**~ bleiben** be left) unsaid.

'ungesalzen *adj* unsalted.

'ungeschehen *adj* **~ machen** undo.

'Ungeschick *n* (-[e]s; *no pl*), **'Ungeschicklichkeit** *f* (-; *no pl*) clumsiness.

'ungeschickt *adj* clumsy.

'ungeschlagen *adj fig.* undefeated.

'ungeschliffen *adj* 1. rough (*diamond*). 2. *fig.* unpolished (*behavio[u]r etc*).

'ungeschminkt *adj* 1. not made up, without makeup. 2. *fig.* unvarnished, *a.* plain (*truth*).

'ungeschoren *adj* 1. unshorn. 2. *fig.* unmolested: **j-n ~ lassen** leave s.o. in peace; **~ davonkommen** get off lightly (*or* F scot-free).

'ungeschrieben *adj* unwritten.

'ungeschützt *adj* unprotected.

'ungesehen *adj and adv* unseen.

'ungesellig *adj* unsociable. **'Ungeselligkeit** *f* (-; *no pl*) unsociableness.

'ungesetzlich *adj* illegal, illicit, unlawful.

'Ungesetzlichkeit *f* (-; *no pl*) illegality.

'ungesittet *adj* uncivilized.

'ungestört *adj and adv* undisturbed.

'ungestraft I *adj* unpunished. II *adv* with impunity: **~ davonkommen** go unpunished, F get off scot-free.

ungestüm ['ʊŋgəʃtyːm] *adj* impetuous.

'Ungestüm *n* (-s; *no pl*) impetuosity.

'ungesund *adj a. fig.* unhealthy.

'ungeteilt *adj a. fig.* undivided.

ungetrübt ['ʊŋgətryːpt] *adj fig.* unspoilt.

Ungetüm ['ʊŋgətyːm] *n* (-s; -e) monster.

'ungeübt *adj* untrained.

'ungewaschen *adj and adv* unwashed.

'ungewiß *adj* uncertain: **j-n im ungewissen lassen** keep s.o. guessing.

'Ungewißheit *f* (-; *no pl*) uncertainty: **in ~ schweben** be (kept) in suspense.

'ungewöhnlich *adj* unusual.

'**ungewohnt** *adj* strange, new (**für** to).
'**ungewollt** *adj* unintentional, unintended (*effect etc*), unwanted (*baby*).
'**ungezählt** *adj* uncounted, countless.
'**ungezähmt** *adj* untamed.
Ungeziefer ['ʊngətsi:fər] *n* (-s; *no pl*) *a. fig.* vermin.
'**ungezogen** *adj* naughty. '**Ungezogenheit** *f* (-; *no pl*) naughtiness.
'**ungezügelt** *fig.* **I** *adj* unbridled. **II** *adv* unrestrainedly.
'**ungezwungen** *adj* relaxed, informal. '**Ungezwungenheit** *f* (-; *no pl*) ease.
'**ungiftig** *adj* nontoxic.
'**Unglaube** *m* unbelief. '**unglaubhaft** → **unglaubwürdig**. '**ungläubig** *adj* incredulous, disbelieving, *a. eccl.* unbelieving. **un'glaublich** *adj* incredible, unbelievable. '**unglaubwürdig** *adj* untrustworthy, implausible (*reasons etc*).
'**ungleich** **I** *adj* **1.** unequal, unlike, dissimilar. **II** *adv* **2.** ~ **lang** (**groß**) unequal in length (size); ~ **verteilt** unevenly distributed. **3.** far *better etc*.
'**Ungleichgewicht** *n* imbalance.
'**Ungleichheit** *f* (-; *no pl*) **1.** dissimilarity, unlikeness. **2.** inequality.
'**ungleichmäßig** *adj* uneven, irregular.
'**Unglück** *n* (-[e]s; -e) a) misfortune, b) bad luck, c) mishap, d) disaster: **es ist** (**weiter**) **kein** ~! it is no tragedy!; **zu allem** ~ to crown it all; ~ **bringen** bring ill (*or* bad) luck; **in sein** ~ **rennen** head for disaster. '**unglücklich** *adj* a) unfortunate, b) unlucky, c) unhappy, miserable: ~ **enden** end badly; ~ **verliebt** crossed in love. '**unglücklicher'weise** *adv* unfortunately. '**unglückselig** *adj* a) unfortunate, b) disastrous, fatal.
'**Unglücks|fall** *m* **1.** accident. **2.** misadventure. **~rabe** *m* unlucky fellow. **~tag** *m* black day. **~zahl** *f* unlucky number.
'**Ungnade** *f* (-; *no pl*) disfavo(u)r: **in** ~ **fallen** fall out of favo(u)r (**bei** with).
'**ungnädig** *adj* ungracious.
'**ungültig** *adj* invalid, (null and) void, *coin:* not legal tender, *vote:* spoilt, *goal:* disallowed: ~ **machen** cancel (*ticket etc*); **et. für** ~ **erklären** invalidate s.th., declare s.th. null and void.
'**Ungültigkeit** *f* (-; *no pl*) invalidity.
'**Ungunst** *f* (-; *no pl*) **zu j-s** ~**en** to s.o.'s disadvantage. '**ungünstig** *adj* unfavo(u)rable, inconvenient (*date etc*).

'**ungut** *adj* bad: **ein** ~**es Gefühl haben** have misgivings (**bei** about); **nichts für** ~! no offen/ce (*Am.* -se) meant.
'**unhaltbar** *adj* **1.** untenable (*arguments etc*). **2.** intolerable (*conditions*). **3.** *sports:* unstoppable (*ball, shot, etc*).
'**unhandlich** *adj* unwieldy.
'**unharˌmonisch** *adj* a. *fig.* discordant.
'**Unheil** *n* (-s; *no pl*) a) harm, b) disaster: ~ **anrichten** wreak havoc.
un'heilbar *adj* incurable: ~ **krank** suffering from an incurable disease.
'**unheilbringend** *adj* fatal. '**unheilvoll** *adj* **1.** disastrous. **2.** sinister (*look etc*).
'**unheimlich** **I** *adj* **1.** uncanny, weird (*both a. fig.*), eerie, F creepy. **2.** F *fig.* tremendous, terrific. **II** *adv* **3.** F *fig.* tremendously, awfully: ~ **gut** terrific, fantastic; ~ **viel** a tremendous lot of.
'**unhöflich** *adj* impolite.
'**Unhöflichkeit** *f* (-; *no pl*) impoliteness.
'**Unhold** *m* (-[e]s; -e) monster, fiend.
un'hörbar *adj* inaudible.
'**unhygiˌenisch** *adj* unhygienic.
Uni ['ʊni] *f* (-; -s) F university.
Uniform [uni'fɔrm] *f* (-; -en) uniform.
uniformiert [-'mi:rt] *adj* in uniform.
Unikum [u'ni:kʊm] *n* (-s; -ka] **1.** unique specimen. **2.** (*pl* -s) F character.
'**uninteresˌsant** *adj* uninteresting, not interesting. '**uninteresˌsiert** *adj* uninterested (**an** *dat* in).
Union [u'nio:n] *f* (-; -en) union: **die** ~ the Christian-Democrat Union (*or* Party).
universal [univer'za:l] *adj* universal.
Univer'sal|erbe *m* sole heir. **~mittel** *n* universal remedy, *a. fig.* panacea.
universell [univer'zɛl] *adj* universal.
Universität [univerzi'tɛ:t] *f* (-; -en) (**auf** *or* **an der** ~ at the) university; **e-e** ~ **besuchen** go to university.
Universiˌtäts... university (*library, hospital, studies, etc*).
Universum [uni'vɛrzʊm] *n* (-s; *no pl*) universe.
unken ['ʊŋkən] *v/i* (h) F *fig.* croak.
'**unkenntlich** *adj* unrecognizable.
'**Unkenntnis** *f* (-; *no pl*) ignorance: **in** ~ (*gen*) unaware of *the danger etc*, ignorant of *the facts etc*; **j-n in** ~ **lassen** keep s.o. in the dark (**über** *acc* about).
'**unklar** *adj* unclear, *pred* not clear, *a.* vague, obscure, muddled; **im** ~**en sein** be in the dark (**über** *acc* about).

'**Unklarheit** f (-; no pl) unclearness, lack of clarity, vagueness.

'**unklug** adj unwise, imprudent.

'**unkompli,ziert** adj uncomplicated.

'**unkontrol,lierbar** adj uncontrollable.

'**unkontrol,liert** adj uncontrolled.

'**Unkosten** pl costs, expenses: **allgemeine** (or **laufende**) ~ running expenses, + overhead; → **stürzen** 6.

'**Unkraut** n (-[e]s; ̈er) weed(s): fig. ~ **vergeht nicht** ill weeds grow apace. ~**vertilgungsmittel** n weed killer.

'**unkritisch** adj uncritical.

'**unkulti,viert** adj uncultivated.

'**unkündbar** adj permanent (post), contract etc: not terminable: **er ist** ~ F he can't be sacked.

'**unlängst** adv lately, recently.

'**unlauter** adj fig. dubious: + ~**er Wettbewerb** unfair competition.

'**unleserlich** adj illegible.

'**unlieb** adj **es ist mir nicht** ~(, **daß**) it suits me quite fine (that).

'**unliebenswürdig** adj unamiable, unfriendly. '**Unliebenswürdigkeit** f (-; no pl) unamiableness, unfriendliness.

unliebsam [ˈʊnliːpzaːm] adj unpleasant.

'**unlini,iert** adj unruled.

'**unlogisch** adj illogical.

un'lösbar adj insoluble (problem etc).

un'löslich adj 🜄 insoluble.

'**Unlust** f (-; no pl) a) listlessness, b) aversion: **mit** ~ with reluctance.

'**unlustig** adj listless, reluctant.

'**unma,nierlich** adj ill-mannered.

'**unmännlich** adj effeminate.

'**unmaßgeblich** adj unauthoritative: iro. **nach m-r** ~**en Meinung** in my humble opinion.

'**unmäßig** adj excessive, immoderate. '**Unmäßigkeit** f (-; no pl) immoderateness, excess.

'**Unmenge** f (-; -n) (**von** of) vast (or enormous) amount (or number), F loads.

'**Unmensch** m monster, brute: F **sei kein** ~! have a heart! '**unmenschlich** adj **1.** inhuman, cruel. **2.** F fig. awful. '**Unmenschlichkeit** f (-; no pl) inhumanity, cruelty.

'**unmerklich** adj imperceptible.

'**unme,thodisch** adj unmethodical.

'**unmißverständlich I** adj unmistakable. **II** adv a) unmistakably, b) plainly.

'**unmittelbar I** adj immediate, direct. **II** adv immediately, directly: ~ **vor** (dat) a) right in front of, b) time: just before; ~ **bevorstehen** be imminent.

'**unmö,bliert** adj unfurnished.

'**unmo,dern** adj outmoded, dated.

'**unmöglich I** adj impossible (a. F fig. person, dress, situation, etc): **Ɂes leisten** (**verlangen**) do (ask) the impossible; fig. ~ **aussehen** look a sight; **sich** ~ **machen** a) compromise o.s., b) make a fool of o.s. **II** adv not possibly: **ich kann es** ~ **tun** I can't possibly do it. '**Unmöglichkeit** f (-; no pl) impossibility.

'**unmo,ralisch** adj immoral.

'**unmoti,viert** adj unmotivated.

'**unmündig** adj under age, minor.

'**unmusi,kalisch** adj unmusical.

'**Unmut** m (-[e]s; no pl) annoyance (**über** acc at).

unnachahmlich [ˈʊnnaːxˈʔaːmlɪç] adj inimitable.

'**unnachgiebig** adj unyielding.

'**unnachsichtig** adj strict, severe.

un'nahbar adj unapproachable.

'**unna,türlich** adj **1.** unnatural (a. fig.). **2.** affected.

'**unnötig** adj unnecessary.

unnütz [ˈʊnnʏts] adj useless, pointless.

'**unordentlich** adj disorderly, untidy.

'**Unordnung** f (-; no pl) disorder, mess: **in** ~ in a mess; **in** ~ **bringen** mess s.th. up.

'**unor,ganisch** adj inorganic.

'**unpar,teilisch** adj impartial. '**Unpar,teiische** m (-n; -n) sports: referee.

'**unpassend** adj **1.** inappropriate, unsuitable. **2.** improper. **3.** untimely.

'**unpas,sierbar** adj impassable.

unpäßlich [ˈʊnpɛslɪç] adj ~ **sein**, **sich** ~ **fühlen** be indisposed, feel unwell. '**Unpäßlichkeit** f (-; -en) indisposition.

'**unpatri,otisch** adj unpatriotic.

'**Unper,son** f (-; -en) nonperson.

'**unper,sönlich** adj impersonal.

'**unpo,litisch** adj apolitical.

'**unpopu,lär** adj unpopular.

'**unpraktisch** adj impractical.

'**unproble,matisch** adj unproblematic.

'**unproduk,tiv** adj unproductive, + nonproductive.

'**unpünktlich** adj unpunctual. '**Unpünktlichkeit** f (-; no pl) unpunctuality.

'**unqualifi,ziert** adj unqualified.

'**unra,siert** adj unshaven.

Unrat ['ʊnraːt] *m* (-[e]s; *no pl*) rubbish, *Am.* garbage: F **~ wittern** smell a rat.
'**unratio,nell** *adj* inefficient.
'**unratsam** *adj* inadvisable.
'**unrecht** *adj* wrong: *et.* ♀*es tun* do s.th. wrong. '**Unrecht** *n* (-[e]s; *no pl*) wrong, injustice: *j-m* ♀ *tun* do s.o. wrong; *im ~ sein,* ♀ *haben* be (in the) wrong, *a.* be mistaken; *j-m* ♀ *geben* disagree with s.o., *fig.* result *etc*: prove s.o. wrong; *j-n ins ~ setzen* put s.o. in the wrong; *zu ~* wrong(ful)ly, unjustly; *nicht zu ~* not without good reason.
'**unrechtmäßig** *adj* wrongful, unlawful.
'**unredlich** *adj* dishonest.
'**Unredlichkeit** *f* (-; *no pl*) dishonesty.
'**unre,ell** *adj* dishonest.
'**unregelmäßig** *adj* irregular. '**Unregelmäßigkeit** *f* (-; -en) irregularity.
'**unreif** *adj* **1.** unripe. **2.** *fig.* immature.
'**unrein** *adj* impure (*a. fig.*), bad (*skin*).
'**Unreinheit** *f* (-; -en) impurity.
'**unreinlich** *adj* unclean.
'**unren,tabel** *adj* unprofitable.
un'rettbar *adj* irrecoverable: *~ verloren* irretrievably lost, *person:* beyond help.
'**unrichtig** *adj* incorrect, wrong.
'**Unrichtigkeit** *f* (-; -en) **1.** *no pl* incorrectness. **2.** mistake, error.
'**Unruh** *f* (-; -en) balance wheel.
'**Unruhe** *f* (-; *no pl*) **1.** restlessness. **2.** uneasiness, anxiety. **3.** commotion, tumult: *pol.* *~n* unrest, disturbances.
'**Unruheherd** *m fig.* trouble spot.
'**Unruhestifter(in** *f) m* troublemaker.
'**unruhig** *adj* **1.** restless. **2.** *fig.* troubled (*sleep, times*). **3.** *fig.* uneasy, worried. **4.** *fig.* noisy. **5.** *fig.* choppy (*sea*).
'**unrühmlich** *adj* inglorious.
uns [ʊns] **I** *pers pron* **1.** us, to us: *ein Freund von ~* a friend of ours; *wir sehen ~ selten* we seldom see each other. **II** *reflex pron* **2.** ourselves: *wir waschen ~* we wash (ourselves). **3.** each other, one another.
'**unsachgemäß** *adj* improper, inexpert.
'**unsachlich** *adj* unobjective, irrelevant, *pred* beside the point: *~ werden* become personal.
unsagbar [ʊn'zaːkbaːr], **unsäglich** [ʊn-'zɛːklɪç] *adj* unspeakable.
'**unsanft** *adj* rough: *fig. ein ~es Erwachen* a rude awakening.
'**unsauber** *adj* **1.** dirty. **2.** *fig.* a) sloven-

ly, b) shady, dubious, c) *sports:* unfair.
'**unschädlich** *adj* harmless: *~ machen* render harmless, neutralize, put *s.o.* out of action, lay *criminal* by the heels.
'**unscharf** *adj* **1.** *phot.* blurred: *opt.* *~ (eingestellt)* out of focus. **2.** *fig.* hazy.
un'schätzbar *adj* invaluable.
'**unscheinbar** *adj* insignificant, inconspicuous, plain, *Am.* homely.
'**unschicklich** *adj* unseemly, improper.
un'schlagbar *adj* unbeatable.
'**unschlüssig** *adj* irresolute. '**Unschlüssigkeit** *f* (-; *no pl*) irresolution.
'**unschön** *adj* **1.** unlovely, ugly. **2.** *fig.* a) unkind, *pred* not nice, b) unpleasant.
'**Unschuld** *f* (-; *no pl*) innocence.
'**unschuldig** *adj* innocent (*an dat* of): 🏛 *sich für ~ erklären* plead not guilty.
'**unschwer** *adv* easily, without difficulty.
'**unselbständig** *adj* **1.** dependent (on others), helpless. **2.** employed: *Einkünfte aus ~er Arbeit* wage and salaries income. '**Unselbständigkeit** *f* (- *no pl*) lack of independence.
'**unselig** *adj* unfortunate, fatal.
unser ['ʊnzər] **I** *pos pron* our, ours: *der (die, das) ~e* (*or* uns[e]rige) ours; *wir haben das ~e getan* we have done our bit. **II** *gen of wir:* of us.
'**unsereiner,** '**unsereins,** '**unseresgleichen** *indef pron* F people like us.
'**unser(e)twegen** *adv* **1.** for our sake. **2.** because of us.
'**unseri,ös** *adj* dubious.
'**unsicher** *adj* **1.** unsafe, insecure, risky: F *die Gegend ~ machen criminal etc:* prowl (*humor. tourists etc:* infest) the place. **2.** uncertain. **3.** unsteady, shaky (*a. fig. in dat* in). **4.** insecure, unsure (of o.s.): *j-n ~ machen* make s.o. feel insecure. '**Unsicherheit** *f* (-; *no pl*) **1.** unsafeness, insecurity. **2.** uncertainty. **3.** unsteadiness. **4.** unsureness (of o.s.), insecurity. '**Unsicherheitsfaktor** *m* element of uncertainty.
'**unsichtbar** *adj* invisible.
'**Unsichtbarkeit** *f* (-; *no pl*) invisibility.
'**Unsinn** *m* (-[e]s; *no pl*) **1.** (*~ reden* talk) nonsense (*or* rubbish). **2.** *~ machen* fool around. '**unsinnig** *adj* **1.** unreasonable, absurd. **2.** F tremendous.
'**Unsitte** *f* (-; -n) bad habit.
'**unsittlich** *adj* immoral, indecent.
'**Unsittlichkeit** *f* (-; *no pl*) immorality.

'**unso,lide** *adj* **1.** unsolid. **2.** loose (*life, person, etc*). **3.** dubious (*firm etc*).

'**unsozi,al** *adj* antisocial.

'**unsportlich** *adj* **1.** unathletic. **2.** *fig.* unfair, unsporting.

un'sterblich I *adj* immortal. **II** *adv* F awfully: **~ verliebt** madly in love (*in acc* with). **Un'sterblichkeit** *f* (-; *no pl*) immortality.

'**unstet** *adj* **1.** inconstant. **2.** restless.

un'stillbar *adj* unquenchable (*thirst*), insatiable (*hunger*), *fig.* unappeasable.

'**Unstimmigkeit** *f* (-; -en) *usu. pl* **1.** discrepancy. **2.** disagreement, difference.

'**unstreitig** *adj* indisputable.

'**Unsumme** *f* (-; -n) enormous sum.

'**unsym,metrisch** *adj* asymmetrical.

'**unsym,pathisch** *adj* disagreeable, unpleasant: **er ist mir ~** I don't like him.

'**Untat** *f* (-; -en) atrocity, outrage.

'**untätig** *adj* inactive, idle. '**Untätigkeit** *f* (-; *no pl*) inactivity, idleness.

'**untauglich** *adj* unfit (*a.* ✕), unsuitable.

'**Untauglichkeit** *f* (-; *no pl*) unfitness.

un'teilbar *adj* indivisible.

unten ['ʊntən] *adv* a) below, b) downstairs: **da ~** down there; **nach ~** down(wards), *a.* downstairs; **~ auf der Seite** at the bottom of the page; **siehe ~!** see below; **von oben bis ~** from top to bottom (*person*: to toe); F **er ist bei mir ~ durch** I am through with him.

'**untenerwähnt**, '**untengenannt** *adj* undermentioned, mentioned below.

unter ['ʊntər] *prep* (*dat*) **1.** under, below, *a.* less than: **~ Null** below zero; **~ sich haben** be in charge of; **was versteht man ~ ...?** what is meant by ...?; → **Bedingung, Hand, Träne** *etc.* **2.** among: **einer ~ hundert** one in a hundred; **~ anderem** among other things; **~ uns gesagt** between you and me; **wir sind ganz ~ uns** we are quite alone. **3.** during: **~ s-r Regierung** under (*or* during) his reign.

'**Unter|abteilung** *f* subdivision. **~arm** *m* forearm. **~art** *f* subspecies. **~ausschuß** *m* subcommittee. **~bau** *m* (-[e]s; -ten) **1.** substructure, foundation. **2.** *no pl fig.* base, ✝ *etc* infrastructure.

'**unterbelichten** *v/t* (*insep, no* -ge-, h) underexpose.

'**unterbeschäftigt** *adj* underemployed.

'**unterbesetzt** *adj* understaffed.

'**unterbewerten** *v/t* (*insep, no* -ge-, h) undervalue, *fig. a.* underrate.

'**unterbewußt** *adj* subconscious. '**Unterbewußtsein** *n* (-s; *no pl*) the subconscious: **im ~** subconsciously.

'**unterbezahlt** *adj* underpaid.

unter'bieten *v/t* (*irr, insep, no* -ge-, h, → **bieten**) underbid, undercut (*price*), undersell (*competitors*), beat (*record*).

unter'binden *v/t* (*irr, insep, no* -ge-, h, → **binden**) *fig.* stop, prevent.

unter'bleiben *v/i* (*irr, insep, no* -ge-, sn, → **bleiben**) **1.** be left undone, not to take place. **2.** stop, cease.

Unter'bodenschutz *m mot.* underseal, *Am.* undercoat.

unter'brechen (*irr, insep, no* -ge-, h, → **brechen**) **I** *v/t* interrupt, *teleph.* cut off, hold up (*game*), ⚡ adjourn: **die Fahrt** (*or* **Reise**) **~** break one's journey. **II** **sich ~** pause. **Unter'brechung** *f* (-; -en) interruption, break, *a.* stopover.

unter'breiten *v/t* (*insep, no* -ge-, h) submit (*dat* to).

'**unterbringen** *v/t* (*irr, sep,* -ge-, h, → **bringen**) **1.** accommodate, *a.* put *s.o.* up: **j-n ~ in** put *s.o.* into (⚡ commit *s.o.* to) *an institution etc*; **j-n ~ in** (*or bei*) get *s.o.* a job with *a firm etc*; F *fig.* **ich kann ihn nicht ~** I can't place him. **2.** a) store, b) stow (away): **et. ~ in** (*dat*) get (*or* fit) *s.th.* into, ⊕ install *s.th.* in. **3.** ✝ place capital, orders (**bei** with): **ein Buch bei e-m Verlag ~** have a book accepted by publishers. **Unter'bringung** *f* (-; -en) accommodation, housing, ⚡ committal (**in** *dat* to). '**Unterbringungsmöglichkeit(en** *pl*) *f* accommodation.

'**unterbuttern** *v/t* (*sep*, h) F **j-n ~** push *s.o.* under.

'**Unterdeck** *n* ⚓ lower deck.

unterder'hand *adv* secretly, on the quiet: **~ verkaufen** sell *s.th.* privately.

unter'dessen *adv* in the meantime.

unter'drücken *v/t* (*insep, no* -ge-, h) suppress (*a. publication*), *a.* stifle (*laughter, yawn, etc*), oppress (*people*), put down, quell (*rebellion*). **Unter'drücker** *m* (-s; -) oppressor. **Unter'drückung** *f* (-; -en) suppression, oppression.

'**unterdurchschnittlich** *adj* below average.

'**untere** *adj* lower.

'**untereinander¹** *adv* one below the

other. **unterein'ander**[2] *adv* among one another (*or* each other, themselves, yourselves, *etc*).

'**unterentwickelt** *adj* underdeveloped (*a. phot.*), *a.* backward (*child, country, etc*), *psych.* subnormal.

'**unterernährt** *adj* underfed, undernourished. '**Unterernährung** *f* (-; *no pl*) malnutrition, undernourishment.

Unter'fangen *n* (-s; *no pl*) **1.** venture, undertaking. **2.** attempt.

Unter'führung *f* (-; -en) a) underpass, b) subway, *Am.* pedestrian underpass.

'**Unterfunkti,on** *f* ✱ hypofunction.

'**Untergang** *m* (-[e]s; ⸚e) **1.** *astr.* setting. **2.** ⚓ sinking. **3.** *fig.* (down)fall, decline.

'**Untergattung** *f* subgenus.

Unter'gebene *m, f* (-n; -n) subordinate.

'**untergehen** *v/i* (*irr, sep, -ge-, sn,* → **gehen**) go down, go under (*both a. fig.*), ⚓ *a.* sink, *astr. a.* set: *fig. im Lärm* ~ be drowned out (*or* lost) by the noise.

'**untergeordnet** *adj* **1.** subordinate (*dat* to). **2.** *fig.* secondary (*importance etc*).

'**Unter'geschoß** *n* basement. **~gestell** *n mot.* underframe. **~gewicht** *n* (~ *haben* be) underweight.

unter'|gliedern *v/t* (*insep, no -ge-, h*) subdivide. **~'graben** *v/t* (*irr, insep, no -ge-, h,* → **graben**) *fig.* undermine.

'**Untergrund** *m* (-[e]s; ⸚e) **1.** *geol.* subsoil. **2.** *paint.* ground(ing). **3.** *no pl pol.* (*in den* ~ *gehen* go) underground. **~bahn** *f* underground, *in London: a.* tube, *Am.* subway. **~bewegung** *f pol.* underground movement. **~kämpfer(in** *f) m pol.* underground fighter.

'**unterhalb I** *prep* (*gen*) below, under. **II** *adv* below, underneath.

'**Unterhalt** *m* (-[e]s; *no pl*) **1.** support, maintenance. **2.** → **Lebensunterhalt**.

unter'halten (*irr, insep, no -ge-, h,* → **halten**) **I** *v/t* **1.** maintain, support. **2.** keep up (*correspondence etc*). **3.** amuse, entertain. **II** *sich* ~ **4.** talk (*mit* with, to). **5.** *sich* (*gut*) ~ enjoy o.s., have a good time. **unter'haltend** → **unterhaltsam**. **Unter'halter** *m* (-s; -) entertainer. **unter'haltsam** *adj* entertaining.

'**Unterhalts|anspruch** *m* maintenance claim. **~beihilfe** *f* maintenance grant. **☿berechtigt** *adj* entitled to maintenance. **~kosten** *pl* maintenance costs.

Unter'haltung *f* (-; -en) **1.** entertain-

ment. **2.** conversation, talk. **3.** *no pl* upkeep, maintenance.

Unter'haltungs... entertainment (*concert, film, industry, etc*). **~branche** *f* (*in der* ~ in) show business. **~elek,tronik** *f* video and audio systems. **~litera,tur** *f* light fiction. **~mu,sik** *f* light music. **~ro,man** *m* light novel. **~wert** *m* (-[e]s; *no pl*) entertainment value.

'**Unterhändler** *m* (-s; -) negotiator.

Unter'handlung *f* (-; -en) negotiation.

'**Unterhaus** *n* (-es; *no pl*) *parl. Br.* House of Commons.

'**Unterhemd** *n* vest, *Am.* undershirt.

unter'höhlen *v/t* (*insep, no -ge-, h*) *a. fig.* undermine.

'**Unterholz** *n* (-es; *no pl*) undergrowth.

'**Unterhose** *f* (*e-e* ~ a pair of) underpants.

'**unterirdisch** *adj* subterranean, underground.

unter'jochen *v/t* (*insep, no -ge-, h*) subjugate.

'**unterjubeln** *v/t* (*sep,* h) F *j-m et.* ~ foist s.th. (off) on s.o.

'**Unterkiefer** *m anat.* lower jaw.

'**Unterkleid** *n* (full-length) slip.

'**Unterkleidung** *f* underwear.

'**unterkommen** *v/i* (*irr, sep, -ge-, sn,* → **kommen**) find accommodation (*or* lodgings): ~ *in* (*dat*) find a place in; F ~ *bei* find a job with *a firm etc*.

'**Unterkörper** *m* lower part of the body.

'**unterkriegen** *v/t* (*sep,* h) F *j-n* ~ get s.o. down.

Unter'kühlung *f* (-; -en) ✱ hypothermia.

'**Unterkunft** *f* (-; ⸚e) accommodation, lodging(s), quarters: ~ *und Verpflegung* board and lodgings.

'**Unterlage** *f* (-; -n) **1.** ⚙ base, support. **2.** *fig.* basis. **3.** *pl* a) documents, records, b) data.

'**Unterlaß** *m ohne* ~ incessantly.

unter'lassen *v/t* (*irr, insep, no -ge-, h,* → **lassen**) *et.* ~ a) omit (*or* fail) to do s.th., b) refrain from (doing) s.th.; *unterlaß das!* stop that!

Unter'lassung *f* (-; -en) omission.

Unter'lassungs|klage *f* ⚖ action for injunction. **~sünde** *f* sin of omission.

'**Unterlauf** *m* (-[e]s; ⸚e) lower course.

unter'laufen (*irr, insep, no -ge-,* → **laufen**) **I** *v/t* (h) F dodge. **II** *v/i* (sn) *mir ist ein Fehler* ~ I've made a mistake.

'**unterlegen**[1] *v/t* (*sep*, h) lay (*or* put) *s.th.* under. **unter'legen**[2] *adj* **1.** inferior (*dat* to). **2.** losing, defeated.

Unter'legene *m, f* (-n; -n) loser.

Unter'legenheit *f* (-; *no pl*) inferiority.

'**Unterleib** *m* abdomen, belly.

'**Unterleibs...** abdominal (*pain etc*).

unter'liegen *v/i* (*irr*, *insep*, *no* -ge-, sn, → **liegen**) **1.** (*dat*) be defeated (*or* beaten) (by), lose (to), *fig.* succumb (to). **2.** be subject (*dat to rule etc*): **es unterliegt k-m Zweifel, daß** there is no doubt that.

'**Unterlippe** *f* lower lip.

Unter'malung *f* (-; -en) background.

unter'mauern *v/t* (*insep*, *no* -ge-, h) *a. fig.* underpin.

'**untermengen** *v/t* (*sep*, h) mix in.

'**Untermensch** *m* subhuman creature.

'**Untermiete** *f* (-; *no pl*) **1.** subtenancy: **in** (*or* **zur**) **~ wohnen** be a subtenant (*Am.* roomer), lodge (*bei* with). **2.** sublease: → **untervermieten**. '**Untermieter(in** *f*) *m* subtenant, lodger, *Am.* roomer.

untermi'nieren *v/t* (*insep*, h) undermine.

unter'nehmen *v/t* (*irr*, *insep*, *no* -ge-, h, → **nehmen**) make, go on (*a trip etc*), do (*s.th.*): **et. ~ gegen** a) take action against s.o., b) **et.** do s.th. about s.o.; **er unternahm nichts** he did nothing.

Unter'nehmen *n* (-s; -n) **1.** firm, business, enterprise, company. **2.** undertaking, enterprise, project: (**gewagtes**) **~** venture. **3.** ✕ operation.

Unter'nehmensberater *m* management consultant. **~führung** *f* (-; *no pl*) management.

Unter'nehmer *m* (-s; -) a) entrepreneur b) contractor, c) employer, d) industrialist. **unter'nehmerisch** *adj* entrepreneurial. **Unter'nehmerschaft** *f* (-; *no pl*) the employers, the management.

Unter'nehmertum *n* (-s; *no pl*) **1.** entrepreneurship: **freies ~** free enterprise. **2.** → **Unternehmerschaft**.

unter'nehmungsgeist *m* (spirit of) enterprise, initiative.

unter'nehmungslustig *adj* enterprising.

'**Unteroffizier** *m* a) noncommissioned officer (*abbr.* NCO), b) sergeant, ✔ corporal.

'**unterordnen** (*sep*, h) **I** *v/t* subordinate (*dat* to). **II** *sich* **~** submit (*dat* to).

'**Unterordnung** *f* (-; -en) **1.** *no pl* subordination. **2.** *biol.* suborder.

'**unterprivilegiert** *adj* underprivileged.

Unter'redung *f* (-; -en) talk, conversation.

Unterricht ['ʊntərrɪçt] *m* (-[e]s; *no pl*) instruction, lessons, classes: **j-m ~ (in Deutsch) geben** teach s.o. (German), give (German) lessons to s.o.

unter'richten (*insep*, *no* -ge-, h) **I** *v/t*, *v/i* **1.** teach, give lessons (*dat* to): **j-n (in Deutsch) ~** teach s.o. (German); **Mathematik ~** teach mathematics. **2.** inform (**von**, **über** *acc* of): (**gut**) **unterrichtete Kreise** (well-)informed circles. **II** *sich* **~** inform o.s. (**über** *acc* about).

'**Unterrichtseinheit** *f* teaching unit. **~raum** *m* classroom. **~stunde** *f* lesson.

Unter'richtung *f* (-; -en) **1.** instruction. **2.** (**zu Ihrer ~** for your) information.

'**Unterrock** *m* slip.

unter'sagen *v/t* (*insep*, *no* -ge-, h) forbid, *adm.* prohibit: **j-m ~ zu inf** forbid s.o. to *inf*, prohibit s.o. from *ger*.

'**Untersatz** *m* (-es; -e) stand, (*for glasses*: mat, *for flowerpots*: saucer: F **fahrbarer ~** wheels.

'**Unterschall...** subsonic (*speed etc*).

unter'schätzen *v/t* (*insep*, *no* -ge-, h) underestimate.

unter'scheiden (*irr*, *insep*, *no* -ge-, h, → **scheiden**) **I** *v/t*, *v/i* distinguish (**zwischen** between, **von** from): **et. ~ von** a. tell s.th. apart from; **das unterscheidet ihn von ...** that sets him apart from ... **II** *sich* **~** differ (**von** from, **dadurch daß** in *ger*). **unter'scheidend** *adj* distinctive.

Unter'scheidung *f* (-; -en) **1.** differentiation. **2.** difference. **Unter'scheidungsmerkmal** *n* distinguishing mark.

'**Unterschenkel** *m* *anat.* lower leg.

'**Unterschicht** *f* *sociol.* lower classes.

Unterschied ['ʊntərʃiːt] *m* (-[e]s; -e) difference: **e-n ~ machen** (**zwischen** between) distinguish, **z.** a. discriminate; **das macht k-n ~** that makes no difference; **ohne ~** indiscriminately; **zum ~ von** unlike, in contrast to; **das ist ein großer ~** that makes a great difference.

'**unterschiedlich** *adj* different, varying, variable; **~ behandeln** discriminate between. '**unterschiedslos I** *adj* indiscriminate. **II** *adv* without exception.

unter'schlagen *v/t* (*irr*, *insep*, *no* -ge-, h,

→ *schlagen*) embezzle (*money*), intercept (*letter*), suppress (*last will etc*), hold back (*facts*).

Unter'schlagung *f* (-; -en) embezzlement, interception, suppression.

'**Unterschlupf** *m* (-[e]s; -e) **1.** hiding place, F hideout. **2.** shelter, refuge.

'**unterschlüpfen** *v/i* (*sep*, sn) hide. **2.** take shelter (*bei* with).

unter'schreiben *v/t, v/i* (*irr, insep, no* -ge-, h, → *schreiben*) **1.** sign. **2.** F *fig.* subscribe (to).

unter'schreiten *v/t* (*irr, insep, no* -ge-, h, → *schreiten*) fall short of.

'**Unterschrift** *f* (-; -en) signature: → *setzen* 1. '**Unterschriftenmappe** *f* signature blotting book. '**unterschriftsberechtigt** *adj* authorized to sign.

'**unterschwellig** [-ʃvelɪç] *adj* subliminal.

'**Unterseeboot** *n* submarine.

'**unterseeisch** [-ze:ɪʃ] *adj* submarine.

'**Unterseite** *f* underside, bottom.

untersetzt [-'zetst] *adj* stocky.

'**unterst** *adj* lowest: *das 2e zuoberst kehren* turn everything upside down.

'**Unterstand** *m* shelter, ✕ *a.* dugout.

unter'stehen (*irr, insep, no* -ge-, h, → *stehen*) **I** *v/i j-m* ~ be subordinate (*or* answerable) to s.o., be under s.o.'s supervision. **II** *sich* ~ *zu inf* dare to *inf*; *was ~ Sie sich?* how dare you?

'**unterstellen**[1] (*sep*, h) **I** *v/t* put *s.th.* in(to *in dat*). **II** *sich* ~ take shelter.

unter'stellen[2] *v/t* (*insep, no* -ge-, h) **1.** *j-m j-n* (*et.*) ~ put s.o. in charge of s.o. (s.th.). **2.** *fig. j-m et.* ~ impute s.th. to s.o. **3.** suppose, assume. **Unter'stellung** *f* (-; -en) allegation, suggestion.

unter'streichen *v/t* (*irr, insep, no* -ge-, h, → *streichen*) *a. fig.* underline.

'**Unterstufe** *f* (-; -n) *ped.* lower grades.

unter'stützen *v/t* (*insep, no* -ge-, h) support, back (up), **II** assist, aid, help.

Unter'stützung *f* (-; -en) **I. a)** support, **b)** aid, grant, **c)** subsidy, **d)** benefit: ~ *beziehen* be on social security. **II** *fig.* support, backing, aid, assistance.

unter'suchen *v/t* (*insep, no* -ge-, h) examine (*a.* ✱), investigate (*a.* ⚖), inspect, check, ⚒ *or fig.* analyse (*Am.* -ze): *et.* ~ *auf* (*acc*) test s.th. for.

Unter'suchung *f* (-; -en) examination, ✱ *a.* checkup, investigation, inspection, test, ⚒ *or fig.* analysis.

Unter'suchungs|ausschuß *m* fact-finding committee. **~gefangene** *m, f* prisoner on remand. **~gefängnis** *n* remand prison. **~haft** *f* detention pending trial: *in ~ sein* be on remand. **~richter(in** *f***)** *m* examining magistrate.

Untertan [-ta:n] *m* (-s, -en; -en) subject.

'**Untertasse** *f* saucer.

'**untertauchen** *v/i* (*sep*, sn) **1.** *a. v/t* duck. **2.** *fig.* disappear, go into hiding, *esp. pol.* go underground.

'**Unterteil** *n, m* lower part, base.

unter'teilen *v/t* (*insep, no* -ge-, h) subdivide (*in acc* into). **Unter'teilung** *f* (-; -en) subdivision (*in acc* into).

'**Untertitel** *m* subtitle, *film: a.* caption.

'**Unterton** *m* *a. fig.* undertone.

unter'treiben *v/t, v/i* (*irr, insep, no* -ge-, h, → *treiben*) understate. **Unter'treibung** *f* (-; -en) understatement.

unter'tunneln *v/t* (*insep, no* -ge-, h) tunnel through.

'**untervermieten** *v/t* (*only inf and pp* untervermietet, h) sublet.

'**unterversichert** *adj* underinsured.

unter'wandern *v/t* (*insep, no* -ge-, h) infiltrate.

Unter'wanderung *f* (-; -en) infiltration.

'**Unterwäsche** *f* (-; *no pl*) underwear.

'**Unterwasser...** underwater (*camera, massage, etc*).

unterwegs [ʊntɐ've:ks] *adv* on the (*or* one's) way (*nach* to), away: *immer ~* always on the move.

unter'weisen *v/t* (*irr, insep, no* -ge-, h, → *weisen*) instruct.

Unter'weisung *f* (-; -en) instruction.

'**Unterwelt** *f* (-; *no pl*) underworld.

unter'werfen *v/t* (*irr, insep, no* -ge-, h, → *werfen*) **I** *v/t* **1.** subdue, subjugate. **2.** subject (*dat* to *test etc*). **II** *sich* ~ *a. fig.* submit (*dat* to). **Unter'werfung** *f* (-; -en) **1.** subjugation, subjection. **2.** *fig.* submission (*unter acc* to). **unterworfen** [-'vɔrfən] *adj* subject (*dat* to).

unterwürfig [ʊntɐ'vyrfɪç] *adj* submissive, servile. **Unter'würfigkeit** *f* (-; *no pl*) submissiveness, servility.

unter'zeichnen *v/t, v/i* (*insep, no* -ge-, h) sign. **Unter'zeichner** *m* (-s; -) signer, *the* undersigned, signatory (*gen* to). **Unter'zeichnete** *m, f* (-n; -n) *the* undersigned. **Unter'zeichnung** *f* (-; -en) signing.

'**unterziehen**¹ v/t (irr, sep, -ge-, h, → ziehen) put on underneath.

unter'ziehen² v/t (irr, insep, no -ge-, h, → ziehen) subject (dat to): **sich e-r Operation** ~ undergo an operation; **sich e-r Prüfung** ~ take an examination.

'**Untiefe** f (-; -n) shallow, shoal.

'**Untier** n (-[e]s; -e) a. fig. monster.

un'**tragbar** adj intolerable (conduct etc), prohibitive (prices etc).

un'**trennbar** adj inseparable.

'**untreu** adj (dat to) unfaithful, disloyal.

'**Untreue** f (-; no pl) unfaithfulness, disloyalty, (marital) infidelity.

un'**tröstlich** adj inconsolable.

un**trüglich** [ʊn'try:klɪç] adj **1.** unerring (instinct etc). **2.** sure (sign etc).

'**untüchtig** adj incapable, incompetent.

'**Untugend** f (-; -en) vice, bad habit.

unüber'**brückbar** adj fig. unbridgeable.

'**unüberlegt** adj ill-considered, unwise.

unüber'**sehbar** adj immense, vast.

unüber'**setzbar** adj untranslatable.

'**unübersichtlich** adj **1.** blind (curve etc). **2.** badly arranged, unclear, confused.

unüber'**trefflich** [-'trɛflɪç] adj matchless, unsurpassable. **unüber'troffen** [-'trɔfən] adj unsurpassed, unmatched.

unüber'**windlich** [-'vɪntlɪç] adj invincible, fig. insurmountable, insuperable.

'**unumgänglich** adj unavoidable: ~ (notwendig) indispensable.

'**unumschränkt** [-ʃrɛŋkt] adj unlimited, pol. absolute.

unum'**stößlich** [-'ʃtø:slɪç] adj irrefutable (fact etc), irrevocable (decision etc).

unum'**stritten** adj undisputed.

'**unumwunden** [-vʊndən] adv straight out, frankly.

'**ununterbrochen** [-brɔxən] adj uninterrupted, incessant.

unver'**änderlich** adj unchanging, ling., År invariable. **unver'ändert** adj unchanged.

unver'**antwortlich** adj irresponsible.

unver'**äußerlich** adj inalienable.

unver'**besserlich** adj incorrigible.

'**unverbindlich** adj offer etc without obligation, noncommittal (answer etc).

'**unverblümt** adj plain, blunt.

'**unverbraucht** adj unused, fig. unspent.

'**unverbürgt** adj unconfirmed.

'**unverdächtig** adj unsuspicious.

'**unverdaulich** adj a. fig. indigestible.

'**unverdaut** adj a. fig. undigested.

'**unverdient** adj undeserved. '**unverdienter'maßen** adv undeservedly.

'**unverdorben** adj unspoilt, fig. a. uncorrupted.

'**unverdrossen** adj indefatigable.

'**unverdünnt** adj undiluted.

unver'**einbar** adj incompatible, irreconcilable.

'**unverfälscht** adj unadulterated, pure, fig. a. genuine.

'**unverfänglich** adj harmless.

'**unverfroren** adj brazen, F cheeky.

'**Unverfrorenheit** f (-; no pl) brazenness, impertinence, F cheek.

'**unvergänglich** adj immortal. '**Unvergänglichkeit** f (-; no pl) immortality.

'**unvergessen** adj unforgotten.

'**unvergeßlich** adj unforgettable.

unver'**gleichlich** adj incomparable.

'**unverhältnismäßig** adv disproportionately: ~ **hoch** excessive.

'**unverheiratet** adj unmarried, single.

'**unverhofft** [-hɔft] adj a) unhoped-for, b) unexpected.

'**unverhohlen** [-ho:lən] adj undisguised.

'**unverhüllt** adj fig. undisguised.

'**unverkäuflich** adj unsal(e)able, not for sale. '**unverkauft** adj unsold.

unver'**kennbar** adj unmistakable.

unver'**letzlich** adj fig. inviolable.

'**unverletzt** adj uninjured, unhurt.

unver'**meidlich** [-'maɪt-] adj unavoidable, inevitable (a. iro.): **sich ins Unvermeidliche fügen** bow to the inevitable.

'**unvermindert** adj undiminished.

'**unvermittelt** adj abrupt.

'**Unvermögen** n (-s; no pl) inability.

'**unvermutet** adj unexpected.

'**Unvernunft** f (-; no pl) unreasonableness, folly. '**unvernünftig** adj unreasonable, foolish.

'**unveröffentlicht** adj unpublished.

'**unverrichteter'dinge** adv without having achieved anything.

'**unverschämt** adj **1.** impudent, impertinent. **2.** F barefaced (lie), outrageous (demand, price, etc).

'**Unverschämtheit** f (-; -en) impudence, impertinence: **die ~ haben zu** inf have the cheek to inf.

'**unverschuldet** adj and adv through no fault of one's own.

unversehens ['ʊnfɛrze:əns] *adv* unexpectedly, all of a sudden.

un'versehrt *adj* unharmed, intact.

'unversichert *adj* uninsured.

unver'siegbar *adj* inexhaustible.

unver'söhnlich *adj a. fig.* irreconcilable.

'unverstanden *adj* (*sich ~ fühlen* feel) misunderstood. **'unverständig** *adj* ignorant. **'unverständlich** *adj* (*dat* to) **1.** unintelligible. **2.** incomprehensible, obscure (*reasons etc*): **es ist mir ~, warum** (*wie etc*) I can't understand (F it beats me) why (how *etc*).

'unversteuert *adj* untaxed.

'unversucht *adj nichts ~ lassen* (*um zu inf*) try everything (to *inf*).

'unverträglich *adj* **1.** quarrelsome. **2.** indigestible. **3.** *a.* ✠ incompatible.

unver'wechselbar *adj* unmistakable.

unver'wundbar *adj* invulnerable.

unver'wüstlich [-'vy:stlɪç] *adj* indestructible (*a. fig.*), irrepressible (*humo[u]r*).

'unverzagt *adj* undaunted.

unver'zeihlich *adj* inexcusable.

unver'zichtbar *adj* **1.** unrenounceable. **2.** indispensable.

unver'zinslich *adj* noninterest-bearing: **~es Darlehen** interest-free loan.

'unverzollt *adj* duty unpaid.

unver'züglich [ʊnfɛr'tsy:klɪç] *adj* immediate(ly *adv*), *adv a.* without delay.

'unvollendet *adj* unfinished.

'unvollkommen *adj* imperfect. **'Unvollkommenheit** *f* (-; -en) imperfection.

'unvollständig *adj* incomplete.

'unvorbereitet *adj* unprepared.

'unvoreingenommen *adj* unbias(s)ed, unprejudiced, objective.

'unvorhergesehen *adj* unforeseen.

'unvorschriftsmäßig *adj* irregular, contrary to (the) regulations, improper.

'unvorsichtig *adj* imprudent, rash, careless. **'Unvorsichtigkeit** *f* (-; *no pl*) imprudence, rashness, carelessness.

unvor'stellbar *adj* unimaginable, unthinkable, incredible.

'unvorteilhaft *adj* **1.** unprofitable. **2.** unbecoming (*dress etc*).

'unwahr *adj* untrue.

'Unwahrheit *f* (-; -en) untruth.

'unwahrscheinlich *adj* **1.** improbable, unlikely. **2.** F *fig.* incredible, fantastic. **'Unwahrscheinlichkeit** *f* (-; *no pl*) improbability.

un'wandelbar *adj* unchanging.

unweg'sam ['ʊnve:kza:m] *adj* difficult.

'unweiblich *adj* unfeminine.

unweiger'lich [ʊnvaɪɡər'lɪç] **I** *adj* inevitable. **II** *adv* inevitably, without fail.

'unweit *prep* (*gen*) not far from.

'Unwesen *n* (-s; *no pl*) nuisance: **sein ~ treiben in** (*dat*) terrorize *a place etc*.

'unwesentlich *adj* **1.** irrelevant, unimportant. **2.** negligible.

'Unwetter *n* (-s; -) (thunder)storm.

'unwichtig *adj* unimportant, irrelevant.

un'wider'legbar *adj* irrefutable.

unwiderruflich [-'ru:flɪç] **I** *adj* irrevocable. **II** *adv* irrevocably, definitely: **es steht ~ fest, daß** it is absolutely certain that.

unwiderstehlich [-'ʃte:lɪç] *adj* irresistible.

Unwider'stehlichkeit *f* (-; *no pl*) irresistibility.

unwiederbringlich [-'brɪŋlɪç] *adj* irretrievable.

'Unwille *m* (-ns; *no pl*) indignation.

'unwillig *adj* **1.** (*über acc* at) indignant, annoyed. **2.** unwilling, reluctant.

'unwillkommen *adj* unwelcome.

'unwillkürlich *adj* involuntary.

'unwirklich *adj* unreal.

'unwirksam *adj* ineffective, ✠ inoperative, null and void.

unwirsch ['ʊnvɪrʃ] *adj* disgruntled.

unwirtlich ['ʊnvɪrtlɪç] *adj* a) inhospitable, b) rough (*climate*).

'unwirtschaftlich *adj* uneconomic(al).

'unwissend *adj* ignorant.

'Unwissenheit *f* (-; *no pl*) ignorance.

'unwissenschaftlich *adj* unscientific.

'unwissentlich *adj* unknowing.

'unwohl *adj* **1.** unwell. **2.** *fig.* uneasy.

'Unwohlsein *n* (-s; *no pl*) indisposition.

'unwürdig *adj* unworthy (*gen* of): **das ist s-r ~** that is beneath him.

'Unzahl *f e-e ~ von* a host of.

un'zählig [ʊn'tsɛ:lɪç] *adj* countless.

Unze ['ʊntsə] *f* (-; -n) ounce (*abbr.* oz.).

'unzeitgemäß *adj* old-fashioned.

unzer'brechlich *adj* unbreakable.

unzer'reißbar *adj* untearable.

unzer'störbar *adj* indestructible.

unzertrennlich [-'trɛnlɪç] *adj* inseparable.

'unzivili,siert *adj* uncivilized.

'Unzucht *f* (-; *no pl*) ✠ sexual offen/ce

(*Am.* -se): *gewerbsmäßige ~ prostitution.* '**unzüchtig** *adj* lewd, obscene.
'**unzufrieden** *adj* dissatisfied, discon-
tented. '**Unzufriedenheit** *f* (-; *no pl*)
dissatisfaction, discontent.
'**unzugänglich** *adj* inaccessible (*dat*
to).
'**unzulänglich** *adj* inadequate.
'**Unzulänglichkeit** *f* (-; -en) **1.** *no pl* in-
adequacy. **2.** shortcoming.
'**unzulässig** *adj* inadmissible.
'**unzumutbar** *adj* unreasonable: *das ist
für sie ~ a*) you can't expect that of her,
b) she will never accept that.
'**unzurechnungsfähig** *adj* irresponsible
(for one's actions), insane.
'**Unzurechnungsfähigkeit** *f* (-; *no pl*)
(*zeitweilige ~* temporary) insanity.
'**unzureichend** *adj* insufficient.
'**unzusammenhängend** *adj* a) disconnected, b) incoherent (*speech etc*).
'**unzuständig** *adj* 🏛 (*für*) incompetent
(for), having no jurisdiction (over).
'**unzutreffend** *adj* incorrect: *Unzutref-
fendes bitte streichen!* please delete
where inapplicable.
'**unzuverlässig** *adj* unreliable. '**Unzu-
verlässigkeit** *f* (-; *no pl*) unreliability.
'**unzweckmäßig** *adj* unsuitable.
'**unzweideutig** *adj* unequivocal.
'**unzweifelhaft I** *adj* indubitable. **II** *adv*
doubtless, without a doubt.
üppig ['ʏpɪç] *adj* a) luxurious, b) luxu-
riant (*vegetation, fig. imagination etc*),
c) opulent (*meal*), d) luscious, voluptuous (*figure etc*).
Ur [uːr] *m* (-[e]s; -e) *zo.* aurochs.
'**Urabstimmung** *f* strike ballot.
'**Urahn** *m* **1.** ancestor. **2.** great-grandfather. '**Urahne** *f* (-; -n) **1.** ancestress.
2. great-grandmother.
'**uralt** *adj* ancient (*a. fig. iro.*), F as old as
the hills, *fig.* age-old (*problem etc*).
Uran [u'raːn] *n* (-s; *no pl*) ⚛ uranium.
u'ranhaltig *adj* uranium-bearing.
'**uraufführen** *v/t* (*only inf and pp* urauf-
geführt, h) première, *a.* show *film* for
the first time. '**Uraufführung** *f* première, first night (*or* showing).
urbar ['uːrbaːr] *adj* arable: *~ machen*
cultivate, reclaim. '**Urbarmachung** *f*
(-; -en) cultivation, reclamation.
'**Urbevölkerung** *f* → *Ureinwohner.*
'**Urbild** *n* model, prototype.

'**urdeutsch** *adj* German to the core, *iro.*
very German.
'**ur'eigen** *adj in Ihrem ~sten Interesse*
in your own best interest.
'**Ureinwohner** *pl* original inhabitants, *in
Australia:* Aborigines.
'**Urenkel** *m* great-grandson.
'**Urenkelin** *f* great-granddaughter.
'**Urform** *f* archetype.
'**urge'mütlich** *adj* F very cosy.
'**Urgeschichte** *f* (-; *no pl*) primeval histo-
ry. '**urgeschichtlich** *adj* prehistoric.
'**Urgestein** *n geol.* primary rock.
'**Urgewalt** *f* elemental force.
'**Urgroßeltern** *pl* great-grandparents.
'**Urgroßmutter** *f* great-grandmother.
'**Urgroßvater** *m* great-grandfather.
Urheber ['uːrheːbər] *m* (-s; -) author.
'**Urheberrecht** *n* copyright.
'**urheberrechtlich** *adj* copyright ...: *~
geschützt* (protected by) copyright.
'**Urheberschaft** *f* (-; *no pl*) authorship.
urig ['uːrɪç] *adj* F → *urwüchsig.*
Urin [u'riːn] *m* (-s; -e) urine.
urinieren [uri'niːrən] *v/i* (h) urinate.
U'rinprobe *f* urine specimen.
U'rinuntersuchung *f* urine test.
'**Urknall** *m* (-[e]s; *no pl*) *phys.* big bang.
'**ur'komisch** *adj* F extremely funny.
Urkunde *f* (-; -n) document, deed, record, *a. sports etc:* diploma. '**Urkundenfälschung** *f* forgery of documents.
'**urkundlich** *adj* documentary: *et. ~ belegen* document s.th.
'**Urkundsbeamte** *m* registrar.
Urlaub ['uːrlaʊp] *m* (-[e]s; -e) leave (of
absence) (*a.* ⚔), holiday(s), *esp. Am.*
vacation: *auf ~, im ~* on holiday (vacation, ⚔ leave); *in ~ gehen* (*sein*) go
(be) on holiday (*etc*); *~ nehmen* go on
leave; *e-n Tag ~ nehmen* take a day
off. **Urlauber** ['uːrlaʊbər] *m* (-s; -) holidaymaker, *esp. Am.* vacationist.
'**Urlaubs|anspruch** *m* holiday entitle-
ment, *Am.* vacation privilege. *~geld n*
holiday pay, *Am.* vacation money.
~tag m (a day's) holiday (*esp. Am.*
vacation). *~zeit f* holiday period.
'**Urmensch** *m* primitive man.
Urne ['ʊrnə] *f* (-; -n) **1.** urn. **2.** ballot box.
Urologe [uro'loːgə] *m* (-n; -n) urologist.
Urologie [urolo'giː] *f* (-; *no pl*) urology.
'**ur'plötzlich I** *adj* sudden, abrupt. **II** *adv*
all of a sudden.

'**Ursache** f (-; -n) a) cause, reason, b) occasion: **keine ~!** don't mention it, that's all right. '**ursächlich** adj causal: **~er Zusammenhang** causality.

'**Urschrift** f original (text or copy).

'**Ursprung** m (-[e]s; ⁔e) origin: **s-n ~ haben in** (dat) originate in (or from); **deutschen ~s** of German origin.

ursprünglich ['uːrʃprYŋlɪç] adj original.

'**Ursprungsland** n country of origin.

Urteil ['ʊrtaɪl] n (-s; -e) 1. judg(e)ment, of jury: verdict (a. fig.), criminal court: sentence, divorce: decree: **das ~ verkünden** pronounce judg(e)ment (or sentence); → **fällen** 2. 2. judg(e)ment, opinion: **sich ein ~ bilden** form a judg(e)ment (**über** acc about, on); **darüber kann ich mir kein ~ erlauben!** I am no judge (of that).

urteilen ['ʊrtaɪlən] v/i (h) judge: **über j-n** (et.) ~ judge s.o. (s.th.); **ich urteile darüber anders** I take a different view (of it); **~ Sie selbst!** judge for yourself;

nach s-m Aussehen (**s-n Worten**) **zu** ~ judging by his looks (by what he says).

'**Urteils|begründung** f opinion. **⚲fähig** adj discerning. **~kraft** f (-; no pl) (power of) judg(e)ment. **~spruch** m → **Urteil** 1.

'**Urtext** m original text.

'**Urtrieb** m basic instinct.

urtümlich ['uːrtyːmlɪç] adj **1.** original. **2.** archaic.

'**Urur...** great-great(-grandfather etc).

'**Urvolk** n **1.** pimitive people. **2.** → **Ureinwohner.**

'**Urwald** m **1.** primeval forest. **2.** jungle.

urwüchsig ['uːrvyːksɪç] adj **1.** original, natural. **2.** earthy, robust.

'**Urzeit** f primeval time: **vor ~en** a long, long time ago; **seit ~en** for ages.

'**Urzustand** m original state.

Utensilien [uten'ziːlĭən] pl utensils.

Uterus ['uːterʊs] m (-s; -ri) anat. uterus.

Utopie [uto'piː] f (-; -n) a) utopia, b) wild dream. **utopisch** [u'toːpɪʃ] adj utopian, fantastic.

V

V, v [faʊ] n (-; -) V, v.

Vagabund [vaga'bʊnt] m (-en; -en) vagabond, tramp. **vagabundieren** [vagabʊn'diːrən] v/i (h) lead a vagabond life.

Vagina [va'giːna] f (-; -nen) anat. vagina.

vakant [va'kant] adj vacant.

Vakuum ['vaːkuʊm] n (-s; -kŭa) vacuum. **⚲verpackt** adj vacuum-packed.

Vakzine [vak'tsiːnə] f (-; -n) ⚕ vaccine.

Valenz [va'lɛnts] f (-; -en) valence.

Valuta [va'luːta] f (-; -ten) ✝ valuta, foreign currency.

Vampir ['vampiːr] m (-s; -e) vampire.

Vandale m etc → **Wandale** etc.

Vanille [va'nɪljə] f (-; no pl) ⚘ or gastr. vanilla. **~zucker** m vanilla sugar.

variabel [va'rĭaːbəl] adj variable.

Variable [va'rĭaːblə] f (-; -n) ⅍ variable.

Variante [va'rĭantə] f (-; -n) **1.** variant. **2.** version. **Variation** [varĭa'tsĭoːn] f (-; -en) variation.

Varieté [varĭe'teː] n (-s; -s), **~the|ater** n

variety theatre, music hall, Am. vaudeville (theater).

variieren [vari'iːrən] v/t, v/i (h) vary.

Vasall [va'zal] m (-en; -en) vassal.

Va'sallenstaat m contp. satellite state.

Vase ['vaːzə] f (-; -n) vase.

Vaseline [vaze'liːnə] f (-; no pl) vaseline.

Vater ['faːtər] m (-s; ⁔) father (a. fig.), zo. sire: **er ist ~ von drei Kindern** he is a father of three (children); **er ist ganz der ~** he is a chip off the old block; humor. **~ Staat** the State.

'**Vaterfi|gur** f father figure.

'**Vaterland** n (-[e]s; ⁔er) one's native country. '**Vaterlandsliebe** f love of one's country, patriotism.

väterlich ['fɛːtərlɪç] **I** adj fatherly, paternal. **II** adv like a father. '**väterlicherseits** adv on one's father's side: **Groß-vater** ~ paternal grandfather.

'**Vaterliebe** f paternal love.

'**vaterlos** adj fatherless.

'**Vater|mord** *m*, **~mörder** *m* patricide.
'**Vaterschaft** *f* (-; *no pl*) 👥 paternity:
Feststellung der ~ affiliation.
'**Vaterschaftsklage** *f* 👥 paternity suit.
'**Vater|unser** *n* (-s; -) F daddy, dad.
'**Vatistadt** *f* hometown. **~stelle** *f ~ vertreten** act as father (*bei* to).
Vater|unser *n* (-s; -) Lord's Prayer.
Vati ['fa:ti] *m* (-s; -s) F daddy, dad.
Vatikan [vati'ka:n] *m* (-s), **vati'kanisch** *adj* Vatican. **Vati'kanstadt** *f* Vatican
City.
V-Ausschnitt ['fau-] *m* V-neck: *mit ~* V-necked.

Vegetarier [vege'ta:riər] *m* (-s; -) vegetarian. **vege'tarisch** [-rɪʃ] *adj* vegetarian: *~ leben* be a vegetarian.
Vegetation [vegeta'tsio:n] *f* (-; -en) vegetation. **vegetativ** [-'ti:f] *adj* vegetative: *~es Nervensystem* autonomous nervous system. **vegetieren** [vege'ti:rən] *v/i* (h) *fig.* vegetate.
Vehikel [ve'hi:kəl] *n* (-s; -) F rattletrap.
Veilchen ['failçən] *n* (-s; -) **1.** 🌸 violet:
F *blau wie ein ~* drunk as a lord.
2. F *fig.* black eye. '**veilchenblau** *adj* violet.
Vektor ['vɛktɔr] *m* (-s; -en [-'to:rən]) ⅄ vector. **~rechnung** *f* vector analysis.
Velours [və'lu:r] *m* (- [və'lu:rs]; - [və'lu:rs]) velour(s).
Ve'loursleder *n* suede (leather).
Ve'loursteppich *m* velvet-pile carpet.
Vene ['ve:nə] *f* (-; -n) *anat.* vein.
'**Venenentzündung** *f* 🔬 phlebitis.
venerisch [ve'ne:rɪʃ] *adj* 🔬 venereal.
Venezianer [vene'tsia:nər] *m* (-s; -), **Venezianerin** *f* (-; -nen), **venezi'anisch** *adj* Venetian.
Venezolaner [venetso'la:nər] *m* (-s; -), **Venezo'lanerin** *f* (-; -nen), **venezo'lanisch** *adj* Venezuelan.
venös [ve'nø:s] *adj* 🔬 venous.
Ventil [vɛn'ti:l] *n* (-s; -e) **1.** 🎵, ☼ valve. **2.** *fig.* outlet. **Ventilation** [vɛntila'tsio:n] *f* (-; -en) a) ventilation, b) ventilating system. **Ventilator** [vɛnti'la:tɔr] *m* (-s; -en [-la'to:rən]) (ventilating) fan.
ver'abreden (h) **I** *v/t* agree upon, arrange, *a.* fix (*date, place*): *vorher ~* prearrange. **II** *sich ~* (*mit j-m*) arrange to meet (s.o.), make a date (*or* an appointment) (with s.o.): *ich bin leider schon verabredet* I'm afraid I have a previous engagement. **Ver'abredung** *f*

(-; -en) **1.** date, engagement, appointment. **2.** agreement, arrangement.
ver'abreichen *v/t* (h) *j-m et. ~* give s.o. s.th., ☼ *a.* administer s.th. to s.o.
ver'abscheuen *v/t* (h) abhor, detest.
verabschieden [vɛr'apʃi:dən] (h) **I** *v/t* **1.** say goodbye to. **2.** discharge. **3.** *parl.* pass (*bill etc*), adopt (*budget*). **II** *sich ~ von →* 1. **Ver'abschiedung** *f* (-; -en) **1.** discharge. **2.** *parl.* passing (*of bill etc*), adoption (*of budget*).
ver'achten *v/t* (h) despise, disdain, *a.* scorn: F *nicht zu ~* not to be sneezed at.
ver'achtenswert *adj* contemptible, despicable. **Verächter** [vɛr'ɛçtər] *m* (-s; -) despiser. **ver'ächtlich** *adj* **1.** contemptuous, scornful: *~ machen* run s.o., s.th. down. **2.** → *verachtenswert*.
Ver'achtung *f* (-; *no pl*) contempt, disdain, *a.* scorn: *mit ~ strafen* ignore.
ver'albern *v/t* (h) F *j-n ~* pull s.o.'s leg.
verallgemeinern [fɛr'algə'mainərn] *v/t* (h) generalize. **Verallge'meinerung** *f* (-; -en) generalization.
ver'alten *v/t* (sn) become (out)dated (*or* obsolete, *views etc*: antiquated). **ver'altet** *adj* obsolete, (out)dated, *method etc*: antiquated: *~ sein* be out of date.
Veranda [ve'randa] *f* (-; -den) veranda(h).
ver'änderlich *adj* changeable, *a.* ling, ⅄ variable: ⅄ *~e Größe* variable.
Ver'änderlichkeit *f* (-; -en) changeability, *ling.*, ⅄ variability.
ver'ändern (h) **I** *v/t* **1.** (*an dat* so) alter, change. **II** *sich ~* **2.** change: *sich zu s-m Vorteil (Nachteil) ~* change for the better (worse); *hier hat sich vieles verändert* there have been many changes. **3.** change one's job. **ver'ändert** *adj* changed, different: *sie ist ganz ~* she has changed a lot. **Ver'änderung** *f* (-; -en) change.
verängstigt [-'ɛŋstɪçt] *adj* frightened.
ver'ankern *v/t* (h) ☼, ⚓ anchor: *fig. in der Verfassung verankert* laid down in the constitution.
ver'anlagen *v/t* (h) *taxation:* assess.
ver'anlagt *adj* (*zu, für* to) (🔬 pre)disposed, (naturally) inclined: *künstlerisch ~ sein* have an artistic bent; *er ist praktisch ~* he is practical(ly minded); *romantisch ~ sein* have a romantic disposition. **Ver'anlagung** *f* (-; -en) **1.**

taxation: assessment. **2.** (⚙ pre)disposition. **3.** inclination, *a.* talent(s).

ver'anlassen *v/t* (h) **1.** *et. ~; ~, daß et. getan wird* order (*or* arrange) s.th., see (to it) that s.th. is done; *das Nötige ~* take the necessary steps. **2.** *j-n ~ et. zu tun* cause (*or* get) s.o. to do s.th., make s.o. do s.th.; *sich veranlaßt sehen zu inf* feel compelled to *inf*; *was hat ihn bloß dazu veranlaßt?* whatever made him do that? **Ver'anlassung** *f* (-; -en) **1.** (*zu, für*) cause, motive: *ohne jede ~* without provocation. **2.** *auf ~ von* (*or gen*) at the instigation of.

ver'anschaulichen [fɛr'ʔanʃaulɪçən] *v/t* (h) illustrate: *sich et. ~* visualize s.th. **Ver'anschaulichung** *f* (-; -en) (*zur ~ by* way of) illustration.

ver'anschlagen *v/t* (h) ☆ estimate (*auf acc* at): *zu hoch ~* overestimate; *zu niedrig ~* underestimate.

veranstalten [fɛr'ʔanʃtaltən] *v/t* (h) organize, arrange, stage (*a.* F *fig.*), give (*concert etc*). **Ver'anstalter** *m* (-s; -) organizer, sports: *a.* promoter. **Ver'anstaltung** *f* (-; -en) **1.** arrangement, organization, *fig.* staging. **2.** event, *a.* (public) function, sports: meeting, *Am.* meet, fixture. **Ver'anstaltungska,lender** *m* calendar of events.

ver'antworten (h) **I** *v/t* answer for, take the responsibility for. **II** *sich* (*j-m gegenüber*) *für et. ~* answer (to s.o.) for s.th. **ver'antwortlich** *adj* responsible (*für* for): *j-n ~ machen* hold s.o. responsible (*für* for), *w.s.* blame s.o. (*für* for). **Ver'antwortlichkeit** *f* (-; -en) responsibility. **Ver'antwortung** *f* (-; -en) (*die ~ tragen* bear [the]) responsibility; *auf Ihre eigene ~!* at your own risk; *j-n zur ~ ziehen* call s.o. to account; *~ abwälzen.* **ver'antwortungsbewußt** *adj* responsible. **Ver'antwortungsbewußtsein** *n* sense of responsibility. **ver'antwortungslos** *adj* irresponsible. **ver'antwortungsvoll** *adj* responsible.

ver'äppeln [fɛr'ʔɛpəln] *v/t* (h) F *j-n ~* pull s.o.'s leg.

ver'arbeiten *v/t* (h) process (*a.* data), *physiol. or fig.* digest, use (*in dat, zu* in, for): *et. ~ zu* manufacture s.th. into; *~de Industrie* processing industries. **Ver'arbeitung** *f* (-; -en) **1.** processing, manufacture, treatment. **2.** *physiol. or*

fig. digestion. **3.** workmanship.

ver'ärgern *v/t* (h) annoy.

ver'armen *v/i* (sn) become poor. **ver'armt** *adj* impoverished. **Ver'armung** *f* (-; -en) *a. fig.* impoverishment.

ver'arschen *v/t* (h) V *j-n ~* take the mickey out of s.o., *by satire*: send s.o. up.

verarzten [fɛr'ʔartstən] *v/t* (h) F *j-n ~* fix s.o. up.

ver'ästeln [fɛr'ʔɛstəln] *sich ~* (h) ramify. **Ver'ästelung** *f* (-; -en) ramification.

ver'ausgaben: *sich ~* (h) **1.** overspend. **2.** *fig.* spend o.s.

ver'auslagen *v/t* (h) lay out.

ver'äußern *v/t* (h) sell, dispose of. **Ver'äußerung** *f* (-; -en) sale, disposal.

Verb [vɛrp] *n* (-s; -en) *ling.* verb.

verbal [vɛr'baːl] *adj* verbal. **verbalisieren** [vɛrbali'ziːrən] *v/t* (h) verbalize.

Verband [fɛr'bant] *m* (-[e]s; ⁓e) **1.** ☆ bandage, dressing. **2.** union, federation. **3.** ✕ unit, ✈ formation. **Verband(s)kasten** *m* ☆ first-aid kit. **~materi,al** *n* dressing material. **~mull** *m* surgical gauze.

ver'bannen *v/t* (h) (*aus* from) exile, banish (*a. fig.*). **Ver'bannte** *m,f* (-n; -n) exile. **Ver'bannung** *f* (-; -en) exile, banishment (*a. fig.*).

verbarrikadieren [fɛrbarika'diːrən] *v/t* (h) barricade (*sich* o.s.).

ver'bauen *v/t* (h) **1.** block up, obstruct: *fig. j-m* (*sich*) *den Weg ~* bar s.o.'s (one's own) way (*zu* to). **2.** build up (*area*). **3.** use (*material*).

ver'bauern *v/i* (sn) become countrified.

ver'beamten *v/t* (h) *j-n ~* give s.o. the rank of a civil servant.

ver'beißen (*irr, no -ge-*, h, → *beißen*) **I** *v/t* **1.** suppress (*pain etc*), *a.* bite back (*laughter, tears, etc*): *er konnte sich ein Lächeln nicht ~* he couldn't keep a straight face. **II** *sich ~* (*in acc*) **2.** *dog etc*: sink its teeth into. **3.** *fig. person*: get set on, keep grimly at.

ver'bergen *v/t* (*irr, no -ge-*, h, → *bergen*) conceal, hide.

ver'bessern (h) **I** *v/t* **1.** improve, better (*record*). **2.** correct (*mistake etc*). **II** *sich ~* **3.** improve: *sich finanziell ~* better o.s. **4.** correct o.s.

Ver'besserung *f* (-; -en) **1.** improvement, betterment. **2.** correction.

ver'besserungs|bedürftig *adj* in need

of improvement. **~fähig** *adj* capable of improvement. **2vorschlag** *m* suggestion for improvement.

ver'beugen: sich ~ (h) bow (*vor dat* to). **Ver'beugung** *f* (-; -en) bow (*vor dat* to).

ver'beulen *v/t* (h) batter, dent.

ver'biegen *v/t* (*irr, no* -ge-, h, → **biegen**) twist, bend.

ver'bieten *v/t* (*irr, no* -ge-, h, → **bieten**) **j-m das Haus** (**das Rauchen**) **~** forbid s.o. the house (to smoke); → **verboten**.

ver'billigen *v/t* (h) reduce *s.th.* in price. **ver'billigt** *adj* reduced (*price etc*), (*tickets etc*) at reduced prices.

ver'binden *v/t* (*irr, no* -ge-, h, → **binden**) **1.** 🩹 bandage: **j-n ~** dress s.o.'s wounds; **j-m die Augen ~** blindfold s.o.; → **verbunden 1. 2.** (*a.* **sich ~**) (*mit* with) connect (*a.* ⚗, ✪, *teleph. or fig.*), combine (*a.* 🖐), unite: *teleph.* **ich verbinde Sie** I'll put you through (*mit* to); **das Angenehme mit dem Nützlichen ~** combine business with pleasure; **sich mit j-m ~** associate with s.o. **ver'bindend** *adj fig.* connecting (*text, words, etc*).

verbindlich [fɛr'bɪntlɪç] *adj* **1.** (*für* upon) obligatory, binding: **~e Zusage** definite promise. **2.** obliging, courteous, friendly. **Ver'bindlichkeit** *f* (-; -en) **1.** *no pl* obligation, binding character. **2.** *no pl* obligingness, friendliness. **3.** *pl* courtesies. **4.** *pl* ♦ liabilities.

Ver'bindung *f* (-; -en) **1.** connection (*a.* ✪, *teleph.*), combination: **in ~ mit** a) in conjunction with, b) in connection with; **in ~ bringen mit** connect (*or* associate) *s.o.*, *s.th.* with. **2.** (*bus etc*) connection. **3.** a) union, association, b) students' society, *Am.* fraternity: **e-e ~ eingehen** join together (*mit* with). **4.** contact (*a.* ✕), *pl* connections: **mit j-m ~ aufnehmen** (*or* **in ~ treten**) contact s.o., get in touch with s.o.; **mit j-m in ~ stehen** (**bleiben**) be (keep) in touch with s.o.; **s-e ~en spielen lassen** pull a few strings.

Ver'bindungs... connecting (*cable, line, road, etc*). **~mann** *m* contact. **~offizier** *m* liaison officer. **~stück** *n* ✪ connecting piece, 🔧 connector, *a.* adaptor.

ver'bissen *adj* grim, dogged. **Ver'bissenheit** *f* (-; *no pl*) doggedness.

ver'bitten *v/t* (*irr, no* -ge-, h, → **bitten**) **sich et. ~** not to stand for s.th.; **das**

verbitte ich mir! I won't have that.

ver'bittert *adj* embittered, bitter.

Ver'bitterung *f* (-; *no pl*) bitterness.

verblassen [fɛr'blasən] *v/i* (sn) fade.

ver'bleiben *v/i* (*irr, no* -ge-, sn, → **bleiben**) **1.** remain: **verbleibe ich Ihr ... in** *letter*: (I remain,) Yours faithfully ... **2.** **wir sind so verblieben, daß** we agreed (*or* arranged) that.

verbleit [fɛr'blaɪt] *adj* leaded.

ver'blenden *v/t* (h) **1.** 🔺 face, line. **2.** *fig.* blind: **von Haß verblendet** blind with hatred. **Ver'blendung** *f* (-; -en) **1.** 🔺 facing. **2.** *no pl fig.* blindness.

verblichen [fɛr'blɪçən] *adj* faded.

verblöden [fɛr'bløːdən] F *v/i* (sn) go dotty, go daft (*bei* with). **II** *v/t* (h) dull s.o.'s mind, stultify.

verblüffen [fɛr'blʏfən] *v/t* (h) amaze, baffle. **ver'blüffend** *adj* amazing. **ver'blüfft** *adj* amazed, *pred* taken aback. **Ver'blüffung** *f* (-; *no pl*) amazement.

ver'blühen *v/i* (sn) *a. fig.* fade, wither.

ver'bluten *v/i* (sn) bleed to death.

ver'bocken *v/t* (h) F bungle, botch (up).

ver'bohren: sich ~ (h) F *fig.* become obsessed (*in acc* with). **ver'bohrt** *adj* F *fig.* stubborn, pigheaded.

ver'borgen[1] *v/t* (h) lend (out).

ver'borgen[2] *adj* hidden: **~ halten** conceal; **sich ~ halten** hide (o.s.); **im ~en** in secret, secretly.

Verbot [fɛr'boːt] *n* (-[e]s; -e) prohibition (*gen* of), ban (*gen, von* on). **ver'boten** *adj* a) forbidden, prohibited, banned, b) illegal: **es war uns ~ zu** *inf* we were forbidden (*or* not allowed) to *inf*; **ist das etwa ~?** F is there a law against it?; **Rauchen ~!** no smoking!; F **sie sah ~ aus** she looked a sight. **ver'botenerweise** *adv* **~ et. tun** do s.th. although it is forbidden. **Ver'botsschild** *n* no parking (*or* no smoking etc) sign.

verbrämen [fɛr'brɛːmən] *v/t* (h) **1.** a) border, trim, b) fur. **2.** *fig.* gloss over.

Ver'brauch *m* (-[e]s; *no pl*) consumption (*an dat* of).

ver'brauchen (h) **I** *v/t* consume, use up. **II sich ~** *fig.* exhaust o.s., wear o.s. out.

Ver'braucher *m* (-s; -) consumer. **~markt** *m* hypermarket. **~schutz** *m* consumer protection. **~umfrage** *f* consumer survey. **~verhalten** *n* consumer behavio(u)r.

Ver'brauchsgüter *pl* consumer goods.
ver'braucht *adj a. fig.* used(-)up, spent, worn(-)out: **~e Luft** stale air.
ver'brechen *v/t* (*irr, no* -ge-, h, → **brechen**) F *humor.* perpetrate: **was hat er verbrochen?** what has he done?
Ver'brechen *n* (-s; -) *a. fig.* crime.
Ver'brecher *m* (-s; -) criminal. **~album** *n* rogues' gallery. **~bande** *f* gang of criminals.
Ver'brecherin *f* (-; -nen) criminal.
ver'brecherisch *adj* criminal.
ver'breiten *v/t* (*a. sich ~*) (h) spread (*in dat, auf dat, über acc* over), *a.* disseminate (*ideas etc*): (*weit*) *verbreitet* widespread, *a.* widely held.
verbreitern [fɛrˈbraɪtərn] *v/t* (*a. sich ~*) (h) widen.
Ver'breitung *f* (-; *no pl*) spread(ing), *a.* dissemination.
ver'brennen (*irr, no* -ge-, h, → **brennen**) **I** *v/t* burn, burn up (*calories*), cremate (*corpse*), scorch: **sich den Mund ~** burn one's mouth, *fig.* put one's foot in it; ✗ *verbrannte Erde* scorched earth. **II** *v/i a*) burn, b) be burnt to death.
Ver'brennung *f* (-; -en) **1.** burning, ◎ combustion. **2.** cremation. **3.** ✿ burn: → **Grad**.
Ver'brennungs|motor *m* combustion engine. **~ofen** *m* incinerator.
verbrieft [fɛrˈbriːft] *adj* vested (*right*).
ver'bringen *v/t* (*irr, no* -ge-, h, → **bringen**) spend, pass.
verbrüdern [fɛrˈbryːdərn] *sich ~* (h) fraternize. **Ver'brüderung** *f* (-; -en) fraternization.
ver'brühen (h) **I** *v/t* scald (*sich die Hand* one's hand). **II** *sich ~* scald o.s.
ver'buchen (h) **I** *v/t* **1.** ✝ book. **2.** *fig.* achieve, F notch up (*success etc*).
ver'bummeln *v/t* (h) F **1.** waste, idle away. **2** a) lose, b) clean forget.
Ver'bund *m* (-[e]s; -e) network, (integrated) system: **im ~ arbeiten** cooperate; **~** *Medien-, Verkehrsverbund.* **~bauweise** *f* sandwich construction.
verbunden [fɛrˈbʊndən] *adj* **1.** dressed (*wound*): **mit ~en Augen** blindfold.2. **~ sein mit** a) be connected with, entail (*difficulties, costs, etc*), b) be attached to; **j-m ~ sein für** be obliged to s.o. for.
verbünden [fɛrˈbyndən] *sich ~* (h) (*mit* with) form an alliance, ally o.s. (*a.* to).

Ver'bundenheit *f* (-; *no pl*) (*mit*) attachment (to), bond(s), solidarity (with).
Ver'bündete *m, f* (-n; -n) *a. fig.* ally.
Ver'bundglas *n* laminated glass.
ver'bürgen *v/t* (h) guarantee: **sich ~ für** *a.* answer for. **verbürgt** [-ˈbʏrkt] *adj* authentic, established (*fact etc*).
ver'büßen *v/t* (h) serve (*sentence*).
ver'chromen *v/t* (h) chromium-plate.
Verdacht [fɛrˈdaxt] *m* (-[e]s; -e) (*~ erregen* arouse) suspicion: **j-n im ~ haben** (*et. getan zu haben*) suspect s.o. (of having done s.th.); **in ~ kommen** be suspected; **~ schöpfen** become suspicious, F smell a rat; **bei ihm besteht ~ auf Krebs** he is suspected of having cancer; F *auf* ~ on spec; → **lenken** 3.
verdächtig [fɛrˈdɛçtɪç] *adj* suspicious, suspect, *a.* dubious, F fishy: **des Diebstahls ~ sein** be suspected of theft.
Ver'dächtige *m, f* (-n; -n) suspect.
verdächtigen [fɛrˈdɛçtɪɡən] *v/t* (h) **j-n ~** cast suspicion on s.o., suspect s.o. (*gen* of; *et. getan zu haben* of having done s.th.). **Ver'dächtigung** *f* (-; -en) **1.** casting suspicion (*gen* on). **2.** suspicion.
Ver'dachtsmo ment *n* suspicious fact.
verdammen [fɛrˈdamən] *v/t* (h) (*zu* to) condemn, *a. eccl.* damn. **ver'dammt I** *adj* **1.** damned: **dazu ~ sein zu** *inf* be condemned (*or* doomed) to *inf.* **2.** F damn(ed), blasted, *Br. sl.* bloody: **~** (*nochmal*)*!* damn (it)!, blast it (all)! **II** *adv* F damn(ed), *Br. sl.* bloody: **~ kalt** *a.* beastly cold. **Ver'dammung** *f* (-; -en) condemnation, *a. eccl.* damnation.
ver'dampfen *v/t* (h), *v/i* (sn) evaporate.
ver'danken *v/t* (h) **j-m et. ~** owe s.th. to s.o., be indebted to s.o. for s.th.; **es ist ihr zu ~, daß** it is due to her that.
verdarb [fɛrˈdarp] *pret of* **verderben**.
verdattert [fɛrˈdatərt] *adj* F dazed.
verdauen [fɛrˈdaʊən] *v/t* (h) digest.
ver'daulich *adj* (*leicht ~* easily) digestible; **schwer ~** hard to digest.
Ver'daulichkeit *f* (-; *no pl*) digestibility.
Ver'dauung *f* (-; *no pl*) digestion.
Ver'dauungs|appa rat *m* digestive system. **~beschwerden** *pl* indigestion, digestive trouble.
Ver'deck *n* (-[e]s; -e) (folding) top, hood.
ver'decken *v/t* (h) cover, hide, *a.* ✗ conceal: **verdeckte** (*Polizei*)*Aktion* undercover operation.

ver'denken v/t (irr, no -ge-, h, → **denken**) **ich kann es ihm nicht ~ (, daß)** I can't blame him (if).

verderben [fɛr'dɛrbən] (verdarb, verdorben) **I** v/i (sn) spoil, go bad, perish. **II** v/t (h) spoil, a. ruin, morally: corrupt: **sich den Magen (die Augen) ~** upset one's stomach (ruin one's eyes); **j-m die Freude (den Appetit) ~** spoil s.o.'s fun (appetite); F **es mit j-m ~** fall out with s.o.; **er will es mit niemandem ~** he tries to please everybody.

Ver'derben n (-s; no pl) ruin: **in sein ~ rennen** rush (headlong) into disaster.

verderblich [fɛr'dɛrplɪç] adj **1.** perishable (goods). **2.** fig. ruinous (effect etc), corrupting (influence etc).

ver'deutlichen v/t (h) j-m et. ~ make s.th. clear (or explain s.th.) to s.o.

ver'dichten (h) **I** v/t **1.** ⊚ compress, a. 🔾 condense. **II sich ~ 2.** condense, fog: thicken. **3.** fig. suspicion etc: grow stronger. **Ver'dichtung** f (-; -en) condensation, mot. compression.

ver'dicken v/t (a. **sich ~**) (h) thicken.

ver'dienen (h) **I** v/t **1.** earn, make (money): **sich et. nebenbei ~** make some money on the side. **2.** fig. deserve (punishment, praise, etc): **er hat es nicht besser verdient!** (it) serves him right!; → **verdient. II** v/i **gut ~** earn a good salary (or wage); **an e-r Sache gut ~** make a good profit on s.th.

Ver'diener m (-s; -) (salary or wage) earner, breadwinner.

Ver'dienst[1] n (-[e]s; -e) fig. merit: **es ist ihr ~, daß** it is thanks to her that; → **erwerben.**

Ver'dienst[2] m (-[e]s; -e) income, earnings, wages, salary.

Ver'dienstausfall m lost earnings.

verdienstvoll adj deserving (person), commendable (deed etc).

ver'dient adj fig. **1.** deserving, man etc of merit: **sich ~ machen um** do s.o., s.th. a great service. **2.** a) well-deserved, due (punishment), b) well-earned (victory).

ver'dienter'maßen adv deservedly.

ver'dolmetschen v/t (h) j-m et. ~ translate s.th. for (fig. explain s.th. to) s.o.

ver'donnern v/t (h) F condemn s.o. (**zu** to); **j-n ~, et. zu tun** make s.o. do s.th.

ver'doppeln v/t (a. **sich ~**) (h) double. **Ver'dopplung** f (-; -en) doubling.

verdorben [fɛr'dɔrbən] **I** pp of **verderben. II** adj spoiled (a. fig.), a. bad, fig. a. ruined, morally: a. corrupt: **~er Magen** upset stomach, indigestion.

verdorren [fɛr'dɔrən] v/i (sn) wither.

verdrahten [fɛr'dra:tən] v/t (h) ⚡ wire.

ver'drängen v/t (h) **1.** → **vertreiben** 1. **2.** fig. a) displace (a. ⚓, phys.), b) supersede, replace: **j-n ~** push s.o. out (sports: **vom ersten Platz** from first place); **j-n aus s-r Stellung ~** oust s.o. from his position. **3.** psych. repress, suppress. **4.** dismiss (a problem etc).

Ver'drängung f (-; -en) ousting, displacement (a. ⚓, phys.), fig. replacement, psych. repression, suppression.

verdreckt [fɛr'drɛkt] adj filthy, soiled.

ver'drehen v/t (h) **1.** twist (j-m den Arm s.o.'s arm): **die Augen: ~** roll one's eyes; **j-m den Kopf ~** turn s.o.'s head. **2.** F fig. twist, distort (words etc), pervert (law).

ver'dreht adj F fig. **1.** crazy, cranky. **2.** confused. **Ver'drehung** f (-; -en) twisting, fig. a. distortion (of facts etc).

ver'dreifachen v/t (h) treble.

verdrießen [fɛr'dri:sən] v/t (verdroß, verdrossen, h) annoy.

ver'drießlich adj morose, sullen.

verdrossen [fɛr'drɔsən] adj **1.** sullen. **2.** listless. **Ver'drossenheit** f (-; no pl) **1.** sullenness. **2.** listlessness.

ver'drücken (h) **I** v/t polish off. **II sich ~** slip away, beat it.

Verdruß [fɛr'drʊs] m (-sses; no pl) annoyance: **~ bereiten** cause s.o. trouble.

ver'duften v/i (sn) F beat it, scram.

verdummen [fɛr'dʊmən] **I** v/t (h) dull s.o.'s mind, stultify, brainwash (the people). **II** v/i (sn) become stultified.

ver'dunkeln v/t (h) darken (a. **sich ~**), black out, a. fig. cloud, fig. obscure. **Ver'dunklung** f (-; -en) a) darkening, b) blackout. **Ver'dunklungsgefahr** f ⚖ danger of collusion.

verdünnen [fɛr'dʏnən] v/t (h) dilute, thin (down) (paint). **Ver'dünner** m (-s; -) thinner. **Ver'dünnung** f (-; -en) dilution, thinning (down).

ver'dunsten v/t (h), v/i (sn) evaporate. **Ver'dunster** m (-s; -) humidifier. **Ver'dunstung** f (-; no pl) evaporation.

ver'dursten v/i (sn) die of thirst.

verdüstern [fɛr'dʏstərn] **sich ~** (h) a. fig. darken.

verdutzt [fɛrˈdʊtst] *adj* nonplussed, *pred* taken aback.

ver'ebben *v/i* (sn) *a. fig.* ebb away.

veredeln [fɛrˈʔeːdəln] *v/t* (h) **1.** ennoble. **2.** refine, ⊙ *a.* process, finish. **3.** 🌿 graft, bud. **Ver'edelungsindu‚strie** *f* processing industry.

ver'ehren *v/t* (h) a) revere, *a. fig.* adore, worship, b) admire: **Verehrte Anwesende!** Ladies and Gentlemen! **Ver'ehrer** *m* (-s; -), **Ver'ehrerin** *f* (-; -nen) **1.** admirer. **2.** fan. **Ver'ehrerpost** *f* fan mail. **Ver'ehrung** *f* (-; *no pl*) a) (**~ zollen** pay) reverence (*dat* to), *a. fig.* worship, adoration, b) admiration. **ver'ehrungswürdig** *adj* venerable.

vereidigen [fɛrˈʔaɪdɪɡən] *v/t* (h) (**auf** *acc* on) put *s.o.* under an oath, swear *s.o.* in. **vereidigt** [fɛrˈʔaɪdɪçt] *adj* sworn. **Ver'eidigung** *f* (-; -en) swearing-in.

Ver'ein *m* (-[e]s; -e) **1.** club: F *contp.* **ein netter ~** a fine bunch. **2.** 🕆 society, association. **3.** **im ~ mit** together with.

ver'einbar *adj* (**mit**) compatible, consistent. **ver'einbaren** *v/t* (h) **1.** agree (up)on, arrange: **vorher ~** prearrange. **2.** reconcile (**mit** with). **Ver'einbarkeit** *f* (-; *no pl*) compatibility (**mit** with). **ver'einbart** *adj* agreed: **zur ~en Zeit** at the time agreed upon. **Ver'einbarung** *f* (-; -en) agreement, arrangement: **e-e ~ treffen** reach an agreement; **laut ~** as agreed; **nach ~** by agreement; **Gehalt nach ~** salary negotiable.

ver'einen *v/t* → **vereinigen: mit vereinten Kräften** in a combined effort.

ver'einfachen *v/t* (h) simplify. **Ver'einfachung** *f* (-; -en) simplification.

ver'einheitlichen *v/t* (h) standardize. **Ver'einheitlichung** *f* (-; -en) standardization.

ver'einigen *v/t* (*a.* **sich ~**) (h) a) unite (**zu** into), combine, join (together), 🕆 amalgamate, b) assemble, *a.* rally: **Vereinigte Staaten (von Amerika)** United States (of America) (*abbr.* U.S.[A.]).

Ver'einigung *f* (-; -en) **1.** *no pl* uniting (*etc*), *pol.* unification, 🕆 merger. **2.** association, union.

ver'einnahmen *v/t* (h) F monopolize.

ver'einsamen *v/i* (sn) become isolated (*or* lonely). **Ver'einsamung** *f* (-; *no pl*) (growing) isolation.

Ver'eins|haus *n* clubhouse. **~kame‚rad**

m clubmate. **~kasse** *f* club funds.

ver'einzelt I *adj* isolated, sporadic, *a.* scattered (*showers*). **II** *adv* a) sporadically, now and then, b) here and there.

ver'eisen I *v/t* (h) 🌡 freeze. **II** *v/i* (sn) ice over, 🌿 *etc* ice up, freeze over: **vereiste Straßen** icy roads.

ver'eiteln *v/t* (h) thwart, frustrate (*plan etc*), prevent (*deed*).

ver'eitert *adj* 🌡 septic.

ver'ekeln *v/t* **j-m et. ~** put *s.o.* off *s.th.*

verelenden [fɛrˈʔeːlɛndən] *v/i* (sn) be reduced to poverty. **Ver'elendung** *f* (-; *no pl*) impoverishment.

ver'enden *v/i* (sn) perish, die.

ver'engen *v/t* (*a.* **sich ~**) (h) narrow (*a. fig.*), *pupil:* contract. **Ver'engung** *f* (-; -en) **1.** narrowing, contraction. **2.** narrow part (*in dat* of).

ver'erben (h) **I** *v/t* **j-m et. ~** leave (🌡 transmit) *s.th.* to *s.o.* **II** **sich ~** *a.* 🌡 *or fig.* be passed on (*or* down) (**auf** *acc* to). **vererbt** [-ˈʔɛrpt] *adj* biol. inherited, hereditary. **Ver'erbung** *f* (-; *no pl*) biol. heredity, (hereditary) transmission. **~lehre** *f* genetics.

Ver'erbungs|gesetze *pl* laws of heredity. **~technik** *f* process technology.

verewigen [fɛrˈʔeːvɪɡən] *v/t* (h) immortalize.

ver'fahren[1] (*irr, no* -ge-, → **fahren**) **I** *v/i* (sn) (**nach** on) proceed, act: **~ mit** deal with, treat. **II** *v/t* (h) use up (*petrol*), spend *money, time* driving (around). **III** **sich ~** get lost.

ver'fahren[2] *adj* muddled, tangled: **e-e ~e Sache** a (great) muddle.

Ver'fahren *n* (-s; -) **1.** procedure, method, process. **2.** 🏛 a) procedure, b) proceedings: **ein ~ einleiten** take (legal) proceedings (**gegen** against).

Ver'fahrens|frage *f* 🏛 procedural question. **~technik** *f* process technology. **~weise** *f* → **Verfahren** 1.

Ver'fall *m* (-[e]s; *no pl*) **1.** decay, *a.* dilapidation, ruin, *a.* 🌡 decline, (*moral*) degeneration, corruption. **2.** 🌡 expiry.

ver'fallen[1] *v/i* (*irr, no* -ge-, sn, → **fallen**) **1.** decay, dilapidate, *building etc:* a. go to ruin, *culture, empire, etc:* a. decline, *patient:* waste away. **2.** become addicted (*dat* to): **j-m ~** become *s.o.*'s slave. **3.** (**wieder**) **~ in** (*acc*) fall (back) into. **4.** **~ auf** (*acc*) hit (up)on (*an idea etc*); **wie ist er nur darauf ~?** what on earth made him think (or do) that? **5.** *ticket*: expire, *pawn*: become forfeited. **ver'fallen** *adj* **1.** decayed, a. dilapidated. **2.** *ticket etc*: expired, *pawn*: forfeited. **3.** addicted (*dat* to); **j-m ~ sein** be s.o.'s slave.

Ver'falls|datum *n* best-before (*Am.* pull, *pharm.* sell-by) date. **~erscheinung** *f* sign of decay. **~tag** *m* ✝ expiry date.

ver'fälschen *v/t* (h) **1.** adulterate (*food etc*). **2.** falsify, distort (*facts etc*). **Ver'fälschung** *f* (-; -en) **1.** adulteration. **2.** falsification, distortion.

ver'fangen (*irr, no* -ge-, h, → *fangen*) **I** *v/i* work (*bei* with): *das verfängt bei mir nicht* a. that cuts no ice with me. **II** *sich ~ a.* *fig.* get caught (*in dat* in).

verfänglich [fɛr'fɛnlɪç] *adj* trick (*question*), compromising, awkward (*situation etc*).

ver'färben: sich ~ (h) change colo(u)r, *leaves*: turn.

ver'fassen *v/t* (h) write, compose, draw up. **Ver'fasser** *m* (-s; -), **Ver'fasserin** *f* (-; -nen) author, writer.

Ver'fassung *f* (-; -en) **1.** *no pl* a) state, condition, b) frame of mind: *in guter ~* in good condition (*or* shape), in a good state (of health). **2.** *pol.* constitution.

Ver'fassungs|änderung *f* constitutional amendment. **~beschwerde** *f* constitutional complaint. **~bruch** *m* breach of the constitution. **Ωfeindlich** *adj* anti-constitutional. **~gericht** *n* constitutional court. **~klage** *f* complaint of unconstitutionality. **Ωmäßig, Ωrechtlich** *adj* constitutional. **~schutz** *m* protection of the constitution. **Ωwidrig** *adj* unconstitutional.

ver'faulen *v/i* (sn) rot, decay.

ver'fechten *v/t* (*irr, no* -ge-, h, → *fechten*) stand up for. **Ver'fechter** *m* (-s; -), **Ver'fechterin** *f* (-; -nen) advocate.

ver'fehlen *v/t* (h) miss (*um* by): *s-n Beruf verfehlt haben* have missed one's vocation; → *Wirkung* 1, *Zweck* 1.

ver'fehlt *adj* wrong, misguided.

Ver'fehlung *f* (-; -en) offen/ce (*Am.* -se).

ver'feinden [fɛr'faɪndən] **sich ~** (h) become enemies; *sich mit j-m ~* make an enemy of s.o. **ver'feindet** *adj* hostile: **~ sein** be enemies.

ver'feinern [fɛr'faɪnərn] *v/t* (h) refine. **Ver'feinerung** *f* (-; -en) refinement.

ver'femen *v/t* (h) **1.** ostracize. **2.** ban.

Ver'fettung *f* (-; -en) ✿ adiposis.

ver'feuern *v/t* (h) **1.** a) burn, b) use up. **2.** fire (*ammunition etc*).

ver'filmen *v/t* (h) film, adapt *novel etc* for the screen.

Ver'filmung *f* (-; -en) **1.** filming. **2.** film version, screen adaptation.

ver'filzen *v/i* (h) felt, *hair*: mat.

ver'finstern *v/t* (*a. sich ~*) (h) darken.

ver'flachen *v/i* (sn) **1.** flatten. **2.** *fig.* degenerate (*zu* into).

ver'flechten *v/t* (*irr, no* -ge-, h, → *flechten*) (*a. sich ~*) interweave (*a. fig.*), ✝ interlock: → *verflochten*. **Ver'flechtung** *f* (-; -en) interweaving (*a. fig.*), *fig.* entanglement, ✝ interlocking.

ver'fliegen (*irr, no* -ge-, → *fliegen*) **I** *v/i* (sn) **1.** *alcohol etc*: evaporate. **2.** *fig.* vanish, *time etc*: fly. **II** *sich ~* get lost.

verflixt [fɛr'flɪkst] *adj* F blasted, damn(ed): **~!** blast!, damn (it)!

verflochten [fɛr'flɔxtən] *adj* interwoven (*a. fig.*), *fig.* (en)tangled, ✝ interlocked.

ver'flossen *adj* **1.** past (*time*). **2.** F ex-...

ver'fluchen *v/t* (h) curse.

ver'flucht → *verdammt*.

ver'flüchtigen [fɛr'flʏçtɪɡən] **sich ~** (h) evaporate, *fig.* a. disappear.

ver'flüssigen [fɛr'flʏsɪɡən] *v/t* (*a. sich ~*) (h) liquefy. **Ver'flüssigung** *f* (-; -en) liquefaction.

ver'folgen *v/t* (h) **1.** pursue (*a. fig. policy, career, etc*), chase, *a. hunt.* track: *j-n ~ thought etc*: haunt s.o.; *strafrechtlich ~* prosecute; *gerichtlich ~* take legal steps against. **2.** follow (*trail, a. fig. events, progress, etc*). **3.** *esp. pol.* persecute. **Ver'folger** *m* (-s; -) pursuer, *pol. etc* persecutor. **Ver'folgte** *m, f* (-n; -n) victim of persecution, (political) persecutee. **Ver'folgung** *f* (-; -en) pursuit (*a. cycling or fig.*), *pol. etc* persecution: *strafrechtliche ~* (criminal) prosecution. **Ver'folgungswahn** *m* persecution complex.

ver'formen *v/t* (*a. sich ~*) (h) deform. **Ver'formung** *f* (-; -en) deformation.

ver'frachten *v/t* (h) freight, ⚓ *or Am.* ship: F *j-n ein in Taxi* (*ins Bett*) *~* bundle s.o. off into a taxi (to bed).

ver'fremden [fɛr'frɛmdən] *v/t* (h) alienate. **Ver'fremdung** *f* (-; -en) alienation.

ver'fressen *adj* F greedy.

ver'froren adj ~ sein feel the cold (very easily); ~ aussehen look frozen.
ver'früht adj premature.
verfügbar [fɛr'fy:kba:r] adj available.
Ver'fügbarkeit f (-; no pl) availability.
ver'fugen v/t (h) ☺ point.
ver'fügen (h) I v/t order: testamentarisch ~ decree by will. II v/i ~ über (acc) have s.o., s.th. at s.o.'s disposal, dispose of, possess, have; frei ~ können über (acc) be able to do what one wants with. Ver'fügung f (-; -en) 1. order, adm. decree: laut ~ as ordered; → einstweilig, letztwillig. 2. (über acc of) disposal, 🔧 disposition: zur ~ stehen (stellen) be (make) available, j-m be (place) at s.o.'s disposal; sich zur ~ stellen offer one's services, volunteer (für for); sein Amt zur ~ stellen tender one's resignation. Ver'fügungsgewalt f (-; no pl) control (über acc of).
ver'führen v/t (h) seduce. Ver'führer m (-s; -) seducer. Ver'führerin f (-; -nen) seductress. ver'führerisch adj 1. seductive. 2. fig. tempting. Ver'führung f (-; -en) 1. seduction. 2. fig. temptation. Ver'führungskünste pl powers of seduction.
ver'fünffachen v/t (a. sich ~) (h) quintuple.
ver'füttern v/t (h) feed.
Ver'gabe f (-; -n) placing (of orders etc), awarding (of prizes), allocation (of funds).
vergällen [fɛr'gɛlən] v/t (h) 1. denature (alcohol). 2. fig. sour, spoil.
ver'gammeln F I v/i (sn) rot, person: go to seed. II v/t (h) laze away (time).
ver'gammelt adj F scruffy, seedy.
vergangen [fɛr'gaŋən] adj past: ~e Woche, in der ~en Woche last week.
Ver'gangenheit f (-; no pl) past (a. fig.), ling. past tense: politische ~ political background; → ruhen.
Ver'gangenheitsbewältigung f coming to terms with the past.
vergänglich [fɛr'gɛŋlɪç] adj transitory, transient. Ver'gänglichkeit f (-; no pl) transitoriness, transience.
vergasen [fɛr'ga:zən] v/t (h) 1. 🔧 gasify. 2. gas.
Ver'gaser m (-s; -) mot. carburet(t)or.
vergaß [fɛr'ga:s] pret of vergessen.

Ver'gasung f (-; -en) 1. 🔧 gasification. 2. gassing.
ver'geben[1] (irr, no -ge-, h, → geben) I v/t 1. (an acc) give s.th. away (to), place order etc (with), assign work etc (to), award prize (to), allocate funds (to), grant scholarship (to). 2. j-m et. ~ forgive s.o. (for doing) s.th. 3. e-e Chance ~ miss (or give away) the chance. II v/i 4. j-m ~ forgive s.o. 5. sports: give away the chance, shoot wide. ver'geben[2] adj post: filled, work etc: assigned: noch nicht ~ open, still vacant.
ver'gebens adj pred and adv in vain.
vergeblich [fɛr'ge:plɪç] I adj vain, futile, useless. II adv in vain.
Ver'geblichkeit f (-; no pl) futility.
Ver'gebung f (-; no pl) 1. (j-n um ~ bitten ask s.o.'s) forgiveness. 2. → Vergabe.
vergegenwärtigen [fɛr'ge:gənvɛrtɪgən] v/t (h) sich et. ~ visualize, picture.
ver'gehen (irr, no -ge-, → gehen) I v/i (sn) pass (away) (a. fig.), time: a. go by, pain etc: wear off: wie die Zeit vergeht! how time flies; vor Ungeduld etc ~ be dying of impatience etc; er verging fast vor Angst he was frightened to death; mir ist der Appetit vergangen I've lost my appetite; F da vergeht einem alles! that turns you off completely. II sich ~ (h) a) an j-m commit indecent assault on s.o., rape s.o., b) gegen violate, offend against (law etc).
Ver'gehen n (-s; -) offen/ce (Am. -se).
ver'gelten v/t (irr, no -ge-, h, → gelten) repay (j-m et. s.o. for s.th.).
Ver'geltung f (-; no pl) (als ~ in) retaliation (für for, of): ~ üben retaliate (an dat on). Ver'geltungs... retaliatory (measure, strike, etc).
verge'sellschaften v/t (h) 🌱 socialize.
vergessen [fɛr'gɛsən] v/t (irr (vergaß, vergessen, h) forget (sich o.s.), a. leave behind: ich habe es ~ a. it slipped my mind; ich habe ganz ~, wie I forgot how; das vergesse ich dir nie I won't ever forget it; F das kannst du ~! forget it! Ver'gessenheit f (-; no pl) (in ~ geraten fall into) oblivion.
vergeßlich [fɛr'gɛslɪç] adj forgetful: ~ sein a. keep forgetting things.
Ver'geßlichkeit f (-; no pl) forgetfulness.
vergeuden [fɛr'gɔydən] v/t (h) waste,

squander. **Ver'geudung** f (-; -en) waste, squandering.

vergewaltigen [fɛrgə'valtɪgən] v/t (h) rape, a. fig. violate. **Verge'waltigung** f (-; -en) rape, a. fig. violation.

vergewissern [fɛrgə'vɪsərn] **sich ~** (h) make sure (**e-r Sache** of s.th.).

ver'gießen v/t (irr, no -ge-, h, → **gießen**) **1.** spill. **2.** shed (blood, tears).

ver'giften v/t (h) poison (**sich** o.s.), fig. a. contaminate. **Ver'giftung** f (-; -en) poisoning, fig. a. contamination.

vergilbt [fɛr'gɪlpt] adj yellowed.

Vergißmeinnicht [fɛr'gɪsmaɪnnɪçt] n (-[e]s; -[e]) ❦ forget-me-not.

ver'gittern v/t (h) bar, a. lattice.

verglasen [fɛr'glaːzən] v/t (h) glaze.

Ver'gleich m (-[e]s; -e) **1.** (**im ~** in or by) comparison (**zu** with): **e-n ~ anstellen** draw a comparison; **dem ~ (nicht) standhalten** bear (no) comparison (**mit** with); → **hinken. 2.** ⚖ settlement, with creditors: composition: **gütlicher ~** amicable arrangement; **mit e-m Gläubiger e-n ~ schließen** compound with a creditor. **ver'gleichbar** adj comparable (**mit** to, with). **ver'gleichen** (irr, no -ge-, h, → **gleichen**) **I** v/t compare (**mit** to, with): **das ist nicht zu ~ mit ...** a) that cannot be compared to ..., b) it cannot compare with ... **II sich ~ mit** come to terms (or settle, compound) with. **ver'gleichend** adj comparative. **Ver'gleichs|kampf** m sports: test. **~maßstab** m standard of comparison. **ver'gleichsweise** adv comparatively. **Ver'gleichszahl** f comparative figure.

ver'glühen v/i (sn) fire: smo(u)lder, meteor: burn out, rocket: burn out.

vergnügen [fɛr'gnyːgən] **sich ~** (h) enjoy o.s. **Ver'gnügen** n (-s; -) pleasure, fun: **mit ~** with pleasure; **viel ~!** a. iro. have fun!; **(nur) zum ~** (just) for fun; **vor ~ yell etc** with delight; **sein ~ haben an** (dat) enjoy; **j-m ~ machen** amuse s.o.; **ich wünsche dir viel ~** I hope you'll enjoy yourself; **es war kein (reines) ~!** F it was no picnic; **ein teures ~** a costly affair. **vergnüglich** [-'gnyːklɪç] adj pleasant, amusing. **vergnügt** [-'gnyːkt] adj cheerful: **~ sein** a. be in high spirits. **Ver'gnügung** f (-; -en) usu. pl pleasure, amusement.

Ver'gnügungs|park m amusement

park, fun fair. **~reise** f pleasure trip. **~steuer** f entertainment tax. **⚲süchtig** adj pleasure-seeking. **~viertel** n night-life district.

ver'golden v/t (h) a. fig. gild.

ver'goldet adj gold-plated (watch etc).

ver'gönnen v/t (h) grant: **es war ihr nicht vergönnt zu** inf it was not granted to her to inf.

vergöttern [fɛr'gœtərn] v/t (h) idolize.

ver'graben v/t (irr, no -ge-, h, → **graben**) a. fig. bury (**sich** o.s.).

vergrämt [fɛr'grɛːmt] adj careworn.

ver'graulen v/t (h) F scare off.

ver'greifen (irr, no -ge-, h, → **greifen**) **1. sich ~** make a mistake, ♪ play a wrong note: fig. **sich im Ton ~** strike a false note. **2. sich ~ an** (dat) misappropriate (s.th.); **sich an j-m ~** lay hands on s.o., (sexually) assault s.o.

vergreisen [fɛr'graɪzən] v/i (sn) become senile, a. population: age. **vergreist** [-'graɪst] adj senile. **Ver'greisung** f (-; no pl) (progressive) senility, ag(e)ing.

ver'griffen adj book: out of print.

vergrößern [fɛr'grøːsərn] (h) **I** v/t a) enlarge, phot. a. blow up, opt. magnify, b) expand, extend, c) a. fig. increase. **II sich ~** grow, a. enlarge, expand, increase, organ: become enlarged.

Ver'größerung f (-; -en) **1.** enlargement, expansion, increase. **2.** phot. enlargement, blow-up, opt. magnification.

Ver'größerungs|appa,rat m phot. enlarger. **~glas** n opt. magnifying glass.

Ver'günstigung f (-; -en) privilege, (tax) allowance, (social) benefit.

vergüten [fɛr'gyːtən] v/t (h) **1.** (j-m) et. **~** a) remunerate (or pay) (s.o.) (for) s.th., b) reimburse (s.o.) for s.th., c) compensate (s.o.) for s.th. **2.** ⚙ quench and temper (steel), opt. coat (lenses). **Ver'gütung** f (-; -en) **1.** remuneration, reimbursement, compensation. **2.** ⚙ quenching and tempering, opt. coating.

ver'haften v/t (h) arrest: **Sie sind verhaftet!** you are under arrest!

Ver'haftete m, f (-n; -n) person arrested.

Ver'haftung f (-; -en) arrest.

ver'hallen v/i (sn) die away.

ver'halten¹: sich ~ (irr, no -ge-, h, → **halten**) behave, a. conduct o.s., act, ⚗ a. react: **sich ruhig ~** keep quiet; **ich weiß nicht, wie ich mich ~ soll** I'm not sure what to do; **wenn sich die Sache so verhält** if that is the case.

ver'halten² I *adj* **1.** suppressed (*rage, laughter, etc*), restrained. **2.** → **gedämpft** 1. II *adv* with restraint: ~ **fahren** drive cautiously; *sports:* **er lief ~** he didn't go all out; ~ **spielen** *sports:* play a waiting game, *thea.* underact.

Ver'halten *n* (-s) behavio(u)r, conduct, attitude, reaction.

Ver'haltens|forscher *m* behavio(u)ral scientist. **~forschung** *f* behavio(u)ral science. **2gestört** *adj* disturbed, maladjusted. **~(maß)regeln** *pl* instructions. **~muster** *n* behavio(u)ral pattern. **~thera,pie** *f* behavio(u)r therapy.

Verhältnis [fɛrˈhɛltnɪs] *n* (-ses; -se) **1.** proportion, relation, ratio: **im ~ 1:10** in a ratio of 1:10; **in k-m ~ stehen** be out of all proportion (**zu** to). **2.** (**zu** with) relations, relationship: **ein gutes ~ zu j-m haben** get on well with s.o.; **er hat kein ~ zur Musik** he cannot relate to music. **3.** *pl* conditions, circumstances: **unter diesen ~sen** as matters stand; **in guten ~sen leben** be well off; **über s-e ~se leben** live beyond one's means. **4.** F (love) affair.

ver'hältnismäßig *adv* comparatively, relatively.

Ver'hältnis|wahl *f parl.* proportional representation. **~wort** *n* preposition.

ver'handeln *v/i* I **1.** ~ **über** (*acc*) a) negotiate (about, on, for), b) discuss. **2.** ⚖ hold a hearing (*or* trial). II *v/t* ⚖ hear (*a case*), *criminal law:* try.

Ver'handlung *f* (-; -en) **1.** negotiation (**über** *acc* about, on, for). **2.** ⚖ a) hearing, b) trial: **zur ~ kommen** come up (for trial).

Ver'handlungs|basis *f* basis for negotiation: **✝ ~ 5000 DM** (*price*) DM 5,000 or nearest offer. **2bereit** *adj* ready to negotiate. **~partner** *m* negotiating partner. **~runde** *f* round of negotiations. **~tisch** *m* negotiating table.

verhangen [fɛrˈhaŋən] *adj* cloudy (*sky*).

ver'hängen *v/t* (h) **1.** (**mit** with) cover, drape. **2.** (**über** *acc*) impose *fine etc* (on), declare *state of emergency* (in *a country etc*). **3.** *sports:* award *penalty kick* (**gegen** against).

Ver'hängnis *n* (-ses; -se) a) fate, b) disaster: **j-m zum ~ werden** be s.o.'s un-

doing. **ver'hängnisvoll** *adj* a) fateful (*day etc*), b) disastrous, fatal.

verharmlosen [fɛrˈharmloːzən] *v/t* (h) play *s.th.* down.

verhärmt [fɛrˈhɛrmt] *adj* careworn.

ver'harschen *v/i* (sn) crust.

ver'härten *v/t* (h) *a. fig.* harden (**sich** o.s.). **Ver'härtung** *f* (-; -en) *esp. fig.* hardening, induration (*a.* ⚕).

ver'haspeln: sich ~ (h) F *fig.* get in a muddle.

ver'haßt *adj* hated, *matter: a.* hateful: **er hat sich bei allen ~ gemacht** he has turned everyone against him.

ver'hätscheln *v/t* (h) coddle, pamper.

ver'hauen *v/t* (h) *a. fig.* **1.** beat *s.o.* up, spank. **2.** *fig.* muff.

verheddern [fɛrˈhɛdərn] **sich ~** (h) F **1.** *a. fig.* tangle. **2.** → **verhaspeln**.

verheerend [fɛrˈheːrənd] *adj* disastrous: ~ **wirken auf** (*acc*) play havoc with. **2.** dreadful. **Ver'heerungen** *pl* (~ **anrichten** cause) havoc.

ver'heilen *v/i* (sn) heal (up).

ver'heimlichen *v/t* (h) (*dat* from) hide, conceal, keep *s.th.* a secret.

ver'heiraten *v/t* (h) **j-n ~** marry s.o. (off) (**mit, an** *acc* to); **sich ~** marry, get married; **verheiratet sein** be married (**mit** to, *a.* F *fig.*). **Ver'heiratete** *m, f* (-n; -n) married man (woman).

ver'heißen *v/t* (*irr, no* -ge-, h, → **heißen**), **Ver'heißung** *f* (-; -en) promise.

ver'heißungsvoll *adj* promising.

ver'helfen *v/t* (*irr, no* -ge-, h, → **helfen**) **j-m ~ zu** help s.o. (to) find (*or* get *etc*).

ver'herrlichen *v/t* (h) glorify.

Ver'herrlichung *f* (-; -en) glorification.

ver'hexen *v/t* (h) bewitch, F jinx: **es ist wie verhext!** there is a jinx on it.

ver'hindern *v/t* (h) prevent: (**es**) ~, **daß j-d et. tut** prevent s.o. from doing s.th.

ver'hindert *adj* **1.** ~ **sein** be unable to come. **2.** F *fig.* would-be (*artist etc*).

Ver'hinderung *f* (-; -en) prevention.

ver'höhnen *v/t* (h) deride, mock. **Ver'höhnung** *f* (-; -en) derision, mockery.

verhökern [fɛrˈhøːkərn] *v/t* (h) F *contp.* flog, sell off.

Verhör [fɛrˈhøːr] *n* (-[e]s; -e) ⚖ interrogation, questioning.

ver'hören (h) I *v/t* ⚖ interrogate, question. II **sich ~** mishear.

ver'hüllen *v/t* (h) cover (up), *a. fig.* veil.

ver'hundertfachen v/t (h) centuple.
ver'hungern v/i (sn) die of starvation: **j-n ~ lassen** starve s.o. to death; F **ich bin am Verhungern!** I'm starving.
ver'hüten v/t (h) prevent.
ver'hütten v/t (h) ⊕ smelt (ore).
Ver'hütung f (-; no pl) **1.** prevention. **2.** ⚘ contraception.
Ver'hütungsmittel n ⚘ contraceptive.
verhutzelt [fɛr'hʊtsəlt] adj F wizened.
ver'innerlichen v/t (h) internalize.
ver'irren: sich ~ (h) lose one's way, get lost: fig. **verirrte Kugel** stray bullet.
Ver'irrung f (-; -en) fig. aberration.
ver'jagen v/t (h) a. fig. chase away.
ver'jähren v/i (sn) come under the statute of limitation. **ver'jährt** adj statute-barred. **Ver'jährung** f (-; -en) **1.** limitation. **2.** (negative) prescription.
Ver'jährungsfrist f period of limitation.
ver'jubeln v/t (h) F blow.
verjüngen [fɛr'jʏŋən] (h) **I** v/t **1.** make s.o. (look) younger, rejuvenate: sports: **die Mannschaft ~** build up a younger team. **II sich ~ 2.** grow (or look) younger. **3.** ⊕ taper. **Ver'jüngung** f (-; -en) **1.** rejuvenation. **2.** ⊕ taper.
ver'kabeln v/t (h) connect to a cable TV network.
ver'kalken v/i (h) **1.** calcify, F ⚘ arteries: a. harden, ⊕ a. fur up. **2.** F go senile: **er ist völlig verkalkt** a. he's gone completely gaga.
verkalku'lieren: sich ~ (h) miscalculate.
Ver'kalkung f (-; -en) **1.** calcification, F ⚘ a. hardening of the arteries, ⊕ a. furring up. **2.** F senility.
verkannt [fɛr'kant] adj unrecognized.
ver'kanten v/t (h) edge (ski).
ver'kappt adj disguised, in disguise.
Ver'kauf m (-[e]s; ⁀e) **1.** (zum ~ for) sale. **2.** ✝ sales department. **ver'kaufen** (h) **I** v/t (dat, an acc to) sell (a. F fig.): **zu ~!** for sale! **II sich ~** sell well, badly, etc, fig. sell o.s. **Ver'käufer** m (-s; -) **1.** seller, vendor. **2.** shop assistant, Am. salesclerk. **Ver'käuferin** f (-; -nen) shop assistant, saleslady, Am. salesclerk. **ver'käuflich** adj marketable, sal(e)able, b) for sale: **gut ~** easy to sell; **✝ frei ~** available without prescription.
Ver'kaufs|förderung f sales promotion. **~gespräch** n sales talk. **~leiter** m sales manager. **⚘offen** adj **~er Samstag**

all-day shopping on Saturday. **~preis** m selling price. **~schlager** m F money-spinner. **~stand** m stand. **~wert** m market value. **~ziffer** f sales figure.
Verkehr [fɛr'keːr] m (-s; no pl) **1.** traffic: **öffentlicher ~** public transport(ation). **2.** contact, dealings: **den ~ abbrechen** break off all contact(s). **3.** ✝ a) trade, b) payments, c) circulation: **aus dem ~ ziehen** a. F fig. withdraw from circulation. **4.** (sexual) intercourse.
ver'kehren v/i (h) **1.** (a. sn) bus etc: run, operate. **2. ~ in** (dat) frequent: **bei j-m ~** visit s.o. regularly. **3. ~ mit** associate with; **geschäftlich ~ mit** have business dealings with. **4. (geschlechtlich) ~ mit** have (sexual) intercourse with.
Ver'kehrs|ampel f traffic lights. **~amt** n tourist office. **~aufkommen** n volume of traffic. **~behinderung** f holdup, delay. **~betriebe** pl transport services. **~chaos** n traffic chaos. **~de,likt** n traffic offen/ce (Am. -se). **~dichte** f traffic density. **~durchsage** f traffic announcement. **~erziehung** f road safety education. **~flugzeug** n airliner. **~fluß** m (-sses; no pl) traffic flow. **~frei** adj traffic-free (area etc). **~funk** m information for motorists. **⚘günstig** adv gelegen conveniently placed as regards transport facilities. **~insel** f traffic island. **~kon,trolle** f vehicle spot check. **~lage** f situation on the roads. **~lärm** m traffic noise. **~meldungen** pl traffic news. **~mi,nister** m minister of transport. **~mini,sterium** n ministry of transport. **~mittel** n (means of) transportation: **öffentliche ~** pl public transport(ation Am.). **~netz** n traffic system. **~opfer** n road casualty. **~ordnung** f traffic regulations. **~poli,zei** f traffic police. **~poli,zist** m traffic policeman. **~regel** f traffic regulation. **~regelung** f traffic control. **⚘reich** adj busy. **~schild** n road sign. **⚘sicher** adj mot. roadworthy. **~sicherheit** f road safety, mot. roadworthiness. **~sprache** f lingua franca. **~stau** m, **~stockung** f traffic jam. **~streife** f traffic patrol. **~sünder** m traffic offender. **~teilnehmer** m road user. **~unfall** m traffic accident, (car) crash. **~unterricht** m traffic instruction. **~verbindung** f (road or rail) link. **~verbund** m (integrated) public

transport system. **~verein** m tourist office. **~wert** m ✝ market value. **~wesen** n (-s; no pl) public transport(ation Am.). **⚥widrig** adj contrary to the traffic regulations. **~zählung** f traffic census. **~zeichen** n road sign.

ver'kehrt adj and adv wrong, adv a. the wrong way: **~ herum** a) the wrong way round, b) upside down, c) inside out.

ver'kennen v/t (irr, no -ge-, h, → **kennen**) misjudge; → **verkannt.**

ver'ketten v/t (h) a. fig. link.

Ver'kettung f (-; -en) fig. concatenation.

ver'ketzern v/t (h) denounce.

ver'klagen v/t (h) ⚖ sue (**wegen, auf** acc for).

ver'klappen v/t (h) dump into the sea.

ver'klären v/t (h) fig. idealize.

ver'klärt adj fig. beatific.

ver'kleiden (h) **I** v/t **1.** dress s.o. up, disguise. **2.** ⚙ a) cover, b) line, c) case, d) panel, e) △ case, revet. **II sich ~** dress (o.s.) up, disguise o.s.

Ver'kleidung f (-; -en) **1.** disguise. **2.** ⚙ covering, casing, lining, panel(l)ing, △ facing, mot. cowling, ✈ fairing.

verkleinern [fɛr'klaɪnərn] v/t (h) **1.** make s.th. smaller, reduce (scale etc), diminish. **2.** fig. detract from, belittle.

Ver'kleinerung f (-; -en) reduction.

Ver'kleinerungsform f ling. diminutive.

ver'klemmen: sich ~ (h) get stuck.

ver'klemmt adj psych. inhibited.

ver'klingen v/i (irr, no -ge-, sn, → **klingen**) a. fig. die away.

ver'knacken v/t (h) F **j-n zu zwei Jahren ~** put s.o. inside for two years.

ver'knallen: sich ~ (h) F fall for (**in** j-n s.o.); **verknallt sein in** (acc) a. be madly in love with, have a crush on.

Ver'knappung f (-; -en) shortage.

ver'kneifen v/t (irr, no -ge-, h, → **kneifen**) F **sich et. ~** do (or go) without s.th.; **ich konnte mir ein Lächeln nicht ~** I couldn't help smiling.

ver'kniffen adj pinched (face, mouth).

ver'knöchern v/i (sn) a. fig. ossify: **er ist total verknöchert** F he's an old fossil.

ver'knoten v/t (h) knot, tie (up).

ver'knüpfen v/t (h) **1.** tie (or knot) together. **2.** fig. link: **verknüpft sein mit** involve (costs, difficulties, etc); **eng verknüpft sein mit** be bound up with.

ver'kochen v/i (sn) boil away: gastr. **verkocht sein** be overboiled.

ver'kohlen I v/i (sn) char. **II** v/t (h) F fig. **j-n ~** have s.o. on, pull s.o.'s leg.

ver'kommen¹ v/i (irr, no -ge-, sn, → **kommen**) go to rack and ruin, person: go to seed, morally: sink low, fruit etc: go to waste. **ver'kommen²** adj a) run-down, dilapidated, b) seedy, depraved. **Ver'kommenheit** f (-; no pl) seediness, depravity.

ver'korken v/t (h) cork (up).

verkorksen [fɛr'kɔrksən] v/t (h) F mess s.th. up; **sich den Magen ~** upset one's stomach; **verkorkste Sache** mess.

verkörpern [fɛr'kœrpərn] v/t (h) personify, embody, thea. impersonate, play.

Ver'körperung f (-; -en) personification, embodiment, thea. impersonation.

verköstigen [fɛr'kœstɪgən] v/t (h) feed.

ver'krachen: sich ~ (h) F fall out (**mit** with). **ver'kracht** adj F **1.** mit j-m ~ **sein** have fallen out with s.o. **2.** failed (artist etc): **~e Existenz** failure.

verkraften [fɛr'kraftən] v/t (h) cope with, handle, mentally: bear, take.

ver'krampfen: sich ~ (h) hands: clench, muscles etc: cramp, person: tense (up).

ver'kriechen: sich ~ (irr, no -ge-, h, → **kriechen**) a. fig. hide.

ver'krümeln: sich ~ (h) F sneak off.

ver'krümmt adj ⚕ curved. **Ver'krümmung** f (-; -en) distortion: **~ der Wirbelsäule** curvature of the spine.

ver'krüppeln I v/t (h) cripple. **II** v/i (sn) become crippled (tree: stunted).

ver'krusten v/i (sn) become encrusted.

ver'kümmern v/i (sn) become stunted, a. fig. waste away, atrophy. **ver'kümmert** adj stunted, a. fig. atrophied.

verkünden [fɛr'kʏndən] v/t (h) **1.** announce, adm. proclaim, ⚖ pronounce (sentence), promulgate (law etc). **2.** fig. herald. **ver'kündigen** v/t (h) **1.** lit. for **verkünden. 2.** eccl. preach.

Ver'kündigung f (-; -en) eccl. preaching.

Ver'kündung f (-; -en) announcement, proclamation, ⚖ pronouncement, promulgation.

ver'kupfern v/t (h) copper.

ver'kuppeln v/t (h) F **j-n ~** marry s.o. off (**an** acc to).

ver'kürzen (h) **I** v/t shorten (**um** by), abridge, cut short: **verkürzte Arbeits-**

zeit reduced hours. **II** *v/i* **~ auf** (*acc*) *sports*: shorten to.

Ver'ladebahnhof *m* shipping station.

ver'laden *v/t* (*irr, no -ge-, h,* → *laden*) **1.** load, ship, ♣ embark, ✈ emplane, 🚂 entrain, *mot.* entruck. **2.** F *j-n* **~** take s.o. for a ride, sell s.o.

Ver'ladung *f* (-; -en) loading (*etc*).

Verlag [fɛr'la:k] *m* (-[e]s; -e) publishing house (*or* company), publisher(s): *er-schienen im* **~** *L.* published by L.

ver'lagern *v/t* (h) **1.** (*a.* **sich ~**) *a.* fig. interest, emphasis, *etc*: shift (*auf* acc to). **2.** → *verlegen* [1]. **Ver'lagerung** *f* (-; -en) **1.** shift(ing). **2.** → *Verlegung*.

Ver'lags|anstalt *f* publishing house (*or* company). **~buchhandel** *m* publishing trade. **~buchhändler** *m* publisher. **~pro₁gramm** *n* publisher's list. **~werk** *n* publication. **~wesen** *n* (-s; *no pl*) publishing.

ver'landen *v/i* (sn) silt up.

ver'langen (h) **I** *v/t* **1.** a) ask for, demand, b) expect, c) claim, d) charge: *die Rechnung* **~** ask for the bill; *er verlangt viel* he's very demanding; *das ist* (*nicht*) *zuviel verlangt* that's (that's not) asking too much; *er verlangte den Ge-schäftsführer* he asked to speak to the manager; *Sie werden am Telefon ver-langt* you are wanted on the phone. **2.** require, call for (*patience, time, etc*). **II** *v/i* **~ nach** a) ask for, b) long for.

Ver'langen *n* (-s) **1.** (*nach* for) desire, longing: *heftiges* **~** craving. **2.** demand, request: *auf* **~** on request.

verlängern [fɛr'lɛŋərn] *v/t* (h) **1.** lengthen (*a.* **sich ~**), make *s.th.* longer, *fig.* prolong (*life, period, etc*), extend (*a. credit, membership, etc*), renew (*con-tract etc*). **2.** *sports*: touch *ball etc* on (*zu* to). **Ver'längerung** *f* (-; -en) **1.** a) lengthening, b) prolongation, extension, renewal. **2.** *sports*: a) pass, b) (*in die* **~** *gehen* go into) extra time (*Am.* overtime). **Ver'längerungsschnur** *f* ⚡ extension flex (*Am.* cord).

ver'langsamen *v/t* (*a.* **sich ~**) (h) slacken, slow down (*a. fig. development etc*).

Verlaß [fɛr'las] *m* **es ist** (*kein*) **~ auf** *j-n* (**et.**) s.o. (s.th.) is reliable (unreliable).

ver'lassen¹ (*irr, no -ge-, h,* → *lassen*) **I** *v/t* leave, *a.* abandon, desert: *s-e Kräfte verließen ihn* his strength failed him.

II *sich* **~ auf** (*acc*) rely (*or* count, depend) on; F *verlaß dich drauf!* take my word for it! **ver'lassen²** *adj* **1.** deserted, desolate (*region etc*). **2.** abandoned.

Ver'lassen *n* (-s) abandonment, desertion. **Ver'lassenheit** *f* (-; *no pl*) **1.** loneliness. **2.** desolation.

ver'läßlich *adj* reliable, dependable.

Ver'lauf *m* (-[e]s; ‿e) **1.** course (*of road etc*). **2.** a) course, run, b) progress, development: *im* **~** *von* (*or* gen) in the course of; *im weiteren* **~** in the sequel.

ver'laufen (*irr, no -ge-,* → *laufen*) **I** *v/i* (sn) **1.** *road etc*: run. **2.** go, run, come off: *alles verlief wie geplant* everything went according to plan; *normal* **~** take its normal course; **~ ergebnislos. 3.** *paint*: run, bleed. **4.** *trail*: disappear: → *Sand*. **5.** → *zerlaufen*. **II** *sich* **~** (h) get lost, lose one's way.

ver'laust *adj* full of lice.

ver'lauten *v/i* (sn) be reported: *wie ver-lautet* as reported; **~ lassen** give to understand, hint.

ver'leben *v/t* (h) spend: *e-e schöne Zeit* **~** *a.* have a nice time. **verlebt** [fɛr'le:pt] *adj* dissipated, worn-out (*by a fast life*).

ver'legen¹ (h) **I** *v/t* **1.** (*nach,* in *acc* to) transfer, move. **2.** (*auf* acc) put off (to), postpone (until). **3.** mislay (*key etc*). **4.** lay (*carpet, cable, etc*). **5.** publish (*book etc*). **6.** → *verlagern* [1]. **II** *sich* **~ auf** (*acc*) a) take up, take to *gardening etc*, b) resort to *pleading etc*.

ver'legen² *adj* **1.** embarrassed: **~ ma-chene** embarrass. **2.** (*nie*) **~ um** (never) at a loss for *an answer, excuse, etc*.

Ver'legenheit *f* (-; -en) **1.** *no pl* embarrassment: *j-n in* **~** *bringen* embarrass s.o. **2.** predicament, awkward situation: *j-m aus der* **~** *helfen* help s.o. out. **Ver'legenheits|lösung** *f* makeshift solution. **~pause** *f* awkward silence.

Ver'leger *m* (-s; -) publisher.

ver'legerisch *adj* publisher's (*risk etc*).

Ver'legung *f* (-; -en) **1.** transfer, removal. **2.** postponement. **3.** ⊙ laying.

ver'leiden *v/t* (h) *j-m et.* **~** spoil s.th. for s.o.

Verleih [fɛr'laɪ] *m* (-[e]s; -e) **1.** *no pl* hiring out, *film*: distribution: **~ von Autos** *etc* cars *etc* for hire. **2.** hire (*or* rental) service, *film*: distributors.

ver'leihen *v/t* (*irr, no -ge-, h,* → *leihen*)

1. (*an* *acc* to) a) lend (out), *esp. Am.* loan, b) hire (*Am.* rent) out. **2.** (*dat*) award *prize etc* (to), confer *title etc* (on), grant *s.o. right etc.* **3.** *fig.* give (*dat* to): **s-r Dankbarkeit Ausdruck ~** express one's gratitude. **Ver'leiher** *m* (-s; -) lender, *esp. Am.* loaner, *film:* distributor. **Ver'leihung** *f* (-; -en) **1.** lending (*etc,* → *verleihen* 1). **2.** award(ing), conferment, grant(ing).

ver'leimen *v/t* (h) glue together.

ver'leiten *v/t* (h) *j-n zu et.* ~ make s.o. do s.th., lead s.o. to do s.th., seduce (*or* talk) s.o. into doing s.th.; **sich ~ lassen (zu** *inf*) be seduced (*to inf*).

ver'lernen *v/t* (h) unlearn, forget.

ver'lesen¹ (*irr, no* -ge-, h, → *lesen*) **I** *v/t* read out, call out: **die Namensliste ~** call the roll. **II sich ~** read it wrong.

ver'lesen² *v/t* (*irr, no* -ge-, h, → *lesen*) pick (through).

ver'letzbar, ver'letzlich *adj fig.* vulnerable, touchy. **verletzen** [fɛr'lɛtsən] (h) **I** *v/t* injure, hurt, wound, *fig. a.* offend (*s.o.*), violate (*law etc*), offend against (*good taste etc*): **er wurde tödlich verletzt** he was fatally injured; **j-n tief ~** cut s.o. to the quick; **s-e Pflicht ~** neglect one's duty. **II sich ~** hurt o.s., get hurt; **er hat sich am Arm verletzt** he hurt his arm. **ver'letzend** *adj fig.* offensive. **Ver'letzte** *m, f* (-n; -n) injured person: **die ~n** the injured; **es gab viele ~n** many people were injured. **Ver'letzung** *f* (-; -en) **1.** injury, wound. **2.** *fig.* infringement, violation, breach. **Ver'letzungs|gefahr** *f* danger of injuring o.s. **~pech** *n sports:* **vom ~ verfolgt** injury-ridden.

ver'leugnen *v/t* (h) deny (*fact etc*), renounce (*faith etc*), disown (*friend etc*): **es läßt sich nicht ~, daß** there's no denying that; **sich vor j-m ~ lassen** not to be at home to s.o. **Ver'leugnung** *f* (-; -en) denial.

verleumden [fɛr'lɔymdən] *v/t* (h) calumniate, ⚖ slander, libel. **Ver'leumder** *m* (-s; -), **Ver'leumderin** *f* (-; -nen) slanderer, libel(l)er. **ver'leumderisch** *adj* slanderous, libel(l)ous. **Ver'leumdung** *f* (-; -en) calumny, slander, libel. **Ver'leumdungskam,pagne** *f* smear campaign. **Ver'leumdungsklage** *f* ⚖ action for slander (*or* libel).

ver'lieben: sich ~ (h) fall in love (**in** *acc* with). **verliebt** [fɛr'li:pt] *adj* in love (**in** *acc* with), amorous (*look etc*): **Verliebte** people in love, lovers. **Ver'liebtheit** *f* (-; *no pl*) being in love, amorousness.

verlieren [fɛr'li:rən] (verlor, verloren, h) **I** *v/t* lose, *a.* shed (*leaves, hair*): *fig.* **kein Wort darüber ~** not to say a word about it; F **er hat hier nichts verloren!** he's got no business (to be) here; → **Auge** 1, **Mut, Nerv.** **II** *v/i* lose (**gegen** to, against): *fig.* **an Wert ~** go down in value; → **Reiz** 2. **III sich ~** disappear. **Ver'lierer** *m* (-s; -), **Ver'liererin** *f* (-; -nen) loser. **Ver'liererseite** *f* **auf der ~ sein** be on the losing side.

Verlies [fɛr'li:s] *n* (-es; -e) dungeon.

ver'loben: sich ~ (h) get engaged (**mit** to). **verlobt** [fɛr'lo:pt] *adj* engaged (to be married) (**mit** to). **Ver'lobte** *m, f* (-n; -n) fiancé(e) *f*: **die ~n** the engaged couple. **Ver'lobung** *f* (-; -en) engagement. **Ver'lobungs|anzeige** *f* engagement announcement. **~feier** *f* engagement party. **~ring** *m* engagement ring.

ver'locken *v/t* (h) tempt (**zu et.** into doing s.th.). **ver'lockend** *adj* tempting. **Ver'lockung** *f* (-; -en) temptation.

verlogen [fɛr'lo:gən] *adj* a) lying, b) hypocritical (*morals etc*): **du ~er Kerl!** you damned liar! **Ver'logenheit** *f* (-; -en) a) lying, b) hypocrisy.

verlor [fɛr'lo:r] *pret of* **verlieren.**

ver'loren **I** *pp of* **verlieren.** **II** *adj* lost, *fig. a.* wasted, *a.* forlorn: *gastr.* **~e Eier** poached eggs; *bibl.* **der ~e Sohn** the prodigal son; **auf ~em Posten stehen** fight a losing battle.

ver'lorengehen *v/i* (*irr, sep,* -ge-, sn, → *gehen*) get lost, be lost: **an ihm ist ein Lehrer verlorengegangen** he would have made a good teacher.

ver'losen *v/t* (h) **1.** draw lots for. **2.** raffle (off). **Ver'losung** *f* (-; -en) **1.** drawing lots (*gen* for). **2.** raffle, lottery.

ver'löten *v/t* (h) ⊕ solder (up).

verlottern [fɛr'lɔtərn] → **verwahrlosen.**

Ver'lust *m* (-[e]s; -e) loss (**an** *dat* of, *fig.* **für** to), *a.* bereavement: **~e** losses, *at games:* losings, ✕ casualties; **mit ~** at a loss; **mit ~ arbeiten** *a.* be losing money. **Ver'lust|geschäft** *n* losing deal. **~meldung** *f* report of loss, ✕ casualty report. **~ziffer** *f* ✕ casualty figure.

ver'machen v/t (h) leave (dat to).
Vermächtnis [fɛr'mɛçtnɪs] n (-ses; -se) ₫₫ **1.** will. **2.** a. fig. legacy.
vermählen [fɛr'mɛ:lən] **sich** ~ (h) get married (**mit** to). **Ver'mählte** m, f (-n; -n) newlywed: **die** ~**n** the newly-married couple. **Ver'mählung** f (-; -en) marriage, wedding.
ver'männlichen v/t (h) masculinize.
vermarkten [fɛr'marktən] v/t (h) market, a. fig. sell, fig. commercialize.
Ver'marktung f (-; -en) marketing, fig. commercialization.
vermasseln [fɛr'masəln] v/t (h) F **et.** ~ mess th. up; **j-m die Tour** ~ queer s.o.'s pitch.
vermassen [fɛr'masən] **I** v/i (sn) lose one's individuality. **II** v/t (h) depersonalize. **Ver'massung** f (-; -en) loss of individuality, depersonalization.
ver'mehren (h) **I** v/t **1.** (**um** by) increase, multiply. **2.** biol. breed. **II sich** ~ **3.** → **1. 4.** biol. reproduce, multiply, breed.
Ver'mehrung f (-; -en) **1.** increase. **2.** biol. reproduction, breeding.
vermeidbar [fɛr'maɪtba:r] adj avoidable. **ver'meiden** v/t (irr, no -ge-, h, → **meiden**) avoid, evade, shun: **es läßt sich nicht** ~ it can't be helped.
vermeintlich [fɛr'maɪntlɪç] adj a) supposed, b) alleged.
ver'mengen v/t (h) mix, fig. mix up.
ver'menschlichen v/t (h) humanize.
Vermerk [fɛr'mɛrk] m (-[e]s; -e) note.
ver'merken v/t (h) make a note of.
ver'messen¹ v/t (irr, no -ge-, h, → **messen**) measure, survey (land).
ver'messen² adj presumptuous.
Ver'messenheit f (-; -en) presumption.
Ver'messung f (-; -en) survey(ing).
Ver'messungsingeni,eur m surveyor.
vermiesen [fɛr'mi:zən] v/t (h) F **j-m et.** ~ spoil s.th. for s.o.
ver'mieten v/t (h) (**an** acc to) let, ₫₫ lease, esp. Am. rent (out), hire (Am. rent) out (car etc): **zu** ~ **house:** to let, car: for hire, esp. Am. for rent.
Ver'mieter m (-s; -) **1.** landlord. **2.** lessor. **Ver'mieterin** f (-; -nen) landlady.
Ver'mietung f (-; -en) letting, leasing, esp. Am. renting (out), hiring (out).
ver'mindern → **verringern.**
verminen [fɛr'mi:nən] v/t (h) ✗ mine.
ver'mischen v/t (a. **sich** ~) (h) mix.

ver'mischt adj mixed, miscellaneous.
vermissen [fɛr'mɪsən] v/t (h) miss: **j-n sehr** ~ miss s.o. badly; **vermißt werden** be missing; **ich vermisse m-e Uhr** my watch is missing; ~ **lassen** lack.
Ver'mißte m, f (-n; -n) missing person.
ver'mitteln (h) **I** v/t **1.** **j-m et.** ~ get (or find) s.o. s.th.; **j-n** ~ **an** (acc) find s.o. a place with a firm etc. **2.** arrange, negotiate (deal etc). **3.** (dat to) impart (knowledge etc), convey (impression etc). **II** v/i (**zwischen** between, **in** dat in) a) mediate, b) intervene. **Ver'mittler** m (-s; -) **1.** mediator. **2.** go-between. **3.** ✝ agent. **Ver'mittlung** f (-; -en) **1.** procurement, negotiation (of deal etc), placement (of worker etc), arrangement (of meeting etc): **durch** ~ **von** (or gen) through. **2.** imparting (of knowledge etc), conveyance (of impression etc). **3.** a) mediation, b) intervention. **4.** agency, office. **5.** a) (telephone) exchange, in firm etc: switchboard, b) operator.
Ver'mittlungs|gebühr f ✝ agent's commission. ~**versuch** m attempt at mediation.
ver'modern v/i (sn) mo(u)lder, rot.
Ver'mögen n (-s; -) **1.** a) fortune, b) property, ✝ assets: **sie hat** ~ she is wealthy; F fig. **ein** ~ **kosten** cost a fortune. **2.** no pl (nach bestem ~ to the best of one's ability.
ver'mögend adj wealthy, well-to-do.
Ver'mögens|bildung f wealth formation. ~**steuer** f property tax. ~**verhältnisse** pl (financial) circumstances. ~**verwalter** m custodian. ~**werte** pl assets. ♀**wirksam** adj ~**e Leistung** (employer's) capital-forming payment under the employees' saving scheme.
vermummen [fɛr'mʊmən] v/t (h) **1.** wrap up. **2.** disguise.
ver'murksen v/t (h) F **et.** ~ mess s.th. up.
vermuten [fɛr'mu:tən] v/t (h) **1.** think, suppose, assume, Am. F guess. **2.** expect. **3.** suspect. **ver'mutlich I** adj → **mutmaßlich. II** adv probably: ~**!** I suppose so. **Ver'mutung** f (-; -en) a) supposition, F guess, b) suspicion, c) conjecture, speculation: **s-e** ~ **war richtig** his guess was right; **die** ~ **liegt nahe, daß** it is highly probable that; **das sind reine** ~**en** that's mere guesswork.

vernachlässigen [fɛr'naːxlɛsɪgən] v/t (h) **1.** neglect. **2.** ignore.

Ver'nachlässigung f (-; -en) neglect.

ver'nageln v/t (h) *mit Brettern* ~ board up. **ver'nagelt** adj F fig. dense, thick: *ich war wie* ~ my mind was a blank.

ver'nähen v/t (h) sew up.

ver'narben v/i (sn) **1.** scar over. **2.** fig. heal. **vernarbt** F[-'narpt] adj scarred.

ver'narrt adj ~ *sein in* (acc) F be wild about, *ein Kind* dote on a child.

ver'naschen v/t (h) **1.** spend on sweets. **2.** F a) lay (sl.), b) sports: clobber.

ver'nebeln v/t (h) **1.** ✪ atomize. **2.** ✕ screen. **3.** fig. obscure.

ver'nehmbar adj audible. **ver'nehmen** v/t (irr, no -ge-, h, → *nehmen*) **1.** hear, fig. a. learn. **2.** ⚖ interrogate, examine: *als Zeuge vernommen werden* be called into the witness box (Am. stand).

Ver'nehmen v/n *dem* ~ *nach* from what one hears; *sicherem* ~ *nach* according to reliable reports.

ver'nehmlich adj audible, distinct.

Ver'nehmung f (-; -en) ⚖ interrogation, examination. **ver'nehmungsfähig** adj fit to be examined.

ver'neigen: sich ~ (h) bow (*vor* dat to).

Ver'neigung f (-; -en) bow (*vor* dat to).

verneinen [fɛr'naɪnən] v/t (h) **1.** a. v/i answer in the negative. **2.** a) deny, b) reject. **verneinend** adj a. ling. negative. **Ver'neinung** f (-; -en) **1.** a. ling. negation. **2.** a) denial, b) rejection.

vernetzen [fɛr'nɛtsən] v/t (h) computer: network. **Ver'netzung** f (-; -en) networking.

vernichten [fɛr'nɪçtən] v/t (h) **1.** destroy, annihilate, a. fig. exterminate, wipe out. **2.** fig. dash, shatter (*hopes*).

ver'nichtend adj fig. scathing, devastating (*look*, *criticism*, etc), crushing (*blow*, *defeat*, etc): *j-n* ~ *schlagen* sports: beat s.o. hollow.

Ver'nichtung f (-; -en) destruction, annihilation, a. fig. extermination.

Ver'nichtungs|krieg m war of annihilation. **~lager** n extermination camp. **~potenti,al** n destructive potential. **~schlag** m fig. final blow. **~waffe** f weapon of destruction.

ver'nickeln v/t (h) nickel(-plate).

ver'niedlichen v/t (h) play down.

ver'nieten v/t (h) ✪ rivet.

Vernissage [vɛrnɪ'saːʒə] f (-; -n) private view.

Vernunft [fɛr'nʊnft] f (-; *no pl*) reason: ~ *annehmen* listen to reason; *j-n zur* ~ *bringen* bring s.o. to his senses; *wieder zur* ~ *kommen* come back to one's senses. ⚲**begabt** adj rational. **~ehe** f marriage of convenience. **~gründe** pl *aus* ~*n* for reasons of common sense.

vernünftig [fɛr'nʏnftɪç] **I** adj **1.** sensible, reasonable, level-headed: *sie war* ~ *genug, nein zu sagen* she had the good sense to say no; *sei (doch)* ~*!* be sensible! **2.** F reasonable, decent: *e-n* ~*en Beruf ergreifen* take up a proper career. **II** adv sensibly, reasonably: ~ *reden* talk sense; F ~ *essen* eat properly.

Ver'nunftmensch m rational person.

ver'nunftwidrig adj irrational.

ver'öden I v/t (h) 🩺 sclerose, obliterate. **II** v/i (sn) become deserted.

ver'öffentlichen v/t (h) publish.

Ver'öffentlichung f (-; -en) publication.

ver'ordnen v/t (h) **1.** 🩺 a) order, b) prescribe (*j-m* for s.o.). **2.** adm. decree.

Ver'ordnung f (-; -en) **1.** 🩺 prescription. **2.** adm. ordinance, decree.

ver'pachten v/t (h) lease (*dat*, *an* acc to).

Ver'pächter(in f) m lessor.

Ver'pachtung f (-; -en) lease, leasing.

ver'packen v/t (h) pack (up), ✈ package, wrap up; → *Geschenk*.

Ver'packung f (-; -en) **1.** *no pl* packing, packaging. **2.** wrapping, packing material: ✈ *zuzüglich* ~ plus packing.

Ver'packungs|auto,mat m automatic packaging machine. **~materi,al** n packing material.

ver'passen v/t (h) **1.** miss (*bus* etc), a. lose, waste (*chance*). **2.** F *j-m e-e Uniform* etc ~ fit s.o. with a uniform etc; *j-m ein Ding* ~ land s.o. one, zap s.o.

ver'patzen v/t (h) F et. ~ mess s.th. up, sports, thea. muff s.th.

verpesten [fɛr'pɛstən] v/t (h) pollute: F *die Luft* ~ stink the place out.

ver'petzen v/t (h) F *j-n* ~ sneak on s.o.

ver'pfänden v/t (h) pawn, pledge (a. fig. *one's word*), mortgage.

ver'pfeifen v/t (irr, no -ge-, h, → *pfeifen*) F *j-n* ~ squeal on s.o.; et. ~ let s.th. out.

ver'pflanzen v/t (h) 🌱, 🩺 transplant.

Ver'pflanzung f (-; -en) transplant.

ver'pflegen *v/t* (h) feed, ✕ supply with rations: *sich selbst* ~ cook for o.s.

Ver'pflegung *f* (-; -en) no *pl* catering, food supply. **2.** food, ✕ rations.

ver'pflichten (h) **I** *v/t* **1.** *j-n* ~ oblige (*by contract:* obligate) s.o. (**zu** *inf* to do); *j-n zum Schweigen* ~ bind s.o. to silence; → **verpflichtet. 2.** engage (*artist*), *sports:* sign on (*player etc*). **II** *sich* ~ **3.** commit o.s. (*et. zu tun* to do[ing] s.th.). **4.** *artist, player, etc:* sign on (*für* for). **ver'pflichtet** *adj j-m zu Dank* ~ *sein* be indebted to s.o.; *ich fühle mich* ~, *ihr zu helfen* I feel obliged to help her; *gesetzlich* ~ (*zu inf*) bound by law (to *inf*). **Ver'pflichtung** *f* (-; -en) a) obligation, duty, b) commitment, engagement, ✝, 🛪🛪 liability.

ver'pfuschen *v/t* (h) F botch, mess *s.th.* up, ruin (*a. fig.* one's life *etc*).

ver'planen *v/t* (h) budget (*funds*), plan (*holidays etc*), book up (*time*).

ver'plappern: sich ~ (h) F blab.

verplempern [fɛrˈplɛmpərn] *v/t* (h) F waste, fritter away.

verpönt [fɛrˈpøːnt] *adj* disapproved-of: (*streng*) ~ *sein a.* be frowned upon.

ver'prassen *v/t* (h) squander, F blow.

ver'puffen *v/i* (sn) **1.** 🝆 detonate, blow up. **2.** *fig.* fizzle out, fall flat.

ver'pulvern *v/t* (h) F blow (*money*).

ver'pumpen *v/t* (h) F (*an acc* to) lend, *esp. Am.* loan.

ver'puppen: sich ~ (h) *zo.* pupate.

ver'pusten: sich ~ (h) F get one's breath back.

ver'putzen *v/t* (h) **1.** 🛆 roughcast. **2.** F polish off, put away.

ver'qualmt *adj* smoke-filled, *pred* full of smoke.

verquollen [fɛrˈkvɔlən] *adj* puffed.

ver'ramschen *v/t* (h) F sell *s.th.* off dirt-cheap, remainder (*books*).

Ver'rat *m* (-[e]s; *no pl*) (*an dat* of) betrayal (of), *a.* 🛪🛪, ✕ treason (to), treachery (to): ~ *begehen an* (*dat*) betray.

ver'raten (*irr, no* -ge-, h, → **raten**) **I** *v/t* betray (*a. fig.*), give *s.o., s.th.* away, *fig. a.* show, reveal: F *kannst du mir* (*mal*) ~, *warum?* can you tell me why?; *nicht* ~*!* don't tell!; ~ *und verkauft* sold down the river. **II** *sich* ~ betray o.s., give o.s. away. **Verräter** [fɛrˈrɛːtər] *m* (-s; -) traitor (*fig. an dat* to). **Ver'räterin** *f* (-;

-nen) traitress. **ver'räterisch** *adj* **1.** treacherous, traitorous, 🛪🛪 treasonable. **2.** *fig.* revealing, telltale.

ver'rauchen *v/i* (sn) *fig.* blow over.

ver'räuchert *adj* smoky.

ver'rechnen (h) **I** *v/t* charge (to account), clear (*cheque*): *et.* ~ *mit* offset *s.th.* against. **II** *sich* ~ *a. fig.* make a mistake; *sich um 10 Mark* ~ be out by ten marks; *fig.* da *hast du dich aber leider verrechnet!* you are sadly mistaken there.

Ver'rechnung *f* (-; -en) offset, clearing: *nur zur* ~ *cheque:* for account only.

Ver'rechnungs|**einheit** *f* clearing unit. ~*konto n* offset account. ~*scheck m* collection-only cheque (*Am.* check). ~*verfahren n* clearing (system).

ver'recken *v/i* (sn) F perish, die, croak (*sl.*), *fig.* engine *etc:* conk out.

ver'regnet *adj* rainy.

ver'reiben *v/t* (*irr, no* -ge-, h, → **reiben**) spread *s.th.* by rubbing.

ver'reisen *v/i* (sn) go away: ~ *nach* to; *sie sind verreist* they are away.

ver'reißen *v/t* (*irr, no* -ge-, h, → **reißen**) F tear *s.o., s.th.* to pieces, slate, pan.

verrenken [fɛrˈrɛŋkən] *v/t* (h) contort, 🦴 dislocate (*sich den Arm* one's arm): F *sich den Hals* ~ crane one's neck (*nach* to get a glimpse of), *Am.* rubberneck. **Ver'renkung** *f* (-; -en) contortion, 🦴 dislocation.

ver'rennen: sich ~ (*irr, no* -ge-, h, → **rennen**) *fig.* get stuck (*in acc* on).

ver'richten *v/t* (h) do, carry out, b) say (*prayer*).

ver'riegeln *v/t* (h) bolt, bar.

verringern [fɛrˈrɪŋərn] *v/t* (h) reduce, lower, (*a. sich* ~) diminish, decrease, lessen: *das Tempo* ~ slow down.

Ver'ringerung *f* (-; -en) (*gen*) reduction (of), lowering (of), decrease (in).

verrohen [fɛrˈroːən] *v/i* (sn) become brutalized.

Ver'rohung *f* (-; -en) brutalization.

ver'rosten *v/i* (sn) rust.

ver'rostet *adj* rusty.

verrotten [fɛrˈrɔtən] *v/i* (sn) *a. fig.* rot.

ver'rücken *v/t* (h) move, disarrange.

ver'rückt *adj a.* F *fig.* mad, crazy, wild: ~ *sein a.* be out of one's mind; ~ *sein nach* (or *auf acc*) be wild about; *j-n* ~ *machen* drive s.o. mad; *mach dich* *doch nicht ~!* don't get all worked up!; *~ spielen* act up; *wie ~* like mad; *ich werd' ~!* I'll be blowed!; *es ist zum Verrücktwerden!* it's enough to drive you mad.

Ver'rückte *m, f* (-n; -n) *a.* F *fig.* lunatic, maniac, madman (madwoman).

Ver'rücktheit *f* (-; -en) **1.** *no pl* madness. **2.** folly, craze, F crazy idea (*or* thing).

Ver'ruf *m* in *~ bringen* (*kommen*) bring (fall) into disrepute.

ver'rufen *adj* disreputable, notorious.

ver'rutschen *v/i* (sn) slip.

Vers [fɛrs] *m* (-es; -e) a) verse, b) line.

ver'sachlichen *v/t* (h) de-emotionalize.

ver'sagen (h) **I** *v/t j-m et. ~* refuse (*or* deny) s.o. s.th.; *sich et. ~* deny o.s. s.th., forgo s.th.; → *Dienst* 1. **II** *v/i* fail (*a. person*), ⊙ *a.* break down, *gun:* misfire: *ihr Gedächtnis versagte* her memory failed her. **Ver'sagen** *n* (-s) failure: *menschliches ~* human error. **Ver'sager** *m* (-s; -) failure, F flop.

ver'salzen *v/t* (h) **1.** oversalt. **2.** F *fig.* spoil.

ver'sammeln *v/t* (*a. sich ~*) (h) assemble (*a.* ✕), gather, meet. **Ver'sammlung** *f* (-; -en) assembly, gathering, meeting: *gesetzgebende ~* legislative assembly. **Ver'sammlungs|freiheit** *f* freedom of assembly. *~raum* *m* assembly room.

Versand [fɛr'zant] *m* (-[e]s; *no pl*) ↑ **1.** dispatch, forwarding, shipment. **2.** → *~abteilung* *f* forwarding department.

ver'sanden *v/i* (sn) **1.** silt up. **2.** *fig.* peter out.

ver'sandfertig *adj* ready for dispatch. **Ver'sand|geschäft** *n*, *~handel* *m* mail-order business. *~haus* *n* mail-order firm. *~kosten* *pl* forwarding costs. *~pa,piere* *pl* shipping documents.

versauen [fɛr'zaʊən] *v/t* (h) F mess *s.th.* up, *fig. a.* ruin *s.th.* (*j-m* for s.o.).

ver'sauern *v/i* (sn) F *fig.* rot (away).

ver'saufen *v/t* (*irr, no* -ge-, h, → *saufen*) F spend on booze.

ver'säumen *v/t* (h) **1.** → *verpassen* 1. **2.** neglect (*duty etc*): (*es*) *~ zu inf* fail to *inf.* **Ver'säumnis** *n* (-ses; -se) omission, neglect. **Ver'säumnisurteil** *n* judg(e)ment by default.

ver'schachern *v/t* (h) F flog.

ver'schachtelt *adj* interlocked, *fig.* complicated, *ling.* involved (*sentence*).

ver'schaffen *v/t* (h) **1.** *j-m et. ~* get (*or* find) s.o. s.th. (*or* s.th. for s.o.). **2.** *sich et. ~* get, obtain, secure, raise (*money*); → *Respekt.*

verschalen [fɛr'ʃaːlən] *v/t* (h) △ board, shutter (*concrete*). **Ver'schalung** *f* (-; -en) a) boarding, b) form(s).

verschämt [fɛr'ʃɛːmt] *adj* bashful.

verschandeln [fɛr'ʃandəln] *v/t* (h) F disfigure, spoil.

ver'schanzen: *sich ~* (h) *a. fig.* entrench (*hinter* behind, *in* dat in).

ver'schärfen *v/t* (*a. sich ~*) (h) increase, tighten (up) (*control, law, measures, etc*), aggravate (*crisis etc*), stiffen (*penalty*): *das Tempo ~* increase the pace; *die Spannungen ~ sich* tension is mounting. **Ver'schärfung** *f* (-; -en) increase, tightening (up), aggravation.

ver'scharren *v/t* (h) bury (hurriedly).

ver'schätzen: *sich ~* (h) be out (*um* by).

ver'schaukeln *v/t* (h) F *j-n ~* take s.o. for a ride, outtrick s.o.

ver'schenken *v/t* (h) *a. fig.* give away.

ver'scherzen *v/t* (h) forfeit.

ver'scheuchen *v/t* (h) chase away.

ver'scheuern *v/t* (h) F flog.

ver'schicken *v/t* (h) **1.** dispatch, send, ship. **2.** *j-n ~* send s.o. away.

verschiebbar [fɛr'ʃiːpbaːr] *adj* mov(e)able. **ver'schieben** (*irr, no* -ge-, h, → *schieben*) **I** *v/t* **1.** (re)move, shift. **2.** postpone (*to* a later date): *et.* (*von e-m Tag zum anderen*) *~* put s.th. off (from one day to the next). **3.** F ↑ sell *s.th.* underhand. **II** *sich ~* **4.** shift, get out of place. **5.** be postponed, be put off. **Ver'schiebung** *f* (-; -en) **1.** shift(ing), moving. **2.** postponement.

verschieden [fɛr'ʃiːdən] *adj* **1.** different (*von* from): *~ sein a.* differ, vary; *die beiden Brüder sind sehr ~* the two brothers are quite unlike; *das ist ganz ~* it depends; *~ groß sein* vary in size. **2.** *~e pl* various, several; *~es* various things; *aus den ~sten Gründen* for a variety of reasons. **ver'schiedenartig** *adj* different (kinds of) ..., various. **Ver'schiedenartigkeit** *f* (-; *no pl*) **1.** difference. **2.** variety. **Ver'schiedenheit** *f* (-; -en) **1.** difference (*gen* of, in). **2.** dissimilarity. **3.** diversity, variety. **ver'schiedentlich** *adv* **1.** several times, repeatedly. **2.** occasionally.

ver'schießen (*irr, no* -ge-, → *schießen*) **I** *v/t* (h) **1.** shoot. **2.** *sports*: shoot wide. **II** *v/i* (sn) fade: → *verschossen* 1.

ver'schiffen *v/t* (h) ship.

Ver'schiffung *f* (-; -en) shipment.

ver'schimmeln *v/i* (sn) go mo(u)ldy.

ver'schlafen¹ (*irr, no* -ge-, h, → *schlafen*) **I** *v/i* **1.** oversleep. **II** *v/t* **2.** sleep through. **3.** *F fig.* miss (*chance etc*), forget (*appointment etc*). **ver'schlafen²** *adj a. fig.* sleepy. **Ver'schlafenheit** *f* (-; *no pl*) *a. fig.* sleepiness.

Ver'schlag *m* (-[e]s, ÷e) shed, shack.

ver'schlagen¹ *v/t* (*irr, no* -ge-, h, → *schlagen*) **1.** mishit (*ball*). **2.** lose (*page in book etc*). **3.** *fig.* **es hat mich nach X ~** I ended up in X. **4.** *fig.* **j-m die Stimme** (*or Rede, Sprache*) **~** leave s.o. speechless; **es verschlug mir den Atem** it took my breath away.

ver'schlagen² *adj* sly, shifty.

Ver'schlagenheit *f* (-; *no pl*) shiftiness.

ver'schlampen F **I** *v/i* (h) a) go and lose, b) clean forget. **II** *v/i* (sn) go to seed.

verschlechtern [fɛr'ʃlɛçtərn] (h) **I** *v/t* make worse. **II** *sich ~* get worse, deteriorate; *sich (finanziell) ~* leave s.o. worse off. **Ver'schlechterung** *f* (-; -en) deterioration, *a.* change for the worse.

verschleiern [fɛr'ʃlaɪərn] *v/t* (h) veil.

ver'schleifen *v/t* (*irr, no* -ge-, h, → *schleifen¹*) *ling., ♪* slur.

ver'schleimt *adj* blocked with phlegm.

Verschleiß [fɛr'ʃlaɪs] *m* (-es; *no pl*) wear and tear (*a. fig.*), ⊕ *a.* attrition.

ver'schleißen (verschliß, verschlissen, h) **I** *v/t* wear out. **II** *sich ~* wear o.s. out. **III** *v/i* (sn) wear (out), become worn.

Ver'schleiß|erscheinung *f a. fig.* sign of wear. **≈fest** *adj* wear-resistant. **≈teil** *n* ⊕ working (*or* expendable) part.

ver'schleppen *v/t* (h) **1.** carry off, *pol.* displace, ⚖ kidnap. **2.** delay, protract. **3.** ♯ spread (*epidemic etc*). **4.** neglect (*disease*). **Ver'schleppte** *m, f* (-n; -n) *pol.* displaced person.

Ver'schleppung *f* (-; -en) **1.** *a. pol.* displacement, b) kidnap(p)ing. **2.** protraction, delay(ing). **3.** ♯ spreading (*of epidemic etc*), protraction (*of disease*).

Ver'schleppungstaktik *f* delaying tactics, *parl.* obstructionism.

ver'schleudern *v/t* (h) **1.** waste, squander (away). **2.** ✝ sell at a loss, dump.

ver'schließbar *adj* lockable.

ver'schließen (*irr, no* -ge-, h, → *schließen*) **I** *v/t* a) shut, close, b) lock (up), c) put *s.th.* under lock and key: *die Ohren ~ vor* (*dat*) turn a deaf ear to; → *Auge* 1. **II** *sich ~* (*dat*) shut o.s. off (from); *sich j-s Argumenten etc ~* remain inaccessible to s.o.'s arguments *etc*.

verschlimmern [fɛr'ʃlɪmərn] (h) **I** *v/t* make *s.th.* worse, aggravate. **II** *sich ~* get worse, deteriorate.

Ver'schlimmerung *f* (-; -en) deterioration, change for the worse.

ver'schlingen¹ *v/t* (*irr, no* -ge-, h, → *schlingen²*) wolf (down), devour (*a. book etc*), *fig.* swallow (up) (*money etc*).

ver'schlingen² *v/t* (*a. sich ~*) (*irr, no* -ge-, h, → *schlingen¹*) intertwine.

verschliß [fɛr'ʃlɪs] *pret*, **ver'schlissen** *pp of* **verschleißen**.

verschlossen [fɛr'ʃlɔsən] *adj* a) shut, closed, b) locked (up): *hinter ~en Türen* behind closed doors. **2.** reserved.

Ver'schlossenheit *f* (-; *no pl*) reserve.

ver'schlucken (h) **I** *v/t* swallow. **II** *sich ~* choke, swallow the wrong way.

verschlungen [fɛr'ʃlʊŋən] *adj fig.* intricate (*pattern etc*), tortuous (*path etc*).

Ver'schluß *m* (-sses; ÷sse) **1.** a) fastener, clasp, b) stopper, c) ⚙ lock, seal: *unter ~* under lock and key, *customs*: in bond. **2.** *phot.* shutter **3.** ♯ occlusion.

ver'schlüsseln *v/t* (h) encode: *verschlüsselter Text* code(d) text.

Ver'schlußlaut *m ling.* plosive. **~sache** *f pol.* classified matter.

ver'schmähen *v/t* (h) disdain, scorn.

ver'schmelzen (*irr, no* -ge-, → *schmelzen*) *v/t* (h), *v/i* (sn) (*mit, zu* into) fuse, merge (*both a. ✝, pol.*), *colo[u]rs etc*: blend. **Ver'schmelzung** *f* (-; -en) fusion, ✝, *pol. a.* merger.

ver'schmerzen *v/t* (h) *et. ~* get over s.th.

ver'schmieren *v/t* (h) smear.

verschmitzt [fɛr'ʃmɪtst] *adj* roguish.

ver'schmutzen *v/t* (h) **1.** dirty, soil. **2.** pollute (*air, water, etc*).

Ver'schmutzung *f* (-; -en) **1.** a) soiling, b) dirt. **2.** (*air, water, etc*) pollution.

ver'schnaufen *v/i* (*a. sich ~*) (h) F have a breather.

ver'schneiden *v/t* (*irr, no* -ge-, h, → *schneiden*) blend (*rum etc*).

verschneit [fɛr'ʃnaɪt] *adj* snow-covered.

Ver'schnitt m (-[e]s; -e) blend.
ver'schnörkelt adj a. fig. ornate.
verschnupft [fɛr'ʃnʊpft] adj ~ sein have a cold, F fig. be in a huff.
ver'schnüren v/t (h) tie up.
verschollen [fɛr'ʃɔlən] adj 1. missing, ⚖ presumed dead. 2. (long-)forgotten.
ver'schonen v/t (h) spare: von et. ver-schont bleiben be spared s.th.; ver-schone mich damit! spare me that!
ver'schönen v/t (h) embellish, enhance.
verschönern [fɛr'ʃøːnərn] v/t (h) embellish, a. fig. brighten. **Ver'schönerung** f (-; -en) embellishment.
verschossen [fɛr'ʃɔsən] adj 1. faded. 2. F in j-n ~ sein have a crush on s.o.
verschränken [fɛr'ʃrɛŋkən] v/t (h) 1. fold (arms), cross (legs). 2. ⚙ cross.
ver'schrauben v/t (h) bolt, screw up.
ver'schreiben (irr, no -ge-, h, → schrei-ben) I v/t 1. j-m et. ~ a) ⚕ prescribe s.th. for s.o., b) ⚖ make s.th. over to s.o. II sich ~ 2. make a slip (of the pen). 3. fig. devote o.s. (dat to).
Ver'schreibung f (-; -en) ⚕ prescrip-tion. **ver'schreibungspflichtig** adj ⚕ obtainable on prescription only.
verschroben [fɛr'ʃroːbən] adj eccentric. **Ver'schrobenheit** f (-; -en) eccentricity.
ver'schrotten v/t (h) scrap, a. junk (car).
ver'schrumpeln v/i (sn) F shrivel (up).
verschüchtert [fɛr'ʃʏçtərt] adj intimi-dated, shy.
ver'schulden (h) I v/t be responsible (or to blame) for. II v/i (a. sich ~) get into debt. **Ver'schulden** n (-s) fault: ohne ihr ~ through no fault of hers; uns trifft kein ~ it's not our fault. **ver'schuldet** adj indebted (bei to), property: encum-bered. **Ver'schuldung** f (-; -en) indebt-edness, debts, encumbrance.
ver'schütten v/t (h) 1. spill. 2. bury s.o. alive, block (road).
verschwägert [fɛr'ʃvɛːgərt] adj related by marriage.
ver'schweigen v/t (irr, no -ge-, h, → schweigen) (dat from) keep s.th. (a) secret, hide, withhold.
ver'schweißen v/t (h) weld together.
ver'schwenden [fɛr'ʃvɛndən] v/t (h) (an acc, für, mit on) waste, squander: fig. du verschwendest d-e Worte you are wasting your breath. **Ver'schwender** m (-s; -), **Ver'schwenderin** f (-; -nen)

spendthrift, squanderer. **ver'schwen-derisch** adj wasteful, extravagant, lavish: ~ umgehen mit be lavish with. **Ver'schwendung** f (-; -en) waste, ex-travagance. **Ver'schwendungssucht** f extravagance, squandermania.
verschwiegen [fɛr'ʃviːgən] adj 1. dis-creet. 2. secret, secluded (place). **Ver'schwiegenheit** f (-; no pl) 1. discre-tion, secrecy; → Siegel. 2. seclusion.
ver'schwimmen v/i (irr, no -ge-, sn, → schwimmen) a. fig. become blurred: die Farben ~ the colo(u)rs merge.
ver'schwinden (irr, no -ge-, sn, → schwinden) v/i 1. disappear, vanish: spurlos ~ vanish into thin air; ~d klein infinitely small. 2. F make o.s. scarce: verschwinde! beat it!
Ver'schwinden n (-s) disappearance.
ver'schwitzen v/t (h) 1. soak s.th. with sweat. 2. F et. ~ clean forget about s.th.
ver'schwitzt adj sweaty.
verschwollen [fɛr'ʃvɔlən] adj swollen.
verschwommen [fɛr'ʃvɔmən] adj 1. a. phot. blurred. 2. vague (idea etc), hazy, dim (recollection etc): sich nur ~ erin-nern remember only dimly.
Ver'schwommenheit f (-; no pl) vague-ness, haziness, dimness.
ver'schwören: sich ~ (irr, no -ge-, h, → schwören) 1. conspire (or plot) (mit j-m with s.o.) (gegen against). 2. fig. devote o.s. (dat to). **Ver'schwörer** m (-s; -) conspirator, plotter. **Ver'schwö-rung** f (-; -en) conspiracy, plot.
ver'sehen (irr, no -ge-, h, → sehen) I v/t 1. ~ mit provide (or furnish, equip) s.o., s.th. with; mit Ratschlägen ~ armed with advice; mit Vollmacht ~ author-ize. 2. perform, discharge (duty etc), a. hold (office): er versieht auch das Amt des Richters a. he acts as judge as well. II sich ~ 3. make a mistake. 4. provide (or equip) o.s. (mit with). 5. ehe man sich's versieht F before you know it.
Ver'sehen n (-s; -) oversight, mistake: aus ~ → ver'sehentlich adv inadvert-ently, by mistake.
versehrt [fɛr'zeːrt] adj disabled.
Ver'sehrte m, f (-n; -n) disabled person.
ver'senden v/t (irr, no -ge-, h, → sen-den) send, forward, ship. **Ver'sen-dung** f (-; -en) dispatch, shipment.
ver'sengen v/t (h) scorch, singe.

ver'senken (h) **I** *v/t* sink. **II** *sich ~ in* (*acc*) *fig.* become absorbed in.

Ver'senkung *f* (-; -en) **1.** sinking. **2.** *thea.* trapdoor: F *fig. in der ~ verschwinden* disappear from the scene. **3.** (*mental*) absorption.

versessen [fɛr'zɛsən] *adj ~ auf* (*acc*) mad about; *darauf ~ sein zu inf* be desperate to *inf*.

ver'setzen (h) **I** *v/t* **1.** remove, displace, shift, ✗ transplant. **2.** transfer (*in, auf acc, nach* to), *ped.* move *s.o.* up, *Am.* promote: → *Ruhestand.* **3.** a) pawn, b) sell. **4.** F *j-n ~ a*) stand *s.o.* up, b) *sports*: outtrick *s.o.* **5.** *j-n in die Lage ~ zu inf* put *s.o.* in a position (*or* enable *s.o.*) to *inf*; *j-n in Unruhe ~* disturb *s.o.*; *et. in Schwingungen ~* set *s.th.* vibrating; → *Angst.* **6.** F *j-m e-n Schlag etc ~* give (*or* deal) *s.o.* a blow *etc.* **7.** mix (*mit* with). **8.** ☉ stagger. **II** *sich in j-n* (*j-s Lage*) *~* put *o.s.* in *s.o.'s* place (*or* position).

Ver'setzung *f* (-; -en) **1.** removal, ✗ transplanting. **2.** transfer (*in, auf acc, nach* to). **3.** *ped.* remove, *Am.* promotion.

Ver'setzungs|zeichen *n* ♩ accidental. **~zeugnis** *n ped.* end-of-year report.

ver'seuchen *v/t* (h) contaminate.

Ver'seuchung *f* (-; -en) contamination.

Ver'sicherer *m* (-s; -) ✝ insurer, ⚓ underwriter. **ver'sichern** *v/t* (h) **1.** ✝ insure (*sich* o.s.) (*bei* with, *gegen* against). **2.** declare, protest: *ich kann dir ~, daß* I (can) assure you that. **Ver'sicherte** *m, f* (-n; -n) *the* insured (party). **Ver'sicherung** *f* (-; -en) **1.** insurance: *e-e ~ abschließen* take out insurance (*or* an insurance policy). **2.** insurance company. **3.** assurance.

Ver'sicherungs|anstalt *f* insurance company. **~betrug** *m* insurance fraud. **~dauer** *f* time insured. **~gesellschaft** *f* insurance company. **~mathe,matiker** *m* actuary. **~nehmer** *m* (-s; -) insurant, *the* insured. **~nummer** *f* insurance policy number. **~po,lice** *f* insurance policy. **~prämie** *f* insurance premium. **~schutz** *m* insurance cover(age). **~summe** *f* sum insured. **~vertreter** *m* insurance agent. **~wesen** *n* (-s; *no pl*) insurance (business).

ver'sickern *v/i* (sn) trickle away.

ver'siegeln *v/t* (h) seal.

ver'siegen *v/i* (sn) dry up, run dry.

versiert [vɛr'zi:rt] *adj* (*in dat* in) experienced, (well-)versed.

ver'silbern *v/t* (h) **1.** ☉ silverplate. **2.** F *et. ~* turn *s.th.* into cash, sell *s.th.*

ver'sinken *v/i* (*irr, no* -ge-, sn, → *sinken*) *a. fig.* sink (*in acc* into).

Version [vɛr'zi̯o:n] *f* (-; -en) version.

ver'sklaven *v/t* (h) enslave.

verslumen [fɛr'slamən] *v/i* (sn) become a slum.

'Versmaß *n* metre, *Am.* meter.

versnobt [fɛr'snɔpt] *adj* snobbish.

versoffen [fɛr'zɔfən] *adj* F boozy.

ver'söhnen [fɛr'zø:nən] (h) **I** *v/t* reconcile (*mit* with *s.o.*, *to one's* fate etc) **II** *sich* (*wieder*) *~* be(come) reconciled, make it up. **ver'söhnlich** *adj* conciliatory; *~ stimmen* placate. **Ver'söhnung** *f* (-; -en) reconciliation.

versonnen [fɛr'zɔnən] *adj* pensive.

ver'sorgen *v/t* (h) **1.** (*mit* with) supply, provide. **2.** provide for (*family etc*). **3.** look after, take care of. **4.** ✗ attend to (*s.o.*), see to (*wound*). **Ver'sorgung** *f* (-; *no pl*) **1.** supply. **2.** (*gen*) support (of), provision (for). **3.** care.

Ver'sorgungs|betrieb *m* public utility. **~empfänger(in** *f*) *m* pensioner. **~güter** *pl* supplies. **~leitung** *f* supply line. **~lücke** *f* supply gap. **~netz** *n* supply system. **~technik** *f* utilities engineering.

ver'spannen *v/t* (h) ☉ stay, brace.

ver'spannt *adj* cramped, tense.

ver'späten [fɛr'ʃpɛ:tən] *sich ~* (h) be late.

ver'spätet *adj* late (*arrival etc*), belated (*thanks etc*).

Ver'spätung *f* (-; -en) delay: *bitte entschuldigen Sie m-e ~* please excuse my being late; (*e-e Stunde*) *~ haben* be (an hour) late; *mit* (*e-r Stunde*) *~ abfahren* leave (an hour) behind schedule.

ver'speisen *v/t* (h) eat, consume.

ver'sperren *v/t* (h) bar, block (up), obstruct (*a. view*).

ver'spielen (h) **I** *v/t* lose (at play), *a. fig.* gamble away. **II** *v/i fig.* lose: *fig. bei mir hat er verspielt!* I'm through with him.

ver'spielt *adj* playful.

ver'spotten *v/t* (h) make fun of, ridicule.

ver'sprechen (*irr, no* -ge-, h, → *sprechen*) **I** *v/t* **1.** *a. fig.* promise: *das Wetter verspricht schön zu werden* the weather looks promising. **2.** *sich et. ~*

von expect s.th. of; *ich hatte mir mehr davon versprochen* I had expected better of it. **II** *sich ~* make a slip (of the tongue). **Ver'sprechen** *n* (-s; -) promise. **Ver'sprecher** *m* (-s; -) slip (of the tongue). **Ver'sprechung** (-; -en) *f* promise; *j-m große ~en machen* promise s.o. the earth.

ver'spritzen, ver'sprühen *v/t* (h) spray.

ver'staatlichen *v/t* (h) nationalize. **Ver'staatlichung** *f* (-; -en) nationalization.

verstädtern [fɛr'ʃtɛːtərn] **I** *v/t* (h) urbanize. **II** *v/i* (sn) become urbanized. **Ver'städterung** *f* (-; -en) urbanization.

Ver'stand *m* (-[e]s; *no pl*) a) intellect, mind, b) reason, (common) sense, c) brain(s), intelligence: *scharfer ~* keen mind; *klarer (kühler) ~* clear (cool) head; *den ~ verlieren* go mad; F *hast du den ~ verloren?* are you out of your mind?; F *das geht über m-n ~!* that's beyond me; *all s-n ~ zs.-nehmen* keep all one's wits about one. **ver'standesmäßig** *adj* a) intellectual, b) rational. **Ver'standesmensch** *m* rationalist.

ver'ständig *adj* **1.** intelligent. **2.** reasonable, sensible, understanding.

verständigen [fɛr'ʃtɛndɪgən] (h) **I** *v/t* inform (*von* about, of), call (*police, doctor, etc*). **II** *sich mit j-m ~* a) make o.s. understood by s.o., b) come to an agreement with s.o. (*über acc* on). **Ver'ständigung** *f* (-; -en) **1.** information. **2.** communication: *teleph. die ~ war schlecht* the line was bad. **3.** agreement, understanding. **Ver'ständigungsschwierigkeiten** *pl* communication problems: *ich hatte ~* I had problems to make myself understood.

verständlich [fɛr'ʃtɛntlɪç] *adj* **1.** distinct, clear, audible. **2.** understandable, intelligible: *schwer ~* difficult to understand; *j-m et. ~ machen* explain s.th. to s.o.; *sich j-m ~ machen* make o.s. understood (or heard) by s.o. **ver'ständlicherweise** *adv* understandably.

Verständnis [fɛr'ʃtɛntnɪs] *n* (-ses; *no pl*) **1.** (*gen* of) understanding, comprehension: *zum besseren ~ des Textes* in order to understand the text better. **2.** a) understanding, insight, b) appreciation (*für* of), c) sympathy (*für* with): (*viel*) *~ haben für* (fully) understand; *j-n* show (great) understanding for s.o.;

dafür fehlt mir jedes ~ that's beyond me.

ver'ständnislos *adj* uncomprehending: *~e Blicke* blank looks; *e-r Sache ~ gegenüberstehen* have no understanding (or appreciation) of s.th. **Ver'ständnislosigkeit** *f* (-; *no pl*) lack of understanding (or appreciation).

ver'ständnisvoll *adj* understanding, sympathetic, *a.* knowing (*look*).

ver'stärken *v/t* (h) strengthen, *a.* ✕ reinforce (*both a.* ⊚), ⚡ concentrate, ⚡ amplify, (*a. sich ~*) increase, intensify (*a. phot.*). **Ver'stärkung** *f* (-; -en) a) strengthening, reinforcement(s ✕), b) ⚡ amplification, c) increase, intensification (*a. phot.*).

ver'stauben *v/i* (sn) gather dust.

verstaubt [fɛr'ʃtaʊpt] *adj* **1.** dusty. **2.** *fig.* antiquated.

ver'stauchen *v/t* (h) ⚕ sprain (*sich die Hand etc* one's wrist *etc*).

ver'stauen *v/t* (h) stow away.

Versteck [fɛr'ʃtɛk] *n* (-[e]s; -e) hiding place, hideaway: *~ spielen* play hide-and-seek. **ver'stecken** *v/t* (*a. sich ~*) (h) hide (*vor dat* from). **Ver'steckspiel** *n* (game of) hide-and-seek. **ver'steckt** *adj* hidden: *sich ~ halten* lie low; *~e Kamera* candid camera.

ver'stehen (*irr, no* ge-, h, → *stehen*) **I** *v/t* **1.** hear, get, catch. **2.** understand, comprehend, grasp, catch, F get, realize, see, *a.* appreciate (*work of art etc*): *Spaß ~* take (or see) a joke; *falsch ~* misunderstand; *verstehe mich recht!* don't misunderstand me! **3.** understand, read, take: *was ~ Sie unter ...?* what do you understand by ...?; *wie ~ Sie das?* what do you make of it? **4.** know: *er versteht es zu inf* he knows how to *inf*; *sein Handwerk ~* know one's job; *davon versteht er gar nichts* he doesn't know the first thing about it. **5.** *j-m zu ~ geben* give s.o. to understand. **6.** *sich (or einander) ~* get along (or on) (with each other). **II** *~ sich* **7.** *mit* get on (or along) with. **8.** *auf (acc)* be (very) good at *ger*. **9.** *das versteht sich von selbst* that goes without saying. **III** *v/i ~ Sie?* you see?, F get me?; *ich verstehe!* I see; *verstanden?* F got it?; *wenn ich recht verstanden habe, willst du kommen?* I take it that you will come?

ver'steifen v/t (a. **sich ~**) (h) stiffen: fig. **sich ~ auf** (acc) insist on ger.

Ver'steigerer m (-s; -) auctioneer.

ver'steigern v/t (h) auction (off).

Ver'steigerung f (-; -en) (**zur ~ kommen** be put up for [Am. at]) auction.

ver'steinern v/i (a. **sich ~**) (h) petrify: fig. **wie versteinert vor Schreck** petrified with terror. **Ver'steinerung** f (-; -en) **1.** petrifaction. **2.** fossil.

ver'stellbar adj adjustable. **ver'stellen** (h) **I** v/t **1.** move, shift. **2.** disguise. **3.** misadjust: **wer hat den Wecker verstellt?** who has tampered with the alarm? **4.** obstruct, block. **II sich ~** fig. a) put on an act, b) hide one's feelings.

Ver'stellung f (-; no pl) **1.** ⚙ adjustment. **2.** fig. a) play-acting, b) disguise.

ver'steppen v/i (sn) turn into steppe.

ver'steuern v/t (h) pay tax on: **zu ~(d)** taxable. **ver'steuert** adj tax-paid.

Ver'steuerung f (-; -en) payment of tax (gen, von) on.

verstiegen [fɛr'ʃtiːɡən] adj high-flown.

ver'stimmen v/t (h) **1.** ♪ put s.th. out of tune. **2.** ♪ detune. **3.** j-n ~ annoy s.o., put s.o. in a bad mood. **ver'stimmt** adj **1.** ♪ out of tune. **2.** ♪ off-tune. **3.** annoyed (**über** acc at), in a bad mood. **4.** ♪ **~er Magen** upset stomach.

Ver'stimmung f (-; -en) **1.** ill humo(u)r, ill feeling. **2.** ♪ (stomach) upset.

verstockt [fɛr'ʃtɔkt] adj stubborn, impenitent.

verstohlen [fɛr'ʃtoːlən] adj furtive, surreptitious.

ver'stopfen v/t (h) **1.** stop (up), plug. **2.** a) block (up), obstruct, b) congest, jam (road). **3.** ♪ a) clog, occlude, b) constipate: **m-e Nase ist verstopft** my nose is plugged up; **verstopft sein** be constipated. **Ver'stopfung** f (-; -en) **1.** jam, block(age). **2.** ♪ constipation: **an ~ leiden** a. be constipated.

verstorben [fɛr'ʃtɔrbən] adj deceased, late. **Ver'storbene** m, f (-n; -n) the deceased: **die ~n** a. the dead.

verstört [fɛr'ʃtøːrt] adj badly upset, distraught, wild (look etc). **Ver'störtheit** f (-; no pl) distraction, distraught state.

Ver'stoß m (-es; ⸚e) (gegen) offen(c)e (Am. -se) (against), violation (of).

ver'stoßen (irr, no -ge-, h, → stoßen) **I** v/t reject: **j-n ~ aus** expel s.o. from, cast

s.o. out of. **II** v/i ~ **gegen** offend against, infringe, violate.

ver'streben v/t (h) ⚙ strut.

Ver'strebung f (-; -en) ⚙ strut.

ver'streichen (irr, no -ge-, → streichen) **I** v/i (sn) time: pass, set period: expire. **II** v/t (h) spread (butter, paint, etc).

ver'streuen v/t (h) scatter.

ver'stricken (h) **I** v/t **1.** use (up) (wool). **2.** j-n ~ in (acc) involve s.o. in. **II sich ~ in** (acc) get entangled (or involved) in.

verstümmeln [fɛr'ʃtvmɔln] v/t (h) mutilate, fig. a. garble (text).

Ver'stümmelung f (-; -en) mutilation.

verstummen [fɛr'ʃtomən] v/i (sn) become silent, a. stop talking, conversation, noise, a. rumo(u)rs, etc: stop, die down.

Versuch [fɛr'zuːx] m (-[e]s; -e) **1.** attempt (a. ⚖), trial (both a. sports), F try: **e-n ~ machen mit** try, give s.o., s.th. a try; **beim ersten ~** at the first attempt; **es käme auf e-n ~ an** we might as well try. **2.** 🐾, 🔬, phys. experiment, a. ⚙ test, trial: **~e anstellen** experiment. **3.** essay (**über** acc on).

ver'suchen v/t (h) **1.** try, attempt (a. ⚖): **et. ~** a) try s.th., b) experiment with s.th.; **es ~ mit** try, **j-m** give s.o. a try; **versuch's doch mal!** just (have a) try!, F have a go! **2.** fig. tempt: **ich war versucht zu inf** I was tempted to inf. **3.** taste, try. **Ver'sucher** m (-s; -) tempter.

Ver'sucherin f (-; -nen) temptress.

Ver'suchs|anstalt f research institute. **~bedingung** f test condition. **~bohrung** f trial drilling. **~gelände** n testing ground. **~ingeni,eur** m research engineer. **~ka,ninchen** n F fig. guinea pig. **~ob,jekt** n test object. **~per,son** f test subject (or person). **~pro,jekt** n pilot project. **~reihe** f series of tests. **~stadium** n experimental stage. **~strecke** f mot. test track. **~tier** n experimental (or laboratory) animal.

ver'suchsweise adv a) by way of trial, b) on trial, on a trial basis.

Ver'suchszwecke pl **zu ~n** for experimental purposes.

Ver'suchung f (-; -en) (j-n in ~ führen lead s.o. into) temptation: **in ~ sein** (or **kommen**) be tempted.

ver'sumpfen v/i (sn) **1.** become marshy. **2.** F fig. a) go to seed, b) end up boozing.

versunken [fɛr'zʊŋkən] *adj fig.* **~ in** (*acc*) absorbed in, lost in.

ver'sündigen: sich ~ (h) sin (**an** *dat* against).

ver'süßen *v/t* (h) *fig.* sweeten.

ver'tagen *v/t* (*a.* **sich ~**) (h) adjourn (**auf** *acc* until). **Ver'tagung** *f* (-; -en) adjournment.

vertäuen [fɛr'tɔʏən] *v/t* (h) ⚓ moor.

ver'tauschen *v/t* (h) **1.** exchange (**mit**, **gegen** for): **mit vertauschten Rollen** with reversed roles. **2.** confuse, mix up.

verteidigen [fɛr'taɪdɪɡən] (h) **I** *v/t* a) defend (**sich** o.s.) (**gegen** against, from), b) stand up for: **sich** (**vor Gericht**) **selbst ~** conduct one's own defence (*Am.* -se). **II** *v/i sports:* defend.

Ver'teidiger *m* (-s; -) **1.** defender, *fig. a.* advocate, *soccer: a.* fullback. **2.** ⚖ counsel for the defence (*Am.* -se).

Ver'teidigung *f* (-; -en) defen/ce (*Am.* -se).

Ver'teidigungs|ausgaben *pl* defen/ce (*Am.* -se) expenditure. **~beitrag** *m* defen/ce (*Am.* -se) contribution. **~bereitschaft** *f* preparedness for defen/ce (*Am.* -se). **~bündnis** *n* defensive alliance. **~krieg** *m* defensive war. **~mi͵nister** *m* defen/ce (*Am.* -se) minister, *Br.* Defence Secretary, *Am.* Secretary of Defense. **~mini͵sterium** *n* ministry of defence, *Am.* Department of Defense. **~rede** *f* (speech for the) defen/ce (*Am.* -se), *w.s.* apology. **~waffe** *f* defensive weapon.

ver'teilen (h) **I** *v/t* **1.** distribute, hand out, share out (*all:* **an** *acc* to, **unter** among), allocate, *thea.* cast (*rôles*): **unter sich ~** share; **mit verteilten Rollen lesen** do a play reading of. **2.** (**auf**, **über** *acc* over) distribute, spread, *w.s.* scatter. **II** **sich ~** spread (**auf**, **über** *acc* over), *persons:* scatter, *a.* ✗ spread out.

Ver'teiler *m* (-s; -) **1.** distributor (*a.* ⚡, ⚡, *mot.*). **2.** *office:* distribution list. **~kasten** *m* ⚡ distributing box. **~netz** *n* **1.** ⚡ distribution system. **2.** ⚡ distributing network. **~schlüssel** *m* ✝ **1.** distribution key. **2.** → *Verteiler* **2.** **~tafel** *f* ⚡ distribution switchboard.

Ver'teilung *f* (-; -en) distribution.

ver'teuern (h) **I** *v/t* raise the price of. **II** **sich ~** go up (in price). **Ver'teuerung** *f* (-; -en) rise in price(s) (*or* costs).

ver'teufeln *v/t* (h) denounce, demonize.

ver'teufelt *adj* F devilish, tricky: **~ schwer** damned difficult.

ver'tiefen (h) **I** *v/t* **1.** (*a.* **sich ~**) deepen, *fig. a.* heighten. **2.** extend (*knowledge etc*). **II** **sich ~ in** (*acc*) become absorbed (*or* engrossed) in. **Ver'tiefung** *f* (-; -en) **1.** deepening, *fig. a.* heightening, extension. **2.** depression. **3.** *fig.* absorption.

vertikal [vɛrti'kaːl] *adj* vertical.

Verti'kale *f* (-; -n) vertical (line).

ver'tilgen *v/t* (h) **1.** exterminate, kill. **2.** F polish off (*food*).

Ver'tilgung *f* (-; *no pl*) extermination.

ver'tippen: sich ~ (h) make a (typing) mistake.

vertonen [fɛr'toːnən] *v/t* (h) *et.* **~** set s.th. to music. **Ver'tonung** *f* (-; -en) setting.

Vertrag [fɛr'traːk] *m* (-[e]s; ⁓e) contract, agreement, *pol.* treaty, pact: **mündlicher ~** verbal agreement; **e-n ~** (**ab**)-**schließen** make (*or* enter into) a contract; **j-n unter ~ nehmen** sign s.o. on.

ver'tragen (*irr, no* -ge-, h, → *tragen*) **I** *v/t* **1.** a) *a.* F *fig.* endure, bear, stand, F take, b) be able to eat (*or* drink), tolerate (*medicament*): **ich vertrage k-n Kaffee** coffee doesn't agree with me; **sie verträgt das Klima nicht** she can't stand the climate; **er kann e-e Menge ~** a) he can take a lot, b) he can hold his drink; **kannst du Kritik ~?** can you take criticism?; F **ich könnte e-e Tasse Tee ~** I could do with a cup of tea. **2.** **sich** (**miteinander**) **~** a) get on (well) together, b) *colo(u)rs etc:* go well together. **II** **sich ~ mit** a) *j-m* get on (well) with s.o., b) *fig.* go well with.

ver'traglich I *adj* contractual. **II** *adv* by contract: **sich ~** (**zu et.**) **verpflichten** contract (for s.th. *or* to do s.th.).

verträglich [fɛr'trɛːklɪç] *adj* **1.** sociable: **~ sein** *a.* be easy to get along with. **2.** (easily) digestible, light (*food*), (*a.* **gut ~**) well-tolerated (*medicament*).

Ver'trags|abschluß *m* conclusion of a contract: **bei ~** on entering into the contract. **~bedingungen** *pl* terms of the contract. **~bruch** *m* breach of contract. **2brüchig** *adj* defaulting: **~ werden** commit a breach of contract.

ver'tragschließend *adj* contracting.

Ver'trags|entwurf *m* draft agreement.

⚲gemäß *adv* as stipulated. **~gemeinschaft** *f pol.* contractual union. **~händler** *m* authorized dealer. **~par₁tei** *f*, **~partner** *m* party to an agreement. **~punkt** *m* article of a contract. **~spieler(in** *f)* *m sports*: player under contract. **~strafe** *f* (contractual) penalty. **~werkstatt** *f* authorized repairer.

ver'tragswidrig *adj* contrary to (the terms of) the contract.

ver'trauen *v/i* (h) *(dat)* trust: **~ auf** *(acc)* trust in, rely upon. **Ver'trauen** *n* (-s) *(in, auf acc* in) trust, faith, confidence: *(ganz) im ~ (gesagt)* (strictly) confidentially, F between you and me; *im ~ auf (acc)* trusting in, relying on; **~ haben zu** have confidence in, trust; *er hat wenig ~ zu Ärzten* he has little faith in doctors; *j-n ins ~ ziehen* confide in s.o.; *der Regierung das ~ aussprechen* pass a vote of confidence.

ver'trauenerweckend *adj* inspiring confidence: *(wenig) ~ aussehen* inspire (little) confidence.

Ver'trauens₁arzt *m* (health insurance) medical examiner. **~beweis** *m* mark of confidence. **~bruch** *m* breach of trust. **~frage** *f pol.* **die ~ stellen** propose a vote of confidence. **~mann** *m* (-[e]s; -leute) a) representative, b) *(pl a. ~er)* spokesman. **~per₁son** *f* reliable person. **~sache** *f* confidential matter: *das ist ~* that's a matter of confidence. **⚲selig** *adj* (too) confiding, gullible. **~seligkeit** *f* (-; *no pl)* blind confidence, gullibility. **~stellung** *f* position of trust. **~verlust** *m* loss of confidence. **⚲voll** *adj* trustful, trusting. **~votum** *n* vote of confidence. **⚲würdig** *adj* trustworthy.

ver'traulich *adj* **1.** confidential: *~e Mitteilung a.* confidence. **2.** familiar, *(a. plump ~)* F chummy.

Ver'traulichkeit *f* (-; -en) **1.** *no pl* confidentiality, confidence. **2.** familiarity, *(a. plumpe ~)* F chumminess.

ver'träumt *adj* dreamy.

ver'traut *adj* **1.** close, intimate. **2.** familiar *(dat* to): *~ sein mit* be familiar with; *sich ~ machen mit* acquaint *(or* familiarize) o.s. with; *sich mit dem Gedanken ~ machen* get used to the idea.

Ver'traute *m, f* (-n; -n) confidant(e *f)*.

Ver'trautheit *f* (-; *no pl)* familiarity.

ver'treiben *v/t (irr, no* -ge-, h, → *trei-*

ben) **1.** drive *s.o., s.th.* away: *j-n ~ aus (dat)* drive s.o. out of, expel s.o. from; *sich die Zeit ~* while away the time. **2.** ✝ sell, distribute.

Ver'treibung *f* (-; -en) expulsion.

ver'tretbar *adj* justifiable, acceptable.

ver'treten¹ *v/t (irr, no* -ge-, h, → *treten)* **1.** substitute *(or* stand in, *a. ⚖ act)* for *s.o.* **2.** represent *(s.o., country, etc)*, look after *(s.o.'s interests)*: *j-s Sache ~* plead s.o.'s cause. **3.** support, advocate *(idea etc)*, hold, take *(view etc)*: *e-e andere Ansicht ~* take a different view *(als* from); → *Standpunkt* 2. **4.** *den Fuß ~* sprain one's ankle; F *sich die Beine ~* stretch one's legs.

ver'treten² *adj* **~ sein** a) be represented, b) be present, *esp. things*: be found.

Ver'treter *m* (-s; -), **Ver'treterin** *f* (-; -nen) **1.** substitute, stand-in, deputy. **2.** a) representative, ✝ a. agent; b) sales representative, c) proxy. **3.** exponent. **4.** advocate.

Ver'tretung *f* (-; -en) **1.** representation, ✝ *a.* agency: *in ~ (gen)* a) as representative of, b) (signed) for, c) by proxy; *diplomatische ~* diplomatic mission. **2.** a) substitution, b) stand-in, substitute: *j-s ~ übernehmen* stand in for s.o.

ver'tretungsweise *adv* as a stand-in.

Vertrieb [fεr'tri:p] *m* (-[e]s; *no pl)* **1.** sale, distribution. **2.** sales department.

Vertriebene [fεr'tri:bənə] *m, f* (-n; -n) expellee.

Ver'triebs₁abteilung *f* sales department. **~kosten** *pl* marketing costs. **~leiter** *m* sales manager. **~organisa₁tion** *f* marketing organization. **~weg** *m* distribution channel.

ver'trimmen *v/t* (h) F thrash.

ver'trinken *v/t (irr, no* -ge-, h, → *trinken)* spend on drink.

ver'trocknen *v/i* (sn) dry up.

ver'trödeln *v/t* (h) dawdle away, waste.

ver'trösten *v/t* (h) *j-n ~* feed s.o. with hopes *(auf acc* of); *j-n auf später ~* put s.o. off until later.

ver'trotteln *v/i* (sn) F go gaga.

ver'trottelt *adj* F senile: *~ sein* be gaga.

ver'tun *v/t (irr, no* -ge-, h, → *tun)* waste.

ver'tuschen *v/t* (h) cover up, hush up.

verübeln [fεr'ºy:bəln] *v/t* (h) *j-m et. ~* take s.th. amiss; *j-m ~, daß* take it badly that; *ich kann es ihr nicht ~(, wenn)* I can't blame her (if).

ver'üben *v/t* (h) commit, perpetrate.

ver'ulken *v/t* (h) F make fun of.

verunglimpfen [fɛr'ʔʊnglɪmpfən] *v/t* (h) revile, disparage.

ver'unglücken *v/i* (sn) **1.** have an accident: *tödlich ~* be killed in an accident; *mit dem Auto ~* have a car accident. **2.** F go wrong, be a flop. **Ver'unglückte** *m, f* (-n; -n) injured person, casualty.

ver'unsichern *v/t* (h) *j-n ~* make s.o. feel insecure, F rattle s.o.

verunstalten [fɛr'ʔʊnʃtaltən] *v/t* (h) deface, disfigure.

veruntreuen [fɛr'ʔʊntrɔyən] *v/t* (h) embezzle. **Ver'untreuung** *f* (-; -en) embezzlement.

ver'ursachen *v/t* (h) a) cause, create, give rise to, b) entail.

ver'urteilen *v/t* (h) (*zu* to) ⚖ sentence, *a. fig.* condemn. **Ver'urteilte** *m, f* (-n; -n) convict. **Ver'urteilung** *f* (-; -en) *a. fig.* condemnation.

vervielfältigen [fɛr'fiːlfɛltɪgən] *v/t* (h) **1.** (*a. sich ~*) multiply. **2.** duplicate, copy. **Ver'vielfältigung** *f* (-; -en) **1.** multiplication. **2.** a) duplication, b) duplicate. **Ver'vielfältigungsappa,rat** *m* duplicator.

vervierfachen [fɛr'fiːrfaxən] *v/t* (*a. sich ~*) (h) quadruple.

vervollkommnen [fɛr'fɔlkɔmnən] (h) **I** *v/t* perfect. **II** *sich ~* become perfect. **Ver'vollkommnung** *f* (-; -en) perfection.

vervollständigen [fɛr'fɔlʃtɛndɪgən] *v/t* (h) complete. **Ver'vollständigung** *f* (-; -en) completion.

ver'wachsen¹ *v/i* (*irr, no* -ge-, sn, → *wachsen*) (*miteinander*) *~* grow together, *bones:* unite, *organs:* fuse: *fig. ~ mit* become bound up with *one's job etc,* feel at home in *a town etc.*

ver'wachsen² *adj* deformed, crippled.

ver'wachsen³ *v/t* (h) apply the wrong wax to *skis*.

ver'wackeln *v/t* (h) F *phot.* blur.

ver'wählen: *sich ~* (h) F dial the wrong number.

ver'wahren (h) **I** *v/t* keep (*sicher* in a safe place). **II** *sich ~* protest (*gegen* against).

verwahrlosen [fɛr'vaːrloːzən] *v/i* (sn) be neglected, *person:* go to seed: *~ lassen*

neglect. **ver'wahrlost** [-loːst] *adj* a) neglected, run-down, dilapidated, b) seedy, *a.* dissolute. **Ver'wahrlosung** *f* (-; *no pl*) **1.** neglect. **2.** (moral) decline.

Ver'wahrung *f* (-; *no pl*) a) safekeeping, b) custody (*gen of s.o.*): *in ~ nehmen* take charge of, (*j-m*) *et. in ~ geben* deposit s.th. (with s.o.).

verwaisen [fɛr'vaɪzən] *v/i* (sn) become an orphan, be orphaned. **verwaist** [-'vaɪst] *adj* **1.** orphan (*child etc*). **2.** *fig.* a) deserted, b) vacant (*post*).

ver'walten *v/t* (h) administer, manage, conduct, run. **Ver'walter** *m* (-s; -) administrator, (*a. estate*) manager, trustee. **Ver'walterin** *f* (-; -nen) manageress. **Ver'waltung** *f* (-; -en) **1.** administration, ⚓ management. **2.** administrative authority.

Ver'waltungs|angestellte *m, f* (-n; -n) employee in the administration. **~appa,rat** *m* administrative machinery. **~beamte** *m* civil servant. **~bezirk** *m* administrative district. **~gebäude** *n* administration building. **~gebühr** *f* administrative fee. **~gericht** *n* ⚖ administrative court. **~rat** *m* ⚓ governing board. **£technisch** *adj* administrative. **~weg** *m* *auf dem ~e* through (the) administrative channels.

ver'wandeln *v/t* (h) (*in acc* into) change (*a. sich ~*), transform, turn, convert (*a. sports*): *wie verwandelt* completely changed. **Ver'wandlung** *f* (-; -en) change, transformation, conversion.

verwandt [fɛr'vant] *adj* (*mit*) *a. fig.* related (to), *ling.* cognate (with).

Ver'wandte *m, f* (-n; -n) relative, relation: *der nächste ~* the next of kin.

Ver'wandtschaft *f* (-; *no pl*) **1.** relationship, *fig.* affinity. **2.** relations.

ver'wandtschaftlich *adj* relational: *~e Beziehung(en)* relationship.

Ver'wandtschaftsgrad *m* degree of relationship.

verwanzt [fɛr'vantst] *adj* buggy.

ver'warnen *v/t* (h) warn, *a. sports:* caution. **Ver'warnung** *f* (-; -en) warning, *a. sports:* caution.

ver'waschen *adj* **1.** washed(-)out, *a.* faded. **2.** *fig.* vague, wool(l)y.

ver'wässern *v/t* (h) *a. fig.* water down.

ver'weben *v/t* (h) (*irr, no* -ge-, h, → *weben*) interweave.

ver'wechseln v/t (h) (*mit* with) confuse, mix up: *j-n* (*mit j-m*) ~ mistake s.o. for s.o. else; *sie sehen sich zum ♀ ähnlich* they are like as two peas (in a pod). **Ver'wechslung** f (-; -en) **1.** confusion, mistake, F mix-up. **2.** case of mistaken identity.

ver'wegen adj bold, daring, reckless.

ver'wehen v/t (h) **1.** blow s.th. away, scatter. **2.** cover (up) *traces etc*.

ver'wehren v/t (h) refuse: *j-m den Zutritt* ~ refuse s.o. admittance (*zu* to).

ver'weichlichen I v/t (h) *j-n* ~ make s.o. soft. **II** v/i (sn) go soft.

ver'weichlicht adj soft, effeminate.

ver'weigern (h) **I** v/t refuse: *j-m et.* ~ refuse (*or* deny) s.o. s.th.; *e-n Befehl* ~ disobey an order; *die Nahrung* ~ refuse to eat. **II** v/i *horse*: refuse. **Ver'weigerung** f (-; -en) refusal, denial.

Ver'weildauer f length of stay.

verweilen [fɛr'vaɪlən] v/i (h) **1.** stay. **2.** fig. rest (*auf dat* on). **3.** ~ *bei* dwell on.

verweint [fɛr'vaɪnt] adj tear-stained (*face*), *eyes* red from crying.

Verweis [fɛr'vaɪs] m (-es; -e) **1.** reprimand, rebuke: *j-m e-n* ~ *erteilen* reprimand s.o. (*wegen* for). **2.** reference (*auf acc* to). **ver'weisen** v/t (irr, no -ge-, h, → *weisen*) **1.** refer (*an, auf acc* to). **2.** *j-n von der Schule* ~ expel s.o. from school; *j-n des Landes* ~ expel s.o. (from the country); → *Platz* 5.

ver'welken v/i (sn) a. fig. wither.

verwendbar [fɛr'vɛntba:r] adj usable, suitable. **Ver'wendbarkeit** f (-; no pl) usability, suitability.

ver'wenden (irr, no -ge-, h, → *wenden*) **I** v/t **1.** use, employ, a. make use of, utilize. **2.** (*auf acc*) spend (on), a. devote *effort, time, etc* (to). **II** *sich* (*bei j-m*) *für j-n* ~ use one's influence (with s.o.) on s.o.'s behalf.

Ver'wendung f (-; -en) use, employment: *k-e* ~ *haben für* have no use for; ~ *finden* be used (*bei* in).

Ver'wendungs|bereich m range of use. **~möglichkeit** f use. **~zweck** m use, (intended) purpose.

ver'werfen (irr, no -ge-, h, → *werfen*) **I** v/t reject, turn down (*plan etc*), ⚖ dismiss (*appeal, action, etc*), overrule (*motion*), quash (*sentence*). **II** *sich* ~ a) geol. fault, b) *wood*: warp.

ver'werflich adj reprehensible.

Ver'werfung f (-; -en) **1.** rejection, ⚖ dismissal. **2.** a) geol. fault, b) warping.

ver'wertbar adj usable, ♈ realizable.

Ver'wertbarkeit f (-; no pl) usability.

ver'werten v/t (h) use, utilize, make use of, exploit (*patent etc*), ♈ realize (*property etc*). **Ver'wertung** f (-; -en) use, utilization, exploitation, ♈ realization.

ver'wesen v/i (sn) rot, decay: *halb verwest* putrefying. **Ver'wesung** f (-; no pl) decay, putrefaction.

ver'wetten v/t (h) spend s.th. on betting.

ver'wickeln (h) **I** v/t **1.** tangle s.th. (up). **2.** fig. *j-n* ~ *in* (acc) involve s.o. in, a. drag s.o. into. **II** *sich* ~ **3.** tangle up. **4.** *sich* ~ *in* (acc) fig. get caught in, get tangled up in a web of contradictions etc.

ver'wickelt adj fig. **1.** complicated, complex, intricate. **2.** ~ *sein* (*werden*) *in* (acc) be (get) involved (*or* mixed up) in.

Ver'wicklung f (-; -en) fig. **1.** involvement (*in acc* in). **2.** entanglement, complication.

ver'wildern v/i (sn) run wild, *morals etc*: degenerate. **ver'wildert** adj wild, overgrown (*garden*), fig. degenerate.

Ver'wilderung f (-; no pl) (state of) neglect, fig. degeneration.

ver'wirken v/t (h) forfeit.

ver'wirklichen (h) **I** v/t realize. **II** *sich* ~ be realized, come true; *sich* (*selbst*) ~ fulfil(l) o.s. **Ver'wirklichung** f (-; -en) realization.

ver'wirren (h) **I** v/t **1.** tangle s.th. (up). **2.** fig. confuse, bewilder, muddle. **II** *sich* ~ **3.** get tangled up. **4.** fig. become muddled. **ver'wirrt** adj fig. confused, bewildered, muddled. **Ver'wirrung** f (-; -en) confusion, muddle, a. bewilderment: *es herrschte allgemeine* ~ there was general confusion; *in* ~ *bringen* → *verwirren* 2.

ver'wischen v/t (a. *sich* ~) (h) blur, fig. a. cover (up); → *Spur* 1.

ver'wittern v/i (sn) weather.

ver'wittert adj weather-beaten.

ver'witwet adj widowed.

verwöhnen [fɛr'vø:nən] v/t (h) spoil, pamper. **ver'wöhnt** adj **1.** spoilt. **2.** fastidious. **3.** demanding. **Ver'wöhnung** f (-; no pl) spoiling, pampering.

verworren [fɛr'vɔrən] adj confused,

muddled. **Ver'worrenheit** f (-; no pl) confusion, muddle.

verwundbar [fɛr'vʊntbaːr] adj a. fig. vulnerable. **Ver'wundbarkeit** f (-; no pl) a. fig. vulnerability. **verwunden** [fɛr'vʊndən] v/t (h) a. fig. wound.

ver'wunderlich adj surprising, astonishing. **ver'wundern** (h) I v/t surprise, astonish. II **sich** ~ (**über** acc at) be surprised, be astonished. **ver'wundert** adj surprised, astonished: **j-n** ~ **ansehen** look at s.o. in surprise.

Ver'wunderung f (-; no pl) surprise, astonishment.

Ver'wundete m, f (-n; -n) casualty: **die** ~**n** the wounded.

Ver'wundung f (-; -en) wound, injury.

verwunschen [fɛr'vʊnʃən] adj enchanted.

ver'wünschen v/t (h) curse.
ver'wünscht adj cursed, confounded.
Ver'wünschung f (-; -en) curse.

ver'wurzelt adj fig. (deeply) rooted.
ver'wüsten v/t (h) devastate, ravage.
Ver'wüstung f (-; -en) devastation, ravage(s).

ver'zagen v/i (h) despair (**an** dat of), lose heart. **verzagt** [-'tsaːkt] adj disheartened, despondent.

ver'zählen: **sich** ~ (h) miscount.

ver'zahnt adj ⊙ toothed: **miteinander** ~ a. fig. interlocked.

ver'zapfen v/t (h) **1.** ⊙ mortise. **2.** F dish out: **Unsinn** ~ talk nonsense.

ver'zärteln [fɛr'tsɛːrtəln] v/t (h) pamper, (molly)coddle.

ver'zaubern v/t (h) cast a spell on, fig. a. enchant: **j-n** ~ **in** (acc) turn s.o. into.

ver'zehnfachen v/t (a. **sich** ~) (h) increase tenfold.

Verzehr [fɛr'tseːr] m (-[e]s; no pl) consumption. **ver'zehren** v/t (h) eat, consume (a. fig.). **Ver'zehrzwang** m (-[e]s; no pl) obligation to order.

ver'zeichnen v/t (h) **1.** note (or write) down, register, record: **in e-r Liste** ~ list; **er konnte e-n großen Erfolg** ~ he achieved a great success; **Fortschritte sind nicht zu** ~ no progress has been made. **2.** fig. distort, misrepresent.

Verzeichnis [fɛr'tsaiçnɪs] n (-ses; -se) a) list, catalog(ue Br.), register, record, b) index, c) inventory.

verzeihen [fɛr'tsaiən] (verzieh, verzie-

hen, h) I v/t forgive, excuse, pardon: **j-m et.** ~ forgive s.o. s.th., excuse (or pardon) s.o. (for) s.th.; ~ **Sie die Störung** excuse my interrupting you. II v/i **j-m** ~ forgive s.o.; ~ **Sie!** (I beg your) pardon!, sorry!, Am. excuse me!

ver'zeihlich adj pardonable.

Ver'zeihung f (-; no pl) pardon: **j-n um** ~ **bitten** a) ask s.o.'s forgiveness, b) apologize to s.o.; ~! (I beg your) pardon!, sorry!, Am. excuse me!

ver'zerren (h) I v/t a. fig. distort. II **sich** ~ become distorted.

Ver'zerrung f (-; -en) a. fig. distortion.

ver'zetteln (h) I v/t fritter away. II **sich** ~ waste one's time (or energy) (**in** dat, **mit** on).

Verzicht [fɛr'tsɪçt] m (-[e]s; -e) (**auf** acc of) renunciation, ⚖ a. waiver.

ver'zichten v/i (h) ~ **auf** (acc) do without, F cut out, a. give up, ⚖ renounce, waive; **zu j-s Gunsten** ~ stand aside for s.o.'s benefit.

Ver'zichterklärung f ⚖ waiver.

verzieh [fɛr'tsiː] pret of **verzeihen.**

ver'ziehen¹ pp of **verzeihen.**

ver'ziehen² (irr, no -ge-, → **ziehen**) I v/i (sn) **1.** → **umziehen** I. II v/t (h) **2.** distort, twist (**zu** into): **das Gesicht** ~ (make a) grimace, pull a face; → **Miene. 3.** spoil: → **verzogen.** III **sich** ~ **4.** mouth, face, etc: twist (**zu** into). **5.** wood: warp. **6.** clouds etc: disperse, storm etc: blow over. **7.** F make o.s. scarce: **verzieht euch!** beat it!, get lost!

ver'zieren v/t (h) decorate.

Ver'zierung f (-; -en) decoration.

ver'zinken v/t (h) ⊙ galvanize.

ver'zinnen v/t (h) ⊙ tin(-plate).

verzinsen [fɛr'tsɪnzən] (h) I v/t pay interest on: **e-e Summe mit 5%** ~ pay 5 per cent (or percent) interest on a sum. II **sich** (**mit 5%**) ~ yield (or bear) (5 per cent or percent) interest. **ver'zinslich** adj interest-bearing: ~ **anlegen** put out at interest. **Ver'zinsung** f (-; -en) **1.** (**von**, gen on) a) payment of interest, b) interest yield. **2.** → **Zinssatz.**

verzogen [fɛr'tsoːgən] adj fig. spoilt.

ver'zögern (h) I v/t a) delay, b) slow down, c) protract. II **sich** ~ be delayed. **Ver'zögerung** f (-; -en) delay. **Ver'zögerungstaktik** f delaying tactics.

ver'zollen v/t (h) pay duty on: **haben**

Sie et. zu ~? have you anything to declare? **ver'zollt** *adj* duty-paid.

Ver'zollung *f* (-; -en) payment of duty (*gen* on).

verzückt [fɛr'tsʏkt] *adj* enraptured, ecstatic. **Ver'zückung** *f* (-; -en) rapture, ecstasy: *in ~ geraten* go into raptures (*or* ecstasies) (*über acc* over, about).

Ver'zug *m* (-[e]s; *no pl*) **1.** delay: *ohne ~* without delay, forthwith; **†** *im ~ sein* (*mit*) default (on), be in arrear(s) (for). **2.** *es ist Gefahr im ~* there is danger ahead.

Ver'zugszinsen *pl* interest on arrears.

ver'zweifeln *v/i* (sn) despair (*an dat* of): *es ist zum ~* it's enough to drive you to despair; *ich bin am ~* ♀ I'm desperate.

ver'zweifelt *adj* despairing (*look etc*), desperate (*fight, situation, etc*).

Ver'zweiflung *f* (-; *no pl*) (*j-n zur ~ bringen or treiben* drive s.o. to) despair.

Ver'zweiflungstat *f* act of desperation.

verzweigen [fɛr'tsvaɪɡən] *sich ~* (h) branch out, *esp. fig.* ramify.

ver'zweigt *adj* branching (*network etc*).

ver'zwickt *adj* F tricky, complicated.

Veteran [vete'raːn] *m* (-en; -en) **1.** ✗ ex-serviceman, *Am. and fig.* veteran. **2.** *mot.* vintage car.

Veterinär [veteri'nɛːr] *m* (-s; -e) veterinary surgeon, *Am.* veterinarian, F vet.

Veto ['veːto] *n* (-s; -s) veto: (*s)ein ~ einlegen* put a veto on, veto.

'Vetorecht *n* veto (power).

Vetter ['fɛtər] *m* (-s; -n) cousin.

'Vetternwirtschaft *f* (-; *no pl*) nepotism.

Viadukt [via'dʊkt] *m* (-[e]s; -e) viaduct.

Vibration [vibra'tsi̯oːn] *f* (-; -en) vibration.

vibrieren [vi'briːrən] *v/i* (h) vibrate.

Video ['viːdeo] *n* → *Videotechnik.*

'Video... video (*camera, film, system, etc*). *~aufzeichnung f* video recording. *~band n* video tape. *~gerät n* video recorder. *~kassette f* video cassette. *~re̩corder m* video recorder. *~spiel n* video game. *~technik f* video technology. *~text m* teletext.

Videothek [video'teːk] *f* (-; -en) video-tape library.

Vieh [fiː] *n* (-[e]s; *no pl*) **1.** cattle, livestock. **2.** F *contp.* animal, beast. *~bestand m* livestock. *~futter n* fodder, feed. *~händler m* cattle dealer.

'viehisch *adj* bestial, brutal.

'Vieh|markt *m* cattle market. *~wagen m* 🚃 cattle truck, *Am.* stock car. *~zeug n* F animals. *~zucht f* stockbreeding. *~züchter m* stockbreeder, cattleman.

viel [fiːl] *adj and adv* a) lot (of), plenty (of), F lots of, b) (*as, how, so, too, very, not*) much: (*sehr*) *~e* (a great) many; *sehr ~ Geld* a great deal (*or* plenty) of money; *ziemlich ~* quite a lot (of); *das kommt vom ~en Rauchen* that comes from all that smoking; *ich halte nicht ~ davon* I don't think much of it; *~e hundert* hundreds and hundreds of; *~ besser* (*lieber*) much better (rather); *~ zuviel* far too much; *~ zu wenig* not nearly enough; *in ~em* in many ways.

'vielbeschäftigt *adj* very busy.

'vieldeutig [-dɔʏtiç] *adj* ambiguous.

'vieldisku̩tiert *adj* much-discussed.

'Vieleck *n* (-[e]s; -e) ⟂ polygon.

'vielerlei ['fiːlərlaɪ] *adj* all sorts of.

'vieler'orts *adv* in many places.

'vielfach I *adj and adv* a) *~er Millionär* he is a millionaire many times over; *auf ~en Wunsch* by popular request. **II** *adv* a) in many cases, b) frequently.

'Vielfalt [-falt] *f* (-; *no pl*) (great) variety.

'vielfältig [-fɛltiç] *adj* varied, manifold.

'Vielfraß *m* (-es; -e) a. F *fig.* glutton.

'vielgeliebt *adj* much-loved.

'vielgepriesen *adj* much-vaunted.

'vielköpfig [-kœpfiç] *adj* large (*family*).

vielleicht [fi'laɪçt] *adv* perhaps, maybe, possibly: *hast du ihn ~ gesehen?* have you seen him by any chance?; *~ kommen sie noch* they may yet come; *es ist ~ besser* it might be better; *könnten Sie ~ das Fenster schließen?* would you mind closing the window?; F *das ist ~ ein Trottel!* he really is an idiot!; *ich war ~ aufgeregt!* what a state I was in!; *das ist ~ ein Auto!* that's some car.

'vielmals *adv* many times: *danke ~* many thanks; *sie läßt ~ grüßen* she sends her best regards; *ich bitte ~ um Entschuldigung* I'm terribly sorry.

'vielmehr *adv* rather.

'vielsagend *adj* meaningful, knowing.

'vielschichtig [-ʃiçtiç] *adj fig.* complex.

'vielseitig [-zaɪtiç] *adj* many-sided, versatile (*person*), varied (*interests etc*): *auf ~en Wunsch* by popular request; *sie ist ~ begabt* she has many talents;

er ist ~ interessiert he has varied interests; *~ verwendbar* multi-purpose.

'**Vielseitigkeit** *f* (-; *no pl*) versatility.

'**vielsprachig** [-∫praːxɪç] *adj* polyglot.

'**vielstimmig** [-∫tɪmɪç] *adj ♪* polyphonic.

'**vielversprechend** *adj* (very) promising: *nicht (gerade) ~* unpromising.

Viel'**völkerstaat** *m* multiracial state.

Vielweiberei [fiːlvaɪbəˈraɪ] *f* (-; *no pl*) polygamy.

'**Vielzahl** *f* (-; *no pl*) multitude.

vier [fiːr] *adj* four: *unter ~ Augen* in private; *Gespräch unter ~ Augen* private talk; F *auf allen ~en* on all fours.

Vier *f* (-; -en) four: *ped.* *e-e ~ bekommen* get a D.

'**Vierbeiner** [-baɪnər] *m* (-s; -) F quadruped. '**vierbeinig** *adj* four-legged.

'**vierblätt(e)rig** [-blɛt(ə)rɪç] *adj* four-leaf ..., four-leaved.

'**Viereck** *n* (-[e]s; -e) quadrangle, square. '**viereckig** *adj* quadrangular, square.

Vierer ['fiːrər] *m* (-s; -) *rowing:* four, *golf:* foursome. **~bob** *m* four-seater bob.

'**vierfach** *adj* fourfold.

Vier'farbendruck *m* four-colo(u)r printing (*picture:* print).

'**Vierfüßer** [-fyːsər] *m* (-s; -) *zo.* quadruped. '**vierfüßig** *adj* four-footed.

'**Vierganggetriebe** *n mot.* four-speed gear unit.

'**vierhändig** [-hɛndɪç] *adj* four-handed, for four hands: *~ spielen* play a duet.

vier'hundert *adj* four hundred.

'**vierjährig** [-jɛːrɪç] *adj* **1.** of four years, four-year (*period etc*). **2.** four-year-old.

'**Vierjährige** [-jɛːrɪgə] *m, f* (-n; -n) four-year-old.

'**Vierkant** *n, m* (-[e]s; -e) ⊙ square.

'**vierkantig** *adj* square.

'**Vierlinge** *pl* quadruplets.

'**viermal** *adv* four times.

'**viermotorig** [-moːtoˈrɪç] *adj esp.* ✈ four-engine(d).

'**Vierrad...** four-wheel (*drive, brake*).

'**vierrädrig** [-rɛːdrɪç] *adj* four-wheeled.

'**vierschrötig** [-∫røːtɪç] *adj* square-built, burly.

'**vierseitig** [-zaɪtɪç] *adj* four-sided, *A* quadrilateral.

'**viersilbig** [-zɪlbɪç] *adj* four-syllable.

'**Viersitzer** *m* (-s; -) four-seater.

'**vierspurig** [-∫puːrɪç] *adj* four-lane.

'**vierstellig** [-∫tɛlɪç] *adj A* four-digit.

'**vierstimmig** [-∫tɪmɪç] *adj ♪* four-part: *~ singen* sing in four voices.

'**vierstöckig** [-∫tœkɪç] *adj* four-storeyed, *Am.* four-storied.

'**vierstündig** [-∫tʏndɪç] *adj* four-hour.

viert [fiːrt] *adj* fourth: *sie waren zu ~* there were four of them.

'**Viertaktmotor** *m* four-stroke engine.

'**vier'tausend** *adj* four thousand.

'**Vierte** *m, f* (-n; -n) fourth.

Viertel ['fɪrtəl] *n* (-s; -) quarter, fourth: *es ist ~ vor eins* it is a quarter to one.

'**Viertelfi,nale** *n sports:* quarter final.

'**Viertel'jahr** *n* three months, quarter.

'**vierteljährlich** *adj and adv* quarterly: *~e Kündigung* three months' notice.

'**Vierteliliter** *m, n* (-s; -) quarter of a litre (*Am.* liter).

vierteln ['fɪrtəln] *v/t* (h) quarter.

'**Viertel|note** *f ♪* crotchet, *Am.* quarter note. **~pause** *f ♪* crotchet (*Am.* quarter note) rest. **~pfund** *n* quarter of a pound. **~stunde** *f* quarter of an hour.

'**viertelstündlich** *adj and adv* every quarter of an hour (*or* fifteen minutes).

'**viertens** *adv* fourthly.

Vier'vierteltakt *m ♪* four-four (*or* common) time.

vierzehn ['fɪr-] *adj* fourteen: *~ Tage* a fortnight, *Am.* fourteen days; *in ~ Tagen* in two weeks' time, in a fortnight. **~jährig** [-jɛːrɪç] *adj* fourteen-year-old. **~tägig** [-tɛːgɪç] *adj* two-week.

'**Vierzeiler** [-tsaɪlər] *m* (-s; -) quatrain.

vierzig ['fɪrtsɪç] *adj* forty. '**Vierzig** *f* (-; -en) forty: *sie ist Anfang (der) ~* she is in her early forties. '**vierziger** *adj die ~ Jahre* the forties. '**Vierziger** *m* (-s; -), '**Vierzigerin** *f* (-; -nen) man (woman) of forty (*or* in his [her] forties).

'**vierzigst** *adj* fortieth.

Vietnam [viɛtˈnam] *n* (-s) Vietnam.

Vietnamese [viɛtnaˈmeːzə] *m* (-n; -n), **Vietna'mesin** *f* (-; -nen), **vietna'mesisch** *adj* Vietnamese.

Vikar [viˈkaːr] *m* (-s; -e) curate.

Villa ['vɪla] *f* (-; Villen) villa.

'**Villenviertel** *n* residential area.

Viola ['vioːla] *f* (-; Violen) *♪* viola.

violett [vioˈlɛt] *adj* violet.

Violine [vioˈliːnə] *f* (-; -n) *♪* violin.

Violinist [violiˈnɪst] *m* (-en; -en) violinist.

Vio'linschlüssel *m ♪* treble clef.

Violon'cello [violɔn-] *n ♪* violoncello.

Viper ['vi:pər] f (-; -n) zo. viper, adder.
Virologie [virolo'gi:] f (-; no pl) virology.
virologisch [viro'lo:gɪʃ] adj virological.
virtuos [vɪr'tǔo:s] adj virtuoso. **Virtuose** [vɪr'tǔo:zə] m (-n; -n), **Virtu'osin** f (-; -nen) virtuoso. **Virtuosität** [vɪrtǔozi'tɛːt] f (-; no pl) virtuosity.
virulent [viru'lɛnt] adj virulent.
Virus ['vi:rʊs] m, n (-; Viren) 🖋 virus. **~infekti,on** f virus (or viral) infection.
Visage [vi'za:ʒə] f (-; -n) F mug.
Visier [vi'zi:r] n (-s; -e) **1.** visor. **2.** on rifle: sight. **vi'sieren** v/i (h) take aim.
Vision [vi'zǐo:n] f (-; -en) vision.
visionär [vizǐo'nɛ:r] adj visionary.
Visite [vi'zi:tə] f (-; -n) (doctor's) visit. **Vi'sitenkarte** f (visiting) card.
visuell [vi'zǔɛl] adj visual.
Visum ['vi:zʊm] n (-s; Visa, Visen) visa.
vital [vi'ta:l] adj **1.** vigorous, fit. **2.** vital.
Vitalität [vitali'tɛ:t] f (-; no pl) vitality.
Vitamin [vita'mi:n] n (-s; -e) vitamin: F fig. ~ **B** contacts. **2arm** adj low in vitamins. **~bedarf** m vitamin requirement. **~gehalt** m vitamin content.
vita'minhaltig adj containing vitamins.
vitaminieren [vitami'ni:rən] v/t (h) vitaminize.
Vita'min|mangel m vitamin deficiency. **~präpa,rat** n vitamin preparation. **2reich** adj rich in vitamins. **~stoß** m massive dose of vitamins.
Vitrine [vi'tri:nə] f (-; -n) glass cupboard, 🕊 showcase, display case.
Vize... ['fi:tsə-] vice-(admiral, chancellor, president, etc). **~könig** m viceroy. **~meister(in** f) m sports: runner-up (hinter dat to).
Vogel ['fo:gəl] m (-s; ") **1.** bird: F fig. **e-n ~ haben** have a screw loose; **den ~ abschießen** take the cake; **j-m den ~ zeigen** tap one's forehead at s.o. **2.** F fig. bird, fellow: **ein komischer ~** a queer customer. **~beerbaum** m rowan- (-tree). **~beere** f rowanberry. **~futter** n birdseed. **~haus** n aviary. **~käfig** m birdcage. **~kunde** f (-; no pl) ornithol- ogy. **~mist** m bird droppings.
vögeln ['fø:gəln] v/t, v/i (h) V screw.
'Vogel|nest n bird's nest. **~perspek,tive** f **Berlin aus der ~** a bird's-eye view of Berlin. **~scheuche** f (-; -n) scarecrow. **~schutzgebiet** n bird sanctuary.
Vogel-'Strauß-Poli,tik f ostrich policy.

'Vogelwarte f ornithological station.
'Vogelzug m migration of birds.
Vokabel [vo'ka:bəl] f (-; -n) word. **Vo'kabelheft** n vocabulary book.
Vokal [vo'ka:l] m (-s; -e) vowel.
Vo'kalmu,sik f vocal music.
Volk [fɔlk] n (-[e]s; ") **1.** a) people, nation, b) the masses, contp. mob, rabble, c) crowd: **ein Mann aus dem ~** a man of the people; **sich unters ~ mischen** mingle with the crowd. **2.** zo. swarm (of bees). **3.** hunt. covey.
Völker|kunde ['fœlkər-] f (-; no pl) eth- nology. **~mord** m genocide. **~recht** n (-[e]s; no pl) international law. **2recht- lich** adj relating to (adv under) interna- tional law. **~verständigung** f interna- tional understanding. **~wanderung** f **1.** migration of peoples. **2.** fig. exodus.
'volkreich adj populous.
'Volks|abstimmung f referendum. **~aufstand** m national uprising. **~be- fragung** f public opinion poll. **~be- gehren** n petition for a referendum. **~büche,rei** f public library. **~cha,rak- ter** m national character. **~demokra- ,tie** f people's democracy. **~deutsche** m, f (-n; -n) ethnic German. **2eigen** adj hist. DDR state-owned. **~eigentum** n national property. **~einkommen** n na- tional income. **~entscheid** m referen- dum. **~feind** m public enemy. **~fest** n public festival, fair. **~gruppe** f ethnic group. **~held(in** f) m folk hero(ine f). **~herrschaft** f democracy. **~hochschu- le** f adult evening classes. **~kammer** f hist. DDR People's Chamber. **~kunde** f (-; no pl) folklore. **~lauf** m open cross- -country race. **~lied** n folk song. **~mund** m (im ~ in the) vernacular. **~mu,sik** f folk music. **2nah** adj popu- lar, people-oriented, grassroots (politi- cian). **~poli,zist** m hist. DDR member of the people's police. **~repu,blik** f peo- ple's republic. **~schicht** f social class. **~schule** f → Grund-, Hauptschule. **~seele** f iro. **die ~ kocht** the populace is seething. **~sport** m popular sport. **~sprache** f vernacular. **~stamm** m tribe, race. **~stück** n thea. folk play. **~tanz** m folk dance. **~tracht** f national costume. **~trauertag** m day of national mourning.
'Volkstum n (-s; no pl) folklore.

'**volkstümlich** [-ty:mlıç] *adj* **1.** folkloristic. **2.** *ling.* vernacular. **3.** traditional. **4.**
popular: *sich ~ geben* act folksy.

'**Volks\vermögen** *n* national wealth.
~versammlung *f* public meeting.
~vertreter(in *f*) *m* people's representative. **~vertretung** *f* representation of
the people, parliament. **~wirt** *m* † (political) economist. **~wirtschaft** *f* **1.** political economy. **2.** → **wirtschaftsleh-
re** *f* economics. **~zählung** *f* census.

voll [fɔl] **I** *adj* **1.** full, *a.* filled, *a.* full up:
~(er), ~von, ~mit full of (*a. fig.*), filled
(*or* loaded) with; *e-e Kanne (~) Tee* a
pot of tea; *fig. aus dem ~en schöpfen*
draw on plentiful resources; F *~ sein* a)
be full up, b) be tight. **2.** full, round
(*figure*), thick, rich (*hair*): *~er werden*
a. fill out. **3.** *fig.* full, rich (*scent, voice,
etc*). **4.** full, whole: *der Mond ist ~* the
moon is full; *e-e ~e Stunde* a full (*or*
solid) hour; *~e drei Tage* fully three
days; *et. in ~er Höhe bezahlen* pay the
full amount, pay the amount in full;
mit ~er Lautstärke (at) full blast; *aus
~er Brust, aus ~em Halse* at the top of
one's voice; *aus ~em Herzen* from the
bottom of one's heart; *~es Vertrauen*
complete confidence; *die ~e Wahrheit*
the whole truth. **II** *adv* fully, *a.* in full: *~
und ganz* completely, wholly; *~ arbei-
ten* work full time; *~ beschäftigt* fully
occupied; *~ besetzt* full (up); *Sie müssen ~ bezahlen* you have to pay the
full price; *~ schlagen* clock: strike the
full hour; *j-n nicht für ~ nehmen* not to
take s.o. seriously; F *in die ~en gehen*
go flat out.

'**vollauf** *adv* quite, perfectly.
'**vollauto,matisch** *adj* fully automatic.
'**Vollbad** *n* full bath.
'**Vollbart** *m* full beard.
'**vollbeschäftigt** *adj* employed full-time.
'**Vollbeschäftigung** *f* (-; *no pl*) full employment.
'**Vollbesitz** *m im ~* (*gen*) in full possession of.
'**Vollblut** *n* (-[e]s; *no pl*), '**Vollblüter**
[-bly:tɐ] *m* (-s; -), '**Vollblutpferd** *n*
thoroughbred.
'**Vollbremsung** *f* full braking, crash-
-halt: *e-e ~ machen* F slam on the
brakes.
voll'bringen *v/t* (*irr, insep, no* -ge-, h, →

bringen) a) accomplish, achieve, b)
perform (*miracles etc*).
'**vollbusig** [-bu:zıç] *adj* bosomy, busty.
'**Volldampf** *m mit ~* at full steam, *fig.* at
full blast.
'**vollelek,tronisch** *adj* fully electronic.
voll'enden *v/t* (*insep, no* -ge-, h) **1.** finish, complete. **2.** perfect. **voll'endet** *adj*
perfect, accomplished: *~ schön* of perfect beauty; → *Tatsache.* **voll'endung**
f (-; *no pl*) **1.** completion: *nach* (*or mit*)
~ (gen) on completion of. **2.** perfection.
'**voller** → **voll** I.
Völlerei [fœlə'raɪ] *f* (-; -en) gluttony.
Volleyball(spiel) [ˈvɔli-] *n* volleyball.
'**Vollfettkäse** *m* full-fat cheese.
voll'führen *v/t* (*insep, no* -ge-, h) perform.
'**vollfüllen** *v/t* (*sep*, h) fill (up).
'**Vollgas** *n mot.* full throttle: *mit ~* F full
tilt; *~ geben* F step on the gas.
'**voll\gepackt, ~gepfropft, ~gestopft**
adj crammed (full), F (jam-)packed.
'**vollgießen** *v/t* (*irr, sep,* -ge-, h, → *gießen*) fill (up).
'**Vollgummi** *m, n* solid rubber.
völlig [ˈfœlıç] **I** *adj* total, absolute, complete: *~e Gleichberechtigung* full
equality; *~er Unsinn* utter (*or* perfect)
nonsense; *ein ~er Versager* a complete
failure. **II** *adv* quite, fully (*etc*): *~ richtig*
absolutely right; *~ am Ende sein* be
completely run down; *das ist mir ~
gleichgültig* I don't give a damn.
'**volljährig** [-jɛ:rıç] *adj* of (full legal) age,
major: *~ sein* (*werden*) be (come) of
age; *noch nicht ~* under age.
'**Volljährigkeit** *f* (-; *no pl*) full legal age,
majority.
'**Vollju,rist** *m* fully qualified lawyer.
'**Vollkaskoversicherung** *f* comprehensive insurance.
voll'kommen **I** *adj* perfect, total, absolute. **II** *adv* † → *völlig* II.
Voll'kommenheit *f* (-; *no pl*) perfection.
'**Vollkornbrot** *n* wholemeal bread.
'**vollmachen** *v/t* (*sep*, h) F **1.** fill (up). **2.**
dirty, soil: *die Hosen ~* fill one's pants.
'**Vollmacht** *f* (-; -en) full power(s), authority, ✍ a) power of attorney, b)
proxy: *~ haben* be authorized; *j-m ~
erteilen* authorize s.o.
'**Vollma,trose** *m* able-bodied seaman.

'**Vollmilch** f full-cream milk. **~schoko-**
lade f milk chocolate.
'**Vollmond** m full moon: *heute ist ~*
there is a full moon tonight.
'**vollmundig** [-mʊndɪç] adj **1.** full-bodied
(*wine etc*). **2.** *fig. iro.* pompous.
'**Vollnar,kose** f general an(a)esthesia.
'**vollpacken** v/t (sep, h) pack s.th. full
(*mit* of).
'**Vollpensi,on** f (-; no pl) (full) board and
lodging.
'**vollsaugen: sich ~** (sep, h) become sat-
urated (*mit* with).
'**vollschlagen: sich ~** (irr, sep, -ge-, h, →
schlagen) fill one's belly.
'**vollschlank** adj **~ sein** have a full figure.
'**vollschreiben** v/t (irr, sep, -ge-, h, →
schreiben) fill.
'**vollständig I** adj complete, whole, entire: *~e Anschrift* full address. **II** adv ↔
völlig II. '**Vollständigkeit** f (-; no pl)
completeness.
'**vollstopfen** v/t (sep, h) stuff, cram.
voll'streckbar adj ⚖ enforceable.
voll'strecken (h) **I** v/t **1.** execute, ⚖ a.
enforce. **2.** *sports:* convert (*penalty kick
etc*). **II** v/i *sports:* score. **Voll'strecker**
m (-s; -) ⚖ executor. **Voll'streckung** f
(-; -en) ⚖ execution. **Voll'streckungs-**
befehl m ⚖ writ of execution.
'**vollsyn,thetisch** adj all-synthetic.
'**volltanken** v/t, v/i (sep, h) fill up.
'**Volltreffer** m direct hit, a. fig. bull's-eye.
'**volltrunken** adj completely drunk.
'**Vollversammlung** f plenary assembly.
'**Vollwaise** f orphan. '**Vollwaschmit-**
tel n all-purpose washing powder.
'**vollwertig** adj full, adequate, of high
value. '**Vollwertkost** f natural food.
'**vollzählig** [-tsɛːlɪç] adj **1. ~ sein** be present in full number; **~ erscheinen** assemble in full strength. **2.** complete.
voll'ziehen (irr, insep, no -ge-, h, → **zie-**
hen) **I** v/t a) execute, carry out, b) perform (*marriage ceremony etc*), c) con-
summate (*marriage*): *~de Gewalt* executive. **II** sich **~** take place. **Voll'zieher**
m (-s; -) executor. **Voll'ziehung** f (-; no
pl), **Voll'zug** m (-[e]s; no pl) execution,
performance (*of marriage ceremony
etc*), consummation (*of marriage*).
Voll'zugs|anstalt f penal institution,
prison. **~beamte** m prison officer.
Volontär [volɔn'tɛːr] m (-s; -e), **Volon-**

'**tärin** f (-; -nen) unpaid trainee.
Volt [vɔlt] n (-, -[e]s; -) ⚡ volt.
'**Voltmeter** n (-s; -) voltmeter.
Volumen [vo'luːmən] n (-s; -, -mina) volume, a. capacity. **voluminös** [volumi-
'nøːs] adj voluminous.
von [fɔn] prep **1.** from: *~ der Seite* from
the side; *~ morgen an* from (*adm.* as of)
tomorrow. **2.** a) of, b) by: *e-e Freundin
~ ihr* a friend of hers; *ein Bild ~ Picas-*
so a painting by Picasso; *sie nahm ~
dem Kuchen* she had some of the cake;
9 ~ 10 Leuten 9 out of (*or* in) 10 people;
→ *selbst* I. **3.** of: *ein Mann ~ Bildung* a
man of culture. **4.** of, about: *ich habe ~
ihm gehört* I have heard of him; *weißt
du ~ der Sache?* do you know about
this affair?
vonein'ander adv from each other.
vonstatten [fɔn'ʃtatən] adv **~ gehen** a)
take place, b) go, proceed (*well etc*).
vor [foːr] prep **1.** a) before, in front (*dat*
of), b) outside, c) in the presence (*dat*
of): *~ der Klasse* in front of the class; *~
der Tür* at the door; *~ dem Gesetz*
before the law. **2.** before, ago: *~ 10
Jahren (ein paar Tagen)* ten years (a
few days) ago; *~ dem Essen* before
dinner; *5 Minuten ~ 12* five minutes to
(*Am.* of) 12, *fig.* at the eleventh hour;
j-m liegen be (*or* lie) ahead of s.o.; *et.~
sich haben* have s.th. ahead of one, *b.s.*
be in for s.th.; *das haben wir noch ~
uns* that's still to come. **3.** for, with: *~
Angst* for fear; *~ Kälte* with cold; *~
lauter Arbeit* for all the work. **4.** above,
before: *~ allem, ~ allen Dingen* above
all. **5.** from, against; → **warnen**.
vor'ab adv **1.** first, to begin with. **2.** in
advance.
'**Vorabend** m (am *~* on the) eve (*gen* of).
'**Vorahnung** f premonition, foreboding.
vor'an adv before, at the head, in front:
mit dem Kopf ~ head first.
vor'angehen v/i (irr, sep, -ge-, sn, →
gehen) **1.** lead the way, walk at the
front (*or* head) (*dat* of): *j-n ~ lassen*
let s.o. go first; → **Beispiel**. **2.** precede
(*e-r Sache* s.th.). **3.** fig. get on, get
ahead.
vor'ankommen v/i (irr, sep, -ge-, sn, →
kommen) make progress (*or* headway): *beruflich ~* get on in one's job.
'**Vorankündigung** f previous notice.

'**Voranmeldung** f booking: *teleph.* **Gespräch mit ~** person-to-person call.

vor'antreiben v/t (irr, sep, -ge-, h, → *treiben*) fig. press ahead with.

'**Voranzeige** f preannouncement, *film:* trailer.

'**Vorarbeit** f preparatory work, preparations. '**vorarbeiten** v/i, v/t (sep, h) work in advance: **j-m ~** pave the way for s.o. '**Vorarbeiter** m foreman. '**Vorarbeiterin** f forewoman.

vor'aus¹ adv a. fig. ahead (dat of).

'**voraus²** adv im ~ in advance.

vor'aus|ahnen v/t (sep, h) anticipate. **~berechnen** v/t (sep, h) precalculate. **~bezahlen** v/t (sep, h) prepay, pay s.th. in advance.

Vor'ausexem,plar n advance copy.

vor'aus|fahren v/i (irr, sep, -ge-, sn, → *fahren*) drive ahead (dat of). **~gehen** v/i (irr, sep, -ge-, sn, → *gehen*) **1.** go ahead (dat of). **2.** precede (**e-r Sache** s.th.).

vor'ausgesetzt conj ~, **daß** provided (that), on condition that.

vor'aushaben v/t (irr, sep, -ge-, h, → *haben*) **j-m einige Erfahrung** etc ~ have the advantage of greater experience etc over s.o.

Vor'auskasse f † **gegen ~** cash before delivery.

vor'aus|laufen v/i (irr, sep, -ge-, sn, → *laufen*) run on ahead (dat of). **~planen** v/t, v/i (sep, h) plan s.th. ahead.

Vor'aussage f (-; -n) prediction, forecast. **voraus'sagen** v/t (sep, h) predict, forecast.

vor'ausschauend adj fig. foresighted.

vor'ausschicken v/t (sep, h) **1.** send on ahead. **2. ~, daß** first mention that.

vor'aussehen v/t (irr, sep, -ge-, h, → *sehen*) foresee, expect: **das war vorauszusehen** that was to be expected.

vor'aussetzen v/t (sep, h) **1.** require. **2.** assume, expect: **et. stillschweigend ~** take s.th. for granted; **ich setze diese Tatsachen als bekannt voraus** I assume that these facts are known; → *vorausgesetzt*.

Vor'aussetzung f (-; -en) **1.** condition, prerequisite: **unter der ~, daß** on condition that; **die ~en erfüllen** meet the requirements. **2.** assumption.

Vor'aussicht f (**in weiser ~** with wise) foresight; **aller ~ nach** in all probabili-

ty. **vor'aussichtlich I** adj prospective, expected. **II** adv probably: **er kommt ~ a.** he is likely (or expected) to come.

Vor'auszahlung f advance payment.

'**Vorbau** m (-[e]s; -ten) **1.** front part (of a building). **2.** porch. '**vorbauen** (sep, h) **I** v/t build s.th. in front (or out). **II** v/i fig. take precautions.

'**Vorbedeutung** f (-; -en) omen.

'**Vorbedingung** f (-; -en) condition.

'**Vorbehalt** m (-[e]s; -e) reservation, proviso: **unter dem ~, daß** provided (that); **ohne ~** without reservation.

'**vorbehalten** v/t (irr, sep, h, → *behalten*) reserve: **Änderungen ~** subject to change (without notice); **Irrtümer ~** errors excepted; **alle Rechte ~** all rights reserved; **sich (das Recht) ~ zu** inf reserve the right to inf; **j-m ~ sein** (or **bleiben**) be left to s.o.

'**vorbehaltlich** prep (gen) subject to.

'**vorbehaltlos** adj unreserved.

'**vorbehandeln** v/t (sep, h) pretreat.

vor'bei adv **1. ~ an** (dat) past by: **~!** missed! **2.** a) over, finished, b) gone, c) past: **5 Uhr ~** past five (o'clock); **es ist aus und ~** it's all over and done with.

vor'bei|fahren v/i (irr, sep, -ge-, sn, → *fahren*) **~ an** (dat) drive past. **~gehen** v/i (irr, sep, -ge-, sn, → *gehen*) **1. ~ an** (dat) pass by, fig. miss, pass s.th. by: **im ♀ in** passing. **2.** fig. pass. **3.** shot etc: miss (the mark). **~kommen** v/i (irr, sep, -ge-, sn, → *kommen*) **1. ~ an** (dat) pass by, get past (or round), pass (obstacle etc). **2.** F drop in (bei on). **~lassen** v/t (irr, sep, -ge-, h, → *lassen*) let s.o., s.th. pass. **~mar,schieren** v/i (sep, sn) **~ an** (dat) march past. **~reden** v/i (sep, h) **aneinander ~** talk at cross-purposes; **am Thema ~** miss the point. **~schießen** v/i (irr, sep, -ge-, h, → *schießen*) miss: (**am Tor**) **~** shoot wide. **~ziehen** v/i (irr, sep, -ge-, sn, → *ziehen*) **an j-m ~ 1.** pass (or go past, sports: overtake) s.o. **2.** fig. go through s.o.'s mind.

'**vorbelastet** adj **erblich ~ sein** have a hereditary handicap.

'**Vorbemerkung** f preliminary remark.

'**vorbereiten** v/t (a. **sich ~**) (sep, h) (**für, auf** acc for) prepare, get ready: **sich auf das Schlimmste ~** be prepared for the worst. '**vorbereitend** adj preparatory.

'**Vorbereitung** f (-; -en) preparation

(für, zu, auf *acc* for): **~en treffen** make preparations (*or* prepare) (**für**) for); **in ~** in preparation, being prepared.

'**Vorbericht** *m* preliminary report.

'**vorberuflich** *adj* prevocational.

'**Vorbesprechung** *f* preliminary discussion (*or* talk).

'**vorbestellen** *v/t* (*sep*, h) book *room*, *tickets, etc* in advance, reserve.

'**Vorbestellung** *f* (-; -en) advance booking, reservation.

'**vorbestraft** *adj* **~ sein** have a police record.

'**vorbeugen** (*sep*, h) **I** *v/i* **e-r Sache ~** prevent (*or* guard against) s.th. **II** *sich* **~** bend forward. '**vorbeugend** *adj* preventive, *ꝓ* (*a*. **~es Mittel**) prophylactic.

'**Vorbild** *n* (-[e]s; -er) model, example: **leuchtendes ~** shining example; **sich j-n zum ~ nehmen** follow s.o.'s example; (*j-m*) **ein ~ sein** set an example (to s.o.). '**vorbildlich** *adj* exemplary, model: **er benahm sich ~** he behaved in an exemplary manner.

'**Vorbildung** *f* (-; *no pl*) (previous) training, education(al background).

'**Vorbote** *m* (-n; -n) *fig*. herald (*gen* of).

'**vorbringen** *v/t* (*irr*, *sep*, -ge-, h, → **bringen**) bring forward (*argument etc*), express, state (*wish, claim, etc*), offer (*excuse, reasons, etc*), raise (*objection*), enter (*protest*), *ꝛꝛ* prefer (*charges*).

'**vorchristlich** *adj* pre-Christian.

'**Vordach** *n* canopy.

'**vorda,tieren** *v/t* (*sep*, h) a) postdate, b) antedate.

'**Vordenker** *m* (-s; -) thinker, brain.

vorder ['fɔrdər] *adj* front.

'**Vorder|achse** *f* front axle. **~ansicht** *f* front view. **~bein** *n zo*. foreleg. **~deck** *n* ♧ foredeck. **~fuß** *m zo*. forefoot, front paw (*of cat, dog, etc*).

'**Vordergrund** *m* (-[e]s; *no pl*) foreground: *fig*. **in den ~ rücken** come to the fore; **et. in den ~ stellen** give s.th. special emphasis. '**vordergründig** [-grʏndɪç] *adj* (*adv* on the) surface.

'**Vorder|haus** *n* front building. **~lauf** *m* *hunt*. foreleg. **~mann** *m* (-[e]s; ⸚er) **mein ~** the person in front of me; F **auf ~ bringen** a) *j-n* make s.o. pull his socks up, b) *et*. bring s.th. up to scratch. **~rad** *n* front wheel. **~rad...** front-wheel (*brake, drive, etc*). **~reihe** *f* front row.

~seite *f* front, △, ⊙ *a*. face, obverse (*of coin*). **~sitz** *m* front seat.

vorderst ['fɔrdərst] *adj* front.

'**Vorder|teil** *m, n* front (part). **~tür** *f* front door. **~zahn** *m* front tooth.

'**vordrängen: sich ~** (*sep*, h) a) push forward, b) jump the queue, c) *fig*. put o.s. forward.

'**vordringen** *v/i* (*irr*, *sep*, -ge-, sn, → **dringen**) push (*or* forge) ahead: **~ in** (*acc*) *a*. *fig*. penetrate into; **~ (bis) zu** *a*. *fig*. work one's way through to. '**vordringlich** *adj* urgent, priority (*task etc*): **~ behandelt werden** be given priority.

'**Vordruck** *m* (-[e]s; -e) form, *Am*. blank.

'**vorehelich** *adj* premarital.

'**voreilig** *adj* hasty, rash: **~e Schlüsse ziehen** jump to conclusions. '**Voreiligkeit** *f* (-; *no pl*) rashness, hastiness.

vorein'ander *adv* **1.** one in front of the other. **2. Achtung ~** respect for each other; **sie haben Angst ~** they are afraid of each other.

'**voreingenommen** *adj* (**gegenüber** against) prejudiced, bias(s)ed.

'**Voreingenommenheit** *f* (-; *no pl*) prejudice, bias.

'**vorenthalten** *v/t* (*irr*, *sep*, h, → **enthalten**) *j-m et*. **~** keep s.th. from s.o.

'**Vorentscheidung** *f* preliminary decision.

'**vorerst** *adv* for the time being.

'**Vorex,amen** *n* preliminary examination.

Vorfahr ['fo:rfa:r] *m* (-en; -en) ancestor.

'**vorfahren** *v/i* (*irr*, *sep*, -ge-, sn, → **fahren**) drive up (**vor** *dat* before). '**Vorfahrt** *f* (-; *no pl*) priority, right of way: **~ beachten!** give way! '**vorfahrt(s)berechtigt** *adj* having the right of way.

'**Vorfahrt(s)|schild** *n* sign regulating priority. **~straße** *f* priority road.

'**Vorfall** *m* (-[e]s; ⸚e) **1.** incident, occurrence. **2.** *ꝓ* prolapse. '**vorfallen** *v/i* (*irr*, *sep*, -ge-, sn, → **fallen**) happen, occur.

'**Vorfeld** *n* **1.** ✈ apron. **2.** *fig*. **im ~** (*gen*) in the run-up to.

'**Vorfilm** *m* supporting film.

'**vorfinan,zieren** *v/t* (*sep*, h) prefinance.

'**vorfinden** *v/t* (*irr*, *sep*, -ge-, h, → **finden**) find.

'**Vorfreude** *f* (-; -n) anticipation.

vorfristig ['fo:rfrɪstɪç] *adj and adv* ahead of time.

'**Vorfrühling** m early spring.
'**vorfühlen** v/i (sep, h) **bei j-m ~** sound s.o. out.
'**vorführen** v/t (sep, h) **1.** show, present, model (clothes), demonstrate (machine etc), perform (stunt). **2.** j-n ~ bring s.o. before (**e-m Richter** a judge etc), fig. make s.o. look like a fool.
'**Vorführer** m (-s; -) projectionist.
'**Vorführraum** m projection room.
'**Vorführung** f (-; -en) **1.** showing, presentation, ⊚ demonstration, performance (of stunts etc). **2.** thea. etc show.
'**Vorführwagen** m demonstration car.
'**Vorgabe** f (-; -n) **1.** sports: a) start, handicap, b) stagger. **2.** a) precondition, stipulation, b) target, c) given (or set) data. **3.** → **~zeit** f ⊚ allowed time.
'**Vorgang** m (-[e]s; ¨e) **1.** proceedings, biol., 🐾, ⬚ process. **2.** occurrence, event. **3.** adm. file, record.
Vorgänger ['fo:rgɛŋər] m (-s; -), '**Vorgängerin** f (-; -nen) predecessor.
'**Vorgarten** m front garden, Am. frontyard.
'**vorgeben** v/t (irr, sep, -ge-, h, → **geben**) **1.** sports: give, allow. **2.** allege, claim, pretend. **3.** a) prescribe, stipulate, b) give, set (data etc).
'**Vorgebirge** n foothills.
'**vorgefaßt** adj preconceived.
'**vorgefertigt** adj a. fig. prefabricated.
'**vorgehen** v/i (irr, sep, -ge-, sn, → **gehen**) **1.** go forward, go up (**zu** to), ✕ advance, F lead the way: **m-e Uhr geht (e-e Minute) vor** my watch is (one minute) fast; F **geh schon mal vor!** you go on ahead! **2.** act: ~ **gegen** take action against; **gerichtlich gegen j-n** ~ proceed against s.o.; **hart** ~ **gegen** crack down on. **3.** happen, go on: **was geht hier vor?** what's going on here? **4.** come first, have priority. '**Vorgehen** n (-s) **1.** (line of) action. **2.** procedure.
'**vorgelagert** adj **~e Inseln** offshore islands.
'**Vorgeschichte** f (-; no pl) **1.** prehistory. **2.** (past) history, ⚕ case history.
'**vorgeschichtlich** adj prehistoric.
'**Vorgeschmack** m (-[e]s; no pl) foretaste (**auf** acc, **von** of).
'**Vorgesetzte** m, f (-n; -n) superior.
'**Vorgespräche** pl preliminary talks.
'**vorgestern** adv the day before

yesterday: F **von** ~ → '**vorgestrig** adj **1.** paper etc of the day before yesterday. **2.** fig. antiquated (views etc).
'**vorgreifen** v/i (irr, sep, -ge-, h, → **greifen**) j-m (**e-r Sache**) ~ anticipate s.o. (s.th.). '**Vorgriff** m (**im** ~ in) anticipation (**auf** acc of).
'**vorhaben** v/t (irr, sep, -ge-, h, → **haben**) ~ **zu** inf plan (or have in mind, intend) to inf; **e-e Reise** ~ plan to go on a journey; **was habt ihr heute vor?** what are your plans for today?; **haben Sie heute abend etwas vor?** have you got anything planned for tonight?; **morgen habe ich e-e Menge vor** I've got a lot to do tomorrow; **was hast du damit vor?** what are you going to do with it?; **was hast du jetzt wieder vor?** what are you up to now?
'**Vorhaben** n (-s; -) intention, plan(s), (a. building) project.
'**Vorhalle** f (entrance) hall, vestibule.
'**Vorhalt** m (-[e]s; -e) ♩ suspension.
'**vorhalten** v/t (irr, sep, -ge-, h, → **halten**) j-m et. ~ a) hold s.th. (up) in front of s.o., b) fig. reproach s.o. with s.th.; **mit vorgehaltener Pistole** at pistol point.
'**Vorhaltung** f (-; -en) reproach: j-m ~**en machen** remonstrate with s.o. (**über** acc about).
'**Vorhand** f (-; no pl) tennis etc: forehand.
vorhanden [fo:r'handən] adj existing, available, ⬆ in stock: ~ **sein** exist; **es ist nichts mehr** ~ there is nothing left.
Vor'handensein n (-s) existence.
'**Vorhang** m (-[e]s; ¨e) curtain, drapes.
'**Vorhängeschloß** n padlock.
'**Vorhaut** f anat. foreskin, prepuce.
'**vorher** adv before: **am Abend** ~ the evening before, the previous evening.
vor'herbestimmen v/t (sep, h) a) predetermine, b) predestine.
vor'hergehen v/i (irr, sep, -ge-, sn, → **gehen**) **e-r Sache** ~ precede s.th.
vor'hergehend, vorherig [fo:r'he:rɪç] adj preceding, previous.
'**Vorherrschaft** f (-; no pl) predominance, supremacy.
'**vorherrschen** v/i (sep, h) predominate, prevail. '**vorherrschend** adj predominant, prevailing (opinion etc).
Vor'hersage f (-; -n) prediction, a. 🜂, meteor. forecast.
vor'hersagen v/t (sep, h) predict.

vor'hersehen v/t (irr, sep, -ge-, h, → **sehen**) foresee.

'**vorhin** adv a (short) while ago.

'**Vorhut** f (-; -en) ✕ van(guard).

vorig ['fo:rɪç] adj former, previous: ～e **Woche** last week.

'**vorindustri**‚**ell** adj pre-industrial.

'**Vorjahr** n previous (or last) year.

vorjährig ['fo:rjɛ:rɪç] adj of last year.

'**Vorkämpfer(in** f) m champion.

'**vorkauen** v/t (sep, h) F fig. **j-m et.** ～ spoon-feed s.th. to s.o.

'**Vorkaufsrecht** n right of preemption: **das** ～ **haben** a. have the refusal.

'**Vorkehrung** f (-; -en) measure, precaution: ～**en treffen** a) take measures (or precautions) (**gegen** against), b) make arrangements (**für** for).

'**Vorkenntnisse** pl previous knowledge (or experience).

'**vorknöpfen** v/t (sep, h) F **sich j-n** ～ take s.o. to task.

'**vorkommen** v/i (irr, sep, -ge-, sn, → **kommen**) 1. be found, occur. 2. happen, occur: **so et. ist mir noch nicht vorgekommen!** F well, I never!; **das darf nicht wieder** ～! that must not (or don't let it) happen again! 3. seem: **es kommt mir so vor, als ob** it seems to me as if; **sich dumm** ～ feel silly; **er kommt sich sehr klug vor** he thinks he is very clever; **sie kommt mir bekannt vor** she looks familiar; **das kommt dir nur so vor** you are just imagining it; **es kommt mir merkwürdig vor** it strikes me as (funny) strange. '**Vorkommen** n (-s; -) 1. occurrence. 2. ⚒ deposit(s). '**Vorkommnis** n (-ses; -se) incident: **k-e besonderen** ～**se** no unusual occurrence(s).

'**Vorkriegs...** prewar ...

'**vorladen** v/t (irr, sep, -ge-, h, → **laden**) ⚖ summon. '**Vorladung** f (-; -en) (writ of) summons.

'**Vorlage** f (-; -n) 1. model, pattern: **et. als** ～ **benutzen** copy from s.th. 2. (**gegen** ～ on) presentation (**gen** of). 3. parl. bill. 4. sports: pass.

'**vorlassen** v/t (irr, sep, -ge-, h, → **lassen**) **j-n** ～ a) let s.o. go first, b) let s.o. pass, c) admit s.o. (**bei** to).

'**Vorlauf** m (-[e]s; ⁾e) 1. sports: preliminary heat. 2. ⊙ forward run.

'**Vorläufer** m forerunner (a. skiing).

'**vorläufig I** adj temporary, provisional. **II** adv for the time being.

'**vorlaut** adj pert, cheeky.

'**Vorleben** n (-s; no pl) former life, past.

'**vorlegen** (sep, h) **I** v/t 1. a) (dat to) present, submit, b) produce, show (**document** etc), c) bring out, publish: pol. **den Haushalt** ～ present the budget. 2. put **chain** etc on. 3. F **ein schnelles Tempo** ～ set a fast pace. **II sich** ～ lean forward. '**Vorleger** m (-s; -) rug, mat.

'**vorlehnen: sich** ～ (sep, h) lean forward. '**Vorleistung** f (-; -en) 1. ✝ advance (payment). 2. pol. advance concession.

'**vorlesen** v/t (irr, sep, -ge-, h, → **lesen**) **I** v/t (**j-m**) et. ～ read s.th. (out) (to s.o.). **II** v/i **j-m** ～ read to s.o. (**aus** dat from, out of). '**Vorleser(in** f) m reader.

'**Vorlesung** f (-; -en) (**e-e** ～ **halten** give a) lecture (**über** acc on, **vor** to): ～**en halten** lecture (**über** acc on); ～**en hören** go to lectures. '**Vorlesungsverzeichnis** n program(me Br.) of lectures.

'**vorletzt** adj last but one: ～**e Woche** the week before last.

'**Vorliebe** f (-; -n) (**für** for) preference, special liking: **et. mit** ～ **tun** love doing (or to do) s.th.

'**vorliebnehmen** v/i (irr, sep, -ge-, h, → **nehmen**) make do (**mit** with).

'**vorliegen** v/i (irr, sep, h, → **liegen**) 1. **j-m** ～ lie before s.o.; **der Antrag liegt vor** the application has been submitted; **es liegen k-e Beschwerden vor** there are no complaints; **liegt sonst noch et. vor?** is there anything else? 2. be, exist: **es liegen Gründe vor** there are reasons; **es lag Notwehr vor** it was a case of self-defen/ce (Am. -se); **da muß ein Irrtum** ～ there must be a mistake. 3. be available, be out: **das Ergebnis liegt noch nicht vor** the result is not yet known. '**vorliegend** adj a) existing, present, b) available: **die** ～**en Probleme** the problems at issue; **im** ～**en Falle** in the present case.

'**vorlügen** v/t (irr, sep, -ge-, h, → **lügen**) **j-m et.** ～ lie to s.o.

'**vormachen** v/t (sep, h) F **j-m et.** ～ a) show s.o. how to do s.th., b) fool s.o.; **sich (selbst)** et. ～ fool (F kid) o.s.

'**Vormacht(stellung)** f (-; no pl) supremacy.

vormalig ['fo:rma:lɪç] adj former.

'**vormals** *adv* formerly.

'**Vormarsch** *m* advance: **im** (*or* **auf dem**) **~** advancing, *fig.* on the march.

'**vormerken** *v/t* (*sep*, h) make a note of: **sich ~ lassen** put one's name down (**für** for).

'**Vormieter(in** *f*) *m* previous tenant.

'**vormittag** *adv* **heute** (**gestern**) **~** this (yesterday) morning. '**Vormittag** *m* (-s; -e) (**am ~** in the) morning. '**vormittags** *adv* in the morning: **Montag ~, montags ~** every Monday morning.

'**Vormund** *m* (-[e]s; -e, ⸚er) guardian.

'**Vormundschaft** *f* (-; -en) guardianship.

vorn [fɔrn] *adv* in front, before, ahead: **ganz ~** a) right in front, up front, b) at the beginning; **nach ~** to the front, forward; **von ~** from the front; **~ anfangen** begin at the beginning; (**nochmal**) **von ~ anfangen** start (all over) again; **noch einmal von ~** all over again; **von ~ bis hinten** a) from front to back, b) from beginning to end.

'**Vorname** *m* Christian (*or* first, *esp. Am.* given) name.

vornehm ['fo:rne:m] *adj* **1.** *a. fig.* noble: **~e Gesinnung** high-mindedness. **2.** a) distinguished, b) elegant, fashionable, exclusive: **e-e ~e Dame** a distinguished lady; **e-e ~e Gegend** a fashionable quarter; F **~ tun** give o.s. airs.

'**vornehmen** *v/t* (*irr*, *sep*, -ge-, h, → **nehmen**) **1.** make (*changes etc*), carry out (*work etc*). **2. sich et. ~** plan, make plans for; **sich ~ zu** *inf* decide to *inf*; **sich zuviel ~** take on too much; F **sich j-n ~** take s.o. to task (**wegen** about).

'**Vornehmheit** *f* (-; *no pl*) **1.** nobility. **2.** a) distinction, b) elegance, refinement, exclusiveness: **ihre ~** her distinguished appearance.

'**vornherein** *adv* **von ~** from the start.

vorn'über *adv* forward.

'**Vorort** *m* (-[e]s; -e) suburb. '**Vorort(s)...** suburban (*traffic etc*). **~bewohner(in** *f*) *m* suburbanite. **~zug** *m* suburban (*or* local, commuter) train.

'**Vorplatz** *m* forecourt, square.

'**Vorposten** *m* ✗ outpost.

'**Vorpro,gramm** *n* film: supporting program(me *Br.*). '**vorprogram,mieren** *v/t* (*sep*, h) (pre)program(me *Br.*).

'**Vorprüfung** *f* preliminary examination.

'**vorragen** *v/i* (*sep*, h) project, protrude.

'**Vorrang** *m* (-[e]s; *no pl*) precedence, priority: **den ~ haben vor** (*dat*) take (*or* have) priority (*or* precedence) over.

vorrangig ['fo:rraŋɪç] *adj* priority: **~ behandeln** give s.th. priority treatment.

'**Vorrangstellung** *f* (-; *no pl*) (position of) pre-eminence.

'**Vorrat** *m* (-[e]s; ⸚e) (**an** *dat* of) stock (*a. fig.*), store, supply, provisions, stockpile (*of weapons etc*): **e-n ~ anlegen** lay in a stock (**von** of); **solange der ~ reicht** while stocks last.

vorrätig ['fo:rrɛ:tɪç] *adj* available, ✝ in stock: **nicht (mehr) ~** out of stock; **wir haben ... nicht mehr ~** we are out of ...

'**Vorrats|behälter** *m* storage bin (*or* tank). **~kammer** *f* pantry, larder.

'**Vorraum** *m* anteroom.

'**vorrechnen** *v/t* (*sep*, h) **j-m et. ~** calculate s.th. for s.o.

'**Vorrecht** *n* privilege, prerogative.

'**Vorredner(in** *f*) *m* previous speaker.

'**Vorrichtung** *f* (-; -en) device, F gadget.

'**vorrücken** (*sep*) **I** *v/t* (h) move s.th. forward. **II** *v/i* (sn) move on, ✗ advance.

'**Vorrunde** *f* sports: preliminary round.

'**vorsagen** (*sep*, h) **I** *v/t* **j-m et. ~** tell s.o. s.th. **II** *v/i* **j-m ~** tell s.o. the answer.

'**Vorsai,son** *f* (-; -s) early season.

'**Vorsatz** *m* (-es; ⸚e) resolution, intention, ⚖ (criminal) intent: **mit ~** with intent, wil(l)fully.

vorsätzlich ['fo:rzɛtslɪç] *adj* intentional, deliberate, ⚖ wil(l)ful: **~er Mord** premeditated murder.

'**Vorschau** *f* (-; -en) preview (**auf** *acc* of), *film etc*: trailer(s).

'**Vorschein** *m* **zum ~ bringen** produce, *fig.* bring to light; **zum ~ kommen** come to light, appear, emerge.

'**vorschieben** *v/t* (*irr*, *sep*, -ge-, h, → **schieben**) **1.** push (*or* move) forward, advance. **2.** shoot (*bolt*): → **Riegel** 1. **3.** *fig. et. ~* use s.th. as an excuse; *j-n ~* use s.o. as a dummy.

'**vorschießen** *v/t* (*irr*, *sep*, -ge-, h, → **schießen**) advance (*sum*).

'**Vorschlag** *m* (-[e]s; ⸚e) suggestion, proposal (*a. parl.*), recommendation: **darf ich e-n ~ machen** may I offer a suggestion; **auf ~ von** (*or* **gen**) at the suggestion of. '**vorschlagen** *v/t* (*irr*, *sep*, -ge-, h, → **schlagen**) suggest, propose (*s.o.*): **ich schlage vor, nach**

Hause zu gehen I suggest going (*or* that we go) home.

'**Vorschlußrunde** *f sports*: semifinal.

'**vorschnell** *adj* hasty, rash.

'**vorschreiben** *v/t* (*irr, sep,* -ge-, h, → *schreiben*) *fig.* prescribe, dictate: *ich lasse mir nichts ~!* I won't be dictated to!; *das Gesetz schreibt vor, daß* the law provides that.

'**Vorschrift** *f* (-; -en) a) rule(s), regulation(s), b) direction, instruction: *nach ärztlicher ~* according to doctor's orders; *Dienst nach ~* work-to-rule; *streng nach ~ arbeiten* work to rule.

'**vorschriftsmäßig I** *adj* correct, (as) prescribed, regulation ... **II** *adv* correctly, according to the regulations.

'**vorschriftswidrig** *adj and adv* contrary to the regulations.

'**Vorschub** *m* (-[e]s; ⸚e) **1.** ⊙ feed. **2.** *fig.* ~ *leisten* (*dat*) encourage (*s.th., s.o.*).

'**Vorschulalter** *n* preschool age.

'**Vorschule** *f* preschool.

'**vorschulisch** *adj* preschool.

'**Vorschuß** *m* (-sses; ⸚sse) advance (payment) (*auf acc* on).

'**vorschützen** *v/t* (*sep,* h) *et.* ~ plead s.th. (as an excuse).

'**vorschweben** *v/i* (*sep,* h) *mir schwebt ... vor* I'm thinking of ...

'**vorsehen** (*irr, sep,* -ge-, h, → *sehen*) **I** *v/t* **1.** plan, schedule: *das war nicht vorgesehen* that was not planned. **2.** intend, designate, *a.* earmark (*funds etc*): *j-n für e-n Posten ~* designate s.o. for a post. **II** *sich ~* be careful, watch out (*vor dat* against).

'**Vorsehung** *f* (-; *no pl*) *die* ~ Providence.

'**vorsetzen** *v/t* (*sep,* h) *j-m et.* ~ set s.th. before s.o., *a. fig.* offer s.o. s.th.

'**Vorsicht** *f* (-; *no pl*) caution, care: *~!* watch out!, careful!, (*inscription*) (handle) with care!; *~, Stufe!* mind the step!; *zur ~* as a precaution; *mit äußerster ~* with the utmost caution.

'**vorsichtig** *adj* cautious, careful: *~e Schätzung* conservative estimate; (*sei*) *~!* be careful!; *~ fahren* drive carefully.

'**vorsichtshalber** *adv* as a precaution.

'**Vorsichtsmaßnahme** *f* precaution(ary measure): *~n treffen* take precautions.

'**Vorsilbe** *f ling.* prefix.

'**vorsingen** (*irr, sep,* -ge-, h, → *singen*) **I** *v/t j-m et.* ~ sing s.th. to s.o. **II** *v/i*

audition (*bei* with): *j-n ~ lassen* audition s.o.

'**vorsintflutlich** *adj* F *fig.* antediluvian.

'**Vorsitz** *m* (-es; *no pl*) chair(manship), presidency: *bei e-r Versammlung den ~ haben* (*or* *führen*) preside over (*or* chair, be in the chair at) a meeting; *unter dem ~ von ...* with ... in the chair.

'**Vorsitzende** *m, f* (-n; -n) **1.** president, chairman (chairwoman), chairperson. **2.** ⚖ presiding judge.

'**Vorsorge** *f* (-; *no pl*) provision, precaution: *~ treffen* take precautions (*daß* that), provide (*gegen* against).

'**vorsorgen** *v/i* (*sep,* h) (*für* for) make provisions, provide.

'**Vorsorgeuntersuchung** *f* (preventive) medical checkup.

'**vorsorglich** [-zɔrklɪç] **I** *adj* precautionary. **II** *adv* as a precaution.

'**Vorspann** *m* (-[e]s; -e) **1.** introduction. **2.** *film:* a) (title and) credits, b) pre-title sequence.

'**Vorspeise** *f* hors d'oeuvre, starter: *als ~ a.* for starters.

'**Vorspiegelung** *f* (-; -en) preten/ce (*Am.* -se): *unter ~ falscher Tatsachen* under false preten/ces (*Am.* -ses).

'**Vorspiel** *n* (-[e]s; -e) **1.** (*zu* to) *a. fig.* a) ♪ prelude, b) *thea.* curtain-raiser, prolog(ue *Br.*). **2.** foreplay. '**vorspielen** (*sep,* h) **I** *v/t* play: *j-m et.* ~ play s.th. to s.o., *fig.* put on an act for s.o.'s benefit. **II** *v/i* a) play, b) audition (*bei* with): *j-n ~ lassen* audition s.o.

'**vorsprechen** (*irr, sep,* -ge-, h, → *sprechen*) **I** *v/t* **1.** *j-m et.* ~ pronounce s.th. for s.o. to repeat. **2.** recite. **II** *v/i* **3.** *thea.* audition (*bei* with): *j-n ~ lassen* audition s.o. **4.** call (*bei* at).

'**vorspringen** *v/i* (*irr, sep,* -ge-, sn, → *springen*) **1.** leap forward. **2.** project, jut (out). '**vorspringend** *adj* projecting, jutting, prominent (*a.* nose, chin).

'**Vorsprung** *m* (-[e]s; ⸚e) **1.** △ projection, ledge. **2.** *a. sports:* a) start, b) lead: *ich gebe dir 5 Minuten ~* I'll give you a start of five minutes; *sein ~ beträgt 30 Sekunden* he has a lead of 30 seconds (*vor dat* on); *mit großem ~* by a wide margin; *e-n ~ haben a. fig.* be ahead (*vor dat* of).

'**Vorstadt** *f* suburb.

'**Vorstadtbewohner** *m* suburbanite.

'**vorstädtisch** *adj* suburban.

'**Vorstand** *m* (-[e]s; ⁓e) **1.** ✝ board of directors: *im ⁓ sitzen* be on the board. **2.** managing committee (*of club etc*) **3.** chairman, *Am.* chief executive.

'**Vorstands|e|tage** *f* executive floor. **⁓mitglied** *n* member of the board. **⁓sitzung** *f* board meeting. **⁓vorsitzende** *m, f* (-n; -n) chairman (chairwoman) (of the board), *Am.* chief executive. **⁓wahl** *f* board elections.

'**vorstehen** *v/i* (*irr, sep, -ge-, h, → stehen*) **1.** project, jut out, *eyes*: protrude. **2.** (*dat*) direct, be at the head of, run (*institute etc*). '**vorstehend** *adj* projecting, protruding (*a. eyes, teeth, etc*): ⁓e **Zähne** *a.* bucketeeth. '**Vorsteher** *m* (-s; -) manager, director, head.

'**Vorsteherdrüse** *f anat.* prostate gland.

'**vorstellbar** *adj* conceivable, imaginable. '**vorstellen** (*sep, h*) **I** *v/t* **1.** move *s.th.* forward. **2.** put *clock etc* forward. **3.** *j-n j-m ⁓* introduce s.o. to s.o.: *darf ich Ihnen Herrn X ⁓?* may I introduce you to Mr X, I'd like you to meet Mr X. **4.** ✝ present, introduce (*new product*). **5.** a) represent, b) mean: *was soll das Bild ⁓?* what's that picture supposed to be?; F *er stellt etwas vor* he's quite somebody. **6.** *sich et. ⁓* fancy, imagine, picture, have *s.th.* in mind; F *stell dir vor!* fancy!, just imagine!; *du kannst dir gar nicht ⁓ ...* you've no idea ...; *man kann sich ihre Enttäuschung ⁓* you can picture their disappointment; *so stelle ich mir ... vor* that's my idea of ...; *stellt euch das nicht so leicht vor!* don't think it's so easy; *darunter kann ich mir nichts ⁓* it doesn't mean anything to me. **II** *sich ⁓* introduce o.s. ([*bei*] *j-m* to s.o.), *bei* go for an interview with *a firm etc*.

'**Vorstellung** *f* (-; -en) **1.** introduction, ✝ *a.* presentation (*of new product*). **2.** interview (*bei* with). **3.** *thea. etc* performance, show, *film*: showing. **4.** idea, notion, concept: *falsche ⁓* wrong idea, misconception; *sich e-e ⁓ machen* form an idea (*or* a picture) (*von* of); F *du machst dir k-e ⁓!* you've no idea; *das entspricht nicht m-n ⁓en* that's not what I expected (*or* had in mind). **5.** imagination.

'**Vorstellungsgespräch** *n* interview.

'**Vorstopper** *m* (-s; -) *soccer*: centre (*Am.* center) half.

'**Vorstoß** *m* (-es; ⁓e) ✕ advance, *sports*: attack (*a. fig.*), *pol. or fig.* démarche.

'**vorstoßen** *v/i* (*irr, sep, -ge-, sn, → stoßen*) ✕ advance, *sports*: attack: *fig. ⁓ in* (*acc*) venture into; *⁓ zu* reach.

'**Vorstrafe** *f* previous conviction. '**Vorstrafen(re)gister** *n*) *pl* police record.

'**vorstrecken** *v/t* (*sep, h*) **1.** stretch out, stick *one's head* out. **2.** advance (*sum*).

'**Vorstufe** *f* preliminary stage.

'**vorstürmen** *v/i* (*sep, sn*) rush forward.

'**vortasten**: *sich ⁓* (*sep, h*) grope one's way (*bis zu* to).

'**vortäuschen** *v/t* (*sep, h*) feign, simulate, fake, pretend: *Interesse ⁓* pretend to be interested.

Vorteil ['fɔrtail] *m* (-s; -e) a) advantage (*a. tennis*), b) benefit: *die Vor- und Nachteile e-r Sache gegeneinander abwägen* consider the pros and cons; *im ⁓ sein* have the advantage (*gegenüber* over); *auf s-n eigenen ⁓ bedacht sein* have an eye to the main chance; *⁓ ziehen aus* profit by; *sich zu s-m ⁓ verändern* change for the better.

'**vorteilhaft** *adj* advantageous, profitable, becoming (*dress etc*): *⁓ aussehen* look attractive; *sich ⁓ auswirken* have a favo(u)rable effect (*auf acc* on).

Vortrag ['fo:rtra:k] *m* (-[e]s; ⁓e) **1.** lecture (*über acc* on): *e-n ⁓ halten* (*vor dat* to) give a lecture (*or* talk), read a paper; F *j-m e-n ⁓ halten* lecture s.o. **2.** performance, recitation (*of poetry*), ♪ recital, execution. **3.** ✝ carryover.

'**vortragen** *v/t* (*irr, sep, -ge-, h, → tragen*) **1.** state, present, express. **2.** perform, play, sing, recite. **3.** ✝ carry forward. '**Vortragende** *m, f* (-n; -n) **1.** lecturer, speaker. ♪ *etc* performer.

'**Vortragsreihe** *f* series of lectures.

'**Vortragsreise** *f* lecture tour.

'**vortreten** *v/i* (*irr, sep, -ge-, sn, → treten*) **1.** step (*or* come) forward. **2.** protrude.

'**Vortritt** *m* (-[e]s; *no pl*) (*den ⁓ haben* take) precedence (*vor dat* over): *j-m den ⁓ lassen* let s.o. go first.

vor'übergehen *adv* ⁓ over.

vor'übergehen *v/i* (*irr, sep, -ge-, sn, → gehen*) pass, *fig. a.* go away. **vor'über-**

gehend I *adj* temporary, passing. **II** *adv* temporarily, for a short time.

'**Vorübung** *f* preliminary exercise.

'**Voruntersuchung** *f* ɪ̈ɪ̈, ⚕ preliminary examination.

'**Vorurteil** *n* prejudice: **~e haben gegen** be prejudiced against.

'**vorurteilsfrei**, '**vorurteilslos** *adj* unprejudiced, unbias(s)ed.

'**Vorvergangenheit** *f* ling. past perfect, pluperfect.

'**Vorverhandlung** *f* **1.** ɪ̈ɪ̈ preliminary trial. **2.** *pl* ~en *f*, pol. preliminary negotiations, preliminaries.

'**Vorverkauf** *m* (-[e]s; *no pl*) advance sale (*thea.* booking): **im ~ besorgen** buy (*or* book) *tickets* in advance.

'**Vorverkaufskasse** *f*, '**Vorverkaufsstelle** *f* (advance) booking office.

'**vorverlegen** *v/t* (*sep*, h) advance.

'**Vorverstärker** *m* ⚡ pre-amplifier.

'**Vorvertrag** *m* precontract.

'**vorvorig** *adj the year etc* before last.

'**Vorwahl** *f* **1.** *pol.* preliminary election, *Am.* primary (election). **2.** → '**Vorwählnummer** *f* teleph. dialling (*Am.* area) code.

'**Vorwand** *m* (-[e]s; ⁓e) pretext, excuse: **unter dem ~ von** (*or* **daß**) on the pretext of (*or* that).

'**vorwärmen** *v/t* (*sep*, h) warm, preheat.

'**Vorwarnung** *f* (advance) warning.

'**vorwärts** *adv* forward, onward, on: **~!** let's go!

'**Vorwärtsgang** *m* mot. forward speed.

'**vorwärtsgehen** *v/i* (*irr*, *sep*, -ge-, sn, → **gehen**) F (make) progress.

'**Vorwäsche** *f* (-; -n), '**Vorwaschen** *n* (-s) prewash.

vor'weg *adv* beforehand.

Vor'wegnahme *f* (-; *no pl*) anticipation.

vor'wegnehmen *v/t* (*irr*, *sep*, -ge-, h, → **nehmen**) anticipate: **um es gleich vorwegzunehmen** to come to the point.

'**vorweihnachtlich** *adj* pre-Christmas.

'**Vorweihnachtszeit** *f* Advent season.

'**vorweisen** *v/t* (*irr*, *sep*, h, → **weisen**) produce, show.

'**vorwerfen** *v/t* (*irr*, *sep*, -ge-, h, → **werfen**) **1. e-m Tier et. ~** throw s.th. to an

animal. **2. j-m Faulheit** *etc* **~** reproach s.o. with laziness (*or* for being lazy *etc*): **ich habe mir nichts vorzuwerfen** I have nothing to blame myself for.

'**vorwiegend** *adv* predominantly, mainly, chiefly: **~ sonnig** mainly sunny.

'**Vorwort** *n* (-[e]s; -e) foreword, preface.

'**Vorwurf** *m* (-[e]s; ⁓e) reproach: **j-m Vorwürfe machen** reproach s.o. (**wegen** for). '**vorwurfsvoll** *adj* reproachful.

'**vorzählen** *v/t* (*sep*, h) **j-m et. ~** count s.th. out to s.o.

'**Vorzeichen** *n* **1.** omen. **2.** ♪ accidental. **3.** A⁺ sign: *fig.* **mit umgekehrtem ~** the other way round.

'**vorzeichnen** *v/t* (*sep*, h) **j-m et. ~** draw (*fig.* trace out) s.th. for s.o.

vorzeigbar ['fo:rtsaɪkbaːr] *adj* presentable. '**vorzeigen** *v/t* (*sep*, h) show.

'**Vorzeit** *f* **der Mensch der ~** prehistoric man; *fig.* **in grauer ~** ages and ages ago.

'**vorzeitig** *adj* premature.

'**Vorzen,sur** *f* precensorship: **e-r ~ unterziehen** precensor.

'**vorziehen** *v/t* (*irr*, *sep*, -ge-, h, → **ziehen**) **1.** pull out. **2. die Vorhänge ~** pull the curtains. **3.** advance (*date etc*), deal with *s.th.* first. **4.** prefer (*dat* to): **es ~ zu** *inf* prefer to *inf*; **j-n ~** favo(u)r s.o.

'**Vorzimmer** *n* anteroom, outer office.

'**Vorzimmerdame** *f* receptionist.

'**Vorzug** *m* (-[e]s; ⁓e) **1.** (**vor** *dat* over) priority, preference. **2.** advantage, merit. **3.** privilege. **vorzüglich** [foːrˈtsyːklɪç] *adj* excellent, exquisite, first-rate.

'**Vorzugs|aktien** *pl* preference shares, *Am.* preferred stock. **~milch** *f* full-cream milk. **~preis** *m* special price.

'**vorzugsweise** *adv* **1.** preferably. **2.** chiefly, mainly.

votieren [voˈtiːrən] *v/i* (h) vote.

Votum ['voːtʊm] *n* (-s; -ten, -ta) vote.

Voyeur [vŏaˈjøːr] *m* (-s; -e) voyeur.

vulgär [vʊlˈɡɛːr] *adj* vulgar.

Vulkan [vʊlˈkaːn] *m* (-s; -e) volcano. **~ausbruch** *m* (volcanic) eruption.

vul'kanisch *adj geol.* volcanic.

vulkanisieren [vʊlkaniˈziːrən] *v/t* (h) Ⓞ vulcanize, *mot. a.* recap.

W

W, w [ve:] *n* (-; -) W, w.

Waage ['va:gə] *f* (-; -n) **1.** (pair of) scales, balance (*a. fig.*): *fig.* **sich die ~ halten** balance each other; → **Zünglein. 2.** *astr.* (**er ist** [e-e] **~** he is [a]) Libra.

'waagerecht *adj* horizontal.

Waagschale ['va:k-] *f* scale: *fig.* **in die ~ werfen** bring *s.th.* to bear; **s-e Worte auf die ~ legen** weigh one's words.

wabb(e)lig ['vab(ə)lıç] *adj* flabby.

wabbeln ['vabəln] *v/i* (h) wobble.

Wabe ['va:bə] *f* (-; -n) honeycomb.

'Wabenhonig *m* comb honey.

wach [vax] *adj* **1.** awake: **~ werden** *a. fig.* wake up, awake; **~ liegen** lie awake. **2.** *fig.* alert, wide-awake.

'Wachablösung *f* **1.** ✗ changing of the guard. **2.** *fig. pol.* change of power.

Wache ['vaxə] *f* (-; -n) **1.** guard: **~ halten** → **wachen** 2. **2.** ✗ a) guard, sentry, b) guardroom: **auf ~** on guard, on duty; **~ stehen**, F **~ schieben** be on guard. **3.** police station.

'wachen *v/i* (h) **1. ~ über** (*acc*) watch (over), guard; **darüber ~, daß** see (to it) that. **2. bei j-m ~** sit up with *s.o.*

'Wachhabende *m* (-n; -n) ✗ commander of the guard.

'wachhalten *v/t* (*irr, sep*, -ge-, h, → **halten**) *fig. et.* **~** keep *s.th.* alive.

'Wachhund *m a. fig.* watchdog.

'Wachmannschaft *f* guard.

Wacholder [va'xɔldər] *m* (-s; -) **1.** ♣ juniper. **2.** → **Wa'cholderschnaps** *m* gin.

'Wachposten *m* guard, ✗ *a.* sentry.

'wachrufen *v/t* (*irr, sep*, -ge-, h, → **rufen**) rouse, bring back (*memories etc*).

~rütteln *v/t* (*sep*, h) rouse (*aus* from).

Wachs [vaks] *n* (-es; -e) wax.

'Wachsabdruck *m* wax impression.

'wachsam *adj* watchful, vigilant: **ein ~es Auge haben auf** (*acc*) keep a sharp eye on. **'Wachsamkeit** *f* (-; *no pl*) vigilance, watchfulness.

wachsen[1] ['vaksən] *v/i* (wuchs, gewachsen, sn) grow, *fig. a.* increase (*an dat* in): → **Bart** 1, **gewachsen** II.

'wachsen[2] *v/t* (h) wax (*a.* ski).

'Wachsfi₁gur *f* wax figure, *pl a.* waxwork. **~fi₁gurenkabi₁nett** *n* waxworks.

~kerze *f* wax candle. **~tuch** *n* oilcloth.

'Wachstum *n* (-s; *no pl*) growth (*a.* ✝), *fig. a.* increase, expansion: (*noch*) **im ~ begriffen** still growing.

'wachstums₁fördernd *adj* **1.** ♣ growth-inducing. **2.** ♀ growth-stimulating. **~hemmend** *adj* growth-retarding.

'Wachstums₁indu₁strie *f* growth industry. **~rate** *f* rate of (economic) growth.

'wachs₁weich *adj* **1.** *a. fig.* (as) soft as wax. **2.** medium boiled (*egg*).

Wachtel ['vaxtəl] *f* (-; -n) *zo.* quail.

Wächter ['vεçtər] *m* (-s; -) a) guard, b) attendant, c) watchman.

'Wachtraum *m* daydream.

'Wach(t)turm *m* watchtower.

'Wach- und Schließgesellschaft *f* Security Corps.

wack(e)lig ['vak(ə)lıç] *adj* shaky, wobbly (*a.* F *fig.*), rickety (*chair etc*), loose (*tooth, screw*): *a. fig.* **auf ~en Beinen stehen** stand on shaky legs, be shaky.

'Wackelkon₁takt *m* ⚡ loose contact.

'wackeln ['vakəln] *v/i* (h) a) wobble, *tooth, screw, etc*: *a.* be loose, b) totter, F *fig. government, job, etc*: be shaky: **mit den Ohren ~** waggle one's ears.

Wade ['va:də] *f* (-; -n) calf.

'Wadenkrampf *m* cramp in the leg.

Waffe ['vafə] *f* (-; -n) weapon (*a. fig.*), *pl* arms: **~n tragen** bear arms; **j-n mit s-n eigenen ~n schlagen** beat *s.o.* at his own game.

Waffel ['vafəl] *f* (-; -n) waffle, wafer.

'Waffeleisen *n* waffle iron.

'Waffen₁besitz *m* possession of firearms. **~fa₁brik** *f* arms factory. **~gattung** *f* arm, branch (of the service). **~gewalt** *f* (*mit ~* by) force of arms. **~handel** *m* arms trade. **~händler** *m* arms dealer. **~kammer** *f* armo(u)ry. **~lager** *n* **1.** ✗ ordnance depot. **2.** cache. **~lieferung** *f* supply of arms.

'waffenlos *adj* weaponless, unarmed.

'Waffen₁ruhe *f* cease-fire. **~schein** *m* firearm certificate, *Am.* gun license. **~schmuggel** *m* gun-running. **~stillstand** *m* armistice, cease-fire, truce (*a. fig.*). **~sy₁stem** *n* weapons system.

'wagemutig *adj* daring, bold.

wagen ['va:gən] *v/t* (h) venture (*a. sich ~*), risk, dare: *es ~ take* the plunge; *es ~ mit* try; *sich ~ an* (*acc*) venture on *a task etc*; *wie können Sie es ~* (, *das zu sagen*)? how dare you (say that)?; *wer nicht wagt, der nicht gewinnt* nothing ventured, nothing gained.

'Wagen *m* (-s; -) **1.** a) vehicle, b) car, c) lorry, *Am.* truck, d) van. **2.** wag(g)on, cart: F *j-m an den ~ fahren* tread on s.o.'s toes. **3.** 🚃 carriage, *Am.* car. **4.** *astr. der Große ~* the Great Bear, *Am.* the Big Dipper. **5.** *typewriter:* carriage. **~heber** *m mot.* jack. **~ko̱lonne** *f* column of cars. **~ladung** *f* (cart)load, *Am.* truckload, 🚃 waggonload, *Am.* carload. **~pflege** *f* (car) maintenance. **~typ** *m* model. **~wäsche** *f* (-; -n) car wash.

Waggon [va'gõ:, va'gɔ̃] *m* (-s; -s) **1.** a) (railway) carriage, *Am.* (railroad) car, b) goods waggon, *Am.* freight car. **2.** waggonload, *Am.* carload.

waghalsig ['va:khalziç] *adj* daring.

Wagnis ['va:knıs] *n* (-ses; -se) risk.

Wahl [va:l] *f* (-; -en) **1.** a) choice, alternative, b) selection: ✝ *erste ~* top quality; *zweite ~* second-rate quality, seconds; *die ~ haben* have one's choice; *k-e* (*andere*) ~ *haben* have no choice (*or* alternative) (*als* but); *vor der ~ stehen zu inf* be faced with the choice of *ger*; *s-e ~ treffen* make one's choice; *e-e gute ~ treffen* choose well; *wer die ~ hat, hat die Qual* the wider the choice, the greater the trouble. **2.** *pol.* a) election, b) poll(ing): **~en abhalten** hold elections; *zur ~ gehen* go to the polls; *in die engere ~ kommen* be short-listed.

'Wahlalter *n* voting age.

'wählbar *adj* eligible (for election).

'wahlberechtigt *adj* entitled to vote.

'Wahl|beteiligung *f* turnout (at the election): *hohe* (*geringe*) ~ heavy (poor) polling. **~bezirk** *m* ward, constituency, *Am.* electoral district.

wählen ['vɛ:lən] (h) **I** *v/t* **1.** choose, select. **2.** *esp. pol.* elect, vote for: *j-n zum Präsidenten ~* elect s.o. president; ✝ *j-n in den Vorstand ~* vote s.o. on the board. **3.** *teleph.* dial. **II** *v/i* **4.** choose, make one's choice. **5.** *pol.* vote, (*a. ~ gehen*) go to the polls.

'Wähler *m* (-s; -) voter.

'Wahlergebnis *n* election results.

'Wählerin *f* (-; -nen) voter.

'Wählerinitia,tive *f* voters' initiative.

'wählerisch *adj* particular, choosy: *iro. nicht gerade ~* not too particular (*in dat, mit* about).

'Wählerschaft *f* (-; *no pl*) a) electorate, b) constituency, voters.

'Wahl|fach *n ped.* optional subject, *Am. a.* elective. **2frei** *adj ped.* optional, *Am.* elective. **~gang** *m* (*im ersten ~* at the first) ballot. **~geschenk** *n* campaign promise. **~heimat** *f* adopted country. **~helfer**(**in** *f*) *m* campaign assistant. **~jahr** *n* election year. **~ka,bine** *f* polling booth. **~kampf** *m* electoral battle, election campaign. **~kreis** *m* → *Wahlbezirk*. **~leiter** *m* returning officer. **~liste** *f* electoral register. **~lo,kal** *n* polling station. **~lokomo,tive** *f* F *fig.* (great) vote-catcher.

'wahllos *adj* indiscriminate.

'Wahl|niederlage *f* election defeat. **~ordnung** *f* election regulations. **~pflicht** *f* electoral duty. **~pla,kat** *n* election poster. **~pro,gramm** *n* election platform. **~recht** *n* (-[e]s; *no pl*) a) right to vote, franchise, b) eligibility: *allgemeines ~* universal suffrage. **~rede** *f* electoral address. **~redner** *m* election speaker.

'Wählscheibe *f teleph.* dial.

'Wahl|sieg *m* election victory. **~spende** *f* election (campaign) contribution. **~spruch** *m* motto. **~stimme** *f* vote. **~tag** *m* election day. **~urne** *f* ballot box: *zur ~ gehen* go to the polls. **~versammlung** *f* election meeting. **~versprechen** *n* campaign promise. **~vorschlag** *m* election proposal.

'wahlweise *adv* alternatively: *es gab ~ Fisch oder Fleisch* there was a choice of fish or meat.

Wahn [va:n] *m* (-[e]s; *no pl*) delusion, mania: *in e-m ~ befangen sein* be under a delusion. **~bild** *n* hallucination.

'Wahnsinn *m* (-[e]s; *no pl*) *a.* F *fig.* insanity, madness. **'wahnsinnig I** *adj* **1.** mad, insane. **2.** F *fig.* a) mad, crazy, b) terrible (*shock, pain, etc*), c) terrific. **II** *adv* F *fig.* terribly, awfully: *~ verliebt* madly in love. **'Wahnsinnige** *m, f* (-n; -n) lunatic, madman (madwoman).

'Wahnvorstellung *f* delusion, idée fixe.

'wahnwitzig *adj* mad, crazy.

wahr [va:r] *adj* true, real, genuine: *ein ~er Freund* a true friend; *~e Liebe* true love; *ein ~es Wunder* a real wonder; *so ~ ich lebe!* as sure as I live!; *so ~ mir Gott helfe!* so help me God!; *~ werden* come true; F *das darf doch nicht ~ sein!* I can't believe it!; *das ist nicht das Wahre* that's not the real thing.

wahren ['va:rən] *v/t* (h) preserve, maintain, keep (*a. secret*), protect, safeguard (*interests*): → *Form* 1, *Schein*[1] 2.

während ['vɛːrənt] I *prep* (*gen*) during, in the course of. II *conj* while.

'**wahrhaben**: *nicht ~ wollen* refuse to believe.

'**wahrhaft** I *adj* true, real. II *adv* → **wahr'haftig** *adv* truly, really, indeed.

'**Wahrheit** *f* (-; -en) truth: *in ~* in fact, in reality; *um die ~ zu sagen* to tell the truth; F *j-m mal die ~ sagen* give s.o. a piece of one's mind.

'**wahrheitsgemäß**, '**wahrheitsgetreu** I *adj* truthful, true. II *adv* truthfully. '**Wahrheitsliebe** *f* veracity. '**wahrheitsliebend** *adj* truthful, veracious.

'**wahrlich** *adv* truly, *bibl.* verily.

'**wahrnehmbar** *adj* perceptible, noticeable. '**wahrnehmen** *v/t* (*irr, sep, -ge-, h, → nehmen*) 1. perceive, notice, see, *a.* hear. 2. use, seize (*opportunity etc*), protect, safeguard (*interests etc*), observe (*deadline*). '**Wahrnehmung** *f* (-; -en) 1. a) (*sinnliche ~* sense) perception, b) observation. 2. *j-n mit der ~ s-r Geschäfte* (*Interessen*) *beauftragen* entrust s.o. with the care of one's business (the safeguarding of one's interests). '**Wahrnehmungsvermögen** *n* (-s; *no pl*) perceptive faculty.

'**wahrsagen** (*sep or insep*, h) I *v/t* prophesy. II *v/i* tell fortunes: *j-m ~* tell s.o.'s fortune. '**Wahrsager** *m* (-s; -), '**Wahrsagerin** *f* (-; -nen) fortune-teller.

wahrscheinlich [va:r'ʃaɪnlç] I *adj* probable, likely. II *adv* probably: *er wird ~ nicht kommen* he's not likely to come. **Wahr'scheinlichkeit** *f* (-; -en) (*aller ~ nach* in all) probability (*or* likelihood). **Wahr'scheinlichkeitsrechnung** *f* theory of probabilities.

'**Wahrung** *f* (-; *no pl*) maintenance, protection, safeguarding (*of interests etc*). **Währung** ['vɛːrʊŋ] *f* (-; -en) currency. '**Währungs|abkommen** *n* monetary agreement. **~block** *m* monetary bloc. **~einheit** *f* unit of currency. **~krise** *f* monetary crisis. **~poli,tik** *f* monetary policy. **~re,form** *f* currency reform. **~sy,stem** *n* monetary system. **~uni,on** *f* monetary union.

'**Wahrzeichen** *n* 1. symbol, emblem. 2. landmark.

Waise ['vaɪzə] *f* (-; -n) orphan: (*zur*) *~ werden* be orphaned.

'**Waisen|haus** *n* orphanage. **~kind** *n* orphan. **~knabe** *m fig. gegen ihn sind wir die reinsten ~n* we are mere babes compared to him.

Wal [va:l] *m* (-[e]s; -e) *zo.* whale.

Wald [valt] *m* (-[e]s; ⁻er) wood, forest (*a. fig.*): *er sieht den ~ vor lauter Bäumen nicht* he can't see the wood for the trees. **~bestand** *m* forest stand. **~brand** *m* forest fire. **~gebiet** *n*, **~gegend** *f* wooded area, woodland.

'**Waldhorn** *n* (-[e]s; ⁻er) ♪ French horn.

waldig ['valdç] *adj* wooded.

'**Wald|lauf** *m* cross-country race. **~meister** *m* ♀ woodruff. **~rand** *m* (*am ~* at *or* on the) edge of the forest. **~schäden** *pl* forest damage. **~sterben** *n* dying of forests.

Waldung ['valdʊŋ] *f* (-; -en) wood(land), forest.

'**Walfang** *m* (-[e]s; *no pl*) whaling. '**Walfänger** *m* (-s; -) whaler (*a. ship*).

'**Walfisch** *m* F whale.

Waliser [va'li:zər] *m* (-s; -) Welshman: *die ~* the Welsh. **Wa'liserin** *f* (-; -nen) Welshwoman. **wa'lisisch** *adj* Welsh.

walken ['valkən] *v/t* (h) 1. mill. 2. knead.

Wall [val] *m* (-[e]s; ⁻e) *a. fig.* rampart.

Wallach ['valax] *m* (-[e]s; -e) *zo.* gelding.

'**wallfahren** *v/i* (*insep*, sn) (go on a) pilgrimage. '**Wallfahrer** *m* (-s; -), '**Wallfahrerin** *f* (-; -nen) pilgrim. '**Wallfahrt** *f* (-; -en) pilgrimage. '**Wallfahrtsort** *m* (-[e]s; -e) place of pilgrimage.

'**Wallung** *f* (-; -en) (✿ hot) flush: *fig. j-n in ~ bringen* make s.o.'s blood boil.

Walnuß ['valnʊs] *f* (-; ⁻sse) ♀ walnut.

Walroß ['valrɔs] *n* (-sses; -sse) *zo.* walrus.

walten ['valtən] *v/i* (h) be at work: *s-s Amtes ~* do one's duty; → *schalten* 3.

'**Walzblech** *n* rolled steel plate.

Walze ['valtsə] *f* (-; -n) 1. ✿ roll, roller, cylinder. 2. *typewriter*: platen. 3. *barrel organ*: barrel. '**walzen** *v/t* (h) ✿ roll.

wälzen ['vɛltsən] (h) **I** v/t **1.** roll. **2.** F pore over *books etc*, turn *problem etc* over in one's mind. **II** sich ~ roll, a. wallow (*in mud etc*); **sich hin und her ~** toss about, toss and turn.

'**walzenförmig** adj cylindrical.

'**Walzer** m (-s; -) (a. ~ **tanzen**) waltz.

'**Wälzer** m (-s; -) F huge tome.

'**Walzer|takt** m waltz time.

'**Walz|maschine** f rolling machine. ~**stahl** m rolled steel. ~**straße** f (rolling) mill train. ~**werk** n (rolling) mill.

Wampe ['vampə] f (-; -n) F paunch.

wand [vant] pret of **winden**.

Wand f (-; ⸚e) a) wall (a. fig.), b) side, c) (rock) face: ~ **an** ~ wall to wall; **in s-n vier Wänden** within one's own four walls; F fig. **j-n an die ~ drücken** drive s.o. to the wall; **j-n an die ~ spielen** play s.o. into the ground; F **j-n an die ~ stellen** execute s.o.; **es ist, um die Wände hochzugehen** it's enough to drive you mad.

Wandale [van'da:lə] m (-n; -n) *hist.* Vandal, *fig.* vandal. **Wandalismus** [vanda'lɪsmʊs] m (-; *no pl*) vandalism.

'**Wandbehang** m wall hanging, tapestry.

'**Wandel** ['vandəl] m (-s; *no pl*) change: **der ~ der Zeit** the changing times; **sich im ~ befinden** be changing.

'**wandelbar** adj changeable.

'**Wandelhalle** f at spa: pump room.

'**wandeln** v/t (a. **sich ~**) (h) change.

'**Wander|ausstellung** f touring exhibition. ~**büche,rei** f travel(l)ing library, *Am. a.* bookmobile. ~**bühne** f touring company. ~**düne** f shifting sand dune.

'**Wanderer** m (-s; -), '**Wanderin** f (-; -nen) wanderer, hiker, rambler.

'**Wanderkarte** f hiking map.

'**Wanderleben** n (-s; *no pl*) vagrant life.

wandern ['vandərn] v/i (sn) walk, hike, tramp, a. fig. thoughts etc: wander, a. zo. migrate: ~ **gehen** go hiking; F fig. ~ **in** (acc) end up in, go (in)to. '**Wandern** n (-s) hiking (etc), zo. migration.

'**Wanderpo,kal** m challenge cup.

'**Wanderpreis** m challenge trophy.

'**Wanderschaft** f (-; *no pl*) travels: **auf ~ sein** (**gehen**) be on (take) to the road.

'**Wandertag** m ped. school outing.

'**Wanderung** f (-; -en) walking tour, hike, ramble, a. zo. migration.

'**Wanderverein** m rambling club.

'**Wanderweg** m foothpath.

'**Wand|gemälde** n mural. ~**ka,lender** m wall calendar. ~**karte** f wall map.

'**Wandler** ['vandlər] m (-s; -) converter.

'**Wandleuchte** f wall lamp.

'**Wandlung** f (-; -en) change.

'**wandlungsfähig** adj flexible, versatile.

'**Wand|male,rei** f a) mural painting, b) mural. ~**schrank** m built-in cupboard (*Am.* closet). ~**spiegel** m wall mirror. ~**tafel** f blackboard.

wandte ['vantə] pret of **wenden**.

Wange ['vaŋə] f (-; -n) a. ⊗ cheek: ~ **an** ~ cheek to cheek.

wankelmütig ['vaŋkəlmy:tɪç] adj fickle.

wanken ['vaŋkən] v/i (h) **1.** ~ **machen** 1. 2. fig. falter, waver: **ins Wanken geraten** begin to rock (fig. falter or waver). **3.** → **weichen**[1] 2.

wann [van] adv when, (at) what time: **seit ~?** (for) how long?, since when?; **bis ~?** till when?

Wanne ['vanə] f (-; -n) **1.** tub. **2.** bath(tub). '**Wannenbad** n (tub) bath.

Wanst [vanst] m (-[e]s; ⸚e) F paunch.

Wanze ['vantsə] f (-; -n) **1.** zo. bug, *Am.* bedbug. **2.** F fig. bug: ~**n anbringen in** (dat) bug (a room etc).

Wappen ['vapən] n (-s; -) coat of arms. ~**bild** n heraldic figure. ~**kunde** f (-; *no pl*) heraldry. ~**schild** n escutcheon, blazon. ~**spruch** m heraldic motto. ~**tier** n heraldic animal.

wappnen ['vapnən] **sich ~** (h) (**gegen**) arm (against), prepare (or brace) o.s. (for); → **gewappnet**.

war [va:r] pret of **sein**[1].

warb [varp] pret of **werben**.

Ware ['va:rə] f (-; -n) product, article, *coll. a.* merchandise, *pl a.* goods, commodities.

'**Waren|angebot** n range of goods. ~**bestand** m stock (on hand). ~**börse** f commodity exchange. ~**haus** n department store. ~**lager** n **1.** stock (on hand). **2.** warehouse. ~**probe** f sample. ~**sendung** f consignment, ⊗ trade sample. ~**zeichen** n trademark.

warf [varf] pret of **werfen**.

warm [varm] **I** adj warm (a. fig.), hot (*meal, drink, etc*): **mir ist ~** I feel warm; **et. ~ halten** keep s.th. warm; **sich ~ halten** keep warm; **et. ~ machen** warm s.th. up; ~ **werden** warm up; **es wird**

wärmer it's getting warmer; F *ich kann mit ihr nicht ~ werden* I can't warm to her; → *warmhalten*. **II** *adv* warmly (*a. fig.*): F *die Wohnung kostet ~ ...* the rent for the flat is ... including heating.

'**Warmblüter** [-bly:tər] *m* (-s; -) warm-blooded animal.

Wärme ['vɛrmə] *f* (-; *no pl*) warmth (*a. fig.*), meteor., phys. heat: *zehn Grad ~* ten degrees above zero. ~*behandlung f* **1.** ⊗ heat treatment. **2.** ⚕ thermotherapy. ~*beständig adj* heat-resistant. ~*dämmung f* heat insulation. ~*einheit f* thermal unit. ~*grad m* degree above zero. ~*kraftwerk n* thermoelectric power plant. ~*lehre f* thermodynamics. ~*leiter m* phys. heat conductor.

wärmen ['vɛrmən] (h) **I** *v/t* warm (up), heat (up) (*food etc*): *sich die Füße ~* warm one's feet. **II** *v/i* be warm: *Wolle wärmt* wool keeps you warm. **III** *sich ~* warm o.s.

'**Wärme|pumpe** *f* heat pump. ~*technik f* heat engineering. ~*verlust m* heat loss.

'**Wärmflasche** *f* hot-water bottle.

'**warmhalten** *v/t* (*irr, sep,* -ge-, h, → *halten*) F *fig. sich j-n ~* keep in with s.o.

'**Warmhalteplatte** *f* plate warmer.

'**warmherzig** *adj* warm-hearted.

'**warmlaufen** *v/i* (*irr, sep,* -ge-, sn, → *laufen*) ~ *lassen* run the engine up.

'**Warmluftfront** *f* meteor. warm front.

'**Warmmiete** *f* rent including heating.

'**Warm|wasser|bereiter** *m* water heater. ~*heizung f* hot-water heating. ~*speicher m* hot-water tank. ~*versorgung f* hot-water supply.

'**Warn|anlage** *f* warning device. ~*blinkanlage f* mot. warning flasher. ~*dreieck n* mot. warning triangle.

warnen ['varnən] *v/t, v/i* (h) warn (*vor* against): *davor ~ zu inf* warn against *ger; vor ... wird gewarnt* beware of ...!

'**Warn|kreuz** *n* warning cross. ~*leuchte f*, ~*licht n* warning light. ~*schild n* danger sign. ~*schuß m* (*e-n ~ abgeben* fire a) warning shot. ~*si,gnal n* warning signal. ~*streik m* token strike.

'**Warnung** *f* (-; -en) warning.

'**Warnzeichen** *n* warning sign.

Warte ['vartə] *f fig.* *von hoher ~ aus* from a lofty standpoint; *von s-r ~ aus gesehen* from his point of view.

'**Warteliste** *f* (*auf der ~ stehen* be on

the) waiting list.

warten[1] ['vartən] *v/t* (h) ⊗ service.

'**warten**[2] *v/i* (h) wait (*auf acc* for): *j-n ~ lassen* keep s.o. waiting; *lange auf sich ~ lassen* be a long time in coming; *nicht lange auf sich ~ lassen* not to be long in coming; *warte (mal)!* wait a minute!; *na, warte!* you just wait!; *da kann er lange ~!* he's got a long wait coming; *das kann ...!* that'll keep!; *iro. auf ihn (darauf) haben wir gerade noch gewartet!* he (that) is all we needed. '**Warten** *n* (-s) wait(ing): *nach langem ~* after a long wait.

Wärter ['vɛrtər] *m* (-s, -), '**Wärterin** *f* (-; -nen) attendant, keeper.

'**Wartesaal** *m* 🚂 waiting room.

'**Wartezeit** *f* waiting period.

'**Wartezimmer** *n* waiting room.

'**Wartung** *f* (-; -en) maintenance, servicing.

'**Wartungsanleitung** *f* service manual.

'**wartungsfrei** *adj* maintenance-free.

warum [va'rʊm] *adv* why.

Warze ['vartsə] *f* (-; -n) **1.** ⚕ wart. **2.** → *Brustwarze*.

was [vas] **I** *interrog pron* **1.** what (*a.* F *for wie bitte?, nanu!, nicht wahr?*): ~ *gibt's?* what is it?, F what's up?; ~ *gibt's zum Mittagessen?* what's for lunch?; ~ *kostet das?* how much is it?; ~ *für (ein) ...?* what sort of ...?; ~ *für e-e Farbe?* what colo(u)r?; ~ *für ein Unsinn!* what nonsense! F a) ~ *mußte er auch lügen?* why did he have to lie?, b) ~ *fährt er auch so e-n großen Wagen?* what does he need such a big car for? **II** *rel pron* **3.** what: ~ *auch immer* whatever; *alles, ~ ich brauche* all I need; *ich weiß nicht, ~ ich tun soll* I don't know what to do. **4.** which: *er lachte nur, ~ mich ärgerte* he just laughed, which made me angry. **III** *indef pron* F something (*bad, better, etc*): *das ist ~ anderes* that's different; *ich will dir ~ sagen!* I'll tell you what; *sonst noch ~?* anything else?; *ist ~?* is anything wrong (*or* the matter)?

'**Wasch|anlage** *f mot.* car wash. ~*anleitung f* washing instructions. ~*auto,mat m* washing machine.

'**waschbar** *adj* washable.

'**Waschbär** *m zo.* raccoon.

'**Waschbecken** *n* washbasin.

Wäsche ['vɛʃə] f (-; no pl) **1.** wash(ing), laundry: *in der ~* in the wash; *fig. schmutzige ~ waschen* wash one's dirty linen in public. **2.** (*bed, table*) linen. **3.** (*die ~ wechseln* put on fresh) underwear. **~beutel** m laundry bag.

'**waschecht** adj **1.** a) washable, non-shrink, b) fast. **2.** F fig. true, genuine.

'**Wäsche|klammer** f clothes peg. **~korb** m laundry basket. **~leine** f clothesline.

waschen ['vaʃən] (wusch, gewaschen, h) **I** v/t wash (*sich die Hände etc* one's hands *etc*), launder (a. F fig. money): *Waschen und Legen* shampoo and set. **II** *sich ~* wash (o.s.).

'**Wäsche'rei** f (-; -en) laundry.

'**Wäsche|schleuder** f spin-drier. **~ständer** m clotheshorse. **~tinte** f marking ink. **~trockner** m drier.

'**Wasch|gang** m cycle. **~gelegenheit** f washing facilities. **~küche** f **1.** wash-house. **2.** F fig. pea soup. **~lappen** m **1.** flannel, Am. washcloth. **2.** F fig. sissy. **~lauge** f lye. **~leder** n chamois (leather). **~ma,schine** f washing machine. **2ma,schinenfest** adj machine-washable. **~mittel** n, **~pulver** n washing powder. **~raum** m washroom. **~sa,lon** m launderette, Am. laundromat. **~schüssel** f washbowl. **~straße** f car wash.

'**Waschung** f (-; -en) washing, esp. eccl., 🌿 ablution.

'**Wasch|wasser** n (-s; no pl) washing water. **~zettel** m blurb.

Wasser ['vasər] n (-s; -, -, ¨) water: *fließendes* (*stehendes*) *~* running (stagnant) water; *zu ~ und zu Land* by land and by water; *~ lassen* pass water; *sich über ~ halten* a. fig. keep one's head above water; *unter ~ setzen* flood; *fig. ins ~ fallen* fall flat; *das ist ~ auf s-e Mühle* that's grist to his mill; *da läuft e-m das ~ im Munde zusammen* it makes your mouth water; *er kann ihr nicht das ~ reichen* he's not a patch on her; *er ist mit allen ~n gewaschen* he knows all the tricks (of the trade); *das ~ steht ihm bis zum Hals* he is in bad trouble; *er ist ein stilles ~* he's a deep one; → *Schlag* 1.

'**wasser|abstoßend** adj textil. water-repellent. **~arm** adj dry, arid.

'**Wasser|aufbereitungsanlage** f water-recycling plant. **~bad** n **1.** 🌿, phot.

water bath. **2.** gastr. bain-marie. **~ball** m **1.** beach ball. **2.** → **~ballspiel** n water polo. **~bau** m (-[e]s; no pl) hydraulic engineering. **~behälter** m water container (🚰 tank). **~bett** n water bed. **~bombe** f depth charge.

Wässerchen ['vɛsərçən] n er sah aus, als könne er kein ~ trüben he looked as though butter would not melt in his mouth.

'**Wasser|dampf** m steam. **2dicht** adj waterproof, ⚓, ⚙ a. watertight. **~enthärter** m water softener. **~fahrzeug** n watercraft, vessel. **~fall** m waterfall, falls: F reden wie ein ~ talk nineteen to the dozen. **~farbe** f water colo(u)r. **2fest** adj waterproof. **~flasche** f water bottle. **~flugzeug** n seaplane. **~gehalt** m water content. **2gekühlt** adj water-cooled. **~glas** n **1.** 🔬 water glass. **2.** water glass, tumbler: → *Sturm* 1. **~graben** m ditch, sports: water jump. **~hahn** m tap, Am. faucet.

'**wasserhaltig** adj 🌿 hydrous.

'**Wasserhaushalt** m **1.** water supply. **2.** biol., 🌱 water balance.

wässerig ['vɛsərıç] adj watery, 🌿 aqueous: *j-m den Mund ~ machen* make s.o.'s mouth water (*nach* for).

'**Wasser|kessel** m **1.** kettle. **2.** ⚙ boiler. **~klo,sett** n water closet (abbr. W.C.). **~kraft** f water power. **~kraftwerk** n hydroelectric power plant. **~kühlung** f water cooling (system). **~lauf** m water-course. **~leitung** f water pipe(s). **~linie** f ⚓ water line. **2löslich** adj water-soluble. **~mangel** m water shortage.

'**Wassermann** m (-[e]s; no pl) astr. (er ist [ein] ~ he is [an]) Aquarius.

'**Wasserme,lone** f water melon.

wassern ['vasərn] v/i (h) ✈ touch down, spacecraft: splash down.

wässern ['vɛsərn] v/t (h) **1.** water, irrigate. **2.** soak.

'**Wasser|pfeife** f water pipe. **~pflanze** f aquatic (plant). **~pi,stole** f water pistol. **~ratte** f **1.** zo. water rat. **2.** F enthusiastic swimmer. **~rohr** n water pipe. **~rutschbahn** f water chute. **~schaden** m water damage. **~scheide** f watershed, Am. a. divide. **2scheu** adj afraid of water. **~schildkröte** f turtle.

'**Wasserschutz** m prevention of water

pollution. **~gebiet** n water reserve.
~poli,zei f river police.

'**Wasser|ski** n (-s; no pl) water skiing: **~ laufen** go water-skiing, water-ski. **~speier** m △ gargoyle. **~spiegel** m **1.** surface of the water. **2.** water level. **~sport** m water (or aquatic) sports, aquatics. **~spülung** f a) flush, b) cistern. **~stand** m water level. **~standsanzeiger** m water ga(u)ge.

'**Wasserstoff** m (-[e]s; no pl) hydrogen. **⚵blond** adj F peroxide blond(e). **~bombe** f hydrogen bomb. **~'pero,xid** n, **~'supero,xid** n hydrogen peroxide.

'**Wasser|strahl** m jet of water. **~straße** f waterway. **~sucht** f (-; no pl) ♣ dropsy. **~tier** n aquatic (animal). **~tropfen** m drop of water. **~turm** m water tower.

'**Wasserung** f (-; -en) ✈ touchdown on water, of spacecraft: splashdown.

'**Wasser|verbrauch** m water consumption. **~verdrängung** f (water) displacement. **~verschmutzung** f water pollution. **~versorgung** f water supply. **~vogel** m water bird, of a. waterfowl. **~waage** f spirit level. **~weg** m waterway: **auf dem ~** by water. **~welle** f (hairdo) water wave. **~werfer** m water cannon. **~werk(e** pl) n waterworks. **~zeichen** n watermark.

waten ['va:tən] v/i (sn) wade.

watscheln ['va:tʃəln] v/i (sn) waddle.

Watt¹ [vat] n (-[e]s; -en) geol. mud flats.

Watt² n (-s; -) ⚡ watt.

Watte ['vatə] f (-; -n) cotton wool.

'**Wattebausch** m cotton-wool swab.

'**Wattenmeer** n mud flats.

'**Wattestäbchen** n cotton bud.

wattieren [va'ti:rən] v/t (h) pad, wad.

weben ['ve:bən] v/t, v/i (h) weave.

'**Weber** m (-s; -) weaver. **Webe'rei** f (-; -en) **1.** no pl weaving. **2.** weaving mill.

'**Weberknecht** m zo. daddy longlegs.

'**Web|fehler** ['ve:p-] m film flaw. **~pelz** m woven imitation fur. **~stuhl** m loom. **~waren** pl woven goods.

Wechsel ['vɛksəl] m (-s; -) **1.** change, (a. ♂ crop) rotation. **2.** ♣ draft, bill of (exchange): **e-n ~ (auf j-n) ziehen** draw a bill (on s.o.). **3.** sports: a) (baton) change, b) change of ends. **4. → Wild-wechsel.** **~bäder** pl ♣ alternating hot and cold baths. **~bank** f (-; -en) discount house. **~beziehung** f interrela-

tion. **~fälle** pl vicissitudes, F the ups and downs. **~geld** n (small) change.

'**wechselhaft** adj changeable.

'**Wechseljahre** pl physiol. menopause.

'**Wechselkurs** m rate of exchange.

wechseln ['vɛksəln] (h) **I** v/t **1.** a) change b) exchange (rings, glances, words, etc), c) vary, d) alternate, a. rotate: **den Arbeitsplatz (Arzt etc) ~** change jobs (doctors etc); **→ Besitzer.** **II** v/i **2.** a) change, b) vary. **3.** (sn) deer etc: cross.

'**wechselnd** adj changing, varying.

'**Wechsel|rahmen** m interchangeable picture frame. **~schuld** f ♣ bill debt.

'**wechselseitig** [-zaıtıç] adj mutual, reciprocal: **~e Abhängigkeit** interdependence.

'**Wechselstrom** m ⚡ alternating current (abbr. A.C.). **~motor** m A.C. motor.

'**Wechselstube** f exchange office.

'**Wechselwähler(in** f) m floating voter.

'**wechselweise** adv alternately, in turn.

'**Wechselwirkung** f interaction.

wecken ['vɛkən] v/t (h) wake (up), call, a. fig. rouse, fig. awaken.

'**Wecker** m (-s; -) alarm clock): F **j-m auf den ~ gehen** get on s.o.'s nerves.

'**Weckruf** m teleph. alarm call.

Wedel ['ve:dəl] m (-s; -) ♣ frond.

'**wedeln** v/i (h) **1. ~ mit** wave (s.th.), **dem Schwanz** wag (its tail). **2.** skiing: wedel.

weder ['ve:dər] conj **~ ... noch** neither ... nor.

weg [vɛk] adv F **1.** a) gone, b) not in, c) away: **~ (da)!** get away!, beat it!; **~ damit!** take it away!, w.s. off with it!; **Finger (or Hände) ~!** hands off!; **ich muß ~!** I must be off!; **nichts wie ~!** let's get out of here! **2. ~ sein** a) be out cold, b) be in raptures (over sth.); **über et. ~ sein** have got over s.th.

Weg [ve:k] m (-[e]s; -e) way (a. fig.), path, route, F a. errand: **~ zum Erfolg** the road to success; **auf dem ~(e) der Besserung** on the road to recovery, F on the mend; **auf diesem ~e** this way; **auf diplomatischem ~e** through diplomatic channels; **auf friedlichem (legalem) ~e** by peaceful (legal) means; **auf dem besten ~e sein zu** inf be well on the way to ger; **auf dem richtigen ~e sein** be on the right track; **sich auf den ~ machen** set off; **j-m aus dem ~(e) gehen** get out of s.o.'s way; (dat) **aus**

dem ~e gehen steer clear of; *aus dem ~e räumen* (*or* **schaffen**) get rid of; *s-e eigenen ~e gehen* go one's own way; *den ~ ebnen* pave the way (*dat* for); *et. in die ~e leiten* initiate s.th., start s.th. off; *ich traue ihm nicht über den ~* I don't trust him an inch; *im ~(e) stehen* (*or* **sein**) a) *j-m* be in s.o.'s way, b) *e-r* **Sache** be an obstacle to s.th.; *dem steht nichts im ~e* there are no obstacles to that, F that's all right; → **bahnen, halb** I.

'**wegbekommen** *v/t* (*irr, sep,* h, → **bekommen**) F get s.th. off, move.

'**Wegbereiter** *m* (-s; -) pioneer: *der ~ sein für* pave the way for.

'**wegblasen** *v/t* (*irr, sep,* -ge-, h, → **blasen**) blow s.th. away: *fig. wie weggeblasen sein* be clean gone.

'**wegbleiben** *v/i* (*irr, sep,* -ge-, sn, → **bleiben**) F **1.** stay away. **2.** ☉ fail, *sl.* conk out: → **Luft 1, Spucke.**

'**wegbringen** *v/t* (*irr, sep,* -ge-, h, → **bringen**) take s.o., s.th. away.

wegen ['ve:gən] *prep* (*gen,* F *dat*) **1.** because of, on account of: *~ Diebstahls* for larceny; → **Amt 1, Recht 1. 2.** for the sake of: *er hat es ~ s-r Kinder getan* he did it for his children's sake. **3.** due to. **4.** F *von ~* that's what you think!; *von ~ hübsch!* pretty, my foot!

'**Wegerecht** *n* (-[e]s; *no pl*) right of way.

Wegerich ['ve:gərıç] *m* (-s; -e) plantain.

'**wegfahren** *v/i* (*irr, sep,* -ge-, sn, → **fahren**) leave, drive away.

'**wegfegen** *v/t* (*sep,* h) sweep s.th. away.

Weggang ['vɛk-] *m* (-[e]s; *no pl*) leaving.

'**weggeben** *v/t* (*irr, sep,* -ge-, h, → **geben**) give s.th. away.

'**weggehen** *v/i* (*irr, sep,* -ge-, sn, → **gehen**) **1.** go away (a. F *fig.* pain etc), leave: F *geh weg!* leave me alone!; *von Berlin* (*der Firma*) *~* leave Berlin (the firm). **2.** F *fig.* sell: → **Semmel.**

'**weghaben** *v/t* (*irr, sep,* -ge-, h, → **haben**) F **1. sein Teil** *etc ~* have got one's share *etc.* **2. et.** *~* a) have got the hang of it, b) be good (*in dat* at).

'**wegkommen** *v/i* (*irr, sep,* -ge-, sn, → **kommen**) F **1.** get away. **2.** get lost. **3.** *fig.* **gut** (*schlecht*) *~* come off well (badly) (*bei* at). **4. ~ über** (*acc*) get over.

'**weglassen** *v/t* (*irr, sep,* -ge-, h, → **lassen**) **1.** let s.o. go. **2.** leave s.th. out.

'**Weglassung** ['vɛk-] *f* (-; -en) omission.

'**weglaufen** *v/i* (*irr, sep,* -ge-, sn, → **laufen**) run away.

'**weglegen** *v/t* (*sep,* h) put s.th. aside.

'**wegmüssen** *v/i* (*irr, sep,* -ge-, h, → **müssen**) F *ich muß weg* I must be off; *es muß weg!* it must go!

'**wegnehmen** *v/t* (*irr, sep,* -ge-, h, → **nehmen**) remove, *fig.* take up (*room, time, etc*): (*j-m*) *et.* **~** take s.th. away (from s.o.); → **Gas.**

'**wegrationali,sieren** *v/t* (*sep,* h) cut jobs *etc* (by rationalization).

'**wegräumen** *v/t* (*sep,* h) *a. fig.* remove.

'**wegreißen** *v/t* (*irr, sep,* -ge-, h, → **reißen**) tear s.o., s.th. away.

'**wegscheren: sich ~** (*sep,* h) F clear off.

'**wegschicken** *v/t* (*sep,* h) send s.o., s.th. away (*or* off).

'**wegschleppen** *v/t* (*sep,* h) drag s.o., s.th. off.

'**wegschließen** *v/t* (*irr, sep,* -ge-, h, → **schließen**) lock s.th. away.

'**wegschnappen** *v/t* (*sep,* h) F (*j-m*) *et.* **~** snatch s.th. away (from s.o.).

'**wegsehen** *v/i* (*irr, sep,* -ge-, h, → **sehen**) **1.** look away, *a. fig.* look the other way. **2.** → **hinwegsehen.**

'**wegspülen** *v/t* (*sep,* h) wash away.

'**wegstecken** *v/t* (*sep,* h) put s.th. away.

'**wegtreten** *v/i* (*irr, sep,* -ge-, sn, → **treten**) step aside, ✗ break (the) ranks: *~ lassen* (*weggetreten!*) dismiss(!).

'**Wegweiser** *m* (-s; -) signpost, (road) sign, *in buildings*: directory.

'**wegwerfen** (*irr, sep,* -ge-, h, → **werfen**) **I** *v/t a. fig.* throw s.th. away. **II sich ~** throw o.s. away (*an acc* on).

'**wegwerfend** *adj* disparaging.

Wegwerf|flasche ['vɛk-] *f* throwaway (*or* disposable) bottle. **~gesellschaft** *f contp.* throwaway society.

'**wegwischen** *v/t* (*sep,* h) **1.** wipe s.th. off. **2.** *fig.* brush objection *etc* off.

'**wegzaubern** *v/t* (*sep,* h) spirit away.

'**wegziehen** (*irr, sep,* -ge-, sn, → **ziehen**) **I** *v/t* pull s.o., s.th. away. **II** *v/i* move.

weh [ve:] *adj* sore: (*j-m*) *~ tun* hurt (s.o., *fig.* s.o.'s feelings); *sich* (*am Kopf etc*) *~* hurt o.s. (one's head *etc*); *mir tut der Knöchel ~* my ankle hurts.

wehe ['ve:ə] *int ~* (*dir*), *wenn ...* you'll be sorry if ...

'**Wehe** *f* (-; -n) (*sand, snow*) drift.

wehen ['ve:ən] v/i, v/t (h) flag etc: wave, wind: blow, scent, tune, etc: drift, waft.
'**Wehen** pl ✲ pains, labo(u)r.

'**Wehgeschrei** n a. fig. wailing.

'**wehleidig** adj plaintive, whining: **sei nicht so ~!** don't be such a sissy!

'**Wehmut** f (-; no pl) melancholy, wistfulness, nostalgia. **wehmütig** ['ve:my:tıç] adj melancholy, wistful, nostalgic.

Wehr¹ [ve:r] f **sich zur ~ setzen** → **wehren** I.

Wehr² n (-[e]s; -e) weir, dam.

'**Wehr|beauftragte** m ombudsman (for the Armed Forces). **~bereich** m military district. **~bereichskom,mando** n military district command. **~dienst** m (-[e]s; no pl) (**s-n ~ ableisten** do one's) military service. **~dienstverweigerer** m (-s; -) conscientious objector.

wehren ['ve:rən] (h) **I sich ~** defend o.s. (**gegen** against); **sich ~ gegen** a) resist, fight, b) refuse to accept. **II** v/i **den Anfängen ~** nip things in the bud.

'**Wehrersatzdienst** m (-[e]s; no pl) alternative service (for conscientious objectors).

'**wehrfähig** adj fit for military service.

'**wehrlos** adj defen/celess (Am. -se-), helpless. '**Wehrlosigkeit** f (-; no pl) defen/celessness (Am. -se-), helplessness.

'**Wehrmacht** f (-; no pl) hist. (German) Armed Forces, Wehrmacht.

'**Wehrpaß** m service record (book).

'**Wehrpflicht** f (-; no pl) (**allgemeine**) ~ (universal) compulsory military service, (universal) conscription. '**wehrpflichtig** adj a) liable for military service, b) recruitable (age). '**Wehrpflichtige** m (-n; -n) a) person liable for military service, b) conscript, Am. draftee.

'**Wehrsold** m (service) pay.

'**Wehrübung** f reserve duty training.

Weib [vaip] n (-[e]s; -er) a. contp. woman.

'**Weibchen** n (-s; -) zo. female.

'**Weiber|feind** ['vaibər-] m woman-hater. **~geschichten** pl F affairs, womanizing. **~held** m contp. ladykiller. **~regiment** n petticoat government.

weibisch ['vaibıʃ] adj effeminate.

'**weiblich** adj female, feminine (a. ling.), womanly.

'**Weibsbild** n F contp. female, woman.

weich [vaiç] adj soft (a. ling., phot. or fig.), mellow (voice, colo[u]r, etc), ten-

der (meat), soft-boiled (egg): ~ **machen** soften; ~ **werden** soften, fig. a. give in.

'**Weiche**¹ f (-; -n) anat. flank, side.

'**Weiche**² f (-; -n) 🚃 points, Am. switch: fig. **die ~n stellen** set the course (**für** for).

weichen¹ ['vaiçən] v/i (wich, gewichen, sn) **1.** (dat to) a. fig. give way, yield. **2.** go (away): **j-m nicht von der Seite ~** not to leave s.o.'s side; **er wich und wankte nicht** he didn't budge.

'**weichen**² v/i, v/t (h) (a. ~ **lassen**) soak.

'**weichgekocht** adj soft-boiled (egg).

'**Weichheit** f (-; no pl) softness (etc, → **weich**).

'**weichherzig** adj soft-hearted.

'**Weichkäse** m soft cheese.

'**weichlich** adj fig. soft, effeminate.

'**Weichling** m (-s; -e) F softie, sissy.

'**Weich|macher** m (-s; -) 🧪, ◉ softener. **~spüler** m (-s; -) (fabric) softener. **~teile** pl anat. soft parts. **~tier** n mollusc. **~zeichner** m phot. soft-focus lens.

Weide¹ ['vaidə] f (-; -n) ◈ willow (tree).

'**Weide**² f (-; -n) (**auf der ~** at) pasture.

'**Weideland** n pasturage.

'**weiden** (h) **I** v/i graze. **II** v/t a. ~ **lassen** put out to pasture. **III** v/i **sich ~ an** (dat) a) feast one's eyes on, b) gloat over.

'**Weidenbaum** m willow (tree).

'**Weidenkätzchen** n ◈ catkin.

weidlich ['vaitlıç] adv thoroughly.

Weidmann ['vait-] m (-[e]s; ⸚er) huntsman. '**weidmännisch** [-mɛnıʃ] **I** adj huntsmanlike. **II** adv in a huntsmanlike manner.

Weidmanns'heil n ~**!** good sport!

weigern ['vaigərn] **sich ~** (h) refuse.

'**Weigerung** f (-; -en) refusal.

'**Weihbischof** m suffragan (bishop).

Weihe ['vaiə] f (-; -n) **1.** eccl. a) consecration, b) ordination. **2.** fig. solemnity.

'**weihen** v/t (h) **1.** eccl. a) consecrate, b) ordain as a priest. **2.** (dat to) devote, dedicate (both a. **sich** o.s.): **dem Tode** (or **Untergang**) **geweiht** doomed.

'**Weihnacht** f (-; no pl) → **Weihnachten** pl (**an ~, zu ~** at) Christmas (F Xmas); **Fröhliche ~!** Merry Christmas!

'**weihnachtlich** adj Christmas, F Christmassy.

'**Weihnachts|abend** m Christmas Eve. **~baum** m Christmas tree. **~einkäufe** pl Christmas shopping. **~feiertag** m

Christmas Day (*pl* holidays): **zweiter ~** Boxing Day. **~fest** *n* Christmas. **~geld** *n* Christmas bonus. **~lied** *n* Christmas carol. **~mann** *m* (-[e]s; ⸚er) **1.** Father Christmas, Santa Claus. **2.** F *contp.* dope. **~markt** *m* Christmas fair. **~zeit** *f* Christmas (season).

'Weihrauch *m* (-[e]s; *no pl*) incense.

'Weihwasser *n* (-s; *no pl*) holy water.

weil [vaɪl] *conj* **1.** because. **2.** since, as.

'Weilchen *n* (-s; *no pl*) **ein ~** a little while.

'Weile *f* (-; *no pl*) **e-e ~** a while, a time.

Wein [vaɪn] *m* (-[e]s; -e) **1.** ♀ vine. **2.** wine: **j-m reinen ~ einschenken** tell s.o. the truth. **~bau** *m* (-[e]s; *no pl*) wine growing, viticulture. **~bauer** *m* wine grower. **~baugebiet** *n* wine growing area. **~beere** *f* grape. **~berg** *m* vineyard. **~bergschnecke** *f* (edible) snail. **~blatt** *n* vine leaf. **~brand** *m* (-[e]s; ⸚e) brandy.

weinen ['vaɪnən] *v/i, v/t* (h) weep (**um** over), cry: **j-n zum ♀ bringen** make s.o. cry; **es ist zum ♀** it's a (crying) shame.

weinerlich ['vaɪnərlɪç] *adj* tearful, F weepy, whining (*voice, child, etc*).

'Wein|essig *m* wine vinegar. **~faß** *n* wine cask. **~flasche** *f* wine bottle. **~geist** *m* spirit(s) of wine. **~glas** *n* wine glass. **~gut** *n* wine-growing estate. **~händler** *m* wine merchant. **~handlung** *f* wine shop. **~karte** *f* wine list. **~keller** *m* wine cellar. **~kelter** *f* wine press. **~kenner** *m* wine connoisseur.

'Weinkrampf *m* crying fit.

'Wein|lese *f* grape harvest. **~lo,kal** *n* wine tavern. **~probe** *f* wine tasting. ♀**rot** *adj* wine-red. **~stock** *m* ♀ vine. **~stube** *f* wine tavern. **~traube** *f* a) bunch of grapes, b) *pl* grapes.

weise ['vaɪzə] *adj* wise.

'Weise¹ *m* (-n; -n) wise man, sage.

'Weise² *f* (-; -n) **1.** way: **auf diese ~** (in) this way; **auf jede ~** in every way; **auf die gleiche ~** the same way; **auf die e-e oder andere ~** (in) one way or another; **auf m-e (s-e) ~** my (his) way; **in k-r ~** in no way; **jeder auf s-e ~** everyone after his own fashion. **2.** ♪ tune.

weisen ['vaɪzən] (wies, gewiesen, h) **I** *v/t* **1.** **j-m den Weg ~** show s.o. the way. **2.** **j-n von der Schule ~** expel s.o. (from school). **3.** *et.* (**weit**) **von sich ~** repudiate s.th. (emphatically). **II** *v/i* → **zeigen** II.

'Weisheit *f* (-; -en) wisdom: **mit s-r ~ am Ende sein** be at one's wits' end.

'Weisheitszahn *m* wisdom tooth.

'weismachen *v/t* (*sep*, h) **j-m ~, daß** make s.o. believe that; **mir kannst du nichts ~!** you can't fool me!; **laß dir nichts ~!** don't be fooled!

weiß [vaɪs] *adj* **1.** white: **~ machen** whiten; **~ werden** go white; **~ gekleidet** dressed in white. **2.** *fig.* blank.

Weiß *n* (-[es]; -) *a.* chess etc: white.

'weissagen *v/t* (*insep*, h) prophesy, foretell. **'Weissager** *m* (-s; -) prophet. **'Weissagerin** *f* (-; -nen) prophetess. **'Weissagung** *f* (-; -en) prophecy.

'Weiß|blech *n* tinplate. ♀**blond** *adj* silver-blond(e). **~brot** *n* white bread. **~buch** *n pol.* white paper (*Am.* book). **~dorn** *m* (-[e]s; -e) ♀ whitethorn.

'Weiße *m, f* (-n; -n) white man (woman): **die ~n** the whites, the white man.

'weißen ['vaɪsən] *v/t* (h) **1.** whiten. **2.** whitewash.

'weißglühend *adj* white-hot.

'Weißglut *f* (-; *no pl*) white heat: F **j-n zur ~ bringen** make s.o. see red.

'weißhaarig *adj* white-haired.

'Weiß|kohl *m*, **~kraut** *n* white cabbage.

'weißlich *adj* whitish.

'Weißwein *m* white wine.

'Weisung *f* (-; -en) instruction, order(s). **'Weisungs|befugnis** *f* authority to issue directives. ♀**gemäß** *adv* as directed.

weit [vaɪt] **I** *adj* **1.** a) wide, a full (*skirt etc*), b) *a.* ⊙ loose. **2.** wide, extensive, vast, immense. **3.** *fig.* broad (*concept etc*): **im ~esten Sinne** in the widest sense. **4.** long: **auf ~e** (*or* **aus ~er**) **Entfernung** at a great distance. **5.** ~ **offen** wide open. **6.** far: **sie ist ~ über 60** she is well over sixty; **er ist ~ gereist** he has got around a good deal; **~** (*or* **bei ~em**) **das beste** by far the best; **bei ~em nicht so gut** not nearly so good; **~ gefehlt!** far from it!; F **es ist nicht ~ her mit ihm** he is not up to much; **es ~ bringen** (**im Leben**) go far; **zu ~ gehen** go too far; **das geht zu ~** that's going too far; **ich bin so ~** I'm ready; **wie ~ bist du?** how far have you got?; **wenn es so ~ ist** when the time comes; → **entfernt, kommen** 1, 10.

'weit'ab *adv* far away (**von** from).

'weit'aus *adv* far *better etc*.

'**Weitblick** m (-[e]s; no pl) farsightedness.
'**weitblickend** adj farsighted, farseeing.
'**Weite**[1] f (-; -n) **1.** a. ⊕ a) width, b) breadth, c) size, extent: → **licht** 3. **2.** vastness, expanse. **3.** sports: distance.
'**Weite**[2]: das ~ suchen take to one's heels.
weiten ['vaɪtən] v/t (a. sich ~) (h) widen (a. fig.), stretch (shoes etc).
weiter ['vaɪtər] **I** comp of **weit**. **II** adj further: nach e-r ~en Woche after another week. **III** adv ~! go on!; halt, nicht ~! stop, no further!; immer ~ on and on; nichts (niemand) ~ nothing (no one) else; und so ~ and so on (abbr. etc); das ist nicht ~ schlimm that's no tragedy; das störte sie ~ nicht that didn't really bother her; → **weiterhin** I.
'**weiter|arbeiten** v/i (sep, h) go on working. **~befördern** v/t (sep, h) forward, send on. **~bestehen** → **fortbestehen**.
'**weiterbilden** → **fortbilden**.
'**Weiterbildung** f → **Fortbildung**.
'**weiterbringen** v/t (irr sep, -ge-, h, → **bringen**) das bringt mich (uns etc) nicht weiter that's not much help.
'**Weitere, das** (-n) the rest: bis auf weiteres for the time being, adm. until further notice; ohne weiteres without further ado, easily.
'**weiter|empfehlen** v/t (irr, sep, h, → **empfehlen**) recommend (to others). **~entwickeln** v/t (a. sich ~) (sep, h) develop (further). **~erzählen** v/t (sep, h) tell others, repeat. **~fahren** v/i (irr, sep, -ge-, sn, → **fahren**) go on, drive on. **~führen** v/t (sep, h) continue, carry on. **~geben** v/t (irr, sep, -ge-, h, → **geben**) et. ~ pass s.th. on. **~gehen** v/i (irr, sep, -ge-, sn, → **gehen**) **1.** go on, walk on. **2.** fig. go on, continue: das kann so nicht ~! things can't go on like this!
'**weiter|hin** **I** adv ~ et. tun continue doing (or to do) s.th., go on doing s.th. **II** conj further(more), moreover.
'**weiter|kämpfen** v/i (sep, h) continue fighting. **~kommen** v/i (irr, sep, -ge-, sn, → **kommen**) get on, fig. a. make headway, get somewhere: nicht ~ a. be stuck; so kommen wir nicht weiter this won't get us any further. **~laufen** v/i (irr, sep, -ge-, sn, → **laufen**) payment etc: be continued. **~leben** v/i (sep, h) live on, fig. a. survive. **~leiten** v/t (sep,

h) (an acc to) pass s.th. on, refer. **~lesen** v/t, v/i (irr, sep, -ge-, h, → **lesen**) go on (reading), continue to read. **~machen** v/i, v/t (sep, h) continue, carry (or go) on (with). **~sagen** v/t (sep, h) et. ~ pass s.th. on.
'**Weiterungen** pl complications.
'**weiterverarbeiten** v/t (sep, h) process.
'**Weiterverarbeitung** f (-; no pl) processing.
'**Weiterverkauf** m (-[e]s; no pl) resale.
'**weiterverkaufen** v/t (sep, h) resell.
'**weitgehend** **I** adj extensive, far-reaching, a. wide (powers etc): es herrschte ~e Übereinstimmung there was a large degree of consent. **II** adv largely, to a great extent.
'**weitgereist** adj widely travel(l)ed.
'**weit'her** adv from afar.
'**weit'hergeholt** adj fig. far-fetched.
'**weit'hin** adv **1.** far. **2.** to a large extent.
'**weitläufig** **I** adj **1.** extensive, vast, spacious. **2.** detailed, contp. long-winded. **3.** distant (relatives). **II** adv **4.** at great length. **5.** ~ verwandt distantly related.
'**weitreichend** adj **1.** far-reaching. **2.** ✕ long-range.
'**weitschweifig** [-ʃvaɪfɪç] adj long-winded.
'**weitsichtig** adj long-sighted, a. fig. farsighted. '**Weitsichtigkeit** f (-; no pl) long-sightedness, a. fig. farsightedness.
'**Weitspringer(in** f) m longjumper, Am. broadjumper. '**Weitsprung** m (-[e]s; no pl) long (Am. broad) jump.
'**weit|verbreitet** adj widespread, common. **~verzweigt** adj widely ramified.
'**Weitwinkelobjek,tiv** n wide-angle lens.
Weizen ['vaɪtsən] m (-s; -) wheat: fig. sein ~ blüht he is in clover.
welch [vɛlç] **I** interrog pron what, which: ~er (von beiden)? which (of the two)?; ~ ein Anblick! what a sight! **II** rel pron who, which, that. **III** indef pron some, any: have you got money? ja, ich habe ~es yes, I have some; brauchen Sie ~es? do you need any?
welk [vɛlk] adj withered, faded: ~e Haut wrinkled skin. '**welken** v/i (sn) wither.
'**Wellblech** n corrugated iron.
Welle ['vɛlə] f (-; -n) **1.** a. fig. wave: fig. (hohe) ~n schlagen cause quite a stir. **2.** ⊕ shaft. **3.** gym. circle.

wellen 656

'**wellen** (h) **I** v/t wave (hair). **II sich ~**
hair: be (or go) wavy.
'**Wellen|bad** n swimming pool with arti-
ficially produced waves. **~band** n ♪
wave band. **~bereich** m radio: wave
range. **~brecher** m ⚓ breakwater.
'**wellenförmig** adj wavy.
'**Wellen|länge** f (F fig. **die gleiche ~
haben** be on the same) wavelength.
~linie f wavy line. **~reiten** n surfing.
'**Wellensittich** m zo. budgerigar.
wellig ['vɛlɪç] adj wavy.
'**Wellpappe** f corrugated board.
Welpe ['vɛlpə] m (-n; -n) zo. puppy, pup.
Welt [vɛlt] f (-; -en) world: **die große ~** a)
the big wide world, b) high society; **alle
~** everybody; **auf der ganzen ~** all over
the world; **der längste Fluß der ~** the
longest river in the world, the world's
longest river; **was in aller ~ ...?** what
on earth ...?; **nicht um alles in der ~** not
on your life; **aus der ~ schaffen** a) get
rid of, b) settle (*problem etc*); **in die ~
setzen** a) put *children* into the world,
b) start (*rumo[u]r*); **zur ~ bringen** give
birth to; **zur ~ kommen** be born.
'**Welt|all** n (-s; no pl) universe. **2an-
schaulich** adj ideological. **~anschau-
ung** f philosophy (of life), world view,
a. ideology. **~ausstellung** f world fair.
~bank f (-; no pl) World Bank.
'**welt|bekannt, ~berühmt** adj world-
-famous. **~bewegend** adj worldshak-
ing: *iro.* **nichts Weltbewegendes** nothing to write home about.
'**Weltbild** n world view.
'**Weltbürger(in** f) m cosmopolitan.
'**Weltenbummler(in** f) m globetrotter.
'**Welterfolg** m worldwide success.
'**Weltergewicht** [-vɛltər-] n boxing: welt-
erweight.
'**Welt|firma** f world-renowned firm.
2fremd adj naive, unworldly, ivo-
ry-towered (*scholar etc*). **~frieden** m
world peace. **~geschichte** f (-; no pl)
world history. **2gewandt** adj urbane.
~handel m international trade. **~herr-
schaft** f (-; no pl) world domination.
~karte f map of the world. **~krieg** m
world war: **der Zweite ~** World War II,
the Second World War. **~kugel** f globe.
~lage f (-; no pl) international situation.
'**weltlich** adj **1.** worldly. **2.** secular.

'**Weltlitera,tur** f world literature.
'**Weltmacht** f world power.
'**weltmännisch** [-mɛnɪʃ] adj man-of-the-
-world.
'**Welt|markt** m world market. **~meer** n
ocean. **~meister(in** f) m world champion. **~meisterschaft** f world championship, *esp. soccer*: World Cup.
2offen adj open-minded. **~öffentlich-
keit** f world public. **~poli,tik** f international (or world) politics. **~presse** f
international press. **~rangliste** f world
ranking list: **er steht an dritter Stelle
der ~** he is ranked third in the world.
~raum m (-[e]s; no pl) (outer) space.
~raum... → **Raum...** **~reich** n empire.
~reise f world trip. **~reisende** m, f
globetrotter. **~re,kord** m world record.
~re,kordinhaber(in f) m, **~re,kord-
ler(in** f) m world-record holder. **~reli-
gi,on** f world religion. **~ruf** m (**von ~** of)
worldwide renown. **~schmerz** m (-es;
no pl) world-weariness. **~sicherheits-
rat** m U.N. Security Council. **~spra-
che** f universal language. **~stadt** f metropolis. **~stadt...**, **2städtisch** adj met-
ropolitan. **~untergang** m end of the
world. **~uraufführung** f world première. **~verbesserer** m (-s; -) world
changer. **~währungsfonds** m International Monetary Fund. **2weit** adj
worldwide, global. **~wirtschaft** f (-; no
pl) world economy. **~wirtschaftskrise**
f worldwide economic crisis. **~wunder**
n wonder of the world.
wem [ve:m] pron (to) whom: **von ~** of
whom, by whom.
wen [ve:n] pron whom, F who.
Wende ['vɛndə] f (-; -n) **1.** a. sports: turn.
2. change, pol. change of power. **~hals**
m **1.** zo. wryneck. **2.** pol. contp. quick-
-change artist. **~kreis** m **1.** geogr. trop-
ic. **2.** mot. turning circle.
Wendeltreppe ['vɛndəl-] f spiral staircase.
wenden¹ ['vɛndən] (h) **I** v/t a) turn, b)
turn over (*page, roast, etc*). **II** v/i turn
(around), *sports*: turn: **bitte ~!** please
turn over (*abbr.* p.t.o.). **III sich zum
Guten ~** take a turn for the better.
'**wenden²** (wandte, gewandt, h) **I** v/t **~
an** (*acc*) spend *money* on, devote *time
etc* to. **II sich ~** turn (**nach** to, **gegen**
on, against); **sich ~ gegen** oppose; **sich**

an *j-n* ~ ask (*or* see, consult, contact) s.o.; *sich um Rat (Hilfe)* **an** *j-n* ~ turn to s.o. for advice (help).

'**Wendepunkt** *m a. fig.* turning point.

wendig ['vɛndɪç] *adj* **1.** manoeuvrable, *Am.* maneuverable. **2.** nimble, agile.

'**Wendigkeit** *f* (*-; no pl*) **1.** manoeuvrability, *Am.* maneuverability. **2.** agility.

'**Wendung** *f* (*-; -en*) **1.** turn: *fig.* **e-e un-erwartete** ~ *nehmen* take an unexpected turn. **2.** expression, phrase.

wenig ['ve:nɪç] *indef pron and adv* little, not much: ~**e** *pl* few, not many, *su.* few (people); *nur* ~**e** only few; (*nur*) *einige* ~**e** (only) a few; ~**er** less, *A* minus; *immer* ~**er** less and less, *A* als less than; *nicht* ~**er als** no less than, *pl* no fewer than; *nichts* ~**er als** anything but; ~**er werden** decrease; *das* ~**e** the little; *das* ~**ste** the least; *am* ~**sten** least of all; *ein* ~ a little; *nicht* ~ quite a lot; ~ *beliebt* not very popular; ~ *bekannt* little known; ~ *begeistert* (rather) unenthusiastic; ~ *hilfreich* unhelpful.

'**Wenigkeit** *f* **F m-e** ~ yours truly.

'**wenigstens** *adv* at least: *wenn sie* ~ *zuhörte* if only she would listen.

wenn [vɛn] *conj* **1.** a) when, b) whenever, c) as soon as: ~ *man ihn so reden hört* to hear him (talk). **2.** if: ~ *sie doch* (*or nur*) *käme* if only she would come; ~ *du nicht bezahlst* unless you pay; ~ *ich das gewußt hätte* had I (but) known. **3.** ~ *auch, und* ~ even if; → *schon* 5. **Wenn** *n ohne* ~ *und Aber* no ifs or buts.

wer [ve:r] **I** *interrog pron* who, which: ~ *von euch?* which of you? **II** *rel pron* who, which: ~ (*auch immer*) whoever. **III** *indef pron* a) who, *adm.* any person who, b) F somebody, anybody.

'**Werbe|ab,teilung** *f* publicity department. ~**agen,tur** *f* advertising agency. ~**akti,on** *f* → **Werbekampagne.** ~**fach-mann** *m* advertising expert. ~**fernse-hen** *n* **1.** commercial television. **2.** television (*or* TV) commercials. ~**film** *m* promotion(al) film. ~**funk** *m* **1.** commercial radio. **2.** radio ads (*Am.* commercials). ~**geschenk** *n* promotional gift. ~**graphik** *f* commercial art. ~**gra-phiker** *m* commercial artist. ~**kam,pa-gne** *f* publicity (*or* advertising) campaign. ~**kosten** *pl* advertising costs.

~**leiter** *m* publicity manager. ~**mittel** *pl* advertising media (*or* funds).

werben ['vɛrbən] (warb, geworben, h) **I** *v/t* **1.** enlist (*members*), *a.* recruit (*work-ers etc*), canvass, attract (*votes etc*): *j-n für e-e Sache* ~ win s.o. over to a cause. **II** *v/i* **2.** ~ *für* advertise, promote, F plug, *pol.* campaign (*or* canvass) for. **3.** ~ *um a. fig.* court, woo.

'**Werbe|pro,spekt** *m* publicity brochure. ~**psycholo,gie** *f* psychology of advertising. ~**spot** *m* commercial (spot), spot. ~**spruch** *m* (advertising) slogan. ~**texter** *m* copywriter. ~**trom-mel** *f* **die** ~ *rühren* → **werben** 2.

'**werbewirksam** *adj* effective.

Werbung (*-; no pl*) *f* **1.** enlisting (*etc.*, → **werben** 1), recruitment. **2.** advertising, publicity: *das ist e-e gute* ~ *für ...* that is good publicity for ... **3.** → **Werbeab-teilung.** '**Werbungskosten** *pl taxa-tion*: professional outlays.

'**Werdegang** *m* (*-[e]s; no pl*) develop-ment, *a. fig. or* ⚙ history, *of person*: professional background, *a.* career.

werden ['ve:rdən] (wurde, geworden, sn) **I** *v/i* **1.** a) become, get, grow, b) turn, go (*sour etc*), turn out (*well etc*): *blaß* ~ turn pale; *blind* (*verrückt*) ~ go blind (mad); *böse* ~ get angry; *gesund* ~ get well; *wie sind die Fotos geworden?* how have the photos turned out?; *was will er* (*einmal*) ~? what does he want to be?; *was soll nun* ~? what are we going to do now?; *was ist aus ihm geworden?* what has become of him?; *daraus wird nichts!* a) nothing will come of it, b) nothing doing!; F *es wird schon* (*wieder*) ~! it'll be all right!; F *wird's bald?* get a move on!; → *Mut-ter*[1]. **II** *v/aux* *ich werde fahren* I will (*or* I'll) drive, I am going to drive; *es wird gleich regnen* it's going to rain; *es ist uns gesagt worden* we have been told; *geliebt* ~ be loved; *gebaut* ~ be (being) built.

'**Werden** *n* (*-s*) development, growth, progress: *im* ~ *sein* be in the making.

werfen ['vɛrfən] (warf, geworfen, h) **I** *v/t* **1.** throw (*a. fig. or zo.*), cast (*a. anchor, glance, shadow*): (*v/i mit*) *et.* ~ *nach* throw s.th. at; *Bomben* ~ drop bombs; → *Blick* 1, *Handtuch etc.* **II** *v/i* **2.** throw. **3.** → *schmeißen* 5. **III** *sich* ~ **4.**

◎ buckle, *wood*: warp. **5. sich ~ auf** *(acc)* throw o.s. on *(fig.* into); → **Hals.**

'**Werfer** *m* (-s; -), '**Werferin** *f* (-; -nen) *sports*: thrower.

Werft [verft] *f* (-; -en) **1.** shipyard. **2.** ✈ hangar. **~arbeiter** *m* docker.

Werg [verk] *n* (-[e]s; *no pl*) tow.

Werk [verk] *n* (-[e]s; -e) **1.** work, *of writer etc*: *a.* works, *a.* deed: **am ~ sein** be at work; **ans ~ gehen** set to work; **ein gutes ~ tun** do a good deed; **vorsichtig zu ~e gehen** go about it cautiously; *b.s.* **es war sein ~** it was his work (*or* doing). **2.** factory, works, plant: ☂ **ab ~** ex works. **3.** ◎ works, mechanism.

'**Werk...** works ..., factory ... **~angehörige** *m, f* (-n; -n) (works) employee. **~arzt** *m* works doctor. **~bank** *f* (-; ~e) (work)bench. **☨eigen** *adj* works ..., company(-owned).

werkeln ['verkəln] *v/i* (h) potter about.

werken ['verkən] *v/i* (h) work, *ped.* do handicrafts.

'**Werken** *n* (-s) *ped.* handicrafts.

'**Werkleiter** *m* works manager.

'**Werkmeister** *m* foreman.

'**Werks...** → **Werk...**

'**Werk|schutz** *m* Security. **~spionage** *f* industrial espionage. **~statt** *f* (-; ~en) workshop. **~stoff** *m* material. **~stück** *n* workpiece. **~tag** *m* workday, working day. **☨tags** *adv* on weekdays, during the week. **☨tätig** *adj* working. **~tätige** *m, f* (-n; -n) working person: **die ~n** the working population. **~unterricht** *m* *ped.* handicrafts.

'**Werkzeug** *n* (-[e]s; -e) tool *(a. fig.)*, *coll.* tools. **~kasten** *m* tool box, tool kit. **~macher** *m* toolmaker. **~ma☨schine** *f* machine tool. **~tasche** *f* tool bag.

Wermut ['ve:rmu:t] *m* (-[e]s; *no pl*) **1.** ♣ wormwood. **2.** vermouth. '**Wermutstropfen** *m fig.* drop of bitterness.

wert [ve:rt] *adj* worth: *et.* **~ sein** be worth s.th.; **e-n Versuch (e-e Reise) ~** worth a try (a trip); **e-r Sache ~ sein** be worthy of s.th.; **viel ~** worth a lot, (very) valuable; **nicht viel ~** not up to much; **nichts ~** worthless, no good; **~ getan zu werden** worth doing; **das ist es (mir) nicht ~** not worth it.

Wert *m* (-[e]s; -e) **1.** a) value *(a. ♣, ♠, philos., phys., ◎)*, *fig. a.* merit(s), b) importance, c) F use: **im ~(e) von** to the

value of; **Waren im ~(e) von 400 Dollar** 400 dollars worth of goods; **im ~ sinken (steigen)** lose (go up) in value; **e-r Sache großen ~ beimessen** attach great importance to s.th.; **(großen) ~ legen auf** *(acc)* set (great) store by; **k-n besonderen ~ legen auf** *(acc)* not to care much for; *fig.* **sich unter ~ verkaufen** sell o.s. short; F **es hat k-n ~!** that's no use! **2.** **~e** *pl* a) data, readings, levels, b) ♣ assets, securities, stocks.

'**Wertangabe** *f* **1.** declaration of value. **2.** declared value.

'**Wertarbeit** *f* (high-class) workmanship.

'**wertbeständig** *adj* stable, of stable *(fig.* lasting) value.

werten ['ve:rtən] *v/t* (h) assess, judge, *a. sports*: rate **(als Erfolg** as a success).

'**wertfrei** *adj and adv* value-free.

'**Wertgegenstand** *m* article of value, *pl* valuables.

Wertigkeit ['ve:rtiç-] *f* (-; -en) ♣ valency.

'**wertlos** *adj* worthless *(a. fig.)*, valueless, useless, *pred* (of) no use, no good.

'**Wertlosigkeit** *f* (-; *no pl*) worthlessness.

'**Wertmaßstab** *m* standard (of value).

'**Wertminderung** *f* depreciation.

'**Wertpa☨piere** *pl* securities.

'**Wertsachen** *pl* valuables.

'**Wertsendung** *f* ✉ registered item.

'**Wertsteigerung** *f* ☂ increase in value.

'**Wertung** *f* (-; -en) assessment, *a. sports*: rating, *sports*: score, points.

'**Werturteil** *n* value judgement.

'**Wertverlust** *m* ☂ loss of value.

'**wertvoll** *adj* valuable.

'**Wertvorstellungen** *pl* values.

'**Wertzeichen** *n* (postage) stamp.

'**Wertzuwachs** *m* ☂ increase in value.

Wesen ['ve:zən] *n* (-s; -) **1.** being, creature. **2.** *no pl* a) *philos.* essence, b) character, nature: **ihr heiteres ~** her cheerful disposition. **3.** F **viel ~s von et. machen** make a great fuss about s.th.

'**Wesensart** *f* (-; *no pl*) nature, character.

'**wesensfremd** *adj* alien *(dat* to).

'**Wesenszug** *m* (characteristic) trait.

wesentlich ['ve:zəntliç] **I** *adj* essential **(für** to), substantial: **das Wesentliche** the essence, the essential point; **nichts Wesentliches** nothing (very) important; **im ~en** essentially, on the whole; **der ~e Inhalt** the substance (*of book* *etc.*) **II** *adv* essentially, considerably, a great deal, much: **~ besser** far better.

weshalb [vɛs'halp] **I** *interrog pron* why. **II** *conj* and so, which is why.

Wespe ['vɛspə] *f* (-; -n) *zo.* wasp.

'**Wespennest** *n* wasps' nest: *fig.* **in ein ~ stechen** stir up a hornet's nest.

'**Wespenstich** *m* wasp sting.

wessen ['vɛsən] *interrog pron* **1.** *gen of* **wer**: whose. **2.** *gen of* **was**: **~ beschuldigt man ihn?** what is he accused of?

West [vɛst] *m invar* **1.** West. **2.** west wind.

'**westdeutsch** *adj*, '**Westdeutsche** *m*, *f* (-n; -n) West German.

Weste ['vɛstə] *f* (-; -n) waistcoat, *Am.* vest: F *fig.* **e-e weiße ~ haben** have a clean record.

Westen ['vɛstən] *m* (-s; *no pl*) west, *of country*: West, *of town*: *a.* West End, *pol. the* West: **von ~** from the west; **nach ~** west(wards).

'**Westentasche** *f* waistcoat (*Am.* vest) pocket: F *et. wie s-e ~ kennen* know s.th. like the back of one's hand.

Westfale [vɛst'fa:lə] *m* (-n; -n), **Westfälin** [vɛst'fɛ:lɪn] *f* (-; -nen), **westfälisch** [vɛst'fɛ:lɪʃ] *adj* Westphalian.

'**westlich I** *adj* western, west(erly) (*wind, direction*), *pol.* West(ern). **II** *adv* (to the) west (**von** of). **III** *prep* (*gen*) (to the) west of.

'**Westmächte** *pl pol.* Western powers.

'**westwärts** *adv* west(wards).

'**Westwind** *m* west wind.

'**Wettannahme** *f* betting office.

Wettbewerb ['vɛtbəvɛrp] *m* (-[e]s; -e) competition, *sports: a.* event: **♱ freier** (*unlauterer*) **~** free (unfair) competition; **in ~ stehen** be competing (**mit** with). '**Wettbewerber** *m* competitor.

'**wettbewerbsfähig** *adj* competitive.

'**Wettbüro** *n* betting office.

Wette ['vɛtə] *f* (-; -n) bet: **e-e ~ eingehen** (*or* **abschließen**) make a bet; **was gilt die ~?** what do you bet?; **mit j-m um die ~ laufen** (*or* **fahren**) race s.o.

'**Wetteifer** *m* competition, rivalry.

'**wetteifern** *v/i* (*insep*, ge-, h) (**mit** with, **um** for) vie, compete.

wetten ['vɛtən] *v/t, v/i* (h) bet: (**mit j-m**) **um et. ~** bet (s.o.) s.th.; **ich wette zehn zu eins, daß** I bet you ten to one that; **~ auf** (*acc*) bet on, put one's money on, back (*horse*); F **~, daß ...?** want to bet?

Wetter¹ ['vɛtər] *m* (-s; -) better.

'**Wetter²** *n* (-s; -) **1.** weather, *a.* storm: **bei diesem ~** in a weather like this; **→ Wind. 2.** ⚒ **schlagende ~** firedamp.

'**Wetter|amt** *n* meteorological office. **~aussichten** *pl* weather outlook. **~bedingungen** *pl* weather conditions. **~bericht** *m* weather report. **~dienst** *m* weather service. **~fahne** *f* weather vane. ⛄**fest** *adj* weatherproof. **~frosch** *m humor.* weatherman.

'**wetterfühlig** [-fy:lɪç] *adj* **~ sein** be sensitive to changes in the weather.

'**Wetter|hahn** *m* weathercock. ⛄**hart** *adj* weather-beaten. **~karte** *f* weather map. **~kunde** *f* (-; *no pl*) meteorology. **~lage** *f* weather situation. **~leuchten** *n* (-s) sheet lightning.

wettern ['vɛtərn] *v/i* (h) F storm (**gegen** at).

'**Wetter|satel,lit** *m* weather satellite. **~seite** *f* weather side. **~stati,on** *f* weather station. **~sturz** *m* sudden drop in temperature. **~umschwung** *m* (sudden) change in weather. **~vor,hersage** *f* (-; -n) weather forecast.

'**wetterwendisch** [-vɛndɪʃ] *adj* fickle.

'**Wett|fahrt** *f* race. **~kampf** *m* contest, competition, *sports: a.* event. **~kämpfer(in** *f*) *m* competitor, contestant. **~lauf** *m* race (*fig.* **mit der Zeit** against time). **~läufer(in** *f*) *m* runner.

'**wettmachen** *v/t* (*sep*, h) make up for.

'**Wett|rennen** *n a. fig.* race. **~rüsten** *n* arms race. **~streit** *m* contest.

wetzen ['vɛtsən] **I** *v/t* (h) sharpen, whet. **II** *v/i* (sn) F scoot.

Whisky ['vɪski] *m* (-s; -s) whisky.

wich [vɪç] *pret of* **weichen**.

wichsen ['vɪksən] (h) **I** *v/t* polish. **II** *v/i* V wank, jerk off.

Wichtel ['vɪçtəl] *m* (-s; -), '**Wichtelmännchen** *n* brownie, goblin.

wichtig ['vɪçtɪç] *adj* important (**für j-n** to s.o., **für et.** for s.th.): **~ tun, sich ~ machen** be self-important; *Wichtigeres zu tun haben* have more important things to do; *das Wichtigste* the most important thing; *das Wichtigste zuerst!* first things first.

'**Wichtigkeit** *f* (-; *no pl*) importance.

'**Wichtigtuer** *m* (-s; -) F pompous ass.

Wichtigtue'rei *f* (-; *no pl*) F pomposity.

'**wichtigtuerisch** *adj* pompous.

Wicke ['vɪkə] f (-; -n) ♀ vetch, sweet pea.
Wickel ['vɪkəl] m (-s; -) ✄ compress.
~**kom,mode** f (baby's) changing table.
wickeln ['vɪkəln] (h) **I** v/t **1.** (*um* [a]round) wind, tie, wrap: *et. in Papier* ~ wrap s.th. (up) in paper; → *Finger.* **2.** *ein Baby* ~ change a baby's nappies (*Am.* diapers). **II** *sich* ~ *um* wind (or coil) itself around; *sich in e-e Decke* ~ wrap o.s. up in a blanket.
Wickler ['vɪklər] m (-s; -) curler.
'Wicklung f (-; -en) ⚙ winding.
Widder ['vɪdər] m (-s; -) **1.** *zo.* ram. **2.** *astr.* (*er ist* [*ein*] ~ he is [an]) Aries.
wider ['vi:dər] *prep* against, contrary to: ~ *Erwarten* contrary to (one's) expectation(s); → *Für, Wille.* **wider'fahren** v/i (*irr, insep, no* -ge-, sn, → *fahren*) *j-m* ~ happen to s.o.; *j-m Gerechtigkeit* ~ *lassen* a) do justice to s.o., b) give s.o. his due.
'Widerhaken m (-s; -) barb.
'Widerhall m (-[e]s; -e) echo, *fig. a.* resonance: *k-n* ~ *finden* meet with no response. **'widerhallen** v/i (*sep*, h) (*von* with) echo, resound.
widerlegbar [-'le:kba:r] *adj* refutable.
wider'legen v/t (*insep, no* -ge-, h) refute.
Wider'legung f (-; -en) refutation.
'widerlich *adj* revolting, disgusting.
'widerna,türlich *adj* perverse.
'widerrechtlich *adj* illegal, unlawful: ~ *betreten* trespass (up)on; *sich et. ~ an-eignen* misappropriate s.th.
'Widerrede f (-; -n) contradiction(s), protest: *k-e* ~! no argument!
'Widerruf m (-[e]s; -e) revocation, withdrawal: (*bis*) *auf* ~ until revoked.
wider'rufen v/t (*irr, insep, no* -ge-, h, → *rufen*) revoke, withdraw.
Widersacher [-zaxər] m (-s; -) adversary, opponent.
'Widerschein m reflection.
wider'setzen: *sich* ~ (*insep, no* -ge-, h) put up resistance, (*dat*) oppose (*s.th., s.o.*). **wider'setzlich** *adj* recalcitrant.
'widersinnig *adj* absurd.
'widerspenstig [-ʃpɛnstɪç] *adj* rebellious, unruly (*a. fig.* hair).
'Widerspenstigkeit f (-; *no pl*) rebelliousness, *a. fig.* unruliness.
'widerspiegeln (*sep*, h) **I** v/t *a. fig.* reflect. **II** *sich* ~ be reflected.
wider'sprechen v/i (*irr, insep, no* -ge-, h, → *sprechen*) contradict (*j-m* s.o., *sich*

o.s.), (*dat*) oppose (*suggestion etc*): *sich* (*or einander*) ~ be contradictory, conflict. **'Widerspruch** m (-[e]s; ⁓e) a) contradiction (*in sich* in terms), b) protest, opposition: *im* ~ *zu* in contradiction to; *im* ~ *stehen zu* be inconsistent with, contradict; *auf* ~ *stoßen* meet with protest (*bei* from). **'widersprüchlich** [-ʃprɥçlɪç] *adj* contradictory, inconsistent, conflicting (*feelings*).
'Widerspruchsgeist m (-[e]s; *no pl*) spirit of contradiction.
'widerspruchslos *adj and adv* without contradiction (*or* protest).
'Widerstand m (-[e]s; ⁓e) **1.** *no pl* (*gegen* to) resistance, opposition: ~ *leisten* offer resistance, fight back; *auf* (*heftigen*) ~ *stoßen* meet with (stiff) opposition; *den* ~ *aufgeben* give in; *den Weg des geringsten* ⁓*es wählen* take the line of least resistance. **2.** ⚡ resistor.
'Widerstands|bewegung f *pol.* resistance movement. **⚴fähig** *adj* resistant (*gegen* to), *a.* ⚙ robust. **⁓fähigkeit** f (-; *no pl*) resistance (*gegen* to), robustness. **⁓kämpfer(in** f) m resistance fighter. **⁓kraft** f (powers of) resistance.
'widerstandslos *adv* without resistance.
wider'stehen v/i (*irr, insep, no* -ge-, h → *stehen*) (*dat*) resist (*s.o., s.th.*).
wider'streben v/i (*insep, no* -ge-, h) be repugnant (*dat* to): *es widerstrebt mir zu* *inf* I hate to *inf.* **Wider'streben** n (-s) reluctance. **wider'strebend** *adv* reluctantly.
'Widerstreit m conflict. **'widerstreitend** *adj* conflicting (*feelings etc*).
'widerwärtig [-vɛrtɪç] *adj* repulsive, disgusting, F nasty.
'Widerwille m (-n; *no pl*) (*gegen*) aversion (to), disgust (at). **'widerwillig** *adj* unwilling, reluctant.
widmen ['vɪtmən] (h) (*dat* to) **I** v/t **1.** dedicate. **2.** devote, give (*one's time etc*). **II** *sich* ~ devote o.s.; *sich ganz ...* ~ give one's undivided attention to ...
widrig ['vi:drɪç] *adj* adverse.
widrigenfalls [-'dri:gən-] *adv* failing which, ⚖ in default of which.
wie [vi:] **I** *interrog adv* **1.** how: ~ *macht man das?* how is that done?; ~ *ist er* (*es*)? what is he (it) like?; ~ *nennt man das?* what do you call that?; ~ *sagten Sie?* (sorry,) what did you say?; ~ *wäre*

es mit ...? what about ...? **2. ~ schön!** how beautiful; **~ gut, daß er da war!** lucky for me *etc* that he was there; *und ~!* and how!, F you bet!; → *bitte* **3. II** *conj* **3.** as, like: *stark ~ ein Bär* (as) strong as a bear; *ein Mann ~ er* a man like him; *dumm ~ er ist* fool that he is; *~ gesagt* as I said. **4.** ~ **(zum Beispiel),** *~ etwa* such as. **5.** *time:* F as, when. **6.** *ich sah, ~ er weglief* I saw him running away; *ich hörte, ~ er es sagte* I heard him say so. **7.** ~ *(auch) immer* however, no matter how; *~ dem auch sei* be that as it may; *~ sie auch heißen mögen* whatever they are called.

Wiedehopf ['vi:dəhɔpf] *m* (-[e]s; -e) *zo.* hoopoe.

wieder ['vi:dər] *adv* again: *~ gesund* well again; *immer ~* again and again, time and again; *schon ~?* not again!; *ich bin gleich ~ da!* I'll be back in a minute!; *~ ist ein Tag vorbei!* another day's over.

Wieder|'annäherung *f pol.* rapprochement. *~'aufbau m* (-[e]s; *no pl*) **1.** reconstruction. **2.** recovery. *~'aufbereitung f* reprocessing. *~'aufbereitungsanlage f* reprocessing plant.

wieder|'aufführen *v/t* (*sep,* h) rerun (*film etc*). *~'aufleben v/i* (*sep,* sn) (*a. → lassen*) revive.

Wieder'aufnahme *f* (-; *no pl*) resumption. **Wieder'aufnahmeverfahren** *n* 🏛 a) new hearing, b) retrial.

wieder'aufnehmen *v/t* (*irr, sep,* -ge-, h, → *nehmen*) resume.

Wieder'aufrüstung *f* (-; *no pl*) rearmament.

wieder|'auftauchen *v/i* (*sep,* sn) re-emerge, ⚓ *a.* resurface, *fig.* reappear, turn up again. *~'auftreten v/i* (*irr, sep,* -ge-, sn, → *treten*) reappear.

Wieder'ausfuhr *f* re-exportation.

'Wiederbeginn *m* (-[e]s; *no pl*) recommencement, *of school etc:* reopening.

'wiederbekommen *v/t* (*irr, sep,* h, → *bekommen*) get s.th. back.

'wiederbeleben *v/t* (*sep,* h) resuscitate, *a. fig.* revive. **'Wiederbelebung** *f* (-; *no pl*) resuscitation, *fig.* revival.

'Wiederbelebungsversuch *m* attempt at resuscitation.

'wiederbeschaffen *v/t* (*sep,* h) replace.

'wiederbringen *v/t* (*irr, sep,* -ge-, h, → *bringen*) bring s.o., s.th. back, return.

wieder'einführen *v/t* (*sep,* h) **1.** reintroduce, revive. **2.** ✝ reimport. **Wieder'einführung** *f* (-; *no pl*) **1.** reintroduction, revival. **2.** ✝ reimportation.

Wieder'eingliederung *f* reintegration (*in acc* into), (*social etc*) rehabilitation.

wieder'einsetzen *v/t* (*sep,* h) reinstate (*in acc* in). **Wieder'einsetzung** *f* (-; *no pl*) reinstatement.

'Wiedereintritt *m* re-entry (*in acc* into).

'wiederentdecken *v/t* (*sep,* h) rediscover.

'Wiederergreifung *f* (-; *no pl*) recapture.

'wiedererkennen *v/t* (*irr, sep,* h, → *erkennen*) recognize: *nicht wiederzuerkennen* unrecognizable.

'wiedererlangen *v/t* (*sep,* h) recover, regain.

'wiedereröffnen *v/t* (*sep,* h) reopen.

'Wiedereröffnung *f* reopening.

'wiederfinden *v/t* (*irr, sep,* -ge-, h, → *finden*) find again.

'Wiedergabe *f* (-; *no pl*) **1.** account. **2.** ♪ rendering, interpretation. **3.** reproduction (*a.* ⊙), ♪ playback. *~gerät n* playback unit. *~qualität f* fidelity of reproduction.

'wiedergeben *v/t* (*irr, sep,* -ge-, h, → *geben*) **1.** give s.th. back (*dat* to). **2.** a) describe, b) repeat, c) quote. **3.** ♪ render, interpret. **4.** reproduce (*a.* ⊙), ♪ a. play back.

'Wiedergeburt *f a. fig.* rebirth.

'wiedergewinnen *v/t* (*irr, sep,* h, → *gewinnen*) regain, recover (*a.* ⊙), ⊙ reclaim. **'Wiedergewinnung** *f* (-; *no pl*) recovery, ⊙ *a.* reclamation.

wieder'gutmachen *v/t* (*sep,* h) make up for, compensate for: *nicht wiedergutzumachen(d)* irreparable. **Wieder'gutmachung** *f* (-; -en) reparation.

'wiederhaben *v/t* (*irr, sep,* -ge-, h, → *haben*) F have s.o., s.th. back.

wieder'herstellen *v/t* (*sep,* h) restore, 🏥 *a.* cure, *a.* re-establish (*connections etc*). **Wieder'herstellung** *f* (-; -en) restoration, re-establishment, 🏥 recovery.

wieder|'holbar *adj* repeatable. **wieder-'holen** (*insep, no* -ge-, h) **I** *v/t* a) repeat, say (*or* do) *s.th.* again, sum up, F recap. **II** *sich ~* a) repeat itself (*or* o.s.), b) recur. **wieder'holt** *adj* repeated. **Wieder'holung** *f* (-; -en) repetition, *radio, TV etc:* repeat, *TV, soccer etc:* replay.

Wieder'holungs|impfung *f* booster (shot). **~kurs** *m* refresher course. **~prüfung** *f* resit. **~spiel** *n sports:* replay. **~taste** *f* repeat key.

'**Wiederhören:** *auf* ~**!** goodbye(e)!

'**wiederkäuen** [-kɔvən] (*sep,* h) **I** *v/i zo.* ruminate. **II** *v/t fig.* rehash.

'**Wiederkäuer** *m* (-s; -) *zo.* ruminant.

'**Wiederkehr** [-ke:r] *f* (-; *no pl*) **1.** return. **2.** recurrence. '**wiederkehren** *v/i* (*sep,* sn) **1.** return. **2.** come back. **2.** recur: (*regelmäßig*) ~**d** recurrent.

'**wiederkommen** *v/i* (*irr, sep,* -ge-, sn, → **kommen**) a) come again, b) come back.

'**wiedersehen** *v/t* (*irr, sep,* -ge-, h, → **sehen**) see *s.o., s.th.* again: *sich* ~ meet again. '**Wiedersehen** *n* (-s; -) reunion: ~ *mit London* London revisited; *auf* ~**!** goodbye(e)!, F so long!, bye!

wiederum [ˈviːdərʊm] *adv* **1.** again. **2.** on the other hand.

'**wiedervereinigen** *v/t* (*a. sich* ~) (*sep,* h) reunite. '**Wiedervereinigung** *f* (-; -en) reunion, *pol. a.* reunification.

'**Wieder|verheiratung** *f* (-; -en) remarriage. **~verkäufer** *m* reseller. **~verkaufswert** *m* (-[e]s; *no pl*) resale value. **~verwendung** *f* (-; -en) reuse.

'**wiederverwerten** *v/t* (*sep,* h) recycle. '**Wiederverwertung** *f* (-; -en) recycling.

'**Wiederwahl** *f* (-; *no pl*) re-election. '**wiederwählen** *v/t* (*sep,* h) re-elect.

'**Wiederzulassung** *f* (-; -en) **1.** readmission. **2.** *mot.* relicensing.

Wiege [ˈviːgə] *f* (-; -n) *a. fig.* cradle.

wiegen[1] [ˈviːgən] (h) **I** *v/t* rock, shake (*one's head*), sway (*one's hips*): *j-n in Sicherheit* ~ lull s.o. into a false sense of security. **II** *sich* ~ rock; *sich in den Hüften* ~ sway one's hips; *fig.* *sich in Sicherheit* ~ believe o.s. safe.

wiegen[2] (wog, gewogen, h) **I** *v/t, v/i* weigh: *fig. schwer* ~ carry (a lot of) weight. **II** *sich* ~ weigh o.s.

wiegen[3] *v/t* (h) *gastr.* chop, mince.

'**Wiegenlied** *n* lullaby.

wiehern [ˈviːərn] *v/i* (h) neigh: ~(*d lachen*) heehaw.

Wiener[1] [ˈviːnɐ] *f* (-; -) wiener(wurst).

Wiener[2] *m* (-s; -), '**Wienerin** *f* (-; -nen), '**wienerisch** *adj* Viennese.

wienern [ˈviːnɐn] *v/t* (h) F polish.

wies [viːs] *pret of* **weisen.**

Wiese [ˈviːzə] *f* (-; -n) meadow.

Wiesel [ˈviːzəl] *n* (-s; -) *zo.* weasel.

wieso [viˈzoː] → **warum.**

wieviel [viˈfiːl] *interrog adv* how much: ~(*e*) how many. '**wievielmal** *adv* how many times, how often. **wie'vielt** *adj der* (*die, das*) ~*e* which; *zum* ~*en Male?* how many times?; *den* 2*en haben wir heute?* what's the date today?

wieweit [viˈvait] → **inwieweit.**

Wikinger [ˈviːkiŋɐr] *m* (-s; -) Viking.

wild [vilt] *adj* **1.** wild (*a.* ♀*, zo. or fig.*), *a.* savage (*dog, tribe, etc*): ♂ ~*es Fleisch* proud flesh; ~*e Vermutungen* wild speculation; ~ *wachsen* grow wild. **2.** violent, fierce, wild: *das ist halb so* ~**!** it's not all that bad. **3.** F *fig.* wild, mad: *wie* ~ *work etc* like mad; *j-n* ~ *machen* make s.o. mad; ~ *werden* get mad, see red; *den* ~*en Mann spielen* go berserk. **4.** F *ganz* ~ *sein auf* (*acc*) be wild (*or* crazy) about. **5.** unauthorized (*camping etc*); → **Streik.**

Wild *n* (-[e]s; *no pl*) game, *gastr. a.* venison. **~bach** *m* torrent. **~bahn** *f in freier* ~ in the wild. **~dieb** *m* poacher.

Wilde [ˈvildə] *m, f* (-n; -n) savage.

'**Wildente** *f zo.* wild duck.

Wilderer [ˈvildərɐr] *m* (-s; -) poacher. '**wildern** [ˈvildɐn] *v/i* (h) poach.

'**wild'fremd** *adj* completely strange (*dat* to): ~*er Mensch* complete stranger.

'**Wildgans** *f zo.* wild goose.

'**Wildgehege** *n* game preserve.

'**Wildheit** *f* (-; *no pl*) wildness (*a. fig.*), savagery, fury, *a.* unruliness.

'**Wildhüter** *m* (-s; -) gamekeeper.

'**Wildkatze** *f zo.* wild cat.

'**wildlebend** *adj* wild.

'**Wildleder** *n*, '**wildledern** *adj* suede.

'**Wildnis** *f* (-; -se) wilderness (*a. fig.*): *in der* ~ in the wild.

'**Wild|park** *m* game park. **~sau** *f* wild sow. **~schwein** *n* wild boar. 2**wachsend** *adj* wild. **~wasser** *n* (-s; -) torrent, wildwater. **~wechsel** *m* run.

Wild'westfilm *m* western.

Wille [ˈvilə] *m* (-ns; *no pl*) will, *philos. a.* volition, *a.* intention: *böser* ~ ill will; *guter* ~ good will (*or* intention); *letzter* ~ (last) will, ⚖ last will and testament; *aus freiem* ~*n* of one's own free will; *gegen m-n* ~*n* against my will; *j-m s-n*

~n lassen let s.o. have his (own) way; **ich kann Ihnen beim besten ~n nicht helfen** I can't help you, much as I should like to; **ich kann mich beim besten ~n nicht erinnern** I can't remember for the life of me; **wenn es nach ihrem ~n ginge** if she had her way; **sie mußte wider ~n lachen** she couldn't help laughing; → **durchsetzen[1]** I. **'Willen** m → **Wille.**

'willenlos adj weak, weak-willed: **j-s ~es Werkzeug sein** be s.o.'s slave.

'willens adj **~ sein zu** inf be willing (or prepared) to inf.

'Willens|akt m act of volition. **~anstrengung** f effort of will. **~äußerung** f expression of one's will. **~erklärung** f ⚖ declaration of intention. **~freiheit** f free will. **~kraft** f (-; no pl) **1.** willpower. **2.** strong will. **2schwach** adj weak, weak-willed: **~stark** adj strong-willed. **~stärke** f (-; no pl) strong will.

'willentlich adv deliberately.

willfährig ['vɪlfɛːrɪç] adj compliant.

'willig adj willing.

will'kommen adj welcome (dat to): **j-n ~ heißen** welcome s.o. **Will'kommen** n (-s; -) welcome, reception.

Willkür ['vɪlkyːr] f (-; no pl) arbitrariness: **j-s ~ ausgeliefert sein** be at s.o.'s mercy. **~akt** m arbitrary act. **~herrschaft** f (-; no pl) arbitrary rule, despotism.

'willkürlich adj **1.** arbitrary. **2.** random (selection etc). **3.** physiol. voluntary.

wimmeln ['vɪməln] v/i (h) **~ von** be teeming (F crawling) with.

wimmern ['vɪmərn] v/i (h) whimper.

Wimpel ['vɪmpəl] m (-s; -) pennant.

Wimper ['vɪmpər] f (-; -n) eyelash: **ohne mit der ~ zu zucken** without batting an eyelid.

'Wimpernbürste f eyelash brush.

'Wimperntusche f mascara.

Wind [vɪnt] m (-[e]s; -e) (**günstiger ~** fair) wind; fig. **ein frischer ~** a breath of fresh air; **gegen den ~** into the wind; **mit dem ~** down the wind; **bei ~ und Wetter** in rain or storm; fig. **~ bekommen von** get wind of; F **viel ~ machen** a) make a great fuss (**um** of, about, over), b) act big, talk big; **j-m den ~ aus den Segeln nehmen** take the wind out of s.o.'s sails; **in alle ~e zerstreut** scattered to the four winds; **in den ~ reden**

waste one's breath; **in den ~ schlagen** cast to the winds; **wissen, woher der ~ weht** know how the wind blows; → **Mantel** 1.

'Windbeutel m gastr. cream puff.

Winde[1] ['vɪndə] f (-; -n) ⚙ winch, hoist.

'Winde[2] f (-; -n) ♣ bindweed.

'Windei n wind egg.

Windel ['vɪndəl] f (-; -n) nappy, Am. diaper. **'windelweich** adj **j-n ~ schlagen** beat s.o. to a pulp.

winden ['vɪndən] (wand, gewunden, h) **I** v/t **1.** wind (**um** round). **2.** make, bind (wreath). **II** sich ~ **3.** wriggle, squirm: **sich vor Schmerzen ~** writhe with pain. **4.** wind its way (**durch** through). **5.** sich ~ **um** wind (or coil) itself round.

Windeseile ['vɪndəs-] f **in ~** at lightning speed, in no time; **sich mit ~ verbreiten** rumo(u)r etc: spread like wildfire.

'windgeschützt adj sheltered (from the wind).

'Wind|hose f meteor. whirlwind. **~hund** m **1.** zo. greyhound. **2.** F fig. loose fish.

'windig adj **1.** windy. **2.** F shady (fellow), fishy (business), lame (excuse etc).

'Wind|jacke f windcheater. **~ka₁nal** m ⚙ wind tunnel. **~kraft** f (-; no pl) wind power. **~licht** n storm lantern. **~mühle** f windmill. **~pocken** pl 🦠 chickenpox. **~richtung** f direction of the wind. **~rose** f compass card (or rose). **~sack** m wind sock. **~schatten** m ⚓ lee, ✓ sheltered zone, sports: slipstream. **2schief** adj F crooked. **2schlüpfig** [-'ʃlʏpfɪç], **2schnittig** adj streamlined. **~schutzscheibe** f windscreen, Am. windshield. **~stärke** f wind force. **2still** adj calm. **~stille** f calm, a. lull. **~stoß** m gust (of wind). **~surfen** n (-s) windsurfing. **~surfer** m wind surfer.

Windung ['vɪndʊŋ] f (-; -en) winding, a. anat. convolution, bend (of river etc), whorl (of spiral, shell), ⚙ thread.

Wink [vɪŋk] m (-[e]s; -e) a) sign, fig. hint, tip, b) tip-off, warning: → **Zaunpfahl.**

Winkel ['vɪŋkəl] m (-s; -) **1. 1.** ⅄ angle: **im rechten ~** at right angles (**zu** to); → **tot. 2.** corner. **3.** ✗ chevron. **4.** ⚙ a) square, b) knee, elbow. **~advo₁kat** m contp. pettifogger, Am. F shyster. **~eisen** n ⚙ angle iron. **~funkti₁on** f ⅄ goniometric function. **~hal₁bierende** f (-n; -n) ⅄ bisector of an angle. **~maß** n ⚙ square.

~messer *m* (-s; -) ⚕ protractor, *surv.* goniometer. **~zug** *m* F dodge, evasion.

winken ['vɪŋkən] (h) I *v/i j-m ~* a) wave to s.o., b) reward for s.o.; *mit dem Taschentuch ~* wave one's handkerchief; *e-m Taxi ~* hail a taxi. II *v/t j-n zu sich ~* beckon s.o. (to come).

Winter ['vɪntɐ] *m* (-s; -) (*im ~* in) winter.

'**Winter...** winter (*coat, fashion, holiday, month, semester, etc*). **~ausrüstung** *f* *mot.* winter equipment. 2**fest** *adj* winterproof, ⚕ hardy: **~ machen** winterize. **~garten** *m* conservatory. **~getreide** *n* winter crop. **~halbjahr** *n* winter.

'**winterlich** *adj* wintry.

'**Winter|pause** *f* winter break. **~reifen** *m* *mot.* winter tyre (*Am.* tire). **~schlaf** *m* *zo.* hibernation: **~ halten** hibernate. **~schlußverkauf** *m* winter sales. **~sonnenwende** *f* winter solstice. **~spiele** *pl* **Olympische ~** Winter Olympics. **~sport** *m* winter sport(s). **~sportler(in** *f*) *m* person doing winter sports.

Winzer ['vɪntsɐ] *m* (-s; -) wine grower.

winzig ['vɪntsɪç] *adj* tiny, minute.

Winzling ['vɪntslɪŋ] *m* (-s; -e) F mite.

Wipfel ['vɪpfəl] *m* (-s; -) (tree) top.

Wippe ['vɪpə] *f* (-; -n) seesaw, *Am.* teeter-totter. '**wippen** *v/i* (h) seesaw, rock, *skirt etc:* bob.

wir [viːr] *pers pron* we: **~ beide (alle)** both (all) of us; **~ drei** we three, the three of us.

Wirbel ['vɪrbəl] *m* (-s; -) **1.** whirl, eddy, vortex, turbulence. **2.** *fig.* a) turmoil, whirl, b) F fuss, to-do (*um* about): *e-n ziemlichen ~ verursachen* cause quite a stir. **3.** *anat.* vertebra. **4.** cowlick. **5.** (drum) roll. **6.** peg (*of violin*).

'**Wirbelknochen** *m → Wirbel* 3.

'**wirbellos** *adj zo.* invertebrate.

wirbeln ['vɪrbəln] *v/i* (sn) whirl, swirl.

'**Wirbelsäule** *f* spine, spinal column.

'**Wirbelsturm** *m* cyclone, tornado.

'**Wirbeltier** *n* vertebrate.

wirken ['vɪrkən] (h) I *v/i* **1.** take (*or* have) effect, be effective, work, act: **~ auf** (*acc*) have a *depressing etc* effect on, affect, ⚕, ⚙ act on; **~ gegen** be effective against; *stark ~d* potent, strong; *langsam ~d* slow-acting; *et. auf sich ~ lassen* take s.th. in; F *das wirkt immer!* it never fails (to work); *das hat gewirkt!* a) that did the trick, b) that hit

home. **2.** work (*an dat* at). **3.** seem, look: *jünger ~* look younger; *er wirkt schüchtern* he seems shy; *überzeugend ~* be convincing. II *v/t* **4.** → *bewirken, hinwirken, Wunder.* **5.** ⚙ knit.

'**Wirken** *n* (-s) **1.** activity, work. **2.** ⚕, ⚙ action. '**Wirker** *m* (-s; -) ⚙ knitter.

'**wirklich** I *adj* real, actual, true. II *adv* really, actually: **~?** really?, is that so?

'**Wirklichkeit** *f* (-; *no pl*) (*die rauhe ~* harsh) reality; *in ~* in reality, actually; **~ werden** come true.

'**wirklichkeits|fremd** *adj* unrealistic, starry-eyed. **~getreu** *adj* realistic, faithful (*copy etc*).

'**wirksam** *adj* effective: *sehr ~ a.* powerful, drastic; **~ gegen** good for; **~ werden** take effect, ⚕ come into force.

'**Wirksamkeit** *f* (-; *no pl*) effectiveness.

'**Wirkstoff** *m* (-[e]s; -e) active substance.

'**Wirkung** *f* (-; -en) **1.** (*auf acc* on) a) effect, operation, b) impact: *mit ~ vom* with effect from, as from, as of; *mit sofortiger ~* as of now; **~ erzielen** have an effect, *a. s-e ~ tun* work; *s-e ~ verfehlen* prove ineffective, have no effect; *Ursache und ~* cause and effect. **2.** *phys.* action. **3.** *fig.* appeal (*auf acc* to).

'**Wirkungs|bereich** *m* sphere of activity. **~grad** *m* ⚙ efficiency. **~kraft** *f* (-; *no pl*) efficacy. **~kreis** *m* sphere of activity.

'**wirkungslos** *adj* ineffective: **~ bleiben** have no effect. '**Wirkungslosigkeit** *f* (-; *no pl*) ineffectiveness.

'**wirkungsvoll** *adj* effective.

'**Wirkungsweise** *f* (mode of) operation, function, ⚙ action, effect.

wirr [vɪr] *adj* **1.** dishevel(l)ed (*hair*), tangled (*growth*). **2.** *fig.* confuse, muddle-headed (*person*), wild (*rumo[u]r etc*), incoherent (*speech*): *~es Zeug reden* talk wild; *mir ist ganz ~ im Kopf* my head is spinning. '**Wirren** *pl* turmoil, confusion. '**Wirrkopf** *m* muddlehead.

Wirrwarr ['vɪrvar] *m* (-s; *no pl*) muddle, chaos, F jumble.

Wirsing ['vɪrzɪŋ] *m* (-s; *no pl*), **~kohl** *m* (-[e]s; *no pl*) ⚕ savoy.

Wirt [vɪrt] *m* (-[e]s; -e) a) *biol.* host , b) landlord. '**Wirtin** *f* (-; -nen) a) hostess, b) landlady.

'**Wirtschaft** *f* (-; -en) **1.** ♀, *pol.* a) economy, b) trade and industry. **2.** *no pl* a) management, b) housekeeping: *j-m die*

~ **führen** keep house for s.o. **3.** *no pl* F *contp.* mess. **4.** → *Wirtshaus*.

'**wirtschaften** *v/i* (h) **1.** manage (one's affairs): *sparsam* ~ economize, be economical (*mit* with); *schlecht* ~ mismanage. **2.** be busy. '**Wirtschafterin** *f* (-; -nen) housekeeper. '**wirtschaftlich** *adj* **1.** a) economic, b) financial, c) business ... **2.** economical, efficient: *ein* ~*es Auto* an economical car. **3.** profitable. '**Wirtschaftlichkeit** *f* (-; *no pl*) **1.** profitability, economic efficiency. **2.** economy.

'**Wirtschafts|abkommen** *n* economic (*or* trade) agreement. ~**berater** *m* economic adviser. ~**beziehungen** *pl* economic (*or* trade) relations. ~**führer** *m* leading industrialist. ~**geld** *n* (-[e]s; *no pl*) housekeeping money. ~**gemeinschaft** *f* **Europäische** ~ European Economic Community (*abbr. EEC*). ~**gipfel** *m* economic summit. ~**güter** *pl* economic goods. ~**hilfe** *f* economic aid. ~**jahr** *n* financial year. ~**kriminalität** *f* white-collar crime. ~**krise** *f* economic crisis. ~**macht** *f* economic power. ~**mi̱ni̱ster** *m* minister for economic affairs. ~**mini̱sterium** *n* economics ministry. ~**poli̱tik** *f* economic policy. 2**poli̱tisch** *adj* (politico-)economic. ~**prüfer** *m* chartered (*Am.* certified public) accountant. ~**re̱form** *f* economic reform. ~**spio̱nage** *f* industrial espionage. ~**sy̱stem** *n* economic system. ~**teil** *m* business section. ~**uni̱on** *f* economic union. ~**verband** *m* trade association. ~**wachstum** *n* economic growth. ~**wissenschaft** *f* economics. ~**wissenschaftler** *m* economist. ~**wunder** *n* economic miracle. ~**zweig** *m* branch of industry.

'**Wirtshaus** *n* inn, public house, F pub, *Am.* saloon.

'**Wirtsleute** *pl* landlord and landlady. '**Wirtstier** *n biol.* host.

Wisch [vɪʃ] *m* (-es; -e) scrap of paper. **wischen** ['vɪʃən] *v/t* (h a) wipe (*sich den Mund* one's mouth), b) mop (up). '**Wischer** *m* (-s; -) *mot.* wiper. '**Wischlappen** *m*, '**Wischtuch** *n* cloth. **Wisent** ['vi:zɛnt] *m* (-s; -e) *zo.* bison. **wispern** ['vɪspərn] *v/t, v/i* (h) whisper. **Wißbegier(de)** *f* **1.** thirst for knowledge. **2.** curiosity. '**wißbegierig** *adj* **1.**

eager for knowledge. **2.** curious.

wissen ['vɪsən] *v/t, v/i* (wußte, gewußt, h) know (*von* about): *man kann nie* ~ you never know; *weder ein noch aus* ~ be at one's wits' end; *ich weiß nicht recht* I'm not so sure; *nicht, daß ich wüßte* not that I know of; *woher weißt du das?* how do you know (that)?; *was weiß ich!* how should I know?; *weißt du noch?* (do you) remember?; *ich weiß nicht mehr* I don't remember; *ich will davon nichts* ~ I don't want anything to do with it; *sie will von ihm nichts mehr* ~ she is through with him; → *Bescheid*.

'**Wissen** *n* (-s) knowledge, learning, F know-how: *ohne mein* ~ without my knowing; *m-s* ~ *s* as far as I know; *nach bestem* ~ *und Gewissen* to the best of one's knowledge and belief; *wider besseres* ~ against one's better judgement.

'**wissend** *adj* knowing (*look etc*).
'**Wissenschaft** *f* (-; -en) science.
'**Wissenschaftler** *m* (-s; -) scientist.
'**wissenschaftlich** *adj* **1.** scientific. **2.** academic (*career, work, etc*).

'**Wissens|durst** *m* thirst for knowledge. ~**gebiet** *n* province, field of knowledge. ~**lücke** *f* gap in one's knowledge. ~**stand** *m* level of knowledge: *auf dem neuesten* ~ *sein* be up to date.

'**wissenswert** *adj* worth knowing: *Wissenswertes* interesting facts.

'**wissentlich I** *adj* conscious, deliberate. **II** *adv* knowingly, deliberately.

wittern ['vɪtərn] *v/t* (h) scent, smell, *fig.* sense (*danger*), see (*chance*).

'**Witterung**¹ *f* (-; -en) *hunt.* scent.
'**Witterung**² *f* (-; -en) weather: *bei jeder* ~ in all weathers. '**witterungsbeständig** *adj* weatherproof. '**Witterungseinflüsse** *pl* influence of the weather.

Witwe ['vɪtvə] *f* (-; -n) widow.
'**Witwenrente** *f* widow's pension.
Witwer ['vɪtvər] *m* (-s; -) widower.

Witz [vɪts] *m* (-es; -e) **1.** joke, quip: ~*e machen* (*or reißen*) crack jokes; F *das ist der* ~ *an der Sache* a) that's the funny thing about it, b) that's the whole point; F *mach k-e* ~*e!* you're joking. **2.** *no pl* wit. '**Witzbold** [-bɔlt] *m* (-[e]s; -e) F joker. **Witze'lei** *f* (-; -en) silly jokes. **witzeln** ['vɪtsəln] *v/i* (h) joke (*über acc* about), quip. '**witzig** *adj* witty, funny: *a. iro.* **sehr ~!** very funny!, big joke! **'witzlos** *adj* **1.** unfunny. **2.** F pointless, (of) no use.

wo [vo:] **I** *interrog and rel adv* where. **II** *conj* **wo ... (doch)** when, F although. **III** F *indef adv* somewhere. **IV** F *int* **i wo, ach wo!** nonsense!, nothing of the kind! **wo'anders** *adv* somewhere else, anywhere else. **wo'bei** *interrog adv* **~ bist du gerade?** what are you doing right now? **II** *rel adv* in doing so: **~ mir einfällt** which reminds me.

Woche ['vɔxə] *f* (-; -n) week: **in e-r ~** in a week('s time); **zweimal die ~** twice a week; **auf ~n hinaus** sold out *etc* for weeks (to come); **~ um ~** week after week; F **unter der ~** during the week.

'Wochenbett *n* (-[e]s; *no pl*) childbed.

'Wochenend... weekend (*edition etc*).

'Wochenende *n* (**am ~** at the) weekend.

'Wochenkarte *f* weekly season ticket.

'wochenlang I *adj* lasting several weeks: **nach ~em Warten** after weeks of waiting. **II** *adv* for weeks.

'Wochenlohn *m* weekly wages.

'Wochenschau *f* newsreel.

'Wochentag *m* weekday.

'wochentags *adv* on weekdays.

wöchentlich ['vœçəntlɪç] *adj* weekly: **einmal ~** once a week.

'Wochenzeitung *f* weekly (paper).

Wöchnerin ['vœçnərɪn] *f* (-; -nen) woman in childbed.

Wodka ['vɔtka] *m* (-s; -s) vodka.

wo'durch I *interrog adv* how. **II** *rel adv* by which, through which, whereby.

wo'für I *interrog adv* what for. **II** *rel adv* for which, which ... for.

wog [vo:k] *pret of* **wiegen²**.

Woge ['vo:gə] *f* (-; -n) wave, surge: **die ~n glätten** pour oil on troubled waters.

wo'gegen I *interrog adv* against what, what ... against. **II** *rel adv* against which, which ... against. **III** *conj* → **wohingegen**.

wo'her I *interrog and rel adv* where (...) from: → **wissen**. **II** *int* F **~ denn!** nonsense!

wo'hin *interrog adv* where (... to).

wohin'gegen *conj* whereas.

wohl [vo:l] *adv* **1.** well: **sich ~ fühlen** a) feel fine, feel good, be happy, b) **bei j-m** feel at home with s.o.; **ich fühle mich nicht ~** I don't feel well; F *fig.* **mir ist**

nicht ~ dabei I don't feel happy about it; **~ oder übel** willy-nilly, whether you *etc* like it or not; → **bekommen** II. **2. sehr ~** very well; **ich bin mir dessen sehr ~ bewußt** I am well aware of that; **das kann man ~ sagen!** you can say that again. **3.** probably, I suppose: **das ist ~ möglich** that's quite possible; **ob er es ~ weiß?** I wonder if he knows (that); **~ kaum** hardly. **4. ~ 100 Leute** *etc* about 100 people *etc*. **Wohl** *n* (-[e]s; *no pl*) welfare, good, well-being: **auf j-s ~ trinken** drink to s.o.'s health; **zum ~!** to your health!, F cheers!

wohl'auf *adj* **~ sein** be well, be in good health.

'Wohlbefinden *n* (-s; *no pl*) well-being.

'wohl|behalten *adj* safe (and sound), *object*: safe, undamaged. **~bekannt** *adj* well-known, *b.s.* notorious.

'Wohlergehen *n* (-s; *no pl*) well-being.

'wohlerzogen *adj* well-behaved.

'Wohlfahrt *f* (-; *no pl*) welfare.

'Wohlfahrts|marke *f* charity stamp. **~organisati,on** *f* charitable institution. **~staat** *m* welfare state.

'wohlgeformt *adj* well-shaped, shapely.

'Wohlgefühl *n* (-[e]s; *no pl*) sense of well-being.

'wohlgemeint *adj* well-meant.

'wohlgemerkt *int* mind you!

'wohlgenährt *adj* well-fed.

'wohlgesinnt *adj* well-meaning: **j-m ~ sein** be well disposed towards s.o.

'wohlhabend *adj* well-to-do, prosperous, affluent: **~ sein** be well off.

'wohlig *adj* pleasant, cosy.

'Wohlklang *m* (-[e]s; *no pl*) melodiousness. **'wohlklingend** *adj* melodious.

'wohlmeinend *adj* well-meaning.

'wohlriechend *adj* fragrant.

'wohlschmeckend *adj* tasty.

'Wohlsein: **zum ~!** F cheers!

'Wohlstand *m* (-[e]s; *no pl*) prosperity, affluence: **'Wohlstandsgesellschaft** *f* affluent society.

'Wohltat *f* (-; -en) **1.** good deed. **2.** *no pl* a) relief, b) blessing. **'Wohltäter(in** *f) m* benefactor (benefactress). **'wohltätig** *adj* charitable. **'Wohltätigkeit** *f* (-; *no pl*) charity. **'Wohltätigkeits...** charity (*or* benefit) (*ball, concert, match, etc*).

'wohltuend *adj* **1.** pleasant. **2.** soothing.

'wohltun *v/i* (*irr, sep*, -ge-, h, → **tun**) **j-m**

~ do s.o. good; *das tut wohl* that does you good.

'wohl**überlegt** *adj* well-considered.

'wohl**verdient** *adj* well-deserved.

'Wohl**verhalten** *n* good behavio(u)r.

'wohl**weislich** [-vaisliç] *adv* wisely, for good reason: ~ *tun* be careful to do *s.th.*

'Wohl**wollen** *n* (-s; *no pl*) goodwill, favo(u)r. **'wohlwollend** *adj* benevolent, kind: *e-r Sache ~ gegenüberstehen* take a favo(u)rable view of s.th.

'Wohn|**anlage** *f* housing area. **~bezirk** *m* residential district. **~block** *m* block of flats. **~einheit** *f* housing unit.

wohnen ['vo:nən] *v/i* (h) (*in dat* in, at, *bei* with) a) live, reside, b) stay.

'Wohn|**fläche** *f* living space. **~gebäude** *n* residential building. **~geld** *n* housing subsidy. **~gemeinschaft** *f* flat-sharing community: *in e-r ~ leben* share a flat with s.o. (*or* several other people).

'wohn**haft** *adj* resident (*in dat* in, at).

'Wohn|**haus** *n* residential building. **~heim** *n* hostel, *Am.* rooming house. **~küche** *f* kitchen-cum-living-room.

'wohn**lich** *adj* comfortable, cosy.

'Wohn**mo,bil** *n* (-s; -e) camper.

'Wohn|**ort** *m* (place of) residence. **~raum** *m* **1.** housing, accommodation. **2.** → *Wohnfläche.* **3.** → *Wohnzimmer.*

'Wohn-'**Schlafzimmer** *n* bedsit(ter).

'Wohn**siedlung** *f* housing estate.

'Wohn**sitz** *m* (place of) residence.

'**Wohnung** *f* (-; -en) flat, *Am.* apartment.

'Wohnungs**amt** *n* housing office.

'Wohnungs**bau** *m* (-[e]s; *no pl*) house building. **~mi,nister** *m* housing minister. **~pro,gramm** *n* housing scheme.

'Wohnungs**inhaber(in** *f*) *m* tenant.

'wohnungs**los** *adj* homeless.

'Wohnungs|**markt** *m* housing market. **~not** *f* (-; *no pl*) housing shortage. **~schlüssel** *m* key (to the flat). **~suche** *f* F flat-hunting. **~suchende** *m, f* (-n; -n) F flat-hunter. **~tür** *f* front door. **~wechsel** *m* change of residence.

'Wohn|**verhältnisse** *pl* housing conditions. **~viertel** *n* residential area. **~wagen** *m* caravan, *Am.* trailer. **~zimmer** *n* sitting (*or* living) room.

wölben ['vœlbən] *v/t* (*a.* *sich* ~) (h) arch: → *gewölbt.*

'**Wölbung** *f* (-; -en) **1.** arch. **2.** vault.

Wolf [vɔlf] *m* (-[e]s; ̈e) **1.** *zo.* wolf: *fig. mit*

den Wölfen heulen howl with the wolves; → *Schafpelz.* **2.** mincer. **3.** ̈ intertrigo: *sich e-n ~ laufen* get sore.

Wölfin ['vœlfɪn] *f* (-; -nen) *zo.* she-wolf.

Wolfram ['vɔlfram] *n* (-s; *no pl*) tungsten.

'**Wolfsmilch** *f* ̈ spurge.

'**Wolfsrachen** *m* ̈ cleft palate.

Wolke ['vɔlkə] *f* (-; -n) cloud: *fig. aus allen ~n fallen* be thunderstruck; *in den ~n schweben* have one's head in the clouds.

'Wolken|**bruch** *m* cloudburst. **~decke** *f* cloud cover. **~kratzer** *m* skyscraper.

'wolken**los** *adj* cloudless, clear.

'Wolken**wand** *f* bank of clouds.

'**wolkig** *adj* cloudy (*a.* ̈, *phot. etc*), clouded.

'**Wolldecke** *f* wool(l)en blanket.

Wolle ['vɔlə] *f* (-; -n) wool: F *sich in die ~ kriegen* quarrel, (have a) fight (*mit* with).

'**wollen¹** *adj* wool(l)en.

'**wollen²** **I** *v/t, v/i* (wollte, gewollt, h) a) want, *a.* demand, b) be willing (*or* prepared to), c) want to: *lieber ~* prefer; *ich will lieber* I'd rather; *et. unbedingt ~* insist on s.th.; *ich will nicht* I don't want to; *sie will, daß ich komme* she wants me to come; *was ~ Sie von mir?* what do you want?; *was will du mit e-m Regenschirm?* what do you want an umbrella for?; *Verzeihung, das wollte ich nicht!* sorry, that was unintentional; *ob er will oder nicht* whether he likes it or not; *du weißt nicht, was du willst!* you don't know your own mind!; *mach, was du willst!* do what you like!; *du hast es ja so gewollt!* you asked for it!; *was (wann) du willst* whatever (whenever) you like; *wie du willst* as you like, suit yourself; *ich wollte, ich wäre (hätte) ...* I wish I were (had) ...; F *hier ist nichts zu ~* nothing doing; → *gewollt.* **II** *v/aux* (*pp* wollen) want: *et. haben ~* want (to have) s.th.; *et. tun ~* want (or be going) to do s.th.; *er will es nicht tun* he refuses to do it; *was ~ Sie damit sagen?* what do you mean (by that)?; *er will dich gesehen haben* he says he saw you; → *heißen¹* **I** *etc.*

'**wollig** *adj* wool(l)y.

'Woll|**jacke** *f* cardigan. **~knäuel** *m, n* ball of wool. **~sachen** *pl* wool(l)ens.

~socken pl wool(l)en socks. **~stoff** m wool(l)en fabric, (broad)cloth.

wollte ['vɔltə] pret of **wollen²**.

Wollust ['vɔlʊst] f (-; no pl) voluptuousness, sensuality. **wollüstig** ['vɔlʏstɪç] adj voluptuous, sensual.

'**Wollwaren** pl wool(l)ens.

wo'mit I interrog adv what (...) with: **~ kann ich dienen?** what can I do for you?; **~ hab' ich das verdient?** what did I do to deserve that? II rel adv with which: **~ ich nicht sagen will** by which I don't mean to say.

wo'möglich adv if possible, possibly.

wo'nach I interrog adv after what: **~ fragt er?** what is he asking about? II rel adv what, after (or according to) which.

Wonne ['vɔnə] f (-; -n) delight, bliss: **e-e wahre ~** a real treat; F **mit ~** with relish.

'**wonnig** adj lovely, sweet.

wor'an I interrog adv **~ denken Sie?** what are you thinking about?; **~ arbeitet er?** what is he working on (or at)?; **~ liegt es, daß?** how is it that?; **~ hast du ihn erkannt?** how did you recognize him?; **~ sieht man, welche (ob)?** how can you tell which (if)? II rel adv **ich weiß nicht, ~ ich bin** I don't know where I stand, **mit ihm** I don't know what to make of him; **~ ich dich erinnern möchte** what I want to remind you of; **~ man merkte, daß** which showed that.

wor'auf I interrog adv what: **~ wartest du noch?** what are you (still) waiting for? II rel adv et., **~ ich bestehe** s.th. (which or that) I insist (up)on; **~ er sagte** upon which he said; **~ alle gingen** whereupon everybody left.

wor'aus I interrog adv **~ ist es (gemacht)?** what is it made of?; **~ schließt du das?** what makes you think that? II rel adv **~ zu entnehmen war, daß** from which we understood that.

wor'in I interrog adv **~ liegt der Unterschied?** what (or where) is the difference? II rel adv in which.

Wort [vɔrt] n (-[e]s; -e, ⁓er) **1.** (pl ⁓er) word. **2.** (pl -e) word, eccl. Word, saying: **geflügelte ~e** familiar quotations; **in ~en** with coins: in letters; **~ für ~** word for word; **ein ernstes ~ mit j-m reden** have a good talk with s.o.; **ein gutes ~ einlegen** put in a good word; **das ~ ergreifen** (begin to) speak, parl. a. take the floor; **mir fehlen die ~e** words fail me; **das ~ führen** do the talking; **das große ~ führen** a) do all the talking, b) talk big; **das ~ hat Herr X** the word is with Mr. X; **das letzte ~** the last word (in dat on); **das letzte ~ haben** have the final say; **du willst (or mußt) immer das letzte ~ haben** you always have to have the last word; **kein ~ darüber!** not a word of it!; **kein ~ mehr!** not another word!; **hast du das ~e?** would you believe it?; **ein ~ gab das andere** one thing led to another; **~ abschneiden, entziehen** l. **3.** no pl word (of hono[u]r): **sein ~ geben (brechen, halten)** give (break, keep) one's word; → **Mann. 4. aufs ~ gehorchen (glauben)** obey (believe) implicitly; **j-n beim ~ nehmen** take s.o. at his word; **j-m ins ~ fallen** cut s.o. short; F **hast du die ~e fassen** put into words; **mit anderen ~en** in other words; **mit 'einem ~** in a word; **zu ~e kommen** have one's say; **nicht zu ~e kommen** not to get a word in edgeways.

'**Wortart** f ling. part of speech.

'**Wortbildung** f word formation.

'**wortbrüchig** adj **~ werden** break one's word.

Wörterbuch ['vœrtər-] n dictionary.

'**Wörterverzeichnis** n list of words, vocabulary.

'**Wort|führer** m spokesman. **~gefecht** n battle of words, argument.

'**wortgetreu** adj literal, word-for-word.

'**wortgewandt** adj eloquent.

'**wortkarg** adj taciturn.

Wortklauberei [-klaʊbə'raɪ] f (-; no pl) hairsplitting.

'**Wortlaut** m (-[e]s; no pl) wording, text: **der Brief hat folgenden ~** the letter runs as follows.

wörtlich ['vœrtlɪç] adj literal, word-to-word: **~e Rede** direct speech.

'**wortlos** adj wordless.

'**Wortmeldung** f request to speak.

'**wortreich** adj verbose, wordy.

'**Wortschatz** m (-es; no pl) vocabulary.

'**Wortschöpfung** f coinage, neologism.

'**Wortschwall** m torrent of words.

'**Wortspiel** n play on words, pun.

'**Wortstellung** f word order.

'**Wortwechsel** m argument, dispute.

'wort|wörtlich → wörtlich.

wor'über I *interrog adv* ~ lachst du? what are you laughing about (*or* at)? II *rel adv* et., ~ ich sehr verärgert war s.th. I was very angry about (*or* at); ~ er ärgerlich war which annoyed him.

wor'um I *interrog adv* ~ handelt es sich? what is it about? II *rel adv* et., ~ ich dich bitten möchte s.th (which *or* that) I want to ask you.

wor'unter I *interrog adv* what ... under. II *rel adv* et., ~ ich mir nichts vorstellen kann s.th. which doesn't mean anything to me; ~ ich leide what I suffer from (*or* under).

wo'von I *interrog adv* ~ leben sie? what do they live on?; ~ sprecht ihr? what are you talking about? II *rel adv* et., ~ ich nur zu träumen wage s.th. I can only dream about (*or* of).

wo'vor I *interrog adv* ~ hast du Angst? what are you afraid of? II *rel adv* ~ du dich hüten mußt, ist what you must be careful of is.

wo'zu I *interrog adv* 1. ~ hat er sich entschlossen? what did he decide upon? 2. why. II *rel adv* ~ er bereit ist what (*or* which) he is prepared to do.

Wrack [vrak] *n* (-[e]s; -s) *a. fig.* wreck.

wringen ['vrɪŋən] *v/t* (wrang, gewrungen, h) wring.

Wucher ['vu:xər] *m* (-s; *no pl*) usury.

'Wucherer *m* (-s; -) usurer.

'Wuchermiete *f* rack rent.

wuchern ['vu:xərn] *v/i* (h) 1. 🌿 grow rampant, *a.* 🌿 proliferate, *fig. a.* be rampant. 2. practi|se (*Am.* -ce) usury.

'Wucherpreis *m* exorbitant price.

'Wucherung *f* (-; -en) 🌿 a) excrescence, tumo(u)r, b) (tissue) proliferation.

'Wucherzinsen *pl* usurious interest.

wuchs [vu:ks] *pret of* wachsen[1].

Wuchs *m* (-es; *no pl*) 1. growth. 2. build, physique: klein von ~ of small build.

Wucht [vʊxt] *f* (-; *no pl*) force, *a.* impact: mit voller ~ with full force; F das ist 'ne ~! it's terrific! 'wuchten *v/t* (h) 1. heave. 2. Räder ~ balance wheels.

'wuchtig *adj* heavy (*a. blow*), powerful.

'Wühlarbeit *f fig.* subversive activity.

wühlen ['vy:lən] (h) I *v/i* 1. dig, *animal*: burrow, *pig*: root, grub: ~ in (*dat*) rummage in. 2. *pol.* agitate. II sich ~ in (*acc*) burrow (o.s.) into.

'Wühler *m* (-s; -) *pol.* agitator.

'Wühlmaus *f zo.* vole.

'Wühltisch *m* ✝ rummage counter.

Wulst [vʊlst] *m* (-[e]s; ⸚e) 1. roll. 2. pad. 3. bulge. 4. (*tyre*) bead.

'wulstig *adj* bulging, thick (*lips*).

wund [vʊnt] *adj* sore, raw: ~ reiben chafe; ~e Stelle sore; *fig.* ~er Punkt sore point; sich die Füße ~ laufen get sore feet, *fig.* run from pillar to post.

'Wundbrand *m* (-es; *no pl*) 🌿 gangrene.

Wunde ['vʊndə] *f* (-; -n) wound, cut, gash: *fig.* alte ~n wieder aufreißen open old sores; die Zeit heilt alle ~n time is a great healer.

Wunder ['vʊndər] *n* (-s; -) miracle, wonder: ~ der Technik engineering marvel; (es ist) kein ~(, daß) no wonder (that); ~ tun, ~ wirken perform miracles, *fig.* work wonders; es grenzt an ein ~ it borders on the miraculous; F er wird sein blaues ~ erleben he's in for a shock; wie durch ein ~ miraculously; wunder wie goodness knows how; er glaubt wunder was er getan hat he thinks he's done goodness knows what; → Zeichen 2.

'wunderbar *adj* 1. miraculous. 2. wonderful, marvel(l)ous.

'wunderbarer'weise *adv* miraculously.

'Wunderding *n* wonder.

'Wunderdoktor *m iro.* miracle doctor.

'Wunderglaube *m* belief in miracles.

'wunder'hübsch *adj* lovely.

'Wunderkerze *f* sparkler.

'Wunderkind *n* child prodigy.

'wunderlich *adj* strange, peculiar.

'Wundermittel *n* wonder drug.

wundern ['vʊndərn] (h) I *v/t* surprise: es wundert mich I'm surprised. II sich ~ (über *acc* at) be surprised, wonder; du wirst dich ~! you'll be surprised!

'wunder'schön *adj* very beautiful.

'Wundertäter(in *f*) *m* miracle worker.

'wundervoll → wunderbar 2.

'Wunderwerk *n fig.* wonder, marvel.

'Wundfieber *n* wound fever.

'wundliegen: sich ~ (*irr, sep,* -ge-, h, → liegen) get bedsores.

'Wundmal *n eccl.* stigma.

'Wundschmerz *m* traumatic pain.

'Wundstarrkrampf *m* 🌿 tetanus.

Wunsch [vʊnʃ] *m* (-[e]s; ⸚e) 1. wish, desire, request: auf j-s ~ (hin) at s.o.'s request; *auf eigenen ~* at one's own request; *auf allgemeinen ~* by popular request; *(je) nach ~* as desired; *es ging alles nach ~* everything went as planned; *haben Sie noch e-n ~?* is there anything else I can do for you?; → *ablesen*[2] 3, *fromm* 1. **2. mit den besten Wünschen** with best wishes.

'**Wunschbild** *n* ideal.

'**Wunschdenken** *n* wishful thinking.

Wünschelrute ['vynʃəl-] *f* divining rod.

'**Wünschelrutengänger** [-gɛŋər] *m* (-s; -) diviner.

wünschen ['vynʃən] (h) **I** *v/t* wish, want: *sich et. ~* wish (*or* long) for s.th.; *was ~ Sie?* what can I do for you?; *du darfst dir et. ~* you can make a wish; *ich wünsche mir* I'd like to have; → *gewünscht*. **II** *v/i* **Sie ~?** what can I do for you?; *wie Sie ~* as you wish (*or* like), *iro.* suit yourself; *viel zu ~ übriglassen* leave much to be desired.

'**wünschenswert** *adj* desirable.

'**wunschgemäß** *adv* as requested.

'**Wunsch|kind** *n* planned child. **~konzert** *n* request program(me *Br.*).

'**wunschlos** *adv* **~ glücklich** perfectly happy.

'**Wunschtraum** *m* (*iro.* pipe) dream.

'**Wunschzettel** *m* list of presents.

wurde ['vʊrdə] *pret of* **werden**.

Würde ['vyrdə] *f* (-; -n) dignity, *a.* hono(u)r, *a.* rank, *a.* title: *akademische ~* academic degree; *unter aller ~* beneath contempt; *unter m-r ~* beneath my dignity. '**würdelos** *adj* undignified.

'**Würdenträger** *m* (-s; -) dignitary.

'**würdevoll I** *adj* dignified. **II** *adv* with dignity.

'**würdig** *adj* **1.** dignified. **2.** (*gen* of) worthy, deserving: *ein ~er Nachfolger* a worthy successor; *er ist dessen nicht ~* he doesn't deserve it.

würdigen ['vyrdigən] *v/t* (h) **1.** appreciate, acknowledge, recognize. **2.** *j-n k-s Blickes ~* not to deign to look at s.o.

'**Würdigung** *f* (-; -en) appreciation, acknowledgement: *in ~ s-r Verdienste* in recognition of his merits.

Wurf [vʊrf] *m* (-[e]s; ⁓e) **1.** throw: *fig. glücklicher ~* lucky strike; *großer ~* great success. **2.** *zo.* litter.

'**Wurfdiszi,plin** *f sports*: throwing event.

Würfel ['vyrfəl] *m* (-s; -) **1.** cube. **2.** dice:

die ~ sind gefallen the die is cast.

'**Würfelbecher** *m* (dice) shaker.

'**würfelförmig** *adj* cubic, cube-shaped.

würfeln ['vyrfəln] (h) **I** *v/i* **1.** play dice: *um et. ~* throw dice for s.th. **II** *v/t* **2.** throw. **3.** *gastr.* dice.

'**Würfelspiel** *n* game of dice.

'**Würfelzucker** *m* lump (*or* cube) sugar.

'**Wurf|geschoß** *n* projectile. **~kreis** *m sports*: (throwing) circle. **~pfeil** *m* dart. **~sendung(en** *pl) f* unaddressed advertising matter, *contp.* junk mail. **~spieß** *m* javelin. **~taube** *f sports*: clay pigeon.

'**Würgegriff** *m a. fig.* stranglehold.

würgen ['vyrgən] (h) **I** *v/t* strangle, throttle, choke. **II** *v/i/a*) choke, b) retch: *~ an* (*dat*) choke on.

Wurm[1] [vʊrm] *m* (-[e]s; ⁓er) *zo.* worm (*a. fig.*), *a.* maggot: **⚕** *Würmer haben* suffer from worms; F *j-m die Würmer aus der Nase ziehen* drag it out of s.o.; *da ist der ~ drin* s.th. is wrong (with it).

Wurm[2] *n* (-[e]s; ⁓er), **Würmchen** ['vyrm-çən] *n* (-s; -) F (little) mite.

wurmen ['vʊrmən] *v/t* (h) *j-n ~* gall (*or* get) s.o., rankle with s.o.

'**Wurm|fortsatz** *m anat.* (vermiform) appendix. **~kur** *f* **⚕** deworming. **~mittel** *n* **⚕** vermifuge.

'**wurmstichig** *adj* wormy, worm-eaten.

Wurst [vʊrst] *f* (-; ⁓e) sausage: F *es ist mir (völlig) ~!* I don't care (a damn)!; *jetzt geht's um die ~* now or never.

Würstchen ['vyrstçən] *n* (-s; -) **1.** small sausage: *Frankfurter ~* frankfurter; *Wiener ~* wiener(wurst). **2.** F nobody: *armes ~* poor soul. **~bude** *f*, **~stand** *m* hot-dog stand.

wursteln ['vʊrstəln] *v/i* (h) F muddle along.

'**Wursthaut** *f* sausage skin.

'**Wurstigkeit** *f* (-; *no pl*) F couldn't-care-less attitude.

'**Wurstwaren** *pl* sausages.

Würze ['vyrtsə] *f* (-; -n) **1.** spice (*a. fig.*), seasoning, flavo(u)r. **2.** wort.

Wurzel ['vʊrtsəl] *f* (-; -n) **1.** root (*a. fig.*), *A a.* radical: *A a.* zweite (*dritte*) ~ square (cubic) root; *die ~ (aus) e-r Zahl ziehen* extract the (square) root of a number; *a. fig.* **~n schlagen** take root. **2.** *dial.* carrot. **~behandlung** *f* **⚕** root treatment. **~gemüse** *n* root vegetables. **~größe** *f* *A* radical quantity.

'wurzellos adj a. fig. rootless.
wurzeln ['vʊrtsəln] v/i (h) take root: fig.
~ in (dat) be rooted in, have its roots in.
'Wurzelwerk n (-[e]s; no pl) roots.
'Wurzelzeichen n ⅋ radical sign.
'Wurzelziehen n (-s) ⅋ root extraction.
würzen ['vʏrtsən] v/t (h) a. fig. spice.
'würzig adj spicy, fig. fragrant (air).
'Würzkräuter pl (pot) herbs.
wusch [vuːʃ] pret of **waschen.**
wuschelig ['vʊʃəlɪç] adj F fuzzy.
wußte ['vʊstə] pret of **wissen.**
Wust [vuːst] m (-[e]s; no pl) **1.** tangled
mass. **2.** trash. **3.** jumble.
wüst [vyːst] adj **1.** desert, waste. **2.** a)
wild, dissolute, b) rude, c) vile: **~ aus-**
sehen look a real mess.
Wüste ['vyːstə] f (-; -n) desert, fig. a.
waste: F fig. **j-n in die ~ schicken** give
s.o. the boot.
'Wüsten... desert (sand, wind, etc).
'Wüstling m (-s; -e) libertine, rake.

Wut [vuːt] f (-; no pl) rage; fury: **e-e ~**
bekommen (F **kriegen**), **in ~ geraten**
get furious (F mad), fly into a rage; **j-n**
in ~ bringen enrage (or infuriate) s.o.;
vor ~ kochen (or **schäumen**) seethe
with rage, fume; **e-e ~ auf j-n haben** F
be mad at s.o.; **s-e ~ an j-m auslassen**
take it out on s.o.
'Wutanfall m fit (or outburst) of rage:
e-n ~ bekommen blow one's top.
wüten ['vyːtən] v/i (h) rage (a. fig. storm,
epidemic, etc): **~ gegen** rage at (or
against); **~ unter** create havoc among.
'wütend adj **1.** furious, F mad: **auf**
j-n ~ sein be furious with (F mad at)
s.o.; **über et. ~ sein** be furious at (F
mad about) s.th.; **j-n ~ machen** infuriate (or enrage) s.o. **2.** fig. raging (pain
etc).
'wutentbrannt adj furious, infuriated.
'wutschäumend adj foaming with rage.
'Wutschrei m yell of rage.

X

X, x [ɪks] n (-; -) X, x: F **j-m ein X für ein U**
vormachen fool s.o.; **ich habe x Leute**
gefragt I've asked umpteen people.
'X-Achse f ⅋ x-axis.
Xanthippe [ksanˈtɪpə] f (-; -n) F shrew,
battle-ax(e).
'X-Beine pl knock-knees.
x-beinig ['ɪksbaɪnɪç] adj knock-kneed.
x-be'liebig adj F any (... you like): **jeder**
~e anybody, any Tom, Dick and Har-
ry; **et. ℒes** anything (you like).

'X-Chromo,som n X chromosome.
Xenon ['kseːnɔn] n (-s; no pl) 🜊 xenon.
Xerographie [kserograˈfiː] f (-; no pl)
print. xerography.
'x-fach adv ever so often.
x-förmig ['ɪksfœrmɪç] adj x-shaped.
'x-mal adv F umpteen times.
x-te ['ɪkstə] adj F **zum ~n Mal** for the
umpteenth time.
Xylophon [ksyloˈfoːn] n (-s; -e) ♪ xylo-
phone.

Y

Y, y ['ʏpsilɔn] n (-; -) Y, y.
'Y-Achse f ⅋ y-axis.
'Y-Chromo,som n Y chromosome.

Yen [jɛn] m (-[s]; -[s]) 🜊 yen.
Yoga ['joːga] m, n (-[s]; no pl) yoga.
Yogi ['joːgi] m (-s; -s) yogi.

Z

Z, z [tsɛt] *n* (-; -) Z, z; → *A*.

Zack [tsak] F *auf ~ sein* (*bringen*) be on the ball (bring *s.o., s.th.* up to scratch).

Zacke ['tsakə] *f* (-; -n) a) (sharp) point, jag, ◐ tooth, indentation, b) prong.

zacken ['tsakən] *v/t* (h) a) indent, jag, b) pink (*cloth, paper*), c) tooth.

'**Zacken** *m* (-s; -) *dial.* → *Zacke:* F *er bricht sich k-n ~ aus der Krone, wenn er ihr hilft* it won't kill him to help her.

'**Zackenschere** *f* pinking shears.

'**zackig** *adj* **1.** a) indented, jagged, b) toothed. **2.** F *fig.* snappy.

zaghaft ['tsa:khaft] *adj* timid, cautious.

zäh [tsɛ:] *adj* **1.** tough (*meat*), viscous (*liquid*). **2.** *fig.* a) tough, tenacious, b) stubborn, c) slow, sluggish, slow-moving (*traffic*): *ein ~er Bursche* a tough fellow; *~ festhalten an* (*dat*) stick doggedly to. '**zähflüssig** *adj* **1.** viscous. **2.** *fig.* sluggish, slow-moving (*traffic*).

'**Zähigkeit** *f* (-; *no pl*) *fig.* toughness.

Zahl [tsa:l] *f* (-; -en) a) number (*a. ling.*), b) figure, c) numeral, cipher, d) digit: *genaue ~en* exact figures; *römische ~en* Roman numerals; *sechsstellige ~* six-digit number; *fig. in großer ~* in large numbers; *an ~ übertreffen* outnumber; → *rot*.

'**zahlbar** *adj* payable (*an acc* to, *bei* at, with): *~ nach Erhalt* payable (up)on receipt; → *Lieferung* 1.

'**zählbar** *adj* countable.

'**zählebig** [-le:biç] *adj* tough, tenacious. '**Zählebigkeit** *f* (-; *no pl*) tenacity of life.

zahlen ['tsa:lən] *v/t, v/i* (h) pay: (*Herr Ober,*) *~, bitte!* the bill (*Am.* check), please!

zählen ['tsɛ:lən] (h) **I** *v/t* count, *sports:* score: *s-e Tage sind gezählt* his days are numbered; *ich zähle ihn zu m-n Freunden* I count him as a friend. **II** *v/i* count (*bis zehn* up to ten): *fig. er* (*es*) *zählt nicht* he (it) doesn't count; *~ auf* (*acc*) count on; *~ zu* rank with, belong to (*the best etc*); *er zählt zu m-n Freunden* he is a friend (of mine); → *drei* I.

'**Zahlen|angaben** *pl* figures. *~folge f* order of numbers. *~gedächtnis* *n* memory for figures. *~lotto* *n* → *Lotto* 2.

'**zahlenmäßig** *adj* numerical: *j-m ~ überlegen sein* outnumber s.o.

'**Zahlenschloß** *n* combination lock.

Zahler ['tsa:lər] *m* (-s; -) payer.

Zähler ['tsɛ:lər] *m* (-s; -) **1.** counter, ⚡ *a.* meter. **2.** A numerator. **3.** *sports:* point.

'**Zählerablesung** *f* ⚡ meter reading.

'**Zählerstand** *m* ⚡ count.

'**Zahlgrenze** *f* fare stage.

'**Zahlkarte** *f* ✝ paying-in slip.

'**zahllos** *adj* countless, innumerable.

'**Zahlmeister** *m* **1.** ⚓ purser. **2.** ✗ paymaster.

'**zahlreich** *adj* a) numerous, many, b) large: *~ versammelt sein* be present in large numbers.

'**Zahltag** *m* payday.

'**Zahlung** *f* (-; -en) (*e-e ~ leisten* make a) payment: *et. in ~ geben* trade s.th. in; *et. in ~ nehmen* take s.th. in part exchange.

'**Zählung** *f* (-; -en) count, *a.* census.

'**Zahlungs|abkommen** *n* payments agreement. *~anweisung f* **1.** order to pay. **2.** money order. *~aufforderung f* request for payment. *~aufschub* *m* respite. *~auftrag* *m* of depositor: banker's order. *~bedingungen* *pl* terms of payment. *~bi,lanz f* balance of payments. *~einstellung f* suspension of payment. *~empfänger(in f) m* payee. *~erleichterungen* *pl* easy terms (for payment). *Ωfähig* *adj* able to pay, solvent. *~fähigkeit f* (-; *no pl*) ability to pay, solvency. *~frist f* term of payment. *Ωkräftig adj* F potent, wealthy. *~mittel n* a) means of payment, b) currency: *gesetzliches ~* legal tender. *~schwierigkeiten pl* financial difficulties. *~ter,min* *m* date of payment. *Ωunfähig* *adj* unable to pay, insolvent. *~unfähigkeit f* inability to pay, insolvency. *~verpflichtung f* liability (to pay): *s-n ~en pünktlich nachkommen* be punctual in one's payments. *~verzug* *m* default (of payment): *in ~ geraten* default. *~weise f* mode of payment. *~ziel n* date of payment.

'**Zählwerk** *n* counter.

'**Zahlwort** *n* (-[e]s; *~er*) *ling.* numeral.

'**Zahlzeichen** *n* figure, numeral.
zahm [tsaːm] *adj* tame (*a. fig.*), domesticated, *fig.* tractable. '**zähmbar** *adj* tam(e)able. '**zähmen** ['tsɛːmən] *v/t* (h) **1.** *a. fig.* tame, domesticate. **2.** control, restrain (*sich* o.s.). '**Zahmheit** *f* (-; *no pl*) *a. fig.* tameness. '**Zähmung** *f* (-; *no pl*) taming (*a. fig.*), domestication.
Zahn [tsaːn] *m* (-[e]s; ¨e) **1.** tooth (*a. ⊙*), *zo. a.* fang, *a.* tusk: *Zähne bekommen* → *zahnen* I; *humor.* *die dritten Zähne* (a set of) false teeth; *der ~ der Zeit* the ravages of time; *bis an die Zähne bewaffnet* armed to the teeth; *sich e-n ~ ziehen lassen* have a tooth out; F *fig.* *sich an e-r Sache die Zähne ausbeißen* find s.th. too hard a nut to crack; *j-m auf den ~ fühlen* sound s.o. out; F *et. für den hohlen ~* precious little; → *fletschen, Haar, knirschen, putzen* I. **2.** F speed: *er hatte e-n ziemlichen ~ drauf* he was going at a terrific lick; *e-n ~ zulegen* step on it.
'**Zahn|arzt** *m* dentist, dental surgeon. **~arzthelferin** *f* dentist's assistant. ₂**ärztlich** *adj* dental. **~arztpraxis** *f* dental practice. **~behandlung** *f* dental treatment. **~belag** *m* plaque. **~bett** *n* *anat.* tooth socket. **~bürste** *f* toothbrush. **~creme** *f* toothpaste.
zähne|fletschend ['tsɛː·nə-] *adj and adv* snarling. **~klappernd** *adj and adv* with chattering teeth. **~knirschend** *adv fig.* gritting one's teeth.
zahnen ['tsaːnən] (h) **I** *v/i* teethe, cut one's teeth. **II** *a.* **zähnen** ['tsɛːnən] *v/t* (h) ⊙ tooth.
'**Zahn|ersatz** *m* dentures. **~fäule** *f* tooth decay, caries. **~fleisch** *n* gums: *humor.* *auf dem ~ gehen* be on one's last legs. **~fleischbluten** *n* bleeding of the gums. **~füllung** *f* filling. **~hals** *m* neck of a tooth. **~klinik** *f* dental clinic. **~kranz** *m* ⊙ a) gear rim, b) sprocket (wheel). **~krone** *f* ⚕ crown. **~la¸bor** *n* dental laboratory. **~laut** *m* dental (sound).
'**zahnlos** *adj* toothless.
'**Zahn|lücke** *f* gap (in one's teeth). **~medi¸zin** *f* dentistry. **~medi¸ziner** *m* **1.** dentist. **2.** dental student. **~nerv** *m* nerve of a tooth. **~pasta** *f* toothpaste. **~pflege** *f* dental hygiene. **~pro¸these** *f* dentures.
'**Zahnrad** *n* ⊙ gearwheel, toothed wheel.

~antrieb *m* gearwheel drive. **~bahn** *f* rack railway (*Am.* railroad). **~getriebe** *n* toothed gearing.
'**Zahn|schmelz** *m* (dental) enamel. **~schmerzen** *pl* (*~ haben* have [a]) toothache. **~schutz** *m* *boxing*: gumshield. **~seide** *f* dental floss. **~spange** *f* brace. **~stange** *f* ⊙ rack. **~stein** *m* ⚕ tartar. **~stocher** *m* (-s; -) toothpick. **~stummel** *m* stump. **~technik** *f* dentistry. **~techniker** *m* dental technician. **~wechsel** *m* second dentition. **~weh** *n* → *Zahnschmerzen.* **~wurzel** *f* root (of a tooth). **~ze¸ment** *m* (dental) cement.
Zander ['tsandər] *m* (-s; -) *zo.* zander, pike-perch.
Zange ['tsaŋə] *f* (-; -n) pliers, tongs, *a. zo.* pincers, *⚕, zo.* forceps: *e-e ~* a pair of tongs *etc*; F *fig.* *j-n in die ~ nehmen* put the screws on s.o.; *den würde ich nicht mit der ~ anfassen!* I wouldn't touch him with a bargepole.
Zank [tsaŋk] *m* (-[e]s; *no pl*) quarrel. '**Zankapfel** *m* (-s; *no pl*) bone of contention. '**zanken** *v/i* (h) **1.** (*a. sich ~*) quarrel (*über* *acc* about, *um* about, over). **2.** *dial.* (*mit j-m*) ~ scold (s.o.). **Zanke'rei** *f* (-; -en) bickering.
zänkisch ['tsɛŋkɪʃ] *adj* quarrelsome.
Zäpfchen ['tsɛpfçən] *n* (-s; -) **1.** *anat.* uvula. **2.** ⚕ suppository.
zapfen ['tsapfən] *v/t* (h) **1.** tap, draw (*beer etc*). **2.** ⊙ mortise.
'**Zapfen** *m* (-s; -) **1.** ⚕ cone. **2.** tap, spigot, *Am.* faucet. **3.** ⊙ a) journal, b) pivot, c) tenon, d) peg.
'**Zapfenstreich** *m* ✕ tattoo.
'**Zapfer** *m* (-s; -) tapster.
'**Zapf|hahn** *m* tap, *Am.* faucet. **2.** → **~pi¸stole** *f* *mot.* nozzle. **~säule** *f* *mot.* petrol (*Am.* gasoline) pump.
Zappe'lei *f* (-; *no pl*) F fidgets.
'**zapp(e)lig** *adj* F fidgety: *du machst mich ganz ~!* you give me the fidgets.
zappeln ['tsapəln] *v/i* (h) **1.** struggle, wriggle: F *fig.* *j-n ~ lassen* keep s.o. on tenterhooks. **2.** F fidget (*vor Aufregung* with excitement).
'**Zappelphilipp** [-filɪp] *m* (-s; -e) F fidget.
Zar [tsaːr] *m* (-en; -en) czar, tsar.
Zarge ['tsargə] *f* (-; -n) ⊙ **1.** notch, groove. **2.** frame, case (*of door etc*).
Zarin ['tsaːrɪn] *f* (-; -nen) czarina, tsarina.

zart [tsart] *adj* tender (*meat etc*, *a. fig. age, love, etc*), delicate (*a. child, health, colo[u]r, etc*), frail (*a. fig.*), filmy (*fabric etc*), gentle (*touch etc*), soft (*skin etc*), *a.* sensitive: **das ~e Geschlecht** the gentle sex; **ein ~er Wink** a gentle hint; **nicht für ~e Ohren** not for tender (*or* sensitive) ears: (**nicht gerade**) **~ umgehen mit** handle *s.o.*, *s.th.* (none too) gently.
'zartbesaitet *adj* highly sensitive.
'zartbitter *adj* plain (*chocolate*).
'zartblau *adj* pale-blue.
'zartfühlend *adj* 1. sensitive. 2. tactful, discreet. **'Zartgefühl** *n* (-[e]s; *no pl*) 1. delicacy (of feeling), sensitivity. 2. tact.
'zartgliedrig *adj* delicate, gracile.
'Zartheit *f* (-; *no pl*) tenderness (*a. fig.*), delicacy, fragility, softness, gentleness.
zärtlich ['tsɛːrtlɪç] *adj* tender, affectionate (**zu** with), caressing: **~e Mutter** fond mother. **'Zärtlichkeit** *f* (-; -en) 1. *no pl* tenderness, affection, fondness. 2. endearment, caress.
Zaster ['tsastər] *m* (-s; *no pl*) F dough.
Zäsur [tsɛ'zuːr] *f* (-; -en) 1. *metr.*, ♪ c(a)esura, break. 2. *fig.* turning point.
Zauber ['tsaʊbər] *m* (-s; *no pl*) 1. (**wie durch ~** as if by) magic: F *contp.* **fauler ~** mumbo-jumbo. 2. *fig.* charm, magic, spell. 3. F *contp.* a) fuss, b) nonsense: **der ganze ~** the whole bag of tricks.
Zaube'rei *f* (-; *no pl*) F 1. magic, witchcraft. 2. conjuring trick.
'Zauberer *m* (-s; -) 1. magician, sorcerer, *a. fig.* wizard. 2. → **Zauberkünstler**.
'Zauberformel *f* magic formula.
'zauberhaft *adj* charming, enchanting.
'Zauberin *f* (-; -nen) *a. fig.* sorceress.
'Zauber|kraft *f* magic power. **~kunst** *f* magic (art). **~künstler** *m* conjurer, magician. **~kunststück** *n* conjuring trick.
zaubern ['tsaʊbərn] (h) I *v/t* produce *s.th.* by magic, conjure up. II *v/i* a) perform magic, b) conjure, do conjuring tricks, c) *soccer etc*: put on a brilliant show: **ich kann doch nicht ~!** I can't perform miracles.
'Zauber|spruch *m* charm, spell. **~stab** *m* (magic) wand. **~trank** *m* magic potion. **~wort** *n* (-[e]s; -e) magic word.
'Zauderer *m* (-s; -) waverer.
zaudern ['tsaʊdərn] *v/i* (h) hesitate, waver: **ohne Zaudern** without hesitation.

Zaum [tsaʊm] *m* (-[e]s; ~e) (*a. fig.* **im ~e halten**) bridle.
zäumen ['tsɔʏmən] *v/t* (h) bridle.
'Zaumzeug *n* headgear, bridle.
Zaun [tsaʊn] *m* (-[e]s; ~e) a) fence, b) hoarding: **vom ~ brechen** a) **e-n Streit** pick a quarrel, b) **e-n Krieg** start a war. **~gast** *m* onlooker. **~könig** *m zo.* wren. **~pfahl** *m* pale: F **ein Wink mit dem ~** a broad hint.
zausen ['tsaʊzən] *v/t* (h) ruffle, *a.* tousle.
Zebra ['tseːbra] *n* (-s; -s) *zo.* zebra.
'Zebrastreifen *m* zebra crossing.
Zeche¹ ['tsɛça] *f* (-; -n) ⚒ pit, (coal) mine, colliery.
'Zeche² *f* (-; -n) bill, *Am.* check: **die ~ prellen** leave without paying; *fig.* **die ~ zahlen müssen** F have to pay the piper. **'Zechpreller** *m* (-s; -) bilk. **Zechprelle'rei** *f* (-; -en) bilking.
Zecke ['tsɛkə] *f* (-; -n) *zo.* tick.
Zeder ['tseːdər] *f* (-; -n) ♣ cedar.
'Zedernholz *n* cedar(wood).
Zeh [tseː] *m* (-s; -en) → **Zehe** 1. Zehe ['tseːə] *f* (-; -n) 1. *anat.*, *zo.* toe: **große (kleine) ~** big (little) toe; **j-m auf die ~n treten** *a.* F *fig.* tread on s.o.'s toes. 2. clove (of garlic).
'Zehen|nagel *m* toenail. **~san,dale** *f* flip-flop. **~spitze** *f* tip of one's toe: **auf (den) ~n** on tiptoe.
zehn [tseːn] *adj* ten. **Zehn** *f* (-; -en) (number) ten. **'Zehneck** *n* (-[e]s; -e) decagon.
'Zehner¹ *m* (-s; -) 1. ten. 2. F → **Zehnpfennigstück**, **Zehnmarkschein**.
'Zehner² *f* (-; -) → **Zehnpfennig-(brief)marke**.
'Zehnerkarte *f* ten-trip ticket.
'Zehnerpackung *f* pack(et) of ten.
'Zehnerstelle *f* ♣ tens digit.
'zehnfach *adj and adv* tenfold.
'Zehnfache *n* (-n) ten times the amount: **um das ~ increase etc** tenfold.
Zehn'fingersy,stem *n* touch system.
'zehnjährig [-jɛːrɪç] *adj* 1. ten-year-old: **ein ~er Junge** a boy of ten. 2. **~es Jubiläum etc** ten-year (*or* tenth) anniversary *etc*. 3. **nach ~er Abwesenheit** *etc* after an absence *etc* of ten years.
'Zehnkampf *m sports*: decathlon.
'Zehnkämpfer *m* decathlete.
'zehnmal *adv* ten times.
Zehn'markschein *m* ten-mark note (*Am.* bill), F tenner.

Zehn'pfennig‖(brief)marke f ten-pfennig stamp. **~stück** n ten-pfennig piece.
zehnt adj tenth.
'zehn'tausend adj ten thousand: fig. **die oberen ♀** the upper ten (thousand); **♀e von ...** tens of thousands of ...
Zehntel ['tse:ntəl] n (-s; -) tenth.
'Zehntelse.kunde f tenth of a second.
zehntens ['tse:ntəns] adv tenthly.
zehren ['tse:rən] v/i (h) **1. ~ von** live on (a. fig. memories etc); **von s-m Kapital ~** live off one's capital. **2. ~ an** (dat) weaken, undermine; **an j-s Kräften ~** sap s.o.'s energy.
Zeichen ['tsaçən] n (-s; -) **1.** a) sign, a. mark, a. characteristic, b) signal, c) symbol, computer: character: **chemisches ~** chemical symbol; **j-m ein ~ geben** give s.o. a sign (or signal), signal to s.o.; **er gab das ~ zum Aufbruch** he gave the sign to leave. **2.** fig. sign, a. mark, token, a. omen, a. symptom: **ein ~ für** (or von) a sign of; **zum ~ daß** as a proof that; **als** (or **zum**) **~ m-r Dankbarkeit** as a token of my gratitude; **es ist ein ~ der Zeit** it's a symptom of our times; **es geschehen noch ~ und Wunder** wonders never cease. **3.** punctuation mark. **4.** astr. sign: **im ~ des Löwen** under the sign of Leo; fig. **im ~ stehen von** (or gen) be marked by. **5.** reference (number): **✝ unser** (**Ihr**) **~** our (your) reference. **6. ✝** trademark.
'Zeichen‖block m sketch pad. **~brett** n drawing board. **~dreieck** n set square. **~erklärung** f key (**für, zu** to), on maps etc: legend, in textbooks etc: signs and symbols. **~feder** f drawing pen. **~gerät** n computer: plotter. **~heft** n drawing book. **~kunst** f drawing. **~lehrer** m art teacher. **~pa‚pier** n drawing paper. **~saal** m art room. **~setzung** f (-; no pl) punctuation. **~sprache** f (-; no pl) sign language. **~stift** m pencil, crayon. **~trickfilm** m (animated) cartoon. **~unterricht** m drawing lessons, ped. art.
zeichnen ['tsaçnən] (h) **I** v/t **1.** draw (a. fig.), sketch, a. fig. delineate, design. **2.** mark: **er war von der Krankheit gezeichnet** the illness had left its mark (on him). **3.** sign (letter etc). **4. ✝** subscribe (**für Aktien** etc for shares etc, **für e-n Fonds** to a fund). **II** v/i **5.** draw (**nach der Natur** from nature). **6.** sign:

ich zeichne ... I remain ...; **verantwortlich ~ für** be responsible for.
'Zeichner m (-s; -) **1.** drawer, draughtsman, Am. draftsman. **2. ✝** subscriber (gen for, to). **'Zeichnerin** f (-; -nen) **1.** drawer, draughtswoman, Am. draftswoman. **2. → Zeichner** 2.
'zeichnerisch adj graphic: **~e Begabung haben, ~ begabt sein** have (a) talent for drawing.
'Zeichnung f (-; -en) **1.** a) drawing, ⚙ a. design, diagram, b) sketch, c) illustration. **2.** ♀, zo. marking(s), patterning. **3. ✝** subscription: **e-e Anleihe zur ~ auflegen** invite subscriptions for a loan.
'zeichnungsberechtigt adj authorized to sign, having signatory power.
'Zeigefinger m forefinger, index finger.
zeigen ['tsaigən] (h) **I** v/t show (a. fig.), a. present (film etc), a. display, exhibit, a. indicate, a. demonstrate, point out: **j-m die Stadt ~** show s.o. (around) the town; **er will nur s-e Macht ~** he just wants to demonstrate his power; **großen Mut ~** display great courage; F **dem werd' ich's ~!** I'll show him. **II** v/i (**mit dem Finger**) **~ auf** (acc) point (one's finger) at; **nach Norden ~** point (to the) north; **die Uhr zeigte** (**auf**) **12** the clock said twelve. **III sich ~** show (o.s.), appear, turn up; fig. **sie zeigte sich sehr großzügig** she was very generous; **sich von s-r besten Seite ~** present o.s. to best advantage; **er zeigte sich der Aufgabe nicht gewachsen** it became obvious that he wasn't equal to the task. **IV** v/impers turn out, prove: **es zeigte sich, daß er recht gehabt hatte** (**es richtig gewesen war**) he (it) turned out to have been right; **es wird sich ~, wer recht hat** we'll see who is right in the end.
'Zeiger m (-s; -) hand, ⚙ a. index, pointer, needle (of speedometer etc).
'Zeigestock m pointer.
Zeile ['tsailə] f (-; -n) **1.** line: **j-m ein paar ~n schreiben** drop s.o. a line. **2.** row.
'Zeilen‖abstand m **1.** spacing. **2.** TV line advance. **~anzeige** f computer: line display. **~drucker** m computer: line printer. **~eingabe** f computer: line entry. **~raster** n TV line-scanning pattern. **~schalter** m typewriter: line spacer. **~vorschub** m computer: line feed.

'**zeilenweise** adv by the line.
Zeisig ['tsaɪzɪç] m (-s; -e) zo. siskin.
Zeit [tsaɪt] f (-; -en) **1.** no pl time: ~ **und Raum** space and time; *freie* ~ spare time; *mit der* ~ in course of time, with time; *mit der* ~ *gehen* move with the times. **2.** time, a. period, space (of time), a. era, age, a. season: *schwere* (or *harte*) ~*en* hard times; F *das waren (noch)* ~*en!* those were the days; *die gute alte* ~ the good old days; ~ *aller* ~*en* ... of all time; *seit dieser* ~ since then; *(für) einige* ~ (for) some time; *(für) längere* ~ for quite some time, for a prolonged period; *lange* ~ for a long time; *seit einiger* (or *längerer*) ~ for quite some time (now); *die ganze* ~ *(hindurch)* all the time, all along; *in kurzer* ~ in a short time; *in kürzester* ~ in no time at all; *in letzter* ~ lately, recently; *in nächster* ~ shortly, soon, presently; *die* ~ *ist um!* time's up!; *um diese* ~ *bin ich schon im Bett* I'll be in bed already by that time; *morgen um diese* ~ this time tomorrow; *von* ~ *zu* ~ from time to time, now and then; *in der* ~ *vom ... bis ...* in the time between ... and ...; *vor der* ~ prematurely; *vor langer* ~ a long time ago; *vor nicht allzu langer* ~ not so long ago; *zur* ~ *(gen)* at the time of; *zu* ~*en der Römer* in the days of the Romans; *zu m-r* ~ in my time; *alles zu s-r* ~*!* a) there's a time for everything, b) one thing after another; *es ist (höchste)* ~ *zu gehen* it is (high) time to leave; *ich habe k-e* ~ I'm busy, I'm in a hurry; *das hat* ~ there's no hurry, *bis morgen* that can wait till tomorrow; *laß dir* ~*!* take your time!; *j-m* ~ *lassen* give s.o. time; *sich* ~ *nehmen für* take (the) time for (or to do s.th.); *die* ~ *nutzen* make the most of one's time; *sports*: *auf* ~ *spielen* play for time; F *es wurde aber auch* ~*!* about time too!; *es ist Geld* time is money; *andere* ~*en, andere Sitten* other times, other manners; *kommt* ~, *kommt Rat* time will bring an answer; F *(ach,) du liebe* ~*!* good heavens!; → *schinden* 2, *totschlagen, vertreiben* 1, *Wunde.* **3.** *ling.* tense.
'**Zeit|abschnitt** m period (of time), era. ~**abstand** m interval. ~**alter** n age, era, epoch. ~**angabe** f exact (date and)

time. ~**ansage** f teleph. speaking-clock announcement. ~**arbeit** f temporary work. ~**aufnahme** f phot. time exposure. ~**aufwand** m time spent (*für* on): *mit großem* ~ *verbunden sein* take (up) a great deal of time. **2**aufwendig adj time-consuming. ~**begriff** m conception of time. ~**bombe** f a. fig. time bomb. ~**dauer** f **1.** length of time. **2.** period, duration, term. ~**doku** m document of the times. ~**druck** m (-[e]s; no pl) (time) pressure: *unter* ~ *stehen* be pressed for time. ~**einteilung** f time plan: *sie hat k-e* ~ she doesn't know how to organize her time.
'**Zeitenfolge** f ling. sequence of tenses.
'**Zeit|ersparnis** f saving of time. ~**faktor** m time factor. ~**folge** f chronological order. ~**form** f ling. tense. ~**frage** f **1. es ist e-e** ~ it is a question of time. **2.** topic of the day. ~**gefühl** n (-[e]s; no pl) sense of time. ~**geist** m spirit of the age, zeitgeist.
'**zeitgemäß** adj **1.** up(-)to(-)date, modern. **2.** current, topical.
'**Zeitgenosse** m contemporary: F fig. *er ist ein übler* ~ he's a nasty customer.
'**zeitgenössisch** [-gənœsɪʃ] adj contemporary.
'**Zeit|geschehen** n current events. ~**geschichte** f contemporary history. ~**geschmack** m (-[e]s; no pl) taste (or fashion) of the time(s). ~**gewinn** m (-[e]s; no pl) time gained: *e-n* ~ *von 3 Stunden bedeuten* save three hours. **2**gleich adj sports: with the same time: ~ *ins Ziel kommen* be clocked at the same time. ~**guthaben** n time credit.
'**zeitig** adj and adv early.
'**Zeitkarte** f season (Am. commutation) ticket. '**Zeitkarteninhaber(in** f) m season-ticket holder, Am. commuter.
'**zeitkritisch** adj topical.
'**Zeitlang** f: *e-e* ~ for some time.
'**zeitlebens** adv all one's life.
'**zeitlich I** adj **1.** a) time ..., b) chronological: ~*e Abstimmung* (or *Berechnung*) timing. **2.** a. eccl. temporary, transitory. **II** adv ~ *abstimmen* time, synchronize; ~ *begrenzt* limited in time; *es paßt mir* ~ *nicht* I can't fit it in(to my timetable); *ich schaffe es* ~ *nicht* a) I don't have the time to do it,

b) I can't make it in time; **~ zs.-fallen** coincide.

'zeitlos adj timeless, ageless.

'Zeitlupe f (-; no pl) **1.** slow-motion camera. **2.** → Zeitlupentempo.

~tempo n (im ~ in) slow motion.

'Zeitlupen|aufnahme f slow-motion shot. **~tempo** n (im ~ in) slow motion.

'Zeit|mangel m (aus ~ for) lack of time. **~maß** n tempo, ♩ a. time. **~messer** m ⊚ timekeeper, timer. **~messung** f timing. **Ωnah** adj topical, current. **~nehmer** m (-s; -) timekeeper, ⊚ a. time-study man. **~not** f in ~ sein (geraten) be(come) pressed for time. **~plan** m schedule, timetable. **~punkt** m time, moment: **zum ~** at the time of; **zu e-m späteren ~** at a later date; **der ~ für den Angriff war gut gewählt** the attack was well timed.

'Zeitraffer... time-lapse, quick-motion (camera etc).

'zeitraubend adj time-consuming.

'Zeit|raum m period, space (of time). **~rechnung** f chronology: **unserer ~** of our time. **~schalter** m, **~schaltwerk** n ⊚ time switch, timer. **~schrift** f magazine, periodical. **~spanne** f period, space (of time). **Ωsparend** adj time-saving. **~strafe** f sports: time penalty. **~strömung** f trend. **~stück** n thea. period play. **~studien** pl time(-and-motion) studies. **~tafel** f chronological table. **~umstände** pl prevailing circumstances.

Zeitung ['tsaɪtʊŋ] f (-; -en) (news)paper, journal, adm. gazette: **in der ~ steht, daß** it says in the paper that.

'Zeitungs|abonne,ment n newspaper subscription. **~anzeige** f (newspaper) advertisement, F ad. **~ar,tikel** m newspaper article. **~ausschnitt** m newspaper clipping. **~austräger** m newspaper carrier. **~beilage** f newspaper supplement. **~ente** f F fig. hoax, canard. **~frau** f F **1.** newspaper carrier. **2.** news agent (Am. dealer). **3.** news vendor. **~händler** m news agent (Am. dealer). **~inse,rat** n → Zeitungsanzeige. **~junge** m newsboy. **~kiosk** m newsstand. **~leser** m newspaper reader. **~mann** m F → Zeitungsfrau. **~meldung** f, **~no,tiz** f press item. **~pa,pier** n newspaper, a. newsprint. **~redak,teur** m newspaper editor. **~ro,man** m novel se-

rialized in a newspaper. **~stand** m newsstand. **~ständer** m magazine (or newspaper) rack. **~stil** m journalese. **~verkäufer** m news vendor. **~verleger** m newspaper publisher. **~wesen** n (-s; no pl) journalism, the press. **~wissenschaft** f journalism.

'Zeit|unterschied m time difference, ✈ time lag. **~verlust** m (-[e]s; no pl) loss of time: **den ~ aufholen** make up for lost time. **~verschwendung** f waste of time. **~vertreib** [-fɛrtraɪp] m (-[e]s; -e) pastime: **zum ~** as a pastime, to pass the time.

'zeitweilig [-vaɪlɪç] **I** adj **1.** temporary. **2.** occasional. **II** adv → **'zeitweise** adv **1.** for a time. **2.** from time to time, at times, occasionally.

'Zeit|wert m ⊹ fume (or current) value. **~wort** n (-[e]s; ⸚er) verb. **~zeichen** n radio: time signal. **~zone** f time zone. **~zünder** m time fuse.

zelebrieren [tsele'bri:rən] v/t (h) celebrate (mass etc).

Zell... cellular. **~atmung** f biol. vesicular breathing. **~bau** m (-[e]s; no pl) cell structure. **~bildung** f cell formation.

Zelle ['tsɛlə] f (-; -n) **1.** cell. **2.** airframe. **3.** (telephone) booth.

'Zellgewebe n cell tissue.

'zellig adj, a. **...zellig** biol. cellular.

'Zellkern m biol. nucleus.

Zellophan n → Cellophan.

'Zellstoff m cellulose, paper: pulp.

'Zellteilung f biol. cell division.

zellular [tsɛlu'la:r] adj cellular.

Zellulitis [tsɛlu'li:tɪs] f (-; -litiden [-li'ti:dən]) ⚕ cellulitis.

Zelluloid [tsɛlu'lɔʏt] n (-[e]s; no pl) celluloid.

Zellulose [tsɛlu'lo:zə] f (-; -n) cellulose.

'Zell|wand f biol. cell wall. **~wolle** f rayon staple fib/re (Am. -er).

Zelt [tsɛlt] n (-[e]s; -e) a) tent, of circus: a. big top, b) marquee: **ein ~ aufschlagen (abbrechen)** pitch (strike) a tent; F fig. **s-e ~e aufschlagen (abbrechen)** settle down (pack up). **~bahn** f **1.** tent square. **2.** tarpaulin. **~dach** n **1.** tent roof. **2.** △ pyramid-type roof.

zelten ['tsɛltən] v/i (h) camp: **~ gehen** go camping; Ω **verboten!** no camping!

'Zelt|lager n (tent) camp. **~leine** f guy line. **~leinwand** f canvas. **~pflock** m tent peg. **~plane** f tarpaulin. **~stadt** f tent city. **~stange** f tent pole.

Zement [tse'mɛnt] m (-[e]s; -e) cement.

zementieren [tsemɛn'tiːrən] v/t (h) cement (a. fig.), metall. carburize.

Ze'mentsack m cement bag.

Zenit [tse'niːt] m (-[e]s; no pl) astr. or fig. (**im ~** at the) zenith.

zensieren [tsɛn'ziːrən] v/t (h) **1.** ped. mark, Am. grade. **2.** censor. **Zensor** ['tsɛnzɔr] m (-s; -en [-'zoːrən]) censor. **Zensur** [tsɛn'zuːr] f (-; -en) **1.** ped. mark, Am. grade: **gute ~en haben a.** have a good report. **2.** no pl censorship: **der ~ unterliegen** be censored.

Census ['tsɛnzʊs] m (-; -) census.

Zentimeter [tsɛnti'meːtər] m, n (-s; -) centimet/re (Am. -er).

Zentner ['tsɛntnər] m (-s; -) (metric) hundredweight (abbr. cwt.), centner (50 kg). **~last** f fig. heavy burden: **mir fiel e-e ~ vom Herzen** it was a great weight off my mind. **2schwer** adj fig. very heavy: **es liegt mir ~ auf der Seele** it weighs very heavily on my mind.

zentral [tsɛn'traːl] adj central: **~ gelegen sein** be centrally located; fig. **das ~e Problem** the crucial problem.

Zen'tralbank f (-; -en) central bank.

zen'tralbeheizt adj centrally heated.

Zentrale [tsɛn'traːlə] f (-; -n) **1.** central office, headquarters. **2.** telephone exchange, in firm: switchboard. **3.** ⊕ control room. **4.** fig. centre, Am. center.

Zen'tralheizung f central heating.

zentralisieren [tsɛntrali'ziːrən] v/t (h) centralize. **Zentrali'sierung** f (-; -en) centralization.

Zentralismus [tsɛntra'lɪsmʊs] m (-; no pl) pol. centralism. **zentra'listisch** [-tɪʃ] adj pol. centralist(ic).

Zen'tral|komi,tee n pol. central committee. **~nervensy,stem** n central nervous system. **~or,gan** n official party organ. **~verband** m ✝ etc central association. **~verriegelung** f mot. central locking (system).

zentrieren [tsɛn'triːrən] v/t (h) centre, Am. center.

zentrifugal [tsɛntrifu'gaːl] adj centrifugal. **Zentri'galkraft** f centrifugal force. **Zentrifuge** [tsɛntri'fuːgə] f (-; -n) centrifuge.

zentrisch ['tsɛntrɪʃ] adj centric(al).

Zentrum ['tsɛntrʊm] n (-s; -tren) centre, Am. center: **im ~ von New York** Am. a. (in) downtown New York; **sie stand im ~ des Interesses** she was the centre of interest.

Zepter ['tsɛptər] n (-s; -) sceptre, Am. scepter: humor. **das ~ schwingen** rule the roost.

zer'beißen v/t (irr, no -ge-, h, → **beißen**) bite to pieces, crunch.

zerbeult [-'bɔylt] adj battered.

zerbomben [-'bɔmbən] v/t (h) bomb. **zerbombt** [-'bɔmpt] adj bomb-wrecked.

zer'brechen (irr, no -ge-, h, → **brechen**) **I** v/t break, crack, smash: → **Kopf** 2. **II** v/i break (fig. up): fig. **~ an** (dat) be crushed (or broken) by. **zerbrechlich** [-'brɛçlɪç] adj breakable, a. fig. frail, delicate, fragile: **Vorsicht, ~!** fragile, handle with care! **Zer'brechlichkeit** f (-; no pl) a. fig. fragility, frailness.

zer'bröckeln v/t (h), v/i (sn) crumble.

zer'drücken v/t (h) crush, a. mash (potatoes etc), a. crumple (clothes).

zerebral [tsere'braːl] adj cerebral.

Zeremonie [tseremo'niː] f (-; -n) ceremony. **zeremoniell** [tseremo'niɛl] adj ceremonial. **Zeremoni'ell** n (-s; -e) ceremonial, fig. a. ritual. **zeremoniös** [tseremo'niøːs] adj ceremonious.

Zer'fall m (-[e]s; no pl) disintegration, decay, a. fig. ruin, ↯ decomposition.

zer'fallen¹ v/i (irr, no -ge-, sn, → **fallen**) **1.** disintegrate (**in** acc, **zu** into), decay, ↯ decompose, building etc: crumble (a. fig. empire etc), fall to pieces. **2.** fig. **~ in** (acc) be divided into.

zer'fallen² adj **1.** decayed, in ruins. **2.** **mit j-m ~ sein** be at odds with s.o.; **mit sich und der Welt ~** disgusted with life.

Zer'falls|erscheinung f sign of decay. **~pro,dukt** n nucl. decay product. **~reihe** f nucl. family, decay chain. **~zeit** f nucl. decay period (or time).

zer'fetzen v/t (h) tear s.th. (in)to pieces, shred, slash, mangle.

zerfleddern [-'flɛdərn] v/t (h) tatter.

zerfleischen [-'flaiʃən] (h) **I** v/t mangle, tear s.o., s.th. to pieces: fig. **einander ~** tear each other apart. **II sich ~** fig. torment o.s.

zer'fließen v/i (irr, no -ge-, sn, → **fließen**) a) run, b) melt: **sie zerfloß vor Mitleid** she was melting with pity.

zer'**fressen**[1] v/t (irr, no -ge-, h, → **fressen**) 1. moths: eat (holes into), mice etc: gnaw s.th. to pieces. 2. 🐟, ⊙ corrode.

zer'**fressen**[2] adj von Motten ~ moth-eaten; vom Rost ~ corroded; fig. vom Neid ~ eaten up with envy.

zer**furcht** [-'furçt] adj a. fig. furrowed.

zer'**gehen** v/i (irr, no -ge-, sn, → **gehen**) dissolve, melt; auf der Zunge ~ melt in one's mouth.

zer'**gliedern** v/t (h) analy/se (Am. -ze), dissect, a. parse (sentence).

zer'**hacken** v/t (h) chop (a. 🍴), mince.

zer'**hauen** v/t (h) cut s.th. to pieces.

zer'**kauen** v/t (h) chew (well).

zer**kleinern** [-'klaınərn] v/t (h) reduce s.th. to small pieces, crush, cut s.th. up.

zer**klüftet** [-'klyftət] adj jagged, rugged.

zer'**knautschen** v/t (h) F crumple.

zer**knirscht** [-'knɪrʃt] adj contrite: ~ sein feel remorse (über acc at).

zer**knirschung** f (-; no pl) contrition.

zer'**knittern** v/t (h), v/i (sn) crumple, crease.

zer'**knüllen** v/t (h) crumple up.

zer'**kratzen** v/t (h) scratch.

zer'**krümeln** v/t (h), v/i (sn) crumble.

zer'**lassen** v/t (irr, no -ge-, h, → **lassen**) melt (butter etc).

zer'**laufen** v/i (irr, no -ge-, sn, → **laufen**) butter etc: melt, colo[u]r: bleed.

zer**legbar** [-'le:kba:r] adj dismountable, knock-down ...: ... ist ~ ... can be taken apart. zer'**legen** v/t (h) 1. take s.th. apart, ⊙ a. dismantle, knock down. 2. cut s.th. up, dissect, carve (roast). 3. 🔬 reduce, a. 🐟 decompose; 🔬 in Faktoren ~ factorize. 4. → **zergliedern**.

zer'**lesen** adj well-thumbed (book etc).

zer**löchert** [-'lœçərt] adj full of holes.

zer**lumpt** [-'lʊmpt] adj ragged, tattered.

zer**malmen** [-'malmən] v/t (h) crush.

zer'**martern** v/t (h) sich den Kopf ~ rack one's brain (über acc over).

zer**mürben** [-'myrbən] v/t (h) wear s.o. down, ✕ soften up: ~d trying.

Zer'**mürbungskrieg** m war of attrition.

zer'**nagen** v/t (h) gnaw s.th. to pieces.

zer'**pflücken** v/t (h) pick s.th. to pieces.

zer'**platzen** v/i (sn) burst, explode.

zer'**quetschen** v/t (h) crush (a. ⊙), squash, mash: F 70 Mark und ein paar Zerquetschte 70 marks and some.

'**Zerrbild** n a. fig. caricature, distorted picture, fig. a. travesty.

zer'**reden** v/t (h) flog s.th. to death.

zer'**reiben** v/t (irr, no -ge-, h, → **reiben**) crush, grind: et. zwischen den Fingern ~ rub s.th. between one's fingers.

zer'**reißen** (irr, no -ge-, h, → **reißen**) I v/t tear s.th. up, tear s.th. to pieces (or apart), rip up, break (thread, fetters, fig. ties etc): er hat sich die Hose zerrissen he tore his pants; es zerriß ihr das Herz it broke her heart; F fig. in der Luft ~ a) tear s.o. limb from limb, b) tear s.o., s.th. to pieces. II v/i tear, chain, thread, etc: break, bag etc: burst. III sich (fast) ~ F fig. bend over backwards; ich kann mich doch nicht ~! I can't be in two places at once.

Zer'**reißfestigkeit** f ⊙ tear resistance. ~**probe** f 1. ⊙ tension test. 2. ordeal.

zer**ren** ['tsɛrən] I v/t 1. drag, haul: j-n hinter sich her ~ drag s.o. along; fig. et. an die Öffentlichkeit ~ drag s.th. into the limelight. 2. 🔬 pull, strain (sich e-n Muskel a muscle). II v/i ~ an (dat) pull at, tug at; der Hund zerrte an der Leine the dog strained at its leash.

zer'**rinnen** v/i (irr, no -ge-, sn, → **rinnen**) melt away (a. fig. money etc), fig. dreams etc: fade, vanish, plans etc: come to nothing: wie gewonnen, so zerronnen easy come, easy go.

zer**rissen** [-'rɪsən] adj a. fig. torn: er ist innerlich ~ he is torn by inner conflicts.

Zer'**rissenheit** f (-; no pl) fig. (innere) ~ inner conflicts.

'**Zerrung** f (-; -en) 🔬 strain.

zer**rütten** [-'rytən] v/t (h) ruin, wreck (a. health, marriage, etc), a. unhinge, derange (mind): ihre Nerven sind zerrüttet her nerves are shattered; zerrüttete Ehe (Familienverhältnisse) broken marriage (home).

Zer'**rüttung** f (-; -en) ruin, ruinous state: ⚖ (unheilbare) ~ der Ehe (irretrievable) breakdown of a marriage.

zer'**sägen** v/t (h) saw s.th. up.

zer'**schellen** v/i (sn) smash, be smashed to pieces, ✈ crash, ⚓ be wrecked.

zer'**schießen** v/t (irr, no -ge-, h, → **schießen**) riddle, batter.

zer'**schlagen**[1] (irr, no -ge-, h, → **schlagen**) I v/t smash (a. fig.), smash s.th. to pieces, shatter. II sich ~ hopes, plans, *etc*: come to nothing. **zer'schlagen²** *adj* F *fig.* dead-beat, whacked: *sich wie ~ fühlen* feel washed out.

zerschlissen [-'ʃlɪsən] *adj* worn-out.

zer'schmettern *v/t* (h) smash, shatter.

zer'schneiden *v/t* (*irr, no* -ge-, h, → *schneiden*) cut (*s.th.* up), carve (*roast*), slice, shred.

zer'schrammen *v/t* (h) scratch.

zer'setzen (h) I *v/t* **1.** 🝆 decompose. **2.** *fig.* corrupt, undermine. II *sich ~ a.* 🝆 decay, decompose, disintegrate.

zer'setzend *adj fig.* subversive.

Zer'setzung *f* (-; *no pl*) **1.** decay, *a.* 🝆 decomposition, disintegration. **2.** *fig.* corruption, *pol.* subversion.

zer'siedeln *v/t* (h) spoil (by uncontrolled development). **Zer'sied(e)lung** *f* (-; *no pl*) urban sprawl.

zerspanen [-'ʃpaːnən] *v/t* (h) machine.

zer'splittern I *v/t* (h) shatter, *a. fig.* split (up), splinter: *s-e Kräfte ~* → III a. II *v/i* (sn) shatter, *a. fig.* splinter. III *sich ~ fig. a.*) dissipate one's energies, b) do too many things at once.

zer'springen *v/i* (*irr, no* -ge-, sn, → *springen*) shatter, break.

zer'stampfen *v/t* (h) **1.** crush, pound. **2.** trample (down).

zer'stäuben *v/t* (h) **1.** spray, atomize. **2.** dust, sprinkle (*powder*).

Zer'stäuber *m* (-s; -) atomizer, sprayer.

zer'stechen *v/t* (*irr, no* -ge-, h, → *stechen*) **1.** *j-n ~ insects*: bite s.o. all over. **2.** puncture, pierce.

zer'stören *v/t* (h) *a. fig.* destroy, ruin (*a. health etc*), wreck (*a. marriage etc*): *j-s Hoffnungen ~* shatter s.o.'s hopes.

Zer'störer *m* (-s; -) *a.* ✠ destroyer.

zer'störerisch *adj* destructive.

Zer'störung *f* (-, -en) **1.** destruction (*a. fig.*), devastation. **2.** *pl* ravages.

Zer'störungs|trieb *m psych.* destruction instinct. **~werk** *n* work of destruction. **~wut** *f* destructive frenzy, vandalism.

zer'streuen (h) I *v/t* **1.** disperse, scatter, *a.* diffuse (*light*), *a.* break up (*crowd*). **2.** dispel, dissipate (*doubts etc*). **3.** *j-n ~* amuse s.o. II *sich ~* **4.** → 1. **5.** amuse o.s. **zer'streut** *adj fig.* absent-minded. **Zer'streutheit** *f* (-; *no pl*) *fig.* absent-mindedness. **Zer'streuung** *f* (-; -en) **1.** *no pl* a) dispersion, scattering, *a.* diffu-

sion (*of light*), b) dissipation (*of doubts etc*). **2.** (*zur ~* as a) diversion.

zerstückeln [-'ʃtʏkəln] *v/t* (h) cut *s.th.* up, dismember (*body*).

zer'teilen *v/t* (h) **1.** (*a. sich ~*) divide (*or* split) (*in acc* into). **2.** → *zerlegen* 2. **3.** (*a. sich ~*) disperse, break up (*clouds, fog, etc*). **4.** ✚ resolve (*tumo[u]r*).

Zertifikat [tsɛrtifi'kaːt] *n* (-[e]s; -e) certificate.

zer'trampeln *v/t* (h) trample under foot.

zer'trennen *v/t* (h) **1.** take *s.th.* apart, separate, sever. **2.** undo (*seam*).

zer'treten *v/t* (*irr, no* -ge-, h, → *treten*) crush (*a. fig.*), stamp out (*fire etc*).

zertrümmern [-'trʏmərn] *v/t* (h) demolish, wreck, smash, ✚ crush (*stone*). **Zer'trümmerung** *f* (-; -en) demolition, smashing, ✚ crushing.

Zervelatwurst [tsɛrvə'laːt-] *f* saveloy.

zer'wühlen *v/t* (h) **1.** root up, churn up. **2.** dishevel (*hair*), rumple (*a. bed*).

Zerwürfnis [-'vʏrfnɪs] *n* (-ses; -se) quarrel, split, rupture.

zer'zausen *v/t* (h) ruffle, tousle: *zerzaust* dishevel(l)ed, untidy.

Zeter ['tseːtər] F *~ und Mord(io) schreien* cry blue murder.

zetern ['tseːtərn] *v/i* (h) F **1.** wail. **2.** a) (put up a) squawk, b) nag.

Zettel ['tsɛtəl] *m* (-s; -) slip (of paper), b) note, c) label, *Am.* sticker, d) leaflet, e) card. **~kar|tei** *f* card index. **~kasten** *m* card index (box).

Zeug [tsɔʏk] *n* (-[e]s; *no pl*) **1.** a) things, b) tools, c) (*drinks, food, etc*) stuff, d) *contp.* rubbish: *dummes ~ reden* talk nonsense, drivel. **2.** fabric, stuff: *fig.* **er hat das ~ zum Arzt** he has the makings of a doctor; *sie hat das ~ dazu* she's got what it takes; F *was das ~ hält* like mad; *sich ins ~ legen* put one's back into it, go all out (*für* for); *j-m am ~(e) flicken* find fault with s.o.

Zeuge ['tsɔʏgə] *m* (-n; -n) witness (*der Anklage* for the prosecution): *vor ~n* in the presence of witnesses; *fig. ~n der Vergangenheit* relics of the past.

zeugen¹ ['tsɔʏgən] *v/t* (h) **1.** *biol.* procreate, father. **2.** *fig.* generate, create.

'zeugen² *v/i* (h) **1.** 🜨 give evidence: *fig. ~ von* bespeak, be a sign of, show.

'Zeugen|aussage *f* evidence, testimony, *a.* deposition. **~bank** *f* witness box

(*Am.* stand). **~geld** *n* witness expenses. **~vernehmung** *f* hearing of witnesses.

'**Zeugin** *f* (-; -nen) (female) witness.

'**Zeugnis** ['tsɔʏknɪs] *n* (-ses; -se) **1.** *ped.* a) report (card), b) certificate, diploma: **er hat ein gutes ~** he was given a good report. **2.** a) reference, b) credentials: **gute ~se haben** have good references; **j-m ein gutes ~ ausstellen** a. *fig.* give s.o. a good character. **3.** certificate. **4.** ⚖ *or fig.* testimony (*gen* to), evidence: **zum ~** (*gen*) in witness of; *fig.* **~ ablegen** (*or* **geben**) bear witness (**für** to, **von** of). **~konfe,renz** *f* *ped.* reports conference. **~verweigerungsrecht** *n* ⚖ right to refuse to give evidence.

'**Zeugung** *f* (-; -en) *biol.* procreation.
'**Zeugungsakt** *m* progenitive act.
'**zeugungsfähig** *adj* fertile.
'**Zeugungsfähigkeit** *f* (-; *no pl*) fertility.
'**zeugungsunfähig** *adj* impotent, sterile.
'**Zeugungsunfähigkeit** *f* (-; *no pl*) impotence, sterility.

Zichorie [tsɪ'çoːrɪə] *f* (-; -n) ♣ chicory.

'**Zicke** ['tsɪkə] *f* (-; -n) **1.** *zo.* (she-)goat. **2.** → **Ziege** 2. '**Zicken** *pl* F (**mach k-e ~**) none of your) silly tricks. '**zickig** *adj* F a) prim, prudish, b) silly.

'**Zicklein** *n* (-s; -) *zo.* kid.
'**Zickzack** ['tsɪktsak] *m* (-[e]s; -e) (*a.* **im ~ gehen** *or* **fahren**) zigzag.

'**Ziege** ['tsiːgə] *f* (-; -n) **1.** *zo.* (she-)goat. **2.** F *contp.* (**blöde ~**) silly old cow.

'**Ziegel** ['tsiːgəl] *m* (-s; -) a) brick, b) tile.
'**Ziegeldach** *n* tiled roof.
'**Ziege'lei** *f* (-; -en) brickworks.
'**ziegelrot** *adj* brick-red.
'**Ziegelstein** *m* brick.
'**Ziegen**|**bock** *m* he-goat. **~fell** *n* goatskin. **~käse** *m* goat's cheese. **~leder** *n* goatskin, kid (leather). **~milch** *f* goat's milk. **~peter** *m* (-s; *no pl*) F 🐛 mumps.

'**Ziehbrunnen** *m* draw well.

ziehen ['tsiːən] (zog, gezogen, h) **I** *v/t* **1.** draw, pull, drag, tug, haul: **j-n mit sich ~** drag s.o. along with one; **j-n am Ärmel (Ohr) ~** pull s.o. by the sleeve (ear); **j-n an den Haaren ~** pull s.o.'s hair; **Zigaretten aus e-m Automaten ~** get some cigarettes from a machine; **sie zog den Ring vom Finger** she pulled the ring off (her finger); *mot.* **er zog den Wagen nach links** he pulled the car to the left; **j-n an sich ~** draw s.o. close (to one);

die Aufmerksamkeit (alle Blicke) auf sich ~ attract attention (every eye); **Blasen ~** blister; **auf Flaschen ~** bottle; **den Hut ~** *a. fig.* take off one's hat (**vor j-m** to s.o.); **Perlen auf e-e Schnur ~** thread beads; → **Betracht, Bilanz, Erwägung, Fell** 2, **Länge** 1 *etc.* **2. nach sich ~** have (*consequences etc*), involve, entail (*costs etc*). **3.** draw, pull (out), *a.* extract (*tooth*), 💉 take out, remove (*stitches*): **er zog s-e Brieftasche** he took out his wallet; **er zog die Pistole** he drew his pistol; **j-n aus dem Wasser ~** pull s.o. from the water; → **Affäre, Gewinn** 1, **Los** 1, **Nutzen, Wurzel** 1, **Zahn** 1. **4.** draw (*circle, line, etc*): → **Parallele, Schlußstrich. 5.** ⚙ a) draw, b) stretch, c) rifle (*gun barrel*). **6.** cut, run, dig (*ditch etc*), build, erect (*wall, fence, etc*), put up (*line etc*): → **Leine.** **7.** ♣ cultivate, *zo.* rear, breed. **II** *v/i* **8.** **~ an** (*dat*) pull at, tug at, **e-r Zigarette** *etc.* F (have a) drag at a cigarette *etc.*, **der Leine** strain at its leash; F **laß mich mal ~!** give me a drag! **9.** pipe, stove, *etc.* *a.* coffee, tea: draw: **den Tee drei Minuten ~ lassen** *a.* let the tea stand for three minutes. **10.** move, go, march, wander, migrate, *clouds etc*: drift: **s-s Weges ~** go one's way; *in den Krieg ~* go to war; → **Feld.** **11.** (re)move: **aufs Land ~** move to the country; **zu j-m ~** move in with s.o. **12.** hurt, ache: **~der Schmerz** twinge. **13.** F *fig.* pretext *etc*: work, *publicity etc*: go down (well): **das zieht (bei ihm) nicht!** that won't work (with him); **das zieht immer!** that sort of thing always goes down well (**bei** with); **das zog!** that did the trick. **14.** *chess*: move: **wer zieht?** whose move is it?; **mit dem König ~** move the king (**auf** *acc* to). **15.** draw (one's pistol), pull a gun. **16.** *sports or fig.* set the pace. **III** *sich ~* **17.** (*a.* **sich ~ lassen**) stretch: → **Länge 1.** **18.** → **verziehen²** 5. **19.** stretch, extend, run (*a. motif etc*, **durch** through): F **der Weg zieht sich** the way seems endless. **IV** *v/impers* **20.** **es zieht** there is a draught (*Am.* draft). **21. es zieht j-n zu** s.o. feels attracted (*or* drawn) to; **es zog ihn nach Hause** he felt an urge to return home.

'**Ziehen** *n* (-s) twinge, ache.

'**Ziehhar,monika** *f* ♪ accordion.

'**Ziehung** f (-; -en) drawing, draw.
Ziel [tsi:l] n (-[e]s; -e) **1.** destination. **2.** *sports:* finish(ing line): **als Erster durchs ~ gehen** finish first; **sich ins ~ werfen** lunge into the tape. **3.** *esp.* ✗ mark, aim, *a.* target, *a.* (*tactical*) objective: **das ~ verfehlen** miss; **über das ~ hinausschießen** *a. fig.* overshoot the mark. **4.** *fig.* aim, goal, end, objective, target (*a.* ✝): **sein ~ erreichen** reach one's goal, F get there; (**nicht**) **zum ~ führen** succeed (fail); **sich das ~ setzen zu** *inf* aim to *inf*, aim at *ger*; **sein ~ aus dem Auge verlieren** (**im Auge behalten**) lose (keep) sight of one's goal.
'**Zielanflug** m approach run.
'**Zielband** n *sports:* tape.
'**zielbewußt → zielstrebig.**
'**Zieleinlauf** m *sports:* finish.
zielen ['tsi:lən] v/i (h) (**auf** acc at) (take) aim, level, *fig.* be aimed: → **gezielt.**
'**Ziel|fernrohr** n telescopic sight. **~flug** m homing. **~foto** n *sports:* photo of the finish. **~gerade** f *sports:* home stretch. **⩗gerichtet** adj goal-directed. **~gruppe** f target group. **~kamera** f photo-finish camera. **~kurve** f *sports:* home bend. **~linie** f *sports:* finishing line.
'**ziellos** adj aimless.
'**Ziel|richter** m *sports:* judge (at the finish). **~scheibe** f target, *fig. a.* butt: ~ **des Spottes** laughing-stock.
'**Zielsetzung** f (-; -en) objective, target.
'**zielsicher** adj unerring.
'**Zielsprache** f target language.
'**Zielvorstellung** f objective.
'**zielstrebig** [-ʃtre:biç] adj purposeful, single-minded, determined.
'**Zielstrebigkeit** f (-; no pl) determination, single-mindedness.
ziemlich ['tsi:mlıç] **I** adj **1.** F considerable, quite a lot: **er wird mit ~er Sicherheit kommen** he's fairly certain to come; **das ist e-e ~e Frechheit** that's rather a cheek. **II** adv **2.** rather, quite: ~ **gut** F pretty good; ~ **ausführlich** in some detail; ~ **viel** quite a lot (of); ~ **viele** quite a few; **ich bin ~ sicher** F I'm pretty sure. **3.** almost, just about, F pretty well: **ich bin so ~ fertig** I've more or less finished; **so ~ alles** practically everything; **es ist so ~ dasselbe** F it's pretty much the same thing.
Zierde ['tsi:rdə] f (-; -n) **1.** (**zur ~** for)

decoration. **2.** *fig.* credit (*gen* or **für** to).
zieren ['tsi:rən] (h) **I** v/t adorn, decorate. **II sich ~** make a fuss, *woman:* play coy; **er zierte sich nicht lange** he didn't need much pressing; **komm, zier dich nicht!** come on!
'**Zierfisch** m ornamental fish.
'**Ziergarten** m ornamental garden.
'**Zierleiste** f border (*a. print.*), ornamental mo(u)lding, *mot.* trim.
'**zierlich** adj **1.** delicate, dainty. **2.** graceful, gracile, *woman: a.* petite. '**Zierlichkeit** f (-; no pl) delicateness, daintiness.
'**Zierpflanze** f ornamental plant.
Ziffer ['tsıfər] f (-; -n) **1.** a) figure, number, b) digit: **in ~n** in figures. **2.** ⅔ subparagraph, *in contract etc:* item.
'**Zifferblatt** n dial, face.
zig [tsıç] adj F umpteen.
Zigarette [tsiga'rɛtə] f (-; -n) cigarette, *Am. a.* cigaret.
Ziga'retten|anzünder m *mot.* cigarette lighter. **~auto,mat** m cigarette machine. **~e,tui** n cigarette case. **~marke** f brand of cigarettes. **~packung** f cigarette packet (*Am.* pack). **~pause** f F (**e-e ~ machen**) have a) smoke. **~raucher** m cigarette smoker. **~schachtel** f cigarette packet (*Am.* pack). **~spitze** f cigarette holder. **~stummel** m cigarette end, stub, butt.
Zigarillo [tsiga'rılo] m (-s; -s) cigarillo.
Zigarre [tsi'garə] f (-; -n) cigar.
Zi'garrenabschneider m cigar cutter.
Zi'garrenstummel m cigar end, butt.
Zigeuner [tsi'gɔynər] m (-s; -), **Zi'geunerin** f (-; -nen) gypsy, *Br. a.* gipsy.
Zi'geunerleben n *fig.* gypsy life.
zigst [tsıçst] adj F umpteenth.
Zikade [tsi'ka:də] f (-; -n) *zo.* cicada.
Zimmer ['tsımər] n (-s; -) room. **~an,tenne** f indoor aerial (*Am.* antenna). **~einrichtung** f **1.** furnishing, interior (decoration). **2.** furniture.
'**Zimmerhandwerk** n carpentry.
...zimm(e)rig [-tsım(ə)rıç] ...-roomed.
'**Zimmer|kellner** m room waiter. **~lautstärke** f household noise level: **das Radio auf ~ stellen** turn one's radio down to moderate volume. **~mädchen** n chambermaid.
'**Zimmermann** m (-[e]s; -leute) carpenter. '**zimmern** v/t (h) carpenter (*a. v/i*), *a.* build (of wood), *fig.* shape.

'Zimmer|nachweis *m* accommodation office. **~pflanze** *f* indoor plant. **~re-ser,vierung** *f* room reservation(s). **~schlüssel** *m* room key. **~service** *m* room service. **~suche** *f* (*auf ~ sein* be) room-hunting. **~tempera,tur** *f* room temperature. **~the,ater** *n* small theat/re (*Am.* -er). **~vermittlung** *f* → *Zimmernachweis.*

zimperlich ['tsɪmpərlɪç] *adj* a) soft, over-sensitive, b) squeamish, c) prim, prissy: *sei nicht so ~!* don't be a softie!; F *nicht gerade ~, wenig ~* none too gently, not exactly scrupulous (*in one's methods*). 'Zimperlichkeit *f* (-; *no pl*) a) softness, b) squeamishness, c) primness.

'Zimt [tsɪmt] *m* (-[e]s; -e) **1.** cinnamon. **2.** F *contp.* (*red k-n ~* don't talk) rubbish: *der ganze ~* the whole business.

Zink [tsɪŋk] *n* (-[e]s; *no pl*) zinc. **~blech** *n* a) sheet zinc, b) zinc plate.

Zinke ['tsɪŋkə] *f* (-; -n) **1.** prong. **2.** tooth (*of comb*). 'zinken *v/t* (h) mark (*cards*). 'Zinken *m* (-s; -) **1.** → *Zinke*. **2.** F conk.

Zinn [tsɪn] *n* (-[e]s; *no pl*) **1.** tin. **2.** pewter.

Zinne ['tsɪnə] *f* (-; -n) △ pinnacle, *pl* battlement.

'Zinngeschirr *n* pewter.

Zinnober [tsɪ'no:bər] *m* (-s; -) **1.** *min.* cinnabar. **2.** *no pl* F a) rubbish, b) fuss. **zin'noberrot** *adj* vermilion.

Zins [tsɪns] *m* (-es; -en) interest: **~en tra-gen** (*or* **bringen**) bear interest; *ohne* **~en** ex interest; *zu 4%* **~en** at 4% interest; → *Zinseszins.*
'zinsbringend *adj* interest-bearing.
'Zinseinnahme *f* income from interest.
'Zinsen|dienst ['tsɪnzən-] *m* interest pay-ment. **~last** *f* burden of interest.
'Zinsertrag *m* interest yield.
'Zinseszins *m* compound interest.
'Zinsfuß *m* (-e) interest rate.
'zinsgünstig *adj* low-interest.
'Zinsgutschrift *f* interest credited.
'Zinsku,pon *m* interest coupon.
'zinslos *adj* interest-free.
'Zins|poli,tik *f* interest rate policy. **~rechnung** *f* **1.** calculation of interest. **2.** interest account. **~satz** *m* interest rate. **~senkung** *f* lowering of interest rates. **~verlust** *m* loss of interest.
Zionismus [tsɪo'nɪsmʊs] *m* (-; *no pl*) Zionism. **Zionist** [-'nɪst] *m* (-en; -en), **zio'nistisch** *adj* Zionist.

Zipfel ['tsɪpfəl] *m* (-s; -) a) tip, point, b) end (*of sausage etc*), c) corner.
'Zipfelmütze *f* pointed cap.
Zirbeldrüse ['tsɪrbəl-] *f* pineal gland.
zirka ['tsɪrka] *adv* about, approximately.
'Zirkapreis *m* ✝ approximate price.
Zirkel ['tsɪrkəl] *m* (-s; -) **1.** (*ein ~* a pair of) compasses, dividers. **2.** *a. fig.* circle.
'Zirkelkasten *m* compasses case.
'Zirkelschluß *m philos.* vicious circle.
'Zirkeltraining *n sports:* circuit training.
Zirkulation [tsɪrkula'tsɪo:n] *f* (-; *no pl*) circulation. **zirkulieren** [tsɪrku'li:rən] *v/i* (sn) (*a. ~ lassen*) circulate.
Zirkumflex [tsɪrkʊm'flɛks] *m* (-es; -e) *ling.* circumflex (accent).
Zirkus ['tsɪrkʊs] *m* (-; -se) **1.** circus. **2.** *no pl* F fuss, carry-on.
zirpen ['tsɪrpən] *v/t*, *v/i* (h) chirp (*a. fig.*).
'Zirpen *n* (-s) chirp(ing).
Zirrhose [tsɪ'ro:zə] *f* (-; -n) ✿ cirrhosis.
Zirrus ['tsɪrʊs] *m* (-; -, Zirren), **~wolke** *f* cirrus (cloud).
zischeln ['tsɪʃəln] *v/t*, *v/i* (h) hiss.
zischen ['tsɪʃən] (h) **I** *v/i* **1.** hiss (*a. fig.*), *fat:* sizzle, *bullet etc:* whiz(z). **II** *v/t* **2.** hiss (*words*). **3.** F *e-n ~* knock one back. 'Zischen *n* (-s) **1.** hiss(ing), sizzle. **2.** hisses. 'Zischlaut *m ling.* sibilant.
ziselieren [tsizə'li:rən] *v/t* (h) chase.
Zisterne [tsɪs'tɛrnə] *f* (-; -n) cistern.
Zitadelle [tsita'dɛlə] *f* (-; -n) citadel.
Zitat [tsi'ta:t] *n* (-[e]s; -e) quotation.
Zither ['tsɪtər] *f* (-; -n) ♪ zither.
zitieren [tsi'ti:rən] *v/t* (h) **1.** cite, quote: *falsch ~* misquote. **2.** summon, cite.
Zitronat [tsitro'na:t] *n* (-[e]s; -e) candied lemon peel.
Zitrone [tsi'tro:nə] *f* (-; -n) lemon.
Zi'tronen|falter *m zo.* brimstone. **~limo,nade** *f* lemonade, *Am.* lemon soda. **~saft** *m* lemon juice. **~säure** *f* citric acid. **~schale** *f* lemon peel.
Zitrusfrucht ['tsi:trʊs-] *f* citrus fruit.
zitt(e)rig *adj* shaky.
zittern ['tsɪtərn] *v/i* (h) (*vor* with) tremble, shake, quiver: *vor j-m ~* be terrified of s.o.; *~ um* tremble for; *mir ~ die Knie* my knees are shaking.
'Zittern *n* (-s) tremble, shake, vibration: *fig. mit ~ und Zagen* trembling; F *das große ~ kriegen* get the willies.
'Zitterpappel *f* ❀ (quaking) aspen.
Zitze ['tsɪtsə] *f* (-; -n) teat, dug.

Zivi ['tsi:vi] *m* (-s; -s) F → **Zivildienstleistende**.

zivil [tsi'vi:l] *adj* **1.** a) civil, b) civilian. **2.** *fig.* a) decent, b) reasonable (*price etc*).

Zi'vil *n* (-s; *no pl*) civilian dress, *a.* plain clothes: *in* ~ F *a.* in mufti; *Kriminalbeamter in* ~ plain-clothes policeman. **~beruf** *m* civilian profession (*or* trade). **~bevölkerung** *f* civilian population, *the* civilians. **~cou,rage** *f* (-; *no pl*) courage of one's convictions.

Zi'vildienst *m* alternative (*or* community) service (*in lieu of military service*). **~leistende** *m* (-n; -n) *conscientious objector doing community service*.

Zi'vil|ehe *f* civil marriage. **~fahnder** *m* plain-clothes policeman. **~fahndung** *f* plain-clothes search. **~gericht** *n* civil court.

Zivilisation [tsiviliza'tsio:n] *f* (-; -en) civilization.

zivilisieren [tsivili'zi:rən] *v/t* (h) civilize.

Zivilist [tsivi'lɪst] *m* (-en; -en) civilian.

Zi'vil|kammer *f* ⚖ civil division. **~klage** *f* ⚖ civil suit. **~kleidung** *f* → *Zivil.* **~luftfahrt** *f* civil aviation. **~per,son** *f* civilian. **~pro,zeß** *m* ⚖ civil action. **~pro,zeßordnung** *f* code of civil procedure. **~recht** *n* (-[e]s; *no pl*) civil law. ⚖**rechtlich** *adj* (under) civil law. **~schutz** *m* civil defen/ce (*Am.* -se). **~stand** *m* *Swiss* civil (*or* marital) status. **~trauung** *f* civil marriage.

Zloty ['zlɔti, 'slɔti] *m* (-s; -s) zloty.

Zobel ['tso:bəl] *m* (-s; -) **1.** *zo.* sable. **2.** *a.* '**Zobelfell** *n* sable-skin. **3.** *a.* '**Zobelpelz** sable (fur).

zocken ['tsɔkən] *v/i* (h) F gamble.

Zocker *m* (-s; -) F gambler.

Zoff [tsɔf] *m* (-s; *no pl*) F trouble.

zog [tso:k] *pret of ziehen.*

'**zögerlich** *adj* → *zögernd.* **zögern** ['tsø:gərn] *v/i* (h) hesitate, waver: *ohne zu* ~ without hesitation; *er zögerte mit der Antwort* he was slow to answer; *sie zögerten mit der Entscheidung* they deferred their decision; *nicht* ~ *zu inf* lose no time in *ger.* '**Zögern** *n* (-s) hesitation. '**zögernd** *adj* hesitating, slow.

Zögling ['tsø:klɪŋ] *m* (-s; -e) pupil.

Zölibat [tsøli'ba:t] *n*, *eccl. m* (-[e]s; *no pl*) celibacy.

Zoll¹ [tsɔl] *m* (-[e]s; -) inch.

Zoll² *m* (-[e]s; ⸚e) **1.** (customs) duty. **2.**

customs. **~abfertigung** *f* customs clearance. **~amt** *n* customs office. **~beamte** *m* customs officer. **~behörde** *f* customs authorities. **~bestimmungen** *pl* customs regulations.

'**zollen** *v/t* (h) *Anerkennung* ~ pay tribute (*dat* to); *j-m Beifall* ~ applaud s.o.

'**Zoll|erklärung** *f* customs declaration. **~fahnder** *m* customs investigator. **~fahndung** *f* **1.** customs investigation. **2.** → **~fahndungsstelle** *f* customs investigation office. ⸚**formali,täten** *pl* customs formalities. ⸚**frei** *adj and adv* duty-free. ⸚**freiheit** *f* (-; *no pl*) exemption from duty. **~gebiet** *n* customs territory. **~grenze** *f* customs frontier. **~kon,trolle** *f* customs examination.

Zöllner ['tsœlnər] *m* (-s; -) **1.** customs officer. **2.** *bibl.* publican.

'**Zollpa,piere** *pl* customs documents.

'**zollpflichtig** *adj* liable to duty, dutiable.

'**Zollschranke** *f* customs barrier.

'**Zollstock** *m* ⊕ folding rule.

'**Zoll|ta,rif** *m* (customs) tariff. **~uni,on** *f* customs union. **~vergehen** *n* customs offen/ce (*Am.* -se). **~wert** *m* dutiable (*or* customs) value.

Zone ['tso:nə] *f* (-; -n) **1.** zone. **2.** fare stage.

Zoo [tso:] *m* (-s; -s) zoo.

'**Zoobesucher(in)** *f)m* visitor to the zoo.

'**Zoodi,rektor** *m* zoo director.

Zoologe [tsoo'lo:gə] *m* (-n; -n), **Zoo'login** *f* (-; -nen) zoologist.

Zoologie [tsoolo'gi:] *f* (-; *no pl*) zoology.

zoologisch [tsoo'lo:gɪʃ] *adj* zoologic(al): **~er Garten** zoological garden(s).

Zoomobjek,tiv ['zu:m-] *n* zoom lens.

Zopf [tsɔpf] *m* (-[e]s; ⸚e) **1.** plait, pigtail: F *alter* ~ antiquated custom. **2.** *gastr.* twist. **~stil** *m art*: late rococo (style).

Zorn [tsɔrn] *m* (-[e]s; *no pl*) anger (*auf acc* at), rage, temper, fury: *in* ~ *geraten* become furious, fly into a rage; (*der*) ~ *packte ihn* he was seized with anger.

'**Zornausbruch** *m* fit of anger.

'**zornentbrannt** *adj* incensed, furious.

'**zornig** *adj* (*auf, über acc* at) angry, furious, F mad; → *a. wütend.*

'**Zornröte** *f* flush of anger.

Zote ['tso:ta] *f* (-; -n) dirty joke: ~*n reißen* talk smut.

Zotte ['tsɔtə] *f* (-; -n) *zo.* tuft (of hair).

Zottel ['tsɔtəl] *f* (-; -n) F **1.** → *Zotte.* **2.**

straggly hair. '**zott(e)lig** *adj* F straggly, unkempt (*hair*). '**zottig** *adj* shaggy.

zu [tsu:] **I** *prep* **1.** a) at, b) to; towards: ~ **m-n Füßen** at my feet; ~ **m Friseur gehen** go to the hairdresser; **komm ~ mir!** come to me!; **sich ~ j-m setzen** sit with s.o.; ~ **Wasser und ~ Lande** on land and sea; **von Mann ~ Mann** between men. **2.** *time*: at, *occasion*: for: ~ **Ostern** at Easter; ~ **Beginn** at the beginning; **ein Geschenk ~m Geburtstag** a present for his *etc* birthday; → **bis** 1. **3.** for: **Stoff ~m Kleid** material for a dress; *et.* **~m Essen** s.th. to eat; **der Schlüssel ~m Schrank** the key to the cupboard; **~m Preis von 100 Mark** at a price of 100 marks; **aus Liebe ~ j-m** out of love for s.o. **4.** as: **~m Vergnügen** for fun; **j-n ~m Freund haben** have s.o. as a friend; **j-n ~m Präsidenten wählen** elect s.o. president. **5.** with: **~m Essen Wein** trinken drink wine with one's dinner; **ich nehme k-n Zucker ~m Tee** I don't take sugar with (*or* in) my tea; **Lieder ~r Laute** songs to the lute. **6.** ~ **10 DM das Pfund** at ten marks the pound; **sie gewannen 7:5** they won 7 (to) 5; **wir sind ~ dritt** there are three of us; **~m ersten Mal** for the first time; → **bis** 3. **7.** in(to): **werden ~** turn into, *person*: a. become; **~ Asche verbrennen** burn to ashes; **er hat ihn sich ~m Feind gemacht** he made him his enemy. **II** *adv* **8.** too: ~ **sehr** too much, overmuch; ~ **sehr betonen** overemphasize; ~ **dumm!** too bad!, what a nuisance! **9.** to, towards: **er ging dem Ausgang ~** he went towards the exit. **10.** shut, closed: (**mach die**) **Tür ~!** shut the door! **11.** F **immer ~!, nur ~!** go on! **III** *conj* **j-n bitten ~ kommen** ask s.o. to come; **ich habe ~ arbeiten** I have work to do; **du bist ~ beneiden** you are to be envied; **nicht ~ gebrauchen** useless; **ohne es ~ wissen** unknowingly. **IV** *adj* F a) closed, shut, b) chock-a-block, c) *fig.* bombed, sloshed.

zu'aller'erst *adv* first of all.

zu'aller'letzt *adv* last of all.

'**zubauen** *v/t* (*sep*, h) **1.** build *area etc* up. **2.** block (*a.* view).

'**Zubehör** [-bəhø:r] *n* (-[e]s; -e) accessories: **mit allem ~** with all conveniences.

'**Zubehörteil** *n* fitting, accessory.

'**zubeißen** *v/i* (*irr, sep,* -ge-, h, → **beißen**) bite, *dog:* snap.

'**zubekommen** *v/t* (*irr, sep,* h, → **bekommen**) F *et.* ~ get s.th. shut.

Zuber ['tsu:bər] *m* (-s; -) tub.

'**zubereiten** *v/t* (*sep*, h) prepare, make.

'**Zubereitung** *f* (-; -en) preparation.

'**zubilligen** *v/t* (*sep*, h) grant, concede, *a.* ⚖ allow (*all:* **j-m et.** s.o. s.th.).

'**zubinden** *v/t* (*irr, sep,* -ge-, h, → **binden**) tie (*or* bind) *s.th.* up.

'**zubleiben** *v/i* (*irr, sep,* -ge-, sn, → **bleiben**) F stay closed, stay shut.

'**zublinzeln** *v/t* (*sep*, h) **j-m ~** wink at s.o.

'**zubringen** *v/t* (*irr, sep,* -ge-, h, → **bringen**) spend, pass (*time*).

'**Zubringer** *m* (-s; -) → **Zubringerbus, -dienst, -linie, -straße. ~bus** *m* feeder bus. **~dienst** *m* feeder service. **~linie** *f* feeder line. **~straße** *f* feeder (road).

Zucchino [tsu'ki:no] *m* (-s; -ni) ⚘ courgette, *esp. Am.* zucchini.

Zucht [tsuχt] *f* (-; -en) **1.** breeding, rearing, raising, ⚘ cultivation, growing, culture (*of bees, bacteria, etc*). **2.** breed. **3.** *no pl* (*a.* ~ **und Ordnung**) discipline.

'**Zuchtbuch** *n* studbook.

'**Zuchtbulle** *m* breeding bull.

züchten ['tsʏçtən] *v/t* (h) breed (*a. fig.*), *a.* rear, raise (*animals*), *a.* cultivate, grow (*plants*), *a.* cultivate (*bacteria etc*).

'**Züchter** *m* (-s; -) breeder, *a.* grower.

'**Zuchterfolg** *m* breeding success.

'**Zuchthaus** *n* † prison; → *a.* **Gefängnis.**

'**Zuchthengst** *m* stud horse, stallion.

züchtigen ['tsʏçtɪgən] *v/t* (h) punish, flog. '**Züchtigung** *f* (-; -en) (**körperliche ~** corporal) punishment.

'**zuchtlos** *adj* undisciplined. '**Zuchtlosigkeit** *f* (-; *no pl*) lack of discipline.

'**Zucht|mittel** *n* disciplinary measure. **~perle** *f* cultured pearl. **~stier** *m* breeding bull. **~stute** *f* stock mare. **~tier** *n* breeding animal, *pl a.* breeding stock.

'**Züchtung** *f* (-; -en) → **Zucht** 1, 2.

'**Zuchtvieh** *n* breeding cattle.

'**Zuchtwahl** *f biol.* selection.

zuckeln ['tsʊkəln] *v/i* (sn) F trundle (*mot. etc* chug) along.

zucken ['tsʊkən] *v/i* (h) **1.** jerk, twitch, move convulsively, wince: → **Achsel, Schulter, Wimper. 2.** *lightning etc*: flash, *flames:* flicker.

zücken ['tsʏkən] v/t (h) draw (knife etc), F pull out, produce (wallet etc).

Zucker ['tsʊkər] m (-s; -) **1.** sugar. **2.** F ♬ (er hat ~ he is suffering from) diabetes. **~brot** n F mit ~ und Peitsche with a stick and a carrot. **~dose** f sugar bowl. **~erbse** f ♀ sugar pea. **~guß** m icing, frosting; mit ~ überziehen v/t ice, frost. **~hut** m sugar loaf.

'zuck(e)rig adj sugary.

'zuckerkrank adj, **'Zuckerkranke** m, f diabetic. **'Zuckerkrankheit** f diabetes.

zuckern ['tsʊkərn] v/t (h) sugar.

'Zucker|rohr n (-[e]s; -e) sugar cane. **~rübe** f sugar beet. ♀**süß** adj (as) sweet as sugar, fig. honeyed, sugary. **~watte** f candy floss. **~zange** f sugar tongs.

'Zuckung f (-; -en) a) twitch(ing), jerk, b) convulsion, spasm.

zudecken v/t (sep, h) cover (up): sich ~ cover o.s. (up); F j-n mit Arbeit ~ swamp s.o. with work.

zu'dem adv besides, moreover.

'zudrehen v/t (sep, h) **1.** turn off. **2.** j-m den Rücken ~ turn one's back on s.o.

'zudringlich adj obtrusive, F pushy: e-r Frau gegenüber ~ werden F make a pass at a woman. **'Zudringlichkeit** f (-; -en) **1.** no pl obtrusiveness, F pushiness. **2.** advances, F pass.

'zudrücken v/t (sep, h) close, (press) shut: → Auge 1.

'zueilen v/i (sep, sn) rush up (auf acc to).

zuein'ander adv to each other, to one another: Vertrauen ~ haben trust each other. **~halten** v/i (irr, sep, -ge-, h, → halten) F stick together.

'zuerkennen v/t (irr, sep, h, → erkennen) (dat) award (to), confer (on).

zu'erst adv **1.** first: wer ~ kommt, mahlt ~ first come, first served. **2.** first (of all). **3.** at first, at the beginning. **4.** for the first time, first.

'Zufahrt f (-; -en) **1.** access. **2.** → '**Zufahrtsstraße** f access road.

'Zufall m (-[e]s; ⁚e) chance, accident, a. coincidence: durch ~ by chance; reiner ~ pure chance; glücklicher ~ lucky coincidence, F fluke; unglücklicher ~ bit of bad luck; was für ein ~! what a coincidence!; wie es der ~ wollte as luck would have it; es ist kein ~, daß it's no accident that; et. dem ~ überlassen leave it to chance.

'zufallen v/i (irr, sep, -ge-, sn, → fallen) **1.** eyes etc: close, door etc: slam (shut): mir fallen die Augen zu I can't keep my eyes open. **2.** j-m ~ inheritance etc: fall to s.o., prize etc: be awarded to s.o., task etc: be assigned to s.o.; fig. ihm fällt alles nur so zu everything comes quite naturally to him.

'zufällig I adj accidental, chance: ~es Zs.-treffen a) chance encounter, b) coincidence; jede Ähnlichkeit (mit ...) ist rein ~ any resemblance (to ...) is purely coincidental. **II** adv by chance, accidentally: er war ~ zu Hause he happened to be at home; wir trafen uns ~ we met by chance, F we bumped into each other; ~ stoßen auf (acc) chance (up)on; rein ~ by sheer chance; weißt du ~, wo er ist? do you know by any chance where he is? **'Zufälligkeit** f (-; -en) **1.** no pl coincidence, accidentalness. **2.** fortuity, contingency.

'Zufalls|auswahl f statistics: random selection. **~bekanntschaft** f chance acquaintance. **~treffer** m lucky hit (F fluke) hit, sports: a. lucky goal.

'zufassen v/i (sep, h) **1.** take hold of it, grasp it. **2.** F give a hand, help.

'zufliegen v/i (irr, sep, -ge-, sn, → fliegen) **1.** F door etc: slam (shut). **2.** ~ auf (acc) fly toward(s). **3.** j-m ~ a) bird: fly into s.o.'s home, b) come easily to s.o.

'zufließen v/i (irr, sep, -ge-, sn, → fließen) a. fig. flow into.

'Zuflucht f (-; -en) **1.** refuge, shelter: ~ suchen (finden) seek (find) refuge (bei with, fig. in). **2.** fig. m-e letzte ~ my last) resort: s-e ~ nehmen zu resort to.

'Zufluchtsort m place of refuge, retreat.

'Zufluß m (-sses; ⁚sse) **1.** influx, inflow. **2.** a) inlet, b) tributary.

'zuflüstern v/t (sep, h) whisper (dat to).

zufolge [tsu'fɔlgə] prep (dat) according to, in accordance with (his request etc).

zu'frieden adj (mit with) a) content(ed), b) satisfied, pleased: ein ~es Gesicht machen look pleased; ~es Lächeln contented smile; mit wenig ~ easily satisfied; sie ist nie ~ there is no pleasing her; iro. bist du nun ~? are you satisfied now?; ~ lächeln smile contentedly.

zu'friedengeben: sich ~ (irr, sep, -ge-, h, → geben) content o.s. (mit with).

Zu'friedenheit f (-; no pl) contentment, (**zu m-r** etc **~** to my etc) satisfaction.

zu'friedenlassen v/t (irr, sep, -ge-, h, → **lassen**) leave s.o. alone (or in peace).

zu'friedenstellen v/t (sep, h) satisfy: **sie sind schwer zufriedenzustellen** they are hard to please.

zu'friedenstellend adj satisfactory.

'zufrieren v/i (irr, sep, -ge-, sn, → **frieren**) freeze up (or over).

'zufügen v/t (sep, h) **1.** add (dat to). **2.** **j-m e-n Schaden ~** harm s.o.; **j-m e-e Niederlage** etc **~** inflict defeat etc on s.o.; **j-m (ein) Unrecht ~** wrong s.o.

'Zufuhr f (-; -en) supply, meteor. influx: **die ~ abschneiden** cut off supplies.

'zuführen (sep, h) **I** v/t (dat to) carry, bring, lead, ⚙ feed, supply: **dem Körper Nahrung ~** feed the body; **j-n s-r (gerechten) Strafe** etc **~** punish s.o. (as he deserves). **II** v/i **auf ~** (acc) a. fig. lead to. **'Zuführung** f (-; -en) **1.** no pl conveyance, feeding, delivery. **2.** ⚡ lead.

Zug¹ [tsu:k] m (-[e]s; ⨯e) (**mit dem ~ fahren** go by) train: **im ~** on the train; **wir brachten sie zum ~** we saw her off at the station; F fig. **im Fahrwasser ~ sitzen** be on the wrong track; **der ~ ist abgefahren!** it's too late for that now!

Zug² m (-[e]s; ⨯e) **1.** no pl draw(ing), pull(ing), traction. **2.** ⚙ tension, tensible force. **3.** no pl draught, Am. draft. **4.** a) breath, gulp, F swig, c) drag, puff: **in 'einem ~** a. fig. in one go; **in den letzten Zügen liegen** be breathing one's last, humor. object: be on its last legs; **et. in vollen Zügen genießen** enjoy s.th. to the full. **5.** chess: move: **wer ist am ~?** who is to move?; **~ um ~** a) step by step, b) without delay, c) ✝ concurrently; **er kam nicht zum ~e** F he didn't get a look-in. **6.** stroke (of pen etc), a. writing: fig. **in groben Zügen** in broad outline, roughly. **7.** procession, column, ✗ etc platoon: **endlose Züge von Flüchtlingen** an endless procession of refugees. **8.** passage, migration (of birds), a. flight, movement (of clouds etc). **9.** im ~e (gen) in the course of; **im besten ~e sein** be well under way, person: be going strong. **10.** no pl F **~ bringen in** (acc) bring a class, team, etc up to scratch; **da ist kein ~ drin** it's a slow show, they lack the real drive. **11.**

⚙ flue. **12.** groove, pl rifling. **13.** ped. etc: stream.

Zug³ m (-[e]s; ⨯e) a) feature, b) line, look, c) characteristic, d) trait, b.s. streak, d) bent (**zu** for): **das war kein schöner ~ von ihr** that wasn't nice of her; **der ~ der Zeit** the trend of the times.

'Zugabe f (-; -n) **1.** extra, bonus. **2.** addition, ⚙ makeweight. **3.** ♪ etc encore.

'Zugang m (-[e]s; ⨯e) **1.** access (a. fig.), gate(way) (a. fig.), approach, access road: **ich finde k-n ~ zur modernen Musik** I'm unable to appreciate modern music. **2.** in library etc: accession, in hospital etc: admission, at university etc: intake.

'zugänglich [-gɛŋlɪç] adj a. fig. accessible (**für** to), get-at-able, available: **et.** (**der Allgemeinheit**) **~ machen** open s.th. (to the public); **~ für** open to arguments etc; **er war für neue Methoden ~** he was quite willing to try out new methods; **sie war k-n Vernunftgründen ~** she wasn't amenable to reason. **'Zugänglichkeit** f (-; no pl) (**für** to) accessibility, fig. a. amenability.

'Zugangsstraße f access road.

'Zugbrücke f drawbridge.

'zugeben v/t (irr, sep, -ge-, h, → **geben**) **1.** add (dat to), ✝ give as an extra, F throw in, ♪ give s.th. as an encore. **2.** admit, confess, a. grant, concede: **zugegeben, er hat recht, aber ...** I grant you he's right but ... **3.** allow.

'zugegebener'maßen adv admittedly.

zu'gegen adj **~ sein** be present (**bei** at).

'zugehen (irr, sep, -ge-, sn, → **gehen**) **I** v/i **1.** **~ auf** (acc) go up to, go (or walk) towards, head for; fig. **er geht auf die Achtzig zu** he's getting on for eighty; **dem Ende ~** be drawing to a close; **man muß auf die Leute ~** you have to talk to people (openly). **2.** **j-m ~** reach s.o.; **j-m et. ~ lassen** have s.th. sent to s.o. **3.** F walk faster: **geh zu!** get a move on! **4.** F door, suitcase, etc: shut. **5.** **~ zulaufen** 4. **II** v/impers **6.** **es geht auf 8 Uhr zu** it's getting on for eight (o'clock); **es geht dem Winter zu** winter is drawing near (or is on its way). **7.** happen, go: **wie geht es zu, daß?** how is it that?; F how come ...?; **bei ihnen geht's vielleicht hektisch zu!** things are pretty hectic with them; → **Ding** 2.

'**Zugehörigkeit** f (-; no pl) (**zu**) membership (in), affiliation (to, with).
'**zugeknöpft** adj F fig. reserved, silent.
'**Zügel** ['tsy:gəl] m (-s; -) rein: fig. **die ~ (fest) in der Hand halten** have things (firmly) under control; **die ~ lockern** loosen the reins; **der Phantasie** etc **die ~ schießen lassen** give free rein to one's imagination etc.
'**zügellos** adj fig. **1.** unrestrained. **2.** licentious. '**Zügellosigkeit** f (-; no pl) **1.** lack of restraint. **2.** licentiousness.
'**zügeln** ['tsy:gəln] v/t (h) **1.** rein (up). **2.** fig. curb, check, bridle.
'**Zugereiste** m, f (-n; -n) newcomer.
'**Zugeständnis** n (-ses; -se) concession (**an** acc to). '**zugestehen** v/t (irr, sep, h, → **gestehen**) **1.** (dat to) concede, grant. **2.** admit.
'**zugetan** adj (dat) **~ sein** be fond of.
'**Zugewinn** m (-[e]s; -e) gain(s).
'**Zugfeder** f ⚙ tension spring, of watch: main spring.
'**Zugfestigkeit** f (-; no pl) ⚙ tensile strength.
'**Zugführer** m **1.** 🚆 guard, Am. train conductor. **2.** ✕ platoon leader.
'**Zugfunk** m 🚆 train radio.
'**zugießen** v/t (irr, sep, -ge-, h, → **gießen**) add.
'**zugig** ['tsu:gɪç] adj draughty, Am. drafty.
'**zügig** ['tsy:gɪç] adj quick, speedy: **~ vorankommen** make rapid progress.
'**Zugkraft** f **1.** ⚙ tractive (or tensile) force. **2.** fig. attraction, appeal, of person: magnetism. '**zugkräftig** adj fig. powerful, catchy (slogan), crowd-pulling (actor, film, etc), pol. vote-getting (candidate etc): **~ sein** a. have appeal.
zu'gleich adv at the same time.
'**Zugluft** f (-; no pl) draught, Am. draft.
'**Zugma,schine** f mot. tractor.
'**Zugmittel** n fig. draw, attraction.
'**Zugnummer** f fig. draw(ing card).
'**Zugpferd** n fig. draw, thea. etc crowd-puller, pol. a. (great) vote-getter.
'**Zugpflaster** m 💊 blistering plaster.
'**zugreifen** v/i (irr, sep, -ge-, h, → **greifen**) **1.** → **zufassen**. **2.** help o.s.: **greifen Sie bitte zu!** please help yourself! **3.** fig. seize (or jump at) the opportunity: **du brauchst nur zuzugreifen!** you may have it for the asking. **4.** fig. intervene.

'**Zugriff** m (-[e]s; -e) **1.** intervention: **er entzog sich dem ~ der Polizei** he escaped the police. **2.** computer: access.
'**Zugriffszeit** f computer: access time.
zu'grunde adv **1. ~ gehen** (**an** dat) perish (of), die (of), b) be ruined (by). **2.** (dat) etc. **~ legen** base s.th. on. **3.** (dat) **~ liegen** form the basis of, be based on. **4. ~ richten** ruin, wreck.
'**Zugschaffner** m 🚆 train conductor.
'**Zugstück** n thea. etc draw, hit.
'**Zugtele,fon** n telephone on the train.
'**Zugtier** n draught (Am. draft) animal.
'**zugucken** F → **zusehen**.
zu'gunsten prep (gen) in favo(u)r of.
zu'gute adv **1.** j-m et. **~ halten** a) give s.o. credit for s.th., b) pardon s.o. s.th.; **sie hielten ihm s-e Unerfahrenheit ~** they made allowances for his lack of experience. **2. ~ kommen** (dat) a) go to, be for the benefit of, b) be of advantage to, stand s.o. in good stead. **3.** sich et. **~ halten** (or tun) **auf** (acc) pride o.s. on.
'**Zugverbindung** f 🚆 train connection.
'**Zugverkehr** m train services.
'**Zugvogel** m bird of passage.
'**Zugzwang** m fig. **in ~ geraten** be forced to make a move; **unter ~ stehen** be under pressure to act.
'**zuhaben** v/i (irr, sep, -ge-, h, → **haben**) F be closed.
'**zuhalten** (irr, sep, -ge-, h, → **halten**) **I** v/t **1.** keep s.th. closed. **2.** put (or hold) one's hand(s) over (one's eyes, ears): **sich die Nase ~** hold one's nose. **II** v/i **~ auf** (acc) make for, head for.
'**Zuhälter** ['tsu:hɛltər] m (-s; -) pimp.
'**Zuhälte'rei** f (-; no pl) pimping.
Zuhause [tsu'haʊzə] n (-s; no pl) home.
zu'hilfenahme f unter (ohne) **~ von** (or gen) with (without) the aid of.
zu'hinterst adv at the very end.
'**zuhören** v/i (sep, h) listen (dat to).
'**Zuhörer(in** f) m listener: **die Zuhörer** a. the audience. '**Zuhörerraum** m auditorium. '**Zuhörerschaft** f (-; no pl) audience, radio: a. listeners.
'**zujubeln** v/i (sep, h) (dat) cheer.
'**zuklappen** v/t (sep, h), v/i (sn) shut, close s.th. with a snap.
'**zukleben** v/t (sep, h) seal.
'**zuklinken** v/t (sep, h) latch.
'**zuknallen** v/t (sep, h) slam s.th. (shut).

'**zuknöpfen** v/t (sep, h) button (up); → *zugeknöpft*.

'**zukommen** v/i (irr, sep, -ge-, sn, → *kommen*) **1.** ~ **auf** (acc) approach, come up to; fig. **auf j-n** ~ be in store for s.o.; adm. **wir werden auf Sie** ~ we'll contact you; **die Sache auf sich** ~ **lassen** let the matter take its course, wait and see. **2.** **j-m et.** ~ **lassen** send (or give) s.o. s.th. **3.** **j-m** ~ a) befit s.o., b) be due to s.o.

Zukunft ['tsu:kʊnft] f (-; no pl) **1.** (**in** ~ in) future: **in naher** (**nächster**) ~ in the near (immediate) future; **in die** ~ **blicken** look ahead; **dieser Beruf hat k-e** ~ there is no future in this profession; F **das hat k-e** ~! that has no future; **abwarten, was die** ~ **bringt** wait and see what the future has in store for us. **2.** ling. future (tense). '**zukünftig I** adj future, person: a. prospective, father etc -to-be. **II** adv in (the) future.

Zukunfts|aussichten pl future prospects. ♀**bezogen I** adj forward-looking. **II** adv with a view to the future. ~**forscher** m futurologist. ~**forschung** f futurology. ~**glaube** m faith in the future. ~**mu,sik** f fig. **das ist alles noch** ~ that's all still up in the air. ♀**orien,tiert** adj future-oriented. ~**pläne** pl plans for the future. ♀**reich** adj with a great future, promising. ~**ro,man** m science fiction novel.

'**zukunft(s)weisend** adj advanced.

'**zulächeln** v/i (sep, h) **j-m** ~ smile at s.o.

'**Zulage** f (-; -n) a extra pay, additional allowance, b bonus, c) rise, Am. raise.

'**zulangen** v/i (sep, h) **1.** F → **zugreifen** 2. **2.** → **zupacken**.

'**zulassen** v/t (irr, sep, -ge-, h, → **lassen**) **1.** F leave door etc shut. **2.** admit s.o. (**zu** to), adm. license, a. register (car etc): **amtlich** ~ authorize; **staatlich** ~ register; **j-n als Rechtsanwalt** ~ call (or admit) s.o. to the bar. **3.** a) allow, permit, b) admit (of) (doubt etc).

'**zulässig** adj admissible, permissible, allowable: ~**e** (**Höchst**)**Belastung** maximum permissible (or safe) load; ~**e Höchstgeschwindigkeit** speed limit; **das ist** (**nicht**) ~ that is (not) allowed.

'**Zulassung** f (-; -en) **1.** no pl admission (**zu** to). **2.** mot. a) licen/ce (Am. -se), b) registration.

'**Zulassungs|beschränkung** f restriction on admissions. ~**nummer** f mot. registration number. ~**pa,piere** pl registration papers. ~**prüfung** f entrance exam(ination). ~**stelle** f registration office.

'**Zulauf** m (-[e]s; no pl) **1.** a) run (of customers etc), b) custom, c) approval: **großen** ~ **haben** be much sought after, film etc: be very popular, draw large crowds. **2.** ⚙ supply.

'**zulaufen** v/i (irr, sep, -ge-, sn, → **laufen**) **1.** ~ **auf** (acc) run up to. **2.** **j-m** ~ a) animal: stray to s.o., b) customers etc: flock to s.o.; **zugelaufener Hund** stray dog. **3.** flow in: ~ **lassen** add, run hot water etc in. **4.** **spitz** ~ taper to a point. **5.** F hurry: **lauf zu!** hurry up!

'**zulegen** (sep, h) **I** v/t **1.** F **sich ein Auto** etc ~ buy (or get) o.s. a car etc; fig. **er hat sich e-e Freundin** (**e-n Bart**) **zugelegt** he has got himself a girlfriend (he has grown a beard). **2.** add (dat to): → **Zahn** 2. **II** v/i F a) put on weight, b) increase the pace, c) score gains.

zuleide [tsu'laidə] adv **j-m et.** ~ **tun** harm (or hurt) s.o.; → **Fliege** 1.

'**zuleiten** v/t (sep, h) **1.** ⚙ feed, supply, a. let in (water). **2.** pass s.th. on (dat to).

'**Zuleitung** f (-; -en) **1.** ⚙ supply (or feeding) pipe. **2.** ⚡ a) feeder, b) lead(-in).

zu'letzt adv **1.** last: **du kommst immer** ~ you are alway the last (to arrive); **ganz** ~ last of all. **2.** **bis** ~ to the (very) end. **3.** finally, in the end. **4.** last: **wann haben Sie ihn** ~ **gesehen**? when did you see him last? **5.** **nicht** ~ not least.

zu'liebe adv **mir** etc ~ for my etc sake.

'**Zulieferer** m (-s; -) supplier.

'**Zulieferindu,strie** f ancillary industry.

'**zumachen** (sep, h) F **I** v/t **1.** shut, close (door etc, a. shop etc), stop up (hole), button up, do up (jacket etc), put down (umbrella), seal (envelope etc): **ich habe kein Auge zugemacht** I didn't sleep a wink. **II** v/i **2.** shop etc: a) close, b) close down. **3.** hurry: **mach zu!** hurry up!

zu'mal conj ~ (**da** or **weil**) particularly since. **II** adv particularly, above all.

'**zumauern** v/t (sep, h) wall up.

'**zumessen** v/t (irr, sep, -ge-, h, → **messen**) **1.** (dat to) apportion, allot. **2.** attach (importance etc).

zu'mindest adv at least.

zumute [tsu'muːtə] *adv* **wie ist dir ~?** how do you feel?; **mir ist jämmerlich ~** I feel miserable; **mir ist nicht nach Essen ~** I don't like eating; **mir ist bei dieser Sache gar nicht wohl ~** I don't feel at all happy about it.

zumuten ['tsuːmuːtən] *v/t* (*sep*, h) **j-m et. ~** expect s.th. of s.o; **sich zuviel ~** overdo things, F bite off more than one can chew.

'**Zumutung** *f* (-; -en) a) unreasonable demand, b) cheek: **das ist e-e ~!** that's asking a bit much!, *a.* what a nerve!

zu'nächst *adv* **1.** first (of all), above all. **2.** to begin with, in the first place. **3.** for the present, for the time being.

'**zunageln** *v/t* (*sep*, h) nail up.

'**zunähen** *v/t* (*sep*, h) sew up.

Zunahme ['tsuːnaːmə] *f* (-; -n) increase (*gen* or **an** *dat* in).

'**Zuname** *m* surname, last name.

'**Zündeinstellung** *f mot.* ignition timing.

zünden ['tsyndən] (h) **I** *v/i* **1.** *mot.* ignite. **2.** detonate. **3.** fire (*rocket etc*) **II** *v/i* **4.** catch fire. **5.** ⚡, *mot.* ignite, fire. **6.** *fig.* arouse enthusiasm, *idea etc*: catch on. '**zündend** *adj fig.* rousing (*speech*).

Zunder ['tsundər] *m* (-s; -) (*brennen wie ~* burn like) tinder: F *fig.* **j-m ~ geben** give s.o. hell.

'**Zünder** *m* (-s; -) ⚙ fuse, *Am.* fuze, ⚡ igniter.

'**Zünd|funke** *m mot.* (ignition) spark. **~holz** *n*, **~hölzchen** *n* match. **~kabel** *n mot.* ignition cable. **~kerze** *f mot.* spark(ing) plug. **~punkt** *m* 🔥 ignition point. **~satz** *m* primer. **~schloß** *n mot.* ignition lock. **~schlüssel** *m mot.* ignition key. **~schnur** *f* fuse, *a.* slow match wick. **~spule** *f mot.* ignition coil. **~stoff** *m* (-[e]s; *no pl*) *fig.* dynamite.

'**Zündung** *f* (-; -en) *mot.* ignition.

'**zunehmen** (*irr*, *sep*, -ge-, h, → **nehmen**) **I** *v/i* **1.** increase, grow: **an Wert ~** increase in value; **an Bedeutung ~** gain in importance. **2.** *moon*: wax. **3.** (**stark** or **sehr**) **~** put on (a lot of) weight. **II** *v/t* **sie hat 10 Pfund zugenommen** she has put on (or gained) ten pounds.

'**zunehmend I** *adj* **1.** increasing, growing: **mit ~em Alter** as one gets older; **in ~em Maße ~ II. 2.** waxing: **bei ~em Mond** when the moon is waxing. **II** *adv* increasingly, more and more.

'**zuneigen** (*sep*, h) **I** *v/i* **der Ansicht ~, daß** be inclined to think that. **II** *sich dem Ende ~* draw to a close.

'**Zuneigung** *f* (-; -en) affection (**für, zu** for).

Zunft [tsunft] *f* (-; ⍵e) *hist.* guild.

zünftig ['tsynftɪç] *adj* F proper, good.

Zunge ['tsuŋə] *f* (-; -n) tongue: **mit der ~ anstoßen** (have a) lisp; **sich auf die ~ beißen** bite one's tongue (*fig.* lips); (**j-m**) **die ~ herausstrecken** put one's tongue out (at s.o.); *fig.* **es lag mir auf der ~** I had it on the tip of my tongue; **sie hat e-e lose (scharfe) ~** she has a loose (sharp) tongue; → **zergehen.**

züngeln ['tsyŋəln] *v/i* (h) *snake*: dart tongue, *flames*: lick.

'**Zungen|belag** *m* 🩺 coat(ing) of the tongue. **~brecher** *m* F tongue twister. **2fertig** *adj* glib. **~kuß** *m* French (or deep) kiss. **~laut** *m* lingual (sound). **~spitze** *f* tip of the tongue.

Zünglein ['tsyŋlaɪn] *n fig.* **das ~ an der Waage sein** tip the scales.

zunichte [tsu'nɪçtə] *adv* **~ machen** ruin; **~ werden** come to nothing.

'**zunicken** *v/i* (*sep*, h) nod (*dat* to): **j-m freundlich ~** give s.o. a friendly nod.

zunutze [tsu'nʊtsə] *adv* **sich et. ~ machen** make (good) use of s.th., *a. b.s.* take advantage of s.th.

zu'oberst *adv* (right) at the top.

'**zuordnen** *v/t* (*sep*, h) (*dat*) assign (to) (*a.* Ⓐ), class (with).

'**zupacken** *v/i* (*sep*, h) work hard.

zupfen ['tsupfən] (h) **I** *v/t* pull, pick, *a.* ♪ pluck: **j-n am Ärmel ~** tug at s.o.'s sleeve. **II** *v/i* **~ an** (*dat*) pull at, tug at.

'**Zupfinstru,ment** *n* plucked instrument.

'**zuprosten** ['tsuːproːstən] *v/i* (*sep*, h) raise one's glass (*dat* to).

'**zuraten** *v/i* (*irr*, *sep*, -ge-, h, → **raten**) **j-m ~, et. zu tun** advise s.o. to do s.th.; **auf mein** *etc* **Zuraten** on my *etc* advice.

'**zurechnen** *v/t* (*sep*, h) **1.** → **zuordnen. 2.** add (*dat* to).

'**zurechnungsfähig** *adj* sane, of sound mind, ⚖️ responsible. '**Zurechnungsfähigkeit** *f* (-; *no pl*) ⚖️ (**verminderte ~** diminished ~ responsibility.

zu'rechtbasteln *v/t* (*sep*, h) rig up.

zu'rechtbiegen *v/t* (*irr*, *sep*, -ge-, h, → **biegen**) **1.** bend *s.th.* into shape. **2.** F *fig.* straighten *s.o.*, *s.th.* out.

zu'rechtfinden: *sich* ~ (*irr, sep, -ge-,* → *finden*) find one's way (around), *fig.* cope, manage: *findest du dich darin zurecht?* can you make sense of it all?

zu'rechtkommen *v/i* (*irr, sep, -ge-, sn,* → *kommen*) **1.** arrive in time. **2.** (*mit* with) manage, cope: *mit j-m* (*gut*) ~ get on (well) with s.o.

zu'rechtlegen *v/t* (*sep, h*) **1.** lay *s.th.* ready, arrange. **2.** *fig. sich et.* ~ work (*or* figure) out, have *excuse etc* ready.

zu'rechtmachen (*sep, h*) F **I** *v/t* get *s.th.* ready, prepare, make, *Am.* F *a.* fix (*salad etc*), make up (*bed*). **II** *sich* ~ a) do o.s. up, b) make up.

zu'rechtrücken *v/t* (*sep, h*) adjust, *a. fig.* put *s.th.* straight.

zu'rechtstutzen *v/t* (*sep, h*) *a. fig.* trim.

zu'rechtweisen *v/t* (*irr, sep, -ge-, h,* → *weisen*) rebuke, reprimand. **Zu'rechtweisung** *f* (-; -en) rebuke, reprimand.

'zureden *v/i* (*sep, h*) *j-m* ~ (*, et. zu tun*) encourage (*or* persuade, urge) s.o. (to do s.th.); *auf ihr etc Zureden* upon her *etc* encouragement; *alles Zureden war umsonst* all persuasion was in vain.

'zureiten (*irr, sep, -ge-,* → *reiten*) **I** *v/t* (h) break in (*horse*). **II** *v/i* (sn) ~ *auf* (*acc*) ride up to.

'zurichten *v/t* (*sep, h*) **1.** ◉ a) finish, b) shape. **2.** *print.* make ready. **3.** *übel* ~ injure *s.o.* badly, batter (*s.o., s.th.*).

'zuriegeln *v/t* (*sep, h*) bolt.

zürnen ['tsʏrnən] *v/i* (h) *j-m* ~ be angry with s.o.

Zur'schaustellung *f* (-; -en) exhibition, display, *fig. a.* parading.

zurück [tsu'rʏk] *adv* back: ~ *sein* a) be (*or* have come) back, b) F lag behind (*a. ped.*), *in one's development:* be retarded, be backward; F *mit s-r Arbeit* ~ *sein* be behind (*or* in arrears) with one's work; *sports:* **5 Punkte** (**3 Meter** *etc*) ~ *liegen* be five points down (be three metres *etc*) behind.

Zu'rück *n* *es gibt kein* ~ (*mehr*) there's no turning back (now).

zu'rück|bekommen *v/t* (*irr, sep, h,* → *bekommen*) get *s.th.* back. **~beordern** *v/t* (*sep, h*) order *s.o.* back. **beugen** *v/t* (*a. sich* ~) (*sep, h*) bend back. **bilden:** *sich* ~ (*sep, h*) recede, *biol.* regress. **~bleiben** *v/i* (*irr, sep, -ge-, sn,* → *bleiben*) **1.** stay (*or* be left) behind. **2.** be

left. **3.** lag behind (*a. ped.*), *sports:* a. drop back, *in one's development:* be retarded: *hinter den Erwartungen* ~ fall short of expectations. **~blicken** *v/i* (*sep, h*) look back (*auf acc* at, *fig.* on). **~bringen** *v/t* (*irr, sep, -ge-, h,* → *bringen*) bring (*or* take) *s.o., s.th.* back, return: *j-n ins Leben* ~ bring s.o. back to life. **~datieren** *v/t* (*sep, h*) backdate. **~denken** *v/i* (*irr, sep, -ge-, h,* → *denken*) (*an acc*) think back (to), recall (*s.o., s.th.*). **~drängen** *v/t* (*sep, h*) **1.** push *s.o.* back. **2.** *fig.* repress. **~drehen** *v/t* (*sep, h*) turn (*or* put) back. **~dürfen** *v/i* (*irr, sep, -ge-, h,* → *dürfen*) be allowed back. **~eilen** *v/i* (*sep, sn*) hurry back. **~erobern** *v/t* (*sep, h*) recapture, *fig.* win back. **~erstatten** *v/t* (*sep, h*) refund, reimburse. **~erwarten** *v/t* (*sep, h*) expect *s.o.* back. **~fahren** (*irr, sep, -ge-,* → *fahren*) **I** *v/i* (sn) **1.** drive (*or* travel, go) back, return. **2.** *fig.* recoil (*vor dat* from). **II** *v/t* (h) drive *s.o., s.th.* back. **~fallen** *v/i* (*irr, sep, -ge-, sn,* → *fallen*) **1.** fall back. **2.** fall behind (*a. ped.*), *sports:* a. drop back (*auf den dritten Platz* to third place). **3.** ~ *in* (*acc*) relapse (*or* fall back) into. **4.** *fig.* ~ *auf* (*acc*) reflect on. **~finden** *v/i* (*irr, sep, -ge-, h,* → *finden*) find one's way back (*zu* to). **~fließen** *v/i* (*irr, sep, -ge-, sn,* → *fließen*) flow back. **~fordern** *v/t* (*sep, h*) reclaim, demand *s.th.* back. **~führen** *v/t* (*sep, h*) **1.** lead *s.o.* back. *fig.* repatriate. **2.** *fig.* (*auf acc* to) reduce, trace *s.th.* (back), attribute. **~geben** *v/t* (*irr, sep, -ge-, h,* → *geben*) **1.** give *s.th.* back, return. **2.** *sports:* pass the ball back.

zu'rückgeblieben *adj fig.* retarded, backward.

zu'rückgehen *v/i* (*irr, sep, -ge-, sn,* → *gehen*) **1.** go back, return, retreat: *fig. et.* ~ *lassen* send s.th. back, return s.th.; *bis ins 19. Jh.* ~ go (*or* date) back to the 19th century. **2.** *fig.* go down (*a. ☿*), fall (*or* decrease: *das Geschäft geht zurück* business is falling off. **3.** *fig.* ~ *auf* (*acc*) go back to, have its origin in.

zu'rückgezogen *adj* retired, secluded: ~ *leben* lead a secluded life.

zu'rückgreifen *v/i* (*irr, sep, -ge-, h,* → *greifen*) ~ *auf* (*acc*) fall back on.

zu'rückhalten (*irr, sep, -ge-, h,* → *halten*) **I** *v/t* **1.** hold *s.o., s.th.* back, withhold, *a.* suppress (*tears etc*). **II sich ~ 2.** restrain o.s.; **sich ~ mit** go easy on (*drinks etc*). **3.** be reserved, keep (o.s.) to o.s., *buyer:* hold back: **sich sehr ~** keep very much in the background. **III** *v/i ~ mit* keep back; **mit s-r Meinung ~** reserve judg(e)ment.

zu'rückhaltend *adj* a) reserved (*a.* ♱), b) guarded, cautious, c) reticent, d) unobtrusive: **~ sein mit** be sparing in (*or* with) one's praise *etc*; **er reagierte sehr ~** his reaction was very cool.

Zu'rückhaltung *f* (*-; no pl*) *fig.* a) reserve, b) caution, discretion.

zu'rück|holen *v/t* (*sep, h*) fetch *s.o., s.th.* back. **~kehren** *v/i* (*sep, sn*) come back, return. **~kommen** *v/i* (*irr, sep, -ge-, sn,* → **kommen**) **1.** come back, return. **2. ~ auf** (*acc*) come back to, refer to (*letter etc*): **auf j-s Angebot ~** take s.o. up on his offer. **~können** *v/i* (*irr, sep, -ge-, h,* → **können**) F be able to go back: *fig.* **jetzt kann ich nicht mehr zurück!** I can't go back on my word (*or* decision *etc*) now. **~lassen** *v/t* (*irr, sep, -ge-, h,* → **lassen**) **1.** leave *s.o., s.th.* behind. **2.** F allow *s.o.* back. **~laufen** *v/i* (*irr, sep, -ge-, sn,* → **laufen**) run back. **~legen** (*sep, h*) **I** *v/t* **1. et.** (**an s-n Platz**) ~ put s.th. back (in its place). **2.** a) put *s.th.* aside, b) save, put by, lay aside (*money*): **können Sie mir den Mantel bis morgen ~?** would you keep the coat for me till tomorrow? **3.** cover, *a.* walk (*distance*): **zurückgelegte Strecke** distance covered, *mot. a.* mileage. **II sich ~** lie back. **~lehnen** *v/t* (*a. sich ~*) (*sep, h*) lean back. **~liegen** *v/i* (*irr, sep, -ge-, h,* → **liegen**) **das liegt zwei Jahre zurück** that was two years ago. **~melden: sich ~** (*sep, h*) report back (*bei* to). **~müssen** *v/i* (*irr, sep, -ge-, h,* → **müssen**) F have to go back.

Zu'rücknahme [-na:mə] *f* (*-; no pl*) taking back, ⚖ *a.* withdrawal, retraction.

zu'rück|nehmen *v/t* (*irr, sep, -ge-, h,* → **nehmen**) take *s.th.* back, withdraw (*troops,* ⚖ *action*), revoke (*statement*), cancel (*order etc*). **~prallen** *v/i* (*sep, sn*) **1.** rebound. **2.** *fig.* (**vor** *dat* from) recoil, start back. **~rechnen** *v/i* (*sep, h*) reckon back. **~reichen** (*sep, h*) **I** *v/t* hand *s.th.* back, return. **II** *v/i ~ bis* go (*or* date) back to. **~reisen** *v/i* (*sep, sn*) trav-

el back, return. **~rufen** (*irr, sep, -ge-, h,* → **rufen**) **I** *v/t* call *s.o.* back (*a. teleph.*), recall (*a. defective cars etc*): **ins Gedächtnis ~** recall. **II** *v/i teleph.* call back. **~schalten** *v/i* (*sep, h*) change (*Am.* shift) down. **~scheuen** *v/i* (*sep, h*) shrink (back) (**vor** *dat* from): *fig.* **er scheut vor nichts zurück** he sticks at nothing. **~schicken** *v/t* (*sep, h*) send *s.o., s.th.* back, return. **~schlagen** (*irr, sep, -ge-, h,* → **schlagen**) **I** *v/t* **1.** hit *s.o.* back. **2.** repulse, beat off (*attack, enemy*). **3.** fold back (*cover etc*), turn down (*collar*). **4.** return (*ball*). **II** *v/i* **5.** hit back. **6.** *flames:* flare back. **~schrauben** *v/t* (*sep, h*) F *fig.* cut down, reduce, lower (*expectations etc*). **~schrecken** *v/i* (*sep, sn*) (**vor** *dat* from) recoil, start back: *fig.* **er schreckt vor nichts zurück** he sticks at nothing. **~sehnen: sich ~** (*sep, h*) long to be back.

zu'rücksetzen (*sep, h*) **I** *v/t* **1.** put *s.th.* back, back up (*car*). **2.** *fig. j-n ~* treat s.o. unfairly, slight s.o. **II** *v/i mot.* back (up). **Zu'rücksetzung** *f* (*-; -en*) *fig.* unfair treatment, slight.

zu'rück|spielen *v/t, v/i* (*sep, h*) pass (the ball) back. **~springen** *v/i* (*irr, sep, -ge-, sn,* → **springen**) **1.** jump back. **2.** △ recess. **~spulen** *v/t, v/i* (*sep, h*) rewind. **~stecken** *v/t, v/i* (*sep, h*) F put *s.th.* back. **II** *v/i* F *fig.* come down a peg. **~stehen** *v/i* (*irr, sep, -ge-, h,* → **stehen**) **1.** stand back. **2.** *fig.* a) take second place (**hinter** *j-m* behind s.o.), b) stand down (*or* aside). **~stellen** *v/t* (*sep, h*) **1.** put *s.th.* back. **2.** ✕ defer. **3.** postpone, defer. **4.** put *s.th.* aside (*or* last). **~stoßen** (*irr, sep, -ge-, h,* → **stoßen**) **I** *v/t* push *s.o., s.th.* back. **II** *v/i mot.* back (up). **~stufen** *v/t* (*sep, h*) downgrade. **~treiben** *v/t* (*irr, sep, -ge-, h,* → **treiben**) drive *s.o., s.th.* back. **~treten** *v/i* (*irr, sep, -ge-, sn,* → **treten**) **1.** a) step (*or* stand) back, b) recede. **2.** *government etc:* resign, step down: **von s-m Posten ~** resign one's post; **~ von** withdraw from, back out of (*a deal etc*). **3.** *fig.* be of secondary importance (**gegenüber** in comparison with). **~verfolgen** *v/t* (*sep, h*) *fig.* trace *s.th.* back (**zu** to). **~versetzen** *v/t* (*sep, h*) **1.** move *pupil* down, transfer *official* back. **2.** *fig.* take *s.o.* back (**in** *acc* to): **wir fühlten uns ins Mittelalter zurück-**

versetzt we felt to have stepped back into the Middle Ages. **~weichen** v/i (irr, sep, -ge-, sn, → **weichen**) **1.** step back, ✗ fall back. **2.** fig. **~ vor** (dat) yield to, a. shrink back from.

zu'rückweisen v/t (irr, sep, -ge-, h, → **weisen**) **1.** refuse, reject, repudiate (accusation etc). **2.** j-n ~ turn s.o. back, refuse s.o. entry. **Zu'rückweisung** f (-; -en) refusal, rejection.

zu'rück|werfen v/t (irr, sep, -ge-, h, → **werfen**) **1.** throw s.o., s.th. back, a. reflect (light), a. reverberate (sound). **2.** fig. set s.o. back in one's development, work, etc (**um 10 Jahre** [by] ten years). **~wollen** v/i (irr, sep, -ge-, h, → **wollen**) F want to go back. **~zahlen** v/t (sep, h) a. fig. pay back, repay. **~ziehen** (irr, sep, -ge-, → **ziehen**) **I** v/t (h) pull (or draw) s.o., s.th. back, ✗ or fig. withdraw. **II sich ~** (h) (**aus, von** from) retire, withdraw, ✗ a. retreat; **sich ~ von** a. give up (activity etc); **sich von j-m ~** dissociate o.s. from s.o.; **sich zur Beratung ~** retire for deliberation. **III** v/i (sn) move back. **~zucken** v/i (sep, sn) flinch (**vor** dat at).

'**Zuruf** m (-[e]s; -e) a) shout, b) cheer: **durch ~** by acclamation.

'**zurufen** v/t (irr, sep, -ge-, h, → **rufen**) j-m et. ~ shout s.th. to s.o.

Zusage ['tsuːzaːɡə] f (-; -n) **1.** promise, word. **2.** acceptance (of invitation). **3.** assent, consent. '**zusagen** (sep, h) **I** v/t **1.** promise (**sein Kommen** to come). **2.** F j-m et. auf den Kopf ~ tell s.o. s.th. to his face. **II** v/i **3.** accept an invitation, promise to come. **4.** agree. **5.** j-m ~ a) agree with s.o., b) be to s.o.'s liking.

zusammen [tsu'zamən] adv together, a. jointly: **~ mit** together (or along) with; **alle ~** all of them; **wir alle ~** all of us; **alles ~** all together, (all) in all; **wir haben ~ 100 Mark** we have one hundred marks between us; **das macht ~ ...** that amounts to (or totals) ...

Zu'sammenarbeit f (-; no pl) cooperation, a. collaboration, a. teamwork: **in ~ mit** in cooperation with. **zu'sammenarbeiten** v/i (sep, h) (**mit** with) cooperate, collaborate, work together.

zu'sammen|ballen (sep, h) **I** v/t form into a ball. **II sich ~** mass, gather. **~bauen** v/t (sep, h) ☯ assemble. **~bei-**

ßen v/t (irr, sep, -ge-, h, → **beißen**) a. fig. **die Zähne ~** clench one's teeth. **~bekommen** v/t (irr, sep, h, → **bekommen**) get s.th. together, raise (money). **~binden** v/t (irr, sep, -ge-, h, → **binden**) bind (or tie) s.th. together. **~brauen** v/t (sep, h) concoct (a. fig.): fig. **sich ~** be brewing. **~brechen** v/i (irr, sep, -ge-, -sn, → **brechen**) break down, collapse, traffic: come to a standstill. **~bringen** v/t (irr, sep, -ge-, h, → **bringen**) **1.** bring (or get) s.o., s.th. together, raise (money). **2.** F fig. manage, bring off, remember (poem). **Zu'sammenbruch** m (-[e]s; ~e) breakdown, collapse.

zu'sammen|drängen v/t (sep, h) **1.** (a. **sich ~**) crowd (or huddle) together. **2.** fig. compress, condense. **~drücken** v/t (sep, h) compress. **~fahren** v/i (irr, sep, -ge-, sn, → **fahren**) **1.** → **zusammenstoßen**. **2.** fig. (give a) start (**bei** at). **~fallen** v/i (irr, sep, -ge-, sn, → **fallen**) **1.** fall in, collapse. **2.** coincide. **3.** waste away. **~falten** v/t (sep, h) fold up.

zu'sammenfassen v/t (sep, h) **1.** unite, combine: **in Gruppen ~** group. **2.** (a. v/i) summarize, sum up. **zu'sammenfassend** adj summary: **~ kann man sagen** to sum it up it can be said. **Zu'sammenfassung** f (-; -en) **1.** combination. **2.** summary, résumé, synopsis.

zu'sammen|finden: sich ~ (irr, sep, -ge-, h, → **finden**) meet. **~fließen** v/i (irr, sep, -ge-, sn, → **fließen**) flow together, meet.

Zu'sammenfluß m confluence.

zu'sammen|fügen v/t (sep, h) join (together), ☯ assemble. **~führen** v/t (sep, h) bring persons together: **wieder ~** reunite. **~gehen** v/i (irr, sep, -ge-, sn, → **gehen**) fig. (**mit** with) go together, make common cause.

zu'sammengehören v/i (sep, h) belong together, a. be a pair. **zu'sammengehörig** adj belonging together, a. matching, fig. a. related. **Zu'sammengehörigkeit** f (-; no pl) unity, solidarity. **Zu'sammengehörigkeitsgefühl** n (-[e]s; no pl) (feeling of) solidarity.

zu'sammengesetzt adj ★ composite, a. ling. compound: **~ sein aus** be composed of; **~es Wort** compound (word).

zu'sammengewürfelt adj (bunt) ~ motley: ~e Mannschaft scratch team.

Zu'sammenhalt m (-[e]s; no pl) **1.** a. ⊕ cohesion. **2.** fig. a) bond, b) team spirit. **zu'sammenhalten** (irr, sep, -ge-, h, → halten) **I** v/i hold (F stick) together. **II** v/t hold s.th., persons together.

Zu'sammenhang m (-[e]s; ¨e) a) connection, b) context: in diesem ~ in this connection; et. in ~ bringen mit connect s.th. with; im ~ stehen mit be connected with; nicht im ~ stehen mit have no connection with; et. aus dem ~ reißen divorce s.th. from its context.

zu'sammenhängen v/i (irr, sep, -ge-, h, → hängen) fig. be connected (mit with): wie hängt das zusammen? how is that linked up? **zu'sammenhängend** adj coherent (thoughts, speech, etc), connected (questions etc). **zu'sammenhang(s)los** adj incoherent, disconnected.

zu'sammen|hauen v/t (sep, h) **1.** smash s.th. to pieces: F j-n ~ beat s.o. up. **2.** F fig. knock s.th. together. **~klappbar** adj folding, collapsible. **~klappen** (sep) **I** v/t (h) fold up, shut (knife etc). **II** v/i (sn) F fig. break down, collapse. **~kleben** v/t, v/i (sep, h) stick together. **~knüllen** v/t (sep, h) crumple up. **~kommen** v/i (irr, sep, -ge-, sn, → kommen) **1.** come (or get) together, meet, assemble. **2.** fig. combine: heute kommt mal wieder alles zuammen! it never rains but it pours! **3.** accumulate, mount up, money: be collected: F da kommt ganz schön was zusammen it comes to quite a lot in the end.

Zu'sammenkunft [-kʊnft] f (-; ¨e) get--together, meeting, gathering.

zu'sammenlaufen v/i (irr, sep, -ge-, sn, → laufen) **1.** people: gather. **2.** roads etc: meet, converge. **3.** colo(u)rs: run.

zu'sammenleben **I** v/i (sep, h) live together: mit j-m ~ live with s.o. **II** 2 n (-s) living together: das 2 mit ... life with ...

zu'sammenlegen (sep, h) **I** v/t **1.** fold up. **2.** put things together, club persons together (in one room). **3.** ✝ fuse, combine, centralize. **II** v/i club together (für ein Geschenk for a present).

Zu'sammenlegung f (-; -en) ✝ fusion.

zu'sammen|nehmen (irr, sep, -ge-, h, → nehmen) **I** v/t gather (up): alles

zusammengenommen all things considered; ich mußte all m-n Mut ~ I had to muster up all my courage. **II** sich ~ control o.s., pull o.s. together. **~pakken** v/t (sep, h) pack up. **~passen** (sep, h) **I** v/i harmonize (with each other), colo(u)rs etc: a. go well together, partners: a. be well matched: sie passen nicht zusammen they are mismatched. **II** v/t ⊕ adjust, match. **~pferchen** v/t (sep, h) herd (fig. a. crowd) together.

Zu'sammenprall m (-[e]s; no pl) a. fig. collision, clash. **zu'sammenprallen** v/i (sep, sn) a. fig. collide, clash.

zu'sammen|pressen v/t (sep, h) compress. **~raffen** v/t (sep, h) **1.** gather up. **2.** fig. amass. **~rechnen** v/t (sep, h) add (or sum) s.th. up. **~reimen** v/t (sep, h) fig. sich et. ~ work (or figure) s.th. out, put two and two together. **~reißen:** sich ~ (irr, sep, -ge-, h, →reißen) F pull o.s. together. **~rollen** (sep, h) **I** v/t roll up. **II** sich ~ coil up, cat etc: curl up.

zu'sammenrotten: sich ~ (sep, h) gang up, form a mob. **Zu'sammenrottung** f (-; -en) a) riot(ing), b) riotous mob, ⚖ riotous assembly.

zu'sammen|rücken (sep) **I** v/t (h) move things together (or closer). **II** v/i (sn) move up, make room. **~rufen** v/t (irr, sep, -ge-, h, → rufen) convene, call persons together. **~sacken** v/i (sep, sn) (in sich) ~ slump (down). **~scharen:** sich ~ (sep, h) flock together. **~scharren** v/t (sep, h) scrape s.th. together. **~schiebbar** adj telescopic, sliding. **~schieben** v/t (irr, sep, -ge-, h, → schieben) push things together, (a. sich ~ lassen) telescope. **~schlagen** (irr, sep, -ge-, →schlagen) **I** v/t (h) **1.** clap (hands), click (heels etc). **2.** F smash s.th. to pieces: j-n ~ beat s.o. up. **II** v/i (sn) ~ über (dat) close over, a. fig. engulf. **~schließen** (irr, sep, -ge-, h, → schließen) v/t **1.** lock (or chain) together. **2.** unite, ✝ merge. **II** sich ~ unite, join forces, team up, form an alliance.

Zu'sammenschluß m (-sses; ¨sse) **1.** union (a. pol.), ✝ merger. **2.** alliance.

zu'sammen|schnüren v/t (sep, h) tie s.th. up: der Anblick schnürte ihr das Herz zusammen the sight made her heart bleed. **~schrauben** v/t (sep, h) screw (or bolt) s.th. together. **~schrei-**

ben v/t (irr, sep, -ge-, h, → **schreiben**) **1.** write s.th. in one word: **wird das zusammengeschrieben?** is that one word? **2.** contp. scribble. **~schustern** v/t (sep, h) F contp. cobble together. **~schweißen** v/t (sep, h) a. fig. weld.

Zu'sammensein n (-s) gathering, meeting, get-together.

zu'sammensetzen (sep, h) **I** v/t **1.** put s.th. together, **a.** compose, a. 🐍, ling. compound. **2.** seat persons together. **II sich ~ 3.** sit together. **4.** get together. **5. sich ~ aus** consist of, be composed of.

Zu'sammensetzung f (-; -en) **1.** no pl composition (a. of court, team, etc), assembly. **2.** 🐍, ling. compound.

zu'sammensinken v/i (irr, sep, -ge-, sn, → **sinken**) collapse: **in sich ~** slump (down).

Zu'sammenspiel n (-[e]s; no pl) sports: teamwork.

zu'sammen|stauchen v/t (sep, h) F j-n ~ haul s.o. over the coals. **~stecken** (sep, h) **I** v/t put things together. **II** v/i F **immer ~** be as thick as thieves. **~stehen** v/i (irr, sep, h, → **stehen**) stand (F fig. stick) together.

zu'sammenstellen v/t (sep, h) **1.** put things together. **2.** combine, draw up, compile, make (catalogue etc), make up, form (team etc), arrange: **in e-r Liste ~** list; **ein Menü ~** compose a menu. **Zu'sammenstellung** f (-; -en) **1.** combination, arrangement. **2.** a) survey, synopsis, b) table, c) list.

Zu'sammenstoß m (-[e]s; ⸚e) **1.** mot. collision, crash. **2.** F fig. clash.

zu'sammen|stoßen v/i (irr, sep, sn, → **stoßen**) collide (**mit** with): **~ mit a.** run (or crash) into. **~streichen** v/t (irr, sep, -ge-, h, → **streichen**) F shorten (text etc). **~strömen** v/i (sep, sn) fig. flock together. **~suchen** v/t (sep, h) gather, collect. **~tragen** v/t (irr, sep, -ge-, h, → **tragen**) collect (a. fig.), fig. compile (facts etc). **~treffen I** v/i (irr, sep, -ge-, sn, → **treffen**) **1. mit j-m ~** meet s.o. **2.** coincide. **II** ~ n (-s) meeting, b.s. encounter. **~treiben** v/t (irr, sep, -ge-, h, → **treiben**) round up. **~treten** v/i (irr, sep, -ge-, sn, → **treten**) meet, parl. convene. **~trommeln** v/t (sep, h) F call persons together. **~tun: sich ~** (irr, sep, -ge-, h, → **tun**) (**mit** with) team up, join

forces. **~wachsen** v/i (irr, sep, -ge-, sn, → **wachsen**) grow together. **~wirken I** v/i (sep, h) factors etc: combine. **II** ⸙ n (-s) combination, interplay. **~zählen** v/t (sep, h) add up, sum up. **~ziehen** (irr, sep, -ge-, → **ziehen**) **I** v/t (h) **1.** pull s.th. together, a. 🔧 contract. **2.** concentrate, mass (troops). **II** v/i (sn) **3. mit j-m ~** move in (together) with s.o., go to live with s.o. **III sich ~** (h) **4.** contract. **5.** storm etc: be brewing.

Zu'sammenziehung f (-; -en) **1.** contraction. **2.** 🔬 concentration.

zu'sammenzucken v/i (sep, sn) wince (**bei** at).

'Zusatz m (-es; ⸚e) a) addition, a. additive, admixture, b) addendum, 🏛 rider. **~abkommen** n supplementary agreement. **~batte,rie** f ⚡ booster battery. **~gerät** n ⚙ attachment.

'zusätzlich [-zɛtslɪç] **I** adj a) additional, extra, b) supplementary, c) auxiliary. **II** adv in addition (**zu** to).

'Zusatzversicherung f supplementary insurance.

zuschanden [tsuˈʃandən] adv **~ machen** ruin, destroy (a. hopes etc), thwart (plans etc); **~ fahren** ruin, smash (up).

'zuschanzen v/t (sep, h) j-m et. ~ line s.o. up with s.th.

'zuschauen → **zusehen**.

'Zuschauer m (-s; -) onlooker, sports, thea. etc spectator, TV viewer: **die ~ a.** the audience. **~raum** m auditorium. **~reakti,on** f audience (TV viewer) response. **~sport** m spectator sport.

'zuschicken v/t (sep, h) j-m et. ~ send (or mail, post) s.th. to s.o.

'zuschieben v/t (irr, sep, -ge-, h, → **schieben**) **1.** close, shut. **2.** j-m et. ~ push s.th. over to s.o.; **j-m die Schuld (Verantwortung) ~** put (or shift) the blame (responsibility) on s.o.

'zuschießen (irr, sep, -ge-, → **schießen**) **I** v/t (h) F contribute (money). **II** v/i (sn) **~ auf** (acc) rush towards, dart up to.

'Zuschlag m (-[e]s; ⸚e) **1.** a) extra charge, b) supplementary fare, c) extra pay. **2.** award: **er erhielt den ~** a) at an auction: the object went to him, b) 🔨 he was awarded the contract.

'zuschlagen (irr, sep, -ge-, h, → **schlagen**) **I** v/t **1.** slam door etc (shut), shut, close (book etc). **2.** j-m et. ~ at an auc-

tion: knock s.th. down to s.o.; **† der Auftrag wurde ... zugeschlagen** ... was awarded the contract. **II** *v/i* **3.** (sn) slam shut. **4.** strike (*a. fig. enemy, fate, etc*), hit. **5.** F jump at it, grab it: **schwer ~ when shopping etc**: really go to town (**bei** on), *at dinner etc*: tuck in mightily.

'**zuschließen** *v/t* (*irr, sep, -ge-, h, → schließen*) lock (up).

'**zuschnallen** *v/t* (*sep, h*) buckle (up).

'**zuschnappen** *v/i* (*sep*) **1.** (sn) snap shut. **2.** (h) *dog*: snap.

'**zuschneiden** *v/t* (*irr, sep, -ge-, h, → schneiden*) **1.** cut out *dress etc* (**nach e-m Schnittmuster** from a pattern): *fig.* **zugeschnitten auf** (*acc*) tailored to. **2.** ⊙ cut up, (cut *s.th.* to) size.

'**Zuschneider(in** *f*) *m* cutter.

'**Zuschnitt** *m* (-[e]s; -e) cut, style.

'**zuschnüren** *v/t* (*sep, h*) lace up (*shoes*), tie *s.th.* up: *fig.* **Angst schnürte ihr die Kehle zu** she was choked with fear.

'**zuschrauben** *v/t* (*sep, h*) screw *s.th.* shut.

'**zuschreiben** *v/t* (*irr, sep, -ge-, h, → schreiben*) *j-m et.* ~ ascribe (*or* attribute) s.th. to s.o.; **das Bild wird Dürer zugeschrieben** the painting is ascribed to Dürer; **sie schrieben ihm die Schuld dafür zu** they blamed him for it; **das hast du dir selbst zuzuschreiben!** you've only yourself to blame.

'**Zuschrift** *f* (-; -en) letter, reply (**auf e-e Annonce** to an ad *etc*).

zu'schulden *adv* **sich et. ~ kommen lassen** do (s.th.) wrong.

'**Zuschuß** *m* (-sses; *ⁿsse*) **1.** contribution. **2.** allowance. **3.** subsidy, grant. **~betrieb** *m* subsidized enterprise.

'**zuschütten** *v/t* (*sep, h*) fill *s.th.* up.

'**zusehen** *v/i* (*irr, sep, -ge-, h, → sehen*) **1.** look on, watch: *j-m bei der Arbeit* ~ watch s.o. work(ing) (*or* at work). **2.** (**untätig**) ~ sit back and watch. **3.** ~, **daß** see (to it) that.

zusehends ['tsu:ze:ənts] *adv* **1.** visibly. **2.** rapidly.

'**zusein** *v/i* (*irr, sep, -ge-, sn, → sein*) F be closed; → *a.* **zu** IV.

'**zusetzen** (*sep, h*) **I** *v/t* **1.** add (*dat* to). **2.** *Geld* ~ *bei* lose money on; F *fig.* **er hat nichts mehr zuzusetzen** he has used up all his reserves. **II** *v/i* F *j-m* ~ a) press s.o. (hard), b) *fig. heat, illness, etc*: take

it out of s.o.; *j-m mit Fragen* (**Bitten**) ~ pester s.o. with questions (requests).

'**zusichern** *v/t* (*sep, h*) *j-m et.* ~ assure s.o. of s.th. '**Zusicherung** *f* (-; -en) assurance.

Zu'spätkommende *m, f* (-n; -n) latecomer.

'**Zuspiel** *n* (-[e]s; *no pl*) *sports*: pass(es).

'**zuspielen** *v/t* (*sep, h*) **1.** *j-m den Ball* ~ pass the ball to s.o. **2.** *j-m et.* ~ play s.th. into s.o.'s hands.

'**zuspitzen: sich** ~ (*sep, h*) *fig.* come to a head.

'**zusprechen** (*irr, sep, -ge-, h, → sprechen*) **I** *v/t* **1.** *j-m Trost* ~ comfort s.o.; *j-m Mut* ~ encourage s.o., cheer s.o. up. **2.** *j-m et.* ~ award s.th. to s.o.; ⚖ **die Kinder wurden der Mutter zugesprochen** the mother was granted custody of the children. **II** *v/i j-m freundlich etc* ~ speak gently *etc* to s.o.

'**zuspringen** *v/i* (*irr, sep, -ge-, sn, → springen*) ~ **auf** (*acc*) rush up at.

'**Zuspruch** *m* (-[e]s; *no pl*) **1.** (words of) comfort. **2.** encouragement. **3.** → **Zulauf** 1.

'**Zustand** *m* (-[e]s; *ⁿe*) **1.** condition, state (*a. phys.*), F shape: *ihr seelischer* ~ her mental state; **das Haus ist in gutem** ~ the house is in good condition (*or* repair); **in betrunkenem** ~ while under the influence (of alcohol); F **da kann man ja Zustände kriegen!** it's enough to drive you up the wall. **2.** state of affairs, situation: **es herrschen katastrophale Zustände** conditions are catastrophic; F **das ist doch kein ~!** that's intolerable!

zustande [tsu'ʃtandə] *adv* **1.** ~ **bringen** bring s.th. off, achieve, succeed in doing. **2.** ~ **kommen** a) be achieved, come off, *agreement etc*: be reached, *contract*: be signed, b) take place.

'**zuständig** *adj* relevant, competent (*authority etc*), responsible: *der ~e Beamte* the official in charge; ⚖ ~ **sein** have jurisdiction (**für** over); **dafür ist er ~** that's his job.

'**Zuständigkeit** *f* (-; -en) competence, responsibility, powers, ⚖ jurisdiction (**für** over): **das fällt nicht in s-e ~** that's not within his province.

'**Zuständigkeitsbereich** *m* (sphere of) responsibility, ⚖ jurisdiction.

zustatten [tsu'ʃtatən] *adv* *j-m* (**sehr**) **~ kommen** be (very) useful to s.o.

'**zustecken** *v/t* (*sep*, h) *j-m et.* **~** slip s.o. s.th.

'**zustehen** *v/i* (*irr*, *sep*, -ge-, h, → **stehen**) **1.** *et.* **steht** *j-m* **zu** s.o. is entitled to s.th. **2. es steht ihr etc nicht zu zu** *inf* she *etc* has no right (*or* it's not for her) to *inf*.

'**zusteigen** *v/i* (*irr*, *sep*, -ge-, sn, → **steigen**) get on *a bus etc*.

'**zustellen** *v/t* (*sep*, h) deliver: ⚖ *j-m* **e-e Ladung ~** serve s.o. with a summons.

'**Zusteller** *m* (-s; -) postman.

'**Zustellgebühr** *f* postal delivery fee.

'**Zustellung** *f* (-; -en) delivery, ⚖ service.

'**zusteuern** (*sep*) I *v/t* (h) ~. II *v/i* (sn) **~ auf** (*acc*) a ⚓, *a.* person: make (*or* head) for, b) *fig.* be heading for *a crisis etc*, be driving at *a subject etc*.

'**zustimmen** *v/i* (*sep*, h) (*dat*) agree (to *s.th.*, with *s.o.*), consent (to), approve (of): **~d nicken** nod in approval; **er stimmte mir in diesem Punkt nicht zu** he disagreed with me on this point.

'**Zustimmung** *f* (-; -en) agreement, consent, approval: **allgemeine ~ finden** meet with universal approval.

'**zustöpseln** *v/t* (*sep*, h) stopper.

'**zustoßen** (*irr*, *sep*, -ge-, → **stoßen**) I *v/t* (h) **1.** push *door etc* shut. II *v/i* **2.** (h) thrust, stab. **3.** (sn) *j-m* **~** happen to s.o.; **ihr muß et. zugestoßen sein** she must have had an accident.

'**zustreben** *v/i* (*sep*, sn) (*dat*) make for.

'**Zustrom** *m* (-[e]s; *no pl*) **1.** influx: *meteor.* **~ kühler Meeresluft** inflow of fresh sea air. **2.** rush. '**zuströmen** *v/i* (*sep*, sn) *fig.* throng (*dat* towards).

'**zustürzen** *v/i* (*sep*, sn) **~ auf** (*acc*) rush up to.

zutage [tsu'ta:gə] *adv* **~ bringen**, **~ fördern** *a. fig.* bring *s.th.* to light; **~ treten** a) come to light, be revealed, show, b) *a. klar ~ treten* be evident, be obvious.

'**Zutaten** *pl* **1.** *gastr.* ingredients. **2.** *fashion:* accessories.

zu'teil *adv* *j-m* **~ werden** be given to s.o.; *j-m et.* **~ werden lassen** grant s.o. s.th.

'**zuteilen** *v/t* (*sep*, h) *j-m et.* **~** allot (*or* allocate, apportion) s.th. to s.o.; *j-m* **e-e Aufgabe** *etc* **~** assign s.o. a task *etc*.

'**Zuteilung** *f* (-; -en) **1.** allotment, allocation, assignment. **2.** quota.

zu'tiefst *adv* deeply, most: *fig.* **~ verletzt** deeply hurt, cut to the quick.

'**zutragen** (*irr*, *sep*, -ge-, h, → **tragen**) I *v/t* (*dat* to) **1.** carry. **2.** *fig.* tell, report. II *sich* **~** happen, take place. '**Zuträger** *m* (-s; -) *contp.* informer, talebearer.

zuträglich ['tsu:trɛːklɪç] *adj* good (*dat* for): **der Gesundheit ~** conducive to health; **nicht ~ sein** disagree (*dat* with).

'**zutrauen** *v/t* (*sep*, h) *j-m et.* **~** a) think s.o. capable of s.th., b) credit s.o. with s.th.; **das hätte ich dir nie zugetraut!** I never knew you had it in you; **ihm ist alles zuzutrauen!** he stops at nothing; **das ist ihr glatt zuzutrauen!** I wouldn't put it past her.

'**Zutrauen** *n* (-s) confidence (**zu** in).

'**zutraulich** *adj* trusting, confiding, friendly (*a.* animal). '**Zutraulichkeit** *f* (-; *no pl*) confidingness, friendliness.

'**zutreffen** *v/i* (*irr*, *sep*, -ge-, h, → **treffen**) b) be right, be correct: **~ auf** (*acc*), **~ für** be true of, apply to; **die Beschreibung trifft auf ihn zu** the description fits him.

'**zutreffend** *adj* right, true, correct: **Zutreffendes bitte unterstreichen!** please underline where applicable!

'**zutrinken** *v/i* (*irr*, *sep*, -ge-, h, → **trinken**) (*dat* to) drink, raise one's glass.

'**Zutritt** *m* (-[e]s; *no pl*) access, admission: **sich gewaltsam ~ verschaffen** force one's way (**zu** into); **~ verboten!**, **kein ~!** no entry!; → **Unbefugte.**

zu'tun *v/t* (*irr*, *sep*, -ge-, h, → **tun**) → **Auge** 1. '**Zutun** *n ohne mein* **~** a) without any help from me, b) through no fault of mine; **es geschah ohne mein ~** I had nothing to do with it.

zu'ungunsten *prep* (*gen*) to the disadvantage of.

zu'unterst *adv* right at the bottom.

zuverlässig ['tsu:fɛrlɛsɪç] *adj* a) reliable (*a.* ⚙), safe (*a.* ⚙), b) loyal, faithful: **aus ~er Quelle** from a reliable source. '**Zuverlässigkeit** *f* (-; *no pl*) a) *a.* ⚙ reliability, safety, b) loyalty.

Zuversicht ['tsu:fɛrzɪçt] *f* (-; *no pl*) confidence: **voll(er) ~ sein** be quite confident (**daß** that). '**zuversichtlich** *adj* confident, optimistic: **~ hoffen, daß** be quite confident (that). '**Zuversichtlichkeit** *f* (-; *no pl*) confidence, optimism.

zu'viel *adv* too much: **eine(r) ~** one too many; **viel ~** far too much; **~ des Guten**

too much of a good thing; **was ~ ist, ist ~!** there's a limit to everything.

zu'vor adv **1.** (**kurz ~** shortly) before: **am Tag ~** the day before, (on) the previous day. **2.** first.

zu'vorkommen v/i (irr, sep, -ge-, sn, → **kommen**) anticipate, forestall, F a. beat s.o. to it. **zu'vorkommend** adj obliging, courteous. **Zu'vorkommenheit** f (-; no pl) obligingness, courtesy.

Zuwachs ['tsu:vaks] m (-es; no pl) **1.** (**an** dat in) increase, growth (a. ✝): F **auf ~ kaufen** buy shoes etc on the big side. **2.** F addition to the family, baby.

'zuwachsen v/i (irr, sep, -ge-, sn, → **wachsen¹**) **1.** become overgrown. **2.** ✚ heal up, close.

'Zuwachsrate f ✝ growth rate.

'Zuwanderer m (-s; -) immigrant.

'zuwandern v/i (sep, sn) immigrate.

'Zuwanderung f (-; -en) immigration.

zuwege [tsu've:gə] adv **1. ~ bringen** bring s.th. off, achieve, manage to do. **2.** F (**noch) gut ~ sein** be (still) very fit.

zu'weilen adv at times, occasionally.

'zuweisen v/t (irr, sep, -ge-, h, → **weisen**) assign (dat to).

'zuwenden (irr, sep, h, → **wenden²**) **I** v/t **1.** turn (dat towards): **j-m den Rücken ~** turn one's back on s.o.; **j-m das Gesicht ~** face s.o. **2.** j-m et. **~** give s.o. s.th. **II sich ~** turn to, fig. a. devote o.s. to (a task etc). **'Zuwendung** f (-; -en) **1.** a) grant, b) allowance, c) donation. **2.** no pl love, (loving) care, attention.

zu'wenig indef pron a) too little, b) too few: **das ist ~** that's not enough; **du schläfst ~** you don't get enough sleep.

'zuwerfen v/t (irr, sep, -ge-, h, → **werfen**) **1.** slam s.th. (shut). **2.** (dat to) throw, toss: fig. **j-m e-n Blick ~** dart (or flash) s.o. a look; → **Kußhand.**

zu'wider I adj j-m ist ... **~** s.o. hates (or detests) ... **II** prep (dat) contrary to, against.

zu'widerhandeln v/i (sep, h) (dat) act against, act contrary to, violate, contravene (law etc). **Zu'widerhandelnde** m, f (-n; -n) ⚖ offender. **Zu'widerhandlung** f (-; -en) ⚖ (**gegen**) offen/ce (Am. -se) (against), contravention (of).

zu'widerlaufen v/i (irr, sep, -ge-, sn, → **laufen**) (dat) run counter to.

'zuwinken v/i (sep, h) **j-m ~** wave to s.o.

'zuzahlen v/t (sep, h) pay s.th. extra.

'zuzählen v/t (sep, h) **1.** add. **2.** (dat) count among.

'zuziehen (irr, sep, -ge-, → **ziehen**) **I** v/t (h) **1.** pull noose etc tight, tighten, draw (curtains). **2. sich et. ~** a) catch (disease etc), suffer (injury), b) incur (s.o's hatred etc). **3.** → **hinzuziehen. II** v/i (sn) a) move in, b) settle (down). **'Zuzug** m (-[e]s; ✚e) **1.** move. **2.** → **Zuwanderung.**

zuzüglich ['tsu:tsy:kliç] prep (gen) plus.

zwang [tsvaŋ] pret of **zwingen.**

Zwang m (-[e]s; ✚e) compulsion (a. psych.), constraint, pressure, force: **ohne ~** without being forced to; **unter ~ handeln** ⚖ act under duress; **~ ausüben** exert pressure (**auf** acc on); **gesellschaftliche Zwänge** social constraints; **... ist ~ ...** is compulsory; iro. **tu dir k-n ~ an!** just go ahead!

zwängen ['tsvɛŋən] v/t (h) squeeze.

'zwanglos adj informal, casual, unconstrained, a. free and easy: **in ~er Folge erscheinen** magazine etc: appear at irregular intervals; **sich ~ unterhalten** talk at ease; **es geht bei ihnen sehr ~ zu** things are very informal with them. **'Zwanglosigkeit** f (-; no pl) informality, casualness.

Zwangs|anleihe f compulsory loan. **~arbeit** f (-; no pl) forced labo(u)r. **~arbeiter(in** f) m forced labo(u)r convict. **~aufenthalt** m enforced stay, detention. **~bewirtschaftung** f (economic) control: **die ~ aufheben von** (or gen) decontrol. **~einweisung** f committal (**in** acc to). **⚖ernähren** v/t (h) force-feed. **~ernährung** f force feeding. **~handlung** f compulsive act. **~herrschaft** f despotism, tyranny. **~jacke** f straitjacket. **~lage** f predicament.

'zwangsläufig adj inevitable: **er mußte ~ davon erfahren** he was bound to hear of it.

Zwangs|maßnahme f coercive measure, pol. sanction. **~neu,rose** f obsessional neurosis. **~pause** f enforced break. **~räumung** f eviction. **~umsiedler(in** f) m displaced person. **⚖versteigern** v/t (only inf and pp zwangsversteigert, h) put s.th. up for compulsory auction. **~versteigerung** f compulsory auction. **~verwaltung** f sequestration. **~vollstreckung** f execution. **~vorstel-**

lung f psych. obsession: *von der ~ befallen, daß* obsessed with the idea that.

'**zwangsweise I** adj compulsory. **II** adv compulsorily, by force.

'**Zwangswirtschaft** f government control, controlled economy.

zwanzig ['tsvantsıç] adj (*~ [Jahre alt] sein* be) twenty. '**Zwanzig** f (-; -en) twenty: *sie ist Mitte (der) ~* she is in her mid-twenties. **zwanziger** ['tsvantsıgər] adj *die goldenen ~ Jahre* the roaring twenties. '**zwanzigfach** adj adv twentyfold. '**zwanzigjährig** [-jɛːrıç] adj **1.** twenty-year-old, of twenty. **2.** twentieth (*jubilee etc*). '**Zwanzigjährige** [-jɛːrıgə] m, f (-n; -n) twenty-year-old (person): *die ~n* the twenty-year-olds. '**zwanzigst** adj, '**Zwanzigstel** n (-s; -) twentieth.

zwar [tsvaːr] adv **1.** *~ ..., aber ...* it is true ..., but; *es ist ~ verboten, aber ... a.* it may be forbidden, but ... **2.** *und ~* a) namely, b) in fact.

Zweck [tsvɛk] m (-[e]s; -e) **1.** purpose, object, aim, end, use: *zu diesem ~* a) for that purpose, b) to this end; *ein Mittel zum ~* a means to an end; *der ~ heiligt die Mittel* the end justifies the means; *s-n ~ erfüllen (verfehlen)* serve (defeat) its purpose; *für wohltätige ~e* for charity. **2.** point, use: *es hat k-n ~ zu warten* it's no use waiting; *es hat wenig ~, daß ich hingehe* there's little point in my going; *F das ist ja (gerade) der ~ der Übung!* that's the whole point (of the exercise).

'**Zweck**|**bau** m (-[e]s; -ten) functional building. **~bindung** f earmarking of funds for specific purposes. **~denken** n (-s) pragmatism.

'**zweckdienlich** adj relevant, useful: *~e Hinweise* relevant information.

'**zweckentfremden** v/t (*only inf and pp* zweckentfremdet, h) use *s.th.* for a purpose not intended, misappropriate.

'**zweckentsprechend** adj appropriate.

'**zweckfrei** adj nonutility.

'**zweckfremd** adj foreign to the purpose.

'**zweckgebunden** adj earmarked.

'**zweckgemäß** adj appropriate.

'**zwecklos** adj useless, pointless, futile: *~ sein a.* be no use; *es ist ~, daß ich hingehe* there's no point in my going.

'**Zwecklosigkeit** f (-; *no pl*) uselessness, futility.

'**zweckmäßig** adj **1.** practical, functional. **2.** expedient, advisable.

'**Zweckmäßigkeit** f (-; *no pl*) **1.** practicality, functionality. **2.** advisability.

'**Zweck**|**opti**,**mismus** m calculated optimism. **~pessi**,**mismus** m calculated pessimism.

zwecks prep (*gen*) for the purpose of, with a view to.

'**Zwecksparen** n target saving.

'**zweckwidrig** adj inappropriate.

zwei [tsvaı] adj two: *wir ~* we two, the two of us; *dazu gehören ~* it takes two. **Zwei** f (-; -en) **1.** (number) two. **2.** ped. (*mark, grade*) B.

'**zweiachsig** [-ʔaksıç] adj **1.** ⚭ biaxial. **2.** mot. two-axle.

'**zweia**,**tomig** adj ⚛ diatomic.

'**zweibändig** [-bɛndıç] adj two-volume.

'**Zweibeiner** [-baınər] m (-s; -) F man.

'**Zweibettzimmer** n twin-bedded room.

'**zweideutig** [-dɔʏtıç] adj ambiguous, equivocal, *b.s.* suggestive, off-colo(u)red.

'**Zweideutigkeit** f (-; -en) **1.** *no pl* ambiguity, equivocality, *b.s.* suggestiveness. **2.** a) suggestive remark, b) risqué joke.

Zwei'**drittelmehrheit** f two thirds majority.

'**zweieiig** [-ʔaııç] adj biol. binovular: *~e Zwillinge* fraternal twins.

'**Zweier** m (-s; -) rowing: pair: *~ mit (Steuermann)* coxed pair.

'**Zweierbeziehung** f partnership.

'**Zweierbob** m (-s; -s) two-man bob.

'**zweierlei** adj two different (kinds of): *mit ~ Maß messen* apply double standards.

'**zweifach** adj double, adv a. doubly: *in ~er Ausfertigung* in duplicate.

'**zweifarbig** adj two-colo(u)red.

Zweifa'**milienhaus** n two-family (*Am.* duplex) house.

Zweifel ['tsvaıfəl] m (-s; -) doubt (*an dat, wegen* about): *ohne ~ → zweifellos*; *im ~ sein über* (*acc*) be doubtful (*or* in two minds) about; *ihm kamen ~* he was beginning to have doubts; *es bestehen berechtigte ~ an s-r Ehrlichkeit* there is good reason to doubt his honesty; *sie ließen k-n ~ daran, daß* they made it quite plain that.

'**zweifelhaft** adj doubtful, dubious,

questionable, F shady: **~es Vergnügen** dubious pleasure; **von ~em Wert** of debatable value (*or* merit); **es erscheint ~, ob** it seems doubtful whether.

'**zweifellos** *adv* undoubtedly, doubtless, without (a) doubt.

zweifeln ['tsvaɪfəln] *v/i* (h) doubt: **~ an** (*dat*) doubt (*or* question) *s.th.*; **daran ist nicht zu ~** there's no doubt about it.

'**Zweifelsfall** *m* in case of doubt.

Zweifler ['tsvaɪflər] *m* (-s; -) doubter, sceptic, *Am.* skeptic. '**zweiflerisch** *adj* doubting, sceptical, *Am.* skeptical.

Zweig [tsvaɪk] *m* (-[e]s; -e) branch (*a. fig.*), twig; → **grün** I. **~betrieb** *m* branch. **~bü₂ro** *n* branch (office).

'**zweigeschlechtig** *adj* ⚥ bisexual.

'**zweigeteilt** *adj* divided in(to) two.

'**Zweiggeschäft** *n* branch.

'**zweigleisig** [-glaɪzɪç] *adj* **1.** ⚘ double-tracked. **2.** *fig.* two-track: **~ fahren** leave both one's options open.

'**Zweigniederlassung** *f* (~ **im Ausland** foreign) branch.

'**Zweigstelle** *f* branch (office).

'**zweihändig** [-hɛndɪç] *adj* two-handed, ♪ for two hands.

Zweihundert'jahrfeier *f* bicentenary.

'**zweijährig** [-jɛːrɪç] *adj* **1.** two-year. **2.** two-year-old. '**Zweijährige** [-jɛːrɪgə] *m, f* (-n; -n) two-year-old (child).

'**Zweikampf** *m* duel.

'**Zweika₂nal...** ⚡ two-channel. **~ton** *m* TV *m* with two language channels.

'**zweimal** *adv* twice: **das ließ sie sich nicht ~ sagen** she didn't wait to be told twice. '**zweimalig** *adj* (twice) repeated.

Zwei'markstück *n* two-mark piece.

'**zweimotorig** [-mo₂toːrɪç] *adj* twin-engined.

Zweipar'teiensy₂stem *n* two-party system.

'**zweiphasig** [-faːzɪç] *adj* ⚡ two-phase.

'**zweipolig** [-poːlɪç] *adj* ⚡ two-pole, bipolar, two-pin (*plug*).

'**Zweirad** *n* (-[e]s; ~er) bicycle, F bike.

'**zweirädrig** [-rɛːdrɪç] *adj* two-wheeled.

'**Zweireiher** [-raɪər] *m* (-s; -) double-breasted suit. '**zweireihig** *adj* **1.** in two rows. **2.** double-breasted (*suit*).

'**zweischneidig** *adj a. fig.* double-edged.

'**zweiseitig** [-zaɪtɪç] *adj* **1.** bilateral. **2.** two-page (*letter*), double-page (*ad*).

'**zweisilbig** [-zɪlbɪç] *adj* two-syllable.

'**Zweisitzer** [-zɪtsər] *m* (-s; -) two-seater.

'**zweispaltig** [-ʃpaltɪç] *adj* two-column: **~ gedruckt** printed in two columns.

'**zweisprachig** [-ʃpraːxɪç] *adj* bilingual, *document etc* in two languages. '**Zweisprachigkeit** *f* (-; *no pl*) bilingualism.

'**zweispurig** [-ʃpuːrɪç] *adj* **1.** ⚘ double-tracked. **2.** two-lane (*road etc*).

Zwei'stärken₂glas *n opt.* bifocal lens. **~brille** *f* (pair of) bifocals.

'**zweistellig** [-ʃtɛlɪç] *adj* two-digit (*number*), two-place (*decimal*).

'**zweistimmig** [-ʃtɪmɪç] *adj* ♪ for (*or* in) two voices.

'**zweistöckig** [-ʃtœkɪç] *adj* two-storeyed, *Am.* two-storied.

'**zweistrahlig** [-ʃtraːlɪç] *adj* ✈ twin-jet.

'**zweistufig** [-ʃtuːfɪç] *adj* ⊙ two-stage.

'**zweistündig** [-ʃtʏndɪç] *adj* two-hour, lasting two hours.

zweit *adj* second: **der ~e Band** volume two; **~er Mai** May 2nd, *Am.* May 2; **ein ~er Mozart** another Mozart; **jeder ~e** every other person; **zu ~** in twos, in pairs; **sie waren zu ~** there were two of them; **~er Klasse** *a. fig.* second-class; → **Geige, Hand, Ich, Wahl** 1.

'**Zweitakter** *m*, '**Zweitaktmotor** *m* two-stroke engine.

'**zweitältest** *adj*, **Zweitälteste** *m, f* (-n; -n) second eldest.

'**zwei'tausend** *adj* two thousand.

'**zweitbest** *adj*, '**Zweitbeste** *m, f* (-n; -n) second best.

'**Zweite** *m, f* (-n; -n) second: *sports:* **sie wurde ~ hinter ...** she came in second behind ..., she was runner-up to ...; *fig.* **wie kein Zweiter** like nobody else.

'**Zweiteiler** *m* (-s; -) F **1.** two-piece (suit). **2.** *film, TV* two-parter. '**zweiteilig** [-taɪlɪç] *adj* **1.** two-piece. **2.** in two parts.

'**zweitens** *adv* secondly.

'**Zweitfri₂sur** *f* wig.

'**zweitgrößt** *adj* second largest.

'**zweithöchst** *adj* second highest.

'**zweitklassig** [-klasɪç] *adj* second-class, *contp.* second-rate.

'**zweitletzt** *adj* last but one.

'**zweitrangig** [-raŋɪç] *adj* secondary: **~ sein** be of secondary importance.

'**Zweitschlüssel** *m* spare key.

'**Zweitschrift** *f* (-; -en) duplicate.

'**Zweitstimme** *f pol.* second vote.

'**Zweitstudium** n ein ~ beginnen begin a second course of studies.
'**zweitürig** [-ty:rɪç] adj mot. two-door.
'**Zweitwagen** m second car.
'**Zweitwohnung** f second home.
Zwei'vierteltakt m ♩ two-four time.
'**zweiwertig** [-ve:rtɪç] adj ♞ bivalent.
'**zweiwöchig** [-vœçɪç] adj two-week.
'**zweizeilig** [-tsaɪlɪç] adj double-spaced: ~ schreiben double-space.
Zwei'zimmerwohnung f two-room(ed) flat (Am. apartment).
Zwerchfell ['tsvɛrç-] n diaphragm.
~atmung f abdominal breathing.
Չerschütternd adj fig. sidesplitting.
Zwerg [tsvɛrk] m (-[e]s; -e) dwarf, gnome, fig. a. midget.
'**zwergenhaft** adj dwarfish.
'**Zwergpudel** m miniature poodle.
'**Zwergwuchs** m biol., ♣ dwarfism, ♀ dwarf growth. '**zwergwüchsig** [-vy:k-sɪç] adj dwarfish.
Zwetsch(g)e ['tsvɛtʃ(g)ə] f (-; -n) plum.
'**Zwetsch(g)en|baum** m plum tree.
~wasser n (-s; ~) plum brandy.
Zwickel ['tsvɪkəl] m (-s; -) **1.** gusset. **2.** △ spandrel.
zwicken ['tsvɪkən] v/t, v/i (h) pinch.
'**Zwickmühle** f F fig. (in e-r ~ sein or sitzen be on the horns of a) dilemma.
Zwieback ['tsvi:bak] m (-[e]s; -e) rusk.
Zwiebel ['tsvi:bəl] f (-; -n) **1.** onion. **2.** bulb.
'**Zwiebelkuchen** m onion gateau.
'**Zwiebelmuster** n onion pattern.
zwiebeln ['tsvi:bəln] v/t (h) F j-n ~ give s.o. a hard time.
'**Zwiebel|ringe** pl gastr. onion rings.
~schale f onion skin. **~suppe** f onion soup. **~turm** m △ onion spire.
Zwielicht ['tsvi:-] n (-[e]s; no pl) twilight: fig. ins ~ geraten lay o.s. open to suspicion. '**zwielichtig** [-lɪçtɪç] adj fig. dubious, F shady.
'**Zwiespalt** m (-[e]s; rare -e) conflict.
'**zwiespältig** [-ʃpɛltɪç] adj conflicting: er ist ein ~er Mensch he has a conflicting personality; mein Eindruck war ~ I came away with mixed impressions.
Zwilling ['tsvɪlɪŋ] m (-s; -e) **1.** twin. **2.** pl astr. (er ist [ein] ~ he is [a]) Gemini.
'**Zwillings|bruder** m twin brother.
~paar n pair of twins. **~reifen** m mot.

dual (or double, twin) tyres (Am. tires).
~schwester f twin sister.
Zwinge ['tsvɪŋə] f (-; -n) clamp, cramp.
zwingen ['tsvɪŋən] (zwang, gezwungen, h) **I** v/t force, compel: j-n ~, et. zu tun a. make s.o. do s.th.; j-n zum Rücktritt ~ force s.o. to resign; ich sehe mich gezwungen zu verkaufen I find myself compelled to sell; → a. gezwungen. **II** v/i ~ zu necessitate; die Lage zwingt zu e-r schnellen Entscheidung the situation calls for a quick decision. **III** sich ~ force o.s. (et. zu tun to do s.th.); sie zwang sich zu e-m Lächeln she forced a smile; ich mußte mich dazu ~ it cost me an effort (to do that).
'**zwingend** adj compelling (reason etc), absolute, urgent (necessity etc), cogent, conclusive (argument, evidence, etc).
Zwinger ['tsvɪŋər] m (-s; -) kennel(s).
zwinkern ['tsvɪŋkərn] v/i (h) (mit den Augen) ~ a) blink, b) wink.
zwirbeln ['tsvɪrbəln] v/t (h) twist, twirl.
Zwirn [tsvɪrn] m (-[e]s; -e) twine, twist.
zwischen ['tsvɪʃən] prep (dat, acc) a) between, b) among.
'**Zwischenakt** m, **~mu,sik** f entr'acte.
'**Zwischen|aufenthalt** m stop(over).
~bemerkung f interjection. **~bericht** m interim report. **~bescheid** m provisional reply. **~bi,lanz** f interim balance sheet: fig. e-e ~ ziehen take stock in between. **~blutung** f ♣ bleeding between periods, intermenstrual bleeding. **~deck** n ⚓ between decks.
zwischen'durch adv a) in between, b) in the meantime, c) now and then.
'**Zwischen|ergebnis** n provisional result, sports: interim results (or score). **~fall** m incident: ohne Zwischenfälle without a hitch. **~finan,zierung** f intermediate financing, bridging. **~frage** f (interposed) question. **~gericht** n gastr. entrée. **~geschoß** n △ mezzanine. **~glied** n link. **~größe** f intermediate size. **~händler** m intermediary. **~hoch** n meteor. ridge of high pressure. **~lagerung** f nucl. interim storage. **Չlanden** v/i (only inf and pp zwischengelandet, sn) make an intermediate landing, stop. **~landung** f stop(over): ohne ~ nonstop. **~lauf** m sports: intermediate heat. **~lösung** f interim solution. **~mahlzeit** f snack (between

meals). **⊇menschlich** *adj* interpersonal: **~e Beziehungen** human relations. **~prüfung** *f* intermediate examination (*or* test). **~raum** *m* **1.** space, distance, ⊚ clearance, *a.* gap, *print.* spacing: **e-e Zeile ~ lassen** leave a space. **2.** interval. **~ruf** *m* interruption: **~e** heckling. **~rufer** *m* (-s; -) heckler. **~runde** *f* *sports:* intermediate round. **⊇schalten** *v/t* (*only inf and pp* zwischengeschaltet, h) ⚡ connect *s.th.* in series. **~schaltung** *f* ⚡ insertion. **~speicher** *m* *computer:* buffer store (*or* storage). **~spiel** *n* interlude. **~spurt** *m sports:* (sudden) spurt: **e-n ~ einlegen** put in a burst of speed. **⊇staatlich** *adj* **1.** international, intergovernmental. **2.** interstate. **~stadium** *n* intermediate stage. **~stand** *m* (-[e]s; *no pl*) *sports:* interim score. **~station** *f* stopover, (*a.* place) stop. **~stecker** *m* ⚡ adapter. **~stück** *n* ⚙ intermediary, ⚡ adapter. **~stufe** *f* intermediate stage. **~summe** *f* subtotal. **~text** *m* (inserted) caption. **~tief** *n meteor.* ridge of low pressure. **~töne** *pl fig.* overtones. **~urteil** *n* ⚖ interlocutory judg(e)ment. **~wand** *f* dividing wall, partition. **~zeit** *f* **1.** time in between: **in der ~ →** *zwischenzeitlich.* **2.** *sports:* intermediate time. **⊇zeitlich** *I adj* intermediate, interim. **II** *adv* meanwhile, (in the) meantime. **~zeugnis** *n* intermediate report.

Zwist [tsvɪst] *m* (-[e]s; -e), **'Zwistigkeit** *f* (-; -en) quarrel.

zwitschern ['tsvɪtʃərn] *v/t, v/i* (h) twitter, chirp: F **e-n ~** down one. **'Zwitschern** *n* (-s) twitter(ing), chirp(ing).

Zwitter ['tsvɪtər] *m* (-s; -) hermaphrodite.

zwo [tsvoː] F → *zwei.*

zwölf [tsvœlf] *adj* twelve: **um ~ (Uhr)** at twelve (o'clock), *a.* at noon, *a.* at midnight; *fig.* **fünf Minuten vor ~** at the eleventh hour.

Zwölf'fingerdarm *m anat.* duodenum. **~geschwür** *n* ⚕ duodenal ulcer.

'Zwölfkampf *m gym.* twelve events.

zwölft *adj,* **'Zwölfte** *m, f* (-(n); -n) twelfth.

'Zwölftonmu₁sik *f* twelve-tone music.

Zyankali [tsyaˈnˈkaːli] *n* (-s; *no pl*) 🜨 potassium cyanide.

zyklisch ['tsyːklɪʃ] *adj* cyclic(al).

Zyklon [tsyˈkloːn] *m* (-s; -e) cyclone.

Zyklone [tsyˈkloːnə] *f* (-; -n) cyclone.

Zyklotron ['tsyːklotroːn] *n* (-s; -e) *phys.* cyclotron.

Zyklus ['tsyːklʊs] *m* (-; Zyklen) **1.** cycle. **2.** series (*of lectures etc*).

Zylinder [tsiˈlɪndər] *m* (-s; -) **1.** top hat. **2.** 🜨, ⚗, *mot.* cylinder.

Zy'linderkopf *m mot.* cylinder head. **~dichtung** *f mot.* cylinder-head gasket. **~schraube** *f mot.* cylinder-head stud.

zylindrisch [tsiˈlɪndrɪʃ] *adj* cylindric(al).

Zyniker ['tsyːnikər] *m* (-s; -) cynic.

zynisch ['tsyːnɪʃ] *adj* cynical.

Zynismus [tsyˈnɪsmʊs] *m* (-; -men) cynicism.

Zypern ['tsyːpərn] *n* (-s) Cyprus.

Zyprer ['tsyːprər] *m* (-s; -), **'Zyprerin** *f* (-; -nen) Cypriote.

Zypresse [tsyˈprɛsə] *f* (-; -n) ♣ cypress.

zyprisch ['tsyːprɪʃ] *adj* Cyprian.

Zyste ['tsyːstə] *f* (-; -en) cyst.

Zystoskopie [tsʏstoskoˈpiː] *f* (-; -n) ⚕ cystoscopy.

zytologisch [tsytoˈloːgɪʃ] *adj* cytologic(al). **Zytostatikum** [tsytoˈstaːtikʊm] *n* (-s; -ka) ⚕ cytostatic agent.

German Abbreviations

A

AA *das Auswärtige Amt* Foreign Office; *Anonyme Alkoholiker* Alcoholics Anonymous

Abb. *Abbildung* ill(us)., illustration; fig., figure

Abf. *Abfahrt* dep., departure

Abk. *Abkürzung* abbr., abbreviation

ABM *Arbeitsbeschaffungsmaßnahme* job creation scheme

Abo *Abonnement* subscription

ABS *Antiblockiersystem* anti-lock braking system

Abs. *Absatz* par., paragraph; *Absender* sender

Abschn. *Abschnitt* section; ch., chapter

Abt. *Abteilung* dept, department

abzgl. *abzüglich* less, minus

a. D. *außer Dienst* retd, retired; *an der Donau* on the Danube

ADAC *Allgemeiner Deutscher Automobil-Club* General German Automobile Association

Adr. *Adresse* address

AG *Aktiengesellschaft* Br. PLC, Plc, plc, Ltd, public limited company; *Am.* (stock) corporation

AKW *Atomkraftwerk* nuclear power station *or* plant

allg. *allgemein* gen., general

a. M. *am Main* on the Main

am., amer(ik). *amerikanisch* Am., American

amtl. *amtlich* off., official

Anh. *Anhang* app., appendix

Ank. *Ankunft* arr., arrival

Anl. *Anlage(n)* encl., enclosure(s)

Anm. *Anmerkung* note

anschl. *anschließend* foll., following

AOK *Allgemeine Ortskrankenkasse* compulsory health insurance scheme

a. o. Prof. *außerordentlicher Professor* Br. senior lecturer; *Am.* associate professor

App. *Apparat* ext., extension; telephone

ARD *Arbeitsgemeinschaft der öffentlich-rechtlichen Rundfunkanstalten der Bundesrepublik Deutschland* Working Pool of the Broadcasting Corporations of the Federal Republic of Germany

a. Rh. *am Rhein* on the Rhine

Art. *Artikel* art., article

ASU *Abgassonderuntersuchung* exhaust emission test

Aufl. *Auflage* ed., edition

Ausg. *Ausgabe* ed., edition; copy

Az. *Aktenzeichen* file number

B

B *Bundesstraße* major road, federal highway

b. *bei* at; with; nr., near; c/o, care of

BAföG *Bundesausbildungsförderungsgesetz* student financial assistance scheme

BAT *Bundesangestelltentarif* salary scale for public employees

BBk *Deutsche Bundesbank* German Federal Bank

Bde. *Bände* vols, volumes

BE *Broteinheit* bread unit

beil. *beiliegend* encl., enclosed

BENELUX *Belgien, Niederlande, Luxemburg* Belgium, the Netherlands, and Luxembourg

bes. *besonders* esp., especially

Best.-Nr. *Bestellnummer* ord. no., order number

Betr. *Betreff, betrifft* ✝ re

betr. *betreffend, betreffs* conc., concerning; regarding

Bev. *Bevölkerung* pop., population

Bez. *Bezeichnung* mark; name, designation; *Bezirk* dist., district

BGB *Bürgerliches Gesetzbuch* Civil Code

BGH *Bundesgerichtshof* Federal Supreme Court

BGS *Bundesgrenzschutz* Federal Border Guard

Bhf. *Bahnhof* Sta., station

BLZ *Bankleitzahl* bank code

BND *Bundesnachrichtendienst* Federal Intelligence Service

Bq *Becquerel* Bq., Becquerel

BR *Bayerischer Rundfunk* Bavarian Broadcasting Corporation

BRD *Bundesrepublik Deutschland* FRG, Federal Republic of Germany

brit. *britisch* Br(it)., British

BRT *Bruttoregistertonnen* GRT, gross register tons

bsd. *besonders* esp., especially

Btx *Bildschirmtext* viewdata

BUND *Bund für Umwelt und Naturschutz Deutschland* the German Association for Environment Protection and Nature Conservancy

Bw. *Bundeswehr* Federal Armed Forces

b. w. *bitte wenden* PTO, p.t.o., please turn over

BWV *Bachwerkeverzeichnis* BWV, Bach catalogue

bzgl. *bezüglich* with reference to

bzw. *beziehungsweise* resp., respectively

C

C *Celsius* C, Celsius, centigrade

ca. *circa, ungefähr, etwa* c., ca, circa; about; approx., approximately

cand. *candidatus, Kandidat* cand., candidate

CD *Compact Disc* CD, compact disc

CDU *Christlich-Demokratische Union* Christian Democratic Union

cm *Zentimeter* centimetre(s)

Co. *obs. Compagnie* co., company; *Compagnon* partner

CSU *Christlich-Soziale Union* Christian Social Union

CT *Computertomographie* computer tomography

CVJM *Christlicher Verein Junger Männer* YMCA, Young Men's Christian Association

D

d. Ä. *der Ältere* Sen., sen., Snr, Sr, senior

DAAD *Deutscher Akademischer Austauschdienst* German Academic Exchange Service

DAG *Deutsche Angestelltengewerkschaft* Trade Union of German Employees

DB *Deutsche Bahn* German Railway

DBP *Deutsche Bundespost* German Federal Postal Services

DDR *Deutsche Demokratische Republik* hist. GDR, German Democratic Republic

DFB *Deutscher Fußball-Bund* German Football Association

DGB *Deutscher Gewerkschaftsbund* Federation of German Trade Unions

dgl. *dergleichen, desgleichen* the like

d. Gr. *der or die Große* the Great

d. h. *das heißt* i.e., that is

d. i. *das ist* i.e., that is

Di. *Dienstag* Tues., Tuesday

DIN *Deutsches Institut für Normung* German Institute for Standardization

Dipl. *Diplom* Dip., Dipl., diploma

Dipl.-Ing. *Diplomingenieur* qualified engineer

Dir. *Direktor* Dir., dir., director; *Direktion the* directors *pl*

d. J. *der Jüngere* Jun., jun., Jnr, Jr, junior; *dieses Jahres* of this year

DJH *Deutsches Jugendherbergswerk* German Youth Hostel Association

DKP *Deutsche Kommunistische Partei* German Communist Party

dkr *dänische Krone(n)* Danish crown(s)

DM *Deutsche Mark* German mark(s)

d. M. *dieses Monats* inst., instant

d. O. *der* (*die, das*) *Obige* the above-mentioned

do. *ditto* do., ditto

Do. *Donnerstag* Thurs., Thursday

Doz. *Dozent(in)* lecturer

dpa *Deutsche Presse-Agentur* German Press Agency

DR *Deutsche Reichsbahn* hist. DDR East German railway

Dr. *Doktor* Dr, Doctor; ~ **jur.** *Doktor der Rechte* LLD, Doctor of Laws; ~ **med.** *Doktor der Medizin* MD, Doctor of Medicine; ~ **phil.** *Doktor der Philosophie* DPhil, PhD, Doctor of Philosophy; ~ **rer. nat.** *Doktor der Naturwissenschaften* DSc, ScD, Doctor of Science; ~ **theol.** *Doktor der Theologie* DD, Doctor of Divinity

dt. *deutsch* Ger., German

Dtzd. *Dutzend* doz., dozen(s)

DZ *Doppelzimmer* double (room)

E

E *Eilzug* fast train; *Europastraße* European Highway

ebd. *ebenda* ib(id)., ibidem, in the same place

Ed. *Edition, Ausgabe* ed., edition

ed. *edidit, hat herausgegeben* ed., edited by, published by

EDV *elektronische Datenverarbeitung* EDP, electronic data processing

EEG *Elektroenzephalogramm* EEG, electroencephalogram

e. G. *eingetragene Gesellschaft* registered (*Am.* incorporated) company

EG *Europäische Gemeinschaft hist.* EC, European Community

e.h. *ehrenhalber* hon., honorary

eh(e)m. *ehemals* formerly; *ehemalig* former

eidg. *eidgenössisch* fed., federal, confederate, Swiss

eigtl. *eigentlich* actual(ly), real(ly), *adv a.* strictly speaking

einschl. *einschließlich* incl., inclusive (-ly), including; *einschlägig* relevant

EKD *Evangelische Kirche in Deutschland* Protestant Church in Germany

EKG *Elektrokardiogramm* ECG, electrocardiogram

engl. *englisch* Eng., English

entspr. *entsprechend* corr., corresponding

erb. *erbaut* built, erected

Erw. *Erwachsene pl* adults

EU *Europäische Union* European Union

Euratom *Europäische Atomgemeinschaft* Euratom, European Atomic Energy Community

ev. *evangelisch* Prot., Protestant

e. V. *eingetragener Verein* registered society *or* association

evtl. *eventuell* poss., possibly; perhaps

EWS *Europäisches Währungssystem* EMS, European Monetary System

exkl. *exklusive* exc., except(ed); excl., exclusive, excluding

Expl. *Exemplar* sample, copy

EZ *Einzelzimmer* single (room)

F

Fahrenheit *Fahrenheit* F, Fahrenheit

f. *und folgende Seite* and following *page*

Fa. *Firma* firm; *on letter:* Messrs

Fam. *Familie* family; *on letter:* Mr and Mrs ... (and family)

FC *Fußballclub* FC, Football Club

FCKW *Fluorchlorkohlenwasserstoff*

CFC, chlorofluorocarbon

F.D.P. *Freie Demokratische Partei* Liberal Democratic Party

ff. *und folgende Seiten* and following *pages*

FF *Französischer Franc* FF, French franc

FH *Fachhochschule* advanced technical college

Fig. *Figur* fig., figure; diag., diagram

fig. *figurativ, figürlich, bildlich* fig., figurative(ly)

FKK *Freikörperkultur* nudism

fl. k. u. w. W. *fließend kaltes und warmes Wasser* hot and cold running water

Fmk *Finnmark* fin(n)mark

folg. *folgend(e etc)* foll., following

Forts. *Fortsetzung* continuation; **Forts. f.** *Fortsetzung folgt* to be contd, to be continued

Fr. *Frau* Ms; (*married*) Mrs; *Freitag* Fri., Friday

Frl. *Fräulein* Miss

frz. *französisch* Fr., French

FU *Freie Universität* (*Berlin*) Free University

G

GAU *größter anzunehmender Unfall* MCA, maximum credible accident

geb. *geboren* b., born; *geborene ...* née ...; *gebunden* bd, bound

Gebr. *Gebrüder* Bros., Brothers

gegr. *gegründet* founded; est(ab)., established

gek. *gekürzt* abr., abridged

Ges. *Gesellschaft* assoc., association; co., company; soc., society; *Gesetz* law

gesch. *geschieden* div., divorced

ges. gesch. *gesetzlich geschützt* regd, registered

gest. *gestorben* d., died, deceased

Gew. *Gewicht* w., wt, weight

gez. *gezeichnet* sgd, signed

GG *Grundgesetz* constitution

Ggs. *Gegensatz* contrast; opp., opposite

ggf(s). *gegebenenfalls* should the occasion arise; if necessary; if applicable

GmbH *Gesellschaft mit beschränkter Haftung* limited liability company

GMD *Generalmusikdirektor* (chief) musical director
GUS *Gemeinschaft Unabhängiger Staaten* CIS, Commonwealth of Independent States

H

ha *Hektar* hectare(s)
Hbf. *Hauptbahnhof* cent. sta., central station; main sta., main station
h. c. *honoris causa, ehrenhalber* hon., honorary
HGB *Handelsgesetzbuch* Commercial Code
hins. *hinsichtlich* with regard to, regarding, as to
Hj. *Halbjahr* half-year, six months
hl *Hektoliter* hl, hectolitre(s)
hl. *heilig* holy
HP *Halbpension* half board
hPa *Hektopascal* hPa, hectopascal
HR *Hessischer Rundfunk* Hessian Broadcasting Corporation
Hr(n). *Herr(n)* Mr
H(rs)g. *Herausgeber* ed., editor
h(rs)g. *herausgegeben* ed., edited
Hz *Hertz* Hz, hertz
Hzg. *Heizung* heating

I

i. *im, in* in (the)
i. A. *im Auftrag* p.p., per procurationem, by proxy
i. allg. *im allgemeinen* in general, gen., generally; on the whole
i. b. *im besonderen* in particular
IC *Intercity(-Zug)* inter-city (train)
ICE *Intercity-Expresszug* intercity express (train)
i. D. *im Dienst* on duty; *im Durchschnitt* on av., on average
i. e. *im einzelnen* in detail *or* particular; *id est, das heißt, das ist* i.e., that is
IFO *Institut für Wirtschaftsforschung* Institute for Economic Research
IG *Industriegewerkschaft* industrial union
i. H. *im Hause* on the premises
IHK *Industrie- und Handelskammer* Chamber of Industry and Commerce
i. J. *im Jahre* in (the year)

i. M. *im Monat* in (the month of) *May etc*
inf. *infolge* owing to; as a result of
Ing. *Ingenieur* eng., engineer
Inh. *Inhaber* prop., propr, proprietor; *Inhalt* cont., contents
inkl. *inklusive* incl., including, included; inclusive of
IOK *Internationales Olympisches Komitee* IOC, International Olympic Committee
IQ *Intelligenzquotient* IQ, intelligence quotient
i. R. *im Ruhestand* ret., retd, retired
IRK *Internationales Rotes Kreuz* IRC, International Red Cross
ISBN *Internationale Standardbuchnummer* ISBN, international standard book number
ital. *italienisch* It., Ital., Italian
i. Tr. *in der Trockenmasse percentage of fat* in dry matter
i. V. *in Vertretung* p.p., by proxy; *in Vorbereitung* in prep., in preparation
IWF *Internationaler Währungsfonds* IMF, International Monetary Fund

J

J *Joule* joule(s)
Jan. *Januar* Jan., January
jap. *japanisch* Jap., Japanese
JH *Jugendherberge* Y.H., youth hostel
Jh. *Jahrhundert* c, cent., century
jhrl. *jährlich* yearly, ann., annual(ly)
jr., jun. *junior* Jun., jun., Jnr, Jr, junior
jur. *juristisch* leg., legal
JVA *Justizvollzugsanstalt* prison

K

Kap. *Kapitel* ch(ap)., chapter
Kat *Katalysator* cat., catalytic converter, catalyst
kath. *katholisch* C(ath)., Catholic
KB *Kilobyte(s)* KB, kilobyte(s)
kcal *Kilokalorie(n)* kcal., kilocalorie(s), kilogram(me) calorie(s)
Kffr. *Kauffrau* businesswoman
Kfm. *Kaufmann* merchant; businessman; trader; dlr, dealer; agt, agent
kfm. *kaufmännisch* com(m)., commercial

Kfz *Kraftfahrzeug* motor verhicle
kg *Kilogramm* kg, kilogramme(s)
KG *Kommanditgesellschaft* limited partnership
kgl. *königlich* royal
kHz *Kilohertz* kHz, kilohertz
kJ *Kilojoule* kJ, kilojoule(s)
k.k. *kaiserlich-königlich* imperial and royal
KKW *Kernkraftwerk* nuclear power station *or* plant
Kl. *Klasse* cl., class
km *Kilometer* km, kilometre(s)
KP *Kommunistische Partei* CP, Communist Party
Kripo *Kriminalpolizei* CID, criminal investigation department
KSZE *Konferenz über Sicherheit und Zusammenarbeit in Europa* hist. CSCE, Conference on Security and Cooperation in Europe
Kto. *Konto* acct, a/c, account
KV *Köchelverzeichnis* K, Köchel catalogue
kW *Kilowatt* kW, kilowatt(s)
kWh *Kilowattstunde(n)* kilowatt-hour(s)
KZ *Konzentrationslager* concentration camp

L

l *Liter* litre(s)
l. *links* l., left
lat. *lateinisch* Lat., Latin
l. c. *loco citato, am angegebenen Ort* l.c., in the place cited
led. *ledig* single, unmarried
lfd. *laufend* current, running
lfde. Nr. *laufende Nummer* ser. no., serial number
Lf(r)g. *Lieferung* dely, delivery
LG *Landgericht* district court
Lkw, LKW *Lastkraftwagen* lorry, *esp. Am.* truck
log *Logarithmus* log, logarithm
LP *Langspielplatte* LP, long-playing record
LPG *landwirtschaftliche Produktionsgenossenschaft* hist. DDR collective farm
LSD *Lysergsäurediäthylamid* LSD, lysergic acid dieathylamide
lt. *laut* acc. to, according to; as per
ltd. *leitend* man., managing

Ltg. *Leitung* direction; mangt, management
luth. *lutherisch* Luth., Lutheran
LZB *Landeszentralbank* State Central Bank

M

m *Meter* m, metre(s)
MA *Mittelalter* MA, Middle Ages
M. A. *Magister Artium* MA, Master of Arts
MAD *Militärischer Abschirmdienst* Military Counter-Intelligence Service
Math. *Mathematik* math., mathematics
m. a. W. *mit anderen Worten* in other words
max. *maximal* max., maximum
MAZ *magnetische Bildaufzeichnung* VTR, video tape recording
MB *Megabyte* mb, megabyte
mbH *mit beschränkter Haftung* with limited liability
MdB *Mitglied des Bundestages* Member of the Bundestag
MdL *Mitglied des Landtages* Member of the Landtag
mdl. *mündlich* verbal, oral
m. E. *meines Erachtens* in my opinion
MEZ *mitteleuropäische Zeit* CET, Central European Time
MG *Maschinengewehr* MG, machine gun
mg *Milligramm* milligramme(s)
MHz *Megahertz* MHz, megahertz
Mi. *Mittwoch* Wed., Wednesday
Mill. *Million(en)* m, million
Min., min. *Minute(n)* min., minute(s)
min. *minimal* min., minimum
Mio. *Million(en)* m, million
Mitw. *Mitwirkung* assistance, participation, cooperation
mm *Millimeter* mm, millimetre(s)
Mo. *Montag* Mon., Monday
möbl. *möbliert* furn., furnished
mod. *modern* mod., modern
MP *Maschinenpistole* submachine gun
Mrd. *Milliarde(n)* bn, billion
MS, Ms. *Manuskript* MS, ms, manuscript
MS, m.s. *multiple Sklerose* multiple sclerosis
MT *Megatonne* megaton

MTA *medizinisch-technische Assistentin* medical laboratory assistant
mtl. *monatlich* monthly
m. ü. M. *Meter über (dem) Meer(esspiegel)* metres above sea level
mus. *musikalisch* mus., musical
m. W. *meines Wissens* as far as I know
MwSt., MWSt. *Mehrwertsteuer* VAT, value-added tax

N

N *Nord(en)* N, north
n. *nach* after
N(a)chf. *Nachfolger* successor
nachm. *nachmittags* p.m., pm, in the afternoon
näml. *nämlich* viz, i.e., namely, that is to say
NATO *Nordatlantikpakt-Organisation* NATO, North Atlantic Treaty Organization
NB *notabene* NB, note well
n. Br. *nördlicher Breite* N lat, northern latitude
n. Chr. *nach Christus* AD, anno domini
NDR *Norddeutscher Rundfunk* Northern German Broadcasting Corporation
n. J. *nächsten Jahres* of next year
nkr *norwegische Krone(n)* Nkr, Norwegian crown(s)
n. M. *nächsten Monats* of next month
N. N. *nomen nominandum* name hitherto unknown
NO *Nordost(en)* NE, northeast
No. *Nummer* No., no., number
NOK *Nationales Olympisches Komitee* National Olympic Committee
nördl. *nördlich* N, north, northern
norw. *norwegisch* Norw., Norwegian
Nov. *November* Nov., November
NPD *Nationaldemokratische Partei Deutschlands* National-Democratic Party of Germany
Nr. *Nummer* No., no., number
NS *Nachschrift* PS, postscript; *hist.* *Nationalsozialismus* National Socialism
NVA *Nationale Volksarmee* hist. *DDR*
NW *Nordwest(en)* NW, northwest

O

O *Ost(en)* E, east
o. *oben* above; *oder* or; *ohne* w/o, without
o. a. *oben angeführt* above(-mentioned)
o. ä. *oder ähnlich(e, -es etc)* or the like
ÖAMTC *Österreichischer Automobil-, Motorrad- und Touring-Club* Austrian Automobile, Motorcycling and Touring Association
OB *Oberbürgermeister* mayor
o. B. *ohne Befund* ✚ results negative
Obb. *Oberbayern* Upper Bavaria
ÖBB *Österreichische Bundesbahnen* Austrian Federal Railways
od. *oder* or
offiz. *offiziell* off., official
OHG *offene Handelsgesellschaft* general partnership
OLG *Oberlandesgericht* Higher Regional Court
OP *Operationssaal* operating theatre (*Am.* room)
op. *Opus* ♪ op., opus
o. Prof. *ordentlicher Professor* Prof., prof., (full) professor
ORF *Österreichischer Rundfunk* Austrian Broadcasting Corporation
Orig. *Original* orig., original
orth. *orthodox* Orth., Orthodox
österr. *österreichisch* Aus., Austrian
ÖTV *(Gewerkschaft) Öffentliche Dienste, Transport und Verkehr* the (German) Public Services and Transport Union
ÖVP *Österreichische Volkspartei* Austrian People's Party

P

p. A(dr) *per Adresse* c/o, care of
PC *Personalcomputer* PC, pc, personal computer
PCB *polychlorierte Biphenyle*
PDS *Partei des demokratischen Sozialismus* Party of Democratic Socialism
pers. *persönlich* pers., personal; personally, in person
Pf *Pfennig* pf., pfennig
Pfd. *Pfund* German pound(s)
PGiroA *Postgiroamt* postal giro office
PH *Pädagogische Hochschule* college of education, *Am.* teachers' college

PIN *persönliche Identifikationsnummer* PIN, personal identification number, PIN number

Pkt. *Punkt* pt, point

Pkw, PKW *Personenkraftwagen* (motor)car

Pl. *Platz* Sq., Square; *Plural* pl., plural

PLO *Palästinensische Befreiungsorganisation* PLO, Palestine Liberation Organization

PLZ *Postleitzahl* postcode, *Am.* zip code

pol. *polizeilich* police ...

poln. *polnisch* Pol., Polish

port(ug). *portugiesisch* Port., Portuguese

pp(a). *per Prokura* p.p., per pro(c)., by proxy

PR *Public Relations, Öffentlichkeitsarbeit* PR, public relations

prakt. *praktisch* practical(ly)

Priv.-Doz. *Privatdozent(in)* unsalaried lecturer

Prof. *Professor* Prof., Professor

PS *Pferdestärke(n)* HP, hp, horsepower; *Postskriptum* PS, postscript

Pta(s) *Peseta(s)* pta(s), peseta(s)

PTT *Post, Telefon, Telegraf; Schweizerische Post-, Telefon- und Telegrafenbetriebe* Swiss Postal, Telephone and Telegraph Services

PVC *Polyvinylchlorid* PVC, polyvinyl chloride

Q

qkm *Quadratkilometer* (*obs. for* km²) sq. km, square kilometre(s)

qm *Quadratmeter* (*obs. for* m²) sq. m, square metre(s)

Qual. *Qualität* qual., quality

R

r. *rechts* r., right

RA *Rechtsanwalt* lawyer; *Br.* sol., solr, solicitor; bar., barrister; *Am.* att., atty, attorney

RAF *Rote Armee-Fraktion* Red Army Fraction

RB *Radio Bremen* Broadcasting Corporation of Bremen

Rbl *Rubel* Rbl., rbl., r(o)uble(s)

rd. *rund* roughly

Reg.-Bez. *Regierungsbezirk* administrative district

Rel. *Religion* rel., religion

Rep. *Republik* Rep., Republic

resp. *respektive* resp., respectively

RIAS *Rundfunk im* (*ehemaligen*) *amerikanischen Sektor* (*von Berlin*) Radio in the (*former*) American Sector (*of Berlin*)

rk, r.-k. *römisch-katholisch* RC, Roman Catholic

RNS *Ribonukleinsäure* RNA, ribonucleic acid

röm. *römisch* Rom., Roman

RT *Registertonne(n)* reg. t., register ton(s)

russ. *russisch* Russ., Russian

S

S *Süd(en)* S, south; *Schilling* S., schilling

s *Sekunde(n)* s, sec., second(s)

S. *Seite* p., page

s. *siehe* v., vide, see

s. a. *siehe auch* see also

SB- *Selbstbedienungs-* self-service ...

SBB *Schweizerische Bundesbahnen* Swiss Federal Railways

SC *Sportclub* sports club

schwed. *schwedisch* Swedish

schweiz. *schweizerisch* Swiss

SDR *Süddeutscher Rundfunk* Southern German Broadcasting Corporation

SED *Sozialistische Einheitspartei Deutschlands* *hist. DDR* Socialist Unity Party of Germany

Sek., sek. *Sekunde(n)* s., sec., second(s)

sen. *senior* Sen., sen., Snr, Sr, senior

Sept. *September* Sept., September

SFB *Sender Freies Berlin* Broadcasting Corporation of Free Berlin

sFr., sfr *Schweizer Franken* SF, Sfr, Swiss Franc(s)

Sg. *Singular* sing., singular

SJ *Societate Jesu, Jesuit* Jesuit

skr *schwedische Krone(n)* Kr, Skr, Swedish crown(s)

sm *Seemeile(n)* n. m., nautical mile(s)

SO *Südost(en)* SE, southeast

s.o. *siehe oben* see above

sog. *sogenannt(e, -es etc)* so-called

soz. *sozial* social
span. *spanisch* Span., Spanish
SPD *Sozialdemokratische Partei Deutschlands* Social Democratic Party of Germany
spez. *speziell* special, particular
SPÖ *Sozialistische Partei Österreichs* Austrian Socialist Party
SR *Saarländischer Rundfunk* Broadcasting Corporation of the Saarland
s. R. *siehe Rückseite* see overleaf
SRG *Schweizerische Radio- und Fernsehgesellschaft* Swiss Broadcasting Corporation
SS *Sommersemester* summer semester *or* term
St. *Sankt* St., Saint; *Stück* pc(s)., piece(s)
Std. *Stunde(n)* h., hr(s)., hour(s)
stdl. *stündlich* hourly, every hour
stellv. *stellvertretend* asst, assistant
StGB *Strafgesetzbuch* penal *or* criminal code
StPO *Strafprozeßordnung* Code of Criminal Procedure
Str. *Straße* St, Street; Rd, Road
stud. *studiosus, Student* student
StVO *Straßenverkehrsordnung* (road) traffic regulations, *Br.* Highway Code
s. u. *siehe unten* see below
SW *Südwest(en)* SW, southwest
SWF *Südwestfunk* Southwestern German Broadcasting Corporation

---

T

t *Tonne(n)* t, ton(s)
t(ä)gl. *täglich* daily, a *or* per day
Tb(c) *Tuberkulose* TB, tuberculosis
TEE *Trans-Europ-Express* TEE, Trans--European-Express
Tel. *Telefon* tel., (tele)phone
Telegr. *Telegramm* teleg., telegram
TH *Technische Hochschule* college of technology, technical university
TL *türkische Lira* (*pl* Lire) TL, Turkish lira (*pl* lire *or* liras)
TU *Technische Universität* technical university
TÜV *Technischer Überwachungsverein* Technical Control Board
TV *Turnverein* gymnastics club; *Television* TV, television

U

U *Unterseeboot* sub., submarine
u. *und* and
u. a. *und andere(s)* and others (other things); *unter anderem (anderen)* among other things, inter alia (among others)
u. ä. *und ähnliche(s)* and the like
U. (*or* **u.**) **A. w. g.** *um Antwort wird gebeten* RSVP, please reply
U-Bahn *Untergrundbahn* underground, *Am.* subway
u. d(er)gl. (m.) *und dergleichen (mehr)* and so on; and the like
u. d. M. *unter dem Meeresspiegel* below sea level
ü. d. M. *über dem Meeresspiegel* above sea level
u. E. *unseres Erachtens* in our opinion, as we see it
UFO, Ufo *unbekanntes Flugobjekt* UFO, unidentified flying object
U-Haft *Untersuchungshaft* custody, detention (pending trial)
UKW *Ultrakurzwelle* USW, ultrashort wave; FM, frequency modulation
U/min. *Umdrehungen pro Minute* r.p.m., revolutions per minute
U-Musik *Unterhaltungsmusik* light music
unbek. *unbekannt* unknown
unbez. *unbezahlt* unpaid
unehel. *unehelich* illegit., illegitimate
ung(ar). *ungarisch* Hung., Hungarian
ungebr. *ungebräuchlich* unusual
unverb. *unverbindlich* not binding
unverh. *unverheiratet* unm., unmarried, sgl., single
unvollst. *unvollständig* incomplete
unz. *unzählig* innumerable
urspr. *ursprünglich* orig., original(ly)
US(A) *Vereinigte Staaten (von Amerika)* US(A), United States (of America)
usw. *und so weiter* etc., and so on
u. U. *unter Umständen* poss., possibly; perh., perhaps; if need be
UV *Ultraviolett* UV, ultraviolet
u. W. *unseres Wissens* as far as we know
Ü-Wagen *Übertragungswagen* outside broadcast (OB) van *or* unit

V

V *Volt* V, volt(s)

V. *Vers* v., verse; l., line

v. von, vom of; from; by; *versus*, *gegen* v., vs., versus

VAE *Vereinigte Arabische Emirate* UAE, United Arab Emirates

VB *Verhandlungsbasis* o.n.o., or near-(est) offer

v. Chr. *vor Christus* BC, before Christ

v. D. *vom Dienst* on duty, in charge

VDE *Verein Deutscher Elektrotechniker* Association of German Electricians

VEB *volkseigener Betrieb* hist. *DDR* state-owned enterprise *or* company

Verf. *Verfasser* author

vergr. *vergriffen* out of print

verh. *verheiratet* mar., married

Verl. *Verlag* publishing house *or* company, publishers

Verw. *Verwaltung* admin, administration; mngmt, management

verw. *verwitwet* widowed

vgl. *vergleiche* cf., confer; cp., compare

v. H. *vom Hundert* pc, per cent, percent

VHS *Volkshochschule* adult education program(me); adult evening classes

v. J. *vorigen Jahres* of last year

v. l. n. r. *von links nach rechts* from left to right

v. M. *vorigen Monats* of last month

V-Mann *Vertrauensmann, Verbindungsmann* contact

Vollm. *Vollmacht* full power(s), auth., authority

vollst. *vollständig* complete(ly)

vorl. *vorläufig* temp., temporary

vorm. *vormittags* a.m., am, in the morning; *vormals* formerly

Vors. *Vorsitzende(r)* chairperson, chm., chairman, chw., chairwoman

VP *Vollpension* full board, board and lodging

VR *Volksrepublik* People's Republic

v. T. *vom Tausend* per thousand

VW *Volkswagen* VW, Volkswagen

W

W *West(en)* W, west; *Watt* W, watt(s)

WAA *Wiederaufbereitungsanlage* reprocessing plant

wbl. *weiblich* fem., female

WC *Wasserklosett* WC toilet

Wdh(lg). *Wiederholung* repetition; *TV etc* repeat

WDR *Westdeutscher Rundfunk* Western German Broadcasting Corporation

werkt. *werktags* (on) weekdays

westl. *westlich* west, western

WEU *Westeuropäische Union* WEU, Western European Union

WEZ *westeuropäische Zeit* GMT, Greenwich Mean Time

WG *Wohngemeinschaft* flat share; people sharing a flat (*esp. Am.* an apartment) *or.* a house

Whg. *Wohnung* flat, *esp. Am.* apt., apartment

wirtsch. *wirtschaftlich* econ., economic

wiss. *wissenschaftlich* academic

w. L. *westlicher Länge* W long., Western longitude

WM *Weltmeisterschaft* world championship; *soccer*: World Cup

wö. *wöchentlich* weekly, every week

WS *Wintersemester* winter semester *or* term

WSV *Winterschlußverkauf* winter sales

Wwe. *Witwe* widow

Wz. *Warenzeichen* TM, trademark; *Wasserzeichen* watermark

Z

Z. *Zeile* l., line; *Zahl* number

z. zu, zum, zur at; to

z. B. *zum Beispiel* e.g., for example, for instance

ZDF *Zweites Deutsches Fernsehen* Second Channel *or* Program(me) of German Television Broadcasting

zeitgen. *zeitgenössisch* contemporary

zeitl. *zeitlich* temporal, time ...

zeitw. *zeitweilig, zeitweise* occasionally, from time to time

ZH *Zentralheizung* centr. heat., central heating

z. H(d). *zu Händen* attn, attention (of)

Zi. *Zimmer* rm (no.), room (number); *Ziffer* fig., figure; No., no., number; §§ subparagraph; *in contract etc*: item

ZK *Zentralkomitee* Central Committee

Zl *Zloty* Zl, zloty(s)

Zlg. *Zahlung* payment

ZOB *zentraler Omnibusbahnhof* bus *or* coach station

z. T. *zum Teil* partly

Ztg. *Zeitung* newspaper

Ztr. *Zentner* cwt, hundredweight(s)

Ztschr. *Zeitschrift* mag., magazine

Zub. *Zubehör* accessories, fittings

zul. *zulässig* permissible; ⊚ safe

zur. *zurück* back

zus. *zusammen* tog., together

zw. *zwischen* bet., between; among

Zwgst. *Zweigstelle* branch (office)

z. Z(t). *zur Zeit* at present

Alphabetical List of the German Irregular Verbs
Infinitive — Preterite — Past Participle

backen – backte (buk) – gebacken
bedingen – bedang – (bedingte) – bedungen (*conditional*: bedingt)
befehlen – befahl – befohlen
beginnen – begann – begonnen
beißen – biß – gebissen
bergen – barg – geborgen
bersten – barst – geborsten
bewegen – bewog – bewogen
biegen – bog – gebogen
bieten – bot – geboten
binden – band – gebunden
bitten – bat – gebeten
blasen – blies – geblasen
bleiben – blieb – geblieben
bleichen – blich – geblichen
braten – briet – gebraten
brauchen – brauchte – gebraucht (*v/aux* brauchen)
brechen – brach – gebrochen
brennen – brannte – gebrannt
bringen – brachte – gebracht
denken – dachte – gedacht
dreschen – drosch – gedroschen
dringen – drang – gedrungen
dürfen – durfte – gedürft (*v/aux* dürfen)
empfehlen – empfahl – empfohlen
erlöschen – erlosch – erloschen
erschrecken – erschrak – erschrocken
essen – aß – gegessen
fahren – fuhr – gefahren
fallen – fiel – gefallen
fangen – fing – gefangen
fechten – focht – gefochten
finden – fand – gefunden
flechten – flocht – geflochten
fliegen – flog – geflogen
fliehen – floh – geflohen
fließen – floß – geflossen
fressen – fraß – gefressen
frieren – fror – gefroren
gären – gor (*esp. fig.* gärte) – gegoren (*esp. fig.* gegärt)
gebären – gebar – geboren
geben – gab – gegeben
gedeihen – gedieh – gediehen
gehen – ging – gegangen
gelingen – gelang – gelungen
gelten – galt – gegolten
genesen – genas – genesen

genießen – genoß – genossen
geschehen – geschah – geschehen
gewinnen – gewann – gewonnen
gießen – goß – gegossen
gleichen – glich – geglichen
gleiten – glitt – geglitten
glimmen – glomm – geglommen
graben – grub – gegraben
greifen – griff – gegriffen
haben – hatte – gehabt
halten – hielt – gehalten
hängen – hing – gehangen
hauen – haute (hieb) – gehauen
heben – hob – gehoben
heißen – hieß – geheißen
helfen – half – geholfen
kennen – kannte – gekannt
klimmen – klomm – geklommen
klingen – klang – geklungen
kneifen – kniff – gekniffen
kommen – kam – gekommen
können–konnte–gekonnt (*v/aux* können)
kriechen – kroch – gekrochen
laden – lud – geladen
lassen – ließ – gelassen (*v/aux* lassen)
laufen – lief – gelaufen
leiden – litt – gelitten
leihen – lieh – geliehen
lesen – las – gelesen
liegen – lag – gelegen
lügen – log – gelogen
mahlen – mahlte – gemahlen
meiden – mied – gemieden
melken – melkte (molk) – gemolken (gemelkt)
messen – maß – gemessen
mißlingen – mißlang – mißlungen
mögen – mochte – gemocht (*v/aux* mögen)
müssen–mußte–gemußt (*v/aux* müssen)
nehmen – nahm – genommen
nennen – nannte – genannt
pfeifen – pfiff – gepfiffen
preisen – pries – gepriesen
quellen – quoll – gequollen
raten – riet – geraten
reiben – rieb – gerieben
reißen – riß – gerissen
reiten – ritt – geritten
rennen – rannte – gerannt

riechen – roch – gerochen
ringen – rang – gerungen
rinnen – rann – geronnen
rufen – rief – gerufen
salzen – salzte – gesalzen (gesalzt)
saufen – soff – gesoffen
saugen – sog – gesogen
schaffen – schuf – geschaffen
schallen – schallte (scholl) – geschallt
(*for* erschallen *a.* erschollen)
scheiden – schied – geschieden
scheinen – schien – geschienen
scheißen – schiß – geschissen
schelten – schalt – gescholten
scheren – schor – geschoren
schieben – schob – geschoben
schießen – schoß – geschossen
schinden – schindete – geschunden
schlafen – schlief – geschlafen
schlagen – schlug – geschlagen
schleichen – schlich – geschlichen
schleifen – schliff – geschliffen
schleißen – schliß – geschlissen
schließen – schloß – geschlossen
schlingen – schlang – geschlungen
schmeißen – schmiß – geschmissen
schmelzen – schmolz – geschmolzen
schnauben – schnob – geschnoben
schneiden – schnitt – geschnitten
schrecken – schrak – *obs.* geschrocken
schreiben – schrieb – geschrieben
schreien – schrie – geschrie(e)n
schreiten – schritt – geschritten
schweigen – schwieg – geschwiegen
schwellen – schwoll – geschwollen
schwimmen – schwamm – geschwommen
schwinden – schwand – geschwunden
schwingen – schwang – geschwungen
schwören – schwor – geschworen
sehen – sah – gesehen
sein – war – gewesen
senden – sandte – gesandt
sieden – sott – gesotten
singen – sang – gesungen
sinken – sank – gesunken
sinnen – sann – gesonnen
sitzen – saß – gesessen
sollen – sollte – gesollt (*v/aux* sollen)

spalten – spaltete – gespalten (gespaltet)
speien – spie – gespie(e)n
spinnen – spann – gesponnen
sprechen – sprach – gesprochen
sprießen – sproß – gesprossen
springen – sprang – gesprungen
stechen – stach – gestochen
stecken – steckte (stak) – gesteckt
stehen – stand – gestanden
stehlen – stahl – gestohlen
steigen – stieg – gestiegen
sterben – starb – gestorben
stieben – stob – gestoben
stinken – stank – gestunken
stoßen – stieß – gestoßen
streichen – strich – gestrichen
streiten – stritt – gestritten
tragen – trug – getragen
treffen – traf – getroffen
treiben – trieb – getrieben
treten – trat – getreten
triefen – triefte (troff) – getrieft
trinken – trank – getrunken
trügen – trog – getrogen
tun – tat – getan
verderben – verdarb – verdorben
verdrießen – verdroß – verdrossen
vergessen – vergaß – vergessen
verlieren – verlor – verloren
verschleißen – verschliß – verschlissen
verzeihen – verzieh – verziehen
wachsen – wuchs – gewachsen
wägen – wog (wägte) – gewogen (gewägt)
waschen – wusch – gewaschen
weben – wob – gewoben
weichen – wich – gewichen
weisen – wies – gewiesen
wenden – wandte – gewandt
werben – warb – geworben
werden – wurde – geworden (worden*)
werfen – warf – geworfen
wiegen – wog – gewogen
winden – wand – gewunden
wissen – wußte – gewußt
wollen – wollte – gewollt (*v/aux* wollen)
wringen – wrang – gewrungen
zeihen – zieh – geziehen
ziehen – zog – gezogen
zwingen – zwang – gezwungen

---

* only in connection with the past participles of other verbs, *e.g.*, **er ist gesehen worden** he has been seen.

States of the Federal Republic of Germany

Baden-Württemberg Baden-Württemberg
Bayern Bayern
Berlin Berlin
Brandenburg Brandenburg
Bremen Bremen
Hamburg Hamburg
Hessen Hessen
Mecklenburg-Vorpommern Mecklenburg-Western Pomerania
Niedersachsen Lower Saxony
Nordrhein-Westfalen North Rhine-Westphalia
Rheinland-Pfalz Rhineland-Palatinate
Saarland Saarland
Sachsen Saxony
Sachsen-Anhalt Saxony-Anhalt
Schleswig-Holstein Schleswig-Holstein
Thüringen Thuringia

States of the Republic of Austria

Burgenland Burgenland
Kärnten Carinthia
Niederösterreich Lower Austria
Oberösterreich Upper Austria
Salzburg Salzburg
Steiermark Styria
Tirol Tyrol
Vorarlberg Vorarlberg
Wien Vienna

Cantons of the Swiss Confederation

(Half cantons in brackets)

Aargau Aargau
Appenzell (Inner-Rhoden; Außer-Rhoden) Appenzell (Inner Rhodes; Outer Rhodes)
Basel Basel, Basle
Bern Bern, Berne
Freiburg, Fribourg Fribourg
Genf, Genève Geneva
Glarus Glarus
Graubünden Graubünden, Grisons
Jura Jura
Luzern Lucerne
Neuenburg, Neuchâtel Neuchâtel
St. Gallen St Gallen, St Gall
Schaffhausen Schaffhausen
Schwyz Schwyz
Solothurn Solothurn
Tessin, Ticino Ticino
Thurgau Thurgau
Unterwalden (Obwalden; Nidwalden) Unterwalden (Obwalden; Nidwalden)
Uri Uri
Waadt, Vaud Vaud
Wallis, Valais Valais, Wallis
Zug Zug
Zürich Zurich

Numerals
Cardinal Numbers

0 null *nought, zero*
1 eins *one*
2 zwei *two*
3 drei *three*
4 vier *four*
5 fünf *five*
6 sechs *six*
7 sieben *seven*
8 acht *eight*
9 neun *nine*
10 zehn *ten*
11 elf *eleven*
12 zwölf *twelve*
13 dreizehn *thirteen*
14 vierzehn *fourteen*
15 fünfzehn *fifteen*
16 sechzehn *sixteen*
17 siebzehn *seventeen*
18 achtzehn *eighteen*
19 neunzehn *nineteen*
20 zwanzig *twenty*
21 einundzwanzig *twenty-one*
22 zweiundzwanzig *twenty-two*
23 dreiundzwanzig *twenty-three*
30 dreißig *thirty*
31 einunddreißig *thirty-one*
40 vierzig *forty*

41 einundvierzig *forty-one*
50 fünfzig *fifty*
51 einundfünfzig *fifty-one*
60 sechzig *sixty*
61 einundsechzig *sixty-one*
70 siebzig *seventy*
71 einundsiebzig *seventy-one*
80 achtzig *eighty*
81 einundachtzig *eighty-one*
90 neunzig *ninety*
91 einundneunzig *ninety-one*
100 hundert *a* (or *one*) *hundred*
101 hundert(und)eins *a hundred and one*
200 zweihundert *two hundred*
300 dreihundert *three hundred*
572 fünfhundert(und)zweiund- siebzig *five hundred and seventy-two*
1000 tausend *a* (or *one*) *thousand*
2000 zweitausend *two thousand*
1 000 000 eine Million *a* (or *one*) *million*
2 000 000 zwei Millionen *two million*
1 000 000 000 eine Milliarde *a* (or *one*) *billion*

Ordinal Numbers

1. erste *first*
2. zweite *second*
3. dritte *third*
4. vierte *fourth*
5. fünfte *fifth*
6. sechste *sixth*
7. siebente *seventh*
8. achte *eighth*
9. neunte *ninth*
10. zehnte *tenth*
11. elfte *eleventh*
12. zwölfte *twelfth*
13. dreizehnte *thirteenth*
14. vierzehnte *fourteenth*
15. fünfzehnte *fifteenth*
16. sechzehnte *sixteenth*
17. siebzehnte *seventeenth*
18. achtzehnte *eighteenth*

19. neunzehnte *nineteenth*
20. zwanzigste *twentieth*
21. einundzwanzigste *twenty-first*
22. zweiundzwanzigste *twenty- -second*
23. dreiundzwanzigste *twenty- -third*
30. dreißigste *thirtieth*
31. einunddreißigste *thirty-first*
40. vierzigste *fortieth*
41. einundvierzigste *forty-first*
50. fünfzigste *fiftieth*
51. einundfünfzigste *fifty-first*
60. sechzigste *sixtieth*
61. einundsechzigste *sixty-first*
70. siebzigste *seventieth*
71. einundsiebzigste *seventy-first*
80. achtzigste *eightieth*

81.	einundachtzigste *eighty-first*	**572.**	fünfhundertundzweiund-
90.	neunzigste *ninetieth*		siebzigste *five hundred and*
100.	hundertste *(one) hundredth*		*seventy-second*
101.	hundertunderste *hundred*	**1000.**	tausendste *(one) thousandth*
	and first	**2000.**	zweitausendste *two thousandth*
200.	zweihundertste *two hundredth*	**1 000 000.**	millionste *millionth*
300.	dreihundertste *three hun-*	**2 000 000.**	zweimillionste *two mil-*
	dredth		*lionth*

Fractions and other numerical values

$^1/_2$ ein halb *one* (or *a*) *half*
$1^1/_2$ anderthalb *one and a half*
$2^1/_2$ zweieinhalb *two and a half*
$^1/_2$ Meile *half a mile*
$^1/_3$ ein Drittel *one* (or *a*) *third*
$^2/_3$ zwei Drittel *two thirds*
$^1/_4$ ein Viertel *one* (or *a*) *fourth, one* (or *a*) *quarter*
$^3/_4$ drei Viertel *three fourths, three quarters*
$1^1/_4$ Stunden *one* (or *an*) *hour and a quarter*
$^1/_5$ ein Fünftel *one* (or *a*) *fifth*
$3^4/_5$ drei vier Fünftel *three and four fifths*
0,4 null Komma vier *(nought) point four (0.4)*
2,5 zwei Komma fünf *two point five (2.5)*

Einfach *single*
zweifach *double*
dreifach *treble, triple, threefold*
vierfach *fourfold, quadruple*
fünffach *fivefold etc*

Einmal *once*
zweimal *twice*
drei-, vier-, fünfmal *etc three, four, five times*
zweimal soviel(e) *twice as much (many)*
noch einmal *once more*

Erstens, zweitens, drittens *etc firstly, secondly, thirdly, in the first (second, third) place*

$7 + 8 = 15$ sieben plus (or und) acht ist fünfzehn *seven plus* (or *and*) *eight is fifteen*

$10 - 3 = 7$ zehn minus (or weniger) drei ist sieben *ten minus* (or *less*) *three is seven*

$2 \times 3 = 6$ zweimal drei ist sechs *twice three is six*

$20 : 5 = 4$ zwanzig dividiert (or geteilt) durch fünf ist vier *twenty divided by five is four*

German Weights and Measures

I. Measure of length

1 mm *Millimeter* millimetre
= $^1/_{1000}$ metre
= 0.0010936 yards
= 0.0032809 feet
= 0.03937079 inches

1 cm *Zentimeter* centimetre
= $^1/_{100}$ metre
= 0.3937 inches

1 dm *Dezimeter* decimetre
= $^1/_{10}$ metre
= 3.9370 inches

1 m *Meter* metre
= 1.0936 yards
= 3.2809 feet
= 39.37079 inches

1 km *Kilometer* kilometre
= 1,000 metres
= 1,093.637 yards
= 3,280.8692 feet
= 39,370.79 inches
= 0.62138 British or Statute Miles

1 sm *Seemeile* nautical mile
= 1,852 metres

II. Surface measurements

1 mm² *Quadratmillimeter*
square millimetre
= $^1/_{1\,000\,000}$ square metre
= 0.000001196 square yards
= 0.0000107641 square feet
= 0.00155 square inches

1 cm² *Quadratzentimeter*
square centimetre
= $^1/_{10\,000}$ square metre

1 dm² *Quadratdezimeter*
square decimetre
= $^1/_{100}$ square metre

1 m² *Quadratmeter* square metre
= 1.19599 square yards
= 10.7641 square feet
= 1,550 square inches

1 a *Ar* are
= 100 square metres
= 119.5993 square yards
= 1,076.4103 square feet

1 ha *Hektar* hectare
= 100 ares
= 10,000 square metres
= 11,959.90 square yards
= 107,641.03 square feet
= 2.4711 acres

1 km² *Quadratkilometer*
square kilometre
= 100 hectares
= 1,000,000 square metres
= 247.11 acres
= 0.3861 square miles

III. Solid measures

1 cm³ *Kubikzentimeter*
cubic centimetre
= 1,000 cubic millimetres
= 0.061 cubic inches

1 dm³ *Kubikdezimeter*
cubic decimetre
= 1,000 cubic centimetres
= 61.0253 cubic inches

1 m³ *Kubikmeter*
1 rm *Raummeter* } cubic metre
1 fm *Festmeter*
= 1,000 cubic decimetres
= 1.3079 cubic yards
= 35.3156 cubic feet

1 RT *Registertonne*
register ton
= 2.832 m³
= 100 cubic feet

IV. Measure of Capacity

1 l *Liter* litre
= 10 decilitres
= 1.7607 pints (*Br.*)
= 7.0431 gills (*Br.*)
= 0.8804 quarts (*Br.*)
= 0.2201 gallons (*Br.*)
= 2.1134 pints (*Am.*)
= 8.4534 gills (*Am.*)
= 1.0567 quarts (*Am.*)
= 0.2642 gallons (*Am.*).

1 hl *Hektoliter* hectolitre
= 100 litres
= 22.009 gallons (*Br.*)
= 2.751 bushels (*Br.*)
= 26.418 gallons (*Am.*)
= 2.84 bushels (*Am.*)

V. Weights

1 mg *Milligramm* milligram(me)
= $^1/_{1000}$ gram(me)
= 0.0154 grains

1 g *Gramm* gram(me)
= $^1/_{1000}$ kilogram(me)
= 15.4324 grains

1 Pfd *Pfund* pound (German)
= $^1/_2$ kilogram(me)
= 500 gram(me)s
= 1.1023 pounds (avdp.)
= 1.3396 pounds (troy)

1 kg *Kilogramm, Kilo*
kilogram(me)
= 1,000 gram(me)s
= 2.2046 pounds (avdp.)
= 2.6792 pounds (troy)

1 Ztr. *Zentner* center
= 100 pounds (German)
= 50 kilogram(me)s
= 110.23 pounds (avdp.)
= 0.9842 British hundredweights
= 1.1023 U.S. hundredweights

1 dz *Doppelzentner*
= 100 kilogram(me)s
= 1.9684 British hundredweights
= 2.2046 U.S. hundredweights

1 t *Tonne* ton
= 1,000 kilogram(me)s
= 0.984 British tons
= 1.1023 U.S. tons

Phonetic Alphabet

	German	British English	American English	International	Civil Aviation (ICAO)
A	Anton	Andrew	Abel	Amsterdam	Alfa
Ä	Ärger	—	—	—	—
B	Berta	Benjamin	Baker	Baltimore	Bravo
C	Cäsar	Charlie	Charlie	Casablanca	Charlie
CH	Charlotte	—	—	—	—
D	Dora	David	Dog	Danemark	Delta
E	Emil	Edward	Easy	Edison	Echo
F	Friedrich	Frederick	Fox	Florida	Foxtrot
G	Gustav	George	George	Gallipoli	Golf
H	Heinrich	Harry	How	Havana	Hotel
I	Ida	Isaac	Item	Italia	India
J	Julius	Jack	Jig	Jerusalem	Juliett
K	Kaufmann	King	King	Kilogramme	Kilo
L	Ludwig	Lucy	Love	Liverpool	Lima
M	Martha	Mary	Mike	Madagaskar	Mike
N	Nordpol	Nellie	Nan	New York	November
O	Otto	Oliver	Oboe	Oslo	Oscar
Ö	Ökonom	—	—	—	—
P	Paula	Peter	Peter	Paris	Papa
Q	Quelle	Queenie	Queen	Québec	Quebec
R	Richard	Robert	Roger	Roma	Romeo
S	Samuel	Sugar	Sugar	Santiago	Sierra
Sch	Schule	—	—	—	—
T	Theodor	Tommy	Tare	Tripoli	Tango
U	Ulrich	Uncle	Uncle	Upsala	Uniform
Ü	Übermut	—	—	—	—
V	Viktor	Victor	Victor	Valencia	Victor
W	Wilhelm	William	William	Washington	Whiskey
X	Xanthippe	Xmas	X	Xanthippe	X-Ray
Y	Ypsilon	Yellow	Yoke	Yokohama	Yankee
Z	Zacharias	Zebra	Zebra	Zürich	Zulu

Second Part

English – German

Guide for the User

1. English Headwords.

1.1 The alphabetical order of the headwords has been observed throughout, including the irregular forms.

1.2 Centred dots or stress marks within a headword indicate syllabification,

e.g. **cul·ti·vate ...,** **,cul·ti'va·tion**

1.3 In hyphenated compounds a hyphen coinciding with the end of a line is repeated at the beginning of the next.

1.4 The tilde (**~**, ~) represents the repetition of a headword.

1.4.1 In compounds where the tilde in bold type (**~**) replaces the catchword,

e.g. **af·ter ... '~·birth** (= afterbirth) ...

1.4.2 The simple tilde (~) replaces the headword immediately preceding (which itself may contain a tilde in bold type),

e.g. **dis·tance ...** *at a* ~ = at a distance.
day ... '~·light ... ~ *saving time* = daylight saving time.

1.5 When the initial letter changes from small to capital or vice versa, the usual tilde is replaced by ♀ or ♀,

e.g. **state ...** ♀ *Department* = State Department.

2. Pronunciation.

2.1 The pronunciation of English headwords is given in square brackets by means of the symbols of the International Phonetic Association.

2.2 To save space the tilde (~) has been made use of in many places within the phonetic transcription. It replaces any part of the preceding complete transcription which remains unchanged,

e.g. **gym·na·si·um** [dʒɪm'neɪzjəm] ... **gym·nast** ['~næst] ...

3. Subject Labels.
The field of knowledge from which an English headword or some of its meanings are taken is indicated by figurative or abbreviated labels or other labels written out in full. A figurative or abbreviated label placed immediately after the phonetic transcription of a headword refers to all translations. A label preceding an individual translation refers to this only.

4. Usage Label.
The indication of the level of usage by abbreviations such as F, *sl.* etc refers to the English headword. Wherever possible the same level of usage between headword and translation has been aimed at.

5. Grammatical References.

5.1 When the last element of a compound is a noun with an irregular plural, a reference such as (*irr man*) indicates that the plural form is given under the separate headword (in this case *man*):

fore·man (*irr man*).

5.2 An adjective marked with □ takes the regular adverbial form, i.e. by affixing ...ly to the adjective or by changing ...le into ...ly or ...y into ...ily.

5.3 (~*ally*) means that an adverb is formed by affixing ...ally to the adjective.

5.4 When there is only one adverb for adjectives ending in both ...ic and ...ical, this is indicated in the following way:

ge·o·met·ric, ge·o·met·ri·cal □,
i.e. geometrically is the adverb of both adjectives.

6. Translations.

6.1 The direct and indirect objects of verbs are printed in italics before the translation. Where necessary the subject of an adjective or verb is indicated in italics and in brackets after the translation,

e.g. **a·ban·don** ... **2.** *Hoffnung etc* aufgeben, *Suche etc a.* einstellen ...
a·bate ... abklingen (*Begeisterung, Lärm, Schmerz etc*) ...
ab·ject ... bitter (*Armut etc*) ...

6.2 Prepositions governing an English catchword (verb, adjective, noun) are given in both languages,

e.g. **place** ... **10.** (*with*) *Auftrag* erteilen (*dat*), vergeben (an *acc*), *Bestellung* aufgeben (bei) ...
pose ... **3.** ... *Bedrohung, Gefahr etc* darstellen (**for, to** für) ...

6.3 Where a German preposition may govern the dative or the accusative case, the case is given in brackets,

e.g. **en·ter** ... eindringen in (*acc*) ...

7. Illustrative phrases and their translations follow the translation of the headword. When the translation can easily be gathered from the meanings of the separate words, it has occasionally been omitted, e.g.

gain ... **4.** zunehmen an (*dat*): ~ **speed** schneller werden, ...
a·board ... **1.** ⚓, ✈ an Bord (*gen*): **go** ~; ...

A

A [eɪ] s: *from A to Z* F von A bis Z.

a [ə], *vor vokalischem Anlaut* **an** [ən] *adj od. Artikel* **1.** ein(e): *he is a doctor* er ist Arzt. **2.** der-, die-, dasselbe: *they are of an age* sie sind gleichaltrig. **3.** per, pro, je: *twice a week* zweimal wöchentlich *od.* in der Woche.

a·back [ə'bæk] *adv: taken ~* überrascht, verblüfft; bestürzt.

a·ban·don [ə'bændən] *v/t* **1.** *Frau etc* verlassen. **2.** *Hoffnung etc* aufgeben, *Suche etc a.* einstellen, (*Sport*) *Spiel* abbrechen.

a·base [ə'beɪs] *v/t* erniedrigen, demütigen. **a'base·ment** *s* Erniedrigung *f*, Demütigung *f*.

a·bashed [ə'bæʃt] *adj* beschämt, verlegen: *feel ~* sich schämen.

a·bate [ə'beɪt] *v/i* abklingen (*Begeisterung, Lärm, Schmerz etc*), (*a. Sturm etc*) sich legen.

ab·at·toir ['æbətwɑ:] *s* Schlachthaus *n*, -hof *m*.

ab·bess ['æbes] *s* Äbtissin *f*. **ab·bey** ['æbɪ] *s* Abtei *f*. **ab·bot** ['æbət] *s* Abt *m*.

ab·bre·vi·ate [ə'bri:vɪeɪt] *v/t* (ab-, ver)kürzen: *~d form* Kurzform *f*. **ab·bre·vi·a·tion** *s* (Ab-, Ver)Kürzung *f*.

ABC [,eɪbi:'si:] *s* **1.** *Am. oft pl* Abc *n*, Alphabet *n*: (*as*) *easy as ~* kinderleicht; *~ weapons pl* ⚔ ABC-Waffen *pl*. **2.** *fig.* Abc *n*, Anfangsgründe *pl*.

ab·di·cate ['æbdɪkeɪt] **I** *v/i* abdanken. **II** *v/t Amt* niederlegen: *~ the throne* abdanken. **,ab·di'ca·tion** *s* Abdankung *f*.

ab·do·men ['æbdəmen] *s anat.* Unterleib *m*. **ab·dom·i·nal** [æb'dɒmɪnl] *adj* Unterleibs...

ab·duct [æb'dʌkt] *v/t* entführen. **ab·duc·tion** [æb'dʌkʃn] *s* Entführung *f*.

ab·er·ra·tion [,æbə'reɪʃn] *s* **1.** Abweichung *f*, *ast., biol., phys. a.* Aberration *f*. **2.** geistige Verwirrung.

a·bet [ə'bet] → *aid* 3.

a·bey·ance [ə'beɪəns] *s: fall into ~* außer Gebrauch kommen.

ab·hor [əb'hɔ:] *v/t* verabscheuen.

ab·hor·rence [əb'hɒrəns] *s* Abscheu *m*, *f* (*of* vor *dat*). **ab'hor·rent** *adj* □ **1.** zuwider, verhaßt (*to dat*): *it is ~ to me* es widerstrebt mir zutiefst (*to do* zu tun). **2.** abstoßend.

a·bide [ə'baɪd] **I** *v/i: ~ by* sich halten an (*acc*); *Folgen* tragen. **II** *v/t* ertragen, aushalten: *I cannot ~ him* ich kann ihn nicht ausstehen.

a·bil·i·ty [ə'bɪlətɪ] *s* Fähigkeit *f*: *to pay* Zahlungsfähigkeit; *to the best of one's ~* nach besten Kräften.

ab·ject ['æbdʒekt] *adj* □ **1.** bitter (*Armut etc*), (*a. Verzweiflung etc*) tiefst. **2.** demütig, unterwürfig.

ab·jure [əb'dʒʊə] *v/t* abschwören (*dat*).

a·blaze [ə'bleɪz] *adv u. adj* **1.** *be ~* in Flammen stehen. **2.** *fig. be ~ with light* im Lichterglanz erstrahlen; *his eyes were ~ with anger* s-e Augen funkelten vor Zorn; *his face was ~ with excitement* sein Gesicht glühte vor Aufregung.

a·ble ['eɪbl] *adj* □ fähig, tüchtig, geschickt: *be ~ to* imstande *od.* in der Lage sein zu können; *~ to pay* zahlungsfähig. **~-bod·ied** [,~'bɒdɪd] *adj* körperlich leistungsfähig, kräftig: *~ seaman* ⚓ Vollmatrose *m*.

ab·ne·ga·tion [,æbnɪ'geɪʃn] *s* Selbstverleugnung *f*.

ab·nor·mal [æb'nɔ:ml] *adj* □ anormal, *bsd. ✶* abnorm.

a·board [ə'bɔ:d] *adv u. prp* **1.** ⚓, ✈ an Bord (*gen*): *go ~; all ~! ✶* alle Mann an Bord!; 🚂 alles einsteigen! **2.** in (*ein od. e-m Verkehrsmittel*): *~ a bus*.

a·bode [ə'bəʊd] *s a. place of ~* 🏛 Wohnsitz *m*: *of* (*od. with*) *no fixed ~* ohne festen Wohnsitz.

a·bol·ish [ə'bɒlɪʃ] *v/t* abschaffen, *Gesetz etc a.* aufheben. **a·bol·ish·ment**, **ab·o·li·tion** [,æbəʊ'lɪʃn] *s* Abschaffung *f*, Aufhebung *f*.

'A-bomb *s* Atombombe *f*.

a·bom·i·na·ble [ə'bɒmɪnəbl] *adj* □ abscheulich, scheußlich: *~ snowman*

Schneemensch *m*. **a'bom·i·nate** [~neɪt] *v/t* verabscheuen. **a,bom·i'na·tion** *s* **1.** Abscheu *m, f* (**of** vor *dat*). **2.** Scheußlichkeit *f*.

ab·o·rig·i·nal [,æbə'rɪdʒənl] **I** *adj* □ eingeboren, einheimisch, Ur... **II** *s* Ureinwohner *m, pl* a. Urbevölkerung *f*. **ab·o'rig·i·ne** [~dʒəni] → **aboriginal** II.

a·bort [ə'bɔːt] **I** *v/t* **1.** *Schwangerschaft* abbrechen; *Kind* abtreiben. **2.** *Raumflug etc* abbrechen. **II** *v/i* **3.** e-e Fehlgeburt haben. **4.** *fig*. fehlschlagen, scheitern. **a'bor·tion** *s* **1.** Fehlgeburt *f*; Schwangerschaftsabbruch *m*, Abtreibung *f*: **have an ~** abtreiben (lassen). **2.** *fig*. Fehlschlag *m*. **a'bor·tive** [~tɪv] *adj* □ erfolglos, fehlgeschlagen: **prove ~** sich als Fehlschlag erweisen.

a·bound [ə'baʊnd] *v/i* **1.** reichlich vorhanden sein. **2.** Überfluß haben, reich sein (**in** an *dat*). **3.** voll sein, wimmeln (**with** von).

a·bout [ə'baʊt] **I** *prp* **1.** um (... herum). **2.** herum in (*dat*): **wander ~ the streets** in den Straßen herumwandern. **3.** bei, auf (*dat*), an (*dat*): **I had no money ~ me** ich hatte kein Geld bei mir. **4.** um, gegen: **~ noon** um die Mittagszeit, gegen Mittag. **5.** über (*acc*): **talk ~ business** über Geschäfte reden. **6.** im Begriff, dabei: **he was ~ to go out** er wollte gerade weggehen. **7.** F beschäftigt mit: **what are you ~?** was macht ihr da? **II** *adv* **8.** herum, umher: **all ~** überall. **9.** ungefähr, etwa: **it's ~ right** F es kommt so ungefähr hin. **10.** *be* (**up and**) **~** auf den Beinen sein. **11.** in der Nähe, da: **there was no one ~**

a·bove [ə'bʌv] **I** *prp* **1.** über (*dat od. acc*), oberhalb. **2.** über (*dat od. acc*), mehr als: **~ all** vor allem; **be ~ s.o.** j-m überlegen sein; **it is ~ me** es ist mir zu hoch. **II** *adv* **3.** (dr)oben: **from ~** von oben. **4.** darüber (hinaus). **III** *adj* **5.** a. **~-mentioned** obig, obenerwähnt. **IV** *s* **6.** *das* Obige, *das* Obenerwähnte. **a,bove'board** *adv u. adj* ehrlich, offen.

ab·rade [ə'breɪd] *v/t* **1.** abschaben, -reiben, *Reifen* abfahren. **2.** *Haut etc* abschürfen.

ab·ra·sion [ə'breɪʒn] *s* **1.** Abschaben *n*, -reiben *n*. **2.** (Haut)Abschürfung *f*. **ab'ra·sive** [~sɪv] *s* ⊙ Schleifmittel *n*.

ab·re·act [,æbrɪ'ækt] *v/t psych*. abreagieren.

a·breast [ə'brest] *adv*: **three ~** zu dritt nebeneinander; **keep ~ of** *fig*. Schritt halten mit; **keep ~ of the times** auf dem laufenden bleiben.

a·bridge [ə'brɪdʒ] *v/t* Buch, Rede etc kürzen. **a'bridg(e)·ment** *s* **1.** Kürzung *f*. **2.** Kurzfassung *f*.

a·broad [ə'brɔːd] *adv* **1.** im *od.* ins Ausland: **from ~** aus dem Ausland; **trip ~** Auslandsreise *f*. **2.** überall(hin): **spread ~** (sich) verbreiten; **a rumo(u)r is ~** es geht das Gerücht (um); **get ~** ruchbar werden.

ab·ro·gate ['æbrəʊgeɪt] *v/t* Vertrag etc außer Kraft setzen, Gesetz etc a. aufheben. **,ab·ro'ga·tion** *s* Außerkraftsetzung *f*, Aufhebung *f*.

ab·rupt [ə'brʌpt] *adj* □ **1.** kurz (angebunden), schroff. **2.** plötzlich, abrupt: **come to an ~ stop** plötzlich *od.* mit e-m Ruck anhalten.

ab·scess ['æbsɪs] *s* ⚕ Abszeß *m*.

ab·scond [əb'skɒnd] *v/i* sich heimlich davonmachen; flüchten (**from** vor *dat*).

ab·sence ['æbsəns] *s* **1.** Abwesenheit *f*: **~ of mind** → absent-mindedness. Fernbleiben *n* (**from** von). **3.** (**of**) Fehlen *n* (*gen od.* von), Mangel *m* (an *dat*): **in the ~ of** in Ermangelung (*gen*).

ab·sent **I** *adj* ['æbsənt] **1.** abwesend: **be ~ fehlen** (**from school** in der Schule; **from work** am Arbeitsplatz). **2.** fehlend. **3.** a) (geistes)abwesend (*Blick etc*), b) → **absent-minded**. **II** *v/t* [æb'sent] **4.** **~ o.s.** (**from**) fernbleiben (*dat od.* von); sich entfernen (von, aus). **ab·sen·tee** [,æbsən'tiː] *s* Abwesende *m, f*: **~ ballot** *bsd. Am.* Briefwahl *f*; **~ voter** *bsd. Am.* Briefwähler(in). **,ab·sen'tee·ism** *s* häufiges *od.* längeres (unentschuldigtes) Fehlen (*am Arbeitsplatz, in der Schule*).

,ab·sent·'mind·ed *adj* □ geistesabwesend, zerstreut. **,~·'mind·ed·ness** *s* Geistesabwesenheit *f*, Zerstreutheit *f*.

ab·so·lute ['æbsəluːt] *adj* □ absolut (a. ♠, *ling., phys.*): a) unumschränkt (*Herrscher*), b) vollkommen, völlig, c) ♠ rein, unvermischt. **,ab·so'lu·tion** *s* Lossprechung *f*; *eccl.* Absolution *f*. **'ab·so·lut·ism** *s phls., pol.* Absolutismus *m*.

ab·solve [əbˈzɒlv] v/t frei-, lossprechen (**of** von *Sünde*); entbinden (**from** von *Verpflichtung etc*); *eccl.* die Absolution erteilen (*dat*).

ab·sorb [əbˈsɔːb] v/t **1.** absorbieren, auf-, einsaugen, *a. fig. Wissen etc* aufnehmen. **2.** *fig.* ganz in Anspruch nehmen; fesseln; *~ed in* vertieft in (*acc*). **3.** *Stoß etc* dämpfen. **ab'sorb·ent** *adj* absorbierend: *~ cotton* ✣ *Am.* (Verband-) Watte *f*.

ab·stain [əbˈsteɪn] v/i sich enthalten (**from** *gen*): *~* (**from voting**) sich der Stimme enthalten.

ab·ste·mi·ous [æbˈstiːmjəs] *adj* □ **1.** enthaltsam; mäßig. **2.** bescheiden, kärglich (*Mahlzeit*).

ab·sten·tion [əbˈstenʃn] *s*: *~* (**from voting**) (Stimm)Enthaltung *f*.

ab·sti·nence [ˈæbstɪnəns] *s* Abstinenz *f*, Enthaltsamkeit *f*. **'ab·sti·nent** *adj* □ abstinent, enthaltsam.

ab·stract I *adj* □ [ˈæbstrækt] **1.** abstrakt (*a.* ✞, *paint. etc*): a) theoretisch, b) schwerverständlich. **II** *s* [~] **2.** das Abstrakte: *in the ~* rein theoretisch (betrachtet), an u. für sich. **3.** *a.* ~ *noun ling.* Abstraktum *n*, Begriffswort *n*. **4.** Auszug *m*, Abriß *m*. **III** v/t [æbˈstrækt] **5.** abstrahieren. **6.** entwenden. **7.** e-n Auszug machen von. **ab'stract·ed** *adj* □ *fig.* zerstreut. **ab·strac·tion** [æbˈstrækʃn] *s* **1.** Abstraktion *f*. **2.** Entwendung *f*. **3.** *fig.* Zerstreutheit *f*.

ab·struse [æbˈstruːs] *adj* □ abstrus, schwerverständlich.

ab·surd [əbˈsɜːd] *adj* □ **1.** absurd, widersinnig. **2.** unsinnig, albern, lächerlich.

a·bun·dance [əˈbʌndəns] *s* (**of**) Überfluß *m* (*an dat*), Fülle *f* (von): *in ~* in Hülle u. Fülle. **a'bun·dant** *adj* □ **1.** reichlich (vorhanden). **2.** *~ in* reich an (*dat*).

a·buse I *s* [əˈbjuːs] **1.** Mißbrauch *m*: *~ of drugs* Drogenmißbrauch. **2.** Beschimpfungen *pl*: → *term* 3. **II** v/t [~z] **3.** mißbrauchen. **4.** beschimpfen. **a'bu·sive** [~sɪv] *adj* □ beleidigend: *~ language* Beleidigungen *pl*, Beschimpfungen *pl*.

a·but [əˈbʌt] v/i (an)grenzen (**on** an *acc*). **a'but·ment** *s* △ Strebe-, Stützpfeiler *m*.

a·bys·mal [əˈbɪzml] *adj* □ miserabel. **a·byss** [əˈbɪs] *s* Abgrund *m* (*a. fig.*).

a·ca·cia [əˈkeɪʃə] *s* ✿ Akazie *f*.

ac·a·dem·ic [ˌækəˈdemɪk] **I** *adj* □ **1.** akademisch: a) Universitäts...: *~ freedom* akademische Freiheit; *~ year* Studienjahr *n*, b) (rein) theoretisch: *~ question* akademische Frage. **2.** gelehrt, wissenschaftlich. **II** *s* **3.** Universitätslehrer(in).

a·cad·e·my [əˈkædəmɪ] *s* Akademie *f*: *~ of music* Musikhochschule *f*.

ac·cede [ækˈsiːd] v/i (**to**) **1.** e-m Vorschlag etc beipflichten, zustimmen. **2.** *Amt* antreten, *Macht* übernehmen, *Thron* besteigen.

ac·cel·er·ate [əkˈseləreɪt] **I** v/t beschleunigen. **II** v/i schneller werden, *mot. a.* Gas geben. **ac·cel·er·a·tion** *s* Beschleunigung *f*: *~ lane* mot. Beschleunigungsspur *f*, -streifen *m*. **ac'cel·er·a·tor** *s mot.* Gaspedal *n*.

ac·cent I *s* [ˈæksent] Akzent *m*: a) *ling.* Ton *m*, Betonung *f*, b) *ling.* Betonungs-, Tonzeichen *n*, c) Tonfall *m*, (lokale etc) Aussprache *f* d) *fig.* Nachdruck *m*: *the ~ is on* der Akzent liegt auf (*dat*). **II** v/t [ækˈsent] → *accentuate*.

ac·cen·tu·ate [ækˈsentjʊeɪt] v/t akzentuieren, betonen (*a. fig.*). **ac·cen·tu·a·tion** *s* Akzentuierung *f*, Betonung *f*.

ac·cept [əkˈsept] v/t **1.** an-, entgegennehmen. **2.** *j-n, etc* akzeptieren: a) *et.*, ✞ *Wechsel* annehmen, b) *et.* hinnehmen, sich abfinden mit. **3.** *Verantwortung etc* auf sich nehmen. **4.** aufnehmen (*into* in *acc*). **ac'cept·a·ble** *adj* □ **1.** akzeptabel, annehmbar (*to* für). **2.** angenehm, willkommen. **ac'cept·ance** *s* **1.** Annahme *f*. **2.** Akzeptierung *f*; Hinnahme *f*: *win ~* Anerkennung finden. **3.** Aufnahme *f*. **4.** ✞ Akzept *n*. **ac'cept·ed** *adj* allgemein anerkannt, üblich.

ac·cess [ˈækses] *s* **1.** Zugang *m* (**to** zu) (*a. fig.*): *~ road* Zufahrts- od. Zubringerstraße *f*. **2.** *fig.* Zutritt *m* (**to** bei, zu): *easy of ~* zugänglich (*Person*). **3.** Computer: Zugriff *m* (**to** auf *acc*).

ac·ces·sa·ry → *accessory* 2.

ac·ces·si·ble [əkˈsesəbl] *adj* □ **1.** (leicht) zugänglich (**to** für *od. dat*) (*a. fig.*). **2.** um-, zugänglich (*Person*). **3.** empfänglich (**to** für). **ac·ces·sion** [ækˈseʃn] *s* **1.** Antritt *m* (**to** *e-s Amts*): *~ to power* Machtübernahme *f*; *~ to the throne*

Thronbesteigung f. **2.** (Neu)Anschaffung f (**to** für). **3.** Zustimmung f (**to** zu).

ac·ces·so·ry [əkˈsesəri] s **1.** Zubehörteil n, (Mode) Accessoire n, pl a. Zubehör n. **2.** ⚖ Mitschuldige m, f (**to** an dat).

ac·ci·dence [ˈæksɪdəns] s ling. Formenlehre f.

ac·ci·dent [ˈæksɪdənt] s **1. by** ~ zufällig. **2.** Unfall m, Unglück(sfall m) n, (in Kernkraftwerk) Störfall m: **have** (od. **meet with**) **an** ~ e-n Unfall haben, verunglücken; **be killed in an** ~ bei e-m Unfall ums Leben kommen, tödlich verunglücken; ~ **insurance** Unfallversicherung f; ~**prone** unfallgefährdet. **ac·ci·den·tal** [ˌæksɪˈdentl] adj □ **1.** zufällig. **2.** versehentlich. **3.** Unfall...

ac·claim [əˈkleɪm] **I** v/t **1.** feiern (**as** als). **2.** ~ **s.o. king** j-n zum König ausrufen. **II** s **3.** hohes Lob.

ac·cla·ma·tion [ˌækləˈmeɪʃn] s **1.** lauter Beifall. **2.** hohes Lob. **3. by** ~ pol. durch Zuruf od. Akklamation.

ac·cli·mate [əˈklaɪmət] → **acclimatize.** **ac·cli·ma·tion** [ˌæklaɪˈmeɪʃn] → **acclimatization.**

ac·cli·ma·ti·za·tion [əˌklaɪmətaɪˈzeɪʃn] s Akklimatisierung f. **ac·cli·ma·tize** v/t u. v/i (**to**) (sich) akklimatisieren (an acc), (sich) eingewöhnen (in dat) (beide a. fig.).

ac·cliv·i·ty [əˈklɪvətɪ] s Steigung f.

ac·com·mo·date [əˈkɒmədeɪt] v/t **1.** (**to**) anpassen (dat od. an acc), (in Einklang bringen (mit). **2.** j-m aushelfen (**with** mit). **3.** unterbringen. **4.** Platz haben für, fassen. **ac·com·mo·dat·ing** adj □ gefällig, entgegenkommend. **ac·com·mo·da·tion** s **1.** Anpassung f (**to** an acc). **2.** Gefälligkeit f. **3.** Am. mst pl Unterkunft f, -bringung f; Einrichtung(en pl) f: **sanitary** ~.

ac·com·pa·ni·ment [əˈkʌmpənɪmənt] s ♪ Begleitung f. **ac·com·pa·nist** s ♪ Begleiter(in). **ac·com·pa·ny** v/t begleiten (a. ♪).

ac·com·plice [əˈkʌmplɪs] s Komplice m.

ac·com·plish [əˈkʌmplɪʃ] v/t erreichen, leisten. **ac·com·plished** adj fähig, tüchtig. **ac·com·plish·ment** s Fähigkeit f, Fertigkeit f.

ac·cord [əˈkɔːd] **I** v/t **1.** gewähren, Empfang bereiten. **II** v/i **2.** übereinstimmen (**with** mit). **III** s **3.** Übereinstimmung f:

be in ~ → 2; **with one** ~ einstimmig. **4.** of one's own ~ aus freien Stücken, von selbst. **ac·cord·ance** s: **in** ~ **with** entsprechend (dat), gemäß (dat). **ac·cord·ing: ~ to** prp laut; nach. **ac·cord·ing·ly** adv **1.** (dem)entsprechend. **2.** also, folglich.

ac·cor·di·on [əˈkɔːdjən] s ♪ Akkordeon n, Ziehharmonika f.

ac·cost [əˈkɒst] v/t Frau (in eindeutiger Absicht) ansprechen; j-n anpöbeln.

ac·count [əˈkaʊnt] **I** v/t **1.** ansehen als, halten für. **II** v/i **2.** ~ (**to s.o.**) **for** (j-m) Rechenschaft ablegen über (acc). **3.** ~ **for** (sich) et. erklären, et. begründen: **there's no** ~ **ing for tastes** über Geschmack läßt sich nicht streiten. **4.** ~ **for** der Grund sein für. **III** s **5.** † Konto n (**with** bei): **for** ~ **only** nur zur Verrechnung; **on one's own** ~ fig. auf eigene Faust; auf eigene Gefahr; **settle** (od. **square**) ~**s with** fig. abrechnen mit. **6.** Rechenschaft(sbericht m) f: **bring** (od. **call**) **to** ~ zur Rechenschaft ziehen; **give** (**an**) ~ **of** Rechenschaft ablegen über (acc); **give a good** (**bad**) ~ **of o.s.** sich von s-r guten (schlechten) Seite zeigen; gut (schlecht) abschneiden. **7.** Bericht m, Darstellung f: **by all** ~**s** nach allem, was man hört; **give an** ~ **of** Bericht erstatten über (acc). **8.** of great (**no**) ~ von großer (ohne) Bedeutung; **on** ~ **of** um ... willen, wegen; **on my** ~ meinetwegen; **on no** ~ auf keinen Fall; **leave out of** ~ außer acht lassen; **take into** ~, **take** ~ **of** in Betracht ziehen, berücksichtigen. **9. put** (od. **turn**) **to** (**good**) ~ (aus)nutzen, Kapital schlagen aus. **ac·count·a·ble** adj verantwortlich (**to** dat; **for** für): **hold s.o.** ~ j-n verantwortlich machen. **ac·count·ant** s **1.** Buchhalter(in). **2.** Buchprüfer(in). **3.** Br. Steuerberater(in).

ac·cred·it [əˈkredɪt] v/t Botschafter etc akkreditieren (**to** bei).

ac·crue [əˈkruː] v/i **1.** erwachsen (**to** dat; **from** aus). **2.** anwachsen: ~**d interest** aufgelaufene Zinsen pl.

ac·cu·mu·late [əˈkjuːmjʊleɪt] v/t u. v/i (sich) ansammeln od. anhäufen. **ac·cu·mu·la·tion** s Anhäufung f, Ansammlung f. **ac·cu·mu·la·tor** s ⚡ Akkumulator m.

ac·cu·ra·cy [ˈækjʊrəsɪ] s Genauigkeit f.

ac·cu·rate [ˈækrət] *adj* □ genau: **be ~** genau gehen (*Uhr*).

ac·cu·sa·tion [ˌækjuːˈzeiʃn] *s* **1.** ⚖ Anklage *f* (**bring an ~ of murder) against** (Mord)Anklage erheben gegen. **2.** An-, Beschuldigung *f*. **3.** Vorwurf *m*.

ac·cu·sa·tive [əˈkjuːzətɪv] *s a.* **~ case** *ling.* Akkusativ *m*, 4. Fall *m*.

ac·cuse [əˈkjuːz] *v/t* **1.** ⚖ anklagen (**of** *gen od.* wegen). **2.** ~ **s.o. of doing s.th.** j-n beschuldigen, et. getan zu haben. **3.** ~ **s.o. of s.th.** j-m et. zum Vorwurf machen. **ac·'cused:** *the* ~ ⚖ der *od.* die Angeklagte, die Angeklagten *pl.* **ac·'cus·ing** *adj* □ anklagend, vorwurfsvoll.

ac·cus·tom [əˈkʌstəm] *v/t* gewöhnen (**to** an *acc*): **be ~ed to doing s.th.** (es) gewöhnt *od.* gewohnt sein, et. zu tun; **get ~ed to** sich gewöhnen an (*acc*). **ac·'cus·tomed** *adj* gewohnt: ~ **seat** Stammplatz *m*.

ace [eɪs] I *s* **1.** As *n* (*Spielkarte; a. Tennis etc*); Eins *f* (*auf Würfeln*): **have an ~ in the hole** (*od.* **up one's sleeve**) *fig.* (noch) e-n Trumpf in der Hand haben. **2.** **he came within an ~ of losing** er hätte um ein Haar verloren. **3.** F As *n*, Kanone *f* (**at** in *dat*). II *adj* **4.** F ~ **skier** Spitzenskiläufer(in); ~ **reporter** Starreporter(in). **~** Spitze sein.

ac·e·tate [ˈæsɪteɪt] *s* 🧪 Acetat *n*. **a·ce·tic** [əˈsiːtɪk] *adj* essigsauer: ~ **acid** Essigsäure *f*. **a·cet·y·lene** [əˈsetɪliːn] *s* Acetylen *n*.

ache [eɪk] I *v/i* **1.** schmerzen, weh tun: *I am aching all over* mir tut alles weh. **2.** sich sehnen (**for** nach), darauf brennen (**to do** zu tun). II *s* **3.** anhaltender Schmerz: *he has ~s and pains all over* ihm tut alles weh.

a·chieve [əˈtʃiːv] *v/t* Ziel erreichen, *Erfolg* erzielen. **a·'chieve·ment** *s* Leistung *f*: ~ **test** Leistungstest *n*.

A·chil·les| heel [əˈkɪliːz] *s fig.* Achillesferse *f*. **~ ten·don** *s anat.* Achillessehne *f*.

ac·id [ˈæsɪd] I *adj* **1.** sauer: ~ **drops** *pl* saure Drops *pl*. **2.** *fig.* bissig. **3.** 🧪 säurehaltig, Säure...: ~ **rain** saurer Regen. II *s* **4.** 🧪 Säure *f*. **5.** *sl.* Acid *n* (*LSD*).

ac·knowl·edge [əkˈnɒlɪdʒ] *v/t* **1.** anerkennen. **2.** zugeben: ~ **having done**

s.th. zugeben, et. getan zu haben. **3.** *Brief, Empfang etc* bestätigen. **ac·'knowl·edg(e)·ment** *s* **1.** Anerkennung *f*: **in ~ of** in Anerkennung (*gen*). **2.** (Empfangs)Bestätigung *f*.

ac·me [ˈækmɪ] *s fig.* Gipfel *m*, Höhepunkt *m*.

ac·ne [ˈæknɪ] *s* 🩺 Akne *f*.

a·corn [ˈeɪkɔːn] *s* ♣ Eichel *f*.

a·cous·tic [əˈkuːstɪk] I *adj* (**~ally**) akustisch, Gehör...: ~ **nerve** *anat.* Gehörnerv *m*. II *s pl* Akustik *f* (*e-s Raums*).

ac·quaint [əˈkweɪnt] *v/t* bekannt *od.* vertraut machen (**with** mit): **be ~ed with** j-n, et. kennen; **we are ~ed** wir kennen uns; **become ~ed with** j-n, et. kennenlernen. **ac·'quaint·ance** *s* **1.** Bekanntschaft *f* (**with** mit): **make s.o.'s ~** j-n kennenlernen, j-s Bekanntschaft machen. **2.** Kenntnis *f* (**with** *von od. gen*). **3.** Bekannte *m, f*.

ac·qui·esce [ˌækwɪˈes] *v/i* (zögernd) einwilligen (**in** in acc).

ac·quire [əˈkwaɪə] *v/t* erwerben (*a. fig.*), sich *Wissen etc* aneignen.

ac·qui·si·tion [ˌækwɪˈzɪʃn] *s* **1.** Erwerb *m*. **2.** Anschaffung *f*, Errungenschaft *f*. **ac·quis·i·tive** [əˈkwɪzɪtɪv] *adj* □ habgierig. **ac·'quis·i·tive·ness** *s* Habgier *f*.

ac·quit [əˈkwɪt] *v/t* **1.** ⚖ freisprechen (**of** von). **2.** ~ **o.s. well** s-e Sache gut machen. **ac·'quit·tal** *s* ⚖ Freispruch *m*.

a·cre [ˈeɪkə] *s* Acre *m* (*4047 qm*).

ac·rid [ˈækrɪd] *adj* □ scharf, beißend (*beide a. fig.*).

ac·ri·mo·ni·ous [ˌækrɪˈməʊnjəs] *adj* □ *fig.* bitter; scharf, beißend; erbittert (geführt) (*Diskussion etc*). **ac·ri·mo·ny** [ˈækrɪmənɪ] *s fig.* Bitterkeit *f*; Schärfe *f*.

ac·ro·bat [ˈækrəbæt] *s* Akrobat(in). **ac·ro·'bat·ic** I *adj* (**~ally**) akrobatisch. II *s pl* (*a. sg konstruiert*) Akrobatik *f* (*a. fig.*): **mental ~s** Gedankenakrobatik.

a·cross [əˈkrɒs] I *prp* **1.** (quer) über (*acc*); (quer) durch, mitten durch: **run ~ the road** über die Straße laufen; **swim ~ a river** e-n Fluß durchschwimmen. **2.** jenseits (*gen*): **he lives ~ the street** er wohnt auf der gegenüberliegenden Straßenseite. II *adv* **3.** (quer) hinüber *od.* herüber; (quer) durch; im Durchmesser: **go ~** hinübergehen; **saw ~** durchsägen; **a lake three miles ~** ein 3 Meilen breiter See. **4.** drüben, auf der anderen Seite. **5.** waag(e)recht (*in Kreuzworträtseln*).

a‚cross-the-'board *adj* linear (*Steuersenkung etc*).

act [ækt] **I** *s* **1.** (🕱 *a.* Straf)Tat *f*, Handlung *f*, Akt *m*: **an ~ of God** höhere Gewalt; **catch in the (very) ~** auf frischer Tat ertappen; **catch s.o. in the ~ of doing s.th.** j-n (dabei) ertappen, als er et. tut. **2.** ♀ (*of Parliament, Am. of Congress*) Gesetz *n*. **3.** *thea.* Aufzug *m*, Akt *m*. **4.** (Programm)Nummer *f*; *fig.* T Tour *f*: **put on an ~** Theater spielen. **II** *v/t* **5.** *thea. etc* Rolle spielen, j-n *a.* darstellen, Stück *a.* aufführen: **~ the fool** *fig.* sich wie ein Narr benehmen; den Dummen spielen. **III** *v/i* **6.** (Theater) spielen, *fig.* Theater spielen. **7.** handeln; tätig sein: **~ as** amtieren *od.* fungieren *od.* dienen als; **~ for s.o.** j-n vertreten; **~ on** sich richten nach. **8.** sich verhalten *od.* benehmen (**towards** *j-m* gegenüber): **~ up** F Theater machen; angeben; verrückt spielen (*Gerät etc*). **9.** (ein)wirken (**on** auf *acc*). **'act·ing I** *adj* stellvertretend, amtierend, geschäftsführend. **II** *s thea. etc* Spiel *n*; Schauspielerei *f*.

ac·tion ['ækʃn] *s* **1.** Handlung *f* (*a. thea. etc*), Tat *f*: **man of ~** Mann *m* der Tat; **put into ~** in die Tat umsetzen; **take ~** handeln. **2.** *Film etc*: Action *f*: **~ film.** 3. *bsd* ⊗ Funktionieren *n*: **~ of the heart** *physiol.* Herztätigkeit *f*. **4.** (Ein)Wirkung *f* (**on** auf *acc*). **5.** 🕱 Klage *f*, Prozeß *m*: **bring an ~ against** verklagen. **6.** ✕ Gefecht *n*, Einsatz *m*: **killed in ~** gefallen. **~re·play** *s* Sport, TV: Br. (*bsd.* Zeitlupen)Wiederholung *f* (*e-r Spielszene*).

ac·ti·vate ['æktıveıt] *v/t* **1.** Alarm etc auslösen. **2.** *bsd.* 🦌 aktivieren.

ac·tive ['æktıv] **I** *adj* □ **1.** *allg.* aktiv, (*Vulkan a.*) tätig, (*Phantasie*) lebhaft. **2.** *ling.* aktivisch: **~ voice** → **3. II** *s* **3.** *ling.* Aktiv *n*, Tatform *f*. **ac'tiv·i·ty** *s* **1.** Aktivität *f*. **2.** *mst pl* Aktivität *f*, Betätigung *f*.

ac·tor ['æktə] *s* Schauspieler *m*. **ac·tress** ['æktrıs] *s* Schauspielerin *f*.

ac·tu·al ['æktʃʊəl] *adj* wirklich, tatsächlich; eigentlich. **'ac·tu·al·ly** *adv* **1.** → **actual. 2.** sogar.

ac·tu·ate ['æktʃʊeıt] *v/t*: **be ~d by** *fig.* getrieben werden von.

a·cu·men ['ækjʊmən] *s* Scharfsinn *m*.

ac·u·pres·sure ['ækjʊ‚preʃə] *s* 🦌 Akupressur *f*. **ac·u·punc·ture** ['ækjʊ‚pʌŋktʃə] 🦌 **I** *s* Akupunktur *f*. **II** *v/t* akupunktieren.

a·cute [ə'kju:t] *adj* □ **1.** ∆ spitz (*Winkel*). **2.** scharf (*Gehör etc*). **3.** scharfsinnig. **4.** akut (*Krankheit*). **5.** stark (*Schmerzen*), erheblich (*Mangel etc*).

ad [æd] F → **advertisement.**

Ad·am ['ædəm] *npr.*: **I don't know him from ~** F ich hab' keine Ahnung, wer er ist; **~'s apple** *anat.* Adamsapfel *m*.

ad·a·mant ['ædəmənt] *adj* unnachgiebig: **be ~ that s.o. should do sth.** darauf bestehen, daß j-d et. tut.

a·dapt [ə'dæpt] **I** *v/t* **1.** anpassen (**to** *dat*): **~ o.s.** → **3. 2.** *Text* bearbeiten (**for** für). **II** *v/i* **3.** (**to**) sich anpassen (*dat*); sich gewöhnen (an *acc*). **a'dapt·a·ble** *adj* anpassungsfähig. **a·dap·ta·tion** [‚ædæp'teıʃn] *s* **1.** Anpassung *f* (**to** an *acc*). **2.** Bearbeitung *f*. **a·dap·ter, a·dap·tor** [ə'dæptə] *s* ∮ Adapter *m*.

add [æd] **I** *v/t* **1.** hinzuzählen, -rechnen (**to** *zu*). **2.** hinzufügen (**to** *dat od.* zu; **that** daß): → **fuel. 3.** **~ up** (*od.* **together**) addieren, zs.-zählen. **4.** ✝ *etc* aufschlagen (**to** auf *acc*): **~ 5% to the price. II** *v/i* **5.** **~ to** hinzukommen *od.* beitragen zu, vermehren. **6.** **~ up** ℵ aufgehen, stimmen; *fig.* e-n Sinn ergeben. **7.** **~ up to** sich belaufen auf (*acc*), betragen; *fig.* hinauslaufen auf (*acc*), bedeuten. **'add·ed** *adj* zusätzlich.

ad·den·dum [ə'dendəm] *pl* **-da** [‚~də] *s* Zusatz *m*, Nachtrag *m*.

ad·der ['ædə] *s zo.* Natter *f*.

ad·dict ['ædıkt] *s* (Drogen-, Fernseh- etc) Süchtige(r) *m*, *f*, (*Fußball- etc*)Fanatiker *m*, (*Film- etc*)Narr *m*. **ad·dict·ed** [ə'dıktıd] *adj*: **be ~ to ...** ...süchtig sein. **ad'dic·tion** *s* Sucht *f*, (*Zustand a.*) Süchtigkeit *f*: **~ to alcohol** Alkoholsucht *f*. **ad'dic·tive** *adj* suchterzeugend: **be ~** süchtig machen; **~ drug** Suchtmittel *n*.

add·ing ma·chine ['ædıŋ] *s* Addier-, Additionsmaschine *f*.

ad·di·tion [ə'dıʃn] *s* **1.** Hinzufügung *f*, Zusatz *m*: **in ~** noch dazu, außerdem; **in ~ to** außer (*dat*), zusätzlich zu. **2.** Vermehrung f (**to** gen): **an ~ to the family** Familienzuwachs m. **3.** A Addition f: ~ **sign** Pluszeichen n. **ad·di·tion·al** [~ʃənl] adj □ zusätzlich, Zusatz...

ad·di·tive ['ædɪtɪv] s Zusatz m (a. 🜚).

ad·dress [ə'dres] **I** v/t 1. Worte etc richten (**to** an acc), j-n anreden od. ansprechen (**as** als), Brief etc adressieren (**to** an acc). **2.** e-e Ansprache halten an (acc). **II** s **3.** Anrede f. **4.** Ansprache f, Rede f. **5.** Adresse f, Anschrift f. **ad·dress·ee** [,ædre'siː] s Adressat(in), Empfänger(in).

ad·duce [ə'djuːs] v/t Grund anführen, Beweis erbringen.

ad·e·noids ['ædɪnɔɪdz] s pl 🜚 Polypen pl.

ad·ept ['ædept] **I** adj erfahren, geschickt (**at, in** in dat). **II** s Meister m, Experte m (**at, in** in dat).

ad·e·qua·cy ['ædɪkwəsɪ] s Angemessenheit f. **ad·e·quate** ['~kwət] adj □ **1.** angemessen (**to** dat). **2.** ausreichend: **be ~ for** reichen für.

ad·here [əd'hɪə] v/i 1. (an)kleben, (-)haften (**to** an dat). **2.** fig. (to) festhalten (an dat), bleiben (bei). **ad'her·ence** s **1.** (An)Kleben n, (-)Haften n. **2.** fig. Festhalten n. **ad'her·ent I** adj (an)klebend, (-)haftend. **II** s Anhänger(in).

ad·he·sion [əd'hiːʒn] s **1.** → **adherence**. **2.** phys., 🜚 Adhäsion f, Haftvermögen n.

ad·he·sive [əd'hiːsɪv] **I** adj □ (an)haftend, klebend, Haft..., Kleb(e)...: ~ **plaster** Heftpflaster n; ~ **tape** Klebstreifen m; Am. Heftpflaster n. **II** s Klebstoff m.

ad·ja·cent [ə'dʒeɪsənt] adj □ **1.** angrenzend, -stoßend (**to** an acc). **2.** bsd. A, 🜚 Nachbar..., Neben...

ad·jec·ti·val [,ædʒek'taɪvl] adj □ ling. adjektivisch. **ad·jec·tive** ['ædʒɪktɪv] s Adjektiv n, Eigenschaftswort n.

ad·join [ə'dʒɔɪn] **I** v/t (an)stoßen od. (-)grenzen an (acc). **II** v/i aneinandergrenzen, nebeneinander liegen. **ad·'join·ing** adj angrenzend, -stoßend, Nachbar..., Neben...

ad·journ [ə'dʒɜːn] **I** v/t verschieben, -tagen (**till, until** auf acc; **for** um). **II** v/i sich vertagen. **ad'journ·ment** s Vertagung f, -schiebung f.

ad·judge [ə'dʒʌdʒ] v/t **1.** ⚖ e-e Sache (gerichtlich) entscheiden; j-n für (schul-

dig etc) erklären. **2.** ⚖, Sport: zusprechen, -erkennen (**to** dat).

ad·ju·di·cate [ə'dʒuːdɪkeɪt] → **adjudge**.

ad·junct ['ædʒʌŋkt] s **1.** Zusatz m (**to** zu). **2.** ling. Attribut n, Beifügung f.

ad·ju·ra·tion [,ædʒʊə'reɪʃn] s Beschwörung f. **ad·jure** [ə'dʒʊə] v/t beschwören (**to do** zu tun).

ad·just [ə'dʒʌst] v/t **1.** (**to**) anpassen, -gleichen (dat od. an acc), abstimmen (auf acc). **2.** in Ordnung bringen, regeln. **3.** 🜚 (ein)stellen, regulieren, Gewehr etc justieren, Uhr stellen. **ad'just·a·ble** adj 🜚 ein-, verstellbar, regulierbar. **ad'just·ment** s **1.** Anpassung f, -gleichung f. **2.** Regelung f. **3.** 🜚 Einstellung f, Regulierung f; Einstellvorrichtung f.

ad·ju·tant ['ædʒʊtənt] s ⚔ Adjutant m.

ad-lib [,æd'lɪb] v/t u. v/i F improvisieren.

ad·man ['ædmæn] s (irr **man**) F **1.** Werbetexter m für Zeitungsanzeigen. **2.** Anzeigenvertreter m. **ad·mass** ['ædmæs] s F **1.** Konsumbeeinflussung f. **2.** werbungsmanipulierte Gesellschaft.

ad·min·is·ter [əd'mɪnɪstə] v/t **1.** verwalten, Amt etc ausüben. **2.** Arznei, Schlag verabreichen, Sakrament spenden, Tadel erteilen (**to** dat): ~ **justice** Recht sprechen. **ad,min·is'tra·tion** s **1.** Verwaltung f Ausübung f. **2.** Verabreichung f, Spendung f, Erteilung f: ~ **of justice** Rechtsprechung f. **3.** pol. bsd. Am. Regierung f, Amtsdauer f (e-s Präsidenten etc). **ad'min·is·tra·tive** [~trətɪv] adj Verwaltungs... **ad'min·is·tra·tor** [~treɪtə] s **1.** Verwalter m. **2.** Verwaltungsbeamte m.

ad·mi·ra·ble ['ædmərəbl] adj □ bewundernswert, großartig.

ad·mi·ral ['ædmərəl] s Admiral m.

ad·mi·ra·tion [,ædmə'reɪʃn] s Bewunderung f (**for** für): **she was the ~ of all** sie wurde von allen bewundert.

ad·mire [əd'maɪə] v/t **1.** bewundern (**for** wegen). **2.** verehren. **ad'mir·er** s **1.** Bewunderer m. **2.** Verehrer(in).

ad·mis·si·ble [əd'mɪsəbl] adj zulässig, statthaft. **ad'mis·sion** s **1.** Einlaß m (**to** a. 🜚); Ein-, Zutritt m; Aufnahme f: ~ **free** Eintritt frei; ~ **ticket** Eintrittskarte f. **2.** Eintritt(sgeld n) m. **3.** Zulassung f. **4.** Eingeständnis n: **by** (od. **on**) **his own ~** wie er selbst zugab; ~ **of guilt** Schuldeingeständnis. **5.** Zugeständnis n. **6.** ⊘ (*Luft- etc*)Zufuhr f.

ad·mit [əd'mɪt] **I** v/t **1.** j-n einlassen. **2.** (*into, to*) j-n aufnehmen (in *acc od. dat*), zulassen (zu): → **bar** 9. **3.** zulassen, gestatten. **4.** anerkennen, gelten lassen. **5.** zugeben, (ein)gestehen: ~ *doing s.th.* zugeben, et. getan zu haben. **6.** zugeben, einräumen (*that* daß). **7.** Platz haben für, fassen. **8.** ⊘ einlassen, einführen. **II** v/i **9.** ~ *of* → 3: *it ~s of no excuse* es läßt sich nicht entschuldigen. **10.** ~ *to* → 5. **ad'mit·tance** s Ein-, Zutritt m: *no* ~ (*except on business*) Zutritt (für Unbefugte) verboten. **ad'mit·ted·ly** *adv* zugestandenermaßen.

ad·mix·ture [æd'mɪkstʃə] s Beimischung f, Zusatz m.

ad·mon·ish [əd'mɒnɪʃ] v/t **1.** warnen (*of, against* vor *dat*). **2.** ermahnen (*for* wegen). **ad·mo·ni·tion** [ˌædməʊ'nɪʃn] s **1.** Warnung f. **2.** Ermahnung f.

a·do [ə'duː] s Getue n: *much* ~ *about nothing* viel Lärm um nichts; *without more* (*od. further*) ~ ohne weitere Umstände.

ad·o·les·cence [ˌædəʊ'lesns] s jugendliches Alter. **ˌad·o'les·cent I** *adj* jugendlich, heranwachsend. **II** s Jugendliche m, f.

a·dopt [ə'dɒpt] v/t **1.** adoptieren: ~*ed child* Adoptivkind n; ~*ed country* Wahlheimat f. **2.** *fig.* annehmen, sich zu eigen machen, *Handlungsweise* wählen, *Haltung* einnehmen. **a·'dop·tion** s **1.** Adoption f: *give up for* ~ zur Adoption freigeben. **2.** Annahme f. **a·'dop·tive** *adj* Adoptiv...: ~ *child* (*parents*); ~ *country* Wahlheimat f.

a·dor·a·ble [ə'dɔːrəbl] *adj* □ allerliebst, entzückend. **ad·o·ra·tion** [ˌædə'reɪʃn] s Anbetung f, Verehrung f. **a·dore** [ə'dɔː] v/t anbeten, verehren (*beide a. fig.*); F *et.* entzückend *od.* hinreißend finden.

a·dorn [ə'dɔːn] v/t **1.** schmücken, (ver)zieren (*beide a. fig.*). **2.** *fig.* Glanz verleihen (*dat*). **a'dorn·ment** s Schmuck m, Verzierung f.

a·dren·al·in(e) [ə'drenəlɪn] s **1.** 🐾, *physiol.* Adrenalin n. **2.** *fig.* Aufputschmittel n.

a·droit [ə'drɔɪt] *adj* □ geschickt, gewandt (*at, in* in *dat*). **a'droit·ness** s

Geschicklichkeit f, Gewandtheit f.

ad·u·late ['ædjʊleɪt] v/t j-m schmeicheln. **ˌad·u'la·tion** s Schmeichelei f. **'ad·u·la·tor** s Schmeichler m. **'ad·u·la·to·ry** *adj* schmeichlerisch.

a·dult ['ædʌlt] **I** *adj* **1.** erwachsen. **2.** (*nur*) für Erwachsene (*Film etc*). **II** s **3.** Erwachsene m, f: ~ *education* Erwachsenenbildung f.

a·dul·ter·ate [ə'dʌltəreɪt] v/t *Nahrungsmittel* verfälschen, *Wein* panschen. **a·ˌdul·ter'a·tion** s Verfälschung f. **a·dul·ter·er** [ə'dʌltərə] s Ehebrecher m. **a·'dul·ter·ess** s Ehebrecherin f. **a·'dul·ter·ous** *adj* □ ehebrecherisch. **a·'dul·ter·y** s Ehebruch m.

ad·um·brate ['ædʌmbreɪt] v/t vorausahnen lassen, hindeuten auf (*acc*).

ad·vance [əd'vɑːns] **I** v/t **1.** vorrücken, -schieben, *Fuß* vorsetzen. **2.** *Zeitpunkt* vorverlegen. **3.** *Argument etc* vorbringen, geltend machen. **4.** *Projekt etc* fördern. **5.** j-n befördern, *Stellung etc* verbessern. **6.** *Preis* erhöhen. **7.** *Wachstum etc* beschleunigen. **8.** im voraus liefern; *Geld* vorauszahlen, vorschießen. **II** v/i **9.** vordringen, -rücken (*a. Zeit*). **10.** zunehmen (*in* an *dat*): ~ *in age* älter werden. **11.** vorankommen, Fortschritte machen. **12.** *im Rang* aufrücken, befördert werden. **13.** (an)steigen (*Preise*). **III** s **14.** Vorrücken n. **15.** Beförderung f, (*beruflicher etc*) Aufstieg. **16.** Fortschritt m, Verbesserung f. **17.** Vorsprung m: *in* ~ vorn; im voraus; *in* ~ *of* vor (*dat*); *be in* ~ e-n Vorsprung haben (*of* vor *dat*); *paid in* ~ vorausbezahlt. **18.** Vorschuß m, Vorauszahlung f. **19.** (*Preis*)Erhöhung f. **IV** *adj* **20.** Vor(aus)...: ~ *booking* Vor(aus)bestellung f; *thea. etc* Vorverkauf m; ~ *payment* Vorauszahlung f. **ad'vanced** *adj* **1.** vorgerückt (*Alter, Stunde*): *be* ~ *in years* in fortgeschrittenem Alter sein. **2.** fortgeschritten: ~ *English* Englisch für Fortgeschrittene. **3.** fortschrittlich. **ad'vance·ment** s Fortschritt m, Verbesserung f.

ad·van·tage [əd'vɑːntɪdʒ] s Vorteil m (*a. Sport*): *to* ~ günstig, vorteilhaft; *gain an* ~ *over s.o.* sich j-m gegenüber e-n Vorteil verschaffen; *have an* ~ *over s.o.* j-m gegenüber im Vorteil sein; *have the* ~ (*over s.o.*) (j-m gegenüber) den Vorteil haben (*of being* zu sein); *take ~ of* j-n, et. ausnutzen; *~ law* (*od. rule*) Vorteilsregel *f*. **ad·van·ta·geous** [ˌædvənˈteɪdʒəs] *adj* □ vorteilhaft, günstig.

Ad·vent [ˈædvənt] *s eccl.* Advent *m*.

ad·ven·ture [ədˈventʃə] *s* Abenteuer *n*: *~ holiday* (*bsd. Am. vacation*) Abenteuerurlaub *m*; *~ playground Br.* Abenteuerspielplatz *m*. **ad·ven·tur·er** *s* Abenteurer *m*. **ad·ven·tur·ess** *s* Abenteu(r)erin *f*. **ad·ven·tur·ous** *adj* □ **1.** abenteuerlich. **2.** abenteuerlustig.

ad·verb [ˈædvɜːb] *s ling.* Adverb *n*, Umstandswort *n*. **ad·ver·bi·al** [ədˈvɜːbjəl] *adj* □ adverbial: *~ phrase* Adverbiale *n*, Adverbialbestimmung *f*.

ad·ver·sar·y [ˈædvəsəri] *s* Gegner(in).

ad·verse [ˈⱱːʒs] *adj* □ **1.** widrig. **2.** ungünstig, nachteilig (*to* für): *~ balance of trade* passive Handelsbilanz.

ad·ver·si·ty [ədˈvɜːsəti] *s* **1.** Not *f*, Unglück *n*. **2.** Mißgeschick *n*.

ad·vert [ˈædvɜːt] *s Br.* F *für advertisement.*

ad·ver·tise [ˈædvətaɪz] **I** *v/t* **1.** ankündigen. **2.** *contp.* ausposaunen, an die große Glocke hängen. **II** *v/i* **4.** inserieren, annoncieren: *~ for* durch Inserat suchen. **5.** Reklame machen, Werbung treiben. **ad·ver·tise·ment** [ədˈvɜːtɪsmənt] *s* **1.** Inserat *n*, Annonce *f*. **2.** → *advertising* I. **ad·ver·tis·ing** *s* **I** Werbung *f*, Reklame *f*. **II** *adj* Werbe..., Reklame...: *~ agency* Werbeagentur *f*; *~ campaign* (*od. drive*) Werbekampagne *f*; *~ manager* Werbeleiter *m*; *~ medium* Werbeträger *m*.

ad·vice [ədˈvaɪs] *s* **1.** Rat(schlag) *m*; Ratschläge *pl*: *a piece* (*od. bit*) *of ~* ein Ratschlag; *act* (*od. on*) *s.o.'s ~* auf j-s Rat hin; *take my ~ and ...* hör auf mich u. ...; *take medical ~* e-n Arzt zu Rate ziehen. **2. †** Avis *m*, Anzeige *f*: *letter of ~* Benachrichtigungsschreiben *n*.

ad·vis·a·ble [ədˈvaɪzəbl] *adj* ratsam. **ad·vise** [ədˈvaɪz] **I** *v/t* **1.** j-n raten *od.* empfehlen (*to do* zu tun), j-n beraten: *~ against* j-m abraten von; *be well ~d* gut beraten sein, gut daran tun (*to do* zu tun). **2.** et. empfehlen, raten zu. **3. †** avisieren (*s.o. of s.th.* j-m et.). **ad·vis·ed·ly** [ˌ~ɪdlɪ] *adv* mit Überlegung. **ad·vis·er** *s*

Berater(in), Ratgeber(in). **ad·vi·so·ry** [ˌ~ərɪ] *adj* beratend.

ad·vo·ca·cy [ˈædvəkəsɪ] *s* (*of*) Eintreten *n* (für), Befürwortung *f* (*gen*). **ad·vo·cate** **I** *s* [ˈ~kət] Verfechter *m*, Befürworter *m*. **II** *v/t* [ˈ~keɪt] befürworten, eintreten für.

ae·gis [ˈiːdʒɪs] *s* Schirmherrschaft *f*: *under the ~ of*.

aer·ate [ˈeɪəreɪt] *v/t* **1.** lüften. **2.** mit Kohlensäure anreichern.

aer·i·al [ˈeəriəl] **I** *adj* Luft...: *~ cableway* Seilschwebebahn *f*; *~ camera* Luftkamera *f*; *~ view* Luftbild *n*. **II** *s bsd. Br.* Antenne *f*.

aer·o·drome [ˈeərədrəʊm] *s Br.* Flugplatz *m*. **ˌaer·o·dyˈnam·ic** *phys.* **I** *adj* (*~ally*) aerodynamisch. **II** *s pl* (*sg konstruiert*) Aerodynamik *f*. **aer·o·gram** [ˈ~græm] *s* **1.** Funkspruch *m*. Aerogramm *n*, Luftpostleichtbrief *m*. **ˌaer·o·ˈnau·ti·cal** *adj* □ aeronautisch: *~ engineering* Flugzeugbau *m*. **ˌaer·o·ˈnau·tics** *s* Aeronautik *f*, Luftfahrtkunde *f*. **aer·o·plane** *s bsd. Br.* Flugzeug *n*. **ˈaer·o·space** **I** *s* **1.** Weltraum *m*. **II** *adj* **2.** Raumfahrt...: *~ industry* (*medicine*). **3.** (Welt)Raum...: *~ research* (*vehicle*).

aes·thete [ˈiːsθiːt] *s* Ästhet *m*. **aes·ˈthet·ic**, **aes·ˈthet·i·cal** [iːsˈθetɪk(l)] *adj* □ ästhetisch. **aes·ˈthet·ics** *s pl* (*sg konstruiert*) Ästhetik *f*.

a·far [əˈfɑː] *adv*: *from ~* von weit her, aus weiter Ferne.

af·fa·bil·i·ty [ˌæfəˈbɪlətɪ] *s* Leutseligkeit *f*. **ˈaf·fa·ble** *adj* □ leutselig.

af·fair [əˈfeə] *s* **1.** Angelegenheit *f*, Sache *f*: → *foreign* 1. **2.** F Ding *n*. **3.** Affäre *f*: a) Ereignis *n*, b) Skandal *m*, c) Verhältnis *n*.

af·fect¹ [əˈfekt] *v/t* **1.** e-e Vorliebe haben für. **2.** vortäuschen: *he ~ed not to understand* er tat so, als ob er nicht verstehe.

af·fect² [ˌ~] *v/t* **1.** beeinflussen, in Mitleidenschaft ziehen. **2. ✠** angreifen, befallen. **3.** bewegen, rühren: *be deeply ~ed.*

af·fec·ta·tion [ˌæfekˈteɪʃn] *s* **1.** Vorliebe *f* (*of* für). **2.** Verstellung *f*.

af·fec·tion [əˈfekʃn] *s* **1.** *oft pl* Liebe *f*, Zuneigung *f* (*for, towards* zu); Gefühl *n*: *play on s.o.'s ~s* mit j-s Gefühlen spielen. **2.** Gemütsbewegung f. **af-'fec·tion·ate** [⸝k∫nət] adj □ liebevoll, herzlich: *yours ~ly* Dein Dich liebender (*Briefschluß*).

af·fi·da·vit [ˌæfɪˈdeɪvɪt] s 🕮 *schriftliche* eidliche Erklärung.

af·fil·i·ate [əˈfɪlɪeɪt] I v/t **1.** als Mitglied aufnehmen. **2.** angliedern (*to* dat od. an acc): *~d company* ♀ Tochtergesellschaft f. II v/i **3.** sich anschließen (*with* dat od. an acc). **af,fil·i'a·tion** s **1.** Aufnahme f. **2.** Angliederung f.

af·fin·i·ty [əˈfɪnɪtɪ] s **1.** Verschwägerung f. **2.** (geistige) Verwandtschaft. **3.** 🕮 Affinität f. **4.** Neigung f (*for*, *to* zu).

af·firm [əˈfɜːm] v/t **1.** versichern; beteuern. **2.** bekräftigen, 🕮 *Urteil* bestätigen. **3.** 🕮 an Eides Statt versichern. **af·fir·ma·tion** [ˌæfəˈmeɪ∫n] s **1.** Versicherung f, Beteuerung f. **2.** Bekräftigung f, Bestätigung f. 🕮 Versicherung f an Eides Statt. **af·firm·a·tive** [əˈfɜːmətɪv] I adj bejahend, zustimmend. II s: *answer in the ~* bejahen.

af·fix I v/t [əˈfɪks] **1.** (*to*) befestigen, anbringen (an dat), anheften, -kleben (an acc). **2.** (*to*) Unterschrift setzen (unter acc). II s [ˈæfɪks] **3.** *ling.* Affix n.

af·flict [əˈflɪkt] v/t plagen, heimsuchen: *~ed with* geplagt von, leidend an (dat). **af·flic·tion** s **1.** Kummer m. **2.** Gebrechen n; *pl* Beschwerden pl: *~s of old age* Altersbeschwerden. **3.** Not f, Elend n.

af·flu·ence [ˈæfluəns] s **1.** Überfluß m. **2.** Reichtum m, Wohlstand m. **'af·flu·ent** I adj □ wohlhabend, reich (*in* an dat): *~ society* Wohlstandsgesellschaft f. II s Nebenfluß m.

af·flux [ˈæflʌks] s Zufluß m.

af·ford [əˈfɔːd] v/t **1.** sich leisten: *we can't ~ it* wir können es uns nicht leisten. **2.** aufbringen, *Zeit* erübrigen. **3.** *Schutz etc* gewähren, bieten, *Freude* machen. **af'ford·a·ble** adj **1.** erschwinglich (*Preis*). **2.** finanziell möglich od. tragbar.

af·for·est [æˈfɒrɪst] v/t aufforsten. **af,for·est'a·tion** s Aufforstung f.

af·front [əˈfrʌnt] I v/t beleidigen. II s Beleidigung f.

a·fi·cio·na·do [əˌfɪsjəˈnɑːdəʊ] pl **-dos** s Fan m, Liebhaber m.

a·field [əˈfiːld] adv in der od. die Ferne.

a·fire [əˈfaɪə] adv u. adj in Flammen: *be ~* in Flammen stehen; *fig.* glühen (*with* vor dat); *set ~* in Brand stecken, anzünden; *all ~ fig.* Feuer u. Flamme.

a·flame [əˈfleɪm] → afire.

a·float [əˈfləʊt] adv u. adj **1.** flott, schwimmend: *keep ~* (sich) über Wasser halten (*a. fig.*); *set ~* ♣ flottmachen. **2.** in Umlauf (*Gerücht etc*): *set ~* in Umlauf bringen; *there is a rumo(u)r ~ that* es geht das Gerücht (um), daß. **3.** im Gange: *set ~* in Gang setzen. **4.** überschwemmt: *be ~* unter Wasser stehen.

a·foot [əˈfʊt] → afloat **3.**

a,fore·'men·tioned [əˌfɔː⸜], **~·said** [əˈfɔː⸜] adj obenerwähnt. **~·thought** [əˈfɔː⸜] adj: → malice **3.**

a·fraid [əˈfreɪd] adj: *be ~ of* sich fürchten od. Angst haben vor (dat); *be ~ to do* sich fürchten od. scheuen zu tun; *I'm ~ I must go* leider muß ich jetzt gehen.

a·fresh [əˈfre∫] adv von neuem.

Af·ri·can [ˈæfrɪkən] I adj afrikanisch. II s Afrikaner(in).

af·ter [ˈɑːftə] I adv **1.** nach-, hinterher, darauf: *for months ~* noch monatelang; *during the weeks ~* in den (nach)folgenden Wochen; *shortly ~* kurz danach. II prp **2.** hinter (dat) (... her), nach: *be ~* hersein hinter. **3.** *zeitlich* nach: *~ a week; day ~ day* Tag für Tag; *the month ~ next* der übernächste Monat; *~ all* schließlich, im Grunde; immerhin, dennoch; (also) doch. **4.** nach, gemäß: *named ~ his father* nach s-m Vater genannt. III adj **5.** später: *in ~ years.* **6.** ♣ Achter... IV cj **7.** nachdem. '~·birth s ♀ Nachgeburt f. '~·care s **1.** ♣ Nachbehandlung f, -sorge f. **2.** 🕮 Resozialisierungshilfe f. '~·din·ner adj: *~ speech* Tischrede f; *~ walk* Verdauungsspaziergang m. '~·ef·fect s ♣ Nachwirkung f (a. fig.). '~·glow s Abendrot n. '~·life s **1.** Leben n nach dem Tode. **2.** (zu)künftiges Leben. '~·math [ˈ⸜mæθ] s Folgen pl, Nachwirkungen pl. '~·noon s **1** Nachmittag m: *in the ~* am Nachmittag; *this ~* heute nachmittag; *good ~!* guten Tag! II adj Nachmittags... '~·play s sexuelles Nachspiel.

af·ters [ˈɑːftəz] s pl (sg konstruiert) Br. F

Nachtisch *m*: **for** ~ als *od.* zum Nachtisch.

'**af·ter**‹**-sales ser·vice** *s* Kundendienst *m*. '**~·taste** *s* Nachgeschmack *m* (*a. fig.*). '**~·thought** *s* nachträglicher Einfall. '**~·treat·ment** *s* ✽, ⚙ Nachbehandlung *f*. **~·wards** ['~wədz] *adv* später, nachher, hinterher.

a·gain [ə'gen] *adv* **1.** wieder: ~ **and** ~ immer wieder; → **now** 1, **time** 4. **2.** schon wieder: *that fool* ~*!* 3. außerdem, ferner. **4.** noch einmal: → **much** 1. **5.** and(e)rerseits.

a·gainst [ə'genst] *prp* **1.** gegen: **be** ~ **s.th.** gegen et. sein; e-r Sache zuwiderlaufen. **2.** gegenüber (*dat*): (**over**)~ *the town hall* gegenüber dem Rathaus; *my rights* ~ *the landlord* m-e Rechte gegenüber dem Vermieter. **3.** an (*dat od. acc*), gegen: ~ *the wall.* **4.** *a. as* ~ verglichen mit, im Vergleich zu.

a·gape [ə'geɪp] *adv u. adj* mit (vor Staunen *etc*) offenem Mund.

ag·ate ['ægət] *s min.* Achat *m*.

age [eɪdʒ] **I** *s* **1.** (Lebens)Alter *n*: *at the* ~ *of* im Alter von; *I have a daughter your* ~ in Ihrem Alter; *when I was your* ~ als ich so alt war wie du; *ten years of* ~ zehn Jahre alt; *what is his* ~*?, what* ~ *is he?* wie alt ist er?; *be your* ~*!* sei kein Kindskopf! **2.** Reife *f*: (**come**) **of** ~ mündig *od.* volljährig (werden); *under* ~ minderjährig, unmündig. **3.** vorgeschriebenes Alter (*für ein Amt etc*): **be over** ~ die Altersgrenze überschritten haben. **4.** Zeit(alter *n*) *f*: *in our* ~ in unserer Zeit. **5.** *a.* **old** ~ (hohes) Alter: ~ *before beauty!* *humor.* Alter vor Schönheit! **6.** *oft pl* F Ewigkeit *f*: *I haven't seen him for* ~*s* seit e-r Ewigkeit. **II** *v/t* **7.** alt machen (*Kleid etc*); um Jahre älter machen (*Sorgen etc*). **III** *v/i* **8.** alt werden, altern. ~ **brack·et** → **age group.**

aged[1] ['eɪdʒd] *adj* im Alter von ..., ...jährig, ... Alter: *s.* **twenty.**

a·ged[2] ['eɪdʒɪd] *adj* alt, betagt, bejahrt.

age‹ group *s* Altersgruppe *f*, -klasse *f*. '**~·less** *adj* **1.** nicht alternd, ewig jung. **2.** zeitlos. ~ **lim·it** *s* Altersgrenze *f*.

a·gen·cy ['eɪdʒənsɪ] *s* **1.** (Handels-, Nachrichten- *etc*) Vertretung *f*; (Handels)Vertretung *f*. **2.** *bsd.* Am. Geschäfts-, Dienststelle *f*; Amt *n*, Behörde

f. **3.** Mittel *n*: **by** (*od.* **through**) **the** ~ **of** mit Hilfe von (*od.* gen).

a·gen·da [ə'dʒendə] *s* Tagesordnung *f*: **be on the** ~ auf der Tagesordnung stehen.

a·gent ['eɪdʒənt] *s* **1.** *biol., phys. etc* Agens *n*, Wirkstoff *m*, Mittel *n*. **2.** ♀ Agent *m* (*a. pol.*), Vertreter *m*; (*Grundstücks- etc*)Makler *m*.

ag·glom·er·ate [ə'glɒmərɪt] *v/t u. v/i* (sich) zs.-ballen; (sich) (an)häufen; **ag‹glom·er·a·tion** *s* Zs.-ballung *f*; Anhäufung *f*.

ag·glu·ti·nate [ə'glu:tɪneɪt] *v/t* **1.** zs.-kleben. **2.** *biol., ling.* agglutinieren. **ag‹glu·ti·na·tion** *s* **1.** Zs.-kleben *n*. **2.** zs.-klebende Masse, Klumpen *m*. **3.** *biol., ling.* Agglutination *f*.

ag·gra·vate ['ægrəveɪt] *v/t* **1.** verschlimmern. **2.** F (ver)ärgern. '**ag·gra·vat·ing** *adj* **1.** verschlimmernd. **2.** F ärgerlich. ‚**ag·gra·va·tion** *s* **1.** Verschlimmerung *f*. **2.** F Ärger *m*.

ag·gre·gate I *adj* ['ægrɪgət] **1.** gesamt, Gesamt...: ~ **amount** → 5. **II** *v/t* ['~geɪt] **2.** anhäufen, -sammeln. **3.** sich (insgesamt) belaufen auf (*acc*). **III** *s* ['~gət] **4.** Anhäufung *f*, -sammlung *f*. **5.** Gesamtbetrag *m*, -summe *f*: **in the** ~ insgesamt, alles in allem. **6.** ⚙ *etc* Aggregat *n*. **ag·gre·ga·tion** [‚~'geɪʃn] *s* (An)Häufung *f*, Ansammlung *f*.

ag·gres·sion [ə'greʃn] *s* *bsd.* ✕ Angriff *m*, Aggression *f* (*a. psych.*).

ag·gres·sive [ə'gresɪv] *adj* aggressiv. **ag'gres·sive·ness** *s* Aggressivität *f*. **ag'gres·sor** *s* *bsd.* ✕ Angreifer *m*.

ag·grieve [ə'gri:v] *v/t* **1.** betrüben, -drücken. **2.** kränken.

ag·gro ['ægrəʊ] *s* *Br. sl.* Aggressivität *f*.

a·ghast [ə'gɑ:st] *adv u. adj* entgeistert, entsetzt, bestürzt (**at** über *acc*).

ag·ile ['ædʒaɪl] *adj* □ beweglich, wendig: *have an* ~ *mind* geistig beweglich sein. **a·gil·i·ty** [ə'dʒɪlətɪ] *s* Beweglichkeit *f*, Wendigkeit *f*.

ag·i·tate ['ædʒɪteɪt] **I** *v/t* **1.** schütteln, (um)rühren. **2.** aufregen, -wühlen. **3.** aufwiegeln, -hetzen. **II** *v/i* **4.** agitieren, hetzen (**against** gegen); Propaganda machen (**for** für). ‚**ag·i'ta·tion** *s* **1.** Aufregung *f*. **2.** Agitation *f* (*a. psych.*). '**ag·i·ta·tor** *s* Agitator *m*, Hetzer *m*.

a·glow [ə'gləʊ] *adv u. adj* glühend.

a·go [ə'gəʊ] *adv* vor: *a year ~* vor e-m Jahr; *long ~* vor langer Zeit; *not long ~* (erst) vor kurzem.

a·gog [ə'gɒg] *adv u. adj* erpicht; gespannt (*for acc*): *all ~* ganz aus dem Häuschen; *be ~ to do s.th.* es kaum mehr erwarten können, et. zu tun.

ag·o·nize ['ægənaɪz] *v/i* **1.** mit dem Tode ringen. **2.** sich abquälen, verzweifelt ringen (*over* mit). **'ag·o·niz·ing** *adj* □ qualvoll. **ag·o·ny** ['ˌni] *s* **1.** Qual *f*: *be in an ~ of doubt* von Zweifeln gequält werden; *~ aunt* F Kummerkastentante *f*; *~ column* F Seufzerspalte *f* (*Zeitung*). **2.** Todeskampf *m*.

a·grar·i·an [ə'greərɪən] *adj* landwirtschaftlich, Agrar...: *~ reform* Bodenreform *f*.

a·gree [ə'griː] **I** *v/t* **1.** vereinbaren (*to do* zu tun; *that* daß): *~d!* einverstanden!, abgemacht!; *~ to differ* sich auf verschiedene Standpunkte einigen. **2.** *bsd. Br.* sich einigen auf (*acc*); *Streit* beilegen. **II** *v/i* **3.** (*on, about*) einig werden (über *acc*), sich einigen (auf *acc*), vereinbaren (*acc*). **4.** (*to*) zustimmen (*dat*), einverstanden sein (mit). **5.** sich einig sein, gleicher Meinung sein (*with* wie). **6.** (*with*) übereinstimmen (mit), entsprechen (*dat*). **7.** bekommen (*with dat*) (*Speise etc*). **a·gree·a·ble** [ə'griːəbl] *adj* □ **1.** angenehm (*to dat od.* für): *agreeably surprised* angenehm überrascht. **2.** liebenswürdig. **3.** einverstanden (*to* mit). **a·gree·a·ble·ness** *s* Liebenswürdigkeit *f*; **a·greed** *adj*: *be ~* sich einig sein, gleicher Meinung sein. **a·gree·ment** [ə'griːmənt] *s* **1.** Vereinbarung *f*; *bsd. pol.* Abkommen *n*; Einigung *f*: *come to an ~* sich einigen. **2.** Einigkeit *f*. **3.** Übereinstimmung *f*.

ag·ri·cul·tur·al [ˌægrɪ'kʌltʃərəl] *adj* □ landwirtschaftlich: *~ prices pl* Agrarpreise *pl*. **ag·ri·cul·ture** ['ˌtʃə] *s* Landwirtschaft *f*.

a·ground [ə'graʊnd] *adv u. adj* ⚓ gestrandet: *run ~* auflaufen, stranden; *Schiff* auf Grund setzen; *be ~* aufgelaufen sein; *fig.* auf dem trock(e)nen sitzen.

ah [ɑː] *int* ah!, ach!

a·ha [ɑː'hɑː] **I** *int* aha! **II** *adj*: *~ experience psych.* Aha-Erlebnis *n*.

a·head [ə'hed] *adv u. adj* **1.** vorn, nach

vorn zu. **2.** voraus, vorwärts: *~ of* vor (*dat*), voraus (*dat*).

a·hoy [ə'hɔɪ] *int* ⚓ ahoi!

aid [eɪd] **I** *v/t* **1.** unterstützen, *j-m* helfen (*in* bei). **2.** *Verdauung etc* fördern. **II** *v/i* **3.** *he was accused of ~ing and abetting* er wurde wegen Beihilfe angeklagt. **III** *s* **4.** Hilfe *f* (*to* für), Unterstützung *f*: *by (od. with) (the) ~ of* mit Hilfe von (*od. gen*); *in ~ of* zugunsten von (*od. gen*); *come to s.o.'s ~* j-m zu Hilfe kommen. **5.** Hilfsmittel *n*, -gerät *n*.

AIDS [eɪdz] *s* ⚕ AIDS *n* (*acquired immune deficiency syndrome*).

ail [eɪl] *v/i* kränklich sein, kränkeln (*beide a. fig. Wirtschaft etc*).

ai·le·ron ['eɪlərɒn] *s* ✈ Querruder *n*.

ail·ing ['eɪlɪŋ] *adj* kränkelnd, kränklich (*beide a. fig. Wirtschaft etc*). **'ail·ment** *s* Leiden *n*.

aim [eɪm] **I** *v/i* **1.** zielen (*at* auf *acc*, nach). **2.** beabsichtigen, bezwecken (*at acc*): *~ to do s.th.* vorhaben, et. zu tun. **3.** streben (*at* nach). **4.** abzielen, anspielen (*at* auf *acc*). **II** *v/t* **5.** *Waffe* richten (*at* auf *acc*). **6.** (*at*) *Bemerkung etc* richten (gegen); *Bestrebungen* richten (auf *acc*). **III** *s* **7.** Ziel *n*: *take ~* → 1. **8.** *fig.* Ziel *n*; Absicht *f*. **'aim·less** *adj* □ ziellos.

ain't [eɪnt] F *für are not, am not, is not, have not, has not.*

air¹ [eə] **I** *s* **1.** Luft *f*: *by ~* auf dem Luftweg; *in the open ~* im Freien; *be in the ~* im Umlauf sein (*Gerücht etc*); in der Schwebe sein (*Frage etc*); *take the ~* frische Luft schöpfen; → *light¹* 1, *thin* 1. **2.** *Rundfunk, TV*: Äther *m*: *on the ~* im Rundfunk *od.* Fernsehen; *be on the ~* senden (*Sender*); gesendet werden (*Programm*); im Rundfunk zu hören *od.* im Fernsehen zu sehen sein (*Person*). **3.** Miene *f*, Aussehen *n*: *an ~ of importance* e-e gewichtige Miene. **4.** *mst pl* Getue *n*: *~s and graces* affektiertes Getue; *put on ~s, give o.s. ~s* vornehm tun. **II** *v/t* **5.** lüften. **6.** *Wäsche* zum Trocknen aufhängen. **7.** *et.* an die Öffentlichkeit *od.* zur Sprache bringen.

air² [~] *s* ♪ Lied *n*, Melodie *f*.

air| bag *s mot.* Luftsack *m*. **~ base** *s* Luftstützpunkt *m*. **~ bath** *s* Luftbad *n*. **'~·borne** *adj* **1.** im Flugzeug befördert: *~ radar* Bordradar *m, n*; *~ troops pl* ✗ Luftlandetruppen *pl*. **2.** *be ~* sich in der

Luft befinden, fliegen. ~ **brake** *s* ⊕ Druckluftbremse *f*. '~**bus** *s* ✈ Airbus *m*. ~ **car·go** *s* Luftfracht *f*. '~**con·di·tioned** *adj* mit Klimaanlage, klimatisiert. ~ **con·di·tion·ing** *s* 1. Klimatisierung *f*. 2. Klimaanlage *f*. '~**cooled** *adj* luftgekühlt. ~**craft** *s* Flugzeug *n*; *coll.* Flugzeuge *pl*: ~ **car·rier** Flugzeugträger *m*. ~ **crash** *s* Flugzeugabsturz *m*. ~**cush·ion** *s* Luftkissen *n*. '~**drop** *v/t* mit dem Fallschirm abwerfen; ✗ *Fallschirmjäger etc* absetzen. '~**field** *s* Flugplatz *m*. ~ **force** *s* Luftwaffe *f*. ~ **freight** *s* 1. Luftfracht *f*. 2. Luftfrachtgebühr *f*. ~ **gun** *s* Luftgewehr *n*. ~ **host·ess** *s* Stewardeß *f*.

air·ing ['eərɪŋ] *s* 1. Lüftung *f*: *give s.th. an* ~ et. lüften; *the room needs an* ~ das Zimmer muß (durch)gelüftet werden. 2. Spaziergang *m*: *take an* ~ frische Luft schöpfen. 3. *give s.th. an* ~ → *air¹*

air|jack·et *s* Schwimmweste *f*. '~**less** *adj* 1. luftlos. 2. stickig. ~**let·ter** *s* Luftpost(leicht)brief *m*. '~**lift** *s* Luftbrücke *f*. '~**line** *s* Fluggesellschaft *f*. '~**lin·er** *s* Verkehrsflugzeug *n*. '~**mail** *s* Luftpost *f*. II *v/t* per Luftpost schicken. ~ **pas·sen·ger** *s* Fluggast *m*. ~ **pho·to·graph** *s* Luftbild *n*. ~ **pi·rate** *s* Luftpirat(in). '~ **plane** *s Am.* Flugzeug *n*. ~ **pock·et** *s* ✈ Luftloch *n*. ~ **pol·lu·tion** *s* Luftverschmutzung *f*. '~**port** *s* Flughafen *m*, -platz *m*. ~ **pres·sure** *s* Luftdruck *m*. '~**proof** *adj* luftdicht. ~ **pump** *s* Luftpumpe *f*. ~ **raid** *s* ✗ Luftangriff *m*. '~**raid** *adj*: ~ *precautions pl* Luftschutz *m*; ~ *shelter* Luftschutzbunker *m*, -raum *m*. ~ **shaft** *s* Luftschacht *m*. '~**ship** *s* Luftschiff *n*. '~**sick** *adj* luftkrank. '~**space** *s* Luftraum *m*. '~**strip** *s* (behelfsmäßige) Start- u. Landebahn. ~ **ter·mi·nal** *s* 1. Flughafenabfertigungsgebäude *n*. 2. *Br.* Endstation *f* der Zubringerlinie zum u. vom Flughafen. ~ **tick·et** *s* Flugticket *n*, -schein *m*. '~**tight** *adj* 1. luftdicht. 2. *fig.* hieb- u. stichfest (*Argument etc*). ~ **traf·fic** *s* Flug-, Luftverkehr *m*. '~**traf·fic** *adj*: ~ *control* Flugsicherung *f*; ~ *controller* Fluglotse *m*. '~**way** *s* ✈ Luftstraße *f*. '~**wor·thy** *adj* ✈ flugtüchtig.

air·y ['eərɪ] *adj* □ 1. Luft... 2. luftig. 3. graziös, anmutig. 4. lebhaft, munter. 5. verstiegen, überspannt. 6. vornehmtuerisch. 7. lässig, ungezwungen.

aisle [aɪl] *s* 1. △ Seitenschiff *n*. 2. Gang *m* (*zwischen Bänken etc*).

a·jar [ə'dʒɑː] *adv u. adj* angelehnt (*Tür etc*).

a·kim·bo [ə'kɪmbəʊ] *adv u. adj*: *with arms* ~ die Arme in die Seite gestemmt.

a·kin [ə'kɪn] *adj* 1. verwandt (*to* mit). 2. *fig.* verwandt, ähnlich (*to dat*): *be* ~ sich ähneln; ähneln (*to dat*).

al·a·bas·ter [ˌælə'bɑːstə] *s* Alabaster *m*.

a·lac·ri·ty [ə'lækrətɪ] *s* Bereitwilligkeit *f*, Eifer *m*.

a·larm [ə'lɑːm] I *s* 1. Alarm *m*: *give* (*od.* *raise, sound*) *the* ~ Alarm geben; *fig.* Alarm schlagen. 2. Weckvorrichtung *f* (*e-s Weckers*): ~ (*clock*) Wecker *m*. 3. Alarmvorrichtung *f*, -anlage *f*. 4. Angst *f*, Unruhe *f*. II *v/t* 5. alarmieren. 6. ängstigen, beunruhigen. **a·larm·ist** *s* Bangemacher *m*.

a·las [ə'læs] *int* ach!, leider!

Al·ba·ni·an [æl'beɪnjən] I *adj* albanisch. II *s* Albanier(in).

al·ba·tross ['ælbətrɒs] *s orn.* Albatros *m*, Sturmvogel *m*.

al·bi·no [æl'biːnəʊ] *pl* **-nos** *s biol.* Albino *m*.

al·bum ['ælbəm] *s* Album *n* (*a. Langspielplatte*).

al·bu·men ['ælbjumɪn] *s biol.* Eiweiß *n*.

al·che·my ['ælkəmɪ] *s hist.* Alchimie *f*.

al·co·hol ['ælkəhɒl] *s* Alkohol *m*. ˌal·co·hol·ic [-'hɒl-] *adj* (*~ally*) alkoholisch. II *s* Alkoholiker(in): Ɛs *Anonymous* die Anonymen Alkoholiker. 'al·co·hol·ism *s* Alkoholismus *m*.

al·cove ['ælkəʊv] *s* 1. Alkoven *m*, Nische *f*. 2. *bsd. poet.* (Garten)Laube *f*.

al·der ['ɔːldə] *s* ♣ Erle *f*.

al·der·man ['ɔːldəmən] *s* (*irr man*) Ratsherr *m*, Stadtrat *m*.

ale [eɪl] *s* Ale *n* (*helles, obergäriges Bier*).

a·lert [ə'lɜːt] I *adj* □ 1. auf der Hut (*to* vor *dat*), wachsam. 2. munter, flink. 3. aufgeweckt, (hell)wach: *be* ~ *to* sich *e-r Sache* bewußt sein. II *s* 4. ✗ (Alarm)Bereitschaft *f*: *be on the* ~ in Alarmbereitschaft sein; *fig.* auf der Hut sein. 5. *bsd.* ✈ Alarm(signal *n*) *m*. III *v/t* 6. alarmieren, ✗ *a.* in Alarmzustand versetzen. 7. *fig.* aufrütteln: ~

s.o. to s.th. j-m et. (deutlich) zum Bewußtsein bringen.

al·fres·co ['ælˈfreskəʊ] *adj u. adv* im Freien: **~ lunch; lunch ~.**

al·ga ['ælɡə] *pl* **-gae** ['~dʒiː] *s* ♣ Alge *f.*

al·ge·bra ['ældʒɪbrə] *s* ♣ Algebra *f.* **al·ge·bra·ic** [,~'breɪk] *adj* (**~ally**) algebraisch.

a·li·as ['eɪlɪəs] **I** *adv* alias. **II** *s* Deck-, ☇ Falschname *m.*

al·i·bi ['ælɪbaɪ] *s* ☇ Alibi *n, fig.* F *a.* Ausrede *f,* Entschuldigung *f: give s.o. an ~* j-m ein Alibi geben.

al·ien ['eɪljən] **I** *adj* **1.** ausländisch. **2.** außerirdisch. **3.** *fig.* fremd (**to** dat): *that is ~ to his nature* das ist ihm wesensfremd. **II** *s* **4.** Ausländer(in). **5.** außerirdisches Wesen. **al·ien·ate** ['~eɪt] *v/t* **1.** ☇ veräußern. **2.** befremden; entfremden (**from** dat). **al·ien·a·tion** *s* **1.** ☇ Veräußerung *f.* **2.** Entfremdung *f.*

a·light¹ [ə'laɪt] *adv u. adj* in Flammen: **be ~** in Flammen stehen; *fig.* strahlen (**with** vor dat); **set ~** in Brand stecken, anzünden.

a·light² [~] *v/i (a. irr)* **1.** (**from**) aussteigen (aus), absteigen (von *Fahrrad etc*), absitzen (von *Pferd*). **2.** (**on**) (sanft) fallen (auf acc) (*Schnee*), sich niederlassen (auf dat od. acc) (*Vogel*). **3.** ✓ niedergehen, landen (a. allg.): **~ on one's feet** auf die Füße fallen.

a·lign [ə'laɪn] **I** *v/t* **1.** in e-e (gerade) Linie bringen, ⚙ (aus)fluchten. **2.** ausrichten (**with** nach). **3. ~ o.s. with** *fig.* sich anschließen (dat od. an acc). **II** *v/i* **4.** sich ausrichten (**with** nach). **a'lign·ment** *s* Ausrichtung *f:* **in ~ with** in 'einer Linie mit, *fig. a.* in Übereinstimmung mit.

a·like [ə'laɪk] **I** *adj* gleich; ähnlich (**to** dat). **II** *adv* gleich, ebenso, in gleicher Weise; ähnlich: *treat ~* gleich behandeln.

al·i·men·ta·ry [,ælɪ'mentərɪ] *adj* **1.** Nahrungs... **2.** Ernährungs..., Speise...: **~ canal** Verdauungskanal *m.*

al·i·mo·ny ['ælɪmənɪ] *s* ☇ Unterhalt(szahlung *f*) *m.*

a·live [ə'laɪv] *adj* **1.** lebend, lebendig, am Leben: *his grandparents* **are still ~** leben noch; *be burnt ~* bei lebendigem Leib verbrennen. **2.** in voller Kraft *od.* Wirksamkeit: *keep ~* aufrechterhalten. **3.** lebendig, lebhaft: **~ and kicking** F gesund u. munter; *look ~!* F mach fix! **4. be ~ to** sich e-r *Sache* bewußt sein. **5. be ~ with** wimmeln von.

al·ka·li ['ælkəlaɪ] *s* ♣ Alkali *n,* Laugensalz *n.* **al·ka·line** ['~laɪn] *adj* alkalisch.

all [ɔːl] **I** *adj* **1.** all, gesamt, ganz: **~ day** (**long**) den ganzen Tag (hindurch); **~ the time** die ganze Zeit. **2.** jeder, jede, jedes, alle *pl*: **at ~ hours** zu jeder Stunde. **II** *adv* **3.** ganz, gänzlich: **~ the better** um so besser; **~ in** F total fertig *od.* erledigt; **~ over** überall; *that is John* **~ over** das ist typisch John; **~ right** schon gut; in Ordnung; *it's ~ right for you to talk!* F du hast gut reden!; **~ round** rings- *od.* rundherum; *it's ~ up with him* mit ihm ist's aus; → **there** 1. **III** *pron* **4.** alles: **~ in ~** alles in allem; **~ of it** alles, das Ganze; **~ of us** wir alle; → **above** 2, **after** 3. **IV** *s* **5. his ~** sein Hab u. Gut; sein ein u. alles.

,all-A'mer·i·can *adj* **1.** rein *od.* typisch amerikanisch. **2.** die ganzen USA vertretend.

al·lay [ə'leɪ] *v/t* beschwichtigen; *Schmerzen etc* mildern, lindern.

al·le·ga·tion [,ælɪ'ɡeɪʃn] *s* Behauptung *f.* **al·lege** [ə'ledʒ] *v/t* behaupten. **al'leged** *adj* angeblich.

al·le·giance [ə'liːdʒəns] *s* Treue *f,* Loyalität *f.*

al·le·gor·ic, al·le·gor·i·cal [,ælɪ'ɡɒrɪk(l)] *adj* □ allegorisch. **al·le·go·ry** ['~ɡərɪ] *s* Allegorie *f.*

al·le·lu·ia [,ælɪ'luːjə] *s* Halleluja *n.*

al·ler·gic [ə'lɜːdʒɪk] *adj* (**~ally**) allergisch (**to** gegen) (*a. fig.* F). **al·ler·gy** ['ælədʒɪ] *s* ♣ Allergie *f.*

al·le·vi·ate [ə'liːvɪeɪt] *v/t* mildern, lindern. **al,le·vi·a·tion** *s* Milderung *f,* Linderung *f.*

al·ley ['ælɪ] *s* **1.** Gasse *f:* → **blind alley**. **2.** *Bowling*: Bahn *f: that's down (od. up) my ~* F das ist et. für mich.

All Fools' Day *s* der 1. April.

al·li·ance [ə'laɪəns] *s* **1.** Verbindung *f.* **2.** Bund *m,* Bündnis *n: form an ~* ein Bündnis schließen. **3.** Verschwägerung *f; weitS.* Verwandtschaft *f.* **al·lied** [ə'laɪd; *attr.* 'ælaɪd] *adj* **1.** verbündet. **2.** *fig.* verwandt (**to** mit). **Al·lies** ['ælaɪz] *s pl hist.* die Alliierten *pl.*

al·li·ga·tor ['ælɪɡeɪtə] *s zo.* Alligator *m.*

,all-'in *adj* Gesamt..., Pauschal...

al·lit·er·a·tion [əˌlɪtəˈreɪʃn] s Alliteration f.

al·lo·cate [ˈæləʊkeɪt] v/t zuteilen, zuweisen (**to** dat). **al·lo·ca·tion** s Zuteilung f, Zuweisung f.

al·lop·a·thy [əˈlɒpəθɪ] s 🥼 Allopathie f.

al·lot [əˈlɒt] v/t **1.** zuteilen, zuweisen (**to** dat). **2.** Geld etc bestimmen (**to, for** für). **al·lot·ment** s **1.** Zuteilung f, Zuweisung f. **2.** Parzelle f. **~** (**garden**) bsd. Br. Schrebergarten m.

all-'out adj F **1.** total: **~ effort** äußerste Anstrengung. **2.** Am. kompromißlos, radikal.

al·low [əˈlaʊ] **I** v/t **1.** erlauben, gestatten; bewilligen, gewähren: **be ~ed to do s.th.** et. tun dürfen; **we are ~ed ...** uns stehen ... zu. **2.** Summe geben. **3.** zugeben; anerkennen, gelten lassen. **II** v/i **4. ~ of** erlauben, gestatten: **it ~s of no excuse** es läßt sich nicht entschuldigen. **5. ~ for** in Betracht ziehen, berücksichtigen (acc). **al·low·a·ble** adj □ erlaubt, zulässig. **al·low·ance** s **1.** Erlaubnis f; Bewilligung f. **2.** Anerkennung f. **3.** Zuschuß m, Beihilfe f; Taschengeld n. **4.** 🔧 Nachlaß m, Rabatt m: **~ for cash** Skonto n. **5.** Nachsicht f: **make ~(s) for → allow** 5. **6.** 🔩, ⚙ Toleranz f.

al·loy ⚙ **I** s [ˈælɔɪ] Legierung f. **II** v/t [əˈlɔɪ] legieren.

'all-,pur·pose adj Allzweck..., Universal...; **,~-'round** adj vielseitig, Allround...

All Saints' Day s eccl. Allerheiligen n. **~ Souls' Day** s eccl. Allerseelen n.

'all-,time adj bisher unerreicht, beispiellos: **~ high** Höchstleistung f, -stand m; **~ low** Tiefststand m.

al·lude [əˈluːd] v/i anspielen (**to** auf acc).

al·lure [əˈljʊə] v/t **1.** (an-, ver)locken. **2.** anziehen, verzaubern. **al·lure·ment** s **1.** Verlockung f. **2.** Anziehungskraft f, Zauber m. **al·lur·ing** adj □ (ver)lockend, verführerisch.

al·lu·sion [əˈluːʒn] s Anspielung f (**to** auf acc).

al·lu·vi·al [əˈluːvjəl] adj geol. angeschwemmt, Schwemm...

'all-,weath·er adj Allwetter...

al·ly [əˈlaɪ] **I** v/t verbinden, -einigen (**to, with** mit): **~ o.s.** → **II**; → **allied. II** v/i sich vereinigen od. verbünden (**to, with**

mit). **III** s [ˈælaɪ] Verbündete m, f, Bundesgenosse m: → **Allies.**

al·ma·nac [ˈɔːlmənæk] s Almanach m, Kalender m.

al·might·y [ɔːlˈmaɪtɪ] adj allmächtig: **the ☨ der Allmächtige.**

al·mond [ˈɑːmənd] s ♀ Mandel f.

al·most [ˈɔːlməʊst] adv fast, beinahe.

alms [ɑːmz] s **1.** (mst pl konstruiert) Almosen n. **2.** 🔩 Kollekte f.

al·oe [ˈæləʊ] s ♀ Aloe f.

a·lone [əˈləʊn] **I** adj allein: → **leave¹** 2, **let¹** 1. **II** adv allein, bloß, nur.

a·long [əˈlɒŋ] **I** prp **1.** entlang (dat od. acc), längs (gen, a. dat), an (dat) ... vorbei: **~ the river** am Fluß entlang, entlang dem Fluß. **II** adv **2.** vorwärts, weiter: → **get along**, etc. **3. ~ with** zs. mit: → **take along**, etc. **4.** f. da: **I'll be ~ shortly** ich bin gleich da. **a,long'side I** adv **1.** ⚓ längsseits. **2.** Seite an Seite. **II** prp **3.** neben (dat od. acc).

a·loof [əˈluːf] **I** adv fern, abseits: **hold** (od. **keep**) (**o.s.**) **~, stand ~** sich fernhalten (**from** von), für sich bleiben. **II** adj reserviert, zurückhaltend.

a·loud [əˈlaʊd] adv laut, mit lauter Stimme.

al·pha·bet [ˈælfəbet] s Alphabet n. **,al·pha'bet·ic, ,al·pha'bet·i·cal** adj □ alphabetisch: **in ~ order** in alphabetischer Reihenfolge, alphabetisch (an)geordnet.

Al·pine [ˈælpaɪn] adj **1.** Alpen... **2.** alpin, (Hoch)Gebirgs...

al·read·y [ɔːlˈredɪ] adv bereits, schon.

al·right [ˌɔːlˈraɪt] Br. F u. Am. für **all right** (→ **all** 3).

Al·sa·tian [ælˈseɪʃn] **I** adj **1.** elsässisch. **II** s **2.** Elsässer(in). **3.** a. **~ dog** deutscher Schäferhund.

al·so [ˈɔːlsəʊ] adv auch, ebenfalls. **'~-ran** s **1.** Sport: Teilnehmer an e-m Rennen, der sich nicht plazieren kann: **she was an ~** sie kam unter ,ferner liefen' ein. **2.** F Versager m, Niete f.

al·tar [ˈɔːltə] s eccl. Altar m. **~ boy** s Ministrant m.

al·ter [ˈɔːltə] **I** v/t (ver-, ab-, um)ändern. **II** v/i sich (ver)ändern. **'al·ter·a·ble** adj □ veränderlich. **,al·ter'a·tion** s Änderung f (**to** an dat), Ver-, Ab-, Umänderung f.

al·ter·ca·tion [,ɔːltə'keɪʃn] s heftige Auseinandersetzung.

al·ter·nate I adj [ɔːl'tɜːnət] **1.** abwechselnd: **on ~ days** jeden zweiten Tag. **II** v/t ['ɔːltəneɪt] **2.** abwechseln lassen. **3.** miteinander vertauschen. **4.** ⚡, ☼ (periodisch) verändern. **III** v/i ['ɔːltəneɪt] **5.** abwechseln. **al'ter·nate·ly** adv abwechselnd, wechselweise. **'al·ter·nat·ing** adj abwechselnd, Wechsel...: **~ current** ⚡ Wechselstrom m. **al·ter·na·tion** [,ɔːltə'neɪʃn] s Abwechslung f, Wechsel m. **al·ter·na·tive** [ɔːl'tɜːnətɪv] **I** adj **1.** alternativ, Ersatz...: **~ airport** Ausweichflughafen m; **~ society** alternative Gesellschaft. **2.** ander(er, e, es) (von zweien). **II** s **3.** Alternative f (**to** zu): **have no (other) ~** keine andere Möglichkeit od. Wahl haben (**but to** als zu).

al·though [ɔːl'ðəʊ] cj obwohl, obgleich.

al·tim·e·ter ['æltɪmiːtə] s phys. Höhenmesser m.

al·ti·tude ['æltɪtjuːd] s ast., ✈, ⚘ Höhe f: **at an ~ of** in e-r Höhe von; **~ of the sun** Sonnenstand m.

al·to ['æltəʊ] pl **-tos** ♪ Alt(stimme f) m; Altistin f.

al·to·geth·er [,ɔːltə'geðə] **I** adv **1.** insgesamt. **2.** ganz (u. gar), völlig. **3.** im ganzen genommen. **II** s **4. in the ~** humor. im Adams- od. Evaskostüm.

al·tru·ism ['æltrʊɪzəm] s Altruismus m, Selbstlosigkeit f. **'al·tru·ist** s Altruist(in). **,al·tru'is·tic** adj (**~ally**) altruistisch, selbstlos.

a·lu·min·i·um [,æljʊ'mɪnɪəm], Am. **a·lu·mi·num** [ə'luːmənəm] s ♫ Aluminium n.

a·lum·na [ə'lʌmnə] pl **-nae** [~niː] s Am. ehemalige Schülerin od. Studentin. **a'lum·nus** [~nəs] pl **-ni** [~naɪ] s Am. ehemaliger Schüler od. Student.

al·ways ['ɔːlweɪz] adv immer, stets: **as ~** wie immer.

am [æm] ich bin.

a·mal·gam [ə'mælgəm] s **1.** ♫, ☼ Amalgam n. **2.** fig. Mischung f. **a'mal·gam·ate** [~meɪt] v/t u. v/i **1.** ♫, ☼ (sich) amalgamieren, a. fig. (sich) vereinigen, verschmelzen. **2.** fig. (sich) zs.-schließen, † a. fusionieren. **a·mal·gam'a·tion** s **1.** ♫, ☼ Amalgamieren n, a. fig. Vereinigung f, Verschmelzung f. **2.** fig. Zs.-schluß m, † a. Fusion f.

a·mass [ə'mæs] v/t an-, aufhäufen.

am·a·teur ['æmətə] s Amateur m: a) (Kunst- etc)Liebhaber(in): **~ painter** Sonntagsmaler(in), b) Amateursportler(in): **~ boxer** Amateurboxer m, c) Nichtfachmann m, contp. Dilettant(in): **~ detective** Amateurdetektiv m. **am·a·teur·ish** [,~'tɜːrɪʃ] adj □ amateurhaft, dilettantisch.

a·maze [ə'meɪz] v/t in (Er)Staunen setzen, verblüffen. **a'mazed** adj □ erstaunt, verblüfft (**at** über acc). **a'maze·ment** s (Er)Staunen n, Verblüffung f: **in ~** staunend, verblüfft; **to my ~** zu m-m Erstaunen, zu m-r Verblüffung. **a'maz·ing** adj □ erstaunlich, verblüffend.

Am·a·zon ['æməzən] s **1.** antiq. Amazone f. **2.** ⚲ fig. Amazone f, Mannweib n.

am·bas·sa·dor [æm'bæsədə] s pol. Botschafter m (**to** in dat). **am'bas·sa·dress** [~drɪs] s Botschafterin f.

am·ber ['æmbə] s **1.** min. Bernstein m. **2.** Br. Gelb(licht) n, gelbes Licht (Verkehrsampel): **at ~** bei Gelb; **the lights were at ~** die Ampel stand auf Gelb. **II** adj **3.** Bernstein-. **4.** bernsteinfarben. **5.** **the lights were ~** Br. die Ampel stand auf Gelb.

am·bi·dex·trous [,æmbɪ'dekstrəs] adj □ **1.** beidhändig. **2.** fig. doppelzüngig, falsch.

am·bi·gu·i·ty [,æmbɪ'gjuːətɪ] s Zweideutigkeit f (a. Äußerung), Mehr-, Vieldeutigkeit f. **am'big·u·ous** [~gjʊəs] adj □ zwei-, mehr-, vieldeutig.

am·bi·tion [æm'bɪʃn] s Ehrgeiz m. **am'bi·tious** adj □ ehrgeizig (a. Plan etc): **be ~ to do s.th.** den Ehrgeiz haben, et. zu tun; **be ~ for s.o.** große Dinge mit j-m vorhaben.

am·biv·a·lent [æm'bɪvələnt] adj bsd. psych. ambivalent, doppelwertig.

am·ble ['æmbl] **I** v/i **1.** im Paßgang gehen od. reiten. **2.** fig. schlendern. **II** s **3.** Paßgang m. **4.** fig. gemächlicher Gang.

am·bu·lance ['æmbjʊləns] s Kranken-, Sanitätswagen m.

am·bush ['æmbʊʃ] **I** s Hinterhalt m: **lay an ~** in e-n Hinterhalt legen; (**lie od. wait**) **in ~** → III. **II** v/t aus dem Hinterhalt überfallen; auflauern (dat). **III** v/i im Hinterhalt liegen.

amplifier

a·me·ba *Am.* → **amoeba.**

a·mel·io·rate [ə'mi:ljəreɪt] **I** *v/t* verbessern, ✗ (a)meliorieren. **II** *v/i* besser werden. **a,mel·io·ra·tion** *s* Verbesserung *f*, ✗ (A)Melioration *f*.

a·men [ˌɑː'men] **I** *int* amen! **II** *s* Amen *n*.

a·me·na·ble [ə'mi:nəbl] *adj* □ (**to**) **1.** zugänglich (*dat*). **2.** verantwortlich (*dat*); unterworfen (*dat*).

a·mend [ə'mend] *v/t* **1.** verbessern. **2.** *parl.* Gesetz abändern, ergänzen. **a'mend·ment** *s* **1.** Verbesserung *f*. **2.** *parl.* Abänderungs-, Ergänzungsantrag *m*; *Am.* Zusatzartikel *m* zur Verfassung. **a'mends** *s pl* (*mst sg konstruiert*) (Schaden)Ersatz *m*: **make ~** Schadensersatz leisten, es wiedergutmachen; **make ~ to s.o. for s.th.** j-n für et. entschädigen.

a·men·i·ty [ə'mi:nətɪ] *s* **1.** *oft pl* Liebenswürdigkeit *f*, Höflichkeit *f*: **his ~ of temper** sein angenehmes Wesen. **2.** schöne Lage (*e-s Hauses etc*); *oft pl* Annehmlichkeit(en *pl*) *f*; *pl* (natürliche) Vorzüge *pl od.* Reize *pl* (*e-r Person, e-s Ortes etc*).

A·mer·i·can [ə'merɪkən] **I** *adj* amerikanisch: **~ Dream** der amerikanische Traum; **~ Indian** (*bes.* nordamer.) Indianer(in). **II** *s* Amerikaner(in). **A'mer·i·can·ism** *s* Amerikanismus *m*. **A,mer·i·can·i'za·tion** *s* Amerikanisierung *f*. **A'mer·i·can·ize** *v/t u. v/i* (sich) amerikanisieren.

am·e·thyst ['æmɪθɪst] *s min.* Amethyst *m*.

a·mi·a·bil·i·ty [ˌeɪmjə'bɪlətɪ] *s* Liebenswürdigkeit *f*. **'a·mi·a·ble** *adj* □ liebenswürdig, freundlich.

am·i·ca·ble ['æmɪkəbl] *adj* freund(schaftl)ich, friedlich, *a.* ⚖ gütlich. **'am·i·ca·bly** *adv* in Güte, gütlich: **part ~** im guten auseinandergehen.

a·mid(st) [ə'mɪd(st)] *prp* inmitten (*gen*), (mitten) in *od.* unter (*dat od. acc*).

a·miss [ə'mɪs] *adj u. adv* verkehrt, falsch: **take ~** übelnehmen; **there is s.th. ~ with** et. stimmt nicht mit; **it would not be ~** es würde nicht schaden (**for s.o. to do s.th.** wenn j-d et. täte).

am·i·ty ['æmətɪ] *s* Freundschaft *f*, gutes Einvernehmen.

am·me·ter ['æmɪtə] *s* ⚡ Amperemeter *n*.

am·mo·ni·a [ə'məʊnjə] *s* 🜛 Ammo-

niak *n*: **liquid ~** Salmiakgeist *m*.

am·mu·ni·tion [ˌæmjʊ'nɪʃn] *s* ✕ Munition *f*: **~ dump** Munitionslager *n*.

am·ne·sia [æm'ni:zjə] *s* ✚ Amnesie *f*, Gedächtnisschwund *m*.

am·nes·ty ['æmnəstɪ] **I** *s* Amnestie *f*. **II** *v/t* amnestieren, begnadigen.

a·moe·ba [ə'mi:bə] *s zo.* Amöbe *f*.

a·mok [ə'mɒk] → **amuck.**

a·mong(st) [ə'mʌŋ(st)] *prp* (mitten) unter (*dat od. acc*), zwischen (*dat od. acc*); bei: **from ~** aus ... hervor; **be ~** gehören zu; **~ other things** unter anderem; **they had two pounds ~ them** sie hatten zusammen zwei Pfund.

a·mor·al [ˌeɪ'mɒrəl] *adj* □ amoralisch.

am·o·rous ['æmərəs] *adj* □ **1.** verliebt (**of** in *acc*). **2.** Liebes...: **~ song.**

a·mor·phous [ə'mɔːfəs] *adj* □ form-, gestaltlos.

am·or·ti·za·tion [əˌmɔːtɪ'zeɪʃn] *s* Amortisation *f*, Tilgung *f*, Abschreibung *f*. **am'or·tize** [ˌtaɪz] *v/t* amortisieren: a) *Schuld* tilgen, b) *Anlagewerte* abschreiben.

a·mount [ə'maʊnt] **I** *v/i* **1.** (**to**) sich belaufen (auf *acc*), betragen (*acc*). **2.** *fig.* (**to**) hinauslaufen (auf *acc*), bedeuten (*acc*). **II** *s* **3.** Betrag *m*, Summe *f*; Höhe *f* (*e-r Summe*): **to the ~ of** in Höhe von; bis zum Betrag von. **4.** Menge *f*.

a·mour-pro·pre [ˌæmʊə'prɒprə] *s* Eigenliebe *f*.

amp [æmp] F → **ampere, amplifier.**

am·pere ['æmpeə] *s* Ampere *n*.

am·phet·a·mine [æm'fetəmiːn] *s* 🜪 Amphetamin *n*.

am·phib·i·an [æm'fɪbɪən] **I** *adj* **1.** → **amphibious. II** *s* **2.** *zo.* Amphibie *f*, Lurch *m*. **3.** Amphibienfahrzeug *n*. **am'phib·i·ous** *adj* □ *zo.*, ⊚ amphibisch, Amphibien...

am·phi·the·a·ter, *bsd. Br.* **am·phi·the·a·tre** ['æmfɪˌθɪətə] *s* Amphitheater *n*.

am·ple ['æmpl] *adj* □ **1.** weit, groß, geräumig. **2.** weitläufig, -gehend, ausführlich. **3.** reich(lich), beträchtlich. **4.** stattlich (*Figur etc*).

am·pli·fi·ca·tion [ˌæmplɪfɪ'keɪʃn] *s* **1.** Erweiterung *f*, Vergrößerung *f*, Ausdehnung *f*. **2.** nähere Ausführung *od.* Erläuterung; Weitschweifigkeit *f*. **3.** ⚡, *phys.* Verstärkung *f*. **am·pli·fi·er** [ˌfaɪə] *s* ⚡, *phys.* Verstärker *m*.

'**am·pli·fy** I v/t **1.** erweitern, vergrößern, ausdehnen. **2.** näher ausführen od. erläutern. **3.** ♪, phys. verstärken. II v/i **4.** sich weitläufig auslassen (**on** über acc). **am·pli·tude** ['‿tjuːd] s **1.** Weite f, Umfang m (a. fig.). **2.** Fülle f, Reichtum m. **3.** ♪, phys. Amplitude f, Schwingungsweite f.

am·poule ['æmpuːl] s ♣ Ampulle f.

am·pu·tate ['æmpjʊteɪt] v/t ♣ amputieren, abnehmen. ˌ**am·pu'ta·tion** s Amputation f, Abnahme f.

a·muck [ə'mʌk] adv: **run ~** Amok laufen.

am·u·let ['æmjʊlɪt] s Amulett n.

a·muse [ə'mjuːz] v/t amüsieren; unterhalten; Spaß machen (dat): **be ~d** sich freuen (**at, by** über acc). **a'muse·ment** s Unterhaltung f; Zeitvertreib m: **for ~** zum Vergnügen; **~ arcade** Br. Spielsalon m; **~ park** Vergnügungspark m. **a'mus·ing** adj □ amüsant; unterhaltsam.

an [ən] → **a**.

a·nach·ro·nism [ə'nækrənɪzəm] s Anachronismus m.

an·a·con·da [ˌænə'kɒndə] s zo. Anakonda f, Riesenschlange f.

a·nae·mi·a [ə'niːmjə] s bsd. Br. ♣ Anämie f, Blutarmut f. **a'nae·mic** adj bsd. Br. anämisch, blutarm.

an·aes·the·si·a [ˌænɪs'θiːzjə] s bsd. Br. ♣ Anästhesie f, Narkose f, Betäubung f. **an·aes·thet·ic** [ˌ‿'θetɪk] bsd. Br. I adj (**~ally**) betäubend, Narkose... II s Betäubungsmittel n. **an·aes·the·tist** [æ'niːsθətɪst] s bsd. Br. Anästhesist m, Narkosearzt m. **an'aes·the·tize** v/t bsd. Br. betäuben, narkotisieren.

an·a·log·ic, an·a·log·i·cal [ˌænə'lɒdʒɪk(l)], **a·nal·o·gous** [ə'næləgəs] adj □ analog, entsprechend (**to, with** dat). **a'nal·o·gy** [‿dʒɪ] s Analogie f, Entsprechung f: **on the ~ of, by ~ with** analog, gemäß, entsprechend (dat).

an·a·lyse ['ænəlaɪz] v/t analysieren: a) ⬆ etc zerlegen, b) eingehend untersuchen, c) ling. zergliedern, d) ⅋ auflösen. **a'nal·y·sis** [ə'næləsɪs] pl **-ses** [‿siːz] s **1.** Analyse f, Zerlegung f, gründliche Untersuchung, Zergliederung f, Auflösung f. **2.** ⅋ Analysis f. **3.** Psychoanalyse f. **an·a·lyst** ['ænəlɪst] s **1.** Analytiker m: **public ~** (behördlicher) Lebensmittelchemiker. **2.** Psy-

choanalytiker m. **an·a·lyt·ic, an·a·lyt·i·cal** [ˌænə'lɪtɪk(l)] adj □ **1.** analytisch. **2.** psychoanalytisch.

an·ar·chic, an·ar·chi·cal [æ'nɑːkɪk(l)] adj □ anarchisch. **an·arch·ism** ['ænəkɪzəm] s Anarchismus m. '**an·arch·ist** I s Anarchist(in). II adj anarchistisch. '**an·arch·y** s Anarchie f.

a·nath·e·ma [ə'næθəmə] s **1.** eccl. Bannfluch m, Kirchenbann m. **2. be an ~ to s.o.** fig. j-m verhaßt od. ein Greuel sein. **a'nath·e·ma·tize** v/t in den Bann tun, mit dem Kirchenbann belegen.

an·a·tom·i·cal [ˌænə'tɒmɪkl] adj □ anatomisch. **a·nat·o·mize** [ə'nætəmaɪz] v/t ♣ sezieren, fig. a. zergliedern. **a'nat·o·my** s **1.** ♣ Anatomie f. **2.** fig. Zergliederung f, Analyse f.

an·ces·tor ['ænsestə] s Vorfahr m, Ahn(herr) m: **~ cult** Ahnenkult m. **an·ces·tral** [‿'sestrəl] adj angestammt, Ahnen...: **~ home** Stammsitz m. **an·ces·tress** ['ænsestrɪs] s Ahnfrau f, Ahne f. '**an·ces·try** s **1.** (bsd. vornehme) Abstammung f. **2.** Vorfahren pl, Ahnen(reihe f) pl: **~ research** Ahnenforschung f.

an·chor ['æŋkə] I s **1.** ♣ Anker m: **cast** (od. **drop**) **~** → 5a; **lie** (od. **ride**) **at ~** → 5b; → **weigh** 3. **2.** Rundfunk, TV: Am. Moderator m, Moderatorin f (e-r Nachrichtensendung); Diskussionsleiter(in). II v/t **3.** ♣, ⚙ verankern (a. fig.). **4.** Rundfunk, TV: Am. Nachrichtensendung moderieren; Diskussion leiten. III v/i **5.** ♣ ankern: a) vor Anker gehen, b) vor Anker liegen. '**an·chor·age** s **1.** Ankerplatz m. **2.** a. **~ dues** pl Anker-, Liegegebühr f.

an·chor·man ['æŋkəmən] s (irr **man**), '**~wom·an** s (irr **woman**) → **anchor** 2.

an·cho·vy ['æntʃəvɪ] s ichth. An(s)chovis f, Sardelle f.

an·cient ['eɪnʃənt] I adj **1.** alt, aus alter Zeit. **2.** uralt. **3.** altertümlich. II s **4.** the **~s** pl die Alten f pl (Griechen u. Römer).

an·cil·lar·y [æn'sɪlərɪ] adj untergeordnet (**to** dat), Zusatz...: **~ industries** pl Zulieferbetriebe pl.

and [ænd] cj und: **better ~ better** immer besser; **thousands ~ thousands** Tausende u. aber Tausende; **there are books ~ books** es gibt gute u. schlechte Bücher; **for miles ~ miles** viele Meilen weit; **he ran ~ ran** er lief immer weiter; **bread ~ butter** Butterbrot *n*; **try ~ come** versuche zu kommen; → **nice** 4.

an·ec·do·tal [ˌænekˈdəʊtl] *adj* anekdotenhaft, anekdotisch. **an·ec·dote** [ˈænɪkdəʊt] *s* Anekdote *f*.

a·ne·mi·a, *etc Am*. → **anaemia**, *etc*.

an·e·mom·e·ter [ˌænɪˈmɒmɪtə] *s phys*. Windmesser *m*.

a·nem·o·ne [əˈnemənɪ] *s ♀* Anemone *f*.

an·es·the·si·a, *etc Am*. → **anaesthesia**, *etc*.

a·new [əˈnjuː] *adv* **1.** von neuem, noch einmal. **2.** neu.

an·gel [ˈeɪndʒəl] *s* Engel *m* (*a. fig*.): **you are an ~** du bist ein Schatz. **an·gel·ic**, **an·gel·i·cal** [ænˈdʒelɪk(l)] *adj* □ engelhaft, Engels...

an·ger [ˈæŋgə] **I** *s* Zorn *m*, Ärger *m*, Wut *f* (**at** über *acc*). **II** *v/t* erzürnen, (ver)ärgern.

an·gi·na (**pec·to·ris**) [ænˈdʒaɪnə (ˈpektərɪs)] *s ♂* Angina *f* pectoris.

an·gle¹ [ˈæŋgl] **I** *s* **1.** *bsd. ♣* Winkel *m*: **at an ~** schräg; **at right ~s** to im rechten Winkel zu. **2.** Ecke *f*. **3.** *fig*. Standpunkt *m*. **4.** *fig*. Seite *f*, Aspekt *m*. **II** *v/t* **5.** ab-, umbiegen. **6.** *Bericht etc* färben.

an·gle² [~] *v/i* angeln: ~ **for** *fig*. aussein auf (*acc*); → **compliment** I.

an·gle|·i·ron *s ♂* Winkeleisen *n*. **'~-park** *v/t u. v/i mot*. schräg parken.

an·gler [ˈæŋglə] *s* Angler(in).

An·gles [ˈæŋglz] *s pl hist*. Angeln *pl*.

An·gli·can [ˈæŋglɪkən] *eccl*. **I** *adj* anglikanisch. **II** *s* Anglikaner(in).

An·gli·cism [ˈæŋglɪsɪzəm] *s ling*. Anglizismus *m*.

An·glo|·A·mer·i·can [ˌæŋgləʊəˈmerɪkən] **I** *s* Angloamerikaner(in). **II** *adj* angloamerikanisch. **'~·'Sax·on** **I** *s* Angelsachse *m*. **II** *adj* angelsächsisch.

an·go·ra [æŋˈgɔːrə] *s a*. **~·cat** *zo*. Angorakatze *f*. **~ wool** *s* Angorawolle *f*.

an·gry [ˈæŋgrɪ] *adj* □ (**at**, **about**) ärgerlich (auf, über *acc*), verärgert (über *acc*), böse (auf *j-n*, über *et*.; **with** mit *j-m*).

an·guish [ˈæŋgwɪʃ] *s* Qual *f*, Pein *f*: **be in ~** Ängste ausstehen.

an·gu·lar [ˈæŋgjʊlə] *adj* □ **1.** wink(e)lig, Winkel...: **~ point** ♣ Scheitelpunkt *m*. **2.** knochig. **3.** *fig*. steif: a) linkisch, b) förmlich.

an·i·line [ˈænɪliːn] *s ♣* Anilin *n*.

an·i·mal [ˈænɪml] **I** *s* Tier *n*. **II** *adj* animalisch, tierisch. **~ food** *s* **1.** Fleischnahrung *f*. **2.** Tierfutter *n*. **~ lov·er** *s* Tierfreund(in). **'~·lov·ing** *adj* tierliebend. **~ shel·ter** *s Am*. Tierheim *n*. **~ spir·its** *s pl* Lebenskraft *f*, -geister *pl*.

an·i·mate **I** *v/t* [ˈænɪmeɪt] **1.** beleben, mit Leben erfüllen. **2.** anregen, aufmuntern. **II** *adj* [ˈ~mət] **3.** belebt, lebend. **4.** lebhaft, munter. **an·i·mat·ed** [ˈ~meɪtɪd] *adj* **1.** lebendig: ~ **cartoon** Zeichentrickfilm *m*. **2.** lebhaft, munter. **an·i·ma·tion** [ˌ~ˈmeɪʃn] *s* Lebhaftigkeit *f*, Munterkeit *f*.

an·i·mos·i·ty [ˌænɪˈmɒsɪtɪ] *s* Feindseligkeit *f* (**against**, **toward[s]** gegen[über]; **between** zwischen *dat*).

an·ise [ˈænɪs] *s ♀* Anis *m*. **an·i·seed** [ˈ~siːd] *s* Anis(samen) *m*.

an·kle [ˈæŋkl] *s anat*. (Fuß)Knöchel *m*. **ˌ~·'deep** *adj* knöcheltief. **~ sock** *s Br*. Söckchen *n*.

an·klet [ˈæŋklɪt] *s* **1.** Fußring *m*. **2.** *Am*. Söckchen *n*.

an·nals [ˈænlz] *s pl* **1.** Annalen *pl*, Jahrbücher *pl*. **2.** (Jahres)Bericht *m*.

an·neal [əˈniːl] *v/t* **1.** *metall*. ausglühen, *a. Kunststoffe* tempern. **2.** *Keramik*: einbrennen. **3.** *fig*. härten, stählen.

an·nex **I** *v/t* [əˈneks] **1.** (**to**) beifügen (*dat*), anhängen (an *acc*). **2.** *Gebiet* annektieren, sich einverleiben. **II** *s* [ˈæneks] **3.** Anhang *m*, Zusatz *m*. **4.** Anbau *m*, Nebengebäude *n*. **ˌan·nex'a·tion** *s* Annektierung *f*, Einverleibung *f* (**to** in *acc*).

an·ni·hi·late [əˈnaɪəleɪt] *v/t* vernichten. **an·ˌni·hi·'la·tion** *s* Vernichtung *f*.

an·ni·ver·sa·ry [ˌænɪˈvɜːsərɪ] *s* Jahrestag *m*.

an·no·tate [ˈænəʊteɪt] *v/t* mit Anmerkungen versehen; kommentieren. **ˌan·no·'ta·tion** *s* Anmerkung *f*; Kommentar *m*.

an·nounce [əˈnaʊns] *v/t* **1.** ankündigen. **2.** bekanntgeben, verkünden, *Geburt etc* anzeigen. **3.** *Rundfunk, TV*: ansagen; *über Lautsprecher* durchsagen. **an'nounce·ment** *s* **1.** Ankündigung *f*. **2.** Bekanntgabe *f* (*Geburts- etc*) Anzeige *f*. **3.** *Rundfunk, TV*: Ansage *f*; (Lautsprecher)Durchsage *f*. **an'nounc·er** *s Rundfunk, TV*: Ansager(in).

an·noy [əˈnɔɪ] v/t **1.** ärgern: *be ~ed* sich ärgern (*at s.th.* über et.; *with s.o.* über j-n). **2.** belästigen, stören. **an'noy·ance** s **1.** Ärger m. **2.** Belästigung f, Störung f. **an'noy·ing** adj □ **1.** ärgerlich. **2.** lästig, störend.

an·nu·al [ˈænjʊəl] **I** adj □ **1.** jährlich, Jahres...: ~ *ring* ⚭ Jahresring m. **2.** a. ⚭ einjährig. **II** s **3.** jährlich erscheinende Veröffentlichung. **4.** ⚭ einjährige Pflanze.

an·nu·i·ty [əˈnjuːɪtɪ] s (Jahres-, Leib-) Rente f.

an·nul [əˈnʌl] v/t annullieren, *Gesetz, Ehe etc* aufheben, für ungültig erklären, *Vorschrift etc* abschaffen.

an·nu·lar [ˈænjʊlə] adj □ ringförmig, Ring...

an·nul·ment [əˈnʌlmənt] s Annullierung f, Aufhebung f, Ungültigkeitserklärung f, Abschaffung f.

An·nun·ci·a·tion (Day) [əˌnʌnsɪˈeɪʃn] s eccl. Mariä Verkündigung f.

an·ode [ˈænəʊd] s ⚡ Anode f, positiver Pol.

an·o·dyne [ˈænəʊdaɪn] adj u. s 🕇 schmerzstillend(es Mittel).

a·noint [əˈnɔɪnt] v/t bsd. eccl. salben.

a·nom·a·lous [əˈnɒmələs] adj □ **1.** anomal. **2.** ungewöhnlich. **a'nom·a·ly** s Anomalie f.

a·non·y·mi·ty [ˌænəˈnɪmətɪ] s Anonymität f. **a·non·y·mous** [əˈnɒnɪməs] adj □ anonym.

a·no·rak [ˈænəræk] s Anorak m.

an·oth·er [əˈnʌðə] adj u. pron **1.** ein anderer, e-e andere, ein anderes: ~ *thing* etwas anderes; *one after* ~ e-r nach dem andern; → *one* 6. **2.** noch ein(er, e, es), ein zweiter od. weiterer, e-e zweite od. weitere, ein zweites od. weiteres: ~ *ten years* noch od. weitere zehn Jahre; *tell me* ~! F das kannst du deiner Großmutter erzählen!

an·swer [ˈɑːnsə] **I** s **1.** Antwort f (a. fig. Reaktion) (**to** auf acc): *in ~ to* in Beantwortung (gen); auf (acc) hin; als Antwort auf (acc). **2.** Lösung f (**to** e-s Problems). **II** v/i **3.** antworten (**to** auf acc): ~ *back* freche Antworten geben; widersprechen; sich (*mit Worten etc*) verteidigen od. wehren. **4.** ~ *to* → 10 u. 11. **5.** (**to** *s.o.*) sich (j-m gegenüber) verantworten, (j-m) Rechenschaft ablegen (**for**

für). **6.** verantwortlich sein, haften (**for** für). **7.** ~ *to* hören auf (*e-n Namen*). **III** v/t **8.** j-m antworten: ~ *s.o. back* j-m freche Antworten geben; j-m widersprechen; sich gegen j-n (*mit Worten etc*) verteidigen od. wehren. **9.** antworten auf (*acc*), beantworten. **10.** fig. reagieren auf (*acc*): a) eingehen auf: ~ *the bell* (od. *door*) (*auf das Läuten od. Klopfen*) die Tür öffnen, aufmachen; ~ *the telephone* ans Telefon gehen, b) ◉ *dem Steuer etc* gehorchen, c) *e-m Befehl etc* Folge leisten, gehorchen, d) *Wunsch etc* erfüllen, *Gebet* erhören, e) sich auf *e-e Anzeige* hin melden od. bewerben. **11.** *e-r Beschreibung* entsprechen. **12.** sich *j-m* gegenüber verantworten, *j-m* Rechenschaft ablegen (**for** für). **'an·swer·a·ble** adj **1.** verantwortlich (**to** dat; **for** für). **2.** zu beantworten(d).

ant [ænt] s zo. Ameise f.

an·tag·o·nism [ænˈtægənɪzəm] s Feindschaft f (**between** zwischen dat). **an'tag·o·nist** s Feind(in). **an,tag·o·'nis·tic** adj (~ally) feindlich (**to** gegen). **an'tag·o·nize** v/t **1.** bekämpfen. **2.** sich j-n zum Feind machen.

ant·arc·tic [ænˈtɑːktɪk] **I** adj antarktisch: ♀ *Circle* südlicher Polarkreis. **II** s ♀ Antarktis f.

ant bear s zo. Ameisenbär m.

an·te·ced·ent [ˌæntɪˈsiːdənt] **I** adj **1.** (**to**) vorhergehend (dat), früher (als). **II** s **2.** pl Vorgeschichte f: *his ~s* sein Vorleben; s-e Abstammung. **3.** ling. Bezugswort n.

an·te·cham·ber [ˈæntɪˌtʃeɪmbə] s Vorzimmer n.

an·te·date [ˌæntɪˈdeɪt] v/t *Brief etc* zurückdatieren.

an·te·di·lu·vi·an [ˌæntɪdaɪˈluːvjən] adj vorsintflutlich (a. fig.).

an·te·lope [ˈæntɪləʊp] s zo. Antilope f.

an·te me·rid·i·em [ˌæntɪməˈrɪdɪəm] adv vormittags (abbr. **a.m.**): *3 a.m.* 3 Uhr morgens.

an·te·na·tal [ˌæntɪˈneɪtl] **I** adj □ vor der Geburt: ~ *examination* Mutterschaftsvorsorgeuntersuchung f; ~ *exercises* pl Schwangerschaftsgymnastik f. **II** s f Mutterschaftsvorsorgeuntersuchung f.

an·ten·na [ænˈtenə] s **1.** pl **-nae** [-niː] zo. Fühler m. **2.** pl **-nas** bsd. Am. Antenne f.

an·te·ri·or [æn'tɪərɪə] *adj* **1.** (*to*) vorhergehend (*dat*), früher (als). **2.** vorder.

an·te·room ['æntɪrʊm] *s* Vorzimmer *n*.

an·them ['ænθəm] *s* Hymne *f*.

'ant·hill *s* Ameisenhaufen *m*.

an·thol·o·gy [æn'θɒlədʒɪ] *s* Anthologie *f*, (*bsd.* Gedicht)Sammlung *f*.

an·thra·cite ['ænθrəsaɪt] *s min.* Anthrazit *m*, Glanzkohle *f*.

an·thro·poid ['ænθrəʊpɔɪd] *zo.* **I** *adj* menschenähnlich. **II** *s* Menschenaffe *m*.

an·thro·po·log·i·cal [,ænθrəpə'lɒdʒɪkl] *adj* □ anthropologisch. **an·thro·pol·o·gist** [,~'pɒlədʒɪst] *s* Anthropologe *m*. **an·thro·pol·o·gy** [,~'pɒlədʒɪ] *s* Anthropologie *f*, Menschenkunde *f*.

an·ti... ['æntɪ] *in Zssgn* Gegen..., gegen... eingestellt, anti..., Anti...

an·ti'air·craft *adj* ✕ Flugabwehr...: ~ **gun** Flakgeschütz *n*.

an·ti·bi·ot·ic [,æntɪbaɪ'ɒtɪk] *s* ✚ Antibiotikum *n*.

'an·ti,bod·y *s* ✚ Antikörper *m*, Abwehrstoff *m*.

'An·ti·christ *s eccl.* Antichrist *m*.

an·tic·i·pate [æn'tɪsɪpeɪt] *v/t* **1.** voraussehen, (-)ahnen. **2.** erwarten, erhoffen. **3.** vorwegnehmen. **4.** *j-m, e-m* Wunsch *etc* zuvorkommen. **5.** ✝ vor Fälligkeit bezahlen *od.* einlösen. **an·tic·i'pa·tion** *s* **1.** (Vor)Ahnung *f*. **2.** Erwartung *f*, Hoffnung *f*: **in ~ of** in Erwartung (*gen*). **3.** Vorwegnahme *f*: **in ~** im voraus. **an·tic·i·pa·to·ry** [~pətərɪ] *adj* □ vorwegnehmend.

an·ti'cler·i·cal *adj* □ antiklerikal, kirchenfeindlich.

an·ti'cli·max *s* **1.** *rhet.* Antiklimax *f*. **2.** *fig.* enttäuschendes Abfallen; Enttäuschung *f*.

an·ti'clock·wise *adj u. adv* entgegen dem *od.* gegen den Uhrzeigersinn.

an·ti·cor'ro·sive *adj* **1.** korrosionsverhütend: ~ **agent** Rostschutzmittel *n*. **2.** rostfest.

an·ti'cy·clone *s meteor.* Hoch(druckgebiet) *n*.

an·ti'daz·zle *adj* Blendschutz...: ~ **switch** Abblendschalter *m*.

an·ti·dote ['æntɪdəʊt] *s* Gegengift *n*, -mittel *n* (*a. fig.*) (**against, for, to** gegen).

an·ti'fas·cist I *s* Antifaschist(in). **II** *adj* antifaschistisch.

'an·ti·freeze *s* Frostschutzmittel *n*.

'an·ti,he·ro *s* Antiheld *m*.

an·ti'knock 🔧, *mot.* **I** *adj* klopffest. **II** *s* Antiklopfmittel *n*.

an·tip·a·thy [æn'tɪpəθɪ] *s* Antipathie *f*, Abneigung *f* (**against, to, towards** gegen).

an·tip·o·des [æn'tɪpədiːz] *s pl* **1.** *die* diametral gegenüberliegenden Teile *pl* der Erde. **2.** (*a. sg* konstruiert) *das* (genaue) Gegenteil.

an·ti·pol'lu·tion *adj* umweltschützend: ~ **device** Abgasentgiftungsanlage *f*.

an·ti·quar·i·an [,æntɪ'kweərɪən] **I** *adj* **1.** antiquarisch. **2.** ~ **bookseller** Antiquar *m*; ~ **bookshop** (*bsd. Am.* **bookstore**) Antiquariat *n*. **II** *s* **3.** → **antiquary 1**. **an·ti·quar·y** ['~kwərɪ] *s* **1.** Altertumskenner(in), -forscher(in). **2.** Antiquitätensammler(in). -händler(in). **an·ti·quat·ed** ['~kweɪtɪd] *adj* antiquiert, veraltet.

an·tique [æn'tiːk] **I** *adj* **1.** antik, alt. **2.** F → **antiquated**. **II** *s* **3.** Antiquität *f*: ~ **dealer** Antiquitätenhändler(in); ~ **shop** (*bsd. Am.* **store**) Antiquitätenladen *m*. **an·tiq·ui·ty** [~'tɪkwətɪ] *s* **1.** Altertum *n*. **2.** *die* Antike. **3.** *pl* Altertümer *pl*.

an·ti'rust *adj* Rostschutz...

an·ti'Sem·ite *s* Antisemit(in). **an·ti-Se'mit·ic** *adj* antisemitisch. **an·ti-Sem·i·tism** [~'semɪtɪzəm] *s* Antisemitismus *m*.

an·ti'sep·tic ✚ **I** *adj* □ antiseptisch. **II** *s* Antiseptikum *n*.

an·ti'so·cial *adj* **1.** asozial, gesellschaftsfeindlich. **2.** ungesellig.

an·tith·e·sis [æn'tɪθɪsɪs] *pl* **-ses** [~siːz] *s* Antithese *f*, Gegensatz *m*. **an·ti'thet·ic, an·ti·thet·i·cal** [~'θetɪk(l)] *adj* □ gegensätzlich.

ant·ler ['æntlə] *s* **1.** (Geweih)Sprosse *f*. **2.** *pl* Geweih *n*.

an·to·nym ['æntəʊnɪm] *s ling.* Antonym *n*.

a·nus ['eɪnəs] *s anat.* After *m*.

an·vil ['ænvɪl] *s* Amboß *m* (*a. anat.*).

anx·i·e·ty [æŋ'zaɪətɪ] *s* **1.** Angst *f*, Sorge *f* (**about, for** wegen, um). **2.** ✚, *psych.* Beklemmung *f*: ~ **dream** Angsttraum *m*. **3.** (starkes) Verlangen (**for** nach).

anx·ious ['æŋkʃəs] *adj* □ **1.** ängstlich; besorgt (**about, for** wegen, um). **2.** *fig.*

(for, to inf) begierig (auf acc, zu inf), (ängstlich) bedacht (auf acc, darauf zu inf), bestrebt (zu inf): **I am very ~ to see him** mir liegt (sehr) viel daran, ihn zu sehen.

an·y ['enɪ] **I** adj **1.** (fragend, verneinend) (irgend)ein(e), einige pl, etwas: **not ~** kein. **2.** (bejahend) jeder, jede, jedes (beliebige): **at ~ time** jederzeit; → **case²**, **rate** 2. **II** adv **3.** irgend(wie), (noch) etwas: **~ more?** noch (etwas) mehr? **'~‚bod·y** pron **1.** (irgend) jemand, irgendeine(r). **2.** jeder(mann): **~ who** jeder, der; wer; **hardly ~** kaum j-d, fast niemand; **not ~** niemand, keiner. **'~‚how** adv **1.** irgendwie. **2.** jedenfalls. **'~‚one** pron → **anybody**. **'~‚thing** pron **1.** (irgend) etwas: **not ~** (gar od. überhaupt) nichts; **not ~** um keinen Preis; **take ~ you like** nimm, was du willst. **2.** alles: **~ but** alles andere als. **'~‚way** adv → **anyhow**. **'~‚where** adv **1.** irgendwo(hin): **not ~** nirgendwo(hin); **hardly ~** fast nirgends. **2.** überall.

a·or·ta [eɪ'ɔːtə] s anat. Aorta f, Hauptschlagader f.

a·part [ə'pɑːt] adv **1.** einzeln, für sich: **live ~** getrennt leben; → **take apart**, **tell** 4. **2.** beiseite: → **joking** II.

a·part·heid [ə'pɑːtheɪt] s pol. Apartheid f.

a·part·ment [ə'pɑːtmənt] s **1.** bsd. Am. Wohnung f. **2.** mst pl Gemach n. **~ ho·tel** s Appartementhotel n. **~ house** s Am. Wohnhaus n.

ap·a·thet·ic [ˌæpə'θetɪk] adj (**~ally**) apathisch, teilnahmslos, gleichgültig. **'ap·a·thy** s Apathie f, Teilnahmslosigkeit f, Gleichgültigkeit f (**to** gegenüber).

ape [eɪp] **I** s zo. (bsd. Menschen)Affe m. **II** v/t nachäffen.

a·pe·ri·ent [ə'pɪərɪənt] ℞, pharm. **I** s Abführmittel n. **II** adj abführend.

ap·er·ture ['æpəˌtjʊə] s **1.** Öffnung f. **2.** phot. Blende f.

a·pex ['eɪpeks] pl **'a·pex·es**, **ap·i·ces** ['eɪpɪsiːz] s **1.** (Kegel-, Lungen- etc-) Spitze f. **2.** fig. Gipfel m, Höhepunkt m.

aph·o·rism ['æfərɪzəm] s Aphorismus m.

ap·i·ces ['eɪpɪsiːz] pl von **apex**.

a·piece [ə'piːs] adv pro Stück; pro Kopf od. Person.

ap·ish ['eɪpɪʃ] adj □ äffisch.

a·poc·a·lypse [ə'pɒkəlɪps] s Enthüllung f, Offenbarung f.

a·pol·o·gize [ə'pɒlədʒaɪz] v/i sich entschuldigen (**for** wegen; **to** bei). **a'pol·o·gy** s **1.** Entschuldigung f: **in ~ for** zur od. als Entschuldigung für; **make** (od. **offer**) **s.o. an ~** sich bei j-m entschuldigen (**for** für). **2.** F minderwertiger Ersatz (**for** für): **an ~ for a meal** ein armseliges Essen.

ap·o·plec·tic [ˌæpəʊ'plektɪk] adj: **~ stroke** (od. **fit**) → **apoplexy**. **ap·o·plex·y** ['æpəpleksɪ] s ℞ Schlaganfall m, Gehirnschlag m.

a·pos·tle [ə'pɒsl] s eccl. Apostel m.

a·pos·tro·phe [ə'pɒstrəfɪ] s ling. **1.** Apostroph m, Auslassungszeichen n. **a'pos·tro·phize** v/t apostrophieren.

ap·pal [ə'pɔːl] v/t erschrecken, entsetzen: **be ~ed** entsetzt sein (**at** über acc). **ap'pal·ling** adj □ erschreckend, entsetzlich.

ap·pa·ra·tus [ˌæpə'reɪtəs] pl **-tus**, **-tus·es** s Apparat m, Gerät n, Vorrichtung f.

ap·par·el [ə'pærəl] s Kleidung f.

ap·par·ent [ə'pærənt] adj □ **1.** augenscheinlich, offenbar, -sichtlich: **be ~ from** hervorgehen aus; **with no ~ reason** ohne ersichtlichen Grund. **2.** anscheinend; scheinbar.

ap·pa·ri·tion [ˌæpə'rɪʃn] s Erscheinung f, Gespenst n, Geist m.

ap·peal [ə'piːl] **I** v/i **1.** ⚖ Berufung od. Revision einlegen, a. allg. Einspruch erheben, Beschwerde einlegen (**against**, ⚖ mst **from** gegen; **to** bei). **2.** appellieren, sich wenden (**to** an acc). **3.** sich berufen (**to** auf acc). **4.** (**to**) Anklang finden (bei), gefallen, zusagen (dat), reizen (acc). **5.** ~ **to** j-n dringend bitten (**for** um). **II** s **6.** ⚖ Berufung f, Revision f: **file** (od. **lodge**) **an ~** → 1. **7.** Appell m (**to** an acc). **8.** Berufung f (**to** auf acc). **9.** dringende Bitte (**to** an acc; **for** um). **10.** (**to**) Anziehung(skraft) f, Zugkraft f, Wirkung f (auf acc), Anklang m (bei). **ap'peal·ing** adj □ **1.** bittend, flehend. **2.** reizvoll, gefällig, ansprechend.

ap·pear [ə'pɪə] v/i **1.** erscheinen (a. vor Gericht), (von Büchern etc a.) herauskommen: **~ in public** sich in der Öffentlichkeit zeigen; **~ on television** im

Fernsehen auftreten. **2.** scheinen, aussehen, *j-m* vorkommen: *it ~s to me you are right* mir scheint; *he ~ed calm* er war äußerlich ruhig. **ap'pear·ance** *s* **1.** Erscheinen *n*: *public ~* Auftreten *n* in der Öffentlichkeit; *make an ~ on television* im Fernsehen auftreten. **2.** (äußere) Erscheinung, Aussehen *n*, *das* Äußere: *have an unhealthy ~* ungesund aussehen. **3.** *mst pl* (An)Schein *m*: *to all ~(s)* allem Anschein nach; *there is every ~ that* es hat ganz den Anschein, als ob; *~s are deceptive* der Schein trügt; *keep up (od. save) ~s* den Schein wahren.

ap·pease [ə'pi:z] *v/t* besänftigen, beschwichtigen; *Durst etc* stillen, *Neugier* befriedigen. **ap'pease·ment** *s* Besänftigung *f*, Beschwichtigung *f*: *(policy of) ~* Beschwichtigungspolitik *f*.

ap·pend [ə'pend] *v/t* (*to*) **1.** befestigen, anbringen (an *dat*), anheften (an *acc*). **2.** bei-, hinzufügen (*dat*). **ap'pend·age** *s* Anhang *m*; Anhängsel *n*. **ap·pen·dec·to·my** [ˌæpen'dektəmɪ] *s* ✚ Blinddarmoperation *f*. **ap·pen·di·ci·tis** [əˌpendɪ'saɪtɪs] *s* ✚ Blinddarmentzündung *f*. **ap·pen·dix** [ə'pendɪks] *pl* **-dix·es, -di·ces** [ˌdɪsiːz] *s* **1.** Anhang *m* (*e-s Buchs*). **2.** (*vermiform*) *~* *anat.* Wurmfortsatz *m*, Blinddarm *m*.

ap·per·tain [ˌæpə'teɪn] *v/i* gehören (*to* zu).

ap·pe·tite ['æpɪtaɪt] *s* **1.** Appetit *m* (*for* auf *acc*): *give s.o. an ~* j-m Appetit machen; *have an ~* Appetit haben; *take away (od. spoil) s.o.'s ~* j-m den Appetit nehmen *od.* verderben. **2.** (*for*) Verlangen *n* (nach), Lust *f* (zu). **ap·pe·tiz·er** ['~taɪzə] *s* appetitanregendes Mittel *od.* Getränk *od.* Gericht. **'ap·pe·tiz·ing** *adj* ☐ appetitanregend; appetitlich, lecker (*beide a. fig.*).

ap·plaud [ə'plɔːd] *v/i u. v/t* applaudieren (*dat*), Beifall spenden (*dat*). **ap·plause** [ə'plɔːz] *s* Applaus *m*, Beifall *m*.

ap·ple ['æpl] *s* Apfel *m*: *~ of discord fig.* Zankapfel *m*; *the ~ of s.o.'s eye fig.* j-s Liebling. **'~cart** *s* Apfelkarren *m*: *upset s.o.'s ~ fig.* j-s Pläne über den Haufen werfen. **'~jack** *s Am.* Apfelschnaps *m*. **~ pie** *s* gedeckter Apfelkuchen. **'~·pie or·der** *s*: *in ~* F in Butter, in bester Ordnung. **'~·pol·ish** *v/i Am.* F

radfahren. **~ pol·ish·er** *s Am.* F Radfahrer *m*, Speichellecker *m*. **'~sauce** *s* **1.** Apfelmus *n*. **2.** *Am. sl.* Schmus *m*; Quatsch *m*. **~ tree** *s* Apfelbaum *m*.

ap·pli·ance [ə'plaɪəns] *s* Gerät *n*; *engS.* (elektrisches) Haushaltsgerät.

ap·pli·ca·ble ['æplɪkəbl] *adj* ☐ (*to*) anwendbar (auf *acc*), passend (für): *be ~ (to)* → *apply* 4; *not ~* (*in Formularen*) entfällt. **'ap·pli·cant** *s* Bewerber(in) (*for* um); Antragsteller(in). **ˌap·pli·ca·tion** *s* **1.** (*to*) Anwendung *f* (auf *acc*); Anwendbarkeit *f* (auf *acc*): *have no ~ (to)* nicht zutreffen (auf *acc*), in keinem Zs.-hang stehen (mit). **2.** (*for*) Gesuch *n* (um), Antrag *m* (auf *acc*): *on ~* auf Ersuchen *od.* Verlangen *od.* Wunsch. **3.** Bewerbung *f* (*for* um): *(letter of) ~* Bewerbungsschreiben *n*.

ap·plied [ə'plaɪd] *adj* angewandt: *~ linguistics (psychology, etc)*.

ap·ply [ə'plaɪ] **I** *v/t* **1.** (*to*) auflegen, -tragen (auf *acc*), anbringen (an, auf *dat*). **2.** (*to*) verwenden (auf *acc*, für); anwenden (auf *acc*); betätigen: *~ the brakes* bremsen. **3.** *~ one's mind to* sich beschäftigen mit; *~ o.s. to* sich widmen (*dat*). **II** *v/i* **4.** (*to*) zutreffen (auf *acc*), gelten (für). **5.** (*for*) beantragen (*acc*), nachsuchen (um). **6.** sich bewerben (*for* um).

ap·point [ə'pɔɪnt] *v/t* **1.** ernennen *od.* berufen zu: *~ s.o. as one's heir* j-n als Erben einsetzen. **2.** festsetzen, bestimmen. **3.** ausstatten, einrichten (*with* mit). **ap'point·ment** *s* **1.** Ernennung *f*, Berufung *f*. Amt *n*, Stellung *f*: *hold an ~* e-e Stelle innehaben. **3.** Festsetzung *f*, Bestimmung *f*. **4.** Verabredung *f*, (*geschäftlich, beim Arzt etc*) Termin *m*: *by ~* nach Verabredung; *make an ~* e-e Verabredung treffen, e-n Termin ausmachen; *~ book* Terminkalender *m*. **5.** *mst pl* Ausstattung *f*, Einrichtung *f*.

ap·por·tion [ə'pɔː∫n] *v/t* **1.** zuteilen (*to* dat). **2.** (proportional *od.* gerecht) verteilen; *Kosten* umlegen.

ap·po·site ['æpəʊzɪt] *adj* ☐ passend, angemessen, (*Antwort etc*) treffend.

ap·po·si·tion [ˌæpəʊ'zɪ∫n] *s* Beifügung *f*, *ling. a.* Apposition *f*.

ap·prais·al [ə'preɪzl] *s* (Ab)Schätzung *f*, Taxierung *f*. **ap'praise** *v/t* (ab)schätzen, taxieren: *~d value* Schätzwert *m*.

ap·pre·ci·a·ble [əˈpriːʃəbl] *adj* □ merklich, spürbar. **ap'pre·ci·ate** [~ʃıeıt] **I** *v/t* **1.** (hoch)schätzen, würdigen, zu schätzen *od.* zu würdigen wissen. **2.** Gefallen finden an (*dat*); Sinn haben für. **3.** dankbar sein für. **4.** (richtig) beurteilen *od.* einschätzen. **II** *v/i* **5.** im Wert steigen. **ap,pre·ci'a·tion** *s* **1.** Würdigung *f*. **2.** Sinn *m* (*of, for* für). **3.** Dankbarkeit *f* (*of* für). **4.** (richtige) Beurteilung. **ap·pre·ci·a·tive** [əˈpriːʃjətıv] *adj* □ würdigend: *be ~ of → appreciate* I.

ap·pre·hend [ˌæprıˈhend] *v/t* **1.** festnehmen, verhaften. **2.** *fig.* begreifen, erfassen. **3.** *fig.* (be)fürchten. **ˌap·pre'hen·sion** *s* **1.** Festnahme *f*, Verhaftung *f*. **2.** *fig.* Begreifen *n*, Erfassen *n*; Fassungskraft *f*. **3.** *fig.* Besorgnis *f*, *oft pl* Befürchtung *f*. **ˌap·pre'hen·sive** *adj* □ besorgt (*for* um; *that* daß): *be ~* Bedenken hegen.

ap·pren·tice [əˈprentıs] **I** *s* Auszubildende *m*, *f*, Lehrling *m*. **II** *v/t* in die Lehre geben (*to* bei, zu): *be ~d to* in die Lehre sein bei. **ap'pren·tice·ship** *s* Lehrzeit *f*; Lehre *f*.

ap·pro [ˈæprəʊ] *s*: *on ~* ✝ F zur Ansicht, zur Probe.

ap·proach [əˈprəʊtʃ] **I** *v/i* **1.** sich nähern, (heran)nahen. **II** *v/t* **2.** sich nähern (*dat*). **3.** *fig.* nahekommen (*dat*), (fast) erreichen. **4.** herangehen an (*acc*), *Aufgabe etc* anpacken. **5.** an *j-n* herantreten, sich an *j-n* wenden; *bsd. b.s.* sich an *j-n* heranmachen. **III** *s* **6.** (Heran)Nahen *n*, Annäherung *f* (*a. fig.* an *acc*), ✈ Anflug *m*. **7.** Zugang *m*: *~ (road)* Zufahrtsstraße *f*. **8.** *fig.* (*to*) erster Schritt (zu), (erster) Versuch (*gen*). **9.** Herantreten *n* (*to* an *acc*), *mst pl* Annäherungsversuch *m*: *make ~es to → approach* 5. **10.** Methode *f*, Verfahren *n*; Einstellung *f* (*to* zu); Behandlung *f* (*to* e-s *Themas etc*). **ap'proach·a·ble** *adj* zugänglich (*a. fig.*).

ap·pro·ba·tion [ˌæprəʊˈbeıʃn] *s* (amtliche) Billigung, Genehmigung *f*.

ap·pro·pri·ate I *adj* [əˈprəʊprııt] **1.** (*to, for*) passend (zu), geeignet (für). **II** *v/t* [~eıt] **2.** *bsd. parl.* Geld bewilligen, bereitstellen. **3.** sich *et.* aneignen. **ap,pro·pri'a·tion** [~prıˈeıʃn] *s* **1.** Bewilligung *f*, Bereitstellung *f*. **2.** Aneignung *f*.

ap·prov·al [əˈpruːvl] *s* **1.** Billigung *f*, Genehmigung *f*: *on ~* ✝ zur Ansicht, zur Probe. **2.** Anerkennung *f*, Beifall *m*: *meet with ~* Beifall finden. **ap'prove I** *v/t* billigen, genehmigen. **II** *v/i* (*of*) billigen, genehmigen (*acc*), einverstanden sein (mit), zustimmen (*dat*).

ap·prox·i·mate I *adj* [əˈprɒksımət] □ annähernd, ungefähr: *~ value* Näherungswert *m*. **II** *v/t* [~meıt] sich (e-*m Wert etc*) nähern. **III** *v/i* [~meıt] sich nähern (*to* *dat*). **ap,prox·i'ma·tion** [~ˈmeıʃn] *s* Annäherung *f* (*to* an *acc*).

ap·pur·te·nance [əˈpɜːtınəns] *s mst pl* Zubehör *n*, Ausrüstung *f*.

a·pri·cot [ˈeıprıkɒt] *s* Aprikose *f*.

A·pril [ˈeıprəl] *s* April *m*: *in ~* im April; *make an ~ fool of s.o.* j-n in den April schicken.

a·pron [ˈeıprən] *s* **1.** Schürze *f*. **2.** ✈ (Hallen)Vorfeld *n*. **3.** *thea.* Vorbühne *f*. *~ strings s pl* Schürzenbänder *pl*: *be tied to one's mother's (wife's) ~ fig.* an Mutters Schürzenzipfel hängen (unter dem Pantoffel stehen).

apt [æpt] *adj* □ **1.** passend, geeignet. **2.** treffend (*Bemerkung etc*). **3.** neigend, geneigt (*to do* zu tun): *he is ~ to believe it* er wird es wahrscheinlich glauben; *~ to be overlooked* leicht zu übersehen. **4.** (*at*) geschickt (in *dat*), begabt (für). **ap·ti·tude** [ˈæptıtjuːd] *s* **1.** (*for*) Begabung *f* (für), Geschick *n* (in *dat*): *~ test* Eignungsprüfung *f*. **2.** Neigung *f*, Hang *m* (*for* zu). **3.** Auffassungsgabe *f*.

aq·ua·ma·rine [ˌækwəməˈriːn] *s* **1.** *min.* Aquamarin *m*. **2.** Aquamarinblau *n*.

aq·ua·plan·ing [ˈækwəˌpleınıŋ] *s mot.* Aquaplaning *n*.

aq·ua·relle [ˌækwəˈrel] *s* **1.** Aquarell *n*. **2.** Aquarellmalerei *f*. **ˌaq·ua'rel·list** *s* Aquarellmaler(in).

a·quar·i·um [əˈkweərıəm] *pl* **-i·ums**, **-i·a** [~ıə] *s* Aquarium *n*.

A·quar·i·us [əˈkweərıəs] *s ast.* Wassermann *m*: *be (an) ~* Wassermann sein.

a·quat·ic [əˈkwætık] *adj* Wasser...: *~ plants*; *~ sports pl* Wassersport *m*.

aq·ue·duct [ˈækwıdʌkt] *s* Aquädukt *m*, *a. n*.

a·que·ous [ˈeıkwıəs] *adj* wäßrig, wässerig.

aq·ui·cul·ture [ˈækwıˌkʌltʃə] *s* Hydrokultur *f*.

aq·ui·line ['ækwɪlaɪn] adj Adler..., weitS. a. gebogen: ~ nose Adlernase f.

Ar·ab ['ærəb] **I** s **1.** Araber(in). **2.** zo. Araber m (Pferd). **II** adj **3.** arabisch.

ar·a·besque [͵~'besk] s Arabeske f.

A·ra·bi·an [ə'reɪbjən] **I** adj arabisch: The ~ Nights Tausendundeine Nacht. **II** s → Arab I. **Ar·a·bic** ['ærəbɪk] **I** adj arabisch: ~ numeral arabische Ziffer. **II** s ling. Arabisch n.

ar·a·ble ['ærəbl] adj pflügbar, anbaufähig: ~ land Ackerland n.

ar·bi·ter ['ɑːbɪtə] s **1.** Schiedsrichter m. **2.** Gebieter m (of über acc): be the ~ of fashion die Mode bestimmen od. diktieren. **'ar·bi·tra·ry** adj □ willkürlich: a) beliebig (a. ℞), b) eigenmächtig. **ar·bi·trate** ['͵treɪt] **I** v/t (als Schiedsrichter) entscheiden, schlichten. **II** v/i als Schiedsrichter fungieren. **͵ar·bi·tra·tion** s **1.** Schieds(gerichts)verfahren n. **2.** Schiedsspruch m; Schlichtung f: court of ~ Schiedsgericht n.

ar·bo(u)r ['ɑːbə] s Laube f.

arc [ɑːk] s Bogen m, ℞ a. Arkus m, ∮ a. Lichtbogen.

ar·cade [ɑː'keɪd] s Arkade f, Bogen-, Laubengang m.

arch¹ [ɑːtʃ] **I** s **1.** △ Bogen m. **2.** △ überwölbter Gang, Gewölbe n. **3.** Bogen m, Wölbung f: ~ support Senkfußeinlage f. **II** v/t **4.** a. ~ over überwölben. **5.** wölben, krümmen: ~ one's back e-n Buckel machen (bsd. Katze). **III** v/i **6.** sich wölben.

arch² [͵~] adj □ schalkhaft, schelmisch, spitzbübisch.

arch³ [͵~] adj Erz...

ar·chae·o·log·i·cal [͵ɑːkɪə'lɒdʒɪkl] adj □ bsd. Br. archäologisch. **ar·chae·ol·o·gist** [͵~'ɒlədʒɪst] s bsd. Br. Archäologe m. **͵ar·chae'ol·o·gy** s bsd. Br. Archäologie f.

ar·cha·ic [ɑː'keɪɪk] adj (͵ally) archaisch: a) altertümlich, b) ling. veraltet.

arch·an·gel ['ɑːk͵eɪndʒəl] s Erzengel m. **͵arch'bish·op** s Erzbischof m. **͵arch'bish·op·ric** [͵rɪk] s Erzbistum n. **͵arch'duch·ess** s Erzherzogin f. **͵arch'duch·y** s Erzherzogtum n. **͵arch'duke** s Erzherzog m.

ar·che·o·log·i·cal, etc Am. → archaeological, etc.

arch·er ['ɑːtʃə] s **1.** Bogenschütze m. **2.** ℞

ast. Schütze m: be (an) ℞ Schütze sein. **'arch·er·y** s Bogenschießen n.

ar·che·type ['ɑːkɪtaɪp] s Archetyp(us) m, Urform f.

ar·chi·pel·a·go [͵ɑːkɪ'pelɪgəʊ] pl **-go(e)s** s Archipel m, Inselgruppe f.

ar·chi·tect ['ɑːkɪtekt] s **1.** Architekt(in). **2.** fig. Urheber(in), Schöpfer(in). **͵ar·chi'tec·tu·ral** [͵tʃərəl] adj □ architektonisch, Bau..., baulich. **'ar·chi·tec·ture** s Architektur f, a. Baustil m.

ar·chive ['ɑːkaɪv] s mst pl Archiv n. **ar·chi·vist** ['ɑːkɪvɪst] s Archivar(in).

'arch·way s △ **1.** Bogengang m. **2.** Bogen m (über e-m Tor etc).

arc·tic ['ɑːktɪk] **I** adj arktisch, nördlich, Polar...: ℞ Circle nördlicher Polarkreis; ℞ Ocean Nördliches Eismeer. **II** s Arktis f.

ar·dent ['ɑːdənt] adj □ fig. **1.** heiß, feurig, glühend. **2.** leidenschaftlich, heftig. **3.** eifrig, begeistert. **ar·do(u)r** ['ɑːdə] s **1.** Leidenschaft f, Glut f, Feuer n. **2.** Eifer m, Begeisterung f.

ar·du·ous ['ɑːdjʊəs] adj □ schwierig, mühsam, anstrengend.

are [ɑː] du bist, wir (od. sie od. Sie) sind, ihr seid.

a·re·a ['eərɪə] s **1.** (Boden-, Grund)Fläche f. **2.** Gebiet n (a. fig.), Gegend f: ~ code teleph. Am. Vorwahl(nummer) f. **3.** fig. Bereich m.

a·re·na [ə'riːnə] s Arena f, fig. a. Schauplatz m.

aren't [ɑːnt] F für are not.

Ar·gen·tine ['ɑːdʒəntaɪn], **Ar·gen·tin·e·an** [͵~'tɪnɪən] **I** adj argentinisch. **II** s Argentinier(in).

ar·gu·a·ble ['ɑːgjʊəbl] adj □ **1.** zweifelhaft, fraglich. **2.** it is ~ that man kann durchaus die Meinung vertreten, daß. **ar·gue** ['ɑːgjuː] **I** v/i **1.** argumentieren: ~ for eintreten für; sprechen für (Sache); ~ against Einwände machen gegen; sprechen gegen (Sache). **2.** streiten (with mit; about über acc): don't ~! keine Widerrede! **II** v/t **3.** erörtern, diskutieren. **4.** behaupten (that daß). **5.** j-n überreden (into zu): ~ s.o. out of s.th. j-n von et. abbringen.

ar·gu·ment ['ɑːgjəmənt] s **1.** Argument n. **2.** Erörterung f, Diskussion f. **3.** Streitfrage f. **4.** Wortwechsel m, Auseinandersetzung f. **ar·gu·men·ta·tion**

[ˌɑːmenˈteɪʃn] s 1. Argumentation f, Beweisführung f. 2. → **argument** 2.
ar·gu·men·ta·tive [ˌɑːˈmentətɪv] adj □ 1. streitlustig. 2. streitig, umstritten.
a·ri·a [ˈɑːrɪə] s ♪ Arie f.
ar·id [ˈærɪd] adj dürr, trocken (a. fig.). **a'rid·i·ty** s Dürre f, Trockenheit f.
Ar·ies [ˈeəriːz] s ast. Widder m: **be (an)** ~ Widder sein.
a·rise [əˈraɪz] v/i (irr) 1. (**from, out of**) entstehen, hervorgehen (aus), herrühren, stammen (von). 2. entstehen, sich erheben, auftauchen. **a·ris·en** [əˈrɪzn] pp von **arise**.
ar·is·toc·ra·cy [ˌærɪˈstɒkrəsɪ] s Aristokratie f. **a·ris·to·crat** [ˈærɪstəkræt] s Aristokrat(in). **a·ris·to'crat·ic**, **a·ris·to·'crat·i·cal** adj □ aristokratisch.
a·rith·me·tic [əˈrɪθmətɪk] s Arithmetik f, Rechnen n.
ar·ith·met·ic, **ar·ith·met·i·cal** [ˌærɪθˈmetɪk(l)] adj □ arithmetisch, Rechen...
ark [ɑːk] s: **Noah's** ~ Bibl. die Arche Noah.
arm¹ [ɑːm] s 1. Arm m (a. ⊚ u. fig.): **with open** ~s mit offenen Armen; **within** ~**'s reach** in Reichweite; **the** ~ **of the law** der Arm des Gesetzes; **keep s.o. at** ~**'s length** sich j-n vom Leibe halten; **take s.o. in one's** ~s j-n in die Arme nehmen. 2. Fluß-, Meeresarm m. 3. Ast m. 4. Arm-, Seitenlehne f (e-s Stuhls etc). 5. Ärmel m.
arm² [~] I s 1. mst pl Waffe f (a. fig.): **up in** ~s kampfbereit; fig. in hellem Zorn (**about, over** wegen); **take up** ~s zu den Waffen greifen; ~s **control** Rüstungskontrolle f; ~s **dealer** Waffenhändler m; ~s **race** Wettrüsten n, Rüstungswettlauf m. 2. ✕ Waffen-, Truppengattung f. 3. pl Wappen(schild) n. II v/t 4. bewaffnen. 5. ~ o.s. fig. sich wappnen (**with** mit).
ar·ma·da [ɑːˈmɑːdə] s (hist. ⒉) Armada f.
ar·ma·ment [ˈɑːməmənt] s 1. Kriegsstärke f. 2. Bewaffnung f. 3. Rüstung f: ~ **race** Wettrüsten n, Rüstungswettlauf m. **ar·ma·ture** [~ˌtjʊə] s ⚓ Anker m.
'arm·chair s Lehnstuhl m: ~ **politician** Stammtischpolitiker m.
armed [ɑːmd] adj bewaffnet (**to the teeth** bis an die Zähne): ~ **conflict** bewaffnete Auseinandersetzung; ~ **forces**

pl Streitkräfte pl; ~ **robbery** bewaffneter Raubüberfall.
...-armed [ɑːmd] ...armig, mit ... Armen.
arm·ful [ˈɑːmfʊl] s Armvoll m.
ar·mi·stice [ˈɑːmɪstɪs] s Waffenstillstand m.
ar·mor, etc Am. → **armour**, etc.
ar·mo·ri·al [ɑːˈmɔːrɪəl] adj Wappen...
ar·mour [ˈɑːmə] bsd. Br. I s 1. Rüstung f, Panzer m (a. zo.). 2. ✕ Panzer(fahrzeuge) pl; Panzertruppen pl. II v/t 3. panzern: ~ed car ✕ Panzerkampfwagen m; gepanzertes Fahrzeug (für Geldtransporte etc). '~-clad, '~-plat·ed adj bsd. Br. gepanzert, Panzer...
ar·mour·y [ˈɑːmərɪ] s bsd. Br. Waffenfabrik f.
'arm·pit s Achselhöhle f. '~-rest s Armlehne f.
ar·my [ˈɑːmɪ] s Armee f, Heer n (a. fig.): **be in the** ~ beim Militär sein; **join the** ~ Soldat werden.
a·ro·ma [əˈrəʊmə] s Aroma n. **ar·o·mat·ic** [ˌærəʊˈmætɪk] adj (~**ally**) aromatisch.
a·rose [əˈrəʊz] pret von **arise**.
a·round [əˈraʊnd] I adv 1. (rings)herum, überall(hin), nach od. auf allen Seiten. 2. umher, (in der Gegend) herum: **look** ~ sich umsehen; zurückschauen. 3. F in der Nähe, da. II prp 4. um (... herum), rund um. 5. in (dat) ... herum. 6. F ungefähr, etwa. 7. F (nahe) bei.
a·rouse [əˈraʊz] v/t 1. (auf)wecken. 2. fig. auf-, wachrütteln, Gefühle etc wachrufen, erregen.
ar·range [əˈreɪndʒ] I v/t 1. (an)ordnen, aufstellen; Angelegenheiten ordnen, regeln. 2. festsetzen, -legen. 3. in die Wege leiten, arrangieren. 4. verabreden, vereinbaren. 5. Streit schlichten, beilegen. 6. ♪ arrangieren, a. thea. etc bearbeiten. II v/i 7. sich verständigen (**with** mit; **about** über acc). 8. Vorkehrungen treffen (**for, about** für; **to** inf zu inf): ~ **for s.th. to be there** dafür sorgen, daß et. da ist. **ar'range·ment** s 1. (An)Ordnung f. 2. Festsetzung f. 3. Verabredung f, Vereinbarung f: **make an** ~ e-e Verabredung treffen (**with** mit). 4. Schlichtung f, Beilegung f. 5. ♪ Arrangement n, a. thea. etc Bearbeitung f. 6. pl Vorkehrungen pl: **make** ~s Vorkehrungen treffen.

ar·ray [əˈreɪ] **I** v/t **1.** *Truppen etc* aufstellen. **2.** (**o.s.** sich) kleiden, (heraus)putzen. **II** s **3.** ⚔ Schlachtordnung f. **4.** *fig.* Phalanx f, (stattliche) Reihe. **5.** Kleidung f, Staat m.

ar·rear [əˈrɪə] s *mst pl* Rückstand m, -stände *pl:* **~s of rent** rückständige Miete; **~s of work** Arbeitsrückstände; **be in ~s** im Rückstand od. Verzug sein (**for,** *in* mit).

ar·rest [əˈrest] **I** s **1.** Verhaftung f, Festnahme f; Haft f: **be under ~** verhaftet sein; **in Haft sein;** → **warrant** 2. **II** v/t **2.** an-, aufhalten, hemmen. **3.** *Aufmerksamkeit etc* fesseln. **4.** verhaften, festnehmen.

ar·ri·val [əˈraɪvl] s **1.** Ankunft f: '**~s**' *pl* 'Ankunft' (*Fahrplan etc*). **2.** Erscheinen n, Auftauchen n. **3.** Ankömmling m: **new ~** Neuankömmling, F *a.* Familienzuwachs m. **ar·rive** [əˈraɪv] v/i **1.** (an)kommen, eintreffen. **2.** erscheinen, auftauchen. **3.** *fig.* (**at**) erreichen (*acc*), kommen od. gelangen (zu).

ar·ro·gance [ˈærəgəns] s Arroganz f, Überheblichkeit f. '**ar·ro·gant** *adj* □ arrogant, überheblich.

ar·row [ˈærəʊ] s Pfeil m. '**~·head** s Pfeilspitze f.

arse [ɑːs] s *Br.* V Arsch m (*a. fig. contp.*). '**~·hole** s *Br.* V Arschloch n (*a. fig. contp.*).

ar·se·nal [ˈɑːsənl] s **1.** Arsenal n (*a. fig.*). **2.** Waffen-, Munitionsfabrik f.

ar·se·nic [ˈɑːsnɪk] s ⚗ Arsen n.

ar·son [ˈɑːsn] s ⚖ Brandstiftung f.

art [ɑːt] **I** s **1.** (*bsd.* bildende) Kunst: **work of ~** Kunstwerk n; → **fine**¹ 1. **2.** Kunst(fertigkeit) f: **the ~ of cooking** die hohe Schule des Kochens; **~s and crafts** *pl* Kunstgewerbe n. **3.** *pl univ.* Geisteswissenschaften *pl:* **Faculty of ~s**, *Am.* ~s **Department** philosophische Fakultät; → **bachelor** 2, **master** 5. **4.** *mst pl* Kniff m, Trick m. **II** *adj* Kunst...: **~ critic**, **~ gallery** Gemäldegalerie f.

ar·te·ri·al [ɑːˈtɪərɪəl] *adj* **1.** *anat.* arteriell, Arterien... **2.** ~ **road**, *Am. a.* ~ **highway** Hauptverkehrsstraße f. **ar·te·ri·o·scle·ro·sis** [ɑːˌtɪərɪəʊsklɪəˈrəʊsɪs] s ⚕ Arteriosklerose f, Arterienverkalkung f. **ar·ter·y** [ˈɑːtərɪ] s **1.** *anat.* Arterie f, Schlagader f. **2.**

fig. (Haupt)Verkehrsader f.

ar·te·sian well [ɑːˈtiːzjən] s Artesischer Brunnen m.

art·ful [ˈɑːtfʊl] *adj* □ schlau, listig.

ar·thrit·ic [ɑːˈθrɪtɪk] *adj* ⚕ arthritisch. **ar·thri·tis** [ɑːˈθraɪtɪs] s Arthritis f, Gelenkentzündung f.

ar·ti·choke [ˈɑːtɪtʃəʊk] s ♣ Artischocke f.

ar·ti·cle [ˈɑːtɪkl] **I** s **1.** (*Zeitungs- etc*)Artikel m. **2.** Artikel m, Gegenstand m. **3.** *ling.* Artikel m, Geschlechtswort n. **4.** Artikel m, Paragraph m, Abschnitt m (*e-s Gesetzes etc*); Punkt m, Klausel f (*e-s Vertrags etc*): **~s** *pl* **of apprenticeship** Lehrvertrag m; **~s** *pl* **of association** (*Am.* **incorporation**) Satzung f (*e-r Aktiengesellschaft*). **II** v/t **5.** in die Lehre geben (**to** bei, zu): **be ~d to** in der Lehre sein bei.

ar·tic·u·late I v/t [ɑːˈtɪkjʊleɪt] **1.** artikulieren, deutlich (aus)sprechen. **2.** äußern; zur Sprache bringen. **3.** ⚙ durch Gelenke verbinden. **II** *adj* [~lət] □ **4.** deutlich ausgesprochen, verständlich (*Wörter etc*). **5.** fähig, sich klar auszudrücken. **ar'tic·u·lat·ed** [~leɪtɪd] *adj* ⚙ Gelenk...: **~ lorry** *mot. Br.* Sattelschlepper m. **ar.tic·u·la·tion** s **1.** Artikulation f, deutliche Aussprache. **2.** ⚙ Gelenk(verbindung) f.

ar·ti·fice [ˈɑːtɪfɪs] s **1.** List f. **2.** Kunstgriff m, Kniff m. **ar·ti·fi·cial** [~ˈfɪʃl] *adj* □ Kunst..., künstlich: **~ flower** (**insemination**, **respiration**, *etc*) künstliche Blume (Befruchtung, Beatmung *etc*); **~ person** juristische Person; **~ silk** Kunstseide f; **~ tears** *pl* falsche Tränen *pl*.

ar·til·ler·y [ɑːˈtɪlərɪ] s Artillerie f. **ar'til·ler·y·man** [~mən] s (*irr* **man**) Artillerist m.

ar·ti·san [ˌɑːtɪˈzæn] s (Kunst)Handwerker m.

art·ist [ˈɑːtɪst] s, **art·iste** [ɑːˈtiːst] s Künstler(in), *weitS. a.* Könner(in). **ar·tis·tic**, **ar·tis·ti·cal** [ɑːˈtɪstɪk(l)] *adj* □ **1.** künstlerisch, Künstler..., Kunst... **2.** kunstverständig.

art·less [ˈɑːtlɪs] *adj* □ **1.** aufrichtig, arglos. **2.** naiv.

art·y [ˈɑːtɪ] *adj* F künstlerisch aufgemacht. **,~(-and)-'craft·y** *adj* F gewollt künstlerisch.

Ar·y·an ['eəriən] **I** *adj* arisch. **II** *s* Arier(in).

as [æz] **I** *adv* **1.** (eben-, gerade)so: *I ran ~ fast ~ I could* so schnell ich konnte; *just ~ good* ebenso gut; *twice ~ large* zweimal so groß; *~ well* ebenfalls, auch; → *much* 2. **2.** wie (z. B.): *statesmen, ~ Churchill.* **II** *cj* **3.** (so) wie: *~ follows* wie folgt; *~ requested* wunschgemäß; *~ ... ~* (eben)so ... wie; *(~) soft ~ butter* butterweich; *(~) happy ~ can be* überglücklich; *~ far ~ I know* soviel ich weiß; *~ it were* sozusagen, gleichsam; → *good* 5, *long*¹⁷, *soon*, *though* 3, *word* 1. **4.** als, während: *~ he entered* als er eintrat, bei s-m Eintritt. **5.** da, weil: *~ you are sorry, I'll forgive you.* **6.** *~ for* (*od. to*) was ... (an)betrifft; *~ from* (*vor Zeitangaben*) von ... an, ab; → *against* 4, *per* 3, *yet* 2. **III** *pron* **7.** was, wie: *~ he himself admits.* **IV** *prp* **8.** als: *appear ~ Hamlet* als Hamlet auftreten.

as·bes·tos [æs'bestɒs] *s* Asbest *m*.

as·cend [ə'send] **I** *v/i* **1.** (auf)steigen. **2.** ansteigen. **II** *v/t* **3.** *a. fig.* den Thron besteigen. **as'cend·an·cy** *s* Übergewicht *n*, Überlegenheit *f* (*over* über *acc*). **as'cend·ant I** *s* **1.** *ast.* Aszendent *m*, Aufgangspunkt *m*: *in the ~ fig.* im Aufstieg *od.* Kommen. **II** *adj* **2.** (auf)steigend. **3.** überlegen (*over dat*). **as'cend·en·cy**, **as'cend·ent** → **ascendancy, ascendant.**

as·cen·sion [ə'senʃn] *s* **1.** Aufsteigen *n*. **2.** *the* ♀ Christi Himmelfahrt *f*; ♀ *Day* Himmelfahrtstag *m*.

as·cent [ə'sent] *s* **1.** Aufstieg *m*. **2.** Besteigung *f*. **3.** Steigung *f*, Gefälle *n*.

as·cer·tain [ˌæsə'teɪn] *v/t* ermitteln, feststellen, in Erfahrung bringen. **ˌas·cer'tain·a·ble** *adj* feststellbar. **ˌas·cer'tain·ment** *s* Ermittlung *f*, Feststellung *f*.

as·cet·ic [ə'setɪk] **I** *adj* (*~ally*) asketisch. **II** *s* Asket(in). **as'cet·i·cism** [~tɪsɪzəm] *s* Askese *f*.

as·cor·bic ac·id [ə'skɔːbɪk] *s* 🧪 Ascorbinsäure *f*, Vitamin *n* C.

as·crib·a·ble [ə'skraɪbəbl] *adj* zuzuschreiben(d). **as'cribe** *v/t* (*to*) **1.** zurückführen (auf *acc*), zuschreiben (*dat*). **2.** zuschreiben, beimessen (*dat*).

a·sep·tic [ˌeɪ'septɪk] *adj* (*~ally*) aseptisch, keimfrei.

a·sex·u·al [ˌeɪ'seksjʊəl] *adj* □ *biol.* geschlechtslos.

ash¹ [æʃ] *s* **1.** 🌿 Esche *f*. **2.** Eschenholz *n*.

ash² [~] *s* **1.** *mst pl* Asche *f*: *burn to* (*od. lay in*) *~es* einäschern, niederbrennen. **2.** *pl* Asche *f*, (sterbliche) Überreste *pl*.

a·shamed [ə'feɪmd] *adj* beschämt: *be* (*od. feel*) *~ of* sich e-r *Sache od. j-s* schämen; *be ~ of o.s.* sich schämen; *be* (*od. feel*) *~ to do* (*od. of doing*) *s.th.* sich schämen, et. zu tun.

ash| bin, ~ can *s Am.* **1.** Abfall-, Mülleimer *m.* **2.** Abfall-, Mülltonne *f.*

ash·en¹ ['æʃn] *adj* eschen, aus Eschenholz.

ash·en² [~] *adj* **1.** Aschen... **2.** aschfarben. **3.** aschgrau, -fahl.

a·shore [ə'ʃɔː] *adv u. adj* am *od.* ans Ufer: *go ~* an Land gehen.

'ash|·pan *s* Asche(n)kasten *m*. **'~·tray** *s* Aschenbecher *m*. **~ Wednes·day** *s* Aschermittwoch *m*.

ash·y ['æʃɪ] *adj* **1.** Aschen... **2.** mit Asche bedeckt. **3.** → *ashen²* 2, 3.

A·sian ['eɪʃn], **A·si·at·ic** [ˌeɪʃɪ'ætɪk] **I** *adj* asiatisch. **II** *s* Asiat(in).

a·side [ə'saɪd] **I** *adv* **1.** beiseite, auf die Seite: *step ~* zur Seite treten. **2.** *~ from bsd. Am.* abgesehen von. **II** *s* **3.** *thea.* Aparte *n*.

as·i·nine ['æsɪnaɪn] *adj* **1.** Esels... **2.** *fig.* eselhaft, dumm.

ask [ɑːsk] **I** *v/t* **1.** *j-n* fragen. **2.** *j-n* fragen nach, sich bei *j-m* nach *et.* erkundigen: *~ s.o. the way;* *~ s.o. a question* *j*-m e-e Frage stellen, *j*-n et. fragen. **3.** bitten um, *et.* erbitten: *~ advice;* → *favo(u)r* 4. **4.** *j-n* bitten, fragen (*for* um): *~ s.o. for advice.* **5.** einladen, bitten: *~ s.o. to dinner* j-n zum Essen einladen; *~ s.o. in* j-n hereinbitten; *~ s.o. out* j-n ausführen. **6.** verlangen, fordern (*of* von): *~ a high price for s.th.;* *that is ~ing too much* das ist zuviel verlangt. **II** *v/i* **7.** fragen, sich erkundigen (*for, about, after* nach): *~ for s.o. a.* j-n *od.* nach j-m verlangen, j-n zu sprechen wünschen; *~ around* herumfragen, sich umhören. **8.** bitten (*for* um): *he ~ed for it* (*od. trouble*) *F* er wollte es ja so haben.

a·skance [ə'skæns] *adv: look ~ at s.o.* j-n von der Seite ansehen; *fig.* j-n schief *od.* mißtrauisch ansehen.

a·skew [ə'skjuː] *adv* **1.** schief: *go ~ fig.*

schiefgehen. 2. *look ~ at s.o.* j-n verächtlich ansehen.

ask·ing [ˈɑːskɪŋ] s Fragen n, Bitten n: *to be had for the ~* umsonst *od.* leicht zu haben sein.

a·slant [əˈslɑːnt] **I** *adv u. adj* schräg, quer. **II** *prp* quer über (*acc*) *od.* durch.

a·sleep [əˈsliːp] *adv u. adj* schlafend, (*Fuß etc*) eingeschlafen: *be ~* schlafen; *drop* (*od. fall*) *~* einschlafen.

as·par·a·gus [əˈspærəɡəs] s ♀ Spargel m: *~ tips pl* Spargelspitzen *pl.*

as·pect [ˈæspekt] s **1.** Aussehen n, Erscheinung f. **2.** Aspekt m (*a. ling.*), Seite f, Gesichtspunkt m. **3.** Beziehung f, Hinsicht f.

as·pen [ˈæspən] s ♀ Espe f: *tremble like an ~ leaf* wie Espenlaub zittern.

as·per·i·ty [æˈsperətɪ] s **1.** Rauheit f (*a. fig.*), Unebenheit f. **2.** *fig.* Schärfe f, Schroffheit f.

as·perse [əˈspɜːs] *v/t* verleumden.

as·per·sion s Verleumdung f: *cast ~s on* verleumden.

as·phalt [ˈæsfælt] **I** s Asphalt m. **II** *v/t* asphaltieren.

as·phyx·i·a [əsˈfɪksɪə] s ⚕ Erstickung(stod m) f. **as·phyx·i·ate** [~eɪt] *v/t u. v/i* ersticken: *be ~d* ersticken. **as·phyx·i·a·tion** s Erstickung f.

as·pic [ˈæspɪk] s Aspik m, Gelee n.

as·pir·ant [əˈspaɪərənt] s (*to, after, for*) Bewerber(in) (um *acc*), Anwärter(in) (auf *acc*). **as·pi·ra·tion** [ˌæspəˈreɪʃn] s **1.** Streben n, Bestrebung f (*for, after* nach). **as·pire** [əˈspaɪə] *v/i* streben, trachten (*to, after* nach): *~ to* (*od. after*) *s.th. a.* et. erstreben.

as·pi·rin [ˈæspərɪn] s *pharm.* Aspirin n.

as·pir·ing [əˈspaɪərɪŋ] *adj* □ **1.** ehrgeizig, strebsam. **2.** auf-, emporstrebend.

ass¹ [æs] s *zo.* Esel m (*a. fig.*): *make an ~ of o.s.* sich lächerlich machen *od.* blamieren.

ass² [~], *'~·hole Am.* V → *arse, arsehole.*

as·sail [əˈseɪl] *v/t* **1.** angreifen. **2.** *fig.* bestürmen (*with mit Fragen etc*): *~ed by fear* von Furcht gepackt. **3.** *Aufgabe etc* in Angriff nehmen. **as·sail·a·ble** *adj* angreifbar. **as·sail·ant** s Angreifer m.

as·sas·sin [əˈsæsɪn] s (*bsd.* politischer) Mörder, Attentäter m. **as·sas·si·nate** [~neɪt] *v/t bsd. pol.* ermorden: *be ~d* e-m Attentat zum Opfer fallen. **as·sas·si·na·tion** s (*of*) (*bsd.* politischer) Mord, Ermordung f (*gen*), Attentat n (auf *acc*).

as·sault [əˈsɔːlt] **I** s **1.** Angriff m (*on* auf *acc*) (*a. fig.*). **2.** ⚔ Sturm m: *take by ~* im Sturm nehmen, erstürmen. **3.** *a. ~ and battery* ⚖ tätliche Beleidigung: *criminal* (*od. indecent*) *~* unzüchtige Handlung (*unter Gewaltandrohung od. -anwendung*). **II** *v/t* **4.** angreifen (*a. fig.*). **5.** ⚔ stürmen. **6.** ⚖ tätlich beleidigen. **7.** *euphem.* vergewaltigen.

as·say [əˈseɪ] **I** s **1.** Prüfung f, Untersuchung f. **II** *v/t* **2.** *Metall etc* prüfen, untersuchen. **3.** *fig.* versuchen, probieren.

as·sem·blage [əˈsemblɪdʒ] s **1.** Ansammlung f. **2.** Versammlung f. **3.** ⚙ Montage f. **as·sem·ble** [~] *v/t* **1.** versammeln. **2.** ⚙ montieren, zs.-setzen. **II** *v/i* **3.** sich versammeln. **as·sem·bler** s ⚙ Monteur m. **as·sem·bly** s **1.** Versammlung f. **2.** ⚙ Montage f: *~ line* Fließband n; *~ shop* Montagehalle f.

as·sent [əˈsent] **I** *v/i* (*to*) **1.** zustimmen, beipflichten (*dat*). **2.** billigen, genehmigen (*acc*). **II** s **3.** Zustimmung f, Beipflichtung f: *by common ~* mit allgemeiner Zustimmung. **4.** Billigung f, Genehmigung f.

as·sert [əˈsɜːt] *v/t* **1.** behaupten, erklären. **2.** *Anspruch etc* geltend machen, bestehen auf (*dat*). **3.** *~ o.s.* sich behaupten *od.* durchsetzen; sich zu viel anmaßen. **as·ser·tion** s **1.** Behauptung f, Erklärung f: *make an ~* e-e Behauptung aufstellen. **2.** Geltendmachung f. **as·ser·tive** *adj* □ **1.** ausdrücklich. **2.** anmaßend.

as·sess [əˈses] *v/t* **1.** *Geldstrafe etc* festsetzen. **2.** *Einkommen etc* (*zur Steuer*) veranlagen (*at* mit). **3.** *fig.* ab-, einschätzen, (be)werten. **as·sess·ment** s **1.** Festsetzung f. **2.** (*Steuer*)Veranlagung f. **3.** Steuer(betrag m) f. **4.** *fig.* Ab-, Einschätzung f, (Be)Wertung f: *what is your ~ of ...?* wie beurteilen Sie ... (*acc*)?

as·set [ˈæset] s **1.** ♦ Aktivposten m; *pl* Aktiva *pl*: *~s and liabilities* Aktiva u. Passiva. **2.** *pl* ⚖ Vermögen(smasse f) n; Konkursmasse f. **3.** *fig.* Vorzug m,

Plus n; Gewinn m (**to** für): **be a great ~** viel wert sein.

as·si·du·i·ty [ˌæsɪˈdjuːətɪ] s Fleiß m, Eifer m. **as·sid·u·ous** [əˈsɪdjʊəs] adj □ fleißig, eifrig.

as·sign [əˈsaɪn] v/t **1.** Aufgabe etc zuanweisen, zuteilen (**to** dat). **2.** (**to** j-n bestimmen, einteilen (zu, für e-e Aufgabe etc), beauftragen (zu). **3.** Zeitpunkt etc bestimmen, festsetzen. **4.** et. zuschreiben (**to** dat). **5.** ﷼ abtreten, übertragen (**to** dat). **as'sign·ment** s **1.** Zu-Anweisung f (**to** an acc). **2.** Bestimmung f, Festsetzung f. **3.** Aufgabe f, Arbeit f (beide a. ped.), Auftrag m. **4.** ﷼ Abtretung f, Übertragung f (**to** an acc).

as·sim·i·late [əˈsɪmɪleɪt] **I** v/t **1.** assimilieren: a) angleichen (a. ling.), anpassen (**to, with** dat, an acc), b) biol. (Nahrung) einverleiben, c) sociol. aufnehmen. **II** v/i **2.** sich angleichen od. anpassen (**to, with** dat, an acc). **3.** biol., sociol. sich assimilieren. **as,sim·i'la·tion** s Assimilation f: a) Angleichung f, Anpassung f (**to** an acc), b) biol. Einverleibung f.

as·sist [əˈsɪst] **I** v/t **1.** j-m helfen, beistehen, j-n unterstützen: **~ s.o. in doing s.th.** j-m (dabei) helfen, et. zu tun. **II** v/i **2.** mithelfen, Hilfe leisten (**in** bei). **3.** (**at**) beiwohnen (dat), teilnehmen (an dat). **as'sist·ance** s Hilfe f, Beistand m, Unterstützung f: **come to s.o.'s ~** j-m zu Hilfe kommen. **as'sist·ant I** adj **1.** stellvertretend: **~ editor** Redaktionsassistent m; **~ professor** univ. Am. (etwa) Lehrbeauftragte m, f. **II** s **2.** Assistent(in), Mitarbeiter(in). **3.** Angestellte m, f: (**shop**) **~** Br. Verkäufer(in).

as·so·ci·ate [əˈsəʊʃɪeɪt] **I** v/t **1.** vereinigen, -binden, zs.-schließen (**with** mit): **~ o.s. with** a. sich e-r Partei, j-s Ansichten etc anschließen. **2.** bsd. psych. assoziieren, (gedanklich) verbinden (**with** mit). **II** v/i **3.** sich vereinigen etc, → **1. 4.** verkehren (**with** mit). **III** adj [ˌʃɪət] **5.** verwandt (**with** mit). **6.** beigeordnet, Mit...: **~ editor** Mitherausgeber m. **7.** außerordentlich (Mitglied). **IV** s [ˌʃɪət] **8.** ﷼ Teilhaber m, Gesellschafter m. **9.** Gefährte m, Genosse m. **10.** außerordentliches Mitglied. **as·so·ci·a·tion** [əˌsəʊsɪˈeɪʃn] s **1.** Vereinigung f, -bindung f, Zs.-schluß m: **in ~ with** zusam-

men mit. **2.** Verein(igung f) m. **3.** ﷼ Genossenschaft f, (Handels)Gesellschaft f, Verband m: **~ football** Br. Fußball m. **4.** Umgang m, Verkehr m. **5.** psych. (Ideen-, Gedanken)Assoziation f, Gedankenverbindung f.

as·sort·ed [əˈsɔːtɪd] adj **1.** sortiert, geordnet. **2.** zs.-gestellt, gemischt, verschiedenartig. **as'sort·ment** s bsd. ﷼ (**of**) Sortiment n (von), Auswahl f (an dat).

as·sume [əˈsjuːm] v/t **1.** annehmen, voraussetzen: **assuming that** angenommen od. vorausgesetzt, daß. **2.** Amt, Verantwortung etc übernehmen. **3.** Eigenschaft, Gestalt etc annehmen. **4.** sich Recht etc anmaßen. **as'sum·ing** adj □ anmaßend. **as·sump·tion** [əˈsʌmpʃn] s **1.** Annahme f, Voraussetzung f: **on the ~ that** in der Annahme od. unter der Voraussetzung, daß. **2.** Übernahme f. **3.** Anmaßung f. **4.** ♀ (**Day**) eccl. Mariä Himmelfahrt f.

as·sur·ance [əˈʃʊərəns] s **1.** Ver-, Zusicherung f. **2.** bsd. Br. (Lebens)Versicherung f. **3.** Sicherheit f, Gewißheit f. **4.** Selbstsicherheit f; b.s. Dreistigkeit f. **as·sure** [əˈʃʊə] v/t **1.** j-m versichern (**that** daß): **~ s.o. of s.th.** j-m et. zusichern. **2.** sichern, sicherstellen, bürgen für. **3.** überzeugen (**of** von): **~ o.s.** a. sich vergewissern (**of** gen). **4.** beruhigen. **5.** bsd. Br. Leben versichern: **~ one's life with** e-e Lebensversicherung abschließen bei. **as'sured I** adj **1.** (**of**) überzeugt (von), sicher (gen): **you can rest ~** daß Sie können sicher sein od. sich darauf verlassen, daß. **2.** gesichert. **3.** selbstsicher; b.s. dreist. **II** s **4.** bsd. Br. Versicherte m, f. **as'sur·ed·ly** [ˌrɪdlɪ] adv ganz gewiß.

as·ter [ˈæstə] s ♣ Aster f.

as·ter·isk [ˈæstərɪsk] s typ. Sternchen n.

a·stern [əˈstɜːn] adv ⚓ achtern.

asth·ma [ˈæsmə] s ♨ Asthma n. **asth·mat·ic** [æsˈmætɪk] **I** adj (**~ally**) asthmatisch: **~ attack** Asthmaanfall m; **be ~** Asthma haben. **II** s Asthmatiker(in).

a·stig·ma·tism [əˈstɪɡmətɪzəm] s ♨, phys. Astigmatismus m.

as·ton·ish [əˈstɒnɪʃ] v/t in Erstaunen setzen: **be ~ed** erstaunt od. überrascht sein (**at** über acc; **to** inf zu inf), sich wundern (**at** über acc). **as'ton·ish·ing**

adj □ erstaunlich. **as·ton·ish·ment** *s* (Er)Staunen *n*, Verwunderung *f*: **to one's ~** zu s-r Verwunderung.

as·tound [ə'staʊnd], **as·tound·ing** → **astonish, astonishing.**

a·stray [ə'streɪ] *adv*: **go ~** vom Weg abkommen; *fig.* auf Abwege geraten; **lead ~** *fig.* irreführen.

as·trin·gent [ə'strɪndʒənt] **I** *adj* □ **1.** ⚕ adstringierend, zs.-ziehend. **2.** *fig.* streng, hart. **II** *s* **3.** ⚕ Adstringens *n*.

as·trol·o·ger [ə'strɒlədʒə] *s* Astrologe *m*. **as·tro·log·i·cal** [ˌæstrə'lɒdʒɪkl] *adj* □ astrologisch. **as·trol·o·gy** [ə'strɒlədʒɪ] *s* Astrologie *f*.

as·tro·naut [ˈæstrənɔːt] *s* Astronaut *m*. **'as·tro·naut·ess** *s* Astronautin *f*. **ˌas·tro'nau·tics** *s pl* (*mst sg konstruiert*) Astronautik *f*, Raumfahrt *f*.

as·tron·o·mer [ə'strɒnəmə] *s* Astronom *m*. **as·tro·nom·i·cal** [ˌæstrə'nɒmɪkl] *adj* □ astronomisch. **as·tron·o·my** [ə'strɒnəmɪ] *s* Astronomie *f*.

as·tute [ə'stjuːt] *adj* □ **1.** scharfsinnig. **2.** schlau, gerissen. **as'tute·ness** *s* **1.** Scharfsinn *m*. **2.** Schlauheit *f*.

a·sun·der [ə'sʌndə] *adv* auseinander, entzwei.

a·sy·lum [ə'saɪləm] *s* **1.** Asyl *n*: a) Zufluchtsort *m*, b) *fig.* Zuflucht *f*. **2.** (politisches) Asyl: **ask for ~** um Asyl bitten *od.* nachsuchen; **give s.o. ~** j-m Asyl gewähren; **~ seeker** Asylant(in), Asylbewerber(in).

a·sym·met·ric [ˌeɪsɪ'metrɪk], **ˌa·sym'met·ri·cal** *adj* □ asymmetrisch, ungleichmäßig. **a·sym·me·try** [ˌeɪ'sɪmətrɪ] *s* Asymmetrie *f*, Ungleichmäßigkeit *f*.

at [æt] *prp* **1.** (*Ort*) in (*dat*), an (*dat*), bei, auf (*dat*): **~ a ball** auf e-m Ball; **~ the baker's** beim Bäcker; **~ the door** an der Tür. **2.** (*Richtung*) auf (*acc*), nach, gegen, zu: **he threw a stone ~ the door** er warf e-n Stein gegen die Tür. **3.** (*Beschäftigung*) bei, beschäftigt mit, an (*dat*): **he is still ~ it** er ist noch dabei *od.* damit beschäftigt. **4.** (*Art u. Weise, Zustand*) in (*dat*), bei, zu, unter (*dat*): **~ all** überhaupt; **not ~ all** überhaupt *od.* gar nicht; **not ~ all!** F nichts zu danken!; **nothing ~ all** überhaupt *od.* gar nichts; **no doubts ~ all** keinerlei Zweifel. **5.** (*Preis, Wert etc*) für, um: **~ 6 dollars. 6.**

(*Zeit, Alter*) um, bei: **~ 21** mit 21 (Jahren); **~ 3 o'clock** um 3 Uhr; **~ his death** bei s-m Tod.

ate [et] *pret von* **eat.**

a·the·ism [ˈeɪθɪɪzəm] *s* Atheismus *m*. **'a·the·ist** *s* Atheist(in). **ˌa·the'is·tic**, **ˌa·the'is·ti·cal** *adj* □ atheistisch.

ath·lete [ˈæθliːt] *s* **1.** Athlet *m*: a) Sportler *m*, b) Kraftmensch *m*. **2.** *Br.* Leichtathlet *m*. **ath·let·ic** [æθ'letɪk] *adj* (**~ally**) **1.** athletisch: a) Sport...: **~ field** Sportplatz *m*, b) von athletischem Körperbau. **2.** *Br.* leichtathletisch. **II** *s pl* **3.** (*a. sg konstruiert*) Sport *m*. **4.** (*mst sg konstruiert*) *Br.* Leichtathletik *f*.

at-home [ət'həʊm] *s* zwangloser Empfang: **give an ~.**

a·thwart [ə'θwɔːt] **I** *adv* quer. **II** *prp* (quer) über (*acc*) *od.* durch.

At·lan·tic [ət'læntɪk] *adj* atlantisch.

at·las [ˈætləs] *s* Atlas *m* (*Buch*).

at·mos·phere [ˈætməsfɪə] *s* Atmosphäre *f* (*a. fig.*). **at·mos·pher·ic** [ˌ~'ferɪk] **I** *adj* (**~ally**) atmosphärisch. **II** *s pl* atmosphärische Störungen *pl*.

at·oll [ˈætɒl] *s* Atoll *n*.

at·om [ˈætəm] *s phys.* Atom *n* (*a. fig.*): **not an ~ of truth** kein Körnchen Wahrheit; **~ bomb** Atombombe *f*. **a·tom·ic** [ə'tɒmɪk] *adj* (**~ally**) atomar, Atom...: **~ age** Atomzeitalter *n*; **~ bomb** Atombombe *f*; **~ energy** Atomenergie *f*; **~ nucleus** Atomkern *m*; **~ pile** Atomreaktor *m*; **~ power** Atomkraft *f*; **~ research** Atomforschung *f*; **~-powered** mit Atomkraft betrieben, Atom...; **~ power plant** Atomkraftwerk *n*; **~ waste** Atommüll *m*; **~ weight** Atomgewicht *n*. **at·om·ize** [ˈætəʊmaɪz] *v/t* **1.** atomisieren. **2.** Flüssigkeit zerstäuben. **'at·om·iz·er** *s* Zerstäuber *m* (*Gerät*).

a·tone [ə'təʊn] *v/i*: **~ for** büßen für *et.*, *et.* sühnen. **a'tone·ment** *s* Buße *f*, Sühne *f*.

a·top [ə'tɒp] **I** *adv* oben(auf). **II** *prp a.* **~ of** (oben) auf (*dat*).

a·tro·cious [ə'trəʊʃəs] *adj* □ scheußlich, gräßlich (*beide a. fig.*). **a·troc·i·ty** [ə'trɒsətɪ] *s* **1.** Scheußlichkeit *f*, Gräßlichkeit *f*. **2.** Greueltat *f*.

at·ro·phy [ˈætrəfɪ] ⚕ **I** *s* Atrophie *f*, Verkümmerung *f* (*a. fig.*). **II** *v/i* verkümmern (*a. fig.*).

at·tach [ə'tætʃ] **I** *v/t* **1.** (**to**) befestigen, anbringen (an *dat*), anheften, ankleben (an *acc*). **2.** (**to**) *fig. Sinn etc* verbinden (*mit*); *Wert, Wichtigkeit etc* beimessen (*dat*); *magische Kräfte etc* zuschreiben (*dat*); *Bedingungen* knüpfen (an *acc*). **3.** *fig.* **~ o.s.** sich anschließen (**to** *dat* od. an *acc*): **be ~ed to s.o.** an j-m hängen. **4.** *fig.* (**to**) zuteilen (*dat*), ✗ *a.* abkommandieren (zu). **5.** 🏛 *j-n* verhaften; *et.* beschlagnahmen; pfänden. **II** *v/i* **6.** (**to**) anhaften (*dat*); verknüpft od. verbunden sein mit.

at·ta·ché [ə'tæʃeɪ] *s* Attaché *m:* **~ case** Aktentasche *f*, -koffer *m*.

at·tach·ment [ə'tætʃmənt] *s* **1.** Befestigung *f.* **2.** Anhängsel *n*, Beiwerk *n*; 🔧 Zusatzgerät *n*. **3.** *fig.* (**to**) Anhänglichkeit *f* (an *acc*); Bindung *f* (an *acc*). **4.** 🏛 Verhaftung *f*; Beschlagnahme *f*; Pfändung *f.*

at·tack [ə'tæk] **I** *v/t* **1.** (*a. v/i*) *allg.* angreifen. **2.** *fig. Arbeit etc* in Angriff nehmen, über *e-e Mahlzeit etc* herfallen. **II** *s* Angriff *m.* **4.** 🎺 Anfall *m.* **at'tack·er** *s* Angreifer *m.*

at·tain [ə'teɪn] *v/t* (*u. v/i* **~ to**) *Ziel etc* erreichen, erlangen. **at'tain·a·ble** *adj* erreichbar. **at'tain·ment** *s* **1.** Erreichung *f*, Erlangung *f.* **2.** *pl* Kenntnisse *pl*, Fertigkeiten *pl.*

at·tempt [ə'tempt] **I** *v/t* **1.** versuchen (**to do, doing** zu tun): **~ed suicide** Selbstmordversuch *m.* **2.** sich machen *od.* wagen an (*acc*), in Angriff nehmen. **II** *v/i* **3.** Versuch *m* (**to do, doing** zu tun): **~ at explanation** Erklärungsversuch; **~s pl at resuscitation** 🎺 Wiederbelebungsversuche *pl.* **4.** Anschlag *m:* **an ~ on s.o.'s life** ein Mordanschlag *od.* Attentat auf j-n.

at·tend [ə'tend] **I** *v/t* **1.** *Kranke* pflegen; (*ärztlich*) behandeln. **2.** *fig.* begleiten: **~ed with** (*od.* **by**) verbunden mit. **3.** teilnehmen an (*dat*), *Schule, Versammlung etc* besuchen. **II** *v/i* **4.** (**to**) beachten (*acc*), achten auf (*acc*). **5.** (**to**) sich kümmern (um); erledigen (*acc*). **6.** **~ to** *j-n* (*im Laden*) bedienen: **are you being ~ed to?** werden Sie schon bedient? **7.** anwesend sein; erscheinen. **8.** **~ on** *j-n* bedienen. **at'tend·ance** *s* **1.** Dienst *m*, Bereitschaft *f:* **physician in ~** diensthabender Arzt; **hours pl of ~** Dienststunden *pl.* **2.** Pflege *f* (**on** *gen*), Dienstlei-

stung *f:* **be in ~ on** → **attend** 1. **3.** Anwesenheit *f*, Erscheinen *n:* **~ list** (*od.* **record**) Anwesenheitsliste *f.* **4.** Besucher *pl*, Teilnehmer *pl*; Besuch(erzahl *f*) *m*, Beteiligung *f.* **at'tend·ant I** *adj* **1.** begleitend. **2.** *fig.* verbunden (**on** mit): **~ circumstances** *pl* Begleitumstände *pl.* **3.** anwesend. **II** *s* **4.** Begleiter(in). **5.** Aufseher(in). **6.** *pl* Dienerschaft *f.*

at·ten·tion [ə'tenʃn] *s* **1.** Aufmerksamkeit *f* (*a. fig.*): **attract ~** Aufmerksamkeit erregen; **call** (*od.* **draw**) **~ to** die Aufmerksamkeit lenken auf (*acc*), aufmerksam machen auf (*acc*); **pay ~ to** Beachtung schenken (*dat*), achtgeben auf (*acc*); (**for the**) **~ of** zu Händen von (*od. gen*). **2.** **give** (**prompt**) **~ to s.th.** et. (*rasch*) erledigen. **3.** **~!** ✗ Achtung!; stillgestanden! **at'ten·tive** *adj* □ aufmerksam (**to** auf *acc*; *fig.* gegen).

at·ten·u·ate [ə'tenjʊeɪt] *v/t* **1.** *bsd.* 🎺 verdünnen. **2.** *fig.* vermindern, (ab)schwächen.

at·test [ə'test] *v/t* **1.** beglaubigen, bescheinigen. **2.** zeugen von, bestätigen. **at·tes·ta·tion** [ˌæte'steɪʃn] *s* **1.** Beglaubigung *f*, Bescheinigung *f.* **2.** Zeugnis *n.*

at·tic [ˈætɪk] *s* Dachgeschoß *n*; Dachstube *f*, -kammer *f.*

at·tire [ə'taɪə] **I** *v/t* (be)kleiden. **II** *s* Kleidung *f*, Gewand *n.*

at·ti·tude [ˈætɪtjuːd] *s* **1.** (*Körper*)Haltung *f*, Stellung *f.* **2.** *fig.* Haltung *f:* a) Verhalten *n*, b) Einstellung *f* (**to, toward[s]** zu, gegenüber): **what is your ~ to ...?** wie stehen Sie zu ...?

at·tor·ney [ə'tɜːnɪ] *s* 🏛 **1.** *bsd. Am.* **~** (**at law**) (*Rechts*)Anwalt *m*; **~** (**in fact**) Bevollmächtigte *m.* **2.** (**power of**) **~** Vollmacht *f;* **~ gen·er·al** *pl* **~s gen·er·al**, **gen·er·als** *s* 🏛 **1.** *Br.* erster Kronanwalt. **2.** *Am.* Justizminister *m.*

at·tract [ə'trækt] *v/t* **1.** *phys.* anziehen (*a. fig.*). **2.** *fig. j-n* anlocken, reizen, *j-s Interesse, Blicke etc* auf sich ziehen: **be ~ed to** sich hingezogen fühlen zu; → **attention** 1. **at'trac·tion** [-kʃn] *s* **1.** *phys.* Anziehung(skraft) *f.* **2.** *fig.* a) Anziehungskraft *f*, Reiz *m:* **have little ~ for** wenig anziehend sein für, b) Attraktion *f*, *thea. etc* Zugnummer *f.* **at'trac·tive** *adj* □ **1.** *phys.* anziehend: **~ force** (*od.* **power**) Anziehungskraft *f.* **2.** *fig.* attraktiv: a) anziehend, reizvoll,

b) einnehmend (*Äußeres etc*), c) zugkräftig (*Angebot etc*).

at·trib·ute [ə'trɪbjuːt] **I** v/t [ə'trɪbjuːt] **1.** zuschreiben (**to** dat). **2.** zurückführen (**to** auf acc). **II** s ['ætrɪbjuːt] **3.** Attribut n (a. ling.): a) Eigenschaft f, Merkmal n, b) (Kenn)Zeichen n. **at·trib·u·tive** [ə'trɪb-jʊtɪv] ling. **I** adj □ attributiv. **II** s Attribut n.

at·tri·tion [ə'trɪʃn] s **1.** Abnutzung f, Verschleiß m (*beide a. fig.*). **2.** fig. Zermürbung f.

au·burn ['ɔːbən] adj kastanienbraun (*Haar*).

auc·tion ['ɔːkʃn] **I** s Auktion f, Versteigerung f: **sell** (**buy**) **by** (*Am. at*) ~ versteigern (ersteigern); **sale by** (*Am. at*) ~, ~ **sale** Versteigerung f. **II** v/t mst ~ **off** versteigern. **auc·tion·eer** [,ɔːkʃə'nɪə] s Auktionator m, Versteigerer m: ~**s** pl Auktionshaus n.

au·da·cious [ɔː'deɪʃəs] adj □ **1.** kühn, verwegen. **2.** dreist, unverfroren. **au·dac·i·ty** [ɔː'dæsətɪ] s **1.** Kühnheit f, Verwegenheit f. **2.** Dreistigkeit f, Unverfrorenheit f.

au·di·ble ['ɔːdəbl] adj □ hörbar, vernehmlich.

au·di·ence ['ɔːdjəns] s **1.** Audienz f (**of**, **with** bei). **2.** Publikum n: a) Zuhörer(schaft f) pl, b) Zuschauer (pl), c) Besucher pl, d) Leser(kreis m) pl.

au·di·o·phile ['ɔːdɪəʊfaɪl] s Hi-Fi-Fan m. '~,**typ·ist** s Phonotypistin f. ~**'vis·u·al I** adj □ audiovisuell: ~ **aids** → II. **II** s pl audiovisuelle Unterrichtsmittel pl.

au·dit ['ɔːdɪt] ✝ **I** s Buch-, Rechnungsprüfung f. **II** v/t prüfen.

au·di·tion [ɔː'dɪʃn] **I** s **1.** physiol. Hörvermögen n, Gehör n. **2.** ♩, thea. Vorspiel(en) n; Vorsingen n; Vorsprechen n; Anhörprobe f. **II** v/t u. v/i **3.** ♩, thea. vorspielen od. vorsingen od. vorsprechen (lassen).

au·di·tor ['ɔːdɪtə] s **1.** ✝ Buch-, Rechnungsprüfer m. **2.** univ. Am. Gasthörer(in).

au·di·to·ri·um [,ɔːdɪ'tɔːrɪəm] pl **-ri·ums**, **-ri·a** [~ə] s **1.** Auditorium n, Zuhörer-, Zuschauerraum m. **2.** Am. Vortragssaal m, Konzerthalle f.

aug·ment [ɔːɡ'ment] **I** v/t vermehren, steigern, Gehalt etc aufbessern. **II** v/i

sich vermehren, zunehmen. ,**aug·men·'ta·tion** s Vermehrung f, Zunahme f; Aufbesserung f.

au·gur ['ɔːɡə] **I** v/t vorher-, weissagen. **II** v/i: ~ **well** (**ill**) ein gutes (schlechtes) Zeichen sein (**for** für). **au·gu·ry** ['ɔːɡjʊrɪ] s Vorzeichen n.

Au·gust ['ɔːɡəst] s August m: **in** ~ im August.

auld lang syne [,ɔːldlæŋ'saɪn] schott. die gute alte Zeit.

aunt [ɑːnt] s Tante f.

au·pair [ˌəʊ'peə] Br. **I** s a. ~ **girl** Au-pair-Mädchen n. **II** adv als Au-pair-Mädchen: **work** ~. **III** v/i als Au-pair-Mädchen arbeiten.

au·ra ['ɔːrə] s fig. Aura f.

au·ral ['ɔːrəl] adj □ **1.** Ohren...: ~ **surgeon** Ohrenarzt m. **2.** akustisch, Hör...

au·re·ole ['ɔːrɪəʊl] s ast. Aureole f, Hof m.

au·ri·cle ['ɔːrɪkl] s anat. **1.** Ohrmuschel f. **2.** Herzvorhof m. **au·ric·u·lar** [ɔː'rɪk-jʊlə] adj Ohren...: ~ **confession** eccl. Ohrenbeichte f; ~ **witness** Ohrenzeuge m.

aus·cul·ta·tion [,ɔːskəl'teɪʃn] s ✚ Abhorchen n.

aus·pic·es ['ɔːspɪsɪz] s pl: **under the** ~ **of** unter der Schirmherrschaft von (od. gen). **aus·pi·cious** [ɔː'spɪʃəs] adj □ günstig: a) vielversprechend, b) glücklich: **be** ~ unter e-m günstigen Stern stehen.

Aus·sie ['ɒzɪ] F **I** s Australier(in). **II** adj australisch.

aus·tere [ɒ'stɪə] adj □ **1.** streng, ernst. **2.** enthaltsam; dürftig, karg. **3.** herb, rau, hart. **4.** nüchtern, schmucklos. **aus·ter·i·ty** [ɒ'sterətɪ] s **1.** Strenge f, Ernst m. **2.** Enthaltsamkeit f; Dürftigkeit f. **3.** Herbheit f, Rauheit f. **4.** Nüchternheit f, Schmucklosigkeit f. **II** adj **5.** ✝, pol. Spar...: ~ **budget**; ~ **program**(**me**).

Aus·tra·lian [ɒ'streɪljən] **I** adj australisch. **II** s Australier(in).

Aus·tri·an ['ɒstrɪən] **I** adj österreichisch. **II** s Österreicher(in).

au·tar·kic [ɔː'tɑːkɪk] adj ✝ autark. **au·tar·ky** ['~kɪ] s Autarkie f.

au·then·tic [ɔː'θentɪk] adj (~**ally**) **1.** authentisch: a) echt, verbürgt, b) original, urschriftlich. **2.** ⚖ gültig, rechtskräftig. **au'then·ti·cate** [~keɪt] v/t **1.** beglaubigen. **2.** als echt erweisen, verbürgen. **au,then·ti'ca·tion** *s* Beglaubigung *f.* **,au·then'tic·i·ty** [~sətɪ] *s* **1.** Authentizität *f*, Echtheit *f.* **2.** 🕱 Gültigkeit *f*, Rechtskräftigkeit *f.*

au·thor ['ɔːθə] *s* **1.** Urheber(in). **2.** Autor(in), Verfasser(in), *a. allg.* Schriftsteller(in). **'au·thor·ess** *s* Autorin *f*, Verfasserin *f*, *a. allg.* Schriftstellerin *f.* **au·thor·i·tar·i·an** [ɔː,θɒrɪ'teərɪən] *adj* autoritär.

au'thor·i·ta·tive [~tətɪv] *adj* □ **1.** gebieterisch, herrisch. **2.** autoritativ, maßgebend, -geblich. **au'thor·i·ty** *s* **1.** Autorität *f*, (Amts)Gewalt *f.* **2.** Autorität *f*, Ansehen *n* (**with** bei), Einfluß *m* (**over** auf *acc*). **3.** Vollmacht *f*: ~ **to sign** Unterschriftsvollmacht *f*; **without** ~ unbefugt, unberechtigt. **4.** Quelle *f*, Beleg *m*: **on good** ~ aus glaubwürdiger Quelle. **5.** Autorität *f*, Kapazität *f* (**on** in *e-r* Sache, auf *e-m* Gebiet). **6.** *mst pl* Behörde(n *pl*) *f.*

au·thor·i·za·tion [,ɔːθəraɪ'zeɪʃn] *s* **1.** Ermächtigung *f*, Bevollmächtigung *f*, Befugnis *f.* **2.** Genehmigung *f.* **'au·thor·ize** *v/t* **1.** autorisieren, ermächtigen, bevollmächtigen: ~*d* **to sign** unterschriftsbevollmächtigt. **2.** billigen, genehmigen. **au·thor·ship** ['ɔːθəʃɪp] *s* **1.** Urheberschaft *f.* **2.** Autorschaft *f.*

au·to ['ɔːtəʊ] *pl* **-tos** *s Am.* F Auto *n.* **au·to...** ['ɔːtəʊ] auto..., selbst..., Auto..., Selbst...

'au·to,bi·o'graph·ic, 'au·to,bi·o'graph·i·cal *adj* □ autobiographisch. **,au·to·bi'og·ra·phy** *s* Autobiographie *f.*

au·to·cade ['ɔːtəʊkeɪd] *Am.* → **motorcade.**

'au·to,chang·er *s* Plattenwechsler *m.*

au·toc·ra·cy [ɔː'tɒkrəsɪ] *s pol.* Autokratie *f.* **au·to·crat** ['ɔːtəʊkræt] *s* Autokrat *m:* a) *pol.* diktatorischer Alleinherrscher, b) selbstherrlicher Mensch. **,au·to'crat·ic, ,au·to'crat·i·cal** *adj* □ autokratisch: a) *pol.* unumschränkt, b) selbstherrlich.

au·to·di·dact ['ɔːtəʊdɪ,dækt] *s* Autodidakt(in). **,au·to·di'dac·tic** *adj* autodidaktisch.

au·to·gen·ic [,ɔːtəʊ'dʒenɪk] *adj* 🗶 autogen: ~ **training.**

au·to·graph ['ɔːtəgrɑːf] **I** *s* Autogramm

n: **sign** ~**s** Autogramme geben. **II** *adj* Autogramm...: ~ **album** (**hunter,** *etc*). **III** *v/t* sein Autogramm schreiben in (*acc*) *od.* auf (*acc*), *Buch etc* signieren.

au·to·mat ['ɔːtəʊmæt] *s* **1.** *bsd. Am.* Automatenrestaurant *n.* **2.** (Verkaufs)Automat *m.* **au·to·mate** ['ɔːtəmeɪt] *v/t* automatisieren. **au·to·mat·ic** [,ɔːtə'mætɪk] **I** *adj* (~*ally*) **1.** automatisch: ~ **choke** *mot.* Startautomatik *f.* 🗟 Automat *m.* **3.** Selbstladepistole *f*, -gewehr *n.* **4.** Auto *n* mit Automatik. **au·to·ma·tion** [,ɔːtə'meɪʃn] *s* **1.** Automation *f.* **2.** Automatisierung *f.* **'au·tom·a·tize** [ɔː'tɒmətaɪz] *v/t* automatisieren. **au'tom·a·ton** [~tən] *pl* **-ta** [~tə], **-tons** *s* Automat *m*, Roboter *m* (*a. fig.*).

au·to·mo·bile ['ɔːtəməbiːl] *s* Auto(mobil) *n.* **au·to·mo·tive** [,ɔːtə'məʊtɪv] *adj* **1.** selbstfahrend, mit Eigenantrieb. **2.** Auto(mobil)..., Kraftfahrzeug...

au·ton·o·mous [ɔː'tɒnəməs] *adj* autonom. **au'ton·o·my** *s* Autonomie *f.*

'au·to,pi·lot *s* 🛫 Autopilot *m*, automatische Steuerungsanlage.

au·top·sy ['ɔːtəpsɪ] *s* 🗶 Autopsie *f.*

au·tumn ['ɔːtəm] **I** *s* Herbst *m* (*a. fig.*): **the** ~ **of life;** *in* (**the**) ~ im Herbst. **II** *adj* Herbst... **au·tum·nal** [ɔː'tʌmnəl] *adj* □ herbstlich, Herbst...

aux·il·ia·ry [ɔːg'zɪljərɪ] **I** *adj* **1.** Hilfs..., 🗟 *a.* Zusatz...: ~ **verb** → **3.** **II** *s* **2.** Helfer(in), Hilfskraft *f.* **3.** *ling.* Hilfsverb *n*, -zeitwort *n.*

a·vail [ə'veɪl] **I** *v/t:* ~ **o.s. of** sich *e-r* Sache bedienen, sich *et.* zunutze machen. **II** *v/i* nützen. **III** *s* Nutzen *m:* **of no** ~ nutzlos; **to no** ~ vergeblich. **a,vail·a·'bil·i·ty** *s* Verfügbarkeit *f.* **a'vail·a·ble** *adj* □ **1.** verfügbar, vorhanden: **make** ~ zur Verfügung stellen. **2.** 🕇 lieferbar, vorrätig, erhältlich: **no longer** ~ nicht mehr lieferbar, vergriffen; → **prescription. 3.** erreichbar, abkömmlich.

av·a·lanche ['ævəlɑːntʃ] *s* **1.** Lawine *f.* **2.** *fig.* Flut *f:* **an** ~ **of letters.**

av·a·rice ['ævərɪs] *s* Habsucht *f*, Habgier *f.* **,av·a'ri·cious** *adj* □ habsüchtig, habgierig.

a·venge [ə'vendʒ] *v/t* rächen: ~ **o.s.,** **be** ~**d** sich rächen (**on** an *dat;* **for** für). **a'veng·er** *s* Rächer(in).

av·e·nue ['ævənjuː] *s* **1.** Allee *f.* **2.** Hauptstraße *f.* **3.** *fig.* Weg *m* (**to** zu).

av·er·age ['ævərɪdʒ] **I** s **1.** Durchschnitt m: *be above* (*the*) ~ über dem Durchschnitt liegen; *be below* (*the*) ~ unter dem Durchschnitt liegen; *on* (*an od. the*) ~ durchschnittlich, im Durchschnitt. **2.** ⚓, ⚖ Havarie f, Seeschaden m. **II** adj **3.** durchschnittlich, Durchschnitts... **III** v/t **4.** a. ~ *out* den Durchschnitt ermitteln od. nehmen von (od. gen). **5.** ☇ anteil(s)mäßig aufteilen (*among* unter dat). **6.** durchschnittlich betragen od. haben od. leisten etc. **IV** v/i **7.** ~ *out at* → 6.

a·verse [ə'vɜːs] adj □ abgeneigt (*to*, bsd. Br. a. *from* dat). **a'ver·sion** s **1.** Abneigung f, Aversion f (*to*, *from* gegen). **2.** ... *is my* ~ ... ist mir ein Greuel.

a·vert [ə'vɜːt] v/t abwenden (a. fig.).

a·vi·a·tion [ˌeɪvɪ'eɪʃn] s Luftfahrt f.

av·id ['ævɪd] adj □ gierig (*for*, a. *of* nach): ~ *for fame* ruhmsüchtig. **a·vid·i·ty** [ə'vɪdətɪ] s Gier f.

a·void [ə'vɔɪd] v/t (ver)meiden, ausweichen (dat), aus dem Wege gehen (dat), Pflicht etc umgehen, e-r Gefahr entgehen: ~ *s.o.* j-n meiden; ~ *doing s.th.* es vermeiden, et. zu tun. **a'void·a·ble** adj vermeidbar. **a'void·ance** s (Ver)Meiden n, Umgehung f: *in* ~ *of* um zu vermeiden.

av·oir·du·pois [ˌævədə'pɔɪz] s a. ~ *weight* ☇ Handelsgewicht n (= 16 Unzen).

a·vow [ə'vaʊ] v/t bekennen, (ein)gestehen. **a'vow·al** s Bekenntnis n, (Ein)Geständnis n. **a'vowed** adj erklärt (Gegner, Prinzip etc). **a'vow·ed·ly** [~ɪdlɪ] adv eingestandenermaßen.

a·wait [ə'weɪt] v/t erwarten (a. fig.).

a·wake [ə'weɪk] **I** v/t (irr) **1.** (auf)wecken. **2.** fig. auf-, wachrütteln (*from* aus): ~ *s.o. to s.th.* j-m et. zum Bewußtsein bringen. **II** v/i (irr) **3.** auf-, erwachen. **4.** ~ *to s.th.* fig. sich e-r Sache bewußt werden. **III** adj **5.** wach: *wide* ~ hellwach, fig. a. aufgeweckt: *be* ~ *to s.th.* fig. sich e-r Sache bewußt sein. **a·wak·en** v/t u. v/i 1–4. **a'wak·en·ing** s Erwachen n: *a rude* ~ fig. ein unsanftes od. böses Erwachen.

a·ward [ə'wɔːd] **I** v/t **1.** zuerkennen, zusprechen, Preis etc a. verleihen. **II** s **2.** Urteil n, bsd. Schiedsspruch m. **3.** Auszeichnung f, Preis m. **4.** (Preis- etc)

Verleihung f. **5.** univ. Stipendium n.

a·ware [ə'weə] adj: *be* ~ *of s.th.* et. wissen od. kennen, sich e-r Sache bewußt sein; *become* ~ *of s.th.* et. merken; *make s.o.* ~ *of s.th.* j-m et. bewußt machen. **a'ware·ness** s Bewußtsein n, Kenntnis f.

a·way [ə'weɪ] **I** adv u. adj **1.** weg, fort (*from* von): *go* ~ weg-, fortgehen. **2.** (weit) entfernt od. weg: *six miles* ~ sechs Meilen entfernt. **3.** fort, abwesend, verreist: ~ *on business* geschäftlich unterwegs. **4.** d(a)rauflos, immer weiter (→ Verben). **II** adj **5.** Sport: Auswärts...: ~ *match*.

awe [ɔː] **I** s (Ehr)Furcht f, Scheu f: *hold s.o. in* ~ → II; *stand in* ~ *of* e-e (heilige) Scheu od. gewaltigen Respekt haben vor (dat). **II** v/t j-m (Ehr)Furcht od. großen Respekt einflößen. **'~·in·spir·ing** adj ehrfurchtgebietend.

awe·some ['ɔːsəm] adj □ **1.** furchteinflößend. **2.** ehrfurchtgebietend.

'awe-struck adj von Ehrfurcht ergriffen.

aw·ful ['ɔːfʊl] adj furchtbar, schrecklich (beide a. F). **'aw·ful·ly** adv F furchtbar, schrecklich: ~ *nice* furchtbar od. riesig nett; *thanks* ~! tausend Dank!

awk·ward ['ɔːkwəd] adj □ **1.** ungeschickt, unbeholfen, linkisch: *be* ~ *with* ungeschickt umgehen mit. **2.** verlegen (a. Schweigen etc): *feel* ~ verlegen sein. **3.** peinlich, unangenehm. **4.** unhandlich, sperrig. **5.** unangenehm, schwierig: *an* ~ *customer* F ein unangenehmer Zeitgenosse. **6.** ungünstig (Zeitpunkt etc).

awl [ɔːl] s ⚙ Ahle f, Pfriem m.

awn·ing ['ɔːnɪŋ] s **1.** Plane f. **2.** Markise f. **3.** ⚓ Sonnensegel n. **4.** Vorzelt n.

a·woke [ə'wəʊk] pret u. pp von awake. **a'wok·en** pp von awake.

a·wry [ə'raɪ] adv u. adj schief: *go* ~ fig. schiefgehen.

ax(e) [æks] **I** s Axt f, Beil n: *have an* ~ *to grind* fig. eigennützige Zwecke verfolgen; *get the* ~ F rausfliegen, entlassen werden. **II** v/t F Ausgaben etc rücksichtslos kürzen od. (zs-)streichen; Beamte, Dienststellen abbauen, Leute feuern, entlassen.

ax·es ['æksiːz] pl von axis.

ax·i·om ['æksɪəm] s Axiom n, Grundsatz m.

ax·is [ˈæksɪs] *pl* **ax·es** [ˈ∼siːz] *s* ⚻ etc Achse *f (a. pol.)*.
ax·le [ˈæksl] *s* ◉ (Rad)Achse *f*, Welle *f*.
ay(e) [aɪ] *s parl.* Jastimme *f*: **the ∼s**

have it die Mehrheit ist dafür.
a·zal·ea [əˈzeɪljə] *s* ⚘ Azalee *f*.
az·ure [ˈæʒə] **I** *adj* himmelblau. **II** *s* Himmelblau *n*.

B

baa [bɑː] *v/i* blöken.
Bab·bitt [ˈbæbət] *s Am.* selbstzufriedener Spießer.
bab·ble [ˈbæbl] **I** *v/i* **1.** *a. v/t* stammeln. **2.** *a. v/t* plappern, schwatzen: ∼ *(out)* ausplaudern. **3.** plätschern. **II** *s* **4.** Geplapper *n*, Geschwätz *n*. **5.** Geplätscher *n*.
babe [beɪb] *s* **1.** Baby *n*: → *innocent* b. **2.** *bsd. Am. sl.* Puppe *f (Mädchen)*.
ba·bel [ˈbeɪbl] *s* Wirrwarr *m*, Durcheinander *n*; Stimmengewirr *n*.
ba·boon [bəˈbuːn] *s zo.* Pavian *m*.
ba·by [ˈbeɪbɪ] **I** *s* **1.** Baby *n*, Säugling *m*: *be left holding the ∼* F der Dumme sein; *that's your ∼ sl.* das ist dein Bier *od.* d-e Sache. **2.** Benjamin *m (der Familie etc)*. **3.** *contp.* Kindskopf *m*; Heulsuse *f*. **4.** *sl.* Puppe *(Mädchen)*; Schatz *m*, Liebling *m*. **II** *adj* **5.** Baby..., Säuglings... **6.** Klein... **III** *v/t* **7.** verhätscheln. ∼ *boom s* Babyboom *m*. ∼ *car s* Kleinwagen *m*. ∼ *car·riage s Am.* Kinderwagen *m*.
ba·by·hood [ˈbeɪbɪhʊd] *s* Säuglingsalter *n*. **'ba·by·ish** *adj* **1.** kindisch. **2.** kindlich.
'ba·by|-,mind·er *s Br.* Tagesmutter *f*. **'∼-sit** *v/i (irr sit)* babysitten. **'∼-,sit·ter** *s* Babysitter(in). ∼ *talk s* kindlich-(tuend)es Gebabbel.
bach·e·lor [ˈbætʃələ] *s* **1.** Junggeselle *m*: ∼ *girl* Junggesellin *f*. **2.** *univ.* Bakkalaureus *m*: ☲ *of Arts (Science)* Bakkalaureus der philosophischen Fakultät (der Naturwissenschaften). **bach·e·lor·ette** [ˌ∼ˈret] *s* Junggesellin *f*. **bach·e·lor·hood** [ˈ∼hʊd] *s* **1.** Junggesellenstand *m*. **2.** *univ.* Bakkalaureat *n*.
ba·cil·lus [bəˈsɪləs] *pl* **-li** [ˌ∼laɪ] *s* ⚕ Bazillus *m*.

back [bæk] **I** *s* **1.** *anat., zo.* Rücken *m*: *at the ∼ of* hinter *(dat)*; hinten in *(dat)*; *be at the ∼ of s.th. fig.* hinter et. stecken; *behind s.o.'s ∼ fig.* hinter j-s Rücken; ∼ *to* ∼ Rücken an Rücken; *be on one's ∼* bettlägerig sein; *break s.o.s ∼* j-m das Kreuz brechen *(a. fig.)*; *break the ∼ of s.th. fig.* das Schwierigste hinter sich bringen; *have one's ∼ to the wall fig.* mit dem Rücken zur Wand stehen; *put (od. get) s.o.'s ∼ up fig.* j-n auf die Palme bringen; *put one's ∼ into s.th. fig.* sich in e-e Sache hineinknien; *turn one's ∼ on* den Rücken zuwenden *(dat)*; *fig.* den Rücken kehren *(dat)*. **2.** Hinter-, Rückseite *f (Buch-, Hand- etc)* Rücken *m*, (Rück)Lehne *f (e-s Stuhls)*, linke Seite *(e-s Stoffs)*. **3.** hinterer *od.* rückwärtiger Teil: ∼ *of the head* Hinterkopf *m*; *in the ∼ of the car* auf dem Rücksitz *od.* im Fond des Autos. **4.** Rückenteil *m (e-s Kleidungsstücks)*: *have one's pullover on ∼ to front* den Pullover verkehrt herum anhaben. **5.** *Sport:* Verteidiger *m*. **II** *adj* **6.** rückwärtig, Hinter...: ∼ *entrance.* **7.** fern, abgelegen: ∼ *country* Hinterland *n*. **8.** rückständig *(Zahlung)*. **9.** alt, zurückliegend *(Zeitung etc)*. **III** *adv* **10.** zurück, rückwärts: ∼ *and forth* hin u. her, vor u. zurück; *move ∼* zurückgehen. **11.** (wieder) zurück: *he is ∼ (again)* er ist wieder da. **12.** zurück, vorher: *20 years ∼* vor 20 Jahren; ∼ *in 1900* (noch *od.* schon) im Jahre 1900. **13.** F zurück, im Rückstand: *be ∼ in one's rent* mit der Miete im Rückstand sein. **IV** *v/t* **14.** *a.* ∼ *up* unterstützen, j-m den Rücken stärken, ✝ *Währung etc* stützen. **15.** *a.* ∼ *up* zurückbewegen, rückwärts fahren *od.* laufen lassen: ∼ *the car out of the* *garage* den Wagen rückwärts aus der Garage fahren. **16.** wetten *od.* setzen auf (*acc*). **V** *v/i* **17.** *oft* **~ up** sich rückwärts bewegen, zurückgehen *od.* -fahren, *mot. a.* zurückstoßen: **~ out** (*of*) rückwärts herausfahren (aus). **18. ~ out** (*of*) zurücktreten *od.* abspringen (von), aussteigen (aus).

'**back·ache** *s* Rückenschmerzen *pl.* **~ al·ley** *s Am.* finsteres Seitengäßchen. ‚**~'bench·er** *s parl. Br.* Hinterbänkler *m.* '**~bite** *v/t* (*irr bite*) lästern über *j-n.* '**~bone** *s* Rückgrat *n* (*a. fig.*), Wirbelsäule *f:* **to the ~** *fig.* bis auf die Knochen, durch u. durch. '**~break·ing** *adj* zermürbend, mörderisch. '**~chat** *s* freche Antwort(en *pl*). '**~cloth** *s thea. bsd. Br.* Prospekt *m.* '**~date** *v/t* (zu)rückdatieren. **~ door** *s* Hintertür *f; fig.* Hintertürchen *n.* '**~door** *adj* geheim, heimlich. '**~drop** *s thea.* Prospekt *m:* **be the ~ for** *fig.* den Hintergrund (*gen*) bilden.

back·er ['bækə] *s* Unterstützer(in), Helfer(in); Geldgeber(in).

‚**back'fire** *I v/i* **1.** ⊙ früh-, fehlzünden. **2.** *fig.* fehlschlagen, ins Auge gehen. **II** *s* **3.** ⊙ Früh-, Fehlzündung *f.* **~ for·ma·tion** *s ling.* Rückbildung *f.* '**~gam·mon** *s* Backgammon *n* (*Spiel*). '**~ground** *s* **1.** Hintergrund *m* (*a. fig.*): **against the ~ of** vor dem Hintergrund (*gen*); **keep in the ~** im Hintergrund bleiben; **~ music** musikalische Untermalung, Hintergrundsmusik *f.* **2.** *fig.* Hintergrund *m*, Umstände *pl*; Umwelt *f*, Milieu *n*; Werdegang *m*; Erfahrung *f*, Wissen *n*: **~ information** Hintergrundinformationen (*pl*) *f*; **educational ~** Vorbildung *f.* '**~hand** *I s Sport:* Rückhand(schlag *m*) *f.* **II** *adj* → **backhanded.** ‚**~'hand·ed** *adj Sport:* Rückhand... **2.** indirekt (*Zensur etc*). **3.** unredlich (*Methode etc*). **4.** zweifelhaft (*Kompliment etc*).

back·ing ['bækɪŋ] *s* Unterstützung *f.*

'**back·lash** *s* (heftige) Reaktion (**to** auf *acc*). '**~log** *s* (*Arbeits-, Auftrags etc*)Rückstand *m;* Überhang *m* (**of** an *dat*): **~ demand** Nachholbedarf *m.* **~ num·ber** *s* **1.** alte Nummer (*e-r Zeitung etc*). **2.** F rückständige Person *od.* Sache. '**~pack** *s bsd. Am.* Rucksack *m.* ‚**~'pack·ing** *s bsd. Am.* Rucksacktou-

rismus *m.* ‚**~'ped·al** *v/i pret u. pp -aled, bsd. Br. -alled* **1.** rückwärts treten (*Radfahrer*). **2.** *fig.* e-n Rückzieher machen. **~ seat** *s* Rücksitz *m: take a ~* F in den Hintergrund treten (to gegenüber). '**~-seat driv·er** *s* F Besserwisser(in). ‚**~'side** *s* **1.** Kehr-, Rückseite *f.* **2.** F Hintern *m.* ‚**~'slide** *v/i* (*irr slide*) rückfällig werden. '**~stage** *adj u. adv thea.* hinter den Kulissen (*a. fig.*). '**~stair** → **backstairs** II. ‚**~'stairs I** *s pl* **1.** Hintertreppe *f.* **II** *adj* **2. ~ gossip** (*od. talk*) (bösartige) Anspielungen *pl* (**about** auf *acc*). **3. ~ influence** Protektion *f.* **~ street** *s* Seitenstraße *f.* '**~street** *adj* heimlich: **~ abortion** illegale Abtreibung; **~ abortionist** Engelmacher(in). '**~stroke** *s* Rückenschwimmen *n.* **~ talk** *s bsd. Am.* F freche Antwort(en *pl*). '**~track** *v/i* **1.** denselben Weg zurückgehen. **2.** *fig.* sich zurückziehen (**from** von), e-n Rückzieher machen; e-e Kehrtwendung machen. '**~up** *s* **1.** Unterstützung *f.* **2.** *mot. Am.* (Rück)Stau *m.* **3.** *fig.* Ersatzmann *m* (**on** hinsichtlich). **4.** ⊙ Ersatzgerät *n.*

back·ward ['bækwəd] *I adj* **1.** rückwärts gerichtet, Rückwärts...: **~ flow** Rückfluß *m; a ~ glance* ein Blick zurück *od.* nach hinten. **2.** *in der Entwicklung etc* zurück(geblieben). **3.** rückständig: **be ~ in one's work** mit s-r Arbeit im Rückstand liegen. **II** *adv* **4.** rückwärts, zurück: **~ and forward** hin u. her, vor u. zurück. **back·wards** ['~dz] → **backward** II.

'**back·wash** *s* **1.** Rückströmung *f,* ♧ *a.* Kielwasser *n.* **2.** *fig.* Aus-, Nachwirkung(en *pl*) *f.* '**~wa·ter** *s* **1.** → **backwash** **1. 2.** Stauwasser *n.* **3.** *fig.* Ort *m od.* Zustand *m* der Rückständigkeit u. Stagnation. '**~woods** *s pl* **1.** unerschlossenes Waldgebiet. **2.** *contp.* Provinz *f.* '**~woods·man** ['~mən] *s* (*irr man*) *contp.* Hinterwäldler *m.* ‚**~'yard** *s* **1.** *Br.* Hinterhof *m.* **2.** *Am.* Garten *m* hinter dem Haus.

ba·con ['beɪkən] *s* Frühstücks-, Schinkenspeck *m: bring home the ~* F die Brötchen verdienen; Erfolg haben; **save one's ~** *Br.* F mit heiler Haut davonkommen.

bac·te·ri·al [bæk'tɪərɪəl] *adj* □ bakteriell. **bac·te·ri·o·log·i·cal** [bæk‚tɪərɪə-

'lɒdʒɪkl] *adj* □ bakteriologisch, Bakterien... **bac·te·ri·ol·o·gist** [ˌ͜tɪərɪˈɒlədʒɪst] *s* Bakteriologe *m*. **bac·te·ri·um** [ˌ͜rɪəm] *pl* **-ri·a** [ˌrɪə] *s* Bakterie *f*.

bad [bæd] **I** *adj comp* **worse** [wɜːs] *sup* **worst** [wɜːst] (□ → *badly*) **1.** *allg.* schlecht: a) fehler-, mangelhaft (*Qualität, Zustand etc*): **not ~** nicht schlecht *od.* übel; **~ trip** *sl.* Bad Trip *m* (*Drogenrausch mit Angstzuständen*), b) ungünstig (*Nachricht etc*), c) schädlich, ungesund (**for** für): **~ for one's health** ungesund, d) verdorben (*Nahrungsmittel*): **go ~** schlecht werden, verderben, e) angegriffen (*Gesundheit*), f) widerlich (*Geruch*), g) schwach (**at** in *e-m Fach*). **2.** böse: a) schlimm, schwer (*Verbrechen, Erkältung etc*), b) ungezogen (*Junge etc*). **3.** unanständig, unflätig, (*Wort a.*) häßlich: **~ language** unanständige Ausdrücke *pl*; beleidigende Äußerungen *pl*. **4.** ungedeckt (*Scheck*), ungültig (*Münze etc*): **~ debts** *pl* zweifelhafte Forderungen *pl*. **5.** unangenehm, ärgerlich: **that's too ~** das ist (doch) zu dumm. **6.** unwohl, krank: **she is** (*od.* **feels**) **very ~ today** es geht ihr heute sehr schlecht; **he felt ~ at** (*od.* **about**) **it** er war (sehr) deprimiert darüber. **II** *s* **7.** *das Schlechte*: **go from ~ to worse** immer schlimmer werden; **go to the ~** auf die schiefe Bahn geraten; **be in the ~ with** F schlecht angeschrieben sein bei. **8.** ✝ Defizit *n*: **be £ 100 to the ~** ein Defizit *od.* e-n Verlust von 100 Pfund haben. **III** *adv* **9.** F → *badly*.

bade [bæd] *pret u. pp von* **bid**.

badge [bædʒ] *s* **1.** (✗ *Rang*)Abzeichen *n*. **2.** *fig.* Kennzeichen *n*.

badg·er ['bædʒə] **I** *s zo.* Dachs *m*. **II** *v/t* plagen, *j-m* zusetzen (**for** wegen).

bad·ly ['bædlɪ] *adv* **1.** schlecht, schlimm: **he is ~ off** es geht ihm sehr schlecht; **do ~** schlecht fahren (**in** bei, mit). **2.** dringend, sehr: **~ needed** dringend nötig. **3.** schwer: **~ wounded**.

bad·min·ton ['bædmɪntən] *s* Federball(spiel *n*) *m*, *Sport:* Badminton *n*. **bad·'tem·pered** *adj* schlechtgelaunt.

baf·fle ['bæfl] *v/t* **1.** verwirren, -blüffen: **be ~d** *a.* vor e-m Rätsel stehen. **2.** *Plan etc* durchkreuzen, vereiteln: **it ~s** (**all**) **description** es spottet jeder Beschreibung.

bag [bæg] **I** *s* **1.** Sack *m*; Beutel *m*; Tasche *f*; Tüte *f*: **~ and baggage** mit Sack u. Pack; **~s of** F jede Menge (*Geld etc*). **2.** *hunt.* (Jagd)Beute *f*, Strecke *f*. **3.** (**pair of**) **~s** *pl bsd. Br.* F Hose *f*. **II** *v/t* **4.** in e-n Sack *etc* stecken; in Beutel verpacken *od.* abfüllen. **5.** *hunt.* zur Strecke bringen. **6.** F klauen, stehlen. **III** *v/i* **7.** *a.* **~ out** sich bauschen.

bag·a·telle [ˌbægəˈtel] *s* Bagatelle *f*.

bag·gage ['bægɪdʒ] *s bsd. Am.* (Reise)Gepäck *n*. **~ al·low·ance** *s* ✈ *bsd. Am.* Freigepäck *n*. **~ car** *s* ⊞ *Am.* Gepäckwagen *m*. **~ check** *s bsd. Am.* Gepäckschein *m*. **~ in·sur·ance** *s bsd. Am.* Reisegepäckversicherung *f*. **~ lock·er** *s bsd. Am.* Gepäckschließfach *n*. **~ re-claim** *s* ✈ *bsd. Am.* Gepäckausgabe *f*.

bag·gy ['bægɪ] *adj* **1.** bauschig. **2.** ausgebeult (*Hose*).

'bag|pip·er *s* Dudelsackpfeifer *m*. **'~pipes** *s pl* ♪ Dudelsack *m*. **'~snatch·er** *s* Handtaschenräuber *m*.

bah [bɑː] *int contp.* bah!

bail¹ [beɪl] 🕮 **I** *s* **1.** Bürge(n *pl*) *m*. **2.** (Haft)Kaution *f*, Sicherheitsleistung *f*: **be out on ~** gegen Kaution auf freiem Fuß sein; **go** (*od.* **stand**) **~ for s.o.** für j-n Kaution stellen. **II** *v/t* **3.** **~ s.o. out** j-s Freilassung gegen Kaution erwirken.

bail² [ˌ\] **I** *v/t mst* **~ out** *Wasser, Boot etc* ausschöpfen. **II** *v/i:* **~ out** ✈ aussteigen (*a.* F *fig.* of aus), (mit dem Fallschirm) abspringen.

bail³ [ˌ\] *s* Henkel *m* (*e-s Eimers etc*).

bail·iff ['beɪlɪf] *s Br.* **1.** 🕮 Gerichtsvollzieher *m*. **2.** (Guts)Verwalter *m*.

bait [beɪt] **I** *s* **1.** Köder *m* (*a. fig.*): **rise to** (*od.* **swallow, take**) **the ~** anbeißen (*a. fig.*). **II** *v/t* **2.** mit e-m Köder versehen. **3.** *fig.* ködern. **4.** *hunt.* (mit Hunden) hetzen. **5.** *fig.* quälen, peinigen.

bake [beɪk] **I** *v/t* **1.** backen: **~d beans** *pl* Baked Beans *pl* (*in Tomatensoße gekochte Bohnen*); **~d potatoes** *pl ungeschälte, im Ofen gebackene Kartoffeln*. **2.** dörren, härten; (*Ziegel*) brennen; *Lack* einbrennen. **II** *v/i* **3.** backen, *mst fig.* (*in der Sonne*) braten. **4.** *zs.- od.* festbacken. **'bak·er** *s* Bäcker *m*: **at the ~'s** beim Bäcker; **~'s dozen** dreizehn. **'bak·er·y** *s* Bäckerei *f*; **baking·'hot** *adj* glühendheiß (*Tag etc*).

bak·ing pow·der s Backpulver n.

bal·ance ['bæləns] **I** s **1.** Waage f. **2.** Gleichgewicht n: a) Balance f, b) a. **~ of mind** Fassung f: **in the ~** fig. in der Schwebe; **hold the ~** fig. das Zünglein an der Waage bilden; **keep one's ~** das Gleichgewicht halten; fig. sich nicht aus der Fassung bringen lassen; **lose one's ~** das Gleichgewicht od. (fig.) die Fassung verlieren; **strike a ~ between ... and** fig. e-n Mittelweg finden zwischen (dat) ... u.; **throw s.o. off (his) ~** fig. j-n aus der Fassung bringen; **~ of power** pol. Gleichgewicht der Kräfte. **3.** bsd. fig. (**to**) Gegengewicht n (zu), Ausgleich m (für). **4.** ✝ Bilanz f; Saldo m, Guthaben n; Restbetrag m: **~ of payments** Zahlungsbilanz; **~ of trade** Handelsbilanz; **on ~** fig. alles in allem. **II** v/t **5.** fig. ab-, erwägen. **6.** (o.s. sich) im Gleichgewicht halten; balancieren. **7.** ins Gleichgewicht bringen, ausbalancieren. **8.** ✝ Konten, Rechnungen ausgleichen, saldieren. **III** v/i **9.** sich im Gleichgewicht halten (a. fig.); balancieren. **10.** ✝ sich ausgleichen. '**balanced** adj fig. ausgewogen, -geglichen.

bal·ance| sheet s ✝ Bilanz f. **~ wheel** s ⚙ Unruh f (e-r Uhr).

bal·anc·ing ['bælənsɪŋ] adj Balance..., Balancier...: **~ act** Balanceakt m (a. fig.); **~ pole** Balancierstange f.

bal·co·ny ['bælkənɪ] s Balkon m, thea. a. zweiter Rang.

bald [bɔːld] adj □ **1.** kahl: **go ~** e-e Glatze bekommen, kahl werden. **2.** (völlig) abgefahren (Reifen).

bal·der·dash ['bɔːldədæʃ] s Quatsch m, Unsinn m.

'bald·head s Kahl-, Glatzkopf m; ,**~'head·ed** adj kahl-, glatzköpfig.

bale¹ [beɪl] **I** s ✝ Ballen m: in **~s** ballenweise. **II** v/t in Ballen verpacken.

bale² [~] → **bail²**.

balk [bɔːk] v/i **1.** stocken, stutzen. **2.** scheuen (**at** vor dat) (Pferd). **3.** (**at**) sich sträuben (gegen); zurückschrecken (vor dat).

ball¹ [bɔːl] **I** s **1.** Ball m; Kugel f; Knäuel m, n: **be on the ~** F auf Draht sein; **the ~ is with you** (od. **in your court**) du bist an der Reihe od. am Zug; **have the ~ at one's feet** Br. s-e große Chance haben; **keep the ~ rolling** das Gespräch od. die Sache in Gang halten; **play ~** F mitmachen, spuren; **set** (od. **start**) **the ~ rolling** den Stein ins Rollen bringen. **2.** anat. **~ of the eye** Augapfel m; **~ of the foot** Fußballen m; **~ of the thumb** Handballen m. **3.** pl �V Eier pl (Hoden). **II** v/t u. v/i **4.** (sich) zs.-ballen.

ball² [~] s Ball m (Tanzveranstaltung): **have a ~** bsd. Am. F sich köstlich amüsieren.

bal·lad ['bæləd] s Ballade f.

,**ball-and-'sock·et** adj: **~ joint** anat., ⚙ Kugelgelenk n.

bal·last ['bæləst] bsd. ✈, ⚓ **I** s Ballast m. **II** v/t mit Ballast beladen.

ball| bear·ing s ⚙ Kugellager n. **~ boy** s Sport: Balljunge f.

bal·let ['bæleɪ] s Ballett n. **~ danc·er** s Balletttänzer(in).

bal·lis·tics [bə'lɪstɪks] s pl (meist sg konstruiert) ✗, phys. Ballistik f.

bal·loon [bə'luːn] **I** s **1.** (Frei-, Fessel-, Luft)Ballon m. **2.** Sprech-, Denkblase f. **II** v/i **3.** sich (auf)blähen. **bal'loon·ist** s Ballonfahrer(in).

bal·lot ['bælət] **I** s **1.** Stimmzettel m. **2.** Gesamtzahl f der abgegebenen Stimmen: **large ~** hohe Wahlbeteiligung. **3.** (bsd. geheime) Wahl od. Abstimmung: **have** (od. **hold, take**) **a ~** abstimmen (**on** über acc). **4.** Wahlgang m. **II** v/i **5.** (**for**) stimmen (für), (bsd. in geheimer Wahl) wählen (acc). **~ box** s Wahlurne f. **~ card, ~ pa·per** s Stimmzettel m.

'ball|·point (**pen**) s Kugelschreiber m. '**~room** s Ball-, Tanzsaal m.

bal·ly·hoo [,bælɪ'huː] s F **1.** Wirbel m, Tamtam n, Getue n (**about** um). **2.** marktschreierische Reklame.

balm [bɑːm] s Balsam m (a. fig.). '**balm·y** adj □ **1.** balsamisch. **2.** lind, mild (Wetter). **3.** bsd. Am. sl. bekloppt, verrückt: **go ~** überschnappen.

ba·lo·ney → **boloney**.

bal·us·trade [,bæləs'treɪd] s Balustrade f.

bam·boo [bæm'buː] s Bambus m.

bam·boo·zle [bæm'buːzl] v/t F **1.** betrügen (**out of** um), übers Ohr hauen: **~ s.o. into doing s.th.** j-n so einwickeln, daß er et. tut. **2.** irremachen, verwirren.

ban ['bæn] **I** v/t **1.** verbieten: **~ s.o. from speaking** j-m Rede- od. Sprechverbot erteilen. **2.** Sport: sperren. **II** s **3.** (amtliches) Verbot (**on** _gen_), Sperre _f_ (_a. Sport_): **import ~** Einfuhrverbot, -sperre.

ba·nal [bə'nɑːl] _adj_ □ banal, abgedroschen.

ba·nan·a [bə'nɑːnə] _s_ 1. ✿ Banane _f_. 2. _sl._ **be ~s** bekloppt _od._ verrückt sein; **go ~s** überschnappen. ~ **re·pub·lic** _s_ Bananenrepublik _f_.

band¹ [bænd] I _s_ 1. Schar _f_, Gruppe _f_; _b.s._ (_bsd. Räuber_)Bande _f_. 2. (Musik)Kapelle _f_, (_Jazz-, Rock- etc_)Band _f_: **big ~** Big Band. II _v/i_ 3. _mst_ ~ **together** sich zs.-tun, _b.s._ sich zs.-rotten.

band² [~] I _s_ 1. Band _n_; Gurt _m_; (_Hosen- etc_)Bund _m_; Bauchbinde _f_ (_e-r Zigarre_); _andersfarbiger od. -artiger_ Streifen. 2. _Radio:_ (Frequenz)Band _n_. 3. Ring _m_. 4. ⚙ Treibriemen _m_; Band _n_. II _v/t_ 5. mit e-m Band zs.-binden.

band·age ['bændɪdʒ] I _s_ ⚕ Bandage _f_; Binde _f_; Verband _m_. II _v/t_ bandagieren; verbinden.

'band-aid _s_ Am. Heftpflaster _n_.

ban·dit ['bændɪt] _s_ Bandit _m_.

'band|,lead·er _s_ ♪ Bandleader _m_. '~~,mas·ter** _s_ ♪ Kapellmeister _m_. '~~,wag·(g)on** _s_ Wagen _m_ mit e-r Musikkapelle: **climb** (_od._ **get, jump**) **on the ~** _fig._ zur erfolgreichen Partei umschwenken.

ban·dy¹ ['bændɪ] _v/t_ 1. sich _e-n Ball etc_ zuwerfen. 2. sich _Geschichten etc_ erzählen. 3. sich _Beleidigungen etc_ an den Kopf werfen, sich (gegenseitig) _Komplimente, Vorwürfe_ machen: ~ **blows** sich schlagen; ~ **words** sich streiten. 4. _a._ ~ **about** (_od._ **around**) _Gerücht etc_ in Umlauf setzen; weitererzählen: **he has his name bandied about** sein Name fällt dauernd (**in connection with** in Zs.-hang mit); _b.s._ er ist ins Gerede gekommen.

ban·dy² [~] _adj_ 1. krumm, nach außen gebogen: ~ **legs** _pl_ Säbelbeine _pl_, O-Beine _pl_. 2. → **bandy-legged.** '~~-legged** _adj_ säbelbeinig, O-beinig.

bang [bæŋ] I _s_ 1. heftiger _od._ schallender Schlag. 2. Bums _m_, Krach _m_, Knall _m_: **shut the door with a ~** zuschlagen, zuknallen. 3. _sl._ Schuß _m_ (_Heroin etc_). II _v/t_ 4. knallen mit, _Tür etc_ zuschlagen, zuknallen: ~ **one's fist on the table** mit der Faust auf den Tisch schlagen; ~ **one's head** sich den Kopf anschlagen

(**against, on** an _dat_); ~ **sense into s.o.** _fig._ j-m Vernunft einhämmern. 5. V bumsen. III _v/i_ 6. knallen: a) krachen, b) zuschlagen (_Tür etc_), c) schießen: ~ **away** drauflosknallen; ~ **into** stoßen _od._ prallen gegen _od._ an (_acc_); _fig._ F zufällig treffen. 7. _sl._ sich _e-n_ Schuß (_Heroin etc_) setzen _od._ drücken. 8. V bumsen. IV _adv_ 9. mit lautem Knall: **go ~** explodieren. 10. peng; genau: ~ **in the eye** peng ins Auge. V _int_ 11. peng!, bum(s)! '**bang·er** _s Br._ 1. Feuerwerks-, Knallkörper _m_. 2. F (alter) Klapperkasten (_Auto_). 3. F (Brat)Wurst _f_, Würstchen _n_.

'bang-up _adj bsd. Am._ F prima.

ban·ish ['bænɪʃ] _v/t_ 1. verbannen (_a._ _fig._), ausweisen (**from** aus). 2. _Sorgen etc_ verscheuchen, -treiben. **'ban·ish·ment** _s_ Verbannung _f_, Ausweisung _f_.

ban·is·ters ['bænɪstəz] _s pl_ Treppengeländer _n_.

ban·jo ['bændʒəʊ] _pl_ **-jo(e)s** _s_ ♪ Banjo _n_.

bank¹ [bæŋk] I _s_ 1. ✝ Bank _f_. 2. Bank _f_ (_bei Glücksspielen_): **break** (**be** _od._ **keep**) **the ~** die Bank sprengen (halten). 3. (_Blut-, Daten- etc_)Bank _f_. II _v/i_ 4. ein Bankkonto haben (**with** bei). 5. die Bank halten (_bei Glücksspielen_). 6. ~ **on** bauen _od._ sich verlassen auf (_acc_). III _v/t_ 7. _Geld_ bei e-r Bank einzahlen, auf die Bank bringen.

bank² [~] I _s_ 1. (Erd)Wall _m_; Böschung _f_; Überhöhung _f_ (_e-r Straße etc in Kurven_). 2. (Fluß- etc)Ufer _n_. 3. (Sand-)Bank _f_. Zs.-ballung _f_: ~ **of clouds** Wolkenbank _f_; ~ **of snow** Schneewall _m_, -wächte _f_. II _v/t_ 5. mit e-m Wall umgeben. 6. _Straße etc_ (_in der Kurve_) überhöhen. 7. ~ **up** aufhäufen, zs.-ballen. III _v/i_ 8. ~ **up** sich aufhäufen, sich zs.-ballen. 9. überhöht sein (_Straße, Kurve_).

bank·a·ble ['bæŋkəbl] _adj fig._ zuverlässig, verläßlich.

bank| ac·count _s_ Bankkonto _n_. ~ **bill** _Am._ → **bank note.** '~~-book** _s_ Sparbuch _n._ ~ **card** _s_ Scheckkarte _f_. ~ **clerk** _s_ Bankangestellte _m, f_.

bank·er ['bæŋkə] _s_ 1. ✝ Bankier _m_. 2. Bankhalter _m_ (_bei Glücksspielen_).

bank| hold-up _s_ Banküberfall _m_. ~ **hol·i·day** _s Br._ Bankfeiertag _m_.

bank·ing ['bæŋkɪŋ] ✝ **I** s Bankwesen n. **II** adj Bank...: ~ **hours** pl Öffnungszeiten pl (e-r Bank).

bank| man·ag·er s Bankdirektor m. ~ **note** s Banknote f, Geldschein m. ~ **raid** s Banküberfall m, -raub m. ~ **raid·er** s Bankräuber m. ~ **rate** s ✝ Diskontsatz m. ~ **rob·ber** s Bankräuber m. ~ **rob·ber·y** s Bankraub m, -überfall m.

bank·rupt ['bæŋkrʌpt] ⚖ **I** s **1.** Konkurs-, Gemeinschuldner m: ~'s **estate** (od. **property**) Konkursmasse f. **2.** (betrügerischer) Bankrotteur. **II** adj **3.** bankrott: **go** ~ in Konkurs gehen, Bankrott machen; **declare o.s.** ~ Konkurs anmelden. **bank·rupt·cy** ['~rəptsɪ] s ⚖ Bankrott m, Konkurs m.

ban·ner ['bænə] **I** s **1.** Standarte f; Banner n. **2.** Spruchband n, Transparent n. **3.** a. ~ **headline** Balkenüberschrift f, breite Schlagzeile. **II** adj **4.** Am. hervorragend.

banns [bænz] s pl eccl. Aufgebot n: **have one's** ~ **called** das Aufgebot bestellen.

ban·quet ['bæŋkwɪt] **I** s Bankett n, Festessen n. **II** v/i tafeln.

ban·tam·weight ['bæntəmweɪt] (Sport) **I** s Bantamgewicht(ler m) n. **II** adj Bantamgewichts...

ban·ter ['bæntə] **I** v/t u. v/i necken. **II** s Neckerei f.

bap·tism ['bæptɪzəm] s eccl. Taufe f. **bap·tis·mal** [~'tɪzml] adj Tauf...: ~ **font** Taufbecken n. '**Bap·tist** s Baptist(in). **bap·tize** [~'taɪz] v/t taufen.

bar [ba:] **I** s **1.** Stange f, Stab m: ~s pl Gitter n; **behind** ~s fig. hinter Schloß u. Riegel. **2.** Riegel m. **3.** Schranke f, Sperre f; fig. Hindernis n (**to** für). **4.** Riegel m, Stange f: **a** ~ **of soap** ein Riegel od. Stück Seife; **a** ~ **of chocolate** ein Riegel (weitS. e-e Tafel) Schokolade. **5.** (Gold- etc)Barren m. **6.** (dicker) Strich m. ♪ Taktstrich m; **ein** Takt m. ⚖ (Gerichts)Schranke f: **prisoner at the** ~ Angeklagte m, f. **9.** ⚖ Anwaltsberuf m; coll. Anwaltschaft f. **Br.** Stand m der **barristers: be admitted** (Br. **called**) **to the** ~ als Anwalt (Br. **barrister**) zugelassen werden; **read for the** ~ Br. Jura studieren. **10.** (Tor-, Quer-, Sprung)Latte f. **11.** Bar f; Lokal n, Imbißstube f; Bar f, Theke f. **II** v/t **12.**

verriegeln. **13.** a. ~ **up** vergittern. **14.** a. ~ **in** einsperren: ~ **out** aussperren. **15.** hemmen; (**from**) hindern (an dat), abhalten (von). **II** prp **16.** außer, abgesehen von: ~ **none** (alle) ohne Ausnahme.

barb [ba:b] s **1.** Widerhaken m; Stachel m. **2.** fig. Spitze f.

bar·bar·i·an [ba:'beərɪən] **I** s Barbar(in). **II** adj barbarisch. **bar·bar·ic** [~'bærɪk] adj (~ally) barbarisch. **bar·ba·rism** ['~bərɪzəm] s **1.** Barbarismus m, Sprachwidrigkeit f. **2.** Barbarei f. **bar·bar·i·ty** [~'bærətɪ] s Barbarei f. **bar·ba·rize** ['~bəraɪz] v/t barbarisieren. '**bar·ba·rous** adj □ barbarisch.

bar·be·cue ['ba:bɪkju:] **I** v/t auf dem Rost od. am Spieß braten, grillen. **II** s Barbecue n: a) Grillfest n, b) Bratrost m, Grill m, c) auf dem Rost od. Grill gebratenes Fleisch.

barbed [ba:bd] adj **1.** mit Widerhaken od. Stacheln: ~ **wire** Stacheldraht m. **2.** fig. spitz (Bemerkung etc).

bar·ber ['ba:bə] s (Herren)Friseur m: ~'(s) **shop** Friseurgeschäft n.

bar·bi·tu·rate [ba:'bɪtjʊrət] s ⚗ etc Barbiturat n.

bare [beə] **I** adj (□ → **barely**) **1.** nackt: a) entblößt: **on one's** ~ **feet** barfuß; **in one's** ~ **skin** nackt, b) kahl (Wand etc); c) fig. ungeschminkt: ~ **facts** pl nackte Tatsachen pl. **2.** fig. unverhüllt: ~ **nonsense** blanker Unsinn; **lay** ~ → **II. 3.** ~ **of** arm an (dat); ohne, ...los. **4.** knapp (Mehrheit etc): **earn a** ~ **living** knapp das Nötigste zum Leben verdienen. **5.** bloß: **the** ~ **thought** allein od. schon der Gedanke. **II** v/t **6.** entblößen, weitS. Zähne zeigen. **7.** fig. enthüllen, bloßlegen. '~**back(ed)** adj u. adv ungesattelt, ohne Sattel. '~**faced** adj unverschämt, schamlos. '~**foot**, '~**foot·ed** adj u. adv barfuß, -füßig. '~**head·ed** adj u. adv barhäuptig.

bare·ly ['beəlɪ] adv **1.** kaum, knapp. **2.** ärmlich, spärlich.

bar·gain ['ba:gɪn] **I** s **1.** Handel m, Geschäft n (a. fig.): **it's a** ~! abgemacht!; **into the** ~ noch dazu, obendrein; **make the best of a bad** ~ sich so gut wie möglich aus der Affäre ziehen; **strike a** ~ ein Geschäft abschließen; → **drive** 12. **2.** vorteilhaftes Geschäft, Gelegenheitskauf m. **II** v/i **3.** handeln, feilschen (*for* um). **4.** verhandeln (*for* über *acc*): ~ **on** vereinbaren (*acc*). **5.** (*for*) rechnen (mit), gefaßt sein (auf *acc*). **III** *v/t* **6.** aushandeln. ~ **base·ment** *s* Niedrigpreisabteilung *f* im Tiefgeschoß (*e-s Kaufhauses*). ~ **count·er** *s* Wühltisch *m*. ~ **price** *s* Gelegenheits-, Sonderpreis *m*. ~ **sale** *s* **1.** Verkauf *m* zu herabgesetzten Preisen. **2.** Ausverkauf *m*.

barge [bɑːdʒ] **I** *s* **1.** Last-, Schleppkahn *m*. **II** *v/i* **2.** sich schwerfällig bewegen. **3.** F (*into*) stoßen, prallen, bumsen (gegen, an *acc*). **4.** ~ *in*(*to*) F hereinplatzen (in *acc*); sich einmischen (in *acc*).

bar·i·tone ['bærɪtəʊn] *s* ♪ Bariton *m*.

bark[1] [bɑːk] **I** *s* **1.** (Baum)Rinde *f*, Borke *f*. **II** *v/t* **2.** abrinden. **3.** sich *die Knie etc* auf-, abschürfen: ~ *one's knees*.

bark[2] [~] **I** *v/i* bellen (*a.* F *husten*): ~ *at s.o.* j-n anbellen; *fig.* j-n anschnauzen; ~*ing dogs never bite* Hunde, die bellen, beißen nicht; ~ *up the wrong tree* F auf dem Holzweg sein; an der falschen Adresse sein. **II** *s* Bellen (*a.* F *Husten*): *his* ~ *is worse than his bite* er bellt nur(, aber beißt nicht).

'**bar·keep·er** *s* Barkeeper *m*: a) Barbesitzer *m*, b) Barmann *m*, -mixer *m*.

bar·ley ['bɑːlɪ] *s* ♀ Gerste *f*.

'**bar·maid** *s bsd. Br.* Bardame *f*. ~**man** ['~mæn] *s* (*irr man*) Barmann *m*, -keeper *m*, -mixer *m*.

barm·y ['bɑːmɪ] *adj sl.* bekloppt, verrückt: *go* ~ überschnappen.

barn [bɑːn] *s* **1.** Scheune *f*. **2.** (Vieh-) Stall *m*.

ba·rom·e·ter [bə'rɒmɪtə] *s* Barometer *n* (*a. fig.*).

bar·on ['bærən] *s* **1.** Baron *m*. **2.** (*Industrie- etc*)Baron *m*, Magnat *m*. '**bar·on·ess** *s* Baronin *f*. **bar·on·et** ['~nɪt] *s* Baronet *m*.

ba·roque [bə'rɒk] **I** *adj* barock. **II** *s* Barock *n, m*.

bar·racks ['bærəks] *s pl* (*meist sg konstruiert*) **1.** Kaserne *f*. **2.** *contp.* Mietskaserne *f*.

bar·rage ['bærɑːʒ] *s* **1.** (Stau)Damm *m*, Talsperre *f*. **2.** ✕ Sperrfeuer *n*. **3.** *fig.* Hagel *m*, Schwall *m*.

bar·rel ['bærəl] **I** *s* **1.** Faß *n*, (*Rohölmaß mst*) Barrel *n*: ~*s* (*od.* **a** ~) *of* F in Haufen (*Geld etc*). **2.** (Gewehr)Lauf *m*, (Geschütz)Rohr *n*. **II** *v/t pret u. pp*

-**reled**, *bsd. Br.* -**relled** **3.** in Fässer füllen: ~(*l*)*ed beer* Faßbier *n*. ~ **or·gan** *s* ♪ Drehorgel *f*, Leierkasten *m*.

bar·ren ['bærən] *adj* □ **1.** unfruchtbar (*Lebewesen, Land etc*). **2.** *geistig* unproduktiv. **3.** ~ *of* arm an (*dat*), ...los. **4.** nutzlos, ✝ tot (*Kapital*).

bar·rette [bæ'ret] *s Am.* Haarspange *f*.

bar·ri·cade [ˌbærɪ'keɪd] **I** *s* Barrikade *f*: *go to* (*od. mount*) *the* ~*s* fig. auf die Barrikaden gehen *od.* steigen. **II** *v/t* verbarrikadieren.

bar·ri·er ['bærɪə] *s* **1.** Schranke *f*, Barriere *f*, Sperre *f*. **2.** Schlag-, Grenzbaum *m*. **3.** *phys.* (Schall)Grenze *f*. **4.** *fig.* Hindernis *n* (*to* für). ~ **cream** *s* Schutzcreme *f*.

bar·ring ['bɑːrɪŋ] *prp* ausgenommen, abgesehen von: ~ *a miracle* falls *od.* wenn kein Wunder geschieht.

bar·ris·ter ['bærɪstə] *s* ⚖ **1.** *Br.* Barrister *m* (*vor höheren Gerichten plädierender Anwalt*). **2.** *Am. allg.* Rechtsanwalt *m*.

bar·row ['bærəʊ] *s* (Hand-, Schub)Karre(n *m*) *f*.

'**bar·tend·er** *bsd. Am.* → **barman**.

bar·ter ['bɑːtə] **I** *v/t* (*ein*)tauschen (*against, for* gegen). **II** *v/i* verhandeln (*for* über *acc*). **III** *s* Tausch(handel *m*, -geschäft *n*) *m*.

ba·salt ['bæsɔːlt] *s geol.* Basalt *m*.

base[1] [beɪs] *adj* □ **1.** gemein, niederträchtig. **2.** minderwertig, (*Metall*) unedel.

base[2] [~] **I** *s* **1.** *a. fig.* Basis *f*, Grundlage *f*, Fundament *n* (*a.* △). **2.** Grundstoff *m*, Hauptbestandteil *m*. **3.** *fig.* Ausgangspunkt *m*, -basis *f*. **4.** ✕ Standort *m*; Basis *f*, Stützpunkt *m*. **5.** *Baseball:* Mal *n*. **II** *v/t* **6.** stützen, gründen (*on od. acc*): *be* ~*d on* beruhen *od.* basieren auf (*dat*).

'**base·ball** *s Sport:* Baseball(spiel *n*) *m*. '~**board** *s Am.* Fuß(boden)-, Scheuerleiste *f*. '~**less** *adj* □ grundlos. ~ **line** *s* Grundlinie *f*.

base·ment ['beɪsmənt] *s* Kellergeschoß *n*.

base·ness ['beɪsnɪs] *s* **1.** Gemeinheit *f*, Niedertracht *f*. **2.** Minderwertigkeit *f*.

ba·ses ['beɪsiːz] *pl von* **basis**.

bash [bæʃ] F **I** *v/t* **1.** heftig schlagen, j-n verprügeln: ~ *in* einschlagen. **II** *s* **2.** heftiger Schlag: *give s.o. a* ~ (*on the*

battery

nose) *j-m* ein Ding (auf die Nase) verpassen. **3.** Versuch *m:* **have a ~ at s.th.** es mit et. probieren.

bash·ful ['bæʃfʊl] *adj* □ scheu, schüchtern.

bas·ic ['beɪsɪk] **I** *adj* grundlegend, Grund...: **~ fact** grundlegende Tatsache; **~ fee** (*law, salary, etc*) Grundgebühr *f* (*-gesetz n, -gehalt n etc*). **II** *s pl* Grundlagen *pl.* **'bas·i·cal·ly** *adv* **1.** im Grunde. **2.** im wesentlichen.

ba·sil·i·ca [bə'zɪlɪkə] *s* △ Basilika *f.*

ba·sin ['beɪsn] *s allg.* Becken *n* (*a. geol. etc*); *engS.* Schale *f*, Schüssel *f.*

ba·sis ['beɪsɪs] *pl* **-ses** [-siːz] *s* **1.** ✕ Basis *f*, Stützpunkt *m.* **2.** *fig.* Basis *f*, Grundlage *f:* **on the ~ of** auf der Basis von (*od. gen*); **~ of discussion** Diskussionsgrundlage; **take as a ~** zugrunde legen.

bask [baːsk] *v/i* sich sonnen (*a. fig.*): **~ in the sun** ein Sonnenbad nehmen.

bas·ket ['baːskɪt] *s* Korb *m.* **'~·ball** *s Sport:* Basketball(spiel *n*) *m.*

bass [beɪs] *s* ♪ Baß(stimme *f*) *m;* Bassist *m.*

bas·soon [bə'suːn] *s* ♪ Fagott *n.*

bas·tard ['baːstəd] **I** *s* **1.** Bastard *m* (*a. biol.*). **2.** *sl.* Scheißkerl *m; allg.* Kerl *m:* **poor ~** armes Schwein; **a ~ of a headache** verfluchte Kopfschmerzen *pl.* **II** *adj* **3.** unehelich. **4.** *biol.* Bastard...

baste¹ [beɪst] *v/t* Braten mit Fett begießen.

baste² [~] *v/t* verprügeln.

baste³ [~] *v/t* (an)heften.

bas·tion ['bæstjən] *s* ✕ Bastion *f.*

bat¹ [bæt] *s zo.* Fledermaus *f:* **(as) blind as a ~** stockblind; **have ~s in the belfry** F e-n Vogel haben.

bat² [~] **I** *s* **1.** *Baseball, Kricket:* Schlagholz *n,* Schläger *m:* **off one's own ~** selbständig; auf eigene Faust. **2.** *Br.* F Tempo *n:* **at a fair ~** mit e-m ganz schönen Zahn. **3.** *Am. sl.* Sauferei *f:* **go on a ~** e-e Sauftour machen. **II** *v/i* **4.** *Baseball, Kricket:* am Schlagen sein.

bat³ [~] *v/t:* **without ~ting an eyelid** ohne mit der Wimper zu zucken.

batch [bætʃ] *s* Stapel *m,* Stoß *m.*

bat·ed ['beɪtɪd] *adj:* **with ~ breath** mit angehaltenem Atem, gespannt.

bath [baːθ] **I** *pl* **baths** ['~ðz] *s* **1.** (Wannen)Bad *n:* **have** (*od.* **take**) **a ~** ein Bad nehmen, baden. **2.** Badewanne *f.* **3.** Bad(ezimmer) *n.* **4.** *mst pl* Bad *n:* a) Badeanstalt *f,* b) Badeort *m.* **5.** 🔥, *phot.* Bad *n.* **II** *v/t* **6.** *Br.* baden. **III** *v/i* **7.** *Br.* baden, ein Bad nehmen.

bathe [beɪð] **I** *v/t* **1.** Wunde etc, *bsd. Am. a. Kind etc* baden. **2.** *~d in sunlight* (*sweat, tears*) *fig.* sonnenüberflutet (schweißgebadet, tränenüberströmt). **II** *v/i* **3.** *bsd. Am.* baden, ein Bad nehmen. **4.** baden, schwimmen. **III** *s* **5.** Bad *n* (*im Freien*): **have** (*od.* **take**) **a ~ → 4.**

bath·ing ['beɪðɪŋ] **I** *s* Baden *n.* **II** *adj* Bade...: **~ accident** (*cap, costume od. dress od. suit, trunks*) Badeunfall *m* (*-mütze f od. -kappe f, -anzug m, -hose f*).

'bath·robe *s* **1.** Bademantel *m.* **2.** *Am.* Morgen-, Schlafrock *m.* **~·room** ['~·rʊm] *s* **1.** Badezimmer *n.* **2.** *Am.* Toilette *f.* **~ tow·el** *s* Badetuch *n.* **'~·tub** *s* Badewanne *f.*

ba·tik [bə'tiːk] *s* Batik(druck) *m.*

ba·tiste [bæ'tiːst] *s* Batist *m.*

ba·ton ['bætən] *s* **1.** (Amts-, Kommando)Stab *m.* **2.** ♪ Taktstock *m.* **3.** *Leichtathletik:* (Staffel)Stab *m.* **4.** Schlagstock *m,* Gummiknüppel *m* (*der Polizei*).

bats·man ['bætsmən] *s* (*irr man*) *Kricket:* Schläger *m,* Schlagmann *m.*

bat·tal·ion [bə'tæljən] *s* ✕ Bataillon *f.*

bat·ten¹ ['bætn] **I** *s* Latte *f,* Leiste *f.* **II** *v/t:* **~ down the hatches** ⚓ die Luken schalken; *fig.* alles dichtmachen.

bat·ten² [~] *v/i mst fig.* dick u. fett werden (**on** auf Kosten *gen*).

bat·ter¹ ['bætə] *v/t* **1.** wiederholt heftig schlagen; *Frau, Kind etc* (wiederholt) mißhandeln: **~ down** (*od.* **in**) einschlagen; **~ed wives' refuge** Frauenhaus *n.* **2.** abnutzen. **3.** (arg) lädieren *od.* zerbeulen, *a. fig.* arg in Mitleidenschaft ziehen. **II** *v/i* **4.** wiederholt heftig schlagen *od.* stoßen (**against** gegen; **at** an *acc*): **~ (away) at the door** gegen die Tür hämmern. **III** *s* **5.** *gastr.* Eierkuchenteig *m.*

bat·ter² [~] *s Baseball, Kricket:* Schläger *m,* Schlagmann *m.*

bat·ter·y ['bætərɪ] *s* **1.** ⚡ Batterie *f.* **2.** Batterie *f,* Reihe *f,* Satz *m.* **3.** ✈ Legebatterie *f.* **4.** ⚖ Tätlichkeit *f;* Körper-

verletzung f. **~ hen** s 🐦 Batteriehenne f.
'**~-op·er·at·ed** adj batteriebetrieben,
Batterie...

bat·tle ['bætl] **I** s **1.** ⚔ Schlacht f (of bei).
2. fig. Kampf m (for um). **II** v/i **3.** bsd.
fig. kämpfen: **~ for breath** um Atem
ringen. '**~·ax(e)** s **1.** ⚔ hist. Streitaxt f.
2. F alter Drachen. '**~·field**, '**~·ground**
s ⚔ Schlachtfeld n: **~ country** kriegführendes Land. '**~·ship** s Schlacht-
schiff n.

bat·tue [bæˈtuː] s Treibjagd f.

bat·ty ['bætɪ] adj sl. bekloppt, verrückt.

baulk → **balk**.

baux·ite ['bɔːksaɪt] s min. Bauxit m.

Ba·var·i·an [bəˈveərɪən] **I** adj bay(e)-
risch. **II** s Bayer(in).

bawd·y ['bɔːdɪ] adj unflätig, obszön.

bawl [bɔːl] **I** v/i schreien, brüllen: **~ at**
s.o. j-n anbrüllen; **~ for help** um Hilfe
schreien. **II** v/t oft **~ out** (heraus)schrei-
en, (-)brüllen.

bay¹ [beɪ] s Bai f, Bucht f.

bay² [~] s △ Erker m.

bay³ [~] s ♣ Lorbeer(baum) m.

bay⁴ [~] **I** v/i bellen: **~ at s.o.** j-n anbellen;
fig. j-n anschreien. **II** s Gebell n: **be** (od.
stand) **at ~** gestellt sein (Wild); fig. in
die Enge getrieben sein; **bring to ~** Wild
stellen; fig. in die Enge treiben; **keep**
(od. **hold**) **at ~** j-n in Schach halten;
Krankheit etc von sich fernhalten; Feuer, Seuche etc unter Kontrolle halten.

bay·o·net ['beɪənɪt] s ⚔ Bajonett n, Sei-
tengewehr n.

bay win·dow s **1.** Erkerfenster n. **2.** Am.
humor. Vorbau m (Bauch).

ba·zaar [bəˈzɑː] s (a. Wohltätigkeits)Ba-
sar m.

be [biː] (irr) **I** v/aux **1.** Zustand: sein: **he**
is gone er ist weg. **2.** Passiv: werden: **I**
was cheated ich wurde betrogen. **3.**
sollen, müssen, dürfen, können: **he is**
to be pitied er ist zu bedauern; **it is not**
to be seen es ist nicht zu sehen; **it was**
not to be es sollte nicht sein. **4.** Verlaufsform: **he is reading** er liest (gerade); **he was watching TV when the**
telephone rang er sah gerade fern, als
das Telefon läutete. **5.** nahe Zukunft: **I**
am leaving tomorrow ich reise morgen
ab; → **go** 27. **6.** Kopula: sein: **he is my**
father. **II** v/i **7.** sein, der Fall sein: **how**
is it that ...? wie kommt es, daß ...?; **it is**

I (F **me**) ich bin es. **8.** sein, bestehen: **to**
be or not to be: that is the question
Sein oder Nichtsein, das ist hier die
Frage. **9.** sein, stattfinden (Versammlung etc); gehen, fahren (Bus etc). **10.**
sein, sich befinden: **have you ever**
been to London? sind Sie schon einmal
in London gewesen?; **has anyone**
been? F ist j-d dagewesen? **11.** (beruflich) werden: **I'll be an engineer** ich
werde einmal Ingenieur. **12.** gehören:
this book is mine. 13. sein, stammen
(from aus). **14.** kosten: **how much are**
these gloves? **15.** dauern (Veranstaltung etc).

beach [biːtʃ] **I** s Strand m: **on the ~** am
Strand. **II** v/t Schiff auf den Strand
setzen od. ziehen. '**~·ball** s Wasserball
m. '**~·bug·gy** s mot. Strandbuggy m.
'**~·tow·el** s Bade-, Strandlaken n. '**~·wear**
s Strandkleidung f.

bea·con ['biːkən] s **1.** Leucht-, Signal-
feuer n. **2.** → **Belisha beacon**.

bead [biːd] **I** s **1.** (Glas-, Schweiß-, Tau-
etc)Perle f. **2.** pl eccl. Rosenkranz m:
say (od. **tell**) **one's ~s** den Rosenkranz
beten. **II** v/t **3.** mit Perlen besetzen. **III**
v/i **4.** perlen.

beak [biːk] s **1.** orn. Schnabel m. **2.** ⚙
Tülle f. **beaked** adj **1.** schnabelförmig.
2. vorspringend, spitz.

beak·er ['biːkə] s Becher m.

beam [biːm] **I** s **1.** Balken m. **2.** Strahl m,
🔆, phys. a. Bündel n. **~ of rays** Strahlen-
bündel; **~ of hope** Hoffnungsstrahl. **3.**
Peil-, Leit-, Richtstrahl m: **be off** (the) **~**
✈, ⚓ vom Kurs abgekommen sein; F
auf dem Holzweg sein; **be on** (the) **~** ✈,
⚓ auf Kurs sein; F auf dem richtigen
Weg sein. **4.** strahlendes Lächeln. **II** v/t
5. ausstrahlen (a. phys. u. Rundfunk,
TV). **III** v/i **6.** strahlen (a. fig. with vor
dat): **~ing with joy** freudestrahlend.
'**~·ends** s pl: **be on one's ~** fig. auf
dem letzten Loch pfeifen.

bean [biːn] s **1.** ♣ Bohne f: **be full of ~s**
F aufgekratzt sein; voller Leben(skraft)
stecken; **spill the ~s** F alles ausplaudern. **2.** Am. sl. Birne f (Kopf).

bear¹ [beə] **I** s **1.** zo. Bär m. **2.** fig.
Brummbär m; Tolpatsch m. **3.** ♣ Bais-
sespekulant m. **II** v/i **4.** ♣ auf Baisse
spekulieren.

bear² [~] (irr) **I** v/t **1.** Last, a. fig. Datum,

Verantwortung, Verlust etc tragen: → **fruit** 2a, **interest** 6, **resemblance**, *etc.* **2.** zur Welt bringen, gebären. **3.** *Gefühl* hegen: → **grudge** 3. **4.** *Gehorsam etc* leisten: → **company** 1. **5.** ertragen, aushalten, -stehen: → **comparison** 1. **II** *v/i* **6.** tragen, halten (*Balken, Eis etc*). **7.** (*on*) sich beziehen (auf *acc*), betreffen (*acc*): → **pressure**. **8.** ~ (**to the**) **left** sich links halten.

Verbindungen mit Adverbien:

~ **a·way** *v/t* **1.** forttragen. **2.** *Sieg etc* davontragen. ~ **down I** *v/t* überwinden, -wältigen, *Widerstand* brechen. **II** *v/i* (*on*) sich (schnell) nähern (*dat*); sich stürzen (auf *acc*); *fig.* lasten (auf *dat*), bedrücken (*acc*); *e-r Sache* zu Leibe gehen. ~ **in** *v/t*: *it was borne in on him* es wurde ihm klar (*that* daß). ~ **out** *v/t* bekräftigen, bestätigen; *j-m* recht geben. ~ **up I** *v/t* **1.** ermutigen. **II** *v/i* **2.** (*against, under*) sich behaupten (gegen), (tapfer) ertragen (*acc*). **3.** *Br.* Mut fassen, (wieder) fröhlich werden: ~*!* Kopf hoch!

bear·a·ble ['beərəbl] *adj* □ erträglich.

beard [bɪəd] **I** *s* Bart *m*: *laugh in one's* ~ sich ins Fäustchen lachen. **II** *v/t*: ~ *the lion in his den fig.* sich in die Höhle des Löwen wagen. **'beard·ed** *adj* bärtig. **'beard·less** *adj* bartlos.

bear·er ['beərə] *s* **1.** Träger(in). **2.** Überbringer(in) (*a.* ♣ *e-s Schecks etc*). **3.** ♣ Inhaber(in) (*e-s Wertpapiers*).

bear·ing ['beərɪŋ] *s* **1.** Ertragen *n*: *beyond* (*od. past*) ~ unerträglich. **2.** Betragen *n*, Verhalten *n*. **3.** (Körper)Haltung *f*. **4.** (*on*) Beziehung *f* (zu), Bezug *m* (auf *acc*). **5.** ✈, ⚓ Lage *f*, Position *f* (*a.* Funk)Peilung *f*, *a. fig.* Orientierung *f*: *take one's* ~*s* e-e Peilung vornehmen; sich orientieren; *lose one's* ~(*s*) die Orientierung verlieren; *find* (*od. get*) *one's* ~*s* sich zurechtfinden. **6.** ⚙ (*Achsen-, Kugel- etc*)Lager *n*.

bear·ish ['beərɪʃ] *adj* **1.** bärenhaft. **2.** *fig.* brummig; tolpatschig. **3.** ♣ flau; Baisse...

bear| paw *s Am.* Radkralle *f*, Parkriegel *m.* '~**·skin** *s* Bärenfell *n*.

beast [bi:st] *s* **1.** (*a.* wildes) Tier: ~ *of burden* Lasttier; ~ *of prey* Raubtier. **2.** *fig.* Bestie *f*; F Biest *n*, Ekel *n*. **'beast·ly**

adj **1.** *fig.* tierisch. **2.** F ekelhaft, gemein; scheußlich.

beat [bi:t] **I** *s* **1.** (*Herz-, Trommeletc*)Schlag *m*. **2.** ♪ Takt *m*; (*Jazz*) Beat *m*; Beat(musik *f*) *m*: *in* ~ im Takt; *out of* ~, *off* (**the**) ~ aus dem Takt. **3.** Runde *f*, Revier *n* (*e-s Schutzmanns etc*): *be on one's* ~ s-e *od.* die Runde machen; *that is out of my* ~ *fig.* das schlägt nicht in mein Fach. **4.** F wie erschlagen, fix u. fertig. **5.** ♪ Beat...: ~ *group* (*music, etc*). **III** *v/t* (*irr*) **6.** schlagen, (ver)prügeln. **7.** a) schlagen; *Teppich etc* (aus)klopfen; *Metall* hämmern *od.* schmieden, b) → **beat up** 3. **8.** *Weg* treten, sich bahnen: ~ *it* F abhauen, verduften. **9.** *j-n* schlagen, besiegen (*at* in *dat*); *et.* übertreffen, -bieten: *that* ~*s all* (*od. everything*)! *das* ist doch die Höhe! **10.** verblüffen: *that* ~*s me* das ist mir zu hoch. **IV** *v/i* **11.** schlagen: ~ *at* (*od. on*) *the door* gegen die Tür hämmern.

Verbindungen mit Adverbien:

beat| back *v/t Gegner* zurückschlagen. ~ **down I** *v/t* **1.** *Aufstand etc* niederschlagen. **2.** *Preis* drücken, *a. j-n* herunterhandeln (*to auf acc*). **II** *v/i* **3.** herunterbrennen (*on auf acc*) (*Sonne*); herunter-, niederprasseln (*on auf acc*) (*Regen*). ~ **off** *v/t Angriff, Gegner* zurückschlagen. ~ **in** *v/t Tür* einschlagen. ~ **out** *v/t* Feuer ausschlagen. ~ **up** *v/t* **1.** aufrütteln (*a. fig.*). **2.** *j-n* zs.-schlagen. **3.** *Eier etc* (zu Schaum *od.* Schnee) schlagen.

beat·en ['bi:tn] **I** *pp von* **beat**. **II** *adj* **1.** ⚙ gehämmert: ~ *gold* Blattgold *n*. **2.** vielbegangen (*Weg*): *off the* ~ *track* ungewöhnlich, ungewöhnlich. **'beat·er** *s* **1.** ⚙ Stampfe *f*; Stößel *m*; Klopfer *m*. **2.** *gastr.* Schneebesen *m*. **'beat·ing** *s* Prügel *pl*; *fig.* Niederlage *f*: *give s.o. a sound* ~ j-m e-e tüchtige Tracht Prügel verabreichen; j-m e-e böse Schlappe zufügen.

beat·nik ['bi:tnɪk] *s* Beatnik *m*.

beau·ti·cian [bju:'tɪʃn] *s* Kosmetiker(in).

beau·ti·ful ['bju:təfʊl] *adj* □ schön: *the* ~ *people pl* die Schickeria.

beau·ti·fy ['bju:tɪfaɪ] *v/t* verschönern.

beau·ty ['bju:tɪ] *s* **1.** Schönheit *f* (*a.* Frau). **2.** F das Schön(st)e. **3.** F Gedicht *n*, Prachtstück *n* (**of** von). **~ com-pe·ti·tion**, **~ con·test** *s* Schönheitswettbewerb *m.* **~ farm** *s* Schönheitsfarm *f.* **~ par·lo(u)r** *s* Schönheitssalon *m.* **~ patch** → **beauty spot** 1. **~ queen** *s* Schönheitskönigin *f.* **~ sa·lon**, *Am.* **~ shop** → **beauty parlo(u)r.** **~ sleep** *s* F Schlaf *m* vor Mitternacht. **~ spot** *s* 1. Schönheitspflästerchen *n.* 2. schönes Fleckchen Erde.

bea·ver ['biːvə] *s zo.* Biber *m.*

be·came [bɪ'keɪm] *pret von* become.

be·cause [bɪ'kɒz] I *cj* weil, da. II *prp:* **~ of** wegen (*gen*).

beck [bek] *s:* **be at s.o.'s ~ and call** j-m auf den leisesten Wink gehorchen, nach j-s Pfeife tanzen. **beck·on** ['~ən] *v/t* j-m (zu)winken, j-m ein Zeichen geben.

be·come [bɪ'kʌm] (*irr*) I *v/i* 1. werden: **what has become of him?** was ist aus ihm geworden? II *v/t* 2. sich ziemen für. 3. j-m stehen, passen zu.

be·com·ing *adj* □ 1. passend, kleidsam: **be very ~ to s.o.** j-m sehr gut stehen. 2. schicklich, geziemend.

bed [bed] I *s* 1. (*a. Fluß- etc*)Bett *n:* **go to ~** ins Bett gehen (**with** mit); **keep one's ~** das Bett hüten; **make the ~** das Bett machen; **as you make your ~ so you must lie on it** wie man sich bettet, so liegt man; **put to ~** ins Bett bringen; **take to one's ~** sich (krank) ins Bett legen; **~ and breakfast** Zimmer *n* mit Frühstück. 2. (Garten)Beet *n.* 3. ☉ Bett(ung *f*) *n*, Unterlage *f.* II *v/t* 4. ins Bett bringen. 5. **~ out** auspflanzen, -setzen.

be·daub [bɪ'dɔːb] *v/t* beschmieren: **~ed with clay** lehmbeschmiert.

'**bed|·bug** *s zo.* Wanze *f.* '**~·clothes** *s pl* Bettwäsche *f.* '**~·cov·er** *s* Bettdecke *f.*

bed·ding ['bedɪŋ] *s* Bettzeug *n.*

be·deck [bɪ'dek] *v/t* schmücken.

be·dev·il [bɪ'devl] *v/t pret u. pp* **-iled**, *bsd. Br.* **-illed** durcheinanderbringen, verwirren.

bed·lam ['bedləm] *s fig.* Tollhaus *n.*

bed| lin·en *s* Bettwäsche *f.* '**~·pan** *s* Stechbecken *n*, Bettpfanne *f*, -schüssel *f.* '**~·post** *s* Bettpfosten *m:* → **between** 2.

be·drag·gled [bɪ'dræɡld] *adj* 1. durchnäßt; verdreckt. 2. *fig.* heruntergekom-

men (*Haus etc*); ungepflegt (*Erscheinung etc*).

bed|·rest *s* Bettruhe *f.* '**~·rid·den** *adj* bettlägerig. '**~·rock** *s geol.* Grund-, Muttergestein *n:* **get down to the ~ of a matter** *fig.* e-r Sache auf den Grund gehen. '**~·room** ['~rʊm] *s* Schlafzimmer *n:* **~ suburb** (*od.* **town**) Schlafstadt *f.* '**~·side** *s:* **at the ~** am Bett; **have a good ~ manner** gut mit Kranken umgehen können; **~ lamp** Nachttischlampe *f;* **~ rug** Bettvorleger *m;* **~ table** Nachttisch(chen *n*) *m.* '**~·sit**, ,**~·sit·ter**, ,**~·sit·ting room** *s Br.* 1. möbliertes Zimmer. 2. Einzimmerapartment *n.* '**~·sore** *s ❦* wundgelegene Stelle: **get ~s** sich durch- *od.* wundliegen. '**~·space** *s* Bettenzahl *f*, -kapazität *f* (*in Klinik, Hotel etc*). '**~·spread** *s* Tagesdecke *f.* '**~·stead** *s* Bettgestell *n.* '**~·tick** *s* Inlett *n.* '**~·time** *s* Schlafenszeit *n:* **~ reading** Bettlektüre *f;* **~ story** Gutenachtgeschichte *f.*

bee [biː] *s zo.* Biene *f:* (**as**) **busy as a ~** bienenfleißig; **have a ~ in one's bonnet** F e-n Fimmel *od.* Tick haben.

beech [biːtʃ] *s ❧* Buche *f.* '**~·nut** *s* Bucheicker *f.*

beef [biːf] I *s* 1. Rindfleisch *n.* 2. F (Muskel)Kraft *f.* 3. *sl.* Meckerei *f*, Nörgelei *f.* II *v/i* 4. *sl.* meckern, nörgeln (**about** über *acc*). '**~·bur·ger** ['~bɜːɡə] *s gastr.* Hamburger *m.* '**~·eat·er** *s Br.* Beefeater *m*, Tower-Wächter *m.* ,**~·steak** *s* Beefsteak *n.* **~ tea** *s* (Rind)Fleischbrühe *f*, Bouillon *f.*

beef·y ['biːfɪ] *adj* F bullig.

'**bee·line** *s:* **make a ~ for** schnurstracks zu- *od.* losgehen auf (*acc*).

been [biːn] *pp von* be.

beer [bɪə] *s* Bier *n:* → **small** I. **~ gar·den** *s* Biergarten *m.*

beer·y ['bɪərɪ] *adj* 1. bierselig. 2. nach Bier riechend: **~ breath** Bierfahne *f.*

'**bees·wax** *s* Bienenwachs *n.*

beet [biːt] *s ❧* Runkelrübe *f*, *Am. a.* rote Bete *od.* Rübe.

bee·tle ['biːtl] *s zo.* Käfer *m.*

be·fore [bɪ'fɔː] I *adv* 1. *räumlich:* vorn, voran: **go ~** vorangehen. 2. *zeitlich:* vorher, zuvor: **the year ~** das vorhergehende Jahr. II *prp* 3. *räumlich:* vor (*acc od. dat*): **~ my eyes** vor m-n Augen. 4. vor (*dat*), in Gegenwart von (*od. gen*): **~**

witnesses vor Zeugen. **5.** *zeitlich:* vor (*dat*): *the week ~ last* vorletzte Woche; *~ long* in Kürze, bald. **6.** *Reihenfolge, Rang:* voraus, vor (*acc od. dat*): *be ~ the others* den anderen voraus sein. **III** *cj* **7.** bevor, ehe: *not ~* erst als *od.* wenn.

be'fore·hand *adv* **1.** zu'vor, (im) voraus: *know s.th. ~* et. im voraus wissen. **2.** zuvor, früher. **3.** zu früh, verfrüht.

be·friend [bɪˈfrend] *v/t j-m* behilflich sein; sich *j-s* annehmen.

beg [beg] **I** *v/t* **1.** et. erbitten (*of s.o.* von j-m): *~ leave* (*of s.o.*) (j-n) um Erlaubnis bitten; → *pardon* 3. **2.** erbetteln, betteln um. **3.** *j-n* bitten (*to do* zu tun). **II** *v/i* **4.** betteln: *go ~ging* betteln gehen; *fig.* keinen Interessenten *od.* Abnehmer finden. **5.** (dringend) bitten (*for* um; *of s.o.* j-n). **6.** sich erlauben *od.* gestatten (*to do* zu tun).

be·gan [bɪˈgæn] *pret von* begin.

be·get [bɪˈget] *v/t* (*irr*) **1.** *Kind* zeugen. **2.** *fig.* erzeugen.

beg·gar [ˈbegə] **I** *s* **1.** Bettler(in). **2.** F Kerl *m:* *lucky ~* Glückspilz *m.* **II** *v/t* **3.** an den Bettelstab bringen. **4.** *~ description* sich nicht mit Worten beschreiben lassen; jeder Beschreibung spotten. 'beg·gar·ly *adj* **1.** bettelarm. **2.** *fig.* armselig, kümmerlich. 'beg·gar·y *s* Bettelarmut *f.*

be·gin [bɪˈgɪn] *v/t u. v/i* (*irr*) beginnen, anfangen: *to ~ with* zunächst (einmal); erstens (einmal); *~ on s.th.* et. in Angriff nehmen; *~ (on) a new bottle* e-e neue Flasche anbrechen. be·gin·ner *s* Anfänger(in): *~'s luck* Anfängerglück *n.* be·gin·ning *s* **1.** Beginn *m,* Anfang *m:* *at* (*od. in*) *the ~* am Anfang; *from the ~* (ganz) von Anfang an. **2.** *pl* (erste) Anfänge *pl.*

be·go·ni·a [bɪˈgəʊnjə] *s* ⚘ Begonie *f.*

be·got [bɪˈgɒt] *pret von* beget. be·got·ten [~tn] *pp von* beget.

be·grudge [bɪˈgrʌdʒ] *v/t* **1.** *~ s.o. s.th.* j-m et. mißgönnen. **2.** *~ doing s.th.* et. nur widerwillig tun.

be·guile [bɪˈgaɪl] *v/t* **1.** betrügen (*of, out of* um), täuschen. **2.** verleiten (*into doing* zu tun). **3.** sich *die Zeit* (angenehm) vertreiben (*by, with* mit).

be·gun [bɪˈgʌn] *pp von* begin.

be·half [bɪˈhɑːf] *s:* *on* (*Am. a. in*) *~ of* zugunsten von (*od. gen*), für; im Na-

men *od.* Auftrag von (*od. gen*), für.

be·have [bɪˈheɪv] **I** *v/i* **1.** sich (gut) benehmen. **2.** sich verhalten *od.* benehmen (*to, towards* gegen, gegenüber). **3.** sich verhalten (*Sache*), arbeiten, funktionieren (*Maschine etc*). **II** *v/t* **4.** *~ o.s.* → 1: *~ yourself!* benimm dich! be'hav·io(u)r [~jə] *s* Benehmen *n,* Betragen *n,* Verhalten *n:* *be on one's best ~* sich von s-r besten Seite zeigen; *put s.o. on his best ~* j-m einschärfen, sich gut zu benehmen; *~ pattern psych.* Verhaltensmuster *n.* be'hav·io(u)r·al *adj psych.* Verhaltens...: *~ disturbance* Verhaltensstörung *f.* be'hav·io(u)r·ism *s psych.* Behaviorismus *m.*

be·head [bɪˈhed] *v/t* enthaupten.

be·hind [bɪˈhaɪnd] **I** *prp* **1.** *räumlich u. zeitlich:* hinter (*acc od. dat*): *get s.th. ~ one* et. hinter sich bringen. **2.** *Reihenfolge, Rang:* hinter (*acc od. dat*): *be ~ s.o.* j-m nachstehen (*in in dat*). **II** *adv* **3.** hinten, dahinter: *walk ~* hinterhergehen. **4.** nach hinten: *look ~* zurückblicken. **III** *adj* **5.** hinten. **6.** *~ with* Verzug (*in, with* mit). **IV** *s* **6.** F Hintern *m.* be'hind·hand *adv u. adj* **1.** im Rückstand *od.* Verzug (*with* mit). **2.** rückständig.

beige [beɪʒ] *adj* beige.

be·ing [ˈbiːɪŋ] *s* **1.** (Da)Sein *n,* Existenz *f:* *in ~* existierend, wirklich (vorhanden); *call into ~* ins Leben rufen; *come into being* entstehen. **2.** *j-s* Wesen *n,* Natur *f.* **3.** (Lebe)Wesen *n,* Geschöpf *n.*

be·la·bo(u)r [bɪˈleɪbə] *v/t* mit Worten bearbeiten, *j-m* zusetzen.

be·lat·ed [bɪˈleɪtɪd] *adj* verspätet: *~ best wishes* nachträglich herzlichen Glückwunsch.

belch [beltʃ] **I** *v/i* **1.** aufstoßen, rülpsen. **2.** quellen (*from* aus) (*Rauch etc*). **II** *v/t* **3.** *a.* *~ out* (*od. forth*) Feuer, Rauch etc speien, *a. fig. Beleidigungen etc* ausstoßen. **III** *s* **4.** Aufstoßen *n,* Rülpsen *n;* Rülpser *m.* **5.** *fig.* (Rauch-, Flammen*etc*)Stoß *m.* **6.** *fig.* Schwall *m* (*von Beleidigungen etc*).

bel·fry [ˈbelfrɪ] *s* Glockenstuhl *m;* Glockenturm *m:* → *bat*[1].

Bel·gian [ˈbeldʒən] **I** *adj* belgisch. **II** *s* Belgier(in).

be·lie [bɪˈlaɪ] *v/t* **1.** *j-n, et.* Lügen strafen. **2.** hinwegtäuschen über (*acc*). **3.** *Hoff-*

belief   772

nung etc enttäuschen, *e-r Sache* nicht entsprechen.

be·lief [bɪˈliːf] *s* **1.** Glaube *m* (*in an acc*): **beyond** ∼ unglaublich. **2.** Vertrauen *n* (*in auf e-e Sache*, zu *j-m*). **3.** Anschauung *f*, Überzeugung *f*: **to the best of my** ∼ nach bestem Wissen u. Gewissen.

be·liev·a·ble [bɪˈliːvəbl] *adj* **1.** glaubhaft. **2.** glaubwürdig.

be·lieve [bɪˈliːv] I *v/i* **1.** glauben (*in an acc*), (*in*) vertrauen (auf *acc*), Vertrauen haben (zu). **3.** viel halten (*in* von): **not to** ∼ *in s.th.* nichts *od.* nicht viel davon halten, *et.* zu tun. II *v/t* **4.** glauben: ∼ *it or not!* ob Sie es glauben oder nicht! *would you* ∼ *it!* ist das denn die Möglichkeit!; *he is* ∼*d to be rich* man hält ihn für reich; → *reason* 1. **5.** glauben (*dat*). **be·liev·er** *s* Gläubige *m*, *f*: *be a great* ∼ *in* fest glauben an (*acc*); viel halten von.

Be·li·sha bea·con [bɪˈliːʃə] *s Br.* Blinklicht *n* (*an Fußgängerüberwegen*).

be·lit·tle [bɪˈlɪtl] *v/t* **1.** herabsetzen, schmälern. **2.** verharmlosen, bagatellisieren.

bell [bel] I *s* **1.** Glocke *f*, Klingel *f*, Schelle *f*: *that rings a* ∼ F das kommt mir bekannt vor, das erinnert mich an et. **2.** Glockenzeichen *n*, Läuten *n*, Klingeln *n*: → *answer* 10. **3.** *teleph.* Wecker *m*. **4.** Taucherglocke *f.* II *v/t* **5.** ∼ *the cat fig.* der Katze die Schelle umhängen. '∼·**boy** *s bsd. Am.* (Hotel)Page *m.* '∼·**flow·er** *s* ♀ Glockenblume *f.* '∼·**hop** *s Am.* (Hotel)Page *m.*

bel·li·cose [ˈbelɪkəʊs] *adj* □ **1.** kriegslustig, kriegerisch. **2.** → *belligerent* 3.

bel·lied [ˈbelɪd] *adj* bauchig.

bel·lig·er·ent [bɪˈlɪdʒərənt] I *adj* □ **1.** → *bellicose* **1.** **2.** kriegführend. **3.** *fig.* streitlustig, aggressiv. II *s* **4.** kriegführendes Land.

bel·low [ˈbeləʊ] I *v/i* **1.** brüllen (*with vor dat*). **2.** grölen. II *v/t* **a.** ∼ *out* **3.** Befehl *etc* brüllen, *Lied etc* grölen. III *s* **5.** Brüllen *n.* **6.** Grölen *n.*

bel·lows [ˈbeləʊz] *s pl* (*a. sg konstruiert*) Blasebalg *m.*

bell| **push** *s* Klingelknopf *m.* '∼·**weth·er** *s* Leithammel *m* (*a. fig.*).

bel·ly [ˈbelɪ] I *s* **1.** Bauch *m* (*a. e-s Schiffs etc*). **2.** Magen *m.* II *v/i u. v/t* **3.** *a.* ∼ *out* (an)schwellen (lassen). '∼·**ache** I *s* F

Bauchweh *n.* II *v/i sl.* meckern, nörgeln (*about* über *acc*). ∼ *but·ton n.* F Bauchknöpfchen *n.* ∼ *danc·er s* Bauchtänzerin *f.*

bel·ly·ful [ˈbelɪfʊl] *s* F **1.** *have a* ∼ *of* sich den Bauch vollschlagen mit. **2.** *have had a* (*od. one's*) ∼ *of* die Nase voll haben un.

bel·ly land·ing *s* ✈ Bauchlandung *f.*

be·long [bɪˈlɒŋ] *v/i* **1.** gehören (*to dat*). **2.** gehören (*to* zu; *in acc*). **3.** angehören (*to dat*). **be·long·ings** *s pl* Habseligkeiten *pl*, Habe *f*; F Angehörige *pl.*

be·lov·ed [bɪˈlʌvd; -vɪd] *adj* (innig) geliebt. II *s* Geliebte *m, f.*

be·low [bɪˈləʊ] I *adv* **1.** unten. **2.** hinunter, nach unten. II *prp* **3.** unter (*acc od. dat*), unterhalb (*gen*): ∼ *s.o.* unter j-s Rang, Würde *etc.*

belt [belt] I *s* **1.** Gürtel *m*: *hit below the* ∼ (*Boxen*) tief schlagen, *j-m* e-n Tiefschlag versetzen; → *tighten* 1. **2.** (Sicherheits)Gurt *m.* **3.** Gürtel *m*, Gebiet *n*, Zone *f.* **4.** ⚙ (Treib)Riemen *m.* II *v/t* **5.** ∼ *on* an-, umschnallen. **6.** *a.* ∼ *out Lied etc* schmettern. III *v/i* **7.** ∼ *up mot. etc* sich anschnallen. **8.** *bsd. mot.* F rasen. **9.** ∼ *up! sl.* halt die Schnauze!

be·moan [bɪˈməʊn] *v/t* betrauern, beklagen.

be·mused [bɪˈmjuːzd] *adj* **1.** verwirrt. **2.** gedankenverloren.

bench [bentʃ] *s* **1.** (Sitz)Bank *f.* **2.** Werkbank *f*, -tisch *m.*

bend [bend] I *s* **1.** Biegung *f*, Krümmung *f*, (*e-r Straße a.*) Kurve *f*: *drive s.o. round the* ∼ *Br.* F j-n verrückt machen. II *v/t* (*irr*) **2.** biegen, krümmen: ∼ *out of shape* verbiegen. **3.** *Kopf* neigen, *Knie* beugen. **4.** *Bogen, Feder etc* spannen. **5.** ⚖ *Recht* beugen. **6.** *Blicke, Gedanken etc* richten, *Anstrengungen etc* konzentrieren (*on, to* auf *acc*). III *v/i* (*irr*) **7.** sich biegen *od.* krümmen; e-e Biegung machen (*Fluß*), (*Straße a.*) e-e Kurve machen. **8.** *a.* ∼ *down* sich bücken; sich nach unten biegen; sich verbeugen (*to, before vor dat*).

be·neath [bɪˈniːθ] I *adv* **1.** unten. **2.** darunter. II *prp* **3.** unter (*acc od. dat*), unterhalb (*gen*): ∼ *him* (*od. his dignity*) unter s-r Würde; → *contempt* 1.

ben·e·dic·tion [ˌbenɪˈdɪkʃn] *s eccl.* **1.** Segen *m.* **2.** Segnung *f.*

ben·e·fac·tion [ˌbenɪˈfækʃn] s **1.** Wohltat f. **2.** wohltätige Gabe. **ben·e·fac·tor** [ˈ~tə] s Wohltäter m. **ben·e·fac·tress** [ˈ~trɪs] s Wohltäterin f.

be·nef·i·cence [bɪˈnefɪsns] s Wohltätigkeit f. **be·nef·i·cent** adj □ wohltätig.

ben·e·fi·cial [ˌbenɪˈfɪʃl] adj □ (to) nützlich, zuträglich (dat), vorteilhaft, günstig (für).

ben·e·fit [ˈbenɪfɪt] I s **1.** Vorteil m, Nutzen m, Gewinn m: be of ~ to nützen (dat); for the ~ of zugunsten (gen); de·rive (od. get) ~ (from) → 5; → reap. 2. (Arbeitslosen- etc)Unterstützung f; (Kranken- etc)Geld n; (Sozial-, Versicherungs- etc)Leistung f. **3.** Wohltätigkeitsveranstaltung f. II v/t pret u. pp -ed, bsd. Am. -ted 4. nützen (dat), fördern (acc), im Interesse (gen) sein od. liegen. III v/i 5. (by, from) Vorteil haben (von, durch), Nutzen ziehen (aus).

be·nev·o·lence [bɪˈnevələns] s **1.** Wohltätigkeit f. **2.** Wohlwollen n. **3.** Wohltat f. **be·nev·o·lent** adj □ **1.** wohltätig. **2.** wohlwollend.

be·nign [bɪˈnaɪn] adj □ **1.** gütig, freundlich. **2.** mild: ~ climate. **3.** ✿ gutartig: ~ tumo(u)r.

bent [bent] I pret u. pp von **bend**. II adj **1.** entschlossen (on doing zu tun); erpicht (on auf acc), darauf aus (on doing zu tun). III s **2.** Neigung f, Hang m (for zu): to the top of one's ~ nach Herzenslust. **3.** Veranlagung f: have a ~ for art künstlerisch veranlagt sein; ~ for languages Sprachbegabung f.

be·numbed [bɪˈnʌmd] adj **1.** gefühllos, starr (with cold vor Kälte). **2.** fig. gelähmt.

ben·zene [ˈbenziːn] s 🜊 Benzol n.

ben·zine [ˈbenziːn] s 🜊 Leichtbenzin n.

be·queath [bɪˈkwiːð] v/t hinterlassen, vermachen (s.th. to s.o. j-m et.). **be·quest** [bɪˈkwest] s Vermächtnis n.

be·rate [bɪˈreɪt] v/t auszanken (about, for wegen).

be·reave [bɪˈriːv] v/t (a. irr) berauben (of gen): ~ s.o. of speech j-m die Sprache rauben; the ~d der od. die Hinterbliebene; the Hinterbliebenen pl. **be·reave·ment** s **1.** schmerzlicher Verlust (durch Tod). **2.** Trauerfall m.

be·reft [bɪˈreft] I pret u. pp von **bereave**. II adj mst fig. beraubt (of gen): ~ of all hope.

ber·ry [ˈberɪ] s ♣ Beere f.

ber·serk [bəˈzɜːk] adj: go ~ wild werden; Amok laufen.

berth [bɜːθ] I s **1.** ⚓ Liege-, Ankerplatz m. **2.** ⚓ Koje f. **3.** 🛏 (Schlafwagen)Bett n. **4.** give a wide ~ to e-n großen Bogen machen um. **5.** F Stellung f, Pöstchen n: he's got a good ~. II v/i **6.** ⚓ festmachen, anlegen.

be·seech [bɪˈsiːtʃ] v/t (a. irr) **1.** j-n anflehen (for um; to do zu tun). **2.** et. erflehen (of von). **be'seech·ing** adj flehend. **be'seech·ing·ly** adv flehentlich.

be·set·ting [bɪˈsetɪŋ] adj hartnäckig: ~ sin Gewohnheitslaster n.

be·side [bɪˈsaɪd] prp **1.** neben (acc od. dat). **2.** außerhalb: → point 11. **3.** be ~ o.s. außer sich sein (with vor dat). **be·sides** [~dz] I adv außerdem. II prp außer, neben (dat).

be·siege [bɪˈsiːdʒ] v/t **1.** ⚔ belagern (a. fig.). **2.** fig. bestürmen, bedrängen (with mit).

be·sought [bɪˈsɔːt] pret u. pp von **beseech**.

be·spec·ta·cled [bɪˈspektəkld] adj bebrillt.

be·spoke [bɪˈspəʊk] adj Br. Maß...: ~ tailor Maßschneider m.

best [best] I (sup von **good**) adj **1.** best. **2.** größt, meist: the ~ part of der größte Teil (gen). II (sup von **well²**) adv **3.** am besten: the ~-hated man der meistgehaßte Mann; as ~ they could so gut sie konnten; you had ~ go es wäre das beste, wenn Sie gingen. III s **4.** der, die, das Beste: at ~ bestenfalls, höchstens; do one's ~ sein möglichstes tun; have (od. get) the ~ of übertreffen; F übers Ohr hauen; make the ~ of sich zufriedengeben mit; sich abfinden mit; voll ausnutzen; das Beste machen aus; all the ~! alles Gute!; → ability, belief 3, etc.

bes·tial [ˈbestjəl] adj □ tierisch, fig. a. bestialisch, viehisch. **bes·ti·al·i·ty** [ˌ~tɪˈælətɪ] s **1.** Bestialität f (a. fig.). **2.** Sodomie f.

be·stir [bɪˈstɜː] v/t: ~ o.s. to do s.th. sich dazu aufraffen, et. zu tun.

best man s (irr **man**) Freund des Bräuti-

*gams, der bei der Ausrichtung der Hoch-
zeit e-e wichtige Rolle spielt.*

be·stow [bɪ'stəʊ] *v/t Preis, Titel* verleihen (**on** *dat*). **be'stow·al** *s* Verleihung *f.*

best| sell·er *s* **1.** Bestseller *m.* **2.** Bestsel-
lerautor *m.* '**~·,sell·ing** *adj:* ~ *novel*
Bestseller *m;* ~ *author* Bestseller-
autor *m.*

bet [bet] **I** *s* **1.** Wette *f;* Welteinsatz *m:*
have (*od.* **make**) **a** ~ e-e Wette abschließen *od.* eingehen (**on** auf *acc*). **2. my ~ is
that** ich würde sagen, daß; **it's a safe ~
that** es steht so gut wie fest, daß. **3. your
best ~ is to take the car** F du nimmst
am besten den Wagen. **II** *v/t* (*a. irr*) **4.**
Geld wetten, setzen (**on** auf *acc*): **I'll ~
you £ 10 that** ich wette mit dir (um) 10
Pfund, daß; **you can ~ your boots** (*od.*
bottom dollar, shirt) **that** F du kannst
Gift darauf nehmen, daß. **5.** ~ (*s.o.*)
that fig. (mit j-m) wetten, daß. **III** *v/i* (*a.
irr*) **6.** wetten, setzen (**on** auf *acc*): **you
~!** F das kann man wohl sagen.

be·tray [bɪ'treɪ] *v/t* verraten (**to** *dat od.* an
acc) (*a. fig.*). **be'tray·al** *s* Verrat *m.*

bet·ter¹ [ˈbetə] **I** (*comp von* **good**) *adj*
besser: *I am* ~ es geht mir (*gesundheitlich*) besser; *get* ~ besser werden; sich
erholen. **II** *s das Bessere:* **for** ~ **for
worse** in Freud u. Leid (*Trauformel*);
was auch (*immer*) geschieht; **get the** ~
of *j-n* besiegen, ausstechen; *et.* überwinden. **III** (*comp von* **well²**) *adj* besser: ~ *off* besser daran; (*finanziell*) bessergestellt; *think* ~ *of it* es sich anders
überlegen; *you had* ~ *go* es wäre besser,
du gingest; *you had* ~ *not!* laß das
lieber sein!; → *know* 6, *like²* I. **IV** *v/t
Beziehungen, Rekord etc* verbessern: ~
o.s. sich (*finanziell*) verbessern; sich
weiterbilden. **V** *v/i* besser werden.

bet·ter² [~] *s* Wetter(in).

bet·ter·ment [ˈbetəmənt] *s* **1.** (Ver)Besse-
rung *f.* **2.** ♉ Wertsteigerung *f,* -zu-
wachs *m.*

bet·ting [ˈbetɪŋ] *s* Wetten *n:* ~ *office* (*Br.
shop*) Wettbüro *n.*

be·tween [bɪ'twiːn] **I** *prp* **1.** *räumlich u.
zeitlich:* zwischen (*dat od. acc*): → *devil*
1, *stool* 1. **2.** unter (*dat od. acc*): ~ *you
and me* (*and the bedpost od.* gatepost
od. lamppost F) unter uns *od.* im Vertrauen (gesagt); *we had ten pounds* ~

us wir hatten zusammen zehn Pfund. **II**
adv **3.** dazwischen: *the space* ~ der
Zwischenraum; *in* ~ dazwischen.

bev·el [ˈbevl] **I** *s* Schräge *f,* Abschrägung *f.* **II** *v/t pret u. pp* -**eled,** *bsd. Br.*
-**elled** abschrägen. **III** *adj* abgeschrägt,
schräg.

bev·er·age [ˈbevərɪdʒ] *s* Getränk *n.*

bev·y [ˈbevɪ] *s orn.* Schwarm *m,* Schar *f.*

be·wail [bɪ'weɪl] *v/t* beklagen.

be·ware [bɪ'weə] *v/i* sich hüten, sich
in acht nehmen (**of** vor *dat*): ~ *of the
dog!* Vorsicht, bissiger Hund!; ~ *of pick-
pockets!* vor Taschendieben wird gewarnt!

be·wil·der [bɪ'wɪldə] *v/t* irremachen,
verwirren. **be'wil·der·ment** *s* Verwirrung *f.*

be·witch [bɪ'wɪtʃ] *v/t* bezaubern, be-
hexen.

be·yond [bɪ'jɒnd] **I** *adv* **1.** darüber hinaus. **II** *prp* **2.** jenseits. **3.** über ... (*acc*)
hinaus: *that is* ~ *me* F das ist mir zu
hoch, das geht über m-n Verstand; →
belief 1, *endurance* 1, *measure* 2,
word 1, *etc.*

bi- ... [baɪ] zwei...

,bi'an·nu·al *adj* zweimal jährlich vorkommend *od.* erscheinend. **,bi'an·nu-
al·ly** *adv* zweimal im Jahr.

bi·as [ˈbaɪəs] **I** *s* **1.** Neigung *f,*
Hang *m* (zu); Vorliebe *f* (für). **2.** Vorurteil *n,* ♌ Befangenheit *f:* *free from* ~
unvoreingenommen. **II** *adj u. adv* **3.**
schräg. **III** *v/t pret u. pp* -**as(s)ed 4.**
(*mst ungünstig*) beeinflussen, *j-n* einnehmen (*against* gegen). **'bi·as(s)ed**
adj voreingenommen, ♌ befangen.

bib [bɪb] *s* **1.** Lätzchen *n.* **2.** Schürzen-
latz *m.*

Bi·ble [ˈbaɪbl] *s* Bibel *f.* **bib·li·cal**
[ˈbɪblɪkl] *adj* ☐ biblisch, Bibel...

bib·li·o·graph·ic, **bib·li·o·graph·i·cal**
[ˌbɪblɪəʊˈɡræfɪk(l)] *adj* ☐ bibliogra-
phisch. **bib·li·og·ra·phy** [ˌ~ˈɒɡrəfɪ] *s*
Bibliographie *f.* **bib·li·o·phile** [ˈ~əʊ-
faɪl] *s* Bücherfreund *m,* Bibliophile *m.*

bi·car·bon·ate [~ ♉ Bikarbonat *n:* ~ *of
soda* Natriumbikarbonat.

bi·ceps [ˈbaɪseps] *pl* -**ceps**(-**es**) *s anat.*
Bizeps *m.*

bick·er [ˈbɪkə] **I** *v/i* sich zanken *od.* streiten (*about, over* um). **II** *s* Zank *m,*
Streit *m.* **'bick·er·ing** *s* Gezänk *n.*

bi·cy·cle [ˈbaɪsɪkl] **I** s Fahrrad n. **II** v/i radfahren; mit dem Rad fahren.

bid [bɪd] **I** s 1. † Gebot n (*bei Versteigerungen*); † Angebot n (*bei Ausschreibungen*); † *Am.* Kostenvoranschlag m; *fig.* Bewerbung f (**for** um), Versuch m (**to do** zu tun): *highest* ~ Meistgebot n; *make a* ~ *for* sich bemühen um; ~ *for power* Griff m nach der Macht. **II** v/t (*irr*) 2. † *bei Versteigerungen* bieten. 3. *j-m e-n guten Morgen etc* wünschen: ~ *s.o. good morning;* ~ *farewell* Lebewohl sagen. **III** v/i (*irr*) 4. † *bei Versteigerungen* bieten; † *Am.* e-n Kostenvoranschlag machen; *fig.* sich bemühen (**for** um): ~ *for power* nach der Macht greifen. **'bid·den** pp von **bid**. **'bid·der** s † Bieter m (*bei Versteigerungen*): *highest* ~ Meistbietende m. **'bid·ding** s † Gebot n (*bei Versteigerungen*).

bide [baɪd] v/t (*a. irr*): ~ *one's time* den rechten Augenblick abwarten *od.* abpassen.

bi·en·ni·al [baɪˈenɪəl] adj □ 1. zweijährlich. 2. zweijährig.

bier [bɪə] s (Toten)Bahre f.

bi·fur·cate [ˈbaɪfəkeɪt] **I** v/i sich gabeln. **II** adj gegabelt, gabelförmig. **bi·fur·'ca·tion** s Gabelung f.

big [bɪg] **I** adj 1. *allg.* groß: a) dick, stark: *the* ~*gest party* die stärkste Partei; *earn* ~ *money* F das große Geld verdienen, b) breit, weit: *the coat is too* ~ *for me* der Mantel ist mir zu groß; *get too* ~ *for one's boots* (*od. breeches, bsd. Am. pants*) F größenwahnsinnig werden, c) hoch: ~ *trees,* d) Mords...: ~ *rascal* Erzgauner m; ~ *eater* starker Esser, e) erwachsen, f) wichtig, bedeutend: → *shot* 3. 2. ausgiebig, reichlich: ~ *meal.* 3. F aufgeblasen, eingebildet: *have* ~ *ideas* große Rosinen im Kopf haben; ~ *talk* große Töne pl. 4. *that's very* ~ *of you* das ist sehr großzügig *od.* nobel von Ihnen. 5. *be* ~ *on* F stehen auf (*acc*). **II** adv 6. F mächtig, mordsmäßig. 7. F großspurig: *talk* ~ große Töne spucken.

big·a·mist [ˈbɪgəmɪst] s Bigamist(in).

'big·a·my s Bigamie f, Doppelehe f.

big | **bang** s *Kosmologie:* Urknall m. **'~·,cir·cu·la·tion** adj auflagenstark (*Zeitung*). **'~·mouth** s F Großmaul n.

big·ness [ˈbɪgnɪs] s Größe f.

big·ot [ˈbɪgət] s 1. selbstgerechte *od.* intolerante Person. 2. Frömmler(in). **'big·ot·ed** adj 1. selbstgerecht, intolerant. 2. bigott, frömmlerisch. **'big·ot·ry** s 1. Selbstgerechtigkeit f, Intoleranz f. 2. Bigotterie f, Frömmelei f.

'big·wig s F großes *od.* hohes Tier.

bike [baɪk] F **I** s Rad n (*Fahrrad*); Maschine f (*Motorrad*). **II** v/i radeln, Motorrad fahren; mit dem Motorrad fahren.

bi·lat·er·al adj bilateral, zweiseitig.

bil·ber·ry [ˈbɪlbərɪ] s ❧ Blau-, Heidelbeere f.

bile [baɪl] s 1. *physiol.* Galle f. 2. *fig.* Gereiztheit f; Reizbarkeit f. **'~·stone** s *physiol.* Gallenstein m.

bilge [bɪldʒ] s 1. ⚓ Kielraum m. 2. F Quatsch m, Mist m.

bi·lin·gual adj □ zweisprachig.

bil·ious [ˈbɪljəs] adj □ 1. ⚕ gallig; Gallen...: ~ *attack* Gallenkolik f. 2. *fig.* gereizt; reizbar.

bill¹ [bɪl] **I** s zo. Schnabel m. **II** v/i a. ~ *and coo* (miteinander) turteln.

bill² [~] **I** s 1. *pol.* (Gesetzes)Vorlage f, Gesetzentwurf m. 2. ⚖ (An)Klageschrift f. 3. a. ~ *of exchange* † Wechsel m. 4. Rechnung f: *waiter, the* ~, *please* (Herr) Ober, bitte zahlen! 5. Liste f, Aufstellung f: ~ *of fare* Speise(n)karte f. 6. Bescheinigung f: ~ *of delivery* † Lieferschein m. 7. Plakat n. 8. *thea. etc* Programm(zettel m) n; *weitS.* Programm n: *be on the* ~ auftreten; → *top¹* 12. 9. *Am.* Banknote f, (Geld)Schein m. **II** v/t 10. *j-m* e-e Rechnung ausstellen *od.* schicken: ~ *s.o. for s.th.* j-m et. in Rechnung stellen. 11. (durch Plakate) ankündigen *od.* bekanntgeben.

'bill·board s *bsd. Am.* 1. Reklametafel f. 2. *Film, TV:* Vorspann m.

bil·let [ˈbɪlɪt] **I** s 1. ✕ (Privat)Quartier n. 2. Unterkunft f. **II** v/t 3. ✕ einquartieren (**with, on** bei). 4. unterbringen. **III** v/i 5. ✕ einquartiert sein. 6. (*bsd.* vorübergehend) wohnen.

'bill·fold s *Am.* Scheintasche f; Brieftasche f.

bil·liard [ˈbɪljəd] **I** s pl (*mst sg konstruiert*) Billard(spiel) n. **II** adj Billard...: ~ *ball* (*table*); ~ *cue* Queue f.

bil·lion ['bɪljən] s **1.** Milliarde f. **2.** Br. obs. Billion f.

bil·low ['bɪləʊ] **I** s **1.** Woge f. **2.** (Nebel-, Rauch)Schwaden m. **II** v/i **3.** wogen. **4.** a. ~ **out** sich bauschen od. blähen (Segel, Vorhänge etc). **III** v/t **5.** bauschen, blähen. '**bil·low·y** adj **1.** wogend. **2.** in Schwaden ziehend. **3.** gebauscht, gebläht.

'**bill‖post·er**, '**~stick·er** s Plakatkleber m.

bil·ly ['bɪlɪ] s Am. (Polizei)Knüppel m. ~ **goat** s Ziegenbock m.

‚**bi'month·ly** adj u. adv zweimonatlich.

bin [bɪn] s Behälter m.

bi·na·ry ['baɪnərɪ] adj ∆, ⊙ etc binär, Binär...

bind [baɪnd] **I** v/t (irr) **1.** binden (**to** an acc); ~ **together** zs.-binden; ~ **up** aneinander-, zs.-binden; Wunde verbinden. **2.** Saum einfassen. **3.** 🐝 etc (mit e-m Bindemittel) binden. **4.** Buch (ein)binden. **5.** fig. (a. vertraglich) binden, verpflichten (**to s.th.** zu et.; **to do** zu tun). **II** v/i (irr) **6.** 🐝 etc binden. **7.** fest od. hart werden. **8.** fig. binden(d sein). **III** s **9.** **be in a** ~ F in Schwulitäten sein. '**bind·er** s **1.** (Buch- etc)Binder(in). **2.** (Akten- etc)Deckel m, Umschlag m. **3.** 🐝 etc Bindemittel n. '**bind·ing I** adj □ **1.** fig. bindend, verbindlich (**on** für): **legally** ~ rechtsverbindlich; **not** ~ unverbindlich. **II** s **2.** (Buch)Einband m. **3.** Einfassung f, Borte f. **4.** (Ski)Bindung f. **5.** → **binder** 3.

binge [bɪndʒ] s F Sauf- od. Freßgelage n: **go** (**out**) **on a** ~ e-e Sauf- od. Freßtour machen; **go on a buying** (**shopping, spending**) ~ wie verrückt einkaufen.

bin·go ['bɪŋɡəʊ] s Bingo n (ein Glücksspiel).

bin·oc·u·lars [bɪ'nɒkjʊləz] s pl (**a pair of** ein) Fernglas n.

bi·o·chem·i·cal [‚baɪəʊ'kemɪkl] adj □ biochemisch. ‚**bi·o'chem·ist** s Biochemiker(in). ‚**bi·o'chem·is·try** s Biochemie f.

bi·o·graph·ic, bi·o·graph·i·cal [‚baɪəʊ-'ɡræfɪk(l)] adj □ biographisch. **bi·og·ra·phy** [~'ɒɡrəfɪ] s Biographie f.

bi·o·log·i·cal [‚baɪəʊ'lɒdʒɪkl] adj □ biologisch. **bi·ol·o·gist** [~'ɒlədʒɪst] s Biologe m. **bi'ol·o·gy** s Biologie f.

bi·par·ti·san [‚baɪpɑːtɪ'zæn] adj pol. Zweiparteien...

birch [bɜːtʃ] s 🌿 Birke f.

bird [bɜːd] s **1.** Vogel m: ~ **of passage** Zugvogel (a. fig.); ~ **of prey** Raubvogel; **a** ~ **in the hand is worth two in the bush** besser ein Spatz in der Hand als e-e Taube auf dem Dach; **tell a child about the** ~**s and the bees** ein Kind aufklären; **that's** (**strictly**) **for the** ~**s** F das ist für die Katz; das taugt nichts; **give s.o. the** ~ j-n auspfeifen od. ausbuhen; → **early** 4, **feather** 1, **fly** 1 2, **kill** 1. **2.** F Kerl m: **queer** ~ komischer Kauz. '~**cage** s Vogelkäfig m. '~**house** s Nistkasten m.

bird·ie ['bɜːdɪ] s Vögelchen n.

bird‖ sanc·tu·a·ry s Vogelschutzgebiet n. '~**seed** s Vogelfutter n. '**bird's-eye** adj: ~ **view** (Blick m aus der) Vogelschau; fig. allgemeiner Überblick (**of** über acc); ~ **perspective** Vogelperspektive f. ~ **nest** s Vogelnest n.

bird strike s ✈ Vogelschlag m.

bi·ro ['baɪərəʊ] pl **-ros** (TM) s Br. Kugelschreiber m.

birth [bɜːθ] s **1.** Geburt f: **at** ~ bei der Geburt; **from** (od. **since**) (**one's**) ~ von Geburt an; **give** ~ gebären, zur Welt bringen; fig. hervorbringen, -rufen. **2.** Abstammung f, Herkunft f: **he's a man of** (**good**) ~ er stammt aus gutem Hause; **she's English by** ~ sie ist gebürtige Engländerin. **3.** Ursprung m, Entstehung f. ~ **cer·tif·i·cate** s Geburtsurkunde f. ~ **con·trol** s Geburtenregelung f, -kontrolle f. '~**day** s Geburtstag m: **when is your** ~? wann hast du Geburtstag?; **happy** ~! alles Gute od. herzlichen Glückwunsch zum Geburtstag! **II** adj Geburtstags...: ~ **party** (**present,** etc); ~ **honours** pl Titelverleihungen pl anläßlich des Geburtstags des Königs od. der Königin; **in one's** ~ **suit** im Adams- od. Evaskostüm. '~**mark** s Muttermal n. ~ **pill** s ✞ Antibabypille f. '~**place** s Geburtsort m. '~**rate** s Geburtenziffer f: **falling** ~ Geburtenrückgang m.

bis·cuit ['bɪskɪt] s **1.** Br. Keks m, n. **2.** Am. kleines weiches Brötchen.

bi·sect [baɪ'sekt] v/t **1.** in zwei Teile (zer)schneiden. **2.** 🅰 halbieren. ‚**bi'sec·tion** s 🅰 Halbierung f.

ˌbi'sex·u·al adj □ bisexuell.

bish·op ['bɪʃəp] s **1.** eccl. Bischof m. **2.** Schach: Läufer m. **bish·op·ric** ['ˌrɪk] s eccl. Bistum n.

bit¹ [bɪt] s **1.** Gebiß n (am Pferdezaum): **take the ~ between one's teeth** durchgehen (Pferd); fig. sich reinknien. **2.** ⊕ Backe f, Maul n (e-r Zange etc); (Schlüssel)Bart m. **3.** Mundstück n (e-r Tabakspfeife etc).

bit² [~] s **1.** Bissen m, Happen m. **2.** Stück(chen) n (a. fig.): **fall to ~s** entzweigehen, zerbrechen; **a ~** ein bißchen; ziemlich; **not a ~** überhaupt nicht; **a ~ of a coward** ziemlich feig; **a ~ of a fool** ein bißchen dumm; **~ by ~** Stück für Stück, nach u. nach; **do one's ~** s-e Pflicht (u. Schuldigkeit) tun; s-n Beitrag leisten. **3.** F Augenblick m, Moment m: **after a ~** nach e-m Weilchen. **4.** F kleine Münze.

bit³ [~] s Computer: Bit n.

bit⁴ [~] pret von **bite**.

bitch [bɪtʃ] s **1.** zo. Hündin f. **2.** sl. Schlampe f; Miststück n: → **son** 1.

bite [baɪt] **I** v/t (irr) **1.** beißen: ~ **back** sich e-e Äußerung etc verkneifen; ~ **off** abbeißen; ~ **off more than one can chew** F sich zuviel zumuten; ~ **the dust** (Am. a. **ground**) F ins Gras beißen; ~ **one's nails** an den Nägeln kauen; fig. nervös sein; → **lip** 1, **tongue** 1. **2.** beißen, stechen (Insekt). **II** v/i (irr) **3.** (zu)beißen: ~ **into** (hinein)beißen in (acc). **4.** anbeißen (a. fig.), schnappen (**at** nach) (Fisch). **5.** beißen, stechen (Insekt). **6.** beißen (Rauch, Gewürz etc). **7.** fassen, greifen (Rad, Schraube etc). **8.** fig. beißend od. verletzend sein. **9.** sich (bsd. negativ) auswirken (Maßnahme). **III** s **10.** Biß m, (e-s Insekts a.) Stich m. Biß(wunde f) m. **12.** Bissen m, Happen m (a. weitS. Imbiß, Nahrung). **13.** Fassen n, Greifen n (von Rädern, Schrauben etc): **s.th. has lost its ~** fig. et. greift od. funktioniert nicht mehr. **14.** Schärfe f (a. fig.).

bit·ing ['baɪtɪŋ] adj beißend (Rauch etc), schneidend (Wind, Kälte etc) (beide a. Worte etc).

bit·ten ['bɪtn] **I** pp von **bite**. **II** adj: **once ~ twice shy** (ein) gebranntes Kind scheut das Feuer.

bit·ter ['bɪtə] **I** adj □ **1.** bitter (a. fig.): **to** **the ~ end** bis zum bitteren Ende; **weep ~ly** bitterlich weinen. **2.** fig. scharf, heftig (Kritik etc). **3.** fig. erbittert (Feinde etc); verbittert (**about** wegen). **II** adv **4.** ~ **cold** bitterkalt. **III** s **5.** Bitterkeit f. **6.** fig. das Bittere. **7.** Br. stark gehopftes (Faß)Bier. **8.** mst pl Magenbitter m.

bit·ter·ness ['bɪtənɪs] s **1.** Bitterkeit f (a. fig.). **2.** fig. Verbitterung f.

bi·tu·men ['bɪtjʊmɪn] s min. Bitumen n.

bi·tu·mi·nous [bɪ'tjuːmɪnəs] adj: ~ **coal** Steinkohle f.

biz [bɪz] F für **business**.

bi·zarre [bɪ'zɑː] adj bizarr.

blab [blæb] **I** v/t **1.** oft ~ **out** ausplaudern. **II** v/i **2.** schwatzen. **3.** fig. plaudern.

black [blæk] **I** adj **1.** allg. schwarz (a. fig.): ~ **coffee**; ~ **humo(u)r**; ~ **man** Schwarze m; ~ **in the face** dunkelrot im Gesicht (vor Aufregung etc); **beat s.o. ~ and blue** j-n grün u. blau schlagen; **look ~ at s.o., give s.o. a ~ look** j-n (böse) anfunkeln; **he's not so ~ (od. as) as as he's painted** er ist besser als sein Ruf. **2.** ✝ bsd. Br. boykottiert. **II** s **3.** Schwarz n: **dressed in ~** schwarz od. in Schwarz gekleidet; **be in (od. wear) ~** Trauer tragen. **4.** oft ⊠ Schwarze m, f. **5.** **be in the ~** ✝ mit Gewinn arbeiten; aus den roten Zahlen heraussein. **III** v/t **6.** → **blacken** 1. **7.** ✝ bsd. Br. boykottieren. **8.** ~ **out** abdunkeln, a. ✕ verdunkeln. **9.** ~ **out** Nachrichten etc unterdrücken. **IV** v/i **10.** schwarz werden. **11.** ~ **out** ein Blackout haben. **12.** ~ **out** bewußtlos werden.

black| and white pl **black and whites** s **1.** **in ~** schwarz auf weiß, schriftlich. **2.** Schwarzweißbild n. **3.** **depict s.th. in ~** fig. et. schwarzweißmalen. **~-and- -'white** adj **1.** schriftlich. **2.** Schwarzweiß...: ~ **television**; ~ **depiction** Schwarzweißmalerei f. **~'ball** v/t stimmen gegen. **~·ber·ry** ['ˌbərɪ] s ♣ Brombeere f. **'~·bird** s orn. Amsel f. **'~·board** s (Schul-, Wand)Tafel f. **~ box** s ✈ F Flugschreiber m.

black·en ['blækən] **I** v/t **1.** schwarz machen, schwärzen. **2.** fig. ~ **s.o.'s character** j-n verunglimpfen; ~ **s.o.'s name** (od. **reputation**) j-n schlechtmachen. **II** v/i **3.** schwarz werden.

black| eye s blaues Auge, Veilchen n: **give s.o. a ~** j-m ein blaues Auge schlagen. **~·guard** ['blægɑːd] s Schuft *m*, Lump *m*. **~ ice** s Glatteis *n*.

black·ish ['blækɪʃ] *adj* schwärzlich.

'black·jack s **1.** Siebzehnundvier *n*. **2.** *bsd. Am.* Totschläger *m* (*Waffe*). **~ lead** [led] s *min.* Graphit *m*. **'~·leg** s *bsd. Br.* Streikbrecher *m*. **~·let·ter day** s schwarzer Tag, Unglückstag *m*. **'~·list** **I** s schwarze Liste. **II** v/t auf die schwarze Liste setzen. **~ mag·ic** s Schwarze Magie. **'~·mail I** s Erpressung *f*. **II** v/t *j-n* erpressen (**over** mit). **'~·mail·er** s Erpresser(in). ♀ **Ma·ri·a** [mə'raɪə] s F grüne Minna. **~ mar·ket** s schwarzer Markt, Schwarzmarkt *m*. **~ mar·ket·eer** [ˌmɑːkə'tɪə] s Schwarzhändler(in). **~ mass** s Schwarze Messe.

black·ness ['blæknɪs] s Schwärze *f*.

'black·out s **1.** ✕, ✈, *thea. etc* Blackout *n, m*. **2.** ✚ Ohnmacht *f*, Bewußtlosigkeit *f*. **3.** (*bsd.* Nachrichten)Sperre *f*: **draw a ~ over** e-e Nachrichtensperre verhängen über (*acc*). **~ pud·ding** s Blutwurst *f*. **~ sheep** s (*irr sheep*) *fig.* schwarzes Schaf.

blad·der ['blædə] s *anat.* Blase *f*.

blade [bleɪd] s **1.** ♦ Halm *m*: **~ of grass** Grashalm. **2.** ❀ Blatt *n* (*e-r Säge, e-s Ruders etc*). **3.** ❀ Flügel *m* (*e-s Propellers*); Schaufel *f* (*e-r Turbine etc*). **4.** ❀ Klinge *f* (*e-s Messers etc*).

blah [blɑː], *a.* **,blah'blah** s F Blabla *n*, Geschwafel *n*.

blame [bleɪm] **I** v/t **1.** tadeln (**for** wegen). **2. ~ s.o. for s.th., ~ s.th. on s.o.** j-n verantwortlich machen für et., *j-m* die Schuld geben an et.: **he is to ~ for it** er ist daran schuld; **he has only himself to ~** er hat es sich selbst zuzuschreiben. **II** s **3.** Tadel *m*. **4.** Schuld *f*, Verantwortung *f*: **lay** (*od.* **put, cast**) **the ~ on s.o.** j-m die Schuld geben; **bear** (*od.* **take**) **the ~** die Schuld auf sich nehmen. **'blame·less** *adj* □ **1.** untadelig. **2.** schuldlos (**of** an *dat*).

blanch [blɑːntʃ] **I** v/t **1.** bleichen. **2.** *gastr.* blanchieren. **3.** erbleichen lassen. **II** v/i **4.** erbleichen, bleich werden (**with** vor *dat*).

blanc·mange [blə'mɒndʒ] s Pudding *m*.

blan·dish ['blændɪʃ] v/t *m* schmeicheln, schöntun. **'blan·dish·ment** s *mst pl* Schmeichelei *f*.

blank [blæŋk] **I** *adj* □ **1.** leer, unbe-

schrieben: *leave ~* frei lassen. **2.** ✝, ⚔ Blanko...: **~ check** (*Br.* **cheque**) Blankoscheck *m*, Scheckformular *n*; **~ signature** Blankounterschrift *f*. **3.** inhaltslos, unausgefüllt (*Leben etc*); ausdruckslos (*Gesicht etc*). **4.** verdutzt, verblüfft; verständnislos. **5.** **~ cartridge** → 9. **II** s **6.** freier Raum, Lücke *f*. **7.** unbeschriebenes Blatt (*a. fig.*); Formular *n*, Vordruck *m*. **8.** *Lotterie*: Niete *f*: **draw a ~** e-e Niete ziehen, *fig. a.* kein Glück haben. **9.** ✕ Platzpatrone *f*.

blan·ket ['blæŋkɪt] **I** s (*engS.* Bett)Decke *f*: **~ of snow** (**clouds**) Schnee-(Wolken)decke; → **wet** 1. **II** v/t zudecken: **~ed in** (*od.* **with**) **fog** in Nebel eingehüllt. **III** *adj* umfassend, Gesamt..., Pauschal...

blare [bleə] **I** v/i schmettern (*Trompete*), brüllen, plärren (*Radio etc*). **II** s Schmettern *n*; Brüllen *n*, Plärren *n*.

blar·ney ['blɑːnɪ] **I** s Schmeichelei *f*. **II** v/t *u.* v/i (*j-m*) schmeicheln.

bla·sé ['blɑːzeɪ] *adj* gleichgültig.

blas·pheme [blæs'fiːm] **I** v/t **1.** Gott etc lästern. *allg.* schmähen. **II** v/i **3.** Gott lästern: **~ against** → I. **blas'phem·er** s (Gottes)Lästerer *m*. **blas·phe·mous** ['blæsfəməs] *adj* □ blasphemisch, (gottes)lästerlich. **'blas·phe·my** s **1.** Blasphemie *f*, (Gottes)Lästerung *f*. **2.** *allg.* Schmähung *f*.

blast [blɑːst] **I** s **1.** Windstoß *m*. **2.** (**at**) **full ~** ❀ *u. fig.* auf Hochtouren (*laufen od. arbeiten*). **3.** Explosion *f*, Detonation *f*; Druckwelle *f*. **4.** Sprengung (*f*) Sprengladung *f*. **II** v/t **5.** sprengen. **6.** *fig.* zunichte machen, vereiteln. **7. ~ off** (**into space**) in den Weltraum schießen. **8.** *sl.* verfluchen: **~ed** verdammt, verflucht; **~ed idiot** Vollidiot *m*; **~ it** (**all**)! verdammt (nochmal)!; **~ him!** der Teufel soll ihn holen! **~ fur·nace** s ❀ Hochofen *m*. **'~·off** s Start *m* (*e-r Rakete*).

bla·tant ['bleɪtənt] *adj* □ **1.** lärmend, laut. **2.** marktschreierisch; aufdringlich. **3.** offenkundig, eklatant.

blath·er ['blæðə] **I** v/i quatschen. **II** s Gequatsche *n*.

blaze [bleɪz] **I** s **1.** (lodernde) Flamme: **be in a ~** in hellen Flammen stehen. **2.** Glanz *m* (*a. fig.*): **~ of colo(u)rs** Farbenpracht *f*. **3.** *fig.* plötzlicher Ausbruch: **~ of anger** Wutanfall *m*. **4.** F **go to ~s!** scher dich zum Teufel!; **like ~s** wie verrückt; **what the ~s ...?** was zum Teufel ...? II *v/i* **5.** lodern: **~ up** aufflammen, -lodern, *fig. a.* entbrennen. **6.** *a. fig.* leuchten, glühen (**with** vor *dat*). III *v/t* **7.** *a.* **~ abroad** verkünden, *contp.* ausposaunen. '**blaz·er** *s* Blazer *m*, Klub-, Sportjacke *f*. '**blaz·ing** *adj* **1.** glühend. **2.** auffällig, schreiend, (*Farben a.*) grell.

bla·zon ['bleɪzn] I *s* Wappen *n*. II *v/t mst* **~ abroad** → **blaze** 7.

bleach [bli:tʃ] I *v/t* bleichen. II *s* Bleichmittel *n*.

bleak [bli:k] *adj* □ **1.** kahl, öde. **2.** ungeschützt, windig. **3.** *fig.* trost-, freudlos (*Dasein etc*), trüb, düster (*Aussichten etc*).

blear·y ['blɪərɪ] *adj* **1.** verschwommen. **2.** trüb (*Augen*). '**~-eyed** *adj* **1.** mit trüben Augen. **2.** *fig.* kurzsichtig.

bleat [bli:t] I *v/i* blöken (*Schaf*), meckern (*Ziege*). II *v/t et.* in weinerlichem Ton sagen. III *s* Blöken *n*, Meckern *n*.

bled [bled] *pret u. pp von* **bleed**.

bleed [bli:d] (*irr*) I *v/i* **1.** bluten: **~ to death** verbluten. II *v/t* **2.** *et.* Blut ab lassen. **3.** F schröpfen: **~ s.o. for s.th.** j-m et. abknöpfen. **4.** ◎ **♂** Bremsen entlüften. '**bleed·er** *s* **♂** Bluter *m*: **~'s disease** Bluterkrankheit *f*. '**bleed·ing** I *s* **1.** Blutung *f*: **~ of the nose** Nasenbluten *n*. **2.** **♂** Aderlaß *m*. II *adj u. adv* **3.** *sl.* verdammt, verflucht.

bleep [bli:p] I *s* **1.** Piepton *m*. **2.** F Piepser *m* (*Funkrufempfänger*). II *v/i* **3.** piepen. III *v/t* **4.** *j-n* anpiepsen. '**bleep·er** → **bleep** 2.

blem·ish ['blemɪʃ] I *v/t* verunstalten; *fig.* beflecken. II *s* Fehler *m*, Mangel *m*; *fig.* Makel *m*.

blend [blend] I *v/t* **1.** vermengen, (ver)mischen; e-e (*Tee- etc*)Mischung zs.-stellen aus, *Wein* verschneiden. II *v/i* **2.** (**with**) sich vermischen (mit), gut passen (zu). **3.** verschmelzen, ineinander übergehen (*Farben, Klänge, Kulturen etc*): **~ into** sich vereinigen zu. III *s* **4.** Mischung *f*; Verschnitt *m*.

bless [bles] *v/t* (*a. irr*) **1.** segnen (*a. fig.*): **be ~ed with** gesegnet sein mit; **~ me!**, **~ my soul!** F du m-e Güte!; (**God**) **~ you!** Gesundheit! **2.** **~ o.s.** sich glücklich

schätzen. **3.** **~ him!** *euphem.* der Teufel soll ihn holen! **bless·ed** ['blesɪd] *adj* **1.** gesegnet, selig: **the ♀ Virgin** die heilige Jungfrau. **2.** *euphem.* verwünscht, verflixt: **not a ~ soul** keine Menschenseele. '**bless·ed·ness** *s* Seligkeit *f*. '**bless·ing** *s* Segen *m* (*a. fig.* **to** für): **it turned out to be a ~ in disguise** es stellte sich im nachhinein als Segen heraus.

blest [blest] *pret u. pp von* **bless**.

bleth·er ['bleðə] → **blather**.

blew [blu:] *pret von* **blow**[1].

blight [blaɪt] I *s* **1.** **♣** Mehltau *m*. **2.** *fig.* schädlicher Einfluß. II *v/t* **3.** *fig.* zunichte machen, zerstören. '**blight·er** *s* *Br.* F Kerl *m*: **lucky ~** Glückspilz *m*; **poor ~** armer Hund.

bli·mey ['blaɪmɪ] *int bsd. Br. sl.* Mensch Meier! (*überrascht*); verdammt!

blind [blaɪnd] I *adj* **1.** blind (*a. fig.* **to** gegenüber; **with** vor *dat*): **~ in one eye** auf e-m Auge blind; **turn a ~ eye** ein Auge zudrücken (**to** bei). **2.** unübersichtlich (*Kurve etc*). II *adv* **3.** **~ drunk** F sternhagelvoll. III *v/t* **4.** blenden (*a. fig.*); blind machen (*a. fig.* **to** für, gegen). IV *s* **5.** Rolladen *m*; Rouleau *n*; *bsd. Br.* Markise *f*; ~ **Venetian**. ~ **al·ley** *s* Sackgasse *f* (*a. fig.*): **lead up a ~** in e-e Sackgasse führen. ~ **flight** *s* **✈** Blindflug *m*. '**~·fold** I *adj* mit verbundenen Augen. II *adv fig.* blindlings. III *v/t* *j-m* die Augen verbinden. IV *s* Augenbinde *f*. '**~·man's 'buff** *s* Blindekuh(spiel *n*) *f*.

blind·ness ['blaɪndnɪs] *s* Blindheit *f* (*a. fig.*).

blind| spot *s* **1.** *mot.* toter Winkel (*im Rückspiegel*). **2.** *fig.* schwacher Punkt. '**~·worm** *s* *zo.* Blindschleiche *f*.

blink [blɪŋk] I *v/i* **1.** blinzeln, zwinkern: **~ at** *j-m* zublinzeln, b) *fig.* sich maßlos wundern über (*acc*), c) → **4. 2.** flimmern; blinken. **3.** ~ **one's eyes** mit den Augen zwinkern. **4.** *a.* ~ **away** *fig.* ignorieren. III *s* **5.** Blinzeln *n*. '**blink·er** *s* Blinklicht *n*; *mot.* Blinker *m*. '**blink·ing** *adj u. adv Br.* verdammt.

bliss [blɪs] *s* (Glück)Seligkeit *f*. **bliss·ful** ['~fʊl] *adj* □ (glück)selig.

blis·ter ['blɪstə] I *s* **♂**, ◎ Blase *f*. II *v/t* Blasen hervorrufen auf (*dat*). III *v/i* Blasen ziehen *od.* ◎ werfen.

blith·er·ing [ˈblɪðərɪŋ] *adj Br.* F verdammt: **~ idiot** Vollidiot *m*.

blitz [blɪts] ✕ I *s* **1.** heftiger Luftangriff. **2.** Blitzkrieg *m*. II *v/t* **3.** schwer bombardieren: **~ed** zerbombt.

bliz·zard [ˈblɪzəd] *s* Blizzard *m*, Schneesturm *m*.

bloat·ed [ˈbləʊtɪd] *adj* aufgeblasen (*a. fig. Person*), aufgebläht (*a. fig. Budget etc*), aufgedunsen (*Gesicht etc*).

bloat·er [ˈbləʊtə] *s gastr.* Bückling *m*.

blob [blɒb] *s* Klecks *m*.

bloc [blɒk] *s* ✝, *pol.* Block *m*.

block [blɒk] I *s* **1.** (*a. Motor- etc*)Block *m*, Klotz *m*; Baustein *m*, (Bau)Klötzchen *n* (*für Kinder*). **2.** (*Schreib-, Notiz*)Block *m*. **3.** *bsd. Am.* (Häuser)Block *m*: **~** (*of flats*) *Br.* Wohnhaus *n*. **4.** *fig.* Block *m*, Gruppe *f*. II *v/t* **5.** *a.* **~ up** (ab-, ver)sperren, blockieren, verstopfen. **6.** ✝ *Konto* sperren: **~ed account** Sperrkonto *n*.

block·ade [blɒˈkeɪd] I *s* Blockade *f*. II *v/t* blockieren.

'block|·head *s* Dummkopf *m*. **'~·house** *s* Blockhaus *n*. **~ let·ters** *s pl* Blockschrift *f*.

bloke [bləʊk] *s bsd. Br.* F Kerl *m*.

blond [blɒnd] *adj* **1.** blond (*Haar*), hell (*Haut*). **2.** blond(haarig). **blonde** [blɒnd] I *s* Blondine *f*. II *adj* → **blond**.

blood [blʌd] *s* **1.** Blut *n* (*a. fig.*): **his ~ froze** das Blut erstarrte ihm in den Adern; **related by ~** blutsverwandt; → **cold** 1, **sweat** 2. **2.** Geblüt *n*, Abstammung *f*. **~ al·co·hol** *s* ✻ Blutalkohol *m*. **,~-and-'thun·der** *adj*: **~ novel** Reißer *m*. **~ bank** *s* ✻ Blutbank *f*. **'~·bath** *s* Blutbad *n*. **~ clot** *s* ✻ Blutgerinnsel *n*. **'~·cur·dling** *adj* grauenhaft. **~ do·nor** *s* ✻ Blutspender(in). **~ group** *s* Blutgruppe *f*. **'~·hound** *s* Bluthund *m*.

blood·less [ˈblʌdlɪs] *adj* □ **1.** blutlos, -leer (*a. fig.*). **2.** unblutig (*Kampf etc*).

blood| or·ange *s* Blutorange *f*. **~ poi·son·ing** *s* ✻ Blutvergiftung *f*. **~ pres·sure** *s* ✻ Blutdruck *m*. **~ pud·ding** *s* Blutwurst *f*. **~ re·la·tion**, **~ re·la·tive** *s* Blutsverwandte *m*, *f*. **~ re·venge** *s* Blutrache *f*. **~ sam·ple** *s* ✻ Blutprobe *f*. **'~·shed** *s* Blutvergießen *n*. **'~·shot** *adj* blutunterlaufen. **'~·stained** *adj* blutbefleckt. **'~·suck·er** *s zo.* Blutsauger *m* (*a. fig.*). **~ sug·ar** *s physiol.* Blutzucker *m*.

'~·,thirst·y *adj* blutdürstig. **~ trans·fu·sion** *s* ✻ Bluttransfusion *f*, -übertragung *f*. **~ ves·sel** *s anat.* Blutgefäß *n*.

blood·y [ˈblʌdɪ] *adj* **1.** blutig. **2.** *Br. sl.* verdammt, verflucht: **~ fool** Vollidiot *m*; **not a ~ soul** kein Schwanz. II *adv* **3.** *Br. sl.* → 2: **~ awful** saumäßig.

bloom [bluːm] I *s a.* **blossom** I. II *v/i* blühen (*a. fig.*).

bloom·er [ˈbluːmə] *s bsd. Br.* F grober Fehler, Schnitzer *m*.

bloom·ing [ˈbluːmɪŋ] *adj* **1.** blühend (*a. fig.*). **2.** (*a. adv*) F verflixt.

blos·som [ˈblɒsəm] I *s* **1.** Blüte *f*: **be in full ~** in voller Blüte stehen. **2.** *fig.* Blüte(-zeit) *f*. II *v/i* **3.** blühen (*a. fig.*): **~** (*out*) erblühen (*into* zu).

blot [blɒt] I *s* **1.** Klecks *m*. **2.** *fig.* Makel *m*. II *v/t* **3.** beklecksen. **4.** beflecken. **5.** *Familie, Erinnerungen etc* auslöschen. **6.** *mit Löschpapier* (ab)löschen.

blotch [blɒtʃ] → **blot** 1–3.

blot·ter [ˈblɒtə] *s Am.* Kladde *f*.

blot·ting pa·per [ˈblɒtɪŋ] *s* Löschpapier *n*.

blot·to [ˈblɒtəʊ] *adj sl.* (stink)besoffen.

blouse [blaʊz] *s* Bluse *f*.

blow¹ [bləʊ] I *s* **1.** Blasen *n*, Wehen *n*. **2.** Luftzug *m*. **3.** Blasen *n*: **~ on a whistle** Pfiff *m*; **give one's nose a ~** sich schneuzen. II *v/i* (*irr*) **4.** blasen, wehen. **5.** ertönen (*Pfiff etc*). **6.** keuchen, schnaufen. **7.** explodieren; platzen (*Reifen*); ✻ durchbrennen (*Sicherung*). III *v/t* (*irr*) **8.** blasen, wehen. **9.** *Suppe etc* blasen, *Feuer* anfachen. **10.** (auf-, aus)blasen: **~ bubbles** Seifenblasen machen; **~ glass** Glas blasen; **~ one's nose** sich schneuzen. **11.** **~ one's lid** (*od. top, stack*) F an die Decke gehen. **12.** *sl. Geld* verpulvern (*on* für); *Chance* vergeben.

Verbindungen mit Adverbien:

blow| a·way *v/t* fort-, wegblasen. **~ down** *v/t* um-, herunterwehen. **~ in** *v/i* F hereinschneien (*Besucher*). **~ off** → **blow away**. **~ out** *v/t* **1.** *Licht etc* ausblasen. **2.** *a.* **~ one's brains** F sich e-e Kugel durch den Kopf jagen. **~ up** I *v/t* **1.** (in die Luft) sprengen. **2.** aufblasen, -pumpen. **3.** *phot.* vergrößern. **4.** aufbauschen (*into* zu). **4.** F *j-n* anschnauzen. II *v/i* **5.** in die Luft fliegen; explodieren (*a. fig.* F): **~ at** → 4. **6.** losbrechen (*Sturm etc*), ausbrechen (*Streit etc*).

blow² [~] *s* (*a.* Schicksals)Schlag *m*, Stoß *m*: **at one od. a** [*single*] ~ mit 'einem Schlag; **come to ~s** handgreiflich werden.

'blow·dry *v/t* **1.** j-m die Haare fönen: ~ **s.o.'s hair. 2.** j-m die Haare fönen: ~ **s.o.** ~ **dry·er** *s* Haartrockner *m*.

blow·er *s* ⊙ Gebläse *n*.

'blow·fly *s zo.* Schmeißfliege *f*. **'~·gun** *s* ⊙ Spritzpistole *f*. **'~·lamp** *s* ⊙ Lötlampe *f*.

blown [bləʊn] *pp von* **blow¹**.

'blow·out *s mot.* Reifenpanne *f*. **'~·torch** *s* ⊙ Lötlampe *f*. **'~·up** *s* **1.** Explosion *f* (*a. fig.* F). **2.** F Krach *m*, Streit *m*. **3.** *phot.* Vergrößerung *f*.

blow·y [ˈbləʊɪ] *adj* windig.

blowz·y [ˈblaʊzɪ] *adj* schlampig (*bsd. Frau*).

blub·ber [ˈblʌbə] *v/i* flennen, plärren.

bludg·eon [ˈblʌdʒən] **I** *s* **1.** Knüppel *m*. **II** *v/t* **2.** niederknüppeln. **3.** ~ **s.o. into doing s.th.** j-n zwingen, et. zu tun.

blue [bluː] **I** *adj* **1.** blau: → **moon** I. **2.** F melancholisch, traurig. **3.** unanständig, schlüpfrig: ~ *jokes*; ~ *film* Pornofilm *m*. **4.** F schrecklich: ~ *fear* Heidenangst *f*; → *funk* I, *murder* 1. **II** *s* **5.** Blau *n*: *dressed in* ~ blau od. in Blau gekleidet; *out of the* ~ *fig.* aus heiterem Himmel. **6.** *pl* (*a. sg konstruiert*) F Melancholie *f*: *have* (*od. be in*) *the* ~*s* den Moralischen haben. **7.** → *blues*. **III** *v/t* **8.** blau färben. **~·ber·ry** [ˈ~bərɪ] *s* ♀ Blau-, Heidelbeere *f*. **~·'blood·ed** *adj* blaublütig, adlig. **'~·bot·tle** *s* **1.** *zo.* Schmeißfliege *f*. **2.** ♀ Kornblume *f*. ~ *jeans* *s pl* blue jeans *pl*. ~ *'pen·cil* **1.** Blaustift *m*. **2.** *fig.* Rotstift *m*, Zensur *f*. **~·'pen·cil** *v/t pret u. pp* **-ciled**, *bsd. Br.* **-cilled** zensieren. **'~·print** I *s* **1.** ♦ Blaupause *f*. **2.** *fig.* Plan *m*, Entwurf *m*: ~ *stage* Planungsstadium *n*. **II** *v/t* **3.** e-e Blaupause machen von. **4.** planen, entwerfen.

blues [bluːz] *s pl* **1.** → **blue** 6. **2.** (*a. sg konstruiert*) ♪ Blues *m*.

'blue·stock·ing *s bsd. contp.* Blaustrumpf *m*.

bluff [blʌf] **I** *v/t u. v/i* bluffen. **II** *s* Bluff *m*. **'bluff·er** *s* Bluffer *m*.

blu·ish [ˈbluːɪʃ] *adj* bläulich.

blun·der [ˈblʌndə] **I** *s* **1.** (grober) Fehler. **II** *v/i* **2.** e-n (groben) Fehler machen. **3.** pfuschen, stümpern. **4.** stolpern, tappen (*into* in *acc*) (*beide a. fig.*). **III** *v/t* **5.** verpfuschen, verpatzen. **'blun·der·er** *s* Pfuscher *m*, Stümper *m*. **'blun·der·ing** *adj* stümperhaft.

blunt [blʌnt] *adj* **1.** stumpf. **2.** *fig.* abgestumpft (*to* gegen). **3.** *fig.* ungehobelt. **4.** *fig.* offen, schonungslos. **II** *v/t* **5.** stumpf machen, abstumpfen (*a. fig.* to gegen). **'blunt·ly** *adv fig.* frei heraus: **to put it** ~ um es ganz offen zu sagen; **refuse** ~ glatt ablehnen.

blur [blɜː] **I** *v/t* **1.** verwischen: a) *Schrift etc* verschmieren, b) *a. fig.* undeutlich *od.* verschwommen machen. **2.** *phot.* verwackeln. **3.** *Sinne etc* trüben. **II** *v/i* **4.** verschwimmen (*a. fig. Eindruck etc*). **5.** *fig.* sich verwischen (*Unterschiede etc*).

blurt [blɜːt] *v/t*: ~ **out** herausplatzen mit.

blush [blʌʃ] **I** *v/i* erröten, rot werden (**at** bei): ~ **for** (*od. with*) **shame** schamrot werden. **II** *s* Erröten *n*, (Scham)Röte *f*. **'blush·er** *s* Rouge *n*.

boar [bɔː] *s zo.* Eber *m*, (*Wildschwein*) Keiler *m*.

board [bɔːd] **I** *s* **1.** Brett *n*, Diele *f*, Planke *f*. **2.** (Anschlag-, Schach- *etc*)Brett *n*; (Wand)Tafel *f*: → *sweep* 4. **3.** *pl thea.* Bretter *pl*, Bühne *f*: *tread* (*od. walk*) *the* ~*s* auf den Brettern stehen. **4.** Kost *f*, Verpflegung *f*: ~ *and lodging* Kost u. Logis, Wohnung u. Verpflegung. **5.** Ausschuß *m*, Kommission *f*; Amt *n*, Behörde *f*: ~ *of examiners* Prüfungskommission; ♀ *of Trade Br.* Handelsministerium *n*, *Am.* Handelskammer *f*. **6. on** ~ an Bord (*e-s Schiffs, Flugzeugs*); im Zug *od.* Bus; **go on** ~ **(a) ship** an Bord e-s Schiffs; **go on** ~ an Bord gehen; einsteigen. **7.** Pappe *f*: (*bound*) *in* ~*s* kartoniert. **8.** ♦ dielen, täfeln, verschalen. **9.** an Bord *e-s Schiffs od. Flugzeugs* gehen, ⚓, ✗ entern; einsteigen in (*e-n Zug od. Bus*). **'board·er** *s* **1.** Kostgänger(in); Pensionsgast *m*. **2.** *Br.* Internatsschüler(in).

board game *s* Brettspiel *n*.

board·ing [ˈbɔːdɪŋ] *s* Dielenbelag *m*, Täfelung *f*, Verschalung *f*. ~ *card* *s* ✈ Bordkarte *f*. **~·house** *s* Pension *f*, Fremdenheim *n*. **~·pass** *s* ✈ Bordkarte *f*. ~ *school* *s* Internat *n*, Pensionat *n*.

board room s Sitzungssaal m.

boast [bəʊst] **I** s **1.** Prahlerei f. **2.** Stolz m (*Gegenstand des Stolzes*). **II** v/i **3.** prahlen (**of**, **about** mit). **III** v/t **4.** sich des Besitzes (*gen*) rühmen (können), aufzuweisen haben. '**boast·er** s Prahler(in). '**boast·ful** [-fʊl] adj □ prahlerisch.

boat [bəʊt] **I** s **1.** Boot n; Schiff n: **be in the same ~** fig. im selben Boot sitzen; **burn one's ~s** (**behind one**) fig. alle Brücken hinter sich abbrechen; **take to the ~s** ♣ in die (Rettungs)Boote gehen; → **miss²** 1, **rock²** 2. **2.** (*bsd.* Soßen)Schüssel f. **II** v/i **3.** Boot fahren: **go ~ing** e-e Bootsfahrt machen. '**~house** s Bootshaus n.

boat·ing ['bəʊtɪŋ] s **1.** Bootfahren n. **2.** Bootsfahrt f.

boat¦ race s Bootrennen n. **~swain** ['bəʊsn] s ♣ Bootsmann m. **~ train** s Zug m mit Schiffsanschluß.

bob [bɒb] **I** s **1.** Knicks m. **2.** Sport: Bob m. **II** v/t **3.** Haare etc kurz schneiden, stutzen. **III** v/i **4.** sich auf u. ab bewegen: **~ up** (plötzlich) auftauchen (*a. fig.*). **5.** knicksen (**at**, **before**, **to** vor *dat*).

bob·bin ['bɒbɪn] s Spule f (*a. ⚡*).

bob·by ['bɒbɪ] s Br. F Bobby m (*Polizist*). **~ pin** s bsd. Am. Haarklammer f, -klemme f.

'**bob¦·sled**, '**~·sleigh** s Sport: Bob m.

bode¹ [bəʊd] v/i: **~ ill** Unheil verkünden; **~ well** Gutes versprechen.

bode² [~] pret von **bide**.

bod·ice ['bɒdɪs] s **1.** Mieder n. **2.** Oberteil n (*e-s Kleids etc*).

bod·i·ly ['bɒdɪlɪ] **I** adj **1.** körperlich: **~ harm** (*od.* **injury**) ⚖ Körperverletzung f; **~ needs** (*od.* **wants**) pl leibliche Bedürfnisse pl. **II** adv **2.** leibhaftig. **3.** als Ganzes; geschlossen.

bod·y ['bɒdɪ] s **1.** Körper m, Leib m, engS. Rumpf m. **2.** oft **dead ~** Leiche f. **3.** ♣, ✈ Rumpf m; mot. Karosserie f. **4.** Gesamtheit f: **in a ~** geschlossen, wie ein Mann. **~ of laws** Gesetz(es)sammlung f. **5.** Körper(schaft f) m, Gruppe f, Gremium m: → **diplomatic**, **governing** 2. **6.** fig. Kern m, das Wesentliche. **7.** Haupteil m, Text(teil) m: → **celestial**, **heavenly**. **9.** fig. Körper m, Gehalt m (*von Wein*), (Klang)Fülle f. **~**

build·ing s Bodybuilding n. '**~·guard** s **1.** Leibwächter m. **2.** Leibgarde f, -wache f. **~ lan·guage** s Körpersprache f. **~ o·do(u)r** s (*bsd. unangenehmer*) Körpergeruch. **~ search** s Leibesvisitation f. '**~·work** s mot. Karosserie f.

bog [bɒg] **I** s Sumpf m, Morast m (*beide a. fig.*). **II** v/t: **~ down** fig. zum Stocken bringen; **get ~ged** (**down**) → III. **III** v/i sich festfahren, steckenbleiben (*beide a. fig.*).

bo·gey → **bogy**.

bog·gle ['bɒgl] v/i fassungslos sein: **imagination** (*od.* **the mind**) **~s at the thought** es wird e-m schwindlig bei dem Gedanken.

bog·gy ['bɒgɪ] adj sumpfig, morastig.

bo·gie → **bogy**.

bo·gus ['bəʊgəs] adj **1.** falsch, unecht. **2.** Schwindel..., Schein...

bo·gy ['bəʊgɪ] s Kobold m; (Schreck-) Gespenst n (*a. fig.*).

boil¹ [bɔɪl] s ✱ Geschwür n, Furunkel m, n.

boil² [~] **I** s Kochen n, Sieden n: **bring to the ~** zum Kochen bringen. **II** v/i kochen (*a. fig.* **with** vor *dat*), sieden: → **kettle**, **pot** 1. **III** v/t kochen (lassen). *Verbindungen mit Adverbien:*

boil¦ a·way **I** v/i **1.** kochen, sieden. **2.** verdampfen. **II** fig. abkühlen (*Interesse etc*). **II** v/t **4.** verdampfen lassen. **~ down I** v/t **1.** einkochen lassen. **2.** fig. zs.-fassen (**to a few sentences** in ein paar Sätzen). **II** v/i **3.** einkochen. **4.** **~ to** fig. hinauslaufen auf (*acc*). **~ o·ver** v/i **1.** überkochen, -laufen. **2.** fig. vor Wut kochen. **3.** fig. Situation etc: außer Kontrolle geraten; sich auswachsen (**into** zu).

boil·er ['bɔɪlə] s **1.** ⚙ Dampfkessel m. **2.** Boiler m, Heißwasserspeicher m. **3.** Suppenhuhn n. **~ suit** s Overall m.

boil·ing ['bɔɪlɪŋ] **I** adj siedend, kochend. **II** adv: **~ hot** kochendheiß. **~ point** s Siedepunkt m (*a. fig.*): **reach ~** den Siedepunkt erreichen.

bois·ter·ous ['bɔɪstərəs] adj □ **1.** stürmisch (*Meer, Wetter etc*). **2.** lärmend, laut. **3.** ausgelassen, wild (*Person, Party etc*).

bold [bəʊld] adj □ **1.** kühn: a) mutig, unerschrocken, b) gewagt, c) fortschrittlich. **2.** dreist, frech: **make ~ to**

sich erdreisten *od.* es wagen zu. **3.** scharf hervortretend: *in* ~ *outline* in deutlichen Umrissen.

bole [bəʊl] *s* Baumstamm *m*.

bo·lo·ney [bə'ləʊnɪ] *s sl.* Quatsch *m*.

bol·ster ['bəʊlstə] **I** *s* **1.** Keilkissen *n*; Nackenrolle *f*. **2.** Polster *n*, Kissen *n*, Unterlage *f* (*a.* ☼). **II** *v/t* **3.** (aus)polstern. **4.** *mst* ~ *up fig.* unterstützen.

bolt¹ [bəʊlt] **I** *s* **1.** Bolzen *m*: *he has shot his* ~ *fig.* er hat sein Pulver verschossen. **2.** Blitz(strahl) *m*: *a* ~ *from the blue fig.* ein Blitz aus heiterem Himmel. **3.** ☼ Riegel *m*. **4.** ☼ (Schrauben)Bolzen, Schraube *f* (mit Mutter): ~ *nut* Schraubenmutter *f*. **5.** plötzlicher Satz *od.* Sprung: *he made a* ~ *for the door* er machte e-n Satz zur Tür. **II** *adv* **6.** ~ *upright* bolzen-, kerzengerade. **III** *v/i* **7.** durchbrennen, ausreißen. **8.** durchgehen (*Pferd*). **IV** *v/t* **9.** ver-, zuriegeln. **10.** *oft* ~ *down Essen* hinunterschlingen, *Getränk* hinunterstürzen.

bolt² [⌣] *v/t Mehl* sieben.

bomb [bɒm] **I** *s* Bombe *f*. **II** *v/t* bombardieren: ~*ed out* ausgebombt. ~ *a·lert* *s* Bombenalarm *m*.

bom·bard [bɒm'bɑːd] *v/t* bombardieren (*a. fig.* mit). **bom'bard·ment** *s* Bombardement *n*, Bombardierung *f*.

bom·bast ['bɒmbæst] *s* Bombast *m*, Schwulst *m*. **bom'bas·tic** *adj* (~*ally*) bombastisch, schwülstig.

bombed [bɒmbd] *adj sl.* **1.** besoffen. **2.** high (*im Drogenrausch*).

bomb·er ['bɒmə] *s* **1.** ✈ Bomber *m*. **2.** Bombenleger *m*.

'bomb·proof I *adj* bombensicher: ~ *shelter* → **II**. **II** *s* Bunker *m*. **'~shell** *s*: *be a* ~ wie e-e Bombe einschlagen. **~ threat** *s* Bombendrohung *f*.

bo·nan·za [bəʊ'nænzə] **I** *s fig.* Goldgrube *f*. **II** *adj* einträglich.

bond [bɒnd] **I** *s* **1.** *pl fig.* Bande *pl*: *the* ~*s of love*. **2.** Bund *m*, Verbindung *f*. **3.** ✝ Zollverschluß: *in* ~ unter Zollverschluß. **4.** ✝ Schuldverschreibung *f*, Obligation *f*. **II** *v/t* **5.** ✝ unter Zollverschluß legen: ~*ed warehouse* Zollspeicher *m*. **'~·hold·er** *s* ✝ Obligationshaber *m*.

bone [bəʊn] **I** *s* **1.** Knochen *m*, *pl a.* Gebeine *pl*: *make no* ~*s about* (*od. of*) nicht viel Federlesens machen mit; *feel*

s.th. in one's ~*s* et. in den Knochen *od.* instinktiv spüren; *have a* ~ *to pick with s.o.* mit j-m ein Hühnchen zu rupfen haben; *chilled* (*od. frozen*) *to the* ~ völlig durchgefroren; → *contention* 1. **2.** (*Fisch*)Gräte *f*. **II** *v/t* **3.** entbeinen; *Fisch* entgräten. **III** *v/i* **4.** ~ *up on s.th.* F et. pauken *od.* büffeln. **'~·dry** *adj* knochentrocken. **'~·head** *s* F Holzkopf *m*. **~·'la·zy** *adj* stinkfaul. **'~·shak·er** *s* F Klapperkasten *m* (*Bus etc*).

bon·fire ['bɒn͵faɪə] *s* **1.** Freudenfeuer *n*. **2.** Feuer *n* im Freien (*zum Unkrautverbrennen etc*).

bonk [bɒŋk] *v/t u. v/i sl.* bumsen.

bon·kers ['bɒŋkəz] *adj sl.* übergeschnappt: *go* ~ überschnappen.

bon·net ['bɒnɪt] *s* **1.** ☼ (Schutz)Kappe *f*, Haube *f*. **2.** *mot. Br.* Motorhaube *f*.

bo·nus ['bəʊnəs] *s* **1.** ✝ Bonus *m*, Prämie *f*. **2.** Gratifikation *f*. **3.** ✝ *bsd. Br.* Extradividende *f*.

bon·y ['bəʊnɪ] *adj* **1.** (stark-, grob)knochig. **2.** voll(er) Knochen; voll(er) Gräten (*Fisch*). **3.** knochendürr.

boo [buː] **I** *int* buh! **II** *s* Buh(ruf *n*) *n*. **III** *v/i* buhen. **IV** *v/t* ausbuhen.

boob [buːb] *sl.* **I** *s* **1.** Blödmann *m*, Idiot *m*. **2.** *Br.* Schnitzer *m*. **II** *v/i* **3.** *Br.* e-n Schnitzer machen.

boo·by ['buːbɪ] *s* **1.** Trottel *m*, Dummkopf *m*. **2.** *Sport etc:* Letzte *m*, *f*, Schlechteste *m*, *f*. ~ *hatch* *s Am. sl.* Klapsmühle *f*. ~ *prize s Sport etc:* *Scherzpreis für den Letzten od. Schlechtesten.* ~ *trap s* **1.** versteckte Sprengladung; *Auto etc*, in dem e-e Sprengladung versteckt ist. **2.** grober Scherz (*bsd. über halbgeöffneter Tür angebrachter Wassereimer*).

book [bʊk] **I** *s* **1.** Buch *n*: *the* ♀ die Bibel; *a closed* ~ *fig.* ein Buch mit sieben Siegeln (*to* für); *an open* ~ *fig.* ein offenes *od.* aufgeschlagenes Buch (*to* für); *be at one's* ~*s* über s-n Büchern sitzen; *speak* (*od. talk*) *like a* ~ geschraubt *od.* gestelzt reden; → *suit* 5. **2.** ✝ Geschäftsbuch *n*: *be deep in s.o.'s* ~*s* bei j-m tief in der Kreide stehen. **3.** Liste *f*, Verzeichnis *n*: *be on the* ~*s* auf der (Mitglieder- *etc*)Liste stehen. **4.** Notizbuch *n*, -block *m*; (Schreib-, Schul)Heft *n*: *be in s.o.'s good* (*bad*) ~*s* bei j-m gut (schlecht) angeschrieben sein. **5.**

Heft(chen) *n*: **~ of stamps** (**tickets**) Marken-(Fahrschein)heft(chen); **~ of matches** Streichholzbriefchen *n*. **II** *v/t* **6. 🕈** (ver)buchen; *Auftrag* notieren. **7.** aufschreiben, *Sport*: *a.* verwarnen. **8.** verpflichten, engagieren. **9.** *Zimmer etc* bestellen, *Reise etc* buchen, *Eintritts-, Fahrkarte* lösen: **~ed up** ausgebucht (*Künstler, Hotel, Veranstaltung*). **10.** *Gepäck* aufgeben (**to** nach). **III** *v/i* **11.** *Br. a.* **~ up** e-e (Fahr- *etc*)Karte lösen (**to, for** nach): **~ through** durchlösen (**to** bis, nach). **12.** sich (*für e-e Fahrt etc*) vormerken lassen, e-n Platz *etc* bestellen, buchen. **13. ~ in** *bsd. Br.* sich (*im Hotel*) eintragen: **~ in at** absteigen in (*dat*).

book·a·ble ['bʊkəbl] *adj* im Vorverkauf erhältlich.

'**book**|**bind·er** *s* Buchbinder *m*. '**~·case** *s* Bücherschrank *m*. **~ club** *s* Buchgemeinschaft *f*. **~ end** *s* Bücherstütze *f*.

book·ie ['bʊkɪ] *s* F Buchmacher *m*.

book·ing ['bʊkɪŋ] *s* Buchung *f*, (Vor)Bestellung *f*: **make a** (**firm**) **~** (fest) buchen. **~ clerk** *s* Fahrkartenverkäufer *m*. **~ of·fice** *s* **1.** (Fahrkarten)Schalter *m*. **2.** (*Theater- etc*)Kasse *f*, Vorverkaufsstelle *f*.

book·ish ['bʊkɪʃ] *adj* **1.** belesen. **2.** papieren (*Stil*).

'**book**|**keep·er** *s* 🕈 Buchhalter(in). '**~·keep·ing** *s* 🕈 Buchhaltung *f*, -führung *f*. '**~·mak·er** *s* Buchmacher *m*. '**~·mark, ~·mark·er** *s* Lesezeichen *n*. **~·mo·bile** ['~məʊˌbiːl] *s* *Am*. Wanderbücherei *f*. '**~·sell·er** *s* Buchhändler(in). '**~·shop** *s* Buchhandlung *f*. '**~·stall** *s* **1.** Bücherstand *m*. **2.** *bsd. Br.* Zeitungskiosk *m*, -stand *m*: '**~·store** *s* *bsd. Am.* Buchhandlung *f*. '**~·worm** *s* *zo.* Bücherwurm *m* (*a. fig.*).

boom¹ [buːm] **I** *v/i* dröhnen (*Stimme etc*), donnern (*Geschütz etc*), brausen (*Wellen etc*). **II** *s* Dröhnen, Donner *m*, Brausen *n*.

boom² [~] *s* **1.** ⚓ Baum *m*, Spiere *f*. **2.** ⚙ (*Kran*)Ausleger *m*. **3.** *Film, TV*: (*Mikrophon*)Galgen *m*.

boom³ [~] 🕈 **I** *s* Boom *m*: a) Hochkonjunktur *f*, b) *Börse*: Hausse *f*, c) (plötzlicher) Aufschwung. **II** *v/i* e-n Boom erleben.

boom·er·ang ['buːməræŋ] **I** *s* Bumerang

m (*a. fig.*). **II** *v/i fig.* sich als Bumerang erweisen (**on** für).

boon [buːn] *s fig.* Segen *m* (**to** für).

boor [bʊə] *s* ungehobelter Kerl. '**boor-ish** ['bʊərɪʃ] *adj* □ ungehobelt. '**boor-ish·ness** *s* ungehobeltes Benehmen *od.* Wesen.

boost [buːst] **I** *v/t* **1.** F *Preise* in die Höhe treiben. **2.** F *Auftrieb* geben (*dat*), *Produktion etc* ankurbeln, *Moral* heben. **3.** ⚙ *Druck* erhöhen; ⚡ *Spannung* verstärken. **II** *s* **4.** F Auftrieb *m*. **5.** ⚙ Erhöhung *f*; ⚡ Verstärkung *f*. '**boost·er** *s* **1.** *a.* **~ shot** 💉 Wiederholungsimpfung *f*. **2.** Zündstufe *f* (*e-r Rakete*): **~ rocket** Startrakete *f*.

boot¹ [buːt] **I** *s* **1.** Stiefel *m*: **the ~ is on the other foot** (*od.* **leg**) der Fall liegt umgekehrt; → **bet 4**, **lick 7.** **2.** F (Fuß)Tritt *m*: **give s.o. a ~** → 4; **get the ~** rausgeschmissen (*entlassen*) werden. **3.** *mot. Br.* Kofferraum *m*. **II** *v/t* **4.** F *j-m* e-n (Fuß)Tritt geben: **~** (**out**) rausschmeißen (*entlassen*).

boot² [~] *s*: **to ~** obendrein, noch dazu.

'**boot·black** *s* Schuhputzer *m*.

booth [buːð] *s* **1.** (Markt-, Schau)Bude *f*, (Messe)Stand *m*. **2.** (Telefon)Zelle *f*; (Wahl)Kabine *f*, (-)zelle *f*.

'**boot**|**·lace** *s* Schnürsenkel *m*. '**~·lick** *v/t u. v/i* F (vor *j-m*) kriechen: '**~·lick·er** *s* F Kriecher *m*.

boots [buːts] *pl* **boots** *s* *Br.* Hausdiener *m* (*im Hotel*).

boo·ty ['buːtɪ] *s* (*fig. a.* Aus)Beute *f*.

booze [buːz] F **I** *v/i* saufen. **II** *s* Zeug *n* (*alkoholisches Getränk*); Sauferei *f*; (*Br. a.* **~up**) Sauftour *f*; (*Br. a.* **~up**) Besäufnis *n*. '**booz·er** *s* F **1.** Säufer(in). **2.** Kneipe *f*. '**booz·y** *adj* F versoffen.

bor·der ['bɔːdə] **I** *s* **1.** Rand *m*. **2.** Einfassung *f*, Saum *m*, Umrandung *f*. **3.** (Gebiets-, Landes)Grenze *f*: **~ incident** Grenzzwischenfall *m*. **II** *v/t* **4.** einfassen. **5.** begrenzen, grenzen an (*acc*). **III** *v/i* **6.** grenzen (**on** an *acc*) (*a. fig.*). '**bor·der·er** *s* Grenzbewohner *m*.

'**bor·der**|**·land** *s* Grenzgebiet *n*. '**~·line** **I** *s* **1.** Grenzlinie *f*. **2.** *fig.* Grenze *f*. **II** *adj* **1.** *fig.* Grenz...: **~ case** Grenzfall *m*.

bore¹ [bɔː] **I** *s* **1.** Bohrung *f*: a) Bohrloch *n*, b) Kaliber *n*. **II** *v/t* (*bsd. aus*)bohren. **III** *v/i* bohren (**for** nach).

bore² [~] **I** *s* **1.** langweilige Sache; *bsd.*

Br. lästige Sache. **2.** Langweiler *m*; *bsd. Br.* lästiger Kerl. **II** *v/t* **3.** *j-n* langweilen; *bsd. Br. j-m* lästig sein: **be ~d** sich langweilen; **be ~d stiff** F sich zu Tode langweilen.

bore³ [~] *pret von* **bear²**.

bore·dom ['bɔːdəm] *s* **1.** Lang(e)weile *f*. **2.** Langweiligkeit *f*.

bor·er ['bɔːrə] *s* ⊚ Bohrer *m*.

bo·ric ac·id ['bɔːrɪk] *s* 🔬 Borsäure *f*.

bor·ing ['bɔːrɪŋ] *adj* langweilig.

born [bɔːn] **I** *pp von* **bear²** 2. **II** *adj* geboren (*a. fig.*): **a ~ poet.**

borne [bɔːn] *pp von* **bear²**.

bo·ron ['bɔːrɒn] *s* 🔬 Bor *n*.

bor·ough ['bʌrə] *s* **1.** *Br.* Stadt *f* (*mit Selbstverwaltung*); (*a. parliamentary ~*) Stadt *f od.* städtischer Wahlbezirk mit eigener Vertretung im Parlament; Stadtteil *m* (*von Groß-London*). **2.** *Am.* Stadtbezirk *m* (*in New York*).

bor·row ['bɒrəʊ] **I** *v/t* **1.** (sich) *et.* (aus)borgen *od.* leihen (**from** von). **2.** *fig.* entlehnen (**from** von): *~ed word* Lehnwort *n*. **II** *v/i* **3.** 💰 Kredit aufnehmen. **'bor·row·er** *s* **1.** Entleiher(in). **2.** 💰 Kreditnehmer(in).

bosh [bɒʃ] *s* F Blödsinn *m*, Quatsch *m*.

bos·om ['bʊzəm] *s* **1.** Busen *m* (*a. fig.*): *~ friend* Busenfreund(in). **2.** *fig.* Schoß *m*: *in the ~ of one's family.*

boss¹ [bɒs] *s* Buckel *m*, Knauf *m*.

boss² [~] **I** *s* Boß *m*, Chef *m*. **II** *v/t*: *~ about* (*od. around*) herumkommandieren.

boss·y ['bɒsɪ] *adj* F herrisch.

bo·tan·i·cal [bə'tænɪkl] *adj* □ botanisch: *~ garden(s pl)* botanischer Garten. **bot·a·nist** ['bɒtənɪst] *s* Botaniker(in). **'bot·a·ny** *s* Botanik *f*.

botch [bɒtʃ] **I** *s* Pfusch(arbeit *f*) *m*: *make a ~ of* → **II**. **II** *v/t* verpfuschen. **III** *v/i* pfuschen. **'botch·er** *s* Pfuscher *m*.

both [bəʊθ] **I** *adj u. pron* beide(s): *~ my brothers* m-e beiden Brüder; *~ of them* alle beide; → *sex* 1. **II** *adv od. cj*: *~ ... and* sowohl ... als (auch).

both·er ['bɒðə] **I** *s* **1.** Belästigung *f*, Störung *f*. **II** *v/t* belästigen, stören: *don't ~ me!* laß mich in Ruhe!; *I can't ~ ed* ich habe keine Lust (*to do* zu tun). **III** *v/i* (*about*) sich kümmern (um); sich aufregen (über *acc*).

bot·tle ['bɒtl] **I** *s* Flasche *f*: → *hit* 7. **II** *v/t*

in Flaschen abfüllen: *~d beer* Flaschenbier *n*; *~ up Gefühle etc* unterdrücken; *~d-up* aufgestaut. **'~neck** *s* Flaschenhals *m*, Engpaß *m* (*a. fig.*). **~o·pen·er** *s* Flaschenöffner *m*. **~ post** *s* Flaschenpost *f*.

bot·tom ['bɒtəm] **I** *s* **1.** Boden *m* (*e-s Gefäßes etc*), Fuß *m* (*e-s Bergs etc*), Sohle *f* (*e-s Tals etc*), Unterseite *f*: *at the ~ of the street* am Ende der Straße; *from the ~ of one's heart* aus tiefstem Herzen; *~s up!* F ex! **2.** Boden *m*, Grund *m*: *~ of the sea* Meeresboden, -grund. **3.** Grund(lage *f*) *m*: *be at the ~ of* der Grund sein für, hinter *e-r Sache* stecken; *get to the ~ of s.th.* *e-r Sache* auf den Grund gehen *od.* kommen; *knock the ~ out of s.th.* *et.* gründlich widerlegen. **4.** (Stuhl)Sitz *m*. **5.** F Popo *m*. **II** *adj* **6.** unterst: *~ line* letzte Zeile; → *bet* 4, *rung²*. **'bot·tom·less** *adj* □ *fig.* unergründlich; unerschöpflich.

bough [baʊ] *s* Ast *m*, Zweig *m*.

bought [bɔːt] *pret u. pp von* **buy.**

bouil·lon ['buːjɔːn] *s* Fleischbrühe *f*, Bouillon *f*.

bou·le·vard ['buːləvɑːd] *s* Boulevard *m*.

bounce [baʊns] **I** *s* **1.** Elastizität *f*. **2.** Sprung *m*, Satz *m*. **3.** F Schwung *m*, Schmiß *m*. **4.** F Rausschmiß *m* (*a. Entlassung*): *give s.o. the ~* → 6; *get the ~* rausgeschmissen werden. **II** *v/t* **5.** *Ball etc* aufprallen *od.* aufspringen lassen. **6.** F *j-n* rausschmeißen (*a. entlassen*). **III** *v/i* **7.** aufprallen, -springen (*Ball etc*): *~ off* abprallen (*von*). **8.** federn, elastisch sein (*Gummi etc*); springen (*Ball*). **9.** a) springen, hüpfen (*over über acc*), b) stürmen, stürzen (*into in acc*). **10.** F platzen (*Scheck*). **'bounc·er** *s* F **1.** Rausschmeißer *m*. **2.** ungedeckter Scheck. **'bounc·ing** *adj* stramm (*Baby etc*).

bound¹ [baʊnd] **I** *pret u. pp von* **bind.** **II** *adj*: *be ~ to do sth.* (zwangsläufig) *et.* tun müssen; *he was ~ to be late* er mußte ja zu spät kommen.

bound² [~] *adj* unterwegs (*for* nach): *where are you ~ for?* wohin reisen *od.* gehen Sie?

bound³ [~] **I** *s mst pl* Grenze *f*, *fig. a.* Schranke *f*: *keep within ~s* in (vernünftigen) Grenzen halten; *beyond all ~s* maß-, grenzenlos; *the park is out of ~s*

bound   786

(**to**) das Betreten des Parks ist (für *od. dat*) verboten; **within the ~s of possibility** im Bereich des Möglichen. **II** *v/t* begrenzen.

bound⁴ [~] **I** *s* → **bounce** 2. **II** *v/i* → **bounce** 7, 9 a.

bound·a·ry ['baʊndərɪ] *s* Grenze *f*.

boun·den ['baʊndən] *adj*: **my ~ duty** meine Pflicht u. Schuldigkeit.

bound·less ['baʊndlɪs] *adj* □ grenzenlos (*a. fig.*).

boun·te·ous ['baʊntɪəs], **boun·ti·ful** ['~tɪfʊl] *adj* □ **1.** freigebig (**of** mit). **2.** reichlich.

boun·ty ['baʊntɪ] *s* **1.** Freigebigkeit *f*. **2.** großzügige Spende. **3.** Prämie *f*: a) Belohnung *f*, b) ✝ Zuschuß *m* (**on** auf *acc*, für).

bou·quet [bʊ'keɪ] *s* Bukett *n*: a) (Blumen)Strauß *m*, b) Blume *f* (*von Wein*).

bour·bon ['bɜːbən] *s* Bourbon *m* (*amerikanischer Maiswhisky*).

bout [baʊt] *s* **1.** *fenc.* Gefecht *n*; (*Box-, Ring*)Kampf *m*. **2.** ✿ Anfall *m*: **~ of rheumatism** Rheumaanfall.

bou·tique [buː'tiːk] *s* Boutique *f*.

bo·vine ['baʊvaɪn] *adj* (*a. geistig*) träge, schwerfällig.

bov·ver ['bɒvə] *Br. sl.* **I** *s* Straßenkämpfe *pl* (*bsd. unter Rockerbanden*): **~ boots** *pl* schwere Stiefel, mit denen Rocker aufeinander eintreten; **~ boy** Rocker *m*. **II** *v/i* sich Straßenkämpfe liefern (**with** mit).

bow¹ [baʊ] **I** *s* Verbeugung *f*. **II** *v/t* beugen, *Kopf* neigen. **III** *v/i* sich verbeugen (**to** vor *dat*): **have a ~ing acquaintance with s.o.** j-n flüchtig kennen.

bow² [~] *s* ♉ Bug *m*.

bow³ [baʊ] *s* **1.** (Schieß)Bogen *m*: → **string** 3 a. **2.** ♪ (*Violin- etc*)Bogen *m*. **3.** Knoten *m*, Schleife *f*.

bowd·ler·ize ['baʊdləraɪz] *v/t* Text von anstößigen Stellen reinigen.

bow·el ['baʊəl] *s anat.* Darm *m*, *pl a.* Eingeweide *pl*. **~ move·ment** *s physiol.* Stuhl(gang) *m*.

bowl¹ ['baʊl] *s* **1.** Schüssel *f*; (*Obstetc*)Schale *f*; (*Zucker*)Dose *f*; Napf *m* (*für Tiere etc*). **2.** (*Wasch*)Becken *n*. **3.** (*Pfeifen*)Kopf *m*.

bowl² [~] *s* **1.** (Bowling-, Kegel)Kugel *f*. **2.** Wurf *m*. **II** *v/t* **3.** **~ over** umwerfen, *fig. a.* j-m die Sprache verschlagen.

bow·legged ['baʊlegd] *adj* O-beinig. **~ legs** *s pl* O-Beine *pl*.

bowl·er ['baʊlə] *s* **1.** Bowlingspieler(in); Kegler(in). **2.** *a.* **~ hat** *bsd. Br.* Bowler *m*, Melone *f*.

bowl·ing ['baʊlɪŋ] *s* Bowling *n*; Kegeln *n*. **~ al·ley** *s* Bowling-, Kegelbahn *f*.

bow·man ['baʊmən] *s* (*irr man*) Bogenschütze *m*. **~sprit** ['~sprɪt] *s* ♉ Bugspriet *n*. **~string** *s* Bogensehne *f*. **~ tie** *s* (Frack)Schleife *f*, Fliege *f*.

bow-wow I *int* [ˌbaʊ'waʊ] wauwau! **II** *s* ['baʊwaʊ] *Kindersprache*: Wauwau *m* (*Hund*).

box¹ [bɒks] *s* **1.** Kasten *m*, Kiste *f*. **2.** Schachtel *f*: **~ of chocolates** Bonbonniere *f*. **3.** Büchse *f*, Dose *f*, Kästchen *n*. **4.** Behälter *m*. **5.** ✿ Gehäuse *n*. **6.** Briefkasten *m*; Postfach *n*. **7.** (Wahl)Urne *f*. **8.** *Br.* (Telefon)Zelle *f*. **9.** → **Christmas box. 10.** → **box junction. 11.** *thea. etc* Loge *f*. **12.** ⚖ Zeugenstand *m*; Geschworenenbank *f*. **13.** Box *f*: a) Pferdestand, b) abgeteilter Einstellplatz in e-r Großgarage. **14.** → **box number. 15.** F Kasten *m* (*Fernseher*); Fernsehen *n*: **on the ~** im Fernsehen. **II** *v/t* **16.** *oft* **~ in** (*od.* **up**) in Schachteln *etc* packen, ver-, einpacken; *parkendes Fahrzeug* einklemmen. **17.** *oft* **~ up** einschließen, -sperren.

box² [~] **I** *s* **1.** **~ on the ear** Ohrfeige *f*. **II** *v/t* **2.** **~ s.o.'s ears** j-n ohrfeigen. **3.** *Sport*: boxen mit *od.* gegen. **III** *v/i* **4.** boxen.

box·er ['bɒksə] *s Sport*: Boxer *m* (*a. zo.*).

box·ing ['bɒksɪŋ] *s* Boxen *n*, Boxsport *m*. **~ bout** *s* Boxkampf *m*. **♀ Day** *s Br.* der 2. Weihnachtsfeiertag. **~ gloves** *pl* Boxhandschuhe *pl*. **~ match** *s* Boxkampf *m*.

box| junc·tion *s Br.* gelbmarkierte Kreuzung, in die bei stehendem Verkehr nicht eingefahren werden darf. **~ num·ber** *s* Chiffre(nummer) *f*. **~ of·fice** *s thea. etc* **1.** Kasse *f*. **2.** **be a good ~** ein Kassenerfolg *od.* -schlager sein. **'~·of·fice** *adj*: **~ success** *thea. etc* Kassenerfolg *m*, -schlager *m*.

boy [bɔɪ] *s* Junge *m* (*a. F Sohn*), Knabe *m*.

boy·cott ['bɔɪkɒt] **I** *v/t* boykottieren. **II** *s* Boykott *m*.

'boy·friend *s* Freund *m* (*e-s Mädchens*).

boy·hood ['bɔɪhʊd] s Knabenjahre pl, Jugend(zeit) f.

boy·ish ['bɔɪʃ] adj □ **1.** jungenhaft: *his ~ laughter*. **2.** knabenhaft: *her ~ movements*. **3.** Jungen...: *~ games*.

boy scout s Pfadfinder m.

bra [brɑː] s F BH m (Büstenhalter).

brace [breɪs] **I** s **1.** ⊙ Strebe f, △ a. Stützbalken m. **2.** pl Br. Hosenträger pl. **3.** mst pl ♪ (Zahn)Klammer f, (-)Spange f. **4.** (pl brace) Paar n. **II** v/t **5.** ⊙ verstreben. **6.** fig. (a. v/i) erfrischen; kräftigen, stärken. **7.** ~ *o.s. for* fig. sich gefaßt machen auf (acc).

brace·let ['breɪslɪt] s Armband n.

brack·et ['brækɪt] **I** s **1.** ⊙ Träger m, Stütze f. **2.** ♪, typ. Klammer f: *in ~s; round (square)* ~s runde (eckige) Klammern. **3.** (Alters-, Steuer)Klasse f, (Einkommens- etc)Gruppe f, (-)Stufe f. **II** v/t **4.** einklammern.

brag [bræg] **I** s **1.** Prahlerei f. **2.** Prahler m. **II** v/i **3.** prahlen (*about, of* mit).

brag·gart ['brægət] **I** s Prahler m. **II** adj prahlerisch.

braid [breɪd] **I** v/t **1.** Haar, Bänder flechten. **2.** mit Litze od. Borte besetzen. **II** s **3.** Zopf m. **4.** Borde f, Litze f, bsd. ✕ Tresse f.

braille [breɪl] s Blindenschrift f.

brain [breɪn] s **1.** anat. Gehirn n. **2.** oft pl fig. F Köpfchen n, Grips m, Verstand m: *cudgel (od. rack) one's ~* sich das Hirn zermartern, sich den Kopf zerbrechen; → *blow out* 2. **'~·case** s anat. Hirnschale f, Schädeldecke f. ~ **child** s (irr child) F Geistesprodukt n. ~ **death** s ♪ Hirntod n. ~ **drain** s Brain-Drain m (Abwanderung von Wissenschaftlern ins Ausland). **'~·fag** s geistige Erschöpfung.

brain·less ['breɪnlɪs] adj □ hirn-, geistlos.

'brain|·pan → braincase. **'~·storm** s F **1. have a** ~ Br. geistig weggetreten sein. **2.** Am. a) hirnverbrannte Idee, b) → *brain wave*. **'~·storm·ing** s Brainstorming n (Sammeln von spontanen Einfällen zur Lösung e-s Problems).

brains trust [breɪnz] s Br. **1.** Teilnehmer pl an e-r Podiumsdiskussion. **2.** → *brain trust*.

'brain|·teas·er → brain twister. ~ **trust** s Am. Brain-Trust m (bsd. politische od. wirtschaftliche Beratergruppe). ~ **twist·er** s F harte Nuß. **'~·wash** v/t j-n e-r Gehirnwäsche unterziehen. **'~·wash·ing** s Gehirnwäsche f. ~ **wave** s F Geistesblitz m, tolle Idee. **'~·work·er** s Geistes-, Kopfarbeiter m.

brain·y ['breɪnɪ] adj F gescheit (a. Vorschlag etc).

braise [breɪz] v/t gastr. schmoren.

brake [breɪk] **I** s ⊙ Bremse f. **II** v/t u. v/i bremsen. ~ **flu·id** s Bremsflüssigkeit f. ~ **lin·ing** s Bremsbelag m. ~ **ped·al** s Bremspedal n.

brak·ing dis·tance ['breɪkɪŋ] s Bremsweg m.

bram·ble ['bræmbl] s ♣ bsd. Br. Brombeerstrauch m; Brombeere f.

branch [brɑːntʃ] **I** s **1.** Ast m, Zweig m. **2.** fig. Zweig m, Linie f (e-r Familie). **3.** fig. Zweig m, Sparte f (e-r Wissenschaft etc); ♀ Branche f. **4.** ♀ Filiale f. **5.** → *branch line* 1. **6.** geogr. Arm m (e-s Gewässers); Am. Nebenfluß m. **II** v/i **7.** oft ~ *off* (od. out) sich verzweigen od. verästeln; abzweigen od. sich gabeln (Straße etc). ~ **line** s ♬ Neben-, Zweiglinie f. **2.** Seitenlinie f (e-r Familie). ~ **man·ag·er** s Filialleiter m. ~ **of·fice** s ♀ Filiale f.

brand [brænd] **I** s **1.** ♀ (Handels-, Schutz)Marke f, Warenzeichen n; Markenname m; Sorte f, Klasse f (e-r Ware). **2.** fig. Sorte f, Art f. **3.** Brandmal n, -zeichen n. **II** v/t **4.** mit e-m Warenzeichen etc versehen: *~ed goods* pl Markenartikel pl. **5.** fig. unauslöschlich einprägen (*on s.o.'s mind* j-m).

bran·dish ['brændɪʃ] v/t (bsd. drohend) schwingen.

brand-'new adj (funkel)nagelneu.

bran·dy ['brændɪ] s **1.** Weinbrand m, Kognak m, Brandy m. **2.** Obstwasser n: *plum* ~ Zwetschgenwasser n.

bran-new [ˌbræn'njuː] → brand-new.

brash [bræʃ] adj F **1.** ungestüm; draufgängerisch; unüberlegt; taktlos, ungezogen; frech, unverfroren. **2.** aufdringlich, laut (Musik etc); grell, schreiend (Farben).

brass [brɑːs] s **1.** Messing n. **2.** *the* ~ ♩ das Blech (im Orchester), die Blechbläser pl. **3.** Br. F Knete f (Geld). **4.** F Frechheit f, Unverschämtheit f. ~ **band** s Blaskapelle f.

bras·sière ['bræsɪə] *s* Büstenhalter *m*.

brass tacks *s pl*: *get down to* ~ F zur Sache *od.* auf den Kern der Sache kommen.

bras·sy ['brɑːsɪ] *adj* □ **1.** messingartig *od.* -farben. **2.** blechern (*Klang*). **3.** F frech, unverschämt. **4.** unangenehm laut.

brat [bræt] *s contp.* Balg *m, n,* Gör *n.*

brave [breɪv] **I** *adj* □ tapfer, mutig. **II** *v/t* die Stirn bieten, trotzen (*dat*): ~ *it out* es (tapfer) durchstehen. **'brav·er·y** *s* Tapferkeit *f,* Mut *m.*

bra·vo [‚brɑː'vəʊ] **I** *int* bravo! **II** *pl* **-vos** *f* Bravo(ruf *m*) *n.*

brawl [brɔːl] **I** *v/i* **1.** e-e laute Auseinandersetzung haben. **2.** raufen, sich schlagen. **3.** tosen, rauschen (*Fluß etc*). **II** *s* **4.** laute Auseinandersetzung *f.* **5.** Rauferei *f,* Schlägerei *f.* **6.** Tosen *n,* Rauschen *n.*

brawn [brɔːn] *s* **1.** Muskeln *pl.* **2.** Muskelkraft *f.* **3.** *gastr. Br.* (Schweine)Sülze *f.* **'brawn·y** *adj* muskulös.

bray [breɪ] **I** *v/i* **1.** schreien (*Esel, a. Person*): ~ *at s.o.* j-n anschreien. **2.** schmettern (*Trompete*). **3.** lärmen, tosen (*Verkehr etc*). **II** *s* **4.** Schrei *m.* **5.** Schmettern *n.* **6.** Lärmen *n,* Tosen *n.*

bra·zen ['breɪzn] **I** *adj* □ **1.** Messing... **2.** metallisch (*Klang*). **3.** *fig.* unverschämt, unverfroren. **II** *v/t* **4.** ~ *it out* sich mit großer Unverfrorenheit behaupten. **'~·faced** → **brazen** 3.

breach [briːtʃ] **I** *s* **1.** *fig.* Bruch *m,* Verletzung *f*: ~ *of confidence* Vertrauensbruch; ~ *of contract* 🏛 Vertragsbruch; ~ *of the peace* 🏛 öffentliche Ruhestörung; → *duty* 1, *promise* 1. **2.** ✕ Bresche *f* (*a. fig.*): *fill* (*od. step into*) the ~ in die Bresche springen (*for* für). **II** *v/t* **3.** ✕ e-e Bresche schlagen in (*acc*).

bread [bred] **I** *s* **1.** Brot *n* (*a. Lebensunterhalt*): ~ *and butter* Butterbrot; *earn* (*od. make*) *one's* ~ sein Brot verdienen; *know which side one's* ~ *is buttered* (*on*) F s-n Vorteil (er)kennen; *take the* ~ *out of s.o.'s mouth* j-n brotlos machen. **2.** *sl.* Knete *f* (*Geld*). **II** *v/t* **3.** *gastr.* panieren. **'~·bas·ket** *s* **1.** Brotkorb *m.* **2.** *sl.* Magen *m.* ~ *bin* *s* Brotkasten *m.* ~ *crumb* *s* Brotkrume *f,* -krümel *m*: ~*s pl* Paniermehl *n.* **'~·crumb** → **bread** 3.

breadth [bretθ] *s* Breite *f*: *ten yards in* ~ 10 Yards breit; *what* ~ *is it?* wie breit ist es?

'bread‚win·ner *s* Ernährer *m,* (Geld-)Verdiener *m* (*e-r Familie*).

break [breɪk] **I** *s* **1.** Bruch(stelle *f*) *m.* **2.** *fig.* Bruch *m* (*from, with* mit; *between* zwischen *dat*): *make a* ~ *from* brechen mit. **3.** Pause *f,* Unterbrechung *f*: *without a* ~ ununterbrochen; *take a* ~ *for a cigarette* e-e Zigarettenpause machen. **4.** (plötzlicher) Wechsel, Umschwung *m*: ~ *in the weather* Wetterumschlag *m*; *at* ~ *of day* bei Tagesanbruch. **5.** F *bad* ~ Pech *n*; *lucky* ~ Dusel *m,* Schwein *n.* **6.** F Chance *f*: *give s.o. a* ~ II *v/t* (*irr*) **7.** (ab-, auf-, durch-, zer)brechen; *Schallmauer* durchbrechen: ~ *one's arm* sich den Arm brechen; ~ *s.o.'s resistance* j-s Widerstand brechen; → *heart* 1, *ice* 1. **8.** zerschlagen, -trümmern, kaputtmachen: → *bank¹* 2. **9.** ~ *s.o. of s.th.* j-m et. abgewöhnen. **10.** *Speise, Ware, Geldschein* anbrechen; *Geldschein* kleinmachen, wechseln. **11.** a) *Tiere* zähmen, abrichten, *Pferd* zureiten, *a. j-n* gewöhnen (*to* an *acc*), b) → *break in* 3 b, c. **12.** *Gesetz, Vertrag etc* brechen. **13.** ~ *the bad news gently to s.o.* j-m die schlechte Nachricht schonend beibringen. **14.** *Code etc* knacken, entschlüsseln. **III** *v/i* (*irr*) **15.** brechen (*a. fig.* Widerstand *etc*): ~ *into* einbrechen in (*ein Haus etc*); ~ *with* brechen mit (*j-m, e-r Tradition etc*). **16.** (zer)brechen, (-)reißen, kaputtgehen. **17.** umschlagen (*Wetter*); anbrechen (*Tag*). **18.** *fig.* ausbrechen (*into* in *Tränen etc*). *Verbindungen mit Adverbien:*

break| a·way **I** *v/t* **1.** ab-, losbrechen (*from* von). **II** *v/i* **2.** ab-, losbrechen (*from* von). **3.** *fig.* sich lossagen *od.* trennen (*from* von). ~ *down* **I** *v/t* **1.** ein-, niederreißen, *Haus* abbrechen, abreißen. **2.** *Maschine* zerlegen. **3.** *fig.* aufgliedern, -schlüsseln. **II** *v/i* **4.** zs.--brechen (*a. fig.*). **5.** versagen (*Maschine, Stimme etc*), kaputtgehen, *mot.* e-e Panne haben. **6.** scheitern (*Ehe, Verhandlungen etc*). ~ *in* **I** *v/i* **1.** einbrechen, -dringen: ~ *on* bei *j-m* hereinplatzen; sich in *e-e Unterhaltung etc* einmischen. **II** *v/t* **2.** einschlagen, *Tür* aufbrechen. **3.** a) → *break* 10 a, b) *Auto etc* einfahren, *Schuhe* einlaufen, c) *j-n* einarbeiten, anlernen. **~ off I** v/t **1.** → **break away** 1. **2.** *Rede, Verhandlungen etc* abbrechen, *Verlobung* (auf)lösen: **break it off** sich entlernen. **II** v/i **3.** → **break away** 2. **~ out** v/i ausbrechen (*Gefangener, Krieg etc*): **~ in laughter** (*tears*) in Gelächter (Tränen) ausbrechen; **he broke out in a cold sweat** ihm brach der Angstschweiß aus. **~ through I** v/t **1.** durchbrechen. **II** v/i **3.** **2.** durchbrechen, (*Sonne a.*) hervorkommen. **3.** *fig.* den Durchbruch schaffen. **~ up I** v/t **1.** *Straße, Eis etc* aufbrechen. **2.** *Sitzung etc* aufheben, *Versammlung, Haushalt etc* auflösen. **II** v/i **3.** aufbrechen (*Straße, Eis etc*). **4.** aufgehoben werden (*Sitzung etc*), sich auflösen (*Versammlung*). **5.** zerbrechen, auseinandergehen (*Ehe etc*); sich trennen (*Ehepaar etc*).

break·a·ble ['breɪkəbl] *adj* zerbrechlich. **'break·age** *s* Bruch(stelle *f*) *m*.
'break|·a·way *s* Trennung *f* (**from** von). **'~down** *s* **1.** Zs.-bruch *m* (*a. fig.*): **nervous ~** Nervenzusammenbruch. **2.** *mot.* Panne *f*: **~ service** *Br.* Pannen-, Straßendienst *m*; **~ van** *Br.* Abschleppwagen *m*. **'~fast** ['brekfəst] **I** *s* **1.** Frühstück *n*: **have ~** → **II**; **~ television** Frühstücksfernsehen *n*. **II** v/i frühstücken. **'~in** *s* **1.** ⚡ Einbruch *m*. **2.** Abrichten, Einfahren *n etc* (→ **break** 10 a, **break in** 2 b, c). **'~neck** *adj* halsbrecherisch (*Geschwindigkeit*). **'~out** *s* Ausbruch *m* (*aus dem Gefängnis etc*). **'~through** *s* ✕ Durchbruch *m* (*a. fig.*). **'~up** *s* Aufhebung *f* (*e-r Sitzung etc*), Auflösung *f* (*e-r Versammlung, e-s Haushalts etc*).

breast [brest] **I** *s* Brust *f* (*a. gastr.*): **make a clean ~ of s.th.** sich et. von der Seele reden. **II** v/t: **~ the tape** (*Sport*) das Zielband durchreißen, *weitS.* durchs Ziel gehen. **'~bone** *s anat.* Brustbein *n*. **'~feed** v/t u. v/i (*irr feed*) stillen. **'~pin** *s* Brosche *f*, Anstecknadel *f*. **'~pock·et** *s* Brusttasche *f*. **'~stroke** *s Sport:* Brustschwimmen *n*.

breath [breθ] *s* **1.** Atem(zug) *m*: **bad ~** Mundgeruch *m*; **in the same ~** im gleichen Atemzug; **under** (*od.* **below**) **one's ~** im Flüsterton, leise; **be out of ~** außer Atem sein; **get one's ~ back** wieder zu Atem kommen; **waste one's ~**

in den Wind reden. **2.** *fig.* Hauch *m*, Spur *f*. **3.** *a.* **~ of air** Lufthauch *m*, Lüftchen *n*.

breath·a·lys·er ['breθəlaɪzə] *s mot.* Alkoholtestgerät *n*, Röhrchen *n*.
breathe [briːð] **I** v/i **1.** atmen: **~ in** (**out**) ein-(aus)atmen. **II** v/t **2.** atmen: **~ in** (**out**) ein-(aus)atmen; → **sigh** II. **3.** flüstern, hauchen. **'breath·er** *s F* Atem-, Verschnaufpause *f*: **have** (*od.* **take**) **a ~** verschnaufen. **'breath·ing** *s* Atmen *n*, Atmung *f*: **~ space** Atem-, Verschnaufpause *f*.
breath·less ['breθlɪs] *adj* ☐ atemlos (*a. fig.*).
'breath|·tak·ing *adj* ☐ atemberaubend. **~ test** *s mot. Br.* Alkoholtest *m*.
bred [bred] *pret u. pp von* **breed**.
breech·es ['brɪtʃɪz] *s pl* (**a pair of** e-e) Kniebund-, Reithose *f*.
breed [briːd] **I** v/t (*irr*) **1.** *Tiere, Pflanzen* züchten. **2.** *fig.* hervorrufen, verursachen. **II** v/i (*irr*) **3.** sich fortpflanzen *od.* vermehren. **III** v/ **4.** Rasse *f*, Zucht *f*. **5.** Art *f*, (*Menschen*)Schlag *m*. **'breed·er** *s* **1.** Züchter(in). **2.** Zuchttier *n*. **3.** *phys.* Brüter *m*: **~ reactor** Brutreaktor *m*. **'breed·ing** *s* **1.** Fortpflanzung *f*. **2.** Züchtung *f*, Zucht *f*. **3.** Ausbildung *f*, Erziehung *f*. **4.** (gutes) Benehmen, (gute) Manieren *pl*.
breeze [briːz] **I** *s* Brise *f*. **II** v/i *F* schweben (*Person*): **~ in** hereingeweht kommen. **'breez·y** *adj* ☐ **1.** luftig, windig. **2.** heiter, unbeschwert.
breth·ren ['breðrən] *pl von* **brother** 2.
bre·vi·ar·y ['briːvjəri] *s eccl.* Brevier *n*.
brev·i·ty ['brevəti] *s* Kürze *f*.
brew [bruː] **I** v/t **1.** *Bier* brauen, *Tee a.* zubereiten. **2.** *fig.* aushecken, -brüten. **II** v/i **3.** *fig.* sich zs.-brauen, im Anzug sein (*Gewitter, Unheil*). **III** *s* **4.** Gebräu *n*. **'brew·er** *s* Brauer *m*. **'brew·er·y** *s* Brauerei *f*.
brib·a·ble ['braɪbəbl] *adj* bestechlich.
bribe [braɪb] **I** v/t bestechen. **II** *s* Bestechungsgeld *n*, -geschenk *n*: **accept** (*od.* **take**) **~s** sich bestechen lassen. **'brib·er·y** *s* Bestechung *f*: **open to ~** bestechlich.
bric·a·brac ['brɪkəbræk] *s* Nippsachen *pl*.
brick [brɪk] **I** *s* **1.** Ziegel(stein) *m*, Backstein *m*: **drop a ~** *Br. F* ins Fettnäpfchen treten. **2.** *Br.* Baustein *m*, (Bau)Klötz-

chen *n* (*für Kinder*): *box of* **~s** Baukasten *m*. **3.** F Pfundskerl *m*, feiner Kerl.
II *v/t* **4.** **~** *up* (*od. in*) zumauern.
'**~,lay·er** *s* Maurer *m*.

brid·al ['braɪdl] *adj* Braut...: **~** *dress*
Braut-, Hochzeitskleid *n*; **~** *ceremony*
Hochzeitsfeier *f*.

bride [braɪd] *s* Braut *f*: *give away the* **~**
die Braut zum Altar führen. **~·groom**
['~grom] *s* Bräutigam *m*.

brides·maid ['braɪdzmeɪd] *s* Brautjungfer *f*.

bridge¹ [brɪdʒ] **I** *s* **1.** (*♪ a.* Kommando)Brücke *f*: *burn one's* **~s** (*behind
one*) *fig.* alle Brücken hinter sich abbrechen. **2.** **~** *of the nose anat.* Nasen-
rücken *m*. **II** *v/t* **3.** e-e Brücke schlagen
über (*acc*). **4.** *oft* **~** *over* ⚡ überbrücken
(*a. fig.*).

bridge² [~] *s* Bridge *n* (*Kartenspiel*).
'**bridge·head** *s* ✕ Brückenkopf *m*.

bri·dle ['braɪdl] **I** *s* **1.** Zaum(zeug *n*) *m*;
Zügel *m*. **II** *v/t* **2.** (auf)zäumen. **3.** zügeln, im Zaum halten (*beide a. fig.*). **III**
v/i **4.** *oft* **~** *up* den Kopf zurückwerfen.

brief [briːf] **I** *adj* □ **1.** kurz: *be* **~**! fasse
dich kurz! **2.** kurz angebunden (*with*
mit). **3.** knapp (*Bikini etc*). **4.** **in** **~**
kurz(um). **5.** ⚖ *Br.* schriftliche Beauf-
tragung u. Information (*des Barristers
durch den Solicitor*) zur Vertretung des
Falles vor Gericht, *weitS.* Mandat *n*:
abandon (*od. give up*) *one's* **~** sein
Mandat niederlegen; *hold a* **~** *for j-n
od. j-s Sache vor Gericht vertreten; *fig.*
sich einsetzen für. **6.** *pl* → **briefs.** **II** *v/t*
7. *j-n* instruieren, *j-m* genaue Anweisungen geben. **8.** ⚖ *Br. Barrister* mit
der Vertretung des Falles betrauen;
Anwalt über den Sachverhalt informieren. '**~·case** *s* Aktentasche *f*.

brief·ness ['briːfnɪs] *s* Kürze *f*.

briefs [briːfs] *s pl* (*a pair of* ein) Slip *m*
(*kurze Unterhose*).

bri·gade [brɪ'geɪd] *s* ✕ Brigade *f*.

bright [braɪt] *adj* □ **1.** hell, glänzend,
leuchtend, strahlend. **2.** heiter (*Wetter
etc*). **3.** gescheit, hell. **4.** günstig, vielversprechend (*Aussichten*). '**bright·en**
I *v/t oft* **~** *up* **1.** hell(er) machen, auf-,
erhellen (*a. fig.*). **2.** *j-n* fröhlich stimmen, aufheitern. **II** *v/i* **3.** *oft* **~** *up* sich
aufhellen (*Gesicht, Wetter etc*), auf-
leuchten (*Augen*). '**bright·ness** *s* **1.**

Helligkeit *f* (*a. TV*), Glanz *m*. **2.** Heiterkeit *f*. **3.** Gescheitheit *f*.

bril·liance ['brɪljəns], '**bril·lian·cy** *s* **1.**
Leuchten *n*, Glanz *m*, Helligkeit *f*. **2.**
fig. Brillanz *f*. '**bril·liant** *adj* □ **1.**
leuchtend, glänzend, hell. **2.** *fig.* brill-
lant. **II** *s* **3.** Brillant *m*.

brim [brɪm] **I** *s* **1.** Rand *m* (*bsd. e-s Gefäßes*): *full to the* **~** randvoll. **2.** (Hut-)
Krempe *f*. **II** *v/i* **3.** voll sein: **~** *over*
übervoll sein (*with* von) (*a. fig.*); überfließen (*with* von) (*a. fig.*). ,**brim'ful(l)**
adj randvoll.

brine [braɪn] **I** *s* **1.** Sole *f*; Lake *f*. **2.**
Salzwasser *n*. **II** *v/t* **3.** (ein)salzen.

bring [brɪŋ] *v/t* (*irr*) **1.** (mit-, her)brin-
gen: *what* **~s** *you here?* was führt Sie
zu mir?; → *bacon, home 9, light*¹ le. **2.**
Gewinn etc (ein)bringen. *Kran* nach sich
ziehen, bewirken. **3.** *j-n* dazu bringen
od. bewegen (*to do* zu tun): *I can't* **~**
myself to do it ich kann mich nicht
dazu durchringen(es zu tun).

Verbindungen mit Adverbien:

bring| **a·bout** *v/t* **1.** zustande bringen.
2. bewirken, verursachen. **~** **a·long** *v/t*
mitbringen. **~** **back** *v/t* **1.** zurückbringen. **2.** *Erinnerungen* wachrufen (*of an*
acc); Erinnerungen wachrufen an
(*acc*). **3.** **~** *to life j-n* wieder zu(m) Bewußtsein bringen; (*a.* **~** *to health*) *j-n*
wieder gesund machen. **~** *down* *v/t* **1.**
herunterbringen. **2.** *Regierung etc* zu
Fall bringen, stürzen. **3.** *Preis etc* herabsetzen. **4.** **~** *the house thea. etc* F
stürmischen Beifall auslösen; *Lach-
stürme entfesseln.* **~** *forth v/t* hervorbringen. **~** *for·ward v/t* **1.** *Entschuldigung etc* vorbringen. **2.** † *Betrag* übertragen. **3.** *Versammlung etc* vorverlegen (*to* auf *acc*); *Uhr* vorstellen (*one
hour* um e-e Stunde). **~** *in* *v/t* **1.** herein-
bringen. **2.** *Kapital, Gesetzesvorlage etc*
einbringen. **3.** → *verdict.* **~** *off* *v/t* zustande bringen. **~** *on* *v/t* **1.** *bsd. Krankheit* verursachen. **2.** in Gang bringen. **~**
out *v/t allg., a. Buch, Auto etc* herausbringen. **~** *o·ver* *v/t* **1.** herüberbringen.
2. → *bring round* 3. **~** *round* *v/t* **1.** her-,
vorbeibringen. **2.** a) *Ohnmächtigen*
wieder zu sich bringen, b) *Kranken* wieder auf die Beine bringen. *j-n* umstimmen, herumkriegen. **~** *through* *v/t*
Kranken durchbringen. **~** *to* → *bring*

round 2 a. ~ *up* v/t **1.** heraufbringen. **2.** *Kind* auf-, großziehen; erziehen: ~ *s.o. up to do s.th.* j-n dazu erziehen, et. zu tun. **3.** *et.* (er)brechen. **4.** zum Stillstand *od.* Halten bringen.

bring·er ['brɪŋə] *s* Überbringer(in).

brink [brɪŋk] *s* Rand *m* (*a. fig.*): **be on the ~ of war** am Rande e-s Krieges stehen; **bring s.o. to the ~ of ruin** j-n an den Rand des Ruins bringen. **'~·man·ship** ['~mənʃɪp] *s* Politik *f* des äußersten Risikos.

brin·y ['braɪnɪ] *adj* salzig.

bri·quet(te) [brɪ'ket] *s* Brikett *n.*

brisk [brɪsk] *adj* □ **1.** flott. **2.** lebhaft, munter. **3.** frisch (*Luft etc*).

bris·ket ['brɪskɪt] *s gastr.* Brust(stück *n*) *f.*

bris·tle ['brɪsl] **I** *s* **1.** Borste *f*; (Bart)Stoppel *f.* **II** *v/i* **2.** *a.* ~ *up* sich sträuben. **3.** *a.* ~ *up* zornig werden. **4.** strotzen, wimmeln (*with* von). **'bris·tly** *adj* **1.** borstig; stopp(e)lig: ~ *beard* Stoppelbart *m.* **2.** *fig.* kratzbürstig.

Brit·ish ['brɪtɪʃ] **I** *adj* britisch. **II** *s:* **the ~** *pl* die Briten (*pl*). **'Brit·ish·er** *s Am.* Brite *m*, Britin *f.*

Brit·on ['brɪtn] *s* Brite *m*, Britin *f.*

brit·tle ['brɪtl] *adj* **1.** spröde, zerbrechlich. **2.** brüchig (*Metall etc*) (*a. fig.*).

broach [brəʊtʃ] *v/t* **1.** *Faß* anstechen. **2.** *Thema* anschneiden.

broad [brɔːd] *adj* (□ → **broadly**). **1.** breit. **2.** weit, ausgedehnt. **3.** → **daylight. 4.** weitreichend, -gehend: *in the ~est sense* im weitesten Sinne. **5.** → **broad-minded. 6.** derb; anstößig, schlüpfrig. **7.** klar, deutlich: → **hint** 1. **8.** allgemein: *in ~ outline* in großen Zügen, in groben Umrissen. **9.** breit, stark (*Akzent*). **'~·cast I** *v/t* (*a. irr*) **1.** *Nachricht* verbreiten, *contp.* ausposaunen. **2.** im Rundfunk *od.* Fernsehen bringen; übertragen. **II** *v/i* (*a. irr*) **3.** im Rundfunk *od.* Fernsehen auftreten. **4.** senden. **III** *s* **5.** *Rundfunk, TV:* Sendung *f*; Übertragung *f.* **'~·cast·er** *s* Rundfunk-, Fernsehsprecher(in). **'~·cast·ing** *s* **1.** → **broadcast** 5. **2.** Sendebetrieb *m.* **3.** Rundfunk *m*, Fernsehen *n. od.* **4.** Rundfunk..., Fernsehen...: ~ *station* Sender *m.*

broad·en ['brɔːdn] **I** *v/t* verbreitern: ~ *one's horizons* (*od.* *mind*) s-n Horizont erweitern. **II** *v/i a.* ~ *out* sich verbreitern (*into* zu), sich erweitern (*a. fig.*).

broad| jump *s Leichtathletik: Am.* Weitsprung *m.* ~ **jump·er** *s Am.* Weitspringer(in).

broad·ly ['brɔːdlɪ] *adv* **1.** *a.* ~ *speaking* allgemein (gesprochen). **2.** in großen Zügen.

,broad·'mind·ed *adj* □ großzügig, tolerant. **'~·side** *s ♣* Breitseite *f* (*a. fig.*).

bro·cade [brəʊ'keɪd] *s* Brokat *m.*

bro·chure ['brəʊʃə] *s* Broschüre *f.*

brogue [brəʊg] *s* derber Straßenschuh.

broil[1] [brɔɪl] **I** *v/t* **1.** (auf dem Rost) braten, grillen. **2.** *fig.* vor Hitze fast umkommen. **II** *v/i* **3.** *be ~ing in the sun* in der Sonne schmoren. **4.** vor Wut kochen.

broil[2] [~] *s* laute Auseinandersetzung.

broil·ing ['brɔɪlɪŋ] **I** *adj* glühendheiß: *a ~ day.* **II** *adv:* ~ *hot* glühend heiß.

broke[1] [brəʊk] *pret von* **break.**

broke[2] [~] *adj* F pleite (*a.* 🖅), abgebrannt: *go ~* pleite gehen.

bro·ken ['brəʊkən] **I** *pp von* **break. II** *adj* **1.** zerbrochen, entzwei, kaputt. **2.** gebrochen (*a. fig.*): *a ~ leg* (**promise**, *etc*). **3.** unterbrochen, gestört: ~ *sleep.* **4.** (*seelisch od. körperlich*) gebrochen. **5.** zerrüttet: ~ *marriage*; ~ *health*; ~ *home* zerrüttete Familienverhältnisse *pl.* **6.** *ling.* gebrochen: *speak ~ English* gebrochen Englisch sprechen.

bro·ker ['brəʊkə] *s* **1.** 🖅 Makler *m.* **2.** Vermittler *m.* **'bro·ker·age** *s* Maklergebühr *f.*

brol·ly ['brɒlɪ] *s Br.* F (Regen)Schirm *m.*

bro·mide ['brəʊmaɪd] *s* **1.** 🜪 Bromid *n.* **2.** *fig.* Gemeinplatz *m.* **bro·mine** ['~miːn] *s* 🜪 Brom *n.*

bron·chi ['brɒŋkaɪ] *s pl anat.* Bronchien *pl.* **bron·chi·al** ['~kjəl] *adj anat...,* 🬞 Bronchial... **bron·chi·tis** ['~kaɪtɪs] *s* 🬞 Bronchitis *f.*

bronze [brɒnz] **I** *s* **1.** Bronze *f.* **II** *adj* **2.** bronzefarben. **3.** Bronze...: 🜿 *Age* Bronzezeit *f*; ~ *medal* Bronzemedaille *f*; ~ *medal(l)ist* Bronzemedaillengewinner(in).

brooch [brəʊtʃ] *s* Brosche *f.*

brood [bruːd] **I** *s* Brut *f* (*a. fig. contp.*). **II** *v/t* ausbrüten (*a. fig.*). **III** *v/i* brüten (*a. fig.* **on**, **over**, *about* über *dat*). **IV** *adj*

Brut...: ~ **hen.** '**brood·er** *s* Brutapparat *m*, -kasten *m*.

brook [brʊk] *s* Bach *m*.

broom [bruːm] *s* Besen *m*: *a new ~ sweeps clean* neue Besen kehren gut. '**~·stick** *s* Besenstiel *m*.

broth [brɒθ] *s* (Kraft-, Fleisch)Brühe *f*.

broth·el ['brɒθl] *s* Bordell *n*.

broth·er ['brʌðə] *s* **1.** Bruder *m*: *~s pl and sisters pl* Geschwister *pl*; *Smith ⚲s ✝* Gebrüder Smith. **2.** *eccl. pl* **brethren** Bruder *m*. **broth·er·hood** ['⁓hʊd] *s eccl.* Bruderschaft *f*.

'**broth·er-in-law** *pl* '**broth·ers-in-law** *s* Schwager *m*.

broth·er·ly ['brʌðəlɪ] *adj* brüderlich.

brought [brɔːt] *pret u. pp von* **bring.**

brow [braʊ] *s* **1.** (Augen)Braue *f*. **2.** Stirn *f*. **3.** Miene *f*, Gesichtsausdruck *m*. '**~·beat** *v/t* (*irr beat*) einschüchtern.

brown [braʊn] **I** *adj* braun: *~ bread* Misch-; Vollkorn-; Schwarzbrot *n*; *~ coal* Braunkohle *f*; *~ paper* Packpapier *n*; → *study* 1. **II** *s* Braun *n*: *dressed in ~* braun *od.* in Braun gekleidet. **III** *v/t Haut etc* bräunen, *Fleisch etc* (an)bräunen. **IV** *v/i* braun werden. **brown·ie** ['⁓] *s* Heinzelmännchen *n*. '**brown·ish** *adj* bräunlich.

browse [braʊz] *v/i* **1.** grasen, weiden. **2.** *a. ~ around* sich umsehen: *~ through a book* in e-m Buch schmökern *od.* blättern; *~ in (od. around) a shop* (*bsd. Am.* **store**) sich (unverbindlich) in e-m Laden umsehen.

bruise [bruːz] **I** *v/t* **1.** sich e-n Körperteil quetschen; *Früchte* anstoßen. **II** *v/i* **2.** e-e Quetschung *od.* e-n blauen Fleck bekommen. **III** *s* **3.** Quetschung *f*, blauer Fleck. **4.** Druckstelle *f* (*auf Früchten*).

brunch [brʌntʃ] *s* F Brunch *n* (*spätes reichliches Frühstück*).

bru·nette [bruː'net] **I** *s* Brünette *f*. **II** *adj* brünett.

brunt [brʌnt] *s*: *bear the ~ fig.* die Hauptlast tragen.

brush¹ [brʌʃ] **I** *s* **1.** Bürste *f*. **2.** Pinsel *m*: → *tar* II. **3.** *give s.th. a ~* et. ab- *od.* ausbürsten. **4.** ✕ Scharmützel *n* (*a. fig.*): *have a ~ with s.o.* mit j-m aneinandergeraten. **II** *v/t* **5.** bürsten: *brush one's teeth* sich die Zähne putzen; *~ aside (od. away)* zur Seite schieben,

wegschieben; *fig.* (mit e-r Handbewegung) abtun, wegwischen; *~ away (od. off)* wegbürsten; *~ down* abbürsten; *~ off sl. j-n* abwimmeln; *j-m* e-e Abfuhr erteilen; *~ up Kenntnisse* aufpolieren, -frischen. **6.** streifen, leicht berühren. **III** *v/i* **7.** *~ past s.o.* j-n streifen *od.* leicht berühren; an j-m vorbeihuschen; an j-m (gerade noch) vorbeikommen.

brush² [~], *a.* '**~·wood** *s* Gestrüpp *n*, Unterholz *n*.

brusque [bruːsk] *adj* □ brüsk, barsch, schroff.

Brus·sels sprouts [ˌbrʌsl'spraʊts] *s pl* ⚘ Rosenkohl *m*.

bru·tal ['bruːtl] *adj* □ brutal. **bru·tal·i·ty** [~'tælətɪ] *s* Brutalität *f*. **bru·tal·ize** ['⁓təlaɪz] *v/t* **1.** brutalisieren. **2.** brutal behandeln. **brute** [bruːt] **I** *s* **1.** Vieh *n*, *fig. a.* Untier *n*, Scheusal *n*. **II** *adj* **2.** brutal: *~ force (od. strength)* rohe Gewalt. **3.** hirnlos, dumm. '**brut·ish** *adj* □ → **brute** II.

bub·ble ['bʌbl] **I** *s* **1.** (*Luft- etc*)Blase *f*: *~ bath* Schaumbad *n*; *~ gum* Bubble-gum *m*, Ballon-, Knallkaugummi *m*. **2.** *fig.* Seifenblase *f*. **II** *v/i* **3.** sprudeln, brodeln (*kochendes Wasser etc*); sprudeln, perlen (*Sekt etc*); in Blasen aufsteigen (*Gas*); *~ over* übersprudeln (*a. fig. with vor dat*). '**bub·bly** **I** *adj* **1.** sprudelnd. **2.** *fig.* temperamentvoll. **II** *s* **3.** *bsd. Br.* F Schampus *m*.

buck¹ [bʌk] **I** *s* **1.** *zo.* Bock *m*, *engS.* Rehbock, *allg.* Männchen *n*. **2.** *pass the ~* F den Schwarzen Peter weitergeben; *pass the ~ to s.o.* F j-m den Schwarzen Peter zuschieben. **II** *v/i* **3.** bocken (*Pferd etc*). **4.** *~ up* F aufleben; sich ranhalten: *~ up!* Kopf hoch! **III** *v/t* **5.** *~ up* F j-n aufmuntern; *j-m* Dampf machen.

buck² [~], *s Am. sl.* Dollar *m*.

buck·et ['bʌkɪt] **I** *s* Eimer *m*, Kübel *m*: *kick the ~* F den Löffel weglegen (*sterben*). **II** *v/t* schöpfen: *~ out* ausschöpfen. **III** *v/i*: *it's (od. the rain's) ~ing (down) Br.* F es gießt wie aus *od.* mit Kübeln. **buck·et·ful** ['⁓fʊl] *s ein* Eimer(voll) *m*.

buck·et seat *s mot.* Schalensitz *m*.

buck·le ['bʌkl] **I** *s* **1.** Schnalle *f*, Spange *f*. **II** *v/t* **2.** *a. ~ up* zu-, festschnallen: *~ on* anschnallen. **III** *v/i* **3.** *~ up mot.,* ✈ sich anschnallen. **4.** ~ **down** F sich dahinterklemmen: ~ **down to a task** sich hinter e-e Aufgabe klemmen.

'buck·skin s Wildleder n.

bud [bʌd] **I** s Knospe f: **be in** ~ knospen; **nip in the** ~ fig. im Keim ersticken. **II** v/i knospen: ~**ding lawyer** angehender Jurist.

Bud·dhism ['bʊdɪzəm] s Buddhismus m. **'Bud·dhist I** s Buddhist m. **II** adj buddhistisch.

bud·dy ['bʌdɪ] s bsd. Am. F Kumpel m, Spezi m.

budge [bʌdʒ] mst neg **I** v/i sich (von der Stelle) rühren: ~ **from** fig. von et. abrücken. **II** v/t (vom Fleck) bewegen: ~ **from** fig. j-n abbringen von.

bud·ger·i·gar ['bʌdʒərɪɡɑː] s orn. Wellensittich m.

budg·et ['bʌdʒɪt] s Budget n, Etat m: **for the low** ~ für den schmalen Geldbeutel; ~**conscious** preisbewußt; ~**(-priced)** preisgünstig. **'budg·et·a·ry** adj Budget..., Etat...

bud·gie ['bʌdʒɪ] F → **budgerigar**.

buff [bʌf] s F **1. in the** ~ im Adams- od. Evaskostüm. **2.** in Zssgn ...fan m; ...experte m.

buf·fa·lo ['bʌfələʊ] pl **-lo(e)s** s zo. Büffel m.

buff·er ['bʌfə] s ⊙ Stoßdämpfer m; Puffer m (a. fig.); Prellbock m (a. fig.). ~ **state** s pol. Pufferstaat m. ~ **zone** s ✕ Pufferzone f.

buf·fet¹ ['bʌfɪt] **I** s **1.** (Faust)Schlag m; Ohrfeige f. **II** v/t **2.** j-m e-n (Faust)-Schlag versetzen; j-m e-e Ohrfeige geben. **3.** ankämpfen gegen.

buf·fet² s **1.** ['bʌfɪt] Büfett n, Anrichte f. **2.** ['bʊfeɪ] Büfett n, Theke f.

buf·foon [bəˈfuːn] s Possenreißer m, Hanswurst m (a. fig. contp.).

bug [bʌɡ] s **1.** zo. Wanze f (a. F Minispion); bsd. Am. allg. Insekt n. **2.** F Bazillus m, fig. a. Fieber n: **he got bitten by** (od. **he's got) the** ~ ihn hat's gepackt. **3.** ⊙ F Defekt m, pl Mucken pl. **II** v/t **4.** Am. F j-n wütend machen; j-m auf den Wecker fallen. **5.** F Wanzen anbringen in (dat). **'~bear** s (Schreck-) Gespenst n.

bug·ger ['bʌɡə] V **I** s Scheißkerl m; allg. Kerl m: **poor** ~ armes Schwein. **II** v/t: ~ **up** versauen: ~**ed up** im Arsch. **III** v/i: ~ **off** Br. (mst imp) sich verpissen.

bug·gy¹ ['bʌɡɪ] adj verwanzt.

bug·gy² [~] s mot. Buggy m (geländegängiges Freizeitauto).

bu·gle ['bjuːɡl] s (Wald-, Jagd)Horn n; ✕ Signalhorn n: ~ **call** Hornsignal n. **'bu·gler** s Hornist m.

build [bɪld] **I** v/t (irr) **1.** bauen: a) errichten, b) herstellen: ~ **in(to)** einbauen (in acc). **2.** ~ **up** Gebäude bauen. **3.** ~ **up** Geschäft etc aufbauen: ~ **up a reputation** sich e-n Namen machen. **4.** ~ **up** (in der Presse etc) aufbauen. **5.** ~ **one's hope on** s-e Hoffnung setzen auf (acc). **II** v/i (irr) **6.** bauen: **be** ~**ing** im Bau sein. **7.** ~ **up** bauen (**on** auf acc). **III** s **1.** Körperbau m, Statur f. **'build·er** s **1.** Erbauer m. **2.** Bauunternehmer m. **'build·ing I** s **1.** Bauwesen n. **2.** Gebäude n, Bau(werk n) m. **II** adj **3.** Bau...: ~ **contractor** → **builder** 2; ~ **freeze** Baustopp m; ~ **industry** Baugewerbe n, -wirtschaft f; ~ **site** Baustelle f; ~ **society** Br. Bausparkasse f.

built [bɪlt] pret u. pp von **build**. **,~'in** adj eingebaut, Einbau... **,~'up** adj: ~ **area** bebautes Gelände od. Gebiet; (Verkehr) geschlossene Ortschaft.

bulb [bʌlb] s **1.** ♀ Knolle f, Zwiebel f. **2.** ⚡ Glühbirne f. **'bulb·ous** adj ☐ knollenförmig: ~ **nose** Knollennase f.

Bul·gar·i·an [bʌlˈɡeərɪən] **I** s **1.** Bulgare m, Bulgarin f. **2.** ling. Bulgarisch n. **II** adj **3.** bulgarisch.

bulge [bʌldʒ] **I** s **1.** (Aus)Bauchung f, Ausbuchtung f. **2.** fig. (rapide) Zunahme. **II** v/i **3.** a. ~ **out** sich (aus)bauchen, hervorquellen (a. Augen). **III** v/t **4.** Backen aufblähen. **5.** Taschen etc vollstopfen (**with** mit).

bulk [bʌlk] s **1.** Umfang m, Größe f, Masse f. **2.** Großteil m, Mehrheit f. **3. in** ~ ✝ lose, unverpackt; in gros. **'bulk·y** adj **1.** massig. **2.** unhandlich, sperrig: ~ **refuse** (od. **waste**) Sperrmüll m.

bull [bʊl] **I** s **1.** zo. Bulle m, (Zucht)Stier m: **take the** ~ **by the horns** fig. den Stier bei den Hörnern packen; **like a** ~ **in a china shop** wie ein Elefant im Porzellanladen; → **shoot** 5a. **2.** ✝ Haussespekulant m. **II** v/i **3.** ✝ auf Hausse spekulieren. **'~dog** s zo. Bulldogge f. **'~doze** v/t **1.** planieren. **2.** F einschüchtern;

zwingen (**into doing** zu tun). '**~·doz·er**
s ✿ Bulldozer m, Planierraupe f.
bul·let ['bʊlɪt] s (Gewehr-, Pistolen)Ku-
gel f.
bul·le·tin ['bʊlətɪn] s **1.** Bulletin n: a)
Tagesbericht m, b) ✛ Krankenbericht
m, c) offizielle Bekanntmachung: **~
board** Am. Schwarzes Brett. **2.** Mitteilungsblatt n.
'**bul·let|·proof** adj kugelsicher: **~ glass**
Panzerglas n. **~ wound** s Schußwunde
f, -verletzung f.
'**bull|·fight** s Stierkampf m. '**~·fight·er** s
Stierkämpfer m.
bul·lion ['bʊljən] s (Gold-, Silber)Barren
m.
bull·ish ['bʊlɪʃ] adj ✝ Hausse...
bull·ock ['bʊlək] s zo. Ochse m.
'**bull·ring** s Stierkampfarena f.
'**bull's-eye** ['bʊlzaɪ] s **1.** △, ⚓ Bullauge
n. **2.** Zentrum n, das Schwarze (e-r Zielscheibe): **hit the ~** ins Schwarze treffen
(a. fig.).
'**bull|·shit** s V Scheiß m: **talk ~** Scheiß
reden. **~ ter·ri·er** s zo. Bullterrier m.
bul·ly ['bʊlɪ] **I** s brutaler od. tyrannischer
Kerl. **II** v/t tyrannisieren, schikanieren: **~ about** (od. **around**) j-n herumkommandieren. **III** adj u. int F prima: **~
for you!** na und?; iro. gratuliere!
bul·wark ['bʊlwək] s Bollwerk n.
bum[1] [bʌm] s bsd. Br. F Hintern m.
bum[2] [~] bsd. Am. F **I** s **1.** Gammler m;
Tippelbruder m. **2.** Schnorrer m, Nassauer m. **3.** Saukerl m. **II** v/i **4.** mst **~
about** (od. **around**) herumgammeln. **5.**
schnorren, nassauern (**off** bei). **6.** tip-
peln (**through** durch). **III** adj **7.** mies;
kaputt.
bum·ble·bee ['bʌmblbiː] s zo. Hummel
f.
bump [bʌmp] **I** v/t **1.** (heftig) stoßen. **2.**
mit et. rennen (**against** gegen), et. rammen, auf ein Auto auffahren. **3. ~ off** F
umlegen (umbringen). **II** v/i **4.** (**against,
into**) stoßen, prallen (gegen, an acc),
zs.-stoßen (mit): **~ into** fig. j-n zufällig
treffen. **5.** rumpeln, holpern (Fahr-
zeug). **III** s **6.** heftiger Ruck od. Stoß. **7.**
Beule f. **8.** Unebenheit f.
bump·er[1] ['bʌmpə] **I** s et. Riesiges. **II** adj
riesig: **~ crop** Rekordernte f.
bump·er[2] [~] s **1.** mot. Stoßstange f. 🚗
etc Am. Puffer m.

bump·er| car s (Auto)Skooter m. **~
stick·er** s Autoaufkleber m.
bump·kin ['bʌmpkɪn] s a. **country ~**
contp. Bauer m, Provinzler m.
bump| start s Br. Anschieben n. '**~·start**
v/t Br. Auto anschieben.
bump·tious ['bʌmpʃəs] adj ☐ F aufgeblasen, wichtigtuerisch.
bump·y ['bʌmpɪ] adj ☐ **1.** holp(e)rig,
uneben. **2.** unruhig (Flug).
bun [bʌn] s **1.** süßes Brötchen: **she has a
~ in the oven** F bei ihr ist was unterwegs. **2.** (Haar)Knoten m.
bunch [bʌntʃ] **I** s **1.** Bündel n, Bund n: **~
of flowers** Blumenstrauß m; **~ of
grapes** Weintraube f; **~ of keys** Schlüs-
selbund m, n. **2.** F Verein m, Haufen m.
II v/t **3.** a. **~ up** bündeln. **III** v/i **4.** oft **~
up** (od. **together**) Grüppchen od. Hau-
fen bilden.
bun·combe bsd. Am. → **bunkum.**
bun·dle ['bʌndl] **I** s **1.** Bündel n, Bund n.
2. F (Energie-, Nerven- etc)Bündel n. **II**
v/t **3.** oft **~ up** bündeln. **4.** stopfen (**into**
in acc). **5.** mst **~ off** eilig od. ohne viel
Federlesens fortschaffen. **III** v/i **6.** mst
~ off sich packen od. eilig davonmachen.
bung [bʌŋ] **I** s **1.** a) Spund(zapfen) m, b)
→ **bunghole. II** v/t **2.** Faß verspunden.
3. mst **~ up** F Öffnung etc verstopfen:
my nose is ~ed up m-e Nase ist zu.
bun·ga·low ['bʌŋɡələʊ] s Bungalow m.
'**bung·hole** s Spundloch n.
bun·gle ['bʌŋɡl] **I** v/i pfuschen. **II** v/t
verpfuschen. **III** s Pfusch(arbeit f) m.
'**bun·gler** s Pfuscher(in). '**bun·gling**
adj ☐ stümperhaft.
bunk[1] [bʌŋk] s ⚓ Koje f.
bunk[2] [~] F → **bunkum.**
bunk[3] [~] s: **do a ~** Br. F verduften, türmen.
bunk bed s Etagenbett n.
bunk·er ['bʌŋkə] s ⚓, ✕ Bunker m.
bun·kum ['bʌŋkəm] s Blödsinn m, Gewäsch n.
bun·ny ['bʌnɪ] s Häschen n (a. F attrakti-
ves Mädchen).
buoy [bɔɪ] **I** s **1.** ⚓ Boje f, Bake f. **2.**
Rettungsring m. **II** v/t **3.** mst **~ up** fig.
Auftrieb geben (dat).
buoy·an·cy ['bɔɪənsɪ] s **1.** phys.
Schwimm-, Tragkraft f. **2.** ✈ Auftrieb
m. **3.** fig. Spannkraft f; Schwung m.

'buoy·ant *adj* **1.** federnd (*Schritt*). **2.** schwungvoll.

bur [bɜː] *s* ⚘ Klette *f* (*a. fig.*).

bur·den¹ ['bɜːdn] **I** *s* Last *f*, *fig. a.* Bürde *f*: **~ of proof** ⚖ Beweislast; **be a ~ to** (*od.* **on**) *s.o.* j-m zur Last fallen. **II** *v/t* belasten (*a. fig.*): **~ s.o. with s.th.** j-m et. aufbürden.

bur·den² [~] *s* **1.** Kehrreim *m*, Refrain *m*. **2.** Hauptgedanke *m*.

bur·den·some ['bɜːdnsəm] *adj* lästig, beschwerlich.

bu·reau ['bjʊərəʊ] *pl* **-reaus, -reaux** ['~rəʊz] *s* **1.** *Br.* Schreibtisch *m*, -pult *n*. **2.** *Am.* (*bsd.* Spiegel)Kommode *f*. **3.** Büro *n*. **4.** Auskunfts- *od.* Vermittlungsstelle *f*. **bu·reauc·ra·cy** [~'rɒkrəsɪ] *s* Bürokratie *f*. **bu·reau·crat** ['~kræt] *s* Bürokrat *m*. **bu·reau·crat·ic** *adj* (**~ally**) bürokratisch. **bu·reauc·ra·tize** [~'rɒkrətaɪz] *v/t* bürokratisieren.

burg·er ['bɜːgə] *s gastr. bsd. Am.* F Hamburger *m*.

bur·glar ['bɜːglə] *s* Einbrecher *m*: **we had ~s** bei uns wurde eingebrochen; **~ alarm** Alarmanlage *f*. **bur·glar·ize** ['~raɪz] *Am.* → **burgle**.

'bur·glar·proof *adj* einbruch(s)sicher.

bur·gla·ry ['bɜːglərɪ] *s* Einbruch *m*.

bur·gle ['bɜːgl] *v/t u. v/i* einbrechen (in *acc od. dat*): **he was ~d** bei ihm wurde eingebrochen.

bur·i·al ['berɪəl] *s* Begräbnis *n*, Beerdigung *f*. **~ ground** *s* Friedhof *m*. **~ place** *s* Grabstätte *f*. **~ serv·ice** *s* Trauerfeier *f*.

bur·lesque [bɜː'lesk] **I** *adj* burlesk, possenhaft. **II** *s* Burleske *f*, Posse *f*.

bur·ly ['bɜːlɪ] *adj* stämmig.

burn [bɜːn] **I** *s* **1.** verbrannte Stelle. **2.** ⚕ Verbrennung *f*, Brandwunde *f*. **II** *v/i* (*a. irr*) **3.** *allg.* brennen (*Feuer, Licht, Haus, Wunde etc*): **~ down** ab-, niederbrennen. **4.** *fig.* brennen (**with** vor *dat*): **~ing with anger** wutentbrannt; **be ~ing to do s.th.** darauf brennen, et. zu tun. **5.** ver-, anbrennen (*Speise etc*). **III** *v/t* (*a. irr*) **6.** verbrennen: **~ down** ab-, niederbrennen; **his house was ~t** sein Haus brannte ab; **be ~t to death** verbrennen; → **boat** 1, **bridge** 1, **candle.** 7. verbrennen, -sengen, *Speise* anbrennen (lassen): **~ one's fingers** sich die Finger verbrennen (*a. fig.*); **~ a hole in** ein

Loch brennen in (*acc*). **8.** *Ziegel, Porzellan etc* brennen. **'burn·er** *s* Brenner *m* (*Person u. Gerät*). **'burn·ing** *adj* brennend (*a. fig.*): **take a ~ interest in** brennend interessiert sein an (*dat*); **~ sensation** ⚕ Brennen *n*.

bur·nish ['bɜːnɪʃ] *v/t* polieren.

burnt [bɜːnt] **I** *pret u. pp von* **burn.** **II** *adj*: **~ almonds** *pl* gebrannte Mandeln *pl*.

burp [bɜːp] **I** *v/i* rülpsen, aufstoßen, (*Baby*) ein Bäuerchen machen. **II** *s* Rülpser *m*, Bäuerchen *n*.

burr → **bur**.

bur·row ['bʌrəʊ] **I** *s* (*Fuchs- etc*)Bau *m*. **II** *v/i* (**into**) sich eingraben (in *acc*); *fig.* sich vertiefen (in *acc*).

burst [bɜːst] **I** *v/i* (*irr*) **1.** bersten (*Eis etc*), (zer)platzen (*Luftballon etc*): **~ (open)** aufplatzen (*Wunde etc*), aufspringen (*Tür etc*); → **seam** 1. **2.** explodieren. **3.** *fig.* ausbrechen (**into** *in acc*): **~ into laughter** (**tears**) in Gelächter (Tränen) ausbrechen; **~ into flame(s)** in Flammen aufgehen. **4.** **~ out** *fig.* herausplatzen. **5.** **~ with** zum Bersten voll sein von; *fig.* strotzen vor *od.* von; *fig.* platzen vor (*dat*). **6.** **~ in** (**out**) herein-(hinaus)stürmen; **~ into sight** (*od.* **view**) plötzlich sichtbar werden. **II** *v/t* (*irr*) **7.** (auf)sprengen, zum Platzen bringen: **~ open** aufbrechen; **the car ~ a tire** (*bsd. Br.* **tyre**) ein Reifen am Wagen platzte. **III** *s* **8.** Bersten *n*, Platzen *n*. **9.** Explosion *f*. **10.** Ausbruch *m*: **~ of applause** Beifallssturm *m*; **~ of laughter** Lachsalve *f*. **11.** *a.* **~ of fire** Feuerstoß *m*, Salve *f*.

bur·y ['berɪ] *v/t* **1.** begraben: a) beerdigen, b) verschütten, c) *Streit etc* vergessen: **~ o.s. in** sich vertiefen in (*acc*); **buried in thought(s)** gedankenversunken. **2.** ver-, eingraben, ⚡, ⚙ in die Erde verlegen: → **hatchet**.

bus [bʌs] *pl* **-(s)es** *s* (Omni-, Auto)Bus: → **miss²** 1.

bush¹ [bʊʃ] *s* **1.** Busch *m*, Strauch *m*: **beat about** (*od.* **around**) **the ~** *fig.* wie die Katze um den heißen Brei herumgehen, um die Sache herumreden. **2.** Gebüsch *n*. **3.** Busch *m*; Waldland *n*.

bush² [bʊʃ] *s* ⚙ Buchse *f*.

bush·el ['bʊʃl] *s* Bushel *m*, Scheffel *m* (*Br.* 36, 37 *l*, *Am.* 35, 24 *l*): → **light¹** 1d.

bush·y ['bʊʃɪ] *adj* □ buschig.

busi·ness ['bɪznɪs] *s* **1.** Geschäft *n*, Beruf *m*, Tätigkeit *f*: **on ~** geschäftlich, beruflich. **2.** ♉ Geschäft(sgang *m*) *n*: **how is ~?** wie gehen die Geschäfte? **3.** ♉ Geschäft *n*, Unternehmen *n*. **4.** Arbeit *f*, Beschäftigung *f*: **~ before pleasure** erst die Arbeit, dann das Vergnügen; → **mix** 2. **5.** Sache *f*, Aufgabe *f*: **make it one's ~ to do s.th.** es sich zur Aufgabe machen, et. zu tun. **6.** Angelegenheit *f*, Sache *f*: **get down to ~** zur Sache kommen; **that's none of your ~** das geht Sie nichts an; **send s.o. about his ~** j-m heimleuchten; → **mean³** 1, **mind** 5. **7.** Anlaß *m*, Berechtigung *f*: **have no ~ doing** (*od.* **to do**) kein Recht haben, et. zu tun. **8.** Geschäft *n* (*Notdurft*): **do one's ~** sein Geschäft erledigen *od.* machen. **~ ad·dress** *s* Geschäftsadresse *f*. **~ hours** *s pl* Geschäftsstunden *pl*, -zeit *f*: **after ~** nach Geschäftsschluß. **~ let·ter** *s* Geschäftsbrief *m*. '**~·like** *adj* sachlich, nüchtern. '**~·man** *s* (*irr* **man**) Geschäftsmann *m*. **~ se·cret** *s* Betriebs-, Geschäftsgeheimnis *n*. **~ trip** *s* Geschäftsreise *f*. '**~·wom·an** *s* (*irr* **woman**) Geschäftsfrau *f*. **~ year** *s* ♉ Geschäftsjahr *n*.

bus·ker ['bʌskə] *s Br.* Straßenmusikant(in); -sänger(in).

bus·man ['bʌsmən] *s* (*irr* **man**) (Omni)Busfahrer *m*: **~'s holiday** Urlaub, der mit der üblichen Berufsarbeit verbracht wird. **~ ser·vice** *s* Busverbindung *f*. **~ stop** *s* Bushaltestelle *f*.

bust¹ [bʌst] *s* Büste *f*.

bust² [~] F I *v/i* (*a. irr*) **1.** kaputtgehen. **2.** pleite gehen. II *v/t* (*a. irr*) **3.** kaputtmachen. III *s* **4.** Pleite *f*, *a. weitS.* Reinfall *m.* **5.** Sauferei *f*; Sauftour *f*: **go on a ~** e-e Sauftour machen. IV *adj* **6.** kaputt. **7.** pleite: **go ~** → 2.

bus·tle ['bʌsl] I *v/i* **1.** *a.* **~ about** (*od.* **around**) geschäftig hin u. her eilen. **2.** sich beeilen; eilen, hasten. **3.** **the streets were bustling with life** auf den Straßen herrschte geschäftiges Treiben. II *v/t* **4.** *a.* **~ up** antreiben, hetzen. III *s* **5.** Geschäftigkeit *f*; geschäftiges Treiben. '**bus·tler** *s* geschäftiger Mensch. '**bus·tling** *adj* **1.** geschäftig. **2.** belebt (*Straße etc*).

bus·y ['bɪzɪ] I *adj* □ **1.** beschäftigt: **be ~ doing s.th.** damit beschäftigt sein, et.

zu tun. **2.** geschäftig, fleißig: **get ~!** an die Arbeit!; → **bee.** **3.** *Straße etc*: belebt; verkehrsreich. **4.** arbeitsreich (*Tag etc*). **5.** übereifrig, aufdringlich. **6.** *teleph. bsd. Am.* besetzt: **~ signal** Besetztzeichen *n*. II *v/t* **7.** (**o.s.** sich) beschäftigen (**with mit**): **~ o.s. doing s.th.** sich damit beschäftigen, et. zu tun. '**~·bod·y** *s* j-d, der sich in alles einmischt.

bus·y·ness ['bɪznɪs] *s* Geschäftigkeit *f*.

but [bʌt] I *cj* **1.** aber, jedoch: **~ then** (**again**) and(e)rerseits. **2.** sondern: **not only ... ~ also** nicht nur ..., sondern auch. **3.** als, außer: **~ for** ohne; **~ for my parents** wenn m-e Eltern nicht (gewesen) wären. II *prp* **4.** außer: **nothing ~** nichts als, nur; **the last ~ one** (**two**) der vorletzte (drittletzte); → **anything** 2. **5.** **all ~** fast, beinahe. III *s* **6.** **no ~s about it** kein Aber; → **if** 4.

bu·tane ['bju:teɪn] *s* 🜓 Butan *n*.

butch·er ['bʊtʃə] I *s* **1.** Fleischer *m*, Metzger *m*: **at the ~'s** beim Fleischer. II *v/t* **2.** schlachten. **3.** abschlachten, niedermetzeln. '**butch·er·y** *s* **1.** Fleischer-, Metzgerhandwerk *n*. **2.** Gemetzel *n*.

but·ler ['bʌtlə] *s* Butler *m*.

butt [bʌt] *s* **1.** (*Gewehr- etc*)Kolben *m.* **2.** (*Zigarren-, Zigaretten-, Kerzen-*) Stummel *m*, (*Zigaretten*)Kippe *f*. **3.** *fig.* Zielscheibe *f*. **4.** Kopfstoß *m*; Stoß mit den Hörnern. II *v/t* **5.** j-m e-n Kopfstoß *od.* e-n Stoß mit den Hörnern versetzen. **6.** *Zigarre, Zigarette* ausdrücken. III *v/i* **7.** **~ in** F sich einmischen: **~ in on, ~ into** sich einmischen in (*acc*).

but·ter ['bʌtə] I *s* **1.** Butter *f*: **he looks as if ~ would not melt in his mouth** er sieht aus, als könnte er nicht bis drei zählen *od.* als könnte er kein Wässerchen trüben. II *v/t* **2.** mit Butter bestreichen. **3.** **~ up** F j-m schöntun, j-m Honig ums Maul schmieren. **~ dish** *s* Butterdose *f*, -schale *f*. '**~·fin·gered** *adj* F tolpatschig. '**~·fin·gers** *pl* -**fin·gers** *s* F Tolpatsch *m*. '**~·fly** *s* **1.** *zo.* Schmetterling *m*: **have butterflies in one's stomach** F ein flaues Gefühl in der Magengegend haben. **2.** *a.* **~ stroke** (*Schwimmen*) Schmetterlingsstil *m*. '**~·milk** *s* Buttermilch *f*.

but·tock ['bʌtək] *s anat.* Gesäßbacke *f*: **~s** *pl* Gesäß *n*.

but·ton [ˈbʌtn] **I** s **1.** (*Kleider-*, *a. Klingel-etc*)Knopf m. **2.** (Ansteck)Plakette f, Abzeichen n. **3.** pl (sg konstruiert) bsd. Br. F Hotelpage m. **II** v/t **4.** mst ~ **up** zuknöpfen: **~ed up** F zugeknöpft, zurückhaltend. **III** v/i **5.** hinten etc geknöpft werden. '**~hole** s **1.** Knopfloch n. **2.** bsd. Br. Blume f im Knopfloch.

but·tress [ˈbʌtrɪs] **I** s **1.** △ Strebe-, Stützpfeiler m. **2.** fig. Stütze f. **II** v/t a. ~ **up 3.** stützen. **4.** fig. (unter)stützen.

bux·om [ˈbʌksəm] adj drall.

buy [baɪ] **I** s Kauf m: a good ~. **II** v/t (irr) **2.** (ein)kaufen (**of**, **from** von; **at** bei): ~ s.th. from s.o. j-m et. abkaufen. **3.** Fahrkarte etc lösen. **4.** fig. Sieg etc erkaufen (**with** mit): **dearly bought** teuer erkauft. **5.** j-n kaufen, bestechen. **6.** bsd. Am. F et. glauben: **I won't ~ that!** das kauf' ich dir etc nicht ab!

Verbindungen mit Adverbien:

buy| back v/t zurückkaufen. **~ in** v/i sich eindecken mit. **~ off** → **buy** 5. **~ out** v/t Teilhaber etc abfinden, auszahlen. **~ up** v/t aufkaufen.

buy·er [ˈbaɪə] s Käufer(in).

buzz [bʌz] **I** v/i summen, surren, schwirren: **~ off** F (mst imp) abschwirren, abhauen; **~ for** → II a. **II** v/t a) j-n mit dem Summer rufen, b) teleph. F j-n anrufen. **III** s Summen n, Surren n, Schwirren f: **give s.o. a ~** → II.

buz·zard [ˈbʌzəd] s orn. Bussard m.

buzz·er [ˈbʌzə] s ⚡ Summer m.

'**buzz·word** s Modewort n.

by [baɪ] **I** prp **1.** örtlich: (nahe od. dicht) bei od. an (dat), neben (dat): **side ~ side** Seite an Seite. **2.** vorbei od. vorüber an (dat), an (dat) ... entlang. **3.** Verkehrsmittel: per, mit: → **air'** 1, etc. **4.** zeitlich: bis um od. spätestens: **be here ~ 4.30** sei um 4 Uhr 30 hier; → **now** 1. **5.** Tageszeit: während, bei: → **day** 1, etc.

6. nach, ...weise: **sold by the yard** yardweise verkauft; → **hour** 1, etc. **7.** nach, gemäß: **it is ten ~ my watch** nach od. auf m-r Uhr ist es zehn. **8.** von: → **nature** 2, **trade** 4. **9.** Urheberschaft: von, durch: **a play ~ Shaw** ein Stück von Shaw; → **oneself** 1. **10.** mit Hilfe von, mit, durch: **~ listening** durch Zuhören; → **force** 1, 3, 4. **11.** Größenverhältnisse: um: (**too**) **short ~ an inch** um e-n Zoll zu kurz. **12.** Ⓐ a) mal: **3 ~ 4**; **the size is 9 feet ~ 6** die Größe ist 9 auf 6 (od. 9×6) Fuß; → **multiply** 2, b) durch: **6 ~ 2**; → **divide** 4, 6. **13.** an (dat), bei: → **root'**, etc. **II** adv **14.** nahe: **~ and large** im ganzen; ~ **and** ~ bald, demnächst; nach u. nach; → **close** 9, **hard** 13. **15.** vorbei, vorüber: → **go by**, etc. **16.** beiseite: → **put by**, etc.

by(e)... Neben..., Seiten...

bye [baɪ] → **bye-bye** II.

bye-bye **I** s [ˈbaɪbaɪ]: **go to ~(s)** in die Heia gehen; einschlafen. **II** int [ˈbaɪˈbaɪ] F Wiedersehen!, Tschüs!; teleph. Wiederhören!

'**by|·ef·fect** s Nebenwirkung f. '**~e·lec·tion** s Nachwahl f. '**~gone I** adj vergangen. **II** s: **let ~s be ~s** laß(t) das Vergangene ruhen. '**~law** s bsd. Br. Ortsstatut n, städtische Verordnung. '**~name** s Beiname m. '**~pass** s **1.** Umleitung f, Umgehungsstraße f. **2.** 🎐 Bypass m: ~ **operation** Bypassoperation f. '**~·prod·uct** s Nebenprodukt n (a. fig.). '**~road** s Seiten-, Nebenstraße f. '**~·stand·er** s Umstehende m, f, Zuschauer(in). '**~street** → **byroad.**

byte [baɪt] s Computer: Byte n, Binärwort n.

'**by|·way** → **byroad.** '**~word** s Inbegriff m (**for** gen): **be a ~ for** stehen für, gleichbedeutend sein mit.

C

cab [kæb] s **1.** Taxi n, Taxe f. **2.** 🚃 Führerstand m; Fahrerhaus n (e-s Lastkraftwagens), (a. e-s Krans) Führerhaus n.

cab·a·ret ['kæbəreɪ] s a. ~ **show** Varietédarbietungen pl (in e-m Restaurant od. Nachtklub).

cab·bage ['kæbɪdʒ] s ♣ Kohl m.

cab·bie, cab·by ['kæbɪ] s bsd. Am. F Taxifahrer(in).

'cab,driv·er s bsd. Am. Taxifahrer(in).

cab·in ['kæbɪn] s **1.** Häuschen n, Hütte f. **2.** ⚓ Kabine f, Kajüte f. **3.** ✈ Kabine f (a. e-r Seilbahn etc). ~ **class** s ⚓ Kabinen-, Kajütsklasse f. ~ **cruis·er** s ⚓ Kabinenkreuzer m.

cab·i·net ['kæbɪnɪt] s **1.** oft ⚑ pol. Kabinett n. **2.** Vitrine f. **3.** (Büro-, Kartei-etc)Schrank m. **4.** (Radio- etc)Gehäuse n.

ca·ble ['keɪbl] **I** s **1.** Kabel n (a. ⚡), (Draht)Seil n. **2.** → cablegram. **II** v/t **3.** TV: Gegend etc verkabeln. **4.** j-m et. telegrafieren; j-n telegrafisch benachrichtigen. **5.** j-m Geld telegrafisch an- od. überweisen. **III** v/i **6.** telegrafieren. ~ **ad·dress** s Telegrammadresse f. ~ **car** s Seilbahn: Kabine f; Wagen m.

ca·ble·gram ['keɪblgræm] s (Übersee-) Telegramm n.

ca·ble tel·e·vi·sion s Kabelfernsehen n.

cab·man ['kæbmən] s (irr man) Taxifahrer m.

ca·boo·dle [kə'buːdl] s: the whole ~ F die ganze Chose.

ca·boose [kə'buːs] s ⚓ Kombüse f.

cab| **rank,** '**~stand** s bsd. Am. Taxistand m.

cache [kæʃ] **I** s Versteck n, geheimes Lager. **II** v/t verstecken.

cack·le ['kækl] **I** v/i gackern (Huhn), schnattern (Gans), fig. a. gackernd lachen. **II** s Gegacker n, Geschnatter n, fig. a. gackerndes Lachen.

ca·coph·o·ny [kæ'kɒfənɪ] s ♪ Kakophonie f, Mißklang m.

cac·tus ['kæktəs] pl **-ti** ['~taɪ], **-tus·es** s ♣ Kaktus m.

ca·das·tre [kə'dæstə] s Grundbuch n.

ca·dav·er·ous [kə'dævərəs] adj □ leichenblaß.

cad·die ['kædɪ] s Golf: Caddie m (Schlägerträger).

cad·dy ['kædɪ] s (bsd. Tee)Büchse f, (-)Dose f.

ca·dence ['keɪdəns] s **1.** (Vers-, Sprech-) Rhythmus m. **2.** ♪ Kadenz f.

ca·det [kə'det] s **1.** ✕ Kadett m. **2.** (Polizei- etc)Schüler m: ~ **nurse** Schwesternschülerin f.

cadge [kædʒ] v/t u. v/i schnorren (**from** bei). **'cadg·er** s Schnorrer(in).

cad·mi·um ['kædmɪəm] s 🧪 Cadmium n.

ca·dre ['kɑːdə] s ✕, ✕, pol. Kader m.

Cae·sar·e·an, **Cae·sar·i·an** [siː'zeərɪən] **I** adj: ~ **section** → **II. II** s 🩺 Kaiserschnitt m.

cae·su·ra [sɪ'zjʊərə] s Zäsur f.

ca·fé ['kæfeɪ] s **1.** Café n. **2.** Restaurant n. **3.** Am. Kneipe f; Nachtklub m.

caf·e·te·ri·a [ˌkæfɪ'tɪərɪə] s Cafeteria f, Selbstbedienungsrestaurant n, a. Kantine f, univ. Mensa f.

caf·feine ['kæfiːn] s 🧪 Koffein n.

cage [keɪdʒ] **I** s **1.** Käfig m. **2.** Kabine f (e-s Aufzugs); ✕ Förderkorb m. **II** v/t **3.** in e-n Käfig sperren, einsperren.

cage·y ['keɪdʒɪ] adj □ F **1.** verschlossen. **2.** vorsichtig. **3.** Am. gerissen, schlau.

ca·jole [kə'dʒəʊl] v/t **1.** j-m schmeicheln. **2.** j-n beschwatzen (**into doing** zu tun): ~ **s.o. out of s.th.** j-m et. ausreden; ~ **s.th. out of s.o.** j-m et. abbetteln.

cake [keɪk] **I** s **1.** Kuchen m, Torte f: **go** (od. **sell**) **like hot** ~**s** weggehen wie die warmen Semmeln; **take the** ~ F den Vogel abschießen; **you can't have your** ~ **and eat it** du kannst nur eines von beiden tun od. haben; → **piece** 1. **2.** Tafel f Schokolade, Riegel m Seife. **II** v/i **3.** klumpen.

ca·lam·i·tous [kə'læmɪtəs] adj □ verheerend, katastrophal. **ca'lam·i·ty** s **1.** Katastrophe f: **in the** ~ bei der Katastrophe; ~ **of nature** Naturkatastrophe; ~ **howler** bsd. Am. Schwarzseher(in), Panikmacher(in). **2.** Elend n, Misere f.

cal·cif·er·ous [kæl'sɪfərəs] adj kalkhal-

tig. **cal·ci·fy** ['-faɪ] *v/t u. v/i* verkalken.
cal·ci·um ['-sɪəm] *s* 🜍 Kalzium *n*.
cal·cu·la·ble ['kælkjʊləbl] *adj* □ **1.** berechen-, kalkulierbar: ~ **risk** kalkulierbares Risiko. **2.** verläßlich. **cal·cu·late** ['-leɪt] **I** *v/t* **1.** be-, ausrechnen: ~ **that** damit rechnen, daß. **2.** *Preise, Entfernung etc* kalkulieren, *Chancen etc* abwägen. **3.** *Am.* F vermuten, glauben (**that** daß). **II** *v/i* **4.** ~ **on** rechnen *od.* auf (*acc*), zählen *od.* sich verlassen auf (*acc*). **cal·cu·lat·ed** *adj* **1.** gewollt, beabsichtigt, (*Indiskretion*) gezielt, (*Beleidigung*) bewußt, (*Risiko*) kalkuliert. **2.** gedacht, bestimmt (**for** für; **to do** zu tun): *it was* ~ **to impress** es sollte Eindruck machen. '**cal·cu·lat·ing** *adj* □ **1.** (kühl) überlegend; berechnend. **2.** Rechen...: ~ **machine.** ,**cal·cu'la·tion** *s* **1.** Berechnung *f* (*a. fig.*), Ausrechnung *f*: **be out in one's** ~ sich verrechnet haben. **2.** Kalkulation *f*: ~ **of profits** 🜊 Gewinnkalkulation. **3.** Überlegung *f*: **after much** ~ nach reiflicher Überlegung. '**cal·cu·la·tor** *s* Rechner *m* (*Gerät*). **cal·cu·lus** ['-ləs] *pl* **-li** ['-laɪ], **-lus·es** *s* 🜖 Rechnungsart *f*, (*Differential- etc*)Rechnung *f*: ~ **of probabilities** Wahrscheinlichkeitsrechnung.

cal·en·dar ['kælɪndə] *s* **1.** (*engS.* Termin)Kalender *m*, *fig. a.* Zeitrechnung *f*. **2.** Liste *f*, Register *n*.
cal·ends ['kælɪndz] *s pl*: **on the Greek** ~ am St. Nimmerleinstag.
calf[1] [kɑːf] *pl* **calves** [kɑːvz] *s* **1.** Kalb *n*. **2.** Kalb(s)leder *n*.
calf[2] [~] *pl* **calves** [~] *s anat.* Wade *f*.
calf **love** *s* F jugendliche Schwärmerei.
'~**skin** → **calf**[1] 2.

cal·i·ber *Am.* → **calibre. cal·i·brate** ['kælɪbreɪt] *v/t* ⚙ kalibrieren, eichen.
cal·i·bre ['-bə] *s* Kaliber *n*, *fig. a.* Format *n* (*e-s Menschen*).

call [kɔːl] **I** *v/t* **1.** rufen (**for** nach): ~ **for help** Hilferuf *m*; **within** ~ in Rufweite. **2.** *teleph.* Anruf *m*: **give s.o. a** ~ j-n anrufen; **make a** ~ telefonieren. **3.** (Lock)Ruf *m* (*e-s Tiers*). **4.** *fig.* Ruf *m* (*der Natur etc*). **5.** Berufung *f* (**to** auf *e-n* Lehrstuhl, an *e-e* Universität, in *ein Amt*). **6.** Aufruf *m*: **make a** ~ **for s.th.** zu et. aufrufen. **7.** *thea.* Herausruf *m*, Vorhang *m*. **8.** (kurzer) Besuch (**on**

s.o., **at s.o.'s** [**house**] bei j-m): **make** (*od.* **pay**) **a** ~ **on s.o.** j-n besuchen, j-m e-n Besuch abstatten. **9.** 🜊 Zahlungsaufforderung *f*; Abruf *m*, Kündigung *f* (*von Geldern*). **II** *v/t* **10.** *j-n* (herbei)rufen, *Arzt etc* kommen lassen: → **attention** 1, **being** 1. **11.** zu *e-m* Streik *etc* aufrufen. **12.** *Versammlung etc* einberufen. **13.** *j-n* wecken. **14.** *teleph.* anrufen. **15.** *j-n* berufen (**to** → 5). **16.** *j-n* nennen: **be** ~**ed** heißen; → **spade**[1]. **17.** nennen, bezeichnen (als): **what do you** ~ **this?** wie nennt man *od.* heißt das? **18.** nennen, finden, halten für: **I** ~ **that stupid.** **19.** *j-n et.* schimpfen: **he** ~**ed me a fool.** **III** *v/i* **20.** rufen (*a. fig. Pflicht etc*): ~ **for** um Hilfe rufen; nach *j-m, et.* rufen; *fig.* erfordern. **21.** e-n (kurzen) Besuch machen (**on s.o.**, **at s.o.'s** [**house**] bei j-m): **call on s.o.** j-n besuchen, j-m e-n Besuch abstatten; ~ **for** et. abfordern; *j-n, et.* abholen. **22.** ~ **on** sich wenden an (*acc*) (**for s.th.** um et., wegen e-r Sache); *j-n* bitten (**to do** zu tun). **23.** ~ **at** ⚓ anlegen in (*dat*), *Hafen* anlaufen; 🚂 halten in (*dat*); ✈ *Flughafen* anfliegen. **24.** anrufen, telefonieren.
Verbindungen mit Adverbien:
call | **a·way** *v/t* **1.** wegrufen (**from** von). **2.** *Gedanken etc* ablenken (**from** von). ~ **back I** *v/t* **1.** *a. teleph.* zurückrufen. **2.** *defekte Autos etc* (in die Werkstatt) zurückrufen. **II** *v/i* **3.** *a. teleph.* zurückrufen. **4.** noch einmal vorbeikommen. ~ **down** *v/t* **1.** *Segen etc* herabflehen, -rufen. **2.** sich *j-s Zorn* zuziehen. **II** *v/i* **4.** *Am.* F zs.-stauchen (**for** wegen). ~ **forth** *v/t* hervorrufen, auslösen, *Fähigkeiten etc* wachrufen, wecken. ~ **in I** *v/t* **1.** hinein-, hereinrufen. **2.** *Arzt etc* (hin)zuziehen, zu Rate ziehen. **3.** *Schulden* einfordern, *Forderungen etc* einlösen. **II** *v/i* **4.** (kurz) vorbeischauen (**on s.o.**, **at s.o.'s** [**house**] bei j-m). ~ **off** *v/i* **1.** *j-n* (von s-m Posten) abberufen. **2.** *Streik etc* absagen; abbrechen. ~ **out I** *v/t* **1.** ausrufen, *Namen etc* aufrufen. **2.** *Polizei etc* aufbieten; alarmieren. **3.** *Fähigkeiten etc* wachrufen, wecken. **4.** zum Streik aufrufen. **II** *v/i* **5.** rufen (**for** um *Hilfe*). ~ **o·ver** *v/t* *Namen, Liste etc* verlesen. ~ **up** *v/t* **1.** *teleph.* anrufen. **2.** *Erinnerungen etc* wachrufen, wecken. **3.** ✕ einberufen.

'**call**·**back** s Rückruf(aktion f) m. ~ **box** s Br. Telefonzelle f.

call·er ['kɔːlə] s **1.** Rufer(in). **2.** teleph. Anrufer(in). **3.** Besucher(in). **4.** Abholer(in).

call| **girl** s Callgirl n. '~-**in** Am. → **phone-in**.

call·ing ['kɔːlɪŋ] s **1.** Beruf m: **what is his ~?** was ist er von Beruf? **2.** bsd. eccl. Berufung f: **have a ~ to do s.th.** sich berufen fühlen, et. zu tun. ~ **card** s Am. Visitenkarte f.

cal·lis·then·ics [,kælɪs'θenɪks] s pl Gymnastik f, Freiübungen pl.

cal·los·i·ty [kæ'lɒsətɪ] s **1.** Schwiele f. **2.** fig. Gefühllosigkeit f. '**cal·lous** adj □ **1.** schwielig. **2.** fig. abgestumpft, gefühllos (**to** gegenüber).

'**call-up** s × Einberufung f.

cal·lus ['kæləs] s Schwiele f.

calm [kɑːm] **I** s **1.** Stille f, Ruhe f (a. fig.): **the ~ before the storm**; ~ (**of mind**) Gelassenheit f, Gemütsruhe f. **2.** Windstille f. **II** adj □ **3.** still, ruhig. **4.** windstill. **5.** fig. ruhig, gelassen. **III** v/t **6.** oft ~ **down** beruhigen, besänftigen. **IV** v/i oft ~ **down 7.** sich beruhigen. **8.** sich legen (Sturm, Zorn etc).

cal·o·rie ['kælərɪ] s Kalorie f. '~-,**con·scious** adj □ kalorienbewußt.

ca·lum·ni·ate [kə'lʌmnɪeɪt] v/t verleumden. **ca'lum·ni·a·tor** s Verleumder(in). **ca'lum·ni·ous** adj □ verleumderisch. **cal·um·ny** ['kæləmnɪ] s Verleumdung f.

calve [kɑːv] v/i kalben.

calves [kɑːvz] pl von **calf** [1] u. [2].

ca·lyp·so [kə'lɪpsəʊ] pl -**sos** s ♪ Calypso m.

cam [kæm] s ⚙ Nocken m.

cam·ber ['kæmbə] **I** v/t u. v/i **1.** (sich) wölben. **II** s **2.** (leichte) Wölbung. **3.** mot. Sturz m.

came [keɪm] pret von **come**.

cam·el ['kæml] s zo. Kamel n.

cam·el's| hair ['kæmlz] s Kamelhaar(stoff m) n. '~-**hair** adj Kamelhaar...

cam·er·a ['kæmərə] s **1.** (a. Film-, Fernseh)Kamera f, Fotoapparat m. **2.** **in** ~ ⚖ unter Ausschluß der Öffentlichkeit; fig. geheim. '~-**man** s (irr **man**) **1.** Kameramann m. **2.** Pressefotograf m. '~-**shy** adj kamerascheu.

cam·i·on ['kæmɪən] s Last(kraft)wagen m.

cam·o·mile ['kæməmaɪl] s ⚘ Kamille f: ~ **tea** Kamillentee m.

cam·ou·flage ['kæməflɑːʒ] **I** s ×, zo. Tarnung f, fig. a. Verschleierung f. **II** v/t × tarnen, fig. a. verschleiern.

camp[1] [kæmp] **I** s **1.** (Zelt- etc)Lager n (fig. a. Partei): ~ **bed** (Am. a. **cot**) Feldbett n; Campingliege f; ~ **chair** Klapp-, Campingstuhl m. **II** v/i **2.** sein Lager aufschlagen, kampieren. **3.** oft ~ **out** zelten, campen.

camp[2] [~] F **I** adj **1.** künstlich, gewollt; aufgemotzt, thea. etc a. überzogen. **2.** tuntenhaft. **II** v/i **3.** sich tuntenhaft benehmen. **III** v/t **4.** ~ **it up** a) → 3, b) die Sache aufmotzen, thea. etc a. überziehen.

cam·paign [kæm'peɪn] **I** s **1.** × Feldzug m, fig. a. Kampagne f. **2.** pol. Wahlkampf m: ~ **pledge** (od. **promise**) Wahlversprechen n. **II** v/i **3.** × an e-m Feldzug teilnehmen. **4.** fig. kämpfen (**for** für; **against** gegen). **cam'paign·er** s **1.** × Feldzugteilnehmer m: **old** ~ Veteran m; fig. alter Praktikus. **2.** fig. Kämpfer m.

camp·er ['kæmpə] s **1.** Zeltler(in), Camper(in). **2.** Am. Wohnanhänger m, -wagen m; Wohnmobil n.

'**camp**|**fire** s Lagerfeuer n. '~-**ground** s **1.** Lagerplatz m. **2.** Zelt-, Campingplatz m.

cam·phor ['kæmfə] s ⚘ Kampfer m: ~ **ball** Mottenkugel f.

camp·ing ['kæmpɪŋ] s Camping n, Zelten n: ~ **ground** (od. **site**) → **campground**.

'**camp·site** → **campground**.

cam·pus ['kæmpəs] s Campus m (Gesamtanlage e-r Universität, e-s College od. e-r Schule).

'**cam·shaft** s ⚙ Nockenwelle f.

can[1] [kæn] v/aux (irr) ich kann etc.

can[2] [~] **I** s **1.** (Blech)Kanne f: **have to carry the** ~ F den Kopf hinhalten müssen (**for** für). **2.** (Blech-, Konserven-)Dose f, (-)Büchse f: ~ **opener** Dosen-, Büchsenöffner m. **3.** Kanister m. **4.** Am. Müll-, Abfalleimer m; Müll-, Abfalltonne f. **II** v/t **5.** einmachen, -dosen: → **canned** 1. **6.** F (auf Band etc) aufnehmen: → **canned** 2.

Ca·na·di·an [kə'neɪdjən] **I** *adj* kanadisch. **II** *s* Kanadier(in).

ca·nal [kə'næl] *s* Kanal *m*, *anat. a.* Gang *m*, Röhre *f*. **ca·nal·i·za·tion** [ˌkænəlaɪ'zeɪʃn] *s* Kanalisation *f*, Kanalisierung *f*. **'ca·nal·ize** *v/t* kanalisieren.

can·a·pé ['kænəpeɪ] *s gastr.* Appetit-, Cocktailhappen *m*.

ca·nard [kæ'nɑːd] *s* (Zeitungs)Ente *f*, Falschmeldung *f*.

ca·nar·y [kə'neərɪ] *s* Kanarienvogel *m*.

can·cel ['kænsl] **I** *v/t pret u. pp* **-celed,** *bsd. Br.* **-celled 1.** (durch-, aus)streichen. **2.** *Erlaubnis etc* widerrufen, *Beschluß etc* rückgängig machen, *Abonnement etc* kündigen, *Auftrag etc* stornieren. **3.** *Verabredung etc* absagen, *Veranstaltung etc* ausfallen lassen. **4.** *Briefmarke, Fahrschein* entwerten. **5.** *A* kürzen. **6.** *a.* **~ out** ausgleichen, kompensieren. **II** *v/i* **7.** *A* sich kürzen lassen. **8.** *a.* **~ out** sich (gegenseitig) aufheben.

can·cel·(l)a·tion [ˌ~sə'leɪʃn] *s* **1.** Streichung *f*. **2.** Widerrufung *f*, Rückgängigmachung *f*, Kündigung *f*, Stornierung *f*. **3.** Absage *f*. **4.** Entwertung *f*. **5.** *A* Kürzung *f*.

can·cer ['kænsə] **I** *s* **1.** ❀ Krebs *m*. **2.** *fig.* Krebsgeschwür *n*. **3.** ♋ *astr.* Krebs *m*. **II** *adj* **4.** Krebs...: **~ cells** (**research,** *etc*). **'can·cer·ous** *adj* ❀ krebsbefallen; Krebs...; krebsartig.

can·de·la·bra [ˌkændɪ'lɑːbrə] *s* **1.** *pl* **-bras** → **candelabrum. 2.** *pl von* **candelabrum. ,can·de·la·brum** [~brəm] *pl* **-bra** [~brə], **-brums** *s* Kandelaber *m*, Armleuchter *m*.

can·did ['kændɪd] *adj* □ **1.** offen, aufrichtig. **2.** unvoreingenommen. **3.** *phot.* ungestellt: **~ camera** versteckte Kamera; **~ picture** Schnappschuß *m*.

can·di·da·cy ['kændɪdəsɪ] *s bsd. Am.* Kandidatur *f*, Bewerbung *f*, Anwartschaft *f*. **can·di·date** ['~dət] *s* (**for**) Kandidat(in) (für), Anwärter(in) (auf *acc*), Bewerber(in) (um). **can·di·da·ture** ['~tʃə] *bsd. Br.* → **candidacy.**

can·died ['kændɪd] *adj* **1.** kandiert. **2.** *fig.* honigsüß, schmeichlerisch.

can·dle ['kændl] *s* Kerze *f*: **burn the ~ at both ends** Raubbau mit s-r Gesundheit treiben; **not to be fit** (*od.* **able**) **to hold a ~ to** j-m nicht das Wasser reichen können; **the game is not worth the ~**

die Sache ist nicht der Mühe wert. **'~·light** *s* Kerzenlicht *n*: **by ~** bei Kerzenlicht; **~ dinner** Essen *n* bei Kerzenlicht.

Can·dle·mas ['kændlməs] *s eccl.* (Mariä) Lichtmeß *f*.

'can·dle·stick *s* Kerzenleuchter *m*, -ständer *m*.

can·do(u)r ['kændə] *s* **1.** Offenheit *f*, Aufrichtigkeit *f*. **2.** Unvoreingenommenheit *f*.

can·dy ['kændɪ] **I** *s* **1.** Kandis(zucker) *m*. **2.** *bsd. Am.* Süßigkeiten *pl*: (**hard**) **~** Bonbon *m, n*. **II** *v/t* **3.** kandieren. **'~·floss** *s Br.* Zuckerwatte *f*.

cane [keɪn] **I** *s* **1.** Spazierstock *m*. **2.** (Rohr)Stock *m*. **3.** (*Bambus-, Zucker-, Schilf*)Rohr *n*. **II** *v/t* **4.** (mit dem Stock) züchtigen. **~ sug·ar** *s* Rohrzucker *m*.

ca·nine ['keɪnaɪn] **I** *adj* **1.** Hunde..., Hunds... **2.** *contp.* hündisch: **~ devotion** hündische Ergebenheit. **II** *s* **3.** *a.* **~ tooth** Eckzahn *m*.

can·is·ter ['kænɪstə] *s* Blechbüchse *f*, -dose *f*.

can·ker ['kæŋkə] *s* **1.** 𝄞 Soor *m*; Lippengeschwür *n*. **2.** ❀ Baumkrebs *m*. **3.** *fig.* Krebsgeschwür *n*.

can·na·bis ['kænəbɪs] *s* Cannabis *m*: a) ❀ Hanf *m*, b) Haschisch *n*.

canned [kænd] *adj* **1.** Dosen..., Büchsen...: **~ fruit** Obstkonserven *pl*; **~ meat** Büchsenfleisch *n*. **2.** F **~ music** Musik *f* aus der Konserve; **~ program(me)** (*Rundfunk, TV*) Programmkonserve *f*. **3.** *sl.* blau, betrunken.

can·ni·bal ['kænɪbl] *s* Kannibale *m*, Menschenfresser *m*. **can·ni·bal·ism** ['~bəlɪzəm] *s* Kannibalismus *m*. **,can·ni·bal·is·tic** *adj* (**~ally**) kannibalisch. **'can·ni·bal·ize** *v/t* Auto ausschlachten.

can·non ['kænən] *pl* **-non(s)** *s* ✕ (✔ Bord)Kanone *f*, (-)Geschütz *n*. **can·non·ade** [ˌ~'neɪd] *s* ✕ Kanonade *f*. **'can·non·ball** *s* Kanonenkugel *f*. **~ fod·der** *s* Kanonenfutter *n*.

can·not ['kænɒt] kann *etc* nicht.

can·ny ['kænɪ] *adj* □ schlau, gerissen.

ca·noe [kə'nuː] **I** *s* Kanu *n*, Paddelboot *n*: **paddle one's own ~** *fig.* auf eigenen Beinen *od.* Füßen stehen. **II** *v/i* paddeln.

can·on ['kænən] *s* **1.** Kanon *m* (*a. eccl.*),

Regel f. **2.** Grundsatz m. **3.** ♪ Kanon m.
can·on·i·za·tion [͵~nɑɪˈzeɪʃn] s eccl.
Heiligsprechung f. **'can·on·ize** v/t heiligsprechen.

can·on law s Kirchenrecht n.

ca·noo·dle [kəˈnuːdl] v/i sl. knutschen,
schmusen (**with** mit).

can·o·py [ˈkænəpɪ] s **1.** Baldachin m (a.
△). **2.** △ Vordach n. **3.** ✈ Kabinenhaube f.

cant¹ [kænt] **I** s **1.** Schrägung f. **2.** Neigung f. **II** v/t **3.** kanten, kippen: **~ over**
umkippen. **4.** ⊙ abschrägen. **III** v/i **5.**
a. ~ **over** umkippen.

cant² [~] **I** s **1.** Jargon m. **2.** Kauderwelsch n. **3.** (leere) Phrase(n pl). **II** v/i **4.**
Jargon reden. **5.** Phrasen dreschen.

can't [kɑːnt] F → **cannot.**

can·tan·ker·ous [kænˈtæŋkərəs] adj □
giftig, streitsüchtig.

can·teen [kænˈtiːn] s **1.** bsd. Br. Kan'tine
f. **2.** ✗ Feldflasche f; Kochgeschirr n.
3. Erfrischungsstand m. **4.** Besteckkasten m; Besteck n.

can·ter [ˈkæntə] **I** s Kanter m: **win at a ~**
fig. mühelos siegen. **II** v/i kantern.

can·ti·le·ver [ˈkæntɪliːvə] s **1.** △ Konsole f. **2.** ⊙ Ausleger m.

can·vas [ˈkænvəs] s **1.** Segeltuch n. **2.**
Zeltleinwand f. **3.** paint. Leinwand f.

can·vass [ˈkænvəs] **I** v/t **1.** eingehend
erörtern od. prüfen. **2.** pol. um Stimmen
werben. **3.** ✝ Geschäftsbezirk bereisen;
Aufträge hereinholen, Abonnenten, Inserate sammeln. **II** v/i **4.** pol. e-n Wahlfeldzug veranstalten. **5.** ✝ werben (**for**
um, für), e-n Werbefeldzug durchführen. **III** s **6.** eingehende Erörterung od.
Prüfung. **7.** pol. Wahlfeldzug m. **8.** ✝
Werbefeldzug m. **'can·vass·er** s **1.** ✝
Stimmenwerber m. **2.** ✝ Handelsvertreter m.

can·yon [ˈkænjən] s Cañon m.

caou·tchouc [ˈkaʊtʃʊk] s Kautschuk m.

cap [kæp] **I** s **1.** Mütze f, Kappe f, Haube
f: ~ **in hand** demütig, unterwürfig; **set
one's ~ at** (od. **for**) s.o. F j-n zu angeln
suchen (Frau). **2.** ⊙ (Schutz-, Verschluß)Kappe f, (Abdeck-, Schutz-)
Haube f; Deckel m. **II** v/t **3.** Flasche etc
verschließen. **4.** krönen: a) oben liegen
auf (dat), b) fig. abschließen. **5.** fig.
übertreffen, -trumpfen: ~ **everything**
allem die Krone aufsetzen, alles über-

treffen; **to ~ it all** als Krönung des Ganzen.

ca·pa·bil·i·ty [͵keɪpəˈbɪlətɪ] s **1.** Fähigkeit f (**of** zu). **2.** a. pl Begabung f,
Begabung f. **ca·pa·ble** [ˈ~bl] adj □ **1.**
fähig, tüchtig. **2.** fähig (**of** zu od. gen; **of
doing** zu tun), imstande (**of doing** zu
tun). **3.** **be ~ of s.th.** et. zulassen: ~ **of
being divided** teilbar.

ca·pa·cious [kəˈpeɪʃəs] adj □ **1.** geräumig (Saal, Tasche etc), groß (Flasche,
Topf etc). **2.** aufnahmefähig (Verstand). **ca·pac·i·tate** [kəˈpæsɪtent] v/t
befähigen. **ca·pac·i·tor** [~tə] s ≨ Kondensator m. **ca·pac·i·ty** **I** s **1.**
(Raum)Inhalt m; Fassungsvermögen
n, Kapazität f (a. ≨): **filled to ~** ganz
voll, thea. etc ausverkauft; → **measure**
1. **2.** a. ≨, ⊙ (Leistungs)Fähigkeit f. **3.**
fig. Auffassungsgabe f: **that is beyond
his ~** das ist zu hoch für ihn. **4.** Eigenschaft f, Stellung f: **in his ~ as** in s-r
Eigenschaft als. **II** adj **5.** Höchst..., maximal. **6.** ~ **audience** thea. etc ausverkauftes Haus.

cape¹ [keɪp] s Kap n, Vorgebirge n.

cape² [~] s Cape n, Umhang m.

ca·per¹ [ˈkeɪpə] s Kaper f: ~ **sauce** Kapernsoße f.

ca·per² [~] **I** s Kapriole f: a) Freuden-,
Luftsprung m: **cut ~s** → II, b) übermütiger Streich. **II** v/i Freuden- od. Luftsprünge machen; herumtollen, -hüpfen.

cap·il·lar·y [kəˈpɪlərɪ] **I** adj haarförmig,
-fein: ~ **vessel** → II. **II** s anat. Kapillargefäß n.

cap·i·tal¹ [ˈkæpɪtl] s △ Kapitell n.

cap·i·tal² [~] **I** s **1.** Hauptstadt f. **2.**
Großbuchstabe f. **3.** ✝ Kapital n:
make ~ (out) of → **capitalize** 3. **III** adj
4. Kapital...: ~ **crime** Kapitalverbrechen n; ~ **error** Kapitalfehler m; ~ **punishment** Todesstrafe f. **5.** Haupt...,
wichtigst: ~ **city** → 1. **6.** großartig: **a ~
fellow** ein Prachtkerl. **7.** ~ **letter** → 2; ~
B großes B.

cap·i·tal **as·sets** s pl ✝ Kapitalvermögen n; (Bilanz) Anlagevermögen n. ~
flight s Kapitalflucht f. ~ **goods** s pl
Investitionsgüter pl. **'~·in͵ten·sive** adj
□ kapitalintensiv. ~ **in·vest·ment** s
Kapitalanlage f.

cap·i·tal·ism [ˈkæpɪtəlɪzəm] s Kapitalismus *m*. **'cap·i·tal·ist I** *s* Kapitalist *m*. **II** *adj* kapitalistisch. ˌcap·i·tal·**is·tic** *adj* (~*ally*) kapitalistisch. **'cap·i·tal·ize I** *v/t* **1. ✝** kapitalisieren. **2.** groß schreiben. **II** *v/i* **3.** ~ *on* Kapital schlagen aus.

cap·i·tal mar·ket *s* ✝ Kapitalmarkt *m*.

Cap·i·tol ['kæpɪtl] *s* Kapitol *n* (*Kongreßhaus in Washington*).

ca·pit·u·late [kə'pɪtʃʊleɪt] *v/i* ⚔ kapitulieren (**to** vor *dat*) (*a. fig.*). **ca·pit·u·la·tion** *s* Kapitulation *f*.

ca·price [kə'priːs] *s* **1.** Laune *f*. **2.** Launenhaftigkeit *f*. **ca·pri·cious** [kə'prɪʃəs] *adj* □ launenhaft, launisch, kapriziös.

Cap·ri·corn ['kæprɪkɔːn] *s* *ast.* Steinbock *m*.

cap·size [kæp'saɪz] **I** *v/i* kentern. **II** *v/t* zum Kentern bringen.

cap·sule ['kæpsjuːl] *s* *allg.* Kapsel *f*.

cap·tain ['kæptɪn] *s* **1.** (An)Führer *m*: ~ *of industry* Industriekapitän *m*. **2.** ⚔ Hauptmann *m*. **3.** ⚓ (✈ Flug)Kapitän *m*. **4.** *Sport*: (Mannschafts)Kapitän *m*, Mannschaftsführer *m*. **II** *v/t* **5.** Kapitän (*gen*) sein, Schiff *a.* befehligen.

cap·tion ['kæpʃn] *s* **1.** Überschrift *f*. **2.** Bildunterschrift *f*, -text *m*; (*Film*) Untertitel *m*.

cap·tious ['kæpʃəs] *adj* □ kritt(e)lig, spitzfindig.

cap·ti·vate ['kæptɪveɪt] *v/t fig.* gefangennehmen, fesseln. **'cap·tive I** *adj* gefangen (*a. fig.* **to** von), in Gefangenschaft: *hold* ~ gefangenhalten (*a. fig.*); *take* ~ gefangennehmen (*a. fig.*); ~ *balloon* Fesselballon *m*. **II** *s* Gefangene *m*, *f* (*a. fig.* **to** *od.* von).

cap·ture ['kæptʃə] **I** *v/t* **1.** fangen, gefangennehmen. **2.** ⚔ erobern (*a. fig.*); erbeuten. **3.** ⚓ kapern, aufbringen. **4.** *Stimmung* einfangen. **II** *s* **5.** Gefangennahme *f*. **6.** ⚔ Eroberung *f* (*a. fig.*); Erbeutung *f*. **7.** ⚓ Kapern *n*, Aufbringen *n*; Beute *f*, Prise *f*.

car [kɑː] *s* **1.** Auto *n*, Wagen *m*: *by* ~ mit dem Auto. **2.** 🚌 *Am. allg.* Wagen *m*, Waggon *m*, *Br.* (*nur in Zssgn*) Personenwagen *m*: → *dining car*, *etc.* **3.** (*Straßenbahn- etc*)Wagen *m*; Gondel *f* (*e-s Ballons etc*); Kabine *f* (*e-s Aufzugs*).

ca·rafe [kə'ræf] *s* Karaffe *f*.

car·a·mel ['kærəmel] *s* **1.** Karamel *m*. **2.** Karamelle *f* (*Bonbon*).

car·at ['kærət] *s* Karat *n*: *18-*~ *gold* 18karätiges Gold.

car·a·van ['kærəvæn] *s* **1.** Karawane *f*. **2.** Wohnwagen *m* (*von Schaustellern etc*); *Br.* Caravan *m*, Wohnwagen *m*, -anhänger *m*: ~ *site* (*od. park*) Platz *m* für Wohnwagen. **'car·a·van·(n)er** *s* *Br.* Caravaner *m*.

car·a·way ['kærəweɪ] *s* ♣ Kümmel *m* (*a. Gewürz*).

car·bide ['kɑːbaɪd] *s* 🜋 Karbid *n*.

car·bine ['kɑːbaɪn] *s* Karabiner *m*.

car·bo·hy·drate [ˌkɑːbəʊ'haɪdreɪt] *s* 🜋 Kohle(n)hydrat *n*.

car bomb *s* Autobombe *f*.

car·bon ['kɑːbən] *s* **1.** 🜋 Kohlenstoff *m*: ~ *dioxide* Kohlendioxyd *n*; ~ *monoxide* Kohlenmonoxyd *n*. **2.** a) a. ~ *paper* Kohlepapier *n*, b) a. ~ *copy* Durchschlag *m*. **car·bon·ate** ['~bənɪt] *s* 🜋 Karbonat *n*, kohlensaures Salz. **car·bon·at·ed** ['~bəneɪtɪd] *adj* kohlensäurehaltig. **car·bon·ic** [~'bɒnɪk] *adj* 🜋 kohlenstoffhaltig: ~ *acid* Kohlensäure *f*. **'car·bon·ize** *v/t u. v/i* verkohlen.

car·bu·ret·(t)er, **car·bu·ret·(t)or** [ˌkɑːbə'retə] *s* *mot.* Vergaser *m*.

car·case, **car·cass** ['kɑːkəs] *s* **1.** Kadaver *m*, *contp.* Leiche *f*. **2.** *humor.* Leichnam *m* (*Körper*). **3.** Rumpf *m* (*e-s ausgeweideten Tiers*): ~ *meat* frisches (*Ggs. konserviertes*) Fleisch. **5.** Gerippe *n*, Skelett *n* (*e-s Schiffs etc*).

car| **cem·e·ter·y** *s* Autofriedhof *m*. ~ **chase** *s* Verfolgungsjagd *f* im Auto.

car·ci·no·gen·ic [ˌkɑːsɪnəʊ'dʒenɪk] *adj* ⚕ karzinogen, krebserzeugend. **car·ci·no·ma** [~'nəʊmə] *pl* **-ma·ta** [~mətə], **-mas** *s* Karzinom *n*, Krebsgeschwulst *f*.

card [kɑːd] *s* **1.** (*Spiel-, Post-, Visitenetc*)Karte *f*: *house of* ~*s* Kartenhaus *n* (*a. fig.*); *have a* ~ *up one's sleeve fig.* (noch) e-n Trumpf in der Hand haben; *at* ~*s* beim Kartenspiel; → *stack* 6. **2.** *pl* (Arbeits)Papiere *pl*: *get one's* ~*s* entlassen werden. **'~board** *s* Karton *m*, Pappe *f*: ~ *box* Pappschachtel *f*, -karton *m*. ~ **game** *s* Kartenspiel *n*.

car·di·ac ['kɑːdɪæk] **I** *adj* ⚕, *anat.*, *physiol.* Herz...: ~ *arrest* Herzstillstand *m*; ~ *pacemaker* Herzschrittmacher *m*. **II** *s pharm.* Herzmittel *n*.

car·di·gan ['kɑːdɪɡən] *s* Strickjacke *f*.

car·di·nal ['kɑːdɪnl] **I** *adj* □ **1.** hauptsächlich, Haupt...: **~** *number* → **4.** **2.** scharlachrot. **II** *s* **3.** *eccl.* Kardinal *m.* **4.** Kardinal-, Grundzahl *f.*

'card‚**sharp·er** *s* Falschspieler *m.* **~ trick** *s* Kartenkunststück *n.*

care [keə] **I** *s* **1.** Kummer *m,* Sorge *f:* **be free from ~(s)** keine Sorgen haben. **2.** Sorgfalt *f,* Vorsicht *f:* **have a ~!** Br. F paß (doch) auf!; **take ~** vorsichtig sein, aufpassen; sich Mühe geben; darauf achten, nicht vergessen (**to do** zu tun; **that** daß); **take ~!** F mach's gut! **3.** Obhut *f,* Fürsorge *f,* Betreuung *f:* **~ and custody** ⚖ Sorgerecht *n;* **take ~ of** aufpassen auf (*acc.*). **4.** (*Körperetc*)Pflege *f.* **II** *v/i u. v/t* **5.** sich sorgen (**about** über *acc,* um): **I couldn't ~ less** das ist mir völlig egal. **6. ~ for** sorgen für, sich kümmern um, betreuen. **7.** (**for**) Interesse haben (an *dat*), (*j-n, et.*) gern mögen: **I don't ~ for** ich mache mir nichts aus. **8. I don't ~ if** ich habe nichts dagegen *od.* es macht mir nichts aus, wenn; **I don't ~ if I do!** F von mir aus!

ca·reer [kə'rɪə] *s* **1.** Karriere *f,* Laufbahn *f:* **enter upon a ~** e-e Laufbahn einschlagen; **make a ~ for o.s.** Karriere machen. **2.** Beruf *m:* **~ diplomat** Berufsdiplomat *m;* **~ girl** (*od.* **woman**) Karrierefrau *f.* **ca·reer·ist** [kə'rɪərɪst] *s* Karrieremacher *m.*

'care·free sorgenfrei.

care·ful ['keəfʊl] *adj* □ **1.** vorsichtig, achtsam: **be ~!** paß auf!, gib acht!; **be ~ to do** darauf achten *od.* nicht vergessen zu tun. **2.** sorgfältig, gründlich. **3.** sorgsam, bedacht (**of, for, about** auf *acc*): **be ~ with** Br. sparsam umgehen mit. **'care·ful·ness** *s* **1.** Vorsicht *f.* **2.** Sorgfalt *f,* Gründlichkeit *f.*

care·less ['keəlɪs] *adj* □ **1.** nachlässig. **2.** unüberlegt. **3. be ~ of** nicht achten auf (*acc*), unachtsam umgehen mit. **4.** unvorsichtig, leichtsinnig. **5.** sorglos. **'care·less·ness** *s* **1.** Nachlässigkeit *f.* **2.** Unüberlegtheit *f.* **3.** Unvorsichtigkeit *f,* Leichtsinn *m.* **4.** Sorglosigkeit *f.*

ca·ress [kə'res] **I** *s* Liebkosung *f.* **II** *v/t* liebkosen, streicheln.

'care‚**tak·er** *s* **1** Hausmeister *m;* (*Hausetc*)Verwalter *m.* **II** *adj* Interims...: **~ government** geschäftsführende Re-

gierung. **'~worn** *adj* abgehärmt.

'car‚**fare** *s Am.* Fahrgeld *n* (*für Bus etc*). **~ fer·ry** *s* Autofähre *f.*

car·go ['kɑːgəʊ] **I** *pl* **-go(e)s** *s* Ladung *f,* Fracht *f.* **II** *adj* Fracht...: **~** *plane*...

car·i·ca·ture ['kærɪkəˌtjʊə] **I** *s* Karikatur *f* (*a. fig.*). **II** *v/t* karikieren. **'car·i·ca**‚**tur·ist** *s* Karikaturist *m.*

car·ies ['keərɪːz] *s* ⚕ Karies *f:* a) Knochenfräß *m,* b) Zahnfäule *f.*

car·il·lon ['kærɪljən] *s* (Turm)Glockenspiel *n.*

car·i·ous ['keərɪəs] *adj* ⚕ kariös, von Karies befallen.

car‚ **jack** *s* ⊙ Wagenheber *m.* **'~load** *s* **1.** Wagenladung *f.* **2.** 🚃 *Am.* Waggonladung *f.*

car·mine ['kɑːmaɪn] *adj* karminrot.

car·nage ['kɑːnɪdʒ] *s* Blutbad *n,* Gemetzel *n.*

car·nal ['kɑːnl] *adj* □ fleischlich, sinnlich.

car·na·tion [kɑː'neɪʃn] *s* ⚘ Nelke *f.*

car·ni·val ['kɑːnɪvl] *s* **1.** Karneval *m,* Fasching *m.* **2.** Volksfest *n.*

car·ni·vore ['kɑːnɪvɔː] *s zo.,* ⚘ Fleischfresser *m.* **car·niv·o·rous** [~'nɪvərəs] *adj* □ fleischfressend.

car·ol ['kærəl] **I** *s* Weihnachtslied *n.* **II** *v/i pret u. pp* **-oled,** *bsd.* Br. **-olled** Weihnachtslieder singen.

ca·rot·id [kə'rɒtɪd] *s anat.* Halsschlagader *f.*

car·ou·sel [ˌkærə'sel] *s bsd. Am.* Karussell *n.*

car own·er *s* Autobesitzer(in).

carp¹ [kɑːp] *s ichth.* Karpfen *m.*

carp² [~] *v/i* (herum)nörgeln, (-)kritteln (**at** an *dat*).

car park *s bsd.* Br. **1.** Parkplatz *m.* **2.** Parkhaus *n.* **~ pas·sen·ger** *s* Autoinsasse *m.*

car·pen·ter ['kɑːpəntə] **I** *s* Zimmermann *m,* (Bau)Tischler *m:* **~'s bench** Hobelbank *f.* **II** *v/t u. v/i* zimmern.

car·pet ['kɑːpɪt] **I** *s* **1.** Teppich *m* (*a. fig.*): **sweep** (*od.* **brush**) **under the ~** Br. *fig. et.* unter den Teppich kehren. **II** *v/t* **2.** mit e-m Teppich auslegen. **3.** *bsd.* Br. F *j-n* zs.-stauchen. **'~bag** *s* Reisetasche *f.*

car·pet·ing ['kɑːpɪtɪŋ] *s* **1.** Teppichstoff *m,* -material *n.* **2.** *coll.* Teppiche *pl.*

car·pet **square** *s* Teppichfliese *f.*

sweep·er s Teppichkehrmaschine f. **~ tile** s Teppichfliese f.

car| pool s 1. Fahrbereitschaft f, Fuhrpark m. 2. Fahrgemeinschaft f. **'~port** s Einstellplatz m (im Freien).

car·riage ['kærɪdʒ] s 1. Wagen m, Kutsche f. 2. 🚂 Br. (Personen)Wagen m. 3. Beförderung f, Transport m. 4. ⚓ Transport-, Beförderungskosten pl, Fracht(gebühr) f: **~ free** (od. **paid**) frachtfrei. 5. ⚙ Wagen m (e-r Schreibmaschine etc); Schlitten m (e-r Werkzeugmaschine). 6. (Körper)Haltung f: **~ of head** Kopfhaltung f. **'~way** s Fahrbahn f.

car·ri·er ['kærɪə] s 1. Überbringer m, Bote m. 2. Spediteur m. 3. 🪰 Keimträger m, (Krankheits)Überträger m. 4. Gepäckträger m (am Fahrrad); mot. Dachgepäckträger m. 5. Transportbehälter m. 6. Flugzeugträger m. 7. → carrier pigeon. **~ bag** s Br. Einkaufsbeutel m, -tasche f. **~ pi·geon** s Brieftaube f.

car·ri·on ['kærɪən] I s Aas n. II adj aasfressend, Aas...

car·rot ['kærət] s 1. 🌿 Karotte f, Mohrrübe f. 2. F a) pl rotes Haar, b) Rotkopf m. **'car·rot·y** adj 1. gelbrot. 2. rothaarig.

car·ry ['kærɪ] I v/t 1. tragen. 2. bringen, tragen, befördern: → **coal**. 3. Nachricht etc (über)bringen; Bericht etc bringen (Medien). 4. mitführen, mit od. bei sich tragen: **~ s.th. in one's head** fig. et. im Kopf haben. 5. fig. (an sich od. zum Inhalt) haben: **~ conviction** überzeugen(d sein od. klingen); **~ weight** Gewicht od. Bedeutung haben (**with** bei). 6. fig. nach sich ziehen, zur Folge haben: **~ interest** Zinsen tragen. 7. fig. treiben: **~ s.th. too far** (od. **to excess**) et. übertreiben od. zu weit treiben. 8. fig. erreichen, durchsetzen; parl. Antrag etc durchbringen: **be carried** durchgehen. 9. a) → **carry off** 3, b) siegreich hervorgehen aus (e-r Wahl etc): → **day** 2. 10. Mineralien etc führen. 11. ⚓ Ware führen. II v/i 12. weit tragen, reichen (Stimme, Schußwaffe etc).

Verbindungen mit Adverbien:

car·ry| a·bout v/t herumtragen: **~ with one** mit sich herumtragen, Paß etc bei sich haben. **~ a·way** v/t 1. weg-, forttragen. 2. wegreißen (Sturm etc), (Flut etc a.) wegspülen. 3. fig. mitreißen. **~ for·ward** v/t ⚓ Summe, Saldo vor-, übertragen. **~ off** v/t 1. weg-, forttragen. 2. wegraffen (Krankheit). 3. Preis etc erringen, gewinnen. **~ on** I v/t 1. fortführen, -setzen. 2. Geschäft betreiben. II v/i 3. weitermachen (**with** mit). 4. F e-e Szene machen (**about** wegen). **~ out** v/t Plan etc aus-, durchführen, Drohung wahrmachen. **~ o·ver** → **carry forward**. **~ through** v/t aus-, durchführen.

car·ry| all s bsd. Am. Reisetasche f. **'~cot** s Br. (Baby)Tragetasche f. **'~on** ✈ I s Bordcase n, m. II adj: **~ baggage** (bsd. Br. **luggage**) Bordgepäck n. **'~out** → **takeaway**.

'car·sick adj: **she gets easily ~** ihr wird beim Autofahren leicht übel od. schlecht. **~ sick·ness** s Übelkeit f beim Autofahren. **~ stick·er** s Autoaufkleber m.

cart [kɑːt] s 1. Karren m: **put the ~ before the horse** fig. das Pferd beim Schwanz aufzäumen. 2. (Hand)Wagen m.

car·tel [kɑː'tel] s ⚓ Kartell n.

car·ti·lage ['kɑːtɪlɪdʒ] s anat. Knorpel m.

'cart·load s Fuhre f.

car·tog·ra·pher [kɑː'tɒgrəfə] s Kartograph(in). **car'tog·ra·phy** s Kartographie f.

car·ton ['kɑːtən] s (Papp)Karton m, (-)Schachtel f; Tüte f (Milch); Stange f (Zigaretten).

car·toon [kɑː'tuːn] s 1. Cartoon m, n, Karikatur f. 2. Zeichentrickfilm m. 3. Cartoon m, n, Bilderfortsetzungsgeschichte f. **car'toon·ist** s Cartoonist m, Karikaturist m.

car·tridge ['kɑːtrɪdʒ] s 1. ✗ Patrone f. 2. phot. (Film)Patrone f, (-)Kassette f. 3. Tonabnehmer m (e-s Plattenspielers). 4. Patrone f (e-s Füllhalters). **~ case** s Patronenhülse f.

'cart·wheel s 1. Wagenrad n. 2. Sport: Rad n: **turn ~s** radschlagen. 3. Am. F Silberdollar m.

carve [kɑːv] v/t 1. (in) Holz schnitzen, (in) Stein meißeln: **~ out of stone** aus Stein meißeln od. hauen; **~ one's name on a tree** s-n Namen in e-n Baum schnitzen. **2.** (mit Schnitzereien) verzieren. **3.** *Fleisch etc* zerlegen, tranchieren. **'carv·er** s **1.** (Holz)Schnitzer m, Bildhauer m. **2.** Tranchiermesser n: (*pair of*) **~s** *pl* Tranchierbesteck n. **'carv·ing** s **1.** Schnitzen n, Meißeln n. **2.** Schnitzerei f. **3.** Tranchieren n: **~ knife** Tranchiermesser n.

car wash s **1.** Autowäsche f. **2.** Waschanlage f, -straße f.

cas·cade [kæ'skeɪd] s Kaskade f, (*bsd. mehrstufiger*) Wasserfall.

case¹ [keɪs] **I** s **1.** Kiste f, Kasten m. **2.** *allg.* Behälter m: a) Schachtel f, b) (*Brillen- etc*)Etui n, (-)Futteral n, c) (*Schreib- etc*)Mappe f, d) (*Kissen*)Bezug m, Überzug m. **3.** ⚙ Verkleidung f, Mantel m. **II** v/t **4.** in ein Futteral *etc* stecken. **5.** ⚙ verkleiden, ummanteln.

case² [~] s Fall m (*a.* ♬, ♩♩): *it is a ~ of* es handelt sich um; *in any ~* auf jeden Fall, jedenfalls; *in no ~* auf keinen Fall, keinesfalls; *in ~ (that)* falls; *in ~* of im Falle von (*od. gen*); *in ~ of need* nötigenfalls, im Notfall.

'case·book s ♬ Patientenbuch n. **'~,hard·ened** *adj fig.* hartgesotten. **'~ his·to·ry** s **1.** *bsd.* ♩♩ Vorgeschichte f (*e-s Falls*). **2.** ♬ Krankengeschichte f. **case·ment** ['keɪsmənt] s Fensterflügel m: **~ (window)** Flügelfenster m:

case stud·y s sociol. Fallstudie f.

cash [kæʃ] **I** s **1.** (Bar)Geld n. **2.** † Zahlung f, Kasse f: *for* **~**, *down* gegen bar *od.* Barzahlung; *in* **~** bar; **~** *in advance* gegen Vorauszahlung; **~** *with order* zahlbar bei Bestellung; *be in* (*out of*) **~** (nicht) bei Kasse sein; *short of* **~** knapp bei Kasse; **~** *delivery* ↓ II. **~** *in* **3.** Scheck *etc* einlösen. **4.** zu Geld machen. **III** v/i **5.** **~** *in on* F profitieren von; ausnutzen. **~** *and car·ry* s econ. Cash-and-carry-Geschäft n. **~** *cheque* s † Br. Barscheck m. **~** *desk* s Kasse f (*im Warenhaus etc*). **~** *dis·count* s † Barzahlungsrabatt m. **~** *dis·pens·er* s *bsd. Br.* Geldautomat m.

cash·ier [kæˈʃɪə] s Kassierer(in): **~'s desk** (*od.* **office**) Kasse f.

cash·less ['kæʃlɪs] *adj* bargeldlos.

cash ma·chine s *bsd. Am.* Geldautomat m.

cash·mere [kæʃ'mɪə] s Kaschmir(wolle f) m.

cash| pay·ment s Barzahlung f. **~ price** s Bar(zahlungs)preis m. **~ vouch·er** s Kassenbeleg m, -zettel m.

cas·ing ['keɪsɪŋ] s **1.** → **case¹** 3. **2.** (*Fenster-, Tür*)Futter n. **3.** (*Wurst*)Haut f.

ca·si·no [kəˈsiːnəʊ] *pl* **-nos** s Kasino n.

cask [kɑːsk] s Faß n.

cas·ket ['kɑːskɪt] s **1.** Schatulle f, Kästchen n. **2.** *bsd. Am.* Sarg m.

cas·se·role ['kæsərəʊl] s Kasserolle f.

cas·sette [kəˈset] s (*Film- etc*)Kassette f. **~ deck** s Kassettendeck n. **~ ra·di·o** s Radiorecorder m. **~ re·cord·er** s Kassettenrecorder m.

cas·sock ['kæsək] s eccl. Soutane f.

cast [kɑːst] **I** s **1.** Wurf m. **2.** thea. etc Besetzung f: a) Rollenverteilung f, b) Ensemble n. **3.** Schattierung f, Anflug m (*a. fig.*). **4.** ⚙ Guß(form f) m; Abdruck m. **5.** ♬ Gips(verband) m. **6.** Typ m, Gattung f. **II** v/t (*irr*) **7.** werfen: → **die²** 1, **doubt** 5, **light¹** 1, **spell³** 2, **8.** *Angel, Netz etc* auswerfen. **9.** zo. *Haut, Gehörn* abwerfen. **10.** *Stimmzettel, Stimme* abgeben: → **vote** 2. **11.** *Blick* werfen (*at, on* auf acc); *Schatten etc* werfen (*on* auf acc). **12.** ⚙ *Metall, Statue etc* gießen, formen. **13.** *thea. etc Stück etc* besetzen; *Rollen* verteilen (*to* an acc). **III** v/i (*irr*) **14.** sich werfen (*Holz*).

Verbindungen mit Adverbien:

cast| a·bout, **~ a·round** v/i: **~ for** suchen (nach), *fig. a.* sich umsehen nach. **~ a·side** v/t **1.** *Möbel etc* ausrangieren, *Kleidung a.* ablegen. **2.** *Gewohnheit etc* ablegen, *Freund etc* fallenlassen. **~ a·way** v/t wegwerfen. **~ down** v/t **1.** entmutigen: *be* **~** niedergeschlagen *od.* deprimiert sein. **2.** *Augen* niederschlagen. **~ off** v/t **1.** *Kleidung* ablegen, ausrangieren. **2.** *Freund etc* fallenlassen. **~ out** v/t verstoßen, vertreiben (*from* aus), *Dämonen etc* austreiben. **~ up** v/t **1.** *Augen* aufschlagen. **2.** zs.-zählen, ausrechnen.

'cast·a·way I s et. Ausrangiertes, *bsd.* abgelegtes Kleidungsstück. **II** *adj* ausrangiert (*Möbel etc*), (*Kleidung a.*) abgelegt.

caste [kɑːst] s **1.** Kaste f. **2.** gesellschaftliche Stellung, Ansehen n.

cas·ter → **castor.**

cas·ti·gate ['kæstɪgeɪt] v/t **1.** züchtigen.

2. scharf kritisieren. ˌ**cas·ti·ga·tion** s **1.** Züchtigung f. **2.** scharfe Kritik (*of* an dat).

cast·ing ['kɑːstɪŋ] **I** s **1.** ⊙ Guß(stück n) m. **2.** → cast 2a. **II** adj **3.** Wurf... **4.** entscheidend (*Stimme*).

cast| i·ron s ⊙ Gußeisen n. ˌ**~·'i·ron** adj **1.** gußeisern. **2.** *fig.* eisern (*Wille, Konstitution*), hieb- u. stichfest (*Alibi*).

cas·tle ['kɑːsl] s **1.** Burg f; Schloß n: **build ~s in the air** (*od.* **in Spain**) *fig.* Luftschlösser bauen. **2.** *Schach*: Turm m. **II** v/i **3.** *Schach*: rochieren.

cast·ling ['kɑːslɪŋ] s *Schach*: Rochade f.

ˌ**cast|-'off** adj abgelegt, ausrangiert (*Kleidungsstück*). '**~-off** s abgelegtes *od.* ausrangiertes Kleidungsstück.

cas·tor ['kɑːstə] s **1.** Laufrolle f. **2.** (*Salz- etc*)Streuer m. **~ oil** s Rizinusöl n.

cas·trate [kæ'streɪt] v/t kastrieren. **cas'tra·tion** s Kastrierung f, Kastration f.

cast steel s ⊙ Gußstahl m.

cas·u·al ['kæʒʊəl] adj □ **1.** zufällig. **2.** gelegentlich: **~ customer** Laufkunde m; **~ labo(u)rer** Gelegenheitsarbeiter m. **3.** beiläufig (*Bemerkung*); flüchtig (*Blick*). **4.** lässig (*Art etc*). **5.** sportlich, salopp (*Kleidung*): **~ wear** Freizeitkleidung f.

cas·u·al·ty ['kæʒʊəltɪ] s **1.** Unfall m. **2.** Verunglückte m, f; ✕ Verwundete m, Gefallene m: **casualties** pl Opfer pl (*e-r Katastrophe etc*), ✕ mst Verluste pl. **3.** a. **~ ward** (*od.* **department**) Unfallstation f.

cat [kæt] s **1.** zo. Katze f: **let the ~ out of the bag** die Katze aus dem Sack lassen; **play ~ and mouse with** Katz u. Maus spielen mit; **it is raining ~s and dogs** es gießt in Strömen; **see which way the ~ jumps** sehen, wie der Hase läuft. **2.** *fig.* Katze f, falsches Frauenzimmer: **old ~** boshafte Hexe.

cat [kæt] s **1.** zo. Katze f: **let the ~ out of the bag** die Katze aus dem Sack lassen; **play ~ and mouse with** Katz u. Maus spielen mit; **it is raining ~s and dogs** es gießt in Strömen; **see which way the ~ jumps** sehen, wie der Hase läuft. **2.** *fig.* Katze f, falsches Frauenzimmer: **old ~** boshafte Hexe.

cat·a·comb ['kætəkuːm] s mst pl Katakombe f.

cat·a·logue, Am. a. **cat·a·log** ['kætəlɒg] **I** s **1.** Katalog m. **2.** (*univ. Am.* Vorlesungs)Verzeichnis n, (*Preis- etc*)Liste f. **II** v/t **3.** katalogisieren.

ca·tal·y·sis [kə'tæləsɪs] s 🜊 Katalyse f. **cat·a·lyst** ['kætəlɪst] s Katalysator m (*a. fig.*). **cat·a·lyt·ic** [ˌkætə'lɪtɪk] adj ka-

talytisch (*a. fig.*): **~ converter** mot. Katalysator m.

ˌ**cat-and-'dog** adj: **lead a ~ life** wie Hund u. Katze leben.

cat·a·pult ['kætəpʌlt] **I** s Katapult n, m: **~ seat** ✈ Schleudersitz m. **II** v/t katapultieren.

cat·a·ract ['kætərækt] s **1.** Katarakt m, Wasserfall m. **2.** ✚ grauer Star.

ca·tarrh [kə'tɑː] s ✚ Katarrh m.

ca·tas·tro·phe [kə'tæstrəfɪ] s Katastrophe f. **cat·a·stroph·ic** [ˌkætə'strɒfɪk] adj (**~ally**) katastrophal.

cat| bur·glar s Fassadenkletterer m. '**~·call** s Buh(ruf m) n; Pfiff m. **II** v/i buhen; pfeifen. **III** v/t ausbuhen; -pfeifen.

catch [kætʃ] **I** s **1.** Fangen n. **2.** Fang m, Beute f (*beide a. fig.*). **3.** ⊙ Haken m (*a. fig.*), (*Tür*)Klinke f; Verschluß m (*e-r Brosche etc*). **II** v/t (*irr*) **4.** *allg.* fangen; *Blick, Flüssigkeit* auffangen; *Tier etc* (ein)fangen; → **sight** 2. **5.** kriegen, bekommen, erwischen. **6.** *j-n* einholen. **7.** erwischen, ertappen (**s.o. at** et. bei et.): **~ s.o. lying** j-n bei e-r Lüge ertappen; **~ me** (**doing that**)! *Br.* F denkste! → **nap** 1, **unawares**. **8.** *a. fig.* packen, ergreifen, erfassen: → **hold** 1. **9.** sich *e-e Krankheit etc* holen, sich *e-e Erkältung etc* zuziehen: **~** (**a**) **cold** sich erkälten; **~ it** *sl.* sein Fett (ab)kriegen; → **fire** 1. **10.** *fig.* **~ the ear** ans Ohr dringen; **~ the eye** ins Auge fallen; **~ s.o.'s eye** (*od.* **attention**) j-s Aufmerksamkeit auf sich lenken. **11.** verstehen, mitkriegen. **12.** Gewohnheit, Aussprache annehmen. **13.** hängenbleiben *od.* sich verfangen mit et. (**in** in dat): **my fingers were caught in the door** ich klemmte mir die Finger in der Tür. **III** v/i (*irr*) **14.** **~ at** greifen *od.* schnappen nach, Gelegenheit ergreifen. **15.** einschnappen, -rasten (*Schloß etc*); klemmen, festsitzen. **16.** sich verfangen, hängenbleiben (**on** an dat; **in** in dat). **17.** anspringen (*Motor*).

Verbindungen mit Adverbien:

catch| on v/i F **1.** **~ to s.th.** et. kapieren. **2.** Anklang finden, einschlagen. **~ out** v/t ertappen; überführen. **~ up I** v/t **1.** *Br.* einholen (*a. bei der Arbeit*). **2.** **be caught up in** vertieft sein in (*acc*); verwickelt sein in (*acc*). **II** v/i **3.** aufholen:

~ **with** einholen (*a. bei der Arbeit*); ~ **on** (*od.* **with**) *Arbeitsrückstand etc* aufholen; ~ **on one's sleep** Schlaf nachholen.

'**catch**|**·all** *s bsd. Am.* **1.** Tasche *f od.* Behälter *m* für alles mögliche. **2.** *fig.* Sammelbezeichnung *f*: ~ *term* Sammelbegriff *m*. '**~-as-,catch-'can** *s Sport*: Catchen *n*: ~ *wrestler* Catcher *m*.

catch·er ['kætʃə] *s* Fänger *m*; '**catch·ing** *adj* □ **1.** ∌ ansteckend (*a. fig. Lachen etc*). **2.** *fig.* anziehend, fesselnd. **3.** → **catchy** 1.

catch·ment ['kætʃmənt] *s geol.* Reservoir *n*. ~ **a·re·a** *s* **1.** *geol.* Einzugsgebiet *n* (*e-s Flusses*). **2.** *fig.* Einzugsbereich *m*, -gebiet *n* (*e-s Krankenhauses etc*). ~ **ba·sin** → **catchment area** 1.

'**catch**|**·phrase** *s* Schlagwort *n*. '**~-up** *bsd. Am.* → **ketchup**. '**~-word** *s* **1.** Stichwort *n* (*im Lexikon etc*; *a. thea.*). **2.** Schlagwort *n*.

catch·y ['kætʃɪ] *adj* **1.** eingängig (*Melodie etc*). **2.** → **catching** 2. **3.** Fang...: ~ **question**.

cat·e·chism ['kætɪkɪzəm] *s eccl.* Katechismus *m*.

cat·e·gor·i·cal [,kætə'gɒrɪkl] *adj* □ kategorisch. **cat·e·go·ry** ['~gərɪ] *s* Kategorie *f*, Klasse *f*.

ca·ter ['keɪtə] *v/i* **1.** Speisen u. Getränke liefern (*for* für). **2.** sorgen (*for* für). **3.** *fig.* (*for, to*) befriedigen (*acc*), *bsd. b.s.* Nahrung liefern (*dat*). '**ca·ter·er** *s* Lieferant *m od.* Lieferfirma *f* für Speisen u. Getränke.

cat·er·pil·lar ['kætəpɪlə] *s* **1.** *zo.* Raupe *f*. **2.** (*TM*) ⚙ Raupenfahrzeug *n*.

cat·er·waul ['kætəwɔːl] *I v/i* **1.** jaulen (*Katze*). **2.** *fig.* (sich an)keifen. **II** *s* **3.** Jaulen *n*. **4.** *fig.* Keifen *n*.

'**cat·gut** *s* Darmsaite *f*.

ca·the·dral [kə'θiːdrəl] **I** *s* Dom *m*, Kathedrale *f*. **II** *adj* Dom...

cath·e·ter ['kæθɪtə] *s* ∌ Katheter *m*.

cath·ode ['kæθəʊd] *s* ≶ Kathode *f*.

Cath·o·lic ['kæθəlɪk] *eccl.* **I** *adj* katholisch. **II** *s* Katholik(in). **Ca·thol·i·cism** [kə'θɒləsɪzəm] *s* Katholizismus *m*.

cat·kin ['kætkɪn] *s* ♀ (Blüten)Kätzchen *n*.

'**cat**|**·lick** *s F* Katzenwäsche *f*: **have a** ~ Katzenwäsche machen. ~ **lit·ter** *s* Katzenstreu *f*. '**~-nap** *s* Nickerchen *n*: **have** (*od.* **take**) **a** ~ ein Nickerchen machen.

'**cat's-eye** *s* ⚙ Katzenauge *n*, Rückstrahler *m*; Leuchtnagel *m*.

cat suit *s* einteiliger Hosenanzug.

cat·tish ['kætɪʃ] *adj* □ **1.** katzenhaft. **2.** *fig.* falsch, boshaft.

cat·tle ['kætl] *s coll.* (mst pl konstruiert) (Rind)Vieh *n*: **ten head of** ~ zehn Stück Vieh, zehn Rinder. ~ **breed·ing** *s* Viehzucht *f*.

cat tray *s* Katzenklosett *n*.

cat·ty ['kætɪ] → **cattish**.

'**cat·walk** *s* **1.** ⚙ Laufplanke *f*, Steg *m*. **2.** Laufsteg *m* (*bei Modeschauen*).

caught [kɔːt] *pret u. pp von* **catch**.

caul·dron ['kɔːldrən] *s* großer Kessel.

cau·li·flow·er ['kɒlɪ,flaʊə] *s* ♀ Blumenkohl *m*.

caus·al ['kɔːzl] *adj* □ ursächlich, kausal: ~ **connection** → **causality** 2; ~ **law** Kausalgesetz *n*. **cau·sal·i·ty** [~'zælətɪ] *s* **1.** Ursächlichkeit *f*, Kausalität *f*: **law of** ~ Kausalgesetz *n*. **2.** Kausalzs.-hang *m*. **caus·a·tive** ['~zətɪv] *adj* □ verursachend (*of acc*).

cause [kɔːz] **I** *s* **1.** Ursache *f*: ~ **of death** Todesursache. **2.** Grund *m*, Anlaß *m* (**for** für): ~ **for complaint** Grund zur Klage. **3.** Sache *f*: **make common** ~ **with** gemeinsame Sache machen mit. **4.** ⚖ Rechtsstreit *m*; Gegenstand *m* (*e-s Rechtsstreits*): ~ **of action** Klagegrund *m*. **II** *v/t* **5.** veranlassen. **6.** verursachen, bewirken. **7.** bereiten, zufügen. '**~-less** *adj* □ grundlos, unbegründet.

caus·tic ['kɔːstɪk] **I** *adj* (**~ally**) ∌ ätzend, *fig. a.* beißend, sarkastisch. **II** *s* Ätzmittel *n*.

cau·ter·ize ['kɔːtəraɪz] *v/t* **1.** ∌, ⚙ (aus)brennen, (ver)ätzen. **2.** *fig. Gefühl etc* abstumpfen.

cau·tion ['kɔːʃn] **I** *s* **1.** Vorsicht *f*. **2.** Warnung *f*. **3.** Verwarnung *f*. **II** *v/t* **4.** warnen (**against** vor *dat*). **5.** verwarnen.

cau·tious ['kɔːʃəs] *adj* □ **1.** vorsichtig. **2.** achtsam. **3.** verhalten, gedämpft (*Optimismus etc*).

cav·al·cade [,kævl'keɪd] *s* Kavalkade *f*.

cav·al·ry ['kævlrɪ] *s* ✕ a) *bsd. hist.* Kavallerie *f*, b) Panzertruppe(n *pl*) *f*. ~ **man** [-mən] *s* (*irr man*) ✕ a) *bsd. hist.* Kavallerist *m*, b) Angehörige *m* e-r Panzertruppe.

cave [keɪv] **I** *s* **1.** Höhle *f*. **II** *v/t* **2.** aushöhlen. **3.** *mst* ~ *in* eindrücken, zum Einsturz bringen. **III** *v/i mst* ~ *in* **4.** einstürzen, -sinken. **5.** F zs.-klappen, schlappmachen; nachgeben (**to** *dat*), klein beigeben. ~ **dwell·er** *s* Höhlenbewohner(in).

cav·ern ['kævən] *s* (große) Höhle.

cav·i·ar(e) ['kævɪɑː] *s* Kaviar *m*: ~ **to the general** *fig.* Kaviar fürs Volk.

cav·il ['kævl] **I** *v/i pret u. pp* **-illed**, *bsd. Br.* **-illed** nörgeln: ~ **at** (*od. about*) herumnörgeln an (*dat*). **II** *s* Nörgelei *f*. **'cav·il·(l)er** *s* Nörgler(in).

cav·i·ty ['kævətɪ] *s* **1.** (Aus)Höhlung *f*, Hohlraum *m*. **2.** *anat.* Höhle *f*: *abdominal* → ~ Bauchhöhle; → *oral* 2. **3.** ✗ Loch *n* (*im Zahn*).

ca·vort [kə'vɔːt] *v/i* F herumhüpfen, -tanzen.

cay·enne [keɪ'en], *a.* ~ **pep·per** ['keɪen] *s* Cayennepfeffer *m*.

cease [siːs] **I** *v/i* aufhören, enden. **II** *v/t* aufhören (**to do, doing** zu tun): ~ *fire* ✗ das Feuer einstellen; ~ *payment* ✝ die Zahlungen einstellen. ~**·'fire** *s* ✗ Feuereinstellung *f*; Waffenstillstand *m*. **'~·less** *adj* □ unaufhörlich.

cede [siːd] *v/t* **1.** (**to**) abtreten, abgeben (*dat od. an acc*), überlassen (*dat*). **2.** ~ **a point** in e-m Punkt nachgeben.

ceil [siːl] *v/t e-e* Decke einziehen in (*acc*). **'ceil·ing** *s* **1.** Decke *f* (*e-s Raums*). **2.** Höchstmaß *n*; ✝ Höchstgrenze *f* (*von Preisen etc*), Plafond *m* (*e-s Kredits*): ~ *price* Höchstpreis *m*. **3.** ✈ Gipfelhöhe *f*; Wolkenhöhe *f*.

cel·e·brate ['selɪbreɪt] **I** *v/t* **1.** Fest etc feiern, begehen: → *occasion* 3. **2.** *j-n* feiern. **3.** *eccl.* Messe etc zelebrieren. **II** *v/i* feiern. **'cel·e·brat·ed** *adj* berühmt (**for** für, wegen). **,cel·e·'bra·tion** *s* **1.** Feier *f*. **2.** Feiern *n*: **in** ~ **of** zur Feier (*gen*). **3.** *eccl.* Zelebrieren *n*.

ce·leb·ri·ty [sɪ'lebrətɪ] *s* Berühmtheit *f* (*a. Person*).

cel·er·y ['selərɪ] *s* ♣ Sellerie *m, f*.

ce·les·tial [sɪ'lestjəl] *adj* □ himmlisch, Himmels... (*a. astr.*): ~ *body* Himmelskörper *m*.

cel·i·ba·cy ['selɪbəsɪ] *s* Zölibat *n, m*, Ehelosigkeit *f*. **cel·i·bate** ['~bət] **I** *adj* unverheiratet. **II** *s* Unverheiratete *m, f*.

cell [sel] *s allg.* Zelle *f*, ⚡ *a.* Element *n*.

cel·lar ['selə] **I** *s* **1.** Keller *m*. → *salt-*

---

cellar. **II** *v/t* **3.** *a.* ~ *in* einkellern, -lagern.

cell di·vi·sion *s biol.* Zellteilung *f*.

cel·list ['tʃelɪst] *s* ♪ Cellist(in).

cell nu·cle·us (*mst irr nucleus*) *biol.* Zellkern *m*.

cel·lo ['tʃeləʊ] *pl* **-los** *s* ♪ Cello *n*.

cel·lo·phane ['seləfeɪn] *s* Zellophan *n*.

cell ther·a·py *s* ⚕ Zelltherapie *f*.

cel·lu·lar ['seljʊlə] *adj* Zell(en)...: ~ *therapy* ⚕ Zelltherapie *f*. **cel·lu·loid** ['~jʊlɔɪd] *s* Zelluloid *n*. **cel·lu·lose** ['~jʊləʊs] *s* Zellulose *f*, Zellstoff *m*.

Celt [kelt] *s* Kelte *m*, Keltin *f*. **'Celt·ic** **I** *adj* keltisch. **II** *s ling.* Keltisch *n*.

ce·ment [sɪ'ment] **I** *s* **1.** Zement *m*. **2.** Kitt *m*. **II** *v/t* **3.** zementieren, *fig. a.* festigen. **4.** (ver)kitten. ~ **mix·er** *s* Betonmischmaschine *f*.

cem·e·ter·y ['semɪtrɪ] *s* Friedhof *m*.

cen·ser ['sensə] *s eccl.* Weihrauchfaß *n*.

cen·sor ['sensə] **I** *s* Zensor *m*. **II** *v/t* zensieren. **cen·so·ri·ous** [~'sɔːrɪəs] *adj* □ **1.** kritisch, streng. **2.** kritt(e)lig (**of** gegenüber). **'cen·sor·ship** *s* Zensur *f*: ~ **of the press** Pressezensur.

cen·sure ['senʃə] **I** *s* **1.** Tadel *m*, Rüge *f*: **vote of** ~ Mißtrauensvotum *n*. **2.** (**of**) Kritik *f* (an *dat*), Mißbilligung *f* (*gen*). **II** *v/t* **3.** tadeln (**for** wegen). **4.** kritisieren, mißbilligen.

cen·sus ['sensəs] *s* (*bsd.* Volks)Zählung *f*: *traffic* ~ Verkehrszählung.

cent [sent] *s Am.* Cent *m*.

cen·te·nar·i·an [,sentɪ'neərɪən] **I** *adj* hundertjährig. **II** *s* Hundertjährige *m, f*. **cen·te·nar·y** [sen'tiːnərɪ] **I** *adj* hundertjährig. **II** *s* Hundertjahrfeier *f*, hundertjähriges Jubiläum.

cen·ten·ni·al [sen'tenjəl] **I** *adj* hundertjährig. **II** *s bsd. Am.* → *centenary* II.

cen·ter, *etc Am.* → *centre*, *etc*.

cen·ti·grade ['sentɪɡreɪd] *adj*: ... **degrees** ~ ... Grad Celsius; ~ *thermometer* Celsiusthermometer *n*. **'~gram(me)** *s* Zentigramm *n*. **'~,me·ter**, *bsd. Br.* **'~,me·tre** *s* Zentimeter *m*.

cen·tral ['sentrəl] **I** *adj* □ **1.** zentral (gelegen). **2.** Mittel(punkts)... **3.** Haupt..., Zentral...: ~ *bank* ✝ Zentralbank *f*; ~ *figure* Schlüssel-, Hauptfigur *f*. **II** *s* **4.** (*Am.* Telefon)Zentrale *f*. **2 A·mer·i·can** *adj* zentral-, mittelamerikanisch. **2 Eu·ro·pe·an Time** *s* mitteleuropäische

Zeit. **~ heat·ing** s Zentralheizung f.

cen·tral·ize ['sentrəlaɪz] v/t u. v/i (sich) zentralisieren.

cen·tral‖ lock·ing s mot. Zentralverrieg(e)lung f. **~ ner·vous sys·tem** s physiol. Zentralnervensystem n. **~ re·serve** s Br. Mittelstreifen m (e-r Autobahn). **~ sta·tion** s Hauptbahnhof m.

cen·tre ['sentə] **I** s **1.** Mitte f, a. fig. Zentrum n, Mittelpunkt m: in (od. at) the ~ in der Mitte; **~ of gravity** phys. Schwerpunkt m; **be the ~ of interest** im Mittelpunkt des Interesses stehen. **2.** Fußball: Flanke f. **II** v/t **3.** fig. konzentrieren (**on** auf acc). **4.** ⊙ zentrieren **III** v/i **5.** fig. sich konzentrieren (**in, on** auf acc), sich drehen (**round** um). **6.** Fußball: flanken. **~ for·ward** s Sport: Mittelstürmer(in). **~ half** s Sport: Mittelläufer m.

cen·trif·u·gal [sen'trɪfjʊgl] adj □ phys. zentrifugal: **~ force** Flieh-, Zentrifugalkraft f. **cen·tri·fuge** ['~fjuːdʒ] s ⊙ Zentrifuge f.

cen·tu·ry ['sentʃʊrɪ] s Jahrhundert n.

ce·ram·ic [sɪ'ræmɪk] **I** adj **1.** keramisch. **II** s **2.** Keramik f, pl a. keramische Erzeugnisse pl. **3.** pl (mst sg konstruiert) Keramik f (Technik).

ce·re·al ['sɪərɪəl] **I** adj **1.** Getreide... **II** s **2.** Getreidepflanze f. **3.** Getreide n. **4.** Getreideflocken pl, Frühstückskost f (aus Getreide).

cer·e·bel·lum [ˌserɪ'beləm] s anat. Kleinhirn n.

cer·e·bral ['serɪbrəl] adj anat. Gehirn...: **~ death** ✠ Hirntod m.

ce·re·brum ['serɪbrəm] s anat. Großhirn n.

cer·e·mo·ni·al [ˌserɪ'məʊnjəl] **I** adj □ **1.** zeremoniell, feierlich. **2.** → ceremonious **2, 3. II** s **3.** Zeremoniell n. **cer·e·mo·ni·ous** adj □ **1.** feierlich. **2.** förmlich. **3.** rituell. **4.** umständlich.

cer·e·mo·ny ['serɪmənɪ] s **1.** Zeremonie f, Feier(lichkeit) f: **master of ceremonies** Zeremonienmeister m; thea. etc bsd. Am. Conférencier m. **2.** Förmlichkeit(en pl) f: **without ~** ohne Umstände; → **stand on 2.**

cert [sɜːt] s Br. F sichere Sache: **it's a dead ~ that** es ist todsicher, daß.

cer·tain ['sɜːtn] adj **1.** sicher: a) (mst von Sachen) bestimmt: **it is ~ to happen** es wird mit Sicherheit geschehen; **for ~** mit Sicherheit, b) (mst von Personen) überzeugt: **make ~ of** sich (gen) vergewissern; sich et. sichern; **make ~ (that)** dafür sorgen, daß, c) zuverlässig. **2.** (ganz) bestimmt: **a ~ day. 3.** gewiß: **a ~ Mr Brown; for ~ reasons** aus bestimmten Gründen. **'cer·tain·ly** adv **1.** sicher, bestimmt. **2.** Antwort: aber natürlich. **'cer·tain·ty** s Sicherheit f, Bestimmtheit f: **it is a ~ that** es ist sicher, daß.

cer·tif·i·cate I s [sə'tɪfɪkət] **1.** Bescheinigung f, Attest n: **~ of (good) conduct** Führungszeugnis n. **2.** ped. Zeugnis n. **3.** Gutachten n. **II** v/t [sə'tɪfɪkeɪt] **4.** et. bescheinigen. **5.** j-m e-e Bescheinigung od. ein Zeugnis geben: **~d** (amtlich) zugelassen; diplomiert. **cer·ti·fy** ['sɜːtɪfaɪ] v/t **1.** bescheinigen, attestieren: **this is to ~ that** hiermit wird bescheinigt, daß. **2.** beglaubigen. **3.** amtlich für geisteskrank erklären.

cer·ti·tude ['sɜːtɪtjuːd] s Sicherheit f, Bestimmtheit f.

ces·sa·tion [se'seɪʃn] s Aufhören n, Einstellung f.

ces·sion ['seʃn] s Abtretung f.

cess‖pit ['sespɪt], **'~pool** s Senkgrube f.

chafe [tʃeɪf] **I** v/t **1.** warmreiben, frottieren. **2.** auf-, durchreiben, wund reiben. **3.** fig. ärgern, reizen. **II** v/i **4.** (sich) durch)reiben, scheuern. **5.** fig. sich ärgern (**at, against** über acc).

chaff [tʃɑːf] s Spreu f: → **wheat.**

cha·grin ['ʃægrɪn] **I** v/t verdrießen. **II** s Verdruß m.

chain [tʃeɪn] **I** s allg. Kette f (a. fig.): **~ of evidence** Beweiskette; **~ of mountains** Gebirgskette. **II** v/t (an)ketten (**to** an acc): **~ (up)** Hund an die Kette legen. **~ re·ac·tion** s phys. Kettenreaktion f (a. fig.). **~ smok·er** s Kettenraucher(in). **~ store** s Kettenladen m.

chair [tʃeə] **I** s **1.** (Am. F elektrischer) Stuhl, Sessel m: **on a ~** auf e-m Stuhl; **in a ~** in e-m Sessel; **take a ~** Platz nehmen. **2.** fig. Vorsitz m: **be in the ~** den Vorsitz führen. **3.** univ. Lehrstuhl m (**of** für). **II** v/t **4.** bestuhlen. **5.** den Vorsitz führen bei: **~ed by** unter dem Vorsitz von (od. gen). **~ lift** s Sessellift m.

chair·man ['tʃeəmən] s (irr man) Vorsitzende m. **'chair·man·ship** s Vorsitz m: **under the ~ of** unter dem Vorsitz von (*od. gen*). '**chair‚wom·an** *s* (*irr* **woman**) Vorsitzende *f.*

chal·ice ['tʃælɪs] *s eccl.* (Abendmahls-) Kelch *m.*

chalk [tʃɔːk] **I** *s* **1.** Kreide *f:* (*as*) *different* (*od. like*) *as ~ and cheese* verschieden wie Tag u. Nacht. **II** *v/t* **2.** mit Kreide markieren. **3.** *~ out* Plan *etc* entwerfen, skizzieren.

chal·lenge ['tʃælɪndʒ] **I** *s* **1.** Herausforderung *f* (*to gen od.* an *acc*) (*a. fig.*): *~ cup* (*bsd. Sport*) Wanderpokal *m.* **2.** (schwierige *od.* reizvolle) Aufgabe. **3.** ⚖ Ablehnung *f.* **II** *v/t* **4.** herausfordern. **5.** ⚖ Geschworenen, Richter ablehnen. **6.** *j-n* fordern *od.* reizen (*Aufgabe*). **7.** stark anzweifeln, in Frage stellen. **chal·leng·er** *s bsd. Sport:* Herausforderer *m.* '**chal·leng·ing** *adj* □ **1.** herausfordernd. **2.** schwierig; reizvoll (*Aufgabe*).

cham·ber ['tʃeɪmbə] *s* ⚙, *parl. etc* Kammer *f: ~ of commerce* Handelskammer. '*~maid* *s* Zimmermädchen *n.* *~ mu·sic* *s* Kammermusik *f.* *~ pot* *s* Nachtgeschirr *n,* -topf *m.*

cha·me·le·on [kə'miːljən] *s zo.* Chamäleon *n.*

cham·fer ['tʃæmfə] **I** *s* **1.** △ Auskehlung *f.* **2.** ⚙ Abschrägung *f.* **II** *v/t* **3.** △ auskehlen. **4.** ⚙ abschrägen.

cham·ois ['ʃæmwɑː] *s* **1.** *zo.* Gemse *f.* **2.** *a. ~leather* [*mst* 'ʃæmɪ] Sämischleder *n.* **3.** Polier-, Fensterleder *n.*

champ¹ [tʃæmp] *v/i u. v/t* (heftig *od.* geräuschvoll) kauen: *~ at the bit fig.* ungeduldig sein, es kaum mehr erwarten können (*to do* zu tun).

champ² [‿] F → **champion** 2.

cham·pagne [ʃæm'peɪn] *s* Champagner *m;* Sekt *m.*

cham·pi·on ['tʃæmpjən] **I** *s* **1.** Verfechter *m,* Fürsprecher *m* (*of von od. gen*). **2.** *Sport:* Meister *m.* **II** *v/t* **3.** verfechten, eintreten für. '**cham·pi·on·ship** *s Sport:* Meisterschaft *f.*

chance [tʃɑːns] **I** *s* **1.** Zufall *m:* *by ~* zufällig; *game of ~* Glücksspiel *n.* **2.** Möglichkeit *f,* Wahrscheinlichkeit *f: the ~s are that* es besteht Aussicht, daß. **3.** Chance *f,* (günstige) Gelegenheit; Aussicht *f* (*of auf acc*): *stand a ~* Aussichten haben: e-e Chance haben. *Risiko n: take a ~* es darauf ankommen

lassen, es riskieren (*on* mit); *take no ~s* nichts riskieren (wollen). **II** *v/i* **5.** *I ~d to meet her* ich traf sie zufällig. **6.** *~ on* zufällig begegnen (*dat*) *od.* treffen (*acc*); zufällig stoßen auf (*acc*). **III** *v/t* **7.** riskieren: *~ missing him* es riskieren, ihn zu verfehlen; *~ it* F es darauf ankommen lassen. **IV** *adj* **8.** zufällig, Zufalls...

chan·cel·lor ['tʃɑːnsələ] *s pol.* Kanzler *m:* ⚓ *of the Exchequer Br.* Schatzkanzler *m,* Finanzminister *m.*

chanc·y ['tʃɑːnsɪ] *adj* F riskant.

chan·de·lier [‚ʃændə'lɪə] *s* Kronleuchter *m,* Lüster *m.*

change [tʃeɪndʒ] **I** *v/t* **1.** (ver)ändern, verwandeln (*into* in *acc*): → *subject* 1. **2.** wechseln, (ver)tauschen: *~ one's shirt* ein anderes Hemd anziehen; *~ places with s.o.* mit j-m den Platz tauschen; → *trains* (*planes*) umsteigen; → *hand* 1, *mind* 4. **3.** Bettzeug *etc* wechseln, Bett frisch beziehen, Baby wickeln. **4.** Geld (um)wechseln (*into* in *acc*). **5.** ⚙ Teile (aus)wechseln, Öl wechseln. **6.** *mot.,* ⚙ schalten: *~ over* umschalten; *Maschine, a.* Industrie *etc* umstellen (*to* auf *acc*); → *gear* 1. **II** *v/i* **7.** sich (ver)ändern, wechseln. **8.** sich verwandeln (*to, into* in *acc*). **9.** übergehen (*to* zu). **10.** sich umziehen (*for dinner* zum Abendessen). **11.** 🚂, ✈ umsteigen. **12.** wechseln, umspringen (*from ... to* von ... auf *acc*) (*Verkehrsampel*). **13.** *mot.,* ⚙ schalten: *~ up* (*down*) hinauf- (herunter)schalten; → *gear* 1. **III** *s* **14.** (Ver)Änderung *f,* Wechsel *m, weitS. a.* Umschwung *m: ~ of air* Luftveränderung; *~ of life physiol.* Wechseljahre *pl; ~ in weather* Witterungsumschlag *m;* → *scene* 1a. **15.** (Aus)Tausch *m.* **16.** *et.* Neues, Abwechslung *f: for a ~* zur Abwechslung. **17.** Wechselgeld *n;* Kleingeld *n: can you give me ~ for a pound?* können Sie mir auf ein Pfund herausgeben?; können Sie mir ein Pfund wechseln?; → *small* I. '**change·a·ble** *adj* □ unbeständig: a) wankelmütig (*Person*), b) veränderlich (*Wetter*).

chan·nel ['tʃænl] *s* Kanal *m* (*a. fig.*), (*Rundfunk, TV a.*) Programm *n: switch ~s* umschalten; *through official ~s* auf dem Dienst- *od.* Instanzenweg.

chant [tʃɑːnt] I s 1. Gesang m. 2. Singsang m. 3. Sprechchor m. II v/t 4. singen. 5. herunterleiern. 6. in Sprechchören rufen.

cha·os ['keɪɒs] s Chaos n. **cha·ot·ic** adj (~ally) chaotisch.

chap¹ [tʃæp] I v/t Haut rissig machen. II v/i rissig werden, aufspringen. III s Riß m.

chap² [~] s F Bursche m, Kerl m.

chap·el ['tʃæpl] s Kapelle f.

chap·er·on ['ʃæpərəʊn] I s 1. Anstandsdame f. 2. Aufsichts-, Begleitperson f. II v/t 3. (als Anstandsdame) begleiten. 4. beaufsichtigen.

chap·fall·en ['tʃæpˌfɔːlən] adj niedergeschlagen, bedrückt.

chap·lain ['tʃæplɪn] s Kaplan m.

chapped [tʃæpt], **chap·py** ['tʃæpɪ] adj aufgesprungen, rissig.

chap·ter ['tʃæptə] s Kapitel n (a. fig.).

char¹ [tʃɑː] v/t u. v/i verkohlen.

char² [~] I s Br. F → **charwoman**. II v/i putzen: **go out ~ring** putzen gehen.

char·ac·ter ['kærəktə] I s 1. allg. Charakter m. 2. Ruf m, Leumund m. 3. Eigenschaft f, Stellung f: **in one's ~ as** in s-r Eigenschaft als. 4. Figur f, Gestalt f (e-s Romans etc), pl a. Charaktere pl. 5. Schriftzeichen n, Buchstabe m. II adj 6. Charakter...: **~ actor** (study, etc); **~ assassination** Rufmord m. ˌ**char·ac·ter'is·tic** I adj (~ally) charakteristisch (of für). II s charakteristisches Merkmal. I **'char·ac·ter·ize** v/t charakterisieren.

char·coal ['tʃɑːkəʊl] s Holzkohle f.

charge [tʃɑːdʒ] I v/t 1. Gewehr etc laden, Batterie etc (auf)laden. 2. beauftragen (**with** mit): **~ s.o. to be careful** j-m einschärfen, vorsichtig zu sein. 3. (**with**) j-m (et.) zur Last legen od. vorwerfen, a. ⚖ j-n (e-r Sache) beschuldigen od. anklagen. 4. (**with**) ✝ j-n belasten (mit e-m Betrag), j-m (et.) in Rechnung stellen. 5. berechnen, verlangen, fordern (**for** für). 6. ⚔ angreifen; stürmen. II v/i 7. **~ at** losgehen auf (acc). III s 8. Ladung f (e-s Gewehrs etc). 9. Preis m; Forderung f; Gebühr f; a. pl Unkosten pl, Spesen pl: **free of ~** kostenlos, gratis. 10. Beschuldigung f, a. ⚖ Anklage(punkt m) f: **be on a ~ of murder** unter Mordanklage stehen. 11. Verant-

wortung f: **the person in ~** der od. die Verantwortliche; **be in ~ of** verantwortlich sein für, leiten (acc); **be in** (od. **under**) **s.o.'s ~** von j-m betreut werden; **take ~ of** die Leitung od. Aufsicht (gen) übernehmen. 12. Schützling m, Mündel m, n; j-m anvertraute Sache. **~ ac·count** s ✝ 1. Kundenkreditkonto n. 2. Abzahlungskonto n (bei Teilzahlungen).

char·gé d'af·faires [ˌʃɑːʒeɪdæˈfeə] pl **char·gés d'af·faires** [~ʒeɪz~] s Geschäftsträger m.

charg·er ['tʃɑːdʒə] s ⚡ Ladegerät n.

char·is·ma [kəˈrɪzmə] s Charisma n, Ausstrahlung(skraft) f. **char·is·mat·ic** [ˌkærɪzˈmætɪk] adj charismatisch.

char·i·ta·ble ['tʃærətəbl] adj □ 1. wohltätig, karitativ. 2. gütig, nachsichtig (**to** gegenüber). **char·i·ty** ['~tɪ] s 1. Nächstenliebe f. 2. Wohltätigkeit f. 3. Güte f, Nachsicht f. 4. Almosen n, milde Gabe.

char·la·tan ['ʃɑːlətən] s Scharlatan m. '**char·la·tan·ry** s Scharlatanerie f.

char·ley horse ['tʃɑːlɪ] s Am. F Muskelkater m.

charm [tʃɑːm] I s 1. Charme m, Zauber m. 2. Zauber(formel f; -mittel n) m. 3. Talisman m, Amulett n. II v/t 4. bezaubern, entzücken: 5. verzaubern, Schlangen beschwören: **~ away** wegzaubern, Sorgen etc zerstreuen. '**charm·er** s 1. Zauberer m, Zauberin f. 2. reizvolles Geschöpf (Frau); Charmeur m. '**charm·ing** adj □ charmant, bezaubernd.

chart [tʃɑːt] I s 1. (See-, Himmels-, Wetter)Karte f. 2. Diagramm n, Schaubild n, Kurve(nblatt n) f. 3. pl Charts pl, Hitliste(n pl) f. II v/t 4. auf e-r Karte etc einzeichnen od. verzeichnen.

char·ter ['tʃɑːtə] I s 1. Urkunde f. 2. Konzession f. 3. pol. Charta f. 4. Chartern n. II v/t 5. konzessionieren. 6. chartern: **~ed** Charter... **~ flight** s Charterflug m.

'**char·wom·an** s (irr **woman**) Putzfrau f, Raumpflegerin f.

char·y ['tʃeərɪ] adj □ 1. vorsichtig (**in**, **of** in dat, bei). 2. sparsam, zurückhaltend (**of** mit).

chase¹ [tʃeɪs] I v/t 1. jagen, Jagd machen auf, (a. fig. e-m Traum etc) nachjagen;

F e-m *Mädchen etc* nachlaufen. **2.** *hunt.* hetzen, jagen: ~ **up** (*od.* **down**) *mst fig.* aufstöbern. **3.** *a.* ~ **away** verjagen, -treiben. **II** *v/i* **4.** ~ **after s.o.** j-m nachjagen. **5.** F rasen, rennen. **III** *s* **6.** *hunt.* (Hetz-) Jagd *f*, *fig. a.* Verfolgung(sjagd) *f*: **give** ~ **to** verfolgen (*acc*), nachjagen (*dat*).

chase² [~] *v/t* ziselieren.

chas·er¹ ['tʃeɪsə] *s* Jäger *m*, Verfolger *m*.

chas·er² [~] *s* Ziseleur *m*.

chasm ['kæzəm] *s* **1.** Kluft *f*, Abgrund *m* (*a. fig.*). **2.** Schlucht *f*, Klamm *f*. **3.** Riß *m*, Spalte *f*. **4.** *fig.* Lücke *f*.

chas·sis ['ʃæsɪ] *pl* **-sis** ['~sɪz] *s* ✈, *mot.* Chassis *n*, Fahrgestell *n*.

chaste [tʃeɪst] *adj* □ **1.** keusch, züchtig. **2.** bescheiden, schlicht (*Mahl etc*).

chas·ten ['tʃeɪsn] *v/t* **1.** züchtigen. **2.** *fig.* läutern. **3.** *fig.* ernüchtern, nachdenklich stimmen.

chas·tise [tʃæ'staɪz] *v/t* **1.** züchtigen. **2.** *fig.* geißeln, scharf tadeln.

chas·ti·ty ['tʃæstətɪ] *s* **1.** Keuschheit *f*. **2.** Schlichtheit *f*.

chat [tʃæt] **I** *v/i* plaudern. **II** *v/t* ~ **up** Br. F einreden auf (*acc*); sich ranmachen an (*ein Mädchen etc*), anquatschen. **III** *s* Plauderei *f*: **have a** ~ plaudern.

chat show *s* Br. Talk-Show *f*.

chat·tels ['tʃætlz] *s pl* ⚖ bewegliches Eigentum: → **good 3**.

chat·ter ['tʃætə] **I** *v/i* **1.** schnattern, schwatzen, plappern. **2.** klappern. **II** *s* **3.** Geschnatter *n*, Geplapper *n*. **4.** Klappern *n*. **'~box** *s* Plaudertasche *f*, Plappermaul *n*.

chat·ty ['tʃætɪ] *adj* □ **1.** geschwätzig, gesprächig. **2.** *fig.* wortreich, ausführlich; im Plauderton (geschrieben).

chauf·feur ['ʃəʊfə] **I** *s* Chauffeur *m*, Fahrer *m*. **II** *v/t* chauffieren, fahren: **~ed** mit Chauffeur.

chau·vi ['ʃəʊvɪ] *s* F Chauvi *m*. **'chau·vin·ism** *s* Chauvinismus *m*: **male** ~ männlicher Chauvinismus. **'chau·vin·ist** *s* Chauvinist *m*: **male** ~ männlicher Chauvinist; **male** ~ **pig** F a) *contp.* Chauvischwein *n*, b) *humor.* Chauvi *m*. **,chau·vin·ist·ic** *adj* (**~ally**) chauvinistisch.

cheap [tʃiːp] **I** *adj* □ **1.** billig, Billig... **2.** billig, minderwertig. **3.** schäbig, gemein: **feel** ~ sich schäbig vorkommen. **II** *adv* **4.** billig: **buy s.th.** ~. **III** *s* **5.** **on**

the ~ billig. **'cheap·en** *v/t u. v/i* (sich) verbilligen. **'cheap·ness** *s* Billigkeit *f*. **'cheap·skate** *s* F Knicker *m*, Geizkragen *m*.

cheat [tʃiːt] **I** *s* **1.** Betrüger(in), Schwindler(in). **2.** Betrug *m*, Schwindel *m*. **II** *v/t* **3.** betrügen (**out of, out of** um). **III** *v/i* **4.** betrügen, schwindeln. **5.** ~ **on** F s-e *Frau etc* betrügen. **'cheat·ing** *adj:* ~ **pack** Mogelpackung *f*.

check [tʃek] **I** *s* **1.** Schach(stellung *f*) *n*: **give** ~ Schach bieten; **hold** (*od.* **keep**) **in** ~ *fig.* in Schach halten. **2.** Hemmnis *n*, Hindernis *n* (**on** für). **3.** Einhalt *m*: **give a** ~ **to** Einhalt gebieten (*dat*). **4.** Kontrolle *f*, Überprüfung *f*: **keep a** ~ **on** unter Kontrolle halten (*acc*). **5.** Am. Häkchen *n* (*auf Liste etc*). **6.** ✝ Am. Scheck *m* (**for** über *acc*). **7.** *bsd. Am.* Kassenzettel *m*, Rechnung *f*. **8.** Kontrollabschnitt *m*, -schein *m*. **9.** *bsd. Am.* Garderobenmarke *f*, Gepäckschein *m*. **10.** Schachbrett-, Karomuster *n*; Karo *n*, Viereck *n*; karierter Stoff. **11.** Poker *etc*: Spielmarke *f*; pass (*od.* hand) in one's ~s Am. F den Löffel weglegen (*sterben*). **II** *v/t* **12.** Schach bieten (*dat*). **13.** hemmen, hindern. **14.** ⊙ drosseln, bremsen (*a. fig.*). **15.** zurückhalten, zügeln: ~ **o.s.** sich beherrschen. **16.** checken, kontrollieren, überprüfen (**for** auf *acc* hin). **17.** *Am.* auf Liste *etc* abhaken. **18.** *bsd. Am.* (zur Aufbewahrung *od.* in der Garderobe) abgeben; (als Reisegepäck) aufgeben. **19.** *a.* ~ **out** Am. Geld mittels Scheck abheben. **III** *v/i* **20.** (plötzlich) innehalten, stutzen. **21.** Am. e-n Scheck ausstellen (**for** über *acc*).

Verbindungen mit Adverbien:

check| back *v/i* rückfragen (**with** bei). ~ **in** *v/i* **1.** sich (*in e-m Hotel*) anmelden. **2.** einstempeln. **3.** ✈ (*a. v/t*) einchecken. ~ **off** → **check 17.** ~ **out I** *v/i* **1.** → **check 19. 2.** sich erkundigen nach, sich informieren über (*acc*). **II** *v/i* **3.** *aus e-m Hotel* abreisen. **4.** ausstempeln. ~ **up** *v/i:* ~ **on** *et.* nachprüfen, *et.*, j-n überprüfen.

'check| back *s* Rückfrage *f*. **'~book** *s* Am. Scheckbuch *n*, -heft *n*. ~ **card** *s* Am. Scheckkarte *f*.

checked [tʃekt] *adj* kariert: ~ **pattern** Karomuster *n*.

check·er¹ ['tʃekə] *s* **1.** Am. a) (Dame)Stein m, b) pl (sg konstruiert) Dame(spiel n) f. **2.** Karomuster n.

check·er² [~] s bsd. Am. **1.** Kassiererin f (bsd. im Supermarkt). **2.** Garderobenfrau f. **3.** 🚉 Angestellte m, f in e-r Gepäckaufbewahrung.

'**check·er·board** s Am. Schach-, Damebrett n.

check·ered ['tʃekəd] adj **1.** kariert. **2.** bunt (a. fig.). **3.** fig. wechselvoll, bewegt (Geschichte etc).

'**check·in** s **1.** Anmeldung f (in e-m Hotel). **2.** Einstempeln n. **3.** ✈ Einchecken n: ~ **counter** Abfertigungsschalter m.

check·ing ac·count s ✝ Am. Girokonto n.

check| list s Check-, Kontrolliste f. '**~·mate** I s (Schach)Matt n, Mattstellung f. II v/t (schach)matt setzen (a. fig.). '**~·out** s **1.** Abreise f (aus e-m Hotel): ~ **(time)** Zeit, zu der ein Hotelzimmer geräumt sein muß. **2.** Ausstempeln n. **3.** a. ~ **counter** Kasse f (bsd. im Supermarkt). '**~·point** s Kontrollpunkt m (an der Grenze). '**~·room** s bsd. Am. **1.** 🚉 Gepäckaufbewahrung(sstelle) f. **2.** Garderobe(nraum m) f. '**~·up** s **1.** Überprüfung f. **2.** ✚ Check-up m, Vorsorgeuntersuchung f.

cheek [tʃiːk] I s **1.** Backe f (a. ✪), Wange f: **be ~ by jowl** Tuchfühlung haben (**with** mit) (a. fig.). **2.** F Frechheit f. II v/t **3.** F frech sein zu. '**~·bone** s Backenknochen m.

cheek·y ['tʃiːkɪ] adj □ F frech (**to** zu).

cheep [tʃiːp] I v/i u. v/t piepsen. II s Piepsen n; Pieps(er) m (a. fig.).

cheer [tʃɪə] I s **1.** Beifall(sruf) m, Hoch(ruf m) n: **give three ~s** for sb. j-n dreimal hochleben lassen. **2.** Auf-, Ermunterung f, Aufheiterung f: **words pl of ~** aufmunternde Worte pl; **~s!** → **cheerio**. **3.** (gute) Laune: **be of good ~** guter Laune od. Dinge sein. II v/t **4.** Beifall spenden (dat), hochleben lassen. **5.** a. ~ **on** anspornen, anfeuern. **6.** a. ~ **up** auf-, ermuntern, aufheitern. III v/i **7.** Beifall spenden, jubeln. **8.** mst ~ **up** Mut fassen, (wieder) fröhlich werden: ~ **up!** Kopf hoch!, laß den Kopf nicht hängen! **cheer·ful** ['~fʊl] adj □ **1.** fröhlich (a. Lied etc), vergnügt. **2.** freundlich (Raum, Wetter etc).

cheer·i·o [,tʃɪərɪ'əʊ] int bsd. Br. F **1.** mach's gut!, tschüs! **2.** prost!

'**cheer**,**lead·er** s Sport: Einpeitscher m.

cheer·less ['tʃɪəlɪs] adj □ **1.** freudlos. **2.** unfreundlich (Raum, Wetter etc).

'**cheer·y** adj □ fröhlich, vergnügt.

cheese [tʃiːz] s Käse m: **say ~!** phot. bitte recht freundlich!; **hard ~!** sl. Künstlerpech!; **the ~** sl. genau das Richtige. '**~·cake** s **1.** ein Käsekuchen m. **2.** sl. Zurschaustellung f weiblicher Reize (bsd. auf Fotografien). '**~,par·ing** I s Knauserei f. II adj knaus(e)rig. ~ **spread** s Streichkäse m.

chees·y ['tʃiːzɪ] adj käsig.

chef [ʃef] s Küchenchef m.

chem·i·cal ['kemɪkl] I adj □ chemisch: ~ **fiber** (bsd. Br. **fibre**) Chemie-, Kunstfaser f; ~ **warfare** chemische Kriegsführung. II s Chemikalie f.

chem·ist ['kemɪst] s **1.** Chemiker(in). **2.** Br. Apotheker(in); Drogist(in): ~'**s shop** Apotheke f; Drogerie f. '**chem·is·try** s Chemie f.

chem·o·ther·a·py [,kiːməʊ'θerəpɪ] s 💊 Chemotherapie f.

cheque [tʃek] s ✝ Br. Scheck m. ~ **ac·count** s ✝ Br. Girokonto n. '**~·book** s Br. Scheckbuch n, -heft n. ~ **card** s Scheckkarte f.

cheq·uer, cheq·uer·board, cheq·uered bsd. Br. → **checker¹, checkerboard, checkered.**

cher·ish ['tʃerɪʃ] v/t **1.** j-s Andenken in Ehren halten. **2.** Gefühle hegen. **3.** festhalten an (dat).

che·root [ʃə'ruːt] s Stumpen m (Zigarre ohne Spitzen).

cher·ry ['tʃerɪ] I s 🌿 Kirsche f. II adj kirschrot. ~ **bran·dy** s Cherry Brandy m, Kirschlikör m.

cher·ub ['tʃerəb] pl **-ubs**, **-u·bim** ['~əbɪm] s **1.** Cherub m, Engel m. **2.** geflügelter Engelskopf.

chess [tʃes] s Schach(spiel) n. '**~·board** s Schachbrett n. '**~·man** s (irr **man**), **~ piece** s Schachfigur f.

chest [tʃest] s **1.** Kiste f, Kasten m; Truhe f: ~ **(of drawers)** Kommode f. **2.** anat. Brust(kasten m) f: **get sth. off one's ~** F sich et. von der Seele reden.

chest·nut ['tʃesnʌt] I s **1.** 🌿 Kastanie f: **pull the ~s out of the fire (for s.o.)** fig. (für j-n) die Kastanien aus dem Feuer holen. **2.** F alte *od.* olle Kamelle, alter Witz. **II** *adj* **3.** kastanienbraun.

chest·y ['tʃestɪ] *adj* F **1.** mit viel Holz vor der Hütte (*vollbusig*). **2.** tiefsitzend (*Husten*).

chev·ron ['ʃevrən] *s* ⚔ Winkel *m* (*Rangabzeichen*).

chew [tʃuː] **I** *v/t* **1.** (zer)kauen: ~ *one's nails* an den Nägeln kauen; → *cud* 1, *fat* 3. **II** *v/i* **2.** kauen: ~ *on* herumkauen auf (*dat*). **3.** nachsinnen, grübeln (*on, over* über *acc*).

chew·ing gum ['tʃuːɪŋ] *s* Kaugummi *m, a. n.*

chic [ʃiːk] **I** *s* Schick *m*, Eleganz *f*. **II** *adj* schick, elegant.

chick [tʃɪk] *s* **1.** Küken *n*, junger Vogel. **2.** F Kleine(s) (*Kind; oft Anrede*). **3.** *sl.* Biene *f*, Puppe *f* (*Mädchen*).

chick·en ['tʃɪkɪn] **I** *s* **1.** Küken *n* (*a.* F *junge Person*), Hühnchen *n*, Hähnchen *n*: *she's no* ~ F sie ist (auch) nicht mehr die Jüngste. **2.** Huhn *n*. **3.** F Feigling *m*. **II** *adj* **4.** F feig. **III** *v/i* **5.** ~ *out* F kneifen (*of, on* vor *dat*). ~ **broth** *s* Hühnerbrühe *f*. ~ **farm·er** *s* Geflügelzüchter *m*. ~ **feed** *s* **1.** Hühnerfutter *n*. **2.** *sl. contp.* ein paar Pfennige *pl, a.* Hungerlohn *m*. '~**heart·ed**, '~**liv·ered** *adj* furchtsam, feig. ~ **pox** *s* 🩺 Windpocken *pl.*

chic·o·ry ['tʃɪkərɪ] *s* 🌿 Chicorée *f, a. m.*

chief [tʃiːf] **I** *s* **1.** (Ober)Haupt *n*, (An)Führer *m*, Chef *m*: ~ *of the department* Abteilungsleiter *m*; ~ *of state* Staatschef, -oberhaupt. **2.** Häuptling *m*: ~ *of the tribe* Stammeshäuptling. **II** *adj* **3.** erst, oberst, Ober..., Haupt...: ~ *designer* Chefkonstrukteur *m*. **4.** hauptsächlich, wichtigst. '**chief·ly** *adv* hauptsächlich, vor allem.

chif·fon ['ʃɪfɒn] *s* Chiffon *m*.

chil·blain ['tʃɪlbleɪn] *s* Frostbeule *f*.

child [tʃaɪld] *pl* **chil·dren** ['tʃɪldrən] *s* Kind *n*: *from a* ~ von Kindheit an; *be a good* ~! sei artig *od.* brav!; *that's* ~*'s play* *fig.* das ist ein Kinderspiel. '~**bed** *s*: *be in* ~ im Wochenbett liegen; ~ *fever* 🩺 Kindbettfieber *n*. ~ **ben·e·fit** *s Br.* Kindergeld *n*. '~**birth** *s* Geburt *f*, Niederkunft *f*, Entbindung *f*.

child·hood ['tʃaɪldhʊd] *s* Kindheit *f*: *from* ~ von Kindheit an; → *second*¹ 1.

child·ish ['tʃaɪldɪʃ] *adj* □ **1.** kindlich. **2.** kindisch.

child·less ['tʃaɪldlɪs] *adj* kinderlos.

'**child**|**·like** *adj* kindlich. ~ **mind·er** *s* Tagesmutter *f*. ~ **prod·i·gy** *s* Wunderkind *n*. '~**proof** *adj* kindersicher: ~ *lock* mot. Kindersicherung *f*.

chil·dren ['tʃɪldrən] *pl von* **child**: ~*'s clin·ic* Kinderklinik *f*.

chil·e ['tʃɪlɪ], '**chil·i** *pl* **-ies** 🌿 Chili *m* (*a.* Cayennepfeffer): ~ *sauce* Chili(soße *f*) *m.*

chill [tʃɪl] **I** *s* **1.** Kältegefühl *n*, Frösteln *n*. **2.** Kälte *f*, Kühle *f* (*beide a. fig.*): *take the* ~ *off et.* leicht anwärmen. **3.** Erkältung *f*: *catch a* ~ sich erkälten. **4.** *fig.* gedrückte Stimmung: *cast* (*od.* *put*) *a* ~ *on* (*od.* *over*) → 5. **II** *adj* **5.** kalt, frostig, kühl (*alle a. fig.*). **III** *v/i* **6.** abkühlen. **IV** *v/t* **7.** j-n frösteln lassen; abkühlen (lassen), erkalten *et.* kühlen: ~*ed meat* Kühlfleisch *n*. **8.** *fig.* abkühlen, dämpfen; entmutigen.

chil·li *pl* **-lies** → **chile**.

chil·ly ['tʃɪlɪ] *adj* → **chill** 5: *feel* ~ frösteln.

chime [tʃaɪm] **I** *s* **1.** *oft pl* Glockenspiel *n*, (Glocken)Geläute *n*. **2.** (Glocken-) Schlag *m*. **II** *v/i* **3.** läuten; ertönen; schlagen (*Uhr*). **4.** *fig.* harmonieren, übereinstimmen (*with* mit): ~ *in* sich (ins Gespräch) einmischen, einfallen (*a.* ♪); ~ *in* zustimmen, beipflichten (*with dat*); übereinstimmen mit. **III** *v/t* **5.** Glocken läuten; *die Stunde* schlagen.

chim·ney ['tʃɪmnɪ] *s* Schornstein *m*, Kamin *m*. '~**piece** *s* Kaminsims *m, n.* ~ **sweep** *s* Schornsteinfeger(in), Kaminkehrer(in).

chim·pan·zee [ˌtʃɪmpənˈziː] *s* zo. Schimpanse *m.*

chin [tʃɪn] **I** *s* Kinn *n*: (*keep your*) ~ *up!* F Kopf hoch!, halt die Ohren steif! **II** *v/t*: ~ *o.s.* (*up*), ~ *the bar* e-n Klimmzug machen. **III** *v/i Am.* F schwatzen, plappern.

chi·na ['tʃaɪnə] *s* **1.** Porzellan *n*. **2.** (Porzellan)Geschirr *n*. **2·man** ['~mən] *s* (*irr man*) *mst contp.* Chinese *m*. '**2·town** *s* Chinesenviertel *n*. '~**ware** *s* Porzellan(waren *pl*) *n.*

Chi·nese [ˌtʃaɪˈniːz] **I** *s* **1.** Chinese *m*, Chinesin *f*: *the* ~ *pl* die Chinesen *pl*. **2.** *ling.* Chinesisch *n*. **II** *adj* **3.** chinesisch.

chink¹ [tʃɪŋk] *s* Riß *m*, Ritze *f*, Spalt *m*, Spalte *f.*

chink 816

chink² [~] **I** v/i u. v/t klingen od. klirren (lassen), klimpern (mit). **II** s Klirren n, Klimpern n.

'chin·wag F I s **1.** Plauderei f, Plausch m. **2.** Klatsch m, Tratsch m. **II** v/i **3.** plaudern, plauschen. **4.** klatschen, tratschen.

chip [tʃɪp] **I** s **1.** Splitter m, Span m, Schnitzel n, m: *be a ~ off the old block* ganz der Vater sein; *have a ~ on one's shoulder* F sich ständig angegriffen fühlen; e-n Komplex haben (*about* wegen). **2.** angeschlagene Stelle. **3.** pl Br. Pommes frites pl; Am. (Kartoffel-)Chips pl. **4.** Chip m (a. ⚡), Spielmarke f. **II** v/t **5.** a. *~ off* abbrechen, abbröckeln. **6.** Geschirr etc anschlagen. **7.** *~ in* F im Gespräch einwerfen. **8.** *~ in* F Geld etc beisteuern. **III** v/i **9.** a. *~ off* abbrechen, abbröckeln. **10.** *~ in* F dazu beisteuern: *~ in with* → **8**. **11.** *~ in* F sich (*in ein Gespräch*) einmischen. *~ pan* s Friteuse f.

chi·rop·o·dist [kɪ'rɒpədɪst] s Fußpfleger(in), Pediküre f. **chi'rop·o·dy** s Fußpflege f, Pediküre f.

chi·ro·prac·tor ['kaɪrəʊˌpræktə] s ♂ Chiropraktiker m.

chirp [tʃɜːp] **I** v/i u. v/t **1.** zirpen (*Grille etc*); zwitschern, piepsen (*Vogel*) (*alle a. fig. Person etc*). **II** s **2.** Zirpen n; Zwitschern n, Piepsen n. **3.** Piepser m. **'chirp·y** adj □ F quietschvergnügt.

chir·rup ['tʃɪrəp] → **chirp**.

chis·el ['tʃɪzl] **I** s **1.** Meißel m. **II** v/t pret u. pp **-eled**, bsd. Br. **-elled 2.** (aus)meißeln. **3.** fig. (stilistisch) ausfeilen. **4.** sl. betrügen (*out of* um); et. ergaunern.

chit¹ [tʃɪt] s: *a ~ of a girl* ein junges Ding; contp. ein Fratz.

chit² [~] s **1.** vom Gast abgezeichnete Rechnung. **2.** (kurze) Notiz; beschriebener Zettel.

chit·chat ['tʃɪttʃæt] s **1.** Plauderei f, Plausch m. **2.** Klatsch m, Tratsch m.

chiv·al·rous ['ʃɪvlrəs] adj □ **1.** ritterlich, galant. **2.** tapfer; loyal; großzügig. **'chiv·al·ry** s **1.** Ritterlichkeit f. **2.** hist. Rittertum n; -stand m.

chives [tʃaɪvz] s pl ♣ Schnittlauch m.

chlo·ric ['klɔːrɪk] adj 🜍 chlorhaltig, Chlor... **chlo·rin·ate** ['~rɪneɪt] v/t chloren. **chlo·rine** ['~riːn] s 🜍 Chlor n.

chlo·ro·form ['klɒrəfɔːm] **I** s 🜍 Chloroform n. **II** v/t chloroformieren.

chlo·ro·phyll ['klɒrəfɪl] s ♣ Chlorophyll n, Blattgrün n.

choc ice [tʃɒk] s Br. Eis n mit Schokoladeüberzug.

chock [tʃɒk] **I** s Bremsklotz m. **II** v/t festkeilen. **,~·a·'block** adj vollgestopft (*with* mit). **,~·'full** adj zum Bersten voll (*of* mit).

choc·o·late ['tʃɒkələt] **I** s **1.** Schokolade f (a. Getränk). **2.** Praline f: *~s* pl Pralinen pl, Konfekt n; → **box¹** 2. **II** adj **3.** schokolade(n)braun.

choice [tʃɔɪs] **I** s **1.** (a. freie) Wahl: *make a ~* wählen; *e-e Wahl treffen*; *take one's ~* s-e Wahl treffen, sich et. aussuchen; *at ~* nach Belieben; *have no ~* keine andere Wahl haben. **2.** (große) Auswahl (*of* an dat). **3.** Auslese f, das Beste. **II** adj **4.** auserlesen, ausgesucht (gut). **5.** humor. deftig (*Sprache*): *~ word* Kraftausdruck m.

choir ['kwaɪə] s ♪, △ Chor m.

choke [tʃəʊk] **I** s **1.** Würgen n. **2.** mot. Choke m: *pull out the ~* den Choke ziehen. **II** v/t **3.** würgen. **4.** erwürgen, erdrosseln, a. weitS. Feuer ersticken. **5.** a. *~back* (*od. down*) Bemerkung, Ärger etc unterdrücken, hinunterschlucken, Tränen zurückhalten. **6.** Motor, Strom drosseln; F Motor abwürgen. **7.** a. *~ off* Diskussion etc abwürgen; j-s Redefluß stoppen. **8.** a. *~ up* verstopfen; vollstopfen. **III** v/i **9.** würgen. **10.** ersticken (*on* an dat). **'chok·ing** adj **1.** stickig (*Luft*). **2.** erstickt (*Stimme*). **'chok·y** → **choking** 1.

chol·er·a ['kɒlərə] s ♂ Cholera f. **'chol·er·ic** adj (*~ally*) cholerisch.

cho·les·ter·in [kə'lestərɪn], **cho·les·ter·ol** ['~rɒl] s physiol. Cholesterin n.

choose [tʃuːz] (*irr*) **I** v/t **1.** (aus)wählen, (sich et.) aussuchen. **2.** *~ to do s.th.* es vorziehen od. beschließen, et. zu tun. **II** v/i **3.** wählen: *there are three versions to ~ from* es stehen drei Ausführungen zur Auswahl. **'choos·(e)y** adj F wählerisch, heikel.

chop¹ [tʃɒp] **I** s **1.** Hieb m, Schlag m. **2.** gastr. Kotelett n. **II** v/t **3.** (zer)hacken: *~ wood* Holz hacken; *~ away* (*od. off*) abhacken; *~ down* fällen.

chop² [~] v/i oft *~ about* (*od. round*) plötzlich umschlagen (*Wind etc*): *~ and* *change* dauernd s-e Meinung *od.* s-e Pläne ändern.

chop·per ['tʃɒpə] *s* **1.** Hackmesser *n.* **2.** F Hubschrauber *m.*

chop·py ['tʃɒpi] *adj* **1.** kabbelig (*Meer*). **2.** böig (*Wind*). **3.** *fig.* abgehackt; zusammenhang(s)los.

'**chop·stick** *s* Eßstäbchen *n.*

cho·ral ['kɔːrəl] *adj* □ Chor..., chorartig: ~ **society** Gesangverein *m.* **cho·ral(e)** [kɒ'rɑːl] *s* Cho'ral *m.*

chord[1] [kɔːd] *s* ♪ Saite *f* (*a. fig.*): **strike the right** ~ den richtigen Ton treffen; **does that strike a ~?** erinnert dich das an etwas?

chord[2] [~] *s* ♪ Akkord *m.*

chore [tʃɔː] *s* **1.** *pl* Hausarbeit *f:* **do the ~s** den Haushalt machen. **2.** schwierige *od.* unangenehme Aufgabe.

cho·re·og·ra·pher [ˌkɒrɪ'ɒɡrəfə] *s* Choreograph(in). **ˌcho·re·og·ra·phy** *s* Choreographie *f.*

cho·rus ['kɔːrəs] *s* **1.** Chor *m* (*a. fig.*): ~ **of protest** Protestgeschrei *n*; **in** ~ im Chor. **2.** Tanzgruppe *f* (*bsd.* e-r *Revue*). **II** *v/t u. v/i* **3.** im Chor singen *od.* sprechen *od.* rufen. ~ **girl** *s* (Revue)Tänzerin *f.*

chose [tʃəʊz] *pret von* **choose. cho·sen** ['~zn] *pp von* **choose.**

chow [tʃaʊ] *s* **1.** *zo.* Chow-Chow *m.* **2.** *sl.* Futter *n*, Essen *n.*

chow·der ['tʃaʊdə] *s gastr. bsd. Am.* dikke Suppe *aus* Meeresfrüchten.

Christ [kraɪst] **I** *s* Christus *m:* **before** ~ vor Christi Geburt. **II** *int sl.* verdammt *od.* Herrgott noch mal!

chris·ten ['krɪsn] *v/t j-n, a. Schiff etc* (auf den Namen ...) taufen. '**chris·ten·ing** *s* Taufe *f.*

Chris·tian ['krɪstʃən] **I** *adj* □ christlich: ~ **Era** christliche Zeitrechnung; ~ **name** → **first name. II** *s* Christ(in). **Chris·ti·an·i·ty** [ˌ~tɪ'ænətɪ] *s* **1.** Christenheit *f.* **2.** Christentum *n.* **Chris·tian·ize** ['~tʃənaɪz] *v/t* christianisieren.

Christ·mas ['krɪsməs] *s* Weihnachten *n u. pl:* **at** ~ zu Weihnachten; → **merry** 1. ~ **bo·nus** *s* Weihnachtsgratifikation *f.* ~ **box** *s Br.* Geldgeschenk *n* zu Weihnachten (*für Briefträger etc*). ~ **car·ol** *s* Weihnachtslied *n.* ~ **Day** *s* erster Weihnachtsfeiertag. ~ **Eve** *s* Heiliger Abend. ~ **pud·ding** *s* Plumpudding *m.* '~·**tide,**

'~·**time** *s* Weihnachtszeit *f.* ~ **tree** *s* Christ-, Weihnachtsbaum *m.*

chro·mat·ic [krəʊ'mætɪk] *phys.* **I** *adj* (**~ally**) chromatisch, Farben... **II** *s pl* (*sg konstruiert*) Chromatik *f*, Farbenlehre *f.*

chrome [krəʊm] 🔥 **I** *s* Chrom *n.* **II** *v/t a.* ~·**plate** verchromen.

chro·mi·um ['krəʊmɪəm] *s* 🔥 Chrom *n.* ~·'**plate** *v/t* verchromen.

chro·mo·some ['krəʊməsəʊm] *s biol.* Chromosom *n.*

chron·ic ['krɒnɪk] *adj* (**~ally**) **1.** ständig, (an)dauernd: ~ **unemployment** Dauerarbeitslosigkeit *f.* **2.** eingewurzelt; unverbesserlich **3.** 🩺 chronisch. **4.** *Br.* F scheußlich, miserabel.

chron·i·cle ['krɒnɪkl] **I** *s* Chronik *f.* **II** *v/t* aufzeichnen. '**chron·i·cler** *s* Chronist *m.*

chron·o·log·i·cal [ˌkrɒnə'lɒdʒɪkl] *adj* □ chronologisch: **in** ~ **order,** ~**ly** in chronologischer Reihenfolge. **chro·nol·o·gy** [krə'nɒlədʒɪ] *s* **1.** Chronologie *f*, Zeitrechnung *f.* **2.** Zeittafel *f.* **3.** chronologische Aufstellung.

chrys·an·the·mum [krɪ'sænθəməm] *s* 🌼 Chrysantheme *f.*

chub·by ['tʃʌbɪ] *adj* **1.** dicklich, rundlich: ~ **cheeks** *pl* Pausbacken *pl.* **2.** pausbäckig.

chuck[1] [tʃʌk] **I** *s* **1.** F Wurf *m:* **give s.o. the** ~ *Br.* j-n rausschmeißen (*entlassen*). **II** *v/t* **2.** F schmeißen, werfen. **3.** F *a*) Schluß machen mit (*e-r Freundin etc*): ~ **it!** laß das!, *b*) → **chuck up. 4.** ~ **s.o. under the chin** j-n *od.* j-m zärtlich unters Kinn fassen.

Verbindungen mit Adverbien:

chuck a·way *v/t* F **1.** wegschmeißen. **2.** Geld verschwenden. **3.** Gelegenheit *etc* verpassen, verschenken. ~ **in** → **chuck up.** ~ **out** *v/t* F j-n rausschmeißen, *et.* Altes *etc a.* wegschmeißen. ~ **up** *v/t* F Job *etc* hinschmeißen.

chuck[2] [~] *s* ⚙ **1.** Spann-, Klemmfutter *n.* **2.** Spannvorrichtung *f.*

chuck·er-out [ˌtʃʌkər'aʊt] *s* F Rausschmeißer *m.*

chuck·le ['tʃʌkl] **I** *v/i* **1.** glucksen: ~ (**to o.s.**) (stillvergnügt) in sich hineinlachen. **2.** glucken (*Henne*). **II** *s* **3.** Glucksen *n.*

chug [tʃʌg] **I** s Tuckern n (des Motors). **II** v/i tuckern(d fahren).

chum [tʃʌm] F **I** s Kumpel m: *be great ~s* dicke Freunde sein. **II** v/i: *~ up with s.o.* enge Freundschaft mit j-m schließen.

chump [tʃʌmp] s **1.** Holzklotz m. **2.** dickes Ende (e-r Hammelkeule etc). **3.** F Trottel m. **4.** Br. sl. Birne f (Kopf): *be off one's ~* e-n Vogel haben.

chunk [tʃʌŋk] s F (Holz)Klotz m; (dickes) Stück: *a ~ of bread* ein Runken m.

'chunk·y adj F klobig, klotzig.

church [tʃɜːtʃ] **I** s Kirche f: *at* (od. *in*) *~* in der Kirche; *go to ~* in die Kirche gehen. **II** adj Kirchen..., kirchlich. **'~·go·er** s Kirchgänger(in). **~ wed·ding** s kirchliche Trauung. **'~·yard** s Kirch-, Friedhof m.

churl [tʃɜːl] s **1.** Flegel m. **2.** Geizhals m. **'churl·ish** adj □ **1.** flegelhaft. **2.** geizig.

churn [tʃɜːn] s **1.** Butterfaß n, -maschine f. **2.** Br. Milchkanne f. **II** v/t **3.** zu Butter verarbeiten. **4.** a. *~ up* Flüssigkeiten heftig schütteln, Wellen aufwühlen, peitschen. **III** v/i **5.** buttern. **6.** sich heftig bewegen.

chute [ʃuːt] s **1.** Stromschnelle f. **2.** Rutsche f (a. ⚙). **3.** Rutschbahn f. **3.** Müllschlucker m. **4.** F Fallschirm m.

chut·ney ['tʃʌtnɪ] s gastr. Chutney n (scharf gewürzte Paste aus Früchten).

ci·ce·ro·ne [,tʃɪtʃəˈrəʊnɪ] pl **-ni** [ˌ.niː], **-nes** s Cicerone m, Fremdenführer m.

ci·der ['saɪdə] s (Am. *hard ~*) Apfelwein m: (*sweet*) *~ Am.* Apfelmost m, -saft m.

ci·gar [sɪˈgɑː] s Zigarre f. **~ cut·ter** s Zigarrenabschneider m.

cig·a·rette, Am. a. **cig·a·ret** [ˌsɪgəˈret] s Zigarette f. **~ case** s Zigarettenetui n. **~ end** s Zigarettenstummel m. **~ hold·er** s Zigarettenspitze f. **~ pa·per** s Zigarettenpapier n.

cig·a·ril·lo [ˌsɪgəˈrɪləʊ] pl **-los** s Zigarillo m, n.

ci·gar light·er s mot. Zigarren-, Zigarettenanzünder m.

cinch [sɪntʃ] s sl. todsichere Sache; Kinderspiel n.

cin·der ['sɪndə] s **1.** Schlacke f: *burnt to a ~* verkohlt, verbrannt. **2.** pl Asche f. **Cin·der·el·la** [ˌsɪndəˈrelə] s Aschenbrödel n, -puttel n (a. fig.).

cin·der track s Sport: Aschenbahn f.

cin·e·cam·er·a ['sɪnɪˌkæmərə] s

(Schmal)Filmkamera f. **'cin·e·film** s Schmalfilm m.

cin·e·ma ['sɪnəmə] s **1.** bsd. Br. Kino n. **2.** Film(kunst f) m. **'~·go·er** s bsd. Br. Kinobesucher(in).

cin·na·mon ['sɪnəmən] s Zimt m.

ci·pher ['saɪfə] **I** s **1.** & Null f (Ziffer). **2.** (arabische) Ziffer, Zahl f. **3.** fig. Null f (Person); Nichts n (Sache). **4.** Chiffre f: *in ~* chiffriert. **5.** fig. Schlüssel m (zu e-r Geheimschrift). **II** v/t **6.** chiffrieren, verschlüsseln.

cir·cle ['sɜːkl] **I** s **1.** (a. Familien-, Freundes- etc)Kreis m: *go* (od. *run*) *round in ~s* fig. sich im Kreis bewegen; → *vicious circle*. **2.** thea. Rang m: *upper ~* zweiter Rang; → *dress circle*. **3.** fig. Kreislauf m, Zyklus m. **II** v/t **4.** umringen. **5.** umkreisen. **6.** einkreisen, umzingeln. **7.** einringeln. **III** v/i **8.** kreisen (a. ✈), die Runde machen (a. Pokal etc).

cir·cuit ['sɜːkɪt] **I** s **1.** Umfang m, Umkreis m. **2.** Runde f, Rundreise f, -flug m: *make* (od. *do*) *the* (od. *a*) *~ of* die Runde od. e-e Rundreise machen in (dat). **3.** ⚡ Strom-, Schaltkreis m; Schaltung f, Schaltsystem n: → *closed* 1, *integrate* Ia, *short circuit*. **II** v/t **4.** umkreisen. **~ break·er** s ⚡ Unterbrecher m (a. mot.). **~ di·a·gram** s ⚡ Schaltplan m.

cir·cu·i·tous [səˈkjuːɪtəs] adj □ **1.** gewunden (Flußlauf etc). **2.** fig. weitschweifig, umständlich.

cir·cuit train·ing s Sport: Zirkel-, Circuittraining n.

cir·cu·lar ['sɜːkjʊlə] **I** adj □ **1.** (kreis)rund, kreisförmig. **2.** Kreis..., Rund...: *~ letter* → 4a; *~ saw* ⚙ Kreissäge f. **3.** → *circuitous* 2. **II** s **4.** a) Rundschreiben n, -brief m, b) Umlauf m, c) (Post)Wurfsendung f.

cir·cu·late ['sɜːkjʊleɪt] **I** v/i zirkulieren: a) kreisen, b) im Umlauf sein, kursieren (Geld, Nachricht etc). **II** v/t in Umlauf setzen (a. fig.), zirkulieren lassen. **'cir·cu·lat·ing** adj zirkulierend, kursierend: *~ library* Leihbücherei f. **circu·la·tion** s **1.** (physiol. a. Blut)Kreislauf m, Zirkulation f. **2.** ✟ Umlauf m: *bring* (od. *put*) *into ~* in Umlauf setzen (a. fig.); *withdraw from ~* aus dem Verkehr ziehen; *out of ~* außer Kurs (gesetzt). **3.** Auflage f (e-r Zeitung etc).

ˌcir·cu·la·to·ry adj ⚕, physiol. (Blut-)
Kreislauf...: ~ **collapse** Kreislaufkol-
laps m; ~ **disturbances** pl Kreislaufstö-
rungen pl; ~ **system** Kreislauf m.

cir·cum·cise ['sɜːkəmsaɪz] v/t ⚕, eccl.
beschneiden. **cir·cum·ci·sion** [ˌ~'sɪʒn] s
Beschneidung f.

cir·cum·fer·ence [səˈkʌmfərəns] s ▲
Umfang m.

cir·cum·lo·cu·tion [ˌsɜːkəmləˈkjuːʃn] s **1.**
Umschreibung f. **2.** Umschweife pl;
Weitschweifigkeit f.

cir·cum·nav·i·gate [ˌsɜːkəmˈnævɪɡeɪt]
v/t umschiffen, umsegeln. **'cir·cum-
ˌnav·i·ga·tion** s Umschiffung f, Um-
seg(e)lung f: ~ **of the globe** Weltumseg-
lung.

cir·cum·scribe ['sɜːkəmskraɪb] v/t **1.** begrenzen, einschränken. **2.** umschreiben
(a. ▲); definieren.

cir·cum·scrip·tion [ˌ~'skrɪpʃn] s **1.** Begrenzung f, Einschränkung f. **2.** Umschreibung f. **3.** Umschrift f (e-r Münze
etc).

cir·cum·spect ['sɜːkəmspekt] adj □ **1.**
umsichtig. **2.** vorsichtig. **cir·cum-
spec·tion** [ˌ~'spekʃn] s **1.** Umsicht f. **2.**
Vorsicht f.

cir·cum·stance ['sɜːkəmstəns] s **1.** Umstand m. **2.** mst pl (Sach)Lage f, Umstände pl: **in** (od. **under**) **no** ~**s** unter
keinen Umständen, auf keinen Fall; **in**
(od. **under**) **the** ~**s** unter diesen Umständen. **3.** pl Verhältnisse pl: **live in
easy** ~**s** in gesicherten Verhältnissen
leben. **cir·cum·stan·tial** [ˌ~'stænʃl] adj
□ **1.** umstandsbedingt. **2.** ausführlich.
3. umständlich. **4.** ~ **evidence** 🕸 Indi-
zienbeweis m. **5.** nebensächlich.

cir·cus ['sɜːkəs] s **1.** Zirkus m. **2.** Br.
runder, von Häusern umschlossener
Platz.

cir·rho·sis [sɪˈrəʊsɪs] s ⚕ Zirrhose f.

cir·rus ['sɪrəs] pl -**ri** [ˌ~raɪ] s meteor. Zir-
rus-, Federwolke f.

cis·sy → **sissy**.

cis·tern ['sɪstən] s **1.** Wasserbehälter m,
(in Toilette) Spülkasten m. **2.** Zisterne f.

cit·a·del ['sɪtədəl] s ✕ Zitadelle f.

ci·ta·tion [saɪˈteɪʃn] s **1.** Zitieren n; Zitat
n. **2.** 🕸 Vorladung f. **3.** ✕ lobende
Erwähnung f.

cite [saɪt] v/t **1.** zitieren. **2.** 🕸 vorladen.
3. ✕ lobend erwähnen.

cit·i·zen ['sɪtɪzn] s **1.** Bürger(in). **2.** Städ-
ter(in). **3.** Staatsangehörige m, f.
'cit·i·zen·ship s Staatsangehörigkeit f.

cit·ric ac·id ['sɪtrɪk] s ⚗ Zitronensäure f.

cit·rus ['sɪtrəs] s ♀ Zitrusgewächs n. ~
fruit s Zitrusfrucht f.

cit·y ['sɪtɪ] s (Groß)Stadt f: **the** ⚷ die
(Londoner) City. ~ **cen·tre** s Br. Innenstadt f, City f. ~ **fa·thers** s pl Stadtväter
pl. ~ **hall** s Rathaus n. ~ **plan·ning** s
Stadtplanung f. ~ **state** s Stadtstaat n.

civ·ic ['sɪvɪk] **I** adj (**~ally**) **1.** → **civil** 2. **2.**
städtisch, Stadt... **II** s pl (sg konstruiert)
Staatsbürgerkunde f.

civ·il ['sɪvl] adj □ **1.** staatlich, Staats... **2.**
(a. staats)bürgerlich, Bürger... **3.** zivil,
Zivil... (Ggs. militärisch, kirchlich etc):
~ **aviation** Zivilluftfahrt f; ~ **marriage**
standesamtliche Trauung. **4.** höflich. **5.**
🕸 zivilrechtlich: ~ **case** (od. **suit**) Zivil-
prozeß m. ~ **en·gi·neer** s Bauingenieur
m.

ci·vil·ian [sɪˈvɪljən] **I** s Zivilist m. **II** adj
zivil, Zivil...

civ·i·li·za·tion [ˌsɪvɪlaɪˈzeɪʃn] s Zivilisation f, Kultur f: **disease of a** ~ Zivili-
sationskrankheit f. **'civ·i·lize** v/t zivilisieren: ~**d nations** pl Kulturvölker pl.

civ·il law s **1.** römisches Recht. **2.** Zivil-
recht n, bürgerliches Recht. ~ **rights**
s pl bürgerliche Ehrenrechte pl,
(Staats)Bürgerrechte pl: ~ **activist** Bür-
gerrechtler(in); ~ **movement** Bürgerrechtsbewegung f. ~ **ser·vant** s Staats-
beamte m. ~ **ser·vice** s Staatsdienst m.
~ **war** s Bürgerkrieg m.

clack [klæk] **I** v/i **1.** klappern. **2.** plappern. **II** s **3.** Klappern n. **4.** Geplapper n.

clad [klæd] **I** pret u. pp von **clothe**. **II** adj
gekleidet.

claim [kleɪm] **I** v/t **1.** verlangen, a. Todes-
opfer etc fordern: ~ **back** zurückfor-
dern. **2.** in Anspruch nehmen, (er)for-
dern. **3.** behaupten (**s.th.** et.; **that** daß);
(von sich) behaupten (**to be** zu sein),
Anspruch erheben auf (acc); aufweisen
(können), haben; sich bekennen zu
(e-m Terroranschlag etc). **II** s **4.** Forderung f (**on, against** gegen): **make a** ~
e-e Forderung erheben. **5.** Anrecht n
(**to** auf acc): ~ **for damages** Schadener-

satzanspruch *m*. **6.** Behauptung *f*.
'**claim·ant** *s* **1.** Antragsteller(in): *right·ful* ~ Anspruchsberechtigte *m, f*. **2.** Anwärter(in) (*to* auf *acc*).

clair·voy·ance [kleə'vɔɪəns] *s* Hellsehen *n*. **clair·voy·ant I** *adj* hellseherisch. **II** *s* Hellseher(in).

clam [klæm] *s zo.* eßbare Muschel: *hard* (*od. round*) ~ Venusmuschel.

clam·ber ['klæmbə] **I** *v/i* (mühsam) klettern. **II** *v/t* erklettern.

clam·my ['klæmɪ] *adj* □ feuchtkalt, klamm.

clam·or·ous ['klæmərəs] *adj* □ **1.** lärmend. **2.** *fig.* lautstark (*Forderungen etc*) '**clam·o(u)r I** *s* **1.** Lärm *m*, Geschrei *n*. **2.** *fig.* lautstarker Protest (*against* gegen), fordernder Schrei (*for* nach). **II** *v/i* **3.** lärmen, schreien. **4.** *fig.* lautstark protestieren (*against* gegen), lautstark verlangen (*for* nach).

clamp [klæmp] **I** *s* ⊕ Klemme *f*, Klammer *f*. **II** *v/t* festklemmen, mit Klammern befestigen. **III** *v/i*: ~ *down* F scharf vorgehen (*on* gegen).

clan [klæn] *s* **1.** Clan *m*: a) *schott.* Stamm *m*, b) *allg.* Sippe *f*, Geschlecht *n*. **2.** Gruppe *f, bsd. contp.* Clique *f*.

clan·des·tine [klæn'destɪn] *adj* □ heimlich, verstohlen.

clang [klæŋ] **I** *v/i* klingen, klirren. **II** *v/t* erklingen lassen. **III** *s* Klang *m*, Geklirr *n*. '**clang·er** *s*: *drop a* ~ *Br.* F ins Fettnäpfchen treten. **clang·or·ous** ['klæŋgərəs] *adj* □ klirrend.

clang·o(u)r ['klæŋə] → **clang** III.

clank [klæŋk] **I** *v/i u. v/t* klirren *od.* rasseln (mit). **II** *s* Geklirr *n*, Gerassel *n*.

clap¹ [klæp] **I** *s* **1.** (*a.* Hände-, Beifall)Klatschen *n*. **2.** Klaps *m*. **3.** Krachen *n*: ~ *of thunder* Donnerschlag *m*. **II** *v/t* **4.** zs.-schlagen: ~ *one's hands* in die Hände klatschen. **5.** *j-m* Beifall klatschen, applaudieren, *a. et.* beklatschen. **6.** *j-m auf die Schulter etc* klopfen. **III** *v/i* **7.** klatschen. **8.** (Beifall) klatschen, applaudieren.

clap² [~] *s ⚕ sl.* Tripper *m*.

clap·per ['klæpə] *s* **1.** Klöppel *m* (*e-r Glocke*). **2.** Klapper *f*.

'**clap·trap** *s* F **1.** Effekthascherei *f*. **2.** Gewäsch *n*.

clar·et ['klærət] *s* roter Bordeaux(wein); *allg.* Rotwein *m*.

clar·i·fi·ca·tion [‚klærɪfɪ'keɪʃn] *s* **1.** (Auf)Klärung *f*, Klarstellung *f*. **2.** ⊕ (Abwasser)Klärung *f*, Abklärung *f*: ~ *plant* Kläranlage *f*. **clar·i·fy** ['~faɪ] **I** *v/t* **1.** (auf)klären, klarstellen. **2.** ⊕ (ab)klären. **II** *v/i* **3.** sich (auf)klären, klar werden. **4.** sich abklären.

clar·i·net [‚klærə'net] *s ♪* Klarinette *f*. ‚**clar·i'net·(t)ist** *s* Klarinettist *m*.

clar·i·ty ['klærətɪ] *s* Klarheit *f*.

clash [klæʃ] **I** *v/i* **1.** prallen, stoßen (*into* gegen), (*a. feindlich*) zs.-prallen, -stoßen (*with* mit). **2.** *fig.* kollidieren: a) im Widerspruch stehen (zu), unvereinbar sein (mit), b) (zeitlich) zs.-fallen (mit). **3.** nicht zs.-passen (*with* mit), (*Farben a.*) sich beißen. **II** *s* **4.** (*a. feindlicher*) Zs.-prall *od.* -stoß, Kollision *f* (*a. fig.*): ~ *of interests* Interessenkollision. **5.** *fig.* Widerspruch *m*. **6.** (zeitliches) Zs.-fallen.

clasp [klɑːsp] **I** *v/t* **1.** ein-, zuhaken, zu-, festschnallen. **2.** ergreifen, umklammern: ~ *s.o.'s hand* j-m die Hand drükken; *j-s hand* umklammern; ~ *one's hands* die Hände falten. **II** *s* **3.** Haken *m*, Schnalle *f*; Schloß *n*, Schließe *f* (*e-r Handtasche etc*). **4.** Umklammerung *f*: *by* ~ *of hands* durch Händedruck *od.* Handschlag. ~ *knife s* (*irr knife*) Klapp-, Taschenmesser *n*.

class [klɑːs] **I** *s* **1.** Klasse *f* (*a.* 🚂, *biol. etc*). **2.** (Wert-, Güte)Klasse; *eng S.* F Klasse *f* (*Erstklassigkeit*): *in the same* ~ *with* gleichwertig mit; *in a* ~ *by o.s.* (*od. of one's own*) e-e Klasse für sich; *have* ~ F (große) Klasse sein. **3.** gesellschaftlicher Rang, soziale Stellung; (Gesellschafts)Klasse *f*, (Bevölkerungs)Schicht *f*. **4.** *ped.* (Schul)Klasse *f*; (Unterrichts)Stunde *f*: *attend* ~*es* am Unterricht teilnehmen. **II** *v/t* **5.** klassifizieren: ~ *with* gleichstellen mit; ~ *as* ansehen *od.* betrachten als. ~ **con·flict** *s* Klassenkonflikt *m*. '~**con·scious** *adj* klassenbewußt. ~ **dis·tinc·tion** *s* Klassenunterschied *m*. '~**fel·low** *s* Klassenkamerad(in), Mitschüler(in). ~ **ha·tred** *s* Klassenhaß *m*. ~ **hour** *s ped.* Unterrichtsstunde *f*.

clas·sic ['klæsɪk] **I** *adj* (~*ally*) **1.** klassisch, vollendet: ~ *example* klassisches Beispiel. **2.** klassisch: a) *das klassische Altertum betreffend*, b) *die klassische*

Literatur etc betreffend. **3.** klassisch: a) herkömmlich, b) typisch, c) zeitlos. **II** *s* **4.** Klassiker *m (Person u. Werk).* **5.** *pl* Altphilologie *f.* **clas·si·cal** [ˈ⁓kl] *adj* □ **1.** → **classic** I. **2.** klassisch: a) humanistisch (gebildet), b) *die klassische Kunst od. Literatur etc betreffend:* ⁓ **education** humanistische Bildung; **the ⁓ languages** die alten Sprachen; ⁓ **scholar** Altphilologe *m.* **3.** klassisch *(Musik).*

clas·si·fi·ca·tion [ˌklæsɪfɪˈkeɪʃn] *s* Klassifikation *f,* Klassifizierung *f.* **clas·si·fied** [ˈ⁓faɪd] *adj* **1.** klassifiziert: ⁓ **ad(vertisement)** Kleinanzeige *f;* ⁓ **directory** Branchenverzeichnis *n.* **2.** ✕, *pol.* geheim. **clas·si·fy** [ˈ⁓faɪ] *v/t* **1.** klassifizieren. **2.** ✕, *pol.* für geheim erklären.

class|**·less** [ˈklɑːslɪs] *adj* klassenlos *(Gesellschaft).* '⁓**mate** → **classfellow.** ⁓**room** [ˈ⁓rʊm] *s* Klassenzimmer *n.* ⁓ **strug·gle,** ⁓ **war** *s* Klassenkampf *m.* **class·y** [ˈklɑːsɪ] *adj* F Klasse, Klasse...

clat·ter [ˈklætə] **I** *v/i* **1.** klappern, rasseln. **2.** poltern: ⁓ **about** *(od. around)* herumtrampeln. **II** *v/t* **3.** klappern *od.* rasseln mit. **III** *s* **4.** Geklapper *n,* Gerassel *n.*

clause [klɔːz] *s* **1.** *ling.* Satz(teil) *m.* **2.** ⚖ Klausel *f;* Abschnitt *m,* Absatz *m.*

claus·tro·pho·bi·a [ˌklɔːstrəˈfəʊbjə] *s* 🏥 Klaustrophobie *f,* Platzangst *f.*

clav·i·cle [ˈklævɪkl] *s anat.* Schlüsselbein *n.*

claw [klɔː] **I** *s* **1.** Klaue *f,* Kralle *f (beide a.* ⚙ *u. fig.),* Schere *f (e-s Krebses etc).* **II** *v/t* **2.** zerkratzen. **3.** umkrallen, packen. **III** *v/i* **4.** kratzen. **5.** reißen, zerren *(at an dat).* **6.** greifen *(at, for* nach).

clay [kleɪ] *s* Ton *m,* Lehm *m:* ⁓ **pigeon** *(Sport)* Ton-, Wurftaube *f.* **clay·ey** [ˈ⁓ɪ] *adj* Ton..., Lehm...

clean [kliːn] **I** *adj* □ **1.** rein, sauber: → **breast** I, **heel²** 1, **sweep** 1. **2.** sauber, frisch (gewaschen). **3.** unvermischt, rein. **4.** makellos *(a. fig.):* ⁓ **record** tadellose Vergangenheit. **5.** anständig, sauber: → **living!** bes. **6.** glatt *(Schnitt, Bruch).* **7.** *sl.* clean *(nicht mehr drogenabhängig).* **8.** *sl.* sauber *(unbewaffnet).* **II** *adv* **9.** rein, sauber: **sweep** ⁓ rein ausfegen; → **broom.** **10.** völlig, total. **III** *v/t* **11.** reinigen, säubern, putzen: ⁓ **down** *(od. up)* gründlich reini-

gen. ⁓**'cut** *adj* klar (umrissen), deutlich.

clean·er [ˈkliːnə] *s* **1.** *pl* Reinigung(sanstalt) *f:* **take to the ⁓s** zur Reinigung bringen; F *j-n* ausnehmen. **2.** Rein(e)-machefrau *f,* *(Fenster- etc)*Putzer *m.* **'clean·ing I** *s:* **do the** ⁓ saubermachen, putzen. **II** *adj* Reinigungs...: ⁓ **cloth;** ⁓ **woman** *(od. lady)* Rein(e)machefrau *f.* **clean·li·ness** [ˈklenlɪnɪs] *s* Reinlichkeit *f.* '**clean·ly** *adj* reinlich: a) sauber, b) sauberkeitsliebend.

clean·ness [ˈkliːnnɪs] *s* Reinheit *f,* Sauberkeit *f.*

cleanse [klenz] *v/t* reinigen, säubern, reinwaschen *(from, of* von) *(alle a. fig.).* '**cleans·er** *s* Reinigungsmittel *n.*

ˌ**clean·'shav·en** *adj* glattrasiert.

clear [klɪə] **I** *adj* □ (→ *clearly*) **1.** klar, hell. **2.** klar, heiter *(Wetter etc).* **3.** rein, hell *(Stimme etc).* **4.** klar, verständlich, deutlich: **make s.th.** ⁓ **(to s.o.)** (j-m) et. klarmachen; **make o.s.** ⁓ sich klar ausdrücken, sich verständlich machen. **5.** klar, unvermischt: ⁓ **soup** *gastr.* klare Suppe. **6.** deutlich, scharf *(Foto, Umrisse etc).* **7.** klar, offensichtlich: **a** ⁓ **win** ein klarer Sieg; **for no** ⁓ **reason** ohne ersichtlichen Grund. **8.** klar: a) sicher, b) in Ordnung. **9.** frei *(of* von) *(a. fig.):* ⁓ **of snow** *(debt)* schneefrei (schuldenfrei); **a** ⁓ **conscience** ein reines Gewissen. **10.** ♣ Netto..., Rein...: ⁓ **gain** *(od. profit)* Reingewinn *m.* **II** *adv* **11.** hell, klar. **12.** klar, deutlich: **speak** ⁓. **13.** los, weg *(of* von): **keep** ⁓ **of** sich fernhalten von, meiden; **get** ⁓ **of** loskommen von; **stand** ⁓ **of** Tür etc freihalten. **III** *v/t* **14.** oft ⁓ **away** wegräumen *(from* von), *Geschirr* abräumen. **15.** *Straße etc* freimachen, *Saal etc* räumen. **16.** reinigen, säubern: ⁓ **one's throat** sich räuspern. **17.** frei-, lossprechen *(of* von), *Gewissen* entlasten, *Namen* reinwaschen. **18.** *Verbrechen etc* (auf)klären. **IV** *v/i* **19.** klar *od.* hell werden. **20.** aufklaren *(Wetter).* **21.** *oft* ⁓ **away** sich verziehen *(Nebel etc).* '**clear·ance** *s* Räumung *f:* ⁓ **sale** Räumungs-, Ausverkauf *m.* ˌ**clear**|'**cut** *adj* **1.** scharfgeschnitten. **2.** *fig.* klar, deutlich. ˌ⁓'**head·ed** *adj* klardenkend, intelligent.

clear·ly [ˈklɪəlɪ] *adv* **1.** klar, deutlich. **2.**

offensichtlich. **'clear·ness** *s* **1.** Klarheit *f*. **2.** Reinheit *f*. **3.** Schärfe *f*.

cleav·age ['kli:vɪdʒ] *s* **1.** Spaltung *f*. **2.** Spalt *m*.

cleave [kli:v] (*mst irr*) *v/t* **1.** (zer)spalten. **2.** Luft, Wasser etc durchschneiden. **3.** Weg bahnen.

clef [klef] *s* ♪ (Noten)Schlüssel *m*.

cleft [kleft] **I** *pret u. pp von* **cleave**. **II** *s* **1.** Spalt *m*, Spalte *f*. **2.** *fig.* Kluft *f*. **~ pal·ate** *s* 🦷 Wolfsrachen *m*. **~ stick** *s*: **be in a ~** in der Klemme sitzen *od.* stecken.

clem·en·cy ['klemənsɪ] *s* Milde *f*, Nachsicht *f*. **'clem·ent** *adj* □ mild (*a. Wetter*), nachsichtig.

clench [klentʃ] *v/t* **1.** zs.-pressen, Faust ballen, Zähne zs.-beißen. **2.** fest packen *od.* anfassen.

cler·gy ['klɜːdʒɪ] *s eccl.* Klerus *m*, die Geistlichen *pl*. **~man** ['~mən] *s* (*irr man*) Geistlicher *m*.

cler·i·cal ['klerɪkl] *adj* □ **1.** klerikal, geistlich. **2.** Schreib..., Büro...: **~ error** Schreibfehler *m*; **~ work** Büroarbeit *f*.

clerk [klɑːk] *s* **1.** Schriftführer *m*, Sekretär *m*. **2.** (*Büro- etc*)Angestellte *m*, *f*, (*Bank- etc*)Beamte *m*, (-)Beamtin *f*. **3.** *Am.* Verkäufer(in).

clev·er ['klevə] *adj* □ **1.** clever: a) geschickt, gewandt (*at* in *dat*), b) gerissen, raffiniert (*a. Gerät etc*): **~ dick** *bsd. Br. sl.* Schlaumeier *m*. **2.** gescheit: a) clever, klug, b) geistreich (*Bemerkung etc*). **3.** begabt (*at* in *dat*, für). **'clev·er·ness** *s* **1.** Cleverness *f*. **2.** Gescheitheit *f*.

cli·ché ['kli:ʃeɪ] *s* Klischee *n*, Gemeinplatz *m*.

click [klɪk] **I** *s* **1.** Klicken *n*. **2.** Einschnappen *n*. **3.** ⚙ Sperrklinke *f*, -vorrichtung *f*. **4.** Schnalzer *m*. **II** *v/i* **5.** klicken. **6.** *mit der Zunge* schnalzen. **7.** zu-, einschnappen: **~ shut** ins Schloß fallen. **8.** F einschlagen, Erfolg haben (**with** bei). **9.** F sofort Gefallen aneinander finden; sich sofort ineinander verknallen. **III** *v/t* **10.** klicken *od.* einschnappen lassen: **~ one's heels** die Hacken zs.-schlagen. **11.** **~ glasses** anstoßen. **12.** mit *der Zunge* schnalzen.

cli·ent ['klaɪənt] *s* **1.** ⚖ Klient(in), Mandant(in). **2.** Kunde *m*, Kundin *f*. **cli·en·tele** [,kli:ən'tel] *s* **1.** ⚖ Klientel *f*, Klienten *pl*. **2.** Kundschaft *f*, Kunden *pl*.

cliff [klɪf] *s* **1.** Klippe *f*, Felsen *m*. **2.** steiler Abhang. **'~·hang·er** *s* **1.** spannender Fortsetzungsroman (*der immer im spannendsten Moment aufhört*); (*Rundfunk, TV*) spannender Mehrteiler. **2.** *fig.* spannende Sache.

cli·mac·ter·ic [klaɪ'mæktərɪk] *s physiol.* Wechseljahre *pl*.

cli·mate ['klaɪmɪt] *s* Klima *n*, *fig. a.* Atmosphäre *f*. **cli·mat·ic** [~'mætɪk] *adj* (**~ally**) klimatisch, Klima...

cli·max ['klaɪmæks] **I** *s* Höhepunkt *m*, *physiol. a.* Orgasmus *m*. **II** *v/t* den Höhepunkt bringen. **III** *v/i* den Höhepunkt erreichen.

climb [klaɪm] **I** *s* **1.** Aufstieg *m*, Besteigung *f*. **2.** Berg-, Klettertour *f*. **II** *v/i* **3.** klettern: **~ up (down) a tree** auf e-n Baum klettern (von e-m Baum herunterklettern). **4.** (auf-, empor)steigen. **5.** (an)steigen (*Straße etc*). **III** *v/t* **6.** er-, besteigen, erklettern, klettern auf (*acc*).

clinch [klɪntʃ] **I** *v/t* **1.** Spiel etc entscheiden: **that ~ed it** damit war die Sache entschieden. **2.** ⚙ sicher befestigen; (ver)nieten. **3.** Boxen: umklammern. **II** *v/i* **4.** Boxen: clinchen. **III** *s* **5.** ⚙ Vernietung *f*. **6.** Boxen: Clinch *m* (*a. sl. Umarmung*).

cling [klɪŋ] *v/i* (*irr*) **1.** kleben, haften (**to** an *dat*): **~ together** zs.-halten (*a. fig.*). **2.** *a. fig.* (**to**) hängen (an *dat*), anhaften (*dat*). **3.** *a. fig.* (**to**) sich klammern (an *acc*), festhalten (an *dat*). **4.** sich (an-)schmiegen (**to** an *acc*). **~ film** *s* Frischhaltefolie *f*.

clin·ic ['klɪnɪk] *s* Klinik *f*. **clin·i·cal** [~kl] *adj* □ klinisch: **~ death**; **~ thermometer** Fieberthermometer *n*.

clink¹ [klɪŋk] **I** *v/i* klingen, klirren. **II** *v/t* klingen *od.* klirren lassen: **~ glasses** anstoßen. **III** *s* Klingen *n*, Klirren *n*.

clink² [~] *s sl.* Kittchen *n*: **in ~** im Knast.

clip¹ [klɪp] **I** *v/t* **1.** (be)schneiden, stutzen (*a. fig.*). **2.** *fig.* kürzen, beschneiden. **3.** *a.* **~ off** abschneiden. **4.** *aus der Zeitung* ausschneiden. **5.** Haare schneiden. **6.** Schaf etc scheren. **7.** Fahrschein etc lochen. **8.** Silben verschlucken. **9.** F *j-m* e-n Schlag verpassen. **10.** *sl. j-n* erleichtern (*for um Geld*); *j-n* neppen. **II** *s* **11.** Haarschnitt *m*. **12.** Schur *f*.

clip² [~] **I** *v/t a.* **~ on** anklammern. **II** *s* (Heft-, Büro- etc)Klammer *f*.

clip joint s sl. Nepplokal n.

clip·pers ['klɪpəz] s pl, a. **pair of ~** (Nagel- etc)Schere f, Haarschneidemaschine f.

'clip·ping s **1.** bsd. Am. (Zeitungs)Ausschnitt m. **2.** pl Schnitzel pl, Abfälle pl.

clique [kliːk] s Clique f, Klüngel m.

clit·o·ris ['klɪtərɪs] s anat. Kitzler m.

cloak [kləʊk] **I** s (loser) Mantel, Umhang m: **under the ~ of** fig. unter dem Deckmantel der Freundschaft etc, im Schutz der Dunkelheit etc. **II** v/t fig. bemänteln, verhüllen. **~·room** ['~rʊm] s **1.** Garderobe f: **~ attendant** Garderobenfrau f; **~ ticket** (bsd. Am. **check**) Garderobenmarke f, -zettel m. **2.** Br. Toilette f.

clob·ber¹ ['klɒbə] s Br. sl. Klamotten pl; Plunder m, Kram m.

clob·ber² [~] v/t sl. **1.** zs.-schlagen. **2.** Sport: überfahren (hoch besiegen).

clock [klɒk] s **1.** (Wand-, Turm-, Stand)Uhr f: (a)**round the ~** rund um die Uhr, 24 Stunden (lang); **five o'~** 5 Uhr; **put** (od. **turn**) **the ~ back** fig. das Rad der Zeit zurückdrehen. **2.** F Kontroll-, Stoppuhr f; Fahrpreisanzeiger m (Taxi). **II** v/t **3.** bsd. Sport: (ab)stoppen: **~ (up)** Zeit erreichen f über e-e Distanz). **III** v/i **4. ~ in (out)** einstempeln (ausstempeln). **~ card** s Steckkarte f. **'~·face** s Zifferblatt n. **~ ra·di·o** s Radiowecker m. **'~·wise** adj u. adv im Uhrzeigersinn. **'~·work** s Uhrwerk n: **like ~** wie am Schnürchen, wie geschmiert.

clod [klɒd] s **1.** (Erd)Klumpen m. **2.** Trottel m.

clog [klɒg] **I** s **1.** (Holz)Klotz m. **2.** fig. Hemmschuh m, Klotz m am Bein. **3.** Holzschuh m. **II** v/t **4.** (be)hindern, hemmen. **5.** a. **~ up** verstopfen. **III** v/i **6.** sich verstopfen.

clois·ter ['klɔɪstə] s **1.** Kloster n. **2.** △ Kreuzgang m.

close [kləʊs] **I** adj [kləʊs] ☐ **1.** geschlossen. **2.** verschlossen, verschwiegen. **3.** eng(anliegend). **4.** nah: **~ fight** Handgemenge n, weitS. zähes Ringen; **~ to tears** den Tränen nahe. **5.** eng (Freund); nah (Verwandter). **6.** knapp (Sieg etc): → **shave** 5. **7.** gespannt (Aufmerksamkeit). **8.** gründlich (Untersuchung etc).
II adv [kləʊs] **9.** eng, nahe, dicht: **~ by**

ganz in der Nähe; nahe od. dicht bei; **~ at hand** nahe bevorstehend; **come ~ to** fast ... sein; → **wind¹** 1. **III** s [kləʊz] **10.** Abschluß m: **come** (od. **draw**) **to a ~** sich dem Ende nähern. **IV** v/t [kləʊz] **11.** (ab-, ver-, zu)schließen, zumachen. **12.** Betrieb etc schließen; Straße etc sperren (**to** für). **13.** beenden, beschließen. **V** v/i [kləʊz] **14.** sich schließen (a. Wunde etc). **15.** geschlossen werden. **16.** schließen, zumachen. **17.** enden, aufhören, zu Ende gehen. **18.** schließen (**with the words** mit den Worten). **19.** sich verringern (Abstand etc).
Verbindungen mit Adverbien:

close| down v/t **1.** Betrieb etc schließen, Betrieb stillegen. **II** v/i **2.** schließen, stillgelegt werden. **3.** fig. scharf vorgehen (**on** gegen). **~ in** v/i **1.** sich heranarbeiten (**on** an acc). **2.** kürzer werden (Tage). **3.** hereinbrechen (Dunkelheit, Nacht). **~ up** v/t **1.** → close 11, 12. **2.** abschließen, beenden. **II** v/i **3.** → **close down** 2. **4.** aufschließen, -rücken (Personen).

closed [kləʊzd] adj **1.** geschlossen: **behind ~ doors** hinter verschlossenen Türen; **~ circuit** ⚡ geschlossener Stromkreis; → **book** 1. **2.** gesperrt (**to** für). **'~-down** s Schließung f, Stillegung f. **closed shop** s ✝ gewerkschaftspflichtiger Betrieb.

close·ness ['kləʊsnɪs] s **1.** Nähe f. **2.** Knappheit f. **3.** Gründlichkeit f.

close sea·son s hunt. Schonzeit f.

clos·et ['klɒzɪt] s **1.** (Wand-, Einbau)Schrank m. **2.** Klosett n.

'close-up s phot., Film: Nah-, Großaufnahme f.

clos·ing| date ['kləʊzɪŋ] s letzter Termin (**for** für). **~ time** s Laden-, Geschäftsschluß m; Ende n der Schalterstunden; Polizeistunde f.

clo·sure ['kləʊʒə] s **1.** Schließung f (e-s Betriebs etc). **2.** ⚙ Verschluß m. **3.** Schluß m, Beendigung f (e-r Debatte etc).

clot [klɒt] **I** s **1.** Klumpen m, Klümpchen n: **~ of blood** 🩸 Blutgerinnsel n. **2.** Br. F Trottel m. **II** v/i **3.** gerinnen. **4.** Klumpen bilden.

cloth [klɒθ] s **1.** Tuch n, Stoff m. **2.** Tuch n, Lappen m.

clothe [kləʊð] v/t (a. irr) **1.** (an-, be)kleiden. **2.** einkleiden. **3.** fig. umhüllen, einhüllen.

clothes [kləʊðz] s pl **1.** Kleider pl, Kleidung f: **change one's ~** sich umziehen. **2.** (a. Bett)Wäsche f. **~ bas·ket** s Wäschekorb m. **~ brush** s Kleiderbürste f. **~ hang·er** s Kleiderbügel m. **'~·horse** s Wäscheständer m. **'~·line** s Wäscheleine f. **~ peg** s Br., **'~·pin** s Am. Wäscheklammer f. **~ tree** s Garderoben-, Kleiderständer m.

cloth·ing ['kləʊðɪŋ] s Kleidung f: **~ indus·try** Bekleidungsindustrie f.

cloud [klaʊd] **I** s **1.** Wolke f: **~ of dust** Staubwolke; **have one's head in the ~s** fig. in höheren Regionen schweben; in Gedanken vertieft sein; **be on ~ nine** F im siebten Himmel schweben. **2.** fig. Schatten m: **cast a ~ on** e-n Schatten werfen auf (acc). **II** v/t **3.** be-, umwölken. **4.** fig. verdunkeln, trüben. **III** v/i a. **~ over 5.** sich bewölken. **6.** fig. sich trüben. **~ bank** s Wolkenbank f. **'~·burst** s Wolkenbruch m. **'~·cuck·oo-land** s Wolkenkuckucksheim n.

cloud·less ['klaʊdlɪs] adj □ **1.** wolkenlos. **2.** fig. ungetrübt. **'cloud·y** adj □ **1.** wolkig, bewölkt. **2.** fig. nebelhaft, unklar.

clout [klaʊt] F **I** s **1.** Schlag m: **give s.o. a ~** j-m e-e runterhauen. **2.** bsd. pol. Am. Einfluß m (**with** auf acc). **II** v/t **3.** schlagen: **~ s.o. one** j-m e-e runterhauen.

clove¹ [kləʊv] s (Gewürz)Nelke f.

clove² [~] s: **~ of garlic** Knoblauchzehe f.

clove³ [~] pret von cleave.

clo·ven ['kləʊvn] pp von cleave: **show the ~ foot** (od. hoof) fig. sein wahres Gesicht zeigen.

clo·ver ['kləʊvə] s ♣ Klee m: **be** (od. **live**) **in ~** wie Gott in Frankreich leben. **'~·leaf** s (irr leaf) **1.** Kleeblatt n. **2.** a. **~ intersection** mot. Kleeblatt n.

clown [klaʊn] **I** s Clown m (a. fig.). **II** v/i a. **~ about** (od. around) herumkaspern. **'clown·ish** adj □ clownisch.

club [klʌb] **I** s **1.** Keule f, Knüppel m. **2.** Sport: Schlagholz n; (Golf)Schläger m. **3.** Klub m, Verein m: **join the ~!** bsd. Br. F du auch? **4.** Spielkarten: a) pl Kreuz n, Eichel f (Farbe), b) Kreuz(karte f) n. **II** v/t **5.** einknüppeln auf (acc), (nieder)knüppeln. **6.** sich teilen in (acc); Geld zs.-legen. **III** v/i **7.** mst **~ together** sich zs.-tun: a) e-n Verein etc bilden, b) (Geld) zs.-legen. **~ chair** s Klubsessel m. **'~·foot** s (irr foot) ⚕ Klumpfuß m. **'~·house** s Klub-, Vereinshaus n.

cluck [klʌk] v/i gackern; glucken.

clue [klu:] **I** s **1.** (**to**) Hinweis m (auf acc), Anhaltspunkt m (für), Fingerzeig m. **2.** Schlüssel m (**to** zu e-m Rätsel etc): **I haven't a ~** F ich hab' keinen Schimmer. **II** v/t **3.** **~ in** j-m e-n Hinweis geben. **4.** **~** j-n informieren (**on, about** über acc): **all ~d up** vollkommen im Bild.

clump [klʌmp] **I** s **1.** (Baum-, Häuser)Gruppe f. **2.** (Holz)Klotz m; (Erd etc)Klumpen m. **II** v/i **3.** trampeln: **~ about** (od. around) herumtrampeln. **4.** sich zs.-ballen. **II** v/t **5.** zs.-ballen, anhäufen.

clum·si·ness ['klʌmzɪnɪs] s Plumpheit f. **'clum·sy** adj □ plump: a) ungeschickt, unbeholfen, b) schwerfällig, c) taktlos, d) unförmig.

clung [klʌŋ] pret u. pp von cling.

clus·ter ['klʌstə] **I** s **1.** ♣ Büschel n, Traube f. **2.** Haufen m, Schwarm m, Gruppe f. **II** v/i **3.** e-e Gruppe od. Gruppen bilden, sich versammeln od. drängen (**round** um).

clutch [klʌtʃ] **I** v/t **1.** packen, (er)greifen. **2.** umklammern. **II** v/i **3.** (gierig) greifen (**at** nach): **~ at a straw** ⇒ straw **3.** **I** s **4.** (gieriger) Griff. **5.** zo. Klaue f, Kralle f (beide a. fig.): **in s.o.'s ~es** in j-s Klauen od. Gewalt. **6.** ⊙ Kupplung f: **~ disk** Kupplungsscheibe f; **~ facing** (od. **lining**) Kupplungsbelag m; **~ pedal** Kupplungspedal n.

clut·ter ['klʌtə] **I** v/t **1.** a. **~ up** (unordentlich) vollstopfen. **2.** durcheinanderwerfen, herumstreuen. **II** s **3.** Wirrwarr m, Durcheinander n. **4.** Unordnung f: **in a ~** in Unordnung.

coach [kəʊtʃ] **I** s **1.** Kutsche f. **2.** 🚃 Br. (Personen)Wagen m. **3.** Br. Reisebus m. **4.** Nachhilfe-, Hauslehrer m. **5.** Sport: Trainer m. **II** v/t **6.** j-m Nachhilfeunterricht geben: **~ s.o. in s.th.** j-m et. einpauken. **7.** Sport: trainieren. **'~·man**

['ˌmən] *s* (*irr* **man**) Kutscher *m*. '**ˑwork** *s mot*. Karosserie *f*.

co·ag·u·late [kəʊˈægjʊleɪt] *v/i u. v/t* gerinnen (lassen). **coˌag·u·laˈtion** *s* Gerinnung *f*.

coal [kəʊl] I *s* 1. Kohle *f*; *eng S.* Steinkohle *f*: *carry* (*od. take*) **ˑs to Newcastle** *fig.* Eulen nach Athen tragen; *haul* (*od. drag*) *s.o. over the* **ˑs** *fig.* j-m die Hölle heiß machen.

co·a·li·tion [ˌkəʊəˈlɪʃn] I *s* 1. *pol.* Koalition *f*: *form a* **ˑ** e-e Koalition eingehen *od.* bilden, koalieren. 2. Bündnis *n*, Zs.-schluß *m*. II *adj* 3. *pol.* Koalitions...

coal| **mine**, '**ˑpit** *s* Kohlenbergwerk *n*, -grube *f*, -zeche *f*. **ˑ pow·er sta·tion** *s* Kohlekraftwerk *n*.

coarse [kɔːs] *adj* □ grob: a) rauh, b) grobkörnig, c) *fig.* ungenau, d) *fig.* derb, ungehobelt.

coast [kəʊst] I *s* Küste *f*: *the* **ˑ is clear** *fig.* die Luft ist rein. II *v/i* 2. **ⵜ** die Küste entlangfahren. 3. im Leerlauf (*Auto*) *od.* im Freilauf (*Fahrrad*) fahren. **coast·al** ['ˑtl] *adj* Küsten... '**coast·er** *s* 1. *Am.* Berg-u.-Tal-Bahn *f* (*im Vergnügungspark*). 2. *bes. Am.* Untersatz *m* (*für Gläser etc*).

coast guard *s Br.* Küsten(zoll)wache *f*.

coat [kəʊt] I *s* 1. Jacke *f*, Jackett *n*. 2. Mantel *m*: *turn one's* **ˑ** *fig.* sein Mäntelchen nach dem Wind hängen. 3. *zo.* Pelz *m*, Fell *n*. 4. (*Farb- etc*) Überzug *m*, Anstrich *m*, Schicht *f*. II *v/t* 5. (an)streichen, überstreichen, -ziehen, -schichten. 6. bedecken, umhüllen, umgeben (*with* mit). '**coatˑed** *adj* 1. mit ... überzogen *od.* beschichtet: *sugar-* mit Zuckerüberzug; **ˑ tablet** Dragée *n*. 2. **ⵝ** belegt (*Zunge*).

coat| **hang·er** *s* Kleiderbügel *m*. **ˑ hook** *s* Kleiderhaken *m*.

coat·ing ['kəʊtɪŋ] *s* 1. Mantelstoff *m*. 2. → **coat** 4.

coat of arms *s* Wappen(schild *m*, *n*) *n*.

coax [kəʊks] *v/t* überreden, beschwatzen (*to do*, *into doing* zu tun): **ˑ** *s.th. out of* (*od. from*) *s.o.* j-m et. abschwatzen.

cob [kɒb] *s* Maiskolben *m*.

co·balt [kəʊˈbɔːlt] *s min.* Kobalt *n*: **ˑ** (*blue*) Kobaltblau *n*.

cob·ble¹ ['kɒbl] *s* Kopfstein *m*: **ˑs** *pl* Kopfsteinpflaster *n*. II *v/t* mit Kopf-

steinen pflastern: **ˑd street** Straße *f* mit Kopfsteinpflaster.

cob·ble² [ˈˑ] *v/t* 1. Schuhe flicken. 2. *a.* **ˑ up** zs.-pfuschen, zs.-schustern.

cob·bler ['kɒblə] *s* 1. (Flick)Schuster *m*. 2. Pfuscher *m*.

co·bra ['kəʊbrə] *s zo.* Kobra *f*.

'**cob·web** *s* Spinnwebe *f*, Spinnennetz *n*.

co·cain(e) [kəʊˈkeɪn] *s* Kokain *n*.

cock [kɒk] I *s* 1. *orn.* Hahn *m*. 2. Männchen *n*, Hahn *m* (*von Vögeln*). 3. Wetterhahn *m*. 4. **ˑ of the walk** (*od. roost*) oft *contp.* der Größte. 5. **ⵝ** (*Absperr-, Gewehr- etc*)Hahn *m*. 6. V Schwanz *m* (*Penis*). II *v/t* 7. aufrichten: **ˑ one's ears** die Ohren spitzen; **ˑ one's hat** den Hut schief aufsetzen; → **snook**.

Cock·aigne [kɒˈkeɪn] *s* Schlaraffenland *n*.

ˌ**cock-and-'bull sto·ry** *s* F Ammenmärchen *n*.

cock·a·too [ˌkɒkəˈtuː] *s orn.* Kakadu *m*.

'**cock**ˌ**chaf·er** *s zo.* Maikäfer *m*.

cocked hat [kɒkt] *s* Dreispitz *m*: *knock* (*od. beat*) *into a* **ˑ** *sl.* j-n, et. weit in den Schatten stellen; *Plan etc* völlig über den Haufen werfen.

cock·er¹ ['kɒkə] → **cocker spaniel**.

cock·er² [ˈˑ] *v/t* verhätscheln, verwöhnen: **ˑ up** aufpäppeln.

cock·er span·iel *s zo.* Cockerspaniel *m*.

'**cock**|-**eyed** *adj* F 1. schielend: *be* **ˑ** schielen. 2. blau (*betrunken*). '**ˑfight**, '**ˑfightˑing** *s* Hahnenkampf *m*.

cock·ney ['kɒknɪ] *s* 1. Cockney *m*, waschechter Londoner. 2. Cockney-(dialekt *m*) *n*. '**cock·ney·ism** *s* Cockneyausdruck *m*.

'**cock**|**pit** *s* 1. **ⵝ**, **ⵜ** Cockpit *n* (*a. e-s Rennwagens*). 2. Hahnenkampfplatz *m*. '**ˑroach** *s zo.* (Küchen)Schabe *f*. ˌ**ˑsure** *adj* □ 1. vollkommen überzeugt (*of*, *about* von), ganz sicher. 2. übertrieben selbstsicher. '**ˑtail** *s* Cocktail *m*.

cock·y ['kɒkɪ] *adj* □ F großspurig, anmaßend.

co·co ['kəʊkəʊ] I *pl* **-cos** **ⵯ** Kokospalme *f*; Kokosnuß *f*. II *adj* Kokos...: **ˑ matting** Kokosmatte *f*.

co·coa ['kəʊkəʊ] *s* Kakao(pulver *n*) *m*.

co·co·nut ['kəʊkənʌt] *s* Kokosnuß *f*. ~ **palm** *s* ❀ Kokospalme *f*.

co·coon [kə'ku:n] *s zo.* Kokon *m*, Puppe *f* (*der Seidenraupe*).

cod [kɒd] *s ichth.* Kabeljau *m*, Dorsch *m*.

cod·dle ['kɒdl] *v/t* verhätscheln, verzärteln: ~ *up* aufpäppeln.

code [kəʊd] **I** *s* **1.** Kodex *m*: a) ⚖ Gesetzbuch *n*, b) Regeln *pl*: ~ *of hono(u)r* Ehrenkodex; → *moral* **4. 2.** (Telegramm)Schlüssel *m*. **3.** Code *m*; Chiffre *f*; Code *m*, Schlüssel *m*: ~ *number* Code-, Kennziffer *f*; ~ *word* Code-, Schlüsselwort *n*. **II** *v/t* **4.** verschlüsseln, chiffrieren.

'**cod·fish** → *cod*.

cod·i·fy ['kəʊdɪfaɪ] *v/t* ⚖ kodifizieren.

'**cod·,liv·er oil** *s* Lebertran *m*.

co·ed [,kəʊ'ed] *ped.* F **I** *s* **1.** *Am.* Studentin *f od.* Schülerin *f* e-r gemischten Schule. **2.** *Br.* gemischte Schule. **II** *adj* **3.** gemischt.

co·ed·u·ca·tion [,kəʊedjʊ'keɪʃn] *s ped.* Gemeinschaftserziehung *f*. **,co·ed·u-'ca·tion·al** [~ʃənl] *adj*: ~ *school* gemischte Schule; ~ *teaching* → *coeducation*.

co·ef·fi·cient [,kəʊɪ'fɪʃnt] *s* ℝ, *phys.* Koeffizient *m*.

co·erce [kəʊ'ɜːs] *v/t* **1.** zwingen (*into* zu). **2.** erzwingen. **co·er·cion** [~ʃn] *s* Zwang *m*: *by* ~ → *coercively*. **co·er·cive** [~sɪv] *adj* **1.** Zwangs..., zwingend: ~ *measure* Zwangsmaßnahme *f*. **2.** überzeugend, zwingend (*Gründe etc*). **co·er·cive·ly** *adv* durch Zwang, zwangsweise.

co·ex·ist [,kəʊɪg'zɪst] *v/i* gleichzeitig *od.* nebeneinander bestehen *od.* leben. **,co·ex·ist·ence** *s* Koexistenz *f*: *peaceful* ~ *pol.* friedliche Koexistenz. **,co-ex·ist·ent** *adj* gleichzeitig *od.* nebeneinander bestehend.

cof·fee ['kɒfɪ] *s* Kaffee *m*. ~ *bar s Br.* Café *n*; Imbißstube *f*. ~ *bean s* Kaffeebohne *f*. ~ *break s* Kaffeepause *f*. ~ *cup s* Kaffeetasse *f*. ~ *grind·er s* Kaffeemühle *f*. ~ *grounds s pl* Kaffeesatz *m*. '~·*house s* Kaffeehaus *n*, Café *n*. ~ *ma·chine s* Kaffeeautomat *m*. '~·,*mak·er s* Kaffeemaschine *f*. ~ *mill s* Kaffeemühle *f*. '~·*pot s* Kaffeekanne *f*. ~ *set s* Kaffeeservice *n*. '~·*shop Am.* → *coffee bar*. ~ *ta·ble s* Couchtisch *m*.

cof·fin ['kɒfɪn] *s* Sarg *m*.

cog [kɒg] *s* ❂ (Rad)Zahn *m*; Zahnrad *n*: *be just a* ~ *in the machine* (*od. wheel*) *fig.* nur ein Rädchen im Getriebe sein.

co·gent ['kəʊdʒənt] *adj* □ zwingend, überzeugend (*Gründe etc*).

cogged [kɒgd] *adj* ❂ gezahnt.

cog·i·tate ['kɒdʒɪteɪt] **I** *v/t* nachdenken über (*acc*). **II** *v/i* (nach)denken: ~ *on* (*od. about*) → I.

cog·nate ['kɒgneɪt] *adj* **1.** (bluts)verwandt (*with* mit). **2.** *fig.* (art)verwandt (*with* mit).

cog·ni·tion [kɒg'nɪʃn] *s* Erkenntnis *f*.

cog·ni·zance ['kɒgnɪzəns] *s* **1.** Kenntnis *f*: *have* (*take*) ~ *of s.th.* von et. Kenntnis haben (nehmen). **2.** ⚖ Zuständigkeit *f*: *have* ~ *over* zuständig sein für (*a. weitS*). '**cog·ni·zant** *adj* unterrichtet (*of* über *acc od.* von): *be* ~ *of s.th.* a. von et. Kenntnis haben.

cog·no·men [kɒg'nəʊmen] *pl* **-mens**, **-nom·i·na** [~'nɒmɪnə] *s* **1.** Familien-, Zuname *m*. **2.** Spitz-, Beiname *m*.

'**cog·wheel** *s* ❂ Zahnrad *n*.

co·hab·it [kəʊ'hæbɪt] *v/i* (*unverheiratet*) zs.-leben. **,co·hab·i'ta·tion** *s* Zs.-leben *n*.

co·here [kəʊ'hɪə] *v/i* zs.-hängen (*a. fig*.). **co'her·ence**, **co'her·en·cy** *s* **1.** Zs.-halt *m* (*a. fig*.). **2.** *phys.* Kohärenz *f*. **3.** *fig.* Zs.-hang *m*. **co'her·ent** *adj* □ **1.** zs.-hängend (*a. fig*.). **2.** *phys.* kohärent.

co·he·sion [kəʊ'hi:ʒn] *s* **1.** Zs.-halt *m* (*a. fig*.). **2.** *phys.* Kohäsion *f*. **co'he·sive** *adj* □ **1.** (fest) zs.-haltend (*a. fig*.). **2.** *phys.* Kohäsions..., Binde...

coil [kɔɪl] **I** *v/t* **1.** *a.* ~ *up* aufrollen, (auf)wickeln. **2.** ⚡ wickeln. **II** *v/i* **3.** *a.* ~ *up* sich zs.-rollen. **III** *s* **4.** Spirale *f* (*a.* ❂ *u.* ❀). **5.** Rolle *f*, Spule *f*.

coin [kɔɪn] **I** *s* Münze *f*: *pay s.o. back in his own* (*od. in the same*) ~ *fig.* es j-m mit *od.* in gleicher Münze heimzahlen; *the other side of the* ~ *fig.* die Kehrseite der Medaille. **II** *v/t* Münzen, *fig. Wort etc* prägen: ~ *money* F Geld wie Heu verdienen. '**coin·age** *s* **1.** Prägen *n*. **2.** *coll.* Münzen *pl*. **3.** *fig.* Prägung *f* (*e-s Worts etc*); Neuprägung *f* (*Wort etc*).

'**coin-box tel·e·phone** *s* Münzfernsprecher *m*.

co·in·cide [,kəʊɪn'saɪd] *v/i* **1.** örtlich *od.* zeitlich zs.-treffen, -fallen (*with* mit). **2.**

collector

übereinstimmen, sich decken (**with** mit). **co'in·ci·dence** [~sıdəns] *s* **1.** Zs.-treffen *n*, -fallen *n*. **2.** zufälliges Zs.-treffen, Zufall *m*: **by mere ~** rein zufällig. **co'in·ci·dent** *adj* □ **1.** zs.-fallend, -treffend. **2.** übereinstimmend, sich deckend. **co,in·ci'den·tal** □ **1.** → **coincident 2.** zufällig.

coin|-op ['kɔınɒp] *s* F **1.** Waschsalon *m*. **2.** Münztankstelle *f*. **'~,op·er·at·ed** *adj* mit Münzbetrieb, Münz...

coke[1] [kəʊk] **I** *s* Koks *m*. **II** *v/t u. v/i* verkoken.

coke[2] [~] *s sl.* Koks *m* (*Kokain*).

co·la ['kəʊlə] *pl von* **colon**[1].

col·an·der ['kʌləndə] **I** *s* Sieb *n*, Seiher *m*. **II** *v/t* durchseihen, (durch)sieben.

cold [kəʊld] **I** *adj* □ **1.** kalt: (**as**) **~ as ice** eiskalt; *I feel* (*od. am*) **~** mir ist kalt, ich friere; *in* **~** *blood* kaltblütig; **~** *snap* Kälteeinbruch *m*; *get* **~** *feet* F kalte Füße (*Angst*) bekommen; → *shoulder* 1, *sweat, water* 1. **2.** *fig.* kalt, kühl: a) frostig, unfreundlich (*Empfang etc.*), b) nüchtern, sachlich: **~** *facts* die nackten Tatsachen, c) ruhig, gelassen: *it left me* **~** es ließ mich kalt. **3.** (gefühls)kalt, frigid. **II** *s* **4.** Kälte *f*: *be left out in the* **~** *fig.* kaltgestellt sein, ignoriert werden. **5.** # Erkältung *f*: (*common*) **~**, **~** *in the head* Schnupfen *m*; → *catch* 9. **'~'blood·ed** *adj* □ **1.** *zo.* kaltblütig (*a. fig.*). **2.** F kälteempfindlich: *be* **~** *a.* leicht frieren. **'~'heart·ed** *adj* □ kalt-, hartherzig.

cold·ish ['kəʊldıʃ] *adj* ziemlich kalt. **'cold·ness** *s* Kälte *f* (*a. fig.*).

cold| room *s* Kühlraum *m*. **,~'shoul·der** *v/t* F j-m die kalte Schulter zeigen, j-n kühl *od.* abweisend behandeln. **~ stor·age** *s* Kühlraumlagerung *f*: *put into* **~** *fig.* auf Eis legen. **~ tur·key** *s sl.* radikale Entziehungskur: *go* **~** e-e radikale Entziehungskur machen. **~ war** *s pol.* kalter Krieg. **~ wave** *s* **1.** *meteor.* Kältewelle *f*. **2.** Kaltwelle *f* (*Frisur*).

cole·slaw ['kəʊlslɔ:] *s* Krautsalat *m*.

col·ic ['kɒlık] *s ≉* Kolik *f*.

col·lab·o·rate [kə'læbəreıt] *v/i* **1.** zs.-arbeiten (**with** mit; **in, on** bei), mitarbeiten. **2.** *pol.* kollaborieren. **col·lab·o'ra·tion** *s* **1.** Zs.-arbeit *f*: *in* **~** *with* gemeinsam mit. **2.** *pol.* Kollaboration *f*. **col'lab·o·ra·tor** *s* **1.** Mitar-

beiter(in). **2.** *pol.* Kollaborateur *m*.

col·lage ['kɒlɑ:ʒ] *s Kunst:* Collage *f*.

col·lapse [kə'læps] **I** *v/i* **1.** zs.-brechen, einfallen, -stürzen. **2.** *fig.* zs.-brechen, scheitern. **3.** *moralisch od. physisch* zs.-brechen. **4.** *≉* e-n Kollaps erleiden. **5.** zs.-legbar sein, sich zs.-klappen lassen. **II** *v/t* **6.** zum Einsturz bringen. **7.** zs.-legen, -klappen. **III** *s* **8.** Einsturz *m*. **9.** *fig.* Zs.-bruch *m*. **10.** *≉* Kollaps *m*: *nervous* **~** Nervenzusammenbruch *m*. **col'laps·i·ble** *adj* zs.-klappbar, Klapp...: **~** *chair*.

col·lar ['kɒlə] **I** *s* **1.** Kragen *m*. **2.** (*Hunde-etc*)Halsband *n*. **3.** Hals-, Amts-, Ordenskette *f*. **4.** Kollier *n*: **~** *of pearls* Perlenkollier *n*. **II** *v/t* **5.** j-n beim Kragen packen. **6.** F j-n schnappen, verhaften, festnehmen; sich *etc.* schnappen; sich *et.* unter den Nagel reißen. **'~-bone** *s anat.* Schlüsselbein *n*.

col·lat·er·al [kɒ'lætərəl] *adj* □ **1.** seitlich, Seiten... **2.** parallel (laufend). **3.** begleitend, Neben...: **~** *circumstances pl* Begleit-, Nebenumstände *pl*.

col·league ['kɒli:g] *s* Kollege *m*, Kollegin *f*.

col·lect [kə'lekt] *v/t* **1.** Briefmarken *etc* sammeln. **2.** (ein)sammeln. **3.** auflesen, -sammeln. **3.** *Fakten etc* sammeln, zs.-tragen. **5.** j-n, *et.* abholen. **6.** *Geld etc* (ein)kassieren. **7.** *Gedanken etc* sammeln: **~** *o.s.* sich sammeln *od.* fassen. **8.** versammeln. **II** *v/i* **9.** sich (ver)sammeln. **10.** sich ansammeln. **III** *adj* **11.** *Am.* Nachnahme...: **~** *call teleph.* R-Gespräch *n*. **IV** *adv* **12.** *a.* **~** *on delivery Am.* per Nachnahme: *call* **~** *teleph.* ein R-Gespräch führen. **col'lect·ed** *adj* □ **1.** gesammelt: **~** *works*. **2.** *fig.* gefaßt. **col'lec·tion** *s* **1.** (Ein)Sammeln *n*. **2.** (*Briefmarkenetc*)Sammlung *f*. **3.** Kollekte *f*, (Geld-)Sammlung *f*. **4.** *♥* Inkasso *n*. **5.** *♥* (Muster)Kollektion *f*. **6.** Abholung *f*. **7.** *fig.* Fassung *f*, Gefaßtheit *f*. **col'lec·tive** *adj* **1.** gesammelt, zs.-gefaßt. **2.** kollektiv: **~** *agreement ♥* Tarifabkommen *n*; **~** *bargaining ♥* Tarifverhandlungen *pl*; **~** *noun* Sammelbegriff *m*. **col'lec·tive·ly** *adv* gemeinsam, gemeinschaftlich. **col'lec·tor** *s* **1.** Sammler(in): **~'s** *item* Sammlerstück *n*. **2.** Kassierer *m*. **3.** *⚡* Stromabnehmer *m*.

col·lege [ˈkɒlɪdʒ] s **1.** College n: ~ *of education* Br. pädagogische Hochschule. **2.** Akademie f. **3.** Kollegium n (a. eccl.). **col·le·gi·ate** [kəˈliːdʒɪət] adj □ College..., akademisch: ~ *dictionary* Schulwörterbuch n.

col·lide [kəˈlaɪd] v/i (**with**) kollidieren (mit): a) zs.-stoßen (mit) (a. fig.), b) fig. im Widerspruch stehen (zu).

col·lie [ˈkɒlɪ] s zo. Collie m (langhaariger schottischer Schäferhund).

col·li·sion [kəˈlɪʒn] s **1.** Kollision f, Zs.-stoß m (beide a. fig.): **be on a ~ course** auf Kollisionskurs sein. **2.** fig. Widerspruch m: **bring s.o. into ~ with the law** j-n mit dem Gesetz in Konflikt bringen.

col·lo·qui·al [kəˈləʊkwɪəl] adj □ umgangssprachlich: ~ *English* Umgangsenglisch n. **col·lo·qui·al·ism** s Ausdruck m der Umgangssprache.

col·lu·sion [kəˈluːʒn] s ṡ̌ **1.** geheimes Einverständnis. **2.** Verdunk(e)lung f: **risk** (od. **danger**) **of ~** Verdunklungsgefahr f.

col·ly·wob·bles [ˈkɒlɪˌwɒblz] s pl (a. sg konstruiert): **have the ~** F ein flaues Gefühl in der Magengegend haben.

co·lon[1] [ˈkəʊlən] pl **-lons, -la** [~lə] s anat. Dickdarm m.

co·lon[2] [~] s ling. Doppelpunkt m.

colo·nel [ˈkɜːnl] s ✕ Oberst m.

co·lo·ni·al [kəˈləʊnjəl] adj □ kolonial, Kolonial...: ~ *masters* pl Kolonialherren pl. **co·lo·ni·al·ism** s pol. Kolonialismus m. **col·o·nist** [ˈkɒlənɪst] s Kolonist(in), (An)Siedler(in). **col·o·ni·za·tion** [ˌkɒlənaɪˈzeɪʃn] s Kolonisation f, Besiedlung f. **col·o·nize** [ˈkɒlənaɪz] I v/t **1.** kolonisieren, besiedeln. **2.** ansiedeln. II v/i **3.** sich ansiedeln. **4.** e-e Kolonie bilden.

col·on·nade [ˌkɒləˈneɪd] s △ Säulengang m, Kolonnade f.

col·o·ny [ˈkɒlənɪ] s (a. Ausländer-, Künstler- etc)Kolonie f.

col·or, etc Am. → **colour,** etc.

Col·o·ra·do bee·tle [ˌkɒləˈrɑːdəʊ] s zo. Kartoffelkäfer m.

co·los·sal [kəˈlɒsl] adj □ kolossal, riesig, Riesen... (alle a. fig. F).

co·los·sus [~sɒs] pl **-si** [~saɪ], **-sus·es** [~sɪz] s Koloß m.

col·our [ˈkʌlə] bsd. Br. I s **1.** Farbe f: **what ~ is ...?** welche Farbe hat ...?; **to**

paint in bright (*glowing, gloomy*) ~**s** et. in rosigen (glühenden, düsteren) Farben schildern; *local ~* fig. Lokalkolorit n. **2.** (a. gesunde) Gesichtsfarbe: **lose** (**all**) ~ (ganz) blaß werden. **3.** (bsd. dunkle) Hautfarbe: **people** pl **of ~** Farbige pl. **4.** fig. Färbung f, Ton m. **5.** pl ✕ Fahne f: **call to the ~s** einberufen; **pass** (**fail**) **an examination with flying ~s** e-e Prüfung mit Glanz u. Gloria bestehen (mit Pauken u. Trompeten durch e-e Prüfung fallen). **6.** pl ⚓ Flagge f: **sail under false ~s** unter falscher Flagge segeln (a. fig.); **show one's true ~s** fig. sein wahres Gesicht zeigen; Farbe bekennen. II v/t **7.** färben (a. fig.), kolorieren. III v/i **8.** sich (ver)färben. **9.** a. ~ **up** erröten, rot werden (**with** vor dat). ~ **bar** s Rassenschranke f. '**~-blind** adj 🟥 farbenblind.

col·oured [ˈkʌləd] adj bsd. Br. **1.** farbig, bunt (beide a. fig.): ~ *pencil* Bunt-, Farbstift m. **2.** farbig: **a ~ man** ein Farbiger. **3.** fig. gefärbt.

'**col·our·fast** adj bsd. Br. farbecht. ~ **film** s phot. Farbfilm m.

col·our·ful [ˈkʌləfʊl] adj □ bsd. Br. **1.** farbenfreudig, -prächtig. **2.** fig. farbig, bunt. '**col·our·ing** I s **1.** Färbung f (a. fig.), Farbgebung f. **2.** Gesichtsfarbe f. II adj **3.** Farb...: ~ *matter* Farbstoff m; ~ *book* Malbuch n.

'**col·our·in,ten·sive** adj bsd. Br. farbintensiv.

col·our·less [ˈkʌləlɪs] adj □ bsd. Br. **1.** farblos (a. fig.). **2.** fig. neutral, unparteiisch.

col·our| line s bsd. Br. Rassenschranke f. ~ **or·gan** s Lichtorgel f. ~ **prob·lem** s Rassenproblem n. ~ **set** s Farbfernseher m. ~ **sup·ple·ment** s Farbbeilage f (e-r Zeitung). ~ **tel·e·vi·sion** s Farbfernsehen n.

colt [kəʊlt] s **1.** Fohlen n. **2.** fig. Grünschnabel m.

col·umn [ˈkɒləm] s **1.** △ (a. Rauch-, Wasser- etc)Säule f. **2.** typ. Spalte f: **in double ~s** zweispaltig. **3.** Zeitung: Kolumne f. **4.** 🅰, ✕ Kolonne f. **2.** **co·lum·nar** [kəˈlʌmnə] adj **1.** säulenartig, -förmig. **2.** Säulen... **col·um·nist** [ˈkɒləmnɪst] s Kolumnist(in).

co·ma [ˈkəʊmə] s 🩺 Koma n: **be in a ~** im Koma liegen.

comb [kəʊm] **I** s **1.** Kamm m (a. des Hahns, e-r Welle etc). **II** v/t **2.** kämmen: **~** one's hair (od. o.s.) sich kämmen. **3.** fig. Gegend durchkämmen. **4.** mst **~** out fig. sieben, sichten; aussondern, -suchen.

com·bat ['kɒmbæt] **I** v/t bekämpfen, kämpfen gegen (beide a. fig.). **II** v/i kämpfen (**with** mit) (a. fig.). **III** s Kampf m, ✗ a. Gefecht n. **IV** adj Kampf...

com·bi·na·tion [ˌkɒmbɪ'neɪʃn] s **1.** Verbindung f (a. 🜛), Kombination f: **~** lock Kombinationsschloß n. **2.** ✝ Konzern m; Kartell n, Ring m. **3.** Zs.-schluß m, Bündnis n. **com·bine** [kəm'baɪn] **I** v/t **1.** verbinden (a. 🜛), kombinieren: **~** business with pleasure das Nützliche mit dem Angenehmen verbinden. **2.** in sich vereinigen. **II** v/i **3.** sich verbinden (a. 🜛). **4.** zs.-wirken: everything **~**d against him alles verschwor sich gegen ihn. **III** s ['kɒmbaɪn] **5.** Verbindung f. **6.** pol. Interessengemeinschaft f; ✝ a. Verband m; Konzern m; Kartell n. **com·bined** [kəm'baɪnd] adj gemeinsam, gemeinschaftlich.

com·bus·ti·ble [kəm'bʌstəbl] **I** adj □ **1.** brennbar, (leicht)entzündlich. **2.** fig. leichterregbar. **II** s **3.** Brennstoff m, -material n. **com·bus·tion** [~'bʌstʃən] s Verbrennung f (a. biol., 🜛): **~** engine ⊚ Verbrennungsmotor m.

come [kʌm] **I** v/i (irr) **1.** kommen (a. sl. e-n Orgasmus haben): **s.o. is coming** es kommt j-d; **he came to see us** er besuchte uns. **2.** (dran)kommen, an die Reihe kommen. **3.** kommen, erscheinen: **~** and go kommen u. gehen; erscheinen u. verschwinden. **4.** kommen, gelangen (to zu). **5.** kommen, abstammen (of, from von). **6.** kommen, herrühren (of von). **7.** kommen, geschehen, sich ereignen: **~** what may (od. will) komme, was da wolle; **how ~**s it that ...?, **F** how ~ that ...? wie kommt es, daß ...? **8.** sich erweisen: it ~s expensive es kommt teuer. **9.** vor inf: dahin od. dazu kommen: **~** to know s.o. j-n kennenlernen; **~** to know s.th. et. erfahren; **I have ~** to believe that ich bin zu der Überzeugung gekommen, daß **10.** bsd. vor adj: werden: **~** true sich bewahrheiten od. erfüllen, eintreffen. **11.** to **~** (als adj) zukünftig, kommend: for

all time to **~** für alle Zukunft. **II** v/t (irr) **12.** F sich aufspielen als, j-n, et. spielen. **III** int **13.** na!, komm!: **~**, **~**! nicht so wild!, immer langsam!; na komm schon!, auf geht's!
Verbindungen mit Präpositionen:
come|a·cross v/i zufällig treffen od. finden od. sehen, stoßen auf (acc). **~** at v/i **1.** erreichen, bekommen, Wahrheit etc herausfinden. **2.** losgehen auf (acc). **~** for v/i **1.** et. abholen kommen, kommen wegen. **2.** losgehen auf (acc). **~** in-to v/i **1.** kommen in (acc). **2.** **~** a fortune ein Vermögen erben; **~** fashion 1, own 5, use 5. **~** near v/i **1.** fig. nahekommen (dat). **2.** **~** doing s.th. et. beinahe tun. **~** off v/i **1.** herunterfallen von. **2.** **~** it! F hör schon auf damit! **~** on **→** come upon. **~**, befallen: what has **~** you? was ist mit dir los? **~** through v/i Krankheit etc überstehen, -leben. **~** to v/i **1.** j-m (bsd. durch Erbschaft) zufallen. **2.** when it comes to paying wenn es ans Bezahlen geht. **3.** sich belaufen auf (acc). **~** un·der v/i **1.** unter ein Gesetz etc fallen. **2.** geraten unter (acc). **~** up·on v/i **1.** **→** come over, 2. **→** come across.
Verbindungen mit Adverbien:
come|a·bout v/i geschehen, passieren. **~** a·cross v/i **1.** herüberkommen. **2.** verstanden werden; an-, rüberkommen (Rede etc). **3.** F damit herausrücken: **~** with mit Informationen od. Geld herausrücken. **~** a·long v/i **1.** mitkommen, -gehen: **~**! F dalli! **2.** kommen, sich ergeben (Chance etc). **~** a·part v/i auseinanderfallen. **~** a·way v/i sich lösen, ab-, losgehen (Knopf etc). **~** back v/i **1.** zurückkommen: **~** to s.th. auf e-e Sache zurückkommen; it came back to him es fiel ihm wieder ein. **2.** wieder in Mode kommen. **3.** ein Comeback feiern. **~** by v/i vorbeikommen (Besucher). **~** down v/i **1.** herunterkommen, (Regen, Schnee) fallen. **2.** (ein)stürzen, (ein)fallen. **3.** fig. herunterkommen (Person): she has **~** quite a bit sie ist ganz schön tief gesunken. **4.** überliefert werden. **5.** F sinken (Preise); billiger werden (Ware). **6.** **~** on sich stürzen auf (acc); j-m aufs Dach steigen. **7.** **~** with F Geld herausrücken. **8.** **~** with erkranken an (dat). **9.** **~** to hinaus-

laufen auf (acc). **~ for·ward** v/i sich (freiwillig) melden, sich anbieten. **~ home** v/i **1.** nach Hause kommen, heimkommen. **2. ~ to s.o.** j-m schmerzlich bewußt werden. **~ in** v/i **1.** hereinkommen: **~!** herein!; (Funk) (bitte) kommen! **2.** eingehen, -treffen (Nachricht etc), Sport, ♣ einkommen; 🚗 einlaufen: **~ second** den zweiten Platz belegen. **3.** aufkommen, in Mode kommen. **4.** an die Macht kommen. **5.** sich als *nützlich* etc erweisen: → **handy** 4. **6.** Berücksichtigung finden: **where do I ~?** wo bleibe ich? **7. ~ for** Bewunderung etc erregen, auf Kritik etc stoßen. **8. ~ on** mitmachen bei, sich beteiligen an (dat). **~ off** v/i **1.** → **come away**. **2.** herunterfallen. **3.** auslaufen (Stück), enden (Ausstellung). **4.** F abschneiden; erfolgreich verlaufen, glücken. **~ on** v/i **1.** herankommen: **~!** komm (mit)!; komm her!; los!; F na, na! **2.** an die Reihe kommen. **3.** thea. auftreten; aufgeführt werden. **~ out** v/i **1.** herauskommen. **2. a. ~ on strike** bsd. Br. streiken. **3.** herauskommen: a) erscheinen (Buch etc), b) an den Tag kommen (Wahrheit etc). **4.** ausgehen (Haare, Farbe), herausgehen (Fleck etc). **5.** ausbrechen (Ausschlag): **~ in a rash** e-n Ausschlag bekommen. **6.** phot. etc gut etc werden (Bild); gut etc herauskommen (*in* auf dat). **7. ~ with** F mit der Wahrheit etc herausrücken; Flüche etc vom Stapel lassen. **8. ~ against (for)** sich aussprechen gegen (für). **~ over** → **come across** 1, 2. **~ round** v/i **1.** vorbeikommen (**to** bei). **2.** wieder zu sich kommen; sich erholen. **~ through** v/i durchkommen (Funkspruch, Patient etc). **~ to** → **come round** 2. **~ up** v/i **1.** heraufkommen. **2.** herankommen: **~ to s.o.** auf j-n zukommen. **3.** 🏛 zur Verhandlung kommen. **4. a. ~ for discussion** zur Sprache kommen. **5. ~ for** zur Abstimmung, Entscheidung kommen. **6.** aufkommen, in Mode kommen. **7. ~ to** reichen bis an (acc) od. zu; erreichen (acc); fig. heranreichen an (acc): → **expectation. 8. his supper came up again** das Abendessen kam ihm wieder hoch. **9. ~ with** daherkommen mit, auftischen, präsentieren.

come·|-at·a·ble [ˌkʌmˈætəbl] adj F erreichbar, zugänglich. '**~·back** s Comeback n: **stage** (od. **make**) **a ~** ein Comeback feiern.

co·me·di·an [kəˈmiːdjən] s **1.** Komödienschauspieler m; Komiker m (a. contr.). **2.** Spaßvogel m, Witzbold m (beide a. contr.).

'**come·down** s fig. **1.** Niedergang m, Abstieg m. **2.** F Enttäuschung f.

com·e·dy [ˈkɒmədɪ] s **1.** Komödie f (a. fig.), Lustspiel n. **2.** Komik f.

come·ly [ˈkʌmlɪ] adj attraktiv, schön.

com·er [ˈkʌmə] s Ankömmling m.

com·et [ˈkɒmɪt] s ast. Komet m.

com·fort [ˈkʌmfət] **I** v/t **1.** trösten. **2.** beruhigen. **II** s **3.** Trost m: **cold ~** ein schwacher Trost. **4.** Behaglichkeit f: **to live in ~** sorgenfrei leben. **5.** a. pl Komfort m: **with every modern ~** (od. **all modern ~s**) mit allem Komfort; **~ station** Am. öffentliche Bedürfnisanstalt. '**com·fort·a·ble** adj □ **1.** komfortabel, bequem, behaglich: **make o.s. ~** es sich bequem machen; **are you ~?** haben Sie es bequem?, sitzen od. liegen etc Sie bequem?; **feel ~** sich wohl fühlen. **2.** bequem, sorgenfrei (Leben etc). **3.** ausreichend, recht gut (Einkommen etc): **to be ~** (od. **comfortably off**) einigermaßen wohlhabend sein. '**com·fort·er** s **1.** Tröster m. **2.** bsd. Br. Wollschal m. **3.** Am. Steppdecke f. **4.** bsd. Br. Schnuller m. '**com·fort·ing** adj tröstlich. '**com·fort·less** adj **1.** unbequem. **2.** trostlos.

com·fy [ˈkʌmfɪ] F → **comfortable** 1.

com·ic [ˈkɒmɪk] **I** adj (**~ally**) **1.** Komödien..., Lustspiel...: **~ actor** Komödienschauspieler m; Komiker m; **~ opera** ♪ komische Oper; **~ tragedy** Tragikomödie f (a. fig.). **2.** komisch, humoristisch: **~ paper** Witzblatt n; **~ strips** pl Comics pl. **3.** → **comical** 1. **II** s **4.** → **comedian** 1. **5.** F Witzblatt n: **~s** pl Comics pl. '**com·i·cal** adj □ **1.** komisch, ulkig, spaßig. **2.** F seltsam, sonderbar.

com·ing [ˈkʌmɪŋ] **I** adj kommend: a) zukünftig: **the ~ man** der kommende Mann, b) nächst: **~ week** nächste Woche. **II** s Kommen n, Ankunft f: **the ~s and goings** das Kommen u. Gehen.

com·ma [ˈkɒmə] s Komma n, Beistrich m.

com·mand [kəˈmɑːnd] **I** v/t **1.** befehlen

(*s.o. to do*) j-m zu tun). **2.** fordern, verlangen: ~ *silence* sich Ruhe erbitten. **3.** ✕ kommandieren, befehligen. **4.** *Gefühle, Lage etc* beherrschen. **5.** *Vertrauen etc* einflößen: ~ (*s.o.'s*) *admiration* (j-m) Bewunderung abnötigen; ~ *respect* Achtung gebieten. **6.** zur Verfügung haben, verfügen über (*acc*). **II** *v/i* **7.** befehlen. **8.** ✕ das Kommando führen, den Befehl haben. **III** *s* **9.** Befehl *m*: *at s.o.'s* ~ auf j-s Befehl. **10.** Verfügung *f*: *be at s.o.'s* ~ j-m zur Verfügung stehen; *have at* ~ → 6. **11.** Beherrschung *f* (*e-r Sprache etc*): *have* ~ *of English* s-e Englischkenntnisse *pl*. **12.** ✕ Kommando *n*: a) (Ober)Befehl *m*: *be in* ~ → 8; ~ *module* (*Raumfahrt*) Kommandokapsel *f*, b) Befehl *m*. **com·man·dant** [ˌkɒmənˈdænt] *s* ✕ Kommandant *m*. **com·mand·er** [kəˈmɑːndə] *s* ✕ Kommandeur *m*, Befehlshaber *m*; Kommandant *m*: ~ *in chief* Oberbefehlshaber *m*. **com·mand·ing** *adj* □ **1.** ✕ kommandierend, befehlshabend. **2.** herrisch, gebieterisch. **3.** *die Gegend* beherrschend. **4.** weit (*Aussicht*). **com·mand·ment** *s* Gebot *n*, Vorschrift *f*: *the Ten* ⚍*s Bibl.* die Zehn Gebote. **com·man·do** [~ˈdəʊ] *pl* **-do(e)s** *s* ✕ Kommando *n*: ~ *squad* Kommandotrupp *m*.

com·mem·o·rate [kəˈmeməreɪt] *v/t* **1.** erinnern an (*acc*). **2.** (ehrend) gedenken (*gen*). **com,mem·o·ra·tion** *s* Gedenk-, Gedächtnisfeier *f*: *in* ~ *of* zum Gedenken *od.* Gedächtnis an (*acc*). **com·'mem·o·ra·tive** [~rətɪv] *adj* **1.** *be* ~ *of* erinnern an (*acc*). **2.** Gedenk-, Gedächtnis..., Erinnerungs...: ~ *issue* Gedenkausgabe *f* (*Briefmarken etc*); ~ *plaque* Gedenktafel *f*.

com·mence [kəˈmens] *v/i u. v/t* anfangen, beginnen (*to do, doing* zu tun). **com'mence·ment** *s* Anfang *m*, Beginn *m*.

com·mend [kəˈmend] *v/t* **1.** empfehlen. **2.** loben (*on* wegen). **3.** anvertrauen (*to dat*). **com'mend·a·ble** *adj* □ **1.** empfehlenswert. **2.** lobenswert, löblich. **com·men·da·tion** [ˌkɒmenˈdeɪʃn] *s* **1.** Empfehlung *f*. **2.** Lob *n*. **com'men·da·to·ry** [~dətərɪ] *adj* **1.** Empfehlungs...: ~ *letter* Empfehlungsbrief *m*,

-schreiben *n*. **2.** lobend, anerkennend.

com·men·su·ra·ble [kəˈmenʃərəbl] *adj* □ vergleichbar (*to, with* mit). **com·'men·su·rate** [~rət] *adj* (*to, with*) im Einklang stehend (mit), entsprechend *od.* angemessen (*dat*).

com·ment [ˈkɒment] **I** *s* (*on*) Kommentar *m* (zu): a) Bemerkung *f* (zu): *no* ~*!* kein Kommentar!, b) Anmerkung *f* (zu). **II** *v/i*: ~ *on* e-n Kommentar abgeben zu, *et.* kommentieren. **III** *v/t* bemerken (*that* daß). **com·men·ta·tor** [ˈ~məntertə] *s* Kommentator *m*.

com·merce [ˈkɒmɜːs] *s* Handel *m*. **com·mer·cial** [kəˈmɜːʃl] **I** *adj* □ **1.** Geschäfts..., Handels...: ~ *attaché* Handelsattaché *m*; ~ *correspondence* Geschäfts-, Handelskorrespondenz *f*; ~ *letter* Geschäftsbrief *m*; ~ *travel(l)er* Handlungsreisende *m*. **2.** handelsüblich (*Qualität etc*). **3.** Rundfunk, *TV*: Werbe..., Reklame...: ~ *broadcasting* Werbefunk *m*; kommerzieller Rundfunk; ~ *television* Werbefernsehen *n*; kommerzielles Fernsehen. **4.** kommerziell: a) auf finanziellen Gewinn abzielend, b) finanziell. **II** *s* **5.** Rundfunk, *TV*: Werbespot *m*; von e-m Sponsor finanzierte Sendung. **com'mer·cial·ize** [~ʃəlaɪz] *v/t* kommerzialisieren, vermarkten.

com·mie [ˈkɒmɪ] *s* F Kommunist(in).

com·mis·er·ate [kəˈmɪzəreɪt] *v/t* (*u. v/i* ~ *with*) bemitleiden. **com,mis·er·a·tion** *s* Mitleid *n*.

com·mis·sion [kəˈmɪʃn] **I** *s* **1.** Auftrag *m*. **2.** Kommission *f*, Ausschuß *m*: *be on the* ~ Mitglied der Kommission sein. **3.** ✝ a) Kommission *f*: *on* ~ in Kommission, b) Provision *f*: *on* ~ gegen Provision; *on a* ~ *basis* auf Provisionsbasis. **4.** Begehung *f*, Verübung *f* (*e-s Verbrechens etc*). **II** *v/t* **5.** beauftragen. **6.** *et.* in Auftrag geben: ~*ed work* Auftragsarbeit *f*. **com·mis·sion·aire** [kə,mɪʃəˈneə] *s bsd. Br.* (livrierter) Portier (*Theater, Hotel etc*). **com·mis·sion·er** [~ʃnə] *s* Beauftragte *m*.

com·mit [kəˈmɪt] *v/t* **1.** anvertrauen, übergeben (*to dat*): ~ *to paper* zu Papier bringen. **2.** ⚖ einweisen (*to in acc*). **3.** *Verbrechen etc* begehen, verüben. **4.** (*to*) verpflichten (zu), festlegen (auf *acc*): ~*ted* engagiert (*Schriftsteller etc*).

com'mit·ment s 1. Übergabe f. 2. → committal 2. 3. Begegnung f, Verübung f. 4. Verpflichtung f, Festlegung f, (a. politisches etc) Engagement: without any ~ ganz unverbindlich. com'mit·tal [~tl] s 1. → commitment 1, 3, 4. 2. ⚖ Einweisung f. com'mit·tee [~tɪ] s Komitee n, Ausschuß m: be (od. sit) on a ~ in e-m Ausschuß sein.

com·mode [kəˈməʊd] s (Wasch)Kommode f. com'mo·di·ous [~djəs] adj □ geräumig.

com·mod·i·ty [kəˈmɒdətɪ] s ✝ Ware f, (Handels)Artikel m. ~ ex·change s Warenbörse f.

com·mo·dore [ˈkɒmədɔː] s ⚓ Kommodore m.

com·mon [ˈkɒmən] I adj (□ → commonly) 1. gemeinsam (a. A), gemeinschaftlich: ~ to all allen gemeinsam; ~ room Gemeinschaftsraum m; → cause 3, denominator. 2. allgemein: by ~ consent mit allgemeiner Zustimmung. 3. allgemein (bekannt), alltäglich: it is ~ knowledge (usage) es ist allgemein bekannt (üblich); ~ name häufiger Name; ~ sight alltäglicher od. vertrauter Anblick. 4. bsd. biol. gemein: ~ or garden F Feld-Wald-u.-Wiesen-...; ~ cold 5. 5. gewöhnlich, ohne Rang: the ~ people pl das einfache Volk; ~ soldier einfacher Soldat. II s 6. Gemeinsamkeit f: in ~ gemeinsam (with mit). 7. das Gewöhnliche: out of the ~ außergewöhnlich, -ordentlich. 8. → commons. 'com·mon·er s Bürger(liche) m.

com·mon law s 1. Br. Gewohnheitsrecht n. 2. das anglo-amerikanische Rechtssystem.

com·mon·ly [ˈkɒmənlɪ] adv gewöhnlich, im allgemeinen.

Com·mon| Mar·ket s Gemeinsamer Markt. '~place s 1. Gemeinplatz m. 2. alltägliche Sache. II adj 3. alltäglich, abgedroschen. ~ Prayer s eccl. anglikanische Liturgie.

com·mons [ˈkɒmənz] s pl 1. the ♀ parl. Br. das Unterhaus. 2. be kept on small ~ auf schmale Kost gesetzt sein.

com·mon| sense s gesunder Menschenverstand. '~·wealth s: the ♀ (of Nations) das Commonwealth.

com·mo·tion [kəˈməʊʃn] s 1. Aufregung f. 2. Aufruhr m, Tumult m.

com·mu·nal [ˈkɒmjʊnl] adj □ 1. Gemeinde..., Kommunal... 2. gemeinschaftlich: ~ aerial (bsd. Am. antenna) TV Gemeinschaftsantenne f.

com·mune¹ [kəˈmjuːn] v/i 1. sich (vertraulich) unterhalten (with mit): ~ with o.s. mit sich zu Rate gehen. 2. bsd. Am. → communicate 6.

com·mune² [ˈkɒmjuːn] s Gemeinde f, Kommune f (a. sociol.).

com·mu·ni·ca·ble [kəˈmjuːnɪkəbl] adj □ 1. mitteilbar. 2. 🞄 übertragbar. com'mu·ni·cate [~keɪt] I v/t 1. mitteilen (to dat). 2. 🞄, phys. übertragen (to auf acc) (a. fig.). II v/i 3. kommunizieren, sich besprechen, in Verbindung stehen (with mit). 4. sich in Verbindung setzen (with mit). 5. miteinander (durch e-e Tür etc) verbunden sein: communicating door Verbindungstür f. 6. eccl. das Abendmahl empfangen, kommunizieren. com,mu·ni'ca·tion s 1. Mitteilung f (to an acc): ~ cord 🚆 Br. Notbremse f. 2. Übertragung f: ~ of power phys. Kraftübertragung. 3. Verbindung f: be in ~ with in Verbindung stehen mit. 4. pl bsd. ⚔ Fernmeldewesen n: ~s satellite Nachrichtensatellit m; ~ system Fernmeldenetz n. com'mu·ni·ca·tive [~kətɪv] adj □ mitteilsam, gesprächig, kommunikativ.

com·mun·ion [kəˈmjuːnjən] s 1. (eccl. Religions)Gemeinschaft f. 2. ♀ eccl. Abendmahl n, Kommunion f: go to ~ zum Abendmahl gehen; ~ cup Abendmahlskelch m.

com·mu·ni·qué [kəˈmjuːnɪkeɪ] s Kommuniqué n.

com·mu·nism [ˈkɒmjʊnɪzəm] s Kommunismus m. 'com·mu·nist I s Kommunist(in). II adj kommunistisch. ,com·mu'nis·tic adj (~ally) kommunistisch.

com·mu·ni·ty [kəˈmjuːnətɪ] s 1. Gemeinschaft f: ~ of heirs Erbengemeinschaft; ~ singing gemeinsames Singen; ~ spirit Gemeinschaftsgeist m. 2. Gemeinde f. 3. Gemeinsamkeit f, gemeinsamer Besitz: ~ of goods (od. property) Gütergemeinschaft f. ~ cen·ter, bsd. Br. ~ cen·tre s Gemeinschaftszentrum n. ~ home s Br. Erziehungsheim n.

com·mut·a·ble [kəˈmjuːtəbl] adj umwandelbar. com·mu·ta·tion [ˌkɒmjuː-

'teɪʃn] s 1. Umwandlung f. 2. Ablösung f; Ablöse(summe) f. 3. ⚖ (Straf)Umwandlung f. 4. 🚇, etc Pendeln n: ~ ticket Am. Dauer-, Zeitkarte f. com-mute [kə'mjuːt] I v/t 1. eintauschen (for für). 2. ⚖ Strafe umwandeln (to, into in acc). 3. Verpflichtung etc umwandeln (into in acc), ablösen (for, into durch). II v/i 4. 🚇, etc pendeln. com'mut-er s 4. a) Am. Zeitkarteninhaber(in), b) Pendler(in): ~ train Pendler-, Nahverkehrszug m.

com-pact [kəm'pækt] I adj ☐ 1. kompakt: ~ cassette Kompaktkassette f. 2. eng, klein (Wohnung etc). 3. gedrungen (Gestalt). 4. knapp, gedrängt (Stil etc). II v/t 5. zs.-drängen, fest miteinander verbinden. III s ['kɒmpækt] 6. kompakte Masse. 7. Puderdose f. com-'pact-ness s 1. Kompaktheit f. 2. Knappheit f, Gedrängtheit f.

com-pan-ion [kəm'pænjən] s 1. Begleiter(in) (a. fig.). 2. Kamerad(in), Genosse m, Genossin f. 3. Gesellschafterin f. 4. Gegenstück n, Pendant n. 5. Handbuch n, Leitfaden m. com'pan-ion-a-ble adj ☐ umgänglich, gesellig. com'pan-ion-ship s Begleitung f, Gesellschaft f.

com-pa-ny ['kʌmpənɪ] s 1. Gesellschaft f: in ~ (with) in Gesellschaft od. Begleitung (gen od. von); be in good ~ sich in guter Gesellschaft befinden; keep (od. bear) s.o. ~ j-m Gesellschaft leisten; part ~ (with) sich trennen (von); fig. anderer Meinung sein (als) (on in dat). 2. Gesellschaft f; Besuch m, Gäste pl: be fond of ~ die Gesellschaft lieben; present ~ excepted! Anwesende ausgenommen! 3. Gesellschaft f, Umgang m: keep good ~ guten Umgang pflegen; keep ~ with verkehren mit. 4. ✝ Gesellschaft f, Firma f: ~ car Firmenwagen m; ~ pension Betriebsrente f. 5. ✗ Kompanie f. 6. thea. Truppe f.

com-pa-ra-ble ['kɒmpərəbl] adj ☐ vergleichbar (with, to mit). **com-par-a-tive** [kəm'pærətɪv] I adj 1. vergleichend. 2. verhältnismäßig, relativ. 3. ~ degree → 4. II s 4. ling. Komparativ m. com'par-a-tive-ly adv verhältnismäßig: a) vergleichsweise, b) ziemlich. **com-pare** [~'peə] I v/t 1. vergleichen (with, to mit): ~d with (od. to) im Ver-

gleich zu, gegenüber (dat). 2. vergleichen, gleichsetzen, -stellen: not to be ~d with (od. to) nicht zu vergleichen mit. 3. ling. steigern. II v/i 4. sich vergleichen (lassen): ~ favo(u)rably with den Vergleich mit ... nicht zu scheuen brauchen. III s 5. beyond (od. past, without) ~ unvergleichlich. **com-par-i-son** [~'pærɪsn] s 1. Vergleich m: by ~ vergleichsweise; in ~ with im Vergleich mit od. zu; bear (od. stand) ~ with e-n Vergleich aushalten mit; without ~, beyond (all) ~ unvergleichlich. 2. ling. Steigerung f.

com-part-ment [kəm'pɑːtmənt] s 1. Fach n. 2. 🚇 Abteil n.

com-pass ['kʌmpəs] s 1. Kompaß m. 2. pl, a. pair of ~es Zirkel m.

com-pas-sion [kəm'pæʃn] s Mitleid n, -gefühl n: have (od. take) ~ on (od. for) Mitleid mit j-m haben. **com'pas-sion-ate** [~ʃənət] adj ☐ mitleidsvoll, -fühlend.

com-pat-i-ble [kəm'pætəbl] adj ☐ 1. vereinbar (with mit), miteinander vereinbar. 2. verträglich: be ~ (with) sich vertragen (mit); passen (zu), zs.-passen.

com-pa-tri-ot [kəm'pætrɪət] s Landsmann m, -männin f.

com-pel [kəm'pel] v/t 1. zwingen: be ~led to do (od. into doing) s.th. gezwungen sein, et. zu tun, et. tun müssen. 2. et. erzwingen. 3. a. Bewunderung etc abnötigen (from dat).

com-pen-di-um [kəm'pendɪəm] pl -ums, -a [~ə] s 1. Kompendium n, Handbuch n. 2. Zs.-fassung f, Abriß m.

com-pen-sate ['kɒmpenseɪt] I v/t 1. kompensieren (a. psych.), ausgleichen. 2. j-n entschädigen (for für); et. ersetzen, vergüten, für et. Ersatz leisten (to dat). 3. Am. j-n bezahlen, entlohnen. II v/i 4. Ersatz leisten (for für). 5. ~ for → 1. **com-pen-sa-tion** s 1. Kompensation f, Ausgleich m: in ~ for als Ausgleich für. 2. (Schaden)Ersatz m, Entschädigung f; Vergütung f: pay ~ Schadenersatz leisten; as (od. by way of) ~ als Ersatz. 3. Am. Bezahlung f, Gehalt n, Lohn m. 4. psych. Kompensation f, Ersatzhandlung f.

com-père, com-pere ['kɒmpeə] bsd. Br. I s Conférencier m, Ansager(in). II v/t konferieren, ansagen. III v/i konferieren, als Conférencier fungieren.

com·pete [kəm'pi:t] *v/i* **1.** sich (mit)bewerben (**for** um). **2.** ♥ *u. weitS.* konkurrieren (**with** mit). **3.** wetteifern, sich messen (**with** mit). **4.** *Sport:* (am Wettkampf) teilnehmen; *a. weitS.* kämpfen (**for** um; **against** gegen).

com·pe·tence, com·pe·ten·cy ['kɔmpɪtəns(ı)] *s* **1.** Fähigkeit *f*, Tüchtigkeit *f*. **2.** ⚖ Zuständigkeit *f*, Kompetenz *f* (*beide a. weitS.*); Zulässigkeit *f*. **'com·petent** *adj* □ **1.** fähig (**to do** zu tun), tüchtig. **2.** fach-, sachkundig. **3.** gut(gemacht), gekonnt. **4.** ⚖ zuständig, kompetent (*beide a. weitS.*); zulässig (*Beweise, Zeuge*).

com·pe·ti·tion [ˌkɔmpɪ'tɪʃn] *s* **1.** *allg.* Wettbewerb *m* (**for** um). **2.** ♥ Konkurrenz *f:* a) ♥ Wettbewerb *m*, Konkurrenzkampf *m:* **unfair ~** unlauterer Wettbewerb, b) ♥ Konkurrenzfirma *f*, -firmen *pl*, c) *weitS.* Gegner *pl*, Rivalen *pl.* **3.** Preisausschreiben *n.* **com·pet·itive** [kəm'petətıv] *adj* □ **1.** konkurrierend. **2.** Wettbewerbs..., Konkurrenz..., ♥ *a.* konkurrenzfähig. **com'pet·i·tor** [~tə] *s* **1.** Mitbewerber(in) (**for** um). **2.** *bsd.* ♥ Konkurrent(in). **3.** *bsd. Sport:* Teilnehmer(in).

com·pi·la·tion [ˌkɔmpɪ'leıʃn] *s* Kompilation *f* (*a. Werk*). **com·pile** [kəm'paıl] *v/t Verzeichnis etc* kompilieren, zs.stellen, *Material* zs.-tragen. **com'pil·er** *s* Kompilator *m.*

com·pla·cence, com·pla·cen·cy [kəm'pleısns(ı)] *s* Selbstzufriedenheit *f*, gefälligkeit *f.* **com'pla·cent** *adj* □ selbstzufrieden, -gefällig.

com·plain [kəm'pleın] *v/i* **1.** sich beklagen *od.* beschweren (**of, about** über *acc*; **to** bei): *~ing letter* Beschwerdebrief *m.* **2.** klagen (**of** über *acc*). **3.** ♥ reklamieren: *~ about et.* reklamieren *od.* beanstanden. **com'plaint** *s* **1.** Klage *f*, Beschwerde *f:* **make** (*od.* **lodge**) **a ~** (**about**) → **complain** 1; *~ book* Beschwerdebuch *n.* **2.** ♥ Reklamation *f*, Beanstandung *f.* **3.** ⚕ Leiden *n*, *pl a.* Beschwerden *pl.*

com·plai·sance [kəm'pleızəns] *s* Gefälligkeit *f*, Entgegenkommen *n.* **com'plai·sant** *adj* □ gefällig, entgegenkommend.

com·ple·ment I *s* ['kɔmplımənt] **1.** (**to**

gen) Ergänzung *f* (*a. ling.*); Vervollkommnung *f.* **2.** Ergänzungsstück *n.* **II** *v/t* [~ment] **3.** ergänzen; vervollkommnen. **com·ple·men·ta·ry** [~'mentərı] *adj* □ (sich) ergänzend: *be ~ to s.th. et.* ergänzen; *~ colo(u)rs pl* Komplementärfarben *pl.*

com·plete [kəm'pli:t] **I** *adj* □ **1.** komplett, vollständig. **2.** vollzählig. **3.** beendet, vollendet. **II** *v/t* **4.** vervollständigen. **5.** vollenden, abschließen. **6.** *fig.* vollenden, vollkommen machen. **7.** *Formular* ausfüllen. **com'plete·ness** *s* Vollständigkeit *f.* **com'ple·tion** *s* **1.** Vervollständigung *f.* **2.** Vollendung *f:* **bring to ~** zum Abschluß bringen. **3.** Ausfüllung *f.*

com·plex ['kɔmpleks] **I** *adj* □ **1.** zs.-gesetzt (*a. ling.*). **2.** komplex, vielschichtig. **II** *s* **3.** Komplex *m*, *das Ganze*. **4.** (*Gebäude- etc*)Komplex *m.* **5.** *psych.* Komplex *m.*

com·plex·ion [kəm'plekʃn] *s* **1.** Gesichtsfarbe *f*, Teint *m.* **2.** *fig.* Aussehen *n*, Anstrich *m.* **3.** *fig.* Couleur *f*, (politische) Richtung.

com·plex·i·ty [kəm'pleksətı] *s* **1.** Komplexität *f*, Vielschichtigkeit *f.* **2.** *et.* Komplexes.

com·pli·ance [kəm'plaıəns] *s* **1.** (**with**) Einwilligung *f* (in *acc*); Befolgung *f* (*gen*): *in ~ with e-r Vorschrift etc* gemäß. **2.** Willfährigkeit *f.* **com'pli·ant** *adj* □ willfährig.

com·pli·cate ['kɔmplıkeıt] *v/t* komplizieren. **'com·pli·cat·ed** *adj* □ kompliziert. **,com·pli'ca·tion** *s* **1.** Komplikation *f* (*a.* ⚕). **2.** Kompliziertheit *f.*

com·plic·i·ty [kəm'plısətı] *s* Mitschuld *f*, Mittäterschaft *f* (**in** an *dat*): *~ in murder* ⚖ Beihilfe *f* zum Mord.

com·pli·ment I *s* ['kɔmplımənt] **1.** Kompliment *n:* **angle** (*od.* **fish**) **for ~s** nach Komplimenten fischen; **pay s.o. a ~** j-m ein Kompliment machen. **2.** Empfehlung *f*, Gruß *m:* **with the ~s of the season** mit den besten Wünschen zum Fest. **II** *v/t* [~ment] **3.** *j-m* ein Kompliment *od.* Komplimente machen (**on** wegen). **com·pli·men·ta·ry** [~'mentərı] *adj* □ **1.** höflich, Höflichkeits...: *~ close* Gruß-, Schlußformel *f* (*in Briefen*). **2.** Ehren..., Frei..., Gratis...: *~ ticket* Ehren-, Freikarte *f.*

com·ply [kəmˈplaɪ] v/i (**with**) einwilligen (**in** acc); (e-m Wunsch od. Befehl) nachkommen od. Folge leisten, erfüllen (acc); (e-e Abmachung) befolgen, einhalten: ~ **with the law** sich an die Gesetze halten.

com·po·nent [kəmˈpəʊnənt] I adj Teil...: ~ **part** Bestandteil m. II s (Bestand)Teil m, a. ⚓, phys. Komponente f.

com·pose [kəmˈpəʊz] I v/t 1. zs.-setzen od. -stellen: **be** ~**d of** bestehen od. sich zs.-setzen aus. 2. Satz etc bilden. 3. Gedicht etc verfassen. 4. ♪ komponieren. 5. Gemälde etc entwerfen. 6. typ. (ab)setzen. 7. besänftigen: ~ **o.s.** sich beruhigen od. fassen. 8. Streit etc beilegen, schlichten. 9. Gedanken sammeln. II v/i 10. ♪ komponieren. **com'posed** adj, **com'pos·ed·ly** [~zɪdlɪ] adv ruhig, gelassen. **com'pos·er** s 1. ♪ Komponist m. 2. Verfasser(in). **com·po·site** [ˈkɒmpəzɪt] adj zs.-gesetzt. **,com·po·'si·tion** s 1. Zs.-setzung f. 2. Verfassen n. 3. Schrift(stück n) f. 4. ped. Aufsatz m. 5. Komposition f: a) Musikstück n, b) (künstlerische) Anordnung od. Gestaltung, Aufbau m. 6. Beschaffenheit f, Art f. 7. typ. Setzen n, Satz m. **com·pos·i·tor** [kəmˈpɒzɪtə] s (Schrift-)Setzer m. **com·post** [ˈkɒmpɒst] I s Kompost m: ~ **heap** Komposthaufen m. II v/t kompostieren. **com·po·sure** [kəmˈpəʊʒə] s (Gemüts)Ruhe f, Fassung f, Gelassenheit f.

com·pote [ˈkɒmpɒt] s Kompott n.

com·pound¹ [kəmˈpaʊnd] I v/t 1. zs.-setzen, (ver)mischen. 2. zs.-setzen, -stellen. 3. Streit beilegen; Sache gütlich od. durch Vergleich regeln. II v/i 4. sich vergleichen od. einigen (**with** mit; **for** über acc). III adj [ˈkɒmpaʊnd] 5. zs.-gesetzt: ~ **interest** ⛯ Zinseszinsen pl; ~ **word** → 11. 6. ⚕ kompliziert (Bruch). 7. ⚡, ☉ Verbund... IV s [ˈkɒmpaʊnd] 8. Zs.-setzung f. Mischung f. 9. Mischung f, Masse f. 10. ⚓ Verbindung f. 11. ling. Kompositum n, zs.-gesetztes Wort.

com·pound² [ˈkɒmpaʊnd] s 1. Lager n. 2. Gefängnishof m. 3. (Tier)Gehege n.

com·pre·hend [ˌkɒmprɪˈhend] v/t 1. umfassen, einschließen. 2. begreifen, verstehen. **,com·pre·'hen·si·ble** adj begreiflich, verständlich. **,com·pre·'hen-**

si·bly adv verständlicherweise. **,com·pre·'hen·sion** s 1. Begriffsvermögen n, Verstand m: **past** ~ unfaßbar, unfaßlich. 2. (**of**) Begreifen n (gen), Verständnis n (für). **,com·pre·'hen·sive** I adj □ 1. umfassend: ~ **school** → 3. 2. Begriffs...: ~ **faculty** Fassungskraft f, Begriffsvermögen n. II s 3. Br. Gesamtschule f.

com·press I v/t [kəmˈpres] zs.-drücken, -pressen, phys., ☉ komprimieren (a. fig.), verdichten: ~**ed air** Preß-, Druckluft f. II s [ˈkɒmpres] ⚕ Kompresse f. **com·pres·sion** [kəmˈpreʃn] s 1. Zs.-drücken n, -pressen n. 2. phys., ☉ Druck m; Kompression f, Verdichtung f. **com'pres·sor** [~sə] s ☉ Kompressor m.

com·prise [kəmˈpraɪz] v/t 1. einschließen, umfassen. 2. bestehen od. sich zs.-setzen aus.

com·pro·mise [ˈkɒmprəmaɪz] I s 1. Kompromiß m: **make a** ~ e-n Kompromiß schließen; ~ **formula** Kompromißformel f; ~ **settlement** (od. **solution**) Kompromißlösung f. II v/t 2. Ruf, Leben etc gefährden, aufs Spiel setzen. 3. bloßstellen, kompromittieren. III v/i 4. e-n Kompromiß od. (a. fig. contp.) Kompromisse schließen.

com·pul·sion [kəmˈpʌlʃn] s Zwang m (a. psych.): **under** ~ unter Zwang, zwangsweise. **com'pul·sive** [~sɪv] adj □ 1. zwingend, Zwangs... 2. psych. zwanghaft. **com'pul·so·ry** [~sərɪ] adj □ 1. zwangsweise: ~ **auction** Zwangsversteigerung f; ~ **measures** pl Zwangsmaßnahmen pl. 2. obligatorisch, Pflicht...: ~ **education** allgemeine Schulpflicht; ~ **military service** allgemeine Wehrpflicht; ~ **subject** ped. univ. Pflichtfach n.

com·punc·tion [kəmˈpʌŋkʃn] s Gewissensbisse pl; Reue f; Bedenken pl: **without** ~ a. bedenkenlos.

com·pu·ta·tion [ˌkɒmpjuːˈteɪʃn] s 1. Berechnung f. 2. Schätzung f. **com·pute** [kəmˈpjuːt] v/t 1. berechnen. 2. schätzen, veranschlagen (**at** auf acc). **com'put·er** s Computer m: ~ **centre** (Am. **center**) Rechenzentrum n; ~**-controlled** computergesteuert; ~ **language** Computersprache f; ~ **science** Informatik f. **com'put·er·ize** [~təraɪz] I v/t

Werk etc computerisieren, auf Computer umstellen; *System etc* mit e-m Computer durchführen; computerisieren, mit Hilfe e-s Computers errechnen *od.* zs.-stellen. **II** *v/i* sich auf Computer umstellen.

com·rade ['kɒmreɪd] *s* **1.** Kamerad *m*, Gefährte *m.* **2.** *pol.* (Partei)Genosse *m.* '**com·rade·ship** *s* Kameradschaft *f.*

con¹ [kɒn] **I** *s* **1.** Nein-Stimme *f.* **2.** Gegenargument *n*: → **pro¹.** **II** *adv* **3.** *f* dagegen: **be** ~.

con² [~] *sl.* **I** *adj* betrügerisch: ~ **man** Betrüger *m*; Hochstapler *m*; ~ **game** aufgelegter Schwindel; Hochstapelei *f.* **II** *v/t* betrügen (*out of* um), reinlegen.

con·cat·e·nate [kɒn'kætɪneɪt] *v/t* verknüpfen. **con,cat·e'na·tion** *s* **1.** Verkettung *f.* **2.** Kette *f*, Reihe *f.*

con·cave ['kɒnkeɪv] *adj* □ konkav, hohl: ~ **mirror** Hohlspiegel *m.*

con·ceal [kən'siːl] *v/t* (*from* vor *dat*) verbergen: a) verstecken, b) geheimhalten, c) verschweigen, verheimlichen. **con'ceal·ment** *s* **1.** Verbergung *f*, Geheimhaltung *f*, Verheimlichung *f.* **2.** Verborgenheit *f*: **stay in** ~ sich verborgen halten.

con·cede [kən'siːd] *v/t* zugestehen, einräumen: a) gewähren, bewilligen, b) anerkennen (**a.** *that* daß). **con'ced·ed·ly** *adv* zugestandenermaßen.

con·ceit [kən'siːt] *s* Einbildung *f*, Dünkel *m*: **be full of** ~ völlig von sich eingenommen sein. **con'ceit·ed** *adj* □ eingebildet, dünkelhaft.

con·ceiv·a·ble [kən'siːvəbl] *adj* □ denk-, vorstellbar: **the best plan** ~ der denkbar beste Plan. **con'ceive I** *v/t* **1.** *biol.* Kind empfangen. **2.** begreifen. **3.** sich *et.* vorstellen *od.* denken, sich e-n Begriff *od.* e-e Vorstellung machen von. **4.** ersinnen, ausdenken. **II** *v/i* **5.** *biol.* empfangen, schwanger werden (*Mensch*); aufnehmen, trächtig werden (*Tier*). **6.** ~ **of** → 3.

con·cen·trate ['kɒnsəntreɪt] **I** *v/t* konzentrieren: a) zs.-ziehen, -ballen, massieren, b) *Gedanken etc* richten (**on** auf *acc*), c) 🜨 anreichern. **II** *v/i* sich konzentrieren. **III** *s* Konzentrat *n.* **,con·cen'tra·tion** *s* Konzentration *f*: a) Zs.-ziehung *f*, -ballung *f*, Massierung *f*: ~ **camp** Konzentrationslager *n*, b) ge-

spannte Aufmerksamkeit: **power of** ~ Konzentrationsfähigkeit *f*, c) 🜨 Anreicherung *f.*

con·cen·tric [kən'sentrɪk] *adj* (~*ally*) konzentrisch.

con·cept ['kɒnsept] *s* **1.** *phls.* Begriff *m.* **2.** Gedanke *m*, Auffassung *f.* **con·cep·tion** [kən'sepʃn] *s* **1.** *biol.* Empfängnis *f.* **2.** Begreifen *n*; Begriffsvermögen *n*; Begriff *m*, Vorstellung *f* (*of* von); Konzeption *f*, Idee *f.* **3.** Entwurf *m*, Konzept *n.* **con'cep·tu·al** [~tjʊəl] *adj* begrifflich, Begriffs...

con·cern [kən'sɜːn] **I** *v/t* **1.** angehen: a) betreffen, b) von Wichtigkeit *od.* Interesse sein für. **2.** beunruhigen. **3.** ~ **o.s. with** sich beschäftigen *od.* befassen mit. **II** *s* **4.** Angelegenheit *f*, Sache *f*: **that is no** ~ **of mine** das geht mich nichts an. **5.** 🜨 Geschäft *n*, Unternehmen *n.* **6.** Unruhe *f*, Sorge *f* (**at, about, for** wegen, um). **7.** Wichtigkeit *f*: **a matter of national** ~ ein nationales Anliegen. **8.** Beziehung *f* (**with** zu): **have no** ~ **with** nichts zu tun haben mit. **9.** (**at, about, for, in, with**) Teilnahme *f* (an *dat*), Rücksicht *f* (auf *acc*), Anteil *m* (an *dat*), Interesse *n* (für). **10.** f Ding *n*, Geschichte *f.* **con'cerned** *adj* **1.** betroffen, betreffend. **2.** (**in**) beteiligt, interessiert (an *dat*); verwickelt (in *acc*). **3.** (**with, in**) befaßt, beschäftigt (mit); handelnd (von). **4.** (**about, at, for**) besorgt (um), beunruhigt (wegen). **con'cern·ing** *prp* betreffend, hinsichtlich, was ... (an)betrifft.

con·cert *s* **1.** ['kɒnsət] ♪ Konzert *n*: ~ **hall** Konzertsaal *m*; ~ **pianist** Konzertpianist(in). **2.** ['kɒnsɜːt] *in* ~ **with** in Übereinstimmung *od.* gemeinsam mit. **con·cert·ed** [kən'sɜːtɪd] *adj* gemeinsam: ~ **action** gemeinsames Vorgehen; 🜨, *pol.* konzertierte Aktion. **con·cer·to** [kən-'tʃeətəʊ] *pl* **-tos, -ti** [~tiː] *s* ♪ (Solo)Konzert *n* (*mit Orchesterbegleitung*): **piano** ~ Klavierkonzert.

con·ces·sion [kən'seʃn] *s* **1.** Konzession *f*, Zugeständnis *n.* **2.** Genehmigung *f*, Bewilligung *f*; (amtliche *od.* staatliche) Konzession.

con·cil·i·ate [kən'sɪlɪeɪt] *v/t* **1.** aus-, versöhnen, versöhnlich stimmen. **2.** *Gunst etc* gewinnen. **3.** in Einklang bringen. **con,cil·i'a·tion** *s* Aus-, Versöhnung *f*: ~

committee Schlichtungsausschuß *m.*

con·cil·i·a·tor *s* Schlichter *m*, Vermittler *m.* **con'cil·i·a·to·ry** [~ətəri] *adj* □ versöhnlich, vermittelnd.

con·cise [kən'saɪs] *adj* □ kurz, knapp, prägnant. **con'cise·ness** *s* Kürze *f*, Prägnanz *f*.

con·clave ['kɒŋkleɪv] *s eccl.* Konklave *n.*

con·clude [kən'klu:d] **I** *v/t* **1.** beenden, (be-, ab)schließen (**with** mit): *to be ~d* Schluß folgt. **2.** *Vertrag etc* abschließen. **3.** *et.* folgern, schließen (**from** aus): *~ that* zu dem Schluß kommen, daß. **II** *v/i* **4.** enden, schließen (**with** mit). **con'clud·ing** *adj* abschließend, Schluß...

con·clu·sion [kən'klu:ʒn] *s* **1.** (Ab-) Schluß *m*, Ende *n*: *bring to a ~* zum Abschluß bringen; *in ~* zum Schluß. **2.** Abschluß *m* (*e-s Vertrags etc*). **3.** (Schluß)Folgerung *f*: *come to* (*od.* *arrive at*) *the ~ that* zu dem Schluß kommen, daß; *draw a ~* e-n Schluß ziehen; *jump at* (*od. to*) *~s, leap to ~s, rush at ~s* voreilig(e) Schlüsse ziehen. **con'clu·sive** [~sɪv] *adj* □ **1.** → *concluding.* **2.** schlüssig (*Beweis*).

con·coct [kən'kɒkt] *v/t* **1.** (zs.-)brauen. **2.** *fig.* aushecken, -brüten. **con'coc·tion** *s* **1.** (Zs.-)Brauen *n.* **2.** Gebräu *n* (*a. contp.*). **3.** *fig.* Ausbrüten *n*, -hecken *n.* **4.** *fig.* Erfindung *f.*

con·course ['kɒŋkɔ:s] *s* **1.** Zs.-treffen *n*; Zs.-fluß *m.* **2.** (Menschen)Auflauf *m*, (-)Menge *f.* **3.** freier Platz (*für Versammlungen etc*); *Am.* Bahnhofshalle *f.*

con·crete I *v/t s* **1.** [kən'kri:t] konkretisieren. **2.** ['kɒŋkri:t] betonieren: *~ over* zubetonieren. **II** *adj* [kɒŋkri:t] □ **3.** konkret (*a. ling., ♪ etc*). **4.** betoniert, Beton...: *~ jungle* Betonwüste *f*; *~ mixer* Betonmischmaschine *f*; *~ pile* Betonklotz *m*, -silo *m.* **III** *s* [kɒŋkri:t] **5.** Beton *m.*

con·cu·bine ['kɒŋkjʊbaɪn] *s* Nebenfrau *f.*

con·cur [kən'kɜ:] *v/i* **1.** zs.-fallen, -treffen. **2.** zs.-wirken. **3.** übereinstimmen (**with** mit; *in* in dat): *~ with s.o. a.* j-m beipflichten. **con·cur·rence** [~'kʌrəns] *s* **1.** Zs.-treffen *n.* **2.** Zs.-Wirken *n.* **3.** Übereinstimmung *f.* **con'cur·rent** *adj* □ **1.** zs.-treffend. **2.** zs.-wirkend. **3.** übereinstimmend.

con·cuss [kən'kʌs] *v/t* erschüttern: *be ~ed ♯* e-e Gehirnerschütterung erleiden. **con'cus·sion** [~ʃn] *s* Erschütterung *f*: *~* (*of the brain*) *♯* Gehirnerschütterung.

con·demn [kən'dem] *v/t* **1.** verdammen, verurteilen. **2.** *♯♯* verurteilen (*to death* zum Tode): *~ed cell* Todeszelle. **3.** für unbrauchbar *od.* unbewohnbar *od.* gesundheitsschädlich erklären. **4.** *Kranken* aufgeben. **con·dem·na·tion** [,kɒndem'neɪʃn] *s* Verdammung *f*, Verurteilung *f* (*a. ♯♯*).

con·den·sa·tion [,kɒnden'seɪʃn] *s* **1.** *phys.* Kondensation *f* (*a. ♠*), Verflüssigung *f*; Kondensat *n*, Kondenswasser *n*: *~ trail ✈* Kondensstreifen *m.* **2.** Zs.-fassung *f.* **con·dense** [kən'dens] **I** *v/t* **1.** *phys.* Gase, Dämpfe kondensieren, verflüssigen. **2.** *♠ Milch etc* eindicken, konzentrieren: *~d milk* Kondensmilch *f.* **3.** zs.-fassen, gedrängt darstellen. **II** *v/i* **4.** *phys.* kondensieren, sich verflüssigen. **con'dens·er** *s phys.* Kondensator *m* (*a. ∮*), Verflüssiger *m.*

con·de·scend [,kɒndɪ'send] *v/i* **1.** sich herablassen (*to do* zu tun; *to* zu). **2.** herablassend *od.* gönnerhaft sein (*to* gegen, zu). **con·de'scend·ing** *adj* □ herablassend, gönnerhaft.

con·di·ment ['kɒndɪmənt] *s* Gewürz *n*, Würze *f.*

con·di·tion [kən'dɪʃn] **I** *s* **1.** Bedingung *f*: *on ~ that* unter der Bedingung *od.* vorausgesetzt, daß; *on no ~* unter keinen Umständen, keinesfalls; *make s.th. a ~* et. zur Bedingung machen. **2.** Verfassung *f*: a) Zustand *m*, Beschaffenheit *f*, b) (körperlicher *od.* Gesundheits)Zustand *m*, (*Sport*) Form *f*: *out of ~* in schlechter Verfassung, in schlechtem Zustand; *the ~ of her health* ihr Gesundheitszustand. **3.** *pl* Bedingungen *pl*, Verhältnisse *pl*: *living ~s* Lebensbedingungen, -verhältnisse; *weather ~s* Witterungs-, Wetterverhältnisse. **II** *v/t* **4.** zur Bedingung machen, die Bedingung stellen (*that* daß). **5.** *j-n* programmieren (*to, for* auf acc). **con'di·tion·al** [~ʃənl] *adj* □ **1.** (*on*) bedingt (durch), abhängig (von): *be ~ on* abhängen von; *make ~ on* abhängig machen von. **2.** *ling.* Konditional...: *~ clause* (*od. sentence*) Konditional-, Bedingungssatz *m.* **con·di·tioned** [-∫nd] *adj* **1.** (*on*) bedingt (durch), abhängig (von): *be ~ on* abhängen von; *~ response* (*od.* **reflex**) *psych.* bedingter Reflex. **2.** beschaffen, geartet.

con·dole [kən'dəʊl] *v/i* sein Beileid ausdrücken, kondolieren (*with s.o.* on s.th. j-m zu et.). **con·do·lence** *s* Beileid *n: please accept my ~s* mein herzliches *od.* aufrichtiges Beileid; *register of ~* Kondolenzliste *f.*

con·dom [ˈkɒndəm] *s* Kondom *n, m,* Präservativ *n.*

con·do·min·i·um [ˌkɒndəˈmɪnɪəm] *s Am.* Eigentumswohnanlage *f:* **~** (*apartment*) Eigentumswohnung *f.*

con·done [kən'dəʊn] *v/t* **1.** verzeihen, vergeben: *she ~d his infidelity* sie verzieh ihm s-e Untreue. **2.** wettmachen, wiedergutmachen.

con·duce [kən'djuːs] *v/i* (*to, toward*[s]) beitragen (zu), dienlich *od.* förderlich sein, dienen (*dat*). **con·du·cive** *adj* dienlich, förderlich (*to dat*).

con·duct I *s* [ˈkɒndʌkt] **1.** Führung *f,* Leitung *f.* **2.** Betragen *n,* Verhalten *n:* → *certificate* **1. II** *v/t* [kən'dʌkt] **3.** führen, geleiten: *~ed tour* Führung *f* (*of* durch). **4.** *Prozeß, Verhandlungen etc* führen, *Geschäft a.* betreiben, leiten. **5.** ♪ leiten, dirigieren. **6.** *~ o.s.* sich betragen *od.* verhalten. **7.** *phys.* leiten. **con·duct·i·ble** [kən'dʌktəbl], **con·duc·tive** *adj phys.* leitfähig. **con·duc·tor** *s* **1.** Führer *m,* Leiter *m.* **2.** (*Bus-, Straßenbahn*)Schaffner *m; Am.* Zugbegleiter *m.* **3.** ♪ Dirigent *m.* **4.** *phys.* Leiter *m;* ⚡ *a.* Blitzableiter *m.* **con·duc·tress** *s* Schaffnerin *f.*

cone [kəʊn] **I** *s* **1.** ⚭ *u. fig.* Kegel *m.* **2.** ⚭ (*Tannen- etc*)Zapfen *m.* **3.** kegelförmiger Gegenstand, *z. B.* a) Waffeltüte *f* (*für Speiseeis*), b) Pylon(e *f*) *m,* Leitkegel *m.* **II** *v/t* **4.** *~ off* mit Leitkegeln absperren.

con·fec·tion [kən'fek∫n] *s* Konfekt *n.* **con·fec·tion·er** *s* Konditor *m.* **con·fec·tion·er·y** *s* **1.** Süßwaren *pl.* **2.** Süßwarengeschäft *n;* Konditorei *f.*

con·fed·er·a·cy [kən'fedərəsɪ] *s* **1.** (Staaten)Bund *m.* **2.** Komplott *n,* Verschwörung *f.* **con·fed·er·ate** [~rət] **I** *adj* verbündet (*with* mit), Bundes... **II** *s* Verbündete *m,* Bundesgenosse *m.* **III** *v/t u.*

v/i [~reɪt] (sich) verbünden *od.* zs.-schließen. **con·fed·er·a·tion** *s* **1.** Bund *m,* Bündnis *n.* **2.** (Staaten)Bund *m.*

con·fer [kən'fɜː] **I** *v/t Titel etc* verleihen (*on dat*). **II** *v/i* sich beraten (*with* mit). **con·fer·ence** [ˈkɒnfərəns] *s* Konferenz *f:* a) Tagung *f,* b) Besprechung *f: be in ~* in e-r Besprechung sein.

con·fess [kən'fes] **I** *v/t* **1.** bekennen, (ein)gestehen, zugeben (*a. that* daß). **3.** *eccl.* beichten; j-m die Beichte abnehmen. **II** *v/i* **4.** (*to*) (ein)gestehen (*acc*), sich schuldig bekennen (*gen od. an acc*), sich bekennen (zu): *~ to doing s.th.* (ein)gestehen, et. getan zu haben; *he has ~ed* ⚖ er hat gestanden, er ist geständig. **5.** *eccl.* beichten (*to dat*). **con·fessed** *adj* erklärt. **con·fess·ed·ly** [~ɪdlɪ] *adv* zugestandener-, eingestandenermaßen. **con·fes·sion** [~∫n] *s* **1.** Geständnis *n* (*a.* ⚖): *make a full ~* ein volles Geständnis ablegen. **2.** *eccl.* Beichte *f: go to ~* zur Beichte gehen; → *auricular.* **3.** *eccl.* Konfession *f:* a) Glaubensbekenntnis *n,* b) Glaubensgemeinschaft *f.* **con·fes·sion·al** [~∫ənl] **I** *adj* **1.** konfessionell, Konfessions... **2.** Beicht... **II** *s* **3.** Beichtstuhl *m: secret of the ~* Beichtgeheimnis *n.* **con·fes·sor** [~sə] *s eccl.* Beichtvater *m.*

con·fet·ti [kən'fetɪ] *s pl* (*sg* konstruiert) Konfetti *n.*

con·fi·dant [ˌkɒnfɪ'dænt] *s* Vertraute *f.* **con·fi·dante** [~'dænt] *s* Vertraute *f.*

con·fide [kən'faɪd] **I** *v/i* **1.** sich anvertrauen (*in dat*). **2.** vertrauen (*in dat* auf *acc*). **II** *v/t* **3.** *~ s.th. to s.o.* j-m et. anvertrauen.

con·fi·dence [ˈkɒnfɪdəns] *s* **1.** (*in*) Vertrauen *n* (auf *acc,* zu), Zutrauen *n* (zu): *have ~ in* Vertrauen haben zu; *take s.o. into one's ~* j-n ins Vertrauen ziehen; *in ~,* → *confidentially;* → *strict.* **2.** *a. ~ in o.s.* Selbstvertrauen *n.* **3.** vertrauliche Mitteilung, *pl a.* Vertraulichkeiten *pl. ~* **game** *Am.* → *confidence trick. ~* **man** *s* (*irr man*) Betrüger *m;* Hochstapler *m. ~* **trick** *s* aufgelegter Schwindel; Hochstapelei *f.* **~ trick·ster** → **confidence man.**

con·fi·dent [ˈkɒnfɪdənt] *adj* □ **1.** (*of; that*) überzeugt (von; daß), sicher (*gen;* daß). **2.** *a. ~ in o.s.* selbstsicher. **con·fi·den·tial** [ˌ~ˈden∫l] *adj* **1.** vertrau-

lich, geheim. **2.** vertraut, Vertrauens...:
~ **clerk** ✝ Prokurist(in). ˌcon·fi'den·
tial·ly [~ʃəlɪ] adv vertraulich, im Vertrauen.

con·fine I s ['kɒnfaɪn] **1.** mst pl Grenze f,
Grenzgebiet n, fig. Rand m, Schwelle f.
II v/t [kən'faɪn] **2.** begrenzen, be-, einschränken (**to** auf acc). **3.** einschließen,
einsperren: **~d to bed** ans Bett gefesselt.
4. be ~d (of) niederkommen (mit), entbunden werden (von). con'fine·ment s
1. Be-, Einschränkung f. **2.** Haft f: solitary ~ Einzelhaft. **3.** Niederkunft f,
Entbindung f.

con·firm [kən'fɜːm] v/t **1.** bestätigen. **2.**
Entschluß bekräftigen; j-n bestärken
(**in** in dat). **3.** eccl. konfirmieren; firmen. con·fir·ma·tion [ˌkɒnfə'meɪʃn] s
1. Bestätigung f. **2.** Bekräftigung f; Bestärkung f. **3.** eccl. Konfirmation f; Firmung f. con'firmed adj **1.** fest (Gewohnheit etc). **2.** erklärt, überzeugt: ~
bachelor eingefleischter Junggeselle.

con·fis·cate ['kɒnfɪskeɪt] v/t beschlagnahmen, konfiszieren. ˌcon·fis'ca·tion
s Beschlagnahme f, Konfiszierung f.

con·flict I s ['kɒnflɪkt] s Konflikt m: a)
Zs.-stoß m: → armed, b) Widerstreit
m: come into ~ with in Konflikt geraten mit; ~ of interests Interessenkon-
flikt m, -kollision f. **II** v/i [kən'flɪkt]
(**with**) kollidieren (mit), im Widerspruch od. Gegensatz stehen (zu).
con'flict·ing adj widersprüchlich.

con·form [kən'fɔːm] **I** v/t **1.** anpassen (**to**
dat od. an acc). **2.** in Einklang bringen
(**to** mit). **II** v/i **3.** sich anpassen (**to** dat).
4. übereinstimmen (**to** mit). con'form-
i·ty s **1.** Übereinstimmung f: be in ~
übereinstimmen (**with** mit); in ~ with in
Übereinstimmung mit, gemäß (dat). **2.**
Anpassung f (**to** an acc).

con·found [kən'faʊnd] v/t **1.** verwechseln, durcheinanderbringen (**with** mit).
2. verwirren, durcheinanderbringen. **3.**
~ it! verdammt! con'found·ed adj ☐ F
verdammt.

con·front [kən'frʌnt] v/t **1.** (oft feindlich)
gegenübertreten, -stehen (dat): be ~ed
with Schwierigkeiten etc gegenüberstehen, sich gegenübersehen (dat). **2.**
sich e-r Gefahr etc stellen. **3.** a. 🜨 (with)
konfrontieren (mit), gegenüberstellen
(dat): ~ s.o. with s.th. j-m et. entge-

genhalten. con·fron·ta·tion [ˌkɒnfrʌn-
'teɪʃn] s Konfrontation f (a. pol. etc).

con·fuse [kən'fjuːz] v/t **1.** verwechseln,
durcheinanderbringen (**with** mit). **2.**
verwirren: a) in Unordnung bringen,
b) aus der Fassung bringen, verlegen
machen. con'fused adj **1.** verwirrt: a)
konfus, verworren, wirr, b) verlegen,
bestürzt. **2.** undeutlich, verworren.
con'fu·sion [~ʒn] s **1.** Verwechs(e)lung
f: ~ of names Namensverwechslung. **2.**
Verwirrung f: a) Durcheinander n:
cause ~ Verwirrung stiften od. anrichten; throw everything into → alles
durcheinanderbringen, b) Verlegenheit
f, Bestürzung f: in ~ → confused 1b;
put to ~ in Verlegenheit bringen.

con·fu·ta·tion [ˌkɒnfjuː'teɪʃn] s Widerlegung f. con·fute [kən'fjuːt] v/t widerlegen.

con·geal [kən'dʒiːl] v/t u. v/i gefrieren
od. gerinnen (lassen), erstarren (lassen).

con·gen·ial [kən'dʒiːnjəl] adj ☐ **1.** gleichartig, (geistes)verwandt (**with** mit od.
dat). **2.** sympathisch, angenehm (**to**
dat): be ~ to s.o. j-m zusagen. **3.** zuträglich (**to** dat od. für): ~ to one's health
gesund.

con·gen·i·tal [kən'dʒenɪtl] adj angeboren: ~ defect Geburtsfehler m. con-
'gen·i·tal·ly [~təlɪ] adv **1.** von Geburt
(an). **2.** von Natur (aus).

con·gest·ed [kən'dʒestɪd] adj **1.** verstopft: ~ streets. **2.** überfüllt (**with**
von): ~ area übervölkertes Gebiet,
Ballungsgebiet n. con'ges·tion s **1.** Anhäufung f: ~ of population Übervölkerung f; ~ of traffic Verkehrsstockung f,
-stauung f, -stau m. **2.** 🜨 Blutandrang
m (of the brain zum Gehirn).

con·glom·er·ate I v/t u. v/i [kən-
'glɒməreɪt] (sich) zs.-ballen (**to** zu). **II**
adj [~rət] fig. zs.-gewürfelt. **III** s [~rət]
Konglomerat n, zs.-gewürfelte Masse,
Gemisch n. con·glom·er·a·tion →
conglomerate **III**.

con·grats [kən'ɡræts] int bsd. Br. F gratulieren!

con·grat·u·late [kən'ɡrætʃʊleɪt] v/t j-m
gratulieren, j-n beglückwünschen (**on**
zu). con·grat·u·la·tion s Gratulation f,
Glückwunsch m: ~s! ich gratuliere!,
herzlichen Glückwunsch! con'grat·u·
la·tor s Gratulant(in). con'grat·u·la-

to·ry [ˌ⁀lətəri] *adj* Glückwunsch...: ~ *telegram.*

con·gre·gate [ˈkɒŋgrɪgeɪt] *v/t u. v/i* (sich) versammeln. **ˌcon·greˈga·tion** *s* **1.** Versammlung *f.* **2.** (Kirchen)Gemeinde *f.* **ˌcon·greˈga·tion·al** [ˌ⁀ʃənl] *adj eccl.* Gemeinde...

con·gress [ˈkɒŋgres] *s* **1.** Kongreß *m,* Tagung *f.* **2.** ♀ *pol. Am.* der Kongreß. **♀·man** [ˈ⁀mən] *s (irr man),* **ˈ♀·wom·an** *s (irr woman) pol. Am.* Mitglied *n* des Repräsentantenhauses.

con·gru·ence [ˈkɒŋgrʊəns] *s* **1.** Übereinstimmung *f.* **2.** ♣ Kongruenz *f (a. fig.).* **ˈcon·gru·ent** *adj* □ **1.** übereinstimmend **(to, with** mit). **2.** ♣ kongruent *(a. fig.).* **con·gru·i·ty** [ˈgruːəti] → *congruence.* **con·gru·ous** [ˈ⁀grʊəs] → *congruent.*

con·ic, con·i·cal [ˈkɒnɪk(l)] *adj* □ konisch, kegelförmig: *conic section* ♣ Kegelschnitt *m.*

co·ni·fer [ˈkɒnɪfə] *s* ♣ Nadelbaum *m.* **co·nif·er·ous** [kəˈnɪfərəs] *adj* zapfentragend; Nadel...: → *tree.*

con·jec·tur·al [kənˈdʒektʃərəl] *adj* □ mutmaßlich. **con·jec·ture** I *s* Vermutung *f,* Mutmaßung *f: be reduced to ~* auf Vermutungen angewiesen sein. II *v/t* vermuten, mutmaßen. III *v/i* Vermutungen anstellen, mutmaßen **(of, about** über *acc).*

con·ju·gal [ˈkɒndʒʊgl] *adj* □ ehelich: ~ *life* Eheleben *n.* **con·ju·gate** [ˈ⁀geɪt] *ling.* I *v/t* konjugieren, beugen. II *v/i* konjugiert *od.* gebeugt werden. **ˌcon·juˈga·tion** *s ling.* Konjugation *f,* Beugung *f.*

con·junc·tion [kənˈdʒʌŋkʃn] *s* **1.** Verbindung *f: in ~ with* in Verbindung *od.* zusammen mit. **2.** Zs.-treffen *n (von Ereignissen etc).* **3.** *ling.* Konjunktion *f,* Bindewort *n.* **con·junc·ti·va** [ˌkɒn-dʒʌŋkˈtaɪvə] *pl* **-vas, -vae** [ˌ⁀viː] *s anat.* Bindehaut *f.* **con·junc·ti·vi·tis** [kən-ˌdʒʌŋktuˈvaɪtɪs] *s* ✚ Bindehautentzündung *f.*

con·jure [ˈkʌndʒə] I *v/t* **1.** [kənˈdʒʊə] beschwören **(to do** zu tun). **2.** *Teufel etc* beschwören, anrufen: ~ *up* heraufbeschwören *(a. fig.).* **3.** ~ *away* wegzaubern; ~ *up* hervorzaubern *(a. fig.).* II *v/i* **4.** zaubern. **ˈcon·jur·er** *s* **1.** Zauberer *m.* **2.** Zauberkünstler *m.* **ˈcon·jur·ing**

trick *s* Zauberkunststück *n,* -trick *m.* **ˈcon·jur·or** → *conjurer.*

conk¹ [kɒŋk] *s sl.* Riecher *m (Nase);* Birne *f (Kopf).*

conk² [~] *v/i sl. mst* ~ *out* **1.** streiken, den Geist aufgeben *(Fernseher etc),* absterben *(Motor).* **2.** a) umkippen *(ohnmächtig werden),* b) *vor Erschöpfung etc* zs.-klappen, c) *a.* ~ *off* einpennen. **3.** den Löffel weglegen *(sterben).*

con·nect [kəˈnekt] I *v/t* **1.** verbinden **(with** mit) *(a. fig.).* **2.** *fig.* in Zs.-hang *od.* Verbindung bringen **(with** mit). **3.** ⚙ **(to)** verbinden (mit), *Wagen etc* anhängen, ankuppeln (an *acc).* **4.** ⚡ **(to)** anschließen (an *acc),* zuschalten *(dat).* **5.** *teleph.* verbinden **(to, with** mit): ~ *s.o. further* j-n weiterverbinden. II *v/i* **6.** 🚆 *etc* Anschluß haben **(with** an *acc).* **con·nect·ed** *adj* **1.** verbunden. **2.** (logisch) zs.-hängend. **3.** verwandt: ~ *by marriage* verschwägert; *be well* ~ einflußreiche Verwandte *od.* gute Beziehungen haben. **4. (with)** verwickelt (in *acc),* beteiligt (an *dat).* **con·nect·ing** *adj* Verbindungs...: ~ *door; ~ flight* Anschlußflug *m;* ~ *train* Anschlußzug *m.* **con·nec·tion** *s* **1.** Verbindung *f.* **2.** ⚙ *allg.* Verbindung *f,* Anschluß *m (a.* ⚡, 🚆, *teleph. etc).* **3.** Zs.-hang *m: in this* ~ in diesem Zs.-hang; *in* ~ *with* in Zs.-hang mit; mit Bezug auf *(acc).* **4.** *pl* geschäftliche, gute *etc* Beziehungen *od.* Verbindungen *pl;* Bekannten-, Kundenkreis *m.* **con·nec·tive** I *adj* □ verbindend: ~ *tissue anat.* Bindegewebe *f;* ~ *word* →II. II *s ling.* Bindewort *n.*

con·nex·ion *bsd. Br.* → *connection.*

con·nois·seur [ˌkɒnəˈsɜː] *s (Wein- etc)* Kenner *m.*

con·no·ta·tion [ˌkɒnəʊˈteɪʃn] *s* Nebenbedeutung *f.* **con·note** [kəˈnəʊt] *v/t* (zugleich) bedeuten.

con·quer [ˈkɒŋkə] *v/t* **1.** erobern *(a. fig.).* **2.** besiegen, *fig. a.* bezwingen. **ˈcon·quer·or** *s* Eroberer *m.*

con·quest [ˈkɒŋkwest] *s* **1.** Eroberung *f (a. fig. Person): make a ~ of s.o.* j-n erobern. **2.** Besiegung *f, fig. a.* Bezwingung *f.*

con·san·guin·e·ous [ˌkɒnsæŋˈgwɪnɪəs] *adj* blutsverwandt. **ˌcon·sanˈguin·i·ty** *s* Blutsverwandtschaft *f.*

con·science [ˈkɒnʃəns] *s* Gewissen *n: a*

good (*guilty*) ~ ein gutes (schlechtes) Gewissen; *for ~'s sake* um des Gewissens zu beruhigen; *act on ~* nach s-m Gewissen handeln, s-m Gewissen folgen; *have s.th. on one's ~* Gewissensbisse od. ein schlechtes Gewissen haben wegen an.

con·sci·en·tious [ˌkɒnʃɪˈenʃəs] *adj* □ **1.** gewissenhaft. **2.** Gewissens...: ~ **objector** Kriegs-, Wehrdienstverweigerer *m* (*aus Gewissensgründen*). **ˌcon·sci'en·tious·ness** *s* Gewissenhaftigkeit *f*.

con·scious [ˈkɒnʃəs] *adj* □ **1.** bei Bewußtsein. **2.** *be* ~ *of* sich bewußt sein (*gen*), sich im klaren sein über (*acc*). **3.** bewußt, absichtlich. **'con·scious·ness** *s* Bewußtsein *n*: *lose* ~ das Bewußtsein verlieren; *regain* ~ wieder zu sich kommen; *~-expanding* bewußtseinserweiternd.

con·script ✗ **I** *v/t* [kənˈskrɪpt] **1.** einziehen, -berufen. **II** *s* [ˈkɒnskrɪpt] **2.** Wehr(dienst)pflichtige *m*. **3.** Einberufene *m*. **con·scrip·tion** [kənˈskrɪpʃn] *s* **1.** Einziehung *f*, -berufung *f*. **2.** Wehrpflicht *f*.

con·se·crate [ˈkɒnsɪkreɪt] *v/t* **1.** *eccl.* weihen. **2.** weihen, widmen (*to dat*). **ˌcon·se'cra·tion** *s* **1.** *eccl.* Weihe *f*, Weihung *f*. **2.** Hingabe *f* (*to* an *acc*).

con·sec·u·tive [kənˈsekjʊtɪv] *adj* **1.** aufeinanderfolgend: *for two ~ days* zwei Tage hintereinander. **2.** (fort)laufend (*Nummer*). **3.** ~ *clause ling.* Konsekutiv-, Folgesatz *m*. **con'sec·u·tive·ly** *adv* **1.** nach-, hintereinander. **2.** (fort)laufend.

con·sen·sus [kənˈsensəs] *s a.* ~ *of opinion* (allgemein) übereinstimmende Meinung, (allgemeine) Übereinstimmung.

con·sent [kənˈsent] **I** *v/i* **1.** (*to*) zustimmen (*dat*), einwilligen (in *acc*). **2.** sich bereit erklären (*to do* zu tun). **II** *s* **3.** (*to*) Zustimmung *f* (zu), Einwilligung *f* (in *acc*): *with the ~ of* mit Zustimmung von (*od. gen*); *with one ~* einstimmig, -mütig.

con·se·quence [ˈkɒnsɪkwəns] *s* **1.** Folge *f*, Konsequenz *f*: *in ~* folglich, daher; *in* (*od. as a*) ~ *of* infolge von (*od. gen*); *take the ~s* die Folgen tragen; *with the ~ that* mit dem Ergebnis, daß. **2.** Folgerung *f*, Schluß *m*. **3.** Bedeutung *f*,

Wichtigkeit *f*: *of* (*no*) ~ von (ohne) Bedeutung, (un)bedeutend, (un)wichtig (*to* für); *a person of great* ~ e-e bedeutende *od.* einflußreiche Persönlichkeit. **'con·se·quent** *adj* (*on*) folgend (*dat od.* auf *acc*); sich ergebend (aus). **'con·se·quent·ly** *adv* folglich, daher.

con·ser·va·tion [ˌkɒnsəˈveɪʃn] *s* **1.** Erhaltung *f*, Bewahrung *f*. **2.** Natur- *od.* Umweltschutz *m*: ~ *area* Naturschutzgebiet *n*. **3.** Konservieren *n*, Haltbarmachen *n*. **ˌcon·ser'va·tion·ist** *s* Natur- *od.* Umweltschützer(in). **con·serv·a·tive** [kənˈsɜːvətɪv] **I** *adj* □ **1.** konservativ (*pol. mst* ♘). **2.** vorsichtig (*Schätzung etc*). **II** *s* **3.** *mst* ♘ *pol.* Konservative *m*, *f*. **4.** konservativer Mensch. **con·ser·va·toire** [~twɑː] *s* Konservatorium *n*, Musik(hoch)schule *f*. **con·serv·a·to·ry** [~trɪ] *s* **1.** Treib-, Gewächshaus *n*, *bsd.* Wintergarten *m*. **2.** → *conservatoire*. **con·serve** *v/t* **1.** erhalten, bewahren. **2.** konservieren, haltbar machen, *Obst etc* einmachen. **II** *s* **3.** *mst* ♘ Eingemachte *n*.

con·sid·er [kənˈsɪdə] **I** *v/t* **1.** nachdenken über (*acc*). **2.** betrachten *od.* ansehen als, halten für: ~ *s.th.* (*to be*) *a mistake*; *be* ~*ed rich* als reich gelten. **3.** sich überlegen, erwägen (*doing* zu tun). **4.** berücksichtigen, in Betracht ziehen. **5.** Rücksicht nehmen auf (*acc*), denken an (*acc*). **6.** finden, meinen, denken (*that* daß). **II** *v/i* **7.** nachdenken, überlegen. **con'sid·er·a·ble** *adj* □ **1.** beachtlich, beträchtlich. **2.** bedeutend, wichtig (*beide a.* Person). **con'sid·er·ate** [~rət] *adj* □ aufmerksam, rücksichtsvoll (*to, toward[s]* gegen): *be* ~ *of* Rücksicht nehmen auf (*acc*). **conˌsid·er'a·tion** [~ˈreɪʃn] *s* **1.** Erwägung *f*, Überlegung *f*: *take into* ~ in Erwägung *od.* Betracht ziehen; *leave out of* ~ ausklammern; *on* (*od. under*) *no* ~ unter keinen Umständen. **2.** Berücksichtigung *f*: *in* ~ *of* in Anbetracht (*gen*). **3.** Rücksicht(nahme) *f* (*for, of* auf *acc*): *lack of* ~ Rücksichtslosigkeit *f*. **4.** (zu berücksichtigender) Grund: *money is no* ~ Geld spielt keine Rolle. **con'sid·er·ing I** *prp* in Anbetracht (*acc*). **II** *cj*: ~ *that* in Anbetracht der Tatsache, daß. **III** *adv* F alles in allem.

con·sign [kənˈsaɪn] *v/t* **1.** übergeben (*to*

dat). **2.** ✝ *Waren* übersenden, zusenden (**to** *dat*). **con·sig·nee** [ˌkɒnsaɪˈniː] *s* ✝ Empfänger *m*. **con·sign·er** [kənˈsaɪnə] → **consignor. con·sign·ment** *s* ✝ **1.** Übersendung *f*, Zusendung *f*: **~ note** Frachtbrief *m*. **2.** (Waren)Sendung *f*. **con·sign·or** *s* ✝ Übersender *m*.

con·sist [kənˈsɪst] *v/i* **1. ~ of** bestehen *od.* sich zs.-setzen aus. **2. ~ in** bestehen in (*dat*). **con·sist·ence, con·sist·en·cy** *s* **1.** Konsistenz *f*, Beschaffenheit *f*, (Grad *m* der) Festigkeit *f od.* Dichtigkeit *f*. **2.** *fig.* Konsequenz *f*, Folgerichtigkeit *f*. **3.** *fig.* Übereinstimmung *f*, Einklang *m*. **con·sist·ent** *adj* □ **1.** konsistent, fest, dicht. **2.** *fig.* konsequent, folgerichtig. **3.** *fig.* übereinstimmend, vereinbar, in Einklang stehend (**with** mit). **4.** *fig.* beständig (*Leistung etc*).

con·so·la·tion [ˌkɒnsəˈleɪʃn] *s* Trost *m*: **~ goal** (*Sport*) Ehrentor *n*; **~ prize** Trostpreis *m*. **con·sol·a·to·ry** [kənˈsɒlətərɪ] *adj* tröstend, tröstlich.

con·sole[1] [ˈkɒnsəʊl] *s* **1.** Konsole *f*: **~ table** Konsoltischchen *n*. **2.** (Fernseh-, Musik)Truhe *f*, (Radio)Schrank *m*. **3.** ⚡ Schalt-, Steuerpult *n*.

con·sole[2] [kənˈsəʊl] *v/t* trösten: **~ s.o. for s.th.** j-n über *et.* hinwegtrösten.

con·sol·i·date [kənˈsɒlɪdeɪt] **I** *v/t* **1.** (ver)stärken, festigen (*beide a. fig.*). **2.** ✕ *Truppen* zs.-ziehen. **3.** ✝ *Gesellschaften* zs.-schließen, -legen. **4.** ⚙ verdichten. **II** *v/i* **5.** ✝ sich zs.-schließen. **6.** ⚙ sich verdichten. **con·sol·i·da·tion** *s* **1.** (Ver)Stärkung *f*, Festigung *f*. **2.** ✕ Zs.-ziehung *f*. **3.** ✝ Zs.-legung *f*; Zs.-schluß *m*. **4.** ⚙ Verdichtung *f*.

con·som·mé [kənˈsɒmeɪ] *s* Consommé *f* (*klare Kraftbrühe*).

con·so·nant [ˈkɒnsənənt] **I** *adj* □ **1.** gleichlautend. **2.** übereinstimmend (**with** mit). **II** *s* **3.** *ling.* Konsonant *m*.

con·sort [ˈkɒnsɔːt] *s* Gemahl(in): **prince ~** Prinzgemahl. **con·sor·ti·um** [ˌtjəm] *pl* **-ti·a** [ˌə] *s* ✝ Konsortium *n*: **~ of banks** Bankenkonsortium.

con·spic·u·ous [kənˈspɪkjʊəs] *adj* □ **1.** deutlich sichtbar: **be ~** *a.* in die Augen fallen. **2.** auffallend, -fällig: **make o.s. ~** sich auffällig benehmen, auffallen. **3.** bemerkenswert (**for** wegen): **be ~ by one's absence** durch Abwesenheit glänzen; **render o.s. ~** sich hervortun.

con·spir·a·cy [kənˈspɪrəsɪ] *s* Verschwörung *f*. **con·spir·a·tor** *s* Verschwörer *m*. **con·spire** [ˌˈspaɪə] *v/i* **1.** sich verschwören (**against** gegen) (*a. fig.*). **2.** *fig.* zs.-wirken.

con·sta·ble [ˈkʌnstəbl] *s bsd. Br.* Polizist *m*, Wachtmeister *m*. **con·stab·u·lar·y** [kənˈstæbjʊlərɪ] *s bsd. Br.* Polizei *f* (*e-s Bezirks*).

con·stan·cy [ˈkɒnstənsɪ] *s* **1.** Konstanz *f*, Beständigkeit *f*. **2.** Bestand *m*, Dauer *f*. **3.** *fig.* Standhaftigkeit *f*. **con·stant I** *adj* □ **1.** konstant (*a. phys., ✚ etc*), beständig, gleichbleibend. **2.** (be)ständig, (an)dauernd: **~ rain** anhaltender Regen. **3.** *fig.* standhaft, beharrlich. **II** *s* **4.** *phys., ✚* Konstante *f*.

con·stel·la·tion [ˌkɒnstəˈleɪʃn] *s ast.* Konstellation *f* (*a. fig.*), Sternbild *n*.

con·ster·na·tion [ˌkɒnstəˈneɪʃn] *s* Bestürzung *f*: **in ~** konsterniert, bestürzt; **to my ~** zu m-r Bestürzung.

con·sti·pate [ˈkɒnstɪpeɪt] *v/t* 💊 verstopfen: **be ~d** an Verstopfung leiden. **con·sti·pa·tion** *s* Verstopfung *f*.

con·stit·u·en·cy [kənˈstɪtjʊənsɪ] *s* **1.** Wählerschaft *f*. **2.** Wahlbezirk *m*, -kreis *m*. **con·stit·u·ent I** *adj* **1.** e-n (Bestand)Teil bildend: **~ part** → **4. 2.** *pol.* Wähler..., Wahl...: **~ body** Wählerschaft *f*. **3. ~ assembly** *pol.* verfassunggebende Versammlung. **II** *s* **4.** (wesentlicher) Bestandteil. **5.** *pol.* Wähler(in).

con·sti·tute [ˈkɒnstɪtjuːt] *v/t* **1.** ernennen, einsetzen: **~ s.o. a judge** j-n als Richter einsetzen *od.* zum Richter ernennen. **2.** *Gesetz* erlassen, in Kraft setzen. **3.** einrichten, gründen, *Ausschuß etc* einsetzen. **4.** ausmachen, bilden, darstellen. **con·sti·tu·tion** *s* **1.** Zs.-setzung *f*, (Auf)Bau *m*. **2.** Konstitution *f*, körperliche Veranlagung. **3.** Natur *f*, Wesen *n*: **by ~** von Natur (aus). **4.** Einrichtung *f*, Gründung *f*, Einsetzung *f*. **5.** *pol.* Verfassung *f*. **con·sti·tu·tion·al** [ˌʃənl] **I** *adj* □ **1.** 💊 konstitutionell, anlagebedingt. **2.** *pol.* a) verfassungsgemäß, Verfassungs...: → **monarchy**, b) rechtsstaatlich: **~ state** Rechtsstaat *m*. **II** *s* **3.** F Gesundheitsspaziergang *m*.

con·strain [kənˈstreɪn] *v/t* **1.** j-n zwingen, nötigen: **feel ~ed to do s.th.** sich gezwungen fühlen, et. zu tun. **2.** *et.* erzwingen. **con'straint** [~'streɪnt] *s* Zwang *m*, Nötigung *f*: *under ~* unter Zwang, gezwungen.

con·struct [kən'strʌkt] *v/t* **1.** errichten, bauen. **2.** ⊙ konstruieren (*a. ling.*, ₳). bauen. **3.** *fig.* gestalten, ausarbeiten. **con'struc·tion** [~kʃn] *s* **1.** Errichtung *f*, Konstruktion *f* (*a.* ⊙, ₳, *ling.*): *under ~* im Bau (befindlich); *~ industry* Baugewerbe *n*, -wirtschaft *f*; *~ site* Baustelle *f*. **2.** Bauweise *f*: *steel ~* Stahlkonstruktion *f*. **3.** Bau(werk *n*) *m*. **4.** *fig.* Aufbau *m*, Gestaltung *f*. **con'struc·tion·al** [~ʃənl] *adj* □ Konstruktions..., baulich. **con'struc·tive** *adj* □ **1.** konstruktiv (*a. Kritik*), schöpferisch. **2.** → **constructional**. **con'struc·tor** *s* Erbauer *m*; Konstrukteur *m*.

con·strue [kən'struːʔ] *v/t ling.* konstruieren.

con·sul ['kɒnsəl] *s* Konsul *m*: *~ general* Generalkonsul *m*. **con·su·lar** ['~sjʊlə] *adj* Konsulats..., Konsular..., konsularisch. **con·su·late** ['~lət] *s* Konsulat *n* (*a. Gebäude*): *~ general* Generalkonsulat.

con·sult [kən'sʌlt] **I** *v/t* **1.** um Rat fragen, zu Rate ziehen, konsultieren (*about* wegen). **2.** in *e-m Buch* nachschlagen *od.* -sehen. **3.** berücksichtigen. **II** *v/i* **4.** (sich) beraten (*about* über *acc*). **con'sult·ant** *s* **1.** (fachmännischer) Berater. **2.** ₳ fachärztlicher Berater; Facharzt *m* (*an e-m Krankenhaus*). **con·sul·ta·tion** [ˌkɒnsəl'teɪʃn] *s* Beratung *f*, Konsultation *f*: *on ~ with* nach Rücksprache mit; *~ hour* Sprechstunde *f*. **con'sult·ing** *adj* beratend: *~ room* Sprechzimmer *n*.

con·sume [kən'sjuːm] *v/t* **1.** zerstören, vernichten: *be ~d by fire* ein Raub der Flammen werden. **2.** *fig.* verzehren: *be ~d with hatred* von Haß verzehrt werden. **3.** auf-, verzehren. **4.** auf-, verbrauchen, konsumieren. **5.** verschwenden, -geuden (*on* für). **6.** *Aufmerksamkeit etc* in Anspruch nehmen. **con'sum·er** *s* Verbraucher(in), Konsument(in): *~ goods pl* Konsumgüter *pl*; *~ protection* Verbraucherschutz *m*. **con·sum·mate I** *v/t* ['kɒnsəmeɪt] **1.** vollenden; *Ehe* vollziehen. **2.** vollkommen machen. **II** *adj* [kən'sʌmɪt] **3.** vollendet,

vollkommen. **con'sum·ma·tion** [ˌkɒnsə'meɪʃn] *s* Vollendung *f*; Vollziehung *f*.

con·sump·tion [kən'sʌmpʃn] *s* **1.** Verbrauch *m* (*of* an *dat*), ₊ *a.* Konsum *m*. **2.** Verzehr *m*: (*un*)*fit for human ~* für den menschlichen Verzehr (un)geeignet.

con·tact ['kɒntækt] **I** *s* **1.** Kontakt *m* (*a.* ₰ *u. fig.*), Berührung *f*: *make ~s* Verbindungen anknüpfen *od.* herstellen; *business ~s* Geschäftsverbindungen *pl*; *~ lens* Haftlinse *f*, -schale *f*, Kontaktlinse *f*, -schale *f*. **2.** ₳ Kontaktperson *f*. **3.** *a. ~ man* Verbindungs-, Kontaktmann *m*. **II** *v/t* Kontakt aufnehmen mit, sich in Verbindung setzen mit.

con·ta·gion [kən'teɪdʒən] *s* ₳ Ansteckung *f* (*durch Berührung*); ansteckende Krankheit. **con'ta·gious** *adj* □ ₳ ansteckend (*a. fig.*).

con·tain [kən'teɪn] *v/t* **1.** enthalten. **2.** aufnehmen, fassen. **3.** *fig.* zügeln, zurückhalten: *~ o.s.* (an) sich halten, sich beherrschen. **con'tain·er** *s* **1.** Behälter *m*, (*Benzin- etc*)Kanister *m*. **2.** ₳ Container *m*: *~ ship* Containerschiff *n*. **con'tain·er·ize** *v/t* **1.** auf Containerbetrieb umstellen. **2.** in Containern transportieren.

con·tam·i·nate [kən'tæmɪneɪt] *v/t* **1.** verunreinigen. **2.** infizieren, vergiften (*beide a. fig.*), (*a.* radioaktiv) verseuchen. **con·tam·i·na·tion** *s* **1.** Verunreinigung *f*. **2.** Infizierung *f*, Vergiftung *f* (*beide a. fig.*), (*a.* radioaktiv) Verseuchung.

con·tem·plate ['kɒntempleɪt] **I** *v/t* **1.** (nachdenklich) betrachten. **2.** nachdenken über (*acc*). **3.** erwägen, beabsichtigen (*doing* zu tun). **4.** erwarten, rechnen mit (*a. ~ doing* daß man etwas tut). **II** *v/i* **5.** nachdenken (*about, on* über *acc*). **con·tem·pla·tion** *s* **1.** (nachdenkliche) Betrachtung. **2.** Nachdenken *n*. **3.** Erwägung *f*: *be in ~* erwogen werden. **'con·tem·pla·tive** *adj* □ nachdenklich.

con·tem·po·ra·ne·ous [kənˌtempə'reɪnjəs] *adj* □ gleichzeitig: *be ~ with* zeitlich zs.-fallen mit. **con'tem·po·ra·ry** *I adj* □ **1.** zeitgenössisch. **2.** → **contemporaneous**. **3.** gleichalt(e)rig. **II** *s* **4.** Zeitgenosse *m*, -genossin *f*. **5.** Altersgenosse *m*, -genossin *f*.

con·tempt [kən'tempt] *s* **1.** Verachtung *f*: ~ *of death* Todesverachtung; *feel* ~ *for, hold in* ~ verachten; *feel nothing but* ~ *for* nur Verachtung übrig haben für; *beneath* ~ unter aller Kritik; einfach lächerlich. **2.** Mißachtung *f*: ~ (*of court*) 🏛 Mißachtung des Gerichts. **con'tempt·i·ble** *adj* □ verächtlich, verachtenswert. **con'temp·tu·ous** [~tʃʊəs] *adj* □ verächtlich, geringschätzig: *be* ~ *of s.th.* et. verachten.

con·tend [kən'tend] I *v/i* **1.** kämpfen, ringen (*with* mit; *for* um). **2.** *mit Worten* streiten (*about* über *acc*). **3.** wetteifern, sich bewerben (*for* um). II *v/t* **4.** behaupten (*that* daß).

con·tent[1] ['kɒntent] *s* **1.** *e-s Buchs etc:* a) Gehalt *m*, Aussage *f*, b) *pl* Inhalt *m* (*a. e-r Tasche etc*): (*table of*) ~*s* Inhaltsverzeichnis *n*. **2.** 🧪 Gehalt *m* (*of an dat*): *gold* ~ Goldgehalt.

con·tent[2] [kən'tent] I *adj* zufrieden (*with* mit): *have to be* ~ *with* sich begnügen müssen mit. II *v/t* zufriedenstellen: ~ *o.s. with* sich zufrieden geben *od.* begnügen mit. III *s* Zufriedenheit *f*: → *heart* 1. **con'tent·ed** *adj* □ zufrieden (*with* mit).

con·ten·tion [kən'tenʃn] *s* **1.** Streit *m*, Zank *m*: *bone of* ~ *fig.* Zankapfel *m*. **2.** Streitpunkt *m*. **3.** Behauptung *f*: *my* ~ *is that* ich behaupte, daß. **con'ten·tious** *adj* □ **1.** streitsüchtig. **2.** umstritten, strittig: ~ *point* Streitpunkt *m*.

con·tent·ment [kən'tentmənt] *s* Zufriedenheit *f*.

con·test I *s* ['kɒntest] **1.** (Wett)Kampf *m*; Wettbewerb *m* (*for* um). II *v/t* [kən'test] **2.** kämpfen um, sich bewerben um. **3.** bestreiten, *a.* 🏛 anfechten: ~ *s.o.'s right to do s.th.* j-m das Recht streitig machen, et. zu tun. III *v/i* [kən'test] **4.** wetteifern (*with, against* mit). **con'test·ant** *s* **1.** (Wettkampf-)Teilnehmer(in). **2.** (Mit)Bewerber(in). **con'test·ed** → *contentious* 2.

con·text ['kɒntekst] *s* Zs.-hang *m*, Kontext *m*: *in this* ~ in diesem Zs.-hang; *out of* ~ aus dem Zs.-hang gerissen.

con·ti·nent ['kɒntɪnənt] *s* **1.** Kontinent *m*, Erdteil *m*. **2.** *the* 🌍 *Br.* das (europäische) Festland. **con·ti·nen·tal** [~'nentl] I *adj* **1.** kontinental, Kontinental... **2.** *mst* 🌍 *Br.* kontinental(europä-

isch): ~ *breakfast* kleines Frühstück; ~ *quilt* Federbett *n*. II *s* **3.** 🌍 *Br.* Kontinentaleuropäer(in).

con·tin·gen·cy [kən'tɪndʒənsɪ] *s* **1.** Zufälligkeit *f*. **2.** Möglichkeit *f*, Eventualität *f*: ~ *plan* Notplan *m*. **con'tin·gent** I *adj* □ **1.** (*on*) abhängig (von), bedingt (durch). **2.** möglich, eventuell. **3.** zufällig. II *s* **4.** (✕ Truppen)Kontingent *n*, Anteil *m*.

con·tin·u·al [kən'tɪnjʊəl] *adj* □ **1.** (an)dauernd, ständig. **2.** immer wiederkehrend, sich wiederholend: *a* ~ *knocking* ein wiederholtes Klopfen. **con'tin·u·ance** → *continuation*. **con,tin·u'a·tion** *s* **1.** Fortsetzung *f*. **2.** Fortbestand *m*, -dauer *f*. **con'tin·ue** [~ju:] I *v/t* **1.** fortfahren, weitermachen. **2.** andauern, anhalten. **3.** (fort)bestehen. **4.** (ver)bleiben: ~ *in office* im Amt bleiben. **5.** a) ~ *to do*, ~ *doing* (auch) weiterhin tun: ~ *to sing* weitersingen, b) ~ *to be*, ~ *being* weiterhin *od.* noch immer ... sein. II *v/t* **6.** fortsetzen, -führen, -fahren mit: *to be* ~*d* Fortsetzung folgt. **7.** beibehalten, erhalten. **con·ti·nu·i·ty** [,kɒntɪ'nju:ətɪ] *s* **1.** Kontinuität *f*. **2.** *Film:* Drehbuch *n*; *Rundfunk, TV:* Manuskript *n*: ~ *girl* Scriptgirl *n*. **con·tin·u·ous** [kən'tɪnjʊəs] *adj* □ **1.** ununterbrochen, unaufhörlich. **2.** kontinuierlich: ~ *current* ⚡ Gleichstrom *m*. **3.** ~ *form ling.* Verlaufsform *m*.

con·tort [kən'tɔ:t] I *v/t* **1.** *Glieder* verdrehen, verrenken. **2.** *Gesicht* verzerren, -ziehen (*with vor dat*): ~*ed with pain* schmerzverzerrt. **3.** *fig. Tatsachen etc* verdrehen. II *v/i* **4.** sich verzerren *od.* verziehen (*with vor dat*; *in a grimace* zu e-r Grimasse). **con'tor·tion** *s* **1.** Verrenkung *f.* **2.** Verzerrung *f.* **3.** *fig.* Verdrehung *f.* **con'tor·tion·ist** *s* **1.** Schlangenmensch *m.* **2.** *a. verbal* ~ Wortverdreher(in).

con·tour ['kɒn,tʊə] *s* Kontur *f*, Umriß *m*.

con·tra·band ['kɒntrəbænd] *s* **1.** Schmuggelware *f.* **2.** Schmuggel *m*.

con·tra·cep·tion [,kɒntrə'sepʃn] *s* ⚕ Empfängnisverhütung *f.* **,con·tra'cep·tive** *adj u. s* empfängnisverhütend(es Mittel).

con·tract I *s* ['kɒntrækt] **1.** Vertrag *m*: ~ *of employment* Arbeitsvertrag; ~ *of* *sale* Kaufvertrag; *enter into* (*od. make*) *a* ~ e-n Vertrag abschließen; *by* ~ vertraglich; *be under* ~ unter Vertrag stehen (*with, to* bei). **II** *v/t* [kən'trækt] **2.** *Muskel etc* zs.-ziehen, *Stirn* runzeln. **3.** *Gewohnheit* annehmen; sich *e-e Krankheit* zuziehen. **4.** *Schulden* machen. **5.** *Verpflichtung* eingehen; *Ehe etc* schließen. **III** *v/i* [kən'trækt] **6.** sich zs.-ziehen. **7.** e-n Vertrag abschließen; sich vertraglich verpflichten (*to do* zu tun; *for* zu): ~ *for s.th.* et. vertraglich festsetzen. **con'trac·tion** *s* Zs.-ziehung *f.* **con'trac·tor** *s* (*bsd.* Bau)Unternehmer *m*; (Vertrags)Lieferant *m.* **con'trac·tu·al** [~tʃʊəl] *adj* □ vertraglich, Vertrags...

con·tra·dict [ˌkɒntrə'dɪkt] *v/t* **1.** *j-m, e-r Sache* widersprechen, *et.* bestreiten. **2.** widersprechen (*dat*), im Widerspruch stehen zu, unvereinbar sein mit. **,con·tra'dic·tion** *s* **1.** Widerspruch *m*, -rede *f.* **2.** Unvereinbarkeit *f*: *be in* ~ *to* im Widerspruch stehen zu; ~ *in terms* Widerspruch *m* in sich selbst. **,con·tra'dic·to·ry** *adj* □ **1.** (*to*) widersprechend (*dat*), im Widerspruch stehend (zu), unvereinbar (mit). **2.** sich widersprechend, widersprüchlich.

con·tral·to [kən'træltəʊ] *pl* **-tos** *s* ♪ Alt(stimme *f*) *m*; Altistin *f.*

con·trap·tion [kən'træpʃn] *s* F (komischer) Apparat.

con·tra·ry ['kɒntrərɪ] **I** *adj* **1.** entgegengesetzt (*to dat*). **2.** einander entgegengesetzt, gegensätzlich. **3.** widrig, ungünstig (*Wind, Wetter*). **4.** (*to*) verstoßend (gegen), im Widerspruch (zu). **II** *adv* **5.** im Widerspruch (*to* zu): ~ *to expectations* wider Erwarten; *act* ~ *to* zuwiderhandeln (*dat*); → *law* 1. **III** *s* **6.** Gegenteil *n*: *on the* ~ im Gegenteil; *be the* ~ *to* das Gegenteil sein von; *to the* ~ gegenteilig; *proof to the* ~ Gegenbeweis *m.*

con·trast I *s* ['kɒntrɑːst] **1.** Kontrast *m* (*a. TV etc*), Gegensatz *m* (*between* zwischen *dat*): *form a* ~ e-n Kontrast bilden (*to* zu); *by* ~ *with* im Vergleich mit; *in* ~ *to* (*od. with*) im Gegensatz zu. **II** *v/t* [kən'trɑːst] **2.** entgegensetzen, gegenüberstellen (*with dat*). **III** *v/i* [kən'trɑːst] **3.** sich abheben, abstechen (*with* von, gegen); ~*ing colo(u)rs pl*

Kontrastfarben *pl.* **4.** e-n Gegensatz bilden, im Gegensatz stehen (*with* zu).

con·tra·vene [ˌkɒntrə'viːn] *v/t* **1.** zuwiderhandeln (*dat*), *Gesetz* übertreten, verstoßen gegen. **2.** im Widerspruch stehen zu. **con·tra·ven·tion** [~'venʃn] *s* (*of*) Zuwiderhandlung *f* (gegen), Übertretung *f* (von *od. gen*): *in* ~ *to* entgegen (*dat*).

con·trib·ute [kən'trɪbjuːt] **I** *v/t* **1.** beitragen, -steuern (*to* zu). **2.** *Artikel etc* beitragen (*to* zu *e-r Zeitung*). **3.** spenden (*to* für). **4.** † *Kapital* (*in e-e Firma*) einbringen. **II** *v/i* **5.** (*to*) beitragen, -steuern, e-n Beitrag leisten (zu), mitwirken (an *dat*): ~ *to* (*od. toward*[*s*]) *the expenses* sich an den Unkosten beteiligen; ~ *to a newspaper* für e-e Zeitung schreiben. **5.** spenden (*to* für). **con·tri·bu·tion** [ˌkɒntrɪ'bjuːʃn] *s* **1.** Beitrag *m* (*a. für Zeitung etc*), Beisteuer *f*: ~ *to* (*od. toward*[*s*]) *the expenses* Unkostenbeitrag. **2.** Spende *f*: *a small* ~, *please.* **3.** † Einlage *f.* **con·trib·u·tor** [kən'trɪbjʊtə] *s* **1.** Beitragende *m, f.* **2.** Mitarbeiter(in) (*to a newspaper* bei *od. an* e-r Zeitung). **con'trib·u·to·ry** *adj* beitragend.

con·trite ['kɒntraɪt] *adj* □ zerknirscht, reuevoll. **con·tri·tion** [kən'trɪʃn] *s* Zerknirschung *f*, Reue *f.*

con·triv·ance [kən'traɪvns] *s* **1.** ☼ Vorrichtung *f*; Gerät *n*, Apparat *m.* **2.** Erfindung *f.* **3.** Erfindungsgabe *f.* **4.** Plan *m.* **5.** Kunstgriff *m*, Kniff *m.* **con'trive** *v/t* **1.** erfinden, sich ausdenken. **2.** *et. Böses* ausdenken, *Pläne* schmieden. **3.** zustande bringen; es fertigbringen, es verstehen (*to do* zu tun).

con·trol [kən'trəʊl] **I** *v/t* **1.** beherrschen, die Herrschaft *od.* Kontrolle haben über (*acc*). **2.** in Schranken halten, (erfolgreich) bekämpfen: ~ *o.s.* sich beherrschen. **3.** kontrollieren: a) überwachen, beaufsichtigen, b) (nach)prüfen. **4.** leiten, führen, verwalten. **5.** † *Absatz etc* lenken, *Preise* binden. **6.** ⚡, ☼ steuern, regeln, regulieren. **II** *s* **7.** (*of, over*) Beherrschung *f* (*gen*), Macht *f*, Gewalt *f*, Kontrolle *f*, Herrschaft *f* (über *acc*): *bring* (*od. get*) *under* ~ unter Kontrolle bringen; *get out of* ~ außer Kontrolle geraten; *lose* ~ *of* (*od. over*) die Herrschaft *od.* Kontrolle verlieren über (*acc*); **lose ~ of o.s.** die (Selbst)Beherrschung verlieren. **8.** Aufsicht *f*, Kontrolle *f* (**of, over** über *acc*): **be in ~ of** et. leiten *od.* unter sich haben; **be under s.o.'s ~** j-m unterstehen *od.* unterstellt sein. **9.** Leitung *f*, Verwaltung *f*. **10.** *mst pl* ⚙ Steuerung *f*, Steuervorrichtung *f*; Kontroll-, Betätigungshebel *m*: **be at the ~s** *fig.* das Sagen haben; **sit at the ~s** an den (Schalt)Hebeln der Macht sitzen. **11.** ⚡, ⚙ Reg(e)lung *f*, Regulierung *f*; Regler *m*. ~ **cen·tre** (*Am.* **cen·ter**) *s* Kontrollzentrum *n*. ~ **desk** *s* **1.** ⚡ Schaltpult *n*. **2.** *Rundfunk, TV:* Regiepult *n*.

con·trol·la·ble [kən'trəʊləbl] *adj* **1.** kontrollierbar. **2.** ⚡, ⚙ steuer-, regel-, regulierbar. **con'trol·ler** *s* **1.** Kontrolleur *m*, Aufseher *m*. **2.** ✝ Controller *m* (*Fachmann für Kostenrechnung u. -planung*).

con·trol| le·ver *s* **1.** ⚙ Schalthebel *m*. **2.** → **control stick**. ~ **room** *s Rundfunk, TV:* Regieraum *m*. ~ **stick** *s* ✈ Steuerknüppel *m*. ~ **tow·er** *s* ✈ Kontrollturm *m*, Tower *m*.

con·tro·ver·sial [ˌkɒntrə'vɜːʃl] *adj* □ **1.** strittig, umstritten. **2.** polemisch. **3.** streitsüchtig. **con·tro·ver·sy** ['~sɪ] *s* **1.** Kontroverse *f*, *beyond* ~ unstreitig. **2.** *a. point in* ~ Streitfrage *f*, -punkt *m*.

con·tuse [kən'tjuːz] *v/t* ✚ sich et. quetschen. **con'tu·sion** [~ʒn] *s* Quetschung *f*.

co·nun·drum [kə'nʌndrəm] *s* Scherzfrage *f*, (Scherz)Rätsel *n*.

con·ur·ba·tion [ˌkɒnɜː'beɪʃn] *s* Ballungsraum *m*, -zentrum *n*.

con·va·lesce [ˌkɒnvə'les] *v/i* gesund werden. **con·va'les·cence** *s* Rekonvaleszenz *f*, Genesung *f*. **con·va'les·cent I** *adj* rekonvaleszent, genesend. **II** *s* Rekonvaleszent(in), Genesende *m, f*.

con·vene [kən'viːn] **I** *v/i* zs.-kommen, sich versammeln. **II** *v/t* versammeln, zs.-rufen, *Versammlung* einberufen.

con·ven·ience [kən'viːnjəns] *s* **1.** Annehmlichkeit *f*, Bequemlichkeit *f*: **all** (**modern**) **~s** aller Komfort; **at your ~** wenn es Ihnen gerade paßt; **at your earliest ~** so bald wie möglich. **2.** *bsd. Br.* Toilette *f*. **con'ven·ient** *adj* □ **1.** bequem, praktisch. **2.** günstig, passend: **be ~ for s.o.** j-m passen.

con·vent ['kɒnvənt] *s* (*bsd.* Nonnen)Kloster *n*.

con·ven·tion [kən'venʃn] *s* **1.** Zs.-kunft *f*, Tagung *f*, Versammlung *f*. **2.** a) *pol. Am.* Parteiversammlung *f*, -tag *m*, b) Kongreß *m*: ~ **centre** (*Am.* **center**) Kongreßzentrum *n*. **3.** bilaterales Abkommen; *multilaterales* Übereinkommen, Konvention *f*. **4.** (gesellschaftliche) Konvention, Sitte *f*. **con'ven·tion·al** [~ʃənl] *adj* □ **1.** konventionell, herkömmlich (*beide a.* ✗). **2.** *contp.* schablonenhaft, unoriginell. **3.** konventionell, förmlich.

con·verge [kən'vɜːdʒ] *v/i* zs.-laufen (*Straßen, Flüsse*), 𝒜 konvergieren (*a. fig.*), *fig.* sich annähern. **con'ver·gence**, **con'ver·gen·cy** *s* **1.** Zs.-laufen *n*. **2.** 𝒜 Konvergenz *f* (*a. fig.*). **con'ver·gent** *adj* 𝒜 konvergent, *fig. a.* sich annähernd.

con·ver·sa·tion [ˌkɒnvə'seɪʃn] *s* Konversation *f*, Unterhaltung *f*, Gespräch *n*: **in ~ with** im Gespräch; **get into ~ with s.o.** mit j-m ins Gespräch kommen; **make ~** Konversation machen. **con·ver'sa·tion·al** [~ʃənl] *adj* □ **1.** gesprächig. **2.** Unterhaltungs..., Gesprächs...: **~ English** Umgangsenglisch *n*; **~ tone** Plauderton *m*. **con·ver'sa·tion·al·ly** [~ʃnəlɪ] *adv* im Plauderton. **con·verse** [kən'vɜːs] *v/i* sich unterhalten (**with** mit; **on, about** über *acc*).

con·ver·sion [kən'vɜːʃn] *s* **1.** Um-, Verwandlung *f* (**into, to** in *acc*). **2.** △, ⚙ Umbau *m* (**into** zu). **3.** ⚙, *a.* ✝ Umstellung *f* (**to** auf *acc*). **4.** 𝒜 Umrechnung *f* (**into, to** in *acc*): **~ table** Umrechnungstabelle *f*. **5.** Bekehrung *f*, *eccl. a.* Konversion *f*, Übertritt *m* (*a. pol. etc*) (**to** zu).

con·vert I *v/t* [kən'vɜːt] **1.** *allg.*, *a.* 🛐 um-, verwandeln (**into, to** in *acc*). **2.** △, ⚙ umbauen (**into** zu). **3.** ⚙, *a.* ✝ umstellen (**to** auf *acc*). **4.** 𝒜 umrechnen (**into, to** in *acc*). **5.** *eccl. etc* bekehren (**to** zu). **II** *v/i* [kən'vɜːt] **6.** sich umwandeln *od.* verwandeln (**into, to** in *acc*). **7.** sich bekehren, *eccl. a.* konvertieren, übertreten (*a. pol. etc*) (**to** zu). **III** *s* ['kɒnvɜːt] **8.** Bekehrte *m, f*, *eccl. a.* Konvertit(in). **con'vert·i·ble I** *adj* □ **1.** um-, verwandelbar. **2.** 𝒜 umrechenbar. **II** *s* **3.** *mot.* Kabriolett *n*.

con·vex [kɒn'veks] *adj* □ konvex: ~ *mirror* Konvex-, Wölbspiegel *m*.

con·vey [kən'veɪ] *v/t* **1.** *Waren etc* befördern, transportieren (*beide a.* ☉). **2.** *Grüße etc* überbringen, -mitteln. **3.** *Ideen etc* mitteilen, vermitteln, *Meinung, Sinn* ausdrücken. **con'vey·ance** *s* **1.** Beförderung *f*, Transport *m*. **2.** Transport-, Verkehrsmittel *n*. **3.** Überbringung *f*, -mittlung *f*. **4.** Mitteilung *f*, Vermittlung *f*. **con'vey·er, con'vey·or** *s a.* ~ *belt* ☉ Förderband *n*.

con·vict I *v/t* [kən'vɪkt] **1.** ⚖ überführen, für schuldig erklären (*gen*); verurteilen (*wegen*). **2.** überzeugen (*of* von). II *s* ['kɒnvɪkt] **3.** Verurteilte *m*, *f*. **4.** Strafgefangene *m*, *f*, Sträfling *m*. **con'vic·tion** *s* **1.** ⚖ Überführung *f*, Schuldspruch *m*; Verurteilung *f*: → *previous* 1. **2.** Überzeugung *f*: *from* ~ aus Überzeugung; → *carry* 5.

con·vince [kən'vɪns] *v/t* überzeugen (*of* von; *that* daß). **con'vinc·ing** *adj* □ überzeugend: ~ *proof* schlagender Beweis.

con·voy ['kɒnvɔɪ] I *s* **1.** Geleit *n*, Begleitung *f*. **2.** Konvoi *m*: a) ✕, *a. allg.* (Wagen)Kolonne *f*, b) ⚓ Geleitzug *m*. II *v/t* **3.** Geleitschutz geben (*dat*).

con·vulse [kən'vʌls] I *v/t* **1.** in Zuckungen versetzen: *be ~d with* → 4. **2.** *Muskeln etc* krampfhaft zs.-ziehen: *~d features pl* verzerrte Züge *pl*. **3.** in Lachkrämpfe versetzen. II *v/i* **4.** ~ *with* sich krümmen vor (*Lachen, Schmerzen etc*). **con'vul·sion** *s* **1.** ✚ Krampf *m*, Zuckung *f*: *nervous ~s pl* nervöse Zuckungen *pl*. **2.** *pl* Lachkrampf *m*: *they were in ~s* sie krümmten sich vor Lachen. **con'vul·sive** *adj* □ krampfhaft.

coo [ku:] I *v/i* gurren (*a. fig.*). II *s* Gurren *n*.

cook [kʊk] I *s* **1.** Koch *m*, Köchin *f*: *too many ~s spoil the broth* viele Köche verderben den Brei. II *v/t* **2.** kochen. **3.** *a.* ~ *up* F *Geschichte etc* erfinden, sich ausdenken. **4.** F *Rechnung etc* frisieren. III *v/i* **5.** kochen, gekocht werden: *what's ~ing?* F was ist los? **'~·book** *s bsd. Am.* Kochbuch *n*.

cook·er ['kʊkə] *s* Kocher *m*, Kochgerät *n*; *Br.* Herd *m*: ~ *hood Br.* Abzugshaube *f*. **'cook·er·y** *s* Kochen *n*, Kochkunst *f*: ~ *book bsd. Br.* Kochbuch *n*.

cook·ie ['~ɪ] *s Am.* (süßer) Keks, Plätzchen *n*. **'cook·ing** I *s* **1.** Kochen *n*. **2.** Küche *f*, Art *f* zu kochen: *Italian ~* die italienische Küche. II *adj* **3.** Koch... **'cook·y** → **cookie**.

cool [ku:l] I *adj* □ **1.** kühl, frisch: *get ~* sich abkühlen. **2.** *fig.* kühl: a) gelassen, kalt(blütig): *keep ~* e-n kühlen Kopf behalten, sich nicht aufregen; → *cucumber.* b) gleichgültig, c) abweisend. **3.** F glatt: *a ~ thousand pounds* glatte *od.* die Kleinigkeit von tausend Pfund. **4.** *bsd. Am.* F klasse, prima. II *s* **5.** Kühle *f*, Frische *f* (*der Luft*). **6.** F (Selbst)Beherrschung *f*: *blow* (*od. lose*) *one's ~* die Beherrschung verlieren; *keep one's ~* ruhig bleiben. III *v/t* **7.** (ab)kühlen, abkühlen lassen: ~ *it!* F immer mit der Ruhe!; reg dich ab! IV *v/i* **8.** kühl werden, sich abkühlen: ~ *down* F sich abregen. ~ *bag* *s* Kühltasche *f*. ~ *box* *s* Kühlbox *f*.

cool·er ['ku:lə] *s* **1.** (*Wein- etc*)Kühler *m*. **2.** *sl.* Kittchen *n*.

,cool'head·ed *adj* □ besonnen.

cool·ing ['ku:lɪŋ] *adj* □ **1.** (ab)kühlend. **2.** ☉ Kühl... **'cool·ness** *s* **1.** Kühle *f* (*a. fig.*). **2.** Kaltblütigkeit *f*.

co-op ['kəʊɒp] *s* F Co-op *m* (*Genossenschaft u. Laden*).

co·op·er·ate [kəʊ'ɒpəreɪt] *v/i* **1.** zs.-arbeiten (*with* mit; *in* bei; *to, toward[s]* zu *e-m Zweck*). **2.** (*in*) mitwirken (an *dat*), helfen, behilflich sein (bei). **co,op·er'a·tion** *s* **1.** Zs.-arbeit *f*. **2.** Mitwirkung *f*, Hilfe *f*. **co'op·er·a·tive** [~rətɪv] I *adj* □ **1.** zs.-arbeitend. **2.** mitwirkend. **3.** kooperativ, hilfsbereit. **4.** ⭳ Gemeinschafts...; Genossenschafts...: ~ *society* → 5; ~ *store* → 6. II *s* **5.** Co-op *m*: a) Genossenschaft *f*, b) Konsumverein *m*. **6.** Co-op *m*, Konsumladen *m*.

co·or·di·nate I *v/t* [kəʊ'ɔ:dɪneɪt] koordinieren, bei-, gleichordnen, aufeinander abstimmen. II *adj* [~dnət] □ koordiniert, bei-, gleichgeordnet. III *s* [~dnət] Ⱥ Koordinate *f*. **co,or·di'na·tion** *s* Koordinierung *f*, Koordination *f*, Gleichordnung *f*, Abstimmung *f*.

cop [kɒp] *sl.* I *v/t* **1.** erwischen (*at* bei): ~ *it* sein Fett (ab)kriegen; → *packet* 3. II *s* **2.** *no great ~, not much ~ Br.* nicht so toll. **3.** Bulle *m* (*Polizist*).

co·part·ner [,kəʊ'pɑ:tnə] *s* Teilhaber *m*,

Mitinhaber *m.* ˌco**·part·ner·ship** *s* **1.** Teilhaberschaft *f.* **2.** *Br.* Gewinn- *od.* Mitbeteiligung *f (of labour* der Arbeitnehmer).

cope [kəʊp] *v/i (with)* gewachsen sein *(dat),* fertig werden (mit).

cop·i·er ['kɒpɪə] *s* Kopiergerät *n,* Kopierer *m.*

co·pi·lot ['kəʊˌpaɪlət] *s* ✈ Kopilot *m.*

co·pi·ous ['kəʊpjəs] *adj* □ **1.** reich(lich), ausgiebig. **2.** wortreich, weitschweifig. **3.** produktiv *(Schriftsteller etc).*

cop·per[1] ['kɒpə] **I** *s* **1.** *min.* Kupfer *n.* **2.** Kupfermünze *f:* ⁓*s pl* Kupfergeld *n.* **II** *adj* **3.** kupfern, Kupfer... **4.** kupferrot.

cop·per[2] [⁓] *s sl.* Bulle *m (Polizist).*

cop·per| **ore** *s min.* Kupfererz *n.* '⁓**plate** *s* Kupferstich(platte *f) m: like* ⁓ wie gestochen *(Schrift).* '⁓**smith** *s* Kupferschmied *m.*

cop·u·la ['kɒpjʊlə] *s ling.* Kopula *f.* **cop·u·late** ['⁓leɪt] *v/i* kopulieren: a) koitieren, b) *zo.* sich paaren. ˌcop·u'la·tion *s* Kopulation *f:* a) Koitus *m,* b) Paarung *f.*

cop·y ['kɒpɪ] **I** *s* **1.** Kopie *f,* Abschrift *f: fair (od. clean)* ⁓ Reinschrift *f; rough (od. foul)* ⁓ Rohentwurf *m,* Konzept *n.* **2.** Durchschlag *m,* -schrift *f.* **3.** *phot.* Abzug *m.* **4.** Nachbildung *f,* Kopie *f.* **5.** *typ.* (Satz)Vorlage *f.* **6.** Exemplar *n (e-s Buchs etc).* **7.** (Werbe-, Zeitungs*etc)*Text *m.* **II** *v/t* **8.** abschreiben *(off, from* von), e-e Kopie anfertigen von, *Kassette etc* überspielen. **9.** durch-, abpausen; kopieren. **10.** *phot.* e-n Abzug machen von. **11.** nachbilden. **12.** kopieren, nachahmen, -machen. **III** *v/i* **13.** abschreiben *(from* von). '⁓**cat** F **I** *s (bsd.* sklavischer *od.* gedankenloser) Nachahmer. **II** *v/t (bsd.* sklavisch *od.* gedankenlos) nachahmen *od.* -machen. **III** *adj* ⁓ **ed·i·tor** *s* Zeitungsredakteur(in); Lektor(in).

cop·y·ing| **ma·chine** ['kɒpɪɪŋ] *s* Kopiergerät *n.* ⁓ **pa·per** *s* Kopierpapier *n.*

'**cop·y**|ˌ**read·er** *Am.* → **copy editor.** '⁓**right** ⚖ *s* **1.** Urheberrecht *n,* Copyright *n (in, on, of, for* für, von). **II** *v/t* das Urheberrecht erwerben für *od.* von; urheberrechtlich schützen. **III** *adj* urheberrechtlich geschützt. '⁓ˌ**writ·er** *s* Werbetexter *m.*

cor·al ['kɒrəl] **I** *s* **1.** *zo.* Koralle *f.* **II**
adj **2.** Korallen... **3.** korallenrot.

cord [kɔːd] **I** *s* **1.** Schnur *f (a.* ⚡*),* Kordel *f,* Strick *m.* **2.** gerippter Stoff, *bsd.* Kordsamt *m.* **II** *v/t* **3.** festbinden; ver-, zuschnüren.

cor·dial ['kɔːdjəl] **I** *adj* □ **1.** herzlich. **2.** ✿ belebend, stärkend. **II** *s* **3.** ✿ Stärkungsmittel *n.* **4.** Fruchtsaftgetränk *n.* **5.** Likör *m.* **cor·dial·i·ty** [ˌ⁓dɪ'ælətɪ] *s* Herzlichkeit *f.*

cor·don ['kɔːdn] **I** *s* Kordon *m,* Postenod. Absperrkette *f.* **II** *v/t a.* ⁓ *off* (mit Posten *od.* Seilen) absperren *od.* abriegeln.

cor·du·roy ['kɔːdərɔɪ] *s* **1.** Kordsamt *m.* **2.** *pl. a. pair of* ⁓**s** Kord(samt)hose *f.*

core [kɔː] **I** *s* **1.** ✿ Kerngehäuse *n;* Kern *m.* **2.** *fig.* Kern *m, das Innerste: to the* ⁓ bis ins Innerste; durch *u.* durch. **II** *v/t* **3.** *Obst* entkernen. ⁓ **time** *s* Kernzeit *f.*

cork [kɔːk] **I** *s* **1.** Kork *m.* **2.** Korken *m,* Pfropfen *m.* **II** *v/t* **3.** *oft* ⁓ *up* zu-, verkorken.

'**cork·screw** *s* Korkenzieher *m.*

corn[1] [kɔːn] **I** *s* **1.** Korn *n,* Getreide *n: bsd.* a) *Br.* Weizen *m,* b) *schott., ir.* Hafer *m.* **2.** *a. Indian* ⁓ *Am.* Mais *m.* **II** *v/t* **3.** pökeln: ⁓*ed beef* Corned beef *n,* gepökeltes Rindfleisch.

corn[2] [⁓] *s* ✿ Hühnerauge *n: tread on s.o.'s* ⁓**s** *fig.* j-m auf die Hühneraugen treten.

corn| **bread** *s Am.* Maisbrot *n.* '⁓**cob** *s Am.* Maiskolben *m.*

cor·ne·a ['kɔːnɪə] *pl* **-as, -ae** [ˌ⁓iː] *s* Hornhaut *f (des Auges).*

cor·ner ['kɔːnə] **I** *s* **1.** Ecke *f, bsd. mot.* Kurve *f: take a* ⁓ → 5; *turn the* ⁓ um die Ecke biegen; *he's turned the* ⁓ *fig.* er ist über den Berg. **2.** Winkel *m,* Ecke *f:* ⁓ *of the mouth* Mundwinkel; *look at s.o. from the* ⁓ *of one's eye* j-n aus den Augenwinkeln (heraus) ansehen; *drive (od. force, put) into a* ⁓ → 4; *be in a tight* ⁓ in der Klemme sein *od.* sitzen *od.* stecken. **3.** *Fußball:* Eckball *m,* Ecke *f.* **II** *v/t* **4.** in die Enge treiben. **III** *v/i* **5.** *mot.* e-e Kurve nehmen: ⁓ *well* gut in die Kurve liegen, e-e gute Kurvenlage haben. **IV** *adj* **6.** Eck...: ⁓ *house;* ⁓ *seat* Eckplatz *m.* '**cor·nered** *adj in Zssgn* ...eckig.

cor·ner| **kick** *s Fußball:* Eckstoß *m,*

'**∼stone** *s* **1.** △ Eckstein *m*; Grundstein *m*. **2.** *fig.* Eckpfeiler *m*.
'**corn**|**field** *s* **1.** *Br.* Korn-, Getreidefeld *n*. **2.** *Am.* Maisfeld *n*. '**∼flakes** *s pl* Corn-flakes *pl*. '**∼flow·er** *s* ✿ Kornblume *f*.
Cor·nish [ˈkɔːnɪʃ] *adj* kornisch, aus Cornwall.
corn pop·py *s* ✿ Klatschmohn *m*.
corn·y [ˈkɔːnɪ] *adj sl.* sentimental, schmalzig; kitschig; abgedroschen: *a ∼ joke* ein Witz mit Bart.
cor·o·nar·y [ˈkɒrənərɪ] *adj anat.* Koronar...: *∼ vessel* (Herz)Kranzgefäß *n*.
cor·o·na·tion [ˌkɒrəˈneɪʃn] *s* Krönung(sfeier) *f*.
cor·o·ner [ˈkɒrənə] *s* ⚖ Coroner *m* (*richterlicher Beamter zur Untersuchung der Todesursache in Fällen gewaltsamen od. unnatürlichen Todes*): *∼'s inquest* gerichtliches Verfahren zur Untersuchung der Todesursache.
cor·po·ral¹ [ˈkɔːpərəl] *s* ✕ Unteroffizier *m*.
cor·po·ral² [∼] *adj* □ körperlich, leiblich: *∼ punishment* körperliche Züchtigung.
cor·po·rate [ˈkɔːpərət] *adj* □ **a)** ⚖ körperschaftlich, Körperschafts...: *∼ body* → *corporation* 1, **b)** ✝ *Am.* Gesellschafts..., Firmen...: *∼ planning* Unternehmensplanung *f*. **2.** gemeinsam, kollektiv. **cor·po·ra·tion** [ˌ∼ˈreɪʃn] *s* **1.** ⚖ Körperschaft *f*, juristische Person: *∼ tax* Körperschaftssteuer *f*. **2.** *a.* **stock ∼** ✝ *Am.* Kapital- *od.* Aktiengesellschaft *f*. **3.** *Br.* Innung *f*. **4.** *Br.* Stadtverwaltung *f*. **5.** F Schmerbauch *m*.
corps [kɔː] *pl* **corps** [∼z] *s* **1.** ✕ Korps *n*, Truppe *f*. **2.** Korps *n*: → *diplomatic*.
corpse [kɔːps] *s* Leichnam *m*, Leiche *f*.
cor·pu·lence, **cor·pu·len·cy** [ˈkɔːpjʊləns(ɪ)] *s* Beleibtheit *f*, Korpulenz *f*. '**cor·pu·lent** *adj* □ beleibt, korpulent.
Cor·pus Chris·ti [ˌkɔːpəsˈkrɪstɪ] *s eccl.* Fronleichnam(sfest *n*) *m*.
cor·ral [kəˈrɑːl] *bsd. Am.* I *s* **1.** Pferch *m*. II *v/t* **2.** in e-n Pferch treiben. **3.** *fig.* einpferchen, -sperren. **4.** F sich *et.* schnappen.
cor·rect [kəˈrekt] I *v/t* **1.** korrigieren, verbessern, berichtigen: *I stand ∼ed* ich nehme alles zurück. **2.** *Mängel etc*

abstellen. **3.** zurechtweisen, tadeln; (be)strafen (*for* wegen). II *adj* **4.** korrekt: **a)** richtig: *be ∼* stimmen; recht haben, **b)** einwandfrei (*Benehmen*).
cor·rec·tion *s* **1.** Korrektur *f*, Verbesserung *f*, Berichtigung *f*. **2.** Zurechtweisung *f*, Tadel *m*; Bestrafung *f*.
cor·rec·tive *adj* □ korrigierend, verbessernd, berichtigend. **cor·rect·ness** *s* Korrektheit *f*, Richtigkeit *f*.
cor·re·late [ˈkɒrɪleɪt] I *v/t* **1.** in Wechselbeziehung bringen (*with* mit). **2.** in Übereinstimmung bringen (*with* mit), aufeinander abstimmen. II *v/i* **3.** in Wechselbeziehung stehen (*with* mit), sich aufeinander beziehen. **4.** übereinstimmen (*with* mit). '**cor·re·la·tion** *s* **1.** Wechselbeziehung *f*. **2.** Übereinstimmung *f*.
cor·re·spond [ˌkɒrɪˈspɒnd] *v/i* **1.** (*to*, *with*) entsprechen (*dat*), übereinstimmen (mit). **2.** (*to*) entsprechen (*dat*), das Gegenstück sein (von). **3.** korrespondieren, in Briefwechsel stehen (*with* mit). '**cor·re·spond·ence** *s* **1.** Entsprechung *f*, Übereinstimmung *f*. **2.** Korrespondenz *f*: **a)** Briefwechsel *m*: *be in ∼ (with) ∼ correspond* 3; *∼ course* Fernkurs *m*; *∼ school* Fernlehrinstitut *n*, **b)** Briefe *pl*. '**cor·re·spond·ent** I *s* **1.** Briefpartner(in): *be a good (bad) ∼* fleißig schreiben (schreibfaul sein). **2.** ✝ (auswärtiger) Geschäftsfreund. **3.** Korrespondent(in), Berichterstatter(in) (*e-r Zeitung etc*): *foreign ∼* Auslandskorrespondent(in). II *adj* □ **4.** entsprechend, gemäß (*to dat*). **cor·re-'spond·ing** *adj* □ *correspondent* 4.
cor·ri·dor [ˈkɒrɪdɔː] *s* Korridor *m*, Gang *m*. *∼* **train** *s* D-Zug *m*.
cor·rode [kəˈrəʊd] I *v/t* **1.** 🜍, ⚙ korrodieren, an-, zerfressen, angreifen. **2.** *fig.* zerfressen, untergraben. II *v/i* **3.** korrodieren, rosten: *∼d* rostig. **cor·ro·sion** [∼ʒn] *s* **1.** 🜍, ⚙ Korrosion *f*. **2.** Rostfraß *m*, dünnes *f*. **3.** *fig.* Untergrabung *f*. **cor·ro·sive** [∼sɪv] *adj* □ **1.** 🜍, ⚙ korrodierend, Korrosions... **2.** *fig.* nagend, quälend.
cor·ru·gat·ed [ˈkɒrʊgeɪtɪd] *adj* gewellt: *∼ cardboard* Wellpappe *f*; *∼ iron* (*od.* **sheet**) Wellblech *n*.
cor·rupt [kəˈrʌpt] I *adj* □ **1.** (*moralisch*) verdorben. **2.** unredlich, unlauter. **3.**

korrupt: a) bestechlich, b) Bestechungs... **II** v/t **4.** (*moralisch*) verderben. **5.** korrumpieren, bestechen. **III** v/i **6.** (*moralisch*) verderben, -kommen.

cor·rupt·i·ble → **corrupt** 3a. **cor·rup·tion** s **1.** Verdorbenheit f. **2.** Unredlichkeit f, Unlauterkeit f. **3.** Korruption f: a) Bestechlichkeit f, b) Bestechung f. **cor·rup·tive** adj verderblich (*Einfluß etc*).

cor·set ['kɔːsɪt] s a. pl Korsett n.

cosh [kɒʃ] s Br. F Totschläger m (*Waffe*).

co·sig·na·to·ry [ˌkəʊˈsɪgnətərɪ] s Mitunterzeichner(in).

co·sine ['kəʊsaɪn] s & Kosinus m.

co·si·ness ['kəʊzɪnɪs] s Behaglichkeit f, Gemütlichkeit f.

cos·met·ic [kɒzˈmetɪk] **I** adj (**~ally**) kosmetisch (a. fig.): ~ **surgery** Schönheitschirurgie f. **II** s kosmetisches Mittel. **cos·me·ti·cian** [ˌkɒzməˈtɪʃn] s Kosmetiker(in).

cos·mic ['kɒzmɪk] adj □ kosmisch.

cos·mo·naut ['kɒzmənɔːt] s (Welt-) Raumfahrer m, Kosmonaut m.

cos·mo·pol·i·tan [ˌkɒzməˈpɒlɪtən] **I** adj kosmopolitisch, weltbürgerlich, *weitS*. weltoffen. **II** s Kosmopolit(in), Weltbürger(in).

cos·mos ['kɒzmɒs] s Kosmos m, Weltall n.

cost [kɒst] **I** s **1.** Kosten pl, Aufwand m: ~ **of living** Lebenshaltungskosten. **2.** Kosten pl, Schaden m: *at s.o.'s* ~ auf j-s Kosten; *at the* ~ *of his health* auf Kosten s-r Gesundheit. **3.** Opfer n, Preis m: *at all* ~*s*, *at any* ~ um jeden Preis; *at a heavy* ~ unter schweren Opfern. **4.** ✝ (Selbst-, Gestehungs)Kosten pl: ~ **a·batement** Kostendämpfung f; ~ **in·crease** Kostensteigerung f; ~ **inflation** Kosteninflation f; ~ **price** Selbstkostenpreis m; *at* ~ zum Selbstkostenpreis. **5.** pl ⚖ (Gerichts-, Prozeß)Kosten pl: *with* ~ kostenpflichtig. **II** v/t (irr) **6.** Preis kosten: *it* ~ *me one pound* es kostete mich ein Pfund. **7.** kosten, bringen um: *it* ~ *him his life* es kostete ihn das Leben. **8.** et. Unangenehmes verursachen: *it* ~ *me a lot of trouble* es verursachte mir od. kostete mich große Mühe. **9.** pret u. pp '**cost·ed** ✝ den Preis od. die Kosten kalkulieren von

(od. gen). **III** v/i (irr) **10.** *it* ~ *him dearly* bsd. fig. es kam ihm teuer zu stehen.

co·star ['kəʊstɑː] **I** v/t: *the film* ~*red* X X spielte in dem Film e-e der Hauptrollen. **II** v/i: ~ *with* die Hauptrolle spielen neben (*dat*).

'**cost|-,con·scious** adj □ kostenbewußt. '~**,cov·er·ing** adj □ kostendeckend.

cos·ter(-mon·ger) ['kɒstə(ˌmʌŋgə)] s Br. Straßenhändler(in) für Obst, Gemüse etc.

cost es·ti·mate s Kostenvoranschlag m.

cost·ly ['kɒstlɪ] adj **1.** kostspielig, teuer. **2.** teuer erkauft (*Sieg etc*). **3.** prächtig.

'**cost-of-'liv·ing**| **al·low·ance**, ~ **bo·nus** s ✝ Teuerungszulage f. ~ **in·dex** s (a. irr **index**) ✝ Lebenshaltungs(kosten)index m.

cos·tume ['kɒstjuːm] s **1.** Kostüm n, Kleidung f, Tracht f. **2.** thea. etc Kostüm n: ~ **ball** Kostümball m; ~ **de·signer** Kostümbildner(in); ~ **jew·el(le)ry** Modeschmuck m.

co·sy ['kəʊzɪ] **I** adj □ behaglich, gemütlich. **II** s Wärmer m: → **egg cosy, tea cosy.**

cot [kɒt] s **1.** Feldbett n. **2.** Br. Kinderbett(chen) n.

cot·tage ['kɒtɪdʒ] s **1.** Cottage n, (kleines) Landhaus. **2.** Am. Ferienhaus n, -häuschen n. **3.** Am. Wohngebäude n, (*e-s Krankenhauses etc*) Einzelgebäude n, (*e-s Hotels*) Dependance f. ~ **cheese** s Hüttenkäse m. ~ **in·dus·try** s Heimgewerbe n, -industrie f.

cot·ton ['kɒtn] **I** s **1.** Baumwolle f: → **absorbent. II** adj **2.** baumwollen, Baumwoll... **III** v/i **3.** Am. F (**with**) gut auskommen (mit). sich anfreunden (mit). **4.** F ~ **to** Am. sich anfreunden mit (*e-r Idee etc*); ~ **on to** et. kapieren. ~ **pad** s Wattestäbchen n. ~ **wool** s Br. (Verband)Watte f.

couch [kaʊtʃ] **I** s Couch f, Liege(sofa n) f. **II** v/t abfassen, formulieren; *Gedanken etc* in Worte fassen, ausdrücken.

cou·chette [kuːˈʃet] s 🚆 Platz m (im Liegewagen).

cough [kɒf] **I** s **1.** Husten m: *have a* ~ Husten haben; *give a (slight)* ~ hüsteln, sich räuspern. **2.** Husten n. **3.** mot. Stottern n. **II** v/i **4.** husten. **5.** mot. stottern, husten (*Motor*). **III** v/t **6.** mst

~ out, ~ up aushusten: **~ up blood** Blut husten. **7. ~ up** *sl.* herausrücken mit (*der Wahrheit etc*); Geld herausrücken, ausspucken. **~ drop** *s* Hustenbonbon *m, n*.

cough·ing bout ['kɒfɪŋ] *s* Hustenanfall *m*.

cough| **loz·enge** → **cough drop.** **~ syr·up** *s* Hustensaft *m*, -sirup *m*.

could [kʊd] *v/aux* **1.** *pret von* **can¹. 2.** *konditional, vermutend od. fragend*: könnte *etc*: *that* **~** *be right* das könnte stimmen.

couldn't ['kʊdnt] F *für* **could not.**

coun·cil ['kaʊnsl] *s* **1.** Rat(sversammlung *f*) *m*: *be in* **~** zu Rate sitzen; *family* **~** Familienrat. **2.** Rat *m* (*Körperschaft*); *engS.* Gemeinderat *m*: **⌾** *of Europe* Europarat; *municipal* **~** Stadtrat. **~ es·tate** *s Br.* soziale Wohnsiedlung (*e-r Gemeinde*). **~ house** *s Br.* gemeindeeigenes Wohnhaus (*mit niedrigen Mieten*).

coun·cil·(l)or ['kaʊnsələ] *s* Ratsmitglied *n*, Stadtrat *m.* -rätin *f.*

coun·sel ['kaʊnsl] *s* **1.** Rat(schlag) *m*: *take* **~** *of s.o.* von j-m (e-n) Rat annehmen. **2.** Beratung *f*: *hold* (*od. take*) **~** *with* sich beraten mit; sich Rat holen bei. **3.** 🏛 *Am.* Rechtsberater *m*, -beistand *m*; *Br.* (Rechts)Anwalt *m*: **~** *for the defence* Verteidiger *m*; **~** *for the prosecution* Anklagevertreter *m.* **II** *v/t pret u. pp* **-seled,** *bsd. Br.* **-selled 4.** *j-m* raten, *j-m* e-n Rat geben *od.* erteilen: **~** *s.o. against* j-m abraten von. **5.** zu *et.* raten: **~** *s.th. to s.o.* j-m et. raten. **III** *v/i* **6. ~** *against* abraten von. **¹coun·sel·(l)or** *s* (*Berufs- etc*)Berater(in).

count¹ ['kaʊnt] *s* **1.** Zählen *n*, (Ab-, Auf-, Aus)Zählung *f*: *keep* **~** *of et.* genau zählen (*acc*); *fig.* die Übersicht behalten über (*acc*); *lose* **~** sich verzählen; *fig.* die Übersicht verlieren (*of* über *acc*); *by this* **~** nach dieser Zählung; *a.* Berechnung. **2.** Endzahl *f*, Ergebnis *n*. **3.** 🏛 Anklagepunkt *m*: *on all* **~s** in allen Anklagepunkten; *fig.* in jeder Hinsicht. **4.** *leave out of* **~** unberücksichtigt lassen; *take no* **~** *of* nicht berücksichtigen. **II** *v/t* **5.** (ab-, auf-, aus-, zs.-)zählen, *Wechselgeld* nachzählen. **6.** aus-, berechnen. **7.** zählen bis: **~** *ten.* **8.** (mit)zählen, mit einrechnen: (*not*) **~ing**

the persons present die Anwesenden (nicht) mitgerechnet; *without* (*od. not*) **~ing** abgesehen von. **9.** halten für, betrachten als, zählen (*among* zu): **~** *o.s. lucky* (*od. fortunate*) sich glücklich schätzen. **III** *v/i* **10.** zählen (*fig. among* zu): **~** *up to ten* bis 10 zählen; **~ing from today** von heute an (gerechnet). **11.** (*on*) zählen, sich verlassen (auf *acc*), sicher rechnen (mit). **12.** zählen: a) von Wert sein, ins Gewicht fallen, b) gelten: **~** *for much* viel gelten *od.* wert sein; **~** *against* sprechen gegen; sich nachteilig auswirken auf (*acc*).

Verbindungen mit Adverbien:

count| down *v/t* **1.** Geld hinzählen. **2.** den Countdown durchführen für, *a. weitS.* letzte (Start)Vorbereitungen treffen für. **~ in** *v/t* → **count¹ 8: count me in!** ich bin dabei!, ich mache mit! **~ off** *v/t u. v/i bsd.* ✕ abzählen. **~ out** *v/t* **1.** *Münzen etc* (langsam) abzählen. **2.** ausschließen, unberücksichtigt lassen: *count me out!* ohne mich! **3.** *Boxen, Kinderspiel:* auszählen. **~ o·ver** *v/t* nachzählen. **~ up** *v/t* zs.-zählen.

count² [\~] *s* nichtbritischer Graf.

count·a·ble ['kaʊntəbl] *adj* zählbar (*a. ling.*).

¹count·down *s* Countdown *m, n, a. weitS.* letzte (Start)Vorbereitungen *pl.*

coun·te·nance ['kaʊntənəns] *s* **1.** Gesichtsausdruck *m*, Miene *f*: *change one's* **~** s-n Gesichtsausdruck ändern. **2.** Fassung *f*, Haltung *f*: *in* **~** gefaßt; *keep one's* **~** die Fassung bewahren; *put s.o. out of* **~** j-n aus der Fassung bringen.

count·er¹ ['kaʊntə] *s* **1.** Ladentisch *m*: *under the* **~** unter dem Ladentisch *verkaufen etc*; *fig.* unter der Hand, heimlich. **2.** Theke *f.* **3.** (*Bank-, Post*)Schalter *m.* **II** *adj* **4.** rezeptfrei (*Medikament*).

count·er² [\~] *s* **1.** ⚙ Zähler *m.* **2.** Spielmarke *f*, Jeton *m.*

count·er³ [\~] **I** *adv* **1.** in entgegengesetzter Richtung. **2. ~** *to fig.* wider (*acc*), zuwider (*dat*), entgegen (*dat*): *run* **~** *to* zuwiderlaufen (*dat*). **II** *adj* **3.** Gegen..., entgegengesetzt. **III** *v/t* **4.** entgegenwirken (*dat*). **IV** *v/i* **5.** *bsd. Sport:* kontern.

coun·ter... [kaʊntə] *in Zssgn* Gegen...

¸coun·ter'act *v/t* **1.** entgegenwirken

(dat). **2.** Wirkung kompensieren, neutralisieren. ˌcoun·ter'ac·tive adj □ entgegenwirkend, Gegen...

'coun·ter,ar·gu·ment s Gegenargument n.

'coun·ter·at,tack s Gegenangriff m.

coun·ter·bal·ance fig. I s ['kaʊntə-ˌbæləns] Gegengewicht n (to zu). II v/t [ˌ~'bæləns] ein Gegengewicht bilden zu, ausgleichen.

'coun·ter·blast s heftige Reaktion.

'coun·ter·charge s 1. ₰₷ Gegenklage f. 2. ⚔ Gegenangriff m.

'coun·ter·check I s Gegen-, Nachprüfung f. II v/t gegen-, nachprüfen.

'coun·ter·claim s ✝, ₰₷ Gegenanspruch m, -forderung f.

ˌcoun·ter'clock·wise Am. → anticlockwise.

'coun·ter,dem·on·stra·tion s Gegendemonstration f.

ˌcoun·ter'es·pi·o·nage s Spionageabwehr f.

ˌcoun·ter·ex,am·ple s Gegenbeispiel n.

coun·ter·feit ['kaʊntəfɪt] I adj 1. falsch: a) gefälscht: ~ money Falschgeld n, b) vorgetäuscht. II s 2. Fälschung f. III v/t 3. Geld, Unterschrift etc fälschen. 4. vortäuschen, simulieren.

'coun·ter·foil s bsd. Br. (Kontroll)Abschnitt m.

'coun·ter·in,tel·li·gence s Spionageabwehr(dienst m) f.

coun·ter·mand [ˌkaʊntə'mɑːnd] I v/t 1. Befehl etc widerrufen, rückgängig machen, ✝ Auftrag stornieren: until ~ed bis auf Widerruf. 2. Ware abbestellen. II s 3. Widerrufung f, ✝ Stornierung f.

'coun·ter,meas·ure s Gegenmaßnahme f.

'coun·ter·move s Gegenzug m.

'coun·ter·of,fen·sive s ⚔ Gegenoffensive f.

'coun·ter·of·fer s Gegenangebot n.

'coun·ter,or·der s bsd. ⚔ Gegenbefehl m.

'coun·ter·pane s Tagesdecke f.

'coun·ter·part s 1. Gegenstück n (to zu). 2. Pendant n, genaue Entsprechung. 3. Ebenbild n (Person).

'coun·ter·point s ♪ Kontrapunkt m.

'coun·ter·poise s Gegengewicht n (to zu) (a. fig.).

ˌcoun·ter·pro'duc·tive adj kontrapro-

duktiv: be ~ nicht zum gewünschten Ziel führen, das Gegenteil bewirken.

'coun·ter·pro,pos·al s Gegenvorschlag m.

'coun·ter·rev·o,lu·tion s pol. Konter-, Gegenrevolution f.

'coun·ter·sign v/t gegenzeichnen.

'coun·ter·weight s Gegengewicht n (to zu) (a. fig.).

count·ess ['kaʊntɪs] s Gräfin f.

count·less ['kaʊntlɪs] adj zahllos, unzählig.

coun·try ['kʌntrɪ] I s 1. Gegend f, Landschaft f: flat ~ Flachland n. 2. Land n, Staat m: in this ~ hierzulande; ~ of birth Geburtsland. 3. Land n (Ggs. Stadt): in the ~ auf dem Lande. II adj 4. ländlich, Land... ~ home, ~ house s 1. Landhaus n. 2. Landsitz m. ~·man ['~mən] s (irr man) 1. Landsmann m. 2. Landbewohner m; Bauer m. ~ mu·sic s Country-music f. ~ road s Landstraße f. ~ seat s Landsitz m. '~·side s 1. Landstrich m, (ländliche) Gegend. 2. Landschaft f. ~·'wide adj agi landesweit. '~·ˌwom·an s (irr woman) 1. Landsmännin f. 2. Landbewohnerin f; Bäuerin f.

coun·ty ['kaʊntɪ] s 1. Br. Grafschaft f. 2. Am. (Land)Kreis m (einzelstaatlicher Verwaltungsbezirk).

coup [kuː] s 1. Coup m: make (od. pull off) a ~ e-n Coup landen. 2. Staatsstreich m, Putsch m. ~ d'é·tat [ˌkuː-deɪ'tɑː] pl coups d'é·tat [ˌkuːz·~] → coup 2.

cou·pé ['kuːpeɪ] s mot. Coupé n.

cou·ple ['kʌpl] I s 1. Paar n: a ~ of zwei; I ein paar; in ~s paarweise. 2. (Ehe-, Liebes- etc)Paar n. II v/t 3. (zs.-)koppeln, verbinden (a. fig. with mit). 4. ⚡ koppeln: ~ back rückkoppeln; ~ out auskoppeln.

cou·pon ['kuːpɒn] s 1. Gutschein m, Bon m; Berechtigungsschein m. 2. Kupon m, Bestellzettel m (in Zeitungsinseraten etc). 3. Br. Tippzettel m (Fußballtoto).

cour·age ['kʌrɪdʒ] s Mut m, Tapferkeit f: lose ~ den Mut verlieren; muster up (od. pluck up, take) ~ Mut od. sich ein Herz fassen. cou·ra·geous [kə'reɪdʒəs] adj □ mutig, tapfer.

cour·gette [ˌkɔː'ʒet] s ⚘ Br. Zucchini f.

cour·i·er ['kʊrɪə] s 1. Eilbote m, (a. diplomatischer) Kurier. 2. Reiseleiter m.

course [kɔːs] *s* **1.** ✈, ⚓ Kurs *m* (*a. fig.*): **change one's ~** s-n Kurs ändern; *~* **correction** Kurskorrektur *f*. **2.** *Sport:* (*Renn*)Bahn *f*, (-)Strecke *f*, (*Golf*)Platz *m*. **3.** (*zeitlicher, natürlicher*) (Ver-)Lauf *m*: **in the ~ of** im (Ver)Lauf (*gen*); **in the ~ of time** im Laufe der Zeit; **of ~** natürlich, selbstverständlich; **the ~ of events** der Gang der Ereignisse, der Lauf der Dinge; **take** (*od.* **run**) **its ~** s-n Lauf nehmen; **→ due 6, matter 3. 4.** Gang *m* (*Speisen*): **a four-~ meal** e-e Mahlzeit mit 4 Gängen. **5.** Zyklus *m*, Reihe *f*: **~ of lectures** Vortragsreihe. **6.** Kurs *m*, Lehrgang *m*: **English ~** Englischkurs; **~ of study** *univ.* Kurs; Lehrplan *m*.

court [kɔːt] **I** *s* **1.** Hof *m*: **in the ~** auf dem Hof. **2.** *Sport:* (*Tennis- etc*)Platz *m*; (Spiel)Feld *n*. **3.** (*fürstlicher etc*) Hof: **at ~** bei Hofe. **4. pay** (**one's**) **~ to** a) → 6, b) *j-m* s-e Aufwartung machen. **5.** ⚖ Gericht *n*: **in ~** vor Gericht; **bring into ~** vor Gericht bringen; **come to ~** vor Gericht *od.* zur Verhandlung kommen; **go to ~** vor Gericht gehen; **out of ~** außergerichtlich; → **arbitration 2. II** *v/t* **6.** e-r *Dame* den Hof machen. **7. ~ death** sein s-m Leben spielen; **~ disaster** das Schicksal herausfordern. **III** *v/i* **8.** miteinander gehen: *~ing* **couple** Liebespaar *n*. **~ card** *s* Kartenspiel: Bild(karte *f*) *n*.

cour·te·ous [ˈkɜːtjəs] *adj* □ höflich, liebenswürdig.

cour·te·sy [ˈkɜːtɪsɪ] *s* **1.** Höflichkeit *f*, Liebenswürdigkeit *f*: **by ~** aus Höflichkeit; **~ light** *mot.* Innenbeleuchtung *f*. **~ visit** Höflichkeits-, Anstandsbesuch *m*. **2.** Gefälligkeit *f*: **by ~** aus Gefälligkeit; **by ~ of** mit freundlicher Genehmigung von (*od. gen*).

'**court·house** *s* Gerichtsgebäude *n*. **~ mar·tial** *pl* **court mar·tials, courts mar·tial** *s* Kriegsgericht *n*. **.~-'martial** *v/t pret u. pp* -'**mar·tialed**, *bsd. Br.* -'**mar·tialled** vor ein Kriegsgericht stellen. **~ or·der** *s* ⚖ Gerichtsbeschluß *m*, richterliche Verfügung *f*. '**.~-room** *s* Gerichtssaal *m*. '**.~-yard** → **court 1**.

cous·in [ˈkʌzn] *s* Cousin *m*, Vetter *m*; Cousine *f*.

cov·er [ˈkʌvə] **I** *s* **1.** (*weitS. a.* Schnee-, Wolken- *etc*)Decke *f*, Deckel *m*. **2.** (*Buch*)Deckel *m*, Einband *m*; Umschlag-, Titelseite *f*; (Schutz)Umschlag *m*: **from ~ to ~** von der ersten bis zur letzten Seite. **4.** Hülle *f*, Futteral *n*. **5.** Überzug *m*, Bezug *m*. **6.** Abdeck-, ⊚ Schutzhaube *f*. **7.** Briefumschlag *m*: **under separate ~** mit getrennter Post; **under plain ~** in neutralem Umschlag. **8.** ✕ *u. allg.* Deckung *f* (**from** vor *dat*): **take ~** in Deckung gehen. **9.** Schutz *m* (**from** vor *dat*): **get under ~** sich unterstellen; **under** (**the**) **~ of night** im Schutze der Nacht. **10.** *fig.* Tarnung *f*: **under ~ of** unter dem Deckmantel (*gen*). **11.** Gedeck *n* (*bei Tisch*). **12.** † a) Deckung *f*, Sicherheit *f*, b) → **coverage 2. II** *v/t* **13.** be-, zudecken (**with** mit); *Dach* dekken: *~ed* **with** voll von; *~ed* **court** (*Sport*) Hallenplatz *m*. **14.** Fläche bedecken, sich über e-e Fläche, a. e-n Zeitraum erstrecken. **15.** Seite *etc* vollschreiben. **16.** einwickeln, -schlagen (**in, with** in *acc*). **17.** verbergen (*a. fig.*): **~** (**up**) *fig.* verheimlichen, -tuschen. **18.** decken, schützen (**from, against** vor *dat*, gegen) (*beide a.* ✕ *u. fig.*): **~ o.s.** *fig.* sich absichern. **19.** † a) *ab*)decken; versichern. **20.** *Thema* erschöpfend behandeln. **21.** *Presse, Rundfunk etc:* berichten über (*acc*). **22.** *Strecke* zurücklegen. **23.** *Sport:* Gegenspieler decken. **24.** *j-n* beschatten. **25.** *zo.* decken. **~ ad·dress** *s* Deckadresse *f*.

cov·er·age [ˈkʌvərɪdʒ] *s* **1.** erschöpfende Behandlung (*e-s Themas*). **2.** † Versicherungsschutz *m*, (*Schadens*)Deckung *f*. **3.** *Presse, Rundfunk etc:* Berichterstattung *f* (**of** über *acc*).

cov·er | **charge** *s* pro *Gedeck* berechneter Betrag. **~ girl** *s* Covergirl *n*, Titelblattmädchen *n*.

cov·er·ing [ˈkʌvərɪŋ] *s* **1.** → **cover 4. 2.** (*Fußboden*)Belag *m*. **~ let·ter** *s* Begleitbrief *m*, -schreiben *n*.

cov·er·let [ˈkʌvəlɪt] *s* Tagesdecke *f*.

cov·er sto·ry *s* Titelgeschichte *f*.

cov·ert [ˈkʌvət] *adj* □ heimlich, verborgen.

'**cov·er-up** *s* Vertuschung *f* (**for** *gen*).

cow¹ [kaʊ] *s* ✕ Kuh *f* (*a. fig. contp.*): **till the ~s come home** F bis in alle Ewigkeit.

cow² [.~] *v/t* einschüchtern.

cow·ard [ˈkaʊəd] *s* Feigling *m*. **cow-**

ard·ice ['˷dɪs] s Feigheit f. '**cow·ard·ly** adj feig.

'**cow·boy** s Cowboy m.

cow·er ['kaʊə] v/i **1.** kauern, (zs.-gekauert) hocken. **2.** a. ~ **down** sich ducken.

'**cow·hide** s **1.** Kuhhaut f. **2.** Rind(s)leder n. '**˷house** s Kuhstall m.

cowl [kaʊl] s **1.** Mönchskutte f. **2.** Kapuze f. **3.** Schornsteinkappe f.

'**cow·pat** s Kuhfladen m. '**˷pox** s ♀ Kuh-, Impfpocken pl. '**˷shed** s Kuhstall m. '**˷skin** s **cowhide.** '**˷slip** s ♀ **1.** Br. Schlüsselblume f. **2.** Am. Sumpfdotterblume f.

cox [kɒks] → **coxswain. ˷swain** ['kɒksn] I s **1.** Rudern: Steuermann m. **2.** Boot(s)führer m. II v/t u. v/i **3.** steuern.

coy [kɔɪ] adj □ **1.** schüchtern, scheu. **2.** neckisch-verschämt.

co·zi·ness, co·zy Am. → **cosiness, cosy.**

crab¹ [kræb] s **1.** zo. Krabbe f; Taschenkrebs m: **catch a ~** (Rudern) e-n Krebs fangen. **2.** ⊕ Winde f; Laufkatze f. **3.** → **crab louse.**

crab² [˷] F I s **1.** Nörgler(in); Nörgelei f. II v/i **2.** nörgeln. III v/t **3.** (herum)nörgeln an (dat). **4.** Am. verpatzen.

crab·bed ['kræbɪd] adj □ **1.** mürrisch, verdrießlich. **2.** verworren, unklar. **3.** unleserlich. '**crab·by** → **crabbed** 1.

crab louse s (irr louse) zo. Filzlaus f.

crack [kræk] I s **1.** Krach m, Knall m: **at the ~ of dawn** im Morgengrauen, in aller Frühe; **in a ~** F im Nu; **give s.o. a fair ~ of the whip** F j-m e-e faire Chance geben. **2.** F (heftiger) Schlag: **give s.o. a ~ on the head** j-m eins auf den Kopf geben. **3.** Sprung m, Riß m. **4.** Spalt(e f) m, Ritz(e f) m: **be open a ~** e-n Spalt (breit) offenstehen. **5.** F Knacks m (geistiger Defekt). **6.** sl. Versuch m: **have a ~ at sth., give s.th. a ~** es (einmal) mit et. versuchen. **7.** sl. a) Witz m: **make ˷s about** Witze machen über (acc), b) Seitenhieb m, Stichelei f. **8.** Br. F Crack m, As n (bsd. Sportler). II adj **9.** F erstklassig, großartig: **~ shot** Meisterschütze m. III v/t **10.** krachen, knallen. **11.** (zer)springen, (-)platzen, rissig werden, e-n Sprung od. Sprünge bekommen. **12.** überschnappen (Stimme). **13.** fig.

(F ~ **up**) zs.-brechen. **14. get ˷ing** F loslegen. **15.** ~ **down on** F scharf vorgehen gegen, durchgreifen bei. IV v/t **16.** knallen mit (Peitsche), knacken mit (Fingern) u. **17.** zerbrechen, Ei aufschlagen, e-r Flasche den Hals brechen. **18.** e-n Sprung machen in (dat); sich e-e Rippe etc anbrechen. **19.** F a) schlagen, hauen: ~ **s.o. over the head** j-m eins auf den Kopf geben, b) ein-, zerschlagen. **20.** Nuß, F Code, Safe etc knacken. **21.** ~ **up** F hochjubeln. '**˷brained** adj F verrückt. '**˷down** s F (**on**) scharfes Vorgehen (gegen), Durchgreifen n (bei).

cracked [krækt] adj **1.** gesprungen, rissig: **be ~** e-n Sprung haben. **2.** F verrückt.

crack·er ['krækə] s **1.** Cracker m, Kräkker m: a) ungesüßtes, keksartiges Kleingebäck, b) Schwärmer m, Frosch m (Feuerwerkskörper), c) Knallbonbon m, n. **2.** pl Nußknacker m. **crack·ers** ['˷əz] adj Br. F übergeschnappt: **go ~** überschnappen.

'**crack·jaw** adj zungenbrecherisch. II s Zungenbrecher m.

crack·le ['krækl] I v/i knistern, prasseln, knattern. II s Knistern n, Prasseln n, Knattern n.

'**crack·pot** F I s Verrückte m, Spinner m. II adj verrückt. '**˷up** s fig. F Zs.-bruch m.

crack·y ['krækɪ] → **cracked.**

cra·dle ['kreidl] I s **1.** Wiege f (a. fig.): **from the ~ to the grave** von der Wiege bis zur Bahre; **from the ~** von Kindheit od. von Kindesbeinen an. **2.** teleph. Gabel f: **put the receiver in the ~** den Hörer auf die Gabel legen. II v/t **3.** wiegen, schaukeln: ~ **to sleep** in den Schlaf wiegen. **4.** (zärtlich) halten. **5.** teleph. Hörer auflegen.

craft [krɑːft] s **1.** (Hand- od. Kunst)Fertigkeit f, Geschicklichkeit f: → **art** 2. **2.** Gewerbe n, Beruf m, Handwerk n. **3.** → **craftiness. 4.** Boot(e pl) n, Schiff(e pl) n; Flugzeug(e pl) n. '**craft·i·ness** s Schlauheit f, Verschlagenheit f, List f.

crafts·man ['krɑːftsmən] s (irr **man**) Handwerker m. '**crafts·man·ship** s Kunstfertigkeit f, handwerkliches Können.

craft·y ['krɑːftɪ] *adj* □ schlau, verschlagen, listig.

crag [kræg] *s* Felsenspitze *f*, Klippe *f*. **crag·ged** ['krægɪd] *adj Am.*, '**crag·gy** *adj* **1.** felsig, schroff. **2.** runz(e)lig, zerfurcht (*Gesicht*); knorrig, rauh (*Person*).

cram [kræm] **I** *v/t* **1.** vollstopfen, *a. fig.* vollpacken (**with** mit). **2.** (hinein)stopfen, (-)zwängen (**into** in *acc*). **3.** F a) mit *j-m* pauken *od.* büffeln, b) *mst* ~ **up** *j-n* ein Fach pauken, büffeln. **II** *v/i* **4.** sich vollstopfen. **5.** F pauken, büffeln (für für): ~ *up on* → 3b. **II** *s* **6.** F Pauken *n*, Büffeln *n*: ~ *course* Paukkurs *m*. ,~'**full** *adj* vollgestopft (*of* mit), zum Bersten voll.

cram·mer ['kræmə] *s* F **1.** Paukstudio *n*. **2.** Einpauker *m*. **3.** Paukbuch *n*. **4** *j-d*, der für e-e Prüfung paukt.

cramp[1] [kræmp] *s* $ Krampf *m*.

cramp[2] [~] **I** *s* **1.** ⊕ Krampe *f*, Klammer *f*. **II** *v/t* **2.** ⊕ ankrampen, anklammern. **3.** *a.* ~ *up* einzwängen, -engen: **be** ~*ed* **for space** (*od.* **room**) (zu) wenig Platz haben, räumlich beschränkt sein.

cran·ber·ry ['krænbərɪ] *s* ♣ Preiselbeere *f*.

crane [kreɪn] **I** *s* **1.** *orn.* Kranich *m*. **2.** ⊕ Kran *m*. **II** *v/t* **3.** ~ *one's neck* sich den Hals verrenken (**for** nach), e-n langen Hals machen, den Hals recken. **III** *v/i* **4.** *a.* ~ *forward* den Hals recken. ~ *driv·er* *s* Kranführer *m*.

crank [kræŋk] **I** *s* **1.** ⊕ Kurbel *f*. **2.** F wunderlicher Kauz, Spinner *m*; *Am.* Miesepeter *m*. **3.** F fixe Idee, Marotte *f*. **II** *v/t* **4.** *oft* ~ *up* ankurbeln. '~**·shaft** *s* ⊕ Kurbelwelle *f*.

crank·y ['kræŋkɪ] *adj* □ F **1.** verschroben, wunderlich. **2.** *Am.* reizbar, schlechtgelaunt. **3.** wack(e)lig, unsicher, baufällig.

cran·nied ['krænɪd] *adj* rissig. '**cran·ny** *s* Riß *m*, Ritze *f*, Spalt *m*: → **nook**.

crape [kreɪp] *s* **1.** Krepp *m*. **2.** Trauerflor *m*.

crash [kræʃ] **I** *v/t* **1.** zertrümmern, -schmettern. **2.** F uneingeladen kommen zu, hineinplatzen in (*acc*): ~ *a party*; ~ *the gate* → **gate-crash**. **II** *v/i* **3.** (krachend) zerbersten. **4.** krachend einstürzen, zs.-krachen. **5.** *bsd.* ✈ zs.-brechen. **6.** krachen (**against**, **into** gegen):

~ *open* krachend auffliegen (*Tür*). **7.** stürmen, platzen: ~ *in(to the room)* hereinplatzen. **8.** *mot.* zs.-stoßen, verunglücken; ✈ abstürzen. **III** *s* **9.** Krach(en) *m* **10.** *bsd.* ✝ Zs.-bruch *m*, (Börsen)Krach *m*. **11.** *mot.* Unfall *m*, Zs.-stoß *m*; ✈ Absturz *m*. ~ *bar·ri·er* *s* Br. Leitplanke *f*. ~ *course* *s* Schnell-, Intensivkurs *m*. ~ *di·et* *s* radikale Schlankheitskur. ~ *hel·met* *s* Sturzhelm *m*.

crash·ing ['kræʃɪŋ] *adj* F fürchterlich.

'**crash**-**land** *v/i* ✈ Bruch *od.* e-e Bruchlandung machen, bruchlanden. ~ **land·ing** *s* ✈ Bruchlandung *f*. ~ **pro·gram(me)** *s* Sofortprogramm *n*. ~ **test** *s mot.* Crashtest *m*.

crass [kræs] *adj* □ **1.** grob, kraß (*Fehler etc*). **2.** derb, unfein (*Benehmen etc*).

crate [kreɪt] *s* **1.** (Latten)Kiste *f*. **2.** (Bieretc)Kasten *m*. **3.** *sl.* Kiste *f* (*Auto*, *Flugzeug*).

cra·ter ['kreɪtə] *s* **1.** *geol.* Krater *m*: ~ *lake* Kratersee *m*. **2.** (Bomben-, Granat)Trichter *m*.

cra·vat [krə'væt] *s* Halstuch *n*.

crave [kreɪv] **I** *v/t* **1.** *et.* ersehnen. **2.** (inständig) bitten *od.* flehen um. **II** *v/i* **3.** sich sehnen (**for**, **after** nach). **4.** ~ **for** → 2. '**crav·ing** *s* Sehnsucht *f* (**for** nach).

crawl [krɔːl] **I** *v/i* **1.** kriechen: a) krabbeln, b) *fig.* sich dahinschleppen (*Zeit etc*), c) im Schneckentempo gehen *od.* fahren, d) F unterwürfig sein: ~ *to s.o.* vor *j-m* kriechen. **2.** wimmeln (**with** von). **3.** kribbeln: *the sight made her flesh* ~ bei dem Anblick bekam sie e-e Gänsehaut. **4.** *Schwimmen:* kraulen. **II** *s* **5.** Kriechen *n*: *go at a* ~ → 1c. **6.** *Schwimmen:* Kraul(en) *n*, Kraulstil *m*. '**crawl·er** *s* **1.** Kriechtier *n*. **2.** *Br.* F Kriecher(in). **3.** *Schwimmen:* Krauler(in).

cray·fish ['kreɪfɪʃ] *s zo.* **1.** Flußkrebs *m*. **2.** Languste *f*.

cray·on ['kreɪən] **I** *s* **1.** Zeichenkreide *f*. **2.** Zeichen-, Bunt-, Pastellstift *m*: *blue* ~ Blaustift *m*. **3.** Kreide-, Pastellzeichnung *f*. **II** *v/t* **4.** mit Kreide *etc* zeichnen.

craze [kreɪz] *s* Manie *f*, Verrücktheit *f*: *be the* ~ große Mode sein; *the latest* ~ der letzte Schrei. '**cra·zi·ness** *s* Verrücktheit *f*. '**cra·zy** *adj* □ **1.** *a. fig.*

verrückt, wahnsinnig (**with** vor *dat*): **drive s.o.** ~ j-n wahnsinnig machen; ~ **bone** *Am.* Musikantenknochen *m.* **2** F (**about**) hingerissen (von), vernarrt in (*acc*); versessen, scharf (auf *acc*), wild, verrückt (nach): **be** ~ **to do s.th.** darauf versessen sein, et. zu tun.

creak [kriːk] **I** *v/i* knarren (*Treppe etc*), quietschen (*Bremsen etc*). **II** *s* Knarren *n*, Quietschen *n*. '**creak·y** *adj* knarrend, quietschend.

cream [kriːm] **I** *s* **1.** Rahm *m*, Sahne *f*. Creme(speise) *f*. **3.** (*Haut-*, *Schuh-etc*)Creme *f*. **4.** *fig.* Creme *f*, Auslese *f*, Elite *f*: **the** ~ **of the** ~ die Crème de la crème. (II *v/t* **5.** den Rahm abschöpfen von (*a. fig.*). **6.** zu Schaum schlagen; schaumig rühren. **7.** sich *das Gesicht etc* eincremen: ~ **one's face.** **III** *adj* **8.** creme(farben). ~ **cheese** *s* Rahm-, Vollfettkäse *m*. '~,col·o(u)red → cream 8. ~ puff *s* Windbeutel *m*.

crease [kriːs] **I** *s* **1.** Falte *f*. **2.** Bügelfalte *f*. **3.** Knick *m*, *a.* Eselsohr *n*. **II** *v/t* **4.** falten, knicken. **5.** Falten bügeln in (*e-e Hose*). **6.** zerknittern. **III** *v/i* **7.** knittern. '~-proof, '~-re,sist·ant *adj* knitterfrei, -fest.

cre·ate [kriːˈeɪt] *v/t* **1.** (er)schaffen. **2.** ins Leben rufen, *Arbeitsplätze* schaffen; hervorrufen, verursachen. **3.** *thea. etc*, *Mode*: kreieren. **4.** *j-n* machen *od.* ernennen zu. **cre'a·tion** *s* **1.** (Er)Schaffung *f*. **2.** Hervorrufung *f*, Verursachung *f*. **3.** **the** 2 *eccl.* die Schöpfung. **4.** *thea. etc*, *Mode*: Kreierung *f*. **5.** (*Kunst-*, *Mode*)Schöpfung *f* (*Mode a.*) Kreation *f*. **6.** Ernennung *f*. **cre'a·tive** *adj* □ schöpferisch, kreativ. **cre'a·tor** *s* Schöpfer *m*, Urheber *m*: **the** 2 *eccl.* der Schöpfer.

crea·ture [ˈkriːtʃə] *s* **1.** Geschöpf *n*, (Lebe)Wesen *n*, Kreatur *f*: **dumb** ~ stumme Kreatur; **good** ~ gute Haut; **lovely** ~ süßes Geschöpf; **poor** (**silly**) ~ armes (dummes) Ding; ~ **of habit** Gewohnheitstier *n*. **2.** Produkt *n*: ~ **of the imagination** Phantasieprodukt. ~ **com·forts** *s pl* leibliches Wohl.

crèche [kreɪʃ] *s* **1.** (Kinder)Krippe *f*. **2.** *Am.* (Weihnachts)Krippe *f*.

cre·dence [ˈkriːdəns] *s*: **give** (*od.* **attach**) ~ **to** Glauben schenken (*dat*).

cre·den·tials [krɪˈdenʃlz] *s pl* **1.** Beglau-

bigungs- *od.* Empfehlungsschreiben *n*. **2.** (Leumunds)Zeugnis *n*. **3.** Ausweis-(papiere *pl*) *m*).

cred·i·bil·i·ty [ˌkredəˈbɪlətɪ] *s* Glaubwürdigkeit *f*. '**cred·i·ble** *adj* □ glaubwürdig.

cred·it [ˈkredɪt] **I** *s* **1.** Glaube(n) *m*: **give** ~ **to** Glauben schenken (*dat*). **2.** Ansehen *n*, Achtung *f*: **be in high** ~ **with** in hohem Ansehen stehen bei. **3.** Ehre *f*: **be a** ~ **to s.o., be to s.o.'s** ~ j-m Ehre machen *od.* einbringen; **to his** ~ **it must be said** zu s-r Ehre muß man sagen; ~ **where** ~ **is due** Ehre, wem Ehre gebührt. **4.** Anerkennung *f*, Lob *n*: **get** ~ **for** Anerkennung finden für; **that's very much to his** ~ das ist sehr anerkennenswert *od.* verdienstvoll von ihm. **5.** Verdienst *n*: **give s.o.** (**the**) ~ **for** j-m et. hoch anrechnen; j-m et. zutrauen; j-m et. zuschreiben. **6.** ✝ Kredit *m*: **on** ~ auf Kredit; **give s.o.** ~ **for £ 1,000** j-m e-n Kredit von 1000 Pfund geben; ~ **card** Kreditkarte *f*. **7.** ✝ Guthaben *n*, Kredit(seite *f*) *m*, Haben *n*: **your** ~ **a** Saldo zu Ihren Gunsten; **enter** (*od.* **place**, **put**) **a sum to s.o.'s** ~ j-m e-n Betrag gutschreiben. **II** *v/t* **8.** Glauben schenken (*dat*), glauben (*dat*). **9.** ~ **s.o. with** j-m et. zutrauen; j-m et. zuschreiben. **10.** ✝ *Betrag* gutschreiben (**to s.o.** j-m). '**cred·it·a·ble** *adj* □ (**to**) ehrenvoll (für), anerkennenswert (von). '**cred·i·tor** *s* ✝ Gläubiger *m*.

'**cred·it,wor·thy** *adj* ✝ kreditwürdig.

cre·du·li·ty [krɪˈdjuːlətɪ] *s* Leichtgläubigkeit *f*. **cred·u·lous** [ˈkredjʊləs] *adj* □ leichtgläubig.

creed [kriːd] *s* **1.** *eccl.* Glaubensbekenntnis *n*; Glaube *m*, Konfession *f*. **2.** *fig.* Überzeugung *f*, Weltanschauung *f*.

creek [kriːk] *s* **1.** *Am.* Bach *m*. **2.** *bsd. Br.* kleine Bucht. **3. be up the** ~ F in der Klemme sein *od.* sitzen *od.* stecken.

creep [kriːp] **I** *v/i* (*irr*) **1.** kriechen: a) krabbeln, b) *fig.* sich dahinschleppen (*Zeit etc*), c) im Schneckentempo gehen *od.* fahren, d) unterwürfig sein. **2.** schleichen: ~ **in** (sich) hinein- *od.* hereinschleichen; *fig.* sich einschleichen (*Fehler etc*). **3.** kribbeln: **the sight made her flesh** ~ bei dem Anblick bekam sie e-e Gänsehaut. **II** *s* **4.** Kriechen *n*, Schleichen *n*: **go at a** ~ 1c. **5. the**

sight gave her the ~s F bei dem Anblick bekam sie e-e Gänsehaut. **6.** F Kriecher(in). **'creep·er** s **1.** Kriechtier n. **2.** Kriech- od. Kletterpflanze f. **'creep·ing** adj □ kriechend: *~ inflation* ✝ schleichende Inflation. **'creep·y** adj grus(e)lig.

cre·mate [krɪ'meɪt] v/t bsd. *Leichen* verbrennen, einäschern. **cre'ma·tion** s Verbrennung f, Einäscherung f, Feuerbestattung f. **crem·a·to·ri·um** [ˌkremə-'tɔːriəm] pl **-ums, -a** [~ə], bsd. Am. **cre·ma·to·ry** [~ˈtəri] s Krematorium n.

crept [krept] pret u. pp von **creep**.

cres·cent ['kresnt] s Halbmond m, Mondsichel f.

cress [kres] s ♣ Kresse f.

crest [krest] s **1.** orn. Büschel n, Haube f; Kamm m. **2.** zo. Mähne f. **3.** Bergrücken m, Kamm m. **4.** (*Wellen*)Kamm m: *be riding (along) on the ~ of a wave* fig. im Augenblick ganz oben schwimmen. **5.** fig. Gipfel m, Scheitelpunkt m: *at the ~ of his fame* auf dem Gipfel s-s Ruhms. **'~·fall·en** adj fig. niedergeschlagen, geknickt.

cre·tin ['kretɪn] s ♣ Kretin m (a. fig. contp.).

cre·vasse [krɪ'væs] s **1.** tiefer Spalt od. Riß. **2.** Gletscherspalte f.

crev·ice ['krevɪs] s Riß m, Spalt m, (Fels)Spalte f.

crew¹ [kruː] s **1.** (*Arbeits*)Gruppe f, (*Bauetc*)Trupp m, (*Arbeiter*)Kolonne f. **2.** ⊕ (*Bedienungs*)Mannschaft f. **3.** ✈, ♣ Besatzung f; ♣ engS. Mannschaft f (a. Sport).

crew² [~] pret von **crow²**.

crew cut s Bürstenschnitt m.

crib [krɪb] I s **1.** Kinderbettchen n. **2.** (Futter)Krippe f. **3.** bsd. Br. (Weihnachts)Krippe f. **4.** F kleiner Diebstahl; Anleihe f, Plagiat n. **5.** ped. F Eselsbrücke f, Klatsche f; Spickzettel m. II v/t u. v/i **6.** F klauen (a. fig. plagiieren). **7.** ped. F abschreiben, spicken (*off, from* von).

crick [krɪk] s: *a ~ in one's neck* ein steifer Hals.

crick·et¹ ['krɪkɪt] s zo. Grille f.

crick·et² [~] (Sport) I s Kricket n: *not ~* F nicht fair. II v/i Kricket spielen. **'crick·et·er** s Kricketspieler m.

cri·er ['kraɪə] s Schreier m, Schreihals m.

crime [kraɪm] s **1.** Verbrechen n, coll. a. pl: *~ prevention* Verbrechensverhütung f; *~ syndicate* Verbrechersyndikat n; *~ wave* Welle f von Verbrechen. **2.** → **criminality**. **3.** F Verbrechen n; Jammer m, Zumutung f.

crim·i·nal ['krɪmɪnl] I adj **1.** kriminell, verbrecherisch (beide a. fig. F): *~ act* Straftat f, strafbare Handlung; *~ association* kriminelle Vereinigung; → **record¹ 2.** strafrechtlich, Straf..., kriminal...: *~ code* Strafgesetzbuch n; *~ law* Strafrecht n; *~ proceedings* pl Strafprozeß m, -verfahren n. II s **3.** Verbrecher(in), Kriminelle m, f. **crim·i·nal·i·ty** [ˌ~ˈnæləti] s Kriminalität f, Verbrechertum n. **crim·i·nol·o·gy** [ˌ~-ˈnɒlədʒi] s Kriminologie f.

crimp [krɪmp] v/t **1.** kräuseln. **2.** falten, fälteln. **3.** Haar wellen, locken.

crim·son ['krɪmzn] adj **1.** karmin-, karmesinrot. **2.** puterrot (*from* vor dat).

cringe [krɪndʒ] v/i **1.** sich ducken od. (zs.-)krümmen: *~ at* zurückschrecken vor (dat). **2.** fig. kriechen, katzbuckeln (*to* vor dat). **'cring·ing** adj □ kriecherisch, unterwürfig.

crin·kle ['krɪŋkl] v/i **1.** Falten werfen. **2.** knittern. **3.** rascheln, knistern. II v/t **4.** zerknittern. III s **5.** Falte f, (im Gesicht) Fältchen n.

crip·ple ['krɪpl] I s Krüppel m (a. fig.). II v/t zum Krüppel machen; lähmen, fig. a. lahmlegen.

cri·sis ['kraɪsɪs] pl **-ses** ['~siːz] s Krise f (a. thea., ♣): *economic ~* Wirtschaftskrise; *~ of confidence* Vertrauenskrise; *~ staff* Krisenstab m.

crisp [krɪsp] I adj □ **1.** knusp(e)rig (Gebäck etc). **2.** kraus (Haar). **3.** frisch, knackig, fest (Gemüse). **4.** forsch, schneidig (Benehmen etc). **5.** klar (Stil etc). **6.** scharf, frisch (Luft etc). II s **7.** bsd. Br. (Kartoffel)Chips pl. III v/t **8.** knusp(e)rig backen od. braten. IV v/i **9.** knusp(e)rig werden.

criss·cross ['krɪskrɒs] I adj kreuzweise, Kreuz... II adv kreuzweise, kreuz u. quer. III s Gewirr m. IV v/t kreuz u. quer ziehen durch. V v/i kreuz u. quer (ver)laufen.

cri·te·ri·on [kraɪ'tɪərɪən] pl **-ri·a** [~ə], **-ri·ons** s Kriterium n: a) Maßstab m, b) (Unterscheidungs)Merkmal n.

crit·ic ['krɪtɪk] *s* Kritiker(in): a) Beurteiler(in), b) Rezensent(in), c) Krittler(in). **crit·i·cal** ['᷉kl] *adj* □ kritisch: a) anspruchsvoll, b) mißbilligend, tadelnd (*of acc*): **be ~ of** et. auszusetzen haben an (*dat*), kritisch gegenüberstehen (*dat*), kritisieren (*acc*), c) entscheidend (*Augenblick etc*), d) gefährlich, bedenklich (*Situation etc*): **he is in** (a) **~ condition** *er* sein Zustand ist kritisch. **crit·i·cism** ['᷉sɪzəm] *s* Kritik *f*: a) kritische Beurteilung, b) Tadel *m*, Vorwurf *m*: **open to ~** anfechtbar; **above ~** über jede Kritik *od.* jeden Tadel erhaben, c) → **critique** a. **crit·i·cize** ['᷉saɪz] *v/t* kritisieren: a) kritisch beurteilen, b) Kritik üben an (*dat*), bekritteln, tadeln: **~ s.o. for doing s.th.** j-n kritisieren, weil er et. getan hat, c) besprechen, rezensieren. **cri·tique** [krɪ'tiːk] *s* Kritik *f*: a) Rezension *f*, Besprechung *f*, b) kritische Untersuchung.

croak [krəʊk] **I** *v/i* **1.** quaken (*Frosch*); krächzen (*Rabe etc, a. Mensch*). **2.** *sl.* abkratzen. **II** *s* **3.** Quaken *n*; Krächzen *n*.

cro·chet ['krəʊʃeɪ] **I** *s a.* **~ work** Häkelarbeit *f*, Häkelei *f*: **~ hook** Häkelnadel *f*. **II** *v/t u. v/i* häkeln.

crock[1] [krɒk] *s* irdener Topf *od.* Krug. **crock**[2] [᷉] *s sl.* Wrack *n* (*Person od. Sache*); Klapperkasten *m* (*Auto*). **crock·er·y** ['krɒkərɪ] *s* Steingut *n*, Töpferware *f*.

croc·o·dile ['krɒkədaɪl] *s zo.* Krokodil *n*. **~ tears** *s pl* Krokodilstränen *pl*.

cro·cus ['krəʊkəs] *s* ♀ Krokus *m*.

crook [krʊk] *s* **1.** Haken *m*. **2.** Krümmung *f*, Biegung *f*: **~ of one's arm** Armbeuge *f*. **3.** F Gauner *m*; Gaunerei *f*: **on the ~** auf betrügerische Weise. **II** *v/t u. v/i* **4.** (sich) krümmen *od.* biegen. **crook·ed** ['᷉ɪd] *adj* □ **1.** gekrümmt, gebogen, krumm. **2.** F betrügerisch.

croon [kruːn] *v/t u. v/i* **1.** schmachtend singen. **2.** leise singen *od.* summen. **'croon·er** *s* Schnulzensänger(in).

crop [krɒp] **I** *s* **1.** Ernte *f*: **~ failure** Mißernte. **2.** *fig.* Ertrag *m*, Ausbeute *f* (*of* an *dat*); große Menge, Masse *f*. **3.** kurzer Haarschnitt; kurzgeschnittenes Haar. **II** *v/t* **4.** stutzen, beschneiden. **5.** *Haar* kurz scheren. **III** *v/i* **6.** *mst* **~ up** (*od. out*) *fig.* plötzlich auftauchen *od.*

eintreten. **'crop·per** *s* F **1.** schwerer Sturz: **come a ~** schwer stürzen. **2.** Mißerfolg *m*, Fehlschlag *m*: **come a ~** Schiffbruch erleiden.

cro·quet ['krəʊkeɪ] *s Sport:* Krocket *n*.

cross [krɒs] **I** *s* **1.** *eccl.* Kreuz *n*: **the ♀** das Kreuz (Christi), das Kruzifix. **2.** Kreuz(zeichen) *n*: **make the sign of the ~** sich bekreuzigen; **mark with a ~** ankreuzen. **3.** *fig.* Kreuz *n*, Leiden *n*: **bear** (*od. carry*) **one's ~** sein Kreuz tragen. **4.** Querstrich *m*. **5.** *biol.* Kreuzung(sprodukt *n*) *f*. **6.** *fig.* Mittel-, Zwischending *n*. **II** *v/t* **7.** das Kreuzzeichen machen auf (*acc*) *od.* über (*dat*): **~ o.s.** sich bekreuzigen. **8.** kreuzen: **~ one's arms** die Arme kreuzen *od.* verschränken; *fig.* die Hände in den Schoß legen; **~ one's legs** die Beine kreuzen *od.* über(einander)schlagen; → **finger** I, **sword**. **9.** *Grenze, Meer, Straße etc* überqueren: **~ s.o.'s path** *fig.* j-m in die Quere kommen. **10.** kreuzen, schneiden. **11.** sich kreuzen mit (*Brief*). **12.** ankreuzen. **13.** *oft* **~ off** (*od. out*) aus-, durchstreichen: **~ off** *fig.* abschreiben (**as** als). **14.** *Plan etc* durchkreuzen, vereiteln. **15.** *biol.* kreuzen. **III** *v/i* **16.** sich kreuzen (*a. Briefe*) *od.* schneiden. **17.** *oft* **~ over** (**to**) hinübergehen, -fahren (nach), übersetzen (nach). **18.** *biol.* sich kreuzen (lassen). **IV** *adj* **19.** schräg, Schräg... **20.** (**to**) entgegengesetzt (*dat*), im Widerspruch (zu). **21.** F böse (**with** auf *acc*, mit), mürrisch. **'~·bar** *s Sport:* Tor-, Querlatte *f*. **'~·beam** *s* ⊙ Querträger *m*, -balken *m*. **'~·bones** *s pl* → **skull**. **'~·breed** *biol.* **I** *s* Mischling *m*, Kreuzung *f*. **II** *v/t* (*irr* **breed**) kreuzen. **'~·check** *v/t* von verschiedenen Gesichtspunkten aus überprüfen. **II** *s* Überprüfung *f* von verschiedenen Gesichtspunkten aus. **'~·coun·try** *adj* Querfeldein..., Gelände..., *mot. a.* geländegängig: **~ skiing** Skilanglauf *m*. **'~·cur·rent** *s* Gegenströmung *f* (*a. fig.*). **'~·dress·ing** *s* Transvestismus *m*.

crossed [krɒst] *adj* gekreuzt: **~ cheque** ♣ *Br.* Verrechnungsscheck *m*. **'cross·ex·am·i·na·tion** *s* ♣♣ Kreuzverhör *n*. **'~·ex'am·ine** *v/t* ♣♣ ins Kreuzverhör nehmen. **'~·eyed** *adj* schielend: **be ~** schielen. **'~·fire** *s* ✗ Kreuzfeuer *n* (*a. fig.*). **'~·grained** *adj* **1.** quergefasert.

2. *fig.* widerspenstig (*a. Sache*); kratzbürstig.

cross·ing ['krɒsɪŋ] *s* **1.** Überquerung *f:* ~ **point** Grenzübergang *m.* **2.** ⚓ Überfahrt *f:* **rough** ~ stürmische Überfahrt. **3.** (*Straßen- etc*)Kreuzung *f.* **4.** Straßenübergang *m;* *Br.* Fußgängerüberweg *m:* → **grade** 4, **level** 5. **5.** *biol.* Kreuzung *f.*

'**cross-legged** *adj u. adv* mit gekreuzten *od.* über(einander)geschlagenen Beinen, (*am Boden a.*) im Schneidersitz.

cross·ness ['krɒsnɪs] *s* F Mürrischkeit *f,* schlechte Laune.

'**cross**|-**patch** *s* F Brummbär *m.* ,~-'**pur·pos·es** *s pl:* **talk at** ~ aneinander vorbeireden. ~ **ref·er·ence** *s* Kreuz-, Querverweis *m.* '~**-road** *s* **1.** *Am.* Querod. Seitenstraße *f.* **2.** *pl* (*mst sg konstruiert*) (Straßen)Kreuzung *f;* *fig.* Scheideweg *m.* ~ **sec·tion** *s* ⚓, ☉ *u.* ⚙ Querschnitt *m* (**of** durch). '~**walk** *s Am.* Fußgängerüberweg *m.* '~**ways**, '~-**wise** *adv* quer, kreuzweise. '~-**word** (**puz·zle**) *s* Kreuzworträtsel *n.*

crotch [krɒtʃ] *s* **1.** Gab(e)lung *f.* **2.** Schritt *m* (*der Hose od. des Körpers*).

crotch·et ['krɒtʃɪt] *s* **1.** ♪ *bsd. Br.* Viertelnote *f.* **2.** *fig.* Grille *f,* Marotte *f.* '**crotch·et·y** *adj* **1.** grillenhaft. **2.** F mürrisch.

crouch [kraʊtʃ] **I** *v/i* **1.** *a.* ~ **down** sich bücken *od.* ducken. **2.** hocken; kauern. **II** *s* **3.** Hocke *f:* **in a** ~ gebückt; in der Hocke.

crou·pi·er ['kru:pɪə] *s* Croupier *m.*

crow[1] [krəʊ] *s* **1.** *orn.* Krähe *f:* **as the** ~ **flies** (in der) Luftlinie; **eat** ~ *bsd. Am.* F zu Kreuze kriechen; **have a** ~ **to pluck** (*od.* **pull, pick**) **with** F ein Hühnchen zu rupfen haben mit. **2.** → **crowbar.**

crow[2] [krəʊ] **I** *v/i pret* **crowed** *u.* (*für* 1) **crew** [kru:], *pp* **crowed** **1.** krähen (*Hahn*). **2.** (*fröhlich*) krähen. **3.** jubeln, frohlocken (**over** über *acc*). **4.** protzen, prahlen (**over, about** mit). **II** *s* **5.** Krähen *n.* **6.** Jubel(schrei) *m.*

'**crow·bar** *s* ⚙ Brecheisen *n,* -stange *f.*

crowd [kraʊd] **I** *s* **1.** dichte (Menschen)Menge, Masse *f:* ~**s** *pl of people* Menschenmassen *pl.* **2.** **the** ~ die Masse, das (gemeine) Volk: **one of the** ~ ein Mann aus dem Volk; **follow** (*od.* **move**

with) **the** ~ mit der Masse gehen. **3.** F Gesellschaft *f,* Haufen *m,* Verein *m.* **4.** Ansammlung *f,* Haufen *m.* **II** *v/i* **5.** (zs.-)strömen, sich drängen (*into* in *acc;* *round* um). **III** *v/t* **6.** *Straßen etc* bevölkern. **7.** sich drängen in (*acc od. dat*) *od.* um. **8.** zs.-drängen, -pressen. **9.** hineinpressen, -stopfen (*into* in *acc*). **10.** vollstopfen (**with** mit). '**crowd·ed** *adj* **1.** (**with**) überfüllt (mit), voll (von): ~ **street** stark befahrene *od.* verkehrsreiche Straße. **2.** (zs.-)gedrängt. **3.** *fig.* voll ausgefüllt, ereignisreich.

crowd|**pull·er** *s* Zuschauermagnet *m.* ~ **scene** *s* Film, TV: Massenszene *f.*

crown [kraʊn] *s* **1.** Krone *f* (*a. fig.*), (*Sport a.*) (Meister)Titel *m:* **the** ♔ die Krone, der König, die Königin. **2.** Krone *f* (*Währung*). **3.** Zahnmedizin: Krone *f.* **4.** *fig.* Krönung *f,* Höhepunkt *m.* **II** *v/t* **5.** *j-n* krönen (**king** zum König): ~**ed heads** *pl* gekrönte Häupter *pl.* **6.** *fig.* krönen: a) ehren, auszeichnen, b) schmücken, zieren, c) den Höhepunkt bilden von (*od. gen*): ~ **all** allem die Krone aufsetzen (*a. iro.*); **to it all** zu allem Überfluß *od.* Unglück; d) erfolgreich abschließen: ~**ed with success** von Erfolg gekrönt. **7.** *Zahn* überkronen. ~ **col·o·ny** *s Br.* Kronkolonie *f.*

crown·ing ['kraʊnɪŋ] **I** *adj fig.* krönend. **II** *s* Krönung *f* (*a. fig.*).

crown| **jew·els** *s pl* Kronjuwelen *pl.* ~ **prince** *s* Kronprinz *m* (*a. fig.*). ~ **prin·cess** *s* Kronprinzessin *f.* ~ **wit·ness** *s* ⚖ *Br.* Belastungszeuge *m.*

'**crow's**|-**feet** *s pl* Krähenfüße *pl,* Fältchen *pl.* ~ **nest** *s* ⚓ Krähennest *n.*

cru·ces ['kru:si:z] *pl von* **crux.**

cru·cial ['kru:ʃl] *adj* □ kritisch, entscheidend (**to, for** für): ~ **point** springender Punkt.

cru·ci·fix ['kru:sɪfɪks] *s* Kruzifix *n.* **cru·ci·fix·ion** [ˌ~'fɪkʃn] *s* Kreuzigung *f.* **cru·ci·fy** ['~faɪ] *v/t* kreuzigen.

crude [kru:d] *adj* □ **1.** roh, unver-, unbearbeitet: ~ **oil** Rohöl *n.* **2.** *fig.* roh, grob. **3.** *fig.* nackt, ungeschminkt. '**crude·ness**, **cru·di·ty** ['~dɪtɪ] *s* Roheit *f* (*a. fig.*).

cru·el ['krʊəl] *adj* □ **1.** grausam (**to** zu, gegen). **2.** unmenschlich, unbarmherzig. **3.** schrecklich, mörderisch. '**cru-**

el·ty s Grausamkeit f: ~ **to animals** Tierquälerei f.

cru·et ['kru:ɪt] s **1.** Essig-, Ölfläschchen n. **2.** a. ~ **stand** Menage f, Gewürzständer m.

cruise [kru:z] **I** v/i **1.** ♣ kreuzen, e-e Kreuzfahrt od. Seereise machen. **2.** ✈, mot. mit Reisegeschwindigkeit fliegen od. fahren: **cruising speed** Reisegeschwindigkeit f. **II** v/t **3.** Kreuzfahrt f, Seereise f. ~ **mis·sile** ✕ Marschflugkörper m.

cruis·er ['kru:zə] s **1.** ♣ a) ✕ Kreuzer m (a. allg.), b) Kreuzfahrtschiff n. **2.** Am. (Funk)Streifenwagen m.

crumb [krʌm] **I** s **1.** Krume f, Krümel m, Brösel m. **2.** fig. Brocken m: **a few ~s of information** ein paar Informationsbrocken; ~ **of comfort** Trostpflaster n, -pflästerchen n. **II** v/t **3.** gastr. panieren. **4.** zerkrümeln. **crum·ble** ['~bl] **I** v/t **1.** zerkrümeln, -bröckeln. **II** v/i **2.** a. ~ **away** zerbröckeln, -fallen: ~ **to dust** (od. **nothing**) fig. sich in nichts auflösen. **3.** ✝ abbröckeln (Kurse). **'crum·bling, 'crum·bly** adj **1.** krüm(e)lig, bröck(e)lig. **2.** zerbröckelnd, -fallend.

crum·my ['krʌmɪ] adj sl. lausig, miserabel.

crum·ple ['krʌmpl] **I** v/t **1.** a. ~ **up** zerknittern, -knüllen. **2.** zerdrücken. **II** v/i **3.** knittern. **4.** a. ~ **up** zs.-brechen (a. fig.). **III** s **5.** (Knitter)Falte f.

crunch [krʌntʃ] **I** v/t **1.** knirschend (zer)kauen. **2.** zermalmen. **II** v/i **3.** knirschend kauen. **4.** knirschen. **III** s **5.** Knirschen n. **6. when it comes to the ~, when the ~ comes** F wenn es hart auf hart geht.

cru·sade [kru:'seɪd] **I** s hist. Kreuzzug m (a. fig.). **II** v/i hist. e-n Kreuzzug unternehmen, fig. a. zu Felde ziehen (**against** gegen; **for** für). **cru·sad·er** s **1.** hist. Kreuzfahrer m, -ritter m. **2.** fig. Kämpfer m.

crush [krʌʃ] **I** s **1.** Gedränge n, Gewühl n. **2.** bsd. Br. Getränk aus ausgepreßten Früchten: **orange ~. 3. have a ~ on s.o.** F in j-n verknallt sein. **II** v/t **4.** zerquetschen, -malmen, -drücken: ~ **out** Zigarette etc ausdrücken. **5.** zerdrücken, -knittern. **6.** ⊙ zerkleinern, -mahlen. **7.** auspressen, -drücken, -quetschen: ~

the juice from Zitrone etc auspressen. **8.** fig. nieder-, zerschmettern; Aufstand etc niederwerfen, unterdrücken: ~**ing blow** vernichtender Schlag; ~**ing majority** erdrückende Mehrheit. **III** v/i **9.** zerquetscht werden. **10.** sich drängen (**into** in acc). **11.** (zer)knittern. **'crush·a·ble** adj **1.** knitterfest, -frei. **2.** ~ **zone** mot. Knautschzone f.

crush| bar·ri·er s Br. Barriere f, Absperrung f. **'~re, sist·ant** → **crushable** 1.

crust [krʌst] **I** s **1.** (Brot)Kruste f, (-)Rinde f. **2.** Knust m, hartes od. trockenes Stück Brot. **3.** geol. (Erd)Kruste f. **4.** ❀ Kruste f, Schorf m. **5.** sl. Unverschämtheit f. **II** v/i a. ~ **over 6.** verkrusten. **7.** verharschen: ~**ed snow** Harsch m. **'crust·y** adj □ **1.** verkrustet, krustig. **2.** fig. barsch.

crutch [krʌtʃ] s **1.** Krücke f: **walk on ~es** auf od. an Krücken gehen. **2.** fig. Stütze f, Hilfe f.

crux [krʌks] pl **'crux·es, cru·ces** ['kru:si:z] s Crux f, Schwierigkeit f, Haken m; schwieriges Problem, harte Nuß.

cry [kraɪ] **I** s **1.** Schrei m, Ruf m (**for** nach): ~ **for help** Hilferuf; **within** ~ in Rufweite (**of** von); **a far** (od. **long**) ~ **from** fig. (himmel)weit entfernt von; et. ganz anderes als. **2.** Geschrei n. **3.** Weinen n: **have a good** ~ sich (richtig) ausweinen. **4.** (Schlacht)Ruf m, Schlag-, Losungswort n. **II** v/i **5.** schreien, rufen (**for** nach): ~ **for help** (**vengeance**) um Hilfe rufen (nach Rache schreien). **6.** weinen (**for joy** vor Freude); heulen, jammern (**over** wegen, über acc; **for** um): → **milk** I. **III** v/t **7.** et. schreien, (aus)rufen: → **wolf** 1. **8.** ~ **Tränen** weinen: ~ **o.s. to sleep** sich in den Schlaf weinen; → **eye** 1, **head** 8, **heart** 1.

Verbindungen mit Adverbien:

cry| down v/t **1.** heruntersetzen, -machen. **2.** niederschreien. ~ **off** v/t u. (bsd. Br.) v/i (plötzlich) absagen, zurücktreten (**von**). ~ **out** I v/t ausrufen. II v/i aufschreien: ~ **against** heftig protestieren gegen; ~ **(for)** → **cry** 5. ~ **up** v/t rühmen: **he's not all he's cried up to be** so gut ist er auch wieder nicht. **'cry, ba·by** s Heulsuse f.

cry·ing ['kraɪɪŋ] adj **1.** (himmel)schreiend: **it's a ~ shame** es ist jammerschade *od.* ein Jammer. **2.** dringend (*Bedürfnis etc*).

crypt [krɪpt] *s* △ Krypta *f*. **'cryp·tic** *adj* (*~ally*) **1.** geheim, verborgen. **2.** rätselhaft, dunkel.

crys·tal ['krɪstl] **I** *s* **1.** Kristall *m* (*a.* 🔭, *etc*): (*as*) *clear as* ~ kristallklar; *fig.* sonnenklar. **2.** *a.* ~ *glass* Kristall(glas) *n*. **3.** Uhrglas *n*. **II** *adj* **4.** kristallen: a) Kristall..., b) kristallklar. **crys·tal·li·za·tion** [ˌkrɪstəlaɪ'zeɪʃn] *s* Kristallisation *f*, Kristallbildung *f*. **'crys·tal·lize I** *v/t* **1.** kristallisieren. **2.** *fig.* konkrete *od.* feste Form geben (*dat*). **3.** Früchte kandieren. **II** *v/i* **4.** kristallisieren. **5.** *fig.* konkrete *od.* feste Form annehmen, sich kristallisieren (*into* zu): ~ *out* sich herauskristallisieren.

cub [kʌb] *s* **1.** *zo.* Junge *n* (*des Fuchses, Bären etc*). **2.** *a.* *unlicked* ~ grüner Junge. **3.** Anfänger *m*. **II** *v/i* **4.** (Junge) werfen.

cube [kju:b] **I** *s* **1.** Würfel *m*: ~ *sugar* Würfelzucker *m*. **2.** Å Kubikzahl *f*, dritte Potenz: ~ *root* Kubikwurzel *f*. **II** *v/t* **1.** Å zur dritten Potenz erheben. **2.** würfeln, in Würfel schneiden *od.* pressen. **'cu·bic** *adj* (*~ally*) **1.** Kubik..., Raum...: ~ *content* Rauminhalt *m*; ~ *metre* (*Am.* *meter*) Kubikmeter *m, n*. **2.** würfelförmig, Würfel... **3.** Å kubisch: ~ *equation* Gleichung *f* dritten Grades.

cu·bi·cle ['kju:bɪkl] *s* Kabine *f*.

cuck·old ['kʌkəʊld] **I** *s* betrogener Ehemann. **II** *v/t* j-m Hörner aufsetzen.

cuck·oo ['kuku:] **I** *s* *orn.* Kuckuck *m*. **II** *adj* F bekloppt, plemplem. ~ *clock* *s* Kuckucksuhr *f*.

cu·cum·ber ['kju:kʌmbə] *s* Gurke *f*: (*as*) *cool as a* ~ F eiskalt, kühl u. gelassen.

cud [kʌd] *s* **1.** Klumpen *m* wiedergekäuten Futters: *chew the* ~ wiederkäuen; *fig.* überlegen, nachdenken. **2.** F Streifen *m* (*Kaugummi*).

cud·dle ['kʌdl] **I** *v/t* **1.** an sich drücken, hätscheln. **2.** schmusen mit. **II** *v/i* **3.** ~ *up* sich kuscheln *od.* schmiegen (*to* an *acc*): ~ *up together* sich aneinanderkuscheln. **4.** schmusen. **III** *s* **5.** enge Umarmung.

cudg·el ['kʌdʒəl] **I** *s* Knüppel *m*: *take up the* ~*s for s.o.* *fig.* für j-n eintreten. **II**

v/t pret u. pp **-eled**, *bsd. Br.* **-elled** prügeln: → *brain* 2.

cue¹ [kju:] **I** *s* **1.** *thea. etc, a. fig.* Stichwort *n*, ♪ Einsatz *m*. **2.** Wink *m*, Fingerzeig *m*: *take the* ~ *from s.o.* sich nach j-m richten. **II** *v/t* **3.** *a.* ~ *in* *thea. etc, a. fig.* j-m das Stichwort geben, ♪ j-m den Einsatz geben.

cue² [~] *s* Queue *n*, Billardstock *m*.

cuff¹ [kʌf] *s* **1.** (Ärmel-, *Am. a.* Hosen)Aufschlag *m*, Manschette *f* (*a.* ⚙): ~ *link* Manschettenknopf *m*; *off the* ~ F aus dem Stegreif. **2.** *pl* F Manschetten *pl* (*Handschellen*).

cuff² [~] *v/t* j-m e-n Klaps geben. **II** *s* Klaps *m*.

cui·sine [kwɪ'zi:n] → *cooking* 2.

cul-de-sac ['kʌldəsæk] *pl* **cul-de-sacs**, **culs-de-sac** *s* Sackgasse *f* (*a. fig.*).

cu·li·nar·y ['kʌlɪnərɪ] *adj* kulinarisch, Koch...: ~ *art* Kochkunst *f*; ~ *herbs* *pl* Küchenkräuter *pl*.

cull [kʌl] *v/t* **1.** pflücken. **2.** auslesen, -suchen. **3.** *Minderwertiges* aussortieren.

cul·mi·nate ['kʌlmɪneɪt] *v/i* **1.** *ast.* kulminieren: *culminating point* Kulminations-, *fig. a.* Höhepunkt *m*. **2.** *fig.* den Höhepunkt erreichen; kulminieren, gipfeln (*in* in *dat*). **cul·mi·na·tion** *s* **1.** *ast.* Kulmination *f*. **2.** *fig.* Gipfel *m*, Höhepunkt *m*.

cu·lottes [kju:'lɒts] *s pl* Hosenrock *m*.

cul·pa·ble ['kʌlpəbl] *adj* □ **1.** tadelnswert, sträflich. **2.** 🏛 strafbar, schuldhaft.

cul·prit ['kʌlprɪt] *s* **1.** 🏛 Angeklagte *m, f*; Täter(in), Schuldige *m, f*. **2.** Missetäter(in).

cult [kʌlt] *s* **1.** *eccl.* Kult(us) *m*. **2.** *fig.* Kult *m*.

cul·ti·vate ['kʌltɪveɪt] *v/t* **1.** *Boden* bebauen, bestellen. **2.** *Pflanzen* züchten, anbauen. **3.** *fig.* entwickeln, ausbilden; verfeinern. **4.** *fig.* kultivieren: a) fördern, b) *Freundschaft etc* pflegen, c) sich widmen (*dat*). **5.** freundschaftlichen Verkehr pflegen mit. **'cul·ti·vat·ed** → *cultured* 2. **cul·ti·va·tion** *s* **1.** Bebauung *f*, Bestellung *f*. **2.** Züchtung *f*, Anbau *m*. **3.** *fig.* Kultivierung *f*: a) Förderung *f*, b) Pflege *f*. **4.** → *culture* 4. **'cul·ti·va·tor** *s* Pflanzer *m*, Züchter *m*.

cul·tur·al [ˈkʌltʃərəl] *adj* □ kulturell, Kultur...

cul·ture [ˈkʌltʃə] *s* **1.** → cultivation 1, 2. **2.** (*Tier*) Züchtung *f*, (-)Zucht *f*. **3.** *biol.* Kultur *f*. **4.** Kultur *f*: a) (Geistes)Bildung *f*, b) Kultiviertheit *f*. **5.** Kultur *f*: a) Kulturkreis *m*, b) Kulturform *f*, -stufe *f*. **'cul·tured** *adj* **1.** gezüchtet: ~ **pearl** Zuchtperle *f*. **2.** kultiviert, gebildet.

cum·ber·some [ˈkʌmbəsəm] *adj* □ **1.** lästig, hinderlich. **2.** klobig, unhandlich, sperrig.

cu·mu·la·tive [ˈkjuːmjʊlətɪv] *adj* □ **1.** sich (an)häufend, anwachsend. **2.** ✝ kumulativ. **cu·mu·lus** [ˈ~ləs] *pl* **-li** [ˈ~laɪ] *s* Haufenwolke *f*.

cun·ning [ˈkʌnɪŋ] **I** *adj* □ **1.** klug, geschickt; schlau, listig, gerissen. **2.** *Am.* F niedlich, süß; drollig. **II** *s* **3.** Klugheit *f*, Geschicktheit *f*; Schlauheit *f*, List(igkeit) *f*, Gerissenheit *f*.

cunt [kʌnt] *s* V Fotze *f* (*Vagina*).

cup [kʌp] **I** *s* **1.** Tasse *f*: *that's not my ~ of tea Br.* F das ist nicht mein Fall. **2.** *Sport:* Cup *m*, Pokal *m*: ~ *final* Pokalendspiel *n*; ~ *tie* Pokalspiel *n*, -paarung *f*; ~ *winner* Pokalsieger *m*. **3.** (*Wein etc*)Becher *m*: *be fond of the ~* gern trinken. **4.** *eccl.* Kelch *m*, *fig. a.* Becher *m*. **5.** ♀ Blüten-, Fruchtbecher *m*. **II** *v/t* **6.** *Hand* hohl machen: *~ped hand* hohle Hand. **~·board** [ˈkʌbəd] *s* (Geschirr-, Speise-, *bsd. Br. a.* Kleider-, Wäsche-) Schrank *m*: ~ *bed* Schrankbett *n*. **~·ful** [ˈ~fʊl] *s e-e* Tasse(voll).

cu·po·la [ˈkjuːpələ] *s* △ Kuppel *f*.

cup·pa, cup·per [ˈkʌpə] *s Br.* F Tasse *f* Tee.

cur [kɜː] *s* **1.** Köter *m*. **2.** *fig.* (Schweine)Hund *m*.

cur·a·ble [ˈkjʊərəbl] *adj* heilbar.

curb [kɜːb] **I** *s* **1.** Kandare *f*. **2.** *bsd. Am.* Bord-, Randstein *m*. **II** *v/t* **3.** *Pferd* an die Kandare nehmen. **4.** *fig.* zügeln, im Zaum halten. **'~·stone** → *curb* 2.

curd [kɜːd] *s oft pl* geronnene *od.* dicke Milch, Quark *m*.

cur·dle [ˈkɜːdl] **I** *v/t Milch* gerinnen lassen: ~ *s.o.'s blood* j-m das Blut in den Adern erstarren lassen. **II** *v/i* gerinnen, dick werden (*Milch*): *the sight made my blood ~* bei den Anblick erstarrte mir das Blut in den Adern.

cure [kjʊə] **I** *s* **1.** ❦ Kur *f*, Heilverfahren

n (*for* gegen): *under ~* in Behandlung. **2.** ❦ Heilung *f*: *past ~* unheilbar krank (*Person*); unheilbar (*Krankheit*); *fig.* hoffnungslos (*Lage etc*). **3.** ❦ (Heil-) Mittel *n* (*for* gegen) (*a. fig.*). **II** *v/t* **4.** ❦ *j-n* heilen, kurieren, *fig. a.* abbringen (*of* von); ❦ *Krankheit* heilen; *fig. Mißstände etc* abstellen. **5.** haltbar machen: a) räuchern, b) trocknen, c) einpökeln, -salzen. **III** *v/i* **6.** Heilung bringen, heilen. **'~·all** *s* Allheilmittel *n*.

cur·few [ˈkɜːfjuː] *s* ✕ Ausgangsverbot *n*, -sperre *f*.

cu·ri·o [ˈkjʊərɪəʊ] *pl* **-os** → *curiosity* 2a, c. **cu·ri·os·i·ty** [ˌ~ˈɒsətɪ] *s* **1.** Neugier *f*; Wißbegierde *f*. **2.** Kuriosität *f*: a) Rarität *f*, b) Sehenswürdigkeit *f*, c) Kuriosum *n*. **'cu·ri·ous** *adj* □ **1.** neugierig; wißbegierig: *I am ~ to know if* ich möchte gern wissen, ob. **2.** kurios, seltsam: *~ly enough* merkwürdigerweise. **3.** F komisch, wunderlich.

curl [kɜːl] **I** *v/t* **1.** *Haar etc* locken; kräuseln. **II** *v/i* **2.** sich locken *od.* kräuseln: *~ up* in Ringen hochsteigen (*Rauch*); sich zs.-rollen; *~ up on the sofa* es sich auf dem Sofa gemütlich machen. **3.** *Sport:* Curling spielen. **III** *s* **4.** Locke *f*. **5.** (Rauch)Ring *m*. **'curl·er** *s* **1.** *Sport:* Curlingspieler(in). **2.** Lockenwickel *m*, -wickler *m*. **'curl·ing** *s Sport:* Curling *n*: ~ *stone* Curlingstein *m*. **'curl·y** *adj* gelockt, lockig; gekräuselt, kraus.

cur·rant [ˈkʌrənt] *s* **1.** Korinthe *f*. **2.** ♀ Johannisbeere *f*.

cur·ren·cy [ˈkʌrənsɪ] *s* **1.** Umlauf *m*: *give ~ to Gerücht etc* in Umlauf setzen. **2.** ✝ Währung *f*; Zahlungsmittel *pl*: *foreign ~* Devisen *pl*; ~ *reform* Währungsreform *f*. **3.** ✝, ⚖ Laufzeit *f*. **'cur·rent** **I** *adj* □ **1.** laufend (*Monat*, *Ausgaben etc*): ~ *account* ✝ Girokonto *n*. **2.** gegenwärtig, augenblicklich, aktuell: ~ *events pl* Tagesereignisse *pl*. **3.** üblich, gebräuchlich: *not in ~ use* nicht allgemein üblich. **II** *s* **4.** Strömung *f*, Strom *m* (*beide a. fig.*): *against the ~* gegen den Strom; ~ *of air* Luftstrom, -zug *m*. **5.** ⚡ Strom *m*: ~ *meter* Stromzähler *m*.

cur·ric·u·lum [kəˈrɪkjələm] *pl* **-la** [ˌ~lə], **-lums** *s* Lehr-, Studienplan *m*. ~ **vi·tae** [ˈviːtaɪ] *pl* **-la** - *s* Lebenslauf *m*.

cur·ry¹ [ˈkʌrɪ] **I** *s* Curry *m*, *n*. **II** *v/t* mit

Curry zubereiten: **curried** Curry...

cur·ry² [~] v/t **1.** *Pferd* striegeln. **2.** *Leder* zurichten. **3.** ~ **favo(u)r with s.o.,** ~ **s.o.'s favo(u)r** sich bei j-m lieb Kind machen (wollen).

curse [kɜːs] **I** s **1.** Fluch m: **there is a** ~ **on the house, the house is under a** ~ auf dem Haus lastet *od.* liegt ein Fluch. **2.** Fluch(wort n) m, Verwünschung f. **3.** Fluch m, Unglück n (**to** für). **II** v/t **4.** verfluchen: a) mit e-m Fluch belegen, b) verwünschen, fluchen auf (acc) *od.* über (acc). **5. be** ~**d with** bestraft *od.* geplagt sein mit. **curs·ed** [~sɪd] adj □ verflucht, F a. verdammt.

cur·so·ry [ˈkɜːsərɪ] adj □ flüchtig, oberflächlich.

curt [kɜːt] adj □ **1.** kurz(gefaßt), knapp. **2.** (**with**) barsch, schroff (gegen), kurz angebunden (zu).

cur·tail [kɜːˈteɪl] v/t **1.** (ab-, ver)kürzen. **2.** beschneiden, stutzen. **3.** *fig. Ausgaben etc* kürzen, *Rechte etc* beschneiden, einschränken. **cur'tail·ment** s **1.** (Ab-, Ver)Kürzung f. **2.** *fig.* Beschneidung f, Einschränkung f.

cur·tain [ˈkɜːtn] **I** s **1.** Vorhang m (a. thea. u. fig.), Gardine f: **draw the** ~ die Vorhänge auf- *od.* zuziehen; **the** ~ **rises (falls)** der Vorhang geht auf (fällt); **lift the** ~ den Schleier lüften. **2.** thea. Hervorruf m: **get** (od. **take**) **ten** ~**s** zehn Vorhänge haben. **II** v/t **3.** mit Vorhängen versehen: ~ **off** mit Vorhängen abteilen *od.* abschließen. ~ **call** → **curtain** 2. ~ **lec·ture** s Gardinenpredigt f. ~ **rais·er** s **1.** thea. kurzes Vorspiel. **2.** fig. Vorspiel n, Ouvertüre f (**to** zu).

curt·s(e)y [ˈkɜːtsɪ] **I** s Knicks m: **drop a** ~ (**to**) → **II. II** v/i e-n Knicks machen, knicksen (**to** vor dat).

cur·va·ture [ˈkɜːvətʃə] s Krümmung f: ~ **of the earth** Erdkrümmung f.

curve [kɜːv] **I** s Kurve f (a. ⚡). a) Krümmung f, Biegung f, b) (Straßen)Kurve f, (-)Biegung f, c) Rundung f (pl F a. e-r Frau). **II** v/t u. v/i (sich) krümmen *od.* biegen.

cush·ion [ˈkʊʃn] **I** s **1.** Kissen n, Polster n (a. fig.). **2.** ⚙ Puffer m, Dämpfer m. **II** v/t **3.** polstern (a. fig.). **4.** Stoß, Fall etc dämpfen, a. fig. abmildern. **5.** ⚙ abfedern.

cush·y [ˈkʊʃɪ] adj F gemütlich, ruhig (Job etc).

cuss [kʌs] s F **1.** Fluch m. **2.** Kerl m: **queer** ~ komischer Kauz.

cus·tard [ˈkʌstəd] s Vanillesoße f.

cus·to·di·an [kʌˈstəʊdjən] s **1.** Aufseher m, Wächter m. **2.** (Haus- etc)Verwalter m. **3.** ⚖ (Vermögens)Verwalter m. **cus·to·dy** [ˈ~tədɪ] s **1.** Obhut f, Schutz m: **in s.o.'s** ~ in j-s Obhut. **2.** Aufsicht f (**of** über acc). **3.** ⚖ (a. Untersuchungs)Haft f: **take into** ~ verhaften; → **remand** I. **4.** ⚖ Sorgerecht n.

cus·tom [ˈkʌstəm] **I** s **1.** Brauch m, Gewohnheit f, Sitte f, pl a. Brauchtum n. **2.** ⚖ Gewohnheitsrecht n. **3.** ✝ Kundschaft f: a) Kunden (pl), b) Kundesein n: **get s.o.'s** ~ j-n als Kunden gewinnen; **have withdrawn one's** ~ **from** nicht mehr (ein)kaufen bei. **4.** pl Zoll m: ~**s clearance** Zollabfertigung f; ~**s examination** (od. **inspection**) Zollkontrolle f; ~**s officer** (od. **official**) Zollbeamte m. **II** adj **5.** → **custom-made**. **'cus·tom·ar·y** adj üblich, gebräuchlich. **'cus·tom·er** s **1.** Kunde m, Kundin f. **2.** F Kerl m, Kunde m: → **queer** 1.

,**cus·tom-'made** adj bsd. Am. maßgefertigt, Maß...

cut [kʌt] **I** s **1.** Schnitt m; Schnittwunde f. **2.** Haarschnitt m. **3.** Schnitte f, Stück n (bsd. Fleisch): **cold** ~**s** pl bsd. Am. Aufschnitt m. **4.** F Anteil m (**of, in** an dat). **5.** (Zu)Schnitt m (von Kleidung). **6.** Schnitt m, Schliff m (von Edelsteinen). **7.** Kürzung f, Senkung f: **~ in salary** Gehaltskürzung f. **8.** Kartenspiel: Abheben n; abgehobene Karte(n pl). **II** adj **9.** ge-, beschnitten: ~ **flowers** pl Schnittblumen pl. **III** v/t (irr) **10.** (ab-, be-, durch-, zer)schneiden: ~ **one's finger** sich in den Finger schneiden; ~ **to pieces** zerstückeln; ~ **one's teeth** Zähne schneiden, zahnen; ~ **one's teeth in** (od. **on**) s.th. fig. s-e ersten Erfahrungen mit et. sammeln; → **throat** 1. **11.** Gras mähen, Bäume fällen, Holz hacken. **12.** Hecke etc (be)schneiden, stutzen: ~ **s.o.'s hair** j-m die Haare schneiden. **13.** Kleid etc zuschneiden, et. zurechtschneiden; Stein behauen, Glas, Edelsteine schleifen. **14.** mot. Kurve schneiden. **15.** a) Löhne etc kürzen, *Text etc* a. zs.-streichen (**to** auf *acc*), b) *Film* schneiden. **16.** *Preise* herabsetzen, senken. **17.** (*auf Tonband*) mitschneiden. **18.** *fig. j-m* weh tun, *j-n* kränken. **19.** F *j-n* schneiden: **~ dead** völlig ignorieren. **20.** *ped. univ.* F *Stunde etc* schwänzen. **21.** *Karten* abheben. **22.** *Tennis etc: Ball* (an)schneiden. **23.** F *Gewinne* teilen. **IV** *v/i (irr)* **24.** schneiden (**in**, **into** in *acc*): **~ into** *Kuchen etc* abschneiden; einschneiden in (*acc*) (a. *fig.*); **~ into s.o.'s time** j-n Zeit kosten; **~ into s.o.'s savings** ein Loch in j-s Ersparnisse reißen; **~ into a conversation** sich in ein Gespräch einmischen; *it* **~s both ways** es ist ein zweischneidiges Schwert. **25.** einschneiden (*Kragen etc*). **26.** sich schneiden lassen. **27.** *fig.* weh tun, kränken. **28.** F abhauen. **29.** *Kartenspiel:* abheben. **30.** F die Gewinne teilen.

Verbindungen mit Adverbien:

cut| back I *v/t* **1.** *Hecke etc* beschneiden, stutzen. **2.** → **cut** 15a. **II** *v/i* **3.** *bsd. Am.* (zu)rückblenden (**to** auf *acc*) (*Film, Roman etc*). **4.** **~ on** *et.* einschränken. **~ down I** *v/t* **1.** *Bäume* fällen, *Wald* abholzen. **2.** zurechtschneiden, -stutzen (a. *fig.*): → **size** 2. **3.** *Ausgaben* verringern, einschränken. **4.** *j-n* herunterhandeln (**by** um; **to** auf *acc*). **II** *v/i* **5.** → **cut back** 4. **~ in I** *v/t* **1.** F *j-n* beteiligen (**on** an *dat*). **II** *v/i* **2.** sich einmischen. **3.** **~ on s.o.** *mot.* j-n schneiden. **~ off** *v/t* **1.** abschneiden. **2.** *Strom etc* absperren, abdrehen, *Verbindung, Versorgung, Weg etc* abschneiden: *he* **had his electricity ~** ihm wurde der Strom gesperrt. **3.** *teleph. Teilnehmer* trennen. **~ out I** *v/t* **1.** (her)ausschneiden. **2.** *Kleid etc* zuschneiden. **3.** *be* **~ for** wie geschaffen sein für. **4.** *Rivalen* ausstechen, verdrängen. **5.** *cut it out!* F hör auf (damit)! **6.** F *j-n* betrügen (**of** um *s-n Anteil*). **II** *v/i* **7.** *mot.* ausscheren. **~ un-der** *v/t* ✝ *j-n* unterbieten. **~ up** *v/t* **1.** zerschneiden. **2.** F verreißen.

'cut|·a·way I *adj* Schnitt...: **~ model. II** *s* *a.* **~ coat** Cut(away) *m.* **'~back** *s* **1.** Kürzung *f,* Zs.-streichung *f.* **2.** *Film etc: bsd. Am.* Rückblende *f.*

cute [kju:t] *adj* ☐ F **1.** schlau, clever. **2.** niedlich, süß.

cut·ler·y ['kʌtləri] *s* (Tisch-, Eß)Besteck *n.*

cut·let ['kʌtlɪt] *s* **1.** Schnitzel *n.* **2.** Hacksteak *n.*

'cut|·out *s* **1.** Ausschnitt *m.* **2.** Ausschneidefigur *f.* **,~'price** *adj Br.,* **,~'rate** *adj Am.* ✝ ermäßigt, herabgesetzt: **~ offer** Billigangebot *n.*

cut·ter ['kʌtə] *s* **1.** Zuschneider *m;* (*Glas-, Diamant*)Schleifer *m.* **2.** ⚙ Schneidemaschine *f,* -werkzeug *n.* **3.** *Film:* Cutter(in). **4.** ⚓ Kutter *m.*

'cut·throat I *s* Mörder *m;* (professioneller) Killer. **II** *adj* mörderisch, *fig. a.* halsabschneiderisch: **~ price** Wucherpreis *m.*

cut·ting ['kʌtɪŋ] **I** *s* **1.** (Ab-, Aus-, Be-, Zu)Schneiden *n.* **2.** *bsd. Br.* (Zeitungs)Ausschnitt *m.* **3.** *pl* (*Hobel etc*)Späne *pl;* Abfälle *pl,* Schnitzel *pl.* **II** *adj* **4.** schneidend (*a. fig. Schmerz, Wind*), Schneid(e)..., Schnitt...: **~ blowpipe** (*od.* **torch**) ⚙ Schneidbrenner *m;* **~ edge** Schneide *f;* **~ nippers** *pl* Kneifzange *f.*

cy·a·nide ['saɪənaɪd] *s:* **~ of potash** 🜍 Zyankali *n.*

cy·ber·net·ics [,saɪbə'netɪks] *s pl (sg konstruiert)* Kybernetik *f.*

cyc·la·men ['sɪkləmən] *s* 🜂 Alpenveilchen *n.*

cy·cle ['saɪkl] **I** *s* **1.** Zyklus *m,* Kreis(lauf) *m.* **2.** (*Gedicht-, Lieder*)Zyklus *m.* **3.** a) Fahrrad *n:* **~ lane** (*od.* **path**) Rad(fahr)weg *m;* **~ race** (*Sport*) Radrennen *n,* b) Motorrad *n.* **4.** ⚙ Arbeitsgang *m;* Takt *m:* **four-~ engine** Viertaktmotor *m.* **5.** ⚡, *phys.* (Schwingungs)Periode *f.* **II** *v/i* **6.** radfahren, radeln. **'cy·cler** *Am.* → **cyclist.**

'cy·cle·way *s* Rad(fahr)weg *m.*

cy·clic, cy·cli·cal ['saɪklɪk(l)] *adj* ☐ **1.** zyklisch. **2.** konjunkturbedingt, Konjunktur... **cy·cling** ['-klɪŋ] *s* **1.** Radfahren *n:* **~ tour** Radtour *f.* **2.** Radrennsport *m.* **'cy·clist** *s* Rad- *od.* Motorradfahrer(in).

cy·clone ['saɪkləʊn] *s* Zyklon *m,* Wirbelsturm *m.*

cyl·in·der ['sɪlɪndə] *s* 🜂 Zylinder *m,* ⚙ Walze *f,* Trommel *f.* **cy'lin·dri·cal** [-drɪkl] *adj* ☐ zylindrisch, Zylinder..., ⚙ *a.* walzenförmig.

cyn·ic ['sɪnɪk] **I** *s* Zyniker *m.* **II** *adj* (**~ally**)

zynisch. **cyn·i·cal** ['ˌkl] → **cynic** II.
cyn·i·cism ['ˌsɪzəm] s Zynismus m, a.
zynische Bemerkung.
cy·press ['saɪprəs] s ♣ Zypresse f.
Cyp·ri·ot ['sɪprɪət], **Cyp·ri·ote** ['ˌəʊt] I s
Zyprer(in). II adj zyprisch.
cyst [sɪst] s ✱ Zyste f.

czar [zɑ:] s hist. Zar m.
Czech [tʃek] I s 1. Tscheche m, Tschechin f. 2. ling. Tschechisch n. II adj 3.
tschechisch.
Czech·o·slo·vak [ˌtʃekəʊ'sləʊvæk] I s
Tschechoslowake m, -slowakin f. II adj
tschechoslowakisch.

D

'd F für had, should, would.
dab¹ [dæb] I v/t 1. antippen. 2. be-, abtupfen (**with** mit). 3. Farbe etc (leicht)
auftragen (**on** auf acc). II s 4. Klecks m,
Spritzer m.
dab² [ˌ] s a. ~ **hand** bsd. Br. F Könner m:
be a ~ at et. aus dem Effeff können; ~ at
tennis Tennisas n.
dab·ble ['dæbl] I v/t 1. bespritzen. II v/i
2. plan(t)schen. 3. ~ at (od. in) fig. sich
oberflächlich od. aus Liebhaberei od.
dilettantisch beschäftigen mit: ~ in politics ein bißchen in der Politik mitmischen.
dachs·hund ['dækshʊnd] s zo. Dackel
m.
dad [dæd] s F Vati m, Papa m.
dad·dy ['dædɪ] → **dad**. ~ **long·legs** pl
-dy -legs s zo. F 1. Schnake f. 2. Am.
Weberknecht m.
daf·fo·dil ['dæfədɪl] s ♣ gelbe Narzisse,
Osterglocke f.
daft [dɑ:ft] adj □ F 1. doof, dämlich. 2.
be ~ **about** verrückt sein nach.
dag·ger ['dægə] s Dolch m: be at ~s
drawn auf Kriegsfuß stehen (**with** mit);
look ~s at s.o. j-n mit Blicken durchbohren.
da·go ['deɪgəʊ] pl **-go(e)s** s Schimpfwort
für Italiener, Spanier u. Portugiesen.
dahl·ia ['deɪljə] s ♣ Dahlie f.
dai·ly ['deɪlɪ] I adj 1. täglich (a. adv),
Tage(s)....: ~ **help** → 4; ~ **newspaper**
→ 3; ~ **press** Tagespresse f; → **dozen**.
2. alltäglich: be a ~ **occurrence** an der
Tagesordnung sein. II s 3. Tageszeitung f. 4. Br. Putzfrau f (die jeden Tag
kommt).

dain·ty ['deɪntɪ] I adj 1. zierlich, niedlich,
reizend. 2. wählerisch, verwöhnt (bsd.
im Essen). 3. schmackhaft, lecker. II s
4. Leckerbissen m (a. fig.).
dair·y ['deərɪ] s 1. Molkerei f. 2. Milchgeschäft n. ~ **prod·uce** s Molkereiprodukte pl.
da·is ['deɪɪs] s Podium n.
dai·sy ['deɪzɪ] s ♣ Gänseblümchen n:
push up the daisies sl. sich die Radieschen von unten ansehen od. betrachten.
dal·ly ['dælɪ] I v/i 1. schäkern: ~ **with** a.
spielen mit (j-s Gefühlen). 2. spielen,
liebäugeln (**with** mit e-r Idee etc). 3. a. ~
about (od. **around**) herumtrödeln,
bummeln. II v/t 4. ~ **away** Zeit vertrödeln; Gelegenheit verspielen.
dam [dæm] I s 1. (Stau)Damm m, Talsperre f. 2. Stausee m. II v/t 3. a. ~ **up**
stauen, ab-, eindämmen; Gefühle aufstauen: ~ **back** Tränen zurückhalten.
dam·age ['dæmɪdʒ] I s 1. Schaden m (**to**
an dat). 2. ✴ Schadenersatz m: **sue
for** ~s auf Schadenersatz verklagen. 3.
what's the ~? F was kostet es? II v/t 4.
beschädigen. 5. j-m, j-s Ruf etc schaden.
dam·ask ['dæməsk] s Damast m.
dame [deɪm] s 1. ✷ Br. Ordens- od. Adelstitel. 2. bsd. Am. sl. Weib n.
damn [dæm] F v/t 1. eccl. u. weitS. verdammen. 2. verurteilen. 3. verwerfen,
ablehnen. 4. F ~ **it!**, ~ **me!** verflucht!,
verdammt!; ~ **you!** der Teufel soll dich
holen!; I'll be ~ed if I do that ich denk'
ja gar nicht daran, das zu tun. II s 5. F
I don't care a ~ das ist mir völlig egal;

not worth a ~ keinen Pfifferling wert. **III** *int* **6.** F verflucht!, verdammt! **IV** *adj u. adv* **7.** → **damned** 2, 4.

dam·na·tion I *s* Verdammung *f; eccl.* Verdammnis *f.* **II** *int* → **damn** 6.

damned [dæmd] **I** *adj* **1.** verdammt: *the* ~ *pl eccl.* die Verdammten *pl.* **2.** F verflucht, verdammt: ~ *fool* Vollidiot *m.* **3.** F *Bekräftigung:* **a** ~ *sight better* viel besser. **II** *adj* **4.** F verdammt: ~ *cold.* **5.** F *Bekräftigung:* **he** ~ *well ought to know it* das müßte er wahrhaftig wissen.

Dam·o·cles ['dæməkli:z]: *sword of* ~ Damoklesschwert *n; hang over s.o. like a sword of* ~ über j-m wie ein Damoklesschwert hängen.

damp [dæmp] **I** *adj* □ **1.** feucht, (*Raum etc a.*) klamm: ~ *squib* Br. F Pleite *f,* Reinfall *m.* **II** *s* **2.** Feuchtigkeit *f:* ~ *in the air* Luftfeuchtigkeit. **3.** *fig.* Dämpfer *m: cast* (*od.* **strike**) **a** ~ *on* (*od.* **over**) *et.* dämpfen *od.* lähmen. **III** *v/t* **4.** an-, befeuchten. **5.** *Begeisterung etc* dämpfen; *j-n* entmutigen. **'damp·en** → *damp* **III.** **'damp·er** *s fig.* Dämpfer *m: cast* (*od.* **put, strike**) **a** ~ *on et.* dämpfen *od.* lähmen. **'damp·ness** *s* Feuchtigkeit *f.*

dance [dɑ:ns] **I** *v/i* **1.** tanzen: ~ *to* (*od.* **after**) *s.o.'s pipe* (*od.* **tune, whistle**) *fig.* nach j-s Pfeife tanzen. **2.** tanzen, hüpfen (*with, for* vor *dat*). **II** *v/t* **3.** *Tanz* tanzen: ~ *attendance on s.o.* um j-n scharwenzeln. **III** *s* **4.** Tanz *m: lead s.o. a (pretty)* ~ *Br.* j-n zum Narren halten. **5.** *Tanzveranstaltung f) m.* **IV** *adj* **6.** Tanz...: ~ *music.* **'danc·ing** *s* Tanzen *n.* **II** *adj* Tanz...: ~ *lesson* Tanzstunde *f, pl a.* Tanzunterricht *m;* ~ *master* Tanzlehrer *m;* ~ *partner* Tanzpartner(in); ~ *school* Tanzschule *f.*

dan·de·li·on ['dændɪlaɪən] *s* Löwenzahn *m.*

dan·der ['dændə] *s* F: *get s.o.'s* ~ *up* j-n auf die Palme bringen; *get one's* ~ *up* auf die Palme gehen.

dan·druff ['dændrʌf] *s* (Kopf-, Haar-) Schuppen *pl.*

dan·dy ['dændɪ] **I** *s* Dandy *m.* **II** *adj* F prima.

Dane [deɪn] *s* Däne *m,* Dänin *f.*

dan·ger ['deɪndʒə] **I** *s* Gefahr *f* (*to* für): ~ *of infection* 🗲 Infektionsgefahr; *be in* ~

of one's life in Lebensgefahr sein *od.* schweben; *without* ~ gefahrlos. **II** *adj* Gefahr...: ~ *area* (*od.* **zone**) Gefahrenzone *f,* -bereich *m;* ~ *money* (*od.* **pay**) Gefahrenzulage *f.* **'dan·ger·ous** □ gefährlich (*to, for* für).

dan·gle ['dæŋgl] **I** *v/i* baumeln: *keep s.o. dangling* F j-n im unklaren lassen. **II** *v/t* baumeln lassen: ~ *s.th. before s.o. fig.* j-m et. (verlockend) in Aussicht stellen, j-m mit et. winken.

Dan·ish ['deɪnɪʃ] **I** *adj* **1.** dänisch. **II** *s* **2.** *ling.* Dänisch *n.* **3.** *the* ~ *pl* die Dänen *pl.*

dank [dæŋk] *adj* □ (*unangenehm*) feucht, naß(kalt).

dap·per ['dæpə] *adj* □ **1.** adrett, elegant. **2.** flink, (*a. Benehmen*) gewandt.

dap·ple ['dæpl] *v/t* sprenkeln.

dare [deə] **I** *v/i* es wagen, sich (ge)trauen: *who* ~*s wins* wer wagt, gewinnt; *how* ~ *you!* untersteh dich!; was fällt dir ein!; *how* ~ *you say that?* wie können Sie das sagen?; *don't (you)* ~ *(to) touch it!* rühr es ja nicht an!; *I* ~ *say* ich glaube wohl; allerdings. **II** *v/t et.* wagen, riskieren. **'~,dev·il** *s* Draufgänger *m.*

dar·ing ['deərɪŋ] **I** *adj* **1.** wagemutig, kühn. **2.** gewagt, verwegen (*beide a. fig.*). **3.** unverschämt, dreist. **II** *s* **4.** Wagemut *m,* Kühnheit *f.*

dark [dɑ:k] **I** *adj* **1.** dunkel, finster. **2.** dunkel (*Farbe*). **3.** *fig.* düster, trüb (*Aussichten etc*): *the* ~ *side of things* die Schattenseite der Dinge; *one's* ~*est hour* s-e schwärzeste Stunde. **4.** *fig.* düster, finster (*Blick etc*). **5.** finster, böse (*Gedanken etc*). **6.** *fig.* geheim(nisvoll), verborgen: *keep s.th.* ~ *et.* geheimhalten. **II** *s* **7.** Dunkel(heit *f*) *n,* Finsternis *f:* *in the* ~ im Dunkel(n); *after* ~ nach Einbruch der Dunkelheit. **8.** *fig.* das Ungewisse *od.* Dunkle: *be in the* ~ im dunkeln tappen; *keep s.o. in the* ~ j-n im ungewissen lassen (*about* über *acc*). ♀ **Ag·es** *s pl* das (frühe *od.* finstere) Mittelalter. ♀ **Con·ti·nent** *s* der dunkle Erdteil, Afrika *n.*

dark·en ['dɑ:kən] **I** *v/t* **1.** verdunkeln, -düstern (*beide a. fig.*). **2.** dunkler färben. **II** *v/i* **3.** dunkel werden, sich verdunkeln. **4.** *fig.* sich verdüstern.

dark horse *s* **1.** *Sport:* unbekannte Größe (*Person*). **2.** *pol. Am.* unbeschriebenes Blatt.

dark·ness ['dɑːknɪs] *s* Dunkelheit *f*, Finsternis *f*: *be in complete ~* völlig dunkel sein.

'dark·room *s phot.* Dunkelkammer *f*.

'~-skinned *adj* dunkelhäutig.

dar·ling ['dɑːlɪŋ] **I** *s* Liebling *m.* **II** *adj* reizend, goldig.

darn¹ [dɑːn] → **damn** 4–6.

darn² [~] *v/t* stopfen.

darned [dɑːnd] → **damned** 2–5.

dart [dɑːt] **I** *s* **1.** (Wurf)Pfeil *m.* **2.** Satz *m*, Sprung *m*: *make a ~ for* losstürzen auf (*acc*). **3.** *pl* (*sg konstruiert*) Darts *n* (*Wurfpfeilspiel*). **II** *v/t* **4.** Speer werfen, schleudern, Pfeil schießen: *~ a look at s.o.* j-m e-n Blick zuwerfen. **III** *v/i* **5.** sausen, flitzen: *~ at* losstürzen auf (*acc*). **6.** zucken, schnellen (*Schlange, Zunge etc*), huschen (*Augen, Blick*).

'~-board *s* Dartsscheibe *f*.

dash [dæʃ] **I** *v/t* **1.** schleudern, schmettern: *~ to pieces* zerschmettern. **2.** *~ down* (*od. off*) *Getränk* hinunterstürzen; *Aufsatz, Zeichnung etc* schnell hinhauen. **3.** *Hoffnungen etc* zerstören, zunichte machen; *j-n* deprimieren. **II** *v/i* **4.** stürmen: *~ off* davonstürzen. **III** *s* **5.** Schlag *m*: *at one ~* mit 'einem Schlag (*a. fig.*). **6.** Schuß *m* (*Rum etc*), Prise *f* (*Salz etc*). **7.** *fig.* Anflug *m* (*of* von); Stich *m* (*of green* ins Grüne). **8.** Gedankenstrich *m.* **9.** *make a ~ at* (*od. for*) losstürzen auf (*acc*). **10.** Schwung *m*, Schmiß *m*, Elan *m.* **11.** *Leichtathletik:* Sprint *m*, Kurzstreckenlauf *m*; **'~-board** *s mot.* Armaturen-, ✈ *a.* Instrumentenbrett *n.*

dash·ing ['dæʃɪŋ] *adj* □ schneidig, forsch.

da·ta ['deɪtə] *s pl* **1.** (*oft sg konstruiert*) (*a. technische*) Daten *pl od.* Angaben *pl*: *~ protection* Datenschutz *m.* **2.** *Computer:* Daten *pl*: *~ bank* Datenbank *f*; *~ processing* Datenverarbeitung *f*; *~ transmission* Datenübertragung *f*; *~ typist* Datentypistin *f.*

date¹ [deɪt] *s* ♣ Dattel *f.*

date² [~] **I** *s* **1.** Datum *n*: a) Tag *m*: *what is the ~ today?* der Wievielte ist heute?, welches Datum haben wir heute?, b) Zeit(punkt *m*) *f*: *of recent ~* neu(eren Datums), c) Datumsangabe *f*, d) ✞, ⚒,

Tag *m*, Termin *m*: *~ of delivery* Liefertermin; *~ of maturity* Fälligkeitstag. **2.** heutiges Datum, heutiger Tag: *to ~* bis heute; *out of ~* veraltet, unmodern; *go out of ~* veralten; *(up) to ~* zeitgemäß, modern, auf dem laufenden; *bring up to ~* auf den neuesten Stand bringen, modernisieren. **3.** Verabredung *f*, Rendezvous *n*: *have a ~ with s.o.* mit j-m verabredet sein; *make a ~* sich verabreden. **4.** (Verabredungs)Partner(in): *who is your ~?* mit wem bist du verabredet? **II** *v/t* **5.** datieren. **6.** sich verabreden mit; gehen mit. **III** *v/i* **7.** *~ back to* a) *a. ~ from* stammen aus, entstanden sein in (*dat*), b) bis in *e-e Zeit* zurückreichen, auf *e-e Zeit* zurückgehen. **8.** veralten. **'dat·ed** *adj* **1.** datiert. **2.** veraltet, überholt. **'date·less** *adj* **1.** undatiert. **2.** zeitlos.

date| line *s geogr.* Datumsgrenze *f.* **~ stamp** *s* Datums-, *a.* Poststempel *m.*

da·tive ['deɪtɪv] *s a. ~ case ling.* Dativ *m*, 3. Fall.

daub [dɔːb] **I** *v/t* **1.** be-, verschmieren: *~ed with oil* ölverschmiert. **2.** schmieren (*on* auf *acc*). **3.** *contp. Bild* zs.-klecksen. **II** *s* **4.** *paint. contp.* (Farb-)Kleckserei *f.*

daugh·ter ['dɔːtə] *s* Tochter *f*: *~ (company)* ✝ Tochter(gesellschaft) *f.* **'~-in--law** *pl* **'daugh·ters-in-law** *f* Schwiegertochter *f.*

daunt [dɔːnt] *v/t* **1.** einschüchtern, erschrecken. **2.** entmutigen. **'daunt·less** *adj* □ unerschrocken.

dav·en·port ['dævnpɔːt] *s* **1.** kleiner Schreibtisch. **2.** *Am.* (*bsd.* Bett)Couch *f.*

daw·dle ['dɔːdl] **I** *v/i* (herum)trödeln, (-)bummeln. **II** *v/t oft ~ away* Zeit vertrödeln. **'daw·dler** *s* Trödler(in), Bummler(in).

dawn [dɔːn] **I** *v/i* **1.** dämmern (*Morgen, Tag*). **2.** *~ on fig. j-m* dämmern, klarwerden. **3.** *fig.* sich zu entwickeln beginnen, erwachen. **II** *s* **4.** (Morgen)Dämmerung *f*: *at ~* bei Tagesanbruch. **5.** *fig.* Beginn *m.*

day [deɪ] *s* **1.** Tag *m* (*Ggs. Nacht*): *by ~* bei Tag(e). **2.** Tag *m* (*Zeitraum*): *~ after ~* Tag für Tag; *the ~ after tomorrow, Am. ~ after tomorrow* übermorgen; *~ in, ~ out* tagaus, tagein; *let's call it a ~!*

F Feierabend!, Schluß für heute!; **carry** (*od.* **win**) **the ~** den Sieg davontragen. **3.** (*bestimmter, festgesetzter*) Tag: **~ of delivery** Liefertermin *m.* **4.** *oft pl* (Lebens)Zeit *f*, Zeiten *pl*, Tage *pl*: **in my young ~s** in m-n Jugendtagen; **in those ~s** damals. **5.** *oft pl* (*beste*) Zeit (*des Lebens*), Glanzzeit *f*: **he has had his ~** s-e beste Zeit ist vorüber; **those were the ~s!** das waren noch Zeiten! '**~break** *s* Tagesanbruch *m*: **at ~** bei Tagesanbruch. '**~dream I** *s* Tag-, Wachtraum *m*. **II** *v/i* (*a. irr dream*) (mit offenen Augen) träumen. '**~dream•er** *s* Träumer(in). '**~light** *s* Tageslicht *n*: **by** (*od.* **in**) **~** bei Tag(eslicht); **in broad ~** am hellichten Tag; **beat** (*od.* **knock**) **the** (**living**) **~s out of s.o.** F j-n fürchterlich verdreschen; **~ saving time** Sommerzeit *f.* **~ nurs•er•y** *s* Tagesheim *n*, -stätte *f.* **~ re•turn** (**tick•et**) → **day ticket.** **~ shift** *s* Tagschicht *f*: **be** (*od.* **work**) **on ~** Tagschicht haben. **~ tick•et** *s Br.* Tagesrückfahrkarte *f.* '**~time** *s*: **in the ~** bei Tag(e). ,**~-to-'day** *adj* (tag)täglich.

day| trip *s* Tagesausflug *m*. **~ trip•per** *s* Tagesausflügler(in).

daze [deɪz] **I** *v/t* benommen machen. **II** *s* Benommenheit *f*: **in a ~** benommen.

daz•zle ['dæzl] **I** *v/t* **1.** blenden (*a. fig.*). **II** *s* **2.** Blenden *n*: **in a ~** geblendet. **3.** blendender Glanz.

dea•con ['di:kən] *s eccl.* Diakon *m.* **dea•con•ess** [,~'nes] *s* Diakonisse *f.*

dead [ded] **I** *adj* (□ → **deadly II**) **1.** tot, gestorben: **shoot ~** erschießen; → **body** **2.** *fig.* tot: a) leblos: **~ matter** tote Materie, b) ausgestorben: **~ language** tote Sprache, c) überlebt (*Brauch etc*). **3.** gefühllos, abgestorben (*Finger etc*). **4.** *fig.* (**to**) unempfänglich (für); gleichgültig, abgestumpft (gegen). **5.** *bsd.* ✝ flau. **6.** tot (*Kapital, Wissen etc*). **7.** ✝ tot, stromlos. **8.** erloschen (*Vulkan, Gefühle etc*). **9.** matt, stumpf (*Farben, Blick etc*). **10.** völlig, total: **~ certainty** absolute Gewißheit; **~ silence** Totenstille *f*; **~ cert, earnest** 4, **loss** 1a. **II** *s* **11. the ~** *pl* die Toten *pl.* **12.** in the **~ of night** mitten in der Nacht; **in the ~ of winter** im tiefsten Winter. **III** *adv* **13.** völlig, total: **be ~ asleep** in tiefstem Schlaf liegen; **~ drunk** sinnlos betrunken; **~ slow!** *mot.* Schritt fahren!; **~**

straight schnurgerade; **~ tired** todmüde; **~ set** 8. **14.** plötzlich, abrupt: **stop ~** (**in one's tracks**) plötzlich *od.* abrupt stehenbleiben. **15.** genau, direkt: **~ against** genau gegenüber von (*od. dat*). ,**~-'beat** *adj* F todmüde, völlig kaputt. **~ cen•tre** (*Am.* **cen•ter**) *s* genaue Mitte.

dead•en ['dedn] *v/t* **1.** Geräusch abdämpfen, *a. Schlag etc* abschwächen. **2.** *Schmerz* stillen; *Gefühl* abtöten, abstumpfen (**to** gegen).

dead| end *s* Sackgasse *f* (*a. fig.*): **come to a ~** in e-e Sackgasse geraten. '**~-end** *adj* **1. ~ street** Sackgasse *f.* **2.** ohne Aufstiegschancen (*Stellung*). **~ heat** *s Sport*: totes Rennen. '**~-line** *s* **1.** letzter (Ablieferungs)Termin, Anzeigen-, Redaktionsschluß *m*: **~ pressure** Termindruck *m*; **meet the ~** den Termin einhalten. **2.** Stichtag *m.* '**~-lock I** *s* völliger Stillstand, toter Punkt: **come to a ~** (*od. reach*) **a ~** → **II. II** *v/i* sich festfahren, an e-m toten Punkt anlangen (*Verhandlungen etc*). '**~-locked** *adj* festgefahren.

dead•ly ['dedlɪ] **I** *adj* **1.** tödlich; Tod...: **~ enemy** Todfeind *m*; **~ fight** mörderischer Kampf; **~ sin** Todsünde *f.* **2.** totenähnlich: **~ pallor** Leichen-, Todesblässe *f.* **3.** F schrecklich, äußerst: **~ heat** *Sport*: totes Rennen. '**~-line** **4.** totenähnlich: **~ pale** leichen-, totenblaß. **5.** F schrecklich, äußerst: **be ~ afraid of** e-e Sterbensangst haben vor (*dat*); **~ dull** sterbenslangweilig; **~ tired** todmüde.

dead| march *s* ♩ Trauermarsch *m.* **~ pan** *s* F ausdrucksloses Gesicht. ,**~'pan** *adj* F **1.** ausdruckslos (*Gesicht*); mit ausdruckslosem Gesicht (*Person*). **2.** trocken (*Humor*).

deaf [def] **I** *adj* □ **1.** taub (*a. fig.* **to** gegen); **~ and dumb** taubstumm; **~ in one ear** auf einem Ohr taub; → **ear**[1] **1. 2.** schwerhörig. **II** *s* **3. the ~** *pl* die Tauben *pl.* **~ aid** *s* Hörgerät *n.* ,**~-and-'dumb** *adj* **1.** taubstumm. **2.** Taubstummen...: **~ language.**

deaf•en ['defn] *v/t* taub machen. '**deaf•en•ing** *adj* ohrenbetäubend.

,**deaf-'mute** *adj* taubstumm. **II** *s* Taubstumme *m*, *f.*

deaf•ness ['defnɪs] *s* **1.** Taubheit *f* (*a. fig.* **to** gegen). **2.** Schwerhörigkeit *f.*

deal¹ [di:l] **I** *v/i (irr)* **1.** ~ **with** sich befassen *od.* beschäftigen mit; handeln von, *et.* behandeln *od.* zum Thema haben; *et.* erledigen, mit *et.*, *j-m* fertig werden. **2.** ~ **with** ✝ Handel treiben mit. Geschäfte machen mit. **3.** ~ **in** ✝ handeln *od.* Handel treiben mit: ~ **in paper** Papier führen. **4.** *sl.* dealen (*mit Drogen handeln*). **5.** *Kartenspiel:* geben. **II** *v/t* **6.** *oft* ~ **out** aus-, verteilen, *Karten a.* geben. **III** *s* **7.** F Handlungsweise *f*, Verfahren *n*. **8.** F Geschäft *n*, Handel *m*: *it is a* ~*!* abgemacht!; → **raw** 6. **9.** Abkommen *n*: *make a* ~ ein Abkommen treffen. **10.** *Kartenspiel:* Geben *n*: *it is my* ~ ich muß geben.

deal² [~] *s* Menge *f*: *a great* ~ sehr viel; *a good* ~ e-e ganze Menge, ziemlich viel; *a* ~ *worse* F viel schlechter.

deal·er ['di:lə] *s* **1.** Händler(in): ~ *in antiques* Antiquitätenhändler. **2.** *sl.* Dealer *m* (*Drogenhändler*). **3.** *Kartenspiel:* Geber(in). '**deal·ing** *s* **1.** *mst pl* Umgang *m*, Beziehungen *pl*: *have* ~*s with* zu tun haben mit. **2.** ✝ Handel *m* (*in* in *dat*, mit).

dealt [delt] *pret u. pp von* **deal¹**.

dean [di:n] *s eccl.*, *univ.* Dekan *m*.

dear [diə] **I** *adj* **1.** lieb, teuer (*to* dat): ♀ *Sir*, (*in Briefen*) Sehr geehrter Herr (*Name*); *run for* ~ *life* um sein Leben rennen. **2.** teuer, kostspielig. **II** *adv* **3.** teuer: *it cost him* ~ es kam ihm *od.* ihn teuer zu stehen. **III** *s* **4.** Liebste *m*, *f*, Schatz *m*: *there's a* ~ sei (so) lieb. **IV** *int* **5.** (*oh*) ~*!*, ~ *me!* du liebe Zeit!, ach je! '**dear·ly** *adv* **1.** innig, herzlich. **2.** teuer: → **buy** 4. '**dear·ness** *s* hoher Preis.

dearth [dɜ:θ] *s* Mangel *m* (*of* an *dat*).

death [deθ] *s* **1.** Tod *m*: *to* ~ zu Tode; (*as*) *sure as* ~ todsicher; *catch one's* ~ sich den Tod holen (*engS. durch Erkältung*); *put to* ~ hinrichten. **2.** Todesfall *m*. ~ *ag·o·ny* *s* Todeskampf *m*. '~·*bed* *s* Totenbett *n*. '~·*blow* *s fig.* Todesstoß *m* (*to* für). ~ *cell* *s* Todeszelle *f*. ~ *du·ty* *s Br.* Erbschaftssteuer *f*.

death·less ['deθlɪs] *adj* □ unsterblich (*Ruhm etc*). '**death·like** *adj* totenähnlich: ~ *pallor* Leichen-, Todesblässe *f*; ~ *stillness* Totenstille *f*. '**death·ly** → *deadly:* ~ *silence* eisiges Schweigen; ~ *stillness* Totenstille *f*.

death| mask *s* Totenmaske *f*. ~ **pen·al·ty** *s* Todesstrafe *f*. ~ **rate** *s* Sterblichkeitsziffer *f*.

'**death's-head** *s* Totenkopf *m* (*Symbol*).

death| threat *s* Morddrohung *f*. ~ **toll** *s* Zahl *f* der Toten: *the* ~ *on the roads* die Zahl der Verkehrstoten. ~ **trap** *s* Todesfalle *f*. ~ **war·rant** *s* **1.** ⚖ Hinrichtungsbefehl *m*. **2.** *fig.* Todesurteil *n* (*of* für): *sign one's* ~ sein (eigenes) Todesurteil unterschreiben.

de·ba·cle [deɪ'bɑːkl] *s* Debakel *n*, Zs.-bruch *m*.

de·bar [dɪ'bɑː] *v/t j-n* ausschließen (*from* von).

de·base [dɪ'beɪs] *v/t* **1.** entwürdigen. **2.** im Wert mindern; *Wert* mindern.

de·bat·a·ble [dɪ'beɪtəbl] *adj* strittig, umstritten. **de·bate I** *v/i* **1.** debattieren, diskutieren (*on, about* über *acc*). **II** *v/t* **2.** *et.* debattieren, diskutieren. **3.** *et.* erwägen, sich *et.* überlegen. **III** *s* **4.** Debatte *f*, Diskussion *f*: *be under* ~ zur Debatte stehen.

de·bauch [dɪ'bɔːtʃ] **I** *v/t* sittlich verderben. **II** *s* Ausschweifung *f*, Orgie *f*. **de·bauch·er·y** [~tʃəri] *s* Ausschweifung *f*.

de·ben·ture [dɪ'bentʃə] *s* **1.** Schuldschein *m*. **2.** ✝ a) *Br. a.* ~ *bond* Obligation *f*, Schuldverschreibung *f*, b) *Br.* Pfandbrief *m*.

de·bil·i·tate [dɪ'bɪlɪteɪt] *v/t* schwächen, entkräften. **de·bil·i·ta·tion** *s* Schwächung *f*, Entkräftung *f*. **de·bil·i·ty** *s* Schwäche *f*, Kraftlosigkeit *f*.

deb·it ['debɪt] ✝ **I** *s* **1.** Soll *n*: ~ *and credit* Soll u. Haben *n*. **2.** Belastung *f*: *to the* ~ *of* zu Lasten von (*od. gen*); *charge* (*od. place*) *a sum to s.o.'s* ~ j-s Konto mit e-r Summe belasten; ~ *entry* Lastschrift *f*. **II** *v/t* **3.** *j-n*, *Konto* belasten (*with* mit): ~ *£ 100 against s.o.* ('*s account*) j-n (j-s Konto) mit £ 100 belasten.

de·bouch [dɪ'baʊtʃ] *v/i* sich ergießen, (ein)münden (*into* in *acc*) (*Fluß*).

de·brief [ˌdiː'briːf] *v/t* sich informieren lassen von (*e-m Piloten, Diplomaten etc*).

de·bris ['deɪbriː] *s* Trümmer *pl*, Schutt *m*.

debt [det] *s* Schuld *f*: ~ *of hono(u)r* Ehrenschuld; *be in* ~ Schulden haben, ver-

schuldet sein; *be in ~ to* s.o. *for £ 100*
j-m £ 100 schulden; *be in s.o.'s ~* in j-s
Schuld stehen; *be out of ~* schuldenfrei
sein. **'debt·or** s Schuldner *m*.

de·bug [‚di:'bʌg] *v/t* **1.** entwanzen (*a.* F
von Minispionen befreien). **2.** ☉ F Fehler *e-r Maschine* beheben; (*Computer*)
Programm austesten.

de·bu·reauc·ra·tize [‚di:bjʊə'rɒkrətaɪz]
v/t entbürokratisieren.

de·but ['deɪbju:] *s* Debüt *n*: *make one's
~* sein Debüt geben.

deb·u·tant ['debju:tɑ:ŋ] *s* Debütant
m. **deb·u·tante** ['~tɑ:nt] *s* Debütan-
tin *f*.

dec·ade ['dekeɪd] *s* Jahrzehnt *n*.

de·ca·dence ['dekədəns] *s* Dekadenz *f*.
'de·ca·dent *adj* dekadent.

de·caf·fein·at·ed [‚di:'kæfɪneɪtɪd] *adj*
koffeinfrei (*Kaffee*).

de·cal ['di:kæl] *s bsd. Am.* Abziehbild *n*.

de·camp [dɪ'kæmp] *v/i* F sich aus dem
Staub machen.

de·cant [dɪ'kænt] *v/t* **1.** dekantieren. **2.**
ab-, umfüllen. **de'cant·er** *s* Karaffe *f*.

de·cap·i·tate [dɪ'kæpɪteɪt] *v/t* enthaupten, köpfen. **de‚cap·i'ta·tion** *s* Ent-
hauptung *f*.

de·car·tel·i·za·tion [‚di:‚kɑ:təlaɪ'zeɪʃn] *s*
⊹ Entkartellisierung *f*, Entflechtung *f*.
‚de'car·tel·ize *v/t* entkartellisieren,
entflechten.

de·cath·lete [dɪ'kæθli:t] *s Leichtathletik*:
Zehnkämpfer *m*. **de'cath·lon** [~lɒn] *s*
Zehnkampf *m*.

de·cay [dɪ'keɪ] **I** *v/i* **1.** zerfallen (*a. phys.*),
vermodern. **2.** verfaulen, -wesen; ka-
riös *od.* schlecht werden (*Zahn*). **3.** abnehmen, schwinden; schwach *od.*
kraftlos werden. **4.** zugrunde gehen. **5.**
geol. verwittern. **II** *s* **6.** Zerfall *m* (*a.
phys.*). **7.** Verfaulen *n*. **8.** *geol.* Verwitterung *f*.

de·cease [dɪ'si:s] *s* Ableben *n*. **de-
'ceased I** *adj* verstorben. **II** *s*: *the ~* der
od. die Verstorbene, die Verstorbenen
pl.

de·ceit [dɪ'si:t] *s* Betrug *m*, Täuschung *f*.
de'ceit·ful *adj* □ **1.** betrügerisch. **2.**
falsch, hinterlistig.

de·ceive [dɪ'si:v] *v/t* täuschen (*Person*),
(*Sache a.*) trügen: *be ~d* sich täuschen
(lassen); *be ~d in s.o.* sich in j-m täuschen; *~ o.s.* sich et. vormachen. **II** *v/i*

täuschen, trügen (*Sache*). **de'ceiv·er** *s*
Betrüger(in).

de·cel·er·ate [‚di:'seləreɪt] **I** *v/t* verlang-
samen; die Geschwindigkeit herabset-
zen von (*od. gen*). **II** *v/i* sich verlangsa-
men; s-e Geschwindigkeit verringern.

De·cem·ber [dɪ'sembə] *s* Dezember *m*:
in ~ im Dezember.

de·cen·cy ['di:snsɪ] *s* Anstand *m*, *pl a.*
Anstandsformen *pl*: *for ~'s sake* anstandshalber. **'de·cent** *adj* □ **1.** anständig. **2.** passabel, annehmbar. **3.** F
salonfähig (angezogen).

de·cen·tral·i·za·tion [di:‚sentrəlaɪ'zeɪʃn]
s Dezentralisierung *f*. **de'cen·tral·ize**
v/t dezentralisieren.

de·cep·tion [dɪ'sepʃn] *s* Täuschung *f*.
de'cep·tive *adj* □ täuschend, trügerisch: *be ~* → **deceive** II; → **appearance** 3.

de·cide [dɪ'saɪd] **I** *v/t* **1.** *et.* entscheiden;
et. bestimmen. **2.** ~ *s.o. to do s.th.* j-n
veranlassen *od.* dazu bringen, et. zu
tun. **II** *v/i* **3.** beschließen, sich entscheiden *od.* entschließen (*to do, on doing*
zu tun; *against doing* nicht zu tun): ~
in favo(u)r of (*od. on*) (*against*) sich
entscheiden für (gegen). **4.** entscheiden,
den Ausschlag geben. **de'cid·ed** *adj* □
entschieden, entschlossen. **de'cid·ing**
adj entscheidend, ausschlaggebend.

de·cid·u·ous [dɪ'sɪdjʊəs] *adj*: ~ *tree*
Laubbaum *m*.

dec·i·mal ['desɪml] **I** *adj* □ **1.** dezimal,
Dezimal...: *go* ~ das Dezimalsystem
einführen; ~ *fraction* → 2; ~ *point*
Komma *n* (*in GB u. USA* Punkt) vor
der ersten Dezimalstelle: ~ *system*
Dezimalsystem *n*. **II** *s* **2.** Dezimalbruch
m. **3.** Dezimalzahl *f*. **dec·i·mal·ize**
['~məlaɪz] *v/t* auf das Dezimalsystem
umstellen.

dec·i·mate ['desɪmeɪt] *v/t* dezimieren.

de·ci·pher [dɪ'saɪfə] *v/t* entziffern.

de·ci·sion [dɪ'sɪʒn] *s* **1.** Entscheidung *f*:
make (*od. take*) *a* ~ e-e Entscheidung
treffen (*on, over* über *acc*). **2.** Entschluß *m*: *arrive at* (*od. come to*) *a* ~ zu
e-m Entschluß kommen. **3.** Entschluß-
kraft *f*, Entschlossenheit *f*. **de·ci·sive**
[dɪ'saɪsɪv] *adj* □ **1.** ~ → *deciding*: *be* ~ *of*
et. entscheiden. **2.** → *decided*.

deck [dek] **I** *s* **1.** ♣ Deck *n*: *on* ~ an Deck;
bsd. Am. F auf dem Posten. **2.**

Stock(werk n) m, (e-s Busses a.) Deck n. **3.** bsd. Am. Spiel m, Pack m (Spiel)Karten. **II** v/t **4.** oft ~ **out** herausputzen; schmücken. ~ **chair** s Liegestuhl m.

de·claim [dɪ'kleɪm] v/i **1.** deklamieren, (v/t a.) vortragen. **2.** eifern, wettern (**against** gegen).

dec·la·ra·tion [ˌdeklə'reɪʃn] s **1.** Erklärung f: a) Aussage f: **make a ~** e-e Erklärung abgeben; ~ **of intent** Absichtserklärung f, b) Verkündung f: ~ **of independence** Unabhängigkeitserklärung f; ~ **of war** Kriegserklärung f. **2.** (Zoll)Deklaration f, Zollerklärung f.

de·clare [dɪ'kleə] **I** v/t **1.** erklären, verkünden: ~ **open** für eröffnet erklären; ~ **s.o. the winner** j-n zum Sieger erklären; → **war. 2.** deklarieren: **have you anything to ~?** haben Sie et. zu verzollen? **II** v/i **3.** sich erklären od. entscheiden (**for** für; **against** gegen). **de'clared** adj erklärt.

de·clen·sion [dɪ'klenʃn] s ling. Deklination f.

de·cline [dɪ'klaɪn] **I** v/i **1.** sich neigen od. senken. **2.** zur Neige od. zu Ende gehen. **3.** abnehmen, zurückgehen; fallen, sinken (Preise); verfallen. **4.** (höflich) ablehnen. **II** v/t **5.** (höflich) ablehnen: ~ **doing** (od. **to do**) es ablehnen zu tun. **6.** ling. deklinieren. **III** s **7.** Neigung f, Senkung f. **8.** Neige f: **be on the ~** zur Neige gehen; **im Niedergang begriffen** sein, sinken. **9.** Abnahme f, Rückgang m: ~ **of** (od. **in**) **strength** Kräfteverfall m; ~ **in value** Wertminderung f.

de·cliv·i·tous [dɪ'klɪvɪtəs] adj abschüssig. **de'cliv·i·ty** [~vətɪ] s **1.** Abschüssigkeit f. **2.** (Ab)Hang m.

de·clutch [ˌdiː'klʌtʃ] v/i mot. auskuppeln.

de·code [ˌdiː'kəʊd] v/t entschlüsseln.

dé·colle·tage [ˌdeɪkɒl'tɑːʒ], **dé'colle·té** [~teɪ] s Dekolleté n.

de·com·pose [ˌdiːkəm'pəʊz] **I** v/t **1.** 🐦, phys. zerlegen, spalten. **2.** zersetzen. **II** v/i **3.** sich auflösen, zerfallen (**into** in acc). **4.** sich zersetzen. **de·com·po·si·tion** [ˌdiːkɒmpə'zɪʃn] s **1.** 🐦, phys. Zerlegung f, Spaltung f. **2.** Zersetzung f, Zerfall m.

de·con·tam·i·nate [ˌdiːkən'tæmɪneɪt] v/t entgasen, -seuchen, -strahlen. **'de·con-**

tam·i·na·tion s Entgasung f, -seuchung f, -strahlung f.

de·con·trol [ˌdiːkən'trəʊl] 🏛 **I** v/t freigeben, die Zwangsbewirtschaftung aufheben von (od. gen). **II** s Freigabe f, Aufhebung f der Zwangsbewirtschaftung.

dé·cor, de·cor ['deɪkɔː] s **1.** Ausstattung f (e-s Raums). **2.** thea. Dekor m, n, Ausstattung f, Dekoration f.

dec·o·rate ['dekəreɪt] v/t **1.** schmücken, verzieren; ausschmücken, dekorieren. **2.** tapezieren; (an)streichen. **3.** dekorieren, (mit Orden etc) auszeichnen. **dec·o'ra·tion** s **1.** (Aus)Schmückung f, Dekorierung f. **2.** Schmuck m, Dekoration f, Verzierung f. **3.** Orden m, Ehrenzeichen n. **dec·o·ra·tive** ['dekərətɪv] adj dekorativ, Schmuck...: ~ **plant** Zierpflanze f. **dec·o·ra·tor** ['~reɪtə] s **1.** Dekorateur m: → **interior** 1. **2.** Maler m u. Tapezierer m.

dec·o·rous ['dekərəs] adj □ anständig, schicklich. **de·co·rum** [dɪ'kɔːrəm] s Anstand m, Schicklichkeit f.

de·coy s ['diːkɔɪ] Lockvogel m, fig. a. Köder m. **II** v/t [dɪ'kɔɪ] (an)locken, ködern; fig. a. verleiten (**into** zu).

de·crease [diː'kriːs] **I** v/i abnehmen, sich vermindern od. verringern: ~ **in length** kürzer werden. **II** v/t vermindern, -ringern, herabsetzen. **III** s ['diːkriːs] Abnahme f, Verminderung f, -ringerung f: **be on the ~** → I.; ~ **in value** Wertminderung f.

de·cree [dɪ'kriː] **I** s **1.** Dekret n, Erlaß m, Verfügung f. **2.** 🏛 Entscheid m, Urteil n. **II** v/t **3.** verfügen. ~ **ni·si** ['naɪsaɪ] 🏛 vorläufiges Scheidungsurteil n.

de·crep·it [dɪ'krepɪt] adj altersschwach (Person, Auto etc).

de·cry [dɪ'kraɪ] v/t schlecht-, heruntermachen, herabsetzen.

ded·i·cate ['dedɪkeɪt] v/t **1.** Buch, Leben, Zeit etc widmen (**to** dat). **2.** Am. feierlich eröffnen od. einweihen. **'ded·i·cat·ed** adj treusorgend (Vater etc), einsatzfreudig (Angestellter etc), engagiert (Verfechter etc). **ˌded·i'ca·tion** s **1.** Widmung f. **2.** Hingabe f. **3.** Am. feierliche Eröffnung od. Einweihung.

de·duce [dɪ'djuːs] v/t **1.** folgern, schließen (**from** aus). **2.** ab-, herleiten (**from** von).

de·duct [dɪ'dʌkt] *v/t* (**from**) *Betrag* a) abziehen (von): *after ~ing charges, charges ~ed* nach Abzug der Kosten, b) einbehalten (von), c) (von *der Steuer*) absetzen. **de'duct·i·ble** *adj* (*steuerlich*) absetzbar. **de'duc·tion** *s* **1.** Abzug *m*; Einbehaltung *f*; Absetzung *f*. **2.** ♀ Nachlaß *m*. **3.** (Schluß)Folgerung *f*, Schluß *m*.

deed [diːd] *s* **1.** Tat *f*: *do a good ~* e-e gute Tat vollbringen; → *will* [1] 1, *word* 1. **2.** Helden-, Großtat *f*. **3.** ₰ (Übertragungs)Urkunde *f*.

dee·jay ['diːdʒeɪ] *s* F Diskjockey *m*.

deem [diːm] *v/t* halten *od.* erachten für, betrachten als.

deep [diːp] **I** *adj* □ **1.** tief (*a. fig.*): *~ breath* tiefer Atemzug; *~ disappointment* schwere *od.* bittere Enttäuschung; *~ly disappointed* schwer *od.* bitter enttäuscht; *~ poverty* tiefste Armut; *~ silence* tiefes *od.* völliges Schweigen; *~ sleep* tiefer Schlaf, Tiefschlaf *m*; *~ voice* tiefe *od.* dunkle Stimme; *in ~ water(s)* in Schwierigkeiten. **2.** schwerverständlich, schwierig: *that is too ~ for me* das ist mir zu hoch. **II** *adv* **3.** tief (*a. fig.*): *~ into the night* bis tief in die Nacht (hinein); *~ in thought* in Gedanken (versunken); *~ in winter* im tiefen Winter; → *water* 2. **III** *s* **4.** Tiefe *f*. **5.** *in the ~ of night* mitten in der Nacht; *in the ~ of winter* im tiefen Winter. **'deep·en** *v/t u. v/i* (sich) vertiefen, *fig. a.* (sich) steigern *od.* verstärken.

'deep|-felt *adj* tiefempfunden. **'~-'freeze I** *s* Tiefkühl-, Gefriergerät *n*. **II** *adj* Tiefkühl..., Gefrier...: *~ cabinet* Tiefkühl-, Gefriertruhe *f*. **III** *v/t* (*irr* **freeze**) tiefkühlen, einfrieren: *deep-frozen food* Tiefkühlkost *f*. *~ freez·er* → *deep-freeze* [1]. **'~'fry** *v/t* fritieren. **'~·fry·er**, **'~·fry·ing pan** *s* Friteuse *f*.

deep·ness ['diːpnɪs] *s* Tiefe *f* (*a. fig.*).

'deep|-'root·ed *adj* tief verwurzelt (*a. fig.*). **'~-'sea** *adj* Tiefsee...: *~ fishing* Hochseefischerei *f*. **'~'seat·ed** *adj fig.* tiefsitzend. **'~-'set** *adj* tiefliegend (*Augen*).

deer [dɪə] *pl* **deer(s)** *s zo.* Hirsch *m*; Reh *n*.

de·es·ca·late [ˌdiːˈeskəleɪt] **I** *v/t* **1.** *Krieg etc* deeskalieren. **2.** *Erwartungen etc* herunterschrauben. **II** *v/i* **3.** deeskalieren. **,de·es·ca'la·tion** *s* Deeskalation *f*.

de·face [dɪ'feɪs] *v/t* **1.** entstellen, verunstalten. **2.** aus-, durchstreichen, unleserlich machen.

def·a·ma·tion [ˌdefə'meɪʃn] *s* Verleumdung *f*, Diffamierung *f*. **de·fam·a·to·ry** [dɪ'fæmətərɪ] *adj* □ verleumderisch, diffamierend. **de·fame** [dɪ'feɪm] *v/t* verleumden, diffamieren.

de·fault [dɪ'fɔːlt] **I** *s* **1.** Unterlassung *f*, (Pflicht)Versäumnis *n*. **2.** ♀ Nichterfüllung *f*, Verzug *m*: *be in ~* in Verzug sein (*on* mit). **3.** ₰ Nichterscheinen *n* vor Gericht: *judg(e)ment by ~* Versäumnisurteil *n*. **4.** *Sport*: Nichtantreten *n*. **5.** *in ~ of* in Ermangelung von (*od. gen*), mangels (*gen*). **II** *v/i* **6.** s-n Verpflichtungen nicht nachkommen, ♀ *a.* im Verzug sein: *~ on s.th.* mit et. in Rückstand sein. **7.** ₰ nicht vor Gericht erscheinen. **8.** *Sport*: nicht antreten. **III** *v/t* **9.** *e-r Verpflichtung* nicht nachkommen, in Verzug geraten mit.

de·feat [dɪ'fiːt] **I** *v/t* **1.** *Gegner* besiegen, schlagen. **2.** *Hoffnung, Plan etc* vereiteln, zunichte machen. **II** *s* **3.** Besiegung *f*. **4.** Niederlage *f*: *admit ~* sich geschlagen geben. **5.** Vereit(e)lung *f*.

de·fect I *s* ['diːfekt] **1.** Defekt *m*, Fehler *m*: *~ in character* Charakterfehler *m*; *~ of vision* Sehfehler *m*. **2.** Mangel *m* (*of* an *dat*): *~ of memory* Gedächtnisschwäche *f*. **II** *v/i* [dɪ'fekt] **3.** abtrünnig werden (*from dat*); übergehen, -laufen (*to* zu). **de'fec·tion** *s* Überlaufen *n*. **de'fec·tive** *adj* □ **1.** mangelhaft, unzulänglich: *he is ~ in* es mangelt ihm an (*dat*). **2.** schadhaft, defekt: *mentally ~* schwachsinnig. **de'fec·tor** *s* Überläufer *m*.

de·fence [dɪ'fens] *s Br.* Verteidigung *f* (*a.* ✕, ₰, *Sport*), Schutz *m*: *in ~ of* zur Verteidigung *od.* zum Schutz von (*od. gen*); *come to s.o.'s ~* j-m zu Hilfe kommen; → *counsel* 3, *witness* 1. **de'fence·less** *adj* □ schutz-, wehrlos.

de·fend [dɪ'fend] *v/t* **1.** (**from**, **against**) verteidigen (gegen), schützen (vor *dat*, gegen). **2.** *Meinung etc* verteidigen, rechtfertigen. **de'fend·ant** *s* ₰ Beklagte *m*, *f*; Angeklagte *m*, *f*.

de·fend·er *s* **1.** Verteidiger(in). **2.** *Sport*: Abwehrspieler(in).

de·fense, *etc Am.* → **defence,** *etc.*

de·fen·sive [dɪˈfensɪv] **I** *adj* defensiv, Verteidigungs..., Abwehr... **II** *s* Defensive *f*: **on the ~** in der Defensive.

de·fer¹ [dɪˈfɜː] *v/t* **1.** auf-, verschieben (**to** auf *acc*). **2.** hinausschieben, verzögern. **3.** ✗ *Am.* (vom Wehrdienst) zurückstellen.

de·fer² [~] *v/i* sich fügen (**to** *dat*). **def·er·ence** [ˈdefərəns] *s* **1.** Ehrerbietung *f*, (Hoch)Achtung *f*: **in** (*od.* **out of**) **~ to** aus Achtung vor (*dat*). **2.** Rücksicht(nahme) *f*: **in** (*od.* **out of**) **~ to** mit *od.* aus Rücksicht auf (*acc*). **def·er·en·tial** [~ˈrenʃl] *adj* □ **1.** ehrerbietig. **2.** rücksichtsvoll.

de·fer·ment [dɪˈfɜːmənt] *s* **1.** Aufschub *m*, Verschiebung *f*. **2.** ✗ *Am.* Zurückstellung *f* (*vom Wehrdienst*).

de·fi·ance [dɪˈfaɪəns] *s* **1.** Trotz *m*: **in ~ of** ungeachtet, trotz (*gen*), **e-m Gebot** *etc* zuwider, **j-m** zum Trotz. **2.** Herausforderung *f*. **de·fi·ant** *adj* □ **1.** trotzig. **2.** herausfordernd.

de·fi·cien·cy [dɪˈfɪʃnsɪ] *s* **1.** (**of**) Mangel *m* (*an dat*), Fehlen *n* (*von*): **~ of blood** Blutarmut *f*; **~ disease** 🌱 Mangelkrankheit *f*. **2.** → **deficit. de·fi·cient** *adj* □ unzureichend, mangelhaft, ungenügend: **be ~ in** Mangel leiden an (*dat*); **he is ~ in** ihm fehlt es an (*dat*).

def·i·cit [ˈdefɪsɪt] *s* Defizit *n*, Fehlbetrag *m*.

de·file [dɪˈfaɪl] *v/t* beschmutzen, besudeln (*beide a. fig.*).

de·fine [dɪˈfaɪn] *v/t* **1.** definieren: a) *Wort etc* erklären, b) *Begriff etc* bestimmen. **2.** abgrenzen. **3. ~ itself against** sich scharf *od.* deutlich abheben von *od.* gegen. **def·i·nite** [ˈdefɪnɪt] *adj* **1.** bestimmt (*a. ling.*). **2.** endgültig, definitiv. **ˈdef·i·nite·ly** *adv* ~ **definite:** ~ **not!** ganz bestimmt nicht! **ˌdef·iˈni·tion** *s* Definition *f*: a) Erklärung *f*, b) Bestimmung *f*. **de·fin·i·tive** [dɪˈfɪnɪtɪv] *adj* □ **1.** → **definite. 2.** maßgeblich.

de·flate [dɪˈfleɪt] *v/t* **1.** (die) Luft ablassen aus. **2.** ♥ deflationieren. **de·fla·tion** *s* ♥ Deflation *f*.

de·flect [dɪˈflekt] **I** *v/t* ablenken (**from** von). **II** *v/i* abweichen (**from** ·von) (*a.*

fig.). **de·flec·tion** *s* **1.** Ablenkung *f*. **2.** Abweichung *f*.

de·fo·li·ate [ˌdiːˈfəʊlɪeɪt] *v/t* entblättern, -lauben.

de·for·est [ˌdiːˈfɒrɪst] *v/t* abholzen.

de·form [dɪˈfɔːm] *v/t* **1.** deformieren, verformen (*beide a. phys.*, ⊙). **2.** verunstalten, entstellen: **~ed by anger** wutverzerrt (*Gesicht*). **de·for·ma·tion** [ˌdiːfɔːˈmeɪʃn] *s* **1.** Deformierung *f*, Verformung *f*. **2.** Verunstaltung *f*, Entstellung *f*. **de·form·i·ty** [dɪˈfɔːmətɪ] *s* **1.** Entstelltheit *f*. **2.** Mißbildung *f*.

de·fraud [dɪˈfrɔːd] *v/t* betrügen (**of** um).

de·fray [dɪˈfreɪ] *v/t* *Kosten* tragen, bestreiten.

de·frost [ˌdiːˈfrɒst] **I** *v/t* von Eis befreien, *Windschutzscheibe etc* enteisen, *Kühlschrank etc* abtauen, *Tiefkühlkost etc* auftauen. **II** *v/i* ab-, auftauen.

deft [deft] *adj* □ gewandt, geschickt.

de·fuse [ˌdiːˈfjuːz] *v/t* *Bombe, Lage etc* entschärfen.

de·fy [dɪˈfaɪ] *v/t* **1.** trotzen (*dat*); sich widersetzen (*dat*): **~ description** unbeschreiblich sein, jeder Beschreibung spotten. **2.** herausfordern.

de·gen·er·ate I *v/i* [dɪˈdʒenəreɪt] degenerieren, entarten (**into** zu). **II** *adj* [~rət] degeneriert, entartet. **de·gen·er·a·tion** [~ˈreɪʃn] *s* Degeneration *f*, Entartung *f*.

deg·ra·da·tion [ˌdegrəˈdeɪʃn] *s* **1.** Degradierung *f*. **2.** Erniedrigung *f*. **de·grade** [dɪˈgreɪd] *v/t* **1.** degradieren. **2.** erniedrigen (**into, to** zu).

de·gree [dɪˈgriː] *s* **1.** Grad *m*, Stufe *f*: **by ~s** allmählich, nach u. nach; **by slow ~s** ganz allmählich; **to some** (*od.* **a certain**) **~** ziemlich, bis zu e-m gewissen Grade; **to a high ~** in hohem Maße; **~ of comparison** *ling.* Steigerungsstufe *f*; **~ of priority** Dringlichkeitsstufe *f*. **2.** ᴀ, ⊙, *ast., geogr etc* Grad *m*: **~ of latitude** (**longitude**) Breiten-(Längen)grad. **3.** *univ.* Grad *m*: **take one's ~** e-n akademischen Grad erwerben; → **doctor 2.**

de·hu·man·ize [ˌdiːˈhjuːmənaɪz] *v/t* entmenschlichen.

de·hy·drate [ˌdiːˈhaɪdreɪt] *v/t* das Wasser entziehen (*dat*): **~d vegetables** *pl* Trockengemüse *n*.

de·ice [ˌdiːˈaɪs] *v/t* enteisen.

deign [deɪn] **I** *v/i* sich herablassen, geru-

deity 874

hen (**to do** zu tun). **II** v/t sich herablassen zu.

de·i·ty ['di:ıtı] s Gottheit f.

de·ject·ed [dı'dʒektıd] adj □ niedergeschlagen.

de'jec·tion s Niedergeschlagenheit f.

de·lay [dı'leı] **I** v/t. a) ver-, auf-, hinausschieben: **~ doing s.th.** es verschieben, et. zu tun, b) verzögern, -schleppen: **be ~ed** sich verzögern. **2.** aufhalten: **be ~ed (for two hours)** 🚅, etc (zwei Stunden) Verspätung haben. **II** v/i **3.** zögern. **4.** Zeit zu gewinnen suchen. **III** s **5.** Verschiebung f, Aufschub m; Verzögerung f, Verschleppung f: **without ~** unverzüglich. **6.** 🚅, etc Verspätung f. **de'lay·ing** adj: **~ tactics** pl Hinhalte-, Verzögerungstaktik f.

de·lec·ta·ble [dı'lektəbl] adj □ köstlich (bsd. Speise). **de·lec·ta·tion** [,di:lek-'teıʃn] s Vergnügen n: **for the ~ of** zum Ergötzen (gen).

del·e·gate I s ['delıgət] **1.** Delegierte m, f, bevollmächtigter Vertreter. **II** v/t ['~geıt] **2.** abordnen, delegieren. **3.** Vollmachten etc übertragen (**to** dat). **del·e·ga·tion** [,~'geıʃn] s **1.** Übertragung f. **2.** Abordnung f, Delegation f.

de·lete [dı'li:t] **I** v/t (aus)streichen. **II** v/i: **~ where inapplicable** Nichtzutreffendes bitte streichen. **de·le·tion** [dı'li:ʃn] s Streichung f.

de·lib·er·ate I adj [dı'lıbərət] □ **1.** überlegt. **2.** bewußt, absichtlich, vorsätzlich. **3.** bedächtig, besonnen. **II** v/t [~reıt] **4.** überlegen, erwägen. **III** v/i [~reıt] **5.** nachdenken (**on** über acc), überlegen. **6.** beratschlagen, sich beraten (**on** über acc). **de,lib·er'a·tion** [~'reıʃn] s **1.** Überlegung f. **2.** Beratung f. **3.** Bedächtigkeit f.

del·i·ca·cy ['delıkəsı] s **1.** Zartheit f. Fein-, Zartgefühl n, Takt m. **3.** Empfindlichkeit f. **4. of great ~** sehr heikel. **5.** Delikatesse f, Leckerbissen m. **del·i·cate** ['~kət] adj □ **1.** zart: a) fein (Farben etc), b) zierlich (Figur etc), c) zerbrechlich: **of** (od. **in**) **~ health** von zarter Gesundheit. 2) sanft, leise: **~ hint** zarter Wink. **2.** delikat, heikel (Frage etc). **3.** fein, empfindlich (Instrument etc). **4.** feinfühlig, zartfühlend, taktvoll. **5.** delikat, schmackhaft. **del·i·ca·tes·sen** [,delıkə'tesn] s pl **1.** Deli-

katessen pl, Feinkost f. **2.** (sg konstruiert) Feinkostgeschäft n.

de·li·cious [dı'lıʃəs] adj □ köstlich.

de·light [dı'laıt] **I** s Vergnügen n, Entzücken n: **to my ~** zu m-r Freude; **take ~ in →** III. **II** v/t erfreuen, entzücken. **III** v/i: **~ in** (große) Freude haben an (dat), sich ein Vergnügen machen aus. **de'light·ful** [~fʊl] adj □ entzückend, herrlich.

de·lim·it [di:'lımıt], **de·lim·i·tate** [~teıt] v/t abgrenzen.

de·lin·e·ate [dı'lınıeıt] v/t **1.** skizzieren, entwerfen. **2.** beschreiben, schildern.

de·lin·quen·cy [dı'lıŋkwənsı] s Kriminalität f: **→ juvenile** I. **de'lin·quent** I adj straffällig. **II** s Delinquent(in), Straffällige m, f: **→ juvenile** I.

de·lir·i·ous [dı'lırıəs] adj □ **1.** 🔬 im Delirium, phantasierend. **2.** fig. rasend (**with** vor dat): **~ with joy** in e-m Freudentaumel; **~ly happy** vor Glück außer sich. **de·lir·i·um** [~əm] pl **-i·ums**, **-i·a** [~ıə] s **1.** 🔬 Delirium n: **~ tremens** ['tri:menz] Delirium tremens, Säuferwahn(sinn) m. **2.** fig. Taumel m: **~ of joy** Freudentaumel.

de·liv·er [dı'lıvə] v/t. a. **~ up** (od. **over**) übergeben, ausliefern: **~ o.s. up to s.o.** sich j-m stellen od. ergeben. **2.** Waren liefern; Brief etc zustellen; Nachricht etc bestellen. **3.** Rede etc halten (**to** vor dat). **4.** befreien, erlösen (**from** von, aus). **5. be ~ed** 🔬 entbinden: **be ~ed of** entbunden werden von. **de'liv·er·y** s **1.** † Lieferung f: **on ~** bei Lieferung od. Empfang; **cash** (Am. **collect**) **on ~** per Nachnahme; **~ note** Lieferschein m. **2.** 📮 Zustellung f: **~ charge** Zustellgebühr f. **3.** Halten n (e-r Rede); Vortrag(sweise f) m. **4.** 🔬 Entbindung f: **~ room** Kreißsaal m.

de·louse [,di:'laʊs] v/t entlausen.

del·ta ['deltə] s (Fluß)Delta n.

de·lude [dı'lu:d] v/t **1.** täuschen, irreführen: **~ o.s.** sich et. vormachen. **2.** verleiten (**into** zu).

del·uge ['delju:dʒ] **I** s **1.** Überschwemmung f: **the ♑ Bibl.** die Sintflut. **2.** fig. Flut f, (Un)Menge f. **II** v/t **3.** überschwemmen, -fluten (beide a. fig. **with** mit).

de·lu·sion [dı'lu:ʒn] s **1.** Täuschung f, Irreführung f. **2.** Wahn m (a. psych.):

be **under the** ~ **that** in dem Wahn leben, daß; ~**s** pl **of grandeur** Größenwahn. **de'lu·sive** [~sɪv] adj □ **1.** täuschend, irreführend. **2.** Wahn...

de **luxe** [də'lʌks] adj Luxus..., De-Luxe-...

delve [delv] v/i angestrengt suchen (**for** nach): ~ **into** sich vertiefen in (acc); erforschen.

dem·a·gog·ic [ˌdemə'gɒɡɪk] adj (~**ally**) demagogisch. **dem·a·gogue** ['~ɡɒɡ] s Demagoge m. '**dem·a·gog·y** s Demagogie f.

de·mand [dɪ'mɑːnd] I v/t **1.** fordern, verlangen (**of, from** von). **2.** (fordernd) fragen nach. **3.** fig. erfordern, verlangen. II s **4.** Forderung f (**for** nach): **on** ~ auf Verlangen; **make** ~**s on s.o.** Forderungen an j-n stellen. **5.** (**on**) Anforderung f (an acc), Beanspruchung f (gen): **make great** ~**s on** stark in Anspruch nehmen (acc), große Anforderungen stellen an (acc). **6.** ✝ u. allg. (**for**) Nachfrage f (nach), Bedarf m (an dat): **be in great** ~ sehr gefragt sein. **de'mand·ing** adj anspruchsvoll.

de·mar·cate ['diːmɑːkeɪt] v/t abgrenzen (**from** gegen, von) (a. fig.). ˌ**de·mar·'ca·tion** s Abgrenzung f: ~ **line** Grenz-, pol. Demarkationslinie f; fig. Trennungslinie f, -strich m.

dem·i... [demɪ] in Zssgn Halb..., halb...

'**dem·i·god** s Halbgott m (a. fig.).

'**dem·i·john** s große Korbflasche.

de·mil·i·ta·rize [ˌdiː'mɪlɪtəraɪz] v/t entmilitarisieren.

de·mist [ˌdiː'mɪst] v/t Windschutzscheibe freimachen. ˌ**de'mist·er** s mot. Gebläse n.

dem·o ['deməʊ] pl -os s F Demo f (Demonstration).

de·mo·bi·lize [ˌdiː'məʊbɪlaɪz] v/t demobilisieren.

de·moc·ra·cy [dɪ'mɒkrəsɪ] s Demokratie f. **dem·o·crat** [pol. Am. ♀ 'demə-kræt] s Demokrat(in). ˌ**dem·o'crat·ic**, pol. Am. ♀ adj (~**ally**) demokratisch.

de·mog·ra·phy [diː'mɒɡrəfɪ] s Demographie f.

de·mol·ish [dɪ'mɒlɪʃ] v/t **1.** ab-, ein-, niederreißen, abbrechen. **2.** fig. zerstören. **3.** F Essen verdrücken. **dem·o·li·tion** [ˌdemə'lɪʃn] s **1.** Niederreißen n, Abbruch m. **2.** fig. Zerstörung f.

de·mon ['diːmən] s **1.** Dämon m. **2.** ~ **for work** Arbeitsfanatiker m. **de·mo·ni·ac** [dɪ'məʊnɪæk], **de·mon·ic** [diː'mɒnɪk] adj (~**ally**) dämonisch.

dem·on·strate ['demənstreɪt] I v/t **1.** demonstrieren: a) beweisen, b) darlegen, veranschaulichen, zeigen. **2.** Auto etc vorführen. II v/i **3.** pol. etc demonstrieren. ˌ**dem·on'stra·tion** s **1.** Demonstrierung f, Veranschaulichung f. **2.** Vorführung f: ~ **car** Vorführwagen m. **3.** Demonstration f, Kundgebung f. **de·mon·stra·tive** [dɪ'mɒnstrətɪv] adj □ **1.** anschaulich: **be** ~ **of** → **demonstrate** 1. **2.** **be** ~ s-e Gefühle (offen) zeigen. **3.** demonstrativ, betont. **4.** ~ **pronoun** ling. Demonstrativpronomen n, hinweisendes Fürwort.

dem·on·stra·tor ['demənstreɪtə] s **1.** Vorführer(in), Propagandist(in). **2.** Demonstrant(in).

de·mor·al·ize [dɪ'mɒrəlaɪz] v/t demoralisieren.

de·mo·ti·vate [ˌdiː'məʊtɪveɪt] v/t demotivieren.

den [den] s **1.** zo. Höhle f (a. fig.): ~ **of vice** Lasterhöhle. **2.** F Bude f.

de·na·tion·al·ize [ˌdiː'næʃnəlaɪz] v/t ✝ reprivatisieren, entstaatlichen.

de·na·ture [ˌdiː'neɪtʃə] v/t 🐟 denaturieren.

de·ni·al [dɪ'naɪəl] s **1.** Ablehnung f. **2.** (Ab)Leugnung f: **official** ~ Dementi n.

de·nim ['denɪm] s **1.** Köper m. **2.** pl Jeans pl.

de·nom·i·nate [dɪ'nɒmɪneɪt] v/t nennen, bezeichnen als. **de·nom·i'na·tion** s **1.** Bezeichnung f. **2.** eccl. Konfession f, Bekenntnis n. **3.** ✝ Nennwert m. **de·nom·i·na·tion·al** [~'neɪʃənl] adj □ konfessionell, Konfessions... **de'nom·i·na·tor** s 𝔸 Nenner m: **common** ~ gemeinsamer Nenner (a. fig.); **reduce to a common** ~ auf e-n gemeinsamen Nenner bringen.

de·note [dɪ'nəʊt] v/t **1.** bedeuten, anzeigen. **2.** kenn-, bezeichnen.

de·nounce [dɪ'naʊns] v/t **1.** (öffentlich) anprangern. **2.** j-n anzeigen, contp. denunzieren (**to** bei). **3.** Vertrag kündigen.

dense [dens] adj □ **1.** allg. dicht: ~**ly populated** dichtbevölkert. **2.** fig. beschränkt, begriffsstutzig. '**dense·ness**

s **1.** → **density. 2.** *fig.* Beschränktheit *f*, Begriffsstutzigkeit *f*. **'den·si·ty** *s* Dichte *f*, Dichtheit *f*: ~ *of population* Bevölkerungsdichte; ~ *of traffic* Verkehrsdichte.

dent [dent] **I** *s* Beule *f*, Delle *f*, Einbeulung *f*: *make a* ~ *in fig.* ein Loch reißen in (*Ersparnisse etc*); *j-s Ruf etc* schaden, *j-s Stolz etc* verletzen. **II** *v/t* ein-, verbeulen.

den·tal ['dentl] *adj* **1.** Zahn...: ~ *hygiene* Zahnpflege *f*; ~ *plaque* Zahnbelag *m*; ~ *surgeon* → *dentist*; ~ *treatment* Zahnbehandlung *f*. **2.** Zahnarzt...: ~ *assistant* Zahnarzthelferin *f*. **'den·tist** *s* Zahnarzt *m*, -ärztin *f*. **'den·tist·ry** *s* Zahnmedizin *f*. **den·ture** ['~tʃə] *s mst pl* (Zahn)Prothese *f*.

de·nude [dɪ'njuːd] *v/t* (*of*) entblößen (von *od.* gen); *fig.* berauben (gen).

de·nun·ci·a·tion [dɪˌnʌnsɪ'eɪʃn] *s* **1.** (öffentliche) Anprangerung. **2.** Anzeige *f*, *contp.* Denunziation *f*. **3.** Kündigung *f* (*of e-s Vertrags*).

de·ny [dɪ'naɪ] *v/t* **1.** ab-, bestreiten, dementieren, (ab)leugnen: *it cannot be denied, there is no* ~*ing (the fact)* es läßt sich nicht bestreiten, es ist nicht zu leugnen (*that* daß). **2.** *Bitte etc* ablehnen, *j-m etc.* abschlagen, verweigern. **3.** *Glauben, j-n etc* verleugnen.

de·o·dor·ant [diː'əʊdərənt] **I** *s* De(s)odorant *n*, Deo *n*. **II** *adj* de(s)odorierend. **de·o·dor·ize** *v/t* de(s)odorieren.

de·part [dɪ'pɑːt] *v/i* **1.** abreisen, abfahren (*for* nach). **2.** 🚂, *etc* abfahren, ✈ abfliegen. **3.** abweichen (*from* von *e-r Regel, der Wahrheit etc*). **de'part·ed I** *adj* verstorben. **II** *s: the* ~ der *od.* die Verstorbene, die Verstorbenen *pl.* **de·'part·ment** *s* **1.** Fach *n*, Gebiet *n*. **2.** Abteilung *f*, *univ. a.* Fachbereich *m*. **3.** ~ *store* Kauf-, Warenhaus *n*. **4.** *pol.* Ministerium *n*: ♀ *of Defense Am.* Verteidigungsministerium; ♀ *of the Interior Am.* Innenministerium; ♀ *of State Am.* Außenministerium. **de·part·ment·al** [ˌdiːpɑːt'mentl] *adj* Abteilungs... **de·par·ture** [dɪ'pɑːtʃə] *s* **1.** Abreise *f*. **2.** 🚂, *etc* Abfahrt *f*, ✈ Abflug *m*: ~*s pl* 'Abfahrt' (*Fahrplan etc*); ~ *lounge* Abflughalle *f*. **3.** Abweichen *n*.

de·pend [dɪ'pend] *v/i* **1.** sich verlassen (*on* auf *acc*). **2.** (*on*) abhängen, abhän-

gig sein (von): a) angewiesen sein (auf *acc*), b) ankommen (auf *acc*): *that* ~*s* das kommt darauf an, je nachdem; ~*ing on whether* je nachdem, ob. **de'pend·a·ble** *adj* □ verläßlich, zuverlässig. **de·pen·dance** *Am.* → *dependence*. **de'pen·dant** *s* (Familien)Angehörige *m*, *f*. **II** *adj Am.* → *dependent* **I. de'pen·dence** *s* **1.** Vertrauen *n* (*on* auf *acc*). **2.** (*on*) Abhängigkeit *f* (von), Angewiesensein *n* (auf *acc*). **de'pen·dent I** *adj* (*on*) abhängig (von): a) angewiesen (auf *acc*), b) bedingt (durch): ~ *on weather conditions* wetter-, witterungsbedingt. **II** *s bsd. Am.* → *dependant* **I.**

de·pict [dɪ'pɪkt] *v/t* **1.** (bildlich) darstellen. **2.** schildern, beschreiben.

de·pil·a·to·ry [dɪ'pɪlətərɪ] *s* Enthaarungsmittel *n*.

de·plete [dɪ'pliːt] *v/t* **1.** leeren. **2.** *fig.* Raubbau treiben mit, *Kräfte, Vorräte etc* erschöpfen, *Bestand etc* dezimieren.

de·plor·a·ble [dɪ'plɔːrəbl] *adj* □ **1.** bedauerlich, bedauerns-, beklagenswert. **2.** erbärmlich, kläglich. **de·plore** *v/t* bedauern, beklagen.

de·ploy [dɪ'plɔɪ] *v/t* **1.** ✕ *u. allg.* verteilen, einsetzen. **2.** ✕ *Truppen* stationieren, *Raketen etc a.* aufstellen.

de·pop·u·late [ˌdiː'pɒpjʊleɪt] *v/t u. v/i* (sich) entvölkern.

de·port [dɪ'pɔːt] *v/t* **1.** des Landes verweisen, ausweisen, *Ausländer a.* abschieben. **2.** deportieren. **de·por·ta·tion** [ˌdiːpɔː'teɪʃn] *s* **1.** Ausweisung *f*, Abschiebung *f*. **2.** Deportation *f*.

de·pose [dɪ'pəʊz] **I** *v/t* **1.** *j-n* absetzen: ~ *s.o. from office* *j-n s-s* Amtes entheben. **2.** 🏛 eidlich bezeugen *od.* erklären. **II** *v/i* **3.** ~ *to* → **2.**

de·pos·it [dɪ'pɒzɪt] **I** *v/t* **1.** absetzen, abstellen. **2.** 🪨, *geol.* ablagern, absetzen. **3.** deponieren, hinterlegen. **4.** ✝ *Betrag* anzahlen. **II** *v/i* **5.** 🪨 sich absetzen *od.* ablagern. **III** *s* **6.** 🪨 Ablagerung *f*, *geol. a.* (*Erz- etc*)Lager *n*. **7.** Deponierung *f*, Hinterlegung *f*. **8.** ✝ Anzahlung *f*: *make (od. pay) a* ~ e-e Anzahlung leisten (*on* für). ~ *ac·count* *s bsd. Br.* Sparkonto *n*.

dep·o·si·tion [ˌdepə'zɪʃn] *s* **1.** Absetzung *f*. **2.** 🪨, *geol.* Ablagerung *f*. **3.** 🏛 eidliche Aussage.

de·pot s 1. ['depəʊ] Depot n (a. ✕, ✛). 2. ['di:pəʊ] Am. Bahnhof m.

de·prave [dɪ'preɪv] v/t moralisch verderben. **de·prav·i·ty** [dɪ'prævətɪ] s Verderbtheit f.

dep·re·cate ['deprɪkeɪt] v/t 1. mißbilligen. 2. → **depreciate** 2. '**dep·re·cat·ing** adj □ 1. mißbilligend. 2. entschuldigend. ,**dep·re·ca·tion** s Mißbilligung f. **dep·re·ca·to·ry** ['kətərɪ] → **deprecating**.

de·pre·ci·ate [dɪ'pri:ʃɪeɪt] I v/t 1. geringschätzen, verachten. 2. herabsetzen, herunterwürdigen. 3. im Preis od. Wert herabsetzen; Währung abwerten. II v/i 4. an Wert verlieren. **de'pre·ci·at·ing** adj □ geringschätzig, verächtlich. **de,pre·ci'a·tion** s 1. Geringschätzung f, Verachtung f. 2. Herabsetzung f. 3. ✝ Wertminderung f; Abwertung f.

dep·re·da·tion [,deprɪ'deɪʃn] s Verwüstung f.

de·press [dɪ'pres] v/t 1. Pedal, Taste etc (nieder)drücken. 2. j-n deprimieren, bedrücken. 3. Preis, Stimmung etc drücken. **de'pres·sant** s ✻ Beruhigungsmittel n. **de'pressed** adj 1. deprimiert, niedergeschlagen, bedrückt. 2. gedrückt. 3. ✝ flau (Markt etc), notleidend (Industrie). 4. ~ **area** Notstandsgebiet n. **de'pres·sion** s 1. Depression f, Niedergeschlagenheit f. 2. Senkung f, Vertiefung f; geol. Landsenke f. 3. ✝ Depression f, Flaute f. 4. meteor. Tief(druckgebiet) n.

dep·ri·va·tion [,deprɪ'veɪʃn] s 1. Beraubung f, Entzug m. 2. (empfindlicher) Verlust. **de·prive** [dɪ'praɪv] v/t (of s.th.) j-n od. etw. (e-r Sache) berauben, j-m (et.) entziehen od. nehmen: be ~d of s.th. et. entbehren od. (müssen). **de'prived** adj benachteiligt.

depth [depθ] I s Tiefe f (a. fig.): **at a ~ of** in e-r Tiefe von; **five feet in ~** fünf Fuß tief; **in ~** bis in alle Einzelheiten, eingehend; **in the ~(s) of winter** im tiefsten Winter; **be out of one's ~** nicht mehr stehen können; fig. ratlos od. unsicher sein, schwimmen; **get out of one's ~** den Boden unter den Füßen verlieren (a. fig.); ~ **(of field od. focus)** phot. Tiefenschärfe f. II adj psych. etc Tiefen...: ~ **psychology.**

dep·u·tize ['depjʊtaɪz] I v/t (als Vertre-

ter) ernennen. II v/i: ~ **for** j-n vertreten. '**dep·u·ty** I s 1. (Stell)Vertreter(in). 2. parl. Abgeordnete m, f. 3. a. ~ **sheriff** Am. Hilfssheriff m. II adj 4. stellvertretend, Vize...

de·rail [dɪ'reɪl] I v/t entgleisen lassen: **be ~ed** → II. II v/i entgleisen.

de·range [dɪ'reɪndʒ] v/t in Unordnung bringen, durcheinanderbringen. **de'ranged** adj 1. in Unordnung, durcheinander. 2. a. **mentally ~** geistesgestört. **de'range·ment** s 1. Unordnung f. 2. a. **mental ~** Geistesgestörtheit f.

der·by ['dɑːbɪ] s 1. Sport: Derby n: ~ **local** 1. 2. a. ~ **hat** Am. Bowler m, Melone f.

der·e·lict ['derəlɪkt] adj heruntergekommen, baufällig.

de·ride [dɪ'raɪd] v/t verhöhnen, -spotten. **de·ri·sion** [dɪ'rɪʒn] s Hohn m, Spott m. **de·ri·sive** [dɪ'raɪsɪv] adj □, **de·ri·so·ry** [~sərɪ] adj 1. höhnisch, spöttisch: ~ **laughter** Hohngelächter n. 2. fig. lächerlich.

der·i·va·tion [,derɪ'veɪʃn] s 1. Ab-, Herleitung f. 2. Herkunft f, Abstammung f. **de·riv·a·tive** [dɪ'rɪvətɪv] I adj □ abgeleitet. II s et. Abo od. Hergeleitetes, a. ling. Ableitung f. **de·rive** [dɪ'raɪv] I v/t 1. herleiten (from von): **be ~d (from)**, ~ **itself (from)** → 4. 2. Nutzen ziehen, Gewinn schöpfen (from aus): ~ **pleasure from** Freude finden od. haben an (dat). 3. ling., ✻, etc ableiten. II v/i 4. **(from)** abstammen (von); sich ab- od. herleiten (von).

der·ma·tol·o·gist [,dɜːmə'tɒlədʒɪst] s Dermatologe m, Hautarzt m. ,**der·ma'tol·o·gy** s Dermatologie f.

de·rog·a·to·ry [dɪ'rɒgətərɪ] adj □ 1. **(from, to)** nachteilig (für), abträglich (dat). 2. abfällig, geringschätzig.

der·rick ['derɪk] s 1. Derrick-, Mastenkran m. 2. Bohrturm m.

de·scale [,diː'skeɪl] v/t Boiler etc entkalken.

de·scend [dɪ'send] I v/i 1. herunter-, hinuntersteigen, -gehen, -kommen, -fahren, -fallen. 2. ✈ niedergehen; (mit dem Fallschirm) abspringen. 3. abfallen (Straße etc). 4. abstammen, herkommen **(from** von j-m, aus e-r Familie). 5. **(to)** übergehen, sich vererben (auf acc), zufallen (dat). 6. **(on)** herfallen (über *acc*), sich stürzen (auf *acc*), *a.* *fig.* überfallen (*acc*) (*Besuch etc*). **7.** *ast.* sinken. **II** *v/t* **8.** *Treppe etc* herunter-, hinuntersteigen, -gehen. **9. be ~ed (from)** → **4. de'scend·ant** *s* Nachkomme *m*, Abkömmling *m*.

de·scent [dɪ'sent] *s* **1.** Herunter-, Hinuntersteigen *n*, -gehen *n*, -fahren *n*. **2.** ✈ Niedergehen *n*; (*Fallschirm*)Absprung *m*. **3.** Abfallen *n*, Gefälle *n*. **4.** Abstammung *f*, Herkunft *f*: **of French ~** französischer Herkunft. **5.** Vererbung *f* (**to** auf *acc*). **6.** Überfall *m* (**on** auf *acc*) (*a. fig.*).

de·scribe [dɪ'skraɪb] *v/t* **1.** beschreiben, schildern (**s.th. to s.o.** j-m et.). **2.** bezeichnen (**as** als).

de·scrip·tion [dɪ'skrɪpʃn] *s* **1.** Beschreibung *f* (*a.* ⊙), Schilderung *f*: **beyond ~** unbeschreiblich; → **beggar** 4. **2.** Art *f*, Sorte *f*. **de'scrip·tive** *adj* □ **1.** beschreibend. **2.** anschaulich.

des·e·crate ['desɪkreɪt] *v/t* entweihen.

de·seg·re·gate [ˌdiː'segrɪɡeɪt] *v/t* die Rassentrennung aufheben in (*dat*). **ˌde·seg·re'ga·tion** *s* Aufhebung *f* der Rassentrennung (**of** in *dat*).

de·sen·si·tize [ˌdiː'sensɪtaɪz] *v/t* ✗ unempfindlich *od.* immun machen (**to** gegen).

de·sert[1] [dɪ'zɜːt] *v/t* verlassen, im Stich lassen; ⚖ *Ehegatten* (böswillig) verlassen. **II** *v/i* ✕ desertieren.

de·sert[2] [~] *s mst pl* verdienter Lohn (*a. iro. Strafe*).

des·ert[3] ['dezət] **I** *s* Wüste *f*. **II** *adj* Wüsten...

de·sert·ed [dɪ'zɜːtɪd] *adj* **1.** verlassen, unbewohnt (*Insel etc*), (wie) ausgestorben, menschenleer (*Straßen etc*). **2.** verlassen, einsam (*Person*). **de'sert·er** *s* ✕ Deserteur *m*. **de'ser·tion** *s* **1.** (*a.* ⚖ böswilliges) Verlassen. **2.** ✕ Desertion *f*, Fahnenflucht *f*.

de·serve [dɪ'zɜːv] *v/t* verdienen, verdient haben. **de'serv·ed·ly** [~ɪdlɪ] *adv* verdientermaßen. **de'serv·ing** *adj* verdienstvoll.

des·ic·cat·ed ['desɪkeɪtɪd] *adj*: **~ fruit** Dörrobst *n*; **~ milk** Trockenmilch *f*.

de·sign [dɪ'zaɪn] **I** *v/t* **1.** entwerfen, ⊙ konstruieren. **2.** gestalten, anlegen. **3.** ausdenken, ersinnen. **4.** bestimmen, vorsehen (**for** für; **as** als): **~ed to do**

---

s.th. dafür bestimmt, et. zu tun. **II** *v/i* **5.** Entwürfe machen (**for** für). **III** *s* **6.** Design *n*, Entwurf *m*, (⊙ Konstruktions)Zeichnung *f*. **7.** Design *n*, Muster *n*. **8.** Gestaltung *f*. **9.** (*a.* böse) Absicht: **by ~** mit Absicht; **have ~s on** (*od.* **against**) et. im Schilde führen gegen, *a. humor.* e-n Anschlag vorhaben auf (*acc*).

des·ig·nate ['dezɪɡneɪt] **I** *v/t* **1.** et. bestimmen, festlegen. **2.** j-n designieren, bestimmen (**to, for** für *ein Amt etc*, zu *e-m Amtsträger etc*). **3.** et. bestimmen, vorsehen (**for** für). **II** *adj* **4.** *nachgestellt:* designiert.

de·sign·ed·ly [dɪ'zaɪnɪdlɪ] *adv* absichtlich. **de'sign·er** *s* Designer(in); ⊙ Konstrukteur *m*; (*Mode*)Schöpfer(in).

de·sir·a·ble [dɪ'zaɪərəbl] *adj* □ **1.** wünschenswert, erwünscht. **2.** begehrenswert. **de·sire** [dɪ'zaɪə] **I** *v/t* **1.** wünschen: **if ~d** auf Wunsch; **leave much** (**nothing**) **to be ~d** viel (nichts) zu wünschen übriglassen. **2.** begehren. **II** *s* **3.** Wunsch *m*: **at his ~** auf s-n Wunsch. **4.** Verlangen *n*, Begierde *f* (**for** nach): **~ for knowledge** Wissensdurst *m*. **de·sir·ous** [dɪ'zaɪərəs] *adj*: **be ~ to know s.th.** et. (sehr) gern wissen wollen.

de·sist [dɪ'zɪst] *v/i* Abstand nehmen (**from** von).

desk [desk] **I** *s* **1.** Schreibtisch *m*. **2.** (*Schreib-, Noten- etc*)Pult *n*. **3.** Kasse *f* (*im Restaurant etc*). **4.** Empfang *m*, Rezeption *f* (*im Hotel*): **~ clerk** *Am.* Empfangschef *m*, -dame *f*. **II** *adj* **5.** Schreibtisch...; Büro... '**~top** *adj*: **~ computer** Tischcomputer *m*.

des·o·late ['desələt] *adj* □ **1.** einsam, verlassen. **2.** trostlos. **des·o·la·tion** [~'leɪʃn] *s* **1.** Einsamkeit *f*, Verlassenheit *f*. **2.** Trostlosigkeit *f*.

de·spair [dɪ'speə] **I** *v/i* verzweifeln (**of** an *dat*). **II** *s* Verzweiflung *f* (**at** über *acc*): **a look of ~** ein verzweifelter Blick; **drive s.o. to ~, be the ~ of s.o.** j-n zur Verzweiflung bringen. **de'spair·ing** *adj* □ verzweifelt.

des·patch → **dispatch**.

des·per·ate ['despərət] *adj* □ **1.** verzweifelt (*Mensch, Anstrengung, Lage etc*): **~ deed** Verzweiflungstat *f*; **be ~ for s.th.** et. dringend nötig haben; **be ~ to do s.th.** et. unbedingt tun wollen; →

strait. **2.** F hoffnungslos, schrecklich.

des·per·a·tion [ˌ∼'reɪʃn] s Verzweiflung f: **in** ∼ verzweifelt; **drive s.o. to** ∼ j-n zur Verzweiflung bringen.

des·pi·ca·ble [dɪ'spɪkəbl] adj □ verachtenswert, verabscheuungswürdig.

de·spise [dɪ'spaɪz] v/t verachten, *Speise etc a.* verschmähen: **not to be** ∼**d** nicht zu verachten.

de·spite [dɪ'spaɪt] prp trotz (*gen od. dat*).

de·spond·ent [dɪ'spɒndənt] adj □ mutlos, verzagt.

des·pot ['despɒt] s Despot m. **des'pot·ic** adj (∼*ally*) despotisch. **des·pot·ism** ['∼pətɪzəm] s Despotismus m.

des·sert [dɪ'zɜːt] I s Dessert n, Nachtisch m. II adj Dessert...: ∼ **wine**. **des·'sert-spoon** s Dessertlöffel m.

des·ti·na·tion [ˌdestɪ'neɪʃn] s **1.** Bestimmungsort m; Reiseziel n: **country of** ∼ Bestimmungsland n. **2.** Bestimmung f, (End)Zweck m, Ziel n. **des·tine** ['∼tɪn] v/t bestimmen, vorsehen (**for** für): ∼**d for** unterwegs nach (*Schiff etc*); **be** ∼**d to** (*inf*) dazu bestimmt *od.* dafür vorgesehen sein zu (*inf*); **he was** ∼**d to** (*inf*) er sollte (*früh sterben etc*). **'des·ti·ny** s Schicksal n: **he met his** ∼ sein Schicksal ereilte ihn.

des·ti·tute [destɪtjuːt] adj **1.** mittellos, (völlig) verarmt. **2.** (**of**) bar (*gen*), ohne (*acc*). **ˌdes·ti'tu·tion** s **1.** Mittellosigkeit f, (völlige) Armut. **2.** (völliger) Mangel (**of** an *dat*).

de·stroy [dɪ'strɔɪ] v/t **1.** zerstören, a. *Insekten etc* vernichten. **2.** *Tier* töten, einschläfern. **3.** *j-n, j-s Ruf, Gesundheit etc* ruinieren, *Hoffnungen etc* zunichte machen, zerstören. **de'stroy·er** s **1.** Zerstörer(in), Vernichter(in). **2.** ♃, ✕ Zerstörer m.

de·struc·tion [dɪ'strʌkʃn] s **1.** Zerstörung f, Vernichtung f. **2.** Tötung f, Einschläferung f. **de'struc·tive** adj □ **1.** zerstörend, vernichtend. **2.** schädlich, verderblich: ∼ **to health** gesundheitsschädlich. **3.** destruktiv (*Kritik*). **de·'struc·tive·ness** s zerstörende *od.* vernichtende Wirkung.

des·ul·to·ry ['desəltərɪ] adj □ **1.** unzusammenhängend. **2.** oberflächlich.

de·tach [dɪ'tætʃ] v/t (ab-, los)trennen, (los)lösen, a. ⚙ abnehmen (**from** von). **de'tached** adj □ **1.** (ab)getrennt: **be-**

come ∼ sich (los)lösen. **2.** einzeln, frei-, alleinstehend: ∼ **house** Einzelhaus n. **3.** separat, gesondert. **4.** *fig.* unvoreingenommen; uninteressiert (**about** an *dat*); distanziert. **de'tach·ment** s **1.** (Ab-) Trennung f, (Los)Lösung f. **2.** *fig.* Unvoreingenommenheit f; Distanz f.

de·tail ['diːteɪl] I s **1.** Detail n, Einzelheit f: ∼**s** pl Näheres n; (**down**) **to the smallest** ∼ bis ins kleinste Detail; **in** ∼ ausführlich, in allen Einzelheiten; **go into** ∼ ins einzelne gehen, auf Einzelheiten eingehen. II v/t **2.** ausführlich berichten; einzeln aufzählen *od.* -führen. **3.** ✕ abkommandieren (**for** zu). **'de·tailed** adj detailliert, ausführlich, eingehend.

de·tain [dɪ'teɪn] v/t **1.** *j-n* aufhalten. **2.** a. ∼ **in custody** ⚖ in (Untersuchungs-) Haft behalten. **3.** *ped.* nachsitzen lassen.

de·tect [dɪ'tekt] v/t **1.** entdecken, (heraus)finden, ermitteln. **2.** wahrnehmen. **3.** *Verbrechen etc* aufdecken. **de'tec·tion** s **1.** Entdeckung f, Ermittlung f. **2.** Wahrnehmung f. **3.** Aufdeckung f. **de'tec·tive** I adj Detektiv...: ∼ **story** (*od. novel*) Kriminalroman m. II s Detektiv m, Kriminalbeamte m. **de'tec·tor** s ⚡ Detektor m.

dé·tente [deɪ'tɑːnt] s pol. Entspannung f.

de·ten·tion [dɪ'tenʃn] s **1.** ⚖ Haft f: ∼ (**pending trial**) Untersuchungshaft f. **2.** *ped.* Nachsitzen n: **keep in** ∼ → **detain** 3.

de·ter [dɪ'tɜː] v/t abschrecken (**from** von).

de·ter·gent [dɪ'tɜːdʒənt] s Reinigungs-, Wasch-, Geschirrspülmittel n.

de·te·ri·o·rate [dɪ'tɪərɪəreɪt] I v/i sich verschlechtern, schlechter werden, (*Material*) verderben. II v/t verschlechtern. **de·te·ri·o·ra·tion** s Verschlechterung f.

de·ter·mi·na·ble [dɪ'tɜːmɪnəbl] adj □ bestimmbar. **de'ter·mi·nant** I adj **1.** bestimmend, entscheidend. II s **2.** entscheidender Faktor (**in** bei). **3.** *biol.*, A Determinante f. **de'ter·mi·nate** [∼nət] adj □ bestimmt, festgelegt. **de·ter·mi·na·tion** [∼'neɪʃn] s **1.** Entschluß m. **2.** Bestimmung f, Festsetzung f. **3.** Feststellung f, Ermittlung f. **4.** Bestimmtheit f, Entschlossenheit f. **de·'ter·mine** I v/t **1.** *Streitfrage etc* entscheiden. **2.** *et.* beschließen (*a.* **to do** zu tun), *Zeitpunkt etc* bestimmen, festsetzen. **3.** feststellen, ermitteln, bestimmen. **4.** *j-n* bestimmen, veranlassen (**to do** zu tun). **II** *v/i* **5.** (**on**) sich entscheiden (für), sich entschließen (zu). **de·'ter·mined** *adj* □ entschlossen.

de·ter·rence [dɪ'terəns] *s* Abschreckung *f*. **de·'ter·rent I** *adj* abschreckend, Abschreckungs... **II** *s* Abschreckungsmittel *n* (**to** für).

de·test [dɪ'test] *v/t* verabscheuen, hassen: **~ having to do s.th.** es hassen, et. tun zu müssen. **de·'test·a·ble** *adj* □ abscheulich. **,de·tes·'ta·tion** [,di:~] *s* (**of**) Verabscheuung *f* (*gen*), Abscheu *m* (**vor** *dat*, **gegen**).

de·throne [dɪ'θrəʊn] *v/t* entthronen (*a.* fig.).

det·o·nate ['detəneɪt] **I** *v/t* zünden. **II** *v/i* detonieren, explodieren. **,det·o·'na·tion** *s* Detonation *f*, Explosion *f*; Zündung *f*. **'det·o·na·tor** *s* Zünd-, Sprengkapsel *f*.

de·tour ['di:ˌtʊə] **I** *s* **1.** Umweg *m*: **make a ~** → 3. **2.** Umleitung *f*. **II** *v/i* **3.** e-n Umweg machen. **II** *v/t* **4.** e-n Umweg machen um. **5.** *Verkehr etc* umleiten.

de·tract [dɪ'trækt] **I** *v/t* *Aufmerksamkeit etc* ablenken (**from** von). **II** *v/i* (**from**) Abbruch tun (*dat*), herabsetzen, schmälern (*acc*).

det·ri·ment ['detrɪmənt] *s* Nachteil *m*, Schaden *m* (**to** für): **to the ~ of** zum Nachteil *od.* Schaden (*gen*). **det·ri·men·tal** [,~'mentl] *adj* □ nachteilig, schädlich (**to** für).

de·tri·tus [dɪ'traɪtəs] *s* geol. Geröll *n*, Schutt *m*.

deuce [dju:s] *s* **1.** *Kartenspiel, Würfeln:* Zwei *f*. **2.** *Tennis:* Einstand *m*. **3.** F Teufel *m*: **who** (**what**) **the ~?** wer (was) zum Teufel?

de·val·u·ate [,di:'væljʊeɪt] *v/t* † abwerten (**against** gegenüber). **,de·val·u·'a·tion** *s* Abwertung *f*. **,de·'val·ue** [~ju:] → **devaluate**.

dev·as·tate ['devəsteɪt] *v/t* verwüsten, -nichten. **'dev·as·tat·ing** *adj* □ **1.** verheerend, vernichtend (*a. Kritik etc*). **2.** F toll, phantastisch. **3.** F umwerfend (*Humor etc*). **,dev·as·'ta·tion** *s* Verwüstung *f*.

de·vel·op [dɪ'veləp] **I** *v/t* **1.** *phot. u. fig.*

allg. entwickeln. **2.** *Krankheit, Fieber* bekommen. **3.** *Naturschätze, Bauland* erschließen, *Altstadt etc* sanieren. **II** *v/i* **4.** sich entwickeln (**from** aus; **into** zu). **de·'vel·op·er** *s* **1.** phot. Entwickler *m* (*a. Flüssigkeit*). **2.** late ~ *bsd. ped.* Spätentwickler *m*. **3.** (Stadt)Planer *m*. **de·'vel·op·ing** *adj* Entwicklungs...: **~ country. de·'vel·op·ment** *s* **1.** Entwicklung *f*: **~ aid** † Entwicklungshilfe *f*; **~ country** † Entwicklungsland *n*. **2.** Erschließung *f*, Sanierung *f*.

de·vi·ate ['di:vɪeɪt] *v/i* abweichen (**from** von). **,de·vi·'a·tion** *s* Abweichung *f*. **,de·vi·'a·tion·ist** [~ʃənɪst] *s* pol. Abweichler(in).

de·vice [dɪ'vaɪs] *s* **1.** Vorrichtung *f*, Gerät *n*. **2.** Einfall *m*; Kunstgriff *m*, Trick *m*: **leave s.o. to his own ~s** j-n sich selbst überlassen.

dev·il ['devl] **I** *s* **1.** Teufel *m*: **poor ~** armer Teufel *od.* Schlucker; **be between the ~ and the deep blue sea** sich zwischen zwei Feuern befinden, in e-r bösen Zwickmühle sein *od.* sitzen; **like the ~** F wie der Teufel, wie verrückt; **go to the ~** F vor die Hunde gehen; **go to the ~!** scher dich zum Teufel!; **speak** (*od.* **talk**) **of the ~!** wenn man vom Teufel spricht!; **who** (**what**) **the ~?** F wer (was) zum Teufel? **2.** *a. ~ of a fellow* F Teufelskerl *m*. **II** *v/t* pret *u.* pp **-iled,** *bsd. Br.* **-illed 1.** F schikanieren, piesacken. **'dev·il·ish** *adj* □ **1.** teuflisch. **2.** (*a. adv*) F verteufelt, höllisch.

,dev·il·may·'care *adj* leichtsinnig.

dev·il·ry ['devlrɪ] *s* **1.** Teufelei *f*. **2.** Übermut *m.*

de·vi·ous ['di:vjəs] *adj* □ **1.** abwegig, falsch. **2.** gewunden (*a. fig.*): **~ route** Umweg *m*. **3.** verschlagen, unaufrichtig: **by ~ means** auf krummen Wegen.

de·vise [dɪ'vaɪz] *v/t* (sich) ausdenken, ersinnen.

de·void [dɪ'vɔɪd] *adj*: **~ of** ohne (*acc*), bar (*gen*), ...los.

dev·o·lu·tion [,di:və'lu:ʃn] *s* **1.** Übertragung *f*. **2.** pol. Dezentralisierung *f*. **de·volve** [dɪ'vɒlv] **I** *v/t* *Rechte etc* übertragen (**on** *dat od. auf acc*). **II** *v/i* (**on, to**) übergehen (auf *acc*), zufallen (*dat*).

de·vote [dɪ'vəʊt] *v/t* *Zeit etc* widmen (**to** *dat*): **~ o.s. to** sich *j-m* widmen, sich e-r

Sache widmen *od.* verschreiben. **de-'vot·ed** *adj* □ hingebungsvoll: a) aufopfernd, b) anhänglich, c) eifrig, begeistert. **dev·o·tee** [ˌdevəʊˈtiː] *s* begeisterter Anhänger; glühender Verehrer *od.* Verfechter. **de·vo·tion** [dɪˈvəʊʃn] *s* **1.** Hingabe *f.* a) Aufopferung *f,* b) Anhänglichkeit *f.* **2.** Frömmigkeit *f:* **~s** *pl* Gebet *n,* Andacht *f.*

de·vour [dɪˈvaʊə] *v/t* **1.** Essen, *fig.* Buch *etc* verschlingen. **2.** *fig. j-n* verzehren (*Leidenschaft etc*).

de·vout [dɪˈvaʊt] *adj* □ **1.** fromm. **2.** innig. **3.** herzlich.

dew [djuː] *s* Tau *m.* '**~·drop** *s* **1.** Tautropfen *m.* **2.** *Br. humor.* Nasentropfen *m.*

dew·y [ˈdjuːɪ] *adj* □ taufeucht, *a. fig.* taufrisch. '**~-eyed** *adj* blauäugig, naiv.

dex·ter·i·ty [dekˈsterətɪ] *s* Gewandtheit *f,* Geschicklichkeit *f.* **dex·ter·ous** [ˈ~stərəs] *adj* □ gewandt, geschickt.

dex·trose [ˈdekstrəʊs] *s* Traubenzucker *m.*

dex·trous [ˈdekstrəs] → **dexterous.**

di·a·be·tes [ˌdaɪəˈbiːtiːz] *s* ♂ Diabetes *m,* Zuckerkrankheit *f:* **suffer from ~** Zukker haben. **di·a·bet·ic** [ˌ~ˈbetɪk] **I** *adj* diabetisch: a) zuckerkrank, b) Diabetes...: **~ chocolate** Diabetikerschokolade *f.* **II** *s* Diabetiker(in).

di·a·bol·ic, di·a·bol·i·cal [ˌdaɪəˈbɒlɪk(l)] *adj* □ **1.** diabolisch, teuflisch. **2.** F scheußlich, widerlich.

di·a·dem [ˈdaɪədem] *s* Diadem *n.*

di·ag·nose [ˈdaɪəgnəʊz] *v/t* ♂ diagnostizieren (**as** als) (*a. fig.*). **di·ag·no·sis** [ˌ~sɪs] *pl* **-ses** [ˌ~siːz] *s* Diagnose *f* (*a. fig.*): **give** (*od.* **make**) **a ~** e-e Diagnose stellen.

di·ag·o·nal [daɪˈægənl] **I** *adj* □ diagonal. **II** *s* ♉ Diagonale *f.*

di·a·gram [ˈdaɪəgræm] *s* Diagramm *n,* graphische Darstellung.

di·al [ˈdaɪəl] **I** *s* **1.** *a.* **~ plate** Zifferblatt *n* (*Uhr*). **2.** *a.* **~ plate** ☉ Skala *f,* Skalenscheibe *f.* **3.** *teleph.* Wählscheibe *f.* **4.** *Br. sl.* Visage *f* (*Gesicht*). **II** *v/t pret u. pp* **-aled,** *bsd. Br.* **-alled. 5.** *teleph.* Nummer wählen, *Stadt* anwählen. **III** *v/i* **6.** *teleph.* wählen: **~ direct** durchwählen (**to** nach).

di·a·lect [ˈdaɪəlekt] *s* Dialekt *m,* Mundart *f.* **di·a·lec·tal** [ˌ~ˈlektl] *adj* □ Dialekt..., mundartlich.

di·al·ling| code [ˈdaɪəlɪŋ] *s teleph. Br.* Vorwahl(nummer) *f.* **~ tone** *s teleph. Br.* Wählton *m,* -zeichen *n.*

di·a·logue, *Am. a.* **di·a·log** [ˈdaɪəlɒg] *s* Dialog *m.*

di·al tone *Am.* → **dialling tone.**

di·am·e·ter [daɪˈæmɪtə] *s* Durchmesser *m:* **be ... in ~** e-n Durchmesser von ... haben.

di·a·met·ri·cal [ˌdaɪəˈmetrɪkl] *adj* □ **1.** diametrisch. **2.** *fig.* diametral, genau entgegengesetzt.

di·a·mond [ˈdaɪəmənd] *s* **1.** *min.* Diamant *m:* → **rough** 4. **2.** ♉ Raute *f,* Rhombus *m.* **3.** *Kartenspiel:* a) *pl* Karo *n* (*Farbe*), b) Karo(karte *f*) *n.* **~ cut·ter** *s* Diamantschleifer *m.* **~ wed·ding** *s* diamantene Hochzeit.

di·a·per [ˈdaɪəpə] *s Am.* Windel *f.*

di·a·phragm [ˈdaɪəfræm] *s* **1.** *anat.* Zwerchfell *n.* **2.** *teleph. etc* Membran(e) *f.* **3.** *opt. phot.* Blende *f.*

di·ar·rh(o)e·a [ˌdaɪəˈrɪə] *s* ♂ Durchfall *m.*

di·a·ry [ˈdaɪərɪ] *s* **1.** Tagebuch *n.* **2.** Notizbuch *n,* Taschenkalender *m.* **3.** Terminkalender *m.*

dice [daɪs] **I** *s* **1.** *pl von* **die². 2.** *pl* **dice** → **die².** **II** *v/t* **3.** *gastr.* in Würfel schneiden. **4.** mit *j-m* würfeln *od.* knobeln (**for** um). **III** *v/i* **5.** würfeln, knobeln (**for** um): **~ with death** mit s-m Leben spielen. **~ cup** *s* Würfel-, Knobelbecher *m.*

dic·ey [ˈdaɪsɪ] *adj* F prekär, heikel (*Situation etc*).

dick [dɪk] *s* **1.** *bsd. Br. sl.* Kerl *m:* → **clever** 1. **2.** *bsd. Am. sl.* Schnüffler *m* (*Detektiv*).

dick·ens [ˈdɪkɪnz] *s* F Teufel *m:* **who** (**what**) **the ~?** wer (was) zum Teufel?

dick·er [ˈdɪkə] *v/i* feilschen, schachern (**with** mit; **for** um).

dick·(e)y [ˈdɪkɪ] *adj* F schwach (*Herz*), wack(e)lig (*Leiter etc*).

dic·tate [dɪkˈteɪt] **I** *v/t* (**to** *dat*) **1.** *Brief etc* diktieren. **2.** diktieren: a) vorschreiben, b) aufzwingen. **II** *v/i* **3.** **~ to s.o.** *j-m* Vorschriften machen. **III** *s* [ˈdɪkteɪt] **4.** Gebot *n,* Diktat *m.* **dic·ta·tion** *s* Diktat *n.* **dic·ta·tor** *s* Diktator *m.* **dic·ta·to·ri·al** [ˌ~təˈtɔːrɪəl] *adj* □ diktatorisch. **dic-'ta·tor·ship** *s* Diktatur *f.*

dic·tion [ˈdɪkʃn] *s* Diktion *f,* Ausdrucksweise *f,* Sprache *f.*

dic·tion·ar·y ['dɪkʃənrɪ] s Wörterbuch n.

did [dɪd] pret von **do.**

di·dac·tic [dɪ'dæktɪk] adj (**~ally**) didaktisch.

did·dle ['dɪdl] v/t F betrügen (**out of** um), übers Ohr hauen.

didn't ['dɪdnt] F = **did not.**

die¹ [daɪ] I v/i (pres p **dying**) **1.** sterben (**of** an dat): **~ of hunger** (**thirst**) verhungern (verdursten); **never say ~!** nur nicht nach- od. aufgeben! **2.** eingehen (Pflanze, Tier), verenden (Tier). **3. be dying** (**for; to do**) sich sehnen (nach; danach, zu tun), brennen (auf acc; darauf, zu tun). II v/t **4.** e-s Todes sterben: → **natural** 1, **violent** 2.

Verbindungen mit Adverbien:

die| a·way v/i sich legen (Wind), verhallen, -klingen (Ton). **~ down** v/i **1.** → **die away. 2.** sich legen (Aufregung etc). **~ out** v/i aussterben (a. fig.).

die² [~] pl **dice** [daɪs] s Würfel m (a. gastr. etc): **the ~ is cast** fig. die Würfel sind gefallen.

die·sel ['di:zl] I s Diesel m (Motor, Fahrzeug, Kraftstoff). II adj Diesel...

di·et ['daɪət] I s **1.** Nahrung f, Ernährung f, Kost f. **2.** ♣ Diät f: **be** (**put**) **on a ~** auf Diät gesetzt sein, diät leben (müssen). II v/t **3.** j-n auf Diät setzen: **~ o.s.** → **4.** III v/i **4.** Diät halten, diät leben.

dif·fer ['dɪfə] v/i **1.** sich unterscheiden, verschieden sein (**from** von). **2.** auseinandergehen (Meinungen). **3.** (**from, with**) nicht übereinstimmen (mit), anderer Meinung sein (als): → **agree** 1 **4.** sich nicht einig sein (**on, about, over** über acc). **dif·fer·ence** ['dɪfrəns] s **1.** Unterschied m: a) Unterscheidung f: **make no ~ between** keinen Unterschied machen zwischen (dat); **make no ~** nichts ausmachen (**to** dat), b) Verschiedenheit f: **~ of opinion** Meinungsverschiedenheit, c) Differenz f (a. ♣): **~ in price, price ~** Preisunterschied; **~ split** 2. **2.** Differenz f, Meinungsverschiedenheit f. **3.** Besonderheit f: **with a ~** (von) ganz besonderer Art, mit Pfiff. **'dif·fer·ent** adj □ **1.** verschieden(artig). **2.** (**from**) verschieden (von), anders (als): **he is ~** er ist anders. **dif·fer·en·tial** [,dɪfə'renʃl] I adj □ **1.** unterschiedlich. **2.** ♣, ☉, etc Differential...: **~ calculus** Differentialrechnung f; **~**

gear → **4.** II s **3.** ♣ Differential n. **4.** ☉ Differential-, Ausgleichsgetriebe n. **,dif·fer·en·ti·ate** [~ʃɪeɪt] I v/t **1.** unterscheiden (**from** von); voneinander unterscheiden. II v/i **2.** sich unterscheiden (**from** von). **3.** differenzieren, unterscheiden (**between** zwischen dat). **dif·fer·en·ti·a·tion** s Differenzierung f, Unterscheidung f.

dif·fi·cult ['dɪfɪkəlt] adj schwierig (a. Person), schwer: **it was quite ~ for me to** inf es fiel mir schwer, zu inf. **'dif·fi·cul·ty** s **1.** Schwierigkeit f: a) Mühe f: **with ~** mühsam, (nur) schwer; **have ~** (**in**) **doing s.th.** Mühe haben, et. zu tun, b) schwierige Sache, c) Hindernis n, Widerstand m: **make** (od. **raise**) **difficulties** Schwierigkeiten machen. **2.** oft pl (a. Geld)Schwierigkeiten pl, Verlegenheit f.

dif·fi·dence ['dɪfɪdəns] s Schüchternheit f, Mangel m an Selbstvertrauen. **'dif·fi·dent** adj □ schüchtern, ohne Selbstvertrauen: **be ~ about doing s.th.** et. nur zögernd od. zaghaft tun.

dif·fuse I v/t u. v/i [dɪ'fjuːz] **1.** bsd. fig. (sich) verbreiten: **a widely ~d opinion** e-e weitverbreitete Meinung. **2.** ♠, phys. (sich) zerstreuen. II adj [~s] **3.** diffus: a) weitschweifig, langatmig (Stil, Autor), b) unklar, ungeordnet (Gedanken etc), c) ♠, phys. zerstreut: **~ light** diffuses Licht, Streulicht n. **dif·'fu·sion** [~ʒn] s **1.** bsd. fig. Verbreitung f. **2.** ♠, phys. (Zer)Streuung f.

dig [dɪg] I s **1.** Puff m, Stoß m: **~ in the ribs** Rippenstoß m. **2.** fig. (Seiten)Hieb m (**at** auf acc). **3.** pl Br. F Bude f. II v/t (irr) **4.** Loch etc graben: **~** (**up**) umgraben; **~** (**up** od. **out**) ausgraben (a. fig.); → **grave²**. **5.** j-m e-n Stoß geben: **~ s.o. in the ribs** j-m e-n Rippenstoß geben. **6.** F kapieren. **7.** F stehen od. abfahren auf (acc). III v/i **8.** (**for**) graben (nach); fig. forschen (nach). **9.** **~ in(to)** F reinhauen (in e-n Kuchen etc). **10.** Br. F s-e Bude haben, wohnen.

di·gest [dɪ'dʒest] I v/t verdauen (a. fig.). II v/i sich verdauen lassen: **~ well** leicht verdaulich sein. III s ['daɪdʒest] (**of**) Auslese f (a. Zeitschrift), Auswahl f (aus); Abriß m (gen). **di·gest·i·ble** [dɪ'dʒestəbl] adj verdaulich. **di·gestion** s Verdauung f (a. fig.). **di·ges·tive**

I adj □ **1.** verdauungsfördernd. **2.** Verdauungs...: ~ **system** Verdauungsapparat m; ~ **tract** Verdauungstrakt m. **II** s **3.** ✷ verdauungsförderndes Mittel.

dig·ger ['dɪgə] s **1.** (bsd. Gold)Gräber m; Erdarbeiter m. **2.** Grabgerät n, -maschine f.

dig·it ['dɪdʒɪt] s **1.** anat. zo. Finger m, Zehe f. **2.** ✳ Ziffer f; Stelle f. **dig·i·tal** ['~tl] adj **1.** Finger...: ~ **telephone** Tastentelefon n. **2.** Digital...: ~ **clock** (**watch**); ~ **computer** Digitalrechner m.

dig·ni·fied ['dɪgnɪfaɪd] adj würdevoll, würdig. **dig·ni·fy** ['~faɪ] v/t Würde verleihen (dat).

dig·ni·tar·y ['dɪgnɪtərɪ] s Würdenträger(in). '**dig·ni·ty** s **1.** Rang m, (hohe) Stellung. **2.** Würde f: → **beneath** 3.

di·gress [daɪ'gres] v/i abschweifen (**from** von; **into** in acc). **di·gres·sion** s Abschweifung f.

dike[1] [daɪk] s **1.** Deich m, Damm m. **2.** Graben m. **II** v/t **3.** eindämmen, -deichen.

dike[2] [~] s sl. Lesbe f (Lesbierin).

di·lap·i·dat·ed [dɪ'læpɪdeɪtɪd] adj verfallen, baufällig (Haus etc), klapp(e)rig (Auto etc).

di·late [daɪ'leɪt] **I** v/t u. v/i (sich) ausdehnen od. (-)weiten od. erweitern: **with ~d eyes** mit aufgerissenen Augen; **his eyes ~d with terror** s-e Augen weiteten sich vor Entsetzen. **II** v/i: ~ **on** fig. sich (ausführlich) verbreiten od. auslassen über (acc).

dil·a·to·ry ['dɪlətərɪ] adj □ **1.** verzögernd, hinhaltend: ~ **tactics** pl Verzögerungs-, Verschleppungs-, Hinhaltetaktik f. **2.** langsam: **be ~ in doing s.th.** sich mit et. Zeit lassen.

di·lem·ma [dɪ'lemə] s Dilemma n, Klemme f: **be on the horns of a ~** in e-r Zwickmühle sein od. sitzen.

dil·et·tante [dɪlɪ'tæntɪ] mst contp. **I** pl -ti [~tiː], -tes Dilettant(in). **II** adj dilettantisch.

dil·i·gence ['dɪlɪdʒəns] s **1.** Fleiß m. **2.** Sorgfalt f. '**dil·i·gent** adj □ **1.** fleißig. **2.** sorgfältig, gewissenhaft.

dill [dɪl] s ⚘ Dill m.

dil·ly·dal·ly ['dɪlɪdælɪ] v/i F (herum)trödeln.

di·lute [daɪ'ljuːt] **I** v/t **1.** verdünnen. **2.** fig. verwässern, abschwächen. **II** adj **3.**

verdünnt. **4.** fig. verwässert, abgeschwächt. **di·lu·tion** s **1.** Verdünnung f. **2.** fig. Verwässerung f, Abschwächung f.

dim [dɪm] **I** adj □ **1.** (halb)dunkel, düster (a. fig.): → **view** 4. **2.** undeutlich, verschwommen, schwach. **3.** schwach, trüb (Licht): ~**ly lit** schwacherleuchtet. **4.** matt (Farbe). **5.** fig. schwer von Begriff. **II** v/t **6.** verdunkeln, -düstern. **7.** trüben (a. fig.). **8.** a. ~ **out** Licht abblenden: ~ **the headlights** mot. Am. abblenden. **III** v/i **9.** sich verdunkeln od. -düstern. **10.** undeutlich werden. **11.** sich trüben (a. fig.).

dime [daɪm] s Am. Zehncentstück n: ~ **novel** Groschenroman m.

di·men·sion [dɪ'menʃn] s Dimension f (a. ✳): a) Ausdehnung f, Maß n, Abmessung f, b) pl oft fig. Ausmaß n, Umfang m. **di·men·sion·al** [~ʃənl] adj □ in Zssgn: ...dimensional.

di·min·ish [dɪ'mɪnɪʃ] v/t u. v/i (sich) vermindern od. verringern: ~ **in numbers** weniger werden; ~ **in value** an Wert verlieren. **dim·i·nu·tion** [dɪmɪ'njuːʃn] s Verminderung f, Verringerung f. **di·min·u·tive** [~jʊtɪv] **I** adj **1.** klein, winzig. **2.** ling. Diminutiv..., Verkleinerungs... **II** s **3.** ling. Diminutiv n, Verkleinerungsform f od. -silbe f.

dim·mer ['dɪmə] s **1.** Dimmer m (Helligkeitsregler). **2.** pl mot. Am. Abblendod. Standlicht n. '**dim·ness** s **1.** Dunkelheit f, Düsterkeit f. **2.** Undeutlichkeit f. **3.** Mattheit f.

dim·ple ['dɪmpl] s Grübchen n.

din [dɪn] **I** s Lärm m, Getöse n: **kick up** (od. **make**) **a ~** Krach machen. **II** v/t: ~ **s.th. into s.o.** j-m et. einhämmern. **III** v/i lärmen, (Motoren etc) dröhnen (**in s.o.'s ears** j-m in den Ohren).

dine [daɪn] **I** v/i speisen, essen (**off**, **on** acc): ~ **in** (**out**) zu Hause (auswärts) essen. **II** v/t bewirten. **din·er** s **1.** Speisende m, f. **2.** Gast m (im Restaurant). **3.** 🚃 Speisewagen m. **4.** Am. Eß-, Speiselokal n. **di·nette** [daɪ'net] s Eßecke f.

din·ghy ['dɪŋgɪ] s **1.** ⚓ Ding(h)i n; Beiboot n. **2.** Schlauchboot n.

din·gy ['dɪndʒɪ] adj □ schmutzig, schmudd(e)lig.

din·ing| car ['daɪnɪŋ] s 🚃 Speisewagen

m. ~ **room** *s* Speise-, Eßzimmer *n.* ~ **ta·ble** *s* Eßtisch *m.*

dink·y ['dɪŋkɪ] *adj* F **1.** *Br.* niedlich. **2.** *Am.* klein, unbedeutend.

din·ner ['dɪnə] *s* **1.** (Mittag-, Abend-) Essen *n* (*Hauptmahlzeit*): *after* ~ nach dem Essen, nach Tisch; *at* ~ bei Tisch. **2.** Diner *n*, Festessen *n*: *at a* ~ auf *od.* bei e-m Diner. ~ **coat** *s bsd. Am.*, ~ **jack·et** *s* Smoking *m.* ~ **par·ty** *s* Diner *n*, Abendgesellschaft *f.* ~ **ser·vice**, ~ **set** *s* Speiseservice *n*, Tafelgeschirr *n.* ~ **ta·ble** *s* Eßtisch *m.* '~**time** *s* Essens-, Tischzeit *f.*

di·no·saur ['daɪnəsɔː] *s zo.* Dinosaurier *m.*

di·o·cese ['daɪəsɪs] *s eccl.* Diözese *f.*

di·ode ['daɪəʊd] *s ⚡* Diode *f.*

di·ox·ide [daɪ'ɒksaɪd] *s 🜍* Dioxyd *n.*

dip [dɪp] **I** *v/t* **1.** (ein)tauchen (*in*, *into* in *acc*): ~ *one's hand into one's pocket* in die Tasche greifen. **2.** ~ *the headlights mot. bsd. Br.* abblenden. **II** *v/i* **3.** unter-, eintauchen. **4.** ~ *into* a) sich flüchtig befassen mit, e-n Blick werfen in (*ein Buch etc*), b) *Reserven etc* angreifen: ~ *into one's pocket* (*od. purse*) *fig.* tief in die Tasche greifen. **III** *s* **5.** (Unter-, Ein)Tauchen *n.* **6.** kurzes Bad: *have a* ~ mal schnell ins Wasser springen.

diph·the·ri·a [dɪf'θɪərɪə] *s 𝔐* Diphtherie *f.*

diph·thong ['dɪfθɒŋ] *s* Diphthong *m*, Doppelvokal *m.*

di·plo·ma [dɪ'pləʊmə] *s* Diplom *n.*

di·plo·ma·cy [dɪ'pləʊməsɪ] *s pol.* Diplomatie *f* (*a. fig.*). **dip·lo·mat** ['dɪpləmæt] *s* Diplomat *m.* ,**dip·lo·mat·ic** *adj* (~*ally*) diplomatisch: ~ *corps* (*a. body*) diplomatisches Korps; ~ *relations pl* diplomatische Beziehungen *pl.*

'**dip·stick** *s* (*Öl- etc*) Meßstab *m.*

dire ['daɪə] *adj* **1.** gräßlich, schrecklich. **2.** äußerst, höchst: *be in* ~ *need of s.th.* et. ganz dringend brauchen; → **strait**.

di·rect [dɪ'rekt] **I** *v/t* **1.** *Aufmerksamkeit etc* richten, lenken (*to*, *toward*[s] auf *acc*): ~ *away* *j-n, et.* ablenken (*from* von). **2.** *Betrieb etc* führen, leiten; Regie führen bei (*e-m Film od. Stück*): ~*ed by* unter der Regie von. **3.** *Worte* richten, *Brief etc* adressieren, richten (*to* an *acc*). **4.** anweisen, beauftragen, *j-m* Anweisungen geben (*to do* zu tun).

5. anordnen, verfügen: ~ *s.th. to be done* anordnen, daß et. geschieht. **6.** (*to*) *j-m* den Weg zeigen (zu, nach); *fig. j-n* verweisen (an *acc*). **II** *adj* □ **7.** direkt, gerade. **8.** direkt, unmittelbar: ~ *current ⚡* Gleichstrom *m*; ~ *flight* Direktflug *m*; ~ *train* durchgehender Zug. **9.** direkt, genau: *the* ~ *contrary* das genaue Gegenteil. **10.** *ling.* ~ *speech* (*bsd. Am. discourse*) direkte Rede; ~ *object* direktes Objekt, Akkusativobjekt *n.* **III** *adv* **11.** direkt, unmittelbar: → *dial* **6.** **di'rec·tion** *s* **1.** Richtung *f*: *in the* ~ *of* in Richtung auf (*acc*) *od.* nach; *from* (*in*) *all* ~*s* aus (nach) allen Richtungen *od.* Seiten; *sense of* ~ Orts-, Orientierungssinn *m*; ~ *indicator mot.* (Fahrt)Richtungsanzeiger *m*, Blinker *m.* **2.** Führung *f*, Leitung *f*; (*Film etc*) Regie *f.* **3.** Anweisung *f*, Anleitung *f*: ~*s pl for use* Gebrauchsanweisung. **4.** Anweisung *f*, Anordnung *f*: *by* (*od. at*) ~ *of* auf Anweisung (*od. gen*). **di'rec·tion·al** [~ʃənl] *adj* **1.** Richtungs... **2.** ⚡ Peil...; Richt...: ~ *aerial* (*bsd. Am. antenna*) Richtantenne *f.* **di'rec·tive** *s* Direktive *f*, Anweisung *f.* **di'rec·tor** *s* **1.** Direktor *m* (*a. ✝*), Leiter *m*: ~'*s secretary* Chefsekretärin *f*; ~*general* Generaldirektor *m.* **2.** *Film etc*: Regisseur *m.* **di'rec·to·rate** [~rət] *s* **1.** Direktorat *n*, Direktor-, Direktorenposten *m.* **2.** Direktorium *n.* **di'rec·tor·ship** → *directorate* **1.** **di'rec·to·ry** *s* Adreßbuch *n*; Telefonbuch *n*; Branchenverzeichnis *n.* **di'rec·tress** *s* Direktorin *f*, Leiterin *f.*

dirt [dɜːt] *s* Schmutz *m* (*a. fig.*), Dreck *m*: *fling* (*od. throw*) ~ *at s.o. fig. j-n* mit Schmutz bewerfen; *treat s.o. like* ~ *j-n* wie (den letzten) Dreck behandeln. ,~'**cheap** *adj u. adv* F spottbillig. ~ **road** *s Am.* unbefestigte Straße.

dirt·y ['dɜːtɪ] **I** *adj* □ **1.** schmutzig (*a. fig.*), dreckig: ~ *look* böser Blick; ~ *mind* schmutzige Gedanken *pl*; schmutzige Phantasie; ~ *word* Reizwort *n*; ~ *work* Drecks(arbeit *f* (*a. fig.*); → *linen* **2.** **2.** gemein, niederträchtig: → *trick* **1. 3.** schlecht, *bsd. ⚓* stürmisch (*Wetter*). **II** *v/t* **4.** beschmutzen (*a. fig.*). ~ *one's hands* sich die Hände schmutzig machen (*a. fig.*). **III** *v/i* **5.** schmutzig werden, schmutzen.

discharge

dis·a·bil·i·ty [ˌdɪsə'bɪlətɪ] s 1. Unvermögen n, Unfähigkeit f. 2. Arbeits-, Erwerbsunfähigkeit f, Invalidität f: ~ **benefit** Invalidenrente f. 3. 🞉 Gebrechen n.

dis·a·ble [dɪs'eɪbl] v/t 1. unfähig machen, außerstand setzen (**from doing** zu tun). 2. unbrauchbar od. untauglich machen (**for** für, zu). 3. arbeits- od. erwerbsunfähig machen. **dis'a·bled** adj 1. arbeits-, erwerbsunfähig, invalid. 2. kriegsversehrt. 3. (körperlich od. geistig) behindert. **dis·a·ble·ment** s 1. → **disability** 2. 2. (körperliche od. geistige) Behinderung.

dis·ad·van·tage [ˌdɪsəd'vɑːntɪdʒ] I s Nachteil m (**to** für): **to s.o.'s** ~ zu j-s Nachteil od. Schaden; **be at a** ~ im Nachteil od. benachteiligt sein; **put at a** ~ → II; **sell at a** ~ mit Verlust verkaufen. II v/t benachteiligen. **dis·ad·van·ta·geous** [ˌædvɑːn'teɪdʒəs] adj ⬜ nachteilig, ungünstig, unvorteilhaft (**to** für).

dis·af·fect·ed [ˌdɪsə'fektɪd] adj ⬜ unzufrieden (**to, toward[s]** mit), verdrossen. **dis·af'fec·tion** s Unzufriedenheit f, (a. Staats)Verdrossenheit f.

dis·a·gree [ˌdɪsə'griː] v/i 1. (**with**) nicht übereinstimmen (mit), im Widerspruch stehen (zu, mit). 2. (**with**) anderer Meinung sein (als), nicht zustimmen (dat). 3. (sich) streiten (**on, about** über acc). 4. nicht einverstanden sein (**with** mit). 5. nicht bekommen (**with** dat) (Essen). **dis·a·gree·a·ble** [ˌ~'grɪəbl] adj ⬜ unangenehm. **dis·a'gree·ment** s 1. Unstimmigkeit f, Verschiedenheit f: **be in** ~ (**with**) → **disagree** 1. 2. Widerspruch m (**between** zwischen dat). 3. Meinungsverschiedenheit f (**over, on** über acc).

dis·al·low [ˌdɪsə'laʊ] v/t nicht anerkennen, nicht gelten lassen.

dis·ap·pear [ˌdɪsə'pɪə] v/i verschwinden (**from** von, aus): → **thin** 1. **dis·ap'pear·ance** s Verschwinden n.

dis·ap·point [ˌdɪsə'pɔɪnt] v/t j-n enttäuschen, j-s Hoffnungen etc a. zunichte machen: **be ~ed** enttäuscht sein (**in, at** s.th. von, über acc; **in, with** s.o. von). **dis·ap'point·ment** s Enttäuschung f.

dis·ap·prov·al [ˌdɪsə'pruːvl] s (**of**) Mißbilligung f (gen), Mißfallen n (über

acc): **in** ~ mißbilligend. **dis·ap'prove** I v/t mißbilligen. II v/i dagegen sein: ~ **of** → I.

dis·arm [dɪs'ɑːm] I v/t entwaffnen (a. fig.). II v/i ✗, pol. abrüsten. **dis'ar·ma·ment** s 1. Entwaffnung f. 2. ✗, pol. Abrüstung f. **dis'arm·ing** adj ⬜ fig. entwaffnend.

dis·ar·range [ˌdɪsə'reɪndʒ] v/t in Unordnung bringen, durcheinanderbringen (beide a. fig.).

dis·ar·ray [ˌdɪsə'reɪ] I v/t in Unordnung bringen (a. fig.). II s Unordnung f (a. fig.).

dis·as·sem·ble [ˌdɪsə'sembl] v/t auseinandernehmen, zerlegen, demontieren. **dis·as'sem·bly** s 1. Zerlegung f, Demontage f. 2. zerlegter Zustand.

dis·as·ter [dɪ'zɑːstə] s 1. Unglück n (**to** für). 2. Unglück n, Katastrophe f: ~ **area** Katastrophengebiet n. **dis'as·trous** adj ⬜ katastrophal, verheerend.

dis·be·lief [ˌdɪsbɪ'liːf] s 1. Unglaube m. 2. Zweifel m (**in** an dat). **dis·be·lieve** [ˌ~'liːv] I v/t et. nicht glauben, bezweifeln; j-m nicht glauben. II v/i nicht glauben (**in** an dat). **dis·be'liev·er** s Ungläubige m, f (a. eccl.).

dis·bur·den [dɪs'bɜːdn] v/t entlasten (**of, from** von): ~ **one's mind** sein Herz ausschütten od. erleichtern.

dis·burse [dɪs'bɜːs] v/t 1. Geld aus(be)zahlen. 2. Geld auslegen, verauslagen.

disc, etc → **disk**, etc.

dis·card I v/t [dɪ'skɑːd] 1. Spielkarten ablegen, Kleidung etc a. ausrangieren, Gewohnheit etc a. aufgeben. 2. Freund etc fallenlassen. II s ['dɪskɑːd] 1. abgelegte Karte(n pl). 2. etc Abgelegtes.

dis·cern [dɪ'sɜːn] v/t wahrnehmen, erkennen. **dis'cern·ing** adj ⬜ scharfsichtig, kritisch (urteilend). **dis'cern·ment** s 1. Wahrnehmen n, Erkennen n. 2. Scharfblick m.

dis·charge [dɪs'tʃɑːdʒ] I v/t 1. ausladen: a) Schiff etc entladen, b) Ladung löschen, c) Passagiere ausschiffen. 2. Gewehr, Geschoß etc abfeuern, abschießen. 3. ~ **itself** → 9. 4. ausströmen, -stoßen; 🞉, physiol. absondern: ~ **matter** eitern. 5. Angestellte, Patienten, Strafgefangenen etc entlassen (**from** aus). 6. ⚖ freisprechen (**of** von). 7. befreien, entbinden (**of, from** von; **from**

doing *s.th.* davon, et. zu tun). **8.** *Verpflichtungen etc* erfüllen, nachkommen (*dat*). **II** *v/i* **9.** sich ergießen, münden (*into in acc*). **10.** ⚕ eitern. **11.** ⚡ sich entladen. **III** *s* [ˈ~tʃɑːdʒ] **12.** Entladung *f*; Löschung *f*. **13.** Abfeuern *n*. **14.** ⚕ *physiol.* Absonderung *f*. **15.** Entlassung *f*. **16.** ⚖ Freisprechung *f*. **17.** Befreiung *f*, Entbindung *f*. **18.** Erfüllung *f*.

dis·ci [ˈdɪskaɪ] *pl von* **discus.**

dis·ci·ple [dɪˈsaɪpl] *s Bibl.* Jünger *m*, *fig. a.* Schüler *m*.

dis·ci·pli·na·ry [ˈdɪsɪplɪnərɪ] *adj* disziplinarisch, Disziplinar... '**dis·ci·pline I** *s* **1.** Disziplin *f*: **keep** ~ Disziplin halten. **2.** Disziplin *f*, Wissenschaftszweig *m*. **II** *v/t* **3.** disziplinieren, an Disziplin gewöhnen: **badly** ~**d** disziplinlos, undiszipliniert.

dis·claim [dɪsˈkleɪm] *v/t* **1.** ab-, bestreiten. **2.** jede Verantwortung ablehnen für; *Verantwortung* ablehnen. **3.** widerrufen, dementieren. **4.** ⚖ verzichten *od.* keinen Anspruch erheben auf (*acc*), *Erbschaft* ausschlagen. '**dis·claim·er** *s* **1.** Widerruf *m*, Dementi *n*. **2.** (*of*) Verzicht *m* (auf *acc*), Ausschlagung *f* (*gen*).

dis·close [dɪsˈkləʊz] *v/t* **1.** bekanntgeben, -machen. **2.** enthüllen, aufdecken. **3.** zeigen, verraten. **dis'clo·sure** [~ʒə] *s* **1.** Bekanntgabe *f*. **2.** Enthüllung *f*.

dis·co [ˈdɪskəʊ] *pl* **-cos** F Disko *f* (*Diskothek*).

dis·col·o·u(r) [dɪsˈkʌlə] *v/t u. v/i* (sich) verfärben.

dis·com·fit [dɪsˈkʌmfɪt] *v/t* aus der Fassung bringen, verwirren; in Verlegenheit bringen. **dis'com·fi·ture** [~tʃə] *s* Verwirrung *f*; Verlegenheit *f*.

dis·com·fort [dɪsˈkʌmfət] *s* **1.** Unannehmlichkeit *f*, Verdruß *m*. **2.** Unbehagen *n*.

dis·con·cert [ˌdɪskənˈsɜːt] *v/t* **1.** aus der Fassung bringen, verwirren. **2.** beunruhigen.

dis·con·nect [ˌdɪskəˈnekt] *v/t* **1.** trennen (**from** von) (*a. teleph.* Teilnehmer). **2.** ⚡ *Gerät, Stecker etc* ausstecken. **3.** *Gas, Strom, Telefon* abstellen: **we have been** ~**ed** uns ist das Gas *etc* abgestellt worden. '**dis·con'nect·ed** *adj* □ zs.-hang(s)los.

dis·con·so·late [dɪsˈkɒnsələt] *adj* □ untröstlich (**about, at** über *acc*).

dis·con·tent [ˌdɪskənˈtent] **I** *adj* → **dis-contented.** **II** *s* Unzufriedenheit *f*. **ˌdis·con'tent·ed** *adj* □ unzufrieden (**with** mit).

dis·con·tin·ue [ˌdɪskənˈtɪnjuː] *v/t* **1.** unterbrechen. **2.** einstellen (*a.* ⚖); *Gewohnheit etc* aufgeben; *Beziehungen* abbrechen; *Zeitung etc* abbestellen. **3.** aufhören (**doing** zu tun). **ˌdis·con·'tin·u·ous** [~jʊəs] *adj* □ **1.** unterbrochen. **2.** zs.-hang(s)los.

dis·cord [ˈdɪskɔːd] *s* **1.** Uneinigkeit *f*. **2.** Zwietracht *f*, Zwist *m*: → **apple. 3.** ♪ Mißklang *m* (*a. fig.*), Dissonanz *f*. **dis'cord·ant** *adj* □ **1.** sich widersprechend. **2.** ♪ mißtönend (*a. weitS. u. fig.*).

dis·co·theque [ˈdɪskəʊtek] *s* Diskothek *f*.

dis·count [ˈdɪskaʊnt] **I** *s* **1.** ✝ Preisnachlaß *m*, Rabatt *m*, Skonto *m*, *n* (**on** auf *acc*). **2.** ✝ Diskont *m* (*vom* ~ (**rate**) Diskontsatz *m*. **3.** ✝ Abzug *m* (*vom Nominalwert*): **at a** ~ unter Pari; *fig.* nicht geschätzt *od.* gefragt; **sell at a** ~ mit Verlust verkaufen. **II** *v/t* **4.** ✝ abziehen, abrechnen; e-n Abzug gewähren auf (*acc*). **5.** ✝ *Wechsel* diskontieren. **6.** *Geschichte etc* mit Vorsicht *od.* Vorbehalt aufnehmen.

dis·cour·age [dɪsˈkʌrɪdʒ] *v/t* **1.** entmutigen. **2.** abschrecken, abhalten, *j-m* abraten (**from** von). **dis'cour·age·ment** *s* **1.** Entmutigung *f*. **2.** Abschreckung *f*.

dis·course I *s* [ˈdɪskɔːs] **1.** Unterhaltung *f*, Gespräch *n*. **2.** Vortrag *m*. **II** *v/i* [dɪˈskɔːs] **3.** sich unterhalten (**on** über *acc*). **4.** e-n Vortrag halten (**on** über *acc*).

dis·cour·te·ous [dɪsˈkɜːtjəs] *adj* □ unhöflich. **dis'cour·te·sy** [~tɪsɪ] *s* Unhöflichkeit *f*.

dis·cov·er [dɪsˈkʌvə] *v/t* entdecken, *fig. a.* ausfindig machen, (heraus)finden. **dis'cov·er·er** *s* Entdecker(in). **dis'cov·er·y** *s* Entdeckung *f*.

dis·cred·it [dɪsˈkredɪt] **I** *v/t* **1.** in Verruf *od.* Mißkredit bringen (**with** bei). **2.** anzweifeln, keinen Glauben schenken (*dat*). **II** *s* **3.** Mißkredit *m*: **bring into** ~, **bring** ~ **on** → **1. 4.** Zweifel *m*.

dis·creet [dɪsˈkriːt] *adj* □ **1.** umsichtig, besonnen. **2.** diskret: a) taktvoll, b) verschwiegen, c) dezent, unaufdringlich.

dishearten

dis·crep·an·cy [dɪˈskrepənsɪ] s Diskrepanz f, Widerspruch m.

dis·crete [dɪˈskriːt] adj □ getrennt, einzeln.

dis·cre·tion [dɪˈskreʃn] s 1. Ermessen n, Gutdünken n: **at ~** nach Belieben; **it is at** (od. **within**) **your ~** es steht Ihnen frei; **leave s.th. to s.o.'s ~** j-m et. anheimstellen. **2.** Umsicht f, Besonnenheit f. **3.** Diskretion f.

dis·crim·i·nate [dɪˈskrɪmɪneɪt] **I** v/i (scharf) unterscheiden, e-n Unterschied machen (**between** zwischen dat): **~ between** unterschiedlich behandeln (acc); **~ against** j-n benachteiligen, diskriminieren. **II** v/t (scharf) unterscheiden (**from** von). **dis·crim·i·nat·ing** adj □ scharfsinnig, urteilsfähig. **dis·crim·i·na·tion** s 1. unterschiedliche Behandlung; Diskriminierung f: **~ against s.o.** Benachteiligung f e-r Person. **2.** Scharfsinn m, Urteilsfähigkeit f. **dis·crim·i·na·tive** [~nətɪv], **dis·crim·i·na·to·ry** [~nətərɪ] adj diskriminierend.

dis·cur·sive [dɪˈskɜːsɪv] adj □ weitschweifig.

dis·cus [ˈdɪskəs] pl **-cus·es, -ci** [~kaɪ] s Leichtathletik: a) Diskus m: **~ throw →** b; **~ thrower** Diskuswerfer(in), b) Diskuswerfen n.

dis·cuss [dɪˈskʌs] v/t diskutieren, besprechen, erörtern. **dis·cus·sion** s Diskussion f, Besprechung f, Erörterung f: **be under ~** zur Diskussion stehen; **matter for ~** Diskussionsgegenstand m.

dis·dain [dɪsˈdeɪn] **I** v/t verachten, geringschätzen. **II** s Verachtung f, Geringschätzung f. **dis·dain·ful** [~fʊl] adj □ verächtlich, geringschätzig: **be ~ of** (od. **toward[s]**) → **disdain** I.

dis·ease [dɪˈziːz] s Krankheit f (a. fig.). **dis·eased** adj krank.

dis·em·bark [ˌdɪsɪmˈbɑːk] **I** v/t ✈, ⚓ Passagiere von Bord gehen lassen, ⚓ a. ausschiffen, Waren ausladen. **II** v/i ✈, ⚓ von Bord gehen, a. sich ausschiffen. **dis·em·bar·ka·tion** [~em~] s Ausschiffung f, -ladung f.

dis·en·chant [ˌdɪsɪnˈtʃɑːnt] v/t desillusionieren, ernüchtern.

dis·en·gage [ˌdɪsɪnˈɡeɪdʒ] **I** v/t 1. los-, freimachen, befreien (**from** von). **2.** ⚙ loskuppeln: **~ the clutch** auskuppeln; **~ the gears** in den Leergang schalten. **II**

v/i **3.** sich freimachen, loskommen (**from** von). **dis·en·gaged** adj **1.** frei, unbeschäftigt. **2.** ungebunden. **dis·en·gage·ment** s **1.** Befreiung f. **2.** Ungebundenheit f. **3.** Muße(stunden pl) f.

dis·en·tan·gle [ˌdɪsɪnˈtæŋɡl] **I** v/t **1.** entwirren, -flechten (beide a. fig.). **2.** befreien (**from** von, aus). **II** v/i **3.** sich befreien.

dis·e·qui·lib·ri·um [ˌdɪsekwɪˈlɪbrɪəm] s bsd. ✝ Ungleichgewicht n.

dis·fa·vo(u)r [ˌdɪsˈfeɪvə] s **1.** Mißbilligung f, -fallen n. **2.** Ungnade f: **be in** (**fall into**) **~** in Ungnade stehen (fallen) (**with** bei).

dis·fig·ure [dɪsˈfɪɡə] v/t entstellen, verunstalten (**with** durch).

dis·gorge [dɪsˈɡɔːdʒ] **I** v/t **1.** Essen ausspeien, Lava speien. **2.** (widerwillig) wieder herausgeben. **II** v/i **3.** sich ergießen, fließen (**into** in acc).

dis·grace [dɪsˈɡreɪs] s **1.** Schande f (**to** für): **bring ~ on →** 3. **2. →** **disfavo(u)r** 2. **II** v/t **3.** Schande bringen über (acc). **dis·grace·ful** [~fʊl] adj □ schändlich.

dis·grun·tled [dɪsˈɡrʌntld] adj verärgert, -stimmt (**at** über acc).

dis·guise [dɪsˈɡaɪz] **I** v/t **1.** (o.s. sich) verkleiden (od. maskieren (**as** als). **2.** Handschrift, Stimme verstellen. **3.** Absichten, Fakten etc verschleiern, Gefühle etc verbergen. **II** s **4.** Verkleidung f: **in ~** verkleidet, maskiert; fig. verkappt; **in the ~ of** verkleidet als; → **blessing**. **5.** Verstellung f. **6.** Verschleierung f: **make no ~ of** kein Hehl machen aus.

dis·gust [dɪsˈɡʌst] v/t **1.** anekeln, anwidern: **be ~ed with** (od. **at, by**) Ekel empfinden über (acc). **2.** empören, erbittern: **be ~ed with** empört od. entrüstet sein über (acc). **II** s **3.** Ekel m (**at, for** vor dat). **dis·gust·ing** adj □ ekelhaft, widerlich.

dish [dɪʃ] **I** s **1.** flache Schüssel; (Servier)Platte f; pl Geschirr n: **wash** (od. **do**) **the ~es** abspülen. **2.** Gericht n, Speise f. **II** v/t **3.** oft **~ up** Speisen anrichten; auftragen. **4.** oft **~ up** F Geschichte etc auftischen. **5. ~ out** F austeilen.

dis·har·mo·ny [ˌdɪsˈhɑːmənɪ] s Disharmonie f.

'dish-cloth s Geschirrtuch n.

dis·heart·en [dɪsˈhɑːtn] v/t entmutigen.

di·shev·el(l)ed [dɪˈʃevld] *adj* **1.** zerzaust (*Haar*). **2.** unordentlich, ungepflegt.

dis·hon·est [dɪsˈɒnɪst] *adj* □ unehrlich, unredlich. **dis'hon·es·ty** *s* Unredlichkeit *f:* a) Unehrlichkeit *f*, b) unredliche Handlung.

dis·hon·o(u)r [dɪsˈɒnə] **I** *s* **1.** Unehre *f*, Schande *f* (**to** für). **II** *v/t* **2.** entehren. **3.** † *Wechsel etc* nicht honorieren *od.* einlösen. **dis'hon·o(u)r·a·ble** *adj* □ schändlich, unehrenhaft.

'dish·rag *s Br.*, **~ tow·el** *s bsd. Am.* Geschirrtuch *n.* **'~·wash·er** *s* **1.** Tellerwäscher(in), Spüler(in). **2.** Geschirrspülmaschine *f*, -spüler *m.* **'~·wa·ter** *s* Abwasch-, Spülwasser *n.*

dish·y [ˈdɪʃɪ] *adj bsd. Br.* F dufte, toll (*Person*).

dis·il·lu·sion [ˌdɪsɪˈluːʒn] **I** *s* Ernüchterung *f*, Desillusion *f.* **II** *v/t* ernüchtern, desillusionieren. **¸dis·il'lu·sion·ment** → *disillusion* I.

dis·in·cli·na·tion [ˌdɪsɪnklɪˈneɪʃn] *s* Abneigung *f* (**for** gegen; **to do** zu tun). **dis·in·clined** [ˌ~ˈklaɪnd] *adj* abgeneigt.

dis·in·fect [ˌdɪsɪnˈfekt] *v/t* desinfizieren. **¸dis·in'fect·ant** *s* Desinfektionsmittel *n.* **¸dis·in'fec·tion** *s* Desinfektion *f*, Desinfizierung *f.*

dis·in·gen·u·ous [ˌdɪsɪnˈdʒenjʊəs] *adj* □ unaufrichtig.

dis·in·her·it [ˌdɪsɪnˈherɪt] *v/t* enterben.

dis·in·te·grate [dɪsˈɪntɪɡreɪt] **I** *v/t* **1.** auflösen, *fig. a.* zersetzen. **II** *v/i* **2.** sich auflösen (*a. fig.*). **3.** ver-, zerfallen (*a. fig.*). **4.** *geol.* verwittern. **dis¸in·te'gra·tion** *s* **1.** Auflösung *f.* **2.** Zerfall *m.* **3.** *geol.* Verwitterung *f.*

dis·in·ter·est·ed [dɪsˈɪntrəstɪd] *adj* □ **1.** uneigennützig. **2.** objektiv. **3.** un-, desinteressiert (**in** an *dat*).

dis·joint·ed [dɪsˈdʒɔɪntɪd] *adj* □ zs.-hang(s)los.

disk [dɪsk] *s* **1.** *allg.* Scheibe *f.* **2.** (Schall)Platte *f.* **~ brake** *s* ⊚ Scheibenbremse *f.*

disk·ette [dɪˈsket] *s Computer:* Diskette *f.*

disk jock·ey *s* Diskjockey *m.*

dis·like [dɪsˈlaɪk] **I** *v/t* nicht leiden können, nicht mögen: *~ doing s.th.* et. nicht gern od mögen *od.* (nur) ungern tun; *get o.s. ~d* sich unbeliebt machen. **II** *s* Abneigung *f*, Widerwille *m* (**of, for** gegen):

take a ~ to e-e Abneigung fassen gegen.

dis·lo·cate [ˈdɪsləʊkeɪt] *v/t* **1.** verrücken. **2.** ✻ sich *den Arm etc* ver- *od.* ausrenken. **¸dis·lo'ca·tion** *s* **1.** Verrückung *f.* **2.** ✻ Verrenkung *f*; Dislokation *f.*

dis·loy·al [dɪsˈlɔɪəl] *adj* □ (**to**) untreu (*dat*), treulos (gegen). **¸dis'loy·al·ty** *s* Untreue *f*, Treulosigkeit *f.*

dis·mal [ˈdɪzməl] **I** *adj* □ düster, trüb, trostlos, bedrückend. **II** *s:* **be in the ~s** F Trübsal blasen.

dis·man·tle [dɪsˈmæntl] *v/t* **1.** demontieren, abbauen; *Gebäude* abbrechen; ⚓ abwracken. **2.** zerlegen, auseinandernehmen.

dis·may [dɪsˈmeɪ] **I** *v/t* erschrecken, bestürzen. **II** *s* Schreck(en) *m*, Bestürzung *f:* **in** (*od.* **with**) **~** bestürzt; **to one's ~** zu s-r Bestürzung.

dis·mem·ber [dɪsˈmembə] *v/t* **1.** zerstückeln; *bsd.* ✻ zergliedern. **2.** *Land etc* zersplittern, aufteilen.

dis·miss [dɪsˈmɪs] *v/t* **1.** entlassen, gehen lassen. **2.** entlassen (**from** aus e-m Amt etc). **3.** *Thema etc* fallenlassen; *Frage etc* abtun (**as** als). **4.** *a.* ⚖ abweisen. **dis'miss·al** *s* **1.** Entlassung *f.* **2.** *a.* ⚖ Abweisung *f.*

dis·mount [dɪsˈmaʊnt] **I** *v/i* **1.** absteigen, absitzen (**from** von). **II** *v/t* **2.** *Reiter* abwerfen. **3.** abmontieren.

dis·o·be·di·ence [ˌdɪsəˈbiːdjəns] *s* Ungehorsam *m.* **¸dis·o'be·di·ent** *adj* □ ungehorsam (**to** gegen[über]). **¸dis·o·bey** [ˌ~ˈbeɪ] **I** *v/t* **1.** *j-m* nicht gehorchen. **2.** *Gesetz etc* nicht befolgen, mißachten. **II** *v/i* **3.** nicht gehorchen, ungehorsam sein.

dis·o·blige [ˌdɪsəˈblaɪdʒ] *v/t* ungefällig sein gegen. **¸dis·o'blig·ing** *adj* □ ungefällig, unfreundlich.

dis·or·der [dɪsˈɔːdə] **I** *s* **1.** Unordnung *f*, Durcheinander *n:* **in ~** durcheinander; *throw into ~* → **4.** **2.** Aufruhr *m*, Unruhen *pl.* **3.** ✻ Störung *f:* **mental ~** Geistesstörung *f.* **II** *v/t* **4.** in Unordnung bringen, durcheinanderbringen. **dis·'or·dered** *adj* **1.** unordentlich, durcheinander. **2.** ✻ gestört. **dis'or·der·ly** *adj* **1.** unordentlich. **2.** schlampig, (*a. Leben etc*) liederlich. **3.** ⚖ ordnungswidrig.

dis·or·gan·ize [dɪsˈɔːɡənaɪz] → *disorder* 4.

dis·own [dɪs'əʊn] v/t **1.** nichts zu tun haben wollen mit, ablehnen. **2.** ableugnen.

dis·par·age [dɪ'spærɪdʒ] v/t **1.** herabsetzen, verächtlich machen. **2.** verachten, geringschätzen. **dis'par·age·ment** s **1.** Herabsetzung f, Verächtlichmachung f. **2.** Verachtung f, Geringschätzung f. **dis'par·ag·ing** adj □ herabsetzend, verächtlich, geringschätzig.

dis·pa·rate ['dɪspərət] adj □ ungleich(artig), (grund)verschieden. **dis-par·i·ty** [dɪ'spærətɪ] s Verschiedenheit f: ~ **in** (od. **of**) **age** (zu großer) Altersunterschied.

dis·pas·sion·ate [dɪ'spæʃnət] adj □ leidenschaftslos, kühl, sachlich.

dis·patch [dɪ'spætʃ] I v/t **1.** (ab)senden, (ab)schicken, Telegramm etc **2.** rasch erledigen. **3.** ins Jenseits befördern, töten. **4.** F wegputzen, schnell aufessen. II s **5.** Absendung f, Versand m: ~ **by rail** Bahnversand. **6.** rasche Erledigung. **7.** Tötung f. ~ **box**, ~ **case** s bsd. Br. Aktenkoffer m.

dis·pel [dɪ'spel] v/t Menge etc, a. fig. Befürchtungen etc zerstreuen, Nebel zerteilen.

dis·pen·sa·ble [dɪ'spensəbl] adj □ entbehrlich. **dis'pen·sa·ry** s Werks-, Krankenhausapotheke f. **dis·pen-sa·tion** [ˌ~'seɪʃn] s **1.** Aus-, Verteilung f. **2.** Zuteilung f, Gabe f. **3.** (göttliche) Fügung. **4.** Verzicht m (with auf acc). **dis·pense** [dɪ'spens] I v/t **1.** aus-, verteilen; Sakrament spenden: ~ **justice** Recht sprechen. **2.** Arzneien dispensieren, zubereiten u. abgeben. **3.** befreien, entbinden (from von). II v/i **4.** ~ **with** verzichten auf (acc); überflüssig machen (acc). **dis'pens·er** s **1.** Aus-, Verteiler m. **2.** ☺ Spender m, (für Klebestreifen etc a.) Abroller m, (Briefmarken- etc)Automat m. **dis'pens·ing** adj: ~ **chemist** Br. Apotheker m.

dis·per·sal [dɪ'spɜːsl] s **1.** Zerstreuung f (a. fig.). **2.** Verbreitung f. **dis'perse** I v/t **1.** verstreuen (over über acc). **2.** → dispel. **3.** Nachrichten etc verbreiten. **4.** 🜂, phys. dispergieren, zerstreuen. II v/i **5.** sich zerstreuen (Menge). **6.** sich verteilen. **dis'per·sion** s **1.** → dispersal. **2.** 🜂, phys. Dispersion f, (Zer-) Streuung f.

dis·pir·it·ed [dɪ'spɪrɪtɪd] adj mutlos, niedergeschlagen.

dis·place [dɪs'pleɪs] v/t **1.** versetzen, -rücken, verlegen. **2.** verdrängen (a. ⚓, phys., Sport). **3.** j-n ablösen (as als). **4.** j-n verschleppen: ~**d person** Verschleppte m, f, Zwangsumsiedler(in). **dis'place·ment** s **1.** Versetzung f, -schiebung f. **2.** Verdrängung f. **3.** Ablösung f. **4.** Verschleppung f.

dis·play [dɪ'spleɪ] I v/t **1.** Aktivität etc zeigen, entfalten, an den Tag legen. **2.** Waren auslegen, -stellen. **3.** zur Schau stellen, hervorkehren. II s **4.** Entfaltung f. **5.** Ausstellung f: be on ~ ausgestellt sein. **6.** Display n: a) (Sichtbild)Anzeige f, b) a. ~ **unit** Sichtbildgerät n. III adj **7.** Ausstellungs..., Schau...: ~ **cabinet** (od. **case**) Schaukasten m, Vitrine f; ~ **window** Auslage(n)-, Schaufenster n.

dis·please [dɪs'pliːz] v/t **1.** j-m mißfallen: be ~**d at** (od. **with**) unzufrieden sein mit. **2.** j-n ärgern, verstimmen. **dis-'pleas·ing** adj □ unangenehm. **dis-pleas·ure** [ˌ~'pleʒə] s Mißfallen n (at über acc).

dis·pos·a·ble [dɪs'pəʊzəbl] adj **1.** (frei) verfügbar. **2.** Einweg..., Wegwerf... **dis'pos·al** s **1.** Erledigung f. **2.** Beseitigung f. **3.** Übergabe f, -tragung f: ~ **(by sale)** Veräußerung f, Verkauf m. **4.** Verfügung(srecht n) f (of über acc): be at s.o.'s ~ j-m zur Verfügung stehen; place (od. put) s.th. at s.o.'s ~ j-m et. zur Verfügung stellen; have the ~ of verfügen (können) über (acc). **dis'pose** I v/t **1.** anordnen, aufstellen. **2.** geneigt machen, bewegen (to zu; to do zu tun). II v/i **3.** ~ **of** (frei) verfügen über (acc); (endgültig) erledigen; wegschaffen, beseitigen; verkaufen, veräußern; übergeben, -tragen. **dis'posed** adj **1.** be well ~ to(ward[s]) j-m wohlgesinnt sein, j-m wohlwollen; e-m Plan etc wohlwollend gegenüberstehen; → ill-disposed. **2.** geneigt (to do zu tun): feel ~ to do s.th. et. tun wollen. **dis·po·si·tion** [ˌ~pə'zɪʃn] s **1.** Disposition f, Veranlagung f; Art f. **2.** Neigung f, Hang m (to zu); ⚓ Anfälligkeit f (to für): have a ~ to neigen zu; anfällig sein für. **3.** → disposal 4.

dis·pos·sess [ˌdɪspə'zes] v/t enteignen.

dis·pro·por·tion·ate [ˌdɪsprə'pɔːʃnət] *adj* □ unverhältnismäßig (groß *od.* klein); unangemessen; übertrieben: *be ~ to* in keinem Verhältnis stehen zu.

dis·prove [ˌdɪs'pruːv] *v/t* widerlegen.

dis·pu·ta·ble [dɪ'spjuːtəbl] *adj* □ strittig. **,dis·pu'ta·tion** *s* 1. Disput *m.* 2. Disputation *f.* **,dis·pu'ta·tious** *adj* □ streitsüchtig. **dis'pute** I *v/i* 1. streiten (*on, about* über *acc*). 2. *v/t* 2. streiten über (*acc*). 3. in Zweifel ziehen, bezweifeln; **~d** umstritten. 4. kämpfen um. 5. (an)kämpfen gegen. III *s* 6. Disput *m:* **in** (*od.* **under**) *~* umstritten; **beyond** (*od.* **past, without**) *~* fraglos, unbestritten.

dis·qual·i·fi·ca·tion [dɪsˌkwɒlɪfɪ'keɪʃn] *s* 1. Disqualifikation *f*, Disqualifizierung *f.* 2. Untauglichkeit *f* (**for** für). **dis'qual·i·fy** *v/t* 1. disqualifizieren. 2. untauglich machen (**for** für). 3. für untauglich erklären.

dis·qui·et [dɪs'kwaɪət] I *v/t* beunruhigen. II *s* Unruhe *f*, Besorgnis *f.* **dis'qui·et·ing** *adj* □ beunruhigend, besorgniserregend.

dis·re·gard [ˌdɪsrɪ'gɑːd] I *v/t* 1. nicht beachten, ignorieren. 2. mißachten. II *s* 3. Nichtbeachtung *f*, Ignorierung *f* (**of, for** gen). 4. Mißachtung *f* (**of, for** gen).

dis·re·pair [ˌdɪsrɪ'peə] *s* Baufälligkeit *f:* **be in** (**a state of**) *~* baufällig sein; **fall into** *~* baufällig werden.

dis·rep·u·ta·ble [dɪs'repjʊtəbl] *adj* □ verrufen. **dis·re·pute** [ˌ~rɪ'pjuːt] *s* schlechter Ruf: **be in** *~* in schlechtem Ruf: **bring** (**fall, sink**) **into** *~* in Verruf bringen (kommen).

dis·re·spect [ˌdɪsrɪ'spekt] *s* Respektlosigkeit *f*, **dis·re'spect·ful** [~fʊl] *adj* □ respektlos (**to** gegenüber).

dis·rupt [dɪs'rʌpt] *v/t* 1. auseinanderreißen, (zer)spalten. 2. *Gespräch, Verkehr etc* unterbrechen. 3. *Land etc* zerrütten; *Koalition etc* sprengen. **dis'rup·tion** *s* 1. Spaltung *f.* 2. Unterbrechung *f.* 3. Zerrüttung *f*; Sprengung *f.*

dis·sat·is·fac·tion [ˌdɪsˌsætɪs'fækʃn] *s* Unzufriedenheit *f.* **'dis,sat·is·fac·to·ry** [~tərɪ] *adj* unbefriedigend (**to** für). **,dis'sat·is·fied** [~faɪd] *adj* unzufrieden (**at, with** mit).

dis·sect [dɪ'sekt] *v/t* 1. ✄ sezieren. 2. *fig.* zergliedern.

dis·sem·ble [dɪ'sembl] *v/t* verbergen, -hehlen, sich *et.* nicht anmerken lassen.

dis·sem·i·nate [dɪ'semɪneɪt] *v/t* 1. ausstreuen. 2. *fig.* verbreiten. **dis,sem·i'na·tion** *s* 1. Ausstreuung *f.* 2. *fig.* Verbreitung *f.*

dis·sen·sion [dɪ'senʃn] *s* Meinungsverschiedenheit(en *pl*) *f.*

dis·sent [dɪ'sent] I *v/i* 1. (**from**) anderer Meinung sein (als), nicht übereinstimmen (mit). 2. *eccl.* von der Staatskirche abweichen. II *s* 3. Meinungsverschiedenheit *f.* **dis'sent·er** *s* 1. Andersdenkende *m, f.* 2. *eccl.* Dissident *m*; Dissenter *m.*

dis·ser·ta·tion [ˌdɪsə'teɪʃn] *s* 1. (wissenschaftliche) Abhandlung. 2. *univ.* Diplomarbeit *f.*

dis·ser·vice [ˌdɪs'sɜːvɪs] *s*: **do s.o. a** *~* j-m e-n schlechten Dienst erweisen.

dis·si·dent ['dɪsɪdənt] I *adj* 1. (**from**) andersdenkend (als), abweichend (von). II *s* 2. Andersdenkende *m, f.* 3. *eccl.* Dissident(in), *pol. a.* Regime-, Systemkritiker(in).

dis·sim·i·lar [ˌdɪ'sɪmɪlə] *adj* □ (**to, from**) verschieden (von), unähnlich (*dat*). **dis·sim·i·lar·i·ty** [ˌ~'lærətɪ] *s* Verschiedenheit *f*, Unähnlichkeit *f.*

dis·sim·u·late [dɪ'sɪmjʊleɪt] → **dissemble.**

dis·si·pate ['dɪsɪpeɪt] I *v/t* 1. zerstreuen (*a. fig.*); *Nebel* zerteilen. 2. *Kräfte* verzetteln, -geuden; *Vermögen etc* durchbringen, verschwenden. II *v/i* 3. sich zerstreuen (*a. fig.*); sich zerteilen. **'dis·si·pat·ed** *adj* □ ausschweifend: a) zügellos (*Leben*), b) leichtlebig (*Person*). **,dis·si'pa·tion** *s* 1. Zerstreuung *f* (*a. fig.*); Zerteilung *f.* 2. Vergeudung *f.* 3. Ausschweifung *f*: **a life of** *~* ein ausschweifendes *od.* zügelloses Leben.

dis·so·ci·ate [dɪ'səʊʃɪeɪt] *v/t* 1. trennen (**from** von). 2. *~ o.s.* sich distanzieren, abrücken (**from** von). **dis,so·ci'a·tion** [~sɪ'eɪʃn] *s* Trennung *f.*

dis·so·lute ['dɪsəluːt] → **dissipated.**

dis·so·lu·tion [ˌdɪsə'luːʃn] *s* 1. Auflösung *f* (*a. fig.*). 2. ⚖ Annullierung *f*, Aufhebung *f.*

dis·solve [dɪ'zɒlv] I *v/t* 1. auflösen (*a. fig.*): *~ in the mouth Tablette etc* im Mund zergehen lassen; *~d in tears* in Tränen aufgelöst. 2. ⚖ annullieren, aufheben. **II** v/i **3.** sich auflösen (a. fig.): **~ in the mouth** im Mund zergehen; **~ in(to) tears** in Tränen zerfließen.

dis·so·nance ['dɪsənəns] s Dissonanz f: a) ♪ Mißklang m (a. fig.), b) fig. Unstimmigkeit f. **'dis·so·nant** adj □ **1.** ♪ dissonant. **2.** mißtönend. **3.** fig. unstimmig.

dis·suade [dɪ'sweɪd] v/t **1.** j-m abraten (**from** von; **from doing** [davon], et. zu tun). **2.** abbringen (**from** von; **from doing** davon, et. zu tun). **3.** abraten von.

dis·tance ['dɪstəns] **I** s **1.** Entfernung f: **at a ~** in einiger Entfernung, von weitem, von fern; **from a ~** aus einiger Entfernung; **keep one's ~** Abstand halten (**from** von); fig. Distanz wahren. **2.** Ferne f: **from (in) the ~** aus (in) der Ferne. **3.** Strecke: a) Entfernung f: **go the ~** fig. durchhalten, über die Runden kommen, b) Sport: Distanz f: **~ runner** (Leichtathletik) Langstreckenläufer(in), Langstreckler(in). **4.** (a. zeitlicher) Abstand: **at this ~ of** (od. **in**) **time** nach all dieser Zeit. **II** v/t **5.** überholen, (weit) hinter sich lassen, (Sport a.) distanzieren. **6.** fig. überflügeln, -treffen. **7. ~ o.s.** sich distanzieren (**from** von). **'dis·tant** adj □ **1.** entfernt (a. fig.). **2.** fern (a. zeitlich), Fern...: **~ heating** Fernheizung f. **3.** (weit) voneinander entfernt. **4.** fig. distanziert.

dis·taste [ˌdɪs'teɪst] s **1.** Ekel m (**for** vor dat). **2.** fig. Widerwille m, Abneigung f (**for** gegen). **dis'taste·ful** [∼fʊl] adj □ **1.** ekelerregend. **2.** fig. unangenehm: **be ~ to** j-m zuwider sein.

dis·tend [dɪ'stend] **I** v/t **1.** (aus)dehnen. **2.** Bauch etc aufblähen. **II** v/i **3.** sich (aus)dehnen. **4.** sich aufblähen. **5.** sich weiten (**with** vor dat) (Augen).

dis·til(l) [dɪ'stɪl] v/t **1.** 🜍 destillieren: **~ out** herausdestillieren (**from** aus) (a. fig.). **2.** Branntwein brennen (**from** aus). **dis·til·la·tion** [ˌ∼'leɪʃn] s **1.** 🜍 Destillation f. **2.** 🜍 Destillat n. **3.** Brennen n. **dis'till·er·y** s (Branntwein)Brennerei f.

dis·tinct [dɪ'stɪŋkt] adj □ **1.** verschieden (**from** von): **as ~ from** im Unterschied zu. **2.** ausgeprägt, klar, deutlich. **dis'tinc·tion** s **1.** Unterscheidung f. **2.** Unterschied m: **in ~ from** im Unterschied

zu; **draw** (od. **make**) **a ~ between** e-n Unterschied machen zwischen (dat). **3.** Auszeichnung f, Ehrung f. **4.** (hoher) Rang: **of ~** von Rang (u. Namen). **dis'tinc·tive** adj □ **1.** Unterscheidungs... **2.** kennzeichnend (**of** für): → **mark²** 3.

dis·tin·guish [dɪ'stɪŋgwɪʃ] **I** v/t **1.** unterscheiden (**from** von), auseinanderhalten. **2.** wahrnehmen, erkennen. **3.** kennzeichnen: **~ing mark** Kennzeichen n. **4. ~ o.s.** sich auszeichnen (a. iro.). **II** v/i **5.** unterscheiden, e-n Unterschied machen (**between** zwischen dat). **dis'tin·guished** adj **1.** hervorragend, ausgezeichnet. **2.** vornehm.

dis·tort [dɪ'stɔːt] v/t **1.** verdrehen. **2.** Gesicht etc verzerren: **~ed with** (od. **by**) **pain** schmerzverzerrt. **3.** Tatsachen etc verdrehen, entstellen, verzerren. **dis'tor·tion** s **1.** Verdrehung f. **2.** Verzerrung f. **3.** Entstellung f.

dis·tract [dɪ'strækt] v/t Aufmerksamkeit, Person etc ablenken (**from** von). **dis'tract·ed** adj □ **1.** beunruhigt, besorgt. **2.** (**with, by**) außer sich (vor dat); wahnsinnig (vor dat). **dis'trac·tion** s **1.** Ablenkung f. **2.** oft pl Zerstreuung f, Ablenkung f. **3.** Wahnsinn m: **drive s.o. to ~** j-n zur Raserei od. zum Wahnsinn treiben.

dis·traught [dɪ'strɔːt] → **distracted**.

dis·tress [dɪ'stres] **I** s **1.** Leid n, Kummer m, Sorge f. **2.** Not f, Elend n. **3.** Notlage f, -stand m. **4.** ♣ Seenot f: **in ~** in Seenot; **~ call** SOS-Ruf m. **II** v/t **5.** mit Sorge erfüllen. **dis'tressed** adj **1.** besorgt (**about** um). **2.** notleidend: **~ area** Br. Notstandsgebiet n. **dis'tress·ing** adj □ besorgniserregend.

dis·trib·ute [dɪ'strɪbjuːt] v/t **1.** ver-, austeilen (**among** unter dat od. acc; **to** an acc). **2.** zuteilen (**to** dat). **3.** ✝ Waren vertreiben, absetzen; Filme verleihen; Dividende, Gewinn ausschütten. **dis·tri'bu·tion** s **1.** Ver-, Austeilung f: **~ of seats** parl. Sitzverteilung. **2.** Zuteilung f; Gabe f, Spende f. **3.** ✝ Vertrieb m, Absatz m; Verleih m; Ausschüttung f. **dis'trib·u·tor** s **1.** Verteiler m (a. ⊚). **2.** ✝ Großhändler m; Generalvertreter m; pl (Film)Verleih m.

dis·trict ['dɪstrɪkt] s **1.** Distrikt m, (Verwaltungs)Bezirk m, Kreis m. **2.** (Stadt-)

Bezirk *m*, (-)Viertel *n*. **3.** Gegend *f*, Gebiet *n*.

dis·trust [dɪs'trʌst] **I** *s* Mißtrauen *n*: **with ~** mißtrauisch. **II** *v/t* mißtrauen (*dat*). **dis'trust·ful** [~fʊl] *adj* □ mißtrauisch (**of** gegen).

dis·turb [dɪ'stɜːb] *v/t u. v/i allg.* stören. **dis'turb·ance** *s* **1.** Störung *f* (*a.* ⊕ *etc*). **2.** *politische etc* Unruhe; Ruhestörung *f*: **cause** (*od.* **create**) **a ~** für Unruhe sorgen; ruhestörenden Lärm machen. **dis'turb·er** *s* **1.** Störer(in), Störenfried *m*. **2.** Unruhestifter(in).

dis·u·nite [ˌdɪsjuː'naɪt] *v/t u. v/i* (sich) trennen *od.* entzweien. **ˌdis·u·ni·ty** [~'nʌtɪ] *s* Uneinigkeit *f*, Zwietracht *f*.

dis·use [ˌdɪs'juːs] *s*: **fall into ~** ungebräuchlich werden. **ˌdis'used** [~zd] *adj* nicht mehr benutzt (*Maschine etc*), stillgelegt (*Bergwerk etc*), leerstehend (*Haus*).

ditch [dɪtʃ] **I** *s* **1.** Graben *m*. **II** *v/t* **2.** Gräben ziehen durch *od.* in (*dat*). **3.** *Fahrzeug* in den Straßengraben fahren. **4.** *sl. Wagen etc* stehenlassen; *j-m* entwischen; *dem Freund etc* den Laufpaß geben; *etc* wegschmeißen; *Am. die Schule* schwänzen.

dith·er ['dɪðə] **I** *v/i* **1.** (*bsd.* vor Kälte) zittern. **2.** schwanken, sich nicht entscheiden können (**between** zwischen *dat*). **3.** aufgeregt sein. **II** *s* **4.** Schwanken *n*. **5.** Aufregung *f*: **throw into a ~** in Aufregung versetzen; **be all of a ~, be in a ~,** *bsd. Br.* F **have the ~s** aufgeregt sein.

di·ur·nal [daɪ'ɜːnl] *adj* □ täglich (wiederkehrend).

di·va·gate ['daɪvəgeɪt] *v/i* abschweifen (**from** von), nicht bei der Sache bleiben.

di·van [dɪ'væn] *s* Diwan *m*: **~ (bed)** Bettcouch *f*.

dive [daɪv] **I** *v/i* **1.** tauchen (**for** nach; **into** in *acc*). **2.** (unter)tauchen (*a. U-Boot*). **3.** e-n Hecht- *od.* Kopfsprung machen; (*Wasserspringen*) springen; (*bsd. Sport*) sich werfen, hechten (**for the ball** nach dem Ball): **~ for cover** sich in Deckung werfen. **4.** ✈ e-n Sturzflug machen. **II** *s* **5.** (Unter)Tauchen *n*, ⚓ *a.* Unterwasser-, Tauchfahrt *f*. **6.** Kopfsprung *m*, Hechtsprung *m* (*a. des Tormanns etc*); (*Wasserspringen*) Sprung *m*: **make a ~ for** hechten nach; **make a**

~ for cover sich in Deckung werfen. **7.** ✈ Sturzflug *m*. **8.** F Spelunke *f*. **'div·er** *s* **1.** Taucher(in). **2.** *Sport:* Wasserspringer(in).

di·verge [daɪ'vɜːdʒ] *v/i* **1.** divergieren (*a.* A, *phys.*), auseinandergehen, -laufen. **2.** abweichen (**from** von); voneinander abweichen. **di'ver·gent** *adj* □ **1.** divergierend (*a.* A, *phys.*). **2.** abweichend (**from** von).

di·verse [daɪ'vɜːs] *adj* □ verschieden, ungleich, andersartig. **di,ver·si·fi·ca·tion** [~fɪ'keɪʃn] *s* **1.** abwechslungsreiche Gestaltung. **2.** *a.* **~ of risk** Risikoverteilung *f*. **3.** ✝ Diversifikation *f*, Diversifizierung *f*. **di'ver·si·fy** [~faɪ] *v/t* **1.** abwechslungsreich gestalten. **2.** *Risiko* verteilen. **3.** ✝ *Unternehmen* diversifizieren. **di'ver·sion** [~ʃn] *s* **1.** Ablenkung *f*. **2.** Zerstreuung *f*, Zeitvertreib *m*. **3.** *Br.* (Verkehrs)Umleitung *f*. **di'ver·si·ty** [~sətɪ] *s* Verschiedenheit *f*, Ungleichheit *f*. **di'vert** *v/t* **1.** ablenken, abwenden (**from** von), lenken (**to** auf *acc*). **2.** *Br. Verkehr* umleiten. **3.** zerstreuen, unterhalten (**with** mit, durch).

di·vide [dɪ'vaɪd] **I** *v/t* **1.** teilen (**s.th. with s.o.** et. mit j-m): **~ in halves** halbieren. **2.** (zer)teilen, spalten, *fig. a.* entzweien: **opinion is ~d** die Meinungen sind geteilt (**on** über *acc*). **3.** ver-, austeilen (**among, between** unter *dat od. acc*). **4.** A dividieren, teilen (**by** durch): **20 ~d by 5 is 4** 20 (geteilt) durch 5 ist 4; **~ 5 into 20** 20 durch 5 teilen. **II** *v/i* **5.** sich aufteilen, zerfallen (**into** in *acc*). **6.** A sich dividieren *od.* teilen lassen (**by** durch). **div·i·dend** ['dɪvɪdend] *s* **1.** A Dividend *m*. **2.** ✝ Dividende *f*. **di·vid·ers** [dɪ'vaɪdəz] *s pl*, *a.* **pair of ~** Stechzirkel *m*. **di'vid·ing** *adj* Trennungs-.

div·i·na·tion [ˌdɪvɪ'neɪʃn] *s* Weissagung *f*. **di·vine** [dɪ'vaɪn] **I** *adj* □ **1.** göttlich (*a. fig.* F), Gottes... **II** *v/t* **2.** weissagen. **3.** mit der Wünschelrute suchen (nach). **di'vin·er** *s* **1.** Wahrsager(in). **2.** (Wünschel)Rutengänger(in).

div·ing ['daɪvɪŋ] *s* **1.** Tauchen *n*. **2.** *Sport:* Wasserspringen *n*. **~ bell** *s* Taucherglocke *f*. **~ board** *s* Sprungbrett *n*. **~ hel·met** *s* Taucherhelm *m*. **~ suit** *s* Taucheranzug *m*. **~ tow·er** *s* Sprungturm *m*.

di·vin·ing rod [dɪˈvaɪnɪŋ] s Wünschelrute f.

di·vin·i·ty [dɪˈvɪnətɪ] s **1.** Göttlichkeit f. **2.** Gottheit f. **3.** Theologie f.

di·vis·i·ble [dɪˈvɪzəbl] adj □ teilbar (A by durch). **di·vi·sion** [~ʒn] s **1.** (Ver-, Aus)Teilung f. ~ of labo(u)r Arbeitsteilung. **2.** Zerteilung f, Spaltung f, fig. a. Entzweiung f. **3.** A Division f: ~ sign Teilungszeichen n. **4.** parl. Br.: Abstimmung f durch) Hammelsprung m. **5.** Abteilung f. **6.** ✕ Division f. **7.** Sport: Liga f. **di·vi·sor** [dɪˈvaɪzə] s A Divisor m, Teiler m.

di·vorce [dɪˈvɔːs] I s **1.** ⚖ (Ehe)Scheidung f: get (od. obtain) a ~ geschieden werden, sich scheiden lassen (from von). **2.** fig. (völlige) Trennung f (from von; between zwischen dat). II v/t **3.** ⚖ j-n, Ehe scheiden: ~ s.o. j-s Ehe scheiden; he has ~d his wife er hat sich (von s-r Frau) scheiden lassen. **4.** fig. (völlig) trennen (from von).

diz·zi·ness [ˈdɪzɪnɪs] s Schwindel(anfall) m. **'diz·zy** I adj □ **1.** schwind(e)lig. **2.** schwindelnd, schwindelerregend; schwindelnd hoch. II v/t **3.** schwind(e)-lig machen.

do¹ [duː] (irr) I v/t **1.** tun, machen; ausführen, Arbeiten verrichten; anfertigen, herstellen: ~ one's best sein Bestes tun, sich alle Mühe geben. **2.** j-m et. tun, zufügen, erweisen: → disservice, favo(u)r 4, etc. **3.** Speisen zubereiten; Zimmer aufräumen, machen. **5.** (her)richten: → face 1, hair. **6.** zurücklegen, schaffen: the car does 100 m.p.h. der Wagen fährt 160 km/h. **7.** F besichtigen, die Sehenswürdigkeiten besichtigen von (od. gen). **8.** F betrügen (out of um), übers Ohr hauen. **9.** F Strafe abbrummen: → time 1. II v/i **10.** handeln, sich verhalten. **11.** weiter-, vorankommen: ~ well gut abschneiden (in bei, in dat); s-e Sache gut machen. **12.** sich befinden: ~ well gesund sein; in guten Verhältnissen leben; sich gut erholen; how ~ you ~? guten Tag! (bei Vorstellung). **13.** genügen, reichen (for für). III v/t u. v/i **14.** (Ersatzverb zur Vermeidung von Wiederholungen; mst unübersetzt) you know it as well as I ~ du weißt es so gut wie ich; I take a bath. So ~ I Ich nehme ein Bad. Ich auch; he

works hard, doesn't he? er arbeitet viel, nicht wahr?; Did he buy it? He did Kaufte er es? Ja(wohl); He sold his car. Did he? Er verkaufte sein Auto. Wirklich?, So? IV v/aux **15.** in Fragesätzen: ~ you know him? kennst du ihn? **16.** in verneinten Sätzen: I ~ not believe it ich glaube es nicht. **17.** zur Verstärkung: I did like it mir gefiel es wirklich.

Verbindungen mit Präpositionen:

do| by v/i behandeln, handeln an (dat). ~ for v/i F **1.** erledigen, ruinieren. **2.** j-m den Haushalt führen; putzen bei od. für. **3.** → do¹ 13. ~ with v/t u. v/i F **1.** I can't do anything with him (it) ich kann nichts mit ihm (damit) anfangen; I won't have anything to ~ it ich will nichts damit zu tun od. schaffen haben; it has nothing to ~ you es hat nichts mit dir zu tun. **2.** auskommen od. sich begnügen mit. **3.** F he could ~ the money er kann das Geld (sehr gut) brauchen; I could ~ a glass of beer ich könnte ein Glas Bier vertragen. ~ with·out v/t **1.** auskommen od. sich behelfen ohne. **2.** verzichten auf (acc).

Verbindungen mit Adverbien:

do| a·way with v/i **1.** beseitigen: a) wegschaffen, b) abschaffen. **2.** Geld durchbringen. **3.** umbringen, töten. ~ down v/t Br. F **1.** heruntermachen, schlechtmachen. **2.** → do 8. ~ in v/t F **1.** erledigen: a) erschöpfen: I'm done in ich bin geschafft, b) zugrunde richten, ruinieren, c) um die Ecke bringen, umbringen. **2.** reinlegen, übers Ohr hauen. ~ up v/t **1.** zs.-schnüren; Päckchen etc zurechtmachen, verschnüren; einpacken; Kleid, Reißverschluß etc zumachen: do s.o. up j-m das Kleid etc zumachen; → do o.s. up sich zurechtmachen; → face 1.

do² [~] pl dos, do's [duːz] s **1.** sl. Schwindel m, Gaunerei f. **2.** fair ~s! es soll nicht unfair!; gleiches Recht für alle. **3.** ~s and don'ts F Gebote u. Verbote, (Spiel)Regeln.

doc [dɒk] F → doctor 1.

doc·ile [ˈdəʊsaɪl] adj □ **1.** fügsam, gefügig. **2.** gelehrig. **do·cil·i·ty** [~ˈsɪlətɪ] s **1.** Fügsamkeit f. **2.** Gelehrigkeit f.

dock¹ [dɒk] I s **1.** Dock n. **2.** Hafenbecken n, Anlegeplatz m. **3.** Kai m, Pier m.

4. pl Docks pl, Hafenanlagen pl. **II** v/t **5.** Schiff (ein)docken. **6.** Raumschiffe koppeln. **III** v/i **7.** docken. **8.** im Hafen od. am Kai anlegen. **9.** andocken (Raumschiff).

dock² [~] v/t **1.** Schwanz stutzen; e-m Tier den Schwanz stutzen. **2.** j-s Lohn etc kürzen: ~ £5 off (od. from) s.o.'s **wages** j-s Lohn um 5 Pfund kürzen.

dock³ [~] s 🏛 Anklagebank f: **be in the** ~ auf der Anklagebank sitzen.

dock·er ['dɒkə] s Dock-, Hafenarbeiter m, Schauermann m.

'dock·yard s Werft f.

doc·tor ['dɒktə] **I** s **1.** Doktor m, Arzt m, Ärztin f, (Anrede) Herr (Frau) Doktor: **be under the** ~ F in Behandlung sein (for wegen); ~'s **certificate** ärztliches Attest. **2.** univ. Doktor m: **2 of Divinity** (Laws, Medicine) Doktor der Theologie (Rechte, Medizin); ~'s **degree** Doktortitel m; **take one's** ~'s **degree** promovieren. **II** v/t **3.** (ärztlich) behandeln, verarzten. **4.** zs.-flicken, (notdürftig) ausbessern. **5.** a. ~ **up** F Wein etc (ver)panschen, Abrechnung etc frisieren. **'doc·tor·al** adj: ~ **thesis** → thesis 2. **doc·tor·ate** ['~rət] s Doktorwürde f, -titel m.

doc·tri·naire [ˌdɒktrɪˈneə] adj doktrinär. **doc·trine** ['~trɪn] s Doktrin f: a) Lehre f, b) bsd. pol. Grundsatz m: **party** ~ Parteiprogramm n.

doc·u·ment I s ['dɒkjʊmənt] Dokument n: a) Urkunde f, b) amtliches Schriftstück, pl Akten pl. **II** v/t ['~ment] dokumentieren, dokumentarisch od. urkundlich belegen. **doc·u·men·ta·ry** [ˌ~'mentərɪ] **I** adj ☐ **1.** dokumentarisch, urkundlich. **2.** Dokumentar...: ~ **film** → 3; ~ **novel** Tatsachenroman m. **II** s **3.** Dokumentar-, Tatsachenfilm m. ˌdoc·u·men·ta·tion s Dokumentation f.

dod·der ['dɒdə] v/i F **1.** (bsd. vor Altersschwäche) zittern. **2.** wack(e)lig gehen. **'dod·der·er** s F Tattergreis m. **'dod·der·ing, 'dod·der·y** adj F tatterig.

dodge [dɒdʒ] **I** v/i **1.** (rasch) zur Seite springen, ausweichen. **2.** Ausflüchte machen; sich drücken. **II** v/t **3.** ausweichen (dat). **4.** sich drücken vor (dat). **II** s **5.** Sprung m zur Seite. **6.** Kniff m, Trick m. **dodg·em** (**car**) ['dɒdʒəm] s (Auto)Skooter m. **'dodg·er** s **1.** gerie-

bener Kerl. **2.** Gauner m, Schwindler m. **3.** Drückeberger m. **'dodg·y** adj F **1.** verschlagen, gerieben. **2.** Br. unsicher: ~ wack(e)lig, b) riskant.

doe [dəʊ] s zo. (Reh)Geiß f.

do·er ['duːə] s Tatmensch m, Macher m. **does** [dʌz] er, sie, es tut (→ **do¹**).

'doe·skin s Rehleder n.

doesn't ['dʌznt] F = **does not** (→ **do¹**).

dog [dɒg] **I** s **1.** Hund m; engS. Rüde m: ~ **in the manger** j-d, der anderen et. mißgönnt, womit er selbst gar nichts anfangen kann; ~ **does not eat** ~ e-e Krähe hackt der anderen kein Auge aus; **go to the** ~**s** vor die Hunde gehen; **lead a** ~'**s life** ein Hundeleben führen; **let sleeping** ~**s lie** schlafende Hunde soll man nicht wecken. **2.** contp. Schuft m: **dirty** ~ Mistkerl m. **3.** F Kerl m: **lazy** ~ fauler Hund; **lucky** ~ Glückspilz m. **4.** **the** ~**s** pl Br. F das Windhundrennen. **II** v/t **5.** j-n verfolgen (a. Pech etc). **~ bis·cuit** s Hundekuchen m. **ˌ~·'cheap** adj u. adv spottbillig. **~ col·lar** s **1.** Hundehalsband n. **2.** F steifer, hoher Kragen (e-s Geistlichen). **~ days** s pl Hundstage pl. **~ ear** s Eselsohr n (in Buch etc). **'~·eared** adj mit Eselsohren.

dogged ['dɒgɪd] adj ☐ verbissen, hartnäckig.

dog·gie ['dɒgɪ] → **doggy**. **'dog·gish** adj ☐ **1.** hundeartig, Hunde... **2.** bissig; mürrisch. **dog·go** ['dɒgəʊ] adv: **lie** ~ sl. sich mäuschenstill verhalten; sich versteckt halten. **'dog·gy** s Hündchen n, (Kindersprache) Wauwau m: ~ **bag** Beutel für Essensreste, die aus e-m Restaurant mit nach Hause genommen werden.

dog·ma ['dɒgmə] pl **-mas**, **-ma·ta** ['~mətə] s Dogma n, Glaubens- od. Grund- od. (contp. starrer) Lehrsatz. **dog·mat·ic** [~'mætɪk] adj (~ally) dogmatisch.

ˌdog·'poor adj F bettelarm. **ˌ~·'tired** adj hundemüde.

doi·ly ['dɔɪlɪ] s (Zier)Deckchen n.

do·ing ['duːɪŋ] s **1.** Tun n: **it was your** ~ du hast es getan, das war Ihr Werk. **2.** pl Taten pl, Tätigkeit f, Begebenheiten pl, Vorfälle pl; Treiben n. **3.** pl (sg konstruiert) Br. F Dingsbums n.

ˌdo-it-your'self I s Heimwerken n. **II** adj Heimwerker...: ~ **kit** Heimwerkerausrüstung f; Bausatz m (für Radio etc); **~ movement** Do-it-yourself-Bewegung f. **,do-it-your'self·er** s Heimwerker m.

dol·drums ['dɒldrəmz] s pl: **be in the ~** deprimiert od. niedergeschlagen sein, Trübsal blasen.

dole [dəʊl] I s **1.** milde Gabe. **2.** a. **~ money** Br. F Stempelgeld n: **be** (od. **go**) **on the ~** stempeln gehen. II v/t **3. ~ out** sparsam ver- od. austeilen.

dole·ful ['dəʊlfʊl] adj □ traurig, (Gesicht etc a.) trübselig.

doll [dɒl] I s Puppe f (a. F hübsches, aber dummes Mädchen): **~'s house** Br. F Puppenhaus n; **~'s pram** bsd. Br. F Puppenwagen m. II v/t: **~ o.s. up** → III. III v/i: **~ up** F sich feinmachen, sich in Schale werfen.

dol·lar ['dɒlə] s Dollar m.

doll bug·gy s Am. F, **~ car·riage** s Am. Puppenwagen m. **'~·house** s Am. Puppenhaus n.

dol·lop ['dɒləp] s F **1.** Klumpen m. **2.** Schlag m (Essensportion); Am. Schuß m (Alkohol etc, a. fig. Ironie etc).

doll·y ['dɒlɪ] s **1.** Kindersprache: Püppchen n. **2.** Film, TV: Kamerawagen m. **3.** a. **~ bird** bsd. Br. F Püppchen n (hübsches, aber dummes Mädchen).

dol·phin ['dɒlfɪn] s zo. Delphin m.

dolt [dəʊlt] s Dummkopf m, Tölpel m.

do·main [dəʊ'meɪn] s Domäne f, fig. a. Gebiet n, Bereich m.

dome [dəʊm] s △ Kuppel f.

do·mes·tic [dəʊ'mestɪk] I adj (**~ally**) **1.** häuslich, Haus(halts)...: **~ appliance** Haushaltsgerät n; **~ science** ped. Hauswirtschaftslehre f; **~ servant** (od. **help**) → **6. 2.** häuslich (veranlagt). **3.** Haus...: **~ animal. 4.** inländisch, Inlands...: **~ flight** Inlandsflug m; **~ products** → **7**; **~ trade** Binnenhandel m. **5.** inner, Innen..., innenpolitisch: **~ policy** Innenpolitik f. II s **6.** Hausangestellte m, f, pl a. (Dienst)Personal n. **7.** pl **7** Landesprodukte pl, inländische Erzeugnisse pl. **do'mes·ti·cate** [‿keɪt] v/t **1.** an häusliches Leben gewöhnen. **2.** Tier zähmen.

dom·i·cile ['dɒmɪsaɪl] I s **1.** (**½** ständiger) Wohnsitz. **2. 7** Sitz m (e-r Gesellschaft); Zahlungsort m (für e-n Wechsel). II v/t **3.** ansässig od. wohnhaft machen. **4. 7** Wechsel domizilieren.

'dom·i·ciled adj ansässig, wohnhaft.

dom·i·nance ['dɒmɪnəns] s **1.** (Vor-) Herrschaft f. **2.** Macht f, Einfluß m. **'dom·i·nant** I adj □ **1.** dominierend, (vor)herrschend. **2.** beherrschend: a) bestimmend, tonangebend, b) emporragend, weithin sichtbar. II s **3. ♪** Dominante f. **dom·i·nate** ['‿neɪt] I v/t beherrschen (a. fig.): a) herrschen über (acc), b) emporragen über (acc), c) dominieren od. (vor)herrschen in (dat). II v/i dominieren, vorherrschen: **~ over** herrschen über (acc). **,dom·i'na·tion** s (Vor)Herrschaft f. **dom·i·neer** [‿'nɪə] v/i **1.** (over) despotisch herrschen (über acc). **2.** anmaßend sein od. auftreten. **,dom·i'neer·ing** adj □ **1.** tyrannisch, despotisch. **2.** anmaßend.

do·min·ion [də'mɪnjən] s **1.** (Ober)Herrschaft f; Regierungsgewalt f. **2.** (Herrschafts)Gebiet n. **3.** oft ♀ obs. Dominion n (im Commonwealth).

dom·i·no ['dɒmɪnəʊ] pl **-no(e)s** s a) pl (mst sg konstruiert) Domino(spiel) n, b) Dominostein m.

don [dɒn] v/t et. anziehen, Hut aufsetzen.

do·nate [dəʊ'neɪt] v/t schenken (a. **½**), a. Blut etc spenden (**to s.o.** j-m). **do'na·tion** s Schenkung f, Spende f.

done [dʌn] I pp von do¹. II adj **1.** getan: **it isn't ~** (od. **the ~ thing**) so et. tut man nicht, das gehört sich nicht. **2.** erledigt: **get s.th. ~** erledigen (lassen). **3.** gastr. gar: **well ~** durchgebraten. **4.** F fertig: **have ~ with** fertig sein mit (a. fig.); nichts mehr zu tun haben wollen mit; nicht mehr brauchen. **5. ~!** abgemacht!

don·key ['dɒŋkɪ] s zo. Esel m (a. fig. contp.): **~'s years** Br. F e-e Ewigkeit. **'~·work** s F Dreck(s)arbeit f.

do·nor ['dəʊnə] s Schenker(in) (a. **½**), (a. Blut- etc)Spender(in): **~('s) card** Organspenderausweis m.

don't [dəʊnt] F I = **do not** (→ **do¹**). II s pl → **do²** **3**.

doo·dle ['du:dl] I s Gekritzel n, gedankenlos hingekritzelte Figur(en pl). II v/i Männchen malen.

doom [du:m] I s Schicksal n, Geschick n, Verhängnis n: **he met his ~** sein Schicksal ereilte ihn. II v/t verurteilen, verdammen (beide a. fig.): **~ed to failure** (od. **to fail**) zum Scheitern verurteilt.

dooms·day ['du:mzdeɪ] s Jüngstes Gericht, Jüngster Tag.

door [dɔː] s 1. Tür f: *from ~ to ~* von Haus zu Haus; *out of ~s* ins Freie, hinaus; im Freien, draußen; *two ~s down the street* zwei Häuser weiter; *bang* (od. *close, shut*) *the ~ on* j-n abweisen; *et.* unmöglich machen; *lay s.th. at s.o.'s ~* j-m et. zur Last legen; *show s.o. the ~* j-m die Tür weisen. 2. Tor n, Pforte f (*to* zu) (*beide a. fig.*). '**~·bell** s Türklingel f, -glocke f: *ring the ~* (an der Tür) klingeln *od.* läuten. **~·chain** s Sicherheitskette f. '**~·frame** s Türrahmen m. **~·han·dle** s Türgriff m, -klinke f. '**~·keep·er** s Pförtner m. '**~·knock·er** s Türklopfer m. '**~·man** s (*irr man*) (livrierter) Portier. **~·mat** s (Fuß)Abtreter m. '**~·plate** s Türschild n. '**~·post** s Türpfosten m. '**~·step** s Türstufe f: *at* (*od. on*) *s.o.'s ~* vor j-s Tür (*a. fig.*). **~·to-** adj von Haus zu Haus; *Verkauf* an der Haustür: *~ collection* Haussammlung f; *~ salesman* Hausierer m; Vertreter m. '**~·way** s Türöffnung f. 2. *fig.* Weg m (*to* zu). '**~·yard** s Am. Vorgarten m.

dope [dəʊp] I s 1. F Stoff m (*Rauschgift*). 2. a) *Sport:* Dopingmittel n, b) Betäubungsmittel n. 3. F sl. a) Trottel m, b) *oft inside ~* (vertrauliche) Informationen pl, Geheimtip (s pl) m, b) *allg.* Information(en pl) f, Material n. II v/t 5. F j-m Stoff geben. 6. a) *Sport:* dopen, b) *Getränk etc* präparieren, ein Betäubungsmittel untermischen (*dat*). **~ ad·dict, ~·fiend** s F Rauschgiftsüchtige(r) m, f. **~·test** s *Sport:* Dopingkontrolle f.

dop·ey ['dəʊpɪ] adj F 1. benommen, benebelt. 2. dämlich, doof.

dorm [dɔːm] F → *dormitory.*

dor·mant ['dɔːmənt] adj 1. schlafend. 2. *fig.* ruhend (*a. Vulkan*). untätig. 3. *fig.* schlummernd, verborgen, latent: *lie ~* schlummern.

dor·mer ['dɔːmə] s a) (Dach)Gaupe f, (-)Gaube f, b) *a. ~ window* stehendes Dachfenster.

dor·mi·to·ry ['dɔːmɪtrɪ] s 1. Schlafsaal m. 2. (*bsd.* Studenten)Wohnheim n. **~ sub·urb, ~ town** s Schlafstadt f.

dor·sal ['dɔːsl] adj Rücken...: **~ fin** Rückenflosse f.

dos·age ['dəʊsɪdʒ] s 1. Dosierung f. 2.

→ *dose* 1. **dose** [dəʊs] I s 1. ₰ Dosis f (*a. fig.*). II v/t 2. *Arznei etc* dosieren. 3. *j-m* Arznei geben.

doss [dɒs] *bsd. Br. sl.* I s 1. Schlafplatz m. 2. Schlaf m. 3. Penne f. II v/i 4. *oft ~ down* pennen. '**doss·er** s *bsd. Br. sl.* 1. Pennbruder m. 2. Penne f.

'**doss·house** s *bsd. Br. sl.* Penne f.

dos·si·er ['dɒsɪeɪ] s Dossier n, Akten pl: *keep a ~ on* ein Dossier angelegt haben über (*acc*).

dot [dɒt] I s 1. Punkt m, Pünktchen n; Tupfen m: *on the ~* F auf die Sekunde pünktlich; *at 8 o'clock on the ~* F Punkt 8 Uhr; → *year.* II v/t 2. punktieren, pünkteln: *sign on the ~ted line* unterschreiben; (formell *od.* bedingungslos) zustimmen. 3. sprenkeln, übersäen (*with* mit).

dot·age ['dəʊtɪdʒ] s 1. Senilität f: *be in one's ~* kindisch *od.* senil sein. 2. Vernarrtheit f (*on* in *acc*). **dote** [dəʊt] v/i vernarrt sein (*on* in *acc*). '**dot·ing** adj □ 1. vernarrt (*on* in *acc*). 2. kindisch, senil.

dou·ble ['dʌbl] I adj □ 1. doppelt, Doppel..., zweifach: *~ bottom* doppelter Boden; *~ murder* Doppelmord m. 2. Doppel..., verdoppelt, verstärkt: *~ beer* Starkbier n. 3. Doppel... (*für 2 bestimmt*): *~ bed* Doppelbett n; *~ room* Doppel-, Zweibettzimmer n. 4. zweideutig. II adv 5. doppelt: *~ as long* noch einmal so lang. 6. doppelt, zweifach: *play* (*at*) *~ or quit*(*s*) alles riskieren *od.* aufs Spiel setzen; *see ~* doppelt sehen. III s 7. *das* Doppelte *od.* Zweifache. 8. Doppel n, Duplikat n. 9. Doppelgänger(in). 10. *Film, TV:* Double n. 11. *mst pl Tennis etc:* Doppel n: *a ~s match* ein Doppel; *men's ~s* Herrendoppel. IV v/t 12. verdoppeln. 13. *oft ~ up* Papier etc kniffen, falten, *Bettdecke etc* um-, zurückschlagen; zs.-falten, -legen. 14. ⚓ umschiffen. 15. *Film, TV: j-n* doubeln. V v/i 16. sich verdoppeln. 17. sich (zs.-)falten (lassen): *~ up with* sich krümmen vor (*dat*). 18. plötzlich kehrtmachen; e-n Haken schlagen. '**~·bar·rel(l)ed** adj 1. doppelläufig: *~ gun* Doppelflinte f, Zwilling m. 2. zweifach: *~ name* Doppelname m. 3. zweideutig. **~ bend** s S-Kurve f. **~·breast·ed** adj zweireihig (*Anzug*).

downstream

~ check *s* genaue Nachprüfung. **,~·'check** *v/t u. v/i* genau nachprüfen. **~ chin** *s* Doppelkinn *n*. **~ cross** *s* F doppeltes *od.* falsches Spiel. **,~·'cross** *v/t* F ein doppeltes *od.* falsches Spiel treiben mit. **,~·'deal·er** *s* Betrüger *m*. **,~·'deal·ing** *adj* betrügerisch. **II** *s* Betrug *m*. **,~·'deck·er** *s* **1.** Doppeldecker *m* (*Autobus, Flugzeug etc*). **2.** F Etagenbett *n*; Doppelsandwich *n*. **~ Dutch** *s* F Kauderwelsch *n*. **,~·'edged** *adj* **1.** zweischneidig (*a. fig.*). **2.** *fig.* zweideutig. **'~-faced** *adj* heuchlerisch; doppelzüngig. **~ fea·ture** *s* Doppelprogramm *n* (*2 Spielfilme in jeder Vorstellung*). **~ life** *s* (*irr life*) Doppelleben *n*. **,~·'park** *v/t u. v/i mot.* in zweiter Reihe parken. **,~·'quick I** *s* → **double time**s**1**. **II** *adj*: **in ~ time** → III. **III** *adv* F im Eiltempo, fix. **~ stand·ard** *s*: **apply ~s** mit zweierlei Maß messen. **~ talk** *s* hinhaltendes *od.* nichtssagendes Gerede; doppelzüngiges Gerede; Augen(aus)wischerei *f*. **~ time** *s* **1.** ✕ *Am.* Schnellschritt *m*: **in ~** F im Eiltempo, fix. **2.** doppelter Lohn (*für Feiertagsarbeit etc*).

doubt [daʊt] **I** *v/i* **1.** zweifeln (**of** an e-r Sache). **2.** Bedenken haben. **II** *v/t* **3.** bezweifeln (**a. that** daß), anzweifeln. **4.** mißtrauen (*dat*). **III** *s* **5.** Zweifel *m* (**of** an *dat*; **about** hinsichtlich): **no** (*od.* **without, beyond**) **~** zweifellos, fraglos; **be in ~** Zweifel haben (**about** an *dat*); ungewiß sein; unschlüssig sein; **cast** (*od.* **throw**) **~ on** et. in Zweifel ziehen; **if** (*od.* **when**) **in ~** im Zweifelsfall; **leave no ~s about** keinen Zweifel lassen an (*dat*). **'doubt·er** *s* Zweifler(in). **doubt·ful** [ʹ~fʊl] *adj* □ **1.** *allg.* zweifelhaft. **2. be ~ of** (*od.* **about**) zweifeln an (*dat*), im Zweifel sein über (*acc*). **'doubt·less** *adv* zweifellos, sicherlich.

dough [dəʊ] *s* **1.** Teig *m*. **2.** *bsd. Am. sl.* Kohlen *pl* (*Geld*). **'~·nut** *s* Krapfen *m*, Berliner (Pfannkuchen).

dough·y [ʹdəʊɪ] *adj* **1.** teigig. **2.** *fig.* teigig, wächsern (*Gesicht*).

dour [dʊə] *adj* **1.** mürrisch. **2.** hart, streng. **3.** hartnäckig, halsstarrig.

douse [daʊs] *v/t* **1.** ins Wasser tauchen, eintauchen, *Wäsche etc* einweichen; Wasser schütten über (*acc*). F *Licht* ausmachen.

dove [dʌv] *s* **1.** *orn.* Taube *f*: **~ of peace** *fig.* Friedenstaube *f*. **2.** *pol.* Taube *f* (*gemäßigter Politiker*).

dow·dy [ʹdaʊdɪ] *adj* □ nachlässig gekleidet; unelegant; unmodern.

dow·el [ʹdaʊəl] *s* ◎ Dübel *m*.

down¹ [daʊn] **I** *adv* **1.** nach unten, her-, hinunter, abwärts, (*in Kreuzworträtseln*) senkrecht. **2. go ~ to the country** (*von London*) aufs Land fahren. **3. ~ with ...!** nieder mit ...! **4.** (dr)unten: **~ there** dort unten; **~ under** F in *od.* nach Australien *od.* Neuseeland (→ **down under**). **5.** untergegangen (*Sonne etc*). **6.** gefallen (*Preise, Thermometer etc*): **~ by 10 degrees** um 10 Grad gefallen. **7.** niedergeschlagen, down: → **mouth** 1. **8.** bettlägerig: **be ~ with influenza** mit Grippe im Bett liegen. **9. they were 2 points (goals) ~** (*Sport*) sie lagen 2 Punkte (Tore) zurück. **II** *adj* **10.** nach unten (gerichtet), Abwärts... **11.** von London abfahrend *od.* kommend: **~ platform** Abfahrtsbahnsteig *m* (*in London*). **II** *prp* **12.** her-, hinunter: **~ the river** flußabwärts. **IV** *s* **13. have a ~ on** F *j-n* auf dem Kieker haben. **V** *v/t* **14.** zu Fall bringen (*a. Sport u. fig.*). **15.** niederlegen: **~ tools** die Arbeit niederlegen. **16.** *Flugzeug* abschießen. **17.** F *Getränk* runterkippen.

down² [~] *s* **1.** *orn.* Daunen *pl*: **~ quilt** Daunendecke *f*. **2.** (*a. Bart*)Flaum *m*.

'down·cast *adj* niedergeschlagen: a) gesenkt (*Blick*), b) deprimiert. **'~·fall** *s* **1.** *fig.* Sturz *m*. **2.** starker Regenguß, Platzregen *m*, *a.* starker Schneefall. **'~·grade** *v/t* **1.** niedriger einstufen. **2.** degradieren. **,~·'heart·ed** *adj* □ niedergeschlagen, entmutigt. **,~·'hill I** *adv* **1.** abwärts, bergab (*beide a. fig.*), den Berg hinunter: **he is going ~** es geht bergab mit ihm; **the rest was ~** (**all the way**) alles andere ging wie von selbst. **II** *adj* **2.** abschüssig. **3.** *Skisport:* Abfahrts...: **~ race** Abfahrtslauf *m*. **~ pay·ment** *s* **1.** Barzahlung *f*. **2.** Anzahlung *f*. **'~·pour** *s* Platzregen *m*. **'~·right** *adj u. adv* völlig, absolut, ausgesprochen: **a ~ lie** e-e glatte Lüge. **'~·stairs I** *adv* **1.** die Treppe her- *od.* hinunter, nach unten. **2.** unten, in e-m unteren Stockwerk. **3.** e-e Treppe tiefer. **II** *adj* [ʹ~steəz] **4.** im unteren Stockwerk (gelegen), unter. **,~·'stream** *adv* fluß-

ab(wärts). **~-to-'earth** *adj* realistisch.
~·town *Am.* **I** *adv* [**,~'taʊn**] im *od.* ins
Geschäftsviertel. **II** *adj* [**'~taʊn**] im Geschäftsviertel (gelegen *od.* tätig): **in ~**
Los Angeles in der Innenstadt von Los
Angeles. **III** *s* [**'~taʊn**] Geschäftsviertel
n, Innenstadt *f*, City *f*. **'~,trod·den** *adj*
unterdrückt. **~ un·der** *s* **†** F Australien *n*;
Neuseeland *n*.

down·ward ['daʊnwəd] **I** *adv* **1.** nach
unten: **face ~** mit dem Gesicht nach
unten. **2.** *fig.* abwärts, bergab: **he went
~ in life** es ging bergab mit ihm. **3.** *from
... ~* (*zeitlich*) von ... ab, seit. **II** *adj*
Abwärts..., (*Preise*) sinkend. **down·**
wards ['~wədz] → **downward** I.

down·y ['daʊnɪ] *adj* **1.** Daunen... **2.** flaumig.

dow·ry ['daʊərɪ] *s* Mitgift *f*, Aussteuer *f*.

dowse¹ → **douse**.

dowse² [daʊz] *v/i* mit der Wünschelrute
(Wasser *etc*) suchen. **'dows·er** *s* (Wün-
schel)Rutengänger *m*. **'dows·ing rod** *s*
Wünschelrute *f*.

doy·en ['dɔɪən] *s* **1.** Rangälteste *m*. **2.**
Doyen *m*. **3.** Nestor *m*.

doze [dəʊz] **I** *v/i* dösen, ein Nickerchen
machen *od.* halten: **~ off** einnicken, -dö-
sen. **II** *s* Nickerchen *n*: **have a ~** → I.

doz·en ['dʌzn] *s* Dutzend *n*: **~s of times**
F x-mal; **do one's daily ~** F Früh-
Morgengymnastik machen; **talk nine-
teen** (*od.* **twenty, forty**) **to the ~** *Br.* wie
ein Wasserfall reden; → **baker**.

doz·y ['dəʊzɪ] *adj* □ **1.** schläfrig, verschlafen, dösig. **2.** *Br.* F schwer von
Begriff.

drab [dræb] *adj* **1.** graubraun. **2.** *fig.*
trist: a) grau (*Stadt etc*), b) düster (*Farben etc*), c) langweilig (*Abend etc*), d)
freudlos (*Dasein etc*).

Dra·co·ni·an [drə'kəʊnjən] *adj* drakonisch.

draft [drɑːft] **I** *s* **1.** Entwurf *m*. **2.** (Luft-
etc)Zug *m*: **feel the draught** *Br.* F den
Wind im Gesicht spüren. **3.** **make a ~**
on Geld abheben von; *fig.* in Anspruch
nehmen. **4.** **†** Tratte *f*, Wechsel *m*. **5.**
✕ *Am.* Einberufung *f*, Einziehung *f*. **6.**
→ **draught** I. **II** *v/t* **7.** entwerfen,
Schriftstück abfassen. **8.** ✕ *Am.* einziehen (**into** zu), einberufen.

drafts·man ['drɑːftsmən] *s* (*irr* **man**)
1. j-d, der *et.* entwirft *od.* aufsetzt.

2. ⊚ (Konstruktions)Zeichner *m*.

draft·y ['drɑːftɪ] *adj* zugig.

drag [dræg] **I** *s* **1.** Schleppen *n*, Zerren *n*.
2. Hemmschuh *m* (*a. fig. on* für). **3.** F a)
et. Langweiliges *n*: Lästiges: **be a ~**
langweilig sein; **what a ~!** so ein Mist!,
b) Langweiler *m*; lästiger Kerl. **4.** *Am.* F
Einfluß *m*: **use one's ~** s-e Beziehungen spielen lassen. **5.** F Zug *m* (**at, on** an
e-r Zigarette etc): **give a ~** laß mich
mal ziehen. **6.** F (*von Männern, bsd. von
Transvestiten, getragene*) Frauenklei-
dung. **II** *v/t* **7.** schleppen, zerren, schleifen, ziehen; → **mire, mud** 2. **8.** **~ one's
feet** a) schlurfen, b) *a.* **~ one's heels**
fig. sich Zeit lassen (**over, in, about**
mit, bei). **9.** *fig.* hineinziehen (**into** in
acc). **10.** F j-n langweilen; j-m lästig
sein. **III** *v/i* **11.** (am Boden) schleppen
od. schleifen. **12.** → **drag behind**. **13.**
zerren *od.* ziehen (**at** an). **14.** F ziehen (**at, on**
an *e-r Zigarette etc*).
Verbindungen mit Adverbien:

drag| a·long I *v/t* wegschleppen, -zer-
ren. **II** *v/i* sich dahinschleppen. **~ a·way**
v/t → **drag along** I: **drag o.s. away
from** *fig.* sich losreißen von. **~ be·hind**
v/i zurückbleiben, nachhinken. **~ down**
v/t **1.** herunter-, hinunterziehen; *fig.* in
den Schmutz ziehen. **2.** *fig.* zermürbe
(*Krankheit etc*); entmutigen. **~ in** *v/t* **1.**
herein-, hineinziehen. **2.** *fig.* (mit) hineinziehen. **~ off** *v/t* → **drag along** I:
drag s.o. off to a party j-n auf e-e
Party schleppen. **~ on I** *v/t* weiter-
schleppen. **II** *v/i fig.* sich dahinschleppen; sich in die Länge ziehen: **the
speech dragged on for two hours** die
Rede zog sich über zwei Stunden hin. **~
out** *v/t* **1.** heraus-, hinausziehen. **2.** *fig.*
hinausziehen, in die Länge ziehen. **~ up**
v/t **1.** hochziehen. **2.** F *Kind* lieblos aufziehen. **3.** F *Skandal etc* ausgraben.

dra·gée [dræ'ʒeɪ] *s* Dragée *n* (*a. pharm.*).

'drag·lift *s* Schlepplift *m*. **'~·net** *s* **1.**
Schleppnetz *n*: **~ operation** Schlepp-
netzfahndung *f*. **2.** *fig.* Netz *n* (*der Polizei etc*).

drag·on ['drægən] *s* Drache *m*. **'~·fly** *s*
zo. Libelle *f*.

drain [dreɪn] **I** *v/t* **1.** a. **~ off** (*od.* **away**)
Flüssigkeit abfließen lassen: **~ off** ab-
tropfen lassen; *Gemüse* abgießen. **2.** ✵
Eiter etc drainieren. **3.** austrinken, lee-

ren: → *dreg* 1. **4.** *Land* entwässern. **5.** *Gebäude etc* kanalisieren. **6.** *j-n, Vorräte etc* erschöpfen. **II** *v/i* **7.** ~ **off** (*od. away*) abfließen, ablaufen. **8.** leerlaufen. **9.** abtropfen. **10.** *a.* ~ **away** *fig.* dahinschwinden. **III** *s* **11.** → *drainage* 1–3. **12.** Abzugskanal *m*, Entwässerungsgraben *m*. **13.** *pl* Kanalisation *f*. **14.** *fig.* Abfluß *m*. **15.** *fig.* Belastung *f* (*on gen*). **'drain·age** *s* **1.** Ableitung *f* 2. Abfließen *n*, Ablaufen *n*. **3.** Entwässerung *f*. **4.** Kanalisation *f*. **5.** 🏥 Drainage *f*.

'drain·pipe *s* **1.** Abflußrohr *n*: ~ **trousers** → 3. **2.** Fallrohr *n* (*der Dachrinne*). **3.** *pl, a.* **pair of ~s** F Röhrenhose(n *pl*) *f*.

drake [dreɪk] *s orn.* Enterich *m*, Erpel *m*.

dram [dræm] *s* F Schluck *m* (*Alkohol*): **be fond of a** ~ gern einen trinken.

dra·ma ['drɑːmə] *s* Drama *m* (*a. fig.*): ~ **critic** Theaterkritiker(in); ~ **school** Schauspielschule *f*. **dra·mat·ic** [drə'mætɪk] **I** *adj* (~**ally**) **1.** dramatisch (*a. ♪ u. fig.*), Schauspiel..., Theater...: ~ **critic** Theaterkritiker(in). **2.** *fig.* drastisch (*Veränderungen etc*); aufsehenerregend (*Rede etc*). **II** *s pl* **3.** (*a. sg konstruiert*) Dramaturgie *f*. **4.** theatralisches Getue.

dram·a·tis per·so·nae [ˌdrɑːmətɪspɜː'səʊnaɪ] *s pl* Personen *pl* der Handlung.

dram·a·tist ['dræmətɪst] *s* Dramatiker *m*. **dram·a·tize** ['--taɪz] *v/t* dramatisieren: a) für die Bühne bearbeiten, b) *fig.* aufbauschen, (*a. v/i*) übertreiben.

drank [dræŋk] *pret von* **drink.**

drape [dreɪp] *v/t* **1.** drapieren (**with** mit): a) (mit Stoff) behängen, b) in (dekorative) Falten legen. **2.** *Mantel etc* hängen (**over** über *acc*). **'drap·er** *s Br.* Textilkaufmann *m*. **'drap·er·y** *s* **1.** Textilien *pl.* **2.** *bsd. Am.* Vorhänge *pl*, Vorhangstoffe *pl*.

dras·tic ['dræstɪk] *adj* (~**ally**) drastisch.

draught [drɑːft] **I** *s* **1.** Zug *m*, Schluck *m*: **at a** ~ in einem Zug. **2.** *beer on* ~, ~ *beer* Bier *n* vom Faß, Faßbier. **3.** *Br.a)* *pl* (*sg konstruiert*) Dame(spiel *n*) *f*, b) → *draughtsman* 1. **4.** *a) bsd. Br.* für *draft* 2, b) *selten bsd. Br.* für *draft* 1. **II** *v/t* **5.** *selten bsd. Br.* für *draft* 7. **'~·board** *s Br.* Damebrett *n*.

draughts·man *s* (*irr man*) **1.** ['drɑːfts-

mæn] *Br.* Damestein *m*. **2.** ['drɑːftsmən] *selten bsd. Br.* für **draftsman.**

draught·y ['drɑːftɪ] *bsd. Br.* für **drafty.**

draw [drɔː] **I** *s* **1.** Ziehen *n*; Zug *m* (*a. an der Pfeife etc*). **2.** Ziehung *f*, Verlosung *f*. **3.** *fig.* Zugkraft *f*. **4.** *fig.* Attraktion *f* (*a. Person*), Zugstück *n*. **5.** *Sport:* Unentschieden *n*: **end in a** ~ unentschieden ausgehen. **II** *v/t* (*irr*) **6.** *Waffe, Zahn etc, fig.* Schluß *etc* ziehen; *Vorhänge* auf- *od.* zuziehen; *Bogen* spannen: ~ **s.o. into** *fig.* j-n hineinziehen in (*acc*). **7.** bringen (**on** über *acc*): ~ **s.o's anger on o.s.** sich j-s Zorn zuziehen. **8.** *Atem* holen: ~ **a sigh** aufseufzen. **9.** *Tee* ziehen lassen. **10.** auslosen. **11.** *fig.* anziehen: **feel** ~**n to**(**ward**[**s**]) *s.o.* sich zu j-m hingezogen fühlen. **12.** *Linie, Grenze etc, fig.* Vergleich *etc* ziehen. **13.** zeichnen. **14.** *Schriftstück* abfassen, aufsetzen; *Scheck* ausstellen, *Wechsel a.* ziehen (**on** auf *acc*). **15.** *Geld* abheben (**from** von); *Rente etc* beziehen. **16.** entlocken (**from** *dat*): ~ **applause** Beifall hervorrufen; ~ (**information from**) *s.o.* j-n aushorchen. **17.** entnehmen (**from** *dat*): ~ **consolation from** Trost schöpfen aus; ~ **inspiration from** sich Anregung holen von *od.* bei *od.* durch. **III** *v/i* (*irr*) **18.** ziehen (*a. Tee, Kamin etc*). **19.** (**to**) sich nähern (*dat*), herankommen (**an** *acc*): → *end* 8. **20.** (**on**) in Anspruch nehmen (*acc*), Gebrauch machen (**von**), (*Vorräte etc*) angreifen. **21.** *Sport:* unentschieden kämpfen *od.* spielen (**with** gegen), sich unentschieden trennen. **22.** losen (**for** um).

Verbindungen mit Adverbien:

draw| a·part *v/t* auseinanderziehen. **II** *v/i* sich entfernen (**from** von), sich voneinander entfernen, *fig. a.* sich auseinanderleben. ~ **a·side** *v/t* j-n beiseite nehmen. ~ **a·way I** *v/t* **1.** wegziehen. **2.** *j-s Aufmerksamkeit* ablenken. **II** *v/i* **3.** sich entfernen; (*Sport*) sich lösen (**from** von). ~ **down** *v/t* **1.** herabziehen, *Jalousien* herunterlassen. **2.** → *draw* 7. ~ **in I** *v/t* **1.** *Luft* einziehen, *j-n* (mit) hineinziehen. **II** *v/i* **3.** einfahren (*Zug*), vorfahren (*Wagen etc*). **4.** zu Ende gehen (*Tag*); abnehmen, kürzer werden (*Tage*). ~ **off** *v/t Handschuhe etc* ausziehen. ~ **on** *v/t Handschuhe etc* anziehen. ~ **out I** *v/t* **1.** herausziehen. **2.** *fig.* Aussage *etc* herausholen (*of, from* aus); *j-n* aushorchen. **3.** *fig.* hinausziehen, in die Länge ziehen. **II** *v/i* **4.** länger werden (*Tage*). **~ up I** *v/t* **1.** aufrichten. **2.** *Schriftstück* abfassen, aufsetzen. **II** *v/i* **3.** (an)halten (*Wagen etc*). **4.** vorfahren (**to** vor dat).

'**draw**|**·back** *s* Nachteil *m* (**to** für). '**~·bridge** *s* Zugbrücke *f*.

draw·ee [drɔː'iː] *s* ✝ Bezogene *m*.

draw·er [*1, 2:* drɔː; *3, 4:* 'drɔːə] *s* **1.** Schublade *f*, -fach *n* **2.** *pl, a.* **pair of ~s** Unterhose *f*. **3.** Zeichner *m*. **4.** ✝ Aussteller *m*.

draw·ing ['drɔːɪŋ] *s* **1.** Zeichnen *n*. **2.** Zeichnung *f*. **~·block** *s* Zeichenblock *m*. **~ board** *s* Reiß-, Zeichenbrett *n*: **go back to the ~** *fig.* noch einmal von vorne anfangen. **~ pin** *s Br.* Reißzwecke *f*, -nagel *m*. **~ room** *s* Gesellschaftszimmer *n*, Salon *m*.

drawl [drɔːl] **I** *v/t u. v/i* gedehnt *od.* schleppend sprechen. **II** *s* gedehntes Sprechen.

drawn [drɔːn] **I** *pp von* **draw**. **II** *adj Sport:* unentschieden: **~ game** Unentschieden *n*.

dread [dred] **I** *v/t et., j-n* sehr fürchten, sich fürchten (**to do, doing** zu tun), (große) Angst haben *od.* sich fürchten vor (*dat*). **II** *s* (große) Angst, Furcht *f* (**of** vor *dat*). **dread·ful** ['~fʊl] *adj* □ furchtbar, schrecklich (*beide a. fig.* F). **II** *s* → **penny dreadful.**

dream [driːm] **I** *s* **1.** Traum *m*: **have a ~ about** etwas träumen; *pleasant* **~s!** träum was Schönes! **2.** *fig.* Traum *m*: a) Wunschtraum *m*: **that's beyond my wildest ~s** das übertrifft m-e kühnsten Träume, b) Ideal *n*: **a ~ of a hat** ein Gedicht von e-m Hut; **a perfect ~** traumhaft schön. **II** *v/i* (*a. irr*) **3.** träumen (**of, about** von) (*a. fig.*): **~ of doing s.th.** davon träumen, et. zu tun; daran denken, et. zu tun. **III** *v/t* (*a. irr*) **4.** träumen (*a. fig.*): **~ away** verträumen; **~ up** F sich ausdenken *od.* einfallen lassen. '**dream·er** *s* Träumer(in) (*a. fig.*).

dream read·er *s* Traumdeuter(in).

dreamt [dremt] *pret u. pp von* **dream.**

dream·y ['driːmɪ] *adj* □ **1.** verträumt (*a. Augen*), träumerisch. **2.** dunkel, verschwommen (*Erinnerung*). **3.** zum Träumen: **~ music.**

drear·y ['drɪərɪ] *adj* □ **1.** trübselig (*Ort etc*). **2.** trüb (*Tag etc*). **3.** langweilig (*Person, Arbeit etc*).

dredge¹ [dredʒ] ☉ **I** *s* Bagger *m*. **II** *v/t* ausbaggern.

dredge² [~] *v/t* **1.** bestreuen (**with** mit). **2.** *Mehl etc* streuen (**over** über *acc*).

dredg·er¹ ['dredʒə] *s* ☉ Bagger *m*.

dredg·er² [~] *s* Streubüchse *f*, Streuer *m*.

dreg [dreg] *s mst pl* **1.** (Boden)Satz *m*: **drain to the ~s** bis auf den letzten Tropfen *od.* bis zur Neige leeren. **2.** *fig.* Abschaum *m.*

drench [drentʃ] *v/t* durchnässen: **~ed in tears** in Tränen aufgelöst; → **skin** 1.

dress [dres] **I** *s* **1.** Kleidung *f*. **2.** (Damen)Kleid *n.* **II** *v/t* **1.** an-, bekleiden, anziehen: **~ o.s., get ~ed** sich anziehen; → **kill** 9. **4.**, einkleiden. **5.** schmücken, dekorieren. **6.** zurechtmachen, (her-)richten, *bsd. Speisen* zubereiten; *Salat* anmachen; *Haar* frisieren. **7.** ✚ *Wunde etc* verbinden. **III** *v/i* **8.** sich anziehen: **~ well** (*badly*) *weitS.* sich geschmackvoll (geschmacklos) kleiden.

Verbindungen mit Adverbien:

dress| **down I** *v/t* F *j-m* e-e Standpauke halten, *j-m* aufs Dach steigen. **II** *v/i* sich unauffällig kleiden. **~ up** *v/t* **1.** feinmachen; herausputzen. **2.** *Fakten etc* verpacken (**in** in *acc*); beschönigen; ausschmücken (**with** mit). **II** *v/i* **3.** sich feinmachen; sich herausputzen. **4.** sich kostümieren *od.* verkleiden (**as** als).

dress| **cir·cle** *s thea. etc* erster Rang. **~ coat** *s* Frack *m*.

dress·er ['dresə] *s* **1.** *thea.* Garderobiere *f*. **2.** **be a fashionable ~** immer modisch gekleidet sein. **3.** Küchen-, Geschirrschrank *m*. **4.** → **dressing table.**

dress·ing ['dresɪŋ] *s* **1.** Ankleiden *n*. **2.** Zubereitung *f*. **3.** Dressing *n* (*Salatsoße*). **4.** ✚ Verband *m*. **~·down** *s* F Standpauke *f*: **give** *s.o.* **a ~** → **dress down** I; **get a ~** eins aufs Dach bekommen. **~ gown** *s* Morgenmantel *m*, (*für Damen a.*) Morgenrock *m*. **~ room** *s* Ankleidezimmer *n*; (Künstler)Garderobe *f*; (*Sport*) (Umkleide)Kabine *f*. **~ ta·ble** *s* Toilettentisch *m*, Frisierkommode *f*.

'**dress**| **mak·er** *s* (*bsd.* Damen)Schneider(in). **~ re·hears·al** *s thea.* Generalprobe *f* (*a. fig.*); Kostümprobe *f*. **~ shirt** *s* Frackhemd *n*. ~ **suit** *s* Abend-, Gesellschaftsanzug *m*.

dress·y ['dresɪ] *adj* □ F **1.** geschniegelt, aufgetakelt. **2.** elegant, schick.

drew [druː] *pret von* **draw**.

drib·ble ['drɪbl] I *v/i* **1.** tröpfeln: ~ *away fig.* allmählich zu Ende gehen (*Geld etc*). **2.** sabbern, geifern. **3.** *Sport:* dribbeln: ~ *past j-n* umdribbeln. II *v/t* **4.** tröpfeln lassen, träufeln. III *s* **5.** → **drib(b)let.** **6.** *Sport:* Dribbling *n*.

drib·(b)let ['drɪblɪt] *s* kleine Menge *od.* Summe: **in** (*od.* **by**) ~s in kleinen Mengen *od.* Raten.

dribs and drabs [drɪbz] *s pl:* **in** ~ F kleckerweise.

dried [draɪd] *adj* Dörr..., getrocknet: ~ *fruit* Dörrobst *n*; ~ *milk* Trockenmilch *f.*

dri·er ['draɪə] *s* Trockenapparat *m*, Trockner *m*.

drift [drɪft] I *s* **1.** Treiben *n*; *fig.* (Sich-)Treibenlassen *n*, Ziellosigkeit *f*. **2.** ✓, ⚓ Abtrift *f*. **3.** *fig.* Strömung *f*, Tendenz *f*; Absicht *f*; Gedankengang *m*. **4.** (*Schnee*)Verwehung *f*, (*Schnee-*, *Sand-*)Wehe *f*. II *v/i* **5.** getrieben werden, treiben (*a. fig. mic*: in *e-n Krieg etc*): **let things** ~ den Dingen ihren Lauf lassen. **6.** *fig.* sich (willenlos) treiben lassen. **7.** sich häufen (*Sand, Schnee*). III *v/t* **8.** (dahin)treiben. **'drift·er** *s* ziellos herumwandernder Mensch.

drift| ice *s* Treibeis *n*. **'~·wood** *s* Treibholz *n*.

drill¹ [drɪl] I *s* **1.** ⚙ Bohrer *m*. **2.** ✗ Drill *m* (*a. fig.*); Exerzieren *n*. II *v/t* **3.** *Loch* bohren (*in* in *acc*). **4.** ✗ drillen (*a. fig. in* in *dat*). **5.** ~ *s.th. into s.o.* j-m et. eindrillen *od.* einpauken. III *v/i* **6.** bohren (*for* nach).

drill² [~] *s* Drillich *m*.

drink [drɪŋk] I *s* **1.** Getränk *n*; *coll.* Getränke *pl.* **2.** das Trinken, der Alkohol: **take to** ~ sich das Trinken angewöhnen. **3.** Schluck *m*. II *v/t* (*irr*) **4.** trinken, (*Tier a.*) saufen: ~ *away Geld etc* vertrinken; *Sorgen etc* im Alkohol ertränken; ~ *down j-n* unter den Tisch trinken; ~ *in fig.* (gierig) in sich aufnehmen, verschlingen; ~ *off* (*od.* *up*) austrinken; → *table.* **5.** trinken *od.* anstoßen auf (*acc*): → *health* 3. III *v/i* (*irr*) **6.** trinken, *weitS. a.* (ein) Trinker sein, (*Tier a.*) saufen: ~ *off* (*od.* *up*) austrinken. **7.**

trinken, anstoßen (*to* auf *acc*): ~ *to s.o.* j-m zuprosten *od.* zutrinken; → *health* 3. **'drink·a·ble** *adj* trinkbar, Trink... **'drink·er** *s* **1.** Trinkende *m, f.* **2.** Trinker(in).

drink·ing ['drɪŋkɪŋ] I *s* Trinken *n*. II *adj* Trink...: ~ *song* (*water, etc*); ~ *straw* Trinkhalm *m*.

drip [drɪp] I *v/i* **1.** tropfen (*a. Hahn etc*), tröpfeln. **2.** triefen (*with* von, vor *dat*) (*a. fig.*). II *v/t* **3.** tropfen *od.* tröpfeln lassen. **4.** ~ *sweat* vor Schweiß triefen. III *s* **5.** → *dripping* 1. **6.** ☤ Tropf(infusion *f*) *m*: **be on the** ~ am Tropf hängen. **7.** F Nulpe *f*; Flasche *f.* **'~·'dry** I *adj* bügelfrei. II *v/t* tropfnaß aufhängen.

drip·ping ['drɪpɪŋ] I *s* **1.** Tropfen *n* (*a. Geräusch*), Tröpfeln *n*. **2.** (abtropfendes) Bratenfett. II *adj* **3.** tropfend (*a. Hahn etc*), tröpfelnd. **4.** triefend (*with* von, vor *dat*) (*a. fig.*). **5.** triefend (naß), tropf-, triefnaß. III *adv* **6.** ~ *wet* → 5.

drive [draɪv] I *s* **1.** Fahrt *f*; *engS.* Aus-, Spazierfahrt *f*: **an hour's** ~ e-e Autostunde. **2.** Fahrweg *m*; Zufahrt(sstraße) *f*; (*private*) Auffahrt. **3.** *Golf, Tennis:* Drive *m*, Treibschlag *m*. **4.** *fig.* Kampagne *f*, Feldzug *m*. **5.** *fig.* Schwung *m*, Elan *m*. **6.** *psych.* Trieb *m*. **7.** ⚙ Antrieb *m*. **8.** *mot.* (*Links- etc*) Steuerung *f*. II *v/t* (*irr*) **9.** treiben (*a. fig.*); *Nagel etc* schlagen, *Pfahl* rammen (*into* in *acc*): ~ *s.th. into s.o.* j-m et. einbleuen; → *bend* 1, *corner* 2, *home* 9, *wall* 1, *etc.* **10.** *j-n* veranlassen (*to, into* zu; *to do* zu tun), dazu bringen (*to do* zu tun): *driven by hunger* vom Hunger getrieben. **11.** *Auto etc* lenken, steuern, fahren; (*im Auto etc*) fahren, befördern, bringen (*to* nach). **12.** ⚙ (an)treiben. **13.** zielbewußt durchführen: ~ *a hard bargain* hart verhandeln; überzogene Forderungen stellen. III *v/i* (*irr*) **14.** treiben, getrieben werden. **15.** jagen, stürmen. **16.** (*Auto*) fahren: ~ *into a wall* gegen e-e Mauer fahren. **17.** *fig.* abzielen (*at* auf *acc*): *what is he driving at?* worauf will er hinaus? *Verbindungen mit Adverbien:*

drive| a·way *v/t a. fig. Sorgen etc* vertreiben, -jagen; *Bedenken etc* zerstreuen. ~ *in v/t Nagel etc* einschlagen, *Pfahl* einrammen. ~ *up v/t Preise etc* in die Höhe treiben. **II** v/i (**to**) vorfahren (vor dat); heranfahren (an acc).

'**drive-in I** adj Auto...: ~ **cinema** (Am. **motion-picture theater**) → IIa; ~ **restaurant** → IIb; ~ **window** → IIc. **II** s a) Autokino n, Drive-in-Kino n, b) Drive-in-Restaurant n, c) Autoschalter m, Drive-in-Schalter m (e-r Bank).

driv·el ['drɪvl] **I** v/i pret u. pp -**eled**, bsd. Br. -**elled** 1. sabbern, geifern. **2.** faseln. **II** s **3.** Geifer m. **4.** Gefasel n.

driv·en ['drɪvn] pp von **drive**.

driv·er ['draɪvə] s (Auto- etc)Fahrer m; (Kran- etc, Br. Lokomotiv)Führer m. **~'s cab** s Führerhaus n (e-s Lastwagens od. Krans), ⊕ Br. Führerstand m. **~'s li·cense** s Am. Führerschein m.

'**drive-way** s Zufahrt(sstraße) f; (private) Auffahrt.

driv·ing ['draɪvɪŋ] **I** adj **1.** (an)treibend: ~ **force** treibende Kraft. **2.** ⊕ Treib..., Antriebs... **II** s **3.** Autofahren n. **4.** mot. Fahrweise f, -stil m. ~ **in·struc·tor** s Fahrlehrer(in). ~ **les·son** s Fahrstunde f: **take ~s** Fahrunterricht nehmen, den Führerschein machen. ~ **li·cence** s Br. Führerschein m. ~ **mir·ror** s mot. Rückspiegel m. ~ **school** s Fahrschule f. ~ **test** s Fahrprüfung f: **take one's** ~ die Fahrprüfung od. den Führerschein machen.

driz·zle ['drɪzl] **I** v/impers nieseln. **II** s Sprüh-, Nieselregen m.

droll [drəʊl] adj □ drollig, spaßig.

drom·e·dar·y ['drɒmədərɪ] s zo. Dromedar n.

drone¹ [drəʊn] s zo. Drohne f, fig. a. Schmarotzer m.

drone² [~] **I** v/i **1.** brummen, summen. **II** v/t her(unter)leiern. **III** s Brummen n, Summen n.

drool [druːl] **I** v/i **1.** → **drivel** I. **2.** ~ **over** (od. **about**) sich begeistern für, vernarrt sein in (acc). **II** s **3.** → **drivel** II.

droop [druːp] **I** v/i **1.** (schlaff) herabhängen od. -sinken. **2.** ermatten, erschlaffen (**from, with** vor dat). **3.** sinken (Mut etc), erlahmen (Interesse etc). **4.** den Kopf hängenlassen (a. Blume). **II** v/t **5.** (schlaff) herabhängen lassen. **6.** Kopf hängenlassen. **III** s **7.** Herabhängen n.

drop [drɒp] **I** s **1.** Tropfen m: **a ~ in the bucket** (od. **ocean**) fig. ein Tropfen auf den heißen Stein; **empty to the last** ~ bis auf den letzten Tropfen leeren; **he has had a ~ too much** er hat e-n über den Durst getrunken. **2.** Bonbon m, n: **fruit ~** Drops m. **3.** Fall(tiefe f) m: **a ~ of ten yards** ein Fall aus 10 Yards Höhe. **4.** fig. (Ab)Fall m, Sturz m: **~ in prices** ✝ Preissturz; **~ in (the) temperature** Temperatursturz, -abfall. **5.** Falltür f. **6.** bsd. Am. (Brief- etc)Einwurf m. **II** v/i **7.** (herab)tropfen, herabtröpfeln. **8.** (herunter)fallen. **let s.th.** ~ et. fallen lassen. **9.** sinken, fallen (beide a. Preise etc): ~ **into a chair** sich in e-n Sessel fallen lassen. **10.** a) (ohnmächtig) zu Boden sinken, umfallen: **be fit (od. ready) to** ~ (**with fatigue**) zum Umfallen müde sein, b) a. ~ **dead** tot umfallen: ~ **dead!** sl. geh zum Teufel! **11.** leiser werden (Stimme); sich legen (Wind). **III** v/t **12.** tropfen od. tröpfeln lassen. **13.** fallen lassen: ~ **everything** alles liegen- u. stehenlassen. **14.** (hinein)werfen (**into** in acc). **15.** Bemerkung fallenlassen: ~ **s.o. a line** (a. note) j-m ein paar Zeilen schreiben. **16.** j-n, Absicht etc fallenlassen. **17.** Tätigkeit aufgeben, aufhören mit: ~ **it!** hör auf damit! **18.** Last, a. Passagiere absetzen. **19.** Buchstaben etc auslassen: → **H** 1. **20.** Sport: Punkt etc abgeben (**to** gegen). **21.** Augen, a. Stimme senken (**to a whisper** zu e-m Flüstern).

Verbindungen mit Adverbien:

drop| a·way v/i immer weniger werden. **~ back, ~ be·hind** v/i **1.** zurückfallen. **2.** sich zurückfallen lassen. **~ in** v/i **1.** hereinkommen (a. fig. Aufträge etc). **2.** (kurz) hereinschauen (**on** bei). **~ off** **I** v/i **1.** zurückgehen (Umsatz etc), nachlassen (Interesse etc). **2.** einschlafen; -nicken. **II** v/t **3.** → **drop** 18. **~ out** v/i **1.** aussteigen (**of** aus Politik etc). **2.** die Schule od. das Studium abbrechen.

drop·let ['drɒplɪt] s Tröpfchen n.

'**drop-out** s **1.** Aussteiger m (aus der Gesellschaft). **2.** (Schul-, Studien)Abbrecher m.

drop·pings ['drɒpɪŋz] s pl (Tier)Kot m.

drop·sy ['drɒpsɪ] s ✚ Wassersucht f.

drought [draʊt] s Trockenheit f, Dürre(periode) f.

drove¹ [drəʊv] pret von **drive**.

drove² [~] s Schar f (Menschen): **in ~s** in

(großen *od.* hellen) Scharen, scharen-weise.

drown [draʊn] **I** *v/i* **1.** ertrinken. **II** *v/t* **2.** ertränken: *be drowned* → 1; ~ *one's sorrows* s-e Sorgen im Alkohol ertränken. **3.** überschwemmen: *be ~ed in tears* in Tränen schwimmen *od.* zerfließen. **4.** *a.* ~ *out bsd. Stimme* übertönen.

drowse [draʊz] **I** *v/i* **1.** dösen: ~ *off* eindösen. **II** *v/t* **2.** schläfrig machen. **3.** ~ *away Zeit* verdösen. **III** *s* **4.** Dösen *n*. **'drows·y** *adj* □ **1.** schläfrig; verschlafen. **2.** einschläfernd. **3.** *fig.* verschlafen, -träumt.

drudge [drʌdʒ] **I** *s* **1.** *fig.* Kuli *m*, Last-, Packesel *m*; Arbeitstier *n*. **2.** → *drudgery.* **II** *v/i* **3.** sich (ab)placken *od.* (ab)schinden. **'drudg·er·y** *s* (stumpf-sinnige) Plackerei *pl.* Schinderei.

drug [drʌg] **I** *s* **1.** Arzneimittel *n*, Medikament *n*. **2.** Droge *f* (*a. fig.*), Rausch-gift *n*: *be on* (*off*) ~*s* rauschgift- *od.* drogensüchtig (*clean*) sein. **3.** Betäubungsmittel *n* (*a. fig.*). **4.** ~ *on* (*Am. a. in*) *the market* ✝ schwerverkäufliche Ware, (*im Laden a.*) Ladenhüter *m*. **II** *v/t* **5.** *j-m* Medikamente geben. **6.** *j-n* unter Drogen setzen. **7.** ein Betäubungsmittel beimischen (*dat.*). **8.** betäuben (*a. fig.*): ~ed with sleep schlaftrunken. ~ a·buse *s* **1.** Drogenmißbrauch *m*. **2.** Medikamentenmißbrauch *m*. ~ ad·dict *s* **1.** Drogen-, Rauschgiftsüchtige *m, f*. **2.** Medikamentensüchtige *m, f*. '**~·ad,dict·ed** *adj* **1.** drogen-, rauschgiftsüchtig. **2.** medikamentensüchtig. ~ ad·dic·tion *s* **1.** Drogen-, Rauschgiftsucht *f*. **2.** Medikamentensucht *f*. ~ **clin·ic** *s* Drogenklinik *f*. ~ **deal·er** *s* Drogen-, Rauschgifthändler *m*. ~ de·pend·ence *s* **1.** Drogenabhängigkeit *f*. **2.** Medikamentenabhängigkeit *f*.

drug·gist ['drʌgɪst] *s Am.* Inhaber(in) e-s Drugstores.

'**drug|,push·er** *s* F Pusher *m* (*Rauschgifthändler*). ~ **scene** *s* Drogenszene *f*.

drug·ster ['drʌgstə] → **drug addict** 1.

'**drug·store** *s Am.* Drugstore *m*.

drum [drʌm] **I** *s* **1.** ♪ Trommel *f* (*a. ✍, ☉*): ~*s pl* Schlagzeug *n*. **2.** Trommeln *n* (*a. weitS. des Regens etc*). **3.** *anat.* Mittelohr *n*; Trommelfell *n*. **II** *v/t* **4.** *Rhythmus* trommeln: ~ *s.th. into s.o. fig. j-m*

et. einhämmern. **5.** trommeln auf (*acc*); trommeln mit (*on auf acc*). **6.** ~ *up fig.* zs.-trommeln, (an)werben; *Aufträge etc* hereinholen; sich *et.* ausdenken. **III** *v/i* **7.** *a. weitS.* trommeln (*at an acc*; *on auf acc*). '**~·beat** *s* Trommelschlag *m*. ~ **brake** *s* ☉ Trommelbremse *f*. '**~·fire** *s* Trommelfeuer *n*. '**~·head** *s* ♪, *a. anat.* Trommelfell *n*.

drum·mer ['drʌmə] *s* ♪ Trommler *m*; Schlagzeuger *m*.

'**drum·stick** *s* **1.** Trommelstock *m*, -schlegel *m*. **2.** Unterschenkel *m* (*von zubereitetem Geflügel*).

drunk [drʌŋk] **I** *pp von* **drink**. **II** *adj pred* **1.** betrunken: *get ~* sich betrinken; (*as*) ~ *as a lord* F total blau. **2.** *fig.* berauscht (*with von*): ~ *with joy* freudetrunken. **III** *s* **3.** a) Betrunkene *m, f*, b) → *drunkard.* **drunk·ard** ['~əd] *s* (Gewohnheits)Trinker(in), Säufer(in). '**drunk·en** *adj attr* **1.** betrunken: *a ~ man* ein Betrunkener; ~ *driving* Trunkenheit *f* am Steuer; → *stupor.* **2.** Sauf...: ~ *party.* '**drunk·en·ness** *s* **1.** Betrunkenheit *f*. **2.** Trunksucht *f*.

dry [draɪ] **I** *adj* □ **1.** *allg.* trocken (*a. fig. Humor etc*): *rub* ~ trockenreiben. **2.** F durstig. **3.** durstig machend (*Arbeit*). **4.** trocken (*ohne Aufstrich*). **5.** trocken, langweilig: (*as*) ~ *as dust* F stinklangweilig. **6.** trocken, herb (*Wein etc*). **7.** F trocken, weg vom Alkohol. **II** *v/t* **8.** trocknen. **9.** ~ *o.s.* (*one's hands*) sich (sich die Hände) abtrocknen (*on an dat*). **10.** *oft* ~ *up* Geschirr abtrocknen. **11.** *Obst etc* dörren. **III** *v/i* **12.** trocknen, trocken werden. **13.** ~ *up* ein-, aus-, vertrocknen; F die Klappe halten; F steckenbleiben (*Schauspieler etc*). ~ **bat·ter·y** *s* ⚡ Trockenbatterie *f*. ~ **cell** *s* ⚡ Trockenelement *n*. ~ '**clean** *v/t* chemisch reinigen. ~ **clean·er('s)** *s* chemische Reinigung(sanstalt). ~ **clean·ing** *s* chemische Reinigung.

dry·er → **drier.**

dry| goods *s pl* ✝ Textilien *pl.* ~ **ice** *s* 🔬 Trockeneis *n*.

dry·ness ['draɪnɪs] *s* Trockenheit *f*.

dry nurse *s* Säuglingsschwester *f*.

du·al ['dju:əl] *adj* □ doppelt, zweifach: ~ **carriageway** *mot. Br.* Schnellstraße *f*.

dub¹ [dʌb] *v/t* nennen, *j-m* den (Spitz-)Namen ... geben.

dub 904

dub² [~] v/t Film synchronisieren.

du·bi·ous ['dju:bjəs] adj □ **1.** zweifelhaft: a) unklar, zweideutig, b) ungewiß, unbestimmt, c) fragwürdig, dubios: ~ pleasure zweifelhaftes Vergnügen, d) unzuverlässig. **2.** unschlüssig, schwankend; unsicher, im Zweifel (of, about über acc).

du·cal ['dju:kl] adj □ herzoglich, Herzogs...

duch·ess ['dʌtʃis] s Herzogin f.

duch·y ['dʌtʃi] s Herzogtum n.

duck¹ [dʌk] s **1.** orn. Ente f: look like a dying ~ (in a thunderstorm) F dumm aus der Wäsche schauen. **2.** Br. F Schatz m.

duck² [~] **I** v/i **1.** (rasch) (unter)tauchen. **2.** a. fig. sich ducken (to vor dat). **3.** ~ out F verduften; fig. sich drücken (of vor dat). **II** v/t **4.** (unter)tauchen. **5.** Kopf ducken, einziehen. **6.** F sich drücken vor (dat).

duct [dʌkt] s **1.** ◎ Röhre f, Rohr n, Leitung f. **2.** anat. Gang m, Kanal m.

duc·tile ['dʌktail] adj □ **1.** phys., ◎ dehn-, streckbar. **2.** fig. fügsam.

dud [dʌd] s F **1.** ✕ Blindgänger m (a. fig.). **2.** Niete f, Versager m. **3.** ungedeckter Scheck.

dude [dju:d] s Am. F **1.** Dandy m. **2.** Stadtmensch m.

due [dju:] **I** adj (□ → duly) **1.** ✝ fällig: fall (od. become) ~ fällig werden; when ~ bei Fälligkeit; ~ date Fälligkeitstermin m. **2.** zeitlich fällig: the train is ~ at ... der Zug soll um ... ankommen. **3.** be ~ to zuzuschreiben sein (dat), zurückzuführen sein auf (acc): it is ~ to him es ist ihm zu verdanken. **4.** gebührend, geziemend: be ~ to s.o. j-m gebühren od. zukommen; → credit 3, hono(u)r 4. **5.** gebührend, angemessen: after ~ consideration nach reiflicher Überlegung. **6.** passend, richtig: in ~ course zur rechten od. gegebenen Zeit; in ~ time rechtzeitig, termingerecht; in ~ form ordnungsgemäß, vorschriftsmäßig. **7.** ~ to wegen (gen), infolge od. auf Grund (gen od. von). **II** s **8.** das Gebührende: give s.o. his ~ j-m Gerechtigkeit widerfahren lassen. **9.** pl Gebühren pl.

du·el ['dju:əl] **I** s Duell n (a. fig.). **II** v/i pret. u. pp **-eled,** bsd. Br. **-elled** sich duellieren.

du·et [dju:'et] s ♪ **1.** Duett n. **2.** Duo n.

duff·er ['dʌfə] s F (alter) Trottel.

dug [dʌg] pret u. pp von **dig.** '~·out s **1.** ✕ Unterstand m. **2.** Einbaum m.

du·i ['dju:i:] pl von **duo.**

duke [dju:k] s Herzog m.

dull [dʌl] **I** adj □ **1.** schwer von Begriff, dumm. **2.** schwerfällig, träge. **3.** teilnahmslos. **4.** langweilig, fad(e). **5.** ✝ flau, schleppend. **6.** stumpf (Klinge etc). **7.** matt, glanzlos (Augen, Farben). **8.** dumpf (Klang, Schmerz etc). **II** v/t **9.** abstumpfen. **10.** (ab)schwächen. **11.** mildern, dämpfen. **12.** Schmerz betäuben. **dull·ard** ['~əd] s Dummkopf m. **'dul(l)·ness** s **1.** Dummheit f. **2.** Schwerfälligkeit f. **3.** Teilnahmslosigkeit f. **4.** Langweiligkeit f. **5.** ✝ Flaute f. **6.** Stumpfheit f. **7.** Mattheit f. **8.** Dumpfheit f.

du·ly ['dju:li] adv **1.** ordnungsgemäß. **2.** rechtzeitig.

dumb [dʌm] adj □ **1.** stumm (a. fig.): strike s.o. ~ j-m die Sprache verschlagen od. rauben; (struck) ~ sprachlos (with vor dat); the ~ masses pl die stumme Masse. **2.** bsd. Am. F doof, dumm. '~·bell s **1.** Sport: Hantel f. **2.** bsd. Am. sl. Trottel m. ~'found v/t verblüffen. ~'found·ed adj verblüfft, sprachlos. ~ show s Pantomime f. ,~'wait·er s **1.** stummer Diener, Serviertisch m. **2.** Speiseaufzug m.

dum·found, etc → **dumbfound,** etc.

dum·my ['dʌmi] **I** s **1.** Attrappe f, ✝ a. Leer-, Schaupackung f. **2.** Kleider-, Schaufensterpuppe f. **3.** ✝, ✞ Strohmann m. **4.** Br. Schnuller m. **II** adj **5.** Schein...

dump [dʌmp] **I** v/t **1.** (hin)plumpsen od. (-)fallen lassen, hinwerfen. **2.** Schutt etc auskippen, abladen; Karren etc (um-) kippen, entladen. **3.** ✝ zu Dumpingpreisen verkaufen. **II** v/i **4.** plumpsen. **5.** (s-n) Schutt abladen. **III** s **6.** a) Schutt-, Abfallhaufen m, b) (Schutt-, Müll)Abladeplatz m, Müllkippe f, -halde f. '**dump·er (truck)** s mot. Dumper m, Kipper m. '**dump·ing** s **1.** (Schutt)Abladen n: ~ ground → **dump** 6b. **2.** ✝ Dumping n.

dump·ling ['dʌmpliŋ] s **1.** Knödel m, Kloß m. **2.** F Dickerchen n.

dumps [dʌmps] s pl: (down) in the ~ F down, niedergeschlagen.

dump truck → *dumper* (*truck*).

dun [dʌn] *v/t bsd. Schuldner* mahnen.

dune [dju:n] *s* Düne *f*. ~ **bug·gy** *s mot.* Strandbuggy *m*.

dung [dʌŋ] *s* Mist *m*, Dung *m*.

dun·ga·rees [ˌdʌŋɡəˈriːz] *s pl* Arbeitsanzug *m*: (*pair of*) ~ Arbeitshose *f*.

dun·geon [ˈdʌndʒən] *s* Verlies *n*.

'dung·hill *s* Misthaufen *m*.

dunk [dʌŋk] *v/t Brot etc* eintunken, stippen.

du·o [ˈdjuːəʊ] *pl* **-os, du·i** [ˈ.iː] → *duet*.

du·o·de·num [ˌdjuːəʊˈdiːnəm] *pl* **-na** [.nə], **-nums** *s anat.* Zwölffingerdarm *m*.

dupe [dju:p] **I** *s* Betrogene *m*, *f*. **II** *v/t* betrügen.

du·plex [ˈdjuːpleks] **I** *adj* doppelt, Doppel..., zweifach: ~ *apartment* → IIa; ~ *house* → IIb. **II** *s Am.* a) Maison(n)ette *f*, b) Doppel-, Zweifamilienhaus *n*.

du·pli·cate [ˈdjuːplɪkət] **I** *adj* **1.** doppelt, Doppel..., zweifach. **2.** genau gleich *od.* entsprechend: ~ *key* → 5. **II** *s* **3.** Duplikat *n*, Ab-, Zweitschrift *f*, Kopie *f*: *in* ~ in zweifacher Ausfertigung. **4.** (genau gleiches) Seitenstück, Kopie *f*. **5.** Zweit- *od.* Nachschlüssel *m*. **III** *v/t* [ˈ.keɪt] **6.** ein Duplikat anfertigen von, kopieren, vervielfältigen. **7.** *Experiment etc* (beliebig) wiederholen. **du·pli·ca·tor** [ˈ.keɪtə] *s* Vervielfältigungsapparat *m*.

du·ra·bil·i·ty [ˌdjʊərəˈbɪlətɪ] *s* a) Haltbarkeit *f*, b) Dauerhaftigkeit *f*. **'du·ra·ble I** *adj* □ a) haltbar, b) langlebig: ~ *goods* → II, b) dauerhaft. **II** *s pl* ↑ Gebrauchsgüter *pl*. **du·ra·tion** [ˌ.ˈreɪʃn] *s* Dauer *f*: *for the* ~ *of* für die Dauer von (*od. gen*).

du·ress [djʊəˈres] *s* Zwang *m* (*a. ⚖*).

dur·ing [ˈdjʊərɪŋ] *prp* während.

dusk [dʌsk] *s* (Abend)Dämmerung *f*: *at* ~ bei Einbruch der Dunkelheit. **'dusk·y** *adj* □ dämmerig, düster (*a. fig.*).

dust [dʌst] **I** *s* **1.** Staub *m*: *throw* (*od. cast*) ~ *in s.o.'s eyes fig.* j-m Sand in die Augen streuen; *raise a* ~ a) eine Staubwolke aufwirbeln, b) *a. kick up a* ~ *fig.* viel Staub aufwirbeln; *the* ~ *has settled* die Aufregung hat sich gelegt, die Wogen haben sich geglättet; → *bite* 1, *kiss* 1. **II** *v/t* **2.** abstauben. **3.** bestreuen, bestäuben. **III** *v/i* **4.** Staub wi-

schen. **5.** staubig werden, verstauben. **'~·bin** *s Br.* Abfall-, Mülleimer *m*; Abfall-, Mülltonne *f*. ~ *man* Müllmann *m*. **'~·cart** *s Br.* Müllwagen *m*. ~ *cov·er s* Schutzumschlag *m*.

dust·er [ˈdʌstə] *s* Staubtuch *n*.

dust jack·et → *dust cover*. **~·man** [ˈ.mən] *s* (*irr man*) *Br.* Müllmann *m*. ~ *storm s* Staubsturm *m*. ~ *trap s* Staubfänger *m*. **~·up** *s* F **1.** Krach *m*. **2.** handgreifliche Auseinandersetzung.

dust·y [ˈdʌstɪ] *adj* staubig: *not so* ~ *Br.* F gar nicht so übel.

Dutch [dʌtʃ] **I** *adj* **1.** holländisch, niederländisch. **II** *adv* **2.** *go* ~ getrennte Kasse machen. **III** *s* **3.** *ling.* Holländisch *n*, Niederländisch *n*. **4.** *the* ~ *pl* die Holländer *pl*, die Niederländer *pl*. ~ *cour·age s* F angetrunkener Mut. **~·man** [ˈ.mən] *s* (*irr man*) Holländer *m*, Niederländer *m*. **'~·wom·an** *s* (*irr woman*) Holländerin *f*, Niederländerin *f*.

du·te·ous [ˈdjuːtjəs] *adj* → *dutiful*. **du·ti·a·ble** [ˈ.tjəbl] *adj* zollpflichtig. **du·ti·ful** [ˈ.tɪfʊl] *adj* □ pflichtgetreu, -bewußt.

du·ty [ˈdjuːtɪ] *s* **1.** Pflicht *f*: a) Schuldigkeit *f* (*to, toward[s]* gegenüber), b) Aufgabe *f*: *do one's* ~ s-e Pflicht tun; *breach of* ~ Pflichtverletzung *f*. **2.** Dienst *m*: *be on* ~ Dienst haben, im Dienst sein; *be off* ~ nicht im Dienst sein, dienstfrei haben; *do* ~ *for* benutzt werden *od.* dienen als; *j-n* vertreten. **3.** ✝ Zoll *m*. **II** *adj* **4.** ~ *call* Höflichkeits-, Pflichtbesuch *m*. **5.** ~ *chemist Br.* dienstbereite Apotheke; ~ *doctor* Bereitschaftsarzt *m*; ~ *officer* ✕ Offizier *m* vom Dienst; ~ *roster* Dienstplan *m*. **'~·free** I *adj u. adv* zollfrei: ~ *shop* Duty-free-Shop *m*. II *s pl* F zollfreie Ware(n *pl*).

dwarf [dwɔːf] **I** *pl* **dwarfs, dwarves** [~vz] *s* Zwerg(in) (*a. fig.*). **II** *adj* zwergenhaft, *bsd. ♀, zo.* Zwerg... **III** *v/t* klein erscheinen lassen; *fig.* in den Schatten stellen. **'dwarf·ish** *adj* □ zwergenhaft.

dwarves [dwɔːvz] *pl von* **dwarf**.

dwell [dwel] *v/i* (*mst irr*) **1.** wohnen, leben. **2.** ~ *on fig.* (im Geiste) verweilen bei. **'dwell·er** *s mst in Zssgn* Bewohner(in). **'dwell·ing** *s* Wohnung *f*: ~ *house* Wohnhaus *n*.

dwelt [dwelt] *pret u. pp von* **dwell**.

dwin·dle ['dwɪndl] *v/i* abnehmen, schwinden.

dye [daɪ] I *s* 1. Farbstoff *m*. 2. Färbung *f*: *of the deepest* (*od. blackest*) *~ fig.* von der übelsten Sorte. II *v/t* 3. färben. || *v/t* od. Person *od.* Stück.

,**dyed-in-the-'wool** *adj* eingefleischt, ... durch u. durch.

'**dye·works** *s pl* (*oft sg konstruiert*) Färberei *f*.

dy·ing ['daɪɪŋ] *adj* 1. sterbend: *be* ~ im Sterben liegen. 2. Sterbe...: ~ *hour* Todesstunde *f*; ~ *wish* letzter Wunsch.

dyke → *dike* ¹ *u.* ².

dy·nam·ic [daɪ'næmɪk] I *adj* (*~ally*) dynamisch (*a. fig.*). II *s pl* (*sg konstruiert*) Dynamik *f* (*a. fig.*).

dy·na·mite ['daɪnəmaɪt] I *s* Dynamit *n*. II *v/t* (*mit Dynamit*) sprengen.

dy·na·mo ['daɪnəməʊ] *pl* **-mos** *s* ⚡ Dynamo *m*.

dy·nas·ty ['dɪnəstɪ] *s* Dynastie *f*.

dys·en·ter·y ['dɪsntrɪ] *s* 🏥 Ruhr *f*.

dys·func·tion [dɪs'fʌŋkʃn] *s* 🏥 Funktionsstörung *f*.

E

each [iːtʃ] I *adj* jede(r, -s): ~ *one* jede(r) einzelne. II *pron*: ~ *of us* jede(r) von uns; ~ *other* einander, sich. III *adv* je, pro Person *od.* Stück.

ea·ger ['iːgə] *adj* □ 1. eifrig: ~ *beaver* F Übereifrige *m*, *f*. 2. (*for*) begierig (nach), erpicht, gespannt (auf *acc*): *be ~ to do s.th.* darauf brennen, et. zu tun. 3. gespannt (*Aufmerksamkeit, Blick etc*). '**ea·ger·ness** *s* 1. Eifer *m*. 2. Begierde *f*.

ea·gle ['iːgl] *s orn.* Adler *m*.

ear¹ [ɪə] *s* 1. *anat.* Ohr *n*: *be all ~s* ganz Ohr sein; *be up to the* (*od. one's*) *~s in debt* (*work*) bis über die Ohren in Schulden (Arbeit) sitzen *od.* stecken; *fall on deaf ~s* auf taube Ohren stoßen; *have* (*od. keep*) *an* (*od. one's*) ~ *to the ground* die Ohren offenhalten; *turn a deaf ~ to* die Ohren verschließen vor (*dat*); → *flea, prick* 7, *thick* 1, *wet* 1. 2. *fig.* Gehör *n*, Ohr *n*: *play by ~* nach dem Gehör spielen; *fig.* improvisieren.

ear² [~] *s* (Getreide)Ähre *f*.

ear·ache ['ɪəreɪk] *s* Ohrenschmerzen *pl*. '**~drum** *s anat.* Trommelfell *n*.

earl [ɜːl] *s* britischer Graf.

'**ear·lobe** *s anat.* Ohrläppchen *n*.

ear·ly ['ɜːlɪ] I *adv* 1. früh(zeitig): *as ~ as May* schon im Mai. 2. bald: *as ~ as possible* so bald wie möglich. 3. zu früh; früher. II *adj* 4. früh(zeitig): ~

riser, humor. ~ *bird* Frühaufsteher(in); *the ~ bird catches the worm* Morgenstunde hat Gold im Munde; *Thursday is ~ closing* am Donnerstag schließen die Geschäfte früher; *in his ~ days* in s-r Jugend; *at an ~ hour* zu früher Stunde; ~ *warning system* ✕ Frühwarnsystem *n*; *at the* (*very*) *earliest* (aller-)frühestens; → *convenience* 1. 5. vorzeitig: *his ~ death* sein früher Tod. 6. zu früh: *be ~* zu früh (daran) sein. 7. anfänglich, Früh...: ~ *Christian* frühchristlich. 8. baldig.

'**ear·mark** I *s* 1. Ohrmarke *f* (*e-s Haustiers*). 2. *fig.* Kennzeichen. II *v/t* 3. kennzeichnen. 4. *bsd.* 🏥 bestimmen, vorsehen (*for* für): *~ed* zweckbestimmt, -gebunden (*Mittel*). '**~muff** *s* Ohrenschützer *m*.

earn [ɜːn] *v/t* 1. *Geld etc* verdienen: → *living* 6. 2. *Zinsen etc* einbringen. 3. *fig. j-m et.* einbringen, -tragen.

ear·nest ['ɜːnɪst] I *adj* □ 1. ernst. 2. ernst-, gewissenhaft. 3. ernstlich. II *s* 4. *in ~* im Ernst; *in good* (*od. dead, perfect*) ~ in vollem Ernst; *are you in ~?* ist das dein Ernst?; *be in ~ about* es ernst meinen mit.

earn·ings ['ɜːnɪŋz] *s pl* Verdienst *m*, Einkommen *n*.

'**ear·phones** *s pl, a.* **pair of ~** Kopfhörer *m*. '**~piece** *s teleph.* Hörmuschel *f*. '**~,pierc·ing** → *earsplitting*. '**~plug** *s*

Wattepfropf m. '~**ring** s Ohrring m.
'~**shot** s: **within** (**out of**) ~ in (außer)
Hörweite. '~**split·ting** adj ohrenbetäubend.

earth [ɜːθ] **I** s **1.** Erde f: a) a. ♀ Erdball m,
b) Welt f: **on** ~ auf Erden; **what** (**why**)
on ~? warum (was) in aller Welt? **2.**
Erde f, (Erd)Boden m: **come back** (od.
down) **to** ~ fig. auf den Boden der
Wirklichkeit zurückkehren. **3.** (Fuchs-
etc)Bau m. **4.** ⚡ bsd. Br. Erde f, Erdung
f: ~ **cable** Massekabel n. **II** v/t **5.** ⚡ bsd.
Br. erden. 'earth·en adj irden. 'earth-
en·ware s Steingut(geschirr) n.
'earth·ly adj **1.** irdisch, weltlich. **2.** F
there's no ~ **reason** nicht der
geringste Grund; **of no** ~ **use** völlig
unnütz; **not to have an** ~ (**chance**)
nicht die geringste Chance haben.
'earth|·quake s Erdbeben n. '~**quake**-
proof adj erdbebensicher. '~**shak·ing**,
'~**shat·ter·ing** adj fig. welterschüt-
ternd. ~ **sta·tion** s Raumfahrt: Bodenstation f. ~ **trem·or** s leichtes Erdbeben. '~**worm** s zo. Regenwurm m.
earth·y ['ɜːθɪ] adj **1.** erdig, Erd... **2.** weltlich od. materiell (eingestellt). **3.** derb
(Humor etc).
'ear|·wax s physiol. Ohrenschmalz n.
'~**wig** s zo. Ohrwurm m. ,~'**wit·ness** s
Ohrenzeuge m.

ease [iːz] **I** s **1.** Bequemlichkeit f, Behaglichkeit f. **2.** a. ~ **of mind** (Ge-
müts)Ruhe f, Ausgeglichenheit f: **at**
(**one's**) ~ ruhig, entspannt; unbefan-
gen; **be** (od. **feel**) **at** ~ sich wohl fühlen;
ill at ~ unruhig; befangen; **be** (od. **feel**)
ill at ~ sich (in s-r Haut) nicht wohl
fühlen. **3.** Sorglosigkeit f: **live at** ~ in
guten Verhältnissen leben. **4.** Leichtigkeit f, Mühelosigkeit f: **with** ~ leicht,
mühelos. **5.** Erleichterung f, Befreiung
f: **give s.o.** ~ j-m Erleichterung verschaffen. **II** v/t **6.** erleichtern, beruhigen: ~ **one's mind** sich erleichtern. **7.**
Schmerzen lindern. **III** v/i **8.** mst ~ **off**
(od. **up**) nachlassen, sich abschwächen;
sich entspannen (Lage); (bei der Arbeit) kürzertreten; weniger streng sein
(**on** zu).
ea·sel ['iːzl] s paint. Staffelei f.
eas·i·ly ['iːzɪlɪ] adv **1.** leicht, mühelos. **2.**
ohne Zweifel; mit Abstand; bei weitem.
east [iːst] **I** s **1.** Osten m: **in the** ~ **of** im

Osten von (od. gen); **to the** ~ **of** → 5. **2.**
a. ♀ Osten, östlicher Landesteil: **the** ♀
Br. Ostengland n; Am. die Oststaaten
pl; pol. der Osten; der Orient. **II** adj **3.**
Ost..., östlich. **III** adv **4.** ostwärts, nach
Osten. **5.** ~ **of** östlich von (od. gen).
'~**bound** adj nach Osten gehend od.
fahrend.
East·er ['iːstə] **I** s Ostern n od. pl, Osterfest n: **at** ~ zu Ostern; **happy** ~ frohe
Ostern! **II** adj Oster...: ~ **egg**; ~ **Sunday**
(od. **Day**) Ostersonntag m.
east·er·ly ['iːstəlɪ] adj östlich, Ost... **II**
adv von od. nach Osten. **east·ern**
['iːstən] adj östlich, Ost... 'east·ern·er s
1. Bewohner(in) des Ostens (e-s Landes). **2.** ♀ Am. Oststaatler(in). **east-
ern·most** ['~məʊst] adj östlichst.
east·ward ['iːstwəd] **I** adj östlich,
ostwärts, nach Osten: **in an** ~ **direction**
in östlicher Richtung, Richtung Osten.
east·wards ['~z] adv → **eastward**.
eas·y ['iːzɪ] **I** adj (□ → **easily**) **1.** leicht,
mühelos: **it is** ~ **for him to talk** er hat gut
reden. **2.** leicht, einfach (**for** für): ~
money leichtverdientes Geld. **3.** bequem, angenehm: **live in** ~ **circumstances**, F **be on** ~ **street** in guten Verhältnissen leben. **4.** gemächlich, gemütlich
(Tempo, Spaziergang etc): → **stage** 2.
5. günstig, erträglich (Strafe) leicht:
on ~ **terms** auf Raten. **6.** leichtfertig;
locker, frei (Moral etc). **7.** ungezwungen, natürlich: **be free and** ~ sich ganz
ungezwungen benehmen. **II** adv **8.**
leicht, bequem: **go** ~, **take it** ~ sich Zeit
lassen; sich nicht aufregen; **take it** ~!
immer mit der Ruhe!; keine Bange!; **go**
~ **on** j-n, et. sachte anfassen; schonend
od. sparsam umgehen mit; **easier said
than done** leichter gesagt als getan; ~
come, ~ **go** wie gewonnen, so zerronnen. ~ **chair** s Sessel m. '~**go·ing** adj **1.**
gelassen. **2.** unbeschwert.

eat [iːt] **I** s. pl F Fressalien pl. **II** v/t (irr)
2. essen (Mensch), fressen (Tier): ~
one's words alles(, was man gesagt
hat,) zurücknehmen; **what's** ~**ing him?**
F was hat er denn? ~ **up** aufessen, -fres-
sen; Reserven etc völlig aufbrauchen;
be ~**en up with** fig. sich verzehren vor
(dat), zerfressen werden von; → **cake**
1, **dog** 1, **hat**, **humble** Ia. **3.** zerfressen:
~**en by worms** wurmstichig. **4.** Loch

fressen (*into* in *acc*). **III** *v/i* (*irr*) **5.** essen (*Mensch*), fressen (*Tier*): ~ **out** auswärts essen, essen gehen. **6.** ~ **into** sich (hin)einfressen in (*acc*); *Reserven etc* angreifen. **'eat·a·ble** *I adj* eß-, genießbar. **II** *s pl* Eßwaren *pl*. **eat·en** ['iːtn] *pp von* **eat**. **'eat·er** *s* Esser(in) (*Mensch*), Fresser *m* (*Tier*): → **big** 1d, **small** I. **'eat·ing** *I s* Essen *n*. **II** *adj* Eß...: ~ **apple** *s* Speiseapfel *m*.

eau de Co·logne [,əʊdəkə'ləʊn] *s* Kölnischwasser *n*.

eaves [iːvz] *s pl* Traufe *f*. **'~·drop** *v/i* (heimlich) lauschen *od.* horchen: ~ **on** belauschen. **'~·drop·per** *s* Lauscher(in), Horcher(in).

ebb [eb] *I s* **1.** a. ~ **tide** Ebbe *f*. **2.** *fig.* Tiefstand *m*: **be at a low** ~ auf e-m Tiefpunkt angelangt sein. **II** *v/i* **3.** zurückgehen (*a. fig.*). **4.** a. ~ **away** *fig.* abnehmen, verebben.

eb·on·y ['ebənɪ] *s* Ebenholz *n*.

e·bul·li·ent [ɪ'bʌljənt] *adj* □ *fig.* sprudelnd, überschäumend (**with** von); überschwenglich.

ec·cen·tric [ɪk'sentrɪk] *I adj* (**~ally**) ⚗, ⚙ exzentrisch, *fig. a.* überspannt. **II** *s* Exzentriker(in). **ec·cen·tric·i·ty** [,eksen-'trɪsətɪ] *s* ⚗, ⚙ Exzentrizität *f*, *fig. a.* Überspanntheit *f*.

ec·cle·si·as·ti·cal [ɪ,kliːzɪ'æstɪkl] *adj* □ kirchlich: ~ **law** Kirchenrecht *n*.

ech·e·lon ['eʃəlɒn] ⚓, ✗ *I s* Staffelung *f*: **in** ~ staffelförmig. **II** *v/t* staffeln.

ech·o ['ekəʊ] *I pl* -**oes** *s* **1.** Echo *n*, Widerhall *m* (*beide a. fig.*). **II** *v/i* **2.** widerhallen (**with** von). **3.** nach-, widerhallen, zurückgeworfen werden (*Ton*). **III** *v/t* **4.** a. ~ **back** *Ton* zurückwerfen. **5.** *Worte* nachbeten; *j-m* alles nachbeten. ~ **sound·er** *s* ⚓ Echolot *n*.

é·clat ['eɪklɑː] *s* **1.** durchschlagender Erfolg. **2.** (allgemeiner) Beifall.

e·clipse [ɪ'klɪps] *I s* **1.** *ast.* (Sonnen-, Mond)Finsternis *f*. **2.** *fig.* Niedergang *m*: **be in** ~ im Sinken sein; in der Versenkung verschwunden sein. **II** *v/t* **3.** *ast.* verfinstern. **4.** *fig.* in den Schatten stellen: **be ~d by** verblassen neben (*dat*).

e·co·cide ['iːkəʊsaɪd] *s* Umweltzerstörung *f*. **e·co·cri·sis** ['iːkəʊ,kraɪsɪs] *s* (*irr* **crisis**) Umweltkrise *f*.

e·co·log·i·cal [,iːkə'lɒdʒɪkl] *adj* □ öko-

logisch, Umwelt...: ~ **balance** ökologisches Gleichgewicht; **~·ly beneficial** (**harmful**) umweltfreundlich (umweltfeindlich). **e·col·o·gist** [iː'kɒlədʒɪst] *s* Ökologe *m*. **e·col·o·gy** *s* Ökologie *f*.

e·co·nom·ic [,iːkə'nɒmɪk] *I adj* (**~ally**) **1.** (staats-, volks)wirtschaftlich, Wirtschafts...: ~ **aid** Wirtschaftshilfe *f*. **2.** rentabel, wirtschaftlich. **II** *s pl* (*sg konstruiert*) **3.** Volkswirtschaft(slehre) *f*. **e·co·nom·i·cal** [~kl] *adj* □ **1.** wirtschaftlich, sparsam, (*Person a.*) haushälterisch: **be** ~ **with** → **economize** I. **2.** Spar... **3.** → **economic** I. **e·con·o·mist** [ɪ'kɒnəmɪst] *s* Volkswirt(schaftler) *m*. **e·con·o·mize** I *v/t* sparsam umgehen *od.* wirtschaften mit. **II** *v/i* sparsam wirtschaften: ~ **on** → I. **e·con·o·my** I *s* **1.** Wirtschaftlichkeit *f*, Sparsamkeit *f*. **2.** Sparmaßnahme *f*; Einsparung *f*. **3.** Wirtschaft(ssystem *n*) *f*. **II** *adj* **4.** Spar...: ~ **class** ✈ Economyklasse *f*; ~ **drive** Sparmaßnahmen *pl*; ~ **price** günstiger *od.* niedriger Preis.

e·co·sys·tem ['iːkəʊ,sɪstəm] *s* Ökosystem *n*.

ec·sta·size ['ekstəsaɪz] *I v/t* in Ekstase versetzen. **II** *v/i* in Ekstase geraten. **'ec·sta·sy** *s* Ekstase *f*: **be in an** ~ außer sich sein (**of** vor *dat*); **in an** ~ **of joy** in e-m Freudentaumel; **go into ecstasies over** in Verzückung geraten über (*acc*). **ec·stat·ic** [ɪk'stætɪk] *adj* (**~ally**) ekstatisch, verzückt.

e·cu·men·i·cal [,iːkjuː'menɪkl] *adj* □ ökumenisch.

ec·ze·ma ['eksɪmə] *s* ⚕ Ekzem *n*.

ed·dy ['edɪ] *I s* Wirbel *m*, Strudel *m*. **II** *v/i* wirbeln.

edge [edʒ] *I s* **1.** Schneide *f*; Schärfe *f*: **have no** ~ stumpf sein, nicht schneiden; **take the** ~ **off** *Klinge* stumpf machen; *fig.* e-r *Sache* die Schärfe nehmen. **2.** Ecke *f*, scharfe Kante. **3.** (äußerster) Rand, Saum *m*; **on the** ~ **of** *fig.* kurz vor (*dat*); **be on the** ~ **of despair** am Rande der Verzweiflung sein; **be on the** ~ **of doing s.th.** im Begriff sein; et. zu tun. **4.** Kante *f*, Schmalseite *f*: **set** (**up**) **on** ~ hochkant stellen; **on** ~ nervös; gereizt; **set s.o.'s teeth on** ~ j-n nervös machen. **5.** F Vorteil *m*: **give s.o. an** ~ j-m e-n Vorteil verschaffen; **have the** ~ **on s.o.**

j-m über sein. **II** v/t **6.** schärfen. **7.** umsäumen, einfassen. **8.** schieben, drängen: **~ on** antreiben, drängen. **III** v/i **9.** sich schieben od. drängen. **edged** adj **1.** scharf. **2.** in Zssgn ...schneidig; ...kantig.

'edge|·ways, ~·wise ['∼waız] adv hochkant: **I could hardly get a word in ~** fig. ich bin kaum zu Wort gekommen.

edg·y ['edʒı] adj □ nervös; gereizt.

ed·i·ble ['edıbl] **I** adj eß-, genießbar: **~ oil** Speiseöl n. **II** s pl Eßwaren pl.

e·dict ['iːdıkt] s Erlaß m, hist. Edikt n.

ed·i·fice ['edıfıs] s Gebäude n (a. fig.). **ed·i·fy** ['∼faı] v/t fig. erbauen. **'ed·i·fy·ing** adj □ erbaulich.

ed·it ['edıt] v/t **1.** Texte etc a) herausgeben, b) redigieren. **2.** Film schneiden. **3.** Zeitung etc als Herausgeber leiten. **e·di·tion** [ı'dıʃn] s **1.** Ausgabe f: **first ~** Erstausgabe; **morning ~** Morgenausgabe (Zeitung). **2.** Auflage f. **ed·i·tor** ['edıtə] s **1.** a. **~ in chief** Herausgeber(in) (e-s Buchs etc). **2.** Zeitung: a) a. **~ in chief** Chefredakteur(in): **~ staff** s pl die Redaktion. **3.** Film, TV: Cutter(in). **ed·i·to·ri·al** [∼'tɔːrıəl] **I** adj □ redaktionell, Redaktions...: **~ department** Redaktion f; → **staff** 1. **II** s Leitartikel m.

ed·u·cate ['edʒʊkeıt] v/t **1.** erziehen, (aus)bilden: **he was ∼d at** er besuchte die (Hoch)Schule in (dat). **2.** weitS. (to) erziehen (zu); gewöhnen (an acc). **'ed·u·cat·ed** adj gebildet. **2. ~ guess** mehr als e-e bloße Vermutung. **ed·u·ca·tion** s **1.** Erziehung f, (Aus)Bildung f: → **compulsory** 2, **university** II. **2.** Bildung(sstand m) f: → **general** 2. **3.** Bildungs-, Schulwesen n. **4.** Pädagogik f. **ed·u·ca·tion·al** [∼ʃənl] adj □ **1.** a) pädagogisch, Unterrichts...: **~ film** Lehrfilm m; **~ television** Schulfernsehen n, b) lehrreich (Erfahrung etc), c) pädagogisch wertvoll (Spielzeug). **2.** Bildungs...: **~ level** (od. **standard**) Bildungsniveau n.

eel [iːl] s ichth. Aal m: **(as) slippery as an ~** fig. aalglatt.

ee·rie, ee·ry ['ıərı] adj □ unheimlich, (Schrei etc) schaurig.

ef·face [ı'feıs] v/t wegwischen, -reiben, a. fig. (aus)löschen.

ef·fect [ı'fekt] **I** s **1.** Wirkung f (on auf acc): a) Erfolg m: **of no ~, without ~** erfolg-, wirkungslos, b) Auswirkung f, c) Effekt m, Eindruck m: **have an ~ on** wirken auf (acc), e-n Eindruck hinterlassen bei. **2.** Inhalt m, Sinn m: **a letter to the ~ that** ein Brief des Inhalts, daß; **inform s.o. to that ~** j-n entsprechend informieren. **3.** (Rechts)Wirksamkeit f, (-)Kraft f: **be in ~** in Kraft sein; **take ~, come** (od. **go**) **into ~** in Kraft treten; **with ~ from** mit Wirkung vom. **4. carry into ~, give ~ to** verwirklichen, ausführen; **in ~** in Wirklichkeit, tatsächlich. **5.** ⚙ (Nutz)Leistung f. **6.** pl ♣ Effekten pl; Vermögen(swerte pl) n. **II** v/t **7.** bewirken. **8.** ausführen, tätigen. **ef·fec·tive** adj □ **1.** wirksam, erfolgreich. **2.** eindrucks-, wirkungs-, effektvoll. **3.** (rechts)wirksam, rechtskräftig: **be ~** in Kraft sein; **become ~** in Kraft treten; **~ from** (od. **as of**) mit Wirkung vom. **4.** tatsächlich, effektiv: **~ salary** Effektivgehalt n. **ef·fec·tive·ness** s Wirksamkeit f. **ef·fec·tu·al** [∼tʃʊəl] adj □ **1.** wirksam. **2. ~ effective** 3. **ef·fec·tu·ate** [∼tjʊeıt] v/t bewirken.

ef·fem·i·nate [ı'femınət] adj □ **1.** weibisch, unmännlich. **2.** verweichlicht, weichlich.

ef·fer·vesce [ˌefə'ves] v/i **1.** sprudeln, schäumen, moussieren. **2.** fig. (über-)sprudeln, überschäumen (**with** vor dat). **ef·fer·ves·cent** [∼snt] adj □ **1.** sprudelnd, schäumend, moussierend: **~ powder** Brausepulver n. **2.** fig. (über-)sprudelnd, überschäumend.

ef·fi·ca·cious [ˌefı'keıʃəs] adj □ wirksam. **ef·fi·ca·cy** ['∼kəsı] s Wirksamkeit f.

ef·fi·cien·cy [ı'fıʃənsı] s Effizienz f: a) Tüchtigkeit f, (Leistungs)Fähigkeit f: **~ rating** Leistungsbewertung f; → **principle** 1, b) rationelle Arbeitsweise, Wirtschaftlichkeit f: → **expert** ♣ Rationalisierungsfachmann m. **ef·fi·cient** adj □ effizient: a) tüchtig, (leistungs)fähig, b) rationell, wirtschaftlich.

ef·fi·gy ['efıdʒı] s **1.** Steinplastik f; Bildnis n (auf e-r Münze). **2.** Puppe od. bildhafte Darstellung e-r verhaßten Person: **burn** (**hang**) **s.o. in ~** j-n symbolisch verbrennen (hängen).

ef·fort ['efət] s Anstrengung f: a) Bemühung f, b) Mühe f: **make an ~** sich bemühen od. anstrengen; **make every ~** sich alle Mühe geben; **spare no ~** keine Mühe scheuen; **without ~** mühelos; **~ of will** Willensanstrengung. **'ef·fort·less** adj □ mühelos.

ef·fron·ter·y [ɪ'frʌntərɪ] s Frechheit f, Unverschämtheit f: **have the ~** die Unverschämtheit haben od. besitzen (**to do** zu tun).

ef·fu·sive [ɪ'fjuːsɪv] adj □ überschwenglich.

egg¹ [eg] s Ei n: **in the ~** fig. im Anfangsstadium, im Entstehen; **(as) sure as ~s is** (od. **are**) **~s** F so sicher wie das Amen in der Kirche, todsicher; → **like¹** 1.

egg² [~] v/t mst **~ on** anstacheln, antreiben.

'egg|,beat·er s Schneebesen m. **~ co·sy** (Am. **co·zy**) s Eierwärmer m. **'~·cup** s Eierbecher m. **'~·head** s F Eierkopf m (Intellektueller). **'~·shaped** adj eiförmig. **'~·shell** s Eierschale f. **~ tim·er** s Eieruhr f. **~ whisk** s Schneebesen m. **~ white** s Eiweiß n.

e·go ['egəʊ] pl **-gos** s phls., psych. Ich n, Ego n; weitS. Selbst(wert)gefühl n: **boost s.o.'s ~, give s.o. an ~ boost** F j-s Selbstwertgefühl (an)heben. **e·go·cen·tric** [,~'sentrɪk] adj (**~ally**) egozentrisch. **II** s Egozentriker(in). **'e·go·ism** s Egoismus m. **'e·go·ist** s Egoist(in). **,e·go·is·tic, ,e·go·is·ti·cal** [~kl] adj □ egoistisch. **e·go·tism** ['~tɪzəm] s 1. Egotismus m, Geltungsbedürfnis n, Selbstgefälligkeit f. **2.** → **egoism**. **'e·go·tist** s 1. Egotist(in). **2.** → **egoist**. **,e·go·tis·tic, ,e·go·tis·ti·cal** [~kl] adj □ **1.** egotistisch, geltungsbedürftig, selbstgefällig. **2.** → **egoistic**.

e·go trip s F Egotrip m (Akt geistiger Selbstbefriedigung): **be off on an ~** auf e-m Egotrip sein.

E·gyp·tian [ɪ'dʒɪpʃn] **I** adj ägyptisch. **II** s Ägypter(in).

ei·der ['aɪdə] s 1. → **eider duck. 2.** → **eiderdown 1. '~·down** s 1. coll. Eiderdaunen pl. **2.** Daunendecke f. **~ duck** s orn. Eiderente f.

eight [eɪt] **I** adj 1. acht: **~·hour day** Achtstundentag m. **II** s 2. Acht f (Boot, Mannschaft). **eight·een** [,eɪ'tiːn] adj achtzehn. **,eight'eenth** [~θ] adj acht-

zehnt. **eight·fold** ['~fəʊld] **I** adj achtfach. **II** adv achtfach, um das Achtfache: **increase ~** (sich) verachtfachen.

eighth [eɪtθ] **I** adj 1. acht(er, -s). **II** s 2. der, die, das Achte: **the ~ of May** der 8. Mai. **3.** Achtel n. **'eighth·ly** adv achtens.

eight·i·eth ['~ɪəθ] adj achtzigst.

'eight-time adj achtmalig.

'eight·y ['eɪtɪ] **I** adj achtzig. **II** s Achtzig f: **be in one's eighties** in den Achtzigern sein; **in the eighties** in den achtziger Jahren (e-s Jahrhunderts).

ei·ther ['aɪðə] **I** adj 1. jede(r, -s) (von zweien): **on ~ side** auf beiden Seiten. **2.** irgendein (von zweien): **~ way** auf die e-e od. die andere Art. **II** pron 3. irgendein (von zweien): **I haven't seen ~** ich habe beide nicht gesehen, ich habe keinen (von beiden) gesehen. **4.** beides: **~ is possible. III** cj **5.** ~ ... **or** entweder ... oder. **6.** neg.: ~ ... **or** weder ... noch: **it isn't enough ~ for you or for me** es reicht weder für mich noch für dich. **IV** adj **7.** **not ~** auch nicht.

e·jac·u·late [ɪ'dʒækjʊleɪt] **I** v/t **1.** physiol. Samen ausstoßen. **2.** Worte etc ausstoßen, hervorstoßen. **II** v/i **3.** physiol. ejakulieren, e-n Samenerguß haben. **e,jac·u'la·tion** s 1. physiol. Ejakulation f, Samenerguß m. **2.** Ausruf m; Stoßseufzer m.

e·ject [ɪ'dʒekt] **I** v/t **1.** (**from**) j-n hinauswerfen (aus); vertreiben (aus, von). **2.** entlassen, entfernen (**from** aus e-m Amt). **3.** ⚙ ausstoßen, -werfen. **II** v/i **4.** ⚙ den Schleudersitz betätigen. **e'jec·tion** s 1. Vertreibung f. **2.** Entfernung f. **3.** ⚙ Ausstoßen n, -werfen n: ~ **seat** ⚙ Schleudersitz m. **e'jec·tor** s ⚙ Auswerfer m: ~ **seat** ⚙ Schleudersitz m.

eke [iːk] v/t: ~ **out** Flüssigkeit, Vorräte etc strecken; Einkommen aufbessern (**with** mit): ~ **out a living** sich (mühsam) durchschlagen.

e·lab·o·rate **I** adj [ɪ'læbərət] **1.** sorgfältig od. kunstvoll gearbeitet od. ausgeführt. **2.** (wohl)durchdacht. **3.** umständlich. **II** v/t [~reɪt] **4.** sorgfältig ausarbeiten. **5.** Theorie etc entwickeln. **III** v/i [~reɪt] **6.** nähere Angaben machen: ~ **on** näher eingehen auf (acc).

e·lapse [ɪ'læps] v/i vergehen, -streichen (Zeit), ablaufen (Frist).

e·las·tic [ɪˈlæstɪk] **I** *adj* (**~ally**) **1.** *allg.*
elastisch (*a. fig.*): **~ conscience** weites
Gewissen; **~ word** dehnbarer Begriff. **2.**
Gummi...: **~ band** Gummiring *m*,
-band *n*, (Dichtungs)Gummi *m*; **~
stocking** Gummistrumpf *m*. **II** *s* **3.**
bsd. Am. Gummiring *m*, -band *n*,
(Dichtungs)Gummi *m*. **e·las·tic·i·ty**
[ˌelæˈstɪsətɪ] *s allg.* Elastizität *f* (*a. fig.*).

e·lat·ed [ɪˈleɪtɪd] *adj* □ begeistert (**at**
von), in Hochstimmung. **e·la·tion** *s* Begeisterung *f*, Hochstimmung *f*.

el·bow [ˈelbəʊ] **I** *s* **1.** Ell(en)bogen *m*: **at
one's ~** in Reichweite; *bsd. fig.* an s-r
Seite; **out at ~(s)** schäbig, abgetragen
(*Kleidung*); schäbig gekleidet; *Am.*
knapp bei Kasse. **2.** (scharfe) Biegung
od. Krümmung. **3.** (Rohr)Krümmer *m*,
Kniestück *n*. **II** *v/t* **4.** *mit dem Ellbogen*
stoßen, drängen (*a. fig.*): **~ out** hinaus-
drängen; **~ one's way through** sich e-n
Weg bahnen durch. **~ grease** *s humor.*
1. Armschmalz *n* (*Kraft*). **2.** Schufterei
f. **~room** [ˈ~rʊm] *s* **1.** Ellbogenfreiheit
f. **2.** *fig.* Bewegungsfreiheit *f*, Spielraum *m*.

eld·er¹ [ˈeldə] **I** *adj* **1.** älter (*Bruder,
Schwester etc*). **2. ~ statesman** Staatsmann im Ruhestand, der die politischen
Führer inoffiziell berät; *weitS.* großer
alter Mann (*e-r Berufsgruppe etc*). **II** *s*
3. my ~s Leute, die älter sind als ich.
eld·er² [~] *s* ⚕ Holunder *m*. **'~‚ber·ry**
s Holunderbeere *f*.

eld·er·ly [ˈeldəlɪ] *adj* ältlich, älter.

eld·est [ˈeldɪst] *adj* ältest (*Bruder,
Schwester etc*).

e·lect [ɪˈlekt] **I** *v/t j-n* wählen ([**as, to be**]
president zum Präsidenten). **II** *adj*
(*nachgestellt*) designiert, zukünftig.
e·lec·tion **I** *s* Wahl *f*: → **stand for** 4. **II**
adj Wahl...: **~ campaign** Wahlkampf
m. **e‚lec·tion'eer** [~ʃəˈnɪə] *v/i* Wahlkampf betreiben: **~ for** Wahlpropagan-
da treiben für. **e‚lec·tion'eer·ing** *s*
Wahlkampf *m*; -propaganda *f*. **e'lec-
tive I** *adj* **1.** gewählt, Wahl... **2.** wahlberechtigt. **3.** *ped., univ. bsd. Am.* fakultativ: **~ subject** → 4. **II** *s* 4. *ped. univ. bsd.
Am.* Wahlfach *n*. **e'lec·tor** *s* Wäh-
ler(in); *Am.* Wahlmann *m*. **e·lec·tor·al**
adj Wähler..., Wahl...: **~ college** *Am.*
Wahlmänner *pl*. **e'lec·to·rate** [~tərət] *s*
Wähler(schaft *f*) *pl*.

e·lec·tric [ɪˈlektrɪk] *adj* (**~ally**) **1.** a) elektrisch: **~ chair** elektrischer Stuhl; **~
cushion** Heizkissen *n*; **~ shock** Stromschlag *m*; **~ etc** Elektroschock *m*; **~
torch** *bsd. Br.* Taschenlampe *f*, b) Elektro..., c) Elektrizitäts..., d) elektrotech-
nisch. **2.** *fig.* elektrisierend (*Wirkung
etc*); spannungsgeladen (*Atmosphäre*).
e'lec·tri·cal [~kl] *adj* □ → **electric**: **~
engineer** Elektroingenieur *m*; **~** -techni-
ker *m*; **~ engineering** Elektrotechnik
f.

e·lec·tri·cian [ˌɪlekˈtrɪʃn] *s* Elektrotechniker *m*, Elektriker *m*. **‚e·lec'tric·i·ty**
[~sətɪ] *s* Elektrizität *f*; Strom *m*. **e'lec-
tri·fy** [~faɪ] *v/t* **1.** elektrisieren (*a. fig.*).
2. elektrifizieren.

e·lec·tro·car·di·o·gram [ɪˌlektrəʊˈkɑː-
dɪəʊgræm] *s* ⚕ Elektrokardiogramm *n*.

e·lec·tro·cute [ɪˈlektrəkjuːt] *v/t* **1.** auf
dem elektrischen Stuhl hinrichten. **2.**
be ~d e-n tödlichen Stromschlag erhalten. **e‚lec·tro'cu·tion** *s* Hinrichtung *f*
auf dem elektrischen Stuhl.

e·lec·trode [ɪˈlektrəʊd] *s* ⚡ Elektrode *f*.

e·lec·tron [ɪˈlektrɒn] *phys.* **I** *s* Elektron
n. **II** *adj* Elektronen...: **~ microscope.**
‚e·lec'tron·ic I *adj* (**~ally**) elektronisch:
~ data processing elektronische Datenverarbeitung; **~ flash** *phot.* Elektro-
nenblitz *m*. **II** *s pl* (*sg konstruiert*) Elektronik *f*.

e·lec·tro·plate [ɪˈlektrəʊpleɪt] *v/t* galvanisieren. **e‚lec·tro'ther·a·py** *s* ⚕ Elek-
trotherapie *f*.

el·e·gance [ˈelɪgəns] *s* Eleganz *f*. **'el·e-
gant** *adj* □ elegant.

el·e·ment [ˈelɪmənt] *s* **1.** *allg.* Element *n*.
2. *pl* Anfangsgründe *pl*. **3.** grundlegen-
der Umstand, wesentlicher Faktor: **~ of
uncertainty** Unsicherheitsfaktor; **~ of
surprise** Überraschungselement *n*. **4.**
fig. Körnchen *n*, Fünkchen *n* (*Wahrheit etc*). **5.** (Lebens)Element *n*: **be in
one's ~** in s-m Element sein; **be out of
one's ~** sich fehl am Platz fühlen. **6.** *pl*
Elemente *pl*, Naturkräfte *pl*. **el·e·men-
tal** [~ˈmentl] *adj* □ **1.** elementar: a)
ursprünglich, natürlich, b) urgewaltig,
c) wesentlich, grundlegend. **2.** Elementar-
tar..., Ur... **3.** → **elementary** 2, 3.
‚el·e·men·ta·ry *adj* □ **1.** → **elemental**
1, 2. **2.** elementar, Einführungs...: **~
school** *Am.* Grundschule *f*. **3.** 🌿, 🜨,

phys. Elementar...: **~ particle** Elementarteilchen *n*.

el·e·phant ['elɪfənt] *s zo.* Elefant *m*. **el·e·phan·tine** [ˌ~'fæntaɪn] *adj* **1.** elefantenartig: **an ~ memory** ein Gedächtnis wie ein Elefant. **2.** plump, schwerfällig.

el·e·vate ['elɪveɪt] *v/t* **1.** (hoch-, auf)heben. **2.** *j-n* erheben (**to peerage** in den Adelsstand), befördern (**to** zu). **'el·e·vat·ed** *adj* **1.** erhöht: **~ railway** (*Am. railroad*) Hochbahn *f*. **2.** gehoben (*Position, Stil etc*). **3.** übersteigert (*Meinung etc*). ˌel·e·**'va·tion** *s* **1.** (Boden)Erhebung *f*, (An-)Höhe *f*. **2.** Erhebung *f*, Beförderung *f*. **3.** △, 🏛 Aufriß *m*. **'el·e·va·tor** *s Am.* Aufzug *m*, Fahrstuhl *m*: **~ shaft** Aufzugschacht *m*.

el·e·ven [ɪ'levn] **I** *adj* elf. **II** *s* Elf *f* (*a. Sport*). **e'lev·en·ses** [ˌ~zɪz] *s pl Br.* F zweites Frühstück. **e'lev·enth** [ˌ~θ] *adj* elft: **at the ~ hour** *fig.* in letzter Minute.

elf *pl* **elves** [elvz] *s* **1.** Elf *m*, Elfe *f*. **2.** Kobold *m*: **'elf·ish** *adj* □ **1.** elfenhaft. **2.** koboldhaft, schelmisch.

e·lic·it [ɪ'lɪsɪt] *v/t* **1.** (*from*) *et.* entlocken (*dat*), *Wahrheit etc* herausholen, -lokken (aus). **2.** *Applaus, Gelächter etc* hervorrufen.

el·i·gi·bil·i·ty [ˌelɪdʒə'bɪlətɪ] *s* **1.** Eignung *f*. **2.** Berechtigung *f*. **3.** Wählbarkeit *f*. **'el·i·gi·ble** *adj* □ (**for**) in Frage kommend (für): a) geeignet, annehmbar (für): **~ bachelor** begehrter Junggeselle, b) berechtigt, befähigt (zu), qualifiziert (für): **be ~ for** Anspruch haben auf (*acc*); **~ to vote** wahlberechtigt, c) teilnahmeberechtigt (an *dat*), (*Sport a.*) start- *od.* spielberechtigt (für), d) wählbar (für).

e·lim·i·nate [ɪ'lɪmɪneɪt] *v/t* **1.** beseitigen, entfernen, eliminieren (**from** aus). **2.** 🏛, *physiol.* ausscheiden. **3.** *Gegner* ausschalten: **be ~d** (*Sport*) ausscheiden. **e,lim·i'na·tion** *s* **1.** Beseitigung *f*, Eliminierung *f*. **2.** 🏛, *physiol.* Ausscheidung *f* (*a. Sport*): **~ contest** Ausscheidungswettbewerb *m*. **3.** Ausschaltung *f*.

e·lite, *Br. a.* **é·lite** [eɪ'liːt] *s* Elite *f*.

e·lix·ir [ɪ'lɪksə] *s* Elixier *n*.

elk [elk] *s zo.* Elch *m*.

e·lipse [ɪ'lɪps] *s* 🏛 Ellipse *f*. **el'lip·sis**

[ˌ~sɪs] *pl* **-ses** [ˌ~siːz] *s ling.* Ellipse *f*. **el'lip·tic, el'lip·ti·cal** [ˌ~kl] *adj* □ 🏛, *ling.* elliptisch.

elm [elm] *s* ♣ Ulme *f*, Rüster *f*.

el·o·cu·tion [ˌelə'kjuːʃn] *s* **1.** Vortrag(sweise *f*) *m*. **2.** Vortrags-, Redekunst *f*. **3.** Sprechtechnik *f*.

e·lon·gate ['iːlɒŋgeɪt] *v/t* (*u. v/i* sich) verlängern. **,e·lon'ga·tion** *s* Verlängerung *f*.

e·lope [ɪ'ləʊp] *v/i* **1.** (mit s-m *od.* s-r Geliebten) ausreißen *od.* durchbrennen. **2.** sich davonmachen.

el·o·quence ['eləkwəns] *s* Beredsamkeit *f*, Redegewandtheit *f*. **'el·o·quent** *adj* □ beredt, redegewandt.

else [els] *adv* **1.** (*in Fragen u. Verneinungen*) sonst, weiter, außerdem: **anything ~?** sonst noch etwas?; **what ~ can we do?** was können wir sonst noch tun?; **no one ~** sonst *od.* weiter niemand. **2.** ander: **that's s.th. ~** das ist et. anderes; **everybody ~** alle anderen; **s.o. ~** j-d anders. **3.** *mst* **or ~** sonst, andernfalls. **,~'where** *adv* **1.** sonst-, anderswo. **2.** anderswohin.

e·lu·ci·date [ɪ'luːsɪdeɪt] *v/t Text, Gründe etc* erklären, *Geheimnis etc* aufklären.

e·lu·sive [ɪ'luːsɪv] *adj* □ **1.** schwerfaßbar (*Dieb etc*), ausweichend (*Antwort*). **2.** schwer(er)faßbar *od.* -bestimmbar. **3.** unzuverlässig, schlecht (*Gedächtnis*).

elves [elvz] *pl von* **elf**.

e·ma·ci·at·ed [ɪ'meɪʃɪeɪtɪd] *adj* abgemagert, ausgemergelt.

em·a·nate ['eməneɪt] **I** *v/i* **1.** ausströmen (*Gas etc*), ausstrahlen (*Licht*) (**from** von). **2.** stammen, ausgehen (**from** von). **II** *v/t* **3.** ausströmen, -strahlen (*beide a. fig.*).

e·man·ci·pate [ɪ'mænsɪpeɪt] *v/t* emanzipieren, selbständig *od.* unabhängig machen (**from** von). **e'man·ci·pat·ed** *adj* emanzipiert (*Frau etc*), mündig (*Bürger*). **e,man·ci'pa·tion** *s* Emanzipation *f*.

em·balm [ɪm'bɑːm] *v/t* (ein)balsamieren.

em·bank [ɪm'bæŋk] *v/t* eindämmen, -deichen. **em'bank·ment** *s* **1.** Eindämmung *f*, -deichung *f*. **2.** (Erd)Damm *m*. **3.** (Bahn-, Straßen)Damm *m*.

em·bar·go [em'bɑːgəʊ] **I** *pl* **-goes** *s* **1.** ⚓ Embargo *n*: **lay** (*od.* **place, put**) **an ~ on**

→ 3. **2.** ✞ a) Handelssperre f, -verbot n, b) a. allg. Sperre f, Verbot n (**on** auf dat od. acc): **~ on imports** Einfuhrsperre. **II** v/t **3.** ein Embargo verhängen über (acc).

em·bark [ɪmˈbɑːk] **I** v/t **1.** ✈, ⚓ Passagiere an Bord nehmen, ⚓ a. einschiffen, Waren a. verladen (**for** nach). **II** v/i **2.** ✈, ⚓ an Bord gehen, ⚓ a. sich einschiffen (**for** nach). **3.** anfangen, unternehmen (**on** acc). **em·bar·ka·tion** [ˌembɑːˈkeɪʃn] s Einschiffung f, Verladung f.

em·bar·rass [ɪmˈbærəs] v/t in (Geld)Verlegenheit bringen, verlegen machen. **em·bar·rassed** adj **1.** verlegen. **2.** in Geldverlegenheit. **em·bar·rass·ing** adj □ unangenehm, peinlich (**to** dat). **em·bar·rass·ment** s **1.** a. (Geld)Verlegenheit f: **be an ~ to** j-n in Verlegenheit bringen; j-m peinlich sein.

em·bas·sy [ˈembəsɪ] s pol. Botschaft f.

em·bed [ɪmˈbed] v/t **1.** (ein)betten (**in** in acc): **~ded in concrete** einbetoniert. **2.** verankern (**in** acc od. dat) (a. fig.).

em·bel·lish [ɪmˈbelɪʃ] v/t **1.** verschöne(r)n, (aus)schmücken. **2.** Erzählung etc ausschmücken, Wahrheit beschönigen.

em·ber [ˈembə] s **1.** glühendes Stück Holz od. Kohle. **2.** pl Glut(asche) f.

em·bez·zle [ɪmˈbezl] v/t veruntreuen, unterschlagen. **em·bez·zle·ment** s Veruntreuung f, Unterschlagung f. **em·bez·zler** s Veruntreuer(in).

em·bit·ter [ɪmˈbɪtə] v/t **1.** j-n verbittern. **2.** Lage etc (noch) verschlimmern.

em·blem [ˈembləm] s **1.** Emblem n, Symbol n: **national ~** Hoheitszeichen n. **2.** Kennzeichen n.

em·bod·y [ɪmˈbɒdɪ] v/t **1.** verkörpern: a) konkrete Form geben (dat), b) personifizieren. **2.** umfassen, (in sich) vereinigen: **be embodied in** enthalten od. vereinigt sein in (dat).

em·bo·lism [ˈembəlɪzəm] s ✚ Embolie f.

em·brace [ɪmˈbreɪs] **I** v/t **1.** umarmen. **2.** fig. einschließen, umfassen. **3.** Beruf, Gelegenheit ergreifen; Angebot, Religion etc annehmen. **II** v/i **4.** sich umarmen. **III** s **5.** Umarmung f.

em·broi·der [ɪmˈbrɔɪdə] **I** v/t **1.** Muster sticken; Stoff besticken. **2.** Bericht etc ausschmücken. **II** v/i **3.** sticken.

em·broi·der·y s **1.** Sticken n: **~ needle** Sticknadel f. **2.** Stickerei(arbeit) f: **do ~** sticken. **3.** fig. Ausschmückung f.

em·bry·o [ˈembrɪəʊ] pl **-os** s biol. Embryo m: **in ~** fig. im Entstehen od. Werden. **em·bry·on·ic** [ˌ~ˈɒnɪk] adj **1.** biol. embryonal. **2.** fig. (noch) unentwickelt.

em·cee [ˌemˈsiː] bsd. Am. F **I** s Conférencier m. **II** v/t u. v/i als Conférencier leiten (fungieren).

e·mend [ɪˈmend] v/t bsd. Texte verbessern, korrigieren.

e·mer·ald [ˈemərəld] **I** s min. Smaragd m. **II** adj smaragdgrün.

e·merge [ɪˈmɜːdʒ] v/i **1.** auftauchen (a. fig.). **2.** hervorkommen (**from behind** hinter den Wolken etc). **3.** sich herausstellen od. ergeben (Tatsache). **e·mer·gence** [iːˈm~] s Auftauchen n (a. fig.).

e·mer·gen·cy [ɪˈmɜːdʒənsɪ] s plötzliche Notlage, kritische Lage: **in an ~, in case of ~** im Ernst- od. Notfall; **state of ~** Notstand m, pol. a. Ausnahmezustand m. **~ call** s teleph. Notruf m. **~ door, ~ ex·it** s Notausgang m. **~ land·ing** s ✈ Notlandung f: **make an ~** notlanden. **~ meet·ing** s Dringlichkeitssitzung f. **~ num·ber** s teleph. Notruf(nummer f) m. **~ op·er·a·tion** s ✚ Notoperation f. **~ ra·tion** s eiserne Ration. **~ stop** s mot. Vollbremsung f: **do** (od. **make**) **an ~** e-e Vollbremsung machen.

e·mer·gent [iːˈmɜːdʒənt] adj □ **1.** auftauchend (a. fig.). **2.** fig. (jung u.) aufstrebend: **~ countries** pl Schwellenländer pl.

em·er·y [ˈemərɪ] adj Schmirgel...: **~ paper.**

e·met·ic [ɪˈmetɪk] s Brechmittel n.

em·i·grant [ˈemɪgrənt] s Auswanderer m, bsd. pol. Emigrant(in). **em·i·grate** [ˈ~greɪt] v/i auswandern, bsd. pol. emigrieren (**from** aus, von; **to** nach). **em·i·gra·tion** s Auswanderung f, bsd. pol. Emigration f.

em·i·nence [ˈemɪnəns] s **1.** (An)Höhe f. **2.** Berühmtheit f: **reach** (od. **win**) **~** Bedeutung erlangen (**as** als). **3.** eccl. Eminenz f. **'em·i·nent** adj **1.** hervorragend, berühmt. **2.** bedeutend. **3.** überragend, außergewöhnlich. **'em·i·nent·ly** adv in hohem Maße, überaus.

e·mis·sion [ɪ'mɪʃn] s **1.** Ausstoß m, -strahlung f, Aus-, Verströmen n. **2.** ✝ Ausgabe f, Emission f.

e·mit [ɪ'mɪt] v/t **1.** Lava, Rauch ausstoßen, Licht, Wärme austrahlen, Gas, Wärme aus-, verströmen. **2.** Ton, Meinung von sich geben; Schrei, Fluch etc ausstoßen. **3.** Banknoten ausgeben, Wertpapiere a. emittieren.

e·mo·tion [ɪ'məʊʃn] s **1.** Emotion f, Gefühl n. **2.** Erregung f. **3.** Rührung f, Ergriffenheit f. **e·mo·tion·al** [~ʃənl] adj □ **1.** emotional, emotionell: a) gefühlsmäßig, -bedingt, b) gefühlsbetont, empfindsam, c) Gemüts..., seelisch: ~ balance inneres od. seelisches Gleichgewicht. **2.** gefühlvoll, rührselig. **e·mo·tion·al·ize** [~ʃənlaɪz] v/t emotionalisieren. **e·mo·tion·less** adj gefühllos. **e·mo·tive** [~tɪv] adj □ **1.** gefühlvoll. **2.** gefühlsbetont: ~ term (od. word) emotionsgeladenes Wort; Reizwort n.

em·pa·thy ['empəθɪ] s Einfühlung(svermögen) f: feel ~ for sich hineinversetzen in (acc).

em·per·or ['empərə] s Kaiser m.

em·pha·sis ['emfəsɪs] pl **-ses** [~siːz] s ling. Betonung f, fig. a. Schwerpunkt m; Nachdruck m: lay (od. place, put) ~ on → emphasize; with ~ nachdrücklich, mit Nachdruck. **em·pha·size** ['~saɪz] v/t (nachdrücklich) betonen, Nachdruck legen auf (acc), hervorheben, unterstreichen. **em·phat·ic** [ɪm'fætɪk] adj (~ally) nachdrücklich; eindringlich.

em·pire ['empaɪə] s **1.** Reich n, Imperium n (beide a. ✝ u. fig.). **2.** Kaiserreich n.

em·pir·i·cal [em'pɪrɪkl] adj □ empirisch, Erfahrungs...

em·ploy [ɪm'plɔɪ] I v/t **1.** j-n beschäftigen (as als); an-, einstellen. **2.** Gewalt etc anwenden, gebrauchen. **3.** (in) Energie etc widmen (dat), Zeit verbringen (mit): be ~ed in doing s.th. damit beschäftigt sein, et. zu tun. II s **4.** Dienst(e pl) m, Beschäftigung(sverhältnis n) f: in s.o.'s ~ bei j-m beschäftigt. **em·ploy·ee** [,emplɔɪ'iː] s Arbeitnehmer(in), Angestellte m, f, Arbeiter(in): the ~s pl die Belegschaft. **em·ploy·er** [ɪm'plɔɪə] s Arbeitgeber(in); Unternehmer(in). **em·ploy·ment** s **1.** Beschäftigung f,

Arbeit f, (An)Stellung f: full ~ Vollbeschäftigung; ~ agency Stellenvermittlung(sbüro n) f; ~ contract Arbeitsvertrag m; ~ market Arbeits-, Stellenmarkt m; ~ office Br. Arbeitsamt n. **2.** An-, Einstellung f.

em·pow·er [ɪm'paʊə] v/t bevollmächtigen, ermächtigen (to do zu tun).

em·press ['empris] s Kaiserin f.

emp·ti·ness ['emptɪnɪs] s Leere f (a. fig.). **'emp·ty** I adj □ **1.** allg. leer (a. fig. Versprechungen, Worte etc), (Haus etc a.) leerstehend: feel ~ sich (innerlich) leer fühlen; F Kohldampf schieben; ~ stand ~ leerstehen; ~ of ohne; ~ of meaning nichtssagend; → stomach 1. II v/t **2.** leeren (into in acc), Fach etc a. ausräumen, Glas etc a. austrinken. **3.** Haus etc räumen. III v/i **4.** sich leeren. **5.** sich ergießen, münden (into in acc). IV s **6.** pl Leergut n. **~·'hand·ed** adj mit leeren Händen, unverrichteterdinge.

em·u·late ['emjʊleɪt] v/t **1.** wetteifern mit. **2.** nacheifern (dat), es gleichtun wollen (dat).

e·mul·sion [ɪ'mʌlʃn] s 🜂, etc Emulsion f.

en·a·ble [ɪ'neɪbl] v/t **1.** j-n berechtigen, ermächtigen (to do zu tun). **2.** j-n befähigen, es j-m möglich machen (to do zu tun). **3.** et. möglich machen, ermöglichen: ~ s.th. to be done es ermöglichen, daß et. getan wird.

en·act [ɪ'nækt] v/t **1.** ⚖ Gesetz erlassen; verfügen, -ordnen. **2.** thea. etc Stück aufführen; Person, Rolle darstellen, spielen. **en·act·ment** s Verfügung f, -ordnung f.

en·am·el [ɪ'næml] I s **1.** Email(le f) n. **2.** Glasur f. **3.** anat. Zahnschmelz m. II v/t pret u. pp **-eled**, bsd. Br. **-elled 4.** emaillieren. **5.** glasieren.

en·am·o(u)r [ɪ'næmə] v/t: be ~ed of (od. with) verliebt sein in (acc); fig. gefesselt od. verzaubert sein von.

en·case [ɪn'keɪs] v/t: ~d in gehüllt in (acc), umhüllt von.

en·chant [ɪn'tʃɑːnt] v/t **1.** verzaubern. **2.** fig. bezaubern, entzücken: be ~ed entzückt sein (by, with von). **en·chant·er** s Zauberer m. **en·chant·ing** adj □ bezaubernd, entzückend. **en·chant·ment** s **1.** Verzauberung f. **2.** Zauber m (a.

fig.). **3.** Zauberei *f.* **en'chant·ress** *s* **1.** Zauberin *f.* **2.** *fig.* bezaubernde Frau.

en·ci·pher [ɪn'saɪfə] → *encode.*

en·cir·cle [ɪn'sɜːkl] *v/t* **1.** umgeben: **∼d by** (*od.* **with**) umgeben von. **2.** umfassen. **3.** einkreisen, umzingeln, ✕ *a.* einkesseln. **en'cir·cle·ment** *s* Einkreisung *f*, Umzing(e)lung *f*, ✕ *a.* Einkesselung *f.*

en·close [ɪn'kləʊz] *v/t* **1.** (*in*) einschließen (in *acc od. dat*), umgeben (mit). **2.** umringen. **3.** *mit der Hand etc* umfassen. **4.** beilegen, -fügen (*in*, **with** *dat*): **∼d please find** in der Anlage erhalten Sie. **en'clo·sure** [-ʒə] *s* Anlage *f* (*zu e-m Brief etc*).

en·code [en'kəʊd] *v/t* Text verschlüsseln, chiffrieren.

en·com·pass [ɪn'kʌmpəs] *v/t* **1.** umgeben (**with** mit). **2.** *fig.* umfassen.

en·core **I** *int* [ɒŋ'kɔː] **1.** da capo!; Zugabe! **II** *s* ['ɒŋkɔː] **2.** Dakapo(ruf *m*) *n.* **3.** Wiederholung *f* (*e-r Arie etc*); Zugabe *f.* **III** *v/t* ['ɒŋkɔː] **4.** die Wiederholung (*gen*) verlangen *od.* erzwingen; von *j-m* e-e Zugabe verlangen *od.* erzwingen.

en·coun·ter [ɪn'kaʊntə] **I** *v/t* **1.** *j-m*, *e-r Sache* begegnen, *j-n* treffen, auf *j-n*, *Widerstand etc* stoßen. **2.** mit *j-m* (*feindlich*) zs.-stoßen. **II** *v/i* **3.** sich begegnen *od.* treffen. **III** *s* **4.** Begegnung *f* (**of**, **with** mit). **5.** *feindlicher Zs.-stoß m.*

en·cour·age [ɪn'kʌrɪdʒ] *v/t* **1.** *j-n* ermutigen, ermuntern (**to** zu), *j-m* Mut machen. **2.** *j-n* unterstützen, bestärken (**in** *dat*). **3.** *et.* fördern, unterstützen. **en'cour·age·ment** *s* **1.** Ermutigung *f*, Ermunterung *f.* **2.** Unterstützung *f*, Bestärkung *f.* **3.** Förderung *f.*

en·croach [ɪn'krəʊtʃ] *v/i* **1.** (**on**) eingreifen (in *j-s Besitz od. Recht*), unberechtigt eindringen (in *acc*), sich Übergriffe leisten (in, auf *acc*). **2.** über Gebühr in Anspruch nehmen, mißbrauchen (**on** *acc*). **en'croach·ment** *s* Ein-, Übergriff *m.*

en·crust → *incrust.*

en·cum·ber [ɪn'kʌmbə] *v/t* Grundstück *etc* belasten: **∼ed with mortgages** hypothekarisch belastet. **en'cum·brance** *s* Belastung *f.*

en·cy·clo·p(a)e·di·a [en,saɪkləʊ'piːdjə] *s*

Enzyklopädie *f.* **en,cy·clo'p(a)e·dic** *adj* (**∼ally**) enzyklopädisch.

end [end] **I** *v/t* **1.** beenden, zu Ende bringen *od.* führen. **2.** a) *a.* **∼ up** *et.* ab-, beschließen (**with** mit), b) *den Rest s-r Tage* zu-, verbringen, *s-e Tage* beschließen. **II** *v/i* **3.** enden, aufhören. **4.** *a.* **∼ up** enden: **∼ happily** gut ausgehen; **∼ in disaster** (*od.* **a fiasco**) mit e-m Fiasko enden. **5. ∼ up** a) enden, landen (**in prison** im Gefängnis), b) enden (**as** als). **III** *s* **6.** (*örtlich*) Ende *n*: **go off** (**at**) **the ∼ deep** F hochgehen, wütend werden; **make** (**both**) **∼s meet** durchkommen, finanziell über die Runden kommen. **7.** Ende *n*, Rest *m*: **∼ of** → *thick* 1, *thin* 1. **8.** (*zeitlich*) Ende *n*: **in the ∼** am Ende, schließlich; **at the ∼ of May** Ende Mai; **without ∼** unaufhörlich; **come** (*od.* **draw**) **to an ∼** zu Ende gehen; **make an ∼ of**, **put an ∼ to** e-r *Sache* ein Ende setzen. **9.** Tod *m*, Ende *n.* **10.** *oft pl* Absicht *f*, (End)Zweck *m*, Ziel *n*: **the ∼ justifies** (*od.* **sanctifies**) **the means** der Zweck heiligt die Mittel; **to this ∼** zu diesem Zweck; **to no ∼** vergebens.

en·dan·ger [ɪn'deɪndʒə] *v/t* gefährden.

end con·sum·er *s* ✝ End-, Letztverbraucher *m.*

en·dear·ing [ɪn'dɪərɪŋ] *adj* □ **1.** gewinnend (*Lächeln etc*). **2.** liebenswert (*Eigenschaft etc*). **en'dear·ment** *s*: (**term of**) **∼** Kosename *m*, -wort *n*; **words** *pl* **of ∼**, **∼s** *pl* liebe *od.* zärtliche Worte *pl.*

en·deav·o(u)r [ɪn'devə] **I** *v/t* bemüht *od.* bestrebt sein (**to do** zu tun). **II** *s* Bemühung *f*, Bestrebung *f*: **make every ∼** sich nach Kräften bemühen.

end·ing ['endɪŋ] *s* **1.** Ende *n*, Schluß *m*: **happy ∼** Happy-End *n.* **2.** *ling.* Endung *f.*

en·dive ['endɪv] *s* ♣ (Winter)Endivie *f.*

end·less ['endlɪs] *adj* □ *allg.* endlos.

en·dorse [ɪn'dɔːs] *v/t* **1.** *Erklärung etc* vermerken (**on** auf *dat*); *bsd. Br.* e-e *Strafe* vermerken auf (*e-m Führerschein*). **2.** ✝ *Scheck etc* indossieren, girieren. **3.** *Plan etc* billigen. **en·dor·see** [,endɔː'siː] *s* ✝ Indossat *m.*

en·dorse·ment [ɪn'dɔːsmənt] *s* **1.** Vermerk *m*; *bsd. Br.* Strafvermerk *m* (*auf e-m Führerschein*). **2.** ✝ Indossament *n*,

Giro n. **3.** Billigung f. **en'dors·er** s ✝ Indossant m.

en-dow [ɪn'daʊ] v/t **1.** e-e Stiftung machen (dat). **2.** et. stiften: ~ **s.o. with s.th.** j-m et. stiften. **3.** fig. ausstatten (with mit). **en'dow·ment** s **1.** Stiftung f. **2.** Begabung f, Talent n.

end prod·uct s **1.** ✝, ◎ Endprodukt n. **2.** fig. (End)Produkt n.

en-dur-a-ble [ɪn'djʊərəbl] adj □ erträglich. **en'dur·ance** I s **1.** Standhaftigkeit f, Ausdauer f; Aushalten n, Ertragen n: **beyond** (od. **past**) ~ unerträglich. **2.** ◎ Dauerleistung f. II adj **3.** Dauer...: ~ **test** ◎ Belastungsprobe f. **en'dure** I v/i **1.** andauern, Bestand haben. **2.** durchhalten. II v/t **3.** aushalten, ertragen, erdulden. **4.** neg. ausstehen, leiden.

end us·er → **end consumer**.

en-e-ma ['enɪmə] pl **-mas, -ma·ta** [~mətə] s ⚕ Klistier n, Einlauf m: **give s.o. an ~** j-m e-n Einlauf machen.

en-e-my ['enəmɪ] I s ✕ Feind m, weitS. a. Gegner m (of, to gen): ~ **to reform** Reformgegner; **make an ~ of s.o.** sich j-n zum Feind machen. II adj feindlich, Feind(es)...

en-er-get-ic [ˌenə'dʒetɪk] adj (~ally) energisch. **'en·er·gy** s Energie f (a. phys.): ~**-saving** energiesparend.

en-er-vate ['enɜːveɪt] v/t entkräften, schwächen (a. fig.); entnerven.

en-fee-ble [ɪn'fiːbl] v/t entkräften, schwächen (a. fig.).

en-fold [ɪn'fəʊld] v/t **1.** einhüllen (in in acc), umhüllen (with mit) (beide a. fig.). **2.** umfassen: ~ **s.o. in one's arms** j-n in die Arme schließen.

en-force [ɪn'fɔːs] v/t **1.** Argument, ✝, ⚖ Forderung geltend machen; e-r Sache Geltung verschaffen, Gesetz etc durchführen; Urteil vollstrecken. **2.** durchsetzen, erzwingen: ~ **s.th. on s.o.** et. von j-m erzwingen; j-m et. aufzwingen. **en'force·ment** s **1.** ⚖ Geltendmachung f, ⚖ Vollstreckung f. **2.** Durchsetzung f, Erzwingung f.

en-fran-chise [ɪn'fræntʃaɪz] v/t das Wahlrecht verleihen (dat).

en-gage [ɪn'ɡeɪdʒ] I v/t **1.** (o.s. sich) verpflichten (**to do** zu tun). **2.** become (od. **get**) ~**d** sich verloben (**to** mit). **3.** j-n ein-, anstellen, Künstler etc engagieren

(as als). **4.** fig. j-n in Anspruch nehmen, j-s Aufmerksamkeit a. auf sich ziehen. **5.** ◎ einrasten lassen, Kupplung etc einrücken, Gang einlegen. II v/i **6.** sich verpflichten (**to do** zu tun). **7.** ~ **in** sich einlassen auf (acc) od. in (acc); sich beschäftigen mit. **8.** ◎ einrasten.

en'gaged adj **1.** ~ **a. to be married** verlobt: ~ **to** verlobt mit. **2.** beschäftigt (in, on mit): **be ~ in doing s.th.** damit beschäftigt sein, et. zu tun. **3.** in Anspruch genommen: **my time is fully ~** ich bin zeitlich voll ausgelastet. **4.** teleph. Br. besetzt: ~ **tone** Besetztton m, -zeichen n. **en'gage·ment** s **1.** Verpflichtung f: **without ~** unverbindlich, ✝ a. freibleibend. **2.** Verabredung f: **have an ~** verabredet sein. **3.** Verlobung f (**to** mit): ~ **ring** Verlobungsring m. **4.** (An)Stellung f, thea. etc Engagement n. **en'gag·ing** adj □ einnehmend (Wesen etc), gewinnend (Lächeln etc).

en-gen-der [ɪn'dʒendə] v/t Neid etc erzeugen, hervorrufen (in bei).

en-gine ['endʒɪn] s **1.** Motor m. **2.** 🚂 Lokomotive f. ~ **block** s Motorblock m. ~ **driv·er** s 🚂 Lokomotivführer m. **en-gi-neer** [ˌendʒɪ'nɪə] I s **1.** Ingenieur m; Techniker m; Mechaniker m. **2.** 🚂 Am. Lokomotivführer m. II v/t **3.** fig. (geschickt) in die Wege leiten, organisieren. **en-gi'neer·ing** s allg. Technik f, engS. Ingenieurwesen n, (a. **mechanical ~**) Maschinen- u. Gerätebau m.

Eng-lish ['ɪŋglɪʃ] I adj **1.** englisch. II s **2.** **the ~** pl die Engländer pl. **3.** ling. Englisch n: **in ~** auf englisch; **in plain ~** unverblümt; auf gut deutsch; **Queen's** (od. **King's**) ~ hochsprachliches Englisch. ~**man** ['~mən] s (irr **man**) Engländer m. **'~·wom·an** s (irr **woman**) Engländerin f.

en-grave [ɪn'ɡreɪv] v/t (on) (in Metall, Stein etc) (ein)gravieren, (-)meißeln, (in Holz) einschnitzen: **it is ~d on** (od. **in**) **his memory** (od. **mind**) es hat sich ihm tief od. unauslöschlich eingeprägt. **en'grav·er** s Graveur m: ~ **on copper** Kupferstecher m. **en'grav·ing** s **1.** Gravieren n. **2.** Gravierung f, (Kupfer-, Stahl)Stich m, (Holz)Schnitt m.

en-gross [ɪn'ɡrəʊs] v/t j-s Aufmerksamkeit etc in Anspruch nehmen, Macht, Unterhaltung etc an sich reißen:

en'grossed *adj* (*in*) (voll) in Anspruch genommen (von), vertieft, versunken (in *acc*).

en·gulf [ɪn'gʌlf] *v/t* verschlingen (*a. fig.*).

en·hance [ɪn'hɑːns] *v/t* Wert etc erhöhen, steigern, heben.

e·nig·ma [ɪ'nɪgmə] *s fig.* Rätsel *n*.

en·ig·mat·ic [ˌenɪg'mætɪk] *adj* (**~ally**) rätselhaft.

en·joy [ɪn'dʒɔɪ] *v/t* **1.** Vergnügen *od.* Gefallen finden *od.* Freude haben an (*dat*): **~ doing s.th.** daran Vergnügen finden, et. zu tun; *I* **~ dancing** ich tanze gern, Tanzen macht mir Spaß; *did you* **~ the play?** hat dir das Stück gefallen?; **~ o.s.** sich amüsieren *od.* gut unterhalten; **~ yourself!** viel Spaß! **2.** genießen, sich *et.* schmecken lassen. **3.** sich *e-s Besitzes* erfreuen, *j-s Vertrauen etc* genießen: **~ good health** sich e-r guten Gesundheit erfreuen. en'joy·a·ble *adj* □ angenehm, erfreulich. en'joy·ment *s* **1.** Vergnügen *n*, Freude *f* (**of** an *dat*). **2.** Genuß *m*: **be in the ~ of → enjoy** 3.

en·large [ɪn'lɑːdʒ] **I** *v/t* **1.** vergrößern (*a. phot.*), *Kenntnisse etc* a. erweitern, *Einfluß etc* a. ausdehnen. **II** *v/i* **2.** sich vergrößern *od.* erweitern *od.* ausdehnen. **3.** sich verbreiten *od.* (weitläufig) auslassen (**on** über *acc*). en'large·ment *s* Vergrößerung *f* (*a. phot.*).

en·light·en [ɪn'laɪtn] *v/t* aufklären, belehren (**on, as to** über *acc*). en'light·en·ment *s* Aufklärung *f*.

en·list [ɪn'lɪst] **I** *v/t* **1.** *Soldaten* anwerben, *Rekruten* einstellen. **2.** *fig.* heranziehen, *j-s Dienste* in Anspruch nehmen. **II** *v/i* **3.** ⚔ Soldat werden, sich (freiwillig) melden (**to** zu). **4.** (*in*) mitwirken (bei), sich beteiligen (an *dat*).

en·liv·en [ɪn'laɪvn] *v/t* beleben, in Schwung bringen.

en·mesh [ɪn'meʃ] *v/t*: **be ~ed in one's own lies** sich in s-n eigenen Lügen verstrickt *od.* verfangen haben.

en·mi·ty ['enmɪtɪ] *s* Feindschaft *f*: **be at ~ with** verfeindet sein mit.

e·nor·mous [ɪ'nɔːməs] *adj* □ enorm, ungeheuer, gewaltig.

e·nough [ɪ'nʌf] **I** *adj* ausreichend, genug: **be ~** (aus)reichen, genügen. **II** *s*: *I have had ~, thank you* danke, ich bin satt!; **~ of that!** genug davon!, Schluß damit! **III** *adv* genug, genügend: **be kind** (*od.*

good*) **~ to do this for me sei so freundlich *od.* gut u. erledige das für mich; **curiously** (*od.* **strangely**) **~** merkwürdigerweise.

en·quire, en·quir·y → **inquire, inquiry.**

en·rage [ɪn'reɪdʒ] *v/t* wütend machen. en'raged *adj* wütend, aufgebracht (**at, by** über *acc*).

en·rap·ture [ɪn'ræptʃə] *v/t* hinreißen, entzücken. en'rap·tured *adj* hingerissen, entzückt (**at, by** von).

en·rich [ɪn'rɪtʃ] *v/t* **1.** bereichern (*a. fig.*). **2.** 🔬, *etc* anreichern.

en·rol(l) [ɪn'rəʊl] *v/t* **1.** *j-n, j-s Namen* einschreiben, -tragen (**in** in *dat od. acc*), *univ. j-n* immatrikulieren: **~ o.s. → 3. 2.** *j-n* aufnehmen (**in** in *e-n Verein etc*): **~ o.s. in → 4. II** *v/i* **3.** sich einschreiben (lassen), *univ.* sich immatrikulieren: **~ for a course** e-n Kurs belegen. **4.** **~ in** beitreten (*dat*). en'rol(l)·ment *s* **1.** Einschreibung *f*, -tragung *f*, *univ.* Immatrikulation *f*. **2.** (Gesamt)Zahl *f* der Eingetragenen *od. univ.* Immatrikulierten.

en route [ˌɑːn'ruːt] *adv* unterwegs (**for** nach).

en·sem·ble [ɑːn'sɑːmbl] *s* **1.** das Ganze, Gesamteindruck *m*. **2.** ♪, *thea.*, *Mode:* Ensemble *n*.

en·sign ['ensaɪn] *s* ⚓ (*bsd.* National-) Flagge *f*.

en·slave [ɪn'sleɪv] *v/t* zum Sklaven machen (*a. fig.*), versklaven.

en·snare [ɪn'sneə] *v/t* **1.** in e-r Schlinge fangen. **2.** *fig.* bestricken, umgarnen.

en·sue [ɪn'sjuː] *v/i* **1.** (darauf-, nach)folgen: *the ensuing years* die (darauf)folgenden Jahre. **2.** folgen, sich ergeben (**from** aus).

en·sure [ɪn'ʃɔː] *v/t* **1.** (**against, from**) sichern (vor *dat*, gegen), schützen (vor *dat*). **2.** sicherstellen, garantieren (**s.th.** et.; *that* daß; **so being** daß *j-d* ist). **3.** sorgen für *et.*: **~ that** dafür sorgen, daß.

en·tail [ɪn'teɪl] *v/t* mit sich bringen, zur Folge haben, nach sich ziehen, *Kosten etc* verursachen, erfordern.

en·tan·gle [ɪn'tæŋgl] *v/t* **1.** *Haare, Garn etc* verwirren, -filzen. **2.** (**o.s.** sich) verwickeln, -heddern (**in** in *dat*). **3.** *fig.* verwickeln, -stricken (**in** in *acc*).

en·ter ['entə] **I** *v/t* **1.** (hinein-, herein)gehen, (-)kommen, (-)treten in (*acc*), eintreten, -steigen in (*acc*), betreten; einreisen in (*acc*); ♃, 🚢 einlaufen, -fahren in (*acc*); eindringen in (*acc*): *it ~ed my mind* es kam mir in den Sinn. **2.** *fig.* eintreten in (*acc*), beitreten (*dat*). **3.** *Namen* eintragen, -schreiben, *j-n* aufnehmen, zulassen: *~ one's name* (*od.* **o.s.**) → 7a. **4.** *Sport*: melden, nennen (*for* für): *~ o.s.* → 7b. **5.** *Vorschlag etc* einreichen, -bringen: *~ a protest* Protest erheben *od.* einlegen. **II** *v/i* **6.** eintreten, herein-, hineinkommen, -gehen; *thea.* auftreten: ♀ *Hamlet* Hamlet tritt auf. **7.** a) sich eintragen *od.* -schreiben *od.* anmelden (*for* für), b) (*Sport*) melden, nennen (*for* für).

Verbindungen mit Präpositionen:

en·ter| in·to *v/i* **1.** → *enter* 1, 2. **2.** anfangen, beginnen; sich einlassen auf (*acc*); eingehen auf (*acc*): *~ into correspondence with* in Briefwechsel treten mit. **3.** *Verpflichtung, Partnerschaft etc* eingehen. *~ on* *v/i* **1.** *Thema* anschneiden; sich in *ein Gespräch etc* einlassen. **2.** *Amt, Erbschaft* antreten; *Laufbahn* einschlagen; in *ein neues Stadium etc* treten.

en·ter·i·tis [ˌentəˈraɪtɪs] *s* 🔬 Darmkatarrh *m*.

en·ter·prise [ˈentəpraɪz] *s* **1.** Unternehmen *n*, -nehmung *f*. **2.** ♀ Unternehmen *n*, Betrieb *m*; Unternehmen *n*. **3.** Unternehmungsgeist *m*. **'en·ter·pris·ing** *adj* □ unternehmungslustig.

en·ter·tain [ˌentəˈteɪn] *v/t* **1.** (*angenehm*) unterhalten. **2.** bewirten. **3.** *Furcht, Hoffnung etc* hegen. **4.** *Vorschlag etc* in Betracht *od.* Erwägung ziehen: *~ an idea* sich mit e-m Gedanken tragen. **ˌen·ter·tain·er** *s* Entertainer(in). **ˌen·ter·tain·ing** *adj* □ unterhaltend, -haltsam. **ˌen·ter·tain·ment** *s* **1.** Unterhaltung *f*: *much* (*od.* **greatly**) *to his ~* sehr zu s-r Belustigung. **2.** (*öffentliche*) Unterhaltung, (*professionell dargebotena.*) Entertainment *n*: *~ industry* Unterhaltungsindustrie *f*; *~ tax* Vergnügungssteuer *f*.

en·thral(l) [ɪnˈθrɔːl] *v/t fig.* bezaubern, fesseln.

en·thuse [ɪnˈθjuːz] *v/i* F (*about, over*) begeistert sein (von), schwärmen (von, für).

en·thu·si·asm [ɪnˈθjuːzɪæzəm] *s* Enthusiasmus *m*, Begeisterung *f* (*for* für;

about über *acc*). **en·thu·si·ast** [~æst] *s* Enthusiast(in). **en,thu·si·as·tic** [~ˈæstɪk] (*~ally*) begeistert (*about, over* von), enthusiastisch.

en·tice [ɪnˈtaɪs] *v/t* **1.** locken (*into* in *acc*): *~ away* weglocken (*from* von); ♂ abwerben; *~ s.o.'s girlfriend away* j-m die Freundin abspenstig machen. **2.** verlocken, -leiten, -führen (*into* zu *et.*): *~ s.o. to do* (*od.* **into doing**) *s.th.* j-n dazu verleiten, et. zu tun. **en·tice·ment** *s* **1.** (Ver)Lockung *f*, (An)Reiz *m*. **2.** Verführung *f*, -leitung *f*. **en·tic·ing** *adj* □ verlockend, -führerisch.

en·tire [ɪnˈtaɪə] *adj* **1.** ganz: a) vollzählig, -ständig, b) gesamt, Gesamt..., c) unversehrt, unbeschädigt. **2.** *fig.* voll, uneingeschränkt (*Vertrauen etc*): *be in ~ agreement* voll u. ganz *od.* völlig übereinstimmen mit. **en·tire·ly** *adv* völlig, gänzlich. **en·tire·ty** *s*: *in its ~* in s-r Gesamtheit, als (ein) Ganzes.

en·ti·tle [ɪnˈtaɪtl] *v/t* **1.** *Buch etc* betiteln: *~d ...* mit dem Titel ... **2.** *j-n* berechtigen (*to* zu): *be ~d to* ein Anrecht *od.* (e-n) Anspruch haben auf (*acc*); *be ~d to do s.th.* (dazu) berechtigt sein *od.* das Recht haben, et. zu tun; *~d to vote* wahl-, stimmberechtigt.

en·ti·ty [ˈentɪtɪ] *s* **1.** Einheit *f*. **2.** 🔬 Rechtspersönlichkeit *f*: *legal ~* juristische Person.

en·trails [ˈentreɪlz] *s pl anat.* Eingeweide *pl*.

en·trance¹ [ˈentrəns] *s* **1.** Eintreten *n*, -tritt *m*; ♃, 🚢 Einlaufen *n*, -fahrt *f*. **2.** Ein-, Zugang *m* (*to* zu); Zufahrt *f*: *~ hall* (Eingangs-, Vor)Halle *f*, (Haus-)Flur *m*. **3.** *fig.* Antritt *m* (*on an inheritance* e-r Erbschaft): *~ on an office* Amtsantritt *m*. **4.** Einlaß *m*, Ein-, Zutritt *m*: *~ fee* Eintritt(sgeld *n*); Aufnahmegebühr *f*; *no ~!* Zutritt verboten! **5.** *thea.* Auftritt *m*: *make one's ~* auftreten.

en·trance² [ɪnˈtrɑːns] *v/t* entzücken, hinreißen: *~d* entzückt, hingerissen (*at, by* von).

en·trant [ˈentrənt] *s* **1.** (Berufs)Anfänger(in) (*to* in *dat*). **2.** neues Mitglied. **3.** *Sport*: Teilnehmer(in) (*a. allg. an* e-m Wettbewerb).

en·treat [ɪnˈtriːt] *v/t* **1.** inständig *od.* dringend bitten, anflehen (*for* um). **2.**

et. erflehen (**of** von). **en'treat·ing** *adj* □ flehentlich. **en'treat·y** *s* dringende Bitte: **at s.o.'s ~** auf j-s Bitte (hin).

en·trée ['ɒntreɪ] *s* **1.** *bsd. fig.* Zutritt *m* (**into** zu). **2.** *gastr.* Zwischen-, *Am.* Hauptgericht *n.*

en·trench [ɪn'trentʃ] *v/t* ✗ (**o.s.** sich) verschanzen (**behind** hinter *dat*) (*a. fig.*). **en'trenched** *adj fig.* eingewurzelt.

en·tre·pre·neur [,ɒntrəprə'nɜː] *s* ✝ Unternehmer *m.*

en·trust [ɪn'trʌst] *v/t* **1.** *et.* anvertrauen (**to s.o.** j-m). **2.** *j-n* betrauen (**with** mit).

en·try ['entrɪ] *s* **1.** → **entrance¹** 1. 2. Einreise *f*, Zuzug *m*: **~ visa** Einreisevisum *n.* **3.** → **entrance¹** 5. **4.** Beitritt *m* (**into** zu). **5.** Einlaß *m*, Zutritt *m*: **gain** (*od. obtain*) **~** Einlaß finden; **force an ~ into, make a forcible ~ into** gewaltsam eindringen in (*acc*); **no ~!** Zutritt verboten. **6.** Zu-, Eingang(stür *f*) *m*, Einfahrt(stor *n*) *f*; (Eingangs-, Vor)Halle *f*, (Haus)Flur *m.* **7.** Eintrag(ung *f*) *m*, ✝ *a.* Buchung *f*; Stichwort *n* (*im Lexikon etc*). **8.** *Sport:* a) Nennung *f*, Meldung *f*, b) → **entrant** 3. '**~phone** *s* Türsprechanlage *f.*

en·twine [ɪn'twaɪn] *v/t* winden, schlingen (**[a]round** um), umwinden (**with** mit).

e·nu·mer·ate [ɪ'njuːməreɪt] *v/t* aufzählen. **e,nu·mer'a·tion** *s* Aufzählung *f.*

e·nun·ci·ate [ɪ'nʌnsɪeɪt] *v/t* **1.** ausdrücken, -sprechen. **2.** formulieren. **3.** (*bsd.* deutlich) aussprechen. **II** *v/i* **4. ~ clearly** e-e deutliche Aussprache haben, deutlich sprechen.

en·vel·op [ɪn'veləp] *v/t* **1.** einschlagen, -wickeln, (ein)hüllen (**in** in *acc*). **2.** *fig.* ver-, einhüllen: **~ed in mystery** geheimnisumhüllt. **en·ve·lope** ['envələʊp] *s* **1.** Hülle *f*, Umschlag *m.* **2.** Briefumschlag *m*, Kuvert *n.*

en·vi·a·ble ['envɪəbl] *adj* □ beneidenswert. **'en·vi·er** *s* Neider(in). **'en·vi·ous** *adj* □ neidisch (**of** auf *acc*).

en·vi·ron·ment [ɪn'vaɪərənmənt] *s* **1.** Umgebung *f*, *sociol. a.* Milieu *n.* **2.** Umwelt *f.* **en,vi·ron'men·tal** [,~'mentl] *adj* □ **1.** *sociol.* Milieu-... **2.** Umwelt-...: **~ pollution** Umweltverschmutzung *f*; **~ protection** Umweltschutz *m*; **~ly beneficial** (*harmful*) umweltfreundlich

(-feindlich). **en,vi·ron'men·tal·ist** [,~təlɪst] *s* Umweltschützer(in). **en'vi·rons** *s pl* Umgebung *f* (*e-s Ortes etc*).

en·vis·age [ɪn'vɪzɪdʒ] *v/t* **1.** gedenken (**doing** zu tun), in Aussicht nehmen, ins Auge fassen. **2.** sich *et.* vorstellen. **en·vi·sion** [ɪn'vɪʒn] → **envisage** 2.

en·voy ['envɔɪ] *s* **1.** *pol.* Gesandte *m.* **2.** Abgesandte *m*, Bevollmächtigte *m.*

en·vy ['envɪ] **I** *s* **1.** Neid *m* (**of** auf *acc*). **2.** Gegenstand *m* des Neides: **his car is the ~ of everybody** alle beneiden ihn um s-n Wagen. **II** *v/t* **3.** *j-n* beneiden (**s.th.** um etwas).

en·zyme ['enzaɪm] *s Biochemie:* Enzym *n.*

e·phem·er·al [ɪ'femərəl] *adj* □ flüchtig, kurzlebig.

ep·ic ['epɪk] **I** *adj* (**~ally**) **1.** episch. **2.** heldenhaft. **II** *s* **3.** Epos *n.*

ep·i·cure ['epɪˌkjʊə] *s* **1.** Epikureer *m*, Genußmensch *m.* **2.** Feinschmecker *m.*

ep·i·dem·ic [,epɪ'demɪk] ✖ **I** *adj* (**~ally**) epidemisch (*a. fig.*). **II** *s* Epidemie *f*, Seuche *f* (*beide a. fig.*).

ep·i·der·mis [,epɪ'dɜːmɪs] *s anat.* Oberhaut *f.*

ep·i·gram ['epɪɡræm] *s* Epigramm *n.*

ep·i·lep·sy ['epɪlepsɪ] *s* ✖ Epilepsie *f.* **,ep·i'lep·tic** **I** *adj* (**~ally**) epileptisch: **~ fit** epileptischer Anfall. **II** *s* Epileptiker(in).

ep·i·logue ['epɪlɒɡ] *s* Epilog *m*: a) Nachwort *n* (*e-s Buchs etc*), b) *fig.* Nachspiel *n*, Ausklang *m.*

E·piph·a·ny [ɪ'pɪfənɪ] *s eccl.* Dreikönigsfest *n.*

e·pis·co·pal [ɪ'pɪskəpl] *adj* □ bischöflich, Bischofs-... **e·pis·co·pate** [,~kəʊpət] *s* Episkopat *m*, *n*, Bistum *n.*

ep·i·sode ['epɪsəʊd] *s* **1.** Episode *f.* **2.** *Rundfunk, TV etc:* Folge *f.* **ep·i·sod·ic** [,~'sɒdɪk] *adj* (**~ally**) **1.** episodisch, **2.** episodenhaft.

e·pis·tle [ɪ'pɪsl] *s eccl.* Epistel *f.*

ep·i·taph ['epɪtɑːf] *s* Grabschrift *f.*

ep·i·thet ['epɪθet] *s* **1.** Beiwort *n*, Attribut *n.* **2.** Beiname *m.*

e·pit·o·me [ɪ'pɪtəmɪ] *s* **1.** Auszug *m*, Abriß *m*; kurze Darstellung: **in ~** auszugsweise; in gedrängter Form. **2.** *fig.* Verkörperung *f*, Inbegriff *m.* **e'pit·o·mize** *v/t* verkörpern.

ep·och ['i:pɒk] s Epoche f. '**~·**,**mak·ing** adj epochemachend.

eq·ua·bil·i·ty [,ekwə'bɪlətɪ] s **1.** Gleichförmigkeit f. **2.** Ausgeglichenheit f, Gleichmut m. **'eq·ua·ble** adj □ **1.** gleich(förmig). **2.** ausgeglichen (a. Klima), gleichmütig.

e·qual ['i:kwəl] **I** adj (□ → equally) **1.** gleich: be ~ to gleichen, gleich sein (dat); entsprechen, gleichkommen (dat); ~ opportunities pl Chancengleichheit f; ~ rights pl for women Gleichberechtigung f der Frau; ~ in size, of ~ size (von) gleicher Größe, gleich groß. **2.** be ~ to e-r Aufgabe etc gewachsen sein. **3.** ebenbürtig (to dat), gleichwertig: be on ~ terms (with) auf gleicher Stufe stehen (mit); gleichberechtigt sein (dat). **II** s **4.** Gleichgestellte m, f: your ~s pl deinesgleichen; ~s pl in age Altersgenossen pl; he has no (od. is without) ~ er hat nicht od. sucht seinesgleichen. **III** v/t pret u. pp -qualed, bsd. Br. -qualled **5.** (dat) gleichen, gleichkommen (in an dat). **6.** Sport: Rekord einstellen. **e·qual·i·ty** [ɪ'kwɒlətɪ] s Gleichheit f; ~ (of rights) Gleichberechtigung f; ~ of opportunity (od. opportunities) Chancengleichheit. **e·qual·i·za·tion** [,i:kwəlaɪ'zeɪʃn] s Gleichstellung f. **'e·qual·ize** **I** v/t **1.** gleichmachen, -setzen, -stellen. **2.** ausgleichen. **II** v/i **3.** Sport: ausgleichen. **'e·qual·iz·er** s Sport: Ausgleich(stor n) m. **'e·qual·ly** adv gleich (groß etc).

e·qua·nim·i·ty [,ekwə'nɪmətɪ] s Ausgeglichenheit f, Gleichmut m.

e·quate [ɪ'kweɪt] v/t **1.** gleichsetzen, -stellen (to, with dat). **2.** als gleich(wertig) ansehen od. behandeln. **e·qua·tion** [~ʒn] s **1.** Å Gleichung f. **2.** Gleichsetzung f, -stellung f. **e·qua·tor** [~tə] s Äquator m. **e·qua·to·ri·al** [,ekwə'tɔ:rɪəl] adj äquatorial, Äquator-.

e·ques·tri·an [ɪ'kwestrɪən] **I** adj Reit(er)-...: ~ sports pl Reit-, Pferdesport m; ~ statue Reiterstatue f; -standbild n. **II** s (a. Kunst)Reiter(in).

e·qui·dis·tant [,i:kwɪ'dɪstənt] adj □ gleich weit entfernt. **e·qui·lat·er·al** [~'lætərəl] adj □ bsd. Å gleichseitig.

e·qui·lib·ri·um [,i:kwɪ'lɪbrɪəm] pl **-ri·ums, -ri·a** [~rɪə] s Gleichgewicht n (a. fig.).

e·qui·nox ['i:kwɪnɒks] s Tagundnachtgleiche f.

e·quip [ɪ'kwɪp] v/t **1.** ausrüsten, -statten (with mit), Krankenhaus etc einrichten. **2.** fig. j-m das (geistige od. nötige) Rüstzeug geben (for für): be well ~ped for das nötige Rüstzeug haben für. **e'quip·ment** s **1.** a) Ausrüstung f, -stattung f, b) mst pl Ausrüstung(sgegenstände pl) f, c) ⚙ Einrichtung f, Maschine(n pl) f. **2.** fig. (geistiges od. nötiges) Rüstzeug.

e·qui·poise ['ekwɪpɔɪz] **I** s **1.** Gleichgewicht n (a. fig.). **2.** mst fig. Gegengewicht n (to zu). **II** v/t **3.** im Gleichgewicht halten (a. fig.). **4.** mst fig. ein Gegengewicht bilden zu.

eq·ui·ta·ble ['ekwɪtəbl] adj □ gerecht, (recht u.) billig. **eq·ui·ty** ['ekwətɪ] s **1.** Gerechtigkeit f, Billigkeit f. **2.** a. ~ law ⚖ (ungeschriebenes) Billigkeitsrecht.

e·quiv·a·lence [ɪ'kwɪvələns] s **1.** Gleichwertigkeit f, 🜍 etc a. Äquivalenz f. **e·quiv·a·lent** **I** adj □ **1.** gleichbedeutend (to mit). **2.** gleichwertig, 🜍 etc a. äquivalent: be ~ to gleichkommen, entsprechen (dat). **II** s **3.** (of) Äquivalent n (für), (genaue) Entsprechung (zu).

e·quiv·o·cal [ɪ'kwɪvəkl] adj □ **1.** zweideutig, doppelsinnig. **2.** unbestimmt, ungewiß, fraglich. **3.** fragwürdig.

e·ra ['ɪərə] s Ära f, Zeitalter n.

e·rad·i·cate [ɪ'rædɪkeɪt] v/t ausrotten (a. fig.). **e,rad·i·ca·tion** s Ausrottung f.

e·rase [ɪ'reɪz] v/t **1.** Schrift etc ausstreichen, -radieren, löschen (from von); Tonband(aufnahme) etc, ped. Am. a. Tafel löschen. **2.** fig. (aus)löschen (from aus). **e'ras·er** s Radiergummi m; ped. Am. Tafelwischer m. **e'ra·sure** [~ʒə] s **1.** Ausradieren n; Löschen n. **2.** ausradierte od. gelöschte Stelle.

e·rect [ɪ'rekt] **I** v/t **1.** aufrichten. **2.** Gebäude etc errichten; Maschine etc aufstellen. **II** adj □ **3.** aufgerichtet, aufrecht: with head ~ erhobenen Hauptes. **4.** physiol. erigiert. **e'rec·tion** s **1.** Errichtung f; Aufstellung f. **2.** Bau m, Gebäude n. **3.** physiol. Erektion f.

er·e·mite ['erɪmaɪt] s Eremit m, Einsiedler m.

er·mine ['ɜ:mɪn] s zo. Hermelin n.

e·rode [ɪ'rəʊd] v/t **1.** an-, zer-, wegfressen. **2.** *geol.* erodieren. **3.** *fig.* aushöhlen, untergraben.

e·rog·e·nous [ɪ'rɒdʒɪnəs] *adj physiol.* erogen: **~ zone.**

e·ro·sion [ɪ'rəʊʒn] *s* **1.** *geol.* Erosion *f.* **2.** *fig.* Aushöhlung *f.*

e·rot·ic [ɪ'rɒtɪk] *adj* (**~ally**) erotisch. **e'rot·i·cism** [~sɪzəm], *bsd. Am.* **er·o·tism** ['erətɪzəm] *s* Erotik *f.*

err [ɜː] *v/i* (sich) irren: **to ~ is human** Irren ist menschlich.

er·rand ['erənd] *s* Botengang *m*, Besorgung *f:* **go on** (*od.* **run**) **an ~** e-n Botengang *od.* e-e Besorgung machen. **~ boy** *s* Laufbursche *m.*

er·ra·ta [e'rɑːtə] *pl von* **erratum.**

er·rat·ic [ɪ'rætɪk] *adj* (**~ally**) sprunghaft, unberechenbar.

er·ra·tum [e'rɑːtəm] *pl* **-ta** [~tə] *s* **1.** Druckfehler *m.* **2.** *pl* Errata *pl,* Druckfehlerverzeichnis *n.*

er·ro·ne·ous [ɪ'rəʊnjəs] *adj* irrig, falsch: **~ belief** Irrglaube(n) *m.* **er·ro·ne·ous·ly** *adv* irrtümlicher-, fälschlicherweise.

er·ror ['erə] *s* Irrtum *m,* Fehler *m,* Versehen *n:* **in ~** irrtümlicherweise; **be in ~** im Irrtum sein, sich im Irrtum befinden; **~ of judg(e)ment** falsche Beurteilung; **~s excepted** ✝ Irrtümer vorbehalten.

e·rupt [ɪ'rʌpt] *v/i* ausbrechen (*Ausschlag, Streit, Vulkan etc*): **~ in** (*od.* **with**) **anger** e-n Wutanfall bekommen. **e'rup·tion** *s* **1.** Ausbruch *m:* **angry ~** Wutausbruch. **2.** 🌟 Ausschlag *m.*

es·ca·late ['eskəleɪt] **I** *v/t* **1.** Krieg *etc* eskalieren. **2.** *Erwartungen etc* höherschrauben. **II** *v/i* **3.** eskalieren. **4.** steigen, in die Höhe gehen (*Preise etc*). **,es·ca'la·tion** *s* Eskalation *f.* **'es·ca·la·tor** *s* Rolltreppe *f.*

es·ca·lope [e'skælɒp] *s gastr.* (*bsd.* Wiener) Schnitzel *n.*

es·ca·pade [,eskə'peɪd] *s* Eskapade *f.*

es·cape [ɪ'skeɪp] **I** *v/t* **1.** *j-m* entfliehen, -kommen; *e-r Sache* entgehen: **I cannot ~ the impression that** ich kann mich des Eindrucks nicht erwehren, daß; → **notice** 1. **2.** *fig. j-m* entgehen, übersehen *od.* nicht verstanden werden von. **3.** *dem Gedächtnis* entfallen: **his name ~s me** sein Name ist mir entfallen. **4.** *j-m* entschlüpfen, -fahren (*Fluch etc*). **II** *v/i* **5.** (ent)fliehen, entkommen (**from** aus, *dat*). **6.** sich retten (**from** vor *dat*),

davonkommen (**with a fright** mit dem Schrecken; **with one's life** mit dem Leben). **7.** ausfließen (*Flüssigkeit*); entweichen, ausströmen (**from** aus) (*Gas etc*). **III** *s* **8.** Entkommen *n,* Flucht *f:* **have a narrow** (*od.* **near**) **~** mit knapper Not davonkommen *od.* entkommen; **that was a narrow ~!** das war knapp! **9.** Entweichen *n,* Ausströmen *n.* **~ chute** *s* ✈ Notrutsche *f.*

es·cort I *s* ['eskɔːt] **1.** ✕ Eskorte *f,* Begleitmannschaft *f.* **2.** 🔩, ⚓ Geleit(schutz *m*) *n;* ⚓ Geleitschiff *n.* **3.** Geleit *n,* Schutz *m;* Gefolge *n,* Begleitung *f;* Begleiter(in). **II** *v/t* [ɪ'skɔːt] **4.** ✕ eskortieren. **5.** 🔩, ⚓ *j-m* Geleitschutz geben. **6.** geleiten; begleiten.

Es·ki·mo ['eskɪməʊ] *pl* **-mos** *s* Eskimo *m.*

e·soph·a·gus *Am.* → **oesophagus.**

es·o·ter·ic [,esəʊ'terɪk] *adj* (**~ally**) esoterisch.

es·pe·cial [ɪ'speʃl] *adj* besonder. **es'pe·cial·ly** [~ʃəlɪ] *adv* besonders, hauptsächlich.

Es·pe·ran·to [,espə'ræntəʊ] *s* Esperanto *n.*

es·pi·o·nage ['espɪənɑːʒ] *s* Spionage *f.*

es·pla·nade [,esplə'neɪd] *s* **1.** (*bsd.* Strand-, Ufer)Promenade *f.* **2.** Esplanade *f.*

es·pres·so [e'spresəʊ] *pl* **-sos** *s* **1.** Espresso *m.* **2.** Espressomaschine *f.* **~ bar** *s* Espresso *n.*

Es·quire [ɪ'skwaɪə]: **John Smith, Esq.** *bsd. Br.* (*auf Briefen*) Herrn John Smith.

es·say ['eseɪ] *s* Essay *m, n, a. ped.* Aufsatz *m.* **'es·say·ist** *s* Essayist(in).

es·sence ['esns] *s* **1.** *das* Wesen(tliche), Kern *m* (*e-r Sache*): **in ~** im wesentlichen. **2.** Essenz *f,* Extrakt *m.*

es·sen·tial [ɪ'senʃl] **I** *adj* (□ → **essentially**) **1.** wesentlich: a) grundlegend, b) unentbehrlich, unbedingt erforderlich (**to** für): **~** (**to life**) lebensnotwendig, -wichtig. **2.** 🌿 ätherisch: **~ oil.** **II** *s mst pl* **3.** *das* Wesentliche, Hauptsache *f.* **4.** (wesentliche) Voraussetzung *f* (**to** für). **es'sen·tial·ly** [~ʃəlɪ] *adv* im wesentlichen.

es·tab·lish [ɪ'stæblɪʃ] *v/t* **1.** ein-, errichten, *Konto* eröffnen, *Gesetz etc* einführen, erlassen, *Rekord, Theorie* aufstellen, *Ausschuß etc* bilden, einsetzen, *Verbindung* herstellen, *diplomatische Beziehungen etc* aufnehmen. **2. ~ o.s.** sich (*a. beruflich*) etablieren *od.* niederlassen. **3.** *Ruhm etc* begründen: **~ one's reputation as** sich e-n Namen machen als. **4.** *Ansicht, Forderung etc* durchsetzen, *Ordnung* schaffen. **5.** be-, nachweisen. **es'tab·lished** *adj* **1.** bestehend. **2.** feststehend, unzweifelhaft. **3.** ⚲ *Church* Staatskirche *f*. **es'tab·lish·ment** *s* **1.** Ein-, Errichtung *f*, Einführung *f*, Aufstellung *f*, Bildung *f*, Herstellung *f*, Aufnahme *f*. **2. the** ⚲ das Establishment. **3.** ✝ Unternehmen *n*, Firma *f*; Niederlassung *f*. **4.** Anstalt *f*, (öffentliches) Institut.

es·tate [ɪ'steɪt] *s* **1.** *sociol.* Stand *m*. **2.** ⚖ Besitz(tum *n*) *m*; (Erb-, Konkurs)Masse *f*, Nachlaß *m*; → **real 3. 3.** Landsitz *m*, Gut *n*. **4.** *Br.* (Wohn)Siedlung *f*; Industriegebiet *n*. **~ a·gent** *s Br.* **1.** Grundstücksverwalter *m*. **2.** Grundstücks-, Immobilienmakler *m*. **~ car** *s Br.* Kombiwagen *m*.

es·teem [ɪ'stiːm] **I** *v/t* **1.** achten, (hoch)schätzen. **2.** erachten *od.* ansehen als, *et.* halten für. **II** *s* **3.** Achtung *f* (*for, of* vor *dat*): **hold** in **(high)** **~** → **1**.

es·thete, *etc. Am.* → **aesthete**, *etc.*

es·ti·ma·ble ['estɪməbl] *adj* □ **1.** achtens-, schätzenswert. **2.** (ab)schätzbar.

es·ti·mate ['estɪmeɪt] **I** *v/t* **1.** (ab-, ein)schätzen, veranschlagen (*at* auf *acc*): **~d value** Schätzwert *m*; **an ~d 200 people** schätzungsweise 200 Leute. **2.** beurteilen, bewerten. **II** *v/i* **3.** schätzen. **4.** e-n Kostenvoranschlag machen (*for* für). **III** *s* ['~mət] **5.** Schätzung *f*, Veranschlagung *f*, Kostenvoranschlag *m*: **rough ~** grober Überschlag; **at a rough ~** grob geschätzt. **6.** Beurteilung *f*, Bewertung *f*. **es·ti·ma·tion** [~'meɪʃn] *s* **1.** Meinung *f*: **in my ~** nach m-r Ansicht. **2.** Achtung *f*, Wertschätzung *f*.

es·trange [ɪ'streɪndʒ] *v/t* j-n entfremden (*from dat*): **become ~d** sich entfremden (*from dat*); sich auseinanderleben. **es'trange·ment** *s* Entfremdung *f*.

es·tro·gen *Am.* → **oestrogen**.

es·tu·ar·y ['estjʊərɪ] *s* **1.** (*den Gezeiten ausgesetzte*) Flußmündung *f*. **2.** Meeresbucht *f*, -arm *m*.

et cet·er·a [ɪt'setərə] et cetera, und so weiter.

etch [etʃ] *v/t* **1.** ätzen. **2.** in Kupfer stechen; radieren: *be ~ed on* (*od.* **in**) *s.o.'s memory* sich j-s Gedächtnis (unauslöschlich) eingeprägt haben. **'etch·ing** *s* Kupferstich *m*; Radierung *f*.

e·ter·nal [ɪ'tɜːnl] *adj* □ **1.** ewig. **2.** ewig, unaufhörlich. **e'ter·nal·ize** [~nəlaɪz] *v/t* verewigen (*a. fig.*). **e·ter·ni·ty** *s* Ewigkeit *f* (*a. fig.*).

e·ther ['iːθə] *s* 🜍 Äther *m*. **e·the·re·al** [ɪ'θɪərɪəl] *adj* ätherisch (*a. fig.*).

eth·i·cal ['eθɪkl] *adj* □ **1.** ethisch. **2.** *pharm.* rezeptpflichtig. **'eth·ics** *s pl* **1.** (*sg construiert*) Ethik *f*. **2.** (*Berufs· etc*)Ethos *n*.

eth·nic ['eθnɪk] *adj* (*~ally*) ethnisch: **~ group** Volksgruppe *f*.

eth·yl ['eθɪl] *s* 🜍 Äthyl *n*.

et·i·quette ['etɪket] *s* Etikette *f*, Anstands-, Verhaltensregeln *pl*.

et·y·mo·log·i·cal [ˌetɪmə'lodʒɪkl] *adj* □ etymologisch. **et·y·mol·o·gy** [~'mɒlədʒɪ] *s* Etymologie *f*.

eu·ca·lyp·tus [ˌjuːkə'lɪptəs] *pl* **-ti** [~taɪ], **-tus·es** *s* ♣ Eukalyptus *m*.

eu·lo·gy ['juːlədʒɪ] *s* **1.** Lob(preisung *f*) *n*. **2.** Lobrede *f*, -schrift *f* (*on* auf *acc*).

eu·nuch ['juːnək] *s* Eunuch *m*.

eu·phe·mism ['juːfəmɪzəm] *s* Euphemismus *m*. **,eu·phe'mis·tic** *adj* (*~ally*) euphemistisch, beschönigend, verhüllend.

eu·pho·ri·a [juː'fɔːrɪə] *s* Euphorie *f*. **eu·phor·ic** [~'fɒrɪk] *adj* (*~ally*) euphorisch.

Eu·ro·cheque ['jʊərəʊtʃek] *s Br.* Euroscheck *m*.

Eu·ro·pe·an [ˌjʊərə'piːən] **I** *adj* europäisch: **~ (Economic) Community** Europäische (Wirtschafts)Gemeinschaft; **~ champion** (*Sport*) Europameister(in); **~ championship** (*Sport*) Europameisterschaft *f*. **II** *s* Europäer(in).

Eu·ro·vi·sion ['jʊərəʊˌvɪʒn] *TV* **I** *s* Eurovision *f*. **II** *adj* Eurovisions...

eu·tha·na·si·a [ˌjuːθə'neɪʒə] *s* Sterbehilfe *f*: *active* (*passive*) **~**.

e·vac·u·ate [ɪ'vækjʊeɪt] *v/t* *Personen* evakuieren; *Gebiet etc* räumen, *a. Haus etc* räumen. **e·vac·u'a·tion** *s*

Evakuierung f; Räumung f. **e͵vac-**
-u'ee [ˌ-juːˈiː] s Evakuierte m, f.

e·vade [ɪˈveɪd] v/t **1.** e-m Schlag etc ausweichen. **2.** sich e-r Pflicht etc entziehen, et. umgehen, vermeiden, Steuern
hinterziehen: ~ (answering) a question e-r Frage ausweichen.

e·val·u·ate [ɪˈvæljʊeɪt] v/t **1.** Wert etc
schätzen, Schaden etc festsetzen (at auf
acc). **2.** abschätzen, bewerten. **e͵val-**
u'a·tion s **1.** Schätzung f, Festsetzung f.
2. Abschätzung f, Bewertung f.

e·vap·o·rate [ɪˈvæpəreɪt] v/t **1.** verdampfen od. verdunsten lassen. **2.** ein-
dampfen: **~d milk** Kondensmilch f. **II**
v/i **3.** verdampfen, verdunsten. **4.** fig.
sich verflüchtigen, verfliegen. **e͵vap-**
o'ra·tion s Verdampfung f, Verdun-
stung f.

e·va·sion [ɪˈveɪʒn] s **1.** Umgehung f, Vermeidung f, (Steuer)Hinterziehung f. **2.**
Ausflucht f, Ausrede f. **e·va·sive** [ˌ-sɪv]
adj □ **1.** ausweichend (Antwort): be ~
ausweichen. **2.** schwer feststell- od. faßbar.

eve [iːv] s **1.** mst ⚥ Vorabend m, -tag m
(e-s Festes). **2.** fig. Vorabend m: **on the**
~ **of** am Vorabend von (od. gen), kurz
od. unmittelbar vor (dat).

e·ven¹ [ˈiːvn] adv **1.** sogar, selbst: not ~
he nicht einmal er; ~ if selbst wenn; ~
though obwohl; ~ as a child he was ...
schon als Kind war er ... **2.** noch: ~
better (sogar) noch besser.

e·ven² [ˌ-] **I** adj **1.** eben, flach, gerade. **2.**
auf od. in gleicher Höhe (with mit). **3.**
waag(e)recht. **4.** fig. ausgeglichen: of
an ~ temper ausgeglichen; ~ voice ruhige Stimme. **5.** gleichmäßig (Atmen
etc). **6.** ⚕ ausgeglichen (a. Sport): be ~
with quitt sein mit (a. fig.). **7.** gleich,
identisch. **8.** gerade (Zahl). **II** v/t **9.** a. ~
out (ein)ebnen, glätten; ausgleichen;
(gleichmäßig) verteilen. **10.** ~ up Rechnung aus-, begleichen: ~ things up sich
revanchieren. **III** v/i **11.** a. ~ out eben
werden (Gelände); sich ausgleichen;
sich (gleichmäßig) verteilen.

eve·ning [ˈiːvnɪŋ] s Abend m: in the ~
abends, am Abend; on the ~ of am
Abend (gen); last (this, tomorrow) ~
gestern (heute, morgen) abend. ~
class·es s pl ped. Abendunterricht m.
~ **dress** s **1.** Abendkleid n. **2.** Frack m;

Smoking m. ~ **pa·per** s Abendzeitung
f. ~ **star** s ast. Abendstern m.

e·ven·ness [ˈiːvnnɪs] s **1.** Ausgeglichenheit f. **2.** Gleichmäßigkeit f.

e·vent [ɪˈvent] s **1.** Fall m: at all ~s auf
alle Fälle; in any ~ in jedem Fall; in the
~ of im Falle (gen). **2.** Ereignis n: before
the ~ vorher, im voraus; after the ~
hinterher, im nachhinein. **3.** Sport:
Diziplin f; Wettbewerb m.

͵e·ven-'tem·pered adj ausgeglichen.

e·vent·ful [ɪˈventfʊl] adj □ ereignisreich.

e·ven·tu·al·i·ty [ɪˌventʃʊˈælɪti] s Möglichkeit f, Eventualität f. **e·ven·tu·al·ly**
[ˌ-əlɪ] adv schließlich.

ev·er [ˈevə] adv **1.** immer (wieder), ständig: ~ after(wards) (od. since) seit der
Zeit, seitdem; Yours ~, ... Viele Grüße,
Dein(e) od. Ihr(e) ... (Briefschluß); →
forever. **2.** immer (vor comp): ~ larger.
3. je(mals): have you ~ been to London? bist du schon einmal in London
gewesen?; hardly (od. seldom if) ~ fast
nie. **4.** ~ so bsd. Br. F sehr, noch so: ~ so
simpdd ganz einfach; ~ so many unendlich viele; thank yge ~ so much
tausend Dank! **5.** F denn, überhaupt:
what's° does he want? was ist er denn
überhaupt? **'͵~green** s **1.** ⚘ immergrü-
ne Pflanze. **2.** ♪ Evergreen m, n. **͵~-**
'last·ing adj □ **1.** ewig. **2.** fig. unaufhörlich. **3.** unverwüstlich, unbegrenzt
haltbar. **͵~'more** adj: (for) ~ für immer.

ev·er·y [ˈevrɪ] adv **1.** jede(r, -s): ~ day
jeden Tag, alle Tage; → now **1**, other **4**,
second¹ **1. 2.** jede(r, -s) (einzelne od.
erdenkliche): her ~ wish jeder ihrer od.
alle ihre Wünsche; ~ bit as much F
ganz genau so viel; have ~ reason allen
Grund haben. **~ bo·dy** ~ everyone.
'͵~day adj **1.** (all)täglich. **2.** Alltags... **3.**
gewöhnlich, Durchschnitts... **'͵~one**
pron jeder(mann): in ~'s mouth in aller
Munde; to ~'s amazement zum allgemeinen Erstaunen. **'͵~thing** pron **1.** alles (that was). **2.** F die Hauptsache,
alles (to für). **3.** and ~ F und so. **'͵~-**
where adv überall(hin): ~ he goes wo
er auch hingeht.

ev·i·dence [ˈevɪdəns] s **1.** ⚖ Be-
weis(stück n, -material n) m, Beweise
pl: for lack of ~ mangels Beweisen. **2.**
⚖ (Zeugen)Aussage f: give ~ aussagen (for für; against gegen); give ~ of

aussagen über (*acc*); *fig.* zeugen von; **turn queen's** (*od.* **king's,** *Am.* **state's**) ~ als Kronzeuge auftreten. **3.** (An)Zeichen *n,* Spur *f* (**of** von *od. gen*).
ev·i·dent *adj* □ augenscheinlich, offensichtlich.

e·vil [ˈiːvl] **I** *adj* □ übel, böse, schlimm: ~ **day** Unglückstag *m;* ~ **eye** der böse Blick. **II** *s* Übel *n,* das Böse: **do** ~ Böses tun; **the lesser** ~ das kleinere Übel. ˌ~ˈdo·er *s* Übeltäter(in). ˌ~ˈmind·ed *adj* □ bösartig.

e·voc·a·tive [ɪˈvɒkətɪv] *adj:* **be** ~ **of** erinnern an (*acc*).

e·voke [ɪˈvəʊk] *v/t* **1.** *Geister* beschwören, herbeirufen. **2.** *Bewunderung etc* hervorrufen; *Erinnerungen* wachrufen, wecken.

ev·o·lu·tion [ˌiːvəˈluːʃn] *s* **1.** Entfaltung *f,* -wicklung *f:* **the** ~ **of events** die Entwicklung (der Dinge). **2.** *biol.* Evolution *f.*

e·volve [ɪˈvɒlv] *v/t u. v/i* (sich) entfalten *od.* -wickeln (**into** zu).

ex¹ [eks] *prp* ✝ ab: ~ **works** ab Werk.
ex² [~] *s F* Verflossene *m, f.*

ex- [eks] *in Zssgn* Ex..., ehemalig.

ex·ac·er·bate [ɪɡˈzæsəbeɪt] *v/t* **1.** *j-n* verärgern. **2.** *Krankheit, Schmerzen* verschlimmern, *Situation* verschärfen.

ex·act [ɪɡˈzækt] **I** *adj* (□ → *exactly*) **1.** exakt, genau. **2.** genau, tatsächlich. **3.** methodisch, gewissenhaft (*Person*). **II** *v/t* **4.** *Gehorsam, Geld etc* fordern, verlangen (**from** von). **5.** *Zahlung* eintreiben, -fordern (**from** von). **ex'act·ing** *adj* □ **1.** streng, genau. **2.** aufreibend, anstrengend. **3.** anspruchsvoll: **be** ~ hohe Anforderungen stellen. **ex'act·i·tude** [~tɪtjuːd] → **exactness. ex'act·ly** *adv* **1.** → **exact. 2.** *als Antwort:* ganz recht, genau: **not** ~ nicht ganz *od.* direkt. **3.** *wo, wann etc* genau. **ex'act·ness** *s* **1.** Exaktheit *f,* Genauigkeit *f.* **2.** Gewissenhaftigkeit *f.*

ex·ag·ger·ate [ɪɡˈzædʒəreɪt] *v/t u. v/i* übertreiben. **ex‚ag·ger'a·tion** *s* Übertreibung *f.*

ex·alt [ɪɡˈzɔːlt] *v/t* **1.** *im Rang etc* erheben, erhöhen (**to** zu). **2.** (lob)preisen: ~ **to the skies** in den Himmel heben. **ex·al·ta·tion** [ˌeɡzɔːlˈteɪʃn] *s* **1.** Erhebung *f,* Erhöhung *f.* **2.** Begeisterung *f:* **fill with** ~ in Begeisterung versetzen.

ex·alt·ed [ɪɡˈzɔːltɪd] *adj* **1.** hoch (*Rang, Ideal etc*). **2.** begeistert. **3.** F übertrieben hoch (*Meinung etc*).

ex·am [ɪɡˈzæm] *F* → **examination 2.**
ex·am·i·na·tion [ɪɡˌzæmɪˈneɪʃn] *s* **1.** Untersuchung *f* (*a.* ✚), Prüfung *f:* **on** ~ bei näherer Prüfung; **be under** ~ untersucht *od.* geprüft werden. **2.** *ped. etc* Prüfung *f, bsd. univ.* Examen *n:* ~ **paper** schriftliche Prüfung; Prüfungsarbeit *f.* **3.** ⚖ Vernehmung *f,* Verhör *n.* **ex'am·ine** *v/t* **1.** untersuchen (*a.* ✚), prüfen (**for** auf *acc*). **2.** *ped. etc* prüfen (**in** *dat;* **on** über *acc*). **3.** ⚖ vernehmen; verhören. **ex‚am·i'nee** *s ped. etc* Prüfling *m,* (Prüfungs-, *bsd. univ.* Examens)Kandidat(in). **ex'am·in·er** *s ped. etc* Prüfer(in).

ex·am·ple [ɪɡˈzɑːmpl] *s* **1.** Beispiel *n* (**of** für): **for** ~ zum Beispiel; **without** ~ beispiellos. **2.** Vorbild *n,* Beispiel *n:* **set a good** ~ ein gutes Beispiel geben, mit gutem Beispiel vorangehen; **take** ~ **by, take as an** ~ sich ein Beispiel nehmen an (*dat*); → **hold up 2. 3.** (warnendes) Beispiel: **make an** ~ **of s.o.**) (an j-m) ein Exempel statuieren; **let this be an** ~ **to you** laß dir das e-e Warnung sein.

ex·as·per·ate [ɪɡˈzæspəreɪt] *v/t* aufbringen (**against** gegen), wütend machen. **ex'as·per·at·ed** *adj* wütend, aufgebracht (**at, by** über *acc*). **ex‚as·per'a·tion** *s* Wut *f:* **in** ~ wütend, aufgebracht.

ex·ca·vate [ˈekskəveɪt] *v/t* **1.** aushöhlen. **2.** ausgraben, -baggern. **ex‚ca·va·tion** *s* **1.** Aushöhlung *f.* **2.** Ausgrabung *f.* **'ex·ca·va·tor** *s* Bagger *m.*

ex·ceed [ɪkˈsiːd] *v/t* **1.** *Tempolimit etc* überschreiten. ~ **the limit** den Rahmen sprengen. **2.** hinausgehen über (*acc*): ~ **the limit** den Rahmen sprengen. **3.** *et-, j-n* übertreffen (**in** an *dat*). **ex'ceed·ing·ly** *adv* überaus, äußerst: ~ **kind** überfreundlich.

ex·cel [ɪkˈsel] **I** *v/t* übertreffen (**o.s.** sich selbst). **II** *v/i* sich auszeichnen *od.* hervortun (**in, at** in *dat;* **as** als). **ex·cel·lence** [ˈeksələns] *s* **1.** Vorzüglichkeit *f.* **2.** *pl* Vorzüge *pl.* **'Ex·cel·len·cy** *s* Exzellenz *f* (*Titel*). **'ex·cel·lent** *adj* □ ausgezeichnet, hervorragend, vorzüglich.

ex·cept [ɪkˈsept] **I** *v/t* **1.** ausnehmen, -schließen (**from** von): **present compa·ny ~ed** Anwesende ausgenommen; **no-**

body ~*ed* ohne Ausnahme. **2.** sich *et.* vorbehalten: → **error. II** *prp* **3.** ausgenommen, außer, mit Ausnahme von (*od. gen*): ~ **for** abgesehen von, bis auf (*acc*). **III** *cj* **4.** außer: ~ *that* außer, daß. **ex·cept·ing** *prp* → **except** 3. **ex'cep-tion** *s* **1.** Ausnahme *f* (*to the rule* von der Regel): *by way of* ~ ausnahmsweise; *without* ~ ohne Ausnahme, ausnahmslos; *make an* ~ (*in s.o.'s case*) (bei j-m *od.* in j-s Fall) e-e Ausnahme machen. **2.** Einwand *m* (*to* gegen): *take* ~ *to* Einwendungen machen gegen; Anstoß nehmen an (*dat*). **ex'cep-tion-al** [~ʃənl] *adj* **1.** Ausnahme..., Sonder... **2.** außer-, ungewöhnlich. **ex'cep-tion-al-ly** [~ʃnəlɪ] *adv* **1.** außergewöhnlich. **2.** ausnahmsweise.

ex·cerpt ['eksɜːpt] *s* Exzerpt *n*, Auszug *m* (*from* aus).

ex·cess [ɪk'ses] **I** *s* **1.** Übermaß *n*, -fluß *m* (*of an dat*): *in* ~ *of* mehr als, über (*acc*) (... hinaus); *to* ~ übermäßig; → *carry* 7. **2.** *pl* Exzesse *pl:* a) Ausschweifungen *pl*, b) Ausschreitungen *pl.* **3.** Überschuß *m.* **II** *adj* **4.** überschüssig, Über...: ~ *baggage* (*bsd. Br. luggage*) ✈ Übergepäck *n*; ~ *fare* (Fahrpreis)Zuschlag *m*; ~ *postage* Nachporto *n*, -gebühr *f.* **ex'cess·ive** *adj* □ übermäßig, -trieben.

ex·change [ɪks'tʃeɪndʒ] **I** *v/t* **1.** (*for*) aus-, umtauschen (gegen), vertauschen (mit). **2.** eintauschen, *Geld a.* (um-) wechseln (*for* gegen). **3.** *Blicke, die Plätze etc* tauschen, *Blicke* wechseln, *Gedanken, Gefangene etc* austauschen: ~ *blows* aufeinander einschlagen; ~ *words* e-n Wortwechsel haben. **4.** ⚙ auswechseln. **II** *s* **5.** (Aus-, Um)Tausch *m: in* ~ als Ersatz, dafür; *in* ~ *for* (im Austausch) gegen, (als Entgelt) für; ~ *of letters* Brief-, Schriftwechsel *m*; ~ *of shots* Schußwechsel *m*; ~ *of views* Gedanken-, Meinungsaustausch. **6.** ♀ (Um)Wechseln. *rate of* ~, ~ *rate* Wechselkurs *m*; → *bill²* 3, *foreign* 1. **7.** ♀ Börse *f.* **8.** *a.* ~ *office* Wechselstube *f.* **9.** (Fernsprech)Amt *n*, Vermittlung *f.* **ex'change·a·ble** *adj* **1.** aus-, umtauschbar (*for* gegen). **2.** Tausch...

Ex·cheq·uer [ɪks'tʃekə] *s Br.* Finanzministerium *n:* → *chancellor.*

ex·cit·a·ble [ɪk'saɪtəbl] *adj* reizbar, (leicht) erregbar. **ex'cite** *v/t* **1.** *j-n* er-, aufregen (*über acc*); sich aufregen (*over acc*). **2.** *j-n* (an-, auf)reizen, aufstacheln. **3.** *Interesse etc* erregen, (er-) wecken, *Appetit, Phantasie* anregen. **ex'cit·ed** *adj* □ erregt, aufgeregt. **ex'cite·ment** *s* Er-, Aufregung *f.* **ex'cit·ing** *adj* □ er-, aufregend, spannend.

ex·claim [ɪk'skleɪm] **I** *v/i* (auf)schreien. **II** *v/t et.* (aus)rufen.

ex·cla·ma·tion [ˌeksklə'meɪʃn] *s* Ausruf *m*, (Auf)Schrei *m:* ~ *of pain* Schmerzensschrei; ~ *mark* (*Am. a.* *point*) Ausrufe-, Ausrufungszeichen *n.*

ex·clude [ɪk'skluːd] *v/t j-n, Möglichkeit etc* ausschließen (*from* von, aus). **ex'clud·ing** *prp* ausgenommen, nicht inbegriffen.

ex·clu·sion [ɪk'skluːʒn] *s* Ausschluß *m* (*from* von, aus): *to the* ~ *of* unter Ausschluß von (*od. der gen*). **ex'clu·sive** *adj* **1.** ausschließlich: ~ *of* ausschließlich, abgesehen von; *be* ~ *of s.th.* et. ausschließen; *be mutually* ~ einander ausschließen. **2.** ausschließlich, Allein...; Exklusiv-. **3.** exklusiv. **II** *s* **4.** Exklusivbericht *m.*

ex·com·mu·ni·cate [ˌekskə'mjuːnɪkeɪt] *v/t eccl.* exkommunizieren. **'ex·com·mu·ni'ca·tion** *s* Exkommunikation *f.*

ex·cre·ment ['ekskrɪmənt] *s* Kot *m*, Exkremente *pl.*

ex·crete [ɪk'skriːt] *v/t* absondern, ausscheiden. **ex'cre·tion** *s* Absonderung *f*, Ausscheidung *f.*

ex·cru·ci·at·ing [ɪk'skruːʃɪeɪtɪŋ] *adj* □ qualvoll (*to* für).

ex·cur·sion [ɪk'skɜːʃn] *s* Ausflug *m*, *fig. a.* Abstecher *m* (*into politics* in die Politik): *go on an* ~ e-n Ausflug machen. **ex'cur·sion·ist** *s* Ausflügler(in).

ex·cus·a·ble [ɪk'skjuːzəbl] *adj* □ entschuldbar, verzeihlich. **ex·cuse I** *v/t* [ɪk'skjuːz] **1.** *j-n, et.* entschuldigen, *j-m, et.* verzeihen: ~ *me* entschuldigen Sie!, Verzeihung!; ~ *me for being late*, ~ *my being late* entschuldige mein Zuspätkommen; ~ *o.s.* sich entschuldigen. **2.** *für et.* e-e Entschuldigung finden: *I cannot* ~ *his conduct* ich kann sein Verhalten nicht gutheißen. **3.** ~ *s.o. from s.th.* j-n von et. befreien, j-m et. erlassen: *he begs to be* ~*d* er läßt sich entschuldigen. **II** *s* [ɪk'skjuːs] **4.** Entschuldigung *f*: *offer* (*od.* **make**) *an* ~ sich entschuldigen; *in* ~ *of* als Entschuldigung für. **5.** Entschuldigung(sgrund *m*) *f*, Rechtfertigung *f*: *without* (*good*) ~ unentschuldigt. **6.** Ausrede *f*, -flucht *f*.

ex·di·rec·to·ry [ˌeksdɪ'rektərɪ] *adj*: ~ *number* *teleph.* *Br.* Geheimnummer *f*.

ex·e·cute ['eksɪkjuːt] *v/t* **1.** *Auftrag, Plan etc* aus-, durchführen, *Vertrag* erfüllen. **2.** ♪ vortragen, spielen. **3.** ⚖ *Urteil* vollziehen, -strecken; *j-n* hinrichten (*for* wegen). **ˌex·e·ʹcu·tion** *s* **1.** Aus-, Durchführung *f*, Erfüllung *f*: *carry* (*od.* **put**) *into* ~ *execute* 1. **2.** ♪ Vortrag *m*, Spiel *n*. **3.** ⚖ Vollziehung *f*, -streckung *f*; Hinrichtung *f*. **ˌex·e·ʹcu·tion·er** *s* Henker *m*, Scharfrichter *m*.

ex·ec·u·tive [ɪg'zekjʊtɪv] **I** *adj* ☐ **1.** ausübend, vollziehend, *pol.* Exekutiv...: ~ *power* (*od.* **authority**) → 3. **2.** ✝ geschäftsführend, leitend: ~ *board* Vorstand *m*; ~ *post* (*od.* **position**) leitende Stellung; ~ *staff* leitende Angestellte *pl*. **II** *s* **3.** *pol.* Exekutive *f*. **4.** ✝ *senior* ~ ✝ leitender Angestellter.

ex·em·pla·ry [ɪg'zemplərɪ] *adj* ☐ **1.** exemplarisch: a) beispiel-, musterhaft, b) warnend, abschreckend. **2.** typisch, Muster...

ex·em·pli·fy [ɪg'zemplɪfaɪ] *v/t* veranschaulichen: a) durch Beispiele erläutern, b) als Beispiel dienen für.

ex·empt [ɪg'zempt] **I** *v/t* *j-n* befreien (*from* von *Steuern, Verpflichtungen etc*), freistellen (*from military service* vom Wehrdienst): ~*ed amount* ✝ (Steuer)Freibetrag *m*. **II** *adj* befreit, ausgenommen (*from* von): ~ *from taxation* steuerfrei. **ex·ʹemp·tion** *s* Befreiung *f*, Freistellung *f*: ~ *from taxes* Steuerfreiheit *f*.

ex·er·cise ['eksəsaɪz] **I** *s* **1.** Ausübung *f*, Geltendmachung *f*. **2.** (*körperliche od. geistige*) Übung, (körperliche) Bewegung: *do one's* ~ Gymnastik machen; *take* ~ sich Bewegung machen; ~ *bicycle* Zimmerfahrrad *n*; ~ *therapy* ♣ Bewegungstherapie *f*. **3.** *mst pl* ✗ Übung *f*, Manöver *n*. **4.** Übung(sarbeit) *f*, Schulaufgabe *f*: ~ *book* Schul-, Schreibheft *n*. **5.** ♪ Übung(sstück *n*) *f*. **II** *v/t* **6.** *Amt, Recht, Macht etc* aus-

üben, *Einfluß, Macht etc* geltend machen. **7.** *Körper, Geist* üben, trainieren. **8.** *Geduld etc* üben. **III** *v/i* **9.** sich Bewegung machen. **10.** *Sport etc*: üben, trainieren. **11.** ✗ exerzieren. **ʹex·er·cis·er** *s* Trainingsgerät *n*.

ex·ert [ɪg'zɜːt] *v/t* **1.** *Druck, Einfluß etc* ausüben (*on* auf *acc*), *Autorität* geltend machen. **2.** ~ *o.s.* sich bemühen (*for* um; *to do* zu tun), sich anstrengen. **ex·ʹer·tion** *s* **1.** Ausübung *f*, Geltendmachung *f*. **2.** Anstrengung *f*.

ex·e·unt ['eksɪʌnt] *thea.* Bühnenanweisung: (sie gehen) ab: ~ *omnes* alle ab.

ex·ha·la·tion [ˌekshə'leɪʃn] *s* **1.** Ausatmen *n*. **2.** Verströmen *n*. **3.** Gas *n*; Rauch *m*. **ex·ʹhale** [~'heɪl] *v/t* **1.** (*a. v/i*) ausatmen. **2.** *Gas, Geruch etc* verströmen, *Rauch* ausstoßen.

ex·haust [ɪg'zɔːst] **I** *v/t* erschöpfen: a) *Vorräte* ver-, aufbrauchen, b) *j-n* ermüden, entkräften, c) *j-s Kräfte* strapazieren: ~ *s.o.'s patience* j-s Geduld erschöpfen, d) *Thema* erschöpfend *od.* behandeln: ~ *all possibilities* alle Möglichkeiten ausschöpfen. **II** *s* ⊙ *a.* ~ *fumes* *pl* Auspuff-, Abgase *pl*, b) Auspuff *m*: ~ *pipe* Auspuffrohr *n*. **ex·ʹhaust·ed** *adj* **1.** verbraucht, erschöpft, aufgebraucht (*Vorräte*), vergriffen (*Auflage*). **2.** erschöpft, entkräftet. **ex·ʹhaust·ing** *adj* erschöpfend, strapaziös. **ex·ʹhaus·tion** *s* Erschöpfung *f* a) völliger Verbrauch, b) Entkräftung *f*. **ex·ʹhaus·tive** *adj* ☐ *fig.* erschöpfend.

ex·hib·it [ɪg'zɪbɪt] **I** *v/t* **1.** *Bilder etc* ausstellen. **2.** *fig.* zeigen, an den Tag legen; zur Schau stellen. **II** *v/i* **3.** ausstellen (*at a fair* auf e-r Messe). **III** *s* **4.** Ausstellungsstück *n*, Exponat *n*. **5.** ⚖ Beweisstück *n*. **ex·hi·bi·tion** [ˌeksɪ'bɪʃn] *s* **1.** Ausstellung *f*: *be on* ~ ausgestellt *od.* zu sehen sein; *make an* ~ *of o.s.* sich lächerlich *od.* zum Gespött machen. **2.** *fig.* Zurschaustellung *f*. **3.** *univ. Br.* Stipendium *n*. **ˌex·hi·ʹbi·tion·ism** *s* *psych. u. fig.* Exhibitionismus *m*. **ˌex·hi·ʹbi·tion·ist** *psych. u. fig.* **I** *s* Exhibitionist *m*. **II** *adj* exhibitionistisch. **ex·ʹhib·i·tor** [ɪg'zɪbɪtə] *s* Aussteller *m*.

ex·hort [ɪg'zɔːt] *v/t* ermahnen (*to* zu; *to do* zu tun). **ex·hor·ta·tion** [ˌegzɔː'teɪʃn] *s* Ermahnung *f*.

ex·hu·ma·tion [,ekshju:'meɪʃn] s Exhumierung f. **ex'hume** v/t Leiche exhumieren.

ex·i·gence, ex·i·gen·cy ['eksɪdʒəns(-ɪ)] s 1. Dringlichkeit f. 2. Not(lage) f. 3. mst pl Erfordernis n. **'ex·i·gent** adj 1. dringend, drängend. 2. anspruchsvoll.

ex·ig·u·ous [eg'zɪgjʊəs] adj □ dürftig.

ex·ile ['eksaɪl] I s 1. Exil n; Verbannung f: **go into** ~ ins Exil gehen; **live in** ~ im Exil od. in der Verbannung leben; **send into** ~ → 3; **government in** ~ Exilregierung f. 2. im Exil Lebende m, f; Verbannte m, f. II v/t 3. ins Exil schicken; verbannen (**from** aus), in die Verbannung schicken.

ex·ist [ɪg'zɪst] v/i 1. existieren, vorkommen: **do such things** ~? gibt es so etwas?; **right to** ~ Existenzberechtigung f. 2. existieren, leben (**on** von). 3. existieren, bestehen. **ex'ist·ence** s 1. Existenz f, Vorkommen n: **call into** ~ ins Leben rufen; **come into** ~ entstehen; **be in** ~ → **exist** 3; **remain in** ~ weiterbestehen. 2. Existenz f, Leben n, Dasein n. 3. Existenz f, Bestand m. **ex'ist·ent** adj 1. existierend, bestehend, vorhanden. 2. gegenwärtig, augenblicklich. **ex·is-ten·tial·ism** [,egzɪ'stenʃəlɪzəm] s phls. Existentialismus m.

ex·it ['eksɪt] I s 1. Ausgang m. 2. thea. Abgang m. 3. (Autobahn)Ausfahrt f. 4. Ausreise f: ~ **visa** Ausreisevisum n. II v/i 5. thea. Bühnenanweisung: (er, sie, es geht) ab: ~ **Macbeth** Macbeth ab.

ex·o·dus ['eksədəs] s Ab-, Auswanderung f: **rural** ~ Landflucht f.

ex·on·er·ate [ɪg'zɒnəreɪt] v/t 1. Angeklagten etc entlasten (**from** von). 2. j-n befreien, entbinden (**from** von e-r Pflicht etc). **ex,on·er'a·tion** s 1. Entlastung f. 2. Befreiung f, Entbindung f.

ex·or·bi·tance [ɪg'zɔ:bɪtəns] s Exorbitanz f, Maßlosigkeit f. **ex'or·bi·tant** adj □ unverschämt: a) astronomisch: ~ **price** Phantasiepreis m, b) übertrieben, maßlos (**Forderung** etc).

ex·or·cism ['eksɔ:sɪzəm] s Exorzismus m, Geisterbeschwörung f, Teufelsaustreibung f. **'ex·or·cist** s Exorzist m, Geisterbeschwörer m, Teufelsaustreiber m. **ex·or·cize** [~saɪz] v/t 1. böse Geister austreiben, beschwören. 2. j-n, e-n Ort von bösen Geistern befreien, j-m den Teufel austreiben.

ex·ot·ic [ɪg'zɒtɪk] adj (**~ally**) exotisch (a. fig.).

ex·pand [ɪk'spænd] I v/t 1. ausbreiten, -spannen. 2. ✝, phys. etc, a. fig. ausdehnen, -weiten, erweitern. II v/i 3. ✝, phys. etc, a. fig. sich ausdehnen od. erweitern, ✝ a. expandieren. 4. fig. (vor Stolz etc) aufblühen; aus sich herausgehen. 5. fig. sich auslassen od. verbreiten (**on** über acc). **ex'pand·er** s Sport: Expander m. **ex·panse** [~'spæns] s weite Fläche, Weite f. **ex'pan·sion** s 1. Ausbreitung f. 2. ✝, phys. etc, a. fig. Ausdehnung f, -weitung f, Erweiterung f; pol. Expansion f. **ex'pan·sive** adj □ 1. ausdehnungsfähig. 2. ausgedehnt, weit. 3. fig. mitteilsam.

ex·pa·tri·ate [eks'pætrɪeɪt] I v/t ausbürgern. II adj [~ət] ausgebürgert. III s [~ət] Ausgebürgerte m, f. **ex,pa·tri'a·tion** s Ausbürgerung f.

ex·pect [ɪk'spekt] I v/t 1. j-n, et. erwarten: ~ **s.o. to do s.th.** erwarten, daß j-d et. tut; ~ **s.th. of** (od. **from**) **s.o.** et. von j-m erwarten. 2. F vermuten, glauben: **I** ~ **so** ich nehme es an. II v/i 3. **be** ~**ing** F in anderen Umständen sein. **ex'pec·tan·cy** s Erwartung f: **look of** ~ erwartungsvoller Blick. **ex'pec·tant** adj □ 1. ~ **mother** werdende Mutter. 2. erwartungsvoll. **ex·pec·ta·tion** [,ekspek-'teɪʃn] s Erwartung f: **in** ~ **of** in Erwartung (**gen**); **beyond** (**all**) ~(**s**) über Erwarten; **against all** (od. **contrary to** [**all**]) ~(**s**) wider Erwarten; **come up to** ~**s** den Erwartungen entsprechen; **fall short of s.o.'s** ~**s** hinter j-s Erwartungen zurückbleiben; ~ **of life** Lebenserwartung.

ex·pe·di·ence, ex·pe·di·en·cy [ɪk'spi:-djəns(ɪ)] s 1. Zweckdienlichkeit f, Nützlichkeit f. 2. Eigennutz m. **ex'pe·di·ent** I adj 1. ratsam, angebracht. 2. zweckdienlich, -mäßig, nützlich. 3. eigennützig. II s 4. (Hilfs)Mittel n, (Not)Behelf m. **ex'pe·di·ent·ly** adv zweckmäßigerweise.

ex·pe·dite ['ekspɪdaɪt] v/t beschleunigen. **ex·pe·di·tion** [~'dɪʃn] s 1. Expedition f: **on an** ~ auf e-r Expedition. 2. Eile f, Schnelligkeit f. **,ex·pe'di·tious** adj □ schnell, rasch, prompt.

ex·pel [ɪk'spel] v/t (**from**) 1. vertreiben

(aus). **2.** ausweisen (aus), verweisen (*des Landes*). **3.** ausschließen (aus, von).

ex·pen·di·ture [ɪk'spendɪtʃə] *s* **1.** Aufwand *m*, Verbrauch *m* (**of** an dat). **2.** Ausgaben *pl*, (Kosten)Aufwand *m*.

ex·pense [ɪk'spens] *s* **1.** → *expenditure* 2: **at s.o.'s** ~ auf j-s Kosten (*a. fig.*); **spare no** ~ keine Kosten scheuen. **2.** *pl* Unkosten *pl*, Spesen *pl*: *travel(l)ing* ~*s* Reisespesen; ~ *account* Spesenkonto *n*.

ex·pen·sive *adj* □ teuer, kostspielig.

ex·pe·ri·ence [ɪk'spɪərɪəns] **I** *s* **1.** Erfahrung *f*: a) (Lebens)Praxis *f*: **by** (*od.* **from**) ~ aus Erfahrung; **in my** ~ nach m-r Erfahrung, b) Fach-, Sachkenntnis *f*; Routine *f*. **2.** Erlebnis *n*. **II** *v/t* **3.** erfahren: a) kennenlernen, b) erleben, c) *Schmerzen, Verluste* etc erleiden, erdurchmachen, *Vergnügen* etc empfinden. **ex·pe·ri·enced** *adj* erfahren, routiniert.

ex·per·i·ment [ɪk'sperɪmənt] **I** *s* Experiment *n*, Versuch *m* (**on** an dat; **with** mit): ~ **on animals** Tierversuch. **II** *v/i* [~ment] experimentieren, Versuche anstellen (**on** an dat; **with** mit). **ex·per·i·men·tal** [ek͵sperɪ'mentl] *adj* □ experimentell, Versuchs...: ~ *animal* Versuchstier *n*. **ex͵per·i·men'ta·tion** *s* Experimentieren *n*. **ex·per·i·ment·er** *s* Experimentator *m*.

ex·pert ['ekspɜːt] **I** *adj* **1.** (**at, in** in dat) erfahren; geschickt: **be** ~ **at** Erfahrung haben in. **2.** fachmännisch, fach-, sachkundig: ~ *knowledge* Fach-, Sachkenntnis *f*; ~ *opinion* Gutachten *n*. **II** *s* **3.** (**at, in** in dat; **on** auf dem Gebiet gen) Fachmann *m*, Experte *m*; Sachverständige *m*, Gutachter *m*: ~ **on disarmament** Abrüstungsexperte. **ex·per·tise** [͵~'tiːz] *s* **1.** Expertise *f*, Gutachten *n*. **2.** Fach-, Sachkenntnis *f*.

ex·pi·ate ['ekspɪeɪt] *v/t* sühnen, (ab)büßen. **͵ex·pi'a·tion** *s* Sühne *f*, Buße *f*.

ex·pi·ra·tion [͵ekspɪ'reɪʃn] *s* **1.** Ablauf *m*, Erlöschen *n*, Ende *n*: **at** (*od.* **on**) **the** ~ **of** nach Ablauf (*gen*). **2.** Verfall *m*: ~ *date* Verfallstag *m*, -datum *n*. **3.** † Fälligwerden *n*. **ex·pire** [ɪk'spaɪə] *v/i* **1.** ablaufen (*Frist, Paß* etc), erlöschen (*Konzession, Patent* etc), ungültig werden, verfallen. **3.** † fällig werden. **ex·pi·ry** → *expiration* 1.

ex·plain [ɪk'spleɪn] *v/t* erklären: a) erläutern (**s.th. to s.o.** j-m et.), b) begründen, rechtfertigen: ~ *s.th. away* e-e einleuchtende Erklärung für et. finden; sich aus et. herausreden; ~ *o.s.* sich erklären; sich rechtfertigen.

ex·pla·na·tion [͵eksplə'neɪʃn] *s* Erklärung *f* (**for, of** für *od. gen*): a) Erläuterung *f*: **in** ~ **of** als Erklärung für, b) Begründung *f*, Rechtfertigung *f*. **ex·plan·a·to·ry** [ɪk'splænətərɪ] *adj* □ erklärend, erläuternd.

ex·ple·tive [ɪk'spliːtɪv] *s* **1.** *ling.* Füllwort *n*. **2.** Fluch *m*; Kraftausdruck *m*.

ex·pli·ca·ble [ɪk'splɪkəbl] *adj* erklärbar, erklärlich.

ex·plic·it [ɪk'splɪsɪt] *adj* □ **1.** ausdrücklich, deutlich. **2.** ausführlich. **3.** offen, deutlich (*about, on* in bezug auf *acc*): (*sexually*) ~ freizügig (*Film* etc).

ex·plode [ɪk'spləʊd] **I** *v/t* **1.** zur Explosion bringen; (in die Luft) sprengen. **2.** *Gerüchten* etc den Boden entziehen, *Theorie* etc widerlegen, *Mythos* etc zerstören. **II** *v/i* **3.** explodieren; in die Luft fliegen. **4.** *fig.* ausbrechen (**into, with** in *acc*), platzen (**with, in** vor dat). **5.** *fig.* sprunghaft ansteigen, sich explosionsartig vermehren (*bsd. Bevölkerung*).

ex·ploit I *s* ['eksplɔɪt] **1.** (Helden)Tat *f*. **2.** Großtat *f*, große Leistung. **II** *v/t* [ɪk'splɔɪt] **3.** et. auswerten, *Patent* etc (*kommerziell*) verwerten, *Erzvorkommen* etc ausbeuten, abbauen; *b.s. j-n*, et. ausbeuten. **͵ex·ploi'ta·tion** [͵eks~] *s* **1.** Auswertung *f*, Verwertung *f*, Ausbeutung *f*, Abbau *m*.

ex·plo·ra·tion [͵eksplə'reɪʃn] *s* **1.** Erforschung *f*. **2.** Untersuchung *f*. **ex·plor·a·to·ry** [ek'splɔrətərɪ] *adj* Forschungs...: ~ *talks pl* Sondierungsgespräche *pl*. **ex·plore** [ɪk'splɔː] *v/t* **1.** *Land* erforschen. **2.** erforschen, untersuchen, sondieren. **ex'plor·er** *s* Forscher(in), Forschungsreisende *m, f*.

ex·plo·sion [ɪk'spləʊʒn] *s* **1.** Explosion *f*; Sprengung *f*. **2.** *fig.* Widerlegung *f*, Zerstörung *f*. **3.** *fig.* Ausbruch *m*: ~ *of loud laughter* Lachsalve *f*. **4.** *fig.* sprunghafter Anstieg, (*Bevölkerungs*)Explosion *f*.

ex'plo·sive [~sɪv] **I** *adj* □ **1.** explosiv (*a. fig.*), Spreng...: ~ *problem* explosives Problem. **2.** *fig.* aufbrausend (*Temperament*). **II** *s* **3.** Sprengstoff *m*.

ex·po·nent [ɪk'spəʊnənt] s 1. ₳ Exponent m, Hochzahl f. 2. Vertreter(in); Verfechter(in).

ex·port I v/t u. v/i [ɪk'spɔːt] 1. exportieren, ausführen: **~ing country** Ausfuhrland n; **~ing firm** Exportfirma f. II s ['ekspɔːt] 2. Export m, Ausfuhr f. 3. pl (Gesamt)Export m, (-)Ausfuhr f; Exportgüter pl, Ausfuhrware f. III adj ['eksˌ] 4. Export..., Ausfuhr...: **~ trade** Exportgeschäft n, Ausfuhrhandel m. **ex'port·er** [ɪk'spˌ] s Exporteur m.

ex·pose [ɪk'spəʊz] v/t 1. Kind aussetzen. 2. Waren ausstellen (**for sale** zum Verkauf). 3. **~ to** fig. dem Wetter, e-r Gefahr etc aussetzen, der Lächerlichkeit etc preisgeben: **~ o.s.** sich exponieren; **~ o.s. to ridicule** sich zum Gespött (der Leute) machen. 4. fig. j-n bloßstellen; j-n entlarven, Spion a. enttarnen; et. aufdecken, entlarven, enthüllen. 5. entblößen. 6. phot. belichten. **ex'posed** adj ungeschützt (Haus, Lage etc), a. fig. Stellung etc) exponiert.

ex·po·si·tion [ˌekspəʊ'zɪʃn] s 1. Ausstellung f. 2. Exposition f (e-s Dramas). **ex·po·sure** [ɪk'spəʊʒə] s 1. (Kindes-) Aussetzung f. 2. fig. Aussetzen n, Preisgabe f (**to** dat). 3. fig. Ausgesetztsein n (**to** dat): **die of ~** an Unterkühlung sterben. 4. Bloßstellung f; Entlarvung f, Enttarnung f; Aufdeckung f, Enthüllung f. 5. Entblößung f. 6. ungeschützte od. exponierte Lage. 7. phot. a) Belichtung f: **~ meter** Belichtungsmesser m, b) Aufnahme f. 8. Lage f (e-s Gebäudes): **southern ~** Südlage.

ex·pound [ɪk'spaʊnd] v/t erklären, erläutern, Theorie etc entwickeln (**to** s.o. j-m).

ex·press [ɪk'spres] I v/t 1. ausdrücken, äußern: **~ the hope that** der Hoffnung Ausdruck geben, daß; **~ o.s.** sich äußern; sich ausdrücken. 2. bezeichnen, bedeuten. 3. Br. durch Eilboten od. als Eilgut schicken. II adj □ 4. ausdrücklich. 5. Expreß..., Schnell...: **~ letter** Br. Eilbrief m; **~ train** → 9. adv 6. eigens. 7. Br. durch Eilboten, als Eilgut. IV s 8. Br. Eilbote m; -beförderung f. 9. D-Zug m, Schnellzug m. **ex·pres·sion** [ɪk'spreʃn] s 1. Ausdruck m, Äußerung f: **find ~ in** sich ausdrücken od. äußern in (dat); **give ~ to** e-r Sache Ausdruck

verleihen; **beyond** (od. **past**) **~** unsagbar. 2. Ausdruck m, Redensart f. 3. (Gesichts)Ausdruck m. 4. Ausdruck(skraft f) m. **ex'pres·sion·ism** s Kunst: Expressionismus m. **ex'pres·sion·ist** (Kunst) I s Expressionist(in). II adj expressionistisch. **ex'pres·sion·less** adj ausdruckslos. **ex'pres·sive** adj □ 1. **be ~ of** et. ausdrücken. 2. ausdrucksvoll. **ex'press·way** s bsd Am. Schnellstraße f.

ex·pro·pri·ate [eks'prəʊprɪeɪt] v/t ﹩ enteignen. **ex·pro·pri·a·tion** s Enteignung f.

ex·pul·sion [ɪk'spʌlʃn] s (**from**) 1. Vertreibung f (aus). 2. Ausweisung f (aus). 3. Ausschluß m (aus, von).

ex·qui·site ['ekskwɪzɪt] adj □ 1. exquisit, köstlich, erlesen. 2. gepflegt, erlesen (Wein etc). 3. äußerst fein (Gehör etc). 4. heftig (Schmerz), groß (Vergnügen).

ex·ser·vice·man [ˌeks'sɜːvɪsmən] s (irr man) ✕ bsd. Br. Veteran m.

ex·tant [ek'stænt] adj noch vorhanden od. bestehend.

ex·tem·po·ra·ne·ous [ekˌstempə'reɪnjəs], **ex·tem·po·rar·y** [ɪk'stempərərɪ] adj □ improvisiert, aus dem Stegreif, Stegreif... **ex·tem·po·re** [ek'stempərɪ] adj u. adv improvisiert, aus dem Stegreif. **ex·tem·po·rize** [ɪk'stempəraɪz] v/t aus dem Stegreif darbieten od. vortragen, (a. v/i) improvisieren.

ex·tend [ɪk'stend] I v/t 1. (aus)dehnen, (-)weiten. 2. Betrieb etc vergrößern, erweitern, ausbauen. 3. Hand etc ausstrecken. 4. Besuch, Macht, Vorsprung etc ausdehnen (**to** auf acc), Frist, Paß etc verlängern, ✝ a. prolongieren, Angebot etc aufrechterhalten. **~ o.s.** sich völlig ausgeben. II v/i 6. sich ausdehnen od. erstrecken (**over** über acc; **to** bis zu); hinausgehen (**beyond** über acc).

ex·ten·sion [ɪk'stenʃn] s 1. Ausdehnung f (a. fig.: **to** auf acc). 2. Vergrößerung f, Erweiterung f. 3. (Frist)Verlängerung f, ✝ a. Prolongation f. ₳ Erweiterung f, Anbau m. 5. teleph. Nebenanschluß m, Apparat m. **~ ca·ble** ⚡ bsd. Br. Verlängerungsschnur f. **~ cord** Am. → extension cable. **~ lad·der** s Ausziehleiter f. **~ lead** → extension cable.

ex·ten·sive [ɪk'stensɪv] adj □ 1. ausgedehnt (*a. fig.*). **2.** *fig.* umfassend; eingehend; beträchtlich.

ex·tent [ɪkˈstent] *s* **1.** Ausdehnung *f.* **2.** *fig.* Umfang *m,* (Aus)Maß *n,* Grad *m:* **to a large ~** in hohem Maße, weitgehend; **to some** (*od.* **a certain**) **~** bis zu e-m gewissen Grade; **to such an ~ that** so sehr, daß.

ex·ten·u·ate [ɪkˈstenjʊeɪt] *v/t* abschwächen, mildern: **extenuating circumstances** *pl* ⚖ mildernde Umstände *pl.* **ex,ten·u'a·tion** *s* Abschwächung *f,* Milderung *f.*

ex·te·ri·or [ɪkˈstɪərɪə] I *adj* □ **1.** äußer, Außen... II *s* **2.** *das* Äußere: a) Außenseite *f,* b) äußere Erscheinung (*e-r Person*). **3.** *Film, TV:* Außenaufnahme *f.*

ex·ter·mi·nate [ɪkˈstɜːmɪneɪt] *v/t* ausrotten (*a. fig.*), vernichten, *Ungeziefer, Unkraut etc a.* vertilgen. **ex,ter·mi'na·tion** *s* Ausrottung *f,* Vernichtung *f,* Vertilgung *f.*

ex·ter·nal [ɪkˈstɜːnl] I *adj* □ äußer, äußerlich, Außen...: **for ~ use ✍** zum äußerlichen Gebrauch; **~ to** außerhalb (*gen*). II *s pl* Äußerlichkeiten *pl.*

ex·ter·ri·to·ri·al [ˈeksˌterɪtɔːˈrɪəl] *adj* □ exterritorial.

ex·tinct [ɪkˈstɪŋkt] *adj* **1.** erloschen (*Vulkan*) (*a. fig.*). **2.** ausgestorben (*Pflanze, Tier etc*), untergegangen (*Reich etc*): **become ~** aussterben. **ex'tinc·tion** *s* **1.** Erlöschen *n.* **2.** Aussterben *n,* Untergang *m.*

ex·tin·guish [ɪkˈstɪŋgwɪʃ] *v/t* **1.** *Feuer, Licht* (aus)löschen, *Zigarette* ausmachen. **2.** *Leben, Gefühl* auslöschen, ersticken, *Hoffnungen, Pläne etc* zunichte machen. **3.** *Schuld* tilgen. **ex'tin·guish·er** *s* (*Feuer*)Löscher *m.*

ex·tol [ɪkˈstəʊl] *v/t* (lob)preisen, rühmen: → **sky.**

ex·tort [ɪkˈstɔːt] *v/t* *Geld, Geständnis etc* erpressen (**from** von). **ex'tor·tion** *s* **1.** Erpressung *f.* **2.** Wucher *m.* **ex'tor·tion·ate** [~ʃnət] *adj* □ **1.** erpresserisch. **2.** Wucher...: **~ price.** **ex'tor·tion·er, ex'tor·tion·ist** *s* **1.** Erpresser *m.* **2.** Wucherer *m.*

ex·tra [ˈekstrə] I *adj* **1.** zusätzlich, Extra..., Sonder...: **be ~** gesondert berechnet werden; **~ charge** Zuschlag *m;* **~ charges** *pl* Nebenkosten *pl;* **~ pay** Zulage *f;* **if you pay an ~ two pounds**

wenn Sie noch zwei Pfund dazulegen. **2.** besonder. II *adv* **3.** extra, besonders: **charge ~ for** *et.* gesondert berechnen. III *s* **4.** Sonderleistung *f; bsd. mot.* Extra *n, pl a.* Sonderausstattung *f;* Zuschlag *m:* **be an ~** gesondert berechnet werden. **5.** Extrablatt *n,* -ausgabe *f.* **6.** *Film:* Statist(in).

ex·tract I *v/t* [ɪkˈstrækt] **1.** herausziehen, -holen (**from** aus). **2.** *Zahn,* & *Wurzel* ziehen. **3.** *fig.* (**from**) *Geld, Geständnis etc* herausholen (aus), entlocken (*dat*). II *s* [ˈekstrækt] **4.** ✍, *gastr.* Extrakt *m,* (**from** aus e-m *Buch etc a.*) Auszug *m.* **ex'trac·tion** *s* **1.** ✍, & Ziehen *n.* **2.** Herkunft *f,* Abstammung *f.*

ex·tra·cur·ric·u·lar [ˌekstrəkəˈrɪkjələ] *adj* **1.** *ped. univ.* außerhalb des Stunden- *od.* Lehrplans. **2.** außerplanmäßig.

ex·tra·dite [ˈekstrədaɪt] *v/t Verbrecher* ausliefern. **ex·tra·di·tion** [~ˈdɪʃn] *s* Auslieferung *f.*

ˌex·tra'mar·i·tal *adj* außerehelich.

ex·tra·ne·ous [ɪkˈstreɪnjəs] *adj* **1.** fremd (**to** *dat*): **~ to reality** realitätsfremd. **2.** nicht dazugehörig: **be ~ to** nicht gehören zu.

ex·traor·di·nar·y [ɪkˈstrɔːdnrɪ] *adj* □ **1.** außerordentlich, -gewöhnlich. **2.** ungewöhnlich, seltsam.

ˌex·tra'sen·so·ry *adj:* **~ perception** außersinnliche Wahrnehmung. **ˌ~·ter·'res·tri·al** *adj* außerirdisch. **ˈ~ˌter·ri·to·ri·al** *adj* □ exterritorial. **~ time** *s Sport:* Verlängerung *f:* **after ~** nach Verlängerung; **the game went into ~** das Spiel ging in die Verlängerung.

ex·trav·a·gance [ɪkˈstrævəgəns] *s* **1.** Verschwendung(ssucht) *f.* **2.** Übertriebenheit *f,* Extravaganz *f.* **3.** Ausschweifung *f,* Zügellosigkeit *f.* **ex'trav·a·gant** *adj* □ **1.** verschwenderisch. **2.** übertrieben, -spannt, extravagant. **3.** ausschweifend, zügellos.

ex·treme [ɪkˈstriːm] I *adj* (□ → **extremely**) **1.** äußerst, extrem. **2.** äußerst, höchst: **~ necessity** zwingende Notwendigkeit; **~ penalty** Höchststrafe *f.* **3.** extrem, radikal. II *s* **4.** äußerstes Ende: **at the other ~** am entgegengesetzten Ende. **5.** *das* Äußerste, Extrem *n:* **in the ~** extrem, höchst; **go to ~s** vor nichts zurückschrecken. **ex'treme·ly**

adv äußerst, höchst. **ex'trem·ism** *s bsd. pol.* Extre'mismus *m.* **ex'trem·ist** *bsd. pol.* **I** *s* Extremist(in). **II** *adj* extremistisch. **ex·trem·i·ty** [ɪk'stremətɪ] *s* **1.** äußerstes Ende. **2.** *das* Äußerste: *drive s.o. to extremities* j-n bis zum Äußersten treiben. **3.** *be reduced to extremities* in größter Not sein. **4.** *mst pl* Gliedmaße *f,* Extremität *f.*

ex·tri·cate ['ekstrɪkeɪt] *v/t (from)* herausziehen (aus), befreien (aus, von).

ex·tro·vert ['ekstrəʊvɜ:t] *adj psych.* extra-, extrovertiert.

ex·u·ber·ance [ɪg'zju:bərəns] *s* **1.** *(of)* Fülle *f* (von *od. gen*), Reichtum *m* (an *dat*). **2.** *fig.* Überschwang *m.* **ex·u·ber·ant** *adj* □ **1.** üppig, (über)reich. **2.** *fig.* überschwenglich; (-)sprudelnd.

ex·ude [ɪg'zju:d] *v/t* **1.** ausschwitzen, absondern. **2.** *Duft, Charme etc* verströmen.

ex·ult [ɪg'zʌlt] *v/i* frohlocken, jubeln (*at, over, in* über *acc*). **ex'ult·ant** *adj* □ frohlockend, jubelnd. **ex·ul·ta·tion** [ˌegzʌl'teɪʃn] *s* Frohlocken *n,* Jubel *m.*

eye [aɪ] **I** *s* **1.** Auge *n*: *before* (*od. under*) *s.o.'s* ~*s* vor j-s Augen; *all* ~*s* gespannt *warten etc*; *be up to the* ~*s in work* bis über die Ohren in Arbeit sitzen *od.* stecken; *cry one's* ~*s out* sich die Au-

gen ausweinen; → *peel* I, *skin* I, 5. **2.** *fig.* Blick *m,* Auge(nmerk) *n*: *have an* ~ *for* Sinn *od.* ein (offenes) Auge *od.* e-n Blick haben für; → *catch* 10. **3.** *fig.* Ansicht *f*: *in my* ~*s* in m-n Augen, m-r Ansicht nach. **4.** (*Nadel*)Öhr *n*; Öse *f.* **5.** ♣ Auge *n.* **II** *v/t* **6.** betrachten; mustern. '~·**ball** *s anat.* Augapfel *m.* '~·**black** *s* Wimperntusche *f.* '~·**brow** *s* (Augen-) Braue *f*: *raise one's* ~ (*od. an* ~) die Stirn runzeln (*at* über *acc*). '~·**catch·er** *s* Blickfang *m.* ~ **con·tact** *s* Blickkontakt *m.* **II** *v/t* ~ Auge haben. '~·**glass·es** *s pl, a. pair of* ~ *bsd. Am.* Brille *f.* '~·**lash** *s* Augenwimper *f.* ~ **lev·el** *s*: *on* ~ in Augenhöhe. '~·**lid** *s* Augenlid *n*: → *bat*³. ~ **lin·er** *s* Eyeliner *m.* ~ **o·pen·er** *s*: *be an* ~ *to* (*od. for*) j-m die Augen öffnen. ~ **shad·ow** *s* Lidschatten *m.* '~·**shot** *s* Sicht-, Sehweite *f*: (*with*)*in* (*beyond, out of*) ~ in (außer) Sichtweite. '~·**sight** *s* Sehkraft *f*: *good* (*poor*) ~ gute (schlechte) Augen *pl.* '~·**sore** *s et.* Unschönes, Schandfleck *m.* '~·**strain** *s* Überanstrengung *f* der Augen. ˌ~·**wit·ness I** *s* Augenzeuge *m* (*to gen*): ~ *account* Augenzeugenbericht *m.* **II** *v/t* Augenzeuge sein *od.* werden von (*od. gen*).

F

fa·ble ['feɪbl] *s* **1.** Fabel *f;* Sage *f.* **2.** *fig.* Märchen *n.* **fa·bled** ['~bld] *adj* sagenhaft (*a. fig.*).

fab·ric ['fæbrɪk] *s* **1.** Gewebe *n,* Stoff *m.* **2.** *fig.* Gefüge *n,* Struktur *f.* **fab·ri·cate** ['~keɪt] *v/t* **1.** fabrizieren (*a. fig.*), herstellen. **2.** *fig.* erfinden. ˌ**fab·ri'ca·tion** *s* **1.** Fabrikation *f,* Herstellung *f.* **2.** *fig.* Erfindung *f,* Märchen *n.*

fab·u·lous ['fæbjʊləs] *adj* □ sagenhaft (*a. fig.*).

fa·çade, fa·cade [fə'sɑ:d] *s* △ Fassade *f* (*a. fig.*).

face [feɪs] **I** *s* **1.** Gesicht *n*: *in* (*the*) ~ *of* angesichts; trotz; ~ *to* ~ *with* Auge in

Auge mit; *do* (*up*) *one's* ~ sich schminken; *say s.th. to s.o's* ~ j-m et. ins Gesicht sagen; → *stare* II. **2.** Gesicht(sausdruck *m*) *n,* Miene *f*: *make* (*od. pull*) *a* ~ ein Gesicht machen *od.* schneiden; *have the* ~ *to inf* die Stirn haben *od.* so unverfroren sein zu *inf*; → *straight* 1. **3.** *das* Äußere: *on the* ~ *of it* oberflächlich (betrachtet). **4.** Ansehen *n*: *save one's* ~ das Gesicht wahren; *lose* ~ das Gesicht verlieren. **5.** Bildseite *f* (*e-r Spielkarte*). **6.** Zifferblatt *n.* **7.** → *façade.* **II** *v/t* **8.** ansehen, j-m ins Gesicht sehen. **9.** gegenüberstehen, -liegen, -sitzen (*dat*); nach *Osten etc* blicken *od.* liegen

(*Raum etc*). **10.** j-m, e-r Sache mutig entgegentreten *od.* begegnen, sich stellen: → **music** 1. **11.** *oft* **be ~d with** sich e-r Gefahr *etc* gegenüberstehen, gegenüberstehen: **be ~d with ruin** vor dem Ruin stehen. **III** *v/i* **12.** sich wenden: ~ **about** kehrtmachen; ~ **away** sich abwenden. **13.** blicken, liegen (**to, toward[s]** nach; **south** nach Süden). **14.** ~ **up to** → 10. ~ **card** s Kartenspiel: Bild(karte *f*) *n*. '~'**cloth** s Waschlappen *m*. ~ **cream** s Gesichtscreme *f*. '~,lift(·ing)** s Facelifting *n*, Gesichtsstraffung *f*: **have a ~** sich das Gesicht liften lassen.

fa·ce·tious [fə'siːʃəs] *adj* □ witzig, spaßig.

face val·ue s ✝ Nenn-, Nominalwert *m*: **take s.th. at (its) ~** *fig.* et. unbesehen glauben; et. für bare Münze nehmen.

fa·cial ['feɪʃl] *adj* Gesichts...

fa·cil·i·tate [fə'sɪlɪteɪt] *v/t* erleichtern.

fa·cil·i·ty s **1.** Leichtigkeit *f*. **2.** (günstige) Gelegenheit, Möglichkeit *f* (**for** für). **3.** *pl* Einrichtungen *pl*, Anlagen *pl*. **4.** *pl* Erleichterungen *pl*, Vergünstigungen *pl*.

fac·sim·i·le [fæk'sɪmɪli] s Faksimile *n*.

fact [fækt] s Tatsache *f*, Faktum *n*: **be founded on** ~ auf Tatsachen beruhen; **know s.th. for a** ~ et. (ganz) sicher wissen; **tell s.o. the ~s of life** j-n (*sexuell*) aufklären; → **matter** 3. '~,find·ing** *adj* Untersuchungs...

fac·tion ['fækʃn] s *bsd. pol.* Splittergruppe *f*.

fac·ti·tious [fæk'tɪʃəs] *adj* □ künstlich, (*Freundlichkeit etc a.*) gekünstelt.

fac·tor ['fæktə] s Faktor *m*.

fac·to·ry ['fæktərɪ] s Fabrik *f*. ~ **hand**, ~ **work·er** s Fabrikarbeiter(in).

fac·to·tum [fæk'təʊtəm] s Faktotum *n*, Mädchen *n* für alles.

fac·tu·al ['fæktʃʊəl] *adj* □ **1.** Tatsachen...: ~ **report.** **2.** sachlich.

fac·ul·ty ['fæklti] s **1.** Fähigkeit *f*, Vermögen *n*: ~ **of hearing** Hörvermögen *n*; (**mental**) **faculties** *pl* Geisteskräfte *pl*; **be in possession of one's faculties** im (Voll)Besitz s-r Kräfte sein. **2.** Gabe *f*, Talent *n*. **3.** *univ.* Fakultät *f*.

fad [fæd] s Mode(erscheinung, -torheit) *f*; (vorübergehende) Laune.

fade [feɪd] **I** *v/i* **1.** (ver)welken. **2.** verschießen, -blassen (*Farbe etc*). **3.** *a.* ~ **away** sich auflösen (*Menge*), 🎵 immer schwächer werden (*Person*), verklingen (*Lied etc*), verblassen (*Erinnerung*), verrauchen (*Zorn etc*), zerrinnen (*Hoffnungen*). **4.** *Radio:* schwinden (*Ton, Sender*). **5.** nachlassen (*Bremsen*), (*Sportler a.*) abbauen. **6.** *a.* ~ **out** (*Film, Rundfunk, TV*) aus- *od.* abgeblendet werden (*Ton, Bild*): ~ **in** (*od.* **up**) auf- *od.* eingeblendet werden. **II** *v/t* **7.** (ver)welken lassen. **8.** Farbe *etc* ausbleichen. **9.** *a.* ~ **out** Ton, Bild aus- *od.* abblenden: ~ **in** (*od.* **up**) auf- *od.* einblenden. '**fad·ed** *adj* verwelkt, welk.

fae·ces ['fiːsiːz] *s/pl* Fäkalien *pl*, Kot *m*.

fag¹ [fæg] s F Glimmstengel *m*.

fag² [~] F **I** *v/i* sich abarbeiten *od.* (ab)schinden (**at** mit). **II** *v/t a.* ~ **out** ermüden, fertigmachen. **III** s Schinderei *f*.

fag³ [~] → **faggot²**.

fag end s **1.** letzter *od.* schäbiger Rest. **2.** *Br.* F Kippe *f* (*Zigarettenstummel*).

fag·got¹ ['fægət] *bsd. Am.* **fag·ot** ['fægət] s *gastr.* Frikadelle *f* (*bsd. aus Schweineleber*).

fag·got² [~] s *bsd. Am. sl.* Schwule *m*. '**fag·got·y** *adj bsd. Am. sl.* schwul.

Fahr·en·heit ['færənhaɪt]: **10°** = zehn Grad Fahrenheit.

fail [feɪl] **I** *v/i* **1.** versagen (*a. Stimme, Motor etc*); keinen Erfolg haben; *ped.* durchfallen (**in** *in dat*); ✝ Bankrott machen: **he ~ed in his attempt** sein Versuch schlug fehl. **2.** mißlingen, fehlschlagen, scheitern: **if everything else ~s** wenn alle Stricke reißen. **3.** nachlassen, schwinden (*Kräfte etc*); ausgehen, zu Ende gehen (*Vorräte etc*); abnehmen, schwächer werden (*Sehkraft etc*). **4.** ~ **to** *inf* es unterlassen *od.* versäumen zu *inf*: ~ **to do s.th.** et. nicht tun; **I ~ to see** ich sehe nicht ein. **II** *v/t* **5.** j-m versagen: **his courage ~ed him** ihm sank der Mut; **words ~ me** mir fehlen die Worte (**to** *inf zu inf*). **6.** j-n im Stich lassen. **7.** *ped.* j-n durchfallen lassen; durchfallen in (*e-r Prüfung*). **III** s **8.** **without** ~ mit Sicherheit, ganz bestimmt.

'**fail·ing** *prp* in Ermang(e)lung (*gen*): ~ **this** andernfalls.

'**fail-safe** *adj* störungs-, *a. fig.* pannensicher.

fail·ure ['feɪljə] s **1.** Versagen n. **2.** Unterlassung f, Versäumnis f: ~ *to pay* Nichtzahlung f. **3.** Fehlschlag(en n) m, Mißerfolg m. **4.** *ped.* Durchfallen n (*in* in dat). **5.** ✝ Bankrott m. **6.** Versager m (*Person, Sache*).

faint [feɪnt] **I** adj □ schwach, matt (*Person, Farbe* etc; a. fig.): *I haven't the ~est idea* ich habe nicht die leiseste Ahnung. **II** s Ohnmacht f. **III** v/i ohnmächtig werden, in Ohnmacht fallen (*with, from* vor dat). **,~·'heart·ed** adj □ zaghaft, furchtsam.

fair¹ [feə] **I** adj (□ → *fairly*) **1.** schön, hübsch: → *sex* 1. **2.** hell (*Haut, Haar, Teint*), blond (*Haar*), zart (*Teint, Haut*); hellhäutig. **3.** klar, heiter (*Himmel*), schön, trocken (*Wetter, Tag*). **4.** sauber: → *copy* 1. **5.** reell (*Chance*). **6.** gerecht, fair: → *play* 2. **II** adv **7.** anständig, fair: *play ~* fair spielen, a. fig. sich an die Spielregeln halten. **8.** direkt, genau: ~ *in the face* mitten ins Gesicht.

fair² [~] s **1.** Jahrmarkt m; Volksfest n. **2.** Messe f. **'~·ground** s **1.** Rummelplatz m. **2.** Messegelände n.

fair·ly ['feəlɪ] adv **1.** gerecht(erweise). **2.** ziemlich. **'fair·ness** s Gerechtigkeit f, Anständigkeit f, Fairneß f: *in ~ to him* um ihm Gerechtigkeit widerfahren zu lassen.

'fair·way s **1.** ⚓ Fahrwasser n, -rinne f. **2.** Golf: Fairway n. **'~·weath·er** adj: ~ *friend* Freund m nur in guten Zeiten.

fair·y ['feərɪ] s **1.** Fee f. **2.** sl. Schwule m. **'~·sto·ry, ~·tale** s Märchen n (a. fig.).

faith [feɪθ] s **1.** (*in*) Glaube(n) m (an acc) (a. eccl.), Vertrauen n (auf acc, zu): *have ~ in* e-r Sache Glauben schenken, an et. glauben; zu j-m Vertrauen haben. **2.** Redlichkeit f: *in good ~* in gutem Glauben, gutgläubig (*beide a.* ⚖️). **~·ful** ['~fʊl] adj □ **1.** treu (*to* dat): *Yours ~ly* Hochachtungsvoll (*Briefschluß*). **2.** wahrheits- od. wortgetreu. **3.** eccl. gläubig.

faith heal·ing s Gesundbeten n.

faith·less ['feɪθlɪs] adj □ **1.** treulos (*to* gegenüber). **2.** eccl. ungläubig.

fake [feɪk] **I** v/t **1.** a. ~ *up* Bilanz etc frisieren. **2.** Paß etc fälschen. **3.** Interesse etc vortäuschen, Krankheit a. simulieren. **II** s **4.** Fälschung f. **5.**

Schwindel m. **6.** Schwindler m; Simulant m.

fa·kir ['feɪˌkɪə] s Fakir m.

fal·con ['fɔːlkən] s orn. Falke m.

fall [fɔːl] **I** s **1.** Fall m, Sturz m: *have a (bad od. heavy) ~* (schwer) stürzen. **2.** bsd. Am. Herbst m: *in (the) ~* im Herbst. **3.** (*Regen-, Schnee*)Fall m. **4.** fig. Fallen n, Sinken n: ~ *in temperature* Temperatursturz m. **5.** Gefälle n (*des Geländes*). **6.** Fall m (e-r Stadt etc). **7.** Einbruch m (*der Nacht etc*). **8.** mst pl Wasserfall m. **II** v/i (irr) **9.** (um-, herunter-, hinunter)fallen; (ab)stürzen; (ab)fallen (*Blätter*): *he fell to his death* er stürzte tödlich ab. **10.** a. ~ *apart* zerfallen. **11.** fig. fallen: a) (*im Krieg*) umkommen, b) erobert werden (*Stadt*), c) gestürzt werden (*Regierung*). **12.** fig. fallen, sinken (*Preise, Temperatur* etc): *his face fell* er machte ein langes Gesicht. **13.** abfallen (*Gelände* etc). **14.** hereinbrechen (*Nacht* etc). **15.** krank, fällig etc werden.
Verbindungen mit Präpositionen:

fall| be·hind v/i zurückbleiben hinter (*dat*), zurückfallen hinter (acc) (*beide a. fig.*). ~ **down** v/i die Treppe etc hinunterfallen. ~ **for** v/i **1.** hereinfallen auf (acc). **2.** F sich verknallen in (acc). ~ **in·to** v/i **1.** kommen od. geraten in (acc): ~ *difficulties;* → *line¹* 11, *trap* 2. **2.** sich et. angewöhnen: ~ *a habit* e-e Gewohnheit annehmen. **3.** fallen in (*ein Gebiet od. Fach*). ~ **on** v/i **1.** fallen auf (acc) (a. zeitlich): *his glance fell on me; Christmas falls on a Monday this year;* → *ear¹* 1. **2.** herfallen über (acc). **3.** j-m zufallen (*to do* zu tun). ~ **out of** v/i sich et. abgewöhnen: ~ *a habit* e-e Gewohnheit ablegen. ~ **o·ver** v/i: ~ *o.s. to do s.th.* F sich fast umbringen, et. zu tun. ~ **to** v/i **1.** beginnen mit: ~ *doing s.th.* sich daranmachen, et. zu tun. **2.** → *fall on* 3. ~ **un·der** v/i unter *ein Gesetz* etc fallen.
Verbindungen mit Adverbien:

fall| a·bout v/i: ~ (*laughing od. with laughter*) F sich (vor Lachen) kugeln. ~ **a·way** → *fall off.* ~ **back** v/i **1.** zurückweichen. **2.** an zurückgreifen auf (acc). ~ **be·hind** v/i zurückbleiben, -fallen (*beide a. fig.*): ~ *with (od. on)* in Rückstand od. Verzug geraten mit. ~

down *v/i* **1.** umfallen, einstürzen. **2.** F (**on**) enttäuschen, versagen (bei); Pech haben (mit). **~ in** *v/i* **1.** einfallen, -stürzen. **2. ~ with** beipflichten, zustimmen (*dat*); sich anpassen (*dat*); entsprechen (*dat*). **~ off** *v/i* **1.** zurückgehen (*Geschäfte, Zuschauerzahlen etc*), nachlassen (*Begeisterung etc*). **2.** (**from**) abfallen (von), abtrünnig werden (*dat*). **~ out** *v/i* **1.** *agr etc* ausfallen, -gehen. **2.** sich ereignen, geschehen. **3.** (sich) streiten (**with** mit; **over** über *acc*). **~ o·ver** *v/i* hinfallen (*Person*), umfallen (*a. fig.*). **~ to** *v/i* reinhauen, (tüchtig) zugreifen (*beim Essen*).

fal·la·cious [fəˈleɪʃəs] *adj* □ **1.** trügerisch, irreführend. **2.** irrig, falsch.

fal·la·cy [ˈfæləsɪ] *s* Trugschluß *m*, Irrtum *m*.

fall·en [ˈfɔːlən] I *pp von* **fall.** II *adj* gefallen (*a. Mädchen*).

fall guy *s bsd. Am.* F **1.** Opfer *n* (*e-s Betrügers*); Gimpel *m* (*leichtgläubiger Mensch*). **2.** Sündenbock *m*.

fal·li·ble [ˈfæləbl] *adj* □ fehlbar.

fall·ing star [ˈfɔːlɪŋ] *s* Sternschnuppe *f*.

ˈfall·out Fallout *m*, radioaktiver Niederschlag.

fal·low [ˈfæləʊ] *adj* ↗ brach(liegend) (*a. fig.*): **lie ~** brachliegen.

false [fɔːls] I *adj* □ *allg.* falsch: **~ alarm** falscher *od.* blinder Alarm (*a. fig.*); **~ bottom** doppelter Boden; **~ key** Dietrich *m*, Nachschlüssel *m*; **~ teeth** *pl* (*künstliches*) Gebiß; → **pretence** 2. II *adv*: **play s.o. ~** ein falsches Spiel mit j-m treiben. **ˈfalse·hood** [ˈ~hʊd] *s* **1.** Unwahrheit *f.* **2.** Falschheit *f.* **ˈfalse·ness** *s allg.* Falschheit *f.*

fal·si·fi·ca·tion [ˌfɔːlsɪfɪˈkeɪʃn] *s* (Ver-)Fälschung *f.* **fal·si·fy** [ˈ~faɪ] *v/t* **1.** fälschen. **2.** verfälschen, falsch darstellen *od.* wiedergeben. **3.** widerlegen. **fal·si·ty** [ˈ~ətɪ] → **falsehood.**

fal·ter [ˈfɔːltə] I *v/i* schwanken: a) taumeln, b) zögern, zaudern, c) stocken (*a. Stimme*). II *v/t et.* stammeln.

fame [feɪm] *s* Ruhm *m.* **famed** *adj* berühmt (**for** für, wegen).

fa·mil·iar [fəˈmɪljə] I *adj* □ **1.** vertraut, bekannt, geläufig (**to** *dat*): **a ~ sight** ein

gewohnter Anblick. **2.** vertraut, bekannt (**with** mit): **be ~ with** *a.* sich auskennen in (*dat*); **make o.s. ~ with** sich vertraut machen mit. **3.** a) vertraulich, ungezwungen (*Ton etc*), b) plump-vertraulich, aufdringlich. **4.** vertraut, eng (*Freund etc*): **be on ~ terms with** auf vertrautem Fuß stehen mit. II *s* **5.** Vertraute *m, f.* **fa·mil·i·ar·i·ty** [ˌ~lɪˈærətɪ] *s* **1.** Vertrautheit *f.* **2.** a) Vertraulichkeit *f,* b) *oft pl* plumpe Vertraulichkeit, Aufdringlichkeit *f.* **fa·mil·iar·ize** [ˌ~jəraɪz] *v/t* vertraut *od.* bekannt machen (**with** mit).

fam·i·ly [ˈfæməlɪ] I *s* Familie *f, fig. a.* Herkunft *f:* **a ~ of four** e-e vierköpfige Familie; **of good ~** aus gutem Haus; → **run** 11. II *adj* Familien...: **~ allowance** Kindergeld *n*; **~ doctor** Hausarzt *m*; **~ man** Familienvater *m*; häuslicher Mensch; **~ name** → **surname**; **~ planning** Familienplanung *f*; **~ problems** *pl* familiäre Probleme *pl*; **~ tree** Stammbaum *m.*

fam·ine [ˈfæmɪn] *s* Hungersnot *f.*

fa·mous [ˈfeɪməs] *adj* □ berühmt (**for** wegen, für).

fan¹ [fæn] I *s* **1.** Fächer *m.* **2.** Ventilator *m*: **~ belt** ⊙ Keilriemen *m.* II *v/t* **3.** j-m Luft zufächeln. **4.** anfachen, *fig. a.* entfachen, -flammen. III *v/i* **5.** *oft* **~ out** sich fächerförmig ausbreiten; ausschwärmen.

fan² [~] *s* (*Sport- etc*)Fan *m*: **~ club** Fanklub *m*; **~ mail** Verehrerpost *f.*

fa·nat·ic [fəˈnætɪk] I *s* Fanatiker(in). II *adj* (**~ally**) fanatisch. **fa·nat·i·cism** [ˌ~sɪzəm] *s* Fanatismus *m.*

fan·ci·er [ˈfænsɪə] *s* (*Tier-, Blumen- etc*-)Liebhaber(in) *od.* (-)Züchter(in).

fan·ci·ful [ˈfænsɪfʊl] *adj* □ **1.** phantasiereich. **2.** phantastisch, wirklichkeitsfremd.

fan·cy [ˈfænsɪ] I *s* **1.** Phantasie *f*; Einbildung *f*: → **tickle** I. **2.** Idee *f*, plötzlicher Einfall. **3.** Laune *f*, Grille *f.* **4.** (**for**) Neigung *f* (zu), Vorliebe *f* (für), Gefallen *n* (an *dat*): **have a ~ for** gern haben; Lust haben auf (*acc*); **take a ~ to** (*od.* **for**) Gefallen finden an (*dat*), sympathisch finden. II *adj* **5.** Phantasie..., phantastisch: **~ name** Phantasiename *m*; **~ price** Liebhaberpreis *m.* **6.** phantasie-, kunstvoll. III *v/t* **7.** sich j-n, et.

vorstellen: ~ *that!* stell dir vor!, denk nur!; sieh mal einer an! **8.** annehmen, glauben. **9.** ~ *o.s.* sich einbilden (*to be* zu sein), sich halten ([*as*] für): ~ *o.s.* (*very important*) sich sehr wichtig vorkommen. **10.** gern haben *od.* mögen. **11.** Lust haben (auf *acc*; *doing* zu tun). **12.** Tiere, Pflanzen (aus Liebhaberei) züchten. ~ **ball** s Kostümfest *n*, Maskenball *m*. ~ **dress** s (Masken)Kostüm *n*. '~**dress** *adj*: ~ *ball* → *fancy ball*. ,~'**free** *adj* frei u. ungebunden. ~ **goods** s *pl* **1.** Modeartikel *pl*. **2.** kleine Geschenkartikel *pl*; Nippes *pl*.

fan·fare ['fænfeə] s **1.** ♩ Fanfare *f*, Tusch *m*. **2.** *fig. contp.* Trara *n*, Tamtam *n*.

fang [fæŋ] s Reiß-, Fangzahn *m*, Fang *m* (*e-s Raubtiers etc*), Hauer *m* (*e-s Ebers*), Giftzahn *m* (*e-r Schlange*).

fan·ta·sia [fæn'teɪʒə] s ♩ Fantasie *f*.

fan·tas·tic [~'tæstɪk] *adj* (~*ally*) phantastisch: a) unwirklich, b) absurd, c) F toll. **fan·ta·sy** ['fæntəsɪ] s Phantasie *f*: a) Einbildungskraft *f*, b) Phantasievorstellung *f*, c) Tag-, Wachtraum *m*.

far [fɑː] I *adj* **1.** fern, (weit)entfernt, weit: → **cry** 1. **2.** (*vom Sprecher aus*) entfernter: *at the ~ end* am anderen Ende. II *adv* **3.** fern, weit: ~ *away* (*od. off*) weit weg *od.* entfernt; *as* ~ *as* soweit *od.* soviel (wie); bis (nach); *so* ~ *so good* so weit, so gut. **4.** *fig.* (*from*) weit entfernt (von), alles andere (als): ~ *from completed* noch lange *od.* längst nicht fertig. **5.** ~ *into* weit *od.* tief in (*acc*): ~ *into the night* bis spät *od.* tief in die Nacht (hinein). **6.** *a. by* ~ weit(aus), bei weitem, wesentlich. '~**a·way** → *far* 1.

farce [fɑːs] s *thea.* Farce *f* (*a. fig.*), Posse *f*, Schwank *m*. **far·ci·cal** ['~sɪkl] *adj* □ **1.** farcen-, possenhaft. **2.** *fig.* absurd, lächerlich.

fare [feə] I s **1.** Fahrpreis *m*, -geld *n*; Flugpreis *m*: *what's the ~?* was kostet die Fahrt *od.* der Flug?; *any more ~s, please?* noch j-d zugestiegen?; ~ *dodger* (*od. evader*) Schwarzfahrer(in); ~ *stage Br.* Fahrpreiszone *f*, Teilstrecke *f*. **2.** Fahrgast *m* (*bsd. e-s Taxis*). **3.** Kost *f* (*a. fig.*), Nahrung *f*. II *v/i* **4.** (er)gehen: *how did you ~?* wie ist es dir ergangen?; *he ~d ill, it ~d ill with him* es erging ihm schlecht. ,~'**well** I *int* leb(t)

wohl. II s Lebewohl *n*, Abschied(sgruß) *m*: *make one's ~s* sich verabschieden. III *adj* Abschieds...

,**far-'fetched** *adj fig.* weithergeholt, an den Haaren herbeigezogen.

farm [fɑːm] I s **1.** (*a. Geflügel- etc*)Farm *f*, Bauernhof *m*. II *v/t* **2.** *Land* bebauen, bewirtschaften. **3.** *Geflügel etc* züchten. **4.** ~ *out* ⊕ *Arbeit* vergeben (*to* an *acc*). III *v/i* **5.** Landwirtschaft betreiben. '**farm·er** s **1.** Bauer *m*, Landwirt *m*, Farmer *m*. **2.** (*Geflügel- etc*)Züchter *m*. '**farm·house** s Bauernhaus *n*.

farm·ing ['fɑːmɪŋ] s **1.** Landwirtschaft *f*. **2.** (*Geflügel- etc*)Zucht *f*.

,**far·'off** → *far* 1. ,~'**out** *adj sl.* **1.** toll, super. **2.** exzentrisch. **3.** ← folgenschwer. ,~'**reach·ing** *adj* weitreichend, *fig. a.* folgenschwer. ,~-'**see·ing** *adj* weitblickend, umsichtig. ,~'**sight·ed** *adj* **1.** → *farseeing*. **2.** ✻ weitsichtig.

fart [fɑːt] V I s **1.** Furz *m*. **2.** *fig.* Arschloch *n*. II *v/i* **3.** furzen.

far·ther ['fɑːðə] I *adj* **1.** *comp von* far. **2.** weiter weg liegend, entfernter. **3.** → *further* 5. II *adv* **4.** weiter: *so far and no* ~ bis hierher u. nicht weiter. **5.** → *further* 2. **far·thest** ['~ðɪst] I *adj* **1.** *sup von* far. **2.** weitest, entferntest. **3.** → *furthest* 2. II *adv* **4.** am weitesten *od.* entferntesten. **5.** → *further* 4.

fas·ci·nate ['fæsɪneɪt] *v/t* faszinieren. ,**fas·ci·'na·tion** s Faszination *f*.

fas·cism, *oft* ≗ ['fæʃɪzəm] s *pol.* Faschismus *m*. '**fas·cist**, *a.* ≗ I s Faschist(in). II *adj* faschistisch.

fash·ion ['fæʃn] I s **1.** Mode *f*: *come into* ~ in Mode kommen, modern werden; *go out of* ~ aus der Mode kommen, unmodern werden; ~ *parade* (*od. show*) Mode(n)schau *f*. **2.** Art *f* u. Weise *f*, Stil *m*: *after* (*od. in*) *a* ~ schlecht u. recht, so lala. II *v/t* **3.** formen, gestalten. '**fash·ion·a·ble** *adj* □ **1.** modisch, elegant. **2.** a) in Mode: *be very* ~ große Mode sein (*to do* zu tun), b) Mode...: ~ *complaint* Modekrankheit *f*.

fast¹ [fɑːst] I *adj* **1.** schnell: ~ *train* Schnell-, D-Zug *m*; *my watch is* (*ten minutes*) ~ m-e Uhr geht (10 Minuten) vor. **2.** *phot.* hochempfindlich (*Film*); lichtstark (*Objektiv*). II *adv* **3.** schnell.

fast² [~] I *adj* **1.** fest: *make* ~ festmachen; ~ *friends pl* unzertrennliche Freunde *pl.* **2.** widerstandsfähig (**to** gegen): ~ **colo(u)r** (wasch)echte Farbe; ~ **to light** lichtecht. **II** *adv* **3.** fest: *be ~ asleep* fest *od.* tief schlafen; *play ~ and loose with* Schindluder treiben mit.

fast³ [~] **I** *v/i* **1.** fasten. **II** *s* **2.** Fasten *n.* **3.** Fastenzeit *f.* ~ **day** *(day)* Fastentag *m.*

'**fast·back** *s mot.* (Wagen *m* mit) Fließheck *n.* ~ **breed·er,** ,~·'**breed·er re·ac·tor** *s phys.* schneller Brüter.

fas·ten ['fɑːsn] **I** *v/t* **1.** befestigen, festmachen (**to, on** an *acc*): → *seat belt.* **2.** *a.* ~ **up** (ab-, ver)schließen, *Jacke etc* zuknöpfen, *Paket etc* zu-, verschnüren: ~ *s.o. down to* F j-n festnageln auf (*acc*). **3.** ~ *on* fig. *Blick, Aufmerksamkeit etc* richten auf (*acc*); *j-m e-e Straftat etc* in die Schuhe schieben, anhängen. **II** *v/i* **4.** sich festmachen *od.* schließen lassen.

'**fas·ten·er** *s* Verschluß *m.*

'**fast-food re·stau·rant** Schnellimbiß *m,* -gaststätte *f.*

fas·tid·i·ous [fə'stɪdɪəs] *adj* □ anspruchsvoll, wählerisch, heikel (**about** in *dat*).

'**fast·ness** ['fɑːstnɪs] *s* Widerstandsfähigkeit *f* (**to** gegen), Echtheit *f* (*von Farben*).

fat [fæt] **I** *adj* □ **1.** dick (*a. fig. Bankkonto etc*), *contp.* fett. **2.** fett(ig), fetthaltig. **II** *s* **3.** Fett *n:* *the ~ is in the fire* der Teufel ist los; *chew the ~* F quatschen, plaudern; *live on* (*od.* **off**) *the ~ of the land* in Saus u. Braus *od.* wie Gott in Frankreich leben.

fa·tal ['feɪtl] *adj* □ **1.** tödlich. **2.** fatal, verhängnisvoll (**to** für). **fa·tal·ism** ['~təlɪzəm] *s* Fatalismus *m.* '**fa·tal·ist** *s* Fatalist(in). ,**fa·tal'is·tic** *adj* (*~ally*) fatalistisch. **fa·tal·i·ty** [fə'tæləti] *s* **1.** Verhängnis *n.* **2.** tödlicher Unfall; (Todes)Opfer *n.*

fate [feɪt] *s* **1.** Schicksal *n:* *he met his ~* das Schicksal ereilte ihn; **(as)** *sure as ~ is ~* garantiert, mit Sicherheit; → *tempt* **2. 2.** Verhängnis *n,* Verderben *n.* '**fat·ed** *adj* **1.** *he was ~ to inf* es war ihm (vom Schicksal) bestimmt zu *inf.* **2.** → *fateful* **2. fate·ful** ['~fʊl] *adj* □ **1.** verhängnisvoll. **2.** schicksalhaft, Schicksals...

fa·ther ['fɑːðə] **I** *s* **1.** Vater *m, fig. a.* Begründer *m: like ~ like son* der Apfel fällt nicht weit vom Stamm; ♀'*s Day*

Vatertag *m.* **2.** *pl* Ahnen *pl,* Vorfahren *pl,* Väter *pl.* **3.** *eccl.* a) Pater *m,* b) *the Holy* ♀ der Heilige Vater. **II** *v/t* **4.** *et.* ins Leben rufen. **5.** ~ *s.th. on s.o.* j-m die Schuld für et. zuschreiben. ♀ *Christmas* *s bsd. Br.* der Weihnachtsmann. ~ **fig·ure** *s psych.* Vaterfigur *f.*

fa·ther·hood ['fɑːðəhʊd] *s* Vaterschaft *f.* '**fa·ther-in-law** *pl* '**fa·thers-in-law** *s* Schwiegervater *m.* '**~·land** *s* Vaterland *n.*

fa·ther·less ['fɑːðəlɪs] *adj* vaterlos. '**fa·ther·ly** *adj* väterlich.

fath·om ['fæðəm] *v/t* ♎ ausloten, *fig. a.* ergründen, '**fath·om·less** *adj* □ unergründlich (*a. fig.*).

fa·tigue [fə'tiːg] **I** *s* **1.** Ermüdung *f* (*a. ⊙*). **2.** *pl* Strapazen *pl.* **II** *v/t u. v/i* **3.** ermüden (*a. ⊙*).

fat·less ['fætlɪs] *adj* fettlos. '**fat·ness** *s* Dicke *f, contp.* Fettheit *f.* **fat·ten** ['~tn] **I** *v/t* **1.** *a.* ~ **up** dick *od. contp.* fett machen. **2.** *Tier,* F *a. j-n* mästen. **II** *v/i* **3.** dick *od. contp.* fett werden. '**fat·ty I** *adj* fettig, Fett... **II** *s* F Dickerchen *n.*

fa·tu·i·ty [fə'tjuːəti] *s* Albernheit *f.* **fat·u·ous** ['fætjʊəs] *adj* □ albern.

fau·cet ['fɔːsɪt] *s Am.* (Wasser)Hahn *m.*

fault [fɔːlt] *s* **1.** Schuld *f,* Verschulden *n: it is my ~* es ist m-e Schuld; *be at ~* schuld sein. **2.** Fehler *m* (*a. Tennis etc*): *find ~ with* et. auszusetzen haben an (*dat*); *be at ~* sich irren. **3.** ⊙ Defekt *m.* '**~·find·er** *s* Nörgler(in), Kritt(e)ler(in). '**~·find·ing** *s* Nörgelei *f,* Krittelei *f.* **II** *adj* nörglerisch, kritt(e)lig.

fault·less ['fɔːltlɪs] *adj* □ fehlerfrei, -los. '**fault·y** *adj* □ fehlerhaft, ⊙ *a.* defekt, (*Argumentation etc a.*) falsch.

fau·na ['fɔːnə] *pl* **-nas, -nae** ['~niː] *s* Fauna *f,* Tierwelt *f.*

fa·vo(u)r ['feɪvə] **I** *v/t* **1.** begünstigen: a) favorisieren, bevorzugen, b) günstig sein für, fördern, c) unterstützen, für *et.* sein. **2.** *bsd. Sport:* favorisieren, zum Favoriten erklären. **II** *s* **3.** Gunst *f,* Wohlwollen *n: in ~ of* zugunsten von (*od.* gen); *in my ~* zu m-n Gunsten; *be in ~ of* für *et.* sein; *be in (out of) s.o.'s ~,* *be in (out of) ~ with s.o.* bei j-m gut (schlecht) angeschrieben sein. **4.** Gefallen *m,* Gefälligkeit *f: ask s.o. a ~* (*od.* **a ~ of s.o.**) j-n um e-n Gefallen bitten; *do s.o. a ~* j-m e-n Gefallen tun. '**fa-**

vo(u)r·a·ble *adj* □ günstig: a) vorteilhaft (**to, for** für), b) positiv, zustimmend (*Antwort etc*). **'fa·vo(u)red** *adj* **1.** begünstigt. **2.** bevorzugt, Lieblings... **3.** *bsd. Sport*: favorisiert. **fa·vo(u)r·ite** ['ɔ·rɪt] **I** *s* **1.** Liebling *m*, *contp.* Günstling *m*. **2.** *bsd. Sport*: Favorit(in). **II** *adj* **3.** Lieblings... **~ dish** Lieblingsgericht *n*, Leibspeise *f*. **'fa·vo(u)r·it·ism** *s* Günstlings-, Vetternwirtschaft *f*.

fawn [fɔːn] *v/i:* **~ on** *fig.* katzbuckeln vor (*dat*). **'fawn·ing** *adj* □ kriecherisch.

fax [fæks] *v/t* faxen.

fear [fɪə] **I** *s* **1.** Furcht *f*, Angst *f* (**of** vor *dat*; **that** daß): **for ~ that** aus Furcht, daß; **be in ~ (of** *s.o.*) sich (vor j-m) fürchten, (vor j-m) Angst haben. **2.** Befürchtung *f*, Sorge *f*: **for ~ of hurting him** um ihn nicht zu verletzen. **3.** Ehrfurcht *f* (**of** vor *dat*): **~ of God** Gottesfurcht *f*. **II** *v/t* **4.** fürchten, sich fürchten *od.* Angst haben vor (*dat*). **5.** *das Schlimmste etc* (be)fürchten. **6.** *Gott* fürchten. **III** *v/i* **7. ~ for** fürchten um.

'fear·ful *adj* □ **1.** furchtbar, fürchterlich (*beide a. fig.* F). **2. be ~ in** (großer) Sorge sein, sich ängstigen (**of, for** um; **that** daß). **3.** furchtsam, angsterfüllt: **be ~ of →** *fear* **4.** **'fear·less** *adj* □ furchtlos: **be ~ of** sich nicht fürchten *od.* keine Angst haben vor (*dat*).

fea·si·bil·i·ty [,fiːzə'bɪlətɪ] *s* Machbarkeit *f*, Durchführbarkeit *f*. **'fea·si·ble** *adj* □ machbar, (*Plan etc*) durchführbar.

feast [fiːst] **I** *s* **1.** *eccl.* Fest *n*, Feiertag *m*. **2.** Festessen *n*, -mahl *n*. **3.** *fig.* (Hoch-)Genuß *m*: **~ for the eyes** Augenweide *f*. **II** *v/t* **4.** festlich bewirten (**on** mit). **5.** ergötzen (**on** mit): **~ one's eyes on** s-e Augen weiden an (*dat*). **III** *v/i* **6.** sich gütlich tun (**on** an *dat*). **7.** sich weiden (**on** an *dat*).

feat [fiːt] *s* **1.** Helden-, Großtat *f*. **2.** Kunst-, Meisterstück *n*; Kraftakt *m*. **3.** (*technische etc*) Großtat, große Leistung.

feath·er ['feðə] **I** *s* Feder *f*, *pl* Gefieder *n*: **birds of a ~** Leute vom gleichen Schlag; **birds of a ~ flock together** gleich u. gesellt sich gern; **that is a ~ in his cap** darauf kann er stolz sein; **→** *light²* 1. **II** *v/t* mit Federn polstern *od.* schmücken, *Pfeil* fiedern: **~ one's nest** *fig.* sein(e) Schäfchen ins trockene

bringen. **~ bed** *s* Matratze *f* mit Federod. Daunenfüllung. **'~bed** *v/t* *j-n* verhätscheln. **'~brained** *adj* **1.** hohlköpfig. **2.** leichtsinnig. **'~weight I** *s* **1.** *Sport*: Federgewicht(ler *m*) *n*. **2.** Leichtgewicht *n* (*Person*). **II** *adj* **3.** *Sport*: Federgewichts... **4.** leichtgewichtig.

fea·ture ['fiːtʃə] **I** *s* **1.** (Gesichts)Zug *m*. **2.** Merkmal *n*, Charakteristikum *n*. **3.** (Haupt)Attraktion *f*. **4.** a) a. **~ program(me)** (*Rundfunk, TV*) Feature *n*, b) a. **~ article** (*od. story*) (*Zeitung*) Feature *n*, c) a. **~ film** Feature *n*, Haupt-, Spielfilm *m*. **II** *v/t* **5.** als (Haupt-) Attraktion zeigen *od.* bringen, groß herausbringen *od.* -stellen. **6.** in der Hauptrolle zeigen: **a film featuring X** ein Film mit X in der Hauptrolle. **7.** sich auszeichnen durch.

fe·brile ['fiːbraɪl] *adj* ♣ fieb(e)rig, fieberhaft, Fieber...

Feb·ru·ar·y ['febrʊərɪ] *s* Februar *m*: **in ~** im Februar.

fe·ces *bsd. Am. →* **faeces**.

fed [fed] *pret u. pp von* **feed**.

fed·er·al, *mst* ⊇ ['fedərəl] *adj* *pol.* Bundes...: ⊇ **Bureau of Investigation** *Am.* Bundeskriminalpolizei *f*. **'fed·er·al·ism,** *mst* '⊇ *s pol.* Föderalismus *m*. **'fed·er·al·ist I** *adj* föderalistisch. **II** *s mst* '⊇ Föderalist *m*. **,fed·er·a'tion** *s* **1.** *pol.* Bundesstaat *m*; Föderation *f*, Staatenbund *m*. **2.** (*Sport- etc*)Verband *m*.

fee [fiː] *s* (*Anwalts- etc*)Honorar *n*, (*Mitglieds- etc*)Beitrag *m*, (*Eintritts- etc*) Geld *n*, (*Aufnahme- etc*)Gebühr *f*.

fee·ble ['fiːbl] *adj* □ schwach (*a. fig.*). **~'mind·ed** *adj* □ schwachsinnig, geistesschwach. **'fee·ble·ness** ['fiːblnɪs] *s* Schwäche *f*.

feed [fiːd] **I** *v/t* (*irr*) **1.** *Tier, Kind* füttern (**on, with** mit): **be fed up with** F die Nase voll haben von, *e-r. etc* satt haben. **2.** *Familie etc* ernähren, unterhalten. **3.** ⊙ *Maschine* speisen, beschicken, *a. j-n* versorgen (**with** mit): **~ s.th. into a computer** et. in e-n Computer eingeben *od.* einspeisen. **4. ~ back** a) ⚡, *Kybernetik*: rückkoppeln, b) *Informationen etc* zurückleiten (**to** an *acc*). **5.** *Gefühl* nähren. **II** *v/i* (*irr*) **6.** fressen (*Tier*); F futtern (*Mensch*). **7.** sich ernähren, leben (**on** von). **III** *v/s* **8.** Füttern *n*, Fütterung *f*. **9.** F Mahlzeit *f*. **'~back I** *s* **1.** ⚡,

Kybernetik: Feedback *n*, Rückkopp(e)-lung *f*. **2. a)** *Rundfunk*, *TV*: Feedback *n*, **b)** Zurückleitung *f* (*von Informationen*) (**to** *an acc*).

feed·er ['fiːdə] *s* **1. a heavy ~** ein starker Fresser (*Tier*) *od*. F Esser (*Mensch*). **2.** → **feeding bottle. 3.** *Br.* Lätzchen *n*. **~ road** *s* Zubringerstraße *f*.

feed·ing ['fiːdɪŋ] *s* Füttern *n*, Fütterung *f*. **~ bot·tle** *s* (Säuglings-, Saug)Flasche *f*.

feel [fiːl] **I** *v/t* (*irr*) **1.** (an-, be)fühlen: **~ one's way** sich tasten (**through** durch). **2.** fühlen, (ver)spüren: **make itself felt** spürbar werden, sich bemerkbar machen. **3.** *Freude etc* empfinden. **4. a)** finden, glauben (**that** daß), **b)** halten für: **I ~ it (to be) my duty** ich halte es für m-e Pflicht. **II** *v/i* (*irr*) **5.** fühlen (**whether**, *if* ob; **how** wie): **~ for** tasten nach. **6.** sich fühlen: **~ ill**; **~ up to s.th.** sich e-r Sache gewachsen fühlen; **~ like (doing) s.th.** Lust haben zu e-r *od*. auf e-e Sache (*et*. zu tun); → **cold** 1, **warm** 1. **7. how do you ~ about it?** was meinst du dazu? **8.** sich *weich etc* anfühlen. **III** *s* **9.** *klebriges etc* Gefühl. **10. be soft to the ~, have a soft ~** sich weich anfühlen. **'feel·er** *s zo.* Fühler *m* (*a. fig.*): **put out ~s** (*od*. **a ~**) s-e Fühler ausstrecken. **'feel·ing** *s* Gefühl *n*: **a)** Gefühlssinn *m*, **b)** (Gefühls)Eindruck *m*: **have a ~ that** das Gefühl haben, daß, **c)** Empfindung *f*: **~s pl of guilt** Schuldgefühle *pl*, **d)** Feingefühl *n*: **have a ~ for** Gefühl haben für.

feet [fiːt] *pl von* **foot**.

feign [feɪn] **I** *v/t Interesse etc* vortäuschen, *Krankheit a.* simulieren: **~ death** (*od*. **to be dead**) sich totstellen. **II** *v/i* sich verstellen, simulieren.

feint [feɪnt] *s Sport*: Finte *f* (*a. fig.*).

fell¹ [fel] *pret von* **fall**.

fell² [~] *v/t* **1.** *Baum* fällen. **2.** *Gegner etc* fällen, niederstrecken.

fel·loe ['feləʊ] *s* ⊕ Felge *f*.

fel·low ['feləʊ] **I** *s* **1.** Gefährte *m*, Gefährtin *f*, Genosse *m*, Genossin *f*, Kamerad(in). **2.** Mitmensch *m*, Zeitgenosse *m*. **3.** F Kerl *m*: **old ~** alter Knabe; **a ~** man. **II** *adj* **4.** Mit...: **~ being** Mitmensch *m*; **~ citizen** Mitbürger *m*; **~ countryman** Landsmann *m*; **~ feeling** Mitgefühl *n*; Zs.-gehörigkeitsgefühl *n*;

~ student Studienkollege *m*, Kommilitone *m*; **~ trav·el(l)er** Mitreisende *m*; *pol.* Mitläufer *m*. **'fel·low·ship** *s* **1.** Kameradschaft *f*. **2.** Gesellschaft *f*, Gruppe *f*.

felt¹ [felt] *pret u. pp von* **feel**.

felt² [~] **I** *s* Filz *m*. **II** *adj* Filz... **~ tip**, **'~-tip(ped) pen** *s* Filzschreiber *m*, -stift *m*.

fe·male ['fiːmeɪl] **I** *s* **1.** *contp.* Weib(sbild) *n*. **2.** *zo.* Weibchen *n*. **II** *adj* **3.** weiblich: **~ dog** Hündin *f*; **~ screw** Schraubenmutter *f*. **4.** Frauen...

fem·i·nine ['femɪnɪn] *adj* □ **1.** weiblich (*a. ling.*), Frauen... **2.** fraulich. **3.** weibisch, feminin. **,fem·i'nin·i·ty** *s* **1.** Weiblichkeit *f*. Fraulichkeit *f*. **3.** weibische *od*. feminine Art. **'fem·i·nism** *s* Feminismus *m*, Frauenrechtsbewegung *f*. **'fem·i·nist I** *s* Feminist(in), Frauenrechtler(in). **II** *adj* feministisch.

fe·mur ['fiːmə] *pl* **-murs**, **fem·o·ra** ['femərə] *s anat.* Oberschenkel(knochen) *m*.

fen [fen] *s* Fenn *n*, Sumpf-, Marschland *n*.

fence [fens] **I** *s* **1.** Zaun *m*: **sit on the ~** sich neutral verhalten; unentschlossen sein. **2.** *sl.* Hehler *m*. **II** *v/t* **3. a.** **~ in** einzäunen; **~ off** abzäunen. **III** *v/i* **4.** *Sport*: fechten. **'fenc·er** *s Sport*: Fechter(in). **'fenc·ing I** *s* **1.** Zaun *m*, Einzäunung *f*. **2.** *Sport*: Fechten *n*. **3.** *sl.* Hehlerei *f*. **II** *adj* **4.** *Sport*: Fecht...: **~ master** Fechtmeister *m*.

fend [fend] **I** *v/t* **off** *Angreifer*, *Fragen etc* abwehren. **II** *v/i*: **~ for o.s.** für sich selbst sorgen. **'fend·er** *s mot. Am.* Kotflügel *m*.

fen·nel ['fenl] *s* ♀ Fenchel *m*.

fer·ment [fə'ment] **I** *v/t* **1.** ⚗ in Gärung bringen (*a. fig.*), gären lassen, vergären; *fig.* in Wallung bringen. **II** *v/i* **2.** ⚗ gären, in Gärung sein (*beide a. fig.*). **III** *s* ['fɜːment] **3.** ⚗ Gärstoff *m*, Ferment *n*. **4. a)** ⚗ Gärung *f* (*a. fig.*), **b)** *fig.* innere Unruhe, Aufruhr *m*. **fer·men·ta·tion** [,fɜːmen'teɪʃn] *s* **1.** ⚗ Gärung *f* (*a. fig.*), Gärungsprozeß *m*. **2.** → **ferment** 4b.

fern [fɜːn] *s* ♀ Farn(kraut *n*) *m*.

fe·ro·cious [fə'rəʊʃəs] *adj* □ **1.** wild (*Tier etc*). **2.** wild, grimmig (*Blick etc*), grausam (*Strafe etc*), heftig, scharf (*Auseinandersetzung*).

fer·ret ['ferɪt] **I** s zo. Frettchen n. **II** v/t mst ~ **out** et. ausspüren, -stöbern, *Wahrheit* herausfinden, hinter *ein Geheimnis* kommen. **III** v/i mst ~ **about** (*od.* **around**) herumstöbern (**among** in *dat*; **for** nach).

fer·rous ['ferəs] adj eisenhaltig, Eisen...

fer·ry ['ferɪ] **I** s **1.** Fähre f, Fährschiff n, -boot n. **2.** Fährdienst m, -betrieb m. **II** v/t **3.** (in e-r Fähre) übersetzen. '~**boat** → **ferry** 1. '~**man** ['~mən] s (*irr* **man**) Fährmann m. ~ **serv·ice** → **ferry** 2.

fer·tile ['fɜːtaɪl] adj □ fruchtbar, *fig. a.* produktiv, schöpferisch. **fer·til·i·ty** [fə'tɪlətɪ] s Fruchtbarkeit f, *fig. a.* Produktivität f. **fer·til·i·za·tion** [ˌfɜːtɪlaɪ'zeɪʃn] s **1.** Düngung f. **2.** Befruchtung f (*a. fig.*). '**fer·til·ize** v/t **1.** befruchten (*a. fig.*). **2.** düngen. '**fer·til·iz·er** s (*bsd.* Kunst)Dünger m.

fer·vent ['fɜːvənt], **fer·vid** ['~vɪd] adj □ glühend, leidenschaftlich (*Haß, Verehrer etc*), inbrünstig (*Gebet, Verlangen etc*). '**fer·vo(u)r** s Leidenschaft f, Inbrunst f.

fes·ter ['festə] v/i **1.** eitern. **2.** ~ **in** s.o.'s **mind** an j-m nagen *od.* fressen.

fes·ti·val ['festəvl] s **1.** Fest(tag m) n. **2.** Festival n, Festspiele pl. **fes·tive** ['~tɪv] adj □ festlich, Fest...: ~ **season** Festzeit f, *bsd.* Weihnachtszeit f. **fes'tiv·i·ty** s oft pl Festlichkeit f.

fes·toon [fe'stuːn] **I** s Girlande f. **II** v/t mit Girlanden schmücken.

fetch [fetʃ] v/t **1.** (herbei)holen, (her)bringen: (**go and**) ~ **a doctor** e-n Arzt holen. **2.** *Seufzer etc* ausstoßen. **3.** *Preis etc* erzielen, einbringen. **4.** F j-m e-n Schlag *od.* Tritt versetzen: ~ *s.o.* **one** j-m e-e langen *od.* kleben. '**fetch·ing** adj F bezaubernd: a) reizend, entzückend (*Kleid etc*), b) gewinnend, einnehmend (*Lächeln etc*).

fet·id ['fetɪd] adj □ stinkend.

fet·ish ['fetɪʃ] s Fetisch m (*a. psych.*). '**fe·tish·ism** s Fetischismus m. '**fe·tish·ist** s Fetischist(in).

fet·ter ['fetə] **I** s **1.** Fußfessel f. **2.** pl fig. Fesseln pl. **II** v/t **3.** j-m Fußfesseln anlegen. **4.** fig. behindern.

fet·tle ['fetl] s: **in fine** (*od.* **good**) ~ (gut) in Form.

fe·tus ['fiːtəs] s 🐟 Fötus m.

feud [fjuːd] **I** s Fehde f (*a. fig.*): **be at** ~ (**with**) → **II**. **II** v/i sich befehden, in Fehde liegen (**with** mit) (*beide a. fig.*).

feu·dal ['fjuːdl] adj ~ Feudal..., Lehns... **feu·dal·ism** ['~dəlɪzəm] s Feudalismus m, Feudal-, Lehnssystem n.

fe·ver ['fiːvə] s 🐟 Fieber n (*a. fig.*): **have a** ~ Fieber haben; ~ **blister** Fieberbläschen n; ~ **heat** Fieberhitze f; fig. fieberhafte Auf- *od.* Erregung: **be in a** ~ (**of excitement**) in fieberhafter Aufregung sein, vor Aufregung fiebern. '**fe·ver·ish** adj □ **1.** 🐟 a) fieberkrank: **be** ~ Fieber haben, b) fieb(e)rig, Fieber...: ~ **cold** fiebrige Erkältung. **2.** fig. fieberhaft: **be** ~ **with excitement** vor Aufregung fiebern.

few [fjuː] adj u. pron **1.** wenige: **some** ~ einige wenige. **2. a** ~ einige, ein paar: **a good** ~, **quite a** ~ ziemlich viele, e-e ganze Menge; **every** ~ **days** alle paar Tage.

fi·an·cé [fɪ'ɑːnseɪ] s Verlobte m. **fi·an·cée** [fɪ'ɑːnseɪ] s Verlobte f.

fi·as·co [fɪ'æskəʊ] pl **-cos** f Fiasko n.

fib [fɪb] F **I** s Flunkerei f, Schwindelei f. **II** v/i flunkern, schwindeln. '**fib·ber** s F Flunkerer m, Schwindler m.

fi·ber, *bsd. Br.* **fi·bre** ['faɪbə] s **1.** *biol.*, ⚙ Faser f. **2.** fig. Charakter m; Kraft f: **moral** ~ Charakterstärke f. '~**glass** s ⚙ Fiberglas n.

fib·u·la ['fɪbjʊlə] s anat. Wadenbein n.

fick·le ['fɪkl] adj launenhaft, launisch, unbeständig (*Wetter*), (*Person a.*) wankelmütig.

fic·tion ['fɪkʃn] s **1.** (freie) Erfindung f, Fiktion f. **2.** coll. Prosa-, Romanliteratur f. **fic·tion·al** ['~ʃənl] adj erdichtet, erfunden.

fic·ti·tious [fɪk'tɪʃəs] adj □ (frei) erfunden, fiktiv.

fid·dle ['fɪdl] F **I** s **1.** ♪ Fiedel f, Geige f: **play first** (**second**) ~ fig. die erste (zweite) Geige spielen; (**as**) **fit as a** ~ kerngesund. **II** v/i **2.** a. ~ **away** fiedeln, geigen. **3.** ~ **about** (*od.* **around**) herumtrödeln. **4.** a. ~ **about** (*od.* **around**) (**with**) herumfummeln (an *dat*), spielen (mit). **III** v/t **5.** fiedeln. **6.** Br. frisieren, manipulieren. '**fid·dler** s F **1.** Fiedler m, Geiger m. **2.** Br. Schwindler m, Betrüger m. '**fid·dling** adj F läppisch, geringfügig.

fi·del·i·ty [fɪˈdelətɪ] s **1.** Treue f (**to** gegenüber, zu). **2.** Genauigkeit f (a. e-r Übersetzung). **3.** ♫ Klangtreue f.

fidg·et [ˈfɪdʒɪt] I s **1.** oft pl nervöse Unruhe, Zappelei f: **give s.o. the ~s** → 3; **have the ~s** → 4. **2.** Zappelphilipp m. II v/i **3.** j-n nervös od. zapp(e)lig machen. III v/i **4.** (herum)zappeln, unruhig od. nervös sein. **'fidg·et·y** adj zapp(e)lig, nervös.

fi·du·ci·ar·y [fɪˈdjuːʃjərɪ] ‡‡ I s Treuhänder m. II adj treuhänderisch, Treuhand-.

field [fiːld] I s **1.** ✍ Feld n (a. ♟, phys. etc): **in the ~** auf dem Feld; **~ of vision** Blick-, Gesichtsfeld; fig. Gesichtskreis m, Horizont m. **2.** fig. Bereich m, (Fach-, Sach)Gebiet n: **in his ~** auf s-m Gebiet, in s-m Fach; **~ of application** Anwendungsbereich. **3.** Sport: Spielfeld n, -fläche f; Feld n (Läufer etc). II v/t **4.** Sport: Spieler aufs Feld schicken, bringen; Kandidaten etc ins Rennen schicken. **~ day** s: **have a ~** riesigen Spaß haben (**with** mit); s-n großen Tag haben. **~ e·vents** s pl Leichtathletik: Sprung- u. Wurfdisziplinen pl. **~ glass·es** s pl a. **a pair of ~** Feldstecher m. **~ hock·ey** s Sport: bsd. Am. (Feld)Hockey n. **~ mar·shal** s ✗ Feldmarschall m. **'~·work** s **1.** praktische (wissenschaftliche) Arbeit, (Archäologie etc a.) Arbeit f im Gelände. **2.** Markt-, Meinungsforschung: Befragung f. **~ work·er** s Markt-, Meinungsforschung: Befrager(in), Interviewer(in).

fiend [fiːnd] s **1.** Satan m, Teufel m, fig. a. Unhold m. **2.** F (Frischluft- etc)Fanatiker m. **'fiend·ish** adj □ **1.** teuflisch, unmenschlich. **2.** F verteufelt, höllisch.

fierce [fɪəs] adj □ **1.** wild (Tier etc). **2.** böse, grimmig (Gesicht etc), wild (Blick, Haß etc). **3.** scharf (Rede, Wettbewerb etc); heftig (Angriff, Schmerz etc). **'fierce·ness** s **1.** Wildheit f. **2.** Schärfe f; Heftigkeit f.

fi·er·y [ˈfaɪərɪ] adj □ **1.** brennend, glühend. **2.** feurig, hitzig (Person, Temperament). **3.** feurig, scharf (Gewürz etc). **4.** leidenschaftlich (Rede, Affäre etc).

fif·teen [ˌfɪfˈtiːn] adj fünfzehn. **ˌfif'teenth** [~θ] adj fünfzehnt. **fifth** [fɪfθ] I adj **1.** fünft: **~ column** pol. Fünfte Kolonne; **~**

wheel fig. fünftes Rad am Wagen. II s **2.** der, die, das Fünfte: **the ~ of May** der 5. Mai. **3.** Fünftel n. **'fifth·ly** adv fünftens. **fif·ti·eth** [ˈ~ɪəθ] adj fünfzigst.

fif·ty [ˈfɪftɪ] I adj fünfzig. II s Fünfzig f: **be in one's fifties** in den Fünfzigern sein; **in the fifties** in den Fünfzigern (e-s Jahrhunderts). **ˌ~·'fif·ty** adj u. adv F fifty-fifty: **go ~ (with)** halbe-halbe machen (mit).

fig [fɪg] s ♣ Feige f: **I don't care a ~** F das ist mir völlig egal.

fight [faɪt] I s **1.** Kampf m (**for** um; **against** gegen) (a. fig.): **put up a good ~** sich tapfer schlagen. **2.** a) Boxen: Kampf m, b) Rauferei f, Schlägerei f: **have a ~ (with)** → 7. **3.** Kampf(es)lust f: **show ~** sich zur Wehr setzen. II v/t (irr) **4.** j-n, et. bekämpfen. **5.** kämpfen gegen od. mit: **~ back** (od. **down**) Enttäuschung, Tränen etc unterdrücken; **~ off** j-n, et. abwehren. III v/i (irr) **6.** kämpfen (**for** um; **against** gegen): **~ back** sich zur Wehr setzen od. wehren, zurückschlagen; **~ shy** → 7. **7.** sich raufen od. schlagen od. prügeln (**with** mit). **'fight·er** s **1.** Kämpfer m. **2.** Sport: Boxer m. **3.** Schläger m, Raufbold m. **4.** a. **~ plane** ✈, ✗ Jagdflugzeug n. **'fight·ing** I s Kampf m, Kämpfe pl. II adj Kampf...: **~ chance** reelle Chance (wenn man sich anstrengt); **~ spirit** Kampfgeist m.

fig·ment [ˈfɪgmənt] s oft **~ of the imagination** reine Erfindung.

fig tree s Feigenbaum m.

fig·u·ra·tive [ˈfɪgərətɪv] adj □ bildlich, übertragen.

fig·ure [ˈfɪgə] I s **1.** Zahl f, Ziffer f: **run into three ~s** in die Hunderte gehen; **five-~ income** fünfstelliges Einkommen. **2.** Summe f, Preis m: **at a high** (**low**) **~** teuer (billig). **3.** Figur f (a. Sport etc), Gestalt f. **4.** fig. Figur f, Persönlichkeit f: **~ of fun** komische Figur, contp. Witzfigur; **cut** (od. **make**) **a poor ~** e-e traurige Figur abgeben. **5.** a. **~ of speech** (Rede-, Sprach)Figur f. II v/t **6.** oft **~ to o.s.** sich et. vorstellen od. ausmalen. **7.** **~ out** F ausrechnen; ausknobeln, rauskriegen; kapieren. **8.** Am. F meinen, glauben. III v/i **9.** erscheinen, auftauchen, vorkommen. **10.** **~ on** bsd. Am. F rechnen mit; sich verlassen auf (*acc*). **'~head** *s* ⚓ Galionsfigur *f*, *fig. a.* Aushängeschild *n*. **~ skat·ing** *s* *Sport:* Eiskunstlauf *m*.

filch [fɪltʃ] *v/t* klauen, stibitzen.

file¹ [faɪl] **I** *s* **1.** (Akten- *etc*)Ordner *m*. **2.** *a)* Akte *f:* **keep** (*od.* **have**) **a ~ on** e-e Akte führen über (*acc*); **~ number** Aktenzeichen *n*, b) Akten *pl*, Ablage *f:* **on ~** bei den Akten. **3.** Reihe *f:* → **Indian file, single file. II** *v/t* **4.** *a.* **~ away** Briefe *etc* ablegen, zu den Akten nehmen. **5.** *Antrag etc* einreichen, *Forderung* anmelden.

file² [~] **I** *s* **1.** ⚙ Feile *f.* **II** *v/t* **2.** (zu)feilen, sich *die Nägel* feilen: **~ away** (*od.* **down**) abfeilen. **3.** *fig.* Stil *etc* (zurecht)feilen.

fil·i·al ['fɪljəl] *adj* Kindes...

fil·i·bus·ter ['fɪlɪbʌstə] *parl. bsd. Am.* **I** *s* Obstruktion *f;* Obstruktionspolitiker *m*. **II** *v/i* Obstruktion treiben.

fil·i·gree ['fɪlɪɡriː] *s* Filigran(arbeit *f*) *n*.

fil·ing cab·i·net ['faɪlɪŋ] *s* Aktenschrank *m*.

fil·ings ['faɪlɪŋz] *s pl* Feilspäne *pl*.

fill [fɪl] **I** *s* **1.** **eat one's ~** sich satt essen; **have had one's ~ of** von *et.*, *j-m* genug haben, *et.*, *j-n* satt haben. **2.** Füllung *f.* **II** *v/t* **3.** (an-, aus-, voll)füllen; *Pfeife* stopfen; *Zahn* füllen, plombieren. **4.** erfüllen (**with** mit) (*a. fig.*): **~ed with envy** neiderfüllt. **5.** *Posten, Amt* besetzen; ausfüllen, bekleiden: **~ s.o.'s place** j-s Stelle einnehmen, j-n ersetzen. **6.** *Auftrag, Bestellung* ausführen; *Rezept* ausfertigen. **III** *v/i* **7.** sich füllen. *Verbindungen mit Adverbien:*

fill| in **I** *v/t* **1.** *Loch etc* auf-, ausfüllen. **2.** *Br. Formulare etc* ausfüllen. **3.** *Namen etc* einsetzen; *Fehlendes* ergänzen. **4.** F *j-n* informieren (**on** *über acc*). **II** *v/i* **5.** einspringen (**for** für). **~ out I** *v/t* **1.** *bsd. Am.* → **fill in** 2. *Bericht etc* abrunden. **II** *v/i* **3.** fülliger werden (*Figur*), (*Person a.*) zunehmen, (*Gesicht etc*) runder *od.* voller werden. **~ up I** *v/t* **1.** vollfüllen. **2.** → **fill in** 1, 2. **II** *v/i* **3.** → **fill** 7.

fill·er ['fɪlə] *s* **1.** Trichter *m*. **2.** *Zeitungswesen etc:* Füller *m*, Füllsel *n*. **3.** *ling.* Füllwort *n*.

fil·let ['fɪlɪt] *s gastr.* Filet *n*. **~ steak** *s* Filetsteak *n*.

fill·ing ['fɪlɪŋ] **I** *s* **1.** Füllung *f*, Füllmasse *f*. **2.** *Zahnmedizin:* Füllung *f*, Plombe *f*.

II *adj* **3.** sättigend. **~ sta·tion** *s* Tankstelle *f*.

fil·lip ['fɪlɪp] *s* **1.** Schnalzer *m*, Schnipser *m* (*mit den Fingern*). **2.** *fig.* Ansporn *m*, Auftrieb *m*.

film [fɪlm] **I** *s* **1.** Film *m* (*a. phot.*). **2.** (hauch)dünne Schicht, Film *m*; (Plastik)Folie *f*. **II** *adj* **3.** Film... **III** *v/t* **4.** *Roman etc* verfilmen; *Szene etc* filmen.

fil·ter ['fɪltə] **I** *s* **1.** Filter *m*, ⚙ *etc* mst *n*. **II** *v/t* **2.** filtern. **III** *v/i* **3.** durchsickern (**through** durch). **4.** **~ out** grüppchenweise *od.* e-r nach dem anderen herauskommen (**of** aus). **5.** **~ out** (*od.* **through**) *fig.* durchsickern (*Nachricht etc*). **6.** *mot. Br.* die Spur wechseln; sich einordnen (**to the left** links). **~ tip** *s* **1.** Filter *m*. **2.** Filterzigarette *f*. **'~-tipped** *adj* Filter...: **~ cigarette.**

filth [fɪlθ] *s* **1.** Schmutz *m* (*a. fig.*), Dreck *m*. **2.** unflätige Sprache *od.* Ausdrücke *pl.* **'filth·y** *adj* □ **1.** schmutzig (*a. fig.*), dreckig. **2.** *fig.* unflätig. **3.** *bsd. Br.* ekelhaft, scheußlich: **~ weather** Sauwetter *n*.

fin [fɪn] *s* **1.** *ichth.* Flosse *f*. **2.** Schwimmflosse *f*.

fi·nal ['faɪnl] **I** *adj* (□ → **finally**) **1.** letzt; End..., Schluß...: **~ examination** (Ab-)Schlußprüfung *f;* **~ whistle** (*Sport*) Schluß-, Abpfiff *m*. **2.** endgültig. **II** *s* **3.** *Sport:* Finale *n*. **4.** *mst pl bsd. univ.* (Ab)Schlußexamen *n*, -prüfung *f*. **5.** F Spätausgabe *f* (*e-r Zeitung*). **fi·na·le** [fɪ'nɑːlɪ] *s* ♪, *thea.* Finale *n*. **fi·nal·ist** ['faɪnəlɪst] *s Sport:* Finalist(in). **fi·nal·i·ty** [~'nælətɪ] *s* **1.** Endgültigkeit *f*. **2.** Entschiedenheit *f*. **fi·nal·ize** ['~nəlaɪz] *v/t* **1.** be-, vollenden, abschließen. **2.** endgültige Form geben (*dat*). **'fi·nal·ly** *adv* **1.** endlich, schließlich, zuletzt. **2.** zum (Ab)Schluß. **3.** endgültig.

fi·nance [faɪ'næns] **I** *s* **1.** Finanz(wesen *n*) *f:* **~ company** Finanzierungsgesellschaft *f*. **2.** *pl* Finanzen *pl*. **II** *v/t* **3.** finanzieren. **fi·nan·cial** [~fl] *adj* □ **1.** finanziell, Finanz..., Geld...: **~ year** *Br.* Geschäftsjahr *n*. **fin'an·cier** [~sɪə] *s* Finanzier *m*.

finch [fɪntʃ] *s orn.* Fink *m*.

find [faɪnd] **I** *s* **1.** Fund *m*. **II** *v/t* (*irr*) **2.** *allg.* finden. **3.** bemerken, feststellen, (heraus)finden. **4.** ⚖ für *schuldig* erklären *od.* befinden. **5.** **~ out** *et.* herausfinden; *j-n* ertappen; *j-n, et.* durchschauen. **III** *v/i* (*irr*) **6. ~ out** es herausfinden. **7. ~ against (for) the defendant** ⚖ den Angeklagten verurteilen (freisprechen). **'find·er** *s* Finder(in): **~'s reward** Finderlohn *m*. **'find·ing** *s* **1.** *mst pl* Befund *m* (*a.* ⚕). **2.** ⚖ Feststellung *f* (*des Gerichts*), (*der Geschworenen a.*) Spruch *m*.

fine¹ [faɪn] **I** *adj* □ **1.** *allg.* fein: **~ arts** *pl* die schönen Künste *pl*; **one ~ day** e-s schönen Tages. **2.** großartig, ausgezeichnet. **3.** F fein, schön: **that's all very ~ but** das ist ja alles gut u. schön, aber. **II** *adv* **4.** F sehr gut, bestens: **that will suit me ~** das paßt mir ausgezeichnet.

fine² [~] **I** *s* Geldstrafe *f*, Bußgeld *n*. **II** *v/t* mit e-r Geldstrafe belegen, zu e-r Geldstrafe verurteilen: **he was ~d £50** er mußte 50 Pfund Strafe bezahlen, er wurde zu e-r Geldstrafe von 50 Pfund verurteilt.

fine·ness ['faɪnɪs] *s allg.* Feinheit *f*.

fi·nesse [fɪ'nes] *s* **1.** Finesse *f*. **2.** Raffinesse *f*, Schlauheit *f*.

fin·ger ['fɪŋgə] **I** *s* Finger *m*: **first** (**second, third**) **~** Zeige- (Mittel-, Ring)finger; **fourth** (*od.* **little**) **~** kleiner Finger; **have a** (*od.* **one's**) **~ in the pie** die Hand im Spiel haben; **keep one's ~s crossed for s.o.** j-m die Daumen drücken *od.* halten; **not to lift** (*od.* **raise, stir**) **a ~** keinen Finger rühren; → **burn** 7, **twist** 2. **II** *v/t* betasten, befühlen; herumfingern an (*dat*), spielen mit. **III** *v/i* herumfingern (**at** an *dat*), spielen (**with** mit). **~·al·pha·bet** *s* Fingeralphabet *n*. **'~·mark** *s* Fingerabdruck *m* (*Schmutzfleck*). **'~·nail** *s* Fingernagel *m*. **'~·print I** *s* Fingerabdruck *m*: **take s.o.'s ~s** → **II. II** *v/t* j-m Fingerabdrücke abnehmen, von j-m Fingerabdrücke machen. **'~·tip** *s* Fingerspitze *f*: **have at one's ~s Kenntnisse** parat haben; **et.** aus dem Effeff beherrschen.

fin·ick·y ['fɪnɪkɪ] *adj* **1.** pedantisch. **2.** wählerisch (**about** in *dat*). **3.** geziert, affektiert.

fin·ish ['fɪnɪʃ] **I** *v/t* **1.** beenden, aufhören mit: **~ reading** aufhören zu lesen. **2.** *a.* **~ off** vollenden, zu Ende führen, erledigen, *Buch etc* auslesen. **3.** *a.* **~ off** (*od.*

up) *Vorräte* aufbrauchen; aufessen, austrinken. **4.** *a.* **~ off** *j-n* erledigen, fertigmachen. **5.** *a.* **~ off** (*od.* **up**) vervollkommnen, den letzten Schliff geben (*dat*). **II** *v/i* **6.** *a.* **~ off** (*od.* **up**) enden, aufhören (**with** mit): **have you ~ed?** bist du fertig? **7.** enden, zu Ende gehen. **8. ~ with** mit *j-m, et.* Schluß machen, *et.* aufgeben: **I am ~ed with him** ich bin mit ihm fertig. **9. ~ third** (*Sport*) Dritter werden; *allg.* als dritter fertig sein. **III** *s* **10.** Ende *n*, Schluß *m*. **11.** *Sport:* Endspurt *m*, Finish *n*; Ziel *n*. **12.** Vollendung *f*; letzter Schliff. **'fin·ished** *adj* **1.** beendet, fertig: **~ goods** (*od.* **products**) *pl* Fertigwaren *pl*. **2.** *fig.* vollendet, vollkommen. **'fin·ish·ing** *adj* abschließend: **~ line** (*Sport*) Ziellinie *f*; → **touch** 4.

fink [fɪŋk] *s bsd. Am. sl.* **1.** Streikbrecher *m*. **2.** Spitzel *m*.

Finn [fɪn] *s* Finne *m*, Finnin *f*. **'Finn·ish I** *adj* finnisch. **II** *s ling.* Finnisch *n*.

fiord [fjɔːd] *s geogr.* Fjord *m*.

fir [fɜː] *s* ♀ Tanne *f*; Fichte *f*. **~ cone** *s* Tannenzapfen *m*.

fire ['faɪə] **I** *s* **1.** Feuer *n* (*a.* ✕ *u. fig.*), Brand *m*: **be on ~** in Flammen stehen, brennen; **come under ~** unter Beschuß geraten (*a. fig.*); **catch** (*od.* **take**) **~** Feuer fangen, in Brand geraten; **play with ~** *fig.* mit dem Feuer spielen; **set on ~, set ~ to →** 2; → **chestnut** 1, **Thames**. **II** *v/t* **2.** anzünden, in Brand stecken. **3.** *Kessel* heizen, *Ofen* (be)feuern, beheizen. **4.** *j-n, j-s Phantasie* entflammen, *j-s Phantasie* beflügeln. **5.** *a.* **~ off** *Schußwaffe* abfeuern, abschießen; *Schuß* (ab)feuern, abgeben (**at, on** *od. acc*). **6.** F feuern, rausschmeißen. **III** *v/i* **7.** feuern, schießen (**at** auf *acc*). **8.** zünden (*Motor*). **~ a·larm** *s* Feueralarm *m*. **2.** Feuermelder *m*. **'~·arm** *s* Feuer-, Schußwaffe *f*. **'~·ball** *s* Feuerball *m*. **~ bri·gade** *s Br.* Feuerwehr *f*. **'~·bug** *s* Feuerteufel *m*. **~ de·part·ment** *s Am.* Feuerwehr *f*. **'~·,eat·er** *s* **1.** Feuerschlucker *m*, -fresser *m*. **2.** *fig.* aggressiver Mensch. **~ en·gine** *s* Löschfahrzeug *n*. **~ es·cape** *s* **1.** Feuerleiter *f*, -treppe *f*. **2.** *Br.* Feuerwehrleiter *f*. **~ ex·tin·guish·er** *s* Feuerlöscher *m*. **'fight·er** *s* Feuerwehrmann *m*. **~ house** *s Am.* Feuerwache *f*. **~ hy·drant** *s Br.*

'flag·staff s Fahnenstange f, Fahnen-, Flaggenmast m.

flair [fleə] s **1.** Veranlagung f: **have a ~ for art** künstlerisch veranlagt sein. **2.** (feines) Gespür (**for** für).

flake [fleɪk] **I** s (Schnee- etc)Flocke f; (Haut)Schuppe f. **II** v/i a) mst **~ off** abblättern, b) schuppen. **'flak·y** adj **1.** flockig; schuppig. **2.** blätt(e)rig: **~ pastry** Blätterteig m.

flam·boy·ant [flæm'bɔɪənt] adj □ **1.** extravagant. **2.** grell, leuchtend. **3.** pompös, bombastisch.

flame [fleɪm] **I** s **1.** Flamme f: **be in ~s** in Flammen stehen; **an old ~ of mine** F e-e alte Flamme von mir. **2.** fig. Feuer n, Glut f. **II** v/i **3.** lodern: **~ up** auflodern; in Flammen aufgehen; fig. aufbrausen. **'flam·ing** adj **1.** lodernd, brennend. **2.** fig. flammend, feurig. **3.** Br. F verdammt.

flam·ma·ble ['flæməbl] → **inflammable**.

flan [flæn] s Obst-, Käsekuchen m.

flange [flændʒ] s **⊙ 1.** Flansch m. **2.** Spurkranz m (e-s Rads).

flank [flæŋk] **I** s **1.** Flanke f, Weiche f (e-s Tiers); Seite f (e-s Menschen, Gebäudes etc). **2.** ✗ Flanke f, Flügel m (beide a. Sport). **II** v/t **3.** flankieren (a. ✗).

flan·nel ['flænl] s **1.** Flanell m. **2.** pl, a. **pair of ~s** Flanellhose f. **3.** Br. Waschlappen m. **4.** Br. F Schmus m.

flap [flæp] **I** s **1.** Flattern n, (Flügel)Schlag m. **2.** Schlag m, Klaps m. **3.** Klappe f (e-r Tasche etc). **4.** **be in a ~** F in heller Aufregung sein. **II** v/t **5.** mit den Flügeln etc schlagen. **III** v/i **6.** flattern. **7.** F in heller Aufregung sein; in helle Aufregung geraten. **'~·jack** s bsd. Am. Pfannkuchen m.

flare [fleə] **I** s **1.** Flackern n, Lodern n, Leuchten n. **2.** Leuchtfeuer n; Licht-, Feuersignal n. **3.** → **flare-up**. **II** v/i **4.** flackern (Kerze etc), (Feuer etc a.) lodern, (Licht) leuchten: **~ up** aufflammen, -flackern, -lodern (alle a. fig.); fig. aufbrausen; **~ up** at s.o. j-n anfahren. **'~·'up** s **1.** Aufflammen n, -flackern n, -lodern n (alle a fig.). **2.** fig. Ausbruch m: **~ of fury** Wutausbruch m.

flash [flæʃ] **I** s **1.** Aufblitzen n, -leuchten n, Blitz m: **a ~ of lightning** ein Blitz; **~ of wit** Geistesblitz f; **give s.o. a ~** mot. j-n

anblinken. **2.** Stichflamme f: **~ in the pan** fig. Eintagsfliege f; Strohfeuer n. **3.** Augenblick m: **in a ~** im Nu, sofort. **4.** Rundfunk etc: Kurzmeldung f. **II** v/t **5.** aufleuchten od. (auf)blitzen lassen. **III** v/i **6.** aufflammen, (auf)blitzen; zucken (Blitz). **7.** rasen, flitzen: **it ~ed into** (od. **across, through**) **my mind that** plötzlich schoß es mir durch den Kopf, daß. **8.** **~ back** (in e-m Film etc) zurückblenden (**to** auf acc). **'~·back** s Film etc: Rückblende f. **~ bulb** s phot. Blitz(licht)lampe f. **~ cube** s phot. Blitzwürfel m.

flash·er ['flæʃə] s **1.** mot. Blinker m. **2.** Br. F Exhibitionist m.

'flash·light s **1.** phot. Blitzlicht n: **~ photograph** Blitzlichtaufnahme f. **2.** bsd. Am. Taschenlampe f.

flash·y ['flæʃɪ] adj □ **1.** prunkvoll, protzig. **2.** auffallend. **3.** aufbrausend (Temperament).

flask [flɑːsk] s **1.** Taschenflasche f. **2.** Thermosflasche f.

flat¹ [flæt] **I** s **1.** Fläche f, Ebene f. **2.** flache Seite: **~ of the hand** Handfläche f. **3.** Flachland n, Niederung f. **4.** mot. bsd. Am. Reifenpanne f. **II** adj □ **5.** flach, eben, Flach...; **6.** flach, offen (Hand). **7.** mot. platt (Reifen). **8.** entschieden, kategorisch: **and that's ~** u. damit basta! **9.** einheitlich, Einheits...; Pauschal... **III** adv **10.** **fall ~** der Länge nach hinfallen; fig. F danebengehen, mißglücken; durchfallen (Theaterstück etc). **11.** ♪ zu tief: **sing ~**. **12.** **in five minutes ~** F in sage u. schreibe fünf Minuten. **13.** **~ broke** F total abgebrannt od. pleite.

flat² [~] s bsd. Br. Wohnung f: → **block** 3.

'flat·foot s (irr **foot**) **1.** mst pl ✗ Plattfuß m. **2.** pl a. **-foots** sl. Bulle m (Polizist). **'~·'foot·ed** adj **1.** ✗ plattfüßig: **be ~** Plattfüße haben. **2.** F entschieden.

flat·let ['flætlɪt] s bsd. Br. Kleinwohnung f. **'flat·ness** s Flachheit f. **flat·ten** ['~tn] **I** v/t **1.** (ein)ebnen. **2.** ♪, ⊙ abflachen. **⊙** ausbeulen. **II** v/i **3.** a. **~ out** flach(er) werden.

flat·ter ['flætə] v/t j-m schmeicheln (a. fig. Bild etc): **be ~ed** sich geschmeichelt fühlen (**at, by** durch). **'flat·ter·er** s Schmeichler(in). **'flat·ter·ing** adj □ **1.** schmeichlerisch. **2.** schmeichelhaft (**to**

für). **'flat·ter·y** s Schmeichelei(en pl) f: → obtain I.

flat·u·lence ['flætjʊləns] s ♥ Blähung(en pl) f: **cause** (od. **produce**) ~ blähen.

flaunt [flɔːnt] v/t zur Schau stellen, protzen mit.

flau·tist ['flɔːtɪst] s ♪ Flötist(in).

fla·vo(u)r ['fleɪvə] **I** s **1.** Geschmack m, Aroma n. **2.** fig. Beigeschmack m. **II** v/t **3.** würzen (a. fig.). **'fla·vo(u)r·ing** s Würze f, Aroma n (beide a. fig.).

flaw [flɔː] s **1.** (◎ Material-, 🜨 Form-) Fehler m, ⚙ a. Defekt m. **2.** fig. schwache Stelle. **'flaw·less** □ einwandfrei, tadellos.

flax [flæks] s ♣ Flachs m. **'flax·en** adj **1.** Flachs... **2.** flachsen, flachsfarben.

flay [fleɪ] v/t Tier abhäuten: ~ s.o. **alive** F kein gutes Haar an j-m lassen, j-m gehörig s-e Meinung sagen.

flea [fliː] s zo. Floh m: **send s.o. away with a** ~ **in his ear** F j-m e-n Laufpass geben. **'~·bite** s **1.** Flohbiß m. **2.** fig. Bagatelle f. ~ **cir·cus** s Flohzirkus m. ~ **mar·ket** s Flohmarkt m.

fled [fled] pret u. pp von **flee**.

fledged [fledʒd] adj flügge. **fledg(e)·ling** ['~lɪŋ] s **1.** eben flügge gewordener Vogel. **2.** fig. Grünschnabel m.

flee [fliː] (irr) **I** v/i fliehen, flüchten (**from** vor dat; aus). **II** v/t fliehen vor (dat) od. aus.

fleece [fliːs] **I** s **1.** Vlies n, bsd. Schaffell n. **II** v/t **2.** Schaf etc scheren. **3.** F j-n schröpfen (**of** um), ausnehmen.

fleet¹ [fliːt] s **1.** ⚓ Flotte f. **2.** ~ **of cars** Wagenpark m.

fleet² [~] adj □ schnell, flink.

fleet·ing ['fliːtɪŋ] adj □ flüchtig, vergänglich.

Fleet Street s das Londoner Presseviertel; fig. die (Londoner) Presse.

flesh [fleʃ] s **1.** Fleisch n: **put on** ~ zunehmen; **lose** ~ abmagern, abnehmen; → **creep** 3. **2.** Körper m, Leib m: **my own** ~ **and blood** mein eigen Fleisch u. Blut; **in the** ~ leibhaftig, höchstpersönlich; in natura, in Wirklichkeit. **3.** (Frucht-) Fleisch n. **'~·col·o(u)red** adj fleischfarben. **'~·eat·ing** adj ♥, zo. fleischfressend. ~ **wound** s ♥ Fleischwunde f.

flew [fluː] pret von **fly¹**.

flex [fleks] **I** v/t bsd. anat. biegen, beugen. **II** s ⚡ bsd. Br. (Anschluß-, Verlänge-

rungs)Kabel n, (-)Schnur f. **'flex·i·ble** adj □ flexibel: a) elastisch, b) fig. anpassungsfähig, beweglich.

flex·i·time ['fleksɪtaɪm] s Br. gleitende Arbeitszeit: **be on** ~ gleitende Arbeitszeit haben.

flick [flɪk] **I** s **1.** Klaps m. **2.** Knall m, Schnalzer m. **3.** Schnipser m. **II** v/t **4.** j-m e-n Klaps geben. **5.** schnalzen mit (Fingern), (mit Peitsche a.) knallen mit. **6.** schnippen, schnipsen: ~ **away** (od. **off**) wegschnippen.

flick·er ['flɪkə] **I** v/i **1.** Flackern n. **2.** TV Flimmern n. **II** v/i **3.** flackern. **4.** flimmern (Fernsehbild).

flick knife s (irr **knife**) Br. Schnappmesser n.

flight¹ [flaɪt] s **1.** (a. Gedanken- etc)Flug m: **in** ~ im Flug. **2.** Schwarm m (Vögel): **in the first** ~ fig. in vorderster Front. **3.** a. ~ **of stairs** Treppe f.

flight² [~] s Flucht f: **in his** ~ auf s-r Flucht; **put to** ~ in die Flucht schlagen; **take** (**to**) ~ die Flucht ergreifen; ~ **of capital** ♥ Kapitalflucht.

flight| en·gi·neer s Bordingenieur m. ~ **re·cord·er** s Flug(daten)schreiber m.

flight·y ['flaɪtɪ] adj □ flatterhaft.

flim·sy ['flɪmzɪ] **I** adj □ **1.** dünn, zart. **2.** fig. fadenscheinig (Ausrede). **II** s **3.** Durchschlagspapier n.

flinch [flɪntʃ] v/i **1.** zurückschrecken (**from**, **at** vor dat). **2.** (zurück)zucken, zs.-fahren: **without** ~**ing** ohne mit der Wimper zu zucken.

fling [flɪŋ] **I** s **1.** Wurf m: (**at**) **full** ~ mit voller Wucht. **2.** **have one's** (od. **a**) ~ sich austoben. **3.** F Versuch m: **have** (od. **take**) **a** ~ **at** es versuchen od. probieren mit. **II** v/t (irr) **4.** werfen, schleudern (**at** nach): ~ **open** (**to**) Tür etc aufreißen (zuschlagen); ~ **away** wegwerfen; ~ **o.s.** sich stürzen (**at s.o.** auf j-n; **into s.th.** in od. auf e-e Sache).

flint [flɪnt] s Feuerstein m.

flip [flɪp] **I** v/t **1.** → **flick** 6. **2.** a. ~ **over** Pfannkuchen, Schallplatte etc wenden, umdrehen. **II** v/i **3.** a. ~ **out** bsd. Am. sl. ausflippen, durchdrehen (**for**, **over** bei). **III** s **4.** Schnipser m. **5.** Flip m (Getränk). **'~·flop** s Zehensandale f.

flip·pant ['flɪpənt] adj □ respektlos, schnodd(e)rig.

flow

flip·per ['flɪpə] s **1.** zo. Flosse f. **2.** Schwimmflosse f.

flip side s B-Seite f (e-r Single).

flirt [flɜːt] I v/i flirten, fig. a. spielen, liebäugeln (with mit). II s: **be a ~** gern flirten. **flir'ta·tion** s Flirt m, fig. a. Spielen n, Liebäugeln n. **flir'ta·tious** adj □ kokett.

flit [flɪt] v/i flitzen, huschen.

float [fləʊt] I v/i **1.** (auf dem Wasser) schwimmen, (im Wasser) treiben. **2.** ♃ flott sein od. werden. **3.** schweben, ziehen. **4.** a. ♃ in Umlauf sein. II v/t **5.** schwimmen od. treiben lassen. **6.** ♃ flottmachen. **7.** ♃ Wertpapiere etc in Umlauf bringen; Anleihe auflegen; Gesellschaft f gründen. **8.** ♃ Währung floaten, den Wechselkurs (gen) freigeben. **9.** Gerücht etc in Umlauf setzen. III s **10.** flacher Plattformwagen, bsd. Festwagen m. **'float·er** s pol. Wechselwähler(in). **'float·ing** I adj **1.** treibend, schwimmend: **~ ice** Treibeis n. **2.** ♃ umlaufend (Geld etc); frei konvertierbar (Währung). **3. ~ voter → floater.**

flock [flɒk] I s **1.** Herde f (bsd. Schafe od. Ziegen); Schwarm m (Vögel). **2.** Menge f, Haufen m: **come in ~s** in (hellen) Scharen herbeiströmen. **3.** eccl. Herde f, Gemeinde f. II v/i **4.** fig. strömen: **~ together** zs.-strömen.

floe [fləʊ] s **1.** Treibeis n. **2.** Eisscholle f.

flog [flɒg] v/t **1.** prügeln, schlagen: **~ a dead horse** fig. offene Türen einrennen; s-e Zeit verschwenden. **2.** auspeitschen. **3.** Br. F verkloppen, -scheuern. **'flog·ging** s **1.** Tracht f Prügel. **2.** ⚖ Prügelstrafe f.

flood [flʌd] I s **1.** a. **~ tide** Flut f. **2.** Überschwemmung f (a. fig.), Hochwasser n. **3.** fig. Flut f, Strom m, Schwall m: **~ of tears** Tränenstrom m. II v/t **4.** überschwemmen, -fluten (beide a. fig. with mit). **5.** unter Wasser setzen. **6.** Fluß etc anschwellen od. über die Ufer treten lassen. III v/i **7.** fluten, strömen, sich ergießen (alle a. fig.). **8.** anschwellen; über die Ufer treten. **'~·light** I s Scheinwerfer-, Flutlicht n: **by ~** unter Flutlicht. II v/t (irr **light¹**) (mit Scheinwerfern) beleuchten od. anstrahlen: **floodlit match** (Sport) Flutlichtspiel n.

floor [flɔː] I s **1.** (Fuß)Boden m: → **wipe** II. **2.** Tanzfläche f: **take the ~** auf die Tanzfläche gehen. **3.** Stock(werk n) m, Geschoß n. **4.** parl. Sitzungs-, Plenarsaal m: **take the ~** das Wort ergreifen. II v/t **5.** e-n (Fuß)Boden legen in (dat). **6.** zu Boden schlagen, (Boxen etc) auf die Bretter schicken. **7.** F a) j-n umhauen, j-m die Sprache verschlagen: **~ed** platt, sprachlos, b) j-n schaffen (Problem etc). **'~·board** s Diele f. **~ ex·er·cis·es** s pl Sport: Bodenturnen n. **floor·ing** ['flɔːrɪŋ] s (Fuß)Bodenbelag m. **floor| lamp** s Stehlampe f. **~ lead·er** s parl. Am. Fraktionsführer m. **~ show** s Varietévorstellung f (in Nachtclub etc). **~ wait·er** s Etagenkellner m. **~ vase** s Bodenvase f.

floo·zy ['fluːzɪ] s sl. Flittchen n.

flop [flɒp] I v/i **1.** plumpsen; sich plumpsen lassen (into in acc). **2.** F durchfallen (Prüfling, Theaterstück etc); allg. e-e Pleite od. ein Reinfall sein. II s **3.** Plumps m. **4.** F a) thea. etc Flop m, Durchfall m, b) Reinfall m, Pleite f, c) Versager m. **'flop·py** adj □ **1.** schlaff, schlott(e)rig. **2. ~ disk** (Computer) Diskette f.

flo·ra ['flɔːrə] pl -ras, -rae ['-riː] s ♣ Flora f, Pflanzenwelt f. **'flo·ral** adj Blumen..., Blüten...: **~ pattern** Blumenmuster n.

flor·id ['flɒrɪd] adj □ **1.** blühend (Gesichtsfarbe, Gesundheit). **2.** blumig (Stil).

flo·rist ['flɒrɪst] s **1.** Blumenhändler(in). **2.** Blumenzüchter(in).

flot·sam ['flɒtsəm] s a. **~ and jetsam** ♃ Treibgut n: **~ and jetsam** Strandgut n (a. fig.), Wrackgut n.

floun·der¹ ['flaʊndə] s ichth. Flunder f.

floun·der² [~] v/i **1.** zappeln; strampeln. **2.** fig. sich verhaspeln, ins Schwimmen kommen.

flour [flaʊə] I s Mehl n. II v/t mit Mehl bestreuen.

flour·ish ['flʌrɪʃ] I v/i **1.** gedeihen, fig. a. blühen, florieren. **2.** auf der Höhe s-r Macht od. s-s Ruhms stehen; s-e Blütezeit haben. II v/t **3.** Fahne etc schwenken. III s **4.** ♪ Tusch m. **5.** Schnörkel m.

flout [flaʊt] v/t Befehl etc mißachten.

flow [fləʊ] I v/i **1.** fließen, strömen (beide a. fig.): **~ freely** in Strömen fließen

(*Sekt etc*); ~ **over its banks** über die Ufer treten. **2.** lose herabhängen. **II** *s* **3.** Fluß *m*, Strom *m* (*beide a. fig.*): ~ **of information** Informationsfluß; ~ **of tears** Tränenstrom *m*; ~ **of traffic** Verkehrsfluß, -strom. ~ **chart**, ~ **di·a·gram** *s* Flußdiagramm *n*.

flow·er ['flauə] **I** *s* **1.** Blume *f*. **2.** Blüte(zeit) *f* (*a. fig.*): **be in** ~ in Blüte stehen, blühen. **II** *v/i* **3.** blühen, *fig. a.* in höchster Blüte stehen. ~ **bed** *s* Blumenbeet *n*.

flow·ered ['flauəd] *adj* **1.** geblümt. **2.** *in Zssgn* ...blütig; ...blühend.

flow·er pot *s* Blumentopf *m*.

flow·er·y ['flauəri] *adj* **1.** blumen-, blütenreich. **2.** geblümt. **3.** *fig.* blumig (*Stil*).

flown [fləun] *pp von* **fly¹**.

flu [flu:] *s* **ℱ** F Grippe *f*: **he's got (the)** ~ er hat Grippe.

fluc·tu·ate ['flʌktʃueit] *v/i* schwanken (**between** zwischen *dat*) (*a. fig.*), fluktuieren. **fluc·tu·a·tion** *s* Schwankung *f*, Fluktuation *f*: ~ **in prices ✝** Preisschwankung.

flu·en·cy ['flu:ənsi] *s* **1.** Flüssigkeit *f* (*des Stils etc*). **2.** (*Rede*)Gewandtheit *f*. '**flu·ent** *adj* □ **1.** fließend: **speak ~ German, be ~ in German** fließend Deutsch sprechen. **2.** flüssig (*Stil etc*). **3.** gewandt (*Redner etc*).

fluff [flʌf] **I** *s* **1.** Staubflocke *f*, Fussel(n *pl*) *f*. **2.** Flaum *m* (*a. erster Bartwuchs*). **3.** *thea. etc* F Patzer *m*. **II** *v/t* **4.** *thea. etc* F verpatzen: ~ **one's lines** steckenbleiben. '**fluff·y** *adj* □ flaumig.

flu·id ['flu:id] **I** *s* Flüssigkeit *f*. **II** *adj* □ flüssig (*a. Stil etc*).

fluke [flu:k] *s* F Dusel *m*: **by a** ~ mit Dusel.

flung [flʌŋ] *pret u. pp von* **fling**.

flunk [flʌŋk] *ped. bsd. Am.* F **I** *v/t* **1.** *Schüler* durchrasseln lassen. **2.** durchrasseln in (*dat*). **II** *v/i* **3.** durchrasseln.

flu·o·res·cent [fluə'resnt] *adj* **✎**, *phys.* fluoreszierend, Leucht(stoff)...

flur·ry ['flʌri] **I** *s* **1.** Windstoß *m*. **2.** (*Regen-, Schnee*)Schauer *m*. **3.** *fig.* Hagel *m*, Wirbel *m*: ~ **of blows** Schlaghagel. **4.** *fig.* Aufregung *f*, Unruhe *f*: **in a** ~ aufgeregt, unruhig. **II** *v/t* **5.** aufregen, beunruhigen.

flush [flʌʃ] **I** *s* **1.** Erröten *n*, Röte *f*. **2.**

(*Wasser*)Schwall *m*, Strom *m*. **II** *v/t* **3.** *a.* ~ **out** (aus)spülen: ~ **down** hinunterspülen; ~ **the toilet** spülen. **III** *v/i* **4.** *a.* ~ **up** erröten, rot werden. **5.** spülen (*Toilette[nbenutzer]*).

flus·ter ['flʌstə] **I** *v/t* nervös machen, durcheinanderbringen. **II** *v/i* nervös werden. **III** *s* Nervosität *f*: **get in a** ~ nervös werden; **all in a** ~ ganz durcheinander.

flute [flu:t] **♪ I** *s* Flöte *f*. **II** *v/i* flöten, Flöte spielen. **III** *v/t* flöten, auf der Flöte spielen. '**flut·ist** *s bsd. Am.* Flötist(in).

flut·ter ['flʌtə] **I** *v/i* **1.** flattern (*a.* **✎** *Herz, Puls*). **II** *v/t* **2.** wedeln mit. **3.** → **fluster** I. **III** *s* **4.** Flattern *n* (*a.* **✎**). **5.** → **fluster** III.

flux [flʌks] *s* **1.** Fließen *n*, Fluß *m*. **2.** **✎** Ausfluß *m*. **3.** **in (a state of)** ~ *fig.* im Fluß, in Bewegung.

fly¹ [flai] **I** *s* **1.** Hosenschlitz *m*. **II** *v/i* (*irr*) **2.** fliegen: **the bird is flown** *fig.* der Vogel ist ausgeflogen; ~ **open** auffliegen (*Tür etc*). **3.** fliegen, stieben (*Funken etc*): → **spark** I. **4.** stürmen, stürzen: ~ **at s.o.** auf j-n losgehen; → **temper** 3. **5.** (ver)fliegen (*Zeit*). **6.** flattern, wehen. **III** *v/t* **7.** fliegen lassen: → **kite.** **8.** **✈** *Flugzeug, j-n, et-, Strecke* fliegen; *Ozean etc* überfliegen; mit *e-r Fluggesellschaft* fliegen: ~ **in (out)** ein-(aus)fliegen. **9.** *Fahne* hissen, wehen lassen.

fly² [~] *s zo.* Fliege *f*: **a** ~ **in the ointment** *fig.* ein Haar in der Suppe; **he would not hurt (od. harm) a** ~ er tut keiner Fliege et. zuleide.

fly·ing ['flaiŋ] **I** *adj* **1.** fliegend, Flug...: ~ **saucer** fliegende Untertasse; ~ **squad** *Br.* Überfallkommando *n*; ~ **start** (*Sport*) fliegender Start; → **colour** 5. **2.** kurz, flüchtig (*Eindruck etc*): ~ **visit** Stippvisite *f*, Blitzbesuch *m*. **II** *s* **3.** Fliegen *n*.

'**fly·o·ver** *s Br.* (Straßen-, Eisenbahn-) Überführung *f*. ~ **sheet** *s* Flugblatt *n*, Reklamezettel *m*. '~**swat·ter** *s* → **swatter.** '~**weight** (*Sport*) **I** *s* Fliegengewicht(ler *m*) *n*. **II** *adj* Fliegengewichts...

foal [fəul] **I** *s zo.* Fohlen *n*, Füllen *n*: **in (od. with)** ~ trächtig.

foam [fəum] **I** *s* Schaum *m*. **II** *v/i* schäumen (*a. fig.* **with rage** vor Wut).

~ **rub·ber** s Schaumgummi m, n.

foam·y ['fəʊmɪ] adj schäumend, schaumig.

fob [fɒb] v/t **1.** ~ **s.th. off on s.o.** j-m et. andrehen od. aufhängen. **2.** ~ **s.o. off** j-n abspeisen od. abwimmeln (**with** mit).

fo·cal ['fəʊkl] adj ♠, ⊗, phys. im Brennpunkt stehend (a. fig.), Brenn(-punkt)...: ~ **point** Brennpunkt m (a. fig.). **fo·cus** ['fəʊkəs] **I** pl **-cus·es, -ci** ['-saɪ] s **1.** ♠, ⊗, phys. Brenn-, fig. a. Mittelpunkt m; opt., phot. Scharfeinstellung f: **in** ~ scharf; fig. klar u. richtig; **out of** ~ unscharf, verschwommen (a. fig.); **be the** ~ **of attention** im Mittelpunkt des Interesses stehen; **bring into** ~ a) → 2, b) fig. in den Brennpunkt rücken. **II** v/t pret u. pp **-cus(s)ed 2.** phys. im Brennpunkt vereinigen, Strahlen bündeln; opt., phot. scharf einstellen. **3.** fig. konzentrieren, richten (**on** auf acc). **III** v/i **4.** fig. sich konzentrieren od. richten (**on** auf acc).

fod·der ['fɒdə] s (Trocken)Futter n.

fog [fɒg] **I** s (dichter) Nebel. **II** v/t in Nebel hüllen, einnebeln. **III** v/i a. ~ **up** (sich) beschlagen (Glas). ~ **bank** s Nebelbank m.

fo·gey → **fogy**.

fog·gy ['fɒgɪ] adj □ **1.** neb(e)lig: ~ **day** Nebeltag m. **2.** fig. nebelhaft: **I haven't got the foggiest (idea)** F ich hab' keinen blassen Schimmer.

'**fog·horn** s Nebelhorn n. ~ **lamp**, ~ **light** s mot. Nebelscheinwerfer m, -lampe f.

fo·gy ['fəʊgɪ] s mst **old** ~ verknöcherter (alter) Kerl.

foi·ble ['fɔɪbl] s fig. **1.** (kleine) Schwäche. **2.** (vorübergehende) Laune.

foil[1] [fɔɪl] v/t Plan etc vereiteln, durchkreuzen, j-m e-n Strich durch die Rechnung machen.

foil[2] [~] s **1.** (Metall)Folie f. **2.** fig. Hintergrund m (**to** für).

foil[3] [~] s fenc. Florett n.

foist [fɔɪst] v/t: ~ **s.th. (off) on s.o.** j-m et. andrehen od. aufhängen; ~ **o.s.** (od. **one's company) on s.o.** j-m sich aufdrängen.

fold [fəʊld] **I** v/t **1.** Tuch, Hände falten, Arme verschränken, kreuzen. **2.** oft ~ **up** zs.-legen, -falten; zs.-klappen: ~ **away** zs.-klappen (u. verstauen). **3.** ein-

wickeln, -schlagen (**in** in acc): ~ **s.o. in one's arms** j-n in die Arme nehmen od. schließen. **II** v/i **4.** sich (zs.-)falten od. zs.-legen od. zs.-klappen (lassen). **5.** mst ~ **up** F zs.-brechen (**with** vor dat); ✝ eingehen. **III** s **6.** (anat. Haut-), geol. Boden)Falte f. '**fold·er** s **1.** Faltprospekt m, -blatt n, Broschüre f. **2.** Aktendeckel m, Mappe f. **3.** Schnellhefter m. '**fold·ing** adj zs.-legbar, -faltbar; zs.-klappbar: ~ **bed** Klappbett n; ~ **bi·cycle** Klapprad n; ~ **boat** Faltboot n; ~ **chair** Klappstuhl m; ~ **door(s** pl) Falttür f; ~ **table** Klapptisch m; ~ **umbrella** Taschenschirm m.

fo·li·age ['fəʊlɪɪdʒ] s Laub(werk) n, Blätter(werk n) pl: ~ **plant** Blattpflanze f.

folk [fəʊk] **I** s pl **1.** a. **folks** Leute pl. **2.** (nur **folks**) F m-e etc Leute od. Verwandten od. Angehörigen pl; (bsd. als Anrede) Leute pl, Herrschaften pl. **II** adj Volks...: ~ **dance** (**etymology, music,** etc).

fol·low ['fɒləʊ] **I** v/t **1.** folgen (dat): a) nachfolgen (dat), sich anschließen (dat), b) (zeitlich) folgen auf (acc), nachfolgen (dat), c) Ratschlag etc befolgen, sich richten nach, d) Mode etc mitmachen, e) folgen können (dat), verstehen. **2.** Ziel, Zweck verfolgen: ~ **up** e-r Sache nachgehen; Sache weiterverfolgen. **3.** e-r Beschäftigung etc nachgehen, Beruf ausüben. **II** v/i **4.** (zeitlich od. räumlich) (nach)folgen: **letter to** ~ Brief folgt; **as** ~**s** wie folgt, folgendermaßen; → **footstep** 2. **5.** mst impers folgen, sich ergeben (**from** aus): **it** ~**s from this** hieraus folgt (**that** daß). '**fol·low·er** s Anhänger(in): ~**s** pl → **following** 1. '**fol·low·ing I** s **1.** Gefolge n, Anhang m; Anhänger(schaft f) pl, Gefolgschaft f. **2.** das Folgende; **die** Folgenden pl od. Sg: **the** ~. **II** adj ~ **wind** Rückenwind m. **III** prp **4.** im Anschluß an (acc).

'**fol·low-up** s **1.** Weiterverfolgen n (e-r Sache). **2.** ✻ Nachbehandlung f.

fol·ly ['fɒlɪ] s Torheit f.

fond [fɒnd] adj □ **1.** **be** ~ **of** mögen, gern haben: **be** ~ **of doing s.th.** et. gern tun. **2.** zärtlich, liebevoll. **3.** allzu nachsichtig (**Mutter** etc).

fon·dle ['fɒndl] v/t (liebevoll) streicheln.

fond·ness ['fɒndnɪs] s **1.** Zärtlichkeit f.

2. Zuneigung *f* (**of** zu). **3.** Vorliebe *f* (**for** für).

font [font] *s eccl.* Taufstein *m*, -becken *n*.

food [fuːd] *s* **1.** Nahrung *f* (*a. fig.*), Essen *n*, Verpflegung *f*: ~ **for thought** (*od.* **reflection**) Stoff *m* zum Nachdenken. **2.** Nahrungs-, Lebensmittel *pl.* ~ **poi·son·ing** *s* Lebensmittelvergiftung *f*. '~**stuff** → **food** 2.

fool [fuːl] **I** *s* **1.** Narr *m*, Närrin *f*, Dummkopf *m*: **make a** ~ **of** → 2; **make a** ~ **of o.s.** sich lächerlich machen; **I am a** ~ **to him** gegen ihn bin ich ein Waisenknabe. **II** *v/t* **2.** zum Narren halten. **3.** betrügen (**out of** um); verleiten (**into doing** zu tun). **4.** ~ **away** Zeit, Geld *etc* vergeuden. **III** *v/i* **5.** *a.* ~ **about** (*od.* **around**) Unsinn machen, herumalbern. **6.** *oft* ~ **about** (*od.* **around**) spielen (**with** mit); sich herumtreiben; herumtrödeln. '**fool·er·y** *s* Torheit *f*.

'**fool·har·dy** *adj* □ tollkühn, verwegen.

fool·ish ['fuːlɪʃ] *adj* □ dumm, töricht.

'**fool·proof** *adj* **1.** ⚙ betriebssicher. **2.** todsicher (*Plan etc*). **3.** narren-, idiotensicher (*Gerät etc*).

foot [fʊt] **I** *pl* **feet** [fiːt] *s* **1.** Fuß *m*: **on** ~ zu Fuß; **be on** ~ im Gange sein; **set on** ~ in die Wege leiten, in Gang bringen; **be on one's feet** (**again**) (wieder) auf den Beinen sein; **put one's** ~ **in it** ins Fettnäpfchen treten; → **sweep** 6. **2.** (*pl a.* **foot**) Fuß *m* (= 0,3048 m). **3.** Fuß *m* (*e-s Berges, Strumpfes etc*), Fußende *n* (*e-s Bettes etc*): **at the** ~ **of** am Fuß (*gen*), unten an (*dat*). **II** *v/t* **4.** ~ **it** F zu Fuß gehen. **5.** *Rechnung* bezahlen. ,~**-and-'mouth dis·ease** *s vet.* Maulu. Klauenseuche *f*. '~**ball** (*Sport*) **I** *s* **1.** *Br.* Fußball(spiel *n*) *m*; *Am.* Football(spiel *n*) *m*. **2.** *Br.* Fußball *m*; *Am.* Football-Ball *m*. **II** *adj* **3.** *Br.* Fußball...; *Am.* Football...: ~ **pools** *pl* Fußballtoto *n*, *m*. '~**bridge** *s* Fußgängerbrücke *f*. '~**fall** *s* Schritt *m*, Tritt *m* (*Geräusch*). '~**hills** *s pl* Vorgebirge *n*. '~**hold** *s* Stand *m*: **safe** ~ fester Stand, sicherer Halt; **gain** (*od.* **get**) **a** ~ *fig.* (festen) Fuß fassen (**in** in *dat*; **as** als).

foot·ing ['fʊtɪŋ] *s* **1.** Stand *m*: **lose** (*od.* **miss**) **one's** ~ den Halt verlieren. **2.** *fig.* Basis *f*, Grundlage *f*: **place on a** (*od.* **the same**) ~ gleichstellen (**with** *dat*); **be**

on a friendly ~ auf freundschaftlichem Fuße stehen (**with** mit).

'**foot·lights** *s pl thea.* **1.** Rampenlicht(er *pl*) *n*. **2.** *fig.* die Bühne, *das* Theater.

foot·ling ['fuːtlɪŋ] *adj* F läppisch (*Sache*), (*a. Person*) albern.

'**foot·loose** *adj* frei, ungebunden: ~ **and fancy-free** frei u. ungebunden. '~**note I** *s* Fußnote *f* (**to** zu). **II** *v/t* mit Fußnoten versehen. ~**pas·sen·ger** *s Am.* Fußgänger(in). '~**path** *s* **1.** (Fuß)Pfad *m*, (-)Weg *m*. **2.** *bsd. Br.* Bürgersteig *m*. '~**print** *s* Fußabdruck *m*.

foot·sie ['fʊtsɪ] *s*: **play** ~ F füßeln (**with** mit).

'**foot·slog** *v/i* F latschen. '~**sore** *adj* fußwund, *bsd.* ✗ fußkrank. ~ **spray** *s* Fußspray *m*, *n*. '~**step** *s* **1.** Tritt *m*, Schritt *m*. **2.** Fußstapfe *f*: **follow in s.o.'s** ~**s** *fig.* in j-s Fußstapfen treten. '~**wear** *s* Schuhwerk *n*. '~**work** *s Sport:* Beinarbeit *f*.

for [fɔː] **I** *prp* **1.** für: a) zugunsten von: **a gift** ~ **him** ein Geschenk für ihn, b) (mit der Absicht) zu: **come** ~ **dinner** zum Essen kommen, c) (*passend od. geeignet*) für; (*bestimmt*) für, zu: **tools** *pl* ~ **cutting** Schneidewerkzeuge *pl*; **the right man** ~ **the job** der richtige Mann für diesen Posten, d) (*als Belohnung od. Entgelt*) für, e) (*als Strafe etc*) wegen, f) in Anbetracht (*gen*), im Hinblick auf (*acc*): **he is tall** ~ **his age** er ist groß für sein Alter, g) (*Bezahlung, Preis*) für, (*Hang*) zu, h) (*zeitlich*) auf (*acc*), für die Dauer von, seit: ~ **hours** stundenlang; **he has been here** ~ **a week** er ist schon seit e-r Woche hier, i) an Stelle von (*od.* *gen*), (an)statt; in Vertretung *od.* im Namen von (*od.* *gen*). **2.** (*Wunsch, Ziel*) nach, auf (*acc*). **3.** (*Mittel*) gegen. **4.** dank, wegen: **if it wasn't** ~ **him** wenn er nicht wäre, ohne ihn. **5.** (*Strecke*) weit: **run a mile** e-e Meile (weit) laufen. **6.** nach: **the train** ~ **London.** **7.** trotz: ~ **all that** trotz alledem. **8.** was ... betrifft: **as** ~ **me** was mich betrifft *od.* anbelangt; ~ **all I know** soviel ich weiß. **9.** *nach adj u.* **vor** *inf*: **it is impossible** ~ **me to come** ich kann unmöglich kommen. **10.** *mit s od. pron. u.* **inf**: **it is time** ~ **you to go home** es ist Zeit für dich heimzugehen; **it is** ~ **you to decide** die Entscheidung liegt bei Ihnen. **II** *cj* **11.** denn, weil.

fo·ra ['fɔːrə] *pl von* forum.

for·ay ['fɔreɪ] *s* **1.** Beute-, Raubzug *m.* **2.** *bsd.* ✕ Ein-, Überfall *m.*

for·bad(e) [fə'bæd] *pret von* forbid.

for·bear → forebear.

for·bid [fə'bɪd] (*irr*) **I** *v/t* **1.** verbieten, untersagen: ~ *s.o. the house* j-m das Haus verbieten. **2.** ausschließen, unmöglich machen. **II** *v/i* **3.** *God* (*od. heaven*) ~*! Gott behüte od. bewahre!*

for'bid·den [~dn] *pp von* forbid.

for'bid·ding *adj* □ **1.** abstoßend, abschreckend. **2.** bedrohlich.

force [fɔːs] **I** *s* **1.** Stärke *f,* Kraft *f,* Wucht *f* (*a. fig.*): ~ *of gravity phys.* Schwerkraft; *by* ~ *of* kraft, vermittels; *by* ~ *of arms* mit Waffengewalt; *join* ~*s* sich zs.-tun (*with* mit). **2.** *fig.* Kraft *f:* ~*s pl of nature* Naturkräfte *pl,* -gewalten *pl.* **3.** Gewalt *f: by* ~ gewaltsam. **4.** Zwang *m* (*a.* ⚖): *by* ~ zwangsweise. **5.** (Rechts)Kraft *f,* (-)Gültigkeit *f: come* (*put*) *into* ~ in Kraft treten (setzen). **6.** Einfluß *m,* Wirkung *f:* ~ *of habit* Macht *f* der Gewohnheit. **7.** *pl,* a. *armed* ~*s* ✕ Streitkräfte *pl.* **II** *v/t* **8.** j-n zwingen, nötigen (*to do* zu tun). **9.** *et.* erzwingen, durchsetzen. **10.** zwängen, drängen: ~ *one's way* sich (durch)drängen (*through* durch). **11.** ~ *s.th. on s.o.* j-m et. aufzwingen *od.* -drängen; → *o.s. on s.o.* sich j-m aufdrängen; → throat. **12.** *a.* ~ *up Preise* in die Höhe treiben. **13.** *Tempo* beschleunigen, forcieren. **14.** *a.* ~ *open Tür etc* aufbrechen. **forced** *adj* **1.** erzwungen, Zwangs...: ~ *landing* ✈ Notlandung *f.* **2.** gezwungen, gequält. **force·ed·ly** [~ɪdlɪ] *adv* **1.** → forced **2. 2.** gezwungenermaßen.

'force-feed *v/t* (*irr* feed) zwangsernähren.

force·ful ['fɔːsful] *adj* □ **1.** energisch, kraftvoll (Person). **2.** eindrucksvoll, -dringlich (Rede etc). **3.** zwingend, überzeugend (Argument etc).

for·ceps ['fɔːseps] *pl* -ceps, -ci·pes ['~sɪpiːz] *s* **1.** 💉, *zo.* Zange *f:* ~ *delivery* Zangengeburt *f.* **2.** Pinzette *f.*

for·ci·ble ['fɔːsəbl] *adj* □ **1.** gewaltsam: zwangsweise. **2.** → forceful.

ford [fɔːd] **I** *s* Furt *f.* **II** *v/t* durchwaten.

fore [fɔː] **I** *adj* **1.** vorder, Vorder... **2.** früher. **II** *adv* **3.** ⚓ vorn. **III** *s* **4.** Vor-

derteil *m,* -seite *f,* Front *f: come to the* ~ *fig.* sich hervortun. '~*arm* *s* Unterarm *m.* '~*bear* *s mst pl* Vorfahr *m,* Ahn *m.* ~*'bode* *v/t* **1.** *Schlimmes* ahnen, voraussehen. **2.** ein (böses) Vorzeichen *od.* Omen sein für. ~*'bod·ing* *s* **1.** (böse) (Vor)Ahnung. **2.** (böses) Vorzeichen *od.* Omen. '~*cast* **I** *v/t pret u. pp* -cast(·ed) **1.** voraussagen, vorhersehen. **2.** *Wetter etc* vorhersagen. **II** *s* **3.** Voraussage *f.* **4.** (Wetter)Vorhersage *f.* '~*fa·ther* *s* Ahn *m,* Vorfahr *m.* '~*fin·ger* *s* Zeigefinger *m.* '~*front* *s* vorderste Reihe (*a. fig.*). ~*'go* *v/t u. v/i* (*irr go*) vorangehen (*dat*), (*zeitlich a.*) vorhergehen (*dat*). ~*'go·ing* *adj:* ~ *conclusion* ausgemachte Sache; *be a* ~ *conclusion a.* von vornherein feststehen. '~*ground* *s* Vordergrund *m* (*a. fig.*). '~*hand* (Sport) **I** *s* Vorhand(schlag *m*) *f.* **II** *adj* Vorhand... ~*head* ['fɒrɪd] *s* Stirn *f.*

for·eign ['fɒrən] *adj* **1.** fremd, ausländisch, Auslands...: ~ *affairs pl* Außenpolitik *f,* auswärtige Angelegenheiten *pl;* ~ *currency* (*od. exchange*) 📈 Devisen *pl;* ~ *language* Fremdsprache *f;* ♀ *Office pol. Br.* Außenministerium *n;* ~ *policy* Außenpolitik *f;* ♀ *Secretary pol. Br.* Außenminister *m;* ~ *trade* Außenhandel *m;* ~ *word* Fremdwort *n;* ~ *worker* Gastarbeiter *m;* ~ *correspondent* 📈 **2.** fremd (*to dat*): *this is* ~ *to his nature* das ist ihm wesensfremd; ~ *body* (*od. matter*) 💉 Fremdkörper *m.* '**for·eign·er** *s* Ausländer(in).

,**fore·**|**'knowl·edge** *s* Vorherwissen *n,* vorherige Kenntnis. ~*man* ['~mən] *s* (*irr* man) **1.** Vorarbeiter *m,* (*am Bau*) Polier *m.* **2.** ⚖ Obmann *m* (*der Geschworenen*). '~*most* **I** *adj* **1.** vorderst, erst. **2.** *fig.* herausragendst. **II** *adv* **3.** zuerst. '~*name* *s* Vorname *m.*

fo·ren·sic [fə'rensɪk] *adj* Gerichts...: ~ *medicine.*

'**fore·**|**play** *s* (*sexuelles*) Vorspiel. '~*,run·ner* *s fig.* **1.** Vorläufer *m.* **2.** Vorbote *m;* (*erstes*) Anzeichen. ~*'see* *v/t* (*irr* see[^1]) vorher-, voraussehen. ~*'see·a·ble* *adj:* *in the* ~ *future* in absehbarer Zeit. ~*'shad·ow* *v/t* ahnen lassen, andeuten. '~*sight* *s* Weitblick *m;* (*weise*) Voraussicht *f.* '~*skin* *s anat.* Vorhaut *f.*

[^1]: *(irr see[^1])*

for·est ['fɒrist] s (a. fig. Antennen-etc)Wald m; Forst m.

fore·stall [fɔː'stɔːl] v/t **1.** j-m, e-r Sache zuvorkommen. **2.** Einwand etc vorwegnehmen.

for·est·er ['fɒristə] s Förster m. **'for·est·ry** s Forstwirtschaft f.

'fore|·taste s Vorgeschmack m (of von). **~'tell** v/t (irr tell) vorher-, voraussagen: ~ s.o.'s future j-m die Zukunft vorhersagen.

for·ev·er, Br. a. **for ev·er** [fə'revə] adv **1.** für od. auf immer. **2.** ständig, (an)dauernd.

fore|'warn v/t vorher warnen (of vor dat). **~'wom·an** s (irr woman) Vorarbeiterin f. **'~·word** s Vorwort n (to zu).

for·feit ['fɔːfit] **I** s pl (sg konstruiert) Pfänderspiel n: **play ~s** ein Pfänderspiel machen. **II** v/t verwirken, verlustig gehen (gen); einbüßen. **III** adj verwirkt, verfallen. **for·fei·ture** ['~tʃə] s Verlust m; Einbuße f.

forge[^1] [fɔːdʒ] v/t fälschen.

forge[^2] [~] v/i mst ~ **ahead** sich (mühsam) vorankämpfen: ~ **ahead** fig. allmählich Fortschritte machen.

forg·er ['fɔːdʒə] s Fälscher m. **'forg·er·y** s Fälschung f; Fälschung f: ~ **of a document** ggs. Urkundenfälschung f.

for·get [fə'get] (irr) **I** v/t **1.** allg. vergessen: **I ~ his name** sein Name fällt mir im Moment nicht ein. **2.** ~ **o.s.** sich vergessen. **II** v/i **3.** (nur) an andere denken. **II** v/i **3.** a. ~ **about it** es vergessen. **for'get·ful** [~fʊl] adj □ vergeßlich.

for'get-me-not s ⚘ Vergißmeinnicht n.

for·give [fə'gɪv] v/t (irr give) **1.** j-m et. verzeihen, -geben. **2.** j-m e-e Schuld etc erlassen. **for'giv·ing** adj □ **1.** versöhnlich. **2.** verzeihend.

for·go [fɔː'gəʊ] v/t (irr go) verzichten auf (acc).

for·got [fə'gɒt] pret u. pp von **forget**. **for'got·ten** [~tn] pp von **forget**.

fork [fɔːk] **I** s **1.** Gabel f. **2.** Gab(e)lung f, Abzweigung f. **II** v/t **3.** ~ **out** (od. **up**) F Geld herausrücken, lockermachen. **III** v/i **4.** sich gabeln (Fluß), (Straße a.) abzweigen. **forked** adj gegabelt, (Zunge) gespalten.

'fork-lift (truck) s ⚙ Gabel-, Hubstapler m.

for·lorn [fə'lɔːn] adj **1.** verlassen, einsam.

2. verzweifelt (Versuch): ~ **hope** aussichtsloses od. verzweifeltes Unternehmen.

form [fɔːm] **I** s **1.** Form f, Gestalt f: **take** ~ Form od. Gestalt annehmen (a. fig.); **in the ~ of** in Form von (od. gen); **in tablet ~** in Tablettenform. **2.** ⊕ Form f, Schablone f. **3.** Form f, Art f: ~ **of government** Regierungsform; → **due 6. 4.** a. **printed** ~ Formular n, Vordruck m: ~ **letter** Schemabrief m. **5.** Form f (a. ling.), Fassung f (e-s Textes etc). **6. good (bad)** ~ guter (schlechter) Ton: **it is good (bad)** ~ es gehört sich (nicht). **7.** Formalität f: → **matter 3. 8.** Verfassung f: **in (out of, off one's)** ~ (nicht) in Form. **9.** bsd. Br. (Schul)Klasse f: ~ **master (mistress)** Klassenlehrer(in). **II** v/t **10.** formen, gestalten: ~ **into** zu; **after, on** nach), Regierung etc bilden, Gesellschaft gründen. **11.** Charakter etc formen, bilden. **12.** sich e-e Meinung bilden. **III** v/i **13.** Form od. Gestalt annehmen (a. fig.).

for·mal ['fɔːml] adj □ (→ **formally**) **1.** förmlich, formell: ~ **call** Höflichkeitsbesuch m; ~ **dress** Gesellschaftskleidung f. **2.** formal, formell: ~ **defect** ⚖ Formfehler m. **for·mal·ism** ['~məlɪzəm] s Formalismus m. **for·mal·i·ty** [~'mælətɪ] s **1.** Förmlichkeit f. **2.** Formalität f, Formsache f. **for·mal·ize** ['~məlaɪz] v/t **1.** formalisieren. **2.** e-e feste Form geben (dat). **'for·mal·ly** adv formell, in aller Form.

for·mat ['fɔːmæt] s typ. Aufmachung f; Format n.

for·ma·tion [fɔː'meɪʃn] s **1.** Formung f, Gestaltung f. **2.** ✈, ✕, geol., Sport: Formation f. **form·a·tive** ['~mətɪv] adj □ formend, gestaltend: ~ **years** pl Entwicklungsjahre pl.

for·mer ['fɔːmə] adj **1.** früher, vorig; ehemalig: **in** ~ **times** früher. **2.** erstererwähnt, -genannt: **the** ~, **the latter** ersterer, letzterer. **'for·mer·ly** adv früher, ehemals.

for·mi·da·ble ['fɔːmɪdəbl] adj □ **1.** furchterregend. **2.** gefährlich (Gegner etc), gewaltig, riesig (Schulden etc), schwierig (Frage etc).

form·less ['fɔːmlɪs] adj □ formlos.

for·mu·la ['fɔːmjʊlə] pl **-las, -lae** ['~liː] s **1.** A, mot. etc Formel f (a. fig.). **2.**

pharm. Rezept n (*zur Anfertigung*). **for·mu·late** ['ɔːleɪt] v/t formulieren. **for·mu·la·tion** [ɔːeɪʃn] s Formulierung f.

for·sake [fə'seɪk] v/t (*irr*) **1.** j-n verlassen, im Stich lassen. **2.** et. aufgeben. **for'sak·en** pp von **forsake**. **for·sook** [fə'sʊk] pret von **forsake**.

for·swear [fɔː'sweə] v/t (*irr swear*) **1.** unter Eid verneinen. **2.** abschwören (*dat*). **3. ~ o.s.** e-n Meineid leisten.

fort [fɔːt] s ✕ Fort n: **hold the ~** fig. die Stellung halten.

for·te ['fɔːteɪ] s J-s Stärke f, starke Seite.

forth [fɔːθ] adv **1.** weiter, fort: **and so ~** und so weiter. **2.** (her)vor. **,~'com·ing** adj **1.** bevorstehend, kommend. **2.** in Kürze erscheinend (*Buch*) od. anlaufend (*Film*).

for·ti·eth ['fɔːtɪəθ] adj vierzigst.

for·ti·fi·ca·tion [ˌfɔːtɪfɪ'keɪʃn] s **1.** ✕ Befestigung f: **~s** pl Festungswerk n. **2.** Verstärkung f; Anreicherung f. **3.** fig. Untermauerung f. **for·ti·fy** ['fɔːfaɪ] v/t **1.** ✕ befestigen. **2.** *Wein etc* verstärken; *Nahrungsmittel* anreichern. **3.** *Theorie etc* untermauern (**with** mit).

for·ti·tude ['fɔːtɪtjuːd] s (innere) Kraft od. Stärke.

fort·night ['fɔːtnaɪt] s *bsd. Br.* vierzehn Tage: **in a ~** in 14 Tagen. **'fort·night·ly** *bsd. Br.* **I** adj vierzehntägig, halbmonatlich. **II** adv vierzehntäglich, alle 14 Tage.

for·tress ['fɔːtrɪs] s ✕ Festung f.

for·tu·i·tous [fɔː'tjuːɪtəs] adj □ zufällig.

for·tu·nate ['fɔːtʃnət] adj glücklich: **be ~** Glück haben; **be ~ in having s.th., be ~ enough to have s.th.** das Glück haben, et. zu besitzen. **'for·tu·nate·ly** adv glücklicherweise, zum Glück: **~ for me** zu m-m Glück.

for·tune ['fɔːtʃuːn] s **1.** Vermögen n: **come into a ~** ein Vermögen erben; **make a ~** ein Vermögen verdienen; **marry a ~** e-e gute Partie machen, reich heiraten. **2.** (glücklicher) Zufall, Glück(sfall m) n. **3.** Geschick n, Schicksal n: **good ~** Glück n; **bad** (*od.* **ill**) **~** Unglück n; **tell ~s** wahrsagen; **read s.o.'s ~** j-m die Karten legen; j-m aus der Hand lesen. **4.** *oft 2* Fortuna f, das Glück, die Glücksgöttin. **~ hunt·er** s Mitgiftjäger m. **~ tell·er** s Wahrsager(in).

for·ty ['fɔːtɪ] **I** adj vierzig: **have ~ winks** F ein Nickerchen machen. **II** s Vierzig f: **be in one's forties** in den Vierzigern sein; **in the forties** in den vierziger Jahren (*e-s Jahrhunderts*).

fo·rum ['fɔːrəm] pl **-rums, -ra** [ˌ~rə] s Forum n (*a. fig.*).

for·ward ['fɔːwəd] **I** adv **1.** nach vorn, vorwärts. **II** adj □ **2.** Vorwärts...: **~ planning** Vorausplanung f. **3.** fortschrittlich. **4.** vorlaut, dreist. **III** s **5.** Sport: Stürmer m: **~ line** Stürmreihe f. **IV** v/t **6.** fördern, begünstigen. **7.** (ver)senden, schicken; befördern; *Brief etc* nachsenden. **'for·ward·er** s Spediteur m.

'for·ward·ing s Versand m; Beförderung f; Nachsendung f: **~ address** Nachsendeadresse f; **~ agent** Spediteur m.

'for·ward-,look·ing adj vorausschauend, fortschrittlich.

for·wards ['fɔːwədz] → **forward I**.

fos·sil ['fɒsl] geol. **I** s Fossil n (*a. fig.* F), Versteinerung f. **II** adj fossil (*a. fig.* F), versteinert.

fos·ter ['fɒstə] **I** v/t **1.** *Kind* in Pflege haben *od.* nehmen; *bsd. Br.* in Pflege geben (**with** bei). **2.** *Gefühle, Plan etc* hegen. **II** adj **3.** Pflege...: → **mother**.

fought [fɔːt] pret u. pp von **fight**.

foul [faʊl] **I** adj □ **1.** stinkend, widerlich. **2.** verpestet, schlecht (*Luft*); verdorben, faul (*Lebensmittel etc*). **3.** schmutzig, verschmutzt. **4.** schlecht, stürmisch (*Wetter*). **5.** fig. schmutzig, zotig. **6.** Sport: regelwidrig. **II** adv **7.** **fall ~ of** ⚓ kollidieren mit, *a. fig.* zs.-stoßen mit: **fall ~ of the law** mit dem Gesetz in Konflikt geraten. **III** s **8.** Sport: Foul n: **commit a ~** ein Foul begehen an (*dat*). **IV** v/t **9.** a. **~ up** beschmutzen (*a. fig.*), verschmutzen: **~ one's** (**own**) **nest** das eigene Nest beschmutzen. **10.** Sport: foulen. **11.** **~ up** F verpatzen, -sauen. **~-mouthed** ['~maʊðd] adj unflätig.

found[1] [faʊnd] pret u. pp von **find**.

found[2] [~] v/t **1.** (be)gründen, *Schule etc* stiften. **2.** gründen, stützen (**on** auf acc): **be ~ed on** sich gründen auf (*acc*), beruhen auf (*dat*).

found[3] [~] v/t ⊕ gießen.

foun·da·tion [faʊn'deɪʃn] s **1.** △ Fundament n: **lay the ~**(**s**) **of** fig. den

Grund(stock) legen zu. **2.** Gründung *f.*
3. Stiftung *f.* **4.** Grundlage *f*, Basis *f.* ~
stone *s* **1.** △ Grundstein *m* (*a. fig.*). **2.**
→ **foundation** 4.

found·er¹ ['faʊndə] *s* (Be)Gründer(in),
Stifter(in); ~ **member** Gründungsmit-
glied *n.*

found·er² [~] *s* ☉ Gießer *m.*

found·er³ *v/i* scheitern, (*Koalition etc a.*)
zerbrechen, (*Ehe etc a.*) in die Brüche
gehen.

found·ry ['faʊndrɪ] *s* ☉ Gießerei *f.*

foun·tain ['faʊntɪn] *s* **1.** Quelle *f* (*a. fig.*).
2. Fontäne *f:* a) (*Wasser- etc*)Strahl *m*,
b) Springbrunnen *m.* **3.** Trinkbrunnen
m. ~ **pen** *s* Füll(feder)halter *m.*

four [fɔː] **I** *adj* **1.** vier. **II** *s* **2.** Vier *f:* ~ **of
hearts** Herzvier; **on all** ~**s** auf allen
vieren. **3.** Rudern: Vierer *m.* **four·fold**
['~fəʊld] **I** *adj* vierfach. **II** *adv* vierfach,
um das Vierfache: *increase* ~ (sich)
vervierfachen.

,**four·|-'hand·ed** *adj* □ ♪ vierhändig.
'**~-leaf clo·ver** *s* ✿ vierblätt(e)riges
Kleeblatt. '**~-legged** *adj* vierbeinig.
'**~-let·ter word** *s* unanständiges Wort.
~ **star** *s mot.* Br. F Super *n* (*Benzin*).
'**~-star** *adj:* ~ **petrol** *mot.* Br. Superbenzin *n.*

four·teen [ˌfɔː'tiːn] *adj* vierzehn. ,**four·
'teenth** [~θ] *adj* vierzehnt. **fourth** [fɔːθ]
I *adj* **1.** viert. **II** *s* **2.** der, die, das Vierte:
the ~ **of May** der 4. Mai. **3.** Viertel *n.*
'**fourth·ly** *adv* viertens.

'**four-time** *adj* viermalig.

fowl [faʊl] *s coll.* Geflügel *n.*

fox [fɒks] **I** *s* **1.** *zo.* Fuchs *m.* **2.** *oft sly old*
~ gerissener *od.* verschlagener Kerl *m.*
II *v/t* **3.** verblüffen. **4.** täuschen, reinlegen. ~ **hunt(·ing)** *s* Fuchsjagd *f.* ~ **ter·
ri·er** *s zo.* Foxterrier *m.* '**~-trot** *s* ♪ Foxtrott *m.*

fox·y ['fɒksɪ] *adj* □ gerissen, verschlagen.

foy·er ['fɔɪeɪ] *s* Foyer *n.*

fra·cas ['fræka:] *pl* **-cas** [-ka:z], *Am.*
-cas·es ['freɪkəsɪz] *s* Aufruhr *m*, Tumult *m.*

frac·tion ['frækʃn] *s* **1.** Ⓐ Bruch *m:* ~ **bar**
(*od.* **line, stroke**) Bruchstrich *m.* **2.**
Bruchteil *m.* **frac·tion·al** ['~ʃənl] *adj* □
1. Ⓐ Bruch... **2.** *fig.* minimal, geringfügig.

frac·tious ['frækʃəs] *adj* □ mürrisch,
reizbar.

frac·ture ['fræktʃə] **I** *s* Bruch *m*, ⚕ *a.*
Fraktur *f.* **II** *v/t* (zer)brechen: ~ **one's
arm** sich den Arm brechen; ~**d skull** ⚕
Schädelbruch *m;* **speak** ~**d English** *fig.*
gebrochen Englisch sprechen. **III** *v/i*
(zer)brechen.

frag·ile ['frædʒaɪl] *adj* □ **1.** zerbrechlich
(*a. fig.*). **2.** schwach, zart (*Gesundheit*);
gebrechlich (*Person*). **fra·gil·i·ty** [frə-
'dʒɪlətɪ] *s* **1.** Zerbrechlichkeit *f.* **2.**
Zartheit *f;* Gebrechlichkeit *f.*

frag·ment ['frægmənt] *s* **1.** *literarisches
etc* Fragment. **2.** Bruchstück *n*, -teil *m.*
'**frag·men·ta·ry** *adj* □ fragmentarisch,
bruchstückhaft.

fra·grance ['freɪgrəns] *s* Wohlgeruch *m*,
Duft *m.* '**fra·grant** *adj* □ wohlriechend, duftend.

frail [freɪl] *adj* □ zart, schwach (*Gesundheit, Stimme etc*); gebrechlich (*Person*);
(*charakterlich od. moralisch*) schwach.
'**frail·ty** *s* Zartheit *f;* Gebrechlichkeit *f;*
Schwäche *f.*

frame [freɪm] **I** *s* **1.** (*Bilder- etc*)Rahmen
m. **2.** (*Brillen- etc*)Gestell *n.* **3.** *fig.* Rahmen *m:* **within the** ~ **of** im Rahmen
(*gen*). **4.** *bsd.* ~ **of mind** (Gemüts)Ver-
fassung *f*, (-)Zustand *m.* **II** *v/t* **5.** Bild
etc (ein)rahmen; *fig.* umrahmen. **6.**
Plan schmieden, Politik etc abstecken.
7. *a.* ~ **up** F Sache drehen, schaukeln,
Spiel (vorher) absprechen; *j-m* et. anhängen. **III** *v/i* **8.** sich entwickeln. '**~-up**
s F **1.** Komplott *n*, Intrige *f.* **2.** abgekartetes Spiel, Schwindel *m.* '**~-work** →
frame 3.

franc [fræŋk] *s* Franc *m;* Franken *m.*

fran·chise ['fræntʃaɪz] *s* **1.** *pol.* Wahlrecht *n.* **2.** ✝ *bsd. Am.* Konzession *f.*

Fran·co- ['fræŋkəʊ] *in Zssgn* französisch, franko..

frank [fræŋk] **I** *adj* □ offen(herzig), aufrichtig, frei(mütig): **to be** ~, ~**ly**
(*speaking*) offen gestanden *od.* gesagt;
be ~ **with s.o.** ehrlich zu j-m sein. **II** *v/t*
✉ frankieren, (*maschinell a.*) freistem-
peln: ~**ing machine** Frankiermaschine
f, Freistempler *m.*

frank·furt·er ['fræŋkfɜːtə] *s* Frankfurter
(Würstchen *n*) *f.*

frank·in·cense ['fræŋkɪnˌsens] *s* Weihrauch *m.*

frank·ness ['fræŋknɪs] *s* Offenheit *f*,
Freimütigkeit *f.*

fran·tic ['fræntɪk] *adj* (*~ally*) **1.** außer sich, rasend (**with** *od. dat*.). **2.** verzweifelt. **3.** hektisch.

fra·ter·nal [frə'tɜːnl] *adj* □ brüderlich. **fra'ter·ni·ty** *s* **1.** Brüderlichkeit *f*. **2.** Vereinigung *f*, Zunft *f*: *the medical ~* die Ärzteschaft. **3.** *Am.* (Studenten-) Verbindung *f*. **frat·er·ni·za·tion** [ˌfrætənaɪ'zeɪʃn] *s* Verbrüderung *f*. **'frat·er·nize** *v/i* sich verbrüdern.

fraud [frɔːd] *s* **1.** ✖ Betrug *m* (**on** an *dat*.); arglistige Täuschung: *obtain by ~* sich *et.* erschleichen. **2.** Schwindel *m* (*a. Sache*). **3.** Schwindler *m*, Schwindler *m*. **fraud·u·lence** ['~djʊləns] *s* Betrügerei *f*. **'fraud·u·lent** *adj* □ betrügerisch.

fray[1] [freɪ] **I** *v/t a.* ~ **out** ausfransen, durchscheuern: *~ed nerves pl* verschlissene *od.* strapazierte Nerven *pl.* **II** *v/i a.* ~ **out** ausfransen, sich durchscheuern.

fray[2] [~] *s* Rauferei *f*, Schlägerei *f*.

freak [friːk] **I** *s* **1.** Mißgeburt *f*, Monstrosität *f*. **2.** Grille *f*, Laune *f*. **3.** *sl.* ...freak *m*, ...fanatiker *m*. **4.** *sl.* Freak *m*, irrer Typ. **II** *v/i* **5.** ~ **out** *sl. allg.* ausflippen (**for**, **over** bei).

freck·le ['frekl] *s* Sommersprosse *f*. **'freck·led** *adj* [~ld] sommersprossig.

free [friː] **I** *adj* □ **1.** frei: a) unabhängig, b) selbständig, c) ungebunden, d) ungehindert, e) uneingeschränkt, f) in Freiheit (befindlich): *he is ~ to go* es steht ihm frei zu gehen; *give s.o. a ~ hand* j-m freie Hand lassen; → *set* 13, *will*[1] 1. **2.** frei: a) unbeschäftigt, b) ohne Verpflichtungen, c) unbesetzt. **3.** frei (*nicht wörtlich od. an Regeln gebunden*): *~ translation*; *~ skating* (Eis-, Rollkunstlauf) Kür(laufen *n*) *f*. **4.** (**from**, **of**) frei (von), ohne (*acc*): *~ from error* fehlerfrei. **5.** frei, befreit (**from**, **of** von): *~ from pain* schmerzfrei; *~ of debt* schuldenfrei; *→ charge* 9. **6.** ungezwungen, natürlich; → *easy* 7. **7.** offen(herzig), freimütig; unverblümt; dreist; plump-vertraulich: *make ~ with* sich Freiheiten herausnehmen gegen *j-n*; sich (ungeniert) gütlich tun an *e-r Sache*. **8.** frei, kostenlos, unentgeltlich: *~ copy* Freiexemplar *n*; *for ~* F umsonst. **9.** freigebig: *be ~ with* großzügig sein *od.* umgehen mit. **II** *adv* **10.** *allg.* frei. **III** *v/t* **11.** befreien

(**from** von, aus) (*a. fig.*). **12.** freilassen.

free·bee, **free·bie** ['friːbiː] *s sl. et.*, *was es gratis gibt, z. B.* Freikarte *f*.

'free·boot·er *s* Freibeuter *m*.

free·dom ['friːdəm] *s* **1.** Freiheit *f*: *~ of the press* Pressefreiheit. **2.** Freisein *n*: *~ from pain* Schmerzfreiheit *f*.

free| en·ter·prise *s* freies Unternehmertum. *~ fall s* ✖, *phys.* freier Fall. **~ 'hand·ed** *adj* □ freigebig, großzügig. *~ kick s* Fußball: Freistoß *m*: (in)*direct ~*. **'~·lance I** *s* Freiberufler *m*, Freischaffende *m*; freier Mitarbeiter. **II** *adj* frei(beruflich tätig), freischaffend. **III** *adv* freiberuflich: *work ~ → IV.* **IV** *v/i* freiberuflich arbeiten (**for** für). **'~·lanc·er** → **freelance** I. **'~·load** *v/i Am.* F schnorren (**off**, **of** bei), nassauern. **'~·load·er** *s Am.* F Schnorrer *m*, Nassauer *m*. *~ mar·ket e·con·o·my s* freie Marktwirtschaft. *~ port s* Freihafen *m*. *~·'spo·ken adj* □ freimütig, offen. *~ state s* Freistaat *m*. **'~·style** (Sport) **I** *s* Freistil *m*. **II** *adj* Freistil... *~ trade s* Freihandel *m*. *~·'trade a·re·a s* Freihandelszone *f*.

freeze [friːz] **I** *v/i* (*irr*) **1.** *impers* frieren: *it is freezing hard* es herrscht starker Frost. **2.** frieren: *~ to death* erfrieren; *I am freezing* mir ist eiskalt. **3.** (ge)frieren, zu Eis werden: *~ blood* 1. **4.** *~ up* (*od.* **over**) zufrieren (*See etc*), vereisen (*Windschutzscheibe etc*): *~* (**up**) einfrieren (*Türschloß etc*); *~ to* fest- *od.* anfrieren an (*dat*.). **5.** *fig.* erstarren. **II** *v/t* (*irr*) **6.** zum Gefrieren bringen. **7.** *Fleisch etc* einfrieren, tiefkühlen. **8.** ✖ vereisen. **9.** ✝ *Preise etc*, *pol. diplomatische Beziehungen* einfrieren. **III** *s* **10.** Frost(periode *f*) *m*. **11.** ✝, *pol.* Einfrieren *n*: *~ on wages* Lohnstopp *m*. **'freez·er** *s* a) Tiefkühl-, Gefriergerät *n*, b) Gefrierfach *n* (*e-s Kühlschranks*). **'freez·ing** *adj* **1.** Gefrier-, Kälte...: *~ compartment → freezer* b; *~ point* Gefrierpunkt *m*. **2.** eisig kalt, eiskalt.

freight [freɪt] **I** *s* **1.** Fracht(gebühr) *f*. **2.** ♣ (*Am. a.* ✖, *mot.*) Fracht *f*, Ladung *f*. **II** *v/t* **3.** Schiff, *Am. a.* Güterwagen *etc* befrachten, beladen. **4.** Güter verfrachten. *~ car s* ✚ *Am.* Güterwagen *m*.

freight·er ['freɪtə] *s* Frachter *m*, Frachtschiff *n*; Transportflugzeug *n*.

freight train *s Am.* Güterzug *m*.

French [frentʃ] **I** *adj* **1.** französisch: ~ *beans* pl & bsd. Br. grüne Bohnen pl; ~ *fried potatoes*, F ~ *fries* pl bsd. Am. Pommes frites pl; ~ *kiss* Zungenkuß m; *take* ~ *leave* sich (auf) französisch empfehlen; ~ *letter* Br. F Pariser m (*Kondom*); ~ *window*(*s* pl) Terrassen-, Balkontür f. **II** s **2.** the ~ pl die Franzosen pl. **3.** *ling.* Französisch n: *in* ~ auf französisch. ~*man* ['~mən] s (*irr man*) Franzose m. '~*,wom·an* s (*irr woman*) Französin f.

fre·net·ic [frə'netik] *adj* (~*ally*) **1.** a) ausgelassen, b) → *frenzied* 2. **2.** → *frenzied* 3.

fren·zied ['frenzid] *adj* **1.** außer sich, rasend (*with* vor *dat*). **2.** frenetisch (*Geschrei etc*), (*Beifall a.*) rasend. **3.** wild, hektisch. '**fren·zy** s **1.** helle Aufregung. **2.** wildes od. hektisches Treiben. **3.** Wahnsinn m, Raserei f.

fre·quen·cy ['fri:kwənsi] s **1.** Häufigkeit f. **2.** ⚡, *phys.* Frequenz f. **fre·quent I** *adj* ['fri:kwənt] häufig. **II** *v/t* [fri'kwent] häufig besuchen.

fres·co ['freskəʊ] pl -**co**(**e**)**s** s Fresko(gemälde) n.

fresh [freʃ] **I** *adj* □ **1.** *allg.* frisch: ~ *butter* ungesalzene Butter; ~ *meat* Frischfleisch n; ~ *shirt* sauberes Hemd. **2.** neu: → *ground²* 1, *start* 9. **3.** grün, unerfahren: *be* ~ *to* noch keine Erfahrung haben in (*dat*). **4.** F frech (*with* zu): *don't get* ~ *with me!* werd bloß nicht pampig! **II** *adv* **5.** frisch: ~ *from the oven* ofenfrisch; ~ *from the press* druckfrisch; ~*-laid eggs* pl frisch gelegte Eier pl. '**fresh·en I** *v/t* **1.** *mst* ~ *up* erfrischen: ~ *o.s.* (*up*) sich frisch machen. **2.** ~ *s.o.* (*up*) j-m nachgießen od. -schenken. **II** *v/i* *mst* ~ *up* **3.** sich frisch machen. **4.** auffrischen (*Wind*). '**fresh·er** Br. F → *freshman*.

fresh·man ['freʃmən] s (*irr man*) Student(in) im ersten Jahr.

fresh·ness ['freʃnis] s Frische f.

fret [fret] **I** *v/t* **1.** j-m Sorgen machen. **2.** j-n ärgern, reizen. **3.** abscheuern, abnutzen; reiben od. scheuern an (*dat*): ~ *s.o.'s nerves* an j-s Nerven zerren. **II** *v/i* **4.** sich Sorgen machen (*about, at, for, over* wegen). **5.** sich ärgern (*about, at, for, over* über *acc*): ~ *and fume* vor Wut schäumen. **6.** sich abscheuern od.

abnutzen. **III** s **7.** *be in a* ~ → 4, 5. **fret·ful** ['~fʊl] *adj* □ verärgert, gereizt.

Freud·i·an ['frɔɪdɪən] *adj* Freudsch: ~ *slip* Freudsche Fehlleistung.

fri·a·ble ['fraɪəbl] *adj* bröck(e)lig, krümelig.

fric·as·see ['frikəsi:] s *gastr.* Frikassee n: ~ *of chicken* Hühnerfrikassee.

fric·tion ['frikʃn] s **1.** ☉, *phys.* Reibung f. **2.** *fig.* Reiberei(en pl) f. **fric·tion·al** ['~ʃənl] *adj* ☉, *phys.* Reibungs...

Fri·day ['fraɪdɪ] s Freitag m: *on* ~ (am) Freitag; *on* ~*s* freitags.

fridge [frɪdʒ] s *bsd. Br.* F Kühlschrank m. '~*-freez·er* s *bsd. Br.* F Kühl- u. Gefrierkombination f.

friend [frend] s **1.** Freund(in): *be* ~*s with* befreundet sein mit; *make* ~*s with* sich anfreunden mit; *make* ~*s again* sich wieder vertragen. **2.** Bekannte m, f. '**friend·li·ness** s Freundlichkeit f. '**friend·ly I** *adj* **1.** freundlich (*a. fig.* *Zimmer etc*). **2.** freundschaftlich: ~ *game* (*od. match*) (*Sport*) Freundschaftsspiel n; → *term* 5. **3.** befreundet (*with* mit). **II** s **4.** *Sport:* F Freundschaftsspiel n. '**friend·ship** s Freundschaft f.

frieze [fri:z] s △ Fries m.

frig·ate ['frɪgət] s ⚓ Fregatte f.

frige → *fridge*.

fright [fraɪt] s **1.** Schreck(en) m: *get* (*od. have*) *a* ~ e-n Schreck bekommen, erschrecken; *get off with a* ~ mit dem Schrecken davonkommen; *give s.o. a* ~ j-m e-n Schrecken einjagen, j-n erschrecken. **2.** *look a* ~ F verboten od. zum Abschießen aussehen. '**fright·en** *v/t* **1.** j-n erschrecken (*to death* zu Tode); j-m Angst einjagen: *be* ~*ed* erschrecken (*at, by, of* vor *dat*); Angst haben (*of* vor *dat*). **2.** *mst* ~ *away* (*od. off*) vertreiben, -scheuchen. **II** *v/i* **3.** ~ *easily* leicht erschrecken, schreckhaft sein. **fright·ful** ['~fʊl] *adj* □ schrecklich, fürchterlich (*beide a.* F).

frig·id ['frɪdʒɪd] *adj* □ **1.** kalt, frostig, eisig (*alle a. fig.*). **2.** *psych.* frigid. **fri'gid·i·ty** s **1.** Kälte f, Frostigkeit f (*beide a. fig.*). **2.** *psych.* Frigidität f.

frill [frɪl] s **1.** Krause f, Rüsche f. **2.** pl Verzierungen pl, Kinkerlitzchen pl.

fringe [frɪndʒ] **I** s **1.** Franse f, Besatz m. **2.** Rand m, Einfassung f, Umrandung *f.* **II** *v/t* **3.** mit Fransen besetzen. **4.** umsäumen. **~ ben·e·fits** *s pl* ✝ (Gehalts-, Lohn)Nebenleistungen *pl.* **~ group** *s sociol.* Randgruppe *f.*

frisk [frɪsk] **I** *v/i* herumtollen. **II** *v/t* F *j-n* filzen, durchsuchen. **'frisk·y** *adj* □ **1.** lebhaft, munter. **2.** ausgelassen.

frit·ter ['frɪtə] *v/t* mst **~ away** *Geld, Gelegenheit* vertun, *Zeit a.* vertrödeln, *Geld, Kräfte* vergeuden.

fri·vol·i·ty [frɪ'vɒlətɪ] *s* Frivolität *f:* a) Leichtsinnigkeit *f,* -fertigkeit *f,* Oberflächlichkeit *f,* b) leichtfertige Rede *od.* Handlung. **friv·o·lous** ['~ələs] *adj* □ **1.** frivol, leichtfertig, -sinnig. **2.** nicht ernst zu nehmen(d).

friz·zy ['frɪzɪ] *adj* gekräuselt, kraus: **~ hair** Kraushaar *n.*

fro [frəʊ] *adv:* → **to.**

frock [frɒk] *s* **1.** (Mönchs)Kutte *f.* **2.** (Kinder-, Arbeits)Kittel *m.* **3.** Kleid *n.*

frog [frɒg] *s zo.* Frosch *m:* **have a ~ in the** (*od.* **one's**) **throat** *fig.* e-n Frosch im Hals haben. **~·man** ['~mən] *s* (*irr* **man**) Froschmann *m,* ✗ *a.* Kampfschwimmer *m.*

frol·ic ['frɒlɪk] *v/i pret u. pp* **-icked** *a.* **~ about** (*od.* **around**) herumtollen, -tollen. **frol·ic·some** ['~səm] *adj* □ ausgelassen, übermütig.

from [frɒm] *prp* **1.** von, aus, von ... aus *od.* her: **he took it ~ me** er nahm es mir weg; **~ what he said** nach dem, was er sagte. **2.** von (... an), seit: **~ 2 to 4 o'clock** von 2 bis 4 Uhr; **~ day to day** von Tag zu Tag. **3.** von ... an: **~ £ 5** von 5 Pfund an (aufwärts). **4.** (weg *od.* entfernt) von. **5.** von (*Wandlung*): **~ dishwasher to millionaire** vom Tellerwäscher zum Millionär. **6.** von (*Unterscheidung*): **he does not know black ~ white** er kann Schwarz u. Weiß nicht auseinanderhalten. **7.** von (*Geben etc*): **a letter ~ his son. 8.** aus, von (*dat*), an (*dat*) (*Grund*): **he died ~ fatigue** er starb vor Erschöpfung.

front [frʌnt] **I** *s* **1.** *allg.* Voder-, Stirnseite *f,* Front *f:* **at the ~** auf der Vorderseite, vorn. **2.** △ (Vorder)Front *f,* Fassade *f* (*a. fig.* F): **maintain a ~** den Schein wahren. **3.** ✗ Front *f:* **to the ~** an die Front; **on all ~s** an allen Fronten (*a. fig.*). **4.** Vordergrund *m:* **in ~** an der *od.* die Spitze, vorn; **in ~ of** vor (*dat*); **to the**

~ nach vorn. 5. *fig.* Bereich *m,* Sektor *m:* **on the educational ~** auf dem Erziehungssektor. **6.** *fig.* Frechheit *f,* Unverschämtheit *f:* **have the ~ to do s.th.** die Stirn haben, et. zu tun. **7.** *meteor.* Front *f.* **II** *adj* **8.** Front..., Vorder...: **~ entrance** Vordereingang *m;* **~ row** vorder(st)e Reihe; **~ tooth** Vorderzahn *m.* **III** *v/t* **9.** gegenüberstehen, -liegen: **the windows ~ the street** die Fenster gehen auf die Straße (hinaus). **IV** *v/i* **10.** **~ on** (*od.* **to, toward**[**s**]) → **9.** **'front·age** *s* △ (Vorder)Front *f.* **'fron·tal** *adj* **1.** Frontal... **2.** *anat.,* ◎ Stirn...

,front'bench·er *s parl. Br.* führendes Fraktionsmitglied. **~ door** *s* Haus-, Vordertür *f:* **by** (*od.* **through**) **the ~** *fig.* direkt, ohne Umschweife; legal.

fron·tier ['frʌn,tɪə] *s* Grenze *f* (*a. fig.*). **II** *adj* Grenz...: **~ town.**

front| line *s* ✗ Front(linie) *f:* **be in the ~** an vorderster Front stehen (*a. fig.*). **~ page** *s* erste Seite, Titelseite *f* (*e-r Zeitung*): **hit the ~s** Schlagzeilen machen. **'~-page** *adj* wichtig, aktuell: **~ news.** **~ pas·sen·ger** *s mot.* Beifahrer(in). **'~-,pas·sen·ger seat** *s mot.* Beifahrersitz *m.* **~ rank** *s:* **be in the ~** *fig.* zur Spitze gehören *od.* zählen. **'~-seat pas·sen·ger** *s mot.* Beifahrer(in). **'~-wheel drive** *s* ◎ Vorderrad-, Frontantrieb *m.*

frost [frɒst] **I** *s* **1.** Frost *m.* **2.** Reif *m.* **II** *v/t* **3.** mit Reif überziehen. **4.** ◎ *Glas* mattieren: **~ed glass** Matt-, Milchglas *n.* **5.** *gastr. bsd. Am.* glasieren, mit Zuckerguß überziehen; mit (Puder)Zucker bestreuen. **'~-bite** *s* Erfrierung *f.* **'~-,bit·ten** [,~tn] *adj* erfroren.

frost·ing ['frɒstɪŋ] *s gastr. bsd. Am.* Zuckerguß *m,* Glasur *f.* **'frost·y** *adj* □ **1.** eisig, frostig (*beide a. fig.*). **2.** mit Reif bedeckt. **3.** (eis)grau: **~ hair.**

froth [frɒθ] **I** *s* Schaum *m.* **II** *v/t a.* **~ up** zum Schäumen bringen; zu Schaum schlagen. **III** *v/i* schäumen. **'froth·y** *adj* □ **1.** schaumig; schäumend. **2.** *fig.* seicht.

frown [fraʊn] **I** *v/i* die Stirn runzeln (**at** über *acc*) (*a. fig.*): **~ on** et. mißbilligen. **II** *s* Stirnrunzeln *n:* **with a ~** stirnrunzelnd.

frowst [fraʊst] *s bsd. Br.* F Mief *m:* **there's a ~ in here** hier mieft es.

'frowst·y adj bsd. Br. F miefig, vermieft.

frowz·y ['frauzɪ] adj **1.** schlampig, ungepflegt. **2.** muffig.

froze [frəʊz] pret von freeze. **'fro·zen I** pp von freeze. **II** adj Gefrier...: ~ meat; ~ food Tiefkühlkost f.

fru·gal ['fru:gl] adj □ **1.** sparsam: a) haushälterisch (of mit, in dat), b) wirtschaftlich (Auto etc). **2.** genügsam, bescheiden. **3.** einfach, bescheiden (Mahlzeit).

fruit [fru:t] s **1.** Frucht f. **2.** coll. a) Früchte pl: **bear** ~ Früchte tragen (a. fig.), b) Obst n. **3.** mst pl fig. Früchte pl. '~**cake** s englischer Kuchen. ~ **cock·tail** s Frucht-, Früchtecocktail m.

fruit·er·er ['fru:tərə] s bsd. Br. Obsthändler m. **fruit·ful** ['~fʊl] adj □ **1.** fruchtbar (a. fig.). **2.** fig. erfolgreich.

fru·i·tion [fru:'ɪʃn] s: **bring to** ~ verwirklichen; **come to** ~ sich verwirklichen; Früchte tragen.

fruit knife s (irr knife) Obstmesser n.
fruit·less ['fru:tlɪs] adj □ **1.** unfruchtbar. **2.** fig. frucht-, erfolglos.

fruit| ma·chine s Br. (Geld)Spielautomat m. ~ **sal·ad** s Obstsalat m. ~ **tree** s Obstbaum m.

fruit·y ['fru:tɪ] adj **1.** fruchtartig. **2.** fruchtig (Wein). **3.** Br. F saftig, gepfeffert (Witz etc). **4.** Am. F schmalzig: ~ **song** Schnulze f.

frump [frʌmp] s: old ~ alte Schachtel.

frus·trate [frʌ'streɪt] v/t **1.** Plan etc vereiteln, durchkreuzen; Hoffnungen zunichte machen. **2.** j-n frustrieren. **frus'tra·tion** s **1.** Vereit(e)lung f, Durchkreuzung f. **2.** Frustration f (a. psych.).

fry¹ [fraɪ] v/t u. v/i braten: **fried eggs** pl Spiegeleier pl; **fried potatoes** pl Bratkartoffeln pl.

fry² [~] s: **small** ~ ein kleiner Fisch, kleine Fische pl (Person[en]).

fry·ing pan ['fraɪŋ] s Bratpfanne f: **jump** (od. **leap**) **out of the** ~ **into the fire** fig. vom Regen in die Traufe kommen.

fuck [fʌk] v/t u. v/i ficken, vögeln: ~ **off!** verpiß dich! **'fuck·ing** adj V Scheiß..., verflucht.

fud·dled ['fʌdld] adj F **1.** benebelt. **2.** verwirrt, durcheinander.

fuel ['fjʊəl] s Brennstoff m: a) Heiz-, Brennmaterial n, b) mot. etc Treib-,

Kraftstoff m: ~ **ga(u)ge** Benzinuhr f; ~ **injection engine** Einspritzmotor m; **add** ~ **to the fire** (od. **flames**) fig. Öl ins Feuer gießen.

fug [fʌg], **'fug·gy** → frowst, frowsty.

fu·gi·tive ['fju:dʒɪtɪv] **I** s a) Flüchtige m, b) pol. etc Flüchtling m, c) Ausreißer m. **II** adj flüchtig: a) entflohen, b) fig. vergänglich.

ful·fil, Am. a. **ful·fill** [fʊl'fɪl] v/t Bedingung, Versprechen etc erfüllen, Befehl etc ausführen: ~ **o.s.** sich (selbst) verwirklichen; **be fulfilled** sich erfüllen. **ful'fil(l)·ment** s Erfüllung f, Ausführung f.

full [fʊl] **I** adj (□ → **fully**) **1.** allg. voll: ~ **of** voll von, voller; → **stomach** 1. **2.** voll, ganz: **a** ~ **hour** e-e volle od. geschlagene Stunde. **3.** voll (Gesicht), vollschlank (Figur). **4.** voll, besetzt: ~ (**up**) (voll) besetzt (Bus etc); **house** ~! thea. ausverkauft! **5.** fig. (ganz) erfüllt (**of** von): ~ **of o.s.** (ganz) von sich eingenommen. **6.** reichlich (Mahlzeit). **7.** voll, unbeschränkt: ~ **power** Vollmacht f; **have** ~ **power to do s.th.** bevollmächtigt sein, et. zu tun. **8.** voll(berechtigt): ~ **member** Vollmitglied n. **9.** a. ~ **up** F voll, satt. **II** adv **10.** völlig, ganz: **know** ~ **well that** ganz genau wissen, daß. **11.** ~ **out** mit Vollgas fahren, auf Hochtouren arbeiten. **III** s **12.** **in** ~ vollständig, ganz: **spell** (od. **write**) **in** ~ ausschreiben; **to the** ~ vollständig, bis ins letzte od. kleinste.

full| age s: **of** ~ 🏛 mündig, volljährig. '~**back** s Fußball: (Außen)Verteidiger m. ~**'blood·ed** adj **1.** vollblütig, Vollblut... (beide a. fig.). **2.** eindringlich (Argument etc). ~**'blown** adj **1.** 🏵 ganz aufgeblüht. **2.** voll entwickelt, ausgereift (Idee etc). **3.** ausgemacht (Skandal etc). ~**'fledged** bsd. Am. → **fully fledged.** ~**'grown** adj ausgewachsen. ~**'length** adj **1.** in voller Größe, lebensgroß. **2.** abendfüllend (Film) ausgewachsen (Roman). ~ **moon** s Vollmond m: **at** ~ bei Vollmond.

full·ness ['fʊlnɪs] s (♪ Klang)Fülle f: **feeling of** ~ Völlegefühl n.

'full|·page adj ganzseitig. '~**scale** adj **1.** in Originalgröße, im Maßstab 1:1. **2.** fig. großangelegt, Groß... ~ **stop** s ling. Punkt m. '~**time I** adj ganztägig,

Ganztags... **II** *adv* ganztags: **work ~**.

ful·ly ['fʊlɪ] *adv* voll, völlig, ganz: ~ *automatic* vollautomatisch; ~ *two hours* volle *od.* geschlagene zwei Stunden. ~ *fledged adj* **1.** flügge (*Vogel*). **2.** *fig.* richtig.

ful·mi·nate ['fʌlmɪneɪt] *v/i* donnern, wettern (*against, at* gegen).

ful·ness *bsd. Am.* → **fullness**.

ful·some ['fʊlsəm] *adj* □ übertrieben; überschwenglich (*Lob etc*).

fum·ble ['fʌmbl] **I** *v/i a.* ~ *about* (*od. around*) herumtappen, -tasten; (herum)fummeln (*at* an *dat*); ungeschickt umgehen (*with* mit); tastend suchen (*for, after* nach): ~ *in one's pockets* in s-n Taschen (herum)wühlen; ~ *for words* nach Worten suchen. **II** *v/t* verpatzen. **'fum·bler** *s* Patzer(in).

fume [fjuːm] **I** *s* **1.** *oft pl* Dampf *m*, Rauch *m*. **II** *v/i* **2.** dampfen, rauchen. **3.** *fig.* wütend *od.* aufgebracht sein (*at* über *acc*).

fu·mi·gate ['fjuːmɪgeɪt] *v/t* ausräuchern.

fun [fʌn] *s* Spaß *m*: **for ~** aus *od.* zum Spaß; **in ~** im *od.* zum Scherz; **make ~ of** sich lustig machen über (*acc*); → **poke** 4.

func·tion ['fʌŋkʃn] **I** *s* **1.** *allg.* Funktion *f*: **out of ~** ⊙ außer Betrieb. **II** *v/i* **2.** ~ *as* tätig sein *od.* fungieren als; dienen als (*Sache*). **3.** ⊙ *etc* funktionieren. **'func·tion·al** *adj* □ **1.** *allg.* funktionell, Funktions...: ~ *disorder* ⚕ Funktionsstörung *f*. **2.** zweckbetont, -mäßig, praktisch. **'func·tion·ar·y** *s bsd. pol.* Funktionär *m*.

fund [fʌnd] *s* **1.** ⚕ Kapital *n*, Vermögen *n*; Fonds *m*. **2.** *pl* ⚕ (Geld)Mittel *pl*: *no ~s* (*Scheck*) keine Deckung; *be in* (*out of*) *~s* (nicht) bei Kasse sein, zahlungs(un)fähig sein. **3.** *fig.* Vorrat *m* (*of* an *dat*).

fun·da·men·tal [ˌfʌndə'mentl] **I** *adj* (□ → *fundamentally*) **1.** grundlegend, wesentlich, fundamental (*to* für). **2.** grundsätzlich, elementar. **3.** Grund..., Fundamental...: ~ *research* Grundlagenforschung *f*. **II** *s* **4.** Grundlage *f*, -prinzip *n*, -begriff *m*. **fun·da'men·tal·ly** *adv* im Grunde, im wesentlichen.

fu·ner·al ['fjuːnərəl] **I** *s* Begräbnis *n*, Beerdigung *f*: *that's your ~* F das ist dein Problem. **II** *adj* Begräbnis...: ~ *march*

♪ Trauermarsch *m*; ~ *parlo(u)r* Leichenhalle *f*; ~ *service* Trauergottesdienst *m*.

'fun·fair *s bsd. Br.* Vergnügungspark *m*, Rummelplatz *m*.

fun·gus ['fʌŋɡəs] *pl* **-gi** ['~ɡaɪ], **-gus·es** *s* ♣ Pilz *m*, Schwamm *m*.

fu·nic·u·lar (**rail·way**) [fjuˈnɪkjʊlə] *s* (Draht)Seilbahn *f*.

funk [fʌŋk] F **I** *s* Schiß *m*, Bammel *m*: *be in a blue ~* of e-n mächtigen Schiß *od.* Bammel haben vor (*dat*). **II** *v/t* kneifen *od.* sich drücken vor (*dat*).

fun·nel ['fʌnl] *s* **1.** Trichter *m*. **2.** ♨, 🚂 Schornstein *m*.

fun·nies ['fʌnɪz] *s pl bsd. Am.* F *Zeitung:* Comics *pl*; Comic-Teil *m*.

fun·ny ['fʌnɪ] *adj* □ komisch: a) spaßig, lustig, b) sonderbar, merkwürdig. ~ *bone s anat.* Musikantenknochen *m*.

fur [fɜː] *s* **1.** Pelz *m*, Fell *n*: *make the ~ fly fig.* Stunk machen (*Person*), (*a. Sache*) für helle Aufregung sorgen. **2.** a) Pelzfutter *n*, -besatz *m*: ~ *collar* Pelzkragen *m*, b) a. ~ *coat* Pelzmantel *m*.

fur·bish ['fɜːbɪʃ] **1.** polieren, blank reiben. **2.** *oft* ~ *up* herrichten, *Gebäude etc a.* renovieren; *fig.* Kenntnisse auffrischen.

fu·ri·ous ['fjʊərɪəs] *adj* □ **1.** wütend, zornig (*with* s.o. auf, über *acc*; *at* s.th. über *acc*). **2.** wild, heftig (*Kampf etc*).

furl [fɜːl] *v/t* Fahne, Transparent etc auf-, einrollen, Schirm zs.-rollen.

fur·nace ['fɜːnɪs] *s* ⊙ (Schmelz-, Hoch-) Ofen *m*.

fur·nish ['fɜːnɪʃ] *v/t* **1.** versorgen, ausrüsten, -statten (*with* mit): ~ *s.o. with s.th.* a. j-n mit et. beliefern. **2.** *Informationen etc* liefern: ~ *proof* den Beweis liefern *od.* erbringen. **3.** *Wohnung etc* einrichten, möblieren: *~ed room* möbliertes Zimmer. **'fur·nish·ings** *s pl* Einrichtung *f*, Mobiliar *n*.

fur·ni·ture ['fɜːnɪtʃə] *s* Möbel *pl*: *piece of* ~ Möbelstück *n*; → **stick**¹ 4.

furred [fɜːd] *adj* **1.** Pelz... **2.** mit Pelz besetzt. **3.** ⚕ belegt (*Zunge*).

fur·row ['fʌrəʊ] **I** *s* **1.** ✓ (Acker)Furche *f*. **2.** Runzel *f*, Furche *f*. **II** *v/t* **3.** *Land* furchen; *Wasser* durchfurchen. **4.** *Gesicht, Stirn* furchen, runzeln.

fur·ther ['fɜːðə] **I** *adv* **1.** *comp von* **far**. **2.** *fig.* mehr, weiter. **3.** *fig.* ferner, weiterhin. **4.** → *farther* 4. **II** *adj* **5.** *fig.* weiter: ~ *education* Br. Fort-, Weiterbildung *f;* *anything* ~? (sonst) noch etwas? **6.** → *farther* 2. **III** *v/t* **7.** fördern, unterstützen. **,fur·ther'more** → *further* 3. **'further·most** ['ˌɔɪst] **I** *adj* **1.** *sup von* *far*. **2.** *fig.* weitest, meist: *at (the)* ~ höchstens. **3.** → *farthest* 2. **II** *adv* **4.** *fig.* am weitesten, am meisten. **5.** → *farthest* 4.

fur·tive ['fɜːtɪv] *adj* □ heimlich, (*Blick a.*) verstohlen.

fu·ry ['fjʊərɪ] *s* Wut *f*, Zorn *m: for ~* vor lauter Wut; *fly into a* ~ wütend *od.* zornig werden.

fuse [fjuːz] **I** *s* **1.** Zünder *m.* **2.** ⚡ Sicherung *f:* ~ *box* Sicherungskasten *m.* **II** *v/t* **3.** *phys.,* ⚙ schmelzen. **4.** *fig.* verschmelzen, ✝, *pol. a.* fusionieren. **III** *v/i* **5.** ⚙ schmelzen. **6.** *fig.* verschmelzen, ✝, *pol. a.* fusionieren.

fu·se·lage ['fjuːzəlɑːʒ] *s* (Flugzeug-) Rumpf *m.*

fu·sion ['fjuːʒn] *s* **1.** *phys.,* ⚙ Schmelzen *n.* **2.** *biol., opt., phys.* Fusion *f:* ~ *bomb* Wasserstoffbombe *f.* **3.** *fig.* Verschmelzung *f,* ✝, *pol. a.* Fusion *f.*

fuss [fʌs] **I** *s* **1.** (unnötige) Aufregung:

get into a ~ → 3. **2.** Wirbel *m,* Theater *n: make a* ~ → 4. **II** *v/i* **3.** sich (unnötig) aufregen (*about* über *acc*): *don't* ~! nur keine Aufregung. **4.** viel Wirbel machen (*about, over* um). **5.** ~ *about* (*od.* *around*) herumfuhrwerken. '~**,budg·et** *s Am.* F. '~**·pot** *s* F Kleinlichkeitskrämer *m.* **fuss·y** ['fʌsɪ] *adj* □ **1.** (unnötig) aufgeregt. **2.** kleinlich, pedantisch. **3.** heikel, wählerisch (*about* in *dat*).

fust·y ['fʌstɪ] *adj* □ **1.** mod(e)rig, muffig. **2.** *fig.* verstaubt, -altet; rückständig.

fu·tile ['fjuːtaɪl] *adj* □ **1.** nutzlos, vergeblich. **2.** unbedeutend, geringfügig. **fu·til·i·ty** [~'tɪlətɪ] *s* **1.** Nutzlosigkeit *f.* **2.** Geringfügigkeit *f.*

fu·ture ['fjuːtʃə] **I** *s* **1.** Zukunft *f: in* ~ in Zukunft. **2.** *ling.* Futur *n,* Zukunft *f.* **II** *adj* **3.** (zu)künftig, Zukunfts... **4.** *ling.* futurisch: ~ *perfect* Futurum *n* exaktum, zweites Futur; ~ *tense* → 2.

fuze *bsd. Am.* → *fuse.*

fuzz¹ [fʌz] *s* feiner Flaum.

fuzz² [~] *s sl.* Bulle *m* (*Polizist*): *the* ~ *coll.* die Bullen.

fuzz·y ['fʌzɪ] *adj* □ **1.** flaumig. **2.** kraus, wuschelig. **3.** unscharf, verschwommen.

G

gab [gæb] *s* F Gequassel *n,* Gequatsche *n: have the gift of the* ~ (*Am. of* ~) ein flottes Mundwerk haben.

gab·ble ['gæbl] **I** *v/i* **1.** *a.* ~ *away* brabbeln. **2.** schnattern (*Gänse*). **II** *v/t* **3.** *Gebet etc* herunterleiern, -rasseln. **4.** *et.* brabbeln. **III** *s* **5.** Gebrabbel *n.* **6.** Geschnatter *n.*

gab·er·dine [ˌgæbə'diːn] *s* Gabardine *m.*

ga·ble ['geɪbl] *s* Giebel *m:* ~ *window* Giebelfenster *n.* '**ga·bled** *adj* Giebel...

gad [gæd] *v/i:* ~ *about* (*od.* *around*) (viel) unterwegs sein (in *dat*); (viel) herumkommen (in *dat*); sich herumtreiben (in *dat*).

gadg·et ['gædʒɪt] *s* ⚙ F Apparat *m,* Gerät *n; oft contp.* technische Spielerei.

Gael·ic ['geɪlɪk] **I** *s ling.* Gälisch *n.* **II** *adj* gälisch: ~ *coffee* Irish coffee *m.*

gaff [gæf] *s sl.: blow the* ~ alles verraten, plaudern; *blow the* ~ *on s.th.* et. ausplaudern.

gaffe [gæf] *s* Fauxpas *m, bsd.* taktlose Bemerkung.

gag [gæg] **I** *v/t* **1.** knebeln (*a. fig.*). **2.** *fig.* mundtot machen. **II** *s* **3.** Knebel *m* (*a. fig.*). **4.** F Gag *m.*

ga·ga ['gɑːgɑː] *adj sl.* verkalkt, -trottelt; plemplem.

gage *Am.* → *gauge.*

gag·gle ['gægl] **I** *v/i* **1.** schnattern (*Gänse*) (*a. fig.*). **II** *s* **2.** Geschnatter *n* (*a. fig.*). **3.** Gänseherde *f;* F schnatternde Schar.

gai·e·ty ['geɪətɪ] *s* **1.** Fröhlichkeit *f.* **2.** *oft pl* Vergnügen *f.*

gain [geɪn] **I** *v/t* **1.** Zeit, j-s Vertrauen etc gewinnen: → *ground²* 2, *upper* 1. **2.** erreichen, erwerben, *Erfahrungen* sammeln: → *advantage*. **3.** *j-m et.* einbringen, -tragen. **4.** zunehmen an (*dat*): ~ *speed* schneller werden; *he ~ed 10 pounds* er nahm 10 Pfund zu; → *weight* 1. **5.** vorgehen (um) (*Uhr*). **II** *v/i* **6.** Einfluß *od.* Boden gewinnen. **7.** zunehmen (*in* an *dat*). **8.** vorgehen (*by two minutes* zwei Minuten) (*Uhr*). **III** *s* **9.** Gewinn (*to* für) (*a. ✝*). **10.** Zunahme *f* (*in* an *dat*): ~ *in weight* Gewichtszunahme. **gain·ful** ['geɪnfʊl] *adj* □ einträglich, gewinnbringend: ~ *employment* Erwerbstätigkeit *f*; *~ly employed* erwerbstätig. **'gain·ings** *s pl* Gewinn(e *pl*) *m.*

gait [geɪt] *s* **1.** Gang(art *f*) *m.* **2.** Gangart *f* (*des Pferdes*).

gal [gæl] *s* F Mädchen *n.*

ga·la ['gɑːlə] **I** *adj* **1.** festlich, Gala... **II** *s* **2.** Festlichkeit *f.* **3.** Gala(veranstaltung) *f.*

ga·lac·tic [gə'læktɪk] *adj ast.* Milchstraßen..., galaktisch.

gal·ax·y ['gæləksɪ] *s ast.* Milchstraße *f.*

gale [geɪl] *s* Sturm *m* (*a. fig.* F): *a ~ of laughter* e-e Lachsalve, stürmisches Gelächter.

gall¹ [gɔːl] **I** *s* **1.** wund geriebene *od.* gescheuerte Stelle. **II** *v/t* **2.** wund reiben *od.* scheuern. **3.** *fig.* (ver)ärgern.

gall² [~] *s* **1.** Bitterkeit *f*, Erbitterung *f.* **2.** F Frechheit *f.*

gal·lant ['gælənt] *adj* □ **1.** tapfer. **2.** prächtig, stattlich. **3.** galant. **'gal·lant·ry** *s* **1.** Tapferkeit *f.* **2.** Galanterie *f.*

gall blad·der *s anat.* Gallenblase *f.*

gal·ler·y ['gælərɪ] *s* **1.** △ Galerie *f*, Empore *f* (*in Kirchen*). **2.** *thea.* Galerie *f* (*a. Publikum*): *play to the ~* für die Galerie spielen (*a. weitS.*). **3.** (*Gemälde- etc-*) Galerie *f.*

gal·ley ['gælɪ] *s* **1.** ♣ *hist.* Galeere *f.* **2.** ♣ Kombüse *f.*

Gal·li·cism ['gælɪsɪzəm] *s ling.* Gallizismus *m.*

gal·lon ['gælən] *s* Gallone *f* (*GB: 4,55 l, USA: 3,79 l*).

gal·lop ['gæləp] **I** *v/i* galoppieren (*a. Pferd*), (im) Galopp reiten: *~ing infla-*

tion ✝ galoppierende Inflation. **II** *s* Galopp *m*: *at a ~* im Galopp.

gal·lows ['gæləʊz] *pl* **-lows·es, -lows** *s* Galgen *m.* ~ **bird** *s* F Galgenvogel *m.* ~ **hu·mo(u)r** *s* F Galgenhumor *m.*

'gall·stone *s* ⚕ Gallenstein *m.*

Gal·lup poll ['gæləp] *s* Meinungsumfrage *f.*

ga·lore [gə'lɔː] *adv* F in rauhen Mengen: *money ~* Geld wie Heu.

ga·lumph [gə'lʌmf] *v/i* F stampfen, stapfen.

gal·va·nize ['gælvənaɪz] *v/t* **1.** ⚙ galvanisieren. **2.** *fig.* elektrisieren.

gam·ble ['gæmbl] **I** *v/i* (um Geld) spielen: ~ *with s.th.* mit et. spielen, et. aufs Spiel setzen. **II** *v/t mst* ~ *away* verspielen (*a. fig.*). **III** *s* Hasardspiel *n* (*a. fig.*), Glücksspiel *n.* **'gam·bler** *s* **1.** (Glücks)Spieler *m.* **2.** *fig.* Hasardeur *m.* **'gam·bling** *adj* Spiel...: ~ *casino;* ~ *den* Spielhölle *f.*

gam·bol ['gæmbl] **I** *v/i pret u. pp* **-boled,** *bsd.Br.* **-bolled** (herum)tanzen, (-)hüpfen, Freuden- *od.* Luftsprünge machen. **II** *s* Freuden-, Luftsprung *m.*

game [geɪm] **I** *s* **1.** (Karten-, Ball- etc-) Spiel *n*: *play the ~* sich an die Spielregeln halten (*a. fig.*); → *chance* 1, *skill* 1. **2.** (*einzelnes*) *Spiel*: *a ~ of chess* e-e Partie Schach. **3.** *fig.* Spiel *n*, Plan *m*: *the ~ is up* das Spiel ist aus; *play a double ~* ein doppeltes Spiel treiben; *beat s.o. at his own ~* j-n mit s-n eigenen Waffen schlagen. **4.** F Branche *f*: *be in the advertising ~* in Werbung machen. **5.** *pl ped.* Sport *m.* **6.** Wild(bret) *n.* **II** *adj* □ **7.** mutig. **8.** a) aufgelegt (*for* zu): *be ~ to do s.th.* dazu aufgelegt sein, et. zu tun, b) bereit (*for* zu; *to do* zu tun). '*~keep·er* *s bsd. Br.* Wildhüter *m.* ~ *park s* Wildpark *m.* '*~pre·serve* *s* Wildgehege *n.*

gam·ma rays ['gæmə] *s pl phys.* Gammastrahlen *pl.*

gam·mon ['gæmən] *s* schwachgepökelter *od.* -geräucherter Schinken.

gamp [gæmp] *s Br.* F (*bsd.* großer) Regenschirm.

gam·ut ['gæmət] *s* **1.** ♪ Tonleiter *f.* **2.** *fig.* Skala *f.*

gan·der ['gændə] *s* Gänserich *m.*

gang [gæŋ] **I** *s* **1.** (Arbeiter)Kolonne *f*, (-)Trupp *m.* **2.** Gang *f*, Bande *f.* **3.** Cli-

que *f* (*a. contp.*). **4.** *contp.* Horde *f.* **II** *v/i*
5. *mst* **~ up** sich zs.-tun, *bsd. contp.* sich
zs.-rotten: **~ up against** (*od.* **on**) sich
verbünden *od.* verschwören gegen.

gan·grene ['gæŋgri:n] *s* ✖ Brand *m*.

gang·ster ['gæŋstə] *s* Gangster *m*, Verbrecher *m*.

'gang·way *s* **1.** Durchgang *m*, Passage *f.*
2. ⚓, ✈ Gangway *f.* **3.** *Br. thea. etc*
(Zwischen)Gang *m*.

gaol [dʒeɪl], *etc bsd. Br.* → **jail**, *etc*.

gap [gæp] *s* **1.** Lücke *f* (*a. fig.*): **fill in a ~**
in one's education e-e Bildungslücke
schließen. **2.** *fig.* Kluft *f*.

gape [geɪp] **I** *v/i* **1.** den Mund aufreißen
(*vor Staunen etc*). **2.** (mit offenem
Mund) gaffen *od.* glotzen: **~ at s.o.** j-n
angaffen *od.* anglotzen. **II** *s* **3.** Gaffen
n, Glotzen *n*. **4.** gähnender Abgrund.

'gap·ing *adj* □ **1.** gaffend, glotzend. **2.**
klaffend (*Wunde*), gähnend (*Abgrund*).

ga·rage ['gærɑ:ʒ] **I** *s* **1.** Garage *f.* **2.**
Reparaturwerkstätte *f* (u. Tankstelle
f). **II** *v/t* **3.** Auto in die Garage fahren.

gar·bage ['gɑ:bɪdʒ] *s* **1.** *bsd. Am.* Abfall
m, Müll *m*: **~ can** Abfall-, Mülleimer
m; Abfall-, Mülltonne *f*; **~ chute** Müllschlucker *m*; **~ collection** Müllabfuhr
f; **~ collector** (*od. man*) Müllmann *m*; **~**
truck Müllwagen *m*. **2.** *fig.* Schund *m*;
Unfug *m*.

gar·ble ['gɑ:bl] *v/t* Text etc durcheinanderbringen; (*durch Auslassungen etc*)
verfälschen.

gar·den ['gɑ:dn] **I** *s* **1.** Garten *m*. **2.** *oft pl*
Garten(anlagen *pl*) *m*: → **botanical**,
zoological. II *adj* **3.** Garten...: **~ center**
(*bsd. Br.* **centre**) Gartencenter *n*; **~ city**
Br. Gartenstadt *f*; **~ party** Gartenfest *n*,
-party *f*; **lead s.o. up the ~ path** j-n
hinters Licht führen; **~ suburb** *Br.* Gartenvorstadt *f*. **III** *v/i* **4.** im Garten arbeiten. **'gar·den·er** *s* Gärtner(in).
'gar·den·ing *s* Gartenarbeit *f*.

gar·gan·tu·an [gɑ:ˈgæntjʊən] *adj* riesig,
gewaltig.

gar·gle ['gɑ:gl] **I** *v/t* **1.** gurgeln mit. **II** *v/i*
2. gurgeln (*with* mit). **III** *s* **3.** Gurgeln *n*:
have a ~ gurgeln. **4.** Gurgelmittel *n*.

gar·ish ['geərɪʃ] *adj* □ grell (*Licht*), (*Farben a.*) schreiend, (*Parfüm*) aufdringlich.

gar·land ['gɑ:lənd] **I** *s* Girlande *f*, (*a.*

Sieges)Kranz *m*. **II** *v/t* bekränzen.

gar·lic ['gɑ:lɪk] *s* ♣ Knoblauch *m*.

gar·ment ['gɑ:mənt] *s* Kleidungsstück *n*,
pl a. Kleidung *f*.

gar·net ['gɑ:nɪt] *s min.* Granat *m*.

gar·nish ['gɑ:nɪʃ] **I** *v/t* **1.** (**with** mit)
schmücken, verzieren; *fig.* ausschmücken. **2.** *gastr.* garnieren (**with** mit). **II** *s*
3. Verzierung *f*; *fig.* Ausschmückung *f.*
4. *gastr.* Garnierung *f*.

gar·ret ['gærət] *s* Dachkammer *f*.

gar·ri·son ['gærɪsn] ✖ **I** *s* **1.** Garnison *f*:
~ town Garnison(s)stadt *f*. **II** *v/t* **2.** Ort
mit e-r Garnison belegen. **3.** *Truppen in*
Garnison legen.

gar·ru·li·ty [gæˈruːlətɪ] *s* Geschwätzigkeit *f*. **gar·ru·lous** ['gærələs] *adj* □ geschwätzig.

gar·ter ['gɑ:tə] *s* Strumpfband *n*; Sokkenhalter *m*; *Am.* Strumpfhalter *m*,
Straps *m*.

gas [gæs] **I** *pl* **-(s)es 1.** Gas *n*. **2.** *Am.*
Benzin *n*, Sprit *m*, b) **step on the ~** Gas
geben, auf die Tube drücken (*beide a.*
fig.). **3.** ✿ Gewäsch *n*, Blech *n*. **II** *v/t* **3.**
vergasen: **be ~sed** *a.* e-e Gasvergiftung
erleiden. **II** *v/i* **5.** ✿ faseln. **'~bag** *s*
Quatscher(in). **~ cham·ber** *s* Gaskammer *f*. **~ cook·er** *s* Gasherd *m*.

gas·e·ous ['gæsjəs] *adj* **1.** gasförmig. **2.**
Gas...

gas ex·plo·sion *s* Gasexplosion *f*.

gash [gæʃ] **I** *s* klaffende Wunde, tiefer
Riß *od.* Schnitt. **II** *v/t* j-m e-e klaffende
Wunde beibringen, *Haut* aufreißen,
-schlitzen.

gas heat·ing *s* Gasheizung *f*.

gas·ket ['gæskɪt] *s* ⚙ Dichtung(smanschette) *f*.

'gas·man *s* (*irr man*) Gasmann *m*, -ableser *m*. **~ mask** *s* Gasmaske *f*. **~ me·ter**
s Gasuhr *f*, -zähler *m*.

gas·o·lene, **gas·o·line** ['gæsəʊli:n] *s*
Am. Benzin *n*: **~ attendant** Tankwart
m; **~ bomb** Molotowcocktail *m*; **~ sta·**
tion Tankstelle *f*.

gasp [gɑ:sp] **I** *v/i* **1.** keuchen, schwer
atmen: **~ for breath** nach Luft schnappen. **2.** den Atem anhalten (**with**, **in** *vor*
dat): **make s.o. ~** j-m den Atem nehmen *od.* verschlagen. **II** *v/t* **3.** *mst* **~ out**
Worte keuchen, (keuchend) hervorstoßen. **III** *s* **4.** Keuchen *n*, schweres Atmen: **be at one's last ~** in den letzten

Zügen liegen; **to the last** ~ bis zum letzten Atemzug.

gas| sta·tion s Am. F Tankstelle f. ~ **stove** s Gasofen m, -herd m.

gas·sy ['gæsɪ] adj **1.** gasartig. **2.** kohlensäurehaltig. **3.** F geschwätzig.

gas·tric ['gæstrɪk] adj ♠, physiol. Magen...: ~ **acid** Magensäure f; ~ **ulcer** Magengeschwür n. **gas·tri·tis** [gæ-'straɪtɪs] ♠ Gastritis f, Magenschleimhautentzündung f.

gas·tro·nom·ic [,gæstrə'nɒmɪk] adj (~ally) gastronomisch, feinschmeckerisch. **gas·tron·o·my** [~'strɒnəmɪ] s **1.** Gastronomie f (feine Kochkunst). **2.** fig. Küche f: **the Italian** ~.

'**gas·works** s pl (mst sg konstruiert) Gaswerk n.

gate [geɪt] s **1.** Tor n (a. Skisport), Pforte f. **2.** fig. Tor n, Zugang m (**to** zu). **3.** ♠ Sperre f, Schranke f; ✈ Flugsteig m. **4.** Sport: a) Zuschauer(zahl f) pl, b) (Gesamt)Einnahmen pl. '~**crash** v/i u. v/t F uneingeladen kommen (zu); sich ohne zu bezahlen hineinschmuggeln (in acc). '~**house** s Pförtnerhaus n. '~**keep·er** s **1.** Pförtner m. **2.** Bahn-, Schrankenwärter m. '~**leg(ged) ta·ble** s Klapptisch m. '~**man** ['~mən] s (irr **man**) bsd. Am. → **gatekeeper.** '~**mon·ey** → **gate** 4 b. '~**post** s Torpfosten m: → **between** 2. '~**way** s **1.** Torweg m, Einfahrt f. **2.** → **gate** 2.

gath·er ['gæðə] I v/t **1.** Reichtümer, Erfahrungen etc sammeln, Informationen einholen, -ziehen. **2.** Personen versammeln. **3.** erwerben, gewinnen: ~ **dust** verstauben; ~ **speed** schneller werden. **4.** a. ~ **up** auflesen, (vom Boden) aufheben. **5.** Blumen etc pflücken. **6.** fig. folgern, schließen (**from** aus). II v/i **7.** sich (ver)sammeln od. scharen (**round** s.o. um j-n). **8.** sich (an)sammeln. '**gath·er·ing** s (Menschen)Ansammlung f; Versammlung f, Zs.-kunft f.

gauche [gəʊʃ] adj **1.** linkisch. **2.** taktlos.

gaud·y ['gɔːdɪ] adj ☐ auffällig bunt, (Farben) grell, schreiend, (Einrichtung etc) protzig.

gauge [geɪdʒ] I v/t **1.** (ab-, aus)messen. **2.** ⊙ eichen. **3.** fig. (ab)schätzen, beurteilen. II s **4.** ⊙ Eichmaß n. **5.** fig. Maßstab m, Norm f (of für). **6.** ⊙ Meß-

gerät n, Lehre f. **7.** ⊙ Stärke f, Dicke f (bsd. von Blech od. Draht). **8.** 🚂 Spur(weite) f.

gaunt [gɔːnt] adj ☐ hager; ausgemergelt, -gezehrt.

gaunt·let¹ [~] s fig. Fehdehandschuh m: **fling** (od. **throw**) **down the** ~ (**to** s.o.) (j-m) den Fehdehandschuh hinwerfen, (j-n) herausfordern; **pick** (od. **take**) **up the** ~ den Fehdehandschuh aufnehmen, die Herausforderung annehmen.

gaunt·let² [~]: **run the** ~ Spießruten laufen (a. fig.).

gauze [gɔːz] s Gaze f, ♠ a. (Verband[s])Mull m: ~ **bandage** Mullbinde f. '**gauz·y** adj ☐ gazeartig, hauchdünn.

gave [geɪv] pret von **give.**

gav·el ['gævl] s Hammer m (e-s Auktionators, Vorsitzenden etc).

gawk [gɔːk] v/i glotzen: ~ **at** glotzen auf (acc), anglotzen.

gay [geɪ] I adj ☐ **1.** lustig, fröhlich. **2.** bunt, (farben)prächtig; fröhlich, lebhaft (Farben). **3.** lebenslustig. **4.** F schwul (homosexuell), Schwulen... II s **5.** F Schwule m.

gaze [geɪz] I v/i starren: ~ **at** starren auf (acc), anstarren. II s starrer Blick, Starren n.

ga·zette [gə'zet] s Br. Amtsblatt n, Staatsanzeiger m.

gear [gɪə] I s **1.** mot. a) Gang m: **change** (bsd. Am. **shift**) ~(**s**) schalten; **change** (bsd. Am. **shift**) **into second** ~ den zweiten Gang einlegen, in den zweiten Gang schalten, b) pl Getriebe n. **2.** Vorrichtung f, Gerät n. **3.** F Kleidung f, Aufzug m. II v/t **4.** ~ **up** (**down**) fig. steigern (drosseln). **5.** fig. (**to, for**) anpassen (dat od. an acc), abstimmen (auf acc). '~**box** s mot. Getriebe n. ~ **change** s mot. Br. (Gang)Schaltung f. ~ **le·ver** s mot. Br. Schalthebel m. '~**shift** s mot. Am. **1.** (Gang)Schaltung f. **2.** a. ~ **lever** Schalthebel m. '~**wheel** s ⊙ Getriebe-, Zahnrad n.

gee [dʒiː] int Am. F na so was!, Mann!

geese [giːs] pl von **goose.**

Gei·ger count·er ['gaɪgə] s phys. Geigerzähler m.

gei·sha ['geɪʃə] pl **-sha(s)** s Geisha f.

gel·a·tin ['dʒelətɪn], **gel·a·tine** [~'tiːn] s **1.** Gelatine f. **2.** Gallerte f. **gel·a·ti-**

nous [dʒə'lætinəs] *adj* □ gallertartig.

geld [geld] *v/t (a. irr)* Tier, *bsd.* Hengst kastrieren, verschneiden. **'geld·ing** *s* kastriertes Tier, *bsd.* Wallach *m.*

gelt [gelt] *pret u. pp von* **geld.**

gem [dʒem] *s* **1.** Edelstein *m.* **2.** *fig.* Perle *f,* Juwel *n (beide a. Person),* Prachtstück *n.*

Gem·i·ni ['dʒemɪnaɪ] *s pl (mst sg konstruiert) ast.* Zwillinge *pl.*

gen·der ['dʒendə] *s ling.* Genus *n,* Geschlecht *n:* **what ~ is ...?** welches Genus hat ...? '~**,bend·er** *s sl.* Transvestit *m.*

gene [dʒiːn] *s biol.* Gen *n,* Erbfaktor *m.*

gen·e·a·log·i·cal [,dʒiːnjə'lɒdʒɪkl] *adj* □ genealogisch: **~ tree** Stammbaum *m.*

gen·e·al·o·gy [,dʒiːnɪ'ælədʒɪ] *s* Genealogie *f.*

gen·e·ra ['dʒenərə] *pl von* **genus.**

gen·er·al ['dʒenərəl] **I** *adj* (□ → **generally**) **1.** allgemein (gebräuchlich *od.* verbreitet), üblich, gängig: **as a ~ rule** meistens, üblicherweise. **2.** allgemein, generell: **~ education** *(od. knowledge)* Allgemeinbildung *f;* **the ~ public** die breite Öffentlichkeit; **~ term** Allgemeinbegriff *m.* **3.** allgemein *(nicht spezialisiert):* **the ~ reader** der Durchschnittsleser. **4.** allgemein (gehalten); ungefähr: **a ~ idea** e-e ungefähre Vorstellung. **5.** Haupt..., General...: **~ manager** Generaldirektor *m.* **II** *s* **6.** ✕ General *m.* **7.** *in ~* im allgemeinen, im großen u. ganzen. **~ e·lec·tion** *s* Parlamentswahlen *pl.*

gen·er·al·i·ty [,dʒenə'rælətɪ] *s* **1.** *mst pl* allgemeine Redensart, Gemeinplatz *m.* **2.** Allgemeingültigkeit *f.*

gen·er·al·ize ['dʒenərəlaɪz] *v/t* verallgemeinern.

gen·er·al·ly ['dʒenərəlɪ] *adv a.* **~ speaking** im allgemeinen, allgemein.

gen·er·al| prac·ti·tion·er *s* praktischer Arzt. **~ staff** *s* ✕ Generalstab *m.* **~ strike** *s* ✝ Generalstreik *m.*

gen·er·ate ['dʒenəreɪt] *v/t* **1.** Elektrizität *etc* erzeugen. **2.** *biol.* zeugen. **3.** *fig.* bewirken, erzeugen, verursachen. **,gen·er'a·tion** *s* **1.** Generation *f (a.* ⊚ *etc).* **2.** Erzeugung *f.* **3.** *biol.* Zeugung *f,* Fortpflanzung *f.* **,gen·er'a·tion·al** [~ʃənl] *adj* Generations...: **~ conflict** *(od. clash)* Generationskonflikt *m.*

gen·er·a·tive ['~rətɪv] *adj biol.* Zeu-

gungs..., Fortpflanzungs...: **~ power** Zeugungskraft *f.* **gen·er·a·tor** ['~reɪtə] *s* ⚡ Generator *m.*

ge·ner·ic [dʒɪ'nerɪk] *adj:* **~ term** *(od. name) biol.* Gattungsname *m; allg.* Oberbegriff *m.*

gen·er·os·i·ty [,dʒenə'rɒsətɪ] *s* Großzügigkeit *f,* Freigebigkeit *f.* **'gen·er·ous** *adj* □ **1.** großzügig, freigebig. **2.** reichlich, üppig.

gen·e·sis ['dʒenəsɪs] *pl* **-e·ses** [~siːz] *s* Entstehung *f.*

ge·net·ic [dʒɪ'netɪk] **I** *adj* (**~ally**) genetisch: **~ engineering** Gentechnologie *f;* **~ factor** Erbfaktor *m.* **II** *s pl (sg konstruiert)* Genetik *f,* Vererbungslehre *f.*

ge·ni·al ['dʒiːnjəl] *adj* □ freundlich *(a. fig. Klima etc).* **ge·ni·al·i·ty** [,~nɪ'ælətɪ] *s* Freundlichkeit *f.*

gen·i·tals ['dʒenɪtlz] *s pl* Genitalien *pl,* Geschlechtsteile *pl.*

gen·i·tive ['dʒenɪtɪv] *s a.* **~ case** *ling.* Genitiv *m,* zweiter Fall.

gen·ius ['dʒiːnjəs] *s* **1.** Genie *n:* a) genialer Mensch, Genialität *f.* **2.** (natürliche) Begabung: **have a ~ for languages** sprachbegabt sein.

gen·o·cide ['dʒenəʊsaɪd] *s* Völkermord *m.*

genre ['ʒɑ̃ːŋrə] *s* Genre *n,* Gattung *f.* **~ paint·ing** *s* Genremalerei *f.*

gent [dʒent] *s* **1.** F *od. humor.* für **gentleman: ~'s hairdresser** Herrenfriseur *m.* **2.** *pl (sg konstruiert) Br.* F Herrenklo *n.*

gen·teel [dʒen'tiːl] *adj* □ **1.** vornehm. **2.** vornehm tuend, affektiert.

gen·tle ['dʒentl] *adj* □ **1.** freundlich, liebenswürdig. **2.** sanft, zart: **~ hint** zarter Wink; → **sex** 1. '~**·folk(s)** *s pl* vornehme *od.* feine Leute *pl.*

gen·tle·man ['dʒentlmən] *s (irr man)* **1.** Gentleman *m:* **~'s** *(od. gentlemen's)* **agreement** Gentleman's *(od.* Gentlemen's) Agreement *n.* **2.** Herr *m:* **gentlemen** *(Anrede)* m-e Herren; *(in Briefen)* Sehr geehrte Herren. '**gen·tleman-like,** '**gen·tle·man·ly** *adj* gentlemanlike.

gen·tle·ness ['dʒentlnɪs] *s* **1.** Freundlichkeit *f,* Liebenswürdigkeit *f.* **2.** Sanftheit *f,* Zartheit *f.*

gen·try ['dʒentrɪ] *s* **1.** Oberschicht *f.* **2.** *Br.* niederer Adel.

gen·u·ine ['dʒenjʊɪn] *adj* □ **1.** echt: a)

authentisch (*Unterschrift etc*), b) ernsthaft (*Angebot etc*), c) aufrichtig (*Mitgefühl etc*). **2.** natürlich, ungekünstelt (*Lachen, Person*).

ge·nus ['dʒiːnəs] *pl* **gen·er·a** ['dʒenərə] *s* ♀, *zo.* Gattung *f*.

ge·og·ra·pher [dʒɪ'ɒgrəfə] *s* Geograph(in). **ge·o·graph·ic, ge·o·graph·i·cal** [‚ə'græfɪk(l)] *adj* □ geographisch. **ge·og·ra·phy** [‚'ɒgrəfɪ] *s* Geographie *f*, Erdkunde *f*.

ge·o·log·ic, ge·o·log·i·cal [‚dʒɪə'lɒdʒɪk(l)] *adj* □ geologisch. **ge·ol·o·gist** [‚'ɒlədʒɪst] *s* Geologe *m*. **ge·ol·o·gy** [‚'ɒlədʒɪ] *s* Geologie *f*.

ge·o·met·ric, ge·o·met·ri·cal [‚dʒɪə'metrɪk(l)] *adj* □ geometrisch. **ge·om·e·try** [‚'ɒmɪtrɪ] *s* Geometrie *f*.

ge·ra·ni·um [dʒɪ'reɪnjəm] *s* ♀ Geranie *f*.

ger·i·at·rics [‚dʒerɪ'ætrɪks] *s pl* (*sg konstruiert*) ⚕ Geriatrie *f*, Altersheilkunde *f*.

germ [dʒɜːm] *s* **1.** *biol.*, ♀ Keim *m* (*a. fig.*): **in ~** im Keim, im Werden. **2.** ⚕ Bazillus *m*, Bakterie *f*, (Krankheits)Erreger *m*.

Ger·man ['dʒɜːmən] **I** *adj* **1.** deutsch: **~ measles** (*sg konstruiert*) ⚕ Röteln *pl.* **II** *s* **2.** Deutsche *m*, *f*. **3.** *ling.* Deutsch *n*: **in ~** auf deutsch.

ger·mane [dʒɜː'meɪn] *adj*: **~ to** gehörig zu, betreffend (*acc*).

Ger·man·ic [dʒɜː'mænɪk] *adj* germanisch. **Ger·man·ism** ['‚mənɪzəm] *s* *ling.* Germanismus *m*.

'germ-free *adj* ⚕ keimfrei.

ger·mi·nate ['dʒɜːmɪneɪt] *v/i u. v/t* keimen (lassen) (*a. fig.*).

germ war·fare *s* ✕ bakteriologische Kriegführung.

ger·on·tol·o·gy [‚dʒerɒn'tɒlədʒɪ] *s* ⚕ Gerontologie *f*, Altersforschung *f*.

ger·und ['dʒerənd] *s* *ling.* Gerundium *n*.

ges·ta·tion [dʒe'steɪʃn] *s* Schwangerschaft *f*; *zo.* Trächtigkeit *f*: **~ period** Trag(e)zeit *f*.

ges·tic·u·late [dʒe'stɪkjʊleɪt] *v/i* gestikulieren. **ges‚tic·u·la·tion** *s* Gestikulation *f*.

ges·ture ['dʒestʃə] *s* Geste *f* (*a. fig.*), Gebärde *f*.

get [get] (*irr*) **I** *v/t* **1.** bekommen, erhalten. **2.** sich *et.* verschaffen *od.* besorgen: **~ s.th. for s.o.** j-m et. besorgen.

3. erringen, erwerben, sich *Wissen etc* aneignen. **4.** erwischen; (*a. telefonisch*) erreichen. **5.** holen. **6.** schaffen, bringen. **7.** machen: **~ s.th. ready** et. fertigmachen. **8.** (*mit pp*) lassen: **~ one's hair cut** sich die Haare schneiden lassen. **9.** *j-n* dazu bringen (*to do* zu tun): **~ to speak** j-n zum Sprechen bringen. **10.** **~ going** Maschine etc, fig. Verhandlungen etc in Gang bringen; fig. Schwung bringen in (*acc*). **11.** **have got** haben: **have got to** müssen. **12.** F kapieren, (*a. akustisch*) verstehen: **don't ~ me wrong** versteh mich nicht falsch. **II** *v/i* **13.** kommen, gelangen: **~ home** nach Hause kommen. **14.** dahin kommen (*to do* zu tun): **~ to know s.th.** et. erfahren *od.* kennenlernen. **15.** (*mit pp od. adj*) werden: **~ tired** müde werden, ermüden. **16.** beginnen, anfangen (*doing* zu tun): **~ going** in Gang kommen (*Maschine etc, fig. Verhandlungen etc*); fig. in Schwung kommen.

Verbindungen mit Präpositionen:

get| **at** *v/i* **1.** herankommen an (*acc*), erreichen. **2.** an *j-n* herankommen, *j-m* beikommen. **3.** **what is he getting at?** worauf will er hinaus? **~ off** *v/i* absteigen von; aussteigen aus. **~ o·ver** *v/i* hinwegkommen über (*acc*), *fig. a.* sich erholen von. **~ through** *v/i* **1.** kommen durch (*e-e Prüfung etc*). **2.** Geld durchbringen. **~ to** *v/i* **1.** kommen nach, erreichen. **2.** **~ talking about** zu sprechen kommen auf (*acc*).

Verbindungen mit Adverbien:

get| **a·bout** *v/i* **1.** herumkommen. **2.** sich herumsprechen *od.* verbreiten (*Gerücht etc*). **~ a·cross** *v/i* **1.** verständlich machen; *Idee etc* an den Mann bringen. **II** *v/i* **2.** ankommen; sich verständlich machen. **3.** ankommen, einschlagen; klarwerden (*to s.o.* j-m). **~ a·long** *v/i* **1.** vorwärts-, weiterkommen (*a. fig.*). **2.** auskommen, sich vertragen (*with* mit *j-m*). **3.** zurechtkommen (*with* mit *et.*). **~ a·round** *v/i* **1.** → **get about**. **2.** → **get round** II. **~ a·way** *v/i* **1.** loskommen, sich losmachen. **2.** entkommen, -wischen: **~ with** davonkommen mit. **~ back I** *v/t* **1.** zurückbekommen: **get one's own back** F sich rächen; **get one's own back on s.o.** → 3; → **breath** 1. **II** *v/i* **2.** zurückkommen. **3.** **~ at s.o.** F

sich an j-m rächen, es j-m heimzahlen.
~ be·hind v/i in Rückstand kommen
(**with** mit). **~ by** v/i **1.** aus-, durchkommen (**on** mit). **2.** gerade noch annehmbar sein (*Arbeit etc*), gerade noch ausreichen (*Kenntnisse*). **~ down** I v/t **1.**
Essen etc runterkriegen. II v/i **2.** aus-,
absteigen. **3. ~ to** sich machen an (*acc*):
→ **brass tacks, business** 6. **~ in** I v/t **1.**
Bemerkung etc anbringen. **2.** *Spezia-
listen etc* (hin)zuziehen. II v/i **3.** hinein-,
hereinkommen. **4.** einsteigen. **5. ~ on** F
mitmachen bei. **~ off** v/i **1.** (**from**) absteigen (von), aussteigen (aus). **2.** davonkommen (**with** mit). **~ on** v/i **1.** vor-
wärts-, vorankommen (*a. fig.*): **he is
getting on for sixty** er geht auf die
Sechzig zu; **it is getting on for 5 o'clock**
es geht auf 5 Uhr (zu). **2.** → **get along**
2, 3. **~ out** I v/t **1.** herausbekommen (*a.
fig.*). **2.** *Worte etc* herausbringen. II v/i
3. aussteigen. **4.** *fig.* durchsickern, herauskommen (*Geheimnis etc*). **~ o·ver**
v/t hinter sich bringen. **~ round** I v/t j-n
herumkriegen. II v/i dazu kommen (**to
doing** zu tun). **~ through** I v/t **1.** durchbringen, -bekommen (*a. fig.*). II v/i **2. ~
get over.** II v/i **3.** durchkommen (*a. fig.*). **~
to·geth·er** I v/t **1.** *Menschen etc*
zs.-bringen. **2.** zs.-tragen. II v/i **3.**
zs.-kommen. **~ up** I v/t **1.** j-n herausputzen. **2.** *Buch etc* ausstatten, *Waren*
(hübsch) aufmachen. II v/i **3.** aufstehen, (*von e-m Stuhl etc a.*) sich erheben.
get·|-at-a·ble [get'ætəbl] *adj* F **1.** erreich-
bar (*Ort, Sache*). **2.** zugänglich (*Ort,
Person*). **'~·a·way** s Flucht *f*: **~ car**
Fluchtauto *n*. **'~·to,geth·er** s F (zwang-
lose) Zs.-kunft: **have a ~** sich treffen,
zs.-kommen. **'~·up** s F Aufmachung *f*:
a) Ausstattung *f*, b) Aufzug *m* (*Kleidung*).
gey·ser s **1.** ['gaɪzə] Geysir *m*. **2.** ['giːzə]
Br. Durchlauferhitzer *m*.
ghast·ly ['gɑːstlɪ] I *adj* **1.** gräßlich, entsetzlich (*beide a. fig.* F). **2.** gespenstisch.
II *adv* **3. ~ pale** totenblaß.
gher·kin ['gɜːkɪn] s Gewürz-, Essiggurke *f*.
ghet·to ['getəʊ] *pl* **-to(e)s** s G(h)etto *n*.
~ blast·er s sl. Ghetto-Blaster *m*
(*tragbarer Stereo-Kassettenrecorder*). **~
dwell·er** s G(h)ettobewohner(in).
ghost [gəʊst] s **1.** Geist *m*, Gespenst *n*. **2.**

give up the ~ den Geist aufgeben. **3.**
fig. Spur *f*. **'ghost·ly** *adj* geister-, ge-
spensterhaft.
ghost| **sto·ry** s Geister-, Gespensterge-
schichte *f*. **~ town** s Geisterstadt *f*. **~
train** s Geisterbahn *f*: **go on the ~** Geisterbahn fahren. **~ writ·er** s Ghostwriter *m*.
gi·ant ['dʒaɪənt] I s Riese *m*. II *adj* riesig:
~ slalom (*Skisport*) Riesenslalom *m*.
gib·ber ['dʒɪbə] v/i schnattern (*Affen,
Personen*). **gib·ber·ish** ['~rɪʃ] s Geschnatter *n*.
gibe [dʒaɪb] I v/i: **~ at** (*od. about*) spotten über (*acc*), verhöhnen, -spotten. II
s höhnische Bemerkung.
gib·lets ['dʒɪblɪts] s pl Innereien pl (*vom
Geflügel*).
gid·di·ness ['gɪdɪnɪs] s **1.** Schwindel(gefühl *n*) *m*. **2.** *fig.* Leichtsinn *m*. **'gid·dy**
adj □ **1. I am** (*od. feel*) **~** mir ist
schwind(e)lig. **2.** schwindelerregend (*a.
fig.*). **3.** *fig.* leichtsinnig.
gift [gɪft] I s **1.** Geschenk *n*: **I wouldn't
have it as a ~** das möchte ich nicht
(mal) geschenkt; **at £ 10 it's a ~** für 10
Pfund ist es geschenkt. **2.** *fig.* Begabung *f*, Talent *n* (**for**, *of* für): **~ for
languages** Sprachtalent; → **gab.** II *adj*
3. geschenkt, Geschenk...: **don't look a
~ horse in the mouth** e-m geschenkten
Gaul schaut man nicht ins Maul.
'gift·ed *adj* begabt, talentiert.
gi·gan·tic [dʒaɪˈgæntɪk] *adj* (**~ally**) gigantisch, riesig.
gig·gle ['gɪgl] I v/i kichern. II s Gekicher *n*.
gild [gɪld] v/t (*a. irr*) **1.** vergolden. **2.** *fig.*
versüßen; beschönigen: → **pill** 1.
gill [gɪl] s **1.** *ichth.* Kieme *f*. **2.** ♀ Lamelle *f*.
gilt [gɪlt] I *pret u. pp von* **gild.** II s Vergol-
dung *f*: **take the ~ off the gingerbread**
fig. der Sache den Reiz nehmen. **'~-
-'edged** *adj* **1.** mit Goldschnitt. **2. ~
securities** pl ♣ mündelsichere (Wert-)
Papiere pl.
gim·crack ['dʒɪmkræk] *adj* **1.** wertlos;
kitschig. **2.** wack(e)lig.
gim·mick ['gɪmɪk] s F **1.** → **gadget. 2.**
(*bsd.* Reklame)Trick *m*, (-)Dreh *m*.
gin [dʒɪn] s Gin *m*.
gin·ger ['dʒɪndʒə] I s **1.** Ingwer *m*. **2.** F
Schmiß *m*, Schwung *m*. II *adj* **3.** röt-

lich- *od.* gelblichbraun. **III** *v/t* **4.** mit Ingwer würzen. **5.** *mst* ~ **up** F *j-n* aufmöbeln, -muntern; *et.* ankurbeln, in Schwung bringen. ~ **ale** *s* Ginger-ale *n.* ~ **beer** *s* Ginger-beer *n,* Ingwerbier *n.* '~**bread** *s* Leb-, Pfefferkuchen *m* (*mit Ingwergeschmack*): → **gilt** II.

gin·ger·ly ['dʒɪndʒəlɪ] *adj u. adv* **1.** behutsam, vorsichtig. **2.** zimperlich.

gin·gi·vi·tis [,dʒɪndʒɪ'vaɪtɪs] *s* ❦ Zahnfleischentzündung *f.*

gip·sy ['dʒɪpsɪ] *s* Zigeuner(in).

gi·raffe [dʒɪ'rɑːf] *pl* -'**raffes**, *bsd. coll.* -'**raffe** *s zo.* Giraffe *f.*

gird·er ['ɡɜːdə] *s* ⊙ Balken *m,* Träger *m.*

gir·dle ['ɡɜːdl] *s* **1.** Gürtel *m,* Gurt *m.* **2.** Hüfthalter *m,* -gürtel *m.*

girl [ɡɜːl] *s* **1.** Mädchen *n.* **2.** (Dienst-) Mädchen *n.* '~**friend** *s* Freundin *f* (*e-s Jungen*). ~ **guide** *s Br.* Pfadfinderin *f.*

girl·hood ['ɡɜːlhʊd] *s* Mädchenjahre *pl,* Jugend(zeit) *f.*

girl·ish ['ɡɜːlɪʃ] *adj* □ **1.** mädchenhaft. **2.** Mädchen...: → **games.**

girl scout *s Am.* Pfadfinderin *f.*

gi·ro ['dʒaɪərəʊ] *s Br.* Postgirodienst *m:* ~ **account** Postgirokonto *n;* ~ **cheque** Postscheck *m.*

girth [ɡɜːθ] *s* **1.** (*a.* Körper)Umfang *m.* **2.** (Sattel-, Pack)Gurt *m.*

gist [dʒɪst] *s das* Wesentliche, Kern *m.*

give [ɡɪv] (*irr*) **I** *v/t* **1.** geben; schenken; *Blut etc* spenden. **2.** geben, reichen: ~ *s.o. one's hand* j-m die Hand geben. **3.** *Auskunft, Rat etc* geben, erteilen. **4.** *sein Wort* geben. **5.** *Aufmerksamkeit etc* widmen (**to** *dat*): → **attention** 2. **6.** *sein Leben* hingeben, opfern (**for** für). **7.** geben, gewähren: ~ *s.o. until* j-m bis ... Zeit geben *od.* lassen (**to do** zu tun). **8.** *Befehl, Auftrag etc* geben, erteilen. **9.** *Hilfe* gewähren, leisten; *Schutz* bieten. **10.** *Grüße etc* übermitteln: ~ *him my love* bestelle ihm herzliche Grüße von mir. **11.** *j-m e-n Schlag etc* geben, versetzen. **12.** *j-m e-n Blick* zuwerfen. **13.** *Lebenszeichen etc* von sich geben: ~ *a cry* (*od.* **shout**) e-n Schrei ausstoßen, aufschreien; ~ *a laugh* auflachen. **14.** *Grund etc* (an)geben. **15.** *Konzert etc* geben, veranstalten; *Theaterstück etc* geben, aufführen; *Vortrag* halten. **16.** *Schmerzen etc* bereiten, verursachen.

17. *j-m zu tun etc* geben: *I was ~n to understand* man gab mir zu verstehen. **II** *v/i* **18.** geben, spenden (**to** *dat*). **19.** nachgeben (*a. Preise*). **20.** *what ~s?* *sl.* was gibt's? **21.** führen (**into** in *acc;* **on**[**to**] auf *acc,* nach) (*Straße etc*); gehen (**on**[**to**] nach) (*Fenster etc*).

Verbindungen mit Adverbien:

give| **a·way** *v/t* **1.** her-, weggeben; verschenken: → **bride.** **2.** *j-n, et.* verraten. **3.** *Chance etc* vertun. ~ **back** *v/t* **1.** zurückgeben (*a. fig.*), *Blick* erwidern. **2.** *Schall* zurückwerfen; *Licht etc* reflektieren. ~ **in** **I** *v/t* **1.** *Gesuch etc* einreichen, *Prüfungsarbeit etc* abgeben. **II** *v/i* **2.** (**to**) nachgeben (*dat*); sich anschließen (*dat*). **3.** aufgeben, sich geschlagen geben. ~ **off** *v/t Geruch* verbreiten, ausströmen, *Rauch etc* ausstoßen, *Gas, Wärme etc* aus-, verströmen. ~ **out** **I** *v/t* **1.** aus-, verteilen. **2.** bekanntgeben. **3.** *give o.s. out to be s.th.* sich als et. ausgeben. **4.** → **give off.** **II** *v/i* **5.** zu Ende gehen (*Kräfte, Vorräte*). **6.** versagen (*Maschine, Nieren etc*). ~ **o·ver** **I** *v/t* **1.** übergeben (**to** *dat*). **2.** *et.* aufgeben: ~ *doing s.th.* aufhören, et. zu tun. **3.** *give o.s. over to* sich hingeben (*dat*). **II** *v/i* **4.** aufhören. ~ **up** **I** *v/t* **1.** aufgeben, aufhören mit: ~ *smoking* das Rauchen aufgeben. **2.** *Plan, Patienten etc* aufgeben: → **adoption** 1. **3.** *j-n* ausliefern: *give o.s. up* sich stellen (**to** *dat*). **4.** (**to**) *Posten etc* abgeben, abtreten (an *acc*); *Sitzplatz etc* freimachen (für). **5.** *give o.s. up to* sich hingeben (*dat*); sich widmen (*dat*). **II** *v/i* **6.** → **give in** 3. **7.** resignieren.

,**give**|-**and**-'**take** *s* **1.** beiderseitiges Entgegenkommen *od.* Nachgeben, Kompromiß(bereitschaft *f*) *m.* **2.** Meinungs-, Gedankenaustausch *m.* '**~·a·way** *s bsd. Am.* Werbegeschenk *n.* **II** *adj:* ~ **price** Schleuderpreis *m.*

giv·en ['ɡɪvn] **I** *pp von* **give.** **II** *adj* **1.** gegeben: ~ *name bsd. Am.* → **first name;** *at the* ~ *time* zur festgesetzten Zeit; *within a* ~ *time* innerhalb e-r bestimmten Zeit. **2.** *be* ~ *to* neigen zu: *be* ~ *to doing s.th.* die (An)Gewohnheit haben, et. zu tun. **3.** vorausgesetzt. **4.** in Anbetracht (*gen*): ~ *that* in Anbetracht der Tatsache, daß. '**giv·er** *s* Geber(in), Spender(in).

gla·cé ['glæseɪ] *adj* **1.** glasiert; kandiert. **2.** Glacé...

gla·cial ['gleɪsjəl] *adj* □ **1.** eiszeitlich: **~ epoch** (*od.* **era**) Eiszeit *f*. **2.** eisig (*a. fig.*). **gla·cier** ['glæsjə] *s* Gletscher *m*.

glad [glæd] *adj* (□ → **gladly**) **1.** froh, erfreut (**of, about, at** über *acc*): **be ~ of** sich freuen über; **I am ~ to hear** es freut mich zu hören; **I am ~ to go** ich gehe gern. **2.** freudig, froh, erfreulich. **glad·den** ['~dn] *v/t* erfreuen.

glad·i·a·tor ['glædeɪtə] *s hist.* Gladiator *m*.

glad·i·o·lus [ˌglædɪ'əʊləs] *pl* **-li** [~laɪ], **-lus·es** *s* ♀ Gladiole *f*.

glad·ly ['glædlɪ] *adv* mit Freuden, gern. **'glad·ness** *s* Freude *f*.

glam·or·ize ['glæməraɪz] *v/t* verherrlichen, glorifizieren. **'glam·or·ous** *adj* □ bezaubernd (schön). **glam·our** ['~mə] *s* Zauber *m*, (*contp.* falscher) Glanz: **~ girl** Glamourgirl *n*, Film-, Reklameschönheit *f*.

glance [glɑːns] **I** *v/i* **1.** e-n (schnellen) Blick werfen, (rasch *od.* flüchtig) blicken (**at** auf *acc*): **~ over** (*od.* **through**) **a letter** e-n Brief überfliegen; **~ at a problem** ein Problem streifen. **2.** **~ off** abprallen (von) (*Kugel etc*), abgleiten (von) (*Messer etc*). **II** *s* **3.** (schneller *od.* flüchtiger) Blick (**at** auf *acc*): **at a ~** auf 'einen Blick; **at first ~** auf den ersten Blick; **take a ~ at** → **1**; → **steal 1**.

gland [glænd] *s anat.* Drüse *f*. **glan·du·lar** ['~djʊlə] *adj* Drüsen...

glare [gleə] **I** *v/i* **1.** grell scheinen (*Sonne etc*), grell leuchten (*Scheinwerfer etc*). **2.** wütend starren: **~ at s.o.** j-n wütend anstarren, j-n anfunkeln. **II** *s* **3.** greller Schein, grelles Leuchten. **4.** wütender *od.* funkelnder Blick. **glar·ing** ['~rɪŋ] *adj* □ **1.** grell. **2.** grell, schreiend (*Farben*). **3.** eklatant, kraß (*Fehler, Unterschied etc*), (himmel)schreiend (*Unrecht etc*). **4.** wütend, funkelnd (*Blick*).

glass [glɑːs] **I** *s* **1.** Glas *n*. **2.** *coll.* Glas(waren *pl*) *n*. **3.** (Trink)Glas *n*; Glas(gefäß) *n*. **4.** (Fern-, Opern)Glas. **5.** *pl, a. pair of ~s* Brille *f*. **II** *adj* **6.** Glas...: **~ eye. ~ blow·er** *s* Glasbläser *m*. **~ case** *s* Glaskasten *m*, Vitrine *f*.

glass·ful ['glɑːsfʊl] *s* ein Glasvoll *n*.

'glass·house *s* **1.** *bsd. Br.* Gewächs-, Glas-, Treibhaus *n*. **2.** *people who live*

in ~s should not throw stones wer (selbst) im Glashaus sitzt, soll nicht mit Steinen werfen. **'~ware** *s* Glaswaren *pl*.

glass·y ['glɑːsɪ] *adj* □ **1.** gläsern. **2.** glasig (*Augen*).

glau·co·ma [glɔː'kəʊmə] *s* ♣ grüner Star.

glaze [gleɪz] **I** *v/t* **1.** verglasen: **~ in** einglasen; **~d veranda** Glasveranda *f*. **2.** ⊛, *a. gastr.* glasieren: **~d tile** Kachel *f*. **II** *v/i* **3.** *a.* **~ over** glasig werden (*Augen*). **gla·zier** ['~jə] *s* Glaser *m*. **'glaz·ing** *s* **1.** Verglasung *f*. **2.** ⊛, *a. gastr.* Glasur *f*.

gleam [gliːm] **I** *s* **1.** schwacher Schein, Schimmer *m* (*a. fig.*): **~ of hope** Hoffnungsschimmer. **II** *v/i* scheinen, schimmern.

glean [gliːn] *v/t fig.* sammeln, zs.-tragen; herausfinden, in Erfahrung bringen: **~ from** schließen *od.* entnehmen aus. **'glean·ings** *s pl* das Gesammelte.

glee [gliː] *s* **1.** Freude *f*. **2.** Schadenfreude *f*.

glee·ful ['~fʊl] *adj* □ **1.** fröhlich. **2.** schadenfroh.

glib [glɪb] *adj* □ **1.** schlagfertig (*a. Antwort etc*). **2.** oberflächlich.

glide [glaɪd] **I** *v/i* **1.** gleiten. **2.** ✈ gleiten, e-n Gleitflug machen; segelfliegen. **II** *s* **3.** Gleiten *n*. **4.** ✈ Gleitflug *m*. **'glid·er** *s* ✈ a) Segelflugzeug *n*, b) *a.* **~ pilot** Segelflieger(in). **'glid·ing** *s* ✈ Segelfliegen *n*.

glim·mer ['glɪmə] **I** *v/i* **1.** glimmen. **2.** schimmern. **II** *s* **3.** Glimmen *n*. **4.** Schimmer *m* (*a. fig.*): **~ of hope** Hoffnungsschimmer.

glimpse [glɪmps] **I** *s* flüchtiger Blick: **catch** (*od.* **get**) **a ~ of** → **III. II** *v/i* flüchtig blicken (**at** auf *acc*). **III** *v/t* (nur) flüchtig zu sehen bekommen.

glint [glɪnt] **I** *v/i* glänzen, glitzern. **II** *s* Glanz *m*, Glitzern *n*.

glis·ten ['glɪsn] → **glint**.

glit·ter ['glɪtə] **I** *v/i* **1.** glitzern, funkeln, glänzen: **all that ~s is not gold, all is not gold that ~s** es ist nicht alles Gold, was glänzt. **II** *s* **2.** Glitzern *n*, Funkeln *n*, Glanz *m*. **3.** *fig.* Glanz *m*, Pracht *f*. **'glit·ter·ing** *adj* □ **1.** glitzernd, funkelnd, glänzend. **2.** *fig.* glänzend, prächtig.

gloat [gləʊt] v/i (*over*, *at*) sich weiden (an *dat*): a) verzückt betrachten (*acc*), b) sich hämisch *od.* diebisch freuen (über *acc*). **'gloat·ing** *adj* □ hämisch, schadenfroh.

glob·al ['gləʊbl] *adj* □ global: a) weltumspannend, Welt..., b) umfassend, Gesamt...

globe [gləʊb] s 1. Kugel *f*. 2. Erde *f*, Erdball *m*, -kugel *f*. 3. *geogr*. Globus *m*. **'~‚trot·ter** s Globetrotter(in), Weltenbummler(in).

glob·u·lar ['glɒbjʊlə] *adj* □ kugelförmig: **~ lightning** Kugelblitz *m*. **glob-ule** ['~juːl] s 1. Kügelchen *n*. 2. Tröpfchen *n*.

gloom [gluːm] s 1. Düsterkeit *f*. 2. *fig.* düstere *od.* gedrückte Stimmung: **throw a ~ over** e-n Schatten werfen auf (*acc*). **'gloom·y** *adj* □ 1. düster (*a. fig.*). 2. hoffnungslos: **feel ~ about the future** schwarzsehen.

glo·ri·fi·ca·tion [‚glɔːrɪfɪ'keɪʃn] s 1. Verherrlichung *f*. 2. *eccl.* Lobpreisung *f*. **glo·ri·fied** ['~faɪd] *adj* F besser. **glo·ri-fy** ['~faɪ] v/t 1. verherrlichen, glorifizieren. 2. *eccl.* lobpreisen. 3. F aufmotzen. **'glo·ri·ous** *adj* □ 1. ruhm-, glorreich. 2. herrlich, prächtig. 3. *iro.* schön, großartig.

glo·ry ['glɔːrɪ] I s 1. Ruhm *m*. 2. Zier(de) *f*, Stolz *m*. 3. Herrlichkeit *f*, Glanz *m*. II v/i 4. sich freuen, glücklich sein (*in* über *acc*). 5. sich sonnen (*in* in *dat*). **~ hole** s F Rumpelkammer *f*.

gloss¹ [glɒs] s Glosse *f*, Erläuterung *f*, Anmerkung *f*.

gloss² [~] I s 1. Glanz *m*. 2. *fig.* (äußerer) Glanz. II v/t 3. *mst* **~ over** beschönigen; vertuschen.

glos·sa·ry ['glɒsərɪ] s Glossar *n*.

gloss·y ['glɒsɪ] I *adj* □ glänzend: **be ~** glänzen; **~ magazine** Hochglanzmagazin *n*. II s F Hochglanzmagazin *n*.

glove [glʌv] s Handschuh *m*: **fit (s.o.) like a ~** (j-m) wie angegossen passen; *fig.* (zu j-m *od.* auf j-n) ganz genau passen. **~ box**, **~ com·part·ment** s *mot.* Handschuhfach *n*. **~ pup·pet** s Handpuppe *f*.

glow [gləʊ] I v/i glühen (*a. fig.* **with** vor *dat*). II s Glühen *n*, Glut *f* (*beide a. fig.*).

glow·er ['glaʊə] v/i finster blicken: **~ at**

s.o. j-n finster anblicken. **'glow·er·ing** *adj* □ finster.

'glow·worm s *zo.* Glühwürmchen *n*.

glu·cose ['gluːkəʊs] s 🜄 Glukose *f*, Traubenzucker *m*.

glue [gluː] I s Leim *m*; Klebstoff *m*. II v/t leimen, kleben (*on* auf *acc*; *to* an *acc*): **be ~d to** *fig.* kleben an (*dat*). **'glue·y** *adj* klebrig.

glum [glʌm] *adj* □ bedrückt, niedergeschlagen.

glut [glʌt] I v/t 1. übersättigen (*a. fig.*): **~ o.s. with** (*od.* on) sich überessen mit *od.* an (*dat*). 2. 🜨 *Markt* überschwemmen. II s 3. 🜨 Schwemme *f*.

glu·ti·nous ['gluːtɪnəs] *adj* □ klebrig.

glut·ton ['glʌtn] s 1. Vielfraß *m*. 2. *fig.* Unersättliche *m*, *f*: **~ for books** Leseratte *f*, Bücherwurm *m*; **~ for work** Arbeitstier *n*. **'glut·ton·ous** *adj* □ gefräßig, unersättlich (*a. fig.*). **'glut·ton·y** s Gefräßigkeit *f*, Unersättlichkeit *f* (*a. fig.*).

glyc·er·in(e) ['glɪsərɪn('~riːn)] s 🜄 Glyzerin *n*.

G-man ['dʒiːmæn] s (*irr* **man**) G-man *m*, FBI-Agent *m*.

gnarled [nɑːld] *adj* 1. knorrig. 2. schwielig (*Hände*).

gnash [næʃ] v/t: **~ one's teeth** mit den Zähnen knirschen.

gnat [næt] s *zo.* Br. (Stech)Mücke *f*.

gnaw [nɔː] (*a. irr*) I v/t 1. *Loch etc* nagen (*into* in *acc*). 2. nagen an (*dat*) (*a. fig.*). II v/i 3. nagen (*at* an *dat*) (*a. fig.*).

gnome [nəʊm] s Gnom *m*, Zwerg *m* (*beide a. contp. Mensch*).

go [gəʊ] I s *pl* **goes** 1. F Schwung *m*, Schmiß *m*. 2. *be all the* ~ F große Mode sein. 3. *it's a ~*! F abgemacht! 4. F Versuch *m*: **have a ~ at s.th.** et. probieren; **at one** ~ auf 'einen Schlag, auf Anhieb. II v/i (*irr*) 5. gehen, fahren, reisen (*to* nach): **~ on foot** zu Fuß gehen; **~ by plane** (*od.* **air**) mit dem Flugzeug reisen. 6. (fort)gehen: **I must be ~ing** ich muß gehen *od.* weg. 7. anfangen: **~!** (*Sport*) los! 8. gehen, führen (*to* nach) (*Straße etc*). 9. sich erstrecken, gehen (*to* bis). 10. verkehren, fahren (*Bus etc*). 11. *fig.* gehen: **let it ~ at that** laß es dabei bewenden. 12. gehen, passen (*into* in *acc*). 13. (*to*) gehen (an *acc*) (*Preis etc*), zufallen (*dat*) (*Erbe*). 14. ⚙

gehen, laufen, funktionieren (*alle a. fig.*): *keep* (*set*) *s.th.* ~*ing* et. in Gang halten (bringen); → *get* 10, 16. **15.** werden: ~ *cold*; ~ *blind* erblinden. **16.** (*with*) gehen (mit), sich anschließen (an *acc*): → *tide* 2. **17.** sich halten (*by, on* an *acc*), gehen, sich richten (*on* nach): ~*ing by her clothes* ihrer Kleidung nach (zu urteilen). **18.** kursieren, im Umlauf sein (*Gerücht etc*): *the story* ~*es* es heißt, man erzählt sich. **19.** vergehen, -streichen: *one minute to* ~ noch eine Minute. **20.** gelten (*for* für): *it* ~*es without saying* es versteht sich von selbst. **21.** verkauft werden (*at, for* für): → *cake* 1. **22.** dazu beitragen od. dienen (*to do* zu tun): *it* ~*es to show* dies zeigt, daran erkennt man. **23.** ausgehen, -fallen (*Entscheidung etc*). **24.** (*with*) harmonieren (mit), passen (zu). **25.** lauten (*Worte etc*). **26.** sterben. **27.** (*im pres p mit inf*) *zum Ausdruck e-r Zukunft, bsd.* a) *e-r Absicht,* b) *et. Unabänderlichen*: *it is* ~*ing to rain* es gibt Regen; *she is* ~*ing to have a baby* sie bekommt ein Kind; *I am* ~*ing to tell him* ich werde *od.* will es ihm sagen. **28.** (*mit ger*) gehen: ~ *swimming* schwimmen gehen. **29.** (daran)gehen (*to do* zu tun): *he went to find her* er ging sie suchen; *she went to see him* sie besuchte ihn. **III** *v/t* (*irr*) **30.** Weg, Strecke *etc* gehen: ~ *it alone* F es ganz allein machen.

Verbindungen mit Präpositionen:

go | **a·bout** *v/i* in Angriff nehmen, sich machen an (*acc*). ~ **af·ter** *v/i* **1.** nachlaufen (*dat*). **2.** sich bemühen um. ~ **a·gainst** *v/i* **1.** *j-m* widerstreben. **2.** *e-m Verbot etc* zuwiderhandeln, sich widersetzen (*dat*). ~ **at** *v/i* **1.** losgehen auf (*acc*). **2.** → *go about*. ~ **be·tween** *v/i* vermitteln zwischen (*dat*). ~ **be·yond** *v/i fig.* überschreiten, hinausgehen über (*acc*). ~ **by** → *go* 17. ~ **for** *v/i* **1.** holen (gehen). **2.** Spaziergang *etc* machen. **3.** a) gelten als *od.* für, b) → *go* 20. ~ **in·to** *v/i* **1.** in die Politik *etc* gehen: gehen in (*acc*). **3.** (genau) untersuchen *od.* prüfen. ~ **off** *v/i* aufgeben: *have gone off j-n, et.* nicht mehr mögen. ~ **on** *v/i* **1.** → *go* 17. **2.** → *strike* 1. ~ **o·ver** *v/i* **1.** → *go into* 3. **2.** → *go through* 1. ~ **through** *v/i* **1.** durchgehen, -nehmen,

-sprechen. **2.** → *go into* 3. **3.** erleiden, durchmachen; erleben. ~ *with v/i* **1.** begleiten. **2.** mit *e-m Mädchen etc* gehen. **3.** → *go* 24. ~ *with·out v/i* **1.** auskommen *od.* sich behelfen ohne. **2.** verzichten auf (*acc*).

Verbindungen mit Adverbien:

go | **a·bout** *v/i* **1.** herumgehen, -fahren, -reisen. **2.** a) → *go* 18, b) umgehen (*Grippe etc*). ~ **a·head** *v/i* **1.** voran-, vorausgehen (*of s.o.* j-m): ~*! fig.* nur zu!; ~ *with fig.* weitermachen *od.* fortfahren mit. **2.** vorankommen (*Person, Arbeit*). ~ **a·long** *v/i* **1.** weitergehen. **2.** *fig.* weitermachen, fortfahren. **3.** sich einverstanden sein mit; *j-m* beipflichten. ~ **a·round** *v/i* **1.** → *go about*. **2.** → *go round*. ~ **back** *v/i* **1.** zurückgehen. **2.** (*to*) *fig.* zurückgehen (auf *acc*), zurückreichen (bis). **3.** ~ *on fig.* j-n im Stich lassen; *sein Wort etc* nicht halten; *sein Versprechen etc* rückgängig machen. ~ **by** *v/i* vorbeigehen (*a. Chance etc*); vergehen (*Zeit*). ~ **down** *v/i* **1.** hinuntergehen. **2.** untergehen, sinken (*Schiff, Sonne etc*). **3.** → *go back* 2. **4.** (hinunter)rutschen (*Essen*). **5.** *fig.* (*with*) Anklang finden, ankommen (bei); gebilligt werden (von). **6.** zurückgehen, sinken, fallen (*Fieber, Preise etc*), billiger werden. **7.** ~ *in history* in die Geschichte eingehen. **8.** sich im Niedergang befinden. ~ **in** *v/i* **1.** hineingehen. **2.** verschwinden (*Sonne etc*). **3.** ~ *for* sich befassen mit, betreiben, *Sport* treiben; mitmachen (bei), sich beteiligen an (*dat*), *Prüfung* machen; sich einsetzen für; sich begeistern für. ~ **off** *v/i* **1.** fort-, weggehen. **2.** losgehen (*Gewehr etc*). **3.** verfallen, geraten (*in, into* in *acc*): ~ *in a fit* e-n Anfall bekommen. **4.** nachlassen (*Schmerz etc*). **5.** *gut etc* verlaufen. **6.** verderben (*Nahrungsmittel*). ~ **on** *v/i* **1.** weitergehen, -fahren. **2.** angehen (*Licht etc*). **3.** weitermachen, fortfahren (*doing* zu tun; *with* mit): ~ *talking* weiterreden; *he went on to say* darauf sagte er. **4.** weitergehen (*Verhältnisse etc*). **5.** vor sich gehen, passieren, vorgehen. **6.** *it is going on for 5 o'clock* es geht auf 5 Uhr zu; *he is going on for 60* er geht auf die Sechzig zu. ~ **out** *v/i* **1.** hinausgehen. **2.** ausgehen. **3.** ausgehen, erlöschen (*Licht, Feuer*). **4.** in den Streik

treten, streiken: → **strike** 1. ~ **o·ver** v/i
1. hinübergehen (**to** zu). **2.** fig. übergehen (**into** in acc). **3.** fig. übergehen,
-treten (**from** von; **to** zu). ~ **round** v/i **1.**
herumgehen (a. fig.). **2.** (für alle)
(aus)reichen: **there are enough chairs
to** ~ es sind genügend Stühle da. ~
through v/i **1.** durchgehen, angenommen werden (Antrag). **2.** ~ **with** durchführen, zu Ende führen. ~ **to·geth·er**
v/i **1.** zs.-passen (Farben etc). **2.** F miteinander gehen (Liebespaar). ~ **up** v/i **1.**
hinaufgehen. **2.** steigen (Fieber etc),
(Preise a.) anziehen. **3.** ~ **in flames** in
Flammen aufgehen; ~ **in smoke** in
Rauch aufgehen (u. Flammen aufgehen);
fig. in Rauch aufgehen, sich in Rauch auflösen.

goad [gəʊd] v/t a. ~ **on** anstacheln (**to do
s.th., into doing s.th.** dazu, et. zu tun).

'go-a·head I **I** adj mit Unternehmungsgeist od. Initiative. **II** s: **get the** ~ grünes
Licht bekommen (**on** für).

goal [gəʊl] s **1.** Ziel n (a. fig.). **2.** Sport:
(a. erzieltes) Tor: **keep** ~ im Tor stehen,
das Tor hüten. ~ **a·re·a** s Sport: Torraum m. ~**keep·er** s Torjäger(in).

goal·ie ['gəʊlɪ] F → **goalkeeper**.

'goal·keep·er s Sport: Torwart m,
-mann m, -frau f, -hüter(in). ~ **kick** s
Fußball: Abstoß m. ~ **line** s Sport: Torlinie f. ~ **post** s Sport: Torpfosten m.

goat [gəʊt] s Ziege f (a. fig. od. play)
the (**giddy**) ~ fig. herumalbern, -kas-
pern; **get s.o.'s** ~ F j-n auf die Palme
bringen. ~**ee** s Spitzbart m.

gob·ble ['gɒbl] v/t mst ~ **up** verschlingen
(a. fig. Buch etc), hinunterschlingen.

'go-be·tween s Vermittler(in): **act as a**
~ vermitteln.

gob·lin ['gɒblɪn] s Kobold m.

go-by ['gəʊbaɪ] s: **give s.o. the** ~ F j-n
schneiden od. ignorieren.

'go-cart s **1.** bsd. Am. Laufstuhl m (für
Kinder). **2.** bes. Am. Sportwagen m (für
Kinder). **3.** Sport: Go-Kart m.

god [gɒd] s **1.** Gott m, Gottheit f. **2.** 2
eccl. Gott m: **so help me** 2! so wahr mir
Gott helfe!; **thank** 2 Gott sei Dank; →
act 1, **bless** 1, **forbid** 3, **sake, willing**
1. **'~child** s (irr **child**) Patenkind n.

god·dess ['gɒdɪs] s Göttin f (a. fig.).

'god·fa·ther s Pate m: **stand** ~ **to** Pate
stehen bei (a. fig.). **'2-fear·ing** adj got-

tesfürchtig. **'~·for·sak·en** adj contp.
gottverlassen. **'~·less** adj □ gottlos.
'~·like adj gottähnlich, göttergleich.

god·ly ['gɒdlɪ] adj fromm.

'god·moth·er s Patin f. **'~·par·ent** s
Pate m, Patin f. **'~·send** s Geschenk n
des Himmels.

,go-'get·ter s F Draufgänger m.

gog·gle ['gɒgl] I v/i glotzen: ~ **at s.o.** j-n
anglotzen. **II** s pl, a. **pair of** ~**s** Schutzbrille f. **'~·box** s Br. F Glotze f, Glotzki-
ste f (Fernseher).

go·ing ['gəʊɪŋ] I s **1.** Boden-, Straßenzu-
stand m, (Pferderennsport) Geläuf n;
Tempo n. **II** adj **2.** ~ **concern** gutgehen-
des Geschäft. **3.** ~, ~, **gone!** (bei Versteigerungen) zum ersten, zum zweiten,
zum dritten! **,go-ings-'on** s pl mst b.s.
Treiben n, Vorgänge pl: **there were
strange** ~ es passierten merkwürdige
Dinge.

goi·ter, bsd. Br. goi·tre ['gɔɪtə] s 🏥
Kropf m.

go-kart ['gəʊkɑːt] s Sport: Go-Kart
m.

gold [gəʊld] I s Gold n: → **glitter** 1. **II** adj
golden, Gold... ~ **dig·ger** s **1.** Goldgrä-
ber m. **2.** F Frau, die nur hinter dem Geld
der Männer her ist.

gold·en ['gəʊldən] adj **1.** mst fig. golden:
~ **days** pl glückliche Tage pl; ~ **opportunity** einmalige Möglichkeit; ~ **wedding**
goldene Hochzeit. **2.** golden, goldgelb:
~ **hamster** s Goldhamster m.

'gold·fish s Goldfisch m. ~ **med·al** s
Goldmedaille f. ~ **med·al·(l)ist** s Gold-
medaillengewinner(in). ~ **mine** s Goldgrube f (a. fig.), -mine f, -bergwerk n.
,~-'plat·ed adj vergoldet. **'~·smith** s
Goldschmied(in).

golf [gɒlf] (Sport) I s Golf(spiel) n. **II** v/i
Golf spielen. ~ **ball** s **1.** Sport: Golfball
m. **2.** ⚙ Kugel-, Schreibkopf m (der
Schreibmaschine). ~ **club** s (Sport) **1.**
Golfschläger m. **2.** Golfclub m. ~
course s Sport: Golfplatz m.

golf·er ['gɒlfə] s Sport: Golfer(in), Golf-
spieler(in).

golf links s pl (a. sg konstruiert) Sport:
Golfplatz m.

Go·li·ath [gə'laɪəθ] s fig. Goliath m.

gon·do·la ['gɒndələ] s Gondel f.

gone [gɒn] I pp von **go**. **II** adj **1.** fort,
weg. **2.** F verknallt (**on** in acc). **3.** **she's**

six months ~ F sie ist im 6. Monat (*schwanger*).

gong [gɒŋ] *s* Gong *m*.

gon·or·rh(o)e·a [ˌgɒnəˈrɪə] *s* 🗲 Tripper *m*.

goo [guː] *s* F **1.** Papp *m*, klebriges Zeug. **2.** Schmalz *m*, sentimentales Zeug.

good [gʊd] **I** *s* **1.** Nutzen *m*, Wert *m*: **for one's own** ~ zu s-m eigenen Vorteil; **what** ~ **is it?** wozu soll das gut sein?; **it is no** ~ **trying** es hat keinen Sinn *od.* Zweck, es zu versuchen. **2.** *das* Gute, Gutes *n*: **do s.o.** ~ j-m Gutes tun; j-m guttun; **be up to no** ~ nichts Gutes im Schilde führen. **3.** *pl* bewegliches Vermögen: **~s and chattels** Hab *n* u. Gut *n*; F Siebensachen *pl.* **4.** *pl* 🗲 Güter *pl*, Ware(n) *pl*) *f*: **~s lift** *Br.* Lastenaufzug *m*; **~s train** *Br.* Güterzug *m*. **II** *adj* **5.** *allg.* gut: **as** ~ **as** so gut wie, praktisch; **have a** ~ **time** sich (gut) amüsieren; es sich gutgehen lassen. **6.** gut, lieb: **be so** ~ **as to fetch it** sei so gut u. hol es; → **enough** III **7.** gut, geeignet: **~ for colds** gut gegen *od.* für Erkältungen; ~ **for one's health** gesund. **8.** gut, richtig: **in** ~ **time** zur rechten Zeit, (gerade) rechtzeitig; **all in** ~ **time** alles zu s-r Zeit. **9.** gut, reichlich: **a** ~ **hour** e-e gute Stunde; **a** ~ **many** ziemlich viele. **10.** (*vor adj*) *verstärkend:* **a** ~ **long time** sehr lange (*Zeit*); ~ **and ...** F ganz schön, mordsmäßig; ~ **and tired** F hundemüde. **11.** gut, triftig (*Grund*). **12.** gut, tüchtig (**at** in *dat*). **~·by(e)** I *s* Abschiedsgruß *m*: **wish s.o.** ~, **say** ~ **to s.o.** j-m auf Wiedersehen sagen, sich von j-m verabschieden. **II** *adj* Abschieds...: ~ **kiss.** III *int* auf Wiedersehen!, *teleph.* auf Wiederhören! '**~-for-ˌnoth·ing** I *adj* nichtsnutzig. **II** *s* Taugenichts *m*, Nichtsnutz *m*. ♀ **Fri·day** *s eccl.* Karfreitag *m*. ˌ~·'**hu·mo(u)red** *adj* □ **1.** gutgelaunt. **2.** gutmütig. ˌ~·'**look·ing** *adj* gutaussehend. ˌ~·'**na·tured** *adj* □ gutmütig.

good·ness ['gʊdnɪs] *s* **1.** Güte *f*. **2.** **thank** ~ Gott sei Dank; (**my**) ~!, ~ **gracious!** du m-e Güte!, du lieber Himmel!; ~ **sake.**

ˌ**good·-ˈtem·pered** *adj* □ gutmütig. ˌ~·'**will** *s* **1.** gute Absicht, guter Wille: ~ **tour** *bsd. pol.* Goodwillreise *f*, -tour *f*. **2.** Goodwill *m*: a) guter Ruf (*e-r Instituti-*

---

on etc), b) 🖢 ideeller Firmen- *od.* Geschäftswert.

good·y ['gʊdɪ] **I** *s* F **1.** Bonbon *m, n*: **goodies** *pl* Süßigkeiten *pl.* **2.** *Film, TV etc:* Gute *m*, Held *m*. **3.** Tugendbold *m*. **II** *adj* **4.** F (*betont*) tugendhaft. **III** *int* **5.** *bsd. Kindersprache:* prima! '**~-,good·y** → **goody** 3, 4.

goo·ey ['guːɪ] *adj* F **1.** pappig, klebrig. **2.** schmalzig, sentimental: ~ **song** Schnulze *f*.

goof [guːf] F **I** *s* **1.** Schnitzer *m*. **2.** Trottel *m*. **II** *v/t* **3.** *oft* ~**up** vermasseln. **III** *v/i* **4.** Mist bauen. '**goof·y** *adj* F **1.** vertrottelt. **2.** *Br.* vorstehend (*Zähne*).

goose [guːs] *pl* **geese** [giːs] *s* **1.** *orn.* Gans *f*: **all his geese are swans** bei ihm ist immer alles besser als bei anderen; **cook s.o.'s** ~ F j-m alles kaputtmachen. **2.** *fig.* (dumme) Gans. ~**·ber·ry** ['gʊzbərɪ] *s* **1.** ♣ Stachelbeere *f*. **2.** **play** ~ *bsd. Br.* das fünfte Rad am Wagen sein. ~ **flesh** *s*, ~ **pim·ples** *s pl* Gänsehaut *f*.

goos·(e)y ['guːsɪ] *adj* **1.** **get** ~ e-e Gänsehaut bekommen. **2.** dumm.

Gor·di·an ['gɔːdjən] *adj*: **cut the** ~ **knot** *fig.* den gordischen Knoten durchhauen.

gore [gɔː] *s* Zwickel *m*, Keil *m*.

gorge [gɔːdʒ] **I** *s* **1.** enge Schlucht. **2.** *it makes my* ~ *rise, my* ~ *rises at it* mir wird übel davon *od.* dabei; mir kommt die Galle dabei hoch. **II** *v/i* **3.** schlemmen: ~ **on** (*od.* **with**) → **5.** III *v/t* **4.** gierig verschlingen. **5.** ~ **o.s. on** (*od.* **with**) sich vollstopfen mit.

gor·geous ['gɔːdʒəs] *adj* □ **1.** prächtig, prachtvoll (*beide a. fig.* F). **2.** F großartig, wunderbar.

go·ril·la [gəˈrɪlə] *s zo.* Gorilla *m* (*a. fig.* F *Leibwächter*).

gor·mand·ize ['gɔːməndaɪz] *v/i* schlemmen. '**gor·mand·iz·er** *s* Schlemmer(in).

gor·y ['gɔːrɪ] *adj* □ blutrünstig.

gosh [gɒʃ] *int* F Mensch!, Mann!

ˌ**go·'slow** *s* F *Br.* Bummelstreik *m*.

gos·pel, *mst* ♀ ['gɒspl] *s* Evangelium *n* (*a. fig.*): **gospel truth** reine Wahrheit.

gos·sa·mer ['gɒsəmə] *s* **1.** Altweibersommer *m*. **2.** feine Gaze.

gos·sip ['gɒsɪp] **I** *s* **1.** Klatsch *m*, Tratsch *m*: ~ **column** Klatschspalte *f*. **2.** Plauderei f, Schwatz m: **have a** ~ → 5. **3.** Klatschbase f, -maul n. **II** v/i **4.** klatschen, tratschen. **5.** plaudern, schwatzen (**with** mit; **about** über acc).

got [gɒt] pret u. pp von **get**.

Goth·ic ['gɒθɪk] **I** adj (~ally) **1.** gotisch. **2.** ~ **novel** Schauerroman m. **II** s **3.** ∆ Gotik f.

got·ten ['gɒtn] Am. pp von **get**.

gou·lash ['ɡuːlæʃ] s gastr. Gulasch n.

gourd [ɡʊəd] s ⚘ Kürbis m.

gour·mand ['ɡʊəmənd] s Schlemmer m.

gour·met ['ɡʊəmeɪ] s Feinschmecker m.

gout [ɡaʊt] s ✝ Gicht f.

gov·ern ['ɡʌvn] **I** v/t **1.** regieren (a. ling.). **2.** leiten, verwalten. **3.** fig. bestimmen, regeln: **be ~ed by** sich leiten lassen von. **4.** fig. zügeln, beherrschen (~ **o.s.** (od. **one's temper**) sich beherrschen. **II** v/i **5.** regieren. '**gov·ern·ing** adj **1.** regierend, Regierungs... **2.** leitend, Vorstands...: ~ **body** Leitung f, Direktion f, Vorstand m. **3.** fig. leitend, bestimmend: ~ **idea** Leitgedanke m. '**gov·ern·ment** s **1.** oft ⚚ Regierung f: ~ **spokesman** Regierungssprecher m; → **exile** 1. **2.** Regierung(sform) f. **3.** Leitung f, Verwaltung f. **4.** Staat m: ~ **monopoly** Staatsmonopol n. **gov·ern·men·tal** [~'mentl] adj **1.** Regierungs... **2.** Staats..., staatlich. **gov·er·nor** ['ɡʌvnə] s **1.** Gouverneur m. **2.** Direktor m, Leiter m. **3.** F der Alte: a) alter Herr (Vater), b) Chef m (a. Anrede).

gown [ɡaʊn] s **1.** mst in Zssgn Kleid n. **2.** ⚖, eccl., univ. Talar m, Robe f.

grab [ɡræb] **I** v/t **1.** (hastig od. gierig) ergreifen, packen. **2.** fig. an sich reißen; Gelegenheit beim Schopf ergreifen. **3.** F Zuhörer etc packen, fesseln. **II** v/i **4.** ~ **at** (gierig od. hastig) greifen nach, schnappen nach. **III** s **5.** (hastiger od. gieriger) Griff: **make a** ~ **at** → 1, 4. **6.** **be up for** ~s F (für jeden) zu haben od. zu gewinnen sein.

grace [ɡreɪs] **I** s **1.** Anmut f, Grazie f. **2.** Anstand m. **3.** mst pl gute Eigenschaft: → **saving** 3. **4.** Gunst f, Wohlwollen n: **be in s.o.'s good** (**bad**) ~s in j-s Gunst stehen (bei j-m in Ungnade sein). **5.** (a. göttliche) Gnade, Barmherzigkeit f. **6.** Tischgebet n: **say** ~ das Tischgebet sprechen. **II** v/t **7.** zieren, schmücken.

8. (be)ehren. **grace·ful** ['~fʊl] adj □ **1.** anmutig, graziös. **2.** würde-, taktvoll. '**grace·less** adj □ ungraziös.

gra·cious ['ɡreɪʃəs] adj □ **1.** wohlwollend. **2.** gnädig, barmherzig (Gott). **II** int **3.** **good** ~!, ~ **me!** du m-e Güte!, lieber Himmel!

gra·da·tion [ɡrə'deɪʃn] s Abstufung f.

grade [ɡreɪd] **I** s **1.** Grad m, Stufe f. **2.** ✗ bsd. Am. (Dienst)Grad m. **3.** ✝ Qualität f, Handelsklasse f. **4.** bsd. Am. Steigung f, Gefälle n: **make the** ~ fig. es schaffen, Erfolg haben; ~ **crossing** schienengleicher (Bahn)Übergang. **5.** ped. Am. Klasse f; Note f, Zensur f. **II** v/t **6.** sortieren, einteilen. **7.** abstufen, staffeln. ~ **school** s Am. Grundschule f.

gra·di·ent ['ɡreɪdjənt] s Steigung f, Gefälle n.

grad·u·al ['ɡrædjʊəl] adj □ allmählich, stufen-, schrittweise: ~**ly** a. nach u. nach.

grad·u·ate **I** s ['ɡrædjʊət] **1.** univ. Hochschulabsolvent(in), Akademiker(in); Graduierte(r), f. **2.** Am. Schulabgänger(in). **II** adj ['ɡrædjʊət] **3.** univ. Akademiker...; graduiert. **III** v/i ['~jʊeɪt] **4.** univ. graduieren. **5.** ped. Am. die Abschlußprüfung bestehen (**from** an dat): ~ **from** a. Schule absolvieren. **IV** v/t ['~jʊeɪt] **6.** → **grade** 7. **grad·u·a·tion** [ˌɡrædjʊ'eɪʃn] s **1.** Abstufung f, Staffelung f. **2.** univ. Graduierung f. **3.** ped. Am. Absolvieren n (**from** e-r Schule).

graf·fi·ti [ɡrə'fiːtɪ] s pl Wandschmierereien pl.

graft¹ [ɡrɑːft] ✿ **I** s Transplantat n. **II** v/t Gewebe verpflanzen, transplantieren.

graft² [ɡrɑːft] **F I** s **1.** hard ~ Maloche f. **2.** bsd. Am. Schmiergelder pl. **II** v/i **3.** ~ **hard** schuften. **4.** bsd. Am. Schmiergelder zahlen.

grain [ɡreɪn] s **1.** ⚘ (Samen-, bsd. Getreide)Korn n. **2.** coll. Getreide n, Korn n. **3.** (Sand- etc)Körnchen n, (-)Korn n: → **salt** 1. **4.** fig. Spur f: **not a** ~ **of hope** kein Funke Hoffnung. **5.** Maserung f (vom Holz): **it goes** (od. **is**) **against the** ~ (**with** [od. **for**] **me**) fig. es geht mir gegen den Strich.

gram [ɡræm] s Gramm n.

gram·mar ['ɡræmə] s Grammatik f: **bad** ~ grammatisch falsch; ~ (**book**) Grammatik. **gram·mat·i·cal** [ɡrə'mætɪkl] *adj* □ grammatisch, Grammatik...

gramme [græm] *s bsd. Br.* Gramm *n.*

gram·o·phone ['græməfəʊn] *s Br.* Plattenspieler *m.*

grand [grænd] **I** *adj* □ **1.** großartig, grandios, prächtig. **2.** groß, bedeutend, wichtig. **3.** Haupt...: **~ prize**; **~ total** Gesamt-, Endsumme *f.* **4.** F großartig, glänzend. **II** *s* **5.** ♪ Flügel *m.* **6.** *pl* **grand** *Am. sl.* Riese *m* ($ 1000).

gran·dad → **granddad.**

grand·child ['græntʃaɪld] *s* (*irr* **child**) Enkelkind *n.* '**~dad** *s* F Opa *m* (*a. alter Mann*), Großpapa *m.* '**~daugh·ter** *s* Enkelin *f.*

gran·deur ['grændʒə] *s* **1.** Pracht *f.* **2.** Größe *f*, Wichtigkeit *f.*

'**grand**,**fa·ther** *s* Großvater *m:* **~('s) clock** Standuhr *f.*

gran·dil·o·quent [græn'dɪləkwənt] *adj* □ **1.** schwülstig, hochtrabend. **2.** großsprecherisch.

gran·di·ose ['grændɪəʊs] *adj* □ großartig, grandios.

grand·ma ['grænmɑː] *s* F Oma *f*, Großmama *f.* '**~moth·er** *s* Großmutter *f.* '**~pa** *s* F Opa *m*, Großpapa *m.* '**~par·ents** *s pl* Großeltern *pl.* '**~son** *s* Enkel *m.* **~stand** ['grænd**~**] *s Sport:* Haupttribüne *f.*

gran·ite ['grænɪt] *s geol.* Granit *m.*

gran·ny ['grænɪ] *s* F Oma *f.*

grant [grɑːnt] **I** *v/t* **1.** bewilligen, gewähren. **2.** *Erlaubnis etc* geben, erteilen. **3.** *Bitte etc* erfüllen, *a.* ⚖ *e-m Antrag etc* stattgeben. **4.** ⚖ *(bsd. formell)* übertragen, übereignen. **5.** zugeben, zugestehen: **I ~ you that** ich gebe zu, daß; **take s.th. for ~ed** et. als erwiesen *od.* gegeben ansehen; et. als selbstverständlich betrachten *od.* hinnehmen. **II** *s* **6.** Bewilligung *f*, Gewährung *f.* **7.** Stipendium *n.* **8.** ⚖ Übertragung *f*, Übereignung *f.*

gran·u·lar ['grænjʊlə] *adj* gekörnt, körnig, granuliert. **gran·u·lat·ed** ['~leɪtɪd] *adj* → **granular: ~ sugar** Kristallzucker *m.* **gran·ule** ['~juːl] *s* Körnchen *n.*

grape [greɪp] *s* Weintraube *f*, -beere *f.* '**~fruit** *s* ♥ Grapefruit *f*, Pampelmuse *f.* **~ juice** *s* Traubensaft *m.* **~ sug·ar** *s* Traubenzucker *m.* '**~vine** *s* **1.** ♥ Weinstock *m.* **2. I heard on the ~ that** F mir ist zu Ohren gekommen, daß.

graph [grɑːf] **I** *s* **1.** Diagramm *n*, Schaubild *n*, graphische Darstellung. **2.** *bsd.* ♣ Kurve *f:* **~ paper** Millimeterpapier *n.* **II** *v/t* **3.** graphisch darstellen. '**graph·ic** *adj* (**~ally**) **1.** anschaulich, plastisch. **2.** graphisch: **~ artist** Graphiker(in); **~ arts** *pl* Graphik *f.*

graph·ite ['græfaɪt] *s min.* Graphit *m.*

graph·ol·o·gist [græ'fɒlədʒɪst] *s* Graphologe *m.* **graph'ol·o·gy** *s* Graphologie *f.*

grap·ple ['græpl] *v/i:* **~ with** kämpfen mit, *fig. a.* sich herumschlagen mit.

grasp [grɑːsp] **I** *v/t* **1.** packen, (er)greifen, *Gelegenheit* ergreifen; an sich reißen. **2.** *fig.* verstehen, begreifen. **II** *v/i* **3.** zugreifen, zupacken: **~ at** greifen nach (*a. fig.*). **III** *s* **4.** Griff *m.* **5.** Reichweite *f* (*a. fig.*). **6.** *fig.* Verständnis *n:* **be beyond s.o.'s ~** über j-s Verstand gehen.

grass [grɑːs] **I** *s* **1.** ♥ Gras *n:* **hear the ~ grow** *fig.* das Gras wachsen hören; **not let the ~ grow under one's feet** *fig.* keine Zeit verschwenden. **2.** Rasen *m:* **keep off the ~** Betreten des Rasens verboten! **3.** *sl.* Gras(s) *n* (*Marihuana*). **4.** *Br. sl.* Spitzel *m.* **II** *v/i* **5.** grasen, weiden. **6.** *Br. sl.* singen (**to** bei): **~ on** j-n verpfeifen. **~ blade** *s* Grashalm *m.* '**~hop·per** *s zo.* Heuschrecke *f*, Grashüpfer *m.* **~ roots** *s pl* (*a. sg konstruiert*) **1.** *fig.* Wurzel *f:* **attack a problem at the ~** ein Problem an der Wurzel packen. **2.** *pol.* Basis *f* (*e-r Partei*). **~ snake** *s zo.* Ringelnatter *f.* **~ wid·ow** *s* Strohwitwe *f.* **~ wid·ow·er** *s* Strohwitwer *m.*

grass·y ['grɑːsɪ] *adj* grasbedeckt, Gras...

grate¹ [greɪt] **I** *s* **1.** Gitter *n.* **2.** (Feuer)Rost *m.* **II** *v/t* **3.** vergittern.

grate² [**~**] **I** *v/t* **1.** *Käse etc* reiben, *Gemüse etc a.* raspeln. **2.** knirschen *od.* kratzen mit. **3.** *et.* krächzen(d) sagen). **II** *v/i* **4.** knirschen; kratzen; quietschen. **5.** *fig.* weh tun (**on** a.ob. j-m): **~ on s.o.'s ears** j-m in den Ohren weh tun.

grate·ful ['greɪtfʊl] *adj* □ dankbar (**to s.o. for s.th.** j-m für et.).

grat·er ['greɪtə] *s* Reibe *f*, Reibeisen *n*, Raspel *f.*

grat·i·fi·ca·tion [ˌgrætɪfɪ'keɪʃn] *s* **1.** Befriedigung *f*, Genugtuung *f* (**at** über *acc*). **2.** Freude *f*, Genuß *m.* **grat·i·fy**

['∼faɪ] v/t **1.** *j-n, Verlangen etc* befriedigen. **2.** erfreuen: *be gratified* sich freuen (*at* über *acc*); *I am gratified to hear* ich höre mit Befriedigung *od.* Genugtuung. '**grat·i·fy·ing** *adj* □ erfreulich (*to* für).

grat·ing ['greɪtɪŋ] *s* Gitter(werk) *n*.

gra·tis ['greɪtɪs] **I** *adv* gratis, umsonst. **II** *adj* unentgeltlich, Gratis...

grat·i·tude ['grætɪtjuːd] *s* Dankbarkeit *f*: *in ∼ for* aus Dankbarkeit für.

gra·tu·i·tous [grə'tjuːɪtəs] *adj* □ **1.** → *gratis* II. **2.** freiwillig. **3.** grundlos, unbegründet. **gra'tu·i·ty** *s* **1.** Zuwendung *f*, Gratifikation *f*. **2.** Trinkgeld *n*.

grave[1] [greɪv] *adj* □ ernst (*Angelegenheit, Stimme, Zustand etc*).

grave[2] [∼] *s* Grab *n*: *dig one's own ∼* sich sein eigenes Grab schaufeln; *turn (over) in one's ∼* sich im Grab (her)umdrehen. '**∼·dig·ger** *s* Totengräber *m* (*a. fig.*).

grav·el ['grævl] **I** *s* Kies *m*. **II** *v/t pret u. pp* **-eled**, *bsd. Br.* **-elled** mit Kies bestreuen: ∼*(l)ed path* Kiesweg *m*. ∼ *pit s* Kiesgrube *f*.

'**grave·stone** *s* Grabstein *m*. '**∼·yard** *s* Friedhof *m*.

grav·i·tate ['grævɪteɪt] *v/i*: ∼ *toward(s)* sich hingezogen fühlen zu, neigen zu. **grav·i'ta·tion** *s phys.* Gravitation *f*, Schwerkraft *f*. **grav·i'ta·tion·al** *adj phys.* Gravitations...: ∼ *force* Schwerkraft *f*; ∼ *pull* Anziehungskraft *f*.

grav·i·ty ['grævətɪ] *s* **1.** Ernst *m*. **2.** *phys.* Gravitation *f*, Schwerkraft *f*: → *centre* 1, *force* 1, *specific* 1.

gra·vy ['greɪvɪ] *s* **1.** Braten-, Fleischsaft *m*. **2.** (Braten)Soße *f*. ∼ *boat s* Soßenschüssel *f*.

gray, *etc Am.* → *grey, etc.*

graze[1] [greɪz] *v/i* weiden, grasen.

graze[2] [∼] **I** *v/t* **1.** streifen. **2.** ✷ sich *das Knie etc* (ab-, auf)schürfen *od.* (auf)schrammen. **II** *s* **3.** ✷ Abschürfung *f*, Schramme *f*. **4.** *a.* ∼*grazing shot* Streifschuß *m*.

grease *I s* [griːs] **1.** (*zerlassenes*) Fett. **2.** ✪ Schmierfett *n*, Schmiere *f*. **II** *v/t* [griːz] **3.** (ein)fetten, ✪ (ab)schmieren: *like* ∼*d lightning* F wie ein geölter Blitz; → *palm*[1] 1. **greas·y** ['griːzɪ] *adj* □ fett(ig).

great[1] [greɪt] *adj* (□ → *greatly*) **1.** groß,

beträchtlich: *a ∼ many* sehr viele. **2.** groß, bedeutend, wichtig. **3.** ausgezeichnet, großartig. **4.** F *be ∼ at* gut *od.* groß sein in (*dat*); *be ∼ on* sich begeistern für. **5.** F großartig, herrlich. **∼·'grand·child** *s* (*irr child*) Urenkel(in). **∼·'grand,daugh·ter** *s* Urenkelin *f*. **∼·'grand,fa·ther** *s* Urgroßvater *m*. **∼·'grand,moth·er** *s* Urgroßmutter *f*. **∼·'grand,par·ents** *s pl* Urgroßeltern *pl*. **∼·'grand·son** *s* Urenkel *m*.

great·ly ['greɪtlɪ] *adv* sehr, überaus. '**great·ness** *s* Größe *f*, Bedeutung *f*.

greed [griːd] *s* **1.** Gier *f* (*for* nach): ∼ *for power* Machtgier. **2.** Habgier *f*, -sucht *f*. **3.** Gefräßigkeit *f*. '**greed·i·ness** *s* **1.** Gierigkeit *f*. **2.** Gefräßigkeit *f*. '**greed·y** *adj* □ **1.** gierig (*for* auf *acc*, nach): ∼ *for power* machtgierig. **2.** habgierig, -süchtig. **3.** gefräßig.

Greek [griːk] **I** *s* **1.** Grieche *m*, Griechin *f*. **2.** *ling.* Griechisch *n*: *that's ∼ to me fig.* das sind für mich böhmische Dörfer. **II** *adj* **3.** griechisch.

green [griːn] **I** *adj* □ **1.** grün: *have ∼ fingers fig.* e-e grüne Hand haben; *the lights are ∼* die Ampel steht auf Grün; *give s.o. the ∼ light fig.* j-m grünes Licht geben (*on, to* für); ∼ *with envy* grün *od.* gelb vor Neid. **2.** *fig.* grün, unerfahren. **II** *s* **3.** Grün *n*: *dressed in ∼* grün *od.* in Grün gekleidet; *at ∼* bei Grün; *the lights are at ∼* die Ampel steht auf Grün. **4.** *pl* grünes Gemüse. '**∼·gro·cer** *s bsd. Br.* Obst- u. Gemüsehändler *m*. '**∼·horn** *s* F Grünschnabel *m*; Neuling *m*. '**∼·house** *s* Gewächs-, Treibhaus *n*.

green·ish ['griːnɪʃ] *adj* grünlich.

Green·wich (Mean) Time ['grenɪdʒ] *s* Greenwicher Zeit *f*.

greet [griːt] *v/t* **1.** grüßen. **2.** begrüßen, empfangen. **3.** *Nachricht etc* aufnehmen. '**greet·ing** *s* **1.** Gruß *m*, Begrüßung *f*. **2.** *pl* Grüße *pl*; Glückwünsche *pl*: ∼ *card* Glückwunschkarte *f*. **3.** *Am.* Anrede *f* (*im Brief*).

gre·gar·i·ous [grɪ'geərɪəs] *adj* □ **1.** gesellig. **2.** *zo.* in Herden lebend, Herden...

gre·nade [grə'neɪd] *s* ✕ (*Hand-, Gewehr*)Granate *f*.

grew [gruː] *pret von* **grow.**

grey [greɪ] *bsd. Br.* **I** *adj* □ **1.** grau: ∼

area Grauzone *f*; **~ eminence** graue Eminenz; **~ matter** *anat.* graue Substanz; F Grips *m*. **2.** grau(haarig), ergraut. **3.** *fig.* trüb, düster, grau: **~ prospects** *pl* trübe Aussichten *pl*. **II** *s* **4.** Grau *n*: **dressed in ~** grau *od.* in Grau gekleidet. **III** *v/i* **5.** grau werden, ergrauen; **~ing** angegraut, graumeliert (*Haare*). **~·'haired** *adj* grauhaarig. **'~·hound** *s zo.* Windhund *m*.

grey·ish ['grenʃ] *adj* grau-, gräulich.

grid [grɪd] *s* **1.** Gitter *n*, (Eisen)Rost *m*. **2.** ⚡ *etc* Versorgungsnetz *n*. **3.** *geogr.* Gitter(netz) *n* (*auf Karten*). **4.** Bratrost *m*.

grid·dle ['grɪdl] *s* (rundes) Backblech.

'grid·i·ron *s* Bratrost *m*.

grief [griːf] *s* Gram *m*, Kummer *m*: **come to ~** zu Schaden kommen; fehlschlagen, scheitern.

griev·ance ['griːvns] *s* **1.** Beschwerde(-grund *m*) *f*; Mißstand *m*. **2.** **nurse a ~ against** e-n Groll hegen gegen. **grieve** **I** *v/t* betrüben, bekümmern. **II** *v/i* bekümmert sein, sich grämen (**at, about, over** über *acc*, wegen): **~ for** trauern um. **'griev·ous** *adj* □ **1.** schmerzlich, bitter. **2.** schwer, schlimm (*Fehler, Verlust etc*): **~ bodily harm** ⚖ *Br.* schwere Körperverletzung.

grill [grɪl] **I** *s* **1.** Grill *m*. **2.** Grillen *n*. **3.** Gegrillte *n*: **a ~ of meat** gegrilltes Fleisch. **4.** Grillroom *m*. **II** *v/t* **5.** grillen. **6.** **~ o.s.** → **9. 7.** F *j-n* in die Mangel nehmen (*bsd. Polizei*): **~ s.o. about** *j-n* ausquetschen über (*acc*). **III** *v/i* **8.** gegrillt werden. **9.** sich (*in der Sonne*) grillen (lassen).

grille [grɪl] *s* **1.** (Schalter-, Sprech)Gitter *n*. **2.** *mot.* (Kühler)Grill *m*.

grill-room ['~ruːm] *s* Grillroom *m*.

grim [grɪm] *adj* □ **1.** grimmig. **2.** erbittert, verbissen. **3.** hart, unerbittlich. **4.** grausig.

gri·mace [grɪ'meɪs] **I** *s* Grimasse *f*. **II** *v/i* e-e Grimasse *od.* Grimassen schneiden.

grime [graɪm] **I** *s* (dicker) Schmutz *od.* Ruß. **II** *v/t* beschmutzen. **'grim·y** *adj* □ schmutzig, rußig.

grin [grɪn] **I** *v/i* grinsen: **~ at s.o.** *j-n* angrinsen; **~ and bear it** gute Miene zum bösen Spiel machen. **II** *s* Grinsen *n*.

grind [graɪnd] **I** *v/t* (*irr*) **1.** Messer etc schleifen: → **ax(e)** 1. **2.** *a.* **~ down**

(zer)mahlen, zerreiben, -kleinern. **3.** *Kaffee etc* mahlen; *Fleisch* durchdrehen. **4.** **~ one's teeth** mit den Zähnen knirschen. **II** *v/i* (*irr*) **5.** knirschen. **6.** F schuften; pauken, büffeln (**for** für). **III** *s* **7.** Knirschen. **8.** F Schufterei *f*; Pauken *n*, Büffeln *n*. **'grind·er** *s* **1.** (*Messeretc*)Schleifer *m*. **2.** (*Kaffee*)Mühle *f*; (*Fleisch*)Wolf *m*. **3.** *anat.* Backenzahn *m*.

'grind·stone *s* Schleifstein *m*: **keep** (*od.* **have**) **one's nose to the ~** *fig.* schuften.

grip [grɪp] **I** *s* **1.** Griff *m*: **come** (*od.* **get**) **to ~s with** aneinandergeraten mit; *fig.* sich auseinandersetzen mit. **2.** *fig.* Herrschaft *f*, Gewalt *f*: **have** (*od.* **keep**) **a ~ on** et. in der Gewalt haben, *Zuhörer etc* fesseln. **3.** (Hand)Griff *m* (e-s Koffers etc). **II** *v/t* (*Am. a. irr*) **4.** ergreifen, packen. **5.** *fig. j-n* packen (*Furcht etc*), *Zuhörer etc* fesseln.

gripe [graɪp] **I** *v/t* **1.** *Am.* F ärgern. **II** *v/i* **2.** Bauchschmerzen haben. **3.** F (**about**) meckern (über *acc*), nörgeln (an *dat*, über *acc*): **~ at** *j-n* anmeckern. **III** *s* **4.** *mst pl* Bauchschmerzen *pl*.

grip·ping ['grɪpɪŋ] *adj* □ packend, fesselnd.

gript [grɪpt] *Am. pret u. pp von* **grip**.

gris·ly ['grɪzlɪ] *adj* gräßlich, schrecklich.

grist [grɪst] *s* Mahlgut *n*: **all is ~ that comes to his mill** *fig.* er weiß aus allem Kapital zu schlagen.

gris·tle ['grɪsl] *s* Knorpel *m*. **'gris·tly** *adj* knorp(e)lig.

grit [grɪt] **I** *s* **1.** (grober) Sand, Kies *m*. **2.** Streusand *m*. **3.** *fig.* Mut *m*. **II** *v/t* **4.** *Straße etc* sanden, streuen. **5.** **~ one's teeth** die Zähne zs.-beißen (*a. fig.*).

griz·zle ['grɪzl] *v/i Br.* F **1.** quengeln. **2.** sich beklagen (**about** über *acc*).

griz·zly ['grɪzlɪ] **I** *adj* grau(haarig). **II** *s a.* **~ bear** *zo.* Grizzly(bär) *m*.

groan [grəʊn] **I** *v/i* **1.** stöhnen, ächzen (**with** vor *dat*; *fig.* **under** unter *dat*). **2.** ächzen, knarren (**under** unter *dat*) (*Fußboden etc*). **II** *s* **3.** Stöhnen *n*, Ächzen *n*.

groats [grəʊts] *s pl* Hafergrütze *f*.

gro·cer ['grəʊsə] *s* Lebensmittelhändler *m*. **'gro·cer·y** *s* **1.** Lebensmittelgeschäft *n*. **2.** *pl* Lebensmittel *pl*.

grog [grɒg] *s* Grog *m*.

grog·gy ['grɒgɪ] *adj* F **1.** groggy (*a. Boxen*). **2.** wacklig (*Tisch etc*).

groin [grɔɪn] *s anat.* Leiste(ngegend) *f.*

groom [gruːm] I *s* **1.** Pferdepfleger *m*, Stallbursche *m.* **2.** Bräutigam *m.* II *v/t* **3.** *Pferde* versorgen, pflegen. **4.** *Person, Kleidung* pflegen.

groove [gruːv] I *s* **1.** Rinne *f*, Furche *f.* **2.** ⚙ Rille *f* (*a. e-r Schallplatte*), Nut *f.* **3.** *fig.* ausgefahrenes Gleis. II *v/t* ⚙ rillen, nuten.

grope [grəʊp] I *v/i* tasten (**for** nach): ~ **about** (*od.* **around**) herumtasten, -tasten; ~ **in the dark** *fig.* im dunkeln tappen. II *v/t*: ~ **one's way** sich vorwärtstasten.

gross [grəʊs] I *adj* □ **1.** Brutto...: ~ **national product** Bruttosozialprodukt *n.* **2.** schwer, grob (*Fehler etc*), schreiend (*Ungerechtigkeit*), stark, maßlos (*Übertreibung*): ~ **negligence** 🜊 grobe Fahrlässigkeit. **3.** unfein, derb. **4.** dick, feist. II *s* **5.** *das Ganze*: **in** (**the**) ~ im ganzen. **6.** *pl* **gross** Gros *n* (*12 Dutzend*). III *v/t* brutto verdienen *od.* einnehmen.

gro·tesque [grəʊ'tesk] *adj* □ grotesk.

grot·to ['grɒtəʊ] *pl* **-to(e)s** *s* Grotte *f.*

grouch [graʊtʃ] F I *v/i* nörgeln (*an dat*, *über acc*), meckern (*über acc*). II *s* Nörgler(in). **'grouch·y** *adj* □ F nörglerisch.

ground¹ [graʊnd] I *s* **1.** (Erd)Boden *m*, Erde *f.* II *adj* gemahlen (*Kaffee etc*): ~ **meat** Hackfleisch *n.*

ground² [~] I *s* **1.** (Erd)Boden *m*, Erde *f*: **above** ~ oberirdisch; ⚒ über Tage; **below** ~ ⚒ unter Tage; **break new** (*od.* **fresh**) ~ Land urbar machen, *a. fig.* Neuland erschließen; **fall to the** ~ zu Boden fallen; *fig.* sich zerschlagen, ins Wasser fallen. **2.** Boden *m*, Gebiet *n* (*a. fig.*): **on German** ~ auf deutschem Boden; **gain** ~ (an) Boden gewinnen, *fig. a.* um sich fassen. **3.** Grundbesitz *m.* **4.** *oft pl Sport:* Platz *m.* **5.** *fig.* Standpunkt *m*: **hold** (*od.* **stand**) **one's** ~ sich *od.* s-n Standpunkt behaupten. **6.** *fig.* (Beweg)Grund *m*: **on the** ~(**s**) **of** auf Grund von (*od. gen*); **on** ~**s of age** aus Altersgründen; **on the** ~(**s**) **that** mit der Begründung, daß. **7.** *pl* (Boden)Satz *m.* **8.** 🜊 *Am.* Erde *f*, Erdung *f.* II *v/t* **9.** *fig.* gründen, stützen (**on, in** auf *acc*): ~**ed**

in fact auf Tatsachen beruhend. **10.** 🛩 Startverbot erteilen (*dat*). **11.** 🜊 *Am.* erden. III *v/i* **12.** ⚓ auflaufen.

'ground|-,break·ing *adj* bahnbrechend, wegweisend. ~ **ca·ble** *s* 🜊 *Am.* Massekabel *n.* ~ **crew** *s* 🛩 Bodenpersonal *n.* ~ **floor** *s* Erdgeschoß *n.* ~ **fog** *s* Bodennebel *m.* ~ **frost** *s* Bodenfrost *m.*

ground·less ['graʊndlɪs] *adj* □ grundlos, unbegründet.

'ground|-nut *s* 🜃 Erdnuß *f.* ~ **plan** *s* 🜂 Grundriß *m.* ~ **staff** *s* 🛩 *Br.* Bodenpersonal *n.* ~ **sta·tion** *s Raumfahrt:* Bodenstation *f.* ~ **wa·ter** *s* Grundwasser *n.* '~**wa·ter lev·el** *s* Grundwasserspiegel *m.* '~**work** *s* 🜂 Fundament *n* (*a. fig.*).

group [gruːp] I *s* **1.** Gruppe *f.* ~ **of islands** Inselgruppe. **2.** ✝ Gruppe *f*, Konzern *m.* II *v/t* **3.** eingruppieren (**into** in *acc*). **4.** zu e-r Gruppe zs.-stellen. III *v/i* **5.** sich gruppieren. ~ **dy·nam·ics** *s pl* (*sg konstruiert*) *Sozialpsychologie:* Gruppendynamik *f.* ~ **sex** *s* Gruppensex *m.* ~ **ther·a·py** *s* 🜊, *psych.* Gruppentherapie *f.*

grouse [graʊs] → **grouch** I.

grove [grəʊv] *s* Wäldchen *n*, Gehölz *n.*

grov·el ['grɒvl] *v/i pret u. pp* **-eled**, *bsd. Br.* **-elled**: ~ **before** (*od.* **to**) **s.o.** *fig.* vor j-m kriechen. **'grov·el·(l)er** *s* Kriecher *m.* **'grov·el·(l)ing** *adj* □ kriecherisch.

grow [grəʊ] (*irr*) I *v/i* **1.** wachsen: ~ **up** auf-, heranwachsen; ~ **out of a)** herauswachsen aus (*e-m Kleidungsstück*), **b)** *e-r Angewohnheit etc* entwachsen. **2.** *fig.* zunehmen (**in** an *dat*), anwachsen. **3.** *fig.* (*bsd.* allmählich) werden: ~ **less** sich vermindern. II *v/t* **4.** *Gemüse etc* anbauen, anpflanzen, *Blumen etc* züchten. **5.** ~ **a beard** sich e-n Bart wachsen lassen. **'grow·er** *s* Pflanzer *m*, Züchter *m*, *in Zssgn* ...bauer *m.*

growl [graʊl] I *v/i* **1.** knurren (*Hund*), brummen (*Bär*) (*beide a. Person*): ~ **at** j-n anknurren. **2.** (g)rollen (*Donner*). II *v/t* **3.** *oft* ~ **out** *Worte* knurren, brummen. III *s* **4.** Knurren *n*, Brummen *n.* **5.** (G)Rollen *n.*

grown [grəʊn] *pp von* **grow**. '~**-up** I *adj* [*a.* ˌ~'ʌp] **1.** erwachsen. **2.** (nur) für Erwachsene; Erwachsenen... II *s* **3.** Erwachsene *m*, *f.*

growth [grəʊθ] *s* **1.** Wachsen *n*, Wachstum *n.* **2.** Wuchs *m*, Größe *f.* **3.** *fig.*

Zunahme f, Anwachsen n (**in** gen). **4.** Anbau m. **5.** ✿ Gewächs n, Wucherung f. **~ in·dus·try** s ⚜ Wachstumsindustrie f. **~ rate** s ⚜ Wachstumsrate f.

grub [grʌb] **I** v/i **1.** graben. **2.** stöbern, wühlen (**among, in** in dat; **for** nach). **II** v/t **3.** oft **~ up** (od. **out**) ausgraben, fig. a. aufstöbern. **III** s **4.** zo. Made f, Larve f. **5.** sl. Futter n (Essen).

'grub·by adj schmudd(e)lig, schmutzig.

grudge [grʌdʒ] **I** v/t **1.** mißgönnen (**s.o. s.th.** j-m et.). **2.** **~ doing s.th.** et. nur widerwillig od. ungern tun. **II** s **3.** Groll m: **bear s.o. a ~** e-n Groll auf j-n haben. **'grudg·ing** adj □ **1.** mißgünstig. **2.** widerwillig.

gru·el ['gruəl] s Haferschleim m. **'gru·el·(l)ing** adj fig. aufreibend, zermürbend.

grue·some ['gruːsəm] adj □ grausig, schauerlich.

gruff [grʌf] adj □ **1.** schroff, barsch. **2.** rauh (Stimme).

grum·ble ['grʌmbl] **I** v/i **1.** murren (**at, about, over** über acc). **2.** → **growl** 2. **II** v/t **3.** oft **~ out** et. murren. **III** s **4.** Murren n. **5.** → **growl** 5.

grump·y ['grʌmpɪ] adj □ mißmutig, mürrisch.

grunt [grʌnt] **I** v/i **1.** grunzen (Schwein, a. Person). **2.** murren, brummen (**at** über acc). **II** v/t **3.** oft **~ out** et. grunzen, murren, brummen. **III** s **4.** Grunzen n.

guar·an·tee [ˌgærənˈtiː] **I** s **1.** Garantie f (**on** auf acc, für): **the watch is still under ~** auf der Uhr ist noch Garantie; **~** (**card**) Garantiekarte f, -schein m. **2.** Kaution f, Sicherheit f. **3.** Bürge m, Bürgin f, Garant(in). **II** v/t **4.** (sich ver)bürgen für, Garantie leisten für. **5.** garantieren. **guar·an·tor** [ˌˈtɔː] → **guarantee** 3.

guard [gɑːd] **I** v/t **1.** bewachen, wachen über (acc), behüten, beschützen (**against, from** vor dat): **a closely ~ed secret** ein streng gehütetes Geheimnis. **2.** bewachen, beaufsichtigen. **II** v/i **3.** sich hüten (**against** vor dat). od. in acht nehmen od. schützen (**against** vor dat). **III** s **4.** Wache f, (Wach)Posten m, Wächter m; Aufseher m, Wärter m. **5.** Wache f, Bewachung f: **be on ~** Wache stehen; **keep ~ over** et. bewachen. **6.** 🚂 Br. Schaffner m; Am. Bahnwärter m. **7.**

Garde f: **~ of hono(u)r** Ehrengarde. **8.** fig. Wachsamkeit f: **be on** (**off**) **one's ~** (nicht) auf der Hut sein (**against** vor dat). **9.** Boxen etc: Deckung f. **~ dog** s Wachhund m. **~ du·ty** s Wachdienst m: **be on ~** Wache haben.

guard·ed ['gɑːdɪd] adj □ vorsichtig, zurückhaltend, (Optimismus) verhalten, gedämpft.

guard·i·an ['gɑːdjən] s **1.** Hüter m, Wächter m: **~ angel** Schutzengel m. **2.** ⚖ Vormund m. **'guard·i·an·ship** s ⚖ Vormundschaft f (**of** über acc, für): **be** (**place**) **under ~** unter Vormundschaft stehen (stellen).

'guard·rail s **1.** Handlauf m. **2.** mot. Leitplanke f. **~ rope** s Absperrseil n.

guards·man ['gɑːdzmən] s (irr man) ✗ Gardist m.

gue(r)·ril·la [gəˈrɪlə] s ✗ Guerilla m: **~ war(fare)** Guerillakrieg m.

guess [ges] **I** v/t **1.** schätzen (**at** auf acc). **2.** (er)raten. **3.** ahnen, vermuten. **4.** bsd. Am. F glauben, meinen, annehmen. **II** v/i **5.** schätzen (**at s.th.** et.). **6.** raten: **~ing game** Ratespiel n. **III** s **7.** Schätzung f, Vermutung f: **at a ~** schätzungsweise; **I'll give you three ~es** dreimal darfst du raten; → **educated** 2, **rough** 5, **wild** 5. **'~·work** s (reine) Vermutung(en pl).

guest [gest] **I** s Gast m. **II** adj a) Gast...: **~ speaker** Gastredner m, b) Gäste...: **~ list**. **'~·house** s **1.** Gästehaus n. **2.** Pension f, Fremdenheim n. **~ room** s Gast-, Gäste-, Fremdenzimmer n.

guf·faw [gʌˈfɔː] **I** s schallendes Gelächter. **II** v/i schallend lachen.

guid·ance ['gaɪdns] s **1.** Leitung f, Führung f. **2.** Anleitung f, Unterweisung f: **for your ~** zu Ihrer Orientierung. **3.** (Berufs-, Ehe- etc)Beratung f.

guide [gaɪd] **I** v/t **1.** j-n führen, j-m den Weg zeigen. **2.** fig. lenken, leiten. **3.** et., a. j-n bestimmen: **be ~d by** sich leiten lassen von. **4.** anleiten. **II** s **5.** (Reise-, Berg- etc)Führer m. **6.** (Reise- etc)Führer m (**to** durch, von) (Buch): **~ to London** London-Führer m. **7.** (to) Leitfaden m (gen), Einführung f (**to** acc), Handbuch n (gen). **'~·book** → **guide** 7.

guid·ed ['gaɪdɪd] adj **1.** **~ tour** Führung f (**of** durch). **2.** ✗, ⚙ (fern)gelenkt, (-)gesteuert: **~ missile** Lenkflugkörper m.

guide| dog s Blindenhund m. '**~·lines** s pl Richtlinien pl (**on** gen).

guid·ing ['gaɪdɪŋ] adj leitend: **~ principle** Leitprinzip n.

guild [gɪld] s **1.** hist. Gilde f, Zunft f. **2.** Vereinigung f, Gesellschaft f.

guile [gaɪl] s (Arg)List f, Tücke f. **guile·ful** ['~fʊl] adj □ arglistig, tückisch. '**guile·less** adj □ arglos.

guil·lo·tine [ˌɡɪlə'tiːn] **I** s Guillotine f, Fallbeil n. **II** v/t durch die Guillotine od. mit dem Fallbeil hinrichten.

guilt [gɪlt] s Schuld f: **~ complex** Schuldkomplex m. '**guilt·less** adj □ schuldlos, unschuldig (**of** an dat). '**guilt·y** adj □ **1.** schuldig (**of** gen): → **plea** 2, **plead** 2. **2.** schuldbewußt: **a ~ conscience** ein schlechtes Gewissen (**about** wegen).

guin·ea pig ['gɪnɪ] s **1.** zo. Meerschweinchen n. **2.** fig. Versuchskaninchen n.

guise [gaɪz] s: **in the ~ of** als ... (verkleidet); **under** (od. **in**) **the ~ of** fig. in der Maske (gen), unter dem Deckmantel (gen).

gui·tar [gɪ'tɑː] s ♪ Gitarre f. **gui·tar·ist** s Gitarrist(in).

gulch [gʌlʃ] s bsd. Am. (Berg)Schlucht f.

gulf [gʌlf] s **1.** Golf m, Meerbusen m. **2.** Abgrund m (a. fig.). **3.** fig. Kluft f.

gull [gʌl] s orn. Möwe f.

gul·let ['gʌlɪt] s **1.** anat. Speiseröhre f. **2.** Gurgel f, Kehle f.

gul·li·ble ['gʌləbl] adj □ leichtgläubig.

gul·ly ['gʌlɪ] s **1.** (Wasser)Rinne f. **2.** ⊙ Gully m: **~** (**drain**) Abzugskanal m.

gulp [gʌlp] **I** v/t. oft **~ down** hinunterstürzen, Speise hinunterschlingen. **2.** oft **~ back** Tränen etc hinunterschlucken, unterdrücken. **II** s **3.** (großer) Schluck: **at one ~** auf 'einen Zug.

gum¹ [gʌm] s oft pl anat. Zahnfleisch n.

gum² [~] **I** s **1.** Gummi n, m, Kautschuk m. **2.** Klebstoff m, bsd. Gummilösung f. **II** v/t **3.** gummieren. **4.** (an-, ver)kleben. '**gum·my** adj klebrig.

gump·tion ['gʌmpʃn] s F **1.** Grips m. **2.** Mumm m, Schneid m.

gun [gʌn] **I** s **1.** ⚔ Geschütz n, Kanone f: **stand** (od. **stick**) **to one's ~s** F festbleiben, nicht nachgeben. **2.** Gewehr n; Pistole f, Revolver m. **3.** Sport: Startpistole f; Startschuß m: → **jump** 9. **4.** Tankstelle: Zapfpistole f. **II** v/t **5.** a. **~ to**

death erschießen: **~ down** niederschießen. **~ bat·tle** s Feuergefecht n, Schießerei f, Schußwechsel m. '**~·fight** → **gun battle**. **~ li·cence** (Am. **li·cense**) s Waffenschein m. **~·man** ['~mən] s (irr **man**) **1.** Bewaffnete m. **2.** Revolverheld m. '**~·point** s: **at ~** mit vorgehaltener Waffe, mit Waffengewalt. '**~·pow·der** s Schießpulver n. '**~·run·ner** s Waffenschmuggler m. '**~·run·ning** s Waffenschmuggel m. '**~·shot** s **1.** Schuß m. **2.** a. **~ wound** Schußwunde f, -verletzung f. **3.** Schußweite f: **within** (**out of**) **~** in (außer) Schußweite.

gur·gle ['gɜːɡl] **I** v/i gurgeln: a) gluckern (Wasser), b) glucksen (**with** vor dat) (Person, Stimme). **II** s Gurgeln n, Gluckern n, Glucksen n.

gu·ru ['gʊruː] s Guru m.

gush [gʌʃ] **I** v/i **1.** strömen, schießen (**from** aus). **2.** F schwärmen (**over** von). **II** s **3.** Schwall m, Strom m (beide a. fig.). **4.** F Schwärmerei f. '**gush·er** s **1.** F Schwärmer(in). **2.** Springquelle f (Erdöl). '**gush·ing**, '**gush·y** adj □ F schwärmerisch.

gus·set ['gʌsɪt] s Schneiderei: Zwickel m, Keil m.

gust [gʌst] s **1.** Windstoß m, Bö f. **2.** fig. (Gefühls)Ausbruch m: **~ of anger** Wutanfall m.

gus·to ['gʌstəʊ] s Begeisterung f, Genuß m.

gus·ty ['gʌstɪ] adj □ **1.** böig. **2.** stürmisch (a. fig.).

gut [gʌt] **I** s **1.** pl bsd. zo. Eingeweide pl, Gedärme pl: **hate s.o.'s ~s** F j-n hassen wie die Pest. **2.** anat. Darm m. **3.** oft pl F Bauch m. **4.** pl F Mumm m, Schneid m. **II** v/t **5.** ausweiden, -nehmen. '**gut·less** adj F ohne Mumm od. Schneid f. '**guts·y** adj F **1.** mutig. **2.** verfressen.

gut·ter ['gʌtə] **I** s **1.** Gosse f (a. fig.), Rinnstein m. **2.** Dachrinne f. **II** v/i **3.** tropfen (Kerze). **~ press** s Skandal-, Sensationspresse f. '**~·snipe** s Gassenkind n.

gut·tur·al ['gʌtərəl] **I** adj □ Kehl..., guttural (beide a. ling.), kehlig. **II** s ling. Guttural m, Kehllaut m.

guy [gaɪ] s F Kerl m, Typ m.

guz·zle ['gʌzl] v/t **1.** (a. v/i) saufen; fressen. **2.** oft **~ away** Geld verprassen, bsd. versaufen.

gym [dʒɪm] F → **gymnasium; gymnas·tic:** ~ **shoes** pl Turnschuhe pl.

gym·na·si·um [dʒɪm'neɪzjəm] pl **-si·ums, -si·a** [~zɪə] s Turn-, Sporthalle f.

gym·nast ['dʒnæst] s Turner(in). **gym·'nas·tic I** adj (**~ally**) **1.** turnerisch, Turn..., gymnastisch, Gymnastik... **II** s **2.** pl (sg konstruiert) Turnen n, Gymnastik f. **3.** mental ~s pl Gehirnakrobatik f.

gyn·(a)e·co·log·i·cal [ˌɡaɪnəkə'lɒdʒɪkl] adj □ ♀ gynäkologisch. **gyn·(a)e·** **col·o·gist** [ˌ~'kɒlədʒɪst] s Gynäkologe m, Gynäkologin f, Frauenarzt m, -ärztin f. **ˌgyn·(a)e'col·o·gy** s Gynäkologie f.

gyp [dʒɪp] sl. **I** v/t u. v/i **1.** bescheißen. **II** s **2.** Gauner(in). **3.** Beschiß m.

gyp·sum ['dʒɪpsəm] s min. Gips m.

gyp·sy bsd. Am. → **gipsy.**

gy·rate [ˌdʒaɪə'reɪt] v/i kreisen, sich (im Kreis) drehen. **ˌgy'ra·tion** s Kreisbewegung f, Drehung f. **gy·ra·to·ry** ['ˌ~rətərɪ] adj kreisend, sich (im Kreis) drehend.

H

H [eɪtʃ] pl **H's** ['eɪtʃɪz] s **1.** drop one's **H's** das H nicht aussprechen (Zeichen der Unbildung). **2.** sl. H [eɪtʃ] n (Heroin).

ha [hɑː] int ha!, ah!

ha·be·as cor·pus [ˌheɪbjəs'kɔːpəs] s a. **writ of** ~ ♣ gerichtliche Anordnung e-s Haftprüfungstermins.

hab·er·dash·er ['hæbədæʃə] s **1.** Br. Kurzwarenhändler m. **2.** Am. Herrenausstatter m. **'hab·er·dash·er·y** s **1.** Br. Kurzwarengeschäft n; Kurzwaren pl. **2.** Am. Herrenmodengeschäft n; Herrenbekleidung f.

hab·it ['hæbɪt] s **1.** (An)Gewohnheit f: out of (od. by) ~ aus Gewohnheit; get into (out of) a ~ e-e Gewohnheit annehmen (ablegen); get into (out of) the ~ of smoking sich das Rauchen angewöhnen (abgewöhnen); be in the ~ of doing s.th. die (An)Gewohnheit haben, et. zu tun. **2.** oft ~ of mind Geistesverfassung f. **3.** (bsd. Ordens)Tracht f.

hab·it·a·ble ['hæbɪtəbl] □ bewohnbar.

hab·i·tat ['hæbɪtæt] s ♀, zo. Standort m, Heimat f.

ha·bit·u·al [hə'bɪtjʊəl] adj □ **1.** gewohnheitsmäßig, Gewohnheits...: ~ criminal Gewohnheitsverbrecher m. **2.** gewohnt, ständig: be ~ly late ständig zu spät kommen. **ha'bit·u·ate** [~eɪt] v/t (o.s. sich) gewöhnen (to an acc): ~ o.s. to doing s.th. sich daran gewöhnen, et. zu tun.

hack¹ [hæk] **I** v/t **1.** (zer)hacken: ~ to pieces (od. bits) in Stücke hacken; fig. Ruf etc zerstören. **II** v/i **2.** a. ~ away einhauen (auf acc). **3.** trocken u. stoßweise husten: ~ing cough → **5. III** s **4.** Hieb m. **5.** trockener, stoßweiser Husten.

hack² [~] Am. F **I** s **1.** Taxi n. **II** v/i **2.** in e-m Taxi fahren. **3.** ein Taxi fahren.

hack·ie ['hækiː] s Am. F Taxifahrer(in).

hack·le ['hækl] s: get s.o.'s ~ up j-n wütend machen.

hack·neyed ['hæknɪd] adj abgedroschen.

had [hæd] pret u. pp von **have.**

had·dock ['hædək] pl **-docks,** bsd. coll. **-dock** s ichth. Schellfisch m.

hae·mo·glo·bin [ˌhiːməʊ'ɡləʊbɪn] s physiol. bsd. Br. Hämoglobin n.

hae·mo·phile ['hiːməʊfaɪl] s ♣ bsd. Br. Bluter m. **hae·mo·phil·i·a** [ˌ~'fɪlɪə] s bsd. Br. Bluterkrankheit f.

haem·or·rhage ['hemərɪdʒ] s ♣ bsd. Br. Blutung f. **haem·or·rhoids** ['~rɔɪdz] s pl ♣ bsd. Br. Hämorrhoiden pl.

haft [hɑːft] s Griff m, Heft n (bsd. e-r Stichwaffe), Stiel m (e-r Axt).

hag [hæɡ] s häßliches altes Weib, Hexe f.

hag·gard ['hæɡəd] adj □ **1.** wild (Blick). **2.** abgehärmt; abgespannt; abgezehrt, hager.

hag·gle ['hæɡl] v/i feilschen, handeln, schachern (about, over um).

hail¹ [heɪl] I s **1.** Hagel m (a. fig. von Flüchen, Fragen etc): **~ of bullets** Geschoßhagel. II v/i **2.** impers hageln. **3. ~ down** fig. niederhageln, -prasseln (**on** auf acc).

hail² [~] I v/t **1.** j-m zubrüllen. **2.** j-n, Taxi etc herbeirufen od. -winken. **3.** fig. et. begrüßen. II s **4.** (Zu)Ruf m: **within ~** in Rufweite.

'**hail·stone** s Hagelkorn n, (Hagel-) Schloße f. '**~·storm** s Hagelschauer m.

hair [heə] s (einzelnes) Haar; coll. Haar n, Haare pl: **to a ~** aufs Haar, haargenau; **do one's ~** sich die Haare richten, sich frisieren; **keep your ~ on!** F reg dich ab!; **let one's ~ down** sich ungezwungen benehmen; aus sich herausgehen; **split ~s** Haarspalterei treiben; **tear one's ~ (out)** sich die Haare raufen; **without turning a ~** ohne mit der Wimper zu zucken. **~·breadth** [´~bretθ] s: **by a ~** um Haaresbreite; **have a ~ escape** mit knapper Not entkommen. '**~·brush** s Haarbürste f. '**~·cut** s Haarschnitt m: **have a ~** sich die Haare schneiden lassen. '**~·do** pl **-dos** F Frisur f. '**~·dress·er** s Friseur m, Friseuse f. '**~·dress·ing** s Frisieren n: **~ salon** Friseur-, Frisiersalon m. '**~·dri·er** s Haartrockner m.

haired [heəd] adj **1.** behaart. **2.** in Zssgn ...haarig. '**hair·less** adj unbehaart, kahl.

'**hair**|**·line** s **1.** Haaransatz m. **2.** a. **~ crack** ⊙ Haarriß m. '**~·piece** s Haarteil n (für Frauen), Toupet n (für Männer). '**~·pin** s **1.** Haarnadel f. **2.** a. **~ bend** Haarnadelkurve f. '**~·rais·ing** adj haarsträubend. **~ re·stor·er** s Haarwuchsmittel n. **~ slide** s Br. Haarspange f. '**~·split·ting** I s Haarspalterei f. II adj haarspalterisch. **~ spray** s Haarspray m, n. '**~·style** s Frisur f. '**~·styl·ist** s Hair-Stylist(in).

hair·y [´heərɪ] adj **1.** haarig, behaart. **2.** F haarig, schwierig; gefährlich.

hale [heɪl] adj gesund, kräftig, rüstig: **~ and hearty** gesund u. munter.

half [hɑːf] I adj I s adj. halb: **~ a mile** e-e halbe Meile; **two pounds and a ~, two and a ~ pounds** zweieinhalb Pfund; → **mind** 5. II adv **2.** halb, zur Hälfte: **~ as long** halb so lang; **~ past two** halb drei. **3.** halb(wegs), fast, nahezu: **~ dead** halb-

tot; **not ~ bad** F gar nicht übel; **I ~ suspect** ich vermute fast. III pl **halves** [hɑːvz] s **4.** Hälfte f: **cut in(to) halves** (od. in ~) halbieren; **go halves with s.o. in** (od. **on**) **s.th.** et. mit j-m teilen. **5.** Sport: a) (Spiel)Hälfte f, Halbzeit f, b) (a. **~ of the field** Spielfeld)Hälfte f. '**~·baked** adj F nicht durchdacht, unausgegoren (Plan etc); grün (Person). '**~·breed** s Mischling m, Halbblut n. ~**broth·er** s Halbbruder m. **~·caste** [´~kɑːst] → **half-breed**. **~ face** s paint., phot. Profil n. **~·heart·ed** adj ☐ halbherzig. ,**~·mast** s: **fly at ~** a) a. **put at ~** auf halbmast setzen, b) auf halbmast wehen. **~ meas·ure** s Halbheit f, halbe Sache. **~ moon** s Halbmond m. ~**pen·ny** [´heɪpnɪ] s **1.** pl **half-pence** [´heɪpəns] halber Penny. **2.** pl '**half·pen·nies** Halbpennystück n. ,**~·price** adj u. adv zum halben Preis. '**~·seas o·ver** F blau, betrunken. **~·sis·ter** s Halbschwester f. '**~·tim·ber(ed)** adj △ Fachwerk... ~ **time** s Sport: Halbzeit f (Pause): **at ~** bei od. zur Halbzeit. ,**~·time** I adj **1.** Halbtags... **2.** job. **2.** Sport: Halbzeit...: **~ interval** Halbzeitpause f; **~ score** Halbzeitstand m. II adv **3.** halbtags: **work ~** halbtags arbeiten. ,**~·truth** s Halbwahrheit f. ,**~·way** I adj **1.** auf halbem Weg od. in der Mitte (liegend). **2.** fig. halb, teilweise: **~ measure → half measure.** II adv **3.** auf halbem Weg, in der Mitte: **meet s.o. ~** bsd. fig. j-m auf halbem Weg entgegenkommen. **4.** teilweise, halb(wegs). '**~·wit** s Schwachkopf m, Trottel m. ,**~·'year·ly** adj u. adv halbjährlich.

hal·i·but [´hælɪbət] pl **-buts**, bsd. coll. **-but** s ichth. Heilbutt m.

hal·i·to·sis [͵hælɪ´təʊsɪs] s übler Mundgeruch.

hall [hɔːl] s **1.** Halle f, Saal m. **2.** Diele f, Flur m. **3.** univ. a) → of residence Studentenheim n, b) Speisesaal m.

hal·le·lu·jah [͵hælɪ´luːjə] I s Halleluja n. II int halleluja!

'**hall·mark** I s **1.** Br. Feingehaltsstempel m. **2.** fig. (Kenn)Zeichen n, Merkmal n. II v/t **3.** Br. Gold, Silber stempeln. **4.** fig. kennzeichnen.

hal·lo bsd. Br. → **hello**.

hal·low [´hæləʊ] v/t heiligen.

hall\| **por·ter** s bsd. Br. Hausdiener m (im Hotel). '**~stand** s Garderoben-, Kleiderständer m; (Flur)Garderobe f.

hal·lu·ci·nate [həˈluːsɪneɪt] v/i halluzinieren. **hal**\|**lu·ci'na·tion** s Halluzination f.

ha·lo [ˈheɪləʊ] pl **-lo(e)s** s **1.** Heiligenschein m. **2.** ast. Hof m.

hal·o·gen [ˈhælədʒen] s 🞭 Halogen n.

halt [hɔːlt] I s Halt m: **bring to a ~** → II; **come to a ~** → III. II v/t anhalten, a. fig. zum Stehen od. Stillstand bringen. III v/i anhalten. a. fig. zum Stehen od. Stillstand kommen.

hal·ter [ˈhɔːltə] s **1.** Halfter m, n. **2.** Strick m, Strang m (zum Hängen).

halve [hɑːv] v/t halbieren. **halves** [~z] pl von **half.**

ham [hæm] s **1.** Schinken m: **~ and eggs** Schinken mit (Spiegel)Ei. **2.** a. **~ actor** F Schmierenkomödiant m. **3.** F Funkamateur m, Amateurfunker m.

ham·burg·er [ˈhæmbɜːgə] s gastr. Hamburger m.

ham\|-**'fist·ed** adj bsd. Br. F, **'~-**,**hand-ed** adj F tolpatschig, ungeschickt.

ham·let [ˈhæmlɪt] s Weiler m, Dörfchen n.

ham·mer [ˈhæmə] I s **1.** Hammer m: **come** (od. **go**) **under the ~** unter den Hammer kommen; **go at it ~ and tongs** F sich mächtig ins Zeug legen; (sich) streiten, daß die Fetzen fliegen. **2.** Leichtathletik: Hammer m: **~ throw** Hammerwerfen n; **~ thrower** Hammerwerfer m. II v/t **3.** hämmern: **~ in** einhämmern; **~ s.th. into s.o.'s head** fig. j-m et. einhämmern od. -bleuen III v/i **4.** hämmern (a. Puls etc): **~ at** einhämmern auf (acc).

ham·mock [ˈhæmək] s Hängematte f.

ham·per¹ [ˈhæmpə] v/t (be)hindern.

ham·per² [~] s **1.** (Deckel)Korb m. **2.** Geschenk-, Freßkorb m. **3.** Am. Wäschekorb m.

ham·ster [ˈhæmstə] s zo. Hamster m.

'**ham·string** I s anat. Kniesehne f. II v/t (irr **string**) fig. vereiteln; lähmen.

hand [hænd] I s **1.** Hand f: **at ~** in Reichweite; nahe (bevorstehend); bei der od. zur Hand; **by ~** mit der Hand, manuell; **~s down** spielend, mühelos (gewinnen etc); **~s off!** Hände weg!; **~s up!** Hände hoch!; **be ~ in glove** (**with**) ein Herz u.

e-e Seele sein (mit); unter 'einer Decke stecken (mit); **change ~s** den Besitzer wechseln; **give** (od. **lend**) **a** (**helping**) **~** mit zugreifen, j-m helfen (**with** bei); **have a ~ in** s-e Hand im Spiel haben bei, beteiligt sein an (dat); **hold ~s** Händchen halten; **not to lift** (od. **raise**) **a ~** keinen Finger rühren; **live from ~ to mouth** von der Hand in den Mund leben; **shake ~s with** j-m die Hand schütteln od. geben; → **tie** 7a. **2.** oft pl Hand f, Macht f, Gewalt f: **be entirely in s.o.'s ~s** ganz in j-s Hand sein; **fall into s.o.'s ~s** j-m in die Hände fallen. **3.** pl Hände pl, Obhut f: **in good ~s.** **4.** Seite f: **on the right ~** rechts; **on the one ~ ..., on the other ~** fig. einerseits ..., andererseits. **5.** oft in Zssgn Arbeiter m. **6.** Fachmann m, Routinier m: **an old ~** ein alter Praktikus od. Hase; **be a good ~ at** sehr geschickt od. geübt sein in (dat). **7.** Hand f, Quelle f: **at first ~** aus erster Hand. **8.** Handschrift f. **9.** Unterschrift f: **set one's ~ to** s-e Unterschrift setzen unter (acc), unterschreiben. **10.** Applaus m, Beifall m: **get a big ~** stürmischen Beifall bekommen. **11.** (Uhr)Zeiger m. **12.** Kartenspiel: Spieler m; Blatt n, Karten pl: **show one's ~** fig. s-e Karten aufdecken. II v/t **13.** aushändigen, (über)reichen, (-)reichen.

Verbindungen mit Adverbien:

hand\| **a·round** v/t herumreichen, herumgehen lassen. **~ back** v/t zurückgeben. **~ down** v/t **1.** hinunter-, herunterreichen, -langen (**from** von; **to** dat). **2.** (**to**) Tradition etc weitergeben (an acc), Bräuche etc überliefern (dat). **~ in** v/t **1.** hinein-, hereinreichen, -langen (**to** dat). **2.** Prüfungsarbeit etc abgeben, Gesuch etc einreichen (**to** bei): → **check** 11. **~ on** v/t **1.** weiterreichen, -geben (**to** dat, an acc). **2.** → **hand down** 2. **~ out** v/t **1.** aus-, verteilen (**to** an acc). **2.** Ratschläge, Komplimente etc verteilen. **~ o·ver** v/t (**to** dat) **1.** übergeben. **2.** geben, aushändigen. **~ round** → **hand around.** **~ up** v/t hinauf-, heraufreichen, -langen (**to** dat).

'**hand**\|**bag** s Handtasche f. **~ bag·gage** s bsd. Am. Handgepäck n. '**~-bill** s Handzettel m, Flugblatt n. '**~-book** s **1.** Handbuch n. **2.** Reiseführer m (of durch, von): **a ~ of London** ein London-Führer. ~ **brake** s ⊙ Handbremse f. **~breadth** ['~bretθ] s Handbreit f. **'~-carved** adj handgeschnitzt. ~ **cream** s Handcreme f. **'~cuff** I s mst pl Handschelle f. **II** v/t j-m Handschellen anlegen: ~**ed** in Handschellen.

hand·ful ['hændfʊl] s **1.** e-e Handvoll (a. fig. Personen). **2.** F Plage f (Person, Sache), Nervensäge f.

hand gre·nade s ✗ Handgranate f.

hand·i·cap ['hændıkæp] **I** s Handikap s: a) Vorgabe(rennen n, -spiel n) f, b) fig. Behinderung f, Nachteil m (**to** für): → **mental** 1, **physical** 1. **II** v/t behindern, benachteiligen: → **mentally** 1, **physically.**

hand·i·craft ['hændıkrɑːft] s **1.** Handfertigkeit f. **2.** (bsd. Kunst)Handwerk n. **'hand·i,crafts·man** [~mən] s (irr man) (bsd. Kunst)Handwerker m.

hand·i·work ['hændıwɜːk] s **1.** Handarbeit f. **2.** fig. Werk n.

hand·ker·chief ['hæŋkətʃıf] s Taschentuch n.

han·dle ['hændl] **I** s **1.** (Hand)Griff m; Stiel m; Henkel m; Klinke f, Drücker m: **fly off the ~** F hochgehen, wütend werden. **2.** fig. Handhabe f (**against** gegen). **II** v/t **3.** anfassen, berühren. **4.** hantieren od. umgehen mit, Maschine bedienen. **5.** Thema etc behandeln, erledigen, durchführen; mit et., j-m fertigwerden. **6.** j-n behandeln, umgehen mit: → **kid glove, with care!** Vorsicht, Glas! **'~·bar** s mst pl Lenkstange f.

hand| lug·gage s Handgepäck n. **,~·'made** adj handgearbeitet. **,~·'op-er·at·ed** adj handbedient, Hand... **'~·out** s **1.** Almosen n, milde Gabe. **2.** Prospekt m, Hand-, Werbezettel m. **3.** Handout n (für Pressevertreter etc). **'~·rail** s Handlauf m. **'~·set** s teleph. Hörer m. **'~·shake** s Händedruck m: **give s.o. a firm ~** j-m kräftig die Hand schütteln.

hand·some ['hænsəm] adj □ **1.** gutaussehend (bsd. Mann). **2.** beträchtlich, ansehnlich (Summe etc). **3.** großzügig, nobel.

'hand·stand s Handstand m: **do a ~** e-n Handstand machen. **,~·to-'mouth** adj: **lead a ~ existence** von der Hand in den Mund leben. **'~·work** s Handarbeit

f. **'~,writ·ing** s (Hand)Schrift f. **'~,writ-ten** adj handgeschrieben.

hand·y ['hændı] adj □ **1.** zur od. bei der Hand: **keep s.th. ~** et. griffbereit aufbewahren. **2.** geschickt, gewandt. **3.** handlich, praktisch. **4.** nützlich: **come in ~** sich als nützlich erweisen; (sehr) gelegen kommen. **'~·man** s (irr man) Mädchen n für alles, Faktotum n.

hang [hæŋ] **I** s **1.** Sitz m (e-s Kleids etc). **2. get the ~ of s.th.** F et. rauskriegen od. kapieren. **II** v/t (irr) **3.** (auf)hängen; Tür etc einhängen: ~ **on a hook** an e-n Haken hängen. **4.** pret u. pp **hanged** j-n (auf)hängen: ~ **o.s.** sich erhängen. **5.** Kopf hängen lassen od. senken. **6.** behängen (**with** mit). **7.** Tapeten ankleben. **III** v/i (irr) **8.** hängen (**by, on** an dat): ~ **by a thread** fig. an e-m dünnen od. seidenen) Faden hängen; → **over** fig. hängen od. schweben über (dat). **9.** ~ **about** (od. **around**) herumlungern od. sich herumtreiben in (dat).

Verbindungen mit Adverbien:

hang| **a·bout, ~ a·round** v/i herumlungern, sich herumtreiben. ~ **back** v/i zögern (**from doing** zu tun). ~ **down** v/i hinunter-, herunterhängen (**from** von). ~ **on** v/i **1.** (**to**) sich klammern an (acc) (a. fig.), festhalten (acc). **2.** warten; teleph. am Apparat bleiben. **3.** nicht nachlassen (Krankheit etc). ~ **out** I v/t **1.** (hin-, her)aushängen, Wäsche (draußen) aufhängen. **II** v/i **2.** herausragen. **3.** aushängen, ausgehängt sein. ~ **o·ver** I v/i andauern, existieren (**from** seit). **II** v/t: **be hung over** F e-n Kater haben. ~ **to-geth·er** v/i **1.** zs.-halten (Personen). **2.** e-n (logischen) Zs.-hang haben, zs.-hängen. ~ **up** I v/t **1.** aufhängen. **2.** aufschieben. **3. be hung up on** F e-n Komplex haben wegen; besessen sein von. **II** v/i **4.** teleph. einhängen, auflegen.

hang·ar ['hæŋə] s Hangar m, Flugzeughalle f.

hang·er ['hæŋə] s Kleiderbügel m; Schlaufe f, Aufhänger m.

hang| **glid·er** (Sport) **1.** (Flug)Drachen m. **2.** Drachenflieger(in). ~ **glid·ing** s Drachenfliegen n.

hang·ing ['hæŋıŋ] **I** adj Hänge...: ~ **bridge.** **II** s mst pl Wandbehang m.

hang|·**man** ['hæŋmən] s (irr man) Hen-

ker m. '~nail s ⚕ Nied-, Neidnagel m.
'~o·ver s 1. Überbleibsel n, -rest m. 2.
F Katzenjammer m, Kater m (beide a.
fig.). '~up s F 1. Komplex m. 2. Problem n, Schwierigkeit f.

han·ker ['hæŋkə] v/i sich sehnen, Verlangen haben (**after, for** nach): ~ **to do
s.th.** sich danach sehnen, et. zu tun.
'**han·ker·ing** s Sehnsucht f, Verlangen n.

han·kie, han·ky ['hæŋkɪ] s F Taschentuch n.

han·ky-pan·ky [,hæŋkɪ'pæŋkɪ] s F 1.
Hokuspokus m, fauler Zauber. 2.
Techtelmechtel n.

hap·haz·ard [,hæp'hæzəd] adj □ u. adv
plan-, wahllos, adv a. aufs Geratewohl.

hap·pen ['hæpən] v/i 1. geschehen, sich
ereignen, passieren: **it will not ~ again**
es wird nicht wieder vorkommen. 2.
zufällig geschehen, sich zufällig ergeben: **it ~ed that** es traf od. ergab sich,
daß. **if you ~ to see it** wenn du es
zufällig siehst od. sehen solltest; **it ~ed
to be cold** zufällig war es kalt. 4. ~ **to**
geschehen od. passieren mit (dat. dat),
zustoßen (dat), werden aus. 5. ~ **on**
zufällig begegnen (dat) od. treffen
(acc); zufällig stoßen auf (acc).
hap·pen·ing ['hæpnɪŋ] s 1. Ereignis n.
2. Kunst: Happening n.

hap·pi·ly ['hæpɪlɪ] adv 1. glücklich. 2.
glücklicherweise, zum Glück. '**hap·pi·
ness** s Glück n.

hap·py ['hæpɪ] adj (□ → **happily**) 1. allg.
glücklich (**at, about** über acc; **with** mit):
I am ~ to see you es freut mich (sehr),
Sie zu sehen; → **birthday** I, **Easter** I,
new year 1. 2. F beschwipst. 3. in
Zssgn: a) ...begeistert: → **trigger-hap·
py**, b) F ...süchtig. ,~**go·'luck·y** adj
unbekümmert, sorglos. ~ **hour** s F Zeit,
in der in Pubs etc alkoholische Getränke
verbilligt ausgeschenkt werden.

har·ass ['hærəs] v/t 1. ständig belästigen
(**with** mit). 2. aufreiben, zermürben. 3.
schikanieren.

har·bin·ger ['ha:bɪndʒə] fig. I s Vorläufer m; Vorbote m; (erstes) Anzeichen.
II v/t ankündigen.

har·bo(u)r ['ha:bə] I s 1. Hafen m. 2.
Zufluchtsort m, Unterschlupf m. II v/t
3. j-m Zuflucht od. Unterschlupf gewähren. 4. Gedanken, Groll etc hegen.

hard [ha:d] I adj 1. allg. hart. 2. schwer,
schwierig: ~ **work** harte Arbeit; ~ **to
believe** kaum zu glauben; ~ **to please**
schwer zufriedenzustellen; ~ **to imag·
ine** schwer vorstellbar. 3. heftig, stark:
a ~ blow ein harter Schlag, fig. a. ein
schwerer Schlag. 4. hart (Winter), (a.
Frost) streng (Klima) rauh. 5. hart,
streng: **be ~ on s.o.** j-n hart od. ungerecht behandeln; **it trifft ihn schwer. 7.** hart, nüchtern:
the ~ facts pl die nackten Tatsachen pl.
8. hart (Droge), (Getränk a.) stark. 9. ~
of hearing schwerhörig. 10. ~ **up** f in
(Geld)Schwierigkeiten, in Verlegenheit
(**for** um). II adv 11. hart, fest: **frozen ~**
hartgefroren. 12. hart, schwer: **work ~;
brake ~** scharf bremsen; **think ~** scharf
nachdenken; **try ~** sich große Mühe geben. 13. nahe, dicht: ~ **by** ganz in der
Nähe. '~back s gebundene Ausgabe.
,~·'boiled adj 1. hart(gekocht) (Ei). 2.
fig. hart, unsentimental; nüchtern,
sachlich. ~·core s harter Kern (e-r Bande etc). '~·core adj 1. zum harten Kern
gehörend. 2. hart (Pornographie).
'~·cov·er → hardback. '~·earned adj
hartverdient.

hard·en ['ha:dn] I v/t 1. härten (a. ⊙),
hart machen. 2. fig. hart machen, abstumpfen (**to** gegen): ~ed verstockt, abgebrüht. 3. fig. abhärten (**to** gegen). II
v/i 4. erhärten (a. ⊙), hart werden. 5.
fig. hart werden, abstumpfen (**to** gegen). 6. fig. sich abhärten (**to** gegen). 7.
⚕ anziehen (Preise).

,**hard**|'**head·ed** adj nüchtern, realistisch. ,~·'**heart·ed** adj □ hartherzig. ~
line s 1. bsd. pol. harter Kurs: **follow**
(od. **adopt**) **a** ~ e-n harten Kurs einschlagen. 2. pl bsd. Br. Pech n (**on** für).

hard·ly ['ha:dlɪ] adv 1. kaum, fast nicht:
~ **ever** fast nie. 2. (wohl) kaum, schwerlich. 3. (zeitlich) kaum. '**hard·ness** s 1.
Härte f (a. fig.). 2. Schwierigkeit f.
'**hard·ship** s 1. Not f, Elend n. 2. Härte
f: ~ **case** Härtefall m.

hard| **shoul·der** s mot. Br. Standspur f.
'~·top s mot. Hardtop n, m (a. Wagen).
'~·ware s 1. Metall-, Eisenwaren pl;
Haushaltswaren pl. 2. Computer:
Hardware f. ,~·'wear·ing adj Br. stra-

pazierfähig. ˌ~'**work·ing** adj fleißig, arbeitsam.

har·dy ['hɑːdɪ] adj □ **1.** zäh, ausdauernd, robust; abgehärtet. **2.** ♀ winterfest.

hare [heə] s zo. Hase m: (**as**) **mad as a March** ~ F total verrückt; **play** ~ **and hounds** e-e Schnitzeljagd machen. '~**bell** s ♀ Glockenblume f. '~**brained** adj verrückt. ˌ~'**lip** s ♬ Hasenscharte f.

ha·rem ['hɑːriːm] s Harem m (a. fig. humor.).

harm [hɑːm] I s Schaden m: **there is no** ~ **in doing s.th.** es kann nicht(s) schaden, et. zu tun; **there is no** ~ **in trying** ein Versuch kann nicht schaden; **come to** ~ zu Schaden kommen; **do s.o.** ~ j-m schaden od. et. antun; → **bodily** 1, **mean³** 1. II v/t j-n verletzen (a. fig.), j-m, j-s Ruf etc schaden. **harm·ful** ['~ful] adj □ schädlich (**to** für): ~ **to one's health** gesundheitsschädlich. '**harm·less** adj □ allg. harmlos.

har·mon·ic [hɑː'mɒnɪk] adj (**ally**) harmonisch. **har·mon·i·ca** [~kə] s ♪ Mundharmonika f. **har·mo·ni·ous** [~'məʊnjəs] adj □ harmonisch. **har·mo·ni·um** [~'məʊnjəm] s ♪ Harmonium n. **har·mo·nize** ['~mənaɪz] I v/i harmonieren, zs.-passen, in Einklang sein (**with** mit). II v/t harmonisieren, in Einklang bringen (**with** mit). **har·mo·ny** ['~mənɪ] s ♪ Harmonie f, fig. a. Einklang m, Eintracht f.

har·ness ['hɑːnɪs] I s **1.** (Pferde- etc)Geschirr n: **die in** ~ fig. in den Sielen sterben. **2.** mot. (Sicherheits)Gurt m. II v/t **3.** Pferd etc anschirren; anspannen (**to** an acc).

harp [hɑːp] I s **1.** ♪ Harfe f. II v/i **2.** Harfe spielen. **3.** fig. (**on, about**) herumreiten (auf dat), dauernd reden (von). '**harp·er**, '**harp·ist** s Harfenist(in).

har·poon [hɑː'puːn] I s Harpune f. II v/t harpunieren.

harp·si·chord ['hɑːpsɪkɔːd] s ♪ Cembalo n.

har·row ['hærəʊ] I s **1.** ✐Egge f. II v/t **2.** ✐ eggen. **3.** fig. quälen, peinigen.

harsh [hɑːʃ] adj □ rauh (Stoff, Stimme); grell (Farbe); barsch, schroff (Art etc); streng (Disziplin etc), hart (Worte etc).

har·um-scar·um [ˌheərəm'skeərəm] adj unbesonnen, leichtsinnig.

har·vest ['hɑːvɪst] I s Ernte f: a) Erntezeit f, b) Ernten n, c) (Ernte)Ertrag m. II v/t ernten, fig. a. einheimsen. ~ **fes·ti·val** s Erntedankfest n.

has [hæz] er, sie, es hat. '~**been** s F 1. et. Überholtes. **2.** j-d, der den Höhepunkt s-r Karriere überschritten hat. **3.** pl alte Zeiten pl.

hash¹ [hæʃ] I v/t **1.** a. ~ **up** Fleisch zerhacken, -kleinern. **2.** a. ~ **up** fig. durcheinanderbringen; verpfuschen. II s **3.** gastr. Haschee n. **4.** fig. et. Aufgewärmtes. **5.** **make a** ~ **of** → 2.

hash² [~] s F Hasch n (Haschisch).

hash·ish ['hæʃiːʃ] s Haschisch n.

has·sle ['hæsl] F I s **1.** Krach m, (a. handgreifliche) Auseinandersetzung. **2.** Mühe f: **it was quite a** ~ es war ganz schön mühsam (**doing, to do** zu tun). II v/i **3.** a. e-e (handgreifliche) Auseinandersetzung haben.

haste [heɪst] s Hast f, Eile f: **make** ~ sich beeilen; **more** ~ **less speed** eile mit Weile. **has·ten** ['heɪsn] I v/t j-n antreiben; et. beschleunigen. II v/i (sich be)eilen, hasten. **hast·y** ['heɪstɪ] adj □ **1.** eilig, hastig, (Abreise) überstürzt. **2.** voreilig, -schnell, übereilt.

hat [hæt] s Hut m: **I'll eat my** ~ **if ...** F ich fresse e-n Besen, wenn ...; **talk through one's** ~ F dummes Zeug reden; ~**s off!** Hut ab!, alle Achtung! (**to** vor dat); → **cocked hat, old** 1.

hatch¹ [hætʃ] s **1.** ✈, ⚓ Luke f, allg. a. Bodentür f, -öffnung f. **2.** Durchreiche f.

hatch² [~] I v/t **1.** a. ~ **out** Eier, Junge ausbrüten. **2.** a. ~ **out** (od. **up**) Racheplan etc ausbrüten, -hecken; Programm etc entwickeln. II v/i **3.** brüten. **4.** a. ~ **out** (aus dem Ei) ausschlüpfen. III s **5.** Brut f.

hatch³ [~] v/t schraffieren.

'**hatch·back** s mot. (Wagen m mit) Hecktür f.

hatch·et ['hætʃɪt] s Beil n: **bury** (**take up**) **the** ~ fig. das Kriegsbeil begraben (ausgraben).

hate [heɪt] I v/t **1.** hassen: ~**d** verhaßt. **2.** nicht ausstehen können: → **gut** 1. **3.** nicht wollen od. mögen: ~ **doing** (od. **to do**) **s.th.** et. (nur) äußerst ungern tun.

II s **4.** Haß m (**of, for** auf acc, gegen): **full of ~** haßerfüllt. **5.** et. Verhaßtes: *... is my pet ~* F ... kann ich auf den Tod nicht ausstehen od. leiden.

ha·tred ['heɪtrɪd] → **hate** 4.

hat·ter ['hætə] s Hutmacher m: (**as**) **mad as a ~** total verrückt.

hat trick s Sport: Hattrick m.

haugh·ty ['hɔːtɪ] adj □ hochmütig, überheblich.

haul [hɔːl] **I** s **1.** Ziehen n, Zerren n; kräftiger Zug. **2.** Fischzug m, fig. a. Fang m, Beute f: **make a big ~** e-n guten Fang machen. **3.** a) Beförderung f, Transport m, b) Transportweg m. **II** v/t **4.** ziehen, zerren: **~ down** Flagge etc ein-, niederholen; **~ up** F sich j-n vorknöpfen; j-n schleppen (**before** vor acc); → **coal.** **5.** befördern, transportieren. **III** v/i **6.** **~ away** ziehen, zerren (**at, on** an dat). **'haul·age** s → **haul** 3a. **'haul·er, bes. Br. haul·i·er** ['~jə] s Transportunternehmer m.

haulm [hɔːm] s Halm m, Stengel m.

haunch [hɔːntʃ] s gastr. Lendenstück n, Keule f: **~ of beef** Rindslende f.

haunt [hɔːnt] **I** v/t **1.** spuken od. umgehen in (dat): **this room is ~ed** in diesem Zimmer spukt es; **~ed castle** Spukschloß n. **2.** fig. a) verfolgen, quälen: **~ed look** gehetzter Blick, b) j-m nicht mehr aus dem Kopf gehen, j-n nicht mehr loslassen. **3.** häufig besuchen. **II** s **4.** häufig besuchter Ort. **'haunt·ing** adj □ **1.** quälend. **2.** unvergeßlich: **~ melody** (od. **tune**) Ohrwurm m.

have [hæv] **I** v/t (irr) **1.** allg. haben: **~ on** Kleidungsstück anhaben, Hut aufhaben; → **get** 11. **2.** haben, erleben. **3.** Kind bekommen: **may I ~ it?** s. **5.** Gefühle, Verdacht etc haben, hegen. **6.** erhalten, bekommen: **~ back** zurückbekommen. **7.** essen, trinken: → **breakfast** I, etc. **8.** haben, machen: → **look** 1, **try** 1, **walk** 1, **wash** 1. **9.** a. **~ on** F j-n reinlegen. **10.** **~ on** et. vorhaben. **11.** vor inf: müssen: **I ~ to go now**; → **get** 11. **12.** mit Objekt u. inf: lassen: **I had a suit made** ich ließ mir e-n Anzug machen. **13.** mit Objekt u. inf: (veran)lassen: **I had him sit down** ich ließ ihn Platz nehmen. **14.** **I had rather go than stay** ich möchte lieber gehen als bleiben; **you had best**

go du tätest am besten daran zu gehen. **II** v/aux (irr) **15.** haben, (bei vielen v/i) sein: **I have come** ich bin gekommen. **III** s **16. the ~s and the ~-nots** die Begüterten u. die Habenichtse.

ha·ven ['heɪvn] s **1.** mst fig. (sicherer) Hafen. **2.** fig. Zufluchtsort m.

'have-not s mst pl Habenichts m: → **have** 16.

hav·oc ['hævək] s Verwüstung f, Zerstörung f: **cause ~** schwere Zerstörungen od. (a. fig.) ein Chaos verursachen; **play ~ with, make ~ of** verwüsten, zerstören; fig. verheerend wirken auf (acc).

haw [hɔː] v/i → **hem²** II, **hum** 2.

hawk¹ [hɔːk] s orn. Falke m (a. pol.), Habicht m.

hawk² [~] v/t **1.** hausieren mit; auf der Straße verkaufen. **2.** a. **~ about** (od. **around**) Gerücht etc verbreiten. **'hawk·er** s Hausierer(in); Straßenhändler(in).

haw·ser ['hɔːzə] s ♣ Kabeltau n, Trosse f.

haw·thorn ['hɔːθɔːn] s ♣ Weißdorn m.

hay [heɪ] s Heu n: **make ~ while the sun shines** fig. das Eisen schmieden, solange es heiß ist; **hit the ~** sl. sich in die Falle od. Klappe hauen. **~ fe·ver** s ♣ Heuschnupfen m. **'~wire** adj F kaputt (Gerät); (völlig) durcheinander (Pläne etc); übergeschnappt (Person): **go ~** kaputtgehen; (völlig) durcheinandergeraten; überschnappen.

haz·ard ['hæzəd] **I** s **1.** Gefahr f, Risiko n: **at all ~s** unter allen Umständen; **at the ~ of one's life** unter Lebensgefahr, unter Einsatz s-s Lebens; **~ to health** Gesundheitsrisiko; **~ warning lights** pl mot. Warnblinkanlage f. **2.** Zufall m: **by ~** durch Zufall, zufällig. **II** v/t **3.** riskieren: a) aufs Spiel setzen, b) (zu sagen) wagen, sich e-e Bemerkung etc erlauben. **'haz·ard·ous** adj □ gewagt, gefährlich, riskant.

haze [heɪz] s **1.** Dunst(schleier) m. **2.** fig. Nebel m, Schleier m.

ha·zel ['heɪzl] adj (hasel)nußbraun. **'~-nut** s ♣ Haselnuß f.

ha·zy ['heɪzɪ] adj □ **1.** dunstig, diesig. **2.** fig. verschwommen, nebelhaft (Vorstellung etc): **be rather ~ about** nur e-e ziemlich verschwommene od. vage Vorstellung haben von.

'H-bomb s ✕ H-Bombe f, Wasserstoffbombe f.

he [hi:] **I** pron er: **~ who** wer; derjenige,
welcher. **II** s Er m: a) Junge m, Mann
m, b) zo. Männchen n. **III** adj in Zssgn
zo. ...männchen n: **~-goat** Ziegenbock m.

head [hed] **I** v/t **1.** anführen, an der Spitze stehen von (od. gen). **2.** voraus-,
vorausgehen (dat). **3.** (an)führen, leiten:
~ed by unter der Leitung von. **4.** Fußball: köpfen. **II** v/i **5.** (for) gehen, fahren (nach); sich bewegen (auf acc ...
zu), lossteuern, -gehen (auf acc); ♣
Kurs halten (auf acc). III adj **6.** Kopf...
7. Chef..., Haupt..., Ober...: **~ cook**
Chefkoch m; **~ nurse** Oberschwester f.
IV s **8.** Kopf m: **above** (od. over) s.o.'s
~ zu hoch für j-n; **from ~ to foot** von
Kopf bis Fuß; **~ over heels** kopfüber
(die Treppe hinunterstürzen); bis über
beide Ohren (verliebt sein); **be ~ over
heels in debt** bis über die Ohren in
Schulden stecken; **bury one's ~ in the
sand** den Kopf in den Sand stecken;
cry one's ~ off F sich die Augen ausweinen; **go to s.o.'s ~** j-m in den od. zu
Kopf steigen (Alkohol, Erfolg etc);
keep one's ~ above water sich über
Wasser halten (a. fig.); **lose one's ~**
den Kopf od. die Nerven verlieren; →
snap 5. **9.** (Ober)Haupt n: **~ of the
family** Familienvorstand m, -ober-
haupt; **~ of state** Staatsoberhaupt, →
crown 5. **10.** (An)Führer m, Leiter m: **~
of government** Regierungschef m. **11.**
Spitze f, führende Stellung: **at the ~ of**
an der Spitze (gen). **12.** Kopf(ende n) m
(e-s Bettes etc); Kopf m (e-s Briefs,
Nagels etc). **13.** Kopf m, (einzelne)
Person: **one pound a ~** ein Pfund pro
Kopf od. Person. **14.** fig Vorderseite f
(e-r Münze): **~s or tails?** Wappen od.
Zahl?; **I cannot make ~ or tail of it** ich
kann daraus nicht schlau werden. **15.** ♣
(Salat- etc)Kopf m. **16.** Schaum(krone
f) m (vom Bier etc). **17.** Quelle f (e-s
Flusses). **18.** Überschrift f, Titelkopf m.
19. in Zssgn F ...süchtige m, f: **'~ache**
s Kopfschmerz(en pl) m, -weh n: **be a
bit of a ~** F j-m, F, give s.o. a **~**
F j-m Kopfschmerzen od. Sorgen
machen. **'~band** s Kopf-, Stirn-
band n.

head·er ['hedə] s **1.** Kopfsprung m. **2.**
Fußball: Kopfball m.

head·first → headlong. **'~,hunt·er** s
Kopfjäger m.

head·ing ['hedɪŋ] s **1.** Überschrift f, Ti-
tel(zeile f) m. **2.** Thema n, (Gesprächs)Punkt m.

'head·lamp → headlight. **~·land** ['~-
lənd] s Landspitze f, -zunge f. **'~·light** s
mot. etc Scheinwerfer m: **~ flasher**
Lichthupe f. **'~·line** s **1.** Schlagzeile f:
hit the ~s Schlagzeilen machen. **2.**
Überschrift f. **'~·long** I adv **1.** kopfüber, mit dem Kopf voran. **2.** fig. a)
Hals über Kopf, b) ungestüm, stürmisch. **II** adj **3.** mit dem Kopf voran.
4. fig. a) voreilig, -schnell, b) → 2b.
~'mas·ter s ped. (Di)Rektor m.
~'mis·tress s ped. (Di)Rektorin f. **~-
of·fice** s Hauptbüro n, -sitz m, Zentrale
f. **~·'on** adj **1.** frontal (a. adv), Frontal... **2.** fig. direkt (Art etc). **'~·phones** s
pl Kopfhörer m. **~·'quar·ters** s pl (oft
sg konstruiert) **1.** ✕ Hauptquartier n.
2. (Polizei)Präsidium n. **3.** → head
office. **'~·rest** s Kopfstütze f. **'~·set** s
Kopfhörer m. **'~·shrink·er** s sl. Psychiater m. **'~ start** s Sport: Vorsprung m
(a. fig.): **have a ~ on** (od. over) s.o. j-m
gegenüber im Vorteil sein. **'~·strong**
adj eigensinnig, halsstarrig. **~ voice** s ♪
Kopfstimme f. **~·'wait·er** s Oberkellner
m. **'~·way** s: **make ~ (with)** (gut) vorankommen (mit), Fortschritte machen
(bei). **~ wind** s 🪁, ♣ Gegenwind m.
'~·work s geistige Arbeit.

head·y ['hedɪ] adj □ **1.** → headlong 4a.
2. berauschend (a. fig.).

heal [hi:l] **I** v/t heilen (of von) (a. fig.). **II**
v/i oft **~ up** (od. over) (zu)heilen.
'heal·ing I s Heilung f. **II** adj heilsam
(a. fig.), heilend: **~ process** Heil(ungs)-
prozeß m.

health [helθ] s **1.** Gesundheit f: **~ certificate** ärztliches Attest; **~ club** Fitneß-
club m; **~ food** Reform- od. Biokost f;
on ~ grounds aus gesundheitlichen
Gründen; **~ hazard** Gesundheitsrisiko
n; **~ insurance** Krankenversicherung f;
~ resort Kurort m; **~ service** Gesundheitsdienst m. **2.** a. **state of ~** Gesundheitszustand m: **in good (poor) ~** gesund, bei guter Gesundheit (kränklich,
bei schlechter Gesundheit). **3.** Gesund-

heit f, Wohl n: **drink (to)** (od. **propose**) **s.o.'s ~** auf j-s Wohl trinken; **your (very good) ~!** auf Ihr Wohl! **'health·y** adj □ **1.** allg. gesund (a. fig.). **2.** F gesund, kräftig (Appetit).

heap [hi:p] **I** v/t **1.** Haufen m: **in ~s** haufenweise. **2.** F Haufen m, Menge f: **~s of time** e-e Menge Zeit; **~s of times** unzählige Male; **~s better** sehr viel besser. **II** v/t **3.** häufen: **~ up** auf-, fig. a. anhäufen. **4.** fig. überhäufen (**with** mit).

hear [hɪə] (irr) **I** v/t **1.** hören: **I ~d him laugh(ing)** ich hörte ihn lachen; **make o.s. ~d** sich Gehör verschaffen. **2.** et. hören, erfahren (**about, of** von, über acc). **3.** j-n anhören, j-m zuhören: → **s.o. out** j-n ausreden lassen. **4.** (an)hören, sich et. anhören. **5.** Bitte etc erhören. **6.** Schüler, Gelerntes abhören. **7.** ☆☆ verhören, -nehmen; Fall verhandeln. **II** v/i **8.** hören: ~ **say** sagen hören; **he would not ~ of it** er wollte davon nichts hören od. wissen; **~! ~!** bravo!, sehr richtig!, iro. hört, hört! **9.** hören, erfahren (**about, of** von). **heard** [hɜːd] pret u. pp von **hear.** **'hear·ing** s **1.** Hören n: **within (out of) ~** in (außer) Hörweite; **~ aid** Hörgerät n. **2.** Gehör(sinn m) n: → **hard** 9. **3. gain** (od. **get**) **a ~** sich Gehör verschaffen. **4.** ☆☆ Verhör n, Vernehmung f; Verhandlung f. **5.** bsd. pol. Hearing n, Anhörung f.

'hear·say s: **by ~** vom Hörensagen.

hearse [hɜːs] s Leichenwagen m.

heart [hɑːt] s **1.** anat. Herz n (a. fig. Gemüt, Mitgefühl, Empfindung etc): **by ~** auswendig; **to one's ~'s content** nach Herzenslust; **with all one's** (od. **one's whole**) **~** von ganzem Herzen; **break s.o.'s ~** j-m das Herz brechen; **cry** (od. **sob**) **one's ~ out** sich die Augen ausweinen; **have no ~** kein Herz haben, herzlos sein; **my ~ sank** ich wurde deprimiert; **take s.th. to ~** sich et. zu Herzen nehmen; → **bottom** 1, **stone** 1. **2.** fig. Kern m. **3.** Kartenspiel: a) pl Herz n (Farbe), b) Herz(karte f) n. **'~·ache** s Kummer m, Gram m. **~ at·tack** s ☆ Herzanfall m; Herzinfarkt m. **'~·beat** s physiol. Herzschlag m. **'~·break·ing** adj □ herzzerreißend. **'~·burn** s ☆ Sodbrennen n. **~ con·di·tion** s ☆ Herzleiden n.

heart·en ['hɑːtn] v/t ermutigen.

---

heart| fail·ure s ☆ Herzversagen n. **'~·felt** adj tiefempfunden, aufrichtig.

hearth [hɑːθ] s **1.** Kamin m. **2.** a. **~ and home** fig. häuslicher Herd, Heim n.

heart·i·ly ['hɑːtɪlɪ] adv **1.** herzlich, von Herzen. **2.** herzhaft.

heart·less ['hɑːtlɪs] adj □ herzlos.

,heart|-'lung ma·chine s ☆ Herz-Lungen-Maschine f. **~ pace·mak·er** s ☆ Herzschrittmacher m. **'~,rend·ing** adj □ herzzerreißend. **,~-to- '~** adj aufrichtig, offen. ☆☆ **~ trans·plant** s ☆ Herzverpflanzung f.

heart·y ['hɑːtɪ] adj (□ → **heartily**) **1.** herzlich. **2.** → **hale** 3. herzhaft, kräftig (Appetit, Mahlzeit etc).

heat [hiːt] **I** s **1.** allg. Hitze f; a. phys. Wärme f. **2.** fig. Ungestüm n; Eifer m: **in the ~ of the moment** im Eifer od. in der Hitze des Gefechts; **in the ~ of pas·sion** ☆☆ im Affekt. **3.** Sport: (Einzel)Lauf m: (**preliminary**) ~ Vorlauf. **4. the ~** Am. coll. F die Bullen pl (Polizei). **5.** zo. Läufigkeit f: **in ~** läufig. **II** v/t **6.** a. **~ up** erhitzen, Speisen a. aufwärmen. **7.** heizen. **8. ~ up** Diskussion etc anheizen. **III** v/i **9.** sich erhitzen (a. fig.). **'heat·ed** adj **1.** geheizt. **2.** erhitzt, fig. a. erregt, hitzig. **'heat·er** s Heizgerät n, -körper m.

heath [hiːθ] s **1.** bsd. Br. Heide(land n) f. **2.** ♣ a) Erika f, b) → **heather**.

hea·then ['hiːðn] **I** s **1.** Heide m, Heidin f: **the ~** coll. die Heiden pl. **2.** Barbar m. **II** adj **3.** heidnisch, Heiden... **4.** unzivilisiert, barbarisch. **hea·then·ish** ['~·ənɪʃ] → **heathen** II.

heath·er ['heðə] s ♣ Heidekraut n.

heat·ing ['hiːtɪŋ] **I** s Heizung f. **II** adj Heiz...: **~ pad** Heizkissen n.

heat| light·ning s Wetterleuchten n. **'~·proof** adj hitzebeständig, -fest. **~ rash** s ☆ Hitzeausschlag m. **'~·re,sist·ant** → **heatproof**. **'~·stroke** s ☆ Hitzschlag m. **~ wave** s Hitzewelle f.

heave [hiːv] **I** s **1.** Hochziehen n, -winden n. **2.** F Wurf m. **3.** Wogen n: **~ of the sea** ♣ Seegang m. **II** v/t (bsd. ♣ irr) **4.** (hoch)stemmen, (-)hieven. **5.** hochziehen, -winden, Anker lichten. **6.** F schmeißen, werfen. **7.** Seufzer etc ausstoßen: → **sigh** II. **8.** F auskotzen. **III** v/i (bsd. ♣ irr) **9.** sich heben u. senken, wogen. **10.** F würgen, Brechreiz haben:

~ **(up)** kotzen. **11. ~ to** ⚓ beidrehen.

heav·en ['hevn] s **1.** Himmel(reich n) m: **move ~ and earth** fig. Himmel u. Hölle in Bewegung setzen; **in the seventh ~ (of delight)** fig. im sieb(en)ten Himmel; **thank ~!** Gott sei Dank!; **what in ~ ...?** was in aller Welt ...?; → **forbid 3, sake, stink 1. 2.** ♀ Himmel m, Gott m.

'**heav·en·ly** adj himmlisch (a. fig.): ~ **body** ast. Himmelskörper m.

heav·i·ly ['hevɪlɪ] adv schwer (a. fig.): ~ **armed** schwerbewaffnet; **suffer ~** schwere (finanzielle) Verluste erleiden.

heav·y ['hevɪ] I adj (□ → **heavily**) **1.** allg. schwer. **2.** schwer (Sturz, Verluste etc), stark (Regen, Trinker, Verkehr etc), wuchtig (Schlag), hoch (Geldstrafe, Steuern etc): ~ **current** ⚡ Starkstrom m. **3.** schwer (Wein etc), (Nahrung a.) schwerverdaulich: ~ **beer** Starkbier n. **4.** drückend, lastend (Stille etc). **5.** (**with**) (schwer)beladen (mit); fig. überladen, voll (von): ~ **with meaning** bedeutungsvoll, -schwer. **6.** begriffsstutzig, dumm. **7.** benommen (**with** von): ~ **with sleep** schlaftrunken. **8. with a ~ heart** schweren Herzens. II adv **9. hang ~** dahinschleichen (Zeit); **lie ~ on s.o.** schwer auf j-m lasten. '**~·du·ty** adj **1.** ⚙ Hochleistungs... **2.** strapazierfähig. '**~·weight** (Sport) I s Schwergewicht(ler m) n. II adj Schwergewichts...

heck·le ['hekl] v/t Redner durch Zwischenrufe od. -fragen aus dem Konzept bringen od. in die Enge treiben. '**heck·ler** s Zwischenrufer m.

hec·tic ['hektɪk] adj (**~ally**) hektisch (a. ⚕).

hec·to·li·ter, bsd. Br. **hec·to·li·tre** ['hektəʊˌliːtə] s Hektoliter m, n.

he'd [hiːd] F für **he had**; **he would**.

hedge [hedʒ] I s **1.** Hecke f. **2.** fig. (Ab)Sicherung f (**against** gegen). II v/t **3.** a. ~ **in** (od. **round**) mit e-r Hecke einfassen: ~ **off** mit e-r Hecke abgrenzen od. abtrennen. **4.** fig. (ab)sichern (**against** gegen). III v/i **5.** fig. ausweichen, sich nicht festlegen (wollen). '**~·hog** s zo. Igel m; Am. Stachelschwein n.

heed [hiːd] I v/t beachten, Beachtung schenken (dat). II s: **give** (od. **pay**) **~ to**, **take ~ of** → I. **heed·ful** ['~fʊl] adj □ achtsam: **be ~ of** → **heed** I. '**heed·less**

adj □ achtlos, unachtsam: **be ~ of** nicht beachten, keine Beachtung schenken (dat), Warnung etc in den Wind schlagen.

hee-haw [ˌhiːˈhɔː] I s **1.** Iah n (Eselsschrei). **2.** fig. wieherndes Gelächter, Gewieher n. II v/i **3.** iahen. **4.** fig. wiehernd lachen, wiehern.

heel[^1] [hiːl] v/i ⚓ sich auf die Seite legen, krängen.

heel[^2] [~] I s **1.** anat. Ferse f (a. vom Strumpf etc); Absatz m, Hacken m (vom Schuh): **down at ~** a) mit schiefen Absätzen, b) a. **out at ~s** fig. heruntergekommen (Hotel etc), (Person a.) abgerissen; **on the ~s of** unmittelbar auf (acc), gleich nach; **follow at s.o.'s ~s, follow s.o. at** (od. on) **the ~s** j-m auf den Fersen folgen, sich j-m an die Fersen heften; **show a clean pair of ~s, take to one's ~s** die Beine in die Hand nehmen, unter den Arm nehmen. II v/t **2.** Absätze machen auf (acc). **3.** Fußball: Ball mit dem Absatz kicken.

hef·ty ['heftɪ] adj □ **1.** schwer. **2.** kräftig, stämmig. **3.** F mächtig, gewaltig (Schlag etc), stattlich (Mehrheit etc), saftig (Preise etc).

he·gem·o·ny [hɪˈgemənɪ] s bsd. pol. Hegemonie f.

height [haɪt] s **1.** Höhe f: **10 feet in ~** 10 Fuß hoch. **2.** (Körper)Größe f: **what is your ~?** wie groß sind Sie? **3.** Anhöhe f, Erhebung f. **4.** fig. Höhe(punkt m) f, Gipfel m: **at the ~ of one's fame** auf der Höhe s-s Ruhms; **at the ~ of summer** im Hochsommer. '**height·en** v/t **1.** erhöhen (a. fig.). **2.** fig. vergrößern, steigern. II v/i **3.** fig. sich erhöhen, (an)steigen, zunehmen.

hei·nous ['heɪnəs] adj □ abscheulich, scheußlich.

heir [eə] s ⚖ Erbe m (**to, of** gen): ~ **to the throne** Thronerbe m, -folger m; → **universal 1.** '**heir·ess** s Erbin f.

held [held] pret u. pp von **hold**.

hel·i·cop·ter ['helɪkɒptə] s Hubschrauber m.

hel·i·port ['helɪpɔːt] s Hubschrauberlandeplatz m.

he·li·um ['hiːlɪəm] s 🜂 Helium n.

hell [hel] s Hölle f (a. fig.): **like ~** F wie verrückt arbeiten etc; **a ~ of a noise** F ein Höllenlärm; **what the ~ ...?** F was zum Teufel ...?; **give s.o. ~** F j-m die Hölle heiß machen; **go to ~!** F scher dich zum Teufel!; **raise ~** F e-n Mordskrach schlagen; **suffer ~ on earth** die Hölle auf Erden haben.

he'll [hi:l] F *für he will.*

hell|bent *adj* F ganz versessen, wie wild (**on, for** auf acc). '**~cat** *s* Xanthippe f.

hell·ish ['helɪʃ] *adj* □ 1. höllisch (*a. fig.* F). 2. F verteufelt, scheußlich.

hel·lo [hə'ləʊ] F I *int* 1. hallo!, (*überrascht a.*) nanu! II *pl* **-los** *s* 2. Hallo *n.* 3. Gruß *m*: **say ~** (**to s.o.**) (j-m) guten Tag sagen.

helm [helm] *s* ⚓ Ruder *n* (*a. fig.*), Steuer *n*: **be at the ~** am Ruder *od.* an der Macht sein; **take the ~** das Ruder übernehmen.

helms·man ['helmzmən] *s* (*irr* **man**) ⚓ Steuermann *m* (*a. fig.*).

help [help] I *s* 1. Hilfe f: **come to s.o.'s ~** j-m zu Hilfe kommen. 2. Abhilfe f. 3. (*bsd.* Haus)Angestellte f. II *v/t* 4. j-m helfen *od.* behilflich sein (**in** [*od.* with] bei): **~ s.o. out** j-m aushelfen (**with** mit); → **god** 2. 5. **~ s.o. to s.th.** j-m zu et. verhelfen; **~ o.s.** sich bedienen, zugreifen. 6. *mit can:* **I cannot ~ it** ich kann es nicht ändern; ich kann nichts dafür; **it cannot be ~ed** da kann man nichts machen, es ist nicht zu ändern; **I could not ~ laughing** ich mußte einfach lachen. III *v/i* 7. helfen: **~ out** aushelfen (**with** mit). '**help·er** *s* Helfer(in). **help·ful** ['~fʊl] *adj* □ 1. hilfsbereit. 2. hilfreich. '**help·ing** I *adj* hilfreich: → **hand** 1. II *s* Portion f (*Essen*): **have** (*od.* **take**) **a second ~** sich nachnehmen. '**help·less** *adj* □ hilflos.

hel·ter-skel·ter [,heltə'skeltə] I *adv* holterdiepolter, Hals über Kopf. II *adj* hastig, überstürzt. III *s* (wildes) Durcheinander, (wilde) Hast.

hem¹ [hem] F I *s* 1. Saum *m*. 2. Rand *m*, Einfassung f. II *v/t* 3. Kleid *etc* (ein)säumen. 4. **~ in** a) a. **~ about** (*od.* **around**) umranden, einfassen, b) ✕ einschließen, c) fig. einengen.

hem² [~] I *int* h(e)m! II *v/i* sich (*verlegen*) räuspern: **~ and haw** herumdrucksen, nicht recht mit der Sprache herauswollen.

'**he-man** *s* (*irr* **man**) F He-man *m* (*bsd.* männlich wirkender Mann).

hem·i·sphere ['hemɪ,sfɪə] *s geogr.* Halbkugel f, Hemisphäre f.

'**hem-line** *s* Saum *m*: **~s are going up again** die Kleider werden wieder kürzer.

he·mo·glo·bin, hem·or·rhoids *etc bsd. Am.* → **haemoglobin, haemorrhoids** *etc.*

hemp [hemp] *s* Hanf *m*.

hen [hen] *s orn.* 1. Henne f, Huhn *n*. 2. (*Vogel*)Weibchen *n*.

hence [hens] *adv* 1. **a week ~** in e-r Woche. 2. folglich, daher, deshalb. 3. hieraus, daraus: **it follows that** daraus folgt, daß. '**~forth**, '**~for·ward(s)** *adv* von nun an, fortan.

hench·man ['hentʃmən] *s* (*irr* **man**) *bsd. pol.* Anhänger *m*; *contp.* Handlanger *m*.

hen| par·ty *s* F Damengesellschaft f, Kaffeeklatsch *m*. '**~pecked** *adj* unter dem Pantoffel stehend: **~ husband** Pantoffelheld *m*.

hep [hep] *s* → **hip⁴**.

hep·a·ti·tis [,hepə'taɪtɪs] *s* ✽ Leberentzündung f.

her [hɜː] I *personal pron* 1. sie (*acc von* **she**): **I know ~**. 2. ihr (*dat von* **she**): **I gave ~ the book**. 3. F sie (*nom*): **he's younger than ~**; **it's ~** sie ist es. II *possessive pron* 4. ihr(e). III *reflex pron* 5. sich: **she looked about ~** sie sah sich um.

her·ald ['herəld] I *s* 1. *hist.* Herold *m*. 2. *fig.* Vorbote *m*. II *v/t* 3. ankündigen (*a. fig.*). **he·ral·dic** [he'rældɪk] *adj* (**~ally**) heraldisch, Wappen... **her·ald·ry** ['herəldrɪ] *s* Heraldik f, Wappenkunde f.

herb [hɜːb] *s* ✿ Kraut *n*; *engS.* Heilkraut; Gewürz-, Küchenkraut. **herb·al** ['~bl] *adj* Kräuter..., Pflanzen... **her·bar·i·um** [~'beərɪəm] *s* Herbarium *n*. **her·biv·o·rous** [~'bɪvərəs] *adj* □ *zo.* pflanzenfressend.

herd [hɜːd] I *s* 1. Herde f, (*wildlebender Tiere a.*) Rudel *n* (*a. von Menschen*). 2. *contp.* Herde f, Masse f (*Menschen*): **the** (**common** *od.* **vulgar**) **~** die große *od.* breite Masse. II *v/i* 3. a. **~ together** in Herden leben; sich zs.-drängen (*a. Menschen*). 4. sich zs.-tun (**with** mit). III *v/t* 5. Vieh hüten. 6. Vieh, a. *Menschen* treiben: **~ together** zs.-treiben.

'**herd·er** *s bsd. Am.* Hirt *m*.

herd in·stinct *s zo.* Herdeninstinkt *m*, (*a. bei Menschen*) Herdentrieb *m*.

herds·man ['hɜːdzmən] *s* (*irr man*) *bsd. Br.* Hirt *m*.

here [hɪə] *adv* hier; (hier)her: **come ~** komm her; **~ and there** hier u. da, da u. dort; hier u. dorthin; **~'s to you!** auf dein Wohl!; **~ you** (*od.* **we**) **are!** hier (bitte)! (*da hast du es*). **'~ a·bouts** *adv* hier herum, in dieser Gegend. **,~'af·ter I** *adv* **1.** nachstehend, im folgenden. **2.** künftig, in Zukunft. **II** *s* **3.** Jenseits *n*. **,~'by** *adv* hiermit.

he·red·i·ta·ry [hɪ'redɪtərɪ] *adj* □ **1.** (ver)erblich, Erb...: **~ disease** Erbkrankheit *f*. **2.** *fig.* althergebracht, Erb...: **~ enemy** Erbfeind *m*.

,here|**in** *adv* hierin. **,~'of** *adv* hiervon.

her·e·sy ['herəsɪ] *s* Ketzerei *f*.

her·e·tic ['herətɪk] *s* Ketzer(in). **he·ret·i·cal** [hɪ'retɪkl] *adj* □ ketzerisch.

,here|**·up·on** *adv* hierauf, darauf(hin). **,~'with** *adv* hiermit.

her·it·a·ble ['herɪtəbl] *adj* □ erblich, vererbbar. **'her·it·age** *s* Erbe *n*.

her·maph·ro·dite [hɜː'mæfrədaɪt] *s biol.* Zwitter *m*.

her·met·ic [hɜː'metɪk] *adj* (**~ally**) hermetisch, ◎ luftdicht: **~ally sealed** luftdicht verschlossen.

her·mit ['hɜːmɪt] *s* Einsiedler *m* (*a. fig.*), Eremit *m*. **'her·mit·age** *s* Einsiedelei *f*.

her·ni·a ['hɜːnjə] *s* ✚ Bruch *m*.

he·ro ['hɪərəʊ] *pl* **-roes** *s* Held *m*, *thea. etc a.* Hauptperson *f*. **he·ro·ic** [hɪ'rəʊɪk] *adj* (**~ally**) *s* **1.** heroisch, heldenhaft, Helden... **2.** hochtrabend, bombastisch (*Sprache, Stil*).

her·o·in ['herəʊɪn] *s* Heroin *n*.

her·o·ine ['herəʊɪn] *s* Heldin *f*, *thea. etc a.* Hauptperson *f*. **'her·o·ism** *s* Heldentum *n*.

her·on ['herən] *s orn.* Reiher *m*.

her·pes ['hɜːpiːz] *s* ✚ Herpes *m*.

her·ring ['herɪŋ] *pl* **-rings**, *bsd. coll.* **-ring** *s ichth.* Hering *m*. **'~·bone** *s a.* **~ design** (*od.* **pattern**) Fischgrätenmuster *n*.

hers [hɜːz] *possessive pron*: **it is ~** es gehört ihr; **a friend of ~** e-e Freundin von ihr; **my mother and ~** m-e u. ihre Mutter.

her'self *pron* **1.** *verstärkend*: sie (*nom od. acc*) selbst, ihr (*dat*) selbst: **she did it ~**,

she **~ did it** sie hat es selbst getan. **2.** *reflex* sich: **she killed ~**. **3.** sich (selbst): **she wants it for ~**.

he's [hiːz] *F für* **he is**; **he has**.

hes·i·tate ['hezɪteɪt] *v/i* **1.** zögern, zaudern, Bedenken haben (**to do** zu tun), unschlüssig sein (**over** hinsichtlich). **2.** (*beim Sprechen*) stocken. **,hes·i'ta·tion** *s* **1.** Zögern *n*, Zaudern *n*, Unschlüssigkeit *f*: **without** (**any**) **~** ohne zu zögern. **2.** Stocken *n*.

het·er·o·dox ['hetərəʊdɒks] *adj* heterodox, anders-, irrgläubig. **het·er·o·ge·ne·ous** [,~'dʒiːnjəs] *adj* □ heterogen, ungleichartig, verschiedenartig. **,het·er·o'sex·u·al I** *adj* □ heterosexuell. **II** *s* Heterosexuelle *m, f*.

het' [het] *adj*: **be ~ up** F aufgeregt od. nervös sein (**about** wegen).

het² [~] F **I** *adj* hetero (*heterosexuell*). **II** *s* Hetero *m, f*.

hew [hjuː] *v/t* (*a. irr*) **1.** hauen, hacken: **~ down** umhauen; **~ off** abhauen; **~ up** zerhauen, -hacken. **2.** *Steine etc* behauen. **hewn** [hjuːn] *pp von* **hew**.

hex·a·gon ['heksəgən] *s* Sechseck *n*. **hex·ag·o·nal** [~'sægənl] *adj* □ sechseckig.

hey [heɪ] *int* **1.** → **presto. 2.** he!

hey·day ['heɪdeɪ] *s a*) Höhepunkt *m*, Gipfel *m*: **in the ~ of one's power** auf dem Gipfel der Macht, b) Blüte(zeit) *f*: **in one's ~** in s-r Glanzzeit.

hi [haɪ] *int* F hallo!

hi·ber·nate ['haɪbəneɪt] *v/i* überwintern: a) *zo.* Winterschlaf halten, b) den Winter verbringen. **,hi·ber'na·tion** *s* Überwinterung *f*, Winterschlaf *m*.

hi·bis·cus [hɪ'bɪskəs] *s* ❀ Hibiskus *m*, Eibisch *m*.

hic·cough, hic·cup ['hɪkʌp] **I** *s* **1.** **have** (**the**) **~s** e-n Schluckauf haben. **2.** *fig.* Panne *f*. **II** *v/i* **3.** hicksen.

hick [hɪk] *bsd. Am.* F **I** *s* Bauer *m*, Provinzler *m*. **II** *adj* Bauern..., provinziell: **~ town** (*Provinz*)Nest *n* (*Am.* (Bauern-)Kaff *n*.

hick·o·ry ['hɪkərɪ] *s* **1.** ❀ Hickory(baum) *m*. **2.** Hickory(holz) *n*.

hid [hɪd] *pret u. pp von* **hide². 'hid·den I** *pp von* **hide². II** *adj* □ geheim, verborgen.

hide¹ [haɪd] **I** *s* **1.** Haut *f*, Fell *n* (*beide a. fig.*): **save one's own ~** die eigene Haut retten; *tan s.o.'s* ~ F j-m das Fell gerben. **II** *v/t* **2.** abhäuten. **3.** F verprügeln.

hide² [~] (*irr*) **I** *v/t* (*from*) verbergen (vor *dat*): a) verstecken (vor *dat*), b) verheimlichen (*dat od.* vor *dat*), c) verhüllen, -decken. **II** *v/i a.* ~ *out* (*bsd. Am. up*) sich verbergen od. verstecken. **~-and-'seek** *s* Versteckspiel(en): *play* ~ Verstecke spielen. **'~-a-way** *s* **1.** Versteck *n.* **2.** Zufluchtsort *m.*

hid·e·ous ['hɪdɪəs] *adj* □ abscheulich, scheußlich.

'hide·out *s* Versteck *n.*

hid·ing¹ ['haɪdɪŋ] *s* F Tracht *f* Prügel.

hid·ing² [~] *s a.* ~ *place* Versteck *n*: *be in* ~ sich versteckt halten; *go into* ~ untertauchen.

hi·er·arch·y ['haɪərɑːkɪ] *s* Hierarchie *f.*

hi·er·o·glyph ['haɪərəʊglɪf] → *hieroglyphic* 1, 3. **hi·er·o·'glyph·ic** *s* **1.** Hieroglyphe *f.* **2.** *pl* (*mst sg konstruiert*) Hieroglyphenschrift *f.* **3.** *pl humor.* Hieroglyphen *pl*, unleserliches Gekritzel.

hi·fi ['haɪfaɪ] F **I** *s* **1.** Hi-Fi *n.* **2.** Hi-Fi-Anlage *f;* -Gerät *n.* **II** *adj* **3.** Hi-Fi-...

hig·gle·dy-pig·gle·dy [,hɪgldɪ'pɪgldɪ] F **I** *adv* drunter u. drüber, (wie Kraut u. Rüben) durcheinander. **II** *adj* kunterbunt.

high [haɪ] **I** *adj* (□ → *highly*) **1.** *allg.* hoch; *engS. a.* hochgelegen: → *horse.* **2.** hoch (*Geschwindigkeit, Preise etc*), groß (*Hoffnungen, Lob etc*). **3.** (*rang- od. stellungsmäßig*) hoch: ~ *society* High-Society *f.* **4.** fortgeschritten (*Zeit*): ~ *season* Hochsaison *f;* ~ *summer* Hochsommer *m; it is* ~ *time* es ist höchste Zeit. **5.** hoch, erstklassig (*Qualität etc*). **6.** a) gehoben: → *spirit* 4, b) F blau (*betrunken*), c) F high. **7.** F scharf (*on auf acc*). **II** *adv* **8.** hoch: *aim* ~ *fig.* sich hohe Ziele setzen od. stecken: *search* ~ *and low* überall suchen. **9.** hoch, mit hohem Einsatz (*spielen*). **III** *s* **10.** (An)Höhe *f:* *on* ~ hoch oben, droben; *im* Himmel. **11.** *meteor.* Hoch *n.* **12.** *fig.* Höchststand *m.* **13.** *am.* F High-School *f.* ~ *al·tar* *s* Hochaltar *m.* **,~-'al·ti·tude** *adj* Höhen... ~ *and dry* *adj*: *leave s.o.* ~ j-n im Stich lassen. ~ *and might·y* *adj* F anmaßend, arrogant. **'~ball** *s* Am. Highball *m* (*Whiskycocktail*). ~ *beam* *s mot. Am.* Fern-

licht *n.* **'~·brow** *oft contp.* **I** *s* Intellektuelle *m, f.* **II** *adj* (betont) intellektuell. **'~·chair** *s* (Kinder)Hochstuhl *m.* **♀ Church** *s* anglikanische Hochkirche. **,~-cir·cu'la·tion** *adj* auflagenstark. **,~-'class** *adj* erstklassig. **,~-'du·ty** *adj* **☉** Hochleistungs... **,~-fi·'del·i·ty** *s* High-Fidelity *f.* **,~-fi·'del·i·ty** *adj* High-Fidelity-... **'~-flown** *adj* **1.** bombastisch, hochtrabend (*Worte etc*). **2.** (allzu) hochgesteckt (*Ziele etc*), (allzu) hochfliegend (*Pläne etc*). **,~'grade** *adj* **1.** hochwertig. **2.** a. **♀** erstklassig. **,~-'hand·ed** *adj* □ anmaßend, willkürlich. **,~-'heeled** *adj* hochhackig (*Schuhe*). ~ *jump* *s Leichtathletik:* Hochsprung *m.* ~ *jump·er* *s* Hochspringer(in). *jump* ~ *fig.* (*a. fig.*): **~ talks** *pl* Gespräche *pl* auf höherer Ebene. **'~-light** **I** *s* Höhe-, Glanzpunkt *m; pl* Querschnitt *m* (*of durch e-e Oper etc*). **II** *v/t* hervorheben.

high·ly ['haɪlɪ] *adv* **1.** *fig.* hoch: ~ *gifted* hochbegabt; ~ *interesting* hochinteressant; ~ *paid* hochbezahlt; teuer bezahlt. **2.** lobend, anerkennend: *think* ~ *of* viel halten von.

High⎪ Mass *s eccl.* Hochamt *n.* **♀-'necked** *adj* hochgeschlossen (*Kleid*).

high·ness ['haɪnɪs] *s* **1.** *mst fig.* Höhe *f.* **2.** ♀ Hoheit *f* (*Titel*).

,high⎪-'pow·er(ed) *adj* **1.** **☉** Hochleistungs... **2.** *fig.* dynamisch, energisch. **,~-'pres·sure** *adj* **☉**, *meteor.* Hochdruck... ~ *priest* *s eccl.* Hohepriester *m* (*a. fig.*). **,~-'qual·i·ty** *adj* hochwertig. **'~-rank·ing** *adj* hochrangig: ~ *officer* ✗ hoher Offizier. **'~-rise** *s* Hochhaus *n.* ~ *school* *s Am.* High-School *f.* **,~-'sea** *adj* Hochsee... **'~-,sound·ing** *adj* hochtönend, -trabend. ~ *street* *s* Hauptstraße *f.* ~ *tea* *s Br.* frühes Abendessen. **,~-tech** *adj* F High-Tech-... ~ *tech·nol·o·gy* *s* Hochtechnologie *f.* ~ *ten·sion* *s ≴* Hochspannung *f.* **,~-'ten·sion** *adj* Hochspannungs... ~ *trea·son* *s* Hochverrat *m.* ~ *wa·ter* *s* Hochwasser *n.* **'~-way** *s* Highway *m*, Haupt(verkehrs)straße *f:* → *code* **Br.** Straßenverkehrsordnung *f.*

hi·jack ['haɪdʒæk] **I** *v/t* **1.** Flugzeug entführen. **2.** *j-n, Geldtransport etc* überfallen. **II** *s* **3.** (Flugzeug)Entführung *f.* **4.** Überfall *m.* **'hi·jack·er** *s* **1.** (Flugzeug)Entführer *m*. **2.** Räuber *m*. **'hi·jack·ing → hijack** II.

hike [haɪk] **I** *v/i* wandern. **II** *s* Wanderung *f*: **go on a ~** e-e Wanderung machen. **'hik·er** *s* Wanderer *m*.

hi·lar·i·ous [hɪˈleərɪəs] *adj* □ **1.** vergnügt, ausgelassen, übermütig. **2.** lustig (*Geschichte etc*). **hi·lar·i·ty** [hɪˈlærətɪ] *s* Vergnügtheit *f*, Ausgelassenheit *f*, Übermütigkeit *f*.

hill [hɪl] *s* Hügel *m*, Anhöhe *f*: (**as**) **old as the ~s** uralt, (*Person a*.) steinalt; **be over the ~** F s-e beste Zeit hinter sich haben; *bsd.* ⚔ über den Berg sein. **'~·bil·ly** *s Am.* mst *contp.* Hillbilly *m*, Hinterwäldler *m*.

hill·ock ['hɪlək] *s* kleiner Hügel.

,hill·'side *s* (Ab)Hang *m*. **,~·'top** *s* Hügelspitze *f*. **~ walk** *s* Bergwanderung *f*.

hilt [hɪlt] *s* Heft *n*, Griff *m* (*Schwert, Dolch*): (**up**) **to the ~** bis ans Heft; *fig.* durch u. durch, ganz u. gar.

him [hɪm] **I** *personal pron* **1.** ihn (*acc von* **he**): *I know ~*. **2.** ihm (*dat von* **he**): *I gave ~ the book*. **3.** F er (*nom*): **she's younger than ~; it's ~** er ist es. **II** *reflex pron* **4.** sich: *he looked about ~* er sah sich um.

him·self *pron* **1.** *verstärkend:* er *od*. ihm *od*. ihn selbst: *he did it ~, he ~ did it* er hat es selbst getan. **2.** *reflex von:* *he killed ~*. **3.** sich (selbst): *he wants it for ~*.

hind [haɪnd] *adj* hinter, Hinter...: **~ wheel** Hinterrad *n*.

hind·er ['hɪndə] *v/t* **1.** *j-n, et.* aufhalten (**in** bei); behindern. **2.** (**from**) hindern (**an** *dat*), abhalten (von).

hind·most ['haɪndməʊst] *sup von* **hind**.

,hind·'quar·ters *s pl* Hinterhand *f* (*vom Pferd*); Hinterteil *n*.

hin·drance ['hɪndrəns] *s* **1.** Behinderung *f*: **be a ~ to → hinder** 1. **2.** Hindernis *n* (**to** für).

'hind·sight *s*: **with ~** im nachhinein (betrachtet).

Hin·du [ˌhɪnˈduː] *eccl.* **I** *s* Hindu *m*. **II** *adj* Hindu... **'Hin·du·ism** *s* Hinduismus *m*.

hinge [hɪndʒ] **I** *s* **1.** *a*. **~ joint** ⚙ Scharnier *n*, (Tür)Angel *f*. **2.** *fig.* Angelpunkt *m*. **II** *v/t* **3.** mit (*e-r*) Tür einhängen. **III** *v/i* **4.** (**on**) *fig.* abhängen (von), ankommen (auf *acc*); sich drehen (um).

hint [hɪnt] **I** *s* **1.** Wink *m*, Andeutung *f*:

drop a ~ e-e Andeutung machen; **broad ~** Wink mit dem Zaunpfahl. **2.** Fingerzeig *m*, Tip *m* (**on** für). **3.** Anspielung *f* (**at** auf *acc*). **4.** Anflug *m*, Spur *f* (**of** von). **II** *v/t* **5.** andeuten. **III** *v/i* **6.** (**at**) andeuten (*acc*); anspielen (auf *acc*).

hin·ter·land ['hɪntəlænd] *s* **1.** Hinterland *n*. **2.** Umland *n*.

hip¹ [hɪp] *s anat.* Hüfte *f*.

hip² [~] *s* ♣ Hagebutte *f*.

hip³ [~] *int:* **~, ~, hurrah!** hipp, hipp, hurra!

hip⁴ [~] *adj sl.* **1.** **be ~** alles mitmachen, was gerade in ist. **2.** **be ~** auf dem laufenden sein (**to** über *acc*).

'hip·bath *s* Sitzbad *n*. **'~·bone** *s anat.* Hüftbein *n*, -knochen *m*. **~ flask** *s* Taschenflasche *f*, Flachmann *m*. **~ joint** *s anat.* Hüftgelenk *n*.

hip·pie ['hɪpɪ] *s* Hippie *m*.

hip pock·et *s* Gesäßtasche *f*.

hip·po·pot·a·mus [ˌhɪpəˈpɒtəməs] *pl* **-mus·es, -mi** [~maɪ] *s zo.* Fluß-, Nilpferd *n*.

hip·py → hippie.

hire ['haɪə] **I** *v/t* **1.** *Auto etc* mieten, *Flugzeug etc* chartern: **~d car** Leih-, Mietwagen *m*; **~d plane** Charterflugzeug *n*. **2.** *a*. **~ on** *j-n* ein-, anstellen, ♣ (an)heuern; *j-n* engagieren; *bsd. b.s.* anheuern: **~d killer** gekaufter Mörder, Killer *m*. **3.** *mst* **~ out** vermieten. **II** *s* **4.** Miete *f*: **~ company** Verleih(firma *f*) *m*; **on ~** mietweise; **for ~** zu vermieten; (*Taxi*) frei. **5.** Lohn *m*, Entgelt *n*. **~ pur·chase** *s*: **on ~** *bsd. Br.* auf Abzahlung *od.* Raten.

his [hɪz] *possessive pron:* **it is ~** es gehört ihm; **a friend of ~** ein Freund von ihm; **my mother and ~** m-e u. s-e Mutter.

hiss [hɪs] **I** *v/i* **1.** zischen, (*Katze*) fauchen: **~ at → 2. II** *v/t* **2.** auszischen. **3.** *et.* zische(l)n. **III** *s* **4.** Zischen *n*, Fauchen *n*.

his·to·ri·an [hɪˈstɔːrɪən] *s* Historiker *m*.

his·tor·ic [hɪˈstɒrɪk] *adj* (**~ally**) **1.** historisch, geschichtlich (berühmt *od.* bedeutsam). **2. → historical. 'his·tor·i·cal** [~kl] *adj* □ **1. → historic** 1. **2.** historisch: a) geschichtlich (belegt *od.* überliefert), b) Geschichts..., c) geschichtlich(en Inhalts): **~ novel** historischer Roman. **his·to·ry** ['~tərɪ] *s* **1.** Geschichte f: **contemporary** ~ Zeitgeschichte; ~ **of art** Kunstgeschichte; **go down in** ~ in die Geschichte eingehen; **make** ~ Geschichte machen. **2.** (Entwicklungs-) Geschichte f, Werdegang m. **3.** *allg.*, *a.* ⚕ Vorgeschichte f: → **case history.**

hit [hɪt] **I** s **1.** Hieb m (*a. fig.* at gegen), Schlag m: **that was a** ~ **at me** das ging gegen mich. **2.** Treffer m (*a. Sport u. fig.*): **make** (*od.* **score**) **a** ~ e-n Treffer erzielen; *fig.* gut ankommen (**with** bei). **3.** Hit m (*Buch, Schlager etc*): **it was a big** ~ es hat groß eingeschlagen. **4.** *sl.* Schuß m (*Drogeninjektion*): **give o.s. a** ~ sich e-n Schuß setzen *od.* drücken. **5.** *bsd. Am. sl.* (*von e-m hit man ausgeführter*) Mord. **II** *v/t* (*irr*) **6.** schlagen. **7.** (*a. fig. seelisch, finanziell etc*) treffen: ~ **the nail on the head** *fig.* den Nagel auf den Kopf treffen; ~ **the bottle** F saufen; → **hay, road, sack**[1] **7. 8.** *mot. etc* j-n, et. anfahren, et. rammen: ~ **one's head against** (*od.* **on**) sich den Kopf anschlagen an (*dat*), mit dem Kopf stoßen gegen. **9.** et. erreichen, schaffen: → **front page, headline** 1. **10.** *bsd. fig.* stoßen auf (*acc*), finden. **11.** *a.* ~ **up** *bsd. Am.* F anhauen, anpumpen (**for** um). **12.** F ankommen in (*dat*), erreichen. **13.** *bsd. Am. sl.* j-n umlegen (**hit man**). **III** *v/i* (*irr*) **14.** treffen. **15.** schlagen (**at** nach). **16.** stoßen, schlagen (**against** gegen; **on** *auf acc*). **17.** ~ **on** → 10.
Verbindungen mit Adverbien:

hit | **back** *v/i* zurückschlagen (*a. fig.*). ~ **off** *v/t:* **hit it off** F sich gut vertragen (**with** mit). ~ **out** *v/i* **1.** um sich schlagen: ~ **at s.o.** auf j-n einschlagen. **2.** *fig.* her-, losziehen (**at, against** über *acc*).

hit-and-run *adj:* ~ **accident** Unfall m mit Fahrerflucht; ~ **driver** (unfall-)flüchtiger Fahrer.

hitch [hɪtʃ] **I** s **1.** Ruck m, Zug m. **2.** Schwierigkeit f, Haken m: **without a** ~ glatt, reibungslos. **3.** **get a** ~ F im Auto mitgenommen werden. **II** *v/t* **4.** rücken, ziehen: ~ **up** hochziehen. **5.** befestigen, festhaken (**to** *an acc*): **get** ~**ed** F heiraten. **6.** ~ **a ride** → 3. **III** *v/i* **7.** sich festhaken, hängenbleiben (**on** *an dat*). **8.** F → **hitchhike.**

'hitch·er F → **hitchhiker.**

'hitch·|hike *v/i* per Anhalter fahren,

trampen. **'~·hik·er** s Anhalter(in), Tramper(in).

hith·er ['hɪðə] *adv* hierher. **,~'to** *adv* bisher, bis jetzt.

hit| **list** s: **be on the** ~ *bsd. Am. sl.* auf der Abschußliste stehen (*a. fig.*). ~ **man** s (*irr* **man**) *bsd. Am. sl.* Killer m (*eines Verbrechersyndikats*). ~ **or miss** *adv* aufs Geratewohl, auf gut Glück. ~ **pa·rade** s Hitparade f. ~ **song** s Hit m.

hive [haɪv] **I** s **1.** Bienenkorb m, -stock m. **2.** Bienenvolk n; *fig.* Schwarm m (*Menschen*). **II** *v/i* **2.** *fig.* abschwenken (**from** von); sich selbständig machen; *bsd. Br.* F sich aus dem Staub machen. **4.** sich zs.-drängen.

hives [haɪvz] s pl (*a. sg konstruiert*) ⚕ Nesselausschlag m.

hoard [hɔːd] **I** s Vorrat m (**of** *an dat*). **II** *v/t a.* ~ **up** horten, hamstern. **III** *v/i* hamstern, sich Vorräte anlegen.

hoard·ing ['hɔːdɪŋ] s **1.** Bau-, Bretterzaun m. **2.** *Br.* Reklametafel f.

hoar·frost [,hɔː'frɒst] s (Rauh)Reif m.

hoarse [hɔːs] *adj* □ heiser. **'hoarse-ness** s Heiserkeit f.

hoar·y ['hɔːrɪ] *adj* □ **1.** weiß(grau). **2.** (alters)grau.

hoax [həʊks] **I** s **1.** (Zeitungs)Ente f. **2.** Streich m, (übler) Scherz: **play a** ~ **on s.o.** j-m e-n Streich spielen, sich mit j-m e-n Scherz erlauben. **II** *v/t* **3.** j-m e-n Bären aufbinden.

hob·ble ['hɒbl] *v/i* hinken, humpeln.

hob·by ['hɒbɪ] s Hobby n, Steckenpferd n. ~ **room** s Hobbyraum m.

hob·gob·lin ['hɒbgɒblɪn] s Kobold m.

hob·nob ['hɒbnɒb] *v/i* freundschaftlich verkehren, auf du u. du sein (**with** mit).

ho·bo ['həʊbəʊ] pl **-bo(e)s** s Am. Landstreicher m, Tippelbruder m.

Hob·son's choice ['hɒbsnz] s: **it was** (a **case of**) ~ es gab nur 'eine Möglichkeit; **he had to take** ~ es blieb ihm keine andere Wahl.

hock[1] [hɒk] s weißer Rheinwein.

hock[2] [~] *bsd. Am.* F **I** s: **be in** ~ versetzt sein; Schulden haben (*to* bei); im Kittchen sein *od.* sitzen; **put into** ~ → II. **II** *v/t* versetzen, ins Leihhaus tragen.

hock·ey ['hɒkɪ] s Sport: *bsd. Br.* Hockey n; *bsd. Am.* Eishockey n.

ho·cus-po·cus [,həʊkəs'pəʊkəs] s Hokuspokus m, fauler Zauber.

hodge·podge ['hɒdʒpɒdʒ] → **hotch-potch.**

hoe [həʊ] **I** s Hacke f. **II** v/t Boden hacken: ~ (**up**) Unkraut aushacken.

hog [hɒg] **I** s **1.** (Haus-, Schlacht-) Schwein n: **go the whole ~** F aufs Ganze gehen. **2.** F rücksichtsloser Kerl; gieriger od. gefräßiger Kerl; Schmutzfink m, Ferkel n. **II** v/t **3.** F rücksichtslos an sich reißen: ~ **the road** mot. die ganze Straße für sich brauchen; rücksichtslos fahren.

Hog·ma·nay ['hɒgmənei] s schott. Silvester(abend m) m, n.

'hog·wash s **1.** Schweinefutter n. **2.** fig. Spülwasser n (dünner Kaffee etc). **3.** fig. Gewäsch n, Geschwätz n.

hoi pol·loi [,hɔɪ'pɒlɔɪ] s contp. breite Masse, Pöbel m.

hoist [hɔɪst] **I** v/t **1.** hochziehen; Flagge, Segel hissen. **II** s **2.** Hochziehen n. **3.** ◉ (Lasten)Aufzug m.

hoi·ty-toi·ty [,hɔɪtɪ'tɔɪtɪ] adj hochnäsig, eingebildet.

hold [həʊld] **I** s **1.** Griff m (a. Ringen), Halt m: **catch** (od. **get, take**) ~ **of s.th.** et. ergreifen od. zu fassen bekommen; **get** ~ **of s.o.** j-n erwischen; **keep** ~ **of** festhalten; **let go one's** ~ **of s.th.** et. loslassen. **2.** Halt m, Stütze f: **lose one's** ~ den Halt verlieren. **3.** (**on, over, of**) Gewalt f, Macht f (über acc), Einfluß m (auf acc): **have a (firm)** ~ **on s.o.** j-n in s-r Gewalt haben, j-n beherrschen; **lose** ~ **of o.s.** die Fassung verlieren. **II** v/t (irr) **4.** (fest)halten. **5.** sich die Nase, die Ohren zuhalten: ~ **one's nose (ears)**. **6.** Gewicht etc tragen, (aus)halten. **7.** (in e-m Zustand) halten: ~ **o.s. erect** sich geradehalten; ~ **(o.s.) ready** (sich) bereithalten. **8.** zurück-, abhalten (**from** von): ~ **s.o. from doing s.th.** j-n davon abhalten, et. zu tun; **there was no ~ing him** er war nicht zu halten. **9.** Wahlen, Pressekonferenz etc abhalten; Fest etc veranstalten. **10.** ✕ u. fig. Stellung halten, behaupten: ~ **one's own (with)** sich behaupten (gegen), bestehen (neben). **11.** Aktien, Rechte etc besitzen; Amt etc bekleiden. **12.** Platz etc (inne)haben; Rekord halten; Titel führen. **13.** fassen: a) enthalten, b) Platz bieten für. **14.** Bewunderung, Sympathie etc hegen, haben (**for** für).

15. der Ansicht sein (**that** daß). **16.** halten für: **I ~ him to be a liar** ich halte ihn für e-n Lügner. **17.** halten: ~ **responsible** verantwortlich machen; ~ **contempt** 1, **esteem** 3. **18.** bsd. ⚖ entscheiden (**that** daß). **19.** Publikum, j-s Aufmerksamkeit fesseln. **20.** ~ **s.th. against s.o.** j-m et. vorhalten od. vorwerfen; j-m et. übelnehmen od. nachtragen. **III** v/i (irr) **21.** halten, nicht (zer)reißen od. (zer)brechen. **22.** (sich) festhalten (**by, to** an dat). **23.** a. ~ **good** (weiterhin) gelten, gültig sein od. bleiben. **24.** anhalten, andauern.

Verbindungen mit Adverbien:

hold| back I v/t **1.** zurückhalten. **2.** ~ **in** I **3.** fig. zurückhalten mit, verschweigen. **II** v/i **4.** fig. sich zurückhalten. **5.** nicht mit der Sprache herausrücken. ~ **down** v/t **1.** niederhalten, fig. a. unterdrücken. **2.** F Posten haben; sich in e-r Stellung halten. ~ **in** v/t zügeln, zurückhalten: **hold o.s. in** a) → II, b) den Bauch einziehen. **II** v/i sich zurückhalten od. beherrschen. ~ **off** I v/t **1.** ab-, fernhalten, abwehren. **2.** et. aufschieben, j-n hinhalten. **II** v/i **3.** sich fernhalten (**from** von). **4.** zögern; warten (**from** mit). **5.** ausbleiben (Regen etc). ~ **on** v/i **1.** festhalten (**to** an dat) (a. fig.). **2.** sich festhalten (**to** an dat). **3.** aus-, durchhalten. **4.** andauern, anhalten. **5.** teleph. am Apparat bleiben. ~ **out** I v/t **1.** Hand etc ausstrecken: **hold s.th. out to s.o.** j-m et. hinhalten. **II** v/i **2.** reichen (Vorräte). **3.** aus-, durchhalten. ~ **o·ver** v/t **1.** Sitzung, Entscheidung etc vertagen, -schieben (**till, until** auf acc). **2.** Film etc verlängern (**for** um). ~ **to·geth·er** v/t u. v/i zs.-halten (a. fig.). ~ **up** I v/t **1.** hochhalten. **2.** fig. hinstellen (**as an example** als Beispiel). **3.** j-n, et. aufhalten; et. verzögern: **be held up** sich verzögern. **4.** j-n, Bank etc überfallen. **II** v/i **5.** sich halten (Preise, Wetter etc).

'hold·all s bsd. Br. Reisetasche f.

hold·er ['həʊldə] s **1.** oft in Zssgn Halter m, ◉ a. Halterung f. **2.** Inhaber(in).

'hold·ing s oft pl Besitz m (an Effekten etc): ~ **company** ✝ Holding-, Dachgesellschaft f.

'hold·up s (bewaffneter) (Raub)Überfall.

hole [həʊl] **I** s **1.** Loch n: *be in a ~* F in der Klemme sein *od.* sitzen *od.* stecken; *make a ~ in fig.* ein Loch reißen in (*Vorräte*); *pick* (*od.* *knock*) *~s in fig.* an e-r *Sache* herumkritteln, *Argument etc* zerpflücken; *j-m* am Zeug flicken. **2.** Höhle f, Bau m (*e-s Tiers*), Loch n (*e-r Maus*). **3.** F a) a. *~ in the wall* Loch n, (*Bruch*)Bude f, b) Kaff n, Nest n. **II** v/t **4.** ein Loch *od.* Löcher machen in (*acc*); durchlöchern. **5.** *Golf:* Ball einlochen. **III** v/i **6.** oft *~ out* (*Golf*) einlochen.

hol·i·day [ˈhɒlədeɪ] **I** s **1.** Feiertag m: → *public* 3b. **2.** freier Tag: *take a ~* (sich) e-n Tag frei nehmen. **3.** *mst pl bsd. Br.* Ferien pl, Urlaub m: *be on ~* im Urlaub sein, Urlaub machen. **II** adj **4.** *bsd. Br.* Ferien..., Urlaubs... **III** v/i **5.** *bsd. Br.* Urlaub machen , die Ferien verbringen. **~·mak·er** [ˈ~dɪ~] s *bsd. Br.* Urlauber(in).

hol·ler [ˈhɒlə] v/i u. v/t F schreien, brüllen: *~ for help* um Hilfe schreien; *~ at j-n* anbrüllen.

hol·low [ˈhɒləʊ] **I** s **1.** (Aus)Höhlung f, Hohlraum m: *~ of the hand* hohle Hand. **II** adj □ **2.** hohl: *beat s.o. ~ Br.* F j-n haushoch schlagen; *feel ~* Hunger haben. **3.** hohl, dumpf (*Klang, Stimme*). **4.** *fig.* hohl, leer; falsch, unaufrichtig: → *ring*², 6. **5.** hohl: a) eingefallen (*Wangen*), b) tiefliegend (*Augen*). **III** adv **6.** hohl: *ring ~ fig.* hohl klingen (*Versprechen etc*), unglaubwürdig klingen (*Protest etc*). **IV** v/t **7.** oft *~ out* aushöhlen.

hol·ly [ˈhɒlɪ] s ♀ Stechpalme f.

hol·o·caust [ˈhɒləkɔːst] s ♂ Massenvernichtung f, -sterben n, (*bsd.* Brand)Katastrophe f: *the* ♀ *hist.* der Holocaust.

hol·ster [ˈhəʊlstə] s (Pistolen)Halfter f, n.

ho·ly [ˈhəʊlɪ] adj heilig, (*Hostie etc*) geweiht. ♀ **Ghost** s *eccl.* der Heilige Geist. ♀ **Scrip·ture** s *eccl.* die Heilige Schrift. ♀ **Spir·it** → *Holy Ghost.* ♀ **ter·ror** s F Nervensäge f. ♀ **Thurs·day** s *eccl.* Gründonnerstag m. ♀ **wa·ter** s *eccl.* Weihwasser n. ♀ **Week** s *eccl.* Karwoche f.

hom·age [ˈhɒmɪdʒ] s Huldigung f, Reverenz f: *do* (*od.* *pay*) *~ to s.o.* j-m huldigen, j-m (die *od.* s-e) Reverenz erweisen *od.* bezeigen.

home [həʊm] **I** s **1.** Heim n: a) Haus n, (*eigene*) Wohnung f, b) Zuhause n, Daheim n, c) Elternhaus n: *at ~* zu Hause, daheim (*beide a. Sport*); *~ in fig.* zu Hause in (*dat*), bewandert in (*dat*); *make o.s. at ~* sich bequem machen; *away from ~* abwesend, verreist, (*bsd. Sport*) auswärts; *his ~ is in London* er ist in London zu Hause. **2.** Heimat f (*a. fig.*): *at ~ and abroad* im In- u. Ausland. **3.** Heim n: *~ for the aged* Alters-, Altenheim. **II** adj **4.** häuslich, Haus...: *~ address* Privatanschrift f; *~ life* häusliches Leben, Familienleben n **5.** inländisch, Inlands...: *~ affairs* pl innere Angelegenheiten pl, Innenpolitik f; *~ market* ♂ Inlands-, Binnenmarkt m; *~ trade* ♂ Binnenhandel m. **6.** Heimat...: *~ town.* **7.** *Sport:* Heim...: *~ match.* **III** adv **8.** heim, nach Hause: *way ~* Heimweg m; *that's nothing to write ~ about* F das ist nichts Besonderes; → *come home.* **9.** zu Hause, daheim. **10.** *fig.* ins Ziel: *bring* (*od.* *drive*) *s.th. ~ to s.o.* j-m et. klarmachen; *the thrust went ~* der Hieb saß. **'~·com·ing** s Heimkehr f. **~ com·pu·ter** s Homecomputer m. **'~-grown** adj selbstangebaut (*Obst*), (*Gemüse a.*) selbstgezogen. **'~·land** s Heimatland n.

home·less [ˈhəʊmlɪs] adj **1.** heimatlos. **2.** obdachlos: *be left ~* heimatlos werden. **'home·like** adj wie zu Hause, gemütlich. **'home·ly** adj **1.** einfach (*Mahlzeit, Leute*). **2.** *Am.* unscheinbar, reizlos.

home'made adj haus-, selbstgemacht, Hausmacher...

homeo... → *homoeo...*

Home| Of·fice s *Br.* Innenministerium n. ♀ **rule** s *pol.* Selbstverwaltung f. ♀ **Sec·re·tar·y** s *Br.* Innenminister m. **'♀-sick** adj: *be ~* Heimweh haben. **'♀-sick·ness** s Heimweh n. **'♀-spun** adj schlicht, einfach. ♀ **truth** s unangenehme Wahrheit.

home·ward [ˈhəʊmwəd] **I** adv heimwärts, nach Hause. **II** adj Heim..., Rück... **'~·wards** → *homeward* I.

'home|·work s **1.** ♂ Heimarbeit f. **2.** *ped.* Hausaufgabe(n pl) f: *do one's ~* s-e Hausaufgaben machen (*a. fig.*). **'~·work·er** s ♂ Heimarbeiter (-in).

hom·i·cide [ˈhɒmɪsaɪd] *s* ⚖ Mord *m*; Totschlag *m*.

ho·mo [ˈhəʊməʊ] *pl* **-mos** *s* F Homo *m* (*Homosexuelle*).

ho·moe·o·path [ˈhəʊmjəʊpæθ] *s* ⚕ Homöopath(in). **ho·moe·o·path·ic** [ˌhəʊmɪəʊˈpæθɪk] *adj* (*ally*) homöopathisch. **ho·moe·op·a·thy** [ˌhəʊmɪˈɒpəθɪ] *s* Homöopathie *f*.

ho·mo·ge·ne·ous [ˌhɒməˈdʒiːnjəs] *adj* □ homogen, gleichartig. **ho·mog·e·nize** [hɒˈmɒdʒənaɪz] *v/t* homogenisieren.

hom·o·graph [ˈhɒməʊɡrɑːf] *s* ling. Homograph *n*. **hom·o·nym** [ˈ~nɪm] *s* ling. Homonym *n*. **hom·o·phone** [ˈ~fəʊn] *s* ling. Homophon *n*.

ho·mo·sex·u·al [ˌhɒməʊˈseksjʊəl] I *adj* □ homosexuell. II *s* Homosexuelle *m*, *f*. **ho·mo·sex·u·al·i·ty** [ˌ~ʃʊˈælətɪ] *s* Homosexualität *f*.

hom·y [ˈhəʊmɪ] *adj* F gemütlich, behaglich.

hon·est [ˈɒnɪst] *adj* ehrlich: a) redlich, b) aufrichtig. **'hon·est·ly** I *adv* → **honest**. II *int* F ganz bestimmt!, ehrlich! **'hon·es·ty** *s* Ehrlichkeit *f*: a) Redlichkeit *f*, b) Aufrichtigkeit *f*.

hon·ey [ˈhʌnɪ] *s* 1. Honig *m*: (**as**) **sweet as ~** honigsüß (*a. fig.*). 2. *bsd. Am.* F Liebling *m*, Schatz *m*. **'~·bee** *s* Honigbiene *f*. **'~·dew** *s* Honigtau *m*: **~ melon** Honigmelone *f*.

hon·eyed [ˈhʌnɪd] *adj* honigsüß (*a. fig.*). **'hon·ey·moon** I *s* Flitterwochen *pl*: **~ (trip)** Hochzeitsreise *f*. II *v/i* in den Flitterwochen sein, s-e Flitterwochen verbringen; s-e Hochzeitsreise machen, auf Hochzeitsreise sein. **'~·moon·er** *s* Flitterwöchner *m*; Hochzeitsreisende *m*, *f*.

honk [hɒŋk] *mot.* I *s* Hupsignal *n*. II *v/i* hupen.

hon·or, *etc Am.* → **honour**, *etc*.

hon·or·ar·y [ˈɒnərərɪ] *adj* 1. Ehren... 2. ehrenamtlich.

hon·our [ˈɒnə] *bsd. Br.* I *v/t* 1. ehren, ehren, auszeichnen: **~ s.o. with** j-m mit ... verleihen, j-n beehren mit. 3. ✝ *Scheck etc* honorieren, einlösen. II *s* 4. Ehre *f*: (**sense of**) **~** Ehrgefühl *n*; **~ to whom ~ is due** Ehre, wem Ehre gebührt; **guest of ~** Ehrengast *m*; **do s.o. ~** j-m zur Ehre gereichen, j-m Ehre machen; → **debt**. 5. Ehrung *f*, Ehre(n *pl*) *f*: **in s.o.'s ~** zu

j-s Ehren, j-m zu Ehren. 6. **Your** ⚖ *bsd.* ⚖ Euer Gnaden. **'hon·our·a·ble** *adj* □ *bsd. Br.* 1. achtbar, ehrenwert. 2. ehrenvoll, -haft. ⚖ *der*, *die* Ehrenwerte (*Titel*).

hood [hʊd] *s* 1. Kapuze *f*. 2. *mot. Br.* Verdeck *n*; *Am.* (Motor)Haube *f*. 3. ⚙ (Schutz)Haube *f*.

hood·lum [ˈhuːdləm] *s* F 1. Rowdy *m*; Schläger *m*. 2. Ganove *m*; Gangster *m*. **'hood·wink** *v/t* hinters Licht führen.

hoo·ey [ˈhuːɪ] *s bsd. Am. sl.* Krampf *m*, Quatsch *m*.

hoof [huːf] *pl* **hoofs, hooves** [huːvz] *s zo.* Huf *m*.

hook [hʊk] I *s* 1. Haken *m*: **by ~ or (by) crook** unter allen Umständen, mit allen Mitteln; **on one's own ~** F auf eigene Faust. 2. Angelhaken *m*: **~, line and sinker** F voll (u. ganz); **be on the ~** F in der Patsche sein *od.* sitzen *od.* stecken. 3. *Boxen*: Haken *m*. II *v/t* 4. an-, ein-, fest-, zuhaken. 5. angeln (*a. fig.* F): **~ a husband** sich e-n Mann angeln. 6. **~ it** F Leine ziehen, verschwinden. III *v/i* 7. sich (zu)haken lassen. **hooked** [hʊkt] *adj* 1. hakenförmig, Haken... 2. mit (e-m) Haken (versehen). 3. F süchtig (**on** nach) (*a. fig.*): **~ on TV** fernsehsüchtig. **'hook·er** *s Am. sl.* Nutte *f*. **hook·y** *s*: **play ~** *bsd. Am.* F (die Schule) schwänzen.

hoo·li·gan [ˈhuːlɪɡən] *s* Rowdy *m*. **'hoo·li·gan·ism** *s* Rowdytum *n*.

hoop [huːp] *s allg.* Reif(en) *m*: **put through the ~(s)** *fig.* durch die Mangel drehen, in die Mangel nehmen.

hoo·ray [hʊˈreɪ] → **hurah**.

hoot [huːt] I *v/i* 1. (*höhnisch*) johlen: **~ at s.o.** j-n verhöhnen. 2. *bsd. Br.* heulen (*Fabriksirene etc*); *mot.* hupen. II *v/t* 3. auszischen, -pfeifen: **~ down** niederschreien. III *s* 4. (*höhnischer*, *johlender*) Schrei: **I don't care a ~** (*od.* **two ~s**) F das ist mir völlig egal. 5. *bsd. Br.* Heulen *n*; *mot.* Hupen *n*. **'hoot·er** *s bsd. Br.* Sirene *f*; *mot.* Hupe *f*.

Hoo·ver [ˈhuːvə] *TM* I *s* Staubsauger *m*. II *v/t mst* 2 (staub)saugen, *Teppich etc a.* absaugen: 2 *up* aufsaugen. III *v/i mst* 2 (staub)saugen.

hooves [huːvz] *pl von* **hoof**.

hop¹ [hɒp] I *s* ♀ Hopfen *m*. II *v/t* Bier hopfen.

hop² [~] **I** v/i **1.** hüpfen: ~ off Br. F abschwirren. **2.** F schwofen, tanzen. **II** v/t **3.** hüpfen über (acc): ~ it F abschwirren. **III** s **4.** Sprung m: keep s.o. on the ~ F j-n in Trab halten. **5.** F Schwof m, Tanz(veranstaltung f) m.

hope [həʊp] **I** s Hoffnung f (of auf acc): past (od. beyond) (all) ~ hoffnungs-, aussichtslos; in the ~ auf gut Glück; in der Hoffnung (of getting zu bekommen); no ~ of success keine Aussicht auf Erfolg; ~s pl of victory Siegeshoffnungen pl. **II** v/i hoffen (for auf acc): ~ for the best das Beste hoffen; I ~ so hoffentlich; I ~ not hoffentlich nicht. **III** v/t hoffen (that daß). **hope·ful** ['~fʊl] adj hoffnungsvoll: be ~ that hoffen, daß. **'hope·ful·ly** adv **1.** → hopeful. **2.** hoffentlich. **'hope·less** adj □ hoffnungslos.

hop·ping ['hɒpɪŋ] adv: be ~ mad F e-e Stinkwut (im Bauch) haben.

horde [hɔːd] s Horde f, (wilder) Haufen.

ho·ri·zon [hə'raɪzn] s Horizont m: appear on the ~ am Horizont auftauchen, fig. a. sich abzeichnen; → broaden I. **hor·i·zon·tal** [ˌhɒrɪ'zɒntl] **I** adj horizontal, waag(e)recht: ~ bar (Turnen) Reck n; ~ line → II. **II** s ₳ Horizontale f, Waag(e)rechte f.

hor·mone ['hɔːməʊn] s biol. Hormon n.

horn [hɔːn] **I** s **1.** zo. Horn n, pl a. Geweih n: show one's ~s fig. die Krallen zeigen; → bull **1**, dilemma. **2.** zo. Fühler m, Fühlhorn n. **3.** (Pulver-, Trink)Horn n: ~ of plenty Füllhorn n. **4.** Horn n (Substanz). **5.** ♪ Horn n. **6.** mot. Hupe f. **II** v/i **7.** ~ in sl. sich eindrängen od. einmischen (on in acc).

hor·net ['hɔːnɪt] s zo. Hornisse f: stir up a ~'s nest fig. in ein Wespennest stechen.

'horn-rimmed adj: ~ spectacles pl Hornbrille f.

horn·y ['hɔːnɪ] adj **1.** hornig, schwielig. **2.** aus Horn, Horn-.

hor·o·scope ['hɒrəskəʊp] s Horoskop n: cast a ~ ein Horoskop stellen.

hor·ren·dous [hɒ'rendəs] → horrific.

hor·ri·ble ['hɒrəbl] adj □ schrecklich, furchtbar, scheußlich (alle a. fig. F). **hor·rid** ['hɒrɪd] → horrible. **hor·rif·ic** [hɒ'rɪfɪk] adj (~ally) schrecklich, entsetzlich. **hor·ri·fy** ['~faɪ] v/t entsetzen:

be horrified at (od. by) entsetzt sein über (acc); ~ing → horrible.

hor·ror ['hɒrə] **I** s **1.** Entsetzen n: to one's ~ zu s-m Entsetzen; in ~ entsetzt. **2.** Abscheu f, Horror m (of vor dat). **3.** Schrecken m, Greuel m. **4.** F Greuel m (Person od. Sache). **II** adj Horror...: ~ film. '~·strick·en, '~·struck adj von Entsetzen gepackt.

horse [hɔːs] s Pferd n (a. Turnen): back the wrong ~ fig. aufs falsche Pferd setzen; eat like a ~ wie ein Scheunendrescher essen; get (od. come) off one's high ~ fig. von s-m hohen Roß herunterkommen; a ~ of another (od. a different) colo(u)r fig. et. (ganz) anderes; (straight od. right) from the ~'s mouth F aus erster Hand; → cart **1**, dark horse, flog **1**, gift **3**. '~·back s: on ~ zu Pferd; go on ~ reiten. ~ chest·nut s ₰ Roßkastanie f. '~·hair s Roßhaar n. '~·laugh s wieherndes Gelächter. ~·man ['~mən] s (irr man) (geübter) Reiter. ~ op·er·a s F Western m (Film). '~·pow·er s phys. Pferdestärke f. ~ race s Sport: Pferderennen n. '~·rad·ish s ₰ Meerrettich m. ~ sense s gesunder Menschenverstand. ~·shoe ['hɔːʃʃuː] s Hufeisen n. ~ trad·ing s bsd. pol. F Kuhhandel m. '~·wom·an s (irr woman) (geübte) Reiterin.

hor·ti·cul·tur·al [ˌhɔːtɪ'kʌltʃərəl] adj Garten(bau)...: ~ show Gartenschau f. **'hor·ti·cul·ture** s Gartenbau m.

ho·san·na [həʊ'zænə] **I** int hos(i)anna! **II** s hos(i)anna n.

hose¹ [həʊz] s (pl konstruiert) Strümpfe pl, Strumpfwaren pl.

hose² [~] **I** s Schlauch m. **II** v/t spritzen: ~ down abspritzen.

ho·sier·y ['həʊzɪərɪ] s coll. Strumpfwaren pl.

hos·pice ['hɒspɪs] s Sterbeklinik f.

hos·pi·ta·ble [hɒ'spɪtəbl] adj □ gast(freund)lich (Person); gastlich, gastfrei (Haus etc).

hos·pi·tal ['hɒspɪtl] s Krankenhaus n, Klinik f: in (Am. in the) ~ im Krankenhaus.

hos·pi·tal·i·ty [ˌhɒspɪ'tælətɪ] s Gastfreundschaft f, Gastlichkeit f.

hos·pi·tal·ize ['hɒspɪtəlaɪz] v/t ins Krankenhaus einliefern od. einweisen.

host¹ [həʊst] **I** s **1.** Gastgeber m. **2.** biol.

Wirt *m* (*Tier od. Pflanze*). **3.** Rundfunk, *TV*: Talkmaster *m*; Showmaster *m*; Moderator *m*. **II** *v/t* **4.** *Rundfunk*, *TV*: *Sendung* moderieren.

host² [~] *s* Menge *f*, Masse *f*: **a ~ of questions** e-e Unmenge Fragen.

Host³ [~] *s eccl.* Hostie *f*.

hos·tage ['hɒstɪdʒ] *s* Geisel *f*: **take s.o. ~** j-n als Geisel nehmen.

hos·tel ['hɒstl] *s* **1.** *mst* **youth ~** Jugendherberge *f*. **2.** *bsd. Br.* (*Studenten-, Arbeiter- etc*)Wohnheim *n*.

hos·tess ['həʊstɪs] *s* **1.** Gastgeberin *f*. **2.** Hosteß *f* (*Betreuerin auf Messen etc*). **3.** ✈ Hosteß *f*, Stewardeß *f*. **4.** Animier-, Tischdame *f*.

hos·tile ['hɒstaɪl] *adj* □ **1.** feindlich, Feind(es)... **2.** (**to**) feindselig (gegen), feindlich gesinnt (*dat*): **~ to foreigners** ausländerfeindlich. **hos·til·i·ty** [hɒ'stɪlətɪ] *s* **1.** Feindschaft *f*, Feindseligkeit *f*: **~ to foreigners** Ausländerfeindlichkeit *f*. **2.** *pl* ✕ Feindseligkeiten *pl*.

hot [hɒt] **I** *adj* □ **1.** *allg.* heiß (*a. fig.*): **I am ~** mir ist heiß; **I went ~ and cold** es überlief mich heiß u. kalt; **~ favo(u)rite** F (*bsd. Sport*) heißer *od.* hoher Favorit; **~ music** sl. heiße Musik; **~ tip** F heißer Tip; **be in ~ water** F in Schwulitäten sein. **2.** warm, heiß (*Speisen*): **~ meal** warme Mahlzeit; → **potato. 3.** scharf (gewürzt). **4. be ~ for** (*od.* **on**) F brennen *od.* scharf sein auf (*acc*). **5.** ganz neu *od.* frisch: **~ from the press** frisch aus der Presse (*Nachrichten*), soeben erschienen (*Buch etc*); **~ scent** (*od.* **trail**) *hunt.* warme *od.* frische Fährte *n.* Spur (*a. fig.*). **6.** F toll, großartig, (*Nachrichten*) sensationell. **7.** F heiß (*gestohlen, geschmuggelt etc*). **II** *adv* **8.** heiß: **give it s.o. ~** (**and strong**) F j-m gründlich einheizen; → **track** 1, **trail** 7. **III** *v/t* **9.** *mst* **~ up** *bsd. Br.* heiß machen, *Speisen a.* warm machen, aufwärmen. **10. ~ up** *fig.* F an-, aufheizen; Schwung bringen in (*acc*); *Auto, Motor* frisieren. **IV** *v/i* **11. ~ up** F sich verschärfen; schwungvoller werden. **~ air** *s* **1.** ❂ Heißluft *f.* **2.** F heiße Luft, leeres Geschwätz. **,~'air** *adj* Heißluft... **'~·bed** *s* **1.** ✚ Mist-, Frühbeet *n.* **2.** *fig.* Brutstätte *f.* **,~·'blood·ed** *adj* heißblütig.

hotch·potch ['hɒtʃpɒtʃ] *s* **1.** *gastr.* Eintopf *m, bsd.* Gemüsesuppe *f* mit

Fleisch. **2.** *fig.* Mischmasch *m*, Durcheinander *n*.

hot dog *s* Hot Dog *n, m*.

ho·tel [həʊ'tel] **I** *s* Hotel *n.* **II** *adj* Hotel... **ho·tel·ier** [həʊ'telɪeɪ], **ho'tel,keep·er** *s* Hotelier *m*.

'hot-foot F **I** *adv* schleunigst, schnell. **II** *v/i u. v/t:* **~** (**it**) rennen. **'~·head** *s* Hitzkopf *m.* **,~·'head·ed** *adj* □ hitzköpfig. **'~·house** *s* Treib-, Gewächshaus *n.* **'~·line** *s bsd. pol.* heißer Draht. **~ pants** *s pl* Hot pants *pl*, heiße Höschen *pl*. **'~·plate** *s* **1.** Koch-, Heizplatte *f.* **2.** Warmhalteplatte *f.* **~ rod** *s bsd. Am. sl.* frisierter Wagen. **~ spot** *s* **1.** *bsd. pol.* Unruhe-, Krisenherd *m.* **2.** *bsd. Am.* F Nachtklub *od.* Amüsierbetrieb, in dem *et. los ist:* **,~'wa·ter** *adj* Heißwasser...: **~ bottle** Wärmflasche *f*.

hound [haʊnd] **I** *s* **1.** Jagdhund *m.* **2.** *contp.* Hund *m*, gemeiner Kerl. **II** *v/t* **3.** (*bsd. mit Hunden, a. fig. j-n*) jagen, verfolgen.

hour [aʊə] *s* **1.** Stunde *f*: **by the ~** stundenweise; **for ~s** (**and ~s**) stundenlang; **on the ~** (immer) zur vollen Stunde; **24 ~s a day** Tag u. Nacht. **2.** (*Tages*)Zeit *f*, Stunde *f*: **at all ~s** zu jeder Zeit, jederzeit; **at what ~?** um wieviel Uhr?; → **early** 4, **eleventh** 1, **late** 11, **small** 1. **3.** Zeitpunkt *m*, Stunde *f*. **4.** Stunde *f*, Tag *m*: **the man of the ~** der Mann des Tages. **5.** *pl* (*Arbeits*)Zeit *f*, (*Geschäfts*)Stunden *pl*: **after ~s** nach Geschäftsschluß; nach der Polizeistunde; nach der Arbeit; *fig.* zu spät. **~ hand** *s* Stundenzeiger *m*.

hour·ly ['aʊəlɪ] *adj u. adv* stündlich.

house I *s* [haʊs] *pl* **hous·es** ['haʊzɪz] **1.** Haus *n* (*a.* ✝, *parl., thea.*): → **bring down** 4, **card** 1. **2.** Haus(halt *m*) *n*: **keep ~** den Haushalt führen (**for s.o.** j-m); **put** (*od.* **set**) **one's ~ in order** *fig.* s-e Angelegenheiten in Ordnung bringen. **3.** Haus *n*, Geschlecht *n*: **the ♀ of Hanover** das Haus Hannover. **II** *v/t* [haʊz] **4.** unterbringen; beherbergen (*a. fig. enthalten*). **'~·a·gent** *s* Br. Häusermakler *m.* **~ ar·rest** *s* Hausarrest *m*: **be under ~** unter Hausarrest stehen. **'~·boat** *s* Hausboot *n.* **'~·bound** *adj fig.* ans Haus gefesselt. **'~·break·er** *s* Einbrecher *m.* **'~·break·ing** *s* Einbruch *m.* **'~·bro·ken** *adj* Am. stubenrein (*Hund* *etc*, F *a. Witz etc*). '**~·clean** *v/i* Hausputz machen. '**~·clean·ing** *s* Hausputz *m*. '**~·coat** *s* Morgenrock *m*, -mantel *m*. '**~·fly** *s zo.* Stubenfliege *f*.

house·hold ['haʊshəʊld] **I** *s* **1.** Haushalt *m*. **II** *adj* **2.** Haushalts..., häuslich: **~** *remedy* Hausmittel *n*. **3. ~** *name* (*od word*) (fester *od.* geläufiger) Begriff. '**house·hold·er** *s* Haushaltsvorstand *m*.

'**house|-hunt** *v/i* auf Haussuche sein: *go ~ing* auf Haussuche gehen. '**~·keep·er** *s* Haushälterin *f*, Wirtschafterin *f*. '**~·keep·ing** *s* Haushaltung *f*, Haushaltsführung *f*: **~** (*money*) Haushalts-, Wirtschaftsgeld *n*. '**~·maid** *s* Hausangestellte *f*, -mädchen *n*. **♀** **of Com·mons** *s parl.* Unterhaus *n* (*GB*). **♀** **of Lords** *s parl.* Oberhaus *n* (*GB*). **♀** **of Rep·re·sent·a·tives** *s parl.* Repräsentantenhaus *n* (*USA*). '**~·proud** *adj* übertrieben ordentlich (*Hausfrau*). **~** **rules** *s pl* Hausordnung *f*. '**~·search** *s* ✝ᵗᵃ Haussuchung *f*. '**~-to-'~** *adj* von Haus zu Haus: **~** *collection* Haussammlung *f*; **~** *salesman* Hausierer *m*; Vertreter *m*. '**~·top** *s* Dach *n*: *cry* (*od. proclaim, shout*) *from the* **~***s et.* öffentlich verkünden, *et. Vertrauliches* an die große Glocke hängen. '**~-trained** *adj bsd. Br.* stubenrein (*Hund etc*). '**~·warm·ing** (**par·ty**) *s* Einzugsparty *f* (*im neuen Haus*). '**~·wife** *s* (*irr wife*) Hausfrau *f*. '**~·work** *s* Hausarbeit *f*.

hous·ing ['haʊzɪŋ] *s* **1.** Wohnung *f*: **~** *development bsd. Am.*, **~** *estate Br.* Wohnsiedlung *f*; **~** *market* Wohnungsmarkt *m*; **~** *shortage* Wohnungsnot *f*. **2.** *coll.* Häuser *pl*. **3.** Wohnen *n*: **~** *con·ditions pl* Wohnverhältnisse *pl*.

hove [həʊv] *pret u. pp von* **heave**.

hov·el ['hɒvl] *s contp.* Bruchbude *f*, Loch *n*.

hov·er ['hɒvə] *v/i* **1.** schweben (*a. fig. between* zwischen *Leben u. Tod etc*). **2.** sich herumtreiben (*about* in der Nähe von). **3.** *fig.* schwanken (*between* zwischen *dat*). '**~·craft** *pl* -**craft** *s* Luftkissenfahrzeug *n*.

how [haʊ] *adv* **1.** *fragend:* wie: **~** *are you?* wie geht es dir?; **~** *is your toothache?* was machen *od.* die Zahnschmerzen?; **~** *about ...?* wie steht *od.* wäre es mit ...?; **~** *do you know?* woher wissen Sie das?; **~** *much?* wieviel?; **~** *many?*

wieviel?, wie viele?; → *be* **7**, *come* **7**, *do* **1** **12. 2.** *ausrufend u. relativ:* wie: **~** *absurd!* wie absurd!; *he knows* **~** *to ride* er kann reiten; *I know* **~** *to do* it weiß, wie man es macht; *and* **~**! F u. ob! **~·'ev·er I** *adv* wie auch (immer): **~** *it* (*may*) *be* wie dem auch sei; **~** *you do it* wie du es auch machst. **II** *cj* jedoch.

howl [haʊl] **I** *v/i* **1.** heulen (*Wölfe, Wind etc*). **2.** brüllen, schreien (*in agony* vor Schmerzen; *with laughter* vor Lachen). **II** *v/t* **3.** brüllen, schreien: **~** *down j-n* niederschreien, -brüllen. **III** *s* **4.** Heulen *n*. '**howl·er** *s* F grober Schnitzer. '**howl·ing** *adj* **1.** heulend. **2.** F Mords...: **~** *success* Bombenerfolg *m*.

hub [hʌb] *s* **1.** ✪ (Rad)Nabe *f*. **2.** *fig.* Mittel-, Angelpunkt *m*.

hub·bub ['hʌbʌb] *s* **1.** Stimmengewirr *n*. **2.** Tumult *m*.

'**hub·cap** *s mot.* Radkappe *f*.

huck·le·ber·ry ['hʌklbərɪ] *s* ♣ *Amer.* Heidelbeere *f*.

huck·ster ['hʌkstə] → **hawker**.

hud·dle ['hʌdl] **I** *v/t* **1.** *mst* **~** *together* (*od. up*) zs.-werfen, auf e-n Haufen werfen; zs.-drängen: **~** *s.th. into bsd. Br. et.* stopfen in (*acc*). **II** *v/i* **2.** (sich) kauern: **~** *up* sich zs.-kauern. **3.** *mst* **~** *together* (*od. up*) sich zs.-drängen. **4. ~** (*up*) *against* (*od. to*) sich kuscheln *od.* schmiegen an (*acc*). **III** *s* **5.** (wirrer) Haufen; Wirrwarr *m*, Durcheinander *n*. **6.** *go into a* **~** F die Köpfe zs.-stecken; sich beraten (*with* mit).

hue¹ [hjuː] *s* **1.** Farbe *f*. **2.** (Farb)Ton *m*, Tönung *f*, *a. fig.* Färbung *f*, Schattierung *f*.

hue² [~] *s*: *raise a* **~** *and cry against* lautstark protestieren gegen.

huff [hʌf] **I** *v/i* keuchen, schnaufen. **II** *s*: *be in a* **~** muffeln; *go into a* **~** muff(e)lig werden. '**huff·y** *adj* □ **1.** muff(e)lig. **2.** übelnehmerisch.

hug [hʌg] **I** *v/t* **1.** umarmen, (*a.* **~** *to one*) an sich drücken. **2.** *fig.* (zäh) festhalten an (*dat*). **II** *v/i* **3.** sich umarmen. **III** *s* **4.** Umarmung *f*: *give s.o. a* **~** j-n umarmen.

huge [hjuːdʒ] *adj* riesig, riesengroß (*beide a. fig.*). '**huge·ly** *adv* ungeheuer, gewaltig. '**huge·ness** *s* ungeheure *od.* gewaltige Größe.

hulk [hʌlk] *s* Koloß *m*: a) *Gebilde von gewaltigem Ausmaß*, b) klotziges *od.* sperriges *od.* unhandliches Ding, c) ungeschlachter Kerl, schwerfälliger Riese. **'hulk·ing**, **'hulk·y** *adj* **1.** klotzig, sperrig, unhandlich. **2.** ungeschlacht, schwerfällig.

hull¹ [hʌl] **I** *s* ♀ Schale *f*, Hülse *f*. **II** *v/t* schälen, enthülsen.

hull² [~] *s* ♣ Rumpf *m*.

hul·la·ba·ba(l)·loo [ˌhʌləbə'luː] *s* Lärm *m*, Getöse *n*.

hul·lo → **hello**.

hum [hʌm] **I** *v/i* **1.** *allg.* summen: **my head is** ~**ming** mir brummt der Kopf; ~ **(with activity)** **F** voller Leben *od.* Aktivität sein. **2.** ~ **and haw** herumdrucksen, nicht recht mit der Sprache herauswollen. **II** *v/t* **3.** *Lied* summen. **III** *s* **4.** Summen *n*.

hu·man ['hjuːmən] **I** *adj* (☐ → **human·ly**) menschlich, Menschen...: ~ **being** Mensch *m*; ~ **chain** Menschenkette *f*; ~ **dignity** Menschenwürde *f*; ~ **medicine** Humanmedizin *f*; ~ **race** Menschengeschlecht *n*; ~ **rights** *pl* Menschenrechte *pl*; → **err.** **II** *s* Mensch *m*. **hu·mane** [hjuː'meɪn] *adj* ☐ **1.** human, menschlich. **2.** humanistisch. **hu·man·ism** ['hjuːmənɪzəm] *s* Humanismus *m*. **'hu·man·ist** *s* Humanist(in). ˌ**hu·man·'is·tic** *adj* (~**ally**) humanistisch. **hu·man·i·tar·i·an** [hjuːˌmænɪ'teərɪən] *adj* humanitär, menschenfreundlich. **hu·'man·i·ty** *s* **1.** die Menschheit. **2.** Humanität *f*, Menschlichkeit *f*. **3.** *pl* Altphilologie *f*; Geisteswissenschaften *pl*. **hu·man·ize** ['hjuːmənaɪz] *v/t* **1.** humanisieren, humaner *od.* menschenwürdiger gestalten. **2.** vermenschlichen, personifizieren. **hu·man·kind** [ˌ~'kaɪnd] → **humanity** 1. **'hu·man·ly** *adv*: **do everything** ~ **possible** alles menschenmögliche tun; ~ **speaking** nach menschlichem Ermessen. **hu·man·ly possible** alles menschenmöglichstes tun.

hum·ble ['hʌmbl] **I** *adj* ☐ bescheiden: a) demütig: **in my** ~ **opinion** m-r unmaßgeblichen Meinung nach; **eat** ~ **pie** *fig.* klein beigeben; → **self,** b) anspruchslos, einfach, c) niedrig: **of** ~ **birth** von niederer Geburt. **II** *v/t* demütigen, erniedrigen. **'hum·ble·ness** *s* Bescheidenheit *f*, Demut *f*.

hum·bug ['hʌmbʌg] *s* **1.** Humbug *m*: a)

Schwindel *m*, Betrug *m*, b) Unsinn *m*, dummes Zeug. **2.** *Br.* Pfefferminzbonbon *m*, *n*.

hum·ding·er [ˌhʌm'dɪŋə] *s bsd. Am.* **F 1.** Mordskerl *m*. **2.** tolles Ding.

hum·drum ['hʌmdrʌm] **I** *adj* **1.** eintönig, langweilig. **II** *s* **2.** Eintönigkeit *f*, Langweiligkeit *f*. **3.** eintönige *od.* langweilige Arbeit; Langweiler *m*.

hu·mid ['hjuːmɪd] *adj* ☐ feucht. **hu·'mid·i·fi·er** [ˌ~dɪfaɪə] *s* ♦ (Luft)Befeuchter *m*. **hu·'mid·i·fy** [ˌ~faɪ] *v/t* befeuchten. **hu·'mid·i·ty** *s* Feuchtigkeit *f*: ~ **of the air** Luftfeuchtigkeit.

hu·mil·i·ate [hjuː'mɪlɪeɪt] *v/t* demütigen, erniedrigen. **hu·mil·i·a·tion** *s* Demütigung *f*, Erniedrigung *f*.

hum·ming·bird ['hʌmɪŋbɜːd] *s orn.* Kolibri *m*.

hum·mock ['hʌmək] *s* Hügel *m*.

hu·mor *Am.* → **humour.**

hu·mor·ist ['hjuːmərɪst] *s* **1.** Humorist(in). **2.** Spaßvogel *m*. ˌ**hu·mor·'is·tic** *adj* (~**ally**) humoristisch. **hu·mor·ous** ['hjuːmərəs] *adj* ☐ humorvoll, humorig.

hu·mour ['hjuːmə] *bsd. Br.* **I** *s* **1.** Humor *m*: (a: **good**) **sense of** ~ (Sinn *m* für) Humor. **2.** Komik *f*, das Komische. **3.** (Gemüts)Verfassung *f*: **in a good** (**bad**) ~ (bei) guter (schlechter) Laune; **out of** ~ schlecht gelaunt. **II** *v/t* **4.** *j-m* s-n Willen tun *od.* lassen; *j-n, et.* hinnehmen. **'hu·mour·less** *adj bsd. Br.* humorlos.

hump [hʌmp] **I** *s* **1.** Buckel *m*, (*e-s Kamels*) Höcker *m*. **2.** (kleiner) Hügel: **be over the** ~ *fig.* über den Berg sein. **II** *v/t* **3.** ~ **one's back** e-n Buckel machen. **4.** *bsd. Am.* **F** auf den Rücken *od.* die Schulter nehmen; tragen. **'~·back** *s* **1.** Buckel *m*. **2.** Buck(e)lige *m*, *f*. **'~·backed** *adj* buck(e)lig.

humph [hʌmf] *int* hm!

Hun [hʌn] *s* **1.** *hist.* Hunne *m*. **2.** **F** *contp.* Deutsche *m*.

hu·mus ['hjuːməs] *s* Humus *m*.

hunch [hʌntʃ] **I** *s* **1.** → **hump** 1. **2.** dickes Stück. **3.** (Vor)Ahnung *f*: **have a** ~ **that** das Gefühl *od.* den Verdacht haben, daß. **II** *v/t* **4.** → **hump** 3: ~ **one's shoulders** die Schultern hochziehen. **'~·back** → **humpback.** **'~·backed** → **humpbacked.**

hun·dred ['hʌndrəd] **I** adj **1.** hundert: **a (one) ~** (ein)hundert. **II** s **2.** Hundert n: **~s of times** hundertmal; **~s** pl **of thousands** Hunderttausende pl. **3.** & Hunderter m. **hun·dred·fold** ['~fəʊld] **I** adj u. adv hundertfach. **II** s das Hundertfache. **hun·dredth** ['~tθ] **I** adj **1.** hundertst. **II** s **2.** der, die, das Hundertste. **3.** Hundertstel n: **a ~ of a second** e-e Hundertstelsekunde.

hung [hʌŋ] pret u. pp von **hang**.

Hun·gar·i·an [hʌŋˈgeərɪən] **I** adj **1.** ungarisch. **II** s **2.** Ungar(in). **3.** ling. Ungarisch n.

hun·ger ['hʌŋgə] **I** s Hunger m (a. fig. **for, after** nach): **~ for knowledge** Wissensdurst m. **II** v/i fig. hungern (**for, after** nach). **~ strike** s Hungerstreik m: **go on (a) ~** in den Hungerstreik treten.

hun·gry ['hʌŋgrɪ] adj □ hungrig (a. fig. **for** nach): **be** (od. **feel**) **(very) ~** (sehr) hungrig sein, (großen) Hunger haben; **go ~** hungern; **~ for knowledge** wissensdurstig.

hunk [hʌŋk] s großes Stück.

hunt [hʌnt] **I** s **1.** Jagd f, Jagen n. **2.** fig. Jagd f: a) Verfolgung f, b) Suche f (**for, after** nach): **be on the ~ for** auf der Jagd sein nach. **II** v/t **3.** (a. fig. j-n) jagen, Jagd machen auf (acc): **~ down** erlegen, zur Strecke bringen (a. fig.); **~ed look** gehetzter Blick. **4.** verfolgen. **5. ~ away** (od. **off**) wegjagen, vertreiben. **6. ~ out** (od. **up**) heraussuchen; aufstöbern, -spüren. **III** v/i **7.** jagen: **go ~ing** auf die Jagd gehen; **~ for** Jagd machen auf (acc) (a. fig.). **8.** suchen (**for, after** nach). **'hunt·er** s Jäger m (a. fig.). **'hunt·ing I** s Jagen n, Jagd f. **II** adj Jagd...: **~ licence** (Am. **license**) Jagdschein m; **~ season** Jagdzeit f.

hur·dle ['hɜːdl] s Hürde f (a. Leichtathletik u. fig.): **~ race** Hürdenlauf m. **'hur·dler** m Leichtathletik: Hürdenläufer(in).

hur·dy-gur·dy ['hɜːdɪˌɡɜːdɪ] s Leierkasten m.

hurl [hɜːl] v/t schleudern: **~ down** zu Boden schleudern; **~ o.s.** sich stürzen (**on, at** auf acc); **~ abuse at s.o.** j-m Beleidigungen ins Gesicht schleudern.

hurl·y-burl·y ['hɜːlɪˌbɜːlɪ] s Tumult m, Aufruhr m.

hur·rah [hʊˈrɑː], **hur·ray** [hʊˈreɪ] **I** int hurra! **II** s Hurra(ruf m) n.

hur·ri·cane ['hʌrɪkən] s Hurrikan m, Wirbelsturm m; Orkan m, fig. a. Sturm m: **rise to a ~** zum Orkan anschwellen.

hur·ried ['hʌrɪd] adj □ eilig, hastig, übereilt.

hur·ry ['hʌrɪ] **I** s **1.** Hast f, Eile f: **be in a ~** es eilig haben (**to do** zu tun), in Eile sein; **be in no ~** es nicht eilig haben; **do s.th. in a ~** et. eilig od. hastig tun; **there is no ~** es eilt nicht. **2.** Hetze f. **II** v/t **3.** schnell od. eilig befördern od. bringen. **4.** oft **~ up** j-n antreiben, hetzen; et. beschleunigen. **III** v/i **5.** eilen, hasten: **~ (up)** sich beeilen; **~ up!** (mach) schnell!

hurt [hɜːt] (irr) **I** v/t **1.** (a. fig. j-n, j-s Gefühle etc) verletzen: **~ one's knee** sich das Knie verletzen; **feel ~** sich gekränkt fühlen; → **fly².** **2.** schmerzen, j-m weh tun (beide a. fig.). **3.** schaden (dat). **II** v/i **4.** schmerzen, weh tun (beide a. fig.). **hurt·ful** ['~fʊl] adj □ **1.** verletzend. **2.** schmerzlich. **3.** schädlich (**to** für).

hus·band ['hʌzbənd] **I** s (Ehe)Mann m, Gatte m. **II** v/t haushalten mit, sparsam umgehen mit. **'hus·band·ry** s Landwirtschaft f.

hush [hʌʃ] **I** int still!, pst! **II** v/t **2.** zum Schweigen bringen. **3.** mst **~ up** vertuschen. **III** v/i **4.** still werden, verstummen. **IV** s **5.** Stille f, Schweigen n: **~ money** Schweigegeld n.

husk [hʌsk] **I** s & Hülse f, Schale f, Schote f. **II** v/t enthülsen, schälen.

husk·y¹ ['hʌskɪ] adj □ **1.** heiser, rauh (Stimme). **2.** F stämmig, kräftig.

hus·ky² [~] s zo. Husky m, Eskimohund m.

hus·sy ['hʌsɪ] s **1.** Fratz m, Göre f. **2.** Flittchen n.

hus·tle ['hʌsl] **I** v/t **1.** stoßen, drängen; (an)rempeln. **2.** hetzen, (an)treiben; drängen (**into doing** zu tun). **3.** (in aller Eile) wohin bringen od. schicken. **4.** sich beeilen mit. **5.** bsd. Am. F ergattern; (sich) et. ergaunern. **II** v/i **6.** sich drängen. **7.** hasten, hetzen. **8.** sich beeilen. **III** s **9.** mst **~ and bustle** Gedränge n; Gehetze n; Betrieb m, Wirbel m. **'hus·tler** s bsd. Am. F Nutte f.

hut [hʌt] s Hütte f.

hy·a·cinth [ˈhaɪəsɪnθ] *s* ♀ Hyazinthe *f.*

hy·ae·na → **hyena.**

hy·brid [ˈhaɪbrɪd] *s biol.* Hybride *f, m,* Kreuzung *f.*

hy·dran·gea [haɪˈdreɪndʒə] *s* ♀ Hortensie *f.*

hy·drant [ˈhaɪdrənt] *s* Hydrant *m.*

hy·drate [ˈhaɪdreɪt] *s* 🜍 Hydrat *n.*

hy·drau·lic [haɪˈdrɔːlɪk] **I** *adj* (*ally*) *phys.,* ⊙ hydraulisch. **II** *s pl (sg konstruiert) phys.* Hydraulik *f.*

hy·dro... [ˈhaɪdrəʊ] Wasser...

hy·dro|'car·bon *s* 🜍 Kohlenwasserstoff *m.* **~'chlo·ric** *adj:* **~ acid** 🜍 Salzsäure *f.* **~e'lec·tric** *adj:* **~ power station** Wasserkraftwerk *n.* **~'foil** *s* Tragflächen-, Tragflügelboot *n.*

hy·dro·gen [ˈhaɪdrədʒən] *s* 🜍 Wasserstoff *m:* **~ bomb** ✕ Wasserstoffbombe *f.*

hy·dro|'pho·bi·a *s* **1.** *psych.* Hydrophobie *f.* **2.** *vet.* Tollwut *f.* **~'plane** *s* Wasserflugzeug *n.*

hy·e·na [haɪˈiːnə] *s zo.* Hyäne *f (a. fig.).*

hy·giene [ˈhaɪdʒiːn] *s* Hygiene *f,* Gesundheitspflege *f.* **hy·gien·ic** *adj* (*ally*) hygienisch.

hy·grom·e·ter [haɪˈgrɒmɪtə] *s* Hygrometer *n,* Luftfeuchtigkeitsmesser *m.*

hymn [hɪm] *s* Kirchenlied *n,* Choral *m.* **hym·nal** [ˈ-nəl], **'hymn·book** *s* Gesangbuch *n.*

hy·per... [ˈhaɪpə] hyper..., übermäßig.

hy·per·bo·la [haɪˈpɜːbələ] *pl* **-las, -lae** [-iː] *s* ♈ Hyperbel *f.* **hy'per·bo·le** [-lɪ] *s rhet.* Hyperbel *f,* Übertreibung *f.* **hy·per·bol·ic** [ˌhaɪpəˈbɒlɪk] *adj* (*ally*) ♈ hyperbolisch, *rhet. a.* übertreibend.

hy·per|'crit·i·cal *adj* □ hyperkritisch. **~mar·ket** *s Br.* Groß-, Verbraucher-

markt *m.* **~'sen·si·tive** *adj* □ hypersensibel, *a.* ✍ überempfindlich (**to** gegen). **~'ten·sion** *s* ✍ erhöhter Blutdruck.

hy·phen [ˈhaɪfn] *s* **1.** Bindestrich *m.* **2.** Trennungszeichen *n.* **hy·phen·ate** [ˈ-fəneɪt] *v/t* **1.** mit Bindestrich schreiben. **2.** trennen.

hyp·no·sis [hɪpˈnəʊsɪs] *pl* **-ses** [-siːz] *s* Hypnose *f.* **hyp·not·ic** [-ˈnɒtɪk] *adj* (*ally*) hypnotisch. **hyp·no·tist** [ˈ-nətɪst] *s* Hypnotiseur *m.* **hyp·no·tize** [ˈ-taɪz] *v/t* hypnotisieren.

hy·po... [ˈhaɪpəʊ] Unter..., Sub...

hy·po·chon·dri·a [ˌhaɪpəʊˈkɒndrɪə] *s* Hypochondrie *f.* **hy·po'chon·dri·ac** [-dræk] **I** *adj* □ hypochondrisch. **II** *s* Hypochonder *m.*

hy·poc·ri·sy [hɪˈpɒkrəsɪ] *s* Heuchelei *f.* **hyp·o·crite** [ˈhɪpəkrɪt] *s* Heuchler(in). **hyp·o'crit·i·cal** *adj* □ heuchlerisch.

hy·po·der·mic [ˌhaɪpəʊˈdɜːmɪk] ✍ **I** *adj* (*ally*) subkutan, unter *od.* die Haut: **~ injection** → II. **II** *s* subkutane Injektion *od.* Einspritzung.

hy·po'ten·sion *s* ✍ zu niedriger Blutdruck.

hy·pot·e·nuse [haɪˈpɒtənjuːz] *s* ♈ Hypotenuse *f.*

hy·po·ther·mi·a [ˌhaɪpəʊˈθɜːmɪə] *s* ✍ Unterkühlung *f.*

hy·poth·e·sis [haɪˈpɒθɪsɪs] *pl* **-ses** [-siːz] *s* Hypothese *f.* **hy·po·thet·i·cal** [ˌ-pəˈθetɪkl] *adj* □ hypothetisch.

hys·te·ri·a [hɪˈstɪərɪə] *s* Hysterie *f.* **hys·ter·ic** [hɪˈsterɪk] **I** *s* **1.** Hysteriker(in). **2.** *pl (mst sg konstruiert)* hysterischer Anfall: **go (off) into ~s** hysterisch werden. **II** *adj* **3.** → **hysterical. hys·ter·i·cal** *adj* □ hysterisch.

I

I [aɪ] *pron* ich: **it is ~** ich bin es.

i·bex [ˈaɪbeks] *pl* **i·bex·es, ib·i·ces** [ˈɪbɪsiːz] *s zo.* Steinbock *m.*

ice [aɪs] **I** *s* **1.** **be** (**skating**) **on thin ~** *fig.* sich auf gefährlichem Boden bewegen;

break the ~ *fig.* das Eis brechen; **cut no ~** (**with**) F keinen Eindruck machen (auf *acc*), nicht ziehen (bei); **put on ~** kalt stellen; *fig.* F auf Eis legen. **2.** a) *Am.* Fruchteis *n,* b) *Br.* → **ice cream.**

3. → *icing.* **II** *v/t* **4.** gefrieren lassen. **5.** *Getränk etc* mit *od.* in Eis kühlen. **6.** *gastr.* glasieren. **III** *v/i* **7.** gefrieren. **8.** *mst* ~ **up** (*od.* **over**) zufrieren; vereisen. **9.** ~ **out** auftauen (*Gewässer*). ♀ **Age** *s geol.* Eiszeit *f.* ~ **ax(e)** *s* Eispickel *m.* ~ **bag** *s* ☀ Eisbeutel *m.* **~·berg** ['ɔːbɜːɡ] *s* Eisberg *m* (*a. fig. Person*): **the tip of the** ~ die Spitze des Eisbergs (*a. fig.*). **'~·bound** *adj* eingefroren (*Schiff*); zugefroren (*Hafen*). **'~·box** *s* **1.** Eisfach *n* (*e-s Kühlschranks*). **2.** *Am.* Eis-, Kühlschrank *m.* **'~·break·er** *s* ⚓ Eisbrecher *m.* ~ **buck·et** *s* Eiskübel *m.* **~·'cold** *adj* eiskalt. ~ **cream** *s* (Speise)Eis *n*, Eiscreme *f*: *chocolate* ~ Schokoladeneis. **'~·cream** *adj* Eis...: ~ *parlo(u)r* Eisdiele *f.* ~ **cube** *s* Eiswürfel *m.*

iced *adj* **1.** eisgekühlt. **2.** gefroren. **3.** *gastr.* glasiert, mit Zuckerguß.

ice| **floe** → *floe.* ~ **hock·ey** *s Sport:* Eishockey *n.*

Ice·land·er ['aɪsləndə] *s* Isländer(in). **Ice·lan·dic** [~'lændɪk] **I** *adj* isländisch. **II** *s ling.* Isländisch *n.*

ice| **lol·ly** *s Br.* Eis *n* am Stiel. **'~·man** *s* (*irr man*) *Am.* Eismann *m*, -verkäufer *m.* ~ **pack** *s* **1.** Packeis *n.* **2.** ☀ Eisbeutel *m.* ~ **pail** *s* Eiskübel *m.* ~ **rink** *s* (Kunst)Eisbahn *f.* ~ **wa·ter** *s* Eiswasser *n.*

ich·thy·ol·o·gy [ˌɪkθɪˈɒlədʒɪ] *s* Fischkunde *f.*

i·ci·cle ['aɪsɪkl] *s* Eiszapfen *m.*

i·ci·ness ['aɪsɪnɪs] *s* eisige Kälte (*a. fig.*).

ic·ing ['aɪsɪŋ] *s gastr.* Glasur *f*, Zuckerguß *m.*

i·con ['aɪkɒn] *s* Ikone *f.*

i·cy ['aɪsɪ] *adj* eisig (*a. fig.*).

I'd [aɪd] F *für* **I had; I would.**

i·de·a [aɪˈdɪə] *s* **1.** Idee *f*, Vorstellung *f*, Begriff *m*: *form an* ~ *of* sich *et.* vorstellen, sich e-n Begriff machen von; *have no* ~ keine Ahnung haben; *put* ~*s into s.o.'s head* j-m Flausen in den Kopf setzen. **2.** Absicht *f*, Gedanke *m*, Idee *f*: *the* ~ *is* ... der Zweck der Sache ist, ...; es geht darum, ...; *the* ~ *entered my mind* mir kam der Gedanke. **3.** *I have an* ~ *that* ich habe so das Gefühl, daß; es kommt mir (so) vor, als ob.

i·de·al [aɪˈdɪəl] **I** *adj* (□ *u.* ~*ally*) **1.** ideal. **2.** ideell. **II** *s* **3.** Ideal *n.*

i·de·al·ism *s* Idealismus *m.* **i·de·al·ist** *s*

Idealist(in). **i·de·al·is·tic** *adj* (~*ally*) idealistisch. **i·de·al·ize** *v/t u. v/i* idealisieren. **i·de·al·ly** *adv* **1.** → *ideal* I. **2.** im Idealfall.

i·den·ti·cal [aɪˈdentɪkl] *adj* □ identisch (*to, with*) mit): ~ *twins pl* eineiige Zwillinge *pl.*

i·den·ti·fi·ca·tion [aɪˌdentɪfɪˈkeɪʃn] *s* **1.** Identifizierung *f*: ~ *card* (Personal-)Ausweis *m*; ~ *papers pl* Ausweispapiere *pl*; ~ *parade* 🏛 *Br.* Gegenüberstellung *f.* **2.** Ausweis *m*, Legitimation *f*: *he didn't have any* ~ er konnte sich nicht ausweisen. **i·den·ti·fy** [~faɪ] **I** *v/t* **1.** identifizieren, gleichsetzen (*with* mit): ~ *o.s. with* → **4. 2.** identifizieren, erkennen (*as* als). **3.** ~ *o.s.* sich ausweisen *od.* legitimieren. **II** *v/i* **4.** ~ *with* sich identifizieren mit.

i·den·ti·kit (**pic·ture**) [aɪˈdentɪkɪt] *s* 🏛 *Br.* Phantombild *n.*

i·den·ti·ty [aɪˈdentətɪ] *s* Identität *f*: a) (völlige) Gleichheit, b) Persönlichkeit *f*: *prove one's* ~ → *identify* 3; *loss of* ~ Identitätsverlust *m*; → *mistaken* 2. ~ *card s* (Personal)Ausweis *m.* ~ *cri·sis s* (*irr crisis*) Identitätskrise *f.* ~ *pa·rade s* 🏛 Gegenüberstellung *f.*

i·de·o·log·i·cal [ˌaɪdɪəˈlɒdʒɪkl] *adj* □ ideologisch. **i·de·ol·o·gy** [~'ɒlədʒɪ] *s* Ideologie *f.*

id·i·o·cy ['ɪdɪəsɪ] *s* ☀ Idiotie *f*, *contp. a.* Blödheit *f.*

id·i·om ['ɪdɪəm] *s ling.* Idiom *n*, idiomatischer Ausdruck, Redewendung *f.* **id·i·o·mat·ic** [~'mætɪk] *adj* (~*ally*) idiomatisch.

id·i·ot ['ɪdɪət] *s* ☀ Idiot *m*, *contp. a.* Trottel *m.* **id·i·ot·ic** [~'ɒtɪk] *adj* (~*ally*) *adj* idiotisch, *contp. a.* vertrottelt.

i·dle ['aɪdl] **I** *adj* □ **1.** untätig, müßig. **2.** ruhig, still: ~ *hours pl* Mußestunden *pl.* **3.** faul, träge. **4.** ⚙ stillstehend, außer Betrieb; leer laufend, im Leerlauf: *run* ~ → **8. 5.** nutz-, sinn-, zwecklos; vergeblich. **6.** leer, hohl: ~ *gossip* (*od.* *talk*) leeres Geschwätz. **II** *v/i* **7.** faulenzen: ~ *about* (*od.* *around*) herumtrödeln. **8.** ⚙ leer laufen. **III** *v/t* **9.** *mst* ~ *away* Zeit vertrödeln. **'i·dler** *s* Müßiggänger(in).

i·dol ['aɪdl] *s* Idol *n* (*a. fig.*); Gottesstatue *f*, Götterbild *n*; *contp.* Götze(nbild *n*) *m*: *make an* ~ *of* → *idolize* b.

i·dol·a·trous [aɪˈdɒlətrəs] *adj* □ **1.**

contp. Götzen... **2.** *fig.* abgöttisch. **i·dol·a·try** *s* **1.** *Anbetung e-r kultisch verehrten Figur od. e-s Götterbildes*; *contp.* Götzenanbetung *f*, -dienst *m.* **2.** *fig.* Vergötterung *f.* **i·dol·ize** ['aɪdəlaɪz] *v/t* a) abgöttisch verehren, vergöttern, b) idolisieren, zum Idol machen.

i·dyll ['ɪdɪl] *s* Idyll *n.* **i·dyl·lic** [ɪ'dɪlɪk] *adj* (**~ally**) idyllisch.

if [ɪf] **I** *cj* **1.** wenn, falls: **~ I were you** wenn ich du wäre; **as ~** als wenn *od.* ob; **~ so** gegebenenfalls; wenn ja. **2.** wenn auch, aber. **3.** *indirekt fragend:* ob: **try ~ you can do it; and ~!** F u. ob! **II** *s* **4.** Wenn *n*: **without ~s and buts** ohne Wenn u. Aber.

ig·loo ['ɪɡluː] *s* Iglu *m, n.*

ig·nite [ɪɡ'naɪt] **I** *v/t* **1.** an-, entzünden. **2.** *fig.* entzünden, -flammen. **II** *v/i* **3.** sich entzünden. **4.** *mot.,* ⊙ zünden. **ig·ni·tion** [ɪɡ'nɪʃn] **I** *s* **1.** An-, Entzünden *n.* **2.** *mot.,* ⊙ Zündung *f.* **II** *adj* **3.** *mot.,* ⊙ Zünd...: **~ key; ~ coil** Zündspule *f.*

ig·no·min·i·ous [ˌɪɡnə'mɪnɪəs] *adj* □ schändlich, schimpflich. **ig·no·min·y** ['ɪɡnəmɪnɪ] *s* **1.** Schande *f.* **2.** Schändlichkeit *f.*

ig·no·ra·mus [ˌɪɡnə'reɪməs] *s* Ignorant (-in). **'ig·no·rance** *s* **1.** Unkenntnis *f* (**of** *gen*), Unwissenheit *f:* **from** (*od.* **through**) **~** aus Unwissenheit. **2.** *contp.* Ignoranz *f.* **'ig·no·rant** *adj* **1.** **be ~ of s.th.** et. nicht wissen *od.* kennen, nichts wissen von et. **2.** *contp.* ignorant; ungebildet. **'ig·no·rant·ly** *adv* unwissentlich. **ig·nore** [ɪɡ'nɔː] *v/t* **1.** ignorieren, nicht beachten, keine Notiz nehmen von.

ill [ɪl] **I** *adj* **1.** *pred* krank: **be taken** (*od.* **fall**) **~** erkranken (**with** an *dat*), krank werden. **2.** schlecht, schlimm: → **fortune** 3, **luck** 1, **ick** 1, *etc.* **II** *adv* **3.** schlecht: **speak** (**think**) **~ of** schlecht sprechen (denken) von; → **ease** 2. **III** *s* **4.** a) oft *pl* Übel *n,* ills *pl.* **2.** *contp.* Übles.

I'll [aɪl] F *für* **I will.**

ill-ad·vised *adj* **1.** schlecht beraten. **2.** unbesonnen, unklug. → **timed** 2. **1.** schlechtzogen. **2.** ungezogen. **~dis-'posed** *adj* übelgesinnt: **be ~ to** (*-ward*[*s*]) *j-m* übel gesinnt sein, *j-m* übelwollen; *e-m* Plan *etc* ablehnend gegenüberstehen.

il·le·gal [ɪ'liːɡl] *adj* □ unerlaubt, verbo-

ten; illegal, gesetzwidrig, ungesetzlich: **~ parking** Falschparken *n.* **il·le·gal·i·ty** [ˌɪliː'ɡælətɪ] *s* Gesetzwidrigkeit *f:* a) Illegalität *f,* b) gesetzwidrige Handlung.

il·leg·i·ble [ɪ'ledʒəbl] *adj* □ unleserlich.

il·le·git·i·mate [ˌɪlɪ'dʒɪtɪmət] *adj* □ **1.** gesetzwidrig, ungesetzlich. **2.** nicht-, unehelich.

ill-'fat·ed *adj* unglücklich, Unglücks... **~·'fa·vo(u)red** *adj* □ unschön. **~·'hu·mo(u)red** *adj* schlecht-, übelgelaunt.

il·lib·er·al [ɪ'lɪbərəl] *adj* □ **1.** knaus(e)rig. **2.** engstirnig. **3.** *pol.* illiberal.

il·lic·it [ɪ'lɪsɪt] *adj* □ unerlaubt, verboten: **~ trade** Schwarzhandel *m.*

il·lit·er·a·cy [ɪ'lɪtərəsɪ] *s* **1.** Unbildung *f.* **2.** Analphabetentum *n.* **il·lit·er·ate** [~rət] **I** *adj* □ **1.** ungebildet. **2.** analphabetisch. **II** *s* **3.** Ungebildete *m, f.* **4.** Analphabet(in).

ill-'judged → **ill-advised 2.** **~·'man·nered** *adj* □ ungehobelt, unerzogen. **~·'matched** *adj* schlecht zs.-passend. **~·'na·tured** *adj* **1.** unfreundlich. **2.** → **ill-tempered.**

ill·ness ['ɪlnɪs] *s* Krankheit *f.*

il·log·i·cal [ɪ'lɒdʒɪkl] *adj* □ unlogisch. **ill-'tem·pered** *adj* schlechtgelaunt, übellaunig. **~·'timed** *adj* ungelegen, unpassend.

il·lu·mi·nate [ɪ'luːmɪneɪt] *v/t* **1.** be-, erleuchten, erhellen. **2.** illuminieren, festlich beleuchten. **3.** *fig. etc.* aufhellen, erläutern; *j-n* erleuchten. **il·lu·mi·na·tion** *s* **1.** Beleuchtung *f.* **2.** Illumination *f,* Festbeleuchtung *f.* **3.** *fig.* Erläuterung *f;* Erleuchtung *f.*

il·lu·sion [ɪ'luːʒn] *s* Illusion *f:* a) Sinnestäuschung *f:* → **optical,** b) Einbildung *f:* **be under the ~ that** sich einbilden, daß; **have no ~s** sich keine Illusionen machen (**about** über *acc*). **il·lu·sive** [~sɪv], **il·lu·so·ry** [~sərɪ] *adj* □ illusorisch.

il·lus·trate ['ɪləstreɪt] *v/t* illustrieren a) erläutern, veranschaulichen, b) bebildern. **il·lus·tra·tion** *s* Illustration *f:* a) Erläuterung *f,* Veranschaulichung *f:* **in ~ of** zur Erläuterung (*od. gen*); **by way of ~** als Beispiel, b) Bebilderung *f,* c) Bild *n,* Abbildung *f.* **il·lus·tra·tive** ['ɪləstrətɪv] *adj* □ illustrativ, erläuternd, veranschaulichend. **il·lus·tra·tor** ['ɪləstreɪtə] *s* Illustrator *m.*

il·lus·tri·ous [ɪˈlʌstrɪəs] *adj* □ berühmt.

I'm [aɪm] F *für* **I am.**

im·age [ˈɪmɪdʒ] *s* **1.** Bild *n* (*a. TV etc*). **2.** Ab-, Ebenbild *n*: **he is the very ~ of his father** er ist s-m Vater wie aus dem Gesicht geschnitten, er ist ganz der Vater; → **spitting. 3.** Image *n*. **4.** bildlicher Ausdruck, Metapher *f*: **speak in ~s** in Bildern sprechen.

im·ag·i·na·ble [ɪˈmædʒɪnəbl] *adj* □ vorstellbar: **the greatest difficulty ~** die denkbar größte Schwierigkeit. **im'ag·i·na·ry** *adj* imaginär (*a. A*), eingebildet. **im₁ag·i'na·tion** [~ˈneɪʃn] *s* **1.** Phantasie *f*. **2.** Vorstellung *f*, Einbildung *f*: **pure ~** reine Einbildung. **im'ag·i·na·tive** [~ətɪv] *adj* □ **1.** phantasie-, einfallsreich. **2.** phantasievoll. **im'ag·ine** I *v/t* **1.** sich *j-n, et.* vorstellen: **I ~ him as a tall man** ich stelle ihn mir groß vor; **can you ~ him becoming famous?** kannst du dir vorstellen, daß er einmal berühmt wird? **2.** sich *et.* einbilden: **don't ~ that** bilde dir das nur nicht ein, daß. II *v/i* **3.** *just ~!* iro. stell dir vor!, denk dir nur!

im·bal·ance [ˌɪmˈbæləns] *s* **1.** Unausgewogenheit *f*, Unausgeglichenheit *f*. **2.** *pol. etc* Ungleichgewicht *n*.

im·be·cile [ˈɪmbɪsiːl] I *adj* idiotisch, vertrottelt. II *s* Idiot *m*, Trottel *m*. **im·be·cil·i·ty** [~ˈsɪlətɪ] *s* Idiotie *f*, Blödheit *f*.

im·bibe [ɪmˈbaɪb] *v/t* **1.** *Feuchtigkeit etc* aufsaugen. **2.** *Wissen etc* einsaugen, in sich aufnehmen.

im·bue [ɪmˈbjuː] *v/t fig.* erfüllen (**with** mit): **~d with hatred** haßerfüllt.

im·i·tate [ˈɪmɪteɪt] *v/t* **1.** nachahmen, -machen, imitieren. **2.** fälschen. **im·i·'ta·tion** I *s* Nachahmung *f*, Imitation *f*: **in ~ of** nach dem Muster von (*od. gen*). **2.** Fälschung *f*. II *adj* **3.** unecht, künstlich: **~ leather** Kunstleder *n*. **im·i·ta·tive** [~ˈtɪətɪv] *adj* □ nachahmend, imitierend: **be ~ of** → **imitate** 1. **im·i·ta·tor** [~ˈteɪtə] *s* Nachahmer *m*, Imitator *m*.

im·mac·u·late [ɪˈmækjʊlət] *adj* □ **1.** *fig.* unbefleckt, makellos. **2.** tadel-, fehlerlos.

im·ma·nent [ˈɪmənənt] *adj* innewohnend (**in** *dat*).

im·ma·te·ri·al [ˌɪməˈtɪərɪəl] *adj* □ **1.** unkörperlich, unstofflich. **2.** unwesentlich, unerheblich (**to** für).

im·ma·ture [ˌɪməˈtjʊə] *adj* □ unreif, unausgereift (*beide a. fig.*). **im·ma'tu·ri·ty** *s* Unreife *f*.

im·meas·ur·a·ble [ɪˈmeʒərəbl] *adj* □ unermeßlich, grenzenlos.

im·me·di·ate [ɪˈmiːdjət] *adj* □ **1.** (*räumlich, zeitlich*) unmittelbar: **in the ~ vicinity** in unmittelbarer Nähe; **in the ~ future** in nächster Umgebung; **in the ~ future** in nächster Zukunft. **2.** sofortig, umgehend. **3.** nächst (*Verwandtschaft*): **my ~ family** m-e nächsten Angehörigen *pl*. **im'me·di·ate·ly** *adv* **1.** unmittelbar, direkt. **2.** sofort, umgehend.

im·me·mo·ri·al [ˌɪmɪˈmɔːrɪəl] *adj*: **from** (*od. since*) **time ~** seit undenklichen Zeiten.

im·mense [ɪˈmens] *adj* □ riesig, *fig. a.* enorm, immens. **im'men·si·ty** *s* Riesigkeit *f*.

im·merse [ɪˈmɜːs] *v/t* **1.** (ein)tauchen (**in** in *acc*). **2.** ~ **o.s.** *in fig.* sich vertiefen in (*acc*): **~d in** vertieft in; **~d in thought** gedankenversunken. **im'mer·sion** *s* **1.** Eintauchen *n*: **~ heater** Tauchsieder *m*. **2.** *fig.* Versunkenheit *f*, Vertiefung *f*.

im·mi·grant [ˈɪmɪɡrənt] *s* Einwanderer *m*, Einwanderin *f*, Immigrant(in). **im·mi·grate** [ˈ~ɡreɪt] *v/i* einwandern, immigrieren (**into** in *acc*). **im·mi'gra·tion** *s* Einwanderung *f*, Immigration *f*.

im·mi·nence [ˈɪmɪnəns] *s* nahes Bevorstehen. **'im·mi·nent** *adj* □ **1.** nahe bevorstehend: **his ~ death** sein naher Tod. **2.** drohend (*Gefahr etc*).

im·mo·bile [ɪˈməʊbaɪl] *adj* unbeweglich. **im·mo·bil·i·ty** [~ˈbɪlətɪ] *s* Unbeweglichkeit *f*. **im'mo·bi·lize** [~bɪlaɪz] *v/t* unbeweglich machen, *✗* ruhigstellen: **~d** bewegungsunfähig.

im·mod·er·ate [ɪˈmɒdərət] *adj* □ unmäßig, maßlos.

im·mod·est [ɪˈmɒdɪst] *adj* □ **1.** unbescheiden. **2.** schamlos.

im·mo·late [ˈɪməʊleɪt] *v/t* opfern (*a. fig.*).

im·mor·al [ɪˈmɒrəl] *adj* □ unmoralisch, unsittlich.

im·mor·tal [ɪˈmɔːtl] *adj* □ unsterblich, *fig. a.* unvergänglich. **im·mor·tal·i·ty** [~ˈtælətɪ] *s* Unsterblichkeit *f*, *fig. a.* Unvergänglichkeit *f*. **im'mor·tal·ize** [~təlaɪz] *v/t* unsterblich machen, verewigen.

im·mov·a·ble [ɪˈmuːvəbl] *adj* □ **1.** unbeweglich. **2.** *fig.* fest, unerschütterlich; hart, unnachgiebig. **3.** (*zeitlich*) unveränderlich. ~ *feast eccl.* unbeweglicher Feiertag.

im·mune [ɪˈmjuːn] *adj* 🎗 *u. fig.* (**against, from, to**) immun (gegen), unempfänglich (für). **2.** geschützt, gefeit (**against, from, to** gegen). **3.** befreit, ausgenommen (**from** von). **im·mu·ni·ty** *s* 🎗, 🏛 *u. fig.* Immunität *f*: **diplomatic ~. im·mu·nize** [ˈ~naɪz] *v/t* immunisieren, immun machen (**against** gegen) (*a. fig.*).

im·mu·ta·ble [ɪˈmjuːtəbl] *adj* □ unveränderlich.

imp [ɪmp] *s* **1.** Kobold *m*. **2.** F Racker *m*.

im·pact [ˈɪmpækt] *s* **1.** Zs-, (zusammen)prall *m*; Aufprall *m*; ✕ Auf-, Einschlag *m*. **2.** *fig.* (Ein)Wirkung *f*, (starker) Einfluß (**on** auf *acc*).

im·pair [ɪmˈpeə] *v/t* beeinträchtigen.

im·pale [ɪmˈpeɪl] *v/t* aufspießen (**on** auf *acc*), durchbohren.

im·pal·pa·ble [ɪmˈpælpəbl] *adj* □ **1.** unfühlbar. **2.** äußerst fein. **3.** *fig.* kaum (er)faßbar *od.* greifbar.

im·part [ɪmˈpɑːt] *v/t* (**to** *dat*) **1.** Eigenschaft *etc* verleihen. **2.** mitteilen; Kenntnisse etc vermitteln.

im·par·tial [ɪmˈpɑːʃl] *adj* □ unparteiisch, unvoreingenommen. 'im·par·ti·'al·i·ty** [ˌ~ʃɪˈælɪt] *s* Unparteilichkeit *f*, Unvoreingenommenheit *f*.

im·pass·a·ble [ɪmˈpɑːsəbl] *adj* □ **1.** unpassierbar. **2.** *bsd. fig.* unüberwindbar (*Hindernis etc*).

im·passe [ˈæmpɑːs] *s fig.* Sackgasse *f*: **reach an ~** in e-e Sackgasse geraten.

im·pas·sioned [ɪmˈpæʃnd] *adj* leidenschaftlich.

im·pas·sive [ɪmˈpæsɪv] *adj* □ **1.** teilnahmslos; ungerührt. **2.** gelassen.

im·pa·tience [ɪmˈpeɪʃns] *s* **1.** Ungeduld *f*. **2.** Unduldsamkeit *f*. **im·pa·tient** *adj* □ **1.** ungeduldig: **be ~ with** keine Geduld haben mit. **2.** **be ~ for** *et.* nicht erwarten können; **be ~ to do s.th.** es nicht erwarten können, et. zu tun. **3.** unduldsam (**of** gegenüber).

im·peach [ɪmˈpiːtʃ] *v/t* **1.** 🏛 anklagen (**for, of, with** gen); *Am. bsd.* Präsidenten unter Amtsanklage stellen. **2.** 🏛 anfechten. **3.** in Frage stellen, in Zweifel ziehen. **im·peach·ment** *s* **1.** 🏛 Anklage *f*; *Am.* Impeachment *n*. **2.** 🏛 Anfechtung *f*. **3.** Infragestellung *f*.

im·pec·ca·ble [ɪmˈpekəbl] *adj* □ untadelig, einwandfrei.

im·pede [ɪmˈpiːd] *v/t j-n, et.* (be)hindern: ~ **s.o.'s doing s.th.** j-n daran hindern, et. zu tun. **2.** *et.* erschweren.

im·ped·i·ment [ɪmˈpedɪmənt] *s* **1.** Behinderung *f*. **2.** Hindernis *n* (**to** für). **3.** 🎗 (*bsd.* angeborener) Fehler: ~ **speech 1.**

im·pel [ɪmˈpel] *v/t* **1.** antreiben (*a. fig.*). **2.** zwingen: **I felt ~led** ich sah mich gezwungen *od.* fühlte mich genötigt (**to do** zu tun).

im·pend·ing [ɪmˈpendɪŋ] *adj* **1.** nahe bevorstehend: **his ~ death** sein naher Tod. **2.** drohend (*Gefahr etc*).

im·pen·e·tra·ble [ɪmˈpenɪtrəbl] *adj* □ **1.** undurchdringlich (**by** für) (*a. fig.*). **2.** *fig.* unergründlich, unerforschlich.

im·pen·i·tent [ɪmˈpenɪtənt] *adj* □ verstockt; *eccl.* unbußfertig.

im·per·a·tive [ɪmˈperətɪv] **I** *adj* □ **1.** gebieterisch. **2.** unumgänglich, unbedingt erforderlich. **3.** *ling.* Imperativ..., Befehls...: ~ **mood** → 4. **II** *s* 4. *ling.* Imperativ *m*, Befehlsform *f*.

im·per·cep·ti·ble [ˌɪmpəˈseptəbl] *adj* □ **1.** nicht wahrnehmbar, unmerklich. **2.** verschwindend klein.

im·per·fect [ɪmˈpɜːfɪkt] **I** *adj* □ **1.** unvollkommen: a) unvollständig, b) mangel-, fehlerhaft. **2.** ~ **tense** → 3. **II** *s* 3. *ling.* Imperfekt *n*, unvollendete Vergangenheit. **im·per·fec·tion** [ˌ~pəˈfekʃn] *s* **1.** Unvollkommenheit *f*. **2.** Mangel *m*, Fehler *m*.

im·pe·ri·al [ɪmˈpɪərɪəl] *adj* □ **1.** kaiserlich, Kaiser... **2.** *Br.* gesetzlich (*Maße u. Gewichte*). **im·pe·ri·al·ism** *s pol.* Imperialismus *m*. **im·pe·ri·al·ist** **I** *s* Imperialist *m*. **II** *adj* imperialistisch. **im·pe·ri·al·is·tic** *adj* (**~ally**) imperialistisch.

im·per·il [ɪmˈperəl] *v/t* gefährden.

im·pe·ri·ous [ɪmˈpɪərɪəs] *adj* □ **1.** gebieterisch. **2.** dringend: ~ **necessity** zwingende Notwendigkeit.

im·per·ish·a·ble [ɪmˈperɪʃəbl] *adj* □ **1.** unverderblich. **2.** *fig.* unvergänglich.

im·per·ma·nent [ˌɪmˈpɜːmənənt] *adj* □ vorübergehend, nicht von Dauer.

im·per·me·a·ble [ɪmˈpɜːmjəbl] *adj* □

undurchlässig (**to** für): **~ to water** wasserdicht.

im·per·son·al [ɪmˈpɜːsnl] *adj* □ unpersönlich (*a. ling.*).

im·per·son·ate [ɪmˈpɜːsənət] *v/t* **1.** *thea. etc* verkörpern, darstellen. **2.** j-n imitieren, nachahmen.

im·per·ti·nence [ɪmˈpɜːtɪnəns] *s* **1.** Unverschämtheit *f*, Frechheit *f*. **2.** Belanglosigkeit *f*. **im·per·ti·nent** [~t] *adj* □ **1.** unverschämt, frech. **2.** belanglos (**to** für).

im·per·turb·a·ble [ˌɪmpəˈtɜːbəbl] *adj* □ unerschütterlich.

im·per·vi·ous [ɪmˈpɜːvjəs] *adj* □ **1.** → **impermeable**. **2.** *fig.* unzugänglich (**to** für *od. dat*).

im·pet·u·ous [ɪmˈpetʃʊəs] *adj* □ **1.** heftig, ungestüm. **2.** impulsiv. **3.** übereilt, vorschnell.

im·pe·tus [ˈɪmpɪtəs] *s* **1.** *phys.* Triebkraft *f*, Schwung *m* (*a. fig.*). **2.** *fig.* Impuls *m*: **give an ~ to** Auftrieb *od.* Schwung verleihen (*dat*).

im·pi·e·ty [ɪmˈpaɪətɪ] *s* **1.** Gottlosigkeit *f*. **2.** (**to** gegenüber) Pietätlosigkeit *f*; Respektlosigkeit *f*.

im·pinge [ɪmˈpɪndʒ] *v/i* **1.** auftreffen (**on** auf *acc*). **2.** *fig.* (**on**) sich auswirken (auf *acc*), beeinflussen (*acc*).

im·pi·ous [ˈɪmpɪəs] *adj* □ **1.** gottlos. **2.** (**to** gegenüber) pietätlos; respektlos.

imp·ish [ˈɪmpɪʃ] *adj* □ schelmisch, spitzbübisch.

im·plac·a·ble [ɪmˈplækəbl] *adj* □ unversöhnlich, unnachgiebig.

im·plant I *v/t* [ɪmˈplɑːnt] **1.** 🩺 implantieren, einpflanzen (**in**, **into** *dat*). **2.** *fig.* einprägen (**in**, **into** *dat*): **deeply ~ed hatred** tiefverwurzelter Haß. II *s* [ˈɪmplɑːnt] **3.** 🩺 Implantat *n*.

im·plau·si·ble [ˌɪmˈplɔːzəbl] *adj* □ unglaubwürdig.

im·ple·ment I *s* [ˈɪmplɪmənt] Werkzeug *n* (*a. fig.*), Gerät *n*. II *v/t* [~ment] aus-, durchführen. **im·ple·men·ta·tion** [ˌ~menˈteɪʃn] *s* Aus-, Durchführung *f*.

im·pli·cate [ˈɪmplɪkeɪt] *v/t* **1.** j-n verwickeln, hineinziehen (**in** in *acc*). **2.** → **imply** 1, 3. **im·pli·ca·tion** *s* **1.** Verwicklung *f*. **2.** Folgerung *f*. **3.** Folge *f*, Auswirkung *f*. **4.** Andeutung *f*.

im·plic·it [ɪmˈplɪsɪt] *adj* **1.** → **implied**. **2.** vorbehalt-, bedingungslos: **~ faith** (**obedience**) blinder Glaube (Gehor-

sam). **im·plic·it·ly** *adv* **1.** stillschweigend. **2.** → **implicit** 2.

im·plied [ɪmˈplaɪd] *adj* impliziert, (stillschweigend *od.* mit) inbegriffen.

im·plode [ɪmˈpləʊd] *v/i phys.* implodieren.

im·plore [ɪmˈplɔː] *v/t* **1.** j-n anflehen. **2.** *et.* erflehen, flehen um.

im·plo·sion [ɪmˈpləʊʒn] *s phys.* Implosion *f*.

im·ply [ɪmˈplaɪ] *v/t* **1.** implizieren, (sinngemäß *od.* stillschweigend) beinhalten. **2.** andeuten, zu verstehen geben. **3.** mit sich bringen, zur Folge haben.

im·po·lite [ˌɪmpəˈlaɪt] *adj* □ unhöflich.

im·pol·i·tic [ɪmˈpɒlɪtɪk] *adj* □ undiplomatisch, unklug.

im·pon·der·a·ble [ɪmˈpɒndərəbl] I *adj* unwägbar. II *s pl* Imponderabilien *pl*, Unwägbarkeiten *pl*.

im·port I *v/t u. v/i* [ɪmˈpɔːt] **1.** importieren, einführen: **~ing country** Einfuhrland *n*; **~ing firm** Importfirma *f*. II *s* [ˈɪmpɔːt] **2.** Import *m*, Einfuhr *f*. **3.** *pl* (Gesamt)Import *m*, (-)Einfuhr *f*: Importgüter *pl*, Einfuhrware *f*. III *adj* [ˈɪmpɔːt] **4.** Import..., Einfuhr...: **~ trade** Importgeschäft *n*, Einfuhrhandel *m*.

im·por·tance [ɪmˈpɔːtns] *s* Bedeutung *f*: a) Wichtigkeit *f*: **attach ~ to** Bedeutung beimessen (*dat*); **be of no ~** unwichtig *od.* belanglos sein (**to** für), b) Ansehen *n*, Gewicht *n*: **a person of ~** e-e gewichtige Persönlichkeit. **im·por·tant** *adj* □ bedeutend: a) wichtig, von Belang (**to** für), b) angesehen, gewichtig.

im·port·er [ɪmˈpɔːtə] *s* Importeur *m*.

im·por·tu·nate [ɪmˈpɔːtjʊnət] *adj* □ lästig, zu-, aufdringlich. **im·por·tune** [~tjuːn] *v/t* belästigen, dauernd (*bsd.* mit Bitten) behelligen.

im·pose [ɪmˈpəʊz] I *v/t* **1.** (**on**) *et.* auferlegen, -bürden (*dat*); *Strafe* verhängen (gegen). **2.** (**on**) a) *et.* aufdrängen, -zwingen (*dat*): **~ o.s.** (*od.* **one's presence**) **on s.o.** sich j-m aufdrängen; **~ one's will on s.o.** j-m s-n Willen aufzwingen, b) *et.* (*mit Gewalt*) einführen *od.* durchsetzen (**bei**). II *v/i* **3.** ausnutzen, *b.s. a.* mißbrauchen (**on** *acc*). **4.** (**on**) sich aufdrängen; zur Last fallen. **im·pos·ing** *adj* □ imponierend, imposant. **im·po·si·tion** [ˌɪmpəˈzɪʃn] *s*

1. Auferlegung f, -bürdung f; Verhängung f. **2.** Auflage f, Pflicht f. **3.** Abgabe f, Steuer f. **4.** Ausnutzung f, b.s. a. Mißbrauch m (**on** gen).

im·pos·si·bil·i·ty [ɪmˌpɒsəˈbɪlətɪ] s Unmöglichkeit f. **im'pos·si·ble** adj unmöglich (a. F unglaublich, unerträglich etc): **it is ~ for me to come** ich kann unmöglich kommen. **im'pos·si·bly** adv unglaublich.

im·post·er, im·post·or [ɪmˈpəʊstə] s Betrüger(in), bsd. Hochstapler(in).

im·po·tence [ˈɪmpətəns] s **1.** Unvermögen n, Unfähigkeit f; Hilflosigkeit f, Ohnmacht f. **2.** 🖈 Impotenz f. **'im·po·tent** adj □ **1.** unfähig (**in doing, to do** zu tun); hilflos, ohnmächtig. **2.** 🖈 impotent.

im·pov·er·ish [ɪmˈpɒvərɪʃ] v/t arm machen: **be ~ed** verarmen; verarmt sein.

im·prac·ti·ca·ble [ɪmˈpræktɪkəbl] adj □ **1.** undurchführbar. **2.** unpassierbar (**Straße** etc).

im·prac·ti·cal [ɪmˈpræktɪkl] adj □ **1.** unpraktisch (**Person**). **2.** undurchführbar.

im·preg·nate [ˈɪmpregneɪt] v/t **1.** biol. schwängern; befruchten (a. fig.). **2.** 🖈, 💮 imprägnieren, tränken. **3.** fig. durchdringen, erfüllen (**with** mit).

im·pre·sa·ri·o [ˌɪmprɪˈsɑːrɪəʊ] pl **-os** s Impresario m, Theater-, Konzertagent m.

im·press I v/t [ɪmˈpres] **1.** beeindrucken, Eindruck machen auf (acc), imponieren (dat). **2.** (auf)drücken (**on** auf acc), (ein)drucken (**in, into** in acc). **II** s [ˈɪmpres] **3.** Ab-, Eindruck m. **im'pres·sion** [~ʃn] s **1.** Eindruck m (**of** von): **give s.o. a wrong ~** bei j-m e-n falschen Eindruck erwecken; **make a good** (**bad**) **~** e-n guten (schlechten) Eindruck machen. **2.** Eindruck m, Vermutung f: **I have an** (od. **the**) **~** (od. **I am under the ~**) **that** ich habe den Eindruck, daß; **under the ~ that** in der Annahme, daß. **3.** Abdruck m (a. 🖈). **4.** typ. (bsd. unveränderte) Auflage f, Nachdruck m. **im'pres·sion·a·ble** adj leicht zu beeinflussen(d). **im'pres·sion·ism** s Impressionismus m. **im'pres·sion·ist** s Impressionist(in). **II** adj impressionistisch. **im,pres·sion·is·tic** [~ʃəˈn~] adj (~**ally**) impressioni-

stisch. **im'pres·sive** [~sɪv] adj □ eindrucksvoll.

im·print I s [ˈɪmprɪnt] **1.** Ab-, Eindruck m. **2.** fig. Stempel m, Gepräge n. **3.** typ. Impressum n. **II** v/t [ɪmˈprɪnt] **4.** (auf)drücken (**on** auf acc). **5.** ~ **s.th. on** (od. **in**) **s.o.'s memory** j-m et. ins Gedächtnis einprägen.

im·pris·on [ɪmˈprɪzn] v/t 🔏 inhaftieren, a. weitS. einsperren. **im'pris·on·ment** s a) Freiheitsstrafe f, Gefängnis(strafe f) n, Haft f: **he was given 10 years ~** er wurde zu e-r zehnjährigen Freiheitsstrafe verurteilt, b) Inhaftierung f.

im·prob·a·bil·i·ty [ɪmˌprɒbəˈbɪlətɪ] s Unwahrscheinlichkeit f. **im'prob·a·ble** adj □ unwahrscheinlich.

im·promp·tu [ɪmˈprɒmptjuː] **I** s 🎵 Impromptu n. **II** adj u. adv aus dem Stegreif, Stegreif...

im·prop·er [ɪmˈprɒpə] adj □ **1.** ungeeignet, unpassend. **2.** unanständig, unschicklich. **3.** unrichtig. **4.** 🖈 unecht (**Bruch**). **im·pro·pri·e·ty** [ˌɪmprəˈpraɪətɪ] s **1.** Unschicklichkeit f. **2.** Unrichtigkeit f.

im·prove [ɪmˈpruːv] **I** v/t **1.** verbessern. **2.** Wert etc erhöhen, steigern. **II** v/i **3.** sich (ver)bessern, besser werden, Fortschritte machen (a. Patient), sich erholen (gesundheitlich od. 🖈 Preise etc): **he is improving** (**in health**) es geht ihm besser; ~ **in strength** kräftiger werden. **im'prove·ment** s **1.** (Ver)Besserung f (**in** gen; **on** gegenüber, im Vergleich zu): ~ **in the weather** Wetterbesserung. **2.** Erhöhung f, Steigerung f.

im·prov·i·dent [ɪmˈprɒvɪdənt] adj □ **1.** sorglos: **be ~ of** nicht vorsorgen für. **2.** verschwenderisch.

im·pro·vi·sa·tion [ˌɪmprəvaɪˈzeɪʃn] s Improvisation f. **im·pro·vise** [ˈ~vaɪz] v/t u. v/i improvisieren.

im·pru·dence [ɪmˈpruːdəns] s **1.** Unklugheit f. **2.** Unvorsichtigkeit f. **im'pru·dent** adj □ **1.** unklug. **2.** unvorsichtig.

im·pu·dence [ˈɪmpjʊdəns] s Unverschämtheit f. **'im·pu·dent** adj □ unverschämt.

im·pugn [ɪmˈpjuːn] v/t bestreiten; anfechten.

im·pulse [ˈɪmpʌls] s **1.** phys., 🖈, ⚡ etc Impuls m. **2.** fig. Impuls m: a) Anstoß *m*, Anreiz *m*, b) plötzliche Regung *od.* Eingebung: **act on** ~ impulsiv *od.* spontan handeln; **on the ~ of the moment**, **on** ~ e-r plötzlichen Eingebung folgend. **im'pul·sion** *s* **1.** Triebkraft *f* (*a. fig.*). **2.** *psych.* Zwang *m.* **im'pul·sive** *adj* □ *fig.* impulsiv.

im·pu·ni·ty [ɪm'pjuːnəti] *s* Straflosigkeit *f*: **with** ~ straflos.

im·pure [ɪm'pjʊə] *adj* □ **1.** unrein (*a. eccl.*), unsauber. **2.** *fig.* schlecht, unmoralisch. **im'pur·i·ty** *s* **1.** Unreinheit *f.* **2.** *fig.* Schlechtheit *f.*

im·pu·ta·tion [ˌɪmpjuː'teɪʃn] *s* Bezichtigung *f.* **im'pute** *v/t* zuschreiben (**to** *dat*): a) beimessen, b) anlasten: ~ **s.th. to s.o.** j-n e-r Sache bezichtigen.

in [ɪn] **I** *prp* **1.** räumlich: a) (*wo?*) in (*dat*), an (*dat*), auf (*dat*): ~ **London** in London; → **country** 3, **field** 1, **sky**, **street**, *etc*, b) (*wohin?*) in (*acc*): **put it** ~ **your pocket** steck es in die Tasche. **2.** *zeitlich*: in (*dat*), an (*dat*): ~ **1988** 1988; ~ **two hours** in zwei Stunden; → **April**, **beginning** 1, **evening**, *etc*. **3.** *Zustand*, *Beschaffenheit*, *Art u. Weise*: in (*dat*), auf (*acc*), mit: → **brief** 4, **cash** 2, **English** 3, *etc*. **4.** *Tätigkeit*, *Beschäftigung*: in (*dat*), bei, auf (*dat*): ~ **crossing the river** beim Überqueren des Flusses; → **accident** 2, **search** 4. **5.** bei (*Schriftstellern*): ~ **Shakespeare**. **6.** *Richtung*: in (*acc*, *dat*), auf (*acc*, *dat*), zu: → **confidence** 1, *etc*. **7.** *Zweck*: in (*dat*), zu, als: → **answer** 1, **defence**, *etc*. **8.** *Grund*: in (*dat*), aus, zu: → **honour** 5, **sport** 3, *etc*. **9.** *Hinsicht*, *Beziehung*: in (*dat*), an (*dat*): **the latest thing** ~ das Neueste auf dem Gebiet (*gen*); → **equal** 1, **number** 3, *etc*. **10.** nach, gemäß: → **opinion** 1, **probability**, *etc*. **11.** *Material*: in (*dat*), aus, mit: → **black** 3, **oil** 3, *etc*. **12.** *Zahl*, *Betrag*: in (*dat*), von, aus, zu: **five** ~ **all** insgesamt *od.* im ganzen fünf; **one** ~ **ten Americans** einer von zehn Amerikanern; → **all** 4, **two**, *etc*. **II** *adv* **13.** (dr)innen: **be** ~ **for s.th.** et. zu erwarten haben; **be** ~ **on** eingeweiht sein in (*acc*); beteiligt sein an (*dat*); **know** ~ **and out** in- u. auswendig kennen. **14.** innen; herein: → **come in** 1, *etc*. **15.** da, (an)gekommen. **16.** da, zu Hause. **17.** *pol.* an der Macht, an der Regierung. **III** *adj* **18.** ~

party *pol.* Regierungspartei *f.* **19.** ~ **restaurant** Restaurant, das gerade in ist. **IV** *s* **20. know the** ~**s and outs of** in- u. auswendig kennen.

in·a·bil·i·ty [ˌɪnə'bɪlətɪ] *s* Unfähigkeit *f*, Unvermögen *n*: ~ **to pay** † Zahlungsunfähigkeit.

in·ac·ces·si·ble [ˌɪnæk'sesəbl] *adj* □ unzugänglich (**to** für *od. dat*) (*a. fig.*).

in·ac·cu·ra·cy [ɪn'ækjʊrəsɪ] *s* Ungenauigkeit *f.* **in'ac·cu·rate** [~rət] *adj* □ ungenau: **be** ~ falsch gehen (*Uhr*).

in·ac·tion [ɪn'ækʃn] *s* **1.** Untätigkeit *f.* **2.** Trägheit *f*, Faulheit *f.*

in·ac·tive [ɪn'æktɪv] *adj* □ **1.** untätig. **2.** träge (*a. phys.*), faul. **3.** † lustlos, flau. **in·ac'tiv·i·ty** *s* **1.** → **inaction.** **2.** † Lustlosigkeit *f*, Flauheit *f.*

in·ad·e·quate [ɪn'ædɪkwət] *adj* □ **1.** unzulänglich, ungenügend: **be** ~ **for** nicht reichen für. **2.** unangemessen (**to** *dat*): **feel** ~ **to the occasion** sich der Situation nicht gewachsen fühlen.

in·ad·mis·si·ble [ˌɪnəd'mɪsəbl] *adj* □ unzulässig, unstatthaft.

in·ad·vert·ent [ˌɪnəd'vɜːtənt] *adj* □ unabsichtlich, versehentlich: ~**ly** a. aus Versehen.

in·ad·vis·a·ble [ˌɪnəd'vaɪzəbl] *adj* nicht ratsam *od.* empfehlenswert.

in·al·ien·a·ble [ɪn'eɪljənəbl] *adj* □ unveräußerlich.

in·ane [ɪ'neɪn] *adj* □ geistlos, albern.

in·an·i·mate [ɪn'ænɪmət] *adj* □ **1.** leblos, unbelebt. **2.** *fig.* schwunglos, langweilig.

in·ap·pli·ca·ble [ɪn'æplɪkəbl] *adj* □ nicht anwendbar *od.* zutreffend (**to** auf *acc*): → **delete** II.

in·ap·pre·ci·a·ble [ˌɪnə'priːʃəbl] *adj* □ unmerklich.

in·ap·pro·pri·ate [ˌɪnə'prəʊprɪət] *adj* □ unpassend, ungeeignet (**to**, **for** für).

in·apt [ɪn'æpt] *adj* □ **1.** unpassend, ungeeignet. **2.** ungeschickt. **3.** unfähig, außerstande (**to do** zu tun). **in'apt·i·tude** [~tɪtjuːd] *s* **1.** Ungeschicktheit *f.* **2.** Unfähigkeit *f.*

in·ar·tic·u·late [ˌɪnɑː'tɪkjʊlət] *adj* □ **1.** undeutlich (ausgesprochen), unverständlich. **2.** unfähig(, deutlich) zu sprechen. **3.** unfähig, sich klar auszudrücken. **4.** sprachlos (**with** vor *dat*).

in·as·much as [ˌɪnəzˈmʌtʃ] *cj* da (ja), weil.

in·at·ten·tion [ˌɪnəˈtenʃn] *s* Unaufmerksamkeit *f*. **in·at·ten·tive** [~tɪv] *adj* □ unaufmerksam (**to** gegen).

in·au·di·ble [ɪnˈɔːdəbl] *adj* □ unhörbar.

in·au·gu·ral [ɪnˈɔːɡjʊərəl] I *adj* Einweihungs..., Eröffnungs...: **~ speech** → II. II *s* Antrittsrede *f*. **in·au·gu·rate** [~reɪt] *v/t* **1.** *j-n* (feierlich) (in sein Amt) einführen *od.* einsetzen. **2.** einweihen, eröffnen. **3.** Ära etc einleiten. **in·au·gu·ra·tion** *s* **1.** (feierliche) Amtseinsetzung *od.* -einführung; ≈ **Day** *pol. Am.* Tag *m* des Amtsantritts des Präsidenten (*20. Januar*). **2.** Einweihung *f*, Eröffnung *f*. **3.** Beginn *m*.

in·aus·pi·cious [ˌɪnɔːˈspɪʃəs] *adj* □ ungünstig: **be ~** unter e-m ungünstigen Stern stehen.

in·board [ˈɪnbɔːd] ♣ I *adj* **1.** Innenbord...: **~ motor.** II *adv* **2.** innenbords. III *s* **3.** Innenbordmotor *m*. **4.** Innenborder *m* (*Boot*).

in·born [ˌɪnˈbɔːn] *adj* angeboren.

in·bred [ˌɪnˈbred] *adj* **1.** angeboren. **2.** durch Inzucht erzeugt. **in·breed·ing** [ˈɪnˌbriːdɪŋ] *s* Inzucht *f* (*a. fig.*).

in·cal·cu·la·ble [ɪnˈkælkjʊləbl] *adj* □ **1.** unberechenbar (*a. Person etc*). **2.** unermeßlich.

in·can·des·cent [ˌɪnkænˈdesnt] *adj* □ **1.** (weiß)glühend: **~ lamp** Glühlampe *f*. **2.** *fig.* leuchtend, strahlend.

in·can·ta·tion [ˌɪnkænˈteɪʃn] *s* **1.** Beschwörung *f*. **2.** Zauberformel *f*, -spruch *m*.

in·ca·pa·bil·i·ty [ɪnˌkeɪpəˈbɪlətɪ] *s* Unfähigkeit *f*. **in·ca·pa·ble** [ɪnˈkeɪpəbl] *adj* □ **1.** unfähig (*of zu*, *od. gen*; *of doing* zu tun), nicht imstande (*of doing* zu tun). **2.** nicht zulassend (*of acc*): **a problem ~ of solution** ein unlösbares Problem; **~ of being misunderstood** unmißverständlich.

in·ca·pac·i·tate [ˌɪnkəˈpæsɪtent] *v/t* **1.** unfähig *od.* untauglich machen (**for s.th.** für et.; **for** [*od. from*] **doing** zu tun). **2.** ♣ für rechts- *od.* geschäftsunfähig erklären. **in·ca·pac·i·tat·ed** *adj* **1.** *a.* **~ for work** arbeits- *od.* erwerbsunfähig. **2.** körperlich, geistig behindert. **3.** *a.* **legally ~** rechts-, geschäftsunfähig. **in·ca·pac·i·ty** [~ətɪ] *s* **1.** Unfähigkeit *f*, Untauglichkeit *f*: **~ for work** Arbeits-

od. Erwerbsunfähigkeit *f*. **2.** *a.* **legal ~** Rechts-, Geschäftsunfähigkeit *f*.

in·car·cer·ate [ɪnˈkɑːsəreɪt] *v/t* einkerkern.

in·car·nate [ɪnˈkɑːneɪt] *adj* a) leibhaftig, *ein Teufel etc* in Menschengestalt, b) personifiziert, *die Unschuld etc* in Person. **in·car·na·tion** *s* Verkörperung *f*, Inbegriff *m*.

in·cen·di·a·ry [ɪnˈsendjərɪ] I *adj* **1.** Brand...: **~ bomb. 2.** *fig.* aufwiegelnd: **~ speech** Hetzrede *f*. II *s* **3.** Brandstifter(in). **4.** *fig.* Aufwiegler(in).

in·cense¹ [ˈɪnsens] I *s* Weihrauch *m*. II *v/t* beweihräuchern.

in·cense² [ɪnˈsens] *v/t* erzürnen, erbosen: **~d** zornig (**at** über *acc*).

in·cen·tive [ɪnˈsentɪv] *s* Ansporn *m*, Anreiz *m* (**to** zu): **~ to buy** Kaufanreiz.

in·cer·ti·tude [ɪnˈsɜːtɪtjuːd] *s* Unsicherheit *f*, Ungewißheit *f*.

in·ces·sant [ɪnˈsesnt] *adj* □ unaufhörlich, unablässig.

in·cest [ˈɪnsest] *s* Blutschande *f*, Inzest *m*.

inch [ɪntʃ] I *s* Inch *m*, Zoll *m* (*a. fig.*): **by ~es, ~ by ~** Zentimeter um Zentimeter; *fig.* allmählich, ganz langsam; **every ~** *fig.* jeder Zoll, *ein Gentleman etc* vom Scheitel bis zur Sohle; **come within an ~ of death** beinahe *od.* um Haaresbreite sterben. II *v/t u. v/i* (sich) zentimeterweise *od.* sehr langsam bewegen.

in·ci·dence [ˈɪnsɪdəns] *s* Auftreten *n*, Vorkommen *n*, Häufigkeit *f*: **have a high ~** häufig vorkommen. II **·ci·dent** I *adj* verbunden (**to** mit). II *s* Vorfall *m*, Ereignis *n*, *a. pol.* Zwischenfall *m*: **full of ~s** ereignisreich. **in·ci·den·tal** [~ˈdentl] I *adj* □ **1.** nebensächlich, Nebenbei...: **~ earnings** *pl* Nebenverdienst *m*. **2.** beiläufig. **3.** gelegentlich. **4.** zufällig. II *s* **5.** Nebensächlichkeit *f*. **6.** *pl* † Nebenausgaben *pl*. **in·ci·den·tal·ly** [~tlɪ] *adv* nebenbei bemerkt, übrigens.

in·cin·er·ate [ɪnˈsɪnəreɪt] *v/t u. v/i* verbrennen. **in·cin·er·a·tor** *s* Verbrennungsofen *m* *od.* -anlage *f*.

in·cise [ɪnˈsaɪz] *v/t* **1.** ein-, aufschneiden (*a. ♣*). **2.** *Muster etc* einritzen, -schnitzen, -kerben (**on** in *acc*): **~ s.th. with a pattern** ein Muster in et. einritzen *od.* -schnitzen *od.* -kerben. **in·ci·sion** [~ˈsɪʒn] *s* (Ein)Schnitt *m* (*a. ♣*). **in·ci·sive**

[~'saɪsɪv] *adj* □ **1.** (ein)schneidend. **2.** *fig.* scharf (*Verstand, Ton etc*). **3.** *fig.* prägnant, treffend. **in·ci·sor** [ɪn'saɪzə] *s anat.* Schneidezahn *m.*

in·cite [ɪn'saɪt] *v/t* **1.** aufwiegeln, -hetzen, **st̸s** anstiften (**to** zu). **2.** *Zorn etc* erregen. **in'cite·ment** *s* Aufwieg(e)lung *f,* -hetzung *f,* **st̸s** Anstiftung *f.*

in·ci·vil·i·ty [ˌɪnsɪ'vɪlətɪ] *s* Unhöflichkeit *f* (*a. Bemerkung etc*).

in·clem·ent [ɪn'klemənt] *adj* □ **1.** rauh, unfreundlich (*Klima*). **2.** hart, unerbittlich.

in·cli·na·tion [ˌɪnklɪ'neɪʃn] *s* **1.** Neigung *f, fig. a.* Hang *m.* **2.** *fig.* Zuneigung *f* (*for* zu). **3.** Gefälle *n.* **in·cline** [~'klaɪn] **I** *v/i* **1.** sich neigen (**to, toward[s]** nach). **2.** *fig.* neigen (**to, toward[s]** zu): ~ *to do s.th.* dazu neigen, et. zu tun. **II** *v/t* **3.** *Kopf etc* neigen. **4.** *fig.* veranlassen, bewegen (**to** zu; *to do* zu tun). **III** *s* **5.** Gefälle *n.* **6.** (Ab)Hang *m.* **in'clined** *adj* geneigt (*a. fig.*): *be* ~ *to do s.th.* dazu neigen, et. zu tun; ~ *plane* *phys.* schiefe Ebene.

in·close, in·clo·sure → *enclose, enclosure.*

in·clude [ɪn'kluːd] *v/t* **1.** einschließen, -beziehen, -rechnen (*in in acc*): *tax* ~*d* einschließlich *od.* inklusive Steuer. **2.** erfassen, einbeziehen: *be* ~*d on the list* auf der Liste stehen. **in'clud·ing** *prp* einschließlich.

in·clu·sion [ɪn'kluːʒn] *s* Einschluß *m,* Einbeziehung *f* (*in in acc*). **in'clu·sive** [~sɪv] *adj* □ **1.** einschließlich, inklusive (*of gen*): *be* ~ *of* einschließen (*acc*). **2.** Pauschal...: ~ *price.*

in·cog·ni·to [ɪnkɒg'niːtəʊ] **I** *adv* inkognito. **II** *pl* **-tos** *s* Inkognito *n: preserve* (*disclose, reveal*) *one's* ~ sein Inkognito wahren (lüften).

in·co·her·ent [ˌɪnkəʊ'hɪərənt] *adj* □ (logisch) unzusammenhängend.

in·come [ˈɪŋkʌm] *s* Einkommen *n* (*from* aus): *live within* (*beyond*) *one's* ~ s-n Verhältnissen entsprechend (über s-e Verhältnisse) leben; ~ *brack·et,* ~ *group* *s* Einkommensgruppe *f.* ~ *tax* *s* Einkommensteuer *f.*

in·com·ing [ˈɪnˌkʌmɪŋ] *adj* **1.** hereinkommend. **2.** ankommend (*Telefongespräch etc*), nachfolgend, neu (*Mieter, Regierung etc*). **3.** ✝ eingehend, -lau-

fend: ~ *orders* *pl* Auftragseingänge *pl;* ~ *mail* Posteingang *m.*

in·com·men·su·ra·ble [ˌɪnkə'menʃərəbl] *adj* □ **1.** nicht vergleichbar (*with* mit). **2.** unangemessen, unverhältnismäßig. **in·com'men·su·rate** [~rət] *adj* □ **1.** unangemessen, nicht entsprechend (*with, to dat*). **2.** → *incommensurable.*

in·com·mu·ni·ca·tive [ˌɪnkə'mjuːnɪkətɪv] *adj* □ nicht mitteilsam, verschlossen.

in·com·pa·ra·ble [ɪn'kɒmpərəbl] *adj* □ **1.** unvergleichlich. **2.** unvergleichbar (**with, to** mit).

in·com·pat·i·ble [ˌɪnkəm'pætəbl] *adj* □ **1.** unvereinbar. **2.** unverträglich, **ℱ** *a.* inkompatibel: *be* ~ (*with*) sich nicht vertragen (mit), nicht zs.-passen (mit).

in·com·pe·tence, **in·com·pe·ten·cy** [ɪn'kɒmpɪtəns(ɪ)] *s* **1.** Unfähigkeit *f.* **2.** **st̸s,** *a. weitS.* Nichtzuständigkeit *f,* Inkompetenz *f.* **in'com·pe·tent** *adj* □ **1.** unfähig (*to do* zu tun). **2.** **st̸s,** *a. weitS.* unzuständig, inkompetent.

in·com·plete [ˌɪnkəm'pliːt] *adj* □ **1.** unvollständig. **2.** unvollzählig. **3.** unvollendet.

in·com·pre·hen·si·ble [ɪnˌkɒmprɪ'hensəbl] *adj* □ unbegreiflich, unfaßbar, unverständlich. **in·com·pre·hen·si·bly** *adv* unverständlicherweise. **in·com·pre'hen·sion** *s* Unverständnis *n* (*of* für).

in·con·ceiv·a·ble [ˌɪnkən'siːvəbl] *adj* □ **1.** unbegreiflich, unfaßbar. **2.** undenkbar, unvorstellbar (*to* für): *it is* ~ *to me that* ich kann mir nicht vorstellen, daß.

in·con·clu·sive [ˌɪnkən'kluːsɪv] *adj* □ **1.** nicht überzeugend *od.* schlüssig. **2.** ergebnis-, erfolglos.

in·con·gru·i·ty [ˌɪnkɒŋ'gruːətɪ] *s* **1.** Nichtübereinstimmung *f.* **2.** Unvereinbarkeit *f.* **in'con·gru·ous** [~grʊəs] *adj* □ **1.** nicht übereinstimmend (**to, with** mit). **2.** unvereinbar (**to, with** mit).

in·con·se·quent [ɪn'kɒnsɪkwənt] *adj* □ **1.** inkonsequent, unlogisch. **2.** belanglos.

in·con·sid·er·a·ble [ˌɪnkən'sɪdərəbl] *adj* □ **1.** gering(fügig). **2.** unbedeutend, unwichtig (*a. Person*).

in·con·sid·er·ate [ˌɪnkən'sɪdərət] *adj* □ **1.** rücksichtslos (**to, toward[s]** gegen).

2. unbesonnen, (*Handlung a.*) unüberlegt.

in·con·sist·ent [ˌɪnkənˈsɪstənt] *adj* □ **1.** inkonsequent. **2.** unvereinbar (**with** mit). **3.** widersprüchlich.

in·con·sol·a·ble [ˌɪnkənˈsəʊləbl] *adj* □ untröstlich.

in·con·spic·u·ous [ˌɪnkənˈspɪkjʊəs] *adj* □ unauffällig.

in·con·stant [ɪnˈkɒnstənt] *adj* □ **1.** unbeständig. **2.** wankelmütig.

in·con·test·a·ble [ˌɪnkənˈtestəbl] *adj* □ unanfechtbar.

in·con·ti·nent [ɪnˈkɒntɪnənt] *adj* □ **1.** (*bsd. sexuell*) unmäßig, zügellos. **2.** unaufhörlich.

in·con·tro·vert·i·ble [ˌɪnkɒntrəˈvɜːtəbl] *adj* □ **1.** unbestreitbar, unstreitig. **2.** unanfechtbar.

in·con·ven·ience [ˌɪnkənˈviːnjəns] **I** *s* **1.** Unbequemlichkeit *f*. **2.** Ungelegenheit *f*; Unannehmlichkeit *f*: *put to* ~ → 4. **II** *v/t* **3.** *j-m* lästig sein *od.* zur Last fallen. **4.** *j-m* Ungelegenheiten bereiten *od.* Umstände machen. **in·con·ven·ient** *adj* □ **1.** unbequem (**to** für). **2.** ungelegen, lästig (**to** für): *at an* ~ *time* ungelegen.

in·con·vin·ci·ble [ˌɪnkənˈvɪnsəbl] *adj* nicht zu überzeugen(d).

in·cor·po·rate [ɪnˈkɔːpəreɪt] **I** *v/t* **1.** vereinigen, zs.-schließen. **2.** Staatsgebiet eingliedern; *Ort* eingemeinden. **3.** ✝, ⚖ als (*Am.* Aktien)Gesellschaft eintragen (lassen): *~d company Am.* Aktiengesellschaft *f*; *~d society* eingetragener Verein. **4.** in sich schließen, enthalten. **II** *v/i* **5.** sich zs.-schließen (**with** mit). **in·cor·po·ra·tion** *s* **1.** Vereinigung *f*, Zs.-schluß *m*. **2.** Eingliederung *f*; Eingemeindung *f*. **3.** ✝, ⚖ Eintragung *f* als (*Am.* Aktien)Gesellschaft: → **article** 4.

in·cor·rect [ˌɪnkəˈrekt] *adj* □ inkorrekt: a) unrichtig, b) ungehörig.

in·cor·ri·gi·ble [ɪnˈkɒrɪdʒəbl] *adj* □ unverbesserlich.

in·cor·rupt·i·ble [ˌɪnkəˈrʌptəbl] *adj* □ **1.** unbestechlich. **2.** unverderblich (*Speisen*).

in·crease [ɪnˈkriːs] **I** *v/i* zunehmen, (an)wachsen, (*Preise*) steigen, anziehen: ~ *in price* (*value*) teurer (wertvoller) werden; → **threefold** II, **fourfold** II,

etc. **II** *v/t* vergrößern, -mehren, erhöhen: → **threefold** II, **fourfold** II, *etc.* **III** *s* [ˈɪnkriːs] Vergrößerung *f*, -mehrung *f*, Erhöhung *f*, Zunahme *f*, (An)Wachsen *n*: *be on the* ~ zunehmen; ~ *in population* Bevölkerungszunahme, -zuwachs *m*; ~ *in value* Wertsteigerung *f*, -zuwachs *m*. **in·creas·ing·ly** *adv* immer mehr: ~ *clear* immer klarer.

in·cred·i·ble [ɪnˈkredəbl] *adj* □ **1.** unglaublich (*a.* F *unerhört etc*). **2.** unglaubwürdig.

in·cred·u·lous [ɪnˈkredjʊləs] *adj* □ ungläubig: *be* ~ *of s.th.* e-r Sache skeptisch gegenüberstehen.

in·cre·ment [ˈɪnkrɪmənt] *s* (✝ Gewinn)Zuwachs *m*, Zunahme *f*.

in·crim·i·nate [ɪnˈkrɪmɪneɪt] *v/t* belasten. **in·crim·i·nat·ing**, **in·crim·i·na·to·ry** [~nətərɪ] *adj* belastend, Belastungs...

in·crust [ɪnˈkrʌst] *v/i* **1.** sich ver- *od.* überkrusten. **2.** e-e Kruste bilden.

in·cu·ba·tor [ˈɪnkjʊbeɪtə] *s* ⚕ Brutkasten *m*.

in·cul·cate [ˈɪnkʌlkeɪt] *v/t*: ~ *s.th. in(to)* (*od. on*) *s.o.*, ~ *s.o. with s.th.* j-m et. einschärfen.

in·cur [ɪnˈkɜː] *v/t* sich et. zuziehen, auf sich laden: ~ *debts* Schulden machen; ~ *losses* Verluste erleiden.

in·cur·a·ble [ɪnˈkjʊərəbl] *adj* □ ⚕ unheilbar, *fig. a.* unverbesserlich.

in·cur·sion [ɪnˈkɜːʃn] *s* **1.** (feindlicher) Einfall: *make an* ~ *on* einfallen in (*acc, dat*). **2.** Eindringen *n* (*into* in *acc*) (*a. fig.*).

in·debt·ed [ɪnˈdetɪd] *adj* **1.** verschuldet (**to** bei): *be* ~ *to s.o.* a. bei j-m Schulden haben, j-m Geld schulden. **2.** (zu Dank) verpflichtet (**to** *s.o.* j-m): *I am greatly* ~ *to you* ich bin Ihnen zu großem Dank verpflichtet, ich stehe tief in Ihrer Schuld wegen. **in·debt·ed·ness** *s* **1.** Verschuldung *f*. **2.** Dankesschuld *f* (**to** gegenüber).

in·de·cen·cy [ɪnˈdiːsnsɪ] *s* **1.** Unanständigkeit *f*, Anstößigkeit *f*, ⚖ Unzucht *f* (**with children** mit Kindern). **2.** Zote *f*. **3.** Unschicklichkeit *f*. **in·de·cent** *adj* □ **1.** unanständig, anstößig, ⚖ unzüchtig: → **assault** 3. **2.** unschicklich, ungehörig. **3.** ungebührlich: ~ *haste* unziemliche Hast.

in·de·ci·pher·a·ble [ˌɪndɪˈsaɪfərəbl] *adj*

☐ nicht zu entziffern(d), unentzifferbar.

in·de·ci·sion [ˌɪndɪˈsɪʒn] *s* Unentschlossenheit *f*, Unschlüssigkeit *f*. **in·de·ci·sive** [ˌ~ˈsaɪsɪv] *adj* ☐ **1.** nicht entscheidend; noch nicht entschieden, unentschieden. **2.** unentschlossen, unschlüssig. **3.** unbestimmt, ungewiß.

in·dec·o·rous [ɪnˈdekərəs] *adj* ☐ unschicklich, ungehörig.

in·deed [ɪnˈdiːd] **I** *adv* **1.** in der Tat, tatsächlich, wirklich: *thank you very much* ~ vielen herzlichen Dank. **2.** *fragend*: wirklich?, tatsächlich?: *I saw him yesterday. did you* ~? tatsächlich? **3.** allerdings, freilich; zwar. **II** *int* **4.** ach wirklich?, was Sie nicht sagen! **in·de·fat·i·ga·ble** [ˌɪndɪˈfætɪɡəbl] *adj* ☐ unermüdlich.

in·de·fen·si·ble [ˌɪndɪˈfensəbl] *adj* ☐ **1.** ✗ unhaltbar (*a. fig.*). **2.** nicht zu rechtfertigen(d), unentschuldbar.

in·de·fin·a·ble [ˌɪndɪˈfaɪnəbl] *adj* ☐ unbestimmbar, undefinierbar.

in·def·i·nite [ɪnˈdefɪnət] *adj* ☐ **1.** unbestimmt (*a. ling.*): ~ *article*; ~ *pronoun* Indefinitivpronomen *n*, unbestimmtes Fürwort. **2.** unbegrenzt, unbeschränkt: ~*ly* auf unbestimmte Zeit.

in·del·i·ble [ɪnˈdeləbl] *adj* ☐ unauslöschlich (*a. fig.*): ~ *ink* Zeichen-, Kopiertinte *f*; ~ *pencil* Tintenstift *m*.

in·del·i·cate [ɪnˈdelɪkət] *adj* ☐ **1.** taktlos. **2.** unanständig, anstößig. **3.** unfein, grob.

in·dem·ni·fy [ɪnˈdemnɪfaɪ] *v/t* **1.** entschädigen, *j-m* Schadenersatz leisten (*for* für). **2.** absichern (*from, against* gegen). **in·dem·ni·ty** *s* **1.** Entschädigung *f*. **2.** Absicherung *f*.

in·dent **I** *v/t* [ɪnˈdent] **1.** (ein)kerben, auszacken. **2.** *Zeile* einrücken, -ziehen. **II** *s* [ˈɪndent] **3.** Kerbe *f*, Auszackung *f*. **4.** Einrückung *f*, -zug *m*.

in·de·pend·ence [ˌɪndɪˈpendəns] *s* Unabhängigkeit *f* (*from, of* von) (*a. pol.*), Selbständigkeit *f*: ♀ *Day Am.* Unabhängigkeitstag *m* (*4. Juli*). **in·de·pend·ent** *adj* ☐ **1.** unabhängig (*of* von) (*a. pol.*), selbständig. **2.** finanziell unabhängig: *be* ~ auf eigenen Füßen stehen. **3.** *parl.* partei-, fraktionslos.

in-'depth *adj* tiefschürfend, gründlich.

in·de·scrib·a·ble [ˌɪndɪˈskraɪbəbl] *adj* ☐ unbeschreiblich.

in·de·struct·i·ble [ˌɪndɪˈstrʌktəbl] *adj* ☐ unzerstörbar.

in·de·ter·mi·na·ble [ˌɪndɪˈtɜːmɪnəbl] *adj* ☐ unbestimmbar. **in·de·ter·mi·nate** [ˌ~nət] *adj* ☐ **1.** unbestimmt (*a. ⅍*). **2.** ungewiß, unsicher.

in·dex [ˈɪndeks] **I** *pl* **in·dex·es, in·di·ces** [ˈ~dɪsiːz] **1.** Index *m*, (Stichwort *etc*)Verzeichnis *n*, (Sach)Register *n*. **2.** *a.* ~ *file* Kartei *f*. **3.** ♥ Index *m*. **4.** Å Exponent *m*; Index *m*, Kennziffer *f*. **5.** *fig.* (*of, to*) (An)Zeichen *n* (von *od.* für *od. gen*); Hinweis *m* (auf *acc*); Gradmesser *m* (für *od. gen*): *be an* ~ *of* (*od.* **to**) *a. et.* aufzeigen, hinweisen *od.* -deuten auf (*acc*). **II** *v/t* **6.** in e-m Verzeichnis aufführen. **7.** karteimäßig erfassen. ~ *card* *s* Karteikarte *f*. ~ *fin·ger* *s* Zeigefinger *m*. ~*-'linked* *adj* ♥ indexgebunden, Index...

In·di·an [ˈɪndjən] **I** *adj* **1.** indisch. **2.** indianisch, Indianer... **II** *s* **3.** Inder(in). **4.** Indianer(in). ~ *club* *s Sport*: Keule *f*. ~ *corn* *s* Mais *m*. ~ *file* *s*: *in* ~ → **II**. **II** *adv* im Gänsemarsch. ~ *sum·mer* *s* Altweiber-, Nachsommer *m*.

In·di·a rub·ber [ˈɪndjə] *s* **1.** Kautschuk *m*, Gummi *n, m*. **2.** Radiergummi *m*.

in·di·cate [ˈɪndɪkeɪt] *v/t* **1.** deuten *od.* zeigen auf (*acc*). **2.** *fig.* hinweisen *od.* -deuten auf (*acc*); zu erkennen *od.* verstehen geben: *everything* ~*s that* alles deutet darauf hin, daß. **3.** *be* ~*d* angebracht *od.* angezeigt sein. **4.** ☼ anzeigen.

in·di·ca·tion [ˌɪndɪˈkeɪʃn] *s* **1.** (*of*) (An)Zeichen *n* (für); Hinweis *m* (auf *acc*); Andeutung *f* (*gen*): *there is every* ~ *that* alles deutet darauf hin, daß. **2.** ♥ Indikation *f*. **3.** ☼ Anzeige *f*. **in·dic·a·tive** [ɪnˈdɪkətɪv] *adj* ☐ **1.** *be* ~ *of* → **indicate** 2. **2.** *ling.* indikativisch: ~ *mood* → **II**. **II** *s* **3.** *ling.* Indikativ *m*. **in·di·ca·tor** [ˈ~keɪtə] *s* **1.** *Statistik etc*: Indikator *m*. **2.** ☼ Anzeiger *m*. **3.** *mot.* Blinker *m*.

in·di·ces [ˈɪndɪsiːz] *pl von* **index.**

in·dict [ɪnˈdaɪt] *v/t* ⅍ anklagen (*for* wegen). **in'dict·ment** *s* **1.** Anklage *f*. **2.** *a. bill of* ~ Anklageschrift *f*.

in·dif·fer·ence [ɪnˈdɪfrəns] *s* **1.** Gleichgültigkeit *f*, Indifferenz *f*. **2.** Mittelmäßigkeit *f*. **in'dif·fer·ent** *adj* ☐ **1.** gleichgültig, indifferent (*to* gegen[über]): *he* *is ~ to it* es ist ihm gleichgültig. **2.** mittelmäßig.

in·dig·e·nous [ɪnˈdɪdʒɪnəs] *adj* □ **1.** einheimisch (**to** in *dat*) (a. ♀, *zo.*). **2.** *fig.* angeboren (**to** *dat*).

in·di·gest·i·ble [ˌɪndɪˈdʒestəbl] *adj* □ un-, schwerverdaulich (*a. fig.*). **,in·di-ˈges·tion** *s* ♣ Magenverstimmung *f*, verdorbener Magen.

in·dig·nant [ɪnˈdɪɡnənt] *adj* □ entrüstet, empört (**at** *s.th.*, **with** *s.o.* über *acc*). **,in·dig·ˈna·tion** *s* Entrüstung *f*, Empörung *f*: **to my ~** zu m-r Entrüstung.

in·di·rect [ˌɪndɪˈrekt] *adj* □ *allg.* indirekt: **by ~ means** *fig.* auf Umwegen; **~ object** *ling.* Dativobjekt *n*; **~ speech** (*bsd. Am.* **discourse**) *ling.* indirekte Rede.

in·dis·cern·i·ble [ˌɪndɪˈsɜːnəbl] *adj* □ nicht wahrnehmbar, unmerklich.

in·dis·creet [ˌɪndɪˈskriːt] *adj* □ **1.** unbesonnen, unbedacht. **2.** indiskret. **in·dis·ˈcre·tion** [ˌ~ˈskreʃn] *s* **1.** Unbesonnenheit *f*. **2.** Indiskretion *f*.

in·dis·crim·i·nate [ˌɪndɪˈskrɪmɪnət] *adj* □ **1.** nicht wählerisch; urteils-, kritiklos. **2.** wahl-, unterschiedslos; ungeordnet.

in·dis·pen·sa·ble [ˌɪndɪˈspensəbl] *adj* □ unentbehrlich (*a.* Person), unerläßlich (**to** für).

in·dis·posed [ˌɪndɪˈspəʊzd] *adj* **1.** indisponiert, unpäßlich. **2.** abgeneigt (**for** *dat*; **to do** zu tun): **be ~ to do s.th.** *a.* et. nicht tun wollen. **in·dis·po·si·tion** [ˌɪndɪspəˈzɪʃn] *s* **1.** Unpäßlichkeit *f*. **2.** Abgeneigtheit *f* (**for** gegenüber; **to do** zu tun).

in·dis·pu·ta·ble [ˌɪndɪˈspjuːtəbl] *adj* □ unstrittig, unstreitig.

in·dis·so·lu·ble [ˌɪndɪˈsɒljʊbl] *adj* □ **1.** unlöslich. **2.** *fig.* unauflösbar.

in·dis·tinct [ˌɪndɪˈstɪŋkt] *adj* □ **1.** undeutlich; unscharf. **2.** verschwommen (*Erinnerung etc*).

in·dis·tin·guish·a·ble [ˌɪndɪˈstɪŋgwɪʃəbl] *adj* □ nicht zu unterscheiden(d) (**from** von).

in·di·vid·u·al [ˌɪndɪˈvɪdʒʊəl] **I** *adj* (□ → **individually**) **1.** individuell, einzeln, Einzel...: **~ case** Einzelfall *m*; **~ traffic** Individualverkehr *m*. **2.** individuell, persönlich (*Stil etc*). **II** *s* **3.** Individuum *n* (*a. contp.*), Einzelne *m*, *f*. **,in·di-**

ˈvid·u·al·ism *s* Individualismus *m*. **,in·di·ˈvid·u·a·list** *s* Individualist(in). **II** *adj* individualistisch. **ˈin·di,vid·u·al·ˈis·tic** *adj* (**~ally**) individualistisch. **ˈin·di,vid·u·ˈal·i·ty** [ˌ~ˈælətɪ] *s* Individualität *f*. **,in·di·ˈvid·u·a·lize** [ˌ~əlaɪz] *v/t* **1.** individualisieren. **2.** individuell gestalten. **,in·di·ˈvid·u·al·ly** *adv* **I.** individuell. **2.** einzeln, jede(r, -s) für sich.

in·di·vis·i·ble [ˌɪndɪˈvɪzəbl] *adj* □ unteilbar.

in·doc·tri·nate [ɪnˈdɒktrɪneɪt] *v/t* **1.** *contp. bsd. pol.* indoktrinieren. **2.** unterweisen, schulen (**in** in *dat*). **in,doc·tri·ˈna·tion** *s* **1.** Indoktrination *f*. **2.** Unterweisung *f*, Schulung *f*.

in·do·lence [ˈɪndələns] *s* Trägheit *f*. **ˈin·do·lent** *adj* □ träg; träg machend (*Hitze etc*).

in·dom·i·ta·ble [ɪnˈdɒmɪtəbl] *adj* □ **1.** unbezähmbar, nicht unterzukriegen(d). **2.** unbeugsam.

in·door [ˈɪndɔː] *adj* Haus..., Zimmer..., (*Sport*) Hallen...: **~ aerial** (*bsd. Am.* **antenna**) Zimmerantenne *f*; **~ dress** Hauskleid *n*; **~ plant** Zimmerpflanze *f*; **~ shot** *phot.* Innenaufnahme *f*; **~ swimming pool** Hallenbad *n*. **in·doors** *adv* **1.** im Haus, drinnen. **2.** ins Haus (hinein). **3.** *Sport:* in der Halle.

in·du·bi·ta·ble [ɪnˈdjuːbɪtəbl] *adj* □ unzweifelhaft, *adv a.* zweifel-, fraglos.

in·duce [ɪnˈdjuːs] *v/t* **1.** *j-n* veranlassen, bewegen (**to do** zu tun). **2.** herbeiführen, verursachen, auslösen: **~ labo(u)r** ♣ die Geburt einleiten. **3.** ♀ *etc* induzieren: **~d current** Induktionsstrom *m*. **in·ˈduce·ment** *s* Veranlassung *f*; Anreiz *m*: **~ to buy** Kaufanreiz.

in·duc·tion [ɪnˈdʌkʃn] *s* **1.** Herbeiführung *f*, Auslösung *f*. **2.** ♀ *etc* Induktion *f*.

in·dulge [ɪnˈdʌldʒ] **I** *v/t* **1.** nachsichtig sein gegen: **~ o.s. in s.th.** → 4. **2.** *Kinder* verwöhnen. **3.** *e-r Neigung etc* nachgeben, frönen. **II** *v/i* **4.** **~ in s.th.** sich et. gönnen *od.* leisten. **5.** (**in**) schwelgen (in *dat*), frönen (*dat*). **in·ˈdul·gence** *s* **1.** Nachsicht *f*. **2.** Verwöhnung *f*. **3.** Schwelgen *n* (**in** in *dat*). **4.** Luxus *m*; Genuß *m*. **in·ˈdul·gent** *adj* □ nachsichtig (**to** gegen).

in·dus·tri·al [ɪnˈdʌstrɪəl] *adj* □ **1.** industriell, Industrie...: **~ action** *Br.* Arbeitskampf *m*; **~ disease** Berufskrankheit *f*; **~ espionage** Industrie-, Werkspionage *f*. **2.** industrialisiert, Industrie... **3.** Betriebs...: **~ management** Betriebsführung *f*. **4.** industriell erzeugt, Industrie...: **~ products** *pl* gewerbliche Erzeugnisse *pl*. **in'dus·tri·al·ist** *s* Industrielle *m*, *f*. **in'dus·tri·al·ize** *v/t* industrialisieren.

in·dus·tri·ous [ɪn'dʌstrɪəs] *adj* □ fleißig.

in·dus·try ['ɪndəstrɪ] *s* **1.** Industrie *f*; Industrie(zweig *m*) *f*: **steel ~** Stahlindustrie. **2.** Fleiß *m*.

in·ed·i·ble [ɪn'edəbl] *adj* ungenießbar.

in·ef·fa·ble [ɪn'efəbl] *adj* □ unbeschreiblich, unsagbar.

in·ef·face·a·ble [ˌɪnɪ'feɪsəbl] *adj* □ **1.** unlöschbar. **2.** *fig.* unauslöschlich.

in·ef·fec·tive [ˌɪnɪ'fektɪv], **in·ef·fec·tu·al** [~'fektʃʊəl] *adj* □ **1.** unwirksam, wirkungslos. **2.** unfähig, untauglich.

in·ef·fi·cient [ˌɪnɪ'fɪʃnt] *adj* □ ineffizient: a) untüchtig, b) unrationell, unwirtschaftlich.

in·el·e·gant [ɪn'elɪɡənt] *adj* □ unelegant.

in·el·i·gi·ble [ɪn'elɪdʒəbl] *adj* □ (**for**) nicht in Frage kommend (für): a) ungeeignet, unannehmbar (für) b) nicht berechtigt *od.* befähigt (zu): **be ~ for** keinen Anspruch haben auf (*acc*), c) nicht teilnahmeberechtigt (an *dat*), (*Sport a.*) nicht start- *od.* spielberechtigt (für).

in·ept [ɪ'nept] *adj* □ **1.** unpassend. **2.** ungeschickt, unbeholfen; unfähig.

in·e·qual·i·ty [ˌɪnɪ'kwɒlətɪ] *s* Ungleichheit *f*, Verschiedenheit *f*.

in·eq·ui·ta·ble [ɪn'ekwɪtəbl] *adj* □ ungerecht. **in'eq·ui·ty** [~wətɪ] *s* Ungerechtigkeit *f*.

in·e·rad·i·ca·ble [ˌɪnɪ'rædɪkəbl] *adj* □ unausrottbar (*a. fig.*).

in·ert [ɪ'nɜːt] *adj* □ *phys.* träg (*a. fig.*). **in·er·tia** [ɪ'nɜːʃə] *s* Trägheit *f*.

in·es·cap·a·ble [ˌɪnɪ'skeɪpəbl] *adj* □ unvermeidlich: a) unabwendbar, b) unweigerlich.

in·es·sen·tial [ˌɪnɪ'senʃl] **I** *adj* unwesentlich. **II** *s et.* Unwesentliches, Nebensache *f*.

in·es·ti·ma·ble [ɪn'estɪməbl] *adj* □ unschätzbar.

in·ev·i·ta·ble [ɪn'evɪtəbl] **I** *adj* □ unvermeidlich. **II** *s das* Unvermeidliche.

in·ex·act [ˌɪnɪɡ'zækt] *adj* □ ungenau.

in·ex·cus·a·ble [ˌɪnɪk'skjuːzəbl] *adj* □ unverzeihlich, unentschuldbar.

in·ex·haust·i·ble [ˌɪnɪɡ'zɔːstəbl] *adj* □ unerschöpflich (*Thema etc*).

in·ex·o·ra·ble [ɪn'eksərəbl] *adj* □ unerbittlich.

in·ex·pe·di·ent [ˌɪnɪk'spiːdjənt] *adj* □ **1.** nicht ratsam, unangebracht. **2.** unzweckmäßig.

in·ex·pen·sive [ˌɪnɪk'spensɪv] *adj* □ billig, nicht teuer.

in·ex·pe·ri·ence [ˌɪnɪk'spɪərɪəns] *s* Unerfahrenheit *f*. **in·ex'pe·ri·enced** *adj* unerfahren.

in·ex·pert [ɪn'ekspɜːt] *adj* □ **1.** unerfahren (**at, in** in *dat*). **2.** unfachmännisch. **3.** ungeschickt, unbeholfen (**at, in** in *dat*).

in·ex·pli·ca·ble [ˌɪnɪk'splɪkəbl] *adj* □ unerklärlich.

in·ex·press·i·ble [ˌɪnɪk'spresəbl] *adj* □ unaussprechlich, unsäglich.

in·ex·tin·guish·a·ble [ˌɪnɪk'stɪŋɡwɪʃəbl] *adj* □ **1.** unlöschbar. **2.** *fig.* unauslöschlich.

in·ex·tri·ca·ble [ɪn'ekstrɪkəbl] *adj* □ **1.** unentwirrbar (*a. fig.*). **2.** *fig.* auswegslos.

in·fal·li·bil·i·ty [ɪnˌfælə'bɪlətɪ] *s* Unfehlbarkeit *f* (*a. eccl.*). **in·fal·li·ble** *adj* unfehlbar. **in'fal·li·bly** *adv* **1.** unfehlbar. **2.** F todsicher, ganz bestimmt.

in·fa·mous ['ɪnfəməs] *adj* □ **1.** verrufen, berüchtigt (**for** wegen). **2.** infam, niederträchtig. **'in·fa·my** *s* **1.** Verrufenheit *f*. **2.** Infamie *f*: a) Niederträcht *f*, b) niederträchtige Handlung.

in·fan·cy ['ɪnfənsɪ] *s* frühe Kindheit *f*, *bsd.* Säuglingsalter *n*: **be still in its ~** *fig.* noch in den Anfängen *od.* Kinderschuhen stecken. **'in·fant I** *s* Säugling *m*; kleines Kind. **II** *adj* Säuglings...: **~ mortality** Säuglingssterblichkeit *f*; **~ prodigy** Wunderkind *n*.

in·fan·ti·cide [ɪn'fæntɪsaɪd] *s* **1.** Kind(e)stötung *f*. **2.** Kind(e)s-, Kindermörder(in).

in·fan·tile ['ɪnfəntaɪl] *adj* **1.** infantil, kindisch. **2.** kindlich. **3.** Kinder..., Kindes...

in·fan·try ['ɪnfəntrɪ] *s* ✗ Infanterie *f*. **~·man** ['~mən] *s* (*irr* **man**) Infanterist *m*.

in·farct [ɪnˈfɑːkt] *s* ☞ Infarkt *m*.

in·fat·u·at·ed [ɪnˈfætjoeɪtɪd] *adj* vernarrt (**with** in *acc*).

in·fect [ɪnˈfekt] *v/t* **1.** ☞ infizieren, anstecken (**with** mit; **by** durch): *become* ~*ed* sich anstecken. **2.** *Luft* verpesten; *fig. Atmosphäre* vergiften. **3.** *fig.* anstecken (**with** mit). **in·fec·tion** *s* **1.** ☞ Infektion *f*, Ansteckung *f*. **2.** Verpestung *f*; *fig.* Vergiftung *f*. **in·fec·tious** *adj* □ ☞ ansteckend (*a. fig. Lachen etc*), infektiös: ~ *disease* Infektionskrankheit *f*; **be** ~ *fig.* anstecken.

in·fe·lic·i·tous [ˌɪnfɪˈlɪsɪtəs] *adj* □ unglücklich (*a. fig. Ausdruck etc*).

in·fer [ɪnˈfɜː] *v/t* schließen, folgern (**from** aus). **in·fer·ence** [ˈɪnfərəns] *s* (Schluß-) Folgerung *f*, (Rück)Schluß *m*.

in·fe·ri·or [ɪnˈfɪərɪə] *I adj* **1.** (**to**) untergeordnet (*dat*), niedriger (als): *be* ~ *to s.o.* j-m untergeordnet sein; j-m unterlegen sein. **2.** weniger wert (**to** als). **3.** minderwertig, mittelmäßig. **II** *s* **4.** Untergebene *m*, *f*. **in·fe·ri·or·i·ty** [ˌ~ˈɒrəti] *s* **1.** Unterlegenheit *f*. **2.** Minderwertigkeit *f*, Mittelmäßigkeit *f*: ~ *complex psych.* Minderwertigkeitskomplex *m*.

in·fer·nal [ɪnˈfɜːnl] *adj* □ **1.** höllisch, Höllen..., infernalisch. **2.** teuflisch. **in·fer·no** [~nəʊ] *pl* **-nos** *s* Inferno *n*, Hölle *f*.

in·fer·tile [ɪnˈfɜːtaɪl] *adj* unfruchtbar. **in·fer·til·i·ty** [ˌɪnfəˈtɪləti] *s* Unfruchtbarkeit *f*.

in·fest [ɪnˈfest] *v/t* **1.** verseuchen, befallen (*Parasiten etc*): ~*ed with lice* verlaust. **2.** *fig.* überschwemmen, -laufen: *be* ~*ed with* wimmeln von.

in·fi·del [ˈɪnfɪdəl] *eccl.* **I** *s* Ungläubige *m*, *f*. **II** *adj* ungläubig. **in·fi·del·i·ty** [~ˈdelətɪ] *s* **1.** *eccl.* Unglaube *m*. **2.** (*bsd. eheliche*) Untreue.

in·fight·ing [ˈɪnˌfaɪtɪŋ] *s* **1.** *Boxen:* Infight *m*, Nahkampf *m*. **2.** (*partei- etc*)interne Kämpfe *pl od.* Streitereien *pl*.

in·fil·trate [ˈɪnfɪltreɪt] **I** *v/t* **1.** einsickern in (*acc*). **2.** einschleusen, -schmuggeln (*into* in *acc*). **3.** *pol.* unterwandern. **II** *v/i* **4.** einsickern (*into* in *acc*). **in·fil·tra·tion** *s* **1.** Einsickern *n*. **2.** *pol.* Unterwanderung *f*.

in·fi·nite [ˈɪnfɪnət] *adj* □ **1.** unendlich (*a. A*), grenzenlos (*beide a. fig.*). **2.** gewaltig, ungeheuer. **in·fin·i·tes·i·mal** [ˌ~nɪ-

'tesɪml] *adj* □ **1.** unendlich klein. **2.** *A* infinitesimal: ~ *calculus* Infinitesimalrechnung *f*. **in·fin·i·tive** [~ətɪv] *s ling.* Infinitiv *m*. **in·fin·i·ty** *s* **1.** Unendlichkeit *f*, Grenzenlosigkeit *f* (*beide a. fig.*). **2.** unendliche Menge *od.* Größe (*a. A*): *an* ~ *of people* unendlich viele Leute.

in·firm [ɪnˈfɜːm] *adj* □ schwach, gebrechlich. **in·fir·ma·ry** *s* **1.** Krankenhaus *n*. **2.** Krankenzimmer *n*, -stube *f* (*in Internat etc*). **in·fir·mi·ty** *s* Schwäche *f*, Gebrechlichkeit *f*; Gebrechen *n*.

in·flame [ɪnˈfleɪm] **I** *v/t* **1.** entzünden (*a. &*): *become* ~*d* → **3. 2.** *fig. Gefühle etc* entfachen, -flammen; *j-n* entflammen, erregen: ~ *with rage* wutentbrannt. **II** *v/i* **3.** sich entzünden (*a. &*). **4.** *fig.* entbrennen (*with vor dat*); in Wut geraten.

in·flam·ma·ble [ɪnˈflæməbl] *adj* □ **1.** brennbar, leichtentzündlich; feuergefährlich. **2.** *fig.* reizbar, leicht erregbar.

in·flam·ma·tion [ˌɪnfləˈmeɪʃn] *s &* Entzündung *f*. **in·flam·ma·to·ry** [ɪnˈflæmətərɪ] *adj* **1.** *&* entzündlich, Entzündungs... **2.** *fig.* aufrührerisch, Hetz...

in·flate [ɪnˈfleɪt] *v/t* aufblasen, *Reifen etc* aufpumpen. **in·flat·ed** *adj* **1.** aufgeblasen: ~ *with pride fig.* stolzgeschwellt. **2.** *fig.* schwülstig, bombastisch. **in·fla·tion** [~ʃn] *s* **1.** Aufblasen *n*, -pumpen *n*. **2.** ♥ Inflation *f*: → *creeping, gallop* I, *runaway* **3.** **in·fla·tion·ar·y** *adj* ♥ Inflations..., inflationär.

in·flect [ɪnˈflekt] *v/t* **1.** beugen. **2.** *ling.* flektieren, beugen. **in·flec·tion** *s* **1.** Beugung *f*. **2.** *ling.* Flexion *f*, Beugung *f*.

in·flex·i·ble [ɪnˈfleksəbl] *adj* □ inflexibel: a) unbiegsam, b) *fig.* unbeweglich. **in·flex·ion** *bsd. Br.* → **inflection**.

in·flict [ɪnˈflɪkt] *v/t* **1.** *Leid, Schaden etc* zufügen (*dat*), *Niederlage, Wunde etc* beibringen (*dat*); *Strafe* auferlegen (*dat*), verhängen (*on* über *acc*), aufbürden (*dat*): ~ *o.s. on s.o.* sich j-m aufdrängen. **in·flic·tion** *s* **1.** Zufügung *f*; Auferlegung *f*. **2.** Plage *f*, Last *f*.

'in-flight *adj ✈* **1.** Bord...: ~ *fare* Bordverpflegung *f*. **2.** während des Flugs.

in·flow [ˈɪnfləʊ] → **influx**.

in·flu·ence [ˈɪnflʊəns] **I** *s* Einfluß *m* (**on**, **over** auf *acc*; **with** bei): *be under s.o.'s* ~ unter j-s Einfluß stehen; *under the* ~

of drink (*od.* **alcohol**) unter Alkoholeinfluß; **under the** ~ F alkoholisiert. **II** *v/t* beeinflussen. **in·flu·en·tial** [ˌ~'enʃl] *adj* □ einflußreich.

in·flu·en·za [ˌɪnflʊ'enzə] *s* ✿ Grippe *f*.

in·flux ['ɪnflʌks] *s* Zustrom *m* (*a. fig.*), (✝ *Kapital- etc*)Zufluß *m*: ~ **of visitors** Besucherstrom *m*.

in·fo ['ɪnfəʊ] F → **information.**

in·form [ɪn'fɔːm] **I** *v/t* (**of, about**) benachrichtigen, unterrichten (von), informieren (über *acc*): **keep s.o. ~ed** j-n auf dem laufenden halten; ~ **s.o. that** j-n davon in Kenntnis setzen, daß. **II** *v/i*: ~ **against** (*od.* **on**) **s.o.** j-n anzeigen; *b.s.* j-n denunzieren.

in·for·mal [ɪn'fɔːml] *adj* □ **1.** formlos, ⚖ *a.* formfrei. **2.** zwanglos, ungezwungen. **3.** inoffiziell.

in·for·mant [ɪn'fɔːmənt] *s* **1.** Informant *m*, Gewährsmann *m*. **2.** → *informer.*

in·for·mat·ics [ˌɪnfə'mætɪks] *s pl* (*sg konstruiert*) Informatik *f*.

in·for·ma·tion [ˌɪnfə'meɪʃn] *s* **1.** Benachrichtigung *f*, Unterrichtung *f*; Nachricht *f*, Mitteilung *f*, Bescheid *m*. **2.** Auskünfte *pl*, Auskunft *f*, Information *f*: **for your** ~ zu Ihrer Information *od.* Kenntnisnahme. **3.** *coll.* Nachrichten *pl*, Informationen *pl*: **bit** (*od.* **piece**) **of** ~ Nachricht *f*, Information *f*. **4.** *coll.* Erkundigungen *pl*: **gather** ~ Erkundigungen einziehen. **in·for·ma·tive** [ɪn'fɔːmətɪv] *adj* □ informativ, aufschlußreich. **in'form·er** *s* **1.** Denunziant(in). **2.** Spitzel *m*.

in·fra|·dig [ˌɪnfrə'dɪɡ] *adj*: **it is** ~ **for him** F es ist unter s-r Würde (**to do** zu tun). **'~·red** *adj phys.* infrarot. **'~·struc·ture** *s* Infrastruktur *f*.

in·fre·quent [ɪn'friːkwənt] *adj* □ **1.** selten. **2.** spärlich.

in·fringe [ɪn'frɪndʒ] *v/t u. v/i* (~ **on**) Gesetz, Vertrag etc brechen, verletzen, verstoßen gegen. **in'fringe·ment** *s* Verletzung *f*; Verstoß *m* (**of** gegen).

in·fu·ri·ate [ɪn'fjʊərɪeɪt] *v/t* wütend machen.

in·fuse [ɪn'fjuːz] *v/t* **1.** Tee etc aufgießen; ziehen lassen. **2.** *fig.* Mut etc einflößen (**into** dat); *j-n* erfüllen (**with** mit). **in'fu·sion** [~ʒn] *s* **1.** ✿ Infusion *f*. **2.** Aufguß *m*. **3.** *fig.* Einflößung *f*.

in·gen·ious [ɪn'dʒiːnjəs] *adj* □ genial: a)

erfinderisch, einfallsreich, b) sinnreich, raffiniert. **in·ge·nu·i·ty** [ˌɪndʒɪ'njuːətɪ] *s* Genialität *f*, Einfallsreichtum *m*.

in·gen·u·ous [ɪn'dʒenjʊəs] *adj* □ **1.** offen(herzig), aufrichtig. **2.** naiv, kindlich-unbefangen.

in·gle·nook ['ɪŋɡlnʊk] *s* Br. Kaminecke *f*.

in·glo·ri·ous [ɪn'ɡlɔːrɪəs] *adj* □ unrühmlich, schmählich.

in·go·ing ['ɪnˌɡəʊɪŋ] *adj* **1.** nachfolgend, neu (*Mieter etc*). **2.** ~ **mail** Posteingang *m*.

in·got ['ɪŋɡət] *s* (*Gold- etc*)Barren *m*: ~ **of gold.**

in·gra·ti·ate [ɪn'ɡreɪʃɪeɪt] *v/t*: ~ **o.s. with s.o.** sich bei j-m einschmeicheln.

in·grat·i·tude [ɪn'ɡrætɪtjuːd] *s* Undank (-barkeit *f*) *m*.

in·gre·di·ent [ɪn'ɡriːdjənt] *s* **1.** Bestandteil *m* (*a. fig.*). **2.** *gastr.* Zutat *f*.

in·hab·it [ɪn'hæbɪt] *v/t* bewohnen. **in'hab·it·a·ble** *adj* bewohnbar. **in'hab·it·ant** *s* Einwohner(in) (*e-s Orts, Landes*), Bewohner(in) (*bsd. e-s Hauses*).

in·hale [ɪn'heɪl] **I** *v/t* **1.** einatmen, ✿ *a.* inhalieren. **II** *v/i* **2.** einatmen. **3.** inhalieren, Lungenzüge machen.

in·har·mo·ni·ous [ˌɪnhɑː'məʊnjəs] *adj* □ unharmonisch.

in·here [ɪn'hɪə] *v/i* innewohnen (**in** dat). **in'her·ent** *adj* innewohnend.

in·her·it [ɪn'herɪt] *v/t* erben (**from** von) (*a. fig.*). **in'her·i·tance** *s* Erbe *n* (*a. fig.*).

in·hib·it [ɪn'hɪbɪt] *v/t* **1.** hemmen (*a. psych.*), (ver)hindern. **2.** *j-n* hindern (**from** an dat): ~ **s.o. from doing s.th.** j-n daran hindern, et. zu tun. **in·hi·bi·tion** [ˌɪnhɪ'bɪʃn] *s* *psych.* Hemmung *f*.

in·hos·pi·ta·ble [ɪnhɒ'spɪtəbl] *adj* □ wenig gastfreundlich; ungastlich.

in·hu·man [ɪn'hjuːmən], **in·hu·mane** [ˌ~'meɪn] *adj* □ inhuman, unmenschlich. **in·hu·man·i·ty** [ˌ~'mænɪtɪ] *s* Unmenschlichkeit *f*.

in·im·i·cal [ɪ'nɪmɪkl] *adj* □ **1.** feindselig (**to** gegen). **2.** (**to**) nachteilig (für), abträglich (dat).

in·im·i·ta·ble [ɪ'nɪmɪtəbl] *adj* □ unnachahmlich.

in·iq·ui·tous [ɪ'nɪkwɪtəs] *adj* □ **1.** ungerecht. **2.** schändlich. **in'iq·ui·ty** *s* **1.** Ungerechtigkeit f. **2.** Schändlichkeit f; Schandtat f.

in·i·tial [ɪ'nɪʃl] **I** adj anfänglich, Anfangs... **II** s Initiale f, (großer) Anfangsbuchstabe. **III** v/t pret u. pp **-tialed**, bsd. Br. **-tialled** bezeichnen, pol. paraphieren. **in'i·tial·ly** [~ʃəlɪ] adv anfänglich, am Anfang. **in·i·ti·ate I** v/t [ɪ'nɪʃɪeɪt] **1.** einleiten, ins Leben rufen. **2.** j-n einführen (*into* in acc): a) einweihen, b) aufnehmen, c) einarbeiten. **II** s [~ʃɪət] **3.** Eingeweihte m, f. **in·i·ti·a·tion** s **1.** Einleitung f. **2.** Einführung f: a) Einweihung f, b) Aufnahme f, c) Einarbeitung f. **in'i·ti·a·tive** [~ətɪv] s Initiative f: **take the ~** die Initiative ergreifen; **on one's own ~** aus eigenem Antrieb. **in'i·ti·a·tor** [~eɪtə] s Initiator m, Urheber m.

in·ject [ɪn'dʒekt] v/t ✶ injizieren, einspritzen (a. ⊙): **~ s.th. into s.o., ~ s.o. with s.th.** j-m et. spritzen; fig. j-m et. einflößen. **in'jec·tion** s ✶ Injektion f: a) Einspritzung f (a. ⊙), Spritze f, b) eingespritztes Medikament.

in·ju·di·cious [ˌɪndʒuː'dɪʃəs] adj □ unklug, unvernünftig.

in·junc·tion [ɪn'dʒʌŋkʃn] s **1.** ⚖ gerichtliches Verbot: (*interim*) **~** einstweilige Verfügung. **2.** ausdrücklicher Befehl.

in·jure ['ɪndʒə] v/t **1.** verletzen: **~ one's leg** sich am Bein verletzen. **2.** fig. kränken, verletzen. **3.** fig. schaden (dat), schädigen. **in·ju·ri·ous** [ɪn-'dʒʊərɪəs] adj □ (*to*) schädlich (für), abträglich (dat): **be ~** (dat), schaden (dat). **in·ju·ry** ['ɪndʒərɪ] s **1.** ✶ Verletzung f (*to* an dat): **~ to the head** Kopfverletzung, -wunde f. **2.** fig. Kränkung f, Verletzung f (*to* gen).

in·jus·tice [ɪn'dʒʌstɪs] s Unrecht n, Ungerechtigkeit f: **do s.o. an ~** j-m unrecht tun; **suffer an ~** ungerecht behandelt werden.

ink [ɪŋk] s **1.** Tinte f. **2.** Tusche f. **3.** typ. (Drucker)Schwärze f.

ink·ling ['ɪŋklɪŋ] s **1.** Andeutung f, Wink m. **2.** dunkle Ahnung: **give s.o. an ~ of** (od. **as to**) j-m e-e ungefähre Vorstellung geben von.

'ink|·pad s Stempelkissen n. **~ stain** s Tintenklecks m, -fleck m.

ink·y ['ɪŋkɪ] adj **1.** tinten-, pechschwarz. **2.** tintig, voller Tinte.

in·land I adj ['ɪnlənd] **1.** binnenländisch, Binnen... **2.** inländisch, einheimisch: ℒ **Revenue** Br. F Finanzamt n. **II** adv ['ɪnlænd] **3.** landeinwärts.

in·laws ['ɪnlɔːz] s pl angeheiratete Verwandte pl, engS. Schwiegereltern pl.

in·lay I v/t (irr lay) [ˌɪn'leɪ] **1.** einlegen (*with* mit): **inlaid work** → 3. **2.** parkettieren: **inlaid floor** Parkett(fußboden m) n. **II** s ['ɪnleɪ] **3.** Einlegearbeit f.

in·let ['ɪnlet] s **1.** Eingang m. Einlaß m (a. ⊙). **3.** schmale Bucht; Meeresarm m.

in·mate ['ɪnmeɪt] s Insasse m, Insassin f (e-r Anstalt, e-s Gefängnisses etc).

in·most ['ɪnməʊst] adj innerst, fig. a. tiefst, geheimst.

inn [ɪn] s **1.** Gasthaus n, -hof m. **2.** Wirtshaus n.

in·nards ['ɪnədz] s pl F Eingeweide pl: **his ~ were rumbling** es rumorte in s-m Bauch.

in·nate [ˌɪ'neɪt] adj angeboren (*in* dat).

in·ner ['ɪnə] adj **1.** inner, Innen...: **~ door** Innentür f; **~ life** Innen-, Seelenleben n; **~ man** Seele f; Geist m; humor. Magen m. **2.** fig. tiefer, verborgen (Sinn etc). **in·ner·most** ['~məʊst] → **inmost**.

in·no·cence ['ɪnəsəns] s Unschuld f: a) Schuldlosigkeit f, b) Unberührtheit f: **lose one's ~** s-e Unschuld verlieren, c) Harmlosigkeit f, d) Arglosigkeit f, Naivität f. **in·no·cent** ['~snt] adj □ unschuldig: a) schuldlos (*of* an dat), b) sittlich rein, (Mädchen a.) unberührt (as) **~ as a newborn babe** so unschuldig wie ein neugeborenes Kind, c) harmlos: **~ air** Unschuldsmiene f, d) arglos, naiv.

in·noc·u·ous [ɪ'nɒkjʊəs] adj □ unschädlich, harmlos.

in·no·vate ['ɪnəʊveɪt] v/i Neuerungen einführen (*on, in* bei, in dat). **in·no·va·tion** s Neuerung f.

in·nu·en·do [ˌɪnju:'endəʊ] pl **-do(e)s** s (*about, at*) versteckte Andeutung (über acc) od. Anspielung (auf acc).

in·nu·mer·a·ble [ɪ'njuːmərəbl] adj □ unzählig, zahllos.

in·oc·u·late [ɪ'nɒkjʊleɪt] v/t ✶ impfen (*against* gegen): **~ s.o. with s.th.** fig. j-m et. einimpfen. **in·oc·u·la·tion** s ✶ Impfung f.

in·o·dor·ous [ɪn'əʊdərəs] adj geruchlos.

in·of·fen·sive [ˌɪnəˈfensɪv] *adj* □ harm-los.

in·op·er·a·ble [ɪnˈɒpərəbl] *adj* **1.** un-durchführbar. **2.** 🍎 inoperabel.

in·op·er·a·tive [ɪnˈɒpərətɪv] *adj* un-wirksam: a) wirkungslos, b) 🏛 un-gültig.

in·op·por·tune [ɪnˈɒpətjuːn] *adj* □ un-günstig, unpassend.

in·or·di·nate [ɪnˈɔːdɪnət] *adj* □ un-, übermäßig, (*Forderung etc a.*) überzo-gen.

in·or·gan·ic [ˌɪnɔːˈgænɪk] *adj* (*~ally*) **1.** unorganisch. **2.** 🧪 anorganisch.

in·pa·tient [ˈɪnˌpeɪʃnt] *s* stationärer Pati-ent: *~ treatment* stationäre Behand-lung.

in·put [ˈɪnput] *s* Input *m*: a) 🌱 eingesetz-te Produktionsmittel *pl*, b) ⚡ Eingangs-leistung *f*, c) ⊙ eingespeiste Menge, d) *Computer*: (Daten)Eingabe *f*.

in·quest [ˈɪnkwest] *s* 🏛 gerichtliche Un-tersuchung: → **coroner**.

in·qui·e·tude [ɪnˈkwaɪətjuːd] *s* Unruhe *f*, Besorgnis *f*.

in·quire [ɪnˈkwaɪə] **I** *v/t* **1.** *~ s.th.* (*of s.o.*) sich (bei j-m) nach et. erkundigen. **II** *v/i* **2.** (nach)fragen, sich erkundigen (*of s.o.* bei j-m; *after, for* nach; *about* we-gen): *~ within* Näheres im Hause (zu erfragen). **3.** *~ into* et. untersuchen, prüfen. **in·quir·y** *s* **1.** Erkundigung *f*, (An-, Nach)Frage *f*: *on ~* auf An- od. Nachfrage; *make inquiries* Erkundi-gungen einziehen (*of s.o.* bei j-m; *a-bout, after* über *acc,* wegen). **2.** Unter-suchung *f*, Prüfung *f* (*of, into gen*), Nachforschung *f*, Ermittlung *f*, Re-cherche *f*. **3.** *pl* 📞 *etc* Auskunft *f* (*Büro, Schalter*).

in·qui·si·tion [ˌɪnkwɪˈzɪʃn] *s* **1.** (*a.* ge-richtliche *od.* amtliche) Untersuchung (*into gen*). **2.** ♀ *eccl. hist.* Inquisition *f*. **in·quis·i·tive** [ɪnˈkwɪzətɪv] *adj* □ **1.** wißbegierig. **2.** neugierig.

in·quo·rate [ɪnˈkwɔːrət] *adj* beschlußun-fähig.

in·road [ˈɪnrəud] *s bsd. pl* **1.** *bsd.* ⚔ Ein-fall *m* (*in, into, on* in *acc*). **2.** *fig.* (*in, into, on*) Eingriff *m* (in *acc*), Übergriff *m* (auf *acc*). **3.** *a.* **heavy** *~ fig.* übermä-ßige Inanspruchnahme (*in, into, on* gen): *make ~s on s.o.'s free time* j-s Freizeit stark einschränken; *make ~s*

into s.o.'s savings ein großes Loch in j-s Ersparnisse reißen.

in·rush [ˈɪnrʌʃ] *s* **1.** (Her)Einströmen *n*. **2.** *fig.* Flut *f,* (Zu)Strom *m*: *~ of tourists* Touristenstrom.

in·sa·lu·bri·ous [ˌɪnsəˈluːbrɪəs] *adj* □ ungesund.

in·sane [ɪnˈseɪn] *adj* □ wahn-, irrsinnig, 🍎 *a.* geisteskrank.

in·san·i·tar·y [ɪnˈsænɪtərɪ] *adj* unhygie-nisch, gesundheitsschädlich.

in·san·i·ty [ɪnˈsænətɪ] *s* Wahn-, Irrsinn *m*, 🍎 *a.* Geisteskrankheit *f*.

in·sa·ti·a·ble [ɪnˈseɪʃəbl] *adj* □ unersätt-lich (*Person*), unstillbar (*Durst etc*) (*beide a. fig.*).

in·scrip·tion [ɪnˈskrɪpʃn] *s* **1.** In- *od.* Auf-schrift *f*. **2.** (persönliche) Widmung.

in·scru·ta·ble [ɪnˈskruːtəbl] *adj* □ uner-forschlich, unergründlich.

in·sect [ˈɪnsekt] *s* *zo.* Insekt *n*: *~ spray* Insektenspray *n*. **in'sec·ti·cide** [~tɪ-saɪd] *s* Insektizid *n*, Insektenvernich-tungsmittel *n*.

in·se·cure [ˌɪnsɪˈkjuə] *adj* □ **1.** ungesi-chert, nicht fest. **2.** *fig.* unsicher. **in-se'cu·ri·ty** [~rətɪ] *s* Unsicherheit *f*.

in·sem·i·nate [ɪnˈsemɪneɪt] *v/t biol.* be-fruchten, *zo. a.* besamen. **in,sem·i-'na·tion** *s* Befruchtung *f*, Besamung *f*.

in·sen·si·ble [ɪnˈsensəbl] *adj* □ **1.** un-empfindlich (*to* gegen): *~ to pain* schmerzunempfindlich. **2.** bewußtlos. **3.** *fig.* (*of, to*) unempfänglich (für), gleichgültig (gegen). **4.** unmerklich.

in·sen·si·tive [ɪnˈsensətɪv] *adj* □ **1.** *a. phys.,* ⊙ unempfindlich (*to* gegen): *~ to light* lichtunempfindlich. **2.** → **in-sensible** 1, 3.

in·sep·a·ra·ble [ɪnˈsepərəbl] *adj* □ **1.** untrennbar (*a. ling.*). **2.** unzertrennlich (*from* von).

in·sert **I** *v/t* [ɪnˈsɜːt] **1.** einfügen, -setzen, -schieben, *Instrument etc* einführen, *Schlüssel etc* (hinein)stecken, *Münze etc* einwerfen (*in, into* in *acc*): *~ an advertisement in(to) a newspaper* e-e Anzeige in e-e Zeitung setzen, in e-r Zeitung inserieren. **II** *s* [ˈɪnsɜːt] **3.** → **insertion** 2-4. **in'ser·tion** *s* **1.** Einset-zen *n,* Einführung *f,* Einwurf *m*. **2.** Ein-satz(stück *n*) *m*. **3.** Anzeige *f,* Inserat *n*. **4.** (Zeitungs)Beilage *f,* (Buch)Einlage *f*.

in·shore [ˌɪnˈʃɔː] *adj* an *od.* nahe der

Küste: ~ **fishing** Küstenfischerei f.

in·side I s [ˌɪnˈsaɪd] **1.** Innenseite f; das Innere: **on the ~** innen; **from the ~** von innen; **turn ~ out** umdrehen, umstülpen; fig. (völlig) umkrempeln; **know ~ out** in- u. auswendig kennen. **II** adj [ˈɪnsaɪd] **2.** inner, Innen...: **~ lane** (Sport) Innenbahn f; mot. Br. äußere Fahrspur; **overtake s.o. on the ~ lane** (in GB etc) j-n links überholen, (in Deutschland etc) j-n rechts überholen. **3.** **~ information** (F **stuff**) Insiderinformationen pl, interne od. vertrauliche Informationen pl. **III** adv [ˌɪnˈsaɪd] **4.** im Inner(e)n, (dr)innen. **5.** hinein, herein. **6.** **~ of** a) zeitlich: innerhalb (gen), b) Am. → 7. **IV** prp [ˌɪnˈsaɪd] **7.** innerhalb, im Inner(e)n (gen): **~ the house** im Hause. **ˌin·ˈsid·er** s Insider(in), Eingeweihte m, f.

in·sid·i·ous [ɪnˈsɪdɪəs] adj □ hinterhältig, heimtückisch.

in·sight [ˈɪnsaɪt] s **1.** (into) Einblick m (in acc); Verständnis n (für). **2.** Einsicht f.

in·sig·ni·a [ɪnˈsɪgnɪə] pl **-a**(s) s **1.** Insignie f, Amts-, Ehrenzeichen n. **2.** ✕ Abzeichen n.

in·sig·nif·i·cant [ˌɪnsɪɡˈnɪfɪkənt] adj □ **1.** bedeutungslos. **2.** geringfügig, unerheblich (Betrag). **3.** unbedeutend (Person).

in·sin·cere [ˌɪnsɪnˈsɪə] adj □ unaufrichtig, falsch.

in·sin·u·ate [ɪnˈsɪnjʊeɪt] v/t andeuten, anspielen auf (acc): **are you insinuating that ...?** wollen Sie damit sagen, daß ...? **inˌsin·u·ˈa·tion** s (about) Anspielung f (auf acc), Andeutung f (über acc): **by ~** andeutungsweise.

in·sip·id [ɪnˈsɪpɪd] adj □ fad (a. fig.).

in·sist [ɪnˈsɪst] **I** v/i **1.** darauf bestehen: **~ on bestehen auf** (dat), verlangen (acc); **~ on doing s.th.** darauf bestehen, et. zu tun; et. unbedingt tun wollen. **2.** (on) beharren (auf dat), bleiben bei. **3.** om Gewicht legen (auf acc), (nachdrücklich) betonen (acc). **II** v/t **4.** darauf bestehen (**that** daß). **5.** dabei bleiben (**that** daß). **in·ˈsist·ence** s **1.** Bestehen n, Beharren n (**on** auf dat). **2.** Betonung f (**on** gen): **with great ~** mit großem Nachdruck. **3.** Beharrlichkeit f, Hartnäckigkeit f. **in·ˈsist·ent** adj □ **1.** beharrlich, hartnäckig: **be ~ (on)** →

insist I; **be ~ that** darauf bestehen, daß. **2.** eindringlich, nachdrücklich.

ˌin·soˈfar adv: **~ as** soweit.

in·sole [ˈɪnsəʊl] s **1.** Brandsohle f. **2.** Einlegesohle f.

in·so·lence [ˈɪnsələns] s Unverschämtheit f, Frechheit f. **ˈin·so·lent** adj □ unverschämt, frech.

in·sol·u·ble [ɪnˈsɒljʊbl] adj □ **1.** 🜛 un(auf)löslich. **2.** fig. unlösbar.

in·sol·ven·cy [ɪnˈsɒlvənsɪ] s ✝ Zahlungsunfähigkeit f, Insolvenz f. **in·ˈsol·vent** adj zahlungsunfähig, insolvent.

in·som·ni·a [ɪnˈsɒmnɪə] s Schlaflosigkeit f.

ˌin·soˈmuch adv: **~ that** dermaßen od. so sehr, daß.

in·spect [ɪnˈspekt] v/t **1.** untersuchen, prüfen (**for** auf acc). **2.** besichtigen, inspizieren. **in·ˈspec·tion** s **1.** Untersuchung f, Prüfung f: **on ~** bei näherer Prüfung; **for ~** ✝ zur Ansicht. **2.** Besichtigung f, Inspektion f. **in·ˈspec·tor** s **1.** Inspektor m, Aufsichtsbeamte m, Kontrolleur m (a. 🚇 etc). **2.** police ~ Br. Polizeiinspektor m, -kommissar m.

in·spi·ra·tion [ˌɪnspəˈreɪʃn] s Inspiration f: a) (eccl. göttliche) Eingebung, (plötzlicher) Einfall, b) Anregung f: **be s.o.'s ~, be an ~ to** (od. **for**) s.o. j-n inspirieren. **in·ˈspire** v/t **1.** inspirieren, anregen (**to** zu; **to do** zu tun). **2.** Gefühl etc erwecken, auslösen (**in** in dat). **3.** erfüllen (**with** mit).

in·sta·bil·i·ty [ˌɪnstəˈbɪlətɪ] s **1.** mangelnde Festigkeit od. Stabilität. **2.** Labile 🜛, 🜛 Instabilität f. **3.** fig. Unbeständigkeit f. **4.** (**emotional**) **~** fig. Labilität f.

in·stall [ɪnˈstɔːl] v/t **1.** 🜛 installieren: a) Bad etc einbauen, b) Leitung etc legen, c) Telefon etc anschließen. **2.** j-n einsetzen (**interim president**) als Interimspräsidenten. **in·stal·la·tion** [ˌɪnstəˈleɪʃn] s **1.** 🜛 Installation f, Einbau m, Anschluß m. **2.** 🜛 Anlage f, Einrichtung f. **3.** (Amts)Einsetzung f.

in·stall·ment, bsd. Br. in·stal·ment [ɪnˈstɔːlmənt] s **1.** ✝ Rate f: **by** (od. **in**) **~s** in Raten, ratenweise; **first ~** Anzahlung f (**toward**[s] auf acc); **monthly ~** Monatsrate f; **buy on** (od. **by**) **the ~ plan** Am. auf Raten kaufen. **2.** (Teil)Lieferung f (e-s Buchs etc). **3.** a) Fortsetzung f: **novel by** (od. **in**) **~s** Fortsetzungsroman *m*, b) *Rundfunk*, *TV*: Folge *f*.

in·stance ['ɪnstəns] *s* **1**. (*einzelner*) Fall: *in this ~* in diesem (besonderen) Fall. **2**. Beispiel *n*: *for ~* zum Beispiel; *as an ~ of* als Beispiel für. **3**. *at s.o.'s ~* auf j-s Veranlassung (hin), auf j-s Betreiben *od*. Drängen. **4**. ⚖ Instanz *f*: *in the last ~* in letzter Instanz; *fig*. letztlich; *in the first ~ fig*. in erster Linie; zuerst.

in·stant ['ɪnstənt] **I** *s* **1**. Moment *n*, Augenblick *m*: *in an ~*, *on the ~* sofort, augenblicklich; *at this ~* in diesem Augenblick. **II** *adj* (□ → *instantly*) **2**. sofortig, augenblicklich: *~ camera phot*. Sofortbildkamera *f*; *~ coffee* Pulverkaffee *m*; *~ meal* Fertig-, Schnellgericht *n*. **3**. *the 10th ~* ✝ der 10. dieses Monats. **4**. dringend: *be in ~ need of et*. dringend brauchen.

in·stan·ta·ne·ous [ˌɪnstən'teɪnjəs] *adj* sofortig, augenblicklich: *his death was ~* er war auf der Stelle tot. **,in·stan'ta·ne·ous·ly** *adv* sofort, auf der Stelle.

in·stant·ly ['ɪnstəntlɪ] *adv* sofort, augenblicklich.

in·stead [ɪn'sted] *adv* **1**. *~ of* an Stelle von (*od*. gen), (an)statt (gen): *~ of me* an m-r Stelle; *~ of going* (an)statt zu gehen. **2**. statt dessen, dafür.

in·step ['ɪnstep] *s anat*. Rist *m*, Spann *m*.

in·sti·gate ['ɪnstɪɡeɪt] *v/t* **1**. *j-n* aufhetzen, *a*. ⚖ anstiften (*to* zu; *to do zu* tun). **2**. *et*. *Böses* anstiften, anzetteln; *et*. in Gang setzen, in die Wege leiten. **,in·sti'ga·tion** *s* **1**. Aufhetzung *f*, Anstiftung *f*. **2**. *at s.o.'s ~* → *instance* 3.

in·stil(l) [ɪn'stɪl] *v/t* **1**. einträufeln (*into* dat). **2**. *fig*. einflößen (*into* dat).

in·stinct ['ɪnstɪŋkt] *s* Instinkt *m*: *by* (*od*. *from*) *~* instinktiv; *~ for self-preservation* Selbsterhaltungstrieb *m*. **in'stinc·tive** *adj* □ instinktiv.

in·sti·tute ['ɪnstɪtjuːt] **I** *v/t* **1**. gründen, ins Leben rufen. **2**. in Gang setzen, in die Wege leiten. **II** *s* **3**. Institut *n*. **,in·sti·'tu·tion** *s* **1**. Institution *f*, Einrichtung *f* (*beide a. sociol.*); Institut *n*; Anstalt *f*. **2**. Sitte *f*, Brauch *m*. **3**. Gründung *f*. **,in·sti'tu·tion·al** [~ʃənl] *adj* □ **1**. Instituts...; Anstalts... **2**. *bsd*. *contp*. Einheits... **,in·sti'tu·tion·al·ize** *v/t* **1**. institutionalisieren. **2**. in e-e Anstalt einweisen.

in·struct [ɪn'strʌkt] *v/t* **1**. (*in* in dat) unterrichten; ausbilden, schulen. **2**. informieren, unterrichten. **3**. instruieren, anweisen, beauftragen (*to do* zu tun). **in'struc·tion** *s* **1**. Unterricht *m*, Ausbildung *f*, Schulung *f*. **2**. Informierung *f*, Unterrichtung *f*. **3**. Instruktion *f*, Anweisung *f*, (*Computer*) Befehl *m*: *according to ~s* auftragsgemäß; vorschriftsmäßig; *~s pl for use* Gebrauchsanweisung, -anleitung *f*. **in'struc·tive** *adj* □ instruktiv, lehrreich. **in'struc·tor** *s* Lehrer *m*; Ausbilder *m*. **in'struc·tress** *s* Lehrerin *f*.

in·stru·ment ['ɪnstrəmənt] **I** *s* **1**. ⚙ Instrument *n* (*a*. 🛠): a) Werkzeug *n*: *~ of torture* Foltergerät *n*, -instrument, -werkzeug, b) (*bsd*. Meß)Gerät *n*. **2**. ♪ Instrument *n*. **3**. ✝, ⚖ Dokument *n*, Urkunde *f*. **4**. *fig*. Werkzeug *n*: a) (Hilfs)Mittel *n*, Instrument *n*, b) Handlanger(in). **II** *v/t* **5**. ♪ instrumentieren. **in·stru·men·tal** [~'mentl] *adj* □ **1**. ⚙ Instrumenten... **2**. ♪ Instrumental...: *~ music*. **3**. behilflich, förderlich: *be ~ in* beitragen zu.

in·sub·or·di·nate [ˌɪnsə'bɔːdnət] *adj* □ aufsässig.

in·sub·stan·tial [ˌɪnsəb'stænʃl] *adj* □ **1**. unkörperlich. **2**. unwirklich. **3**. wenig *od*. nicht gehaltvoll (*Essen etc*). **4**. nicht *od*. wenig stichhaltig (*Argument etc*); gegenstandslos (*Befürchtung etc*).

in·suf·fer·a·ble [ɪn'sʌfərəbl] *adj* □ unerträglich, unausstehlich.

in·suf·fi·cien·cy [ˌɪnsə'fɪʃnsɪ] *s* **1**. Unzulänglichkeit *f*. **2**. Untauglich-, Unfähigkeit *f*. **3**. 🩺 Insuffizienz *f*. **,in·suf'fi·cient** *adj* □ **1**. unzulänglich, ungenügend. **2**. untauglich, unfähig (*to do* zu tun).

in·su·lar ['ɪnsjʊlə] *adj* □ **1**. Insel... **2**. *fig*. engstirnig.

in·su·late ['ɪnsjʊleɪt] *v/t* ⚡, ⚙ isolieren (*a*. *fig*. *from* von): *insulating tape Br*. Isolierband *n*. **,in·su'la·tion** *s* Isolierung *f*.

in·su·lin ['ɪnsjʊlɪn] *s* 🩺 Insulin *n*.

in·sult *v/t* [ɪn'sʌlt] beleidigen. **II** *s* ['ɪnsʌlt] Beleidigung *f* (*to* für *od*. gen).

in·su·per·a·ble [ɪn'suːpərəbl] *adj* □ unüberwindlich (*a*. *fig*).

in·sup·port·a·ble [ˌɪnsə'pɔːtəbl] *adj* □ unerträglich, unausstehlich.

in·sur·ance [ɪn'ʃɔːrəns] *s* **1**. ✝ Versicherung f: ~ **agent** Versicherungsvertreter m; ~ **company** Versicherung(sgesellschaft f); ~ **policy** Versicherungspolice f, -schein m. **2.** ✝ Versicherungssumme f; -prämie f. **3.** fig. (Ab)Sicherung f (**against** gegen). **in'sure** v/t ✝ versichern (**against** gegen; **for** mit e-r Summe). **in'sured** s Versicherte m, f, Versicherungsnehmer(in). **in'sur·er** s Versicherer m, Versicherungsträger m: ~s pl Versicherung(sgesellschaft) f.

in·sur·mount·a·ble [ˌɪnsəˈmaʊntəbl] adj □ fig. unüberwindlich.

in·sur·rec·tion [ˌɪnsəˈrekʃn] s Aufstand m, Revolte f.

in·sus·cep·ti·ble [ˌɪnsəˈseptəbl] adj □ **1.** unempfindlich (**to** gegen): ~ **to pain** schmerzunempfindlich. **2.** unempfänglich (**to** für).

in·tact [ɪnˈtækt] adj intakt: a) unversehrt, unbeschädigt, b) ganz, vollständig.

in·take [ˈɪnteɪk] s **1.** ⊕ Einlaß(öffnung f) m. **2.** (Nahrungs- etc)Aufnahme f. **3.** aufgenommene Menge, Zufuhr f; (Neu)Aufnahme(n pl) f, (Neu)Zugänge pl.

in·tan·gi·ble [ɪnˈtændʒəbl] adj □ **1.** nicht greifbar. **2.** fig. unbestimmt, vage.

in·te·ger [ˈɪntɪdʒə] s ⅍ ganze Zahl.

in·te·gral [ˈɪntɪɡrəl] adj □ **1.** integral (Bestandteil etc). **2.** ganz, vollständig. **3.** ⅍ Integral...: ~ **calculus** Integralrechnung f.

in·te·grate [ˈɪntɪɡreɪt] **I** v/t integrieren: a) zs.-schließen (**into** zu): ~**d circuit** ⚡ integrierter Schaltkreis, b) eingliedern (**into** in acc), c) einbeziehen, einbauen (**into, with** in acc). **II** v/i sich integrieren (→ Ia, b); sich einbeziehen od. einbauen lassen. **in·te·gra·tion** s Integration f, Integrierung f.

in·te·gri·ty [ɪnˈteɡrətɪ] s **1.** Integrität f. **2.** Vollständigkeit f; Einheit f.

in·tel·lect [ˈɪntəlekt] s Intellekt m, Verstand m. **in·tel·lec·tu·al** [ˌ~ˈtjʊəl] **I** adj □ intellektuell: a) geistig, Geistes...: → **property** 1, b) verstandesbetont. **II** s Intellektuelle m, f.

in·tel·li·gence [ɪnˈtelɪdʒəns] s **1.** Intelligenz f: ~ **quotient** Intelligenzquotient m; ~ **test** Intelligenztest m. **2.** nachrichtendienstliche Informationen pl. **3.** a. ~ **service** Nachrichten-, Geheimdienst m. **in'tel·li·gent** adj □ **1.** intelligent. **2.**

vernünftig. **in·tel·li·gent·si·a** [ˌ~ˈdʒentsɪə] s (pl konstruiert) coll. die Intelligenz, die Intellektuellen pl.

in·tel·li·gi·ble [ɪnˈtelɪdʒəbl] adj □ verständlich (**to** für od. dat).

in·tem·per·ate [ɪnˈtempərət] adj □ unmäßig.

in·tend [ɪnˈtend] v/t **1.** beabsichtigen, vorhaben (**s.th.** et.; **doing, to do** zu tun): **was this ~ed?** war das Absicht? **2.** bestimmen (**for** für, zu): **it was ~ed for you** es war für dich (bestimmt od. gedacht). **3.** sagen wollen, meinen (**by** mit). **4.** bedeuten, sein wollen: **it was ~ed for** (od. **as, to be**) **a compliment** es sollte ein Kompliment sein. **in'tend·ed I** adj **1.** beabsichtigt. **2.** absichtlich. **3.** her ~ **husband** F ihr Zukünftiger. **II** s **4.** F Zukünftige m, f.

in·tense [ɪnˈtens] adj □ intensiv: a) stark, heftig: ~ **heat** starke Hitze, b) hell, grell (Licht), c) satt (Farben), d) durchdringend (Geräusch, Geruch), e) angestrengt, f) sehnlich, dringend. **in'tense·ness** s Intensität f.

in·ten·si·fi·ca·tion [ɪnˌtensɪfɪˈkeɪʃn] s Verstärkung f, Intensivierung f. **in'ten·si·fy** [~faɪ] v/t (a. v/i sich) verstärken, intensivieren.

in·ten·sive [ɪnˈtensɪv] adj □ intensiv: a) → **intense** a, b) gründlich, erschöpfend: ~ **course** Intensivkurs m; **be in** (od. **at**) **the** ~ **care unit** ✚ auf der Intensivstation liegen.

in·tent [ɪnˈtent] **I** s **1.** Absicht f, Vorsatz m (a. ⚖ǚ): **with** ~ absichtlich, mit Absicht, **bsd.** ⚖ǚ vorsätzlich. **II** adj □ **2.** **be** ~ **on doing s.th.** fest entschlossen sein, et. zu tun; et. unbedingt tun wollen. **3.** aufmerksam, gespannt (Blick etc). **in'ten·tion** s Absicht f, Vorsatz m (**of doing, to do** zu tun): **with the best** (**of**) ~s in bester Absicht; **good** ~s pl gute Vorsätze pl. **in'ten·tion·al** [~ʃənl] adj absichtlich, **bsd.** ⚖ǚ vorsätzlich: ~**ly** a. mit Absicht.

in·ter... [ˈɪntə] Zwischen...; Wechsel...

in·ter'act v/i aufeinander (ein)wirken. **in·ter'ac·tion** s Wechselwirkung f.

in·ter'breed v/t u. v/i (irr **breed**) biol. (sich) kreuzen.

in·ter·ca·lar·y [ɪnˈtɜːkələrɪ] adj Schalt...: ~ **day**; ~ **year.**

in·ter·cede [ˌɪntəˈsiːd] v/i sich verwenden *od.* einsetzen (**with** bei; **for, on be-half of** für).

in·ter·cept [ˌɪntəˈsept] *v/t* Brief, Boten, Funkspruch etc abfangen. **ˌin·terˈcep·tion** *s* Abfangen *n*. **ˌin·terˈcep·tor** *s a.* **~ plane** ✈, ✕ Abfangjäger *m*.

in·ter·ces·sion [ˌɪntəˈseʃn] *s* Fürsprache *f*.

in·ter·change I *v/t* [ˌ~ˈtʃ~] **1.** gegen- *od.* untereinander austauschen, auswechseln. **2.** Geschenke, Meinungen etc austauschen, Briefe wechseln (**with** mit). **II** *s* [ˈ~tʃ~] **3.** Austausch *m*: **~ of ideas** Gedankenaustausch. **4.** *mot.* Autobahnkreuz *n*. **5.** *a.* **~ station** Umsteig(e)bahnhof *m*, -station *f*.

ˌin·terˈcit·y *s* 📧 *Br.* Intercity *m*: **~ train** Intercityzug *m*.

in·ter·com [ˈɪntəkɒm] *s* (Gegen-, Haus-, ⚓, ✈ Bord)Sprechanlage *f*.

ˌin·terˈcom·mu·ni·cate *v/i* **1.** miteinander in Verbindung stehen. **2.** miteinander (durch e-e Tür *etc*) verbunden sein.

ˈin·terˌcon·tiˈnen·tal *adj* interkontinental, Interkontinental...: **~ ballistic missile** ✕ Interkontinentalrakete *f*.

ˈin·ter·course *s* **1.** Verkehr *m*, Umgang *m* (**with** mit): **commercial ~** Geschäfts-, Handelsverkehr. **2.** (Geschlechts)Verkehr *m*.

ˈin·terˌde·nomˈi·na·tion·al *adj* interkonfessionell, konfessionsübergreifend.

ˌin·ter·deˈpend·ence *s* gegenseitige Abhängigkeit. **ˌin·ter·deˈpend·ent** *adj* voneinander abhängig.

in·ter·dict I *s* [ˈɪntədɪkt] (amtliches) Verbot. **II** *v/t* [ˌɪntəˈdɪkt] (amtlich) verbieten.

in·ter·est [ˈɪntrəst] **I** *s* **1.** Interesse *n* (**in** an *dat*, für): **take** (*od.* **have**) **an ~ in** sich interessieren für. **2.** Reiz *m*, Interesse *n*: **be of ~** (**to**) reizvoll sein (für), interessieren (*acc*). **3.** Wichtigkeit *f*, Bedeutung *f*: **of great** (**little**) **~** von großer Wichtigkeit (von geringer Bedeutung). **4.** *bsd.* ♰ Beteiligung *f*, Anteil *m* (**in** an *dat*): **have an ~ in s.th.** an et. beteiligt sein. **5.** Interesse *n*, Vorteil *m*, Nutzen *m*: **be in** (*od.* **to**) **s.o.'s ~** in j-s Interesse liegen; **in your** (**own**) **~** zu Ihrem (eigenen) Vorteil. **6.** ♰ Zins(en *pl*) *m*: **bear** (*od.* **carry**) **~** Zinsen tragen, sich verzinsen (**at 4%** mit 4%); **~ rate, rate of ~**

Zinssatz *m*. **II** *v/t* **7.** interessieren (**in** für). **ˈin·ter·est·ed** *adj* interessiert (**in** an *dat*): **be ~ in** sich interessieren für. **ˈin·ter·est·ing** *adj* □ interessant.

ˈin·ter·face *s* ⚡ Schnittstelle *f*, (*Computer a.*) Nahtstelle *f*.

in·ter·fere [ˌɪntəˈfɪə] *v/i* **1.** (**in** in *acc*) eingreifen; sich einmischen. **2.** **~ with** j-n, et. stören, behindern; sich zu schaffen machen an (*dat*). **ˌin·terˈfer·ence** *s* **1.** Eingriff *m*; Einmischung *f*. **2.** Störung *f*, Behinderung *f* (**with** *gen*).

in·ter·im [ˈɪntərɪm] **I** *s*: **in the ~** in der Zwischenzeit, inzwischen. **II** *adj* Interims..., Zwischen...: **~ aid** Überbrückungshilfe *f*; **~ government** Interimsregierung *f*; **~ report** Zwischenbericht *m*.

in·te·ri·or [ɪnˈtɪərɪə] **I** *adj* **1.** inner..., Innen...: **~ decorator** a) Innenausstatter(in), b) *a.* **~ designer** Innenarchitekt(in). **2.** binnenländisch, Binnen...; inländisch, Inlands... **II** *s* **3.** oft *pl* das Innere. **4.** Innenraum *m*, -seite *f*. **5.** *phot.* Innenaufnahme *f*, (*Film, TV a.*) Studioaufnahme *f*. **6.** Binnenland *n*, das Innere. **7.** *pol.* innere Angelegenheiten *pl*: → **department** 3.

in·ter·ject [ˌɪntəˈdʒekt] *v/t* Bemerkung etc dazwischen-, einwerfen. **ˌin·terˈjec·tion** *s ling.* Interjektion *f*.

ˌin·terˈlace I *v/t* **1.** verflechten, -schlingen, *a. fig.* verweben. **2.** durchflechten (**with** mit) (*a. fig.*). **II** *v/i* **3.** sich verflechten.

in·ter·loc·u·tor [ˌɪntəˈlɒkjʊtə] *s* Gesprächspartner *m*.

in·ter·lop·er [ˈɪntələʊpə] *s* Eindringling *m*.

in·ter·lude [ˈɪntəluːd] *s* **1.** (*kurze*) Zeit, Periode *f*. **2.** Unterbrechung *f* (*in gen*). **3.** *thea.*, ♪ Zwischenspiel *n*, Intermezzo *n* (*beide a. fig.*).

ˌin·terˈmar·riage *s* **1.** Mischehe *f*. **2.** Heirat *f* innerhalb der Familie *od.* zwischen Blutsverwandten. **ˌin·terˈmar·ry** *v/i* **1.** e-e Mischehe eingehen; untereinander heiraten. **2.** innerhalb der Familie heiraten.

in·ter·me·di·ar·y [ˌɪntəˈmiːdjərɪ] **I** *adj* **1.** → **intermediate**. **2.** vermittelnd. **II** *s* **3.** Vermittler(in), Mittelsmann *m*. **4.** ♰ Zwischenhändler *m*. **ˌin·terˈme·di·ate** [~djət] *adj* □ **1.** Zwischen... **2.**

ped. für fortgeschrittene Anfänger.

in·ter·mez·zo [ˌɪntəˈmetsəʊ] _pl_ **-zi** [ˌtsiː],
-zos _s_ ♩ Intermezzo _n,_ Zwischenspiel _n._

in·ter·mi·na·ble [ɪnˈtɜːmɪnəbl] _adj_ □
endlos.

ˌin·ter'min·gle _v/t u. v/i_ (sich) vermischen.

ˌin·ter'mis·sion _s_ Pause _f (a. thea. etc),_
Unterbrechung _f: without ~_ pausenlos.

in·ter·mit·tent [ˌɪntəˈmɪtənt] _adj_ □ mit
Unterbrechungen, periodisch (auftre-
tend), ✻ _etc_ intermittierend: _~ fever_ ✻
Wechselfieber _n._

in·tern [ɪnˈtɜːn] _v/t_ internieren.

in·ter·nal [ɪnˈtɜːnl] _adj_ □ **1.** inner, Innen...: _~ injury (medicine)_ innere Verletzung (Medizin); _he was bleeding
~ly_ er hatte innere Blutungen. **2.** ✻,
pharm. innerlich anzuwenden(d). **3.**
einheimisch, Inlands...: _~ trade_ Binnenhandel _m._ **4.** _pol._ innenpolitisch, Innen...: _~ affairs pl_ innere Angelegenheiten _pl._ **5.** (✝ _a._ betriebs)intern.

in·ter·nal-com·bus·tion en·gine _s_ ◎
Verbrennungsmotor _m._

in·ter·nal·ize [ɪnˈtɜːnəlaɪz] _v/t_ verinnerli-
chen.

ˌin·ter'na·tion·al I _adj_ □ **1.** international: _~ law_ Völkerrecht _n;_ 2 _Monetary
Fund_ Internationaler Währungsfonds;
~ reply coupon ✍ internationaler Antwortschein. **2.** Auslands...: _~ call_
teleph. Auslandsgespräch _n; ~ flight_
Auslandsflug _m._ **II** _s_ **3.** _Sport:_ Internationale _m, f,_ Nationalspieler(in); Länderkampf _m,_ -spiel _n._ **ˌin·ter'na·tion-
·al·ize** _v/t_ internationalisieren.

in·tern·ee [ˌɪntɜːˈniː] _s_ Internierte _m, f._

in·tern·ist [ɪnˈtɜːnɪst] _s_ ✻ Internist(in).

in·tern·ment [ɪnˈtɜːnmənt] _s_ Internie-
rung _f: ~ camp_ Internierungslager _n._

'in·ter·phone → **intercom.**

ˌin·ter'plan·e·ta·ry _adj_ interplane-
tar(isch).

'in·ter·play _s_ Wechselspiel _n._

in·ter·pret [ɪnˈtɜːprɪt] **I** _v/t_ **1.** auslegen,
interpretieren (_as_ als). **2.** dolmetschen.
3. _Daten etc_ auswerten. **II** _v/i_ **4.** dolmetschen (_for s.o._ j-m). **in·ter·pre·ta·tion** _s_
1. Auslegung _f,_ Interpretation _f._ **2.**
Dolmetschen _n._ **3.** Auswertung _f._ **in-
'ter·pret·er** _s_ Dolmetscher(in).

ˌin·ter·re'lat·ed _adj_ in Wechselbezie-

hung stehend, zs.-hängend. **ˌin·ter·re-
'la·tion** _s_ Wechselbeziehung _f._

in·ter·ro·gate [ɪnˈterəʊgeɪt] _v/t_ verhören, -nehmen. **in·ter·ro·ga·tion** _s_ **1.**
Verhör _n,_ Vernehmung _f._ **2.** Frage _f (a.
ling.): ~ mark (od. point)_ Fragezeichen
_n._ **in·ter·rog·a·tive** [ˌɪntəˈrɒgətɪv] _adj_
□ **1.** fragend. **2.** _ling._ Interrogativ...,
Frage...: _~ pronoun_ Interrogativpro-
nomen _n,_ Fragefürwort _n._ **ˌin·ter'rog-
·a·to·ry** [ˌtərɪ] _adj_ fragend.

in·ter·rupt [ˌɪntəˈrʌpt] **I** _v/t_ unterbrechen
(_a._ ⚡), _j-m_ ins Wort fallen. **II** _v/i: don't
~!_ unterbrich mich _etc_ nicht! _v/i:_ **ˌin·ter-
'rupt·ed·ly** _adv_ mit Unterbrechungen.
ˌin·ter'rupt·er _s_ ⚡ Unterbrecher _m._
ˌin·ter'rup·tion _s_ Unterbrechung _f:
without ~_ ununterbrochen.

in·ter·sect [ˌɪntəˈsekt] **I** _v/t_ (durch-)
schneiden, (-)kreuzen. **II** _v/i_ sich
schneiden _od._ kreuzen. **ˌin·ter'sec·tion**
_s_ **1.** ✱ Schnitt _m:_ (_point of_) ~ Schnittpunkt _m._ **2.** (Straßen)Kreuzung _f._

in·ter·sperse [ˌɪntəˈspɜːs] _v/t_ **1.** einstreuen. **2.** durchsetzen (_with_ mit).

'in·ter·state _adj Am._ zwischenstaatlich:
~ highway (zwei _od._ mehrere _Bundes-
staaten_ verbindende) Autobahn.

in·ter·stice [ɪnˈtɜːstɪs] _s_ **1.** Zwischenraum _m._ **2.** Lücke _f,_ Spalt _m._

ˌin·ter'twine, ˌin·ter'twist _v/t u. v/i_ (sich)
verflechten _od._ verschlingen.

ˌin·ter'ur·ban _adj_ zwischen mehreren
Städten (bestehend _od._ verkehrend): _~
traffic_ Überlandverkehr _m._

in·ter·val ['ɪntəvl] _s_ **1.** (_zeitlicher od.
räumlicher_) Abstand, (_zeitlich a._) Intervall _n: at regular ~s_ in regelmäßigen
Abständen. **2.** _Br._ Pause _f (a. thea. etc),_
Unterbrechung _f: ~ signal_ (_Rundfunk,
TV_) Pausenzeichen _n._ **3.** ♩, ✱ Intervall _n._

in·ter·vene [ˌɪntəˈviːn] _v/i_ **1.** eingreifen,
-schreiten, _bsd._ ✕, _pol._ intervenieren.
2. (_zeitlich_) dazwischenliegen. **3.** sich
inzwischen ereignen; dazwischenkom-
men: _if nothing ~s_ wenn nichts dazwi-
schenkommt. **in·ter·ven·tion** [ˌ~'ven-
ʃn] _s_ Eingreifen _n,_ -schreiten _n,_ Intervention _f._

in·ter·view ['ɪntəvjuː] **I** _s_ **1.** Interview _n:
give s.o. an ~._ **2.** Einstellungsgespräch
_n._ **II** _v/t_ **3.** interviewen. **4.** ein Einstellungsgespräch führen mit. **in·ter·view-**

ee [~'i:] s Interviewte m, f. 'in·ter·
,view·er s Interviewer(in).

in·ter'weave v/t (irr weave) 1. (miteinander) verweben od. verflechten (a.
fig.). 2. vermengen, -mischen (with mit)
(beide a. fig.).

in·tes·tate [in'testeit] adj: die ~ ɪ̌ɪ̌ ohne
Hinterlassung e-s Testaments sterben.

in·tes·tine [in'testin] s anat. Darm m: ~s
pl Gedärme pl; large ~ Dickdarm;
small ~ Dünndarm.

in·ti·ma·cy ['intiməsi] s Intimität f: a)
Vertrautheit f, b) (a. contp. plumpe)
Vertraulichkeit f, c) intime (sexuelle) Be-
ziehungen pl, d) Gemütlichkeit f.

in·ti·mate¹ ['intimət] adj □ intim: a) vertraut, eng (Freund etc), b) vertraulich
(Mitteilung etc), contp. a. plump-vertraulich, c) in sexuellen Beziehungen
stehend (with mit), d) anheimelnd, gemütlich (Atmosphäre etc), e) innerst
(Wünsche etc), f) gründlich, genau
(Kenntnisse etc): be on ~ terms (with)
auf vertrautem Fuße stehen (mit); intime Beziehungen haben (zu).

in·ti·mate² ['intimeit] v/t 1. andeuten: ~
to s.o. that j-m zu verstehen geben,
daß. 2. ankündigen; mitteilen. ,in·ti·
'ma·tion s 1. Andeutung f. 2. Ankündigung f; Mitteilung f.

in·tim·i·date [in'timideit] v/t einschüchtern: ~ s.o. into doing s.th. j-n nötigen,
et. zu tun. in,tim·i'da·tion s Einschüchterung f.

in·to ['intu] prp 1. in (acc), in (acc) ...
hinein. 2. gegen: → crash 6, etc. 3.
Zustandsänderung: zu: make water →
ice. 4. ⅋ in (acc): → divide 4. 5. be ~ F
stehen auf (acc).

in·tol·er·a·ble [in'tɔlərəbl] adj □ unerträglich. in'tol·er·ance s Intoleranz f.
in'tol·er·ant adj □ intolerant (of gegenüber): be ~ of s.th. et. nicht dulden
od. tolerieren.

in·to·na·tion [,intəu'neiʃn] s 1. ling. Intonation f, Satzmelodie f. 2. Tonfall m. 3.
♪ Intonation f. in'tone v/t ♪ intonieren: a) Lied etc anstimmen, b) Ton angeben.

in·tox·i·cant [in'tɔksikənt] I adj berauschend (a. fig.). II s Rauschmittel n,
bsd. berauschendes Getränk. in'tox·
i·cate [~keit] v/t berauschen (a. fig.).
in,tox·i·ca·tion s Rausch m (a. fig.).

in·trac·ta·ble [in'træktəbl] adj □ 1. eigensinnig. 2. hartnäckig (Krankheit,
Problem etc).

in·tran·si·gent [in'trænsidʒənt] adj □
unnachgiebig.

in·tran·si·tive [in'trænsətiv] adj □ ling.
intransitiv.

in·tra·ve·nous [,intrə'vi:nəs] adj □
anat., ⚕ intravenös.

in·trep·id [in'trepid] adj □ unerschrok-
ken.

in·tri·ca·cy ['intrikəsi] s 1. Kompliziertheit f. 2. Verworrenheit f. in·tri·cate
['~kət] adj □ 1. verwickelt, kompliziert. 2. verworren.

in·trigue [in'tri:g] I v/t faszinieren; interessieren; neugierig machen. II v/i intrigieren (against gegen). III s Intrige f.
in'tri·guer s Intrigant(in). in'tri·guing
adj □ 1. faszinierend; interessant. 2.
intrigant.

in·trin·sic [in'trinsik] adj 1. inner. 2. wesentlich.

in·tro·duce [,intrə'dju:s] v/t 1. neue Methode etc einführen. 2. (to) j-n bekannt
machen (mit), vorstellen (dat). 3. (to)
j-n einführen (in e-n Fach etc), bekannt
machen (mit). 4. Redner, Programm
etc ankündigen. 5. Gedanken, Gesetz-
zesvorlage etc einbringen (into in acc).
6. (into in acc) einfügen; (hinein)stek-
ken, einführen. in·tro·duc·tion [~'dʌk-
ʃn] s 1. Einführung f. 2. Vorstellung f.
3. Einleitung f, Vorwort n. 4. Leitfaden
m (to gen). 5. Einbringung f. ,in·tro·
'duc·to·ry [~təri] adj 1. Einführungs...:
~ price. 2. einleitend, Einleitungs...

in·tro·spec·tion [,intrəu'spekʃn] s Selbst-
beobachtung f. ,in·tro'spec·tive [~tiv]
adj □ introspektiv.

in·tro·vert ['intrəuvə:t] adj psych. introvertiert.

in·trude [in'tru:d] I v/t 1. ~ o.s. → 3. 2.
aufdrängen (s.th. on s.o. j-m et.; o.s.
on s.o. sich j-m). II v/i 3. sich eindrängen (into in acc) (a. fig.). 4. sich aufdrängen (on dat). 5. stören (on s.o. j-n).
in'trud·er s 1. Eindringling m. 2. Störenfried m.

in·tru·sion [in'tru:ʒn] s Störung f (on
gen). in'tru·sive [~siv] adj □ aufdringlich.

in·tu·i·tion [,intju:'iʃn] s Intuition f.
in'tu·i·tive [~tiv] adj □ intuitiv.

in·un·date [ˈɪnʌndeɪt] v/t überschwemmen, -fluten (*beide a.* fig.). **,in·un'da·tion** s Überschwemmung f, -flutung f.

in·ure [ɪˈnjʊə] v/t (*to*) abhärten (gegen), fig. a. gewöhnen (an acc).

in·vade [ɪnˈveɪd] v/t **1.** einfallen *od.* eindringen in (acc), ✕ a. einmarschieren in (acc). **2.** sich ausbreiten über (acc) *od.* in (dat), erfüllen. **3.** fig. überlaufen, -schwemmen. **4.** j-s Privatsphäre etc verletzen, in j-s Rechte eingreifen. **in'vad·er** s **1.** Eindringling m. **2.** pl ✕ Invasoren pl.

in·va·lid¹ [ˈɪnvəlɪd] **I** adj **1.** krank, gebrechlich; invalid, arbeits-, erwerbsunfähig; kriegsbeschädigt. **2.** Kranken... **II** s **3.** Kranke m, f, Gebrechliche m, f; Invalide m, Arbeits-, Erwerbsunfähige m, f; Pflegefall m. **III** v/t [ˈɪnvəliːd] **4.** zum Invaliden machen.

in·val·id² [ɪnˈvælɪd] adj □ (rechts)ungültig, unwirksam. **in'val·i·date** [ˌdeɪt] v/t für ungültig erklären. **in,val·i'da·tion** s Ungültigkeitserklärung f.

in·va·lid·i·ty¹ [ˌɪnvəˈlɪdətɪ] s Invalidität f, Arbeits-, Erwerbsunfähigkeit f.

in·va·lid·i·ty² [∼] s (Rechts)Ungültigkeit f.

in·val·u·a·ble [ɪnˈvæljʊəbl] adj □ unschätzbar, von unschätzbarem Wert (*beide a.* fig.): **be ~ to s.o.** für j-n von unschätzbarem Wert sein.

in·var·i·a·ble [ɪnˈveərɪəbl] adj □ unveränderlich, gleichbleibend.

in·va·sion [ɪnˈveɪʒn] s **1.** (*of*) Einfall m (in acc), Eindringen n (in acc), ✕ a. Invasion f (gen), Einmarsch m (in acc): **~ of tourists** Touristeninvasion. **2.** fig. (*of*) Verletzung f (gen), Eingriff m (in acc).

in·vec·tive [ɪnˈvektɪv] s Beschimpfung(en pl) f, Schmähung(en pl) f.

in·veigh [ɪnˈveɪ] v/i (*against*) schimpfen (über *od.* auf acc), herziehen (über acc).

in·vei·gle [ɪnˈveɪgl] v/t verleiten, -führen (*into* zu; *into doing s.th.* dazu, et. zu tun).

in·vent [ɪnˈvent] v/t erfinden, et. Unwahres a. erdichten. **in'ven·tion** s Erfindung f. **in'ven·tive** [∼tɪv] adj □ **1.** erfinderisch. **2.** einfallsreich. **in'ven·tor** s Erfinder(in).

in·ven·to·ry [ˈɪnvəntrɪ] ✝ **I** s **1.** Inventar n: a) Bestandsliste f: **make** (*od.* **take**) **an ~ of** → 3, b) (Waren-, Lager)Bestand m. **2.** Inventur f. **II** v/t **3.** e-e Bestandsliste machen von.

in·verse [ˌɪnˈvɜːs] adj □ umgekehrt: *in ~ order* in umgekehrter Reihenfolge. **in'ver·sion** s **1.** Umkehrung f. **2.** ♫, ling. etc Inversion f.

in·vert [ɪnˈvɜːt] v/t **1.** umkehren: *~ed commas* pl bsd. Br. Anführungszeichen pl. **2.** umwenden, umstülpen: *~ s.th. over* et. stülpen über (acc).

in·ver·te·brate [ɪnˈvɜːtɪbreɪt] zo. **I** adj wirbellos. **II** s wirbelloses Tier.

in·vest [ɪnˈvest] **I** v/t **1.** ✝ (*in*) investieren (in acc *od.* dat), anlegen (in dat). **2.** *~ s.o. with* j-m et. verleihen; j-n mit Befugnissen etc ausstatten. **II** v/i **3.** *~ in a)* ✝ investieren in (acc *od.* dat), sein Geld anlegen in (dat), b) F sich et. kaufen *od.* zulegen.

in·ves·ti·gate [ɪnˈvestɪgeɪt] **I** v/t Verbrechen etc untersuchen, Ermittlungen *od.* Nachforschungen anstellen über (acc), Fall recherchieren, j-n, Anspruch etc überprüfen, e-r Beschwerde etc nachgehen, Gebiet etc (wissenschaftlich) erforschen. **II** v/i ermitteln, recherchieren, Ermittlungen *od.* Nachforschungen anstellen (*into* über acc): *investigating committee* Untersuchungsausschuß m. **in,ves·ti'ga·tion** s Untersuchung f (*into*, *of* gen), Nachforschung f, Recherche f, Überprüfung f: *be under ~* untersucht werden.

in·vest·ment [ɪnˈvestmənt] s ✝ Investition f, (Kapital)Anlage f; Anlagekapital n: *~ adviser* (*od.* **consultant**) Anlageberater(in); *~ trust* Kapitalanlagegesellschaft f. **in'vest·or** s Investor m, Kapitalanleger m.

in·vet·er·ate [ɪnˈvetərət] adj □ **1.** eingewurzelt, unausrottbar. **2.** ♣ hartnäckig; chronisch. **3.** eingefleischt, unverbesserlich.

in·vid·i·ous [ɪnˈvɪdɪəs] adj □ gehässig, boshaft.

in·vig·or·ate [ɪnˈvɪgəreɪt] v/t stärken, kräftigen; beleben, anregen; er-, aufmuntern.

in·vin·ci·ble [ɪnˈvɪnsəbl] adj □ **1.** ✕, Sport: unbesiegbar. **2.** fig. unüberwindlich.

in·vis·i·ble [ɪnˈvɪzəbl] adj □ unsichtbar (*to* für).

in·vi·ta·tion [ˌɪnvɪˈteɪʃn] s **1.** Einladung f

(**to** an *acc*; zu): **at the ~ of** auf Einladung von (*od. gen*). **2.** (höfliche) Aufforderung, Ersuchen *n*. **3.** Herausforderung *f*: **be an ~ for → invite** 4. **in·vite** *v/t* **1.** einladen (**to dinner** zum Essen). **2.** (höflich) auffordern, ersuchen (**to do** zu tun). **3.** bitten *od*. ersuchen um, erbitten. **4.** herausfordern (zu), einladen zu.

in·vo·ca·tion [ˌɪnvəˈkeɪʃn] *s* **1.** Anrufung *f* (**to** gen). **2.** Beschwörung *f*.

in·voice [ˈɪnvɔɪs] † **I** *s* (Waren)Rechnung *f*, Faktura *f*. **II** *v/t* fakturieren, in Rechnung stellen.

in·voke [ɪnˈvəʊk] *v/t* **1.** flehen um, erflehen. **2.** *Gott etc* anrufen. *Geist etc* beschwören.

in·vol·un·tar·y [ɪnˈvɒləntərɪ] *adj* □ **1.** unfreiwillig. **2.** unabsichtlich. **3.** unwillkürlich.

in·volve [ɪnˈvɒlv] *v/t* **1.** a) *j-n* verwickeln, hineinziehen (**in** in *acc*): **~d in an accident** in e-n Unfall verwickelt, b) *j-n, et.* angehen, betreffen: **the persons ~d** die Betroffenen. **2. be ~d** zu tun haben (**with** mit). **3.** zur Folge haben, nach sich ziehen; verbunden sein mit; erfordern, nötig machen. **in·volved** *adj* kompliziert; verworren.

in·vul·ner·a·ble [ɪnˈvʌlnərəbl] *adj* □ **1.** unverwundbar (*a. fig*). **2.** *fig*. unanfechtbar, hieb- u. stichfest.

in·ward [ˈɪnwəd] **I** *adv* **1.** einwärts, nach innen. **2. → inwardly** 1, 2. **II** *adj* **3.** innerlich, inner (*beide a. fig*), Innen... **'in·ward·ly** *adv* **1.** innerlich, im Inner(e)n (*beide a. fig*). **2.** *fig*. im stillen, insgeheim. **3. → inward** 1. **in·wards** [~z] *→* **inward** I.

i·o·dine [ˈaɪəʊdiːn] *s* ⁊ Jod *n*.

i·on [ˈaɪən] *s* ⁊, *phys*. Ion *n*. **i·on·ic** [aɪˈɒnɪk] *adj* Ionen...

i·o·ta [aɪˈəʊtə] *s fig* Jota *n*: **not an ~ of truth** kein Körnchen Wahrheit.

IOU [ˌaɪəʊˈjuː] *s* Schuldschein *m* (= *I owe you*).

i·ras·ci·ble [ɪˈræsəbl] *adj* □ jähzornig, reizbar.

i·rate [aɪˈreɪt] *adj* zornig, wütend.

ir·i·des [ˈaɪrɪdiːz] *pl von* **iris**.

ir·i·des·cent [ˌɪrɪˈdesnt] *adj* □ (*in den Regenbogenfarben*) schillernd.

i·ris [ˈaɪərɪs] *pl* **'i·ris·es**, **ir·i·des** [ˈaɪrɪdiːz] *s* **1.** *anat*. Iris *f*, Regenbogen-

haut *f*. **2.** ⚘ Iris *f*, Schwertlilie *f*.

I·rish [ˈaɪərɪʃ] **I** *adj* **1.** irisch: **~ coffee** Irish Coffee *m*. **II** *s* **2. the ~** *pl* die Iren *pl*. **3.** *ling*. Irisch *n*. **~·man** [ˈ~mən] *s* (*irr* **man**) Ire *m*. **'~·wom·an** *s* (*irr* **woman**) Irin *f*.

irk [ɜːk] *v/t* **1.** ärgern, verdrießen. **2.** ermüden, langweilen. **irk·some** [ˈɜːksəm] *adj* □ **1.** ärgerlich, verdrießlich. **2.** ermüdend, langweilig.

i·ron [ˈaɪən] **I** *s* **1.** Eisen *n*: **have several ~s in the fire** *fig*. mehrere Eisen im Feuer haben; **strike while the ~ is hot** *fig*. das Eisen schmieden, solange es heiß ist; **will of ~** eiserner Wille. **2.** Bügeleisen *n*. **II** *adj* **3.** eisern (*a. fig*), Eisen...: ⚷ **Curtain** *pol*. Eiserner Vorhang; **~ lung** ⚚ eiserne Lunge; **~ ore** *min*. Eisenerz *n*. **III** *v/t* **4.** bügeln: **~ out** ausbügeln; *fig. Meinungsverschiedenheiten etc* aus der Welt schaffen, beseitigen.

i·ron·ic, i·ron·i·cal [aɪˈrɒnɪk(l)] *adj* □ ironisch.

i·ron·ing board [ˈaɪənɪŋ] *s* Bügelbrett *n*.

'i·ron·work *s* **1.** Eisenbeschläge *pl*. **2.** *pl* (*oft sg konstruiert*) Eisenhütte *f*.

i·ro·ny [ˈaɪərənɪ] *s* Ironie *f*: **~ of fate** Ironie des Schicksals.

ir·ra·tion·al [ɪˈræʃənl] *adj* □ **1.** irrational, unvernünftig. **2.** Ⅰ irrational.

ir·rec·og·niz·a·ble [ɪˈrekəgnaɪzəbl] *adj* □ nicht zu erkennen(d) *od*. wiederzuerkennen(d), unkenntlich.

ir·rec·on·cil·a·ble [ɪˈrekənsaɪləbl] *adj* □ **1.** unvereinbar (**with** mit). **2.** unversöhnlich.

ir·re·cov·er·a·ble [ˌɪrɪˈkʌvərəbl] *adj* □ nicht wiedergutzumachen(d), unersetzlich, -bar (*Verlust etc*).

ir·re·deem·a·ble [ˌɪrɪˈdiːməbl] *adj* □ **1.** † unkündbar (*Obligation etc*). **2.** nicht wiedergutzumachen(d) (*Verlust etc*).

ir·ref·u·ta·ble [ɪˈrefjʊtəbl] *adj* □ unwiderlegbar.

ir·reg·u·lar [ɪˈregjʊlə] *adj* □ **1.** unregelmäßig (*a. ling*). **2.** regel- *od*. vorschriftswidrig. **ir·reg·u·lar·i·ty** [~ˈlærətɪ] *s* **1.** Unregelmäßigkeit *f*. **2.** Regel- *od*. Vorschriftswidrigkeit *f*.

ir·rel·e·vance, ir·rel·e·van·cy [ɪˈreləvəns(ɪ)] *s* Irrelevanz *f*, Unerheblichkeit *f*, Belanglosigkeit *f*. **ir·rel·e·vant** *adj* □ irrelevant, unerheblich, belanglos (**to** für).

ir·re·me·di·a·ble [ˌɪrɪˈmiːdjəbl] *adj* ☐ nicht behebbar *od.* abstellbar.

ir·re·mis·si·ble [ˌɪrɪˈmɪsəbl] *adj* ☐ unverzeihlich.

ir·re·mov·a·ble [ˌɪrɪˈmuːvəbl] *adj* ☐ unabsetzbar.

ir·rep·a·ra·ble [ɪˈrepərəbl] *adj* ☐ irreparabel, nicht wieder gutzumachen(d).

ir·re·place·a·ble [ˌɪrɪˈpleɪsəbl] *adj* ☐ unersetzlich, -bar.

ir·re·press·i·ble [ˌɪrɪˈpresəbl] *adj* ☐ un(be)zähmbar.

ir·re·proach·a·ble [ˌɪrɪˈprəʊtʃəbl] *adj* ☐ untadelig, tadellos.

ir·re·sist·i·ble [ˌɪrɪˈzɪstəbl] *adj* ☐ unwiderstehlich.

ir·res·o·lute [ɪˈrezəluːt] *adj* ☐ unentschlossen, unschlüssig.

ir·re·spec·tive [ˌɪrɪˈspektɪv] *adj* ☐: **~ of** ohne Rücksicht auf (*acc*).

ir·re·spon·si·ble [ˌɪrɪˈspɒnsəbl] *adj* ☐ **1.** verantwortungslos: a) unzuverlässig, b) unverantwortlich. **2.** ⚖ unzurechnungsfähig; nicht haftbar (**for** für).

ir·re·triev·a·ble [ˌɪrɪˈtriːvəbl] *adj* ☐ unersetzlich, -bar.

ir·rev·er·ence [ɪˈrevərəns] *s* Respektlosigkeit *f*. **ir·rev·er·ent** *adj* ☐ respektlos.

ir·re·vers·i·ble [ˌɪrɪˈvɜːsəbl] → **irrevocable.**

ir·rev·o·ca·ble [ɪˈrevəkəbl] *adj* ☐ unwiderruflich, unumstößlich.

ir·ri·gate [ˈɪrɪgeɪt] *v/t* **1.** 🖉 bewässern. **2.** ⚕ *Wunde etc* ausspülen. **ir·ri·ga·tion** *s* **1.** 🖉 Bewässerung *f*: **~ ditch** Bewässerungsgraben *m*. **2.** ⚕ Ausspülung *f*.

ir·ri·ta·ble [ˈɪrɪtəbl] *adj* ☐ reizbar. **ir·ri·tate** [ˈ~teɪt] *v/t* reizen, (ver)ärgern: **~d at** (**by**, **with**) verärgert *od.* ärgerlich über (*acc*). **ir·ri·tat·ing** *adj* ☐ ärgerlich. **ir·ri·ta·tion** *s* Verärgerung *f*; Ärger *m* (**at** über *acc*).

is [ɪz] *er, sie, es* ist.

Is·lam [ˈɪzlɑːm] *s* Islam *m*. **Is·lam·ic** [ɪzˈlæmɪk] *adj* islamisch.

is·land [ˈaɪlənd] *s* **1.** Insel *f*. **2.** Verkehrsinsel *f*. **'is·land·er** *s* Inselbewohner(in).

isn't [ˈɪznt] *F* für **is not.**

i·so·late [ˈaɪsəleɪt] *v/t* **1.** a. ⚕ isolieren, absondern (**from** von). **2.** 🔬 *etc* isolieren. **3.** *fig.* a) isoliert *od.* einzeln betrachten, b) trennen (**from** von). **'i·so·lat·ed** *adj* **1.** isoliert, abgesondert. **2.**

einzeln, vereinzelt: **~ case** Einzelfall *m*. **3.** abgeschieden. **i·so·la·tion** *s* **1.** Isolierung *f*, Absonderung *f*: **~ ward** ⚕ Isolierstation *f*. **2.** 🔬 *etc* → **isolate** 3a. **3.** Abgeschiedenheit *f*: **live in ~** zurückgezogen leben.

i·so·met·rics [ˌaɪsəʊˈmetrɪks] *s pl* (*a. sg konstruiert*) Isometrik *f*.

i·sos·ce·les [aɪˈsɒsɪliːz] *adj* Å gleichschenk(e)lig (*Dreieck*).

i·so·tope [ˈaɪsəʊtəʊp] *s phys.* Isotop *n*.

Is·rae·li [ɪzˈreɪlɪ] **I** *adj* israelisch. **II** *s* Israeli *m, f*.

is·sue [ˈɪʃuː] **I** *s* **1.** Ausgabe *f*, Erlaß *m*. **2.** 🕀 Ausgabe *f*, Emission *f*, Begebung *f*, Auflegung *f*, Ausstellung *f*. **3.** Ausgabe *f* (*e-r Zeitung etc*). **4.** Streitfrage *f*, -punkt *m*: **be at ~** zur Debatte stehen; **point at ~** strittige Frage. **5.** Ausgang *m*, Ergebnis *n*: **bring to an ~** zur Entscheidung bringen; **force an ~** e-e Entscheidung erzwingen. **6.** ⚖ Nachkommen(schaft *f) pl*: **die without ~** kinderlos sterben. **II** *v/t* **7.** *Befehle etc* ausgeben, *a.* ⚔ *Haftbefehl* erlassen. **8.** 🕀 *Banknoten, Wertpapiere etc* ausgeben, *Anleihe* begeben, auflegen, *Dokument, Wechsel etc* ausstellen. **9.** *Zeitung etc* herausgeben. **10.** *bsd.* ⚔ *Munition etc* ausgeben. **III** *v/i* **11.** heraus-, hervorkommen. **12.** herausfließen, -strömen. **13.** herrühren (**from** von).

isth·mus [ˈɪsməs] *pl* **-mus·es, -mi** [ˈ~maɪ] *s* Landenge *f*, Isthmus *m*.

it [ɪt] *pron* **1.** es (*nom od. acc*). **2.** *auf schon Genanntes bezogen:* er, ihm, ihn, sie. **3.** *unpersönliches od. grammatisches Subjekt:* es: **~ is raining; oh, ~ was you** oh, Sie waren es *od.* das. **4.** *unbestimmtes Objekt (oft unübersetzt)* es: → **foot** 4, *etc.* **5.** *verstärkend:* **~ is to him that you should turn** an ihn solltest du dich wenden.

I·tal·ian [ɪˈtæljən] **I** *adj* **1.** italienisch. **II** *s* **2.** Italiener(in). **3.** *ling.* Italienisch *n*.

i·tal·ic [ɪˈtælɪk] *typ.* **I** *adj* kursiv. **II** *s oft pl* Kursivschrift *f*: **in ~s** kursiv. **i'tal·i·cize** [ˈ~saɪz] *v/t* kursiv drucken.

itch [ɪtʃ] **I** *s* **1.** Jucken *n*, Juckreiz *m*. **2.** ⚕ Krätze *f*. **3.** *fig.* Verlangen *n* (**for** nach): **have** (*od.* **feel**) **an ~ to** *od.* **~ to do s.th.** große Lust haben *od.* darauf brennen, et. zu tun. **II** *v/i* **4.** jucken, (*Pullover etc* a.) kratzen. **5.** *fig.* F **be ~ing for s.th.** et.

unbedingt (haben) wollen; *he's ~ing to try it* es reizt *od.* juckt ihn, es zu versuchen. **III** *v/t* **6.** *j-n* jucken, kratzen. **itch·y** *adj* juckend; kratzend: → **palm¹** 1.

i·tem ['aɪtəm] *s* **1.** Punkt *m* (*der Tagesordnung etc*), (*Bilanz- etc*)Posten *m.* **2.** (Waren)Artikel *m; weitS.* Gegenstand *m,* Ding *m.* **3.** (*Presse-, Zeitungs*)Notiz *f,* (*a. Rundfunk, TV*) Nachricht *f,* Meldung *f.* **i·tem·ize** ['~maɪz] *v/t* Rechnungsposten einzeln aufführen, *a.* Rechnung spezifizieren, *Kosten etc* aufgliedern.

i·tin·er·ant [ɪ'tɪnərənt] *adj* □ (*beruflich*) reisend, Reise..., Wander... **i·tin·er·ar·y** [aɪ'tɪnərərɪ] *s* **1.** Reiseweg *m,* -route *f;* Reiseplan *m.* **2.** Reiseführer *m* (*Buch*). **i·tin·er·ate**

[ɪ'tɪnəreɪt] *v/i* (herum)reisen.

it'll ['ɪtl] F *für it will.*

its [ɪts] *pron* sein, s-e, ihr, ihre.

it's [ɪts] F *für it is; it has.*

it·self [ɪt'self] *pron* **1.** *reflex* sich. **2.** sich selbst. **3.** *verstärkend:* selbst: *by ~* (für sich) allein; von allein *od.* selbst.

it·sy-bit·sy [ˌɪtsɪ'bɪtsɪ] *adj* F klitzeklein, winzig.

I've [aɪv] F *für I have.*

i·vo·ry ['aɪvərɪ] **I** *s* **1.** Elfenbein *n.* **2.** *pl sl.* (*bsd.* Klavier)Tasten *pl: tickle the ivories* (auf dem Klavier) klimpern. **II** *adj* **3.** elfenbeinern, Elfenbein...: *live in an ~ tower fig.* in e-m Elfenbeinturm leben *od.* sitzen.

i·vy ['aɪvɪ] *s* ♀ Efeu *m:* ♀ *League* Eliteuniversitäten im Osten der USA.

J

jab [dʒæb] **I** *v/t* **1.** (hinein)stechen, (-)stoßen (*into in acc*). **2.** stechen, stoßen (*at* nach; *with* mit). **III** *s* **3.** Stich *m,* Stoß *m.* **4.** *Boxen:* Jab *m.* **5.** ✍ F Spritze *f.*

jab·ber ['dʒæbə] **I** *v/t a. ~ out* (daher)plappern, *Gebet etc* herunterrasseln. **II** *v/i a. ~ away* plappern, schwatzen. **III** *s* Geplapper *n,* Geschwätz *n.*

jack [dʒæk] **I** *s* **1.** ♀ F *für John: before you could say* ♀ *Robinson* im Nu, im Handumdrehen; *every man ~* jeder, alle. **2.** *Kartenspiel:* Bube *m: ~ of hearts* Herzbube *m.* **3.** ⚙ Hebevorrichtung *f:* (*car*) *~* Wagenheber *m.* **II** *v/t* **4.** hochheben, *Auto* aufbocken.

jack·al ['dʒækɔːl] *s zo.* Schakal *m.*

'jack·ass *s* **1.** (männlicher) Esel. **2.** *fig.* Esel *m,* Dummkopf *m.* **'~boot** *s* **1.** Stulp(en)stiefel *m.* **2.** Wasserstiefel *m.* **'~daw** ['~dɔː] *s orn.* Dohle *f.*

jack·et ['dʒækɪt] *s* **1.** Jacke *f,* Jackett *n.* **2.** ⚙ Mantel *m.* **3.** (Schutz)Umschlag *m,* (*Buch-, Am. a. Schallplatten*)Hülle *f.* **4.** Schale *f: potatoes pl* (*boiled*) *in their*

~s, ~ potatoes pl Pellkartoffeln *pl.* *~ crown s* ⚙ Jacketkrone *f.*

'jack\|ham·mer *s* ⚙ Preßlufthammer *m.* **'~-in-the-box** *pl* **'~-in-the-ˌbox·es,** **'~-s-in-the-box** *s* Schachtelmännchen *n,* -teufel *m.* **'~knife** *s* (*irr knife*) Klappmesser *n.* **ˌ~-of-'all-trades** *s a. contp.* Hansdampf *m* in allen Gassen. **'~pot** *s Poker etc:* Jackpot *m: hit the ~* F den Jackpot gewinnen; *fig.* das große Los ziehen (*with* mit).

jade [dʒeɪd] *s min.* Jade *m, f.*

jad·ed ['dʒeɪdɪd] *adj* **1.** erschöpft, ermattet. **2.** abgestumpft, übersättigt. **3.** schal, reizlos geworden.

jag [dʒæg] **I** *s* **1.** Zacke *f.* **2.** Loch *n,* Riß *m.* **II** *v/t* **3.** e-n Loch reißen in (*acc.*). **jag·ged** ['~gɪd], **'jag·gy** *adj* □ **1.** (aus)gezackt, zackig. **2.** zerklüftet (*Steilküste etc*).

jag·uar ['dʒægjʊə] *s zo.* Jaguar *m.*

jail [dʒeɪl] **I** *s* Gefängnis *n: in ~* im Gefängnis; *put in ~* → **II.** **II** *v/t* einsperren. **'~bird** *s* F Knastbruder *m,* Knacki *m.* **'~break** *s* Ausbruch *m* (aus dem Gefängnis). **'~ˌbreak·er** *s* Ausbrecher *m*

jail·er ['dʒeɪlə] s Gefängniswärter m, -aufseher m.

ja·lop·(p)y [dʒə'lɒpɪ] s F alte Kiste od. Mühle (Auto, Flugzeug).

jam¹ [dʒæm] s Marmelade f.

jam² [~] I v/t **1.** (hinein)pressen, (-)quetschen, (-)zwängen, Menschen a. (-)pferchen (into in acc): **~ in** hineinpressen etc. **2.** (ein)klemmen, (-)quetschen: **he ~med his finger** od. **got his finger ~med) in the door** er quetschte sich den Finger in der Tür; **be ~med in** eingekeilt sein (between zwischen dat). **3.** a. **~ up** blockieren, verstopfen. **4.** a. **~ up** (Funk etc) Empfang (durch Störsender) stören. **5. ~ on the brakes** voll auf die Bremse treten. II v/i **6.** sich (hin ein)drängen od. (-)quetschen od. (-)zwängen (into in acc): **~ in** sich hin eindrängen etc. **7.** ⊙ sich verklemmen, (Bremsen) blockieren; Ladehemmung haben (Pistole etc). III s **8.** Gedränge n. **9.** Verstopfung f: → traffic jam. **10.** ⊙ Verklemmung f, Blockierung f; Ladehemmung f. **11.** F Klemme f: **be in a ~** in der Klemme sein od. sitzen od. stecken.

Ja·mai·ca (rum) [dʒə'meɪkə] s Jamaikarum m.

jamb [dʒæm] s (Tür-, Fenster)Pfosten m.

jam·bo·ree [,dʒæmbə'riː] s **1.** Jamboree n, (internationales) Pfadfindertreffen. **2.** große (Partei- etc)Veranstaltung. **3.** F ausgelassene Feier.

jam·my ['dʒæmɪ] adj Br. sl. **1.** (kinder)leicht. **2.** Glücks...: **~ fellow** Glückspilz m.

jam-'packed adj F vollgestopft (with mit), (Stadion etc) bis auf den letzten Platz besetzt.

jan·gle ['dʒæŋgl] I v/i klimpern (Münzen etc), klirren, rasseln (Ketten etc). II v/t klimpern od. klirren mit. III s Klimpern n, Klirren n.

jan·i·tor ['dʒænɪtə] s **1.** Pförtner m. **2.** bsd. Am. Hausmeister m.

Jan·u·ar·y ['dʒænjʊərɪ] s Januar m: **in ~** im Januar.

Jap [dʒæp] s F Japs m (Japaner).

Jap·a·nese [,dʒæpə'niːz] I s **1.** pl **-nese** Japaner(in). **2.** ling. Japanisch n. II adj **3.** japanisch.

jar¹ [dʒɑː] s **1.** (irdenes od. gläsernes) Gefäß, Krug m. **2.** (Marmelade-,

Einmach)Glas n. **3.** Br. F Glas n Bier.

jar² [~] I v/i **1.** kratzen, kreischen, quietschen (on auf dat). **2.** sich beißen (Farben); sich widersprechen (Meinungen etc); ♪ dissonieren: **~ring tone** Mißton m (a. fig.). **3. ~ on** weh tun (dat) (Farbe, Geräusch etc), Auge etc beleidigen. **4.** wackeln: **~ loose** sich lockern. II v/t **5.** kratzen od. quietschen mit. **6.** erschüttern, fig. a. er-, aufregen. **7.** → **14.** III s **8.** Kratzen n etc (→ 1). **9.** Erschütterung f (a. fig.); Stoß m. **10.** ♪ Mißklang m, Dissonanz f (a. fig.).

jar·gon ['dʒɑːgən] s Jargon m.

jas·min(e) ['dʒæsmɪn] s ♣ Jasmin m.

jas·per ['dʒæspə] s min. Jaspis m.

jaun·dice ['dʒɔːndɪs] s **1.** ♣ Gelbsucht f. **2.** fig. Neid m, Eifersucht f. '**jaundiced** adj **1.** ♣ gelbsüchtig. **2.** fig. neidisch, eifersüchtig.

jaunt [dʒɔːnt] I v/i e-n Ausflug od. e-e Spritztour machen. II s Ausflug m, mot. Spritztour f: **go for** (od. **on**) **a ~** → I.

jaun·ty ['dʒɔːntɪ] adj □ **1.** fesch, flott (Hut etc). **2.** unbeschwert, unbekümmert (Einstellung, Person). **3.** flott, schwungvoll (Melodie).

jave·lin ['dʒævlɪn] s Leichtathletik: Speer m: **~ throw** Speerwerfen n; **~ thrower** Speerwerfer(in).

jaw [dʒɔː] I s **1.** anat. Kiefer m: **lower ~** Unterkiefer; **upper ~** Oberkiefer. **2.** mst pl Mund m; zo. Rachen m (a. fig.), Maul n. **3.** ⊙ (Klemm)Backe f; Klaue f. **4.** F Geschwätz n. II v/i **5.** F schwatzen. '**~·bone** s anat. Kieferknochen m. '**~·break·er** s F Zungenbrecher m.

jay [dʒeɪ] s orn. Eichelhäher m. '**~·walk·er** s unachtsamer Fußgänger.

jazz [dʒæz] I s **1.** ♪ Jazz m. **2. and all that ~** F u. so ein Zeug(s). II adj **3.** ♪ Jazz... III v/t **4.** oft **~ up** ♪ verjazzen. **5.** mst **~ up** F Schmiß od. Schwung bringen in (acc); j-n, et. aufmöbeln. '**jaz·zy** adj □ **1.** ♪ jazzartig. **2.** F knallig (Farben), (a. Kleidung etc) poppig.

jeal·ous ['dʒeləs] adj □ **1.** eifersüchtig (of auf acc). **2.** neidisch (of auf acc): **be ~ of s.o.'s success** j-m s-n Erfolg mißgönnen. **3.** eifersüchtig besorgt (of um). '**jeal·ous·y** s **1.** Eifersucht f; pl Eifersüchteleien pl. **2.** Neid m.

jeans [dʒiːnz] s pl Jeans pl.

jeep [dʒiːp] s mot. Jeep m.

jeer [dʒɪə] **I** v/i **(at)** höhnische Bemerkungen machen (über acc); höhnisch lachen (über acc); ~ **at** → a. **II. II** v/t verhöhnen. **III** s höhnische Bemerkung; Hohngelächter n. '**jeer·ing** adj □ höhnisch: ~ **laughter** Hohngelächter n.

Je·ho·va's Wit·ness [dʒɪ'həʊvəz] s eccl. Zeuge m Jehovas.

jell [dʒel] **I** v/i **1.** gelieren **2.** fig. Gestalt annehmen. **II** v/t **3.** gelieren lassen, zum Gelieren bringen.

jel·lied ['dʒelɪd] adj in Aspik od. Sülze.

jel·ly ['dʒelɪ] **I** s Gallert(e f) n; Gelee n; Aspik n, Sülze f; Götterspeise f. **II** v/i → **jell I. III** v/t n → **jell II.** ~ **ba·by** s Br. Gummibärchen n. '**~fish** s **1.** zo. Qualle f. **2.** fig. f Waschlappen m.

jem·my ['dʒemɪ] Br. s Brech-, Stemmeisen n. **II** v/t a. ~ **open** aufbrechen, -stemmen.

jeop·ard·ize ['dʒepədaɪz] v/t j-n, et. gefährden, in Gefahr bringen, et. in Frage stellen. '**jeop·ard·y** s Gefahr f: **put** (od. **place**) **in** ~ → **jeopardize**.

jerk [dʒɜːk] **I** s **1.** Ruck m; Sprung m, Satz m: **by** ~ ruckweise; **give a** ~ rucken, e-n Satz machen (Auto etc), zs.-zucken (Person). **2.** ⚕ Zuckung f; (bsd. Knie)Reflex m. **3.** Am. sl. Trottel m. **II** v/t **4.** ruckartig ziehen an (dat): ~ **o.s. free** sich losreißen. **III** v/i **5.** sich ruckartig od. ruckweise bewegen: ~ **to a stop** ruckweise od. mit e-m Ruck stehenbleiben. **6.** (zs.-)zucken. '**jerk·y** adj □ **1.** ruckartig, (Bewegungen) fahrig; stoß-, ruckweise. **2.** Am. sl. blöd.

jer·ry ['dʒerɪ] s Br. F Pott m (Nachttopf). '**~built** adj schlampig gebaut: ~ **house** Bruchbude f.

jer·sey ['dʒɜːzɪ] s **1.** Pullover m. **2.** Sport: Trikot n. **3.** Jersey m (Stoff).

jest [dʒest] **I** s Spaß m: **in** ~ im od. zum Scherz. **II** v/i spaßen: ~ **with** (s-n) Spaß treiben mit. '**jest·er** s **1.** Spaßmacher m. **2.** hist. (Hof)Narr m. '**jest·ing** adj spaßend; spaßhaft. '**jest·ing·ly** adv im od. zum Scherz.

Jes·u·it ['dʒezjʊɪt] s eccl. Jesuit m. ,**Jes·u·it·ic,** ,**Jes·u·it·i·cal** adj □ jesuitisch, Jesuiten...

jet [dʒet] **I** s **1.** (Feuer-, Wasseretc)Strahl m. **2.** ⚙ Düse f. **3.** ✈ Jet m. **II** v/i **4.** (heraus-, hervor)schießen

(from aus). **5.** ✈ jetten. **~·age** s Düsenzeitalter n. **~·en·gine** s Strahlmotor m, -triebwerk n. **~ fight·er** s ✈, ⚔ Düsenjäger m. **~ lag** s Störung des gewohnten Alltagsrhythmus durch die Zeitverschiebung bei Langstreckenflügen. '**~·lin·er** s Jetliner m, Düsenverkehrsflugzeug n. **~ plane** s Düsenflugzeug n. '**~·pro·pelled** adj bsd. ✈ mit Düsen- od. Strahlantrieb. **~·pro·pul·sion** s bsd. ✈ Düsen-, Strahlantrieb m.

jet·sam ['dʒetsəm] s ⚓ **1.** Seewurfgut n. **2.** Strandgut n: → **flotsam.**

jet **set** s Jet-set m. '**~·set·ter** s Angehörige m, f des Jet-set.

jet·ti·son ['dʒetɪsn] v/t **1.** ⚓ über Bord werfen (a. fig.). **2.** ✈ (im Notwurf) abwerfen, Treibstoff ablassen. **3.** ausgebrannte Raketenstufe absprengen.

jet·ty ['dʒetɪ] s ⚓ **1.** Hafendamm m, Mole f. **2.** Strombrecher m (an Brücken).

Jew [dʒuː] s Jude m, Jüdin f.

jew·el ['dʒuːəl] **I** s **1.** Juwel n (a. fig.), Edelstein m: → **box** Schmuckkassette f. **2.** ⊙ Stein m (e-r Uhr). **II** v/t pret u. pp **-eled,** bsd. Br. **-elled 3.** mit Juwelen schmücken od. besetzen. '**jew·el·(l)er** s Juwelier m. '**jew·el·ry,** bsd. Br. **jew·el·le·ry** ['~əlrɪ] s Juwelen pl, weitS. Schmuck m: **piece of** ~ Schmuckstück n.

Jew·ish ['dʒuːɪʃ] adj jüdisch, Juden...

jib¹ [dʒɪb] s **1.** ⚓ Klüver m. **2.** ⊙ Ausleger m (e-s Krans).

jib² [~] v/i **1.** scheuen, bocken (**at** vor dat). **2.** fig. störrisch od. bockig sein: ~ **at** sich sträuben gegen; streiken bei.

jif·fy ['dʒɪfɪ] s F Augenblick m: **in a** ~ in Nu, im Handumdrehen.

jig·gered ['dʒɪgəd] adj F **1.** I'm ~ **if** der Teufel soll mich holen, wenn. **2.** **be** ~ Br. baff od. platt sein: **well, I'm** ~! da bin ich aber baff!

jig·gle ['dʒɪgl] **I** v/t wackeln mit; schütteln; rütteln an (dat). **II** v/i wackeln.

jig·saw (**puz·zle**) ['dʒɪgsɔː] s Puzzle (-spiel) n.

jilt [dʒɪlt] v/t Mädchen sitzenlassen (**for** wegen e-s anderen Mädchens); e-m Liebhaber, e-m Mädchen den Laufpaß geben.

jim-jams ['dʒɪmdʒæmz] s pl F **1.** Säuferwahn m. **2.** → **jitter I.**

jim·my ['dʒɪmɪ] *Am.* → **jemmy.**

jin·gle ['dʒɪŋgl] **I** *v/i* klimpern (*Münzen etc*), bimmeln (*Glöckchen etc*). **II** *v/t* klimpern mit, bimmeln lassen. **III** *s* Klimpern *n*, Bimmeln *n*.

jin·go ['dʒɪŋgəʊ] *pl* **-goes** *s* Chauvinist(in). **'jin·go·ism** *s* Chauvinismus *m*. **,jin·go'is·tic** *adj* (⁓ally) chauvinistisch.

jinks [dʒɪŋks] *s pl:* **high** ⁓ Ausgelassenheit *f;* **they were having high** ⁓ bei ihnen ging es hoch her.

jinx [dʒɪŋks] F **I** *s* **1.** Unglücksbringer *m*. **2.** Unglück *n:* **put a** ⁓ **on** → 3. **II** *v/t* **3.** Unglück bringen (*dat*); verhexen.

jit·ter ['dʒɪtə] F **I** *s:* **the** ⁓**s** *pl* Bammel *m*, e-e Heidenangst (*about od. at:* vor *dat*): **have the** ⁓**s** → II. **II** *v/i* Bammel *od.* e-e Heidenangst haben; furchtbar nervös sein. **'jit·ter·y** *adj* F furchtbar nervös.

jiu-jit·su [dʒjuː'dʒɪtsuː] → **jujitsu.**

job¹ [dʒɒb] **I** *s* **1.** (einzelne) Arbeit: **make a good** (**bad**) ⁓ **of s.th.** et. gut (schlecht) machen; ⁓ **odd** 5. **2.** *a.* ⁓ **work** Akkordarbeit *f:* **by the** ⁓ im Akkord. **3.** Stellung *f*, Tätigkeit *f*, Arbeit *f*, Job *m*; Arbeitsplatz *m:* ⁓ **creation** Arbeits(platz)beschaffung *f;* ⁓ **description** Arbeits(platz)beschreibung *f;* **computers are** ⁓ **killers** Computer vernichten Arbeitsplätze; **know one's** ⁓ s-e Sache verstehen. **4.** Sache *f:* a) Aufgabe *f*, Pflicht *f*, b) Geschmack *m:* **this is not everybody's** ⁓ das ist nicht jedermanns Sache, das liegt nicht jedem. **5.** F Sache *f*, Angelegenheit *f:* **make the best of a bad** ⁓ gute Miene zum bösen Spiel machen; das Beste daraus machen. **6.** F Ding *n*, krumme Sache: **pull a** ⁓ ein Ding drehen. **II** *v/t* **7.** Gelegenheitsarbeiten machen, jobben. **8.** (im) Akkord arbeiten. **III** *v/t* **9.** *a.* ⁓ **out** Arbeit in Auftrag geben; im Akkord vergeben.

Job² [dʒəʊb] *npr Bibl.* Hiob *m:* **have the patience of** ⁓, **be** (**as**) **patient as** ⁓ e-e Engelsgeduld haben; ⁓**'s comforter** *j-d*, *der durch s-n Trost alles nur noch schlimmer macht.*

job·ber ['dʒɒbə] *s* **1.** Gelegenheitsarbeiter *m*, Jobber *m*. **2.** Akkordarbeiter *m*. **3.** *Börse:* Br. Jobber *m*.

'job·hunt *v/i* auf Arbeitssuche sein: **go** ⁓**ing** auf Arbeitssuche gehen.

jock·ey ['dʒɒkɪ] **I** *s* **1.** *Pferderennsport:* Jockey *m*. **II** *v/t* **2.** Pferd (*als Jockey*)

reiten. **3.** manövrieren (*a. fig.*): ⁓ **out of** *j-n* hinausbugsieren aus (*e-r Stellung etc*); *j-n* betrügen um (*e-r Sache etc*). **III** *v/i* **4.** ⁓ **for** rangeln um (*a. fig.*): ⁓ **for position** (*Sport etc, a. fig.*) sich e-e günstige (Ausgangs)Position zu verschaffen suchen.

jo·cose [dʒəʊ'kəʊs], **joc·u·lar** ['dʒɒkjʊlə] *adj* □ **1.** ausgelassen (*Person*). **2.** witzig, spaßig (*Bemerkung etc*).

jog [dʒɒg] **I** *v/t* **1.** stoßen an (*acc*) *od.* gegen, *j-n* anstoßen, stupsen: ⁓ **s.o.'s memory** *fig.* j-s Gedächtnis nachhelfen. **II** *v/i* **2.** trotten (*Person, Tier*), zuckeln (*Bus etc*); (*Sport*) joggen. **III** *s* **3.** Stoß *m*, Stups *m*. **4.** Trott *m;* (*Sport*) Trimmtrab *m*. **'jog·ger** *s Sport:* Jogger(in). **'jog·ging** *s Sport:* Joggen *n*, Jogging *n*.

jog| trot *s* gemächlicher Trab, Trott *m* (*a. fig.*). **'⁓-trot** *v/i* gemächlich traben (*bsd. Pferd*), trotten (*Person, Tier*).

john [dʒɒn] *s Am.* F Klo *n:* **in the** ⁓ auf dem *od.* im Klo. **⁓ Bull** *s* England *n*, die Engländer *pl;* ein typischer Engländer. **⁓ Han·cock** ['hænkɒk] *s Am.* F Friedrich Wilhelm *m* (*Unterschrift*).

join [dʒɔɪn] **I** *v/t* **1.** *et.* verbinden, -einigen, zs.-fügen (**to** mit): ⁓ **hands** die Hände falten; sich die Hand *od.* die Hände reichen; *fig.* sich zs.-tun (**with** mit). **2.** *Personen* vereinigen, zs.-bringen (**with, to** mit). **3.** sich anschließen (*dat od. an acc*), stoßen *od.* sich gesellen zu: **I'll** ⁓ **you later** ich komme später nach. **4.** eintreten in (*e-e Firma, e-n Verein etc*). **5.** teilnehmen *od.* sich beteiligen an (*dat*), mitmachen bei. **6.** einmünden in (*acc*) (*Fluß, Straße*). **II** *v/i* **7.** sich vereinigen *od.* verbinden (**with** mit). **8.** ⁓ **in** a) teilnehmen, sich beteiligen, mitmachen, b) → 5. **9.** zs.-kommen (*Straßen*), (*Flüsse a.*) zs.-fließen. **'join·er** *s* Tischler, Schreiner *m:* ⁓**'s bench** Hobelbank *f*. **'join·er·y** *s* **1.** Tischler-, Schreinerhandwerk *n*. **2.** Tischler-, Schreinerarbeit *f*.

joint [dʒɔɪnt] **I** *s* **1.** Verbindung(sstelle) *f*, *bsd.* a) (Löt)Naht *f*, Nahtstelle *f*, b) *anat.*, ⊙ Gelenk *n:* **out of** ⁓ ausgerenkt, *fig.* aus den Fugen; **put out of** ⁓ sich *et.* ausrenken; → **nose** 1. **2.** *gastr.*

Braten(stück *n*) *m*. **3.** *sl.* Laden *m*, Bude *f* (*Lokal, Firma etc*): → **clip joint. 4.** *sl.* Joint *m* (*Haschisch- od. Marihuanazigarette*). **II** *adj* □ **5.** gemeinsam, gemeinschaftlich: **take ~ action** gemeinsam vorgehen; **~ venture †** Gemeinschaftsunternehmen *n*. **,~'stock com·pa·ny** *s* **1.** *Br.* Kapital- *od.* Aktiengesellschaft *f*. **2.** *Am.* Offene Handelsgesellschaft *f*.

joist [dʒɔɪst] *s* △ **1.** Deckenträger *m*, -balken *m*. **2.** I-Träger *m*.

joke [dʒəʊk] **I** *s* **1.** Witz *m*: **crack ~s** Witze reißen. **2.** a) Scherz *m*, Spaß *m*: **in** (*od.* **for a**) **~** im *od.* zum Spaß; **that's going beyond a ~** das ist kein Spaß mehr, das ist nicht mehr lustig; **he can't take a ~** er versteht keinen Spaß, b) *mst* **practical ~** Streich *m*: **play a ~ on s.o.** j-m e-n Streich spielen. **II** *v/i* **3.** scherzen, Witze *od.* Spaß machen: **I'm not joking** ich meine das ernst; **you must be joking, are you joking?** das ist doch nicht dein Ernst! **'jok·er** *s* **1.** Spaßvogel *m*, Witzbold *m*. **2.** Joker *m* (*Spielkarte*). **3.** *sl.* Typ *m*, Kerl *m*. **'jok·ing I** *adj* □ scherzhaft, spaßend: **~ly a.** im Spaß. **II** *s* Witze *pl*: **~ apart** Scherz *od.* Spaß beiseite.

jol·li·fi·ca·tion [,dʒɒlɪfɪ'keɪʃn] *s* *f* (feucht)fröhliches Fest, Festivität *f*.

jol·ly¹ ['dʒɒlɪ] **I** *adj* □ **1.** lustig, fröhlich, vergnügt. **2.** F angeheitert: **be ~** e-n Schwips haben. **II** *adv* **3.** *Br.* F ganz schön, ziemlich: **a ~ good fellow** ein prima Kerl.

jol·ly² [~], **~ boat** *s* ⚓ Jolle *f*.

Jol·ly Rog·er [,dʒɒlɪ'rɒdʒə] *s* Totenkopf-, Piratenflagge *f*.

jolt [dʒəʊlt] **I** *v/t* **1.** e-n Ruck *od.* Stoß geben (*dat*); *Passagiere* durchrütteln, -schütteln. **2.** *fig. j-m* e-n Schock versetzen; *j-n* auf- *od.* wachrütteln: **~ s.o. out of a.** j-n reißen aus. **II** *v/i* **3.** e-n Ruck machen; rütteln, holpern (*Fahrzeug*). **III** *s* **4.** Ruck *m*, Stoß *m*. **5.** *fig.* Schock *m*: **give s.o. a ~** j-m e-n Schock versetzen.

josh [dʒɒʃ] *v/t Am.* F *j-n* aufziehen, veräppeln.

joss stick [dʒɒs] *s* Räucherstäbchen *n*.

jos·tle ['dʒɒsl] **I** *v/t* **1.** anrempeln. **2.** dränge(l)n: **~ one's way through** sich (durch)drängen durch. **II** *v/i* **3.** **~**

against rempeln gegen, anrempeln (*acc*). **4.** (sich) dränge(l)n.

jot [dʒɒt] **I** *s fig.* Spur *f*: **not a ~ of truth** kein Funke *od.* Körnchen Wahrheit. **II** *v/t mst* **~ down** sich *et.* notieren. **'jot·ter** *s* Notizbuch *n*, -block *m*. **'jot·ting** *s mst* *pl* Notiz *f*.

joule [dʒuːl] *s phys.* Joule *n*.

jour·nal ['dʒɜːnl] *s* **1.** Journal *n*, Zeitschrift *f*. **2.** Tagebuch *n*. **3.** *Buchhaltung:* Journal *n*: **cash ~** Kassenbuch *n*. **4.** ⚓ Logbuch *n*. **jour·nal·ese** [,~nə'liːz] *s* Zeitungsstil *m*. **'jour·nal·ism** *s* Journalismus *m*. **'jour·nal·ist** *s* Journalist(in). **jour·nal·is·tic** *adj* (**~ally**) journalistisch.

jour·ney ['dʒɜːnɪ] *s* **1.** Reise *f*: **go on a ~** verreisen. **2.** Reise *f*, Entfernung *f*: **a two days' ~** zwei Tagesreisen (**to** nach). **~·man** ['~mən] *s* (*irr man*) Geselle *m*: **~ tailor** Schneidergeselle.

jo·vi·al ['dʒəʊvjəl] *adj* □ lustig, fröhlich, vergnügt. **jo·vi·al·i·ty** [,~vɪ'ælətɪ] *s* Lustigkeit *f*, Fröhlichkeit *f*.

jowl [dʒaʊl] *s* **1.** (Unter)Kiefer *m*. **2.** Wange *f*, Backe *f*; Hängebacke *f*: → **cheek** 1.

joy [dʒɔɪ] *s* **1.** Freude *f* (**at** über *acc*; **in** *dat*): **for ~** vor Freude *weinen etc*; **tears** *pl* **of ~** Freudentränen *pl*; **to s.o.'s ~** zu j-s Freude. **2.** *Br.* F Erfolg *m*: **I didn't have any ~** ich hatte kein Glück. **'joy·ful** ['~fʊl] *adj* □ **1.** freudig, erfreut: **be ~** sich freuen, froh sein. **2.** erfreulich, freudig (*Ereignis etc*). **'joy·less** *adj* □ **1.** freudlos. **2.** unerfreulich. **'joy·ous →** **joyful.**

joy| ride *s* F Spritztour *f* (*bsd. in e-m gestohlenen Wagen*): **go on a ~** e-e Spritztour machen. **~ stick** *s* F **1.** ✈ Steuerknüppel *m*. **2.** *Computer:* Joystick *m*.

ju·bi·lant ['dʒuːbɪlənt] *adj* □ **1.** überglücklich. **2.** jubelnd: **~ shout** Jubelschrei *m*. **ju·bi·late** ['~leɪt] *v/i* jubilieren, jubeln. **ju·bi·la·tion** *s* Jubel *m*. **ju·bi·lee** ['~liː] *s* Jubiläum *n*.

judge [dʒʌdʒ] **I** *s* **1.** ⚖ Richter *m*: → **sober** I. **2.** Schiedsrichter *m*; Preisrichter *m*; (*Sport a.*) Kampfrichter *m*, (*Boxen*) Punktrichter *m*. **3.** Kenner *m*: **a** (**good**) **~ of wine** ein Weinkenner *m*. **II** *v/t* **4.** ⚖ *Fall* verhandeln; die Verhandlung führen gegen. **5.** *Wettbewerbsteil-*

nehmer, Leistungen etc beurteilen (**on** nach); als Schiedsrichter (*etc*, → 2) fungieren bei. **6.** entscheiden (**s.th.** et; *that* daß). **7.** beurteilen, einschätzen (**by** nach). **III** *v/i* **8.** als Schiedsrichter (*etc*, → 2) fungieren (**at** bei). **9.** urteilen (**of** über *acc*): *judging by his words* s-n Worten nach zu urteilen.

judg(e)·ment ['dʒʌdʒmənt] *s* **1.** ⚖ Urteil *n*. **2.** Urteilsvermögen *n*: *against* (*one's*) *better* ~ wider bessere Einsicht. **3.** Meinung *f*, Ansicht *f*, Urteil *n* (**on** über *acc*): *in my* ~ m-s Erachtens; *form a* (*final*) ~ **on** sich ein (abschließendes *od.* endgültiges) Urteil bilden über. **4.** göttliches (Straf)Gericht: *Day of* ♌, ♌ *Day* Jüngster Tag.

ju·di·ca·ture ['dʒuːdɪkətʃə] *s* ⚖ **1.** Rechtsprechung *f*, Rechtspflege *f*. **2.** Gerichtswesen *n*. **3.** → *judiciary* 3.

ju·di·cial [dʒuːˈdɪʃl] *adj* □ ⚖ gerichtlich, Gerichts...: ~ *error* Justizirrtum *m*; ~ *murder* Justizmord *m*. **2.** ⚖ richterlich. **3.** kritisch.

ju·di·ci·a·ry [dʒuːˈdɪʃərɪ] ⚖ **I** *adj* **1.** → *judicial* 1, 2. **II** *s* **2.** → *judicature* 3. *coll.* Richter(schaft *f*) *pl*.

ju·di·cious [dʒuːˈdɪʃəs] *adj* □ **1.** vernünftig, umsichtig. **2.** wohlüberlegt.

ju·do ['dʒuːdəʊ] *s Sport:* Judo *n*. **ju·do·ka** ['~kɑː] *s* Judoka *m*.

jug [dʒʌɡ] *s* **1.** Krug *m*; *bsd. Br.* Kanne *f*; Kännchen *n*. **2.** *sl.* Knast *m* (*Gefängnis*). **II** *v/t* **3.** *sl.* einlochen.

jug·ger·naut ['dʒʌɡənɔːt] *s* **1.** *mot. Br.* Schwerlastzug *m*. **2.** *fig.* Moloch *m*.

jug·gins ['dʒʌɡɪnz] *s bsd. Br.* F Trottel *m*.

jug·gle ['dʒʌɡl] **I** *v/t* **1.** jonglieren (mit). **2.** *fig.* jonglieren mit (*Fakten, Worten etc*); *Fakten, Worte etc* verdrehen; *Konten etc* fälschen, frisieren. **II** *v/i* **3.** jonglieren. **4.** ~ *with* → 2. '**jug·gler** *s* **1.** Jongleur *m*. **2.** ~ *of words* Wortverdreher *m*. **3.** Schwindler *m*.

Ju·go·slav → *Yugoslav*.

juice [dʒuːs] **I** *s* **1.** Saft *m*: *let s.o. stew in his own* ~ F j-n im eigenen Saft schmoren lassen. **2.** *sl.* ⚡ Saft *m*; *mot.* Sprit *m*. **II** *v/t* **3.** entsaften. '**juic·y** *adj* □ **1.** saftig. **2.** F knackig (*Mädchen*); saftig (*Gewinn etc*); lukrativ (*Vertrag etc*); pikant (*Einzelheiten etc*).

ju·jit·su [dʒuːˈdʒɪtsuː] *s Sport:* Jiu-Jitsu *n*.

juke·box ['dʒuːkbɒks] *s* Jukebox *f*, Musikautomat *m*.

Ju·ly [dʒuːˈlaɪ] *s* Juli *m*: *in* ~ im Juli.

jum·ble ['dʒʌmbl] **I** *v/t a.* ~ *together* (*od.* *up*) *Sachen durcheinanderwerfen*; *Fakten etc* durcheinanderbringen. **II** *s* Durcheinander *n*. ~ *sale* *s Br.* Wohltätigkeitsbasar *m*.

jum·bo ['dʒʌmbəʊ] **I** *pl* **-bos** *s* **1.** Koloß *m* (*Sache, Person*). **2.** ✈ Jumbo *m*. **II** *adj* riesig, Riesen...: ~ *jet* ✈ Jumbo-Jet *m*. '~**-sized** → *jumbo* 2.

jump [dʒʌmp] **I** *s* **1.** Sprung *m*: *make* (*od.* *take*) *a* ~ e-n Sprung machen; *have the* ~ *on s.o.* F j-m vorausein. **2.** *Sport:* (*Hoch-, Ski- etc*)Sprung *m*. **3.** *give a* ~ → 6; *it gives me the* ~*s* es macht mich ganz nervös *od.* unruhig; *have the* ~*s* F ganz nervös *od.* aufgeregt sein. **II** *v/i* **4.** springen: ~ *at* *fig.* sich stürzen auf (*acc*); ~ *off* abspringen (von); ~ *out of one's skin* *fig.* aus der Haut fahren; ~ *to one's feet* aufspringen; → *conclusion* 5. **5.** hüpfen, springen: ~ *for joy* Freudensprünge machen. **6.** zs.-zucken, auf-, zs.-fahren (**at** bei). **7.** *fig.* abrupt übergehen, überspringen, -wechseln (**to** zu). **III** *v/t* **8.** springen über (*acc*). **9.** *fig.* überspringen, auslassen: ~ *the gun* (*Sport*) e-n Fehlstart verursachen; *fig.* voreilig sein *od.* handeln; ~ *the line* (*bsd. Br.* queue) sich vordräng(el)n (*beim Schlangestehen u. fig.*); *mot.* aus e-r Kolonne ausscheren u. überholen; → *light*[1] 3. **10.** (heraus)springen aus: → *rail*[1] 3, *track* 3.

jump·er[1] ['dʒʌmpə] *s Sport:* (Hoch-etc)Springer(in).

jump·er[2] [~] *s* **1.** *bsd. Br.* Pullover *m*. **2.** *Am.* Trägerrock *m*, -kleid *n*.

jump·er ca·bles *s pl Am.* → *jump leads*.

jump leads [liːdz] *s pl Br. mot.* Starthilfekabel *n*. ~ *rope* *s Am.* Spring-, Sprungseil *n*. ~ *seat* *s* Klapp-, Notsitz *m*. ~ *suit* *s* Overall *m*.

jump·y ['dʒʌmpɪ] *adj* □ nervös; schreckhaft.

junc·tion ['dʒʌŋkʃn] *s* **1.** Verbindung *f*, -einigung *f*. **2.** 🚂 Knotenpunkt *m*. **3.** (Straßen)Kreuzung *f*, (-)Einmündung *f*.

junc·ture ['dʒʌŋktʃə] *s*: *at this* ~ in die-

sem Augenblick, zu diesem Zeitpunkt.
June [dʒuːn] *s* Juni *m*: **in** *~* im Juni.

jun·gle [ˈdʒʌŋgl] *s* Dschungel *m* (*a. fig.*).
jun·ior [ˈdʒuːnjə] **I** *adj* **1.** junior. **2.** (*to*)
jünger (als); untergeordnet (*dat*): *~*
partner ✝ Junior(partner) *m*; → **man·**
agement 2. **3.** *ped. ~* **high** (**school**) *Am.*
die unteren Klassen der High-School; ~
school *Br.* Grundschule *f* (*für Kinder*
von 7-11). **4.** *Sport:* Junioren... **II** *s* **5.**
Jüngere *m, f*: **he is my** *~* **by two years,**
he is two years my *~* er ist 2 Jahre
jünger als ich. **6.** *Sport:* Junior(in).
ju·ni·per [ˈdʒuːnipə] *s* ♀ Wacholder *m*.
junk¹ [dʒʌŋk] *s* ♣ Dschunke *f*.
junk² [~] **I** *s* **1.** Trödel *m*; Altmaterial *n*;
Schrott *m*. **2.** Gerümpel *n*, Abfall *m*. **3.**
contp. Schund *m*, Mist *m*. **4.** *sl.* Stoff *m*,
bsd. Heroin *n*. **II** *v/t* **5.** *et.* unbrauchbar
Gewordenes ausrangieren, Auto etc verschrotten.
jun·ket [ˈdʒʌŋkɪt] *s* (Sahne)Quark *m*;
Dickmilch *f*.
junk food *s* Junk-food *m* (*kalorienreiche*
Nahrung von geringem Nährwert).
junk·ie [ˈdʒʌŋkɪ] *s sl.* Junkie *m* (*Rausch-*
giftsüchtiger), *bsd.* H-Fixer *m*.
ʼjunkˈyard *s* Schuttabladeplatz *m*;
Schrottplatz *m*.
jun·ta [ˈdʒʌntə] *s pol.* Junta *f*.
ju·rid·i·cal [ˌdʒʊəˈrɪdɪkl] *adj* □ **1.**
gerichtlich, Gerichts... **2.** juristisch,
Rechts...
ju·ris·dic·tion [ˌdʒʊərɪsˈdɪkʃn] *s* Ge-
richtsbarkeit *f*; (*örtliche u. sachliche*)
Zuständigkeit *f* (**of, over** für): **come** (*od.*
fall) **under** (*od.* **within**) **the** *~* **of** unter
die Zuständigkeit fallen von (*od. gen*);
have *~* **over** zuständig sein für.
ju·ris·pru·dence [ˌdʒʊərɪsˈpruːdəns] *s*
Rechtswissenschaft *f*.
ju·rist [ˈdʒʊərɪst] *s* **1.** Jurist *m*, Rechtsge-
lehrte *m*. **2.** *Br.* Rechtsstudent *m*. **3.**
Am. Rechtsanwalt *m*.
ju·ror [ˈdʒʊərə] *s* **1.** ⚖ Geschworene *m,*
f. **2.** Preisrichter(in).
ju·ry [ˈdʒʊərɪ] *s* **1.** ⚖ *die* Geschworenen
pl: → **trial** 1. **2.** Jury *f*, Preis-, (*Sport a.*)

Kampfgericht *n*. *~* **box** *s* ⚖ Geschworenenbank *f*. *~ˈman* [ˈ~mən] *s* (*irr* **man**)
⚖ Geschworene *m*. *ˈ~ˌwom·an* *s* (*irr*
woman) Geschworene *f*.
just [dʒʌst] **I** *adj* (□ → **justly**) **1.** gerecht
(**to** gegen). **2.** gerecht, angemessen: **it**
was only *~* es war nur recht u. billig. **3.**
rechtmäßig (*Anspruch etc*); berechtigt,
gerechtfertigt (*Zorn etc*). **II** *adv* **4.** gerade, (so)eben: *~* **now** 3. **5.** gerade, genau, eben: *~* **as** gerade als; **that is** *~* **like**
you das sieht dir ähnlich; → **well¹** 1.
6. gerade (noch), ganz knapp. **7.** nur,
lediglich, bloß: → **moment** 1, *etc* **8.** *~*
about ungefähr, etwa; gerade noch.
jus·tice [ˈdʒʌstɪs] *s* **1.** Gerechtigkeit *f* (**to**
gegen): **do** *~* **to** gerecht werden (*dat*); *et.*
richtig würdigen. **2.** ⚖ Gerechtigkeit
f, Recht *n*: **do** *~* **to** der Gerechtigkeit
Genüge tun; **bring to** *~* vor den Richter bringen; → **administer** 2. **3.** ⚖
Richter *m*: *~* **of the peace** Friedensrichter.
jus·ti·fi·a·ble [ˈdʒʌstɪfaɪəbl] *adj* zu recht-
fertigen(d), berechtigt, vertretbar. **ʼjus·**
ti·fi·a·bly *adv* berechtigterweise, mit
gutem Grund, mit Recht.
jus·ti·fi·ca·tion [ˌdʒʌstɪfɪˈkeɪʃn] *s* Rechtfertigung *f*: **in** *~* **of** zur Rechtfertigung
von (*od. gen*).
jus·ti·fy [ˈdʒʌstɪfaɪ] *v/t* rechtfertigen (**be-**
fore, to vor *dat*, gegenüber): **be justi-**
fied in doing s.th. et. mit gutem Recht
tun; berechtigt sein, et. zu tun.
just·ly [ˈdʒʌstlɪ] *adv* mit *od.* zu Recht.
jut [dʒʌt] *v/i a.* *~* **out** vorspringen; herausragen.
jute [dʒuːt] *s* Jute(faser) *f*.
ju·ven·ile [ˈdʒuːvənaɪl] **I** *adj* jugendlich;
Jugend...: *~* **court** Jugendgericht *n*; *~*
delinquency Jugendkriminalität *f*; *~*
delinquent (*od.* **offender**) straffälliger
Jugendlicher. **II** *s* Jugendliche *m, f*.
jux·ta·pose [ˌdʒʌkstəˈpəʊz] *v/t* neben-
einanderstellen (*a. fig.*). **jux·ta·po·si·**
tion [ˌ~pəˈzɪʃn] *s* **1.** Nebeneinanderstel-
lung *f*. **2.** Nebeneinanderstehen *n*: **be**
in *~* nebeneinanderstehen.

K

kale [keɪl] *s* **1.** ♀ Grün-, Braunkohl *m*. **2.** *Am. sl.* Kies *m* (*Geld*).

ka·lei·do·scope [kəˈlaɪdəskəʊp] *s* Kaleidoskop *n* (*a. fig.*).

kan·ga·roo [ˌkæŋɡəˈruː] *s zo.* Känguruh *n*.

ka·put [kæˈpʊt] *adj pred* F kaputt.

kar·at *bsd. Am.* → **carat**.

ka·ra·te [kəˈrɑːtɪ] *s* Karate *n*: ~ **chop** Karateschlag *m*.

kar·ma [ˈkɑːmə] *s* Buddhismus, Hinduismus: Karma(n) *n*.

ka·yak [ˈkaɪæk] *s* Kajak *m*, *n* (*a. Sport*).

keck [kek] *v/i bsd. Am.* **1.** würgen (*beim Erbrechen*). **2.** *fig.* es ekeln (*at* vor *dat*).

keel [kiːl] ♣ **I** *s* Kiel *m*: **on an even ~** *fig.* gleichmäßig, ruhig. **II** *v/i mst* ~ **over** (*od.* **up**) umschlagen, kentern.

keen [kiːn] *adj* □ **1.** scharf (*geschliffen*). **2.** schneidend (*Kälte*), scharf (*Wind*). **3.** scharf (*Sinne, Verstand etc*). **4.** ✝ scharf (*Wettbewerb*); lebhaft, stark (*Nachfrage*). **5.** heftig, stark (*Gefühl*): ~ **interest** starkes *od.* lebhaftes Interesse. **6.** begeistert, leidenschaftlich (*Schwimmer etc*). **7.** versessen, scharf (**on, about** auf *acc*): **be** ~ **on a.** begeistert sein von; **be** ~ **on doing** (*od.* **to do**) **s.th.** et. unbedingt tun wollen.

keep [kiːp] **I** *s* **1.** (Lebens)Unterhalt *m*. **2.** **for ~s** F für *od.* auf immer, endgültig: **it's yours for ~s** du kannst *od.* darfst es behalten. **II** *v/t* (*irr*) **3.** (be)halten. **4.** *j-n, et.* lassen, (*in e-m bestimmten Zustand*) (er)halten: ~ **closed** Tür etc geschlossen halten; ~ **s.th. a secret** et. geheimhalten (**from** vor *dat*); → **wait** 1, etc. **5.** (*im Besitz*) behalten: ~ **the change** der Rest (*des Geldes*) ist für Sie; ~ **your seat, please** bitte behalten Sie Platz. **6.** *j-n* aufhalten: **don't let me ~ you** laß dich nicht aufhalten. **7.** aufheben, -bewahren: **can you ~ a secret?** kannst du schweigen? **8.** *Beziehungen etc* unterhalten (**with** zu). **9.** *Ware* führen. **10.** *Laden etc* haben, betreiben. **11.** *Versprechen, Wort* halten. **12.** *Bett, Haus, Zimmer* hüten. **13.** ernähren, er-, unterhalten: **have a family to ~** e-e Fami-

lie ernähren müssen. **14.** *Tiere* halten; sich *ein Auto etc* halten. **III** *v/i* (*irr*) **15.** bleiben: ~ **in sight** in Sicht(weite) bleiben; ~ **still** stillhalten. **16.** sich halten, (*in e-m bestimmten Zustand*) bleiben: ~ **friends** (weiterhin) Freunde bleiben. **17.** *mit ger* weiter...: ~ **smiling!** immer nur lächeln!; ~ (**on**) **trying** es weiterversuchen, es immer wieder versuchen.
Verbindungen mit Präpositionen:

keep| **at** *v/i* **1.** weitermachen mit. **2.** *j-m* zusetzen (**to do** zu tun). ~ **from** I *v/t* **1.** abhalten von: **keep s.o. from doing s.th.** j-n davon abhalten, et. zu tun. **2.** bewahren vor (*dat*). **3.** *j-m et.* vorenthalten, verschweigen. **II** *v/i* **4.** vermeiden (*acc*): ~ **doing s.th.** es vermeiden *od.* sich davor hüten, et. zu tun; **I could hardly ~ laughing** ich konnte mir kaum das Lachen verkneifen. ~ **off** *v/t u. v/i* (sich) fernhalten von: **keep your hands off it!** Hände weg (davon)!; → **grass** 2. ~ **on** *v/i* leben *od.* sich ernähren von. ~ **to** I *v/t* **1.** bleiben in (*dat*): → **left²** 3, **right** 9. **2.** *fig.* festhalten an (*dat*), bleiben bei. **II** *v/t* **3.** keep s.th. to a (*od.* **the**) **minimum** et. auf ein Minimum beschränken. **4.** **keep s.th. to o.s.** et. für sich behalten.
Verbindungen mit Adverbien:

keep| **a·way** *v/t u. v/i* (sich) fernhalten (**from** von). ~ **back** *v/t* **1.** zurückhalten: **keep s.o. back from doing s.th.** j-n davon abhalten *od.* daran hindern, et. zu tun. **2.** *fig.* zurückhalten: a) *Lohn etc* einbehalten, b) *Tränen etc* unterdrücken, c) *et.* verschweigen. ~ **down** I *v/t* **1.** *Kopf etc* unten behalten. **2.** *Kosten etc* niedrig halten. **3.** unter Kontrolle halten, *Volk, Gefühle etc a.* unterdrücken. **4.** *Nahrung etc* bei sich behalten. **II** *v/i* **5.** unten bleiben; sich geduckt halten. ~ **in** I *v/t* **1.** nicht heraus- *od.* hinauslassen; *ped.* nachsitzen lassen. **2.** *Atem* anhalten. **3.** *Gefühle* zurückhalten, unterdrücken. **II** *v/i* **4.** drin bleiben, nicht herauskommen. **5.** sich mit *j-m* gut stellen. ~ **off** *v/t u. v/i* (sich) fernhalten: **keep your hands off!** Hände weg!; ~**!** Berühren verboten!; Betreten verbo-

ten! ~ **on** I v/t **1.** *Kleidungsstück* anbehalten, anlassen, *Hut* aufbehalten: →
shirt. 2. *Licht* brennen lassen, anlassen.
II v/i **3.** a) weitermachen, b) nicht lok-
kerlassen, c) → **keep** 17. **4.** ~ **at** → keep
at 2. ~ **out** I v/t **1.** (of) nicht hinein- od.
hereinlassen (in *acc*), fern-, abhalten
(von). **2.** *fig.* heraushalten (**of** aus). II
v/i **3.** draußen bleiben: ~! Zutritt verboten! **4.** *fig.* sich heraushalten (**of** aus): ~
of sight sich nicht blicken lassen. ~
to·geth·er I v/t *Dinge, fig.* Mannschaft
etc zs.-halten. II v/i zs.-bleiben (a. *fig.
Mannschaft etc*), zs.-halten (a. *fig.
Freunde etc*). ~ **up** I v/t **1.** oben halten,
hochhalten, c) → **chin** I. **2.** *fig.* aufrechterhalten, *Brauch etc* a. weiterpflegen,
Tempo halten, *Preise etc* (hoch)halten,
Mut nicht sinken lassen: → **appearance** 3. **3.** in gutem Zustand od. in
Ordnung halten. II v/i **4.** oben bleiben.
5. *fig.* sich halten, (*Preise etc a.*) sich
behaupten; andauern, nicht nachlas-
sen. **6.** ~ **with** a) Schritt halten mit (a.
fig.): ~ **with the Joneses** es den Nachbarn gleichtun (wollen); → **time** 1, b)
sich auf dem laufenden halten über
(*acc*), c) in Kontakt bleiben mit.
keep·er ['ki:pə] s **1.** Wächter m, Aufseher m. **2.** *mst in Zssgn* Inhaber m, Besitzer m; Halter m, Züchter m. **3.** Betreuer
m, Verwalter m.
keep-'fresh bag s Frischhaltebeutel m.
keep·ing ['ki:pɪŋ] s **1.** Verwahrung f: **put
in s.o.'s** ~ j-n in j-s Obhut geben; j-m
et. zur Aufbewahrung geben. **2. be in
(out of)** ~ **with** (nicht) übereinstimmen
mit; (nicht) passen zu; (nicht) entsprechen (*dat*).
keep·sake ['ki:pseɪk] s (*Geschenk zum*)
Andenken n: **as** (od. **for**) **a** ~ als od. zum
Andenken.
keg [keg] s Fäßchen n.
ken [ken] s: **this is beyond** (od. **outside**)
my ~ das entzieht sich m-r Kenntnis;
das ist mir zu hoch.
ken·nel ['kenl] s **1.** Hundehütte f. **2.** *oft
pl* (*sg konstruiert*) Hundezwinger m;
Hundeheim n.
kept [kept] *pret u. pp von* **keep.**
kerb [kɜːb] s, **'~·stone** s Br. Bord-, Randstein m.
ker·chief ['kɜːtʃɪf] s Hals-, Kopftuch n.
ker·nel ['kɜːnl] s **1.** Kern m (a. *fig.*).

2. (*Hafer-, Mais- etc*)Korn n.
ker·o·sene ['kerəsiːn] s 🇺🇸 Kerosin n.
ketch·up ['ketʃəp] s Ketchup m, n.
ket·tle ['ketl] s Kessel m: **a pretty** (od.
fine) ~ **of fish** iro. e-e schöne Besche-
rung; **that's a different** ~ **of fish** das ist
et. ganz anderes; **keep the** ~ **boiling**
sich über Wasser halten; die Sache in
Schwung halten.
key [ki:] I s **1.** Schlüssel m (a. *fig.* **to** zu).
2. Taste f (*e-s Klaviers, e-r Schreibmaschine etc*). **3.** ♪ Tonart f: **major** (**minor**) ~ Dur n (Moll n); **off** (od. **out of**) ~
falsch *singen etc.* II *adj* **4.** Schlüssel...
(a. *fig.*). III v/t **5.** ♪ stimmen. **6.** ~ **in**
(*Computer*) *Daten* eintasten, -tippen.
~ (**up**) **to**, ~ **in with** *fig.* abstimmen auf
(*acc*). **8.** ~ **up** j-n in nervöse Spannung
versetzen: ~**ed up** nervös, aufgeregt
(**about** wegen). **'~·board** s **1.** Tastatur f
(*e-s Klaviers, e-r Schreibmaschine etc*):
~ **instrument** Tasteninstrument n. **2.**
Schlüsselbrett n. **'~·hole** s Schlüssel-
loch n. **'~·man** s (*irr man*) **1.** Schlüssel-
figur f. **2.** Mann m in e-r Schlüsselstellung. **'~·note** s **1.** ♪ Grundton m. **2.**
fig. Grund-, Leitgedanke m: ~ **address**
(od. **speech**) *pol.* programmatische
Rede. **'~·phone** s Br. Tastentelefon n. ~
sig·na·ture s ♪ Vorzeichen n u. *pl*
'~·stone s **1.** △ Schlußstein m. **2.** *fig.*
Grundpfeiler m.
khak·i ['kɑːkɪ] I s **1.** Khaki n (*Farbe*). **2.**
Khaki m (*Stoff*); *mst pl* Khakiuniform
f. II *adj* **3.** Khaki...: a) khakifarben, b)
aus Khaki.
kib·itz·er ['kɪbɪtsə] s F **1.** Kiebitz m. **2.**
fig. Besserwisser m.
kick [kɪk] I s **1.** (Fuß)Tritt m, Stoß m:
give s.o. a ~ j-m e-n Tritt geben od.
versetzen; **get the** ~ F (raus)fliegen (*entlassen werden*). **2.** Fußball: Schuß m. **3.**
Schwimmen: Beinschlag m. **4.** F
Schwung m: **give s.th. a** ~ et. in
Schwung bringen. **5.** F Kitzel m, (*an
Spaß; **he gets a** ~ **out of it** es macht ihm
e-n Riesenspaß. II v/t **6.** (mit dem Fuß)
stoßen, treten, e-n Tritt geben od. versetzen (*dat*): **I could have** ~**ed myself**
ich hätte mich arg geärgert od. mir in den
Hintern beißen können; → **bucket** 1. **7.**
loskommen von (*e-r Droge, Gewohnheit etc*). III v/i **8.** (mit dem Fuß) stoßen, treten (**at** nach); strampeln; aus-

schlagen (*Pferd etc*) → **trace²**. **9.** ~ **about** (*od*. **around**) F sich herumtreiben in (*dat*). **10.** F meutern, rebellieren (**against**, **at** gegen).
Verbindungen mit Adverbien:
kick| a·bout, ~ **a·round** F **I** *v/t* **1.** *j-n* herumkommandieren. **2.** *j-n*, *et*. umstoßen, -schubsen. **II** *v/i* **3.** sich herumtreiben. ~ **back** *v/i* **1.** zurücktreten. **2.** *fig*. unangenehme Folgen haben (**at** für); zurückschlagen. ~ **in** *v/t* **1.** Tür eintreten. **2.** *Am*. F *et*. beisteuern (**for** zu). ~ **off** **I** *v/i* **1.** Fußball: anstoßen. **2.** F anfangen. **II** *v/t* **3.** *et*. wegtreten, *Schuhe* wegschleudern. ~ **out** **I** *v/i* um sich treten; losgehen (*Pferd etc*). **II** *v/t* F *j-n* rausschmeißen (**of** aus) (*a. fig*.). ~ **o·ver** *v/t* mit dem Fuß umstoßen. ~ **up** *v/t* mit dem Fuß hochschleudern, *Staub* aufwirbeln: → **din** I, **dust** 1, **row³** I, *etc*.

'**kick|·back** *s* unangenehme Folge(n *pl*). '~**·off** *s* Fußball: Anstoß *m*. '~**·out** *s* F Rausschmiß *m* (*a. fig*.). '~**·start·er** *s* Kickstarter *m* (*e-s Motorrads*).

kid¹ [kɪd] *s* **1.** Zicklein *n*, Kitz *n*. **2.** *a*. ~ **leather** Ziegen-, Glacéleder *n*. **3.** F a) Kind *n*: **my** ~ **brother** mein kleiner Bruder, b) *bsd. Am*. Jugendliche *m*, *f*.

kid² [~] F **I** *v/t* *j-n* auf den Arm nehmen. **II** *v/i* albern; Spaß machen; schwindeln: **he was only** ~**ding** er hat nur Spaß gemacht, er hat es nicht ernst gemeint; **no** ~**ding?** im Ernst?, ehrlich?

kid glove *s* Glacéhandschuh *m*: **handle s.o. with** ~**s** *fig*. *j-n* mit Samt- *od*. Glacéhandschuhen anfassen.

kid·nap ['kɪdnæp] *v/t pret od. pp* **-naped**, *bsd. Br*. **-napped** kidnappen, entführen. '**kid·nap·(p)er** *s* Kidnapper *m*, Entführer *m*. '**kid·nap·(p)ing** *s* Kidnapping *n*, Entführung *f*.

kid·ney ['kɪdnɪ] *s* **1.** *anat*. Niere *f*. **2.** *fig*. Art *f*, Schlag *m*. ~ **bean** *s* ♀ Weiße Bohne. ~ **ma·chine** *s* ♥ künstliche Niere: **put on a** ~ *j-n* an e-e künstliche Niere anschließen. ~ **stone** *s* ♥ Nierenstein *m*. ~ **trans·plant** *s* ♥ Nierenverpflanzung *f*.

kill [kɪl] **I** *v/t* **1.** töten, umbringen, ermorden: ~ **two birds with one stone** *fig*. zwei Fliegen mit 'einer Klappe schlagen; **be** ~**ed** *a*. ums Leben kommen, umkommen; → **accident** 2, **action** 6. **2.**

Tier schlachten. **3.** (fast) umbringen: **my feet are** ~**ing me** m-e Füße bringen mich (noch) um. **4.** *a*. ~ **off** *Knospen*, *Rost etc* vernichten. **5.** *Gefühle* (ab)töten, ersticken; *Schmerzen* stillen. **6.** *Zeit* totschlagen. **7.** F *Flasche etc* vernichten, austrinken. **II** *v/i* **8.** töten. **9.** *dressed to* ~ F todschick gekleidet, *contp*. aufgedonnert. '**kill·er** **I** *s* **1.** Mörder *m*, (*kaltblütiger*, *professioneller*) Killer *m*. **2.** *bsd. in Zssgn* Vertilgungs-*od*. Vernichtungsmittel *n*. **II** *adj* **3.** tödlich: ~**whale** *zo*. Schwert-, Mordwal *m*. '**kill·ing** *adj* □ **1.** tödlich. **2.** vernichtend (*a. fig. Blick*), mörderisch (*a. fig. Tempo etc*). **3.** F umwerfend, hinreißend.

'**kill·joy** *s* Spielverderber(in), Miesmacher(in).

kiln [kɪln] *s* Brenn- *od*. Trockenofen *m*.

ki·lo ['kiːləʊ] *pl* **-los** *s* Kilo *n*.

ki·lo·gram(me) ['kɪləʊgræm] *s* Kilogramm *n*. '~**·me·ter**, *bsd. Br*. '~**·me·tre** *s* Kilometer *m*. '~**·watt** *s* ⚡ Kilowatt *n*.

kilt [kɪlt] *s* Kilt *m*, Schottenrock *m*.

ki·mo·no [kɪˈməʊnəʊ] *pl* **-nos** *s* Kimono *m*.

kin [kɪn] *s coll.* (*pl konstruiert*) Blutsverwandtschaft *f*, Verwandte *pl*: **be of no** ~ **to** nicht verwandt sein mit; → **next** 5.

kind¹ [kaɪnd] *s* **1.** Art *f*, Sorte *f*: **all** ~**s of** alle möglichen, allerlei; **nothing of the** ~ nichts dergleichen. **2.** Art *f*, Wesen *n*: **different in** ~ der Art *od*. dem Wesen nach verschieden. **3.** ~ **of** F ein bißchen, irgendwie: **I've** ~ **of promised it** ich habe es halb u. halb versprochen. **4.** **in** ~ in Naturalien *zahlen*.

kind² [~] *adj* (□ → **kindly** II) **1.** freundlich, liebenswürdig, nett (**to** zu): ~ **to animals** tierlieb; **would you be so** ~ **as to do this for me?** sei so gut *od*. freundlich u. erledige das für mich, erledige das doch bitte für mich; → **enough** III. **2.** herzlich: → **regard** 4.

kin·der·gar·ten ['kɪndəˌgɑːtn] *s* Kindergarten *m*: ~ **teacher** Kindergärtnerin *f*. ,**kind'heart·ed** *adj* □ gütig, gutherzig.

kin·dle ['kɪndl] **I** *v/t* **1.** an-, entzünden. **2.** *Haß etc* entfachen, -flammen, *Interesse etc* wecken. **II** *v/i* **3.** sich entzünden, Feuer fangen. **4.** *fig*. entbrennen, -flammen.

kin·dling ['kɪndlɪŋ] *s* Anzündmaterial *n*.

kind·ly ['kaɪndlɪ] **I** adj **1.** freundlich, liebenswürdig. **II** adv **2.** → **kind²** 1. **3.** freundlicher-, liebenswürdiger-, netterweise: ~ *tell me* sagen Sie mir bitte. **4.** *take ~ to* sich mit et. an- od. befreunden.

kind·ness ['kaɪndnɪs] s **1.** Freundlichkeit f, Liebenswürdigkeit f. **2.** Gefälligkeit f: *do s.o. a ~* j-m e-e Gefälligkeit erweisen.

kin·dred ['kɪndrɪd] **I** s **1.** (Bluts)Verwandtschaft f. **2.** coll. (pl konstruiert) Verwandte pl, Verwandtschaft f. **II** adj **3.** (bluts)verwandt. **4.** fig. verwandt, ähnlich.

ki·net·ic [kɪ'netɪk] phys. **I** adj (~ally) kinetisch. **II** s pl (sg konstruiert) Kinetik f.

king [kɪŋ] s **1.** König m (a. Schach u. Kartenspiel): ~ *of hearts* Herzkönig; → *English* 3, *evidence* 2. **2.** Damespiel: Dame f. **'king·dom** s **1.** Königreich n. **2.** a. ♀ eccl. Reich n (Gottes). **3.** fig. Reich n: *animal* (*mineral, vegetable od. plant*) ~ Tier-(Mineral-, Pflanzen)reich. **'king·ly** adj königlich.

'king·pin s F wichtigster Mann; Drehu. Angelpunkt m. **'~-size(d)** adj Riesen...: ~ *cigarettes* pl King-size-Zigaretten pl.

kink [kɪŋk] s **1.** Knick m (in Draht etc). **2.** fig. Spleen m, Tick m. **3.** *have a ~ in one's back* (*neck*) e-n steifen Rücken (Hals) haben. **'kink·y** adj **1.** kraus (Haar). **2.** fig. spleenig. **3.** F abartig, pervers.

kins·folk ['kɪnzfəʊk] s pl Verwandtschaft f, (Bluts)Verwandte pl.

kin·ship ['kɪnʃɪp] s (Bluts)Verwandtschaft f.

kins·man ['kɪnzmən] s (irr *man*) (Bluts)Verwandte m. **'kins·wom·an** s (irr *woman*) (Bluts)Verwandte f.

ki·osk ['kiːɒsk] s **1.** Kiosk m. **2.** Br. Telefonzelle f.

kip [kɪp] sl. **I** s **1.** Schlaf m: *have a ~* pennen. **2.** Schlafstelle f. **II** v/i **3.** pennen. **4.** ~ *down* sich hinhauen.

kip·per ['kɪpə] s Kipper m (Räucherhering).

kiss [kɪs] **I** s **1.** Kuß m: ~ *of life* Br. Mund-zu-Mund-Beatmung f. **II** v/t **2.** küssen: ~ *s.o. good night* j-m e-n Gutenachtkuß geben; ~ *the dust* F ins Gras

beißen. **3.** leicht berühren. **III** v/i **4.** sich küssen. **5.** sich leicht berühren. **'kiss·er** s sl. Schnauze f, Fresse f; Visage f. **'kiss-proof** adj kußecht.

kit [kɪt] **I** s **1.** (Reise-, Reit- etc)Ausrüstung f, (-)Sachen pl. **2.** ✗ Montur f; Gepäck n. **3.** Arbeitsgerät n, Werkzeug(e pl) n; Werkzeugtasche f, -kasten m. **4.** Baukasten m; Bastelsatz m. **5.** a. *press* ~ Pressemappe f. **II** v/t **6.** oft ~ *out* (od. *up*) ausstatten (*with* mit). ~ *bag* s **1.** ✗ Kleider-, Seesack m. **2.** Reisetasche f.

kitch·en ['kɪtʃɪn] **I** s Küche f. **II** adj Küchen...: ~ *knife* (*table*, etc); ~ *garden* (Obst- u.) Gemüsegarten m; ~ *help* Küchenhilfe f; ~ *sink* Ausguß m, Spüle f; *with everything but the ~ sink* humor. mit Sack u. Pack. **kitch·en·et(te)** [͵~'net] s Kochnische f.

kite [kaɪt] s Drachen m: *fly a ~* e-n Drachen od. fig. e-n Versuchsballon steigen lassen.

kith [kɪθ] s: *with ~ and kin* mit Kind u. Kegel.

kit·ten ['kɪtn] s Kätzchen n: *have ~s* Br. F Zustände kriegen. **'kit·ten·ish** adj **1.** (kindlich) verspielt od. ausgelassen. **2.** kokett.

kit·ty ['kɪtɪ] s Kätzchen n.

ki·wi ['kiːwiː] **I** s **1.** orn. Kiwi m. **2.** ♀ Kiwi f. **3.** mst ♀ F Neuseeländer(in). **II** adj **4.** mst ♀ F neuseeländisch.

klax·on ['klæksn] s mot. Hupe f.

klep·to·ma·ni·a [͵kleptəʊ'meɪnjə] s psych. Kleptomanie f. **͵klep·to'ma·ni·ac** [͵~nɪæk] s Kleptomane m, -manin f.

knack [næk] s **1.** Kniff m, Trick m: *get the ~ of doing s.th.* dahinterkommen od. herausbekommen, wie man et. tut; *have the ~ of s.th.* den Dreh von od. bei et. heraushaben. **2.** Geschick n: *have the* (od. *a*) ~ *of doing s.th.* Geschick od. das Talent haben, et. zu tun.

knack·er ['nækə] s Br. **1.** Abdecker m: *~'s yard* Abdeckerei f. **2.** Abbruchunternehmer m. **'knack·ered** adj Br. F geschlaucht, kaputt. **'knack·er·y** s Br. Abdeckerei f.

knag [næg] s Knorren m.

knap·sack ['næpsæk] s **1.** ✗ Tornister m. **2.** Rucksack m.

knave [neɪv] s **1.** obs. Schurke m. **2.** Kar-

tenspiel: **Bube** *m*: **~ of hearts** Herzbube *m*.

knead [niːd] *v/t* Teig etc (durch)kneten, *Muskeln a.* massieren.

knee [niː] *s* **1.** Knie *n*: **on one's ~s** kniefällig, auf Knien; **bring s.o. to his ~s** j-n auf *od.* in die Knie zwingen; **go (down** (*od.* **fall)** *on one's ~s to* niederknien vor (*dat*), *fig. a.* in die Knie gehen vor (*dat*). **2.** ⚙ Knie(stück) *n*; (Rohr)Krümmer *m.* **~ bend** *s* Kniebeuge *f.* '**~ cap** *s anat.* Kniescheibe *f.* **,~'deep**, **,~'high** *adj* knietief, -hoch. **~ joint** *s anat.*, ⚙ Kniegelenk *n*.

kneel [niːl] *v/i* (*mst irr*) **1.** *a.* **~ down** (sich) hinknien, niederknien (**to** vor *dat*). **2.** knien, auf den Knien liegen (**before** vor *dat*).

'**knee·pad** *s* Knieschützer *m.* '**~pan** → *kneecap.* '**~room** *s* ✈, mot. Kniefreiheit *f*.

knelt [nelt] *pret u. pp von* **kneel**.

knew [njuː] *pret von* **know**.

knick·er·bock·ers ['nɪkəbɒkəz] *s pl, a.* **pair of ~** Knickerbocker *pl*.

knick·ers ['nɪkəz] *s pl, a.* **pair of ~ 1.** → **knickerbockers. 2.** *bsd. Br.* (Damen)Schlüpfer *m*: **get one's ~ in a twist** F, *oft humor.* sich ins Hemd machen.

knick-knack ['nɪknæk] *s* **1.** Nippsache *f.* **2.** billiges Schmuckstück. **3.** Spielerei *f*, Schnickschnack *m*.

knife [naɪf] **I** *pl* **knives** [naɪvz] *s* Messer *n*: **before you can say ~** *bsd. Br.* F im Nu, im Handumdrehen; **to the ~** bis aufs Messer, bis zum Äußersten; **have one's ~ into s.o.** j-n auf dem Kieker haben; **go under the ~** ⚕ unters Messer kommen. **II** *v/t* mit e-m Messer stechen *od.* verletzen; **~ (to death)** erstechen. **~ blade** *s* Messerklinge *f.* **~ edge** *s* Messerschneide *f*: **be balanced on a ~** *fig.* auf des Messers Schneide stehen. **~ point** *s* Messerspitze *f*: **at ~** mit vorgehaltenem Messer.

knight [naɪt] **I** *s* **1.** *hist.* Ritter *m* (*Br. a. Adelsstufe*). **2.** *Schach:* Springer *m*, Pferd *n.* **II** *v/t* **3.** zum Ritter schlagen. '**knight·ly** *adj u. adv* ritterlich.

knit [nɪt] (*a. irr*) **I** *v/t* **1.** stricken. **2.** *a.* **~ together** zs.-fügen, verbinden (*a. fig.*). **3.** *fig.* verknüpfen. **4.** *Stirn* runzeln; *Augenbrauen* zs.-ziehen. **II** *v/i* **5.** stricken. '**knit·ting** *s* **1.** Stricken *n.* **2.**

Strick·arbeit *f*, -zeug *n.* **II** *adj* **3.** **Strick...**: **~ needle.**

'**knit·wear** *s* Strickwaren *pl*.

knives [naɪvz] *pl von* **knife**.

knob [nɒb] *s* **1.** (*runder*) Kniff, Knauf *m.* **2.** Beule *f*, Höcker *m.* **3.** *bsd. Br.* Stück(chen) *n* (*Zucker etc*).

knock [nɒk] **I** *s* **1.** Schlag *m*, Stoß *m.* **2.** Klopfen *n* (*a. mot.*): **there is a ~ (at** [*Am.* **on**] **the door)** es klopft. **II** *v/t* **3.** schlagen, stoßen: **~ one's head against** sich den Kopf anschlagen an (*dat*); **~ one's head against a brick wall** *fig.* mit dem Kopf gegen die Wand rennen. **III** *v/i* **4.** schlagen, klopfen: **~ at** (*Am.* **on**) **the door** an die Tür klopfen. **5.** schlagen, prallen, stoßen (**against**, **into** gegen; **on** auf *acc*). **6.** ⚙ klopfen (*Motor, Brennstoff*) *n* (*Zucker etc*). **7.** ⚙ klopfen (*Motor, Brennstoff*) *n* (*Zucker etc*). **7.** ~ **about** (*around*) F sich herumtreiben in (*dat*); herumliegen in (*dat*) (*Gegenstand*).

Verbindungen mit Adverbien:

knock **a·bout**, **~ a·round I** *v/t* **1.** herumstoßen. **II** *v/i* **2.** F sich herumtreiben: **~ with** *a.* gehen mit (*e-m Mädchen etc*). **3.** F herumliegen (*Gegenstand*). **~ back** *v/t* **1.** Stuhl zurückstoßen. **2.** *bsd. Br.* F *Getränk* runterkippen. **~ down** *v/t* **1.** a) umstoßen, umwerfen, b) niederschlagen, c) an-, umfahren; überfahren, d) F umhauen, sprachlos machen. **2.** *Gebäude etc* abreißen, abbrechen. **3.** (*to auf acc; £2 um 2 Pfund*) *j-n, Preis* herunterhandeln; mit *dem Preis* heruntergehen. **4.** **knock s.th. down to s.o.** (*Auktion*) j-m et. zuschlagen (**at, for** für). **~ in** *v/t* *Nagel* einschlagen. **~ off** *v/t* **1.** herunter-, abschlagen. **2.** F aufhören mit: **knock it off!** hör auf (damit)!; **~ work(ing)** → 6b. **3.** F *Arbeit* erledigen. **4.** F *j-n* umlegen. **5.** F *Essen* wegputzen. **II** *v/i* **6.** F a) allg. aufhören, b) Feierabend *od.* Schluß machen. **~ out** *v/t* **1.** herausschlagen, -klopfen (**of** aus), *Pfeife* ausklopfen: **→ bottom** 3. **2.** a) bewußtlos schlagen, b) *Boxen:* k.o. schlagen, ausknocken, c) betäuben (*Droge etc*), d) F umhauen (*sprachlos machen, hinreißen*). **~ to·geth·er** *v/t* **1.** (*a. v/i*) aneinanderstoßen, -schlagen. **2.** F et. schnell zs.-zimmern, *Essen etc* (*her*)zaubern. **~ o·ver** *v/t* **1.** umwerfen, umstoßen. **2.** überfahren. **~ up I** *v/t* **1.** hochschlagen, in die Höhe schlagen. **2.**

Br. F herausklopfen, (*durch Klopfen*) wecken. **3.** *Br.* F Geld verdienen. **4.** *sl.* Mädchen anbumsen. **II** *v/i* **5.** *Tennis etc:* sich einschlagen *od.* einspielen.

'knock·a·bout *adj* **1.** strapazierfähig (*Kleidung etc*). **2.** *thea. etc* Klamauk...: **~ comedy** Klamaukstück *n.* **'~-down I** *adj* **1.** niederschmetternd (*a. fig.*). **2.** **~ price** Schleuderpreis *m:* **at a ~** spottbillig. **II** *s* Boxen: Niederschlag *m.*

knock·er ['nɒkə] *s* **1.** (Tür)Klopfer *m.* **2.** *pl sl.* Titten *pl.*

‚knock·|-'kneed *adj* X-beinig: **be ~** X-Beine haben. **‚~-'knees** *s pl* X-Beine *pl.* **'~-out I** *s* **1.** Boxen: K.o. *m:* **win by a ~** durch K.o. gewinnen. **2.** F tolle Person *od.* Sache; Attraktion *f;* Bombenerfolg *m.* **II** *adj* **3.** Boxen: K.-o.-...: **~ system** (*Sport*) K.-o.-System *n.* **'~-up** *s* Tennis *etc:* Einschlagen *n,* -spielen *n.*

knoll [nəʊl] *s* Hügel *m.*

knot [nɒt] **I** *s* **1.** Knoten *m:* **make** (*od.* **tie**) **a ~** e-n Knoten machen; **tie s.o.** (**up**) **in ~s** F j-n völlig durcheinanderbringen. **2.** Astknoten *m,* Knorren *m.* **3.** ♣ Knoten *m,* Seemeile *f.* **4.** *fig.* Knoten *m,* Schwierigkeit *f:* **cut the ~** den Knoten durchhauen. **II** *v/t* **5.** (e-n) Knoten machen in (*acc*). **6.** (ver)knoten, (-)knüpfen. **II** *v/i* **7.** sich verknoten. **'knot·ty** *adj* **1.** knotig. **2.** knorrig (*Holz*). **3.** *fig.* verwickelt, kompliziert.

know [nəʊ] **I** *v/t* (*irr*) **1.** *allg.* wissen. **2.** können: **~ how to do s.th.** et. tun können. **3.** kennen: a) sich auskennen in (*dat*), b) vertraut sein mit, c) bekannt sein mit. **4.** erfahren, erleben: **he has ~n better days** er hat schon bessere Tage gesehen. **5.** (wieder)erkennen (**by** an *dat*); unterscheiden (können) (**from** von): **~ apart** auseinanderhalten. **II** *v/i* (*irr*) **6.** wissen (**of** von, um), Bescheid wissen (**about** über *acc*): **you never ~** man kann nie wissen; **~ better than to do s.th.** sich davor hüten, et. zu tun. **III** *s* **7. be in the ~** Bescheid wissen. **'~-all** *s* Besserwisser *m.* **'~-how** *s* Know-how *n* (*a.* ✝): **industrial ~** praktische Betriebserfahrung.

know·ing ['nəʊɪŋ] *adj* **1.** klug, gescheit. **2.** schlau, durchtrieben. **3.** verständnisvoll, wissend (*Blick*). **'know·ing·ly** *adv* **1.** → **knowing. 2.** wissentlich, bewußt, absichtlich.

knowl·edge ['nɒlɪdʒ] *s* **1.** Kenntnis *f:* **bring s.th. to s.o.'s ~** j-n von et. in Kenntnis setzen; **it has come to my ~** ich habe erfahren (**that** daß); (**not**) **to my ~** m-s Wissens (nicht); **without my ~** ohne mein Wissen. **2.** Wissen *n,* Kenntnisse *pl:* **have a good ~ of** viel verstehen von, sich gut auskennen in (*dat*).

known [nəʊn] **I** *pp von* **know. II** *adj* bekannt (**as** als; **for** für; **to s.o.** j-m): **~ to the police** polizeibekannt; **make ~** bekanntmachen; **make o.s. ~ to s.o.** sich j-m vorstellen.

knuck·le ['nʌkl] **I** *s* **1.** *anat.* (Finger)Knöchel *m:* → **rap**[1], 3. **2.** (*Kalbs-, Schweins*)Haxe *f,* (-)Hachse *f:* **near the ~** F reichlich gewagt (*Witz etc*). **II** *v/i* **3. ~ down** sich anstrengen *od.* dahinterklemmen: **~ down to work** sich an die Arbeit machen, sich hinter die Arbeit klemmen. **4. ~ under** sich unterwerfen *od.* beugen (**to** dat), klein beigeben. **'~·dust·er** *s* Schlagring *m.*

kook [kuːk] *s Am.* F Spinner *m.*

Ko·ran [kɒˈrɑːn] *s eccl.* Koran *m.*

kraut [kraʊt] *s sl. contp.* Deutsche *m, f.*

Krem·lin ['kremlɪn] *npr* Kreml *m.*

L

lab [læb] *s* F Labor *n.*

la·bel ['leɪbl] **I** *s* **1.** Etikett *n,* (Klebe-, Anhänge)Zettel *m,* (-)Schild(chen) *n.* **II** *v/t pret u. pp* **-beled,** *bsd. Br.* **-belled**

2. etikettieren, beschriften. **3.** als ... bezeichnen, zu ... stempeln: **be ~(l)ed a criminal** zum Verbrecher gestempelt werden.

la·bi·al ['leɪbjəl] s ling. Lippen-, Labiallaut m.

la·bor ['leɪbə] Am. I → labour, etc. II adj **1.** Gewerkschafts... **2.** ~ **union** Gewerkschaft f.

la·bor·a·to·ry [ləˈbɒrətərɪ] s Labor(atorium) n: ~ **assistant** Laborant(in).

la·bo·ri·ous [ləˈbɔːrɪəs] adj □ **1.** mühsam. **2.** schwerfällig (Stil). **3.** arbeitsam, fleißig.

la·bour ['leɪbə] bsd. Br. I s **1.** (schwere) Arbeit. **2.** Mühe f, Plage f: lost ~ vergebliche Mühe. **3.** ✝ Arbeiterschaft f; Arbeiter pl, Arbeitskräfte pl. **4.** ♀ pol. die Labour Party (Großbritanniens etc). **5.** ✿ Wehen pl: be in ~ in den Wehen liegen. II v/i **6.** (schwer) arbeiten (at an dat), sich bemühen (for um), sich anstrengen od. abmühen (to do zu tun). **7.** a. ~ along sich mühsam fortbewegen: ~ through sich kämpfen durch (Schlamm, Buch etc). **8.** (under) zu leiden haben (unter dat), zu kämpfen haben (mit); befangen sein (in dat). **9.** ✝ in den Wehen liegen. III v/t **10.** ausführlich od. umständlich behandeln, breitwalzen. IV Hilfs)Arbeiter m. **11.** Arbeits...; ~ **Party** Labour Party f. 'la·bour·er s bsd. Br. (bsd. Hilfs)Arbeiter m.

'la·bour|-in,ten·sive adj □ bsd. Br. arbeitsintensiv. '~-,sav·ing adj bsd. Br. arbeitssparend.

lab·y·rinth ['læbərɪnθ] s Labyrinth n, fig. a. Gewirr n.

lace [leɪs] s **1.** Textilwesen: Spitze f. **2.** Litze f, Tresse f, Borte f. **3.** Schnürband n, -senkel m. **4.** Schuß m Alkohol (in Getränken): with a ~ of rum mit e-m Schuß Rum. II v/t **5.** a. ~ up (zu-, zs.-)schnüren. **6.** mit Spitzen od. Litzen besetzen. **7.** ~ one's tea with rum sich e-n Schuß Rum in den Tee geben; ~ s.o.'s beer with vodka j-m heimlich Wodka ins Bier schütten; tea ~d with rum Tee m mit e-m Schuß Rum. III v/i **8.** ~ into s.o. F über j-n herfallen (a. mit Worten).

lac·er·ate ['læsəreɪt] v/t Gesicht etc aufreißen; zerschneiden; zerkratzen. ˌlac·er'a·tion s Riß-; Schnitt-, Kratzwunde f.

lach·ry·mal ['lækrɪml] adj **1.** Tränen...: ~ gland anat. Tränendrüse f. **2.** → lach-

rymose 1, 2. **lach·ry·mose** ['~məʊs] adj □ **1.** tränenreich. **2.** weinerlich. **3.** traurig, ergreifend.

lack [læk] I s **1.** Mangel m (of an dat): ~ of sleep fehlender Schlaf; for (od. through) ~ of time aus Zeitmangel. II v/t **2.** nicht haben, Mangel haben od. leiden an (dat): we ~ coal es fehlt uns an Kohle. **3.** es fehlen lassen an (dat). III v/i **4.** a) be ~ing fehlen, b) ~ in Mangel haben od. leiden an (dat): he is ~ing in courage ihm fehlt der Mut. **5.** ~ for nothing von allem genug haben: he ~s for nothing es fehlt ihm an nichts.

lack·a·dai·si·cal [ˌlækəˈdeɪzɪkl] adj □ **1.** lustlos. **2.** nachlässig (about in dat).

lack·ey ['lækɪ] s Lakai m (a. fig. contp.).

lack·ing ['lækɪŋ] adj **1.** be found ~ sich nicht bewähren. **2.** Br. F beschränkt, dumm.

'lack|,lus·ter adj Am., '~,lus·tre adj bsd. Br. glanzlos, matt.

la·con·ic [ləˈkɒnɪk] adj (~ally) **1.** lakonisch. **2.** wortkarg.

lac·quer ['lækə] I s **1.** (Farb)Lack m. **2.** (Haar)Festiger m. II v/t **3.** lackieren.

la·crosse [ləˈkrɒs] s Sport: Lacrosse n (Ballspiel).

lad [læd] s **1.** junger Kerl od. Bursche. **2.** a bit of a ~ Br. F ein ziemlicher Draufgänger.

lad·der ['lædə] s **1.** Leiter f (a. fig.). **2.** bsd. Br. Laufmasche f. II v/i **3.** bsd. Br. Laufmaschen bekommen. '~-proof adj maschenfest.

lad·en ['leɪdn] adj **1.** (schwer) beladen (with mit). **2.** fig. bedrückt (with von): ~ with guilt schuldbeladen.

la·di·da [ˌlɑːdɪˈdɑː] adj F affektiert, affig.

la·dies'| choice s Damenwahl f. ~ man s (irr man) Frauenheld m. ~ room s Damentoilette f.

la·dle ['leɪdl] I s **1.** Schöpflöffel m, -kelle f. **2.** ❂ Schaufel f (e-s Baggers etc). II v/t **3.** a. ~ out (aus)schöpfen. **4.** a. ~ out austeilen (a. fig.).

la·dy ['leɪdɪ] I s **1.** Dame f: ladies and gentlemen m-e Damen u. Herren. **2.** ♀ Lady f (Titel). **3.** Our ♀ eccl. Unsere Liebe Frau, die Mutter Gottes. **4.** La·dies pl (sg konstruiert) Damentoilette f. II adj **5.** weiblich: ~ doctor Ärztin f. '~-bird, Am. a. '~-bug s zo. Marienkäfer m. ˌ~-in-'wait·ing pl ˌla·dies-in-

-'**wait·ing** s Hofdame f. '**~·,kill·er** s F Ladykiller m, Herzensbrecher m. '**~ -like** adj damenhaft.

la·dy's man → **ladies' man.**

lag[1] [læg] **I** v/i **1.** mst ~ behind zurückbleiben, nicht mitkommen (beide a. fig.): ~ behind s.o. hinter j-m zurückbleiben. **2.** mst ~ behind sich verzögern. **II** s **3.** → time lag.

lag[2] [læg] v/t ⊙ verschalen; isolieren, ummanteln.

la·ger ['lɑːgə] s Lagerbier n.

la·goon [lə'guːn] s Lagune f.

laid [leɪd] pret u. pp von **lay**[1].

lain [leɪn] pp von **lie**[2].

lair [leə] s **1.** zo. Lager n; Bau m; Höhle f. **2.** Versteck n.

la·i·ty ['leɪətɪ] s Laien pl.

lake [leɪk] s See m. ~ **dwell·ings** s pl Pfahlbauten pl.

lam [læm] sl. **I** v/t verdreschen, -möbeln. **II** v/i: ~ into s.o. auf j-n eindreschen; über j-n herfallen (a. mit Worten).

la·ma ['lɑːmə] s eccl. Lama m.

lamb [læm] **I** s **1.** Lamm n: (as) gentle (od. meek) as a ~ lammfromm. **2.** Lamm n: a) gastr. Lammfleisch n: ~ **chop** Lammkotelett n, b) → **lambskin**. **II** v/i **3.** lammen.

lam·baste [læm'beɪst] v/t sl. **1.** → **lam** I. **2.** fig. herunterputzen, zs.-stauchen.

'**lamb·like** adj lammfromm. '**~·skin** s **1.** Lammfell n. **2.** Schafleder n.

lamb's wool s Lambswool f, Lammwolle f.

lame [leɪm] **I** adj □ **1.** a) lahm: walk ~ly hinken, (Tier a.) lahmen, b) gelähmt. **2.** fig. lahm: a) faul (Ausrede), b) schwach (Argument), c) matt, schwach (Anstrengungen). **II** v/t **3.** lähmen (a. fig.). ~ **duck** s F **1.** Niete f, Versager m (a. Sache). **2.** pol. Am. nicht wiedergewähltes Kongreßmitglied bis zum Ablauf s-r Amtszeit.

la·mel·la [lə'melə] pl -**lae** [~liː], -**las** s Lamelle f.

lame·ness ['leɪmnɪs] s Lahmheit f (a. fig.).

la·ment [lə'ment] **I** v/i **1.** jammern, (weh)klagen, contp. lamentieren (for, over um). **2.** trauern (for, over um). **II** v/t **3.** beklagen: a) bejammern, bedauern, b) betrauern **III** s **4.** Jammer m, (Weh)Klage f. **5.** Klagelied n.

lam·en·ta·ble ['læməntəbl] adj □ **1.** beklagenswert, bedauerlich. **2.** contp. erbärmlich, kläglich. **lam·en·ta·tion** [~men'teɪʃn] s **1.** (Weh)Klage f. **2.** contp. Lamento n, Lamentieren n.

lam·i·nat·ed ['læmɪneɪtɪd] adj ⊙ laminiert, geschichtet: ~ **glass** Verbundglas n.

lamp [læmp] s Lampe f, (Straßen)Laterne f.

lam·poon [læm'puːn] **I** s Spott-, Schmähschrift f. **II** v/t (schriftlich) verspotten.

'**lamp-post** s Laternenpfahl m: → **between** 2.

'**lamp·shade** s Lampenschirm m.

lance [lɑːns] **I** s Lanze f. **II** v/t ✻ Geschwür etc (mit e-r Lanzette) öffnen.

lan·cet ['lɑːnsɪt] s **1.** ✻ Lanzette f. **2.** △ a) a. ~ **arch** Spitzbogen m, b) a. ~ **win·dow** Spitzbogenfenster n.

land [lænd] **I** s **1.** Land n (Ggs. Wasser, Luft): by ~ auf dem Landweg; by ~ and sea zu Wasser u. zu Lande; see (od. find out) how the ~ lies fig. die Lage peilen; sich e-n Überblick verschaffen. **2.** Land n, Boden m: ploughed ~ Akkerland. **3.** Land n, Staat m. **4.** fig. Land n, Reich n: → **milk** I. **II** v/i **5.** ✔ landen, ♦ a. anlegen. **6.** oft ~ **up** landen, (an)kommen: ~ **up in prison** im Gefängnis landen. **III** v/t **7.** Personen, Güter, Flugzeug landen, Güter ausladen, ♦ a. löschen. **8.** j-n bringen: ~ **o.s.** (od. be ~ed) in trouble in Schwierigkeiten geraten od. kommen. **9.** F Schlag, Treffer landen, anbringen: he ~ed him one er knallte ihm eine. **10.** F j-n, et. kriegen, erwischen, Preis ergattern. **11.** ~ **s.o. s.th.** F j-m et. einbringen.

land·ed ['lændɪd] adj Land..., Grund...: ~ **property** Land-, Grundbesitz m.

land forc·es s pl ✗ Landstreitkräfte pl.

land·ing ['lændɪŋ] s **1.** ✔ Landung f, Landen n, ♦ a. Anlegen n. **2.** (Treppen)Absatz m. ~ **ap·proach** s ✔ Landeanflug m. ~ **field** s ✔ Landeplatz m. ~ **gear** s ✔ Fahrgestell n, -werk n. ~ **per·mit** s ✔ Landeerlaubnis f.

land|·la·dy ['læn,leɪdɪ] s (Haus-, Gast-, Pensions)Wirtin f. '**~·lord** ['læn~] s **1.** Grundeigentümer m, -besitzer m. **2.** (Haus-, Gast-, Pensions)Wirt m. '**~·lub·ber** ['lænd,~] s ♦ Landratte f. '**~·mark** s

1. Grenzstein *m*, -zeichen *n*. **2.** ⚓ Landmarke *f*, Seezeichen *n*. **3.** Wahrzeichen *n* (*e-r Stadt etc*). **4.** *fig.* Mark-, Meilenstein *m*. **~ of·fice** *s Am.* Grundbuchamt *n*. **'~‚own·er** *s* Grundbesitzer(in), -eigentümer(in). **~ reg·is·ter** *s Br.* Grundbuch *n*. **~ reg·is·try** *s Br.* Grundbuchamt *n*. **‚~scape** ['lænskeɪp] *s* Landschaft *f* (*a. paint.*): **~ architect** Landschaftsarchitekt *m*; **~ gardener** Landschaftsgärtner *m*; **~ painter** Landschaftsmaler *m*. **'~‚slide** *s* **1.** Erdrutsch *m*. **2.** *a.* **~ vic·tory** (*od. win*) *pol.* überwältigender Wahlsieg.

land·ward(s) ['lændwəd(z)] *adv* land(ein)wärts.

lane [leɪn] *s* **1.** (Feld)Weg *m*. **2.** Gasse *f*: a) Sträßchen *n*, b) Durchgang *m* (*zwischen Menschenreihen etc*): **form a ~** Spalier stehen, e-e Gasse bilden. **3.** Schneise *f*. **4.** ⚓ Fahrrinne *f*. **5.** ✈ Flugschneise *f*. **6.** *mot.* (Fahr)Spur *f*: **change ~s** die Spur wechseln; **get in ~** sich einordnen. **7.** *Sport:* (*einzelne*) Bahn *f*.

lan·guage ['læŋgwɪdʒ] *s* **1.** Sprache *f*. **2.** Sprache *f*, Ausdrucks-, Redeweise *f*: → **bad** 3, **strong** 7. **3.** (Fach)Sprache *f*. **~ course** *s* Sprachkurs *m*. **~ la·bor·a·to·ry** *s* Sprachlabor *n*. **~ school** *s* Sprachenschule *f*.

lan·guid ['læŋgwɪd] *adj* □ **1.** schwach, matt. **2.** *fig.* lau, interesselos.

lan·guish ['læŋgwɪʃ] *v/i* **1.** ermatten, erschlaffen. **2.** erlahmen (*Interesse etc*). **3.** sich sehnen, schmachten (**for** nach). **'lan·guish·ing** *adj* □ sehnsüchtig, schmachtend (*Blick etc*).

lan·guor ['læŋgə] *s* **1.** Schwachheit *f*, Mattigkeit *f*. **2.** *fig.* Lauheit *f*, Interesselosigkeit *f*. **3.** einschläfernde Schwüle. **'lan·guor·ous** *adj* □ **1.** → **languid. 2.** einschläfernd schwül.

lank [læŋk] *adj* □ **1.** hager, mager. **2.** glatt (*Haar*). **'lank·y** *adj* □ schlaksig.

lan·tern ['læntən] *s* Laterne *f*.

lap¹ [læp] *s* Schoß *m* (*a. fig.*): **drop** (*od. fall*) **into s.o.'s ~** j-m in den Schoß fallen.

lap² [~] **I** *v/t* **1.** wickeln ([**a**]**round** um). **2.** einschlagen, -wickeln (**in** in *acc*). **3.** hinausragen über (*acc*). **4.** *Sport:* überrunden. **II** *v/i* **5.** überstehen, hinausragen (**over** über *acc*). **6.** sich überlappen. **III**

s **7.** *Sport:* Runde *f*: **~ of hono(u)r** Ehrenrunde.

lap³ [~] **I** *v/t* **1.** (sch)lecken: **~ up** a) auf(sch)lecken, b) *fig.* F fressen, schlucken (*kritiklos glauben*), c) *fig.* F Komplimente *etc* gierig aufnehmen. **II** *v/i* **3.** (Sch)Lecken *n*: **take a ~ at** (sch)lecken an (*dat*). **4.** Plätschern *n*.

lap belt *s* ✈, *mot.* Beckengurt *m*.

la·pel [lə'pel] *s* Aufschlag *m*, Revers *n*, *m*.

lapse [læps] *s* **1.** Versehen *n*, (kleiner) Fehler *od.* Irrtum. **2.** Vergehen *n*, Entgleisung *f*. **3.** Zeitspanne *f*. **4.** ⚖ Verfall *m*, Erlöschen *n*. **II** *v/i* **5.** vergehen, -streichen (*Zeit*); ablaufen (*Frist*). **6.** verfallen, -sinken (**into** in *acc*). **7.** ⚖ verfallen, erlöschen (*Anspruch etc*).

lar·ce·ny ['lɑːsənɪ] *s* ⚖ Diebstahl *m*: **grand** (**petty**) **~** schwerer (einfacher) Diebstahl.

larch [lɑːtʃ] *s* ⚘ Lärche *f*.

lard [lɑːd] **I** *s* **1.** Schweinefett *n*, -schmalz *n*. **2.** einfetten. **3.** *Fleisch* spicken: **~ing needle** (*od. pin*) Spicknadel *f*. **4.** *fig.* spicken, (aus)schmücken (**with** mit).

lard·er ['lɑːdə] *s* **1.** Speisekammer *f*. **2.** Speiseschrank *m*.

large [lɑːdʒ] **I** *adj* (□ → **largely**) **1.** *allg.* groß: (**as**) **~ as life** in voller Lebensgröße; **~r than life** überlebensgroß. **2.** groß (*Familie etc*), (*Einkommen etc a.*) beträchtlich, (*Mahlzeit*) ausgiebig, reichlich. **3.** umfassend, weitgehend (*Vollmachten etc*). **4.** Groß...: **~ consumer** Großverbraucher *m*. **5.** F großspurig. **II** *adv* **6.** **talk** **~** F große Töne spucken. **III** *s* **7.** **at ~** a) in Freiheit, auf freiem Fuß: **set at ~** auf freien Fuß setzen, b) (sehr) ausführlich, c) in der Gesamtheit: **the nation at ~** die ganze Nation.

'large·ly *adv* **1.** großen-, größtenteils. **2.** allgemein.

‚large-'mind·ed *adj* □ aufgeschlossen, tolerant.

large·ness ['lɑːdʒnɪs] *s* **1.** Größe *f*. **2.** F Großspurigkeit *f*.

'large-scale *adj* groß(angelegt), Groß...: **~ experiment** Großversuch *m*.

lar·gess(e) [lɑː'dʒes] *s* Freigebigkeit *f*, Großzügigkeit *f*.

lar·go ['lɑːgəʊ] *pl* **-gos** *s* ♪ Largo *n*.

lar·i·at ['læriət] *s bsd. Am.* Lasso *n, m.*

lark[1] [lɑːk] *s orn.* Lerche *f.*

lark[2] [~] **I** *s* Jux *m,* Ulk *m:* **for a ~** zum Spaß, aus Jux. **II** *v/i mst* **~ about** (*od.* **around**) Blödsinn machen, herumalbern.

lark·spur ['lɑːkspɜː] *s* ⚜ Rittersporn *m.*

lar·va ['lɑːvə] *pl* **-vae** ['~viː] *s zo.* Larve *f.*

lar·yn·gi·tis [ˌlærɪn'dʒaɪtɪs] *s* ⚕ Kehlkopfentzündung *f.* **lar·ynx** ['lærɪŋks] *pl* **la·ryn·ges** [lə'rɪndʒiːz], **'lar·ynx·es** *s anat.* Kehlkopf *m.*

las·civ·i·ous [lə'sɪvɪəs] *adj* □ **1.** geil, lüstern. **2.** lasziv, schlüpfrig.

la·ser ['leɪzə] *s phys.* Laser *m.* **~ beam** *s* Laserstrahl *m.*

lash[1] [læʃ] **I** *s* **1.** Peitschenschnur *f.* **2.** Peitschenhieb *m.* **3.** *fig.* (Peitschen-)Hieb *m* (**at** gegen). **4.** Peitschen *n* (*a. fig.*). **5.** (Augen)Wimper *f.* **II** *v/t* **6.** (aus)peitschen. **7.** *fig.* a) peitschen, b) peitschen an (*acc*) *od.* gegen. **8.** peitschen mit: **~ its tail** mit dem Schwanz um sich schlagen. **9.** *fig.* aufpeitschen (**into** zu): **~ o.s. into a fury** sich in Wut hineinsteigern. **10.** *fig.* geißeln, vom Leder ziehen gegen. **III** *v/i* **11.** **~ against** → 7b; **~ down** niederprasseln (*Regen*). **12.** schlagen (**at** nach): **~ a·bout** (*od.* **around**) (wild) um sich schlagen; **~ into** a) einschlagen auf (*acc*), b) *fig. j-n* zs.-stauchen; **~ out** (wild) um sich schlagen; ausschlagen (*Pferd*); **~ out at** a) einschlagen auf (*acc*), b) *a.* **~ out against** → 10.

lash[2] [~] *v/t* **1.** *a.* **~ down** (fest)binden (**to, on** an *dat*). **2.** ⚓ (fest)zurren.

lash·ing ['læʃɪŋ] *s* **1.** Auspeitschung *f.* **2.** *pl bsd. Br.* F e-e Unmenge (**of** von, an *dat*): **~s of** (*od.* **to**) **drink** jede Menge zu trinken.

lass [læs], **las·sie** ['læsɪ] *s* **1.** Mädchen *n.* **2.** Freundin *f,* Schatz *m.*

las·si·tude ['læsɪtjuːd] *s* Mattigkeit *f,* Abgespanntheit *f.*

las·so [læ'suː] **I** *pl* **-so(e)s** *s* Lasso *n, m.* **II** *v/t* mit e-m Lasso (ein)fangen.

last[1] [lɑːst] **I** *adj* (□ → **lastly**) **1.** letzt: **~ but one** vorletzt; **~ but two** drittletzt. **2.** letzt, vorig: **~ Monday** (am) letzten *od.* vorigen Montag; **~ night** gestern abend; letzte Nacht. **3.** letzt (*allein übrigbleibend*): **my ~ hope.** **4.** letzt (*am wenigsten erwartet od. geeignet*): **the ~ thing I would do** das letzte, was ich tun würde. **II** *adv* **5.** zuletzt, an letzter Stelle: **he came ~** er kam als letzter; **~ but not least** nicht zuletzt, nicht zu vergessen. **6.** zuletzt, zum letzten Mal. **7.** *in Zssgn:* **~-mentioned** letztgenannt, -erwähnt. **III** *s* **8.** **at ~** endlich, schließlich, zuletzt. **9.** *der, die, das* Letzte: **the ~ to arrive** der letzte, der ankam; **to the ~** bis zum äußersten; bis zum Ende *od.* Schluß.

last[2] [~] *v/i* **1.** (an-, fort)dauern. **2.** *a.* **~ out** durch-, aushalten. **3.** (sich) halten. **4.** *a.* **~ out** (aus)reichen (*Geld etc*). **II** *v/t* **5.** *j-m* reichen (*Geld etc*). **6.** *mst* **~ out** überdauern, -leben.

last[3] [~] *s* Leisten *m:* **stick to one's ~** *fig.* bei s-m Leisten bleiben.

'last-ditch *adj* allerletzt: **~ attempt** *a.* letzter verzweifelter Versuch.

last·ing ['lɑːstɪŋ] *adj* □ **1.** dauerhaft: a) andauernd, beständig: **~ peace** dauerhafter Friede; **~ effect** anhaltende Wirkung; **~ memories** *pl* bleibende Erinnerungen *pl,* b) haltbar. **2.** nachhaltig (*Eindruck etc*).

last·ly ['lɑːstlɪ] *adv* zuletzt, zum Schluß.

latch [lætʃ] **I** *s* **1.** Schnappriegel *m.* **2.** Schnappschloß *n.* **II** *v/t* **3.** ein-, zuklinken. **III** *v/i* **4.** einschnappen. **5.** **~ on** F kapieren: **~ on to** (*od.* **onto**) **s.th.** et. kapieren. **'~·key** *s* Haus-, Wohnungsschlüssel *m:* **~ child** (F **kid**) Schlüsselkind *n.*

late [leɪt] **I** *adj* (□ → **lately**) **1.** spät: **at a ~ hour** spät (*a. fig.*), zu später Stunde; **~ shift** ⚒ Spätschicht *f;* **it's getting ~** es ist schon spät. **2.** vorgerückt, Spät...: **~ summer** Spätsommer *m.* **3.** verspätet: **be ~** zu spät kommen (**for dinner** zum Essen), sich verspäten; Verspätung haben (*Zug etc*). **4.** **the latest fashion** die neueste Mode. **5.** letzt, früher, ehemalig; verstorben. **II** *adv* **6.** spät: **as ~ as last year** erst *od.* noch letztes Jahr; **see you ~** auf bald, bis später; **~ or** soon später; → **sleep** II. **7.** zu spät: **the train came ~** der Zug hatte Verspätung. **'~·com·er** *s* Zuspätkommende *m, f;* Zuspätgekommene *m, f.*

late·ly ['leɪtlɪ] *adv* **1.** vor kurzem, kürzlich. **2.** in letzter Zeit, neuerdings. **'late·ness** *s* **1.** späte Zeit: **the ~ of his arrival**

s-e späte Ankunft. **2.** Verspätung *f*, Zuspätkommen *n*.

la·tent ['leɪtənt] *adj* □ latent (*a.* ⚡ *etc*), verborgen.

lat·er·al ['lætərəl] *adj* seitlich, Seiten... '**lat·er·al·ly** *adv* **1.** seitlich, seitwärts. **2.** von der Seite.

la·test ['leɪtɪst] *I adj u. adv sup von* **late. II** *s* **at the ~** spätestens.

lath [lɑ:θ] *s* **1.** Latte *f*, Leiste *f*: (**as**) **thin as a ~** spindeldürr. **2.** *coll.* Latten *pl*, Leisten *pl*.

lathe [leɪð] *s* ⚙ Drehbank *f*.

lath·er ['lɑ:ðə] *I s* **1.** (Seifen)Schaum *m*. **2. get in a ~, work o.s. up into a ~** F außer sich geraten (**over** wegen). **II** *v/t* **3.** einseifen. **4.** F verprügeln. **III** *v/i* **5.** schäumen.

Lat·in ['lætɪn] *ling.* **I** *adj* lateinisch. **II** *s* Latein(isch) *n*. **~ A·mer·i·can I** *adj* lateinamerikanisch. **II** *s* Lateinamerikaner(in).

Lat·in·ism ['lætɪnɪzəm] *s ling.* Latinismus *m*.

lat·i·tude ['lætɪtjuːd] *s* **1.** *geogr.* Breite *f*: **in these ~s** in diesen Breiten *od.* Gegenden; → **degree** 2, **parallel** 3. **2.** *fig.* Spielraum *m*, (Bewegungs)Freiheit *f*.

la·trine [lə'triːn] *s* Latrine *f*.

lat·ter ['lætə] *adj* **1.** letzterwähnt, -genannt (*von zweien*): → **former** 2. **2.** letzt, später: **the ~ half of June** die zweite Junihälfte.

lat·tice ['lætɪs] *I s* Gitter(werk) *n*. **II** *v/t* vergittern.

laud·a·ble ['lɔːdəbl] *adj* □ löblich, lobenswert. **laud·a·to·ry** ['~dətərɪ] *adj* lobend: **~ speech** Lobrede *f*, Laudatio *f*.

laugh [lɑːf] **I** *s* Lachen *n*, Gelächter *n*: **with a ~** lachend; **have a good ~** herzlich lachen; **have the last ~** am Ende recht haben. **II** *v/i* lachen (**at** über *acc*): **~ at s.o.** j-n auslachen; **~ to o.s.** in sich hineinlachen; **~ out** auf- *od.* herauslachen; → **beard**, **sleeve** 1. **III** *v/t*: **~ away** (*od.* **off**) *et.* lachend *od.* mit e-m Scherz abtun. '**laugh·a·ble** *adj* □ lächerlich, lachhaft. '**laugh·er** *s* Lacher(in).

laugh·ing ['lɑːfɪŋ] **I** *s* **1.** Lachen *n*, Gelächter *n*. **II** *adj* □ **2.** lachend. **3.** lustig: **it is no ~ matter** es ist nicht(s) zum Lachen. **~ gas** *s* 🜹 Lachgas *n*. '**~·stock** *s* Zielscheibe *f* des Spotts: **make s.o.**

the ~ of j-n zum Gespött (*gen*) machen.

laugh·ter ['lɑːftə] *s* Lachen *n*, Gelächter *n*.

launch¹ [lɔːntʃ] *I v/t* **1.** *Boot* zu Wasser lassen; *Schiff* vom Stapel lassen: **be ~ed** vom Stapel laufen. **2.** *Geschoß, Torpedo* abschießen, *Rakete, Raumfahrzeug a.* starten. **3.** *Rede, Kritik etc* vom Stapel lassen; *Drohungen etc* ausstoßen. **4.** *Projekt etc* in Gang setzen, starten. **5. ~ o.s. on a task** (**into work**) sich auf e-e Aufgabe (in die Arbeit) stürzen. **II** *v/i* **6. ~ out** *fig.* sich stürzen (**into** in *acc*). **III** *s* **7.** ⚓ Stapellauf *m*. **8.** Abschuß *m*, Start *m*.

launch² [~] *s* ⚓ Barkasse *f*.

launch·ing ['lɔːntʃɪŋ] → **launch** III. **~ pad** *s* Abschußrampe *f*. **~ site** *s* Abschußbasis *f*.

laun·der ['lɔːndə] **I** *v/t* *Wäsche* waschen (u. bügeln). **II** *v/i* sich waschen (lassen).

laun·der·ette [~'ret] *s* Waschsalon *m*.

laun·dro·mat ['lɔːndrəmæt] *s bsd. Am.* Waschsalon *m*.

laun·dry ['lɔːndrɪ] *s* **1.** Wäscherei *f*. **2.** Wäsche *f*. **~ bas·ket** *s* Wäschekorb *m*.

lau·rel ['lɒrəl] *s* **1.** ♣ Lorbeer(baum) *m*. **2.** Lorbeerkranz *m*. **3. rest on one's ~s** *fig.* (sich) auf s-n Lorbeeren ausruhen.

lav [læv] *s* F Klo *n*: **in the ~** auf dem *od.* im Klo.

la·va ['lɑːvə] *s* Lava *f*.

lav·a·to·ry ['lævətərɪ] *s* **1.** Waschraum *m*. **2.** Toilette *f*, Klosett *n*: **in the ~** in *od.* auf der Toilette. **~ at·tend·ant** *s* Toilettenfrau *f*. **~ pa·per** *s* *Br.* Toiletten-, Klosettpapier *n*.

lav·en·der ['lævəndə] *s* ♣ Lavendel *m*.

lav·ish ['lævɪʃ] **I** *adj* □ **1.** sehr freigebig, verschwenderisch (**of** mit; **in** in *dat*): **be ~ of** *a.* verschwenderisch umgehen mit. **2.** überschwenglich (*Lob etc*), großzügig (*Geschenk etc*), luxuriös, aufwendig (*Einrichtung etc*). **II** *v/t* **3.** verschwenden: **~ s.th. on s.o.** j-n mit *et.* überhäufen.

law [lɔː] *s* **1.** (*objektives*) Recht, Gesetz(*e pl*) *n*: **contrary to ~, against the ~** gesetz-, rechtswidrig; **under German ~** nach deutschem Recht; **~ and order** Recht *od.* Ruhe u. Ordnung. **2.** (*einzelnes*) Gesetz. **3.** Recht *n*: a) Rechtssystem *n*, b) (*einzelnes*) Rechtsgebiet: → **international** 1. **4.** Rechtswissenschaft *f*, Jura *pl*: **read** (*od.* **study**) ~ Jura studieren. **5.** Gericht *n*, Rechtsweg *m*: **at** ~ vor Gericht; **go to** ~ vor Gericht gehen, prozessieren; **go to** ~ **with** *j-n* verklagen, belangen. **6.** F Bullen *pl* (*Polizei*); Bulle *m* (*Polizist*). **7.** *allg.* Gesetz *n*, Vorschrift *f*. **8.** a) ~ **of nature, natural** ~ Naturgesetz *n*, b) (wissenschaftliches) Gesetz, c) (Lehr)Satz *m*. '~**a,bid·ing** *adj* gesetzestreu. '~**,break·er** *s* Gesetzesübertreter(in), Rechtsbrecher(in). ~ **court** *s* Gerichtshof *m*.

law·ful ['lɔːful] *adj* □ **1.** gesetzlich, legal. **2.** rechtmäßig, legitim. **3.** gesetzlich anerkannt, rechtsgültig. '**law·less** *adj* □ **1.** gesetzlos. **2.** rechts-, gesetzwidrig. **3.** zügellos.

lawn [lɔːn] *s* Rasen *m*. ~ **chair** *s Am.* Liegestuhl *m*. ~ **mow·er** *s* Rasenmäher *m*.

'**law·suit** *s* 🏛 (Zivil)Prozeß *m*, Verfahren *n*.

law·yer ['lɔːjə] *s* **1.** (Rechts)Anwalt *m*. **2.** Jurist *m*.

lax [læks] *adj* □ **1.** schlaff, lose, locker. **2.** *fig.* lax, lasch (*Einstellung etc*), locker (*Sitten etc*). **3.** *fig.* unklar, verschwommen (*Vorstellung etc*). **lax·a·tive** ['~ətɪv] *s pharm.* mildes Abführmittel. '**lax·i·ty, 'lax·ness** *s* **1.** Schlaffheit *f*. **2.** Laxheit *f*, Laschheit *f*.

lay¹ [leɪ] (*irr*) **I** *v/t* **1.** legen, *Teppich* verlegen. **2.** *Eier* legen. **3.** *fig.* *Hinterhalt etc* legen, *Hoffnungen etc* setzen (**on** auf *acc*). **4.** (her)richten, *Tisch* decken. **5.** be-, auslegen (**with** mit). **6.** (**before**) vorlegen (*dat*), bringen (vor *dat*). **7.** *Anspruch etc* geltend machen. **8.** *Schuld etc* zuschreiben, zur Last legen (**to** *dat*). **II** *v/i* **9.** (Eier) legen. **10.** ~ **about one** → **lay about**; ~ **into s.o.** über *j-n* herfallen (*a. mit Worten*). **11.** ~ **off** F *j-n*, *et.* in Ruhe lassen; aufhören mit: ~ **off it!** hör auf (damit)!

Verbindungen mit Adverbien:

lay | **a·bout** *v/i* (wild) um sich schlagen (**with** mit). ~ **a·side** *v/t* **1.** beiseite legen, weglegen. **2.** *Angewohnheit etc* ablegen, aufgeben. **3.** (*für die Zukunft*) beiseite *od.* auf die Seite legen, zurücklegen. ~ **a·way** *v/t* **1.** → **lay aside** 3. **2.** *angezahlte Ware* zurücklegen. ~ **down** *v/t* **1.** hinlegen. **2.** *Amt, Waffen etc* niederle-

gen. **3.** *sein Leben* hingeben, opfern. **4.** planen, entwerfen; *Straße etc* anlegen. **5.** *Grundsatz etc* aufstellen, *Regeln etc* festlegen, -setzen, *Bedingungen* (*in e-m Vertrag*) niederlegen, verankern. ~ **in** *v/t* sich eindecken mit; einlagern. ~ **off I** *v/t* **1.** *Arbeiter etc* (*bsd. vorübergehend*) entlassen. **2.** *Arbeit* einstellen. **3.** F aufhören mit: ~ **smoking** *a.* das Rauchen aufgeben. **II** *v/i* **4.** F Feierabend machen; Ferien machen, ausspannen; aufhören; e-e Pause machen. ~ **on** *v/t* **1.** *Farbe etc* auftragen: **lay it on** F dick auftragen; → **thick** 6, **trowel.** **2.** *Br.* Gas *etc* installieren. **3.** *Br. Busse etc* einsetzen. ~ **o·pen** *v/t* **1.** bloß-, freilegen. **2.** *fig.* offen darlegen; aufdecken, enthüllen. ~ **out** *v/t* **1.** ausbreiten, -legen. **2.** ausstellen. **3.** *Toten* aufbahren. **4.** planen, entwerfen. **5.** *typ.* aufmachen, das Layout (*gen*) machen. **6.** *lay o.s. out* F sich mächtig anstrengen. ~ **o·ver** *Am.* **I** *v/i* Zwischenstation machen. **II** *v/t* verschieben, -tagen (*until* auf *acc*, bis). ~ **to** *v/i* ♣ beidrehen. ~ **up** *v/t* **1.** anhäufen, (an)sammeln: ~ **trouble for o.s.** sich Schwierigkeiten einbrocken *od.* einhandeln. **2.** *be laid up* das Bett hüten müssen, bettlägerig sein: *be laid up with influenza* mit Grippe im Bett liegen.

lay² [~] *pret von* **lie².**

lay³ [~] *adj* Laien...: ~ **preacher** Laienprediger *m*, b) laienhaft, nicht fachmännisch.

'**lay** | **·a·bout** *s bsd. Br.* F Faulenzer *m*, Tagedieb *m*. '~**·a,way** *s* angezahlte u. zurückgelegte Ware. '~**·by** *s mot. Br.* Park-, Rastplatz *m* (*Autobahn*), Parkbucht *f* (*Landstraße*).

lay·er ['leɪə] **I** *s* **1.** Schicht *f* (*a. geol.*), Lage *f*: **in ~s** schicht-, lagenweise. **2.** *in Zssgn* ...leger *m*. **3.** 🌱, 🐓 Ableger *m*. **II** *v/t* **4.** schicht- *od.* lagenweise anordnen, schichten.

lay·ette [leɪ'et] *s* Babyausstattung *f*.

lay·|·man ['leɪmən] *s* (*irr man*) Laie *m*. '~**·off** *s* **1.** (*bsd. vorübergehende*) Entlassung. **2.** F Pause *f*. '~**·out** *s* **1.** Grundriß *m*, Lageplan *m*. **2.** *typ.* Layout *n*. '~**·o·ver** *s Am.* Zwischenstation *f*.

laze [leɪz] **I** *v/i* faulenzen. **II** *v/t* mst ~ **away** *Zeit* vertrödeln. '**la·zi·ness** *s* Faulheit *f*; Trägheit *f*.

la·zy ['leɪzɪ] *adj* □ **1.** faul; träg. **2.** träg, langsam. '**∼bones** *s pl* (*sg* konstruiert) F Faulpelz *m*.

lead¹ [led] **I** *s* **1.** ⚒ Blei *n*. **2.** ⚓ Senkblei *n*, Lot *n*. **3.** (Bleistift)Mine *f*. **4.** Blei *n*, Kugeln *pl*. **II** *v/t* **5.** verbleien; ∼ed verbleit, (*Benzin a.*) bleihaltig. **6.** mit Blei beschweren.

lead² [li:d] **I** *s* **1.** Führung *f*: a) Leitung *f*: *under s.o.'s ∼*, b) führende Stelle, Spitze *f*: *be in the ∼* an der Spitze stehen, führend sein, (*Sport etc*) in Führung liegen, führen; *take the ∼* die Führung übernehmen, sich an die Spitze setzen (*from* vor *dat*) (*beide a. Sport*). **2.** Vorsprung *m* (*over* vor *dat*) (*a. Sport*). **3.** Vorbild *n*, Beispiel *n*: *follow s.o.'s ∼* j-s Beispiel folgen; *give s.o. a ∼* j-m ein gutes Beispiel geben. **4.** Hinweis *m*, Wink *m*; Anhaltspunkt *m*. **5.** *thea. etc* Hauptrolle *f*; Hauptdarsteller(in). **6.** (Hunde)Leine *f*: *keep on the ∼* an der Leine führen *od.* halten. **II** *adj* **7.** Leit..., Führungs...: *∼ guitarist* ♪ Leadgitarrist *m*. **III** *v/t* (*irr*) **8.** führen: *∼ the way* vorangehen; → *garden* 3, *nose* 1, 9. **9.** führen, bringen (*a. Straße etc*). **10.** dazu bringen, veranlassen (*to do* zu tun). **11.** (an)führen, leiten. **12.** *Leben* führen. **IV** *v/i* (*irr*) **13.** führen: a) vorangehen, b) die erste Stelle einnehmen, c) (*Sport*) an der Spitze *od.* in Führung liegen. **14.** führen (*Straße etc*): *∼ to fig.* führen zu.

Verbindungen mit Adverbien:

lead| a·stray *v/t fig.* irreführen; verführen. **∼ a·way** *v/t* **1.** wegführen, Verhafteten *etc* abführen. **2.** *fig.* abbringen (*from* von). **∼ off** **I** *v/t* **1.** → *lead away*. **2.** einleiten, beginnen (*with mit*). **II** *v/i* **3.** anfangen, beginnen. **∼ on** *v/t* j-m *et.* vor- *od.* weismachen: *lead s.o. on to think that* j-n glauben machen, daß. **∼ up** *v/i fig.* (*to*) (allmählich) führen (zu); hinauswollen (auf *acc*).

lead·en ['ledn] *adj* □ bleiern: a) Blei..., b) bleigrau, c) *fig.* schwer: *∼ limbs pl* bleischwere Glieder *pl*; *∼ sleep* bleierner Schlaf.

lead·er ['li:də] *s* **1.** Führer(in). **2.** (An)Führer *m*, (*Delegations-, Oppositions- etc*)Führer *m*. **3.** ♪ *a. bsd. Am.* Leiter *m*, Dirigent *m*, b) *bsd. Br.* Konzertmeister *m*, c) (*Band*)Leader *m*. **4.**

bsd. Br. Leitartikel *m*. **5.** *Sport etc*: Spitzenreiter *m*. **6.** ⚓ Zug-, Lockartikel *m*. '**lead·er·ship** *s* **1.** Führung *f*, Leitung *f*. **2.** a. *∼ qualities pl* Führungsqualitäten *pl*.

lead-free ['led∼] *adj* bleifrei (*Benzin*).

lead·ing ['li:dɪŋ] *adj* **1.** führend: a) Leit..., leitend, b) Haupt..., erst. **2.** erst. *∼ ar·ti·cle* → *leader* 4. *∼ la·dy s thea. etc* Hauptdarstellerin *f*. *∼ light s* führende *od.* wichtige Persönlichkeit. *∼ man s* (*irr man*) *thea. etc* Hauptdarsteller *m*. *∼ ques·tion s* Suggestivfrage *f*. *∼ strings s pl Am.* Gängelband *n* (*a. fig.*): *keep s.o. in ∼* j-n am Gängelband führen *od.* haben *od.* halten.

leaf [li:f] **I** *pl* **leaves** [li:vz] *s* **1.** ♣ Blatt *n*: *come into ∼* ausschlagen. **2.** Blatt *n* (*Buch*): *take a ∼ out of s.o.'s book fig.* sich an j-m ein Beispiel nehmen; *turn over a new ∼ fig.* ein neues Leben beginnen. **3.** (*Fenster-, Tür*)Flügel *m*; (*Tisch*)Klappe *f*; Ausziehplatte *f* (*e-s Tischs*): *pull out the leaves* den Tisch ausziehen. **II** *v/t* **4.** *Am.* durchblättern. **III** *v/i* **5.** *∼ through* durchblättern.

leaf·let ['∼lɪt] *s* Flugblatt *n*, Hand-, Reklamezettel *m*; Prospekt *m*.

league [li:g] *s* **1.** Liga *f*, Bund *m*. **2.** Bündnis *n*, Bund *m*: *be in ∼ with* gemeinsame Sache machen mit. **3.** *Sport*: Liga *f*: *∼ game* Punktspiel *n*.

leak [li:k] **I** *s* **1.** a) ⚓ Leck *n* (*a. in Tank etc*): *spring a ∼* ein Leck bekommen, b) undichte Stelle (*a. fig.*). **2.** Auslaufen *n*; *fig.* Durchsickern *n*. **II** *v/i* **3.** lecken, leck sein. **4.** tropfen (*Wasserhahn*). **5.** *∼ out* auslaufen, -treten; *fig.* durchsickern. **III** *v/t* **6.** *fig.* durchsickern lassen. '**leak·age** [∼ɪdʒ] *s* **1.** → *leak* 2. **2.** ⚓ Leckage *f*. '**leak·y** *adj* leck, undicht (*a. fig.*).

lean¹ [li:n] **I** *adj* □ mager (*a.* ⚙ *u. fig.*). **II** *s* das Magere (*des Fleisches*).

lean² [∼] **I** *v/i* (*bsd. Br. a. irr*) **1.** sich neigen, schief sein *od.* stehen. **2.** sich beugen (*over* über *acc*): *∼ back* sich zurücklehnen; *∼ forward* sich vorbeugen; *∼ over backward(s)* F sich fast umbringen (*to do* zu tun). **3.** (*against*) sich lehnen (an *acc*, gegen); lehnen (an *dat*). **4.** (*on*) sich stützen (auf *acc*); sich verlassen (auf *acc*). **5.** *∼ to(ward[s])* *fig.* (hin)neigen *od.* tendieren zu. **II** *v/t* (*bsd. Br. a. irr*) **6.** lehnen (*against* an *acc*, gegen). **III** *s* **7.** Neigung *f.* **'lean·ing I** *adj* schräg, schief. **II** *s fig.* Neigung *f*, Tendenz *f* (**to**, **toward[s]** zu).

leant [lent] *bsd. Br.* pret u. pp von **lean²**.

leap [li:p] **I** *v/i* (*a. irr*) springen; **~** *at fig.* sich stürzen auf (*ein Angebot etc*); **~** *for joy* Freudensprünge machen; **~** (*in*)**to fame** schlagartig berühmt werden; **~** *out* ins Auge springen (**to s.o.** j-m); **~** *up* aufspringen; *fig.* sprunghaft anwachsen; **→ conclusion** 3. **II** *v/t* (*a. irr*) überspringen (*a. fig.*), springen über (*acc*). **III** *s* Sprung *m* (*a. fig.*): **take a ~** e-n Sprung machen; **by** (*od.* **in**) **~s and bounds** *fig.* sprunghaft. **IV** *adj* Schalt...: **~ year.** **'~·frog I** *s* Bockspringen. **II** *v/i* bockspringen.

leapt [lept] *pret u. pp von* **leap.**

learn [lɜ:n] (*a. irr*) **I** *v/t* **1.** (er)lernen: **~** (*how*) *to swim* schwimmen lernen. **2.** (*from*) erfahren, hören (von); ersehen, entnehmen (aus *e-m Brief etc*). **II** *v/i* **3.** lernen. **4.** hören, erfahren (*about*, *of* von). **learn·ed** ['lɜ:nɪd] *adj* gelehrt (*Mensch*), (*Abhandlung etc a.*) wissenschaftlich. **'learn·er** [~ə] *s* **1.** Anfänger(in). **2.** Lernende *m*, *f*: *be a fast* (*slow*) **~** schnell (langsam) lernen. **learnt** [lɜ:nt] *pret u. pp von* **learn.**

lease [li:s] **I** *s* **1.** Pacht-, Mietvertrag *m*. **2.** Verpachtung *f*, Vermietung *f* (**to** an *acc*); Pacht *f*, Miete *f*: **put out to** (*od.* **let out on**) **~** → 4; **take on ~** → 5. **3.** Pacht-, Mietzeit *f*. **II** *v/t* **4.** **~** *out* verpachten, -mieten (**to** an *acc*). **5.** pachten, mieten, leasen.

leash [li:ʃ] *s* (Hunde)Leine *f*: *keep on the* **~** an der Leine halten *od.* führen; *keep* (*od.* *hold*) *in* **~** *fig.* im Zaum halten; **→ strain** 5.

least [li:st] **I** *adj* (*sup von* **little**) **1.** geringst, mindest, wenigst: **→ resistance** 1. **2.** geringst, unbedeutendst: *at the* **~** *thing* bei der geringsten Kleinigkeit. **II** *s* **3.** *das Mindeste, das Wenigste*: *at* **~** wenigstens, zumindest; *at* (*the*) **~** mindestens; *not in the* **~** nicht im geringsten *od.* mindesten; *to say the* **~** (*of it*) gelinde gesagt. **III** *adv* **4.** am wenigsten: **~** *of all* am allerwenigsten.

leath·er ['leðə] **I** *s* Leder *n* (*a. humor.* Haut; *a. Sport*: Ball): **→ tough** 1. **II** *v/t*

F versohlen. '**~·neck** *s* ╳ *Am. sl.* Ledernacken *m.*

leath·er·y ['leðərɪ] *adj* lederartig, zäh.

leave¹ [li:v] (*irr*) **I** *v/t* **1.** verlassen: a) von j-m, *e-m Ort etc* fort-, weggehen, b) abreisen, abfahren *etc* von, c) von *der Schule* abgehen, d) j-n, *ein* Im Stich lassen, *et.* aufgeben: *she left him for another man* sie verließ ihn wegen e-s anderen Mannes. **2.** lassen: **~** *alone* allein lassen; j-n, *et.* in Ruhe lassen; **~** *it at that* es dabei belassen *od.* (bewenden) lassen; **~** *s.o. to himself* j-n sich selbst überlassen; **→ cold** 4, **lurch²**. **3.** übriglassen: *be left* übrigbleiben *od.* übrig sein. **4.** *Narbe etc* zurücklassen, *Nachricht*, *Spur etc* hinterlassen. **5.** hängen-, liegen-, stehenlassen, vergessen. **6.** überlassen, anheimstellen (**to s.o.** j-m). **7.** vermachen, -erben. **II** *v/i* **8.** (fort-, weg)gehen, abreisen, abfahren (**for** nach). **9.** gehen (*die Stellung aufgeben*).

Verbindungen mit Adverbien:

leave| *be·hind v/t* **1.** zurücklassen. **2.** **→ leave¹** 4, 5. **3.** *Gegner etc* hinter sich lassen (*a. fig.*). **~** *on v/t Radio etc* anlassen, *Kleidungsstück a.* anbehalten. **~** *out v/t* **1.** draußen lassen. **2.** aus-, weglassen (*of* von, bei). **~·o·ver** *v/t Br.* **1.** **→ leave¹** 3. **2.** verschieben (*until* auf *acc*, bis).

leave² [~] *s* **1.** Erlaubnis *f*, Genehmigung *f*: *ask* **~** *of s.o.*, *ask s.o.'s* **~** j-n um Erlaubnis bitten. **2.** Urlaub *m*: *on* **~** auf Urlaub. **3.** Abschied *m*: *take* (*one's*) **~** Abschied nehmen (*of* von).

leav·en ['levn] **I** *s* **1.** Sauerteig *m*; Treibmittel *n*. **II** *v/t* **2.** *Teig* säuern; (auf)gehen lassen. **3.** *fig.* auflockern (*with* mit, durch).

leaves [li:vz] *pl von* **leaf.**

leav·ing ['li:vɪŋ] *s* **1.** *mst pl* Überbleibsel *n*, Rest *m*. **2.** *pl* Abfall *m.*

lech·er ['letʃə] *s* Lüstling *m.* '**lech·er·ous** *adj* □ geil, lüstern. '**lech·er·y** *s* Geilheit *f*, Lüsternheit *f.*

lec·ture ['lektʃə] **I** *s* **1.** (*on* über *acc*; *to* vor *dat*) Vortrag *m*; *univ.* Vorlesung *f*: **~** *hall* (*od.* *theater*, *bsd. Br. theatre*) Hörsaal *m.* **2.** Strafpredigt *f*: *give* (*od.* *read*) *s.o. a* **~** → 4. **II** *v/i* **3.** (*on* über *acc*; *to* vor *dat*) e-n Vortrag *od.* Vorträge halten; *univ.* e-e Vorlesung *od.* Vor-

lesungen halten. **III** v/t **4.** j-m e-e Strafpredigt halten. **'lec·tur·er** s **1.** Vortragende m, f. **2.** univ. Dozent(in).

led [led] pret u. pp von **lead²**.

ledge [ledʒ] s Leiste f, Sims m, n.

ledg·er ['ledʒə] s ✝ Hauptbuch n.

lee [liː] s ♘ Lee(seite) f.

leech [liːtʃ] s **1.** Blutegel m. **2.** fig.
Klette f; Blutsauger m.

leek [liːk] s ♣ Lauch m, Porree m.

leer [lɪə] **I** s höhnisches od. boshaftes od.
anzügliches Grinsen; lüsterner Seitenblick. **II** v/i höhnisch od. boshaft od.
anzüglich grinsen; lüstern schielen (**at**
nach).

lees [liːz] s pl Bodensatz m.

lee·ward ['liːwəd] adv ♘ leewärts.

'lee·way s **1.** ✈, ♘ Abtrift f. **2.** fig.
Rückstand m, Zeitverlust m: **make up**
~ (den Rückstand od. Zeitverlust) aufholen. **3.** fig. Spielraum m.

left¹ [left] pret u. pp von **leave¹**.

left² [~] **I** adj **1.** link, Links... **II** s **2.** die
Linke, linke Seite: **on** (od. **at, to**) **the ~**
(**of**) links (von), linker Hand (von); **on
our ~** zu unserer Linken; **the second
turning to** (od. **on**) **the ~** die zweite
Querstraße links; **keep to the ~** sich
links halten; mot. links fahren. **3. the ~**
pol. die Linke. **III** adv **4.** links (**of** von):
turn ~ (nach links wenden; mot.
links abbiegen. **'~-hand** adj **1.** link: **~
bend** Linkskurve f. **2.** ⚙ linksgängig,
-läufig: **~ drive** Linkssteuerung f. **,~-
'hand·ed** adj **1.** linkshändig: **be ~**
Linkshänder(in) sein. **2.** linkisch, ungeschickt. **3.** zweifelhaft, fragwürdig
(Kompliment etc). **,~-'hand·er** s Links-
händer(in).

left·ist ['leftɪst] adj pol. linksgerichtet,
-stehend.

,left-'lug·gage lock·er s 🛄 Br. (Gepäck)Schließfach n. **,~-'lug·gage office** s 🛄 Br. Gepäckaufbewahrung(s-
stelle) f. **'~,o·ver** s mst pl Überbleibsel
n, Rest m.

'left-wing adj pol. dem linken Flügel angehörend, links...

leg [leg] **I** s **1.** (a. Hosen-, Stuhl- etc)Bein
n: **be on one's last ~** auf dem letzten
Loch pfeifen; **give s.o. a ~ up** j-m
(hin)aufhelfen; fig. j-m unter die Arme
greifen; **pull s.o.'s ~** F j-n auf den Arm
nehmen; **stretch one's ~s** sich die Bei-

ne vertreten; → **shake** 7. **2.** (Hammel-
etc)Keule f: **~ of mutton.** 3. ⚘ Kathete
f, Schenkel m (e-s Dreiecks). **4.** Etappe
f, Abschnitt m (e-r Reise etc). **II** v/i **5.**
mst **~ it** F zu Fuß gehen.

leg·a·cy ['legəsɪ] s ⚖ Vermächtnis n,
fig. a. Erbe n.

le·gal ['liːgl] adj □ **1.** gesetzlich, rechtlich: **~ holiday** Am. gesetzlicher Feiertag; → **tender²** 4. **2.** legal, gesetzmäßig,
rechtsgültig. **3.** Rechts..., juristisch: **~
adviser** Rechtsberater m; **~ aid** Pro-
zeßkostenhilfe f. **4.** gerichtlich: **take ~
action** (od. **steps**) **against s.o.** gerichtlich gegen j-n vorgehen. **le·gal·i·ty**
[liː'gælətɪ] s Legalität f. **le·gal·i·za·tion**
[,liːgəlaɪ'zeɪʃn] s Legalisierung f. **'le·
gal·ize** v/t legalisieren.

le·ga·tion [lɪ'geɪʃn] s Gesandtschaft f.

leg·end ['ledʒənd] s **1.** Legende f (a. fig.),
Sage f. **2.** Legende f: a) erläuternder
Text, Bildunterschrift f, b) Zeichener-
klärung f (auf Karten etc), c) Inschrift f
(auf Münzen etc).

leg·er·de·main [,ledʒədə'meɪn] s **1.**
Taschenspielerei f (a. fig.). **2.** Schwindel m.

leg·gy ['legɪ] adj langbeinig.

leg·i·ble ['ledʒəbl] adj □ leserlich, lesbar.

le·gion ['liːdʒən] s Legion f. **'le·gion-
ar·y** s Legionär m.

leg·is·late ['ledʒɪsleɪt] v/i Gesetze erlassen. **,leg·is'la·tion** s Gesetzgebung f.
leg·is·la·tive ['~lətɪv] **I** adj □ **1.** gesetz-
gebend, legislativ: **~ assembly** gesetzgebende Versammlung; **~ body** → 3b; **~
power** → 3a. **2.** gesetzgeberisch, Legis-
latur...: **~ period** Legislaturperiode f. **II**
s **3.** Legislative f: a) gesetzgebende Gewalt, b) gesetzgebende Körperschaft.
leg·is·la·tor ['~leɪtə] s Gesetzgeber m.
leg·is·la·ture ['~leɪtʃə] → **legislative**
3b.

le·git·i·ma·cy [lɪ'dʒɪtɪməsɪ] s Legitimität
f: a) Gesetzmäßigkeit f, Gesetzlichkeit
f, b) Rechtmäßigkeit f, Berechtigung f,
c) Ehelichkeit f. **le'git·i·mate** [~mət]
adj □ legitim: a) gesetzmäßig, gesetzlich, b) rechtmäßig, berechtigt, c) ehelich. **le'git·i·mize** v/t legitimieren.

leg·room ['legrʊm] s ✈, mot. Beinfrei-
heit f.

leg·ume ['legjuːm] s ♣ Hülsenfrucht f.

lei·sure ['leʒə] **I** s freie Zeit: **at ~** mit Muße, in (aller) Ruhe; frei, unbeschäftigt; **at your ~** wenn es Ihnen (gerade) paßt, bei Gelegenheit. **II** adj Freizeit...: **~ activities** pl Freizeitgestaltung f; **~ facilities** pl Freizeiteinrichtungen pl; **~ hours** pl Mußestunden pl; **~ occupation** Freizeitbeschäftigung f; **~ time** Freizeit f; **~ wear** Freizeitkleidung f. **'lei·sure·ly** adj u. adv gemächlich, gemütlich.

lem·on ['lemən] **I** s **1.** Zitrone f. **2.** sl. Niete f (Sache, Person). **II** adj **3.** Zitronen...: **~ juice; ~ soda** Am. Zitronenlimonade f; **~ squash** Br. Getränk aus Zitronenkonzentrat u. Wasser; **~ squeezer** Zitronenpresse f. **4.** zitronengelb.

lend [lend] v/t (irr) **1.** (ver-, aus)leihen (**to** dat). **2.** fig. Nachdruck, Würde etc verleihen (**to** dat). **3.** fig. leihen, gewähren: **~ o.s. to s.th.** sich etc hergeben; **~ itself to s.th.** sich für od. zu et. eignen; → **hand** 1. **'lend·er** s Aus-, Verleiher(in). **'lending** adj: **~ library** Leihbücherei f.

length [leŋθ] s **1.** Länge f: **a)** Dimension: **two feet in ~** 2 Fuß lang; **what ~ is it?** wie lang ist es?, **b)** Strecke f: **go to great ~s** sich sehr bemühen; **c)** Umfang m (e-s Buchs etc), **d)** Dauer f: **at ~** ausführlich; **at full ~** in allen Einzelheiten. **2.** Bahn f (Stoff etc). **3.** Sport: Länge f (Vorsprung). **'length·en I** v/t verlängern, länger machen, Kleidungsstück a. auslassen. **II** v/i sich verlängern, länger werden. **'length·ways, length·wise** ['~waɪz] adv der Länge nach, längs. **'length·y** adj □ ermüdend lang, langatmig.

le·ni·ence, le·ni·en·cy ['liːnjəns(ɪ)] s Milde f, Nachsicht f. **'le·ni·ent** adj □ mild, nachsichtig (**to, toward[s]** gegenüber).

lens [lenz] s **1.** anat., phot., phys. Linse f: **~ aperture** phot. Blende f. **2.** phot., phys. Objektiv n. **3.** (einzelnes) Glas (e-r Brille).

lent [lent] pret u. pp von **lend**.

Lent² [~] s Fastenzeit f.

len·til ['lentɪl] s ♀ Linse f.

Leo ['liːəʊ] s ast. Löwe m.

leop·ard ['lepəd] s zo. Leopard m.

le·o·tard ['liːəʊtɑːd] s **1.** Trikot n. **2.** Gymnastikanzug m.

les·bi·an ['lezbɪən] **I** adj lesbisch. **II** s Lesbierin f.

lese maj·es·ty [ˌliːz'mædʒɪstɪ] s **1.** Majestätsbeleidigung f (a. fig.). **2.** Hochverrat m.

le·sion ['liːʒn] s Verletzung f, Wunde f.

less [les] **I** adv (comp von **little**) weniger: **~ and ~** immer weniger; **the ~ so as** (dies) um so weniger, als. **II** adj (comp von **little**) geringer, kleiner, weniger: **in ~ time** in kürzerer Zeit; **no ~ a man than** kein geringerer als. **III** s weniger, e-e kleinere Menge od. Zahl: **little ~ than** so gut wie, schon fast; **no ~ than** nicht weniger als. **IV** prp weniger, minus, abzüglich.

less·en ['lesn] **I** v/i **1.** sich vermindern od. verringern, abnehmen. **II** v/t **2.** vermindern, verringern. **3.** fig. herabsetzen, schmälern, bagatellisieren.

less·er ['lesə] adj kleiner, geringer: → **evil** 2.

les·son ['lesn] s **1.** Lektion f (a. fig.): → **teach** 2. **2.** (Lehr-, Unterrichts)Stunde f; pl Unterricht m, Stunden pl: **give ~s** Unterricht erteilen, unterrichten; **take ~s from** Stunden od. Unterricht nehmen bei. **3.** fig. Lehre f: **this was a ~ to me** das war mir e-e Lehre.

lest [lest] cj **1.** (mst mit folgendem should) daß od. damit nicht: **he ran away ~ he should be seen** er lief weg, um nicht gesehen zu werden. **2.** (nach Ausdrücken des Befürchtens) daß.

let¹ [let] (irr) **I** v/t **1.** lassen: **~ alone** et. seinlassen; j-n, et. in Ruhe lassen; geschweige denn, ganz zu schweigen von; **~ s.th. go** et. loslassen; **~ o.s. go** sich gehenlassen; aus sich herausgehen; **~ it go at that** laß es dabei bewenden; **~'s go** gehen wir!; **~ s.o. know** j-n wissen lassen, j-m Bescheid geben; **~ into** (her-, hin)einlassen in (acc); j-n einweihen in (ein Geheimnis). **2.** bsd. Br. vermieten, -pachten (**to** an acc; **for** auf ein Jahr etc): **"to ~"** „zu vermieten". **II** v/i **3.** **~ go** loslassen (**of s.th.** et.). **4.** **~ into** über j-n herfallen.

Verbindungen mit Adverbien:

let| by v/t vorbeilassen. **~ down** v/t **1.** hinunter-, herunterlassen: → **hair.** **2.** im Stich lassen; enttäuschen. **~ in** v/t **1.** (her-, hin)einlassen. **2.** Stück etc einlassen, -setzen. **3.** j-n einweihen (**on in ein**

Geheimnis). **4. let o.s. in for s.th.** sich einbrocken, sich auf et. einlassen. **~ off** *v/t* **1.** *Feuerwerk* abbrennen, *Gewehr etc* abfeuern. **2.** *Gas etc* ablassen: → **steam** 1. **~ on** F I *v/i* **1.** sich et. anmerken lassen (**about** von). **II** *v/t* **2.** zugeben (**that** daß). **3.** vorgeben. **~ out** I *v/t* **1.** heraus-, hinauslassen (**of** aus). **let the air out of** die Luft lassen aus. **2.** *Kleidungsstück* auslassen. **3.** *Schrei etc* ausstoßen. **4.** *Geheimnis* ausplaudern, verraten. **5.** → **let¹** 2. **II** *v/i* **6.** herfallen (**at** über *acc*) (*a.* mit Worten). **~ through** *v/t* durchlassen. **~ up** *v/i* F nachlassen; aufhören.

let² [~] *s* Tennis: Netzaufschlag *m*: **~!** Netz!

'let-down *s* Enttäuschung *f*.

le·thal ['li:θl] *adj* □ tödlich; Todes...

le·thar·gic [lə'θɑːdʒɪk] *adj* (**~ally**) lethargisch, teilnahmslos. **leth·ar·gy** ['leθədʒɪ] *s* Lethargie *f*, Teilnahmslosigkeit *f*.

let's [lets] F *für* **let us**.

let·ter ['letə] I *s* **1.** Buchstabe *m*: **to the ~** wortwörtlich, buchstäblich; *fig.* peinlich genau. **2.** Brief *m*, Schreiben *n* (**to** an *acc*): **by ~** brieflich; **~ of application** Bewerbungsschreiben *n*; **~ of complaint** Beschwerdebrief; **~ to the editor** Leserbrief. **3.** *typ.* Letter *f*, Type *f*. **4.** *pl* (*a.* sg konstruiert) (schöne) Literatur; Bildung *f*. **II** *v/t* **5.** beschriften. **~ bomb** *s* Briefbombe *f*. **~ box** *s bsd. Br.* Briefkasten *m*. **~ file** *s* Briefordner *m*. **'~ head** *s* (gedruckter) Briefkopf *m*. **~ o·pen·er** *s* Brieföffner *m*. **~ pa·per** *s* Briefpapier *n*. **~ scales** *s pl* Briefwaage *f*. **'~ weight** *s* Briefbeschwerer *m*.

let·tuce ['letɪs] *s* 🍴 (*bsd.* Kopf)Salat *m*.

'let·up *s* F Nachlassen *n*; Aufhören *n*.

leu·co·cyte ['luːkəʊsaɪt] *s* 🔬 Leukozyt *m*.

leu·k(a)e·mi·a [luːˈkiːmɪə] *s* 🔬 Leukämie *f*.

lev·el ['levl] I *s* **1.** ⚙ Libelle *f*, Wasserwaage *f*. **2.** Ebene *f* (*a. fig.*), ebene Fläche *f*: **at government ~** auf Regierungsebene. **3.** Höhe *f* (*a. geogr.*), (*Wasseretc*)Spiegel *m*, (-)Stand *m*, (-)Pegel *m*; *fig.* (*a. geistiges*) Niveau, Stand *m*, Stufe *f*: **~ of sound** Geräuschpegel, Tonstärke *f*; **be on a ~ with** auf gleicher Höhe sein mit; genauso hoch sein wie;

fig. auf dem gleichen Niveau *od.* auf der gleichen Stufe stehen wie. **II** *adj* □ **4.** eben (*Straße etc*): **a ~ teaspoon** ein gestrichener Teelöffel(voll). **5.** gleich (*a. fig.*): **~ crossing** *Br.* schienengleicher (Bahn)Übergang; **be ~ on points** (*Sport*) punktgleich sein; **be ~ with** auf gleicher Höhe sein; genauso hoch sein wie; *fig.* auf dem gleichen Niveau *od.* auf der gleichen Stufe stehen wie; **draw ~** (*Sport*) ausgleichen; **draw ~ with** *j-n* einholen; **make ~ with the ground →** 9b. **6.** a) gleichmäßig: **~ stress** *ling.* schwebende Betonung, b) ausgeglichen (*Rennen etc*). **7. do one's ~ best** sein möglichstes tun. **8. have (keep) a ~ head** e-n kühlen Kopf haben (bewahren), sich nicht aus der Ruhe bringen lassen; **give s.o. a ~ look** *j-n* ruhig *od.* fest anschauen. **III** *v/t pret u. pp* **-eled**, *bsd. Br.* **-elled** **9.** a) (ein)ebnen, planieren, b) *a.* **~ to** (*od.* **with**) **the ground** dem Erdboden gleichmachen. **10.** *fig.* gleichmachen, nivellieren; *Unterschiede* beseitigen, ausgleichen. *Verbindungen mit Adverbien:*

lev·el| down *v/t* Preise, Löhne *etc* drücken, herabsetzen. **~ off** I *v/t* **1.** → **level** 9a, 10. **2.** Flugzeug abfangen. **II** *v/i* **3.** flach werden *od.* auslaufen (*Gelände etc*). **4.** *fig.* sich stabilisieren *od.* einpendeln (**at** bei). **~ out** I *v/t* **1.** → **level** 10. **2.** → **level off** 2. **II** *v/i* **3.** → **level off** II. **~ up** *v/t* Preise, Löhne *etc* hinaufschrauben.

,lev·el-'head·ed *adj* □ vernünftig.

le·ver ['liːvə] I *s* **1.** *phys.*, ⚙ Hebel *m*. **2.** Brechstange *f*. **3.** Anker *m* (*e-r Uhr*). **4.** *fig.* Druckmittel *n*. **II** *v/t* **5. ~ out (of)** herausstemmen (aus); *fig. j-n* verdrängen (aus).

lev·i·ty ['levətɪ] *s* Leichtfertigkeit *f*.

lev·y ['levɪ] I *s* **1.** ✝ Erhebung *f*. **2.** ✝ Steuer *f*, Abgabe *f*. **3.** ✗ Aushebung *f*. **II** *v/t* **4.** Steuern *etc* a) erheben, b) (**on**) legen (auf *acc*), auferlegen (*dat*). **5.** ✗ Truppen ausheben.

lewd [ljuːd] *adj* □ **1.** geil, lüstern. **2.** unanständig, obszön. **'lewd·ness** *s* **1.** Geilheit *f*, Lüsternheit *f*. **2.** Unanständigkeit *f*, Obszönität *f*.

lex·i·cog·ra·pher [ˌleksɪˈkɒɡrəfə] *s* Lexikograph(in). **lex·i·co·graph·ic** [ˌ~kəʊˈɡræfɪk] *adj* (**~ally**) lexikographisch.

lex·i·cog·ra·phy [ˌ~'kɒɡrəfɪ] s Lexikographie f.

li·a·bil·i·ty [ˌlaɪə'bɪlətɪ] s **1.** ✝, ⚖ Verpflichtung f, Verbindlichkeit f; Haftung f, Haftpflicht f: ~ **insurance** Haftpflichtversicherung f; → **limit** 4. **2.** pl → **Passiva** pl. **3.** allg. Verantwortung f, Verantwortlichkeit f. **4.** ~ **to penalty** Strafbarkeit f; ~ **to taxation** Steuerpflicht f. **5.** (**to**) Hang m, Neigung f (zu), Anfälligkeit f (für).

li·a·ble ['laɪəbl] adj **1.** ✝, ⚖ haftbar, -pflichtig (**for** für): be ~ **for** a. haften für. **2.** unterworfen (**to s.th.** e-r Sache): be ~ **to s.th.** a. e-r Sache unterliegen; ~ **to penalty** strafbar; ~ **to taxation** steuerpflichtig. **3.** be ~ **to** neigen zu, anfällig sein für. **4.** be ~ **to do s.th.** et. gern od. leicht tun; et. wahrscheinlich tun: he is ~ **to come** er kommt wahrscheinlich; that is ~ **to happen** das kann durchaus od. leicht passieren.

li·aise [lɪ'eɪz] v/i **1.** Verbindung aufnehmen (**with** mit). **2.** sich verbünden (**with** mit). **3.** zs.-arbeiten (**with** mit). **li·ai-son** [lɪ'eɪzɒn] s **1.** Verbindung f: ~ **man** Verbindungsmann m. **2.** Bündnis n. **3.** Zs.-arbeit f. **4.** Liaison f, (Liebes)Verhältnis n.

li·ar ['laɪə] s Lügner(in).

li·bel ['laɪbl] ⚖ **I** s (schriftliche) Verleumdung od. Beleidigung (**of, on** gen). **II** v/t pret u. pp -**beled**, bsd. Br. -**belled** (schriftlich) verleumden od. beleidigen. **'li·bel·(l)ous** adj □ verleumderisch.

lib·er·al ['lɪbərəl] **I** adj □ **1.** liberal, aufgeschlossen. **2.** mst ♙ pol. liberal. **3.** großzügig: a) freigebig (**of** mit), b) reichlich (bemessen): ~ **gift** großzügiges Geschenk. **4.** ~ **arts** pl Geisteswissenschaften pl. **II** s **5.** mst ♙ pol. Liberale m, f. **'lib·er·al·ism** s Liberalismus m. **lib·er·al·i·ty** [ˌ~'rælətɪ] s **1.** Liberalität f. **2.** Großzügigkeit f. **lib·er·al·ize** ['lɪbərəlaɪz] v/t liberalisieren.

lib·er·ate ['lɪbəreɪt] v/t **1.** befreien (**from** von, aus) (a. fig.); Sklaven etc freilassen. **2.** Gase etc, fig. Kräfte etc freisetzen: be ~**d** a. frei werden. **ˌlib·er·'a·tion** s **1.** Befreiung f; Freilassung f. **2.** Freisetzung f.

lib·er·tine ['lɪbətiːn] s Wüstling m.

lib·er·ty ['lɪbətɪ] s **1.** Freiheit f: a) persönliche etc Freiheit f: **religious** ~ Religionsfreiheit; ~ **of the press** Pressefreiheit; ~ **of speech** Redefreiheit; **at** ~ frei, in Freiheit, auf freiem Fuß, b) freie Wahl, Erlaubnis f: be **at** ~ **to do s.th.** et. tun dürfen, c) mst pl Privileg n, Vorrecht n. **2.** Dreistigkeit f, (plumpe) Vertraulichkeit f: **take liberties with** sich Freiheiten gegen j-n herausnehmen; willkürlich mit et. umgehen.

li·bid·i·nous [lɪ'bɪdɪnəs] adj □ libidinös, triebhaft. **li·bi·do** [lɪ'biːdəʊ] s Libido f, Geschlechtstrieb m.

Li·bra ['laɪbrə] s ast. Waage f.

li·brar·i·an [laɪ'breərɪən] s Bibliothekar(in). **li·brar·y** ['~brərɪ] s **1.** Bibliothek f: a) öffentliche Bücherei: ~ **ticket** Leserausweis m, b) private Büchersammlung, c) Bibliothekszimmer n. **2.** (Bild-, Zeitungs)Archiv n: ~ **picture** Archivbild n.

li·bret·tist [lɪ'bretɪst] s Librettist m, Textdichter m. **li·bret·to** [~təʊ] pl -**tos**, -**ti** [~tɪ] s Libretto n: a) Textbuch n, b) (Opern- etc)Text m.

lice [laɪs] pl von **louse** 1.

li·cence ['laɪsəns] **I** s **1.** Lizenz f, Konzession f, behördliche Genehmigung; (Führer-, Jagd-, Waffen- etc)Schein m: ~ **number** mot. Kennzeichen n. **2.** dichterische Freiheit. **3.** Zügellosigkeit f. **II** v/t **4.** Am. → **license** I.

li·cense ['laɪsəns] **I** v/t **1.** lizensieren, konzessionieren, behördlich genehmigen: **fully ~d** voll mit voller Schankkonzession. **2.** j-m e-e Lizenz od. Konzession erteilen; (es) j-m (offiziell) erlauben (**to do** zu tun). **II** s **3.** Am. → **licence** I: ~ **plate** mot. Nummern-, Kennzeichenschild n.

li·cen·tious [laɪ'senʃəs] adj □ ausschweifend, zügellos.

li·chen ['laɪkən] s **1.** ♣ Flechte f. **2.** ♬ Knötchenflechte f.

lick [lɪk] **I** v/t **1.** (ab)lecken: ~ **up** (**out**) auf-(aus)lecken; ~ **s.o.'s boots** fig. vor j-m kriechen; ~ **one's lips** sich die Lippen lecken (a. fig.). **2.** F verprügeln, -dreschen; übertreffen: **this ~s me** das geht über m-n Horizont. **II** v/i **3.** lecken (**at** an dat). **III** s **4.** Lecken n: **give s.th.** a ~ an etwas lecken. **5.** F Tempo n: **at full** ~ mit voller Geschwindigkeit. **'lick·ing** s F Prügel pl, Dresche f.

lic·o·rice ['lɪkərɪs] s ♣ Lakritze f.

lid [lɪd] *s* **1.** Deckel *m*: *put the ~ on* Br. F *e-r Sache* die Krone aufsetzen; *e-r Sache* ein Ende machen. **2.** (Augen-)Lid *n*.

li·do ['liːdəʊ] *pl* **-dos** *s* Br. Frei- *od.* Strandbad *n*.

lie[1] [laɪ] **I** *s* Lüge *f*: *tell ~s* (*od. a ~*) lügen; *give the ~ to et., j-n* Lügen strafen; → *white lie*. **II** *v/i* lügen: *~ to s.o.* j-n be-*od.* anlügen.

lie[2] [~] **I** *s* **1.** Lage *f* (*a. fig.*): *the ~ of the land fig.* Br. die Lage (der Dinge). **II** *v/i* (*irr*) **2.** liegen: a) *allg.* im Bett, im Hinterhalt *etc* liegen; *ausgebreitet, tot etc* daliegen, b) begraben sein, ruhen, c) gelegen sein, sich befinden: *the town ~s on a river* die Stadt liegt an e-m Fluß; *~ second* (*Sport etc*) an zweiter Stelle liegen, d) begründet liegen (*in* in *dat*). **3.** a) *~ heavy on s.o.'s stomach* j-m schwer im Magen liegen, b) *fig.* lasten (*on auf der Seele etc*). **4.** *fig.* stecken (*behind* hinter *dat*).

Verbindungen mit Adverbien:

lie| a·bout, *v/i* herumliegen. **~ a·head** *v/i*: *what lies ahead of us* was vor uns liegt, was uns bevorsteht. **~ a·round** → *lie about*. **~ back** *v/i* sich zurücklegen *od.* -lehnen; *fig.* sich ausruhen. **~ down** *v/i* **1.** sich hin- *od.* niederlegen: *~ on* sich legen auf (*acc*). **2.** *take lying down* Beleidigung *etc* widerspruchslos hinnehmen, sich *e-e* Beleidigung *etc* gefallen lassen. **~ in** *v/i* Br. (*morgens*) lang im Bett bleiben. **~ low** *v/i* sich verstecken *od.* versteckt halten; sich ruhig verhalten. **~ o·ver** *v/i* liegenbleiben, unerledigt bleiben; aufgeschoben *od.* zurückgestellt werden. **~ up** *v/i* **1.** das Bett *od.* das Zimmer hüten (müssen). **2.** nicht benutzt werden, (*Maschine etc*) außer Betrieb sein.

'**lie-a·bed** *s* Langschläfer(in).

lie de·tec·tor *s* Lügendetektor *m*.

'**lie|-down** *s* F Schläfchen *n*: *have a ~* ein Schläfchen machen; sich (*kurz*) hinlegen. '**~-in** *s*: *have* (*od. take*) *a ~* F → *lie in*.

lieu [ljuː] *s*: *in ~* statt dessen; *in ~ of* an Stelle von (*od. gen*), (an)statt (*gen*); → *oath* 1.

lieu·ten·ant [lef'tenənt] *s* ✗ a) Leutnant *m*, b) Br. (*Am. first ~*) Oberleutnant *m*.

life [laɪf] *pl* **lives** [laɪvz] *s* **1.** Leben *n*: a)

organisches Leben, b) Lebenskraft *f*, c) Lebewesen *pl*, d) Menschenleben *n*: *they lost their lives* sie kamen ums Leben; *a matter of ~ and death* e-e lebenswichtige Angelegenheit; *early in ~* in jungen Jahren; *late in ~* in vorgerücktem Alter, e) Lebenszeit *f*, -dauer *f*: *all his ~* sein ganzes Leben lang; *for ~* fürs (*ganze*) Leben, für den Rest s-s Lebens; *bsd.* ⚖, *pol.* lebenslänglich, auf Lebenszeit, f) menschliches Tun u. Treiben, g) Lebensweise *f*, -wandel *m*, h) Schwung *m*: *full of ~* voller Leben. **2.** ⚖ Laufzeit *f* (*e-s Wechsels, Vertrags etc*); ⚓ Haltbarkeit *f*, Lagerfähigkeit *f*. **3.** ⚖ F lebenslängliche Freiheitsstrafe: *he is doing ~* er sitzt lebenslänglich; *he got ~* er bekam lebenslänglich. **~ an·nu·i·ty** *s* ⚖ Leibrente *f*. **~ as·sur·ance** *s bsd.* Br. Lebensversicherung *f*. '**~-boat** *s* ⚓ Rettungsboot *n*. **~ buoy** *s* ⚓ Rettungsring *m*. **~ ex·pect·an·cy** *s* Lebenserwartung *f*. '**~-guard** *s* Rettungsschwimmer *m*; Bademeister *m*. **~ im·pris·on·ment** *s* ⚖ lebenslängliche Freiheitsstrafe. **~ in·sur·ance** *s* Lebensversicherung *f*. **~ jack·et** *s* ⚓ Rettungs-, Schwimmweste *f*.

life·less ['laɪflɪs] *adj* □ **1.** leblos: a) tot, b) unbelebt. **2.** *fig.* matt, schwunglos.

'**life·like** *adj* lebensecht, naturgetreu. '**~-line** *s* **1.** ⚓ Rettungsleine *f*. **2.** *fig.* Rettungsanker *m*. **3.** Lebenslinie *f* (*in der Hand*). '**~-long** *adj* lebenslang. '**~-mem·ber** *s* Mitglied *n* auf Lebenszeit. **~ peer** *s* Peer *m* auf Lebenszeit. **~ pre·serv·er** *s* **1.** ⚓ *Am.* Rettungs-, Schwimmweste *f*; Rettungsgürtel *m*. **2.** *bsd.* Br. Totschläger *m* (*Waffe*).

lif·er ['laɪfə] *s* ⚖ F Lebenslängliche *m, f*.

life| raft *s* ⚓ Rettungsfloß *n*. '**~-sav·er** *s* **1.** Lebensretter *m*. **2.** → *lifeguard*. **3.** F rettender Engel; Rettung *f*. '**~-sav·ing** *adj* lebensrettend. **~ sen·tence** *s* ⚖ lebenslängliche Freiheitsstrafe. '**~-size**(**d**) *adj* lebensgroß, in Lebensgröße. '**~-time I** *s* Lebenszeit *f*: *once in a ~* sehr selten, einmal im Leben; *during* (*od. in*) *s.o.'s ~* zu j-s Lebzeiten *od.* Zeit; in j-s Leben. **II** *adj* auf Lebenszeit, lebenslang: *~ post* Lebensstellung *f*. '**~-work** *s* Lebenswerk *n*.

lift [lɪft] **I** *s* **1.** (Hoch-, Auf)Heben *n*. **2.** ⚙ Hub(höhe *f*) *m*. **3.** Luftbrücke *f*. **4.** ✈, *phys.* Auftrieb *m, fig. a.* Aufschwung *m*: **give s.o. a ~** → 10. **5. give s.o. a ~** j-n (in Auto) mitnehmen; **get a ~ from s.o.** von j-m mitgenommen werden; → **thumb** II. **6.** *bsd. Br.* Lift *m*, Aufzug *m*, Fahrstuhl *m*. **7.** (*Ski- etc*)Lift *m*. **8.** ⚓ Lift *m, n,* Lifting *n*: **have a ~** sich liften lassen. **II** *v/t* **9.** *a.* **~ up** (hoch-, auf)heben; *Stimme etc* erheben: **~ one's eyes** aufschauen, -blicken; → **finger** 1, **hand** 1. **10.** *a.* **~ up** j-n aufmuntern, j-m Auftrieb *od.* Aufschwung geben. **11.** F klauen (*a. plagiieren*). **12.** *Gesicht etc* liften, straffen. **13.** *Embargo, Verbot etc* aufheben. **III** *v/i* **14.** sich heben, steigen (*a. Nebel*): **~ off** starten (*Rakete*); abheben (*Flugzeug*). **15.** sich (hoch)heben lassen. '**~boy** *s bsd. Br.* Liftboy *m*. '**~·man** *s* (*irr man*) *Br.* Fahrstuhlführer *m*. '**~·off** *s* Start *m* (*e-r Rakete*); Abheben *n* (*e-s Flugzeugs*).

lig·a·ment ['lɪɡəmənt] *s anat.* Band *n*.

lig·a·ture ['lɪɡətʃə] *s typ.,* ♩ Ligatur *f*.

light¹ [laɪt] **I** *s* **1.** Licht *n*: a) Helligkeit *f*: **stand** (*od. be*) **in s.o.'s ~** j-m im Licht (*fig.* im Weg) stehen, b) Beleuchtung *f*: **in subdued ~** bei gedämpftem Licht, c) Schein *m*: **by the ~ of a candle** bei Kerzenschein, d) Lichtquelle *f*: **hide one's ~ under a bushel** sein Licht unter den Scheffel stellen, e) Sonnen-, Tageslicht *n*: **bring** (**come**) **to ~** *fig.* ans Licht bringen (kommen); **see the ~** (**of day**) das Licht der Welt erblicken; *fig.* herauskommen, auf den Markt kommen, f) *fig.* Aspekt *m*: **in the ~ of** unter dem Aspekt *od.* in Anbetracht (*gen*), g) *fig.* Erleuchtung *f*: **cast** (*od.* **shed, throw**) **~ on** Licht auf *e-e Sache* werfen; zur Lösung *e-r Sache* beitragen; **I see the ~** mir geht ein Licht auf. **2.** *mot.* Scheinwerfer *m*. **3.** *Br. mst pl* (Verkehrs)Ampel *f*: **jump** (*od.* **shoot**) **the ~s** bei Rot über die Kreuzung fahren; → **amber** 2, **5, green** 1, 3, **red** 1, 3, **yellow** 3. **4.** Feuer *n* (*zum Anzünden*), *bsd.* Streichholz *n*: **have you got a ~?** haben Sie Feuer? **5.** *a. shining ~ fig.* Leuchte *f*, großes Licht (*Person*): → **leading light**. **II** *adj* **6.** hell, licht: **~ red** Hellrot *n*. **III** *v/t* (*a. irr*) **7.** *a.* **~ up** anzünden: **~ a cigarette** sich e-e Zigarette anzünden. **8.** be-, erleuchten,

erhellen: **~ up** hell beleuchten. **9.** j-m leuchten. **IV** *v/i* (*a. irr*) **10.** *a.* **~ up** sich entzünden. **11.** *mst* **~ up** *fig.* aufleuchten (*Augen etc*). **12.** **~ up** Licht machen; *mot.* die Scheinwerfer einschalten; F sich e-e (*Zigarette etc*) anzünden.

light² [~] **I** *adj* (□ → **lightly**) **1.** *allg.* leicht (*z. B. Last; Kleidung; Mahlzeit, Wein; Schlaf; Fehler, Strafe*): (**as**) **~ as air** (*od.* **a feather**) federleicht; **~ current** ⚡ Schwachstrom *m*; **no ~ matter** keine Kleinigkeit; **~ metal** Leichtmetall *n*; **~ reading** Unterhaltungslektüre *f*; **make ~ of** auf die leichte Schulter nehmen; verharmlosen, bagatellisieren. **2.** locker (*Erde, Schnee*), locker gebacken (*Brot etc*). **3.** *Sport:* Halb...: **~ heavyweight** Halb-, Leichtschwergewicht(ler *m*) *n*. **II** *adv* **4.** **travel ~** mit leichtem Gepäck reisen.

light bar·ri·er *s* ⚡ Lichtschranke *f*. **~ bulb** *s* ⚡ Glühbirne *f*.

light·en¹ ['laɪtn] **I** *v/i* **1.** sich aufhellen, hell(er) werden. **2.** *impers.* blitzen. **II** *v/t* **3.** (*a.* blitzartig) erhellen.

light·en² [~] **I** *v/t* **1.** leichter machen, erleichtern (*beide a. fig.*): **~ s.o.'s heart** j-m das Herz leichter machen. **2.** j-n aufheitern. **II** *v/i* **3.** leichter werden: **her heart ~ed** *fig.* ihr wurde leichter ums Herz.

light·er ['laɪtə] *s* **1.** Anzünder *m* (*a. Gerät*). **2.** Feuerzeug *n*.

'**light-**‚**fin·gered** *adj* **1.** fingerfertig, geschickt. **2.** langfinge(e)rig, diebisch. '**~-**‚**foot·ed** *adj* □ leichtfüßig. '**~-**‚**head·ed** *adj* □ **1.** leichtsinnig, -fertig. **2. feel ~** (leicht) benommen sein; wie auf Wolken schweben. '**~-**‚**heart·ed** *adj* □ unbeschwert. '**~house** *s* Leuchtturm *m*.

light·ing ['laɪtɪŋ] *s* Beleuchtung *f*.

light·ly ['laɪtlɪ] *adv* **1.** leicht. **2.** wenig: **eat ~**. **3.** leichthin. **4.** geringschätzig.

‚**light-'mind·ed** *adj* □ leichtfertig, -sinnig; unbeständig, flatterhaft.

light·ness¹ ['laɪtnɪs] *s* Helligkeit *f*.

light·ness² [~] *s* **1.** Leichtheit *f*, Leichtigkeit *f* (*a. fig.*). **2.** Lockerheit *f*.

light·ning ['laɪtnɪŋ] **I** *s* Blitz *m*: (**as**) **quick as ~** blitzschnell; **struck by ~** vom Blitz getroffen; **like ~** wie der Blitz; → **flash** 1, **grease** 3, **streak** 1, **stroke** 2. **II** *adj* blitzschnell, Blitz...: **with ~ speed** mit

Blitzesschnelle. **~ con·duc·tor, ~ rod** s ⚡ Blitzableiter m.

light| pen s Computer: Lichtstift m. '**~proof** adj lichtundurchlässig.

lights [laɪts] s pl zo. Lunge f.

'**light|·ship** s ⚓ Feuer-, Leuchtschiff n. '**~weight I** adj leicht(gewichtig). **II** s Sport: Leichtgewicht(ler m) n. **~ year** s ast. Lichtjahr n.

lig·ne·ous ['lɪgnɪəs] adj holzig, holzartig, Holz...

lik·a·ble ['laɪkəbl] adj liebenswert, -würdig, sympathisch.

like¹ [laɪk] **I** adj u. prp **1.** gleich (dat), wie (a. adv): **a man ~ you** ein Mann wie du; **what is he ~?** wie ist er?; **what does it look ~?** wie sieht es aus?; → **feel** 6. **2.** ähnlich (dat), bezeichnend für: **that is just ~ him!** das sieht ihm ähnlich. **3.** gleich (Menge etc): **in ~ manner** auf gleiche Weise; gleichermaßen. **4.** ähnlich: **they are (as) ~ as two eggs** sie gleichen sich wie ein Ei dem anderen. **~** ähnlich, gleich-, derartig. **II** s **6.** der, die, das gleiche: **his ~** seinesgleichen; **the ~** dergleichen; **the ~s** pl of me **I** meinesgleichen, Leute pl wie ich.

like² [~] **I** v/t gern haben, mögen: **I ~ it** es gefällt mir; **I ~ him** ich kann ihn gut leiden; **how do you ~ it?** wie gefällt es dir?, wie findest du es?; **what do you ~ better?** was hast du lieber?, was gefällt dir besser?; **~ doing** (bsd. Am. a. **to do**) s.th. et. gern tun; **I should** (od. **would**) **~ to know** ich möchte gern wissen. **II** v/i wollen: **(just) as you ~** (ganz) wie du willst; **do as you ~** mach, was du willst; **if you ~** wenn du willst. **III** s Neigung f, Vorliebe f: **~s** pl **and dislikes** pl Neigungen pl u. Abneigungen pl.

like·a·ble → **likable**.

like·li·hood ['laɪklɪhʊd] s Wahrscheinlichkeit f: **in all ~** aller Wahrscheinlichkeit nach; **it is** highst wahrscheinlich. '**like·ly I** adj **1.** wahrscheinlich, voraussichtlich: **he is** (**not**) **~ to come** er kommt wahrscheinlich (es ist unwahrscheinlich, daß er kommt). **2.** glaubhaft: **a ~ story!** iro. das soll glauben, wer mag! **3.** in Frage kommend, geeignet. **II** adv **4.** wahrscheinlich: **most ~** höchstwahrscheinlich; (**as**) **~ as not** (sehr) wahrscheinlich; **not ~!** F wohl kaum!

'**like-'mind·ed** adj □ gleichgesinnt.

lik·en ['laɪkən] v/t vergleichen (**to** mit).

like·ness ['laɪknɪs] s **1.** Ähnlichkeit f (**between** zwischen dat; **to** mit). **2.** Abbild n (**of** gen).

like·wise ['laɪkwaɪz] adv desgleichen, ebenso.

lik·ing ['laɪkɪŋ] s Vorliebe f (**for** für): **this is not** (**to**) **my ~** das ist nicht nach m-m Geschmack.

li·lac ['laɪlək] **I** s ♣ Flieder m. **II** adj lila(farben).

Lil·li·pu·tian [ˌlɪlɪ'pjuːʃn] **I** adj winzig, zwergenhaft; Liliput..., Klein(st)... **II** s Liliputaner(in).

li·lo ['laɪləʊ] pl **-los** s Br. F Luftmatratze f.

lilt [lɪlt] s flotter Rhythmus; flotte od. schwungvolle Melodie.

lil·y ['lɪlɪ] s ♣ Lilie f: **~ of the valley** Maiglöckchen n. '**~-liv·ered** adj feig.

limb [lɪm] s **1.** (Körper)Glied n, pl a. Gliedmaßen pl. **2.** Hauptast m (e-s Baums): **be out on a ~** F in e-r gefährlichen Lage sein; Br. allein (da)stehen.

lim·ber ['lɪmbə] **I** adj **1.** biegsam, geschmeidig. **2.** beweglich, gelenkig. **II** v/t **3.** mst **~ up** biegsam od. geschmeidig machen, Muskeln a. auflockern: **~ o.s. up** → **4.** **III** v/i **4.** mst **~ up** sich auflockern, Lockerungsübungen machen.

lime¹ [laɪm] **I** s ♠ Kalk m. **II** v/t kalken.

lime² [~] s ♣ Linde f.

lime³ [~] s ♣ Limonelle f (Baum); Limone f, Limonelle f (Frucht).

lime·light s: **be in the ~** im Rampenlicht od. im Licht der Öffentlichkeit stehen.

lim·er·ick ['lɪmərɪk] s Limerick m.

'**lime|·stone** s geol. Kalkstein m. '**~-wash I** v/t kalken, weißen, tünchen. **II** s (Kalk)Tünche f.

lim·it ['lɪmɪt] **I** s **1.** fig. Grenze f, Beschränkung f, (Zeit- etc)Limit n: **to the ~** bis zum Äußersten od. Letzten; **within ~s** in (gewissen) Grenzen; **there is a ~ to everything** alles hat s-e Grenzen; **off ~s** Zutritt verboten (**to** für); **that's the ~!** F das ist (doch) die Höhe! **2.** ♠, ◎ Grenzwert m. **3.** ♈ Limit n, Preisgrenze f. **II** v/t **4.** beschränken, begrenzen (**to** auf acc); Auflage, Preise etc limitieren: **~ed in time** befristet; **~ed** (**liability**) **company** ♈ Br. Aktiengesellschaft f. ˌ**lim·i'ta·tion** s **1.** fig. Grenze f: **know one's (own) ~s** s-e Grenzen kennen. **2.** Begrenzung f, Beschränkung f: **~ of liability** ⚖️ Haftungsbeschränkung. **3.** ⚖️ Verjährung f: **~ (period)** Verjährungsfrist f.

lim·ou·sine ['lɪməzi:n] s mot. **1.** Br. Luxuslimousine f. **2.** Am. Kleinbus m.

limp¹ [lɪmp] **I** v/i hinken (a. fig. Vers etc), humpeln. **II** s Hinken n: **walk with a ~** hinken, humpeln.

limp² [~] adj schlaff, schlapp: **go ~** erschlaffen.

lim·pet ['lɪmpɪt] s zo. Napfschnecke f: **hold on** (od. **hang on, cling**) **to s.o. like a ~** fig. wie e-e Klette an j-m hängen.

lim·pid ['lɪmpɪd] adj □ klar (a. fig. Stil etc), durchsichtig.

lim·y ['laɪmɪ] adj kalkig, Kalk...

lin·age ['laɪndʒ] s **1.** Zeilenzahl f. **2.** Zeilenhonorar n.

linch·pin ['lɪntʃpɪn] s **1.** ⚙️ Achsnagel m. **2.** fig. Stütze f.

lin·den ['lɪndən] s ♣ Linde f.

line¹ [laɪn] **I** s **1.** Linie f (a. Sport), Strich m: → **toe** II. **2.** a) (Hand- etc)Linie f, b) Falte f, Runzel f: **~s** pl of worry Sorgenfalten pl, c) Zug m (im Gesicht). **3.** Zeile f (a. TV): **read between the ~s** fig. zwischen den Zeilen lesen; → **hot line**. **4.** pl thea. etc Rolle f, Text m. **5.** pl (mst sg konstruiert) bsd. Br. F Trauschein m. **6.** Linie f, Richtung f: **~ of sight** Blickrichtung. **7.** pl Grundsätze pl, Richtlinien pl: **along these ~s** nach diesen Grundsätzen; folgendermaßen. **8.** Art f u. Weise f, Methode f: **~ of thought** Auffassung f; Gedankengang m; **take a strong ~** energisch auftreten od. werden (**with s.o.** gegenüber j-m). **9.** Grenze f (a. fig.), Grenzlinie f: **draw the ~** die Grenze ziehen, haltmachen (**at** bei). **10.** Reihe f, Kette f; bsd. Am. (Menschen-, a. Auto)Schlange f: **stand in ~** anstehen, Schlange stehen (**for** um, nach); **drive in ~** mot. Kolonne fahren. **11.** Reihe f, Linie f: **be in** (**out of**) **~** fig. (nicht) übereinstimmen (**with** mit); **bring** (od. **get**) **into ~** fig. in Einklang bringen (**with** mit) auf Vordermann bringen; **fall into ~** sich einordnen; fig. sich anschließen (**with** dat); **keep s.o. in ~** fig. j-n bei der Stange halten. **12.** (Abstammungs)Linie f: **in the direct ~** in direkter Linie. **13.** Fach n, Gebiet n: **~ (of business)** Branche f; **that's not in my ~** das schlägt nicht in mein Fach; das liegt mir nicht. **14.** (Verkehrs-, Eisenbahn- etc)Linie f, Strecke f, Route f, engS. 🚂 Gleis n: **the end of the ~** fig. das (bittere) Ende. **15.** (Flug- etc)Gesellschaft f **16.** bsd. teleph. Leitung f: **the ~ is busy** (Br. engaged) die Leitung ist besetzt; **hold the ~** bleiben Sie am Apparat; → **hot line**. **17.** ⚙️ (Rohr)Leitung f. **18.** ✕ a) Linie: **behind the enemy ~s** hinter den feindlichen Linien, b) Front f: **all along the ~, down the ~** fig. auf der ganzen Linie. **19.** geogr. Längen- od. Breitenkreis m: **the ⚓ der Äquator. 20.** Leine f; Schnur f; Seil n. **II** v/i **21.** → **line up** I. **III** v/t **22.** lini(i)eren. **23.** zeichnen; skizzieren. **24.** Gesicht (zer)furchen. **25.** Straße etc säumen.

Verbindungen mit Adverbien:

line| off v/t abgrenzen. **~ up I** v/i **1.** sich in e-r Reihe od. Linie aufstellen, (Sport) sich aufstellen. **2.** bsd. Am. sich anstellen (**for** um, nach). **II** v/t **3.** in e-r Reihe od. Linie aufstellen. **4.** F auf die Beine stellen, organisieren.

line² [~] v/t **1.** Kleid etc füttern. **2.** bsd. ⚙️ auskleiden, -schlagen (**with** mit), Bremsen, Kupplung belegen. **3.** (an)füllen: **~ one's pocket(s)** (od. **purse**) sich bereichern.

lin·e·age¹ ['lɪnɪdʒ] s **1.** geradlinige Abstammung f. **2.** Stammbaum m. **3.** Geschlecht n.

line·age² → **linage**.

lin·e·al ['lɪnɪəl] adj □ geradlinig, direkt (Nachkomme etc).

lin·e·a·ment ['lɪnɪəmənt] s mst pl (Gesichts)Zug m.

lin·e·ar ['lɪnɪə] adj □ **1.** 📐, ⚙️ etc linear. **2.** Längen...

lin·en ['lɪnɪn] **I** s **1.** Leinen n. **2.** (Bett-, Unter- etc)Wäsche f: **wash one's dirty ~ in public** fig. s-e schmutzige Wäsche in der Öffentlichkeit waschen. **II** adj **3.** Leinen... **~ bas·ket** s bsd. Br. Wäschekorb m.

lin·er ['laɪnə] s **1.** ⚓ Linienschiff n. **2.** ✈ Verkehrsflugzeug n. **3.** → **eye liner**.

lines·man ['laɪnzmən] s (irr man) Sport: Linienrichter m. **~·wom·an** s (irr woman) Linienrichterin f.

'line·up s **1.** Sport: Aufstellung f. **2.** bsd. Am. (Menschen)Schlange f.

lin·ger ['lɪŋgə] v/i **1.** verweilen, sich aufhalten (*beide a.* fig. **over, on** bei e-m *Thema etc*): **~ on** noch dableiben; nachklingen (*Ton*); fig. fortleben, -bestehen (*Tradition etc*). **2.** fig. (zurück)bleiben (*Verdacht etc*). **3.** trödeln: **~ about** (*od.* **around**) herumtrödeln. **'lin·ger·ing** adj □ **1.** nachklingend. **2.** schleichend (*Krankheit*).

lin·go ['lɪŋgəʊ] pl **-goes** s F **1.** Kauderwelsch n. **2.** (Fach)Jargon m.

lin·gual ['lɪŋgwəl] adj Zungen...

lin·guist ['lɪŋgwɪst] s **1.** Linguist(in), Sprachwissenschaftler(in). **2.** Sprachkundige m, f: **be a good ~** (sehr) sprachbegabt sein. **lin'guis·tic** I adj (**~ally**) **1.** linguistisch, sprachwissenschaftlich. **2.** Sprach(en)... II s pl (*mst sg konstruiert*) **3.** Linguistik f, Sprachwissenschaft f.

lin·i·ment ['lɪnɪmənt] s ✹ Einreibemittel n.

lin·ing ['laɪnɪŋ] s **1.** Futter(stoff m) n. **2.** bsd. ⊙ Auskleidung f, (*Brems-, Kupplungs*)Belag m.

link [lɪŋk] I s **1.** (Ketten)Glied n; fig. Glied n (*in e-r Kette von Ereignissen etc*); Bindeglied n; Verbindung f, Zs.-hang m. **2.** Manschettenknopf m. II v/t **3.** a. **~ up** verketten, -binden (**to, with** mit): **~ arms** sich unter- od. einhaken (**with** bei). **4.** a. **~ up** fig. in Verbindung od. Zs.-hang bringen (**with** mit), e-n Zs.-hang herstellen zwischen (*dat*). III v/i **5.** a. **~ up** sich verketten od. verbinden (**to, with** mit). **6.** a. **~ up** fig. sich zs.-fügen.

links [lɪŋks] → **golf links**.

'link·up s Verbindung f, Zs.-hang m.

li·no·le·um [lɪ'nəʊljəm] s Linoleum n.

lin·seed ['lɪnsiːd] s ♣ Leinsamen m. **~ oil** s Leinöl n.

lin·tel ['lɪntl] s △ Oberschwelle f, (Tür-, Fenster)Sturz m.

li·on ['laɪən] s **1.** zo. Löwe m (a. ast. ♌): **go into the ~'s den** fig. sich in die Höhle des Löwen wagen; **the ~'s share** der Löwenanteil; → **beard** II. **2.** fig. Größe f, Berühmtheit f (*Person*). **li·on·ess** ['~es] s Löwin f.

lip [lɪp] s **1.** anat. Lippe f: **lower (upper) ~** Unter-(Ober)lippe f; **keep a stiff upper ~** fig. Haltung bewahren; sich nichts anmerken lassen; **bite one's ~** fig. sich

auf die Lippen beißen; → **smack²** 1. **2.** F Unverschämtheit f: **none of your ~!** sei nicht so unverschämt od. frech! **3.** Rand m (*e-r Wunde, e-s Kraters etc*). **'~-read** v/t u. v/i (*irr read*) von den Lippen ablesen. **~ ser·vice** s Lippenbekenntnis n. **'~-stick** s Lippenstift m: **put on ~** sich die Lippen schminken.

liq·ue·fy ['lɪkwɪfaɪ] v/t u. v/i **1.** (sich) verflüssigen. **2.** schmelzen.

li·queur [lɪ'kjʊə] s Likör m.

liq·uid ['lɪkwɪd] I adj □ **1.** flüssig. **2.** Flüssigkeits...: **~ measure** Flüssigkeitsmaß n. **3.** ✝ liquid, flüssig. II s **4.** Flüssigkeit f.

liq·ui·date ['lɪkwɪdeɪt] v/t **1.** ✝ liquidieren: a) *Gesellschaft* auflösen, b) *Sachwerte etc* realisieren, zu Geld machen, c) *Schulden etc* tilgen. **2.** fig. j-n liquidieren, beseitigen. **,liq·ui'da·tion** s **1.** ✝ Liquidation f: a) Auflösung f, b) Realisierung f, c) Tilgung f. **2.** fig. Liquidierung f, Beseitigung f.

li·quid·i·ty [lɪ'kwɪdətɪ] s **1.** flüssiger Zustand. **2.** ✝ Liquidität f, Flüssigkeit f.

liq·ui·dize ['lɪkwɪdaɪz] v/t **1.** (v/i sich) verflüssigen. **2.** (im Mixer) zerkleinern od. pürieren. **'liq·ui·diz·er** s Mixer m, Mixgerät n.

liq·uor ['lɪkə] s a) Br. alkoholische Getränke pl, Alkohol m: **hard ~** → b, b) Am. Schnaps m, Spirituosen pl: **~ cabi·net** Hausbar f.

liq·uo·rice → **licorice**.

li·ra ['lɪərə] pl **-re** [~'riː], **-ras** s Lira f.

lisp [lɪsp] I v/i lispeln (a. v/t), mit der Zunge anstoßen. II s Lispeln n: **speak with a ~** → I.

list¹ [lɪst] I s **1.** Liste f, Verzeichnis n: **be on the ~** auf der Liste stehen; **~ price** Listenpreis m. II v/t **2.** (in e-r Liste) verzeichnen, erfassen, registrieren: **~ed building** Br. Gebäude n unter Denkmalschutz. **3.** in e-e Liste eintragen.

list² [~] ♣ I s Schlagseite f. II v/i Schlagseite haben od. bekommen.

lis·ten ['lɪsn] v/i **1.** hören, horchen (**to** acc): **~ to** a) j-m zuhören, j-n anhören: **~!** hör mal!), b) auf j-n, j-s Rat hören, c) *e-m Rat etc* folgen; **~ in** Radio hören. **2.** **~ in** Radio hören: **~ in to a concert** im Konzert im Radio anhören. **'lis·ten·er** s **1.** Horcher(in). **2.** Zuhörer(in): **be a**

good ~ (gut) zuhören können. **3.** *Radio:* Hörer(in).

list·less ['lɪstlɪs] *adj* □ lust-, teilnahmslos.

lit [lɪt] *pret u. pp von* **light**¹.

lit·a·ny ['lɪtənɪ] *s eccl.* Litanei *f (a. fig.).*

li·ter *Am.* → **litre.**

lit·er·a·cy ['lɪtərəsɪ] *s* **1.** Fähigkeit *f* zu lesen u. zu schreiben. **2.** (literarische) Bildung, Belesenheit.

lit·er·al ['lɪtərəl] *adj* □ **1.** wörtlich (*Übersetzung etc*): *take s.th. ~ly* et. wörtlich nehmen. **2.** genau, wahrheitsgetreu. **3.** nüchtern, trocken, prosaisch. **4.** wörtlich, eigentlich (*Bedeutung e-s Worts etc*). **5.** buchstäblich: *he did ~ly nothing.*

lit·er·ar·y ['lɪtərərɪ] *adj* □ **1.** literarisch, Literatur...: *~ critic* Literaturkritiker(in); *~ history* Literaturgeschichte *f.* **2.** gewählt, hochgestochen (*Ausdruck etc*).

lit·er·ate ['lɪtərət] *adj* □ **1.** *be ~* lesen u. schreiben können. **2.** (literarisch) gebildet, belesen. **lit·er·a·ture** ['~ətʃə] *s* **1.** Literatur *f.* **2.** F Informationsmaterial *n.*

lith·o·graph ['lɪθəʊɡrɑːf] *s* Lithographie *f,* Steindruck *m.*

lit·i·gant ['lɪtɪɡənt] ⚖ **I** *adj* streitend, prozeßführend. **II** *s* Prozeßführende *m, f,* streitende Partei. **lit·i·gate** ['~ɡeɪt] *v/i* (*u. v/t*) prozessieren *od.* streiten (um). **‚lit·i'ga·tion** *s* Rechtsstreit *m,* Prozeß *m.*

li·to·tes ['laɪtəʊtiːz] *s rhet.* Litotes *f.*

li·tre ['liːtə] *s bsd. Br.* Liter *m, a. n.*

lit·ter ['lɪtə] **I** *s* **1.** (herumliegender) Abfall. **2.** Streu *f (für Tiere),* (*a. für Pflanzen*) Stroh *n.* **3.** *zo.* Wurf *m.* **4.** Trage *f;* Sänfte *f.* **II** *v/t* **5.** Abfall herumliegen lassen in (*dat*) *od.* auf (*dat*); *Park etc* verschandeln (*with* mit). **6.** *mst ~ down* (mit) Streu legen für; *Stall* einstreuen. **7.** *Pflanzen* mit Stroh abdecken. **8.** *zo. Junge* werfen. **III** *v/i* **9.** *zo.* (Junge) werfen. *~ bas·ket,* '*~·bin s* Abfallkorb *m.* '*~·bug s bsd. Am.* F, *~ lout s bsd. Br.* F *j-d, der Straßen etc mit Abfall verschandelt.*

lit·tle ['lɪtl] **I** *adj* **1.** klein (*Kind etc*): *the ~ ones pl* die Kleinen *pl;* → *finger* I. **2.** kurz (*Strecke od. Zeit*). **3.** wenig (*Hoffnung etc*): *a ~ jam* ein wenig *od.* ein

bißchen Marmelade. **4.** klein, gering(fügig). **II** *adv* **5.** wenig, kaum: *think ~ of* wenig halten von; *for as ~ as £ 10* für nur 10 Pfund. **6.** wenig, selten: *I see him very ~.* **III** *s* **7.** Kleinigkeit *f,* das wenige, *das* bißchen: *a ~* ein wenig, ein bißchen; *~ by ~* (ganz) allmählich, nach u. nach. **8.** *in ~* im kleinen, in kleinem Maßstab.

lit·ur·gy ['lɪtədʒɪ] *s eccl.* Liturgie *f.*

liv·a·ble ['lɪvəbl] *adj* **1.** wohnlich, bewohnbar. **2.** lebenswert (*Leben*). **3.** *a. ~ with* erträglich (*Schmerzen etc*): *not ~ (with)* unerträglich. **4.** *~ with* umgänglich (*Person*).

live¹ [lɪv] *v/i* leben: a) am Leben sein, b) am Leben bleiben: *~ through the night* die Nacht überleben; *you ~ and learn* man lernt nie aus; *~ on bsd. fig.* weiter-, fortleben, c) sich ernähren (*on* von): *he ~s on his wife* er lebt auf Kosten *od.* von (den Einkünften) s-r Frau, d) ein *ehrliches etc* Leben führen: *~ honestly; ~ up to s-n Grundsätzen etc* gemäß leben, *s-m Ruf etc* gerecht werden, *den Erwartungen etc* entsprechen, e) wohnen (*with* bei): *~ with* zs.-leben mit; *~ together* zs.-leben, f) das Leben genießen: *~ and let* ~ leben u. leben lassen. **II** *v/t* ein bestimmtes Leben führen.

live² [laɪv] **I** *adj* **1.** lebend, lebendig: *~ weight* Lebendgewicht *n; a real ~ lord* F ein richtiger *od.* echter Lord. **2.** aktuell (*Frage etc*). **3.** scharf (*Munition etc*). **4.** ⚡ stromführend: *~ wire* F Energiebündel *n.* **5.** *Rundfunk, TV:* Direkt..., Original..., Live-... **II** *adv* **6.** direkt, original, live.

live·a·ble → **livable.**

live·li·hood ['laɪvlɪhʊd] *s* Lebensunterhalt *m:* *earn* (*od.* **gain, make**) *a* (*od.* **one's**) *~* s-n Lebensunterhalt verdienen.

live·li·ness ['laɪvlɪnɪs] *s* **1.** Lebhaftigkeit *f.* **2.** Lebendigkeit *f.* '**live·ly** *adj* □ **1.** lebhaft (*Interesse, Person, Phantasie etc*). **2.** lebendig (*Schilderung etc*). **3.** aufregend (*Zeiten*): *make it* (*od.* **things**) *~ for s.o., give s.o. a ~ time* (kräftig) einheizen. **4.** schnell, flott (*Tempo etc*).

liv·en ['laɪvn] *mst ~ up* **I** *v/t* beleben, Leben bringen in (*acc*). **II** *v/i* in Schwung kommen.

liv·er¹ ['lɪvə] s anat. Leber f (a. gastr.).

liv·er² [~] s: **be a ~** ein flottes Leben führen; **loose ~** liederlicher Mensch.

liv·er·ied ['lɪvərɪd] adj livriert.

liv·er·ish ['lɪvərɪʃ] adj **1. be ~** F es mit der Leber haben. **2.** mürrisch.

liv·er| sau·sage s Leberwurst f. **~ spot** s Leberfleck m. **~·wurst** ['~wɜːst] s bsd. Am. Leberwurst f.

liv·er·y ['lɪvərɪ] s Livree f: **in ~** in Livree.

lives [laɪvz] pl von **life**.

live·stock ['laɪvstɒk] s Vieh(bestand m) n.

liv·id ['lɪvɪd] adj □ **1.** blau, bläulich (verfärbt). **2.** bleifarben, graublau. **3.** fahl, aschgrau, bleich (**with** vor dat). **4.** F fuchsteufelswild.

liv·ing ['lɪvɪŋ] **I** adj **1.** lebend (a. Sprache): **while ~** bei od. zu Lebzeiten; **within ~ memory** seit Menschengedenken; → **daylight**. **2.** Lebens...: **~ conditions** pl Lebensbedingungen pl. **II** s **3.** **the ~** pl die Lebenden pl. **4.** das Leben: → **cost** 1. **5.** Leben(sweise f) n: **loose ~** lockerer Lebenswandel; → **clean** 5. **6.** Lebensunterhalt m: **earn** (od. **gain**, **get**, **make**) **a ~** s-n Lebensunterhalt verdienen (**as** als; **out of** durch, mit). **~ room** s Wohnzimmer n. **~ space** s Wohnfläche f, -raum m.

liz·ard ['lɪzəd] s zo. Eidechse f.

lla·ma ['lɑːmə] s zo. Lama n.

load [ləʊd] **I** s **1.** Last f, fig. a. Bürde f: **his decision took a ~** off my mind es fiel mir ein Stein vom s-r Entscheidung Herzen. **2.** Ladung f (a. e-r Schußwaffe): **get a ~** off F sich et. ansehen od. anhören; et. zu sehen od. zu hören bekommen; **get a ~** of this! F hör od. schau dir das mal an! **3.** pl F Massen pl (von Geld etc): e-e Unmasse (Leute etc): **there were ~s to eat** es gab massenhaft zu essen. **4.** ⚡, ⚙ Belastung f. **II** v/t **5.** a. **~ up** Fahrzeug etc beladen (**with** mit). **6.** Gegenstand etc laden (**into** in acc; **onto** auf acc), Güter verladen. **7.** Schußwaffe laden: **~ the camera** e-n Film (in die Kamera) einlegen. **8.** j-n überhäufen (**with** mit Arbeit, Vorwürfen etc). **9.** beschweren, schwerer machen, engS. Würfel einseitig beschweren, präparieren. **III** v/i **10.** mst **~ up** (auf-, ein)laden. **11.** (das Gewehr etc) laden, phot. e-n Film einlegen.

'load·ed adj **1.** be-, geladen etc, → **load** II. **2. ~ question** Fang- od. Suggestivfrage f; **~ word** emotionsgeladenes Wort; vorbelastetes Wort; Reizwort n. **3.** F stinkreich: **be ~** a. Geld wie Heu haben.

loaf¹ [ləʊf] pl **loaves** [ləʊvz] s **1.** Laib m (Brot); weitS. Brot n. **2.** a. **meat ~** gastr. Hackbraten m. **3.** **use one's ~** Br. sl. sein Hirn anstrengen, (nach)denken.

loaf² [~] F **I** v/i **1.** a. **~ about** (od. **around**) herumlungern: **~ about** (od. **around**) **the streets** auf den Straßen herumlungern. **2.** faulenzen. **II** v/t **3. ~ away** Zeit verbummeln. **'loaf·er** s F **1.** Müßiggänger(in). **2.** Faulenzer(in). **3.** bsd. Am. leichter Slipper.

loam [ləʊm] s Lehm m. **'loam·y** adj lehmig, Lehm...

loan [ləʊn] s **1.** (Ver)Leihen n: **on ~** leihweise; **a book on ~** ein geliehenes Buch; **may I have the ~ of ...?** darf ich (mir) ... (aus)leihen? **2.** ✝ Anleihe f (a. fig.): **take up a ~** e-e Anleihe aufnehmen (**on** auf acc). **3.** ✝ Darlehen n, Kredit m. **4.** Leihgabe f (für e-e Ausstellung). **II** v/t **5.** bsd. Am. (**to**) (aus)leihen (dat), ver-, ausleihen (an acc). **~ shark** s F Kredithai m. **'~word** s ling. Lehnwort n.

loath [ləʊθ] adj: **be ~ to do s.th.** et. (sehr) ungern od. widerwillig tun.

loathe [ləʊð] v/t verabscheuen, hassen: **~ doing s.th.** es hassen, et. zu tun. **'loath·ing** s Abscheu m. **'loath·some** ['~səm] adj □ widerlich, abscheulich.

loaves [ləʊvz] pl von **loaf**.

lob [lɒb] (bsd. Tennis) **I** s Lob m. **II** v/t a) **~ a ball** → III, b) Gegner überlobben. **III** v/i lobben, e-n Lob spielen od. schlagen.

lob·by ['lɒbɪ] **I** s **1.** Vor-, Eingangshalle f; Wandelhalle f; thea. Foyer n. **2.** pol. Lobby f, Interessengruppe f, -verband m. **II** v/t **3.** a. **~ through** Gesetzesvorlage mit Hilfe e-r Lobby durchbringen. **4.** Abgeordnete beeinflussen. **'lob·by·ist** s Lobbyist m.

lobe [ləʊb] s ♀, anat. Lappen m: **~ (of the ear)** Ohrläppchen n.

lob·ster ['lɒbstə] s zo. Hummer m: **(as) red as a ~** krebsrot.

lo·cal ['ləʊkl] **I** adj □ **1.** lokal, örtlich: **~ call** teleph. Ortsgespräch n; **~ derby**

(*Sport*) Lokalderby *n*; **~ elections** *pl* Kommunalwahlen *pl*; **~ hero** (*bsd. Sport*) Lokalmatador *m*; **~ news** Lokalnachrichten *pl*; **~ time** Ortszeit *f*; **~ traffic** Lokal-, Orts-, Nahverkehr *m*; → **colour** 1. **2.** Orts..., ansässig, hiesig. **3.** lokal, örtlich (beschränkt): **~ an(a)esthesia** örtliche Betäubung; **~ custom** ortsüblicher Brauch. **II** *s* **4.** *mst pl* Ortsansässige *m, f*, Einheimische *m, f*. **5.** *Br.* F (nächstgelegene) Kneipe, *bsd.* Stammkneipe *f*.

lo·cale [ləʊˈkɑːl] *s* Schauplatz *m*, Szene *f*.

lo·cal·i·ty [ləʊˈkælətɪ] *s* **1.** a) Örtlichkeit *f*, Ort *m*: **sense of ~** Ortssinn *m*, b) Gegend *f*. **2.** (*örtliche*) Lage.

lo·cal·ize [ˈləʊkəlaɪz] *v/t* lokalisieren (**to** auf *acc*).

lo·cate [ləʊˈkeɪt] **I** *v/t* **1.** ausfindig machen, aufspüren; ♣ *etc* orten; ✕ *Ziel* ausmachen. **2.** *Büro etc* errichten. **3.** (*an e-m bestimmten Ort*) an- od. unterbringen; (*an e-n Ort*) verlegen: **be ~d** gelegen sein, liegen, sich befinden. **II** *v/i* **4.** *Am.* sich niederlassen. **lo·ca·tion** *s* **1.** Ausfindigmachen *n*; ♣ *etc* Ortung *f*; ✕ Ausmachen *n*. **2.** Stelle *f*, Platz *m*; Lage *f*, Standort *m*. **3.** *Film, TV:* Gelände *n* für Außenaufnahmen: **~ shooting**, **shooting on ~** Außenaufnahmen *pl*.

loch [lɒx] *s schott.* **1.** See *m*. **2.** Bucht *f*.

lock[1] [lɒk] **I** *s* **1.** (*Tür-, Gewehr- etc-*) Schloß *n*: **under ~ and key** hinter Schloß u. Riegel; unter Verschluß; **~, stock and barrel** *fig.* mit allem Drum u. Dran; mit Stumpf u. Stiel; mit Sack u. Pack. **2.** Verschluß *m*; Sperrvorrichtung *f*. **3.** Schleuse(nkammer) *f*. **II** *v/t* **4.** *a.* **~ up** zu-, verschließen, zu-, versperren. **5.** *a.* **~ up** einschließen, (ein)sperren (*in, into* in *acc*): **~ away** wegschließen; **~ out** ausschließen (*a.* ✝). **6.** umschlingen, umfassen, *in die Arme* schließen. **7.** ☺ sperren. **III** *v/i* **8.** schließen: **~ up** abschließen. **9.** ab- *od.* verschließbar sein. **10.** *mot. etc* blockieren (*Räder*).

lock[2] [~] *s* (*Haar*)Locke *f*, (~)Strähne *f*.

lock·er [ˈlɒkə] *s* **1.** Schließfach *n*. **2.** Spind *m, n*.

lock·et [ˈlɒkɪt] *s* Medaillon *n*.

'lock·jaw *s* 𝕊 **1.** Kiefersperre *f*. **2.** Wundstarrkrampf *m*. **~ keep·er** *s* Schleusenwärter *m*. **'~·out** *s* ✝ Aus-

sperrung *f*. **'~·up** *s* **1.** Arrestzelle *f*; F Kittchen *n*. **2.** *bsd. Br.* (Einzel)Garage *f*.

lo·co [ˈləʊkəʊ] *bes. Am. sl.* verrückt (*a. Ideen etc*).

lo·co·mo·tion [ˌləʊkəˈməʊʃn] *s* Fortbewegungs... **'lo·co·mo·tive** [~tɪv] **I** *adj* Fortbewegungs... **II** *s* 🚂 Lokomotive *f*.

lo·cust [ˈləʊkəst] *s zo.* Heuschrecke *f*.

lo·cu·tion [ləʊˈkjuːʃn] *s* **1.** Ausdrucks-, Redeweise *f*. **2.** Redewendung *f*, Ausdruck *m*.

lodge [lɒdʒ] **I** *s* **1.** Sommer-, Gartenhaus *n*; (*Jagd- etc*)Hütte *f*; Gärtner-, Pförtnerhaus *n*. **2.** Portier-, Pförtnerloge *f*. **II** *v/t* **3.** logieren, (*bsd.* vorübergehend *od.* in Untermiete) wohnen. **4.** übernachten. **5.** stecken(bleiben) (*Kugel, Bissen etc*). **II** *v/t* **6.** aufnehmen, beherbergen, (für die Nacht) unterbringen. **7.** *Antrag, Beschwerde etc* einreichen, *Anzeige* erstatten, *Berufung, Protest* einlegen (**with** bei). **'lodg·er** *s* Untermieter(in): **take ~s** Zimmer vermieten. **'lodg·ing** *s* **1.** Wohnen *n.* **2.** *a. pl* Unterkunft *f*: **night's ~, ~ for the night** Nachtquartier *n*; **~ house** Fremdenheim *n*, Pension *f*; → **board** 4. **3.** *pl* möbliertes Zimmer: **live in ~s** möbliert wohnen.

loft [lɒft] *s* **1.** Dachboden *m*; Speicher *m*. **2.** 🏛 Empore *f*, (*Orgel*)Chor *m.* **'loft·y** *adj* □ **1.** hoch(ragend). **2.** hochfliegend (*Pläne etc*), hochgesteckt (*Ziele etc*), erhaben (*Gedanken, Stil etc*). **3.** stolz, hochmütig.

log [lɒg] **I** *s* **1.** (Holz)Klotz *m*; (*gefällter*) Baumstamm; (*großes*) (Holz)Scheit: → **sleep** II. **2.** → **logbook. II** *v/t* **3.** *a.* **~ up** in das Logbuch *etc* eintragen; *allg. Ereignisse etc* aufzeichnen, festhalten.

log·a·rithm [ˈlɒgərɪðəm] *s* ♯ Logarithmus *m*.

'log·book *s* **1.** ♣ Logbuch *n*. **2.** ✈ Flugbuch *n*. **3.** *mot.* Bord-, Fahrtenbuch *n.* **4.** *mot. Br.* Kraftfahrzeugbrief *m.* **~ cab·in** *s* Blockhaus *n*, -hütte *f.*

log·ger·heads [ˈlɒgəhedz] *s pl*: **be at ~** Streit haben (**with** mit), sich in den Haaren liegen.

log·ic [ˈlɒdʒɪk] *s phls. u. allg.* Logik *f*. **'log·i·cal** *adj* □ logisch.

lo·gis·tics [ləʊˈdʒɪstɪks] *s pl* (*oft sg konstruiert*) ✕, ✝ Logistik *f*.

loin [lɔɪn] *s* **1.** *mst pl anat.* Lende *f*. **2.**

gastr. Lende(nstück *n*) *f.* **'~cloth** *s* Lendenschurz *m.*

loi·ter ['lɔɪtə] I *v/i* 1. bummeln: a) schlendern, b) trödeln. 2. *a.* ~ **about** (*od.* **around**) herumlungern. II *v/t* 3. ~ **away** *Zeit* vertrödeln. **'loi·ter·er** *s* Bummler(in).

loll [lɒl] I *v/i* 1. sich rekeln *od.* räkeln: ~ **about** (*od.* **around**) herumlümmeln. 2. ~ **out** heraushängen (*Zunge*). II *v/t* 3. ~ **out** *Zunge* heraushängen lassen.

lol·li·pop ['lɒlɪpɒp] *s* 1. Lutscher *m.* 2. *Br.* Eis *n* am Stiel. ~ **man** *s* (*irr* **man**) *Br.* F (*etwa*) Schülerlotse *m.* ~ **wom·an** *s* (*irr* **woman**) *Br.* F (*etwa*) Schülerlotsin *f.*

lol·lop ['lɒləp] *v/i* hoppeln (*Hase, Fahrzeug*), latschen (*Person*).

lol·ly ['lɒlɪ] *s* 1. F → **lollipop** 1. 2. → **lollipop** 2. 3. *Br. sl.* Kies *n* (Geld).

Lon·don·er ['lʌndənə] *s* Londoner(in).

lone [ləʊn] *adj* 1. einzeln: **play a ~ hand** *fig.* e-n Alleingang machen; → **wolf** 1. 2. alleinstehend, einzeln (*Haus etc*). **lone·li·ness** ['~lɪnɪs] *s* Einsamkeit *f.* **'lone·ly** *adj* einsam. **'lon·er** *s* Einzelgänger *m* (*a. zo.*). **lone·some** ['~səm] *adj* □ *bsd. Am.* einsam.

long¹ [lɒŋ] I *adj* 1. *allg.* lang (*a. fig.*): → **run** 1. 2. weit, lang (*Weg*), weit (*Entfernung*). 3. zu lang: **the coat is ~ on him** der Mantel ist ihm zu lang. 4. weitreichend (*Gedanken*), gut (*Gedächtnis*). 5. ✝ langfristig. 6. **be ~ on** F e-e Menge ... haben. II *adv* 7. lang(e): ~ **dead** schon lange tot; **as** (*od.* **so**) ~ **as** solange wie; vorausgesetzt, daß; falls; ~ **after** lange danach; **as ~ ago as 1900** schon 1900; **so ~!** F bis dann!; → **ago, all** 7. III *s* 8. (e-e) lange Zeit: **at (the) ~est** längstens; **for ~** lange (Zeit); **take ~** (**to do s.th.**) lange brauchen(, um et. zu tun); → **before** 5.

long² [~] *v/i* sich sehnen (**for** nach): ~ **to do s.th.** sich danach sehnen, et. zu tun.

,long·'dis·tance *adj* 1. Fern...: ~ **call** *teleph.* Ferngespräch *n;* ~ **driver** Fernfahrer *m.* 2. ✓. *Sport:* Langstrecken... ~ **drink** *s* Longdrink *m.* **,~'haired** *adj* langhaarig.

long·ing ['lɒŋɪŋ] I *adj* □ sehnsüchtig. II *s* Sehnsucht *f* (**for** nach).

long·ish ['lɒŋɪʃ] *adj* 1. ziemlich lang. 2. länglich.

lon·gi·tude ['lɒndʒɪtjuːd] *s geogr.* Länge *f:* → **degree** 2.

long| johns *s pl* F lange Unterhose. ~ **jump** *s Leichtathletik: bsd. Br.* Weitsprung *m.* ~ **jump·er** *s Leichtathletik: bsd. Br.* Weitspringer(in). **,~'lived** *adj* 1. langlebig. 2. dauerhaft. **'~,play·ing rec·ord** *s* Langspielplatte *f.* **,~'range** *adj* 1. ✕, ✓ Fern...; Langstrecken... 2. langfristig. **~shore·man** ['~mən] *s* (*irr* **man**) *bsd. Am.* Dock-, Hafenarbeiter *m.* ~ **shot** *s* 1. *Sport:* Weitschuß *m.* 2. *fig.* riskante Angelegenheit. 3. **not by a ~** *fig.* bei weitem nicht, nicht im entferntesten. **,~'sight·ed** *adj* □ ✣ weitsichtig, *fig. a.* weitblickend. **,~'standing** *adj* seit langer Zeit bestehend, alt. **'~term** *adj* langfristig: ~ **memory** Langzeitgedächtnis *n.* **'~time** → **long-standing.** ~ **wave** *s* ⚡, *phys.* Langwelle *f.* **'~wave** *adj* ⚡, *phys.* Langwellen... **~wind·ed** [,~'wɪndɪd] *adj* □ 1. ausdauernd (*Person*). 2. langatmig, weitschweifig (*Erzählung etc*), (*a. Person*) umständlich.

loo·[luː] *s bsd. Br.* F Klo *n:* **in the ~** auf dem *od.* im Klo; ~ **attendant** Klofrau *f;* ~ **paper** Klopapier *n.*

look [lʊk] I *s* 1. Blick *m* (**at** auf *acc*): **cast** (*od.* **throw**) **a ~ at** e-n Blick werfen auf; **give s.o. an angry ~** j-m e-n wütenden Blick zuwerfen, j-n wütend ansehen; **have a ~ at s.th.** (sich) et. ansehen; **have a ~ round** sich umschauen in (*dat*). 2. Miene *f,* (Gesichts)Ausdruck *m:* **the ~ on his face** sein Gesichtsausdruck. 3. *oft pl* Aussehen *n:* **have the ~ of** aussehen wie. II *v/i* 4. schauen: **don't ~!** nicht hersehen!; ~ **who is coming!** schau (mal), wer da kommt. 5. (nach-)schauen, nachsehen. 6. ausschauen, -sehen (*beide a. fig.*): ~ **well on so.** j-m stehen (*Hut etc*); **it ~s like snow(ing)** es sieht nach Schnee aus. 7. liegen *od.* (hinaus)gehen nach: **the room ~s north.** III *v/t* 8. j-m (*in die Augen etc*) sehen *od.* schauen *od.* blicken: ~ **s.o. in the eyes.** 9. aussehen wie: **she does not ~ her age** man sieht ihr ihr Alter nicht an; ~ **an idiot** *fig.* wie ein Idiot dastehen. 10. durch Blicke ausdrücken: ~ **one's surprise** überrascht blicken *od.* dreinschauen; → **dagger.**

Verbindungen mit Präpositionen:

look| a·bout → **look around.** ~ **af·ter** *v/i* 1. nachblicken, -schauen, -sehen (*dat*). 2. aufpassen auf (*acc*), sich kümmern um. ~ **a·round** *v/i* 1. sich umschauen *od.* umsehen in (*dat*). 2. ~ **one** sich umsehen *od.* umblicken. ~ **at** *v/i* 1. ansehen, anschauen, betrachten: **to ~ one's watch** auf die Uhr schauen; **to ~ him** wenn man ihn (so) ansieht. 2. sich *et.* anschauen, *et.* prüfen. ~ **for** *v/i* suchen (nach). ~ **in·to** *v/i* 1. (hinein-) schauen *od.* -sehen in (*acc*): ~ **the mirror** in den Spiegel schauen; ~ **s.o.'s eyes** j-m in die Augen schauen. 2. untersuchen, prüfen. ~ **on** *v/i* nachsehen, betrachten (**as** als). ~ **on·to** *v/i* (hinaus)gehen auf (*acc*) *od.* nach: **my room looks onto the garden.** ~ **o·ver** *v/i* 1. schauen *od.* blicken über (*acc*). 2. (sich) *et.* (flüchtig) ansehen *od.* anschauen, *et.* (flüchtig) überprüfen. ~ **round** → **look around.** ~ **through** *v/i* 1. blicken durch. 2. (hin)durchsehen *od.* (-)durchschauen durch. 3. *fig. j-n, et.* durchschauen. 4. *et.* (flüchtig) durchsehen *od.* -schauen. ~ **to** *v/i* 1. achten *od.* achtgeben auf (*acc*): ~ **it that** achte darauf, daß; sieh zu, daß. 2. ~ **s.o. to do s.th.** von j-m erwarten, daß er et. tut: **I ~ you to help me** (*od. for help*) ich erwarte Hilfe von dir. ~ **to·ward(s)** → **look** 7.

Verbindungen mit Adverbien:

look| a·bout → **look around.** ~ **a·head** *v/i* 1. nach vorne sehen *od.* blicken *od.* schauen. 2. *fig.* vorausschauen (**two years** um zwei Jahre). ~ **a·round** *v/i* sich umblicken *od.* -sehen *od.* -schauen (**for** nach). ~ **a·way** *v/i* wegblicken, -sehen, -schauen. ~ **back** *v/i* 1. sich umsehen. 2. *a. fig.* zurückblicken, -sehen, -schauen (**on, to** auf *acc*). ~ **down** *v/i* 1. hinunterblicken, -sehen, -schauen, herunterblicken, -sehen, -schauen (**on** auf *acc*): ~ **on** *fig.* a) herabschauen auf (*acc*), b) → **look onto.** 2. zu Boden blicken. ~ **for·ward** *v/i* sich freuen (**to** auf *acc*): ~ **to doing s.th.** sich darauf freuen, et. zu tun. ~ **in** *v/i* 1. hineinsehen, -schauen, hereinsehen, -schauen. 2. e-n kurzen Besuch machen, vorbeischauen (**on** bei). ~ **on** *v/i* zusehen, zuschauen. ~ **out** I *v/i* 1. hinausblicken, -sehen, -schauen, herausblicken, -sehen, -schauen (**of**

zu): ~ **of the window** aus dem Fenster blicken. 2. (**for**) aufpassen (auf *acc*), auf der Hut sein (vor *dat*): ~**!** paß auf!, Vorsicht! 3. Ausschau halten (**for** nach). 4. ~ **on** (*od.* **over**) → **look onto.** II *v/t* 5. *bsd. Br. et.* heraussuchen; sich *et.* aussuchen: **look s.th. out for s.o.** j-m et. aussuchen. ~ **o·ver** *v/t* (sich) *et.* (flüchtig) ansehen *od.* anschauen, *et.* (flüchtig) (über)prüfen. ~ **round** → **look around.** ~ **through** *v/t et.* (flüchtig) durchsehen *od.* -schauen. ~ **up** I *v/i* 1. hinaufblicken, -sehen, -schauen, heraufblicken, -sehen, -schauen. 2. aufblicken, -sehen, -schauen (**from** von; *fig. to* zu). 3. *Wort etc* nachschlagen (**in** in *dat*). 4. *look s.o. up and down* j-n von oben bis unten mustern.

'look·a, like *s* 1. Doppelgänger(in). 2. (genaues) Gegenstück.

look·er ['lʊkə] *s*: **she's a real** ~ F sie sieht einfach klasse aus. ~**·'on** *pl* **, look·ers·'on** *s* Zuschauer(in).

'look-in *s* 1. kurzer Besuch. 2. F (Erfolgs- *etc*)Chance *f*: **I don't get a** ~ ich hab' keine Chance.

look·ing glass ['lʊkɪŋ] *s* Spiegel *m*.

'look·out *s* 1. **be on the** ~ (**for**) → **look out** 3. 2. Wache *f*, Beobachtungsposten *m*: **act as** ~ Schmiere stehen. 3. a) *bsd.* ✕ Beobachtungsstand *m*: ~ **tower** Wachturm *m*, b) ♣ Krähennest *n*. 4. F Angelegenheit *f*, Sache *f*. '~**·o, ver** *s*: **give s.th. a** ~ → **look over** (*adv*). '~**·through** *s*: **give s.th. a** ~ → **look through** (*adv*).

loom¹ [luːm] *s* Webstuhl *m*.

loom² [~] *v/i* 1. *a.* ~ **up** undeutlich *od.* drohend sichtbar werden; *fig.* bedrohlich näherrücken. 2. *a.* ~ **up** (drohend) aufragen: ~ **large** *fig.* sich auftürmen (*Schwierigkeiten etc*); e-e große Rolle spielen.

loon·y ['luːnɪ] *sl.* I *adj* bekloppt, verrückt. II *s* Verrückte *m, f.* ~ **bin** *s sl.* Klapsmühle *f*.

loop [luːp] I *s* 1. Schlinge *f*, Schleife *f*. 2. Schleife *f*, Windung *f* (*e-s Flusses etc*). 3. Schlaufe *f*; Öse *f*. 4. ✔ Looping *m, a. n.* II *v/t* 5. *Schnur etc* schlingen ([*a*]*round* um). 6. ~ **the** ~ ✔ loopen, e-n Looping fliegen *od.* ausführen. III *v/i* 7. sich schlingen ([*a*]*round* um). 8. → 6. '~**·hole** *s* 1. ✕ Schießscharte *f*. 2. *fig.*

Schlupfloch *n*, Hintertürchen *n*: **~ in the law, legal ~** Gesetzeslücke *f*.

loose [luːs] **I** *adj* □ **1.** los(e), locker; frei, nicht angebunden *od.* eingesperrt: **break ~** sich losreißen (**from** von); **come** (*od.* **get**) **~** abgehen (*Knopf etc*), sich lockern (*Schraube etc*), sich ablösen, abblättern (*Farbe etc*); **let ~** *Hund* von der Leine lassen, *a. Flüche etc* loslassen, *s-m Ärger etc* Luft machen, freien Lauf lassen; **~ connection** ⚡ Wackelkontakt *m*; → **screw** 1. **2.** a) lose (*Haar, Geldscheine etc*): **~ money** Kleingeld *n*, Münzen *pl*, b) offen, lose, unverpackt (*Ware*). **3.** lose sitzend, weit (*Kleidungsstück*). **4.** *fig.* lose (*Abmachung, Zs.-hang etc*); frei, ungenau (*Übersetzung etc*); unkonzentriert, nachlässig (*Spielweise etc*); unkontrolliert: **have a ~ tongue** den Mund nicht halten können. **5.** locker (*Moral, Lebenswandel etc*): → **liver²**, **living** 5. **II** *s* **6. be on the ~** a) auf freiem Fuß sein, b) *a.* **go on the ~** F auf den Putz hauen. '**~-fit·ting** → **loose** 3. '**~-leaf** *adj* Loseblatt...: **~ binder** Schnellhefter *m*.

'**loos·en I** *v/t* **1.** Knoten, Fesseln etc, *a.* 🏥 *Husten*, *fig. Zunge* lösen: **~ s.o.'s tongue** j-m die Zunge lösen. **2.** *Schraube, Griff etc*, *a. fig. Disziplin etc* lockern: **~ one's hold of** et. loslassen. **3.** *a.* **~ up** *Muskeln etc*, *a. fig. j-n* auflockern. **II** *v/i* **4.** sich lösen *od.* lockern. **5. ~ up** (*bsd. Sport*) sich auflockern.

loot [luːt] **I** *s* (Kriegs-, Diebes)Beute *f*. **II** *v/t* plündern.

lop [lɒp] *v/t* **1.** *Baum etc* beschneiden, (zu)stutzen. **2.** *oft* **~ off** abhauen, abhacken. '**~·sid·ed** *adj* **1.** schief, nach 'einer Seite hängend, ⚓ mit Schlagseite. **2.** *fig.* einseitig.

lo·qua·cious [ləʊˈkweɪʃəs] *adj* □ geschwätzig, redselig.

lord [lɔːd] **I** *s* **1.** Herr *m*, Gebieter *m* (**of** über *acc*). **2.** *fig.* Magnat *m*. **3. the** ♀ a) *a.* ♀ **God** Gott *m* (der Herr): ♀ (**only**) **knows where ...** Gott *od.* der Himmel weiß, wo ..., b) *a.* **our** ♀ (Christus *m* der Herr): ♀**'s Prayer** Vaterunser *m*; ♀**'s Supper** (heiliges) Abendmahl. **4.** *Br.* Lord *m*: **the** ♀**s** das Oberhaus; → **drunk** 1. **II** *v/t* **5. ~ it** den Herren spielen (**over s.o.** j-m gegenüber). ♀ **Chan·cel·lor** *s*

Br. Lordkanzler *m*. ♀ **May·or** *s* Br. Oberbürgermeister *m*.

lor·ry [ˈlɒrɪ] *s* Br. Last(kraft)wagen *m*, Lastauto *n*.

lose [luːz] (*irr*) **I** *v/t* **1.** *Sache, Interesse etc* verlieren, *Geld, Stellung etc a.* einbüßen: **~ o.s.** sich verirren; **~ 10 pounds** 10 Pfund abnehmen; → **life** 1d, **sight** 1, *etc.* **2.** *Spiel, Prozeß etc* verlieren. **3.** *Zug etc*, *fig. Chance etc* versäumen, -passen. **4.** *Gelerntes* vergessen. **5.** *5 Minuten etc* nachgehen (*Uhr*). **6.** *Gewohnheit, Krankheit etc* loswerden, *Verfolger a.* abschütteln. **7. ~ s.o. s.th.** j-n et. kosten, j-n um et. bringen. **II** *v/i* **8. ~ out** (**to** verlieren (gegen), unterliegen (*dat*). **9. ~ out** verlieren, draufzahlen (**on** bei). **10.** nachgehen (*Uhr*). '**los·er** *s* Verlierer(in): **good** (**bad**) **~**: **be a bad ~** a. nicht verlieren können; **be a born ~** der geborene Verlierer sein. '**los·ing** *adj* **1.** verlustbringend, Verlust... **2.** verloren, aussichtslos: **fight a battle** *fig.* auf verlorenem Posten stehen.

loss [lɒs] *s* **1.** Verlust *m*: a) Einbuße *f*: **~ of blood** (**memory, time**) Blut-(Gedächtnis-, Zeit)verlust; **dead ~** Totalverlust; *fig.* hoffnungsloser Fall (*Person*); **sell s.th. at a ~** et. mit Verlust verkaufen; **work at a ~** mit Verlust arbeiten; → **identity**, b) Schaden *m*, c) *verlorene Sache od. Person*, d) Abnahme *f*, Schwund *m*: **~ in weight** Gewichtsverlust, -abnahme. **2.** *pl* ✕ Verluste *pl*, Ausfälle *pl*. **3. be at a ~** in Verlegenheit sein (**for** um): **be at a ~ for words** keine Worte finden.

lost [lɒst] **I** *pret u. pp von* **lose**. **II** *adj* **1.** verloren: **~ cause** *fig.* aussichtslose Sache; **be a ~ cause** a. aussichtslos sein. **2.** verloren(gegangen): **be ~** verlorengehen (*a. fig. Arbeitsplätze etc*); **give up for** (*od.* **as**) **~** verloren geben; → **property** 1. **3.** verirrt: **be ~** sich verirrt haben, sich nicht mehr zurechtfinden (*a. fig.*); **get ~** sich verirren; **get ~!** F hau ab! **4. be ~ on s.o.** keinen Eindruck auf j-n machen, j-n kaltlassen. **5. ~ in** vertieft *od.* versunken in (*acc*): **~ in thought** in Gedanken versunken, *bsd. adv a.* gedankenverloren, -verloren. '**~-and-'found** (**of·fice**) *s* Am. Fundbüro *n*.

lot [lɒt] s **1.** Los n: **cast** (od. **draw**) ~**s** losen (**for** um); **the** ~ **fell on** (od. **to**) me das Los fiel auf mich. **2.** Los n, Schicksal n. **3.** Anteil m. **4.** Parzelle f, Grundstück n. **5.** ♣ Partie f, Posten m. **6.** Gruppe f, Gesellschaft f: **the whole** ~ a) die ganze Gesellschaft, b) → **7. 7. the** ~ alles, das Ganze. **8.** F Menge f, Haufen m: **a** ~ **of**, ~**s of** viel, e-e Menge; **a** ~ (od. ~**s**) **better** (sehr) viel besser. **9. a bad** ~ F ein mieser Typ; ein mieses Pack.

loth → **loath.**

lo·tion ['ləʊʃn] s Lotion f, (Haut-, Rasier)Wasser n.

lot·ter·y ['lɒtərɪ] s **1.** Lotterie f: ~ **ticket** Lotterielos n. **2.** fig. Glückssache f, Lotteriespiel n.

lo·tus ['ləʊtəs] s ♣ Lotos(blume f) m.

loud [laʊd] adj □ **1.** (a. adv) laut. **2.** fig. grell, schreiend (Farben), auffallend (Kleidung, Benehmen). '~·mouth s F Großmaul n. ~·speak·er s Lautsprecher m.

lounge [laʊndʒ] **I** s **1.** Wohnzimmer n. **2.** Gesellschaftsraum m, Salon m (e-s Hotels, Schiffs). **3.** Foyer n (e-s Theaters). **4.** Wartehalle f (e-s Flughafens). **5.** Br. vornehmerer u. teurerer Teil e-s Lokals. **II** v/i **6.** → **loll II. III** v/t **7.** mst ~ **away** Zeit vertrödeln, -bummeln. ~ **bar** → **lounge 5.** ~ **chair** s Klubsessel m. ~ **suit** s bsd. Br. Straßenanzug m.

lour, lour·ing → **lower¹, lowering.**

louse I s [laʊs] **1.** pl **lice** [laɪs] zo. Laus f. **2.** pl **lous·es** sl. Scheißkerl m. **II** v/t [laʊz] **3.** ~ **up** sl. versauen, -murksen.

lous·y ['laʊzɪ] adj □ **1.** verlaust. **2.** sl. fies, hundsgemein; lausig, mies. **3. be** ~ **with** sl. wimmeln von; strotzen vor (dat) od. von: **be** ~ **with money** vor Geld stinken.

lout [laʊt] s Flegel m, Rüpel m. '**lout·ish** adj □ flegel-, rüpelhaft.

lov·a·ble ['lʌvəbl] adj □ liebenswert, reizend.

love [lʌv] **I** s **1.** Liebe f (**of**, **for**, **to toward**[s] zu): ~ herzliche Grüße (Briefschluß); **be in** ~ verliebt sein (**with** in acc); **fall in** ~ sich verlieben (**with** in acc); **not for** ~ **or money** nicht für Geld u. gute Worte; um nichts in der Welt; **make** ~ sich (körperlich) lieben; **make** ~ **to s.o.** j-n (körperlich) lieben; **there is no** ~ **lost between them** sie können

sich nicht leiden; ~ **of adventure** Abenteuerlust f; ~ **of one's country** Vaterlandsliebe; → **give 10. 2.** F a) (Anrede, oft unübersetzt) Schatz, b) Schatz m: **he's a real** ~ er ist ein richtiger Schatz; **a** ~ **of a car** ein süßer Wagen. **3.** bsd. Tennis: null. **II** v/t **4.** j-n (a. körperlich) lieben, liebhaben. **5.** et. lieben, gerne mögen: ~ **doing** (bsd. Am. a. **to do**) **s.th.** et. sehr gern tun.

love·a·ble → **lovable.**

love| **af·fair** s (Liebes)Affäre f, (-)Verhältnis n. ~ **bite** s F Knutschfleck m. ~ **du·et** s ♪ Liebesduett n. ,~'**hate (re·la·tion·ship)** s Haßliebe f.

love·less ['lʌvlɪs] adj □ **1.** lieblos. **2.** ungeliebt.

love| **let·ter** s Liebesbrief m. ~ **life** s (irr **life**) Liebesleben n.

love·ly ['lʌvlɪ] adj □ **1.** (wunder)schön. **2.** nett, reizend. **3.** F prima, großartig. '**love**|**mak·ing** s **1.** (körperliche) Liebe. **2.** Liebeskunst f. ~ **match** s Liebesheirat f. ~ **po·em** s Liebesgedicht n.

lov·er ['lʌvə] s **1.** Liebhaber m, Geliebte m; Geliebte f. **2.** pl Liebende pl, Liebespaar n: **they are** ~**s** sie lieben sich. **3.** (Musik- etc)Liebhaber(in), (-)Freund (-in): ~ **of music, music** ~.

love| **scene** s thea. etc Liebesszene f. '~·**sick** adj liebeskrank: **be** ~ Liebeskummer haben. ~ **song** s Liebeslied n. ~ **sto·ry** s Liebesgeschichte f, (bsd. rührselige a.) Love-Story f.

lov·ing ['lʌvɪŋ] adj □ liebevoll, zärtlich: **your** ~ **father** Dein Dich liebender Vater (Briefschluß).

low¹ [ləʊ] **I** adj u. adv **1.** allg. niedrig (a. fig. Löhne etc): ~ **in fat** fettarm; → **lie low, profile 1. 2.** tief (a. fig.): **a** ~ **bow** e-e tiefe Verbeugung; ~ **shot** (Sport) Flachschuß m; **the sun is** ~ die Sonne steht tief; **sunk thus** ~ fig. so tief gesunken. **3.** tiefgelegen. **4.** knapp (Vorrat etc): **get** (od. **run**) ~ knapp werden, zur Neige gehen; **we are getting** (od. **running**) ~ **on money** uns geht allmählich das Geld aus; ~ **on funds** knapp bei Kasse. **5.** schwach (a. Puls); niedergeschlagen, deprimiert: **feel** ~ in gedrückter Stimmung sein; sich elend fühlen; → **spirit 4. 6.** gering(schätzig): ~ **opinion 2. 7.** ordinär, vulgär (Ausdruck etc); gemein, niederträchtig (Trick etc):

feel ~ sich gemein vorkommen. **8.** tief (*Ton etc*); leise (*Ton, Stimme etc*): **in a ~ voice** leise. **II** *s* **9.** *meteor.* Tief *n.* **10.** *fig.* Tief(punkt *m, -*stand *m*) *n*: **be at a new ~** e-n neuen Tiefpunkt erreicht haben.

low² [\~] **I** *v/i* brüllen, muhen (*Rind*). **II** *s* Brüllen *n,* Muhen *n.*

,**low**|'**bred** *adj* ungebildet, gewöhnlich. '**~brow I** *s* geistig Anspruchslose *m, f,* Unbedarfte *m, f.* **II** *adj* geistig anspruchslos, unbedarft. ,**~'cal·o·rie** *adj* kalorienarm. **~ com·e·dy** *s* Posse *f,* (derber) Schwank. '**~cost** *adj* kostengünstig. '**~down** *adj* F lies, hundsgemein. '**~down** *s* F: **give s.o. the ~** j-n aufklären (**on** über *acc*); **get the ~** aufgeklärt werden (**on** über *acc*).

low·er¹ ['lauə] *v/i* **1.** finster *od.* drohend blicken: **~ at s.o.** j-n finster *od.* drohend ansehen. **2.** sich auftürmen (*Wolken*); sich mit schwarzen Wolken überziehen (*Himmel*).

low·er² ['ləuə] **I** *v/t* **1.** niedriger machen. **2.** *Augen, Preis, Stimme etc* senken. **3.** *fig.* erniedrigen: **~ o.s.** sich herablassen. **4.** herunter-, herablassen, *Fahne, Segel* niederholen, strecken. **II** *v/i* **5.** niedriger werden. **6.** *fig.* sinken, fallen.

low·er³ ['ləuə] **I** *comp. von* **low¹.** **II** *adj* **1.** niedriger (*a. fig.*). **2.** unter, Unter...: **the ~ class** (es *pl*) *sociol.* die Unterschicht; **~ court** ⚖ untergeordnetes Gericht; **~ deck** ⚓ Unterdeck *n*; → **jaw** 1, **lip** 1.

low·est ['ləuist] **I** *sup von* **low¹.** **II** *adj* **1.** niedrigst (*a. fig.*): **~ bid** † Mindestgebot *n.* **2.** unterst. **III** *s* **3. at the ~** wenigstens, mindestens.

'**low**|**fat** *adj* fettarm. ,**~'in·come** *adj* einkommensschwach. ,**~'key(ed)** *adj* **1.** gedämpft (*Farbe*), (*Ton a.*) leise. **2.** zurückhaltend (*Empfang etc*). **~land** ['~lənd] *s* Tief-, Flachland *n.* ⚑ **Mass** *s eccl.* Stille Messe. ,**~'necked** *adj* tief ausgeschnitten, mit tiefem Ausschnitt (*Kleid*). ,**~'noise** *adj* rauscharm (*Tonband etc*). ,**~'pres·sure** *adj*: **~ area** Tiefdruckgebiet *n.* '**~rise** *s* Flachbau *m.* ⚓ **sea·son** *s* Vor- *od.* Nachsaison *f.* '**~shoe** *s* Halbschuh *m.* '**~spir·it·ed** *adj* □ niedergeschlagen, deprimiert.

loy·al ['lɔiəl] *adj* □ **1.** loyal (**to** gegenüber). **2.** (ge)treu (**to** *dat*). '**loy·al·ty** *s* Loyalität *f* (**to** zu).

loz·enge ['lɒzindʒ] *s* **1.** ♈ Raute *f,*

Rhombus *m.* **2.** *pharm.* Pastille *f,* Tablette *f.*

lub·ber ['lʌbə] *s* Flegel *m,* Rüpel *m*; Trottel *m*; Tolpatsch *m.*

lu·bri·cant ['lu:brikənt] *s* ⚙ Schmiermittel *n.* **lu·bri·cate** ['~keit] *v/t* schmieren. ,**lu·bri·ca·tion** *s* Schmieren *n.*

lu·cid ['lu:sid] *adj* □ klar (*Auskunft, Gedanke, Verstand etc*); hell, (*geistig*) klar: **~ interval** (*od. moment*) *bsd. psych.* heller *od.* lichter Augenblick.

luck [lʌk] *s* **1.** Schicksal *n,* Zufall *m*: **as ~ would have it** wie es der Zufall wollte, (un)glücklicherweise; **bad** (*od.* **hard, ill**) **~** Pech *n* (**on** für), Unglück *n*; **good ~** Glück *n*; **good ~!** viel Glück! **2.** Glück *n*: **for ~** als Glücksbringer; **be in** (**out of**) **~** (kein) Glück haben; **try one's ~** sein Glück versuchen. '**luck·i·ly** *adv* zum Glück, glücklicherweise: **~ for me** zu m-m Glück. '**luck·less** *adj* □ glück-, erfolglos. '**luck·y** *adj* □ (*adv* **luckily**) **1.** Glücks..., glücklich: **be** (**very**) **~** (großes) Glück haben; **~ day** Glückstag *m*; **~ fellow** Glückspilz *m.* **2.** Glück bringend, Glücks...: **be ~** Glück bringen; **~ penny** Glückspfennig *m*; → **star** 1.

lu·cra·tive ['lu:krətiv] *adj* □ einträglich, lukrativ.

lu·cre ['lu:kə] *s*: **filthy ~** *oft humor.* schnöder Mammon.

lu·di·crous ['lu:dikrəs] *adj* □ lächerlich, absurd.

lu·do ['lu:dəu] *s Br.* Mensch, ärgere dich nicht *n* (*Spiel*).

lug [lʌg] *v/t* zerren, schleifen; schleppen.

lug·gage ['lʌgidʒ] *s* (Reise)Gepäck *n.* **~ al·low·ance** *s* ✈ Freigepäck *n.* **~ com·part·ment** *s mot. Br.* Kofferraum *m.* **~ in·sur·ance** *s* Reisegepäckversicherung *f.* **~ lock·er** *s* Gepäckschließfach *n.* **~ re·claim** *s* ✈ Gepäckausgabe *f.*

luke·warm [,lu:k'wɔ:m] *adj* □ lau(warm) (*a. fig.* Zustimmung *etc*), (*Unterstützung etc a.*) halbherzig, (*Applaus etc*) lau, mäßig.

lull [lʌl] **I** *v/t* **1.** *mst* **~ to sleep** einlullen. **2.** *fig.* j-n beruhigen, beschwichtigen, j-s *Argwohn* zerstreuen: **~ s.o. into** (**a false sense of**) **security** j-n in Sicherheit wiegen. **II** *v/i* **3.** sich legen, nachlassen (*Sturm*). **III** *s* **4.** (Ruhe)Pause *f* (**in** in *dat*): **~** (**in the wind**) Flaute *f*; **the ~**

before the storm die Stille vor dem Sturm (*a. fig.*).

lull·a·by ['lʌləbaɪ] *s* Wiegenlied *n.*

lum·ba·go [lʌm'beɪgəʊ] *s* ☞ Hexenschuß *m.*

lum·ber[1] ['lʌmbə] **I** *s* **1.** *bsd. Am.* Bau-, Nutzholz *n.* **2.** Gerümpel *n.* **II** *v/t* **3.** *a.* ~ *up* Zimmer etc vollstopfen, *a. Erzählung etc* überladen (**with** mit). **4.** ~ *s.o.* *with s.th. Br.* F j-m et. aufhängen *od.* aufhalsen.

lum·ber[2] [~] *v/i* sich (dahin)schleppen, schwerfällig gehen; (dahin)rumpeln (*Wagen*).

'**lum·ber·|jack** *s bsd. Am.* Holzfäller *m,* -arbeiter *m.* ~ **mill** *s bsd. Am.* Sägewerk *n.* ~ **room** *s* Rumpelkammer *f.*

lu·mi·nar·y ['luːmɪnərɪ] *s fig.* Leuchte *f.*

lu·mi·nos·i·ty [ˌ~'nɒsətɪ] *s* **1.** Leuchtkraft *f; ast., phys.* Lichtstärke *f,* Helligkeit *f.* **2.** *fig.* Brillanz *f.* '**lu·mi·nous** *adj* □ **1.** leuchtend: ~ *paint* Leuchtfarbe *f.* **2.** *fig.* intelligent, brillant; klar, einleuchtend.

lump[1] [lʌmp] **I** *s* **1.** Klumpen *m:* **have a** ~ **in one's** (*od.* **the**) **throat** *fig.* e-n Kloß im Hals haben. **2.** Schwellung *f,* Beule *f;* ☞ Geschwulst *f,* (*in der Brust*) Knoten *m.* **3.** Stück *n* Zucker etc. **4.** *fig.* Gesamtheit *f,* Masse *f:* **in the** ~ in Bausch u. Bogen, pauschal; im großen u. ganzen. **5.** F Klotz *m* (*ungeschlachter, dummer Mensch*). **II** *adj* **6.** Stück...: ~ **sugar** Würfelzucker *m.* **7.** Pauschal... **III** *v/t* **8.** *oft* ~ **together** zs.-ballen; *fig.* zs.-werfen, in 'einen Topf werfen (**with** mit). **IV** *v/i* **9.** Klumpen bilden, klumpen.

lump[2] [~] *v/t:* ~ **it** F sich damit abfinden.

lu·na·cy ['luːnəsɪ] *s* ☞ Wahnsinn *m* (*a. fig.*).

lu·nar ['luːnə] *adj* Mond...: ~ **eclipse** *ast.* Mondfinsternis *f;* ~ **landing** Mondlandung *f;* ~ **module** Mond(lande)fähre *f.*

lu·na·tic ['luːnətɪk] **I** *adj* a) ~ wahnsinnig, geistesgestört: ~ **asylum** *contp.* Irrenanstalt *f,* b) *fig.* verrückt. **II** *s* a) ☞ Wahnsinnige *m, f,* Geistesgestörte *m, f,* b) *fig.* Verrückte *m, f.*

lunch [lʌntʃ] **I** *s* Mittagessen *n:* **have** ~ → II; ~ **hour** a) ~ **break** Mittagspause *f,* b) → **lunchtime.** **II** *v/i* (zu) Mittag essen: ~ **out** auswärts *od.* im Restaurant zu Mittag essen.

lunch·eon| meat ['lʌntʃən] *s* Frühstücksfleisch *n.* ~ **vouch·er** *s* Essen(s)bon *m.*

'**lunch·time** *s* Mittagszeit *f:* **at** ~ zur Mittagszeit; ~ **train** Mittagszug *m.*

lung [lʌŋ] *s anat.* Lungenflügel *m:* ~*s pl* Lunge *f.*

lunge [lʌndʒ] **I** *s* a) *bsd. fenc.* Ausfall *m,* b) *Sprung m* vorwärts, Satz *m:* **make a** ~ → II. **II** *v/i* a) ~ **out** *bsd. fenc.* e-n Ausfall machen, b) *a.* ~ **out** e-n Sprung vorwärts *od.* e-n Satz machen, c) sich stürzen (**at** auf *acc*).

lurch[1] [lɜːtʃ] **I** *s* **1.** Taumeln *n,* Torkeln *n.* **2.** ⚓ Schlingern *n.* **3.** Ruck *m:* **give a** ~ → **II. II** *v/i* **4.** taumeln, torkeln. **5.** ⚓ schlingern. **6.** rucken, e-n Ruck machen.

lurch[2] [~] *s:* **leave in the** ~ im Stich lassen.

lure [lʊə] **I** *s* **1.** Köder *m* (**to** für) (*a. fig.*). **2.** *fig.* Lockung *f,* Reiz *m.* **II** *v/t* **3.** (an)locken, ködern (*beide a. fig.*): ~ **away** weglocken; ~ **into** locken in (*acc*); verlocken *od.* -führen zu.

lu·rid ['lʊərɪd] *adj* □ **1.** fahl, gespenstisch (*Beleuchtung etc*). **2.** grell (*Farben*). **3.** gräßlich, schauerlich.

lurk [lɜːk] *v/i* **1.** lauern (*a. fig.*): ~ **for s.o.** j-m auflauern. **2.** schleichen: ~ **about** (*od.* **around**) herumschleichen.

lus·cious ['lʌʃəs] *adj* □ **1.** köstlich, lecker; süß (*u. saftig*). **2.** sinnlich (*Lippen etc*), üppig (*Figur, Frau etc*), knackig (*Mädchen*).

lush [lʌʃ] *adj* □ saftig (*Gras etc*), üppig (*Vegetation*).

lust [lʌst] **I** *s* **1.** sinnliche Begierde. **2.** Gier *f* (*of,* **for** nach): ~ **for power** Machtgier *f.* **II** *v/i* **3.** gieren (**for, after** nach).

lus·ter *Am.* → **lustre.**

lust·ful ['lʌstfʊl] *adj* □ lüstern.

lus·tre ['lʌstə] *s bsd. Br.* **1.** Glanz *m* (*a. fig.*). **2.** Lüster *m,* Kronleuchter *m.*

lus·trous ['lʌstrəs] *adj* □ **1.** glänzend (*a. fig.*). **2.** *fig.* illuster.

lust·y ['lʌstɪ] *adj* □ **1.** kräftig, robust. **2.** tatkräftig.

lute[1] [luːt] *s* ♪ Laute *f.*

lute[2] [~] **I** *s* Kitt *m.* **II** *v/t* (ver)kitten.

lux·ate ['lʌkseɪt] *v/t* ☞ sich *die Schulter etc* aus- *od.* verrenken: **he** ~**d his left**

shoulder. **lux·a·tion** s Luxation f, Aus-, Verrenkung f.

lux·u·ri·ant [lʌɡˈʒʊəriənt] adj □ **1.** üppig (Vegetation) (a. fig.). **2.** fig. (über)reich, verschwenderisch, (Phantasie) blühend. **lux·u·ri·ate** [~eit] v/i schwelgen (in in dat). **lux·u·ri·ous** adj □ **1.** luxuriös, Luxus... **2.** verschwenderisch, genußsüchtig. **lux·u·ry** [ˈlʌkʃəri] **I** s **1.** allg. Luxus m. **2.** Luxusartikel m. **II** adj **3.** Luxus..., der Luxusklasse.

lye [lai] s 🔧 Lauge f.

ly·ing [ˈlaiiŋ] **I** pres p von **lie¹**. **II** adj lügnerisch, verlogen.

lymph [limf] s physiol. Lymphe f. **~ gland,** **~ node** s anat. Lymphknoten m.

lynch [lintʃ] v/t lynchen. **~ law** s Lynchjustiz f.

lynx [liŋks] s zo. Luchs m. **'~-eyed** adj fig. mit Augen wie ein Luchs.

lyr·ic [ˈlirik] **I** adj (~ally) **1.** lyrisch (a. fig. gefühlvoll). **II** s **2.** lyrisches Gedicht: ~s pl Lyrik f. **3.** pl (Lied)Text m. **lyr·i·cal** adj □ **1.** → **lyric. 2.** schwärmerisch: **get ~** ins Schwärmen geraten. **lyr·i·cist** [ˈ~sist] s **1.** Lyriker(in). **2.** Texter(in), Textdichter(in).

M

ma [mɑː] s F Mama f, Mutti f.

ma'am [mæm] F → **madam.**

mac [mæk] F → **mackintosh.**

ma·ca·bre [məˈkɑːbrə] adj □ makaber.

mac·(c)a·ro·ni [ˌmækəˈrəʊni] s pl (sg konstruiert) Makkaroni pl.

mace¹ [meis] s Amtsstab m.

mace² [~] s Muskatblüte f.

Mach [mæk] s: **fly at ~ two** ✈, phys. mit e-r Geschwindigkeit von zwei Mach fliegen.

ma·che·te [məˈtʃeti] s Machete f, Buschmesser n.

ma·chine [məˈʃiːn] **I** s **1.** Maschine f (F a. Flugzeug, Motorrad etc). **2.** Apparat m; Automat m. **3.** pol. (Partei- etc)Apparat m. **II** v/t **4.** maschinell herstellen. **~ gun** s Maschinengewehr n.

ma·chine|-made adj maschinell hergestellt. **~,read·a·ble** adj maschinell lesbar, maschinenlesbar.

ma·chin·er·y [məˈʃiːnəri] s **1.** Maschinen pl; Maschinerie f. **2.** fig. a) Maschinerie f, Räderwerk n, b) → **machine** 3.

ma·chine| tool s ⚙ Werkzeugmaschine f. **~ trans·la·tion** s maschinelle Übersetzung.

ma·chin·ist [məˈʃiːnist] s **1.** Maschinenschlosser m. **2.** Maschinist m.

ma·chis·mo [məˈtʃizməʊ] s Machismo m, Männlichkeitswahn m. **ma·cho** [ˈmætʃəʊ] pl **-chos** s Macho m.

mack·er·el [ˈmækrəl] pl **-el** s ichth. Makrele f.

mack·in·tosh [ˈmækintɒʃ] s bsd. Br. Regenmantel m.

mac·ro·cosm [ˈmækrəʊkɒzəm] s Makrokosmos m, Weltall n.

mad [mæd] adj (□ → **madly**) **1.** wahnsinnig, verrückt (beide a. fig.): **go ~** verrückt werden; **drive s.o. ~** j-n verrückt machen; **like ~** wie verrückt. **2.** (after, about, for, on) wild, versessen (auf acc), verrückt (nach), vernarrt (in acc): **~ about soccer** fußballverrückt. **3.** F außer sich, verrückt (with vor dat). **4.** bsd. Am. F wütend (at, about über acc, auf acc). **5.** wild (geworden) (Stier etc). **6.** vet. tollwütig.

mad·am [ˈmædəm] s gnädige Frau (Anrede, oft unübersetzt).

'mad·cap I s verrückter Kerl. **II** adj verrückt.

mad·den [ˈmædn] v/t verrückt machen (a. fig.). **'mad·den·ing** adj □ unerträglich: **it is ~** es ist zum Verrücktwerden.

made [meid] **I** pret u. pp von **make.** **II** adj: **a ~ man** ein gemachter Mann. **,~-to-'meas·ure** adj **1.** nach Maß angefertigt, Maß...: **~ suit** maßgeschneiderter Anzug, Maßanzug m. **,~-to-'or·der** adj **1.** → **made-to-measure. 2.** fig.

maßgeschneidert, nach Maß. '**~·up** adj
1. (frei) erfunden. **2.** geschminkt.

'**mad·house** s Irrenhaus n, fig. a. Tollhaus n.

mad·ly ['mædlɪ] adv **1.** wie verrückt. **2.** F
wahnsinnig, schrecklich.

mad·man ['mædmən] s (irr **man**) Verrückte m.

mad·ness ['mædnɪs] s **1.** Wahnsinn m (a.
fig.): **sheer ~** heller od. blanker Wahnsinn. **2.** bsd. Am. F Wut f.

'**mad,wom·an** s (irr **woman**) Verrückte f.

mael·strom ['meɪlstrɒm] s Strudel m,
Sog m (beide a. fig.).

Ma·fi·a ['mæfɪə] s Mafia f (a. fig.).
ma·fi·o·so [ˌ~'əʊsəʊ] pl **-sos, -si** [ˌ~sɪ] s
Mafioso m (a. fig.).

mag [mæg] F → **magazine** 3.

mag·a·zine [ˌmægə'ziːn] s **1.** Magazin n
(e-r Feuerwaffe, e-s Fotoapparats). **2.**
Magazin n, Lagerhaus n. **3.** Magazin n,
Zeitschrift f. **II ~ rack** s Zeitungsständer m.

mag·got ['mægət] s zo. Made f. '**mag·got·y** adj madig.

Ma·gi ['meɪdʒaɪ] s pl: **the** (**three**) **~** die
(drei) Weisen aus dem Morgenland, die
Heiligen Drei Könige.

mag·ic ['mædʒɪk] **I** s **1.** Magie f, Zauberei f: **as if by ~, like ~** wie durch Zauberei. **2.** Zauber(kraft f) m, magische
Kraft (a. fig.). **II** adj (**~ally**) **3.** magisch,
Zauber...: **~ carpet** fliegender Teppich;
~ eye ⚡ magisches Auge; **~ trick** Zaubertrick m, -kunststück n; **~ wand** Zauberstab m. **4.** zauberhaft. **ma·gi·cian**
[mə'dʒɪʃn] s **1.** Magier m, Zauberer m.
2. Zauberkünstler m.

mag·is·trate ['mædʒɪstreɪt] s ⚖ Richter
m (an e-m **magistrates' court**): **~s'
court** Br., **~'s court** Am. erstinstanzliches Gericht für Straf- u. Zivilsachen
niederer Ordnung.

mag·na·nim·i·ty [ˌmægnə'nɪmətɪ] s
Großmut f. **mag·nan·i·mous** [~'næn-
ɪməs] adj □ großmütig.

mag·nate ['mægnɪt] s Magnat m.

mag·ne·sia [mæg'niːʃə] s ⚗ Magnesia f.
mag·ne·si·um [~'niːzɪəm] s ⚗ Magnesium n.

mag·net ['mægnɪt] s Magnet m (a. fig.).
mag·net·ic [~'netɪk] adj (**~ally**) **1.** magnetisch, Magnet...: **~ field** phys. Ma-

gnetfeld n; **~ pole** phys. magnetischer
Pol, Magnetpol m. **2.** fig. magnetisch,
faszinierend. **mag·net·ism** ['~nɪtɪzəm]
s **1.** phys. Magnetismus m. **2.** fig. Anziehungskraft f. '**mag·ne·tize** v/t **1.** magnetisieren. **2.** fig. anziehen, fesseln.

mag·nif·i·cence [mæg'nɪfɪsns] s Großartigkeit f, Herrlichkeit f. **mag·nif·i·cent** adj □ großartig, prächtig, herrlich (alle a. fig. F).

mag·ni·fy ['mægnɪfaɪ] v/t **1.** (a. v/i) vergrößern: **~ing glass** Vergrößerungsglas n, Lupe f. **2.** fig. aufbauschen.

mag·ni·tude ['mægnɪtjuːd] s Größe(nordnung) f, fig. a. Ausmaß n, Schwere
f: **of the first ~** von äußerster Wichtigkeit.

mag·no·lia [mæg'nəʊljə] s ⚘ Magnolie f.

mag·pie ['mægpaɪ] s **1.** orn. Elster f. **2.**
fig. Schwätzer(in). **3.** Br. fig. sammelwütiger Mensch.

ma·hog·a·ny [mə'hɒgənɪ] s Mahagoni(holz) n.

maid [meɪd] s **1.** old **~** alte Jungfer; **~ of
hono(u)r** Hofdame f; Am. (erste)
Brautjungfer. **2.** (Dienst)Mädchen n,
Hausangestellte f: **~ of all work** bsd. fig.
Mädchen für alles.

maid·en ['meɪdn] adj **1.** **~ name** Mädchenname m (e-r Frau). **2.** unverheiratet. **3.** Jungfern...: **~ flight** ✈ Jungfernflug m; **~ speech** parl. Jungfernrede f; **~
voyage** ⚓ Jungfernfahrt f.

mail [meɪl] **I** s Post(sendung) f: **by ~** bsd.
Am. mit der Post; → **incoming** 3, **outgoing** 2. **II** v/t bsd. Am. aufgeben, Brief
einwerfen; (zu)schicken (to dat). '**~·box**
s bsd. Am. Briefkasten m. **~ car·ri·er** s
bsd. Am., '**~·man** s (irr **man**) bsd. Am.
Postbote m, Briefträger m. '**~·or·der**
adj: **~ catalog(ue)** Versandhauskatalog
m; **~ firm** (od. **house**) Versandhaus n.

maim [meɪm] v/t verstümmeln (a. fig.
Text).

main [meɪn] **I** adj (□ → **mainly**) **1.**
Haupt..., wichtigst: **~ clause** ling.
Hauptsatz m; **~ office** Hauptbüro n,
Zentrale f; **~ reason** Hauptgrund m; **~
thing** Hauptsache f. **II** s **2.** mst pl
Haupt(gas-, -wasser)leitung f; (Strom-)
Netz n: **~s cable** Netzkabel n. **3.** in
(Am. a. **for**) **the ~** hauptsächlich, in der
Hauptsache. '**~·land** ['~lənd] s Festland n.

main·ly ['meɪnlɪ] *adv* hauptsächlich, vorwiegend.

'**main·spring** *s fig.* (Haupt)Triebfeder *f.* '**~·stay** *s fig.* Hauptstütze *f.*

main·tain [meɪn'teɪn] *v/t* **1.** *Zustand* (aufrecht)erhalten, beibehalten, (be-)wahren; ☀ *Preis* halten. **2.** instand halten, pflegen, ⊙ *a.* warten. **3.** (*in e-m bestimmten Zustand*) lassen. **4.** *Familie etc* unterhalten, versorgen. **5.** behaupten (*that* daß; *to inf* zu *inf*). **6.** *Meinung, Recht etc* verfechten; auf *e-r Forderung* bestehen: *~* one's ground *bsd. fig.* sich behaupten.

main·te·nance ['meɪntənəns] *s* **1.** (Aufrecht)Erhaltung *f,* Beibehaltung *f.* **2.** Instandhaltung *f,* Pflege *f,* ⊙ *a.* Wartung *f:* *~free* wartungsfrei. **3.** Unterhalt *m:* *~* grant Unterhaltszuschuß *m.*

mai·son·(n)ette [ˌmeɪzə'net] *s* **1.** Maison(n)ette *f.* **2.** Einliegerwohnung *f.*

maize [meɪz] *s* ❦ *bsd. Br.* Mais *m.*

ma·jes·tic [mə'dʒestɪk] *adj* (*~ally*) majestätisch. **maj·es·ty** ['mædʒəstɪ] *s* Majestät *f* (*a. fig.*): *His* (*Her*) ♙ Seine (Ihre) Majestät.

ma·jor ['meɪdʒə] *I s* **1.** ✗ Major *m.* **2.** *univ. Am.* Hauptfach *n.* **3.** ☆ Volljährige *m, f:* become a *~* volljährig werden. **4.** ♪ Dur *n.* **II** *adj* **5.** größer, *fig. a.* bedeutend, wichtig. **6.** ☆ volljährig. **III** *v/i* **7.** ~ in *univ. Am.* als *od.* im Hauptfach studieren. **ma·jor·i·ty** [mə'dʒɒrətɪ] *s* **1.** Mehrheit *f:* by a large *~* mit großer Mehrheit; in the *~* of cases in der Mehrzahl der Fälle; *~* of votes Stimmenmehrheit; be in the (*od.* a) *~* in der Mehrzahl sein; *~* decision Mehrheitsbeschluß *m.* **2.** ☆ Volljährigkeit *f:* reach one's *~* volljährig werden.

make [meɪk] *I s* **1.** Machart *f,* Ausführung *f;* Erzeugnis *n,* Fabrikat *n,* Produkt *n.* **II** *v/t* (*irr*) **2.** *allg. z. B. Reise, Versuch* machen: *~* a speech e-e Rede halten. **3.** machen: a) anfertigen, herstellen, erzeugen (*from, of, out of* von, aus), b) verarbeiten, formen (*to, into* in acc, zu), c) *Tee etc* zubereiten. **4.** (er)schaffen: *he is made for this job* er ist für diese Arbeit wie geschaffen. **5.** ergeben, bilden. **6.** verursachen: a) *Geräusch, Schwierigkeiten etc* machen, b) bewirken, (mit sich) bringen. **7.** machen *od.* ernennen zu: *~* s.o. (a) gen-

eral j-n zum General ernennen. **8.** *mit adj, pp etc:* machen: *~* angry zornig machen, erzürnen. **9.** sich erweisen als (*Person*): *he would ~ a good teacher* er würde e-n guten Lehrer abgeben. **10.** *mit inf:* j-n lassen, veranlassen *od.* bringen zu: *~* s.o. wait j-n warten lassen; *~* s.o. talk j-n zum Sprechen bringen; *~* s.th. do, *~* do with s.th. mit et. auskommen, sich mit et. behelfen. **11.** *~* much of viel Wesens machen um; viel halten von. **12.** sich e-e Vorstellung machen von, halten für: *what do you ~ of it?* was halten Sie davon? **13.** schätzen auf (*acc*). **14.** sich *Vermögen etc* erwerben, *Geld, Profit* machen, *Gewinn* erzielen. **15.** schaffen: a) *Strecke* zurücklegen, b) *Geschwindigkeit* erreichen, machen. **16.** F *Zug* erreichen: *~* it es schaffen. **17.** sich belaufen auf (*acc*), ergeben: *two and two ~ four* 2 u. 2 macht *od.* ist 4. **III** *v/i* (*irr*) **18.** ~ as if (*od.* as though) so tun als *ob od.* als wenn: *~* believe (*that; to do*) vorgeben (daß; zu tun). *Verbindungen mit Präpositionen:*

make| at *v/i* losgehen *od.* sich stürzen auf (*acc*). ~ for *v/i* **1.** zugehen *od.* lossteuern auf (*acc*); sich aufmachen nach; sich stürzen auf (*acc*). **2.** förderlich sein, dienen (*dat*), beitragen zu. *Verbindungen mit Adverbien:*

make| a·way *v/i* sich davonmachen (*with* mit). ~ off → make away. ~ out **I** *v/t* **1.** *Scheck etc* ausstellen; *Urkunde etc* ausfertigen; *Liste etc* aufstellen. **2.** ausmachen, erkennen. **3.** aus *j-m, e-r Sache* klug werden. **4.** make s.o. out to be bad (a liar) j-n als schlecht (als Lügner) hinstellen. **II** *v/i* **5.** *bsd. Am.* auskommen (*with* mit *j-m*). **6.** *bsd. Am.* F *gut etc* zurechtkommen. ~ o·ver *v/t* *Eigentum* übertragen, vermachen (*to* dat). **2.** umarbeiten; umbauen (*into* zu). ~ up **I** *v/t* **1.** bilden: *be made up of* bestehen *od.* sich zs.-setzen aus. **2.** *Schriftstück etc* abfassen, aufsetzen; *Liste etc* anfertigen, *Tabelle* aufstellen; *Arznei, Bericht etc* zs.-stellen. **3.** sich *e-e Geschichte etc* ausdenken, *a. b.s.* erfinden. **4.** *Paket etc* (ver)packen, (-)schnüren. **5.** → mind **5.** **6.** *Versäumtes* nachholen, wettmachen. **7.** make it up sich versöhnen *od.* wieder vertragen (*with* mit). **II** *v/i* **8.** sich schminken. **9.** ~

for wiedergutmachen, wettmachen. **10.** → 7. **11.** ~ *to s.o.* F j-m schöntun; sich an j-n heranmachen.

'**make-be,lieve** *adj* Phantasie..., Schein...: → *world.*

mak·er ['meɪkə] *s* **1.** ✝ Hersteller *m*, Erzeuger *m*. **2. the** ⚲ *eccl.* der Schöpfer.

'**make·shift** I *s* Notbehelf *m*. II *adj* behelfsmäßig, provisorisch, Behelfs... '~**up** *s* **1.** Make-up *n*: *without* ~ *a.* ungeschminkt. **2.** Aufmachung *f*, (Ver)Kleidung *f*. **3.** *Film etc:* Maske *f*. **4.** Zs.-setzung *f*.

mak·ing ['meɪkɪŋ] *s* **1.** Erzeugung *f*, Herstellung *f*, Fabrikation *f*: *be in the* ~ im Werden od. Kommen sein; noch in Arbeit sein. **2. have the** ~**s of** das Zeug haben zu.

mal·ad·just·ed [,mælə'dʒʌstɪd] *adj psych.* nicht angepaßt, milieugestört.

mal·ad·min·is·tra·tion ['mæləd,mɪnɪ'streɪʃn] *s* schlechte Verwaltung.

mal·a·droit [,mælə'drɔɪt] *adj* □ **1.** ungeschickt. **2.** taktlos.

ma·laise [mæ'leɪz] *s* **1.** Unpäßlichkeit *f*, Unwohlsein *n*. **2.** *fig.* Unbehagen *n*.

ma·lar·i·a [mə'leərɪə] *s* ✠ Malaria *f*.

mal·con·tent ['mælkən,tent] I *adj* unzufrieden. II *s* Unzufriedene *m*, *f*.

male [meɪl] I *adj* männlich: ~ *choir* Männerchor *m*; ~ *cousin* Vetter *m*; ~ *model* Dressman *m*; ~ *nurse* (Kranken)Pfleger *m*; ~ *prostitute* Strichjunge *m*; → *chauvinism, chauvinist.* II *s* Mann *m*; *zo.* Männchen *n*.

male·dic·tion [,mælɪ'dɪkʃn] *s* Fluch *m*, Verwünschung *f*.

ma·lev·o·lence [mə'levələns] *s* Böswilligkeit *f*. **ma'lev·o·lent** *adj* □ übelwollend (*to dat*), böswillig.

mal·for·ma·tion [,mælfɔː'meɪʃn] *s bsd.* ✠ Mißbildung *f*.

mal·func·tion [,mæl'fʌŋkʃn] I *s* **1.** ✠ Funktionsstörung *f*. **2.** ⚙ schlechtes Funktionieren *od.* Arbeiten; Versagen *n*. II *v/i* **3.** ⚙ schlecht funktionieren *od.* arbeiten; versagen.

mal·ice ['mælɪs] *s* **1.** Böswilligkeit *f*. Groll *m*: *bear s.o.* ~ e-n Groll auf j-n haben *od.* gegen j-n hegen, j-m grollen. **3.** ⚖ böse Absicht, Vorsatz *m*: *with* ~ (*aforethought*) vorsätzlich.

ma·li·cious [mə'lɪʃəs] *adj* □ **1.** böswillig, ⚖ *a.* vorsätzlich. **2.** arglistig.

ma·lig·nant [mə'lɪgnənt] *adj* □ **1.** bösartig (*a.* ✠), böswillig. **2.** arglistig.

ma·lin·ger [mə'lɪŋgə] *v/i* sich krank stellen, simulieren. **ma'lin·ger·er** *s* Simulant(in).

mall [mɔːl] *s* **1.** Allee *f*. **2.** *Am.* Einkaufszentrum *n*.

mal·le·a·ble ['mælɪəbl] *adj* **1.** ⚙ verformbar. **2.** *fig.* formbar.

mal·let ['mælɪt] *s* Holzhammer *m*, Schlegel *m*.

mal·low ['mæləʊ] *s* ⚘ Malve *f*.

mal·nu·tri·tion [,mælnjuː'trɪʃn] *s* **1.** Unterernährung *f*. **2.** Fehlernährung *f*.

mal·o·dor·ous [mæl'əʊdərəs] *adj* □ übelriechend.

mal·prac·tice [,mæl'præktɪs] *s* Vernachlässigung *f* der beruflichen Sorgfalt; (ärztlicher) Kunstfehler.

malt [mɔːlt] I *s* Malz *n*. II *v/t* mälzen.

Mal·tese [,mɔːl'tiːz] I *s* Malteser(in): *the* ~ *pl* die Malteser *pl*. II *adj* maltesisch: ~ *cross* Malteserkreuz *n*.

mal·treat [,mæl'triːt] *v/t* **1.** schlecht behandeln. **2.** mißhandeln. ,**mal'treat·ment** *s* **1.** schlechte Behandlung. **2.** Mißhandlung *f*.

mam·mal ['mæml] *s zo.* Säugetier *n*.

mam·mon ['mæmən] *s* Mammon *m*.

mam·moth ['mæməθ] I *s zo.* Mammut *n*. II *adj* Mammut..., Riesen...

man [mæn] I *pl* **men** [men] *s* **1.** Mensch *m*. **2.** *oft* ⚲ *coll.* der Mensch, die Menschen *pl*. **3.** Mann *m*: *the* ~ *in* (*Am. a. on*) *the street* der Mann auf der Straße; ~ *of straw fig.* Strohmann; *be one's own* ~ sein eigener Herr sein. **4.** *weitS.* Mann *m*, Person *f*; jemand; man: *every* ~ jeder(mann); *no* ~ niemand; ~ *by* ~ Mann für Mann; *to a* ~ bis auf den letzten Mann; → *jack* 1. **5.** (*Dame*)Stein *m*, (*Schach*)Figur *f*. II *v/t* **6.** (*Raum*)Schiff *etc* bemannen.

man·age ['mænɪdʒ] I *v/t* **1.** *Betrieb etc* leiten, führen. **2.** *Künstler, Sportler etc* managen. **3.** *et.* zustande bringen, bewerkstelligen; es fertigbringen (*to do* zu tun). **4.** umgehen können mit (*Werkzeug, Tieren etc*); mit *j-m, et.* fertig werden, *j-n, et.* zu nehmen wissen. **5.** F *Arbeit, Essen etc* bewältigen, schaffen. II *v/i* **6.** auskommen (*with* mit; *without* ohne). **7.** F es schaffen, zurechtkommen; es einrichten *od.* ermöglichen. '**man·age-**

a·ble adj □ **1.** lenk-, fügsam. **2.** handlich. **'man·age·ment** s **1.** (*Haus- etc*) Verwaltung f. **2.** ♣ Management n, Unternehmensführung f: *junior* (*middle, top*) ~ untere (mittlere, obere) Führungskräfte pl; ~ *consultant* Betriebs-, Unternehmensberater m. **3.** ♣ Geschäftsleitung f, Direktion f: *under new* ~ unter neuer Leitung, (*Geschäft etc*) neu eröffnet. **'man·ag·er** s **1.** (*Haus- etc*)Verwalter m. **2.** ♣ Manager m; Führungskraft f; Geschäftsführer m, Leiter m, Direktor m. **3.** Manager m (*e-s Schauspielers etc*). **4.** *be a good* ~ gut od. sparsam wirtschaften können. **5.** *Fußball:* (Chef)Trainer m. **man·ag·er·ess** [~'res] s **1.** (*Haus- etc*)Verwalterin f. **2.** ♣ Managerin f; Geschäftsführerin f, Leiterin f, Direktorin f. **3.** Managerin f (*e-s Schauspielers etc*). **man·a·ger·i·al** [~ə'dʒɪərɪəl] adj ♣ geschäftsführend, leitend: ~ *position* leitende Stellung; ~ *staff* leitende Angestellte pl. **man·ag·ing** ['~ɪdʒɪŋ] adj ♣ geschäftsführend, leitend: ~ *director* Generaldirektor m, leitender Direktor.

man·da·rin(e) ['mændərɪn] s ⚘ Mandarine f.

man·date ['mændeɪt] s **1.** ⚖ Mandat n, (Prozeß)Vollmacht f. **2.** *parl.* Mandat n, Auftrag m. **man·da·to·ry** ['~dətərɪ] adj □ obligatorisch, zwingend, verbindlich.

man·di·ble ['mændɪbl] s *anat.* Unterkiefer(knochen) m.

man·do·lin ['mændəlɪn], **man·do·line** [~'li:n] s ♪ Mandoline f.

mane [meɪn] s ⚘ Mähne f (a. fig. e-s Menschen).

'man-,eat·er s **1.** Menschenfresser m. **2.** menschenfressendes Tier. **3.** F männermordendes Wesen (*Frau*).

ma·neu·ver, *etc Am.* → **manoeuvre**, *etc*.

man·ga·nese ['mæŋgəni:z] s 🜍 Mangan n.

mange [meɪndʒ] s *vet.* Räude f.

man·ger ['meɪndʒə] s Krippe f, Futtertrog m: → *dog* 1.

man·gle¹ ['mæŋgl] I s (Wäsche)Mangel f. II v/t mangeln.

man·gle² [~] v/t **1.** zerfleischen, -reißen, -fetzen. **2.** *fig.* Text verstümmeln.

man·go ['mæŋgəʊ] pl **-go(e)s** s ⚘ **1.**

Mango(frucht, -baum) f. **2.** Mangobaum m.

man·gy ['meɪndʒɪ] adj □ **1.** *vet.* räudig. **2.** *fig.* schmutzig, eklig. **3.** *fig.* schäbig, heruntergekommen.

'man·,han·dle v/t **1.** mißhandeln. **2.** mit Menschenkraft bewegen. **'~·hole** s Kanal-, Einsteigschacht m: ~ *cover* Schachtdeckel m.

man·hood ['mænhʊd] s **1.** Mannesalter n: *reach* ~ ins Mannesalter kommen. **2.** *euphem.* Manneskraft f.

'man|-hour s Arbeitsstunde f. **'~·hunt** s (Groß)Fahndung f.

ma·ni·a ['meɪnjə] s **1.** ⚕ Manie f, Wahn(sinn) m: → *persuasion* 1. **2.** *fig.* (*for*) Sucht f (nach), Leidenschaft f (für), Manie f, Fimmel m: *collector's* ~ Sammelwut f, -leidenschaft; ~ *for cleanliness* Sauberkeitsfimmel m; *have a* ~ *for* verrückt sein nach. **ma·ni·ac** ['~nɪæk] I s **1.** ⚕ Wahnsinnige m, f, Verrückte m, f. **2.** *fig.* (*Sport etc*)Fanatiker(in): *car* ~ Autonarr m. II adj (~*ally*) **3.** ⚕ wahnsinnig, verrückt.

man·ic-de·pres·sive [,mænɪkdɪ'presɪv] *psych.* I adj manisch-depressiv. II s Manisch-Depressive m, f: *be a* ~ manisch-depressiv sein.

man·i·cure ['mænɪˌkjʊə] I s Maniküre f. II v/t maniküren.

man·i·fest ['mænɪfest] I adj □ offenkundig, augenscheinlich. II v/t offenbaren, manifestieren. III s ✈ *bsd. Am.* Passagierliste f. **,man·i·fes·ta·tion** s **1.** Offenbarung f, Manifestation f. **2.** Anzeichen n, Symptom n. **,man·i·fes·to** [~təʊ] pl **-to(e)s** s Manifest n.

man·i·fold ['mænɪfəʊld] I adj □ **1.** mannigfaltig, vielfältig. **2.** ⚙ Mehr-, Vielfach...; Kombinations... II s **3.** ⚙ Verteiler m. III v/t **4.** vervielfältigen.

ma·nip·u·late [mə'nɪpjʊleɪt] v/t **1.** j-n, Preise etc manipulieren. **2.** ⚙ bedienen, betätigen. **3.** Konten etc frisieren. **ma·nip·u·la·tion** s **1.** Manipulation f. **2.** ⚙ Bedienung f, Betätigung f. **3.** Frisieren n. **ma·nip·u·la·tor** s Manipulator m (a. Zauberkünstler).

man·kind [mæn'kaɪnd] s die Menschheit, die Menschen pl. **'man·ly** adj männlich; Männer...

'man-made adj vom Menschen geschaffen od. verursacht; künstlich: ~ *fibers* (*bsd. Br.* **fibres**) *pl* Kunst-, Chemiefasern *pl.*

man·ne·quin ['mænıkın] *s* **1.** Mannequin *n.* **2.** Kleider- *od.* Schaufensterpuppe *f.*

man·ner ['mænə] *s* **1.** Art *f* (u. Weise *f*): *in this* ~ auf diese Art *od.* Weise, so; *in such a* ~ (*that*) so *od.* derart (daß); *adverb of* ~ Umstandswort *n* der Art u. Weise, Modaladverb *n*; *in a* ~ *of speaking* sozusagen. **2.** Betragen *n*, Auftreten *n*: *it's just his* ~ das ist so s-e Art. **3.** *pl* Benehmen *n*, Umgangsformen *pl*, Manieren *pl*: *it is bad* ~*s* es gehört sich nicht (*to do* zu tun). **4.** *pl* Sitten *pl* (u. Gebräuche *pl*). **'man·ner·ism** *s* **1.** *paint. etc* Manierismus *m.* **2.** Manieriertheit *f.* **3.** manierierte Wendung (*in Rede etc*).

ma·noeu·vra·ble [mə'nu:vrəbl] *adj bsd. Br.* manövrierfähig; lenk-, steuerbar; *weitS.* wendig (*Fahrzeug*). **ma'noeu·vre** [~və] **I** *s* **1.** *a. pl* ♋, ✗ Manöver *n*: *be on* ~*s* im Manöver sein; *room for* ~ *fig.* Handlungsspielraum *m.* **2.** Manöver *n*, Schachzug *m*, List *f.* **II** *v/i* **3.** ♋, ✗ manövrieren (*a. fig.*). **III** *v/t* **4.** manövrieren (*a. fig.*): ~ *s.o. into s.th.* j-n in et. hineinmanövrieren.

man·or ['mænə] *s Br.* (Land)Gut *n*: ~ (*house*) Herrenhaus *n.*

'man,pow·er *s* **1.** menschliche Arbeitskraft *od.* -leistung. **2.** (verfügbare) Arbeitskräfte *pl*: ~ *shortage* Arbeitskräftemangel *m.*

'man,ser·vant *pl* **'men,ser·vants** *s* Diener *m.*

man·sion ['mænʃn] *s* **1.** herrschaftliches Wohnhaus. **2.** *pl bsd. Br.* (großes) Mietshaus.

'man,slaugh·ter *s* ✝✝ Totschlag *m.*

man·tel·piece ['mæntl~] *s*, **'~·shelf** *s* (*irr shelf*) Kaminsims *m.*

,man|-to-'man *adj* von Mann zu Mann: **'~·trap** *s* Fußangel *f.*

man·u·al ['mænjʊəl] **I** *adj* □ **1.** Hand..., manuell: ~ *work* körperliche Arbeit; ~ *worker* (Hand)Arbeiter(in). **2.** handschriftlich. **II** *s* **3.** Handbuch *n*, Leitfaden *m.*

man·u·fac·ture [,mænjʊ'fæktʃə] **I** *s* **1.** Fertigung *f*, Erzeugung *f*, Herstellung *f*: *year of* ~ Herstellungs-, Baujahr *n.* **2.** Erzeugnis *n*, Fabrikat *n.* **II** *v/t* **3.** erzeu-

gen, herstellen. **4.** verarbeiten (*into* zu). **5.** *fig. Ausrede etc* erfinden. **,man·u·'fac·tur·er** *s* Hersteller *m*, Erzeuger *m.* **,man·u·'fac·tur·ing** *adj* Herstellungs...: ~ *cost* Herstellungskosten *pl.*

ma·nure [mə'njʊə] **I** *s* (*bsd. natürlicher*) Dünger. **II** *v/t* düngen.

man·u·script ['mænjʊskrıpt] *s* Manuskript *n.*

man·y ['menı] **I** *adj* **1.** viel(e): ~ *times* oft; *as* ~ *as forty* nicht weniger als vierzig; *we had one chair too* ~ wir hatten e-n Stuhl zuviel. **2.** ~ *a* manch (ein): ~ *a time* so manches Mal. **II** *s* **3.** viele: ~ *of us* viele von uns; *a good* ~ ziemlich viel(e); *a great* ~ sehr viele. **,~'sid·ed** *adj* **1.** vielseitig (*a. fig.*). **2.** *fig.* vielschichtig (*Problem etc*).

map [mæp] **I** *s* **1.** (Land- *etc*)Karte *f*; (*Stadt- etc*)Plan *m*: *be off the* ~ F hinter dem Mond liegen; *put on the* ~ F *Stadt etc* bekannt machen. **II** *v/t* **2.** e-e Karte machen von, *Gebiet* kartographisch erfassen; in e-e Karte eintragen. **3.** *mst* ~ *out fig.* (bis in die Einzelheiten) (vor-aus)planen.

ma·ple ['meıpl] *s* ♣ Ahorn *m.*

mar [mɑː] *v/t* **1.** beschädigen; verunstalten. **2.** *fig. Pläne etc* stören, beeinträchtigen; *Spaß etc* verderben.

mar·a·thon ['mærəθn] (*Leichtathletik*) **I** *s a.* ~ *race* Marathonlauf *m.* **II** *adj* Marathon..., *fig.* Dauer...

ma·raud [mə'rɔːd] **I** *v/i* plündern. **II** *v/t* (aus)plündern. **ma'raud·er** *s* Plünderer *m.*

mar·ble ['mɑːbl] **I** *s* **1.** Marmor *m.* **2.** a) Murmel *f*, b) *pl* (*sg konstruiert*) Murmelspiel *n*: *play* ~*s* (mit) Murmeln spielen. **II** *adj* **3.** marmorn (*a. fig.*).

March¹ [mɑːtʃ] *s* März *m*: *in* ~ im März.

march² [~] **I** *v/i* **1.** ✗ *etc* marschieren: ~ *off* abrücken; ~ *past* (*s.o.*) (an j-m) vorbeiziehen *od.* -marschieren; *time is ~ing on* es wird schon spät; → *time* **1.** **II** *v/t* **2.** *Strecke* marschieren, zurücklegen. **3.** ~ *s.o. off* j-n abführen. **III** *s* **4.** ✗ Marsch *m* (*a.* ♪); *allg.* (Fuß)Marsch *m.* **5.** Marsch(strecke *f*) *m*: *a day's* ~ ein Tage(s)marsch; *steal a* ~ *on s.o. fig.* j-m zuvorkommen. **6.** *fig.* (Ab)Lauf *m*, (Fort)Gang *m.*

march·ing or·ders ['mɑːtʃɪŋ] *s pl* ✗ Marschbefehl *m*: *get one's* ~ *fig.* F den

Laufpaß bekommen (*von Firma od. Freundin*); (*Sport*) vom Platz fliegen.

mare [meə] *s zo.* Stute *f*: **~'s nest** *fig.* Windei *n, a.* (Zeitungs)Ente *f.*

mar·ga·rine [‚maːdʒəˈriːn] *s*, **marge** [maːdʒ] *s Br.* F Margarine *f.*

mar·gin [ˈmaːdʒɪn] *s* **1.** Rand *m* (*a. fig.*). **2.** (Seiten)Rand *m*: **in the ~** am Rand. **3.** Grenze *f* (*a. fig.*): **~ of income** Einkommensgrenze. **4.** *fig.* Spielraum *m*: **allow** (*od.* **leave**) **a ~ for** Spielraum lassen für. **5.** ✝ (*Gewinn-, Verdienst-*)Spanne *f.* **6.** *Sport:* Abstand *m,* (*a.* Punkt)Vorsprung *m*: **by a wide ~** mit großem Vorsprung. **mar·gin·al** [ˈ‚nl] *adj* **1.** Rand...: **~ note** Randbemerkung *f.* **2.** Grenz... (*a. fig.*). **3.** *fig.* geringfügig. **mar·gin·al·ly** [ˈ‚əlɪ] *adv fig.* **1.** geringfügig. **2.** (nur) am Rand.

mar·gue·rite [‚maːɡəˈriːt] *s* ♀ **1.** Gänseblümchen *n.* **2.** Margerite *f.*

mar·i·hua·na, mar·i·jua·na [‚mærɪˈjuːɑːnə] *s* Marihuana *n.*

ma·ri·nade [‚mærɪˈneɪd] *s* Marinade *f.* **mar·i·nate** [ˈ‚neɪt] *v/t* marinieren.

ma·rine [məˈriːn] **I** *adj* **1.** a) See...: **~ chart** Seekarte *f,* b) Meeres...: **~ animal.** **II** *s* **2.** Marine *f.* **3.** ✗ Marineinfanterist *m*: **tell that to the ~s!** F das kannst du deiner Großmutter erzählen!

mar·i·o·nette [‚mærɪəˈnet] *s* Marionette *f*: **~ play** Puppenspiel *n.*

mar·i·tal [ˈmærɪtl] *adj* □ ehelich, Ehe...: **~ duties** *pl* (**rights** *pl*) eheliche Pflichten *pl* (Rechte *pl*); **~ status** Familienstand *m.*

mar·i·time [ˈmærɪtaɪm] *adj* **1.** See...: **~ blockade** Seeblockade *f.* **2.** seefahrend. **3.** Küsten...

mar·jo·ram [ˈmaːdʒərəm] *s* ♀ Majoran *m.*

mark¹ [maːk] *s* (deutsche) Mark.

mark² [‚] **I** *s* **1.** Markierung *f, bsd.* ☉ Marke *f.* **2.** *fig.* Zeichen *n*: **~ of confidence** Vertrauensbeweis *m*; **~ of respect** Zeichen der Hochachtung. **3.** (Kenn)Zeichen *n,* Merkmal *n*: **distinctive ~** Kennzeichen. **4.** Narbe *f* (*a. fig.*); Kerbe *f,* Einschnitt *m.* **5.** Ziel *n* (*a. fig.*): **hit the ~** (das Ziel) treffen; *fig.* ins Schwarze treffen; **miss the ~** das Ziel verfehlen, danebenschießen (*a. fig.*); **be off** (**wide of**) **the ~** (weit) danebenschießen; *fig.* sich (gewaltig) irren; (weit)

danebenliegen (*Schätzung etc*). **6.** *fig.* Norm *f*: **be up to the ~** den Anforderungen gewachsen sein (*Person*) *od.* genügen (*Leistungen etc*); *gesundheitlich* auf der Höhe sein. **7.** a) (*Fuß-, Brems-etc*)Spur *f* (*a. fig.*): **leave one's ~ on** s-n Stempel aufdrücken (*dat*); bei *j*-m s-e Spuren hinterlassen, b) Fleck *m.* **8.** ✝ (*Fabrik-, Waren*)Zeichen *n,* (*Schutz-, Handels*)Marke *f.* **9.** *ped.* Note *f* (*a. Sport*), Zensur *f*: **get** (*od.* **obtain**) **full ~s** die beste Note bekommen, die höchste Punktzahl erreichen. **10.** a) *Fußball:* Elfmeterpunkt *m,* b) *Laufsport:* Startlinie *f*: **on your ~s!** auf die Plätze!; **be quick** (**slow**) **off the ~** e-n guten (schlechten) Start haben; *fig.* schnell (langsam) schalten *od.* reagieren. **II** *v/t* **11.** markieren, anzeichnen, *a. fig.* kennzeichnen; *Wäsche* zeichnen; *Waren* auszeichnen; *Preis* festsetzen; *Temperatur etc* anzeigen; *fig.* ein Zeichen sein für: **to ~ the occasion** zur Feier des Tages, aus diesem Anlaß; **~ time** ✗ auf der Stelle treten (*a. fig.*); *fig.* abwarten. **12.** Spuren hinterlassen auf (*dat*); *fig. j*-n zeichnen (*Krankheit etc*). **13.** bestimmen (**for** für). **14.** *ped.* benoten, zensieren, (*Sport*) bewerten. **15.** *Sport:* *Gegenspieler* decken, markieren. **III** *v/i* **16.** **~ easily** leicht schmutzen.

Verbindungen mit Adverbien:

mark| down *v/t* **1.** ✝ (*im Preis*) herunter-, herabsetzen. **2.** bestimmen, vormerken (**for** für). **~ off** *v/t* **1.** abgrenzen, abstecken. **2.** (*auf e-r Liste*) abhaken. **~ out** *v/t* **1.** → **mark²** 13. **2.** abgrenzen, markieren. **~ up** *v/t* ✝ (*im Preis*) hinauf-, heraufsetzen.

'mark·down *s* ✝ Preissenkung *f* (**of** um).

marked [maːkt] *adj* deutlich, merklich, ausgeprägt. **mark·ed·ly** [ˈ‚kɪdlɪ] *adv* deutlich, ausgesprochen.

mark·er [ˈmaːkə] *s* **1.** Markierstift *m.* **2.** Lesezeichen *n.* **3.** *Sport:* Bewacher(in).

mar·ket [ˈmaːkɪt] ✝ **I** *s* **1.** Markt *m*: a) *Handel:* **be on the ~** auf dem Markt *od.* im Handel sein; **put** (*od.* **place**) **on the ~** auf den Markt od. in den Handel bringen; zum Verkauf anbieten, b) *Handelsmenge,* c) Marktplatz *m*: **in the ~** auf dem Markt, d) Wochen-, Jahrmarkt *m,* e) *Absatzgebiet:* **hold the ~** den Markt beherrschen, f) Absatz *m,* Verkauf *m*:

meet with a ready ~ schnellen Absatz finden; *there is no* ~ *for* ... lassen sich nicht absetzen. **2.** *Am.* (Lebensmittel)Geschäft *n*, Laden *m*. **II** *v/t* **3.** auf den Markt *od.* in den Handel bringen. **4.** vertreiben. **III** *adj* **5.** Markt... ~ **a·nal·y·sis** *s* (*irr analysis*) Marktanalyse *f*. ~ **e·con·o·my** *s*: *free* (*social*) ~ freie (soziale) Marktwirtschaft.

mar·ket·ing ['mɑːkɪtɪŋ] *s* ✝ Marketing *n*: ~ *research* Absatzforschung *f*.

mar·ket| place *s* Marktplatz *m*. ~ **re·search** *s* Marktforschung *f*.

mark·ing ['mɑːkɪŋ] *s* **1.** Markierung *f*, *a.* *fig.* Kennzeichnung *f*. **2.** *zo.* Musterung *f*, Zeichnung *f*. **3.** *ped.* Benotung *f*, Zensierung *f*, (*Sport*) Bewertung *f*. **4.** *Sport*: Deckung *f*.

marks·man ['mɑːksmən] *s* (*irr man*) guter Schütze.

'**mark·up** *s* ✝ Preiserhöhung *f* (*of* um).

mar·ma·lade ['mɑːməleɪd] *s* (*bsd.* Orangen)Marmelade *f*.

mar·mot ['mɑːmət] *s* *zo.* Murmeltier *n*.

ma·roon [mə'ruːn] *adj* kastanienbraun.

mar·quee [mɑː'kiː] *s* großes Zelt.

mar·riage ['mærɪdʒ] *s* **1.** Heirat *f*, Vermählung *f*, Hochzeit *f* (*to* mit). **2.** Ehe *f*: *by* ~ angeheiratet; *related by* ~ verschwägert. ~ **bu·reau** (*a. irr bureau*) Heiratsinstitut *n*. ~ **cer·tif·i·cate** *s* Trauschein *m*. ~ **guid·ance cen·ter** (*bsd. Br.* **cen·tre**) *s* Eheberatungsstelle *f*. ~ **lines** *s pl* (*mst sg konstruiert*) *bsd. Br.* Trauschein *m*.

mar·ried ['mærɪd] *adj* verheiratet, ehelich, Ehe...: ~ *couple* Ehepaar *n*; ~ *life* Eheleben *n*.

mar·row ['mærəʊ] *s* **1.** *anat.* (Knochen)Mark *n*: *be frozen to the* ~ völlig durchgefroren sein. **2.** *fig.* Mark *n*, Kern *m*, *das* Innerste.

mar·ry ['mærɪ] **I** *v/t* **1.** heiraten: *be married* verheiratet sein (*to* mit); heiraten. **2.** *a.* ~ *off* Tochter *etc.* verheiraten (*to an acc*, mit). **3.** Paar trauen. **II** *v/i* **4.** heiraten: ~ *into* einheiraten in (*acc*).

Mars [mɑːz] *s ast.* Mars *m*.

marsh [mɑːʃ] *s* Sumpf(land *n*) *m*, Marsch *f*.

mar·shal ['mɑːʃl] **I** *s* **1.** ✕ Marschall *m*. **2.** *Am.* Bezirkspolizeichef *m*. **II** *v/t pret u. pp* **-shaled**, *bsd. Br.* **-shalled** **3.** (an)ordnen, arrangieren.

marsh·y ['mɑːʃɪ] *adj* sumpfig, Sumpf...

mar·ten ['mɑːtɪn] *s zo.* Marder *m*.

mar·tial ['mɑːʃl] *adj* ☐ **1.** kriegerisch. **2.** Kriegs..., Militär...: ~ *law* Kriegsrecht *n*. **3.** ~ *arts pl* asiatische Kampfsportarten *pl*.

Mar·tian ['mɑːʃn] *s* Marsmensch *m*, -bewohner(in).

mar·ti·ni [mɑː'tiːnɪ] *s* Martini *m* (*Cocktail*).

Mar·tin·mas ['mɑːtɪnməs] *s* Martinstag *m* (*11. November*).

mar·tyr ['mɑːtə] **I** *s* **1.** Märtyrer(in): *make a* ~ *of o.s.* sich (auf)opfern; *iro.* den Märtyrer spielen. **II** *v/t* **2.** zum Märtyrer machen. **3.** zu Tode martern. '**mar·tyr·dom** *s* Martyrium *n* (*a. fig.*).

mar·vel ['mɑːvl] **I** *s* Wunder *n* (*of an dat*): *work* (*od. do*) ~*s* Wunder wirken. **II** *v/i pret u. pp* **-veled**, *bsd. Br.* **-velled** sich wundern, staunen (*at* über *acc*).

mar·vel·(l)ous ['mɑːvələs] *adj* ☐ **1.** erstaunlich, wunderbar. **2.** F fabelhaft, phantastisch.

Marx·ism ['mɑːksɪzəm] *s* Marxismus *m*. '**Marx·ist** *s* Marxist(in). **II** *adj* marxistisch.

mar·zi·pan [ˌmɑːzɪ'pæn] *s* Marzipan *n*, *m*.

mas·ca·ra [mæ'skɑːrə] *s* Wimperntusche *f*.

mas·cot ['mæskət] *s* Maskottchen *n*: a) Glücksbringer(in), b) Talisman *m*.

mas·cu·line ['mæskjʊlɪn] *adj* ☐ **1.** männlich (*a. ling.*), Männer... **2.** unfraulich, maskulin.

mash [mæʃ] **I** *s* **1.** breiige Masse, Brei *m*. **2.** *Br.* F Kartoffelbrei *m*. **II** *v/t* **3.** zerdrücken, -quetschen: ~*ed potatoes pl* Kartoffelbrei *m*.

mask [mɑːsk] **I** *s* **1.** *allg.* Maske *f* (*a. fig.*): *throw off the* ~ die Maske fallen lassen, sein wahres Gesicht zeigen. **II** *v/t* **2.** maskieren: ~*ed ball* Maskenball *m*. **3.** *fig.* verschleiern: ~*ed advertising* ✝ Schleichwerbung *f*.

mas·o·chism ['mæsəʊkɪzəm] *s psych.* Masochismus *m*. '**mas·o·chist** *s* Masochist(in). ˌ**mas·o·chis·tic** *adj* (~*ally*) masochistisch.

ma·son ['meɪsn] *s* **1.** Steinmetz *m*. **2.** *oft* ♁ Freimaurer *m*.

mas·quer·ade [ˌmæskə'reɪd] *s* Maskerade *f* (*a. fig.*).

match point

mass¹ [mæs] *s eccl.* Messe *f*: **go to ~** zur Messe gehen.

mass² [~] I *s* **1.** *allg.* Masse *f* (*a. phys.*): **a ~ of errors** e-e (Un)Menge Fehler; **~es *pl* of ice** Eismassen *pl*; **the ~es *pl*** die (breite) Masse. **2.** Mehrzahl *f*, überwiegender Teil. II *v/t u. v/i* **3.** (sich) (an)sammeln *od.* (an)häufen. III *adj* **4.** Massen...: **~ demonstration,** etc.

mas·sa·cre ['mæsəkə] I *s* Massaker *n.* II *v/t* niedermetzeln.

mas·sage ['mæsɑːʒ] I *s* Massage *f.* II *v/t* massieren.

mas·seur [mæ'sɜː] *s* Masseur *m.* **mas·seuse** [~'sɜːz] *s* Masseurin *f*, Masseuse *f.*

mas·sive ['mæsɪv] *adj □ allg.* massiv (*a. fig.*): **on a ~ scale** in ganz großem Rahmen.

mass| me·di·a *s pl* (*a. sg* konstruiert) Massenmedien *pl.* **'~pro,duce** *v/t* serienmäßig herstellen. **~ pro·duc·tion** *s* Massen-, Serienproduktion *f.*

mast¹ [mɑːst] *s ♣* (*a.* Antennen- *etc*-) Mast *m.*

mast² [~] *s* Mast(futter *n*) *f.*

mas·ter ['mɑːstə] I *s* **1.** Meister *m*, Herr *m*: **be ~ of sth.** et. (*a. e-e Sprache etc*) beherrschen; **be ~ of the situation** Herr der Lage sein; **be one's own ~** sein eigener Herr sein; **find one's ~** s-n Meister finden (**in s.o.** in j-m). **2.** ✝ Lehrherr *m*, Meister *m*; (Handwerks)Meister *m*: **~ tailor** Schneidermeister. **3.** *bsd. Br.* Lehrer *m*. **4.** *paint. etc* Meister *m*: **an old ~** ein alter Meister. **5.** *univ.* Magister *m*: ♀ *of Arts* Magister Artium *od.* der Geisteswissenschaften; ♀ *of Science* Magister der Naturwissenschaften. **6.** → **ceremony** 1. II *v/t* **7.** Herr sein über (*acc*), *a.* Sprache *etc* beherrschen. **8.** *Aufgabe, Schwierigkeit etc* meistern, *Temperament etc* zügeln. III *adj* **9.** meisterhaft, -lich, Meister... **10.** Haupt...: **~ cop·y** *s* Originalkopie *f* (*a. e-s Films etc*).

mas·ter·ful ['mɑːstəfʊl] *adj □* **1.** herrisch, gebieterisch. **2.** → **master** 9.

mas·ter| fuse *s ⚡* Hauptsicherung *f.* **~ key** *s* Hauptschlüssel *m.*

mas·ter·ly ['mɑːstəlɪ] → **master** 9.

'mas·ter·mind I *s* **1.** überragender Geist, Genie *n.* **2.** (führender) Kopf: **be the ~ behind** stecken hinter (*dat*). II *v/t*

3. der Kopf (*gen*) sein, stecken hinter (*dat*). **'~piece** *s* **1.** Haupt-, Meisterwerk *n.* **2.** Meisterstück *n.* **~ plan** *s* Gesamtplan *m.* **'~stroke** *s* Meisterstück *n*, -leistung *f.*

mas·ter·y ['mɑːstərɪ] *s* **1.** Herrschaft *f*, Gewalt *f* (*of, over* über *acc*): **gain the ~ over** die Oberhand gewinnen über. **2.** Beherrschung *f* (*e-r Sprache etc*).

mas·ti·cate ['mæstɪkeɪt] *v/t* (zer)kauen. **mas·ti·ca·tion** *s* (Zer)Kauen *n.*

mas·tiff ['mæstɪf] *s zo.* Bulldogge *f.*

mas·tur·bate ['mæstəbeɪt] *v/i* masturbieren, onanieren. **mas·tur·ba·tion** *s* Masturbation *f*, Onanie *f.*

mat¹ [mæt] I *s* **1.** Matte *f* (*a.* Ringen *etc*). **2.** Untersetzer *m*, -satz *m.* **3.** Vorleger *m*, Abtreter *m.* **4.** verfilzte Masse. II *v/i* **5.** sich verfilzen.

mat² [~] I *adj* matt (*a. phot.*), mattiert. II *v/t* mattieren.

match¹ [mætʃ] *s* Streich-, Zündholz *n.*

match² [~] I *s* **1.** der, die, das gleiche *od.* Ebenbürtige: **his ~** seinesgleichen; sein Ebenbild; j-d, der es mit ihm aufnehmen kann: **be a (no) ~ for s.o.** j-m (nicht) gewachsen sein; **find (*od.* meet) one's ~** s-n Meister finden (**in s.o.** in j-m). **2.** (dazu) passende Sache *od.* Person, Gegenstück *n.* **3.** (zs.-passendes) Paar, Gespann *n* (*a. fig.*): **they are an excellent ~** sie passen ausgezeichnet zueinander. **4.** (*Fußball- etc*)Spiel *n*, (*Box- etc*)Kampf *m.* **5.** Heirat *f*; *gute etc* Partie (*Person*). II *v/t* **6.** j-m, e-r Sache ebenbürtig *od.* gewachsen sein, gleichkommen: **no one can ~ her in cooking** niemand kann so gut kochen wie sie; **... cannot be ~ed** ... ist unerreicht *od.* nicht zu übertreffen. **7.** j-m, e-r Sache (*a. farblich etc*) entsprechen, passen zu. **8.** j-n, et. vergleichen (**with** mit): **~ one's strength against s.o.('s)** s-e Kräfte mit j-m messen. III *v/i* **9.** zs.-passen, übereinstimmen (**with** mit), entsprechen (**to** *dat*).

'match·box *s* Streich-, Zündholzschachtel *f.*

match·ing ['mætʃɪŋ] *adj* (dazu) passend. **'match·less** *adj □* unvergleichlich, einzigartig.

'match| mak·er *s* **1.** Ehestifter(in). **2.** *b.s.* Kuppler(in). **~ point** *s* Tennis *etc*: Matchball *m.*

mate¹ [meɪt] → **checkmate**.

mate² [~] **I** s **1.** (Arbeits)Kamerad m, (-)Kollege m; (Anrede) Kamerad!, Kumpel! **2.** zo., bsd. orn. Männchen n od. Weibchen n. **3.** ♣ Maat m. **II** v/t **4.** Tiere paaren. **III** v/i **5.** zo. sich paaren.

ma·te·ri·al [məˈtɪərɪəl] I adj □ **1.** materiell, physisch; Material...: ~ **damage** Sachschaden m; ~ **defect** Materialfehler m. **2.** materiell: a) leiblich (Wohlergehen), b) wirtschaftlich: ~ **wealth** materieller Wohlstand. **3.** wesentlich, ausschlaggebend (**to** für); ✠ erheblich, relevant. **II** s **4.** Material n, Stoff m (beide a. fig. **for** zu e-m Buch etc). **ma·ˈte·ri·al·ism** s Materialismus m. **ma·ˈte·ri·al·ist** s Materialist(in). **ma·ˌte·ri·al·ˈis·tic** adj (~ally) materialistisch. **ma·ˈte·ri·al·ize** I v/t **1.** et. verwirklichen. **II** v/i **2.** sich verwirklichen. **3.** erscheinen, sich materialisieren (Geist).

ma·ter·nal [məˈtɜːnl] adj □ **1.** mütterlich, Mutter... **2.** Großvater etc mütterlicherseits.

ma·ter·ni·ty [məˈtɜːnətɪ] I s Mutterschaft f. **II** adj: ~ **allowance** (od. **benefit**) Mutterschaftsbeihilfe f; ~ **dress** Umstandskleid n; ~ **leave** Mutterschaftsurlaub m; ~ **ward** Entbindungsstation f.

mat·ey [ˈmeɪtɪ] adj kameradschaftlich: **be** ~ **with** s.o. mit j-m auf du u. du stehen.

math [mæθ] s Am. F Mathe f.

math·e·mat·i·cal [ˌmæθəˈmætɪkl] adj □ mathematisch; Mathematik... **math·e·ma·ti·cian** [ˌmæθəˈtɪʃn] s Mathematiker(in). **math·e·mat·ics** [ˌmæθəˈmætɪks] s pl (mst sg konstruiert) Mathematik f.

maths [mæθs] s pl (mst sg konstruiert) Br. F Mathe f.

mat·i·née [ˈmætɪneɪ] s thea. Nachmittagsvorstellung f.

mat·ing [ˈmeɪtɪŋ] s zo. Paarung f: ~ **season** Paarungszeit f.

ma·tri·arch·y [ˈmeɪtrɪɑːkɪ] s sociol. Matriarchat n.

ma·tri·ces [ˈmeɪtrɪsiːz] pl von **matrix**.

ma·tric·u·late I v/t u. v/i [məˈtrɪkjʊleɪt] (sich) immatrikulieren. **II** s [~lət] Immatrikulierte m, f. **ma·ˌtric·u·ˈla·tion** s Immatrikulation f.

mat·ri·mo·ni·al [ˌmætrɪˈməʊnjəl] adj □ ehelich, Ehe...: ~ **agency** Heiratsinsti-

tut n. **mat·ri·mo·ny** [ˈmætrɪmənɪ] s Ehe(stand m) f.

ma·trix [ˈmeɪtrɪks] pl **ma·tri·ces** [ˈmeɪtrɪsiːz], **ˈma·trix·es** s **1.** ⦿ Matrize f. **2.** ✕ Matrix f.

ma·tron [ˈmeɪtrən] s **1.** Matrone f. **2.** Br. Oberschwester f, Oberin f. **ˈma·tron·ly** adj matronenhaft.

mat·ter [ˈmætə] I s **1.** Materie f (a. phys.), Substanz f, Stoff m. **2.** ✠ Eiter m. **3.** Sache f, Angelegenheit f: **this is an entirely different** ~ das ist et. ganz anderes; **a** ~ **of course** e-e Selbstverständlichkeit; **as a** ~ **of course** selbstverständlich, natürlich; **a** ~ **of fact** e-e Tatsache; **as a** ~ **of fact** tatsächlich, eigentlich; **a** ~ **of form** e-e Formsache; **as a** ~ **of form** der Form halber; **a** ~ **of taste** (e-e) Geschmackssache; **a** ~ **of time** e-e Frage der Zeit; **it is a** ~ **of life and death** es geht um Leben u. Tod; → **laughing 3.** **4.** pl die Sache, die Dinge pl: **to make** ~**s worse** was die Sache noch schlimmer macht; **as** ~**s stand** wie die Dinge liegen. **5.** **what's the** ~ (**with him**)? was ist los (mit ihm)?; **it's no** ~ **whether** es spielt keine Rolle, ob; **no** ~ **what he says** ganz gleich, was er sagt; **no** ~ **who** gleichgültig, wer. **II** v/i **6.** von Bedeutung sein (**to** für): **it doesn't** ~ es macht nichts; **it hardly** ~**s to me** es macht mir nicht viel aus; **it little** ~**s** es spielt kaum e-e Rolle. **7.** ✠ eitern. ~**of-**ˈ**course** adj selbstverständlich, natürlich. ~**of-**ˈ**fact** adj sachlich, nüchtern.

mat·tress [ˈmætrɪs] s Matratze f.

ma·ture [məˈtjʊə] I adj □ **1.** allg. reif (a. fig.). **2.** fig. ausgereift (Pläne etc): **after** ~ **reflection** nach reiflicher Überlegung. **3.** ✞ fällig (Wechsel). **II** v/t **4.** reifen lassen (a. fig.). **III** v/i **5.** (heran)reifen (**into** zu), reif werden (beide a. fig.). **6.** ✞ fällig werden. **ma·ˈtur·i·ty** s **1.** Reife f (a. fig.). **2.** ✞ Fälligkeit f.

maud·lin [ˈmɔːdlɪn] adj **1.** weinerlich (Stimme). **2.** rührselig.

maul [mɔːl] v/t **1.** j-n, et. übel zurichten. **2.** fig. herunter-, verreißen (Kritiker).

Maun·dy Thurs·day [ˈmɔːndɪ] s Gründonnerstag m.

mau·so·le·um [ˌmɔːsəˈlɪəm] pl **-le·ums**, **-le·a** [~ˈlɪə] s Mausoleum n.

mauve [məʊv] adj malvenfarbig, mauve.

mav·er·ick [ˈmævərɪk] s pol. (abtrünniger) Einzelgänger; *allg.* Außenseiter *m*.

mawk·ish ['mɔːkɪʃ] *adj* □ **1.** (unangenehm) süßlich. **2.** *fig.* rührselig, süßlich.

max·im ['mæksɪm] *s* Maxime *f*, Grundsatz *m*.

max·i·ma ['mæksɪmə] *pl von* **maximum**.

max·i·mal ['∼ml] *adj* □ → **maximum** II. '**max·i·mize** *v/t* ✝, ✿ maximieren.

max·i·mum ['∼məm] **I** *pl* **-ma** ['∼mə], **-mums** *s* Maximum *n*. **II** *adj* maximal, Maximal..., Höchst...: ∼ (**permissible**) **speed** (zulässige) Höchstgeschwindigkeit.

May¹ [meɪ] *s* Mai *m*: **in** ∼ im Mai.

may² [∼] *v/aux* (*irr*) **1.** Möglichkeit, Gelegenheit: *ich kann, du kannst etc, ich mag, du magst etc*: **it** ∼ **happen any time** es kann jederzeit geschehen; **it might happen** es könnte geschehen; **you** ∼ **be right** du magst recht haben, vielleicht hast du recht. **2.** *Erlaubnis*: *ich kann, du kannst etc, ich darf, du darfst etc*. **3.** *you* ∼ *well say so* du hast gut reden; **we might as well go** da könnten wir (auch) ebensogut gehen. **4.** *ungewisse Frage*: **how old** ∼ **she be?** wie alt mag sie wohl sein? **5.** *Aufforderung*: **you might help me** du könntest mir (eigentlich) helfen.

may·be ['meɪbɪ] *adv* vielleicht.

May| bee·tle, ∼ bug *s zo.* Maikäfer *m*. ∼ **Day** *s* Erster Mai. '**∼·day** *int* ✈, ⚓ Mayday! (*internationaler Funknotruf*).

may·hem ['meɪhem] *s* **1.** ⚖ *bsd. Am.* schwere Körperverletzung. **2.** *fig.* Chaos *n*: **cause** (*od.* **create**) ∼ ein Chaos auslösen.

may·on·naise [ˌmeɪə'neɪz] *s* Mayonnaise *f*.

may·or [meə] *s* Bürgermeister *m*.

'**may·pole** *s* Maibaum *m*.

maze [meɪz] *s* Irrgarten *m*, Labyrinth *n* (*a. fig.*): ∼ **of streets** Straßengewirr *n*; **be in a** ∼ verwirrt sein.

me [miː] **I** *personal pron* **1.** mich (*acc von* **I**): **he knows** ∼. **2.** mir (*dat von* **I**): **he gave** ∼ **the book. 3.** F ich (*nom*): **he's younger than** ∼; **it's** ∼ ich bin's. **II** *reflex pron* **4.** mich: **I looked about** ∼ ich sah mich um.

mead·ow ['medəʊ] *s* Wiese *f*, Weide *f*: **in the** ∼ auf der Wiese *od.* Weide.

mea·ger *Am.*, **mea·gre** *bsd. Br.* ['miːgə]

adj □ **1.** mager, dürr, (*Gesicht*) hager. **2.** *fig.* dürftig, kärglich: ∼ **attendance** spärlicher Besuch.

meal¹ [miːl] *s* Mahl(zeit *f*) *n*, Essen *n*: ∼**s** *pl* **on wheels** Essen auf Rädern.

meal² [∼] *s* Schrotmehl *n*.

'**meal·time** *s* Essenszeit *f*.

meal·y ['miːlɪ] *adj* mehlig. '**∼·mouthed** ['∼maʊðd] *adj* schönfärberisch, heuchlerisch (*Person*), (*Äußerung etc a.*) verschlüsselt.

mean¹ [miːn] *adj* □ **1.** gemein, niederträchtig. **2.** schäbig, geizig. **3.** F (*charakterlich*) schäbig: **feel** ∼ sich schäbig *od.* gemein vorkommen (**about** wegen).

mean² [∼] **I** *adj* **1.** mittler, Mittel..., durchschnittlich, Durchschnitts... **II** *s* **2.** Mitte *f*, Mittel(weg *m*) *n*, Durchschnitt *m*. **3.** *pl* (*a. sg konstruiert*) Mittel *n od. pl*, Weg *m*: **by all** ∼**s** auf alle Fälle, unbedingt; **by no** ∼**s** keineswegs, auf keinen Fall; **by** ∼**s of** mittels, durch, mit; **find the** ∼**s** Mittel u. Wege finden; **a** ∼**s of communication** ein Kommunikationsmittel; → **end** 10. **4.** *pl* Mittel *pl*, Vermögen *n*: **live within** (**beyond**) **one's** ∼**s** s-n Verhältnissen entsprechend (über s-e Verhältnisse) leben.

mean³ [∼] (*irr*) **I** *v/t* **1.** beabsichtigen, vorhaben; ∼ **to do s.th.** et. tun wollen; **I** ∼ **it** es ist mir Ernst damit; ∼ **business** es ernst meinen; ∼ **no harm** es nicht böse meinen; **no harm** ∼**t** nichts für ungut! **2. be** ∼**t for** bestimmt sein für, (*Bemerkung etc*) gemünzt sein auf (*acc*). **3.** meinen, sagen wollen: **what do you** ∼ **by this?** was wollen Sie damit sagen?; was verstehen Sie darunter? **4.** *e-e Menge Arbeit etc* bedeuten. **5.** bedeuten, heißen (*Wort etc*): **does this** ∼ **anything to you?** ist Ihnen das ein Begriff?, sagt Ihnen das et.? **II** *v/i* **6.** ∼ **well** (**ill**) **by** (*od.* **to**) **s.o.** j-m wohlgesinnt (übel gesinnt) sein. **7.** ∼ **everything** (**little**) **to s.o.** j-m alles (wenig) bedeuten.

me·an·der [mɪ'ændə] *v/i* sich winden *od.* schlängeln.

mean·ing ['miːnɪŋ] **I** *s* **1.** Sinn *m*, Bedeutung *f*: **full of** ∼ → 3; **do you get** (*od.* **take**) **my** ∼**?** verstehst du, was ich meine? **2.** Sinn *m*, Inhalt *m*: **give one's life a new** ∼ s-m Leben e-n neuen Sinn geben. **II** *adj* □ **3.** bedeutungsvoll, bedeutsam (*Blick etc*). **mean·ing·ful**

['~fʊl] *adj* □ **1.** bedeutungsvoll (*Blick, Ereignis etc*). **2.** sinnvoll (*Arbeit etc*). **'mean·ing·less** *adj* □ sinnlos.

mean·ness ['mi:nnɪs] *s* **1.** Gemeinheit *f*, Niederträchtigkeit *f*. **2.** Schäbigkeit *f*, Geiz *m*.

meant [ment] *pret u. pp von* **mean**³.

,mean|'time I *adv* inzwischen, unterdessen, in der Zwischenzeit. **II** *s*: **in the ~** → I. **,~'while** → **meantime** I.

mea·sles ['mi:zlz] *s pl* (*mst sg konstruiert*) 🎗 Masern *pl*: → **German** 1.

meas·ur·a·ble ['meʒərəbl] *adj* □ **1.** meßbar. **2.** merklich.

meas·ure ['meʒə] **I** *s* **1.** Maß(einheit *f*) *n*: **~ of capacity** Hohlmaß; **~ of length** Längenmaß. **2.** *fig.* (richtiges *od.* vernünftiges) Maß, Ausmaß *n*: **set ~s to** Grenzen setzen (*dat*); **know no ~** kein Maß kennen; **beyond** (*all*) **~** über alle Maßen, grenzenlos; **in a great** (*od.* **large**) **~** in großem Maße; großenteils; **in some ~, in a** (*certain*) **~** bis zu e-m gewissen Grade. **3.** Maß *n*, Meßgerät *n*: **weigh with two ~s** *fig.* mit zweierlei Maß messen. **4.** ♪ Takt *m*. **5.** *Metrik*: Versmaß *n*. **6.** Maßnahme *f*: **take ~s** Maßnahmen treffen *od.* ergreifen. **II** *v/t* **7.** (ver)messen, ab-, ausmessen: **~ s.o.** j-m Maß nehmen (**for** für); **~ one's length** *fig.* der Länge nach hinfallen. **8.** *fig.* messen (**by** an *dat*). **9.** *fig.* vergleichen, messen (**against, with** mit): **~ one's strength with** s-e Kräfte messen mit. **III** *v/i* **10.** messen, groß sein: **it ~s 7 inches** es mißt 7 Zoll, es ist 7 Zoll lang. **'meas·ure·ment** *s* **1.** (Ver)Messung *f*. **2.** Maß *n*; *pl a.* Abmessungen *pl*: **take s.o.'s ~s** j-m Maß nehmen (**for** für). **'meas·ur·ing** *adj* Meß...: **~ instrument** Meßgerät *n*.

meat [mi:t] *s* **1.** Fleisch *n*: **cold ~** kalter Braten. **2.** *fig.* Substanz *f*, Gehalt *m*. **'~·ball** *s* Fleischklößchen *n*.

me·chan·ic [mɪ'kænɪk] *s* Mechaniker *m*. **me'chan·i·cal** *adj* □ mechanisch (*a. fig.*): **~ engineering** Maschinenbau *m*; **~ pencil** *Am.* Drehbleistift *m*.

mech·a·nism ['mekənɪzm] *s* Mechanismus *m* (*a. fig.*). **'mech·a·nize** *v/t* mechanisieren.

med·al ['medl] *s* **1.** Medaille *f*. **2.** Orden *m*. **med·al·ist** *Am.* → **medallist**. **me·dal·lion** [mɪ'dæljən] *s* Medaillon *m*.

med·al·list ['medlɪst] *s bsd. Br.* Medaillengewinner(in).

med·dle ['medl] *v/i* sich einmischen (**with, in** in *acc*). **med·dle·some** ['~səm] *adj* aufdringlich.

me·di·a ['mi:djə] **I** *pl von* **medium**. **II** *s pl* (*a. sg konstruiert*) Medien *pl*: **~ event** Medienereignis *s*; **~·shy** medienscheu.

me·di·ae·val → **medieval**.

me·di·ate ['mi:dɪeɪt] **I** *v/i* vermitteln (**between** zwischen *dat*). **II** *v/t* (durch Vermittlung) zustande bringen *od.* beilegen. **,me·di'a·tion** *s* Vermittlung *f*. **'me·di·a·tor** *s* Vermittler *m*.

med·ic ['medɪk] → **medico**.

med·i·cal ['medɪkl] *adj* □ **1.** medizinisch, ärztlich, Kranken...: **~ certificate** ärztliches Attest; **~ examination** ärztliche Untersuchung; **on ~ grounds** aus gesundheitlichen Gründen; **~ student** Medizinstudent(in). **2.** internistisch: **~ ward** innere Abteilung (*e-r Klinik*). **II** *s* **3.** F ärztliche Untersuchung.

me·dic·a·ment [mə'dɪkəmənt] *s* Medikament *n*.

med·i·cate ['medɪkeɪt] *v/t* medizinisch *od.* medikamentös behandeln. **,med·i-'ca·tion** *s* medizinische *od.* medikamentöse Behandlung.

me·dic·i·nal [mə'dɪsɪnl] *adj* □ heilkräftig, Heil...: **~ herbs** *pl* Heilkräuter *pl*.

med·i·cine ['medsɪn] *s* **1.** Medizin *f*, Arznei *f*: **give s.o. a dose** (*od.* **taste**) **of his own ~** *fig.* es j-m in *od.* mit gleicher Münze heimzahlen. **2.** Medizin *f*, Heilkunde *f*; innere Medizin. **~ ball** *s Sport*: Medizinball *m*. **~ chest** *s* Hausapotheke *f*. **~ man** *s* (*irr* **man**) Medizinmann *m*.

med·i·co ['medɪkəʊ] *pl* **-cos** *s* F Mediziner *m* (*Arzt u. Student*).

me·di·e·val [,medɪ'i:vl] *adj* □ mittelalterlich.

me·di·o·cre [,mi:dɪ'əʊkə] *adj* mittelmäßig. **me·di·oc·ri·ty** [,~'ɒkrətɪ] *s* Mittelmäßigkeit *f*.

med·i·tate ['medɪteɪt] **I** *v/i* (**on**) nachdenken (über *acc*), grübeln (über *acc, dat*), *a. engS.* meditieren (über *acc*). **II** *v/t* erwägen: **~ revenge** auf Rache sinnen. **,med·i'ta·tion** *s* Nachdenken *n*, Grübeln *n*; *engS.* Meditation *f*.

me·di·um ['mi:djəm] **I** *pl* **-di·a** ['~djə],

-di·ums s 1. *fig.* Mitte f, Mittelweg m. 2. *biol. etc* Medium n, Träger m. 3. ☩ (*a. künstlerisches etc*) Medium n, Mittel n: → **advertising** II. 4. *Hypnose, Parapsychologie:* Medium n. II *adj* 1. mittler, Mittel..., *a.* mittelmäßig. 6. *gastr.* englisch (*Steak*). '**~-priced** *adj* der mittleren Preislage. '**~-range** *adj:* ~ **missile** ✗ Mittelstreckenrakete f. '**~-size(d)** *adj* mittelgroß: ~ **car** mot. Mittelklassewagen m. '**~-term** *adj* mittelfristig (*Planung etc*). ~ **wave** s ⚡ Mittelwelle f: **on** ~ auf Mittelwelle.

med·ley ['medlı] s 1. Gemisch n, *contp.* Mischmasch m, Durcheinander n. 2. ♪ Medley n, Potpourri n.

meek [mi:k] *adj* □ 1. sanft(mütig). 2. bescheiden; *contp.* unterwürfig: **be** ~ **and mild** sich alles gefallen lassen. '**meek·ness** s 1. Sanftmut f. 2. Bescheidenheit f; *contp.* Unterwürfigkeit f.

meet [mi:t] (*irr*) I *v/t* 1. begegnen (*dat*); treffen, sich treffen mit. 2. *j-n* kennenlernen: **when I first met him** als ich s-e Bekanntschaft machte; **pleased to** ~ **you** F sehr erfreut, (Sie kennenzulernen). 3. *j-n* abholen (**at the station** von der Bahn). 4. → **halfway** 3. 5. (*feindlich*) zs.-treffen mit, (*Sport a.*) treffen auf (*acc*): → **fate** 6. *fig.* entgegentreten (*dat*). 7. münden in (*acc*) (*Straße acc*); stoßen *od.* treffen auf (*acc*): **there is more to it than ~s the eye** da steckt mehr dahinter. 8. *j-s* Wünschen entgegenkommen, entsprechen, *e-r* Forderung, Verpflichtung nachkommen, *Unkosten* bestreiten, decken. II *v/i* 9. zs.-kommen, -treten. 10. sich begegnen, sich (*a. verabredungsgemäß*) treffen: ~ **again** sich wiedersehen; **our eyes met** unsere Blicke trafen sich. 11. (*feindlich*) zs.-stoßen, (*Sport*) aufeinandertreffen. 12. sich kennenlernen: **we have met before** wir kennen uns schon. 13. sich vereinigen (*Straßen etc*); sich berühren (*a. Interessen etc*). 14. genau zs.-passen, sich decken: → **end** 6. 15. ~ **with** zs.-treffen mit; sich treffen mit; erleben, erleiden: ~ **with an accident** e-n Unfall erleiden, verunglücken; ~ **with a refusal** auf Ablehnung stoßen; → **approval** 2.

meet·ing ['mi:tıŋ] s 1. Begegnung f,

Zs.-treffen n, -kunft f. 2. Versammlung f, Konferenz f, Tagung f: **at a** ~ auf e-r Versammlung; ~ **of members** Mitgliederversammlung. 3. *Sport:* Veranstaltung f. ~ **place** s 1. Tagungs-, Versammlungsort m. 2. Treffpunkt m.

meg·a·lo·ma·ni·a [ˌmegələʊ'meınjə] s Größenwahn m. ˌ**meg·a·lo·ma·ni·ac** [ˌ~nıæk] *adj* größenwahnsinnig.

meg·a·phone ['megəfəʊn] s Megaphon f.

mel·an·chol·y ['melənkəlı] I s 1. Melancholie f, Schwermut f. II *adj* 2. melancholisch, schwermütig. 3. traurig, schmerzlich (*Pflicht etc*).

mel·low ['meləʊ] I *adj* □ 1. reif, weich (*Obst*). 2. ausgereift, lieblich (*Wein*). 3. sanft, mild (*Licht*), zart (*Farbton*). 4. *fig.* gereift, abgeklärt (*Person*). 5. angeheitert, beschwipst. II *v/t* 6. reifen lassen (*a. fig.*). III *v/i* 7. reifen (*a. fig.*).

me·lo·di·ous [mı'ləʊdjəs] *adj* □ melodisch, melodiös.

mel·o·dra·ma ['meləʊˌdrɑːmə] s Melodrama(n) n (*a. fig.*). **mel·o·dra·mat·ic** [ˌ~drə'mætɪk] *adj* (**~ally**) melodramatisch.

mel·o·dy ['melədɪ] s Melodie f.

melt [melt] (*a. irr*) I *v/i* 1. (zer)schmelzen, sich auflösen: ~ **in the mouth** auf der Zunge zergehen; ~ **away** *fig.* sich auflösen (*Menge*); dahinschmelzen (*Geld*); ~ **into tears** *fig.* in Tränen zerfließen; ~ **butter** 1. 2. verschmelzen (*Farben, Ränder etc*): ~ **into** übergehen in (*acc*). II *v/t* 3. schmelzen, *Butter* zerlassen: ~ **down** einschmelzen. 4. *fig. j-s Herz* erweichen.

melt·ing ['meltıŋ] *adj* weich, angenehm (*Stimme*). ~ **fur·nace** s ⚙ Schmelzofen m. ~ **point** s *phys.* Schmelzpunkt m. ~ **pot** s Schmelztiegel m (*a. fig.*).

mem·ber ['membə] s 1. Mitglied n, Angehörige m, f: ~ **of the family** Familienmitglied; ♀ **of Parliament** Br. Unterhausabgeordnete m, f; ♀ **of Congress** Am. Mitglied des Repräsentantenhauses; ~ **only** (Zutritt) nur für Mitglieder; ~ **country** Mitgliedsland n. 2. *anat.* Glied(maße f) n; (männliches) Glied. '**mem·ber·ship** s 1. (**of**) Mitgliedschaft f (bei), Zugehörigkeit f (zu): ~ **card** Mitgliedsausweis m; ~ **fee** Mitgliedsbeitrag m. 2. Mitgliederzahl f: **have**

a ~ *of 200* 200 Mitglieder haben.

mem·brane ['membreɪn] *s* Membran(e) *f.*

mem·o ['meməʊ] *pl* **-os** *s* F Memo *n* (→ **memorandum** 1).

mem·oirs ['memwɑːz] *s pl* Memoiren *pl.*

mem·o·ra·ble ['memərəbl] *adj* □ **1.** denkwürdig. **2.** einprägsam. **3.** unvergeßlich.

mem·o·ran·dum [,memə'rændəm] *pl* **-da** [~də], **-dums** *s* **1.** (*a.* Akten)Vermerk *m*, (-)Notiz *f*; (*geschäftliche*) Kurzmitteilung. **2.** *pol.* Memorandum *n*, Denkschrift *f.*

me·mo·ri·al [mə'mɔːrɪəl] **I** *adj* **1.** Gedenk..., Gedächtnis...: ☨ **Day** *Am.* Gedenktag *m* für die Gefallenen (*30. Mai*); ~ **service** Gedenkgottesdienst *m.* **II** *s* **2.** Denk-, Ehrenmal *n*, Gedenkstätte *f* (*to* für). **3.** Gedenkfeier *f* (*to* für).

mem·o·rize ['meməraɪz] *v/t* auswendig lernen, sich *et.* einprägen.

mem·o·ry ['memərɪ] *s* **1.** Gedächtnis *n*: *from* (*od.* **by**) ~ aus dem Gedächtnis, auswendig; ~ *for* **names** Namensgedächtnis; *to the best of my* ~ soweit ich mich erinnern kann; *call to* ~ sich *et.* ins Gedächtnis zurückrufen; → *sieve* I. **2.** Andenken *n*, Erinnerung *f* (*of an acc*): *in* ~ *of* zum Andenken an. **3.** *mst pl* Erinnerung *f*: *childhood memories* Kindheitserinnerungen. **4.** *Computer:* Speicher *m.*

men [men] *pl von* **man**: ~'*s magazine* Herrenmagazin *n*; ~'*s room Am.* Herrentoilette *f.*

men·ace ['menəs] **I** *v/t* bedrohen. **II** *s* Drohung *f*; Bedrohung *f* (*to gen*).

mend [mend] **I** *v/t* **1.** ausbessern, reparieren, flicken, *Strümpfe etc* flicken; *fig. Freundschaft etc* kitten. **2.** (ver)bessern: ~ *one's ways* sich bessern. **II** *v/i* **3.** sich bessern (*a. Person*). **4.** *be ~ing* auf dem Weg der Besserung sein. **III** *s* **5.** Besserung *f*: *be on the* ~ → 4. **6.** ausgebesserte Stelle.

men·da·cious [men'deɪʃəs] *adj* □ lügnerisch, verlogen. **men·dac·i·ty** [~'dæsətɪ] *s* Verlogenheit *f.*

me·ni·al ['miːnjəl] *adj* □ untergeordnet, niedrig (*Arbeit*).

men·in·gi·tis [,menɪn'dʒaɪtɪs] *s* ✠ Hirnhautentzündung *f.*

men·o·pause ['menəʊpɔːz] *s* physiol.

Wechseljahre *pl*: *go through the* ~ in den Wechseljahren sein.

men·stru·ate ['menstrʊeɪt] *v/i* physiol. menstruieren. **,men·stru'a·tion** *s* Menstruation *f.*

men·tal ['mentl] *adj* (□ → **mentally**) **1.** geistig, Geistes...: ~ **arithmetic** Kopfrechnen *n*; ~ **deficiency** (*od.* **derangement**) Geistesstörung *f*; ~ **disease** (*od.* **illness**) Geisteskrankheit *f*; ~ **handicap** geistige Behinderung; ~ **hospital** psychiatrische Klinik, Nervenheilanstalt *f*; *make a* ~ *note of s.th.* sich *et.* (vor)merken; ~ **state** Geisteszustand *m.* **2.** seelisch, psychisch: ~ **cruelty** ⚖ seelische Grausamkeit (*als Scheidungsgrund*); ~ **Mentalität** *f.* **men·tal·i·ty** ['~təlɪ] *adv* **1.** geistig, geistes...: ~ **deficient** (*od.* **deranged**) geistesgestört; ~ **handicapped** geistig behindert; ~ **ill** geisteskrank. **2.** im Geist, in Gedanken.

men·thol ['menθɒl] *s* 🜋 Menthol *n.*

men·tion ['menʃn] **I** *s* Erwähnung *f*: *get* (*od.* **be given**) *a* ~ erwähnt werden. **II** *v/t* erwähnen (*to* gegenüber); *don't* ~ *it!* bitte (sehr)!, gern geschehen!; *not to* ~ ganz abgesehen *od.* zu schweigen von; nicht zu vergessen; → *worth* I.

men·u ['menjuː] *s* Speise(n)karte *f.*

mer·can·tile ['mɜːkəntaɪl] *adj* Handels...: ~ **law** Handelsrecht *n.*

mer·ce·nar·y ['mɜːsɪnərɪ] *s* ✕ Söldner *m.*

mer·chan·dise ['mɜːtʃəndaɪz] *s* Ware(n *pl*) *f.*

mer·chant ['mɜːtʃənt] **I** *s* (Groß)Händler *m*, (Groß)Kaufmann *m.* **II** *adj* Handels...: ~ **ship**.

mer·ci·ful ['mɜːsɪfʊl] *adj* □ (*to*) barmherzig (gegen), gnädig (*dat*). '**mer·ci·less** *adj* □ unbarmherzig, erbarmungslos.

mer·cu·ri·al [mɜː'kjʊərɪəl] *adj* □ **1.** Quecksilber... *fig.* quecksilb(e)rig, quicklebendig; sprunghaft.

mer·cu·ry ['mɜːkjʊrɪ] *s* **1.** ☿ *ast., myth.* Merkur *m.* **2.** 🜍 Quecksilber *n.*

mer·cy ['mɜːsɪ] *s* **1.** Barmherzigkeit *f*, Erbarmen *n*, Gnade *f*: *without* ~ → *merciless*; *be at s.o.'s* ~ j-m (auf Gedeih u. Verderb) ausgeliefert sein; *have* ~ *on* Mitleid *od.* Erbarmen haben mit. **2.** (wahres) Glück, (wahrer) Segen. ~ **kill·ing** *s* Sterbehilfe *f.*

mere [mɪə] *adj* bloß, nichts als: *a* ~ *ex-*

cuse nur e-e Ausrede; **~ imagination** bloße od. reine Einbildung. '**mere·ly** *adv* bloß, nur, lediglich.

merge [mɜːdʒ] **I** *v/i* **1. (in, into)** verschmelzen (mit), aufgehen (in *dat*). **2.** zs.-laufen (*Straßen etc*). **3.** ✝ fusionieren. **II** *v/t* **4.** verschmelzen (*in, into* mit). **5.** ✝ fusionieren. '**merg·er** ✝ Fusion *f*.

me·rid·i·an [məˈrɪdɪən] *s* **1.** *geogr*. Meridian *m*, Längenkreis *m*. **2.** *ast*. Kulminationspunkt *m*; *fig*. Gipfel *m*, Zenit *m*, Höhepunkt *m*.

mer·it [ˈmerɪt] **I** *s* **1.** Verdienst *n*: **a man of ~** ein verdienter od. verdienstvoller Mann. **2.** Wert *m*; Vorzug *m*: **work of ~** bedeutendes Werk; **of artistic ~** von künstlerischem Wert. **II** *v/t* **3.** Lohn, Strafe etc verdienen. **mer·i·toc·ra·cy** [ˌ~ˈtɒkrəsɪ] *s* Leistungsgesellschaft *f*.

mer·maid [ˈmɜːmeɪd] *s* Meerjungfrau *f*, Nixe *f*.

mer·ri·ment [ˈmerɪmənt] *s* **1.** Fröhlichkeit *f*, Lustigkeit *f*, Ausgelassenheit *f*. **2.** Gelächter *n*, Heiterkeit *f*.

mer·ry [ˈmerɪ] *adj* □ **1.** lustig (*a. Streich etc*), fröhlich, ausgelassen: **~ Christmas!** fröhliche od. frohe Weihnachten! **2.** F beschwipst, angeheitert: **get ~** sich e-n andudeln.

mesh [meʃ] **I** *s* **1.** Masche *f*. **2.** *mst pl fig*. Netz *n*, Schlingen *pl*: **~ of lies** Lügennetz, -gespinst *n*; **be caught in the ~es of the law** sich in den Schlingen des Gesetzes verfangen (haben). **II** *v/t* **3.** in e-m Netz fangen. **III** *v/i* **4.** ineinandergreifen (*Zahnräder; a. fig.*). **5.** *fig.* passen (**with** zu), zs.-passen.

mess [mes] **I** *s* **1.** Unordnung *f*, *a. fig.* Durcheinander *n*; Schmutz *m*; *fig.* Patsche *f*, Klemme *f*: **in a ~** in Unordnung; schmutzig; **be in a nice ~** ganz schön in der Klemme sein od. sitzen od. stecken; **make a ~ of →** 3. **2.** ✕ Messe *f*: **officers' ~** Offiziersmesse, -kasino *n*. **II** *v/t* **3.** **~ up** in Unordnung bringen, *a. fig.* durcheinanderbringen; schmutzig machen; *fig.* verpfuschen, *Pläne etc* über den Haufen werfen. **III** *v/i* **4. ~ about** (*od. around*) herumspielen, *b.s. a.* herumbasteln (**with** an *dat*).

mes·sage [ˈmesɪdʒ] *s* **1.** Mitteilung *f*, Nachricht *f*: **can I give him a ~?** kann ich ihm et. ausrichten?; **leave a ~ (for**

s.o.) (j-m) e-e Nachricht hinterlassen; **can I take a ~?** kann ich et. ausrichten?; **get the ~** F kapieren. **2.** *fig*. Anliegen *n* (*e-s Künstlers etc*); Aussage *f* (*e-s Romans etc*).

mes·sen·ger [ˈmesɪndʒə] *s* **1.** Bote *m*: **by ~** durch Boten. **2.** *fig*. (Vor)Bote *m*. **~ boy** *s* Laufbursche *m*, Botenjunge *m*.

Mes·si·ah [mɪˈsaɪə] *s eccl*. der Messias.

'**mess-up** *s* Durcheinander *n* (*a. fig.*).

mess·y [ˈmesɪ] *adj* □ **1.** schmutzig (*a. fig.*). **2.** *fig*. verfahren.

met [met] *pret u. pp von* **meet**.

met·a·bol·ic [ˌmetəˈbɒlɪk] *adj physiol*. Stoffwechsel... **me·tab·o·lism** [meˈtæbəlɪzəm] *s* Stoffwechsel *m*.

met·al [ˈmetl] **I** *s* Metall *n*. **II** *adj* → **metallic**. **1. me·tal·lic** [mɪˈtælɪk] *adj* (**~ally**) **1.** metallen, Metall... **2.** metallisch (glänzend od. klingend). **met·al·lur·gy** [meˈtælədʒɪ] *s* Metallurgie *f*, Hüttenkunde *f*.

'**met·al·pro·cess·ing** *adj* metallverarbeitend.

met·a·mor·pho·sis [ˌmetəˈmɔːfəsɪs] *pl* **-ses** [ˌ~siːz] *s* Metamorphose *f*, Verwandlung *f*.

met·a·phor [ˈmetəfə] *s* Metapher *f*. **met·a·phor·i·cal** [ˌ~ˈfɒrɪkl] *adj* □ metaphorisch, bildlich.

met·a·phys·i·cal [ˌmetəˈfɪzɪkl] *adj* □ **1.** *phls*. metaphysisch. **2.** übersinnlich. **met·a·phys·ics** *s pl* (*sg konstruiert*) *phls*. Metaphysik *f*.

me·tas·ta·sis [məˈtæstəsɪs] *pl* **-ses** [ˌ~siːz] *s* 🩺 Metastase *f*; Metastasenbildung *f*.

me·te·or [ˈmiːtɪə] *s ast*. Meteor *m*. **me·te·or·ic** [ˌmiːtɪˈɒrɪk] *adj* (**~ally**) **1.** *ast*. meteorisch, Meteor... **2.** *fig*. kometenhaft (*Aufstieg etc*). **me·te·or·ite** [ˈmiːtjəraɪt] *s ast*. Meteorit *m*.

me·te·or·o·log·i·cal [ˌmiːtjərəˈlɒdʒɪkl] *adj* □ meteorologisch, Wetter..., Witterungs...: **~ office** Wetteramt *n*. **me·te·or·ol·o·gist** [ˌ~ˈrɒlədʒɪst] *s* Meteorologe *m*. **me·te·or·ol·o·gy** [ˌ~dʒɪ] *s* Meteorologie *f*.

me·ter¹ [ˈmiːtə] *Am.* → **metre**.

me·ter² [ˌ~] *s* ⚙ Meßgerät *n*, Zähler *m*: **~ maid** *bsd. Am.* F Politesse *f*; **~ reader** Gas- od. Stromableser *m*.

meth·od [ˈmeθəd] *s* **1.** Methode *f*, Verfahren *n*: **the ~ of doing s.th.** die Art u. Weise, et. zu tun. **2.** Methode *f*, System *n*, Planmäßigkeit *f*: **work with ~** methodisch arbeiten. **me·thod·i·cal** [mɪ-ˈθɒdɪkl] *adj* □ methodisch, systematisch, planmäßig.

meth·yl [ˈmeθɪl] *s* ℞ Methyl *n*: **~ alcohol** Methylalkohol *m*.

me·tic·u·lous [mɪˈtɪkjʊləs] *adj* □ peinlich genau, akribisch.

me·tre [ˈmiːtə] *s bsd. Br.* **1.** Meter *m, n*. **2.** Versmaß *n*.

met·ric [ˈmetrɪk] **I** *adj* (**~ally**) metrisch: **~ system** metrisches (Maß- u. Gewichts)System. **II** *s pl* (*sg konstruiert*) Metrik *f*, Verslehre *f*.

me·trop·o·lis [mɪˈtrɒpəlɪs] *s* Metropole *f*, Hauptstadt *f*. **met·ro·pol·i·tan** [ˌmetrəˈpɒlɪtən] *I adj* ... der Hauptstadt. **II** *s* Bewohner(in) der Hauptstadt.

met·tle [ˈmetl] *s* Mut *m*; Eifer *m*, Feuer *n*: **put s.o. on his ~** j-n zur Aufbietung all s-r Kräfte zwingen. **met·tle·some** [ˈ~səm] *adj* mutig; eifrig, feurig.

mew [mjuː] *v/i* miauen.

Mex·i·can [ˈmeksɪkən] **I** *adj* mexikanisch. **II** *s* Mexikaner(in).

mez·za·nine [ˈmetsəniːn] *s* △ Zwischen-, Halbgeschoß *n*.

mi·aow [miːˈaʊ] *v/i* miauen.

mice [maɪs] *pl von* **mouse**.

mick·ey [ˈmɪkɪ] *s*: **take the ~ out of s.o.** *bsd. Br.* F j-n auf den Arm nehmen.

mi·cro... [ˈmaɪkrəʊ] *in Zssgn* Mikro..., (sehr) klein.

mi·crobe [ˈmaɪkrəʊb] *s biol.* Mikrobe *f*.

'**mi·cro·chip** *s* ⚡ Mikrochip *m*. '**~·com·put·er** *s* Mikrocomputer *m*. **~·fiche** [ˈ~fiːʃ] *s* Mikrofiche *m*. '**~·film I** *s* Mikrofilm *m*. **II** *v/t* auf Mikrofilm aufnehmen. **~·or·gan·ism** *s biol.* Mikroorganismus *m*.

mi·cro·phone [ˈmaɪkrəfəʊn] *s* Mikrophon *f*: **at the ~** am Mikrophon.

mi·cro·scope [ˈmaɪkrəskəʊp] *s* Mikroskop *n*. **II** *v/t* mikroskopisch untersuchen. **mi·cro·scop·ic** [ˌ~ˈskɒpɪk] *adj* (**~ally**) **1.** mikroskopisch. **2.** mikroskopisch klein.

mi·cro·wave [ˈmaɪkrəweɪv] *s* ⚡ Mikrowelle *f*: **~ oven** Mikrowellenherd *m*.

mid [mɪd] *adj attr. od. in Zssgn* mittler..., Mittel...: **in ~·April** Mitte April; **be in one's ~·forties** Mitte vierzig sein. '**~·air** *s*: **in ~** in der Luft; **~ collision** Zs.-stoß *m* in der Luft. '**~·day I** *s* Mit-

tag *m*. **II** *adj* mittägig, Mittag(s)...

mid·dle [ˈmɪdl] **I** *adj* **1.** mittler, Mittel...: **~ classes** *pl* Mittelstand *m*; **~ ear** *anat.* Mittelohr *n*; **~ finger** Mittelfinger *m*; **~ name** zweiter Vorname; → **management 2. II** *s* **2.** Mitte *f*: **in the ~** in der Mitte; **in the ~ of** in der Mitte (*gen*), mitten in (*dat*); **in the ~ of July** Mitte Juli; **in the ~ of the street** mitten auf der Straße. **3.** Taille *f*. **4.** mittlerer Teil, Mittelstück *n*. '**~·age** *s* mittleres Alter: **be in ~** mittleren Alters sein. '**~·'aged** *adj* mittleren Alters. ♀ **Ag·es** *s pl das* Mittelalter *n*. '**~·'dis·tance** *adj* Sport: Mittelstrecken... ♀ **East** *s geogr.* der Nahe Osten. '**~·man** *s* (*irr* man) **1.** Mittelsmann *m*. **2.** ♀ Zwischenhändler *m*. '**~·of-the-'road** *adj bsd. pol.* gemäßigt. '**~·weight** *s* Sport: Mittelgewicht(ler *m*) *n*.

mid·dling [ˈmɪdlɪŋ] **I** *adj* von mittlerer Größe *od.* Güte, mittelmäßig (*a. contp.*): **how are you? fair to ~** so einigermaßen, mittelprächtig. **II** *adv* F leidlich, einigermaßen.

'**mid·field** *s bsd. Fußball*: Mittelfeld *n*: **in ~** im Mittelfeld; **~ man** (*od.* **player**) Mittelfeldspieler *m*.

midge [mɪdʒ] *s zo.* Mücke *f*.

midg·et [ˈmɪdʒɪt] **I** *s* Zwerg *m*, Knirps *m*. **II** *adj* Zwerg..., Miniatur..., Kleinst...

'**mid·land** [ˈmɪdlənd] *s*: **the ♀s** *pl* Mittelengland *n*. '**~·life cri·sis** *s* (*irr* crisis) *psych.* Midlife-crisis *f*. '**~·night I** *s* Mitternacht *f*: **at ~** um Mitternacht. **II** *adj* Mitternachts...: **~ sun; burn the ~ oil** bis spät in die Nacht arbeiten *od.* aufbleiben. '**~·point** *s*: **be at ~** die Hälfte hinter sich haben. '**~·sum·mer I** *s* **1.** Hochsommer *m*. **2.** *ast.* Sommersonnenwende *f*. **II** *adj* **3.** hochsommerlich, Hochsommer... '**~·way** *adj a. fig.* auf halbem Weg (**between** zwischen *dat*). '**~·wife** *s* (*irr* wife) Hebamme *f*. '**~·'win·ter** *s* **1.** Mitte *f* des Winters. **2.** *ast.* Wintersonnenwende *f*.

might¹ [maɪt] *s*: **with ~ and main** mit aller Kraft *od.* Gewalt.

might² [~] *pret von* **may²**.

might·y [ˈmaɪtɪ] **I** *adj* □ mächtig, gewaltig (*beide a. fig.*). **II** *adv* F ungeheuer: **~ easy** kinderleicht; **~ fine** prima.

mi·graine [ˈmiːɡreɪn] *s* ✚ Migräne *f*.

mi·grant [ˈmaɪɡrənt] → **migratory**.

mi·grate [maɪˈɡreɪt] *v/i* (ab-, aus)wandern, (*a. orn.* fort)ziehen. **mi·ˈgra·tion** *s* **1.** Wanderung *f* (*a.* 🐦, *zo.*). **2.** Abwandern *n*, Fortziehen *n*. **mi·gra·to·ry** [ˈ~ɡrətərɪ] *adj* Wander..., Zug...: **~ bird** Zugvogel *m*; **~ worker** Wanderarbeiter *m*.

mike [maɪk] *s* F Mikro *n* (*Mikrophon*).

mild [maɪld] *adj* □ mild (*Strafe, Wein, Wetter etc*), (*Licht etc a.*) sanft, (*Fieber, Zigarre etc a.*) leicht: **to put it ~ly** gelinde gesagt; **that's putting it ~ly** das ist gar kein Ausdruck.

mil·dew [ˈmɪldjuː] I *s* **1.** 🌿 Mehltau *m*. **2.** Schimmel *m*, Moder *m*. II *v/i* **3.** schimm(e)lig *od.* mod(e)rig werden.

mild·ness [ˈmaɪldnɪs] *s* Milde *f*.

mile [maɪl] *s* Meile *f*: **~s apart** meilenweit auseinander; *fig.* himmelweit (voneinander) entfernt; **~s better** F wesentlich besser; **for ~s** meilenweit; **it sticks out a ~** F wie ein Blinder; **talk a ~ a minute** F wie ein Maschinengewehr *od.* Wasserfall reden.

mile·age [ˈmaɪlɪdʒ] *s* **1.** zurückgelegte Meilenzahl *od.* Fahrtstrecke, Meilenstand *m*: **~ indicator** (*od. recorder*) *mot.* Meilenzähler *m*. **2.** **~ allowance** Meilengeld *n*.

mile·om·e·ter [maɪˈlɒmɪtə] *s mot.* Meilenzähler *m*.

'mile·stone *s* Meilenstein *m* (*a. fig.*).

mil·i·tant [ˈmɪlɪtənt] I *adj* □ **1.** kriegführend. **2.** militant. II *s* **3.** militante Person, militantes Mitglied. **mil·i·ta·rism** [ˈ~tərɪzəm] *s* Militarismus *m*. **'mil·i·ta·rist** *s* Militarist *m*. **ˌmil·i·taˈris·tic** *adj* (**~ally**) militaristisch. **'mil·i·tar·y** I *adj* □ militärisch, Militär...: **~ academy** Militärakademie *f*; **of ~ age** in wehrpflichtigem Alter; **~ cemetery** Soldatenfriedhof *m*; **~ dictatorship** Militärdiktatur *f*; **~ government** Militärregierung *f*; **~ police** Militärpolizei *f*; **do one's ~ service** s-n Militärdienst ableisten. II *s* (*pl konstruiert*): **the ~** das Militär.

mi·li·tia [mɪˈlɪʃə] *s* Miliz *f*, Bürgerwehr *f*. **mi·ˈli·tia·man** [~mən] *s* (*irr man*) Milizsoldat *m*.

milk [mɪlk] I *s* Milch *f* (*a.* 🌿, 🐦): **land of ~ and honey** *fig.* Schlaraffenland *n*; **it's no use crying over spilt ~** geschehen ist geschehen. II *v/t* melken (*a. fig.*). III *v/i*

Milch geben. **~ bar** *s* Milchbar *f*. **~ choc·o·late** *s* Vollmilchschokolade *f*. **~ float** *s* Br. Milchwagen *m*. **~ glass** *s* Milchglas *n*. **~man** [ˈ~mən] *s* (*irr man*) Milchmann *m*. **~ pow·der** *s* Milchpulver *n*, Trockenmilch *f*. **~ shake** *s* Milchshake *m*. **'~sop** *s* Weichling *m*, Muttersöhnchen *n*. **~ tooth** *s* (*irr tooth*) Milchzahn *m*.

milk·y [ˈmɪlkɪ] *adj* □ **1.** milchig. **2.** mit (viel) Milch (*Kaffee etc*). ♀ **Way** *s ast.* Milchstraße *f*.

mill [mɪl] I *s* **1.** *allg.* Mühle *f*: **go through the ~** *fig.* e-e harte Schule durchmachen; **put s.o. through the ~** *fig.* j-n hart rannehmen. **2.** Fabrik *f*, Werk *n*: → **rolling mill, spinning mill.** II *v/t* **3.** Korn etc mahlen. **4.** ⚙ *allg.* verarbeiten. III *v/i* **5.** *a.* **~ about** (*od. around*) herumlaufen; **~ing crowd** wogende Menge, (Menschen)Gewühl *n*.

mil·len·ni·um [mɪˈlenɪəm] *pl* **-ums, -a** [~ə] *s* Jahrtausend *n*.

mil·le·pede [ˈmɪlɪpiːd] *s zo.* Tausendfüßer *m*.

mill·er [ˈmɪlə] *s* Müller *m*.

mil·li·gram(me) [ˈmɪlɪɡræm] *s* Milligramm *n*.

mil·li·me·ter *Am.*, **mil·li·me·tre** *bsd. Br.* [ˈmɪlɪˌmiːtə] *s* Millimeter *m*, *n*.

mil·lion [ˈmɪljən] *s* Million *f*: **feel like a ~ dollars** F sich ganz prächtig fühlen. **mil·lion·aire** [ˌ~ˈneə] *s* Millionär(in).

'mill·pond *s* Mühlteich *m*: (**as**) **smooth as a ~** spiegelglatt (*Meer etc*). **'~stone** *s* Mühlstein *m*: **be a ~ round s.o.'s neck** *fig.* j-m ein Klotz am Bein sein.

mime [maɪm] I *s* **1.** Pantomime *f*. **2.** Pantomime *m*. II *v/t* **3.** (panto)mimisch darstellen. **4.** mimen, nachahmen. III *v/i* **5.** *TV etc* Playback singen *od.* spielen. **'mim·ic·ry** *s* **1.** Nachahmung *f*. **2.** *zo.* Mimikry *f*.

mim·ing [ˈmaɪmɪŋ] *s TV etc* Playback *n*.

mim·ic [ˈmɪmɪk] I *adj* **1.** mimisch. **2.** nachgeahmt, Schein... II *s* **3.** Nachahmer *m*, Imitator *m*. III *v/t* *pret u. pp* **-icked 4.** nachahmen (*a. biol.*).

mi·mo·sa [mɪˈməʊzə] *s* ♀ Mimose *f*.

min·a·ret [ˈmɪnəret] *s* ◬ Minarett *n*.

mince [mɪns] I *v/t* durchdrehen, (zer-)schneiden: **~ meat** Fleisch durchdrehen, Hackfleisch machen; **~d meat** Hackfleisch *n*; **not to ~ matters** (*od.*

one's words) *fig.* kein Blatt vor den Mund nehmen. **II** *v/i* geziert *od.* affektiert sprechen; tänzeln, trippeln. **III** *s bsd. Br.* Hackfleisch *n*. **'~meat** *s* **1.** Hackfleisch *n*: **make ~ of** *fig.* aus j-m Hackfleisch machen; *Argument etc* (in der Luft) zerreißen. **2.** Pastetenfüllung *f*. **~ pie** *s* gefüllte Pastete.

minc·er ['mɪnsə] *s* Fleischwolf *m*. **'minc·ing** *adj* □ **1. ~ machine** Fleischwolf *m*. **2.** geziert, affektiert; tänzelnd, trippelnd.

mind [maɪnd] **I** *s* **1.** Sinn *m*, Gemüt *n*, Herz *n*: **have s.th. on one's ~** et. auf dem Herzen haben. **2.** Verstand *m*, Geist *m*: **before one's ~'s eye** vor s-m geistigen Auge; **be out of one's ~** nicht (recht) bei Sinnen sein; **enter s.o.'s ~** j-m in den Sinn kommen; **lose one's ~** den Verstand verlieren; **put s.th. out of one's ~** sich et. aus dem Kopf schlagen; **read s.o.'s ~** j-s Gedanken lesen; → **presence**. **3.** Kopf *m*, Geist *m* (*Person*). **4.** Ansicht *f*, Meinung *f*: **to my ~** m-r Ansicht nach, m-s Erachtens; **change one's ~** es sich anders überlegen, s-e Meinung ändern; **give s.o. a piece of one's ~** j-m gründlich die Meinung sagen; **speak one's ~ (to s.o.)** (j-m) s-e Meinung sagen. **5.** Neigung *f*, Lust *f*, Absicht *f*: **have s.th. in ~** et. im Sinn haben; **have a good (half a) ~ to do s.th.** gute (nicht üble) Lust haben, et. zu tun; **make up one's ~** sich entschließen, e-n Entschluß fassen; zu der Überzeugung kommen (*that* daß), sich klarwerden (*about* über *acc*). **6.** Erinnerung *f*, Gedächtnis *n*: **bear** (*od.* **keep**) **in ~** (immer) denken an (*acc*), et. nicht vergessen; → **stick²** 7. **II** *v/t* **7.** achtgeben auf (*acc*): **~ the step!** Vorsicht, Stufe!; **~ your head!** stoß dir den Kopf nicht an! **8.** sehen nach, aufpassen auf (*acc*): **~ your own business!** kümmere dich um deine eigenen Dinge! **9.** et. haben gegen: **do you ~ my smoking** (*od.* **if I smoke**)**?** haben Sie et. dagegen *od.* stört es Sie, wenn ich rauche?; **would you ~ coming?** würden Sie so freundlich sein zu kommen? **III** *v/i* **10.** aufpassen: **~ (you)** wohlgemerkt; allerdings; **never ~!** macht nichts!, ist schon gut! **11.** et. dagegen haben: **I don't ~** meinetwegen, von mir aus

(gern). **'~,bend·ing** *adj* F (nahezu) unfaßbar *od.* unverständlich. **'~,blow·ing**, **'~,bog·gling** *adj* F irr(e).

mind·ed ['maɪndɪd] *adj* in Zssgn ...gesinnt; *religiös, technisch etc* veranlagt; ...begeistert. **'mind·er** *s* Aufseher *m*; Aufpasser *m*.

'mind-ex,pand·ing *adj* bewußtseinserweiternd.

mind·ful ['maɪndfʊl] *adj* □ **1.** aufmerksam, achtsam: **be ~ of** achten auf (*acc*). **2.** eingedenk (*of gen*): **be ~ of** denken an (*acc*), bedenken. **'mind·less** *adj* □ **1.** (*of*) unbekümmert (um), ohne Rücksicht (auf *acc*). **2.** gedankenlos, blind.

mind read·er *s* Gedankenleser(in).

mine¹ [maɪn] *possessive pron*: **it is ~** es gehört mir; **a friend of ~** ein Freund von mir; **his mother and ~** s-e u. m-e Mutter.

mine² [~] **I** *v/i* **1.** schürfen, graben (*for* nach). **II** *v/t* **2.** Erz, Kohle abbauen, gewinnen. **3.** ⚓, ✗ verminen. **4.** *fig.* untergraben, -minieren. **II** *s* **5.** Bergwerk *n*, Zeche *f*, Grube *f*. **6.** ⚓, ✗ Mine *f*. **7.** *fig.* Fundgrube *f* (*of* an *dat*): **he is a ~ of information** er ist e-e gute *od.* reiche Informationsquelle. **~ de·tec·tor** *s* ✗ Minensuchgerät *n*.

min·er ['maɪnə] *s* Bergmann *m*, Kumpel *m*.

min·er·al ['mɪnərəl] **I** *s* **1.** Mineral *n*. **2.** *mst pl Br.* Mineralwasser *n*. **II** *adj* **3.** Mineral...: **~ oil;** **~ water;** **~ coal** Steinkohle *f*; **~ resources** *pl* Bodenschätze *pl*.

min·er·al·og·i·cal [,mɪnərə'lɒdʒɪkl] *adj* □ mineralogisch. **min·er·al·o·gist** [~'rælədʒɪst] *s* Mineraloge *m*. **,min·er·'al·o·gy** [~dʒɪ] *s* Mineralogie *f*.

min·gle ['mɪŋgl] **I** *v/i* **1.** sich (ver)mischen (*with* mit). **2.** sich (ein)mischen (*in* in *acc*); sich mischen (*among, with* unter *acc*). **II** *v/t* **3.** (ver)mischen (*with* mit).

min·i... ['mɪnɪ] in Zssgn Mini...

min·i·a·ture ['mɪnətʃə] **I** *s* **1.** Miniatur(gemälde *n*) *f*. **2.** *fig.* Miniaturausgabe *f*: **in ~** en miniature, im kleinen. **II** *adj* **3.** Miniatur...

'min·i·bus *s* Kleinbus *m*. **'~dress** *s* Minikleid *n*.

min·im ['mɪnɪm] *s* ♩ halbe Note.

min·i·ma ['mɪnɪmə] *pl von* **minimum.**

min·i·mal ['⌣ml] *adj* □ **1.** minimal. **2.** → *minimum* II. **'min·i·mize** *v/t* **1.** auf ein Minimum herabsetzen, möglichst gering halten. **2.** bagatellisieren, herunterspielen. **min·i·mum** ['⌣məm] *pl* **-ma** ['⌣mə] *s* Minimum *n*: *with a ~ of* mit e-n Minimum an (*dat*); → *keep to* 3. II *adj* Minimal..., Mindest...

min·ing ['maɪnɪŋ] I *s* Bergbau *m*. II *adj* Bergwerks..., Berg(bau)...: *~ disaster* Grubenunglück *n*.

'min·i·skirt *s* Minirock *m*.

min·is·ter ['mɪnɪstə] I *s* **1.** *eccl*. Geistliche *m*, Pfarrer *m*. **2.** *pol*. *bsd*. *Br*. Minister *m*: **♀** *of Defence* Verteidigungsminister. II *v/i* **3.** *~* *to s.o.* sich um j-n kümmern, für j-n sorgen. **min·is·te·ri·al** [,⌣'stɪərɪəl] *adj* □ **1.** *eccl*. geistlich. **2.** *pol*. *bsd*. *Br*. ministeriell, Minister...

min·is·tra·tion [,mɪnɪ'streɪʃn] *s mst pl* Dienst *m* (*to* an *dat*).

min·is·try ['mɪnɪstrɪ] *s* **1.** *eccl*. geistliches Amt. **2.** *pol*. *bsd*. *Br*. Ministerium *n*: **♀** *of Defence* Verteidigungsministerium.

mink [mɪŋk] *s zo*. Nerz *m*.

mi·nor ['maɪnə] I *s* **1.** *univ*. *Am*. Nebenfach *n*. **2.** **♁** Minderjährige *m*, *f*. **3.** **♪** Moll *n*. II *adj* **4.** kleiner, *fig*. *a*. unbedeutend, unwichtig. **5.** **♁** minderjährig. III *v/i* **6.** *~* *in univ*. *Am*. als *od*. im Nebenfach studieren. **mi·nor·i·ty** [maɪ'nɒrətɪ] *s* **1.** Minderheit *f*: *be in the* (*od*. *a*) *~* in der Minderheit sein; *~ government* Minderheitsregierung *f*. **2.** **♁** Minderjährigkeit *f*.

mint¹ [mɪnt] *s* **1.** **♣** Minze *f*: *~ sauce* Minzsoße *f*. **2.** Pfefferminz *n* (*Bonbon*).

mint² [⌣] I *s* **1.** Münze *f*, Münzanstalt *f*. **2.** *a ~* (*of money*) F ein Heidengeld. II *adj* **3.** ungebraucht (*Münze*), postfrisch (*Briefmarke*): *in ~ condition* in einwandfreiem *od*. tadellosem Zustand. III *v/t* **4.** Geld, *a. fig*. Wort *etc* prägen.

min·u·et [,mɪnjʊ'et] *s* **♪** Menuett *n*.

mi·nus ['maɪnəs] I *prp* **1.** **♣** minus, weniger. **2.** F ohne. II *adj* **3.** Minus...: *~ amount* → 5a; *~ sign* → 4. III *s* **4.** Minus(zeichen) *n*. **5.** Minus *n*: a) Fehlbetrag *m*, b) Nachteil *m*, c) Mangel *m* (*of* an *dat*).

min·ute¹ ['mɪnɪt] I *s* **1.** Minute *f*: *to the ~* auf die Minute (genau); *I won't be a ~* ich bin gleich wieder da; ich bin gleich fertig; *ten-~* zehnminütig; → *silence* I.

2. Augenblick *m*: *at the last ~* in letzter Minute; *in a ~* sofort; *just a ~!* Moment mal! **3.** *pl* (Sitzungs)Protokoll *n*: *keep the ~s* das Protokoll führen. II *v/t* **4.** protokollieren.

mi·nute² [maɪ'njuːt] *adj* □ **1.** winzig. **2.** peinlich genau, minuziös.

min·ute| hand *s* Minutenzeiger *m* (*e-r Uhr*). *~ steak* *s gastr*. Minutensteak *n*.

minx [mɪŋks] *s* (kleines) Biest.

mir·a·cle ['mɪrəkl] *s* Wunder *n* (*a. fig*. *of* an *dat*): *as if by* (*a*) *~* wie durch ein Wunder; *work* (*perform*) *~s* Wunder tun (vollbringen). **mi·rac·u·lous** [mɪ'rækjʊləs] *adj* wunderbar (*a. fig*.), Wunder... **mi·rac·u·lous·ly** *adv* wie durch ein Wunder.

mi·rage ['mɪrɑːʒ] *s* **1.** *phys*. Luftspieg(e)lung *f*, Fata Morgana *f* (*a. fig*.). **2.** *fig*. Illusion *f*.

mire ['maɪə] *s* Schlamm *m*: *drag through the ~* *fig*. in den Schmutz ziehen.

mir·ror ['mɪrə] I *s* **1.** Spiegel *m*: *hold up the ~ to s.o. fig*. j-m den Spiegel vorhalten. **2.** *fig*. Spiegel(bild *n*) *m*. II *v/t* **3.** (wider)spiegeln (*a. fig*.): *be ~ed* sich spiegeln (*in* in *dat*); *~ im·age s* Spiegelbild *n*. **'~-in,vert·ed** *adj* seitenverkehrt. *~ writ·ing s* Spiegelschrift *f*.

mirth [mɜːθ] *s* Fröhlichkeit *f*, Heiterkeit *f*, Freude *f*. **mirth·ful** ['⌣fʊl] *adj* □ fröhlich, heiter, lustig. **'mirth·less** *adj* □ freudlos.

mis... [mɪs] *in Zssgn* miß..., falsch.

,mis·ad'ven·ture *s* **1.** Unfall *m*, Unglück(sfall *m*) *n*. **2.** Mißgeschick *n*: *he's had a ~* ihm ist ein Mißgeschick passiert.

mis·an·thrope ['mɪsənθrəʊp] *s* Menschenfeind(in), -hasser(in). **mis·an·throp·ic** [,⌣'θrɒpɪk] *adj* (*~ally*) menschenfeindlich. **mis·an·thro·py** [mɪ'sænθrəpɪ] *s* Menschenfeindlichkeit *f*, -haß *m*.

,mis·ap'ply *v/t* **1.** falsch verwenden. **2.** → *misappropriate* 1.

'mis·ap·pre'hend *v/t* mißverstehen. **'mis·ap·pre'hen·sion** *s* Mißverständnis *n*: *be* (*od*. *labo[u]r*) *under a ~* sich in e-m Irrtum befinden.

,mis·ap'pro·pri·ate *v/t* **1.** unterschlagen, veruntreuen. **2.** zweckentfremden. **'mis·ap,pro·pri'a·tion** *s* **1.** Unterschla-

gung f, Veruntreuung f. **2.** Zweckent-
fremdung f.

mis·be·have v/i sich schlecht benehmen, sich danebenbenehmen, (Kind)
ungezogen sein. **mis·be·hav·io(u)r**
s schlechtes Benehmen, Ungezogenheit f.

mis·cal·cu·late I v/t falsch berechnen,
sich verrechnen in (dat). **II** v/i sich verrechnen od. verkalkulieren. **mis·cal-
cu·la·tion** s Rechenfehler m, Fehlkal-
kulation f.

mis·car·riage s **1.** Fehlschlag(en n) m,
Mißlingen n: **~ of justice** ⚖ Fehlurteil
n, Justizirrtum m. **2.** ⚕ Fehlgeburt f.
mis·car·ry v/i **1.** fehlschlagen, mißlingen. **2.** ⚕ e-e Fehlgeburt haben.

mis·cel·la·ne·ous [ˌmɪsəˈleɪnjəs] adj □
ge-, vermischt; verschiedenartig. **mis·
cel·la·ny** [mɪˈselənɪ] s **1.** Gemisch n. **2.**
Sammlung f, Sammelband m.

mis·chance s: **by ~** durch e-n unglücklichen Zufall.

mis·chief ['mɪstʃɪf] s **1.** Unheil n, Schaden m: **do ~** Unheil od. Schaden anrichten; **make ~** Unfrieden stiften (**between** zwischen dat); **mean ~** Böses im
Schilde führen. **2.** Unfug m, Dummheiten pl: **be up to ~** et. aushecken. **3.**
Übermut m, Ausgelassenheit f: **be full
of ~** immer zu Dummheiten aufgelegt
sein. **'~·,mak·er** s Unruhestifter(in).

mis·chie·vous ['mɪstʃɪvəs] adj □ **1.** boshaft, mutwillig. **2.** schelmisch.

mis·con·ceive v/t falsch auffassen,
mißverstehen. **mis·con·cep·tion** s
Mißverständnis n.

mis·con·duct I v/t [ˌmɪskənˈdʌkt] **1.**
schlecht führen. **2. ~ o.s.** sich schlecht
benehmen. **II** s [ˌmɪsˈkɒndʌkt] **3.**
schlechte Führung. **4.** schlechtes Benehmen. **5.** Verfehlung f.

mis·con·struc·tion s Mißdeutung f, falsche Auslegung. **mis·con·strue** v/t
mißdeuten, falsch auslegen.

mis·count I v/t falsch (aus)zählen. **II** v/i
sich verzählen.

mis·deal v/t u. v/i (irr deal): **~ (the
cards)** (Kartenspiel) sich vergeben.

mis·deed s Missetat f.

mis·de·mean·o(u)r [ˌmɪsdɪˈmiːnə] s ⚖
Vergehen n.

mis·di·rect v/t **1.** j-n, et. fehl-, irrelei-
ten (a. fig.), j-m den falschen Weg zei-

gen. **2.** Brief etc falsch adressieren.

mi·ser ['maɪzə] s Geizhals m.

mis·er·a·ble ['mɪzərəbl] adj □ **1.** jämmerlich, erbärmlich, kläglich, contp. a.
miserabel. **2.** traurig, unglücklich.

mi·ser·ly ['maɪzəlɪ] adj geizig.

mis·er·y ['mɪzərɪ] s **1.** Elend n, Not f. **2.**
Trübsal f, Jammer m.

mis·fire I v/i **1.** versagen (Schußwaffe).
2. mot. fehlzünden, aussetzen. **3.** fig.
danebengehen (Witz etc), fehlschlagen
(Plan etc). **II** s **4.** mot. Fehlzündung f.

mis·fit s **1.** schlechtsitzendes Kleidungsstück. **2.** Außenseiter(in).

mis·for·tune s **1.** schweres Schicksal,
Unglück n. **2.** Unglücksfall m; Mißgeschick n.

mis·giv·ing s Befürchtung f, Zweifel m.

mis·gov·ern v/t schlecht regieren od.
verwalten.

mis·guid·ed adj irrig (Entscheidung
etc), unangebracht (Optimismus etc).

mis·han·dle v/t **1.** et. falsch behandeln
od. handhaben. **2.** fig. falsch anpacken.

mis·hap ['mɪshæp] s Unglück(sfall m) n;
Mißgeschick n: **he's had a ~** ihm ist ein
Mißgeschick passiert; **without ~** ohne
Zwischenfälle.

mis·hear (irr hear) **I** v/t falsch hören. **II**
v/i sich verhören.

mish·mash ['mɪʃmæʃ] s Mischmasch m.

mis·in·form v/t j-n falsch informieren
(**about** über acc). **mis·in·for·ma·tion** s
Fehlinformation f.

mis·in·ter·pret v/t mißdeuten, falsch
auffassen od. auslegen. **mis·in·ter·-
pre·ta·tion** s Mißdeutung f, falsche
Auslegung.

mis·judge v/t **1.** falsch beurteilen, verkennen. **2.** falsch einschätzen.

mis·lay v/t (irr lay) et. verlegen.

mis·lead v/t (irr lead) **1.** irreführen,
täuschen: **be misled** sich täuschen lassen. **2.** verführen, -leiten (**into doing** zu
tun).

mis·man·age v/t schlecht verwalten od.
führen. **mis·man·age·ment** s Mißwirtschaft f.

mis·no·mer [ˌmɪsˈnəʊmə] s falsche Be-
nennung od. Bezeichnung.

mi·sog·a·mist [mɪˈsɒɡəmɪst] s Ehe-
feind m.

mi·sog·y·nist [mɪˈsɒdʒɪnɪst] s Frauen-
feind m.

‚**mis'place** v/t **1.** et. verlegen. **2.** et. an e-e falsche Stelle legen od. setzen: **~d** fig. unangebracht, deplaziert.

mis·print I v/t [‚mɪs'prɪnt] verdrucken. **II** s ['mɪsprɪnt] Druckfehler m.

‚**mis·pro'nounce** v/t falsch aussprechen. '**mis·pro‚nun·ci·a'tion** s falsche Aussprache.

‚**mis·quo'ta·tion** s falsches Zitat. ‚**mis·'quote** v/t falsch zitieren.

‚**mis'read** v/t (irr read) **1.** falsch lesen. **2.** mißdeuten.

‚**mis·re·pre'sent** v/t **1.** falsch darstellen. **2.** entstellen, verdrehen. '**mis‚rep·re·sen'ta·tion** s **1.** falsche Darstellung. **2.** Entstellung f, Verdrehung f.

miss¹ [mɪs] s **1.** ♀ (mit folgendem Namen) Fräulein n: ♀ **Smith**; ♀ **America** Miß f Amerika. **2.** (ohne folgendem Namen) Fräulein n (Anrede für Lehrerinnen, Kellnerinnen etc).

miss² [~] **I** v/t **1.** Chance, Zug etc verpassen, Beruf, Ziel etc verfehlen, sich et. entgehen lassen: **~ the boat** (od. **bus**) F den Anschluß od. s-e Chance verpassen; **~ doing s.th.** versäumen, et. zu tun. **2.** a. **~ out** auslassen, übergehen, -springen. **3.** überhören; übersehen; nicht bemerken; nicht verstehen od. begreifen. **4.** vermissen: **we ~ her very much** sie fehlt uns sehr. **II** v/i **5.** nicht treffen: a) danebenschlagen etc, b) danebengehen (Schuß etc). **6.** mißglücken, -lingen. **7.** **~ out** on et. versäumen; et. weglassen od. nicht berücksichtigen. **III** s **8.** Fehlschuß m, -wurf m etc. **9.** Verpassen n, Verfehlen n: → **near** 9.

‚**mis'shap·en** adj mißgebildet, ungestalt.

mis·sile ['mɪsaɪl] s **1.** (Wurf)Geschoß n. **2.** ✗ Rakete f: **~ base** (od. **site**) Raketen(abschuß)basis f.

miss·ing ['mɪsɪŋ] adj **1.** fehlend: **be ~** fehlen; verschwunden od. weg sein. **2.** (✗ a. **~ in action**) vermißt: **be ~** vermißt sein od. werden.

mis·sion ['mɪʃn] s **1.** (Militär- etc)Mission f. **2.** bsd. pol. Auftrag m, Mission f. **3.** eccl. Mission f. **4.** (innere) Berufung: **~ in life** Lebensaufgabe f; **sense of ~** Sendungsbewußtsein n. **5.** ✈, ✗ Einsatz m.

‚**mis'spell** v/t (a. irr spell) falsch schrei-

---

ben. ‚**mis'spell·ing** s Rechtschreibfehler m.

‚**mis'state** v/t falsch angeben. ‚**mis·'state·ment** s falsche Angabe.

mist [mɪst] **I** s **1.** (feiner) Nebel. **2.** fig. Nebel m, Schleier m: **see things through a ~** alles wie durch e-n Schleier sehen; **through a ~ of tears** durch e-n Tränenschleier. **3.** Beschlag m (auf Glas). **II** v/i **4.** a. **~ up** (od. **over**) (sich) beschlagen (Glas).

mis·tak·a·ble [mɪ'steɪkəbl] adj **1.** leicht zu verwechseln(d). **2.** mißverständlich. **mis'take I** v/t (irr take) **1.** verwechseln (**for** mit); verkennen, sich irren in (dat). **2.** falsch verstehen, mißverstehen. **II** s **3.** Irrtum m, Versehen n, Fehler m: **by ~** irrtümlich, aus Versehen; **make a ~** einen Fehler machen; **and no ~** F (Rechen- etc)Fehler m. **mis'tak·en I** pp von **mistake. II** adj **1.** **be ~** sich irren: **be ~ in s.o.** sich in j-m täuschen; **unless I am very much ~** wenn mich nicht alles täuscht. **2.** irrig, falsch (Meinung etc), unangebracht (Freundlichkeit etc): **a case of ~ identity** e-e (Personen)Verwechslung.

‚**mis'time** v/t e-n schlechten Zeitpunkt wählen für.

mis·tle·toe ['mɪsltəʊ] s ♣ **1.** Mistel f. **2.** Mistelzweig m.

‚**mis·trans'late** v/t falsch übersetzen. ‚**mis·trans'la·tion** s Übersetzungsfehler m.

mis·tress ['mɪstrɪs] s **1.** Herrin f (a. fig.). **2.** bsd. Br. Lehrerin f. **3.** Mätresse f, Geliebte f.

‚**mis'trust I** s Mißtrauen n (**of** gegen). **II** v/t mißtrauen (dat). mis'trust·ful [~fʊl] adj □ mißtrauisch (**of** gegen).

mist·y ['mɪstɪ] adj □ **1.** (leicht) neb(e)lig. **2.** fig. unklar, verschwommen (Vorstellung etc): **have only ~ memories of s.th.** sich nur schwach od. undeutlich an et. erinnern können. **3.** beschlagen (Glas).

‚**mis·un·der'stand** v/t (irr stand) **1.** mißverstehen: **don't ~ me** versteh mich nicht falsch. **2.** j-n nicht verstehen: **his wife ~s him.** ‚**mis·un·der'stand·ing** s Mißverständnis n, weitS. a. Meinungsverschiedenheit f, Differenz f.

mis·use I s [‚mɪs'juːs] **1.** Mißbrauch m: **~ of power** Machtmißbrauch. **2.** falscher

Gebrauch. **II** v/t [~'juːz] **3.** mißbrauchen. **4.** falsch od. zu unrechten Zwecken gebrauchen.

mite¹ [maɪt] s zo. Milbe f.

mite² [~] s **1.** kleines Ding, Würmchen n. **2.** a ~ F ein bißchen.

mit·i·gate ['mɪtɪgeɪt] v/t Schmerzen etc lindern, Strafe etc mildern, Zorn etc besänftigen: **mitigating circumstances** pl ⅄ mildernde Umstände pl. **,mit·i·ga·tion** s Linderung f, Milderung f, Besänftigung f.

mitt [mɪt] s **1.** Halbhandschuh m. **2.** Baseball: Fanghandschuh m. **3.** → **mitten** 1. **4.** sl. Flosse f, Pfote f (Hand). **5.** sl. Boxhandschuh m.

mit·ten ['mɪtn] s **1.** Fausthandschuh m, Fäustling m. **2.** → **mitt** 5.

mix [mɪks] **I** v/t **1.** (ver)mischen, vermengen (**with** mit), Cocktail etc mischen, Teig anrühren: ~ **into** mischen in (acc), beimischen (dat); ~ **up** zs.-, durcheinandermischen; gründlich mischen; (völlig) durcheinanderbringen; verwechseln (**with** mit); **be** ~**ed up** verwickelt sein od. werden (**in** in acc); (geistig) ganz durcheinander sein. **2.** fig. verbinden: ~ **business with pleasure** das Angenehme mit dem Nützlichen verbinden. **II** v/i **3.** sich (ver)mischen. **4.** sich mischen lassen. **5.** ~ **well** kontaktfreudig sein: ~ **well with s.o.** gut mit j-m auskommen. **6.** verkehren (**with** mit; **in** in dat). **III** s **7.** (a. Back- etc)Mischung f. **8.** F Durcheinander n. **mixed** [mɪkst] adj gemischt (a. fig. Gefühle etc): ~ **blessing** zweifelhaftes Vergnügen; ~ **double(s** pl) (Tennis etc) gemischtes Doppel, Mixed n; **a** ~ **doubles match** ein gemischtes Doppel; ~ **grill** Mixed grill m; ~ **pickles** pl Mixed Pickles pl, Mixpickles pl. **'mix·er** s **1.** Mixer m (a. Küchengerät). **2.** ⚙ Mischmaschine f. **3.** TV etc Mischpult m. **4. be a good (bad)** ~ F kontaktfreudig (kontaktarm) sein. **mix·ture** ['~tʃə] s Mischung f, a. ⚗ Gemisch n (**of** ... **and** aus ... u.): ~ **of teas** Teemischung.

'mix-up s F **1.** Durcheinander n. **2.** Verwechslung f. **3.** Handgemenge n.

mne·mon·ic [niːˈmɒnɪk] s Gedächtnishilfe f, -stütze f.

mo [məʊ] pl **mos** s F Moment m, Augenblick m.

moan [məʊn] **I** v/i stöhnen, ächzen. **II** s Stöhnen n, Ächzen n.

moat [məʊt] s (Burg-, Stadt)Graben m.

mob [mɒb] **I** s **1.** Mob m. **2.** Pöbel m, Gesindel n. **3.** sl. (Verbrecher)Bande f. **II** v/t **4.** herfallen über (acc); Filmstar etc bedrängen, belagern.

mo·bile ['məʊbaɪl] adj allg. beweglich, ⚙ a. fahrbar, ⚔ a. motorisiert: ~ **home** Wohnwagen m; ~ **library** Wander-, Autobücherei f. **mo·bil·i·ty** [~'bɪlətɪ] s Beweglichkeit f. **mo·bi·li·za·tion** [,~bɪlaɪ'zeɪʃn] s Mobilisierung f, ⚔ a. Mobilmachung f. **'mo·bi·lize I** v/t mobilisieren, ⚔ a. mobil machen. **II** v/i ⚔ mobil machen.

moc·ca·sin ['mɒkəsɪn] s Mokassin m.

mo·cha ['mɒkə] s Mokka m.

mock [mɒk] **I** v/t **1.** verspotten, lächerlich machen. **2.** nachäffen. **II** v/i **3.** sich lustig machen, spotten (**at** über acc). **III** adj **4.** nachgemacht, Schein... **'mock·er** s **1.** Spötter(in). **2.** Nachäffer(in). **'mock·er·y** s **1.** Spott m, Hohn m: **hold up to** ~ j-n lächerlich machen; et. ins Lächerliche ziehen. **2.** fig. Hohn m (**of** auf acc). **3.** Gespött n: **make a** ~ **of** j-n zum Gespött (der Leute) machen; ad absurdum führen. **'mock·ing** adj □ spöttisch.

'mock-up s Modell n (in natürlicher Größe), Attrappe f.

mod·al ['məʊdl] **I** adj □ ling. etc modal: ~ **auxiliary** modales Hilfsverb. **II** s ling. F modales Hilfsverb. **mo·dal·i·ty** [~'dælətɪ] s Modalität f.

mode [məʊd] s **1.** (Art f u.) Weise f: ~ **of address** Anrede f; ~ **of life** Lebensweise. **2.** ling. Modus m, Aussageweise f.

mod·el ['mɒdl] **I** s **1.** Muster n, Vorbild n (**for** für): **after** (od. **on**) **the** ~ **of** nach dem Muster von (od. gen); **he is a** ~ **of self-control** er ist ein Muster an Selbstbeherrschung. **2.** (fig. Denk)Modell n. **3.** Muster n, Vorlage f. **4.** paint. etc Modell n. **5.** Mode: Modell n, Typ(e f) m. **II** adj **7.** vorbildlich, musterhaft: ~ **husband** Mustergatte m. **8.** Mode: Mannequin n. **6.** Modell n (Kleidungsstück). **6.** Modellbauer m. **III** v/t pret u. pp **-eled**, bsd. Br. **-elled 9.** modellieren. **10.** fig. formen (**after**, **on** nach [dem Vorbild gen)): ~ **o.s. on** sich j-n zum Vorbild nehmen. **11.** *Kleider etc* vorführen. **IV** *v/i* **12.** Modell stehen *od.* sitzen (*for dat*). **13.** als Mannequin *od.* Dressman arbeiten.

mod·er·ate ['mɒdərət] **I** *adj* □ **1.** mäßig: a) gemäßigt (*a. pol.*), maßvoll, b) mittelmäßig, c) gering: **~ly successful** mäßig erfolgreich, d) vernünftig, angemessen: **~ demands** *pl* maßvolle Forderungen *pl* **2.** mild (*Strafe, Winter etc*). **II** *s* **3.** *bsd. pol.* Gemäßigte *m, f.* **III** *v/t* ['~reɪt] **4.** mäßigen: **~ one's language** sich mäßigen. **mod·er·a·tion** [~'reɪʃn] *s* Mäßigung *f*: **in ~** *in od.* mit Maßen, maßvoll.

mod·ern ['mɒdən] *adj* □ modern. **'mod·ern·ize** *v/t* modernisieren.

mod·est ['mɒdɪst] *adj* □ bescheiden: a) zurückhaltend, b) anspruchslos, c) maßvoll, vernünftig. **'mod·es·ty** *s* Bescheidenheit *f*: a) Zurückhaltung *f*: **in all ~** bei aller Bescheidenheit, b) Anspruchslosigkeit *f.*

mod·i·cum ['mɒdɪkəm] *s* kleine Menge: **a ~ of sense** ein Funke Verstand.

mod·i·fi·a·ble ['mɒdɪfaɪəbl] *adj* modifizierbar. **mod·i·fi·ca·tion** [~fɪ'keɪʃn] *s* Modifikation *f*, (Ab-, Ver)Änderung *f.* **'mod·i·fy** ['~faɪ] *v/t* **1.** (ab-, ver)ändern, modifizieren. **2.** *ling.* näher bestimmen.

mod·u·lar ['mɒdjʊlə] *adj* ⊚ Modul... **mod·u·late** ['mɒdjʊleɪt] *v/t u. v/i* ♩ *etc* modulieren. **mod·u·la·tion** *s* Modulation *f.*

mod·ule ['mɒdju:l] *s* **1.** ⊚ Modul *n, ♩ a.* Baustein *m.* **2.** *Raumfahrt*: (*Kommando- etc*)Kapsel *f.*

mo·hair ['məʊheə] *s* Mohair *m.*

Mo·ham·med·an [məʊ'hæmɪdən] **I** *adj* mohammedanisch. **II** *s* Mohammedaner(in).

moist [mɔɪst] *adj* □ feucht (**with** von): **~ with tears** tränenfeucht. **moisten** ['mɔɪsn] **I** *v/t* an-, befeuchten. **II** *v/i* feucht werden. **mois·ture** ['~tʃə] *s* Feuchtigkeit *f.* **mois·tur·iz·er** ['~tʃəraɪzə] *s* ⊚ Luftbefeuchter *m.*

mo·lar ['məʊlə] **I** *adj*: **~ tooth** → **II. II** *s* Backenzahn *m.*

mo·las·ses [məʊ'læsɪz] *s pl Am.* Sirup *m.*

mold, *etc Am.* → **mould**, *etc.*

mole¹ [məʊl] *s zo.* Maulwurf *m* (F *a.* Spionage).

mole² [~] *s* Muttermal *n*, Leberfleck *m.*

mole³ [~] *s* Mole *f*, Hafendamm *m.*

mo·lec·u·lar [məʊ'lekjʊlə] *s* 🐿, *phys.* Molekular... **mol·e·cule** ['mɒlɪkju:l] *s* Molekül *n.*

'mole·hill *s* Maulwurfshügel *m*: → **mountain I.**

mo·lest [məʊ'lest] *v/t* (*a. unsittlich*) belästigen. **mo·les·ta·tion** [~le'steɪʃn] *s* Belästigung *f.*

moll [mɒl] *s sl.* **1.** Gangsterbraut *f.* **2.** Nutte *f.*

mol·li·fy ['mɒlɪfaɪ] *v/t* besänftigen, beschwichtigen.

mol·lusc, *a. mol·lusk* ['mɒləsk] *s zo.* Molluske *f*, Weichtier *n.*

mol·ly·cod·dle ['mɒlɪˌkɒdl] **I** *s* Weichling *m.* **II** *v/t* verhätscheln.

Mo·lo·tov cock·tail ['mɒlətɒf] *s* Molotowcocktail *m.*

mol·ten ['məʊltən] *pp von* **melt.**

mom [mɒm] *s bsd. Am.* F Mami *f*, Mutti *f.* **'~·and·'pop store** *s Am.* F Tante-Emma-Laden *m.*

mo·ment ['məʊmənt] *s* **1.** Moment *m*, Augenblick *m*: **at the ~** im Augenblick; **at the last ~** im letzten Augenblick; (**not**) **for a ~** (k)einen Augenblick (lang); **just a ~!** a) a. **wait a ~!** Moment mal!, b) Augenblick!; **the ~ of truth** die Stunde der Wahrheit. **2.** Bedeutung *f*, Belang *m* (**to** für): **of great** (**little**) **~** von großer (geringer) Bedeutung; **of no ~** bedeutungs-, belanglos. **3.** *phys.* Moment *n*: **~ of inertia** Trägheitsmoment *n.*

mo·men·tar·i·ly ['~tərəlɪ] *adv* **1.** momentan, e-n Augenblick (lang). **2.** jeden Augenblick. **'mo·men·tar·y** *adj* momentan. **mo·men·tous** [~'mentəs] *adj* □ bedeutsam, folgenschwer. **mo·'men·tum** [~təm] *s* **1.** *phys.* Moment *n*, Impuls *m.* **2.** Wucht *f*, Schwung *m*: **gather** (*od.* **gain**) **~** in Fahrt kommen; *fig. a.* an Boden gewinnen (*Bewegung etc*); **lose ~** an Schwung verlieren (*a. fig.*).

mon·arch ['mɒnək] *s* Monarch(in), Herrscher(in). **mo·nar·chic** [mɒ'nɑ:kɪk] *adj* (**~ally**) **1.** monarchisch. **2.** monarchistisch. **mon·arch·ism** ['mɒnəkɪzəm] *s* Monarchismus *m.* **'mon·arch·ist I** *s* Monarchist(in). **II** *adj* monarchistisch. **'mon·arch·y** *s* Monarchie f: **constitutional** ~ konstitutionelle Monarchie.

mon·as·ter·y ['mɒnəstərɪ] s (Mönchs-) Kloster n. **mo·nas·tic** [mə'næstɪk] adj (~ally) **1.** klösterlich, Kloster... **2.** mönchisch, Mönchs...

Mon·day ['mʌndɪ] s Montag m: **on** ~ (am) Montag; **on** ~**s** montags.

mon·e·tar·y ['mʌnɪtərɪ] adj □ **1.** Währungs...: → **reform. 2.** Geld..., finanziell.

mon·ey ['mʌnɪ] s Geld n: **be out of** ~ kein Geld (mehr) haben; **be in the** ~ F reich od. vermögend sein; **be short of** ~ knapp bei Kasse sein; **I'll bet you any** ~ **that** F ich wette mit dir um jeden Betrag, daß; **get one's money's worth** et. für sein Geld bekommen; **have** ~ **to burn** F Geld wie Heu haben; **for** ~ **reasons** aus finanziellen Gründen; → **roll** 7. '~·**bags** s pl (sg konstruiert) F Geldsack m (reiche Person). ~ **box** s Sparbüchse f. '~·**chang·er** s **1.** (Geld-) Wechsler m. **2.** bsd. Am. Wechselautomat m.

mon·eyed ['mʌnɪd] adj wohlhabend, vermögend.

'**mon·ey**|·**lend·er** s Geldverleiher m. '~·**mak·er** s **1.** guter Geschäftsmann. **2.** gutes Geschäft, einträgliche Sache. ~ **or·der** s Post- od. Zahlungsanweisung f. ~ **spin·ner** F bsd. Br. → **money-maker** 2.

mon·ger ['mʌŋɡə] s in Zssgn **1.** ...händler m. **2.** fig. contp. → **scandalmonger, scaremonger,** etc.

mon·go·li·an [mɒŋ'ɡəʊljən] adj ✻ mongoloid.

mon·gol·ism ['mɒŋɡəlɪzəm] s ✻ Mongolismus m. '**mon·gol·oid** adj ✻ mongoloid.

mon·grel ['mʌŋɡrəl] s biol. Bastard m, bsd. Promenadenmischung f.

mon·i·tor ['mɒnɪtə] I s **1.** Monitor m: a) Abhörgerät n, b) Kontrollgerät n, -schirm m. II v/t **2.** abhören. **3.** überwachen.

monk [mʌŋk] s Mönch m.

mon·key ['mʌŋkɪ] I s **1.** zo. Affe m: **make a** ~ **(out) of s.o.** F j-n zum Deppen machen. **2.** (kleiner) Schlingel m. II v/i **3.** ~ **about** (od. **around**) herumalbern. **4.** a. ~ **about** (od. **around**) (**with**) F herumspielen (mit), herumpfuschen an (dat). ~ **busi·ness** s F **1.** krumme Tour. **2.**

Blödsinn m, Unfug m. ~ **wrench** s ⊕ Engländer m: **throw a** ~ **into s.th.** Am. et. behindern od. beeinträchtigen.

mon·o ['mɒnəʊ] I pl -**os** s **1.** Mono n. **2.** F Monogerät n od. -schallplatte f. II adj **3.** Mono...

mon·o... [~] in Zssgn ein..., mono...

mon·o·cle ['mɒnəkl] s Monokel n.

mo·nog·a·mous [mɒ'nɒɡəməs] adj □ monogam(isch). **mo'nog·a·my** s Monogamie f, Einehe f.

mon·o·gram ['mɒnəɡræm] s Monogramm n.

mon·o·lith ['mɒnəʊlɪθ] s Monolith m. ,**mon·o'lith·ic** adj (~ally) **1.** monolithisch (a. fig.). **2.** fig. gigantisch.

mon·o·logue ['mɒnəlɒɡ] s Monolog m, Selbstgespräch n.

mo·nop·o·lize [mə'nɒpəlaɪz] v/t **1.** ✝ monopolisieren. **2.** fig. a) an sich reißen, Unterhaltung a. ganz allein bestreiten, b) j-n, et. mit Beschlag belegen. **mo'nop·o·ly** s ✝ Monopol n (of auf acc) (a. fig.).

,**mon·o·syl'lab·ic** adj (~ally) ling. einsilbig (a. fig. Antworten etc).

mo·not·o·nous [mə'nɒtnəs] adj □ monoton, eintönig, fig. a. einförmig. **mo'not·o·ny** [~tnɪ] s Monotonie f, Eintönigkeit f, fig. a. Einförmigkeit f, (ewiges) Einerlei.

mon·ox·ide [mɒ'nɒksaɪd] s 🔬 Monoxyd n.

mon·soon [,mɒn'suːn] s Monsun m.

mon·ster ['mɒnstə] I s **1.** Monster n, Ungeheuer n (beide a. fig.). **2.** Monstrum n (a. fig.). II adj **3.** Riesen..., Monster...: ~ **film** Monsterfilm m.

mon·strance ['mɒnstrəns] s eccl. Monstranz f.

mon·stros·i·ty [mɒn'strɒsətɪ] s **1.** Ungeheuerlichkeit f. **2.** → **monster** 2. **mon·strous** ['~strəs] adj □ monströs: a) ungeheuer, riesig, b) unförmig, ungestalt, c) fig. ungeheuerlich, scheußlich.

month [mʌnθ] s Monat m: **we haven't seen each other in a** ~ **of Sundays** F wir haben uns schon seit einer Ewigkeit nicht mehr gesehen. '**month·ly** II adj **1.** (a. adv) monatlich. **2.** Monats...: ~ **sea·son ticket** Monatskarte f. II s **3.** Monatsschrift f.

mon·u·ment ['mɒnjʊmənt] s a. fig. Mo-

nument *n*, Denkmal *n* (**to** für *od. gen*).

mon·u·men·tal [͵ˈmentl] *adj* □ **1.** monumental (*a. fig.*). **2.** F kolossal: **~ stupidity** Riesendummheit *f*.

moo [muː] **I** *v/i* muhen. **II** *s* Muhen *n*.

mood¹ [muːd] *s ling.* Modus *m*.

mood² [~] *s* **1.** Stimmung *f*, Laune *f*: **be in a good (bad) ~** gute (schlechte) Laune haben, gut (schlecht) aufgelegt sein; **be in the (in no) ~ to do** (nicht) dazu aufgelegt sein zu tun, (keine) Lust haben zu tun; **be in the ~ for** aufgelegt sein zu; **I am in no laughing** (*od. ~ for laughing*) mir ist nicht nach *od.* zum Lachen zumute. **2. be in a ~** schlechte Laune haben, schlecht aufgelegt sein; **he is in one of his ~s again** er hat wieder einmal schlechte Laune.

mood·y [ˈmuːdɪ] *adj* □ **1.** launisch, launenhaft. **2.** schlechtgelaunt.

moon [muːn] **I** *s* Mond *m*: **there is a (no) ~** der Mond scheint (nicht); **be over the ~** F überglücklich sein (**about, at** über *acc*); **cry for the ~** nach et. Unmöglichem verlangen; **promise s.o. the ~** j-m das Blaue vom Himmel (herunter)versprechen; **once in a blue ~** F alle Jubeljahre (einmal). **II** *v/i*: **~ about** (*od. around*) herumtrödeln; ziellos herumstreichen. **III** *v/t*: **~ away** Zeit vertrödeln, -träumen. '**~·beam** *s* Mondstrahl *m*. '**~·light** *s* Mondlicht *n*, -schein *m*: **~ walk** Mondscheinspaziergang *m*. **II** *v/i* F schwarzarbeiten. '**~·light·er** *s* F Schwarzarbeiter(in). '**~·lit** *adj* mondhell: **~ night** Mondnacht *f*. '**~·shine** *s* **1.** Mondschein *m*. **2.** F Unsinn *m*, Quatsch *m*.

moon·y [ˈmuːnɪ] *adj* □ F verträumt.

moor¹ [mɔː] *s* (Hoch)Moor *n*.

moor² [~] *v/t* ✲ vertäuen, festmachen.

moo·rings [ˈmɔːrɪŋz] *s pl* ✲ **1.** Vertäuung *f*. **2.** Liegeplatz *m*.

moose [muːs] *pl* **moose** *s zo.* Elch *m*.

moot [muːt] *adj* strittig (*Punkt*): **~ question** Streitfrage *f*.

mop [mɒp] **I** *s* **1.** Mop *m*. **2.** (Haar)Wust *m*. **II** *v/t* **3.** wischen: **~ up** aufwischen; **~ one's face** sich das Gesicht (ab)wischen. **4.** *Blut etc* abtupfen (**from** von).

mope [məʊp] *v/i* den Kopf hängen lassen: **~ about** (*od. around*) mit e-r Leichenbittermiene herumlaufen.

mo·ped [ˈməʊped] *s Br.* Moped *n*.

mo·raine [mɒˈreɪn] *s geol.* Moräne *f*.

mor·al [ˈmɒrəl] **I** *adj* □ **1.** moralisch: a) sittlich, b) geistig, innerlich: **~ obligation** moralische Verpflichtung; **~ support** moralische Unterstützung; **~ victory** moralischer Sieg, c) sittenstreng, tugendhaft. **2.** Moral..., Sitten...: **~ theology** Moraltheologie *f*. **II** *s* **3.** Moral *f* (*e-r Geschichte etc*): **draw the ~ from** die Lehre ziehen aus. **4.** *pl* Moral *f*, Sitten *pl*: **code of ~s** Sittenkodex *m*. **mo·rale** [mɒˈrɑːl] *s* Moral *f*, Stimmung *f*: **raise (lower)** the **~** die Moral heben (senken). **mor·al·ist** [ˈmɒrəlɪst] *s* Moralist(in). **mo·ral·i·ty** [məˈrælɪtɪ] *s* **1.** Moral *f*, Tugend(haftigkeit) *f*. **2.** Ethik *f*, Moral *f*. **mor·al·ize** [ˈmɒrəlaɪz] *v/i* moralisieren (**about, on** über *acc*).

mor·a·to·ri·um [͵mɒrəˈtɔːrɪəm] *pl* **-ri·a** [~rɪə], **-ri·ums** ✝, ✕, *pol.* Moratorium *n*.

mor·bid [ˈmɔːbɪd] *adj* □ **1.** morbid, krankhaft (*beide a. fig.*). **2.** gräßlich, grauenerregend. **3.** trübsinnig; pessimistisch. **mor·bid·i·ty** *s* **1.** Morbidität *f*, Krankhaftigkeit *f* (*beide a. fig.*). **2.** Trübsinn *m*; Pessimismus *m*.

mor·dant [ˈmɔːdənt] *adj* □ *fig.* ätzend, beißend.

more [mɔː] **I** *adj* **1.** mehr: **they are ~ than we are** sie sind zahlreicher als wir. **2.** mehr, noch (mehr): **some ~ tea** noch et. Tee; **two ~ miles** noch zwei Meilen. **II** *adv* **3.** mehr: **~ and ~** immer mehr; **~ and ~ difficult** immer schwieriger; **~ or less** mehr *od.* weniger; ungefähr; **the ~ so because** um so mehr, da. **4.** *zur Bildung des comp:* **~ important** wichtiger; **~ often** öfter. **5.** noch: **once ~** noch einmal. **III** *s* **6.** Mehr *n* (**of** an *dat*). **7.** **some ~** noch et. (mehr); **a little ~** et. mehr; **what ~ do you want?** was willst du denn noch?

mo·rel [mɒˈrel] *s* ✿ Morchel *f*.

mo·rel·lo [məˈreləʊ] *pl* **-los** *s a.* **~ cherry** ✿ Morelle *f*.

more·o·ver [mɔːˈrəʊvə] *adv* außerdem, überdies, weiter, ferner.

morgue [mɔːg] *s* **1.** Leichenschauhaus *n*. **2.** F Archiv *n* (*e-s Zeitungsverlags etc*).

Mor·mon [ˈmɔːmən] **I** *s* Mormone *m*, Mormonin *f*. **II** *adj* mormonisch.

morn·ing [ˈmɔːnɪŋ] **I** *s* Morgen *m*; Vormittag *m: in the ~* morgens, am Morgen; vormittags, am Vormittag; *early in the ~* frühmorgens, früh am Morgen; *this ~* heute morgen *od.* vormittag; *tomorrow ~* morgen früh *od.* vormittag. **II** *adj* Morgen...; Vormittags...; Früh... **~ coat** *s* Cut(away) *m.* **~ pa·per** *s* Morgenzeitung *f.* **~ star** *s ast.* Morgenstern *m.*

mo·rose [məˈrəʊs] *adj* □ mürrisch, verdrießlich.

mor·pheme [ˈmɔːfiːm] *s ling.* Morphem *n.*

mor·phi·a [ˈmɔːfjə], **mor·phine** [ˈmɔːfiːn] *s* Morphium *n.*

mor·pho·log·i·cal [ˌmɔːfəˈlɒdʒɪkl] *adj* □ *biol., ling.* morphologisch. **mor·phol·o·gy** [ˌˈfɒlədʒɪ] *s* Morphologie *f.*

Morse code [mɔːs] *s* Morsealphabet *n.*

mor·sel [ˈmɔːsl] *s* **1.** Bissen *m*, Happen *m.* **2. a.** *fig.* ein bißchen: *a ~ of sense* ein Funke Verstand.

mor·tal [ˈmɔːtl] **I** *adj* □ **1.** sterblich. **2.** tödlich (*to* für). **3.** Tod(es)...: *~ fear* Todesangst *f; ~ hour* Todesstunde *f; ~ sin* Todsünde *f.* **4.** *auf* Leben u. Tod: *~ enemy* Todfeind *m; ~ hatred* tödlicher Haß. **5.** F *of no ~ use* absolut zwecklos; *every ~ thing* alles menschenmögliche; *I'm in a ~ hurry* ich hab's furchtbar eilig. **6.** F ewig (lang): *three ~ hours pl* drei endlose Stunden *pl.* **II** *s* **7.** Sterbliche *m, f: an ordinary ~* ein gewöhnlicher Sterblicher. **mor·tal·i·ty** [ˌˈtælətɪ] *s* **1.** Sterblichkeit *f.* **2. a.** *~ rate* Sterblichkeit(sziffer) *f.*

mor·tar¹ [ˈmɔːtə] *s* **1.** Mörser *m.* **2.** ⨯ Granatwerfer *m.*

mor·tar² [ˌˈ] *s* Mörtel *m.*

mort·gage [ˈmɔːgɪdʒ] **I** *s* Hypothek *f: raise a ~* e-e Hypothek aufnehmen (*on* auf *acc*). **II** *v/t* mit e-r Hypothek belasten, e-e Hypothek aufnehmen auf (*acc*).

mor·ti·cian [mɔːˈtɪʃən] *s Am.* Leichenbestatter *m.*

mor·ti·fi·ca·tion [ˌmɔːtɪfɪˈkeɪʃn] *s* **1.** Demütigung *f*, Kränkung *f.* **2.** Ärger *m*, Verdruß *m: to one's ~* zu s-m Verdruß. **3.** Kasteiung *f.* **4.** Abtötung *f.* **5.** Absterben *n.* **mor·ti·fy** [ˈˌfaɪ] **I** *v/t* **1.** demütigen, kränken. **2.** ärgern, verdrießen. **3.** *Fleisch etc* kasteien. **4.** Leidenschaften abtöten. **II** *v/i* **5.** ⚕ absterben (*Gewebe*).

mor·tu·ar·y [ˈmɔːtʃʊərɪ] **I** *s* Leichenhalle *f.* **II** *adj* Begräbnis..., Leichen...

mo·sa·ic [məʊˈzeɪk] *s* Mosaik *n.*

Mos·lem [ˈmɒzləm] **I** *s* Moslem *m.* **II** *adj* moslemisch.

mosque [mɒsk] *s* Moschee *f.*

mos·qui·to [məˈskiːtəʊ] *pl* **-to(e)s** *s zo.* Moskito *m; allg.* Stechmücke *f.* **~ net** *s* Moskitonetz *n.*

moss [mɒs] *s* Moos *n.* **'moss·y** *adj* moosig, bemoost.

most [məʊst] **I** *adj* **1.** meist, größt: *for the ~ part* größten-, meistenteils. **2.** (*vor e-m s im pl, mst ohne Artikel*) die meisten: *~ people* die meisten Leute. **II** *s* **3.** das meiste, *das* Höchste: *at (the) ~* höchstens, bestenfalls; *make the ~ of et.* nach Kräften ausnützen, das Beste herausholen aus. **4.** das meiste, der größte Teil: *he spent ~ of his time there* er verbrachte die meiste Zeit dort. **5.** die meisten *pl: better than ~* besser als die meisten; *~ of my friends* die meisten m-r Freunde. **III** *adv* **6.** am meisten: *~ of all* am allermeisten. **7.** *zur Bildung des sup:* *the ~ important point* der wichtigste Punkt. **8.** (*vor adj*) höchst, äußerst: *~ agreeable* äußerst angenehm; *he is ~ likely to come* er kommt höchstwahrscheinlich. **'most·ly** *adv* **1.** größtenteils. **2.** meist(ens).

MOT [ˌeməʊˈtiː] *s Br.* a.) *~ test* (*etwa*) TÜV-Prüfung *f: my car has failed* (*od. hasn't got through*) *its* (*od. the*) *~* mein Wagen ist nicht durch den TÜV gekommen, b) a.) *~ certificate* (*etwa*) TÜV-Bescheinigung *f.*

mo·tel [məʊˈtel] *s* Motel *n.*

moth [mɒθ] *s zo.* **1.** Nachtfalter *m.* **2.** Motte *f.* **'~·ball** *s* Mottenkugel *f: put in ~s* einmotten (*a. fig.*). **'~·eat·en** *adj* **1.** mottenzerfressen. **2.** *fig.* veraltet.

moth·er [ˈmʌðə] *s* Mutter *f* (*a. fig.*): ♀*'s Day* Muttertag *m;* ~*'s milk* Muttermilch *f; a ~ of four* e-e Mutter von vier Kindern. **II** *adj* Mutter...; ~ *ship.* **III** *v/t* bemuttern. **~ coun·try** *s* **1.** Mutterland *n.* **2.** Vater-, Heimatland *n.*

moth·er·hood [ˈmʌðəhʊd] *s* Mutterschaft *f.*

'moth·er|-in-law *pl* **'moth·ers-in-law** *s* Schwiegermutter *f.* **~ joke** Schwieger-

membrane *anat.* Schleimhaut *f.* **mu·cus** ['mju:kəs] *s* Schleim *m.*

mud [mʌd] *s* **1.** Schlamm *m,* Matsch *m.* **2.** Schmutz *m* (*a. fig.*): **drag through the** ~ *fig.* in den Schmutz ziehen *od.* zerren; **sling** (*od.* **throw**) ~ **at s.o.** *fig.* j-n mit Schmutz bewerfen.

mud·dle ['mʌdl] **I** *s* Durcheinander *n,* Unordnung *f;* Verwirrung *f:* **be in a** ~ durcheinander sein (*Dinge*), (*Person a.*) konfus sein; **get in(to) a** ~ durcheinandergeraten (*Dinge*), konfus werden (*Person*); **make a** ~ **of** → IIa. **II** *v/t* **1.** durcheinanderbringen: a) in Unordnung bringen, b) konfus machen, c) verwechseln (**with** mit). **III** *v/i:* ~ **through** sich durchwursteln. '~**,head·ed** *adj* wirr(köpfig), konfus.

mud·dy ['mʌdɪ] *adj* □ **1.** schlammig, trüb. **2.** schmutzig. **3.** *fig.* wirr; unklar, verschwommen.

'mud·guard *s mot.* Kotflügel *m;* Schutzblech *n* (*e-s Fahrrads*). ~ **pack** *s* ✻ Fango-, Schlammpackung *f.* '~**,sling·er** *s* Verleumder(in). '~**,sling·ing** *s* Verleumdung *f.*

muf·fin ['mʌfɪn] *s* Muffin *n:* a) *Br.* Hefeteigsemmel *f,* b) *Am. kleine süße Semmel.*

muf·fle ['mʌfl] *v/t* **1.** *oft* ~ **up** einhüllen, -wickeln. **2.** *Ton etc* dämpfen: ~**d voices** *pl* gedämpfte Stimmen *pl.* '**muf·fler** *s* **1.** dicker Schal. **2.** *mot. Am.* Auspufftopf *m.*

muf·ti ['mʌftɪ] *s:* **in** ~ in Zivil.

mug [mʌg] **I** *s* **1.** Krug *m;* Becher *m;* große Tasse. **2.** *sl.* Visage *f* (*Gesicht*); Fresse *f* (*Mund*). **II** *v/t* **3.** (*bsd. auf der Straße*) überfallen u. ausrauben. **4.** *a.* ~ **up** *Br. et.* büffeln. **III** *v/i* **5.** *Br.* F büffeln. '**mug·ger** *s* F (*bsd. Straßen*)Räuber *m.* '**mug·ging** *s* F Raubüberfall *m, bsd.* Straßenraub *m.*

mug·gy ['mʌgɪ] *adj* □ schwül.

mule¹ [mju:l] *s zo.* Maultier *n;* Maulesel *m:* (**as**) **stubborn** (*od.* **obstinate**) **as a** ~ (so) störrisch wie ein Maulesel.

mule² [~] *s* Pantoffel *m.*

mul·ish ['mju:lɪʃ] *adj* □ störrisch, stur.

mull¹ [mʌl] *s* (✻ Verband[s])Mull *m.*

mull² [~] *v/i u. v/t:* ~ **over** *s.th.,* ~ *s.th.* **over** nachdenken *od.* -grübeln über (*acc*).

mulled [mʌld] *adj:* ~ **wine** Glühwein *m.*

mul·ti... ['mʌltɪ] *in Zssgn* viel..., mehr..., Mehrfach..., Multi...

mul·ti·far·i·ous [ˌmʌltɪˈfeərɪəs] *adj* □ mannigfaltig, vielfältig.

mul·ti·lat·er·al [ˌmʌltɪˈlætərəl] *adj* □ **1.** vielseitig. **2.** *pol.* multilateral, mehrseitig. **mul·ti·lin·gual** *adj* mehrsprachig. **mul·ti·mil·lion·aire** *s* Multimillionär *m.* **mul·ti·na·tion·al** ✝ **I** *adj* multinational (*Konzern*). **II** *s* F Multi *m.*

mul·ti·ple ['mʌltɪpl] **I** *adj* □ **1.** viel-, mehrfach: ~ **sclerosis** ✻ multiple Sklerose. **2.** mannigfaltig, vielfältig. **3.** ⚡, ⦿ Mehr(fach)..., Vielfach... **II** *s* **4.** *das* Vielfache (*a. ℞*).

mul·ti·pli·ca·tion [ˌmʌltɪpl'keɪʃn] *s* **1.** Vermehrung *f* (*a. biol.*). **2.** ℞ Multiplikation *f:* ~ **sign** Mal-, Multiplikationszeichen *n;* ~ **table** Einmaleins *n.* **mul·ti·plic·i·ty** [ˌ~'plɪsətɪ] *s* **1.** Vielfalt *f.* **2.** Vielzahl *f.* **mul·ti·pli·er** ['~plaɪə] *s* ℞ Multiplikator *m.* **mul·ti·ply** ['~plaɪ] **I** *v/t* **1.** vermehren, -vielfachen. **2.** ℞ multiplizieren, malnehmen (**by** mit): **6 multiplied by 5 is 30** 6 mal 5 ist 30. **II** *v/i* **3.** sich vermehren (*a. biol.*), sich vervielfachen.

mul·ti·pur·pose *adj* Mehrzweck... **mul·ti·sto·r(e)y** *adj* vielstöckig: ~ **car park** Park(hoch)haus *n.*

mul·ti·tude ['mʌltɪtju:d] *s* **1.** große Zahl, Vielzahl *f:* **for a** ~ **of reasons** aus vielerlei Gründen. **2.** **the** ~(**s** *pl*) die Masse. **mul·ti·tu·di·nous** [ˌ~'tju:dɪnəs] *adj* □ zahlreich.

mum¹ [mʌm] **I** *int:* ~**'s the word** Mund halten!, kein Wort darüber! **II** *adj:* **keep** ~ nichts verraten (**about, on** von), den Mund halten.

mum² [~] *s bsd. Br.* F Mami *f,* Mutti *f.*

mum·ble ['mʌmbl] *v/t u. v/i* (vor sich hin) murmeln.

mum·bo jum·bo [ˌmʌmbəʊˈdʒʌmbəʊ] *s* **1.** Hokuspokus *m,* fauler Zauber. **2.** Kauderwelsch *n.*

mum·mi·fi·ca·tion [ˌmʌmɪfɪˈkeɪʃn] *s* Mumifizierung *f.* **mum·mi·fy** ['~faɪ] **I** *v/t* mumifizieren. **II** *v/i* vertrocknen.

mum·my¹ ['mʌmɪ] *s* Mumie *f.*

mum·my² [~] → **mum.**

mumps [mʌmps] *s pl* (*sg konstruiert*) ✻ Mumps *m,* Ziegenpeter *m.*

munch [mʌntʃ] *v/t u. v/i* mampfen: ~ **away at** *et.* mampfen.

mun·dane [ˌmʌn'deɪn] *adj* □ **1.** weltlich. **2.** alltäglich, profan; prosaisch, sachlich-nüchtern.

mu·nic·i·pal [mjuː'nɪsɪpl] *adj* □ städtisch, Stadt..., kommunal, Gemeinde...; **~ council** Stadt-, Gemeinderat *m*; **~ elections** *pl* Kommunalwahlen *pl*. **mu,nic·i'pal·i·ty** [~'pælətɪ] *s* **1.** Gemeinde *f*. **2.** Kommunalbehörde *f*, -verwaltung *f*.

mu·ral ['mjʊərəl] **I** *adj* Mauer..., Wand...: **~ painting** → II. **II** *s* Wandgemälde *n*.

mur·der ['mɜːdə] **I** *s* **1.** (**of**) Mord *m* (an *dat*), Ermordung *f* (*gen*): **cry** (*od.* **scream**) **blue ~** F zetermordio schreien; **get away with ~** F sich alles erlauben können. **II** *adj* **2.** Mord...: **~ trial** Mordprozeß *m*; **~ victim** Mordopfer *n*; **~ weapon** Mordwaffe *f*. **III** *v/t* **3.** ermorden. **4.** *fig.* verschandeln, verhunzen. **'mur·der·er** *s* Mörder *m*. **'mur·der·ess** *s* Mörderin *f*. **'mur·der·ous** *adj* □ mörderisch (*a. fig.*).

murk·y ['mɜːkɪ] *adj* □ dunkel, finster (*beide a. fig.*).

mur·mur ['mɜːmə] **I** *s* **1.** Murmeln *n*. **2.** Murren (*without a ~** ohne zu murren. **II** *v/i* **3.** murmeln. **4.** murren (**at**, **against** gegen). **III** *v/t* **5.** *et.* murmeln.

mus·cle ['mʌsl] **I** *s anat.* Muskel *m*: **not to move a ~** *fig.* nicht mit der Wimper zucken. **II** *v/i*: **~ in on** *fig.* F sich eindrängen in (*acc*). **'~·man** *s* (*irr* **man**) Muskelmann *m*, -paket *n*.

mus·cu·lar ['mʌskjʊlə] *adj* □ **1.** Muskel...: **~ atrophy** ✠ Muskelschwund *m*. **2.** muskulös.

muse [mjuːz] *v/i* (nach)sinnen, (-)grübeln (**on**, **over** über *acc*).

mu·se·um [mjuː'zɪəm] *s* Museum *n*.

mush [mʌʃ] *s* **1.** Brei *m*, Mus *n*. **2.** *Am.* Maisbrei *m*.

mush·room ['mʌʃrʊm] **I** *s* **1.** ✿ (eßbarer) Pilz, *engS.* Champignon *m*. **2.** *Am.* Pilz...; pilzförmig: **~ cloud** Atompilz *m*. **III** *v/t* **3.** Pilze sammeln: **go ~ing** in die Pilze gehen. **4.** *oft* **~ up** *fig.* wie Pilze aus dem Boden schießen.

mush·y ['mʌʃɪ] *adj* □ **1.** breiig, weich. **2.** F rührselig.

mu·sic ['mjuːzɪk] *s* **1.** Musik *f*: **that's ~ to my ears** das ist Musik in m-n Ohren; **face the ~** F dafür geradestehen; **put**

(*od.* **set**) **to ~** vertonen. **2.** Noten *pl*. **'mu·si·cal** **I** *adj* □ **1.** Musik...: **~ instrument**. **2.** musikalisch. **II** *s* **3.** Musical *n*.

mu·sic| book *s* Notenheft *n*, -buch *n*. **~ cen·tre** (*Am.* **cen·ter**) *s* Kompaktanlage *f*. **~ hall** *s bsd. Br.* Varieté(theater) *n*.

mu·si·cian [mjuː'zɪʃn] *s* Musiker(in).

mu·sic| pa·per *s* Notenpapier *n*. **~ stand** *s* Notenständer *m*. **~ stool** *s* Klavierstuhl *m*.

muss [mʌs] *Am.* F **I** *s* Durcheinander *n*, Verhau *m*. **II** *v/t oft* **~ up** durcheinanderbringen, *Haar* zerwühlen.

mus·sel ['mʌsl] *s* (Mies)Muschel *f*.

must¹ [mʌst] **I** *v/aux ich muß, du mußt etc:* **you ~ not smoke here** du darfst hier nicht rauchen. **II** *s* Muß *n*: **this book is an (a absolute) ~** dieses Buch muß man (unbedingt) gelesen haben.

must² [~] *s* Most *m*.

mus·tache *Am.* → **moustache**.

mus·tang ['mʌstæŋ] *s zo.* Mustang *m*.

mus·tard ['mʌstəd] *s* Senf *m*.

mus·ter ['mʌstə] **I** *v/t* **1.** ✠ (zum Appell) antreten lassen; *allg.* zs.-rufen, versammeln. **2.** *j-n, et.* aufbieten. **3.** *a.* **~ up** *fig. s-e Kraft etc* aufbieten: → **courage**. **II** *v/i* **4.** ✠ (zum Appell) antreten; *allg.* sich versammeln. **III** *s* **5.** ✠ (Antreten *n* zum) Appell: **pass ~** *fig.* durchgehen (**with** bei); ganz passabel sein, den Anforderungen genügen.

mustn't ['mʌsnt] F *für* **must not**.

mus·ty ['mʌstɪ] *adj* □ **1.** muffig. **2.** mod(e)rig.

mu·ta·tion [mjuː'teɪʃn] *s* **1.** (Ver)Änderung *f*. **2.** Umwandlung *f*. **3.** *biol.* Mutation *f*.

mute [mjuːt] **I** *adj* □ **1.** stumm (*a. ling.*), *weitS. a.* sprachlos. **II** *s* **2.** Stumme *m, f*. **3.** ♪ Dämpfer *m*. **II** *v/t* **4.** ♪ dämpfen.

mu·ti·late ['mjuːtɪleɪt] *v/t* verstümmeln (*a. fig.*). **,mu·ti'la·tion** *s* Verstümm(e)lung *f*.

mu·ti·neer [ˌmjuːtɪ'nɪə] **I** *s* Meuterer *m*. **II** *v/i* meutern. **'mu·ti·nous** *adj* □ **1.** meuternd. **2.** meuterisch. **'mu·ti·ny I** *s* Meuterei *f*. **II** *v/i* meutern.

mut·ter ['mʌtə] **I** *v/i* **1.** murmeln: **~ (away) to o.s.** vor sich hin murmeln. **2.** murren (**about** über *acc*). **II** *v/t* **3.** murmeln. **III** *s* **4.** Murmeln *n*. **5.** Murren *n*.

mut·ton ['mʌtn] *s* Hammelfleisch *n*: (**as**

dead as ~ F mausetot. ~ *chop* s Hammelkotelett *n*. ‚~'chops *s pl* Koteletten *pl*.

mu·tu·al ['mjuːtʃʊəl] *adj* □ **1.** gegen-, wechselseitig: *be* ~ auf Gegenseitigkeit beruhen; *by* ~ *consent* (*od*. *agreement*) in gegenseitigem Einvernehmen. **2.** gemeinsam.

muz·zle ['mʌzl] **I** *s* **1.** *zo*. Maul *n*, Schnauze *f*. **2.** Maulkorb *m* (*a. fig.*). **3.** Mündung *f* (*e-r Feuerwaffe*). **II** *v/t* **4.** e-n Maulkorb anlegen (*dat*), *fig. a.* mundtot machen.

my [maɪ] *possessive pron* mein(e).

my·o·pi·a [maɪˈəʊpjə] 🞔 Kurzsichtigkeit *f* (*a. fig.*). **my·op·ic** [~ˈɒpɪk] *adj* (~*ally*) 🞔 kurzsichtig (*a. fig.*).

myr·i·ad ['mɪrɪəd] **I** *s* Myriade *f*, *fig. a.* Unzahl *f* → **II** *adj: a* ~ unzählige, zahllose.

myrrh [mɜː] *s* 🞔 Myrrhe *f*.

myr·tle ['mɜːtl] *s* 🞔 Myrte *f*.

my·self [maɪˈself] *pron* **1.** *verstärkend*: ich, mich *od*. mir selbst: *I did it* ~, *I* ~ *did it* ich habe es selbst getan. **2.** *reflex* mich: *I cut* ~. **3.** mich (selbst): *I want it for* ~.

mys·te·ri·ous [mɪˈstɪərɪəs] *adj* mysteriös: a) geheimnisvoll: *be very* ~ *about* ein großes Geheimnis machen aus, b) rätsel-, schleierhaft, unerklärlich. **mys-'te·ri·ous·ly** *adv* auf mysteriöse Weise, unter mysteriösen Umständen.

mys·ter·y ['mɪstəri] *s* **1.** Geheimnis *n*, Rätsel *n* (*to* für *od. dat*): *it is a* (*complete*) ~ *to me* es ist mir (völlig) schleierhaft; *make a* ~ *of* ein Geheimnis machen aus; *wrapped in* ~ in geheimnisvolles Dunkel gehüllt. **2.** *eccl.* Mysterium *n*.

mys·tic ['mɪstɪk] **I** *adj* (~*ally*) mystisch. **II** *s* Mystiker(in). **'mys·ti·cal** → *mystic* I. **mys·ti·cism** ['~sɪzəm] *s* Mystizismus *m*; Mystik *f*.

mys·ti·fy ['mɪstɪfaɪ] *v/t* verwirren, vor ein Rätsel stellen: *be mystified* vor e-m Rätsel stehen.

myth [mɪθ] *s* Mythos *m*, Mythus *m*, *fig. a.* Märchen *n*. **myth·i·cal** ['mɪθɪkl] *adj* □ mythisch, sagenhaft, *fig. a.* erdichtet.

myth·o·log·i·cal [ˌmɪθəˈlɒdʒɪkl] *adj* □ mythologisch. **my·thol·o·gy** [mɪˈθɒlədʒɪ] *s* Mythologie *f*.

N

nab [næb] *v/t* F **1.** schnappen, erwischen. **2.** sich *et.* schnappen.

na·bob ['neɪbɒb] *s* Nabob *m*, Krösus *m*.

na·dir ['neɪdɪə] *s* **1.** *ast.* Nadir *m*, Fußpunkt *m*. **2.** *fig.* Tief-, Nullpunkt *m*: *reach its* ~ den Nullpunkt erreichen.

nag [næg] *v/t* **1.** herumnörgeln an (*dat*). **2.** ~ *s.o. for s.th.* j-m wegen et. in den Ohren liegen; ~ *s.o. into doing s.th.* j-m so lange zusetzen, bis er et. tut; ~ *s.o. to do s.th.* j-m zusetzen, damit er et. tut. **II** *v/i* **3.** nörgeln: ~ *at* → 1. **III** *s* **4.** Nörgler(in). **'nag·ger** *s* Nörgler(in). **'nag·ging I** *s* **1.** Nörgelei *f*. **II** *adj* □ **2.** nörgelnd. **3.** *fig.* nagend, bohrend (*Schmerzen etc*).

nail [neɪl] **I** *s* **1.** (Finger-, Zehen)Nagel *m*. **2.** ⊕ Nagel *m*: (*as*) *hard as* ~*s* a) *a.* (*as*)

tough as ~*s* von eiserner Gesundheit, b) eisern, unerbittlich; → *hit* 7. **II** *v/t* **3.** (an)nageln (*on* auf *acc*; *to* an *acc*): ~*ed to the spot fig.* wie angenagelt; ~ *down* ver-, zunageln; *fig.* j-n festnageln (*to* auf *acc*). ~ *bed s anat.* Nagelbett *n*. ~ *brush s* Nagelbürste *f*. ~ *file s* Nagelfeile *f*. ~ *pol·ish s* Nagellack *m*. ~ *scis·sors s pl*, *a. pair of* ~ Nagelschere *f*. ~ *var·nish s bsd. Br.* Nagellack *m*.

na·ive, na·ïve [naɪˈiːv] *adj* □ naiv (*a. Kunst*). **na·ive·ty** *s* Naivität *f*.

na·ked ['neɪkɪd] *adj* □ *allg.* nackt (*a. fig. Wahrheit etc*), (*Wand etc a.*) kahl: *with the* ~ *eye* mit bloßem Auge. **'na·ked·ness** *s* Nacktheit *f*.

nam·by-pam·by [ˌnæmbɪˈpæmbɪ] **I** *adj* **1.** sentimental. **2.** verweichlicht. **II**

s **3.** Mutterkind *n*, -söhnchen *n*.

name [neɪm] **I** *v/t* **1.** (be)nennen (**after**, *Am. a.* **for** nach): **~d** genannt, namens. **2.** beim Namen nennen. **3.** nennen, erwähnen. **4.** ernennen zu; nominieren, vorschlagen (**for** für); wählen zu; benennen, bekanntgeben. **5.** *Datum etc* festsetzen, bestimmen. **II** *s* **6.** Name *m*: **what is your ~?** wie heißen Sie?; **by ~** mit Namen, namentlich; dem Namen nach; **in the ~ of** im Namen des Gesetzes etc; auf *j-s* Namen *bestellen etc*; **put one's ~ down for** kandidieren für; sich anmelden für; sich vormerken lassen für. **7.** Name *m*, Bezeichnung *f*. **8.** Schimpfname *m*: **call s.o. ~s** *j*-n beschimpfen *od.* verspotten. **9.** Name *m*, Ruf *m*: **get a bad ~** in Verruf kommen; **have a bad ~** in schlechtem Ruf stehen. **10.** (berühmter) Name, (guter) Ruf: **a man of ~** ein Mann von Ruf; **have a ~ for being ...** im Rufe stehen; **make a ~ for o.s.** sich e-n Namen machen (**as** als). **~ day** *s* Namenstag *m*. **'~-drop-per** *s* F *j-d*, *der dadurch Eindruck schindet*, *daß er ständig (angeblich) prominente Bekannte erwähnt*.

name·less ['neɪmlɪs] *adj* □ **1.** namenlos, unbekannt. **2.** ungenannt, unerwähnt. **3.** *fig.* namenlos, unbeschreiblich; unaussprechlich.

name·ly ['neɪmlɪ] *adv* nämlich.

name| plate *s* Namensschild *n*. **'~·sake** *s* Namensvetter *m*, -schwester *f*. **~ tag** *s* (*am Revers etc getragenes*) Namensschild.

nan·ny ['nænɪ] *s bsd. Br.* **1.** Kindermädchen *n*. **2.** Oma *f*, Omi *f*. **~ goat** *s* Geiß *f*, Ziege *f*.

nap [næp] **I** *v/i* ein Schläfchen *od.* Nickerchen machen: **catch s.o. ~ping** *j*-n überrumpeln *od.* -raschen. **II** *s* Schläfchen *n*, Nickerchen *n*: **have** (*od.* **take**) **a ~** → I.

na·palm ['neɪpɑːm] *s* Napalm *n*: **~ bomb** ⚔ Napalmbombe *f*.

nape [neɪp] *s mst* **~ of the neck** Genick *n*.

nap·kin ['næpkɪn] *s* **1.** Serviette *f*: **~ ring** Serviettenring *m*. **2.** *bsd. Br.* Windel *f*.

nap·py ['næpɪ] *s bsd. Br.* F Windel *f*.

nar·cis·si [nɑːˈsɪsaɪ] *pl von* **narcissus**.

nar·cis·sism ['nɑːsɪsɪzəm] *s psych.* Narzißmus *m*. **'nar·cis·sist** *s* Narziß(in).

nar·cis'sis·tic *adj* (**~ally**) narzißtisch.

nar·cis·sus [nɑːˈsɪsəs] *pl* **-'cis·sus·es**, **-'cis·si** [~saɪ] *s* ♣ Narzisse *f*.

nar·co·sis [nɑːˈkəʊsɪs] *pl* **-ses** [~siːz] ✚ Narkose *f*.

nar·cot·ic [nɑːˈkɒtɪk] **I** *adj* (**~ally**) **1.** narkotisch, betäubend, einschläfernd (*a. fig.*). **2.** Rauschgift...: **~ addiction** Rauschgiftsucht *f*. **II** *s* **3.** Narkotikum *n*, Betäubungsmittel *n*. **4.** *oft pl* Rauschgift *n*.

nark [nɑːk] *Br. sl.* **I** *s* (Polizei)Spitzel *m*. **II** *v/t* ärgern.

nar·rate [nəˈreɪt] *v/t* **1.** erzählen. **2.** berichten, schildern. **nar'ra·tion** *s* Erzählung *f*. **nar·ra·tive** ['nærətɪv] **I** *s* **1.** Erzählung *f*. **2.** Bericht *m*, Schilderung *f*. **II** *adj* **3.** erzählend: **~ perspective** Erzählperspektive *f*. **4.** Erzählungs...

nar·row ['nærəʊ] **I** *adj* □ **~ a. narrow·ly**) **1.** eng, schmal. **2.** eng (*a. fig.*), (*räumlich*) beschränkt: **in the ~est sense** im engsten Sinne. **3.** zs.-gekniffen (*Augen*). **4.** *fig.* eingeschränkt, beschränkt. **5.** *fig.* knapp, dürftig (*Einkommen etc*). **6.** *fig.* knapp (*Mehrheit*, *Sieg etc*): **by a ~ margin** knapp, mit knappem Vorsprung; **win by a ~ majority** knapp gewinnen; → **escape** 8, **squeak** 6. **7.** *fig.* gründlich, eingehend (*Untersuchung etc*). **II** *v/i* **8.** enger *od.* schmäler werden, sich verengen ([*in*]*to* zu): **his eyes ~ed to slits** s-e Augen wurden zu Schlitzen. **9.** *fig.* knapp(er) werden, zs.-schrumpfen (**to** auf *acc*). **10.** *fig.* sich annähern (*Standpunkte etc*). **III** *v/t* **11.** enger *od.* schmäler machen, verenge(r)n, *Augen* zs.-kneifen. **12.** *a.* **~ down** *fig.* be-, einschränken (**to** auf *acc*); eingrenzen. **'nar·row·ly** *adv* mit knapper Not: **he ~ escaped death** er ist gerade noch mit dem Leben davongekommen; **he ~ escaped drowning** er wäre beinahe *od.* um ein Haar ertrunken.

na·sal ['neɪzl] **I** *adj* □ **1.** *anat.* Nasen...: **~ bone** Nasenbein *n*. **2.** a) näselnd (*Stimme*): → **twang**, b) *ling.* nasal, Nasal... **II** *s* **3.** *ling.* Nasal(laut) *m*.

nas·ty ['nɑːstɪ] *adj* □ **1.** ekelhaft, eklig, widerlich (*Geschmack etc*); abscheulich (*Verbrechen*, *Wetter etc*). **2.** schmutzig, zotig (*Buch etc*). **3.** bös, schlimm (*Unfall etc*). **4.** a) häßlich (*Charakter*, *Benehmen etc*), b) gemein, fies (*Person*,

Trick etc), c) übelgelaunt: **turn** ~ unangenehm werden. **II** *s* **5.** *Br.* F *pornographische od. gewaltverherrlichende Videokassette.*

na·tal ['neɪtl] *adj* Geburts...

na·tion ['neɪʃn] *s* Nation *f:* a) Volk *n,* b) Staat *m.*

na·tion·al ['næʃənl] **I** *adj* □ **1.** national, National..., Landes..., Volks...: ~ *anthem* Nationalhymne *f;* ~ *championship* (*Sport*) Landesmeisterschaft *f;* ~ *currency* ✝ Landeswährung *f;* ⚺ *Guard Am.* Nationalgarde *f;* ~ *language* Landessprache *f;* ~ *park* Nationalpark *m;* ~ *team* (*Sport*) Nationalmannschaft *f.* **2.** staatlich, öffentlich, Staats...: ⚺ *Health Service Br.* Staatlicher Gesundheitsdienst. **3.** landesweit (*Streik etc*), überregional (*Sender, Zeitung etc*); inländisch: ~ *call* teleph. Inlandsgespräch *n.* **II** *s* **4.** Staatsangehörige *m, f.* **na·tion·al·ism** ['næʃnəlɪzəm] *s* Nationalismus *m.* '**na·tion·al·ist** *I s* Nationalist(in). **II** *adj* nationalistisch. ˌ**na·tion·al'is·tic** *adj* (⟨⟨*ally*⟩) nationalistisch. **na·tion·al·i·ty** [ˌnæʃə'nælətɪ] *s* **1.** Nationalität *f,* Staatsangehörigkeit *f:* **have French** ~ die französische Staatsangehörigkeit besitzen *od.* haben. ˌ**na·-tion·al·i·za·tion** [ˌnæʃnəlaɪ'zeɪʃn] *s* ✝ Verstaatlichung *f.* '**na·tion·al·ize** *v/t* ✝ verstaatlichen.

'**na·tion-wide** *adj u. adv* landesweit.

na·tive ['neɪtɪv] **I** *adj* □ **1.** eingeboren, Eingeborenen... **2.** einheimisch, inländisch, Landes... **3.** heimatlich, Heimat...: ~ *country* Heimat *f,* Vaterland *n;* ~ *language* Muttersprache *f;* ~ *speaker* Muttersprachler(in); ~ *speaker of English* englischer Muttersprachler; ~ *town* Heimat-, Vaterstadt *f.* **II** *s* **4.** Eingeborene *m, f.* **5.** Einheimische *m, f:* **a** ~ **of London** ein gebürtiger Londoner; **are you a** ~ **here?** sind Sie von hier?

Na·tiv·i·ty [nə'tɪvətɪ] *s die* Geburt Christi (*a. Kunst*): ~ *play* Krippenspiel *n.*

nat·ter ['nætə] *bsd. Br.* F **I** *v/i a.* ~ *away* schwatzen, plaudern. **II** *s* Schwatz *m,* Plausch *m:* **have a** ~ e-n Schwatz *od.* Plausch halten.

nat·u·ral ['nætʃrəl] **I** *adj* (□ → *naturally*) **1.** natürlich, Natur...: ~ *blonde* echte Blondine; *die a* ~ *death* e-s natürlichen

Todes sterben; ~ *disaster* Naturkatastrophe *f;* ~ *gas* Erdgas *n;* ~ *resources pl* Naturschätze *pl;* ~ *science* Naturwissenschaft *f;* ~ *scientist* Naturwissenschaftler(in). **2.** naturgemäß, -bedingt. **3.** angeboren, eigen (**to** *dat*): ~ *talent* natürliche Begabung. **4.** natürlich, selbstverständlich. **5.** natürlich, ungekünstelt (*Benehmen etc*). **6.** naturgetreu, natürlich wirkend. **7.** Natur..., Roh..., (*Lebensmittel*) naturbelassen. **8.** leiblich (*Eltern etc*). **II** *s* **9.** ♪ Auflösungszeichen *n.* **10.** F Naturtalent *n* (*Person*). '**nat·u·ral·ism** *s* Naturalismus *m.* '**nat·u·ral·ist** *I s* Naturalist(in). **II** *adj* naturalistisch. ˌ**nat·u·ral'is·tic** *adj* (⟨⟨*ally*⟩) naturalistisch. **nat·u·ral·i·za·tion** [ˌnætʃrəlaɪ'zeɪʃn] *s* Naturalisierung *f,* Einbürgerung *f.* '**nat·u·ral·ize** *v/t* **1.** naturalisieren, einbürgern: **become ~d** *fig.* sich einbürgern (*Wort etc*). **2.** ♀, *zo.* heimisch machen: **become** ~ heimisch werden. '**nat·u·ral·ly** *adv* **1.** *a. int* natürlich. **2.** von Natur (aus). **3.** instinktiv, spontan: *learning comes* ~ *to him* das Lernen fällt ihm leicht. **4.** auf natürlichem Wege.

na·ture ['neɪtʃə] *s* **1.** *allg.* Natur *f:* **back to** ~ zurück zur Natur. **2.** Natur *f,* Wesen *n,* Veranlagung *f:* **by** ~ von Natur (aus); *it is (in) her* ~ es liegt in ihrem Wesen; → *alien* 3, *second*¹ 1. **3.** Art *f,* Sorte *f:* **of a grave** ~ ernster Natur. **4.** (natürliche) Beschaffenheit.

naught·y ['nɔːtɪ] *adj* □ **1.** ungezogen, unartig. **2.** unanständig (*Witz etc*).

nau·se·a ['nɔːsjə] *s* Übelkeit *f,* Brechreiz *m.* **nau·se·ate** ['~sɪeɪt] *v/t* Übelkeit erregen in (*dat*); *fig.* anwidern.

nau·ti·cal ['nɔːtɪkl] *adj* □ nautisch, See(fahrts)...: ~ *mile* Seemeile *f.*

na·val ['neɪvl] *adj* **1.** Flotten..., Marine...: ~ *base* Flottenstützpunkt *m;* ~ *officer* Marineoffizier *m;* ~ *power* Seemacht *f;* ~ *review* Flottenparade *f.* **2.** See..., Schiffs...: ~ *battle* Seeschlacht *f.*

nave [neɪv] *s* △ Mittel-, Hauptschiff *n.*

na·vel ['neɪvl] *s anat.* Nabel *m, fig. a.* Mittelpunkt *m.* ~ *or·ange s* Navelorange *f.*

nav·i·ga·ble ['nævɪɡəbl] *adj* ⚓ schiffbar.

nav·i·gate ['~ɡeɪt] *v/t* **1.** ⚓ befahren; durchfahren. **2.** ✈, ⚓ steuern, lenken. ˌ**nav·i'ga·tion** *s* **1.** Schiffahrt *f,* Seefahrt f. 2. ✎, ⚓ Navigation f. **'nav·i·ga·tor** s ✎, ⚓ Navigator m.

nav·vy ['nævɪ] s Erd- od. Bauarbeiter m.

na·vy ['neɪvɪ] s 1. (Kriegs)Marine f. 2. Kriegsflotte f. ~ **blue** s Marineblau n.

nay [neɪ] s parl. Gegen-, Neinstimme f: **the ~s have it** die Mehrheit ist dagegen.

near [nɪə] **I** adv 1. a. ~ **at hand** nahe, (ganz) in der Nähe. 2. a. ~ **at hand** nahe (bevorstehend) (Zeitpunkt etc). 3. nahezu, beinahe, fast: ~ **impossible; she came ~ to tears** sie war den Tränen nahe; → **nowhere** 1. **II** adj (□ ~ **nearly**) 4. nahe(gelegen): ⌖ **East** geogr. der Nahe Osten. 5. kurz, nahe (Weg). 6. nahe (Zukunft etc). 7. nahe (verwandt): **the ~est relations** pl die nächsten Verwandten pl. 8. eng (befreundet): **a ~ friend** ein guter od. enger Freund. 9. knapp: ~ **miss** ✎ Beinahezusammenstoß m; **be a ~ miss** knapp scheitern; **that was a ~ thing** F das hätte ins Auge gehen können, das ist gerade noch einmal gutgegangen. 10. genau, wörtlich (Übersetzung etc). **III** prp 11. nahe (dat), in der Nähe von (od. gen): ~ **here** nicht weit von hier; hier in der Nähe. **IV** v/t u. v/i 12. sich nähern, näherkommen (dat): **be ~ing completion** der Vollendung entgegensehen. ~**by I** adj [nɪə'baɪ] in der Nähe. **II** adj ['nɪəbaɪ] nahe(gelegen).

near·ly ['nɪəlɪ] adv 1. beinahe, fast. 2. annähernd: **not ~** bei weitem nicht, nicht annähernd.

near'sight·ed adj □ ✦ kurzsichtig. ~'**sight·ed·ness** s Kurzsichtigkeit f.

neat [niːt] adj □ 1. sauber: a) ordentlich, reinlich: **keep ~** et. sauberhalten, b) übersichtlich, c) geschickt: **a ~ solution** e-e saubere od. elegante Lösung. 2. pur: **drink one's whisky ~; two ~ whiskies** zwei Whisky pur.

neb·u·lous ['nebjʊləs] adj □ fig. verschwommen, nebelhaft.

nec·es·sar·i·ly ['nesəsərəlɪ] adv 1. notwendigerweise. 2. **not ~** nicht unbedingt. '**nec·es·sar·y I** adj 1. notwendig, nötig, erforderlich (**to, for** für): **it is ~ for me to do it** ich muß es tun; **a ~ evil** ein notwendiges Übel; **if ~** nötigenfalls. 2. unvermeidlich, zwangsläufig, notwendig (Konsequenz etc). **II** s 3. **necessaries** pl **of life** Lebensbedürfnisse pl.

ne·ces·si·tate [nɪ'sesɪteɪt] v/t et. notwendig od. erforderlich machen, erfordern: ~ **doing s.th.** es notwendig machen, et. zu tun. **ne·ces·si·ty** s 1. Notwendigkeit f: **of** (od. **by**) ~ notgedrungen; **be under the ~ of doing s.th.** gezwungen sein, et. zu tun. 2. (dringendes) Bedürfnis: **necessities** pl **of life** lebensnotwendiger Bedarf; **be a ~ of life** lebensnotwendig sein. 3. Not f: ~ **is the mother of invention** Not macht erfinderisch; **in case of** ~ im Notfall; → **virtue** 2.

neck [nek] **I** s 1. Hals m (a. e-r Flasche etc): **be ~ and ~** Kopf an Kopf liegen (a. fig.); **be up to one's ~ in debt** bis an den Hals in Schulden stecken; **it is ~ or nothing** es geht um alles od. nichts; **risk one's ~** Kopf u. Kragen riskieren; **save one's ~** den Kopf aus der Schlinge ziehen; **stick out one's ~** einiges riskieren. 2. Genick n: **break one's ~** sich das Genick brechen; **get it in the ~** F eins aufs Dach bekommen. 3. → **neckline**. 4. gastr. Halsstück n (**of lamb** vom Lamm). **II** v/i 5. F knutschen, schmusen. ~**-and-'~** adj: ~ **race** Kopf-an-Kopf-Rennen n (a. fig.).

neck·lace ['neklɪs] s Halskette f. **neck·let** ['~lɪt] s Halskettchen n. '**neck·line** s Ausschnitt m (e-s Kleids etc): **with a low** (od. **plunging**) ~ tief ausgeschnitten. '~**tie** s Am. Krawatte f, Schlips m.

nec·tar ['nektə] s ⚘ Nektar m.

née, nee [neɪ] adj bei Frauennamen: geborene.

need [niːd] **I** s 1. (**of, for**) (dringendes) Bedürfnis (nach), Bedarf m (an dat): **in ~ of help** hilfs-, hilfebedürftig; **in ~ of repair** reparaturbedürftig; **be in ~ of s.th.** et. dringend brauchen. 2. Mangel m (**of, for** an dat). 3. dringende Notwendigkeit: **there is no ~ for you to come** du brauchst nicht zu kommen. 4. Not(lage) f: **in ~** notleidend, in Not. 5. Armut f, Not f: **in ~** in Not. 6. pl Bedürfnisse pl, Erfordernisse pl. **II** v/t 7. benötigen, brauchen: **your hair ~s cutting** du mußt dir wieder einmal die Haare schneiden lassen. 8. erfordern. **III** v/aux 9. brauchen, müssen: **she need not do it** sie braucht es nicht zu tun; **you ~ not have come** du hättest nicht zu kommen brauchen.

nee·dle ['niːdl] **I** s **1.** allg. Nadel f, ☼ a. Zeiger m: **a ~ in a haystack** fig. e-e Stecknadel im Heuhaufen. **II** v/t **2.** F j-n aufziehen, hänseln (**about** wegen). **3. ~ one's way through** sich (durch-) schlängeln durch.

need·less ['niːdlɪs] adj unnötig, überflüssig: **~ to say** selbstverständlich, natürlich. '**need·less·ly** adv unnötig(erweise).

'**nee·dle·work** s Hand-, Nadelarbeit f: **do ~** handarbeiten; **~ magazine** Handarbeitsheft n.

neg [neg] s phot. F Negativ n.

ne·gate [nɪ'ɡeɪt] v/t **1.** verneinen. **2.** Wirkung etc neutralisieren, aufheben. **ne·ga·tion** s **1.** Verneinung f. **2.** Neutralisierung f, Aufhebung f.

neg·a·tive ['neɡətɪv] **I** adj □ **1.** negativ (a. ⚡, ♈, ♂ etc): a) verneinend: **he was ~** ♈ sein Befund war negativ; **~ pole** ⚡ Minuspol m; **~ sign** Minuszeichen n, negatives Vorzeichen n, b) abschlägig, ablehnend. **II** s **2.** Verneinung f (a. ling.): **answer in the ~** verneinen; **his answer was in the ~** s-e Antwort fiel negativ aus. **3.** abschlägige Antwort. **4.** negative Eigenschaft. **5.** phot. Negativ n.

ne·glect [nɪ'ɡlekt] **I** v/t **1.** vernachlässigen: **~ed** ungepflegt (Erscheinung etc), verwahrlost (Kind etc). **2.** es versäumen od. unterlassen (**doing, to do** zu tun). **II** s **3.** Vernachlässigung f: **be in a state of ~** vernachlässigt od. verwahrlost sein. **4.** Versäumnis n, Unterlassung f: **~ of duty** Pflichtversäumnis n. **ne·glect·ful** [~fʊl] → **negligent** 1.

neg·li·gee, neg·li·gé(e) ['neɡlɪʒeɪ] s Negligé n.

neg·li·gence ['neɡlɪdʒəns] s **1.** Nachlässigkeit f, Unachtsamkeit f: **dress with ~** sich nachlässig kleiden. **2.** ♈ Fahrlässigkeit f. '**neg·li·gent** adj □ **1.** nachlässig, unachtsam: **be ~ of** j-n od. et. vernachlässigen, et. außer acht lassen. **2.** ♈ fahrlässig. **3.** lässig, salopp.

neg·li·gi·ble ['neɡlɪdʒəbl] adj □ **1.** nebensächlich, unwesentlich. **2.** geringfügig, unbedeutend, nicht der Rede wert.

ne·go·ti·a·ble [nɪ'ɡəʊʃjəbl] adj □ **1.** ♈ verkäuflich; übertragbar, begebbar. **2.** passier-, befahrbar (Straße etc).

ne·go·ti·ate [nɪ'ɡəʊʃɪeɪt] **I** v/i **1.** verhan-

deln (**with** mit; **for, about, on** über acc): **negotiating skills** pl Verhandlungsgeschick n; **negotiating table** Verhandlungstisch m. **II** v/t **2.** Vertrag etc aushandeln (**with** mit). **3.** verhandeln über (acc). **4.** ♈ verkaufen; Wechsel begeben. **5.** Straße etc passieren, Hindernis etc überwinden, Steigung etc schaffen; Musikstück etc meistern. **ne·go·ti·a·tion** s **1.** Verhandlung f: **by way of ~** auf dem Verhandlungsweg; **it is still under ~** darüber wird noch verhandelt. **2.** Aushandeln n. **3.** ♈ Verkauf m; Begebung f. **4.** Passieren n, Überwindung f.

Ne·gress ['niːɡrɪs] s Negerin f. **Ne·gro** ['niːɡrəʊ] pl **-groes** s Neger m.

neigh [neɪ] **I** v/i wiehern. **II** s Wiehern n.

neigh·bo(u)r ['neɪbə] **I** s Nachbar(in): **~ at table** Tischnachbar(in). **II** v/t (a. v/i **~ on**) (an)grenzen an (acc). '**neigh·bo(u)r·hood** [~hʊd] s **1.** Nachbarschaft f (a. Nachbarn pl): **in the ~ of** in der Umgebung von (od. gen); fig. um (... herum). **2.** Gegend f, Viertel n. '**neigh·bo(u)r·ing** adj benachbart, angrenzend; Nachbar... '**neigh·bo(u)r·ly** adj **1.** (gut)nachbarlich. **2.** Nachbarschafts...: → **help**.

nei·ther ['naɪðə] **I** adj u. pron **1.** kein (von beiden): **~ of you** keiner von euch (beiden). **II** cj **2.** ~ ... nor weder ... noch. **3.** auch nicht: **he does not know, ~ do I** er weiß es nicht, u. ich auch nicht.

ne·ol·o·gism [niː'ɒlədʒɪzəm] s ling. Neologismus m, Neuwort n.

ne·on ['niːən] s ♈ Neon n: **~ lamp** Neonlampe f; **~ sign** Neon-, Leuchtreklame f.

neph·ew ['nevjuː] s Neffe m.

ne·phri·tis [nɪ'fraɪtɪs] s ♈ Nierenentzündung f.

nep·o·tism ['nepətɪzəm] s Vetternwirtschaft f.

nerve [nɜːv] **I** s **1.** Nerv m: **get on s.o.'s ~s** j-m auf die Nerven gehen od. fallen; **get ~s** F Nerven bekommen; **have ~s of iron (steel)** eiserne Nerven (Nerven aus Stahl) haben; **hit (od. touch) a ~** e-n wunden Punkt treffen; **get (od. bundle) of ~s** F Nervenbündel n. **2.** fig. Stärke f, Energie f; Mut m; Selbstbeherrschung f; F Frechheit f: **have the ~ to do s.th.** den Nerv haben, et. zu tun; **lose one's ~** den Mut od. die Nerven verlieren. **II** v/t **3.** ~ **o.s.** sich moralisch od. seelisch vorbereiten (**for** auf acc). ~ **cell** s Nervenzelle f. ~ **cen·tre** (Am. **cen·ter**) s **1.** Nervenzentrum n. **2.** fig. Schaltzentrale f.

nerve·less ['nɜːvlɪs] adj □ **1.** kraft-, energielos; mutlos. **2.** ohne Nerven, kaltblütig. '**nerve-ˌrack·ing** adj nervenaufreibend.

nerv·ous ['nɜːvəs] adj □ **1.** Nerven..., nervös: ~ **system** Nervensystem n; ~ **breakdown** 1, **collapse** 10. **2.** nervös: **make s.o.** ~ j-n nervös machen (**with** mit). '**nerv·ous·ness** s Nervosität f.

nerv·y ['nɜːvɪ] adj □ F **1.** Br. nervös, ängstlich. **2.** Am. frech, unverfroren.

nest [nest] **I** s **1.** orn., zo. Nest n: ~ **feather** II, **foul** 9. **2.** fig. Brutstätte f. **3.** Serie f, Satz m (ineinanderpassender Dinge). **II** v/i **4.** nisten. ~ **egg** s **1.** Nestei n. **2.** fig. Spar-, Notgroschen m.

nes·tle ['nesl] **I** v/i **1.** a. ~ **down** sich behaglich niederlassen, es sich bequem machen (**in** in dat). **2.** sich schmiegen od. kuscheln (**against, to** an acc). **II** v/t **3.** schmiegen, kuscheln (**against, to** an acc).

net¹ [net] **I** s **1.** Netz n (a. fig.): ~ **curtain** Store m. **II** v/t **2.** mit e-m Netz fangen. **3.** fig. einfangen. **4.** mit e-m Netz abdecken.

net² [~] † **I** adj **1.** netto, Netto..., Rein... **II** v/t **2.** netto einbringen. **3.** netto verdienen od. einnehmen.

net·ting ['netɪŋ] s Netz(werk) n, Geflecht n.

net·tle ['netl] **I** s ♣ Nessel f: **grasp the** ~ fig. den Stier bei den Hörnern packen. **II** v/t ärgern, reizen (**with** mit). ~ **rash** s ♣ Nesselausschlag m.

'**net·work** s **1.** Netz(werk) n, Geflecht n. **2.** fig. (Händler-, Straßen- etc)Netz n: ~ **social** ~ soziales Netz. **3.** Rundfunk, TV: Sendernetz n.

neu·ral·gia [ˌnjʊəˈrældʒə] s ♣ Neuralgie f. ˌ**neu·ral·gic** adj (ˌ**ally**) neuralgisch.

neu·ri·tis [ˌnjʊəˈraɪtɪs] s ♣ Nervenentzündung f.

neu·ro·log·i·cal [ˌnjʊərəˈlɒdʒɪkl] adj ♣ neurologisch. **neu·rol·o·gist** [~ˈrɒlədʒɪst] s Neurologe m, Nervenarzt m. ˌ**neu·rol·o·gy** s Neurologie f.

neu·ro·sis [ˌnjʊəˈrəʊsɪs] pl **-ses** [~siːz] s ♣ Neurose f. **neu·rot·ic** [~ˈrɒtɪk] **I** adj

(~**ally**) neurotisch (a. contp.). **II** s Neurotiker(in).

neu·ter ['njuːtə] **I** adj **1.** ling. neutral, sächlich. **2.** biol. geschlechtslos, ungeschlechtlich. **II** s **3.** ling. Neutrum n. **III** v/t **4.** zo. kastrieren.

neu·tral ['njuːtrəl] **I** adj □ **1.** allg. neutral. **II** s **2.** Neutrale m, f. **3.** mot. Leerlaufstellung f: **the car is in** ~ es ist kein Gang eingelegt; **put the car in** ~ den Gang herausnehmen. **neu·tral·i·ty** [~ˈtrælətɪ] s Neutralität f. **neu·tral·i·za·tion** [ˌ~trəlaɪˈzeɪʃn] s Neutralisierung f, a. ♠ Neutralisation f. '**neu·tral·ize** v/t neutralisieren; ~ **each other** sich gegenseitig aufheben.

neu·tron ['njuːtrɒn] s phys. Neutron n: ~ **bomb** ✗ Neutronenbombe f.

nev·er ['nevə] adv **1.** nie(mals): → **die¹** 1. **2.** durchaus nicht, ganz u. gar nicht: → **mind** 10. '~ˌ**end·ing** adj endlos, nicht enden wollend. ˌ~·'**nev·er** s: **buy s.th. on the** ~ Br. F et. auf Pump od. Stottern kaufen.

ˌ**nev·er·the·less** adv nichtsdestoweniger, dennoch, trotzdem.

new [njuː] adj (□ → **newly**) allg. neu: **nothing** ~ nichts Neues; **this is not** ~ **to me** das ist mir nichts Neues; **be** ~ **to s.o.** j-m neu od. ungewohnt sein; **be** ~ **to s.th.** (noch) nicht vertraut sein mit et.; **feel a** ~ **man** sich wie neugeboren fühlen; ~ **moon** Neumond m; ~ **publications** pl Neuerscheinungen pl; ~ **snow** Neuschnee m; ♀ **Testament** das Neue Testament; ♀ **World** die Neue Welt; → **broom, leaf** 2. '~·**born** adj neugeboren. '~ˌ**com·er** s **1.** Neuankömmling m. **2.** Neuling m (**to** auf e-m Gebiet). '~·**fan·gled** ['~ˌfæŋgld] adj contp. neumodisch.

new·ly ['njuːlɪ] adv **1.** kürzlich, jüngst: ~ **married** jungverheiratet, -vermählt. **2.** neu: ~ **arranged furniture** umgestellte Möbel pl; ~ **raised hope** neuerweckte Hoffnung. '~·**weds** s pl die Jungverheirateten pl od. -vermählten pl.

news [njuːz] s pl (sg konstruiert) Neuigkeit(en pl) f, Nachricht(en pl) f: **a bit** (od. **piece**) **of** ~ e-e Neuigkeit od. Nachricht; **at this** ~ bei dieser Nachricht; **what's the** ~? was gibt es Neues?; **this is** ~ **to me** das ist mir (ganz) neu; **have** ~ **from s.o.** Nachricht von j-m haben; **I**

haven't had any ~ *from her for two months* ich habe schon seit zwei Monaten nichts mehr von ihr gehört; *I heard it on the* ~ ich hörte es in den Nachrichten. ~ **a·gen·cy** s Nachrichtenagentur f. '~**a·gent** s Zeitungshändler(in).

black·out s Nachrichtensperre f: *order a* ~ *on* e-e Nachrichtensperre verhängen über (acc). '~**boy** s Zeitungsjunge m. '~**cast** s Rundfunk, TV: Nachrichtensendung f. '~**cast·er** s Rundfunk, TV: Nachrichtensprecher(in). ~ **con·fer·ence** → **press conference**. ~ **deal·er** s Am. Zeitungshändler(in). ~ **flash** s Rundfunk, TV: Kurzmeldung f. '~**let·ter** s Rundschreiben n, Mitteilungsblatt n. ~ **mag·a·zine** s Nachrichtenmagazin n. ~**pa·per** [ˈnjuːzˌpeɪpə] s Zeitung f: ~ **publisher** Zeitungsverleger(in); ~ **rack** Zeitungsständer m. '~**read·er** → **newscaster**. '~**stand** s Zeitungskiosk m, -stand m. ~ **ven·dor** s Zeitungsverkäufer(in).

new| year s oft **New Year** das neue Jahr: *happy New Year!* gutes neues Jahr!, Prosit Neujahr! ♀ **Year's Day** s Neujahr(stag m) n. ♀ **Year's Eve** s Silvester(abend m) m, n.

next [nekst] **I** adj **1.** allg. nächst: (the) ~ **day** am nächsten Tag; ~ **door** nebenan, im nächsten Raum od. Haus; **be** ~ **door to** fig. grenzen an (acc); ~ **month** nächsten Monat; ~ **time** das nächste Mal; ~ **but one** übernächst; ~ **to** a) gleich neben (dat od. acc); gleich nach (Rang, Reihenfolge); beinahe, fast unmöglich etc, so gut wie nichts etc, praktisch zwecklos etc. **II** adv **2.** als nächste(r, -s): **you will be** ~ du wirst der nächste sein. **3.** demnächst, das nächste Mal. **4.** dann, darauf. **III** s **5.** der, die, das nächste: **the next** pl **of kin** die nächsten Angehörigen pl od. Verwandten pl. '~**door** adj (von) nebenan: **we are** ~ **neighbo(u)rs** wir wohnen Tür an Tür.

NHS [ˌenertʃˈes] Br. **I** s Staatlicher Gesundheitsdienst: **get s.th. on the** ~ **I** auf Krankenschein od. Rezept bekommen. **II** adj a) Kassen...: ~ **glasses**, b) Behandlung etc auf Krankenschein: ~ **treatment**.

nib·ble [ˈnɪbl] **I** v/t **1.** knabbern an (dat). **2.** Loch etc knabbern, nagen (**in** in acc). **II** v/i **3.** knabbern (**at** an dat): ~ **at one's**

food im Essen herumstochern. **III** s **4.** Knabbern n.

nice [naɪs] adj **1.** fein (Unterschied etc). **2.** fein, lecker (Speise etc). **3.** nett, freundlich (**to** zu j-m). **4.** nett, hübsch, schön: ~ **and warm** schön warm; → **mess** 1. '**nice·ly** adv **1.** gut, fein: **that will do** ~ das genügt vollauf; das paßt ausgezeichnet; **she is doing** ~ es geht ihr gut od. besser, sie macht gute Fortschritte. **2.** genau, sorgfältig. **ni·ce·ty** [ˈnaɪsətɪ] s **1.** Feinheit f. **2.** peinliche Genauigkeit: **to a** ~ peinlich od. äußerst genau. **3.** pl feine Unterschiede pl, Feinheiten pl.

niche [nɪtʃ] s **1.** Nische f. **2.** fig. Platz m, wo man hingehört: **he has finally found his** ~ **in life** er hat endlich s-n Platz im Leben gefunden.

nick [nɪk] **I** s **1.** Kerbe f, Einkerbung f. **2.** **in the** ~ **of time** gerade noch rechtzeitig, im letzten Moment. **3.** Br. F Kittchen n: **in the** ~ im Kittchen. **4. be in good** ~ Br. F gut in Schuß sein. **II** v/t **5.** a) (ein)kerben: ~ **o.s. while shaving** sich beim Rasieren schneiden, b) j-n streifen (Kugel). **6.** Br. F klauen. **7.** Br. F j-n schnappen. **8.** ~ **s.o. (for)** $ 100 Am. F j-m 100 Dollar abknöpfen.

nick·el [ˈnɪkl] **I** s **1.** 🜍, min. Nickel n. **2.** Am. Fünfcentstück n. **II** v/t pret u. pp **-eled**, bsd. Br. **-elled 3.** vernickeln. '~**plate** v/t vernickeln.

nick·name [ˈnɪkneɪm] **I** s Spitzname m. **II** v/t j-m den Spitznamen ... geben.

nic·o·tine [ˈnɪkətiːn] s Nikotin n.

niece [niːs] s Nichte f.

niff [nɪf] s Br. F Gestank m. '**niff·y** adj Br. F stinkend: **be** ~ stinken.

nif·ty [ˈnɪftɪ] adj □ F **1.** flott, fesch (Kleidung, Person). **2.** praktisch (Gerät).

nig·gard [ˈnɪɡəd] s Knicker(in), Geizhals m. '**nig·gard·ly** adj **1.** geizig, knick(e)rig. **2.** schäbig, kümmerlich.

nig·gle [ˈnɪɡl] v/i **1.** herumnörgeln (**a·bout, over** an dat). **2.** ~ **at** fig. nagen an (dat), plagen, quälen.

night [naɪt] s **1.** Nacht f: **at** (od. **by, in the**) ~ in der od. bei Nacht, nachts; ~ **and day** Tag u. Nacht; **have a good** (**bad**) ~ gut (schlecht) schlafen; **make a** ~ **of it** bis zum Morgen feiern, durchmachen; **stay the** ~ übernachten (**at** in dat; **at s.o.'s** bei j-m). **2.** Abend m: **last** ~ gestern abend; **the** ~ **before last** vorgestern nacht; *on the ~ of May 5th* am Abend des 5. Mai. **3.** Nacht *f*, Dunkelheit *f*. **~ bird** *s* **1.** orn. Nachtvogel *m*. **2.** *fig.* Nachtmensch *m*; Nachtschwärmer *m*. **'~blind** *adj* 🐟 nachtblind. **~ blindness** *s* 🐟 Nachtblindheit *f*. **'~cap** *s* Schlummertrunk *m*. **'~club** *s* Nachtklub *m*, -lokal *n*. **'~dress** *s* Nachthemd *n*. **'~fall** *s*: *at ~* bei Einbruch der Dunkelheit. **~ flight** *s* Nachtflug *m*. **'~gown** *s* Nachthemd *n*.

night·ie ['naɪtɪ] *s* F Nachthemd *n*.

night·in·gale ['naɪtɪŋgeɪl] *s* orn. Nachtigall *f*.

night life *s* Nachtleben *n*.

night·ly ['naɪtlɪ] I *adj* (all)nächtlich; (all)abendlich. II *adv* jede Nacht; jeden Abend.

night·mare ['naɪtmeə] *s* Alptraum *m* (*a. fig.*).

night| nurse *s* Nachtschwester *f*. **~ owl** *s* F Nachteule *f*, -mensch *m*; Nachtschwärmer *m*. **~ por·ter** *s* Nachtportier *m*. **~ school** *s* Abendschule *f*. **~ shift** *s* Nachtschicht *f*: *be* (*od. work*) *on ~* Nachtschicht haben. **'~shirt** *s* Nachthemd *n*. **'~spot** *s* → **nightclub**. **'~stick** *s Am.* Gummiknüppel *m*, Schlagstock *m* (*der Polizei*). **'~time** *s*: *in the* (*od. at*) *~* zur Nachtzeit, nachts. **~ watch** *s* Nachtwache *f*. **~ watch·man** *s* (*irr man*) Nachtwächter *m*.

ni·hil·ism ['naɪlɪzəm] *s* Nihilismus *m*. **'ni·hil·ist** I *s* Nihilist(in). II *adj* nihilistisch. **,ni·hil'is·tic** *adj* (*~ally*) nihilistisch.

nil [nɪl] *s*: *our team won three to ~* (*od. by three goals to ~*) (*3-0*) unsere Mannschaft gewann drei zu null (3 : 0).

nim·bi ['nɪmbaɪ] *pl von* **nimbus**.

nim·ble ['nɪmbl] *adj* □ **1.** flink, gewandt. **2.** *fig.* geistig beweglich: *~ mind* beweglicher Geist.

nim·bus ['nɪmbəs] *pl* **-bi** [-baɪ], **-bus·es** *s* Nimbus *m*, Heiligenschein *m*.

nin·com·poop ['nɪŋkəmpuːp] *s* Einfaltspinsel *m*, Trottel *m*.

nine [naɪn] I *adj num*: *~ times out of ten* in neun von zehn Fällen, fast immer; *~ wonder* 5. II *s* Neun *f*: *~ of hearts* Herzneun; *be dressed* (*up*) *to the ~s* F in Schale sein. **nine·fold** ['~fəʊld] I *adj* neunfach. II *adv* neunfach, um das Neunfache: *increase ~* (sich) verneun-

fachen. **nine·teen** [,~'tiːn] *adj* neunzehn: → **dozen**. **,nine'teenth** [-θ] *adj* neunzehnt. **nine·ti·eth** ['~tɪɪθ] *adj* neunzigst. **'nine-time** *adj* neunmalig. **nine·ty** ['naɪntɪ] I *adj* neunzig. II *s* Neunzig *f*: *be in one's nineties* in den Neunzigern sein; *in the nineties* in den neunziger Jahren (*e-s Jahrhunderts*).

nin·ny ['nɪnɪ] *s* F Dussel *m*, Dummkopf *m*.

ninth [naɪnθ] I *adj* **1.** neunt. II *s* **2.** der, die, das Neunte: *the ~ of May* der 9. Mai. **3.** Neuntel *n*. **'ninth·ly** *adv* neuntens.

nip¹ [nɪp] I *v/t* **1.** kneifen, zwicken: *~ off* abzwicken; *~ one's finger in the door* sich den Finger in der Tür einzwicken. **2.** *Pflanzen* schädigen (*Frost etc*): → **bud** I. II *v/i* **3.** *Br.* F sausen, flitzen: *~ in mot.* einscheren. III *s* **4.** *there's a ~ in the air today* heute ist es ganz schön kalt. **5.** Kniff *m*.

nip² [~] *s* Schlückchen *n* (*Whisky etc*).

nip·pers ['nɪpəz] *s pl*, *a. pair of ~* (Kneif)Zange *f*.

nip·ple ['nɪpl] *s* **1.** anat. Brustwarze *f*. **2.** (Gummi)Sauger *m* (*e-r Saugflasche*). **3.** ⚙ (Schmier)Nippel *m*.

nip·py ['nɪpɪ] *adj* **1.** frisch, kühl, kalt. **2.** *be ~ bsd. Br.* F sich beeilen.

nit [nɪt] *s* zo. Nisse *f*, Niß *f*.

ni·ter *Am.* → **nitre**.

'nit|pick·er *s* F pingeliger *od.* kleinlicher Mensch. **'~pick·ing** *adj* F pingelig, kleinlich.

ni·trate ['naɪtreɪt] *s* 🜄 Nitrat *n*.

ni·tre ['naɪtə] *s bsd. Br.* 🜄 Salpeter *m*.

ni·tric ac·id ['naɪtrɪk] *s* 🜄 Salpetersäure *f*.

ni·tro·gen ['naɪtrədʒən] *s* 🜄 Stickstoff *m*. **ni·trog·e·nous** [~'trɒdʒɪnɪs] *adj* stickstoffhaltig.

ni·tro·glyc·er·in(e) [,naɪtrəʊ'glɪsəriːn] *s* 🜄 Nitroglyzerin *n*.

nit·ty-grit·ty [,nɪtɪ'grɪtɪ] *s*: *go down* (*od. come*) *to the ~ sl.* zur Sache kommen.

nit·wit ['nɪtwɪt] *s* F Schwachkopf *m*.

no [nəʊ] I *adv* **1.** nein: *say ~ to* nein sagen zu. **2.** *beim comp*: um nichts, nicht: *they ~ longer live here* sie wohnen nicht mehr hier; *~ longer ago than yesterday* erst gestern. II *adj* **3.** kein: *~ one* keiner, niemand; *in ~ time* im Nu *od.* Handumdrehen. **4.** *vor ger*: → **deny** 1,

please 4. **III** *pl* **noes** *s* **5.** Nein *n*: **a clear ~** ein klares Nein (**to** auf *acc*). **6.** *parl.* Gegen-, Neinstimme *f*: **the ~es have it** der Antrag ist abgelehnt.

No·bel prize [nəʊ'bel] *s* Nobelpreis *m*: **Nobel peace prize** Friedensnobelpreis; **~ winner** Nobelpreisträger(in).

no·bil·i·ty [nəʊ'bɪlətɪ] *s* **1.** (Hoch)Adel *m*. **2.** *fig.* Adel *m*.

no·ble ['nəʊbl] *adj* □ **1.** adlig, von Adel. **2.** *fig.* edel, nobel. **3.** prächtig, stattlich (*Gebäude etc*). **4.** Edel...: **~ metal.** **'~·man** ['~mən] *s* (*irr* **man**) (hoher) Adliger. **'~·wom·an** *s* (*irr* **woman**) (hohe) Adlige.

no·bod·y ['nəʊbədɪ] **I** *pron* keiner, niemand. **II** *s fig.* Niemand *m*, Null *f*.

noc·tur·nal [nɒk'tɜːnl] *adj* □ nächtlich, Nacht...

nod [nɒd] **I** *v/i* **1.** nicken: **~ at** (*od.* **to**) **s.o.** j-m zunicken; **have a ~ding acquaintance with s.o.** j-n flüchtig kennen. **2. ~ off** einnicken. **II** *v/t* **3. ~ one's head** mit dem Kopf nicken. **III** *s* **4.** Nicken *n*: **give a ~** nicken; **give s.o. a ~** j-m zunikken.

node [nəʊd] *s* Knoten *m* (*a.* ✱).

nod·ule ['nɒdjuːl] *s* ♀, ✱ Knötchen *n*.

noise [nɔɪz] **I** *s* **1.** Krach *m*, Lärm *m*: **not to make any ~** keinen Krach machen; **make a lot of ~ about s.th.** *fig.* viel Tamtam um et. machen. **2.** Geräusch *n*: **what's that ~?** was ist das für ein Geräusch? **3.** *Radio etc*: Rauschen *n*. **II** *v/t* **4. ~ about** (*od.* **abroad, around**) *Gerücht etc* verbreiten: **it is being ~d about that** man erzählt sich, daß. **'noise·less** *adj* □ geräuschlos.

nois·y ['nɔɪzɪ] *adj* □ laut.

no·mad ['nəʊmæd] *s* Nomade *m*, Nomadin *f*. **no'mad·ic** *adj* (*~ally*) nomadisch, Nomaden...

'no-man's-land *s* Niemandsland *n* (*a. fig.*).

no·men·cla·ture [nəʊ'menklətʃə] *s* **1.** Nomenklatur *f*. **2.** (Fach)Terminologie *f*.

nom·i·nal ['nɒmɪnl] *adj* □ **1.** nominal, nominell (*beide a.* ✝): **~ income** Nominaleinkommen *n*; **~ value** Nominalwert *m*. **2.** *ling.* nominal, Nominal...

nom·i·nate ['nɒmɪneɪt] *v/t* **1.** (**to**) ernennen (zu), einsetzen (in *acc*): **be ~d** (**as** *od.* **to be**) ... als ... eingesetzt werden. **2.**

(**for**) nominieren (für), vorschlagen (als), als Kandidaten aufstellen (für). ,**nom·i'na·tion** *s* **1.** Ernennung *f*, Einsetzung *f*. **2.** Nominierung *f*: **place s.o.'s name in ~** j-n vorschlagen.

nom·i·na·tive ['nɒmɪnətɪv] *s a.* **~ case** *ling.* Nominativ *m*, erster Fall.

non... [nɒn] nicht..., Nicht..., un...

,**non·ac'cept·ance** *s* Annahmeverweigerung *f*, Nichtannahme *f*.

,**non·ag'gres·sion pact** *s pol.* Nichtangriffspakt *m*.

,**non·al·co'hol·ic** *adj* alkoholfrei.

,**non·a'ligned** *adj pol.* blockfrei.

,**non·ap'pear·ance** *s* Nichterscheinen *n* (*vor Gericht etc*).

,**non·at'tend·ance** *s* Nichtteilnahme *f*.

nonce word [nɒns] *s ling.* Ad-hoc-Bildung *f*.

non·cha·lance ['nɒnʃələns] *s* Nonchalance *f*, Lässigkeit *f*, Unbekümmertheit *f*. **'non·cha·lant** *adj* □ nonchalant, lässig, unbekümmert.

,**non·com'mis·sioned** *adj*: **~ officer** ✕ Unteroffizier *m*.

,**non·com'mit·tal** [~tl] *adj* □ zurückhaltend, (*Antwort etc*) unverbindlich: **be ~** sich nicht festlegen wollen.

,**non·com'pli·ance** *s* (**with**) Zuwiderhandlung *f* (gegen), Nichtbefolgung *f* (*gen*).

non com·pos men·tis [,nɒn'kɒmpəs'mentɪs] *adj* 🟐 unzurechnungsfähig.

,**non·con'form·ist** **I** *s* Nonkonformist (-in). **II** *adj* nonkonformistisch. ,**non·con'form·i·ty** *s* mangelnde Übereinstimmung (**with** mit).

non·de·script ['nɒndɪskrɪpt] *adj* unbestimmbar; unauffällig.

none [nʌn] **I** *pron s a.* (*mst pl konstruiert*) kein, niemand: **~ of them are** (*od.* **is**) **here** keiner von ihnen ist hier; **~ of your tricks!** laß deine Späße!; **~ but** niemand *od.* nichts außer, nur; → **business** 6. **II** *adv* in keiner Weise, nicht im geringsten: **~ too high** keineswegs zu hoch; **~ too soon** kein bißchen zu früh.

non·en·ti·ty [nɒ'nentətɪ] *s contp.* Null *f* (*Person*).

,**non·es'sen·tial** *adj* unwesentlich (**to** für).

none·the'less *adv* nichtsdestoweniger, dennoch, trotzdem.

,**non·e'vent** *s* F Reinfall *m*, Pleite *f*.

ˌnon·exˈist·ence s Nichtvorhandensein n, Fehlen n. ˌnon·exˈist·ent adj nicht existierend.

ˌnonˈfic·tion s Sachbücher pl.

ˌnon·fulˈfil(l)·ment s Nichterfüllung f.

ˌnon·in·terˈfer·ence, ˈnon·in·terˈven·tion s pol. Nichteinmischung f.

ˈnon·i·ron adj bügelfrei.

ˈnon·mem·ber s Nichtmitglied n.

ˌnon·obˈserv·ance s Nichtbefolgung f, -beachtung f.

ˌno-ˈnon·sense adj nüchtern, sachlich, (Warnung) unmißverständlich.

ˌnon·parˈti·san adj 1. pol. überparteilich. 2. unparteiisch.

ˌnonˈpay·ment s bsd. ✝ Nicht(be)zahlung f.

ˌnonˈplus v/t pret u. pp -ˈplused, bsd. Br. -ˈplussed verblüffen.

ˌnon·pol·ˈlut·ing adj umweltfreundlich.

ˌnonˈprof·it adj Am., ˌnon-ˈprof·it-ˌmak·ing adj gemeinnützig.

ˈnon·proˌlif·erˈa·tion s pol. Nichtweitergabe f von Atomwaffen. ~ treaty Atomsperrvertrag m.

ˌnonˈres·i·dent I adj 1. nicht (orts)ansässig. 2. nicht im Hause wohnend. II s 3. Nichtansässige m, f. 4. nicht im Hause Wohnende m, f.

ˌnon·reˈturn·a·ble adj Einweg...: ~ bot·tle.

non·sense [ˈnɒnsəns] s Unsinn m, dummes Zeug: make (a) ~ of ad absurdum führen; illusorisch machen; stand no ~ sich nichts gefallen lassen, nicht mit sich spaßen lassen. non·sen·si·cal [~ˈsensɪkl] adj □ unsinnig.

ˌnonˈsmok·er s 1. Nichtraucher(in). 2. 🚬 Br. Nichtraucherwagen m. ˌnon-ˈsmok·ing adj: ~ compartment 🚬 Nichtraucher(abteil n) m.

ˌnonˈstan·dard adj ling. nicht hochsprachlich.

ˌnonˈstart·er s: be a ~ keine od. kaum e-e Chance haben (Person, Sache).

ˌnonˈstick adj mit Antihaftbeschichtung (Pfanne etc).

ˌnonˈstop I adj durchgehend (Zug etc), ohne Unterbrechung (Reise etc), ohne Zwischenlandung (Flug): ~ flight 1. Nonstopflug m. II adv nonstop, ohne Unterbrechung od. Zwischenlandung: talk ~ ununterbrochen reden.

ˌnonˈun·ion adj ✝ nicht organisiert.

ˌnonˈvi·o·lence s Gewaltlosigkeit f. ˌnonˈvi·o·lent adj □ gewaltlos.

noo·dle [ˈnuːdl] s Nudel f: ~ soup Nudelsuppe f.

nook [nʊk] s Winkel m, Ecke f: search for s.th. in every ~ and cranny nach et. in jedem Winkel od. in allen Ecken suchen.

noon [nuːn] I s Mittag(szeit f) m: at ~ am od. zu Mittag, engS. um 12 Uhr (mittags). II adj mittägig, Mittags...

noose [nuːs] s Schlinge f: put one's head in(to) the ~ fig. den Kopf in die Schlinge stecken.

nope [nəʊp] adv F nein.

nor [nɔː] cj 1. → neither 2. 2. auch nicht: he does not know, ~ do I er weiß es nicht, u. ich auch nicht.

norm [nɔːm] s Norm f. Nor·mal [ˈ~ml] adj (□ → normally) normal, Normal... II s Normalzustand m: be back to ~ sich normalisiert haben, wieder normal sein; go back (od. return) to ~ sich normalisieren; be above (below) ~ über (unter) dem Durchschnitt od. Normalwert liegen. nor·mal·ize [ˈ~məlaɪz] I v/t 1. normalisieren. 2. normen, vereinheitlichen. II v/i 3. sich normalisieren. nor·mal·ly [ˈ~məlɪ] adv normalerweise, (für) gewöhnlich.

Nor·man [ˈnɔːmən] I s hist. Normanne m, Normannin f. II adj normannisch.

nor·ma·tive [ˈnɔːmətɪv] adj □ normativ.

north [nɔːθ] I s 1. Norden m: in the ~ of im Norden von (od. gen): to the ~ of → 5. 2. a. �î Norden m, nördlicher Landesteil: the �î Br. Nordengland n; Am. die Nordstaaten pl. II adj 3. Nord..., nördlich: ♎ Pole Nordpol m; ♎ Star ast. Polarstern m. III adj 4. nordwärts, nach Norden. 5. ~ of nördlich von (od. gen). '~bound adj nach Norden gehend od. fahrend. ˌ~ˈeast I s Nordosten m. II adj nordöstlich, Nordost... III adv nordöstlich, nach Nordosten.

north·er·ly [ˈnɔːðəlɪ] I adj nördlich, Nord... II adv von od. nach Norden. north·ern [ˈ~ðn] adj nördlich, Nord... north·ern·er [ˈ~ðənə] s 1. Bewohner(in) des Nordens (e-s Landes). 2. ♎ Am. Nordstaatler(in). north·ern·most [ˈ~ðənməʊst] adj nördlichst. north·ward [ˈ~wəd] adj u. adv nördlich, nordwärts, nach Norden: in a ~ direction in nördlicher Richtung, Richtung Norden. **'north·wards** adv → **northward.**

¸north'west I s Nordwesten m. **II** adj nordwestlich, Nordwest... **III** adv nordwestlich, nach Nordwesten.

Nor·we·gian [nɔːˈwiːdʒən] **I** adj **1.** norwegisch. **II** s **2.** Norweger(in). **3.** ling. Norwegisch n.

nose [nəʊz] **I** s **1.** Nase f: **bite** (od. **snap**) **s.o.'s ~ off** j-n anschnauzen; **cut off one's ~ to spite one's face** sich ins eigene Fleisch schneiden; **follow one's ~** immer der Nase nach gehen; s-m Instinkt folgen; **lead s.o. by the ~** j-n unter s-r Fuchtel haben; **look down one's ~ at s.o.** die Nase rümpfen über (acc), auf j-n, et. herabblicken; **poke** (od. **put, stick, thrust**) **one's ~ into** s-e Nase stecken in (acc); **put s.o.'s ~ out of joint** j-n ausstechen; j-n vor den Kopf stoßen; **under s.o.'s (very) ~** direkt vor j-s Nase; vor j-s Augen; → **grindstone, pick** 7, **rub** 3. **2.** fig. Nase f, Riecher m (**for** für). **3.** bsd. ⚙ Nase f, Vorsprung m; ⚓ Bug m; ✈ Nase f. **II** v/t **4.** Auto etc vorsichtig fahren. **5.** ~ **out** fig. ausschnüffeln. **III** v/i **6.** a. ~ **about** (od. **around**) fig. herumschnüffeln (in dat) (**for** nach). **~·bleed** s Nasenbluten n: **have a ~** Nasenbluten haben. **~ dive** s ✈ Sturzflug m. **'~-dive** v/i **1.** ✈ e-n Sturzflug machen. **2.** F purzeln (Preise etc). **~ drops** s pl ⚕ Nasentropfen pl. **'~·gay** s Sträußchen n. **'~·pick·ing** s Nasenbohren n.

nosh [nɒʃ] sl. **I** s **1.** bsd. Br. Essen n: **have a ~** (et.) essen; **have a quick ~** schnell et. essen. **2.** Am. Bissen m, Happen m: **have a ~** e-n Happen essen. **II** v/i **3.** bsd. Br. essen. **4.** Am. e-n Bissen od. Happen essen.

nos·tal·gia [nɒˈstældʒə] s Nostalgie f; weitS. Sehnsucht f (**for** nach). **nos'tal·gic** [~dʒɪk] adj (~ally) nostalgisch.

nos·tril ['nɒstrəl] s Nasenloch n, bsd. zo. Nüster f.

nos·trum ['nɒstrəm] s Allheilmittel n, Patentrezept n.

nos·y ['nəʊzɪ] adj □ F neugierig: ~ **park·er** Br. neugierige Person, Schnüffler(in).

not [nɒt] adv **1.** nicht: ~ **that** nicht, daß; **it is wrong, is it ~** (F **isn't it?**) es ist falsch, nicht wahr?; → **yet** 2. **2.** ~ **a** kein(e).

no·ta·ble ['nəʊtəbl] **I** adj **1.** beachtens-, bemerkenswert. **2.** beträchtlich (Unterschied etc). **3.** angesehen, bedeutend. **II** s **4.** bedeutende od. prominente Persönlichkeit. **'no·ta·bly** adv besonders, vor allem.

no·ta·ry ['nəʊtərɪ] s mst ~ **public** Notar m.

no·ta·tion [nəʊˈteɪʃn] s ♪ Notenschrift f.

notch [nɒtʃ] **I** s **1.** Kerbe f. **2.** Am. Engpaß m. **3.** fig. Grad m: **be a ~ above** e-e Klasse besser sein als. **II** v/t **4.** (ein)kerben. **5.** oft ~ **up** F Sieg, Einnahmen etc erzielen: ~ **s.o. sth.** j-m et. einbringen.

note [nəʊt] **I** s **1.** Bedeutung f: **man of ~** bedeutender Mann. **2.** take ~ **of sth.** von et. Notiz od. et. zur Kenntnis nehmen; et. beachten **3** mst pl Notiz f, Aufzeichnung f: **make a ~ of sth.** sich et. notieren od. vormerken; **take ~s (of)** sich Notizen machen (über acc); **speak without ~s** frei sprechen; → **mental** 1. **4.** (diplomatische) Note. **5.** Briefchen n, Zettel m. **6.** Anmerkung f; Vermerk m, Notiz f. **7.** Banknote f, Geldschein m. **8.** ♪ Note f. **9.** fig. Ton(art f) m: **strike the right (a false) ~** den richtigen Ton treffen (sich im Ton vergreifen). **II** v/t **10.** (besonders) beachten. achten auf (acc). **11.** bemerken. **12.** oft ~ **down** (sich) et. aufschreiben od. notieren. **'~·book** s Notizbuch n.

not·ed ['nəʊtɪd] adj bekannt, berühmt (**for** wegen).

'note·pa·per s Briefpapier n. **'~·wor·thy** adj □ bemerkenswert.

noth·ing ['nʌθɪŋ] **I** pron nichts (**of** von): **as if ~ had happened** als ob nichts passiert sei; **~ doing** F das kommt nicht in Frage; nichts zu machen; ~ **much** nicht (sehr) viel, nichts Bedeutendes; **that's ~ to** das ist nichts gegen od. im Vergleich zu; **that's ~ to me** das bedeutet mir nichts; **there is ~ like** es geht nichts über (acc); **there is ~ to** (od. **in**) **it** da ist nichts dran; an der Sache ist nichts dran; **I can make ~ of** ich kann nichts anfangen mit, ich werde nicht klug aus; **to say ~ of** ganz zu schweigen von; **think ~ of** nichts halten von; sich nichts machen aus; → **but** 4. **II** s Nichts n: **for ~** umsonst; **end in ~** sich in nichts auflösen. **III** adv durchaus nicht, keinesfalls: ~ **like complete** alles andere als *od.* längst nicht vollständig.

no·tice ['nəʊtɪs] **I** *s* **1.** Beachtung *f*, Wahrnehmung *f*: **bring s.th. to s.o.'s ~** j-m et. zur Kenntnis bringen; **escape ~** unbemerkt bleiben; **escape s.o.'s ~** j-m *od.* j-s Aufmerksamkeit entgehen; **take (no) ~ (of** (keine) Notiz nehmen von, (nicht) beachten. **2.** Ankündigung *f*, Bekanntgabe *f*, Mitteilung *f*: **give s.o. ~ of s.th.** j-n von et. benachrichtigen. **3.** Kündigung(sfrist) *f*: **give s.o. (his) ~ (for Easter)** j-m (zu Ostern) kündigen; **give the company one's ~** kündigen; **at short ~** kurzfristig; **till (**od.**) until) further ~** bis auf weiteres; **without ~** fristlos. **II** *v/t* **4.** bemerken: **~ s.o. do(ing) s.th.** bemerken, daß j-d et. tut. **5.** (besonders) beachten *od.* achten auf (*acc*). **III** *v/i* **6.** es bemerken. **'no·tice·a·ble** *adj* □ **1.** erkennbar, wahrnehmbar. **2.** bemerkenswert, beachtlich.

notice board *s bsd. Br.* Anschlagtafel *f*, Schwarzes Brett.

no·ti·fi·a·ble ['nəʊtɪfaɪəbl] *adj* meldepflichtig (*bsd. Krankheit*). **no·ti·fi·ca·tion** [ˌnəʊtɪfɪ'keɪʃn] *s* Meldung *f*, Mitteilung *f*, Benachrichtigung *f*. **no·ti·fy** ['~faɪ] *v/t* **1.** melden, mitteilen (*s.th. to s.o.* j-m et.). **2.** j-n benachrichtigen (**of** von, **that** daß).

no·tion ['nəʊʃn] *s* **1.** Begriff *m* (*a. R, phls.*), Vorstellung *f*: **not to have the faintest (**od.** vaguest) ~** nicht die leiseste Ahnung haben von. **2.** Idee *f*: **take (have) a ~ to do s.th.** Lust bekommen (haben), et. zu tun. **no·tion·al** ['~ʃənl] *adj* □ fiktiv, angenommen.

no·to·ri·e·ty [ˌnəʊtə'raɪətɪ] *s* traurige Berühmtheit. **no·to·ri·ous** ['~'tɔːrɪəs] *adj* □ berüchtigt (**for** für).

not·with·stand·ing [ˌnɒtwɪθ'stændɪŋ] **I** *prp* ungeachtet, trotz. **II** *adv* nichtsdestoweniger, dennoch.

nou·gat ['nuːgɑː] *s (etwa)* Türkischer Honig.

nought [nɔːt] *s*: **bring (come) to ~** zunichte machen (werden).

noun [naʊn] *s ling.* Substantiv *n*, Hauptwort *n*.

nour·ish ['nʌrɪʃ] *v/t* **1.** (er)nähren (**on** von). **2.** *Gefühl* nähren, hegen. **'nour·ish·ing** *adj* □ nahrhaft. **'nour·ish·ment** *s* **1.** Ernährung *f*. **2.** Nahrung *f*:

take ~ Nahrung zu sich nehmen.

nov·el ['nɒvl] **I** *adj* (ganz) neu(artig). **II** *s* Roman *m*. **nov·el·ette** [ˌnɒvə'let] *s* Kurzroman *m*; *contp. bsd. Br.* Groschenroman *m*. **'nov·el·ist** *s* Romanschriftsteller(in). **no·vel·la** [nəʊ'velə] *pl* **-las, -le** [~liː] *s* Novelle *f*. **nov·el·ty** ['nɒvltɪ] *s* **1.** Neuheit *f*: a) *das Neue, weitS. der Reiz des Neuen* b) *et.* Neues. **2.** *pl* (billige) Neuheiten *pl.*

No·vem·ber [nəʊ'vembə] *s* November *m*: **in ~** im November.

nov·ice ['nɒvɪs] *s* **1.** *eccl.* Novize *m*, Novizin *f*. **2.** Anfänger(in), Neuling *m* (**at** auf *e-m Gebiet*).

now [naʊ] **I** *adv* **1.** nun, jetzt: **~ and again, ~ (every) ~ and then** von Zeit zu Zeit, dann u. wann; **by ~** mittlerweile, inzwischen; **from ~ (on)** von jetzt an; **up to ~** bis jetzt. **2.** sofort. **3.** *just* ~ gerade eben. **II** *cj* **4.** *a.* **~ that** nun da, jetzt wo.

now·a·days ['naʊədeɪz] *adv* heutzutage.

no·where ['nəʊweə] *adv* **1.** nirgends, nirgendwo: **have ~ to live** kein Zuhause haben; **~ near** bei weitem nicht, auch nicht annähernd. **2.** nirgendwohin: **get ~ (fast)** überhaupt nicht weiterkommen, überhaupt keine Fortschritte machen; **this will get us ~** damit *od.* so kommen wir auch nicht weiter, das bringt uns auch nicht weiter.

nox·ious ['nɒkʃəs] *adj* □ schädlich (**to** für): **~ substance** Schadstoff *m.*

noz·zle ['nɒzl] *s* ☺ Schnauze *f*; Stutzen *m*; Düse *f*; Zapfpistole *f.*

nu·ance ['njuːɑːns] *s* Nuance *f.*

nub [nʌb] *s* springender Punkt.

nu·cle·ar ['njuːklɪə] *adj* **1.** *biol. etc* Kern... **2.** *phys.* Kern..., Atom...: **~ energy** Atom-, Kernenergie *f*; **~ fission** Kernspaltung *f*; **~-free** atomwaffenfrei; **~ fusion** Kernfusion *f*, -verschmelzung *f*; **~ physics** *pl (sg konstruiert)* Kernphysik *f*; **~ power** Atom-, Kernkraft *f*; *pol.* Atommacht *f*; **~ power plant** Atom-, Kernkraftwerk *n*; **~ reactor** Atom-, Kernreaktor *m*; **~ scientist** Atomwissenschaftler *m*: **~ test** Atomtest *m*; **~ war(fare)** Atomkrieg(führung *f*) *m*; **~ warhead** Atomsprengkopf *m*; **~ weapons** *pl* Atom-, Kernwaffen *pl.* **3.** *a.* **~-powered** atomgetrieben: **~ submarine** Atom-U-Boot *n*. **nu·cle·us** ['~klɪəs] *pl* **-cle·i** [~aɪ] *s* **1.** (*Atom-,*

Zell- etc)Kern *m.* **2.** *fig.* Kern *m.*

nude [nju:d] **I** *adj* **1.** nackt: **~ *beach*** Nacktbadestrand *m*, FKK-Strand *m*; **~ *model*** Aktmodell *n*; **~ *photograph*** Aktaufnahme *f*; **~ *swimming*** Nacktbaden *n.* **II** *s* **2.** *Kunst:* Akt *m.* **3.** *in the* **~** nackt.

nudge [nʌdʒ] **I** *v/t* j-n anstoßen, stupsen. **II** *s* Stups *m.*

nud·ism ['nju:dɪzəm] *s* Nudismus *m*, Freikörper-, Nacktkultur *f.* **'nud·ist** *s* Nudist(in), Anhänger(in) der Freikörperkultur, FKK-Anhänger(in): **~ *beach*** Nacktbadestrand *m*, FKK-Strand *m.*

nug·get ['nʌgɪt] *s* Nugget *n*: **~s** *pl of information* fig. bruchstückhafte Information(en *pl*).

nui·sance ['nju:sns] *s* **1.** Plage *f*, Belästigung *f*, Mißstand *m*: *what a* **~***!* wie ärgerlich!; *public* **~** �425 öffentliches Ärgernis (*a. fig.*). **2.** Landplage *f*, Nervensäge *f*, Quälgeist *m*: *be a* **~** *to s.o.* j-m lästig fallen, j-n nerven; *make a* **~** *of o.s* den Leuten auf die Nerven gehen *od.* fallen.

nukes [nju:ks] *s pl bsd. Am.* F Atom-, Kernwaffen *pl.*

null [nʌl] *adj*: **~** *and void bsd.* �425 null u. nichtig. **nul·li·fy** ['nʌlɪfaɪ] *v/t* **1.** *bsd.* �425 für null u. nichtig erklären. **2.** aufheben.

numb [nʌm] **I** *adj* □ **1.** starr (*with* vor *Kälte etc*), taub (*empfindungslos*). **2.** *fig.* wie betäubt (*with* vor *Schmerz etc*). **II** *v/t* **3.** starr *od.* taub machen. **4.** *fig.* betäuben.

num·ber ['nʌmbə] **I** *s* **1.** Zahl *f*; Ziffer *f*: *be good at* **~s** gut rechnen können. **2.** (*Haus-, Telefon- etc*)Nummer *f*: *be* **~** *one fig.* die Nummer Eins sein; *look after* (*od. take care of*) **~** *one* F (vor allem) an sich selbst denken; *have s.o.'s* **~** F j-n durchschaut haben; *his* **~** *is* (*od. has come*) *up* F jetzt ist er dran. **3.** (An)Zahl *f*: *a* (*great*) **~** *of people* mehrere (sehr viele) Leute; *five in* **~** fünf an der Zahl; **~s** *of times* zu wiederholten Malen; *in large* **~s** in großen Mengen, in großer Zahl. **4.** Nummer *f*, Ausgabe *f* (*e-r Zeitschrift etc*): → *back number.* **5.** *thea. etc* (Programm)Nummer *f*; ♩ Nummer *f*, Stück *n.* **II** *v/t* **6.** *his days are* **~***ed* s-e Tage sind gezählt.

7. numerieren. **8.** **~** *s.o.* *among* (*od. with*) j-n zählen *od.* rechnen zu. **9.** sich belaufen auf (*acc*). **III** *v/i* **10.** **~** *in* sich belaufen auf (*acc*). **11.** **~** *among* (*od. with*) *fig.* zählen zu. **'num·ber·ing** *s* Numerierung *f.* **'num·ber·less** *adj* unzählig, zahllos.

'num·ber·plate *s mot. Br.* Nummern-, Kennzeichenschild *n.*

numb·ness ['nʌmnɪs] *s* **1.** Starr-, Taubheit *f.* **2.** *fig.* Betäubung *f.*

nu·mer·al ['nju:mərəl] *s* **1.** Ziffer *f.* **2.** *ling.* Zahlwort *n.*

nu·mer·i·cal [nju:'merɪkl] *adj* □ numerisch: a) Zahlen..., b) zahlenmäßig.

nu·mer·ous ['nju:mərəs] *adj* □ zahlreich.

nu·mis·mat·ics [ˌnju:mɪz'mætɪks] *s pl* (*sg konstruiert*) Numismatik *f*, Münzkunde *f.*

num·skull ['nʌmskʌl] *s* F Dummkopf *m.*

nun [nʌn] *s eccl.* Nonne *f.*

nun·ci·o ['nʌnsɪəʊ] *pl* **-os** *s eccl.* Nuntius *m.*

nun·ner·y ['nʌnərɪ] *s* Nonnenkloster *n.*

nup·tial ['nʌpʃl] **I** *adj* Hochzeits... **II** *s* Trauung *f.*

nurse [nɜːs] **I** *s* **1.** (Kranken)Schwester *f*: → *male* I. **2.** Kindermädchen *n.* **II** *v/t* **3.** *Baby* säugen, stillen, *e-m Baby* die Brust geben. **4.** *Kranke* pflegen: **~** *s.o. back to health* j-n gesund pflegen. **5.** *Krankheit* auskurieren. **6.** *Stimme etc* schonen. **7.** *fig.* Gefühl hegen, nähren. **8.** die Brust nehmen, trinken (*Baby*). **9.** als Krankenschwester (*od.* als Krankenpfleger arbeiten). **'~maid** → *nurse* 2.

nurs·er·y ['nɜːsərɪ] *s* **1.** Tagesheim *n*, -stätte *f.* **2.** Pflanz-, Baumschule *f.* **3.** Kinderzimmer *n.* **~** *rhyme* *s* Kinderreim *m*, -vers *m.* **~** *school* *s* Kindergarten *m*: **~** *teacher* Kindergärtnerin *f.*

nurs·ing ['nɜːsɪŋ] *s* **1.** Stillen *n.* **2.** Krankenpflege *f.* **~** *bot·tle* *s bsd. Am.* Saugflasche *f.* **~** *home* *s* **1.** Pflegeheim *n.* **2.** *bsd. Br.* Privatklinik *f.*

nut [nʌt] *s* **1.** ♣ Nuß *f*: *a hard* (*od. tough*) **~** *to crack fig.* e-e harte Nuß. **2.** (Schrauben)Mutter *f.* **3.** Birne *f* (*Kopf*): *be* (*go*) *off one's* **~** (anfangen zu) spinnen. **4.** *pl* V Eier *pl* (*Hoden*). **'~crack·er** *s a. fig.* Nußknacker *m*: *a* (*pair of*) **~(s)** ein Nußknacker. **'~**

house s bsd. Br. sl. Klapsmühle f.

nut·meg ['nʌtmeg] s ♉ Muskatnuß f.

nu·tri·ent ['njuːtrɪənt] **I** adj nahrhaft. **II** s Nährstoff m.

nu·tri·tion [njuːˈtrɪʃn] s Ernährung f. **nu'tri·tious** adj □ nahrhaft.

nuts [nʌts] adj F: **be ~** spinnen; **be ~ about** (od. **on**) verrückt sein nach; wild od. scharf sein auf (acc).

'nut·shell s ♉ Nußschale f: (**to put it**) **in a**

nut·ty ['nʌtɪ] adj **1.** Nuß... **2.** F verrückt (a. Idee etc): **be ~** spinnen; **be ~ about** (od. **on**) verrückt sein nach, wild od. scharf sein auf (acc).

ny·lon ['naɪlɒn] s Nylon n.

nymph [nɪmf] s Nymphe f.

nym·pho·ma·ni·ac [ˌnɪmfəʊˈmeɪniæk] **I** adj nymphoman, mannstoll. **II** s Nymphomanin f.

O

O [əʊ] pl **O's, Os** s Null f (Ziffer, a. teleph.).

oaf [əʊf] s Lümmel m, Flegel m. **'oaf·ish** adj □ lümmel-, flegelhaft.

oak [əʊk] s ♉ Eiche f. **oak·en** ['~ən] adj eichen, Eichen...

oar [ɔː] s Ruder n, Riemen m: **put** (od. **shove, stick**) **one's ~s in** F sich einmischen, s-n Senf dazugeben; **rest on one's ~s** fig. ausspannen.

oars·man ['ɔːzmən] s (irr **man**) Sport: Ruderer m. **'~wom·an** s (irr **woman**) Sport: Ruderin f.

o·a·sis [əʊˈeɪsɪs] pl **-ses** [~siːz] s Oase f (a. fig.).

oath [əʊθ] pl **oaths** [əʊðz] s **1.** Eid m, Schwur m: **~ of office** Amts-, Diensteid; **on** (od. **under**) **~** unter Eid, eidlich; **be on** (od. **under**) **~** unter Eid stehen; **swear** (od. **take**) **an ~** e-n Eid leisten od. ablegen, schwören (**on, to** auf acc); **in lieu of an ~** an Eides Statt. **2.** Fluch m.

oat·meal ['əʊtmiːl] s Hafermehl n, -grütze f.

oats [əʊts] s pl ♉ Hafer m: **he feels his ~** F ihn sticht der Hafer; **be off one's ~** F keinen Appetit haben; **he's gone off his ~** F ihm ist der Appetit vergangen; **sow one's wild ~** sich die Hörner abstoßen.

ob·du·ra·cy ['ɒbdjʊrəsɪ] s Starrsinn m, Verstocktheit f. **ob·du·rate** ['~rət] adj □ starrsinnig, verstockt.

o·be·di·ence [əˈbiːdjəns] s Gehorsam m (**to** gegen[über]), Folgsamkeit f. **o'be-**

di·ent adj □ gehorsam (**to** dat), folgsam: **be ~ to s.o.** a. j-m folgen.

ob·e·lisk ['ɒbəlɪsk] s Obelisk m.

o·bese [əʊˈbiːs] adj fettleibig. **o'bes·i·ty** s Fettleibigkeit f.

o·bey [əˈbeɪ] **I** v/t **1.** j-m gehorchen, folgen. **2.** Befehl etc befolgen. **II** v/i **3.** gehorchen, folgen.

ob·fus·cate ['ɒbfʌskeɪt] v/t fig. **1.** verwirren. **2.** vernebeln.

o·bit·u·ar·y [əˈbɪtjʊərɪ] s **1.** Nachruf m. **2.** a. **~ notice** Todesanzeige f.

ob·ject¹ [əbˈdʒekt] **I** v/t **1.** einwenden (**that** daß). **II** v/i **2.** Einspruch erheben (**to** gegen). **3.** et. dagegen haben: **if you don't ~** wenn du nichts dagegen hast; **~ to s.th.** et. beanstanden; **do you ~ to my smoking?** haben Sie et. dagegen, wenn ich rauche?

ob·ject² ['ɒbdʒɪkt] s **1.** Objekt n, Gegenstand m (a. fig. des Mitleids etc): **money (is) no ~** Geld od. der Preis spielt keine Rolle. **2.** Ziel n, Zweck m, Absicht f: **with the ~ of doing s.th.** mit der Absicht, et. zu tun. **3.** ling. Objekt n.

ob·jec·tion [əbˈdʒekʃn] s Einspruch m (a. ⚖️), Einwand m (**to** gegen); Abneigung f (**to** gegen): **if you have no ~s** wenn du nichts dagegen hast; **I have no ~ to him** ich habe nichts an ihm auszusetzen; **raise an ~ to s.th.** gegen et. e-n Einwand erheben. **ob'jec·tion·a·ble** adj □ **1.** unangenehm. **2.** anstößig.

ob·jec·tive [əbˈdʒektɪv] **I** adj □ **1.** objektiv, sachlich. **2.** objektiv, tatsächlich. **II** s **3.** opt. Objektiv n. **4.** Ziel n. **ob·jec·tiv·i·ty** [‚ɒbdʒek'tɪvətɪ] s Objektivität f.

'**ob·ject les·son** s **1.** ped. Anschauungsunterricht m. **2.** fig. Parade-, Schulbeispiel n (in für).

ob·jec·tor [əb'dʒektə] s Gegner(in) (**to** gen): → **conscientious** 2.

ob·li·gate ['ɒblɪgeɪt] v/t: **feel ‿d to do s.th.** sich verpflichtet fühlen, et. zu tun. ‚**ob·li'ga·tion** s Verpflichtung f: **‿ to buy** Kaufzwang m; **without ‿** unverbindlich; **be under an ‿ to do s.th.** verpflichtet sein, et. zu tun. **ob·lig·a·to·ry** [ə'blɪgətərɪ] adj □ verpflichtend, verbindlich, obligatorisch (**on** für): **at·tendance is ‿** Anwesenheit ist Pflicht.

o·blige [ə'blaɪdʒ] v/t **1.** nötigen, zwingen: **be ‿d to do s.th.** a. et. tun müssen. **2.** fig. (a. zu Dank) verpflichten: **feel ‿d to do s.th.** sich verpflichtet fühlen, et. zu tun; **(I am) much ‿d (to you)** ich bin Ihnen sehr zu Dank verpflichtet, besten Dank; **would you ‿ me by** (ger)? wären Sie so freundlich, zu (inf)? **3.** j-m gefällig sein, j-m e-n Gefallen tun. **o'blig·ing** adj □ entgegenkommend, gefällig.

ob·lique [ə'bliːk] adj □ **1.** bsd. Å schief, schiefwink(e)lig, schräg: **at an ‿ angle to** im spitzen Winkel zu. **2.** fig. indirekt.

ob·lit·er·ate [ə'blɪtəreɪt] v/t **1.** unkenntlich od. unleserlich machen. **2.** vernichten, völlig zerstören. **3.** Sonne etc verdecken. **ob‚lit·er'a·tion** s **1.** Unkenntlichmachung f. **2.** Vernichtung f.

o·bliv·i·on [ə'blɪvɪən] s: **fall** (od. **sink**) **into ‿** in Vergessenheit geraten. **o'bliv·i·ous** adj: **be ‿ to** (od. **of**) **s.th.** sich e-r Sache nicht bewußt sein; et. nicht bemerken od. wahrnehmen.

ob·long ['ɒblɒŋ] **I** adj rechteckig. **II** s Rechteck n.

ob·nox·ious [əb'nɒkʃəs] adj □ widerwärtig, widerlich.

o·boe ['əʊbəʊ] s ♪ Oboe f. '**o·bo·ist** s Oboist(in).

ob·scene [əb'siːn] adj □ obszön, unanständig, unzüchtig. **ob·scen·i·ty** [əb'senətɪ] s Obszönität f (a. Wort etc), Unanständigkeit f, Unzüchtigkeit f.

ob·scure [əb'skjʊə] **I** adj □ **1.** a) dunkel, unklar, (Motive etc a.) undurchsichtig:

for some ‿ reason aus e-m unergründlichen Grund, b) unbestimmt, undeutlich (Gefühl). **2.** obskur, unbekannt, unbedeutend. **II** v/t **3.** Sonne etc verdecken. **4.** nicht klarmachen. **ob·scu·ri·ty** s **1.** Unklarheit f. **2.** Unbekanntheit f.

ob·se·quies ['ɒbsɪkwɪz] s Trauerfeierlichkeit(en pl) f.

ob·se·qui·ous [əb'siːkwɪəs] adj □ unterwürfig. **ob'se·qui·ous·ness** s Unterwürfigkeit f.

ob·serv·a·ble [əb'zɜːvəbl] adj □ wahrnehmbar, merklich. **ob'ser·vance** s Beachtung f, Befolgung f, Einhaltung f. **ob'ser·vant** adj □ aufmerksam, achtsam. **ob·ser·va·tion** [‚ɒbsə'veɪʃn] s **1.** Beobachtung f, Überwachung f: **keep s.o. under ‿** j-n beobachten (lassen). **2.** Bemerkung f (**on** über acc). **ob·ser·va·to·ry** [əb'zɜːvətrɪ] s Observatorium n. **ob·serve** v/t **1.** beobachten: a) überwachen, b) studieren, c) bemerken: **he was ‿d entering the house** er wurde beim Betreten des Hauses beobachtet. **2.** Vorschrift etc beachten, befolgen, einhalten; Fest feiern, begehen. **3.** bemerken, äußern (**that** daß). **ob'serv·er** s Beobachter(in). **ob'serv·ing** → **observant**.

ob·sess [əb'ses] v/t: **be ‿ed by** (od. **with**) besessen sein von. **ob·ses·sion** [əb'seʃn] s **1.** Besessenheit f: **have an ‿ with** → **obsess.** **2.** fixe Idee, psych. Zwangsvorstellung f. **ob'ses·sion·al** [‿ʃnl] adj □ psych. zwanghaft: **‿ neuro·sis** Zwangsneurose f.

ob·so·les·cent [‚ɒbsə'lesnt] adj □ veraltend: **be ‿** veralten. **ob·so·lete** ['ɒbsəliːt] adj □ veraltet.

ob·sta·cle ['ɒbstəkl] s Hindernis n (**to** für) (a. fig.): **be an ‿ to s.th.** et. behindern, e-r Sache im Weg stehen; **put ‿s in s.o.'s way** j-m Steine in den Weg legen. **‿ race** s Sport: Hindernisrennen n.

ob·ste·tri·cian [‚ɒbstə'trɪʃn] s ♯ Geburtshelfer(in). **ob·stet·rics** [ɒb'stetrɪks] s pl (mst sg konstruiert) Geburtshilfe f.

ob·sti·na·cy ['ɒbstɪnəsɪ] s Hartnäckigkeit f (a. fig.), Halsstarrigkeit f. **ob·sti·nate** ['ɒbstənət] adj □ hartnäckig (a. fig.), halsstarrig.

ob·strep·er·ous [əb'strepərəs] *adj* □ **1.** lärmend. **2.** aufsässig.

ob·struct [əb'strʌkt] *v/t* **1.** Straße etc blockieren, versperren, *a. Röhre, Arterie etc* verstopfen. **2.** *Aussicht etc* versperren, die Sicht versperren auf *(acc)*: ~ **s.o.'s view** j-m die Sicht nehmen. **3.** *Straßenverkehr, fig. Fortschritt etc* behindern, aufhalten, *Gesetzesvorlage etc* blockieren, sich *e-m Plan etc* in den Weg stellen. **ob'struc·tion** *s* **1.** Blockierung *f*, Versperrung *f*, Verstopfung *f*. **2.** Behinderung *f*. **3.** *pol.* Obstruktion *f*. **ob'struc·tion·ism** [~ʃənɪzəm] *s pol.* Obstruktionspolitik *f*. **ob'struc·tive** [~tɪv] *adj* □ hinderlich (**to** für): **be ~ to s.th.** *a.* et. behindern.

ob·tain [əb'teɪn] **I** *v/t* erhalten, bekommen, sich et. verschaffen: ~ *by flattery* sich et. erschmeicheln; ~ *s.th. for s.o.* j-m et. beschaffen *od.* besorgen. **II** *v/i* bestehen; Geltung haben. **ob'tain·a-ble** *adj* erhältlich: *no longer* ~ nicht mehr lieferbar, vergriffen.

ob·trude [əb'truːd] **I** *v/t* aufdrängen (**on** *dat*): ~ **o.s.** → **II. II** *v/i* sich aufdrängen (**on** *dat*). **ob'tru·sive** [~sɪv] *adj* □ aufdringlich.

ob·tuse [əb'tjuːs] *adj* □ **1.** *Å* stumpf *(Winkel)*. **2.** *fig.* begriffsstutzig, beschränkt.

ob·vi·ous ['ɒbvɪəs] *adj* □ offensichtlich, klar, einleuchtend: *it is (very)* ~ *that* es liegt (klar) auf der Hand, daß.

oc·ca·sion [ə'keɪʒn] **I** *s* **1.** (günstige) Gelegenheit, richtiger Zeitpunkt *(for* für): *take the* ~ *to do s.th.* die Gelegenheit ergreifen, et. zu tun. **2.** (besondere) Gelegenheit, Anlaß *m*: *on this* ~ bei dieser Gelegenheit; *on the* ~ *of* anläßlich *(gen); for the* ~ eigens zu diesem Zweck *od.* Anlaß. **3.** *(bsd.* festliches) Ereignis: *to celebrate the* ~ zur Feier des Tages; *rise to the* ~ sich der Lage gewachsen zeigen; → *mark²* 11. **4.** Anlaß *m*, Anstoß *m*: *give* ~ *to* Anlaß *od.* den Anstoß geben zu. **5.** Grund *m*, Veranlassung *f (for* zu). **II** *v/t* **6.** veranlassen, verursachen. **oc'ca·sion·al** [~ʒənl] *adj* gelegentlich, Gelegenheits...; vereinzelt: *smoke an* ~ *cigarette* gelegentlich *od.* hin u. wieder e-e Zigarette rauchen. **oc'ca·sion·al·ly** [~ʒnəlɪ] *adv* gelegentlich, hin u. wieder.

Oc·ci·dent ['ɒksɪdənt] *s der* Westen, *poet. das* Abendland. **oc·ci·den·tal** [~'dentl] *adj* □ abendländisch, westlich.

oc·cult [ɒ'kʌlt] **I** *adj* □ okkult: a) geheimnisvoll, verborgen, b) übersinnlich, c) geheim, Geheim... **II** *s: the* ~ das Okkulte. **oc·cult·ism** ['ɒkəltɪzəm] *s* Okkultismus *m*.

oc·cu·pant ['ɒkjʊpənt] *s* **1.** Bewohner(in): *the* ~*s pl of the house* die Hausbewohner *pl.* **2.** Insasse *m*, Insassin *f: the* ~*s pl of the car* die Autoinsassen *pl.* **oc·cu·pa·tion** *s* **1.** Besitznahme *f*, -ergreifung *f*. **2.** ✕, *pol.* Besetzung *f*: ~ *troops pl* Besatzungstruppen *pl.* **3.** Beschäftigung *f*. **4.** Beruf *m*: *by* ~ von Beruf. **oc·cu·pa·tion·al** [~ʃənl] *adj* □ Berufs...: ~ *accident* Arbeitsunfall *m*; ~ *disease* Berufskrankheit *f*; ~ *hazard* Berufsrisiko *n*. **2.** Beschäftigungs...: ~ *therapy*. **oc·cu·pi·er** ['~paɪə] → *occupant* 1. **oc·cu·py** ['~paɪ] *v/t* **1.** in Besitz nehmen, Besitz ergreifen von; ✕, *pol.* besetzen. **2.** *be occupied* bewohnt sein; besetzt sein *(Platz).* **3.** Amt bekleiden, innehaben. **4.** *Raum* einnehmen; *Zeit* in Anspruch nehmen. **5.** *j-n* beschäftigen: ~ *o.s. with (od. in) s.th.* sich mit et. beschäftigen.

oc·cur [ə'kɜː] *v/i* **1.** sich ereignen, vorkommen. **2.** vorkommen (*in bei Shakespeare etc*). **3.** zustoßen (**to** *dat*). **4.** einfallen, in den Sinn kommen (**to** *dat*): *it* ~*red to me that* es fiel mir ein *od.* mir kam der Gedanke, daß. **oc·cur·rence** [ə'kʌrəns] *s* **1.** Vorkommen *n*. **2.** Ereignis *n*, Vorfall *m*, Vorkommnis *n*: *be an everyday* ~ et. (ganz) Alltägliches sein.

o·cean ['əʊʃn] *s* **1.** Ozean *m*, Meer *n*: ~ *climate* Meeres-, Seeklima *n*; ~ *liner* Ozeandampfer *m*. **2.** ~*s pl of* F e-e Unmenge von. '~·go·ing *adj* hochseetüchtig, Hochsee...

o·cher *Am.*, **o·chre** *bsd. Br.* ['əʊkə] **I** *s min.* Ocker *m*, *n*. **II** *adj* ockerfarben, -gelb.

o'clock [ə'klɒk] *adv* ... Uhr: *five* ~.

oc·ta·gon ['ɒktəgən] *s* Achteck *n*. **oc·tag·o·nal** [ɒk'tægənl] *adj* □ achteckig.

oc·tane ['ɒkteɪn] *s* 🜍 Oktan *n*: ~ *number (od. rating)* Oktanzahl *f*.

oc·tave ['ɒktɪv] *s* ♪ Oktave *f*.

Oc·to·ber [ɒkˈtəʊbə] s Oktober m: **in ~** im Oktober.

oc·to·pus [ˈɒktəpəs] pl **-pus·es, -pi** [~paɪ] s zo. Krake f.

oc·u·lar [ˈɒkjʊlə] adj Augen... **'oc·u·list** s Augenarzt m.

odd [ɒd] adj (□ → **oddly**) **1.** sonderbar, seltsam, merkwürdig. **2.** nach Zahlen: **50 ~** (et.) über 50, einige 50. **3.** ungerade (Zahl). **4.** Einzel..., einzeln (Schuh etc). **5.** gelegentlich, Gelegenheits...: **~ jobs** pl Gelegenheitsarbeiten pl. **'~·ball** s bsd. Am. F komischer Kauz.

odd·i·ty [ˈɒdɪtɪ] s **1.** Merkwürdigkeit f. **2.** komische Person od. Sache.

'odd·job man s (irr man) Mädchen n für alles.

odd·ly [ˈɒdlɪ] adv **1.** → **odd** 1. **2.** a. **~ enough** seltsamer-, merkwürdigerweise.

odds [ɒdz] s pl **1.** (Gewinn)Chancen pl: **the ~ are 10 to 1** die Chancen stehen 10 zu 1; **the ~ are that he will come** er kommt wahrscheinlich; **the ~ are in our favo(u)r** (od. on us) (against us) unsere Chancen stehen gut (schlecht); **against all ~** wider Erwarten, entgegen allen Erwartungen; → **stack** 6. **2. be at ~ uneins sein (with** mit): **be at ~ with** a. im Widerspruch stehen zu. **3. it makes no ~** Br. es spielt keine Rolle, es macht keinen Unterschied. **4. ~ and ends** Krimskrams m. **'~·on** adj aussichtsreichst (Kandidat etc), hoch, klar (Favorit): **it's ~ that he will come** er kommt höchstwahrscheinlich.

o·di·ous [ˈəʊdjəs] adj □ **1.** abscheulich. **2.** widerlich, ekelhaft.

o·dom·e·ter [əʊˈdɒmɪtə] s mot. Am. Meilenzähler m.

o·dor, etc Am. → **odour**, etc.

o·dor·if·er·ous [ˌəʊdəˈrɪfərəs] adj □ duftend.

o·dour [ˈəʊdə] s bsd. Br. **1.** Geruch m, bsd. Duft m. **2. be in bad ~ with** fig. schlecht angeschrieben sind sein. **'o·dour·less** adj bsd. Am. geruchlos.

od·ys·sey [ˈɒdɪsɪ] s Odyssee f.

oec·u·men·i·cal → **ecumenical**.

oe·de·ma [iːˈdiːmə] pl **-ma·ta** [~mətə] s ☞ Ödem m.

Oe·di·pus com·plex [ˈiːdɪpəs] s psych. Ödipuskomplex m.

oe·soph·a·gus [ɪˈsɒfəgəs] pl **-gi** [~gaɪ],

-gus·es s anat. bsd. Br. Speiseröhre f.

oes·tro·gen [ˈiːstrəʊdʒən] s biol. bsd. Am. Östrogen n.

of [ɒv] prp **1.** allg. von. **2.** zur Bezeichnung des Genitivs: **the tail ~ the dog** der Schwanz des Hundes. **3.** Ort: bei: **the Battle ~ Hastings** die Schlacht bei Hastings. **4.** Entfernung, Trennung, Befreiung: a) von: **south ~ London** südlich von London; → **cure** 4, etc, b) gen: → **rob**, etc, c) um: → **cheat** 3, etc. **5.** Herkunft: von, aus: **Mr X ~ London** Mr X aus London; → **family** I, etc. **6.** Eigenschaft: von, mit: **a man ~ courage** ein mutiger Mann, ein Mann mit Mut; → **importance**, etc. **7.** Stoff: aus, von: **a dress ~ silk** ein Kleid aus Seide, ein Seidenkleid; **(made) ~ steel** aus Stahl (hergestellt). **8.** Urheberschaft, Art u. Weise: von: **the works ~ Shakespeare**; **it was clever ~ him.** **9.** Ursache, Grund: a) an (dat): → **think** 1, etc, b) auf (acc): → **proud** 1, etc, c) vor (dat): → **afraid**, etc, d) nach: → **smell** 2, etc. **10.** Thema: an (acc): → **think** 6, etc. **11.** Apposition, unübersetzt: a) **the city ~ London** die Stadt London; **the month ~ April** der Monat April, b) Maß: **a glass ~ wine** ein Glas Wein; **a piece ~ meat** ein Stück Fleisch. **12.** Zeit: a) von: **your letter ~ March 3rd** Ihr Schreiben vom 3. März, b) Am. vor: **ten (minutes) ~ three**.

off [ɒf] **I** adv **1.** fort(...), weg(...): **be ~** (Sport) gestartet sein; **I must be ~** ich muß gehen od. weg; **~ with you!** fort mit dir!; → **go off** 1, etc. **2.** ab(...): → **cut off**, **hat**, etc. **3.** weg, entfernt: **three miles ~. 4. ~ and on** ab u. zu, hin u. wieder. **5.** ✝ 5% ~ 5% Nachlaß; → **take off** 5. **6.** aus(...), aus-, abgeschaltet: → **switch** 5, 6, etc. **7. be ~** ausfallen, nicht stattfinden: **their engagement is ~** sie haben ihre Verlobung gelöst. **8.** aus(gegangen), alle. **9. she is ~ today** sie hat heute ihren freien Tag; **give s.o. the afternoon ~** j-m den Nachmittag freigeben; **take a day ~** sich e-n Tag frei nehmen. **10.** nicht mehr frisch, verdorben (Nahrungsmittel): → **go off** 6. **11. well (badly) ~** gut (schlecht) d(a)ran od. gestellt od. situiert: **how are you ~ for ...?** wie sieht es bei dir mit ... aus? **II** prp **12.** weg von, von (... weg od. ab od.

herunter): *jump ~ the bus* vom Bus abspringen; → *get off, grass* 2, *etc.* **13.** abseits von (*od. gen*), von ... weg: *a street ~ Piccadilly* e-e Seitenstraße von Piccadilly. **14.** *be ~ duty* nicht im Dienst sein, dienstfrei haben. **15.** *be ~ s.th.* et. nicht mehr mögen; von et. kuriert sein: → *drug* 2. **16.** ♣ *vor der Küste etc*. **III** *adj* **17.** (arbeits-, dienst)frei. **18.** schlecht (*Tag etc*): *this is an ~ day for me* heute geht mir alles schief, das ist heute nicht mein Tag; *an ~ year for fruit* ein schlechtes Obstjahr. **19.** *on the ~ chance* auf gut Glück; in der Hoffnung (*of getting* zu bekommen); *~ season* Nebensaison *f*.

of·fal ['ɒfl] *s gastr.* Innereien *pl.*

'off·beat *adj* F ausgefallen, unkonventionell. **,~'col·o(u)r** *adj* **1.** *be* (*od. feel*) *~* sich nicht wohl fühlen. **2.** gewagt (*Witz etc*).

of·fence [ə'fens] *s* **1.** *allg.* Vergehen *n*, Verstoß *m* (*against* gegen). **2.** ⚖️ Straftat *f*; Vergehen *n*. **3.** Beleidigung *f*, Kränkung *f*: *give* (*od. cause*) *~* Anstoß *od.* Ärgernis erregen (*to* bei); *take ~* Anstoß nehmen (*at an dat*); *be quick* (*od. swift*) *to take ~* schnell beleidigt sein; *no ~* (*meant od. intended*) nichts für ungut!; *no ~* (*taken*) (es) ist schon gut! **4.** Angriff *m*.

of·fend [ə'fend] **I** *v/t* beleidigen, kränken: *be ~ed at* (*od. by*) sich beleidigt fühlen durch. **II** *v/i* verstoßen (*against* gegen). **of·fend·er** *s* (Übel-, Misse)Täter(in): *first ~* ⚖️ nicht Vorbestrafte *m*, *f*, Ersttäter(in).

of·fense *Am.* → offence.

of·fen·sive [ə'fensɪv] **I** *adj* □ **1.** beleidigend, anstößig: *~* **2.** widerlich (*Geruch etc*). **3.** ✗, *Sport:* Angriffs..., Offensiv... **II** *s* **4.** *allg.* Offensive *f*: *take the ~* die Offensive ergreifen.

of·fer ['ɒfə] **I** *v/t* **1.** anbieten: → *resistance* 1. **2.** a) ✝ Ware anbieten (*for sale* zum Verkauf), offerieren, b) ✝ *Preis, Summe* bieten, c) *Preis, Belohnung* aussetzen. **3.** *Entschuldigung etc* vorbringen, *Vorschlag* machen. **4.** sich bereit erklären (*to do* zu tun): *~ to help* s-e Hilfe anbieten. **II** *v/i* **5.** es *od.* sich anbieten. **III** *s* **6.** Angebot *n*: *make s.o. an ~ of s.th.* j-m et. anbieten; *his ~ of help*

sein Angebot zu helfen, s-e angebotene Hilfe. **7.** ✝ (An)Gebot *n*, Offerte *f* (*of* über *acc*): *on ~* zu verkaufen; im Angebot; *or near ~* Verhandlungsbasis.

,off'hand **I** *adv* **1.** auf Anhieb, so ohne weiteres. **II** *adj* **2.** improvisiert, Stegreif... **3.** lässig (*Art etc*), hingeworfen (*Bemerkung*).

of·fice ['ɒfɪs] *s* **1.** Büro *n*, (e-r *Institution*) Geschäftsstelle *f*, (*Anwalts*)Kanzlei *f*: *at the ~* im Büro. **2.** *mst* ⓩ *bsd. Br.* Ministerium *n*: → *foreign* 1, *Home Office*. **3.** (*bsd.* öffentliches) Amt, Posten *m*: *be in* (*out of*) *~* (nicht mehr) im Amt sein; (nicht mehr) an der Macht sein. **~ block** *s* Bürogebäude *n*. **~ boy** *s* Bürogehilfe *m*. **~ cli·mate** *s* Betriebsklima *n*. **~ girl** *s* Bürogehilfin *f*. **'~,hold·er** *s* Amtsinhaber(in). **~ hours** *pl Dienst*zeit *f*; Geschäfts-, Öffnungszeiten *pl.*

of·fi·cer ['ɒfɪsə] *s* **1.** ✗ Offizier *m*. **2.** (*Polizei- etc*)Beamte *m*.

of·fi·cial [ə'fɪʃl] **I** *adj* □ **1.** offiziell, amtlich, dienstlich: *~ duties pl* Amtspflichten *pl*; *~ language* Amtssprache *f*; *~ secret* Amts-, Dienstgeheimnis *n*; *~ trip* Dienstreise *f*; → *channel*, *residence* 1. **II** *s* **2.** Beamte *m*, Beamtin *f*. **3.** (*Gewerkschafts- etc*)Funktionär (-in). **of·fi·cial·dom** *s* Beamtentum *n*, *die Beamten pl.* **of,fi·cial'ese** [,ʃə'liːz] *s* Amtsenglisch *n*, Behördensprache *f*.

of·fi·cious [ə'fɪʃəs] *adj* □ übereifrig, übertrieben dienstbeflissen.

off·ing ['ɒfɪŋ] *s*: *be in the ~* sich abzeichnen, in Sicht sein.

'off- **,li·cence** *s Br.* Wein- u. Spirituosenhandlung *f*. **'~-peak** *adj*: *~ electricity* Nachtstrom *m*; *~ hours pl* verkehrsschwache Stunden *pl.* **'~,put·ting** *adj* *Br.* F unangenehm, störend; unsympathisch (*Person, Wesen*). **~-set I** *s* ['ɒfset] **1.** Ausgleich *m*: *as an ~* als Ausgleich (*to* für). **2.** *typ.* Offsetdruck *m*. **II** *v/t* [ɒf'set] (*irr set*) ausgleichen. **'~-shoot** *s* ⚘ Ableger *m* (*a. fig.*), Sprößling *m*. **'~-shore I** *adv* vor der Küste. **II** *adj* küstennah: *~ boring* Off-shore-Bohrung *f*; *~ fishing* Küstenfischerei *f*. **'~-side** *adj u. adv Sport:* abseits: *be ~* abseits *od.* im Abseits stehen; *~ position* Abseitsposition *f*, -stellung *f*. **~ trap** Abseitsfalle *f.* **'~-spring** *s* **1.** Nachkommen(schaft *f*) *pl.* **2.** *pl offspring*

Abkömmling *m*, Nachkomme *m*. ˌ~-the-'rec·ord *adj u. adv* nicht für die Öffentlichkeit bestimmt, inoffiziell.

of·ten ['ɒfn] *adv* oft(mals); häufig: *more* ~ öfters; *as* ~ *as* jedesmal wenn; *as* ~ *as* (*od. more* ~ *than*) *not* sehr oft; *ever so* ~ öfters, von Zeit zu Zeit.

o·gle ['əʊgl] *v/t* (*a. v/i:* ~ *at*) *j-m* (schöne) Augen machen; *contp.* begaffen.

oh [əʊ] *int.* oh!: → *dear* 5, *yes* I.

ohm [əʊm] *s ⚡* Ohm *n*.

oil [ɔɪl] **I** *s* 1. Öl *n*: *pour* ~ *on troubled waters fig.* Öl auf die Wogen gießen; → *midnight* II. 2. (Erd)Öl *n*: *strike* ~ auf Öl stoßen; *fig.* Glück *od.* Erfolg haben, *a.* fündig werden. 3. *mst pl* Ölfarbe *f*: *paint in* ~*s* in Öl malen. **II** *v/t* 4. (ein)ölen, schmieren: ~ *the wheels fig.* für *e-n* reibungslosen Ablauf sorgen; → *palm*¹ 1. ~ *change* *s mot.* Ölwechsel *m*: *do an* ~ *e-n* Ölwechsel machen. ~ **col·o(u)r** *s* Ölfarbe *f*. ~ **cri·sis** *s* (*irr crisis*) Ölkrise *f*. ~ **dip·stick** *s mot.* Ölmeßstab *m*. '~**field** *s* Ölfeld *n*. '~ˌ**fired** *adj*: ~ *central heating* Ölzentralheizung *f*. ~ **lamp** *s* Öl-, Petroleumlampe *f*. ~ **lev·el** *s mot.* Ölstand *m*. ~ **paint** *s* Ölfarbe *f*. ~ **paint·ing** *s* 1. Ölmalerei *f*. 2. Ölgemälde *n*: *she's no* ~ *F* sie ist keine strahlende Schönheit. '~-pro-ˌduc·ing coun·try *s* Ölförderland *n*. ~ **rig** *s* (Öl)Bohrinsel *f*. ~ **sheik(h)** *s* Ölscheich *m*. ~ **slick** *s* Ölteppich *m*. ~ **tank·er** *s* (Öl)Tanker *m*. ~ **well** *s* Ölquelle *f*.

oil·y ['ɔɪlɪ] *adj* 1. ölig. 2. *fig.* schleimig.

oint·ment ['ɔɪntmənt] *s* Salbe *f*.

OK, o·kay [ˌəʊ'keɪ] F **I** *adj u. int* okay(!), o.k.(!), in Ordnung(!). **II** *v/t* genehmigen, *e-r* Sache zustimmen. **III** *s* Okay *n*, O.K. *n*, Genehmigung *f*, Zustimmung *f*.

old [əʊld] **I** *adj* 1. *allg.* alt: *grow* ~ alt werden, altern; *I'm getting* ~ ich werde alt!; *ten years* ~ zehn Jahre alt; *a ten-year-*~ *boy* ein zehnjähriger Junge; ~ *boy Br.* ehemaliger Schüler, Ehemalige *m*; ~ *girl Br.* ehemalige Schülerin, Ehemalige *f*; *be* ~ *hat* F ein alter Hut sein; *the* (*od. his*) ~ *lady* (*od. woman*) F *s-e* Alte; *s-e* alte Dame; *the* (*od. her*) ~ *man* F ihr alter Herr; ~ *people's home* Alten-, Altersheim *n*; *of the* ~ *school Gentleman etc.* der alten Schule; ⚹ *Testament das Alte*

Testament; ~ *wives' tale* Ammenmärchen *n*; ⚹ *World die* Alte Welt; → *flame* 1, *hand* 6, *maid* 1. 2. *sl.* (*verstärkend*) *have a fine* ~ *time* sich köstlich amüsieren; *I can use any* ~ *thing* ich hab' für alles Verwendung; *come any* ~ *time* komm, wann du *dir gerade paßt*. **II** *s* 3. *the* ~ *pl* die Alten *pl*. ~ *age s* (hohes) Alter: *in one's* ~ im Alter; *die of* (*od. from*) ~ an Altersschwäche sterben. '~-**age** *adj* Alters...: ~ *pension* Rente *f*, Pension *f*; ~ *pensioner* Rentner(in), Pensionär(in). ˌ~-**es'tab·lished** *adj* alteingesessen (*Firma etc.*), alt (*Brauch etc.*). ˌ~-'**fash·ioned** *adj* 1. altmodisch. 2. *Br.* F mißbilligend (*Blick etc.*). ˌ~-'**maid·ish** *adj* □ altjüngferlich.

old·ster ['əʊldstə] *s* F ältere Person.

ˌ**old-'tim·er** *s* F 1. alter Hase. 2. *bsd. Am.* → *oldster*.

o·le·an·der [ˌəʊlɪ'ændə] *s* ♣ Oleander *m*.

ol·fac·to·ry [ɒl'fæktərɪ] *adj* Geruchs...

ol·i·garch ['ɒlɪgɑːk] *s* Oligarch *m*.

ol·i·gar·chy ['ɒlɪgɑːkɪ] *s* Oligarchie *f*.

ol·ive ['ɒlɪv] **I** *s* 1. *a.* ~ *tree* Oliven-, Ölbaum *m*. 2. Olive *f*. ~ *oil* Olivenöl *n*. **II** *adj* 3. olivgrün.

O·lym·pi·ad [əʊ'lɪmpɪæd] *s* Olympiade *f*. **O·lym·pic** I *adj* olympisch: ~ *champion* Olympiasieger(in); ~ *Games* → II; *Summer* (*Winter*) ~ *Games pl* Olympische Sommer-(Winter)spiele *pl*. **II** *s pl* Olympische Spiele *pl*.

om·buds·man ['ɒmbʊdzmən] *s* (*irr man*) *s pol.* Ombudsmann *m*.

om·e·lett *s Am.*, **om·e·lette** *s bsd. Br.* ['ɒmlɪt] Omelett *n*.

o·men ['əʊmen] *s* Omen *n*, Vorzeichen *n*.

om·i·nous ['ɒmɪnəs] *adj* □ ominös, unheilvoll: *that's* ~ das läßt nichts Gutes ahnen.

o·mis·sion [ə'mɪʃn] *s* 1. Aus-, Weglassung *f*. 2. Unterlassung *f*, Versäumnis *n*: *sin of* ~ Unterlassungssünde *f*.

o·mit [ə'mɪt] *v/t* 1. aus-, weglassen (*from* aus). 2. ~ *doing* (*od. to do*) *s.th.* versäumen *od.* es unterlassen, et. zu tun.

om·ni·bus ['ɒmnɪbəs] *s* Sammelband *n*.

om·nis·ci·ent [ɒm'nɪsɪənt] *adj* □ allwissend.

on [ɒn] **I** *prp* 1. auf (*acc od. dat*). 2. getragen von: auf (*dat*), an (*dat*), in (*dat*): *find s.th.* ~ *s.o.* et. bei *j-m* finden; *have you got some money* ~ *you?* hast du Geld bei dir?; → *foot* 1, *etc.* 3. fest-

gemacht od. sehr nahe: an (*dat*): **the dog is ~ the chain;** ~ **the Thames. 4.** *Richtung, Ziel:* auf (*acc*) ... (hin), an (*acc*): **drop s.th.** ~ **the floor** et. zu Boden fallen lassen; **hang s.th.** ~ **a peg** et. an e-n Haken hängen; → **board** 6, *etc.* **5.** *fig. auf der Grundlage von:* auf (*acc*) ... (hin): ~ **this theory** nach dieser Theorie; → **condition** 1, *etc.* **6.** *aufeinanderfolgend:* auf (*acc*), über (*acc*): **loss** ~ **loss** Verlust auf *od.* über Verlust; **be** ~ **one's second glass** beim zweiten Glas sein. **7.** (*gehörig*) zu, (*beschäftigt*) bei: **be** ~ **a committee** zu e-m Ausschuß gehören. **8.** *Zustand:* in (*dat*), auf (*dat*): **be** ~ **Medikament** *etc* ständig nehmen; *b.s.* ...abhängig od. ...süchtig sein; → **duty** 2, *etc.* **9.** *gerichtet:* auf (*acc*): **a joke** ~ **s.o.** ein Spaß auf j-s Kosten; **the next round is** ~ **me** F die nächste Runde geht auf m-e Rechnung. **10.** *Thema:* über (*acc*): **talk** ~ **a subject. 11.** *Zeitpunkt:* an (*dat*): ~ **June 3rd** am 3. Juni; ~ **the morning of July 1st** am Morgen des 1. Juli. **II** *adv* **12.** an..., auf...: ~ **put on** 1, **keep on** 1, *etc.* **13.** weiter(...): **and so** ~ u. so weiter; ~ **and** ~ immer weiter; ~ **and off** ab u. zu; **from that day** ~ von dem Tage an. **III** *adj* **14. be** ~ a) vor sich gehen: **what's** ~? was ist los?, b) an sein (*Licht, Radio etc*), c) *thea.* gegeben werden (*Stück*), laufen (*Film*), (*Rundfunk, TV*) gesendet werden. **15. be always** ~ **at s.o.** F j-m dauernd in den Ohren liegen (*about* wegen).

once [wʌns] **I** *adv* **1.** einmal: ~ **again** (*od. more*) noch einmal; ~ **or twice** ein paarmal; ~ **in a while** ab u. zu, hin u. wieder; ~ **and for all** ein für allemal; not ~ kein einziges Mal; → **lifetime** I, **moon** I. **2.** einmal, einst: ~ **upon a time there was** es war einmal. **II** *s* **3. the** ~ einmal, ein einziges Mal; **this** ~ dieses 'eine Mal. **at** ~ a) auf einmal, gleichzeitig, b) sofort: **all at** ~ mit 'einem Mal. **III** *cj* **5.** sobald *od.* wenn (einmal).

'~-,o·ver *s:* **give s.th. the** (*od. a*) ~ F et. kurz mustern.

on·com·ing ['ɒn,kʌmɪŋ] *adj* entgegenkommend: ~ **traffic** Gegenverkehr *m.*

one [wʌn] **I** *adj* **1.** ein(e): → **hundred** 1, **thousand** 1. **2.** betont: einzig: **they were all of** ~ **mind** sie waren alle 'einer

Meinung; **his** ~ **thought** sein einziger Gedanke; **my** ~ **and only hope** m-e einzige Hoffnung; **the** ~ **and only ...** der einzigartige *od.* unvergleichliche ... **3.** ein gewisser, e-e gewisse, ein gewisses: ~ **day** e-s Tages; ~ **John Smith** ein gewisser John Smith. **II** *s* **4.** Eins *f*, Eins *n:* **at** ~ um eins; **be** ~ **up on s.o.** j-m voraus sein; → **number** 2. **5.** *der, die, das* einzelne: ~ **by** ~, ~ **after the other** e-r nach dem andern; **I for** ~ ich zum Beispiel; ~ **another** 1. **III** *pron* **6.** ein(e): **the** ~ **who** der(jenige), welcher; ~ **another** sich (gegenseitig), einander. **7.** Stützwort, *mst unübersetzt:* **the little** ~**s** die Kleinen; **a red pencil and a blue** ~ ein roter Bleistift u. ein blauer. **8.** man. **9.** ~'**s** sein: **break** ~ **leg** sich das Bein brechen. **,~'armed** *adj:* ~ **bandit** F einarmiger Bandit. **,~'eyed** *adj* einäugig. **,~'hand·ed** *adj u. adv* einhändig. **,~'horse** *adj* einspännig: ~ **town** F Nest *n*, Kaff *n*. **,~'legged** *adj* einbeinig. **'~-man** *adj* Einmann...: ~ **band** Einmannkapelle *f*; ~ **play** *thea.* Personenstück *n*; ~ **show** One-man-Show *f*. **'~-night** *adj:* ~ **stand** *thea. etc* einmaliges Gastspiel. **'~-piece** *adj* einteilig.

on·er·ous ['ɒnərəs] *adj* □ lästig, beschwerlich (**to** für).

one'self *pron* **1.** *reflex* sich (selbst *od.* selber): (**all**) **by** ~ ganz allein; **cut** ~ sich schneiden. **2.** sich selbst *od.* selber. **3.** man selbst *od.* selber: **be** ~ sich normal *od.* natürlich benehmen *od.* geben; **not to be** ~ nicht auf der Höhe sein; nicht ganz bei Verstand sein; **be** ~ **again** wieder der ganz der alte sein.

,one-l'sid·ed *adj* □ einseitig (*a. fig.*). **'~-time** *adj* ehemalig, früher. **'~-track** *adj* 🚆 eingleisig: **have a** ~ **mind** *fig.* immer nur dasselbe im Kopf haben. **'~-way** *adj* **1.** Einbahn...: ~ **street. 2.** ~ **ticket** *Am.* einfache Fahrkarte, 🎫 einfaches Ticket. **3.** *fig.* einseitig.

'on,go·ing *adj* laufend (*Verhandlungen etc*).

on·ion ['ʌnjən] *s* Zwiebel *f:* **know one's** ~**s** F sein Geschäft verstehen.

'on,look·er *s* Zuschauer(in).

on·ly ['əʊnlɪ] **I** *adj* **1.** einzig: ~ **child** Einzelkind *n*; → **one** 2. **II** *adv* **2.** nur, bloß: **if** ~ **he would leave!** wenn er doch nur endlich ginge!; → **but** 2. **3.** erst: ~ **yes-**

terday; ~ *just* eben erst, gerade. **III** *cj* **4.** nur, bloß.

'on|·rush *s* Ansturm *m*. **'~·set** *s* Einbruch *m*, Beginn *m* (*des Winters*); Ausbruch *m* (*e-r Krankheit*). **~·slaught** ['~slɔːt] *s* (heftiger) Angriff (*a. fig.*).

,~·the-'job *adj* praktisch (*Ausbildung*).

on·to ['ɒntu] *prp* **1.** auf (*acc*). **2. *be* ~ *s.o.*** F j-m auf die Schliche gekommen sein.

on·ward(s) ['ɒnwəd(z)] *adv* vorwärts, weiter: *from today* ~ von heute an.

oo·dles ['uːdlz] *s pl* F: ~ *of money* Geld wie Heu; ~ *of time* jede Menge *od.* massenhaft Zeit.

ooze [uːz] **I** *v/i* (ein-, durch)sickern, (-)dringen (*a. Licht, Geräusch etc*): ~ *away* versickern; *fig.* schwinden (*Mut etc*); ~ *out* aussickern; entweichen (*Luft, Gas*); *fig.* durchsickern (*Geheimnis etc*). **II** *v/t* absondern; *fig.* Charme ausstrahlen, *Optimismus, gute Laune etc a.* verströmen; von *Sarkasmus etc* triefen.

o·pal ['əʊpl] *s min.* Opal *m*.

o·paque [əʊ'peɪk] *adj* □ **1.** undurchsichtig. **2.** *fig.* unverständlich.

o·pen ['əʊpən] **I** *adj* □ **1.** *allg.* offen (*Buch, Fenster, Flasche etc*): *the door is* ~ die Tür ist *od.* steht offen; *hold the door* ~ *for s.o.* j-m die Tür aufhalten; *keep one's eyes* ~ *fig.* die Augen offenhalten; → *arm*[1] 1, *book* 1. **2.** offen (*Gelände, Meer*), frei (*Feld*): → *air*[1] 1. **3.** geöffnet, offen (*Laden etc*). **4.** *fig.* offen (**to** für); öffentlich: ~ *letter* offener Brief; ~ *tournament* → 13. **5.** *fig.* zugänglich, aufgeschlossen (**to** für *od.* dat). **6.** *fig.* ausgesetzt, unterworfen (**to** dat): ~ *to question* anfechtbar; *that is* ~ *to argument* darüber läßt sich streiten. **7.** *fig.* offen, unentschieden (*Frage etc*). **8.** *fig.* a) offen, freimütig: *be* ~ *with s.o.* offen mit j-m reden, b) offen(kundig), unverhüllt: ~ *secret* offenes Geheimnis. **9.** ~ *cheque* ✝ *Br.* Barscheck *m*. **10.** ~ *season* Jagdzeit *f*. **11.** *ling.* offen (*Vokal*). **II** *s* **12.** *in the* ~ im Freien: *bring into the* ~ *fig.* an die Öffentlichkeit bringen; *come into the* ~ *fig.* Farbe bekennen; an die Öffentlichkeit treten (*with* mit). **13.** *Golf, Tennis:* offenes Turnier. **III** *v/t* **14.** *allg.* öffnen, aufmachen, *Buch etc a.* aufschlagen. **15.** *Debatte, Feuer, Konto etc* eröffnen, *neuen*

Markt etc erschließen: ~ *to traffic* Straße *etc* dem Verkehr übergeben. **16.** *fig.* Gefühle, Gedanken enthüllen: ~ *o.s. to s.o.* sich j-m mitteilen. **IV** *v/i* **17.** sich öffnen, aufgehen. **18.** öffnen, aufmachen (*Laden etc*). **19.** führen, gehen (*onto* auf *acc* [... hinaus]) (*Tür, Fenster*). **20.** anfangen, beginnen; anlaufen (*Film*).

Verbindungen mit Adverbien:

o·pen| out *I v/t* ausbreiten, *Stadtplan etc* auseinanderfalten. **II** *v/i* auftauen, mitteilsam werden. ~ **up** *I v/t* **1.** aufmachen, -schließen. **2.** *neuen Markt etc* erschließen, *Möglichkeiten etc* eröffnen. **II** *v/i* **3.** aufmachen, -schließen. **4.** *fig.* a) loslegen (**with** mit), b) → **open out** II.

,o·pen-'air *adj im Freien:* ~ *festival* Open-air-Festival *n*; ~ *swimming pool* Freibad *n*; ~ *theater* (*bsd. Br.* **theatre**) Freilichttheater *n*. **,~-'end·ed** *adj* zeitlich unbegrenzt: ~ *discussion* Open-end-Diskussion *f*.

o·pen·er ['əʊpnə] *s* **1.** (*Dosen-, Flaschen-*)Öffner *m*. **2.** *Am.* Eröffnungsnummer *f* (*e-r Show etc*).

,o·pen-'eyed *adj* mit großen Augen, staunend. **,~-'hand·ed** *adj* □ freigebig.

o·pen·ing ['əʊpnɪŋ] *I s* **1.** Öffnung *f*. **2.** ✝ freie Stelle. **3.** Eröffnung *f* (*e-r Debatte, des Feuers, e-s Kontos etc*), Erschließung *f* (*e-s neuen Markts etc*). **II** *adj* **4.** Eröffnungs...: ~ *ceremony* **; ~ *night* *thea.* Eröffnungsvorstellung *f*. **5.** Öffnungs...: ~ *time*; ~ *time is at* ... das Geschäft *etc* ist ab ... geöffnet.

,o·pen-'mind·ed *adj* □ aufgeschlossen. **,~-'mouthed** *adj* sprachlos. **,~-'plan** *adj*: ~ *office* Großraumbüro *n*. ~ *shop* *s* ✝ Betrieb, der auch Nichtgewerkschaftsmitglieder beschäftigt. **⚲ U·ni·ver·si·ty** *s Br.* Fern(seh)universität *f* (*deren Kurse a. ohne entsprechenden Schulabschluß belegt werden können*).

op·er·a[1] ['ɒpərə] *s ♪* Oper *f*: *go to the* ~ in die Oper gehen.

op·er·a[2] [~] *pl von* **opus**.

op·er·a·ble ['ɒpərəbl] *adj* □ **1.** durchführbar. **2.** ⚙ betriebsfähig. **3.** 𝒔 operabel, operierbar.

op·er·a| glass·es *s pl, a. pair of* ~

Opernglas n. ~ **house** s Opernhaus n, Oper f.

op·er·ate ['ɒpəreɪt] **I** v/i **1.** bsd. ◎ arbeiten, in Betrieb sein, laufen (*Maschine etc*). **2.** wirksam sein od. werden; sich auswirken (**against** gegen; **in s.o.'s favo[u]r** zu j-s Gunsten). **3.** ✻ operieren (**on s.o.** j-n): ~ **on s.o. for appendicitis** j-n am Blinddarm operieren. **4.** ✝ tätig sein. **5.** ✕ operieren. **II** v/t **6.** ◎ *Maschine* bedienen, *Schalter, Bremse etc* betätigen. **7.** *Unternehmen, Geschäft* führen.

op·er·at·ic [ˌɒpəˈrætɪk] adj ♪ Opern...

op·er·at·ing ['ɒpəreɪtɪŋ] adj **1.** bsd. ◎ Betriebs..., Arbeits...: ~ **instructions** pl Bedienungs-, Betriebsanleitung f. **2.** ✝ betrieblich, Betriebs...: ~ **costs** (od. **expenses**) pl Betriebskosten pl. **3.** ✻ Operations...: ~ **room** Am., ~ **theatre** Br. Operationssaal m; ~ **table** Operationstisch m. ˌop·er'a·tion s **1.** bsd. ⚖ Wirksamkeit f, Geltung f: **be in ~** in Kraft sein; **come into ~** in Kraft treten. **2.** bsd. ◎ Betrieb m, Lauf m (e-r *Maschine etc*): **in ~** in Betrieb; **put** (od. **set**) **in** (**out of**) ~ in (außer) Betrieb setzen. **3.** ◎ Bedienung f, Betätigung f. **4.** ◎ etc Wirkungs-, Arbeitsweise f; Arbeitsgang m. **5.** ✝ Geschäft n, (*Börse*) Transaktion f. **6.** ✻ Operation f: ~ **for appendicitis** Blinddarmoperation f; **have an ~ on one's arm** am Arm operiert werden. **7.** ✕ Operation f, Unternehmen n. ˌop·er'a·tion·al adj [ˌ~ʃənl] adj **1.** bsd. ◎ Betriebs..., Arbeits...; ◎ betriebsbereit. **2.** ✝ betrieblich, Betriebs... **3.** ✕ Operations..., Einsatz... **op·er·a·tive** ['ɒpərətɪv] adj **1.** wirksam: **become ~** bsd. ⚖ in Kraft treten: **the ~ word** genau das richtige Wort. **2.** ✻ operativ. **op·er·a·tor** ['~reɪtə] s **1.** (Maschinen)Arbeiter(in), (*Kran- etc*-)Führer(in); (*Computer*) Operator m. **2.** teleph. Vermittlung f, Fräulein n (vom Amt). **3.** (*Reise*)Veranstalter(in). **4.** a **clever** (od. **smooth**) ~ F ein raffinierter Kerl.

op·er·et·ta [ˌɒpəˈretə] s ♪ Operette f.

oph·thal·mic [ɒfˈθælmɪk] adj Augen...

o·pi·ate ['əʊpɪət] s pharm. **1.** Opiat n, Opiumpräparat n. **2.** Schlaf- od. Beruhigungsmittel n.

o·pin·ion [əˈpɪnjən] s **1.** Meinung f, An-

sicht f: **in my ~** m-s Erachtens, m-r Meinung od. Ansicht nach; **be of the ~ that** der Meinung od. Ansicht sein, daß; **be of s.o.'s ~** j-s Meinung od. Ansicht sein; **that is a matter of ~** das ist Ansichtssache; **public ~** die öffentliche Meinung. **2.** Meinung f: **form an ~ of** sich e-e Meinung bilden von; **have a good** (od. **high**) (**bad, low**) ~ **of** e-e (keine) hohe Meinung haben von. **3.** Gutachten n (**on** über acc). **o'pin·ion·at·ed** [ˌ~eɪtɪd] adj □ starr-, eigensinnig.

o·pin·ion| poll s Meinungsumfrage f. ~ **re·search** s Meinungsforschung f.

o·pi·um ['əʊpjəm] s Opium n.

o·pos·sum [əˈpɒsəm] s zo. Opossum n, Beutelratte f.

op·po·nent [əˈpəʊnənt] s Gegner(in), Gegenspieler(in) (beide a. Sport).

op·por·tune ['ɒpətjuːn] adj □ **1.** günstig, passend. **2.** rechtzeitig. 'op·por·tun·ism s Opportunismus m. 'op·por·tun·ist **I** s Opportunist(in). **II** adj opportunistisch. ˌop·por'tu·ni·ty s Gelegenheit f, Möglichkeit f, Chance f (**of doing, to do** zu tun; **for s.th.** für od. zu et.): **at the first** (od. **earliest**) ~ bei der erstbesten Gelegenheit; → **equal 1, equality**.

op·pose [əˈpəʊz] v/t sich widersetzen (dat), angehen gegen. **op'posed** adj **1.** entgegengesetzt: **as ~ to** im Gegensatz zu. **2.** **be ~ to** ablehnend gegenüberstehen (dat), sein gegen. **op'pos·ing** adj Sport: gegnerisch (Mannschaft). **op·po·site** ['ɒpəzɪt] **I** adj □ **1.** gegenüberliegend. **2.** entgegengesetzt (Richtung). **3.** gegensätzlich, entgegengesetzt: → **sex 1. 4.** gegnerisch, Gegen...: ~ **number** (Amts)Kollege m. **II** s **5.** Gegenteil n, -satz m: **be completely** (od. **just**) **the ~** genau das Gegenteil sein. **III** adv **6.** gegenüber (**to** dat). **IV** prp **7.** gegenüber (dat). ˌop·po'si·tion s **1.** Widerstand m, Opposition f (**to** gegen). **2.** Gegensatz m: **be in ~ to** im Gegensatz stehen zu. **3.** oft ⚷ parl. Opposition f: **be in ~** in der Opposition sein; ~ **politician** Oppositionspolitiker(in).

op·press [əˈpres] v/t **1.** bedrücken, (a. Hitze etc) lasten auf (dat). **2.** unterdrücken, tyrannisieren. **op·pres·sion** [əˈpreʃn] s **1.** Bedrücktheit f. **2.** Unterdrückung f, Tyrannisierung f. **op'pres·sive** [ˌ~sɪv] adj □ **1.** bedrückend. **2.**

drückend (*Hitze, Steuern* etc). **3.** tyrannisch. **op'pres·sor** *s* Unterdrücker *m*, Tyrann *m*.

opt [ɒpt] *v/i* sich entscheiden (**for** für; **against** gegen; **to do** zu tun): **~ out** sich dagegen entscheiden; abspringen, zurücktreten (**of** von).

op·tic ['ɒptɪk] **I** *adj* (**~ally**) Augen..., Seh...: **~ nerve** Sehnerv *m*. **II** *s pl* (*sg konstruiert*) Optik *f*. **'op·ti·cal** *adj* □ optisch: **~ illusion** optische Täuschung. **op'ti·cian** [~ʃn] *s* Optiker(in).

op·ti·ma ['ɒptɪmə] *pl von* **optimum. op·ti·mal** ['~ml] *adj* □ → **optimum** II.

op·ti·mism ['ɒptɪmɪzəm] *s* Optimismus *m*. **'op·ti·mist** *s* Optimist(in). **op·ti-'mis·tic** *adj* (**~ally**) optimistisch. **'op·ti-mize** *v/t* optimieren.

op·ti·mum ['ɒptɪməm] **I** *pl* **-ma** [~mə], **-mums** *s* Optimum *n*. **II** *adj* optimal, bestmöglich: **in ~ condition** in Bestzustand.

op·tion ['ɒpʃn] *s* **1.** Wahl *f*: **I had no ~ but to** ich hatte keine andere Wahl als zu, mir blieb nichts anderes übrig als zu; **leave one's ~s open** sich alle Möglichkeiten offenlassen. **2.** Option *f*, Vorkaufsrecht *n* (**on** auf *acc*). **3.** *bsd. mot.* Extra *n*, *pl a.* Sonderausstattung *f*. **op·tion·al** ['~ʃənl] *adj* □ freiwillig, fakultativ: **be an ~ extra** *bsd. mot.* gegen Aufpreis erhältlich sein; **~ subject** *ped.* Wahlfach *n*.

op·u·lence ['ɒpjʊləns] *s* Reichtum *m*: **live in ~** im Überfluß leben. **'op·u·lent** *adj* □ **1.** wohlhabend, reich. **2.** üppig, (*Mahlzeit a.*) opulent.

o·pus ['əʊpəs] *pl* **op·er·a** ['ɒpərə] *bsd. ♪* Opus *n*, Werk *n*.

or [ɔː] *cj* **1.** oder: **in a day ~ two** in ein bis zwei Tagen; **~ so I believe** glaube ich zumindest; → **either** 5, 6, **else** 3, **so** 3. **2.** *nach neg*: noch, u. auch nicht.

or·a·cle ['ɒrəkl] *s* Orakel *n*. **o·rac·u·lar** [ɒ'rækjʊlə] *adj* □ orakelhaft.

o·ral ['ɔːrəl] **I** *adj* □ **1.** mündlich. **2.** Mund...: **~ cavity** *anat.* Mundhöhle *f*. **II** *s* **3.** *ped.* mündliche Prüfung, *das* Mündliche.

or·ange ['ɒrɪndʒ] **I** *s* **⚲** Orange *f*, Apfelsine *f*: **~ squash** *Br.* Getränk *aus* Orangenkonzentrat *u.* Wasser. **II** *adj* orange, orange(n)farben. **or·ange·ade** [~'eɪd]

s Orangeade *f*, (*mit Kohlensäure a.*) Orangenlimonade *f*.

o·rang·u·tan [ɔːˌræŋuːˈtæn] *s zo.* Orang-Utan *m*.

o·ra·tion [ɔːˈreɪʃn] *s* Rede *f*, Ansprache *f*. **or·a·tor** ['ɒrətə] *s* Redner(in). **or·a·tor·i·cal** [ˌ~ˈtɒrɪkl] *adj* □ rednerisch. **or·a·to·ri·o** [ˌɒrəˈtɔːrɪəʊ] *pl* **-os** *s ♪* Oratorium *n*.

or·bit ['ɔːbɪt] **I** *s* **1.** *ast.* Kreis-, Umlaufbahn *f*: **put into ~** 4. **2.** *fig.* (Macht-) Bereich *m*, Einflußsphäre *f*. **II** *v/t* **3.** *Erde etc* umkreisen. **4.** *Satelliten etc* in e-e Umlaufbahn bringen.

or·chard ['ɔːtʃəd] *s* Obstgarten *m*; Obstplantage *f*.

or·ches·tra ['ɔːkɪstrə] *s ♪* Orchester *n*: **~ pit** *thea.* Orchestergraben *m*. **or·ches·tral** [ɔːˈkestrəl] *adj* Orchester... **or·ches·trate** ['ɔːkɪstreɪt] *v/t* orchestrieren.

or·chid ['ɔːkɪd] *s* **⚲** Orchidee *f*.

or·dain [ɔːˈdeɪn] *v/t*: **~ s.o.** (*priest*) *eccl.* j-n ordinieren *od.* zum Priester weihen.

or·deal [ɔːˈdiːl] *s* **1.** *hist.* Gottesurteil *n*. **2.** *fig.* Martyrium *n*, Tortur *f*.

or·der ['ɔːdə] **I** *s* **1.** Ordnung *f*: **in ~** in Ordnung (*a. fig.*); **put in ~** in Ordnung bringen. **2.** (öffentliche) Ordnung: → **law** 1. **3.** Ordnung *f*, System *n*. **4.** (An)Ordnung *f*, Reihenfolge *f*: **in ~ of importance** nach Wichtigkeit; → **alphabetic**. **5.** Ordnung *f*, Aufstellung *f*. **6.** *parl. etc* (Geschäfts)Ordnung *f*: **be the ~ of the day** auf der Tagesordnung stehen (*a. fig.*). **7.** Befehl *m*, Anordnung *f*: **by ~ of** auf Befehl von; **be under** (*od.* **have**) **~s to do s.th.** Befehl haben, et. zu tun; → **marching orders. 8.** **⚲** Bestellung *f* (*a. im Restaurant*), Auftrag *m* (**for** für): **make to ~** auf Bestellung *od.* nach Maß anfertigen; **last ~s, please** Polizeistunde!; → **check** Auftragsbuch *n*; **~ form** Bestellschein *m*. **9.** **in ~ to** um zu. **10.** **out of ~** nicht in Ordnung, defekt. **11.** (Größen)Ordnung *f*: **of** (*od.* **in**) (*Am.* **on**) **the ~ of** in der Größenordnung von. **12.** *eccl. etc* Orden *m*. **II** *v/t* **13.** *j-m* befehlen (**to do** zu tun), et. befehlen, anordnen: **~ about** (*od.* **around**) *j-n* herumkommandieren. **14.** *j-n* ausschicken, beordern (**to** nach): **~ back** zurückbeordern (**to** nach); **~ in** hinein- *od.* hereinkommen lassen; **~ off**

(*Sport*) vom Platz stellen; **~ out** hinausweisen. **15.** ✗ *j-m et.* verordnen: **~ s.o. to (stay in) bed** j-m Bettruhe verordnen. **16.** ✝ bestellen (*a. im Restaurant*). **17.** *fig.* ordnen, in Ordnung bringen: **~ed life** geordnetes Leben. **III** *v/i* **18.** bestellen (*im Restaurant*): **are you ready to ~?** haben Sie schon gewählt? **'or·der·ly** [~lɪ] **I** *adj* **1.** ordentlich, geordnet. **2.** *fig.* gesittet, friedlich (*Menge etc*). **II** *s* **3.** ✗ Hilfspfleger *m*. **4.** ✗ (Offiziers)Bursche *m*.

or·di·nal (num·ber) ['ɔːdɪnl] *s* ⅍ Ordnungszahl *f*.

or·di·nar·i·ly ['ɔːdnrəlɪ] *adv* **1.** normalerweise, gewöhnlich. **2.** wie gewöhnlich *od.* üblich, normal.

or·di·nar·y ['ɔːdnrɪ] **I** *adj* **1.** üblich, gewöhnlich, normal: **in the ~ way** → *dinarily* 1. **2.** alltäglich, mittelmäßig, Durchschnitts... **3.** ordentlich (*Gericht, Mitglied*). **II** *s* **4.** **out of the ~** ungewöhnlich, unüblich: **nothing out of the ~** nichts Ungewöhnliches.

ore [ɔː] *s min.* Erz *n*.

or·gan ['ɔːgən] *s* **1.** *anat.* Organ *n*: **~s** *pl* **of speech** Sprechwerkzeuge *pl*. **2.** *fig.* Organ *n*: a) Werkzeug *n*, Instrument *n*, b) Sprachrohr *n*: **party ~** Parteiorgan *n*. **3.** ♪ Orgel *f*. **~ grind·er** *s* Leierkastenmann *m*.

or·gan·ic [ɔːˈgænɪk] *adj* (**~ally**) organisch (*a. fig.*): **~ chemistry** organische Chemie. **or·gan·ism** [ˈɔːgənɪzəm] *s* biol. Organismus *m* (*a. fig.*).

or·gan·ist ['ɔːgənɪst] *s* ♪ Organist(in).

or·gan·i·za·tion [ˌɔːgənaɪˈzeɪʃn] *s allg.* Organisation *f*. **ˌor·gan·i'za·tion·al** *adj* □ organisatorisch, Organisations... **'or·gan·ize** [~aɪz] *v/t allg.* organisieren: **~d crime** das organisierte Verbrechen; **~d tour** Gesellschaftsreise *f*. **II** *v/i* sich (gewerkschaftlich) organisieren. **'or·gan·iz·er** *s* Organisator(in).

or·gasm ['ɔːgæzəm] *s physiol.* Orgasmus *m*.

or·gy ['ɔːdʒɪ] *s* Orgie *f* (*a. fig.*).

o·ri·ent I *s* ['ɔːrɪənt] ⅍ der Orient, *poet.* das Morgenland. **II** *v/t* [~ent] *fig. et.* ausrichten (**toward[s]** auf *acc*): **~ o.s.** sich orientieren (**by** an *dat*, nach) (*a. fig.*); **~ o.s. to a new situation** sich auf e-e neue Situation einstellen. **o·ri·en·tal** [~ˈentl] **I** *adj* □ orientalisch, *poet.*

morgenländisch: **~ carpet** (*od.* **rug**) Orientteppich *m*. **II** ⅍ Orientale *m*, Orientalin *f*. **o·ri·en·tate** ['~enteɪt] → *orient* II. **ˌo·ri·en·ta·tion** *s* Orientierung *f*, *fig. a.* Ausrichtung *f*.

or·i·fice ['ɒrɪfɪs] *s bsd. anat.* Öffnung *f*.

or·i·gin ['ɒrɪdʒɪn] *s* Ursprung *m*, Abstammung *f*, Herkunft *f*: **country of ~** Ursprungsland *n*; **have its ~ in** zurückgehen auf (*acc*); (her)stammen von (*acc*). aus.

o·rig·i·nal [əˈrɪdʒənl] **I** *adj* (□ → *originally*) **1.** Original..., Ur...: **~ text** Ur*od.* Originaltext *m*. **2.** originell. **II** *s* **3.** Original *n*: **in the ~** im Original *od.* Urtext. **4.** Original *n* (*Person*). **o‚rig·i'nal·i·ty** [~ˈnælətɪ] *s* Originalität *f*. **o'rig·i·nal·ly** [~nəlɪ] *adv* **1.** ursprünglich. **2.** originell.

o·rig·i·nate [əˈrɪdʒəneɪt] **I** *v/i* **1.** (**from**) zurückgehen (auf *acc*), (her)stammen (von *od.* aus). **2.** ausgehen (**from, with** von *j-m*). **II** *v/t* **3.** schaffen, ins Leben rufen. **o'rig·i·na·tor** *s* Urheber(in).

or·na·ment I *s* ['ɔːnəmənt] **1.** Ornament(e *pl*) *n*, Verzierung(en *pl*) *f*, Schmuck *m*. **2.** *fig.* Zier(de) *f* (**to** für *od.* gen). **II** *v/t* ['~ment] **3.** verzieren, schmücken (**with** mit). **or·na·men·tal** [~ˈmentl] *adj* □ dekorativ, schmückend, Zier...: **~ plant** Zierpflanze *f*. **ˌor·na·men'ta·tion** [~menˈ~] *s* Ausschmückung *f*, Verzierung *f*.

or·nate [ɔːˈneɪt] *adj* □ **1.** reichverziert *od.* -geschmückt. **2.** *fig.* überladen (*Stil etc*).

or·ni·thol·o·gist [ˌɔːnɪˈθɒlədʒɪst] *s* Ornithologe *m*, Ornithologin *f*. **ˌor·ni'thol·o·gy** *s* Ornithologie *f*, Vogelkunde *f*.

or·phan ['ɔːfn] **I** *s* Waise(nkind *n*) *f*. **II** *adj* Waisen... **III** *v/t*: **be ~ed** verwaisen, Waise werden. **or·phan·age** ['ɔːfənɪdʒ] *s* Waisenhaus *n*.

or·tho·dox ['ɔːθədɒks] *adj* □ *eccl. u. allg.* orthodox: ⅍ **Church** griechisch-orthodoxe Kirche.

or·tho·graph·ic [ˌɔːθəˈgræfɪk], **or·tho·graph·i·cal** [~l] *adj* □ orthographisch. **or·thog·ra·phy** [ɔːˈθɒgrəfɪ] *s* Orthographie *f*, Rechtschreibung *f*.

or·tho·pae·dic *bsd. Br.*, **or·tho·pe·dic** *Am.* [ˌɔːθəʊˈpiːdɪk] ✗ **I** *adj* (**~ally**) orthopädisch. **II** *s pl* (*oft sg konstruiert*)

Orthopädie f. **｡or·tho'p(a)e·dist** s Orthopäde m, Orthopädin f.

Os·car ['ɒskə] s Oscar m (amerikanischer Filmpreis).

os·cil·late ['ɒsɪleɪt] v/i **1.** bsd. phys. oszillieren, schwingen. **2.** fig. schwanken (**between** zwischen dat.). **｡os·cil'la·tion** s **1.** bsd. phys. Oszillation f, Schwingung f. **2.** fig. Schwanken n.

os·si·fy ['ɒsɪfaɪ] v/i verknöchern (a. fig.).

os·ten·si·ble [ɒ'stensəbl] adj □ **1.** scheinbar. **2.** an-, vorgeblich.

os·ten·ta·tion [｡ɒsten'teɪʃn] s **1.** (protzige) Zurschaustellung. **2.** Protzerei f, Prahlerei f. **｡os·ten'ta·tious** adj □ **1.** protzend, prahlerisch: **be ~ about s.th.** mit et. protzen od. prahlen. **2.** ostentativ, demonstrativ.

os·tra·cism ['ɒstrəsɪzəm] s Ächtung f. **os·tra·cize** ['~saɪz] v/t ächten.

os·trich ['ɒstrɪtʃ] s orn. Strauß m.

oth·er ['ʌðə] **I** adj **1.** ander. **2.** vor s im pl: andere, übrige: **the ~ guests. 3.** ander, weiter, sonstig: **the ~ two** die anderen beiden, die beiden anderen; **any ~ questions?** sonst noch Fragen? **4.** zweit (nur in): **every ~** jeder (jede, jedes) zweite; **every ~ day** jeden zweiten Tag, alle zwei Tage. **5. the ~ day** neulich, kürzlich; **the ~ night** neulich abend. **II** pron **6.** ander (die (der (die, das) andere; **the two ~s** die anderen beiden, die beiden anderen; → **each** II. **III** adj **7.** anders (**than** als). **oth·er·wise** ['~waɪz] adv **1.** a. cj sonst, andernfalls. **2.** sonst, im übrigen. **3.** anderweitig: **be ~ engaged** anderweitig beschäftigt sein; **unless you are ~ engaged** wenn Sie nichts anderes vorhaben. **4.** anders (als): **think ~** anderer Meinung sein; **X, ~ (called)** Y X, a. Y genannt; **or ~** od. sonst irgendwie; od. nicht.

ot·ter ['ɒtə] s zo. Otter m.

ought [ɔːt] v/aux ich sollte, du solltest etc: **he ~ to do it** er sollte es (eigentlich) tun.

ounce [aʊns] s **1.** Unze f. **2.** fig. Körnchen n (Wahrheit), Funke m (Verstand).

our ['aʊə] possessive pron unser: ♀ **Father** eccl. Vaterunser n. **ours** ['aʊəz] possessive pron: **it is ~** es gehört uns; **a friend of ~** ein Freund von uns; **their children and ~** ihre Kinder u. unsere. **our-**

selves [｡~'selvz] pron **1.** verstärkend: wir od. uns selbst: **we did it ~, we ~ did it** wir haben es selbst getan. **2.** reflex uns: **we cut ~. 3.** uns (selbst): **we want it for ~.**

oust [aʊst] v/t fig. verdrängen (**from** aus).

out [aʊt] **I** adv **1.** hinaus(...), heraus(...); aus(...): **way ~** Ausgang m; **on the way ~** beim Hinausgehen; **have a tooth ~** e-n Zahn gezogen bekommen. **2.** außen, draußen. **3.** nicht zu Hause, ausgegangen. **4. be ~** ♣ streiken; → **come out** 2, go out 4. **5.** ins Freie; draußen, im Freien. **6.** (aus dem Gefängnis etc) entlassen. **7.** heraus: a) erschienen (Buch etc) b) enthüllt (Geheimnis): **~ with it!** F heraus damit!, heraus mit der Sprache! **8.** pol. nicht (mehr) im Amt od. an der Macht. **9.** aus der Mode, out. **10.** weit u. breit: **~ and away** bei weitem. **11.** aus, vorbei, vorüber: **before the week is ~** vor Ende der Woche. **12.** aus, erloschen: → **go out** 3. **13.** aus(verkauft): → **go out** 3. **14. be ~ for** aussein auf (acc): **be ~ to do s.th.** darauf aussein, et. zu tun. **15. ~ of** a) aus (... heraus); zu ... hinaus, b) aus, von: **two ~ of three Americans** zwei von drei Amerikanern, c) außer Reichweite etc, d) außer Atem, Übung etc: **be ~ of** kein ... mehr haben; **we are ~ of oil** uns ist das Öl ausgegangen, e) aus der Mode etc, f) außerhalb von (od. gen), g) um et. betrügen, h) aus Bosheit, Mitleid etc. **II** prp **16.** → 15a. **｡~-and-'out** adj absolut, ausgesprochen: **an ~ lie** e-e faustdicke Lüge. **｡~'bal·ance** v/t überwiegen. **｡~'bid** v/t (irr bid) überbieten. **'~board** ♣ **I** adj **1.** Außenbord...: **~ motor. II** adv **2.** außenbords. **III** s **3.** Außenbordmotor m. **4.** Außenborder m (Boot). **'~break** s Ausbruch m: **~ of anger** Zornausbruch; **at the ~ of war** bei Kriegsausbruch. **'~build·ing** s Nebengebäude n. **'~burst** s (Zorn- etc)Ausbruch m. **'~cast I** adj ausgestoßen, verstoßen. **II** s Ausgestoßene m, f, Verstoßene m, f. **'~class** v/t weit überlegen sein (dat), (Sport a.) deklassieren. **'~come** s Ergebnis n, Resultat n: **what was the ~ of the talks?** was ist bei den Gesprächen herausgekommen? **'~cry** s fig. Aufschrei m, Schrei m der Entrüstung. **~'dat·ed** adj überholt, veraltet. **~'dis·tance** v/t hinter sich lassen. **~'do** v/t (irr **do**) **1.** (in) übertreffen (in od. in dat), ausstechen (in dat). **2.** schlagen, besiegen (in in dat). **'~·door** adj: **~ games** pl Spiele pl für draußen; **~ sea·son** (Sport) Freiluftsaison f; **~ shoes** pl Straßenschuhe pl; **~ shot** phot. Außenaufnahme f. **~'doors** adv draußen, im Freien; hinaus, ins Freie.

out·er ['aʊtə] adj äußer, Außen...: **~ gar·ments** pl Oberbekleidung f; **~ space** Weltraum m; **~ wall** Außenwand f. **~·most** ['~məʊst] adj äußerst.

'out|·fit s **1.** Ausrüstung f, Ausstattung f, ⊙ a. Gerät(e pl) n, Werkzeug(e pl) n. **2.** F Verein m, Laden m. **'~·fit·ter** s Ausrüster m: (**men's**) **~** Herrenausstatter m. **'~·flow** s Ausfluß m, bsd. ✝ Abfluß m. **~'fox** v/t überlisten. **'~·go·ing I** adj **1.** scheidend, aus dem Amt scheidend. **2.** **~ mail** Postausgang m. **II** s pl **3.** Ausgaben pl. **~'grow** v/t (irr **grow**) **1.** j-m über den Kopf wachsen. **2.** herauswachsen aus (e-m Kleidungsstück); e-r Angewohnheit etc entwachsen. **'~·house** s Nebengebäude n.

out·ing ['aʊtɪŋ] s Ausflug m: **go for an ~** e-n Ausflug machen.

out|·land·ish adj □ befremdend, befremdlich. **~'last** v/t überdauern, -leben. **'~·law I** s **1.** hist. Geächtete m/f. **2.** Bandit m. **II** v/t **3.** hist. ächten, für vogelfrei erklären. **4.** für ungesetzlich erklären, verbieten. **'~·lay** s Auslagen pl, Ausgaben pl (**on, for** für). **'~·let** s **1.** Abfluß(öffnung f) m, Abzug(söffnung f) m. **2.** ✝ Verkaufsstelle f. **3. seek an ~ for** fig. ein Ventil suchen für. **'~·line I** s **1.** Umriß m, Kontur f, pl a. Silhouette f. **2.** fig. Ab-, Grundriß m. **II** v/t **3.** umreißen, fig. a. in Umrissen darlegen. **~'live** v/t überleben: **have ~d its usefulness** ausgedient haben (Maschine etc). **'~·look** s **1.** (Aus)Blick m, (Aus-) Sicht f (**from** von; **onto** auf acc). **2.** fig. (Zukunfts)Aussichten pl (**for** für). **3.** fig. Einstellung f (**on** zu): **~ on life** Lebensauffassung f. **~'ly·ing** adj abgelegen, entlegen. **~·ma'neu·ver** Am., **~·ma'noeu·vre** bsd. Br. v/t ✗ ausmanövrieren (a. fig.). **~'mod·ed** [~'məʊdɪd] adj veraltet, überholt. **~·most** ['~məʊst] adj äußerst. **~'num·ber** v/t

j-m zahlenmäßig überlegen sein: **be ~ed by s.o.** j-m zahlenmäßig unterlegen sein. **~·of-'date** adj veraltet, überholt. **~·of-the-'way** adj **1.** abgelegen, entlegen. **2.** fig. ungewöhnlich, ausgefallen; wenig bekannt. **'~·pa·tient** s ambulanter Patient: **~s' department** Ambulanz f; **~ treatment** ambulante Behandlung. **~'play** v/t Sport: j-m spielerisch überlegen sein. **'~·post** s ✗ Vorposten m (a. fig.). **'~·pour·ing** s (Gefühls)Erguß m. **'~·put** s Output m: a) ✝, ⊙ Arbeitsertrag m, -leistung f, b) ✝ Ausstoß m, Ertrag m, Produktion f, c) ⚡ Ausgangsleistung f, d) Computer: (Daten)Ausgabe f.

out·rage ['aʊtreɪdʒ] **I** s **1.** Greueltat f: **an ~ against** ein Verbrechen an (dat) od. gegen; fig. e-e grobe Verletzung (gen). **2.** a. **sense of ~** Empörung f, Entrüstung f (**at** über acc). **II** v/t **3.** Gefühle, Anstand etc grob verletzen; mit Füßen treten. **4.** j-n empören, schockieren. **out'ra·geous** adj □ **1.** abscheulich, verbrecherisch. **2.** empörend, unerhört.

'out|·rig·ger s ⚓ Ausleger m; Auslegerboot n. **~'right I** adj [~'raɪt] **1.** völlig, gänzlich, total, (Lüge etc) glatt. **II** adv [~'raɪt] **2.** ohne Umschweife, unumwunden. **3.** auf der Stelle, sofort. **~'ri·val** v/t übertreffen, -bieten (in an od. in dat), ausstechen. **~'run** v/t (irr **run**) **1.** schneller laufen als; j-m davonlaufen. **2.** fig. übersteigen. **~'set** s Anfang m, Beginn m: **at the ~** am Anfang; **from the ~** (gleich) von Anfang an. **~'shine** v/t (irr **shine**) überstrahlen, fig. a. in den Schatten stellen. **~'side I** s **1.** Außenseite f: **from the ~** von außen; **on the ~** auf der Außenseite, außen. **2. at the (very) ~** (aller)höchstens, äußerstenfalls. **3.** Sport: Außenstürmer(in): **~ right** Rechtsaußen m. **II** adj **4.** äußer, Außen...: **~ broadcast** (Rundfunk, TV) Außenübertragung f; **~ lane** (Sport) Außenbahn f; mot. Br. innere Fahrspur. **5. ~ chance** kleine od. geringe Chance; (Sport) Außenseiterchance f. **III** adv **6.** draußen. **7.** heraus, hinaus. **8. ~ of** a) → 9, b) Am. F außer. **IV** prp **9.** außerhalb (gen). **~'sid·er** s Außenseiter(in). **'~·size I** s Übergröße f. **II** adj übergroß. **'~·skirts** s pl Stadtrand *m*, Peripherie *f*: **on the ~ of** London am Stadtrand von London. ,~'**smart** F → **outwit.** ,~'**spo·ken** *adj* □ 1. offen(herzig), freimütig: **be ~** kein Blatt vor den Mund nehmen. 2. unverblümt. ,~'**spread** *v/t* (*irr* **spread**) ausbreiten, *Arme a.* ausstrecken: **with arms ~** mit ausgestreckten Armen. ,~'**stand·ing** *adj* □ 1. hervorragend. 2. *bsd.* ✝ unerledigt, rückständig, (*Forderungen etc*) ausstehend. ,~'**stay** *v/t* länger bleiben als: → **welcome** 6. ,~'**stretched** *adj* ausgestreckt. ,~'**strip** *v/t* 1. überholen. 2. *fig.* übertreffen (**in** an *dat*). ,~'**vote** *v/t* überstimmen: **be ~d** e-e Abstimmungsniederlage erleiden.

out·ward ['aʊtwəd] **I** *adj* 1. äußerlich, äußer (*beide a. fig.*), Außen...: **his ~ cheerfulness** s-e zur Schau getragene Fröhlichkeit. **II** *adv* 2. auswärts, nach außen. 3. → **outwardly.** '**out·ward·ly** *adv* äußerlich (*a. fig.*).

out·wards ['~z] → **outward** II.

,**out**'**weigh** *v/t* überwiegen, (ge)wichtiger sein als. ,~'**wit** *v/t* überlisten, reinlegen. '**~·work** *s* ✝ Heimarbeit *f*. ,**~·work·er** *s* ✝ Heimarbeiter(in). '**~·worn** *adj* veraltet, überholt.

o·va ['əʊvə] *pl von* **ovum.**

o·val ['əʊvl] **I** *adj* □ oval. **II** *s* Oval *n*.

o·va·ry ['əʊvərɪ] *s* 1. *anat.* Eierstock *m*. 2. ✿ Fruchtknoten *m*.

o·va·tion [əʊ'veɪʃn] *s* Ovation *f*: **give s.o. a standing ~** j-m stehend e-e Ovation bereiten.

ov·en ['ʌvn] *s* Backofen *m*, Bratofen *m*, -röhre *f*. **~ cloth** *s* Topflappen *m*. **~ glove, ~ mitt** *s* Topfhandschuh *m*. '**~·read·y** *adj* bratfertig.

o·ver ['əʊvə] **I** *prp* 1. *Lage*: über (*dat*): **the lamp ~ his head.** 2. *Richtung, Bewegung*: über (*acc*), über (*acc*) ... (hin)weg: **he jumped ~ the fence;** → **get over,** *etc*. 3. über (*dat*), auf der anderen Seite von (*od. gen*): **~ the street** auf der anderen (Straßen)Seite. 4. über *s-r* Arbeit einschlafen *etc*, bei *e-m* Glas Wein *etc*. 5. *Herrschaft, Rang*: über (*acc od. dat*): **be ~ s.o.** über j-m stehen. 6. über (*acc*), mehr als: **~ a mile; ~ 10 dollars; ~ a week** über *od.* länger als e-e Woche. 7. *zeitlich*: über (*acc*), während: **~ many years** viele Jahre hindurch. **II** *adv* 8. hinüber, her-

über (**to** zu). 9. drüben: **~ there** da drüben. 10. *allg.* über...: → **hand over** 1, **think** 2, *etc*. 11. um...: → **fall over, turn over,** *etc*. 12. (*all*) **~ again** noch einmal; **~ and ~** immer wieder. 13. darüber, mehr: **children of 10 years and ~** Kinder von 10 Jahren u. darüber; **5 ounces and ~** 5 Unzen u. mehr; **~ and above** obendrein, überdies. 14. zu Ende, vorüber, vorbei: **get s.th. ~ (with)** F et. hinter sich bringen. ,~'**act** *thea. etc* **I** *v/t* Rolle überziehen. **II** *v/i* übertreiben (*a. weitS.*). ,~'**age** *adj* zu alt. ,~'**all** **I** *adj* ['~rɔːl] 1. gesamt, Gesamt...: **~ length** Gesamtlänge *f*. **II** *adv* [,~r'ɔːl] 2. allgemein. 3. insgesamt. **III** *s* ['~rɔːl] 4. *Br.* Arbeitsmantel *m*, Kittel *m*. 5. *Am.* Overall *m*. 6. *pl a*) *Br.* Overall *m*, b) *Am.* → **dungarees.** ,~'**bal·ance** **I** *v/t* umstoßen, umkippen. **II** *v/i* Übergewicht bekommen, das Gleichgewicht verlieren, umkippen. ,~'**bear·ing** *adj* □ anmaßend. ,~'**bid** *v/t* (*irr* **bid**) überbieten. '**~·board** *adv* ✡ über Bord: **fall ~** über Bord gehen; **throw ~** über Bord werfen (*a. fig.*). ,~'**book** *v/t* Flug, Hotel *etc* überbuchen. ,~'**cast** *adj* bewölkt, bedeckt. ,~'**charge** **I** *v/t* 1. *j-m* zuviel berechnen *od.* abverlangen: → **s.o.** (**by**) **£10** j-m 10 Pfund zuviel berechnen. 2. *Betrag* zuviel verlangen. 3. überlasten, ⚡ *a.* überladen (*a. fig.*). **II** *v/i* 4. zuviel berechnen *od.* verlangen (**for** für). '**~·coat** *s* Mantel *m*. ,~'**come** (*irr* **come**) **I** *v/t* überwältigen, -winden (*beide a. fig.*), *Gefahren* bestehen: **be ~ with emotion** von s-n Gefühlen übermannt werden. **II** *v/i* siegen. ,~'**crowd·ed** *adj* überfüllt; überlaufen (*a. Beruf*). ,~'**do** *v/t* (*irr* **do**) 1. übertreiben: → **it** (*od.* **things**) zu weit gehen, des Guten zuviel tun. 2. zu lange braten *od.* kochen: **overdone** zu stark gebraten. '**~·dose** *s* Überdosis *f*. '**~·draft** *s* ✝ (Konto)Überziehung *f*: **have an ~ of £100** sein Konto um 100 Pfund überzogen haben. ,~'**draw** *v/t* (*irr* **draw**) ✝ *Konto* überziehen (**by** um): **be ~n** sein Konto überzogen haben. ,~'**dress** *v/t u. v/i* (sich) zu vornehm anziehen: **~ed** *a.* overdressed. '**~·drive** *s mot.* Overdrive *m*, Schongang *m*. ,~'**due** überfällig: **she is ~** sie müßte (schon) längst hier sein. ,~'**es·ti·mate** *v/t* 1. zu hoch schätzen *od.* veranschlagen. **2.** *fig.* überschätzen, überbewerten. **,~ex'pose** *v/t phot.* überbelichten. **,~'flow** I *v/i* **1.** überlaufen, -fließen, (*Fluß etc*) über die Ufer treten: *full to ~ing* zum Überlaufen voll; (*Raum*) überfüllt. **2.** überquellen (*with* von) (*a. fig.*). II *v/t* **3. ~ *its banks*** über die Ufer treten. III *s* ['~fləʊ] **4.** Überlaufen *n*, -fließen *n.* **5. ⚙** Überlauf *m*: **~ *valve*** Überlaufventil *n*. **6.** Überschuß *m* (*of* an *dat*): **~ *of population*** Bevölkerungsüberschuß. **,~'grown** *adj* **1.** überwachsen, -wuchert (*with* von). **2.** übergroß, (*Junge etc*) hoch aufgeschossen. **~haul** I *v/t* [,~'hɔːl] **1. ⚙** überholen: *~ completely* generalüberholen. **2.** *fig.* Pläne *etc* überprüfen. **3.** *j-n, Fahrzeug etc* überholen. II *s* ['~hɔːl] **4. ⚙** Überholung *f*: *complete ~* Generalüberholung. **5.** *fig.* Überprüfung *f.* **'~head** I *adj* **1.** oberirdisch, Frei..., Hoch...: **~ *line ⚡*** Oberleitung *f*; **~ *projector*** Overhead-, Tageslichtprojektor *m*. **2.** allgemein: **~ *costs*** (*od. expenses*) *pl* → **3.** *Sport:* Überkopf...: **~ *kick*** (*Fußball*) (Fall)Rückzieher *m*; **~ *stroke*** → **5.** II *s* **4.** **~** (*s pl Br.*) *Am.* **✝** laufende (Geschäfts)Kosten *pl.* **5.** *Tennis:* Überkopfball *m*. III *adv* [,~'hed] **6.** (dr)oben; über uns. **,~'hear** *v/t* (*irr hear*) zufällig hören. **,~'heat** I *v/t Motor* überhitzen, *Raum* überheizen. II *v/i* **⚙** heißlaufen. **,~in'dulge** I *v/t* **1.** zu nachsichtig behandeln, *j-m* zuviel durchgehen lassen. **2.** *e-r Leidenschaft etc* übermäßig frönen. II *v/i* **3. ~ *in television*** zuviel fernsehen. **,~joyed** [,~'dʒɔɪd] *adj* überglücklich. **'~kill** *s* **✗** Overkill *n*. **~land** I *adv* [,~'lænd] über Land, auf dem Landweg. II *adj* ['~lænd] (Über-) Land... **,~'lap** *v/i* **1.** (sich) überlappen. **2.** *fig.* sich überschneiden. **~'leaf** *adv* umseitig, umstehend. **,~'load** *v/t* überlasten (*a. ⚡*), -laden.

o·ver·ly ['əʊvəlɪ] *adv* übermäßig, allzu: *he wasn't ~ enthusiastic* s-e Begeisterung hielt sich in Grenzen.

,over'manned *adj* (personell) überbesetzt. **,~'much** I *adj* (all)zuviel. II *adv* übermäßig: *I don't like him ~* ich mag ihn nicht besonders. **,~'night** I *adv* über Nacht (*a. fig.*): *stay ~* über Nacht bleiben; *stay ~ with s.o.* (*od. at s.o.'s place*) bei *j-m* übernachten. II *adj*

Nacht...: **~ *bag*** Reisetasche *f*; **~ *stay*** (*od. stop*) Übernachtung *f.* **'~pass** *s bsd. Am.* (Straßen-, Eisenbahn)Überführung *f.* **,~'pay** *v/t* (*irr pay*) **1.** zu teuer bezahlen, zuviel bezahlen für. **2.** *j-m* zuviel zahlen, *j-n* überbezahlen. **,~'play** *v/t* **a)** *→ overact* I, **b)** hochspielen. **2. ~ *one's hand*** sich überreizen *od.* übernehmen. **,~'pop·u·lat·ed** *adj* übervölkert. **~pop·u'la·tion** *s* **1.** Übervölkerung *f.* **2.** Überbevölkerung *f.* **,~'pow·er** *v/t* überwältigen, -mannen (*beide a. fig.*). **,~'pow·er·ing** *adj fig.* überwältigend, (*Geruch*) aufdringlich, penetrant. **,~'rate** *v/t* überbewerten (*a. Sport*), -schätzen. **,~'reach** *v/t* sich übernehmen. **,~re'act** *v/i* überreagieren, überzogen reagieren (*to* auf *acc*). **,~re'ac·tion** *s* Überreaktion *f*, überzogene Reaktion. **,~'ride** *v/t* (*irr ride*) sich hinwegsetzen über (*acc*). **,~'rid·ing** *adj* vordringlich, -rangig: *his ~ concern was* es ging ihm vor allem darum (*to do* zu tun). **,~'rule** *v/t* *Entscheidung etc* aufheben, *Einspruch etc* abweisen. **,~'run** (*irr run*) **1. be ~ with** überlaufen sein von. **2. 🚂** *Signal* überfahren. II *v/i* **3.** länger dauern als vorgesehen. **,~'seas** I *adv* nach *od.* in Übersee. II *adj* überseeisch, Übersee..., aus Übersee. **,~'see** *v/t* (*irr see*) beaufsichtigen, überwachen. **~·se·er** *s* ['~siə] *s* Aufseher(in). **,~'shad·ow** *v/t fig.* **1.** in den Schatten stellen. **2.** überschatten, e-n Schatten werfen auf (*acc*). **,~'shoot** *v/t* (*irr shoot*) hinausschießen über (*ein Ziel*) (*a. fig.*). **'~sight** *s* Versehen *n*: *by* (*od. through an*) *~* aus Versehen. **,~'sim·pli·fy** *v/t* (zu) grob vereinfachen, vergröbern. **,~'size(d)** *adj* übergroß, mit Übergröße. **,~'sleep** *v/i* (*irr sleep*) verschlafen. **,~'staffed** *adj* (personell) überbesetzt. **,~'state** *v/t* übertreiben, übertrieben darstellen. **,~'state·ment** *s* Übertreibung *f.* **,~'stay** *v/t* länger bleiben als: *~ welcome* **6.** **,~'step** *v/t fig.* überschreiten. **,~'take** *v/t* (*irr take*) **1.** einholen (*a. fig.*). **2.** (*a. v/i*) *bsd. Br.* überholen. **3.** *fig.* überraschen. **,~'tax** *v/t* **1.** zu hoch besteuern. **2.** überbeanspruchen, *Geduld etc* strapazieren: *~ one's strength* (*od. o.s.*) sich übernehmen. **~·throw** I *v/t* [,~'θrəʊ] (*irr throw*) **1.** *Regierung etc* stürzen. **2.** besiegen. II

s ['ˌθrəʊ] **3.** Sturz *m.* **4.** Niederlage *f.*
'**∼time I** *s* **1.** ✝ a) Überstunden *pl;* **be on** (*od.* **do**) **∼** Überstunden machen, b) *a.* **∼ pay** Überstundenlohn *m.* **2.** *Sport:* Am. Verlängerung *f; the game went into* **∼** das Spiel ging in die Verlängerung. **II** *adv* **3. work ∼** ✝ Überstunden machen.

o·ver·ture ['əʊvəˌtjʊə] *s* ♪ Ouvertüre *f* (*to* zu).

∼turn I *v/t* **1.** umwerfen, -stoßen, -kippen. **2.** *fig.* Regierung *etc* stürzen. **II** *v/i* **3.** umkippen, ⏃ kentern. '**∼view** *s fig.* Überblick *m.* (*of* über *acc*). **∼weight I** *s* ['∼weɪt] Übergewicht *n* (*a. fig.*). **II** *adj* [ˌ∼'weɪt] übergewichtig (*Person*), zu schwer (**by** um) (*Gegenstand*): **be ∼ by five kilos, be five kilos ∼** fünf Kilo Übergewicht haben. **∼whelm I** ['∼welm] *v/t* **1.** überwältigen (*a. fig.*). **2.** *fig.* überhäufen, -schütten (**with** mit). **∼whelm·ing** *adj* überwältigend: **∼ly** mit überwältigender Mehrheit. **∼work** *v/t* überstrapazieren (*a. fig.*), überanstrengen: **∼ed** a. gestreßt; **∼ o.s.** → **II. II** *v/i* sich überarbeiten.

o·vi·duct ['əʊvɪdʌkt] *s anat.* Eileiter *m.*

o·vip·a·rous [əʊ'vɪpərəs] *adj* □ *zo.* eierlegend.

o·vu·la·tion [ˌɒvjʊ'leɪʃn] *s biol.* Eisprung *m.*

o·vum ['əʊvəm] *pl* **o·va** ['əʊvə] *s biol.* Ei(zelle *f*) *n.*

owe [əʊ] *v/t* **1.** *j-m et.* schulden, schuldig sein (**for** für). **2.** bei *j-m* Schulden haben, *j-m* Geld schulden. **3.** *et.* verdanken, zu verdanken haben.

ow·ing ['əʊɪŋ] *adj* **1.** unbezahlt: *how much is still* **∼** *to you?* wieviel bekommst du noch?; *there is still* **£1,000 ∼** es stehen noch 1000 Pfund aus. **2. ∼ to** infolge, wegen.

owl [aʊl] *s orn.* Eule *f.* '**owl·ish** *adj* □ eulenhaft (*Aussehen etc*).

own [əʊn] **I** *v/t* **1.** besitzen: *who* **∼s** *this car?* wem gehört dieser Wagen? **2.** zugeben, (ein)gestehen (*that* daß). **II** *v/i* **3. ∼ up** es zugeben: **∼** (**up**) **to s.th.** et. zugeben *od.* (ein)gestehen; **∼** (**up**) **to doing s.th.** zugeben *od.* (ein)gestehen, et. getan zu haben. **III** *adj* **4.** eigen: **∼ goal** (*Sport*) Eigentor *n* (*a. fig.*). **IV** *s* **5. my ∼** mein Eigentum: *a car of one's* **∼** ein eigenes Auto; *on one's* **∼** allein; *come into one's* **∼** zur Geltung kommen; → *get back* 1, *hold* 10.

own·er ['əʊnə] *s* Eigentümer(in), Besitzer(in). **∼-'oc·cu·pied** *adj* eigengenutzt (*Haus, Wohnung*).

own·er·ship ['əʊnəʃɪp] *s* Besitz *m.*

ox [ɒks] *pl* **ox·en** ['∼n] *s zo.* Ochse *m.*

Ox·bridge ['ɒksbrɪdʒ] *s* (die Universitäten) Oxford *u.* Cambridge *pl.*

ox·en ['ɒksn] *pl von* **ox.**

ox·ide ['ɒksaɪd] *s* 🜊 Oxyd *n.* **ox·i·dize** ['ɒksɪdaɪz] *v/t u. v/i* oxydieren.

'**ox·tail** *s* Ochsenschwanz *m:* **∼ soup.**

ox·y·gen ['ɒksɪdʒən] *s* 🜊 Sauerstoff *m.* **∼ mask** *s* ⚕ Sauerstoffmaske *f.* **∼ tent** *s* ⚕ Sauerstoffzelt *n.*

oys·ter ['ɔɪstə] *s zo.* Auster *f.* **∼ bed** *s* Austernbank *f.*

o·zone ['əʊzəʊn] *s* 🜊 Ozon *n.* **∼ lay·er, ∼ shield** *s* Ozonschicht *f* (*der Atmosphäre*).

P

P [piː] *s: mind one's p's and q's* F sich anständig aufführen.

pace [peɪs] **I** *s* **1.** Tempo *n* (*a. fig.*), Geschwindigkeit *f: at a* (*very*) *slow* **∼** (ganz) langsam; *keep* **∼ with** Schritt halten *fig.* mitkommen mit (*a. fig.*); *keep* **∼ with the times** mit der Zeit gehen; *set the* **∼** das Tempo angeben (*a. fig.*), (*Sport*) das Tempo machen. **2.** Schritt *m.* **3.** Gangart *f* (*e-s Pferdes*): *put s.o. through his* **∼s** *fig.* j-n auf Herz u. Nieren prüfen; *show one's* **∼s** *fig.* zeigen, was man kann. **II** *v/t* **4.** *Sport:* j-m Schrittmacherdienste leisten. **5.** *a.* **∼**

out (*od.* **off**) ab-, ausschreiten. **6.** *Zimmer etc* durchschreiten. **III** *v/i* **7.** ~ *about* (*od.* **around**) hin u. her laufen; ~ *up and down* auf u. ab gehen. '~ₗmak-er s **1.** *Sport:* Schrittmacher(in) (*a. fig.*). **2.** ⚕ (*Herz*)Schrittmacher *m.* '~ₗset·ter → pacemaker 1.

pach·y·derm ['pækɪdɜːm] *s zo.* Dickhäuter *m.*

pa·cif·ic [pə'sɪfɪk] *adj* (~ally) friedlich, friedfertig, friedliebend.

pac·i·fi·er ['pæsɪfaɪə] *s* **1.** Friedensstifter(in). **2.** *Am.* Schnuller *m.*

pac·i·fism ['pæsɪfɪzəm] *s* Pazifismus *m.* 'pac·i·fist *s* Pazifist(in). **II** *adj* pazifistisch.

pac·i·fy ['pæsɪfaɪ] *v/t* **1.** *Land* befrieden. **2.** besänftigen, beschwichtigen.

pack [pæk] **I** *s* **1.** Pack(en) *m,* Bündel *n.* **2.** Paket *n* (*Waschpulver etc*), *bsd. Am.* Packung *f,* Schachtel *f* (*Zigaretten*). **3.** Rudel *n* (*Wölfe etc*); *hunt.* Meute *f.* **4.** *contp.* Pack *n,* Bande *f:* ~ *of thieves* Diebesbande; *a* ~ *of lies* ein Sack voll Lügen. **5.** (Karten)Spiel *n.* **6.** ⚕, *Kosmetik:* Packung *f.* **II** *v/t* **7.** *oft* ~ *up* ein-, zs.-, ab-, verpacken: ~ *s.o. sth.* j-m et. einpacken. **8.** *a.* ~ *up* Schluß machen mit: ~ *it in!* hör endlich auf (damit)! **III** *v/i* **13.** packen: ~ *up* zs.-packen. **14.** (sich) drängen (*into* in *acc*). **15.** *mst* ~ *off* F sich packen *od.* davonmachen: *send s.o.* ~*ing* j-n fort- *od.* wegjagen. **16.** fest werden. **17.** *a.*) *mst* ~ *up* (*od.* **in**) aufhören, Feierabend machen, b) ~ *up* absterben (*on s.o.* j-m) (*Motor*), s-n Geist aufgeben (*Waschmaschine etc*).

pack·age ['pækɪdʒ] **I** *s* **1.** Paket *n* (*a. fig.*). **2.** Packung *f* (*Spaghetti etc*). **II** *v/t* **3.** verpacken; zu e-m Paket abpacken. ~ *deal s* Pauschalarrangement *n.* ~ *tour s* Pauschalreise *f.*

pack an·i·mal *s* Pack-, Last-, Tragtier *n.*

pack·er ['pækə] *s* Packer(in).

pack·et ['pækɪt] *s* Päckchen *n:* *a* ~ *of cigarettes* e-e Packung *od.* Schachtel Zigaretten. **2.** *Br. sl.* *cost a* ~ ein Hei-

dengeld kosten; *make a* ~ ein Schweinegeld verdienen. **3.** *catch* (*cop, get, stop*) *a* ~ *Br. sl.* in Schwulitäten kommen; eins aufs Dach kriegen (*from von*).

pack ice *s* Packeis *n.*

pack·ing ['pækɪŋ] *s* **1.** Packen *n:* *do one's* ~ packen. **2.** Verpackung *f.*

pact [pækt] *s* Pakt *m:* *make a* ~ *with s.o.* mit j-m e-n Pakt schließen.

pad¹ [pæd] *v/i* trotten.

pad² [~] **I** *s* **1.** Polster *n.* **2.** *Sport:* (*Knie-etc*)Schützer *m.* **3.** (*Schreib- etc*)Block *m.* **4.** (*Stempel*)Kissen *n.* **5.** *zo.* Ballen *m.* **6.** (*Abschuß*)Rampe *f.* **7.** *sl.* Bude *f* (*Wohnung, Zimmer*). **II** *v/t* **8.** *a.* ~ *out* (aus)polstern: ~*ded cell* Gummizelle *f.* **9.** *oft* ~ *out* *Rede etc* aufblähen (*with mit*). '**pad·ding** *s* **1.** Polsterung *f.* **2.** *fig.* Füllsel *n.*

pad·dle¹ ['pædl] **I** *s* **1.** Paddel *n.* **2.** ⚓ Schaufel *f;* Schaufelrad *n.* **II** *v/i* **3.** paddeln (*a. schwimmen*). **III** *v/t* **4.** paddeln: → *canoe* I.

pad·dle² [~] *v/i* (herum)planschen (*in in dat*).

pad·dle steam·er *s* Raddampfer *m.*

pad·dling pool ['pædlɪŋ] *s* Planschbecken *n.*

pad·dock ['pædək] *s* **1.** (*Pferde*)Koppel *f;* (*Pferderennsport:*) Sattelplatz *m.* **2.** *Motorsport:* Fahrerlager *n.*

pad·dy¹ ['pædɪ] *s a.* ~ *field* Reisfeld *n.*

pad·dy² [~] *s Br.* F Koller *m:* *be in a* ~ e-n Koller haben.

Pad·dy³ [~] *s* F Paddy *m,* Ire *m.*

pad·dy wag·on ['pædɪ] *s Am.* F grüne Minna.

pad·lock ['pædlɒk] **I** *s* Vorhängeschloß *n.* **II** *v/t* mit e-m Vorhängeschloß verschließen.

pae·di·a·tri·cian [ˌpiːdɪə'trɪʃn] *s bsd. Br.* Kinderarzt *m.* **pae·di·at·rics** [~'ætrɪks] *s pl* (*sg konstruiert*) Kinderheilkunde *f.*

pa·gan ['peɪɡən] **I** *s* Heide *m,* Heidin *f.* **II** *adj* heidnisch. '**pa·gan·ism** *s* Heidentum *n.*

page¹ [peɪdʒ] **I** *s* **1.** Page *m, hist.* a. Edelknabe *m.* **II** *v/t* **2.** j-n ausrufen (lassen): *paging Mr X* Herr X, bitte! **3.** mit j-m über Funkrufempfänger Kontakt aufnehmen, j-n anpiepsen.

page² [~] **I** *s* Seite *f* (*e-s Buchs etc*): *be on*

~ 10 auf Seite 10 stehen; **four-~** vierseitig. **II** v/t paginieren.

'page·boy s Page m.

pag·er ['peɪdʒə] s Funkrufempfänger m, Piepser m.

pag·i·nate ['pædʒɪneɪt] v/t paginieren.

ˌpag·i·'na·tion s Paginierung f.

pa·go·da [pə'gəʊdə] s Pagode f.

paid [peɪd] **I** pret u. pp von **pay**. **II** adj: **put ~ to** bsd. Br. F ein Ende machen (dat), Hoffnungen etc zunichte machen.

pail [peɪl] s Eimer m, Kübel m.

pain [peɪn] **I** s **1.** Schmerz(en pl) m: **be in ~** Schmerzen haben; **I have a ~ in my back** mir tut der Rücken weh; **be a ~ (in the neck)** F e-m auf den Wecker gehen. **2.** Schmerz m, Kummer m: **cause** (od. **give**) **s.o. ~** j-m Kummer machen. **3.** pl Mühe f, Bemühungen pl: **be at** (**great**) **~s to do sth.** sich (große) Mühe geben, et. zu tun; **spare no ~s** keine Mühe scheuen; **take ~s** sich Mühe geben (**over, with** mit; **to do** zu tun). **II** v/t **4.** bsd. fig. schmerzen. **pain·ful** ['~fʊl] adj □ **1.** schmerzend, schmerzhaft. **2.** fig. schmerzlich; unangenehm; peinlich.

'pain·kill·er s Schmerzmittel n.

pain·less ['peɪnlɪs] adj □ **1.** schmerzlos. **2.** F leicht, einfach.

pain thresh·old s Schmerzschwelle f.

'pains·tak·ing adj □ sorgfältig, gewissenhaft.

paint [peɪnt] **I** v/t **1.** Bild, j-n malen: **~ a gloomy** (**vivid**) **picture of s.th.** fig. et. in düsteren (glühenden) Farben malen od. schildern; **→ black** 1. **2.** anmalen, bemalen, (an)streichen, Auto etc lackieren: **~ out** (od. **over**) übermalen; **~ one's face** contp. sich anmalen; **~ the town red** F e-n draufmachen. **3.** (aus)pinseln (**with** mit). **II** v/i **4.** malen. **III** s **5.** Farbe f; Lack m; contp. Schminke f: **wet ~** frisch gestrichen! **'~box** s Malkasten m. **'~brush** s Pinsel m.

paint·er ['peɪntə] s **1.** a. (Kunst)Maler(in), Anstreicher(in). **2.** (Auto- etc-) Lackierer(in). **'paint·ing** s **1.** Malerei f. **2.** Gemälde n, Bild n.

'paint·work s Lack m (e-s Autos etc).

pair [peə] **I** s **1.** Paar n (Stiefel etc): **in ~s** paarweise. **2.** et. Zweiteiliges, mst unübersetzt: **a ~ of trousers** e-e Hose. **3.** Paar n, Pärchen n (Mann u. Frau, zo.

Männchen u. Weibchen): **~ skating** (Eis-, Rollkunstlauf) Paarlauf(en n) m. **4. where is the ~ to this shoe?** wo ist der andere od. zweite Schuh? **5.** Rudern: Zweier m. **II** v/t **6.** a. **~ off** (od. **up**) paarweise anordnen, in Zweiergruppen einteilen: **~ off** zwei (junge) Leute zs.-bringen, verkuppeln. **III** v/i **7.** zo. sich paaren. **8.** a. **~ off** (od. **up**) Paare bilden.

pa·ja·mas Am. → **pyjamas**.

Pa·ki·stan·i [ˌpɑːkɪ'stɑːnɪ] **I** s Pakistani m, Pakistaner(in). **II** adj pakistanisch.

pal [pæl] F **I** s Kumpel m: **listen, ~, ...** bsd. Am. hör mal, Freundchen, ... **II** v/i mst **~ up** sich anfreunden (**with** mit).

pal·ace ['pælɪs] s Palast m (a. weitS.).

pal·at·a·ble ['pælətəbl] adj □ schmackhaft (a. fig.): **make s.th. ~ to s.o.**

pal·a·tal ['pælətl] s ling. Gaumenlaut m.

pal·ate ['pælət] s **1.** anat. Gaumen m. **2.** fig. for s.o.'s **~** für j-s Geschmack: **have no ~ for** keinen Sinn haben für.

pa·la·tial [pə'leɪʃl] adj □ palastartig.

pa·lav·er [pə'lɑːvə] s F **1.** Palaver n, endloses Gerede. **2.** Theater n.

pale¹ [peɪl] **I** adj □ **1.** blaß, bleich: **turn ~ → 3. 2.** hell, blaß (Farbe). **II** v/i **3.** blaß od. bleich werden. **4.** fig. verblassen (**before, beside** neben dat).

pale² [~] s Pfahl m: **go beyond the ~** fig. die Grenzen des Anstandes überschreiten.

pale·ness ['peɪlnɪs] s Blässe f.

Pal·es·tin·i·an [ˌpælə'stɪnɪən] **I** s Palästinenser(in). **II** adj palästinensisch.

pall¹ [pɔːl] s **1.** Sargtuch n, Sarg m (bsd. während der Beerdigung). **2.** fig. (Dunst-etc)Glocke f.

pall² [~] v/i s-n Reiz verlieren (**on** für): **~ on s.o.** a. j-n langweilen.

'pall·bear·er s Sargträger m; j-d, der neben dem Sarg geht.

pal·let ['pælɪt] s ⊚ Palette f. **~ truck** s Gabelstapler m.

pal·li·ate ['pælɪeɪt] v/t **1.** ✷ lindern. **2.** fig. bemänteln, beschönigen. **pal·li·a·tive** ['~ətɪv] **I** adj □ **1.** ✷ lindernd. **2.** fig. beschönigend. **II** s **3.** ✷ Linderungsmittel n.

pal·lid ['pælɪd] adj □ blaß (a. fig.), bleich. **pal·lor** ['pælə] s Blässe f.

pal·ly ['pælɪ] adj F befreundet (**with** mit): **they are very ~** sie sind dicke Freunde.

palm¹ [pɑːm] **I** s **1.** Handfläche f, -teller

m: **grease** (*od.* **oil**) **s.o.'s ~** F j-n schmieren (*with* mit); **have an itching** (*od.* **itchy**) **~** F e-e offene Hand haben (*bestechlich sein*); **have** (*od.* **hold**) **s.o. in the ~ of one's hand** j-n völlig in der Hand *od.* in s-r Gewalt haben. **II** *v/t* **2.** *et.* in der Hand verschwinden lassen (*Zauberkünstler*). **3.** F **~ s.th. off as** et. an den Mann bringen als; **~ s.th. off on(to) s.o.** j-m et. andrehen; **~ s.o. off with s.th.** j-m et. andrehen; j-n mit et. abspeisen.

palm² [~] *s* ♣ Palme *f*.
palm·ist ['pɑːmɪst] *s* Handleser(in). **'palm·is·try** *s* Handlesekunst *f*.
Palm| **Sun·day** *s eccl.* Palmsonntag *m*. ♀ **tree** *s* ♣ Palme *f*.
pal·pa·ble ['pælpəbl] *adj* □ **1.** fühl-, greif-, tastbar. **2.** *fig.* augenfällig, deutlich; offensichtlich.
pal·pi·tate ['pælpɪteɪt] *v/i* **1.** klopfen, pochen (*Herz*). **2.** zittern (**with** vor *dat*). **pal·pi'ta·tion** *s a. pl* Herzklopfen *n*.
pal·sy ['pɔːlzɪ] *s* ♣ Lähmung *f*.
pal·try ['pɔːltrɪ] *adj* □ armselig, schäbig: **a ~ £10** lumpige 10 Pfund.
pam·per ['pæmpə] *v/t* verwöhnen, *Kind a.* verhätscheln.
pam·phlet ['pæmflɪt] *s* **1.** Broschüre *f*, Druckschrift *f*. **2.** Flugblatt *n*, -schrift *f*.
pan¹ [pæn] **I** *s* **1.** Pfanne *f*, Topf *m*. **2.** (Waag)Schale *f*. **3.** *bsd. Br.* (Klosett)Schüssel *f*. **II** *v/t* **4.** F *Theaterstück etc* verreißen. **III** *v/i* **5. ~ out** F klappen: **~ out well** hinhauen.
pan² [~] **I** *s* (Kamera)Schwenk *m*. **II** *v/t Filmkamera* schwenken. **III** *v/i* schwenken.
pan·a·ce·a [ˌpænə'sɪə] *s* Allheilmittel *n*, *fig. a.* Patentrezept *n*.
Pan-A'mer·i·can *adj* panamerikanisch.
'pan·cake *s* Pfannkuchen *m*.
pan·cre·as ['pæŋkrɪəs] *s anat.* Bauchspeicheldrüse *f*.
pan·da ['pændə] *s zo.* Panda *m*. ♀ **car** *s Br.* (Funk)Streifenwagen *m*.
pan·de·mo·ni·um [ˌpændɪ'məʊnjəm] *s* Chaos *n*, Tumult *m*.
pan·der ['pændə] *v/i*: **~ to** e-m *Laster etc* Vorschub leisten, *j-s Bedürfnisse etc* befriedigen.
pane [peɪn] *s* (Fenster)Scheibe *f*.
pan·el ['pænl] **I** *s* **1.** Tafel *f*, Platte *f*; (vertieftes) Feld. **2.** ♀, ✪ (Schalt-, Kon-

troll- *etc*)Tafel *f*. **3.** ⚖ Liste *f* der Geschworenen. **4.** Diskussionsteilnehmer *pl*, -runde *f*; Rateteam *n*. **II** *v/t pret u. pp* **-eled**, *bsd. Br.* **-elled 5.** täfeln. **~ dis·cus·sion** *s* Podiumsdiskussion *f*. **~ game** *s* Rundfunk, *TV*: Ratespiel *n*.
pan·el·(l)ing ['pænlɪŋ] *s* Täfelung *f*.
pan·el·(l)ist ['~əlɪst] *s* Diskussionsteilnehmer(in).
pang [pæŋ] *s* stechender Schmerz: **~s pl of hunger** nagender Hunger; **feel a ~ of conscience** Gewissensbisse haben.
pan·ic ['pænɪk] **I** *adj* **1.** panisch: **~ buying** Angstkäufe *pl*; **be at ~ stations** rotieren; **push the ~ button** F panisch reagieren. **II** *s* **2.** Panik *f*: **be in a ~** in Panik sein; **get into a ~** → 5; **throw into a ~** → 4. **3.** **be a ~** *Am.* F zum Totlachen sein. **III** *v/t pret u. pp* **-icked 4.** in Panik versetzen, e-e Panik auslösen unter (*dat*). **IV** *v/i* **5.** in Panik geraten: **don't ~!** nur keine Panik! **'pan·ick·y** *adj* F **1.** überängstlich. **2. get ~** → **panic** 5.
'pan·ic-ˌstrick·en *adj* von panischem Schrecken erfaßt *od.* ergriffen.
pan·o·ra·ma [ˌpænə'rɑːmə] *s* **1.** Panorama *n*. **2.** *fig.* (allgemeiner) Überblick (*of* über *acc*). **pan·o·ram·ic** [ˌpænə'ræmɪk] *adj* (**~ally**) panoramisch, Panorama...: **~ view** a) Rundblick *m* (*of* über *acc*), b) → **panorama** 2.
pan·sy ['pænzɪ] *s* **1.** ♣ Stiefmütterchen *n*. **2.** F Weichling *m*.
pant [pænt] **I** *v/i* **1.** keuchen: **~ for breath** nach Luft schnappen. **2. be ~ing** *fig.* lechzen (**after, for** nach; **to do s.th.** danach, et. zu tun). **II** *v/t* **3. ~ out** *Worte* (hervor)keuchen. **III** *s* **4.** Atemstoß *m*.
pan·the·ism ['pænθiːɪzm] *s* Pantheismus *m*. **'pan·the·ist** *s* Pantheist(in). **II** *adj* pantheistisch. **ˌpan·the'is·tic** *adj* (**~ally**) pantheistisch.
pan·ther ['pænθə] *s zo.* Panther *m*.
pant·ies ['pæntɪz] *s pl, a.* **pair of ~** Höschen *n* (*für Kinder*), (*für Damen a.*) Schlüpfer *m*, Slip *m*.
pan·to·mime ['pæntəmaɪm] *s* **1.** *Br.* Weihnachtsspiel *n* (*für Kinder*). **2.** *thea.* Pantomime *f*.
pan·try ['pæntrɪ] *s* Speise-, Vorratskammer *f*.
pants [pænts] *s pl, a.* **pair of ~ 1.** *Br.* Unterhose *f*. **2.** *bsd. Am.* Hose *f*: **catch s.o. with his ~ down** F j-n überrum-

peln; **talk the ~ off s.o.** F j-m ein Loch *od.* Löcher in den Bauch reden; → **wear** 3.

pant-suit ['pæntsu:t] *s bsd. Am.* Hosenanzug *m.*

pan-ty hose ['pænti] *s bsd. Am.* Strumpfhose *f.*

pap [pæp] *s* Brei *m.*

pa-pal ['peɪpl] *adj* □ päpstlich.

pa-per ['peɪpə] **I** *s* **1.** Papier *n:* **on ~** *fig.* auf dem Papier. **2.** Tapete *f.* **3.** Zeitung *f:* **be in the ~s** in der Zeitung stehen. **4.** *pl (Ausweis)*Papiere *pl;* Akten *pl,* Unterlagen *pl.* **5.** *ped.* Arbeit *f, univ.* Klausur(arbeit) *f.* **6.** Referat *n:* **give** *(od.* **read) a ~** ein Referat halten, referieren **(to** vor *dat;* on über *acc).* **II** *v/t* **7.** tapezieren. **8. ~ over** *(od.* **up)** *fig.* Differenzen *etc* (notdürftig) übertünchen. '**~-back** *s* Paperback *n,* Taschenbuch *n:* **in ~** als Taschenbuch. **~ bag** *s* (Papier)Tüte *f.* '**~-boy** *s* Zeitungsjunge *m.* **~ chase** *s* Schnitzeljagd *f.* **~ clip** *s* Büro-, Heftklammer *f.* **~ cup** *s* Pappbecher *m.* **~ hand-ker-chief** *s* Papiertaschentuch *n.* '**~,hang-er** *s* Tapezierer(in). **~ knife** *s (irr knife)* Brieföffner *m.* **~ mon-ey** *s* Papiergeld *n.* **~ plate** *s* Pappteller *m.* '**~-thin** *adj* hauchdünn (*a. fig.*), papierdünn. **~ ti-ger** *s fig.* Papiertiger *m, (Person a.)* Gummilöwe *m.* '**~-weight** *s* **1.** Briefbeschwerer *m.* **2.** *Sport:* Papiergewicht(ler *m*) *n.* '**~-work** *s* Schreibarbeit *f.*

pa-pier-mâ-ché [,pæpjeɪ'mæʃeɪ] *s* Pappmaché *n.*

pap-ri-ka ['pæprɪkə] *s* Paprika *m.*

pa-py-rus [pə'paɪərəs] *pl* **-ri** [~raɪ], **-rus-es** *s* **1.** ♀ Papyrus(staude *f*) *m.* **2.** *antiq.* Papyrus(rolle *f*) *m.*

par [pɑː] **I** *s* **1.** ✝ Nennwert *m:* **at ~** zum Nennwert, al pari. **2. be on a ~** auf gleicher Stufe stehen **(with** wie): **be on a ~ with** *a.* j-m ebenbürtig sein; **I'm feeling below** *(od.* **under) ~ today** F ich bin heute nicht (ganz) auf dem Posten. **3.** *Golf:* Par *n:* **that's ~ for the course** F das ist ganz normal **(for** für). **II** *adj* **4. ~ value** ✝ Nennwert *m.*

par-a-ble ['pærəbl] *s* Parabel *f,* Gleichnis *n.*

pa-rab-o-la [pə'ræbələ] *s* ৯ Parabel *f.* **par-a-bol-ic** [,pærə'bɒlɪk] *adj (~ally)* **1.** ৯ parabolisch, Parabel... **2. ~ mirror** ⚙ Parabolspiegel *m.*

par-a-chute ['pærəʃuːt] **I** *s* Fallschirm *m:* **~ jump** Fallschirmabsprung *m.* **II** *v/t* mit dem Fallschirm absetzen *od.* abwerfen. **III** *v/i* (mit dem Fallschirm) abspringen. '**par-a-chut-ist** *s* Fallschirmspringer(in); ✕ Fallschirmjäger *m.*

pa-rade [pə'reɪd] **I** *s* **1.** Umzug *m, bsd.* ✕ Parade *f:* **be on ~** e-e Parade abhalten. **2.** *fig.* Zurschaustellung *f:* **make a ~ of** → 4. **II** *v/t* **3.** stolzieren durch. **4.** *fig.* zur Schau stellen. **III** *v/i* **5.** ziehen **(through** durch), *bsd.* ✕ paradieren. **6.** stolzieren **(through** durch). **~ ground** *s* ✕ Exerzierplatz *m.*

par-a-digm ['pærədaɪm] *s* **1.** Musterbeispiel *n* **(of** für). **2.** *ling.* Paradigma *n.*

par-a-dise, *eccl. mst* ৫ ['pærədaɪs] *s* Paradies *n* (*a. fig.*).

par-a-dox ['pærədɒks] *s* Paradox(on) *n.* ,**par-a'dox-i-cal** *adj* □ paradox: **~ly (enough)** paradoxerweise.

par-af-fin ['pærəfɪn] *s* **1.** *Br.* Petroleum *n.* **2.** *a.* **~ wax** Paraffin *n.*

par-a-gon ['pærəgɒn] *s* Muster *n* **(of** an *dat):* **~ of virtue** *bsd. iro.* Ausbund *m* an Tugend.

par-a-graph ['pærəgrɑːf] *s* **1.** Absatz *m,* Abschnitt *m.* **2.** (Zeitungs)Notiz *f.*

par-a-keet ['pærəkiːt] *s orn.* Sittich *m.*

par-al-lel ['pærəlel] **I** *adj* **1.** parallel **(to, with** zu) (*a. fig.*): **~ bars** *pl (Turnen)* Barren *m;* **~ case** Parallelfall *m.* **II** *s* **2.** ৯ Parallele *f* **(to, with** zu) (*a. fig.*): **without ~** ohne Parallele, ohnegleichen; **draw a ~ between** e-e Parallele ziehen zwischen *(dat);* **have close ~s** e-e starke Ähnlichkeit haben **(with** mit). **3.** *a.* **~ of latitude** *geogr.* Breitenkreis *m.* **III** *v/t pret u. pp* **-leled,** *Br. a.* **-lelled** **4.** gleichkommen *(dat),* entsprechen *(dat).* '**par-al-lel-ism** *s* **1.** Parallelität *f* (*a. fig.*). **2.** *ling.* Parallelismus *m.* ,**par-al-'lel-o-gram** [~əʊɡræm] *s* ৯ Parallelogramm *n.*

par-a-lyse ['pærəlaɪz] *v/t bsd. Br.* ৶ lähmen, *fig. a.* lahmlegen, zum Erliegen bringen: **~d with** *fig.* starr *od.* wie gelähmt vor *(dat).* **pa-ral-y-sis** [pə'ræləsɪs] *pl* **-ses** [~siːz] *s* ৶ Lähmung *f, fig. a.* Lahmlegung *f.* **par-a-lyt-ic** [,pærə'lɪtɪk] **I** *adj* (**~ally**) **1.** ৶ Lähmungs...; gelähmt. **2.** *Br.* F sternhagelvoll. **II** s 3. ✻ Gelähmte m, f. **par·a-lyze** Am. → **paralyse**.

pa·ram·e·ter [pə'ræmɪtə] s 1. A Parameter m. 2. mst pl fig. Rahmen m: **within the ~s of** im Rahmen (gen).

par·a·mil·i·tar·y [ˌpærə'mɪlɪtərɪ] adj paramilitärisch.

par·a·mount ['pærəmaʊnt] adj: **of ~ importance** von (aller)größter Bedeutung.

par·a·noi·a [ˌpærə'nɔɪə] s ✻ Paranoia f. **par·a·noi·ac** [~æk] **I** adj (~ally) paranoisch. **II** s Paranoiker(in). **'par·a-noid** adj paranoid: **be ~ about** ständig Angst haben vor (dat).

par·a·pet ['pærəpɪt] s Brüstung f.

par·a·pher·na·li·a [ˌpærəfə'neɪljə] s pl (a. sg konstruiert) **1.** (persönliche) Sachen pl. **2.** F bsd. Br. Schererei(en) f.

par·a·phrase ['pærəfreɪz] **I** s Paraphrase f, Umschreibung f. **II** v/t paraphrasieren, umschreiben.

par·a·ple·gi·a [ˌpærə'pli:dʒə] s ✻ Querschnitt(s)lähmung f. **par·a·ple·gic** **I** adj querschnitt(s)gelähmt. **II** s Querschnitt(s)gelähmte m, f.

par·a·psy·chol·o·gy [ˌpærəsaɪ'kɒlədʒɪ] s Parapsychologie f.

par·a·site ['pærəsaɪt] s biol. Schmarotzer m, Parasit m (beide a. fig.). **par·a·sit·ic** [~'sɪtɪk] adj (~ally) biol. parasitär, parasitisch, fig. a. schmarotzerhaft: **be ~ on** schmarotzen von.

par·a·troop·er ['pærəˌtru:pə] s ✕ Fallschirmjäger m. **'par·a·troops** s pl Fallschirmjägertruppe f.

par·a·ty·phoid (fe·ver) [ˌpærə'taɪfɔɪd] s ✻ Paratyphus m.

par·boil ['pɑ:bɔɪl] v/t halbgar kochen, ankochen.

par·cel ['pɑ:sl] **I** s 1. Paket n. 2. Parzelle f. **II** v/t pret u. pp **-celed,** bsd. Br. **-celled** 3. mst ~ **up** (als Paket) verpacken. 4. mst ~ **out** aufteilen, Land parzellieren.

parch [pɑ:tʃ] v/t u. v/i ausdörren, -trocknen, a. verdörren, -trocknen.

parch·ment ['pɑ:tʃmənt] s Pergament n.

par·don ['pɑ:dn] **I** v/t 1. et. verzeihen; **s.o. (for) s.th.** j-m et. vergeben od. verzeihen; **~ me** a) → 3a, c, b) Am. → 3b; **me for interrupting you** verzeihen od. entschuldigen Sie, wenn ich Sie unterbreche; **if you'll ~ the expression** wenn

ich so sagen darf. **2.** ⅜⅜ begnadigen. **II** s 3. **I beg your ~** a) Entschuldigung!, Verzeihung!, b) a. F **~?** (wie) bitte?, c) erlauben Sie mal!, ich muß doch sehr bitten! **4.** ⅜⅜ Begnadigung f. **'par·don·a·ble** adj □ entschuldbar, verzeihlich.

pare [peə] v/t 1. sich die Nägel schneiden: **~ down** fig. einschränken. **2.** Apfel etc schälen: **~ away** (od. **off**) abschälen.

par·ent ['peərənt] **I** s Elternteil n: **~s** pl Eltern pl. **II** adj: **~ company** ✝ Muttergesellschaft f. **'par·ent·age** s Abstammung f, Herkunft f. **pa·ren·tal** [pə'rentl] adj □ elterlich, Eltern...

pa·ren·the·sis [pə'renθɪsɪs] pl **-ses** [~si:z] s 1. ling. Parenthese f, Einschaltung f. 2. mst pl (runde) Klammer: **put in parentheses** einklammern.

par·ent·hood ['peərənthʊd] s Elternschaft f. **'par·ent·less** adj elternlos.

'par·ents-in-law s pl Schwiegereltern pl.

par·ings ['peərɪŋz] s pl Schalen pl.

par·ish ['pærɪʃ] s 1. eccl. Pfarrbezirk m, a. coll. Gemeinde f: **~ church** Pfarrkirche f; **~ register** Kirchenbuch n, -register n. 2. a. civil ~ pol. Br. Gemeinde f: **~ council** Gemeinderat m. **pa·rish·ion·er** [pə'rɪʃənə] s eccl. Gemeinde(mit-) glied n.

par·i·ty ['pærətɪ] s Gleichheit f (with mit).

park [pɑ:k] **I** s 1. Park m. **II** v/t 2. mot. parken, abstellen: **a ~ed car** ein parkender Wagen; **he's ~ed over there** er parkt dort drüben; **~ o.s.** F sich hinhocken od. pflanzen. 3. F abstellen, lassen. **III** v/i 4. parken: **a place to ~** ein Parkplatz. 5. einparken.

par·ka ['pɑ:kə] s Parka m, f.

park·ing ['pɑ:kɪŋ] s 1. Parken n: **"no ~"** „Parken verboten". 2. Einparken n. 3. Parkplätze pl, -fläche f. ~ **disc** s Parkscheibe f. ~ **fee** s Parkgebühr f. ~ **ga·rage** s bsd. Am. Park(hoch)haus n. ~ **lot** s Am. Parkplatz m. ~ **me·ter** s Parkuhr f. ~ **place** s Parkplatz m, -lücke f. ~ **space** s 1. → **parking place**. 2. Abstellfläche f. ~ **tick·et** s Strafzettel m (wegen Falschparkens).

Par·kin·son's dis·ease ['pɑ:kɪnsnz] s ✻ Parkinsonsche Krankheit, Schüttellähmung f.

'park·keep·er s Parkwächter m.

par·ky ['pɑːkı] *adj Br.* F kühl, frisch (*Luft etc*).

par·lance ['pɑːləns] *s*: *in common ~* einfach *od.* verständlich ausgedrückt; *in legal ~* in der Rechtssprache.

par·lia·ment ['pɑːləmənt] *s* Parlament *n.* **par·lia·men·tar·i·an** [ˌ~men'teərıən] *s* (erfahrener) Parlamentarier. **par·lia·men·ta·ry** [ˌ~'mentərı] *adj* parlamentarisch.

par·lor *Am.*, **par·lour** *bsd. Br.* ['pɑːlə] *s mst in Zssgn* Salon *m.* **~ game** *s* Gesellschaftsspiel *n.*

pa·ro·chi·al [pə'rəʊkjəl] *adj* □ **1.** Pfarr..., Gemeinde... **2.** *fig.* beschränkt, engstirnig.

par·o·dist ['pærədıst] *s* Parodist(in). **'par·o·dy** *I s* **1.** Parodie *f* (*of, on* auf *acc*). **2.** *fig.* Abklatsch *m* (*of, on gen*). **II** *v/t* **3.** parodieren.

pa·role [pə'rəʊl] ⚖ **I** *s* bedingte (Haft)Entlassung; Hafturlaub *m*: *put s.o. on ~* → **II.** **II** *v/t* j-n bedingt entlassen; *j-m* Hafturlaub gewähren.

par·quet ['pɑːkeı] *s* **1.** Parkett *n.* **2.** *thea. Am.* Parkett *n.* **~ floor** *s* Parkett(fuß)boden *m.*

par·rot ['pærət] **I** *s orn.* Papagei *m* (*a. fig.*). **II** *v/t et.* (wie ein Papagei) nachplappern. **'~·fash·ion** *adv*: *learn ~ et.* stur *od.* mechanisch lernen; *repeat ~* → *parrot* II.

par·ry ['pærı] **I** *v/t* Frage parieren, Schlag, Stoß *a.* abwehren. **II** *s fenc.* Parade *f.*

par·si·mo·ni·ous [ˌpɑːsı'məʊnjəs] *adj* □ geizig. **par·si·mo·ny** ['~mənı] *s* Geiz *m.*

pars·ley ['pɑːslı] *s* ♥ Petersilie *f.*

pars·nip ['pɑːsnıp] *s* ♥ Pastinake *f*, Pastinak *m.*

par·son ['pɑːsn] *s* Pastor *m*, Pfarrer *m*: *~'s nose* F Bürzel *m.* **'par·son·age** *s* Pfarrhaus *n.*

part [pɑːt] **I** *s* **1.** *allg.* Teil *m*: (a) *~ of his money* ein Teil s-s Geldes; *it is good in ~*(*s*), *~s of it are good, ~ of it is good* es ist zum Teil *od.* teilweise gut; *for the most ~* größtenteils; meistens; *be ~ of s.th.* zu et. gehören; *be ~ and parcel of* e-n wesentlichen Bestandteil bilden von (*od. gen*); *~ of the body* Körperteil; *~ of speech* Wortart *f*; *three-~* dreiteilig. **2.** ⊕ (Bau-, Ersatz)Teil *n.* **3.** Teil *m*, Folge *f*, Fortsetzung *f* (*e-s Ro-*

mans, e-r Fernsehserie etc); Lieferung *f* (*e-s Buchs etc*). **4.** Anteil *m*: *take ~* teilnehmen, sich beteiligen (*in an dat*). **5.** *fig.* Teil *m*, Seite *f*: *on the ~ of* von seiten, seitens (*gen*); *on my ~* von m-r Seite, von mir; *take s.th. in good ~* et. nicht übelnehmen. **6.** *fig.* Seite *f*, Partei *f*: *take s.o.'s ~*, *take ~ with s.o.* für j-n *od.* j-s Partei ergreifen. **7.** *thea. etc* Rolle *f* (*a. fig.*): *act* (*od.* *play*) *the ~ of* die Rolle (*gen*) spielen; *play a ~ in* e-e Rolle spielen bei *od.* in (*dat*). **8.** ♪ (Sing- *od.* Instrumental)Stimme *f*, Partie *f*: *for* (*od. in*) *several ~s* mehrstimmig. **9.** Gegend *f*, Teil *m* (*e-s Landes etc*): *in these ~s* hier(zulande). **10.** *Am.* (Haar)Scheitel *m.* **II** *v/t* **11.** trennen (*from*); *Streitende* trennen; *Vorhang* aufziehen; *Haar* scheiteln: → *company*. **III** *v/i* **12.** sich trennen (*from* von): *~* (*as*) *friends* in Freundschaft auseinandergehen; *~ with et.* aufgeben, sich von *j-m, et.* trennen. **13.** sich zerteilen, aufreißen (*Wolken*). **IV** *adj* **14.** Teil...: *give s.th. in ~ exchange* et. in Zahlung geben; *~ owner* Miteigentümer(in); *give s.o. £100 in ~ payment* j-m 100 Pfund als Abschlagszahlung geben. **V** *adv* **15.** *~ ..., ~* teils ..., teils.

par·tial ['pɑːʃl] *adj* (□ → *partially*) **1.** teilweise, Teil...: *~ success* Teilerfolg *m.* **2.** parteiisch, voreingenommen: *be ~ to s.th.* F e-e Schwäche *od.* besondere Vorliebe für et. haben. **par·ti·al·i·ty** [ˌ~ʃı'ælətı] *s* **1.** Parteilichkeit *f*, Voreingenommenheit *f.* **2.** F Schwäche *f*, besondere Vorliebe (*for* für). **par·tial·ly** ['~ʃəlı] *adv* teilweise, zum Teil: *be ~ to blame for* mitschuld sein an (*dat*).

par·tic·i·pant [pɑː'tısıpənt] *s* Teilnehmer(in). **par·tic·i·pate** [~peıt] *v/i* teilnehmen, sich beteiligen (*in an dat*). **par,tici·'pa·tion** *s* Teilnahme *f*, Beteiligung *f.*

par·ti·ci·ple ['pɑːtısıpl] *s ling.* Partizip *n*, Mittelwort *n*: → *past* 2, *present* 3.

par·ti·cle ['pɑːtıkl] *s* **1.** Teilchen *n*, *phys. a.* Partikel *f*: *there is not a ~ of truth in it fig.* daran ist nicht ein einziges Wort wahr. **2.** *ling.* Partikel *f.*

par·tic·u·lar [pə'tıkjʊlə] **I** *adj* (□ → *particularly*) **1.** besonder, speziell: *this ~ case* dieser spezielle Fall; *be of no ~ importance* nicht besonders wichtig sein; *for no ~ reason* aus keinem besonderen Grund. **2. *be very ~ about*** (*od.* **over**) es sehr genau nehmen mit, großen Wert legen auf (*acc*); sehr heikel *od.* wählerisch sein in (*dat*). **II** s **3.** Einzelheit *f*: *~s pl* nähere Umstände *pl od.* Angaben *pl*; *in ~* insbesondere; *in every ~, in all ~s* in allen Einzelheiten; *enter* (*od.* **go**) *into ~s* ins einzelne gehen; *further ~s from* Näheres bei. **4.** *pl* Personalien *pl*. **par'tic·u·lar·ize** *v/t* spezifizieren, einzeln aufführen. **par-'tic·u·lar·ly** *adv* besonders: *not ~ a.* nicht sonderlich.

part·ing ['pɑːtɪŋ] **I** *adj* **1.** Abschieds...: *~ kiss.* **2.** Abschied *m*. **3.** *bsd. Br.* (Haar)Scheitel *m*.

par·ti·san [ˌpɑːtɪ'zæn] **I** s **1.** Parteigänger(in). **2.** ✕ Partisan(in). **II** *adj* **3.** parteiisch. **4.** ✕ Partisanen-.

par·ti·tion [pɑː'tɪʃn] **I** s **1.** Teilung *f*. **2.** *a.* *~ wall* Trennwand *f*. **II** *v/t* **3.** *Land etc* teilen: *~ off* abteilen, abtrennen.

part·ly ['pɑːtlɪ] → **partially**.

part·ner ['pɑːtnə] **I** s **1.** *allg.* Partner(in). **2.** † Gesellschafter(in), Partner(in), Teilhaber(in). **II** *v/t* **3.** *j-n* zum Partner haben, *j-s* Partner sein. **4.** *oft ~ up* (als Partner) zs.-bringen (*with* mit). **III** *v/i* **5.** *oft ~ up* sich (als Partner) zs.-tun (*with* mit). **'part·ner·ship** s **1.** Partnerschaft *f*: *go into ~* sich (als Partner) zs.-tun (*with* mit). **2.** † Personen-, Personalgesellschaft *f*: *(general od. ordinary) ~* offene Handelsgesellschaft; *limited* (*Am.* **special**) *~* Kommanditgesellschaft *f*.

par·tridge ['pɑːtrɪdʒ] s *orn.* Rebhuhn *n*.

part-'time I *adj* Teilzeit..., Halbtags...: *~ worker* Teilzeitbeschäftigte *m, f*, Halbtagskraft *f*. **II** *adv* halbtags.

par·ty ['pɑːtɪ] s **1.** *pol.* Partei *f*: *within the ~* innerparteilich, parteiintern. **2.** Gesellschaft, Gruppe *f*: *we were a ~ of three* wir waren zu dritt. **3.** (*Rettungs- etc*)Mannschaft *f*; ✕ Kommando *n*, Trupp *m*. **4.** Gesellschaft *f*, Party *f*: *give a ~.* **5.** ⚖ (*Prozeß-, Vertrags*)Partei *f*: *a third ~* ein Dritter. **6.** Teilnehmer(in), Beteiligte *m, f*: *be a ~ to* beteiligt sein an (*dat*), *et.* mitmachen. **7.** F Person *f*, Kerl *m*. *~ line* s **1.** *teleph.* Gemeinschaftsanschluß *m*. **2.** *pol.* Parteilinie *f*: *follow the ~* linientreu sein.

par·ve·nu ['pɑːvənjuː] s Emporkömmling *m*, Parvenü *m*.

pass [pɑːs] **I** s **1.** (*Gebirgs*)Paß *m*. **2.** Passierschein *m*: *free ~* (Dauer)Freikarte *f*, 🚋 *etc* (Dauer)Freifahrkarte *f*, -schein *m*. **3.** *get a ~ in physics ped.* die Physikprüfung bestehen. **4. *things have come to such a ~ that*** die Dinge haben sich derart zugespitzt, daß. **5.** *Sport:* Paß *m*, Zuspiel *n*. **6.** *make a ~ at* F Annäherungsversuche machen bei. **II** *v/t* **7.** vorbeigehen, -fahren an (*dat*). **8.** überholen. **9.** *Prüfung* bestehen: *Prüfling* durchkommen lassen. **10.** *fig.* hinausgehen über (*acc*), übersteigen, -treffen: *~ s.o.'s comprehension* (*od.* *understanding*) über *j-s* Verstand *od.* Horizont gehen. **11. *~ one's hand over*** (sich) mit der Hand fahren über (*acc*). **12.** *j-m et.* reichen, geben, *et.* weitergeben: → *buck* 2. **13.** *Sport:* Ball abspielen, passen (*to* zu). **14.** *Gesetz* verabschieden. **15.** *Zeit* ver-, zubringen: *~ the time reading* sich die Zeit mit Lesen vertreiben. **16.** *Urteil* abgeben, fällen, ⚖ *a.* sprechen (*on* über *acc*). **III** *v/i* **17.** vorbeigehen, -fahren (*by* an *dat*): *let s.o. ~ j-n* vorbeilassen. **18.** (*to*) übergehen (auf *acc*), fallen (an *acc*). **19.** vergehen (*Schmerz etc*), (*Zeit a.*) verstreichen. **20.** durchkommen, (*die Prüfung*) bestehen. **21.** (*as, for*) gelten (als), gehalten *od.* angesehen werden (für). **22.** durchgehen, unbeanstandet bleiben: *let s.th. ~ et.* durchgehen lassen. **23.** *Sport:* (den Ball) abspielen *od.* passen (*to* zu). **24.** *Kartenspiel:* passen (*a. fig.*): *I ~ on that* da muß ich passen. **25. *~ over s.th.*** et. übergehen *od.* ignorieren (*in silence* stillschweigend). *Verbindungen mit Adverbien:* **pass| a·way** I *v/t* **1.** → *pass* 15. **II** *v/i* **2.** → *pass* 19. **3.** verscheiden, sterben. *~* **by** I *v/i* **1.** vorbeigehen, -fahren. **2.** → *pass* 19. **II** *v/t* **3.** *et., j-n* übergehen. *~* **down** *v/t* (*to*) *Tradition etc* weitergeben (*dat od.* an *acc*), *Bräuche etc* überliefern (*dat*). *~* **off** I *v/t* **1.** *j-n, et.* ausgeben (*as* als). **II** *v/i* **2.** *gut etc* vorübergehen, verlaufen. **3.** vergehen (*Schmerz etc*). *~* **on** I *v/t* **1.** weitergeben (*to dat od.* an *acc*) (*a. fig.*); *Krankheit* übertragen. **II** *v/i* **2.** übergehen (*to* zu *e-m anderen Thema etc*). **3.** → *pass away* 3. *~* **o·ver**

pass by 3. **~ round I** *v/t* herumreichen; *Gerücht etc* in Umlauf setzen: **be passed round** *a.* die Runde machen. **II** *v/i* herumgereicht werden, *a. fig.* die Runde machen, *fig.* in Umlauf sein. **~ up** *v/t* sich *e-e* Chance etc entgehen lassen.

pass·a·ble ['pɑːsəbl] *adj* □ **1.** passierbar, befahrbar. **2.** *fig.* passabel.

pas·sage ['pæsɪdʒ] *s* **1.** Durchfahrt *f*, -reise *f*: → **bird** 1. **2.** Passage *f*, (Durch-, Verbindungs)Gang *m*. **3.** (See-, Flug-) Reise *f*: → **rough** 2. **4.** with the **~ of time** mit der Zeit. **5.** Verabschiedung *f* (*e-s Gesetzes*). **6.** Passage *f*, Stelle *f* (*e-s Texts*). **'~·way** → **passage** 2.

pas·sen·ger ['pæsɪndʒə] *s* Passagier *m*, Fahr-, Fluggast *m*, (*Auto- etc*)Insasse *m*. **~ train** *s* Personenzug *m*.

,pass·er·'by *pl* **,pass·ers·'by** *s* Passant(in).

pass·ing ['pɑːsɪŋ] **I** *s* **1.** with the **~ of time** mit der Zeit. **2.** → **passage** 5. **3.** in **~** beiläufig, nebenbei. **II** *adj* **4.** flüchtig (*Blick, Gedanke etc*).

pas·sion ['pæʃn] *s* **1.** Leidenschaft *f*, *weitS. a.* Passion *f*: **be a ~ with s.o.** e-e Leidenschaft bei j-m sein, j-s Leidenschaft sein; **have a ~ for s.th.** e-e Leidenschaft für et. haben; **~s ran high** die Erregung schlug hohe Wellen; → **heat** 2. **2.** **fly into a ~** e-n Wutanfall bekommen. **3.** ♀ *eccl.* Passion *f*: ♀ **play** Passionsspiel *n*. **pas·sion·ate** ['~ʃənət] *adj* □ leidenschaftlich.

pas·sive ['pæsɪv] **I** *adj* □ **1.** passiv: **~ resistance** passiver Widerstand; **~ smoking** passives Rauchen, Passivrauchen *n*; **~ vocabulary** passiver Wortschatz. **2.** *ling.* passivisch: **~ voice** → 3. **II** *s* **3.** *ling.* Passiv *n*, Leideform *f*. **pas·siv·i·ty** *s* Passivität *f*.

'pass·key *s* Hauptschlüssel *m*.

Pass·o·ver ['pɑːsˌəʊvə] *s eccl.* Passah *n*.

pass·port ['pɑːspɔːt] *s* **1.** (Reise)Paß *m*: **hold a British ~** e-n britischen Paß haben; **~ picture** Paßbild *n*. **2.** *fig.* Schlüssel *m* (**to** zu).

'pass·word *s* Kennwort *n*, Parole *f*.

past [pɑːst] **I** *adj* **1.** vergangen: **be ~** vorüber *od.* vorbei sein; **for some time ~** seit einiger Zeit; **learn from ~ mistakes** aus Fehlern in der Vergangenheit lernen. **2.** *ling.* **~ participle** Partizip

n Perfekt, Mittelwort *n* der Vergangenheit; **~ perfect** Plusquamperfekt *n*, Vorvergangenheit *f*; **~ tense** Vergangenheit *f*, Präteritum *n*. **3.** früher, ehemalig. **II** *s* **4.** Vergangenheit *f* (*a. ling.*): **in the ~** in der Vergangenheit, früher. **III** *adv* **5.** vorbei, vorüber: **run ~** vorbeilaufen. **IV** *prp* **6.** *Zeit:* nach, über (*acc*): **half ~ seven** halb acht; **she is ~ forty** sie ist über vierzig. **7.** an ... (*dat*) vorbei *od.* vorüber. **8.** über ... (*acc*) hinaus: **I'm ~ caring** das kümmert mich nicht mehr; **be ~ it** F es nicht mehr bringen; **I wouldn't put it ~ him** F das traue ich ihm glatt *od.* ohne weiteres zu; → **cure** 2, **hope** I, *etc.*

pas·ta ['pæstə] *s* Teigwaren *pl.*

paste [peɪst] **I** *s* **1.** (*Fisch-, Zahn- etc*)Paste *f*. **2.** Kleister *m*. **3.** *Am.* → **pastry**. **II** *v/t* **4.** kleben (**to, on** an *acc*): **~ up** ankleben. **'~·board** *s* Karton *m*, Pappe *f*.

pas·tel *s* [pæ'stel] **1.** Pastellstift *m*. **2.** Pastell(zeichnung *f*) *n*. **3.** Pastellfarbe *f*, -ton *m*. **II** *adj* ['pæstl] **4.** Pastell... **5.** pastellfarben.

pas·teur·ize ['pɑːstʃəraɪz] *v/t* pasteurisieren, keimfrei machen.

pas·time ['pɑːstaɪm] *s* Zeitvertreib *m*, Freizeitbeschäftigung *f*: **as a ~** zum Zeitvertreib.

pas·tor ['pɑːstə] *s* Pastor *m*, Pfarrer *m*. **'pas·to·ral** **I** *adj* □ **1.** pastoral, ländlich, idyllisch. **2.** pastoral, seelsorgerisch: **~ letter** → 4. **II** *s* **3.** ♪ Pastorale *n*, *f*. **4.** *eccl.* Hirtenbrief *m*.

pas·try ['peɪstrɪ] *s* **1.** (*Blätter-, Mürbeetc*)Teig *m*. **2.** *Br. oft pl* (Fein)Gebäck *n*.

pas·ture ['pɑːstʃə] **I** *s* Weide(land *n*) *f*. **II** *v/t* weiden (lassen). **III** *v/i* grasen, weiden.

past·y[1] ['peɪstɪ] *adj* blaß, käsig.

past·y[2] ['pæstɪ] *s bsd. Br.* (Fleisch)Pastete *f*.

pat[1] [pæt] **I** *s* **1.** Klaps *m*: **give s.o.** (**o.s.**) **a ~ on the back** *fig.* F j-m (sich selbst) auf die Schulter klopfen. **2.** Portion *f* (*bsd. Butter*). **3.** (*Kuh*)Fladen *m*. **4.** Trappeln *n*. **II** *v/t* **5.** tätscheln; abtupfen (**with** mit): **~ s.o. on the head** (**shoulder**) j-m den Kopf tätscheln (auf die Schulter klopfen); **~ s.o.** (**o.s.**) **on the back** *fig.* F j-m (sich selbst) auf die Schulter klopfen; **~ down** Haar etc an-,

festdrücken, *Erde etc* festklopfen. **III**
v/i **6.** trappeln.

pat² [~] **I** *adv* **1. have** (*od.* **know**) **s.th.**
(**off**) ~ et. aus dem Effeff *od.* wie am
Schnürchen können. **2.** wie aus der Pistole
geschossen: *answer* ~; *the answer
came* ~. **II** *adj* **3.** glatt (*Antwort
etc*).

patch [pætʃ] **I** *s* **1.** Fleck *m*; Flicken *m*:
~*es pl of mist* Nebelschwaden *pl*; *in* ~*es
fig.* stellenweise; *not to be a* ~ *on Br.* F
nichts sein gegen. **2.** Beet *n*. **3. go
through a bad** (**difficult**) ~ e-e Pechsträhne
haben (*a* e-e schwierige Zeit
durchmachen). **II** *v/t* **4.** flicken: ~ *up*
zs.-flicken (*a. fig.*); *fig.* Streit beilegen;
~ *things up* sich zs.-raufen. ~ *pock·et s*
aufgesetzte Tasche. '~*work s* Patchwork
n: ~ *blanket* Flickendecke *f*.

patch·y ['pætʃɪ] *adj* □ **1.** fleckig. **2.** *fig.*
lückenhaft; unterschiedlich.

pat·ent ['peɪtənt] **I** *adj* □ **1.** offenkundig,
-sichtlich. **2.** patentiert; Patent...: ~ *office*
Patentamt *n*. **3.** *Br.* F patent (*Methode
etc*). **II** *s* **4.** Patent *n*: *protected by*
~ patentrechtlich geschützt; *take out a*
~ *on* → 5. **III** *v/t* **5.** et. patentieren
lassen. ~ *leath·er s* Lackleder *n*.

pa·ter·nal [pə'tɜːnl] *adj* □ **1.** väterlich,
Vater... **2.** *Großvater etc* väterlicherseits.

pa·ter·ni·ty [pə'tɜːnətɪ] *s* Vaterschaft *f*: ~
suit ⚖ Vaterschaftsprozeß *m*.

path [pɑːθ] *pl* **paths** [pɑːðz] *s* **1.** Weg *m*
(*a. fig.* to zu), Pfad *m*: *stand in s.o.'s* ~
j-m im Weg stehen; → *cross* 9. **2.** *phys.*,
⚙ Bahn *f*.

pa·thet·ic [pə'θetɪk] *adj* (~*ally*) **1.** mitleiderregend:
~ *sight* Bild *n* des Jammers.
2. *Br.* kläglich (*Versuch etc*), erbärmlich,
miserabel (*Leistung etc*).

path·o·log·i·cal [ˌpæθə'lɒdʒɪkl] *adj* □
pathologisch, krankhaft. **pa·thol·o·gist**
[pə'θɒlədʒɪst] *s* Pathologe *m*.
pa·thol·o·gy *s* Pathologie *f*.

pa·thos ['peɪθɒs] *s das* Mitleiderregende.

'**path·way** → **path** 1.

pa·tience ['peɪʃns] *s* **1.** Geduld *f*: *lose
one's* ~ die Geduld verlieren (**with** mit);
→ *saint* 1. **2.** *bsd. Br.* Patience *f* (*Kartenspiel*):
play ~ Patiencen *od.* e-e Patience
legen. '**pa·tient** [~] *adj* □ geduldig
(**with** mit). **II** *s* Patient(in).

pat·i·na ['pætɪnə] *s* Patina *f*.

pa·ti·o ['pætɪəʊ] *pl* **-os** *s* **1.** Patio *m*,
Innenhof *m*. **2.** Veranda *f*, Terrasse
f.

pa·tri·arch ['peɪtrɪɑːk] *s* Patriarch *m*.
ˌ**pa·tri·ar·chal** [~kl] *adj* □ patriarchalisch.
pa·tri·arch·ate ['~kɪt] *s* Patriarchat
n.

pa·tri·ot ['pætrɪət] *s* Patriot(in). **pa·tri·ot·ic**
[ˌ~'ɒtɪk] *adj* (~*ally*) patriotisch.
pa·tri·ot·ism ['~ətɪzəm] *s* Patriotismus
m.

pa·trol [pə'trəʊl] **I** *s* **1.** ✕ Patrouille *f*,
(*Polizei*)Streife *f*. **2.** Patrouille *f*, Streife
f, Runde *f*: *on* ~ auf Patrouille *od.* Streife;
~ *car* (Funk)Streifenwagen *m*; ~
wagon Am. (Polizei)Gefangenenwagen
m. **II** *v/t* **3.** abpatrouillieren (*Soldaten*),
auf Streife sein in (*dat*) (*Polizist*),
s-e Runde machen in (*dat*) (*Wachmann*).
pa'trol·man *s* (*irr man*) **1.** Am.
Streifenpolizist *m*. **2.** *Br.* motorisierter
Pannenhelfer.

pa·tron ['peɪtrən] *s* **1.** Schirmherr *m*. **2.**
Gönner *m*, Förderer *m*. **3.** (Stamm-)
Kunde *m*; Stammgast *m*. **pa·tron·age**
['pætrənɪdʒ] *s* **1.** Schirmherrschaft *f*:
under the ~ *of* unter der Schirmherrschaft
von (*od. gen*). **2.** Kundschaft *f*.
pa·tron·ess ['peɪtrənɪs] *s* **1.** Schirmherrin
f. **2.** Gönnerin *f*, Förderin *f*. **pa·tron·ize**
['pætrənaɪz] *v/t* **1.** fördern. **2.**
(Stamm)Kunde *od.* Stammgast sein in
(*dat*). **3.** gönnerhaft *od.* herablassend
behandeln. '**pa·tron·iz·ing** *adj* □ gönnerhaft,
herablassend.

pa·tron saint *s* Schutzheilige *m, f*.

pat·ter¹ ['pætə] **I** *v/i* **1.** prasseln (*Regen
etc*). **2.** trappeln. **II** *s* **3.** Prasseln *n*. **4.**
Trappeln *n*.

pat·ter² [~] *s* **1.** Sprüche *pl* (*e-s Vertreters
etc*). **2.** Jargon *m*: *thieves'* ~ Gaunersprache
f.

pat·tern ['pætən] **I** *s* **1.** (*a. Schnitt-,
Strick*)Muster *n*; *fig.* Muster *n*, Vorbild
n. **2.** ✿ Muster *n*, (Waren)Probe *f*. **3.**
(*Stoff- etc*)Muster *n*. **4.** *fig.* Muster *n*,
Schema *n*: *follow its usual* ~ nach dem
üblichen Schema *od.* wie üblich verlaufen.
II *v/t* **5.** mustern. **6.** bilden, gestalten
(**after, on** nach): ~ *o.s.* **on s.o.** sich
j-n zum Vorbild nehmen.

paunch [pɔːntʃ] *s* (dicker) Bauch, Wanst
m. '**paunch·y** *adj* dickbäuchig.

pau·per ['pɔːpə] *s* Arme *m, f*.

pause [pɔ:z] I *s* Pause *f: without a ~* ohne Pause. II *v/i* innehalten.

pave [peɪv] *v/t* pflastern: *~ the way for* fig. den Weg ebnen (*dat*). **'pave·ment** *s* 1. (Straßen)Pflaster *n*. 2. Br. Bürger-, Gehsteig *m: ~ artist* Pflastermaler(in); *~ café* Straßencafé *n*. 3. Am. Fahrbahn *f*.

pa·vil·ion [pə'vɪljən] *s* Pavillon *m*.

pav·ing stone ['peɪvɪŋ] *s* Pflasterstein *m*.

paw [pɔ:] I *s* 1. Pfote *f* (*a. F* Hand), Tatze *f*. II *v/t* 2. *Boden* scharren, scharren an (*der Tür etc*). 3. F betatschen. III *v/i* 4. scharren (*at* an *dat*).

pawn¹ [pɔ:n] *s* 1. *Schach:* Bauer *m*. 2. *fig.* Schachfigur *f*.

pawn² [~] I *s: be in ~* verpfändet *od.* versetzt sein. II *v/t* verpfänden, versetzen. **'~,brok·er** *s* Pfandleiher *m*. **'~-shop** *s* Leih-, Pfandhaus *n*. **~ tick·et** *s* Pfandschein *m*.

pay [peɪ] I *s* 1. Bezahlung *f*, Gehalt *n*, Lohn *m*. II *v/t* 2. *Betrag* zahlen, entrichten, *Rechnung* (be)zahlen, beigleichen: *~ into* einzahlen auf (*ein Konto*). 3. *j-n* bezahlen. 4. *fig.* Aufmerksamkeit schenken, *Besuch* abstatten, *Kompliment* machen: *~ attention* 1, *etc.* III *v/i* (*irr*) 5. zahlen: *~ for et.* bezahlen (*a. fig.*); *he had to ~ dearly for it fig.* es kam ihn teuer zu stehen, er mußte teuer dafür bezahlen. 6. *fig.* sich lohnen, sich bezahlt machen.

Verbindungen mit Adverbien:

pay| back → **repay:** → **coin** I. *~* **in** *v/t* einzahlen. *~* **off** I *v/t* 1. *j-n* auszahlen. 2. *et.* ab(be)zahlen, tilgen. II *v/i* 3. → **pay** 6. *~* **out** *v/t* ausgeben, bezahlen (*for* für). *~* **up** I *v/t* *j-n*, *et.* voll *od.* sofort bezahlen. II *v/i* zahlen.

pay·a·ble ['peɪəbl] *adj* zahlbar, fällig: *be ~ to* ausgestellt sein auf (*acc*).

pay| bed *s Br.* Privatbett *n* (*in Klinik*). **'~-day** *s* Zahltag *m*. **~ en·ve·lope** *s Am.* Lohntüte *f*.

pay·ing ['peɪɪŋ] *adj* 1. *~ guest* zahlender Gast. 2. lohnend, rentabel. *~'in slip* *s* Einzahlungsschein *m*.

pay·ment ['peɪmənt] *s* (Be)Zahlung *f: in ~ of* als Bezahlung für; *on ~ of* gegen Zahlung von (*od. gen*).

'pay|·off *s* F Pointe *f*. **~ pack·et** *s Br.* Lohntüte *f*. **~ phone** *s* Münzfernspre-

cher *m*. **~ rise** *s* Lohn-, Gehaltserhöhung *f*. **'~·roll** *s* Lohnliste *f: be on s.o.'s ~* bei j-m beschäftigt sein. **~ slip** *s* Lohn-, Gehaltsstreifen *m*. **~ sta·tion** *s Am.* Münzfernsprecher *m*.

pea [pi:] *s* ♀ Erbse *f: they are (as) like as two ~s (in a pod)* sie gleichen sich wie ein Ei dem anderen.

peace [pi:s] *s* 1. Friede(n) *m: the two countries are at ~* zwischen den beiden Ländern herrscht Frieden; *make one's ~ with* sich aus- *od.* versöhnen mit. 2. ⚖ öffentliche Ruhe *u.* Ordnung: *keep the ~* die öffentliche Ordnung aufrechterhalten; → *breach* 1. 3. Ruhe *f: ~ of mind* Seelenfrieden *m*; *in ~ and quiet* in Ruhe u. Frieden. II *adj* 4. Friedens...: *~ conference* Friedenskonferenz *f*; *~ movement* Friedensbewegung *f*; *~ pipe* Friedenspfeife *f*; *~ treaty* Friedensvertrag *m*. **'peace·a·ble** *adj* □ friedlich (*Diskussion etc*), (*Person a.*) friedfertig. **peace·ful** ['pi:sfʊl] *adj* □ friedlich.

'peace-,lov·ing *adj* friedliebend. **'~-time** I *s* Friedenszeiten *pl*. II *adj* in Friedenszeiten.

peach [pi:tʃ] *s* 1. ♀ Pfirsich *m*; Pfirsichbaum *m*. 2. F prima *od.* klasse Person *od.* Sache: *a ~ of a girl* ein süßes Mädchen; *a ~ of a hat* ein Gedicht von e-m Hut.

pea·cock ['pi:kɒk] *s orn.* Pfau *m:* (*as*) *proud as a ~* stolz wie ein Pfau.

peak [pi:k] I *s* 1. Spitze *f*, (*e-s Bergs a.*) Gipfel *m*. 2. Schirm *m* (*e-r Mütze*). 3. *fig.* Höhepunkt *m*, Höchststand *m: be at its ~* am höchsten sein. II *v/i* 4. e-n Höchststand erreichen. III *adj* 5. Höchst..., Spitzen...: *~ hours pl* Hauptverkehrs-, Stoßzeit *f*; ⚡ Hauptbelastungszeit *f*. **peaked** [pi:kt] *adj: ~ cap* Schirmmütze *f*. **'peak·y** *adj* F blaß, kränklich.

peal [pi:l] I *s* 1. (*Glocken*)Läuten *n*. 2. (*Donner*)Schlag *m: ~s pl of laughter* schallendes *od.* dröhnendes Gelächter. II *v/i a. ~* **out** 3. läuten. 4. krachen (*Donner*).

'pea·nut *s* ♀ Erdnuß *f: ~s pl* F lächerliche Summe. **~ but·ter** *s* Erdnußbutter *f*.

pear [peə] *s* ♀ a) Birne *f*, b) *a. ~* **tree** Birnbaum *m*.

pearl [pɜ:l] I *s* 1. Perle *f*. 2. Perlmutter *f*,

n, Perlmutt *n*. **II** *adj* **3.** Perlen... **4.** Perlmutt(er)...

peas·ant ['peznt] *s* **1.** Kleinbauer *m*. **2.** *fig*. F Bauer *m*.

pea·soup·er [,pi:'su:pə] *s* F Waschküche *f* (*dicker, gelber Nebel*).

peat [pi:t] *s* Torf *m*: *cut* (*od. dig*) *~* Torf stechen.

peb·ble ['pebl] *s* Kiesel(stein) *m*: *you are not the only ~ on the beach* F ich *etc* kann auch ohne dich auskommen. **'peb·bly** *adj* Kiesel...: *~ beach.*

pec·ca·dil·lo [,pekə'dıləʊ] *pl* **-lo(e)s** *s* **1.** kleine Sünde. **2.** Kavaliersdelikt *n*.

peck [pek] **I** *v/t* **1.** picken. **2.** F *j-m* e-n flüchtigen Kuß geben (*on* auf *acc*). **II** *v/i* **3.** picken, hacken (*at* nach): *~ at one's food* im Essen herumstochern. **III** *s* **4.** F flüchtiger Kuß. **'peck·er** *s* **1.** *Am. sl.* Schwanz *m* (*Penis*). **2.** *keep one's ~ up* F die Ohren steifhalten. **'peck·ing** *adj*: *~ order orn.* Hackordnung *f* (*a. fig.*).

pec·to·ral ['pektərəl] *adj* Brust...

pe·cu·li·ar [pı'kju:ljə] *adj* (□ → *peculiarly*) **1.** eigen(tümlich) (*to* dat): *be ~ to a.* typisch sein für. **2.** eigenartig, seltsam. **pe,cu·li·ar·i·ty** [ˌlı'ærətı] *s* **1.** Eigenheit *f*, Eigentümlichkeit *f*: *be a ~ of a.* typisch sein für. **2.** Eigenartigkeit *f*, Seltsamkeit *f*. **pe'cu·li·ar·ly** *adv* **1.** → *peculiar.* **2.** besonders.

pe·cu·ni·ar·y [pı'kju:njərı] *adj* geldlich, Geld...: *~ difficulties pl* finanzielle Schwierigkeiten *pl*.

ped·a·gog·ic, ped·a·gog·i·cal [,pedə'gɒdʒık(l)] *adj* (□) pädagogisch. **ped·a·gogue** ['~gɒg] *s contp.* Schulmeister (-in), Pedant(in). **ped·a·go·gy** ['~gɒdʒı] *s* Pädagogik *f*.

ped·al ['pedl] **I** *s* **1.** Pedal *n*. **II** *v/i pret u. pp* **-aled**, *bsd. Br.* **-alled 2.** das Pedal treten. **3.** (mit dem Rad) fahren, strampeln. *~ bin s* Treteimer *m*. *~ boat s* Tretboot *n*.

ped·ant ['pedənt] *s* Pedant(in). **pe·dan·tic** [pı'dæntık] *adj* (*~ally*) pedantisch (*about* wenn es um ... geht). **ped·ant·ry** ['pedəntrı] *s* Pedanterie *f*.

ped·dle ['pedl] *v/t* hausieren (gehen) mit (*a. fig.*): *~ drugs* mit Drogen handeln. **'ped·dler** *s* **1.** Drogenhändler(in). **2.** *Am.* → *pedlar.*

ped·es·tal ['pedıstl] *s* Sockel *m*: *place*

(*od. put, set*) *s.o. on a ~ fig.* j-n aufs Podest erheben; *knock s.o. off his ~ fig.* j-n von s-m Sockel stoßen.

pe·des·tri·an [pı'destrıən] **I** *adj* **1.** Fußgänger...: *~ crossing Br.* Fußgängerüberweg *m*; *~ precinct* (*od. zone*) Fußgängerzone *f*. **2.** *fig.* prosaisch, trocken; phantasielos. **II** *s* **3.** Fußgänger(in).

pe·di·a·tri·cian, pe·di·at·rics *Am.* → **paediatrician, paediatrics.**

ped·i·cure ['pedɪˌkjʊə] *s* Pediküre *f*.

ped·i·gree ['pedıgri:] **I** *s* **1.** Stammbaum *m*. **2.** Ab-, Herkunft *f*. **II** *adj* **3.** *zo.* reinrassig.

ped·lar ['pedlə] *s* Hausierer(in).

pee [pi:] F **I** *v/i* pinkeln. **II** *s*: *have* (*go for*) *a ~* pinkeln (gehen).

peek [pi:k] **I** *v/i* kurz *od.* verstohlen gukken (*at* auf *acc*). **II** *s*: *have* (*od. take*) *a ~ at* e-n kurzen *od.* verstohlenen Blick werfen auf (*acc*).

peel [pi:l] **I** *v/t* Kartoffeln *etc* schälen: *~* (*off*) Tapete *etc* abziehen, ablösen; *Kleider* abstreifen; *keep one's eyes ~ed* F die Augen offenhalten. **II** *v/i a. ~ off* sich lösen (*Tapete etc*), abblättern (*Farbe etc*), sich schälen (*Haut*). **III** *s* Schale *f*. **'peel·er** *s* (*Kartoffel- etc*)Schäler *m*. **'peel·ings** *s pl* (*Kartoffel- etc*)Schalen *pl*.

peep¹ [pi:p] **I** *v/i* **1.** piep(s)en. **II** *s* **2.** Piep(s)en *n*. **3.** F Piepser *m* (*Ton*).

peep² [~] **I** *v/i* **1.** → *peek* **I. 2.** *mst ~ out* vorschauen (*from under* unter dat). **II** *s* **3.** → *peek* **II. 'peep·er** *s mst pl* F Gucker *m* (*Auge*).

'peep·hole *s* Guckloch *n*, (*in Tür*) Spion *m*.

Peep·ing Tom ['pi:pıŋ] *s* Spanner *m*, Voyeur *m*.

peep show *s* Peep-Show *f*.

peer¹ [pıə] *v/i* angestrengt schauen, spähen: *~ at s.o.* j-n anstarren.

peer² [~] *s* **1.** *Br.* Peer *m*. **2.** Gleichgestellte *m*, *f*, Ebenbürtige *m*, *f*, Altersgenosse *m*, -genossin *f*: *one's ~s pl* seinesgleichen. **'peer·age** *s Br.* Peerage *f*: *raise to the ~* in den Adelsstand erheben. **'peer·ess** *s Br.* Peereß *f*. **'peer·less** *adj* □ unvergleichlich, einzigartig.

peeved [pi:vd] *adj* F sauer (*about, at* über *acc*).

pee·vish ['pi:vıʃ] *adj* □ gereizt; reizbar.

peg [peg] **I** *s* **1.** Pflock *m*; (*Holz*)Nagel *m*, (-)Stift *m*; (*Zelt*)Hering *m*: **be a square ~ in a round hole** *fig.* am falschen Platz sein; **take s.o. down a ~ (or two)** F j-m e-n Dämpfer aufsetzen. **2.** (Kleider-) Haken *m*: **off the ~** von der Stange (*Anzug*). **3.** *Br.* (*Wäsche*)Klammer *f*. **II** *v/t* **4.** anpflocken. **5.** *a.* **~ out** (*od.* **up**) *Br. Wäsche* (an der Leine) anklammern. **6.** ✝ *Preise etc* stützen, halten. **III** *v/i* **7. ~ away at** F dranbleiben an (*e-r Arbeit*). **8. ~ out** *bsd. Br.* F den Löffel weglegen (*sterben*).

pe·jo·ra·tive [pɪ'dʒɒrətɪv] *adj* □ pejorativ, abschätzig, herabsetzend.

Pe·kin·ese [ˌpiːkɪ'niːz] *pl* **-ese** *s zo.* Pekinese *m*.

pel·i·can ['pelɪkən] *s orn.* Pelikan *m.* **~ cross·ing** *s Br.* Ampelübergang *m*.

pel·let ['pelɪt] *s* **1.** Kügelchen *n*. **2.** Schrotkorn *n*.

pelt¹ [pelt] *s* Fell *m*, Pelz *m*.

pelt² [~] **I** *v/t* **1.** bewerfen, *a. fig.* bombardieren (**with** mit). **II** *v/i* **2. it is ~ing (down),** **it is ~ing with rain** es gießt in Strömen. **3.** stürmen, stürzen. **III** *s* **4.** (**at**) **full ~** mit voller Geschwindigkeit.

pel·vic ['pelvɪk] *adj anat.,* ✻ Becken...: **~ fin** *ichth.* Bauchflosse *f*.

pel·vis ['pelvɪs] *pl* **-ves** [~viːz] *s anat.* Becken *n*.

pen¹ [pen] *s* (*Schreib*)Feder *f*; Füller *m*; Kugelschreiber *m*.

pen² [~] *s* **1.** Pferch *m*, (*Schaf*)Hürde *f*. **2.** (*Lauf*)Gitter *n*, (-)Stall *m*. **II** *v/t* (*a. irr*) *a.* **~ in** (*od.* **up**) **3.** *Tiere* einpferchen. **4.** *Personen* zs.-pferchen.

pe·nal ['piːnl] *adj* □ **1.** Straf...: **~ code** Strafgesetzbuch *n*; **~ colony** Strafkolonie *f*; **~ law** Strafrecht *n*; **~ reform** Strafrechtsreform *f*. **2.** strafbar: **~ act** strafbare Handlung. **pe·nal·ize** ['piːnəlaɪz] *v/t* **1.** bestrafen, *weitS. a.* benachteiligen. **2.** *et.* unter Strafe stellen. **pen·al·ty** ['penltɪ] *s* **1.** Strafe *f*: **pay the ~ for s.th.** *et.* bezahlen *od.* büßen (**with** mit). **2.** Nachteil *m*. **3.** *Fußball:* Elfmeter *m*: **~ area** (*od.* **box**) Strafraum *m*; **~ kick** Strafstoß *m*.

pen·ance ['penəns] *s eccl.* Buße *f*: **do ~** Buße tun (**for** für).

pen-and-ink draw·ing *s* Federzeichnung *f*.

pence [pens] *pl* von **penny**.

pen·chant ['pɑ̃ːŋʃɑ̃ːŋ] *s* (**for**) Neigung *f*, Hang *m* (zu); Vorliebe *f* (für).

pen·cil ['pensl] *s* **1.** Bleistift *m*. **2.** ✻, *phys.* (*Strahlen- etc*)Bündel *n*. **II** *v/t pret u. pp* **-ciled,** *bsd. Br.* **-cilled 3.** mit Bleistift markieren *od.* schreiben *od.* zeichnen. **4.** *Augenbrauen etc* nachziehen. **~ case** *s* Federmäppchen *n.* **~ sharp·en·er** *s* (Bleistift)Spitzer *m*.

pen·dant ['pendənt] *s* Anhänger *m* (*Schmuckstück*).

pen·dent ['pendənt] *adj* **1.** Hänge...: **~ lamp.** **2.** überhängend (*Felsen etc*).

pend·ing ['pendɪŋ] **I** *adj* **1.** *bsd.* ⚖ schwebend, anhängig. **2.** bevorstehend. **II** *prp* **3.** bis zu.

pen·du·lum ['pendjʊləm] *s* Pendel *n* (*a. fig.*).

pen·e·trate ['penɪtreɪt] **I** *v/t* eindringen in (*acc*) (*a. fig.*); durchdringen, dringen durch. **II** *v/i* eindringen (**into** in *acc*) (*a. fig.*); durchdringen; ~ **through** *a.* dringen durch. **'pen·e·trat·ing** *adj* □ **1.** durchdringend; (*Verstand*) scharf. **2.** scharfsinnig. **,pen·e·'tra·tion** *s* **1.** Ein-, Durchdringen *n*. **2.** Scharfsinn *m*.

pen friend *s* Brieffreund(in).

pen·guin ['peŋgwɪn] *s orn.* Pinguin *m*.

pen·i·cil·lin [ˌpenɪ'sɪlɪn] *s* ✻ Penicillin *n*.

pen·in·su·la [pə'nɪnsjʊlə] *s* Halbinsel *f*. **pen·in·su·lar** *adj* Halbinsel...; halbinselförmig.

pe·nis ['piːnɪs] *pl* **-nis·es, -nes** ['~niːz] *s anat.* Penis *m*.

pen·i·tence ['penɪtəns] *s* Buße *f*: a) *eccl.* Bußfertigkeit *f*, b) Reue *f*. **'pen·i·tent, pen·i·ten·tial** [ˌ~'tenʃl] *adj* □ a) *eccl.* bußfertig, b) reuig. **pen·i·ten·tia·ry** [ˌ~'tenʃərɪ] *s Am.* (Staats)Gefängnis *n*. **~ name** *s* Schriftstellername *m*.

'pen|·knife *s* (*irr* **knife**) Taschenmesser *n*. **~ name** *s* Schriftstellername *m*.

pen·nant ['penənt] *s* Wimpel *m*.

pen·ni·less ['penɪlɪs] *adj* □ (völlig) mittellos: **be ~ a.** keinen Pfennig Geld haben.

pen·ny ['penɪ] *pl* **-nies,** *coll.* **pence** [pens] *s Br.* Penny *m*: **in for a ~, in for a pound** wer A sagt, muß auch B sagen; **a pretty ~** F ein hübsches Sümmchen; **count (the) pennies** jeden Pfennig umdrehen; **the ~('s) dropped** F der Groschen ist gefallen; **spend a ~** F mal verschwinden. **~ dread·ful** *pl* **-fuls** *s Br.* F Groschenroman *m*. **~ pinch·er** *s* F

Pfennigfuchser(in). '~‚**pinch·ing** adj F knick(e)rig.

pen pal F → **pen friend.**

pen·sion ['penʃn] I s Rente f, Pension f: ~ **scheme** Rentenversicherung f. II v/t: ~ **off** j-n pensionieren, in den Ruhestand versetzen; fig. F Maschine etc ausrangieren. '**pen·sion·a·ble** adj: **of** ~ **age** im Renten- od. Pensionsalter. **pen·sion·er** ['~ʃənə] s Rentner(in), Pensionär(in).

pen·sive ['pensɪv] adj □ **1.** nachdenklich. **2.** trübsinnig.

pent [pent] pret u. pp von **pen²**.

pen·ta·gon ['pentəgən] s Fünfeck n: **the** ♀ das Pentagon. **pen·tag·o·nal** [~'tægənl] adj □ fünfeckig.

pen·tath·lete [pen'tæθliːt] s Sport: Fünfkämpfer(in). **pen'tath·lon** [~lɒn] s Fünfkampf m.

Pen·te·cost ['pentɪkɒst] s eccl. Pfingsten n, a. pl.

pent·house ['penthaʊs] s Penthouse n, -haus n.

‚**pent-'up** adj an-, aufgestaut (Gefühle).

pe·nul·ti·mate [pe'nʌltɪmət] adj vorletzt.

pe·o·ny ['pɪənɪ] s ♀ Pfingstrose f.

peo·ple ['piːpl] I s **1.** (pl konstruiert) die Menschen pl, die Leute pl; Leute pl, Personen pl: **my** ~ F m-e Angehörigen pl od. Leute. **2.** (pl konstruiert) man: ~ **say that** man sagt, daß. **3.** (pl konstruiert) **the** ~ a) das (gemeine) Volk: **a man of the** (**common**) ~ ein Mann des Volks, b) die Bürger pl od. Wähler pl, die Bevölkerung: ~'**s front** Volksfront f; ~'**s republic** Volksrepublik f. **4.** Volk n, Nation f. II v/t **5.** besiedeln, bevölkern (**with** mit).

pep [pep] F I s Pep m, Schwung m. II v/t: ~ **up** j-n aufmöbeln: ~ **things up** Schwung in den Laden bringen.

pep·per ['pepə] I s Pfeffer m; Paprikaschote f. II v/t pfeffern, fig. a. spicken (**with** mit). '~**box** Am. → **pepper pot.** '~**corn** s Pfefferkorn n. '~**mill** s Pfeffermühle f. '~**mint** I s **1.** ♀ Pfefferminze f. **2.** Pfefferminz n (Bonbon). II adj **3.** Pfefferminz... ~ **pot** s Pfefferstreuer m.

pep·per·y ['pepərɪ] adj □ **1.** pfeff(e)rig. **2.** fig. hitzig (Person).

pep‖pill s F Aufputschpille f. ~ **talk** s F aufmunternde Worte pl: **give s.o. a** ~

j-m ein paar aufmunternde Worte sagen.

pep·tic ['peptɪk] adj: ~ **ulcer** ♂ Magengeschwür n.

per [pɜː] prp **1.** per, durch. **2.** pro, je. **3.** mst **as** ~ laut, gemäß.

per·am·bu·la·tor [pə'ræmbjʊleɪtə] s bsd. Br. Kinderwagen m.

per cap·i·ta [pə'kæpɪtə] I adj Pro-Kopf-... II adv pro Kopf.

per·ceive [pə'siːv] v/t **1.** wahrnehmen. **2.** begreifen, erkennen.

per cent Br., **per·cent** bsd. Am. [pə'sent] I adj u. adv ...prozentig. II s Prozent n.

per'cent·age s **1.** Prozentsatz m; Teil m: **what** ~ **of ...?** wieviel Prozent von ...?; **in** ~ **terms** prozentual (ausgedrückt). **2. there's no** ~ **in doing s.th.** F es bringt nichts, et. zu tun.

per·cep·ti·ble [pə'septəbl] adj □ wahrnehmbar, merklich. **per'cep·tion** s **1.** Wahrnehmung f. **2.** Auffassung(sgabe) f. **per'cep·tive** adj □ scharfsinnig.

perch¹ [pɜːtʃ] s ichth. Flußbarsch m.

perch² [~] I s **1.** (Sitz)Stange f (für Vögel): **knock s.o. off his** ~ F j-n von s-m Sockel stoßen. **2.** F hochgelegener Platz od. Standort. II v/i **3.** (**on**) sich niederlassen (auf acc, dat), sich setzen (auf acc) (Vogel). **4.** F hocken (**on** auf dat). III v/t **5.** → **o.s.** F sich hocken (**on** auf acc).

per·co·late ['pɜːkəleɪt] I v/t Kaffee filtern, weitS. kochen, machen. II v/i durchsickern (a. fig.), (Kaffee) durchlaufen '**per·co·la·tor** s Kaffeemaschine f.

per·cus·sion [pə'kʌʃn] I s **1.** Schlag m, Stoß m; Erschütterung f. **2.** ♪ Schlagzeug n. II adj **3.** ~ **instrument** Schlaginstrument n; ~ **section** → **2.** **per'cus·sion·ist** s Schlagzeuger m.

per·emp·to·ry [pə'remptərɪ] adj □ **1.** gebieterisch, herrisch. **2.** kategorisch (Befehl etc).

per·en·ni·al [pə'renjəl] adj □ **1.** ewig, immerwährend. **2.** ♀ mehrjährig.

per·fect ['pɜːfɪkt] I adj □ **1.** perfekt: a) vollkommen, vollendet: ~ **crime** perfektes Verbrechen, b) fehler-, makellos. **2.** gänzlich, völlig: ~ **fool** ausgemachter Narr; ~ **nonsense** kompletter Unsinn; ~ **strangers** pl wildfremde Leute pl. **3.** ~ **tense** → **4.** II s **4.** ling.

Perfekt *n*: → *future* 4, *past* 2, *present* 3. **III** *v/t* [pə'fekt] **5.** vervollkommnen, perfektionieren. **per·fec·tion** [pə'fekʃn] *s* **1.** Vervollkommnung *f*, Vollendung *f*. **2.** Vollkommenheit *f*, Perfektion *f*: **bring to ~** vervollkommnen; **to ~** vollkommen, perfekt. **per'fec·tion·ism** *s* Perfektionismus *m*. **per'fec·tion·ist I** Perfektionist(in). **II** *adj* perfektionistisch.

per·fid·i·ous [pə'fɪdɪəs] *adj* □ treulos, verräterisch. **per·fi·dy** ['pɜ:fɪdɪ] *s* Treulosigkeit *f*.

per·fo·rate ['pɜ:fəreɪt] *v/t* **1.** durchbohren, -löchern. **2.** perforieren, lochen. **‚per·fo'ra·tion** *s* **1.** Durchbohrung *f*, -löcherung *f*. **2.** Perforation *f*.

per·form [pə'fɔ:m] **I** *v/t* **1.** *Arbeit, Dienst etc* verrichten, *Pflicht, a. Vertrag* erfüllen, *❦ Operation* durchführen. **2.** *Theaterstück etc* aufführen, spielen, *a. Konzert* geben, *Musikstück, Lied etc* vortragen, *Kunststück etc* vorführen, *Rolle* spielen. **II** *v/i* **3. ~ well** (*bsd. Sport*) e-e gute Leistung zeigen; *ped.* gut abschneiden. **4. ❂** funktionieren, arbeiten (*Maschine etc*). **5.** *thea. etc* e-e Vorstellung geben, auftreten, spielen. **per'form·ance** *s* **1.** Verrichtung *f*, Erfüllung *f*, Durchführung *f*. **2.** *♪, thea.* Aufführung *f*, Vorstellung *f*, Vortrag *m*. **3.** Leistung *f* (*a. ❂*): **~ principle** *sociol.* Leistungsprinzip *n*. **per'form·er** *s* Darsteller(in), Künstler(in). **per'form·ing** *adj* dressiert (*Tier*).

per·fume I *s* ['pɜ:fju:m] **1.** Duft *m*. **2.** Parfüm *n*. **II** *v/t* [pə'fju:m] **3.** parfümieren.

per·func·to·ry [pə'fʌŋktərɪ] *adj* □ flüchtig (*Blick etc*), (*a. Person*) oberflächlich.

per·haps [pə'hæps] *adv* vielleicht.

per·il ['perəl] *s* Gefahr *f*: **be in ~ of one's life** sich in Lebensgefahr befinden; **at one's ~** auf eigene Gefahr. **'per·il·ous** *adj* □ gefährlich.

pe·ri·od ['pɪərɪəd] **I** *s* **1.** Periode *f*, Zeit (-dauer *f*, -raum *m*, -spanne *f*) *f*, Frist *f*: **for a ~ of** für die Dauer von. **2.** Zeit(alter *n*) *f*, Epoche *f*. **3.** *physiol.* Periode *f*. **4.** *ped.* (Unterrichts)Stunde *f*. **5.** *ling. bsd. Am.* Punkt *m*. **II** *adj* **6.** zeitgenössisch, historisch; Stil...: **~ furniture** Stilmöbel *pl*. **pe·ri·od·ic** [‚~'ɒdɪk] *adj*

(**~ally**) periodisch, regelmäßig wiederkehrend. **‚pe·ri'od·i·cal I** *adj* → *periodic*. **II** *s* Zeitschrift *f*.

pe·riph·er·y [pə'rɪfərɪ] *s* Peripherie *f*, *a. fig.* Rand *m*: **on the ~ of the town** am Stadtrand.

per·i·scope ['perɪskəup] *s* Periskop *n*, Sehrohr *n*.

per·ish ['perɪʃ] **I** *v/i* **1.** umkommen: **be ~ing** (**with cold**) F vor Kälte umkommen. **2.** brüchig werden, verschleißen (*Material*), schlecht werden, verderben (*Lebensmittel*). **II** *v/t* **3. be ~ed** (**with cold**) F ganz durchgefroren sein. **'perish·a·ble** *adj* leichtverderblich. **'perish·ing** *bsd. Br.* F **I** *adj* saukalt. **II** *adv*: **~ly cold** → I.

per·i·to·ni·tis [‚perɪtəʊ'naɪtɪs] *s* ❦ Bauchfellentzündung *f*.

per·jure ['pɜ:dʒə] *v/t*: **~ o.s.** e-n Meineid leisten. **'per·ju·ry** *s* Meineid *m*: **commit ~** → *perjure*.

perk¹ [pɜ:k] F **I** *v/t* → *percolate* I. **II** *v/i* durchlaufen (*Kaffee*).

perk² [~] F **I** *v/t*: **~ up** j-n aufmöbeln. **II** *v/i*: **~ up** aufleben, neuen Schwung bekommen.

perk³ [~] F → *perquisite*.

perk·y ['pɜ:kɪ] *adj* □ F **1.** munter, lebhaft. **2.** keck, selbstbewußt.

perm [pɜ:m] F **I** *s* Dauerwelle *f*: **give s.o. a ~** → **II** *v/t*: **~ s.o.'s hair** j-m e-e Dauerwelle machen.

per·ma·nence ['pɜ:mənəns], **'per·ma·nen·cy** *s* Beständigkeit *f*, Dauerhaftigkeit *f*. **'per·ma·nent I** *adj* □ beständig, dauerhaft, Dauer...: **~ address** ständiger Wohnsitz; **~ wave** Dauerwelle *f*. **II** *s Am.* Dauerwelle *f*.

per·me·a·ble ['pɜ:mjəbl] *adj* □ durchlässig (**to** für). **per·me·ate** ['~mɪeɪt] **I** *v/t* durchdringen (*a. fig.*). **II** *v/i* dringen (**into** in *acc*, **through** durch).

per·mis·si·ble [pə'mɪsəbl] *adj* □ zulässig, statthaft, erlaubt. **per·mis·sion** [pə'mɪʃn] *s* Erlaubnis *f*: **by ~ of** mit Genehmigung (*gen*); **without ~** unerlaubt, unbefugt; **ask s.o.'s ~, ask s.o. ~** j-n um Erlaubnis bitten; **give s.o. ~ to do s.th.** j-m die Erlaubnis geben *od.* j-m erlauben, et. zu tun. **per'mis·sive** [~sɪv] *adj* □ liberal; (*sexuell*) freizügig: **~ society** tabufreie Gesellschaft.

per·mit [pə'mɪt] **I** *v/t* **1.** *et.* erlauben, gestatten: **not ~ted** a. verboten; **~ s.o. to do s.th.** j-m erlauben, et. zu tun. **II** v/i **2.** es erlauben od. gestatten: **weather ~ting** wenn es das Wetter erlaubt. **3. ~ of** et. zulassen. **III** s ['pɜːmɪt] **4.** Genehmigung f.

per·ni·cious [pə'nɪʃəs] adj □ schädlich, verderblich.

per·nick·et·y [pə'nɪkətɪ] adj F **1.** pingelig, pedantisch. **2.** kitz(e)lig (Angelegenheit etc).

per·pen·dic·u·lar [ˌpɜːpən'dɪkjʊlə] **I** adj □ senkrecht, rechtwink(e)lig (**to** zu). **II** s Senkrechte f.

per·pe·trate ['pɜːpɪtreɪt] v/t Verbrechen etc begehen, verüben; humor. Buch etc verbrechen. **'per·pe·tra·tor** s Täter(in).

per·pet·u·al [pə'petʃʊəl] adj □ fortwährend, ständig, ewig. **per'pet·u·ate** [~eɪt] v/t verewigen. **per·pe·tu·i·ty** [ˌpɜːpɪ'tjuːətɪ] s: **in ~** auf ewig, für immer.

per·plex [pə'pleks] v/t verwirren, verblüffen: **~ed** a. perplex. **per'plex·i·ty** s Verwirrung f, Verblüffung f.

per·qui·site ['pɜːkwɪzɪt] s mst pl Vergünstigung f.

per·se·cute ['pɜːsɪkjuːt] v/t **1.** bsd. pol., eccl. verfolgen. **2.** belästigen. **'per·se·'cu·tion** s **1.** Verfolgung f: **~ complex** (od. **mania**) psych. Verfolgungswahn m. **2.** Belästigung f.

per·se·ver·ance [ˌpɜːsɪ'vɪərəns] s Ausdauer f, Beharrlichkeit f. **per·se·vere** [~'vɪə] v/i beharrlich weitermachen (**at, in, with** mit). **per·se'ver·ing** adj □ ausdauernd, beharrlich.

Per·sian ['pɜːʃn] **I** adj **1.** persisch: **~ carpet** Perser(teppich) m. **II** s **2.** Perser(in). **3.** ling. Persisch n.

per·sist [pə'sɪst] v/i **1. ~ in doing s.th.** et. unbedingt tun wollen; darauf bestehen, et. zu tun; et. auch od. noch weiterhin tun. **2. ~ with** hartnäckig od. unbeirrt fortfahren mit. **3.** anhalten, fortdauern. **per'sist·ence** s **1.** Hartnäckigkeit f, Unbeirrtheit f. **2.** Fortdauer f. **per'sist·ent** adj □ **1.** unbeirrt (Person), (a. Gerücht etc) hartnäckig. **2.** anhaltend, fortdauernd.

per·snick·et·y [pə'snɪkətɪ] Am. → **pernickety.**

per·son ['pɜːsn] s Person f (a. ling.), Mensch m: **in ~** persönlich. **'per·son**-

a·ble adj von sympathischem od. angenehmem Äußeren. **'per·son·age** s (bedeutende od. prominente) Persönlichkeit. **'per·son·al** adj □ **1.** persönlich, Personal...: **~ column** (Zeitung) Persönliches n; **~ computer** Personal Computer m, Personalcomputer m; **~ file** Personalakte f; **~ pronoun** ling. Personalpronomen n, persönliches Fürwort. **2.** persönlich, privat (Angelegenheit etc). **3.** äußer, körperlich: **~ hygiene** Körperpflege f. **4.** persönlich, anzüglich (Bemerkung etc): **get ~** persönlich werden. **per·son·al·i·ty** [ˌpɜːsə'nælətɪ] s **1.** Persönlichkeit f (a. e·s Menschen): **~ cult** Personenkult m. **2.** pl persönliche od. anzügliche Bemerkungen pl, Persönliches n. **per·son·i·fi·ca·tion** [pəˌsɒnɪfɪ'keɪʃn] s Personifizierung f: **be the ~ of avarice** die Habgier in Person sein. **per'son·i·fy** [~faɪ] v/t personifizieren: **be avarice personified** die Habgier in Person sein. **per·son·nel** [ˌpɜːsə'nel] s **1.** Personal n, Belegschaft f: **~ manager** Personalchef m. **2.** die Personalabteilung.

per·spec·tive [pə'spektɪv] s Perspektive f (a. fig.): **in ~** perspektivisch richtig; fig. in od. aus der richtigen Perspektive; **the houses are out of ~** bei den Häusern stimmt die Perspektive nicht.

per·spex ['pɜːspeks] (TM) s Br. Plexiglas n.

per·spi·ra·tion [ˌpɜːspə'reɪʃn] s **1.** Transpirieren n, Schwitzen n. **2.** Schweiß m. **per·spire** [pə'spaɪə] v/i transpirieren, schwitzen.

per·suade [pə'sweɪd] v/t **1.** j-n überreden (**into doing, to do** zu tun): **~ s.o. out of s.th.** j-m et. ausreden. **2.** j-n überzeugen (**of** von; **that** [davon,] daß).

per·sua·sion [pə'sweɪʒn] s **1.** Überredung f. **2.** a. **powers** pl **of ~** Überredungskunst f. **3.** Überzeugung f: **be of the ~ that** der Überzeugung sein, daß. **per'sua·sive** [~sɪv] adj □ überzeugend.

pert [pɜːt] adj □ keck (a. Hut etc), keß.

per·tain [pə'teɪn] v/i: **~ to s.th.** et. betreffen; zu et. gehören.

per·ti·na·cious [ˌpɜːtɪ'neɪʃəs] adj □ **1.** hartnäckig, zäh. **2.** beharrlich.

per·ti·nent ['pɜːtɪnənt] adj □ relevant (**to** für); sachdienlich.

pert·ness ['pɜːtnɪs] s Keckheit f, Keßheit f.

per·turb [pə'tɜːb] v/t beunruhigen.

pe·ruse [pə'ruːz] v/t sorgfältig durchlesen.

per·vade [pə'veɪd] v/t durchdringen, erfüllen. **per'va·sive** [~sɪv] adj □ weitverbreitet.

per·verse [pə'vɜːs] adj □ **1.** eigensinnig, querköpfig. **2.** pervers, widernatürlich. **per'ver·sion** s **1.** Pervertierung f, Verdrehung f, Entstellung f. **2.** Perversion f, Perversität f. **1.** Eigensinn m, Querköpfigkeit f. **2.** Perversität f.

per·vert I v/t [pə'vɜːt] pervertieren; verdrehen, entstellen: **~ the course of justice** das Recht beugen. **II** s ['pɜːvɜːt] perverser Mensch.

pes·ky ['peskɪ] adj □ bsd. Am. F lästig.

pes·sa·ry ['pesərɪ] s ♣ Pessar n.

pes·si·mism ['pesɪmɪzəm] s Pessimismus m. **'pes·si·mist** s Pessimist(in). **,pes·si'mis·tic** adj (~ally) pessimistisch.

pest [pest] s **1.** Schädling m: **~ control** Schädlingsbekämpfung f. **2.** F Nervensäge f, Plage f. **'pes·ter** ['~tə] v/t F j-n belästigen (**with** mit), j-m keine Ruhe lassen (**for** wegen), j-n drängeln (**to do** zu tun): **~ s.o. into doing s.th.** j-n so lange quälen, bis er et. tut.

pes·ti·cide ['pestɪsaɪd] s Schädlingsbekämpfungsmittel n.

pet [pet] **I** s **1.** Heimtier n. **2.** a) oft contp. Liebling m, b) Schatz m. **II** adj **3.** Lieblings...: **~ name** Kosename m; → **hate** 5. **4.** Tier...: **~ food** Tiernahrung f; **~ shop** Tierhandlung f, Zoogeschäft n, -handlung f. **III** v/t **5.** streicheln. **IV** v/i **6.** F Petting machen.

pet·al ['petl] s ♣ Blütenblatt n.

pe·ter ['piːtə] v/i: **~ out** versickern (Bach etc), allmählich zu Ende gehen (Vorräte etc), versanden (Unterhaltung etc), sich verlieren (Erinnerung etc), sich totlaufen (Verhandlungen).

pe·tite [pə'tiːt] adj zierlich (Frau).

pe·ti·tion [pə'tɪʃn] **I** s Eingabe f, Gesuch n, (schriftlicher) Antrag: **~ for divorce** ♣♣ Scheidungsklage f. **II** v/t ersuchen (**for** um; **to do** zu tun). **III** v/i einkommen, nachsuchen (**for** um): → **for divorce** ♣♣ die Scheidung einreichen.

pe'ti·tion·er s Antragsteller(in), ♣♣

Kläger(in) (im Scheidungsprozeß).

pet·ri·fy ['petrɪfaɪ] **I** v/t: **petrified with horror** vor Entsetzen wie versteinert, starr od. wie gelähmt vor Entsetzen; **be petrified of** panische Angst haben vor (dat). **II** v/i versteinern, fig. a. sich versteinern.

pet·rol ['petrəl] Br. **I** s Benzin n. **II** adj Benzin...: **~ bomb** Molotowcocktail m; **~ coupon** Benzingutschein m; **~ pump** Benzinpumpe f; Tank-, Zapfsäule f; **~ station** Tankstelle f.

pe·tro·le·um [pə'trəʊljəm] s Erdöl n.

pet·ti·coat ['petɪkəʊt] s Unterrock m.

pet·ti·fog·ging ['petɪfɒgɪŋ] adj **1.** kleinlich, pedantisch. **2.** belanglos, unwichtig.

pet·ting ['petɪŋ] s F Petting f.

pet·tish ['petɪʃ] adj □: sich wegen jeder Kleinigkeit aufregen; **don't be so ~!** sei doch nicht so kindisch.

pet·ty ['petɪ] adj □ **1.** belanglos, unbedeutend, (Vergehen) geringfügig: **~ cash** Portokasse f. **2.** engstirnig.

pet·u·lant ['petjʊlənt] adj → **pettish**.

pew [pjuː] s **1.** (Kirchen)Bank f. **2.** Br. F (Sitz)Platz m: **take a ~** sich setzen.

pew·ter ['pjuːtə] s **1.** Zinn n. **2.** a. **~ ware** coll. Zinn(geschirr) n.

pha·lanx ['fælæŋks] pl **-lanx·es, -lan·ges** [fæ'lændʒiːz] s **1.** Phalanx f. **2.** anat. Finger- od. Zehenglied n.

phal·li ['fælaɪ] pl von **phallus.**

phal·lic ['fælɪk] adj phallisch: **~ symbol** Phallussymbol n.

phal·lus ['fæləs] pl **-li** ['~laɪ] s Phallus m.

phan·tom ['fæntəm] **I** s **1.** Phantom n, Trugbild n. **2.** Geist m (e-s Verstorbenen). **II** adj **3. ~ (limb) pain** Phantomschmerz m; **~ pregnancy** Scheinschwangerschaft f.

phar·i·sa·ic [,færɪ'seɪɪk] adj (~ally) pharisäerhaft, pharisäisch. **phar·i·see** ['~siː] s Pharisäer(in).

phar·ma·ceu·ti·cal [,fɑːmə'sjuːtɪkl] adj □ pharmazeutisch. **,phar·ma'ceu·tics** s pl (sg konstruiert) → **pharmacy** 1.

phar·ma·cist ['~sɪst] s **1.** Pharmazeut(in). **2.** Apotheker(in). **'phar·ma·cy** s **1.** Pharmazeutik f, Pharmazie f. **2.** Apotheke f.

pha·ryn·ges [fə'rɪndʒiːz] pl von **pharynx.**

phar·yn·gi·tis [,færɪn'dʒaɪtɪs] s ♣ Rachenkatarrh m.

phar·ynx ['færɪŋks] *pl* **'phar·ynx·es, pha·ryn·ges** [fə'rɪndʒiːz] *s anat.* Rachen *m*.

phase [feɪz] I *s* **1.** *allg.* Phase *f*: **~s** *pl of the moon* Mondphasen *pl*. II *v/t* **2.** schritt- *od.* stufenweise planen *od.* durchführen: **~d** schritt-, stufenweise; **~ in** schritt- *od.* stufenweise einführen; **~ out** auslaufen lassen.

pheas·ant ['feznt] *s orn.* Fasan *m*.

phe·nom·e·na [fə'nɒmɪnə] *pl von* **phenomenon. phe'nom·e·nal** [~nl] *adj* □ phänomenal. **phe'nom·e·non** [~nən] *pl* **-na** [~nə] *s allg.* Phänomen *n*.

phew [fjuː] *int* puh!

phi·al ['faɪəl] *s* (*bsd.* Arznei)Fläschen *n*.

phil·an·throp·ic [ˌfɪlən'θrɒpɪk] *adj* (**~ally**) philanthropisch, menschenfreundlich. **phi·lan·thro·pist** [fɪ'lænθrəpɪst] *s* Philanthrop(in), Menschenfreund(in). **phi'lan·thro·py** *s* Philanthropie *f*, Menschenfreundlichkeit *f*.

phil·a·tel·ic [ˌfɪlə'telɪk] *adj* (**~ally**) philatelistisch. **phi·lat·e·list** [fɪ'lætəlɪst] *s* Philatelist(in). **phi'lat·e·ly** *s* Philatelie *f*.

phil·har·mon·ic [ˌfɪlɑː'mɒnɪk] *adj* philharmonisch.

phi·lis·tine ['fɪlɪstaɪn] *s* Spießer *m*, Banause *m*.

phil·o·log·i·cal [ˌfɪlə'lɒdʒɪkl] *adj* □ philologisch. **phi·lol·o·gist** [fɪ'lɒlədʒɪst] *s* Philologe *m*, -login *f*. **phi'lol·o·gy** *s* Philologie *f*.

phi·los·o·pher [fɪ'lɒsəfə] *s* Philosoph (-in). **phil·o·soph·i·cal** [ˌfɪlə'sɒfɪkl] *adj* □ philosophisch, *fig. a.* abgeklärt, gelassen. **phi·los·o·phize** [fɪ'lɒsəfaɪz] *v/i* philosophieren (**about, on** über *acc*). **phi'los·o·phy** *s* Philosophie *f*, *fig. a.* (Welt)Anschauung *f*.

phle·bi·tis [flɪ'baɪtɪs] *s* 🏥 Venenentzündung *f*.

phlegm [flem] *s* **1.** *physiol.* Schleim *m*. **2.** *fig.* Phlegma *n*. **phleg·mat·ic** [fleg'mætɪk] *adj* (**~ally**) phlegmatisch.

pho·bi·a ['fəʊbjə] *s psych.* Phobie *f*, krankhafte Angst (**about** vor *dat*).

phone [fəʊn] I *s* **1.** Telefon *n*: **by ~** telefonisch; **be on the ~** Telefon(anschluß) haben; am Telefon sein. **2.** Hörer *m*. II *v/t* **3.** telefonieren, anrufen: **~ back** zurückrufen. III *v/t* **4.** **~ up** anrufen: **~ back** zurückrufen; **~ s.th. to s.o.** j-m et.

telefonisch durchgeben. IV *adj* **5.** Telefon...: **~ book** Telefonbuch *n*; **~ booth** (*Br. box*) Telefonzelle *f*; **~ call** Anruf *m*, Gespräch *n*; **~ number** Telefonnummer *f*. **'~·in** *s Rundfunk, TV: Br.* Sendung *f* mit telefonischer Zuhörer- *od.* Zuschauerbeteiligung.

pho·neme ['fəʊniːm] *s ling.* Phonem *n*.

pho·net·ic [fəʊ'netɪk] I *adj* (**~ally**) phonetisch: **~ character** (*od.* **symbol**) Lautzeichen *n*; **~ transcription** Lautschrift *f*. II *s pl* (*mst sg konstruiert*) Phonetik *f*.

pho·n(e)y ['fəʊnɪ] F I *adj* □ **1.** falsch: a) gefälscht (*Geld, Paß etc*), b) unecht (*Schmuck, Gefühle etc*), c) erfunden (*Geschichte etc*), faul (*Sache, Entschuldigung etc*), Schein..., Schwindel...(*-firma etc*), d) verlogen (*Moral etc*). II *s* **2.** Fälschung *f*. **3.** Schwindler(in).

phos·phate ['fɒsfeɪt] *s* 🧪 Phosphat *n*.

phos·pho·res·cent [ˌfɒsfə'resnt] *adj* □ phosphoreszierend.

phos·pho·rus ['fɒsfərəs] *s* 🧪 Phosphor *m*.

pho·to ['fəʊtəʊ] *pl* **-tos** s F Foto *n*, Bild *n*: **in the ~** auf dem Foto; **take a ~** ein Foto machen (**of** von); **~ album** Fotoalbum *n*; **~ safari** Fotosafari *f*. **'~·cell** 🔧 Photozelle *f*. **'~·cop·i·er** *s* Fotokopierer *m*, -kopiergerät *n*. **'~·cop·y** I *s* Fotokopie *f*: **make** (*od.* **take**) **a ~ of** e-e Fotokopie machen von. II *v/t* fotokopieren. **~ fin·ish** *s Sport:* Fotofinish *n*.

pho·to·gen·ic [ˌfəʊtəʊ'dʒenɪk] *adj* (**~ally**) fotogen.

pho·to·graph ['fəʊtəɡrɑːf] I *s* Fotografie *f*, Aufnahme *f*: **in the ~** auf der Fotografie; **take a ~** e-e Aufnahme machen (**of** von). II *v/t* fotografieren. III *v/i* sich *gut* etc fotografieren (lassen). **pho·tog·ra·pher** [fə'tɒɡrəfə] *s* Fotograf(in). **pho·to·graph·ic** [ˌfəʊtə'ɡræfɪk] *adj* (**~ally**) fotografisch: **~ memory** fotografisches Gedächtnis; **~ studio** Fotostudio *n*. **pho·tog·ra·phy** [fə'tɒɡrəfɪ] *s* Fotografie *f* (*Verfahren etc*).

ˌpho·to|'sen·si·tive *adj* lichtempfindlich. **ˌ~·syn·the·sis** *s biol.* Photosynthese *f*.

phras·al ['freɪzl] *adj:* **~ verb** *ling.* Verb in Verbindung mit e-m Adverb u./*od.* e-r Präposition.

phrase [freɪz] I *s* **1.** *ling.* Phrase *f*, Satzteil *m*. **2.** (Rede)Wendung *f*, Redensart *f*. **3.** *contp*. Phrase *f*: *empty* ~*s pl* leere Phrasen *pl*. **II** *v/t* **4.** ausdrücken, formulieren. '~**book** *s* Sprachführer *m*.

phra·se·ol·o·gy [ˌfreɪzɪˈɒlədʒɪ] *s* Ausdrucksweise *f*, Sprache *f*; Jargon *m*.

phut [fʌt] *adv*: *go* ~ F kaputtgehen (*a. fig. Ehe etc*); *fig*. platzen (*Pläne etc*).

phys·i·cal [ˈfɪzɪkl] **I** *adj* (□ → *physical·ly*) **1.** physisch, körperlich: ~ *education* (*od. training*) *ped*. Leibeserziehung *f*, Sport *m*; ~ *examination* → 3; ~ *handi·cap* Körperbehinderung *f*; ~ *jerks pl Br*. F Gymnastik *f*; ~ *strength* Körperkraft *f*. **2.** physikalisch. **II** *s* **3.** ärztliche Untersuchung. **phys·i·cal·ly** [ˈ~kəlɪ] *adv* → *physical*: ~ *handicapped* körperbehindert; ~ *impossible* F völlig unmöglich. **phy·si·cian** [fɪˈzɪʃn] *s* Arzt *m*, Ärztin *f*. **phys·i·cist** [ˈ~sɪst] *s* Physiker(in). **phys·ics** [ˈfɪzɪks] *s pl* (*mst sg konstruiert*) Physik *f*.

phys·i·og·no·my [ˌfɪzɪˈɒnəmɪ] *s* Physiognomie *f*, Gesichtsausdruck *m*.

phys·i·o·log·i·cal [ˌfɪzɪəˈlɒdʒɪkl] *adj* □ physiologisch. **phys·i·ol·o·gy** [ˌ~ˈɒlə·dʒɪ] *s* Physiologie *f*.

phys·i·o·ther·a·py [ˌfɪzɪəʊˈθerəpɪ] *s* Physiotherapie *f*.

phy·sique [fɪˈziːk] *s* Körperbau *m*, Statur *f*.

pi·an·ist [ˈpɪənɪst] *s* Pianist(in).

pi·an·o [pɪˈænəʊ] *pl* **-os** *s* ♪ Klavier *n*.

pick [pɪk] **I** *s* **1.** (Zahn)Stocher *m*. **2.** (Spitz)Hacke *f*, Pickel *m*. **3.** (Aus)Wahl *f*: *have one's* ~ *of* auswählen können aus; *take one's* ~ sich et. aussuchen; *the* ~ *of the bunch* das (Aller)Beste, das Beste vom Besten. **II** *v/t* **4.** (auf)hacken, (-)picken: → *hole* 1. **5.** Körner aufpicken; auflesen; (auf)sammeln; *Blumen, Obst* pflücken. **6.** *Knochen* abnagen; *Am. Hühner etc* rupfen: → *bone* 1. **7.** ~ *one's nose* in der Nase bohren, popeln; ~ *one's teeth* in den Zähnen (herum)stochern. **8.** *Schloß* mit e-m Dietrich *etc* öffnen, knacken. **9.** *Streit* vom Zaun brechen (*with* mit). **10.** (aus)wählen, aussuchen: ~ *one's way* (*od. steps*) sich s-n Weg suchen, mit vorsichtigen Schritten gehen (*through* durch); ~ *a winner fig*. das Große Los ziehen; ~ *one's words* s-e Worte genau wählen. **11.** zerpflücken,

-reißen: → *piece* 1. **III** *v/i* **12.** ~ *and choose* wählerisch sein; sich bei der Auswahl Zeit lassen.

Verbindungen mit Präpositionen:

pick| at *v/i* **1.** ~ *one's food* im Essen herumstochern. **2.** herumnörgeln an (*dat*); herumhacken auf (*dat*). ~ **on** *v/i* **1.** → *pick at* 2. **2.** j-n (für et. Unangenehmes) aussuchen.

Verbindungen mit Adverbien:

pick| out *v/t* **1.** (sich) auswählen. **2.** ausmachen, erkennen. ~ **up I** *v/t* **1.** aufheben, -lesen: *pick o.s. up* sich aufrappeln (*a. fig.*); → *gauntlet*¹, *thread* 1. **2.** F *Passagiere* aufnehmen; j-n abholen. **3.** F *Mädchen* aufgabeln, -lesen; *Anhalter* mitnehmen; sich *e-e Krankheit* holen *od.* einfangen. **4.** *Funkspruch etc* auffangen. **5.** *Kenntnisse, Informationen etc* aufschnappen. **6.** zunehmen an (*dat*): ~ *speed* schneller werden. **II** *v/i* **7.** sich (wieder) erholen (*a.* ♥). **8.** stärker werden (*Wind etc*).

pick·a·back [ˈpɪkəbæk] **I** *adv* huckepack: *carry s.o.* ~ → II. **II** *s*: *give s.o. a* ~ j-n huckepack tragen.

'**pick·ax(e)** → *pick* 1.

pick·er [ˈpɪkə] *s* Pflücker(in).

pick·et [ˈpɪkɪt] **I** *s* **1.** Pfahl *m*. **2.** Streikposten *m*: ~ *line* Streikpostenkette *f*. **II** *v/t* **3.** Streikposten aufstellen vor (*dat*), durch Streikposten blockieren. **III** *v/i* **4.** Streikposten stehen.

pick·ings [ˈpɪkɪŋz] *s pl* Ausbeute *f*: *there are easy* ~ *in this job* bei diesem Job kann man leicht ein paar Mark (dazu)verdienen.

pick·le [ˈpɪkl] **I** *s* **1.** Salzlake *f*; Essigsoße *f*. **2.** a) *Am*. Essig-, Gewürzgurke *f*, b) *mst pl* Pickles *pl*: → *mixed*. **3.** *be in a* (*pretty*) ~ F (ganz schön) in der Patsche sein *od.* stecken. **II** *v/t* **4.** *gastr.* einlegen. '**pick·led** *adj* **1.** eingelegt. **2.** F blau (*betrunken*).

'**pick|·lock** *s* **1.** Einbrecher *m*. **2.** Dietrich *m*. '~**·me-up** *s* F Muntermacher *m*, Anregungsmittel *n*. '~**·pock·et** *s* Taschendieb(in). '~**·up** *s* **1.** Tonabnehmer *m*, Pick-up *m* (*am Plattenspieler*): ~ *arm* Tonarm *m*. **2.** a. ~ *truck* kleiner Lieferwagen, Kleintransporter *m*. **3.** F (Zufalls)Bekanntschaft *f*. **4.** *mot.* F Beschleunigung(svermögen *n*) *f*: *have good* ~ gut beschleunigen.

pick·y ['pɪkɪ] *adj* □ F heikel, wählerisch: *be a very ~ eater* im Essen sehr heikel sein.

pic·nic ['pɪknɪk] **I** *s* Picknick *n*: *go on (od. for) a ~ in the country* zum Picknick aufs Land fahren; *have a ~* Picknick machen; *it's no ~* F es ist kein Honiglecken (*doing* zu tun). **II** *v/i pret u. pp* **-nicked** picknicken.

pic·to·ri·al [pɪk'tɔːrɪəl] **I** *adj* □ **1.** bebildert, illustriert: *~ report* Bildbericht *m.* **2.** bildhaft (*Sprache etc*). **II** *s* **3.** Illustrierte *f.*

pic·ture ['pɪktʃə] **I** *s* **1.** Bild *n* (*a. TV*): a) Abbildung *f*, Illustration *f*: *in the ~* auf dem Bild, b) Gemälde *n*: (*as*) *pretty as a ~* sehr hübsch; *be a ~* e-e Pracht od. ein Gedicht sein; *be the ~ of health* aussehen wie das blühende Leben; *his face was a ~* du hättest sein Gesicht sehen sollen; → *paint* 1, c) *phot.* Aufnahme *f*: *take a ~* e-e Aufnahme machen (*of* von), d) *fig.* Vorstellung *f*: *be in (out of) the ~* (nicht) im Bild sein; *put in the ~* ins Bild setzen; *get the ~?* F kapiert? **2.** a) Film *m*, b) *pl bsd. Br.* Kino *n*: *go to the ~s* ins Kino gehen. **II** *v/t* **3.** darstellen, malen. **4.** *fig.* sich *j-n, et.* vorstellen (*as* als). **~ book** *s* Bilderbuch *n.* **~ card** *s* Kartenspiel: Bild(karte *f*) *n.* **~ de·fi·ni·tion** *s phot., TV* Bildschärfe *f.* **~ frame** *s* Bilderrahmen *m.* **~ gal·ler·y** *s* Gemäldegalerie *f.* **~ post·card** *s* Ansichtskarte *f.* **~ tube** *s TV* Bildröhre *f.*

pic·tur·esque [ˌpɪktʃə'resk] *adj* □ malerisch.

pid·dle ['pɪdl] F **I** *v/i* pinkeln, (*Kind*) Pipi machen. **II** *v/t*: ~ *away* Zeit vertrödeln. **'pid·dling** *adj* F unwichtig.

pidg·in Eng·lish ['pɪdʒɪn] *s* Pidgin-English(c)h *n.*

pie [paɪ] *s gastr.* Pie *f*: a) (*Fleisch- etc*)Pastete *f*, b) (*mst* gedeckter) (*Apfeletc*)Kuchen: (*as*) *easy as ~* F kinderleicht; → *finger* 1, *humble* 1.

piece [piːs] **I** *s* **1.** Stück *n*: ~ *of cake* Stück Kuchen; *fig.* F Kinderspiel *n*: *a ~* das Stück; *~ by ~* Stück für Stück; *by the ~* stückweise; *in ~s* entzwei, kaputt; (*all*) *in one ~* F ganz, unbeschädigt; heil, unverletzt; *break (od. fall) to ~s* zerbrechen, entzweigehen; *go to ~s* F zs.-brechen (*Person*); *pull (od. pick, tear) to ~s*

in Stücke reißen; *fig.* Äußerung *etc* zerpflücken; → **1**, *furniture*, *mind* 4, *news*. **2.** Teil *n* (*e-r Maschine etc*): *take to ~s* auseinandernehmen, zerlegen. **3.** Teil *m* (*e-s Services etc*): *a 30-~ service* ein 30teiliges Service. **4.** (Geld)Stück *n*, Münze *f.* **5.** (*Schach*) Figur *f*; (*Dame etc*) Stein *m.* **6.** (Zeitungs)Artikel *m.* **II** *v/t* **7.** ~ *together* zs.-stücke(l)n; *fig.* zs.-fügen. **'~·meal I** *adv* **1.** schrittweise. **II** *adj* **2.** schrittweise. **3.** unsystematisch. **'~·work** *s* Akkordarbeit *f*: *be on (od. do) ~* im Akkord arbeiten.

pie-'eyed *adj* F blau (*betrunken*).

pier [pɪə] *s* **1.** Pier *m*, ⚓ *a. f*, Landungsbrücke *f*, -steg *m.* **2.** (*Brücken- etc*)Pfeiler *m.*

pierce [pɪəs] *v/t* **1.** durchbohren, -stoßen: ~ *s.o.'s ears* j-m die Ohren durchstechen. **2.** *fig.* durchdringen: *a cry ~d the silence* ein Schrei zerriß die Stille. **'pierc·ing** *adj* □ durchdringend, (*Kälte etc a.*) schneidend, (*Blick, Schmerz etc a.*) stechend, (*Schrei a.*) gellend.

pi·e·ty ['paɪətɪ] *s* Frömmigkeit *f.*

pif·fle ['pɪfl] *s* F Quatsch *m.* **'pif·fling** *adj* F albern.

pig [pɪg] *s* **1.** Schwein *n*: *buy a ~ in a poke fig.* die Katze im Sack kaufen; *make a ~'s ear of s.th. Br. sl. et.* vermasseln. **2.** F *contp.* Schwein *n*; Freßsack *m.* **3.** *sl.* Bulle *m* (*Polizist*).

pi·geon ['pɪdʒɪn] *s orn.* Taube *f*: *that's not my ~ fig.* F das ist nicht mein Bier. **'~·hole I** *s* **1.** (Ablege)Fach *n*: *put in ~s* → **3.** **II** *v/t* **2.** (in Fächern) ablegen. **3.** *fig.* einordnen, klassifizieren. **4.** *fig.* zurückstellen. **'~·toed** *adv*: *walk ~* über den großen Onkel gehen.

pig·gish ['pɪgɪʃ] *adj* □ schweinisch; gefräßig.

pig·gy ['pɪgɪ] **I** *s* **1.** *Kindersprache:* Schweinchen *n.* **II** *adj* **2.** Schweins...: ~ *eyes.* **3.** gefräßig (*bsd. Kind*). **'~·back** → *pickaback.* **~ bank** *s* Sparschwein *n.*

ˌpig·'head·ed *adj* □ dickköpfig, stur. **~ i·ron** *s* Roheisen *n.*

pig·let ['pɪglɪt] *s* Ferkel *n*, Schweinchen *n.*

pig·ment ['pɪgmənt] *s* Pigment *n.*

pig·my → *pygmy.*

'pig·pen *bsd. Am.* → *pigsty.* **'~·skin** *s* Schweinsleder *n.* **'~·sty** *s* Schweinestall *m, fig. a.* Saustall *m.* '**~·tail** *s* Zopf *m.*

pike¹ [paɪk] *pl* **pikes,** *bsd. coll.* **pike** *s ichth.* Hecht *m.*

pike² [~] *s* ✗ *hist.* Pike *f,* Spieß *m.*

pike³ [~] → **turnpike.**

'**pike·staff** *s:* **(as) plain as a ~** deutlich sichtbar; *fig.* sonnenklar.

pile¹ [paɪl] **I** *s* **1.** Stapel *m,* Stoß *m.* **2.** Scheiterhaufen *m.* **3.** Gebäude(komplex *m*) *n.* **4.** (Atom)Reaktor *m.* **5.** ~s (*od.* **a** ~) **of** ... F ein Haufen ..., e-e *od.* jede Menge ... **6. a ~** (**of money**) F e-e Menge Geld: **make a** (*od.* **one's**) ~ (**from**) e-e Menge Geld machen (bei), sich gesundstoßen (an *dat,* mit). **II** *v/t* **7. a.** ~ **up** (an-, auf)häufen, aufstapeln: ~ **it on** F dick auftragen. **8.** laden, aufhäufen (**on, onto** auf *acc*); überhäufen, -laden (**with** mit). **III** *v/i* **9.** *mst* ~ **up** sich (auf *od.* an)häufen, sich ansammeln (*beide a. fig.*). **10.** F (sich) drängen (**into** in *acc*): ~ **in** (sich) hinein- *od.* hereindrängen. **11.** ~ **up** *mot.* F aufeinander auffahren.

pile² [~] *s* Pfahl *m.*

piles [paɪlz] *s pl* ✱ Hämorrhoiden *pl.*

'**pile-up** *s mot.* F Massenkarambolage *f.*

pil·fer ['pɪlfə] *v/t u. v/i* stehlen, klauen. '**pil·fer·er** *s* Dieb(in).

pil·grim ['pɪlɡrɪm] *s* Pilger(in), Wallfahrer(in): **the** ⚥ **Fathers** *pl hist.* die Pilgerväter *pl.* '**pil·grim·age** *s* Pilger-, Wallfahrt *f:* **go on** (*od.* **make**) **a** ~ e-e Pilger*od.* Wallfahrt machen. **II** *v/i* pilgern, wallfahr(t)en.

pill [pɪl] *s* **1.** Pille *f,* Tablette *f:* **a bitter ~** (**for s.o.**) **to swallow** *fig.* e-e bittere Pille (für j-n); **gild** (*od.* **sugar, sweeten**) **the ~** *fig.* die bittere Pille versüßen. **2. the ~** F die (Antibaby)Pille: **be on the ~** die Pille nehmen.

pil·lage ['pɪlɪdʒ] **I** *v/t u. v/i* plündern. **II** *s* Plünderung *f.*

pil·lar ['pɪlə] *s* Pfeiler *m;* Säule *f* (*a. fig.*): **from ~ to post** *fig.* von Pontius zu Pilatus. ~ **box** *s Br.* Briefkasten *m.*

pil·lion ['pɪljən] **I** *s mot.* Sozius(sitz) *m.* **II** *adv:* **ride** ~ auf dem Sozius(sitz) (mit)fahren. ~ **pas·sen·ger** *s* Soziusfahrer(in).

pil·lo·ry ['pɪlərɪ] **I** *s hist.* Pranger *m:* **be in the** ~ am Pranger stehen. **II** *v/t hist.* an den Pranger stellen; *fig.* anprangern.

pil·low ['pɪləʊ] **I** *s* (Kopf)Kissen *n.* **II** *v/t*

bsd. Kopf betten (**on** auf *acc*). '**~·case** *s* (Kopf)Kissenbezug *m.* ~ **fight** *s* Kissenschlacht *f.* ~ **slip** → **pillowcase.** ~ **talk** *s* Bettgeflüster *n.*

pi·lot ['paɪlət] **I** *s* **1.** ✈ Pilot(in): ~**'s licence** (*Am.* **license**) Flug-, Pilotenschein *m.* **2.** ⚓ Lotse *m,* Lotsin *f.* **II** *v/t* **3.** ✈ steuern, fliegen. **4.** ⚓ lotsen, *fig. a.* führen, leiten. **III** *adj* Versuchs..., Probe...: ~ **film** *TV* Pilotfilm *m;* ~ **scheme** Versuchs-, Pilotprojekt *n;* ~ **study** Pilot-, Leitstudie *f.* **6.** ~ **lamp** Kontrollampe *f.*

pimp [pɪmp] **I** *s* Zuhälter *m.* **II** *v/i* von Zuhälterei leben: ~ **for s.o.** j-s Zuhälter sein.

pim·ple ['pɪmpl] *s* Pickel *m,* Pustel *f.* '**pim·pled** *adj* pick(e)lig.

pin [pɪn] **I** *s* **1.** (Steck)Nadel *f.* **2.** (Haar-, Krawatten- *etc*)Nadel *f.* **3.** *bsd. Am.* Brosche *f;* (Ansteck)Nadel *f.* **4.** ⚙ Bolzen *m,* Stift *m;* ✆ Nagel *m.* **5.** (Reiß)Nagel *m,* (-)Zwecke *f.* **6.** *Am.* (Wäsche)Klammer *f.* **7.** *pl* F Gestell *n* (Beine). **8.** Bowling: Kegel *m.* **II** *v/t* **9.** *a.* ~ **up** (**to, on**) heften, stecken (an *acc*), festmachen, befestigen (an *dat*): ~ **s.th. on s.o.** *fig.* j-m et. in die Schuhe schieben; j-m et. anhängen; ~ **one's hopes on** s-e Hoffnung setzen auf (*acc*). **10.** ~ **down** zu Boden drücken; *fig.* j-n festlegen, -nageln (**to** auf *acc*).

pin·a·fore ['pɪnəfɔː] *s* **1.** Schürze *f.* **2.** *a.* ~ **dress** Trägerkleid *n,* Kleiderrock *m.*

'**pin·ball** *s* Flippern *n:* **play** ~ flippern. ~ **ma·chine** *s* Flipper *m.*

pin·cers ['pɪnsəz] *s pl, a.* **pair of** ~ Kneifzange *f.*

pinch [pɪntʃ] **I** *v/t* **1.** kneifen, zwicken: ~ **s.o.'s** (*od.* **s.o. on the**) **arm** j-n in den Arm zwicken; ~ **one's fingers in the door** sich die Finger in der Tür (ein)klemmen. **2. be ~ed for money** (**time**) knapp bei Kasse sein (wenig Zeit haben). **3.** F klauen. **4.** F j-n hopsnehmen (**for** wegen). **II** *v/i* **5.** drücken (Schuh): → **shoe**. **6.** ~ **and scrape** (*od.* **save**) *fig.* sich sehr einschränken, sich nichts gönnen. **III** *s* **7.** Kneifen *n,* Zwicken *n:* **give s.o. a** ~ j-n kneifen *od.* zwicken. **8.** Prise *f* (Salz *etc*): → **salt** 1. **9.** *fig.* Not(lage) *f:* **at** (*Am. in*) **a** ~ zur Not, notfalls; **feel the** ~ die schlechte Lage zu spüren bekommen.

'**pin**,**cush·ion** *s* Nadelkissen *n*.

pine¹ [paɪn] *s* ♀ Kiefer *f*.

pine² [~] *v/i* **1.** sich sehnen (*for* nach). **2.** *mst* ~ *away* vor Gram vergehen.

'**pine**|,**ap·ple** *s* ♀ Ananas *f*. ~ *tree* → **pine¹**.

ping-pong ['pɪŋpɒŋ] *s* F Pingpong *n* (*Tischtennis*).

'**pin·head** *s* **1.** Stecknadelkopf *m*. **2.** F Dummkopf *m*.

pin·ion ['pɪnjən] *s* ⚙ Ritzel *n*.

pink [pɪŋk] I *s* **1.** ♀ Nelke *f*. **2.** Rosa *n*. **3.** *be in the* ~ vor Gesundheit strotzen. II *adj* **4.** rosa: *see* ~ *elephants* weiße Mäuse sehen; → *tickle* I. **5.** *pol.* rot angehaucht.

'**pin**|·**point** I *s* **1.** Nadelspitze *f*. **2.** (winziger) Punkt: ~ *of light* Lichtpunkt *m*. II *v/t* **3.** genau zeigen. **4.** *fig.* genau festlegen *od.* bestimmen. III *adj* **5.** (haar)genau. '~**prick** *s* **1.** Nadelstich *m*. **2.** *fig.* Stichelei *f*. '~**stripe(d)** *adj*: ~ *suit* Nadelstreifenanzug *m*.

pint [paɪnt] *s* **1.** Pint *n*. **2.** *Br.* F Halbe *f* (*Bier*): *meet for a* ~ sich auf ein Bier treffen.

pin|**ta·ble** *s* Flipper *m*. '~**up** *s* **1.** *a.* ~ *girl* Pin-up-Girl *n*. **2.** Pin-up-Foto *n*.

pi·o·neer [,paɪə'nɪə] I *s* Pionier *m, fig. a.* Bahnbrecher *m*, Wegbereiter *m*. II *v/i u. v/t fig.* den Weg bahnen (für), Pionierarbeit leisten (für).

pi·ous ['paɪəs] *adj* □ fromm: ~ *hope* frommer Wunsch.

pip¹ [pɪp] *s*: *give s.o. the* ~ *Br.* F j-m auf die Nerven gehen, j-n nerven.

pip² [~] *s* **1.** (*Apfel- etc*)Kern *m*. **2.** Auge *n* (*auf Spielkarten*), Punkt *m* (*auf Würfeln etc*). **3.** ✕ *bsd. Br.* F Stern *m* (*Rangabzeichen*). **4.** Ton *m* (*e-s Zeitzeichens etc*).

pip³ [~] *v/t Br.* F knapp besiegen *od.* schlagen: ~ *s.o. at the post* (*Sport*) j-n im Ziel abfangen; *fig.* j-m um Haaresbreite zuvorkommen.

pipe [paɪp] I *s* **1.** ♪ Rohr *n*, Röhre *f*. **2.** (*Tabaks*)Pfeife *f*. **3.** (*Orgel*)Pfeife *f*. **4.** *pl* Dudelsack *m*. II *v/t* **5.** durch Rohre *od.* Kabel leiten: ~**d** *music contp.* Musikberies(e)lung *f*; ~**d** *water* Leitungswasser *n*. **6.** *Torte etc* spritzen. III *v/i* **7.** ~ *down* die Luft anhalten, den Mund halten; ~ *up* loslegen (*Sänger, Band etc*); den Mund aufmachen, losreden. ~

clean·er *s* Pfeifenreiniger *m*. ~ *dream* *s* Hirngespinst *n*, Luftschloß *n*. '~**line** *s* Rohrleitung *f*, (*für Erdöl, Erdgas*) Pipeline *f*: *in the* ~ *fig.* in Vorbereitung (*Pläne etc*), im Kommen (*Entwicklung etc*), im Anrollen (*Aktion etc*).

pip·er ['paɪpə] *s* Dudelsackpfeifer *m*: *pay the* ~ F die für die Kosten aufkommen.

pipe smok·er *s* Pfeifenraucher *m*.

pip·ing ['paɪpɪŋ] I *s* **1.** Rohrleitung *f*, -netz *n*. **2.** *gastr.* Spritzguß *m*. II *adv* **3.** ~ *hot* kochendheiß.

'**pip·squeak** *s* F *contp.* Würstchen *n* (*Person*).

pi·quant ['pi:kənt] *adj* □ pikant (*a. fig.*).

pique [pi:k] I *v/t* kränken, verletzen: *be* ~**d** pikiert sein (*at* über *acc*). II *s*: *in a fit of* ~ gekränkt, verletzt, pikiert.

pi·ra·cy ['paɪərəsɪ] *s* **1.** Seeräuberei *f*, Piraterie *f*. **2.** Raubdruck *m*; Raubpressung *f*. **pi·rate** ['~rət] I *s* **1.** Pirat *m*, Seeräuber *m*. II *adj* **2.** Piraten-..., Seeräuber...: ~ *ship.* **3.** ~ *copy* Raubkopie *f*; ~ *edition* Raubdruck *m*; ~ *record* Raubpressung *f*; ~ *(radio) station* Piraten-, Schwarzsender *m*. III *v/t* **4.** unerlaubt kopieren *od.* nachdrucken *od.* nachpressen: ~**d** *copy* (*edition, record*) → **3.**

pir·ou·ette [,pɪru'et] *s* Pirouette *f*: *do a* ~ e-e Pirouette drehen.

Pis·ces ['paɪsi:z] *s pl* (*sg konstruiert*) *ast.* Fische *pl*: *be a* ~ Fisch sein.

piss [pɪs] V I *v/i* **1.** pissen: *it is* ~*ing down bsd. Br.* es schifft. **2.** ~ *off!* verpiß dich! II *v/t* **3.** anpissen, pissen in (*acc*). **4.** ~ *off* ankotzen: *be* ~**ed** *off with* die Schnauze voll haben von. III *s* **5.** Pisse *f*: *take the* ~ *out of s.o.* j-n verarschen. **6.** Pissen *n*: *have* (*go for*) *a* ~ pissen (gehen).

pissed *adj* V **1.** *Br.* blau (*betrunken*). **2.** *Am.* (stock)sauer (*at auf acc*).

pis·ta·chi·o [pɪ'stɑ:ʃɪəʊ] *pl* -**os** ♀ Pistazie *f*.

pis·til ['pɪstɪl] *s* ♀ Stempel *m*.

pis·tol ['pɪstl] *s* Pistole *f*.

pis·ton ['pɪstən] *s* ⚙ Kolben *m*. ~ *ring* *s* Kolbenring *m*. ~ *rod* *s* Kolbenstange *f*. ~ *stroke* *s* Kolbenhub *m*.

pit¹ [pɪt] I *s* **1.** Grube *f*: ~ *of the stomach anat.* Magengrube. **2.** Grube *f*, Zeche *f*: ~ *closure* Zechenstillegung *f*; ~ *disaster* Grubenunglück *n*. **3.** *thea.* a) *bsd.*

Br. Parkett *n*, *b*) (*Orchester*)Graben *m*.
4. *mst pl Motorsport:* Box *f*: **~ stop** Boxenstopp *m*. **5.** (*bsd. Pocken*)Narbe *f*. **II** *v/t* **6. ~ted with smallpox** pockennarbig. **7. ~** *one's wits* (*strength*) *against* sich (geistig) (s-e Kräfte) messen an (*dat*).

pit² [~] *Am.* → *stone* 2, 6.

pitch¹ [pɪtʃ] *s* Pech *n*: (*as*) *black as* ~ → *pitch-black*.

pitch² [~] **I** *v/t* **1.** Lager, Zelt etc aufschlagen. **2.** werfen, schleudern. **II** *v/i* **3.** stürzen, fallen. **4. ♨** stampfen. **5.** sich neigen (*Dach etc*). **6. ~ in** F sich ins Zeug legen; kräftig zulangen (*beim Essen*); zu Hilfe kommen, anpacken (*with* mit). **III** *s* **7.** *Sport:* *Br.* (Spiel)Feld *n*. **8. ♪** Tonhöhe *f*. **9.** *fig.* Grad *m*, Stufe *f*. **10.** *bsd. Br.* (Verkaufs)Stand *m*: *queer s.o.'s* ~ *fig.* F j-m die Tour vermasseln, j-m e-n Strich durch die Rechnung machen. **11. ♨** Stampfen *n*. **12.** Neigung *f* (*e-s Dachs etc*). **13.** → *sales pitch*.

‚pitch-'black, **‚~-'dark** *adj* pechschwarz; stockdunkel.

pitch·er¹ [ˈpɪtʃə] *s* Baseball: Werfer *m*.

pitch·er² [~] *s* Krug *m*.

'pitch-fork *s* **1.** Heugabel *f*. **II** *v/t* **2.** Heu gabeln. **3.** *fig.* j-n (*unversehens od. gegen s-n Willen*) (hinein)drängen (*into* in *acc*).

'pit·fall *s fig.* Falle *f*, Fallstrick *m*.

pith [pɪθ] *s* **1. ♣** Mark *n*. **2.** weiße Haut (*e-r Orange etc*). **3.** *fig.* Kern *m*. ~ **hel·met** *s* Tropenhelm *m*.

pith·y [ˈpɪθɪ] *adj* □ markig, prägnant.

pit·i·a·ble [ˈpɪtɪəbl] → *pitiful*. **pit·i·ful** [ˈ~fʊl] *adj* □ **1.** mitleiderregend (*Anblick etc*), bemitleidenswert (*Person, Zustand etc*). **2.** erbärmlich, jämmerlich, kläglich. **'pit·i·less** *adj* □ unbarmherzig, mitleid(s)los.

'pit·man [ˈpɪtmən] *s* (*irr man*) Bergmann *m*.

pit·tance [ˈpɪtəns] *s* Hungerlohn *m*.

pi·tu·i·tar·y (*gland*) [pɪˈtjʊɪtərɪ] *s anat.* Hirnanhang(drüse *f*) *m*.

pit·y [ˈpɪtɪ] **I** *s* **1.** Mitleid *n*: *out of* ~ aus Mitleid; *feel* ~ *for, have* ~ *on* Mitleid haben mit; *take* ~ *on* Mitleid bekommen mit. **2.** *it is a* (*great*) ~ es ist (sehr) schade; *it is a thousand pities* es ist jammerschade; *what a* ~! wie schade! **II** *v/t* **3.** bemitleiden, bedauern: *I* ~ *him*

er tut mir leid. **'pit·y·ing** *adj* □ mitleid(s)voll, mitleidig.

piv·ot [ˈpɪvət] **I** *s* **1. ⚙** Drehzapfen *m*. **2.** *fig.* Dreh- u. Angelpunkt *m*. **II** *v/i* **3.** sich drehen: ~ *on fig.* abhängen von. **piv·ot·al** [ˈ~tl] *adj fig.* zentral: ~ *position* Schlüsselstellung *f*.

pix·ie, pix·y [ˈpɪksɪ] *s* Elf(e *f*) *m*; Kobold *m*.

piz·za [ˈpiːtsə] *s* Pizza *f*. **piz·ze·ri·a** [‚piːtsəˈriːə] *s* Pizzeria *f*.

pla·card [ˈplækɑːd] **I** *s* **1.** Plakat *n*; Transparent *n*. **II** *v/t* **2.** mit Plakaten bekleben. **3.** Plakatwerbung machen für.

pla·cate [pləˈkeɪt] *v/t* beschwichtigen, besänftigen.

place [pleɪs] **I** *s* **1.** Ort *m*, Stelle *f*, Platz *m*: *from* ~ *to* ~ von Ort zu Ort; *in* ~ stellenweise; *in* ~ *of* an Stelle von (*od. gen*); *in* ~ an s-m (richtigen) Platz; *out of* ~ nicht an s-m (richtigen) Platz; fehl am Platz; unangebracht; *if I were in your* ~ *I would ...* an Ihrer Stelle würde ich ...; *put o.s. in s.o.'s* ~ sich in j-s Lage versetzen; *put s.o. back in his* ~ j-n in die *od.* s-e Schranken verweisen; *take* ~ stattfinden; *take s.o.'s* ~ j-s Stelle einnehmen. **2.** Ort *m*, Stätte *f*: ~ *of birth* Geburtsort; ~ *of work* Arbeitsstätte. **3.** Haus *n*, Wohnung *f*: *at his* ~ bei ihm (zu Hause). **4.** Wohnort *m*, Ort(schaft *f*) *m*: *in this* ~ hier. **5.** Stelle *f* (*in e-m Buch etc*): *lose one's* ~ die Stelle verblättern; die Zeile verlieren. **6.** *Reihenfolge:* Platz *m*, Stelle *f*: *in the first* ~ erstens; in erster Linie; überhaupt (erst). **7.** *Sport:* Platz *m*: *in third* ~ auf dem dritten Platz. **8.** (*Arbeits-, Lehr-*) Stelle *f*; Platz *m* (*in e-m Heim etc*); (*Studien- etc*)Platz *m*. **II** *v/t* **9.** stellen, setzen, legen: ~ *in* in e-e Lage etc versetzen. **10.** (*with*) Auftrag erteilen (*dat*), vergeben (*an acc*), Bestellung aufgeben (*bei*). **11.** *I can't* ~ *him* ich weiß nicht, wo ich ihn unterbringen *od.* wohin ich ihn tun soll (*woher ich ihn kenne*). **12.** *be* ~*d* (*Sport*) sich placieren (*third* an dritter Stelle), placiert sein.

pla·ce·bo [pləˈsiːbəʊ] *pl* **-bo(e)s** *s ♣* Placebo *n*.

place| card *s* Tischkarte *f*. ~ **mat** *s* Set *n*, *m*, Platzdeckchen *n*. ~ **name** *s* Ortsname *m*. ~ **set·ting** *s* Gedeck *n*.

plac·id ['plæsɪd] *adj* □ **1.** ruhig, gelassen. **2.** ruhig, friedlich.

pla·gia·rism ['pleɪdʒjərɪzəm] *s* Plagiat *n.* **'pla·gia·rist** *s* Plagiator(in). **'pla·gia·rize** *v/t u. v/i* plagiieren (**from** von).

plague [pleɪg] **I** *s* **1.** ✺ Seuche *f;* Pest *f.* **2.** (*Insekten- etc*)Plage *f:* ~ **of insects. II** *v/t* **3.** plagen (**with** mit): **be** ~**d by** geplagt werden von.

plaice [pleɪs] *pl* **plaice** *s ichth.* Scholle *f.*

plaid [plæd] *s* Plaid *n.*

plain [pleɪn] **I** *adj* □ **1.** einfach, schlicht: ~ **clothes** *pl* Zivil(kleidung *f*) *n;* **in** ~ **clothes** in Zivil; ~ **chocolate** zartbittere Schokolade; ~ **cooking** gutbürgerliche Küche. **2.** unscheinbar, reizlos. **3.** klar (u. deutlich), unmißverständlich: **the** ~ **truth** die nackte Wahrheit; **make s.th.** ~ et. klarstellen; **make s.th.** ~ **to s.o.** j-m et. klarmachen. **4.** offen (u. ehrlich): **be** ~ **with s.o.** j-m gegenüber offen sein. **5.** ausgesprochen, rein, völlig: ~ **nonsense** barer Unsinn. **II** *adv* **6.** F (ganz) einfach. **III** *s* **7.** Ebene *f,* Flachland *n.* **'~-clothes** *adj* in Zivil.

plain·ness ['pleɪnnɪs] *s* **1.** Einfachheit *f,* Schlichtheit *f.* **2.** Unscheinbarkeit *f.* **3.** Klarheit *f.* **4.** Offenheit *f.*

,**plain-'spo·ken** *adj* offen, freimütig: **be** ~ *a.* sagen, was man denkt.

plain·tiff ['pleɪntɪf] *s* ⚖ Kläger(in). **plain·tive** ['~tɪv] *adj* □ klagend, kläglich; (*Lied etc*) schwermütig.

plait [plæt] **I** *s* Zopf *m.* **II** *v/t* flechten.

plan [plæn] **I** *s* **1.** (*Arbeits- etc*)Plan *m:* **according to** ~ planmäßig, -gemäß; **make** ~**s** (**for the future**) (Zukunfts)Pläne machen. **2.** Plan *m,* Absicht *f:* **change one's** ~**s** umdisponieren. **3.** (*Stadt-, Sitz- etc*)Plan *m.* **4.** ⊕ Grundriß *m.* **II** *v/t* **5.** planen: ~**ned economy** Planwirtschaft *f.* **6.** planen, beabsichtigen (**to do** zu tun). **III** *v/i* **7.** planen: ~ **ahead** vorausplanen; ~ **for** (*od.* **on**) einplanen, rechnen mit. **8.** ~ **on doing s.th.** planen *od.* beabsichtigen, et. zu tun.

plane¹ [pleɪn] **I** *adj* **1.** eben (*a.* Å); ⊕ plan, Plan... **II** *s* **2.** Å Ebene *f:* → **inclined. 3.** *fig.* Ebene *f,* Stufe *f:* **on the same** ~ **as** auf dem gleichen Niveau wie. **4.** Hobel *m.* **III** *v/t* **5.** hobeln: ~ **down** abhobeln.

plane² [~] *s* Flugzeug *n:* **by** ~ mit dem Flugzeug; **go by** ~ fliegen.

plan·et ['plænɪt] *s ast.* Planet *m.*

plan·e·tar·i·um [,plænɪ'teərɪəm] *pl* **-i·ums, -i·a** [~ɪə] *s* Planetarium *n.* **plan·e·tar·y** ['~tərɪ] *adj* planetarisch, Planeten...

plank [plæŋk] *s* **1.** Planke *f,* Bohle *f,* Brett *n:* (**as**) **thick as two** (**short**) ~**s** *Br.* F strohdumm. **2.** *pol.* Schwerpunkt *m* (*e-s Parteiprogramms*). **'plank·ing** *s* Planken *pl.*

plank·ton ['plæŋktən] *s zo.* Plankton *n.*

plant [plɑːnt] **I** *s* **1.** Pflanze *f:* ~ **louse** *zo.* Blattlaus *f.* **2.** Werk *n,* Betrieb *m.* **II** *v/t* **3.** (an-, ein)pflanzen: ~ **out** auspflanzen (**with** mit). **4.** *Garten etc* anlegen. **5.** *Polizisten etc* aufstellen, postieren; *Bombe* legen. **6.** *Messer etc* stoßen (**into** in *acc*): ~ **a kiss on s.o.'s lips** j-m e-n Kuß auf die Lippen drücken. **7.** ~ **s.th. on s.o.** F j-m et. (*Belastendes*) unterschieben *od.* -jubeln. **plan·ta·tion** [plæn'teɪʃn] *s* **1.** Plantage *f,* Pflanzung *f.* **2.** Schonung *f.* **plant·er** ['plɑːntə] *s* **1.** Plantagenbesitzer(in), Pflanzer(in). **2.** Pflanzmaschine *f.* **3.** Übertopf *m.*

plaque [plɑːk] *s* **1.** Gedenktafel *f.* **2.** ✺ (*Zahn*)Belag *m.*

plas·ma ['plæzmə] *s* Plasma *n.*

plas·ter ['plɑːstə] **I** *s* **1.** ✺ Pflaster *n.* **2.** (Ver)Putz *m.* **3.** *a.* ~ **of Paris** Gips *m:* **have one's arm in** ~ *a.* den Arm in Gips haben; **put in** ~ eingipsen; ~ **cast** Gipsabguß *m,* -modell *n;* ✺ Gipsverband *m.* **II** *v/t* **4.** verputzen; (ver)gipsen: ~ **over** *fig.* übertünchen. **5.** bekleben (**with** mit); *Plakate etc* kleben (**on** an *od.* auf *acc*). **'plas·tered** *adj sl.* blau (*betrunken*): **get** ~ sich vollaufen lassen.

plas·tic ['plæstɪk] **I** *adj* (~**ally**) **1.** plastisch: ~ **surgery** ✺ plastische Chirurgie. **2.** plastisch, formbar: ~ **bomb** Plastikbombe *f.* **3.** Plastik..., Kunststoff...: ~ **bag** Plastikbeutel *m,* -tüte *f;* ~ **bullet** Plastikgeschoß *n;* ~ **film** Kunststofffolie *f;* ~ **money** → **5. II** *s* **4.** Plastik *n,* Kunststoff *m.* **5.** Kreditkarten *pl,* Plastikgeld *n.* **'plas·tics I** *s pl* Kunststoffe *pl.* **II** *adj* Plastik..., Kunststoff...: ~ **film** Kunststofffolie *f;* ~ **industry** Kunststoffindustrie *f.*

plate [pleɪt] **I** *s* **1.** Teller *m*: **hand s.o. s.th. on a ~** F j-m et. auf dem Tablett servieren; **have a lot on one's ~** viel am Hals haben. **2.** Platte *f*. **3.** (*Namens-, Tür- etc*)Schild *n*. **4.** (Bild)Tafel *f* (*in e-m Buch etc*). **5.** Gegenstände *pl* aus Edelmetall. **6.** Doublé *n*, Dublee *n*. **II** *v/t* **7.** panzern. **8.** d(o)ublieren, plattieren: **~d with gold** vergoldet.

pla·teau ['plætəʊ] *pl* **-teaus**, **-teaus** ['-təʊz] *s* Plateau *n*, Hochebene *f*.

plate·ful ['pleɪtfʊl] *pl* **-fuls** *s ein* Teller(voll) *m*.

plate rack *s* Geschirrständer *m*.

plat·form ['plætfɔːm] *s* **1.** Plattform *f*; Podium *n*, Tribüne *f*. **2.** 🚄 Bahnsteig *m*. **3.** *pol.* Plattform *f*.

plat·i·num ['plætɪnəm] *s chem.* Platin *n*.

plat·i·tude ['plætɪtjuːd] *s* Platitüde *f*, Plattheit *f*.

pla·ton·ic [plə'tɒnɪk] *adj* (**~ally**) platonisch: **~** *love.*

pla·toon [plə'tuːn] *s* ✕ Zug *m*.

plat·ter ['plætə] *s* Servierplatte *f*.

plau·si·ble ['plɔːzəbl] *adj* □ **1.** plausibel, glaubhaft. **2.** geschickt (*Lügner*).

play [pleɪ] **I** *s* **1.** Spiel *n*: **at ~** beim Spiel(en), spielend (*Kinder etc*); **be at ~** spielen; **in (out of) ~** im Spiel (im Aus) (*Ball*). **2.** Spiel(weise *f*) *n*: **fair ~** (*Sport*) Fair play *n*, Fairneß *f* (*beide a. fig.*). **3.** *fig.* Spiel *n*: **bring into ~** ins Spiel bringen, *Routine etc* aufbieten; **come into ~** ins Spiel kommen. **4.** *fig.* Wortspiel *n*: **~ on words** Wortspiel; **in ~** im Scherz. **5.** *thea.* Schauspiel *n*, (Theater)Stück *n*. **6.** ⚙ Spiel *n*; *fig.* Spielraum *m*: **allow** (*od.* **give**) **full** (*od.* **free**) **~ to** freien Lauf lassen (*dat*). **II** *v/i* **7.** spielen (*a. Sport, thea. etc*): **~ at** Karten, Indianer etc spielen; *fig.* sich nur so nebenbei beschäftigen mit; **~ for money** um Geld spielen; **~ for time** Zeit zu gewinnen suchen; (*Sport*) auf Zeit spielen; **~ with** spielen mit (*a. fig.*); **~ safe** F auf Nummer Sicher gehen. **III** *v/t* **8.** Karten, Rolle, Stück etc, (*Sport*) Spiel austragen: **~** (*s.th. on*) **the piano** (et. auf dem) Klavier spielen; **~ it safe** auf Nummer Sicher gehen; **→ trick** 2, *etc.* **9.** *Sport*: spielen gegen: **~ s.o. at chess** gegen j-n Schach spielen. **10.** *Karte* spielen: **→ trump**[1]. **11.** *thea. etc* spielen *od.* Vorstellungen geben in (*dat*).

Verbindungen mit Adverbien:

play| **back** *v/t Tonband etc* abspielen: **play s.th. back to s.o.** j-m et. vorspielen. **~ down** *v/t* herunterspielen, bagatellisieren. **~ off** I *v/t* j-n ausspielen (*against* gegen). II *v/i Sport*: ein Entscheidungsspiel austragen (*for* um). **~ up** I *v/i* **1.** *Br.* F verrückt spielen, Schwierigkeiten machen (*Auto, Bein etc*). **2. ~ to** j-m schöntun. II *v/t* **3.** hochspielen, aufbauschen. **4.** *Br.* F j-m auf die Palme bringen; *j-m* Schwierigkeiten machen (*Bein etc*).

play·a·ble ['pleɪəbl] *adj Sport*: bespielbar (*Platz*).

'play·act *v/i contp.* schauspielern. **'~back** *s* Wiedergabe *f*, Abspielen *n*. **'~boy** *s* Playboy *m*.

play·er ['pleɪə] *s* **1.** ♪, *Sport*: Spieler(in). **2.** (*Platten*)Spieler *m*.

'play·fel·low → **playmate.**

play·ful ['pleɪfʊl] *adj* □ **1.** verspielt. **2.** schelmisch, neckisch.

'play·go·er *s* Theaterbesucher(in). **'~ground** *s* **1.** Schulhof *m*. **2.** Spielplatz *m*. **3.** *fig.* Tummelplatz *m*. **~ group** *s bsd. Br.* Spielgruppe *f*. **'~house** *s* **1.** Schauspielhaus *n*. **2.** Spielhaus *n*.

play·ing| **card** ['pleɪɪŋ] *s* Spielkarte *f*. **~ field** *s* Sportplatz *m*.

'play·mak·er *s Sport*: Spielmacher(in). **'~mate** *s* Spielkamerad(in). **'~off** *s Sport*: Entscheidungsspiel *n*. **'~pen** *s* Laufgitter *n*, -stall *m*. **~room** ['-rʊm] *s* Spielzimmer *n*. **'~school** → **play group.** **'~thing** *s* Spielzeug *n* (*a. fig.*): **~s** *pl* Spielsachen *pl*, -zeug *n*. **'~time** *s ped.* große Pause. **~wright** ['~raɪt] *s* Dramatiker(in).

plea [pliː] *s* **1.** (dringende) Bitte, Gesuch *n* (*for* um): **make a ~ for mercy** um Gnade bitten. **2.** ⚖ **enter a ~ of** (*not*) **guilty** sich schuldig bekennen (s-e Unschuld erklären); **make a ~ of s.th.** et. geltend machen.

plead [pliːd] (*bsd. schott. u. Am. irr*) **I** *v/i* **1.** (dringend) bitten (*for* um): **~ with s.o.** j-n bitten (*to do* zu tun). **2.** ⚖ **~ guilty** sich schuldig bekennen (*to doing s.th.* et. getan zu haben); **~ not guilty** s-e Unschuld erklären. **II** *v/t* **1.** ⚖ *u. allg.* zu s-r Verteidigung *od.* Entschuldigung anführen, geltend machen. **4. ~ s.o.'s**

case 🎵 j-n vertreten; *allg.* sich für j-n einsetzen.

pleas·ant ['pleznt] *adj* □ **1.** angenehm, (*Nachricht etc a.*) erfreulich: → **dream** 1. **2.** freundlich.

please [pli:z] **I** *v/i* **1.** gefallen. **2. as you ~** wie Sie wünschen; *if you ~* wenn ich bitten darf, *iro. a.* gefälligst. **II** *v/t* **3.** *j-n* gefallen *od.* zusagen, *j-n* erfreuen: *be ~d about* (*od. at*) sich freuen über (*acc*); *I am ~d with it* es ist gefällig mir; *I am ~d to hear* es freut mich zu hören. **4.** zufriedenstellen: (*only*) *to ~ you* (nur) dir zuliebe; *there is no pleasing him, you can't ~ him* man kann es ihm nicht recht machen; *~ o.s.* tun, was man will; *~ yourself!* mach, was du willst!; *be ~d with* zufrieden sein mit; → **hard** 2. **III** *int* **5.** bitte. **'pleas·ing** *adj* □ angenehm.

pleas·ur·a·ble ['pleʒərəbl] *adj* □ angenehm.

pleas·ure ['pleʒə] *s* **1.** Vergnügen *n*: *for ~* zum Vergnügen; *with ~* mit Vergnügen; *give s.o. ~* j-m Vergnügen *od.* Freude *od.* Spaß machen; *have the ~ of doing s.th.* das Vergnügen haben, *etc.* zu tun; *take ~ in* Vergnügen *od.* Freude finden an (*dat*); *he takes no ~ in it* es macht ihm keinen Spaß. **2.** *at* (*one's*) *~* nach Belieben.

pleat [pli:t] *s* Falte *f*. **'pleat·ed** *adj*: *~ skirt* Faltenrock *m*.

pleb [pleb] *s* F *contp.* Prolet(in).

ple·be·ian [plɪ'bi:ən] *contp.* **I** *adj* proletenhaft. **II** *s* Prolet(in).

pleb·i·scite ['plebɪsɪt] *s* Volksabstimmung *f*, -entscheid *m*.

pled [pled] *bsd. schott. u. Am.* pret *u.* pp *von* **plead.**

pledge [pledʒ] **I** *s* **1.** Pfand *n*: *as a ~* als Pfand. **2.** *fig.* Unterpfand *n*: *as a ~ of* zum Zeichen (*gen*). **3.** Versprechen *n*, Zusicherung *f*: *make a* (*firm*) *~* (fest) versprechen *od.* zusichern (*to do* zu tun). **II** *v/t* **4.** verpfänden: *~ one's word fig.* sein (Ehren)Wort geben. **5.** versprechen, zusichern (*to do* zu tun, *that* daß). **6.** → *s.o. to s.th.* j-n zu et. verpflichten, j-m et. auferlegen; *~ o.s.* sich verpflichten (*to do* zu tun).

ple·na·ry ['pli:nərɪ] *adj* **1. ~ session** Plenarsitzung *f*, Vollversammlung *f*. **2. ~ powers** *pl* unbeschränkte Vollmacht.

plen·i·po·ten·ti·a·ry [ˌplenɪpəʊ'tenʃərɪ] **I**

s **1.** (General)Bevollmächtigte *m*, *f*. **II** *adj* **2.** (general)bevollmächtigt. **3. ~ powers** *pl* Generalvollmacht *f*.

plen·ti·ful ['plentɪfʊl] *adj* □ reichlich.

plen·ty ['plentɪ] **I** *s* **1.** Überfluß *m*: *live in ~* im Überfluß leben; *... in ~* ...im Überfluß, ... in Hülle u. Fülle; → **horn** 3. **2.** e-e Menge: *that is ~* das ist reichlich; *there are ~ more* es gibt noch viel mehr; *~ of ...* e-e Menge ..., viel(e) ... **II** *adv* **3.** F ganz schön.

ple·o·nasm ['plɪəʊnæzəm] *s ling.* Pleonasmus *m*. **ple·o·nas·tic** [ˌplɪə'næstɪk] *adj* (*~ally*) pleonastisch.

pleu·ri·sy ['plʊərəsɪ] *s* 🏥 Brustfell-, Rippenfellentzündung *f*.

pli·a·ble ['plaɪəbl], **pli·ant** ['~ənt] *adj* □ **1.** biegsam. **2.** *fig.* flexibel. **3.** *fig.* leicht beeinflußbar.

pli·ers ['plaɪəz] *s pl, a. pair of ~* Beißzange *f*.

plight [plaɪt] *s* Not(lage) *f*.

plim·soll ['plɪmsəl] *s Br.* Turnschuh *m*.

plod [plɒd] *v/i* **1.** trotten. **2.** *mst ~ away fig.* sich abmühen *od.* abplagen (*at* mit), schuften. **'plod·der** *s fig.* Arbeitstier *n*.

plonk [plɒŋk] *v/t* F schmeißen, knallen: *~ down* hinschmeißen.

plop [plɒp] **I** *v/i* plumpsen, (*ins Wasser*) platschen: *~ into a chair* sich in e-n Sessel plumpsen lassen. **II** *s* Plumps *m*, Platsch *m*.

plot [plɒt] **I** *s* **1.** Grundstück *n*; Parzelle *f*; Beet *n*. **2.** △ *bsd. Am.* Grundriß *m*. **3.** Handlung *f* (*e-s Films etc*). **4.** Komplott *n*, Verschwörung *f*. **II** *v/i* **5.** sich verschwören (*against* gegen). **III** *v/t* **6.** aushecken, planen. **7.** (*in e-e Karte etc*) einzeichnen. **'plot·ter** *s* Verschwörer(in).

plough [plaʊ] **I** *s* Pflug *m*. **II** *v/t a. ~ up* (um)pflügen: *~ back* Gewinne reinvestieren (*into* in *acc*). **III** *v/i* pflügen: *~ through* sich en-n Weg bahnen durch; ♣ sich pflügen durch; *~ through a book* F ein Buch durchackern.

plow [plaʊ] → **plough.**

ploy [plɔɪ] *s* Masche *f*, Tour *f*.

pluck [plʌk] **I** *s* **1.** Ruck *m*. **2.** Innereien *pl*. **3.** *fig.* Mut *m*. **II** *v/t* **4.** *Geflügel* rupfen. **5.** *mst ~ out* ausreißen, -rupfen, -zupfen; → **courage.** **III** *v/i* **6.** zupfen (*at* an *dat*): *~ at s.o.'s sleeve* j-n am

Ärmel zupfen. 'pluck·y *adj* ☐ mutig.

plug [plʌg] **I** *s* **1.** Stöpsel *m*. **2.** ⚡ Stecker *m*; Steckdose *f*. **3.** *mot.* (Zünd)Kerze *f*. **II** *v/t* **4.** *a.* ~ *up* zustöpseln; zu-, verstopfen. **5.** ~ *in* ⚡ anschließen, einstecken. **III** *v/i* **6.** ~ *away at* F sich abschuften mit. '~**hole** *s* Abfluß(loch *n*) *m*.

plum [plʌm] *s* **1.** Pflaume *f*; Zwetsch(g)e *f*. **2.** *fig.* F a) Rosine *f*, b) *a.* ~ *job* Bombenjob *m*.

plum·age ['pluːmɪdʒ] *s* Gefieder *n*.

plumb [plʌm] **I** *s* **1.** (Blei)Lot *n*, Senklot *n*: *out of* ~ aus dem Lot, nicht senkrecht. **II** *adj* **2.** lot-, senkrecht. **III** *adv* F **3.** (haar)genau. **4.** *bsd. Am.* komplett, total. **IV** *v/t* **5.** ⚓ ausloten, *fig. a.* ergründen. **6.** ~ *in bsd. Br.* Waschmaschine *etc* anschließen. '**plumb·er** *s* Installateur *m*. '**plumb·ing** *s* **1.** Installaturarbeit *f*. **2.** Rohre *pl*, Rohrleitungen *pl*.

plumb‖**line** *s* **1.** ⚓ Lotschnur *f*, -leine *f*. **2.** → *plumb rule*. ~ **rule** *s* △ Setzlatte *f*, Richtscheit *n*.

plume [pluːm] **I** *s* **1.** (Schmuck)Feder *f*; Federbusch *m*. **2.** (*Rauch*)Fahne *f*. **II** *v/t* **3.** ~ *its feathers* sich *od.* sein Gefieder putzen.

plum·my ['plʌmɪ] *adj* **1.** affektiert (*Stimme*). **2.** F prima, toll: ~ *job* Bombenjob *m*.

plump¹ [plʌmp] **I** *adj* drall, mollig, rund(lich). **II** *v/t*: ~ *up* Kissen aufschütteln.

plump² [plʌmp] **I** *v/i* **1.** *mst* ~ *down* fallen, plumpsen (*on* auf *acc*): ~ *down into a chair* sich in e-n Sessel fallen lassen. **2.** ~ *for bsd. Br.* sich entscheiden für. **II** *v/t* **3.** fallen *od.* plumpsen lassen (*on* auf *acc*).

plum pud·ding *s* Plumpudding *m*.

plun·der ['plʌndə] **I** *v/t* **1.** (aus)plündern. **2.** *et.* rauben. **II** *v/i* **3.** plündern. **III** *s* **4.** Plünderung *f*. **5.** Beute *f*. '**plun·der·er** *s* Plünderer *m*.

plunge [plʌndʒ] **I** *v/t* **1.** ~ *a knife into s.o.'s back* j-m ein Messer in den Rükken stoßen. **2.** ~ *into* in *Schulden*, e-n *Krieg etc* stürzen: *be ~d into darkness* in Dunkel gehüllt sein. **II** *v/i* **3.** ~ *into* ins *Zimmer etc* stürzen; sich ins *Wasser*, in *e-e Tätigkeit*, in *Schulden etc* stürzen. **4.** stürzen (*Preise, Kurse*). **5.** ⚓ stampfen. **III** *s* **6.** (Kopf)Sprung *m*: *take the* ~ *fig.* den Sprung *od.* den ent-

scheidenden Schritt wagen. '**plung·ing** *adj* tief (*Ausschnitt*): *with a* ~ *neckline* tief ausgeschnitten.

plu·per·fect [ˌpluːˈpɜːfɪkt] *s a.* ~ *tense* ling. Plusquamperfekt *n*, Vorvergangenheit *f*.

plu·ral ['plʊərəl] *ling.* **I** *adj* Plural..., Mehrzahl... **II** *s* Plural *m*, Mehrzahl *f*. '**plu·ral·ism** *s sociol.* Pluralismus *m*. ˌ**plu·ral·is·tic** *adj* (~*ally*) pluralistisch.

plus [plʌs] **I** *prp* **1.** & plus, und, *bsd.* ✝ zuzüglich. **II** *adj* **2.** Plus...: ~ *sign* → 3. **III** *s* **3.** Plus(zeichen) *n*. **4.** *fig.* Plus *n*, Vorteil *m*.

plush [plʌʃ] **I** *s* **1.** Plüsch *m*. **II** *adj* **2.** Plüsch... **3.** F feudal: ~ *restaurant* Nobelrestaurant *n*.   nium *n*.

plu·to·ni·um [pluːˈtəʊnɪəm] *s* 🜍 Pluto-

ply¹ [plaɪ] **I** *v/i* **1.** verkehren (*between* zwischen *dat*). **II** *v/t* **2.** verkehren auf (*dat*), befahren. **3.** *fig.* j-n überhäufen (*with* mit *Fragen*).

ply² [~] *s* Lage *f*, Schicht *f*. '~**wood** *s* Sperrholz *n*.

pneu·mat·ic [njuːˈmætɪk] *adj* (~*ally*) pneumatisch, Luft... ; ⊙ Druck-, Preßluft... : ~ *brake* Druckluftbremse *f*; ~ *drill* Preßluftbohrer *m*; ~ *hammer* Preßlufthammer *m*.

pneu·mo·ni·a [njuːˈməʊnjə] *s* 💊 Lungenentzündung *f*.

poach¹ [pəʊtʃ] **I** *v/t* **1.** wildern. **2.** *Arbeitskräfte* abwerben (*from* dat). **II** *v/i* **3.** wildern.

poach² [~] *v/t* Eier pochieren: ~*ed eggs pl a.* verlorene Eier *pl*.

poach·er ['pəʊtʃə] *s* Wilderer *m*.

PO Box [ˌpiːˈəʊ] *s* Postfach *n*.

pock [pɒk] *s* 💊 **1.** Pocke *f*, Blatter *f*. **2.** → *pockmark*. **pocked** → *pockmarked*.

pock·et ['pɒkɪt] *s* **1.** (*Hosen- etc*)Tasche *f*: *with nothing in one's* ~ *except* nichts in der Tasche als; *have in one's* ~ *fig.* j-n, *et.* in der Tasche haben. **2.** *fig.* Geldbeutel *m*: *pay for s.th. out of one's own* ~ *et.* aus eigener Tasche bezahlen; *to suit every* ~ für jeden Geldbeutel. **3.** (*Nebel*)Bank *f*; (*Widerstands- etc*)Nest *n*. **4.** Billard: Loch *n*; ✈ (*Luft*)Loch *n*. **II** *adj* **5.** Taschen... : ~ *calculator* Taschenrechner *m*; ~ *edition* Taschenausgabe *f*; ~ *money* Taschengeld *n*. **III** *v/t* **6.** einstecken, in die Tasche stecken; *fig.* in die eigene Tasche stecken. **7.**

Billard: einlochen. '**~book** *s* **1.** Notizbuch *n.* **2.** *Am.* Brieftasche *f.* '**~knife** *s* (*irr* **knife**) Taschenmesser *n.*

'**pock·mark** *s* Pockennarbe *f.* '**~marked** *adj* pockennarbig; *fig.* übersät (**with** mit).

pod [pɔd] **I** *s* ♀ Hülse *f,* Schote *f.* **II** *v/t* aus-, enthülsen.

po·di·um ['pəʊdjəm] *pl* -**di·ums**, -**di·a** ['~djə] *s* Podium *n,* Podest *n.*

po·em ['pəʊɪm] *s* Gedicht *n.*

po·et ['pəʊɪt] *s* Dichter *m.* '**po·et·ess** *s* Dichterin *f.* **po·et·ic** [~'etɪk] *adj* (**~ally**) dichterisch: **~** *justice fig.* ausgleichende Gerechtigkeit; **~** *licence* (*Am.* **license**) dichterische Freiheit. **po'et·i·cal** → *poetic.* **po·et·ry** ['pəʊɪtrɪ] *s* Dichtung *f;* Gedichte *pl.*

poign·ant ['pɔɪnjənt] *adj* □ **1.** schmerzlich (*Erinnerungen etc*). **2.** scharf (*Verstand*).

point [pɔɪnt] **I** *s* **1.** (*Messer-, Nadel- etc*) Spitze *f.* **2.** *geogr.* Landspitze *f.* **3.** *ling.* *Am.* Punkt *m.* **4.** *four* **~** *three* (*4.3*) 4,3. **5.** Punkt *m* (*a.* A*;*); Grad *m* (*e-r Skala*): **~** *of contact* Berührungspunkt (*a. fig.*); **~** *of intersection* Schnittpunkt; → *freezing* 1, *etc.* **6.** Punkt *m,* Ort *m:* **~** *up to a* **~** *fig.* bis zu e-m gewissen Punkt *od.* Grad; **~** *of view fig.* Gesichts-, Standpunkt. **7.** ♂ *Br.* Steckdose *f.* **8.** *Sport etc:* Punkt *m:* **win on ~s** nach Punkten gewinnen; **winner on ~s** Punktsieger *m.* **9.** *a.* **~** *of time* Zeitpunkt *m,* Augenblick *m:* **be on the ~ of doing s.th.** im Begriff sein, et. zu tun. **10.** Punkt *m* (*e-r Tagesordnung etc*), (*Einzel-, Teil*)Frage *f:* **~** *of interest* interessante Einzelheit. **11.** Kernpunkt *m,* -frage *f,* springender Punkt: **be to** (**beside**) **the ~** (nicht) zur Sache gehören; **come to the ~** zur Sache kommen; **keep** (*od.* **stick**) **to the ~** bei der Sache bleiben; **make a ~ of doing s.th.** Wert darauf legen, et. zu tun; **get** (*od.* **see, take**) **s.o.'s ~** verstehen, was j-d meint; **miss the ~** nicht verstehen, worum es geht; **that's not the ~** darum geht es nicht; **that's the** (**whole**) **~** *!* genau (das ist es)! **12.** Ziel *n,* Absicht *f:* **carry** (*od.* **gain**) **one's ~** sich *od.* s-e Absicht durchsetzen. **13.** Sinn *m,* Zweck *m:* **what's the ~?** wozu?; **what's the ~ of** (*od.* **in**) **waiting?** was hat es für e-n Sinn

zu warten?; **there's no ~ in that** das hat keinen Zweck. **14.** (hervorstechende) Eigenschaft, (Vor)Zug *m:* **strong** (**weak**) **~s** starke (schwache) Seite; **it has its ~s** es hat s-e Vorzüge. **II** *v/t* **15.** (an-, zu)spitzen. **16.** *Waffe etc* richten (**at** auf *acc*): **~** *one's finger at s.o.* (mit dem Finger) auf j-n deuten *od.* zeigen. **17.** zeigen: **~** *the way* den Weg weisen (*a. fig.*); **~** *out* zeigen; *fig.* hinweisen *od.* aufmerksam machen auf (*acc*); **~** *out to s.o. that* j-n darauf aufmerksam machen, daß. **III** *v/i* **18.** (mit dem Finger) deuten *od.* zeigen (**at, to** auf *acc*): **~** *to* nach e-r Richtung weisen *od.* liegen (*Haus etc*); *fig.* hinweisen *od.* -deuten auf (*acc*). **~'blank** *adj u. adv* **1.** *a.* **at ~ range** aus kürzester Entfernung. **2.** *fig.* unverblümt.

point·ed ['pɔɪntɪd] *adj* □ **1.** spitz: **~** *arch* △ Spitzbogen *m.* **2.** *fig.* scharf (*Bemerkung etc*). **3.** *fig.* ostentativ. '**point·er** *s* **1.** Zeiger *m* (*e-s Meßgeräts*). **2.** Zeigestock *m.* **3.** F Fingerzeig *m,* Tip *m.* '**point·less** *adj* □ sinn-, zwecklos.

poise [pɔɪz] **I** *s* **1.** (*Körper*)Haltung *f.* **2.** *fig.* Gelassenheit *f;* (Selbst)Sicherheit *f.* **II** *v/t* **3.** balancieren: **be ~d** *fig.* schweben (**between** zwischen *dat*). **poised** *adj* gelassen; (selbst)sicher.

poi·son ['pɔɪzn] **I** *s* Gift *n* (**to** für) (*a. fig.*): **hate like ~** wie die Pest hassen; **what's your ~?** F was willst du trinken? **II** *v/t* vergiften (*a. fig.*). **III** *adj* Gift...: **~** *gas;* **~** *fang zo.* Giftzahn *m.* '**poi·son·ing** *s* Vergiftung *f.* '**poi·son·ous** *adj* □ giftig (*a. fig.*), Gift...

poke [pəʊk] **I** *v/t* **1.** *j-n* (an)stoßen: **~** *s.o.* **in the ribs** j-m e-n Rippenstoß geben. **2.** *a.* **~** *up* Feuer schüren. **3.** *et.* strecken, *Kopf etc a.* strecken: → *nose* 1. **4.** **~** *fun* **at** sich lustig machen über (*acc*). **II** *v/i* **5.** **~** *about* (*od.* **around**) (herum)stöbern, (-)wühlen (**in** in *dat*). **III** *s* **6.** Stoß *m:* **~** **in the ribs** Rippenstoß.

pok·er¹ ['pəʊkə] *s* Feuerhaken *m.*

po·ker² [~] *s* Poker(spiel) *n.* **~** *face s* Pokergesicht *n,* Pokerface *n.*

pok·y ['pəʊkɪ] *adj* winzig (*Zimmer etc*).

po·lar ['pəʊlə] *adj* □ polar (*a. fig.*), Polar...: **~** *bear zo.* Eisbär *m;* **~** *circle geogr.* Polarkreis *m.* '**po·lar·ize** *v/t* ♀ *phys.* polarisieren (*a. fig.*).

Pole¹ [pəʊl] *s* Pole *m,* Polin *f.*

pole² [~] *s geogr.*, ⚡, *etc* Pol *m*: **they are ~s apart** *fig.* zwischen ihnen liegen Welten.

pole³ [~] *s* Pfosten *m*; (*Fahnen-, Leitungs*)Mast *m*; (*Bohnen- etc*)Stange *f*; (*Leichtathletik*) (Sprung)Stab *m.* '**~cat** *s zo.* Iltis *m.*

po·lem·ic [pə'lemɪk] **I** *adj* (**~ally**) **1.** polemisch. **II** *s* **2.** *a. pl* (*sg konstruiert*) Polemik *f.* **3.** polemische Äußerung. **po'lem·i·cal** *p* → **polemic 1.**

pole star *s ast.* Polarstern *m.*

pole vault *s Leichtathletik:* Stabhochsprung *m.* **~ vault·er** *s* Stabhochspringer *m.*

po·lice [pə'liːs] **I** *s* (*pl konstruiert*) Polizei *f.* **II** *v/t* (polizeilich) überwachen. **III** *adj* polizeilich, Polizei...: **~ constable** → **constable; ~ force** Polizei *f*; **~ offi·cer** Polizeibeamte *m*; **~ protection** Polizeischutz *m*; **~ record** Strafregister *n*; **have a ~ record** vorbestraft sein; **~ state** Polizeistaat *m*; **~ station** Polizeirevier *n*, -wache *f.* **po'lice·man** [~mən] *s* (*irr man*) Polizist *m.* **po'lice,wom·an** *s* (*irr woman*) Polizistin *f.*

pol·i·cy¹ ['pɒləsɪ] *s* **1.** Verfahren(sweise *f*) *n*, Taktik *f*, Politik *f*: **it is our ~** es ist unser Grundsatz (**to do** zu tun). **2.** (*Außen-, Wirtschafts- etc*)Politik *f.* **3.** Klugheit *f*: **be good (bad) ~** (un)klug *od.* (un)vernünftig sein.

pol·i·cy² [~] *s* (*Versicherungs*)Police *f*: **take out a ~** e-e Versicherung abschließen.

po·li·o ['pəʊlɪəʊ] *s* ⚕ F Polio *f.* **po·li·o·my·e·li·tis** [~maɪə'laɪtɪs] *s* ⚕ (spinale) Kinderlähmung.

Pol·ish¹ ['pəʊlɪʃ] **I** *adj* polnisch. **II** *s ling.* Polnisch *n.*

pol·ish² ['pɒlɪʃ] **I** *v/t* **1.** polieren, ⊙ *etc a.* (ab)schleifen, *Fußboden* bohnern: **~ off** F *Arbeit* wegschaffen; *Essen* wegputzen; **~ up** aufpolieren (*a. fig.*). **II** *s* **2.** Politur *f*, Glanz *m.* **3.** (*Möbel*)Politur *f*; (*Schuh*)Creme *f*; (*Bohnerwachs n*; (*Nagel*)Lack *m.* **4.** *fig.* Schliff *m.* '**pol·ished** *adj* **1.** poliert, glänzend. **2.** *fig.* geschliffen; brillant.

po·lite [pə'laɪt] *adj* □ höflich: **to be ~** aus Höflichkeit. **po'lite·ness** *s* Höflichkeit *f.*

po·lit·i·cal [pə'lɪtɪkl] *adj* □ politisch: **~ economy** Volkswirtschaft *f*; **~ science**

Politologie *f*; **~ scientist** Politologe *m*, -login *f.* **pol·i·ti·cian** [,pɒlɪ'tɪʃn] *s* Politiker(in). **po·lit·i·cize** [pə'lɪtɪsaɪz] *v/t* politisieren. **pol·i·tics** ['pɒlətɪks] *s pl* (*mst sg konstruiert*) Politik *f*: **what are his ~?** wo steht er politisch?; **go into ~** in die Politik gehen; **talk ~** über Politik reden, politisieren.

pol·ka ['pɒlkə] *s* ♪ Polka *f.* '**~-dot** *s* gepunktet, getupft (*Kleid etc*).

poll [pəʊl] **I** *s* **1.** (*Meinungs*)Umfrage *f.* **2.** *a. pl* Stimmabgabe *f*, Wahl *f*: **be defeated at the ~s** e-e Wahlniederlage erleiden; **go to the ~s** zur Wahl gehen. **3.** Wahlbeteiligung *f.* **II** *v/t* **4.** befragen: **65% of those ~ed** 65% der Befragten. **5.** *Stimmen* erhalten, auf sich vereinigen.

pol·len ['pɒlən] *s* ⚘ Pollen *m*, Blütenstaub *m.*

poll·ing ['pəʊlɪŋ] **I** *s* → **poll 2, 3.** **II** *adj* Wahl...: **~ booth** Wahlkabine *f*, -zelle *f*; **~ day** Wahltag *m*; **~ place** *Am.*, **~ station** *bsd. Br.* Wahllokal *n.*

poll·ster ['pəʊlstə] *s* Meinungsforscher (-in).

pol·lut·ant [pə'luːtənt] *s* Schadstoff *m.*

pol·lute [pə'luːt] *v/t* **1.** *Umwelt* verschmutzen, *Flüsse etc a.* verunreinigen. **2.** (*moralisch*) verderben. **pol'lut·er** *s* (*Umwelt*)Verschmutzer(in). **pol'lu·tion** *s* (*Umwelt*)Verschmutzung *f*, Verunreinigung *f.*

po·lo ['pəʊləʊ] *s Sport:* Polo *n.* **~ neck** *s* Rollkragen(pullover) *m.* '**~-neck** *adj* Rollkragen... **~ shirt** *s* Polohemd *n.*

pol·yg·a·mist [pə'lɪgəmɪst] *s* Polygamist *m.* **po'lyg·a·mous** *adj* □ polygam (*a.* ⚘, *zo.*). **po'lyg·a·my** *s* Polygamie *f* (*a.* ⚘, *zo.*).

pol·y·glot ['pɒlɪglɒt] *adj* polyglott, vielmehrsprachig.

pol·y·gon ['pɒlɪgən] *s* ⅄ Vieleck *n.*

pol·yp ['pɒlɪp] *s* ⚕, *zo.* Polyp *m.*

pol·y·syl·lab·ic [,pɒlɪsɪ'læbɪk] *adj* (**~ally**) *ling.* viel-, mehrsilbig. **pol·y·syl·la·ble** ['~,sɪləbl] *s* vielsilbiges Wort.

pol·y·tech·nic [,pɒlɪ'teknɪk] *s* (*etwa*) Technische Hochschule.

pol·y·va·lent [,pɒlɪ'veɪlənt] *adj* ⚗ mehrwertig.

po·made [pə'meɪd] *s* Pomade *f.*

pome·gran·ate ['pɒmɪ,grænɪt] *s* ⚘ Granatapfel *m.*

pom·mel ['pʌml] s **1.** (*Sattel- etc*)Knopf m. **2.** *Turnen:* (*Pferd*)Pausche f: ~ **horse** Seitpferd n.

pomp [pɒmp] s Pomp m. '**pomp·ous** adj □ **1.** aufgeblasen, wichtigtuerisch. **2.** bombastisch, schwülstig (*Sprache*).

ponce [pɒns] s Br. sl. **1.** Zuhälter m. **2.** Tunte f.

pond [pɒnd] s Teich m, Weiher m.

pon·der ['pɒndə] I v/i nachdenken (**on, over** über acc). II v/t überlegen, nachdenken über (acc): ~ **doing s.th.** erwägen, et. zu tun. '**pon·der·ous** adj □ **1.** massig, schwer. **2.** fig. schwerfällig.

pong [pɒŋ] Br. F I s Gestank m. II v/i stinken. '**pong·y** adj Br. F stinkend, stinkig.

pon·toon [pɒn'tu:n] s Ponton m. ~ **bridge** s Ponton-, Schiffsbrücke f.

po·ny ['pəʊni] s zo. Pony n. '~**tail** s Pferdeschwanz m (*Frisur*).

poo·dle ['pu:dl] s zo. Pudel m.

poof [pu:f] s Br. sl. Schwule m.

pooh [pu:] int pah! ,**pooh-'pooh** v/t geringschätzig abtun.

pool[1] [pu:l] s **1.** Teich m, Tümpel m. **2.** Pfütze f, (*Blut- etc*)Lache f. **3.** (*Schwimm*)Becken n, (*Swimming-*) Pool m.

pool[2] [~] I s **1.** (gemeinsame) Kasse, (*Kartenspiel a.*) Pot m. **2.** pl Br. (*Fußball*)Toto n, m: **win** (**on**) **the** ~**s** im Toto gewinnen; **win on the** ~**s** Totogewinn m. **3.** Am. Poolbillard n: **shoot** ~ Poolbillard spielen. **4.** ✞ bsd. Am. Pool m, Kartell n. **5.** (*Arbeits-, Fahr*)Gemeinschaft f; (*Mitarbeiter- etc*)Stab m; (*Fuhr*)Park m; (*Schreib*)Pool m. II v/t **6.** Geld etc zs.-legen; fig. Kräfte etc vereinen.

poop [pu:p] s ⚓ **1.** Heck n. **2.** a. ~ **deck** (erhöhtes) Achter- od. Hinterdeck.

pooped (**out**) [pu:pt] adj Am. F erledigt, kaputt.

poor [pɔ:] I adj (□ → **poorly** II) **1.** arm, mittellos. **2.** arm, bedauernswert. **3.** fig. arm (**in** an dat); dürftig, mangelhaft, schwach: ~ **consolation** ein schwacher Trost; → **health** 2. II s **4. the** ~ pl die Armen pl. '**poor·ly** I adj **1.** unpäßlich, kränklich. II adv **2.** ärmlich: **he is** ~ **off** es geht ihm schlecht. **3.** fig. dürftig, mangelhaft, schwach: ~ **gifted** schwachbegabt; ~ **paid** schlechtbe-

zahlt; **be** ~ **off for** knapp sein an (dat); **do** ~ **in** schlecht abschneiden bei; **think** ~ **of** nicht viel halten von. '**poor·ness** s **1.** Armut f. **2.** fig. Dürftigkeit f, Mangelhaftigkeit f.

pop[1] [pɒp] I v/i **1.** knallen. **2.** (zer)platzen: ~ **open** aufplatzen, -springen. **3.** F ballern, schießen (**at** auf acc). **4.** F sausen: ~ **in** auf e-n Sprung vorbeikommen; ~ **off** den Löffel weglegen (*sterben*); ~ **up** (plötzlich) auftauchen (a. fig.). II v/t **5.** zerknallen. **6.** F (schnell) stecken: ~ **on** Hut aufstülpen. **7.** he's ~**ped the question** F er hat ihr e-n (Heirats)Antrag gemacht. III s **8.** Knall m. **9.** F Limo f.

pop[2] [~] I s Pop m. II adj a) Schlager...: ~ **singer**; ~ **song** Schlager m, b) Pop...: ~ **concert** (**group, singer,** etc).

pop[3] [~] s bsd. Am. Papa m, Vati m.

'**pop·corn** s Popcorn n, Puffmais m.

pope [pəʊp] s eccl. Papst m: ~**'s nose** Am. F Bürzel m.

'**pop-eyed** adj F glotzäugig. '~**gun** s Spielzeuggewehr n, -pistole f.

pop·lar ['pɒplə] s ♀ Pappel f.

pop·lin ['pɒplin] s Popelin m.

pop·per ['pɒpə] s bsd. Br. F Druckknopf m.

pop·py ['pɒpi] s ♀ Mohn m. '~**cock** s F Quatsch m.

pop·u·lar ['pɒpjʊlə] adj (□ → **popular·ly**) **1.** populär, beliebt: **make o.s.** ~ **with** sich bei j-m beliebt machen. **2.** weitverbreitet. **3.** populär, volkstümlich; allgemein- od. leichtverständlich: ~ **etymology** ling. Volksetymologie f; ~ **music** volkstümliche Musik; ~ **press** Boulevardpresse f. **4.** volkstümlich (*Preise*): ~ **edition** Volksausgabe f. **5.** bsd. pol. Volks...: ~ **front** Volksfront f. **pop·u·lar·i·ty** [,~'lærəti] s Popularität f: a) Beliebtheit f, b) Volkstümlichkeit f. **pop·u·lar·ize** ['~ləraiz] v/t **1.** populär machen. **2.** allgemeinverständlich darstellen. '**pop·u·lar·ly** adv allgemein.

pop·u·late ['pɒpjʊleit] v/t bevölkern, besiedeln. ,**pop·u·la·tion** s **1.** Bevölkerung f; Einwohnerschaft f: ~ **density** Bevölkerungsdichte f; ~ **explosion** Bevölkerungsexplosion f. **2.** (Gesamt)Bestand m (**an** Tieren etc).

pop·u·lous ['pɒpjʊləs] adj □ dichtbesiedelt, -bevölkert, (*Stadt*) einwohnerstark.

por·ce·lain ['pɔːsəlɪn] *s* Porzellan *n*.

porch [pɔːtʃ] *s* **1.** überdachter Vorbau, Vordach *n*, (*e-r Kirche etc*) Portal *n*. **2.** *Am.* Veranda *f*.

por·cu·pine ['pɔːkjʊpaɪn] *s zo.* Stachelschwein *n*.

pore¹ [pɔː] *s* Pore *f*.

pore² [ˑ] *v/i*: ~ *over* vertieft sein in (*acc*), über ~*n Büchern etc* hocken.

pork [pɔːk] *s* Schweinefleisch *n*. ~ *chop s* Schweinekotelett *n*. ~ *cut·let s* Schweineschnitzel *n*.

pork·y ['pɔːkɪ] *adj* F fett, dick.

porn [pɔːn] → *porno*.

por·no ['pɔːnəʊ] **I** *pl* **-nos** *s* **1.** Porno *m*. **2.** Porno(film) *m*. **II** *adj* **3.** Porno...

por·no·graph·ic [ˌpɔːnəʊ'græfɪk] *adj* (~*ally*) pornographisch. **por·nog·ra·phy** [ˑ'nɒgrəfɪ] *s* Pornographie *f*.

po·rous ['pɔːrəs] *adj* □ porös.

por·poise ['pɔːpəs] *s zo.* Tümmler *m*.

por·ridge ['pɒrɪdʒ] *s* Porridge *n*, *m*, Haferbrei *m*.

port¹ [pɔːt] *s* **1.** Hafen *m*: *come into* ~ einlaufen; *leave* ~ auslaufen; *any* ~ *in a storm fig.* in der Not frißt der Teufel Fliegen; ~ *of call* Anlaufhafen *m*. **2.** *a.* ~ *city* Hafenstadt *f*.

port² [ˑ] *s* ✈, ⚓ Backbord *n*.

port³ [ˑ] *s* Portwein *m*.

port·a·ble ['pɔːtəbl] **I** *adj* tragbar: ~ *radio* (*set*) → IIa; ~ *television set* → IIb; ~ *typewriter* → IIc. **II** *s* a) Kofferradio *n*, b) Portable *n*, tragbares Fernsehgerät, c) Koffer-, Reiseschreibmaschine *f*.

por·tal ['pɔːtl] *s* Portal *n*.

por·tend [pɔː'tend] *v/t* bedeuten, ankündigen.

por·ter¹ ['pɔːtə] *s* a) Pförtner *m*: ~*'s lodge* Pförtnerloge *f*, b) *bsd. Br.* Portier *m*.

por·ter² [ˑ] *s* **1.** (Gepäck)Träger *m*. **2.** 🚂 *Am.* Schlafwagenschaffner(in).

'por·ter·house (steak) *s* Porterhousesteak *n*.

port·fo·li·o [ˌpɔːt'fəʊljəʊ] *pl* **-os** *s* **1.** (Akten-, Dokumenten)Mappe *f*. **2.** *pol.* Portefeuille *n*, Geschäftsbereich *m*.

'port·hole *s* ⚓ Bullauge *n*.

por·ti·co ['pɔːtɪkəʊ] *pl* **-co(e)s** *s* Säulenhalle *f*.

por·tion ['pɔːʃn] **I** *s* **1.** Teil *m*. **2.** Anteil *m* (*of* an *dat*). **3.** Portion *f* (*Essen*). **II** *v/t* **4.**

~ *out* auf-, verteilen (**among, between** unter *acc*).

port·ly ['pɔːtlɪ] *adj* beleibt, korpulent.

port·man·teau word [ˌpɔːt'mæntəʊ] *s* ling. Kurzwort *n*.

por·trait ['pɔːtreɪt] *s* paint. Porträt *n*, *phot. a.* Porträtaufnahme *f*: ~ *painter* Porträtmaler(in). **'por·trait·ist** *s* Porträtist(in), Porträtmaler(in) *od.* -fotograf(in). **por·trai·ture** ['ˑtrɪtʃə] *s* Porträtmalerei *f od.* -fotografie *f*.

por·tray [pɔː'treɪ] *v/t* **1.** porträtieren. **2.** *fig.* schildern, darstellen (*as* als). **3.** *thea. etc* darstellen, verkörpern. **por·'tray·al** *s* **1.** Schilderung *f*, Darstellung *f*. **2.** *thea. etc* Verkörperung *f*.

Por·tu·guese [ˌpɔːtʃʊ'giːz] **I** *adj* **1.** portugiesisch. **II** *s* **2.** Portugiese *m*, Portugiesin *f*: *the* ~ *pl* die Portugiesen *pl*. **3.** *ling.* Portugiesisch *n*.

pose [pəʊz] **I** *s* **1.** Pose *f* (*a. fig.*), Positur *f*. **II** *v/t* **2.** aufstellen, in Positur stellen *od.* setzen. **3.** *fig. Problem, Frage* aufwerfen, *Bedrohung, Gefahr etc* darstellen (*for, to* für). **III** *v/i* **4.** sich aufstellen, sich in Positur stellen *od.* setzen. **5.** *paint.* Modell stehen *od.* sitzen (*for dat*); als (*Maler- od.* Foto)Modell arbeiten. **6.** sich ausgeben (*as* als). **posed** *adj* gestellt (*Aufnahme*). **'pos·er** *s* **1.** F harte Nuß. **2.** Wichtigtuer(in).

posh [pɒʃ] *adj* F piekfein, feudal: ~ *hotel* Nobelhotel *n*.

po·si·tion [pə'zɪʃn] **I** *s* **1.** Position *f*, Lage *f*, Standort *m*: ~ *of the sun ast.* Sonnenstand *m*; *in* (*out of*) ~ an der richtigen (falschen) Stelle. **2.** (*Körper*)Stellung *f*, Position *f*. **3.** Stelle *f*, Stellung *f* (*with, in* bei). **4.** a) Position *f* (*in e-m Beruf, Wettbewerb etc*), (Rang)Stellung *f*: *be in third* ~ in dritter Position *od.* auf dem dritten Platz liegen, b) (gesellschaftliche *od.* soziale) Stellung: *people pl of* ~ Leute *pl* von Rang. **5.** *fig.* Lage *f*, Situation *f*: *be in a* ~ *to do s.th.* in der Lage sein, et. zu tun. **6.** *fig.* (Sach)Lage *f*, Stand *m* (der Dinge): *le·gal* ~ Rechtslage. **7.** *fig.* Einstellung *f* (*on* zu): *what is your* ~ *on ...?* wie stehen Sie zu ...?; *take the* ~ *that* den Standpunkt vertreten, daß. **II** *v/t* **8.** (auf)stellen; *Polizisten etc* postieren.

pos·i·tive ['pɒzətɪv] **I** *adj* □ **1.** *allg.* positiv: *he was* ~ 🩺 sein Befund war positiv; ~ **pole** ⚡ Pluspol *m.* **2.** ausdrücklich (*Befehl etc*), definitiv, fest (*Versprechen etc*). **3.** sicher, eindeutig (*Beweis etc*). **4.** greifbar, konkret; konstruktiv. **5.** *be* ~ sicher sein (*that* daß): *be* ~ *about* sich sicher sein (*gen*). **6.** F ausgesprochen, absolut. **II** *s* **7.** *phot.* Positiv *n.* **8.** *ling.* Positiv *m.*

pos·sess [pə'zes] *v/t* **1.** besitzen (*a. fig.*). **2.** *fig.* beherrschen (*Gedanke, Gefühl etc*): **~ed with** (*od. by*) beherrscht *od.* erfüllt von; besessen von; *like a man* ~*ed* wie ein Besessener. **pos·ses·sion** [pə'zeʃn] *s* **1.** Besitz *m*: *be in s.o.'s* ~ in j-s Besitz sein; *be in* (*od. have*) ~ *of* im Besitz sein von (*od. gen*); *come* (*od. get*) *into* ~ *of* in den Besitz gelangen von (*od. gen*); *take* ~ *of* Besitz ergreifen von, in Besitz nehmen. **2.** Besitz(tum *n*) *m.* **3.** *fig.* Besessenheit *f.* **pos·ses·sive** [~sɪv] *adj* □ **1.** besitzgierig; (*Mutter etc*) besitzergreifend. **2.** *ling.* ~ *case* Genitiv *m*, zweiter Fall; ~ *adjective* attributives Possessivpronomen (*z. B.* my *car*); ~ *pronoun* substantivisches Possessivpronomen (*z. B.* it *is* mine). **pos·ses·sor** *s* Besitzer(in).

pos·si·bil·i·ty [ˌpɒsə'bɪlətɪ] *s* Möglichkeit *f* (*of doing* zu tun). **'pos·si·ble** *adj* möglich: *do everything* ~ alles tun, was e-m möglich ist; *make s.th.* ~ *for s.o.* j-m et. möglich machen *od.* ermöglichen; *if* ~ falls möglich. **'pos·si·bly** *adv* **1.** möglicherweise, vielleicht. **2.** *when I* ~ *can* wenn ich irgend kann; *I can't* ~ *do this* ich kann das unmöglich tun; *how can I* ~ *do it?* wie kann ich es nur *od.* bloß machen?

pos·sum ['pɒsəm] F → **opossum**: *play* ~ sich tot- *od.* schlafend *od.* dumm stellen.

post¹ [pəʊst] **I** *s* **1.** (*Tür-, Tor-, Ziel- etc*)Pfosten *m*, (*Laternen*)Pfahl *m*, (*Telegrafen- etc*)Mast *m*: → **pip³**. **II** *v/t* **2.** *a.* ~ *up* Plakat *etc* anschlagen, ankleben. **3.** et. durch Aushang bekanntgeben: ~ (*as*) *missing* ✈, ⚓ als vermißt melden.

post² [~] **I** *s* **1.** ✕ Posten *m*; Standort *m*, Garnison *f.* **2.** Posten *m*, Platz *m*: *at one's* ~ auf s-m Posten. **3.** Posten *m*, Stelle *f.* **II** *v/t* **4.** *Polizisten etc* aufstellen, postieren. **5.** *bsd. Br.* versetzen, ✕ abkommandieren (*to* nach).

post³ [~] **I** *s* **1.** *bsd. Br.* Post *f*: *by* ~ mit der *od.* per Post; *has the* ~ *been yet?* ist die Post schon da? **II** *v/t* **2.** *bsd. Br.* aufgeben; einwerfen; mit der Post (zu)senden. **3.** *keep s.o.* ~*ed* j-n auf dem laufenden halten.

post·age ['pəʊstɪdʒ] *s* Porto *n*: *what is the* ~ *for a letter to ...?* wieviel kostet ein Brief nach ...? ~ *stamp* *s* Postwertzeichen *n*, Briefmarke *f.*

post·al ['pəʊstəl] **I** *adj* postalisch, Post...: ~ *card* *Am.* Postkarte *f*; ~ *charges* *pl* Postgebühren *pl.* **II** *s* *Am.* F Postkarte *f.* **'post·box** *s* *bsd. Br.* Briefkasten *m.* **'~card** *s* Postkarte *f.* **'~code** *s* *Br.* Postleitzahl *f.*

post·er ['pəʊstə] *s* Plakat *n*; Poster *m, n.*

poste res·tante [ˌpəʊst'restɑːnt] *bsd. Br.* **I** *s* Abteilung *f* für postlagernde Sendungen. **II** *adv* postlagernd.

pos·te·ri·or [pɒ'stɪərɪə] *s* *humor.* Allerwerteste *m.*

pos·ter·i·ty [pɒ'sterətɪ] *s* die Nachwelt.

post·free *adj u. adv bsd. Br.* portofrei. ~ **horn** *s* *hist.* Posthorn *n.*

post·hu·mous ['pɒstjʊməs] *adj* □ post(h)um.

pos·til·(l)ion [pə'stɪljən] *s* *hist.* Postillion *m.*

post·man ['pəʊstmən] *s* (*irr* **man**) *bsd. Br.* Briefträger *m*, Postbote *m.* '~**mark** **I** *s* Poststempel *m.* **II** *v/t* (ab)stempeln: *be* ~*ed London* in London abgestempelt sein. '~**mas·ter** *s* Postamtsvorsteher *m*: ♀ *General* Postminister *m.*

post **me·rid·i·em** [ˌpəʊstmə'rɪdɪəm] *adv* nachmittags (*abbr. p.m.*): *3 p.m.* 15 Uhr. **~·mor·tem** [~'mɔːtem] *s* *a.* ~ *examination* Autopsie *f*, Obduktion *f.*

post **of·fice** *s* Post(amt *n*) *f*: ~ **box** Postfach *n.* **~'paid** → **post-free.**

post·pone [ˌpəʊst'pəʊn] *v/t* verschieben (*to* auf *acc*), aufschieben (*to* auf *acc*; *till, until* bis): *he* ~*ed seeing his doctor* er verschob s-n Arztbesuch. **post-'pone·ment** *s* Verschiebung *f*, Aufschub *m.*

post·script ['pəʊsskrɪpt] *s* **1.** Postskript(um) *n*, Nachschrift *f.* **2.** Nachbemerkung *f* (*zu e-r Rede etc*).

pos·tu·late *v/t* ['pɒstjʊleɪt] postulieren, (als gegeben) voraussetzen. **II** *s* ['~lət] Postulat *n*, Voraussetzung *f.*

pos·ture ['pɒstʃə] **I** *s* **1.** (Körper)Haltung f; Positur f, Stellung f. **2.** fig. Haltung f (**on** in dat, zu). **II** v/i **3.** sich in Positur stellen od. setzen. **4.** fig. sich aufspielen.

post·war [ˌpəʊstˈwɔː] adj Nachkriegs...

pot [pɒt] **I** s **1.** (Blumen-, Koch- etc)Topf m: **big ~** F großes od. hohes Tier; **a ~ of money** F e-e Menge Geld; **he's got ~s of money** F er hat Geld wie Heu; **go to ~** F auf den Hund kommen (Person etc); immer schlechter werden (Sprachkenntnisse etc); ins Wasser fallen (Pläne etc); **keep the ~ boiling** fig. sich über Wasser halten; die Sache in Schwung halten. **2.** (Kaffee-, Tee)Kanne f; Kännchen n, Portion f (Tee etc). **3.** Sport: F Pokal m. **4.** Poker: Pot m, Kasse f. **5.** F → **potbelly. 6.** sl. Pot n (Marihuana). **II** v/t **7.** Pflanze eintopfen: **~ed plant** Topfpflanze f. **8.** Fleisch einmachen, Fisch einlegen. **9.** Billard: Br. einlochen. **10.** F Kind aufs Töpfchen setzen.

po·ta·ble [ˈpəʊtəbl] adj trinkbar, Trink...

po·tas·si·um [pəˈtæsɪəm] s 🜞 Kalium n. **~ cy·a·nide** s Zyankali n.

po·ta·to [pəˈteɪtəʊ] pl **-toes** s Kartoffel f: **hot ~** F heißes Eisen. **~ bee·tle**, bsd. Am. **~ bug** s zo. Kartoffelkäfer m. **~ chips** s pl Am., **~ crisps** s pl Br. Kartoffelchips pl. **~ sal·ad** s Kartoffelsalat m.

'pot|·bel·ly s Schmerbauch m. **'~,boil·er** s contp. rein kommerzielle Arbeit (Buch etc).

po·ten·cy [ˈpəʊtənsɪ] s **1.** Stärke f; Wirksamkeit f, Wirkung f. **2.** physiol. Potenz f. **'po·tent** adj □ **1.** stark (Medikament etc). **2.** fig. überzeugend, zwingend (Argument etc). **3.** physiol. potent. **po·ten·tate** [ˈ~teɪt] s Potentat m. **po·ten·tial** [ˈ~ˈtenʃl] **I** adj **1.** potentiell, möglich. **II** s **2.** Potential n, Leistungsfähigkeit f: **have the ~ to be a top manager** das Zeug zu e-m Spitzenmanager haben. **3.** 🗲 Spannung f. **po·ten·tial·ly** [ˈ~ˈtenʃəlɪ] adv potentiell, möglicherweise.

'pot|·hole s mot. Schlagloch n. **'~·holed** adj voller Schlaglöcher.

po·tion [ˈpəʊʃn] s Trank m.

'pot|·luck s: **take ~** mit dem vorliebnehmen, was es gerade (zu essen) gibt; fig. es probieren. **~ plant** s Topfpflanze f.

pot·pour·ri [ˌpəʊˈpʊərɪ] s ♪ Potpourri n, fig. a. Allerlei n, Kunterbunt n.

pot·ter¹ [ˈpɒtə] v/i **1.** schlendern. **2.** a. **~ about** (od. **around**) herumwerkeln, -hantieren.

pot·ter² [ˈ~] s Töpfer(in): **~'s wheel** Töpferscheibe f. **'pot·ter·y** s **1.** Töpferei f. **2.** Töpferware(n pl) f.

pot·ty¹ [ˈpɒtɪ] adj bsd. Br. F verrückt (**a·bout** nach).

pot·ty² [ˈ~] s Töpfchen n. **'~-trained** adj sauber.

pouch [paʊtʃ] s Beutel m (a. zo.); anat. (Tränen)Sack m; zo. (Backen)Tasche f.

poul·tice [ˈpəʊltɪs] s 🩹 (warmer) (Senfetc)Umschlag od. (-)Wickel.

poul·try [ˈpəʊltrɪ] s Geflügel n.

pounce [paʊns] **I** v/i sich stürzen (**on** auf acc) (a. fig). **II** s Sprung m, Satz m.

pound¹ [paʊnd] s Pfund n (Gewichts- u. Währungseinheit): **by the ~** pfundweise; **five-~ note** Fünfpfundschein m.

pound² [ˈ~] s **1.** Tierheim n. **2.** Abstellplatz m für (polizeilich) abgeschleppte Fahrzeuge.

pound³ [ˈ~] **I** v/t **1.** zerstoßen, -stampfen (**to** zu). **2.** trommeln od. hämmern auf (acc) od. an (acc) od. gegen. **II** v/i **3.** hämmern (**with** vor dat) (Herz): **~ at** (od. **on**) → 2. **4.** stampfen.

pour [pɔː] **I** v/t **1.** gießen, schütten: **~ s.th. on o.s.** sich mit et. übergießen; **~ s.o. a cup of tea** j-m e-e Tasse Tee eingießen; **~ out** ausgießen, -schütten; Getränke eingießen, -schenken; fig. Sorgen etc ausbreiten (**to** vor dat), Herz ausschütten (**to** dat). **II** v/i **2.** strömen (a. fig.). **3.** **it is ~ing down** (od. **~ing with rain**) es gießt in Strömen; **in the ~ing rain** im strömenden Regen.

pout [paʊt] **I** v/i e-n Schmollmund machen od. ziehen; schmollen. **II** v/t Lippen schürzen. **III** s Schmollmund m; Schmollen n: **with a ~** schmollend; **be in a ~, have the ~s** schmollen.

pov·er·ty [ˈpɒvətɪ] s Armut f (a. fig. **of** an dat): **~ of ideas** Ideenarmut. **~ line** s Armutsgrenze f. **'~,strick·en** adj arm, notleidend.

pow·der [ˈpaʊdə] **I** s **1.** (Back-, Schießetc)Pulver n. **2.** (Gesichts- etc)Puder m. **II** v/t **3.** pulverisieren: **~ed milk** Milchpulver n, Trockenmilch f; **~ed sugar** Am. Puderzucker m. **4.** Baby etc (ein-)

pudern, sich *die Nase etc* pudern: **~ one's nose** *a. euphem.* mal verschwinden. **~ keg** *s fig.* Pulverfaß *n.* **~ puff** *s* Puderquaste *f.* **~ room** *s* Damentoilette *f.*

pow·der·y ['paʊdərɪ] *adj* **1.** pulv(e)rig: **~ snow** Pulverschnee *m.* **2.** (ein)gepudert.

pow·er ['paʊə] **I** *s* **1.** Kraft *f,* Macht *f,* Vermögen *n:* **do all in one's ~** alles tun, was in s-r Macht steht; **it was out of** (*od.* **not** [**with**]**in, beyond**) **his ~** es stand nicht in s-r Macht (**to do** zu tun). **2.** Kraft *f,* Energie *f, weitS.* Wucht *f,* Gewalt *f.* **3.** *mst pl* hypnotische *etc* Kräfte *pl,* geistige *etc* Fähigkeiten *pl,* (Denk-, Konzentrations- *etc*)Vermögen *n.* **4.** Macht *f,* Gewalt *f* (**over** über *acc*): **be in ~** *pol.* an der Macht sein; **be in s.o.'s ~** in j-s Gewalt sein; **come into ~** *pol.* an die Macht kommen. **5.** *pol.* Gewalt *f* (**als** Staatsfunktion): **→ separation** 2. **6.** *pol.,* ⚖ *etc* (Amts)Gewalt *f;* Befugnis *f:* **give** (**have**) **full ~s** Vollmacht geben (haben); **→ attorney** 2. **7.** *mst pl pol.* Macht *f* (Staat). **8.** Macht(faktor *m*) *f,* einflußreiche Stelle *od.* Person: **the ~s** *pl that be* F die *pl* da oben. **9.** ⚟ Potenz *f:* **raise to the third ~** in die dritte Potenz erheben. **10.** ⚡ Strom *m.* **II** *v/t* **11.** ⚙ antreiben. **'~·as,sist·ed** *adj mot.* Servo... **'~·boat** *s* Rennboot *n.* **~ brake** *s mot.* Servobremse *f.*

pow·er·ful ['paʊəfʊl] *adj* □ **1.** stark (*a. fig.*), kräftig. **2.** mächtig, einflußreich. **'pow·er·less** *adj* □ **1.** kraftlos. **2.** machtlos: **be ~ to do s.th.** nicht in der Lage sein, et. zu tun; **be ~ to prevent s.th.** nichts tun können, um et. zu verhindern.

pow·er| pack *s* ⚡ Netzteil *n.* **~ plant** *s* **power station.** **~ point** *s* ⚡ *Br.* Steckdose *f.* **~ sta·tion** *s* Kraft-, Elektrizitätswerk *n.* **~ steer·ing** *s mot.* Servolenkung *f.*

pow·wow ['paʊwaʊ] *s* F Besprechung *f.*

pox [pɒks] *s* ⚕ F Syph *f* (Syphilis).

prac·ti·ca·ble ['præktɪkəbl] *adj* □ **1.** durchführbar. **2.** passierbar (Straße *etc*).

prac·ti·cal ['præktɪkl] *adj* **1.** *allg.* praktisch: **→ purpose** 1. **2.** praktisch denkend *od.* veranlagt. **3.** **~ joke** Streich *m:* **play a ~ joke on s.o.** j-m e-n Streich

spielen. **prac·ti·cal·ly** ['~klɪ] *adv* praktisch, so gut wie.

prac·tice ['præktɪs] **I** *s* **1.** Praxis *f:* **in ~** in der Praxis; **put in(to)** **~** in die Praxis umsetzen. **2.** Übung *f:* **in** (**out of**) **~** in (aus) der Übung; **keep in ~** in der Übung bleiben; **~ makes perfect** Übung macht den Meister. **3.** (*Arzt- etc*)Praxis *f.* **4.** Brauch *m,* Gewohnheit *f:* **~s** *pl contp.* Praktiken *pl;* **it is common ~** es ist allgemein üblich; **make it a ~** es sich zur Gewohnheit machen (**to do** zu tun). **II** *adj* **5.** Übungs..., Probe... **III** *v/t u. v/i* **6.** *Am.* → **practise.**

prac·tise ['præktɪs] *bsd. Br.* **I** *v/t* **1.** als Beruf ausüben: **~ law** (**medicine**) als Anwalt (Arzt) praktizieren. **2.** (ein-) üben. **3.** *Grundsätze etc* praktizieren, *Geduld etc* üben. **II** *v/i* **4.** (*als Anwalt od. Arzt*) praktizieren: **practising Catholic** praktizierender Katholik. **5.** üben. **'prac·tised** *adj* **1.** geübt (**at, in** in *dat*): **be ~ at doing s.th.** darin geübt sein, et. zu tun. **2.** eingeübt, *contp. a.* gekünstelt.

prac·ti·tion·er [præk'tɪʃnə] *s:* **medical ~ → general practitioner.**

prag·mat·ic [præg'mætɪk] *adj* (**~ally**) pragmatisch. **prag·ma·tist** ['~mətɪst] *s* Pragmatiker(in).

prai·rie ['preərɪ] *s* Prärie *f.* **~ schoon·er** *s hist. Am.* Planwagen *m.*

praise [preɪz] **I** *v/t* loben (**for** wegen): → **sky.** **II** *s* Lob *n.* **'~·wor·thy** *adj* □ lobenswert, löblich.

pram [præm] *s bsd. Br.* F Kinderwagen *m.*

prance [prɑːns] *v/i* **1.** tänzeln (Pferd, Person). **2.** stolzieren.

prank [præŋk] *s* Streich *m:* **play a ~ on s.o.** j-m e-n Streich spielen.

prate [preɪt] *v/i* schwafeln (**about, on** von).

prat·tle ['prætl] *v/i a.* **~ on** plappern (**about** von).

prawn [prɔːn] *s zo.* Garnele *f.*

pray [preɪ] *v/i* beten (**to** zu; **for** für, um).

prayer [preə] *s* **1.** Gebet *n:* **~ book** Gebetbuch *n;* **~ mat** (*od.* **rug**) Gebetteppich *m.* **2.** *oft pl* Andacht *f.*

preach [priːtʃ] **I** *v/t* predigen (**to** zu, vor *dat*): **~ to the converted** *fig.* offene Türen einrennen; **~ at** (*od.* **to**) **s.o.** *fig.* j-m e-e Predigt halten (**about** wegen). **II** *v/t*

predigen (*a. fig.*); *Predigt* halten.
'**preach·er** *s* Prediger(in).
pre·am·ble [priː'æmbl] *s* Einleitung *f*,
🜚 Präambel *f* (*to* zu).
pre·ar·range [ˌpriːə'reɪndʒ] *v/t* vorher
abmachen *od.* vereinbaren.
pre·car·i·ous [prɪ'keərɪəs] *adj* □ prekär,
unsicher.
pre·cau·tion [prɪ'kɔːʃn] *s* Vorkehrung *f*,
Vorsichtsmaßnahme *f* (*against* gegen):
as a ~ zur Vorsicht, vorsichtshalber.
pre·cau·tion·ar·y *adj* vorbeugend,
Vorsichts...
pre·cede [ˌpriː'siːd] *v/t* **1.** voraus-, vorangehen (*dat*). **2.** (den) Vorrang haben
vor (*dat*). **3. ~ s.th. with** (*od. by*) **s.th.** et.
mit et. einleiten, et. e-r Sache vorausschicken. **prec·e·dence** ['presɪdəns] *s*
Vorrang *m*: **have** (*od. take*) **~ over →
precede** 2; **give ~ to** (den) Vorrang
geben (*dat*). **prec·e·dent** ['presɪdənt]
s 🜚 Präzedenzfall *m* (*a. fig.*): *without*
~ ohne Beispiel, noch nie dagewesen; **set a ~** e-n Präzedenzfall schaffen.
pre·cept ['priːsept] *s* Regel *f*, Richtlinie *f*.
pre·cinct ['priːsɪŋkt] *s* **1.** *pl* Gelände *n*;
Umgebung *f*. **2.** (*Fußgänger*)Zone *f*,
(*Einkaufs*)Viertel *n*. **3.** *Am.* (*Polizei*)Revier *n*; (*Wahl*)Bezirk *m*.
pre·cious ['preʃəs] **I** *adj* □ **1.** kostbar,
wertvoll (*beide a. fig.*). **2.** Edel...: **~
stone; ~ metals.** **II** *adv* **3. ~ little** F
herzlich wenig.
prec·i·pice ['presɪpɪs] *s* Abgrund *m* (*a.
fig.*).
pre·cip·i·tate [prɪ'sɪpɪteɪt] **I** *v/t* **1.** (hinunter-, herunter)schleudern; *fig.* stürzen
(*into* in *acc*). **2.** *fig. Ereignis* beschleunigen. **3.** 🜚 ausfällen. **II** *v/i* **4.** 🜚 ausfallen. **III** *adj* [~tət] **5.** überstürzt. **IV** *s* **6.**
🜚 Niederschlag *m*. **pre·cip·i·ta·tion** *s*
1. Überstürzung *f*. **2.** *meteor.* Niederschlag *m*. **3.** 🜚 Ausfällung *f*. **pre·cip·i·tous** *adj* □ **1.** steil (*abfallend*). **2.**
fig. überstürzt.
pré·cis ['preɪsiː] **I** *pl* **-cis** ['~siːz] *s* Zs.-fassung *f*. **II** *v/t* zs.-fassen.
pre·cise [prɪ'saɪs] *adj* **1.** genau, präzis: *to
be ~* genau gesagt. **2.** gewissenhaft.
pre·cise·ly *adv* **1.** → **precise. 2. ~!**
genau! **pre·ci·sion** [~'sɪʒn] *s* Genauigkeit *f*, *a.* 🜚 Präzision *f*. **II** *adj* 🜚 Präzi-

sions..., Fein...: **~ instrument** Präzisionsinstrument *n*.
pre·clude [prɪ'kluːd] *v/t* **1.** *et.* ausschließen. **2. ~ s.o. from doing s.th.** j-n (daran) hindern, et. zu tun.
pre·co·cious [prɪ'kəʊʃəs] *adj* □ frühreif. **pre·co·cious·ness, pre·coc·i·ty**
[~'kɒsɪtɪ] *s* Frühreife *f*.
pre·con·ceived [ˌpriːkən'siːvd] *adj* vorgefaßt. **pre·con·cep·tion** [~'sepʃn] *s*
vorgefaßte Meinung (*about* über
acc).
pre·con·di·tion [ˌpriːkən'dɪʃn] *s* Vorausbedingung *f*, Voraussetzung *f*.
pre·cook [ˌpriː'kʊk] *v/t* vorkochen.
pre·cur·sor [ˌpriː'kɜːsə] *s* (*of, to gen*) **1.**
Vorläufer *m*. **2.** Vorbote *m*.
pre·date [priː'deɪt] *v/t* *Brief etc* zurückdatieren.
pred·a·to·ry ['predətərɪ] *adj* räuberisch:
~ animal Raubtier *n*.
pre·de·ces·sor ['priːdɪsesə] *s* Vorgänger(in): **~ in office** Amtsvorgänger(in).
pre·des·ti·na·tion [priːˌdestɪ'neɪʃn] *s*
eccl. u. weitS. Prädestination *f*, Vorherbestimmung *f*. **pre·des·tined** [~] *adj* prädestiniert, vorherbestimmt (*to* für, zu):
be ~ to failure (*od. fail*) (von vornherein) zum Scheitern verurteilt sein; *he
was ~ to do s.th.* es war ihm vorherbestimmt, et. zu tun.
pre·de·ter·mine [ˌpriːdɪ'tɜːmɪn] *v/t* **1.**
vorherbestimmen. **2.** → **prearrange.**
pre·dic·a·ment [prɪ'dɪkəmənt] *s* mißliche Lage, Zwangslage *f*.
pred·i·cate ['predɪkət] *s ling.* Prädikat *n*,
Satzaussage *f*. **pred·i·ca·tive** [prɪ'dɪkətɪv] *adj* □ prädikativ.
pre·dict [prɪ'dɪkt] *v/t* vorher-, voraussagen. **pre·dic·tion** *s* **1.** Voraussage *f*: *against all ~s* entgegen allen Voraussagen.
pre·di·lec·tion [ˌpriːdɪ'lekʃn] *s* Vorliebe
f (*for* für).
pre·dis·pose [ˌpriːdɪ'spəʊz] *v/t* **1.** geneigt machen, einnehmen (*in favo[u]r
of* für). **2.** *bsd.* 🜚 anfällig machen (*to*
für). **pre·dis·po·si·tion** [~pə'zɪʃn] *s*
(*to*) Neigung *f* (zu), *bsd.* 🜚 *a.* Anfälligkeit *f* (für).
pre·dom·i·nant [prɪ'dɒmɪnənt] *adj* □
(vor)herrschend, überwiegend. **pre·dom·i·nate** [~neɪt] *v/i* **1.** vorherrschen,
-wiegen, überwiegen. **2.** überlegen sein;

die Oberhand *od.* das Übergewicht haben (**over** über *acc*).

pre·em·i·nent [ˌpriːˈemɪnənt] *adj* □ hervor-, überragend.

pre·emp·tive [ˌpriːˈemptɪv] *adj* **1. ~ right** Vorkaufsrecht *n*. **2. ~ strike** ⚔ Präventivschlag *m*.

preen [priːn] *v/t* sich, *das Gefieder* putzen (*Vogel*): **~ o.s.** sich herrichten (*Person*).

pre·fab [ˈpriːfæb] *s* F Fertighaus *n*. **pre·fab·ri·cate** [ˌ~rɪkeɪt] *v/t* vorfabrizieren, -fertigen: **~d house** Fertighaus *n*.

pref·ace [ˈprefɪs] **I** *s* Vorwort *n* (**to** zu). **II** *v/t* *Rede, Buch etc* einleiten (**with** mit).

pre·fer [prɪˈfɜː] *v/t* vorziehen (**to** *dat*), lieber mögen (**to** als), bevorzugen: **I ~ meat to fish** Fleisch ist mir lieber als Fisch; **~ listening to talking** lieber zuhören als reden; **I'd ~ to stay at home** ich bliebe lieber zu Hause; **I'd ~ you not to go** es wäre mir lieber, wenn du nicht gingst. **pref·er·a·ble** [ˈprefərəbl] *adj*: **be ~ (to)** vorzuziehen sein (*dat*), besser sein (als). **'pref·er·a·bly** *adv* vorzugsweise, lieber, am liebsten. **'pref·er·ence** *s* **1.** Bevorzugung *f*, Vorzug *m*: **give s.o. ~ (over)** j-m den Vorzug geben (gegenüber); **what is your ~?** was möchtest du lieber? **2.** Vorliebe *f* (**for** für). **pref·er·en·tial** [ˌ~ˈrenʃl] *adj* □ bevorzugt, Vorzugs...

pre·fix 1. [ˈpriːfɪks] *ling.* Präfix *m*, Vorsilbe *f*. **II** *v/t* [ˌpriːˈfɪks] **2.** *ling.* e-m *Wort* e-e Vorsilbe voranstellen. **3.** *Bemerkung etc* voranstellen (**to** *dat*).

preg·nan·cy [ˈpregnənsɪ] *s* Schwangerschaft *f*; *zo.* Trächtigkeit *f*: **~ test** Schwangerschaftstest *m*. **'preg·nant** *adj* □ schwanger; *zo.* trächtig: **she's four months ~** sie ist im vierten Monat schwanger; **~ with meaning** *fig.* bedeutungsschwer, -voll.

pre·heat [ˌpriːˈhiːt] *v/t* *Bratröhre* vorheizen.

pre·his·tor·ic [ˌpriːhɪˈstɒrɪk] *adj* (**~ally**) prähistorisch, vorgeschichtlich.

pre·judge [ˌpriːˈdʒʌdʒ] *v/t* j-n vorverurteilen: **~ the issue** sich vorschnell e-e Meinung bilden.

prej·u·dice [ˈpredʒʊdɪs] **I** *s* **1.** Vorurteil *n*, Voreingenommenheit *f*, *bsd.* 🏛 Befangenheit *f*: **have a ~ against** Vorurteile haben *od.* voreingenommen sein

gegen. **2. to the ~ of** zum Nachteil *od.* Schaden (*gen*); **without ~ to** *bsd.* 🏛 unbeschadet. **II** *v/t* **3.** einnehmen (**in favo[u]r of** für; **against** gegen): **~d** (vor)eingenommen, *bsd.* 🏛 befangen. **4.** schaden (*dat*), beeinträchtigen. **prej·u·di·cial** [ˌ~ˈdɪʃl] *adj* □ (**to**) abträglich (*dat*), schädlich (für): **be ~ to → prejudice 4; ~ to health** gesundheitsschädlich.

pre·lim·i·nar·y [prɪˈlɪmɪnərɪ] **I** *adj* Vor...: **~ discussion** Vorbesprechung *f*; **~ measures** *pl* vorbereitende Maßnahmen *pl*; **~ round** (*Sport*) Vorrunde *f*. **II** *s pl* Vorbereitungen *pl*, vorbereitende Maßnahmen *pl*.

prel·ude [ˈprljuːd] *s* ♪ Vorspiel *n* (**to** zu) (*a. fig.*); Präludium *n*.

pre·mar·i·tal [ˌpriːˈmærɪtl] *adj* □ vorehelich.

pre·ma·ture [ˈpremətjʊə] *adj* □ **1.** vorzeitig, verfrüht: **be four weeks ~** vier Wochen zu früh auf die Welt kommen; **~ baby** Frühgeburt *f*. **2.** *fig.* voreilig.

pre·med·i·tat·ed [ˌpriːˈmedɪteɪtɪd] *adj* vorsätzlich. **pre·med·i·ta·tion** *s* Vorsatz *m*: **with ~** vorsätzlich.

pre·mi·er [ˈpremjə] *s* Premier(minister) *m*.

prem·i·ere, prem·i·ère [ˈpremɪeə] **I** *s* Premiere *f*, Ur-, Erstaufführung *f*. **II** *v/t* ur-, erstaufführen.

prem·is·es [ˈpremɪsɪz] *s pl* Gelände *n*, Grundstück *n*; Räumlichkeiten *pl*, (*Geschäfts*)Räume *pl*: **on the ~** an Ort u. Stelle, im Haus *od.* Lokal.

pre·mi·um [ˈpriːmjəm] *s* **1.** Prämie *f*, Bonus *m*: **be at a ~** *fig.* hoch im Kurs stehen; **put a ~ on** *fig.* sehr viel Wert legen auf (*acc*); fördern. **2.** *mot. Am.* Super *n*. **~ gas·o·line** *s mot. Am.* Superbenzin *n*.

pre·mo·ni·tion [ˌpreməˈnɪʃn] *s* (böse) Vorahnung.

pre·na·tal [ˌpriːˈneɪtl] → **antenatal.**

pre·oc·cu·pa·tion [priːˌɒkjʊˈpeɪʃn] *s* Beschäftigung *f* (**with** mit): **he's got so many ~s that** er hat so viele Dinge im Kopf, daß. **pre·oc·cu·pied** [ˌ~paɪd] *adj* gedankenverloren, geistesabwesend. **pre·oc·cu·py** [ˌ~paɪ] *v/t* (stark) beschäftigen.

pre·or·dain [ˌpriːɔːˈdeɪn] *v/t* vorherbestimmen: **his success was ~ed, he**

was ~*ed to succeed* sein Erfolg war ihm vorherbestimmt.

prep [prep] *s Br.* F Hausaufgabe(n *pl*) *f*: *do one's* ~ s-e Hausaufgaben machen.

pre·paid [,pri:'peɪd] *adj* 🕯 frankiert, freigemacht: ~ *envelope* Freiumschlag *m*.

prep·a·ra·tion [,prepə'reɪʃn] *s* **1.** Vorbereitung *f* (*for* auf *acc,* für): *be in* ~ in Vorbereitung sein; *make* ~*s* Vorbereitungen treffen. **2.** Zubereitung *f*. **3.** ♞, ♟ Präparat *n*.

pre·par·a·to·ry [prɪ'pærətərɪ] *adj* □ **1.** vorbereitend, Vor(bereitungs)... **2.** ~ *to* vor (*dat*): ~ *to doing s.th.* bevor *od.* ehe man et. tut. ~ *school s Br. private Vorbereitungsschule auf das College; Am. private Vorbereitungsschule auf die High-School.*

pre·pare [prɪ'peə] **I** *v/t* **1.** *Fest, Rede etc* vorbereiten; *j-n* (*a. seelich*) vorbereiten (*for* auf *acc*): ~ *o.s. for* sich gefaßt machen auf. **2.** anfertigen; *Speise etc* zubereiten. **II** *v/i* **3.** ~ *for* sich vorbereiten auf (*acc*); Vorbereitungen treffen für; sich gefaßt machen auf (*acc*). **pre'pared** *adj* **1.** vorbereitet (*Erklärung etc*). **2.** bereit, gewillt (*to do* zu tun). **3.** gefaßt, vorbereitet (*for* auf *acc;* *to do* darauf, zu tun). **pre'pared·ness** *s* Bereitschaft *f*.

pre·pon·der·ance [prɪ'pɒndərəns] *s fig.* Übergewicht *n*. **pre'pon·der·ant** *adj* □ überwiegend: *be* ~ → *preponderate*. **pre'pon·der·ate** [~reɪt] *v/i* überwiegen; überlegen sein (*over* dat).

prep·o·si·tion [,prepə'zɪʃn] *s ling.* Präposition *f*, Verhältniswort *n*.

pre·pos·sess [,pri:pə'zes] *v/t*: *be* ~*ed by* eingenommen sein von. **pre·pos'sess·ing** *adj* □ einnehmend.

pre·pos·ter·ous [prɪ'pɒstərəs] *adj* □ **1.** absurd. **2.** lächerlich, lachhaft.

prep school F → **preparatory school**.

pre·puce ['pri:pju:s] *s anat.* Vorhaut *f*.

pre·re·cord·ed [,pri:rɪ'kɔ:dɪd] *adj* bespielt (*Musik-, Videokassette*).

pre·req·ui·site [,pri:'rekwɪzɪt] *s* Vorbedingung *f*, Voraussetzung *f* (*for, of, to* für).

pre·rog·a·tive [prɪ'rɒgətɪv] *s* Vorrecht *n*.

Pres·by·te·ri·an [,prezbɪ'tɪərɪən] **I** *adj* presbyterianisch. **II** *s* Presbyterianer (-in).

pre·school [,pri:'sku:l] *adj* vorschulisch:

of ~ *age* im Vorschulalter; ~ *child* Vorschulkind *n*.

pre·scribe [prɪ'skraɪb] *v/t* **1.** *et.* vorschreiben. **2.** ♟ *j-m et.* verschreiben, -ordnen (*for* gegen).

pre·scrip·tion [prɪ'skrɪpʃn] *s* **1.** Vorschrift *f*. **2.** ♟ verordnete Medizin; Rezept *n*: *available only on* ~ rezeptpflichtig. ~ *charge s* Rezeptgebühr *f*.

pres·ence ['prezns] *s* Gegenwart *f*, Anwesenheit *f*: *in the* ~ *of* in Gegenwart *od.* in Anwesenheit *od.* im Beisein von (*od. gen*), vor *Zeugen*; *make one's* ~ *felt fig.* sich bemerkbar *od.* auf sich aufmerksam machen; ~ *of mind* Geistesgegenwart *f*.

pres·ent¹ ['preznt] **I** *adj* (□ → *presently*) **1.** anwesend (*at* bei); vorhanden: → *company* **2.** gegenwärtig, jetzig, derzeitig: *at the* ~ *moment* zum gegenwärtigen Zeitpunkt; *in the* ~ *case* im vorliegenden Fall. **3.** *ling.* ~ *participle* Partizip *n* Präsens, Mittelwort *n* der Gegenwart; ~ *perfect* Perfekt *n*, zweite Vergangenheit; ~ *tense* Präsens *n*, Gegenwart *f*. **II** *s* **4.** Gegenwart *f, ling. a.* Präsens *n*: *at* ~ gegenwärtig, zur Zeit; *for the* ~ vorerst, -läufig, einstweilen.

pre·sent² [prɪ'zent] *v/t* **1.** präsentieren (*to* dat): a) (über)reichen, (-)bringen, (-)geben: ~ *s.th. to s.o.,* ~ *s.o. with s.th. a.* j-m et. schenken, b) vorbringen, -legen, unterbreiten, c) zeigen, vorführen, *thea. etc* aufführen, d) schildern, darstellen, e) *j-n, Produkt etc* vorstellen, f) *Programm etc* moderieren. **2.** *Sicht, Ziel, Möglichkeit etc* bieten, *Schwierigkeit etc* darstellen, bieten: *if the chance* ~*s itself* wenn sich die Chance bietet; *this* ~*s no problem (to him)* das ist kein Problem (für ihn). **3.** ~ *o.s.* sich einfinden (*Person*); ~ *itself* sich einstellen (*Gedanke etc*).

pres·ent³ ['preznt] *s* Geschenk *n*: *make s.o. a* ~ *of s.th.* j-m et. schenken (*a. fig.*).

pre·sent·a·ble [prɪ'zentəbl] *adj* □ vorzeigbar (*Person*): *be* ~ sich sehen lassen können (*a. Sache*); *make o.s.* ~ sich zurechtmachen.

pres·en·ta·tion [,prezən'teɪʃn] *s* Präsentation *f*: a) Überreichung *f*, -gabe *f*, b) Unterbreitung *f*, c) Vorführung *f, thea. etc* Aufführung *f*, d) Schilderung *f,*

Darstellung *f*, e) Vorstellung *f*, f) *Rundfunk*, *TV*: Moderation *f*.

‚pres·ent·'day *adj* heutig, gegenwärtig.

pre·'sent·er [prɪ'zentə] *s Rundfunk*, *TV*: *Br.* Moderator(in).

pre·sen·ti·ment [prɪ'zentɪmənt] *s* (böse) Vorahnung.

pres·ent·ly ['prezntlɪ] *adv* **1.** in Kürze, bald. **2.** *bsd. Am.* gegenwärtig, derzeit.

pres·er·va·tion [ˌprezə'veɪʃn] *s* **1.** Bewahrung *f*; Erhaltung *f*: *in a good state of ~* gut erhalten; *there is a ~ order on this building bsd. Br.* dieses Gebäude steht unter Denkmalschutz. **2.** Konservierung *f*. **pre·serv·a·tive** [prɪ'zɜːvətɪv] *s* Konservierungsmittel *n*.

pre·serve [prɪ'zɜːv] **I** *v/t* **1.** bewahren, (be)schützen (*from* vor *dat*). **2.** bewahren, erhalten. **3.** konservieren, (ein)machen, -kochen. **II** *s* **4.** *mst pl* Eingemachte *n*: *strawberry ~s* eingemachte Erdbeeren *pl*. **5.** (*Jagd*)Revier *n*. **6.** *fig.* Revier *n*, Ressort *n*.

pre·side [prɪ'zaɪd] *v/i* den Vorsitz führen *od.* haben (*at, over* bei): *~ at a meeting* e-e Versammlung leiten.

pres·i·den·cy ['prezɪdənsɪ] *s pol.* Präsidentschaft *f*; Amtszeit *f* (*e-s Präsidenten*). **'pres·i·dent** *s* **1.** Präsident *m* (*a. pol.*). **2.** Vorsitzende *m*, *f*. **3.** *univ. bsd. Am.* Rektor(in). **pres·i·den·tial** [ˌ~'denʃl] *adj pol.* Präsidenten..., Präsidentschafts...

press [pres] **I** *v/t* **1.** drücken, pressen: *~ s.o.'s hand* j-m die Hand drücken. **2.** drücken auf (*e-n Knopf etc*), *Pedal etc* niederdrücken. **3.** *Frucht* (aus)pressen. **4.** *Schallplatte* pressen. **5.** bügeln; *Blumen* pressen. **6.** (*zurück- etc*)drängen: *~ back*. **7.** j-n (be)drängen (*to do* zu tun): *be ~ed for time* unter Zeitdruck stehen, in Zeitnot sein. **8.** *~ s.th. on s.o.* j-m et. aufdrängen *od.* -nötigen. **9.** bestehen auf (*dat*): *~ the point* darauf bestehen; *~ home Forderung etc* durchsetzen; *Vorteil* ausnützen. **II** *v/i* **10.** drücken. **11.** drängen (*Zeit etc*): *~ for* drängen auf (*acc*). **12.** (sich) (*vorwärts- etc*)drängen: *~ forward*; *~ on* (*od. ahead*) *fig.* weitermachen (*with* mit). **III** *s* **13.** (*Frucht- etc*)Presse *f*; Spanner *m* (*für Tennisschläger etc*). **14.** (*Drucker*)Presse *f*: *be in* (*the*) *~* in Druck sein; *go to ~* in Druck gehen. **15.** *give s.th. a ~* et.

drücken. **16.** Presse *f*: *have a good* (*bad*) *~* e-e gute (schlechte) Presse haben. *~* **a·gen·cy** *s* Presseagentur *f*. *~* **box** *s* Pressetribüne *f*: *in the ~* auf der Pressetribüne. *~* **card** *s* Presseausweis *m*. *~* **clip·ping** *s bsd. Am.* Zeitungsausschnitt *m*. *~* **con·fer·ence** *s* Pressekonferenz *f*: *at a ~* auf e-r Pressekonferenz. *~* **cut·ting** *s bsd. Br.* Zeitungsausschnitt *m*. *~* **gal·ler·y** *s parl.* Pressetribüne *f*: *in the ~* auf der Pressetribüne.

press·ing ['presɪŋ] *adj* □ **1.** dringend. **2.** eindringlich.

press‖ pho·tog·ra·pher *s* Pressefotograf(in). *~* **stud** *s bsd. Br.* Druckknopf *m*. **'~-up** *s* Liegestütz *m*: *do a ~* e-n Liegestütz machen.

pres·sure ['preʃə] **I** *phys.*, ⚙, *etc* Druck *m*: *under ~ fig.* unter Druck; *bring ~ to bear on, put ~ on fig.* Druck ausüben auf (*acc*); *work at high ~ fig.* mit Hochdruck arbeiten. **II** *v/t bsd. Am.* → **pressurize** 2. *~* **cab·in** *s* ✈ Druck(ausgleichs)kabine *f*. *~* **cook·er** *s* Schnellkochtopf *m*. *~* **group** *s pol.* Interessengruppe *f*. **'~·sen·si·tive** *adj* □ & *etc* druckempfindlich.

pres·sur·ize ['preʃəraɪz] *v/t* **1.** *~d cabin* → **pressure cabin. 2.** *fig. bsd. Br.* j-n unter Druck setzen (*to do s.th.* damit er et. tut): *~ s.o. into doing s.th.* j-n so lange unter Druck setzen, bis er et. tut.

pres·tige [pre'stiːʒ] *s* Prestige *n*, Ansehen *n*. **pres·tig·ious** [pre'stɪdʒəs] *adj* □ renommiert.

pres·to ['prestəʊ] *adv*: *hey ~* Hokuspokus (Fidibus).

pre·sum·a·ble [prɪ'zjuːməbl] *adj* □ vermutlich. **pre·'sume I** *v/t* **1.** annehmen, vermuten. **2.** sich erdreisten *od.* anmaßen (*to do* zu tun). **II** *v/i* **3.** → **1. 4.** anmaßend *od.* aufdringlich sein: *~ on* et. ausnützen *od.* mißbrauchen. **pre·'sum·ing** *adj* □ anmaßend.

pre·sump·tion [prɪ'zʌmpʃn] *s* **1.** Annahme *f*, Vermutung *f*. **2.** Anmaßung *f*. **pre·'sump·tu·ous** [ˌ~tʃʊəs] *adj* □ anmaßend.

pre·sup·pose [ˌpriːsə'pəʊz] *v/t* voraussetzen (*that* daß). **pre·sup·po·si·tion** [ˌ~sʌpə'zɪʃn] *s* Voraussetzung *f*.

pre·tence [prɪ'tens] *s* **1.** Heuchelei *f*, Verstellung *f*: *his friendliness is only ~* s-e Freundlichkeit ist nur gespielt;

make a ~ of doing s.th. so tun, als tue man et. **2. *under false ~s*** unter falschen Voraussetzungen. **3.** Anspruch *m* (*to* auf *acc*): ***make no ~ to*** keinen Anspruch erheben auf.

pre·tend [prɪˈtend] **I** *v/t* **1.** vorgeben, -schützen, -täuschen: ***~ sleep*** (*od.* **to be asleep**) sich schlafend stellen. **2.** behaupten (**to do** zu tun). **II** *v/i* **3.** sich verstellen: *he's only ~ing* er tut nur so. **4.** Anspruch erheben (**to** auf *acc*). **pre·tend·ed** *adj* vorgetäuscht, gespielt.

pre·tense *Am.* → **pretence**.

pre·ten·sion [prɪˈtenʃn] *s* **1.** *oft pl* Anspruch *m* (**to** auf *acc*): **make no ~s to** keinen Anspruch erheben auf. **2.** Anmaßung *f*.

pre·ten·tious [prɪˈtenʃəs] *adj* □ anmaßend. **pre·ten·tious·ness** *s* Anmaßung *f*.

pret·er·ite [ˈpretərət] *s ling.* Präteritum *n*, (erste) Vergangenheit.

pre·text [ˈpriːtekst] *s* Vorwand *m*: **on** (*od.* **under**) **the ~** unter dem Vorwand (**of doing** zu tun).

pret·ty [ˈprɪtɪ] **I** *adj* □ hübsch, *iro. a.* schön: → **penny**. **II** *adv* F ziemlich, ganz schön: **~ cold; ~ good** recht od. ganz gut; **~ much the same thing** so ziemlich dasselbe; **be sitting ~** F (*finanziell etc*) gut dastehen.

pre·vail [prɪˈveɪl] *v/i* **1.** vorherrschen, weit verbreitet sein. **2.** (**over**, **against**) siegen (über *acc*), sich durchsetzen (gegen). **3. ~ on s.o. to do s.th.** j-n dazu bewegen, et. zu tun. **pre·vail·ing** *adj* (vor)herrschend.

prev·a·lence [ˈprevələns] *s* Vorherrschen *n*, weite Verbreitung. **'prev·a·lent** *adj* □ vorherrschend, weitverbreitet.

pre·var·i·cate [prɪˈværɪkeɪt] *v/i* Ausflüchte machen. **pre·var·i·ca·tion** *s* Ausflucht *f*.

pre·vent [prɪˈvent] *v/t* **1.** verhindern, -hüten, *e-r Sache* vorbeugen. **2.** (**from**) j-n hindern (an *dat*), abhalten (von): **~ s.o.** (**from**) **doing s.th.** j-n (daran) hindern *od.* davon abhalten, et. zu tun. **pre·ven·tion** *s* (**of**) Verhinderung *f*, -hütung *f* (von), Vorbeugung *f* (gegen): **~ of accidents** Unfallverhütung *f*; **~ is better than cure** Vorbeugen ist besser

als Heilen. **pre·ven·tive** *adj* vorbeugend.

pre·view [ˈpriːvjuː] *s* **1.** *Film, TV:* Voraufführung *f*; Vorbesichtigung *f* (*e-r Ausstellung etc*), *paint.* Vernissage *f*. **2.** *Film, TV, a. allg.* Vorschau *f* (**of** auf *acc*).

pre·vi·ous [ˈpriːvjəs] *adj* **1.** vorher-, vorausgehend, vorherig: **~ conviction** 🏛 Vorstrafe *f*; **have a ~ conviction** vorbestraft sein; **on the ~ day** am Tag davor, am Vortag; **on a ~ occasion** bei e-r früheren Gelegenheit; **~ owner** Vorbesitzer(in). **2. ~ to** vor (*dat*): **~ to doing s.th.** bevor man et. tut. **'pre·vi·ous·ly** *adv* früher, vorher.

pre·war [ˌpriːˈwɔː] *adj* Vorkriegs...

prey [preɪ] **I** *s* Beute *f*, Opfer *n* (*e-s Raubtiers*; *a. fig.*): **be easy** (*od.* **fair**) **~ to** leichte Beute sein für; → **beast** 1, **bird** 1. **II** *v/i:* **~ on** a) *zo.* Jagd machen auf (*acc*), b) *fig.* nagen an (*dat*): **~ on s.o.'s mind** j-m keine Ruhe lassen, c) *fig.* j-n ausnehmen.

price [praɪs] **I** *s* **1.** Preis *m* (*a. fig.*), (*Börse*) Kurs *m*: **what is the ~ of ...?** was *od.* wieviel kostet ...?; **at the ~ of** zum Preis von; **at a ... price** zu e-m **günstigen** etc Preis; **at a ~** für entsprechendes Geld; (**not**) **at any ~** *bsd. fig.* um jeden (keinen) Preis; **be above** (*od.* **beyond**, **without**) **~** *fig.* unbezahlbar sein; **pay a high ~ for** *fig.* e-n hohen Preis bezahlen für; **put a ~ on s.o.'s head** e-n Preis auf j-s Kopf aussetzen. **2.** *Wetten:* Quote *f*. **II** *v/t* **3.** den Preis festsetzen für; auszeichnen (**at** mit). **4.** F nach dem Preis (**gen**) fragen. **'~·con·scious** *adj* □ preisbewußt. **'~·con·trolled** *adj* preisgebunden. **~ cut** *s* Preissenkung *f*. **~ freeze** *s* Preisstopp *m*.

price·less [ˈpraɪslɪs] *adj* unbezahlbar (*a. fig.*).

price| list *s* Preisliste *f*. **~ range** *s* Preisklasse *f*, -kategorie *f*. **~ tag, ~ tick·et** *s* Preisschild *n*.

pric·ey [ˈpraɪsɪ] *adj* F teuer.

prick [prɪk] **I** *s* **1.** (*Insekten-, Nadel- etc*) Stich *m*; Einstich *m*. **2.** stechender Schmerz, Stich *m*: **~s pl of conscience** *fig.* Gewissensbisse *pl*. **3.** V Schwanz *m* (*Penis*). **4.** *fig.* V Arschloch *n*. **II** *v/t* **5.** (an-, auf-, durch)stechen, stechen in (*acc*): **~ one's finger** sich in den Finger stechen (**on** an *dat*; **with** mit); *his con-science* ~*ed him fig.* er hatte Gewissensbisse. **6.** prickeln auf *od.* in (*dat*). **7.** ~ *up one's ears* die Ohren spitzen (*a. fig.*). **III** *v/i* **8.** stechen (*a. schmerzen*).

prick·le ['prɪkl] **I** *s* **1.** Stachel *m*, ♀ *a.* Dorn *m*. **2.** Prickeln *n*, Kribbeln *n*. **II** *v/i* **3.** prickeln, kribbeln. '**prick·ly** *adj* **1.** stach(e)lig, ♀ *a.* dornig. **2.** prickelnd, kribbelnd. **3.** *fig.* unangenehm.

'**pric·y** → **pricey**.

pride [praɪd] **I** *s* Stolz *m* (*a. Gegenstand des Stolzes*); *b.s.* Hochmut *m*: *take* (*a*) ~ *in* → **II. II** *v/t*: ~ *o.s. on* stolz sein auf (*acc*).

priest [priːst] *s eccl.* Priester *m.* **priest·hood** ['~hʊd] *s* **1.** Priesteramt *n*, -würde *f.* **2.** *coll.* Priesterschaft *f.* '**priest·ly** *adj* priesterlich.

prig [prɪg] *s* Tugendbold *m.* '**prig·gish** *adj* □ tugendhaft.

prim [prɪm] *adj* □ *a.* ~ *and proper* etepetete; prüde.

pri·ma·cy ['praɪməsɪ] *s* Vorrang *m* (*over* vor *dat*); Vorrangstellung *f.*

pri·mae·val *bsd. Br.* → **primeval.**

pri·mal ['praɪml] *adj* **1.** ursprünglich, Ur... **2.** → **primary 1.**

pri·ma·ri·ly ['praɪmərəlɪ] *adv* in erster Linie, vor allem. '**pri·ma·ry I** *adj* **1.** wichtigst, Haupt...: ~ *accent* (*od.* **stress**) *ling.* Hauptakzent *m*; *of* ~ *importance* von höchster Wichtigkeit. **2.** Anfangs..., Ur... **3.** grundlegend, elementar, Grund...: ~ *colo(u)r* Grundfarbe *f.* **II** *s* **4.** *pol. Am.* Vorwahl *f.*

prime [praɪm] **I** *adj* □ **1.** wichtigst, Haupt...: *of* ~ *importance* von höchster Wichtigkeit; ~ *minister* Premierminister(in), Ministerpräsident(in); ~ *mover* ⊕ Kraft-, Antriebsmaschine *f*; *fig.* treibende Kraft; ~ *suspect* Hauptverdächtige(r) *m, f*; ~ *time TV* Hauptsendezeit *f.* **2.** erstklassig: *in* ~ *condition* in Bestzustand. **3.** ~ *number* → **5. II** *s* **4.** *in the* ~ *of life* in der Blüte s-r Jahre; *be past one's* ~ s-e besten Jahre hinter sich haben; (*Künstler etc*) den Zenit überschritten haben. **5.** ♪ Primzahl *f.* **III** *v/t* **6.** grundieren. **7.** *j-n* instruieren, vorbereiten.

prim·er[1] ['praɪmə] *s* **1.** Grundierfarbe *f*, -lack *m.* **2.** ✗ *etc* Zünder *m.*

prim·er[2] [~] *s* Fibel *f.*

pri·me·val [praɪˈmiːvl] *adj* □ urzeitlich, Ur...: ~ *forest* Urwald *m.*

prim·i·tive ['prɪmɪtɪv] *adj* □ primitiv (*a. contp.*).

pri·mor·di·al [praɪˈmɔːdjəl] *adj* □ uranfänglich, ursprünglich.

prim·rose *s* ♀ Primel *f*, *bsd.* Schlüsselblume *f.*

prim·u·la ['prɪmjʊlə] *s* ♀ Primel *f.*

prince [prɪns] *s* **1.** Fürst *m.* **2.** *Prince Charming fig.* Märchenprinz; → **consort.** '**prince·ly** *adj* fürstlich (*a. fig.*). **prin·cess** [~'ses, *vor npr* '~ses] *s* **1.** Fürstin *f.* **2.** Prinzessin *f.*

prin·ci·pal ['prɪnsəpl] **I** *adj* (□ → **principally**) **1.** wichtigst, hauptsächlich, Haupt...: ~ *character* Hauptfigur *f*, -person *f* (*e-s Romans etc*); ~ *parts pl ling.* Stammformen *pl* (*e-s Verbs*). **II** *s* **2.** *ped.* Rektor(in). **3.** *thea.* Hauptdarsteller(in); ♪ Solist(in).

prin·ci·pal·i·ty [ˌprɪnsɪˈpælətɪ] *s* Fürstentum *n.*

prin·ci·pal·ly ['prɪnsəplɪ] *adv* in erster Linie, hauptsächlich.

prin·ci·ple ['prɪnsəpl] *s* **1.** Prinzip *n*, Grundsatz *m*: *man of* ~*s* Mann *m* mit Grundsätzen; *in* ~ im Prinzip, an sich; *on* ~ prinzipiell, grundsätzlich; ~ *of efficiency* Leistungsprinzip. **2.** *phys. etc* Prinzip *n*, (Natur)Gesetz *n.*

print [prɪnt] **I** *v/t* **1.** *typ.* drucken: ~*ed matter* ✉ Drucksache *f.* **2.** Rede *etc* abdrucken. **3.** Stoff *etc* bedrucken. **4.** in Druckbuchstaben schreiben: ~*ed characters pl* Druckbuchstaben *pl.* **5.** *a.* ~ *off phot.* abziehen. **6.** ~ *out* ausdrucken (*Computer*). **II** *v/i* **6.** *typ.* drucken. **7.** *be* ~*ing* im Druck sein. **III** *s* **8.** (*Finger- etc*)Abdruck *m.* **9.** *typ.* Druck *m*: *out of* ~ vergriffen; *in* ~ gedruckt; ~ *run* Auflage *f.* **10.** Gedruckte *n*: → **small I. 11.** *Kunst:* Druck *m*; *phot.* Abzug *m.* '**print·a·ble** *adj* druckfähig, -reif. '**print·er** *s* Drucker *m* (*a. Gerät*): ~*'s error* Druckfehler *m*; ~*'s ink* Druckerschwärze *f.* '**print·ing** *s* **1.** *typ.* Drucken *n*: ~ *ink* Druckerschwärze *f*; ~ *press* Druck(er)presse *f*; ~ *works pl* (*oft sg konstruiert*) Druckerei *f.* **2.** Auflage *f.* '**print·out** *s Computer:* Ausdruck *m.*

pri·or ['praɪə] *adj* **1.** vorherig, früher. **2.** vorrangig. **3.** ~ *to* vor (*dat*). **pri·or·i·tize** [~'ɒrətaɪz] *v/t* den Vorrang geben *(dat)*, vorrangig behandeln. **pri'or·i·ty** s **1.** Priorität f, Vorrang m: *give ~ to* → **prioritize**; *have (od. take)* ~ den Vorrang haben *(over od. vor dat)*, vorgehen. **2.** vordringliche *od.* vorrangige Sache: *a top* ~ e-e Angelegenheit von äußerster Dringlichkeit. **3.** *mot.* Vorfahrt f: *have* ~.

prise *bsd. Br.* → **prize².**

prism ['prɪzəm] s A, *phys. etc* Prisma n.

pris·mat·ic [~'mætɪk] adj (**~ally**) prismatisch, Prismen...

pris·on ['prɪzn] s Gefängnis n: *be in* ~ im Gefängnis sein *od.* sitzen, einsitzen; ~ *cell* Gefängniszelle f; ~ *sentence* Gefängnis-, Freiheitsstrafe f. **'pris·on·er** s Gefangene m, f, Häftling m: *hold (od. keep)* ~ gefangenhalten; *take* ~ gefangennehmen; *~ of war* Kriegsgefangene; → **bar** 8.

pris·sy ['prɪsɪ] adj □ F etepetete, zimperlich.

pri·va·cy ['praɪvəsɪ] s **1.** Ungestörtheit f: *there is no* ~ *here* hier ist man nie ungestört. **2.** Geheimhaltung f: *in strict* ~ streng vertraulich.

pri·vate ['praɪvɪt] **I** adj □ **1.** privat, Privat...: ~ (*limited*) *company* ✝ *Br.* Gesellschaft f mit beschränkter Haftung; ~ *detective* Privatdetektiv(in); ~ *lessons* pl Privatunterricht m; ~ *life* Privatleben n; ~ *matter* Privatangelegenheit f; ~ *patient* Br. Privatpatient(in); ~ *school* Privatschule f; *~ly owned* in Privatbesitz. **2.** ungestört *(Ort):* *be a very ~ person* sehr zurückgezogen leben. **3.** geheim; vertraulich: *keep s.th.* ~ et. geheimhalten *od.* vertraulich behandeln. **4.** ~ *soldier* → 6. **II** s **5.** *in* ~ privat; unter vier Augen. **6.** ✗ Gefreite m.

pri·va·tion [praɪ'veɪʃn] s Entbehrung f.

pri·vat·ize ['praɪvɪtaɪz] v/t staatlichen Betrieb *etc* privatisieren.

priv·i·lege ['prɪvɪlɪdʒ] **I** s Privileg n, Vorrecht n; (besondere) Ehre. **II** v/t privilegieren, bevorrechtigen: *be ~d* den Vorzug genießen (*to do* zu tun).

priv·y ['prɪvɪ] adj: *be ~ to* eingeweiht sein in *(acc).*

prize¹ [praɪz] **I** s **1.** (Sieger-, Sieges)Preis m; *(Lotterie- etc)*Gewinn m. **II** adj **2.** preisgekrönt. **3.** F *contp.* Riesen...: ~

idiot Vollidiot m. **III** v/t **4.** (hoch)schätzen.

prize² [~] v/t: ~ *open* aufbrechen, -stemmen.

'prize|,win·ner s Preisträger(in); Gewinner(in). **'~,win·ning** adj preisgekrönt: ~ *ticket* Gewinnlos n.

pro¹ [prəʊ] pl **pros** s **1.** Ja-Stimme f. **2.** *the ~s and cons* pl das Für u. Wider, das Pro u. Kontra.

pro² [~] F I pl **pros** s Profi m. II adj Profi...

prob·a·bil·i·ty [,probə'bɪlətɪ] s Wahrscheinlichkeit f: *in all* ~ aller Wahrscheinlichkeit nach, höchstwahrscheinlich. **'prob·a·ble** adj □ wahrscheinlich.

pro·ba·tion [prə'beɪʃn] s Probe(zeit) f; ⚖ Bewährung(sfrist) f: *he's still on* ~ er ist noch in der Probezeit; *put s.o. on* ~ *(for two years)* j-s (Rest)Strafe (auf zwei Jahre) zur Bewährung aussetzen; ~ *officer* Bewährungshelfer(in). **pro'ba·tion·a·ry** adj: ~ *period* Probezeit f; ⚖ Bewährungsfrist f. **pro'ba·tion·er** s **1.** Lernschwester f. **2.** ⚖ j-d, dessen *(Rest)Strafe* zur Bewährung ausgesetzt *wurde.*

probe [prəʊb] **I** s **1.** ⚕, ◎ Sonde f. **2.** *fig.* Untersuchung f (*into* gen). **II** v/t **3.** ⚕ sondieren. **4.** *fig.* erforschen, (gründlich) untersuchen. **III** v/i **5.** ~ *into* → II.

prob·lem ['probləm] s **1.** Problem n: *without any* ~ (völlig) problemlos; ~ *child* Problemkind n; ~ *drinker* *euphem.* Alkoholiker(in). **2.** A *etc* Aufgabe f: *do a* ~ e-e Aufgabe lösen. **prob·lem·at·ic** [,problə'mætɪk] adj (**~ally**) problematisch.

pro·ce·dur·al [prə'siːdʒərəl] adj □ Verfahrens..., verfahrenstechnisch; ⚖ verfahrensrechtlich. **pro'ce·dure** s Verfahren(sweise f) n, Vorgehen n.

pro·ceed [prə'siːd] v/i **1.** (weiter)gehen, (-)fahren; sich begeben *(to* nach, zu). **2.** *fig.* weitergehen *(Handlung etc).* **3.** *fig.* fortfahren (*with* mit): ~ *with one's work* s-e Arbeit fortsetzen. **4.** *fig.* vorgehen, verfahren: ~ *with et.* durchführen; ~ *to do s.th.* sich anschicken *od.* daranmachen, et. zu tun. **5.** ~ *from* herrühren *od.* kommen von. **6.** ~ *against* ⚖ (gerichtlich) vorgehen gegen. **pro'ceed·ing** s **1.** → **procedure**. **2.** pl Vor-

gänge *pl*, Geschehnisse *pl*. **3. start** (*od.*
take) **~s against** → **proceed** 6.
pro·ceeds ['prəʊsiːdz] *s pl* Erlös *m*,
Ertrag *m*, Einnahmen *pl*.

pro·cess ['prəʊses] **I** *s* Prozeß *m*: a) Verfahren *n*, b) Vorgang *m*: **in the ~** dabei;
be in ~ im Gange sein; **be in the ~ of
doing s.th.** (gerade) dabei sein, et. zu
tun; **~ of thinking** Denkprozeß. **II** *v/t*
⚙, *a.* Anträge *etc* bearbeiten; *Daten*
verarbeiten; (*chemisch etc*) behandeln;
Film entwickeln; *Lebensmittel* haltbar
machen, *Milch etc* sterilisieren: **~ into**
verarbeiten zu. **'pro·cess·ing** *s* Be-,
Verarbeitung *f*: **~ industry** verarbeiten-
de Industrie.

pro·ces·sion [prə'seʃn] *s* Prozession *f*;
(Um)Zug *m*.

pro·ces·sor ['prəʊsesə] *s* Computer:
Prozessor *m*; (*Wort-, Text*)Verarbei-
tungsgerät *n*.

pro·claim [prə'kleɪm] *v/t* proklamieren,
verkünd(ig)en: **~ s.o. king** j-n zum König ausrufen. **proc·la·ma·tion** [ˌprɒk-
lə'meɪʃn] *s* Proklamation *f*, Verkünd-
(ig)ung *f*.

pro·cliv·i·ty [prə'klɪvətɪ] *s* Neigung *f*,
Hang *m* (**to, toward**[**s**] *zu*).

pro·cras·ti·nate [prəʊ'kræstɪneɪt] *v/i*
zaudern, zögern.

pro·cre·ate ['prəʊkrɪeɪt] *biol.* **I** *v/t* zeugen. **II** *v/i* sich fortpflanzen. **pro·cre-
'a·tion** *s* Zeugung *f*; Fortpflanzung *f*.

pro·cure [prə'kjʊə] *v/t* **1.** (sich) *et.* beschaffen *od.* besorgen: **~ s.o. s.th.** j-m
et. beschaffen. **2.** verkuppeln (**for** *dat*).
pro'cure·ment *s* Beschaffung *f*, Besorgung *f*. **2.** Verkupplung *f*. **pro'cur-
-er** *s* Kuppler *m*. **pro'cur·ess** *s* Kupplerin *f*.

prod [prɒd] **I** *v/t* **1.** stoßen: **~ s.o. in the
ribs** j-m e-n Rippenstoß geben. **2.** *fig.*
anspornen, anstacheln (**into** *zu*). **II** *v/i*
3. stoßen (**at** *nach*). **III** *s* **4.** Stoß *m*: **~ in
the ribs** Rippenstoß *m*.

prod·i·gal ['prɒdɪgl] **I** *adj* □ verschwenderisch: **be ~ of** verschwenderisch umgehen mit. **II** *s* Verschwender(in).

pro·di·gious [prə'dɪdʒəs] *adj* □ erstaunlich, großartig, wunderbar. **prod·i·gy**
['prɒdɪdʒɪ] *s* Wunder *n*: → **child prodigy, infant** II.

pro·duce[1] [prə'djuːs] *v/t* **1.** *allg.* erzeugen; ✝ *Waren* produzieren, herstellen,

erzeugen; *Theaterstück etc* inszenieren;
Film produzieren. **2.** ✝ *Gewinn etc*
(ein)bringen, abwerfen. **3.** *fig.* erzeugen, bewirken, hervorrufen, *Wirkung*
erzielen. **4.** hervorziehen, -holen (**from**
aus *der Tasche etc*); *Ausweis etc*
(vor)zeigen, vorlegen; *Beweise, Zeugen
etc* beibringen. **II** *v/i* **5.** produzieren:
begin to ~ die Produktion aufneh-
men.

pro·duce[2] ['prɒdjuːs] *s* (*bsd. Agrar*)Pro-
dukt(e *pl*) *n*, (-)Erzeugnis(se *pl*) *n*.

pro·duc·er [prə'djuːsə] *s* **1.** Produzent
(-in), Hersteller(in). **2.** *thea.* Regisseur
(-in); (*Film*) Produzent(in).

prod·uct ['prɒdʌkt] *s* Produkt *n* (*a.* 🔬,
Å, *fig.*), Erzeugnis *n*. **pro·duc·tion**
[prə'dʌkʃn] *s* **1.** *allg.* Erzeugung *f*; ✝
Produktion *f*, Herstellung *f*, Erzeugung *f*; *thea.* Inszenierung *f*; (*Film*)
Produktion *f*: **go into ~** ✝ die Produktion aufnehmen; in Produktion gehen; **~
line** Fertigungsstraße *f*, Fließband *n*. **2.**
fig. Erzeugung *f*, Bewirkung *f*. **3.** Vorzeigen, -legen *n* (*e-s Ausweises etc*); Bei-
bringung *f* (*von Beweisen, Zeugen etc*).
pro·duc·tive *adj* □ produktiv (*a. fig.*),
ergiebig, rentabel; *fig.* schöpferisch.
pro·duc·tiv·i·ty [ˌprɒdʌk'tɪvətɪ] *s* Produktivität *f* (*a. fig.*), Ergiebigkeit *f*,
Rentabilität *f*.

prof [prɒf] *s F* Prof *m* (*Professor*).

prof·a·na·tion [ˌprɒfə'neɪʃn] *s* Entwei-
hung *f*. **pro·fane** [prə'feɪn] **I** *adj* □ **1.**
weltlich, profan, Profan... **2.** (gottes)lä-
sterlich. **II** *v/t* **3.** entweihen.

pro·fess [prə'fes] *v/t* **1.** vorgeben, -täu-
schen; behaupten (**to be** *zu* sein). **2.**
erklären, bekunden: **~ o.s. (to be) satisfied** s-e Zufriedenheit bekunden.
pro'fessed *adj* **1.** erklärt (*Gegner etc*).
2. angeblich. **pro'fess·ed·ly** [~sɪdlɪ] *adv*
1. erklärtermaßen. **2.** angeblich.
pro·fes·sion [prə'feʃn] *s* **1.** (*bsd. akademischer*) Beruf: **by ~** von Beruf. **2.** Be-
rufsstand *m* (*bsd. akademischer*): **the
medical ~** die Ärzte-
schaft, die Mediziner *pl*. **pro'fes·sion-
al** [~ʃənl] **I** *adj* □ **1.** Berufs..., beruflich.
2. Fach..., fachlich. **3.** professionell,
Berufs... (*beide a. Sport*): **turn ~** ins
Profilager überwechseln. **4.** fachmännisch, gekonnt. **II** *s* **5.** Berufssportler-
(in), -spieler(in), Profi *m*. **6.** Fachmann *m*, Profi *m*. **pro'fes·sion·al·ism**

[~'nəlɪzəm] s *Sport:* Professionalismus m (*a. allg.*), Profitum n.

pro·fes·sor [prə'fesə] s Professor(in). **pro'fes·sor·ship** s Professur f.

prof·fer ['prɒfə] v/t: ~ *s.o. s.th.* j-m et. anbieten.

pro·fi·cien·cy [prə'fɪʃnsɪ] s Können n, Tüchtigkeit f. **pro'fi·cient** adj □ tüchtig (**at, in** in dat).

pro·file ['prəʊfaɪl] I s 1. *allg.* Profil n: **in** ~ im Profil; **keep a low** ~ *fig.* Zurückhaltung üben. 2. *fig.* Porträt n. II v/t 3. im Profil darstellen. 4. *fig.* porträtieren.

prof·it ['prɒfɪt] I s 1. Gewinn m, Profit m: **sell at a** ~ mit Gewinn verkaufen; ~ **margin** Gewinnspanne f; ~ **sharing** Gewinnbeteiligung f. 2. *fig.* Nutzen m, Vorteil m: **turn s.th. to** ~ aus et. Nutzen ziehen. II v/i 3. (**by, from**) Nutzen od. Gewinn ziehen (aus), profitieren (von). **'prof·it·a·ble** adj □ 1. gewinnbringend, einträglich, rentabel 2. *fig.* vorteilhaft, nützlich. **prof·it·eer** [~'tɪə] s Profitmacher(in), (*Kriegs*)Gewinnler (-in). **,prof·it'eer·ing** s Wuchergeschäfte pl.

prof·li·gate ['prɒflɪgət] adj □ 1. lasterhaft, verworfen. 2. verschwenderisch.

pro·found [prə'faʊnd] adj □ 1. *fig.* tief (*Eindruck, Schweigen etc*). 2. tiefgründig, -sinnig. 3. völlig (*Blindheit etc*).

pro·fuse [prə'fju:s] adj □ 1. üppig, (*Blutung*) stark. 2. (*oft allzu*) freigebig, verschwenderisch (**in, of** mit). **pro·fu·sion** [~'fju:ʒn] s Überfülle f (**of** an dat): **in** ~ in Hülle u. Fülle.

prog·no·sis [prɒg'nəʊsɪs] pl **-ses** [~si:z] s ♣, *a. allg.* Prognose f.

prog·nos·ti·cate [prɒg'nɒstɪkeɪt] v/t voraus-, vorhersagen, *bsd.* ♣ prognostizieren.

pro·gram ['prəʊgræm] I s 1. *Computer:* Programm n. 2. *Am.* → **programme** 1. II *pret u. pp* **-grammed,** *Am. a.* **-gramed** 3. *Computer* programmieren. 4. *Am.* → **programme** 3.

pro·gram·er, pro·gram·ing *Am.* → **programmer, programming.**

pro·gramme ['prəʊgræm] I s 1. *allg.* Programm n, (*Rundfunk, TV a.*) Sendung f: **be on the** ~ auf dem Programm stehen. 2. *Br.* → **program** 1. II v/t 3. ein Programm aufstellen für. 4. *Br.* → **program** 3.

pro·gram·mer ['prəʊgræmə] s *Computer:* Programmierer(in). **'pro·gram·ming** adj: ~ *language* Programmiersprache f.

pro·gress I s ['prəʊgres] 1. **make slow** ~ (nur) langsam vorankommen. 2. *fig.* Fortschritt(e pl) m: **make** ~ → 6. 3. **be in** ~ im Gange sein. II v/i [prəʊ'gres] 4. sich vorwärts bewegen. 5. *fig.* fortschreiten: **as the day** ~ed im Laufe des Tages. 6. *fig.* Fortschritte machen.

pro·gres·sion [prəʊ'greʃn] s *Steuer:* Progression f, ♣ *a.* Reihe f. **pro'gres·sive** [~sɪv] adj □ 1. progressiv, fortschrittlich. 2. fortschreitend, ♣ *a.* progressiv. 3. *ling.* progressiv (*a. Steuern*): ~ **form** Verlaufsform f.

pro·hib·it [prə'hɪbɪt] v/t 1. *et.* verbieten, untersagen: ~ *s.o. from doing s.th.* j-m verbieten od. untersagen, et. zu tun. 2. *et.* verhindern: ~ *s.o. from doing s.th.* j-n daran hindern, et. zu tun. **pro·hi·bi·tion** [,prəʊɪ'bɪʃn] s Verbot n: ~ *of smoking* Rauchverbot; **the** ♀ *hist. Am.* die Prohibition. **pro·hib·i·tive** [prə'hɪbɪtɪv] adj □ unerschwinglich (*Preis*).

proj·ect¹ ['prɒdʒekt] s Projekt n, Vorhaben n.

pro·ject² [prə'dʒekt] I v/t 1. werfen, schleudern: ~ *into space* in den Weltraum schießen. 2. planen, in Aussicht nehmen. 3. *Bild etc* projizieren, werfen (*onto* auf *acc*). II v/i 4. vorspringen, -stehen, (*Ohren*) abstehen.

pro·jec·tile [prə'dʒektaɪl] s Projektil n, Geschoß n.

pro·jec·tion [prə'dʒekʃn] s 1. Vorsprung m, vorspringender Teil. 2. Werfen n, Schleudern n. 3. Planung f. 4. Projektion f. **pro'jec·tion·ist** s Filmvorführer(in). **pro'jec·tor** s Projektor m.

pro·le·tar·i·an [,prəʊlɪ'teərɪən] I adj proletarisch, Proletarier... II s Proletarier(in). **pro·le'tar·i·at** [~rɪət] s Proletariat n.

pro·lif·e·rate [prəʊ'lɪfəreɪt] v/i sich stark od. schnell vermehren. **pro·lif·er·a·tion** s starke od. schnelle Vermehrung.

pro·lif·ic [prəʊ'lɪfɪk] adj □ (~*ally*) *biol.* fruchtbar, (*Schriftsteller etc a.*) (sehr) produktiv.

pro·lix ['prəʊlɪks] adj □ weitschweifig.

pro·log *Am.* → **prologue.**

pro·logue ['prəʊlɒg] *s* Prolog *m*; *fig.* Auftakt *m* (**to** zu).

pro·long [prəʊ'lɒŋ] *v/t* Aufenthalt *etc* verlängern (**by** um), Diskussion *etc* in die Länge ziehen, ✝ *Wechsel* prolongieren. **pro'longed** *adj* anhaltend (*Applaus etc*), länger (*Abwesenheit etc*). **pro·lon·ga·tion** [ˌ∼'geɪʃn] *s* Verlängerung *f*, ✝ Prolongierung *f*.

prom [prɒm] *bsd. Br. F* → **promenade** I, **promenade concert.**

prom·e·nade [ˌprɒmə'nɑːd] I *s* (Strand-)Promenade *f*. II *v/i u. v/t* promenieren (auf *dat*). ∼ **con·cert** *s* Konzert in ungezwungener Atmosphäre. ∼ **deck** *s* ⚓ Promenadendeck *n*.

prom·i·nence ['prɒmɪnəns] *s* **1.** Vorsprung *m*, vorstehender Teil. **2.** *fig.* Prominenz *f*, Bekannt-, Berühmtheit *f*: **come into** (*od.* **rise to**) ∼ bekannt *od.* berühmt werden. **'prom·i·nent** *adj* □ **1.** vorspringend, (*a. Zähne etc*) vorstehend. **2.** *fig.* prominent, bekannt, berühmt.

prom·is·cu·i·ty [ˌprɒmɪ'skjuːətɪ] *s* häufiger Partnerwechsel. **pro·mis·cu·ous** [prə'mɪskjʊəs] *adj* □ (sexuell) ausschweifend (*Leben*): ∼ **girl** Mädchen, das häufig den Partner wechselt; **be** ∼ häufig den Partner wechseln.

prom·ise ['prɒmɪs] I *s* **1.** Versprechen *n*: **a** ∼ **is a** ∼ versprochen ist versprochen; **make a** ∼ ein Versprechen geben; **breach of** ∼ Wortbruch *m*. **2.** *fig.* Hoffnung *f*, Aussicht *f* (**of** auf *acc*): **show great** ∼ zu den besten Hoffnungen berechtigen. II *v/t* **3.** versprechen (*a. fig.*): **I** ∼ **you** ich warne dich; → **moon** I. III *v/i* **4.** ∼ es versprechen. **'prom·is·ing** *adj* □ vielversprechend.

prom·on·to·ry ['prɒməntrɪ] *s* Vorgebirge *n*.

pro·mote [prə'məʊt] *v/t* **1.** *j-n* befördern, *ped.* versetzen: **be** ∼**d** (*Sport*) aufsteigen (**to** in *acc*); **be** ∼**d to** (*the rank of*) **general**, **be** ∼**d general** zum General befördert werden. **2.** *Boxkampf, Konzert etc* veranstalten. **3.** ✝ werben für. **4.** *et.* fördern: ∼ **health** gesundheitsförderlich sein. **pro'mot·er** *s* **1.** Promoter(in), Veranstalter(in). **2.** → **sales promoter.** **pro'mo·tion** *s* **1.** Beförderung *f*, *ped.* Versetzung *f*, (*Sport*) Aufstieg *m*: **get** ∼ befördert werden;

chances *pl* of ∼, ∼ prospects *pl* Aufstiegschancen *pl*. **2.** Veranstaltung *f*. **3.** ✝ Werbung *f*: → **sales promotion.**

prompt [prɒmpt] I *adj* □ **1.** prompt, unverzüglich, umgehend: **be** ∼ **to do** (*od.* **in doing**) **s.th.** *et.* schnell tun. **2.** pünktlich: ∼**ly at two o'clock** pünktlich um *od.* Punkt zwei Uhr. II *adv* **3.** **at two o'clock** ∼ F pünktlich um *od.* Punkt zwei Uhr. III *v/t* **4.** führen zu, *Gefühle etc* wecken. **5.** *j-n* veranlassen (**to do** zu tun). **6.** *j-m* ein-, vorsagen; *thea.* *j-m* soufflieren. IV *s* **7.** *thea.* Soufflieren *n*: ∼ **box** Souffleurkasten *m*. **'prompt·er** *s thea.* Souffleur *m*, Souffleuse *f*. **promp·ti·tude** ['∼tɪtjuːd], **'prompt·ness** *s* Promptheit *f*, Pünktlichkeit *f*.

pro·mul·gate ['prɒmlgeɪt] *v/t* **1.** *Gesetz etc* verkünd(ig)en. **2.** *Lehre etc* verbreiten. **pro·mul·ga·tion** *s* **1.** Verkünd(ig)ung *f*. **2.** Verbreitung *f*.

prone [prəʊn] *adj* □ **1.** auf dem Bauch *od.* mit dem Gesicht nach unten liegend: ∼ **position** Bauchlage *f*. **2.** **be** ∼ **to** *fig.* neigen zu, anfällig sein für: **be** ∼ **to colds** erkältungsanfällig sein; **be** ∼ **to do s.th.** dazu neigen, *et.* zu tun. **'prone·ness** *s* (**to**) Neigung *f* (zu), Anfälligkeit *f* (für).

prong [prɒŋ] *s* Zacke *f*, Zinke *f* (*e-r Gabel*); (*Geweih*)Sprosse *f*.

pro·noun ['prəʊnaʊn] *s ling.* Pronomen *n*, Fürwort *n*.

pro·nounce [prə'naʊns] I *v/t* **1.** aussprechen. **2.** erklären *od.* für. **3.** *Urteil* verkünden. II *v/i* **4.** Stellung nehmen (**on** zu): ∼ **in favo(u)r of** (*od.* **for**) (**against**) **s.th.** sich für (gegen) *et.* aussprechen. **pro'nounced** *adj* **1.** bestimmt, entschieden (*Ansicht etc*). **2.** ausgesprochen, geprägt, deutlich. **pro'nounce·ment** *s* **1.** Erklärung *f*. **2.** (*Urteils*)Verkündung *f*.

pron·to ['prɒntəʊ] *adv* F fix, schnell.

pro·nun·ci·a·tion [prəˌnʌnsɪ'eɪʃn] *s* Aussprache *f*.

proof [pruːf] I *s* **1.** Beweis(e *pl*) *m*, Nachweis *m*: **as** (*od.* **in**) ∼ **of** als *od.* zum Beweis für (*od.* gen); **give** ∼ **of** *et.* be- *od.* nachweisen; ∼ **of age** Altersnachweis *m*; → **contrary** 6. **2.** Probe *f* (*a.* ℞), Prüfung *f*: **put to the** ∼ auf die Probe stellen. II *adj* **3.** (**against**) geschützt (vor *dat*), undurchlässig (für); *fig.* unempfindlich (gegen), unempfänglich (für): → **heatproof, waterproof** I, *etc.* III *v/t* **4.** imprägnieren. '**~,read·er** s Korrektor(in).

prop¹ [prɒp] I s Stütze *f* (*a. fig.*): **be a ~ to s.o.** j-m e-e Stütze *od.* ein Halt sein. II *v/t a.* **~ up** (ab)stützen: ~ *up fig.* stützen; **~ against** lehnen gegen *od.* an (*acc*).

prop² [~] s *thea. etc* Requisit *n*.

prop·a·gan·da [,prɒpə'gændə] s Propaganda *f.* ,**prop·a'gan·dist** s Propagandist(in).

prop·a·gate ['prɒpəgeɪt] I *v/i biol.* sich fortpflanzen *od.* vermehren. II *v/t* verbreiten, propagieren. ,**prop·a'ga·tion** s **1.** Fortpflanzung *f*, Vermehrung *f.* **2.** Verbreitung *f*, Propagierung *f.*

pro·pane ['prəʊpeɪn] s 🔥 Propan(gas) *n.*

pro·pel [prə'pel] *v/t* (an)treiben. **pro·'pel·lant, pro·pel·lent** s Treibstoff *m*; Treibgas *n.* **pro·'pel·ler** s ✈ Propeller *m*, ♨ *a.* Schraube *f.* **pro·'pel·ling** *adj*: ~ **pencil** *Br.* Drehbleistift *m.*

pro·pen·si·ty [prə'pensətɪ] s Hang *m*, Neigung *f* (**for, to** zu): **have a ~ for doing** (*od.* **to do**) **s.th.** dazu neigen, et. zu tun.

prop·er ['prɒpə] *adj* **1.** richtig, passend, geeignet: **in ~ form** in gebührender *od.* angemessener Form; **in the ~ place** am rechten Platz; **in ~ time** rechtzeitig. **2.** echt, wirklich, richtig: ~ **fraction** 🅰 echter Bruch. **3.** anständig, schicklich (*Benehmen etc*). **4.** *oft nachgestellt*: eigentlich. **5.** eigen(tümlich) (**to** *dat*). **6.** ~ **noun** (*od.* **name**) *ling.* Eigenname *m.* **7.** F richtig (*Feigling etc*), anständig, gehörig (*Tracht Prügel etc*). '**prop·er·ly** *adv* richtig (*etc,* → **proper**): ~ **speaking** eigentlich, genau-, strenggenommen.

prop·er·ty ['prɒpətɪ] s **1.** Eigentum *n*, Besitz *m*: **be s.o.'s ~** j-m gehören; **intellectual ~** geistiges Eigentum; **lost ~** Fundsachen *pl*; **lost ~ office** *Br.* Fundbüro *n.* **2.** Land-, Grundbesitz *m*; Grundstück *n.* **3.** *phys. etc* Eigenschaft *f.* **4.** *thea. etc* Requisit *n.*

proph·e·cy ['prɒfɪsɪ] s Prophezeiung *f.* **proph·e·sy** ['~saɪ] *v/t* prophezeien.

proph·et ['prɒfɪt] s Prophet *m*: ~ **of doom** Schwarzseher *m.* '**proph·et·ess** s Prophetin *f.* **pro·phet·ic** [prə'fetɪk] *adj* (**~ally**) prophetisch.

pro·phy·lac·tic [,prɒfɪ'læktɪk] I *adj* (**~ally**) **1.** *bsd.* 🩺 prophylaktisch, vorbeugend. II *s* **2.** 🩺 Prophylaktikum *n*, vorbeugendes Mittel. **3.** Präservativ *n.* ,**pro·phy'lax·is** [~ksɪs] s Prophylaxe *f.*

pro·pi·ti·ate [prə'pɪʃɪeɪt] *v/t* versöhnen, besänftigen.

pro·pi·tious [prə'pɪʃəs] *adj* □ günstig, vorteilhaft (**for, to** für).

pro·po·nent [prə'pəʊnənt] s Befürworter(in).

pro·por·tion [prə'pɔːʃn] I s **1.** Verhältnis *n* (*of ... to* von ... zu); *pl* Größenverhältnisse *pl*, Proportionen *pl*: **in ~ to** im Verhältnis zu; **out of all ~** unverhältnismäßig; **be out of all ~ to** in keinem Verhältnis stehen zu; **the painting is out of ~** die Proportionen des Bildes stimmen nicht. **2.** (An)Teil *m*: **in ~ to** anteilig. II *v/t* **3.** (**to**) in das richtige Verhältnis bringen (mit, zu), anpassen (*dat*). **4.** anteilmäßig verteilen. **pro·'por·tion·al** [~ʃənl] I *adj* □ **1.** → **proportionate. 2.** proportional, verhältnismäßig. **3.** anteilmäßig: ~ **representation** *pol.* Verhältniswahl(system *n*) *f.* II *s* **4.** 🅰 Proportionale *f.* **pro·'por·tion·ate** [~ʃnət] *adj* □ (**to**) im richtigen Verhältnis (stehend) (zu), entsprechend (*dat*).

pro·pos·al [prə'pəʊzl] s **1.** Vorschlag *m*: **make s.o. a ~** j-m e-n Vorschlag machen. **2.** (Heirats)Antrag *m*: **she had a ~** sie bekam e-n Heiratsantrag; **make s.o. a ~** j-m e-n Antrag machen. ~ **form** s Antrag(sformular *n*) *m.*

pro·pose [prə'pəʊz] I *v/t* **1.** vorschlagen (**s.th. to s.o.** j-m et; **s.o. for** j-n für *od.* als; *that* daß; *doing* zu tun): ~ **marriage to →** 4. **2.** beabsichtigen, vorhaben (**to do** zu tun). **3.** *Toast* ausbringen (**to** *auf acc*): → **health** 3. II *v/i* **4.** ~ **to** j-m e-n (Heirats)Antrag machen. **prop·o·si·tion** [,prɒpə'zɪʃn] s **1.** Behauptung *f.* **2.** *Vorschlag m*: **make s.o. a ~** j-m e-n Vorschlag machen; j-m ein eindeutiges Angebot machen. **3.** 🅰 (Lehr)Satz *m.* **4.** F *Sache f*: **an easy ~** e-e Kleinigkeit.

pro·pound [prə'paʊnd] *v/t Theorie etc* vertreten; *Problem etc* zur Debatte stellen.

pro·pri·e·tar·y [prə'praɪətərɪ] *adj* **1.** gesetzlich *od.* patentrechtlich geschützt: ~

article Markenartikel *m.* **2.** *fig.* besitzergreifend. **pro'pri·e·tor** *s* Eigentümer *m*, Besitzer *m*. **pro'pri·e·tress** [~trıs] *s* Eigentümerin *f*, Besitzerin *f*.

pro·pri·e·ty [prə'praɪətɪ] *s* **1.** Anstand *m.* **2.** *pl* Anstandsformen *pl*, -regeln *pl*. **3.** Richtigkeit *f*.

pro·pul·sion [prə'pʌlʃn] *s* ⊕ Antrieb *m*.

pro·ro·ga·tion [,prəʊrə'geɪʃn] *s parl.* Vertagung *f*. **pro·rogue** [prə'rəʊg] *v/t u. v/i* (sich) vertagen.

pro·sa·ic [prəʊ'zeɪık] *adj* (**~ally**) prosaisch, nüchtern, sachlich.

pro·scribe [prəʊ'skraɪb] *v/t* **1.** *bsd.* ⚖ verbieten. **2.** *hist.* ächten.

pro·scrip·tion [prəʊ'skrɪpʃn] *s* **1.** *bsd.* ⚖ Verbot *m.* **2.** *hist.* Ächtung *f*.

prose [prəʊz] *s* **1.** Prosa *f.* **2.** *ped. bsd. Br.* Übersetzung *f* in e-e Fremdsprache, Hinübersetzung: **an Italian ~** e-e Übersetzung ins Italienische; **do a ~** e-e Hinübersetzung machen.

pros·e·cute ['prɒsɪkjuːt] **I** *v/t* **1.** ⚖ strafrechtlich verfolgen, (gerichtlich) belangen (**for** wegen). **2.** *Untersuchung etc* durchführen. **II** *v/i* **3.** ⚖ die Anklage vertreten: **Mr X, prosecuting, ...** Mr X, der Vertreter der Anklage, ... **,pros·e'cu·tion** *s.* ⚖ strafrechtliche Verfolgung, Strafverfolgung *f*. **2.** *the ~* ⚖ die Staatsanwaltschaft, die Anklage(behörde) *f*: → **witness** 1. **3.** Durchführung *f*. **'pros·e·cu·tor** *s a.* **public ~** Staatsanwalt *m*, -anwältin *f*.

pros·pect I *s* ['prɒspekt] **1.** (Aus)Sicht *f*, (-)Blick *m* (**of** auf *acc*; **over** über *acc*). **2.** *fig.* Aussicht *f* (**of** auf *acc*): **have s.th. in ~** et. in Aussicht haben. **3.** Interessent *m*, ⚹ möglicher Kunde, potentieller Käufer. **II** *v/t* [prə'spekt] **4.** *Gebiet* untersuchen (**for** nach *Gold etc*). **III** *v/i* [prə'spekt] **5.** suchen, bohren (**for** nach). **pro'spec·tive** *adj* □ voraussichtlich: **~ buyer** Kaufinteressent *m*, potentieller Käufer. **pro'spec·tus** [~təs] *s* Prospekt *m*.

pros·per ['prɒspə] *v/i* gedeihen; ⚹ blühen, florieren. **pros·per·i·ty** [~'sperətɪ] *s* Wohlstand *m*. **pros·per·ous** ['~pərəs] *adj* □ **1.** gedeihend; ⚹ blühend, florierend. **2.** wohlhabend.

pros·tate ['prɒsteɪt] *s a.* **~ gland** *anat.* Prostata *f*, Vorsteherdrüse *f*.

pros·the·sis ['prɒsθɪsɪs] *pl* **-ses** ['~siːz] ⚹ Prothese *f*.

pros·ti·tute ['prɒstɪtjuːt] **I** *s* Prostituierte *f*, Dirne *f*: → **male** I. **II** *v/t*: **~ o.s.** sich prostituieren (*a. fig.*). **,pros·ti'tu·tion** *s* Prostitution *f*.

pros·trate I *adj* ['prɒstreɪt] *adj* **1.** hingestreckt. **2.** *fig.* am Boden liegend; erschöpft: **~ with grief** gramgebeugt. **II** *v/t* [prɒ'streɪt] **3.** niederwerfen. **4.** *fig.* erschöpfen. **pros'tra·tion** *s* **1.** Fußfall *m.* **2.** *fig.* Erschöpfung *f*.

pros·y ['prəʊzɪ] *adj* □ **1.** → **prosaic.** **2.** langweilig; weitschweifig.

pro·tag·o·nist [prəʊ'tægənɪst] *s* **1.** *thea. etc* Hauptfigur *f*, Held(in). **2.** *fig.* Vorkämpfer(in).

pro·tect [prə'tekt] *v/t* (be)schützen (**from** vor *dat*; **against** gegen), *Interessen etc* wahren: **pro'tec·tion** *s* **1.** Schutz *m.* **2.** *a.* **~ money** Schutzgeld *n*. **pro'tec·tion·ism** [~ʃənɪzəm] *s* ⚹ Protektionismus *m*. **pro'tec·tive** *adj* □ **1.** Schutz...: **~ clothing** Schutzkleidung *f*; **~ custody** ⚖ Schutzhaft: **take into ~ custody** in Schutzhaft nehmen; **~ duty** (*od.* **tariff**) ⚹ Schutzzoll *m.* **2.** fürsorglich (**toward**[**s**] gegenüber). **pro'tec·tor** *s* **1.** Beschützer *m.* **2.** Schutz *m*, (*Knieetc*)Schützer *m*, (-)Schoner *m*. **pro'tec·to·rate** [~rət] *s pol.* Protektorat *n*.

pro·test I *s* ['prəʊtest] **1.** Protest *m*: **in** (*od.* **as a**) **~** aus Protest (**against** gegen); **under ~** unter Protest; **without ~** ohne Protest, widerspruchslos; **make a ~** Protest einlegen *od.* erheben (**to** bei); **~ march** Protestmarsch *m*. **II** *v/i* [prə'test] **2.** protestieren (**against, about** gegen; **to** bei). **III** *v/t* [prə'test] **3.** *Am.* protestieren gegen. **4.** beteuern.

Prot·es·tant I *s* Protestant (-in). **II** *adj* protestantisch, evangelisch. **'Prot·es·tant·ism** *s* Protestantismus *m*.

prot·es·ta·tion [,prɒte'steɪʃn] *s* **1.** Beteuerung *f*: **~s** *pl* **of innocence** Unschuldsbeteuerungen *pl*. **2.** Protest *m* (**against** gegen).

pro·to·col ['prəʊtəkɒl] *s* Protokoll *n*: **~ demands that** das Protokoll verlangt, daß.

pro·ton ['prəʊtɒn] *s phys.* Proton *n*.

pro·to·plasm ['prəʊtəʊplæzəm] *s biol.* Protoplasma *n*.

pro·to·type ['prəʊtəʊtaɪp] *s* Prototyp *m*.

pro·tract [prəˈtrækt] v/t in die Länge ziehen, hinausziehen. **proˈtract·ed** adj länger, langwierig. **proˈtrac·tion** s Hinausziehen n. **proˈtrac·tor** s ⚙ Winkelmesser m.

pro·trude [prəˈtruːd] v/i herausragen, vorstehen (**from** aus). **proˈtrud·ing** adj vorstehend (a. Zähne etc), vorspringend (Kinn). **proˈtru·sion** [-ʒn] s **1.** Herausragen n, Vorstehen n. **2.** Vorsprung m, vorstehender Teil.

pro·tu·ber·ance [prəˈtjuːbərəns] s Vorsprung m; Schwellung f. **proˈtu·ber·ant** adj □ vorstehend, -tretend.

proud [praʊd] **I** adj □ **1.** allg. stolz (**of** auf acc): **be too ~ to do s.th.** zu stolz sein, um et. zu tun. **2.** hochmütig. **II** adv **3. do s.o. ~** j-n fürstlich bewirten.

prov·a·ble [ˈpruːvəbl] adj □ be-, nachweisbar. **prove** [pruːv] (a. irr) **I** v/t be-, nachweisen; unter Beweis stellen: **~ o.s.** (**to be**) → **II. II** v/i: **~** (**to be**) sich erweisen od. herausstellen als. **prov·en** [ˈvn] **I** pp von **prove. II** adj bewährt.

prov·e·nance [ˈprɒvənəns] s Herkunft f.

prov·erb [ˈprɒvɜːb] s Sprichwort n. **prover·bi·al** [prəˈvɜːbjəl] adj □ sprichwörtlich (a. fig.).

pro·vide [prəˈvaɪd] **I** v/t **1.** versehen, -sorgen, beliefern (**with** mit). **2.** zur Verfügung stellen, bereitstellen (**for s.o.** j-m). **3.** vorsehen, -schreiben (**that** daß) (Gesetz etc). **II** v/i **4. ~ against** a) Vorkehrungen od. Vorsorge treffen gegen, b) verbieten (Gesetz etc); **~ for** a) sorgen für: **she has two children to ~ for** sie hat zwei Kinder zu versorgen, b) vorsorgen für, c) et. vorsehen (Gesetz etc). **proˈvid·ed** cj a. **~ that** vorausgesetzt(, daß).

prov·i·dence [ˈprɒvɪdəns] s Vorsehung f: **→ tempt 2.** **ˈprov·i·dent** adj □ vorausblickend, vorsorglich. **prov·i·den·tial** [ˌvɪˈdenʃl] adj glücklich (Geschick etc). **ˌprov·iˈden·tial·ly** [ˌʃəlɪ] adv glücklicherweise.

pro·vid·er [prəˈvaɪdə] s Ernährer(in).

prov·ince [ˈprɒvɪns] s **1.** Provinz f (Verwaltungseinheit). **2. the ~s** pl die Provinz (Ggs. Stadt). **3.** fig. (Aufgaben-, Wissens)Bereich m, (-)Gebiet n: **this is outside** (od. **not within**) **my ~** dafür bin ich nicht zuständig.

pro·vin·cial [prəˈvɪnʃl] **I** adj □ **1.** Provinz... **2.** contp. provinziell, provinzlerisch. **II** s **3.** Provinzbewohner(in). **4.** contp. Provinzler(in).

pro·vi·sion [prəˈvɪʒn] **I** s **1.** Vorkehrung f: **make ~s** Vorkehrungen od. Vorsorge treffen (**against** gegen; **for** für). **2.** Bestimmung f, Vorschrift f: **with the ~ that** unter der Bedingung, daß. **3.** Bereitstellung f. **4.** pl Proviant m, Verpflegung f. **II** v/t **5.** verproviantieren (**for** für). **pro·vi·sion·al** [ˌʒənl] adj □ provisorisch, vorläufig.

pro·vi·so [prəˈvaɪzəʊ] pl **-sos** s Vorbehalt m, Bedingung f: **with the ~ that** unter der Bedingung, daß.

prov·o·ca·tion [ˌprɒvəˈkeɪʃn] s Provokation f: **at the slightest ~** beim geringsten Anlaß. **pro·voc·a·tive** [prəˈvɒkətɪv] adj □ provozierend, (sexuell a.) aufreizend.

pro·voke [prəˈvəʊk] v/t j-n, et. provozieren, j-n, Tier reizen: **~ s.o. into doing** (od. **to do**) **s.th.** j-n so provozieren, daß er et. tut. **proˈvok·ing** → **provocative**.

prov·ost [ˈprɒvəst] s schott. Bürgermeister(in).

prowl [praʊl] **I** v/i a. **~ about** (od. **around**) herumschleichen, -streifen. **II** v/t durchstreifen. **III** s Herumstreifen n: **be on the ~ → I**; **~ car** Am. (Funk)Streifenwagen m. **ˈprowl·er** s Herumtreiber(in).

prox·im·i·ty [prɒkˈsɪmətɪ] s Nähe f: **in the ~ of** in der Nähe (od. gen).

prox·y [ˈprɒksɪ] s **1.** (Handlungs)Vollmacht f. **2.** (Stell)Vertreter(in), Bevollmächtigte m, f: **by ~** durch e-n Bevollmächtigten.

prude [pruːd] s prüder Mensch: **be a ~** prüde sein.

pru·dence [ˈpruːdns] s **1.** Klugheit f, Vernunft f. **2.** Umsicht f, Besonnenheit f. **ˈpru·dent** adj □ **1.** klug, vernünftig. **2.** umsichtig, besonnen.

prud·er·y [ˈpruːdərɪ] s Prüderie f. **ˈprud·ish** adj □ prüde.

prune¹ [pruːn] s Backpflaume f.

prune² [pruːn] v/t **1.** a. **~ back** Hecke etc (be)schneiden. **2.** a. **~ away** Äste etc wegschneiden. **3.** a. **~ down** fig. Text etc zs.-streichen.

pru·ri·ence [ˈprʊərɪəns] s Lüsternheit f. **ˈpru·ri·ent** adj □ lüstern.

prus·sic ac·id [ˈprʌsɪk] s 🜊 Blausäure f.

pry¹ [praɪ] *bsd. Am.* → **prize²**.

pry² [~] *v/i* neugierig sein: ~ *into* s-e Nase stecken in (*acc.*). '**pry·ing** *adj* □ neugierig.

psalm [sɑːm] *s* Psalm *m*.

pseu·do·nym ['sjuːdənɪm] *s* Pseudonym *n*: *under the* ~ *of XY* unter dem Pseudonym XY.

psych [saɪk] *v/t* F **1.** ~ *out j-n, et.* durchschauen; *j-n* psychologisch fertigmachen. **2.** ~ *up* auf-, hochputschen.

psy·che ['saɪkɪ] *s* Psyche *f*, Seele *f*.

psy·chi·at·ric [ˌsaɪkɪˈætrɪk] *adj* (~*ally*) psychiatrisch (*Behandlung etc*); psychisch (*Störung etc*). **psy·chi·a·trist** [~ˈkaɪətrɪst] *s* Psychiater(in). **psy'chi·a·try** *s* Psychiatrie *f*.

psy·chic ['saɪkɪk] **I** *adj* (~*ally*) **1.** psychisch, seelisch. **2.** übersinnlich. **3.** ~ *research* Parapsychologie *f*. **4.** medial (begabt *od.* veranlagt). **II** *s* **5.** medial veranlagte Person, Medium *n*. '**psy·chi·cal** → *psychic* I.

psy·cho·a·nal·y·sis [ˌsaɪkəʊəˈnæləsɪs] *s* Psychoanalyse *f*. **psy·cho·an·a·lyst** [~ˈænəlɪst] *s* Psychoanalytiker(in).

psy·cho·log·i·cal [ˌsaɪkəˈlɒdʒɪkl] *adj* □ psychologisch: ~ *moment* psychologisch richtiger Augenblick; ~ *terror* Psychoterror *m*; ~ *warfare* psychologische Kriegführung. **psy·chol·o·gist** [~ˈkɒlədʒɪst] *s* Psychologe *m*, Psychologin *f*. **psy'chol·o·gy** *s* **1.** Psychologie *f*. **2.** psychologisches Geschick *od.* Gespür.

psy·cho·path ['saɪkəʊpæθ] *s* Psychopath(in). ,**psy·cho'path·ic** *adj* (~*ally*) psychopathisch.

psy·cho·sis [saɪˈkəʊsɪs] *pl* **-ses** [~siːz] *s* ✽ Psychose *f*.

psy·cho·so·mat·ic [ˌsaɪkəʊsəʊˈmætɪk] *adj* (~*ally*) psychosomatisch.

psy·cho·ther·a·pist [ˌsaɪkəʊˈθerəpɪst] *s* Psychotherapeut(in). ,**psy·cho'ther·a·py** *s* Psychotherapie *f*.

pub [pʌb] *s bsd. Br.* Pub *n*, Kneipe *f*. ~ **crawl** *s bsd. Br.* F Kneipenbummel *m*: *go on a* ~ e-n Kneipenbummel machen.

pu·ber·ty ['pjuːbətɪ] *s* Pubertät *f*: *be going through* ~ in der Pubertät sein.

pu·bic ['pjuːbɪk] *adj anat.* Scham...

pub·lic ['pʌblɪk] **I** *adj* □ **1.** öffentlich (*Versammlung etc*). **2.** öffentlich, allgemein bekannt: ~ *figure* Persönlichkeit *f*

des öffentlichen Lebens; *go* ~ sich an die Öffentlichkeit wenden; *make* ~ bekanntmachen, publik machen. **3.** a) öffentlich (*Einrichtung, Sicherheit, Verkehrsmittel etc*): ~ *bar* Br. Ausschank *m*, Schenke *f*; ~ (*limited*) *company* ✝ *Br.* Aktiengesellschaft *f*; ~ *convenience Br.* öffentliche Bedürfnisanstalt; ~ *house bsd. Br.* Gaststätte *f*; ~ *relations pl* Public Relations *pl*, Öffentlichkeitsarbeit *f*; ~ *school Br.* Public School *f*; *Am.* staatliche Schule; ~ *utility* öffentlicher Versorgungsbetrieb; → *nuisance* 1, b) Staats..., staatlich: ~ *holiday* gesetzlicher Feiertag; → *prosecutor*, c) Volks...: ~ *library* Volksbücherei *f*. **II** *s* **4.** Öffentlichkeit *f*: *in* ~ in der Öffentlichkeit, öffentlich. **5.** Publikum *n*, Öffentlichkeit *f*: *exclude the* ~ ✽✝ die Öffentlichkeit ausschließen. ,~**ad'dress sys·tem** *s* Lautsprecheranlage *f*.

pub·li·can ['pʌblɪkən] *s bsd. Br.* (Gast-) Wirt(in).

pub·li·ca·tion [ˌpʌblɪˈkeɪʃn] *s* **1.** Bekanntgabe *f*, -machung *f*. **2.** Publikation *f*, Veröffentlichung *f* (*beide a. Werk*).

pub·li·cist ['pʌblɪsɪst] *s* **1.** Publizist(in). **2.** Werbeagent(in). **pub·lic·i·ty** [~ˈlɪsətɪ] *s* **1.** Publicity *f*, Bekanntheit *f*. **2.** Publicity *f*, Reklame *f*, Werbung *f*: ~ *agent* Werbeagent(in); ~ *campaign* Werbefeldzug *m*; ~ *stunt* Werbegag *m*. **pub·li·cize** ['~saɪz] *v/t* **1.** bekanntmachen, publik machen. **2.** Publicity *od.* Reklame machen für.

pub·lish ['pʌblɪʃ] *v/t* **1.** bekanntgeben, -machen. **2.** publizieren, veröffentlichen, *Leserbrief a.* abdrucken. **3.** *Buch etc* verlegen, herausbringen: ~*ed weekly* erscheint wöchentlich. '**pub·lish·er** *s* **1.** Verleger(in), Herausgeber(in). **2.** *pl* Verlag(shaus *n*) *m*.

puck [pʌk] *s* Eishockey: Puck *m*, Scheibe *f*.

puck·er ['pʌkə] **I** *v/t* **1.** *a.* ~ *up Gesicht, Mund* verziehen, *Stirn* runzeln. **II** *v/i a.* ~ *up* **2.** sich verziehen, sich runzeln. **3.** Falten werfen. **III** *s* **4.** Falte *f*.

pud [pʊd] *Br.* F → *pudding*.

pud·ding ['pʊdɪŋ] *s* a) *Br.* Nachspeise *f*, -tisch *m*, b) (*Reis- etc*)Auflauf *m*, c) Pudding *m* (*im Wasserbad gekochte Mehlspeise*), d) (*Blut*)Wurst *f*.

pud·dle ['pʌdl] *s* Pfütze *f*.

pu·er·ile ['pjʊəraɪl] *adj* □ infantil, kindisch.

puff [pʌf] **I** *s* **1.** *Rauchen:* Zug *m*: **take a ~ at** ziehen an (*dat*). **2.** (*Luft-, Wind-*) Hauch *m*, (-)Stoß *m*: **~ of air. 3.** *gastr.* (*Wind*)Beutel *m*. **4.** F Puste *f*: **out of ~** aus der od. außer Puste. **5.** (*Puder*)Quaste *f*. **6.** F Anpreisung *f*: **give s.th. a ~** et. hochjubeln. **II** *v/t* **7.** *Rauch* blasen (**in s.o.'s face** j-m ins Gesicht): **~ out** Kerze etc ausblasen; *Rauch etc* ausstoßen; *Brust* herausdrücken; *Gefieder* aufplustern; **be ~ed up** (**with pride**) aufgeblasen sein. **III** *v/i* **8.** schnaufen (*a. Lokomotive etc*), keuchen. **9.** *a.* **~ away** paffen (**at** an *e-r Zigarette etc*). **10.** **~ up** (an)schwellen. **puffed** *adj* F aus der *od*. außer Puste.

puff|·paste *s Am.*, **~·pas·try** *s* Blätterteig *m*. **~·sleeve** *s* Puffärmel *m*.

puff·y ['pʌfɪ] *adj* (an)geschwollen, verschwollen.

pug [pʌg] *s zo.* Mops *m*.

pug·na·cious [pʌg'neɪʃəs] *adj* □ kampf(es)lustig; streitsüchtig. **pug·nac·i·ty** [~'næsətɪ] *s* Kampf(es)lust *f*; Streitsucht *f*.

puke [pjuːk] *sl.* **I** *v/i* kotzen. **II** *v/t* auskotzen. **III** *s* Kotze *f*.

pull [pʊl] **I** *s* **1.** Ziehen *n*; Zug *m*, Ruck *m*: **give the rope a** (**good**) **~** (kräftig) am Seil ziehen. **2.** Anziehungskraft *f* (*a. fig.*). **3.** Anstieg *m*, Steigung *f*. **4.** Zug(griff *m*, -leine *f*) *m*. **5.** F Beziehungen *pl* (**with** zu). **II** *v/t* **6.** ziehen: **→ string** 1. **7.** ziehen an (*dat*): **~ s.o.'s hair** j-n an den Haaren ziehen; **~ a muscle** sich e-e Muskelzerrung zuziehen, sich et. zerren; → **face** 2, **leg** 1, *etc.* **8.** reißen: → **piece** 1. **9.** a) *Zahn* ziehen, *Pflanze* ausreißen, b) *Messer, Pistole* ziehen: **~ a gun on s.o.** j-n mit der Pistole bedrohen, c) *bsd. Br.* Bier zapfen. **10.** *fig.* anziehen. **11.** **~ one's punches** (*Boxen*) verhalten schlagen; *fig.* sich zurückhalten; **not to ~ one's punches, ~ no punches** kein Blatt vor den Mund nehmen. **12.** F *Banküberfall etc* machen: **~ a big one** ein großes Ding drehen; **→ job**[1] 6. **III** *v/i* **13.** ziehen (**at, on** an *dat*).

Verbindungen mit Adverbien:

pull|·a·head *v/i* vorbeiziehen (**of** an

dat) (*Auto etc*) (*a. fig.*). **~·a·way** *v/i* **1.** anfahren (*Bus etc*). **2.** sich absetzen (**from** von), (*Sport a.*) sich freimachen. **~·down** *v/t* **1.** *Gebäude* abreißen. **2.** j-n mitnehmen, schwächen. **~·in** **I** *v/t* **1.** *Bauch etc* einziehen. **2.** → **pull** 10. **3.** *bsd. Br.* F j-n einkassieren. **4.** F kassieren: **he's pulling in quite a bit** er verdient ganz schön. **II** *v/i* **5.** einfahren (*Zug*). **6.** anhalten. **~·off** *v/t* **1.** *Schuhe etc* ausziehen; sich *die Kleider* vom Leib reißen. **2.** F et. schaffen, schaukeln. **~·on** *v/t* *Kleid etc* anziehen, (sich) überziehen. **~·out** **I** *v/t* **1.** a) herausziehen (**of** aus): → **chestnut** 1, **stop** 4, b) → **pull** 9a, c) *Tisch* ausziehen. **II** *v/i* **2.** abfahren (*Zug*). **3.** ausscheren (*Fahrzeug*). **4.** *fig.* sich zurückziehen, (*a. Sport*) aussteigen (**of** aus). **~·through** **I** *v/t* **1.** durchziehen. **2.** *fig.* *Kranken, Kandidaten etc* durchbringen. **II** *v/i* **3.** *fig.* durchkommen. **~·to·geth·er** **I** *v/t* **1.** *pull o.s. together* sich zs.-reißen. **2.** *Partei etc* zs.-schweißen. **II** *v/i* **3.** an 'einem Strang ziehen. **~·up** **I** *v/t* **1.** hochziehen. **2.** *Fahrzeug* anhalten. **3.** j-n korrigieren; zurechtweisen (**for** wegen). **4.** einholen. **5.** **~ to** (*od.* **with**) (*Sport*) j-n einholen.

pul·ley ['pʊlɪ] *s* ☼ Flaschenzug *m*.

'pull·in *s Br.* Rasthaus *n*, -stätte *f*. **'~·out** *adj* ausziehbar: → **table** Ausziehtisch *m*. **'~·o·ver** *s* Pullover *m*. **'~·up** *s* Klimmzug *m*: **do a ~** e-n Klimmzug machen.

pul·mo·nar·y ['pʌlmənərɪ] *adj anat.*, 🌸 Lungen...

pulp [pʌlp] **I** *s* **1.** Fruchtfleisch *n*. **2.** Brei *m*, breiige Masse: **beat to a ~** *fig.* j-n zu Brei schlagen. **II** *adj* **3.** Schund...: **~ novel** Schundroman *m*. **III** *v/t* **4.** *Bücher etc* einstampfen.

pul·pit ['pʊlpɪt] *s* Kanzel *f*: **in the ~** auf der Kanzel.

pulp·y ['pʌlpɪ] *adj* □ breiig.

pul·sate [pʌl'seɪt] *v/i* pulsieren, *a. fig.* vibrieren (**with** vor *dat*).

pulse[1] [pʌls] **I** *s* **1.** Puls(schlag) *m*: **feel** (*od.* **take**) **s.o.'s ~** j-m den Puls fühlen. **2.** ⚡, *phys.* Impuls *m*. **II** *v/i* **3.** pulsieren (**through** durch) (*a. fig.*).

pulse[2] [~] *s mst pl* Hülsenfrüchte *pl*.

pul·ver·ize ['pʌlvəraɪz] *v/t* **1.** pulverisieren. **2.** *fig.* F j-n auseinandernehmen.

pu·ma ['pjuːmə] *s zo.* Puma *m*.

pum·ice ['pʌmɪs] *s a.* ~ **stone** Bimsstein *m.*

pum·mel ['pʌml] *v/t pret u. pp* **-meled,** *bsd. Br.* **-melled** eintrommeln auf (*acc*).

pump [pʌmp] **I** *s* **1.** Pumpe *f*; (*Zapf*)Säule. **II** *v/t* **2.** pumpen: ~ **up** aufpumpen; ~ **s.o.'s stomach** ♣ j-m den Magen auspumpen; ~ **money into** *fig.* Geld hineinpumpen in (*acc*). **3.** F j-*n* ausholen (**for** über *acc*). **III** *v/i* **4.** pumpen (*a. Herz*). **5.** herausschießen (**from** aus) (*Blut etc.*). ~ **at·tend·ant** *s* Tankwart *m.*

pump·kin ['pʌmpkɪn] *s* ♣ Kürbis *m.*

pun [pʌn] **I** *s* Wortspiel *n.* **II** *v/i* Wortspiele *od.* ein Wortspiel machen.

Punch[1] [pʌntʃ] *s* Kasper *m*, Kasperle *n*, *m*: **be (as) pleased as** ~ F sich freuen wie ein Schneekönig.

punch[2] [~] **I** *s* **1.** (Faust)Schlag *m*: **give s.o. a** ~ j-m e-n Schlag versetzen; → **pull** 11. **2.** *fig.* Schwung *m.* **II** *v/t* **3.** (mit der Faust) schlagen.

punch[3] [~] ⊙ **I** *s* Locher *m*; Lochzange *f*; Locheisen *n.* **II** *v/t* lochen; *Loch* stanzen (**in** in *acc*): ~**ed card** Lochkarte *f*; ~**ed tape** Lochstreifen *m.*

punch[4] [~] *s* Punsch *m.*

‚Punch-and-'Ju·dy show ['dʒuːdɪ] *s* Kasperletheater *n.*

punch| card *s* Lochkarte *f.* ~ **line** *s* Pointe *f.* '~**·up** *s Br.* F Schlägerei *f.*

punc·til·i·ous [pʌŋk'tɪlɪəs] *adj* □ peinlich genau.

punc·tu·al ['pʌŋktʃʊəl] *adj* □ pünktlich: **be** ~ pünktlich kommen (**for** zu). **punc·tu·al·i·ty** [~'ælətɪ] *s* Pünktlichkeit *f.*

punc·tu·ate ['pʌŋktʃʊeɪt] *v/t* **1.** interpunktieren. **2.** *fig.* (**with**) unterbrechen (durch, mit); durchsetzen (mit). **3.** *fig.* unterstreichen, betonen. **‚punc·tu·'a·tion** *s* **1.** Interpunktion *f*: ~ **mark** Satzzeichen *n.* **2.** *fig.* Unterbrechung *f*; Durchsetzung *f.* **3.** *fig.* Unterstreichung *f*, Betonung *f.*

punc·ture ['pʌŋktʃə] **I** *v/t* **1.** durchstechen, -bohren. **2.** ♣ punktieren. **II** *v/i* **3.** ein Loch bekommen, platzen. **III** *s* **4.** (Ein)Stich *m.* **5.** *mot.* Reifenpanne *f.* **6.** ♣ Punktion *f.*

pun·dit ['pʌndɪt] *s oft humor.* Weise *m, f.*

pun·gen·cy ['pʌndʒənsɪ] *s* Schärfe *f* (a.

fig.). **'pun·gent** *adj* □ scharf (*Geschmack, Geruch*), (*Bemerkung etc a.*) bissig.

pun·ish ['pʌnɪʃ] *v/t* **1.** j-*n* (be)strafen (**for** für, wegen). **2.** *et.* bestrafen. **'pun·ish·a·ble** *adj* □ strafbar: ~ **act** (*od. offence, Am. offense*) strafbare Handlung; **murder is** ~ **by death** auf Mord steht die Todesstrafe. **'pun·ish·ing** *adj* □ vernichtend (*Kritik etc*), mörderisch, zermürbend (*Rennen etc*). **'pun·ish·ment** *s* **1.** Bestrafung *f.* **2.** Strafe *f*: **as a** ~ als *od.* zur Strafe (**for**).

pu·ni·tive ['pjuːnɪtɪv] *adj* □ **1.** Straf... **2.** extrem hoch (*Steuern etc*).

punk [pʌŋk] *s* **1.** Punk *m* (*Bewegung u. Anhänger*). **2.** ♪ Punk *m*; Punker *m.* ~ **rock** *s* ♪ Punkrock *m.* ~ **rock·er** *s* ♪ Punkrocker *m.*

punt [pʌnt] **I** *s* Stechkahn *m.* **II** *v/t u. v/i* staken.

pu·ny ['pjuːnɪ] *adj* □ schwächlich.

pup [pʌp] → **puppy.**

pu·pa ['pjuːpə] *pl* **-pae** ['~piː], **-pas** *s zo.* Puppe *f.*

pu·pil[1] ['pjuːpl] *s* Schüler(in).

pu·pil[2] [~] *s anat.* Pupille *f.*

pup·pet ['pʌpɪt] *s* Puppe *f*: a) Handpuppe *f*, b) Marionette *f* (*a. fig.*): ~ **government** *fig.* Marionettenregierung *f*; ~ **show** Marionettentheater *n*, Puppenspiel *n.* **pup·pet·eer** [~'tɪə] *s* Puppenspieler(in).

pup·py ['pʌpɪ] *s* Welpe *m*, junger Hund. ~ **fat** *s Br.* F Babyspeck *m.* ~ **love** *s* F jugendliche Schwärmerei.

pur·chas·a·ble ['pɜːtʃəsəbl] *adj* käuflich. **'pur·chase I** *v/t* **1.** kaufen, erstehen. **2.** *fig.* erkaufen (**at the expense of** *an*). **II** *s* **3.** Kauf *m.* **4.** *pl* Einkäufe *pl*: **make** ~**s** Einkäufe machen. **'pur·chas·er** *s* Käufer(in). **'pur·chas·ing** *adj*: ~ **power** ✝ Kaufkraft *f.*

pure [pjʊə] *adj* □ **1.** rein: a) pur, unvermischt, b) sauber, c) anstandfrei, fehlerlos, d) pur, völlig (*Unsinn etc*): **by** ~ **accident** rein zufällig. **2.** ehrlich (*Absicht*). '~**·bred** *adj* reinrassig, rasserein. **II** *s* reinrassiges Tier.

pu·ree ['pjʊəreɪ] *s* Püree *n.* **II** *v/t* pürieren.

pur·ga·tive ['pɜːgətɪv] ♣ **I** *adj* □ abführend. **II** *s* Abführmittel *n.*

pur·ga·to·ry ['pɜːgətərɪ] *s eccl.* Fegefeuer

n: *it is ~ having to do s.th.* es ist die Hölle, et. tun zu müssen.

purge [pɜ:dʒ] **I** *v/t* Partei etc säubern (*of* von). **II** *s pol.* Säuberung(saktion) *f*.

pu·ri·fi·ca·tion [ˌpjʊərɪfɪˈkeɪʃn] *s* Reinigung *f*. **pu·ri·fi·er** [ˈ‿faɪə] *s* ⊙ Reiniger *m*. **pu·ri·fy** [ˈ‿faɪ] *v/t* reinigen.

pur·ism [ˈpjʊərɪzəm] *s* Purismus *m*. **'pur·ist** *s* Purist(in).

Pu·ri·tan [ˈpjʊərɪtən] *hist., fig. mst* ♀ **I** *s* Puritaner(in). **II** *adj* puritanisch. **pu·ri·tan·i·cal** [ˌ‿ˈtænɪkl] *adj* □ *fig.* puritanisch. **Pu·ri·tan·ism** [ˈ‿tənɪzəm] *s hist., fig. mst* ♀ Puritanismus *m*.

pu·ri·ty [ˈpjʊərɪtɪ] *s* **1.** Reinheit *f*. **2.** Ehrlichkeit *f*.

pur·loin [pɜːˈlɔɪn] *v/t oft humor.* entwenden.

pur·ple [ˈpɜːpl] *adj* purpurn, pupurrot: *his face turned ~* sein Gesicht verfärbte sich blau; *~ heart bsd. Br.* F Amphetamintablette *f*; ♀ *Heart* ⚔ *Am.* Verwundetenabzeichen *n*.

pur·port [ˈpɜːpət] **I** *s* Tenor *m*. **II** *v/t*: *~ to be s.th.* vorgeben, et. zu sein; et. sein sollen.

pur·pose [ˈpɜːpəs] **I** *s* **1.** Zweck *m*, Ziel *n*; Absicht *f*, Vorsatz *m*: *for all practical ~s* praktisch; *on ~* absichtlich; mit der Absicht (*to do* zu tun); *answer (od. serve) the same ~* denselben Zweck erfüllen; *put to a good ~* gut anwenden *od.* nützen. **2.** *to no ~* vergeblich, umsonst. **3.** Entschlossenheit *f*, Zielstrebigkeit *f*. **II** *v/t* **4.** beabsichtigen, vorhaben (*doing, to do* zu tun). **pur·pose·ful** [ˈ‿fʊl] *adj* □ entschlossen, zielstrebig. **'pur·pose·less** *adj* □ **1.** zwecklos. **2.** ziel-, planlos. **'pur·pose·ly** *adv* absichtlich.

purr [pɜː] **I** *v/i* schnurren (*Katze*); surren (*Motor etc*). **II** *s* Schnurren *n*; Surren *n*.

purse [pɜːs] **I** *s* **1.** a) Geldbeutel *m*, Portemonnaie *n*: *be beyond s.o.'s ~* fig. j-s Finanzen übersteigen; *hold the ~ strings* fig. die Finanzen verwalten, b) *Am.* Handtasche *f*. **2.** *Sport:* Siegprämie *f*; (*Boxen*) Börse *f*. **II** *v/t* **3.** *a. ~ up Lippen* schürzen. **'purs·er** *s* **1.** ⊕ Proviant- *od.* Zahlmeister *m*. **2.** ✈ Purser *m* (*leitender Steward*).

pur·su·ance [pəˈsjʊəns] *s*: *in (the) ~ of one's duty* in Ausübung s-r Pflicht.

pur·sue [pəˈsjuː] *v/t* **1.** verfolgen: *be ~d by bad luck* vom Pech verfolgt werden. **2.** *fig. s-m Studium etc* nachgehen; *Absicht, Politik etc* verfolgen; *Angelegenheit etc* weiterführen. **pur'su·er** *s* Verfolger(in). **pur'suit** [pəˈsjuːt] *s* **1.** Verfolgung *f*: *be in ~ of s.o.* j-n verfolgen. **2.** *fig.* Verfolgung *f*; Weiterführung *f*: *in (the) ~ of* im *od.* in Verfolg (*gen*). **3.** Beschäftigung *f*.

pu·ru·lent [ˈpjʊərʊlənt] *adj* □ eiternd, eit(e)rig.

pus [pʌs] *s* ⚕ Eiter *m*.

push [pʊʃ] **I** *s* **1.** Stoß *m*: *give s.o. a ~* j-m e-n Stoß versetzen; *give s.o. the ~ Br.* F j-n rausschmeißen (*entlassen*); *get the ~ Br.* F fliegen; *at a ~* F im Notfall, notfalls; *if (od. when) it comes to the ~* F wenn es darauf ankommt. **2.** (*Werbe*)Kampagne *f*. **3.** F Draufgängertum *n*. **II** *v/t* **4.** stoßen, schubsen; schieben; *Taste etc* drücken: *~ one's way* sich drängen (*through* durch); *he's ~ing 70* er geht auf die 70 zu. **5.** *fig.* j-n drängen (*to do* zu tun): *be ~ed (for time)* F es eilig haben; in Zeitnot sein; *be ~ed for money* F knapp bei Kasse sein. **6.** *fig.* Reklame machen für, die Trommel rühren für. **7.** F *Heroin etc* pushen. **III** *v/i* **8.** stoßen, schubsen; schieben, drücken: *~ past s.o.* sich an j-m vorbeidrängen. **9.** *~ for fig.* drängen auf (*acc*).

Verbindungen mit Adverbien:

push| **a·bout** → *push around.* **~ a·head** *v/i*: *~ with Plan etc* vorantreiben. **~ a·long** *v/i* F sich auf die Socken machen. **~ a·round** *v/t* herumschubsen (*a. fig.* F). **~ for·ward** *v/t*: *push o.s. forward fig.* sich in den Vordergrund drängen *od.* schieben. **II** *v/i* → *push ahead.* **~ in** *v/i* F sich vordrängeln. **~ off** *v/i* **1.** sich abstoßen (*from* von). **2.** *mst imp* abhauen, Leine ziehen. **~ on** → *push ahead.* **~ out** *v/t fig.* j-n hinausdrängen. **~ up** *v/t* **1.** → *daisy.* **2.** *Preise etc* hochtreiben.

'push·bike *s Br.* F Fahrrad *n*. **~ but·ton** *s* Druckknopf *m*, -taste *f*. **'~·but·ton** *adj* Druckknopf...: *~ telephone* Tastentelefon *n*. **'~·cart** *s* **1.** (Hand)Karren *m*. **2.** *Am.* Einkaufswagen *m*. **'~·chair** *s Br.* Sportwagen *m* (*für Kinder*).

push·er [ˈpʊʃə] *s* F **1.** Draufgänger *m*. **2.**

Pusher *m* (*Rauschgifthändler*). **'push-ing** → **pushy**.

'push|o-ver *s* F **1.** *fig.* Kinderspiel *n.* **2.** **be a ~ for** nicht widerstehen können (*dat*); immer wieder hereinfallen auf (*acc*). **'~-up** *s Am.* Liegestütz *m:* **do a ~** e-n Liegestütz machen.

push-y ['pʊʃi] *adj* □ draufgängerisch.

pu-sil-lan-i-mous [ˌpjuːsɪ'lænɪməs] *adj* □ kleinmütig, verzagt.

puss [pʊs] *s* F Mieze *f.*

puss-y ['pʊsɪ] *s Kindersprache:* Miezekatze *f.* **'~-cat** → **pussy.** **'~-foot** *v/i a.* **~ about** (*od.* **around**) F um den (heißen) Brei herumreden; sich nicht festlegen wollen.

pus-tule ['pʌstjuːl] *s 🐝* Pustel *f.*

put [pʊt] **I** *adj* **1. stay ~** sich nicht (vom Fleck) rühren. **II** *v/t* (*irr*) **1.** legen, setzen, stellen, tun: **~ s.th. before s.o.** *fig.* j-m et. vorlegen; **~ a tax on s.th.** et. besteuern. **2.** *Hand etc, fig.* Geld, Zeit stecken (**in**[**to**]) (in *acc*). **3.** j-n in e-e unangenehme Lage etc, et. auf den Markt, in Ordnung etc bringen. **5.** *et. in Kraft, in Umlauf etc* setzen. **6.** unterwerfen, -ziehen (**to** *dat*). **7.** übersetzen (**into French** ins Französische). **8.** *et.* ausdrücken, in Worte fassen: → **mild.** **9.** schätzen (**at** auf *acc*). **10.** Geld setzen (**on** auf *acc*). **11.** Schuld geben (**on** *dat*). **III** *v/i* (*irr*) **12. ~ to sea 🐟** in See stechen. **13. ~ upon s.o.** *bsd. Br.* j-m Ungelegenheiten bereiten.

Verbindungen mit Adverbien:

put| a-bout I *v/t* Gerücht verbreiten, in Umlauf setzen. **II** *v/i* 🐟 den Kurs ändern. **~ a-cross** *v/t et.* verständlich machen (**to** *dat*). **~ a-head** *v/t* Sport: in Führung bringen. **~ a-side** *v/t* **1.** beiseite legen. **2.** *Ware* zurücklegen. **3.** *fig.* beiseite schieben. **4.** → **put away** 3. **~ a-way** *v/t* **1.** weglegen, -stecken, -tun. **2.** auf-, wegräumen. **3.** → **put by.** **4.** F *Speisen* verdrücken, *Getränke* schlucken. **~ back** *v/t* **1.** zurücklegen, -stellen, -tun. **2.** *Uhr* zurückstellen (**by** um): → **clock 1. 3.** *fig.* verschieben (**two days** um zwei Tage; **to** auf *acc*). **~ by** *v/t* Geld zurücklegen, auf die hohe Kante legen. **~ down** I *v/t* **1.** hinlegen, -stellen, -setzen. **2.** *Aufstand etc* niederwerfen. **3.** *Fahrgast* absetzen. **4.** *et.* aufschreiben: **put s.o.('s name) down for**

j-n anmelden *od.* eintragen für. **5.** *Betrag* anzahlen. **6.** *Flugzeug* landen. **7.** j-n halten (**as** für). **8.** *et.* zuschreiben (**to** *dat*). **II** *v/i* ✈ landen. **~ for-ward** *v/t* **1.** *Plan etc* vorlegen: **put s.o.('s name) forward as** j-n vorschlagen als. **2.** *Uhr* vorstellen (**by** um). **3.** *fig.* vorverlegen (**two days** um zwei Tage; **to** auf *acc*). **~ in I** *v/t* **1.** herein-, hineinlegen, -stecken, -stellen, *Kassette etc* einlegen. **2.** *Gesuch etc* einreichen, *Forderung etc a.* geltend machen. **3.** *Arbeit, Zeit* verbringen (**with** mit). **4.** *Bemerkung* einwerfen; *ein gutes Wort* einlegen (**for** für). **II** *v/i* **5.** 🐟 einlaufen (**at** in *acc*): **~ at** a. anlaufen (*acc*). **6.** sich bewerben (**for** um). **~ off** *v/t* **1.** *et.* verschieben (**till, until** auf *acc*); j-m absagen. **2.** j-n hinhalten (**with** mit). **3.** aus dem Konzept bringen; j-m den Appetit *od.* die Lust *od.* die Laune verderben. **4.** → **put down.** **~ on** *v/t* **1.** *Mantel etc* anziehen, *Hut, Brille* aufsetzen; *Rouge etc* auflegen: → **lipstick. 2.** *Licht, Radio etc* anmachen, einschalten. **3.** *einige Pfund* zunehmen: → **weight 1. 4.** *Sonderzug etc* einsetzen. **5.** *thea. Stück etc* herausbringen. **6.** *Bremse* anziehen. **7.** *Essen, Topf etc* aufsetzen. **8.** *Schallplatte etc* auflegen, *Kassette etc* einlegen. **9.** vortäuschen, heucheln: **put it on** so tun als ob. **10.** F j-n auf den Arm nehmen. **~ out I** *v/t* **1.** heraus-, hinauslegen, -stellen. **2.** *Hand etc* ausstrecken: → **feeler, tongue 1. 3.** *Feuer* löschen; *Licht, Radio, Zigarette etc* ausmachen, abschalten. **4.** veröffentlichen, herausgeben; (*Rundfunk, TV*) bringen, senden. **5.** aus der Fassung bringen; verstimmen, -ärgern; j-m Ungelegenheiten bereiten. **6.** 🐝 sich *den Arm etc* ver- *od.* ausrenken. **II** *v/i* **7.** 🐟 auslaufen: **~ to sea** in See stechen. **~ o-ver** → **put across. ~ through** *v/t* **1.** *teleph.* j-n verbinden (**to** mit). **2.** durch-, ausführen. **~ to-geth-er** *v/t* **1.** zs.-setzen, *Gerät etc* zs.-bauen; *Mannschaft, Rede etc* zs.-stellen. **2. he is cleverer than all his friends ~** er ist cleverer als alle s-e Freunde zusammen. **~ up I** *v/t* **1.** herauf-, hinauflegen, -stellen. **2.** *Hand (hoch)heben etc.* **3.** *Bild etc* aufhängen; *Plakat, Bekanntmachung etc* anschlagen. **4.** *Schirm* aufspannen. **5.** *Zelt etc* aufstellen, *Gebäude* errich-

ten. **6.** *j-n* unterbringen. **7.** *Widerstand* leisten: → **fight** 1. **8.** *Preis etc* erhöhen. **9.** *j-n* anstiften (**to** zu). **II** *v/i* **10.** absteigen (**at** in *dat*). **11.** ~ **with** sich abfinden mit; sich gefallen lassen.
pu·ta·tive ['pju:tətɪv] *adj* □ mutmaßlich.
'**put**|**·off** *s bsd. Am.* F (faule) Ausrede. '**~·on** *s Am.* F Bluff *m*, Schwindel *m*.
pu·tre·fy ['pju:trɪfaɪ] *v/i* (ver)faulen, verwesen.
pu·trid ['pju:trɪd] *adj* □ **1.** verfault, -west; (*Geruch*) faulig. **2.** F miserabel, saumäßig.
putsch [pʊtʃ] *s pol.* Putsch *m*.
putt [pʌt] *v/t u. v/i Golf:* putten.
putt·er ['pʌtə] *Am.* → **potter**[1].
put·ty ['pʌtɪ] **I** *s* **1.** Kitt *m:* **he was (like)** ~ **in her hands** *fig.* er war Wachs in ihren Händen. **II** *v/t* kitten.
'**put-up job** *s* F abgekartetes Spiel.
puz·zle ['pʌzl] **I** *s* **1.** Rätsel *n* (*a. fig.*); Geduld(s)spiel *n:* **it is a** ~ **to me** es ist mir ein Rätsel *od.* rätselhaft; → **jigsaw**

(**puzzle**). **II** *v/t* **2.** vor ein Rätsel stellen; verdutzen, -blüffen: **be** ~**d** vor e-m Rätsel stehen. **3.** ~ **out** *et.* ausknobeln, herausbringen. **III** *v/i* **4.** sich den Kopf zerbrechen (**about, over** über *dat*).
'**puz·zler** *s* F harte Nuß.
pyg·my ['pɪgmɪ] **I** *s* **1.** ♀ Pygmäe *m*, Pygmäin *f*. **2.** Zwerg(in) (*a. fig. contp.*). **II** *adj* **3.** *bsd. zo.* Zwerg...
py·ja·mas [pə'dʒɑːməz] *s pl, a. pair of* ~ Schlafanzug *m*, Pyjama *m*.
py·lon ['paɪlən] *s* Hochspannungsmast *m*.
pyr·a·mid ['pɪrəmɪd] *s* Pyramide *f*.
pyre ['paɪə] *s* Scheiterhaufen *m*.
py·ro·ma·ni·a [ˌpaɪrəʊ'meɪnɪə] *s* Pyromanie *f*. ,**py·ro'ma·ni·ac** [~æk] *s* Pyromane *m*, -manin *f*.
Pyr·rhic vic·to·ry ['pɪrɪk] *s* Pyrrhussieg *m*.
py·thon ['paɪθn] *s zo.* Python(schlange) *f*.
pyx [pɪks] *s eccl.* Pyxis *f*, Hostienbehälter *m*.

Q

quack[1] [kwæk] **I** *v/i* quaken (*Ente*). **II** *s* Quaken *n*.
quack[2] [~] *s a.* ~ **doctor** Quacksalber *m*, Kurpfuscher *m*. **quack·er·y** ['~ərɪ] *s* Quacksalberei *f*, Kurpfuscherei *f*.
quad [kwɒd] *s* F Vierling *m*.
quad·ran·gle ['kwɒdræŋgl] *s* Viereck *n*. **quad'ran·gu·lar** [~gjʊlə] *adj* □ viereckig.
quad·ra·phon·ic [ˌkwɒdrə'fɒnɪk] *adj* (~**ally**) ♪, *phys.* quadrophon(isch).
quad·ri·lat·er·al [ˌkwɒdrɪ'lætərəl] **I** *adj* vierseitig. **II** *s* Viereck *n*.
quad·ro·phon·ic → **quadraphonic**.
quad·ru·ped ['kwɒdrʊped] *s zo.* Vierfüß(l)er *m*.
quad·ru·ple ['kwɒdrʊpl] **I** *adj* □ vierfach. **II** *v/t u. v/i* (sich) vervierfachen.
quad·ru·plet ['~plɪt] *s* Vierling *m*.
quag·mire ['kwæg maɪə] *s* Morast *m*, Sumpf *m*.

quail[1] [kweɪl] *pl* **quails**, *bsd. coll.* **quail** *s orn.* Wachtel *f*.
quail[2] [~] *v/i* verzagen.
quaint [kweɪnt] *adj* □ idyllisch, malerisch.
quake [kweɪk] **I** *v/i* zittern, beben (**with** vor *dat*; **at** bei *e-m Gedanken*). **II** *s* F Erdbeben *n*.
Quak·er ['kweɪkə] *s eccl.* Quäker(in).
qual·i·fi·ca·tion [ˌkwɒlɪfɪ'keɪʃn] *s* **1.** Qualifikation *f*, Befähigung *f*, Eignung *f* (**for** für, zu). **2.** Vorbedingung *f*, Voraussetzung *f* (**of, for** für). **3.** Abschluß(zeugnis *n*) *m*. **4.** Einschränkung *f*, Vorbehalt *m*. **5.** *ling.* nähere Bestimmung. **qual·i·fied** ['~faɪd] *adj* **1.** qualifiziert, geeignet, befähigt (**for** für). **2.** berechtigt: ~ **to vote** wahlberechtigt. **3.** bedingt, eingeschränkt. **qual·i·fy** ['~faɪ] **I** *v/t* **1.** qualifizieren, befähigen (**for** für, zu). **2.** berechtigen (**to do** zu tun). **3.** *ling.* näher bestimmen. **II** *v/i* **4.** sich

qualifizieren *od.* eignen, die Bedingungen erfüllen (**for** für; **as** als). **5.** *Sport:* sich qualifizieren (**for** für). **6.** s-e Ausbildung abschließen (**as** als).

qual·i·ta·tive [ˈkwɒlɪtətɪv] *adj* □ qualitativ. **qual·i·ty** [ˈ⁓ətɪ] *s* **1.** Qualität *f*, ✝ *a.* Güteklasse *f:* ⁓ *of life* Lebensqualität; ⁓ *of sound TV etc* Tonqualität; ⁓ *goods pl* Qualitätswaren *pl;* ⁓ *newspaper* seriöse Zeitung. **2.** Eigenschaft *f:* → *leadership* 2.

qualms [kwɑːmz] *s pl* Bedenken *pl,* Skrupel *pl:* **have no** ⁓ **about doing s.th.** keine Bedenken haben, et. zu tun.

quan·da·ry [ˈkwɒndərɪ] *s* Dilemma *n,* Verlegenheit *f:* **be in a** ⁓ **about what to do** nicht wissen, was man tun soll.

quan·ta [ˈkwɒntə] *pl von* **quantum.**

quan·ti·ta·tive [ˈkwɒntɪtətɪv] *adj* □ quantitativ. **quan·ti·ty** [ˈ⁓tətɪ] *s* **1.** Quantität *f;* Menge *f:* **in small quantities** in kleinen Mengen; ⁓ *discount (od. allowance)* ✝ Mengenrabatt *m.* **2.** ℞ Größe *f:* → *unknown.*

quan·tum [ˈkwɒntəm] *phys.* **I** *pl* **-ta** [ˈ⁓tə] *s* Quant *n.* **II** *adj* Quanten...

quar·an·tine [ˈkwɒrəntiːn] **I** *s* Quarantäne *f:* **put in** ⁓ → **II. II** *v/t* unter Quarantäne stellen.

quar·rel [ˈkwɒrəl] **I** *s* **1.** Streit *m,* Auseinandersetzung *f* (**with** mit). **2.** *have no* ⁓ *with* nichts auszusetzen haben an (*dat*). **II** *v/i pret u. pp* **-reled,** *bsd. Br.* **-relled 3.** (sich) streiten (**with** mit; *about, over* über *acc*). **4.** ⁓ *with* et. auszusetzen haben an (*dat*). **quar·rel·some** [ˈ⁓səm] *adj* □ streitsüchtig.

quar·ry¹ [ˈkwɒrɪ] *s* Steinbruch *m.*

quar·ry² [⁓] *s hunt.* Beute *f, a. fig.* Opfer *n.*

quart [kwɔːt] *s* Quart *n* (*Hohlmaß*): **you can't put a** ⁓ **into a pint pot** F das geht einfach nicht.

quar·ter [ˈkwɔːtə] **I** *s* **1.** Viertel *n:* **a** ⁓ *of an hour* e-e Viertelstunde. **2.** *it's (a)* ⁓ *to (Am. a. of) six* es ist Viertel vor sechs *od.* drei Viertel sechs; *at (a)* ⁓ *past (Am. a. after) six* um Viertel nach sechs *od.* Viertel sieben. **3.** Quartal *n,* Vierteljahr *n:* **by the** ⁓ vierteljährlich. **4.** *Am.* Vierteldollar *m.* **5.** (Himmels)Richtung *f;* Gegend *f,* Teil *m* (*e-s Landes etc*): **from all** ⁓**s** von überall(her). **6.** (Stadt)Viertel *n.* **7.** *pl* Quartier *n,* Unterkunft *f*

(*beide a.* ✕). **8.** *fig.* Seite *f,* Stelle *f:* **in the highest** ⁓**s** an höchster Stelle; *from official* ⁓**s** von amtlicher Seite. **II** *v/t* **9.** vierteln. **10.** *bsd.* ✕ einquartieren (*on* bei). 'ˈ⁓**·deck** *s* ⚓ Achterdeck *n.* ˌ⁓ˈ**fi·nals** *s pl Sport:* Viertelfinale *n.*

quar·ter·ly [ˈkwɔːtəlɪ] *adj u. adv* vierteljährlich.

quar·ter note *s* ♩ *bsd. Am.* Viertelnote *f.*

quar·tet(te) [kwɔːˈtet] *s* ♩ Quartett *n.*

quartz [kwɔːts] *s min.* Quarz *m.* ⁓ *clock,* ⁓ *watch s* Quarzuhr *f.*

quash [kwɒʃ] *v/t* **1.** ⚖ *Urteil etc* annullieren, aufheben. **2.** *Aufstand etc* niederschlagen, unterdrücken.

qua·ver [ˈkweɪvə] **I** *v/i* **1.** zittern (*Stimme*). **2.** ♩ tremolieren. **II** *v/t* **3.** *et.* mit zitternder Stimme sagen. **III** *s* **4.** Zittern *n.* **5.** ♩ Tremolo *n.* **6.** ♩ *Br.* Achtelnote *f.*

quay [kiː] *s* ⚓ Kai *m.*

quea·sy [ˈkwiːzɪ] *adj: I feel* ⁓ mir ist übel.

queen [kwiːn] **I** *s* **1.** (*a. Schönheitsetc*)Königin *f:* ⁓ *bee* zo. Bienenkönigin; ⁓ *mother* Königinmutter *f;* → *English* 3, *evidence* 2. **2.** *Kartenspiel, Schach:* Dame *f:* ⁓ *of hearts* Herzdame. **3.** F Schwule *m.* **II** *v/t* **4.** *Schach:* Bauern in e-e Dame verwandeln. **5.** ⁓ *it* F die große Dame spielen. 'ˈ**queen·ly** *adj* königlich.

queer [kwɪə] **I** *adj* □ **1.** komisch, seltsam: ⁓ *customer* F komischer Kauz; *be a bit* ⁓ *in the head* F sie nicht alle haben. **2.** F schwul. **II** *s* **3.** F Schwule *m.* **III** *v/t* **4.** → *pitch²* 10.

quell [kwel] *v/t Aufstand etc* niederschlagen, unterdrücken; *Zweifel etc* beseitigen.

quench [kwentʃ] *v/t Durst* löschen, stillen.

quer·u·lous [ˈkwerʊləs] *adj* □ nörgelrisch.

que·ry [ˈkwɪərɪ] **I** *s* Frage *f.* **II** *v/t* in Frage stellen, in Zweifel ziehen.

quest [kwest] **I** *s* Suche *f* (**for** nach): **in** ⁓ *of* auf der Suche nach. **II** *v/i* suchen (**after, for** nach).

ques·tion [ˈkwestʃən] **I** *s* **1.** Frage *f:* ⁓ *mark* Fragezeichen *n;* ⁓ *master Br.* Quizmaster *m;* → *ask* 1, *pop¹* 7. **2.** Frage *f,* Problem *n:* **this is not the point in** ⁓ darum geht es nicht. **3.** Frage *f,* Sache _f: only a ~ of time_ nur e-e Frage der Zeit. **4.** Frage _f_, Zweifel _m_: _there is no ~ that, it is beyond ~ that_ es steht außer Frage, daß; _there is no ~ about this_ daran besteht kein Zweifel; _be out of the ~_ nicht in Frage kommen; _call into ~_ → **6. II** _v/t_ **5.** _(about)_ befragen (über _acc_), ⚖ verhören, -nehmen (zu). **6.** bezweifeln, in Zweifel ziehen, in Frage stellen. **'ques·tion·a·ble** _adj_ □ **1.** fraglich, zweifelhaft. **2.** fragwürdig. **'ques·tion·er** _s_ Fragesteller(in). **'ques·tion·ing I** _adj_ □ fragend (_Blick etc_). **II** _s_ Befragung _f_, ⚖ Verhör _n_, Vernehmung _f_. **ques·tion·naire** [ˌkwestʃəˈneə] _s_ Fragebogen _m_.

queue [kju:] _bsd. Br._ **I** _s_ Schlange _f_: _stand in a ~_ → IIa; → _jump_ 9. **II** _v/i mst ~ up (for_ nach, um) a) Schlange stehen, anstehen, b) sich anstellen. **'~·jump·er** _s_ j-d, der sich vordräng(el)t; _mot._ Kolonnenspringer(in).

quib·ble ['kwɪbl] **I** _v/i_ sich herumstreiten (_with_ mit; _about, over_ wegen). **II** _s_ kleinliche Beschwerde, Kleinigkeit _f_.

quick [kwɪk] **I** _adj_ □ **1.** schnell, rasch: _be ~!_ mach schnell!, beeil dich!; _be ~ to learn (at learning)_ schnell lernen; _a ~ one_ F ein Gläschen auf die Schnelle; → _offence_ 3, _uptake_. **2.** kurz (_Reise etc_). **3.** aufbrausend, hitzig (_Temperament_). **II** _adv_ **4.** schnell, rasch. **III** _s_ **5.** _cut s.o. to the ~ fig._ j-n tief treffen (_with_ mit). **'~·act·ing** _adj_ schnell wirkend (_Medikament_). **'~·change** _adj_: _~ artist thea._ Verwandlungskünstler(in).

quick·en ['kwɪkən] _v/t u. v/i_ (sich) beschleunigen; _v/i a._ schneller werden.

quick·ie ['kwɪkɪ] _s_ F _et._ Schnelles _od._ Kurzes, _z. B._ Gläschen _n_ auf die Schnelle, kurze Frage.

'quick·sand _s_ Treibsand _m._ **'~·tempered** _adj_ aufbrausend, hitzig. **'~·witted** _adj_ □ aufgeweckt; schlagfertig; geistesgegenwärtig.

quid [kwɪd] _pl_ **quid** _s Br._ F Pfund _n_ (_Währung_).

qui·et ['kwaɪət] **I** _adj_ □ **1.** ruhig, still: _~, please_ Ruhe, bitte. **2.** ruhig (_Leben etc_). **3.** geheim, heimlich: _keep s.th. ~_ et. für sich behalten. **II** _s_ **4.** Ruhe _f_, Stille _f_: → _peace_ 3. **5.** _on the ~_ F heimlich. **III** _v/t u. v/i_ **6.** → _quieten_. **'qui·et·en I** _v/t_ **1.** a. _~ down_ j-n beruhigen. **2.**

Befürchtungen etc zerstreuen. **II** _v/i_ **3.** a. _~ down_ sich beruhigen.

quill [kwɪl] _s_ **1.** _orn._ (Schwanz-, Schwung)Feder _f_. **2.** a. _~ pen hist._ Federkiel _m_. **3.** _zo._ Stachel _m_.

quilt [kwɪlt] _s_ Steppdecke _f_. **'quilt·ed** _adj_ Stepp...

quin [kwɪn] _s Br._ F Fünfling _m_.

quince [kwɪns] _s_ ♀ Quitte _f_.

qui·nine [kwɪˈniːn] _s pharm._ Chinin _n_.

quint [kwɪnt] _s Am._ F Fünfling _m_.

quint·es·sence [kwɪnˈtesns] _s_ **1.** Quintessenz _f_. **2.** Inbegriff _m_.

quin·tet(te) [kwɪnˈtet] _s_ ♪ Quintett _n_.

quin·tu·plet ['kwɪntjʊplɪt] _s_ Fünfling _m_.

quip [kwɪp] **I** _s_ geistreiche _od._ witzige Bemerkung. **II** _v/i_ witzeln.

quirk [kwɜːk] _s_ **1.** Eigenart _f_, Schrulle _f_. **2.** _by some ~ of fate_ durch e-n verrückten Zufall.

quit [kwɪt] (_mst irr_) F **I** _v/t_ **1.** aufhören mit: _~ doing s.th._ aufhören, et. zu tun; _~ one's job_ kündigen; _~ smoking_ das Rauchen aufgeben. **II** _v/i_ **2.** aufhören. **3.** kündigen.

quite [kwaɪt] _adv_ **1.** ganz, völlig: _be ~ right_ völlig recht haben; _~ (so) bsd. Br._ genau, ganz recht. **2.** ziemlich: _a ~ disappointment_ e-e ziemliche Enttäuschung; _a few_ ziemlich viele; _~ good_ ganz _od._ recht gut. **3.** _it was ~ a (od. some) sight_ das war vielleicht ein Anblick; _she's ~ a girl_ sie ist ein tolles Mädchen.

quits [kwɪts] _adj_ quitt (_with_ mit): _call it ~_ F es gut sein lassen.

quit·ter ['kwɪtə] _s: he's a (no) ~_ F er gibt (nicht so) schnell auf.

quiv·er¹ ['kwɪvə] **I** _v/i_ zittern (_with_ vor _dat_; _at_ bei e-m Gedanken _etc_). **II** _s_ Zittern _n_.

quiv·er² [~] _s_ Köcher _m_.

quix·ot·ic [kwɪkˈsɒtɪk] _adj_ (_~ally_) weltfremd-idealistisch.

quiz [kwɪz] **I** _pl_ **'quiz·zes** _s_ Quiz _n_. **II** _v/t_ ausfragen (_about_ über _acc_). **'~·mas·ter** _s_ Quizmaster _m_.

quiz·zi·cal ['kwɪzɪkl] _adj_ □ wissend (_Blick etc_).

quoit [kɔɪt] _s_ **1.** Wurfring _m._ **2.** _pl_ (_sg konstruiert_) Wurfringspiel _n_.

quo·rate ['kwɔːreɪt] _adj_ beschlußfähig.

quo·rum ['kwɔːrəm] _s_ zur Beschlußfähigkeit erforderliche Teilnehmerzahl.

quo·ta ['kwəʊtə] s Kontingent n, Quote f, ✝ a. Soll n.

quo·ta·tion [kwəʊ'teɪʃn] s **1.** Zitat n (*from* aus). **2.** ✝ Notierung f. **3.** ✝ (*verbindlicher*) Kosten(vor)anschlag: *get a ~* e-n Kostenvoranschlag einholen. **~ marks** s pl Anführungszeichen pl: *put* (*od. place*) *in ~* in Anführungszeichen setzen.

quote [kwəʊt] I v/t **1.** zitieren (*from* aus); *Beispiel etc* anführen: *he was ~d as saying that* er soll gesagt haben, daß. **2.** *be ~d at* ✝ notieren mit. II v/i **3.** ~ *from* zitieren. III s **F 4.** → **quotation** 1, 2. **5.** pl Gänsefüßchen pl: *put* (*od. place*) *in ~s* in Gänsefüßchen setzen. IV adv **6.** ~ *...* *unquote* Zitat ... Zitat Ende.

quo·tient ['kwəʊʃnt] s ℞ Quotient m.

R

r [ɑː]: *the three R's* (= *reading, writing, arithmetic*) Lesen n, Schreiben n u. Rechnen n.

rab·bi ['ræbaɪ] s eccl. Rabbiner m.

rab·bit ['ræbɪt] s Kaninchen n. **~ punch** s Genickschlag m.

rab·ble ['ræbl] s **1.** Pöbel m, Mob m. **2.** sociol. contp. Pöbel m. **'~,rous·ing** adj aufwieglerisch, Hetz...

rab·id ['ræbɪd] adj □ **1.** vet. tollwütig. **2.** fanatisch.

ra·bies ['reɪbiːz] s vet. Tollwut f.

rac·coon → **racoon**.

race¹ [reɪs] s **1.** Rasse f. **2.** Rasse(nzugehörigkeit) f. **3.** (*Menschen*)Geschlecht n.

race² [~] I s **1.** Sport: Rennen n (a. fig. for um), Lauf m: ~ *against time* fig. Wettlauf mit der Zeit. II v/i **2.** an (e-m) Rennen teilnehmen; um die Wette laufen od. fahren (*against, with* mit). **3.** rasen, rennen. **4.** durchdrehen (*Motor*). III v/t **5.** um die Wette laufen od. fahren mit. **6.** rasen mit: ~ *s.o. to hospital* mit j-m ins Krankenhaus rasen.

'race·course s Pferdesport: Rennbahn f. **'~·horse** s Rennpferd n. **~·meet·ing** s Pferdesport: Rennveranstaltung f.

rac·er ['reɪsə] s **1.** Rennpferd n. **2.** Rennrad n, -wagen m.

'race·track s **1.** Automobilsport etc: Rennstrecke f. **2.** bsd. Am. → **racecourse**.

ra·cial ['reɪʃl] adj □ rassisch, Rassen...: ~ *discrimination* Rassendiskriminie-

rung f; ~ *segregation* Rassentrennung f. **ra·cial·ism** ['reɪʃəlɪzəm], **'ra·cial·ist** → **racism, racist**.

rac·ing ['reɪsɪŋ] adj Renn...: ~ *bicycle* Rennrad n; ~ *car* Rennwagen m; ~ *cyclist* Radrennfahrer(in); ~ *driver* Rennfahrer(in).

ra·cism ['reɪsɪzəm] s Rassismus m. **'ra·cist** I s Rassist(in). II adj rassistisch.

rack¹ [ræk] I s **1.** Gestell n, (*Geschirr-, Zeitungs- etc*)Ständer m, 🚂 (*Gepäck*)Netz n, mot. (*Dach*)Gepäckträger m. **2.** hist. Folter(bank) f: *put s.o. on the ~* j-n auf die Folter spannen (a. fig.). II v/t **3.** *be ~ed by* (od. with) geplagt od. gequält werden von. **4.** → **brain** 2.

rack² [~] s: *go to ~ and ruin* verfallen (*Gebäude, Person*), dem Ruin entgegentreiben (*Land, Wirtschaft*).

rack·et¹ ['rækɪt] s Tennis etc: Schläger m.

rack·et² [~] s F **1.** Krach m, Lärm m: *make a ~* Krach machen. **2.** Schwindel m, Gaunerei f; (*Drogen- etc*)Geschäft n; organisierte Erpressung; Beruf m, Branche f: *what's his ~?* was macht er beruflich? **rack·et·eer** [,rækə'tɪə] s F Gauner m; Erpresser m.

ra·coon [rə'kuːn] s zo. Waschbär m.

rac·y ['reɪsɪ] adj □ **1.** spritzig (*Geschichte etc*). **2.** gewagt.

ra·dar ['reɪdɑː] I s Radar m, n. II adj Radar...: ~ *screen* Radarschirm m; ~ (*speed*) *trap* Radarkontrolle f; ~ *station* Radarstation f.

ra·di·al ['reɪdjəl] I adj □ radial, Radial..., strahlenförmig: **~ tire** (*bsd. Br.* **tyre**) → II. **II** *s mot.* Gürtelreifen *m.*

ra·di·ant [ˈreɪdjənt] *adj* □ strahlend (*a. fig.* with *od* dat): **be ~ with joy** vor Freude strahlen.

ra·di·ate [ˈreɪdɪeɪt] **I** *v/t* Licht, Wärme *etc* ausstrahlen, *Optimismus etc a.* strömen. **II** *v/i* strahlenförmig ausgehen (**from** von). **,ra·di·'a·tion** *s* **1.** Ausstrahlung *f, fig. a.* Verströmen *n.* **2.** *phys.* (*engS.* radioaktive) Strahlung: **~ sickness** ♯ Strahlenkrankheit *f.* **ra·di·a-tor** [ˈ⌐eɪtə] *s* **1.** Heizkörper *m.* **2.** *mot.* Kühler *m:* **~ grill** Kühlergrill *m.*

rad·i·cal [ˈrædɪkl] **I** *adj* □ **1.** radikal (*a. pol.*). **2.** ⅋ Wurzel...: **~ sign** Wurzelzeichen *n.* **3.** *pol.* Radikale *etc, fig.* **4.** ⅋, *ling.* Wurzel *f.* **rad·i·cal·ism** [ˈⁿkəlɪzəm] *s bsd. pol.* Radikalismus *m.* **'rad·i·cal·ize** *v/t bsd. pol.* radikalisieren.

ra·di·i [ˈreɪdɪaɪ] *pl von* **radius.**

ra·di·o [ˈreɪdɪəʊ] **I** *pl* **-os** *s* **1.** Radio *n,* Rundfunkgerät *n;* Funkgerät *n.* **2.** Radio *n,* Rundfunk *m:* **on the ~** im Radio; **be in ~** beim Rundfunk sein. **3.** Funk *m:* **by ~** per *od.* über Funk. **II** *v/t* **4.** *Nachricht etc* funken, durchgeben. **5.** *j-n, Ort* anfunken. **III** *v/i* **6.** **~ for help** per *od.* über Funk um Hilfe bitten. **,~·'ac·tive** *adj* □ radioaktiv: **~ waste** Atommüll *m,* radioaktiver Abfall. **,~·ac·'tiv·i·ty** *s* Radioaktivität *f.* **~ a·larm** *s* Radiowecker *m.* **~ car** *s Am.* Funk-(streifen)wagen *m.* **~ con·tact** *s* Funkkontakt *m,* -verbindung *f:* **be in ~ with** in Funkkontakt stehen mit. **,~·con-'trolled** *adj* funkgesteuert.

ra·di·o·gram [ˈreɪdɪəʊgræm] *s* **1.** Funkspruch *m.* **2.** → **radiograph. ra·di·o·graph** [ˈ⌐grɑːf] *s* ♯ Röntgenbild *n.*

ra·di·o· ham → **ham** 3. **~ mes·sage** *s* Funkspruch *m.* **~ op·er·a·tor** *s* Funker *m.* **~ set** → **radio** 1. **~ sig·nal** *s* Funksignal *n.* **~ sta·tion** *s* Rundfunksender *m,* -station *f.* **,~·'ther·a·py** *s* ♯ Strahlen-, Röntgentherapie *f.* **~ traf·fic** *s* Funkverkehr *m.*

rad·ish [ˈrædɪʃ] *s* ⅋ **1.** Rettich *m.* **2.** Radieschen *n.*

ra·di·um [ˈreɪdɪəm] *s* ♬ Radium *n.*

ra·di·us [ˈreɪdɪəs] *pl* **-di·i** [ˈ⌐dɪaɪ] *s* **1.** ⅋ Radius *m,* Halbmesser *f.* **2.** **within a three-mile ~** im Umkreis von drei

Meilen (**of** um). **3.** *anat.* Speiche *f.*

raf·fle [ˈræfl] **I** *s* Tombola *f.* **II** *v/t oft* **~ off** verlosen.

raft [rɑːft] *s* Floß *n.*

raft·er [ˈrɑːftə] *s* (Dach)Sparren *m.*

rag [ræg] *s* **1.** Fetzen *m,* Lumpen *m;* Lappen *m:* **in ~s** in Fetzen (*Stoff etc*); zerlumpt (*Person*); **be (like) a red ~ to a bull to s.o.** *Br.* F wie ein rotes Tuch für j-n sein *od.* auf j-n wirken; **feel like a wet ~** F total k. o. sein. **2.** F *contp.* Käseblatt *n.* **'~·bag** *s* Sammelsurium *n* (*of* von).

rage [reɪdʒ] **I** *s* **1.** Wut *f,* Zorn *m:* **be in a ~** wütend sein; **fly into a ~** wütend werden. **2.** F **the latest ~** große Mode sein; **be all the ~** große Mode sein. **II** *v/i* **3.** wettern (**against, at** gegen); *fig.* wüten (*Krankheit, Sturm*), toben (*Meer, Sturm*): **a raging headache** rasende Kopfschmerzen *pl.*

rag·ged [ˈrægɪd] *adj* □ **1.** zerlumpt (*Kleidung, Person*). **2.** struppig, zottig (*Bart etc*). **3.** *fig.* dilettantisch, stümperhaft.

ra·gout [ˈræguː] *s gastr.* Ragout *n.*

raid [reɪd] *s* **1.** (**on**) Überfall *m* (auf *acc*), ✕ *a.* Angriff *m* (gegen). **2.** Razzia *f* (**on** in *dat*): **make a ~ on** → 4. **II** *v/t* **3.** überfallen, ✕ *a.* angreifen. **4.** e-e Razzia machen in (*dat*).

rail¹ [reɪl] **I** *s* **1.** Geländer *n.* **2.** (*Handtuch*)Halter *m.* **3.** ♠ Schiene *f, pl a.* Gleis *n:* **go off the ~s** a) *a.* **jump the ~s** entgleisen, b) *fig.* auf die schiefe Bahn geraten. **4.** (Eisen)Bahn *f:* **by ~** mit der Bahn. **II** *v/t* **5.** **~ in** einzäunen; **~ off** abzäunen.

rail² [~] *v/i* schimpfen (**against, at** über *acc*)

rail·ing [ˈreɪlɪŋ] *s oft pl* (Gitter)Zaun *m.*

rail·road [ˈreɪlrəʊd] **I** *s* **1.** *Am.* → **railway. II** *v/t* F **2.** *Gesetzesvorlage etc* durchpeitschen (**through** in *dat*). **3.** **~ s.o. into doing s.th.** j-n rücksichtslos drängen, *etc.* zu tun.

rail·way [ˈreɪlweɪ] *s bsd. Br.* Eisenbahn *f:* **~ station** Bahnhof *m.*

rain [reɪn] **I** *s* **1.** Regen *m:* **in the ~** im Regen; **the ~s** *pl* die Regenzeit (*in den Tropen*); **~ pour** 3. (*Schlag-etc*)Hagel *m,* (*Funken*)Regen *m.* **II** *v/i* **3.** *impers* regnen: **it is ~ing.** **4.** **~ down on** *fig.* niederprasseln auf (*acc*) (*Schläge* etc). **III** v/t **5.** → **cat** 1. **6.** fig. ~ *blows on s.o.* j-n mit Schlägen eindecken; ~ *abuse on s.o.* j-n mit Beschimpfungen überschütten. **7.** be ~**ed off** (Am. *out*) wegen Regens abgesagt od. abgebrochen werden. '~**bow** s Regenbogen m. '~**coat** s Regenmantel m. '~**drop** s Regentropfen m. '~**fall** s Niederschlag(smenge f) m. ~ **for·est** s Regenwald m. '~**proof** adj regen-, wasserdicht. '~**storm** s heftiger Regenguß. '~**wa·ter** s Regenwasser n.

rain·y ['reɪnɪ] adj regnerisch, verregnet, Regen...: *the* ~ *season* die Regenzeit (*in den Tropen*); *put away* (od. *save*) s.th. *for a* ~ *day* et. für schlechte Zeiten zurücklegen, et. auf die hohe Kante legen.

raise [reɪz] **I** v/t **1.** Arm, gesunkenes Schiff etc heben; Vorhang etc hochziehen: ~ *one's hat* den Hut ziehen (*to s.o.* vor j-m; a. fig.) od. lüften; → **eyebrow**. **2.** Denkmal etc errichten. **3.** a) Protest etc hervorrufen: ~ *a laugh* Gelächter ernten, b) Erwartungen (er)wecken: ~ *s.o.'s hopes* in j-m Hoffnung erwecken; ~ *a suspicion* Verdacht erregen, c) Gerücht etc aufkommen lassen, d) Schwierigkeiten machen. **4.** Staub etc aufwirbeln: → **dust** 1. **5.** Frage aufwerfen, et. zur Sprache bringen. **6.** An-spruch geltend machen, Forderung stellen. **7.** Kinder auf-, großziehen; Tiere züchten; Getreide etc anbauen. **8.** Moral, Stimmung heben. **9.** Gehalt etc erhöhen, Geschwindigkeit etc a. steigern: → **power** 9. **10.** Hypothek etc aufnehmen (*on* auf acc); Geld zs.-bringen, beschaffen. **11.** Blockade etc, a. Verbot aufheben. **II** s **12.** bsd. Am. Lohn- od. Gehaltserhöhung f.

rai·sin ['reɪzn] s Rosine f.

rake [reɪk] **I** s **1.** Rechen m, Harke f. **II** v/t **2.** rechen, harken: ~ *in* F Geld kassieren; ~ *it in* F das Geld nur so scheffeln; ~ *out* F et. herausfinden; ~ *up* Laub etc zs.-rechen, -harken; F Leute auftreiben, Geld a. zs.-kratzen; F alte Geschichten etc aufwärmen. **3.** Gelände etc absuchen (*with* mit Fernglas etc). **III** v/i **4.** a. *about* (od. *around*) herumstöbern (*in* in dat). '~**off** s F (Gewinn)Anteil m, Prozente pl.

rak·ish ['reɪkɪʃ] adj □ flott, verwegen.

ral·ly ['rælɪ] **I** s **1.** Kundgebung f, (Massen)Versammlung f. **2.** Motorsport: Rallye f. **3.** Tennis etc: Ballwechsel m. **II** v/t **4.** Truppen etc (wieder) sammeln. **III** v/i **5.** sich (wieder) sammeln: ~ *round* fig. sich zs.-tun; ~ *round s.o.* fig. sich um j-n scharen. **6.** sich erholen (*from* von) (a. ✝).

ram [ræm] **I** s **1.** zo. Widder m, Schafbock m. **2.** ⊙ Ramme f. **II** v/t **3.** Pfahl, Zeug etc rammen. **4.** Pfosten etc rammen (*into* in acc): ~ *down* Erde etc feststampfen, -treten; → **throat**.

ram·ble ['ræmbl] **I** v/i **1.** wandern. **2.** a. ~ *on* contp. faseln (*about* von, über acc). **II** s **3.** Wanderung f: *go for* (od. *on*) a ~ e-e Wanderung machen. '**ram·bling** adj □ **1.** ♣ Kletter...: ~ *rose*. **2.** fig. weitschweifig, unzusammenhängend. **3.** weitläufig (Gebäude).

ram·i·fi·ca·tion [ˌræmɪfɪˈkeɪʃn] s Verzweigung f, -ästelung f (beide a. fig.). **ram·i·fy** ['ræmɪfaɪ] v/i sich verzweigen (a. fig.).

ramp [ræmp] s Rampe f.

ram·page [ræmˈpeɪdʒ] **I** v/i: ~ *through* a) (wild od. aufgeregt) trampeln durch (Elefant etc), b) randalierend ziehen durch. **II** s: *go on the* ~ randalieren; *go on the* ~ *through* → Ib.

ramp·ant ['ræmpənt] adj □ **1.** wuchernd (Pflanze): *be* ~ wuchern. **2.** fig. grassierend: *be* ~ *in* grassieren in (dat).

ram·shack·le ['ræmʃækl] adj baufällig; klapp(e)rig (Fahrzeug).

ran [ræn] pret von **run**.

ranch [rɑːntʃ] s **1.** Ranch f. **2.** (Geflügeletc)Farm f. '**ranch·er** s **1.** Rancher m. **2.** (Geflügel- etc)Züchter m. **3.** Rancharbeiter m.

ran·cid ['rænsɪd] adj □ ranzig: *go* ~ ranzig werden.

ran·cor Am. → **rancour**.

ran·cor·ous ['ræŋkərəs] adj □ voller Groll (*toward[s]* gegen).

ran·cour ['ræŋkə] s bsd. Br. Groll m, Erbitterung f.

ran·dom ['rændəm] **I** adj aufs Geratewohl, zufällig, Zufalls...: ~ *sample* Stichprobe f; *take* ~ *samples* Stichproben machen. **II** s: *at* ~ aufs Geratewohl.

rand·y ['rændɪ] adj F scharf, geil.

rang [ræŋ] pret von **ring**².

range [reɪndʒ] **I** s **1.** (Berg)Kette f. **2.**
(Koch-, Küchen)Herd m. **3.** (Schieß-)
Stand m, (-)Platz m. **4.** Entfernung f: **at
close** (**od. short**) ~ aus kurzer od. kürzester Entfernung, aus nächster Nähe.
5. Reich-, Schuß-, Tragweite f. **6.** fig.
Bereich m, Spielraum m, Grenzen pl. **7.**
✝ Kollektion f, Sortiment n. **8.** fig.
Bereich m, Gebiet n. **II** v/i **9.** schwanken, sich bewegen (**from ... to, between
... and** zwischen ... u.). **III** v/t **10.** aufstellen, anordnen. ~ **find·er** s phot. etc
Entfernungsmesser m.

rang·er ['reɪndʒə] s **1.** Förster m. **2.** Am.
Ranger m.

rank[1] [ræŋk] **I** s **1.** Reihe f; ✗ Glied n:
close the ~s die Reihen schließen; fig.
sich zs.-schließen. **2.** bsd. ✗ Rang m: **in
~** im Rang, rangmäßig; **he is above me
in ~** er ist ranghöher als ich; **of the first**
(**od. front, top**) ~ fig. erstklassig; **the ~s**
pl (Unteroffiziere pl u.) Mannschaften
pl; fig. das Heer, die Masse (der Arbeitslosen etc); **the ~ and file** der Mann-
schaftsstand; fig. die Basis (e-r Partei
etc); **pull ~** F den Vorgesetzten heraus-
kehren (**on** gegenüber); **rise from the
~s** vom Mannschaftsrang zum Offizier
aufsteigen; fig. sich hocharbeiten. **3.**
Rang m, (soziale) Stellung. **II** v/t **4.**
rechnen, zählen (**among** zu); stellen
(**above** über acc): **be ~ed 2nd in the
world** an 2. Stelle der Weltrangliste stehen. **5.** ✗ Am. ranghöher sein als. **III**
v/i **6.** zählen, gehören (**among** zu); gelten (**as** als); rangieren (**above** über
acc).

rank[2] [~] adj □ **1.** üppig wuchernd. **2.**
übel(riechend od. -schmeckend). **3.** fig.
kraß (Außenseiter), blutig (Anfänger),
blühend (Unsinn).

rank·ing ['ræŋkɪŋ] adj **1.** ✗ Am. rang-
höchst (Offizier). **2.** ~ **list** (Sport) Rangliste f.

ran·kle ['ræŋkl] v/i fig. (**on**) nagen (an
dat), weh tun (dat).

ran·sack ['rænsæk] v/t **1.** durchwühlen.
2. plündern.

ran·som ['rænsəm] **I** s Lösegeld n: **hold
s.o. to ~** j-n bis zur Zahlung e-s Löse-
gelds gefangenhalten; fig. j-n erpressen; ~ **demand** Lösegeldforderung f. **II**
v/t auslösen, freikaufen.

rant [rænt] v/i a. ~ **on**, ~ **and rave** (**about**

eifern (gegen), sich in Tiraden ergehen
(über acc).

rap[1] [ræp] **I** s **1.** Klopfen n; Klaps m:
give s.o. a ~ over the knuckles j-m auf
die Finger klopfen (a. fig.). **2. take the
~** F den Kopf hinhalten (**for** für). **II** v/t
3. klopfen an (acc) od. auf (acc): ~ **s.o.
over the knuckles** j-m auf die Finger
klopfen (a. fig.). **4.** mst ~ **out** Befehl etc
bellen, Fluch etc ausstoßen. **III** v/i **5.**
klopfen (**at** an acc; **on** auf acc).

rap[2] [~] s: **I don't care a ~** (**for it**) das ist
mir völlig egal.

ra·pa·cious [rə'peɪʃəs] adj □ **1.** habgierig. **2.** räuberisch. **3.** orn., zo. Raub...
ra·pac·i·ty [rə'pæsətɪ] s Habgier f.

rape[1] [reɪp] **I** s Vergewaltigung f, ⚖
Notzucht f. **II** v/t vergewaltigen.

rape[2] [~] s ♀ Raps m: ~ **oil** Rapsöl n.

rap·id ['ræpɪd] **I** adj □ schnell, rasch. **II** s
pl Stromschnellen pl. '~-**fire** adj **1.** ✗
Schnellfeuer... **2.** fig. schnell (aufeinanderfolgend).

ra·pid·i·ty [rə'pɪdətɪ] s Schnelligkeit f.

rap·ist ['reɪpɪst] s Vergewaltiger m.

rap·port [ræ'pɔː] s harmonisches Verhältnis (**between** zwischen dat; **with**
zu).

rap·proche·ment [ræ'prɒʃmãːŋ] s bsd.
pol. (Wieder)Annäherung f (**between**
zwischen dat).

rapt [ræpt] adj: **with ~ attention** mit ge-
spannter Aufmerksamkeit.

rap·ture ['ræptʃə] s, a. pl Entzücken n,
Verzückung f: **be in ~s** entzückt od.
hingerissen sein (**about, at, over** von);
go into ~s in Verzückung geraten
(**about, at, over** über acc). '**rap·tur·ous**
adj □ **1.** entzückt, hingerissen. **2.** stürmisch (Applaus etc).

rare[1] [reə] adj □ **1.** selten, rar. **2.** dünn
(Luft). **3.** F Mords...: **give s.o. a ~
fright** j-m e-n Mordsschreck(en) einjagen.

rare[2] [~] adj blutig (Steak).

rar·e·fied ['reərɪfaɪd] adj **1.** dünn (Luft).
2. fig. exklusiv.

rar·ing ['reərɪŋ] adj: **be ~ to do s.th.** F es
kaum mehr erwarten können od. ganz
wild darauf sein, et. zu tun.

rar·i·ty ['reərətɪ] s Seltenheit f, (Briefmarke etc A.) Rarität f.

ras·cal ['rɑːskəl] s **1.** Gauner m. **2.** humor. Schlingel m.

rash¹ [ræʃ] *adj* □ voreilig, -schnell.

rash² [~] *s* **1.** ✚ (Haut)Ausschlag *m*: → **come out** 5. **2.** *fig.* Flut *f*.

rash·er ['ræʃə] *s* dünne Scheibe (*Frühstücksspeck etc*).

rasp [rɑːsp] **I** *s* **1.** Raspel *f*. **2.** Kratzen *n*. **II** *v/t* **3.** raspeln: **~ off** abraspeln.

rasp·ber·ry ['rɑːzbəri] *s* ♣ Himbeere *f*.

rasp·ing ['rɑːspiŋ] *adj* □ kratzend (*Geräusch*); kratzend (*Stimme*).

rat [ræt] **I** *s zo.* Ratte *f* (*a.* F *contp.*): **smell a ~** *fig.* Lunte *od.* den Braten riechen; **~s!** F Mist[iəu] *od.* Unsinn! **II** *v/i* **~ on** F *j-n* im Stich lassen; *j-n* verpfeifen; aussteigen aus (*e-m Projekt etc*).

rate [reit] **I** *s* **1.** Quote *f*, (*Inflations-etc*)Rate *f*, (*Geburten-, Sterbe-*)Ziffer *f*. **2.** (*Steuer-, Zins-* etc)Satz *m*, (*Wechsel*)Kurs *m*; **at any ~** *fig.* auf jeden Fall. **3.** *mst pl Br.* Gemeinde-, Kommunalsteuer *f*. **4.** Geschwindigkeit *f*, Tempo *n*. **II** *v/t* **5.** einschätzen (**highly** hoch), halten (**as** für): **be ~d as** gelten als. **6.** *Lob etc* verdienen.

rath·er ['rɑːðə] **I** *adv* **1.** ziemlich: **~ a success** ein ziemlicher Erfolg; **~ a cold night, a ~ cold night** e-e ziemlich kalte Nacht. **2. I would** (*od.* **had**) **~ stay at home** ich möchte lieber zu Hause bleiben. **3. or ~** (*od.*) vielmehr. **II** *int* **4.** *bsd. Br.* F freilich!, und ob!

rat·i·fi·ca·tion [ˌrætifiˈkeiʃn] *s pol.* Ratifizierung *f*. **rat·i·fy** ['~fai] *v/t* ratifizieren.

rat·ing ['reitiŋ] *s* **1.** Einschätzung *f*. **2.** *Rundfunk, TV:* Einschaltquote *f*.

ra·ti·o ['reiʃiəu] *pl* **-os** *s* ♣ *etc* Verhältnis *n* (**of ... to** von ... zu).

ra·tion ['ræʃn] *s* **1.** Ration *f*. **II** *v/t* **2.** *et.* rationieren. **3. ~ out** zuteilen (**to** dat).

ra·tion·al ['ræʃənl] *adj* □ rational: a) vernunftbegabt, b) vernünftig. **ra·tion·al·ism** ['ræʃnəlizəm] *s* Rationalismus *m*. **'ra·tion·al·ist** *s* Rationalist(in). **II** *adj* rationalistisch. **ˌra·tion·al·is·tic** *adj* (**~ally**) rationalistisch. **ˌra·tion·al·i·za·tion** *s* ✝ Rationalisierung *f*. **'ra·tion·al·ize** *v/t* **1.** rational erklären. **2.** ✝ rationalisieren.

rat| **poi·son** *s* Rattengift *n*. **~ race** *s* F endloser Konkurrenzkampf.

rat·tle ['rætl] **I** *v/i* **1.** klappern (*Fenster etc*); rasseln, klirren (*Ketten*); klimpern (*Münzen etc*); prasseln (**on** auf *acc*)

(*Regen etc*); knattern (*Fahrzeug*): **~ at** rütteln an (*dat*); **~ on** F quasseln (*about* über *acc*); **~ through** Rede etc herunterrasseln; *Arbeit* in Windeseile erledigen. **II** *v/t* **2.** rasseln *od.* klimpern mit; rütteln an (*dat*): **~ off** *Gedicht etc* herunterrasseln. **3.** F *j-n* verunsichern. **III** *s* **4.** Klappern *n* (*etc, →* 1). **5.** Rassel *f*, Klapper *f* (*Spielzeug*), Knarre *f*, Schnarre *f* (*Lärminstrument*): '**~snake** *s zo.* Klapperschlange *f*. '**~trap** *s* F Klapperkasten *m* (*Auto*).

'**rat·trap** *s Am.* F Bruchbude *f*, Hundehütte *f*.

rat·ty ['ræti] *adj* F **1.** *Am.* schäbig (*Kleidungsstück*). **2.** gereizt: **there's no need to be ~** sei doch nicht gleich so gereizt.

rau·cous ['rɔːkəs] *adj* □ heiser, rauh.

rav·age ['rævidʒ] **I** *v/t* verwüsten. **II** *s pl* Verwüstungen *pl*, *a. fig.* verheerende Auswirkungen *pl*.

rave [reiv] *v/i* **1.** phantasieren, irrereden. **2.** toben; wettern (**against, at** gegen). **3.** schwärmen (**about** von).

rav·el ['rævl] *pret u. pp* **-eled,** *bsd. Br.* **-elled I** *v/t* **1.** *a.* **~ up** verwickeln, -wirren. **2.** *oft* **~ out** ausfransen; auftrennen; *a. fig.* entwirren. **II** *v/i* **3.** *a.* **~ up** sich verwickeln *od.* -wirren. **4.** *oft* **~ out** ausfransen; auftrennen.

ra·ven ['reivn] *s orn.* Rabe *m*.

rav·en·ous ['rævənəs] *adj* □ **1.** ausgehungert, heißhungrig. **2. ~ hunger** Bären-, Wolfshunger *m*.

ra·vine [rəˈviːn] *s* Schlucht *f*, Klamm *f*.

rav·ing ['reiviŋ] *adj* □ **1.** tobend. **2.** phantasierend. **3.** F toll (*Erfolg*), hinreißend (*Schönheit*). **II** *adv* **~ mad** F völlig *od.* total übergeschnappt. **III** *s pl* **5.** Phantasien *pl*, irres Gerede.

rav·i·o·li [ˌræviˈəuli] *s pl* (*sg konstruiert*) Ravioli *pl*.

rav·ish ['ræviʃ] *v/t* hinreißen. '**rav·ish·ing** *adj* □ hinreißend.

raw [rɔː] *adj* □ **1.** roh (*Gemüse etc*). **2.** ✝, ⚙ roh, Roh...: **~ material** Rohstoff *m*. **3.** unerfahren, grün. **4.** wund (*Haut*). **5.** naßkalt (*Wetter, Tag etc*). **6. get a ~ deal** F benachteiligt *od.* ungerecht behandelt werden. **II** *s* **7. in the ~** im Natur- *od.* Urzustand; F nackt. **ˌ~boned** *adj* hager, knochig.

ray¹ [rei] *s* Strahl *m*: **sun's ~s** *pl* Sonnenstrahlen *pl*; **~ of light** Lichtstrahl; **~ of hope** Hoffnungsstrahl, -schimmer *m*.

ray² [~] *s ichth*. Rochen *m*.

ray·on ['reɪɒn] *s* Kunstseide *f*.

raze [reɪz] *v/t*: **~ to the ground** dem Erdboden gleichmachen.

ra·zor ['reɪzə] *s* Rasiermesser *n*; -apparat *m*: **be on a ~'s edge → razor edge**. **~ blade** *s* Rasierklinge *f*. **~ edge** *s*: **be on a ~** *fig.* auf des Messers Schneide stehen. **,~'sharp** *adj* messerscharf (*a. fig. Verstand*).

raz·zle ['ræzl] *s*: **go on the ~** F auf den Putz hauen.

re [riː] *prp*: **your letter of ...** ✝ Betr.: Ihr Schreiben vom ...

reach [riːtʃ] **I** *v/t* **1.** *j-n, et., Ort, Alter etc* erreichen. **2. ~ out** *Arm etc* ausstrecken. **3. ~ down** herunter-, hinunterreichen (**from** aus). **4.** reichen *od.* gehen bis an (*acc*) *od.* zu. **II** *v/i* **5.** *a.* **~ out** greifen, langen (**for** nach) (*beide a. fig.*). **6. ~ out** die Hand ausstrecken. **7.** reichen, gehen, sich erstrecken (**as far as, to** bis an *acc od.* zu): **as far as the eye can ~** soweit das Auge reicht. **III** *s* **8.** Reichweite *f* (*a.* Boxen): **within** (**out of**) *s.o.'s* **~** in (außer) j-s Reichweite; **be within easy ~** leicht zu erreichen sein (*Instrument etc*); **she lives within easy ~ of the shops** (*bsd. Am.* **stores**) von ihrer Wohnung aus sind die Geschäfte leicht zu erreichen.

re·act [rɪ'ækt] *v/i* **1.** reagieren (**to** auf *acc*): **~ against** sich wehren gegen. **2.** 🐾 reagieren (**with** mit).

re·ac·tion [rɪ'ækʃn] *s* Reaktion *f* (*a.* 🐾, *pol. etc*). **re·ac·tion·ar·y** *pol.* **I** *adj* reaktionär. **II** *s* Reaktionär(in).

re·ac·ti·vate [rɪ'æktɪveɪt] *v/t* reaktivieren (*a.* 🐾).

re·ac·tive [rɪ'æktɪv] *adj* 🐾 reaktiv, reaktionsfähig. **re'ac·tor** *s phys.* Reaktor *m*.

read¹ [riːd] **I** *v/t* (*irr*) **1.** lesen: **~ in** (*Computer*) einlesen; **~ s.th. into** et. hineinlesen in (*acc*); **~ out** verlesen; **~ s.th. to s.o., ~ s.o. s.th.** j-m et. vorlesen; **read over** (*od.* **through**) (sich) *et.* durchlesen; **~ up** nachlesen; **we can take it as ~ that** wir können davon ausgehen, daß. **2.** Zähler etc ablesen. **3.** (an)zeigen, stehen auf (*dat*) (*Thermometer etc*). **4.** *univ.* studieren. **5.** deuten, verstehen

(**as** als). **II** *v/i* (*irr*) **6.** lesen: **I've ~ about it** ich habe darüber *od.* davon gelesen; **~ to s.o.** j-m (et.) vorlesen (**from** aus); **→ line¹** 3. **7. ~ as follows** folgendermaßen lauten. **8.** sich *gut etc* lesen. **9.** sich vorbereiten (**for** auf *e-e* Prüfung): **~ up on** et. nachlesen; **→ bar** 9. **III** *s* **10. be a good ~** *bsd. Br.* sich gut lesen.

read² [red] *pret u. pp von* **read¹**.

read·a·ble ['riːdəbl] *adj* ☐ lesbar: a) lesenswert, b) leserlich.

re·ad·dress [,riːə'dres] *v/t* Brief etc umadressieren.

read·er ['riːdə] *s* **1.** Leser(in). **2.** Lektor(in). **3.** *ped.* Lesebuch *n*. **'read·er·ship** *s* **1.** Leserschaft *f*, -schaft *f*) *pl*.

read·i·ly ['redɪlɪ] *adv* **1.** bereitwillig. **2.** leicht, ohne weiteres. **'read·i·ness** *s* **1.** Bereitschaft *f*: **~ to help** Hilfsbereitschaft. **2.** Gewandtheit *f*.

read·ing ['riːdɪŋ] **I** *s* **1.** Lesen *n*. **2.** Lesung *f* (*a. parl.*). **3.** *be* (*od.* **make**) *good* **~** sich gut lesen. **4.** Deutung *f*, Auslegung *f*. **5.** 🔧 Anzeige *f*, (*Barometeretc*)Stand *m*. **II** *adj* **6.** Lese...: **~ glasses** *pl* Lesebrille *f*; **~ lamp** Leselampe *f*; **~ matter** Lesestoff *m*, Lektüre *f*; **~ room** Lesezimmer *n*, -saal *m*.

re·ad·just [,riːə'dʒʌst] **I** *v/t* 🔧 nachstellen, korrigieren: **~ o.s. →** II. **II** *v/i* (**to**) sich wiederanpassen (*an acc*), sich wiedereinstellen (auf *acc*). **,re·ad'just·ment** *s* **1.** Nachstellung *f*, Korrektur *f*. **2.** (**to**) Wiederanpassung *f* (an *acc*), Wiedereinstellung *f* (auf *acc*).

read·y ['redɪ] **I** *adj* (☐ → **readily**). bereit, fertig (**for s.th.** für et.; **to do** zu tun): **~ for takeoff** ✈ startbereit, -klar; **get** (*od.* **make**) **~** (sich) bereit- *od.* fertigmachen; **get ~ for an examination** sich auf *e-e* Prüfung vorbereiten. **2.** **be ~ to do s.th.** bereit *od.* willens sein, et. zu tun; schnell bei der Hand sein, et. zu tun: **~ to help** hilfsbereit, -willig. **3.** schnell, schlagfertig: **~ wit** Schlagfertigkeit *f*. **4.** im Begriff, nahe daran (**to do** zu tun): **→ drop** 10. **5. ~ money** (*od.* **cash**) Bargeld *n*. **II** *s* **6. the ~** F Bargeld *n*: **be a bit short of the ~** knapp bei Kasse sein. **'~-made** *adj* **1.** Konfektions...: **~ suit** Konfektionsanzug *m*. **2.** *fig.* passend, geeignet (*Entschuldigung etc*): **~ solution** Patentlösung *f*. **,~-to- -'wear → ready-made** 1.

re·af·firm [ˌriːəˈfɜːm] v/t nochmals versichern od. bestätigen.

re·af·for·est [ˌriːəˈfɒrɪst] v/t wieder aufforsten. **'re·af,for·es·ta·tion** s Wiederaufforstung f.

re·a·gent [riːˈeɪdʒənt] s 🜚 Reagens n.

re·al [rɪəl] **I** adj (□ → **really**) **1.** echt (Gold, Gefühl etc). **2.** real, tatsächlich, wirklich: **taken from ~ life** aus dem Leben gegriffen; **his ~ name** sein richtiger Name; **the ~ reason** der wahre Grund. **3. ~ estate** Grundeigentum n, Immobilien pl; **~ estate agent.** → **estate agent. II** adv **4.** bsd. Am. F sehr: **I'm ~ sorry** tut mir echt leid. **III** s **5. for ~** F echt, im Ernst: **be for ~** ernst gemeint sein.

re·al·ism [ˈrɪəlɪzəm] s Realismus m. **'re·al·ist** s Realist(in). **,re·al'is·tic** adj (**~ally**) realistisch.

re·al·i·ty [rɪˈælətɪ] s Realität f, Wirklichkeit f: **in ~** in Wirklichkeit; **become (a) ~** wahr werden.

re·al·i·za·tion [ˌrɪəlaɪˈzeɪʃn] s **1.** Erkenntnis f. **2.** Realisation f (a. ✝), Realisierung f, Verwirklichung f. **'re·al·ize** v/t **1.** erkennen, begreifen, einsehen: **he ~d that** a. ihm wurde klar, daß. **2.** realisieren, verwirklichen. **3.** ✝ realisieren, zu Geld machen.

re·al·ly [ˈrɪəlɪ] adv **1.** wirklich, tatsächlich: **~?** a. im Ernst? **2.** eigentlich: **not ~** eigentlich nicht. **3. well, ~!** ich muß schon sagen! **4. you ~ must come** du mußt unbedingt kommen.

realm [relm] s, a. pl fig. Reich n: **be within the ~s of possibility** im Bereich des Möglichen liegen.

re·an·i·mate [ˌriːˈænɪmeɪt] v/t **1.** 🜚 wiederbeleben. **2.** fig. neu beleben. **,re·an·i'ma·tion** s **1.** 🜚 Wiederbelebung f. **2.** fig. Neubelebung f.

reap [riːp] v/t Getreide etc schneiden, ernten; Feld abernten: **~ the benefit(s) of** fig. die Früchte (gen) ernten.

re·ap·pear [ˌriːəˈpɪə] v/i wiedererscheinen od. -auftauchen.

re·ap·prais·al [ˌriːəˈpreɪzl] s Neubewertung f, -beurteilung f. **,re·ap'praise** v/t neu bewerten od. beurteilen.

rear¹ [rɪə] **I** v/t **1.** Kind, Tier auf-, großziehen. **2.** Kopf heben, aufwerfen. **II** v/i **3.** sich aufbäumen (Pferd).

rear² [~] **I** s **1.** Hinter-, Rückseite f, mot.

Heck n: **at** (Am. **in**) **the ~ of** hinter (dat); **in the ~** hinten, im Heck. **2.** F Hintern m. **3. bring up the ~** die Nachhut bilden. **II** adj **4.** hinter, Hinter..., Rück..., mot. a. Heck...: **~ axle** Hinterachse f; **~ exit** Hinterausgang m; **~ window** Heckscheibe f; **~ wiper** Heckscheibenwischer m. **'~guard** s ✕ Nachhut f.

re·arm [ˌriːˈɑːm] v/i ✕ wieder aufrüsten. **re·ar·ma·ment** [rɪˈɑːməmənt] s Wiederaufrüstung f.

rear·most [ˈrɪəməʊst] adj hinterst.

re·ar·range [ˌriːəˈreɪndʒ] v/t Pläne etc ändern; Möbel etc umstellen; die Möbel umstellen in (dat).

'rear-view mir·ror s mot. Innen-, Rückspiegel m.

rear·ward [ˈrɪəwəd] **I** adj hinter, rückwärtig. **II** adv rückwärts.

'rear·wards → **rearward** II.

rea·son [ˈriːzn] **I** s **1.** Grund m (**for** für): **by ~ of** wegen; **for ~s of** health aus Gesundheitsgründen; **with ~** zu Recht; **without any ~, for no ~** ohne Grund, grundlos; **there is every ~ to believe that** alles spricht dafür, daß; **have every ~** guten Grund haben (**to do** zu tun). **2.** Verstand m. **3.** Vernunft f: **listen to ~** Vernunft annehmen. **II** v/i **4.** logisch denken. **5.** vernünftig reden (**with** mit). **III** v/t **6.** folgern (**that** daß). **7. ~ s.o. into** (**out of**) **s.th.** j-m et. ein(aus)reden. **'rea·son·a·ble** adj **1.** vernünftig. **2.** ganz gut, nicht schlecht. **3.** F billig, günstig. **'rea·son·a·bly** adv **1.** vernünftig. **2.** ziemlich, einigermaßen. **'rea·son·ing** s **1.** logisches Denken. **2.** Gedankengang m; Argumentation f.

re·as·sem·ble [ˌriːəˈsembl] v/t ⚙ wieder zs.-bauen.

re·as·sur·ance [ˌriːəˈʃɔːrəns] s Beruhigung f. **,re·as'sure** v/t beruhigen.

re·bate [ˈriːbeɪt] s **1.** Rabatt m, (Preis-)Nachlaß m. **2.** Rückzahlung f, -vergütung f.

reb·el¹ [ˈrebl] **I** s Rebell(in). **II** adj a) → **rebellious**, b) Rebellen...

re·bel² [rɪˈbel] v/i rebellieren, sich auflehnen (**against** gegen). **re'bel·lion** [~ʒən] s Rebellion f, Aufstand m. **re'bel·lious** [~ʒəs] adj □ rebellisch (a. Jugendlicher etc), aufständisch.

re·birth [ˌriːˈbɜːθ] s Wiedergeburt f (a. fig.).

re·bound I v/i [rı'baʊnd] **1.** ab-, zurückprallen (**from** von). **2.** fig. zurückfallen (**on** auf acc). II s ['ri:baʊnd] **3.** Sport: Abpraller m, (Basketball) Rebound m.

re·buff [rı'bʌf] I v/t schroff abweisen. II s schroffe Abweisung: **meet with a ~** schroff abgewiesen werden.

re·build [,ri:'bıld] v/t (irr build) **1.** wieder aufbauen. **2.** umbauen. **3.** fig. wiederaufbauen.

re·buke [rı'bju:k] I v/t rügen, tadeln (**for** wegen). II s Rüge f, Tadel m.

re·bus ['ri:bəs] s Rebus m, n, Bilderrätsel n.

re·cal·ci·trant [rı'kælsıtrənt] adj □ aufsässig.

re·call [rı'kɔ:l] I v/t **1.** j-n zurückrufen, Botschafter etc a. abberufen; defekte Autos etc (in die Werkstatt) zurückrufen. **2.** a) sich erinnern an (acc): **I can't ~ seeing her** ich kann mich nicht daran erinnern, sie gesehen zu haben, b) erinnern an (acc). II s **3.** Zurückrufung f, Abberufung f; Rückruf(aktion f) m. **4.** Gedächtnis n: **have total ~** das absolute Gedächtnis haben. **5. be beyond** (od. **past**) **~** für immer vorbei sein; **be lost beyond** (od. **past**) **~** unwiederbringlich verloren sein.

re·cap[1] ['ri:kæp] F → **recapitulate, recapitulation**.

re·cap[2] [,ri:'kæp] v/t Am. Reifen runderneuern.

re·ca·pit·u·late [,ri:kə'pıtjʊleıt] v/t u. v/i rekapitulieren, (kurz) zs.-fassen. '**re·ca,pit·u·la·tion** s Rekapitulation f, (kurze) Zs.-fassung.

re·cap·ture [,ri:'kæptʃə] I v/t **1.** Tier wieder einfangen, ausgebrochenen Häftling a. wieder fassen. **2.** ⚔ zurückerobern. II s **3.** Wiedereinfangen n, Wiederergreifung f. **4.** ⚔ Zurückeroberung f.

re·cast [,ri:'kɑ:st] v/t (irr cast) **1.** umformen (a. fig.); ⚙ umgießen. **2.** thea. etc neu besetzen, umbesetzen.

re·cede [rı'si:d] v/i **1.** schwinden (Hoffnung etc). **re'ced·ing** adj fliehend (Kinn, Stirn).

re·ceipt [rı'si:t] s **1.** bsd. ✝ Empfang m, Erhalt m, (a. von Waren) Eingang m: **on ~ of** nach Empfang (gen). **2.** bsd. ✝ Empfangsbescheinigung f, -bestäti-

gung f, Quittung f. **3.** pl ✝ Einnahmen pl.

re·ceive [rı'si:v] v/t **1.** bekommen, empfangen, erhalten; Aufmerksamkeit finden. **2.** j-n empfangen; Vorschlag etc aufnehmen. **3.** j-n aufnehmen (**into** in acc). **4.** Funkverkehr, Rundfunk, TV: empfangen: **are you receiving me?** hören Sie mich? **re'ceiv·er** s **1.** Empfänger(in). **2.** teleph. Hörer m. **3.** a. **official ~** ⚖ Br. Konkursverwalter(in). **4.** Hehler(in). **re'ceiv·ing** s Hehlerei f. II adj: **be on the ~ end of** F derjenige sein, der et. ausbaden muß; et. abkriegen.

re·cent ['ri:snt] adj jüngst (Ereignisse etc); neuer (Foto etc). '**re·cent·ly** adv kürzlich, vor kurzem; in letzter Zeit.

re·cep·ta·cle [rı'septəkl] s Behälter m.

re·cep·tion [rı'sepʃn] s **1.** (a. offizieller) Empfang: **give** (od. **hold**) **a ~** e-n Empfang geben; **give s.o. an enthusiastic ~** j-m e-n begeisterten Empfang bereiten. **2.** Hotel: Rezeption f: a) a. **~ desk** Empfang m: **at ~** am od. beim Empfang, b) Empfangshalle f: **in ~** in der Empfangshalle. **3.** Aufnahme f (**into** in acc). **4.** Funkverkehr, Rundfunk, TV: Empfang m. **re'cep·tion·ist** [,ʃənıst] s **1.** Empfangsdame f, -chef m. **2.** ⚕ Sprechstundenhilfe f.

re·cep·tive [rı'septıv] adj □ aufnahmefähig; empfänglich (**to** für).

re·cess [rı'ses] I s **1.** Pause f (Am. a. ped.), Unterbrechung f, parl. Ferien pl. **2.** Nische f. II v/t **3.** in e-e Nische stellen. **4.** einbauen: **~ed** Einbau...

re·ces·sion [rı'seʃn] s ✝ Rezession f.

re·cid·i·vist [rı'sıdıvıst] s Rückfalltäter(in).

rec·ipe ['resıpı] s gastr. Rezept n (**for** für) (a. fig.). **~ book** s Kochbuch n.

re·cip·i·ent [rı'sıpıənt] s Empfänger(in).

re·cip·ro·cal [rı'sıprəkl] adj □ wechsel-, gegenseitig; ling., ⚖ reziprok. **re'cip·ro·cate** [,keıt] I v/t Einladung, Gefühle etc erwidern. II v/i sich revanchieren (**for** für). **re,cip·ro'ca·tion** s Erwiderung f.

re·cit·al [rı'saıtl] s **1.** Vortrag m, (Klavier- etc)Konzert n, (Lieder)Abend m. **2.** Schilderung f. **rec·i·ta·tion** [,resı-'teıʃn] s **1.** Auf-, Hersagen n. **2.** Rezitation f, Vortrag m. **rec·i·ta·tive** [,resıtə-

'ti:v] *s* ♪ Rezitativ *n*. **re·cite** [rɪ'saɪt] *v/t* **1.** auf-, hersagen. **2.** rezitieren, vortragen. **3.** aufzählen.

reck·less ['reklɪs] *adj* □ rücksichtslos. **'reck·less·ness** *s* Rücksichtslosigkeit *f*.

reck·on ['rekən] **I** *v/t* **1.** aus-, berechnen: ~ *in* ein-, mitrechnen; ~ *up* zs.-rechnen. **2.** ~ *s.o.* (*to be*) *clever* j-n für clever halten: *he is* ~*ed* (*to be*) *clever* er gilt als clever. **3.** rechnen, zählen (*among* zu). **4.** glauben, schätzen (*that* daß). **II** *v/i* **5.** ~ *on* rechnen auf (*acc*) od. mit; ~ *with* rechnen mit; *he's a man to be* ~*ed with* mit ihm muß man rechnen; *you'll have me to* ~ *with* du wirst es mit mir zu tun bekommen; ~ *without* nicht rechnen mit. **'reck·on·ing** *s* Berechnung *f*: *by my* ~ nach m-r (Be)Rechnung; *be out in one's* ~ sich verrechnen haben.

re·claim [rɪ'kleɪm] *v/t* **1.** zurückfordern, -verlangen (*from* von); *Gepäck etc* abholen. **2.** ~ *land from the sea* dem Meer Land abgewinnen. **3.** ⚙, ⚒ wiedergewinnen (*from* aus). **rec·la·ma·tion** [ˌreklə'meɪʃn] *s* **1.** Rückforderung *f*. **2.** ⚙, ⚒ Wiedergewinnung *f*.

re·cline [rɪ'klaɪn] *v/i* sich zurücklehnen: ~*ing seat* mot. *etc*-Ruhesitz *m*.

re·cluse [rɪ'klu:s] *s* Einsiedler(in).

rec·og·ni·tion [ˌrekəg'nɪʃn] *s* **1.** (Wieder)Erkennen *n*: *be burnt beyond* (*od. out of all*) ~ bis zur Unkenntlichkeit verbrennen; *the town has changed beyond* ~ die Stadt ist nicht wiederzuerkennen. **2.** Anerkennung *f*: *in* (*od. as a*) ~ *of* als Anerkennung für, in Anerkennung (*gen*); *gain* (*od. get, win*) ~ Anerkennung finden. **rec·og·niz·a·ble** ['naɪzəbl] *adj* □ (wieder)erkennbar: *be hardly* ~ kaum zu erkennen sein. **re·cog·nize** ['rekəgnaɪz] *v/t* **1.** (wieder)erkennen (*by* an *dat*). **2.** anerkennen (*a. pol.*). **3.** eingestehen, zugeben (*that* daß).

re·coil **I** *v/i* [rɪ'kɔɪl] **1.** zurückschrecken (*from* vor *dat*) (*a. fig.*): ~ *from doing s.th.* davor zurückschrecken, et. zu tun. **2.** zurückstoßen (*Gewehr etc*). **3.** ~ *on fig.* zurückfallen auf (*acc*). **II** *s* ['ri:kɔɪl] **4.** Rückstoß *m*.

rec·ol·lect [ˌrekə'lekt] **I** *v/t* sich erinnern

an (*acc*): ~ *doing s.th.* sich daran erinnern, et. getan zu haben. **II** *v/i*: *as far as I* (*can*) ~ soweit ich mich erinnere. **rec·ol·lec·tion** *s* Erinnerung *f* (*of* an *acc*): *to the best of my* ~ soweit ich mich erinnere.

rec·om·mend [ˌrekə'mend] *v/t* **1.** empfehlen (*as* als; *for* für): ~ *doing s.th.* empfehlen *od.* raten, et. zu tun. **2.** sprechen für: *he has little to* ~ *him* es spricht wenig für ihn. **rec·om·mend·a·ble** *adj* empfehlenswert; ratsam. **rec·om·men·da·tion** [ˌmen'deɪʃn] *s* Empfehlung *f*: *on s.o.'s* ~ auf j-s Empfehlung.

rec·om·pense ['rekəmpens] **I** *v/t* entschädigen (*for* für). **II** *s* Entschädigung *f*: *as a* (*od. in*) ~ als Entschädigung (*for* für).

rec·on·cile ['rekənsaɪl] *v/t* **1.** ver-, aussöhnen (*with* mit): *they are* ~*d again* sie haben sich wieder versöhnt; *become* ~*d to s.th. fig.* sich mit et. abfinden. **2.** in Einklang bringen (*with* mit). **rec·on·cil·i·a·tion** [ˌsɪlɪ'eɪʃn] *s* **1.** Ver-, Aussöhnung *f* (*between* zwischen *dat*; *with* mit). **2.** Einklang *m*.

rec·on·dite ['rekəndaɪt] *adj* □ abstrus, schwerverständlich.

re·con·di·tion [ˌri:kən'dɪʃn] *v/t* ⚙ (general)überholen: ~*ed engine* Austauschmotor *m*.

re·con·nais·sance [rɪ'kɒnɪsəns] *s* ✕ Aufklärung *f*, Erkundung *f*: ~ *flight* *s* Aufklärungsflug *m*. ~ *plane* *s* Aufklärungsflugzeug *n*, Aufklärer *m*.

rec·on·noi·ter *Am., bsd. Br..* **rec·on·noi·tre** [ˌrekə'nɔɪtə] *v/t* ✕ erkunden, auskundschaften.

re·con·quer [ˌri:'kɒŋkə] *v/t* zurückerobern. **'re·con·quest** [~kwest] *s* Zurückeroberung *f*.

re·con·sid·er [ˌri:kən'sɪdə] *v/t* noch einmal überdenken. **'re·con,sid·er·a·tion** *s* nochmaliges Überdenken.

re·con·struct [ˌri:kən'strʌkt] *v/t* **1.** wieder aufbauen; *fig.* wiederaufbauen. **2.** *fig.* Fall *etc* rekonstruieren. **re·con·struc·tion** *s* **1.** Wiederaufbau *m*. **2.** *fig.* Rekonstruktion *f*.

rec·ord ['rekɔːd] **I** *s* **1.** Aufzeichnung *f*, Niederschrift *f*, ⚖ Protokoll *n*: *off the* ~ inoffiziell; *on* ~ aktenkundig; geschichtlich verzeichnet, schriftlich belegt; *fig.* aller Zeiten; **he is** (*od.* **went**) **on ~ as having said that** er hat sich offiziell dahingehend geäußert, daß; **keep a ~ of** Buch führen über (*acc*); **to set the ~ straight** um das klarzustellen. **2.** Vergangenheit *f*; *gute etc* Leistungen *pl* (*in der Vergangenheit*): **have a criminal ~** vorbestraft sein. **3.** (Schall)Platte *f*: **make a ~** e-e Platte aufnehmen. **4.** *Sport etc*: Rekord *m.* **II** *adj* **5.** (Schall)Platten...: **~ player** Plattenspieler *m.* **6.** *Sport etc*: Rekord...: **~ holder** Rekordhalter(in), -inhaber(in); **in ~ time** in Rekordzeit.

re·cord² [rɪˈkɔːd] *v/t* **1.** schriftlich niederlegen, aufzeichnen, -schreiben; ⚖️ protokollieren, zu Protokoll *od.* zu den Akten nehmen. **2.** (*auf Tonband etc*) aufnehmen, *Programm a.* aufzeichnen, mitschneiden: **~ed broadcast** (*Rundfunk, TV*) Aufzeichnung *f.* **3.** *Meßwerte* registrieren.

'rec·ord-ˌbreak·ing *adj Sport etc*: Rekord...

re·cord·er [rɪˈkɔːdə] *s* **1.** (*Kassetten*)Recorder *m*, (*Tonband*)Gerät *n.* **2.** ♪ Blockflöte *f.* **re'cord·ing** *s* Aufnahme *f*, Aufzeichnung *f*, Mitschnitt *m*: **~ studio** Aufnahme-, Tonstudio *n.*

re·count¹ [rɪˈkaʊnt] *v/t* erzählen.

re·count² **I** *v/t* [ˌriːˈkaʊnt] nachzählen. **II** *s* ['riːkaʊnt] Nachzählung *f.*

re·coup [rɪˈkuːp] *v/t* **1.** *Verlust etc* wiedereinbringen, sich *Ausgaben etc* zurückholen (**from** von). **2.** *j-n* entschädigen (**for** für).

re·course [rɪˈkɔːs] *s*: **have ~ to** greifen *od.* Zuflucht nehmen zu.

re·cov·er [rɪˈkʌvə] **I** *v/t et. Verlorenes* wiederfinden; *Bewußtsein etc* wiedererlangen; *Kosten etc* wiedereinbringen; *Fahrzeug, Verunglückten etc* bergen: **~ one's composure** sich wieder fangen *od.* fassen; **~ consciousness** *a.* wieder zu sich kommen. **II** *v/i* sich erholen (**from** von) (*a. fig.*): **he has fully ~ed** er ist wieder ganz gesund. **re'cov·er·y** *s* **1.** Wiederfinden *n*; Wiedererlangen *n*; Wiedereinbringung *f*; Bergung *f.* **2.** Erholung *f* (*a. fig.*): **make a complete ~** völlig gesund werden; **make a quick** (*od.* **speedy**) **~** sich schnell erholen; **wish s.o. a speedy ~** j-m gute Besserung wünschen.

rec·re·a·tion [ˌrekrɪˈeɪʃn] *s* Entspannung *f*, Erholung *f*; Unterhaltung *f*, Freizeitbeschäftigung *f*: **~ ground** Spielplatz *m.* **ˌrec·re'a·tion·al** [-ʃənl] *adj* Erholungs-...; Freizeit...: **~ activities** *pl* Freizeitgestaltung *f*; **~ value** Freizeitwert *m.*

re·crim·i·nate [rɪˈkrɪmɪneɪt] *v/i* Gegenbeschuldigungen vorbringen (**against** gegen). **re·ˌcrim·i'na·tion** *s* Gegenbeschuldigung *f*: **their ~(s** *pl*) ihre gegenseitigen Beschuldigungen *pl.*

re·cruit [rɪˈkruːt] **I** *s* **1.** ✗ Rekrut *m.* **2.** (**to**) Neue *m*, *f* (*in dat*); neues Mitglied (*gen od.* **in** *dat*). **II** *v/t* **3.** ✗ rekrutieren; *Personal* einstellen; *Mitglieder* werben. **re'cruit·ment** *s* ✗ Rekrutierung *f*; Einstellung *f*; Werbung *f.*

rec·ta ['rektə] *pl von* **rectum.**

rec·tan·gle ['rektæŋgl] *s* A Rechteck *n.* **rec'tan·gu·lar** [-ɡjʊlə] *adj* □ rechteckig; rechtwink(e)lig.

rec·ti·fi·ca·tion [ˌrektɪfɪˈkeɪʃn] *s* **1.** Berichtigung *f*, Korrektur *f.* **2.** 🍶 Rektifikation *f.* **3.** ⚡ Gleichrichtung *f.* **rec·ti·fy** ['-faɪ] *v/t* **1.** berichtigen, korrigieren. **2.** 🍶 rektifizieren. **3.** ⚡ gleichrichten.

rec·ti·lin·e·ar [ˌrektɪˈlɪnɪə] *adj* □ geradlinig.

rec·ti·tude ['rektɪtjuːd] *s* Redlichkeit *f*, Rechtschaffenheit *f.*

rec·tor ['rektə] *s* Pfarrer *m.* **'rec·to·ry** *s* Pfarrhaus *n.*

rec·tum ['rektəm] *pl* **-tums, -ta** ['-tə] *s* *anat.* Mastdarm *m.*

re·cu·per·ate [rɪˈkuːpəreɪt] **I** *v/i* sich erholen (**from** von) (*a. fig.*). **II** *v/t Verluste etc* wettmachen. **re·ˌcu·per'a·tion** *s* **1.** Erholung *f* (*a. fig.*). **2.** Wettmachen *n.*

re·cur [rɪˈkɜː] *v/i* wiederkehren, wiederauftreten (*Problem, Symptom etc*), (*Schmerz a.*) wiedereinsetzen: **~ to s.o.** j-m wiederkommen (*Erinnerung etc*). **re·cur·rence** [rɪˈkʌrəns] *s* Wiederkehr *f*, Wiederauftreten *n*, Wiedereinsetzen *n.* **re'cur·rent** *adj* □ wiederkehrend, wiederauftretend, wiedereinsetzend.

re·cy·cle [ˌriːˈsaɪkl] *v/t* wiederverwerten. **ˌre'cy·cling** *s* Recycling *n*, Wiederverwertung *f.*

red [red] **I** *adj* **1.** rot: **the lights are ~** die Ampel steht auf Rot; **go** (*od.* **turn**) **~** rot werden; → **flag¹** 1, **paint** 2, **rag** 1. **2.** *oft* ♀ *pol.* rot. **II** *s* **3.** Rot *n*: **at ~** bei Rot; **the**

lights are at ≈ die Ampel steht auf Rot; *dressed in* ≈ rot *od.* in Rot gekleidet; *see* ≈ *fig.* rotsehen; *be in the* ≈ ✝ in den roten Zahlen sein, rote Zahlen schreiben. **4.** *oft* ⚩ *pol.* Rote m, f. ≈ **car·pet** s roter Teppich. ‚≈'**car·pet** adj: *give s.o. the* ≈ *treatment* j-n mit großem Bahnhof empfangen. ⚩ **Cross** s Rotes Kreuz.

red·den ['redn] **I** v/t röten, rot färben. **II** v/i rot werden (*with* vor dat). '**red·dish** adj □ rötlich.

re·dec·o·rate [ˌriːˈdekəreɪt] v/t Zimmer etc neu streichen *od.* tapezieren.

re·deem [rɪˈdiːm] v/t **1.** *Pfand, Versprechen etc* einlösen. **2.** *Ruf etc* wiederherstellen: ≈ *o.s.* sich rehabilitieren. **3.** *Gefangene etc* los-, freikaufen. **4.** *Hypothek, Schulden etc* abzahlen, tilgen. **5.** *schlechte Eigenschaft etc* ausgleichen, wettmachen. **6.** *bsd. eccl.* erlösen (*from* von). **Re'deem·er** s *eccl.* Erlöser m, Heiland m.

re·demp·tion [rɪˈdempʃn] s **1.** Einlösung f. **2.** Wiederherstellung f. **3.** Los-, Freikauf m. **4.** Abzahlung f, Tilgung f. **5.** Ausgleich m. **6.** *bsd. eccl.* Erlösung f (*from* von). **7.** *beyond* (*od. past*) ≈ hoffnungslos.

re·de·vel·op [ˌriːdɪˈveləp] v/t *Gebäude, Stadtteil* sanieren. ‚**re·de'vel·op·ment** s Sanierung f.

‚**red**|-'**hand·ed** adj: *catch s.o.* ≈ j-n auf frischer Tat ertappen. ‚≈'**head·ed** adj rothaarig. ≈ **her·ring** s **1.** Bückling m. **2.** *fig.* Ablenkungsmanöver n; falsche Fährte *od.* Spur. ‚≈'**hot** adj **1.** rotglühend (*Metall*); glühendheiß. **2.** *fig.* glühend, überschwenglich (*Begeisterung*). **3.** *fig.* brandaktuell (*Nachricht etc*). ⚩ **In·di·an** s Indianer(in).

re·di·rect [ˌriːdɪˈrekt] v/t *Brief etc* nachschicken, -senden (*to s.o.* j-m; *to a new address* an e-e neue Adresse).

re·dis·cov·er [ˌriːdɪsˈkʌvə] v/t wiederentdecken. ‚**re·dis'cov·er·y** s Wiederentdeckung f.

re·dis·trib·ute [ˌriːdɪˈstrɪbjuːt] v/t neu verteilen, umverteilen. '**re‚dis·tri'bu·tion** [-ˈbjuːʃn] s Neu-, Umverteilung f.

‚**red**|-'**let·ter day** s Freuden-, Glückstag m (*for* für). ≈ **light** s **1.** rotes Licht (*Warnsignal etc*): *see the* ≈ *fig.* die Gefahr erkennen. **2.** Rotlicht n: *go*

through the ≈ bei Rot über die Kreuzung fahren. ‚≈'**light dis·trict** s Rotlichtbezirk m, Bordellviertel n.

red·ness ['rednɪs] s Röte f.

re·do [ˌriːˈduː] v/t (*irr do*) **1.** nochmals tun *od.* machen: ≈ *one's hair* sich die Haare in Ordnung bringen. **2.** → **redecorate**.

re·dou·ble [ˌriːˈdʌbl] v/t *bsd. Anstrengungen* verdoppeln.

re·dress [rɪˈdres] **I** v/t *Unrecht* wiedergutmachen; *Mißstand etc* abstellen, beseitigen; *Gleichgewicht* wiederherstellen. **II** s Wiedergutmachung f; Abstellung f, Beseitigung f: *seek* ≈ *for* Wiedergutmachung verlangen für.

red tape s Amtsschimmel m, Bürokratismus m.

re·duce [rɪˈdjuːs] v/t **1.** *Foto etc* verkleinern, *Steuern etc* senken, *Geschwindigkeit, Risiko etc* verringern, *Preis, Waren* herabsetzen, reduzieren (*from ... to* von ... auf acc), *Gehalt etc* kürzen. **2.** (*to*) verwandeln (in acc), machen (zu): ≈ *to a nervous wreck* aus j-m ein Nervenbündel machen. **4.** ≈ *s.o. to silence* (*tears*) j-n zum Schweigen (Weinen) bringen. **5.** reduzieren, zurückführen (*to* auf acc). **6.** 🔬 reduzieren. **7.** → **denominator**. **re·duc·tion** [rɪˈdʌkʃn] s **1.** Verkleinerung f. **2.** Senkung f, Verringerung f, Herabsetzung f, Reduzierung f, Kürzung f. **3.** 🔬 Reduktion f.

re·dun·dan·cy [rɪˈdʌndənsɪ] s **1.** ✝ Freistellung f, -setzung f. **2.** *ling.* Redundanz f. **re'dun·dant** adj □ **1.** ✝ freigestellt, -gesetzt: *be made* ≈ freigestellt *od.* -gesetzt werden. **2.** *ling.* redundant.

red wine s Rotwein m.

re·ech·o [riːˈekəʊ] v/i widerhallen (*with* von).

reed [riːd] s Schilf(rohr) n, Ried n; (*einzelnes*) Schilfrohr.

re·ed·u·cate [ˌriːˈedʒʊkeɪt] v/t umerziehen. '**re-‚ed·u'ca·tion** s Umerziehung f.

reed·y ['riːdɪ] adj □ **1.** schilfig. **2.** piepsig (*Stimme*).

reef[1] [riːf] s (Felsen)Riff n.

reef[2] [≈] v/t ⚓ *Segel* reffen. ≈ **knot** s Kreuz-, Weberknoten m.

reek [ri:k] **I** s Gestank m: **there was a ~ of garlic** es stank nach Knoblauch. **II** v/i stinken (**of** nach).

reel¹ [ri:l] s (*Kabel-, Schlauch- etc*)Rolle f, (*Film-, Garn- etc*)Spule f. **II** v/t: ~ **off** abrollen, abspulen; *fig.* herunterrasseln; ~ **up** aufrollen, -spulen.

reel² [~] v/i **1.** sich drehen: **my head ~ed** mir drehte sich alles, mir wurde schwindlig; **the room ~ed before my eyes** das Zimmer drehte sich vor m-n Augen. **2.** wanken, taumeln, (*Betrunkener a.*) torkeln.

re-e-lect [,ri:ɪ'lekt] v/t wiederwählen. **re-e-lec-tion** s Wiederwahl f: **seek ~** sich erneut zur Wahl stellen.

re-en-ter [,ri:'entə] v/t wieder eintreten in (acc) (a. *Raumfahrt*), wieder betreten. **re-en-try** s Wiedereintreten n, -eintritt m (**into** in acc).

ref [ref] s *Sport:* F Schiri m; (*Boxen*) Ringrichter m.

re-fec-to-ry [rɪ'fektərɪ] s *univ.* Mensa f.

re-fer [rɪ'fɜ:] **I** v/t **1.** j-n ver-, hinweisen (**to** auf acc). **2.** j-n (*um Auskunft etc*) verweisen (**to** an acc). **3.** (**to**) *et.* übergeben (dat), a. *Patienten* überweisen (an acc): ~ **back** zurückverweisen. **II** v/i **4.** ver-, hinweisen (**to** auf acc). **5.** (**to**) sich berufen *od.* beziehen (auf acc); anspielen (auf acc); erwähnen (acc). **6.** (**to**) nachschlagen in (dat), konsultieren (acc). **ref-er-ee** [,refə'ri:] **I** s **1.** 🏀, *Sport:* Schiedsrichter m, (*Boxen*) Ringrichter m. **2.** *Br.* → **reference** 5b. **II** v/i **3.** 🏀, *Sport:* als Schiedsrichter fungieren, (*Sport a.*) pfeifen, (*Boxen*) als Ringrichter fungieren. **III** v/t **4.** 🏀, *Sport:* als Schiedsrichter fungieren bei, (*Sport a.*) Spiel pfeifen, (*Boxen*) Kampf leiten. **ref-er-ence** [*refrəns*] s **1.** Verweis m, Hinweis m (**to** auf acc): (*list of*) ~**s** pl Quellenangabe f. **2.** Verweisstelle f; Beleg m, Unterlage f: ~ **number** Aktenzeichen n. **3.** (**to**) Bezugnahme f (auf acc); Anspielung f (auf acc); Erwähnung f (gen): **make** (a) ~ **to** → **refer** 5. **4.** (**to**) Nachschlagen n (in dat), Konsultieren n (gen): ~ **book** Nachschlagewerk n; ~ **library** Handbibliothek f. **5.** Referenz f: a) Empfehlung f, b) Auskunftgeber m: **act as a ~ for s.o.** j-m als Referenz dienen.

ref-er-en-dum [,refə'rendəm] pl **-dums**, **-da** [~də] s *pol.* Referendum n, Volksabstimmung f, -entscheid m.

re-fill I v/t [,ri:'fɪl] **1.** wieder füllen, nach-, auffüllen. **II** s ['ri:fɪl] **2.** (*Füller*)Patrone f, (*Kugelschreiber- etc*)Mine f. **3.** **would you like a ~?** F darf ich nachschenken?

re-fine [rɪ'faɪn] **I** v/t **1.** *Öl, Zucker* raffinieren. **2.** *fig.* verfeinern, kultivieren. **II** v/i **3.** ~ **on** *fig.* verbessern, -feinern. **re'fined** adj **1.** raffiniert: ~ **sugar** Raffinade f. **2.** *fig.* kultiviert, vornehm. **re'fine-ment** s **1.** Raffination f, Raffinierung f. **2.** Verbesserung f, -feinerung f. **3.** *fig.* Kultiviertheit f, Vornehmheit f. **re'fin-er-y** s Raffinerie f.

re-flect [rɪ'flekt] **I** v/t **1.** *Strahlen etc* reflektieren, zurückwerfen, -strahlen, *Bild etc* reflektieren, (wider)spiegeln (a. acc): **be ~ed in** sich (wider)spiegeln in (dat) (a. *fig.*); ~ (**dis**)**credit on** ein gutes (schlechtes) Licht werfen auf (acc); ~**ing telescope** Spiegelteleskop n. **II** v/i *fig.* **2.** nachdenken (**on** über acc). **3.** ~ (**badly**) **on** sich nachteilig auswirken auf (acc); ein schlechtes Licht werfen auf (acc). **re'flec-tion** s **1.** Reflexion f, Zurückwerfung f, -strahlung f, (Wider)Spieg(e)lung f (a. *fig.*). **2.** Spiegelbild n. **3.** *fig.* Überlegung f: **on ~** nach einigem Nachdenken; **wenn ich etc es mir recht überlege. 4.** mst pl *fig.* Betrachtung f (**on** über acc). **re'flec-tive** adj □ **1.** reflektierend, (wider)spiegelnd. **2.** *fig.* nachdenklich. **re'flec-tor** s **1.** Reflektor m. **2.** Rückstrahler m.

re-flex ['ri:fleks] s a. ~ **action** Reflex m. ~ **cam-er-a** s *phot.* Spiegelreflexkamera f.

re-flex-ive [rɪ'fleksɪv] adj □ *ling.* reflexiv, rückbezüglich: ~ **pronoun** Reflexivpronomen n, rückbezügliches Fürwort; ~ **verb** reflexives Verb, rückbezügliches Zeitwort.

re-for-est [,ri:'fɒrɪst], **re,for-es'ta-tion** → **reafforest, reafforestation.**

re-form [rɪ'fɔ:m] **I** s **1.** *pol. etc* Reform f. **2.** Besserung f. **II** v/t **3.** j-n bessern. **ref-or-ma-tion** [,refə'meɪʃn] s **1.** Reformierung f: **the ≳** *eccl.* die Reformation. **2.** Besserung f. **re-form-a-to-ry** [rɪ'fɔ:mətərɪ] adj Reform... **re'form-er** s

1. *pol. etc* Reformer *m*. **2.** *eccl.* Reformator *m*.

re·fract [rɪˈfrækt] *v/t phys.* Strahlen, Wellen brechen. **re'frac·tion** *s* Refraktion *f*, Brechung *f*.

re·frac·to·ry [rɪˈfræktərɪ] *adj* □ **1.** eigensinnig, störrisch. **2.** 🌡 hartnäckig.

re·frain¹ [rɪˈfreɪn] *v/i* (**from**) absehen (von), sich enthalten (*gen*), unterlassen (*acc*): ~ *from doing s.th.* es unterlassen, et. zu tun.

re·frain² [~] *s* Kehrreim *m*, Refrain *m*.

re·fresh [rɪˈfreʃ] *v/t* (**o.s.** sich) erfrischen; *fig.* Gedächtnis auffrischen. **re'fresh·er** *s* **1.** Erfrischung *f* (*Getränk etc*). **2.** ~ *course* Auffrischungskurs *m*. **re'fresh·ing** *adj* □ erfrischend (*a. fig.*). **re'fresh·ment** *s* Erfrischung *f* (*a. Getränk etc*).

re·frig·er·ate [rɪˈfrɪdʒəreɪt] *v/t* ⊙ kühlen. **re,frig·er'a·tion** *s* Kühlung *f*. **re'frig·er·a·tor** *s* Kühlschrank *m*: ~*freezer* Kühl-u. Gefrierkombination *f*.

re·fu·el [ˌriːˈfjʊəl] *v/t u. v/i pret u. pp* **-eled**, *bsd. Br.* **-elled** ✈, *mot.* auftanken.

ref·uge [ˈrefjuːdʒ] *s* Zuflucht *f* (**from** vor *dat*) (*a. fig.*): *place of* ~ Zufluchtsort *m*; *seek* ~ Zuflucht suchen; *take* ~ *in* Zuflucht nehmen zu, sich flüchten in (*acc*). **ref·u·gee** [ˌrefjʊˈdʒiː] *s* Flüchtling *m*: ~ *camp* Flüchtlingslager *n*.

re·fund *v/t* [riːˈfʌnd] Geld zurückzahlen, -erstatten, *Auslagen* ersetzen: ~ *s.o. his money* j-m sein Geld zurückzahlen. **II** [ˈriːfʌnd] Rückzahlung *f*, -erstattung *f*.

re·fur·bish [ˌriːˈfɜːbɪʃ] *v/t* **1.** aufpolieren (*a. fig.*). **2.** renovieren.

re·fus·al [rɪˈfjuːzl] *s* **1.** Ablehnung *f*; Verweigerung *f*: → *meet* 15. **2.** Weigerung *f* (**to do** zu tun).

re·fuse¹ [rɪˈfjuːz] **I** *v/t* **1.** Kandidaten etc ablehnen, *Angebot a.* ausschlagen: ~ *s.o. s.th.* j-m et. ausschlagen *od.* verweigern. **2.** sich weigern, es ablehnen (**to do** zu tun). **II** *v/i* **3.** ablehnen. **4.** sich weigern.

ref·use² [ˈrefjuːs] *s* Abfall *m*, Abfälle *pl*, Müll *m*. ~ *dump s* Müllabladeplatz *m*, -deponie *f*.

ref·u·ta·ble [ˈrefjʊtəbl] *adj* □ widerlegbar. **ref·u·ta·tion** [ˌ~juˈteɪʃn] *s* Wider-

legung *f*. **re·fute** [rɪˈfjuːt] *v/t* widerlegen.

re·gain [rɪˈgeɪn] *v/t* wieder-, zurückgewinnen: ~ *one's health* (**strength**) wieder gesund werden (wieder zu Kräften kommen).

re·gal [ˈriːgl] *adj* □ **1.** königlich. **2.** *fig.* hoheits-, würdevoll.

re·gale [rɪˈgeɪl] *v/t* **1.** fürstlich bewirten (**with** mit). **2.** erfreuen, ergötzen (**with** mit).

re·ga·li·a [rɪˈgeɪljə] *s pl* Insignien *pl*.

re·gard [rɪˈgɑːd] **I** *s* **1.** Achtung *f*: *hold s.o. in high* (**low**) ~ j-n hochachten (geringachten). **2.** Rücksicht *f*: *without* ~ *to* (*od.* **for**) ohne Rücksicht auf (*acc*); *have no* ~ *for, pay no* ~ *to* keine Rücksicht nehmen auf (*acc*). **3.** *in this* ~ in dieser Hinsicht; *in* ~ *to* im Hinblick auf (*acc*). **4.** *give him my* (**best**) ~*s* grüße ihn (herzlich) von mir; *with kind* ~*s* mit freundlichen Grüßen. **II** *v/t* **5.** betrachten, ansehen. **6.** *fig.* betrachten (**with** mit): ~ *as* betrachten als, halten für; *he ~ed as* gelten als. **7.** *as ~s* ... was ... betrifft. **re'gard·ing** *prp* bezüglich, hinsichtlich. **re'gard·less I** *adj*: ~ *of* ohne Rücksicht auf (*acc*). **II** *adv* F trotzdem.

re·gat·ta [rɪˈgætə] *s Sport:* Regatta *f*.

re·gen·cy [ˈriːdʒənsɪ] *s* Regentschaft *f*.

re·gen·er·ate [rɪˈdʒenəreɪt] *v/t u. v/i* (sich) regenerieren *od.* erneuern. **re,gen·er'a·tion** *s* Regenerierung *f*, Erneuerung *f*.

re·gent [ˈriːdʒənt] *s* Regent(in).

re·gime [reɪˈʒiːm] *s* **1.** *pol.* Regime *n*. **2.** → *regimen*.

reg·i·men [ˈredʒɪmen] *s* Lebensweise *f*; *engS.* Diät *f*.

reg·i·ment I *s* [ˈredʒɪmənt] **1.** ✗ Regiment *n*. **2.** *fig.* Schar *f*. **II** *v/t* [ˈ~ment] **3.** reglementieren, gängeln, bevormunden. **reg·i·men·tal** [ˌ~ˈmentl] *adj* ✗ Regiments... **reg·i·men·ta·tion** [ˌ~menˈteɪʃn] *s* Reglementierung *f*, Gängelung *f*, Bevormundung *f*.

re·gion [ˈriːdʒən] *s* Gebiet *n*, Gegend *f*, Region *f*: *in the* ~ *of the heart* in der Herzgegend; *in the* ~ *of £50* um die *od.* ungefähr 50 Pfund. **re·gion·al** [ˈ~dʒənl] *adj* □ regional.

reg·is·ter [ˈredʒɪstə] **I** *s* **1.** Register *n*, Verzeichnis *n*, (*Wähler- etc*)Liste *f*:

keep a ~ of Buch führen über (*acc*). **2.** ✪ Registrierer *n*. **3.** Sprach-, Stilebene *f*. **II** *v/t* **4.** registrieren, eintragen (lassen). **~ed trademark** eingetragenes Warenzeichen. **5.** Meßwerte registrieren, anzeigen; *fig.* Empfindung zeigen. **6.** ✒ *Brief etc* einschreiben lassen: **~ed letter** Einschreib(e)brief *m*, Einschreiben *n*; **send s.th. by ~ed mail** (*bsd. Br.* **post**) et. eingeschrieben schicken. **III** *v/i* **7.** sich eintragen (lassen). **8.** *he told me who he was* **but it didn't ~** F aber ich habe es nicht registriert *od.* zur Kenntnis genommen. **~ of·fice** *s bsd. Br.* Standesamt *n*.

reg·is·trar [ˌredʒɪˈstrɑː] *s bsd. Br.* Standesbeamter *m*, -beamtin *f*. **reg·is·tra-tion** [ˌ~ˈstreɪʃn] *s* Registrierung *f*, Eintragung *f*: **~ document** *mot. Br.* (*etwa*) Kraftfahrzeugbrief *m*; **~ number** *mot.* (polizeiliches) Kennzeichen. **'reg·is·try** *s* Registratur *f*: **~ office** *bsd. Br.* Standesamt *n*.

re·gress [rɪˈgres] *v/i* **1.** sich rückläufig entwickeln (*Gesellschaft*). **2.** *biol., psych.* sich zurückentwickeln. **re·gres-sion** [rɪˈgreʃn] *s* **1.** rückläufige Entwicklung. **2.** *biol., psych.* Regression *f*, Rückentwicklung *f*. **re'gres·sive** [~sɪv] *adj* □ regressiv, rückläufig.

re·gret [rɪˈgret] **I** *v/t* **1.** bedauern; bereuen: **~ doing s.th.** es bedauern *od.* bereuen, et. getan zu haben; **we ~ to inform you that** wir müssen Ihnen leider mitteilen, daß. **2.** *j-m, e-r Sache* nachtrauern. **II** *s* **3.** Bedauern *n* (**at** über *acc*); Reue *f*: **with great ~** mit großem Bedauern; **have no ~s** nichts bereuen; **have no ~s about doing s.th.** es nicht bedauern *od.* bereuen, et. getan zu haben. **re'gret·ful** [~fʊl] *adj* bedauernd: **~ly** mit Bedauern. **re'gret·ta·ble** *adj* bedauerlich. **re'gret·ta·bly** *adv* bedauerlicherweise.

re·group [ˌriːˈgruːp] *v/t u. v/i* (sich) umgruppieren.

reg·u·lar [ˈregjʊlə] **I** *adj* □ **1.** (*zeitlich*) regelmäßig: **~ customer** Stammkunde *m*, -kundin *f*; Stammgast *m*; **at ~ inter-vals** in regelmäßigen Abständen (*a. örtlich*). **2.** regelmäßig (*in Form od. Anordnung*). **3.** regelmäßig (*Atmen etc*): **at ~ speed** mit gleichbleibender Geschwindigkeit. **4.** geregelt, geordnet

(*Leben etc*): **be in ~ employment** fest angestellt sein. **5.** *ling.* regelmäßig. **6.** *Sport:* Stamm...: **~ player**. **7.** **~ gaso-line** *mot. Am.* Normalbenzin *n*. **II** *s* F **8.** Stammkunde *m*, -kundin *f*; Stammgast *m*. **9.** *Sport:* Stammspieler(in). **10.** *mot. Am.* Normal *n*. **reg·u·lar-i·ty** [ˌ~ˈlærətɪ] *s* Regelmäßigkeit *f*. **reg·u·lar·ize** [ˈ~ləraɪz] *v/t* regulieren.

reg·u·late [ˈregjʊlet] *v/t* **1.** regeln, regulieren. **2.** ✪ einstellen, regulieren. **reg-u·la·tion** *s* **1.** Reg(e)lung *f*, Regulierung *f*. **2.** ✪ Einstellung *f*. **3.** Vorschrift *f*. **'reg·u·la·tor** *s* ✪ Regler *m*.

re·ha·bil·i·tate [ˌriːəˈbɪlɪteɪt] *v/t* **1.** Schwerbehinderte rehabilitieren. **2.** Strafentlassene resozialisieren. **3.** *j-s Ruf etc* wiederherstellen: **be ~d** rehabilitiert werden (*Person*). **re·ha·bil·i·ta-tion** *s* **1.** Rehabilitation *f*: **~ center** (*bsd. Br.* **centre**) Rehabilitationszentrum *n*. **2.** Resozialisierung *f*. **3.** Wiederherstellung *f*.

re·hash **I** *v/t* [ˌriːˈhæʃ] *alte Fakten etc* neu auftischen. **II** *s* [ˈriːhæʃ] Neuauftischung *f*.

re·hears·al [rɪˈhɜːsl] *s* ♪, *thea.* Probe *f*. **re'hearse** *v/t u. v/i* proben.

reign [reɪn] **I** *s* Herrschaft *f* (*a. fig.*): **~ of terror** Schreckensherrschaft. **II** *v/i* herrschen (**over** über *acc*) (*a. fig.*): **si-lence ~ed** es herrschte Schweigen; **the ~ing world champion** (*Sport etc*) der amtierende Weltmeister.

re·im·burse [ˌriːɪmˈbɜːs] *v/t* *Auslagen* erstatten, vergüten: **~ s.o. (for) s.th.** j-m et. erstatten. **re·im'burse·ment** *s* Erstattung *f*, Vergütung *f*.

rein [reɪn] **I** *s* Zügel *m*: **give free ~ to one's imagination** s-r Phantasie freien Lauf *od.* die Zügel schießen lassen; **keep a tight ~ on** *fig. j-n, et.* streng kontrollieren; **take the ~s** *fig.* die Zügel *od.* das Heft in die Hand nehmen. **II** *v/t*: **~ in** *Pferd etc* zügeln; *fig.* bremsen.

re·in·car·nate [riːˈɪnkɑːneɪt] *v/t*: **be ~ed** wiedergeboren werden (**as** als). **re·in-car'na·tion** *s* Reinkarnation *f*, Wiedergeburt *f*.

rein·deer [ˈreɪnˌdɪə] *pl* **-deers**, *bsd. coll.* **-deer** *s zo.* Ren(tier) *n*.

re·in·force [ˌriːɪnˈfɔːs] *v/t allg.* verstärken, *fig. a.* untermauern: **~d concrete** ✪ Stahlbeton *m*. **re·in'force·ment** *s*

Verstärkung f, fig. a. Untermauerung f: **~s** pl ✕ Verstärkung f.

re·in·state [,ri:in'steit] v/t j-n wiedereinstellen (**as** als; **in** in dat). ,**re·in'state·ment** s Wiedereinstellung f.

re·in·sur·ance [,ri:in'ʃɔ:rəns] s † Rückversicherung f. ,**re·in'sure** v/t rückversichern.

re·is·sue [,ri:'iʃu:] I v/t **1.** Buch neu auflegen. **2.** Briefmarken etc neu herausgeben. II s **3.** Neuauflage f. **4.** Neuausgabe f.

re·it·er·ate [ri:'itəreit] v/t (ständig) wiederholen. **re,it·er'a·tion** s (ständige) Wiederholung.

re·ject [ri'dʒekt] I v/t **1.** j-n, et. ablehnen, Angebot a. ausschlagen, Bitte abschlagen, Plan etc verwerfen. **2.** verpflanztes Organ etc abstoßen. **re'jec·tion** s **1.** Ablehnung f, Ausschlagung f, Abschlagen n, Verwerfung f. ✗ Abstoßung f.

re·joice [ri'dʒɔis] v/i (hoch) erfreut sein; jubeln (**at, over** über acc). **re'joic·ing** s, a. pl Jubel m.

re·join¹ [,ri:'dʒɔin] v/t sich wieder anschließen (dat) od. an (acc), wieder eintreten in (acc).

re·join² [ri'dʒɔin] v/t erwidern. **re'join·der** s Erwiderung f.

re·ju·ve·nate [ri'dʒu:vəneit] v/t verjüngen. **re,ju·ve'na·tion** s Verjüngung f.

re·kin·dle [,ri:'kindl] v/t **1.** wieder anzünden. **2.** fig. wieder entfachen.

re·lapse [ri'læps] I v/i **1.** zurückfallen, wieder verfallen (**into** in acc). **2.** a) rückfällig werden, b) ✗ e-n Rückfall bekommen od. erleiden. II s **3.** Rückfall m: **have a ~** → 2b.

re·late [ri'leit] I v/t **1.** erzählen, berichten (**to s.o.** j-m): **strange to ~** so seltsam es klingt. **2.** in Verbindung od. Zs.-hang bringen (**to** mit). II v/i **3.** sich beziehen (**to** auf acc). **4.** zs.-hängen (**to** mit). **re'lat·ed** adj **1.** verwandt (**to** mit): → **marriage** 2. **2.** fig. verwandt: **be ~ to** zs.-hängen mit.

re·la·tion [ri'leiʃn] s **1.** Verwandte m, f. **2.** Beziehung f, Verhältnis n (**between** zwischen dat; **with** zu): **bear no ~ to** in keiner Beziehung stehen zu; **in** (od. **with**) **~ to** in bezug auf (acc). **3.** pl diplomatische, geschäftliche etc Beziehungen pl (**between** zwischen dat; **with** zu). **4.** Erzählung f, Bericht m.

re·la·tion·ship s **1.** Verwandtschaft f: **there is no ~ between them** sie sind nicht miteinander verwandt. **2.** Beziehung f, Verhältnis n (**between** zwischen dat; **to** zu): **have a ~ with s.o.** ein Verhältnis mit j-m haben.

rel·a·tive ['relətiv] I adj **1.** relativ: **~ly** adv verhältnismäßig. **2. ~ to** bezüglich, hinsichtlich. **3.** ling. relativ, Relativ...: **~ clause** Relativsatz m; **~ pronoun** Relativpronomen n, bezügliches Fürwort. II s **4.** Verwandte m, f. **rel·a'tiv·i·ty** s Relativität f: **theory of ~** phys. Relativitätstheorie f.

re·lax [ri'læks] I v/t **1.** j-n, Muskeln etc entspannen. **2.** Griff, Bestimmungen etc lockern. **3.** fig. nachlassen in (dat). II v/i **4.** sich entspannen, fig. a. ausspannen. **5.** sich lockern. ,**re·lax'a·tion** [,ri:~] s **1.** Entspannung f. **2.** Lockerung f. **re'laxed** adj entspannt, (Atmosphäre a.) zwanglos.

re·lay I s ['ri:lei] **1.** [a. ,ri:'lei] ⚡ Relais n. **2.** Ablösung f (Arbeiter etc): **work in ~s** in Schichten arbeiten. **3.** a. **~ race** (Sport) Staffel(lauf m) f: **~ (team)** Staffel f. **4.** Rundfunk, TV: Übertragung f. II v/t [ri:'lei] **5.** (**to**) Nachricht weiterleiten, weitergeben (an acc). **6.** Rundfunk, TV: übertragen.

re·lay [,ri:'lei] v/t (irr **lay**) Kabel, Teppich neu verlegen.

re·lease [ri'li:s] I v/t **1.** entlassen (**from** aus), freilassen: **~ (one's hold on)** j-n, et. loslassen. **2.** fig. (**from**) befreien, erlösen (von); entbinden (von): **~ s.o. from a contract** j-n aus e-m Vertrag entlassen. **3.** Film, Leiche etc freigeben; Schallplatte herausbringen; Statistik etc veröffentlichen. **4.** mot. Handbremse lösen. II s **5.** Entlassung f, Freilassung f. **6.** Befreiung f, Erlösung f; Entbindung f. **7.** Freigabe f; Veröffentlichung f: **be on general ~** überall zu sehen sein (Film).

rel·e·gate ['religeit] v/t et. verbannen (**to** in acc): **be ~d** (Sport) absteigen (**to** in acc). ,**rel·e'ga·tion** s Verbannung f; (Sport) Abstieg m.

re·lent [ri'lent] v/i **1.** nachgeben (Person). **2.** nachlassen (Schmerz, Wind etc). **re'lent·less** adj □ **1.** unnachgiebig. **2.** anhaltend (Wind, Schmerz etc).

rel·e·vant ['reləvənt] adj □ **1.** relevant,

bedeutsam, wichtig (**to** für). **2.** sachbezogen, sach-, zweckdienlich.

re·li·a·bil·i·ty [rɪˌlaɪə'bɪlətɪ] s Zuverlässigkeit f, Verläßlichkeit f; Vertrauenswürdigkeit f. **re'li·a·ble** adj □ zuverlässig, verläßlich; vertrauenswürdig.

re·li·ance [rɪ'laɪəns] s **1.** Vertrauen n: **place complete ~ on** volles Vertrauen setzen in (acc). **2.** Abhängigkeit (**on** von). **re'li·ant** adj: **be ~ on** angewiesen sein von, angewiesen sein auf (acc).

rel·ic ['relɪk] s **1.** Relikt n, Überbleibsel n. **2.** eccl. Reliquie f.

re·lief [rɪ'liːf] s **1.** Erleichterung f (a. ⚕): **give** (od. **bring**) **s.o. some ~** ⚕ j-m Erleichterung verschaffen; **~ of pain** Schmerzlinderung f; **to my great ~** zu m-r großen Erleichterung; **in** (od. **with**) **~** erleichtert; → **sigh** I, II. **2.** Unterstützung f, Hilfe f; Am. Sozialhilfe f: **be on ~** Sozialhilfe beziehen. **3.** Br. (Steuer)Erleichterung f. **4.** Ablösung f (Person[en]). **5.** Entlastung f. **6.** Relief n: **stand out in bold** (od. **sharp**) **~ against** sich deutlich abheben gegen. **~ bus** s Einsatzbus m. **~ fund** s Hilfsfonds m. **~ map** s Reliefkarte f. **~ road** s Entlastungsstraße f.

re·lieve [rɪ'liːv] v/t **1.** Schmerzen, Not lindern, j-n, Gewissen erleichtern: **~ one's feelings** s-n Gefühlen Luft machen; **she was ~d to hear that** sie war erleichtert, als sie hörte, daß; **~ o.s.** euphem. sich erleichtern. **2.** ~ **s.o. of** j-m ein schweres Gepäckstück, e-e Arbeit etc abnehmen; humor. j-n um s-e Brieftasche erleichtern. **3.** j-n ablösen.

re·li·gion [rɪ'lɪdʒən] s Religion f: **soccer is a ~ with him, he makes a ~ of soccer** für ihn gibt es nur Fußball, Fußball ist sein ein u. alles.

re·li·gious [rɪ'lɪdʒəs] adj □ **1.** religiös, Religions...: **~ instruction** ped. Religion(sunterricht m) f; **~ liberty** Religionsfreiheit f. **2.** religiös, fromm. **3.** fig. gewissenhaft: **with ~ care** mit peinlicher Sorgfalt.

re·lin·quish [rɪ'lɪŋkwɪʃ] v/t **1.** aufgeben, verzichten auf (acc). **2.** (**to**) Besitz, Recht abtreten (dat od. an acc), überlassen (dat).

rel·ish ['relɪʃ] I v/t **1.** genießen, sich et. schmecken lassen. **2.** fig. Gefallen od. Geschmack finden an (dat): **not to ~ the**

idea nicht begeistert sein von der Aussicht (**of doing** zu tun); **not to ~ having to do s.th.** nicht davon begeistert sein, et. tun zu müssen. II s **3.** with ~ mit Genuß. **4.** fig. Gefallen m, Geschmack m (**for** an dat). **5.** gastr. Würze f; Soße f.

re·lo·cate [ˌriːlə(ʊ)'keɪt] v/t umsiedeln (a. v/i), verlegen. **ˌre·lo'ca·tion** s Umsiedlung f, Verlegung f.

re·luc·tance [rɪ'lʌktəns] s Widerwillen m: **with ~** widerwillig, ungern. **re'luc·tant** adj widerwillig: **~ly** a. ungern; **be ~** sehr zögern.

re·ly [rɪ'laɪ] v/i: **~ on** sich verlassen auf (acc); **~ on s.o. to do s.th.** sich darauf verlassen, daß j-d et. tut; **have to ~ on** abhängig sein von, angewiesen sein auf (acc).

re·main [rɪ'meɪn] I v/i **1.** allg. bleiben. **2.** (übrig)bleiben: **a lot ~s to be done** es bleibt noch viel zu tun; **it ~s to be seen whether** es bleibt abzuwarten, ob. II s pl **3.** (Über)Reste pl. **re'main·der** [~də] s Rest m (a. ♠). **re'main·ing** adj übrig, restlich.

re·make I v/t (irr make) [ˌriː'meɪk] wieder od. neu machen. II s ['riː'meɪk] Remake n, Neuverfilmung f.

re·mand [rɪ'mɑːnd] ♉ I v/t: **be ~ed in custody** in Untersuchungshaft bleiben. II s: **on ~** in Untersuchungshaft sein; **prisoner on ~, ~ prisoner** Untersuchungsgefangene m, f, -häftling m.

re·mark [rɪ'mɑːk] I v/t **1.** bemerken, äußern (**that** daß). II v/i **2.** ~ **on** sich äußern über j-n, et. od. zu et. III s **3.** Bemerkung f (**about, on** über acc): **make a ~** e-e Bemerkung machen. **4.** **worthy of ~** bemerkenswert. **re'mark·a·ble** adj □ bemerkenswert, beachtlich.

re·mar·riage [ˌriː'mærɪdʒ] s Wiederverheiratung f, -heirat f. **ˌre'mar·ry** v/i wieder heiraten.

re·me·di·a·ble [rɪ'miːdjəbl] adj □ behebbar, abstellbar. **re'me·di·al** adj: **~ exercises** pl Heilgymnastik f.

rem·e·dy ['remədɪ] I s **1.** ⚕ (Heil)Mittel n (**for, against** gegen). **2.** fig. (Gegen)Mittel n (**for, against** gegen): **be beyond** (od. **past**) **~** hoffnungslos od. nicht mehr zu beheben sein. II v/t **3.** Mangel, Schaden beheben; Situation bereinigen; Mißstand abstellen.

re·mem·ber [rɪˈmembə] **I** v/t **1.** sich erinnern an (acc): ~ **doing s.th.** sich daran erinnern, et. getan zu haben; **suddenly he ~ed that** plötzlich fiel ihm ein, daß. **2.** denken an (acc): ~ **to do s.th.** daran denken, et. zu tun; **I must ~ this** das muß ich mir merken. **3.** ~ **s.o. in one's will** j-n in s-m Testament bedenken. **4. please ~ me to your wife** grüßen Sie bitte Ihre Frau von mir; **he asked to be ~ed to you** er läßt Sie grüßen. **II** v/i **5. I can't ~** ich kann mich nicht erinnern; **if I ~ right(ly)** wenn ich mich recht erinnere od. entsinne. **re·mem·brance** s Erinnerung f (**of** an acc): **in ~ of** zur Erinnerung an; ♀ **Day** (od. **Sunday**) Br. Volkstrauertag m.

re·mind [rɪˈmaɪnd] v/t j-n erinnern (**of** an acc; **that** daran, daß): ~ **s.o. to do s.th.** j-n daran erinnern, daß er et. tut. **re·mind·er** s Mahnung f.

rem·i·nisce [ˌremɪˈnɪs] v/i in Erinnerungen schwelgen, sich in Erinnerungen ergehen (**about, on** an acc). **rem·i·nis·cence** [~ˈnɪsns] s mst pl Erinnerung f (**of** an acc). **rem·i·nis·cent** adj: **be ~ of** erinnern an (acc).

re·miss [rɪˈmɪs] adj nachlässig: **be ~ in one's duties** s-e Pflichten vernachlässigen.

re·mis·sion [rɪˈmɪʃn] s **1.** 🏛 a. (Straf-)Erlaß m: **he was given three months' ~** ihm wurden drei Monate (von s-r Strafe) erlassen (wegen). **2.** Vergebung f (der Sünden). **3.** 🩺 vorübergehende Besserung.

re·mit [rɪˈmɪt] v/t **1.** Schulden, Strafe erlassen; Sünden vergeben. **2.** Geld überweisen (**to** dat od. an acc). **3.** 🏛 zurückverweisen (**to** an acc). **re·mit·tance** s Überweisung f (**to** an acc).

rem·nant [ˈremnənt] s **1.** (Über)Rest m (a. fig.). **2.** 🧵 (Stoff)Rest m: ~ **sale** Resteverkauf m.

re·mod·el [ˌriːˈmɒdl] v/t pret u. pp **-eled**, bsd. Br. **-elled** umgestalten.

re·mold Am. → remould.

re·mon·strance [rɪˈmɒnstrəns] s Protest m, Beschwerde f. **re·mon·strate** [ˈremənstreɪt] v/i protestieren (**with** bei; **against** gegen), sich beschweren (**with** bei; **about** über acc).

re·morse [rɪˈmɔːs] s Gewissensbisse pl, Reue f: **feel ~** Gewissensbisse haben.

re·morse·ful [~fʊl] adj □ reumütig, reuig. **re·morse·less** adj □ unbarmherzig (a. fig.).

re·mote [rɪˈməʊt] adj **1.** räumlich: fern, (weit) entfernt; abgelegen, entlegen. **2.** zeitlich: fern: **in the ~ future** in ferner Zukunft. **3.** fig. entfernt (Zs.-hang), (Verwandte a.) weitläufig. **4.** fig. entfernt (Möglichkeit), gering (Chance): **I haven't got the ~st idea** ich habe keine blasse od. nicht die geringste Ahnung. **5.** fig. distanziert, unnahbar. ~ **con·trol** s ⊙ **1.** Fernlenkung f, -steuerung f. **2.** Fernbedienung f. **re·mote-con·trolled** adj **1.** ferngelenkt, -gesteuert. **2.** mit Fernbedienung.

re·mould bsd. Br. **I** v/t [ˌriːˈməʊld] Reifen runderneuern. **II** s [ˈriːməʊld] runderneuerter Reifen.

re·mount [ˌriːˈmaʊnt] **I** v/t Pferd etc wieder besteigen; Treppen wieder hinaufgehen: ~ **one's bicycle** wieder auf sein Fahrrad steigen. **II** v/i wieder aufsitzen.

re·mov·a·ble [rɪˈmuːvəbl] adj abnehmbar. **re·mov·al** [~vl] s **1.** Entfernung f; Abnahme f. **2.** Umzug m: ~ **van** Möbelwagen m. **re·move I** v/t **1.** entfernen (**from** von); Deckel, Hut etc abnehmen; Kleidung ablegen. **2.** fig. Schwierigkeiten etc beseitigen, Hindernisse aus dem Weg räumen; Zweifel etc zerstreuen. **II** v/i **3.** (um)ziehen (**from** von; **to** nach). **III** s **4.** fig. **be** (**at**) **only one ~ from** nicht weit entfernt sein von; **be several ~s from** weit entfernt sein von. **re·mov·er** s (Flecken- etc)Entferner m.

re·mu·ner·ate [rɪˈmjuːnəreɪt] v/t **1.** j-n entlohnen (**for** für). **2.** j-n entschädigen (**for** für). **re·mu·ner·a·tion** s **1.** Entlohnung f. **2.** Entschädigung f. **re·mu·ner·a·tive** [~rətɪv] adj □ einträglich, lohnend.

Ren·ais·sance [rəˈneɪsəns] s hist. Renaissance f.

re·nal [ˈriːnl] adj anat. Nieren...: ~ **fail·ure** ♀ Nierenversagen n.

re·name [ˌriːˈneɪm] v/t umbenennen (**in** acc).

ren·der [ˈrendə] v/t **1.** berühmt etc machen: ~ **s.o. unable to do s.th.** es j-m unmöglich machen, et. zu tun. **2.** Hilfe leisten, Dienst a. erweisen. **3.** Gedicht etc vortragen. **4.** übersetzen, -tragen (**into** in acc). **5.** mst ~ **down** Fett auslassen. **'ren·der·ing** s **1.** Vortrag m. **2.** Übersetzung f, -tragung f.

ren·dez·vous ['rɒndɪvuː] **I** pl **-vous** ['ˌvuːz] s **1.** Rendezvous n, Verabredung f; Treffen n, Zs.-kunft f. **2.** Treffpunkt m. **II** v/i pret u. pp **-voused** ['ˌvuːd] **3.** sich treffen (**with** mit).

ren·di·tion [ren'dɪʃn] bsd. Am. → **rendering**.

re·new [rɪ'njuː] v/t erneuern: **~ one's efforts** erneute Anstrengungen machen; **~ one's visa** sein Visum erneuern lassen; **give s.o. ~ed hope** j-m neue Hoffnung geben; **with ~ed strength** mit neuen Kräften. **re'new·a·ble** adj: **be ~** erneuert werden können od. müssen. **re'new·al** s Erneuerung f.

re·nounce [rɪ'naʊns] v/t **1.** verzichten auf (acc). **2.** s-m Glauben etc abschwören.

ren·o·vate ['renəʊveɪt] v/t renovieren. **ˌren·o'va·tion** s Renovierung f.

re·nown [rɪ'naʊn] s Berühmtheit f, Ruhm m: **win ~** berühmt werden. **re'nowned** adj berühmt (**for** wegen, für).

rent¹ [rent] **I** s **1.** Miete f; Pacht f: **for ~** bsd. Am. zu vermieten od. verpachten. **2.** bsd. Am. Leihgebühr f: **for ~** zu vermieten od. verleihen. **II** v/t **3.** mieten; pachten (**from** von). **4.** a. **~ out** bsd. Am. vermieten; verpachten (**to** an acc). **5.** bsd. Am. Auto etc mieten: **~ed car** Leih-, Mietwagen m.

rent² [ˌ] s Riß m (a. fig.).

'rent-a-ˌcar (**ser·vice**) s bsd. Am. Autoverleih m.

rent·al ['rentl] s **1.** Miete f; Pacht f. **2.** bsd. Am. Leihgebühr f.

rent·er ['rentə] s **1.** Mieter(in); Pächter(in). **2.** bsd. Am. Vermieter(in); Verpächter(in).

ˌrent-'free adj miet- od. pachtfrei.

re·nun·ci·a·tion [rɪˌnʌnsɪ'eɪʃn] s **1.** Verzicht m (**of** auf acc). **2.** Abschwören n.

re·o·pen [ˌriː'əʊpən] **I** v/t **1.** Geschäft etc wiedereröffnen. **2.** Verhandlungen etc wiederaufnehmen; Fall wiederaufrollen. **II** v/i **3.** wiedereröffnen. **4.** wiederaufgenommen od. wiederaufgerollt werden.

re·or·ga·ni·za·tion ['riːˌɔːgənaɪ'zeɪʃn] s Umorganisation f; Umstellung f. **ˌre·'or·gan·ize** v/t umorganisieren; Möbel

umstellen, die Möbel umstellen in (dat).

re·pair [rɪ'peə] **I** v/t **1.** reparieren; ausbessern. **2.** fig. wiedergutmachen. **II** s **3.** Reparatur f; Ausbesserung f: **beyond ~** nicht mehr zu reparieren; **be under ~** in Reparatur sein. **4.** **be in good** (**bad**) **~** in gutem (schlechtem) Zustand sein. **5.** fig. Wiedergutmachung f.

rep·a·ra·ble ['repərəbl] adj □ reparabel, wiedergutzumachen(d). **ˌrep·a'ra·tion** s **1.** Wiedergutmachung f: **make ~ for** et. wiedergutmachen. **2.** pl pol. Reparationen pl.

rep·ar·tee [ˌrepɑː'tiː] s Schlagfertigkeit f; schlagfertige Antwort(en pl): **be good at ~** schlagfertig sein.

re·pa·tri·ate [riː'pætrɪeɪt] v/t repatriieren, in den Heimatstaat zurückführen. **ˌre·pa·tri'a·tion** s Repatriierung f.

re·pay [riː'peɪ] v/t (irr. **pay**) **1.** Geld etc zurückzahlen: **~ s.o.'s expenses** j-m s-e Auslagen erstatten; **I'll ~ you some time** ich gebe dir das Geld irgendwann einmal zurück; fig. ich werde mich irgendwann einmal erkenntlich zeigen; das zahle ich dir schon noch heim. **2.** Besuch etc erwidern. **3.** a) (positiv) sich für et. erkenntlich zeigen: **~ s.o. for his help** j-n für s-e Hilfe belohnen od. entschädigen, b) (negativ) et. vergelten, lohnen (**with** mit): **~ s.o.'s meanness**, **~ s.o. for his meanness** j-m s-e Gemeinheit heimzahlen. **re'pay·a·ble** adj rückzahlbar: **be ~** zurückgezahlt werden können od. müssen (**over two years** in e-m Zeitraum von zwei Jahren). **re'pay·ment** s **1.** Rückzahlung f. **2.** Erwiderung f. **3.** Vergeltung f.

re·peal [rɪ'piːl] **I** v/t Gesetz etc aufheben. **II** s Aufhebung f.

re·peat [rɪ'piːt] **I** v/t **1.** wiederholen: **~ o.s.** sich wiederholen; **~ s.th. after s.o.** j-m et. nachsprechen; **his answer doesn't bear ~ing** s-e Antwort läßt sich nicht wiederholen. **2.** et. weitererzählen, -sagen. **3.** aufstoßen (**on s.o.** j-m) (Speise). **III** s **4.** Rundfunk, TV: Wiederholung f. **5.** ♪ Wiederholungszeichen n. **re'peat·ed** adj □ wiederholt.

re·pel [rɪ'pel] v/t **1.** Angriff, Feind zurückschlagen. **2.** Wasser etc, fig. j-n abstoßen. **re·pel·lent** *adj* □ *fig.* abstoßend: *be ~ to* abstoßend wirken auf (*acc*).

re·pent [rɪˈpent] *v/t* bereuen: *~ having done s.th.* es bereuen, et. getan zu haben.

re·per·cus·sion [ˌriːpəˈkʌʃn] *s mst pl* Auswirkung *f* (*on* auf *acc*).

rep·er·toire [ˈrepətwɑː] *s thea. etc* Repertoire *n*: *have a large ~ of jokes* viele Witze auf Lager haben.

rep·e·ti·tion [ˌrepɪˈtɪʃn] *s* Wiederholung *f*: *his answer doesn't bear ~* s-e Antwort läßt sich nicht wiederholen.

re·place [rɪˈpleɪs] *v/t* **1.** zurücklegen, -stellen: *~ the receiver teleph.* den (Hörer) auflegen. **2.** *j-n, et.* ersetzen (*with, by* durch); *j-n* vertreten. **3.** ⚙ austauschen, ersetzen. **re·place·ment** *s* **1.** Ersatz *m*; Vertretung *f*. **2.** ⚙ Austausch *m*.

re·plant [ˌriːˈplɑːnt] *v/t* **1.** umpflanzen. **2.** neu bepflanzen.

re·play (*Sport*) **I** *s* [ˈriːpleɪ] **1.** Wiederholungsspiel *n*. **2.** → *action replay*. **II** *v/t* [ˌriːˈpleɪ] **3.** Spiel wiederholen.

re·plen·ish [rɪˈplenɪʃ] *v/t* (wieder) auffüllen.

re·plete [rɪˈpliːt] *adj* □ **1.** gesättigt, satt. **2.** angefüllt (*with* mit).

rep·li·ca [ˈreplɪkə] *s* **1.** *Kunst:* Replik *f*, Originalkopie *f*. **2.** Kopie *f*, Nachbildung *f*.

re·ply [rɪˈplaɪ] **I** *v/t* antworten, erwidern (*that* daß). **II** *v/i* antworten (*to* auf *e-n Brief etc*; *to s.o.* j-m): *~ to a letter* a. e-n Brief beantworten. **III** *s* Antwort *f*, Erwiderung *f* (*to* auf *acc*): *in ~* (als Antwort) auf; *give no ~* keine Antwort geben, nicht antworten.

re·port [rɪˈpɔːt] **I** *s* **1.** *allg.* Bericht *m* (*on* über *acc*). **2.** Gerücht *n*: *~ has it that* es geht das Gerücht, daß. **3.** *ped. Br.* Zeugnis *n*. **4.** Knall *m*. **II** *v/t* **5.** berichten (*to s.o.* j-m); berichten über (*acc*): *it is ~ed that* es heißt, daß; *he is ~ed to have said* er soll gesagt haben; *~ed speech ling.* indirekte Rede. **6.** *j-n, Unfall, Verbrechen etc* melden (*to s.o.* j-m): *~ s.o.* (*to the police*) j-n anzeigen (*for* wegen); *the car is ~ed stolen* der Wagen ist als gestohlen gemeldet. **III** *v/i* **7.** berichten, Bericht erstatten (*on* über *acc*). **8.** sich melden (*to* bei): *sick* sich krank melden; *~ for work* sich zur Arbeit melden. *~ card Am.* → *report* 3.

re·port·er [rɪˈpɔːtə] *s* Reporter(in), Berichterstatter(in).

re·pose [rɪˈpəʊz] *s* **1.** Ruhe *f*. **2.** *fig.* Gelassenheit *f*.

rep·re·hen·si·ble [ˌreprɪˈhensəbl] *adj* □ tadelnswert, verwerflich.

rep·re·sent [ˌreprɪˈzent] *v/t* **1.** *j-n, Br. a. Wahlbezirk* vertreten. **2.** darstellen (*a. fig.*). **3.** dar-, hinstellen (*as, to be* als): *~ o.s. as* (*od. to be*) sich ausgeben für. **4.** *Beschwerden etc* vorbringen (*to* bei). **rep·re·sen·ta·tion** *s* **1.** Vertretung *f*. Darstellung *f*: *be a ~ of s.th.* et. darstellen. **3.** *make ~s to* vorstellig werden bei (*about* wegen). **rep·re·sen·ta·tion·al** [~ʃənl] *adj* gegenständlich (*Kunst*). **rep·re·sent·a·tive** [~tətɪv] **I** *s* **1.** (Stell)Vertreter(in); (Handels)Vertreter(in). **2.** *parl.* Abgeordnete *m, f:* → *House of Representatives*. **II** *adj* □ **3.** repräsentativ (*of* für). **4.** *pol.* repräsentativ: *~ government* Repräsentativsystem *n*.

re·press [rɪˈpres] *v/t* **1.** *Volk, Gefühle etc* unterdrücken. **2.** *psych.* verdrängen. **re·pres·sion** [~ʃn] *s* **1.** Unterdrückung *f*. **2.** *psych.* Verdrängung *f*. **re·pres·sive** *adj* □ repressiv.

re·prieve [rɪˈpriːv] ⅈⅈ **I** *s* Begnadigung *f*; Vollstreckungsaufschub *m*. **II** *v/t:* *he was ~d* er wurde begnadigt; s-e Urteilsvollstreckung wurde ausgesetzt.

rep·ri·mand [ˈreprɪmɑːnd] **I** *v/t* rügen, tadeln (*for* wegen). **II** *s* Rüge *f*, Tadel *m*.

re·print I *v/t* [ˌriːˈprɪnt] neu auflegen, nachdrucken. **II** *s* [ˈriːprɪnt] Neuauflage *f*, Nachdruck *m*.

re·pris·al [rɪˈpraɪzl] *s bsd.* ✕, *pol.* Repressalie *f*, Vergeltungsmaßnahme *f: in* (*od. as a*) *~ for* als Vergeltung für; *take ~s* Repressalien ergreifen (*against* gegen).

re·proach [rɪˈprəʊtʃ] **I** *s* **1.** Vorwurf *m*: *above* (*od. beyond*) *~* über jeden Tadel erhaben; *look of ~* vorwurfsvoller Blick. **2.** *fig.* Schande *f* (*to* für). **II** *v/t* **3.** *j-m* Vorwürfe machen (*for* wegen).

rep·ro·bate [ˈreprəʊbeɪt] *s* verkommenes Subjekt.

re·pro·cess [ˌriːˈprəʊses] *v/t Kernbrennstoffe* wiederaufbereiten. **re'pro·cess-**

ing plant s Wiederaufbereitungsanlage f.

e·pro·duce [ˌriːprə'djuːs] **I** v/t **1.** ~ **o.s.** → 4. **2.** Bild etc reproduzieren. **3.** Ton etc wiedergeben. **II** v/i **4.** biol. sich fortpflanzen od. vermehren. **re·pro·duc·tion** [ˌ~'dʌkʃn] s **1.** biol. Fortpflanzung f. **2.** Reproduktion f. **3.** Wiedergabe f. ˌre·pro'duc·tive adj biol. Fortpflanzungs...

e·proof [rɪ'pruːf] s Rüge f, Tadel m.

e·prove [rɪ'pruːv] v/t rügen, tadeln (**for** wegen).

ep·tile ['reptaɪl] s zo. Reptil n, Kriechtier n.

e·pub·lic [rɪ'pʌblɪk] s pol. Republik f. **re'pub·li·can,** pol. Am. 2 ⍰ I adj republikanisch. **II** s Republikaner(in).

e·pu·di·ate [rɪ'pjuːdɪeɪt] v/t **1.** Angebot, Behauptung etc zurückweisen. **2.** Schuld etc nicht anerkennen. **re·pu·di·a·tion** s **1.** Zurückweisung f. **2.** Nichtanerkennung f.

e·pug·nance [rɪ'pʌgnəns] s: **in** (od. **with**) ~ angewidert. **re'pug·nant** adj ⍰ widerlich, widerwärtig.

e·pulse [rɪ'pʌls] **I** v/t **1.** Angriff, Feind zurückschlagen. **2.** j-n, Angebot etc abweisen, zurückweisen. **II** s **3.** Zurückschlagen n. **4.** Ab-, Zurückweisung f. **re'pul·sion** s **1.** Abscheu m, f: **with** ~ voller Abscheu. **2.** phys. Abstoßung f. **re'pul·sive** adj □ phys. abstoßend, fig. a. widerlich, widerwärtig.

e·pur·chase [ˌriːˈpɜːtʃəs] **I** v/t zurückkaufen. **II** s Rückkauf m.

ep·u·ta·ble ['repjʊtəbl] adj □ angesehen. ˌrep·u'ta·tion s (engS. guter) Ruf: **have the** (od. **a**) ~ **of being** im Ruf stehen, et. zu sein; **make o.s. a** ~ **as** sich e-n Namen machen als. **re·pute** [rɪ'pjuːt] **I** s (engS. guter) Ruf: **of** ~ angesehen; **be held in high** ~ hohes Ansehen genießen. **II** v/t: **be** ~**d to be** gelten als. **re'put·ed·ly** adv angeblich, dem Vernehmen nach.

e·quest [rɪ'kwest] **I** s **1.** (**for**) Bitte f (um), Wunsch m (nach): **at s.o.'s** ~ auf j-s Bitte hin; **on** ~ auf Wunsch; **make a** ~ **for s.th.** um et. bitten. **II** v/t **2.** bitten od. ersuchen um. **3.** j-n bitten, ersuchen (**to do** zu tun). ~ **stop** s Br. Bedarfshaltestelle f.

re·qui·em ['rekwɪəm] s Requiem n.

re·quire [rɪ'kwaɪə] v/t **1.** erfordern: **be** ~**d** erforderlich sein; **if** ~**d** wenn nötig. **2.** benötigen, brauchen. **3.** verlangen (**that** daß; **s.th. of s.o.** et. von j-m): ~ **s.o. to do s.th.** von j-m verlangen, daß er et. tut; **be** ~**d to do s.th.** et. tun müssen. **re'quired** adj erforderlich, notwendig: ~ **reading** ped., univ. Pflichtlektüre f. **re'quire·ment** s **1.** Anforderung f: **meet the** ~**s** den Anforderungen entsprechen. **2.** Erfordernis n, Bedürfnis n.

req·ui·site ['rekwɪzɪt] **I** adj erforderlich, notwendig (**for** für). **II** s mst pl Artikel m: **camping** ~**s** pl Campingzubehör n. ˌreq·ui'si·tion **I** s **1.** Anforderung f: **make a** ~ **for** et. anfordern. **2.** ✕ Requisition f, Beschlagnahme f. **II** v/t **3.** anfordern. **4.** ✕ requirieren, beschlagnahmen.

re·quit·al [rɪ'kwaɪtl] s Vergeltung f. **re·quite** [rɪ'kwaɪt] v/t et. vergelten (**with** mit).

re·run **I** v/t (irr run) [ˌriː'rʌn] **1.** TV wiederholen. **2.** **be** ~ (Sport) wiederholt werden (Lauf). **II** s ['riːrʌn] **3.** TV Wiederholung f (a. allg.).

re·scind [rɪ'sɪnd] v/t 🕮 Gesetz, Urteil etc aufheben. **re·scis·sion** [rɪ'sɪʒn] s Aufhebung f.

res·cue ['reskjuː] **I** v/t retten (**from** aus, vor dat). **II** s Rettung f: **come to s.o.'s** ~ j-m zu Hilfe kommen; ~ **operations** pl Rettungsarbeiten pl; ~ **party** (od. **squad, team**) Rettungsmannschaft f. **res·cu·er** [ˈ~kjʊə] s Retter(in).

re·search [rɪ'sɜːtʃ] **I** s Forschung f (**on** auf dem Gebiet gen): **carry out** (od. **do**) ~ **into** et. erforschen. **II** v/i forschen (**on** auf dem Gebiet gen): ~ **into** et. erforschen. **III** v/t et. erforschen. **IV** adj Forschungs...: ~ **team** Forscherteam n; ~ **worker** Forscher(in). **re'search·er** s Forscher(in).

re·sem·blance [rɪ'zembləns] s Ähnlichkeit f (**to** mit; **between** zwischen dat): **there is a strong** ~ **between them** sie sind sich sehr ähnlich; **bear a strong** ~ **to** starke Ähnlichkeit haben mit. **re·sem·ble** [~bl] v/t ähnlich sein, ähneln (dat).

re·sent [rɪ'zent] v/t übelnehmen, sich ärgern über (acc). **re'sent·ful** [~fʊl] adj □

ärgerlich. **re'sent·ment** *s* Ärger *m*
(**against, at** über *acc*).
res·er·va·tion [ˌrezəˈveɪʃn] *s* **1.** *bsd. Am.*
(*Wild*)Reservat *n*; *Am.* (*Indianer*)Re-
servat *n*, (-)Reservation *f*. **2.** Reservie-
rung *f*, Vorbestellung *f*: **make a ~** ein
Zimmer etc bestellen. **3.** Vorbehalt *m*:
with ~(s) unter Vorbehalt; **without ~**
vorbehaltlos.
re·serve [rɪˈzɜːv] **I** *s* **1.** Reserve *f* (**of** an
dat): **keep s.th. in ~** et. in Reserve hal-
ten. **2.** *a. pl* ✕ Reserve *f*. **3.** *Sport*:
Reservespieler(in). **4.** (*Naturschutz-,
Wild*)Reservat *n*. **5.** Reserviertheit *f*,
Zurückhaltung *f*. **6.** **without ~** vorbehaltlos. **II** *v/t* **7.** (sich) et. aufsparen (**for**
für). **8. ~ the right to do s.th.** sich (das
Recht) vorbehalten, et. zu tun. **9.** reservieren (lassen), vorbestellen. **re'served**
adj reserviert, zurückhaltend.
re·serv·ist [rɪˈzɜːvɪst] *s* ✕ Reservist *m*.
res·er·voir [ˈrezəvwɑː] *s* Reservoir *n* (*a.
fig.* **of** an *dat*).
re·set [ˌriːˈset] *v/t* (*irr* **set**) **1.** Edelstein
neu fassen. **2.** Uhr umstellen; Zeiger etc
zurückstellen (**to** auf *acc*).
re·set·tle [ˌriːˈsetl] *v/t* umsiedeln. **ˌre-
ˈset·tle·ment** *s* Umsiedlung *f*.
re·shuf·fle [ˌriːˈʃʌfl] **1.** Karten neu
mischen. **2.** Kabinett etc umbilden. **II** *s*
[ˈriːʃʌfl] **3.** Umbildung *f*.
re·side [rɪˈzaɪd] *v/i* **1.** wohnen, s-n
Wohnsitz haben; residieren. **2. ~ in** *fig.*
liegen od. ruhen bei *j-m*. **res·i·dence**
[ˈrezɪdəns] *s* **1.** Wohnsitz *m*; Residenz *f*:
official ~ Amtssitz *m*; **take up ~** sich
niederlassen. **2.** Aufenthalt *m*: **~ permit**
Aufenthaltsgenehmigung *f*, -erlaubnis
f. **ˈres·i·dent I** *adj* ansässig, wohnhaft:
be ~ abroad *a.* im Ausland wohnen. **II**
s Bewohner(in) (*e-s Hauses*), (*e-r Stadt
etc a.*) Einwohner(in), *mot.* Anlie-
ger(in), (*Hotel*)Gast *m*. **res·i·den·tial**
[ˌrezɪˈdenʃl] *adj* Wohn...
re·sid·u·al [rɪˈzɪdjʊəl] *adj* übrig(geblieben), restlich, Rest... **re·si·due** [ˈrezɪ-
djuː] *s bsd.* 🜍 Rest *m*, Rückstand *m*.
re·sign [rɪˈzaɪn] **I** *v/t* **1.** aufgeben; verzichten auf (*acc*). **2.** Amt etc niederlegen. **3. ~ o.s. to** sich fügen in (*acc*), sich
abfinden mit; **be ~ed to** sich abgefun-
den haben mit. **II** *v/i* **4.** zurücktreten
(**from** von), sein Amt niederlegen.
res·ig·na·tion [ˌrezɪgˈneɪʃn] *s* **1.** Rück-

tritt *m*, Amtsniederlegung *f*: **hand in ~**
(*od.* **send in, submit, tender**) one's ~
s-n Rücktritt einreichen. **2.** Ergebenheit *f*; Resignation *f*.
re·sil·i·ence [rɪˈzɪlɪəns] *s* **1.** Elastizität *f*,
Strapazierfähigkeit *f*. **2.** *fig.* Zähigkeit
f. **re·sil·i·ent** *adj* □ **1.** elastisch; strapazierfähig. **2.** *fig.* zäh: **be ~** nicht unter-
zukriegen sein.
res·in [ˈrezɪn] *s* Harz *n*. **ˈres·in·ous** *adj*
□ harzig; Harz...
re·sist [rɪˈzɪst] **I** *v/t* **1.** *j-m*, *e-r Sache*
widerstehen: **I could not ~ doing it** ich
mußte es einfach tun. **2.** Widerstand
leisten (*dat od.* gegen), sich widersetzen
(*dat*). **II** *v/i* **3.** Widerstand leisten, sich
widersetzen. **re'sist·ance** *s* **1.** Widerstand *m* (**to** gegen): **offer** (*od.* **put up**)
(**a**) **stubborn ~** hartnäckig(en) Widerstand leisten (**to** *dat*); **without offering ~**
widerstandslos; **take the line of least ~**
den Weg des geringsten Widerstandes
gehen. **2.** *a.* **power of ~** Widerstands-
kraft *f* (**to** gegen) (*a.* 🩺). **3.** (*Hitze-
etc*)Beständigkeit *f*, (*Stoß- etc*)Festig-
keit *f*. **4.** ⚡ Widerstand *m* (*a. Bauteil*).
re'sist·ant *adj* □ (*hitze- etc*)beständig,
(*stoß- etc*)fest. **re'sis·tor** *s* ⚡ Widerstand *m* (*Bauteil*).
re·sit *ped., univ. Br.* **I** *v/t* (*irr* **sit**) [ˌriːˈsɪt]
Prüfung wiederholen. **II** *s* [ˈriːsɪt] Wie-
derholungsprüfung *f*.
re·sole [ˌriːˈsəʊl] *v/t* neu besohlen.
res·o·lute [ˈrezəluːt] *adj* □ resolut, entschlossen. **ˈres·o·lute·ness** *s* → **resolution** 3.
res·o·lu·tion [ˌrezəˈluːʃn] *s* **1.** Beschluß
m, *parl. etc a.* Resolution *f*. **2.** Vorsatz
m: **make good ~s** gute Vorsätze fassen.
3. Resolutheit *f*, Entschlossenheit *f*. **4.**
Lösung *f*, Überwindung *f*. **5.** 🜍 *etc*
Auflösung *f*, Zerlegung *f* (**into** in *acc*).
re·solve [rɪˈzɒlv] **I** *v/t* **1.** beschließen
(**that** daß; **to do** zu tun). **2.** Problem etc
lösen, Schwierigkeit etc überwinden. **3.**
🜍 *etc* auflösen, zerlegen (**into** in *acc*).
II *v/i* **4.** (**into** in *acc*) 🜍 *etc* sich auflösen; *fig.* zerfallen. **III** *s* **5.** → **resolution**
2, 3.
res·o·nance [ˈrezənəns] *s* **1.** *phys.* Resonanz *f*. **2.** voller Klang. **ˈres·o·nant** *adj*
□ **1.** *phys.* Resonanz... **2.** voll (*Klang*),
volltönend, sonor (*Stimme*). **3. be ~
with** widerhallen von.

re·sort [rɪ'zɔːt] **I** s **1.** Urlaubsort m: → **health** 1, **seaside. 2. have ~ to** → 3; **as a last ~** notfalls, wenn alle Stricke reißen; **as a last ~ he went ...** als er nicht mehr weiterwußte, ging er ... **II** v/i **3. ~ to** greifen od. Zuflucht nehmen zu.

re·sound [rɪ'zaʊnd] v/i widerhallen (**with** von).

re·source [rɪ'sɔːs] s **1.** pl (Geld)Mittel pl; (Boden-, Natur)Schätze pl. **2.** Mittel n, Zuflucht f; Ausweg m: **leave s.o. to his own ~s** j-n sich selbst überlassen. **3.** Einfallsreichtum m, Findigkeit f. **re·'source·ful** [~fʊl] adj □ einfallsreich, findig.

re·spect [rɪ'spekt] **I** s **1.** Achtung f, Respekt f (**for** vor dat): **have ~ for** Respekt haben vor. **2.** Rücksicht f (**for** auf acc): **out of ~ for** aus Rücksicht auf; **have no ~ for** keine Rücksicht nehmen auf; **without ~ to** ohne Rücksicht auf (acc); ungeachtet (gen). **3.** Beziehung f, Hinsicht f: **in many ~s** in vieler Hinsicht; **in some ~** in gewisser Hinsicht; **with ~ to** was ... anbelangt od. betrifft. **4.** pl Empfehlungen pl: **give my ~s to your wife** e-e Empfehlung an Ihre Gemahlin. **5. pay one's ~s to** j-m s-e Aufwartung machen; **pay one's last ~s to** j-m die letzte Ehre erweisen. **II** v/t **6.** respektieren, achten. **7.** respektieren, berücksichtigen. **re·'spect·a·ble** adj □ **1.** ehrbar, geachtet. **2.** gesellschaftsfähig (Person), (Kleidung, Benehmen a.) korrekt: **it is not ~** es gehört sich nicht (**to do** zu tun). **3.** respektabel, beachtlich. **re·'spect·ful** [~fʊl] adj □ respektvoll. **re·'spect·ing** prp bezüglich (gen). **re·'spec·tive** adj jeweilig: **they went to their ~ places** jeder von ihnen ging zu s-m Platz. **re·'spec·tive·ly** adv beziehungsweise.

res·pi·ra·tion [ˌrespə'reɪʃn] s Atmung f.

res·pi·ra·tor ['respəreɪtə] s Atemschutzgerät n. **re·spir·a·to·ry** [~'spaɪərətərɪ] adj Atem..., Atmungs...: **~ arrest** Atemstillstand m; **~ disease** ☛ Erkrankung f der Atemwege; **~ passages** pl (od. **tract**) anat. Atemwege pl; **~ system** Atmungsorgane pl.

res·pite ['respaɪt] s **1.** Aufschub m. **2.** Pause f: **without ~** ohne Pause od. Unterbrechung.

re·splend·ent [rɪ'splendənt] adj □ glänzend, strahlend.

re·spond [rɪ'spɒnd] **I** v/i **1.** antworten (**to** auf acc): **~ to a letter** a. e-n Brief beantworten. **2.** fig. reagieren (**to** auf acc; **with** mit), ⚙ etc a. ansprechen (**to** auf acc). **II** v/t **3.** antworten (**that** daß). **re·'spond·ent** s ⚖ Beklagte m, f (in e-m Scheidungsprozeß).

re·sponse [rɪ'spɒns] s **1.** Antwort f (**to** auf acc): **give no ~** keine Antwort geben, nicht antworten. **2.** fig. Reaktion f (**to** auf acc).

re·spon·si·bil·i·ty [rɪˌspɒnsə'bɪlətɪ] s **1.** Verantwortung f: **a position of great ~** e-e verantwortungsvolle Position; **on one's own ~** auf eigene Verantwortung; **claim ~ for** die Verantwortung übernehmen für (e-n Terroranschlag etc); **have ~ for** die Verantwortung haben für; **take (full) ~ for** die (volle) Verantwortung übernehmen für; **take no ~ for** nicht haften für. **2.** oft pl Verpflichtung f, Pflicht f. **re·'spon·si·ble** adj □ **1.** verantwortlich (**for** für): **be ~ to s.o. for s.th.** j-m (gegenüber) für et. verantwortlich sein; **not to be ~ for** nicht haften für. **2.** (**for**) verantwortlich (für), schuld (an dat): **hold s.o. ~ for** j-n verantwortlich machen für. **3.** verantwortungsbewußt. **4.** verantwortungsvoll (Position). **re·'spon·sive** adj □ **1.** leichtgängig (Kupplung etc), elastisch (Motor): **be ~ to** reagieren auf (acc), ⚙ etc a. ansprechen auf (acc); empfänglich sein für. **2.** mitteilsam: **he wasn't very ~** a. aus ihm war nicht viel herauszuholen.

rest[1] [rest] **I** s **1.** Ruhe(pause) f; Erholung f: **have** (od. **take**) **a ~** sich ausruhen; **have a good night's ~** gut schlafen; **lay to ~** zur letzten Ruhe betten; fig. ad acta legen; **set s.o.'s mind at ~** j-n beruhigen. **2.** ⚙ Auflage f, Stütze f; teleph. Gabel f. **II** v/i **3.** (sich aus)ruhen: **let s.th. ~** fig. et. auf sich beruhen lassen; **he will not ~ until** fig. er wird nicht eher ruhen, bis; → **laurel** 3. **4.** lehnen (**against**, **on** an dat): **~ on** bsd. ⚙ ruhen auf (dat); fig. (a. fig. Blick); fig. beruhen auf (dat), sich stützen auf (acc); **~ with** fig. bei j-m liegen. **III** v/t **5.** ausruhen (lassen). **6.** lehnen (**against** gegen; **on** an acc).

rest 1204

rest² [~] s Rest m: *the ~ of us* wir übrigen; *all the ~ of them* alle übrigen; *for the ~* im übrigen.

res·tau·rant ['restərɔ̃ːŋ] s Restaurant n, Gaststätte f. **~ car** s 🚂 Br. Speisewagen m.

rest·ful ['restfʊl] adj □ **1.** ruhig, friedlich. **2.** erholsam.

rest home s Alten-, Alters- od. Pflegeheim n.

rest·ing place ['restɪŋ] s: *(last) ~* (letzte) Ruhestätte.

res·ti·tu·tion [ˌrestɪ'tjuːʃn] s Rückgabe f, (*von Geld a.*) Rückerstattung f (*to* an *acc*): *make ~ of sth. to s.o.* j-m et. zurückgeben *od.* -erstatten.

res·tive ['restɪv] adj □ unruhig, nervös. **'res·tive·ness** s Unruhe f, Nervosität f.

rest·less ['restlɪs] adj □ **1.** ruhe-, rastlos. **2.** unruhig (*Person, Nacht*): *I had a ~ night* ich habe nicht gut geschlafen.

re·stock [ˌriː'stɒk] v/t Regal etc wieder auffüllen.

res·to·ra·tion [ˌrestə'reɪʃn] s **1.** Wiederherstellung f. **2.** Restaurierung f. **3.** Rückgabe f, Rückerstattung f (*to* an *acc*).

re·store [rɪ'stɔː] v/t **1.** Ordnung etc wiederherstellen: *be ~d (to health)* wiederhergestellt *od.* wieder gesund sein. **2.** Gemälde etc restaurieren. **3.** zurückgeben, Geld a. zurückerstatten (*to* dat). **re'stor·er** s **1.** Restaurator(in). **2.** → *hair restorer*.

re·strain [rɪ'streɪn] v/t (*from*) zurückhalten (von), hindern an (*dat*): *~ s.o. from doing sth.* j-n davon zurückhalten *od.* daran hindern, et. zu tun; *I had to ~ myself* ich mußte mich beherrschen (*from doing sth.* um nicht et. zu tun). **re'strained** adj **1.** beherrscht. **2.** dezent (*Farbe etc*). **re'straint** [rɪ'streɪnt] s **1.** Beherrschung f. **2.** Be-, Einschränkung f (*on gen*).

re·strict [rɪ'strɪkt] v/t beschränken (*to* auf *acc*), einschränken. **re'stric·tion** s Be-, Einschränkung f: *without ~s* uneingeschränkt. **re'stric·tive** adj □ be-, einschränkend.

rest room s Am. Toilette f (*in Restaurant etc*).

re·struc·ture [ˌriː'strʌktʃə] v/t umstrukturieren.

re·sult [rɪ'zʌlt] I s **1.** Ergebnis n, Resultat n: *without ~* ergebnislos. **2.** Erfolg m. **3.** Folge f: *as a ~ of* als Folge von (*od. gen*). II v/i **4.** resultieren, sich ergeben (*from* aus): *~ in* zur Folge haben (*acc*), führen zu; *~ing* → *resultant*. **re'sult·ant** adj daraus resultierend.

ré·su·mé ['rezjuːmeɪ] s **1.** Resümee n, Zs.-fassung f. **2.** Am. (*bsd. tabellarischer*) Lebenslauf.

re·sume [rɪ'zjuːm] I v/t **1.** Arbeit wiederaufnehmen, Diskussion, Reise etc fortsetzen. **2.** Platz wieder einnehmen; Mädchennamen etc wieder annehmen. II v/i **3.** weitermachen, fortfahren. **re'sump·tion** [rɪ'zʌmpʃn] s Wiederaufnahme f, Fortsetzung f.

re·sur·face [ˌriː'sɜːfɪs] I v/t **1.** Straße neu belegen. II v/i **2.** wieder auftauchen (*U-Boot*). **3.** fig. wiederauftleben.

re·sur·gence [rɪ'sɜːdʒəns] s Wiederaufleben n. **re'sur·gent** adj wiederauftlebend.

res·ur·rect [ˌrezə'rekt] v/t Brauch etc wiederaufleben lassen, Gesetz etc wieder einführen. **res·ur'rec·tion** s **1.** Wiedereinführung f. **2.** ♀ eccl. Auferstehung f.

re·sus·ci·tate [rɪ'sʌsɪteɪt] v/t 🩺 wiederbeleben. **re·sus·ci'ta·tion** s Wiederbelebung f.

re·tail ['riːteɪl] I s **1.** Einzelhandel m: *by (Am. at) ~* → III. II adj **2.** Einzelhandels...: *~ price; ~ dealer* → *retailer*. III adv **3.** im Einzelhandel, einzeln. IV v/t [riː'teɪl] **4.** im Einzelhandel verkaufen (*at, for* für). **5.** fig. Gerücht etc verbreiten. V v/i [riː'teɪl] **6.** im Einzelhandel verkauft werden (*at, for* für): *it ~s at £2 a.* es kostet im Einzelhandel zwei Pfund. **re'tail·er** s Einzelhändler(in).

re·tain [rɪ'teɪn] v/t **1.** Gleichgewicht halten; Eigenschaft, Fassung etc behalten, bewahren. **2.** Wasser stauen (*Damm*), speichern (*Boden*); Wärme speichern. **re'tain·er, re'tain·ing fee** s (Honorar)Vorschuß m (*für Anwalt*).

re·take [ˌriː'teɪk] v/t (*irr take*) **1.** ⚔ zurückerobern. **2.** Film, TV: Szene etc nochmals drehen.

re·tal·i·ate [rɪ'tælɪeɪt] v/i **1.** Vergeltung üben, sich revanchieren (*against* an *dat*); *engS.* zurückschlagen, -treten. **2.** Sport, a. in Diskussion etc: kontern (**with** mit). **re·tal·i·a·tion** s Vergeltung(smaßnahmen pl) f, Revanche f: **in ~ for** als Vergeltung für. **re'tal·i·a·to·ry** [~ətərɪ] adj Vergeltungs..., Revanche...

re·tard [rɪ'tɑːd] v/t verzögern, hemmen. **re'tard·ed** adj: (**mentally**) ~ (geistig) zurückgeblieben. **re·tar·da·tion** [ˌriːtɑː'deɪʃn] s Verzögerung f.

retch [retʃ] v/i würgen.

re·ten·tion [rɪ'tenʃn] s 1. Bewahrung f. 2. Stauung f; Speicherung f. **re'ten·tive** adj gut (Gedächtnis).

re·think [ˌriː'θɪŋk] v/t (irr think) noch einmal überdenken.

ret·i·cence ['retɪsəns] s Schweigsamkeit f. **'ret·i·cent** adj □ schweigsam: **he was very ~ about it** von ihm war nur sehr wenig darüber zu erfahren.

ret·i·na ['retɪnə] pl **-nas, -nae** ['~niː] s anat. Netzhaut f.

ret·i·nue ['retɪnjuː] s Gefolge n.

re·tire [rɪ'taɪə] I v/i 1. allg. sich zurückziehen (a. fig. **from business** aus dem Geschäftsleben; **from competition** vom aktiven Sport): ~ **from business** a. sich zur Ruhe setzen. 2. in Rente od. Pension gehen, sich pensionieren lassen. 3. Sport: aufgeben. II v/t 4. in den Ruhestand versetzen, pensionieren. **re'tired** adj pensioniert, im Ruhestand (lebend): **be ~** a. in Pension od. Rente sein; ~ **general** General m außer Dienst. **re'tire·ment** s 1. Rückzug m. 2. Pensionierung f; Ruhestand m: ~ **age** Pensions-, Rentenalter n. 3. Sport: Aufgabe f. **re'tir·ing** adj □ zurückhaltend.

re·tort¹ [rɪ'tɔːt] I s (scharfe) Entgegnung. II v/t (scharf) entgegnen.

re·tort² [~] s 🝫 Retorte f.

re·touch [ˌriː'tʌtʃ] v/t phot. retuschieren.

re·trace [rɪ'treɪs] v/t Tathergang etc rekonstruieren: ~ **one's steps** denselben Weg zurückgehen.

re·tract [rɪ'trækt] v/t 1. Krallen etc, ✈ Fahrgestell einziehen. 2. Angebot etc zurückziehen, Behauptung etc zurücknehmen, Geständnis etc widerrufen. **re'tract·a·ble** adj einziehbar. **re'trac·tion** s 1. Einziehen n. 2. Zurücknahme f, Widerruf m.

re·train [ˌriː'treɪn] I v/t umschulen. II v/i umschulen, umschulen lassen. **ˌre'train·ing** s Umschulung f.

re·tread I v/t [ˌriː'tred] Reifen runderneuern. II s ['riːtred] runderneuerter Reifen.

re·treat [rɪ'triːt] I s 1. ✕ Rückzug m: **beat a** (**hasty**) ~ fig. abhauen. 2. Zufluchtsort m. II v/i 3. ✕ sich zurückziehen. 4. zurückweichen (**from** vor dat).

re·trench·ment [rɪ'trentʃmənt] s: **policy of ~** Sparpolitik f.

re·tri·al [ˌriː'traɪəl] s ⚖ Wiederaufnahmeverfahren n.

ret·ri·bu·tion [ˌretrɪ'bjuːʃn] s Vergeltung f. **re·trib·u·tive** [rɪ'trɪbjʊtɪv] adj Vergeltungs...

re·triev·al [rɪ'triːvl] s 1. Zurückholen n. 2. Wiedergutmachen n, Wettmachen n; Rettung f: **beyond** (od. **past**) ~ hoffnungslos (Situation). 3. hunt. Apportieren n.

re·trieve [rɪ'triːv] v/t 1. zurückholen. Fehler wiedergutmachen, Verlust a. wettmachen; Situation retten. 3. (a. v/i) hunt. apportieren.

ret·ro·ac·tive [ˌretrəʊ'æktɪv] adj □ rückwirkend.

ret·ro·grade ['retrəʊgreɪd] adj rückschrittlich: ~ **step** Rückschritt m.

ret·ro·gres·sive [ˌretrəʊ'gresɪv] adj □ rückschrittlich.

ret·ro·spect ['retrəʊspekt] s: **in ~** rückschauend, im Rückblick. **ˌret·ro'spec·tion** s Rückblick m, -schau f. **ˌret·ro'spec·tive** adj □ 1. rückblickend, -schauend. 2. rückwirkend.

re·trous·sé [rə'truːseɪ] adj: ~ **nose** Stupsnase f.

re·try [ˌriː'traɪ] v/t ⚖ 1. Fall erneut verhandeln. 2. neu verhandeln gegen j-n.

re·turn [rɪ'tɜːn] I v/i 1. zurückkehren, -kommen; zurückgehen; fig. wiederauftreten: ~ **to** fig. auf ein Thema, Vorhaben zurückkommen; in e-e Gewohnheit etc zurückfallen; in e-n Zustand zurückkehren; → **normal** II. 2. ~ **to sender** ✎ zurück an Absender. II v/t 3. (**to**) zurückgeben (dat); zurückbringen (dat); zurückschicken, -senden (dat od. an acc). 4. zurücklegen, -stellen. 5. Besuch, Kompliment etc erwidern. 6. Gewinn, Zinsen abwerfen. 7. **be ~ed** (**to Parliament**) Br. gewählt werden. 8. → **verdict** 1. III s 9. Rückkehr f; fig. Wiederauftreten n: **on one's ~** bei s-r Rückkehr; **by ~** (**of post**) Br. postwendend, umgehend; **many happy ~s** (*of the day*) herzlichen Glückwunsch zum Geburtstag. **10.** Rückgabe *f*; Zurückbringen *n*; Zurückschicken *n*, -senden *n*. **11.** Zurücklegen *n*, -stellen *n*. **12.** Erwiderung *f*. **13.** *a. pl* ✝ Gewinn *m*. **14. in ~** als Gegenleistung (*for* für): **expect nothing in ~** keine Gegenleistung erwarten. **15.** (*Steuer*)Erklärung *f*. **16.** *Tennis etc*: Return *m*, Rückschlag *m*. **IV** *adj* **17.** Rück...: **~ game** (*Sport*) Rückspiel *n*; **~ journey** Rückreise *f*; **by ~ mail** *Am*. postwendend, umgehend; **~ ticket** *Br*. Rückfahrkarte *f*; Rückflugticket *n*. **V** *adv* **18. the price is £10 ~** *Br*. der Preis beträgt 10 Pfund hin u. zurück. **re'turn·a·ble** *adj* **1. ~ bottle** Pfandflasche *f*. **2. be ~** zurückgegeben *od*. zurückgeschickt werden müssen.

re·un·ion [ˌriːˈjuːnjən] *s* **1.** Treffen *n*, Wiedersehensfeier *f*. **2.** Wiedervereinigung *f*. **re·u·nite** [ˌriːjuːˈnaɪt] *v/t* Land wiedervereinigen, *Familie etc* wieder vereinigen.

rev [rev] *mot*. F I *s* Umdrehung *f*: **number of ~s** Drehzahl *f*; **~ counter** Drehzahlmesser *m*. II *v/t a*. **~ up** Motor aufheulen lassen. III *v/i a*. **~ up** aufheulen (*Motor*).

re·val·u·a·tion [ˌriːˌvæljʊˈeɪʃn] *s* Aufwertung *f*. **ˌre'val·ue** [~ˈjuː] *v/t* Dollar *etc* aufwerten.

re·vamp [riːˈvæmp] *v/t* F Haus *etc* aufmöbeln, *Theaterstück etc* aufpolieren, *Firma etc* auf Vordermann bringen.

re·veal [rɪˈviːl] *v/t* **1.** den Blick freigeben auf (*acc*); zeigen. **2.** Geheimnis *etc* enthüllen, aufdecken. **re'veal·ing** *adj* □ **1.** offenherzig (*Kleid etc*). **2.** *fig*. aufschlußreich.

rev·el [ˈrevl] *v/i pret u. pp* **-eled**, *bsd. Br*. **-elled 1.** (lärmend *od*. ausgelassen) feiern. **2.** (*in*) schwelgen (in *dat*); *b. s.* sich weiden (an *dat*).

rev·e·la·tion [ˌrevəˈleɪʃn] *s* **1.** Enthüllung *f*, Aufdeckung *f*. **2.** *eccl*. Offenbarung *f*.

rev·el·(l)er [ˈrevlə] *s* Feiernde *m*, *f*. **ˈrev·el·ry** *s* (lärmendes *od*. ausgelassenes) Feiern.

re·venge [rɪˈvendʒ] I *s* **1.** Rache *f*: **in ~** aus Rache (*for* für); **take (one's) ~ on s.o.** (*for s.th.*) → 4; **give s.o. a chance to get his ~** j-m Revanche geben. II *v/t*

3. *et*. rächen. **4. ~ o.s. on s.o.** (*for s.th.*) sich an j-m (für *et*.) rächen. **re'venge·ful** [~fʊl] *adj* □ rachsüchtig.

rev·e·nue [ˈrevənjuː] *s a. pl* Staatseinnahmen *pl*, -einkünfte *pl* → **inland** 2.

re·ver·ber·ate [rɪˈvɜːbəreɪt] I *v/i* nachwiderhallen. II *v/t* Schall zurückwerfen. **re,ver·ber'a·tion** *s* **1.** Nach-, Widerhall *m*. **2.** Zurückwerfen *n*.

re·vere [rɪˈvɪə] *v/t* verehren; *Andenken* hochhalten. **rev·er·ence** [ˈrevərəns] *s* Verehrung *f*; Ehrfurcht *f* (*for* vor *dat*): **with ~** ehrfürchtig; **hold in ~** verehren. **rev·er·end** *s eccl*. Hochwürden *m*.

rev·er·ent [ˈrevərənt], **rev·er·en·tial** [ˌ~ˈrenʃl] *adj* □ ehrfürchtig, ehrfurchtsvoll.

rev·er·ie [ˈrevərɪ] *s* (Tag)Träumerei *f*: **fall into a ~** ins Träumen geraten.

re·ver·sal [rɪˈvɜːsl] *s* **1.** Umstoßung *f*, 𝕤 Aufhebung *f*. **2.** Rückschlag *m*. **re'verse** I *s* **1.** Gegenteil *n*: **quite the ~** ganz im Gegenteil. **2.** Rückschlag *m*. **3.** Kehr-, Rückseite *f* (*e-r Münze*). **4.** *mot*. Rückwärtsgang *m*: **put the car into ~** den Rückwärtsgang einlegen. II *adj* □ **5.** umgekehrt; (*Richtung*) entgegengesetzt: **~ gear** → 4; **in ~ order** in umgekehrter Reihenfolge; **~ side** linke (*Stoff*)Seite. III *v/t* **6.** Wagen im Rückwärtsgang *od*. rückwärts fahren: **one's car out of the garage** *a*. rückwärts aus der Garage fahren. **7.** Reihenfolge *etc* umkehren: **~ the charges** *teleph. Br*. ein R-Gespräch führen. **8.** *Entscheidung etc* umstoßen; 𝕤 *Urteil* aufheben. **9.** *Blatt etc* umdrehen; *Mantel etc* wenden. IV *v/i* **10.** *mot*. im Rückwärtsgang *od*. rückwärts fahren.

re·vert [rɪˈvɜːt] *v/i*: **~ to** auf *ein Thema* zurückkommen; in *e-e Gewohnheit etc* zurückfallen; in *e-n Zustand* zurückkehren.

re·view [rɪˈvjuː] I *s* **1.** Überprüfung *f*: **be under ~** überprüft werden. **2.** Besprechung *f*, Kritik *f*, Rezension *f*: **~ copy** Rezensionsexemplar *n*. **3.** ✗ Parade *f*. **4.** → **revue**. **5.** *ped. Am*. (Stoff)Wiederholung *f* (*for* für → *e-e Prüfung*). II *v/t* **6.** überprüfen. **7.** besprechen, rezensieren. **8.** ✗ besichtigen, inspizieren. **9.** *ped. Am*. *Stoff* wiederholen (*for* für → *e-e Prüfung*). **re'view·er** *s* Kritiker(in), Rezensent(in).

re·vile [rɪ'vaɪl] v/t schmähen, verunglimpfen.

re·vise [rɪ'vaɪz] v/t 1. revidieren: a) *Ansicht* ändern, b) *Buch etc* überarbeiten. 2. *Br.* → **review** 9.

re·vi·sion [rɪ'vɪʒn] s 1. Revidierung f, Änderung f; Revision f, Überarbeitung f. 2. überarbeitete Ausgabe. 3. *Br.* → **review** 5.

re·vi·tal·ize [ˌriː'vaɪtəlaɪz] v/t neu beleben.

re·viv·al [rɪ'vaɪvl] s 1. Wiederbelebung f (a. fig.). 2. *thea.* Wiederaufnahme f. 3. Wiederaufleben n (a. fig.). **re·vive** I v/t 1. *j-n* wiederbeleben; beleben. 2. *Brauch etc* wiederbeleben, wiederaufleben lassen; *Erinnerungen* wachrufen. 3. *thea. Stück* wiederaufnehmen. II v/i 4. wieder zu sich kommen; wieder aufleben. 5. wiederaufleben (*Brauch etc*).

rev·o·ca·tion [ˌrevə'keɪʃn] s Aufhebung f, Rückgängigmachung f, Widerruf m. **re·voke** [rɪ'vəʊk] v/t *Gesetz etc* aufheben, *Entscheidung, Erlaubnis etc* rückgängig machen, widerrufen.

re·volt [rɪ'vəʊlt] I s 1. Revolte f, Aufstand m: **be in ~** (**against**) → 3. 2. → **revulsion**. II v/i 3. revoltieren (**against** gegen). 4. *fig.* Abscheu empfinden, empört sein (**against, at, from** über *acc*). III v/t 5. mit Abscheu erfüllen, abstoßen. **re·volt·ing** adj □ abscheulich, abstoßend.

rev·o·lu·tion [ˌrevə'luːʃn] s 1. Umdrehung f: **number of ~s** mot. Drehzahl f; **~ counter** mot. Drehzahlmesser m. 2. *ast.* Umlauf m (**round** um). 3. *pol.* Revolution f, *fig. a.* Umwälzung f. **rev·o·lu·tion·ar·y** [~ərɪ] I adj □ *pol.* revolutionär, *fig. a.* umwälzend. II s *pol.* Revolutionär(in) (a. fig.). **rev·o·lu·tion·ize** v/t fig. revolutionieren.

re·volve [rɪ'vɒlv] v/i sich drehen (**on an axis** um e-e Achse; **round the Earth** um die Erde): **~ around** fig. sich drehen um; **he thinks the whole world ~s around him** er glaubt, alles dreht sich nur um ihn. **re·volv·er** s Revolver m. **re·volv·ing** adj Dreh...: **~ door(s** pl) Drehtür(f). **~ stage** thea. Drehbühne f.

re·vue [rɪ'vjuː] s thea. Revue f; Kabarett n.

re·vul·sion [rɪ'vʌlʃn] s Abscheu f: **in ~** angewidert.

re·ward [rɪ'wɔːd] I s (a. ausgesetzte) Belohnung f: **as a ~** (**for**) als Belohnung (für); → **finder**. II v/t belohnen. **re·'ward·ing** adj lohnend, (*Aufgabe etc a.*) dankbar.

re·word [ˌriː'wɜːd] v/t umformulieren.

re·write [ˌriː'raɪt] v/t (*irr* **write**) umschreiben.

rhap·so·dize ['ræpsədaɪz] v/i schwärmen (**about, over** von). **'rhap·so·dy** s 1. ♪ Rhapsodie f. 2. fig. Schwärmerei f: **go into rhapsodies** ins Schwärmen geraten (**about, over** von).

Rhe·sus fac·tor ['riːsəs] s ♣ Rhesusfaktor m.

rhet·o·ric ['retərɪk] s 1. Rhetorik f. 2. *contp.* Phrasendrescherei f. **rhe·tor·i·cal** [rɪ'tɒrɪkl] adj □ rhetorisch: **~ question** rhetorische Frage.

rheu·mat·ic [ruː'mætɪk] ♣ I adj (~ally □) rheumatisch: **~ fever** rheumatisches Fieber. II s 2. Rheumatiker(in). 3. pl (sg konstruiert) bsd. *Br.* F Rheuma n. **rheu·ma·tism** ['ruːmətɪzəm] s ♣ Rheuma(tismus m) n.

rhi·no ['raɪnəʊ] pl **-nos** s zo. F, **rhi·noc·er·os** [~'nɒsərəs] s zo. Rhinozeros n, Nashorn n.

rho·do·den·dron [ˌrəʊdə'dendrən] s ♣ Rhododendron m, n.

rhom·bus ['rɒmbəs] pl **-bus·es, -bi** [~baɪ] s ♣ Rhombus m, Raute f.

rhu·barb ['ruːbɑːb] s 1. ♣ Rhabarber m. 2. bsd. *Am.* F Krach m, Streit m.

rhyme [raɪm] I s 1. Reim m (**for** auf *acc*): **do s.th. without ~ or reason** et. aus unerklärlichen Gründen tun. 2. Reim m, Vers m. II v/i 3. sich reimen (**with** auf *acc*). III v/t 4. reimen (**with** auf *acc*, mit).

rhythm ['rɪðəm] s Rhythmus m: **break s.o.'s ~** j-n aus dem Rhythmus bringen. **rhyth·mic, rhyth·mi·cal** ['rɪðmɪk(l)] adj □ rhythmisch, (*Atmen etc*) gleichmäßig.

rib [rɪb] I s 1. *anat.* Rippe f (a. ♣ etc): → **dig** 1, 5, **poke** 1, 6. 2. Speiche f (e-s Regenschirms). II v/t 3. F aufziehen, hänseln (**for** wegen).

rib·bon ['rɪbən] s 1. (a. Farb-, Ordens-) Band n. 2. Streifen m; Fetzen m: **tear to ~s** zerfetzen.

rib cage s anat. Brustkorb m.

rice [raɪs] s ♣ Reis m. **~ pad·dy** s Reisfeld

n. ~ **pud·ding** *s* Milchreis *m.* ~ **wine** *s* Reiswein *m.*

rich [rɪtʃ] **I** *adj* □ **1.** reich (*a. fig.*): ~ **in** reich an (*dat*); ~ **in contrasts** kontrastreich. **2.** prächtig, kostbar (*Schmuck etc*). **3.** schwer (*Speise*). **4.** ertragreich, fett (*Boden*). **5.** voll (*Töne*), (*Farben a.*) satt. **6.** *that's* ~*!* F *iro.* na prima! **II** *s* **7.** *the* ~ *pl* die Reichen *pl.* **rich·es** ['~ɪz] *s pl* Reichtümer *pl.* **'rich·ness** *s* **1.** Reichtum *m* (*a. fig.*). **2.** Prächtigkeit *f*, Kostbarkeit *f.* **3.** Schwere *f.* **4.** Fettheit *f.* **5.** Fülle *f*, Sattheit *f.*

rick·ets ['rɪkɪts] *s pl* (*sg konstruiert*) ✷ Rachitis *f.* **rick·et·y** ['~əti] *adj* **1.** ✷ rachitisch. **2.** schwach (*auf den Beinen*); gebrechlich. **3.** wack(e)lig (*Möbelstück etc*).

rick·shaw ['rɪkʃɔ:] *s* Riksha *f.*

ric·o·chet ['rɪkəʃeɪ] **I** *s* Querschläger *m.* **II** *v/i* abprallen (*off* von).

rid [rɪd] *v/t* (*mst irr*) befreien (*of* von): *get* ~ *of* loswerden. **'rid·dance** *s: good* ~ (*to him*)*!* F den sind wir Gott sei Dank los!; *get out and good* ~ auf Nimmerwiedersehen.

rid·den ['rɪdn] **I** *pp von* **ride. II** *adj in Zssgn* geplagt *od.* heimgesucht von.

rid·dle¹ ['rɪdl] *s* Rätsel *n* (*a. fig.*): *speak* (*od. talk*) *in* ~*s* in Rätseln sprechen.

rid·dle² [~] **I** *s* **1.** (Schüttel)Sieb *n.* **II** *v/t* **2.** sieben. **3.** ~ *with bullets* mit Kugeln durchlöchern *od.* -sieben; ~*d with holes* (*mistakes*) voller Löcher (Fehler).

ride [raɪd] **I** *s* **1.** Ritt *m*: *give s.o. a* ~ *on one's shoulders* j-n auf s-n Schultern reiten lassen. **2.** Fahrt *f*: *give s.o. a* ~ j-n (*im Auto etc*) mitnehmen; *go for a* ~ *in the car* e-e Autofahrt machen; *take s.o. for a* ~ F j-n reinlegen *od.* übers Ohr hauen. **II** *v/i* (*irr*) **3.** reiten (*a. rittlings sitzen*) (*on auf dat*): ~ *roughshod.* **4.** fahren (*on auf e-m Fahrrad etc, in e-m Bus etc*). **5.** ~ *up* hochrutschen (*Rock etc*). **III** *v/t* **6.** reiten (*auf dat*). **7.** Fahr-, Motorrad fahren, fahren auf (*dat*): *can you* ~ *a bicycle?* kannst du radfahren? **'rid·er** *s* **1.** Reiter(in). **2.** (Motorrad-, Rad)Fahrer(in).

ridge [rɪdʒ] *s* **1.** (Gebirgs)Kamm *m*, (-)Grat *m.* **2.** (Dach)First *m.*

rid·i·cule ['rɪdɪkju:l] **I** *s* Spott *m*: *for fear of* ~ aus Angst, sich lächerlich zu ma-

chen; *hold up to* ~ → **II. II** *v/t* lächerlich machen, spotten über (*acc*). **ri·dic·u·lous** [~jʊləs] *adj* □ lächerlich: *don't be* ~ mach dich nicht lächerlich.

rid·ing ['raɪdɪŋ] *adj* Reit...: ~ *school*; ~ *breeches* Reithose *f.*

rife [raɪf] *adj*: ~ *with* voll von, voller.

riff·le ['rɪfl] *v/i*: ~ *through s.th.* et. durchblättern.

riff·raff ['rɪfræf] *s* Gesindel *n*, Pack *n.*

ri·fle¹ ['raɪfl] *v/t* durchwühlen.

ri·fle² [~] *s* Gewehr *n.* ~ **range** *s* Schießstand *m.*

rift [rɪft] *s* **1.** Spalt(e *f*) *m.* **2.** *fig.* Riß *m.*

rig¹ [rɪg] *v/t* Wahl *etc* manipulieren.

rig² [~] **I** *s* **1.** ⚓ Takelage *f*, Takelung *f.* **2.** Bohrinsel *f.* **3.** F Aufmachung *f*: *in full* ~ in voller Montur. **4.** *Am.* F Sattelschlepper *m.* **II** *v/t* **5.** Schiff auftakeln. **6.** ~ *out* F j-n ausstaffieren (*as* als); auftakeln. **7.** ~ *up* F provisorisch zs.-bauen (*from* aus).

right [raɪt] **I** *adj* (□ → *rightly*) **1.** richtig, recht: *the* ~ *thing* das Richtige; → *all* 3. **2.** richtig: a) korrekt, b) wahr: *is your watch* ~*?* geht deine Uhr richtig?; *be* ~ recht haben. **3.** richtig, geeignet: *the* ~ *man in the* ~ *place* der rechte Mann am rechten Platz. **4.** richtig, in Ordnung: *put* (*od. set*) ~ in Ordnung bringen; j-n aufklären (*on* über *acc*); *Irrtum* richtigstellen. **5.** recht, Rechts... **6.** ~ *angle* ⟨ rechter Winkel. **II** *s* **7.** Recht *n*: *know* ~ *from wrong* Recht von Unrecht unterscheiden können. **8.** Recht *n*; Anrecht *n* (*to* auf *acc*): *by* ~*s* von Rechts wegen; *it is my* ~ *of way* mot. ich habe Vorfahrt; *know one's* ~*s* s-e Rechte kennen. **9.** *die Rechte*, rechte Seite: *on* (*od. at, to*) *the* ~ (*of*) rechts (von), rechter Hand (von); *on our* ~ zu unserer Rechten; *the second turning to* (*od. on*) *the* ~ die zweite Querstraße rechts; *keep to the* ~ sich rechts halten; *mot.* rechts fahren. **10.** *the* ~ *pol.* die Rechte. **III** *adv* **11.** richtig, recht: *if I get you* ~ wenn ich Sie richtig verstehe; *guess* ~ richtig (er)raten; → *serve* 8. **12.** genau, direkt. **13.** ~ *away* (*od. off*) sofort; ~ *now* im Moment; sofort. **14.** ganz, völlig. **15.** rechts (*of* von): *turn* ~ (sich) nach rechts wenden; *mot.* rechts abbiegen; ~ *and left*; ~, *left and center* (*bsd. Br. centre*) *fig.* F überall; in jeder Hinsicht. **IV** *v/t*

16. aufrichten. **17.** *Unrecht* wiedergutmachen. '~-**an·gled** *adj* ℞ rechtwink(e)lig.

right·eous ['raɪtʃəs] *adj* gerecht (*Zorn* etc).

right·ful ['raɪtfʊl] *adj* □ rechtmäßig. '~-**hand** *adj* **1.** recht: ~ **bend** Rechtskurve *f*; ~ **man** *fig. j-s* rechte Hand. **2.** ⚙ rechtsgängig, -läufig: ~ **drive** Rechtssteuerung *f*. ~-'**hand·ed** *adj* □ rechtshändig: **be** ~ Rechtshänder(in) sein. ~-'**hand·er** *s* Rechtshänder(in).

right·ist ['raɪtɪst] *adj pol.* rechtsgerichtet, -stehend. '**right·ly** *adv* **1.** richtig. **2.** mit Recht: ~ **or wrongly** zu Recht od. Unrecht. **3.** F *I don't* ~ *know* ich weiß nicht sicher; *I can't* ~ *say* ich kann nicht mit Sicherheit sagen.

'**right-wing** *adj pol.* dem rechten Flügel angehörend, Rechts...

rig·id ['rɪdʒɪd] *adj* □ **1.** starr (*a. Person*: **with** vor *dat*), steif. **2.** *fig.* streng (*Disziplin* etc); starr (*Prinzipien* etc); genau, strikt (*Kontrolle* etc). **ri·gid·i·ty** *s* **1.** Starre *f*, Starrheit *f*, Steifheit *f*. **2.** *fig.* Strenge *f*; Genauigkeit *f*, Striktheit *f*.

rig·ma·role ['rɪgmərəʊl] *s* F **1.** Geschwätz *n*. **2.** Theater *n*, Zirkus *m*.

rig·or *Am.* → **rigour**.

ri·gor mor·tis [ˌraɪgɔː'mɔːtɪs] *s* ☤ Leichenstarre *f*.

rig·or·ous ['rɪgərəs] *adj* □ **1.** streng (*Kontrolle* etc). **2.** (peinlich) genau, gründlich.

rig·our ['rɪgə] *s bsd. Br.* **1.** Strenge *f*: **the full** ~ **of the law** die volle Härte des Gesetzes. **2.** *pl* Unbilden *pl*.

'**rig-out** *s Br.* F Aufmachung *f*.

rile [raɪl] *v/t* F ärgern, reizen.

rim [rɪm] *s* **1.** Rand *m* (*e-r Tasse* etc), (*e-s Huts a.*) Krempe *f*. **2.** ⚙ Felge *f*.

rind [raɪnd] *s* (*Zitronen-* etc)Schale *f*; (*Käse*)Rinde *f*; (*Speck-* etc)Schwarte *f*.

ring¹ [rɪŋ] **I** *s* **1.** *allg.* Ring *m*: **at the** ~**s** (*Turnen*) an den Ringen; **form a** ~ e-n Kreis bilden; **he's got** ~**s round his eyes** er hat Ringe unter den Augen; **make** (*od.* **run**) ~**s round s.o.** *fig.* j-n in die Tasche stecken. **2.** (*Zirkus*) Manege *f*; (*Boxen*) Ring *m*. **3.** ✝ Ring *m*, Kartell *n*; (*Spionage-* etc)Ring *m*. **II** *v/t* **4.** *Vogel* etc beringen. **5.** umringen, (*Polizei* etc) umstellen: *Stelle in e-m Buch* etc einkreisen.

ring² [~] **I** *s* **1.** Läuten *n*; Klingeln *n*. **2.** *fig.* **that has a familiar** ~ **to me** das kommt mir (irgendwie) bekannt vor; **have a hollow** ~ hohl klingen (*Versprechen* etc), unglaubwürdig klingen (*Protest* etc). **3.** *teleph. bsd. Br.* Anruf *m*: **give s.o. a** ~ j-n anrufen. **II** *v/i* (*irr*) **4.** läuten; klingeln: **the bell is** ~**ing** es läutet *od.* klingelt; ~ **for** nach *j-m, et.* läuten. **5.** *teleph. bsd. Br.* anrufen: ~ **for** *Arzt* etc rufen. **6.** klingen (*a. fig.*): ~ **in s.o.'s ears** j-m im Ohr klingen; ~ **hollow** hohl klingen (*Versprechen* etc), unglaubwürdig klingen (*Protest* etc). **III** *v/t* (*irr*) **7.** läuten: → **bell 1, doorbell. 8.** *teleph. bsd. Br.* j-n anrufen.

Verbindungen mit Adverbien:

ring| back *v/t u. v/i teleph. bsd. Br.* zurückrufen. ~ **in** *v/i* **1.** *bsd. Br.* sich telefonisch melden (**to** bei). **2.** *Am.* (*bei Arbeitsbeginn*) einstempeln. ~ **off** *v/i teleph. bsd. Br.* (den Hörer) auflegen, Schluß machen. ~ **out** *v/i* **1.** erklingen, ertönen. **2.** *Am.* (*bei Arbeitsende*) ausstempeln. ~ **round** *v/i bsd. Br.* herumtelefonieren. ~ **up** *v/t* **1.** → **ring²** 8. **2.** *Preis, Ware* (*in die Kasse*) eintippen.

ring| bind·er *s* Ringbuch *n*. ~ **fin·ger** *s* Ringfinger *m*. '~**lead·er** *s* Rädelsführer(in). '~**mas·ter** *s* Zirkusdirektor *m*. ~ **road** *s bsd. Br.* Umgehungsstraße *f*. '~**side** *s*: **at the** ~ (*Boxen*) am Ring; ~ **seat** (*Boxen*) Ringplatz *m*; (*Zirkus*) Manegenplatz *m*.

rink [rɪŋk] *s* (Kunst)Eisbahn *f*; Rollschuhbahn *f*.

rinse [rɪns] *v/t* **1.** *a.* ~ **out** (aus)spülen, *Wäsche* spülen: ~ **one's mouth out** sich den Mund ausspülen (**with** mit); ~ **the soap out of one's hair** sich die Seife aus dem Haar spülen. **2.** sich *das Haar* tönen. **II** *s* **3.** Spülung *f*: **give s.th. a** ~ → 1. **4.** Tönung(smittel *n*) *f*.

ri·ot ['raɪət] **I** *s* **1.** Aufruhr *m*, Krawall *m*, Tumult *m*: **run** ~ randalieren, randalierend ziehen (**through** durch); **his imagination ran** ~ s-e Phantasie ging mit ihm durch; **read s.o. the** ~ **act** *oft humor.* j-m die Leviten lesen; ~ **police** Bereitschaftspolizei *f*; ~ **squad** Überfallkommando *n*; ~ **shield** Schutzschild *m*. **2.** ~ **of colo(u)r** Sinfonie *f* von *od.* Orgie *f* in Farben. **3.** **be a** ~ F zum Schreien (komisch) sein. **II** *v/i* **4.** an e-m

Aufruhr teilnehmen; randalieren. **'ri·ot·er** s Aufrührer *m*; Randalierer *m*. **'ri·ot·ous** *adj* □ **1.** aufrührerisch; randalierend. **2.** ausgelassen, wild.

rip [rɪp] **I** *v/t* **1.** *a.* ~ **up** zerreißen: ~ **s.th.** sich et. zerreißen (**on** an *dat*); ~ **s.th. from s.o.'s hand** j-m et. aus der Hand reißen; ~ **off one's shirt** sich das Hemd herunter- *od.* vom Leibe reißen; ~ **open** aufreißen. **2.** ~ **off** F neppen; mitgehen lassen, klauen. **II** *v/i* **3.** (zer)reißen. **4.** **let her** ~*!* *mot.* F volle Pulle! **III** *s* **5.** Riß *m*.

'rip·cord s Reißleine *f* (*am Fallschirm*).

ripe [raɪp] *adj* □ reif (*a. fig.*): **live to a ~ old age** ein hohes Alter erreichen; **the time is ~ for** die Zeit ist reif für; **~ for development** baureif. **rip·en** ['~ən] **I** *v/i* reifen. **II** *v/t* reifen lassen.

'rip-off s F Nepp *m*; Diebstahl *m*.

ri·poste [rɪ'pɒst] **I** s **1.** *fenc.* Riposte *f*. **2.** (schlagfertige *od.* scharfe) Entgegnung. **II** *v/t* **3.** (schlagfertig *od.* scharf) entgegnen.

rip·ple ['rɪpl] **I** s **1.** kleine Welle. **2.** Plätschern *n*. **II** *v/t* **3.** Wasser kräuseln. **III** *v/i* **4.** sich kräuseln. **5.** plätschern.

'rip-,roar·ing *adj* **1.** ausgelassen (*Party etc*). **2.** toll (*Erfolg etc*).

rise [raɪz] **I** *v/i* (*irr*) **1.** aufstehen (*a. am Morgen*), sich erheben. **2.** aufsteigen (*Rauch etc*); sich heben (*Vorhang*): **his spirits rose** s-e Stimmung hob sich. **3.** ansteigen (*Straße, Wasser etc*), anschwellen (*Fluß etc*). **4.** (an)steigen (**by** um) (*Temperatur etc*), (*Preise etc a.*) anziehen. **5.** aufgehen (*Sonne, Teig etc*). **6.** entspringen (*Fluß etc*); *fig.* entstehen (**from, out of** aus). **7.** *a.* ~ **up** sich erheben (**against** gegen). **8.** (**above**) erhaben sein (über *acc*), stehen (über *dat*): → **occasion** 3. **9.** (*beruflich od. gesellschaftlich*) aufsteigen: → **rank** 1. **II** s **10.** Steigung *f*; Anhöhe *f*. **11.** *ast.* Aufgang *m*. **12.** *fig.* Anstieg *m* (**in** gen): **~ in population** Bevölkerungszunahme *f*; **the ~ and fall** das Auf u. Ab. **13.** *fig.* Aufstieg *m* (**to** zu): **the ~ and fall** der Aufstieg u. Fall. **14.** *bsd. Br.* Lohn- *od.* Gehaltserhöhung *f*. **15.** **give ~ to** verursachen, führen zu; Anlaß geben zu. **ris·en** ['rɪzn] *pp von* rise. **'ris·er** s *arch.* **earl·y** ~ Frühaufsteher(in); **late** ~ Langschläfer(in). **'ris·ing** s **1.** Aufstand *m*,

Erhebung *f*. **II** *adj* **2.** heranwachsend, kommend (*Generation*). **3.** aufstrebend (*Politiker etc*). **III** *prp* **4.** **be** ~ **ten** *bsd. Br.* fast zehn sein.

risk [rɪsk] **I** s Gefahr *f*, Risiko *n*: **at one's own** ~ auf eigene Gefahr, auf eigenes Risiko; **at the** ~ **of** (*ger*) auf die Gefahr hin zu (*inf*); **be at** ~ gefährdet sein; **put at** ~ gefährden; **run** (*od.* **take**) **a** ~ ein Risiko eingehen; **run the** ~ **of doing s.th.** Gefahr laufen, et. zu tun; ~ **group** Risikogruppe *f*. **II** *v/t* riskieren: a) *sein Leben etc* aufs Spiel setzen, b) *Sprung etc* wagen, c) es ankommen lassen auf *e-e Verletzung etc*; ~ **doing s.th.** es wagen *od.* riskieren, et. zu tun; → **neck** 1. **'risk·y** *adj* □ riskant.

ri·sot·to [rɪ'zɒtəʊ] *pl* **-tos** *s gastr.* Risotto *m*.

ris·qué ['rɪːskeɪ] *adj* gewagt (*Witz etc*).

rite [raɪt] *s* Ritus *m*: **perform the last** ~**s over** *eccl.* j-m die Sterbesakramente spenden.

rit·u·al ['rɪtʃʊəl] **I** s **1.** Ritual *n*. **II** *adj* □ **2.** Ritual...: ~ **murder** Ritualmord *m*. **3.** rituell.

ritz·y ['rɪtsɪ] *adj* F stinkvornehm, feudal.

ri·val ['raɪvl] **I** s **1.** Rivale *m*, Rivalin *f*, Konkurrent(in): ~ (**in love**) Nebenbuhler(in). **II** *adj* **2.** rivalisierend, konkurrierend: ~ **firm** Konkurrenzfirma *f*. **III** *v/t pret u. pp* **-valed**, *bsd. Br.* **-valled 3.** rivalisieren *od.* konkurrieren mit. **4.** es aufnehmen mit (**for** an *dat*). **'ri·val·ry** s Rivalität *f*; Konkurrenz(kampf *m*) *f*.

riv·er ['rɪvə] *s* Fluß *m*; Strom *m*: **down the** ~ flußabwärts; **up the** ~ flußaufwärts; **sell s.o. down the** ~ F j-n verraten u. verkaufen; ~**s** *pl* **of blood** Blutströme *pl*. ~ **ba·sin** *s* Flußbecken *n*. **'~·bed** *s* Flußbett *n*. **'~·side** *s* Flußufer *n*: **by the** ~ am Fluß.

riv·et ['rɪvɪt] **I** *s* **1. ⦿** Niet *m*. **II** *v/t* **2. ⦿** (ver)nieten: **stand** ~**ed to the spot** *fig.* wie festgenagelt stehen(bleiben). **3.** *fig.* Aufmerksamkeit richten, Augen, Blick *a.* heften (**on** auf *acc*); *j-s Aufmerksamkeit* fesseln.

road [rəʊd] *s* (Land)Straße *f*: **on the** ~ auf der Straße; **be on the** ~ mit dem Auto unterwegs sein; *thea. etc* auf Tournee sein; **be on the right** ~ *fig.* auf dem richtigen Weg sein; **hit the** ~ F sich auf den Weg machen, aufbrechen; **one**

for the ~ F e-n (*Schnaps etc*) zum Abschied *od.* für unterwegs; → *Rome.* **ac·ci·dent** *s* Verkehrsunfall *m.* '~-**block** *s* Straßensperre *f.* **~ hog** *s* F Verkehrsrowdy *m.* '~,**hold·ing** *s* mot. Straßenlage *f.* '~**house** *s* Rasthaus *n.* **~man** ['~mən] *s* (*irr man*) Straßenarbeiter *m.* **~ roll·er** *s* ⊙ Straßenwalze *f.* **~ safe·ty** *s* Verkehrssicherheit *f.* '~**side** *s* Straßenrand *m:* **at** (*od.* **by**) **the ~** am Straßenrand. **~ test** *s mot.* Probefahrt *f:* **do a ~** e-e Probefahrt machen. '~**test** *v/t Auto* probefahren, e-e Probefahrt machen mit. **~us·er** *s* Verkehrsteilnehmer(in). '~**way** *s* Fahrbahn *f.* '~,**works** *s pl* Straßenbauarbeiten *pl.* '~,**wor·thy** *adj* verkehrssicher.

roam [rəʊm] **I** *v/i* wandern. **II** *v/t* wandern durch.

roar [rɔː] **I** *v/i* **1.** brüllen (**with** vor *dat*): **~** (**with laughter**) vor Lachen brüllen; **~ at s.o.** j-n anbrüllen. **2.** donnern (*Fahrzeug, Geschütz*). **II** *v/t* **3.** *a.* **~ out** *et.* brüllen. **III** *s* **4.** Brüllen *n*, Gebrüll *n:* **~s** *pl* **of laughter** brüllendes Gelächter. **5.** Donnern *n.* '**roar·ing** I *adj* □ **1.** brüllend. **2.** donnernd. **3.** **~ success** F Bombenerfolg *m.* **II** *adv* **4.** **~ drunk** F sternhagelvoll. **III** *s* **5.** → **roar** 4, 5.

roast [rəʊst] **I** *v/t Fleisch* braten; *Kaffee etc* rösten. **II** *v/i* braten: **I'm ~ing** ich komme vor Hitze fast um. **III** *s* Braten *m.* **IV** *adj* gebraten: **~ beef** Rinder-, Rindsbraten *m;* **~ chicken** Brathuhn *n*, -hühnchen *n;* **~ pork** Schweine-, Schweinsbraten *m;* **~ veal** Kalbsbraten *m.* '**roast·ing** F **I** *adj* glühend-, knallheiß (*Tag etc*). **II** *adv:* **~ hot** → I. **III** *s:* **give s.o. a** (*real*) **~** j-n zs.-stauchen (*for* wegen).

rob [rɒb] *v/t Bank etc* überfallen; *j-n* berauben: **~ s.o. of s.th.** j-m *et.* rauben. '**rob·ber** *s* Räuber *m.* '**rob·ber·y** *s* Raub(überfall) *m*, (*Bank*)Raub *m*, (-)Überfall *m.*

robe [rəʊb] *s a. pl* Robe *f*, Talar *m.*

rob·in ['rɒbɪn] *s orn.* Rotkehlchen *n.*

ro·bot ['rəʊbɒt] *s* ⊙ Roboter *m* (*a. fig.*).

ro·bust [rəʊ'bʌst] *adj* □ **1.** robust (*Person, Gesundheit, Material etc*); *fig.* gesund (*Firma etc*). **2.** *fig.* nachdrücklich.

rock¹ [rɒk] *s* **1.** Fels(en) *m;* *coll.* Felsen *pl;* *geol.* Gestein *n.* **2.** Felsbrocken *m;* *Am.* Stein *m.* **3.** *pl* Klippen *pl:* **on the ~s**

on the rocks, mit Eis (*bsd. Whisky*); in ernsten Schwierigkeiten (*Ehe etc*); **their marriage is on the ~s** in ihrer Ehe kriselt es gewaltig.

rock² [~] **I** *v/t* **1.** wiegen, schaukeln: **~ a child to sleep** ein Kind in den Schlaf wiegen. **2.** erschüttern (*a. fig.*): **~ the boat** *fig.* alles kaputtmachen. **II** *v/i* **3.** schaukeln. **4.** schwanken: **~ with laughter** F sich vor Lachen biegen. **5.** ♪ rocken. **III** *s* **6.** → **rock 'n' roll. 7.** *a.* ♪ **music** Rock(musik *f*) *m:* **~ group** Rockgruppe *f;* **~ singer** Rocksänger (-in).

rock| and roll *s* ♪ Rock and Roll *m.* **~ bot·tom** *s:* **fall to** (*od.* **hit, reach**) **~** e-n *od.* s-n Tiefpunkt erreichen. **~'bot·tom** *adj* allerniedrigst, äußerst (*Preise*). **~ crys·tal** *s min.* Bergkristall *m.*

rock·er ['rɒkə] *s* **1.** Kufe *f* (*e-s Schaukelstuhls etc*): **off one's ~** F übergeschnappt. **2.** *Am.* Schaukelstuhl *m.* **3.** *Br.* Rocker *m.*

rock·er·y ['rɒkərɪ] *s* Steingarten *m.*

rock·et ['rɒkɪt] **I** *s* **1.** Rakete *f.* **2.** **give s.o. a ~** *fig.* F e-e Zigarre verpassen. **II** *v/i* **3.** *a.* **~ up** hochschnellen, in die Höhe schießen (*Preise*). **4.** rasen, schießen.

'**rock|·fall** *s* Steinschlag *m.* **~ gar·den** *s* Steingarten *m.*

rock·ing| chair ['rɒkɪŋ] *s* Schaukelstuhl *m.* **~ horse** *s* Schaukelpferd *n.*

rock 'n' roll [ˌrɒkən'rəʊl] *s* ♪ Rock 'n' Roll *m.*

rock·y¹ ['rɒkɪ] *adj* □ **1.** felsig. **2.** steinhart.

rock·y² [~] *adj* □ F wack(e)lig.

ro·co·co [rəʊ'kəʊkəʊ] *s* Rokoko *n.*

rod [rɒd] *s* **1.** (*a. Angel*)Rute *f.* **2.** ⊙ Stab *m*, Stange *f.* **3. rule with a ~ of iron** mit eiserner Faust regieren. **4.** *Am. sl.* Schießeisen *n*, Kanone *f.*

rode [rəʊd] *pret von* **ride.**

ro·dent ['rəʊdənt] *s* Nagetier *n.*

ro·de·o [rəʊ'deɪəʊ] *pl* -**os** *s* Rodeo *m*, *n.*

roe¹ [rəʊ] *s a.* **hard ~** *ichth.* Rogen *m;* **soft ~** Milch *f.*

roe² [~] *pl* **roe** *s zo.* Reh *n.* '~**buck** *s* Rehbock *m.* '~ **deer** *s* Reh *n.*

rog·er ['rɒdʒə] *int Funkverkehr:* roger!, verstanden!

rogue [rəʊg] *s* **1.** Gauner *m:* **~s' gallery** Verbrecheralbum *n.* **2.** *oft humor.*

Schlingel *m*, Spitzbube *m*. **'ro·guer·y** *s* **1.** Gaunerei *f*. **2.** Spitzbüberei *f*. **'ro·guish** *adj* □ schelmisch.

role [rəʊl] *s thea. etc* Rolle *f* (*a. fig.*).

roll [rəʊl] **I** *s* **1.** Rolle *f*; (*Fett*)Wulst *f*. **2.** Anwesenheits-, Namenliste *f*: **call the ~** die Anwesenheitsliste verlesen. **3.** Brötchen *n*, Semmel *f*. **4.** *Würfeln*: Wurf *m*. **5.** ♪ Schlingern *n*. **6.** (G)Rollen *n* (*des Donners*); (*Trommel*)Wirbel *m*. **II** *v/i* **7.** rollen; sich wälzen: **tears were ~ing down her cheeks** Tränen rollten ihr über die Wangen; **heads will ~** *fig.* es werden einige Köpfe rollen; **be ~ing in money** (*od. it*) F im Geld schwimmen; → **ball¹** 1. **8.** rollen, fahren. **9.** würfeln. **10.** (sch)wanken (*Person*); ♪ schlingern. **11.** (g)rollen (*Donner*). **III** *v/t* **12.** *et.* rollen: **~ the dice** würfeln; **~ one's eyes** die Augen rollen *od.* verdrehen. **13.** auf-, zs.-rollen: **~ itself into** sich zs.-rollen zu (*Tier*); **~ a cigarette** sich e-e Zigarette drehen; **~ed into one** *fig.* in einem. **14.** *Rasen etc* walzen; *Teig* ausrollen.

Verbindungen mit Adverbien:

roll| down *v/t* **1.** *Ärmel* herunterkrempeln. **2.** *mot. Fenster* herunterkurbeln. **~ in** *v/i* hereinströmen (*Angebote etc*). **~ on** *v/i*: **~, Saturday!** *Br.* wenn es doch nur schon Samstag wäre! **~ out** *v/t* **1.** *Teig, Teppich* ausrollen. **~ up I** *v/t* **1.** auf-, zs.-rollen (*a. fig.*). **2.** *Ärmel* hoch-, aufkrempeln (*a. fig.*). **3.** *mot. Fenster* hochkurbeln. **II** *v/i* **4.** sich zs.-rollen (*into* zu) (*Tier*). **5.** F antanzen. **6.** **~!** (*Rummelplatz etc*) hereinspaziert!

roll| bar *s mot.* Überrollbügel *m*. **~ call** *s* Namensaufruf *m*: **have a ~** die Namen aufrufen.

roll·er ['rəʊlə] *s* **1.** ⚙ Rolle *f*; Walze *f*. **2.** Lockenwickler *m*. **~ blind** *s* Rolladen *m*, Rollo *n*. **~ coast·er** *s* Achterbahn *f*. **~ skate** *s* Rollschuh *m*. **'~·skate** *v/i* Rollschuh laufen. **~ skat·er** *s* Rollschuhläufer(in). **~ skat·ing** *s* Rollschuhlaufen *n*. **~ tow·el** *s* Rollhandtuch *n*.

roll·ing| mill ['rəʊlɪŋ] *s* ⚙ Walzwerk *n*. **~ pin** *s* Nudelholz *n*, -rolle *f*, Teigrolle *f*.

'roll-on *s* Deoroller *m*.

ro·ly-po·ly [ˌrəʊlɪ'pəʊlɪ] F **I** *s* Dickerchen *n*. **II** *adj* dick u. rund.

Ro·man ['rəʊmən] **I** *adj* römisch: **~ nu-** ***meral*** römische Ziffer. **II** *s* Römer(in). **~ Cath·o·lic I** *adj* (römisch-)katholisch. **II** *s* Katholik(in).

ro·mance¹ [rəʊˈmæns] *s* **1.** Liebes- *od.* Abenteuerroman *m*. **2.** Romanze *f*, Liebesverhältnis *n*. **3.** Romantik *f*.

Ro·mance² [~] *adj* romanisch (*Sprache*).

Ro·man·esque [ˌrəʊmə'nesk] *adj* romanisch (*Baustil*).

ro·man·tic [rəʊˈmæntɪk] **I** *adj* (**~ally**) (*Kunst etc oft* ♫) romantisch. **II** *s* (*Kunst etc oft* ♫) Romantiker(in). **ro'man·ti·cism** [~sɪzəm] *s* **1.** *oft* ♫ *Kunst etc*: Romantik *f*. **2.** romantische Vorstellungen *pl*. **ro'man·ti·cist** → **romantic** II. **ro'man·ti·cize** *v/t* romantisieren.

Ro·ma·ny ['rɒmənɪ] *s* **1.** Zigeuner(in). **2.** Romani *n*, Zigeunersprache *f*.

Rome [rəʊm] *npr Rom n*: **~ was not built in a day** Rom ist nicht an *od.* in 'einem Tag erbaut worden; **all roads lead to ~** alle Wege führen nach Rom.

romp [rɒmp] *v/i* **1.** *a.* **~ about** (*od. around*) herumtollen. **2.** **~ through** F *et.* spielend schaffen.

ron·do ['rɒndəʊ] *pl* **-dos** *s* ♪ Rondo *n*.

roof [ruːf] **I** *s* Dach *n*; *mot.* Verdeck *n*: **go through the ~** F an die Decke gehen (*Person*); ins Unermeßliche steigen (*Kosten etc*); **have no ~ over one's head** kein Dach über den Kopf haben; **live under the same ~** unter 'einem Dach leben *od.* wohnen (*as* mit). **II** *v/t* bedachen: **~ in** (*od. over*) überdachen. **~ gar·den** *s* Dachgarten *m*. **'~·rack** *s mot.* Dachgepäckträger *m*. **'~·top** *s*: **scream** (*od.* **shout**) **s.th. from the ~s** *fig.* et. ausposaunen *od.* an die große Glocke hängen.

rook¹ [rʊk] *v/t* F *j-n* betrügen (*of* um).

rook² [~] *s Schach*: Turm *m*.

room [ruːm] **I** *s* **1.** Raum *m*, Zimmer *n*. **2.** Raum *m*, Platz *m*: **make ~ for s.o.** j-m Platz machen. **3.** *fig.* Spielraum *m*: **there is ~ for improvement** es ließe sich noch manches besser machen; **leave little ~ for doubt as to** kaum e-n Zweifel übriglassen an (*dat*). **II** *v/i* **4.** *Am.* → **lodge** 3. **'room·er** *s Am.* → **lodger**. **'room·ing** *adj*: **~ house** *Am.* Fremdenheim *n*, Pension *f*.

'room·mate *s* Zimmergenosse *m*, -genossin *f*. **~ ser·vice** *s* Zimmerservice *m*:

ring for ~ nach dem Zimmerkellner klingeln.

room·y ['ruːmɪ] *adj* □ geräumig.

roost [ruːst] **I** *s* (Hühner)Stange *f*: *come home to* ~ *fig.* sich rächen (*Fehler etc*); → *rule* 5. **II** *v/i* auf der Stange sitzen *od.* schlafen. '**roost·er** *s bsd. Am.* Hahn *m.*

root¹ [ruːt] **I** *s anat.*, ⚓, ⚡ & Wurzel *f* (*a. fig.*): ~ *and branch fig.* mit Stumpf u. Stiel; *get to the* ~ *of fig.* e-r Sache auf den Grund gehen; *have its* ~*s in fig.* wurzeln in (*dat*), s-n Ursprung haben in (*dat*); *pull out by the* ~ mit der Wurzel ausreißen *od.* (*fig.*) ausrotten; *put down (new)* ~*s fig.* Fuß fassen; *take* ~ Wurzeln schlagen (*a. fig.*). **II** *v/i* Wurzeln schlagen (*a. fig.*). **III** *v/t:* ~ *up* mit der Wurzel ausreißen; ~ *out fig.* (mit der Wurzel) ausrotten.

root² [~] **I** *v/i a.* ~ *about* (*od. around*) herumwühlen (*among* in *dat*). **II** *v/t:* ~ *out* aufstöbern.

root³ [~] *v/i:* ~ *for bsd. Am.* F a) *Sport:* j-n anfeuern, b) *fig.* j-m den Daumen drücken *od.* halten; j-n (tatkräftig) unterstützen.

root beer *s Am. Limonade aus Wurzelextrakten.*

root·ed ['ruːtɪd] *adj*: *be* ~ *in fig.* wurzeln in (*dat*), s-n Ursprung haben in (*dat*); *stand* ~ *to the spot* wie angewurzelt dastehen.

rope [rəʊp] **I** *s* **1.** Seil *n*, ⚓ Tau *n*; Strick *m*: *give s.o. plenty of* ~ *fig.* j-m viel Freiheit *od.* Spielraum lassen; *know the* ~*s* F sich auskennen; *jump* ~ *Am.* seilhüpfen, -springen; *show s.o. the* ~*s* F j-n anlernen *od.* einarbeiten *od.* einweihen. **2.** (*Perlen- etc*)Schnur *f.* **II** *v/t* **3.** festbinden (*to an dat, a. acc*). **4.** ~ *off* (durch ein Seil) abgrenzen *od.* absperren. ~ **lad·der** *s* Strickleiter *f.*

rop·(e)y ['rəʊpɪ] *adj* □ F miserabel.

ro·sa·ry ['rəʊzərɪ] *s* (*Gebete oft* ♱) *eccl.* Rosenkranz *m.*

rose¹ [rəʊz] **I** *s* **1.** ⚡ Rose *f*: *life is not all* ~*s* das Leben hat nicht nur angenehme Seiten. **2.** Brause *f* (*e-r Gießkanne etc*). **II** *adj* **3.** rosa-, rosenrot.

rose² [~] *pret von* **rise.**

ro·sé ['rəʊzeɪ] *s* Rosé *m* (*Wein*).

'**rose·bush** *s* ⚡ Rosenstock *m*, -strauch *m.* '~**,col·o(u)red** *adj* rosa-, rosenrot: *see things through* ~ *glasses* (*od.*

spectacles) *fig.* die Dinge durch e-e rosa(rote) Brille sehen. '~**·hip** *s* ⚡ Hagebutte *f.*

rose·mar·y ['rəʊzmərɪ] *s* ⚡ Rosmarin *m.*

ro·sette [rəʊ'zet] *s* Rosette *f* (*a.* △).

ros·in ['rɒzɪn] **I** *s* Kolophonium *n*, Geigenharz *n.* **II** *v/t* mit Kolophonium einreiben.

ros·ter ['rɒstə] *s* Dienstplan *m.*

ros·trum ['rɒstrəm] *pl* **-tra** [ˈ~trə], **-trums** *s* Redner-, Dirigentenpult *m.*

ros·y ['rəʊzɪ] *adj* □ rosig (*a. fig.*).

rot [rɒt] **I** *v/i a.* ~ *away* (ver)faulen, (*bsd. Holz a.*) verrotten, morsch werden. **II** *v/t* (ver)faulen *od.* verrotten lassen, morsch machen. **III** *s* Fäulnis(prozeß *m*) *f.*

ro·ta ['rəʊtə] *s bsd. Br.* Dienstplan *m.*

ro·ta·ry ['rəʊtərɪ] **I** *adj* rotierend, Rotations..., Dreh... **II** *s Am.* Kreisverkehr *m.* **ro·tate** [~'teɪt] *v/i* **1.** rotieren, sich drehen. **2.** turnusmäßig wechseln. **II** *v/t* **3.** rotieren lassen, drehen. **4.** *Personal* turnusmäßig auswechseln. **ro·ta·tion** *s* **1.** Rotation *f*, Drehung *f.* **2.** *in* ~ der Reihe nach, nacheinander.

rote [rəʊt] *s*: *learn s.th. by* ~ et. (mechanisch) auswendig lernen.

ro·tor ['rəʊtə] *s* ⚙, ⚡ Rotor *m.*

rot·ten ['rɒtn] *adj* □ **1.** verfault, faul, (*bsd. Holz a.*) verrottet, morsch. **2.** F miserabel: *feel* ~ sich mies fühlen (*a. fig.*).

ro·tund [rəʊ'tʌnd] *adj* □ rund u. dick.

rouge [ruːʒ] *s* Rouge *n.*

rough [rʌf] **I** *adj* (□ → **roughly**) **1.** uneben (*Straße etc*), rauh (*Haut etc, a. Stimme*). **2.** stürmisch (*Meer, Überfahrt, Wetter*): *he had a* ~ *passage fig.* ihm ist es (e-e Zeitlang) nicht gutgegangen. **3.** a) grob (*Person, Behandlung etc*): *be* ~ *with* grob umgehen mit, b) *Sport:* hart (*Spielweise etc*). **4.** roh, Roh...: ~ *diamond* Rohdiamant *m*; *be a* ~ *diamond fig.* e-e rauhe Schale haben; ~ *draft* Rohfassung *f*; → *copy* 1. **5.** *fig.* grob, ungefähr: *at a* ~ *guess* grob geschätzt; *I have a* ~ *idea where it is* ich kann mir ungefähr vorstellen, wo es ist; → *estimate* 5. **6.** *feel* ~ *Br.* F sich mies fühlen. **II** *s* **7.** *Golf:* Rough *n.* **8.** Rowdy *m.* **9.** *take the* ~ *with the smooth* die Dinge nehmen, wie sie kommen. **III** *adv* **10.** *sleep* ~ im Freien übernachten. **11. play** (*it*) ~ (*Sport*) hart spielen. **IV** *v/t* **12.** ~ *it* F primitiv leben. **13.** ~ *out* entwerfen, skizzieren. **14.** ~ *up* F *j-n* zs.-schlagen. **'rough·age** *s biol.* Ballaststoffe *pl.*

‚rough|-and-'tum·ble *s* Balgerei *f:* **have a** ~ sich balgen. **'~cast** *s* △ Rauhputz *m.*

rough·en ['rʌfn] **I** *v/t* Haut etc rauh machen. **II** *v/i* rauh werden. **'rough·ly** *adv* **1.** grob (*a. fig.*). **2.** *fig.* ungefähr: ~ **speaking** grob geschätzt, über den Daumen gepeilt.

'rough·neck *s bsd. Am.* F Grobian *m;* Schläger *m.*

rough·ness ['rʌfnɪs] *s* **1.** Unebenheit *f,* Rauheit *f.* **2.** Grobheit *f.*

'rough·shod *adv:* ride ~ **over** sich rücksichtslos hinwegsetzen über (*acc*).

rou·lette [ru:'let] *s* Roulett(e) *n.*

round [raʊnd] **I** *adj* (□ → **roundly**) **1.** *allg.* rund. **2.** rund(lich), dick(lich) (*Körperteil*). **3.** rund: a) voll, ganz: **a ~ dozen** ein rundes Dutzend, b) ab- *od.* aufgerundet: **the house cost £100,000 in ~ figures** das Haus kostete rund(er) 100 000 Pfund. **II** *adv* (→ **Verben,** *z. B.* **turn round**) **4.** ~ *all* (**the**) **year** ~ das ganze Jahr lang *od.* hindurch *od.* über. **6.** ~ **about** F ungefähr. **7.** be three **yards** ~ e-n Umfang von drei Yards haben. **III** *prp* **3.** (rund) um, um (... herum): **trip ~ the world** Weltreise *f;* **do you live ~ here?** wohnen Sie hier in der Gegend?; → **bend** 1, **clock** 1, **look** 1. **9.** ungefähr. **IV** *s* **10.** Runde *f,* Rundgang *m:* **do** (*od.* **be out on**) **one's ~s** Se-Runde machen, (*Arzt*) Hausbesuche machen; **go the ~s** *fig.* umgehen (*Gerücht etc*), (*Krankheit a.*) grassieren (*of* in *dat*); **the daily ~** *fig.* der tägliche Trott. **11.** Lage *f,* Runde *f* (*Bier etc*): **it's my ~** die Runde geht auf mich. **12.** *Boxen, Turnier, Verhandlungen etc:* Runde *f.* **13.** ✕ *etc* Schuß *m.* **14.** ♪ Kanon *m.* **V** *v/t* **15.** rund machen, (ab)runden, *Lippen* spitzen. **16.** umfahren, fahren um, *Kurve* nehmen.

Verbindungen mit Adverbien:

round| down *v/t* Preis etc abrunden (**to** auf *acc*). ~ **off** *v/t* **1.** *Mahlzeit etc* abrunden, beschließen (**with** mit). **2.** Preis etc auf- *od.* abrunden (**to** auf *acc*). ~ **out I** *v/t* Ausbildung etc abrunden (**with** mit,

durch). **II** *v/i* rundlich werden (*Person*). ~ **up** *v/t* **1.** *Vieh* zs.-treiben. **2.** F *Verbrecher* hochnehmen; *Leute* zs.-trommeln, *a. et.* auftreiben. **3.** *Preis etc* aufrunden (**to** auf *acc*).

'round·a·bout I *s* **1.** *Br.* Kreisverkehr *m.* **2.** *Br.* Karussell *n:* **go on the ~** Karussell fahren. **II** *adj* **3.** ~ **route** e-n Umweg machen; **in a ~ way** *fig.* auf Umwegen.

round·ly ['raʊndlɪ] *adv* **1.** gründlich, gehörig. **2.** rundweg, -heraus.

round rob·in *s* **1.** Petition *f,* Denkschrift *f* (*bsd. e-e mit im Kreis herum geschriebenen Unterschriften*). **2.** *Sport: Am.* Turnier, *in dem jeder gegen jeden antritt.*

rounds·man ['raʊndzmən] *s* (*irr man*) *Br.* Ausfahrer *m,* Austräger *m.*

'round|-ta·ble *adj:* ~ **conference** Round-table-Konferenz *f,* Konferenz *f* am runden Tisch. **~-the-clock** *adj* 24stündig, rund um die Uhr. **~ trip** *s* Hin- u. Rückfahrt *f,* ✈ Hin- u. Rückflug *m.* **'~-trip** *adj:* **~ ticket** *Am.* Rückfahrkarte *f,* ✈ Rückflugticket *n.*

rouse [raʊz] *v/t* **1.** *j-n* wecken (**from, out of** aus). **2.** *fig. j-n* auf-, aufschütteln (**from, out of** aus); **~ s.o. to action** *j-n* so weit bringen, daß er (*endlich*) et. tut *od.* unternimmt. **3.** *a.* ~ **to anger** *j-n* erzürnen, reizen. **'rous·ing** *adj* □ mitreißend, zündend (*Rede etc*).

rout [raʊt] **I** *s:* **put to ~** → **II**. **II** *v/t* ✕ in die Flucht schlagen.

route [ru:t] *s* Route *f,* Strecke *f,* Weg *m,* (*Bus*)Linie *f.*

rou·tine [ru:'ti:n] **I** *s* Routine *f* (*a. Computer*). **II** *adj* Routine..., routinemäßig.

roux [ru:] *pl* **roux** [ru:z] *s gastr.* Mehlschwitze *f,* Einbrenne *f.*

row¹ [rəʊ] *s* Reihe *f:* **four times in a ~** viermal nach- *od.* hintereinander; ~ **house** *Am.* Reihenhaus *n.*

row² [~] **I** *v/i u. v/t* rudern. **II** *s* Kahnfahrt *f:* **go for a ~** rudern gehen.

row³ [raʊ] F **I** *s* Krach *m:* a) Krawall *m:* **kick up** (*od.* **make**) **a ~** Krach schlagen, b) Streit *m:* **have a ~ with** Krach haben mit. **II** *v/i* (sich) streiten (**with** mit; **about** über *acc*).

row·boat ['rəʊbəʊt] *s Am.* Ruderboot *n.*

row·dy ['raʊdɪ] *adj* □ **1.** rowdyhaft. **2.** ausgelassen, laut (*Party*).

row·er ['rəʊə] s Ruderer *m*, Ruderin *f*. **'row·ing** *adj* Ruder...: ~ **boat** bsd. Br. Ruderboot *n*.

roy·al ['rɔɪəl] **I** *adj* □ **1.** königlich, Königs...: *Her ♀ Highness* Ihre Königliche Hoheit; ~ **road** fig. bequemer od. leichter Weg (*to* zu). **2.** fig. großartig, prächtig. **II** s **3.** ♀ Mitglied *n* des Königshauses. **'roy·al·ist I** *adj* royalistisch. **II** s Royalist(in). **'roy·al·ty** s **1.** die königliche Familie. **2.** mst pl Tantieme *f* (*on* auf acc).

rub [rʌb] **I** s **1.** *give s.th. a* ~ et. abreiben od. polieren. **2.** *there's the* ~ F da liegt der Hase im Pfeffer. **II** v/t **3.** reiben: ~ *dry* trockenreiben; ~ *s.th. into* et. einreiben in (acc); ~ *one's hands* (*together*) sich die Hände reiben (*with* vor dat); ~ *s.o.'s nose in s.th.* F j-m et. unter die Nase reiben; ~ *salt into s.o.'s wound*(*s*) fig. j-m Salz auf od. in die Wunde streuen; ~ *shoulders with* F verkehren mit (*Prominenten* etc). **4.** abreiben; polieren. **III** v/i **5.** reiben, scheuern (*against, on* an dat): ~ *against s.th.* et. streifen.
Verbindungen mit Adverbien:
rub| a·long v/i Br. F **1.** sich durchschlagen. **2.** *a.* ~ *together* recht gut miteinander auskommen; ~ *with* recht gut auskommen mit. ~ **down** v/t **1.** ab-, trockenreiben. **2.** abschmirgeln, abschleifen. ~ **in** v/t abreiben: *rub* (*it*) *in that* F darauf herumreiten, daß. ~ **off I** v/t abreiben. **II** v/i abgehen (*Farbe, Schmutz* etc): ~ **on**(*to*) fig. abfärben auf (acc). ~ **out** v/t **1.** Br. ausradieren. **2.** Am. sl. umlegen (*töten*). ~ **up** v/t: *rub s.o. up the wrong way* F j-n verschnupfen.

rub·ber ['rʌbə] s **1.** Gummi *n*, *m*; Kautschuk *m*. **2.** Br. Radiergummi *m*. **3.** Wischtuch *n*. **4.** F Gummi *m* (*Kondom*). ~ **band** s Gummiband *n*, -ring *m*, (*Dichtungs*)Gummi *m*. ~ **din·ghy** s Schlauchboot *n*. '~**neck** bsd. Am. F **I** s Gaffer(in), Schaulustige *m*, *f*. **II** v/i neugierig gaffen, sich den Hals verrenken. ~ **plant** s ♀ Gummibaum *m*. ~ **stamp** s Stempel *m*. **1.** '~·'**stamp** v/t **1.** (ab)stempeln. **2.** F (automatisch) genehmigen.

rub·bing al·co·hol ['rʌbɪŋ] s Am. Wundbenzin *n*.

rub·bish ['rʌbɪʃ] s **1.** Abfall *m*, Abfälle pl, Müll *m*: ~ **bin** → **dustbin. 2.** fig. Blödsinn *m*, Quatsch *m*. **'rub·bish·y** *adj* F blödsinnig.

rub·ble ['rʌbl] s Schutt *m*; Trümmer pl.

ru·bel·la [rʊ'belə] s ♂ Röteln pl.

ru·by ['ruːbɪ] **I** s min. Rubin *m*. **II** *adj* rubinrot.

ruck[1] [rʌk] s: *get out of the* (*common*) ~ sich über den Durchschnitt erheben.

ruck[2] [~] v/i: ~ **up** Falten werfen.

ruck·sack ['rʌksæk] s Rucksack *m*.

ruc·tion ['rʌkʃn] s oft pl F Krach *m*, Stunk *m*.

rud·der ['rʌdə] s ✈, ⚓ Ruder *n*.

rud·dy ['rʌdɪ] **I** *adj* □ **1.** frisch, gesund (*Gesichtsfarbe*), rot (*Backen*). **2.** Br. sl. verdammt. **II** *adv* **3.** → **2.**

rude [ruːd] *adj* □ **1.** unhöflich; grob (*to* zu). **2.** unanständig (*Witz* etc). **3.** bös (*Schock* etc): → **awakening. 4.** *be in* ~ *health* vor Gesundheit strotzen.

ru·di·men·ta·ry [ˌruːdɪ'mentərɪ] *adj* □ **1.** elementar, Anfangs... **2.** primitiv. **3.** rudimentär (*a. biol.*). **ru·di·ments** ['ruːmənts] s pl Anfangsgründe pl, Grundlagen pl: *learn the* ~ *of* sich Grundkenntnisse aneignen in (dat).

rue [ruː] v/t: ~ **the day** ... den Tag verwünschen, an dem ... **rue·ful** ['ruːful] *adj* □ reuevoll, reumütig.

ruff [rʌf] s Halskrause *f* (*a. orn.*).

ruf·fle ['rʌfl] **I** s **1.** Rüsche *f*. **II** v/t **2.** Wasser kräuseln; *Haar* zerzausen: ~ (*up*) *its feathers* orn. sich aufplustern. **3.** *Seiten* (rasch) durchblättern. **4.** *j-n* verärgern: ~ *s.o.'s composure* j-n aus der Fassung bringen.

rug [rʌg] s **1.** Brücke *f*, (*Bett*)Vorleger *m*: *pull the* ~ (*out*) *from under s.o.* fig. j-m den Boden unter den Füßen wegziehen; *sweep under the* ~ Am. fig. et. unter den Teppich kehren. **2.** bsd. Br. dicke Wolldecke.

rug·by ['rʌgbɪ] s *a.* ~ **football** (*Sport*) Rugby *n*.

rug·ged ['rʌgɪd] *adj* □ **1.** zerklüftet (*Felsen*), felsig (*Landschaft*). **2.** zerfurcht (*Gesicht*). **3.** robust, stabil (*Gerät* etc). **4.** fig. rauh (*Sitten* etc).

ru·in ['ruːɪn] **I** s **1.** Ruine *f*: ~**s** pl Ruinen pl, Trümmer pl; *a castle in* ~**s** eine Burgruine; *be* (*od. lie*) *in* ~**s** in Trümmern liegen; fig. zerstört sein. **2.**

Verfall *m*: **fall into ~** verfallen. **3.** Ruin *m*; Ende *n* (*von Hoffnungen etc*). **II** *v/t* **4.** *Gebäude, Gesundheit, Hoffnungen, Leben etc* zerstören, *j-n, Kleidung, Gesundheit, Ruf etc* ruinieren: **~ one's eyes** sich die Augen verderben. **ru·in·'a·tion** *s*: **be the ~ of s.o.** j-s Ruin sein. **'ru·in·ous** *adj* ruinös. **'ru·in·ous·ly** *adv*: **~ expensive** extrem od. sündhaft teuer.

rule [ru:l] **I** *s* **1.** Regel *f*, Normalfall *m*: **as a ~** in der Regel; **make it a ~** es sich zur Regel machen *od*. gemacht haben (**to do** zu tun); **~ exception 1.** **2.** Regel *f*; Bestimmung *f*, Vorschrift *f*: **against the ~s** regelwidrig; verboten; **as a ~ of thumb** aus Faustregel; **do s.th. by ~ of thumb** et. nach Gefühl tun; **bend** (*od*. **stretch**) **the ~s** es (mit den Vorschriften) nicht so genau nehmen; **work to ~** Dienst nach Vorschrift tun. **3.** Herrschaft *f*. **4.** → **ruler 2. II** *v/t* **5.** herrschen über (*acc*): **~ the roost** *fig*. das Regiment führen; **be ~d by** *fig*. sich leiten lassen von; beherrscht werden von. **6.** *bsd*. ⚖ entscheiden (**that** daß). **7.** ~ *out* et. ausschließen; *et*. unmöglich machen. **8.** *Papier* lin(i)ieren; *Linie* ziehen. **III** *v/i* **9.** herrschen (**over** über *acc*). **10.** *bsd*. ⚖ entscheiden (**against** gegen; **in favo[u]r of** für; **on** in *dat*). **'rul·er** *s* **1.** Herrscher(in). **2.** Lineal *n*; Maßstab *m*. **'rul·ing I** *s bsd*. ⚖ Entscheidung *f*; Verfügung *f*: **give a ~ that** entscheiden, daß.

rum [rʌm] *s* Rum *m*.

Ru·ma·nian [ru:'meɪnjən] **I** *adj* **1.** rumänisch. **II** *s* **2.** Rumäne *m*, Rumänin *f*. **3.** *ling*. Rumänisch *n*.

rum·ble ['rʌmbl] **I** *v/i* **1.** (g)rollen (*Donner*); rumpeln (*Fahrzeug*); knurren (*Magen*). **II** *v/t* **2.** F *j-n, et*. durchschauen. **III** *s* **3.** (G)Rollen *n*; Rumpeln *n*; Knurren *n*. **4.** *Am. sl.* Straßenschlacht *f*.

rum·bus·tious [rʌm'bʌstɪəs] *adj* □ F wild, ausgelassen.

ru·mi·nant ['ru:mɪnənt] *s zo*. Wiederkäuer *m*. **ru·mi·nate** ['~neɪt] *v/i* **1.** *zo*. wiederkäuen. **2.** *fig*. grübeln (**on, over** über *acc, dat*). **ru·mi·na·tive** ['~nətɪv] *adj* □ grüblerisch.

rum·mage ['rʌmɪdʒ] **I** *v/i a*. **~ about**

(*od*. **around**) herumstöbern, -wühlen (**among, in, through** in *dat*). **II** *s* Ramsch *m*. **~ sale** *s Am*. Wohltätigkeitsbasar *m*.

rum·my ['rʌmɪ] *s* Rommé *n* (*Kartenspiel*).

ru·mo(u)r ['ru:mə] **I** *s* Gerücht(e *pl*) *n*: **~ has it that** es geht das Gerücht, daß. **II** *v/t*: **it is ~ed that** es geht das Gerücht, daß; **he is ~ed to be** man munkelt, er sei. '~**mon·ger** *s* Gerüchtemacher(in).

rump [rʌmp] *s* **1.** *zo*. Hinterbacken *pl*; *orn*. Bürzel *m*. **2.** *humor*. Hinterteil *n*. **3.** *fig*. (kümmerlicher) Rest.

rum·ple ['rʌmpl] *v/t* zerknittern, -knüllen; *Haar* zerzausen.

rump steak *s gastr*. Rumpsteak *n*.

rum·pus ['rʌmpəs] → **row³ I. ~ room** *s Am*. F Hobby- *od*. Partyraum *m*.

run [rʌn] **I** *s* **1.** Lauf *m* (*a. Sport*): **at a ~** im Laufschritt; **in the long ~** *fig*. auf (die) Dauer; auf lange *od*. weite Sicht, langfristig; **in the short ~** *fig*. zunächst; auf kurze Sicht, kurzfristig; **on the ~** auf der Flucht (**from the police** vor der Polizei); **~ of good** (**bad**) **luck** Glückssträhne *f* (Pechsträhne *f*). **2.** Fahrt *f*: **go for a ~ in the car** e-e Spazierfahrt machen. **3.** *thea. etc* Laufzeit *f*: **the play had a ~ of six months** das Stück lief ein halbes Jahr lang. **4.** Ansturm *m*, † *a*. Run *m* (**on** auf *acc*). **5.** **have the ~ of** et. benutzen dürfen. **6.** *Am*. Laufmasche *f*. **7.** Auflage *f* (*e-r Zeitung etc*). **8.** **have the ~s** *bsd. Br*. F den flotten Otto haben. **II** *v/i* (*irr*) **9.** laufen (*a. Sport*), rennen. **10.** fahren (*Fahrzeug*); fahren, verkehren (*Bus etc*). **11.** laufen, fließen: **tears were ~ning down her face** Tränen liefen ihr übers Gesicht; **his nose was ~ning** ihm lief die Nase; **it ~s in the family** *fig*. das liegt bei ihm *etc* in der Familie; **~ cold 1. 12.** zerfließen, -laufen (*Butter, Farbe etc*). **13.** ☼ laufen (*a. fig*.): **with the engine ~ning** mit laufendem Motor. **14.** (ver)laufen (*Straße etc*). **15.** *bsd*. ⚖ gelten, laufen (**for two years** zwei Jahre). **16.** *thea. etc* laufen (**for six months** ein halbes Jahr). **17.** *mit Adjektiven:* → **low³ 4. 18.** *pol. bsd. Am*. kandidieren. **19.** gehen, lauten (*Vers etc*). **III** *v/t* (*irr*) **20.** *Strecke, Rennen* laufen: → **course 3, errand, temperature. 21.** *j-n, et*. fahren, bringen. **22.** *Wasser etc* laufen lassen: ~ *s.o.* **a bath** j-m ein Bad einlaufen lassen. **23.** *Geschäft* führen, *Hotel etc a.* leiten. **24.** ⊚ *Maschine etc* laufen lassen. **25.** abdrucken, bringen (*Zeitung etc*). **26.** schmuggeln.

Verbindungen mit Präpositionen:

run| a·cross *v/i* **1.** *j-n* zufällig treffen. **2.** stoßen auf (*acc*). ~ **af·ter** *v/i* nachlaufen (*dat*) (*a. fig.*). ~ **a·gainst** *v/i pol. bsd. Am.* kandidieren gegen. ~ **for** *v/i* **1.** ~ **it!** lauf, was du kannst!; ~ **one's life** um sein Leben laufen. **2.** *pol. bsd. Am.* kandidieren für. ~ **in·to** I *v/i* **1.** laufen *od.* fahren gegen. **2.** *j-n* zufällig treffen. **3.** *fig.* geraten in (*acc*). **4.** *fig.* sich belaufen auf (*acc*), gehen in (*acc*). II *v/t* **5.** *run a knife into s.o.'s back* j-m ein Messer in den Rücken stoßen *od.* rennen. ~ **off** *v/i:* ~ **the road** von der Straße abkommen (*Wagen etc*). ~ **on** *v/i* ⊚ fahren mit: ~ **electricity** elektrisch betrieben werden. ~ **o·ver** → **run through** 1. ~ **through** *v/i* **1.** *Szene etc* durchspielen. **2.** *Notizen etc* durchgehen. **3.** *Vermögen etc* durchbringen. **4.** *j-n* durchlaufen (*Schauder etc*); ~ **s.o.'s mind** j-m durch den Kopf gehen. ~ **to** *v/i bsd. Br.* (aus)reichen für.

Verbindungen mit Adverbien:

run| a·bout → **run around.** ~ **a·long** *v/i:* ~*!* ab mit dir! ~ **a·round** *v/i* sich herumtreiben (**with** mit). ~ **a·way** *v/i* davonlaufen (**from** vor *dat*) (*a. fig.*): ~ **from home** von zu Hause ausreißen; ~ **with** durchbrennen mit; *fig.* durchgehen mit (*Phantasie etc*); **don't** ~ **with the idea that** glaube bloß nicht, daß. ~ **back** *v/t* Band, Film zurückspulen. ~ **down** I *v/t* **1.** *mot.* an-, umfahren. **2.** schlechtmachen. **3.** ausfindig machen. II *v/i* **4.** ablaufen (*Uhr*), leer werden (*Batterie*). ~ **in** *v/t* **1.** *Wagen etc* einfahren. **2.** F *Verbrecher etc* schnappen. ~ **on** *v/i* **1.** weitergehen, sich hinziehen (*until* bis). **2.** unaufhörlich reden (*a·bout* über *acc*, von). ~ **out** *v/i* ablaufen (*Vertrag, Zeit etc*), ausgehen, zu Ende gehen (*Vorräte etc*): **I've** ~ **of money** mir ist das Geld ausgegangen. ~ **steam** 1. ~ **o·ver** I *v/t mot.* überfahren. II *v/i* überlaufen. ~ **up** I *v/t* **1.** *Flagge etc* aufziehen, hissen. **2.** hohe Rechnung, Schulden machen. II *v/i* **3.** ~

against stoßen auf (*starken Widerstand etc*).

'run|·a·bout *s mot.* Stadtwagen *m.* **'~·a·round** *s: give s.o. the* ~ F j-n hinhalten; j-n an der Nase herumführen. **'~·a·way** I *s* **1.** Ausreißer(in). II *adj* **2.** ausgerissen: ~ **child** (kleiner) Ausreißer. **3.** außer Kontrolle geraten: ~ **inflation** ✝ galoppierende Inflation. **'~ down** I *adj* **1.** abgespannt. **2.** baufällig; heruntergekommen. **3.** abgelaufen (*Uhr*), leer (*Batterie*). II *s* **4.** F (genauer) Bericht (**on** über *acc*).

rung[1] [rʌŋ] *pp von* **ring**[2].

rung[2] *s* Sprosse *f* (*e-r Leiter*): **start on the bottom** (*od.* **first**) ~ **of the ladder** *fig.* ganz unten *od.* klein anfangen.

'run-in *s: have a* ~ **with** F in Konflikt kommen mit (**dem** *Gesetz etc*).

run·ner ['rʌnə] *s* **1.** *Sport:* Läufer(in); Rennpferd *n.* **2.** *mst in Zssgn* Schmuggler(in). **3.** (*Schlitten- etc*)Kufe *f.* ~ **bean** ⚹ *Br.* grüne Bohne. **~·'up** *pl* **~s-'up** *s* Zweite *m, f,* (*Sport a.*) Vizemeister(in) (**to** hinter *dat*).

run·ning ['rʌnɪŋ] I *s* **1.** Laufen *n,* Rennen *n:* **be still in the** ~ *fig.* noch gut im Rennen liegen (**for** um); **be out of the** ~ *fig.* aus dem Rennen sein (**for** um); **make the** ~ (*Sport*) das Rennen machen (*a. fig.*). **2.** Führung *f,* Leitung *f.* II *adj* **3.** *Sport:* Lauf...; ~ **shoes**; ~ **track** Laufbahn *f.* **4.** fließend (*Wasser*); ⚹ eiternd (*Wunde*). **5.** **four times** (**for three days**) ~ viermal (drei Tage) hinter- *od.* nacheinander. **6.** ~ **costs** *pl* Betriebskosten *pl,* laufende Kosten *pl.* **7.** ~ **mate** *pol. Am.* Kandidat(in) für die Vizepräsidentschaft.

run·ny ['rʌnɪ] *adj* **1.** flüssig. **2.** laufend (*Nase*), tränend (*Augen*).

,run|-of-the-'mill *adj mst contp.* durchschnittlich, mittelmäßig. **'~-up** *s* **1.** *Sport:* Anlauf *m.* **2. in the** ~ **to** *fig.* im Vorfeld (*gen*). **'~·way** *s* ✈ Start- und Landebahn *f,* Rollbahn *f,* Piste *f.*

rup·ture ['rʌptʃə] I *s* Bruch *m* (*a.* ⚹ *u. fig.*), Riß *m.* II *v/t* zerspringen, (-)reißen, platzen. III *v/t* zersprengen, -reißen: ~ **o.s.** ⚹ sich e-n Bruch heben *od.* zuziehen.

ru·ral ['rʊərəl] *adj* □ ländlich: ~ **population** Landbevölkerung *f;* → **exodus.**

ruse [ruːz] *s* List *f.*

rush¹ [rʌʃ] s ♣ Binse f: **~ mat** Binsenmatte f.

rush² [~] **I** v/i **1.** hasten, hetzen, stürmen, (a. Fahrzeug) rasen: **~ at** losstürzen od. sich stürzen auf (acc); **~ into** fig. sich stürzen in (acc); et. überstürzen; **the blood ~ed to his face** das Blut schoß ihm ins Gesicht; → **conclusion 3. II** v/t **2.** antreiben, drängen, hetzen: **be ~ed (off one's feet)** auf Trab sein. **3.** auf dem schnellsten Weg wohin bringen od. schaffen. **4.** schnell erledigen; Essen hinunterschlingen: **don't ~ it** laß dir Zeit dabei; **~ a bill (through)** e-e Gesetzesvorlage durchpeitschen. **5.** losstürmen auf (acc). **III** s **6.** Ansturm m (for auf acc, nach): **there was a ~ for the door** alles drängte zur Tür. **7.** Hast f, Hetze f: **what's all the ~?** wozu diese Hast? **~ hour** s Rush-hour f, Hauptverkehrs-, Stoßzeit f. **'~-hour** adj: **~ traffic** Stoßverkehr m.

rusk [rʌsk] s Zwieback m.

Rus·sian ['rʌʃn] **I** s **1.** Russe m, Russin f. **2.** ling. Russisch n. **II** adj **3.** russisch:

~ roulette russisches Roulett(e).

rust [rʌst] **I** s Rost m. **II** v/i (ein-, ver)rosten.

rus·tic ['rʌstɪk] adj (**~ally**) **1.** ländlich, bäuerlich. **2.** rustikal (Möbel): **~ furniture** a. Bauernmöbel pl.

rus·tle ['rʌsl] **I** v/i **1.** rascheln (Papier etc), (a. Seide) knistern. **II** v/t **2.** rascheln mit. **3.** **~ up** F Geld, Hilfe etc organisieren, auftreiben; Essen zaubern.

'rust·proof adj rostfrei, nichtrostend.

rust·y ['rʌstɪ] adj □ **1.** rostig. **2.** fig. eingerostet (Kenntnisse): **I'm very ~** ich bin ganz aus der Übung.

rut¹ [rʌt] zo. **I** s Brunft f. **II** v/i brunften.

rut² [~] **I** s **1.** (Rad)Spur f, Furche f. **2.** fig. (alter) Trott: **get into a ~** in e-n Trott verfallen. **II** v/t **3.** furchen: **~ted** ausgefahren.

ruth·less ['ru:θlɪs] adj □ unbarmherzig; rücksichtslos; hart.

rye [raɪ] s ♣ Roggen m. **~ bread** s Roggenbrot n. **~ whis·ky** s Roggenwhisky m.

S

Sab·bath ['sæbəθ] s eccl. Sabbat m.

sa·ber Am. → **sabre.**

sa·ble ['seɪbl] s **1.** zo. Zobel m. **2.** Zobelpelz m.

sab·o·tage ['sæbətɑ:ʒ] **I** s Sabotage f: **act of ~** Sabotageakt m. **II** v/t e-n Sabotageakt verüben gegen; sabotieren. **sab·o·teur** [~'tɜ:] s Saboteur(in).

sa·bre ['seɪbə] s bsd. Br. Säbel m (a. fenc.). **~ rat·tling** s fig. Säbelrasseln n.

sac·cha·rin ['sækərɪn] s ♠ Saccharin n. **sac·cha·rine** ['~raɪn] adj **1.** unangenehm süß. **2.** fig. honig-, zuckersüß.

sack¹ [sæk] **I** s **1.** Sack m. **2.** F **get the ~** rausgeschmissen (entlassen) werden; **give s.o. the ~** → 5. **3. hit the ~** F sich in die Falle od. Klappe hauen. **II** v/t **4.** einsacken, in Säcke abfüllen. **5.** F j-n rausschmeißen (entlassen).

sack² [~] **I** v/t plündern. **II** s Plünderung f.

'sack·cloth s Sackleinen n: **in (od. wearing) ~ and ashes** fig. in Sack u. Asche.

sack·ing ['sækɪŋ] s Sackleinen n.

sack rac·ing s Sackhüpfen n.

sac·ra·ment ['sækrəmənt] s eccl. Sakrament n.

sa·cred ['seɪkrɪd] adj □ **1.** geistlich (Musik etc). **2.** heilig (to dat) (a. fig.): **~ cow** heilige Kuh (a. fig.).

sac·ri·fice ['sækrɪfaɪs] **I** s Opfer n (a. fig.): **make a ~ of** j-n, et. opfern; **make great ~s** große Opfer bringen. **II** v/t opfern (to dat) (a. fig.). **sac·ri·fi·cial** [~'fɪʃl] adj Opfer...

sac·ri·lege ['sækrɪlɪdʒ] s Sakrileg n; allg. Frevel m. **sac·ri·le·gious** [~'lɪdʒəs] adj □ sakrilegisch; allg. frevlerisch.

sac·ris·ty ['sækrɪstɪ] s eccl. Sakristei f.

sac·ro·sanct ['sækrəʊsæŋkt] *adj* sakrosankt.

sad [sæd] *adj* (□ → *sadly*) *allg.* traurig; schmerzlich (*Verlust*); bedauerlich (*Irrtum etc*): ~ *to say* bedauerlicherweise, leider; *be* ~*der but wiser* um e-e schmerzliche Erfahrung reicher sein.

sad·den ['~dn] *v/t* traurig machen *od.* stimmen, betrüben.

sad·dle ['sædl] **I** *s* (*Reit-, Fahrrad- etc*)Sattel *m*: *be in the* ~ im Sattel sitzen; *fig.* im Amt *od.* an der Macht sein. **II** *v/t* satteln: ~ *up* aufsatteln; ~ *s.o. with s.th. fig.* j-m et. aufhalsen *od.* -bürden; *be* ~*d with s.th. fig.* et. am Hals haben. **III** *v/i:* ~ *up* aufsatteln. '~·bag *s* Satteltasche *f*.

sad·ism ['seɪdɪzəm] *s* Sadismus *m*. '**sad·ist** *s* Sadist(in). **sa·dis·tic** [sə'dɪs-tɪk] *adj* (~*ally*) sadistisch.

sad·ly ['sædlɪ] *adv* **1.** traurig; schmerzlich: *be* ~ *mistaken* e-m bedauerlichen Irrtum unterliegen. **2.** bedauerlicherweise, leider. '**sad·ness** *s* Traurigkeit *f*.

sa·fa·ri [sə'fɑːrɪ] *s* Safari *f*. ~ *park s* Safaripark *m*.

safe [seɪf] **I** *adj* □ *allg.* sicher (*from* vor *dat*): *be* ~ in Sicherheit sein (*with s.o.* sicher bei j-m aufgehoben sein; *be in* ~ *hands* in sicheren Händen sein; *to be on the* ~ *side*, *just to be on the* ~ *side* um ganz sicher zu gehen; *it is* ~ *to say* man kann mit Sicherheit sagen; *keep s.th. in a* ~ *place* et. an e-m sicheren Ort aufbewahren; *he has* ~*ly arrived* er ist gut angekommen; → *play* 7, 8. **II** *s* Safe *m*, Tresor *m*, Geld-, Panzerschrank *m*. '~·**blow·er**, '~·**break·er**, '~·**crack·er** *s* Geldschrankknacker *m*. ,~·**de'pos·it box** *s* Bankschließfach *n*, (*a. in Hotel etc*) Tresorfach *n*. '~·**guard** *s* Schutz *m* (*against* gegen, vor *dat*). **II** *v/t* schützen (*against, from* gegen, vor *dat*); *Interessen* wahren. ,~·'**keep·ing** *s* sichere Verwahrung: *give s.o. s.th. for* ~ j-m et. zur Verwahrung geben.

safe·ty ['seɪftɪ] *s allg.* Sicherheit *f*: *jump* (*swim*) *to* ~ sich durch e-n Sprung (schwimmend) in Sicherheit bringen. ~ **belt** → *seat belt*. ~ **cur·tain** *s thea.* eiserner Vorhang. ~ **glass** *s* Sicherheitsglas *n*. ~ **is·land** *s Am.* Verkehrsinsel *f*. ~ **lock** *s* Sicherheitsschloß *n*. ~ **meas·ure** *s* Sicherheitsmaßnahme *f*. ~

net *s* Zirkus *etc:* Fangnetz *n*. ~ **pin** *s* Sicherheitsnadel *f*. ~ **pre·cau·tion** *s* Sicherheitsvorkehrung *f*. ~ **ra·zor** *s* Rasierapparat *m*. ~ **valve** *s* **1.** ⚙ Sicherheitsventil *n*. **2.** *fig.* Ventil *n* (für).

saf·fron ['sæfrən] **I** *s* Safran *m*. **II** *adj* safrangelb.

sag [sæg] **I** *v/i* **1.** sich senken, absacken; durchhängen (*Leitung etc*). **2.** (herab)hängen. **3.** *fig.* sinken, nachlassen (*Interesse etc*); abfallen (*Roman etc*); ↓ nachgeben (*Preise etc*). **II** *s* **4.** Durchhängen *n: there is a* ~ *in the ceiling* die Decke hängt durch. **5.** ↓ Nachgeben *n* (*in gen*).

sa·ga ['sɑːgə] *s* **1.** Saga *f*. **2.** *a. family* ~ Familienroman *m*. **3.** *contp.* Geschichte *f*.

sa·ga·cious [sə'geɪʃəs] *adj* □ scharfsinnig, klug. **sa·gac·i·ty** [sə'gæsətɪ] *s* Scharfsinn *m*, Klugheit *f*.

sage [seɪdʒ] *s* ♣ Salbei *m*.

Sa·git·tar·i·us [,sædʒɪ'teərɪəs] *s ast.* Schütze *m*: *be* (*a*) ~ Schütze sein.

said [sed] *pret u. pp von* **say**.

sail [seɪl] **I** *s* **1.** Segel *n*: *set* ~ auslaufen (*for* nach). **2.** Segelfahrt *f*, -partie *f*: *go for a* ~ segeln gehen. **II** *v/i* **3.** ↓ fahren; segeln (*a. fig.*): *go* ~*ing* segeln gehen. **4.** ↓ auslaufen (*for* nach). **5.** gleiten: *she* ~*ed into the room* sie schwebte ins Zimmer; ~ *through an examination* e-e Prüfung spielend schaffen. **6.** ~ *into s.o.* F über j-n herfallen (*a. mit Worten*). **III** *v/t* **7.** *Boot* segeln, *Schiff* steuern. **8.** durchsegeln; befahren. '~·**boat** *s Am.* Segelboot *n*.

sail·ing ['seɪlɪŋ] *s* **1.** Segeln *n*; Segelsport *m*: *everything was plain* ~ *fig.* es ging alles glatt. **2.** *when is the next* ~ *to ...?* wann fährt das nächste Schiff nach ...? ~ **boat** *s bsd. Br.* Segelboot *n*. ~ **ship** *s* Segelschiff *n*.

sail·or ['seɪlə] *s* **1.** Seemann *m*; Matrose *m*. **2.** Segler(in). **3.** *be a good* (*bad*) ~ seefest sein (leicht seekrank werden). ~ **suit** *s* Matrosenanzug *m*.

'**sail·plane** *s* Segelflugzeug *n*.

saint [seɪnt] *s* **1.** Heilige *m*, *f*: *you need the patience of a* ~ man braucht e-e Engelsgeduld. **2.** *vor Eigennamen* ♀, *abbr.* **St** [snt]: *St Andrew* der heilige Andreas. '**saint·ly** *adj* heiligmäßig.

sake [seɪk] *s: for the* ~ *of* um ... willen,

j-m, e-r Sache zuliebe; **for your ~** dir zuliebe, deinetwegen; **for God's (goodness, heaven's) ~** F um Gottes willen; Herrgott noch mal; **for the ~ of peace** um des lieben Friedens willen; **for the ~ of simplicity** der Einfachheit halber.

sal·a·ble *adj. Am.* → **saleable**.

sa·la·cious [səˈleɪʃəs] *adj* □ schlüpfrig, anstößig.

sal·ad [ˈsæləd] *s* Salat *m.* ~ **dress·ing** *s* Dressing *n*, Salatsoße *f*.

sal·a·man·der [ˈsæləˌmændə] *s zo.* Salamander *m*.

sa·la·mi [səˈlɑːmɪ] *s* Salami *f*.

sal·a·ried [ˈsælərɪd] *adj:* ~ **employee** Gehaltsempfänger(in), Angestellte *m*, *f*. **'sal·a·ry** *s* Gehalt *n*.

sale [seɪl] *s* **1.** Verkauf *m:* **for ~** zu verkaufen; **not for ~** unverkäuflich; be on ~ verkauft werden, erhältlich sein; *bsd. Am.* im Angebot sein; **be up for ~** zum Verkauf stehen. **2.** *a. pl* ✝ Umsatz *m:* **large ~** großer Umsatz. **3.** ✝ Schlußverkauf *m*. **4.** Auktion *f*, Versteigerung *f*. **'sale·a·ble** *adj bsd. Br.* **1.** verkäuflich. **2.** ✝ absatzfähig.

'sales|·clerk *s Am.* (Laden)Verkäufer (-in). **'~·girl** *s* (Laden)Verkäuferin *f*. **~·man** [ˈ~mən] *s (irr man)* **1.** Verkäufer *m*. **2.** (Handels)Vertreter *m*. **'~·man·ship** *s* ✝ **1.** Verkaufstechnik *f*; Verkaufsgeschick *n*. **2.** *fig.* Überzeugungskunst *f*. **~ pitch** *s* ✝ F Verkaufsmasche *f*. **~ pro·mot·er** *s* ✝ Sales-promoter *m*, Verkaufsförderer *m*. **~ pro·mo·tion** *s* ✝ Sales-promotion *f*, Verkaufsförderung *f*. **~ slip** *s Am.* Kassenbeleg *m*, -zettel *m*. **~ talk** *s* ✝ Verkaufsgespräch *n*. **'~·wom·an** *s (irr woman)* **1.** Verkäuferin *f*. **2.** (Handels)Vertreterin *f*.

sa·li·ent [ˈseɪljənt] *adj* □ *fig.* hervorstechend, wichtigst.

sa·line [ˈseɪlaɪn] *adj* salzig, Salz...: **~ so·lution** Salzlösung *f*.

sa·li·va [səˈlaɪvə] *s physiol.* Speichel *m*. **sal·i·var·y** [ˈsælɪvərɪ] *adj* Speichel...: **~ gland** Speicheldrüse *f*.

sal·low [ˈsæləʊ] *adj* □ (ungesund) gelblich (Gesichtsfarbe etc).

salm·on [ˈsæmən] **I** *pl* **-ons**, *bsd. coll.* **-on** *s ichth.* Lachs *m*. **II** *adj* lachsfarben.

sal·on [ˈsælɔːŋ] *s* (Friseur-, Schönheits-etc)Salon *m*.

sa·loon [səˈluːn] *s* **1.** *mot. Br.* Limousine

f. **2.** → **saloon bar. 3.** *hist. Am.* Saloon *m.* **4.** ♣ Salon *m.* ~ **bar** *s Br. vornehmerer u. teurerer Teil e-s Pubs.* ~ **car** → **saloon** 1.

salt [sɔːlt] **I** *s* **1.** Salz *n:* **take s.th. with a grain (od. pinch) of ~** *fig.* et. nicht ganz für bare Münze nehmen; **no composer worth his ~** kein Komponist, der et. taugt *od.* der diesen Namen verdient; → **rub 3. II** *v/t* **2.** salzen. **3.** *a.* ~ **down** (ein)pökeln, einsalzen. **4.** Straße *etc* (mit Salz) streuen. **5.** ~ **away** F Geld auf die hohe Kante legen, *b.s.* auf die Seite schaffen. **III** *adj* **6.** gepökelt, Salz... **'~·cel·lar** *s Br.* Salzstreuer *m*. **'~-free** *adj* salzlos. ~ **lake** *s* Salzsee *m*. **~·pe·ter** *s Am.*, **~·pe·tre** *s bsd. Br.* [ˌ~ˈpiːtə] *s* 🜍 Salpeter *m*. **~ shak·er** *s Am.* → **saltcellar.** ~ **wa·ter** *s* Salzwasser *n.* **'~·wa·ter** *adj* Salzwasser..., Meeres...

salt·y [ˈsɔːltɪ] *adj* salzig.

sa·lu·bri·ous [səˈluːbrɪəs] *adj* □ **1.** gesund (*Klima etc*). **2.** vornehm (*Wohngegend etc*).

sal·u·tar·y [ˈsæljʊtərɪ] *adj* gesund; *fig.* heilsam, lehrreich.

sal·u·ta·tion [ˌsæljuːˈteɪʃn] *s* **1.** Begrüßung *f*, Gruß *m:* **in ~** zum Gruß. **2.** Anrede *f* (*im Brief*).

sa·lute [səˈluːt] **I** *v/t* **1.** ✕ salutieren vor (*dat.*). **2.** (be)grüßen. **II** *v/i* **3.** ✕ salutieren. **III** *s* **4.** ✕ a) Ehrenbezeigung *f:* **give a smart ~** zackig salutieren; **take the ~** die Parade abnehmen, b) Salut *m:* **a 21-gun ~** 21 Salutschüsse.

sal·vage [ˈsælvɪdʒ] **I** *v/t* **1.** bergen (**from** aus). **II** *s* **2.** Bergung *f*. **3.** Bergungsgut *n*.

sal·va·tion [sælˈveɪʃn] *s* **1.** Rettung *f*. **2.** *eccl.* (Seelen)Heil *n;* Erlösung *f:* ☿ **Army** Heilsarmee *f*. **Sal'va·tion·ist** *s* Mitglied *n* der Heilsarmee.

salve [sælv] **I** *s* (Heil)Salbe *f*. **II** *v/t fig.* Gewissen beruhigen.

sal·ver [ˈsælvə] *s* Tablett *n*, Präsentierteller *m*.

sal·vo [ˈsælvəʊ] *pl* **-vo(e)s** *s* ✕ Salve *f* (*a. fig.*): ~ **of applause** Beifallssturm *m*.

Sa·mar·i·tan [səˈmærɪtən] *s* Samariter (-in): **good ~** *Bibl.* barmherziger Samariter (*a. fig.*).

same [seɪm] **I** *adj:* **the ~** der-, die-, dasselbe, der *od.* die *od.* das gleiche: **the film with the ~ name** der gleichnamige

Film; **amount** (*od.* **come**) **to the ~ thing** auf dasselbe hinauslaufen; → **story** 1, **time** 1. **II** *pron:* **the ~** der-, die-, dasselbe, der *od.* die *od.* das gleiche: **it is all the ~ to me** es ist mir ganz egal; **(the) ~ again** noch mal das gleiche; **~ to you** (danke) gleichfalls!; **all** (*od.* **just**) **the ~** dennoch, trotzdem. **III** *adv:* **the ~** gleich; **~ as** F genauso wie. **'same·y** *adj* Br. F eintönig.

sam·ple ['sɑːmpl] **I** *s* **1.** ✝ Muster *n*, (*a.* *Blut- etc*)Probe *f*: **~ bottle** Probe-, Probierfläschchen *n*. **2.** (*of*) Kostprobe *f* (*gen*), *fig. a.* (typisches) Beispiel (für). **II** *v/t* **3.** kosten (*a. fig.*), probieren.

san·a·to·ri·um [ˌsænəˈtɔːrɪəm] *pl* **-ri·ums**, **-ri·a** [~rɪə] *s* Sanatorium *n*.

sanc·ti·fy ['sæŋktɪfaɪ] *v/t* **1.** heiligen. **2.** *fig.* sanktionieren: → **end** 10.

sanc·ti·mo·ni·ous [ˌsæŋktɪˈməʊnjəs] *adj* □ frömmelnd, frömmlerisch.

sanc·tion ['sæŋkʃn] **I** *s* **1.** Billigung *f*, Zustimmung *f*. **2.** *mst pl* Sanktion *f*: **take ~s against, impose ~s on** Sanktionen verhängen über (*acc*). **II** *v/t* **3.** sanktionieren.

sanc·ti·ty ['sæŋktətɪ] *s* Heiligkeit *f*.

sanc·tu·ar·y ['sæŋktʃʊərɪ] *s* **1.** (*Vogel- etc*)Schutzgebiet *n*. **2.** Zuflucht *f*: **seek ~ with** Zuflucht suchen bei.

sand [sænd] **I** *s* **1.** Sand *m*. **2.** *pl* Sand(fläche *f*) *m*. **II** *v/t* **3.** *Weg etc* sanden, mit Sand streuen. **4.** schmirgeln: **~ down** abschmirgeln.

san·dal ['sændl] *s* Sandale *f*.

'sand|·bag I *s* Sandsack *m*. **II** *v/t* mit Sandsäcken befestigen *od.* schützen. **'~·bank** *s* Sandbank *f*. **'~·blast** *v/t* ⊚ sandstrahlen. **'~·box** *s Am.* Sandkasten *m*. **'~·cas·tle** *s* Sandburg *f*. **~ dune** *s* Sanddüne *f*. **'~·man** *s* (*irr man*) Sandmännchen *n*. **'~·pa·per I** *s* Sand-, Schmirgelpapier *n*. **II** *v/t* (ab)schmirgeln. **'~·pit** *s* **1.** *bsd. Br.* Sandkasten *m*. **2.** Sandgrube *f*. **'~·stone** *s* geol. Sandstein *m*. **'~·storm** *s* Sandsturm *m*.

sand·wich ['sænwɪdʒ] **I** *s* Sandwich *n*. **II** *v/t:* **be ~ed between** eingekeilt sein zwischen (*dat*); **~ s.th. in between** *fig. et.* einschieben zwischen (*acc, a. dat*). **~ course** *s. ped. etc* Kurs, bei dem sich theoretische u. praktische Ausbildung abwechseln. **~ man** *s* (*irr man*) Sandwichman *m*.

sand·y ['sændɪ] *adj* **1.** sandig, *pred a.* voller Sand: **~ beach** Sandstrand *m*. **2.** rotblond (*Haar*).

sane [seɪn] *adj* □ **1.** geistig gesund, normal, ⚖ zurechnungsfähig. **2.** vernünftig.

sang [sæŋ] *pret von* **sing.**

san·guine ['sæŋgwɪn] *adj* □ zuversichtlich, optimistisch.

san·i·tar·i·um [ˌsænɪˈteərɪəm] *Am.* → **sanatorium. san·i·tar·y** ['~tərɪ] *adj* □ **1.** hygienisch, Gesundheits...: **~ facilities** *pl* sanitäre Einrichtungen *pl*. **~ napkin** *Am.*, **~ towel** *Br.* (Damen)Binde *f*. **2.** hygienisch (einwandfrei), gesund.

san·i·to·ri·um [ˌsænɪˈtɔːrɪəm] *Am.* → **sanatorium.**

san·i·ty ['sænɪtɪ] *s* geistige Gesundheit, ⚖ Zurechnungsfähigkeit *f*.

sank [sæŋk] *pret von* **sink.**

San·ta Claus ['sæntəklɔːz] *s* der Weihnachtsmann, der Nikolaus.

sap¹ [sæp] *s* **1.** ♀ Saft *m*. **2.** F Einfaltspinsel *m*, Trottel *m*.

sap² [~] *v/t* schwächen.

sap·phire ['sæfaɪə] *s min.* Saphir *m*.

sap·py ['sæpɪ] *adj* □ **1.** ♀ saftig. **2.** F einfältig, trottelig.

sar·casm ['sɑːkæzəm] *s* Sarkasmus *m*. **sar·cas·tic** (*od.* ~**al·ly**) sarkastisch.

sar·coph·a·gus [sɑːˈkɒfəgəs] *pl* **-gi** [~gaɪ], **-gus·es** *s* Sarkophag *m*.

sar·dine [sɑːˈdiːn] *s ichth.* Sardine *f*: **be packed like ~s** wie die Heringe sitzen *od.* stehen.

sar·don·ic [sɑːˈdɒnɪk] *adj* (~**al·ly**) boshaft, höhnisch (*Lachen etc*).

sark·y ['sɑːkɪ] *Br.* F → **sarcastic.**

sar·nie ['sɑːnɪ] *s Br.* F Sandwich *n*.

sash¹ [sæʃ] *s* Fensterrahmen *m* (*e-s Schiebefensters*).

sash² [~] *s* Schärpe *f*.

sash win·dow *s* Schiebefenster *n*.

sass [sæs], **'sass·y** *Am.* F → **sauce** 2, **saucy.**

sat [sæt] *pret u. pp von* **sit.**

Sa·tan ['seɪtən] *s* der Satan. **sa·tan·ic** [sə'tænɪk] *adj* (~**al·ly**) satanisch. **'Sa·tan·ism** *s* Satanismus *m*, Satanskult *m*.

satch·el ['sætʃəl] *s* (Schul)Ranzen *m*.

sat·el·lite ['sætəlaɪt] *s* **1.** *ast.* (*a.* künstlicher) Satellit: **~ picture** Satellitenbild *n*; **~ transmission** *TV* Satellitenübertragung f. **2.** a) a. ~ **nation** (od. **state**) Satellit(enstaat) m, b) a. ~ **town** Satellitenstadt f.

sa·ti·ate ['seɪʃɪeɪt] v/t (über)sättigen.

sat·in ['sætɪn] s Satin m.

sat·ire ['sætaɪə] s Satire f (**on** auf acc).

sa·tir·i·cal [sə'tɪrəkl] adj □ satirisch.

sat·i·rist ['sætərɪst] s Satiriker(in).

'sat·i·rize v/t satirisch darstellen.

sat·is·fac·tion [,sætɪs'fækʃn] s **1.** Befriedigung f, Zufriedenstellung f. **2.** (**at**, **with**) Zufriedenheit f (mit), Genugtuung f (über acc): **to s.o.'s** ~ zu j-s Zufriedenheit.

sat·is·fac·to·ry [,sætɪs'fæktərɪ] adj □ befriedigend, zufriedenstellend.

sat·is·fy ['sætɪsfaɪ] v/t **1.** j-n befriedigen, zufriedenstellen: **be satisfied with** zufrieden sein mit; **a satisfied smile** ein zufriedenes Lächeln. **2.** Bedürfnis, Neugier etc befriedigen; Bedingungen etc erfüllen. **3.** j-n überzeugen (**of** von): **be satisfied that** davon überzeugt sein, daß.

sat·u·rate ['sætʃəreɪt] v/t **1.** (durch)tränken (**with** mit): ~**d with** (od. **in**) **blood** blutgetränkt. **2.** 🜂 sättigen (a. fig.). **,sat·u·ra·tion** s Sättigung f: ~ **point** 🜂 Sättigungspunkt m; **reach** a ~ **point** fig. s-n Sättigungsgrad erreichen.

Sat·ur·day ['sætədɪ] s Sonnabend m, Samstag m: **on** ~ (am) Samstag; **on** ~**s** samstags.

Sat·urn ['sætən] s ast. Saturn m.

sauce [sɔːs] s **1.** Soße f. **2.** F Frechheit f: **none of your** ~! werd bloß nicht frech! **'~-pan** s Kochtopf m.

sauc·er ['sɔːsə] s Untertasse f.

sau·ci·ness ['sɔːsɪnɪs] s F Frechheit f. **'sau·cy** adj □ F frech.

sau·er·kraut ['sauəkraut] s Sauerkraut n.

sau·na ['sɔːnə] s Sauna f: **have a** ~ in die Sauna gehen.

saun·ter ['sɔːntə] **I** v/i bummeln, schlendern. **II** s Bummel m: **have** (od. **take**) **a** ~ e-n Bummel machen.

sau·sage ['sɒsɪdʒ] s Wurst f.

sav·age ['sævɪdʒ] **I** adj □ wild: a) unzivilisiert, b) gefährlich (Tier), c) brutal, d) schonungslos. **II** s Wilde m, f. **III** v/t anfallen (Tier).

sa·van·na(h) [sə'vænə] s geogr. Savanne f.

save [seɪv] **I** v/t **1.** retten (**from** vor dat): ~ **s.o.'s life** j-m das Leben retten; → **bacon**, **face** 4, **neck** 1, **skin** 1. **2.** Geld, Zeit etc (ein)sparen; ebf. aufheben, -sparen (**for** für): ~ **s.th. for s.o.** j-m et. aufheben; ~ **one's strength** s-e Kräfte schonen. **3.** j-m et. ersparen: **you can** ~ **your excuses** du kannst dir d-e Ausreden sparen; ~ **s.o. doing s.th.** es j-m ersparen, et. zu tun. **4.** Sport: Schuß halten, parieren, a. Matchball etc abwehren; Tor verhindern. **II** v/i **5.** a. ~ **up** sparen (**for** auf acc). **6.** ~ **on** et. (ein)sparen. **III** s **7.** Sport: Parade f. **'sav·er** s **1.** Retter(in). **2.** Sparer(in). **3.** in Zssgn: **be a real time** ~ e-e Menge Zeit sparen. **'sav·ing** s **1.** Ersparnis f (**on** gegenüber). **2.** pl Ersparnisse pl: ~**s account** Am. Sparkonto n; ~**s and loan association** Am. Bausparkasse f; ~**s bank** Sparkasse f. **II** adj **3.** **his** (**only**) ~ **grace** das einzig Gute an ihm. **sav·io(u)r** ['~jə] s Retter(in): **the** 2 eccl. der Heiland od. Erlöser.

sa·vo(u)r ['seɪvə] **I** s **1.** (**of**) Geruch m (nach, von), Geschmack m (nach): ~ **of garlic** Knoblauchgeruch m. **2.** fig. Reiz m. **II** v/t **3.** mit Genuß essen od. trinken. **III** v/i **4.** ~ **of** fig. e-n Beigeschmack haben von. **'sa·vo(u)r·y** adj □ schmackhaft.

sa·voy [sə'vɔɪ] s ♣ Wirsing(kohl) m.

sav·vy ['sævɪ] s sl. Grips m, Köpfchen n.

saw¹ [sɔː] pret von **see**.

saw² [~] **I** s Säge f. **II** v/t (mst irr) sägen: ~ **off** absägen; ~ **up** zersägen. **'~·dust** s Sägespäne pl. **'~·mill** s Sägewerk n.

sawn [sɔːn] pp von **saw²**.

Sax·on ['sæksn] hist. **I** s (Angel)Sachse m, (-)Sächsin f. **II** adj (angel)sächsisch.

sax·o·phone ['sæksəfəun] s ♪ Saxophon n. **sax·o·phon·ist** [~'sɒfənɪst] s Saxophonist(in).

say [seɪ] **I** v/t (irr) **1.** sagen (**to** zu): **they** ~ **he is rich, he is said to be** ~ man sagt, er sei reich; er soll reich sein; **what does your watch** ~? wie spät ist es auf deiner Uhr?; **you can** ~ **that again!** das kannst du laut sagen!; ~, **haven't I ...?** Am. F sag mal, habe ich nicht ...?; → **easy** 8, **jack** 1, **knife** I, **nothing** 1, **when** 5. **2.** Gebet sprechen, Vaterunser etc beten: → **grace** 6. **3.** annehmen: (**let's**) ~ **this happens** angenommen od. nehmen wir einmal an, das geschieht; *a sum of,* **~,** **£500** e-e Summe von sagen wir 500 Pfund. **4.** (be)sagen, bedeuten: *that is to ~* das heißt. **II** *v/i* (*irr*) **5.** es sagen: *I can't ~* das kann ich nicht sagen; *you don't ~ (so)!* was du nicht sagst!; *it goes without ~ing* es versteht sich von selbst (*that* daß). **III** *s* **6.** Mitspracherecht *n* (*in* bei). **7.** *have one's ~* s-e Meinung äußern, zu Wort kommen: *he always has to have his ~* er muß immer mitreden. **'say·ing** *s* Sprichwort *n*, Redensart *f*: *as the ~ goes* wie man (so) sagt.

'say-so *s* F **1.** *just on his ~* auf s-e bloße Behauptung hin, nur weil er es sagt. **2.** *on his ~* mit s-r Erlaubnis.

scab [skæb] *s* **1.** ✿ Grind *m*, Schorf *m*. **2.** *vet.* Räude *f*. **3.** *sl.* Streikbrecher(in). **'scab·by** *adj* **1.** grindig, schorfig. **2.** ✿ krätzig; *vet.* räudig.

scab·i·es ['skeibiiz] *s* ✿ Krätze *f*.

scaf·fold ['skæfəʊld] *s* **1.** (Bau)Gerüst *n*. **2.** Schafott *n*. **scaf·fold·ing** ['~fəldıŋ] → **scaffold** 1.

scal·a·wag ['skæləwæg] *bsd. Am.* → **scallywag**.

scald [skɔ:ld] **I** *v/t* **1.** sich *die Finger etc* verbrühen (*on, with* mit): *be ~ed to death* tödliche Verbrühungen erleiden (*by* durch). **2.** *bsd.* Milch abkochen. **II** *s* **3.** Verbrühung *f.* **'scald·ing** *adj u. adv*: *~ (hot)* kochendheiß.

scale¹ [skeil] **I** *s* **1.** *zo.* (*a. Haut*)Schuppe *f*: *the ~s fell from my eyes fig.* es fiel mir wie Schuppen von den Augen. **2.** Kesselstein *m*. **II** *v/t* **3.** Fisch (ab)schuppen.

scale² [~] *s* **1.** Waagschale *f.* *mst pl, a. pair of ~s* Waage *f*: *tip the ~s fig.* den Ausschlag geben (*in favo[u]r of* für). **3.** **2**s *pl* (*sg konstruiert*) *ast.* Waage *f.*

scale³ [~] **I** *s* **1.** Skala *f* (*a. fig.*), Grad- od. Maßeinteilung *f.* Æ, ⊙ Maßstab *m*: *to ~* maßstab(s)gerecht, -getreu; *~ model* maßstab(s)gerecht od. -getreues Modell. **3.** ♪ Skala *f*, Tonleiter *f.* **4.** *fig.* Ausmaß *n*, Maßstab *m*, Umfang *m*: *on a large ~* in großem Umfang. **II** *v/t* **5.** erklettern. **6.** *~ down (up) fig.* verringern (erhöhen).

scal·lop ['skɒləp] *s zo.* Kammuschel *f.*

scal·ly·wag ['skæliwæg] *s bsd. Br.* Schlingel *m*, (kleiner) Strolch.

scalp [skælp] **I** *s* **1.** *anat.* Kopfhaut *f.* **2.** Skalp *m*: *be out for s.o.'s ~ fig.* auf j-s Skalp aussein. **II** *v/t* **3.** skalpieren.

scal·pel ['skælpəl] *s* ✿ Skalpell *n.*

scal·per ['skælpə] *s Am.* Kartenschwarzhändler(in).

scamp [skæmp] *s* Schlingel *m*, (kleiner) Strolch.

scam·per ['skæmpə] *v/i* trippeln (*Kind etc*); huschen (*Maus etc*).

scan [skæn] **I** *v/t* **1.** *et.* absuchen (*for* nach). **2.** Zeitung etc überfliegen. **3.** *Metrik:* skandieren. **4.** *Computer, Radar, TV:* abtasten. **II** *s* **5.** ✿ etc Scanning *n.*

scan·dal ['skændl] *s* **1.** Skandal *m*. **2.** Skandalgeschichten *pl*, Klatsch(geschichten *pl*) *m*. **scan·dal·ize** ['~dəlaız] *v/t:* *he was ~d* er war empört *od.* entrüstet (*by, at* über *acc*; *to* hear als er hörte).

'scan·dal,mon·ger *s* Klatschmaul *n.*

scan·dal·ous ['skændələs] *adj* □ **1.** skandalös: *be ~ a.* ein Skandal sein (*that* daß). **2.** Skandal...

Scan·di·na·vi·an [,skændı'neıvjən] **I** *s* Skandinavier(in). **II** *adj* skandinavisch.

scant [skænt] *adj* □ dürftig, gering.

scant·y ['skæntı] *adj* □ dürftig, kärglich (*Mahlzeit*); knapp (*Bikini etc*).

scape·goat ['skeıpgəʊt] *s* Sündenbock *m.*

scar [skɑ:] **I** *s* Narbe *f*; Schramme *f*, Kratzer *m.* **II** *v/t* Narben *od.* e-e Narbe hinterlassen auf (*dat*); *fig.* j-n zeichnen.

scarce [skeəs] *adj* **1.** knapp (*Ware*): *make o.s. ~* F sich dünnmachen. **2.** selten. **'scarce·ly** *adv* **1.** kaum. **2.** kaum, schwerlich. **'scarce·ness**, **'scar·ci·ty** *s* **1.** Knappheit *f*, Mangel *m* (*of* an *dat*). **2.** Seltenheit *f.*

scare [skeə] **I** *v/t* **1.** erschrecken, j-m e-n Schreck(en) einjagen: *be ~d* Angst haben (*of* vor *dat*). **2.** *~ away* (*od. off*) verjagen, -scheuchen; *fig.* j-n ab-, verschrecken. **II** *v/i* **3.** *~ easily* schreckhaft sein. **III** *s* **4.** Schreck(en) *m*: *give s.o. a ~* → 1. Panik *f.* **'~·crow** *s* Vogelscheuche *f* (*a. fig.*). **'~·mon·ger** *s* Panikmacher(in).

scarf [skɑ:f] *pl* **scarfs**, **scarves** [skɑ:vz] *s* Schal *m*; Hals-, Kopf-, Schultertuch *n.*

scar·let ['skɑːlət] *adj* scharlachrot: **~ fever** ✶ Scharlach *m*.

scar·per ['skɑːpə] *v/i Br. sl.* abhauen, verduften.

scarred [skɑːd] *adj* narbig.

scarves [skɑːvz] *pl von* **scarf**.

scar·y ['skeərɪ] *adj* F **1.** unheimlich (*Gegend etc*); grus(e)lig (*Geschichte etc*): **~ film** Gruselfilm *m*. **2.** furchtsam; schreckhaft.

scath·ing ['skeɪðɪŋ] *adj* □ ätzend, vernichtend (*Kritik etc*).

scat·ter ['skætə] **I** *v/t* **1.** *a.* **~ about** (*od. around*) ver-, ausstreuen: **~ money all over the place** überall herumliegen; **~ money around** *fig.* mit dem Geld um sich werfen. **2.** *Menge etc* zerstreuen, *Vögel etc* auseinanderscheuchen. **II** *v/i* **3.** sich zerstreuen (*Menge etc*), auseinanderstieben (*Vögel etc*), sich zerteilen (*Nebel etc*). '**~·brain** *s* F Schussel *m*. '**~·brained** *adj* F schusselig, schußlig.

scat·tered ['skætəd] *adj* **1.** ver- *od.* zerstreut (liegend) (*Häuser etc*). **2.** vereinzelt (*Schauer etc*).

scav·enge ['skævɪndʒ] **I** *v/i* **1.** **~ on** *zo.* leben von (*Abfällen, Aas*). **2.** *a.* **~ for food** (nach) Nahrung suchen: **~ in** herumwühlen in (*dat*). **II** *v/t* **3.** → 1. **4.** *et.* ergattern. '**scav·en·ger** *s zo.* Aasfresser *m.*

sce·nar·i·o [sɪ'nɑːrɪəʊ] *pl* **-os** *s* Film, thea., TV: Szenario *n* (*a. fig.*), Szenarium *n.*

scene [siːn] *s* **1.** *thea. etc* a) Szene *f*: **change of ~** Szenenwechsel *m*; *fig.* Tapetenwechsel *m*, b) Bühnenbild *n*, Kulissen *pl*: **behind the ~s** hinter den Kulissen (*a. fig.*), c) Ort *m* der Handlung, Schauplatz *m* (*a. e-s Romans etc*). **2.** Schauplatz *m*: **~ of accident** (*crime, crash*) Unfallort *m* (Tatort *m*, Absturzstelle *f*); **be on the ~** zur Stelle sein; **come on(to) the ~** auf der Bildfläche erscheinen, auftauchen. **3.** Szene *f*, Anblick *m*: **~ of destruction** Bild *n* der Zerstörung. **4.** Szene *f*, (heftiger) Auftritt *m*: **make a ~** (j-m) e-e Szene machen. **5.** F (*Drogen-, Pop- etc*)Szene *f*. **6.** ... **is not my ~** F ... ist nicht mein Fall.

scen·er·y ['~ərɪ] *s* **1.** Landschaft *f*, Gegend *f*. **2.** *thea.* Bühnenbild *n*, Kulissen *pl.*

sce·nic ['siːnɪk] *adj* (**~ally**) **1.** landschaft-lich, Landschafts... **2.** landschaftlich schön, malerisch: **~ road** landschaftlich schöne Strecke. **3.** *thea.* Bühnen...

scent [sent] **I** *s* **1.** Duft *m*, Geruch *m.* **2.** *bsd. Br.* Parfüm *n*. **3.** *hunt.* Witterung *f*: **be on the ~ of** *fig.* e-r Sache auf der Spur sein; **follow a wrong ~** *fig.* e-e falsche Spur verfolgen. **II** *v/t* **4.** wittern (*a. fig.*). **5.** **be ~ed with** vom Duft (*gen*) erfüllt sein. **6.** *bsd. Br.* parfümieren. '**scent·less** *adj* geruchlos.

scep·ter *Am.* → **sceptre**.

scep·tic ['skeptɪk] *s Br.* Skeptiker(in). '**scep·ti·cal** *adj* □ skeptisch: **be ~ about** (*od. of*) **s.th.** e-r Sache skeptisch gegenüberstehen. **scep·ti·cism** ['~sɪzəm] *s* Skepsis *f.*

scep·tre ['septə] *s bsd. Br.* Zepter *n.*

sched·ule ['ʃedjuːl] **I** *s* **1.** Aufstellung *f*, Verzeichnis *n*. **2.** (*Arbeits-, Stunden-, Zeit- etc*)Plan *m*; Programm *n*; Fahr-, Flugplan *m*: **three months ahead of ~** drei Monate früher als vorgesehen; **be behind ~** Verspätung haben, *weitS.* im Verzug *od.* Rückstand sein; **on ~** (fahr)planmäßig, pünktlich. **II** *v/t* **3.** *et.* ansetzen (**for** auf *acc*, für); **it is ~d to take place tomorrow** es soll morgen stattfinden; **~d departure** (fahr)planmäßige Abfahrt; **~d flight** Linienflug *m.*

sche·mat·ic [skɪ'mætɪk] *adj* (**~ally**) schematisch.

scheme [skiːm] **I** *s* **1.** Schema *n*, System *n*. **2.** *bsd. Br.* Programm *n*, Projekt *n*. **3.** Intrige *f*, *pl a.* Machenschaften *pl*. **II** *v/i* **4.** intrigieren (**against** gegen): **~ for** hinarbeiten auf (*acc*). '**schem·er** *s* Intrigant(in). '**schem·ing** *adj* □ intrigant.

schist [ʃɪst] *s geol.* Schiefer *m.*

schiz·o·phre·ni·a [ˌskɪtsəʊ'friːnjə] *s psych.* Schizophrenie *f.* **schiz·o·phren·ic** [ˌ~'frenɪk] **I** *adj* (**~ally**) schizophren. **II** *s* Schizophrene *m, f.*

schmal(t)z [ʃmɒlts] *s bsd. ♩* F Schmalz *m.* '**schmal(t)z·y** *adj* F schmalzig.

schnit·zel ['ʃnɪtsl] *s gastr.* Wiener Schnitzel *n.*

schol·ar ['skɒlə] *s* **1.** Gelehrte *m, f, bsd.* Geisteswissenschaftler(in). **2.** *univ.* Stipendiat(in). '**schol·ar·ly** *adj* **1.** gelehrt. **2.** wissenschaftlich. '**schol·ar·ship** *s* **1.** Gelehrsamkeit *f.* **2.** *univ.* Stipendium *n*: **~ holder** → **scholar** 2.

school¹ [sku:l] *s* Schule *f*, Schwarm *m* (*Delphine, Heringe* etc).

school² [~] **I** *s* **1.** *allg.* Schule *f* (*a. fig.*): **at** (*Am.* **in**) ~ auf od. in der Schule; **go to** ~ in die od. zur Schule gehen; **there is no** ~ **today** heute ist schulfrei od. kein Unterricht; → **old 1**. **2.** *Am.* Hochschule *f*. **3.** *univ.* Fakultät *f*; Fachbereich *m*. **II** *v/t* **4.** *j-n* schulen, unterrichten (**in** in dat); *Tier* dressieren: ~ **o.s. to do s.th.** es sich angewöhnen, et. zu tun. ~ **age** *s* schulpflichtiges Alter: **be of** ~ schulpflichtig od. im schulpflichtigen Alter sein. '**~·age** *adj* schulpflichtig, im schulpflichtigen Alter. '**~·boy** *s* Schuljunge *m*, Schüler *m*. ~ **bus** *s* Schulbus *m*. '**~·child** *s* (*irr child*) Schulkind *n*. ~ **days** *s pl* Schulzeit *f*. '**~,fel·low** → **schoolmate**. '**~·girl** *s* Schulmädchen *n*, Schülerin *f*.

school·ing ['sku:lɪŋ] *s* (Schul)Ausbildung *f*.

school| **leav·er** *s bsd. Br.* Schulabgänger(in). '**~·mate** *s* Schulkamerad(in), Mitschüler(in). ~ **ship** *s* Schulschiff *n*. '**~,teach·er** *s* (Schul)Lehrer(in).

schoon·er ['sku:nə] *s* **1.** ♱ Schoner *m*. **2.** *Br.* großes Sherryglas; *Am.* großes Bierglas.

sci·at·ic [saɪ'ætɪk] *adj* ♱ Ischias...: ~ **nerve.** **sci·at·i·ca** [~kə] *s* ♱ Ischias *m, n, f*.

sci·ence ['saɪəns] *s* **1.** Wissenschaft *f*. **2.** *a.* **natural** ~ Naturwissenschaft(en *pl*) *f*. **3.** *fig.* Kunst *f*, Lehre *f*. ~ **fic·tion** *s* Science-fiction *f*.

sci·en·tif·ic [,saɪən'tɪfɪk] *adj* (*~ally*) **1.** (*engS.*) (natur)wissenschaftlich. **2.** *fig.* systematisch. '**sci·en·tist** *s* (*engS.* Natur)Wissenschaftler(in).

sci-fi [,saɪ'faɪ] *s* F Science-fiction *f*.

scin·til·lat·ing ['sɪntɪleɪtɪŋ] *adj* sprühend (*Geist, Witz*), geistsprühend (*Unterhaltung* etc).

scis·sors ['sɪzəz] *s pl, a.* **pair of** ~ Schere *f*.

scle·ro·sis [,sklɪə'rəʊsɪs] *s* ♱ Sklerose *f*.

scoff¹ [skɒf] **I** *v/i* spotten (**at** über *acc*). **II** *s* spöttische Bemerkung.

scoff² [~] *v/t* F Kuchen etc verdrücken, wegputzen.

scoff·er ['skɒfə] *s* Spötter(in).

scold [skəʊld] *v/t* ausschelten, -schimpfen, schimpfen mit (**for** wegen). '**scold-**

---

ing *s* Schelte *f*: **give** *s.o.* **a** ~ → **scold**.

scol·lop ['skɒləp] → **scallop**.

sconce [skɒns] *s* Wandleuchte *f*.

scone [skɒn] *s* kleiner runder Kuchen, mit Butter serviert.

scoop [sku:p] **I** *s* **1.** Schöpfkelle *f*, Schöpfer *m*; (*Mehl- etc*)Schaufel *f*; (*Eis*)Portionierer *m*. **2.** Kugel *f* (*Eis*). **3.** *Presse, Rundfunk, TV*: (sensationelle) Erstmeldung. **II** *v/t* **4.** schöpfen; schaufeln.

scoot [sku:t] *v/i* F abhauen; rennen.

scoot·er ['sku:tə] *s* **1.** (Kinder)Roller *m*. **2.** (*Motor*)Roller *m*.

scope [skəʊp] *s* **1.** Bereich *m*: **be within** (**beyond**) **the** ~ **of** sich im Rahmen (*gen*) halten (den Rahmen [*gen*] sprengen). **2.** (Spiel)Raum *m*, (Entfaltungs)Möglichkeit(en *pl*) *f* (**for** für).

scorch [skɔ:tʃ] **I** *v/t* **1.** an-, versengen, verbrennen. **2.** ausdörren. **II** *v/i* **3.** *mot.* F rasen. **III** *s* **4.** *a.* ~ **mark** angesengte Stelle, Brandfleck *m*. '**scorch·er** *s* F glühendheißer Tag. '**scorch·ing** *adj* F glühendheiß (*Tag etc*), sengend (*Hitze*).

score [skɔ:] **I** *s* **1.** (Spiel)Stand *m*; (Spiel-) Ergebnis *n*: **what is the** ~? wie steht es od. das Spiel?; **the** ~ **stood at** (od. **was**) **2–1** das Spiel stand 2:1; **keep (the)** ~ anschreiben. **2.** *Sport*: Torerfolg *m*. **3.** ♪ Partitur *f*; Filmmusik *f* (*zu e-m Film etc*). **4. on that** ~ deshalb, in dieser Hinsicht. **5. have a** ~ **to settle with** *s.o.* e-e alte Rechnung mit *j-m* zu begleichen haben. **6.** ~**s** *pl* e-e Menge. **7.** *a.* ~ **mark** Kerbe *f*, Rille *f*. **II** *v/t* **8.** *Sport*: Treffer etc erzielen, Tor *a.* schießen; *a. allg.* Erfolg, Sieg erringen. **9.** *Sport*: *j-m* Punkte, Note geben. **10.** ♪ in Partitur setzen; instrumentieren, setzen (**for** für); die Musik schreiben zu od. für. **11.** einkerben. **12.** ~ **out** (od. **through**) aus-, durchstreichen. **III** *v/i* **13.** *Sport*: e-n Treffer etc erzielen, ein Tor schießen: **he** ~**d twice** er war zweimal erfolgreich. **14.** erfolgreich sein, Erfolg haben (**with** mit): ~ **off** *s.o.* *j-n* als dumm hinstellen od. lächerlich machen; ~ **with a girl** *sl.* ein Mädchen ins Bett kriegen. '**~·board** *s Sport*: Anzeigetafel *f*.

scor·er ['skɔ:rə] *s* (*Sport*) **1.** Torschütze *m*, -schützin *f*. **2.** Anschreiber(in).

scorn [skɔ:n] *s* Verachtung *f* (**for** für, **gegen**): **pour** ~ **on** et. verächtlich abtun.

scorn·ful ['.ful] *adj* □ verächtlich.
Scor·pi·o ['skɔːpɪəʊ] *s ast.* Skorpion *m*: **be (a) ~** Skorpion sein.
scor·pi·on ['skɔːpjən] *s zo.* Skorpion *m*.
Scot [skɒt] *s* Schotte *m*, Schottin *f*.
Scotch [skɒtʃ] **I** *adj* schottisch (*Whisky etc*). **II** *s* Scotch *m* (*schottischer Whisky*).
scot-free [ˌskɒt'friː] *adj*: **get off ~** ungeschoren davonkommen.
Scots [skɒts] *adj* schottisch. **~·man** ['.mən] *s* (*irr* **man**) Schotte *m*. **'~·wom·an** *s* (*irr* **woman**) Schottin *f*.
Scot·tish ['skɒtɪʃ] *adj* schottisch.
scoun·drel ['skaʊndrəl] *s* Schurke *m*, Schuft *m*.
scour¹ ['skaʊə] *v/t* Topf *etc* scheuern, *Fußboden etc* a. schrubben.
scour² *v/t Gegend etc* absuchen, abkämmen (*for* nach).
scourge [skɜːdʒ] **I** *s* Geißel *f* (*a. fig.*). **II** *v/t* geißeln, *fig. a.* heimsuchen.
scout [skaʊt] **I** *s* **1.** *oft* ♀ Pfadfinder *m*; *Am.* Pfadfinderin *f*. **2.** ✕ Kundschafter *m*, Späher *m*. **3.** *Br.* motorisierter Pannenhelfer (*e-s Automobilklubs*). **4.** *bsd. Sport:* Talentsucher(in). **II** *v/i* **5.** *~ a-bout* (*od. around*) sich umsehen (*for* nach). **III** *v/t* **6.** *a.* **~ out** ✕ auskundschaften, erkunden.
scowl [skaʊl] **I** *v/i* ein böses Gesicht machen: *~ at* j-n bös anschauen. **II** *s* böses Gesicht.
scrab·ble ['skræbl] *v/i mst* **~ about** (*od. around*) herumsuchen, -wühlen (*for* nach).
scrag·gy ['skrægɪ] *adj* □ dürr, knochig.
scram [skræm] *v/i* F *oft imp* abhauen, Leine ziehen.
scram·ble ['skræmbl] **I** *v/i* **1.** klettern; krabbeln. **2.** sich raufen (*a. fig.*), (*bsd. Kinder*) sich balgen (*for* um); sich drängeln (*for* zu). **II** *v/t* **3.** *Ei* verrühren: *~d eggs pl* Rührei(er *pl*) *n*. **4.** *Funkspruch etc* verschlüsseln. **III** *s* **5.** Kletterei *f*. **6.** Rauferei *f*, Balgerei *f*; Drängelei *f*. **'scram·bler** *s* ⊙ Zerhacker *m*.
scrap¹ [skræp] *s* **1.** Stückchen *n*, Fetzen *m*: *there is not a ~ of evidence* es gibt nicht den geringsten Beweis; *there is not a ~ of truth in it* daran ist kein Wort wahr. **2.** *pl* (Speise)Reste *pl*. **3.** Altmaterial *n*; Altmetall *n*, Schrott *m*: *sell*

s.th. for ~ et. als Schrott verkaufen. **II** *v/t* **4.** *unbrauchbar Gewordenes* ausrangieren; *Plan etc* aufgeben, fallenlassen, *Methode etc* a. zum alten Eisen werfen. **5.** verschrotten.
scrap² [~] F **I** *v/i* sich streiten; sich balgen. **II** *s* Streiterei *f*; Balgerei *f*.
'scrap·book *s* Sammelalbum *n*.
scrape [skreɪp] **I** *v/t* **1.** (ab)kratzen, (ab)schaben (*from* von); *Schuhe etc* abkratzen; *Karotten etc* schaben: *~ off* abkratzen *od.* abschaben (von); *~ to-gether* (*od. up*) *Geld* zs.-kratzen; *~ a living fig.* sich gerade so über Wasser halten. **2.** sich *die Knie etc* ab- *od.* aufschürfen (*on auf dat*); *Wagen etc* ankratzen. **II** *v/i* **3.** scheuern (*against* an *dat*): *~ along the ground* am Boden schleifen. **4.** *fig. ~ along* (*od. by*) über die Runden kommen (*on* mit); *~ through an examination* mit Ach u. Krach durch e-e Prüfung kommen. **III** *s* **5.** Kratzen *n*. **6.** Aufschürfung *f*, Schürfwunde *f*. **7.** *be in a ~* F in Schwulitäten sein. **'scrap·er** *s* ⊙ Kratzer *m*, Schaber *m*.
scrap| heap *s* Schrotthaufen *m*: *be on the ~ fig.* zum alten Eisen gehören. **~ met·al** *s* Altmetall *n*, Schrott *m*. **~ pa·per** *s bsd. Br.* Schmierpapier *n*.
scrap·py ['skræpɪ] *adj* □ zs.-gestoppelt.
scrap| val·ue *s* Schrottwert *m*. **'~·yard** *s* Schrottplatz *m*.
scratch [skrætʃ] **I** *v/t* **1.** (zer)kratzen, *Wagen etc* ankratzen: *~ one's arm on a nail* sich den Arm an e-m Nagel aufreißen. **2.** a) (ab)kratzen (*from* von): *~ off* abkratzen (von), b) *s-n Namen etc* einkratzen (*on* in *acc*). **3.** *j-n, sich* kratzen: *~ one's nose* sich an der Nase kratzen; *~ one's head* sich den Kopf kratzen (*vor Verlegenheit etc*). **II** *v/i* **4.** kratzen (*at* an *dat*). **5.** sich kratzen. **III** *s* **6.** Kratzer *m*. **7.** *fig. start from ~* ganz von vorn anfangen; *be* (*od. come*) *up to ~* den Anforderungen *od.* Erwartungen entsprechen. **IV** *adj* **8.** (bunt) zs.-gewürfelt (*Mannschaft etc*). **'~·pad** *s bsd. Am.* Schmierblock *m*. **~ pa·per** *s Am.* Schmierpapier *n*.
scratch·y ['skrætʃɪ] *adj* □ **1.** kratzend (*Geräusch*). **2.** zerkratzt (*Schallplatte*). **3.** kratzig (*Pullover etc*).
scrawl [skrɔːl] **I** *v/t* **1.** (hin)kritzeln.

scurrilous

II **s** 2. Gekritzel *n*. **3.** Klaue *f*.
scraw·ny ['skrɔ:nɪ] *adj* □ dürr.

scream [skri:m] I *v/i* **1.** schreien (*with*
vor *dat*): ~ *with laughter* vor Lachen
brüllen. II *v/t* **2.** a. ~ *out* schreien: ~ *o.s.*
hoarse sich heiser schreien; ~ *the place*
down F zetermordio schreien; → *roof-*
top. III *s* **3.** Schrei *m*: ~*s pl of laughter*
brüllendes Gelächter. **4. be a ~** F zum
Schreien (komisch) sein.

scree [skri:] *s* Geröll *n*.

screech [skri:tʃ] I *v/i u. v/t* kreischen (*a.*
Bremsen etc), (gellend) schreien. II *s*
Kreischen *n*; (gellender) Schrei.

screed [skri:d] *s* langatmige Rede *etc*,
Roman *m*.

screen [skri:n] I *s* **1.** Wandschirm *m*. **2.**
Film: Leinwand *f*: *adapt for the ~* für
den Film bearbeiten. **3.** *Radar, TV etc*:
(Bild)Schirm *m*. **4.** *fig*. Tarnung *f*. II *v/t*
5. abschirmen. **6.** ~ *off* abtrennen. **7.**
Film zeigen, *Fernsehprogramm a.* senden. **8.** *fig*. j-n überprüfen. '~·**play** *s*
Film: Drehbuch *n*. ~ *test s Film*: Probe-
aufnahmen *pl*.

screw [skru:] I *s* **1.** ⚙ Schraube *f*: *he has*
a ~ loose F bei ihm ist e-e Schraube
locker; *put the ~ on s.o. fig.* j-m (die)
Daumenschrauben anlegen *od.* ansetzen.
II *v/t* **2.** (an)schrauben (*to* an *acc*):
~ *together* zs.-, verschrauben. **3.** *a.* ~ *up*
Papier *etc* zs., zerknüllen. **4.** ~ *up* d-e
Augen zs.-kneifen, *Gesicht* verziehen,
b) F Plan *etc* vermasseln. **5.** ~ *sth. out*
of s.o. et. aus j-m herauspressen. **6.** (*a.*
v/i) V bumsen, vögeln. '~·**ball** *s bsd.*
Am. F Spinner(in). '~·**driv·er** *s* ⚙
Schraubenzieher *m*. ~ *top s* Schrauben-
verschluß *m*.

screw·y ['skru:ɪ] *adj* F verrückt.

scrib·ble ['skrɪbl] I *v/t* (hin)kritzeln. II *s*
Gekritzel *n*. '**scrib·bler** *s humor. od.*
contp. Schreiberling *m*.

scrim·age ['skrɪmɪdʒ] *s* Handgemenge *n*.

scrimp [skrɪmp] *v/i* den Gürtel enger
schnallen: ~ *and scrape* jeden Pfennig
zweimal umdrehen.

script [skrɪpt] *s* **1.** Manuskript *n* (*e-r*
Rede etc); (*Film, TV*) Drehbuch *n*,
Skript *n*; *thea*. Text(buch *n*) *m*. **2.**
Schrift(zeichen *pl*) *f*. **3.** Schreibschrift *f*.
4. *ped. univ. Br.* (schriftliche) Prüfungs-
arbeit.

Scrip·ture ['skrɪptʃə] *s, a. the ~s pl* die
(Heilige) Schrift.

'**script, writ·er** *s Film, TV*: Drehbuchau-
tor(in).

scroll [skrəʊl] *s* Schriftrolle *f*.

scrooge [skru:dʒ] *s* Geizhals *m*.

scro·tum ['skrəʊtəm] *pl* -**tums, -ta** ['-tə]
s anat. Hodensack *m*.

scrounge [skraʊndʒ] F I *v/i* schnorren
(*off* bei). II *v/t et.* schnorren (*off* von,
bei). '**scroung·er** *s* F Schnorrer(in).

scrub¹ [skrʌb] *s* Gebüsch *n*, Gestrüpp
n.

scrub² [~] I *v/t* **1.** et. schrubben, scheuern. **2.** F streichen, ausfallen lassen. II *s*
3. Schrubben *n*, Scheuern *n*: *give s.th.*
a ~ → **1**.

scrub·bing brush ['skrʌbɪŋ] *s*, *Am. a.*
scrub brush *s* Scheuerbürste *f*.

scrub·by ['skrʌbɪ] *adj* gestrüppreich.

scruff [skrʌf] *s*: ~ *of the neck* Genick *n*.

scruff·y ['skrʌfɪ] *adj* ⬚ schmudd(e)lig.

scrump·tious ['skrʌmpʃəs] *adj* ⬚ F fabelhaft, lecker (*Speise*).

scrunch [skrʌntʃ] I *v/t a.* ~ *up* Papier *etc*
zs.-knüllen. II *v/i* knirschen.

scru·ple ['skru:pl] I *s* Skrupel *m*: *have*
no ~s about doing s.th. → II; *without ~*
skrupellos. II *v/t: not to ~ to do s.th.*
keine Skrupel haben, et. zu tun. **scru·**
pu·lous ['~pjʊləs] *adj* ⬚ gewissenhaft.

scru·ti·nize ['skru:tɪnaɪz] *v/t* **1.** genau
prüfen. **2.** mustern. '**scru·ti·ny** *s* **1.** genaue Prüfung. **2.** musternder *od.* prü-
fender Blick.

scu·ba ['sku:bə] *s* Tauchgerät *n*: ~ *diving*
(Sport)Tauchen *n*.

scuff [skʌf] *v/t* **1.** ~ *one's feet* schlurfen.
2. abwetzen.

scuf·fle ['skʌfl] I *v/i* (sich) raufen (*for*
um). II *s* Rauferei *f*, Handgemenge *n*.

scull [skʌl] (*Rudersport*) I *s* **1.** Skull *n*. **2.**
Skullboot *n*, Skuller *m*. II *v/t u. v/i* **3.**
skullen. '**scull·er** *s* Skuller(in).

sculp·tor ['skʌlptə] *s* Bildhauer *m*.

sculp·ture ['skʌlptʃə] I *s* Skulptur *f*, Plastik *f*, (*Kunst a.*) Bildhauerei *f*. II *v/t*
Figur *etc* hauen (*in* in *dat*, aus).

scum [skʌm] *s* **1.** Schaum *m*. **2.** *fig.* Abschaum *m*: *the ~ of the earth* der Abschaum der Menschheit.

scurf [skɜ:f] *s* (Kopf)Schuppen *pl*.

'**scurf·y** *adj* schuppig.

scur·ril·ous ['skʌrələs] *adj* ⬚ **1.** beleidigend; verleumderisch. **2.** derb (*Witz etc*).

scur·ry ['skʌrɪ] I *v/i* **1.** huschen. **2.** trippeln. II *s* **3.** Getrippel *n*.

scut·tle ['skʌtl] → **scurry** I.

scythe [saɪð] I *s* Sense *f*. II *v/t a.* ~ **down** Wiese *etc* mähen.

sea [si:] *s* Meer *n* (*a. fig.*), See *f*: **at** ~ auf See; **be all at** ~ *fig.* völlig ratlos sein; **by** ~ auf dem Seeweg; **by the** ~ am Meer; **go to** ~ zur See gehen; → **put** 12. ~ **an·i·mal** *s* Meerestier *n*. '~**bed** *s* Meeresboden *m*, -grund *m*. '~**board** *s* Küste *f*. '~**food** *s* Meeresfrüchte *pl*. ~ **go·ing** *adj* hochseetüchtig, Hochsee... '~**gull** *s orn.* Seemöwe *f*.

seal¹ [si:l] *pl* ~**s**, *bsd. coll.* ~ *s zo.* Seehund *m*, Robbe *f*.

seal² [~] I *s* **1.** Siegel *n*. **2.** Siegel *n*, Versieg(e)lung *f*; Plombe *f*. **3.** ⊕ Dichtung *f*. **4.** 🐾 Aufkleber *m*. II *v/t* **5.** siegeln. **6.** versiegeln; plombieren; *Briefumschlag etc* zukleben: ~**ed envelope** verschlossener Briefumschlag *m*. **7.** ⊕ abdichten. **8.** ~ **off** *Gegend etc* abriegeln. **9.** *fig.* besiegeln: ~ **s.o.'s fate** *j-s* Schicksal besiegeln.

sea lev·el *s*: **above** (**below**) ~ über (unter) dem Meeresspiegel, über (unter) Meereshöhe.

seal·ing wax ['si:lɪŋ] *s* Siegellack *n*.

sea li·on *s zo.* Seelöwe *m*.

'**seal·skin** *s* Seal(skin) *m*, *n*, Seehundfell *n*.

seam [si:m] *s* **1.** Saum *m*: **burst at the** ~**s** *bsd. fig.* aus allen Nähten platzen. **2.** Fuge *f*. **3.** *geol.* Flöz *n*.

sea·man ['si:mən] *s* (*irr man*) Seemann *m*. ~ **mile** *s* Seemeile *f*.

seam·stress ['semstrɪs] *s* Näherin *f*.

seam·y ['si:mɪ] *adj*: ~ **side** *fig.* Schattenseite(n *pl*) *f*.

'**sea·plane** *s* See-, Wasserflugzeug *n*. '~**port** *s* Seehafen *m*, Hafenstadt *f*. ~ **pow·er** *s* Seemacht *f*.

sear [sɪə] *v/t* **1.** *Fleisch* rasch anbraten. **2.** brennen in (*dat*) (*Geruch etc*). **3.** *Pflanzen* vertrocknen lassen.

search [sɜ:tʃ] I *v/i* **1.** suchen (**for** nach): ~ **through** durchsuchen; → **high** 7. II *v/t* **2.** *j-n*, *et.* durchsuchen (**for** nach): ~ **me!** F keine Ahnung! **3.** ~ **out** *j-n* ausfindig machen; *et.* herausfinden. III *s* **4.** Suche *f* (**for** nach): **in** ~ **of** auf der Suche

nach. **5.** Durchsuchung *f*. '**search·light** *s* (Such)Scheinwerfer *m*. ~ **par·ty** *s* Suchmannschaft *f*, -trupp *m*. ~ **war·rant** *s* ⚖️ Haussuchungs-, Durchsuchungsbefehl *m*.

sear·ing ['sɪərɪŋ] *adj* stechend (*Schmerz*).

'**sea·sick** *adj* seekrank. '~**sick·ness** *s* Seekrankheit *f*. '~**side** *s*: **at** (*od. by*) **the** ~ am Meer; **go to the** ~ ans Meer fahren; ~ **resort** Seebad *n*.

sea·son ['si:zn] I *s* **1.** Jahreszeit *f*: → **rainy**. **2.** *allg.* Saison *f*, *thea. a.* Spielzeit *f*, (*Jagd-*, *Urlaubs- etc*)Zeit *f*: **in** (**out of**) ~ in (außerhalb der) (Hoch)Saison; **ℰ's Greetings!** Frohe Weihnachten!; → **close season, compliment** 2, **high** 4, **low season, open** 10, **silly** 1. **3.** F → **season ticket**. II *v/t* **4.** *Speise* würzen. **5.** *Holz* ablagern. '**sea·son·a·ble** *adj* □ der Jahreszeit entsprechend. '**sea·son·al** ['~zənl] *adj* □ saisonbedingt; Saison... '**sea·soned** *adj* erfahren, routiniert. '**sea·son·ing** *s* Gewürz *n*.

sea·son tick·et *s* **1.** 🚂 *etc* Dauer-, Zeitkarte *f*. **2.** *thea.* Abonnement *n*.

seat [si:t] I *s* **1.** Sitz(gelegenheit *f*) *m*; (Sitz)Platz *m*: **take a** ~ Platz nehmen; **take one's** ~ s-n Platz einnehmen. **2.** Sitz(fläche *f*) *m* (*e-s Stuhls etc*); Hosenboden *m*; Hinterteil *n*: **do s.th. by the** ~ **of one's pants** F et. nach Gefühl u. Wellenschlag tun. **3.** (*Geschäfts-*, *Regierungs- etc*)Sitz *m*. II *v/t* **4.** *j-n* setzen: **be** ~**ed** sitzen; **please be** ~**ed** bitte nehmen Sie Platz; **remain** ~**ed** sitzen bleiben. **5.** Sitzplätze bieten für, Platz bieten (*dat*): ~ **500 persons** *a.* 500 Sitzplätze haben. ~ **belt** *s* ✈️, *mot.* Sicherheitsgurt *m*: **fasten one's** ~ sich anschnallen; **wear a** ~ angegurtet od. angeschnallt sein.

seat·er ['si:tə] *s* ✈️, *mot.* ...sitzer *m*. '**seat·ing** *s* **1.** Sitzgelegenheit(en *pl*) *f*. II *adj*: **a** ~ **capacity of 200** 200 Sitzplätze.

sea ur·chin ['ɜ:tʃɪn] *s zo.* Seeigel *m*. '~**weed** *s* 🌿 (See)Tang *m*. '~**worth·y** *adj* seetüchtig.

sec [sek] F → **second²** 2.

sec·a·teurs [ˌsekə'tɜ:z] *s pl*, *a.* **pair of** ~ *Br.* Gartenschere *f*.

se·cede [sɪˈsiːd] *v/i pol. etc* sich abspalten (**from** von).

se·ces·sion [sɪˈseʃn] *s pol. etc* Abspaltung *f* (**from** von).

se·clud·ed [sɪˈkluːdɪd] *adj* abgelegen, abgeschieden (*Haus etc*); zurückgezogen (*Leben*). **se·clu·sion** [-ʒn] *s* Abgelegenheit *f*, Abgeschiedenheit *f*; Zurückgezogenheit *f*.

sec·ond¹ [ˈsekənd] **I** *adj* (□ → **second·ly**) **1.** zweit: *he is going through his ~ childhood* er fühlt sich wieder wie ein (richtiges) Kind; *at ~ hand* aus zweiter Hand; *it has become ~ nature for* (*od.* **to**) *him* es ist ihm in Fleisch u. Blut übergegangen; *a ~ Shakespeare* ein zweiter Shakespeare; *a ~ time* noch einmal; *every ~ day* jeden zweiten Tag, alle zwei Tage; *be ~ to none* unerreicht *od.* unübertroffen sein (*as* als); → **fiddle** 1, **thought²** 2, **wind¹** 2. **II** *s* **2.** der, die, das Zweite: *the ~ of May* der 2. Mai. **3.** *mot.* zweiter Gang. **4.** *Boxen, Duell:* Sekundant *m*: *~s out* Ring frei. **5.** *pl* ✝ Waren *pl* zweiter Wahl. **6.** *pl* F Nachschlag *m* (*zweite Portion*). **III** *adv* **7.** als zweiter(er, e, es). **IV** *v/t* **8.** Antrag *etc* unterstützen.

sec·ond² [~] *s* **1.** Sekunde *f* (*a. ♈, ♪*). **2.** *fig.* Augenblick *m*, Sekunde *f*: *just a ~* Augenblick(, bitte)!; *I won't be a ~* ich komme gleich (wieder); *have you got a ~?* hast du e-n Moment Zeit (für mich)?

sec·ond³ [sɪˈkɒnd] *v/t Br. j-n* (*bsd.* vorübergehend) versetzen (**to** in *acc*).

sec·ond·ar·y [ˈsekəndərɪ] *adj* □ **1.** sekundär, zweitrangig, nebensächlich. **2.** *✝ etc* sekundär, Sekundär... **3.** *ped.* höher (*Schule etc*).

ˌsec·ond-ˈbest I *adj* zweitbest. **II** *adv*: *come off ~* den kürzeren ziehen. **ˌ~- ˈclass I** *adj* **1.** zweitklassig, -rangig. **2.** 🚂 *etc* zweiter Klasse. **II** *adv* **3.** 🚂 *etc* zweite(r) Klasse. **ˌ~-deˈgree** *adj* Verbrennungen zweiten Grades. **~ hand** *s* Sekundenzeiger *m*. **ˌ~-ˈhand I** *adj* **1.** (*a. adv*) aus zweiter Hand. **2.** gebraucht, Gebraucht..., (*Kleidung a.*) getragen, (*Bücher*) antiquarisch: *~ bookshop* Antiquariat *n*.

sec·ond·ly [ˈsekəndlɪ] *adv* zweitens.

ˌsec·ond-ˈrate → **second-class** 1.

se·cre·cy [ˈsiːkrəsɪ] *s* **1.** Geheimhaltung *f*: *in* (*od.* **amid**) *great ~* unter großer Geheimhaltung. **2.** Verschwiegenheit *f*.

se·cret [ˈsiːkrɪt] **I** *adj* (□ → **secretly**) **1.** geheim, Geheim...: *keep s.th. ~* et. geheimhalten (**from** vor *dat*); *~ agent* Geheimagent(in); *~ service* Geheimdienst *m*. **2.** heimlich (*Bewunderer etc*). **3.** verschwiegen. **II** *s* **4.** Geheimnis *n*: *in* (*~ a*) in Vertrauen, b) *~ secretly*; *have no ~s from s.o.* keine Geheimnisse vor j-m haben; *make no ~ of* kein Geheimnis *od.* Hehl machen aus: → *keep* 4, 7.

se·cre·tar·y [ˈsekrətrɪ] *s* **1.** Sekretär(in) (**to** *gen*). **2.** *pol.* Minister(in): *~ of State Br.* Minister(in); *Am.* Außenminister (-in). **ˌ~·ˈgen·er·al** *pl* **ˌsec·re·tar·ies· ˈgen·er·al** *s* Generalsekretär *m*.

se·crete [sɪˈkriːt] *v/t physiol.* absondern. **se·cre·tion** [-ʃn] *s* Absonderung *f*; Sekret *n*.

se·cre·tive [ˈsiːkrətɪv] *adj* □ heimlichtuerisch: *be ~ about s.th.* mit et. geheimtun.

sect [sekt] *s* Sekte *f*. **sec·tar·i·an** [~ˈteərɪən] *adj* konfessionsbedingt, Konfessions...

sec·tion [ˈsekʃn] **I** *s* **1.** Teil *m*. **2.** Abschnitt *m* (*e-s Buchs etc*); ⚖ Paragraph *m*. **3.** Abteilung *f*. **4.** ♈, ⊙ Schnitt *m*: *in ~* im Schnitt. **II** *v/t* **5.** teilen. **sec·tion·al** [ˈ~ʃənl] *adj* ♈, ⊙ Schnitt...

sec·tor [ˈsektə] *s allg.* Sektor *m*.

sec·u·lar [ˈsekjʊlə] *adj* □ weltlich, profan. **ˈsec·u·lar·ize** *v/t* säkularisieren, verweltlichen.

se·cure [sɪˈkjʊə] **I** *adj* □ **1.** *allg.* sicher (**against, from** vor *dat*): *feel ~* sich sicher fühlen; *financially ~* finanziell abgesichert. **II** *v/t* **2.** Tür *etc* fest verschließen; sichern. **3.** sichern (**against, from** vor *dat*). **4.** sich *et.* sichern *od.* beschaffen; *et.* erreichen.

se·cu·ri·ty [sɪˈkjʊərətɪ] *s* **1.** *allg.* Sicherheit *f*: *♈ Council* Sicherheitsrat *m* (*der UNO*); *for ~ reasons* aus Sicherheitsgründen; *~ risk* Sicherheitsrisiko *n*. **2.** *pl* ✝ Effekten *pl*, Wertpapiere *pl*.

se·dan [sɪˈdæn] *s mot. Am.* Limousine *f*.

se·date [sɪˈdeɪt] **I** *adj* □ ruhig, gelassen; (*Tempo*) gemütlich. **II** *v/t j-m* ein Beruhigungsmittel geben. **se·da·tion** *s*: *be under ~* unter den Einfluß von Beruhigungsmitteln stehen; *put under ~* → *sedate* II. **sed·a·tive** [ˈsedətɪv] **I** *adj*

beruhigend: **~ shot** Beruhigungsspritze
f. **II** s Beruhigungsmittel n (etc).
sed·en·tar·y ['sedntəri] adj □ **1.** sitzend
(Beschäftigung etc). **2.** seßhaft.
sed·i·ment ['sedimənt] s (Boden)Satz m.
se·duce [sɪ'djuːs] v/t verführen, weitS. a.
verleiten (**into** zu; **into doing s.th.** dazu,
et. zu tun). **se'duc·er** s Verführer(in).
se·duc·tion [sɪ'dʌkʃn] s **1.** Verführung
f. **2.** mst pl Verlockung f. **se'duc·tive**
adj □ verführerisch, weitS. a. verlok-
kend.
see¹ [siː] (irr) **I** v/t **1.** sehen: **I saw him
come** (od. **coming**) ich sah ihn kom-
men. **2.** (ab)sehen, erkennen. **3.** ersehen, entnehmen (**from** aus der Zeitung
etc). **4.** (ein)sehen, verstehen: **as I ~ it**
wie ich es sehe, in m-n Augen. **5.** sich et.
ansehen, besuchen. **6.** a) j-n besuchen:
go (**come**) **to ~ s.o.** j-n besuchen (gehen
od. kommen), b) Anwalt etc aufsuchen,
c) zum Arzt gehen, d) j-n sprechen (**on
business** geschäftlich). **7.** j-n empfangen. **8.** j-n begleiten, bringen (**to the
station** zum Bahnhof). **II** v/i **9.** sehen:
you'll ~ du wirst schon sehen. **10.** verstehen: **I ~** (ich) verstehe!, aha!, ach so!;
you ~ weißt du. **11.** nachsehen. **12. let
me ~** warte mal!, laß mich überlegen!
we'll ~ mal sehen.
Verbindungen mit Präpositionen:
see| a·bout v/i sehen nach, sich küm-
mern um: **I'll ~ it** ich werde mich darum
kümmern; sich will mal sehen; **we'll
(soon) ~ that!** F das wollen wir mal
sehen! **~ o·ver, ~ round** v/i sich ein
Haus etc ansehen. **~ through** v/t j-m
durchschauen. **II** v/t j-m hinweghelfen über (acc). **~ to** v/i: **~ it that** dafür
sorgen, daß.
Verbindungen mit Adverbien:
see| off v/t **1.** j-n verabschieden (**at am
Bahnhof etc). **2.** verjagen, -scheuchen. **~
out** v/t **1.** j-n hinausbringen, -begleiten.
2. bis zum Ende (gen) reichen (Vorräte).
see² [~] s **1.** Bistum n, Diözese f. **2. Holy
⌷** der Heilige Stuhl.
seed [siːd] **I** s **1.** ♀ Same(n) m; ✒
Saat(gut n) f: **go** (od. **run**) **to ~** schießen;
fig. herunterkommen (Person); **→ sow**
1. 2. (Orangen- etc)Kern m. **3.** Sport:
gesetzter Spieler. **II** v/t **4.** besäen. **5.**
Sport: Spieler setzen. **III** v/i **6.** ♀ schie-

ßen. **'~bed** s **1.** Saatbeet n. **2.** fig. Brutstätte f.
seed·less ['siːdlɪs] adj kernlos (Orangen
etc).
'seed·y adj □ vergammelt.
see·ing ['siːɪŋ] cj a. **~ that** da.
seek [siːk] (irr) **I** v/t **1.** Schutz, Zuflucht,
Wahrheit etc suchen: **~ s.o.'s advice,
advice from s.o.** j-n um Rat bitten, Rat
bei j-m suchen. **2.** streben nach. **3.**
(ver)suchen (**to do** zu tun). **II** v/i **4. ~
after** (od. **for**) suchen (nach).
seem [siːm] v/i **1.** scheinen: **it ~s impossible to me** das (er)scheint mir unmöglich. **2.** impers **it ~s that** es scheint, daß;
anscheinend; **it ~s as if** (od. **though**) es
sieht so aus od. scheint so, als ob.
'seem·ing adj scheinbar. **'seem·ing·ly**
adv **1.** scheinbar. **2.** anscheinend.
seen [siːn] pp von **see¹.**
seep [siːp] v/i sickern.
see-saw ['siːsɔː] s Wippe f, Wippschau-
kel f.
seethe [siːð] v/i fig. kochen: **he was
seething with rage** er kochte od.
schäumte vor Wut.
'see-through adj durchsichtig (Bluse
etc).
seg·ment I s ['segmənt] Teil m, n; Stück
n; biol., ⅋ etc Segment n. **II** v/t
[seg'ment] zerlegen, -teilen.
seg·re·gate ['segrɪgeɪt] v/t (a. nach Rassen, Geschlechtern) trennen. **,seg·re-
'ga·tion** s Trennung f: **~ racial.**
seis·mic ['saɪzmɪk] adj seismisch, Erdbeben...
seis·mo·graph ['saɪzməɡrɑːf] s Seismograph m, Erdbebenmesser m. **seis·
mol·o·gist** [~'mɒlədʒɪst] s Seismologe
m, Seismologin f. **seis'mol·o·gy** s Seis-
mologie f, Seismik f, Erdbebenkunde f.
seize [siːz] **I** v/t **1.** j-n, et. packen (**by** an
dat); Gelegenheit ergreifen; Macht etc
an sich reißen. **2.** j-n festnehmen; et.
beschlagnahmen. **II** v/i **3.** sich
festfressen; (Verkehr) zum Erliegen
kommen. **sei·zure** ['~ʒə] s **1.** Festnahme f; Beschlagnahme f. **2.** ♠ Anfall
m.
sel·dom ['seldəm] adv selten: **~, if ever**
(nur) äußerst selten, kaum jemals.
se·lect [sɪ'lekt] **I** v/t **1.** (aus)wählen (**from**
aus). **II** adj **2.** ausgewählt. **3.** exklusiv.
se'lec·tion s **1.** (Aus)Wahl f. **2.** ✝ etc

Auswahl f (*of* an *dat*). **se'lec·tive** *adj* □ wählerisch (*in* in *dat*).

self [self] *pl* **selves** [selvz] *s* Ich *n*, Selbst *n*: *my humble ~* m-e Wenigkeit; *one's true ~* sein wahres Wesen; *he is back to his old ~* er ist wieder (ganz) der alte. ˌ~·**ab'sorbed** *adj* mit sich selbst beschäftigt. ˌ~·**ad'dressed** *adj*: *~ envelope* Rückumschlag *m*. ˌ~·**as'sured** *adj* selbstbewußt. ˌ~·**ca·ter·ing** *adj* für Selbstversorger, mit Selbstverpflegung. ˌ~·**cen·tered** *adj Am.*, ˌ~·**cen·tred** *adj bsd. Br.* ichbezogen, egozentrisch. ˌ~·**con·fi·dence** *s* Selbstbewußtsein *n*, -vertrauen *n*. ˌ~·**con·fi·dent** *adj* □ selbstbewußt. ˌ~·**con·scious** *adj* □ befangen, gehemmt. ˌ~·**con'tained** abgeschlossen (*Wohnung, Folge* e-r *Fernsehserie* etc). ˌ~·**con'trol** *s* Selbstbeherrschung *f*. ˌ~·**con'trolled** *adj* selbstbeherrscht. ˌ~·**crit·i·cal** *adj* □ selbstkritisch. ˌ~·**crit·i·cism** *s* Selbstkritik *f*. ˌ~·**de'fence** *s Br.*, ˌ~·**de'fense** *s Am.* Selbstverteidigung *f*; 🏛 Notwehr *f*: *in ~* in od. aus Notwehr. '~·**de·ter·mi·na·tion** *s pol.* Selbstbestimmung *f*. ˌ~·**ed·u·cat·ed** *adj*: *~ person* Autodidakt(in). ˌ~·**ef'fac·ing** *adj* □ zurückhaltend. ˌ~·**em'ployed** *adj* (*beruflich*) selbständig. ˌ~·**es'teem** *s* Selbstachtung *f*. ˌ~·**ev·i·dent** *adj* □ **1.** selbstverständlich: *be ~* sich von selbst verstehen. **2.** offensichtlich. ˌ~·**gov·ern·ment** *s pol.* Selbstverwaltung *f*. ˌ~·'**help** *s* Selbsthilfe *f*: *~ group* Selbsthilfegruppe *f*. ˌ~·**im'por·tance** *s* Eigendünkel *m*, Überheblichkeit *f*. ˌ~·**im'por·tant** *adj* □ dünkelhaft, überheblich. ˌ~·**in'vit·ed** *adj* ungebeten (*Gast*).

self·ish ['selfɪʃ] *adj* □ selbstsüchtig, egoistisch. '**self·ish·ness** *s* Selbstsucht *f*, Egoismus *m*.

self·less ['selflɪs] *adj* □ selbstlos. '**self·less·ness** *s* Selbstlosigkeit *f*.

ˌ**self·|·'made** *adj*: *~ man* Selfmademan *m*. ˌ~·**pit·y** *s* Selbstmitleid *n*. ˌ~·**pos'sessed** *adj* □ selbstbeherrscht. ˌ~·**pos·ses·sion** *s* Selbstbeherrschung *f*. ˌ~·**praise** *s* Eigenlob *n*. '~·**pres·er·va·tion** *s* Selbsterhaltung *f*: → **instinct**. ˌ~·**re'li·ant** *adj* □ selbständig. ˌ~·**re'spect** *s* Selbstachtung *f*. ˌ~·**re'spect·ing** *adj*: *no ~ businessman* kein

Geschäftsmann, der et. auf sich hält. ˌ~·**'right·eous** *adj* □ selbstgerecht. ˌ~·**'sat·is·fied** *adj* selbstzufrieden. ˌ~·**'seal·ing** *adj* selbstklebend (*Briefumschlag*). ˌ~·**'ser·vice** **I** *s* Selbstbedienung *f*. **II** *adj* Selbstbedienungs..., mit Selbstbedienung. ˌ~·**'suf'fi·cient** *adj* □ ✝ autark. ˌ~·**'sup'port·ing** *adj* **1.** finanziell unabhängig: *be ~ a.* sich selbst tragen. **2.** ⚙ freitragend (*Mast*); selbsttragend (*Mauer*). ˌ~·**'willed** *adj* eigensinnig, -willig.

sell [sel] (*irr*) **I** *v/t* **1.** verkaufen (*to* an *acc*; *for* für), ✝ *a.* a) absetzen, b) führen, vertreiben: *~ o.s.* sich verkaufen (*a. contp.*); → *river*. **2.** verkaufen, e-n guten Absatz sichern (*dat*). **3.** F et. schmackhaft machen (*to s.o.* j-m); *j-n* begeistern, gewinnen (*on s.th.* für et.): *be sold on* begeistert sein von. **II** *v/i* **4.** verkaufen: *~ by ...* mindestens haltbar bis ... **5.** verkauft werden (*at, for* für): *~ at £5 a.* 5 Pfund kosten. **6.** sich *gut* etc verkaufen (lassen), gehen: → *cake* 1. *Verbindungen mit Adverben:*

sell off *v/t* (*bsd.* billig) abstoßen. *~ out* **I** *v/t* **1.** ausverkaufen: *be sold out* ausverkauft sein (*a. Stadion* etc); *we are sold out of umbrellas* Schirme sind ausverkauft. **II** *v/i* **2.** *the umbrellas sold out in two days* die Schirme waren in zwei Tagen ausverkauft. **3.** F *contp.* sich verkaufen (*to* an *acc*). *~ up Br.* **I** *v/t* sein *Geschäft* etc verkaufen. **II** *v/i* sein Geschäft etc verkaufen.

'sell-by date *s* Mindesthaltbarkeitsdatum *n*.

sell·er ['selə] *s* **1.** Verkäufer(in). **2.** *be a good ~* sich gut verkaufen, gut gehen.

'sell-out *s* ausverkaufte Veranstaltung.

selves [selvz] *pl von* **self.**

se·man·tic [sɪ'mæntɪk] *ling.* **I** *adj* (*~ally*) semantisch. **II** *s pl* (*mst sg* konstruiert) Semantik *f*.

sem·blance ['sembləns] *s* Anschein *m* (*of* von).

se·men ['siːmen] *s physiol.* Samen(flüssigkeit *f*) *m*, Sperma *n*.

se·mes·ter [sɪ'mestə] *s univ.* Semester *n*.

semi... ['semɪ] halb..., Halb...

sem·i ['semɪ] *s Br.* → *semidetached* II. **2.** *Am.* → *semitrailer*.

semi·|·breve ['semɪbriːv] *s* ♪ *Br.* ganze Note. '~·**cir·cle** *s* Halbkreis *m*. ˌ~·**cir-**

cu·lar adj □ halbkreisförmig. ˌ∿'**colon** s ling. Semikolon n, Strichpunkt m. ˌ∿·**con'duc·tor** s ⚡ Halbleiter m. ˌ∿·**de'tached** I adj: ∼ **house** → II. II s Doppelhaushälfte f. ˌ∿'**fi·nals** s pl Sport: Semi-, Halbfinale n.

sem·i·nar ['seminɑː] s univ. Seminar n.

sem·i·nar·y ['seminəri] s Priesterseminar n.

ˌ**sem·i·of'fi·cial** adj □ halbamtlich, offiziös. ˌ∿·**pre·cious** adj: ∼ **stone** Halbedelstein m. ˌ∿'**skilled** adj angelernt (Arbeiter).

Sem·ite ['siːmaɪt] s Semit(in). **Se·mit·ic** [sɪ'mɪtɪk] adj semitisch.

sem·o·li·na [ˌsemə'liːnə] s Grieß m.

sen·ate ['senɪt] s Senat m. **sen·a·tor** ['senətə] s Senator m.

send [send] (irr) I v/t **1.** j-n schicken (**to bed** ins Bett; **to prison** ins Gefängnis): ∼ **s.o. after s.o.** j-n j-m nachschicken. **2.** (**to**) et., a. Grüße, Hilfe etc senden, schicken (dat od. an acc), Ware etc versenden, -schicken (an acc). **3.** mit adj od. pres p: machen: ∼ **s.o. mad** j-n wahnsinnig machen; → **pack** 15. II v/i **4.** ∼ **for** a) nach j-m schicken, j-n kommen lassen, b) sich et. kommen lassen, et. anfordern.

Verbindungen mit Adverbien:

send| **a·way** I v/t **1.** fort-, wegschicken. **2.** Brief etc absenden, abschicken. II v/i **3.** ∼ **for** → send 4b. ∼ **back** v/t **1.** zurückschicken, Speise a. zurückgehen lassen. ∼ **down** v/t **1.** hinunter-, herunterschicken. **2.** univ. Br. relegieren. **3.** fig. Preise, Temperatur etc fallen lassen. ∼ **in** v/t einsenden, einschicken, einreichen: → **resignation** 1. ∼ **off** I v/t **1.** → send away 1. **2.** j-n verabschieden. **3.** Sport: vom Platz stellen. II v/i **4.** → send away II. ∼ **on** v/t **1.** Gepäck etc vorausschicken. **2.** Brief etc nachschicken, -senden (**to** an e-e Adresse). ∼ **out** I v/t **1.** hinausschicken. **2.** Wärme etc ausstrahlen. **3.** Einladungen, Prospekte etc verschicken. II v/i **4.** ∼ **for s.th.** et. holen lassen. ∼ **up** v/t **1.** hinauf-, heraufschicken. **2.** fig. Preise, Temperatur etc steigen lassen. **3.** Br. F parodieren, verulken.

send·er ['sendə] s Absender(in): → **return** 2.

'**send**·**off** s F Verabschiedung f. '∿·**up** s

Br. F (**of**) Parodie f (auf acc), Verulkung f (gen): **do a** ∼ **of** → send up 3.

se·nile ['siːnaɪl] adj senil. **se·nil·i·ty** [sɪ'nɪlətɪ] s Senilität f.

sen·ior ['siːnjə] I adj **1.** senior. **2.** älter (**to** als): ∼ **citizens** pl Senioren pl. **3.** dienstälter; ranghöher (**to** als): ∼ **partner** ✝ Senior(partner) m. **4.** ∼ **high** (**school**) Am. die oberen Klassen der High-School. II s **5.** Ältere m, f: **he is my** ∼ **by two years, he is two years my** ∼ er ist zwei Jahre älter als ich. **6.** Am. Student(in) im letzten Jahr. **sen·ior·i·ty** [ˌsiːnɪ'ɒrɒtɪ] s **1.** (höheres) Alter. **2.** (höheres) Dienstalter; (höherer) Rang.

sen·sa·tion [sen'seɪʃn] s **1.** Empfindung f; Gefühl n: ∼ **of thirst** Durstgefühl. **2.** Sensation f: **cause** (od. **create**) **a** ∼ großes Aufsehen erregen, für e-e Sensation sorgen. **sen'sa·tion·al** [∿ʃənl] adj □ **1.** sensationell, Sensations... **2.** F phantastisch, sagenhaft. **sen'sa·tion·al·ism** [∿ʃnəlɪzəm] s **1.** Sensationsgier f. **2.** Sensationsmache f.

sense [sens] I s **1.** physiol. Sinn m: ∼ **of hearing** (**sight, smell, taste, touch**) Gehör-(Gesichts-, Geruchs-, Geschmacks-, Tast)sinn; → **sixth** 1. **2.** pl (klarer) Verstand m: **bring s.o. to his** ∼**s** j-n zur Besinnung od. Vernunft bringen; **come to one's** ∼**s** zur Besinnung od. Vernunft kommen. **3.** Vernunft f, Verstand m: **have the** ∼ **to do s.th.** so klug sein, et. zu tun; → **common sense, horse sense. 4.** Gefühl n, Empfindung f: ∼ **of security** Gefühl der Sicherheit. **5.** Sinn m, Gefühl n (**of** für): ∼ **of duty** Pflichtgefühl; → **humour** 1. **6.** Sinn m, Bedeutung f: **in a** ∼ in gewisser Hinsicht. **7.** Sinn m (et. Vernünftiges): **make** ∼ e-n Sinn ergeben; vernünftig sein; **I could make no** ∼ **of it** ich konnte mir darauf keinen Reim machen. II v/t **8.** fühlen, spüren. '**sense·less** adj □ **1.** besinnungs-, bewußtlos. **2.** sinnlos, unsinnig.

sense or·gan s Sinnesorgan n, -werkzeug n.

sen·si·bil·i·ty [ˌsensɪ'bɪlətɪ] s **1.** Empfindlichkeit f: ∼ **to pain** Schmerzempfindlichkeit. **2.** Feingefühl n, Zartgefühl n. **sen·si·ble** [∿səbl] adj □ **1.** vernünftig. **2.** spürbar, merklich. **3.** praktisch (Kleidungsstück).

sen·si·tive ['sensɪtɪv] *adj* □ **1.** sensibel, empfindsam; empfindlich: **be ~ to** empfindlich reagieren auf (*acc*). **2.** einfühlsam. **3.** empfindlich (*a.* ◉): **~ to pain** schmerzempfindlich. **4.** heikel (*Thema etc*).

sen·sor ['sensə] *s* ⚡, ◉ Sensor *m.*

sen·so·ry ['sensərɪ] *adj* sensorisch, Sinnes...

sen·su·al ['sensjʊəl] *adj* □ sinnlich. **'sen·su·al·ist** *s* sinnlicher Mensch. **sen·su·al·i·ty** [,~'ælətɪ] *s* Sinnlichkeit *f.*

sen·su·ous ['sensjʊəs] *adj* □ sinnlich.

sent [sent] *pret u. pp von* **send.**

sen·tence ['sentəns] I *s* **1.** *ling.* Satz *m.* **2.** ⚖ Strafe *f*; Urteil *n*: **pass ~** das Urteil fällen (**on** über *acc*). II *v/t* **3.** ⚖ verurteilen (**to** zu).

sen·ten·tious [sen'tenʃəs] *adj* □ moralisierend.

sen·tient ['senʃnt] *adj* □ empfindungsfähig.

sen·ti·ment ['sentɪmənt] *s* **1.** Gefühle *pl*; Sentimentalität *f.* **2.** *a.* **pl** Ansicht *f*, Meinung *f.* **sen·ti·men·tal** [,~'mentl] *adj* □ gefühlvoll, gefühlsbetont; sentimental: **for ~ reasons** aus Sentimentalität; **~ value** Erinnerungswert *m.* **sen·ti·men·tal·i·ty** [,~men'tælətɪ] *s* Sentimentalität *f.*

sen·try ['sentrɪ] *s* ✕ Wache *f*, (Wach[t]-) Posten *m*. **~ box** *s* Wachhäuschen *n.*

sep·a·ra·ble ['sepərəbl] *adj* □ trennbar. **sep·a·rate** I *v/t* ['sepəreɪt] **1.** *allg.* trennen (**from** von); **be ~d** getrennt leben (**from** von). **2.** (auf-, ein-, zer)teilen (**into** in *acc*). II *v/i* ['sepəreɪt] **3.** sich trennen (*a. Ehepaar*). III *adj* □ ['seprət] **4.** getrennt, separat. **5.** einzeln, gesondert, Einzel...: **charge s.th. ~ly** et. extra berechnen. **6.** verschieden. **sep·a·ra-tion** [,sepə'reɪʃn] *s* **1.** Trennung *f.* **2.** (Auf-, Ein-, Zer)Teilung *f*: **~ of powers** *pol.* Gewaltenteilung *f.* **sep·a·ra·tism** ['~rətɪzəm] *s pol.* Separatismus *m.* **'sep·a·ra·tist** *pol.* I *s* Separatist(in). II *adj* separatistisch.

Sep·tem·ber [sep'tembə] *s* September *m*: **in ~** im September.

se·quel ['si:kwəl] *s* **1.** Nachfolgefilm *m*, -roman *m.* **2.** *fig.* Folge *f* (**to** von *od.* gen); Nachspiel *n.*

se·quence ['si:kwəns] *s* **1.** (Aufeinander)Folge *f*: **the ~ of events** der Ablauf

der Ereignisse; **~ of tenses** Zeitenfolge. **2.** (Reihen)Folge *f*: **in ~** der Reihe nach. **3.** Folge *f*, Reihe *f*, Serie *f*: **~ of wins** Siegesserie. **4.** *Film, TV*: Sequenz *f*, Take *m, n.*

se·quoi·a [sɪ'kwɔɪə] *s* ♀ Mammutbaum *m.*

se·ra ['sɪərə] *pl von* **serum.**

ser·e·nade [,serə'neɪd] ♪ I *s* Serenade *f*; Ständchen *n.* II *v/t* j-m ein Ständchen bringen.

se·rene [sɪ'ri:n] *adj* □ **1.** heiter, klar (*Himmel, Wetter etc*). **2.** heiter, gelassen (*Person, Gemüt etc*). **3.** *His* ♀ *Highness* S-e Durchlaucht. **se·ren·i·ty** [sɪ'renətɪ] *s* Heiterkeit *f*; Gelassenheit *f.*

serf [sɜːf] *s hist.* Leibeigene *m, f.*

ser·geant ['sɑːdʒənt] *s* **1.** ✕ Feldwebel *m.* **2.** Wachtmeister *m.*

se·ri·al ['sɪərɪəl] I *s* **1.** (Rundfunk-, Fernseh)Serie *f*; Fortsetzungsroman *m.* II *adj* □ **2.** Serien...: **~ novel** Fortsetzungsroman *m.* **3.** serienmäßig, Serien...: **~ number** Seriennummer *f*; ✝ Fabrikationsnummer *f.* **'se·ri·al-ize** *v/t* in Fortsetzungen veröffentlichen *od.* senden.

se·ries ['sɪərɪːz] *pl* **-ries** *s* **1.** Serie *f*, Reihe *f*, Folge *f.* **2.** (Rundfunk-, Fernseh- *etc*)Serie *f*, (Buch-, Vortrags- *etc*-) Reihe *f.*

se·ri·ous ['sɪərɪəs] *adj* **1.** ernst. **2.** ernsthaft, (*Angebot etc a.*) seriös; (*Ratschlag etc*) ernstgemeint: **are you ~?** ist das dein Ernst?; meinst du das im Ernst?; **be ~ about doing s.th.** et. wirklich tun wollen. **3.** ernsthaft, ernstlich (*Schwierigkeiten*), schwer (*Krankheit, Schaden, Verbrechen etc*), schwer, ernstlich (*Bedenken*); ernstzunehmend (*Rivale etc*). **'se·ri·ous·ly** *adv* ernst(haft, -lich); im Ernst: **~ ill** ernstlich *od.* schwer krank; **take ~** j-n, et. ernst nehmen. **'se·ri·ous·ness** *s* **1.** Ernst *m.* **2.** Ernsthaftigkeit *f*, Seriosität *f.* **3.** Schwere *f.*

ser·mon ['sɜːmən] *s* **1.** *eccl.* Predigt *f.* **2.** (Moral-, Straf)Predigt *f.* **'ser·mon·ize** *v/i* Moralpredigten halten.

ser·rat·ed [sɪ'reɪtɪd] *adj* gezackt.

se·rum ['sɪərəm] *pl* **-rums, -ra** ['~rə] *s* Serum *n.*

ser·vant ['sɜːvənt] *s* Diener(in) (*a. fig.*); Dienstbote *m*, -mädchen *n*: → **civil servant.**

serve [sɜ:v] **I** v/t **1.** j-m, s-m Land etc dienen. **2.** j-n, et. versorgen (**with** mit). **3.** a. ~ **up** Essen servieren; Alkohol ausschenken: ~ **s.o.** (**with**) **s.th.** j-m et. servieren. **4.** j-n (im Laden) bedienen: **are you being ~d?** werden Sie schon bedient? **5.** Amtszeit etc durchlaufen; ⚖ Strafe verbüßen. **6.** e-m Zweck dienen, Zweck erfüllen. **7.** ⚖ Vorladung etc zustellen (**on s.o.** j-m). **8.** ~ **s.o. right** F j-m (ganz) recht geschehen. **II** v/i **9.** bsd. ✕ dienen (**under** unter dat): ~ **on a committee** e-m Ausschuß angehören. **10.** servieren. **11.** dienen (**as, for** als): ~ **to do s.th.** dazu dienen, et. zu tun. **12.** Tennis etc: aufschlagen: **XY to** ~ Aufschlag XY. **III** s **13.** Tennis etc: Aufschlag m. **'serv·er** s **1.** Servierlöffel m: (**pair of**) **salad ~s** pl Salatbesteck n. **2.** eccl. Meßdiener m, Ministrant m. **3.** Tennis etc: Aufschläger(in).

ser·vice ['sɜ:vɪs] **I** s **1.** a) Dienst m (**to** an dat): **can I be of any ~ to you?** kann ich Ihnen irgendwie helfen?; **do s.o. a ~** j-m e-n Dienst erweisen; **give good ~** gute Dienste leisten; b) Dienstleistung f (a. ✝). **2.** Service m; Bedienung f. **3.** (Post-, Staats-, Telefon- etc) Dienst m: → **civil service, secret** 1. **4.** pl ✕ Streitkräfte pl. **5.** Betrieb m: **be out of ~** außer Betrieb sein. **6.** eccl. Gottesdienst m. **7.** (Kaffee- etc)Service n. **8.** ⊙ Wartung f, mot. Inspektion f: **put one's car in for a ~** s-n Wagen zur Inspektion bringen. **9.** ⚖ Zustellung f (e-r Vorladung etc). **10.** Tennis etc: Aufschlag m. **II** v/t **11.** ⊙ warten: **my car is being ~d** mein Wagen ist bei der Inspektion. **'ser·vice·a·ble** adj □ **1.** brauchbar. **2.** strapazierfähig.

ser·vice| a·re·a s Br. (Autobahn)Raststätte f. ~ **charge** s Bedienung(szuschlag m) f. **~·man** ['~mən] s (irr **man**) **1.** Militärangehörige m. **2.** Wartungstechniker m. ~ **sta·tion** s **1.** (Reparatur)Werkstatt f. **2.** Tankstelle f.

ser·vi·ette [,sɜ:vɪ'et] s bsd. Br. Serviette f.

ser·vile ['sɜ:vaɪl] adj □ servil, unterwürfig; (Gehorsam) sklavisch. **ser·vil·i·ty** [~'vɪlətɪ] s Servilität f, Unterwürfigkeit f.

serv·ing ['sɜ:vɪŋ] s Portion f.

ser·vi·tude ['sɜ:vɪtjuːd] s Knechtschaft f.

ses·a·me ['sesəmɪ] s ♧ Sesam m.

ses·sion ['seʃn] s **1.** ⚖, parl. a) Sitzung f: **be in ~** tagen, b) Sitzungsperiode f. **2.** (einzelne) Sitzung, ✍ a. (einzelne) Behandlung.

set [set] **I** s **1.** Satz m (Briefmarken, Werkzeuge etc), (Möbel- etc)Garnitur f, (Tee- etc)Service n. **2.** (Fernseh-, Rundfunk)Apparat m, (-)Gerät n. **3.** thea. Bühnenbild n: ~ **designer** Bühnenbildner(in). **4.** Tennis etc: Satz m: ~ **point** Satzball m. **5.** (Personen)Kreis m. **6.** (Kopf- etc)Haltung f. **II** adj **7.** festgesetzt, -gelegt: ~ **books** pl (od. **reading**) ped. Pflichtlektüre f; ~ **lunch** (od. **meal**) Br. Menü n. **8.** **be ~ on doing s.th.** (fest) entschlossen sein, et. zu tun; **be dead ~ against s.th.** strikt gegen et. sein. **9.** bereit, fertig: **be all ~** startklar sein; **be all ~ for the journey** reisefertig sein. **10.** starr (Ansichten, Lächeln etc). **III** v/t (irr) **11.** stellen, setzen, legen: → **fire** 1, **music** 1, **trap** 1. **12. the novel is ~ in** der Roman spielt in (dat). **13.** in e-n Zustand versetzen: ~ **s.o. free** j-n auf freien Fuß setzen, j-n freilassen; → **right** 4, etc. **14.** veranlassen (**doing** zu tun): ~ **going** in Gang setzen; ~ **s.o. thinking** j-m zu denken geben; j-m e-n Denkanstoß od. Denkanstöße geben; → **ball**[1] 1. **15.** ⊙ einstellen, Uhr stellen (**by** nach), Wecker stellen (**for** auf acc). **16.** Tisch decken. **17.** Preis, Termin etc festsetzen, -legen; Rekord aufstellen; Präzedenzfall schaffen: → **example** 1. **18.** Edelstein fassen (**in** in dat); Ring etc besetzen (**with** mit). **19.** ✍ Knochen einrichten. **20.** Aufgabe, Frage stellen. **IV** v/i (irr) **21.** untergehen (Sonne etc). **22.** fest werden (Flüssiges), (Zement etc a.) erstarren.

Verbindungen mit Präpositionen:

set| a·bout v/i **1.** sich machen an (acc), et. in Angriff nehmen: ~ **doing s.th.** sich daranmachen, et. zu tun. **2.** F herfallen über (acc). ~ **a·gainst** v/t **1. set one's face** (od. **o.s.**) **against s.th.** sich e-r Sache widersetzen. **2.** j-n aufhetzen gegen. **3.** fig. et. gegenüberstellen (dat): ~ **im** Vergleich zu. ~ **on** v/t Hund, Polizei hetzen auf (acc).

Verbindungen mit Adverbien:

set| a·part v/t j-n unterscheiden, abheben (**from** von). ~ **a·side** v/t **1.** Geld beiseite legen; Zeit reservieren, einpla-

severity

nen. **2.** *Plan etc* fallenlassen. **3.** ⚖️ *Urteil etc* aufheben. **~ back** *v/t* **1.** verzögern; *j-n, et.* zurückwerfen (**by two months** um zwei Monate). **2. the car set me back £500** F der Wagen hat mich 500 Pfund gekostet *od.* um 500 Pfund ärmer gemacht. **~ by** → **set aside** 1. **~ down** *v/t* **1.** *Last* absetzen, abstellen, *Fahrgast* absetzen, aussteigen lassen. **2.** (schriftlich) niederlegen. **~ in** *v/i* einsetzen (*Winter etc*). **~ off I** *v/t* **1.** hervorheben, betonen, besser zur Geltung bringen. **2.** *Alarm, Lawine, Streik etc* auslösen. **3.** *Sprengladung* zur Explosion bringen; *Feuerwerk* abbrennen. **II** *v/i* **4.** → **set out** 3. **~ out I** *v/t* **1.** arrangieren, herrichten, *a. Schachfiguren etc* aufstellen. **2.** (schriftlich) darstellen. **II** *v/i* **3.** aufbrechen, sich aufmachen. **4. ~ to do s.th.** sich daranmachen, et. zu tun. **~ up I** *v/t* **1.** *Denkmal, Straßensperren etc* errichten; *Gerät etc* aufbauen. **2.** *Firma etc* gründen: → **shop** 1. **3.** *et.* auslösen, verursachen. **4.** *j-n* versorgen (**with** mit): **be well ~ with** (*od.* **for**) **reading** mit Lektüre eingedeckt sein. **5.** *Rekord* aufstellen. **6.** F in e-e Falle locken, reinlegen. **7. set o.s. up** → 9. **8. set o.s. up as** sich ausgeben für *od.* als; sich aufspielen als. **II** *v/i* **9.** sich niederlassen (**as** als).

'**set|·back** *s* Rückschlag *m* (**to** für). **~ square** *s* Winkel *m*, Zeichendreieck *n*.

set·tee [se'ti:] *s* Sofa *n*.

set·ting ['setɪŋ] *s* **1.** (*Gold- etc*)Fassung *f*. **2.** Untergang *m* (*der Sonne etc*). **3.** Umgebung *f*; Schauplatz *m* (*e-s Films etc*): **the novel has its ~ in** → **set** 12.

set·tle ['setl] **I** *v/i* **1.** (**on**) sich niederlassen (auf *acc, dat*) *od.* setzen (auf *acc*). **2.** sich beruhigen (*Person, Magen etc*), sich legen (*Aufregung etc*): → **dust** 1. **3.** sich niederlassen (**in** in e-r Stadt etc). **4.** sich einigen. **5.** sich setzen (*Kaffee etc*); sich senken (*Boden etc*). **6. ~ for** sich zufriedengeben *od.* begnügen mit. **7. ~ into** sich eingewöhnen in (*dat*). **8. ~ on** sich einigen auf (*acc*). **II** *v/t* **9. ~ o.s.** → 1. **10.** *j-n, Nerven etc* beruhigen. **11.** vereinbaren; *Frage etc* klären, entscheiden: **that ~s it** damit ist der Fall erledigt. **12.** *Streit etc* beilegen. **13.** *Land* besiedeln; *Leute* ansiedeln. **14.** *Rechnung* begleichen, bezahlen; *Konto*

ausgleichen; *Schaden* regulieren: → **account** 12. **15.** *s-e Angelegenheiten* in Ordnung bringen.

Verbindungen mit Adverbien:

~ down I *v/i* **1.** → **settle** 1, 2. **2.** seßhaft werden. **3. ~ in** → **settle** 7. **II** *v/t* **4.** → **settle** 10. **5. settle o.s. down** → **settle** 1. **~ in** *v/i* sich eingewöhnen; sich einleben. **~ up** *v/i* **1.** (be)zahlen. **2.** abrechnen (**with** mit).

set·tled ['setld] *adj* **1.** beständig (*Wetter*). **2.** fest (*Ansichten etc*).

set·tle·ment ['setlmənt] *s* **1.** Vereinbarung *f*; Klärung *f*. **2.** Beilegung *f*. **3.** Einigung *f*: **reach a ~** sich einigen (**with** mit). **4.** Siedlung *f*; Besiedlung *f*. **5.** Begleichung *f*, Bezahlung *f*; Ausgleich *m*; Regulierung *f*.

set·tler ['setlə] *s* Siedler(in).

'**set·up** *s* **1.** Aufbau *m*, Organisation *f*. **2.** Zustände *pl*. **3.** F abgekartete Sache; Falle *f*.

sev·en ['sevn] **I** *adj* sieben. **II** *s* Sieben *f*: **~ of hearts** Herzsieben. **sev·en·fold** ['~fəʊld] **I** *adj* siebenfach. **II** *adv* siebenfach, um das Siebenfache: **increase ~** (sich) versiebenfachen. **sev·en·teen** [,~'ti:n] *adj* siebzehn. **sev·en·teenth** [~θ] *adj* siebzehnt. **sev·enth** ['sevnθ] **I** *adj* **1.** siebente(r, -s), siebte(r, -s). **II** *s* **2.** der, die, das Sieb(en)te: **the ~ of May** der 7. Mai. **3.** Sieb(en)tel *n*. '**sev·enth·ly** *adv* sieb(en)tens. **sev·en·ti·eth** ['~tɪəθ] *adj* siebzigst.

'**sev·en·time** *adj* siebenfach.

sev·en·ty ['sevntɪ] *adj* siebzig. **II** *s* Siebzig *f*: **be in one's seventies** in Siebzigern sein; **in the seventies** in den siebziger Jahren (*e-s Jahrhunderts*).

sev·er ['sevə] **I** *v/t* **1.** durchtrennen; abtrennen (**from** von). **2.** *Beziehungen etc* abbrechen. **II** *v/i* **3.** (zer)reißen.

sev·er·al ['sevrəl] **I** *adj* mehrere. **II** *s* mehrere *pl*: **~ of you**.

sev·er·ance ['sevərəns] *s* **1.** Durch-, Abtrennung *f*. **2.** *fig.* Abbruch *m*. **~ pay** *s* ✝ Abfindung *f*.

se·vere [sɪ'vɪə] *adj* □ **1.** schwer (*Verletzung, Rückschlag etc*), stark (*Schmerzen*), hart, streng (*Winter*). **2.** streng (*Person, Disziplin etc*). **3.** scharf (*Kritik*): **his ~st critic** a. sein ärgster Kritiker. **se·ver·i·ty** [sɪ'verətɪ] *s* **1.** Schwere *f*, Stärke *f*, Härte *f*, Strenge *f*. **2.** Schärfe *f*.

sew [səʊ] (*mst irr*) **I** *v/t* nähen: **~ on** annähen; **~ up** ver-, zunähen; F *Handel etc* perfekt machen. **II** *v/i* nähen.

sew·age ['suːɪdʒ] *s* Abwasser *n*.

sew·er [sʊə] *s* Abwasserkanal *m*, Kloake *f*. **'sew·er·age** *s* Kanalisation *f*.

sew·ing ['səʊɪŋ] **I** *s* **1.** Nähen *n*. **2.** Näharbeit *f*, Näherei *f*. **II** *adj* **3.** Näh...: **~ machine**.

sewn [səʊn] *pp von* **sew**.

sex [seks] **I** *s* **1.** Geschlecht *n*: **of both ~es** beiderlei Geschlechts; **the fair** (**gentle** *od.* **weaker, opposite, stronger**) **~** das schöne (schwache *od.* zarte, andere, starke) Geschlecht. **2.** Sex *m*: a) Sexualität *f*, b) Sex-Appeal *m*, c) Geschlechtsverkehr *m*: **have ~ with** schlafen mit. **II** *adj* **3.** a) Sexual...: **~ crime** (**life**, *etc*); **~ object** Sexual-, Lustobjekt *n*, b) Geschlechts...: **~ organ**, *etc* c) Sex...: **~ bomb** (**film**, *etc*); **~ appeal** Sex-Appeal *m*.

sex·ism ['seksɪzəm] *s* Sexismus *m*. **'sex·ist** *s* **I** Sexist(in). **II** *adj* sexistisch.

sex·tet(te) [seks'tet] *s* ♩ Sextett *n*.

sex·ton ['sekstən] *s eccl.* Küster *m* (u. Totengräber *m*).

sex·u·al ['seksʊəl] *adj* □ sexuell, Sexual..., geschlechtlich, Geschlechts...: **~ intercourse** Geschlechtsverkehr *m*. **sex·u·al·i·ty** [‿'ælɪtɪ] *s* Sexualität *f*.

sex·y ['seksɪ] *adj* □ F sexy, (*a. Gang etc*) aufreizend.

shab·by ['ʃæbɪ] *adj* □ *allg.* schäbig.

shack [ʃæk] **I** *s* Hütte *f*, Baracke *f*. **II** *v/i*: **~ up** F zs.-leben (**with** mit).

shack·les ['ʃæklz] *s pl* Fesseln *pl*, Ketten *pl* (*beide a. fig.*).

shade [ʃeɪd] **I** *s* **1.** Schatten *m*: **put in(to) the ~** *fig.* in den Schatten stellen. **2.** (*Lampen*)Schirm *m*. **3.** *pl*, *a.* **pair of ~s** F Sonnenbrille *f*. **4.** (*Farb*)Ton *m*. **5.** *fig.* Nuance *f*: **~ of meaning** Bedeutungsnuance *f*. **6.** *a.* **~** *fig.* ein bißchen: **a ~ (too) loud** e-e Spur zu laut. **II** *v/t* **7.** abschirmen (**from** gegen *Licht etc*). **III** *v/i* **8.** *a.* **~ off** (allmählich) übergehen (**into** in *acc*).

shad·ow ['ʃædəʊ] **I** *s* **1.** Schatten *m*: **be in s.o.'s ~** *fig.* in j-s Schatten stehen; **be only a ~ of one's former self** *fig.* nur noch ein Schatten s-r selbst sein; **cast a**

~ over (*od.* **on**) *fig.* e-n Schatten werfen auf (*acc*). **2.** *fig.* Schatten *m* (*Person*). **3.** **there's not a** (*od.* **the**) **~ of doubt about it** *fig.* daran besteht nicht der geringste Zweifel. **II** *v/t* **4.** *j-n* beschatten. **~ cab·i·net** *s pol.* Schattenkabinett *n*.

shad·ow·y ['ʃædəʊɪ] *adj* **1.** schattig, dunkel. **2.** *fig.* geheimnisvoll, -umwittert.

shad·y ['ʃeɪdɪ] *adj* **1.** schattig; schattenspendend. **2.** F zwielichtig (*Person*), zweifelhaft (*Geschäft etc*).

shaft [ʃɑːft] *s* **1.** (*Pfeil- etc*)Schaft *m*. **2.** (*Hammer- etc*)Stiel *m*. **3.** (*Aufzugs-, Bergwerks- etc*)Schacht *m*.

shag·gy ['ʃægɪ] *adj* □ zottig, zott(e)lig.

shake [ʃeɪk] **I** *s* **1.** Schütteln *n*: **with a ~ of one's head** mit e-m Kopfschütteln; **give s.th. a good ~** et. gut durchschütteln; **in two ~s**, **in half a ~** F sofort. **2.** Shake *m*, Mixgetränk *n*. **3.** **he's got the ~s** F er hat den *od.* e-n Tatterich. **4.** **be no great ~s** F nicht gerade umwerfend sein (**at** in *dat*; **as** als). **II** *v/i* (*irr*) **5.** wackeln; zittern (**with** vor *dat*): **~ with laughter** sich vor Lachen schütteln; **let's ~ on it** F Hand drauf! **III** *v/t* (*irr*) **7.** schütteln: **~ one's head** den Kopf schütteln; **~ one's fist at s.o.** j-m mit der Faust drohen; **~ a leg** F Dampf *od.* Tempo machen; → **hand** 1. **8.** *fig. a*) *j-n* erschüttern: **he was badly ~n by the accident** der Unfall hat ihn arg mitgenommen, b) *j-s Glauben etc* erschüttern.

Verbindungen mit Adverbien:

shake| down F **I** *v/i* **1.** sich eingewöhnen *od.* einleben. **2.** kampieren (**on the floor** auf dem Fußboden). **II** *v/t* **3.** *bsd. Am. j-n* ausnehmen *od.* erpressen. **4.** *Am. j-n* filzen, durchsuchen (**for** nach). **~ off** *v/t* Staub, Verfolger *etc* abschütteln, *Besucher, Erkältung etc* loswerden. **~ out** *v/t* ausschütteln. **~ up** *v/t* **1.** Kissen *etc* aufschütteln. **2.** Flasche *etc* durchschütteln. **3.** → **shake** 8a.

'shake-down *s* **1.** (Not)Lager *n*. **2.** *bsd. Am.* Gaunerei *f*; Erpressung *f*. **3.** *Am.* Filzung *f*, Durchsuchung *f*.

shak·en ['ʃeɪkən] *pp von* **shake**. **'shak·er** *s* Shaker *m*, Mixbecher *m*; *Am.* (*Salz-*)Streuer *m*.

'shake-up *s*: **there's been a big ~ in our firm** in unserer Firma ist kräftig aufgeräumt worden □

shak·y ['ʃeɪkɪ] adj □ wack(e)lig (*Person, Stuhl etc*).

shale [ʃeɪl] s geol. Schiefer m.

shall [ʃæl] v/aux (irr) **1.** Futur: *ich werde, wir werden*. **2.** in (*Entscheidungs*)*Fragen*: *soll ich ...?*, *sollen wir ...?*: **~ we go?** gehen wir?

shal·low ['ʃæləʊ] **I** adj □ seicht, flach (*beide a. fig.*). **II** s, oft pl seichte od. flache Stelle, Untiefe f.

sham [ʃæm] **I** s **1.** Farce f. **2.** Heuchelei f. **II** adj **3.** unecht, falsch (*Juwelen etc*), vorgetäuscht, geheuchelt (*Mitgefühl etc*). **III** v/t **4.** *Mitgefühl etc* vortäuschen, heucheln, *Krankheit etc* simulieren. **IV** v/i **5.** sich verstellen, heucheln: **he's only ~ming** er tut nur so.

sham·bles ['ʃæmblz] s pl (*mst sg konstruiert*): **the room was (in) a ~** F das Zimmer war das reinste Schlachtfeld.

shame [ʃeɪm] **I** s **1.** Scham(gefühl n) f: **have you got no ~?** schämst du dich vor gar nichts? **2.** Schande f: **~!** pfui!; **~ on you!** schäm dich!; pfui!; **put to ~** → 4, 5. **3. what a ~!** (wie) schade!; **it's a ~** (es ist) schade; → **crying 1. II** v/t **4.** Schande machen (*dat*). **5.** beschämen. **~'faced** adj □ betreten, verlegen.

shame·ful ['ʃeɪmfʊl] adj □ **1.** beschämend. **2.** schändlich. **'shame·less** adj □ **1.** schamlos. **2.** unverschämt.

sham·poo [ʃæm'puː] **I** s Shampoo(n) n, Schampon n, Schampun n (*alle a. für Teppiche etc*), Haarwaschmittel n. **II** v/t Teppich etc shampoonieren, schamponieren, schampunieren: **~ one's hair** sich den Kopf od. die Haare waschen.

sham·rock ['ʃæmrɒk] s Shamrock m, Kleeblatt n (*Wahrzeichen Irlands*).

shan·dy ['ʃændɪ] s Bier n mit Zitronenlimonade.

shang·hai [ˌʃæŋ'haɪ] v/t: **~ s.o. into doing s.th.** F j-n zwingen od. mit e-m Trick dazu bringen, et. zu tun.

shank [ʃæŋk] s **1.** ⚙ Schaft m (*e-s Bohrers etc*). **2.** Hachse f (*beim Schlachttier*).

shan't [ʃɑːnt] F *für* shall not.

shan·ty¹ ['ʃæntɪ] s Hütte f, Baracke f.

shan·ty² [~] s Shanty n, Seemannslied n. **'shan·ty·town** s Bidonville n (*Slumviertel*).

shape [ʃeɪp] **I** s **1.** Form f: **in the ~ of** in Form (*gen*) (*a. fig.*); **triangular in ~**

dreieckig; **take ~** fig. Gestalt annehmen. **2.** Gestalt f (*Person*). **3. be in good (bad) ~** (*körperlich, geistig*) in guter (schlechter) Verfassung sein; in gutem (schlechtem) Zustand sein (*Gebäude etc*). **II** v/t **3.** Ton etc formen (**into** zu); et. formen (**from** aus); fig. j-n, j-s *Charakter etc* formen, prägen: **~d like a ~** ...förmig. **III** v/i **4.** mst **~ up** F sich gut etc machen (*Person*): **things are shaping up nicely** es sieht nicht schlecht aus. **shaped** adj geformt, ...förmig. **'shape·less** adj □ **1.** weit; ausgebeult (*Kleidungsstück*). **2.** unförmig (*Person, Gegenstand*). **'shape·ly** adj wohlgeformt (*Beine etc*), wohlproportioniert (*Figur*).

shard [ʃɑːd] s Scherbe f.

share [ʃeə] **I** s **1.** Anteil m (**in, of** an dat): **go ~s** F teilen; **have a (no) ~ in** (nicht) beteiligt sein an (*dat*). **2.** † bsd. Br. Aktie f. **II** v/t **3.** et. teilen (*a. fig.*), sich et. teilen (**with** mit): **~ an apartment** (*bsd. Br. a flat*) wir leben in e-r Wohngemeinschaft; **they ~d second place** sie kamen gemeinsam auf den zweiten Platz. **4.** mst **~ out** verteilen (**among, between** an acc, unter acc). **III** v/i **5.** teilen: **~ in** sich teilen in (*acc*). **shared** adj gemeinsam, Gemeinschafts...

'share|·hold·er s † bsd. Br. Aktionär(in). **'~·out** s Verteilung f.

shark [ʃɑːk] s **1.** ichth. Hai(fisch) m. **2.** F (*Kredit- etc*)Hai m.

sharp [ʃɑːp] **I** adj □ **1.** scharf (*Messer etc, a. Gesichtszüge, Kurve etc*); spitz (*Nadel, Nase etc*). **2.** fig. scharf: a) deutlich (*Gegensatz, Umrisse etc*), b) herb (*Geschmack*), c) schneidend (*Befehl, Stimme*), d) heftig (*Schmerz etc*), (*a. Frost, Wind*) schneidend, e) spitz (*Bemerkung, Zunge*), f) schnell (*Tempo etc*), g) jäh, plötzlich: **brake ~** F scharf bremsen. **3.** fig. scharf (*Augen, Verstand etc*); scharfsinnig, gescheit (*Person etc*). **4.** ~ **practice** unsaubere Geschäfte pl. **II** adv **5. at three o'clock ~** Punkt 3 (Uhr). **6.** ♪ zu hoch: **sing ~. 7. look ~** F sich beeilen: **look ~!** Tempo! **sharp·en** ['~ən] v/t **1.** Messer etc schärfen, schleifen. **2.** Bleistift etc spitzen. **'sharp·en·er** s (*Bleistift*)Spitzer m. **'sharp·ness** s **1.** Schärfe f (*a. fig.*). **2.** fig. Scharfsinn m.

'**sharp,shoot·er** s Scharfschütze m.

shat [ʃæt] pret u. pp von **shit**.

shat·ter ['ʃætə] I v/t 1. zerschmettern, -schlagen, -trümmern. 2. fig. Hoffnungen, Träume etc zerstören. 3. j-n schocken. 4. F j-n schlauchen. II v/i 5. zerspringen, (Glas a.) zersplittern. '**_,proof** adj splitterfrei, -sicher.

shave [ʃeɪv] I v/i 1. sich rasieren. II v/t 2. j-n rasieren. 3. sich die Beine etc rasieren: ~ off sich den Bart abrasieren; Holz abhobeln. 4. j-n, et. streifen. III s 5. Rasur f: **have a** ~ → 1; **that was a close** ~ das war knapp, das hätte ins Auge gehen können. '**shav·en** adj kahlgeschoren. '**shav·er** s (bsd. elektrischer) Rasierapparat. '**shav·ing** s 1. Rasieren n. 2. pl Späne pl. II adj 3. Rasier...: ~ **brush** Rasierpinsel m; ~ **cream** Rasiercreme f; ~ **foam** Rasierschaum m; ~ **soap** Rasierseife f.

shawl [ʃɔːl] s 1. Umhängetuch n. 2. Kopftuch n.

she [ʃiː] I pron sie. II s Sie f: a) Mädchen n, Frau f, b) zo. Weibchen n. III adj in Zssgn zo. ...weibchen n: ...~**bear** Bärin f.

sheaf [ʃiːf] pl **sheaves** [ʃiːvz] s 1. ↗ Garbe f. 2. (Papier- etc)Bündel n.

shear [ʃɪə] I v/t (mst irr) Schaf scheren. II s pl, a. **pair of ~s** (große) Schere.

sheath [ʃiːθ] pl **sheaths** [ʃiːðz] s 1. (Schwert- etc)Scheide f. 2. Kondom n, m. 3. → **sheathing**. **sheathe** [ʃiːð] v/t 1. Schwert etc in die Scheide stecken. 2. ✪ umhüllen, verkleiden, Kabel, Rohr ummanteln. '**sheath·ing** s ✪ Umhüllung f, Verkleidung f, Mantel m.

sheath knife s (irr **knife**) Fahrtenmesser n.

sheaves [ʃiːvz] pl von **sheaf**.

she-bang [ʃɪ'bæŋ] s: **the whole** ~ bsd. Am. F der ganze Laden; die ganze Chose.

shed[1] [ʃed] v/t (irr) 1. Blut, Tränen etc vergießen. 2. → **light**[1] 3. biol. Blätter etc verlieren, a. Geweih abwerfen: ~ **its skin** sich häuten; ~ **a few pounds** ein paar Pfund abnehmen. 4. fig. Gewohnheit, Hemmungen etc ablegen.

shed[2] [~] s (Geräte etc)Schuppen m; (Kuh- etc)Stall m.

she'd [ʃiːd] F für **she had; she would**.

sheen [ʃiːn] s Glanz m.

sheep [ʃiːp] pl **sheep** s zo. Schaf n (a. fig. Person): **make** ~'s **eyes at s.o.** j-n anschmachten. '~**dog** s Schäferhund m.

sheep·ish ['ʃiːpɪʃ] adj □ verlegen.

'**sheep·skin** s Schaffell n.

sheer [ʃɪə] I adj 1. bloß, rein: **by** ~ **coincidence** rein zufällig. 2. steil, (fast) senkrecht. 3. hauchdünn (Stoff). II adv 4. → 2.

sheet [ʃiːt] s 1. Bettuch n, (Bett)Laken n, Leintuch n: (**as**) **white as a** ~ kreidebleich. 2. Bogen m, Blatt n (Papier). 3. (Glas)Scheibe f. 4. **the rain was coming down in** ~**s** es regnete in Strömen. 5. weite (Eis- etc)Fläche. ~ **light·ning** n. ~ **mu·sic** s Notenblätter pl.

sheik(h) [ʃeɪk] s Scheich m. '**sheik(h)·dom** s Scheichtum n.

shelf [ʃelf] pl **shelves** [ʃelvz] s (Bücheretc)Brett n, (-)Bord n: **shelves** of Regal n; **she has been left on the** ~ fig. F sie ist sitzengeblieben. ~ **life** s ↑ Haltbarkeit f.

shell [ʃel] I s 1. (Austern-, Eier- etc)Schale f, (Erbsen- etc)Hülse f, Muschel(schale) f, (Schnecken)Haus n, (Schildkröten- etc)Panzer m: **come out of one's** ~ fig. aus sich herausgehen. 2. ✗ Granate f. 3. ✔, ♫ Rumpf m. 4. Rohbau m; Gemäuer n, Außenmauern pl. II v/t 5. schälen, enthülsen. 6. ✗ mit Granaten beschießen. 7. (a. v/i) ~ **out** F blechen.

she'll [ʃiːl] F für **she will**.

'**shell-fish** s pl **-fish** s zo. Schal(en)tier n.

shel·ter ['ʃeltə] I s 1. Unterstand m; ✗ Bunker m; Wartehäuschen n (an Bushaltestelle etc); (Obdachlosen- s.o.)Unterkunft f: → **air-raid**. 2. Schutz m; Unterkunft f: **provide** ~ **for** Obdach bieten od. gewähren (dat); **run for** ~ Schutz suchen; **take** ~ sich unterstellen (**under** unter dat). II v/t 3. schützen (**from** vor dat): **a** ~**ed life** ein behütetes Leben. III v/i 4. sich unterstellen.

shelve [ʃelv] v/t 1. Bücher (in ein Regal) einstellen. 2. fig. Plan etc aufschieben, zurückstellen.

shelves [ʃelvz] pl von **shelf**.

shelv·ing ['ʃelvɪŋ] s Regale pl.

she-nan·i·gans [ʃɪ'nænɪgənz] s pl F Blödsinn m, Unfug m.

shep·herd ['ʃepəd] **I** s Schäfer m. **II** v/t j-n führen.

sher·bet ['ʃɜːbət] s 1. Brausepulver n. 2. bsd. Am. → **sorbet** 1.

sher·iff ['ʃerɪf] s Sheriff m.

sher·ry ['ʃerɪ] s Sherry m.

shield [ʃiːld] **I** s Schild m. **II** v/t j-n schützen (**from** vor dat); b.s. j-n decken.

shift [ʃɪft] **I** v/i **1.** sich bewegen: ~ **on one's chair** (ungeduldig etc) auf s-m Stuhl hin u. her rutschen. **2.** umspringen (Wind). **3.** fig. sich verlagern od. verschieben od. wandeln. **4.** F rasen. **5.** → **gear** 1. **II** v/t **6.** et. bewegen, schieben, Möbelstück a. (ver)rücken. **7.** Schuld, Verantwortung (ab)schieben, abwälzen (**onto** auf acc). **8.** Fleck etc entfernen; et. loswerden. **9.** → **gear** 1. **III** s **10.** fig. Verlagerung f, Verschiebung f, Wandel m. **11.** ✞ Schicht f (Zeit u. Arbeiter). ~ **key** s Umschalttaste ♪ (e-r Schreibmaschine). ~ **work·er** s Schichtarbeiter(in).

shift·y ['ʃɪftɪ] adj ☐ verschlagen (Blick etc); zwielichtig (Charakter).

shil·ling ['ʃɪlɪŋ] s Br. hist. Schilling m.

shil·ly-shal·ly ['ʃɪlɪˌʃælɪ] v/i F sich nicht entscheiden können.

shim·mer ['ʃɪmə] **I** v/i schimmern; (Luft) flimmern. **II** s Schimmer m; Flimmern n.

shin [ʃɪn] **I** s anat. Schienbein n. **II** v/i: ~ **up** (**down**) Baum etc hinauf-(herunter)klettern. '~**bone** → **shin** 1.

shine [ʃaɪn] **I** v/i (irr) **1.** scheinen (Sonne etc), leuchten (Lampe etc). **2.** glänzen (**with** vor dat; fig. **at** in dat). **3.** fig. pret u. pp **shined** Schuhe etc polieren. **4.** ~ **a torch** (bsd. Am. **flashlight**) **into** mit e-r Taschenlampe leuchten in (acc). **II** s **5.** Glanz m: **give one's shoes a** ~ s-e Schuhe polieren; **take a** ~ **to s.o.** F j-n gern mögen.

shin·gle[1] ['ʃɪŋɡl] **I** s (Dach)Schindel f. **II** v/t mit Schindeln decken.

shin·gle[2] [~] s grobe Kieselsteine: ~ **beach** Kieselstrand m.

shin·gles ['ʃɪŋɡlz] s pl (sg konstruiert) ✱ Gürtelrose f.

shin·gly ['ʃɪŋɡlɪ] adj kieselig: ~ **beach** Kieselstrand m.

shin·y ['ʃaɪnɪ] adj glänzend, (Ärmel etc a.) abgewetzt, blank.

ship [ʃɪp] **I** s (a. Raum)Schiff n: **when**

my ~ **comes home** (od. **in**) fig. wenn ich das große Los ziehe. **II** v/t verschiffen; allg. verfrachten, -senden. '~**board** s: **on** ~ an Bord. '~**build·er** s Schiff(s)bauer m.

ship·ment s 1. Ladung f. 2. Verschiffung f; allg. Verfrachtung f, Versand m.

'**ship·own·er** s Reeder m, (bsd. Binnenschiffahrt a.) Schiffseigner m.

ship·per ['ʃɪpə] s Spediteur m. '**ship·ping** s 1. → **shipment** 2. **2.** a) Schiffahrt f: ~ **forecast** Seewetterbericht m, b) coll. Schiffsbestand m (e-s Landes).

'**ship**|**·shape** adj tadellos in Ordnung. '~**·wreck** **I** s a) Schiffbruch m: **in a** ~ bei e-m Schiffbruch; **suffer** ~ Schiffbruch erleiden (a. fig.), b) Wrack n. **II** v/t: **be** ~**ed** Schiffbruch erleiden; ~**ed** schiffbrüchig. '~**yard** s (Schiffs)Werft f.

shirk [ʃɜːk] v/i u. v/t sich drücken (vor dat). '**shirk·er** s Drückeberger(in).

shirt [ʃɜːt] s Hemd n: **keep one's** ~ **on** F sich nicht aufregen; → **bet** 4. '~**·sleeve** **I** adj hemdsärmelig. **II** s pl: **in one's** ~**s** in Hemdsärmeln, hemdsärmelig.

shirt·y ['ʃɜːtɪ] adj F: **get** ~ **with s.o.** j-n anschnauzen; **there's no need to get** ~ du mußt mich nicht gleich anschnauzen.

shit [ʃɪt] **I** s **1.** V Scheiße f: **be in the** ~ fig. in der Scheiße sitzen. **2.** **have** (**go for**) **a** ~ V scheißen (gehen). **3.** **he's got the** ~**s** V er hat Dünnschiß od. die Scheißerei. **4.** fig. V Scheiß m: **talk** ~ Scheiß reden. **5.** fig. V Arschloch m. **6.** sl. Shit m (Haschisch). **II** v/i (mst irr) **7.** V scheißen. **III** v/t (mst irr) **8.** V vollscheißen, scheißen in (acc): ~ **o.s.** sich vollscheißen; fig. sich vor Angst fast in die Hosen scheißen.

shiv·er ['ʃɪvə] **I** v/i zittern (**with** vor dat). **II** s Schauer m: **the sight sent** ~**s** (**up and**) **down my spine** bei dem Anblick überlief es mich eiskalt; **he's got the** ~**s** er hat Schüttelfrost; **spiders give me the** ~**s** F ich hab' e-n Horror vor Spinnen.

shoal[1] [ʃəʊl] s Schwarm m (Fische): ~**s pl of** Schwärme pl von (Touristen etc).

shoal[2] [~] s Untiefe f; Sandbank f.

shock[1] [ʃɒk] **I** s **1.** Wucht f (e-r Explosion, e-s Schlags etc). **2.** Schock m (a. ✱): **be in a state of** (od. **suffer from**) ~ unter Schock stehen; **come as** (od. **be**) **a** ~ **to**

s.o. ein Schock für j-n sein. **3.** ✂ Schlag m, (a. ⚡ Elektro)Schock m. **II** v/t **4.** schockieren, empören. **5.** j-m e-n Schock versetzen: be ~ed at (od. by) erschüttert sein über (acc).

shock² [~] s (~ of hair Haar)Schopf m.

shock ab·sorb·er s mot. Stoßdämpfer m.

shock·er ['ʃɒkə] s F Schocker m (Film, Person etc). **'shock·ing** adj □ **1.** schockierend, anstößig. **2.** erschütternd. **3.** F scheußlich.

'shock|·proof adj stoßfest, -sicher. **~ ther·a·py, ~ treat·ment** s ✂ Schocktherapie f. **~-behandlung** f. **~ wave** s Druckwelle f; send ~s through fig. erschüttern.

shod [ʃɒd] pret u. pp von shoe.

shod·dy ['ʃɒdɪ] adj □ **1.** minderwertig (Ware), schlampig (Arbeit). **2.** gemein, schäbig (Trick etc).

shoe [ʃuː] **I** s **1.** Schuh m: be in s.o.'s ~s fig. in j-s Haut stecken; know where the ~ pinches fig. wissen, wo der Schuh drückt; step into (od. fill) s.o.'s ~s fig. j-s Stelle einnehmen. **2.** (Huf)Eisen n. **II** v/t (mst irr) **3.** Pferd beschlagen. **'~·black** s Schuhputzer m. **'~·box** s Schuhkarton m, -schachtel f. **'~·horn** s Schuhlöffel m. **'~·lace** s Schnürsenkel m. **'~·mak·er** s Schuhmacher m, Schuster m. **'~·string** s Schnürsenkel m: start on a ~ fig. praktisch mit nichts anfangen. **'~·tree** s Schuhspanner m.

shone [ʃɒn] pret u. pp von shine.

shoo [ʃuː] v/t j-n, Vögel etc (ver)scheuchen.

shook [ʃʊk] pret von shake.

shoot [ʃuːt] **I** s **1.** Schuß m. **2.** ⚘ Trieb m. **2.** Jagd f; Jagd(revier n) f. **II** v/t (irr) **3.** schießen mit (e-m Gewehr etc). **4.** Pfeil etc abfeuern, abschießen (at auf acc): shoot a glance at e-n schnellen Blick werfen auf (acc); ~ questions at s.o. j-n mit Fragen bombardieren; → bolt¹ 1. **5.** a) hunt. schießen, erlegen: ~ the bull Am. F plaudern, plauschen, b) anschießen, c) niederschießen, d) a. ~ dead erschießen: ~ o.s. sich erschießen. **6.** Riegel vorschieben. **7.** Film etc drehen, a. phot. j-n aufnehmen. **8.** → light¹ 3. **III** v/i (irr) **9.** schießen (at auf acc): ~ at goal (Sport) aufs Tor schießen. **10.** go somewhere to ~ wohin auf die Jagd gehen. **11.** schießen, rasen. **12.** drehen, filmen. **13.** ⚘ treiben.

Verbindungen mit Adverbien:

shoot| down v/t **1.** j-n niederschießen. **2.** j-n, Flugzeug etc abschießen. **3.** F Antrag etc abschmettern, j-n a. abfahren lassen. **~ off** v/t Waffe abfeuern, -schießen: ~ one's mouth F quatschen (Geheimnisse verraten); blöd daherreden. **~ out** v/t: shoot it out sich e-e Schießerei liefern (with mit). **~ up** v/i in die Höhe schießen (Flammen, Kind etc), in die Höhe schnellen (Preise).

shoot·er ['ʃuːtə] s bsd. Br. sl. Schießeisen n.

shoot·ing ['ʃuːtɪŋ] **I** s **1.** Schießen n; Schießerei f. **2.** Erschießung f; Anschlag m. **3.** Film, TV: Dreharbeiten pl, Aufnahmen pl. **II** adj **4.** stechend (Schmerz). **~ gal·ler·y** s Schießbude f. **~ match** s: the whole ~ F die ganze Chose. **~ range** s Schießstand m. **~ star** s ast. Sternschnuppe f.

shop [ʃɒp] **I** s **1.** Laden m, Geschäft n: set up ~ as F sich niederlassen als; shut up ~ F (den Laden) dichtmachen. **2.** Werkstatt f. **3.** Betrieb m, Werk n: talk ~ fachsimpeln; ~ closed (open) shop. **II** v/i **4.** go ~ping einkaufen gehen; ~ around sich informieren, die Preise vergleichen; ~ for sich umsehen nach. **III** v/t **5.** bsd. Br. sl. j-n verpfeifen. **~ as·sist·ant** s Br. Verkäufer(in). **~ floor** s Arbeiter pl (Ggs. Management). **'~·keep·er** s Ladenbesitzer(in), -inhaber(in). **'~·lift·er** s Ladendieb(in). **'~·lift·ing** s Ladendiebstahl m.

shop·per ['ʃɒpə] s Käufer(in). **'shop·ping I** s **1.** Einkaufen n: do one's ~ einkaufen, (s-e) Einkäufe machen. **2.** Einkäufe pl (Sachen). **II** adj **3.** Einkaufs...: ~ bag Einkaufsbeutel m, -tasche f; ~ center (bsd. Br. centre) Einkaufszentrum n; ~ list Einkaufsliste f, -zettel m; ~ mall Am. Einkaufszentrum n; ~ street Geschäfts-, Ladenstraße f; → spree.

'shop|-soiled adj bsd. Br. Ware: angestaubt (a. fig. Ansichten etc). **~ stew·ard** s ✝ gewerkschaftlicher Vertrauensmann. **'~·talk** s Fachsimpelei f. **~ win·dow** s Schaufenster n, Auslage f. **'~·worn** Am. → shop-soiled.

shore¹ [ʃɔː] s Küste f; (*See*)Ufer n: **on ~** ⚓ **an** Land; **~ leave** ⚓ Landurlaub m.

shore² [~] **I** s Stützbalken m, Strebe(balken m) f. **II** v/t mst **~ up** (ab)stützen; fig. Währung etc stützen.

shorn [ʃɔːn] pp von **shear**.

short [ʃɔːt] **I** adj (□ → **shortly**) **1.** räumlich, zeitlich: kurz: **a ~ time ago** vor kurzer Zeit, vor kurzem; **~ and sweet** F kurz u. bündig; **~ holiday** (bsd. Am. **vacation**) Kurzurlaub m; **~ story** Short story f, Kurzgeschichte f; Novelle f; **be ~ for** die Kurzform sein von; **cut ~** Urlaub etc abbrechen; → **notice** 3, **run** 1, **shrift**, **story** 1, **work** 1. **2.** klein (Person). **3. be ~ of** nicht genügend ... haben; **be in ~ supply** ⚓ knapp sein; **~ cash** 2, **money**. **4.** barsch (**with** zu), kurz angebunden. **II** adv **5.** plötzlich, abrupt: **be caught** (od. **taken**) **~** bsd. Br. F dringend mal (verschwinden) müssen; **stop ~ of** (od. **at**) zurückschrecken vor (dat); **stop ~ of doing s.th.** davor zurückschrecken, et. zu tun. **6. fall ~ of** et. nicht erreichen, den Anforderungen etc nicht entsprechen; **run ~** knapp werden, zur Neige gehen; **we are running ~ of bread** uns geht das Brot aus. **sell ~** j-n, et. unterschätzen. **7. ~ of** a) räumlich vor (dat): **three miles ~ of London**, b) fig. außer. **III** s **8. he is called Bill for ~** er wird kurz Bill genannt; **in ~** kurz(um). **9.** pl, a. **pair of ~s** Shorts pl; bsd. Am. (Herren)Unterhose f. **10.** Br. F Kurze m, Schnaps m. **11.** ⚡ F Kurze m. **12.** F Kurzfilm m. **IV** v/t **13.** ⚡ F e-n Kurzen verursachen in (dat); kurzschließen. **V** v/i **14.** ⚡ F e-n Kurzen haben. **'short-age** s Knappheit f, Mangel m (**of** an dat).

short|**-change** v/t **1.** j-m zuwenig (Wechselgeld) herausgeben. **2.** F j-n übers Ohr hauen. **~ cir-cuit** s ⚡ Kurzschluß m. **~ -'cir-cuit I** v/t **1.** ⚡ e-n Kurzschluß verursachen in (dat); kurzschließen. **2.** fig. et. umgehen. **II** v/i **3.** ⚡ e-n Kurzschluß haben. **~ 'com-ings** s pl Unzulänglichkeiten pl, Mängel pl, (a. e-r Person) Fehler pl. **~ cut** s **1.** Abkürzung(sweg m) f: **take a ~** abkürzen. **2.** fig. abgekürztes Verfahren.

short-en [ˈʃɔːtn] **I** v/t kürzen, Kleidungsstück a. kürzer machen, Text a.

zs.-streichen, Leben etc verkürzen. **II** v/i kürzer werden.

'short|**-fall** s Defizit n. **~-'haired** adj kurzhaarig. **'~-hand** s Kurzschrift f, Stenographie f: **do ~** stenographieren; **take down in ~** et. (mit)stenographieren; **~ typist** Stenotypistin f. **~-'hand-ed** adj knapp an Personal od. Arbeitskräften.

short-ie [ˈʃɔːtɪ] s Kleine m, f, contp. Zwerg m.

short| **list** s: **be on the ~** Br. in der engeren Wahl sein. **'~-list** v/t Br. in die engere Wahl nehmen. **'~-lived** adj kurzlebig, fig. a. von kurzer Dauer.

short-ly [ˈʃɔːtlɪ] adv **1.** bald: **~ after** kurz danach. **2.** in kurzen Worten. **3.** barsch. **'short-ness** s **1.** Kürze f. **2.** Barschheit f. **3.** → **shortage**.

short|**-'range** adj **1.** ✕, ✈ Nah..., Kurzstrecken... **2.** kurzfristig. **~-'sight-ed** adj □ ⚕ kurzsichtig (a. fig.). **~-'sleeved** adj kurzärm(e)lig. **~-'staffed** → **shorthanded**. **~-'tempered** adj aufbrausend, hitzig. **'~-term** adj kurzfristig, -zeitig: **~ memory** Kurzzeitgedächtnis n. **~ time** s ⚓ Kurzarbeit f: **be on** (od. **work**) **~** kurzarbeiten. **~ wave** s ⚡, phys. Kurzwelle f. **'~-wave** adj Kurzwellen... **~-wind-ed** [ˌ~ˈwɪndɪd] adj □ kurzatmig.

short-y → **shortie**.

shot¹ [ʃɒt] **I** pret u. pp von **shoot**. **II** adj: **be** (od. **get**) **~ of** F j-n, et. los sein (loswerden).

shot² [~] s **1.** Schuß m: **like a ~** blitzschnell; sofort; **~ across the bows** Schuß vor den Bug (a. fig.); **~ in the dark** fig. Schuß ins Blaue; **~ in the leg** Beinschuß; **call the ~s** F das Sagen haben. **2.** (Fußball etc) Schuß m, (Basketball etc) Wurf m, (Tennis etc) Schlag m. **3.** guter etc Schütze: **big ~** F hohes Tier. **4.** Schrot m, n. **5.** Kugelstoßen: Kugel f. **6.** F Versuch m: **at the first ~** beim ersten Versuch; **I'll have a ~ at it** ich probier's mal. **7.** a) Film, TV: Aufnahme f; Einstellung f, b) phot. F Schnappschuß m, Aufnahme f. **8.** ⚕ F Spritze f. **'~-gun** s Schrotflinte f: **~ wed-ding** F Mußheirat f. **~ put** s Leichtathletik: Kugelstoßen n. **'~-put-ter** s Kugelstoßer(in).

should [ʃʊd] **1.** pret von **shall**, a. allg. ich

sollte, *du* solltest *etc*: *he ~ be home by then* er müßte bis dahin wieder zu Hause sein. **2.** *konditional*: *ich würde, wir würden*: *I ~ go if ...*; → *like*² 1.

shoul·der [ˈʃəʊldə] I s **1.** Schulter *f*: ~ *to* ~ Schulter an Schulter (*a. fig.*); *a ~ to cry on* e-e Schulter zum Ausweinen; *give s.o. the cold ~* j-m die kalte Schulter zeigen; *put one's ~ to the wheel fig.* sich mächtig ins Zeug legen; → *chip* 1, *rub* 3. II *v/t* **2.** schultern; *fig. Kosten, Verantwortung etc* übernehmen. **3.** (mit der Schulter) stoßen; ~ *one's way through* sich e-n Weg bahnen durch. ~ **bag** *s* Schulter-, Umhängetasche *f*. ~ **blade** *s anat.* Schulterblatt *n*. ~ **strap** *s* Träger *m* (*e-s Kleids etc*); Tragriemen *m*.

shouldn't [ˈʃʊdnt] F *für* **should not**.

shout [ʃaʊt] I *v/i* rufen, schreien (*for* nach; *for help* um Hilfe): ~ *at s.o.* j-n anschreien. II *v/t* rufen, schreien: ~ *down* j-n niederbrüllen; ~ *o.s. hoarse* sich heiser schreien; → *rooftop*. III *s* Ruf *m*, Schrei *m*: ~*s pl of joy* Freudengeschrei *n*; *it's my ~ Br.* F das ist m-e Runde, ich bin dran. **'shout·ing** *s* Schreien *n*, Geschrei *n*: *it's all over bar the ~ Br.* F die Sache ist so gut wie gelaufen.

shove [ʃʌv] I *v/t* **1.** stoßen, schubsen: ~ *about* (*od. around*) j-n herumschubsen (*a. fig.*). **2.** *et.* schieben, stopfen (*into in acc*). II *v/i* **3.** stoßen, schubsen: ~ *off* (vom Ufer) abstoßen; ~ *off!* F schieb ab!; ~ *over bsd. Br.* F rutschen. III *s* **4.** Stoß *m*, Schubs *m*.

shov·el [ˈʃʌvl] I *s* Schaufel *f*. II *v/t pret u. pp* **-eled**, *bsd. Br.* **-elled** schaufeln: ~ *food into one's mouth* Essen in sich hineinschaufeln.

show [ʃəʊ] I *s* **1.** *thea. etc* Vorstellung *f*, Show *f*; (*Rundfunk, TV*) Sendung *f*: *steal the ~ from s.o. fig.* j-m die Schau stehlen. **2.** Ausstellung *f*: *be on* ~ ausgestellt *od.* zu besichtigen sein. **3.** Zurschaustellung *f*, Demonstration *f*. **4.** *by ~ of hands* durch Handzeichen. **5.** Schau *f*: *make a ~ of* Anteilnahme *etc* heucheln; *make a ~ of interest* sich interessiert geben. **6.** F *gute etc* Leistung: *put up a poor ~* e-e schwache Leistung zeigen. **7.** F Laden *m*: *run the ~* den Laden schmeißen. II *adj* **8.** Mu-

ster...: ~ *house*. III *v/t* (*mst irr*) **9.** *a. fig.* Gefühle *etc* zeigen, *Fahrkarte etc* a. vorzeigen, *Zeit etc* anzeigen (*Uhr etc*): ~ *s.o. how to do s.th.* j-m zeigen, wie man et. macht; ~ *s.o. to* sich erweisen als; ~ *s.o. to door* 1, *etc*. **10.** *j-n* bringen, führen (*to* zu): ~ *s.o. (a)round* (*od. over*) *the house* j-n durchs Haus führen, j-m das Haus zeigen. **11.** ausstellen, zeigen. **12.** zeigen: a) *thea. etc* vorführen, b) *TV* bringen. IV *v/i* (*mst irr*) **13.** zu sehen sein: *it ~s* man sieht es. **14.** *be ~ing* gezeigt werden, laufen.

Verbindungen mit Adverbien:

show| a·round *v/t* herumführen. ~ **in** *v/t* herein-, hineinführen, -bringen. ~ **off** I *v/t* **1.** angeben *od.* protzen mit (*to* vor *dat.*). **2.** Figur *etc* vorteilhaft zur Geltung bringen. II *v/i* **3.** angeben, protzen. ~ **out** *v/t* heraus-, hinausführen, -bringen. ~ **round** → **show around.** ~ **up** I *v/t* **1.** herauf-, hinaufführen, -bringen. **2.** sichtbar machen. **3.** *j-n* entlarven; *et.* aufdecken. **4.** *bsd. Br.* j-n in Verlegenheit bringen. II *v/i* **5.** zu sehen sein. **6.** F kommen; aufkreuzen, -tauchen.

show| biz *s* F, ~ **busi·ness** *s* Showbusineß *n*, -geschäft *n*. **'~·case** *s* Schaukasten *m*, Vitrine *f*. **'~·down** *s* Kraft-, Machtprobe *f*.

show·er [ˈʃaʊə] I *s* **1.** (*Regen- etc*)Schauer *m*; (*Funken-, Kugel- etc*)Regen *m*; (*Geschoß-, Stein*)Hagel *m*; (*Wasser-, Wort- etc*)Schwall *m*. **2.** Dusche *f*: *have* (*od. take*) *a* ~ duschen. II *v/i* **3.** duschen. III *v/t* **4.** ~ *s.o. with s.th.*, ~ *s.th. on s.o.* j-n mit et. überschütten, *fig. a.* j-n mit et. überhäufen. ~ **cab·i·net** *s* Duschkabine *f*. ~ **cur·tain** *s* Duschvorhang *m*.

'show·girl *s* Revuegirl *n*. ~ **jump·er** *s Sport:* Springreiter(in). ~ **jump·ing** *s* Springreiten *n*. **'~·man** [~mən] *s* (*irr man*) **1.** *thea. etc* Produzent *m*. **2.** Schausteller *m*. **3.** *fig.* Showman *m*.

shown [ʃəʊn] *pp von* **show.**

'show|-off *s* F Angeber(in). **'~·piece** *s* **1.** Ausstellungsstück *n*. **2.** Parade-, Prunkstück *n*. **'~·room** [ˈ~rʊm] *s* Ausstellungsraum *m*.

show·y [ˈʃəʊɪ] *adj* □ auffallend (*Person*), (*Farben, Kleidung etc a.*) auffällig.

shrank [ʃræŋk] *pret von* **shrink.**

shred [ʃred] **I** s **1.** Fetzen m: *be in ~s* zerfetzt sein; *fig.* ruiniert sein (*Ruf etc*); *tear to ~s* zerfetzen; *fig. Argument etc* zerpflücken, -reißen; *Stück etc* verreißen. **2.** Schnitzel m, m, Stückchen n. **3.** *fig.* not a ~ of doubt nicht der geringste Zweifel; *there is not a ~ of truth in this story* an dieser Geschichte ist kein Wort wahr. **II** v/t (a. irr) **4.** zerfetzen; in den Papier- od. Reißwolf geben. **5.** in (schmale) Streifen schneiden, (*Gemüse a.* schnitzeln, *Fleisch a.* schnetzeln. 'shred·der s **1.** Papier-, Reißwolf m. **2.** Schnitzelmaschine f; Schnitzelwerk n.

shrewd [ʃruːd] adj □ scharfsinnig, klug, (*Beobachter*) scharf: *that was a ~ guess* das war gut geraten.

shriek [ʃriːk] **I** s (schriller) Schrei: ~ *of terror* Entsetzensschrei; ~s pl *of laughter* kreischendes Gelächter. **II** v/i (gellend) aufschreien (*with* vor dat): ~ *with laughter* vor Lachen kreischen.

shrift [ʃrɪft] s: *give s.o. short ~* kurzen Prozeß mit j-m machen.

shrill [ʃrɪl] adj □ **1.** schrill. **2** *fig.* heftig, scharf (*Kritik etc*).

shrimp [ʃrɪmp] s **1.** zo. Garnele f. **2.** *fig. contp.* Knirps m.

shrine [ʃraɪn] s (Reliquien)Schrein m.

shrink [ʃrɪŋk] **I** v/i (irr) **1.** (zs.-, ein)schrumpfen (a. *fig.*), (*Stoff etc a.*) einlaufen, -gehen. **2.** *fig.* abnehmen. **3.** *fig.* zurückschrecken (*from* vor dat): ~ *from doing s.th.* davor zurückschrecken, et. zu tun. **II** v/t (irr) **4.** (zs.-, ein)schrumpfen lassen, *Stoff etc a.* einlaufen lassen. **III** s **5.** F Klapsdoktor m. 'shrink·age s **1.** Schrumpfung f (a. *fig.*), Einlaufen n, -gehen n. **2.** *fig.* Abnahme f. 'shrink·ing adj: ~ *violet* F schüchternes Pflänzchen.

shriv·el ['ʃrɪvl] v/i u. v/t pret u. pp -*eled*, *bsd. Br.* -*elled* runz(e)lig werden (lassen): ~(*l*)*ed* runz(e)lig.

shroud [ʃraʊd] **I** s **1.** Leichentuch n. **2.** *fig.* Schleier m (*of secrecy* des Geheimnisses). **II** v/t **3.** *be ~ed in* in *Nebel etc* gehüllt sein: *be ~ed in mystery* geheimnisumwittert sein.

Shrove Tues·day [ʃrəʊv] s Faschings-, Fastnachtsdienstag m.

shrub [ʃrʌb] s Busch m, Strauch m. 'shrub·ber·y s Busch-, Strauchwerk n.

shrug [ʃrʌg] **I** v/t **1.** ~ *one's shoulders*

→ 3. **2.** ~ *off fig. et.* mit e-m Achsel- od. Schulterzucken abtun, achselzuckend hinweggehen über (*acc*). **II** v/i **3.** mit den Achseln od. Schultern zucken. **III** s **4.** a. ~ *of one's shoulders* Achsel-, Schulterzucken n: *give a* ~ → 3.

shrunk [ʃrʌŋk] pret u. pp von *shrink*.

shuck [ʃʌk] *bsd. Am.* **I** s Hülse f, Schote f; Schale f. **II** v/t enthülsen; schälen. **III** s: ~s! F Quatsch!; Mist!

shud·der ['ʃʌdə] **I** v/i schaudern (*at* bei): ~ *to think of* mit Schaudern denken an (*acc*). **II** s Schauder m.

shuf·fle ['ʃʌfl] **I** v/t **1.** ~ *one's feet* → 3. **2.** *Karten* mischen. **II** v/i **3.** schlurfen. **4.** *Kartenspiel:* mischen. **III** s **5.** Schlurfen n, schlurfender Gang. **6.** Mischen n. '~·board s Shuffleboard n (*Spiel*).

shun [ʃʌn] v/t j-n, et. meiden.

shunt [ʃʌnt] v/t **1.** *Zug etc* rangieren, verschieben. **2.** ~ *off* F j-n abschieben (*to* in *acc, nach*).

shut [ʃʌt] (irr) **I** v/t **1.** *Fenster, Tür etc* zumachen, a. *Fabrik etc* schließen: → *mouth* 1, *trap* 2. **2.** *j-n* einschließen (*in* in *acc, dat*): ~ *one's finger in the door* sich den Finger in der Tür einklemmen. **II** v/i **3.** schließen (a. *Laden etc*), zugehen.

Verbindungen mit Adverbien:

shut| **a·way** v/t **1.** et. wegschließen. **2.** ~ *o.s. away* sich einigeln (*in* in *dat*). ~ *down* v/t *Fabrik etc* schließen, (*für immer a.*) stillegen. **II** v/i schließen (*Fabrik etc*). ~ *off* v/t **1.** *Gas, Maschine etc* abstellen. **2.** abtrennen; fernhalten (*from* von). **II** v/i schließen, abschalten. ~ *out* v/t *Gedanken, Schmerz etc* verdrängen. ~ *up* **I** v/t **1.** *Geschäft* schließen: → *shop* 1. **2.** *j-n* einsperren (*in* in *acc, dat*). **3.** F *j-m* den Mund stopfen. **II** v/i **4.** ~! F halt die Klappe!

'shut·down s Schließung f, (*für immer a.*) Stillegung f. '~·eye s F Schlaf m: *get some* ~ ein paar Stunden schlafen.

shut·ter ['ʃʌtə] s **1.** Fensterladen m. **2.** *phot.* Verschluß m: ~ *speed* Belichtung(szeit) f. 'shut·tered adj: ~ *windows* pl Fenster pl mit Fensterläden; geschlossene Fensterläden; ~ *room* Zimmer n mit geschlossenen Fensterläden.

shut·tle ['ʃʌtl] **I** s **1.** → *shuttle bus* (*service, train*). **2.** (*Raum*)Fähre f,

(-)Transporter *m*. **3.** → *shuttlecock*. **II** *v/t* **4.** hin- u. herbefördern. **~ bus** *s* im Pendelverkehr eingesetzter Bus. '**~-cock** *s* Federball *m*. **~ ser·vice** *s* Pendelverkehr *m*. **~ train** *s* Pendelzug *m*.

shy [ʃaɪ] **I** *adj* □ **1.** scheu (*Tier*), (*Lächeln, Mensch a.*) schüchtern (*of* gegenüber): *fight* **~** *of e-r Sache* aus dem Weg gehen; *fight* **~** *of doing s.th.* sich hüten, et. zu tun. **II** *v/i* **2.** scheuen (*at* vor *dat*) (*Pferd etc*). **3. ~ away** *fig.* zurückschrecken (*from* vor *dat*): **~ away from doing s.th.** davor zurückschrecken, et. zu tun. '**shy·ness** *s* Scheu *f*, Schüchternheit *f*.

shy·ster ['ʃaɪstə] *s Am.* F Winkeladvokat *m*.

Si·a·mese twins [ˌsaɪə'miːz] *s pl* siamesische Zwillinge *pl*.

sick [sɪk] **I** *adj* **1.** krank: *be off* **~** krank (geschrieben) sein; *report* **~** sich krank melden. **2.** *be ~ bsd. Br.* sich übergeben; *he was* (*od. felt*) **~** ihm war schlecht; *be* **~** *of s.th.* F et. satt haben; *be* **~** (*and tired*) *of doing s.th.* F es (gründlich) satt haben, et. zu tun; *it makes me* **~** mir wird schlecht davon, *a. fig.* es ekelt *od.* widert mich an. **3.** makaber (*Witz etc*), abartig (*Person etc*). **II** *s* **4.** *the* **~** *pl* die Kranken *pl*. **5.** *Br.* F Kotze *f*. **~ bag** *s* ✈ Spucktüte *f*. **~ bay** *s* Krankenzimmer *n* (*e-r Schule etc*), ♣ (*Schiffs*)Lazarett *n*. '**~-bed** *s* Krankenbett *n*.

sick·en ['sɪkən] **I** *v/t j-n* anekeln, anwidern (*beide a. fig.*). **II** *v/i* krank werden: *be* **~***ing for s.th.* et. ausbrüten.

sick·le ['sɪkl] *s* ✦ Sichel *f*.

sick leave *s: be on* **~** krank (geschrieben) sein.

sick·ly ['sɪklɪ] *adj* **1.** kränklich. **2.** matt (*Lächeln*). **3.** widerwärtig (*Geruch etc*). '**sick·ness** *s* **1.** Krankheit *f*. **2.** Übelkeit *f*.

sick·room ['~rʊm] *s* Krankenzimmer *n*.

side [saɪd] **I** *s* **1.** *allg.* Seite *f* (*a. fig.*): *at the* **~** *of the road* am Straßenrand; *at* (*od. by*) *s.o.'s* **~** an j-s Seite; *by* **~** nebeneinander; *on the* **~** nebenbei *verdienen etc*; *his* **~** *of the story* s-e Version der Geschichte; *be on s.o.'s* **~** auf j-s Seite sein *od.* stehen; *be on the right* (*wrong*) **~** *of 50* noch nicht (über) 50 sein; *have s.th. on one's* **~** et. auf s-r Seite haben; *put to one* **~** Geld auf die

Seite legen; *take* **~***s* → 4; *take to one* **~** *j-n* beiseite nehmen; → *safe* 1, *seamy*, *split* 1, *sunny*. **2.** *Sport:* Mannschaft *f*. **II** *adj* **3.** Seiten...: **~ door** (*road, etc*). **III** *v/i* **4.** Partei ergreifen (*with* für; *against* gegen). '**~board** *s* **1.** Sideboard *n*. **2.** *pl Br.* Koteletten *pl*. '**~burns** *Am.* → *sideboard* 2. '**~car** *s* Bei-, Seitenwagen *m*. **~ dish** *s* Beilage *f*. **~ ef·fect** *s* Nebenwirkung *f*. **~ is·sue** *s* Randproblem *n*. '**~-line** *s* **1.** Nebenbeschäftigung *f*. **2.** *Sport:* Seitenlinie *f*. '**~-long** *adj u. adv:* **~ glance** Seitenblick *m*; *look at s.o.* **~** *j-n* von der Seite anschauen. '**~sad·dle I** *s* Damensattel *m*. **II** *adv* im Damensitz. '**~split·ting** *adj* zwerchfellerschütternd. **~ step** *s* Seitenschritt *m*, (*Boxen*) Seitschritt *m*, Sidestep *m*. '**~step I** *v/t* **1.** *e-m Schlag* (durch *e-n* Seit[en]schritt) ausweichen. **2.** *fig. e-r Frage etc* ausweichen. **II** *v/i* **3.** *e-n* Seit(en)schritt machen. '**~swipe I** *s:* *take a* **~** *at* F *j-m* e-n Seitenhieb versetzen. **II** *v/t mot. Am. geparktes Fahrzeug etc* streifen. '**~track** *v/t j-n* ablenken; *et.* abbiegen. '**~walk** *bsd. Am.* → *pavement* 2.

side·ward ['saɪdwəd] **I** *adj* seitlich: **~ jump** Sprung *m* zur Seite. **II** *adv* seitwärts, nach der *od.* zur Seite. **side·wards** ['~dz] → *sideward* II. '**~ways** → *sideward*.

si·dle ['saɪdl] *v/i* (sich) schleichen (*out of* aus): **~ up to s.o.** sich an j-n heranschleichen.

siege [siːdʒ] *s* ✕ Belagerung *f*: *lay* **~** *to* belagern (*a. fig.*).

si·er·ra [sɪ'erə] *s* Sierra *f*.

si·es·ta [sɪ'estə] *s* Siesta *f*: *have* (*od. take*) *a* **~** Siesta halten.

sieve [sɪv] **I** *s* Sieb *n*: *put through a* **~** (durch)sieben; *he's got a memory like a* **~** F er hat ein Gedächtnis wie ein Sieb. **II** *v/t* (durch)sieben: **~ out** aussieben (*from* aus).

sift [sɪft] **I** *v/t* **1.** (durch)sieben: **~ out** *fig.* herausfinden (*from* aus). **2.** *fig. Material etc* sichten, durchsehen. **II** *v/i* **3.** **~ through** → 2.

sigh [saɪ] **I** *v/i* (auf)seufzen: **~ with relief** erleichtert aufatmen. **II** *s* Seufzer *m*: **~ of relief** Seufzer der Erleichterung; *breathe* (*od. heave*) *a* **~ of relief** erleichtert aufatmen.

sight [saɪt] **I** s **1.** Sehvermögen n: **have good ~** gute Augen haben, gut sehen; **lose one's ~** das Augenlicht verlieren. **2.** (An)Blick m: **at the ~ of** beim Anblick von (od. gen); **at first ~** auf den ersten Blick; **a ~ for sore eyes** F e-e Augenweide; **you're a ~ for sore eyes** F schön, dich zu sehen; **be** (od. **look**) **a ~** F verboten od. zum Abschießen aussehen; **buy ~ unseen** et. unbesehen kaufen; **catch ~ of** erblicken; **know by ~** j-n vom Sehen kennen; **lose ~ of** aus den Augen verlieren. **3.** Sicht(weite) f: **be** (**with**)**in ~** in Sicht sein (a. fig.); **come into ~** in Sicht kommen; **keep out of ~!** paß auf, daß dich niemand sieht!; **let out of one's ~** j-n, et. aus den Augen lassen. **4.** mst pl Sehenswürdigkeit f. **5.** oft pl Visier n: **set one's ~s on** fig. et. ins Auge fassen. **6.** **a ~** F um einiges, viel besser etc. **II** v/t **7.** sichten. **'sight·ed** adj sehend.

'sight|-read v/t u. v/i (irr read) ♩ vom Blatt singen od. spielen. **'~see** v/i: **go ~ing** sich die Sehenswürdigkeiten anschauen. **'~see·ing** s Sightseeing n, Besichtigung f von Sehenswürdigkeiten: **~ bus** Sightseeing-Bus m; **~ tour** Sightseeing-Tour f, (Stadt)Rundfahrt f.

sign [saɪn] **I** s **1.** allg. Zeichen n, ℞, ♪. Vorzeichen n, fig. a. Anzeichen n: **~s pl of fatigue** Ermüdungserscheinungen pl; **all the ~s are that** dies deutet darauf hin, daß; **there was no ~ of him** von ihm war keine Spur zu sehen; **show ~s of** Anzeichen zeigen von (od. gen); **show only faint ~s of life** nur schwache Lebenszeichen von sich geben. **2.** (Hinweis-, Warn-)Schild n. **3.** (Stern-, Tierkreis)Zeichen n. **II** v/t **4.** unterschreiben, -zeichnen, Bild, Buch signieren; Scheck ausstellen; sich eintragen in (acc): → **autograph** I. 5. Sport: Spieler verpflichten, unter Vertrag nehmen. **III** v/i **6.** unterschreiben, -zeichnen: **~ for** den Empfang (gen) (durch s-e Unterschrift) bestätigen; → **dot** 2. **7.** Sport: unterschreiben (**for, with** bei).
Verbindungen mit Adverbien:
sign| a·way v/t (schriftlich) verzichten auf (acc). **~ in** v/t sich (in e-e Anwesenheitsliste etc) eintragen. **~ off** v/i **1.**

Rundfunk, TV: sein Programm beenden. **2.** Schluß machen (im Brief, a. allg.). **~ on I** v/t **1.** a) → **sign** 5, b) j-n an-, einstellen, ♣ anheuern. **II** v/i **2.** a) → **sign** 7, b) (e-n Arbeitsvertrag) unterschreiben, ♣ anheuern. **3.** Rundfunk, TV: sein Programm beginnen. **~ out** v/i sich (aus e-r Anwesenheitsliste etc) austragen. **~ o·ver** v/t et. überschreiben (**to** dat). **~ up** → **sign on** 1, 2.

sig·nal ['sɪɡnl] **I** s **1.** Signal n, Zeichen n (beide a. fig.): → **busy** 6. **II** adj □ **2.** beachtlich, un-, außergewöhnlich. **III** v/t pret u. pp **-naled**, bsd. Br. **-nalled 3.** ~ s.o. to do s.th. j-m (ein) Zeichen geben, et. zu tun. **4.** fig. Bereitschaft etc signalisieren. **IV** v/i **5.** ~ for a taxi e-m Taxi winken. **~ box** s ♣ Br., **~ tow·er** s ♣ Am. Stellwerk n.

sig·na·ture ['sɪɡnətʃə] s Unterschrift f, (e-s Bildes, Buchs) Signatur f. **~ tune** s Rundfunk, TV: Erkennungs-, Kennmelodie f.

'sign·board s (Aushänge)Schild n.
sign·er ['saɪnə] s Unterzeichnete m, f.
'sig·net ring ['sɪɡnɪt] s Siegelring m.
sig·nif·i·cance [sɪɡ'nɪfɪkəns] s Bedeutung f, Wichtigkeit f: **be of great ~ to** von großer Bedeutung sein für. **sig'nif·i·cant** adj □ **1.** bedeutend, bedeutsam, wichtig. **2.** vielsagend; bezeichnend.
sig·ni·fy ['sɪɡnɪfaɪ] v/t **1.** bedeuten. **2.** Meinung etc kundtun.
sign| lan·guage s Zeichensprache f. **'~post** s Wegweiser m.

si·lence ['saɪləns] **I** s Stille f; Schweigen n: **~!** Ruhe!; **in ~** schweigend; **a one--minute ~** e-e Schweigeminute. **II** v/t zum Schweigen bringen (a. fig.). **'si·lenc·er** s **1.** Schalldämpfer m. **2.** mot. Br. Auspufftopf m.
si·lent ['saɪlənt] adj □ still, (Gebet, a. ling. Buchstabe) stumm; ruhig; schweigsam: **~ film** Stummfilm m; **the ~ majority** die schweigende Mehrheit; **~ partner** ♥ Am. stiller Teilhaber; **be ~ on** sich ausschweigen über (acc); **re·main ~** schweigen.

sil·hou·ette [ˌsɪluːˈet] **I** s Silhouette f. **II** v/t: **be ~d against** sich (als Silhouette) abheben gegen.

sil·i·con ['sɪlɪkən] s ♣ Silizium n. **sil·i·cone** ['sɪlɪkəʊn] s ♣ Silikon n.
sil·i·co·sis [ˌsɪlɪˈkəʊsɪs] s ♣ Staublunge f.

silk [sɪlk] **I** s Seide f. **II** adj Seiden...
'**~worm** s zo. Seidenraupe f.
silk·y ['sɪlkɪ] adj □ seidig (Fell, Haare etc), samtig (Stimme).
sill [sɪl] s (Fenster)Bank f, (-)Brett n.
sil·li·ness ['sɪlɪnɪs] s Albernheit f, Dummheit f.
sil·ly ['sɪlɪ] **I** adj albern, dumm: **don't be ~!** red doch keinen Unsinn!; **~ billy** → II; **~ season** (Journalismus) Sauregurkenzeit f. **II** s F Dummkopf m, Dummerchen n.
si·lo ['saɪləʊ] pl **-los** s **1.** Silo m, n. **2.** ✕ Startsilo m, n.
sil·ver ['sɪlvə] **I** s **1.** 🜛 Silber n (a. Besteck, Geschirr). **2.** Silber(geld n, -münzen pl) n: **three pounds in ~** drei Pfund in Silber. **II** adj **3.** silbern, Silber... **III** v/t **4.** versilbern. '**~fish** s zo. Silberfischchen n. **~ foil** s Silber-, Alu(minium)folie f; Silberpapier n. '**~haired** adj silberhaarig. **~ ju·bi·lee** s 25jähriges Jubiläum. **~ med·al** s Silbermedaille f. **~ med·al·(l)ist** s Silbermedaillengewinner(in). **~ mine** s Silbergrube f, -mine f, -grube f. **~ pa·per** s Silberpapier n. '**~plat·ed** adj versilbert. '**~smith** s Silberschmied(in). '**~ware** s Silber(besteck, -geschirr) n. **~ wed·ding** s silberne Hochzeit.
sil·ver·y ['sɪlvərɪ] adj silb(e)rig, (Lachen) silberhell.
sim·i·lar ['sɪmɪlə] adj ähnlich (to dat). **sim·i·lar·i·ty** [ˌsɪmɪ'lærətɪ] s Ähnlichkeit f (to mit). '**sim·i·lar·ly** adv ähnlich. **2.** entsprechend.
sim·i·le ['sɪmɪlɪ] s Simile n, Vergleich m.
sim·mer ['sɪmə] **I** v/i **1.** köcheln, leicht kochen: **~ with** fig. kochen vor (Zorn etc), fiebern vor (Aufregung etc); **~ down** F sich abregen. **2.** fig. gären, schwelen. **II** s **3.** Köcheln n: **bring to a ~** zum Köcheln bringen.
sim·per ['sɪmpə] **I** v/i albern od. affektiert lächeln. **II** s albernes od. affektiertes Lächeln.
sim·ple ['sɪmpl] adj (□ → **simply**) **1.** allg. einfach, (Aufgabe etc a.) simpel, leicht, (Lebensweise, Person, Stil etc a.) schlicht, (✿ Bruch a.) glatt: **for the ~ reason that** aus dem einfachen Grund, weil. **2.** einfältig; naiv; leichtgläubig. '**~mind·ed** adj □ → **simple** 2.
sim·plic·i·ty [sɪm'plɪsətɪ] s **1.** Einfachheit

f, Schlichtheit f: **be ~ itself** die einfachste Sache der Welt sein. **2.** Einfältigkeit f; Naivität f, Leichtgläubigkeit f.
sim·pli·fi·ca·tion [ˌsɪmplɪfɪ'keɪʃn] s Vereinfachung f. **sim·pli·fy** ['sɪmplɪfaɪ] v/t vereinfachen.
sim·plis·tic [sɪm'plɪstɪk] adj (**~ally**) stark vereinfachend.
sim·ply ['sɪmplɪ] adv **1.** einfach (etc, → **simple** 1): **to put it ~** in einfachen Worten. **2.** bloß, nur. **3.** F einfach großartig etc.
sim·u·late ['sɪmjʊleɪt] v/t **1.** vortäuschen, heucheln, bsd. Krankheit simulieren. **2.** ⊛ etc simulieren. ˌ**sim·u'la·tion** s **1.** Vortäuschung f, Simulieren n; Heuchelei f. **2.** ⊛ etc Simulierung f. '**sim·u·la·tor** s **1.** Heuchler(in), Simulant(in). **2.** ⊛ Simulator m.
si·mul·ta·ne·ous [ˌsɪməl'teɪnjəs] adj □ simultan, gleichzeitig: **~ interpreter** Simultandolmetscher(in).
sin [sɪn] **I** s Sünde f: **live in ~** humor. in Sünde leben; **(as) ugly as ~** häßlich wie die Nacht; → **deadly** 1, **mortal** 3. **II** v/i sündigen: **~ against** fig. sündigen gegen, sich versündigen an (dat); verstoßen gegen.
since [sɪns] **I** adv **1.** a. **ever ~** seitdem, -her. **2.** inzwischen. **II** prp **3.** seit. **III** cj **4.** seit(dem). **5.** da.
sin·cere [sɪn'sɪə] adj □ aufrichtig: **Yours ~ly** Mit freundlichen Grüßen (Briefschluß). **sin·cer·i·ty** [ˌ~'serətɪ] s Aufrichtigkeit f: **in all ~** in aller Offenheit.
sine [saɪn] s Ⓐ Sinus m.
sin·ew ['sɪnjuː] s anat. Sehne f. '**sin·ew·y** adj sehnig, (Fleisch a.) flechsig.
sin·ful ['sɪnfʊl] adj □ sündig, sündhaft.
sing [sɪŋ] (irr) **I** v/i **1.** singen. **2.** pfeifen (Kugel, Wind etc). **II** v/t **3.** et. singen: **~ s.o. s.th.** j-m et. (vor)singen; **~ a baby to sleep** ein Baby in den Schlaf singen.
singe [sɪndʒ] **I** v/t (sich et.) an- od. versengen. **II** s ange- od. versengte Stelle.
sing·er ['sɪŋə] s Sänger(in). '**sing·ing** **I** s Singen n, Gesang m. **II** adj: **~ lesson** Sing-, Gesangsstunde f; **~ voice** Singstimme f.
sin·gle ['sɪŋɡl] **I** adj □ **1.** einzig: **not a ~ one** kein einziger; **2.** einzeln; einzeln, Einzel...: **~ room** Einzelzimmer n; **~ ticket** → 6. **3.** alleinstehend, unverhei-

ratet: **~ mother** alleinerziehende Mutter. **II** *s* **4.** Single *f* (*Schallplatte*). **5.** Single *m* (*Person*). **6.** *Br.* einfache Fahrkarte, ✓ einfaches Ticket. **7.** *mst pl Tennis etc*: Einzel *n*: **a ~s match** ein Einzel; **men's ~s** Herreneinzel. **III** *v/t* **8. ~ out** sich j-n herausgreifen. ,~-'breast·ed *adj* einreihig (*Anzug*). ~file *s u. adv:* (**in**) ~ im Gänsemarsch. ,~'hand·ed *adj u. adv* eigenhändig, (ganz) allein. ,~'mind·ed *adj* □ zielstrebig, -bewußt.

sin·glet ['sɪŋglɪt] *s bsd. Br.* ärmelloses Unterhemd, (*Sport*) ärmelloses Trikot.
'sing·song *s* Singsang *m*.
sin·gu·lar ['sɪŋgjʊlə] **I** *adj* □ **1.** *ling.* Singular..., Einzahl... **2.** *fig.* einzigartig, einmalig. **II** *s* **3.** *ling.* Singular *m*, Einzahl *f*.
sin·is·ter ['sɪnɪstə] *adj* □ finster, unheimlich.

sink [sɪŋk] **I** *v/i* (*irr*) **1.** sinken, untergehen: **leave s.o. to ~ or swim** j-n sich selbst überlassen. **2.** sich senken (*Gebäude etc*); sinken, zurückgehen (*Hochwasser etc, fig. Zahl etc*): → **heart** 1, **spirit** 4. **3.** sinken (**into a chair** in e-n Sessel; **to the ground** zu Boden; **to the knees** auf die Knie; **into a deep sleep** in e-n tiefen Schlaf): → **oblivion.** **4. ~ in** eindringen (*Flüssigkeit, a. fig. Nachricht etc*). **II** *v/t* (*irr*) **5.** Schiff *etc* versenken. **6.** *Graben etc* ausheben, *Brunnen etc* bohren. **7.** *Zähne etc* vergraben, -senken (**into** in *acc*). **8.** Pläne *etc* zunichte machen. **9.** *Streit etc* beilegen, begraben. **10.** *Geld, Arbeit etc* investieren (**in, into** in *acc*). **III** *s* **11.** Spülbecken *n*, Spüle *f*; *bsd. Am.* Waschbecken *n*. **'sink·er** *s* Grundgewicht *n* (*e-s Fischnetzes*). **'sink·ing** *adj*: **I got that ~ feeling when** F mir wurde ganz anders, als.
sin·ner ['sɪnə] *s* Sünder(in).
si·nus ['saɪnəs] *s anat.* (Nasen)Nebenhöhle *f*. **si·nus·i·tis** [,~'saɪtɪs] *s* ✚ (Nasen)Nebenhöhlenentzündung *f*.
Sioux [su:] *pl* **Sioux** [su:z] *s* Sioux *m, f*.
sip [sɪp] **I** *v/t* **1.** schlückchen *n*: **take a ~ of** → IIa. **II** *v/t* a) nippen an (*dat*) *od.* von, b) schlückchenweise trinken. **III** *v/i*: **~ at** → IIa.
si·phon ['saɪfn] **I** *s* **1.** Siphon(flasche *f*) *m*. **2.** 🜂 Saugheber *m*. **II** *v/t* **3.** *a.* **~ off**

absaugen, *Benzin* abzapfen; *fig. Geld, Personal etc* abziehen.
sir [sɜ:] *s* **1.** mein Herr (*Anrede, oft unübersetzt*): **Dear ~s** Sehr geehrte Herren (*Anrede in Briefen*). **2.** ♀ *Br.* (*Adelstitel*): ♀ **Winston** (**Churchill**).
si·ren ['saɪərən] *s* Sirene *f*.
sir·loin steak ['sɜ:lɔɪn] *s* Lendensteak *n*.
sis·sy ['sɪsɪ] *s* F Weichling *m*.
sis·ter ['sɪstə] **I** *s* **1.** Schwester *f*. **2.** *eccl.* (Ordens)Schwester *f*: ♀ **Mary** Schwester Mary. **3.** ✚ *Br.* Oberschwester *f*. **4.** ✝ Schwester(gesellschaft) *f*. **II** *adj* **5.** Schwester...: **~ ship,** *etc.* **~hood** ['~hʊd] *s eccl.* Schwesternschaft *f*.
'sis·ter-in-law *pl* **'sis·ters-in-law** *s* Schwägerin *f*.
sis·ter·ly ['sɪstəlɪ] *adj* schwesterlich.
sit [sɪt] (*irr*) **I** *v/i* **1.** sitzen: **~ fence** 1, **pretty** II, **tight** 8. **2.** sich setzen. **3.** babysitten. **4.** tagen. **II** *v/t* **5.** j-n setzen. **6.** *Br.* → **sit for** 1.
Verbindungen mit Präpositionen:
sit| for *v/i* **1.** *Prüfung* ablegen, machen. **2.** *j-m* (*Modell*) sitzen: **~ one's portrait** sich porträtieren lassen. **~ on** *v/i* **1.** *~ a committee* e-m Ausschuß angehören. **2.** *fig.* sitzen auf (*dat*). **3.** F *j-n* unterbuttern.
Verbindungen mit Adverbien:
sit| a·bout, ~ a·round *v/i* herumsitzen. **~ back** *v/i* sich zurücklehnen, *fig. a.* die Hände in den Schoß legen. **~ down I** *v/i* sich setzen; sitzen: **sitting down** sich hinsetzen. **II** *v/t j-n* absetzen. **~ in** *v/i* **1. ~ for** *j-n* vertreten. **2. ~ on** als Zuhörer teilnehmen an (*dat*). **3.** ein Sit-in veranstalten; an e-m Sit-in teilnehmen. **~ out** *v/t* **1.** *Tanz* auslassen. **2.** bis zum Ende e-r *Veranstaltung etc* bleiben. **3.** das Ende (*gen*) abwarten; *Krise etc* aussitzen. **~ up I** *v/i* **1.** sich aufrichten *od.* -setzen; aufrecht sitzen: **make s.o. ~ (and take notice)** F j-n aufhorchen lassen. **2.** aufbleiben. **3. ~ (at** *od.* **to table** bei Tisch) Platz nehmen. **II** *v/t* **4.** *j-n* aufrichten *od.* -setzen.
sit|·com ['sɪtkɒm] F → **situation comedy.** '**~down** *s* **1.** *a.* **~ strike** → **sit-in.** **2.** *a.* **~ demonstration** Sitzblockade *f*. **3.** F Verschnaufpause *f*: **have a ~** e-e Verschnaufpause machen.
site [saɪt] **I** *s* **1.** Platz *m*, Ort *m*, Stelle *f*; *engS.* Standort *m*; (*Ausgrabungs*)Stätte

f. **2.** Baustelle *f.* **II** *v/t* **3.** placieren, ✕ Raketen *etc* stationieren: *be ~d* gelegen sein, liegen.

'**sit-in** *s* Sit-in *n*, Sitzstreik *m*: *stage a ~ in Gebäude etc* besetzen.

sit·ter ['sɪtə] *s* **1.** *paint. etc* Modell *n*. **2.** Babysitter(in). '**sit·ting** **I** *s* **1.** Sitzung *f* (*a. paint. etc*). **2.** *read s.th. at one* (*od. a single*) ~ et. in 'einem Zug durchlesen. **II** *adj* **3.** ~ *duck* *fig.* leichte Beute; ~ *room* Wohnzimmer *n*.

sit·u·at·ed ['sɪtjʊeɪtɪd] *adj* **1.** *be* ~ gelegen sein, liegen. **2.** *fig.* *be badly* ~ in e-r schwierigen Lage sein; *be well* ~ gut situiert sein; ohne weiteres in der Lage sein (*to do* zu tun).

sit·u·a·tion [ˌsɪtjʊ'eɪʃn] *s* **1.** *fig.* Lage *f*, Situation *f*. **2.** Lage *f* (*e-s Hauses etc*). **3.** *~s pl vacant* (*wanted*) Stellenangebote *pl* (Stellengesuche *pl*). ~ **com·e·dy** *s* *Rundfunk, TV*: humorvolle Serie.

six [sɪks] **I** *adj* sechs. **II** *s* Sechs *f*: ~ *of hearts* Herzsechs; *be all at ~es and sevens* F nicht mehr wissen, wo e-m der Kopf steht. **six·fold** ['~fəʊld] **I** *adj* sechsfach. **II** *adv* sechsfach, um das Sechsfache: *increase* ~ (sich) versechsfachen.

'**six-pack** *s* Sechserpackung *f*.

six·teen [ˌsɪks'tiːn] *adj* sechzehn. ˌ**six-'teenth** [~θ] *adj* sechzehnt. **sixth** [sɪksθ] **I** *adj* **1.** sechste(r, -s): ~ *sense* *fig.* sechster Sinn. **II** *s* **2.** der, die, das Sechste: *the ~ of May* der 6. Mai. **3.** Sechstel *n*. '**sixth·ly** *adv* sechstens. **six·ti·eth** ['~tɪəθ] *adj* sechzigst.

'**six-time** *adj* sechsmalig.

six·ty ['sɪkstɪ] **I** *adj* sechzig. **II** *s* Sechzig *f*: *be in one's sixties* in den Sechzigern sein; *in the sixties* in den sechziger Jahren (*e-s Jahrhunderts*).

size [saɪz] **I** *s* **1.** Größe *f*, *fig. a.* Ausmaß *n*, Umfang *m*: *what is the ~ of ...?* wie groß ist ...? **2.** (*Kleider-, Schuh- etc*) Größe *f*, Nummer *f*: *what ~ do you take?* welche Größe tragen Sie?; *I'll cut him down to* ~ F dem werd' ich's zeigen. **II** *v/t* **3.** *mst* ~ *up* j-n, *et.* abschätzen.

size·a·ble ['saɪzəbl] *adj* beträchtlich (*Summe etc*).

siz·zle ['sɪzl] **I** *v/i* brutzeln. **II** *s* Brutzeln *n*. '**siz·zler** *s* F glühendheißer Tag.

skate [skeɪt] **I** *s* **1.** Schlittschuh *m*; Roll-

schuh *m*. **II** *v/i* Schlittschuh laufen, eislaufen; Rollschuh laufen: ~ *over* (*od. round*) *s.th. fig.* hinweggehen über (*acc*); → *ice* 1. '**~·board** *s* Skateboard *n*.

skat·er ['skeɪtə] *s* Eis-, Schlittschuhläufer(in); Rollschuhläufer(in). '**skat·ing** *adj*: ~ *rink* (Kunst)Eisbahn *f*; Rollschuhbahn *f*.

ske·dad·dle [skɪ'dædl] *v/i* F türmen, abhauen.

skel·e·ton ['skelɪtn] **I** *s* **1.** Skelett *n*, Gerippe *n* (*beide a. fig. Person etc*): ~ *in the cupboard* (*Am. closet*) *fig.* dunkler Punkt (*in j-s Vergangenheit etc*); *have a ~ in the cupboard* e-e Leiche im Keller haben. **2.** △, ✓, ⚓ Skelett *n*. **3.** *fig.* Entwurf *m*; Rahmen *m*. **II** *adj* **4.** Rahmen...: ~ *plan*, *etc.* **5.** Not...: ~ *service* Notdienst *m*. **6.** ~ *key* Hauptschlüssel *m*.

skep·tic *etc bsd. Am.* → **sceptic**, *etc.*

sketch [sketʃ] **I** *s* **1.** *Kunst etc* Skizze *f*. **2.** *thea. etc* Sketch *m*. **II** *v/t* **3.** skizzieren. **4.** *oft* ~ *in* (*od. out*) *fig.* skizzieren, umreißen. '**sketch·y** *adj* □ flüchtig, oberflächlich, (*Erinnerung etc*) bruchstückhaft.

skew [skjuː] **I** *s*: *on the* ~ schief; schräg. **II** *v/t* *fig.* verzerren.

skew·er [skjʊə] **I** *s* (Fleisch)Spieß *m*. **II** *v/t* Fleisch aufspießen.

ski [skiː] **I** *s* Ski *m*. **II** *adj* Ski...: ~ *lift*, *etc.* **III** *v/i* Ski fahren *od.* laufen.

skid [skɪd] *v/i* **1.** *mot.* schleudern. **II** *s* **2.** *go into a* ~ *mot.* ins Schleudern kommen. **3.** ⚙ Rolle *f*: *he's on the ~s* F mit ihm geht es abwärts.

ski·er ['skiːə] *s* Skifahrer(in), -läufer(in).

skiff [skɪf] *s* ⚓ Skiff *n*, (*Rudersport a.*) Einer *m*.

ski·ing ['skiːɪŋ] *s* Skifahren *n*, -laufen *n*, -sport *m*.

skil·ful ['skɪlfʊl] *adj* □ geschickt.

skill [skɪl] *s* **1.** Geschick *n*: *game of* ~ Geschicklichkeitsspiel *n*. **2.** Fertigkeit *f*. **skilled** [~ld] *adj* **1.** geschickt (*at, in* dat). **2.** ~ *worker* Facharbeiter(in).

skil·let ['skɪlɪt] *s bsd. Am.* Bratpfanne *f*.

skill·ful *Am.* → **skilful**.

skim [skɪm] **I** *v/t* **1.** *a.* ~ *off* Fett *etc* abschöpfen (*from* von). **2.** Milch entrahmen: *~med milk* Magermilch *f*. **3.** *Bericht etc* überfliegen. **II** *v/i* **4.** ~ *over* (od. **through**) → 3. ~ **milk** s Magermilch f.

kimp [skɪmp] **I** v/t sparen an (dat). **II** v/i: ~ **on** → **I**. '**skimp·y** adj dürftig (Mahlzeit, Beweise etc); knapp (Kleidungsstück).

skin [skɪn] **I** s **1.** Haut f (a. e-r Wurst, auf Milch etc): **by the** ~ **of one's teeth** F mit Ach u. Krach, gerade noch; **be all** ~ **and bone(s)** nur noch Haut u. Knochen sein; **that's no** ~ **off my nose** F das juckt mich nicht; **be drenched** (od. **soaked**) **to the** ~ bis auf die Haut durchnäßt od. naß sein; **get under s.o.'s** ~ F j-m unter die Haut gehen; j-m auf den Wecker fallen; **save one's** ~ F s-e Haut retten. **2.** Haut f; Fell n. **3.** (Bananen-, Zwiebel- etc)Schale f. **II** v/t **4.** Tier abhäuten: ~ **alive** F j-n zur Schnecke machen. **5.** Zwiebel etc schälen: **keep one's eyes** ~**ned** Br. die Augen offenhalten. **6.** sich das Knie etc aufschürfen. ~**·deep** adj fig. oberflächlich. ~ **div·ing** s Schnorcheln n, Schnorcheltauchen n. ~ **flick** s F Sexfilm m. '~**·flint** s Geizhals m.

skin·ful ['skɪnfʊl] s: **he's had a** ~ F er hat schwer geladen (ist betrunken).

skin| **graft** s Hauttransplantation f, -verpflanzung f. '~**·head** s bsd. Br. Skinhead m.

skin·ny ['skɪnɪ] adj dürr.

skint [skɪnt] adj Br. F blank, pleite.

skin-tight adj hauteng.

skip [skɪp] **I** v/i **1.** hüpfen. **2.** Br. seilhüpfen, -springen. **3.** fig. springen (**from one subject to another** von 'einem Thema zum andern): ~ **over** et. überspringen, auslassen. **4.** a. ~ **off** F abhauen, türmen. **II** v/t **5.** et. überspringen, auslassen; Vorlesung etc schwänzen; Mahlzeit ausfallen lassen. **III** s **6.** Hüpfer m.

skip·per ['skɪpə] s **1.** ♣ Kapitän m. **2.** Sport: Mannschaftsführer(in).

skip·ping rope ['skɪpɪŋ] s Br. Spring-, Sprungseil n.

skir·mish ['skɜːmɪʃ] s ✕ Geplänkel n (a. fig.).

skirt [skɜːt] **I** s Rock m. **II** v/t → **III**. **III** v/i: ~ (**a**)**round** fig. Problem etc umgehen. '**skirt·ing** adj: ~ **board** Br. Fuß(boden)-, Scheuerleiste f.

skit [skɪt] s Parodie f (**on** auf acc): **do a** ~ **on** j-n, et. parodieren.

skive [skaɪv] v/i Br. F blaumachen.

skul·dug·ger·y [skʌl'dʌgərɪ] s F fauler Zauber.

skulk [skʌlk] v/i sich herumdrücken, herumschleichen.

skull [skʌl] s anat. Schädel m: ~ **and crossbones** Totenkopf m (Symbol); **can't you get it into that thick** ~ **of yours that ...?** F will es denn nicht in deinen Schädel, daß ...?

skunk [skʌŋk] s **1.** zo. Skunk m, Stinktier n. **2.** F Saukerl m.

sky [skaɪ] s, a. pl Himmel m: **in the** ~ am Himmel; **the** ~'s **the limit** F nach oben sind keine Grenzen gesetzt; **extol** (od. **praise**) **to the skies** j-n, et. in den Himmel heben. ~**·blue** adj himmelblau. '~**·div·er** s Sport: Fallschirmspringer(in). '~**·div·ing** s Fallschirmspringen n. ~**·high** adj u. adv himmelhoch: **blow** ~ in die Luft jagen; fig. Theorie etc über den Haufen werfen, Argument etc widerlegen, Mythos zerstören. '~**·jack** → **hijack** 1, 3. '~**·jack·er** → **hijacker** 1. '~**·jack·ing** → **hijack** 3. '~**·light** s Dachfenster n. '~**·line** s Skyline f, Silhouette f (e-r Stadt). '~**·rock·et** → **rocket** 3. '~**·scrap·er** s Wolkenkratzer m.

slab [slæb] s **1.** (Stein- etc)Platte f. **2.** dickes Stück (Kuchen etc).

slack [slæk] **I** adj □ **1.** locker (Seil etc). **2.** fig. lax (Disziplin etc). **3.** fig. lasch, nachlässig. **4.** ♥ flau. **II** v/i **5.** bummeln. **6.** ~ **off** (od. **up**) → **slacken** 3. '**slack·en I** v/t **1.** lockern. **2.** fig. verringern: ~ **speed** langsamer werden. **II** v/i **3.** locker werden. **4.** a. ~ **off** fig. nachlassen, (Person a.) abbauen.

slag [slæg] s **1.** Schlacke f. **2.** Br. sl. Schlampe f.

slain [sleɪn] pp von **slay**.

slake [sleɪk] v/t Kalk löschen: ~**d lime** Löschkalk m.

sla·lom ['slɑːləm] s Sport: Slalom m.

slam [slæm] **I** v/t **1.** a. ~ **shut** Tür etc zuknallen, zuschlagen. **2.** a. ~ **down** F et. knallen (**on** auf acc): ~ **the brakes on** mot. auf die Bremse steigen. **3.** fig. scharf kritisieren. **II** v/i **4.** a. ~ **shut** zuknallen, zuschlagen.

slan·der ['slɑːndə] **I** s Verleumdung f. **II**

v/t verleumden. **'slan·der·er** *s* Verleumder(in). **'slan·der·ous** *adj* □ verleumderisch.

slang [slæŋ] **I** *s* Slang *m*; Jargon *m*. **II** *v/t bsd. Br.* F *j-n* wüst beschimpfen. **'slang·ing** *adj*: **they had a ~ match** *bsd. Br.* F sie beschimpften sich wüst.

slant [slɑːnt] **I** *v/t* **1. be ~ed toward(s)** (*od.* **in favo[u]r of**) *fig.* (einseitig) ausgerichtet sein auf (*acc*). **II** *s* **2. at** (*od.* **on**) **a ~** schräg. **3.** *fig.* Einstellung *f* (**on** zu); Ausrichtung *f*. **'slant·ing** *adj* schräg.

slap [slæp] **I** *s* **1.** Schlag *m*, Klaps *m*: **a ~ in the face** e-e Ohrfeige, *bsd. fig.* ein Schlag ins Gesicht (**for** für). **II** *v/t* **2.** schlagen: **~ s.o.'s face** *j-n* ohrfeigen, *j-m* e-e runterhauen (**on** auf *acc*). **3.** *a.* **~ down** *et.* klatschen (**on** auf *acc*). **III** *v/i* **4.** klatschen (**against** gegen) (*Wellen etc*). **IV** *adv* **5.** F direkt, genau. **~·'bang** → **slap** 5. **'~·dash** *adj* schlampig, schlud(e)rig. **'~·stick** *s thea. etc* Slapstick *m*, Klamauk *m*: **~ comedy** Slapstickkomödie *f*. **'~·up** *adj Br.* F toll (*Essen*).

slash [slæʃ] **I** *v/t* **1.** auf-, zerschlitzen: **~ one's wrists** sich die Pulsadern aufschneiden. **2.** *fig.* Preise drastisch herabsetzen; *Ausgaben etc* drastisch kürzen. **II** *v/i* **3. ~ at** schlagen nach. **II.** peitschen (**against** an *acc*, gegen) (*Regen*). **III** *s* **5.** Hieb *m*. **6.** Schlitz *m* (*in Kleid etc*). **7.** *a.* **~ mark** Schrägstrich *m*. **8. have** (**go for**) **a ~** *Br. sl.* schiffen (gehen).

slate¹ [sleɪt] **I** *s* **1.** *geol.* Schiefer *m*. **2.** Schieferplatte *f*. **3.** Schiefertafel *f*: **put on the ~** *fig. et.* anschreiben; **wipe the ~ clean** *fig.* reinen Tisch machen. **4.** *pol. Am.* Kandidatenliste *f*. **II** *v/t* **5.** Dach mit Schiefer decken. **6.** *Am. j-n* vorschlagen (**for, to be** als). **7.** *Am. et.* ansetzen, planen (**for** für).

slate² [~] *v/t* *bsd. Br.* F *Theaterstück etc* verreißen.

slaugh·ter ['slɔːtə] **I** *s* **1.** Schlachten *n*: **ready for ~** schlachtreif. **2.** Gemetzel *n*. **II** *v/t* **3.** *Tier* schlachten. **4.** *Menschen* niedermetzeln. **'~·house** *s* Schlachthaus *n*, -hof *m*.

slave [sleɪv] **I** *s* Sklave *m*, Sklavin *f* (*beide a. fig. of, to* gen). **II** *v/i* *a.* **~ away** sich abplagen. **~ driv·er** *s* F Sklaventreiber *m*, Leuteschinder *m*. **~ la·bo(u)r** *s* Sklavenarbeit *f* (*a. fig.*).

slav·er ['slævə] *v/i* geifern.

slav·er·y ['sleɪvərɪ] *s* Sklaverei *f*.

slave| trade, ~ traf·fic *s* Sklavenhandel *m*.

slav·ish ['sleɪvɪʃ] *adj* □ sklavisch.

slaw [slɔː] *s bsd. Am.* Krautsalat *m*.

slay [sleɪ] *v/t Am.* ermorden, umbringen. **'slay·er** *s* Mörder(in).

slea·zy ['sliːzɪ] *adj* □ schäbig, heruntergekommen; anrüchig.

sled [sled] → **sledge**.

sledge [sledʒ] **I** *s* (*a.* Rodel)Schlitten *m*. **II** *v/i* Schlitten fahren, rodeln.

'sledge·ham·mer *s* ⊙ Vorschlaghammer *m*.

sleek [sliːk] *adj* □ **1.** geschmeidig (*Haar etc*). **2.** schnittig (*Auto*).

sleep [sliːp] **I** *s* Schlaf *m*: **in one's ~** in Schlaf; **I couldn't get to ~** ich konnte nicht einschlafen; **go to ~** einschlafen (F *a.* Bein etc); **put to ~** Tier einschläfern (F *a. j-n* narkotisieren). **II** *v/i* (*irr*) schlafen: **~ late** lang *od.* länger schlafen; **~ like a log** (*od.* **top**) F wie ein Murmeltier schlafen; **~ on** Problem *et.* überschlafen; **~ through** Gewitter *etc* verschlafen; **~ with s.o.** mit *j-m* schlafen. **III** *v/t* (*irr*) Schlafgelegenheit bieten für: **this tent ~s four people** in diesem Zelt können vier Leute schlafen.

Verbindungen mit Adverbien:

sleep| a·round *v/i* F rumbumsen. **~ in** *v/i* lang *od.* länger schlafen. **~ off** *v/t* **sleep it off** F *s-n* Rausch ausschlafen. **~ to·geth·er** *v/i* miteinander schlafen.

sleep·er ['sliːpə] *s* **1.** Schlafende *m*, *f*, Schläfer(in): **be a light** (**heavy** *od.* **sound**) **~** e-n leichten (festen) Schlaf haben. **2.** ⛊ *Br.* Schwelle *f*. **3.** ⛊ Schlafwagen *m*; Schlafwagenplatz *m*.

sleep·ing| bag ['sliːpɪŋ] *s* Schlafsack *m*. **~ car** *s* ⛊ Schlafwagen *m*. **~ part·ner** *s* ✝ *Br.* stiller Teilhaber. **~ pill** *s* Schlaftablette *f*. **~ po·lice·man** *s* (*irr man*) *mot. Br.* Rüttelschwelle *f*. **~ sick·ness** *s* 🦟 Schlafkrankheit *f*. **~ tab·let** *s* Schlaftablette *f*.

sleep·less ['sliːplɪs] *adj* □ schlaflos (*Nacht etc*).

'sleep·walk *v/i* schlaf-, nachtwandeln. **'~·walk·er** *s* Schlaf-, Nachtwandler(in).

sleep·y ['sliːpɪ] *adj* □ **1.** schläfrig, müde

2. *fig.* verschlafen, verträumt (*Städtchen etc*). '**~head** s F Schlafmütze *f*.

sleet [sli:t] s Schneeregen *m*.

sleeve [sli:v] s **1.** Ärmel *m*: **have** (*od. keep*) **s.th. up one's ~** et. auf Lager *od.* in petto haben; **laugh up one's ~** *fig.* sich ins Fäustchen lachen. **2.** ⚙ Manschette *f*, Muffe *f*. **3.** *bsd. Br.* (*Platten*)Hülle *f*. '**sleeve·less** *adj* ärmellos.

sleigh [sleɪ] s (*bsd.* Pferde)Schlitten *m*.

sleight of hand [slaɪt] s **1.** Fingerfertigkeit *f*. **2.** *fig.* Taschenspielertrick *m*.

slen·der ['slendə] *adj* □ **1.** schlank. **2.** *fig.* mager (*Aussichten, Einkommen etc*).

slept [slept] *pret u. pp von* **sleep.**

sleuth [slu:θ] s F Spürhund *m*, Detektiv *m*.

slew [slu:] *pret von* **slay.**

slice [slaɪs] I s **1.** Scheibe *f* (*Brot etc*), Stück (*Kuchen etc*); *fig.* Anteil *m* (**of** an *dat*). **2.** *Br.* (*Braten*)Wender *m*. **3.** *Golf, Tennis:* Slice *m*. II *v/t* **4. ~ up** in Scheiben *od.* Stücke schneiden: **~ off** Stück abschneiden (**from** von). **5.** *Golf, Tennis:* Ball slicen.

slick [slɪk] I *adj* □ **1.** gekonnt (*Vorstellung etc*). **2.** geschickt, raffiniert. **3.** glatt (*Straße etc*). II s **4.** (*Öl*)Teppich *m*. **5.** *Motorsport:* Slick *m* (*Trockenreifen*). **6.** *Am.* F Hochglanzmagazin *n*. '**slick-er** s *Am.* Regenmantel *m*.

slid [slɪd] *pret u. pp von* **slide.**

slide [slaɪd] I *v/i* (*irr*) **1.** gleiten; rutschen: **let things ~** *fig.* die Dinge schleifen lassen. **2.** schleichen. II *v/t* (*irr*) **3.** schieben; gleiten lassen. III s **4.** Rutsche *f*, Rutschbahn *f*. **5.** (*Erd- etc*)Rutsch *m*. **6.** *Br.* (*Haar*)Spange *f*. **7.** Dia *n*. '**~ lec·ture** s Lichtbildervortrag *m*. '**~ pro·jec·tor** s Diaprojektor *m*. '**~ rule** s Rechenschieber *m*, -stab *m*.

slid·ing door ['slaɪdɪŋ] s Schiebetür *f*.

slight [slaɪt] I *adj* □ leicht (*Schmerz etc*), geringfügig (*Änderung etc*): **I haven't got the ~est idea** ich habe nicht die geringste Ahnung; **not in the ~est** nicht im geringsten. II *v/t* j-n beleidigen, kränken. III s Beleidigung *f* (**on, to** *gen*).

slim [slɪm] I *adj* □ **1.** schlank. **2.** *fig.* gering (*Chance, Hoffnung etc*). II *v/i* **3.** e-e Schlankheitskur machen. III *v/t* **4.** **a. ~ down** *fig.* verringern.

slime [slaɪm] s Schleim *m*.

slim·ming ['slɪmɪŋ] I s Abnehmen *n*. II *adj* Schlankheits...: **be on a ~ diet →** **slim** 3.

slim·y ['slaɪmɪ] *adj* □ schleimig (*a. fig.*).

sling¹ [slɪŋ] I s **1.** ✚ Schlinge *f*: **have one's arm in a ~** den Arm in der Schlinge tragen. **2.** Trag(e)riemen *m* (*für Gewehr*); Trag(e)tuch *n* (*für Baby*). II *v/t* (*irr*) **3.** aufhängen.

sling² [~] *v/t* (*irr*) schleudern: → **mud** 2.

slink [slɪŋk] *v/i* (*irr*) (sich) schleichen.

slip¹ [slɪp] I s **1.** Versehen *n*: **~ of the tongue** Versprecher *m*. **2.** Unterkleid *n*, -rock *m*. **3.** (*Kissen*)Bezug *m*. **4. give s.o. the ~** F j-m entwischen. II *v/i* **5.** rutschen, (*auf Eis a.*) schlittern: **~ out of s.o.'s hand** j-m aus der Hand rutschen; **he let ~ that** *fig.* ihm ist herausgerutscht, daß; **let an opportunity ~** (**through one's fingers**) sich e-e Gelegenheit entgehen lassen. **6.** ausrutschen. **7.** *allg.* schlüpfen. **8.** sich vertun. **9.** *fig.* nachlassen, (*Gewinne etc*) zurückgehen. III *v/t* **10. ~ s.th. into s.o.'s hand** j-m et. in die Hand schieben; **~ s.o. s.th.** j-m et. zuschieben. **11.** sich losreißen von. **12. ~ s.o.'s attention** j-m od. j-s Aufmerksamkeit entgehen; **~ s.o.'s memory** (*od.* **mind**) j-m entfallen. **13. he has ~ped a disc, he has a ~ped disc** ✚ er hat e-n Bandscheibenvorfall.

Verbindungen mit Adverbien:

slip by *v/i* verstreichen (*Zeit*). **~ off** *v/t* schlüpfen aus (*e-m Kleidungsstück*). **~ on** *v/t* Kleidungsstück überstreifen, schlüpfen in (*acc*). **~ out** *v/i*: **it just slipped out** es ist mir *etc* so herausgerutscht. **~ past → slip by. ~ up →** **slip** 8.

slip² [~] s **a. ~ of paper** Zettel *m*.

'**slip·case** s Schuber *m*. '**~·cov·er** s *Am.* Schonbezug *m*. '**~·on** I *adj*: **~ shoe →** II. II s Slipper *m*.

slip·per ['slɪpə] s Hausschuh *m*, Pantoffel *m*.

slip·per·y ['slɪpərɪ] *adj* **1.** glatt, rutschig, (*a. Fisch, Seife etc*) glitschig. **2.** *fig.* zwielichtig.

slip·py *adj*: **look ~!** *Br.* F mach fix!

slip road s *Br.* Autobahn: Abfahrt *f*; Zubringer(straße *f*) *m*. '**~·shod** *adj* schlampig, schlud(e)rig. '**~·stream**

(*Sport*) **I** *s* Windschatten *m*. **II** *v/i* im Windschatten fahren. '**~-up → slip¹** 1.

slit [slɪt] **I** *s* Schlitz *m* (*a*. im Rock etc). **II** *v/t* (*irr*) Rock etc schlitzen: **~** (**open**) aufschlitzen.

sliv·er ['slɪvə] *s* (*Glas- etc*)Splitter *m*: **~ of glass**.

slob·ber ['slɒbə] *v/i* sabbern.

slog [slɒg] F **I** *v/i* 1. **~ away at** sich abschleifen mit. **2.** sich schlagen (**through** durch). **II** *s* 3. Schufterei *f*.

slo·gan ['sləʊgən] *s* Slogan *m*.

slop [slɒp] **I** *v/t* 1. verschütten: **~ s.th. over one's trousers** sich et. über die Hose schütten. **II** *v/i* 2. überschwappen; schwappen (**over** über acc). 3. **~ about** (*od*. **around**) F herumhängen (*Person*). **III** *s* 4. *a*. *pl* contp. schlabb(e)riges Zeug.

slope [sləʊp] **I** *s* 1. (Ab)Hang *m*. 2. Neigung *f*, Gefälle *n*. **II** *v/i* 3. sich neigen, abfallen. 4. **~ off** Br. F abhauen.

slop·py ['slɒpɪ] *adj* □ 1. schlampig, schlud(e)rig. 2. F vergammelt (*Kleidungsstück*). 3. F schmalzig.

slosh [slɒʃ] F **I** *v/i* 1. **~ about** (*od*. **around**) herumschwappen. 2. **~ about** (*od*. **around**) (herum)planschen (in in dat). **II** *v/t* 3. Wasser etc verspritzen.

sloshed [~ʃt] *adj* F blau (*betrunken*).

slot [slɒt] *s* Schlitz *m*, (*e-s Automaten etc a*.) Einwurf *m*. **~ ma·chine** *s* (Waren-, Spiel)Automat *m*.

slouch [slaʊtʃ] **I** *s* 1. krumme Haltung; latschiger Gang. 2. **be no ~ at** nicht schlecht sein in (*dat*); **be no ~ at doing s.th.** et. nicht ungern tun. **II** *v/i* 3. krumm dasitzen *od*. dastehen; latschen. **~ hat** *s* Schlapphut *m*.

slough [slʌf] *v/t* Haut abstreifen (*Schlange*).

slov·en·ly ['slʌvnlɪ] *adj* schlampig, schlud(e)rig.

slow [sləʊ] **I** *adj* □ 1. *allg.* langsam, (*Person a*.) begriffsstutzig: **be ~ to do s.th.** sich mit et. Zeit lassen; **be** (**five minutes**) **~** (fünf Minuten) nachgehen (*Uhr*); **~ lane** *mot*. Kriechspur *f*; **in ~ motion** in Zeitlupe; **~ poison** langsam wirkendes Gift; **~ly but surely** langsam, aber sicher; **→ uptake** 2. **~** schleppend. **II** *v/t* 3. *oft* **~ down** (*od*. **up**) Geschwindigkeit verringern; Projekt etc verzögern: **~ the car down** langsamer

fahren. **III** *v/i* 4. *oft* **~ down** (*od*. **up**) langsamer fahren *od*. gehen *od*. werden. '**~·coach** *s* F Langweiler(in). '**~·down** *s* ✝ Am. Bummelstreik *m*. '**~·mov·ing** *adj* kriechend (*Verkehr*).

slow·ness ['sləʊnɪs] *s* Langsamkeit *f*, (*e-r Person a*.) Begriffsstutzigkeit *f*.

'**slow·poke** Am. → **slowcoach.** '**~·worm** *s zo.* Blindschleiche *f*.

sludge [slʌdʒ] *s* Schlamm *m*.

slug¹ [slʌg] *s bsd. Am.* F 1. ✗ etc Kugel *f*. 2. Schluck *m* (*Whisky etc*).

slug² [~] *s zo.* Nacktschnecke *f*.

slug³ [~] *bsd. Am.* **I** *v/t* j-m e-n Faustschlag versetzen. **II** *s* Faustschlag *m*.

slug·gish ['slʌgɪʃ] *adj* □ 1. träge (*Person*), träge fließend (*Fluß etc*). 2. ✝ schleppend.

sluice [sluːs] **I** *s* Schleuse *f*. **II** *v/t*: **~ down** abspritzen; **~ out** ausspritzen. **III** *v/i*: **~ out** herausschießen (*Wasser*). **~ gate** *s* Schleusentor *n*.

slum [slʌm] *s*, *mst pl* Slums *pl*, Elendsviertel *n*. **~ dwell·er** *s* Slumbewohner(in).

slump [slʌmp] **I** *v/i* 1. **~ into a chair** sich in e-n Sessel plumpsen lassen; **sit ~ed over** zs.-gesunken sitzen über (*dat*). 2. ✝ stürzen (*Preise*), stark zurückgehen (*Umsatz etc*). **II** *s* 3. ✝ starker Konjunkturrückgang: **~ in prices** Preissturz *m*.

slung [slʌŋ] *pret u. pp von* **sling¹** *u.* ².

slunk [slʌŋk] *pret u. pp von* **slink.**

slur¹ [slɜː] *s*: **on s.o.'s reputation** Rufschädigung *f*.

slur² [~] *v/t* 1. **~ one's speech** undeutlich sprechen, (*Betrunkener a.*) lallen. 2. ♪ Töne binden.

slurp [slɜːp] *v/t u. v/i* F schlürfen.

slush [slʌʃ] *s* 1. Schneematsch *m*. 2. F rührseliges Zeug. '**slush·y** *adj* □ 1. matschig (*Schnee*). 2. F rührselig.

slut [slʌt] *s* Schlampe *f*.

sly [slaɪ] **I** *adj* □ 1. gerissen, schlau: **you're a ~ one!** du bist mir vielleicht einer! 2. verschmitzt (*Lächeln etc*). **II** *s* 3. **on the ~** heimlich.

smack¹ [smæk] *v/i*: **~ of** *fig.* schmecken *od*. riechen nach.

smack² [~] **I** *v/t* 1. j-m e-n Klaps geben: **~ s.o.'s bottom, ~ s.o. on the bottom** j-m eins hinten draufgeben; **~ s.o.'s face** j-m e-e runterhauen. 2. **~ one's lips** sich die Lippen lecken. **3.** ~ *down* et. hinklatschen. **II** s **4.** Klaps *m*: *give s.o. a* ~ *in the face* F j-m e-e runterhauen. **5.** klatschendes Geräusch. **6.** F Schmatz *m*. **7.** *have a* ~ *at* F es mit et. versuchen. **III** *adv* **8.** F genau, direkt.

smack·er ['smækə] *s* F **1.** Schmatz *m*. **2.** *Br.* Pfund *m*, *Am.* Dollar *m*. **'smack·ing** *s* F Tracht *f* Prügel.

small [smɔːl] **I** *adj* *allg.* klein: ~ *ad Br.* Kleinanzeige *f*; ~ *arms pl* Handfeuerwaffen *pl*; ~ *beer* F ein kleiner Fisch, kleine Fische *pl*; ~ *change* Kleingeld *n*; *that's* ~ *change to him fig.* das ist ein Taschengeld für ihn; ~ *eater* schlechter Esser; *in the* ~ *hours* in den frühen Morgenstunden; ~ *print* das Kleingedruckte (*e-s Vertrags etc*); ~ *talk* Small talk *m*, *n*, Geplauder *n*; *make* ~ *talk* plaudern; ~ *town* Kleinstadt *f*; *feel* ~ sich klein (u. häßlich) vorkommen; → *wonder* **5.** **II** *adv* klein. **III** *s*: ~ *of the back anat.* Kreuz *n*. '~**mind·ed** *adj* □ **1.** engstirnig. **2.** kleinlich. '~**pox** *s* ℳ Pocken *pl*. '~**time** *adj fig.* klein, Klein...

smarm·y ['smɑːmɪ] *adj* F schmierig, schmeichlerisch.

smart [smɑːt] **I** *adj* □ **1.** smart (*Person*), (*a. Auto, Kleidung etc*) schick. **2.** smart, schlau, clever. **3.** vornehm (*Restaurant, Wohngegend etc*). **II** *v/i* **4.** weh tun; brennen. **III** *s* **5.** (brennender) Schmerz. ~**·al·eck** F [ˈælɪk] *s* F Besserwisser(in). ~**·ass** *s Am.* V Klugscheißer(in).

smart·en ['smɑːtn] *v/t mst* ~ *up* et. verschönern; ~ *o.s. up* → **II.** **II** *v/i mst* ~ *up* sich schick machen; sich et. Anständiges anziehen. '**smart·ness** *s* **1.** Schick *m*. **2.** Schlauheit *f*, Cleverneß *f*.

smash [smæʃ] **I** *v/t* **1.** *a.* ~ *up* zerschlagen; *Wagen* zu Schrott fahren; → *smithereens.* **2.** schmettern (*a. Tennis etc*): ~ *one's fist down on the table* mit der Faust auf den Tisch hauen. **3.** *fig.* Aufstand etc niederschlagen, Spionagering etc zerschlagen. **II** *v/i* **4.** zerspringen: → *smithereens.* **5.** ~ *into* prallen an (*acc*) od. gegen, krachen gegen. **III** *s* **6.** Schlag *m*; (*Tennis etc*) Schmetterball *m*. **7.** → *smash-up.* '~**·and-'grab** (*raid*) *s bsd. Br.* Schaufenstereinbruch *m*.

smashed [smæʃt] *adj* F blau (*betrun-*

ken): *get* ~ *on* sich vollaufen lassen mit. '**smash·er** *s* F Klassefrau *f*, toller Typ; tolles Ding.

smash hit → *smash* 8.

smash·ing ['smæʃɪŋ] *adj* F toll.

'**smash-up** *s mot.* schwerer Unfall.

smat·ter·ing ['smætərɪŋ] *s*: *a* ~ *of English* ein paar Brocken Englisch.

smear [smɪə] **I** *s* **1.** Fleck *m*. **2.** ℳ (*entnommener*) Abstrich. **3.** Verleumdung *f*. **II** *v/t* **4.** *Farbe etc* verschmieren, *Schrift a.* verwischen. **5.** *Creme etc* schmieren (*on, over* auf *acc*): *Haut etc* einschmieren (*with* mit). **6.** *Glas etc* beschmieren, verschmieren (*with* mit): ~*ed with blood* blutbeschmiert, -verschmiert. **7.** verleumden. **III** *v/i* **8.** schmieren (*Farbe etc*), sich verwischen (*Schrift*). ~ *campaign* *s* Verleumdungskampagne *f.* ~ *test* *s* ℳ Abstrich *m.*

smell [smel] **I** *v/i* (*mst irr*) **1.** riechen (*at* an *dat*). **2.** riechen, *b.s.* stinken (*of* nach) (*beide a. fig.*): *his breath* ~*s* er riecht aus dem Mund. **II** *v/t* (*mst irr*) **3.** et. riechen; *fig.* wittern: ~ *out hunt.* aufspüren (*a. fig.*); *Zimmer etc* verpesten. **4.** riechen an (*dat*). **III** *s* **5.** Geruch *m*, *b.s.* Gestank *m*: ~ *of gas* Gasgeruch; *there's a* ~ *of garlic here* hier stinkt es nach Knoblauch. **6.** *have* (*od. take*) *a* ~ *at* riechen an (*dat*). ~ *salts pl* Riechsalz *n*. '**smell·y** *adj* stinkend: ~ *feet pl* Schweißfüße *pl*.

smelt¹ [smelt] *pret u. pp von* **smell.**

smelt² [~] *v/t Erz* schmelzen.

smile [smaɪl] **I** *v/i* lächeln (*about* über *acc*): ~ *at* j-n anlächeln, j-m zulächeln; *j-n, et.* belächeln, lächeln über (*acc*); → *keep* 17. **II** *v/t*: ~ *one's approval* beifällig *od.* zustimmend lächeln. **III** *s* Lächeln *n*: *with a* ~ lächelnd; *be all* ~*s* (übers ganze Gesicht) strahlen; *give a* ~ lächeln; *give s.o. a* ~ j-n anlächeln, j-m zulächeln.

smirk [smɜːk] *v/i* (selbstgefällig *od.* schadenfroh) grinsen.

smite [smaɪt] *v/t* (*irr*): *be smitten by* (*od. with*) *fig.* gepackt werden von.

smith [smɪθ] *s* Schmied *m*.

smith·er·eens [ˌsmɪðəˈriːnz] *s pl*: *smash to* ~ in tausend Stücke schlagen *od.* zerspringen.

smith·y ['smɪðɪ] *s* Schmiede *f*.

smit·ten ['smɪtn] *pp von* **smite.**

smock [smɒk] s Kittel m.

smog [smɒg] s Smog m.

smoke [sməʊk] **I** v/i **1.** rauchen. **II** v/t **2.** rauchen. **3.** Fisch, Fleisch etc räuchern: ~ **out** ausräuchern. **III** s **4.** Rauch m: **there's no ~ without fire** fig. kein Rauch ohne Flamme; → **go up** 3. **5.** **have a ~** eine rauchen. **6.** F Glimmstengel m, Zigarette f. ~ **bomb** s Rauchbombe f.

smoked [sməʊkt] adj **1.** geräuchert, Räucher... **2.** ~ **glass** Rauchglas n. '**smok·er** s **1.** Raucher(in): ~ **'s cough** Raucherhusten m. **2.** 🚃 Raucherwagen m.

'**smoke·stack** s Schornstein m.

'**smok·ing** ['sməʊkɪŋ] **I** s Rauchen n: **no** ~ Rauchen verboten. **II** adj: ~ **compartment** Raucher(abteil n) m. '**smok·y** adj **1.** rauchig, verräuchert. **2.** rauchig (Geschmack etc). **3.** rauchfarben, -farbig.

smol·der Am. → **smoulder**.

smooch [smuːtʃ] v/i F knutschen, schmusen (**with** mit).

smooth [smuːð] **I** adj □ **1.** glatt (Fläche, Haut etc). **2.** ruhig (Flug etc). **3.** fig. glatt, reibungslos. **4.** fig. (aal)glatt. **II** v/t **5.** a. ~ **out** glätten, Tischtuch etc a. glattstreichen: ~ **away** Falten etc glätten; fig. Schwierigkeiten etc aus dem Weg räumen; ~ **over** fig. Spannungen etc ausgleichen. **III** s **6.** → **rough** 9.

smote [sməʊt] pret von **smite**.

smoth·er ['smʌðə] v/t **1.** j-n, Aufstand, Feuer etc ersticken. **2.** Gähnen etc unterdrücken. **3.** fig. j-n überschütten (**with** mit Zuneigung etc).

smoul·der ['sməʊldə] v/i bsd. Br. glimmen, schwelen (beide a. fig.).

smudge [smʌdʒ] **I** s **1.** Fleck m. **II** v/t **2.** Farbe etc verschmieren, Schrift a. verwischen. **3.** Glas etc be-, verschmieren (**with** mit). **III** v/i **4.** schmieren (Farbe etc), sich verwischen (Schrift). '**smudg·y** adj verschmiert, -wischt.

smug [smʌg] adj □ selbstgefällig.

smug·gle ['smʌgl] **I** v/t schmuggeln (**into** nach Deutschland; **in** acc): ~ **in** (out) ein-(heraus)schmuggeln. **II** v/i schmuggeln. '**smug·gler** s Schmuggler(in). '**smug·gling** s Schmuggel m.

smut [smʌt] s **1.** Rußflocke f. **2.** fig. Schmutz m. '**smut·ty** adj fig. schmutzig.

snack [snæk] s Snack m, Imbiß m: **have a ~** e-e Kleinigkeit essen. ~ **bar** s Snackbar f, Imbißstube f.

snaf·fle ['snæfl] v/t bsd. Br. et. mitgehen lassen.

snag [snæg] **I** s fig. Haken m. **II** v/t mit et. hängenbleiben (**on** an dat).

snail [sneɪl] s zo. Schnecke f: **at a ~'s pace** im Schneckentempo. ~ **shell** s Schneckenhaus n.

snake [sneɪk] **I** s zo. Schlange f: ~ **in the grass** fig. falsche Schlange (Frau); hinterlistiger Kerl (Mann). **II** v/t u. v/i: ~ (**one's way**) **through** sich schlängeln durch. '~**bite** s Schlangenbiß m. ~ **charm·er** s Schlangenbeschwörer m. '~**skin** s Schlangenhaut f; -leder n.

snak·y ['sneɪkɪ] adj gewunden (Straße etc).

snap [snæp] **I** v/i **1.** (zer)brechen, (-)reißen: **my patience ~ped** mir riß die Geduld od. der Geduldsfaden. **2.** a. ~ **shut** zuschnappen. **3.** ~ **at** schnappen nach (a. fig.); j-n anfahren. **4.** F ~ **out of it!** Kopf hoch!; ~ **to it!** mach fix! **II** v/t **5.** zerbrechen: ~ **off** abbrechen; → **s.o.'s head off** F j-m ins Gesicht springen. **6.** mit den Fingern schnalzen: ~ **one's fingers at** fig. keinen Respekt haben vor (dat), sich hinwegsetzen über (acc). **7.** phot. F knipsen. **8.** ~ **up** et. schnell entschlossen kaufen; fig. Gelegenheit beim Schopf ergreifen: ~ **it up!** Am. F mach fix! **III** s **9.** phot. F Schnappschuß m. **10.** Am. Druckknopf m. **11.** (Kälte-) Einbruch m. **12.** F Schwung m: **come on, put some ~ into it!** häng dich mal ein bißchen rein! **IV** adj **13.** spontan. '~**,drag·on** s 🌻 Löwenmaul n. ~ **fas·ten·er** s Am. Druckknopf m.

snap·pish ['snæpɪʃ] adj □ fig. bissig. '**snap·py** adj □ F **1.** modisch, schick. **2.** **make it ~!**, Br. a. **look ~!** F mach fix! '**snap·shot** s phot. Schnappschuß m.

snare [sneə] **I** s **1.** Falle f, Schlinge f, fig. a. Fallstrick m. **II** v/t **2.** in der Schlinge fangen. **3.** F et. ergattern.

snarl¹ [snɑːl] **I** v/i knurren (Hund, a. Person): ~ **at s.o.** j-n anknurren. **II** v/t et. knurren. **III** s Knurren n.

snarl² [~] v/t: **the traffic was ~ed** (**up**) es entstand ein Verkehrschaos. '~**up** s Verkehrschaos n.

snatch [snætʃ] **I** v/t **1.** et. packen: ~ **s.o.'s**

handbag j-m die Handtasche entreißen; ~ **s.th. from s.o.'s hand** j-m et. aus der Hand reißen. **2.** *fig.* Gelegenheit ergreifen; *ein paar Stunden Schlaf etc* ergattern. **II** *v/i* **3.** ~ **at** greifen nach; *fig.* Gelegenheit ergreifen. **III** *s* **4. make a ~ at** greifen nach. **5.** (*Gesprächs*)Fetzen *m*: ~ **of conversation.**

snaz·zy ['snæzɪ] *adj* □ F schick; *contp.* protzig.

sneak [sniːk] **I** *v/i* **1.** (sich) schleichen, sich stehlen; ~ **up on s.o.** (sich) an j-n heranschleichen. **2.** *Br.* F petzen: ~ **on s.o.** j-n verpetzen. **II** *v/t* **3.** F stibitzen: ~ **a look at** heimlich e-n Blick werfen auf (*acc*). **III** *s* **4.** *Br.* F Petzer(in), Petze *f.* **'sneak·er** *s Am.* Turn- *od.* Wanderschuh *m.* **'sneak·ing** *adj* heimlich, (*Verdacht a.*) leise. **'sneak·y** *adj* □ **1.** heimlich. **2.** gerissen.

sneer [snɪə] **I** *v/i* **1.** höhnisch *od.* spöttisch grinsen (**at** über *acc*). **2.** spotten (**at** über *acc*). **II** *s* **3.** höhnisches *od.* spöttisches Grinsen. **4.** höhnische *od.* spöttische Bemerkung.

sneeze [sniːz] **I** *v/i* niesen: *not to be ~d at* F nicht zu verachten. **II** *s* Niesen *n*; Nieser *m.*

snick·er ['snɪkə] *bsd. Am.* → **snigger.**

snide [snaɪd] *adj* □ abfällig.

sniff [snɪf] **I** *v/i* **1.** schniefen, die Nase hochziehen. **2.** schnüffeln (**at** an *dat*). **3.** ~ **at** *fig.* die Nase rümpfen über (*acc*): *not to be ~ed at* nicht zu verachten. **II** *v/t* **4.** durch die Nase einziehen; *Klebstoff etc* schnüffeln, *Kokain etc* schnupfen. **5.** ~ **out** aufspüren (*a. fig.*). **III** *s* **6.** Schniefen *n.*

snif·fle ['snɪfl] **I** *v/i* → **sniff** 1. **II** *s* Schniefen *n:* **he's got the ~s** F ihm läuft dauernd die Nase.

snif·ter ['snɪftə] *s Am.* Kognakschwenker *m.*

snig·ger ['snɪgə] *bsd. Br.* **I** *v/i* kichern (**at** über *acc*). **II** *s* Kichern *n.*

snip [snɪp] **I** *v/t* **1.** durchschnippeln: ~ **off** abschnippeln. **II** *s* **2.** Schnitt *m.* **3.** *Br.* F Gelegenheitskauf *m.*

snipe [snaɪp] **I** *pl* **snipes**, *bsd. coll.* **snipe** *s orn.* Schnepfe *f.* **II** *v/i:* ~ **at** aus dem Hinterhalt schießen auf (*acc*); *fig.* aus dem Hinterhalt angreifen (*acc*). **'snip·er** *s* Heckenschütze *m.*

snip·pet ['snɪpɪt] *s:* ~ **of conversation**

Gesprächsfetzen *m*; ~**s** *pl* **of information** bruchstückhafte Informationen *pl.*

snitch [snɪtʃ] *v/i:* ~ **on s.o.** F j-n verpetzen *od.* verpfeifen.

sniv·el ['snɪvl] *v/i pret u. pp* **-eled,** *bsd. Br.* **-elled** greinen, jammern.

snob [snɒb] *s* Snob *m.* **'snob·ber·y** *s* Snobismus *m.* **'snob·bish** *adj* □ snobistisch, versnobt.

snog [snɒg] *v/i Br.* F knutschen, schmusen (**with** mit).

snook [snuːk] *s:* **cock a ~ at** *Br.* F j-m zeigen, was man von ihm hält.

snook·er ['snuːkə] **I** *s Billard:* Snooker Pool. **II** *v/t:* **be ~ed** F völlig machtlos sein.

snoop [snuːp] *v/i:* ~ **about** (*od.* **around**) F herumschnüffeln (**in** in *dat*). **'snoop·er** *s* F Schnüffler(in).

snoot·y ['snuːtɪ] *adj* □ F hochnäsig.

snooze [snuːz] F **I** *v/i* ein Nickerchen machen. **II** *s* Nickerchen *n:* **have a ~** → I.

snore [snɔː] **I** *v/i* schnarchen. **II** *s* Schnarchen *n.* **'snor·er** *s* Schnarcher(in).

snor·kel ['snɔːkl] **I** *s* Schnorchel *m.* **II** *v/i* schnorcheln.

snort [snɔːt] **I** *v/i* (*a.* verächtlich *od.* wütend) schnauben. **II** *v/t* schnauben. **III** *s* Schnauben *n:* **give a ~ of derision** verächtlich schnauben.

snot [snɒt] *s* F Rotz *m.* **'snot·ty** *adj* F **1.** Rotz...: → **nose.** **2.** *fig.* aufgeblasen.

snout [snaʊt] *s zo.* Schnauze *f*, (*e-s Schweins etc a.*) Rüssel *m.*

snow [snəʊ] **I** *s* **1.** Schnee *m* (*a. sl. Kokain, Heroin*): (**as**) **white as ~** schneeweiß. **2.** Schneefall *m.* **II** *v/impers* **3.** schneien. **III** *v/t* **4. be ~ed in** (*od.* **up**) eingeschneit sein; **be ~ed under with work** mit Arbeit überhäuft sein. **'~ball** *s* Schneeball *m:* ~ **fight** Schneeballschlacht *f.* **'~-blind** *adj* schneeblind. **'~-capped** *adj* schneebedeckt (*Berggipfel*). **'~drift** *s* Schneewehe *f.* **'~-drop** *s* ♀ Schneeglöckchen *n.* **'~fall** *s* Schneefall *m.* **'~flake** *s* Schneeflocke *f.* **'~line** *s* Schneegrenze *f.* **'~man** *s* (*irr man*) Schneemann *m:* → **abominable.** **'~plough** *s,* **'~plow** *s Am.* Schneepflug *m* (*a. beim Skifahren*). **'~storm** *s* Schneesturm *m.* ‚**~'white** *adj* schneeweiß.

snow·y ['snəʊɪ] *adj* schneereich (*Tag etc*), (*Gegend a.*) verschneit.

snub¹ [snʌb] *v/t j-n* brüskieren, *j-m* über den Mund fahren.

snub² [~] *adj* Stups...: **~ nose. '~-nosed** *adj* stupsnasig.

snuff¹ [snʌf] *s* Schnupftabak *m.*

snuff² [~] *v/t* Kerze ausdrücken: **~ out** *fig. Leben* auslöschen; **~** *it Br.* F den Löffel weglegen (*sterben*).

snuf·fle ['snʌfl] → **sniffle.**

snug [snʌg] **I** *adj* □ **1.** behaglich, gemütlich. **2.** gutsitzend (*Kleidungsstück*): **be a ~ fit** gut passen. **II** *s* **3.** *Br.* kleines Nebenzimmer (*e-s Pubs*).

snug·gle ['snʌgl] *v/i:* **~ up to s.o.** sich an j-n kuscheln; **~ down in bed** sich ins Bett kuscheln.

so [səʊ] **I** *adv* **1.** so, dermaßen: **he is ~ stupid (that) he ...** er ist so dumm, daß er ... **2.** (ja) so: **I am ~ glad. 3.** so, in dieser Weise: **is that ~?** wirklich?; **~ as to** so daß, um zu; **a mile or ~** etwa e-e Meile; → **forth** 1, **if** 1, **on** 13. **4.** verkürzend: **He is tired. 2 am I** Ich auch; → **hope** 11, **think** 6, *etc.* **II** *cj* **5.** deshalb. **6. ~ what?** F na und?

soak [səʊk] **I** *v/t* **1.** einweichen (*in* in *dat*). **2. ~ up** Flüssigkeit aufsaugen; *fig. Neuigkeiten etc* in sich aufsaugen. **3.** durchnässen: → **skin** 1. **4.** F *j-n* ausnehmen, neppen. **II** *v/i* **5.** sickern. **'soak-ing** *adj u. adv:* **~ (wet)** tropfnaß.

'so-and-so *pl* **-sos** *s* F **1.** Herr *od.* Frau *od.* Frl. Soundso *od.* Sowieso: **a Mr ~** ein Herr Soundso. **2.** *euphem.* blöder Hund.

soap [səʊp] **I** *s* **1.** Seife *f.* **2.** F → **soap opera. II** *v/t* **3.** (sich) *et.* einseifen. **~ bub·ble** *s* Seifenblase *f.* **~ dish** *s* Seifenschale *f.* **~ op·er·a** *s* Rundfunk, *TV:* Seifenoper *f.* **'~-suds** *s pl* Seifenschaum *m.*

soap·y ['səʊpɪ] *adj* □ **1.** Seifen...: **~ water. 2.** seifig. **3.** F schmeichlerisch.

soar [sɔː] *v/i* **1.** aufsteigen: **~ into the sky** zum Himmel emporsteigen. **2.** hochragen. **3.** *fig.* in die Höhe schnellen (*Preise etc*).

sob [sɒb] **I** *v/i* schluchzen. **II** *v/t* schluchzen: **~ out** schluchzend erzählen. **III** *s* Schluchzen *n;* Schluchzer *m.*

so·ber ['səʊbə] **I** *adj* □ nüchtern (*a. fig.*): **(as) ~ as a judge** stocknüchtern. **II** *v/t*

mst **~ up** ausnüchtern, wieder nüchtern machen. **III** *v/i mst* **~ up** (sich) ausnüchtern, wieder nüchtern werden: **have a ~ing effect on s.o.** *fig.* auf j-n ernüchternd wirken.

sob sto·ry *s* F rührselige Geschichte.

,so-'called *adj* sogenannt.

soc·cer ['sɒkə] *s* Fußball *m* (*Spiel*).

so·cia·ble ['səʊʃəbl] *adj* □ gesellig (*Person, a. Abend etc*); zutraulich (*Tier*).

so·cial ['səʊʃl] *adj* □ **1.** gesellschaftlich, Gesellschafts..., sozial, Sozial...: **have a busy ~ life** oft ausgehen *od.* Besuch haben; **~ science** Sozialwissenschaft *f.* **2.** sozial, Sozial...: **~ insurance** Sozialversicherung *f;* **~ security** *Br.* Sozialhilfe *f; be on ~ security* Sozialhilfe beziehen; **~ worker** Sozialarbeiter(in). **3.** *pol.* Sozial...: **~ democrat** Sozialdemokrat(in). **4.** *biol.* gesellig (*Wesen*). **5.** F gesellig (*Person*).

so·cial·ism ['səʊʃəlɪzəm] *s* Sozialismus *m.* **'so·cial·ist I** *s* Sozialist(in). **II** *adj* sozialistisch.

so·cial·ize ['səʊʃəlaɪz] *v/i:* **I don't ~ much** ich gehe nicht oft aus; **~ with** (gesellschaftlich) verkehren mit.

so·ci·e·ty [sə'saɪətɪ] *s* Gesellschaft *f.*

so·ci·o·log·i·cal [,səʊsjə'lɒdʒɪkl] *adj* □ soziologisch. **so·ci·ol·o·gist** [,~sɪ'ɒlə-dʒɪst] *s* Soziologe *m,* Soziologin *f.* **,so·ci'ol·o·gy** *s* Soziologie *f.*

sock¹ [sɒk] *s* Socke(n *m*) *f:* **pull one's ~s up** *Br.* F sich am Riemen reißen; **put a ~ in it!** *Br.* F hör doch auf, Mensch!

sock² [~] F **I** *v/t:* **~ s.o. on the jaw** j-m e-n Kinnhaken verpassen. **II** *s* (*Faust-*) Schlag *m;* **give s.o. a ~ on the jaw** → **1.**

sock·et ['sɒkɪt] *s* **1.** *anat.* (*Augen*)Höhle *f.* **2.** *⚡* Steckdose *f;* Fassung *f* (*e-r Glühbirne*); (*Kopfhörer- etc*)Anschluß *m.*

sod [sɒd] *bsd. Br. sl.* **I** *s* blöder Hund: **poor ~** armes Schwein. **II** *v/t:* **~ it!** Scheiße! **III** *v/i:* **~ off!** verpiß dich!

so·da ['səʊdə] *s* **1.** Soda *n:* **two whisky and ~s** zwei Whisky mit Soda. **2.** *bsd. Am.* (*Orangen- etc*)Limonade *f.*

sod·den ['sɒdn] *adj* durchnäßt, (*Boden*) aufgeweicht.

so·di·um ['səʊdɪəm] *s* 🜓 Natrium *n.*

so·fa ['səʊfə] *s* Sofa *n.*

soft [sɒft] *adj* □ **1.** *allg.* weich: **be ~ in the head** F e-e weiche Birne haben; → **spot** 4. **2.** leise (*Stimme, Musik* *etc*); gedämpft, dezent (*Beleuchtung, Farbe, Musik*). **3.** sanft (*Berührung, Brise etc*). **4.** gutmütig; nachsichtig (**with** gegen *j-n*). **5.** ruhig (*Job etc*). **6.** verweichlicht: **get ~** verweichlichen. **7.** weich (*Droge*): **~ drink** Soft Drink *m*, alkoholfreies Getränk. **,~·'boiled** *adj* weich(gekocht) (*Ei*).

soft·en ['sɒfn] **I** *v/t* **1.** weich machen; *Wasser* enthärten. **2.** Ton, Licht *etc* dämpfen. **3. ~ up** *F j-n* weichmachen. **II** *v/i* **4.** weich werden. **'soft·en·er** *s* (*Wasser*)Enthärter *m*.

soft'heart·ed *adj* □ weichherzig.

soft·ie **~ softy.**

soft·ly·'ped·al *v/t* F *et.* herunterspielen. **'~·soap** *v/t* F *j-m* um den Bart gehen. **'~·ware** *s* Computer: Software *f*.

soft·y ['sɒftɪ] *s* F Softie *m*, Softy *m*, Weichling *m*.

sog·gy ['sɒgɪ] *adj* □ aufgeweicht (*Boden etc*), (*a. Gemüse etc*) matschig, (*Brot etc*) teigig, glitschig.

soil¹ [sɔɪl] *s* Boden *m*, Erde *f*.

soil² [~] *v/t* beschmutzen, schmutzig machen.

sol·ace ['sɒləs] *s* Trost *m*: **be a ~ to s.o.** *j-m* ein Trost sein; **find ~ in** Trost finden in (*dat*).

so·lar ['səʊlə] *adj* Sonnen...: **~ eclipse** *ast.* Sonnenfinsternis *f*; **~ energy** Sonnen-, Solarenergie *f*; **~ system** Sonnensystem *n*.

so·lar·i·um [səʊ'leərɪəm] *pl* **-i·a** [~ɪə], **-i·ums** *s* Solarium *n*.

so·lar plex·us ['pleksəs] *s* anat. Solarplexus *m*; Magengrube *f*.

sold [səʊld] *pret u. pp von* **sell.**

sol·der ['sɒldə] *v/t* (ver)löten. **'sol·der·ing** *adj*: **~ iron** Lötkolben *m*.

sol·dier ['səʊldʒə] **I** *s* Soldat *m*. **II** *v/i*: **~ on** *bsd. Br.* (unermüdlich) weitermachen.

sole¹ [səʊl] *adj* (□ → **solely**) einzig; alleinig, Allein...

sole² [~] **I** *s* (Fuß-, Schuh)Sohle *f*. **II** *v/t* *Schuh* besohlen.

sole³ [~] *s* ichth. Seezunge *f*.

sole·ly ['səʊllɪ] *adv* (einzig u.) allein, ausschließlich.

sol·emn ['sɒləm] *adj* □ **1.** feierlich: **give** *s.o.* **one's ~ pledge** (*od.* **word**) **that** *a.* *j-m* hoch u. heilig versprechen, daß. **2.** ernst.

so·lic·it [sə'lɪsɪt] **I** *v/t* *et.* erbitten, bitten um: **~ s.o.'s help** *j-n* um Hilfe bitten. **II** *v/i* Männer ansprechen (*Prostituierte*).

so·lic·i·tor [sə'lɪsɪtə] *s* ⚖ *Br.* Solicitor *m*.

so·lic·it·ous [sə'lɪsɪtəs] *adj* □ **1.** dienstbeflissen. **2.** besorgt (**about, for** um).

sol·id ['sɒlɪd] **I** *adj* □ **1.** allg. fest. **2.** stabil, massiv. **3.** massiv: **a ~ gold watch** e-e Uhr aus massivem Gold. **4.** fig. einmütig, geschlossen (**for** für; **against** gegen). **5.** fig. gewichtig, triftig (*Grund etc*), stichhaltig (*Argument etc*). **6. I waited for a ~ hour** F ich wartete e-e geschlagene Stunde. **II** *s* 🔬 A Körper *m*. **8.** *pl* feste Nahrung.

sol·i·dar·i·ty [,sɒlɪ'dærɪtɪ] *s* Solidarität *f*: **in ~ with** aus Solidarität mit; **declare one's ~ with** sich solidarisch erklären mit.

so·lid·i·fy [sə'lɪdɪfaɪ] **I** *v/t* **1.** fest werden lassen. **2.** fig. festigen. **II** *v/i* **3.** fest werden. **4.** fig. sich festigen.

,sol·id·'state *adj* volltransistor(is)iert.

so·lil·o·quy [sə'lɪləkwɪ] *s* **1.** thea. Monolog *m*. **2.** Selbstgespräch *n*.

sol·i·taire [,sɒlɪ'teə] *s* **1.** Solitär *m*. **2.** *bsd. Am.* → **patience** 2.

sol·i·tar·y ['sɒlɪtərɪ] **I** *adj* □ **1.** einsam, (*Leben a.*) zurückgezogen, (*Ort etc a.*) abgelegen: → **confinement** 2. **2.** einzig. **II** *s* **3.** F Einzelhaft *f*.

so·lo ['səʊləʊ] **I** *pl* **-los** *s* ♪ Solo *n*. **II** *adj* ♪ Solo...: **~ flight** ✈ Alleinflug *m*. **III** *adv* ♪ solo: **fly ~** ✈ e-n Alleinflug machen. **'so·lo·ist** *s* ♪ Solist(in).

sol·stice ['sɒlstɪs] *s* ast. Sonnenwende *f*.

sol·u·ble ['sɒljʊbl] *adj* **1.** 🔬 löslich: **~ in water** wasserlöslich. **2.** fig. lösbar.

so·lu·tion [sə'luːʃn] *s* **1.** fig. Lösung *f* (**to** gen). **2.** 🔬 Lösung *f*; Auflösung *f*.

solv·a·ble ['sɒlvəbl] *adj* fig. lösbar.

solve [sɒlv] *v/t* Fall, Rätsel *etc* lösen.

sol·ven·cy ['sɒlvənsɪ] *s* ✝ Solvenz *f*, Zahlungsfähigkeit *f*. **'sol·vent I** *adj* □ ✝ solvent, zahlungsfähig. **II** *s* 🔬 Lösungsmittel *n*.

som·ber *Am.* → **sombre.**

som·bre ['sɒmbə] *adj* □ düster (*Farben, Raum etc*, fig. Miene etc).

som·bre·ro [sɒm'breərəʊ] *pl* **-ros** *s* Sombrero *m*.

some [sʌm] **I** *adj* **1.** (irgend)ein: **~ day** eines Tages; **~ day** (**or other**) irgendwann (einmal). **2.** *vor pl*: einige, ein paar: → **few** 1. **3.** manche. **4.** gewiß: → **extent** 2. **5.** etwas, ein wenig *od.* bißchen: **take ~ more** nimm noch et.; **would you like ~ more cake?** möchtest du noch ein Stück Kuchen? **6.** ungefähr: **~ 30 people.** II *pron* **7.** (irgend)ein. **8.** etwas. **9.** einige, ein paar. **'~·bod·y** ['~bədɪ] I *pron* jemand. II *s*: **be ~** et. vorstellen, j-d sein. **'~·day** *adv* eines Tages. **'~·how** *adv* irgendwie. **'~·one** → **somebody**. **'~·place** *Am.* → **somewhere** 1.

som·er·sault ['sʌməsɔːlt] *s* Salto *m*; Purzelbaum *m*: **do** (*od.* **turn**) **a ~** e-n Salto machen; e-n Purzelbaum schlagen.

'some·|·thing ['sʌmθɪŋ] I *pron* **1.** etwas: **or ~** F od. so. II *adv* **2. ~ like** F ungefähr; **look ~ like** so ähnlich aussehen wie; **~ over £200** et. mehr als 200 Pfund. **3. be ~ of a pianist** so et. wie ein Pianist sein. III *s* **4. a little ~** e-e Kleinigkeit (*Geschenk*); **a certain ~** ein gewisses Etwas. **'~·time** *adv* irgendwann. **'~·times** *adv* manchmal. **'~·way** *adv Am.* irgendwie. **'~·what** *adv* ein bißchen *od.* wenig: **~ of a shock** ein ziemlicher Schock. **'~·where** *adv* **1.** irgendwo; irgendwohin. **2.** *fig.* **~ between 30 and 40 people** so zwischen 30 u. 40 Leute; **~ in the region of £100** um 100 Pfund herum.

som·nam·bu·list [sɒmˈnæmbjʊlɪst] *s* Nacht-, Schlafwandler(in).

som·no·lent ['sɒmnələnt] *adj* □ **1.** schläfrig. **2.** einschläfernd.

son [sʌn] *s* **1.** Sohn *m*: **~ of a bitch** *bsd. Am. sl.* Scheißkerl *m*. **2.** *Anrede:* F junger Mann.

so·na·ta [səˈnɑːtə] *s* ♪ Sonate *f*.

song [sɒŋ] *s* **1.** Lied *n*: **buy s.th. for a ~** F et. für ein Butterbrot kaufen; **make a ~ and dance about** F ein furchtbares Theater machen wegen. **2.** Gesang *m* (*a. von Vögeln*): **burst into ~** zu singen anfangen; → **bird** 1. **'~·bird** *s* Singvogel *m*. **'~·book** *s* Liederbuch *n*.

son·ic ['sɒnɪk] *adj phys.* Schall...: **~ bang** (*od.* **boom**) ✈ Überschallknall *m*.

'son-in-law *pl* **'sons-in-law** *s* Schwiegersohn *m*.

son·net ['sɒnɪt] *s* Sonett *n*.

so·no·rous ['sɒnərəs] *adj* □ sonor, klangvoll, volltönend.

soon [suːn] *adv* bald: **as ~ as** sobald; **as ~ as possible** so bald wie möglich; **at the ~est** frühestens; **I don't want to speak too ~** ich will es nicht berufen. **'soon·er** *adv* **1.** eher, früher: **the ~ the better** je früher, desto besser *od.* lieber; **~ or later** früher *od.* später; **no ~ said than done** gesagt, getan. **2. I would ~ ... than** ich würde lieber ... als.

soot [sʊt] *s* Ruß *m*.

soothe [suːð] *v/t* **1.** *a.* **~ down** j-n beschwichtigen, *a.* j-s Nerven beruhigen. **2.** *Schmerzen* lindern, mildern.

soot·y ['sʊtɪ] *adj* rußig, Ruß...

sop [sɒp] I *s* Beschwichtigungsmittel *n* (**to** für). II *v/t*: **~ up** aufsaugen.

soph·ism ['sɒfɪzəm] *s* Sophismus *m*, Scheinbeweis *m*, Trugschluß *m*.

so·phis·ti·cat·ed [səˈfɪstɪkeɪtɪd] *adj* □ **1.** kultiviert. **2.** ⊕ hochentwickelt. **3.** *contp.* intellektuell.

soph·o·more ['sɒfəmɔː] *s Am.* Student(in) im zweiten Jahr.

so·po·rif·ic [ˌsɒpəˈrɪfɪk] I *adj* (**~ally**) einschläfernd: **~ drug** → II. II *s* Schlafmittel *n*.

sop·ping ['sɒpɪŋ] *adj u. adv*: **~** (**wet**) F patschnaß. **'sop·py** *adj* □ *Br.* F schmalzig, rührselig.

so·pra·no [səˈprɑːnəʊ] *pl* **-nos** *s* Sopran *m* (*Tonlage, Stimme*), (*Sängerin a.*) Sopranistin *f*.

sor·bet ['sɔːbeɪ] *s bsd. Br.* Fruchteis *n*.

sor·cer·er ['sɔːsərə] *s* Zauberer *m*, Hexenmeister *m*, Hexer *m*. **'sor·cer·ess** *s* Zauberin *f*, Hexe *f*. **'sor·cer·y** *s* Zauberei *f*, Hexerei *f*.

sor·did ['sɔːdɪd] *adj* □ schmutzig (*a. fig.*).

sore [sɔː] I *adj* **1.** weh, wund; entzündet: **he is ~ all over** ihm tut alles weh; **my legs are ~** mir tun die Beine weh; **~ throat** Angina *f*, Halsentzündung *f*; **have a ~ throat** a. Halsschmerzen haben; → **sight** 2, **thumb** I. **2.** *fig.* wund (*Punkt*). **3.** *bsd. Am.* F sauer (**about** wegen). II *s* **4.** wunde Stelle, Wunde *f*. **'sore·ly** *adv*: **~ missed** schmerzlich vermißt; **~ needed** dringend gebraucht.

so·ror·i·ty [səˈrɒrətɪ] *s Am.* Studentinnenverbindung *f*.

sor·rel ['sɒrəl] *s* ♣ Sauerampfer *m*.

sor·row ['sɒrəʊ] *s* **1.** (**at, over**) Kummer *m* (über *acc*, um), Trauer *f* (um); Traurigkeit f. **2.** Sorge f: → **drown** 2. **sor·row·ful** ['sɒrəful] adj □ traurig, kummervoll.

sor·ry ['sɒrɪ] **I** adj **1.** be (od. feel) ~ **for s.o.** j-n bedauern od. bemitleiden: **I'm** ~ **for him** er tut mir leid; **I'm** ~ → 3; **I am** ~ **to say** ich muß leider sagen. **2.** traurig, jämmerlich. **II** int **3.** a) (es) tut mir leid, b) Entschuldigung!, Verzeihung!: **say** ~ sich entschuldigen (*to s.o.* bei j-m; *for s.th.* für et.). **4.** *bsd. Br.* wie bitte?

sort [sɔːt] **I** s **1.** Sorte f, Art f, ♥ a. Marke f: **all** ~**s of things** alle mögliche. **2.** Art f: **nothing of the** ~ nichts dergleichen; **what** ~ **of (a) man is he?** wie ist er?; **I had a** ~ **of (a) feeling that** ich hatte das unbestimmte Gefühl, daß; **I** ~ **of expected it** F ich habe es irgendwie od. beinahe erwartet. **3.** **of a** ~, **of a** ~**s** contp. so et. Ähnliches wie. **4.** **be out of** ~**s** F nicht auf der Höhe od. auf dem Damm sein. **5.** F guter etc Kerl. **II** v/t **6.** sortieren: ~ **out** aussortieren; *Problem etc* lösen, *Frage etc* klären; *Br.* F j-n zur Schnecke machen. **III** v/i **7.** ~ **through** et. durchsehen.

sor·tie ['sɔːtiː] s **1.** ✕ Ausfall m; ✈ Einsatz m. **2.** *fig.* Ausflug m (**into** in *acc*).

SOS [,esəʊ'es] s ♣ SOS n: ~ **message** SOS-Ruf m.

'so·so adj u. adv F so lala.

souf·flé ['suːfleɪ] s gastr. Soufflé n, Auflauf m.

sought [sɔːt] pret u. pp von **seek**. '~-**,af·ter** adj begehrt (*Person*), (*Sache a.*) gesucht.

soul [səʊl] s **1.** Seele f (a. *fig.*). **2.** Gefühl n; (künstlerischer) Ausdruck. **3.** **be the** ~ **of generosity** die Großzügigkeit selbst od. in Person sein. **4.** ♪ Soul m. '~-**de,stroy·ing** adj geisttötend (*Arbeit etc*).

soul·ful ['səʊlful] adj □ gefühlvoll (*Musik etc*), seelenvoll (*Blick*).

soul| mu·sic s Soulmusik f. '~-**,search·ing** s Gewissensprüfung f.

sound[1] [saʊnd] **I** s **1.** Geräusch n; *phys.* Schall m; (*Radio, TV etc*) Ton m; ♪ Klang m, (*Rockmusik etc a.*) Sound m; *ling.* Laut m: **I don't like the** ~ **of it** *fig.* die Sache gefällt mir nicht. **II** v/i **2.** erklingen, ertönen: **the bell** ~**ed for lunch** es klingelte zum Mittagessen. **3.** *fig.* klingen. **4.** ~ **off** F tönen (**about**, **on**

von). **III** v/t **5.** ~ **one's horn** mot. hupen; ~ **alarm** 1. **6.** *ling.* (aus)sprechen.

sound[2] [~] **I** adj □ **1.** gesund; intakt, in Ordnung. **2.** *fig.* klug, vernünftig (*Person, Rat etc*). **3.** *fig.* gründlich (*Ausbildung etc*). **4.** *fig.* gehörig (*Tracht Prügel*); vernichtend (*Niederlage*). **5.** *fig.* fest, tief (*Schlaf*). **II** adv **6.** ~ **sleeper** 1. **II** adv **6.** be ~ **asleep** fest od. tief schlafen.

sound[3] [~] v/t **1.** ♣ (aus)loten. **2.** ~ **out** j-n ausholen (**about, on** über *acc*); *j-s Ansichten etc* herausfinden.

sound| bar·ri·er s *phys.* Schallmauer f, -grenze f. **~ film** s Tonfilm m.

sound·less ['saʊndlɪs] adj □ lautlos. '**sound·ness** s **1.** Gesundheit f; Intaktheit f. **2.** *fig.* Klugheit f, Vernünftigkeit f. **3.** *fig.* Gründlichkeit f.

'**sound|·proof** adj □ schalldicht. **II** v/t schalldicht machen. ~ **track** s **1.** *Film:* Tonspur f. **2.** Filmmusik f. ~ **wave** s *phys.* Schallwelle f.

soup [suːp] **I** s Suppe f: **be in the** ~ F in der Patsche (od. Tinte) sitzen. **II** v/t: ~ **up** F *Auto, Motor* frisieren. ~**plate** s Suppenteller m. ~ **spoon** s Suppenlöffel m.

sour ['saʊə] **I** adj □ **1.** sauer: ~ **cream** Sauerrahm m, saure Sahne; **go** ~ sauer werden. **2.** *fig.* mürrisch. **II** v/i **3.** sauer werden. **III** v/t **4.** sauer werden lassen; säuern: ~**ed cream** *Br.* Sauerrahm m, saure Sahne.

source [sɔːs] s Quelle f, *fig. a.* Ursache f, Ursprung m: **from a reliable** ~ aus zuverlässiger Quelle. ~ **lan·guage** s *ling.* Ausgangssprache f.

sour·puss ['saʊəpʊs] s F Miesepeter m.

soused [saʊst] adj F blau (*betrunken*).

sou·tane [suː'tɑːn] s *eccl.* Soutane f.

south [saʊθ] **I** s **1.** Süden m: **in the** ~ **of** im Süden von (*od. gen*); **to the** ~ **of** → 5. **2.** a. ⌖ Süden m, südlicher Landesteil: **the** ⌖ *Br.* Südengland m; *Am.* die Südstaaten pl. **II** adj **3.** Süd..., südlich: ⌖ **Pole** Südpol m. **III** adv **4.** südwärts, nach Süden. **5.** ~ **of** südlich von (*od. gen*). ⌖ **A·mer·i·can I** adj südamerikanisch. **II** s Südamerikaner(in). '~**bound** adj nach Süden gehend od. fahrend. ~**east I** s Südosten m. **II** adj südöstlich, Südost... **III** adv südöstlich, nach Südosten.

south·er·ly ['sʌðəlɪ] **I** adj südlich, Süd... **II** adv von od. nach Süden. **south·ern**

['~ən] *adj* südlich, Süd... **'south·ern·er** *s* **1.** Bewohner(in) des Südens (*e-s Landes*). **2.** ♀ *Am.* Südstaatler(in). **south·ern·most** ['~məʊst] *adj* südlichst.

'south·paw *s Boxen:* Rechtsauslager *m.*

south·ward ['saʊθwəd] *adj u. adv* südlich, südwärts, nach Süden: **in a ~ di-rection** in südlicher Richtung, Richtung Süden. **'south·wards** *adv* → **southward.**

,south·'west I *s* Südwesten *m.* **II** *adj* südwestlich, Südwest... **III** *adv* südwestlich, nach Südwesten.

sou·ve·nir [suːvə'nɪə] *s* Andenken *n* (**of** an *acc*), Souvenir *n.*

sov·er·eign ['sɒvrɪn] **I** *s* Landesherr(in), Monarch(in). **II** *adj* souverän (*Staat*). **sov·er·eign·ty** ['~rəntɪ] *s* Souveränität *f.*

So·vi·et ['səʊvɪət] **I** *s*: **the ~s** pl die Sowjets *pl.* **II** *adj* sowjetisch, Sowjet...

sow¹ [saʊ] *s zo.* Sau *f.*

sow² [səʊ] *v/t (mst irr)* **1.** *Getreide etc* säen, *Samen* aussäen: **~ the seeds of** discord *fig.* Zwietracht säen; → **oats.** **2.** *Feld* besäen (**with** mit).

so·ya bean ['sɔɪə] *s* ♀ Sojabohne *f.*

soz·zled ['sɒzld] *adj Br.* F blau (*betrunken*).

spa [spɑː] *s* (Heil)Bad *n.*

space [speɪs] **I** *s* **1.** Raum *m*: **stare into ~** ins Leere starren. **2.** Platz *m*, Raum *m.* **3.** (Welt)Raum *m.* **4.** Lücke *f,* Platz *m,* Stelle *f.* **5.** Zwischenraum *m.* **6.** Zeitraum *m.* **II** *v/t* **7.** *a.* **~ out** in Abständen anordnen: **~ the chairs two feet apart** die Stühle im Abstand von zwei Fuß aufstellen. **'~·bar** *s* Leertaste *f* (*e-r Schreibmaschine*). **'~·craft** *s* (*irr* **craft**) (Welt)Raumfahrzeug *n.* **'~·flight** *s* (Welt)Raumflug *m.* **'~ heat·er** *s* Heizapparat *m,* -gerät *n.* **'~·lab** *s* Raumlabor *n.* **'~·man** *s* (*irr* **man**) **1.** Raumfahrer *m.* **2.** Außerirdische *m.* **'~·ship** *s* Raumschiff *n.* **~ shut·tle** *s* Raumfähre *f,* -transporter *m.* **~ sta·tion** *s* (Welt)Raumstation *f.* **~ suit** *s* Raumanzug *m.* **~ trav·el** *s* (Welt)Raumfahrt *f.* **'~·wom·an** *s* (*irr* **woman**) **1.** Raumfahrerin *f.* **2.** Außerirdische *f.*

spac·ing ['speɪsɪŋ] *s*: **type s.th. in** (*od.* **with**) **single** (**double**) **~** et. mit einzeiligem (zweizeiligem) Abstand tippen.

spa·cious ['speɪʃəs] *adj* □ geräumig (*Zimmer etc*), weiträumig angelegt, weitläufig (*Garten etc*).

spade¹ [speɪd] *s* Spaten *m*: **call a ~ a ~** *fig.* das Kind beim Namen nennen.

spade² [~] *s Kartenspiel:* a) *pl* Pik *n* (*Farbe*), b) Pik(karte *f*) *n.*

'spade·work *s fig.* (mühevolle) Vorarbeit.

spa·ghet·ti [spə'getɪ] *s pl* (*sg konstruiert*) Spaghetti *pl.*

span [spæn] **I** *s* **1.** ✈, *orn.* (Flügel-) Spannweite *f.* **2.** Zeitspanne *f.* **3.** (*Lebens*)Spanne *f,* (*Gedächtnis*)Umfang *m.* **II** *v/t* **4.** *Fluß etc* überspannen (*Brücke*). **5.** *fig.* sich erstrecken über (*acc*).

span·gle ['spæŋgl] **I** *s* Paillette *f.* **II** *v/t* mit Pailletten besetzen; *fig.* übersäen (**with** mit).

Span·iard ['spænjəd] *s* Spanier(in).

span·iel ['spænjəl] *s zo.* Spaniel *m.*

Span·ish ['spænɪʃ] **I** *adj* **1.** spanisch. **II** *s* **2.** die **~** pl die Spanier *pl.* **3.** *ling.* Spanisch *n.*

spank [spæŋk] *v/t* j-m den Hintern versohlen. **'spank·ing I** *adj* flott, scharf (*Tempo*). **II** *adv* F: **~ clean** blitzsauber; **~ new** funkelnagelneu. **III** *s*: **give s.o. a ~ →** **spank.**

span·ner ['spænə] *s* ⊙ *bsd. Br.* Schraubenschlüssel *m*: **put** (*od.* **throw**) **a ~ in the works** F j-m in die Quere kommen.

spar [spɑː] *v/i* **1.** *Boxen:* sparren (**with** mit). **2.** sich ein Wortgefecht liefern (**with** mit).

spare [speə] **I** *v/t* **1.** *j-n, et.* entbehren. **2.** *Geld, Zeit etc* übrig haben: **can you ~ me a cigarette** (**10 minutes**)? hast du e-e Zigarette (10 Minuten Zeit) für mich (übrig)? **3.** *keine Kosten, Mühen etc* scheuen. **4.** **~ s.o. s.th.** j-m et. ersparen, j-n mit et. verschonen. **II** *adj* **5.** Ersatz...: **~ part** ⊙ Ersatzteil *n, m;* **~ tire** (*bsd. Br.* **tyre**) *mot.* Ersatz-, Reservereifen *m; Br. fig. humor.* Rettungsring *m.* **6.** überschüssig: **~ bedroom** Gästezimmer *n;* **~ time** Freizeit *f;* **have you got 10 ~ minutes?** hast du 10 Minuten Zeit (übrig)? **III** *s* **7.** *mot.* Ersatz-, Reservereifen *m.* **8.** ⊙ *bsd. Br.* Ersatzteil *n, m.* **'~·ribs** *s pl gastr.* Spareribs *pl* (*gegrillte Rippenstücke vom Schwein*).

spar·ing ['speərɪŋ] *adj* □ sparsam: **be ~ with s.th.,** **use s.th. ~ly** sparsam mit et. umgehen.

spark [spɑːk] **I** s Funke(n) m (a. fig.): *whenever they meet the ~s fly* immer, wenn sie zs.-kommen, fliegen die Fetzen. **II** v/i Funken sprühen: *~ing plug* mot. Br. Zündkerze f. **III** v/t a) *~ off Krawalle etc* auslösen, b) bsd. Am. j-s Interesse etc wecken.

spar·kle ['spɑːkl] **I** v/i funkeln, *(Augen a.)* blitzen *(with* vor *dat).* **II** s Funkeln n, Blitzen n. **spar·kling** ['~klɪŋ] *adj* **1.** funkelnd, blitzend. **2.** *~ wine* Perl- od. Schaumwein m; Sekt m. **3.** fig. sprühend *(Witz);* geistsprühend *(Dialog etc);* schwungvoll *(Vortrag etc).*

spark plug s mot. Zündkerze f.

spar·ring ['spɑːrɪŋ] *adj: ~ partner (Boxen)* Sparringspartner m.

spar·row ['spærəʊ] s orn. Spatz m, Sperling m.

sparse [spɑːs] *adj* □ spärlich: *~ly populated* dünnbesiedelt, -bevölkert.

spar·tan ['spɑːtən] *adj* spartanisch *(Lebensweise etc).*

spasm ['spæzəm] s **1.** ☤ Krampf m. **2.** *(Husten-, Lach- etc)*Anfall m. **spas·mod·ic** [~'mɒdɪk] *adj* (*~ally*) **1.** ☤ krampfartig. **2.** fig. sporadisch, unregelmäßig.

spas·tic ['spæstɪk] ☤ **I** *adj* (*~ally*) spastisch. **II** s Spastiker(in).

spat [spæt] *pret u. pp von* spit².

spate [speɪt] s **1.** *be (od. run) in ~* Hochwasser führen. **2.** fig. Flut f, *(von Unfällen etc)* Serie f.

spa·tial ['speɪʃl] *adj* □ räumlich: *~ ability* räumliches Vorstellungsvermögen.

spat·ter ['spætə] **I** v/t **1.** j-n, etc. bespritzen *(with* mit). **2.** et. spritzen *(in s.o.'s face* j-m ins Gesicht; *over* über *acc).* **II** v/i **3.** spritzen. **III** s **4.** Spritzer m. **5.** a ~ of applause kurzer Beifall; *there was a ~ of rain* es spritzte, es regnete ein paar Tropfen.

spat·u·la ['spætjʊlə] s Spachtel m, f, bsd. ☤ Spatel m, f.

spawn [spɔːn] **I** s zo. Laich m. **II** v/i zo. laichen. **III** v/t fig. hervorbringen, produzieren.

spay [speɪ] v/t weibliches Tier sterilisieren.

speak [spiːk] *(irr)* **I** v/i **1.** sprechen, reden *(to, with* mit; *about* über *acc):* *~ing!* teleph. am Apparat!; *~ for* sprechen für; *this ~s for itself* das spricht für sich

selbst; *~ of fig.* hindeuten auf *(acc);* zeugen von; *we don't ~ (to each other)* wir sprechen od. reden nicht miteinander; *so to ~* sozusagen; → *devil* 1, *generally, ill* 3, *roughly* 2, *soon, strict.* **2.** sprechen *(to* vor *dat; about, on* über *acc).* **3.** sich aussprechen *(in favo[u]r of* für; *against* gegen). **II** v/t **4.** sprechen, sagen; → *mind* 4, *volume* 1. **5.** *Sprache* sprechen.

Verbindungen mit Adverbien:

speak| out v/i: *~ against* sich klar u. deutlich aussprechen gegen. *~ up* v/i **1.** lauter sprechen. **2.** *~ for* sich klar u. deutlich aussprechen für.

speak·er ['spiːkə] s **1.** Sprecher(in), Redner(in). **2.** ♀ parl. Speaker m, Präsident m. **3.** a ~ of English j-d, der Englisch spricht. **4.** ♫ Lautsprecher m. '**speak·ing I** s: → *manner* 1. **II** *adj: ~ clock* teleph. Br. Zeitansage f; *we are not on ~ terms* wir sprechen od. reden nicht miteinander.

spear [spɪə] **I** s Speer m. **II** v/t aufspießen; durchbohren. '*~head* **I** s **1.** Speerspitze f. **2.** ✗ Angriffsspitze f; *(Sport)* (Sturm-, Angriffs)Spitze f. **3.** fig. Anführer(in). **II** v/t **4.** fig. anführen. '*~mint* s ♣ Grüne Minze.

spec [spek] s: *on ~ Br.* F auf gut Glück.

spe·cial ['speʃl] **I** *adj* (□ → *specially*) **1.** speziell, besonder. **2.** speziell, Spezial...: *~ knowledge* Fachkenntnisse pl, -wissen n. **3.** Sonder...: *~ school (train, etc)* Sonder... **II** s **5.** Sonderbus m od. -zug m; *(Rundfunk, TV)* Sondersendung f; ♥ Sonderangebot n: *be on ~ Am.* im Angebot sein. **spe·cial·ist** ['~ʃəlɪst] **I** s Spezialist(in), ☤ a. Facharzt m, -ärztin f *(in* für). **II** *adj* Fach... **spe·ci·al·i·ty** [~ʃɪ'ælətɪ] s **1.** Spezialität f: *~ of the house* Spezialität des Hauses. **2.** Spezialgebiet f. **spe·cial·i·za·tion** [~ʃəlaɪ'zeɪʃn] s Spezialisierung f. '**spe·cial·ize** v/i sich spezialisieren *(in auf acc).* '**spe·cial·ly** *adv* **1.** besonders. **2.** speziell, extra. **spe·cial·ty** ['~ʃltɪ] *Am.* → *speciality.*

spe·cies ['spiːʃiːz] *pl* -cies s biol. Spezies f, Art f *(beide a. allg.).*

spe·cif·ic [spə'sɪfɪk] **I** *adj* **1.** spezifisch *(a. phys.),* speziell, besonder: *~ gravity* spezifisches Gewicht. **2.** konkret, präzis. **3.** eigen *(to dat).* **II** s *pl* **4.** Einzelheiten pl. **spe·cif·i·cal·ly** adv 1. speziell, besonders. 2. ausdrücklich.

spec·i·fi·ca·tion [ˌspesɪfɪˈkeɪʃn] s genaue Angabe od. Beschreibung. **spec·i·fy** [ˈspesɪfaɪ] v/t genau beschreiben od. festlegen.

spec·i·men [ˈspesɪmən] s 1. Exemplar n. 2. Muster n; Probe f. 3. F contp. Typ m (Person).

spe·cious [ˈspiːʃəs] adj □ trügerisch: ~ argument Scheinargument n.

speck [spek] s kleiner Fleck, (Staub-) Korn n; Punkt m (**on the horizon** am Horizont).

speck·led [ˈspekld] adj gesprenkelt.

specs [speks] → **spectacle** 3.

spec·ta·cle [ˈspektəkl] s 1. Schauspiel n (a. fig.): **make a ~ of o.s.** sich lächerlich machen. 2. Anblick m. 3. pl, a. **pair of ~s** Brille f.

spec·tac·u·lar [spekˈtækjʊlə] I adj □ spektakulär. II s Show f der Superlative.

spec·ta·tor [spekˈteɪtə] s Zuschauer(in).

spec·ter Am. → **spectre**.

spec·tra [ˈspektrə] pl von **spectrum**.

spec·tral [ˈspektrəl] adj □ 1. geisterhaft, gespenstisch. 2. phys. Spektral...

spec·tre [ˈspektə] s bsd. Br. (fig. a. Schreck)Gespenst n.

spec·trum [ˈspektrəm] pl **-tra** [ˈ~trə] s phys. Spektrum n (a. fig.): **a wide ~ of opinion(s)** ein breites Meinungsspektrum.

spec·u·late [ˈspekjʊleɪt] v/i 1. spekulieren, Vermutungen anstellen (**about, on** über acc): ~ **that** vermuten, daß. 2. ✝ spekulieren (**in** mit). **spec·u·la·tion** [ˈ~leɪʃn] s Spekulation f (a. ✝), Vermutung f. **spec·u·la·tive** [ˈ~lətɪv] adj □ spekulativ, ✝ a. Spekulations... **spec·u·la·tor** [ˈ~leɪtə] s ✝ Spekulant(in).

sped [sped] pret u. pp von **speed**.

speech [spiːtʃ] s 1. Sprache f (Sprechvermögen, Ausdrucksweise): ~ **defect** (**impediment**) Sprachfehler m. 2. Rede f, Ansprache f (**to** vor dat), ⚖ Plädoyer n. **speech·i·fy** [ˈ~faɪ] v/i contp. Reden od. e-e Rede schwingen. **speech·less** adj □ sprachlos (**with** vor dat).

speed [spiːd] s 1. Geschwindigkeit f, Schnelligkeit f, Tempo n: **at a ~ of** mit e-r Geschwindigkeit von; **at full** (od. **top**) **speed** mit Höchstgeschwindig-

keit. 2. mot. etc Gang m: **five-~ gearbox** Fünfganggetriebe f. 3. phot. Lichtempfindlichkeit f. II v/t (irr) 4. rasch bringen od. befördern. 5. ~ **up** (pret u. pp **-ed**) beschleunigen. III v/i 6. rasen: ~ **by** wie im Flug vergehen (Zeit); **be ~ing** mot. zu schnell fahren, die Geschwindigkeitsbegrenzung überschreiten. 7. ~ **up** (pret u. pp **-ed**) beschleunigen (Fahrer etc), (a. Wachstum etc) schneller werden. ~ **bump** s mot. Rüttelschwelle f.

speed·ing [ˈspiːdɪŋ] s mot. zu schnelles Fahren, Geschwindigkeitsüberschreitung f.

speed lim·it s mot. Geschwindigkeitsbegrenzung f, Tempolimit n.

speed·o [ˈspiːdəʊ] pl **-os** s mot. F Tacho m.

speed·om·e·ter [spɪˈdɒmɪtə] s mot. Tachometer m, n.

speed·y [ˈspiːdɪ] adj □ schnell, (Antwort etc a.) prompt: → **recovery** 2.

spell¹ [spel] (mst irr) I v/t 1. a) ~ **out** buchstabieren: ~ **out** klarmachen (**for s.o.** j-m), b) (orthographisch richtig) schreiben. 2. Unglück etc bedeuten. II v/i 3. (richtig) schreiben.

spell² [~] s 1. Weile f: **for a ~** e-e Zeitlang; **cold ~** meteor. Kälteperiode f. 2. (Husten- etc)Anfall m.

spell³ [~] s 1. Zauber(spruch) m. 2. Zauber m (a. fig.): **be under s.o.'s ~** in j-s Bann stehen; **cast a ~ over s.o.** j-n verzaubern, fig. a. j-n in s-n Bann ziehen.

'**spell**|**bind·ing** adj fesselnd. '**~bound** adj u. adv wie gebannt: **hold s.o. ~** j-n fesseln.

spell·er [ˈspelə] s 1. **be a good** (**bad**) ~ gut (schlecht) in Rechtschreibung sein. 2. Computer: ~ Rechtschreibsystem n. '**spell·ing** s 1. Rechtschreibung f: ~ **mistake** (Recht)Schreibfehler m. 2. Schreibung f, Schreibweise f.

spelt [spelt] pret u. pp von **spell¹**.

spend [spend] v/t (irr) 1. Geld ausgeben (**on** für): → **penny** 1. 2. Urlaub, Zeit verbringen: ~ **an hour doing s.th.** e-e Stunde damit verbringen, et. zu tun. '**spend·er** s: **he's a big ~** über s.o. läßt das Geld locker. '**spend·ing** I s Ausgaben pl. II adj: ~ **money** Taschengeld n; → **spree**.

spend·thrift ['spendθrɪft] **I** s Verschwender(in). **II** adj verschwenderisch.

spent [spent] **I** pret u. pp von **spend**. **II** adj verbraucht.

sperm [spɜːm] s biol. Sperma n, Samen(flüssigkeit f) m.

spew [spjuː] **I** v/t **1.** a. ~ **out** Rauch etc ausstoßen, Lava etc spucken. **2.** a. ~ **up** sl. auskotzen. **II** v/i **3.** a. ~ **out** hervorquellen (**from** aus). **4.** sl. kotzen.

sphere [sfɪə] s **1.** Kugel f. **2.** fig. (Einfluß- etc)Sphäre f, (-)Bereich m: **in the ~ of** auf dem Gebiet (gen). **spher·i·cal** ['sferɪkl] adj □ **1.** kugelförmig. **2.** A- Kugel..., sphärisch.

sphinc·ter ['sfɪŋktə] s anat. Schließmuskel m.

spice [spaɪs] s **1.** Gewürz n. **2.** fig. Würze f. **II** v/t **3.** würzen (**with** mit) (a. fig.). ~ **rack** s Gewürzständer m.

spick-and-span [ˌspɪkən'spæn] adj blitzsauber.

spic·y ['spaɪsɪ] adj □ **1.** gutgewürzt, würzig. **2.** fig. pikant.

spi·der ['spaɪdə] s zo. Spinne f. ~ **web** s Am. Spinnwebe f, Spinnennetz n.

spiel [ʃpiːl] s F mst contp. Masche f.

spike [spaɪk] **I** s **1.** Spitze f; Stachel m: ~ **heel** Pfennigabsatz m. **2.** Sport: a) Spike m, Dorn m, b) pl Spikes pl, Rennschuhe pl. **II** v/t **3.** aufspießen. **4.** → **lace** 7. **'spik·y** adj □ **1.** spitz(ig); stach(e)lig. **2.** Br. F leicht eingeschnappt.

spill [spɪl] **I** v/t (mst irr) a. ~ **out** aus-, verschütten: **I've spilt my coffee over my trousers** ich habe mir m-n Kaffee über die Hose geschüttet; → **bean** 1, **milk** I. **II** v/i (mst irr) verschüttet werden; sich ergießen (**over** über acc); strömen (**out of** aus) (Menschen): ~ **over** überlaufen; fig. übergreifen (**into** auf acc). **III** s Sturz m. Sport: F Sturz m (vom Pferd, [Motor]Rad): **have a ~** stürzen.

spilt [spɪlt] pret u. pp von **spill**.

spin [spɪn] **I** v/t (irr) **1.** drehen; Wäsche schleudern; Münze hochwerfen. **2.** Fäden, Wolle etc spinnen (→ **yarn** 2). **3.** a. ~ **out** Arbeit etc in die Länge ziehen, Geld etc strecken. **II** v/i (irr) **4.** sich drehen: ~ **round** herumwirbeln; **my head was ~ning** mir drehte sich alles. **5.** mst ~ **along** mot. F (dahin)rasen. **III** s **6.**

Sport: Effet m: **put ~ on a ball** e-m Ball Effet geben. **7.** mot. F Spritztour f: **go for a ~** e-e Spritztour machen. **8.** bsd. Br. F **be in a (flat) ~** am Rotieren sein; **send** (od. **throw**) **s.o. in a (flat) ~** j-n zum Rotieren bringen.

spin·ach ['spɪnɪdʒ] s ♀ Spinat m.

spi·nal ['spaɪnl] adj: ~ **column** Rückgrat n, Wirbelsäule f; ~ **cord** Rückenmark n.

spin·dle ['spɪndl] s ⊙ Spindel f. **'spin·dly** adj spindeldürr.

ˌspin·\|-'dri·er s (Wäsche)Schleuder f. ˌ~-'dry** v/t Wäsche schleudern. ˌ~'dry·er → **spin-drier**.

spine [spaɪn] s **1.** anat. Rückgrat n, Wirbelsäule f. **2.** zo. Stachel m, ♀ a. Dorn m. **3.** (Buch)Rücken m. **'spine·less** adj □ fig. rückgratlos.

spin·na·ker ['spɪnəkə] s ⚓ Spinnaker m.

spin·ney ['spɪnɪ] s Br. Dickicht n.

spin·ning **mill** ['spɪnɪŋ] s Spinnerei f. ~ **wheel** s Spinnrad n.

'spin-off s **1.** Neben-, Abfallprodukt n. **2.** fig. (positiver) Nebeneffekt.

spin·ster ['spɪnstə] s ältere unverheiratete Frau, contp. alte Jungfer, spätes Mädchen. **'spin·ster·ish** adj altjüngferlich.

spin·y ['spaɪnɪ] adj zo. stach(e)lig, ♀ a. dornig.

spi·ral ['spaɪərəl] **I** adj □ spiralenförmig, spiralig, Spiral...: ~ **staircase** Wendeltreppe f. **II** s (a. ✝ Preis- etc)Spirale f.

spire ['spaɪə] s (Kirch)Turmspitze f.

spir·it ['spɪrɪt] s **1.** allg. Geist m: **in ~** im Geiste; ~ **of the age** (od. **times**) Zeitgeist. **2.** Stimmung f, Einstellung f. **3.** Schwung m, Elan m. **4.** pl Laune f, Stimmung f: **be in high ~s** in Hochstimmung sein; ausgelassen od. übermütig sein; **be in low ~s** niedergeschlagen sein; **lift** (od. **raise**) **s.o.'s ~s** j-s Stimmung heben; **my ~s sank** ich wurde deprimiert. **5.** mst pl Spirituose f. **6.** ♣ Spiritus m. **'spir·it·ed** adj □ beherzt (Versuch etc); erregt (Auseinandersetzung).

spir·it lev·el s ⊙ Wasserwaage f.

spir·it·u·al ['spɪrɪtʃʊəl] adj □ **1.** geistig. **2.** geistlich. **II** s **3.** ♪ Spiritual n. **'spir·it·u·al·ism** s Spiritismus m. **'spir·it·u·al·ist** s Spiritist(in). ˌspir·it·u·al'is·tic** adj (**~ally**) spiritistisch.

spit¹ [spɪt] **I** v/i (irr) **1.** a) spucken: ~ **at**

s.o. j-n anspucken, b) ausspucken. **2.** *it is ~ting* (*with rain*) es sprüht. **3.** knistern (*Feuer*), brutzeln (*Fleisch etc*). II *v/t* (*irr*) **4.** *Blut etc* spucken: *~ out* ausspucken; *~ it out! fig.* F spuck's aus! **5.** *a. ~ out et.* fauchen. III *s* **6.** Spucke *f*.

spit² [~] *s* **1.** (*Brat*)Spieß *m*. **2.** *geogr.* Landzunge *f*.

spite [spaɪt] I *s* **1.** Boshaftigkeit *f*, Gehässigkeit *f*: *out of* (*od. from*) *pure ~* aus reiner Bosheit. **2.** *in ~ of* trotz. II *v/t* **3.** ärgern. **spite·ful** ['~fʊl] *adj* □ boshaft, gehässig.

spit·ting ['spɪtɪŋ] *adj*: *the bus stop is within ~ distance* F bis zur Bushaltestelle ist es nur ein Katzensprung; *she is the ~ image of her mother* sie ist ganz die Mutter, sie ist ihrer Mutter wie aus dem Gesicht geschnitten.

spit·tle ['spɪtl] *s* Spucke *f*.

splash [splæʃ] I *v/i* **1.** spritzen; (*Regen*) klatschen (*against* gegen). **2.** a) planschen (*in* in *dat*), b) platschen (*through* durch): *~ down* wassern (*Raumkapsel*). **3.** *~ out* bsd. *Br.* F tief in die Tasche greifen für. II *v/t* **4.** bespritzen (*with* mit): *~ one's face with cold water* sich kaltes Wasser ins Gesicht schütten. **5.** *Wasser etc* spritzen (*on* auf *acc*; *over* über *acc*): *~ one's money about* bsd. *Br.* F mit Geld um sich werfen. **6.** F in großer Aufmachung bringen (*Zeitung etc*). III *s* **7.** Spritzer *m*, Spritzfleck *m*: *~ of paint* Farbspritzer. **8.** bsd. *Br.* Spritzer *m*, Schuß *m* (*Soda etc*). **9.** *make* (*quite*) *a ~* F Furore machen. '**~·down** *s* Wasserung *f*.

splat [splæt] *v/i* F klatschen (*against* gegen).

splat·ter ['splætə] → *spatter* 1–3.

splay [spleɪ] *v/t a. ~ out* Finger, Zehen spreizen.

spleen [spliːn] *s anat.* Milz *f*.

splen·did ['splendɪd] *adj* □ großartig, herrlich, prächtig. '**splen·do(u)r** *s* Pracht *f*.

splice [splaɪs] *v/t* miteinander verbinden, *Film, Tonband etc* (zs-)kleben: *get ~d* F heiraten.

splint [splɪnt] ⚕ I *s* Schiene *f*. II *v/t* schienen.

splin·ter ['splɪntə] I *s* Splitter *m*. II *v/t* zersplittern. III *v/i* (zer)splittern: *~ off* absplittern; *fig.* sich absplittern *od.* ab-

spalten (*from* von). *~ group s* Splittergruppe *f*.

split [splɪt] I *v/t* (*irr*) **1.** (zer)spalten; zerreißen: *~ one's sides* F sich vor Lachen biegen; *be ~ fig.* gespalten sein (*on an issue* in e-r Frage); *~ personality psych.* gespaltene Persönlichkeit; *~ second* Bruchteil *m* e-r Sekunde; → *hair.* **2.** *a. ~ up* aufteilen (*between* unter *acc*; *into* in *acc*); sich *et.* teilen: *~ three ways* dritteln; *~ the difference fig.* sich auf halbem Wege einigen. II *v/i* (*irr*) **3.** sich spalten; zerreißen. **4.** sich teilen (*into* in *acc*). **5.** *a. ~ up* (*with*) Schluß machen (mit), sich trennen (von). II *s* **6.** Riß *m*; Spalt *m*. **7.** *fig.* Bruch *m*; Spaltung *f*. **8.** Aufteilung *f*. **9.** *pl* Spagat *m*: *do the ~s* (e-n) Spagat machen. **10.** (*Bananen*)Split *m*. '**split·ting** *adj* rasend (*Kopfschmerzen*).

splodge [splɒdʒ] *s bsd. Br.*, **splotch** [splɒtʃ] *s bsd. Am.* Fleck *m*, Klecks *m*: *~ of paint* Farbklecks.

splurge [splɜːdʒ] F I *v/i*: *~ on* tief in die Tasche greifen für. II *v/t Geld* verschwenden (*on* für). III *s*: *have a ~* tief in die Tasche greifen.

splut·ter ['splʌtə] I *v/i* **1.** stottern (*a. mot.*). **2.** zischen (*Feuer etc*). **3.** prusten. II *v/t* **4.** stottern.

spoil [spɔɪl] I *v/t* (*a. irr*) **1.** verderben. **2.** *j-n* verwöhnen, *Kind a.* verziehen: *be ~t for choice* die Qual der Wahl haben. II *v/i* (*a. irr*) **3.** verderben, schlecht werden (*Nahrungsmittel*). **4.** *be ~ing for a fight* Streit suchen. III *s* **5.** *mst pl* Beute *f*.

'**spoil·er** *s mot.* Spoiler *m*.

'**spoil·sport** *s* Spielverderber(in).

spoilt [spɔɪlt] *pret u. pp von* **spoil**.

spoke¹ [spəʊk] *pret von* **speak**.

spoke² [~] *s* Speiche *f*: *put a ~ in s.o.'s wheel fig.* j-m (e-n) Knüppel zwischen die Beine werfen.

spo·ken ['spəʊkən] *pp von* **speak**.

spokes·man ['spəʊksmən] *s* (*irr man*) Sprecher *m*. '**~·wom·an** *s* (*irr woman*) Sprecherin *f*.

sponge [spʌndʒ] I *s* **1.** Schwamm *m*: *throw in the ~ fig.* das Handtuch werfen. **2.** → *sponge cake.* **3.** *fig.* Schnorrer(in). II *v/t* **4.** *a. ~ down* (mit e-m Schwamm) abwaschen; *~ (up)* aufwischen (*from* von). **5.** *fig.* schnorren

(from, off, on von, bei). III *v/i* **6.** *fig.*
schnorren *(from, off, on* bei): ~ *off s.o.*
a. j-m auf der Tasche liegen. ~ **bag** *s Br.*
Kulturbeutel *m*, Toilettentasche *f.* ~
cake *s* Biskuitkuchen *m.*

spong·er ['spʌndʒə] → **sponge** 3.
'**spong·y** *adj* □ **1.** schwammartig. **2.**
weich, *b.s.* teigig (*Brot etc*). **3.** nachgiebig (*Boden etc*).

spon·sor ['spɒnsə] I *s* **1.** Sponsor(in)
(*a. Rundfunk, TV*), Geldgeber(in). **2.**
Spender(in). **3.** Bürge *m*, Bürgin *f.* II *v/t*
4. sponsern. **5.** bürgen für.

spon·ta·ne·ous [spɒn'teɪnjəs] *adj* □
spontan.

spoof [spuːf] *s F* Parodie *f* (*of, on* auf
acc).

spook [spuːk] F I *s* Gespenst *n.* II *v/t Am.*
j-m e-n Schrecken einjagen. '**spook·y**
adj □ F unheimlich.

spool [spuːl] *s* Spule *f.*

spoon [spuːn] *s* Löffel *m.* '~·**feed** *v/t* (*irr*
feed) **1.** *Kind etc* füttern. **2.** *fig.* j-m alles
vorkauen: ~ *s.o.* with *s.th.*, ~ *s.th.* to
s.o. j-m et. vorkauen.

spoon·ful ['spuːnfʊl] *s* ein Löffel(voll) *m.*

spo·rad·ic [spə'rædɪk] *adj* (~*ally*) sporadisch, gelegentlich.

spore [spɔː] *s biol.* Spore *f.*

spor·ran ['spɒrən] *s* Schottentracht:
Felltasche *f.*

sport [spɔːt] I *s* **1.** a) Sport(art *f*) *m*, b) *oft*
pl allg. Sport *m.* **2.** *a. good* ~ F feiner *od.*
anständiger Kerl: *be a* ~ sei kein Spielverderber. **3.** *in* ~ zum Scherz, im Spaß.
II *adj* **4.** *Am.* Sport... III *v/t* **5.** protzen
mit; mit *e-m blauen Auge* herumlaufen.
'**sport·ing** *adj* □ **1.** Sport... **2.** fair (*a.*
Chance), anständig, sportlich.

sports [spɔːts] *adj* Sport...: ~ *car* Sportwagen *m*; ~ *jacket* Sakko *m*, *n.* ~·**man**
['~mən] *s* (*irr* **man**) **1.** Sportler *m.* **2.**
feiner *od.* anständiger Kerl. ~**-like** *adj* sportlich, fair, anständig.
'~·**man·ship** *s* Sportlichkeit *f*, Fairneß
f, Anständigkeit *f.* '~·**wom·an** *s* (*irr*
woman) Sportlerin *f.*

sport·y ['spɔːtɪ] *adj* □ F **1.** sportlich,
sportbegeistert. **2.** flott (*Kleidungsstück*).

spot [spɒt] I *s* **1.** Punkt *m*, Tupfen *m*;
Fleck *m.* **2.** ✤ Pickel *m.* **3.** Ort *m*, Platz
m, Stelle *f*: *on the* ~ zur Stelle; an Ort u.
Stelle, vor Ort; auf der Stelle, sofort;

put on the ~ j-n in die Enge treiben; j-n
in Verlegenheit bringen; *be in a* ~ F in
Schwulitäten sein; → **rooted. 4.** *fig.*
soft ~ Schwäche *f* (*for* für); **tender** ~
empfindliche Stelle; **weak** ~ schwacher
Punkt; Schwäche *f.* **5.** *a* ~ *of Br.* F ein
bißchen. **6.** *Rundfunk, TV*: (Werbe)Spot *m.* **7.** F Spot *m* (*Spotlight*). II
v/t **8.** entdecken, sehen. III *v/i* **9.** *it is*
~*ting* (**with rain**) *Br.* es tröpfelt. ~
check *s* Stichprobe *f*. ,~'**check** *v/t*
stichprobenweise überprüfen (*for* auf
acc).

spot·less ['spɒtlɪs] *adj* □ **1.** tadellos sauber. **2.** *fig.* untad(e)lig.

'**spot·light** *s* **1.** Spotlight *n*, Scheinwerfer(licht *n*) *m*: *be in the* (*political*) ~ im
Brennpunkt des (politischen) Interesses stehen. **2.** (*a. irr light*) anstrahlen; *fig.* aufmerksam machen auf (*acc*).
,~'**on** *adj u. adv Br.* F genau richtig.

spot·ted ['spɒtɪd] *adj* getüpfelt; fleckig.
'**spot·ty** *adj* □ **1.** pick(e)lig. **2.** *fig.* uneinheitlich, unterschiedlich.

spouse [spaʊz] *s* Gatte *m*, Gattin *f*, Gemahl(in).

spout [spaʊt] I *v/t* **1.** *Wasser etc* (heraus)spritzen. II *v/i* **2.** spritzen (*from*
aus). III *s* **3.** (*Wasser- etc*)Strahl *m.* **4.**
Schnauze *f*, Tülle *f.* **5.** *be up the* ~ F im
Eimer sein (*Wagen etc*); in Schwulitäten sein (*Person*): *she's up the* ~ bei ihr
ist was unterwegs.

sprain [spreɪn] ✦ I *v/t* sich *den Knöchel*
etc verstauchen: ~ *one's ankle.* II *s*
Verstauchung *f.*

sprang [spræŋ] *pret von* **spring.**

sprat [spræt] *s ichth.* Sprotte *f.*

sprawl [sprɔːl] I *v/i* **1.** *a.* ~ *out* ausgestreckt liegen *od.* sitzen. **2.** *b.s.* sich
ausbreiten (*Stadt etc*). II *v/t* **3.** *be* ~*ed*
(*out*) → 1.

spray [spreɪ] I *v/i* **1.** sprühen, spritzen. II
v/t **2.** besprühen, spritzen (**with** mit);
sich *die Haare* sprayen; *et.* sprühen,
spritzen (*on* auf *acc*); *Parfüm etc* versprühen, zerstäuben. III *s* **3.** Sprühnebel *m*; Gischt *f.* **4.** Spray *m, n.* **5.**
Sprüh-, Spraydose *f*; Zerstäuber *m.*
'**spray·er** → **spray** 5.

spray gun *s* ◎ Spritzpistole *f.*

spread [spred] I *v/t* (*irr*) **1.** *a.* ~ *out* ausbreiten, *Arme a.* ausstrecken; *Finger*
etc spreizen. **2.** *Butter etc* streichen (**on**

auf *acc*); *Brot etc* (be)streichen (**with** mit). **3.** *Furcht, Krankheit, Nachricht etc* verbreiten, *Gerücht a.* ausstreuen. **II** *v/i* (*irr*) **4.** *a.* ~ **out** sich ausbreiten. **5.** sich (*räumlich od. zeitlich*) erstrecken (**over** über *acc*). **6.** sich streichen lassen (*Butter etc*). **7.** sich verbreiten (*Furcht, Krankheit, Nachricht etc*), übergreifen (**to** auf *acc*) (*Feuer, Epidemie etc*): → **wildfire. III** *s* **8.** ✔, *orn.* Spannweite *f*. **9.** (Brot)Aufstrich *m*, Paste *f*. **10.** Verbreitung *f*, Ausstreuung *f*. **11.** *fig.* Spektrum *n*. **12.** F Festessen *n*.

spree [spri:] *s* F: **go** (**out**) **on a ~** e-n draufmachen; e-e Sauftour machen; **go on a buying** (*od.* **shopping, spending**) **~** wie verrückt einkaufen.

sprig [sprɪg] *s* Zweig *m*.

spright·ly ['spraɪtlɪ] *adj* rüstig (*alter Mensch*).

spring [sprɪŋ] **I** *v/i* (*irr*) **1.** springen: **~ at** sich stürzen auf (*acc*); **~ to one's feet** aufspringen. **2.** springen, schnellen: **~ back** zurückschnellen; **~ open** aufspringen (*Deckel etc*). **3.** *~ up* aufkommen (*Wind*); aus dem Boden schießen (*Gebäude etc*). **4.** *~ from* herrühren von. **II** *v/t* (*irr*) **5.** ~ **s.th. on s.o.** j-n mit et. überraschen. **6.** → **leak** 1a. **III** *s* **7.** Frühling *m*, Frühjahr *n*: **in** (**the**) **~** im Frühling. **8.** Quelle *f*. **9.** Sprung *m*: **make a ~ at** sich stürzen auf (*acc*). **10.** ⚙ Feder *f*. **11.** Elastizität *f*; Federung *f*. **IV** *adj* **12.** Frühlings...: **~ flowers.** '**~·board** *s* Sprungbrett *n* (*a. fig.* **for, to** für). **~ chick·en** *s*: **he's no ~** F er ist nicht mehr der jüngste. ,**~·'clean** *v/t u. v/i* gründlich putzen, *engS.* Frühjahrsputz machen (**in** *dat*). **~ fe·ver** *s* Frühjahrsmüdigkeit *f*; Frühlingsgefühle *pl*. **~ tide** *s* Springflut *f*, -tide *f*. '**~·time** *s* Frühling(szeit *f*) *m*, Frühjahr *n*.

spring·y ['sprɪŋɪ] *adj* □ elastisch, federnd.

sprin·kle ['sprɪŋkl] **I** *v/t* **1.** *Wasser etc* sprengen (**on** auf *acc*); *Salz etc* streuen (**on** auf *acc*); *et.* (be)sprengen *od.* bestreuen (**with** mit). **II** *v/i* **2.** *it is sprinkling* es sprüht (*regnet fein*). **III** *s* **3.** (Be)Sprengen *n*; (Be)Streuen *n*. **4.** Sprühregen *m*. '**sprin·kler** *s* **1.** (*Rasen*)Sprenger *m*; Sprinkler *m*, Berieselungsanlage *f*. **2.** *eccl.* Weihwasserwe-

del *m*. '**sprin·kling** *s*: **a ~ of** ein bißchen, ein paar.

sprint [sprɪnt] (*Sport*) **I** *v/i* **1.** sprinten; *a. allg.* spinten, spurten. **II** *s* **2.** *a.* ~ **race** Sprint *m*. **3.** Sprint *m*, Spurt *m* (*beide a. allg.*): **make** (*od.* **put on**) **a ~** e-n Spurt hinlegen. '**sprint·er** *s* *Sport*: Sprinter(in).

sprite [spraɪt] *s* Geist *m*, Kobold *m*.

sprout [spraʊt] **I** *v/i* **1.** sprießen (*Knospen etc*), keimen (*Kartoffeln, Saat etc*). **II** *v/t* **2.** ~ **a beard** sich e-n Bart wachsen lassen. **III** *s* **3.** Sproß *m*; Trieb *m*; Keim *m*. **4.** *pl* Rosenkohl *m*.

spruce¹ [spru:s] **I** *adj* □ adrett. **II** *v/t u. v/i*: ~ (**o.s.**) **up** F sich feinmachen, sich in Schale werfen.

spruce² [~] *s* ♣ Fichte *f*.

sprung [sprʌŋ] *pp u. Am. pret von* **spring.**

spry [spraɪ] *adj* □ rüstig (*ältere Person*).

spud [spʌd] *s* F Kartoffel *f*.

spun [spʌn] *pret u. pp von* **spin.**

spunk [spʌŋk] *s* F Mumm *m*. '**spunk·y** *adj* □ F mutig.

spur [spɜ:] **I** *s* **1.** Sporn *m* (*a. zo.*). **2.** *fig.* Ansporn *m* (**to** zu): **on the ~ of the moment** spontan. **II** *v/t* **3.** *e-m Pferd* die Sporen geben. **III** *v/t* **4.** *oft* ~ **on** *fig.* anspornen (**to** zu).

spu·ri·ous ['spjʊərɪəs] *adj* □ **1.** Pseudo..., Schein... **2.** geheuchelt, unecht.

,**spur-of-the-'mo·ment** *adj* spontan.

spurt¹ [spɜ:t] **I** *s* **1.** *Sport*: Spurt *m*, Sprint *m* (*beide a. allg.*): **put on a ~** e-n Spurt hinlegen. **2.** (*Arbeits*)Anfall *m*, (*Gefühls*)Aufwallung *f*. **II** *v/i* **3.** *Sport*: spurten, sprinten (*beide a. allg.*).

spurt² [~] **I** *v/i* spritzen (**from** aus). **II** *s* (*Wasser- etc*)Strahl *m*.

sput·ter ['spʌtə] **I** *v/i* **1.** stottern (*a. mot.*). **2.** zischen (*Feuer etc*). **II** *v/t* **3.** stottern.

spy [spaɪ] **I** *v/i* spionieren, Spionage treiben (**for** für): ~ **into** *fig.* herumspionieren in (*dat*); ~ **on** *j-m* nachspionieren. **II** *v/t*: ~ **out** ausspionieren; ausfindig machen: ~ **out the land** *fig.* die Lage peilen. **III** *s* Spion(in). ~ **ring** *s* Spionagering *m*.

squab·ble ['skwɒbl] **I** *v/i* (sich) streiten (**about, over** um, wegen). **II** *s* Streit *m*.

squad [skwɒd] *s* **1.** Mannschaft *f*, Trupp *m*. **2.** (*Überfall- etc*)Kommando *n* (*der Polizei*); Dezernat *n*. **3.** *Sport*: Kader *m.* **~ car** *s bsd. Am.* (Funk)Streifenwagen *m.*

squad·ron ['skwɒdrən] *s* ✗, ✈ Staffel *f*; ⚓ Geschwader *n.*

squal·id ['skwɒlɪd] *adj* □ **1.** verwahrlost (*Gebäude etc*); erbärmlich (*Verhältnisse etc*). **2.** *fig.* schmutzig (*Geschichte etc*).

squall[1] [skwɔːl] **I** *v/i* schreien. **II** *s* Schrei *m.*

squall[2] [~] *s* Bö *f.* **'squall·y** *adj* böig.

squal·or ['skwɒlə] *s* Verwahrlosung *f:* **live in ~** in erbärmlichen Verhältnissen leben.

squan·der ['skwɒndə] *v/t* Geld, Zeit *etc* verschwenden (**on** an *acc,* auf *acc,* für, mit), *Chance* vertun.

square [skweə] **I** *s* **1.** Quadrat *n.* **2.** Feld *n* (*e-s Brettspiels*): **be back to ~ one** *fig.* wieder ganz am Anfang stehen. **3.** (*öffentlicher*) Platz. **4.** Ⓐ Quadrat(zahl *f*) *n.* **5.** ⊙ Winkel(maß *n*) *m.* **II** *adj* **6.** quadratisch; Quadrat...: **three yards ~** drei Yards im Quadrat; **~ root** Ⓐ Quadratwurzel *f;* **~ peg** 1. **7.** rechtwink(e)lig; eckig (*Schultern etc*). **8.** fair, gerecht. **9. be** (*all*) **~** quitt sein. **10.** F anständig, ordentlich (*Mahlzeit*). **III** *adv* **11.** → **squarely. IV** *v/t* **12.** *a.* **~ off** (*od.* **up**) quadratisch *od.* rechtwink(e)lig machen. **13.** *a.* **~ off** in Quadrate einteilen: **~d paper** kariertes Papier. **14.** Ⓐ *Zahl* quadrieren, ins Quadrat erheben: **4 ~d equals 16** 4 hoch 2 ist 16. **15.** *Konto* ausgleichen; *Schulden* begleichen: → **account** 5. **16. ~ s.th. with one's conscience** et. mit s-m Gewissen vereinbaren *od.* in Einklang bringen. **V** *v/i* **17.** übereinstimmen, in Einklang stehen (*with* mit). **18.** → **up** abrechnen. **19. ~ up to** sich *j-m, e-m Problem etc* stellen. **'square·ly** *adv* **1.** → **square** 6–8. **2.** direkt, genau.

squash [skwɒʃ] **I** *v/t* **1.** zerdrücken, -quetschen: **~ flat** flachdrücken. **2.** quetschen, zwängen (*into* in *acc*). **3.** *j-n* zum Schweigen bringen (*with* mit); *Gerücht etc* ersticken. **II** *v/i* **4.** sich quetschen *od.* zwängen (*into* in *acc*). **III** *s* **5.** Gedränge *n.* **6.** → **lemon** 3, **orange** I. **7.** *Sport:* Squash *m.* **'squash·y** *adj* □ **1.** weich (*Frucht*). **2.** aufgeweicht (*Boden*).

squat [skwɒt] **I** *v/i* **1.** hocken, kauern: **~ down** sich (hin)hocken *od.* (-)kauern. **2. ~ in a house** ein Haus besetzt haben. **II** *adj* **3.** gedrungen, untersetzt. **III** *s* **4.** Hocke *f.* **5.** besetztes Haus. **'squat·ter** *s* Hausbesetzer(in).

squaw [skwɔː] *s* Squaw *f* (*Indianerfrau*).

squawk [skwɔːk] *v/i* F lautstark protestieren (*about* gegen).

squeak [skwiːk] **I** *v/i* **1.** piep(s)en (*Maus etc*). **2.** quietschen (*Tür etc*). **3. ~ through** s gerade noch schaffen. **II** *s* **4.** Piep(s)en *n;* Piep(s)*m,* Piepser *m; fig.* F Piep *m.* **5.** Quietschen *n.* **6. that was a narrow ~** F das war knapp, das hätte ins Auge gehen können. **'squeak·y** *adj* □ **1.** piepsig: **~ voice** a. Piepsstimme *f.* **2.** quietschend.

squeal [skwiːl] *v/i* **1.** kreischen (*with* vor *dat*). **2.** *fig.* F singen: **~ on s.o.** j-n verpfeifen.

squeam·ish ['skwiːmɪʃ] *adj* □ empfindlich, zartbesaitet.

squeeze [skwiːz] **I** *v/t* **1.** drücken; *Orangen etc* auspressen, -quetschen: **~ out** *Schwamm etc* ausdrücken; *Saft etc* auspressen (*of* aus). **2.** quetschen, zwängen (*into* in *acc*). **II** *v/i* **3.** sich quetschen *od.* zwängen (*into* in *acc*). **III** *s* **4. give s.th. a ~** et. drücken; **put the ~ on s.o.** F j-n unter Druck setzen. **5.** Gedränge *n.* **'squeez·er** *s* Presse *f.*

squelch [skwelt∫] *v/i* p(l)atschen.

squib [skwɪb] *s* Knallfrosch *m:* **~ damp** 1.

squint [skwɪnt] **I** *v/i* **1.** schielen. **2.** blinzeln. **II** *s* **3.** Schielen *n:* **have a ~** schielen.

squirm [skwɜːm] *v/i* sich winden (*with* vor *dat*) (*a. fig.*).

squir·rel ['skwɪrəl] *s zo.* Eichhörnchen *n.*

squirt [skwɜːt] **I** *v/i* spritzen (*from* aus). **II** *v/t* bespritzen (*with* mit). **III** *s* Strahl *m.*

stab [stæb] **I** *v/t* **1.** *j-m* e-n Stich versetzen; *j-n* niederstechen: **~ (to death)** erstechen; **he was ~bed in the stomach** er bekam e-n Stich in den Magen; **~ s.o. in the back** *fig.* j-m in den Rücken fallen. **2. ~ one's finger at** mit dem Finger stoßen nach (*od.* auf *acc*). **II** *v/i* **3.** stechen (*at* nach; *with* mit). **III** *s* **4.** Stich *m:* **~ (wound)** Stichverletzung *f,* -wunde *f;* **~ in the back** *fig.* Dolchstoß *m.* **5. feel a ~ of pain** (*remorse*) e-n stechenden Schmerz verspüren (Gewis-

sensbisse fühlen). **6. have** (*od.* **make**) **a**
~ at s.th. F et. probieren. '**stab·bing** *adj*
stechend (*Schmerz*).

sta·bil·i·ty [stə'bılətı] *s* **1.** Stabilität *f* (*a.*
fig.). **2.** *fig.* Dauerhaftigkeit *f.* **3.** *fig.*
Ausgeglichenheit *f.*

sta·bi·li·za·tion [͵steıbəlaı'zeıʃn] *s* Stabi-
lisierung *f* (*a. fig.*).

sta·bi·lize ['steıbəlaız] *v/t u. v/i* (sich)
stabilisieren (*a. fig.*). '**sta·bi·liz·er** ⊚
Stabilisator *m.*

sta·ble¹ ['steıbl] *adj* □ **1.** stabil (*a. fig.*).
2. *fig.* dauerhaft (*Beziehung etc*). **3.** *fig.*
ausgeglichen (*Person*).

sta·ble² [~] *s* Stall *m* (*a. fig.*).

stack [stæk] **I** *s* **1.** Stapel *m*, Stoß *m.* **2. ~s**
(*od. a* **~**) *of* F jede Menge *Zeit etc.* **3. →**
blow¹ 11. **II** *v/t* **4.** stapeln: **~ up** aufstapeln. **5.** vollstapeln (**with** mit). **6. the**
cards (*od.* **odds**) **are ~ed against us**
unsere Chancen sind gleich Null. **III** *v/i*
7. ~ up against *bsd. Am.* F sich halten
gegen.

sta·di·um ['steıdjəm] *s Sport:* Stadion *n.*

staff [stɑːf] **I** *s* **1.** Mitarbeiter(stab *m*) *pl*;
Personal *n*, Belegschaft *f*; Lehrkörper
m, Kollegium *n*; ✕ Stab *m*: *editorial* **~**
Redaktion *f*; *be on the* **~** zur Belegschaft gehören. **2.** (*Amts*)Stab *m*; (*Fah-*
nen)Stange *f.* **II** *v/t* **3.** besetzen (**with**
mit). **~ man·a·ger** *s* Personalchef *m.* **~**
of·fi·cer *s* ✕ Stabsoffizier *m.* **~ room** *s*
Lehrerzimmer *n.*

stag [stæg] *s zo.* Hirsch *m.*

stage [steıdʒ] **I** *s* **1.** *thea.* Bühne *f* (*a. fig.*):
go on the **~** zum Theater gehen; *set the*
~ for die Voraussetzungen schaffen für.
2. Etappe *f* (*a. Radsport u. fig.*), (*Rei-*
se)Abschnitt *m*: *by* (*easy*) **~s** etappen-
weise, *fig. a.* Schritt für Schritt. **3.** Stadium *n*, Stufe *f*, Phase *f.* **4.** ⊚ Stufe *f*
(*e-r Rakete*). **II** *v/t* **5.** *thea.* auf die Bühne bringen. **6.** *Ausstellung, Demonstra-*
tion etc veranstalten: **→ comeback.**
'**~·coach** *s hist.* Postkutsche *f.* **~ di·**
rec·tion *s* Bühnen-, Regieanwei-
sung *f.* **~ door** *s* Bühneneingang *m.* **~**
fright *s* Lampenfieber *n.* **~ name** *s*
Künstlername *m.*

stag·ey → stagy.

stag·ger ['stægə] **I** *v/i* **1.** (sch)wanken,
taumeln, (*Betrunkener a.*) torkeln. **II**
v/t **2.** *j-n* sprachlos machen, umwerfen.
3. *Arbeitszeit etc* staffeln. '**stag·ger-**

-ing *adj* □ umwerfend (*Nachricht etc*),
schwindelerregend (*Preis etc*).

stag·nant ['stægnənt] *adj* □ **1.** stehend
(*Gewässer*). **2.** *bsd.* ✝ stagnierend.
stag·nate [~'neıt] *v/i bsd. Am.* ✝ stagnieren. **stag'na·tion** *s* Stagnation *f.*

stag par·ty *s* F (*mst feuchtfröhlicher*)
Herrenabend.

stag·y ['steıdʒı] *adj* □ theatralisch.

staid [steıd] *adj* □ **1.** gesetzt, seriös,
contr. verknöchert (*Person*). **2.** altbak-
ken (*Ansichten*).

stain [steın] **I** *s* **1.** Fleck *m.* **2.** *fig.* Makel
m. **3.** ⊚ Färbemittel *n*; (*Holz*)Beize *f.* **II**
v/t **4.** beflecken. **5.** (ein)färben; *Holz*
beizen: **~ed glass** Farbglas *n.* **III** *v/i* **6.**
flecken. '**stain·less** *adj* nichtrostend,
rostfrei (*Stahl*).

stair [steə] *s* **1.** (Treppen)Stufe *f.* **2.** *pl*
Treppe *f*: **→ flight¹** 3. **~·car·pet** *s* Trep-
penläufer *m.* '**~·case** *s*, '**~·way** *s* Treppe *f*; Treppenhaus *n.*

stake¹ [steık] **I** *s* **1.** Pfahl *m*, Pfosten *m.* **2.**
hist. Marterpfahl *m*; Scheiterhaufen *m.*
II *v/t* **3.** *oft* **~ off** (*od.* **out**) abstecken: **~**
(**out**) **a** (*od.* **one's**) **claim** *fig.* Ansprüche anmelden (**to** auf *acc*). **4.** *mst* **~ out**
bsd. Am. F überwachen (*Polizei*).

stake² [~] **I** *s* **1.** Einsatz *m*: *be at* **~** *fig.* auf
dem Spiel stehen; *play for high* **~s** hoch
od. um hohe Einsätze spielen. **2.** Anteil
m, Beteiligung *f* (**in** an *dat*) (*beide a.* ✝):
have a **~ in** beteiligt sein an (*dat*). **II** *v/t*
3. *Geld, Hoffnung* setzen (**on** auf *acc*);
Ruf etc riskieren, aufs Spiel setzen.

'**stake-out** *s bsd. Am.* F (polizeiliche)
Überwachung.

stal·ac·tite ['stæləktaıt] *s geol.* Stalaktit
m. **stal·ag·mite** ['stæləgmaıt] *s geol.*
Stalagmit *m.*

stale [steıl] *adj* □ alt(backen) (*Brot etc*);
abgestanden (*Luft etc*), (*Bier etc a.*)
schal; *fig.* abgedroschen (*Witz etc*).

stale·mate ['steılmeıt] **I** *s* **1.** *Schach:*
Patt *n.* **2.** *fig.* Patt(situation *f*) *n*, Sackgasse *f*: *end in* (*a*) **~** in e-r Sackgasse
enden. **II** *v/t* **3.** *Schach:* patt setzen. **4.**
fig. in e-e Sackgasse führen.

stalk¹ [stɔːk] *s* Stengel *m*, Stiel *m*;
Halm *m.*

stalk² [~] *v/i* stolzieren; staksen,
steif(beinig) gehen.

stall¹ [stɔːl] **I** *s* **1.** (*Obst- etc*)Stand *m.* **2.**
pl thea. Br. Parkett *n.* **3.** *pl eccl.* Chor-

gestühl n. **4.** Box f (im Stall). **II** v/t **5.** Motor abwürgen. **III** v/i **6.** absterben (Motor).

stall² [~] **I** v/i Ausflüchte machen; Zeit schinden. **II** v/t j-n hinhalten; et. hinauszögern.

stal·lion ['stæljən] s (Zucht)Hengst m.

stal·wart ['stɔːlwət] **I** adj □ **1.** kräftig, robust. **2.** bsd. pol. treu (Anhänger). **II** s **3.** bsd. pol. treuer Anhänger.

stam·i·na ['stæmɪnə] s Stehvermögen n, (physisch a.) Kondition f.

stam·mer ['stæmə] **I** v/i stottern. **II** v/t a. ~ out stottern, stammeln. **III** s ✺ Stottern n: have (od. speak with) a ~ stottern. **'stam·mer·er** s ✺ Stotterer m, Stotterin f.

stamp [stæmp] **I** v/t **1.** ~ one's foot aufstampfen; ~ out Feuer austreten; Übel ausrotten. **2.** Paß etc (ab)stempeln; Datum etc aufstempeln (on auf acc): ~ s.o. as fig. j-n abstempeln als od. zu. **3.** Brief etc frankieren: ~ed envelope Freiumschlag m. **4.** ~ out ✽ ausstanzen. **II** v/i **5.** sta(m)pfen, trampeln. **III** s **6.** (Brief)Marke f (Rabatt-, Steuer- etc) Marke f. **7.** Stempel m (a. Abdruck). ~ **al·bum** s (Brief)Markenalbum n. ~ **col·lec·tion** s (Brief)Markensammlung f. ~ **col·lec·tor** s (Brief)Markensammler(in).

stam·pede [stæm'piːd] **I** s **1.** wilde Flucht (von Tieren); wilder Ansturm (for auf acc): there was a ~ for the door alles stürzte zur Tür. **2.** fig. (Massen-)Ansturm m (for auf acc). **II** v/t **3.** in wilde Flucht jagen. **4.** ~ s.o. into doing s.th. j-n so überrumpeln, daß er et. tut. **III** v/i **5.** durchgehen.

stamp·ing ground ['stæmpɪŋ] s fig. F Tummelplatz m; Jagdrevier n.

stance [stæns] s **1.** bsd. Sport: Stellung f. **2.** fig. Einstellung f, Haltung f (on zu).

stand [stænd] **I** s **1.** (Obst-, Messe- etc)Stand m. **2.** (Kleider-, Schirm- etc)Ständer m. **3.** Sport etc: Tribüne f: in the ~ auf der Tribüne. **4.** ⚖ Am. Zeugenstand m: take the ~ in den Zeugenstand treten. **5.** (Taxi)Stand(platz) m. **6.** fig. Einstellung f (on zu): take a ~ Position beziehen (on zu). **II** v/i (irr) **7.** allg. stehen: ~ still stillstehen; as matters (od. things) ~ nach Lage der Dinge, so wie die Dinge stehen; my offer still ~s

mein Angebot steht od. gilt noch; ~ or fall by fig. stehen u. fallen mit; → awe **I**, **correct 1**, **clear 14**, **firm¹ II. 8.** aufstehen. **III** v/t (irr) **9.** stellen (on auf acc): ~ s.th. on its head fig. et. auf den Kopf stellen. **10.** Beanspruchung, Hitze etc aushalten, ertragen; e-r Prüfung etc standhalten. **11.** I can't ~ him (it) ich kann ihn (das) nicht ausstehen od. leiden. **12.** ~ s.o. a drink fig. j-m e-n Drink spendieren. **13.** Chance haben. **14.** → **trial 1. 15.** → **bail¹ 2**, **surety**.

Verbindungen mit Präpositionen:

stand| by v/i **1.** zu j-m halten. **2.** zu s-m Wort etc stehen, s-n Prinzipien etc treu bleiben. ~ **for** v/i **1.** stehen für, bedeuten. **2.** eintreten für, vertreten. **3.** sich et. gefallen lassen, dulden. **4.** bsd. Br. kandidieren für: ~ election speziell kandidieren, sich zur Wahl stellen. ~ **on** v/i **1.** stehen auf (dat): ~ one's hands (head) e-n Handstand (Kopfstand) machen; **standing on one's head** F mit links. **2.** ~ **ceremony** förmlich sein. ~ **o·ver** v/i überwachen, aufpassen auf (acc).

Verbindungen mit Adverbien:

stand| a·bout, ~ a·round v/i herumstehen. ~ **back** v/i zurücktreten. ~ **by** v/i **1.** danebenstehen; **stand idly by** tatenlos zusehen (a. fig.). ~ **down** v/i **1.** ⚖ den Zeugenstand verlassen. **2.** verzichten; zurücktreten (in favo[u]r of zugunsten). ~ **in** v/i einspringen (for für): ~ **for s.o.** a. j-n vertreten. ~ **out** v/i **1.** hervorstechen: ~ **against** (from) sich abheben von. **2.** sich hartnäckig wehren (**against** gegen). ~ **to·geth·er** v/i zs.-halten, -stehen. ~ **up** v/i **1.** aufstehen: **standing up** im Stehen. **2.** ~ **for** eintreten od. sich einsetzen für. **3.** ~ **to** Beanspruchung etc aushalten; j-m die Stirn bieten. **II** v/t **4.** F j-n versetzen.

stand·ard¹ ['stændəd] **I** s **1.** Norm f; Maßstab m: set high ~s (of) viel verlangen (von), hohe Anforderungen stellen (an acc); be up to (below) ~ den Anforderungen (nicht) genügen od. entsprechen; by present-day ~s nach heutigen Begriffen. **2.** Standard m, Niveau n: ~ of living Lebensstandard m. **II** adj **3.** normal, Normal...; durchschnittlich, Durchschnitts...; Standard..., ⊚ a. Serien..., serienmäßig. **4.** maßgebend,

Standard...: **~ English** korrektes Englisch.

stand·ard² [~] I s Standarte f, (an Wagen) Stander m; ✕ hist. Banner n. II adj: **~ lamp** Br. Stehlampe f.

stand·ard·i·za·tion [ˌstændədaɪˈzeɪʃn] s Standardisierung f, Normung f, Vereinheitlichung f. **'stand·ard·ize** v/t bsd. ⊕ standardisieren, normen, a. allg. vereinheitlichen.

'stand|-by I pl **-bys** s 1. Reserve f. 2. **be on ~** in Bereitschaft stehen. II adj 3. Reserve..., Not... 4. ✔ Stand-by-... **'~-in** s 1. Film, TV: Double n. 2. Ersatzmann m; Vertreter(in).

stand·ing [ˈstændɪŋ] I adj 1. stehend: **~ room only** nur (noch) Stehplätze; → **ovation.** 2. fig. ständig: **~ order** ✝ Dauerauftrag m. II s 3. Rang m, Stellung f; Ansehen n, Ruf m: **of high ~** hochangesehen, von hohem Ansehen. 4. Dauer f: **of long ~** seit langem bestehend, alt.

stand|-off·ish [ˌstændˈɒfɪʃ] adj ☐ F hochnäsig. **'~point** s fig. Standpunkt m: **from my ~** von m-m Standpunkt aus. **'~still** s Stillstand m (a. fig.): **be at a ~** stehen (Auto etc); ruhen (Produktion etc); **bring to a ~** Auto etc zum Stehen bringen; Produktion etc zum Erliegen bringen. **'~-up** adj 1. a.) Steh...: **~ collar** Stehkragen m, b) im Stehen (eingenommen) (Mahlzeit). 2. **~ fight** wüste Schlägerei.

stank [stæŋk] pret von **stink.**

stan·za [ˈstænzə] s Strophe f.

sta·ple¹ [ˈsteɪpl] I s Heftklammer f; Krampe f. II v/t heften: **~ together** zs.-heften.

sta·ple² [~] I s 1. ✝ Haupterzeugnis n (e-s Landes etc). 2. Hauptnahrungsmittel n. II adj 3. Haupt... 4. üblich.

sta·pler [ˈsteɪplə] s (Draht)Hefter m.

star [stɑː] I s 1. Stern m: ⚹s and Stripes pl (sg konstruiert) das Sternenbanner (Staatsflagge der USA); **see ~s** Sterne sehen; **you can thank your lucky ~s that** du kannst von Glück reden od. sagen, daß. 2. typ. Sternchen n. 3. Star m (Person). II adj 4. Haupt...; Star... III v/t 5. Wort etc mit e-m Sternchen kennzeichnen. 6. **a film ~ring ...** ein Film mit ... in der Hauptrolle od. den Hauptrollen; **~ring ...** in der Hauptrol-

le od. den Hauptrollen ... IV v/i 7. die od. e-e Hauptrolle spielen (**in** in dat). **~board** [ˈ~bəd] s ✔, ⚓ Steuerbord n.

starch [stɑːtʃ] I s 1. (Kartoffel-, Wäsche- etc)Stärke f. 2. pl stärkereiche Nahrungsmittel pl; engS. Kohle(n)hydrate pl. II v/t 3. Wäsche stärken. **'starch·y** adj ☐ 1. stärkehaltig, -reich. 2. fig. F steif.

star·dom [ˈstɑːdəm] s (Star)Ruhm m.

stare [steə] I v/i starren; große Augen machen: **~ after** j-m nachstarren; **~ at** j-n anstarren; → **space** 1. II v/t: **~ s.o. out** (od. **down**) j-n so lange anstarren, bis er verlegen wird; **~ s.o. in the face** j-m ins Gesicht starren; vor j-s Augen liegen; fig. klar auf der Hand liegen. III s (starrer) Blick, Starren n.

'star·fish s zo. Seestern m.

stark [stɑːk] I adj nackt (Tatsachen etc): **be in ~ contrast to** in krassem Gegensatz stehen zu. II adv F: **~ naked** splitternackt; **~ staring** (od. **raving**) **mad** total verrückt.

stark·ers [ˈstɑːkəz] adj Br. F splitternackt.

star·let [ˈstɑːlɪt] s Starlet n, Filmsternchen n.

'star·light s Sternenlicht n.

star·ling [ˈstɑːlɪŋ] s orn. Star m.

'star·lit adj stern(en)klar.

star·ry [ˈstɑːrɪ] adj Stern(en)...(en). **~-'eyed** adj blauäugig, naiv.

'Star-,Span·gled 'Ban·ner s 1. die Nationalhymne (der USA). 2. das Sternenbanner (Staatsflagge der USA).

start [stɑːt] I v/i 1. a. **~ off** anfangen, beginnen: **~ doing** (od. **to do**) **s.th.** anfangen, et. zu tun; **~ (in) on doing s.th.** damit anfangen, et. zu tun; **try ~** am anfangs, zunächst; erstens; → **scratch** 7. 2. a. **~ off** (od. **out**) aufbrechen (**for** nach): **~ back for home** sich auf den Heimweg machen. 3. abfahren (Bus, Zug), ablegen (Boot), ✔ abfliegen, starten; (Sport) starten: **~ing from Monday** ab Montag. 4. a. **~ up** anspringen (Motor etc). 5. zs.-fahren, -zucken (**at** bei). II v/t 6. a. **~ off** anfangen, beginnen. 7. a. **~ up** Aktion starten, Geschäft, Familie etc gründen, Gerücht in Umlauf setzen. 8. Motor etc anlassen, starten. III s 9. Anfang m, Beginn m, (bsd. Sport) Start m: **at the ~** am

Anfang; (*Sport*) am Start; **for a** ~ erstens; *from* ~ **to finish** von Anfang bis Ende; (*Sport*) vom Start bis zum Ziel; *make a fresh* ~ (*in life*) e-n neuen Anfang machen, noch einmal von vorn anfangen; *make a* ~ *on s.th.* mit et. anfangen. **10.** Aufbruch *m*. **11.** *give a* ~ → 5; *wake up with a* ~ aus dem Schlaf aufschrecken. **12.** Vorsprung *m* (*on, over* vor *dat*). '**start·er** *s* **1.** *Sport*: Starter(in) (*Kampfrichter[in]* u. *Wettkampfteilnehmer[in]*). **2.** *mot.* Starter *m*, Anlasser *m*. **3.** F Vorspeise *f*: *as a* ~ als Vorspeise. **4.** *for* ~s F zunächst einmal: *that's just for* ~s das ist nur der Anfang. '**start·ing** *adj bsd. Sport*: Start...: ~ *point* Ausgangspunkt *m* (*a. fig.*).

star·tle ['stɑːtl] *v/t* **1.** erschrecken. **2.** *fig.* überraschen, bestürzen.

star·va·tion [stɑːˈveɪʃn] *s* Hungern *n*: *die of* ~ verhungern; ~ *diet* F Fasten-, Hungerkur *f*; ~ *wages pl* Hungerlohn *m*, -löhne *pl*.

starve [stɑːv] **I** *v/i* **1.** hungern: ~ (*to death*) verhungern; *I'm starving* F ich komme fast um vor Hunger. **II** *v/t* **2.** hungern lassen: ~ (*to death*) verhungern lassen; ~ (*out*) aushungern. **3.** *be* ~*d of* knapp sein an (*dat*).

star wars *s pl* ✕ F Krieg *m* der Sterne.

state [steɪt] **I** *s* **1.** *oft* ♀ *pol.* Staat *m*. **2.** *pol. Am.* (Bundes-, Einzel)Staat *m*: *the* ♀*s pl* F die (*Vereinigten*) Staaten *pl*; → *evidence* 2. **3.** Zustand *m*: ~ *of mind* Geistes-, Gemüts)Verfassung *f*, (-)Zustand *m*; *be in a* ~ *of war with* sich im Kriegszustand befinden mit; *get in(to)* a ~ *bsd. Br.* F sich aufregen; nervös werden; → *emergency, health* 2. **4.** Stand *m*, Lage *f*. **II** *adj* **5.** staatlich, Staats...: ♀ *Department pol. Am.* Außenministerium *n*. **III** *v/t* **6.** angeben, nennen. **7.** erklären, 🏛 aussagen (*that* daß). **8.** festlegen, -setzen: *on the* ~*d date* zum festgesetzten Termin. '**state·less** *adj pol.* staatenlos. '**state·ly** *adj* **1.** gemessen (*Tempo etc*). **2.** prächtig. '**state·ment** *s* **1.** Statement *n*, Erklärung *f*; Angabe *f*; 🏛 Aussage *f*: *make a* ~ e-e Erklärung abgeben (**to** vor *dat*). **2.** ✝ (*Bank-, Konto*)Auszug *m*.

,**state-of-the-'art** *adj* neuest, auf dem neuesten Stand der Technik stehend.

states·man ['steɪtsmən] *s* (*irr* **man**)

Staatsmann *m*. '**states·man·like** *adj* staatsmännisch.

stat·ic ['stætɪk] **I** *adj* (~*ally*) **1.** *phys.* statisch (*a. fig.*). **2.** *fig.* gleichbleibend, konstant. **II** *s* **3.** *Radio, TV*: atmosphärische Störungen *pl*. **4.** *pl* (*sg konstruiert*) *phys.* Statik *f*.

sta·tion ['steɪʃn] **I** *s* **1.** (*a. Bus-, U-*)Bahnhof *m*, Station *f*. **2.** (*Forschungs-, Unfall- etc*)Station *f*, Tankstelle *f*, (*Feuer-*)Wache *f*, (*Polizei*)Revier *n*, (-)Wache *f*, (*Wahl*)Lokal *n*. **3.** *Rundfunk, TV*: Station *f*, Sender *m*. **II** *v/t* **4.** aufstellen, postieren; ✕ stationieren.

sta·tion·ar·y ['steɪʃnərɪ] *adj* stehend (*Fahrzeug etc*): *be* ~ stehen.

sta·tion·er ['steɪʃnə] *s* Schreibwarenhändler(in). '**sta·tion·er·y** *s* Schreibwaren *pl*; Briefpapier *n*.

sta·tion| house *s Am.* (Polizei)Revier *n*, (-)Wache *f*. '~·**mas·ter** *s* Bahnhofsvorsteher *m*. ~ **wag·on** *s mot. Am.* Kombiwagen *m*.

sta·tis·ti·cal [stəˈtɪstɪkl] *adj* □ statistisch. **sta·tis·tics** [stəˈtɪstɪks] *s* (*pl*) **1.** Statistik (*pl*); *f*: → *vital* 2. **2.** (*sg konstruiert*) Statistik *f* (*Wissenschaft, Methode*).

stat·ue ['stætjuː] *s* Statue *f*, Standbild *n*.

stat·ure ['stætʃə] *s* **1.** Statur *f*, Wuchs *m*. **2.** *fig.* Format *n*.

sta·tus ['steɪtəs] *s* **1.** Status *m*, Rechtsstellung *f*. **2.** → *marital*. **3.** Status *m*, Stellung *f*; Prestige *n*. ~ *quo* [kwəʊ] *s* Status *m* quo. ~ *sym·bol* *s* Statussymbol *n*.

stat·ute ['stætjuːt] *s* **1.** Gesetz *n*: *by* ~ gesetzlich. **2.** Statut *n*, *pl a.* Satzung *f*. ~ **book** *s* Gesetzbuch *n*. ~ *law* *s* Gesetzesrecht *n*.

stat·u·to·ry ['stætjʊtərɪ] *adj* □ **1.** gesetzlich (garantiert *od.* vorgeschrieben). **2.** satzungsgemäß.

staunch[1] [stɔːntʃ] *v/t* Blut stillen.

staunch[2] [~] *adj* □ **1.** treu, zuverlässig. **2.** standhaft, fest.

stay [steɪ] **I** *s* **1.** Aufenthalt *m*: ~ *in hospital* Krankenhausaufenthalt. **2.** 🏛 Aussetzung *f*, Aufschub *m*: *he was given* (*od. granted*) (a) ~ *of execution* s-e Hinrichtung wurde ausgesetzt. **II** *v/i* **3.** bleiben (*for od. to lunch* zum Mittagessen). **4.** wohnen (*with friends* bei Freunden): ~ *the night at a hotel* im Hotel übernachten. **III** *v/t* **5.** ~ *the* *course* (*Sport*) durchhalten (*a. fig.*). *Verbindungen mit Adverbien:*

stay| a·way *v/i* wegbleiben, sich fernhalten (*from* von). **~ down** *v/i* unten bleiben (*a. fig.*). **~ in** *v/i* zu Hause od. drinnen bleiben. **~ on** *v/i:* **~ as chairman** (weiterhin) Vorsitzender bleiben; **~ at school** (mit der Schule) weitermachen. **~ out** *v/i* draußen bleiben: **~** (*on strike*) streiken. **~ up** *v/i* aufbleiben.

'stay-at-home *s* Stubenhocker(in).

stay·ing pow·er ['steɪɪŋ] *s* Stehvermögen *n*, Ausdauer *f*.

stead [sted] *s:* **in s.o.'s ~** an j-s Stelle.

stead·fast ['stedfɑːst] *adj* **1.** treu, zuverlässig. **2.** fest, unverwandt (*Blick*).

stead·y ['stedɪ] **I** *adj* **1.** (stand)fest, stabil. **2.** ruhig (*Auge, Hand*), gut (*Nerven*). **3.** gleichmäßig. **4.** fest (*Arbeitsplatz, Freundin etc*). **II** *v/t* **5.** j-n, Nerven beruhigen. **III** *v/i* **6.** sich beruhigen. **IV** *int* **7.** *a.* **~ on!** *Br.* Vorsicht!

steak [steɪk] *s* Steak *n*; (*Fisch*)Filet *n*.

steal [stiːl] (*irr*) **I** *v/t* **1.** stehlen (*a. fig.*), *Gemälde etc* rauben: **~ s.o.'s girlfriend** j-m die Freundin ausspannen; **~ a glance at** e-n verstohlenen Blick werfen auf (*acc*); → **march²** 5, **show** 1, **thunder** I. **II** *v/i* **2.** stehlen. **3.** sich stehlen, (sich) schleichen (*out of* aus).

stealth [stelθ] *s:* **by ~** *→* **stealthy**.
'stealth·y *adj* □ heimlich, verstohlen.

steam [stiːm] **I** *s* **1.** Dampf *m:* **full ~ ahead!** ♣ volle Kraft *od.* Volldampf voraus!; **under one's own ~** *fig.* auf eigene Faust; **let off ~** Dampf ablassen, *fig.* a. sich Luft machen; **run out of ~** *fig.* s-n Schwung verlieren; **he ran out of ~** *a.* ihm ging die Puste aus. **2.** Dampf *m*, Dunst *m.* **II** *v/i* **3.** dampfen (*a.* ♣, 🐟): **~ing hot** dampfend heiß. **4.** **~ up** beschlagen. **III** *v/t* **5.** *gastr.* dämpfen, dünsten. **6.** **~ open** *Brief* über Dampf öffnen. **7. get ~ed up** beschlagen; *fig.* F sich aufregen (*about* über *acc*). **'~·boat** *s* Dampfboot *n*, Dampfer *m.*

steam·er ['stiːmə] *s* **1.** Dampfer *m*, Dampfschiff *n.* **2.** Dampf(koch)-, Schnellkochtopf *m.*

steam| i·ron *s* Dampfbügeleisen *n.* **'~·roll·er** *s* Dampfwalze *f.* **'~·ship** *→* **steamer** 1.

steel [stiːl] **I** *s* Stahl *m:* **~ nerve** I. **II** *v/t:* **~ o.s. for** sich wappnen gegen, sich ge-

faßt machen auf (*acc*). **~ wool** *s* Stahlwolle *f.* **'~·work·er** *s* Stahlarbeiter *m.* **'~·works** *s pl* (*oft sg konstruiert*) Stahlwerk *n.*

steel·y ['stiːlɪ] *adj* **1.** **~ blue** stahlblau. **2.** *fig.* hart (*Blick*); eisern (*Entschlossenheit*).

steep¹ [stiːp] *adj* □ **1.** steil. **2.** *fig.* stark (*Preisanstieg etc*). **3.** F happig (*Forderung*), (*Preis a.*) gepfeffert, gesalzen.

steep² [~] **I** *v/t* eintauchen (*in* acc); *Wäsche* einweichen: **~ed in history** geschichtsträchtig. **II** *v/i* weichen.

steep·en ['stiːpən] *v/i* steiler werden.

stee·ple ['stiːpl] *s* Kirchturm *m.* **'~·chase** *s Pferdesport:* Hindernis-, Jagdrennen *n; Leichtathletik:* Hindernislauf *m.*

steer¹ [stɪə] *s* (junger) Ochse.

steer² [~] **I** *v/t* **1.** steuern, lenken. **2.** *Kurs* steuern (*a. fig.*). **3.** *j-n* lotsen, bugsieren. **II** *v/i* **4. ~ for** ♣ ansteuern, *Kurs* nehmen auf (*acc*); *fig.* zusteuern auf (*acc*); → **clear** 13. **'steer·ing** *s* Steuerung *f*, Lenkung *f.* **II** *adj:* **~ column** *mot.* Lenksäule *f;* **~ wheel** *mot.* Lenk-, *a.* ♣ Steuerrad *n.*

stein [staɪn] *s* Maßkrug *m.*

stel·lar ['stelə] *adj* Stern(en)...

stem¹ [stem] **I** *s* **1.** ♀ Stiel *m* (*a. e-s Sektglases etc*), Stengel *m.* **2.** *ling.* Stamm *m.* **II** *v/i* **3.** **~ from** stammen *od.* herrühren von.

stem² [~] *v/t Blutung* stillen; *fig.* eindämmen, stoppen.

stench [stentʃ] *s* Gestank *m.*

sten·cil ['stensl] *s* Schablone *f; typ.* Matrize *f.*

ste·nog·ra·pher [stə'nɒgrəfə] *s Am.* Stenotypistin *f.*

step [step] **I** *s* **1.** Schritt *m* (*a. Geräusch*): **~ by ~** Schritt für Schritt (*a. fig.*); **take a ~** e-n Schritt machen; **it's just a ~** (od. **a few ~s**) **to the shop** es sind nur ein paar Schritte zum Laden; → **watch** 4. **2.** Stufe *f;* Sprosse *f:* (*pair of*) **~s** *pl* → **stepladder**; → **mind** 7. **3. be in** (**out of**) **~** *bsd.* ✗ im Gleichschritt *od.* Tritt (aus dem Tritt) sein; (*beim Tanzen*) im Takt (aus dem) Takt sein; **be out of ~ with** *fig.* nachhinken (*dat*), zurück sein hinter (*dat*); **keep (in) ~ with** *fig.* sich richten nach. **4.** *fig.* Schritt *m:* **take ~s** Schritte *od.* et. unternehmen; **a ~ in the right**

direction ein Schritt in die richtige Richtung; → *legal* 4. **5.** *fig.* Schritt *m*, Stufe *f*: *three-~ plan* Dreistufenplan *m*. **II** *v/i* **6.** gehen; treten (*in* in *acc*; *on* auf *acc*): *~ on it* mot. F Gas geben, auf die Tube drücken (*beide a. fig.*); → *gas* 2b.

Verbindungen mit Adverbien:

step| a·side *v/i* **1.** zur Seite treten. **2.** *fig.* Platz machen (*in* favo[u]r *of* für), zurücktreten (*as* als; *in* favo[u]r *of* zugunsten). *~ back* *v/i* zurücktreten. *~ down* *v/i* **1.** herunter-, hinuntersteigen. **2.** → *step aside* 2. *~ for·ward* *v/i* **1.** vortreten, nach vorne treten. **2.** *fig.* sich melden (*Zeugen etc*). *~ in* *v/i* **1.** eintreten. **2.** *fig.* einschreiten; sich einmischen. *~ out* *v/i* **1.** heraus-, hinaustreten; *bsd. Am.* weggehen. **2.** *~ on Am.* F Ehepartner betrügen. *~ up* *v/i* herauf-, hinaufsteigen. **II** *v/t* Produktion *etc* steigern.

step... ['step] Stief...: *~father*, *~mother*, *etc.*

step-by-step *adj fig.* schrittweise. **'~-lad·der** *s* Tritt- *od.* Stufenleiter *f*.

steppe [step] *s, oft pl geogr.* Steppe *f*.

step·ping stone Trittstein *m*; *fig.* Sprungbrett *n* (*to* für).

ster·e·o ['steriəʊ] **I** *s* **1.** Stereo *n*: *in ~.* **2.** Stereogerät *n*, *-anlage f*. **II** *adj* **3.** Stereo...: → *unit* Stereoanlage *f*.

ster·e·o·type ['steriətaip] *s* Klischee(vorstellung *f*) *n.* **'ster·e·o·typed** *adj* klischeehaft; stereotyp.

ster·ile ['sterail] *adj* **1.** ✻ steril, keimfrei. **2.** *biol.* steril, (*a. Boden*) unfruchtbar. **3.** *fig.* steril, unoriginell. **ster·il·i·ty** [stə'riləti] *s* Sterilität *f* (*a. fig.*); Unfruchtbarkeit *f*.

ster·i·li·za·tion [,sterəlai'zeiʃn] *s* ✻ Sterilisation *f*, Sterilisierung *f*. **'ster·i·lize** *v/t* sterilisieren.

ster·ling ['stɜːlɪŋ] **I** *s* das Pfund Sterling. **II** *adj*: *~ silver* Sterlingsilber *n*.

stern¹ [stɜːn] *adj* □ streng (*Person*, *Blick*, *Disziplin etc*).

stern² [~] *s* ♻ Heck *n*.

ster·num ['stɜːnəm] *pl* **-na** ['~nə], **-nums** *s anat.* Brustbein *n*.

steth·o·scope ['steθəskəʊp] *s* ✻ Stethoskop *n*.

stet·son ['stetsn] *s* Stetson *m*, Cowboyhut *m*.

ste·ve·dore ['stiːvədɔː] *s* ♻ *bsd. Am.* Schauermann *m*, Stauer *m*.

stew [stjuː] **I** *v/t Fleisch, Gemüse* schmoren, *Obst* dünsten: *~ed apples pl* Apfelkompott *n.* **II** *v/i* schmoren, dünsten: → *juice* 1. **III** *s* Eintopf *m*.

stew·ard [stjʊəd] *s* **1.** ✈, ♻ Steward *m*. **2.** Ordner *m*. **'stew·ard·ess** *s* ✈, ♻ Stewardeß *f.*

stewed [stjuːd] *adj* F blau (*betrunken*).

stick¹ [stik] *s* **1.** Stock *m*, ([*Eis*]Hockey *a.*) Schläger *m*; (*Besen- etc*)Stiel *m*; (*a.* ✈ *Steuer*)Knüppel *m*: *walk with a ~* am Stock gehen; *get* (*hold*) *of the wrong end of the ~* F die Sache in den falschen *od.* verkehrten Hals bekommen; → *cleft stick.* **2.** (trockener) Zweig, *fig. a.* Brennholz *n.* **3.** Stück *n* (*Kreide etc*), Stange *f* (*Dynamit, Sellerie etc*), (*Lippen*)Stift *m*, (*Räucher*)Stäbchen *n*, Streifen *m* (*Kaugummi*). **4.** *a. ~ of furniture* F Möbelstück *n.* **5.** *live out in the ~s* F im finstersten Provinz leben.

stick² [~] (*irr*) **I** *v/t* **1.** mit e-r *Nadel etc* stechen (*into* in *acc*). **2.** *etc.* kleben (*on* auf *acc*, *an acc*); an-, festkleben (*with* mit). **3.** stecken: → *nose* 1. **4.** F tun, stellen, setzen, legen: *bsd. Br.* F → *stand* 11. **II** *v/i* **6.** kleben, halten; klebenbleiben (*to* an *dat*). **7.** steckenbleiben: *~ in s.o.'s mind fig.* j-m im Gedächtnis bleiben. **8.** *~ at nothing* vor nichts zurückschrecken. **9.** *~ to* (F *by*) bei s-r *Ansicht etc* bleiben, zu s-m *Wort etc* stehen; *~ to* (F *by, with*) zu j-m halten; → *gun* 1, *point* 11.

Verbindungen mit Adverbien:

stick| out *v/i* **1.** vorstehen, (*Ohren etc*) abstehen. **2.** *fig.* auffallen: → *mile*, *thumb* 1. **3.** *~ for* bestehen auf (*dat*). **II** *v/t* **4.** aus-, vorstrecken: *stick one's tongue out at s.o.* j-m die Zunge herausstrecken; → *neck* 1. **5.** durchhalten, *-stehen.* *~ to·geth·er* *v/i* **1.** (*a. v/t*) zs.-kleben. **2.** *fig.* zs.-halten. *~ up* *v/t* **1.** F j-*n, Bank etc* überfallen. **2.** stick *'em up!* F Hände hoch! **II** *v/i* **3.** *~ for* j-*n* verteidigen (*a.* mit Worten).

stick·er ['stikə] *s* Aufkleber *m.* **'stick·ing** *adj*: *~ plaster* Heftpflaster *n*; *~ point* *fig.* unüberwindliches Hindernis (*bei Verhandlungen etc*).

'stick-in-the-mud *s* F Rückschrittler(in).

stick·ler ['stɪklə] s: **be a ~ for** es ganz genau nehmen mit, großen Wert legen auf (*acc*).

'**stick|-on** *adj*: **~ label** (Auf)Klebeetikett n. '**~pin** s *Am*. Krawattennadel f. '**~-up** s F (Raub)Überfall m.

stick·y ['stɪkɪ] *adj* □ **1**. a) klebrig (**with** von), b) → **stick-on**. **2**. schwül, drükkend (*Wetter*). **3**. F heikel, unangenehm (*Lage*): **he'll come to** (*od*. **meet**) **a ~ end** mit ihm wird es ein böses Ende nehmen. **4. be ~ about doing s.th.** F et. nur ungern tun.

stiff [stɪf] **I** *adj* □ **1**. *allg*. steif: **beat until ~** steif schlagen; → *bore²*, *lip* 1. **2**. *fig*. stark (*alkoholisches Getränk, Medizin*). **3**. schwer, schwierig (*Aufgabe*); hart (*Strafe*); scharf (*Konkurrenz*); hartnäckig (*Widerstand*). **4**. F happig, gepfeffert, gesalzen (*Preis*). **II** s **5**. *sl*. Leiche f. '**stiff·en** **I** *v/t* **1**. *Wäsche* stärken, steifen. **2**. *fig*. verschärfen. **II** *v/i* **3**. steif werden. **4**. *fig*. sich verschärfen.

sti·fle ['staɪfl] **I** *v/t* ersticken, *fig*. a. unterdrücken. **II** *v/i* ersticken.

stig·ma ['stɪgmə] s **1**. *fig*. Stigma n. **2**. *pl* **-ta** ['~tə] *eccl*. Stigma n, Wundmal n. '**stig·ma·tize** *v/t* *fig*. brandmarken (**as** als).

sti·let·to [stɪ'letəʊ] *pl* **-tos** (*od*. **-toes**) s Stilett n. **~ heel** s Bleistift-, Pfennigabsatz m.

still¹ [stɪl] **I** *adj* **1**. *allg*. still: → *keep* 15, *stand* 7, *water* 2. **2**. ohne Kohlensäure (*Getränk*). **II** s **3**. *Film, TV*: Standfoto n.

still² [~] **I** *adv* **1**. (immer) noch, noch immer. **2**. *beim comp*: noch. **II** *cj* **3**. dennoch, trotzdem.

still³ [~] s 🝆 Destillationsapparat m; Destillierkolben m.

'**still|-birth** s Totgeburt f. '**~-born** *adj* totgeboren. '**~-life** *pl* **lifes** s paint. Stilleben n.

stilt [stɪlt] s **1**. Stelze f. **2**. △ Pfahl m. '**stilt·ed** *adj* gestelzt, gespreizt, geschraubt.

stim·u·lant ['stɪmjʊlənt] s 🝆 Stimulans n, Anregungsmittel n; *fig*. Anreiz m, Ansporn m (**to** für). **stim·u·late** ['~leɪt] *v/t* **1**. 🝆 *j-n*, *Kreislauf etc* stimulieren, anregen, *fig*. *a*. *j-n* anspornen (**to do** zu tun); *physiol*. reizen. **2**. *Produktion etc* ankurbeln. **stim·u·lus** ['~ləs] *pl* **-li** ['~laɪ] s **1**. *physiol*. Reiz m. **2**. *fig*. Anreiz m, Ansporn m (**to** für).

sting [stɪŋ] **I** *v/t* (*irr*) **1**. *j-n* stechen (*Biene etc*). **2**. brennen auf (*dat*) *od*. in (*dat*): **~ s.o. into action** *fig*. *j-n* aktiv werden lassen. **3**. F *j-n* neppen (**for** um). **II** *v/i* **4**. stechen (*Bienen etc*). **5**. brennen (**from** von) (*Augen etc*). **III** s **6**. Stachel m. **7**. Stich m. **8**. Brennen n, brennender Schmerz: **take the ~ out of s.th.** *fig*. e-r Sache den Stachel nehmen. '**sting·ing** *adj*: **~ nettle** ❀ Brennessel f.

stin·gy ['stɪndʒɪ] *adj* □ F knick(e)rig (*Person*), mick(e)rig (*Mahlzeit etc*): **be ~ with** knickern mit.

stink [stɪŋk] **I** *v/i* (*irr*) **1**. stinken (**of** nach): **~ to high heaven** wie die Pest stinken; *fig*. zum Himmel stinken. **2**. F hundsmiserabel sein. **II** *v/t* **3**. **~ out** F *Zimmer etc* verstänkern. **III** s **4**. Gestank m: **there's a ~ of garlic in here** hier stinkt es nach Knoblauch. **5. cause** (*od*. **kick up, raise**) **a ~** F Stunk machen (**about** wegen). **~ bomb** s Stinkbombe f.

stink·ing ['stɪŋkɪŋ] **I** *adj* **1**. stinkend. **2**. F scheußlich; blöd. **II** *adv* **3**. **~ rich** F stinkreich.

stint [stɪnt] s a) Pensum n, b) Zeit f: **he did a three-year ~ in the army** er war drei Jahre lang beim Militär.

stip·u·late ['stɪpjʊleɪt] *v/t* **1**. zur Auflage *od*. Bedingung machen. **2**. festsetzen, vereinbaren. '**stip·u·la·tion** s **1**. Auflage f, Bedingung f. **2**. Festsetzung f, Vereinbarung f.

stir [stɜː] **I** *v/t* **1**. (um)rühren: **~ up** *Staub* aufwirbeln, *Schlamm* aufwühlen. **2**. *Glied etc* bewegen, rühren: **~ o.s.** sich beeilen; → *finger* 1, *stump* 1. **3**. *Blätter etc* leicht bewegen, *Wasser* kräuseln (*Wind*). **4**. *fig*. *j-n* aufwühlen, bewegen. **5. ~ up** *fig*. *Unruhe* stiften, *Streit* entfachen; *Erinnerungen* wachrufen. **II** *v/i* **6**. sich rühren: **~ from** sich fort- *od*. wegrühren von. **7**. *fig*. sich rühren, wach werden. **III** s **8. give s.th. a ~** et. (um-)rühren. **9. cause** (*od*. **create**) **a ~** *fig*. für Aufsehen sorgen. '**stir·ring** *adj* □ aufwühlend, bewegend.

stir·rup ['stɪrəp] s Steigbügel m.

stitch [stɪtʃ] **I** s **1**. *Nähen etc*: Stich m: **the wound needed eight ~es** die Wunde mußte mit acht Stichen genäht werden;

he had his **~es out yesterday** ihm wurden gestern die Fäden gezogen. **2.** *Stricken etc:* Masche *f:* **drop a ~** e-e Masche fallen lassen. **3. have a** *(od.* **the)** **~** Seitenstechen haben; **be in ~es** F sich kaputtlachen. **4. he hadn't got a ~ on** F er war splitterfasernackt. **II** *v/t* **5.** *a.* **~ up** zunähen, *Wunde* nähen: **~ on** *(to)* *Knopf etc* annähen *(an acc).* **6.** *Buch* broschieren, heften.

stock [stɒk] **I** *s* **1.** Vorrat *m (of* an *dat):* **have s.th. in ~** et. vorrätig *od.* auf Lager haben; **take ~** Inventur machen; **take ~ of** *fig.* sich klarwerden über *(acc).* **2.** ♣ a) *bsd. Am.* Aktie(n *pl) f,* b) *pl* Aktien *pl,* c) *pl* Wertpapiere *pl.* **3.** *gastr.* Brühe *f.* **4.** Viehbestand *m.* **5.** *(Gewehr)*Schaft *m.* **6.** *fig.* Abstammung *f,* Herkunft *f.* **II** *v/t* **7.** ♣ *Ware* vorrätig haben, führen. **8. be well ~ed (up) with** gut versorgt sein mit. **III** *v/i* **9. ~ up** sich eindecken **(on,** with mit). **IV** *adj* **10.** ♣ **~ model** Serienmodell *n;* **~ size** Standardgröße *f.* **11.** *contp.* Standard..., stereotyp *(Ausrede etc).* '**~,breed·er** *s* Viehzüchter *m.* '**~,breed·ing** *s* Viehzucht *f.* '**~,brok·er** *s* ♣ Börsenmakler *m.* **~ cor·po·ra·tion** *s* ♣ *Am.* Kapital*od.* Aktiengesellschaft *f.* **~ cube** *s* Brühwürfel *m.* **~ ex·change** *s* ♣ Börse *f.* '**~,hold·er** *s* ♣ *bsd. Am.* Aktionär(in).

stock·ing [stɒkɪŋ] *s* Strumpf *m.* **~ mask** *s* Strumpfmaske *f.*

'**stock·in·trade** *s:* **be part of s.o.'s ~** *fig.* zu j-s Rüstzeug gehören. **~ mar·ket** *s* ♣ Börse *f.* '**~,pile I** *s* Vorrat *m (of* an *dat).* **II** *v/t* e-n Vorrat anlegen an *(dat);* *Lebensmittel etc* hamstern, horten. '**~,room** *s* Lager(raum *m) n.* '**~,still** *adv* regungslos. '**~,tak·ing** *s* ♣ Inventur *f; fig.* Bestandsaufnahme *f.*

stock·y [stɒkɪ] *adj* □ stämmig, untersetzt.

sto·i·cal [stəʊɪkl] *adj* □ stoisch, gelassen. **sto·i·cism** [ˈ~ˌsɪzəm] *s* Gelassenheit *f.*

stoke [stəʊk] **I** *v/t a.* **~ up** *Feuer,* Haß *etc* schüren. **II** *v/i:* **~ up** F sich vollstopfen **(on,** with mit). '**stok·er** *s* Heizer *m.*

stole¹ [stəʊl] *pret von* **steal.**

stole² [~] *s* Stola *f.*

sto·len [stəʊlən] *pp von* **steal.**

stol·id [stɒlɪd] *adj* □ phlegmatisch.

stom·ach [stʌmək] **I** *s* **1.** Magen *m:* **on**

an empty ~ auf leeren *od.* nüchternen Magen *rauchen etc,* mit leerem *od.* nüchternem Magen *schwimmen gehen etc;* **on a full ~** mit vollem Magen; **turn s.o.'s ~** j-m den Magen umdrehen. **2.** Bauch *m.* **3. (for)** Appetit *m* (auf *acc); fig.* Lust *f* (auf *acc,* zu). **II** *v/t* **4.** vertragen *(a. fig.).* **~ache** [ˈ~ˌeɪk] *s* **1.** Magenschmerzen *pl.* **2.** Bauchschmerzen *pl,* -weh *n.* **~ up·set** *s* Magenverstimmung *f.*

stomp [stɒmp] *v/i* sta(m)pfen, trampeln.

stone [stəʊn] **I** *s* **1.** *(a. Edel-,* ♣ *Gallenetc)*Stein *m:* **it's only a ~'s throw (away) from** es ist nur e-n Katzensprung entfernt von; **have a heart of ~** ein Herz aus Stein haben; **leave no ~ unturned** *fig.* nichts unversucht lassen. **2.** ♣ Kern *m,* Stein *m.* **3.** *(Hagel)*Korn *n.* **4.** *pl* **stone(s)** *Br.* Gewichtseinheit *(= 6,35 kg).* **II** *v/t* **5.** mit Steinen bewerfen: **~ (to death)** steinigen. **6.** entkernen, -steinen. ♀ **Age** *s* Steinzeit *f.* '**~-broke** *Am.* → **stony-broke.** '**~-cold** I *adj* eiskalt. **II** *adv:* **~ sober** F stocknüchtern.

stoned [stəʊnd] *adj sl.* **1.** stinkbesoffen. **2.** stoned *(unter Drogeneinwirkung).*

stone-dead *adj* mausetot. **~-deaf** *adj* stocktaub. **~ fruit** *s* Steinfrucht *f,* coll. Steinobst *n.* '**~,ma·son** *s* Steinmetz *m.* '**~ware** *s* Steingut *n.*

ston·y [stəʊnɪ] *adj* □ **1.** steinig. **2.** *fig.* steinern *(Gesicht,* Herz *etc),* eisig *(Schweigen).* **~-broke** *adj bsd. Br.* F total abgebrannt *od.* pleite.

stood [stʊd] *pret u. pp von* **stand.**

stooge [stuːdʒ] *s* F *contp.* Handlanger *m.*

stool [stuːl] *s* **1.** *(Bar-, Klavier- etc)*Hocker *m, (Klavier- etc)*Stuhl *m,* (-)Schemel *m:* **fall between two ~s** *fig.* sich zwischen zwei Stühle setzen. **2.** *physiol.* Stuhl *m.* '**~,pi·geon** *s* F (Polizei)Spitzel *m.*

stoop [stuːp] *v/i* **1.** *a.* **~ down** sich bücken. **2.** gebeugt gehen. **3. ~ to** *fig.* sich herablassen *od.* hergeben zu: **~ to doing s.th.** sich dazu herablassen *od.* hergeben, et. zu tun. **II** *s* **4.** gebeugte Haltung: **walk with a ~** → **2.**

stop [stɒp] **I** *s* **1.** Halt *m:* **come to a ~** anhalten, stoppen, *weitS.* aufhören; **put a ~ to** e-r *Sache* ein Ende machen *od.* setzen. **2.** *(Bus)*Haltestelle *f.* **3.** *ling.*

bsd. Br. Punkt *m*. **4. pull out all the ~s** *fig.* alle Register ziehen. **II** *v/i* **5.** stehenbleiben (*a. Uhr etc*), (an)halten, stoppen: ~ **by s.o.'s place** bei j-m vorbeischauen; → **dead** 14, **thief. 6.** aufhören: ~ **at nothing** vor nichts zurückschrecken (**to get s.th.** um et. zu bekommen); → **short** 5. **7.** *bsd. Br.* bleiben (**for supper** zum Abendessen). **III** *v/t* **8.** anhalten, stoppen; *Maschine etc* abstellen. **9.** aufhören mit: ~ **doing s.th.** aufhören, et. zu tun. **10.** ein Ende machen *od.* setzen (*dat*); *Blutung* stillen; *Arbeiten, Verkehr etc* zum Erliegen bringen; (*Boxen*) *Kampf* abbrechen. **11.** *et.* verhindern; *j-n* hindern (**from** von), hindern (**from** an *dat*): ~ *s.o.* (**from**) **doing s.th.** j-n davon abhalten *od.* daran hindern, et. zu tun. **12.** *Rohr etc* verstopfen; *Zahn* füllen, plombieren: ~ *s.o.'s* **mouth** F j-m den Mund stopfen. **13.** *Scheck* sperren (lassen).
Verbindungen mit Adverbien:

stop| by *v/i* vorbeischauen. ~ **in** *v/i* **1.** vorbeischauen (**at** bei). **2.** *bsd. Br.* zu Hause bleiben. ~ **off** *v/i* F, ~ **o∙ver** *v/i* Zwischenstation machen (**in** *dat*). ~ **round** *v/i* *bsd. Am.* F vorbeischauen. ~ **up I** *v/t* Leitung *etc* verstopfen. **II** *v/i bsd. Br.* aufbleiben.

'stop|∙cock *s* ⚙ Absperrhahn *m*. **'~∙gap I** *s* Notbehelf *m*, Übergangslösung *f*; (*Person*) Aushilfe *f*, *contp.* Lückenbüßer *m*. **II** *adj*: ~ **measure** Überbrückungsmaßnahme *f*; ~ **secretary** Aushilfssekretärin *f*. **'~∙o∙ver** *s* Zwischenstation *f*; ✈ Zwischenlandung *f*.

stop∙page ['stɒpɪdʒ] *s* **1.** Arbeitseinstellung *f*. **2.** ⚙ Verstopfung *f* (*a.* ⚕). **3.** *bsd. Br.* (Gehalts-, Lohn)Abzug *m*. **'stop∙per** *s* **1.** Stöpsel *m*. **II** *v/t a.* ~ **up** ver-, zustöpseln.

stop| press *s bsd. Br.* letzte Meldungen *pl* (**in** *e-r Zeitung*). **'~∙watch** *s* Stoppuhr *f*.

stor∙age ['stɔːrɪdʒ] *s* **1.** (Ein)Lagerung *f*. **2.** Lager(raum *m*) *n*: **be in** ~ eingelagert sein. **3.** Lagergeld *n*.

store ['stɔː] **I** *s* **1.** Vorrat *m*, *pl a.* Bestände *pl* (**of** an *dat*): **there's a shock in** ~ **for you** auf dich wartet e-e unangenehme Überraschung; **have s.th. in** ~ et. vorrätig *od.* auf Lager haben; **have a surprise in** ~ **for s.o.** e-e Überraschung

für j-n haben. **2.** *bsd. Am.* Laden *m*, Geschäft *n*; *bsd. Br.* Kauf-, Warenhaus *n*. **3.** Lager(halle *f*, -haus *n*) *n*: **be in** ~ *Br.* eingelagert sein. **4. set great** (**little**) ~ **by** *fig.* großen (wenig) Wert legen auf (*acc*). **II** *v/t* **5.** *a.* ~ **up** sich e-n Vorrat anlegen an (*dat*). **6.** *Kohle etc* lagern; *Möbel etc* einlagern; *Daten, Energie etc* speichern. ~ **de∙tec∙tive** *s* Kaufhausdetektiv *m*. **'~∙house** *s* **1.** Lagerhaus *n*. **2.** *fig.* Fundgrube *f* (**of** von): **be a** ~ **of good ideas** voller guter Ideen stecken. **'~∙keep∙er** *s bsd. Am.* Ladenbesitzer(in), -inhaber(in). **~∙room** ['~rʊm] *s* Lagerraum *m*.

sto∙rey ['stɔːrɪ] *s bsd. Br.* Stock(werk *n*) *m*, Etage *f*: **a six-~ building** → **storeyed**. **'sto∙reyed** *adj bsd. Br.*, **'sto∙ried** *adj Am.*: **a six-~ building** ein sechsstöckiges Gebäude.

stork [stɔːk] *s* orn. Storch *m*.

storm [stɔːm] **I** *s* **1.** Unwetter *n*; (*a. fig. Protest- etc*)Sturm *m*: **a** ~ **in a teacup** *Br. fig.* ein Sturm im Wasserglas. **2. take by** ~ ✕ im Sturm nehmen *od.* (*a. fig.*) erobern. **II** *v/t* **3.** ✕ *etc* stürmen. **III** *v/i* **4.** stürmen, stürzen. ~ **cloud** *s* Gewitterwolke *f*: **the ~s are gathering** *fig.* es braut sich et. zusammen.

storm∙y ['stɔːmɪ] *adj* □ stürmisch (*a. fig.*).

sto∙ry¹ ['stɔːrɪ] *s* **1.** Geschichte *f*; Märchen *n* (*a. fig.* F): **his side of the** ~ s-e Version; **it's the same old** ~ es das alte Lied; **to cut a long** ~ **short** um es kurz zu machen, kurz u. gut; → **go** 18. **2.** Story *f*, (Lebens-, Entwicklungs)Geschichte *f*. **3.** Story *f*, Handlung *f*. **4.** *Journalismus*: Story *f*, Bericht *m* (**on** über *acc*).

sto∙ry² [~] *Am.* → **storey.**

'sto∙ry|∙book *s* ... wie im Märchen. ~ **line** → **story¹** 3.

stoup [stuːp] *s eccl.* Weihwasserbecken *n*.

stout [staʊt] **I** *adj* □ **1.** korpulent, (*Frau a.*) vollschlank. **2.** *fig.* hartnäckig. **II** *s* **3.** Stout *m* (*dunkles Bier mit starkem Hopfengeschmack*).

stove [stəʊv] *s* Ofen *m*, (*zum Kochen a.*) Herd *m*.

stow [stəʊ] *v/t a.* ~ **away** verstauen. **'stow∙a∙way** *s* ✈, ⚓ blinder Passagier.

strad∙dle ['strædl] *v/t* breitbeinig *od.* mit

gespreizten Beinen stehen über (*dat*); rittlings sitzen auf (*dat*).

strag·gle ['strægl] *v/i*: **~ in** einzeln eintrudeln. **'strag·gler** *s* Nachzügler(in). **'strag·gly** *adj* struppig (*Haar*).

straight [streɪt] **I** *adj* **1.** gerade, (*Haar*) glatt: **~ line** gerade Linie, *A* Gerade *f*; **keep one's face ~** ernst bleiben. **2. get** (*od. put*) **s.th. ~** et. in Ordnung bringen, Zimmer etc a. aufräumen; **set s.o. ~ about s.th.** *fig.* j-m et. klarmachen. **3.** offen, ehrlich (**with** zu). **4.** ohne Unterbrechung: **in ~ sets** (*Tennis etc*) ohne Satzverlust; **his third ~ win** (*Sport*) sein dritter Sieg hintereinander *od.* in Folge. **5.** pur: **drink one's whisky ~; two ~ whiskies** zwei Whisky pur. **6.** *sl.* a) hetero (*heterosexuell*), b) clean, sauber (*nicht mehr drogenabhängig*): **I'm ~** ich nehm' grundsätzlich keine Drogen. **II** *adv* **7.** gerade: **~ ahead** geradeaus. **8.** genau, direkt. **9. a. ~ off** sofort. **10.** klar sehen, denken. **11.** F *a.* **~ out** offen, ehrlich. **12. ~ up?** *Br.* F ehrlich? **III** *s* **13.** *Sport*: **Gegen-, Ziel**Gerade *f*. **~·a·'way** *adv* sofort.

straight·en ['streɪtn] **I** *v/t* **1.** *a.* **~ up** geradebiegen, -legen *etc*, Krawatte *etc* geraderücken. **2. ~ out** *fig.* Angelegenheit *etc* in Ordnung bringen, Mißverständnis klären; F j-m (wieder) auf die Beine helfen; j-n (wieder) auf die richtige Bahn bringen. **3. ~ up** in Ordnung bringen, aufräumen. **II** *v/i* **4.** *a.* **~ out** gerade werden (*Straße etc*). **5. ~ up** sich aufrichten.

straight·for·ward [‚streɪt'fɔːwəd] *adj* □ **1.** aufrichtig. **2.** einfach, unkompliziert. **3.** glatt (*Absage etc*). **~'out** *adj* *bsd. Am.* F offen, ehrlich.

strain [streɪn] **I** *v/t* **1.** Seil *etc* (an)spannen: **~ one's ears** (**eyes**) die Ohren spitzen (genau hinschauen). **2.** sich, Augen etc überanstrengen; sich e-n Muskel etc zerren: **~ a muscle** a. sich e-e Muskelzerrung zuziehen. **3.** Gemüse, Tee etc abgießen. **II** *v/i* **4.** sich anstrengen. **5. ~ at** zerren *od.* ziehen an (*dat*): **~ at the leash** an der Leine zerren (*Hund*); *fig.* es nicht mehr erwarten können. **III** *s* **6.** Spannung *f* (*a. ⚡ u. pol. etc*). **7.** *fig.* Belastung *f* (**on** für): **put a great ~ on s.o.** j-n stark belasten. **strained** *adj* **1.** gezerrt: **~ muscle** a.

Muskelzerrung *f*. **2.** gezwungen (*Lächeln etc*). **3.** gespannt (*Beziehungen*). **4. look ~** abgespannt aussehen. **'strain·er** *s* Sieb *n*.

strait [streɪt] *s* a. *pl* Meerenge *f*, Straße *f*: **be in desperate** (*od.* **dire**) **~s** *fig.* in e-r ernsten Notlage sein. **'strait·ened** *adj*: **live in ~ circumstances** in beschränkten Verhältnissen leben.

'strait·jack·et *s* Zwangsjacke *f*: **put in a ~** j-n in e-e Zwangsjacke stecken. **‚~-'laced** *adj* prüde.

strand [strænd] *s* (*Haar*)Strähne *f*; (*Woll- etc*)Faden *m*, (*Kabel*)Draht *m*; *fig.* Faden *m* (*e-r Handlung etc*).

strand·ed ['strændɪd] *adj*: **be ~** *⚓* gestrandet sein; **be** (**left**) **~** *fig.* festsitzen (**in** in *dat*) (*Person*).

strange [streɪndʒ] *adj* □ **1.** merkwürdig, seltsam, sonderbar: **~ to say** so merkwürdig es auch klingen mag; **~ly** (**enough**) merkwürdiger-, seltsamer-, sonderbarerweise. **2.** fremd (**to s.o.** j-m). **3. be ~ to** nicht vertraut sein mit. **'stran·ger** *s* **1.** Fremde *m*, *f*: **I'm a ~ here** ich bin hier fremd; → **perfect** 2. **2. be a ~ to** → **strange** 3.

stran·gle ['stræŋgl] *v/t* erwürgen, erdrosseln. *fig.* abwürgen, ersticken. **'~-hold** *s* Würgegriff *m*: **have a ~ on** *fig.* j-n, et. vollkommen beherrschen.

stran·gu·late ['stræŋgjʊleɪt] *v/t* *⚕* abschnüren, abbinden. **‚stran·gu·'la·tion** *s* **1.** Erwürgung *f*, Erdrosselung *f*. **2.** *⚕* Abschnürung *f*, Abbindung *f*.

strap [stræp] **I** *s* **1.** Riemen *m*, Gurt *m*; Haltegriff *m*, Schlaufe *f* (*in Bus etc*); Träger *m* (*an Kleid etc*); (*Uhr*)(Arm-)Band *n*. **II** *v/t* **2.** festschnallen (**to** an *dat*): **be ~ped in** *✈*, *mot.* angeschnallt sein. **3. ~ up** F Bein *etc* bandagieren. **4. be ~ped** (**for cash**) F knapp bei Kasse sein; abgebrannt *od.* pleite sein. **'~-hang·er** *s* F **1.** Stehplatzinhaber(in) (*in Bus etc*). **2.** Pendler(in).

strap·less ['stræplɪs] *adj* schulterfrei (*Kleid*), (*a.* Badeanzug) trägerlos.

stra·ta ['strɑːtə] *pl von* **stratum**.

strat·a·gem ['strætədʒəm] *s* (✗ Kriegs)List *f*.

stra·te·gic [strə'tiːdʒɪk] *adj* (**~ally**) strategisch; strategisch wichtig. **strat·e·gist** ['strætɪdʒɪst] *s* Stratege *m*. **strat·e·gy** ['~dʒɪ] *s* Strategie *f*.

strat·i·fied ['strætɪfaɪd] *adj* vielschichtig (*Gesellschaft*).

strat·o·sphere ['strætəʊˌsfɪə] *s meteor.* Stratosphäre *f*.

stra·tum ['strɑːtəm] *pl* **-ta** ['ˌtə] *s geol.*, *sociol.* Schicht *f*.

straw [strɔː] *s* **1.** Stroh *n*: → **man** 3. **2.** Stroh-, *a.* Trinkhalm *m*: **the ~ that breaks the camel's back, the last ~** *fig.* der Tropfen, der das Faß zum Überlaufen bringt; **clutch at ~s** *fig.* sich an e-n Strohhalm klammern. **~·ber·ry** ['ˌbərɪ] *s* Erdbeere *f*. **~ hat** *s* Strohhut *m*. **~ man** *s* (*irr* **man**) Strohmann *m*. **~ poll, ~ vote** *s pol.* Probeabstimmung *f*.

stray [streɪ] **I** *v/i* **1.** sich verirren. **2.** *fig.* abschweifen (**from** von) (*Gedanken etc*). **II** *adj* **3.** verirrt (*Kugel, Tier*); streunend (*Tier*). **4.** vereinzelt. **III** *s* **5.** verirrtes *od.* streunendes Tier.

streak [striːk] *s* **1.** Streifen *m*; Strähne *f* (*im Haar*): **a ~ of lightning** ein Blitz *m*; **like a ~ of lightning** wie der Blitz. **2.** *fig.* (Charakter)Zug *m.* **3.** *fig.* (un)lucky ~ Glückssträhne *f* (Pechsträhne *f*); **win·ning** (**losing**) ~ (*a. Sport*) Siegesserie (Niederlagenserie) *f*; **be on a lucky ~** e-e Glückssträhne haben. **'streak·y** *adj* streifig; durchwachsen (*Frühstücksspeck*).

stream [striːm] **I** *s* **1.** Bach *m.* **2.** Strömung *f*: **go against the ~** *fig.* gegen den Strom schwimmen. **3.** (*Besucher-, Blut-, Verkehrs- etc*)Strom *m*; *fig.* Flut *f*, Schwall *m* (*von Verwünschungen etc*). **4.** *ped. Br.* Leistungsgruppe *f*. **II** *v/i* **7.** *ped. Br. Klasse* in Leistungsgruppen einteilen. **'stream·er** *s* Luft-, Papierschlange *f*. **'stream·ing** *adj*: **he's got a ~ cold** er hat e-n fürchterlichen Schnupfen. **'stream|·line** *v/t* rationalisieren. **'~·lined** *adj* stromlinienförmig, windschnittig, -schlüpf(r)ig.

street [striːt] *s* Straße *f*: **in** (*bsd. Am.* **on**) **the ~** auf der Straße; **be** (**right**) **up s.o.'s ~** *fig.* j-m zusagen; **he's not in the same ~ as me, I'm ~s ahead of him** F ich bin ihm haushoch überlegen; **walk**

the ~s durch die Straßen laufen; auf den Strich gehen; → **man** 3. **~ bat·tle** *s* Straßenschlacht *f*. **~ lamp, ~ light** *s* Straßenlaterne *f*. **~ map** *s* Stadtplan *m*. **~ par·ty** *s* Straßenfest *n*. **~ val·ue** *s* (Straßen)Verkaufswert *m* (*von Drogen*). **~ vend·er, ~ vend·or** *s* Straßenhändler(in). **'~·walk·er** *s* Straßen-, Strichmädchen *n*.

strength [streŋθ] *s* **1.** Stärke *f* (*a. fig.*), Kraft *f*, Kräfte *pl*: **~ of character** Charakterfestigkeit *f*, -stärke; **~ of will** Willenskraft, -stärke; **on the ~ of** auf *j*-s Rat *etc* hin; **he hasn't got enough ~** er ist nicht kräftig genug; **go from ~ to ~** von Erfolg zu Erfolg eilen. **2.** Macht *f*. **3.** (An)Zahl *f*: **in ~** in großer Zahl, zahlreich; **at full ~** vollzählig; **below** (*od.* **under**) **~** nicht vollzählig; unterbesetzt; **be on the ~** F zur Belegschaft gehören. **'strength·en I** *v/t* **1.** verstärken. **2.** *fig.* stärken: **~ s.o.'s resolve** j-n in s-m Vorsatz bestärken. **II** *v/i* **3.** stärker werden, sich verstärken (*Wind etc*).

stren·u·ous ['strenjʊəs] *adj* □ **1.** anstrengend. **2.** unermüdlich.

stress [stres] **I** *s* **1.** *fig.* Streß *m*: **~ of examinations** Prüfungsstreß; **be under ~** unter Streß stehen, im Streß sein; **~ disease** Streß-, Managerkrankheit *f*. **2.** *ling.* Betonung *f*: **lay ~ on** *fig.* → 5; **~ mark** Akzent *m*, Betonungszeichen *n*. **3.** *phys.*, ⊙ Beanspruchung *f*, Belastung *f*; (mechanische) Spannung *f*. **II** *v/t* **4.** **be ~ed** gestreßt sein. **5.** *ling.* betonen, *fig. a.* Wert legen auf (*acc*). **'stress·ful** ['ˌfʊl] *adj* stressig, aufreibend.

stretch [stretʃ] **I** *v/t* **1.** **~ out** Arm *etc* ausstrecken; → **leg** 1. **2.** *Seil etc* spannen: **be fully ~ed** *fig.* richtig gefordert werden. **3.** *Schuhe etc* (aus)weiten. **4.** *fig.* es nicht so genau nehmen mit: **~ a point** ein Auge zudrücken. **II** *v/i* **5.** sich dehnen, *a.* länger *od.* weiter werden. **6.** sich dehnen *od.* strecken: **~ out** sich ausstrecken. **7.** sich (*räumlich*) erstrecken (**to** bis zu); sich hinziehen (*räumlich*: **to** bis zu; *zeitlich*: **into** bis in *acc*); *fig.* reichen (**to** für) (*Vorräte etc*). **III** *s* **8.** **have a ~** → 6; **be at full ~** *fig.* sich sehr viel Mühe geben müssen; **not by any ~ of the imagination** nie u. nimmer. **9.** Dehnbarkeit *f*, Elastizität *f*. **10.**

Strecke f (e-r Straße); (Sport) (Gegen-, Ziel)Gerade f. **11.** Zeit(raum m, -spanne f) f: **at a ~** hintereinander; **do a three-year ~** F drei Jahre absitzen. **IV** adj **12.** → **stretchy.** '**stretch·er** s Trage f. '**stretch·y** adj dehnbar, elastisch.

stri·at·ed ['straɪeɪtɪd] adj gestreift.

strick·en ['strɪkən] adj **1.** leidgeprüft (Person), schwerbetroffen (Gegend etc). **2. ~ with** befallen od. ergriffen von: → **panic-stricken.**

strict [strɪkt] adj □ streng (Person, Disziplin, Gesetze etc), (Anweisungen etc a.) strikt: **be ~ with** streng sein mit od. zu od. gegen; **in ~ confidence** streng vertraulich; **~ly** (speaking) streng-, genaugenommen.

strid·den ['strɪdn] pp von **stride.**

stride [straɪd] **I** v/i (irr) **1.** schreiten, mit großen Schritten gehen. **II** s **2.** (großer) Schritt: **get into one's ~** fig. (richtig) in Fahrt od. Schwung kommen; **take s.th. in one's ~** fig. et. mühelos verkraften. **3.** fig. Fortschritt m: **make great ~s** große Fortschritte machen.

stri·dent ['straɪdnt] adj □ schrill (Stimme etc).

strife [straɪf] s Streit m.

strike [straɪk] **I** s **1. ☛** Streik m: **be (out) on ~** streiken, im Streik stehen; **go (out) on ~** streiken, in den Streik treten. **2.** (Öl- etc)Fund m. **3. ✕** Angriff m. **II** v/i (irr) **4. ~ at** s.o. → **strike out** 2. **5.** einschlagen (Blitz). **6.** schlagen (Uhr): **two o'clock has just struck** es hat gerade zwei Uhr geschlagen. **7. ☛** streiken (for für). **8. ~ on** fig. kommen auf e-n Plan etc. **III** v/t (irr) **9.** schlagen: **~ s.o. a blow** j-m e-n Schlag versetzen; → **dumb** 1. **10.** treffen; einschlagen in (acc) (Blitz): → **lightning** I. **11.** Streichholz anzünden. **12. ♪** auflaufen auf (acc). **13.** streichen (from, off aus e-m Verzeichnis etc, von e-r Liste etc). **14.** fig. stoßen auf (Öl, e-e Straße, Schwierigkeiten etc): → **oil** 2. **15.** → **balance** 1, **bargain** 1. **16. be struck by** beeindruckt sein von; **how does the house ~ you?** wie findest du das Haus?; **it struck me as rather strange that** es kam mir ziemlich seltsam vor, daß. **17.** j-m einfallen, in den Sinn kommen. **18.** Münze etc prägen. **19.** Saite etc an-

schlagen: → **chord¹, note** 9. **20.** Lager, Zelt abbrechen.

Verbindungen mit Adverbien:

strike| back v/i zurückschlagen (a. fig.). **~ down** v/t **1.** niederschlagen. **2.** fig. niederwerfen (Krankheit); dahinraffen. **~ off** v/t **1.** (aus)streichen. **2.** Br. Solicitor von der Anwaltsliste streichen, e-m Arzt die Approbation entziehen. **~ out I** v/t **1.** (aus)streichen. **II** v/i **2. ~ at** s.o. auf j-n einschlagen. **3. ~ on one's own** fig. s-e eigenen Wege gehen, **☛** sich selbständig machen. **III** v/t durchstreichen. **~ up I** v/t **1.** Lied etc anstimmen. **2.** Bekanntschaft, Freundschaft schließen, Gespräch anknüpfen (**with** mit). **II** v/i **3. ♪** einsetzen.

strike| bal·lot s **☛** Urabstimmung f. '**~bound** adj durch Streik lahmgelegt. '**~break·er** s **☛** Streikbrecher(in). **~ call** s **☛** Streikaufruf m. **~ pay** s **☛** Streikgeld(er pl) n.

'**strik·er** s **1. ☛** Streikende m, f. **2.** Fußball: Stürmer(in). '**strik·ing** adj □ **1.** auffallend, (Ähnlichkeit, Vorschlag etc) verblüffend. **2. be within ~ distance of** fig. kurz vor e-m Erfolg etc stehen.

string [strɪŋ] **I** s **1.** Schnur f, Bindfaden m; (Schürzen-, Schuh- etc)Band n; (Puppenspiel) Faden m, Draht m: **with no ~s attached** fig. ohne Bedingungen; **have s.o. on a ~** fig. j-n am Gängelband führen od. haben; **pull the ~s** fig. die Fäden ziehen; **pull a few ~s** fig. ein paar Beziehungen spielen lassen. **2.** (Perlen- etc)Schnur f. **3.** a) Saite f (e-r Gitarre, e-s Tennisschlägers etc; (Bogen)Sehne f: **have two ~s** (od. **a second ~, another ~**) **to one's bow** fig. zwei od. mehrere Eisen im Feuer haben, b) **the ~s pl ♪** die Streichinstrumente pl; die Streicher pl. **4.** fig. Reihe f, Serie f. **II** adj **5. ♪** Streich... **III** v/t **6.** Perlen etc aufreihen. **7.** Gitarre etc besaiten, Tennisschläger etc bespannen.

Verbindungen mit Adverbien:

string| a·long F I v/t j-n hinhalten. **II** v/i sich anschließen (**with** mit). **~ up** v/t **1.** aufhängen. **2.** F j-n aufknüpfen.

string bean s **♣** bsd. Am. grüne Bohne.

stringed in·stru·ment [strɪŋd] s Saiten-, Streichinstrument n.

strin·gent ['strɪndʒənt] adj □ streng (Kontrolle, Regeln etc).

string·y ['strɪŋɪ] *adj* **1.** fas(e)rig (*Bohnen, Fleisch etc*). **2.** sehnig (*Arm etc*).

strip [strɪp] **I** *v/i* **1.** *a.* **~ off** sich ausziehen (**to** bis auf *acc*), (*beim Arzt*) sich freimachen; strippen: **~ to the waist** den Oberkörper freimachen. **II** *v/t* **2.** Farbe *etc* abkratzen, Tapete *etc* abreißen (**from, off** von). **3.** ~ *s.o.* of *s.th.* j-m *et.* rauben *od.* wegnehmen: **he was ~ped of his title** ihm wurde sein Titel aberkannt. **4.** a) *a.* **~ down** *Motor etc* auseinandernehmen, zerlegen, b) *Wagen etc* ausschlachten. **III** *s* **5.** (*Land-, Papier-*)Streifen *m*. Strip *m*: **do a ~** strippen. **7.** *Fußball: Br.* Dreß *m*. ~ **car-toons** *s pl Br.* Comics *pl*.

stripe [straɪp] **1.** Streifen *m*. **2.** ✕ (Ärmel)Streifen *m*, Winkel *m*. **striped** *adj* gestreift: ~ *pattern* Streifenmuster *n*.

strip light·ing *s* Neonbeleuchtung *f*, -licht *n*.

'strip-tease *s* Striptease *m*, *n*: **do a ~** e-n Striptease vorführen.

strip·y ['straɪpɪ] → **striped**.

strive [straɪv] *v/i (irr)* **1.** sich bemühen (**to** *do* zu tun). **2.** streben (**for, after** nach). **3.** (an)kämpfen (**against** gegen).

striv·en ['strɪvn] *pp von* **strive**.

strode [strəʊd] *pret von* **stride**.

stroke [strəʊk] **I** *v/t* **1.** streicheln: ~ *s.o.'s hair* ihm übers Haar streichen. **II** *s* **2.** Schlag *m* (*a. Tennis, e-r Uhr etc*), Hieb *m*: *a ~ of lightning* ein Blitz *m*; *a ~ of genius fig.* ein glänzender Einfall; *a ~ of luck fig.* ein glücklicher Zufall; *at a ~ fig.* auf 'einen Schlag; *on the ~ of ten* Punkt *od.* Schlag zehn (Uhr). **3.** *give s.o. a ~* j-n streicheln. **4.** ✕ Schlag(anfall) *m*. **5.** (*Pinsel*)Strich *m*: *with a ~ of the pen* mit e-m Federstrich (*a. fig.*); *he hasn't done a ~ (of work) yet fig.* er hat noch keinen Strich getan. **6.** *Schwimmen:* Zug *m*; Stil(art *f*) *m*: *backstroke, breaststroke*. **7.** ⊙ (*Kolben*)Hub *m*; Takt *m*: *four-~ engine* Viertaktmotor *m*. **8.** *Rudern:* Schlagmann *m*, -frau *f*.

stroll [strəʊl] **I** *v/i* bummeln, spazieren. **II** *s* Bummel *m*, Spaziergang *m*: *go for a ~* e-n Bummel *od.* Spaziergang machen. **'stroll·er** *s* **1.** Bummler(in), Spaziergänger(in). **2.** *bsd. Am.* Sportwagen *m* (*für Kinder*).

strong [strɒŋ] **I** *adj* □ (→ *a.* **strongly**) **1.** stark, kräftig (*Person, Arme etc*); *fig.* mächtig (*Land etc*), stark (*Persönlichkeit etc*): → **sex** 1. **2.** stabil (*Möbel etc*), (*Schuhe etc a.*) fest; robust (*Person, Gesundheit*), kräftig, (*Herz, Nerven*) stark; *fig.* unerschütterlich (*Beweise*), stark (*Verdacht*): → **point** 14. **3.** stark (*Strömung*), (*Wind etc a.*) kräftig. **4.** kräftig (*Geruch, Geschmack*), (*a. Eindruck, Ähnlichkeit etc*) stark. **5.** überzeugt (*Anhänger etc*). **6.** stark (*Getränk, Medikament etc*). **7.** ~ *language* Kraftausdrücke *pl*. **8.** groß, hoch (*Chance etc*), aussichtsreich (*Kandidat etc*). **9.** *a nine-~ team* ein neun Mann starkes Team; *an 8,000-~ community* e-e 8000-Seelen-Gemeinde; *our club is 500 ~* unser Club hat 500 Mitglieder. **II** *adv* **10.** *be still going ~* noch gut in Schuß sein (*alte Person, altes Gerät etc*). **'~arm** *adj*: ~ *methods* (*od. tactics*) *pl* Gewaltmethoden *pl*. **'~box** *s* (Geld-, Stahl)Kassette *f*. **'~hold** *s* **1.** ✕ Festung *f*; Stützpunkt *m*. **2.** *fig.* Hochburg *f*.

strong·ly ['strɒŋlɪ] *adv*: *I ~ advised him against it* ich riet ihm dringend davon ab.

,strong-'mind·ed *adj* □ willensstark. ~ *room* *s* Tresor(raum) *m*, Stahlkammer *f*.

strove [strəʊv] *pret von* **strive**.

struck [strʌk] *pret u. pp von* **strike**.

struc·tur·al ['strʌktʃərəl] *adj* □ **1.** strukturell (bedingt), Struktur... **2.** ⊙ Bau..., Konstruktions... **'struc·ture I** *s* **1.** Struktur *f*; (Auf)Bau *m*, Gliederung *f*. **2.** Bau *m*, Konstruktion *f*. **II** *v/t* **3.** strukturieren; *Aufsatz etc* aufbauen, strukturieren.

strug·gle ['strʌgl] **I** *v/i* **1.** kämpfen (**with** mit; **for** um), *fig. a.* sich abmühen (**with** mit; **to do** zu tun): ~ *for words* um Worte ringen. **2.** zappeln; um sich schlagen *od.* treten. **3.** sich quälen: ~ *to one's feet* mühsam aufstehen, sich aufrappeln. **II** *s* **4.** Kampf *m* (*a. fig.*), Handgemenge *n*: ~ *for survival* Überlebenskampf, Kampf ums Überleben.

strum [strʌm] **I** *v/t* a) klimpern auf e-r Gitarre etc, b) Melodie klimpern. **II** *v/i*: ~ *on* → Ia.

strung [strʌŋ] *pret u. pp von* **string**.

strut[1] [strʌt] *v/i* stolzieren.

strut² [~] ⊕ **I** s Strebe f; Stütze f. **II** v/t verstreben; (ab)stützen.

strych·nine ['strɪkniːn] s ⚗, pharm. Strychnin n.

stub [stʌb] **I** s **1.** (Bleistift-, Zigaretten- etc)Stummel m. **2.** Kontrollabschnitt m (e-r Eintrittskarte etc). **II** v/t **3.** sich die Zehe anstoßen (**against, on** an dat). **4.** ~ **out** Zigarette ausdrücken.

stub·ble ['stʌbl] s Stoppeln pl. '**stub·bly** adj stoppe(e)lig, Stoppel...

stub·born ['stʌbən] adj □ **1.** eigensinnig, stur. **2.** hartnäckig (Fleck, Widerstand etc).

stub·by ['stʌbɪ] adj: ~ **fingers** pl Wurstfinger pl.

stuc·co ['stʌkəʊ] s △ Stuck m. '**stuc·coed** adj Stuck...

stuck [stʌk] pret u. pp von **stick²**. **II** adj **1. be** ~ klemmen; fig. F hängen, nicht weiterkommen: **be** ~ **with** F j-n, et. am Hals haben. **2. be** ~ **on** F verknallt sein in (acc). **3.** Br. F **get** ~ **in** reinhauen (beim Essen); **get** ~ **into** sich stürzen auf (ein Essen) od. in (e-e Arbeit). ',~-'**up** adj F hochnäsig.

stud¹ [stʌd] **I** s **1.** Beschlag- od. Ziernagel m. **2.** (Kragen-, Manschetten)Knopf m. **3.** Stollen m (e-s Fußballschuhs etc). **II** v/t **4. be** ~**ded with** besetzt sein mit; übersät sein mit.

stud² [~] s Gestüt n (Pferde).

stu·dent ['stjuːdnt] s Student(in), ped. bsd. Am. u. allg. Schüler(in).

stud farm s Gestüt n.

stud·ied ['stʌdɪd] adj □ wohlüberlegt, b.s. wohlberechnet (Antwort etc).

stu·di·o ['stjuːdɪəʊ] pl **-os** s **1.** allg. Studio n, (e-s Künstlers etc a.) Atelier n. **2.** Studio n, Einzimmerappartement n. ~ **a·part·ment** bsd. Am. → **studio** 2. ~ **couch** s Schlafcouch f. ~ **flat** bsd. Br. → **studio** 2.

stu·di·ous ['stjuːdjəs] adj □ fleißig.

stud·y ['stʌdɪ] **I** s **1.** a. pl Studium n: **be in a brown** ~ in Gedanken versunken od. geistesabwesend sein. **2.** Studie f, Untersuchung f (**of** über acc): **make a** ~ **of** et. untersuchen. **3.** bsd. paint. Studie f (**of** zu). **4.** ♪ Etüde f. **5.** Arbeitszimmer n. **II** v/t **6.** Medizin etc, weitS. Landkarte, j-s Gesicht etc studieren. **III** v/i **7.** studieren (**under** s.o. bei j-m), weitS. lernen (**for** für e-e Prüfung):

~ **to be a doctor** Medizin studieren.

stuff [stʌf] **I** s **1.** F allg. Zeug n: **do** ~ **good** ~ et. Gutes sein; **that's the** ~! so ist's richtig!; genau!; **do one's** ~ zeigen, was man kann; **know one's** ~ sich gut auskennen. **II** v/t **2.** (**with** mit) Hohlraum, Tier ausstopfen; Kissen etc stopfen, füllen; sich die Taschen vollstopfen: ~**ed full of** gestopft voll von; ~ **o.s.** F sich vollstopfen. **3.** et. stopfen (**into** in acc). **4.** gastr. Ente etc füllen: **get** ~**ed!** Br. sl. du kannst mich mal! **5.** ~ **up** Loch etc ver-, zustopfen (**with** mit): **my nose is** ~**ed up** m-e Nase ist verstopft od. zu.

stuffed adj: ~ **shirt** F Fatzke m. '**stuff·ing** s Füllung f (a. gastr.): **knock the** ~ **out of** j-n fertigmachen. '**stuff·y** adj □ **1.** stickig. **2.** fig. prüde; spießig.

stum·ble ['stʌmbl] **I** v/i **1.** stolpern (**on, over, at, on** über acc): ~ **across** (od. **on**) fig. stoßen auf (acc); ~ **through** Rede etc herunterstottern. '**stum·bling** adj: ~ **block** fig. Hindernis n (**to** für).

stump [stʌmp] **I** s **1.** (Baum-, Bein-, Kerzen-) Stummel m, (Bleistift-, Kerzen-, Zahn-, Zigarren-)Stummel m: **stir one's** ~**s** F Tempo machen. **II** v/t **2.** I'**m** ~**ed, you've got me** ~**ed there** F da bin ich überfragt. **3.** ~ **up** F Geld herausrücken. **III** v/i **4.** sta(m)pfen. '**stump·y** adj □ kurz u. dick (Arme etc).

stun [stʌn] v/t betäuben; fig. sprachlos machen: **he was** ~**ned by the news** die Nachricht hat ihm die Sprache verschlagen.

stung [stʌŋ] pret u. pp von **sting**.

stunk [stʌŋk] pret u. pp von **stink**.

stun·ner ['stʌnə] s: **she's a real** ~ F sie ist e-e klasse Frau. '**stun·ning** adj □ **1.** phantastisch. **2.** unglaublich (Nachricht).

stunt¹ [stʌnt] s **1.** (gefährliches) Kunststück; (Film) Stunt m (gefährliche Szene, in der ein Stuntman die Rolle des Darstellers übernimmt): **do a** ~ ein Kunststück vorführen od. zeigen; e-n Stunt ausführen. **2.** (Werbe)Gag m.

stunt² [~] v/t Wachstum hemmen; das Wachstum (gen) hemmen): ~**ed** verkümmert.

stunt| fly·ing s Kunstflug m. ~ **man** s (irr **man**) Film: Stuntman m, Double n. ~ **wom·an** s (irr **woman**) Film: Stuntwoman n, Double n.

stu·pen·dous [stju:'pendəs] *adj* □ phantastisch.

stu·pid ['stju:pɪd] *adj* □ **1.** dumm. **2.** *fig.* F blöd. **stu'pid·i·ty** *s* Dummheit *f* (*a. Handlung* etc).

stu·por ['stju:pə] *s*: **in a drunken ~** im Vollrausch.

stur·dy ['stɜ:dɪ] *adj* □ **1.** stämmig (*Beine* etc). **2.** *fig.* hartnäckig (*Widerstand* etc).

stur·geon ['stɜ:dʒən] *s ichth.* Stör *m.*

stut·ter ['stʌtə] **I** *v/i* ⚙ stottern (*a. Motor*). **II** *v/t* → **stammer** II. **III** *s* → **stammer** III. '**stut·ter·er** → **stammerer.**

sty¹ [staɪ] → **pigsty.**

sty² [~] *s* ⚙ Gerstenkorn *n.*

style [staɪl] **I** *s* **1.** *allg.* Stil *m*: **~ of leadership** Führungsstil; **in ~** in großem Stil; **that's not my ~** F das ist nicht m-e Art. **2.** Ausführung *f*, Modell *n.* **II** *v/t* **3.** entwerfen; gestalten.

sty·li ['staɪlaɪ] *pl von* **stylus.**

styl·ish ['staɪlɪʃ] *adj* □ **1.** stilvoll. **2.** modisch, elegant.

styl·ist ['staɪlɪst] *s* **1.** Stilist(in). **2.** a) Modeschöpfer(in), b) → **hair stylist.** **sty'lis·tic** *adj* (**~ally**) stilistisch, Stil...

styl·ize ['staɪlaɪz] *v/t* stilisieren.

sty·lus ['staɪləs] *pl* **-li** ['~laɪ], **-lus·es** *s* Nadel *f* (*e-s Plattenspielers*).

sty·mie ['staɪmɪ] *v/t* F Gegner matt setzen; *Plan* etc vereiteln.

styp·tic ['stɪptɪk] ⚕ **I** *adj* blutstillend. **II** *s* blutstillendes Mittel.

suave [swɑːv] *adj* □ verbindlich, *contp.* aalglatt.

sub [sʌb] F **I** *s* **1.** → **subeditor, submarine** I, **subscription** 1. **2.** *Sport:* Auswechselspieler(in). **3.** *Br.* Vorschuß *m.* **II** *v/i* **4.** → **substitute** IV. **III** *v/t* **5.** → **subedit. 6.** *Br. j-m* e-n Vorschuß geben. '**sub·com,mit·tee** *s* Unterausschuß *m.*

,**sub'con·scious I** *adj* unterbewußt: **~ly** im Unterbewußtsein; F unbewußt. **II** *s* Unterbewußtsein *n*: **in one's ~** im Unterbewußtsein.

,**sub'con·ti·nent** *s* Subkontinent *m.* '**sub,cul·ture** *s sociol.* Subkultur *f.*

sub·cu·ta·ne·ous [,sʌbkju:'teɪnjəs] *adj* □ subkutan, unter der od. die Haut.

,**sub·di'vide** *v/t* unterteilen. '**sub·di,vi·sion** *s* **1.** Unterteilung *f.* **2.** Unterabteilung *f.*

sub·due [səb'dju:] *v/t* Land etc unterwerfen; *Ärger* etc unterdrücken. **sub'dued** *adj* **1.** gedämpft (*Stimme*), (*Farben, Licht a.*) dezent. **2.** (merkwürdig) ruhig *od.* still (*Person*).

,**sub'ed·it** *v/t* redigieren. ,**sub'ed·i·tor** *s* Redakteur(in).

'**sub,head·ing** *s* Untertitel *m.*

,**sub'hu·man** *adj* unmenschlich.

sub·ject ['sʌbdʒɪkt] **I** *s* **1.** Thema *n*: **on the ~ of** über (*acc*); **be the ~ of much criticism** von verschiedenen Seiten kritisiert werden; **change the ~** das Thema wechseln, von et. anderem reden. **2.** *ped., univ.* Fach *n.* **3.** *ling.* Subjekt *n*, Satzgegenstand *m.* **4.** **be the ~ of, be a ~ for** Anlaß *od.* Grund geben zu. **5.** Untertan(in); Staatsangehörige *m, f*, -bürger(in). **6.** Versuchsperson *f*, -tier *n.* **II** *adj* **7.** **~ to** anfällig für: **be ~ to** a. neigen zu. **8.** **be ~ to** unterliegen (*dat*); abhängen von: **be ~ to the approval of** (erst noch) genehmigt werden müssen von; **prices ~ to change** Preisänderungen vorbehalten. **III** *v/t* [səb'dʒekt] **9.** Land etc unterwerfen. **10.** **~ to** e-m Test etc unterziehen; *der Kritik* etc aussetzen. **sub·jec·tion** [səb'dʒekʃn] *s* **1.** Unterwerfung *f.* **2.** Abhängigkeit *f* (**to** von). **sub'jec·tive** *adj* □ subjektiv.

sub·ject mat·ter *s* Stoff *m*; Inhalt *m.*

sub·ju·gate ['sʌbdʒʊgeɪt] *v/t* unterjochen, -werfen.

sub·junc·tive (mood) [səb'dʒʌŋktɪv] *s ling.* Konjunktiv *m.*

,**sub'lease** *v/t* unter-, weitervermieten, unter-, weiterverpachten (**to** an *dat*).

,**sub'let** *v/t* (*irr let*) unter-, weitervermieten (**to** an *dat*).

sub·li·mate ⚗ **I** *v/t* ['sʌblɪmeɪt] sublimieren. **II** *s* ['~mət] Sublimat *n.*

sub·lime [sə'blaɪm] *adj* □ **1.** großartig. **2.** *iro.* großzügig (*Mißachtung*), allumfassend (*Unkenntnis*).

sub·lim·i·nal [,sʌb'lɪmɪnl] *adj* □ *psych.* unterschwellig.

,**sub·ma'chine gun** *s* Maschinenpistole *f.*

,**sub·ma'rine I** *s* Unterseeboot *n*, U-Boot *n.* **II** *adj* untermeerisch, -seeisch.

sub·merge [səb'mɜ:dʒ] **I** *v/t* (ein)tauchen (**in** in *acc*): **be ~d in work** bis über die Ohren in Arbeit stecken. **II** *v/i* tauchen (*U-Boot*).

sub·mis·sion [səb'mɪʃn] *s* **1.** Einreichung *f.* **2.** *Boxen etc:* Aufgabe *f.*

sub·mis·sive [səb'mɪsɪv] *adj* □ unterwürfig.

sub·mit [səb'mɪt] **I** *v/t* **1.** *Gesuch etc* einreichen (**to** *dat od.* bei). **2.** ~ **o.s.** sich fügen (**to** *dat od.* in *acc*). **II** *v/i* **3.** *Boxen etc:* aufgeben.

sub·nor·mal *adj* □ **1.** unterdurchschnittlich. **2.** unterdurchschnittlich intelligent.

sub·or·di·nate [sə'bɔːdnət] **I** *adj* □ untergeordnet (**to** *dat*): **be** ~ **to** a. zurückstehen hinter (*dat*); ~ **clause** *ling.* Nebensatz *m.* **II** *s* Untergebene *m, f.* **III** *v/t* [∟dɪneɪt] (*to*) unterordnen (*dat*), zurückstellen (hinter *acc*).

'sub·plot *s* Nebenhandlung *f.*

sub·poe·na [səb'piːnə] ⚖ **I** *s* Vorladung *f.* **II** *v/t* Zeugen vorladen.

sub·scribe [səb'skraɪb] **I** *v/i* **1.** ~ **to** *Zeitschrift etc* abonnieren; abonniert haben. **2.** ~ **to** *karitative Organisation etc* regelmäßig unterstützen. **3.** ~ **to** *Ansicht etc* billigen. **II** *v/t* **4.** *Geld* geben, spenden (**to** für). **sub'scrib·er** *s* Abonnent(in); (*Fernsprech*)Teilnehmer (-in).

sub·scrip·tion [səb'skrɪpʃn] *s* **1.** (Mitglieds)Beitrag *m.* **2.** Abonnement *n:* **take out a ~ to** *Zeitschrift etc* abonnieren.

'sub·sec·tion *s* Unterabteilung *f.*

sub·se·quent ['sʌbsɪkwənt] *adj* □ später.

sub·ser·vi·ent [səb'sɜːvjənt] *adj* □ **1.** unterwürfig. **2.** untergeordnet (**to** *dat*): **be** ~ **to** a. zurückstehen hinter (*dat*).

sub·side [səb'saɪd] *v/i* **1.** sich senken (*Gebäude, Straße etc*); ~ **into a chair** in e-n Sessel sinken. **2.** zurückgehen (*Überschwemmung, Nachfrage etc*), sich legen (*Sturm, Zorn etc*).

sub·sid·i·ar·y [səb'sɪdjərɪ] **I** *adj* Neben...: ~ **company** → **II**; ~ **question** Zusatzfrage *f;* ~ **subject** *ped., univ.* Nebenfach *n.* **II** *s* ✝ Tochtergesellschaft *f.*

sub·si·dize ['sʌbsɪdaɪz] *v/t* subventionieren.

sub·si·dy ['∟dɪ] *s* Subvention *f.*

sub·sist [səb'sɪst] *v/i* existieren, leben (**on** von). **sub'sist·ence** *s* Existenz *f:* **live at ~ level** am Existenzminimum leben.

sub'son·ic *adj* ✓, *phys.* Unterschall...:

at ~ speed mit Unterschallgeschwindigkeit.

sub·stance ['sʌbstəns] *s* **1.** Substanz *f,* Stoff *m,* Masse *f.* **2.** *fig.* Substanz *f:* **in ~** im wesentlichen.

sub'stand·ard *adj* minderwertig; *ling.* inkorrekt.

sub·stan·tial [səb'stænʃl] *adj* □ **1.** solid (*Schrank etc*). **2.** *fig.* beträchtlich (*Gehalt etc*), (*Änderungen etc a.*) wesentlich: **~ly** a. im wesentlichen. **3.** *fig.* kräftig (*Mahlzeit*).

sub·stan·ti·ate [səb'stænʃɪeɪt] *v/t* beweisen, erhärten.

sub·stan·tive ['sʌbstəntɪv] *s ling.* Substantiv *n,* Hauptwort *n.*

sub·sti·tute ['sʌbstɪtjuːt] **I** *s* Ersatz *m;* Ersatz(mann) *m,* Vertretung *f,* (*Sport*) Auswechselspieler(in). **II** *adj* Ersatz... **III** *v/t:* ~ **A for B** B durch A ersetzen, B gegen A austauschen *od.* auswechseln. **IV** *v/i:* ~ **for** einspringen für, *j-n* vertreten.

'sub·struc·ture *s* △ Fundament *n,* Unterbau *m* (*beide a. fig.*).

sub'ten·ant *s* Untermieter(in).

sub·ter·fuge ['sʌbtəfjuːdʒ] *s* List *f.*

sub·ter·ra·ne·an [ˌsʌbtə'reɪnjən] *adj* □ unterirdisch.

'sub·ti·tle *s* Untertitel *m.*

sub·tle ['sʌtl] *adj* □ **1.** fein (*Unterschied etc*), (*Aroma etc a.*) zart. **2.** raffiniert (*Plan etc*). **3.** scharf (*Verstand*), scharfsinnig (*Person*).

'sub·to·tal *s* Zwischen-, Teilsumme *f.*

sub·tract [səb'trækt] *v/t* ℞ abziehen, subtrahieren (**from** von). **sub'trac·tion** *s* Abziehen *n,* Subtraktion *f.*

sub'trop·i·cal *adj* subtropisch.

sub·urb ['sʌbɜːb] *s* Vorort *m:* **live in the ~s** am Stadtrand wohnen. **sub·ur·ban** [sə'bɜːbən] *adj* Vorort..., vorstädtisch, Vorstadt... **sub'ur·ban·ite** *s* Vorstädter(in). **sub'ur·bi·a** [∟bɪə] *s* **1.** Vorstadt *f:* **live in ~** am Stadtrand wohnen. **2.** Vorstadtleben *n.*

sub·ver·sion [səb'vɜːʃn] *s pol.* Subversion *f.* **sub'ver·sive** [∟sɪv] **I** *adj* □ subversiv, umstürzlerisch. **II** *s* Umstürzler(in).

sub·vert [sʌb'vɜːt] *v/t Regierung* zu stürzen versuchen.

'sub·way *s* **1.** Unterführung *f.* **2.** *Am.* U-Bahn *f.*

suc·ceed [sək'si:d] **I** v/i **1.** Erfolg haben, erfolgreich sein (*Person*), (*Plan etc* a.) gelingen: *he ~ed in doing it* es gelang ihm, es zu tun. **2.** ~ *to* in e-m Amt nachfolgen: ~ *to the throne* dem Thron folgen. **II** v/t **3.** j-m nachfolgen, *j-m od.* auf *j-n* folgen: ~ *s.o. as* j-s Nachfolger werden als.

suc·cess [sək'ses] s Erfolg m: *without ~* ohne Erfolg, erfolglos. **suc'cess·ful** [~fʊl] adj □ erfolgreich: *be ~ → suc·ceed* 1; *he was ~ in doing it* es gelang ihm, es zu tun.

suc·ces·sion [sək'seʃn] s **1.** Folge f: *three times in ~* dreimal nach- *od.* hintereinander; *in quick ~* in rascher Folge. **2.** Nachfolge f: ~ *to the throne* Thronfolge. **suc'ces·sive** [~sɪv] adj □ aufeinanderfolgend: *on three ~ days* a. drei Tage nach- *od.* hintereinander. **suc'ces·sor** [~sə] s Nachfolger(in) (*to* in e-m Amt): ~ *in office* Amtsnachfolger(in); ~ *to the throne* Thronfolger(in).

suc·cinct [sək'sɪŋkt] adj □ kurz (u. bündig), knapp.

suc·cu·lent ['sʌkjʊlənt] adj □ saftig (*Steak etc*).

suc·cumb [sə'kʌm] v/i: ~ *to* e-r Krankheit, der Versuchung *etc* erliegen.

such [sʌtʃ] **I** adj solch, derartig: ~ *a man* ein solcher *od.* ein Mann; *no ~ thing* nichts dergleichen. **II** adv so, derart: ~ *a nice day* so ein schöner Tag; ~ *a long time* e-e so lange Zeit; ~ *is life* so ist das Leben. **III** pron. solch: ~ *as* wie (zum Beispiel); *man as ~* der Mensch als solcher. **'~·like I** adj solche. **II** pron dergleichen.

suck [sʌk] **I** v/t **1.** saugen. **2.** lutschen (an *dat*). **3.** ~ *under* hinunterziehen (*Strudel etc*). **II** v/i **4.** saugen (*at* an *dat*). **5.** ~ *away at et.* lutschen. **6.** ~ *up to s.o.* Br. F sich bei j-m lieb Kind machen wollen. **III** s **7.** *take a ~ at* saugen *od.* ziehen an (*dat*); lutschen an (*dat*). **'suck·er** s **1.** zo. Saugnapf m, -organ n. **2.** ⚙ Saugfuß m. **3.** Am. Lutscher m. **4.** F Gimpel m, leichtgläubiger Kerl: *be a ~ for* immer wieder reinfallen auf (*acc*); verrückt sein nach. **'suck·ing** adj: ~ *pig* Spanferkel n.

suck·le ['sʌkl] v/t säugen (a. zo.), stillen.

suc·tion ['sʌkʃn] s Saugwirkung f. ~ **pump** s ⚙ Saugpumpe f.

sud·den ['sʌdn] **I** adj □ plötzlich: *be very ~* sehr plötzlich kommen. **II** s: *all of a ~* ganz plötzlich, auf einmal.

suds [sʌdz] s pl Seifenschaum m.

sue [su:] ⚖ **I** v/t *j-n* verklagen (*for acc, wegen*). **II** v/i klagen (*for* auf *acc*).

suede, suède [sweɪd] s Wildleder n; Velour(s)leder n.

su·et ['sʊɪt] s Nierenfett n, Talg m.

suf·fer ['sʌfə] **I** v/i **1.** leiden (*from* an *dat*; *weitS.* unter *dat*). **2.** darunter leiden. **II** v/t **3.** Niederlage, Rückschlag, Verlust *etc* erleiden; Folgen tragen. **'suf·fer·er** s: *a cancer ~* ein Krebskranker; *a headache ~* j-d, der an Kopfschmerzen leidet. **'suf·fer·ing** s Leiden n; Leid n.

suf·fice [sə'faɪs] **I** v/i genügen, (aus)reichen (*for* für). **II** v/t j-m genügen, reichen.

suf·fi·cient [sə'fɪʃnt] adj □ genügend, genug, ausreichend: *be ~ → suffice* **I**.

suf·fix ['sʌfɪks] s ling. Suffix n, Nachsilbe f.

suf·fo·cate ['sʌfəkeɪt] v/i u. v/t ersticken.

suf·frage ['sʌfrɪdʒ] s pol. Wahl-, Stimmrecht n.

suf·fuse [sə'fju:z] v/t: *be ~d with* durchdrungen sein von.

sug·ar ['ʃʊɡə] **I** s **1.** Zucker m. **2.** bsd. Am. F Schatz (*Anrede*). **II** v/t **3.** zuckern: → *pill* 1. ~ **beet** s ♀ Zuckerrübe f. ~ **bowl** s Zuckerdose f. ~ **cane** s ♀ Zuckerrohr n. ~ **dad·dy** s F alter Knakker, der ein junges Mädchen aushält.

sug·ar·y ['ʃʊɡərɪ] adj **1.** zuck(e)rig, Zucker... **2.** fig. zuckersüß.

sug·gest [sə'dʒest] v/t **1.** j-n vorschlagen (*as* als), *et.* a. anregen: *I ~ going (od. that we go) home* ich schlage vor heimzugehen. **2.** hindeuten auf, -weisen auf (*acc*), schließen lassen auf (*acc*): *that darauf hindeuten od.* -weisen, daß; *darauf schließen lassen, daß.* **3.** andeuten: *I am not ~ing that* ich will damit nicht sagen, daß. **sug'gest·i·ble** adj beeinflußbar. **sug'ges·tion** s **1.** Vorschlag m, Anregung f: *at s.o.'s ~* auf j-s Vorschlag hin; *make (od. offer) a ~* e-n Vorschlag machen. **2.** Anflug m, Spur f. **3.** Andeutung f. **4.** psych. Suggestion f. **sug'ges·tive** adj □ **1.** *be ~ of →* *suggest* 2. **2.** zweideutig (*Bemer-*

kung etc), vielsagend (*Blick etc*).

su·i·cid·al [sʊɪˈsaɪdl] *adj* □ **1.** selbstmörderisch (*a. fig.*): **~ *thoughts*** *pl* Selbstmordgedanken *pl*. **2.** selbstmordgefährdet. **su·i·cide** ['-saɪd] *s* **1.** Selbstmord *m* (*a. fig.*): *commit* **~** Selbstmord begehen; *he tried to commit* **~** er unternahm e-n Selbstmordversuch; → *attempt* Selbstmordversuch *m*; → *attempt* 1. **2.** Selbstmörder(in).

suit [suːt] **I** *s* **1.** Anzug *m*; Kostüm *n*. **2.** *Kartenspiel*: Farbe *f*: *follow* **~** (Farbe) bedienen; *fig.* dasselbe tun, nachziehen. **3.** → *lawsuit*. **II** *v/t* **4.** *j-m* stehen (*Farbe etc*). **5.** *j-m* passen (*Termin etc*): *that* **~***s me fine* das paßt mir gut, läßt es mir sehr recht; **~** *s.o.'s book* F j-m ins Zeug passen. **6.** **~** *s.th.*, *be* **~***ed to s.th.* geeignet sein *od.* sich eignen für: *they are well* **~***ed (to each other)* sie passen gut zusammen. **7.** **~** *yourself!* mach, was du willst! **8.** *et.* anpassen (*to dat*). **'suit·a·ble** *adj* □ passend, geeignet (*for, to* für).

'suit·case *s* Koffer *m*.

suite [swiːt] *s* **1.** (*Möbel*)Garnitur *f*. **2.** Suite *f*, Zimmerflucht *f*. **3.** ♪ Suite *f*.

sul·fa drug, sul·fate, sul·fide, sul·fon·a·mide, sul·fur *Am.* → *sulpha drug, sulphate, sulphide, sulphonamide, sulphur*.

sulk [sʌlk] **I** *v/i* schmollen. **II** *s: have the* **~***s* → I. **'sulk·y** **I** *adj* □ **1.** schmollend. **2.** schnell schmollend. **II** *s* **3.** *Trabrennen:* Sulky *n*.

sul·len ['sʌlən] *adj* □ mürrisch, verdrossen.

sul·pha drug ['sʌlfə] *s bsd. Br. pharm.* Sulfonamid *n*.

sul·phate ['sʌlfeɪt] *s* 🜍 *bsd. Br.* Sulfat *n*.

sul·phide ['sʌlfaɪd] *s* 🜍 *bsd. Br.* Sulfid *n*.

sul·phon·a·mide [sʌlˈfɒnəmaɪd] *s* → *sulpha drug*.

sul·phur ['sʌlfə] *s* 🜍, *min. bsd. Br.* Schwefel *m*. **sul·phu·ric** [-ˈfjʊərɪk] *adj*: **~** *acid* Schwefelsäure *f*. **sul·phur·ous** ['-fərəs] *adj* schwef(e)lig, Schwefel...

sul·tan ['sʌltən] *s* Sultan *m*.

sul·try ['sʌltrɪ] *adj* □ **1.** schwül. **2.** aufreizend (*Blick etc*).

sum [sʌm] **I** *s* **1.** Summe *f* (*a.* Ⓐ), Betrag *m*: *in* **~** *fig.* mit 'einem Wort. **2.** (einfa-

che) Rechenaufgabe: *do* **~***s* rechnen. **II** *v/t* **3.** **~** *up* zs.-fassen. **4.** **~** *up* *j-n*, *et.* abschätzen. **III** *v/i* **5.** **~** *up* zs.-fassen: *to* **~** *up* zs.-fassend.

sum·ma·rize ['sʌməraɪz] *v/t u. v/i* zs.-fassen. **'sum·mar·y** *s* Zs.-fassung *f*. **II** *adj* summarisch (*a.* 🝐); fristlos (*Entlassung*).

sum·mer ['sʌmə] **I** *s* Sommer *m*: *in* (*the*) **~** im Sommer. **II** *adj* Sommer... '**~house** *s* Gartenhaus *n*. '**~time** *s* Sommer(zeit *f*) *m*: *in* (*the*) **~** im Sommer. **~** *time s bsd. Br.* Sommerzeit *f* (*Uhrzeit*).

sum·mer·y ['sʌmərɪ] *adj* sommerlich, Sommer...

sum·mit ['sʌmɪt] **I** *s* Gipfel *m* (*a.* 🝐, *pol.*), *fig.* Höhepunkt *m*. **II** *adj bsd.* 🝐, *pol.* Gipfel...: **~** *conference*.

sum·mon ['sʌmən] *v/t* **1.** *j-n* zitieren (*to* in *acc*); auffordern (*to do* zu tun). **2.** *Versammlung etc* einberufen. **3.** **~** *up* *Kraft*, *Mut etc* zs.-nehmen. **sum·mons** ['-z] 🝐 **I** *s* Vorladung *f*. **II** *v/t* *j-n* vorladen.

sump [sʌmp] *s mot.*, ⊚ *bsd. Br.* Ölwanne *f*.

sump·tu·ous ['sʌmptʃʊəs] *adj* □ luxuriös.

sun [sʌn] **I** *s* Sonne *f*. **II** *v/t:* **~** *o.s.* sich sonnen. '**~bathe** *v/i* sonnenbaden, sich sonnen. '**~beam** *s* Sonnenstrahl *m*. '**~burn** *s* Sonnenbrand *m*. '**~burned**, '**~burnt** *adj*: *be* **~** e-n Sonnenbrand haben.

sun·dae ['sʌndeɪ] *s* Eisbecher *m*.

Sun·day ['sʌndɪ] *s* Sonntag *m*: *on* **~** (am) Sonntag; *on* **~***s* sonntags. **~** *best s* Sonntagsstaat *m*. **~** *school s* Sonntagsschule *f*.

'sun|·di·al *s* Sonnenuhr *f*. '**~down** → *sunset*. '**~down·er** *s bsd. Br.* F Dämmerschoppen *m*.

sun·dries ['sʌndrɪz] *s pl* Diverses *n*, Verschiedenes *n*. **sun·dry** ['-drɪ] *adj* diverse, verschiedene: *all and* **~** jedermann, *contp.* Hinz u. Kunz.

'sun·flow·er *s* 🌿 Sonnenblume *f*. **~** *oil s* Sonnenblumenöl *n*.

sung [sʌŋ] *pp von* **sing**.

'sun|·glass·es *s pl, a. pair of* **~** Sonnenbrille *f*. **~** *god s* Sonnengott *m*. '**~hel·met** *s* Tropenhelm *m*.

sunk [sʌŋk] *pret u. pp von* **sink**.

sunk·en ['sʌŋkən] *adj* **1.** ge-, versunken;

versenkt. **2.** eingefallen (*Wangen*), (*a. Augen*) eingesunken.

sun| lamp s Höhensonne *f*, Quarzlampe *f*. '**~light** s Sonnenlicht *n*. '**~lit** *adj* sonnenbeschienen.

sun·ny ['sʌnɪ] *adj* □ sonnig (*a. fig. Wesen etc*), *fig.* fröhlich (*Lächeln etc*): **~side** Sonnenseite *f* (*a. fig. des Lebens*); **~side up** nur auf 'einer Seite gebraten (*Ei*).

'**sun|·rise** s Sonnenaufgang *m*: **at ~** bei Sonnenaufgang. '**~roof** s **1.** *mot.* Schiebedach *n*. **2.** Dachterrasse *f*. '**~set** s Sonnenuntergang *m*: **at ~** bei Sonnenuntergang. '**~shade** s Sonnenschirm *m*: **~ lotion** (*od. oil*) Sonnenöl *n*: **~ tanned** *adj* braungebrannt. '**~up** → **sunrise**. **~ vi·sor** s *mot.* Sonnenblende *f*.

su·per ['su:pə] *adj* F super, klasse.

su·per... ['su:pə] Über..., über...

su·per·a·bun·dant *adj* □ überreichlich.

su·per·an·nu·at·ed [ˌsu:pə'rænjʊeɪtɪd] *adj* **1.** pensioniert, im Ruhestand. **2.** *fig.* überholt, veraltet.

su·perb [su:'pɜːb] *adj* □ ausgezeichnet.

su·per·cil·i·ous [ˌsu:pə'sɪlɪəs] *adj* □ hochnäsig.

su·per·fi·cial [ˌsu:pə'fɪʃl] *adj* □ oberflächlich (*a. fig.*). **su·per·fi·ci·al·i·ty** ['~fɪʃɪ'ælɪtɪ] s Oberflächlichkeit *f*.

su·per·flu·ous [su:'pɜːflʊəs] *adj* □ überflüssig.

su·per|'hu·man *adj* □ übermenschlich. **~im'pose** *v/t* Bild etc einblenden (**on** in *acc*).

su·per·in·tend·ent [ˌsu:pərɪn'tendənt] s **1.** Aufsicht(sbeamte *m*) *f*. **2.** *Br.* Kriminalrat *m*.

su·pe·ri·or [su:'pɪərɪə] I *adj* □ **1.** (**to**) überlegen (*dat*), besser (als): **be ~ in number(s) to** j-m zahlenmäßig überlegen sein. **2.** ranghöher (**to** als): **be ~ to** a. höher stehen als. **3.** ausgezeichnet, hervorragend. **4.** *b.s.* überheblich, -legen. II s **5.** Vorgesetzte *m*, *f*. **su·pe·ri'or·i·ty** [~'ɒrətɪ] s **1.** Überlegenheit *f* (**over** gegenüber): **~ in number(s)** zahlenmäßige Überlegenheit. **2.** Überheblichkeit *f*.

su·per·la·tive [su:'pɜːlətɪv] I *adj* □ **1.** unübertrefflich, überragend: **~ly happy**

unsagbar glücklich. **2.** **~ degree** → **3.** II s **3.** *ling.* Superlativ *m*.

'**su·per|·man** s (*irr man*) Supermann *m*. '**~mar·ket** s Supermarkt *m*. **~nat·u·ral** I *adj* □ übernatürlich. II s: **the ~** das Übernatürliche.

su·per·nu·mer·a·ry [ˌsu:pə'nju:mərərɪ] *adj* überzählig.

'**su·per|·pow·er** s *pol.* Supermacht *f*.

su·per·sede [ˌsu:pə'si:d] *v/t et.* ablösen, ersetzen, an die Stelle treten von (*od. gen*).

'**su·per|'son·ic** *adj* ✈, *phys.* Überschall...: **at ~ speed** mit Überschallgeschwindigkeit. '**~star** s Sport etc: Superstar *m*.

su·per·sti·tion [ˌsu:pə'stɪʃn] s Aberglaube *m*, *pl* abergläubische Vorstellungen *pl*. **su·per·sti·tious** [~'stɪʃəs] *adj* □ abergläubisch.

'**su·per|·struc·ture** s △ Oberbau *m*, ⚓ (Deck)Aufbauten *pl*; *fig.* Überbau *m*. '**~tank·er** s ⚓ Supertanker *m*.

su·per·vene [ˌsu:pə'vi:n] *v/i* dazwischenkommen.

su·per·vise ['su:pəvaɪz] *v/t* beaufsichtigen. **su·per·vi·sion** [~'vɪʒn] s Beaufsichtigung *f*; **under s.o.'s ~** unter j-s Aufsicht. **su·per·vi·sor** ['~vaɪzə] s Aufseher(in), Aufsicht *f*.

su·per ['sʌpə] s Abendessen *n*: **have ~** zu Abend essen; → **lord** 3.

sup·plant [sə'plɑ:nt] *v/t* j-n, *et.* verdrängen.

sup·ple ['sʌpl] *adj* □ gelenkig (*Körper etc*), (*a. Material*) geschmeidig, (*Material*) biegsam, elastisch.

sup·ple·ment I s ['sʌplɪmənt] **1.** Ergänzung *f* (**to** gen *od.* zu). **2.** Nachtrag *m*, Anhang *m* (**to** zu e-m Buch); Ergänzungsband *m*. **3.** Beilage *f* (*zu e-r Zeitung*). II *v/t* ['~ment] **4.** ergänzen, (*Einkommen, Einkünfte*) aufbessern (**with** mit). **sup·ple·men·ta·ry** [~'mentərɪ] *adj* ergänzend, zusätzlich: **~ benefit** *Br.* Sozialhilfe *f*.

sup·pli·er [sə'plaɪə] s ✝ Lieferant(in), *a. pl* Lieferfirma *f*.

sup·ply [sə'plaɪ] I *v/t* **1.** liefern; stellen; sorgen für. **2.** j-n, *et.* versorgen, ✝ beliefern (**with** mit). **3.** e-m Bedürfnis etc abhelfen. II s **4.** Lieferung *f* (**to** an *acc*). **5.** Versorgung *f*. **6.** ✝ Angebot *n*: **~ and demand** Angebot u. Nachfrage; →

short 2. **7.** *mst pl* Vorrat *m* (**of** an *dat*), *pl a.* Proviant *m*, ✕ Nachschub *m*. **8.** *pl* (*Büro- etc*)Bedarf *m*.

sup·port [sə'pɔːt] **I** *v/t* **1.** (ab)stützen; *Gewicht etc* tragen; *fig.* Währung stützen. **2.** *j-n* (*a.* finanziell), *Forderung etc* unterstützen, *Familie* unterhalten: **~ Tottenham** ein Tottenham-Anhänger sein. **3.** *Hobby etc* finanzieren. **4.** *Theorie etc* beweisen, erhärten. **5.** *et.* aushalten, ertragen. **II** *s* **6.** Stütze *f*, ⚙ *a.* Stützbalken *m*, -pfeiler *m*. **7.** *fig.* Unterstützung *f*: **in ~ of** zur Unterstützung (*gen*); **have s.o.'s full ~** j-s volle Unterstützung haben. **sup'port·a·ble** *adj* □ erträglich. **sup'port·er** *s* Anhänger(in) (*a.* Sport), Befürworter(in). **sup'port·ing** *adj* **1.** **~ wall** tragende Wand. **2.** *fig.* unterstützend: **~ materials** *pl ped.* Begleitmaterial *n*; **~ part** (*od.* role) *thea. etc* Nebenrolle *f*; **~ program(me)** (*Film*) Beiprogramm *n*. **sup'port·ive** *adj*: **he was very ~ when I ...** er war mir e-e große Stütze, als ich ...

sup·pose [sə'pəʊz] *v/t* **1.** annehmen, vermuten: **I ~ I must have fallen a-sleep** ich muß wohl eingeschlafen sein. **2.** *he is ~d* (**to be**) *rich* er soll reich sein; **you are not ~d to smoke here** du darfst hier nicht rauchen; **aren't you ~d to be at work?** solltest du nicht (eigentlich) in der Arbeit sein?; **what is that ~d to mean?** was soll denn das? **3.** *et.* voraussetzen. **II** *v/i* **4.** *I ~* **so** ich nehme es an, wahrscheinlich, vermutlich. **III** *cj* **5.** angenommen. **6.** wie wäre es, wenn: **~ we went home?** wie wäre es, wenn wir nach Hause gingen? **sup'posed** *adj* □ angeblich. **sup'pos·ing** *cj* **1.** → *suppose* 5, 6. **2.** vorausgesetzt.

sup·po·si·tion [ˌsʌpə'zɪʃn] *s* Annahme *f*, Vermutung *f*: **act on the ~ that** von der Annahme ausgehen, daß.

sup·pos·i·to·ry [sə'pɒzɪtərɪ] *s* ✚ Zäpfchen *n*.

sup·pu·rate ['sʌpjʊəreɪt] *v/i* eitern.

su·pra·na·tion·al [ˌsuːprə'næʃənl] *adj* □ übernational.

su·prem·a·cy [sʊ'preməsɪ] *s* Vormachtstellung *f*.

su·preme [sʊ'priːm] *adj* **1.** höchst, oberst. **2.** höchst, größt. **su'preme·ly** *adv* höchst, absolut.

sur·charge I *s* ['sɜːtʃɑːdʒ] Auf-, Zu-

schlag *m* (**on** auf *acc*); 📧 Nach-, Strafporto *n* (**on** auf *acc*). **II** *v/t* [sɜː'tʃɑːdʒ] Nachporto *od.* e-n Zuschlag erheben auf (*acc*).

sure [ʃɔː] **I** *adj* (□ → *surely*) **1.** *allg.* sicher: **~ of o.s.** selbstsicher; **~ of victory** (*od.* winning) siegessicher; **for ~** ganz sicher *od.* bestimmt; **~ thing!** *bsd. Am.* **1.** (aber) klar!; **be** (*od.* feel) **~** sicher sein; **you are ~ to like this play** dir wird das Stück sicher gefallen; **be ~ to lock the door** vergiß nicht abzuschließen; **to be ~** sicher(lich); **make ~ that** sich (davon) überzeugen, daß; **make ~** dafür sorgen, daß; **make ~ of s.th.** sich von et. überzeugen; sich et. sichern. **II** *adv* **2.** F sicher, klar. **3.** **~ enough** tatsächlich. **'~·fire** *adj* F (tod)sicher.

sure·ly ['ʃɔːlɪ] *adv* **1.** sicher: **~ slow 1. 2.** sicher(lich), bestimmt. **sure·ty** ['ʃɔːrətɪ] *s* bsd. ⚖ Bürgschaft *f*, Sicherheit *f*; Bürge *m*, Bürgin *f*: **stand ~ for s.o.** für j-n bürgen.

surf [sɜːf] **I** *s* Brandung *f*. **II** *v/i* surfen.

sur·face ['sɜːfɪs] **I** *s* **1.** Oberfläche *f* (*a. fig.*): **on the ~** äußerlich; vordergründig; oberflächlich betrachtet. **2.** (*Straßen*)Belag *m*, (-)Decke *f*. **II** *adj* **3.** Oberflächen...: **~ mail** gewöhnliche Post (*Ggs. Luftpost*); **~ tension** *phys.* Oberflächenspannung *f*. **4.** *fig.* oberflächlich. **III** *v/i* **5.** auftauchen (*a. fig.*). **IV** *v/t* **6.** Straße mit e-m Belag versehen. **'surf·board** *s* Surfbrett *n*, -brett *n*.

sur·feit ['sɜːfɪt] **I** *s* Übergebot *n* (**of** an *dat*). **II** *v/t*: **~ o.s. with** sich übersättigen an (*dat*).

surf·er ['sɜːfə] *s* Surfer(in), Wellenreiter(in). **'surf·ing** *s* Surfen *n*, Wellenreiten *n*.

surge [sɜːdʒ] **I** *s* **1.** **a ~ of people** e-e wogende Menschenmenge; **there was a sudden ~ forward** plötzlich drängte alles nach vorn. **2.** *fig.* Welle *f*, Woge *f* (*der Begeisterung*); (*Gefühls*)Aufwallung *f*, Anwandlung *f*. **II** *v/i* **3.** drängen, strömen (*Menschenmenge*). **4.** *mst* **~ up** *fig.* aufwallen (**in** in *dat*) (*Zorn etc*).

sur·geon ['sɜːdʒən] *s* Chirurg(in). **sur·ger·y** ['sɜːdʒərɪ] *s* **1.** Chirurgie *f*. **2.** **he needs ~** er muß operiert werden; **re-move by ~** operativ entfernen. **3.** *Br.* Sprechzimmer *n*; Sprechstunde *f*: **~ hours** *pl* Sprechstunden *pl*. **sur·gi·cal**

['ɪkl] *adj* □ **1.** chirurgisch; operativ; Operations...: ~ **spirit** *Br.* Wundbenzin *n.* **2.** ~ **stocking** Stützstrumpf *m.*

sur·ly ['sɜːlɪ] *adj* □ griesgrämig, sauertöpfisch.

sur·mise I *s* ['sɜːmaɪz] Vermutung *f.* II *v/t* [sɜː'maɪz] vermuten.

sur·mount [sɜː'maʊnt] *v/t Schwierigkeit etc* überwinden. **sur'mount·a·ble** *adj* überwindbar.

sur·name ['sɜːneɪm] *s* Familien-, Nach-, Zuname *m*: **what is his ~?** wie heißt er mit Familiennamen?

sur·pass [sə'pɑːs] *v/t Erwartungen etc* übertreffen.

sur·plus ['sɜːpləs] I *s* Überschuß *m* (*of* an *dat*). II *adj* überschüssig: **be ~ to requirements** zuviel sein.

sur·prise [sə'praɪz] I *s* **1.** Überraschung *f*: **in** ~ überrascht; **take by** ~ überraschen; → **much** 2. II *adj* überraschend, Überraschungs... III *v/t* überraschen: **be ~d at** (*od.* **by**) überrascht sein über (*acc*); **I wouldn't be ~d if** es würde mich nicht wundern, wenn. **sur'pris·ing** *adj* □ überraschend. **~ly** (*enough*) überraschenderweise.

sur·re·al·ism [sə'rɪəlɪzəm] *s Kunst:* Surrealismus *m.* **sur're·al·ist** I *s* Surrealist(in). II *adj* surrealistisch. **sur,re·al'is·tic** *adj* (**~ally**) surrealistisch.

sur·ren·der [sə'rendə] I *v/i* **1.** (**to**) ✕ sich ergeben (*dat*), kapitulieren (vor *dat*) (*beide a. fig.*): ~ **to the police** sich der Polizei stellen. II *v/t* **2.** *et.* übergeben, ausliefern (**to** *dat*): ~ **o.s. to the police** sich der Polizei stellen. **3.** *Anspruch etc* aufgeben, verzichten auf (*acc*). III *s* **4.** ✕ Kapitulation *f* (**to** vor *dat*) (*a. fig.*). **5.** (*of*) Aufgabe *f* (*gen*), Verzicht *m* (auf *acc*).

sur·rep·ti·tious [,sʌrəp'tɪʃəs] *adj* □ heimlich, verstohlen.

sur·ro·gate ['sʌrəgeɪt] *adj*: ~ **mother** Leihmutter *f.*

sur·round [sə'raʊnd] *v/t* **1.** umgeben. **2.** *Haus etc* umstellen. **sur'round·ing** I *adj* umliegend. II *s pl* Umgebung *f.*

sur·veil·lance [sɜː'veɪləns] *s* Überwachung *f*: **be** (**keep**) **under** ~ überwacht werden (überwachen).

sur·vey I *v/t* [sɜː'veɪ] **1.** (sich) *et.* betrachten (*a. fig.*). **2.** *Land* vermessen. **3.** *Haus etc* begutachten. II *s* ['sɜːveɪ] **4.** Umfra-

ge *f.* **5.** Überblick *m* (**of** über *acc*). **6.** Vermessung *f.* **7.** Begutachtung *f.* **sur'vey·or** *s* **1.** Land(ver)messer(in). **2.** Gutachter(in).

sur·viv·al [sə'vaɪvl] *s* **1.** Überleben *n* (*a. fig.*): ~ **training** Überlebenstraining *n.* **2.** Überbleibsel *n* (from aus *e-r* Zeit).

sur·vive I *v/t* **1.** *j-n, et.* überleben; *Erdbeben etc* überstehen (*Haus etc*); *Jahrhundert etc* überdauern (*Brauch etc*). II *v/i* **2.** überleben (*a. fig.*), am Leben bleiben. **3.** erhalten bleiben *od.* sein. **sur'vi·vor** *s* Überlebende *m, f* (**from, of** *gen*).

sus·cep·ti·ble [sə'septəbl] *adj* □ **1.** empfänglich (**to** für). **2.** anfällig (**to** für). **3.** leicht zu beeindrucken.

sus·pect I *v/t* [sə'spekt] **1.** *j-n* verdächtigen (**of** *gen*): ~ **s.o. of doing s.th.** *j-n* im *od.* in Verdacht haben, et. zu tun; **be ~ed of doing s.th.** im *od.* unter dem Verdacht stehen, et. zu tun. **2.** et. vermuten. **3.** *et.* an-, bezweifeln. II *s* ['sʌspekt] **4.** Verdächtige *m, f.* III *adj* ['sʌspekt] **5.** verdächtig, suspekt.

sus·pend [sə'spend] *v/t* **1.** aufhängen (**from** an *dat*). **2.** *Verkauf, Zahlungen etc* (vorübergehend) einstellen; ⛫ *Strafe* zur Bewährung aussetzen: **he was given a two-year ~ed sentence** er bekam zwei Jahre mit Bewährung. **3.** *j-n* suspendieren (**from duty** vom Dienst); vorübergehend ausschließen (**from** aus); (*Sport*) sperren (**for two games** für zwei Spiele). **sus'pend·er** *s* **1.** *Br.* Strumpfhalter *m*, Straps *m*: ~ **belt** Strumpf(halter)-, Strapsgürtel *m.* **2.** *pl, a.* **pair of ~s** *Am.* Hosenträger *pl.*

sus·pense [sə'spens] *s* Spannung *f*: **in** ~ gespannt, voller Spannung; **full of** ~ spannend; **keep s.o. in** ~ *j-n* auf die Folter spannen. **sus'pen·sion** *s* **1.** *mot. etc* Aufhängung *f*: ~ **bridge** Hängebrücke *f.* **2.** (vorübergehende) Einstellung. **3.** Suspendierung *f*; vorübergehender Ausschluß; (*Sport*) Sperre *f*: **he received a two-game** ~ er wurde für zwei Spiele gesperrt.

sus·pi·cion [sə'spɪʃn] *s* **1.** Verdacht *m* (**of** gegen): **be above** (*od.* **beyond**) ~ über jeden Verdacht erhaben sein; **be under** ~ **of murder** unter Mordverdacht stehen. **2.** *a. pl* Verdacht *m*, Argwohn *m*, Mißtrauen *n* (**of** gegen): **with** ~ argwöhnisch, mißtrauisch. **3.** Verdacht *m*, Vermutung *f*. **4.** *fig.* Hauch *m*, Spur *f*. **sus·pi·cious** *adj* □ **1.** verdächtig. **2.** argwöhnisch, mißtrauisch (*of* gegen): **become** ~ *a.* Verdacht schöpfen.

sus·tain [sə'steɪn] *v/t* **1.** *j-n* (*a.* moralisch) stärken. **2.** *Interesse etc* aufrechterhalten. **3.** *Schaden, Verlust* erleiden. **4.** ♩ *Ton* (aus)halten. **5.** 🏛 *e-m Einspruch etc* stattgeben. **6.** *Gewicht* aushalten, tragen. **sus'tained** *adj* anhaltend.

su·ture ['suːtʃə] ✚ **I** *s* Naht *f*. **II** *v/t* Wunde nähen.

svelte [svelt] *adj* gertenschlank (*Frau*).

swab [swɒb] ✚ **I** *s* **1.** Tupfer *m*. **2.** Abstrich *m*: **take** *a* ~ e-n Abstrich machen. **II** *v/t* **3.** *Wunde* abtupfen.

swad·dle ['swɒdl] *v/t Baby* wickeln.

swag·ger ['swæɡə] **I** *v/i* stolzieren. **II** *s*: **walk with a** ~ → **I**.

swal·low¹ ['swɒləʊ] *s orn.* Schwalbe *f*.

swal·low² [~] **I** *v/t* **1.** schlucken (*a. fig. F* glauben, hinnehmen): ~ **one's words** zugeben, daß man sich geirrt hat; ~ **up** *Betrieb, Gewinn etc* schlucken, verschlingen; → **bait** 1. **2.** *Ärger, Tränen etc* hinunterschlucken, *s-n Stolz* vergessen. **II** *v/i* **3.** schlucken: ~ **hard** *fig.* kräftig schlucken. **III** *s* **4.** Schluck *m*.

swam [swæm] *pret von* **swim.**

swamp [swɒmp] **I** *s* Sumpf *m*. **II** *v/t* überschwemmen: **be** ~**ed with** *fig.* überschwemmt werden mit. **'swamp·y** *adj* sumpfig.

swan [swɒn] *s orn.* Schwan *m*.

swank [swæŋk] F **I** *v/i* **1.** angeben. **II** *s* **2.** Angeber(in). **3.** Angabe *f*. **'swank·y** *adj* □ F **1.** piekfein. **2.** angeberisch.

'swan·song *s fig.* Schwanengesang *m*.

swap [swɒp] F **I** *v/t* **1.** *et.* tauschen (*with* mit), (ein)tauschen (*for* für, gegen): ~ **places** die Plätze tauschen. **II** *v/i* **2.** tauschen: ~ **over** (*od.* **round**) die Plätze tauschen. **III** *s* **3.** Tausch *m*: **do a** ~ tauschen; **do** (*od.* **get**) **a good** (**bad**) ~ e-n guten (schlechten) Tausch machen. **4.** Tauschobjekt *n*.

swarm [swɔːm] **I** *s* **1.** Schwarm *m* (*Bienen, Touristen etc*). **II** *v/i* **2.** schwärmen (*Bienen*), (*Menschen a.*) strömen. **3.** ~ **with** wimmeln von: **the square was** ~**ing with people** auf dem Platz wimmelte es von Menschen.

swarth·y ['swɔːðɪ] *adj* dunkel (*Haut*), dunkelhäutig (*Person*).

swash·buck·ling ['swɒʃˌbʌklɪŋ] *adj* verwegen (*Person*), abenteuerlich (*Film etc*).

swas·ti·ka ['swɒstɪkə] *s* Hakenkreuz *n*.

swat [swɒt] **I** *v/t Fliege etc* totschlagen. **II** *s* → **swatter**. **'swat·ter** *s* Fliegenklappe *f*, -klatsche *f*.

sway [sweɪ] **I** *v/i* **1.** sich wiegen (**in the wind** im Wind) (*Bäume etc*), schaukeln (*Schiff etc*): ~ **between** *fig.* schwanken zwischen (*dat*). **II** *v/t* **2.** hin- u. herbewegen, *s-n Körper* wiegen, *Fahne etc* schwenken. **3.** *j-n* beeinflussen; umstimmen. **III** *s* **4.** Schaukeln *n*.

swear [sweə] (*irr*) **I** *v/i* **1.** schwören (**on the Bible** auf die Bibel; **to God** bei Gott): ~ **by** *fig.* F schwören auf (*acc*); **I couldn't** ~ **to it** ich kann es nicht beschwören. **2.** fluchen: ~ **at s.o.** j-n wüst beschimpfen. **II** *v/t* **3.** schwören (**to** zu tun; **that** daß): ~ **s.th. to s.o.** j-m et. schwören; → **oath** 1. **4.** ~ **in** *Minister, Zeugen etc* vereidigen; **I was sworn to secrecy** ich mußte hoch u. heilig versprechen, kein Wort darüber zu sagen. **'~·word** *s* Fluch *m*; Kraftausdruck *m*.

sweat [swet] **I** *v/i* schwitzen (**with** vor *dat*) (*a. fig.* F). **II** *v/t* (*Am. a. irr*) **1.** schwitzen: ~ **it out** F durchhalten; ~ **blood** F sich abrackern (**over** mit). **III** *s* **3.** Schweiß *m*: **cold** ~ kalter Schweiß, Angstschweiß; **no** ~*!* F kein Problem!; **get in(to) a** ~ *fig.* F ins Schwitzen geraten *od.* kommen (**about** wegen). **4.** F Schufterei *f*. **'~·band** *s Sport:* Schweißband *n*.

sweat·er ['swetə] *s* Pullover *m*.

sweat' gland *s anat.* Schweißdrüse *f*. **'~·shirt** *s* Sweatshirt *n* (*weiter Baumwollpullover*).

sweat·y ['swetɪ] *adj* □ **1.** schweißig, verschwitzt. **2.** nach Schweiß riechend, Schweiß... **3.** schweißtreibend.

Swede [swiːd] *s* Schwede *m*, Schwedin *f*. **Swed·ish** ['swiːdɪʃ] **I** *adj* **1.** schwedisch. **II** *s* **2.** *ling.* Schwedisch *n*. **3. the** ~ *pl* die Schweden *pl*.

sweep [swiːp] **I** *s* **1. give the floor a** ~ den Boden kehren *od.* fegen; **make a clean** ~ *fig.* gründlich aufräumen; (*Sport etc*) gründlich abräumen. **2.** Hieb *m*, Schlag

m. **3.** Schornsteinfeger(in), Kaminkehrer(in). **II** *v/t (irr)* **4.** Fußboden, Krümel *etc* kehren, fegen: ~ *the board* (*Sport etc*) gründlich abräumen; → *carpet* 1, *rug* 1. **5.** fegen über (*acc*) (*Sturm etc*); *fig. Land etc* überschwemmen (*Protestwelle etc*). **6.** ~ *along* mitreißen; ~ *s.o. off his feet fig.* j-s Herz im Sturm erobern. **7.** *Horizont etc* absuchen (*for* nach). **III** *v/i (irr)* **8.** kehren, fegen: → *broom.* **9.** rauschen (*Person*): ~ *past s.o.* an j-m vorbeirauschen.
Verbindungen mit Adverbien:

sweep|a·side *v/t Einwände etc* beiseite schieben. ~ **a·way** *v/t* **1.** aufräumen mit. **2.** *be swept away by fig.* mitgerissen werden von. ~ **up** *v/t* **1.** (*a. v/i*) zs.-kehren, -fegen. **2.** *j-n* hochreißen.

sweep·er ['swiːpə] *s* **1.** (*Straßen*)Kehrer(in). **2.** Kehrmaschine *f.* **3.** *Fußball:* Libero *m.* '**sweep·ing I** *adj* □ **1.** durchgreifend (*Änderung etc*). **2.** pauschal. **II** *s pl* **3.** Kehricht *m.*

sweet [swiːt] **I** *adj* □ **1.** süß (*a. fig.*): ~ *nothings pl* Zärtlichkeiten *pl;* ~ *potato* ❦ *Batate f,* Süßkartoffel *f; revenge is* ~ Rache ist süß; ~ *talk F* Schmeichelei(en *pl) f; have a* ~ *tooth* gern naschen. **2.** lieblich (*Musik etc*). **3.** lieb. **II** *s* **4.** *Br.* Bonbon *m, n,* Süßigkeit *f.* **5.** *Br.* Nachtisch *m: for* ~ als *od.* zum Nachtisch. '**sweet**|**-and-'sour** *adj gastr.* süß-sauer.

sweet·en ['swiːtn] **I** *v/t* **1.** süßen. **2.** *fig.* besänftigen; freundlicher stimmen. **3.** *a.* ~ *up* F *j-n* schmieren. **II** *v/i* **4.** süß(er) werden. '**sweet·en·er** *s* **1.** Süßstoff *m.* **2.** *F* Schmiergeld *n.*

'**sweet·heart** *s* Schatz *m* (*Anrede*).

sweet·ie ['swiːtɪ] *s* F **1.** *Br.* Bonbon *m, n.* **2.** *be a* ~ *fig.* süß sein.

'**sweet·talk** *v/t* F *j-m* schmeicheln.

swell [swel] **I** *v/i* (*mst irr*) **1.** *a.* ~ *up* ✿ (an)schwellen. **2.** *a.* ~ *out* ✿ sich blähen (*Segel*). **3.** *fig.* anschwellen (*into* zu) (*Geräusch*); anwachsen (*Zahl etc*). **II** *v/t* (*mst irr*) **4.** ✿ Segel blähen (*Wind*). **5.** *fig. Zahl etc* anwachsen lassen. **III** *s* **6.** ♇ Dünung *f.* **IV** *adj* **7.** *Am.* F klasse. '**swell·ing** *s* ✿ Schwellung *f.*

swel·ter ['sweltə] *v/i* vor Hitze fast umkommen. '**swel·ter·ing** *adj* drückend, schwül.

swept [swept] *pret u. pp von* **sweep.**

swerve [swɜːv] **I** *v/i* **1.** schwenken (*to the left* nach links), e-n Schwenk machen. **2.** *fig.* abweichen (*from* von). **II** *s* **3.** Schwenk(ung *f) m, mot. etc a.* Schlenker *m.*

swift [swɪft] *adj* □ schnell: *be* ~ *to do s.th.* et. schnell tun. '**swift·ness** *s* Schnelligkeit *f.*

swig [swɪg] F **I** *v/t Getränk* hinunterkippen. **II** *s: take a* ~ *at the bottle* e-n Zug aus der Flasche tun; *take a* ~ *of beer* e-n kräftigen Schluck Bier nehmen.

swill [swɪl] *v/t u. v/i contr.* saufen.

swim [swɪm] **I** *v/i (irr)* **1.** schwimmen: → *tide* 2. **2.** *fig.* verschwimmen (*before s.o.'s eyes* vor j-s Augen); *my head was* ~*ming* mir drehte sich alles. **II** *v/t (irr)* **3.** *Strecke* schwimmen; *Gewässer* durchschwimmen. **III** *s* **4.** *go for a* ~ schwimmen gehen. '**swim·mer** *s* Schwimmer(in). '**swim·ming I** *s* Schwimmen *n.* **II** *adj* Schwimm…: ~ *bath(s pl) Br.* Schwimm-, *bsd.* Hallenbad *n;* ~ *cap* Badekappe *f,* -mütze *f;* ~ *costume* Badeanzug *m;* ~ *pool* Swimmingpool *m,* Schwimmbecken *n;* (*pair of*) ~ *trunks pl* Badehose *f.* '**swim·suit** *s* Badeanzug *m.*

swin·dle ['swɪndl] **I** *v/t j-n* beschwindeln (*out of* um): ~ *s.o. out of s.th. a.* j-m et. abschwindeln. **II** *s* Schwindel *m.* '**swin·dler** *s* Schwindler(in).

swine [swaɪn] *s* **1.** *pl* ~ *zo.* Schwein *n.* **2.** *pl* ~(*s*) *sl. contr.* Schwein *n.*

swing [swɪŋ] **I** *v/i* (*irr*) **1.** (hin- u. her)schwingen. **2.** sich schwingen; einbiegen, -schwenken (*into* in *acc*): ~ *round* sich ruckartig umdrehen; ~ *shut* zuschlagen (*Tor etc*). **3.** ♪ schwungvoll spielen (*Band etc*); Schwung haben (*Musik*). **II** *v/t* **4.** et., *die Arme etc* schwingen. **III** *s* **5.** Schwingen *n.* **6.** Schaukel *f.* **7.** *Boxen:* Schwinger *m.* **8.** *fig.* Schwung *m: be in full* ~ in vollem Gang sein. **9.** *fig.* Umschwung *m:* ~ *in opinion* Meinungsumschwung. ~ *door s* Pendeltür *f.*

swinge·ing ['swɪndʒɪŋ] *adj bsd. Br.* einschneidend (*Kürzungen etc*), extrem hoch (*Besteuerung etc*).

swing·ing ['swɪŋɪŋ] *adj* □ **1.** schwingend: ~ *door* bes. *Am.* Pendeltür *f.* **2.** *fig.* schwungvoll. **3.** *fig.* lebenslustig.

swin·ish ['swaɪnɪʃ] *adj* □ ekelhaft.

synonymous

swipe [swaɪp] **I** s Schlag m: *take a ~ at* →
II. **II** v/i: *~ at* schlagen nach. **III** v/t F
klauen.

swirl [swɜːl] **I** v/i wirbeln. **II** s Wirbel m.

swish [swɪʃ] **I** v/i **1.** sausen, zischen. **2.**
rascheln (*Seide etc*). **II** v/t **3.** mit *dem
Schwanz* schlagen. **III** s **4.** Sausen n,
Zischen n. **5.** Rascheln n. **IV** adj **6.** F
feudal.

Swiss [swɪs] **I** s Schweizer(in): *the ~* pl
die Schweizer pl. **II** adj schweizerisch,
Schweizer(...).

switch [swɪtʃ] **I** s **1.** ⚡, ⚙ Schalter m. **2.**
Gerte f, Rute f. **3.** 🚂 Am. Weiche f. **4.**
fig. Umstellung f. **II** v/t **5.** a. *~ over* ⚡,
⚙ (um)schalten; *Produktion etc* umstellen (*to* auf acc): *~ off* ab-, ausschalten; *~ on* an-, einschalten. **III** v/i **6.** a. *~
over* ⚡, ⚙ (um)schalten (*to* auf acc),
fig. überwechseln (*to* zu): *~ off* abschalten (*a. fig.* F *Person*), ausschalten; *~ on*
an-, einschalten. '**~back** s **1.** Gebirgs-, Serpenti-
nenstraße f. **2.** Achterbahn f. '**~blade** s
Am. Schnappmesser n. '**~board** s **1.** ⚡
Schalttafel f. **2.** (Telefon)Zentrale f: ~
operator Telefonist(in).

swiv·el [ˈswɪvl] **I** v/i pret u. pp *-eled, bsd.
Br. -elled* sich drehen: *~ round* sich
herumdrehen. *~ chair* s Drehstuhl m.

swol·len [ˈswəʊlən] pp von **swell.** '*~
-'head·ed* adj fig. aufgeblasen.

swoop [swuːp] **I** v/i **1.** a. *~ down* herab-
stoßen (*on* auf acc) (*Raubvogel*). **2.** fig.
zuschlagen (*Polizei etc*): *~ on* herfallen
über (acc); e-e Razzia machen in (*dat*).
II s **3.** Razzia f.

swop → **swap.**

sword [sɔːd] s Schwert n: *cross ~s* die
Klingen kreuzen (*with* mit) (*a. fig.*); →
Damocles.

swore [swɔː] pret von **swear.**

sworn [swɔːn] **I** pp von **swear. II** adj **1.** *~
enemies* pl Todfeinde pl. **2.** ⚖ eidlich.

swot [swɒt] Br. F **I** v/i büffeln, pauken
(*for* für). **II** v/t: *~ up* → **I. III** s Büf-
fler(in); Streber(in).

swum [swʌm] pp von **swim.**

swung [swʌŋ] pret u. pp von **swing.**

syl·la·bi [ˈsɪləbaɪ] pl von **syllabus.**

syl·lab·ic [sɪˈlæbɪk] adj Silben...; ...silbig.
syl·la·ble [ˈsɪləbl] s Silbe f.

syl·la·bus [ˈsɪləbəs] pl *-bus·es, -bi*
[ˈ~baɪ] s ped., univ. Lehrplan m.

syl·lo·gism [ˈsɪlədʒɪzəm] s Syllogis-
mus m.

sym·bi·o·sis [ˌsɪmbɪˈəʊsɪs] s biol. Symbiose f.

sym·bol [ˈsɪmbl] s Symbol n (a. ✝).
sym·bol·ic [~ˈbɒlɪk] adj (~ally) symbolisch: *be ~ of* etc. symbolisieren. **sym·
bol·ism** [ˈ~bəlɪzəm] s Symbolik f. **sym·
bol·ize** [ˈ~bəlaɪz] v/t symbolisieren.

sym·met·ri·cal [sɪˈmetrɪkl] adj □ symmetrisch. **sym·me·try** [ˈsɪmɪtrɪ] s Symmetrie f.

sym·pa·thet·ic [ˌsɪmpəˈθetɪk] adj (~ally)
1. mitfühlend: *~ strike* ✝ Sympathie-
streik m. **2.** verständnisvoll; wohlwollend: *be ~ of* etc. (od. *toward*[s]) wohlwollend gegenüberstehen (*dat*). '**sym·pa·
thize** v/i **1.** mitfühlen (*with* mit). **2.**
(*with*) Verständnis haben (für); wohlwollend gegenüberstehen (*dat*); sympathisieren (mit). '**sym·pa·thiz·er** s Sym-
pathisant(in). '**sym·pa·thy** s **1.** Mitgefühl n: *in ~* mitfühlend; *letter of ~* Bei-
leidsschreiben n; *~ strike* ✝ Sympathie-
streik m. **2.** Verständnis n; Wohlwollen
n: *be in ~ with* sympathisieren mit. **3.** pl
Sympathien pl: *my sympathies are*
(*od. lie*) *with* sein e-e Sympathien gehören
(*dat*). **4.** pl Beileid n, Teilnahme f.

sym·phon·ic [sɪmˈfɒnɪk] adj (~ally) ♪
sinfonisch, symphonisch. **sym·pho·ny**
[ˈ~fənɪ] s Sinfonie f, Symphonie f: ~
orchestra Sinfonieorchester n.

sym·po·si·um [sɪmˈpəʊzɪəm] pl *-si·ums,
-si·a* [~zjə] s Symposium n, Sympo-
sion n.

symp·tom [ˈsɪmptəm] s ⚕ Symptom n,
Anzeichen n (*of* für, von) (*beide a. fig.*).
symp·to·mat·ic [ˌ~ˈmætɪk] adj (~ally)
symptomatisch (*of* für).

syn·a·gogue [ˈsɪnəgɒg] s eccl. Synagoge f.

syn·chro·nize [ˈsɪŋkrənaɪz] **I** v/t aufeinander abstimmen; *Film, Uhren* synchronisieren. **II** v/i synchron sein
(*Film*) od. gehen (*Uhren*).

syn·di·cate [ˈsɪndɪkət] s ✝ Konsortium n.

syn·drome [ˈsɪndrəʊm] s ⚕ Syndrom n.

syn·od [ˈsɪnəd] s eccl. Synode f.

syn·o·nym [ˈsɪnənɪm] s ling. Synonym n.
syn·on·y·mous [sɪˈnɒnɪməs] adj □
synonym: *be ~ with* fig. gleichbedeutend sein mit.

syn·op·sis [sɪ'nɒpsɪs] *pl* **-ses** [ˌˑsiːz] *s* Zs.-fassung *f*.

syn·tac·tic [sɪn'tæktɪk] *adj* (ˌˑally) *ling*. syntaktisch. **syn·tax** ['sɪntæks] *s* Syntax *f*, Satzlehre *f*.

syn·the·sis ['sɪnθəsɪs] *pl* **-ses** ['ˑsiːz] *s* Synthese *f*. **syn·the·size** ['ˑsaɪz] *v/t* 🐎 synthetisch *od*. künstlich herstellen. '**syn·the·siz·er** *s* Synthesizer *m* (*Gerät zur elektronischen Musik-, Sprach- u. Geräuscherzeugung*).

syn·thet·ic [sɪn'θetɪk] *adj* (ˌˑally) 🐎 synthetisch, Kunst...

syph·i·lis ['sɪfɪlɪs] *s* 🗡 Syphilis.

sy·phon → **siphon**.

syr·inge ['sɪrɪndʒ] *s* 🗡 Spritze *f*.

syr·up ['sɪrəp] *s* **1.** Sirup *m*. **2.** 🗡 (*Husten*)Sirup *m*, (-)Saft *m*. '**syr·up·y** *adj* **1.** sirupartig. **2.** *fig*. zuckersüß.

sys·tem ['sɪstəm] *s* **1.** *allg*. System *n*: ~ *of government* Regierungssystem; ˌˑs *analyst* Systemanalytiker(in); → *digestive* 2, *nervous* 1, *respiratory*. **2.** (*Straßen- etc*)Netz *n*. **3.** Organismus *m*: *get s.th. out of one's* ~ *fig*. sich et. von der Seele reden. **sys·tem·at·ic** [ˌˑtə'mætɪk] *adj* (ˌˑally) systematisch. **sys·tem·a·tize** ['ˑtɪmətaɪz] *v/t* systematisieren.

T

T [tiː] *s*: F *that's him to a T* das ist er, wie er leibt u. lebt; *fit to a T* wie angegossen passen *od*. sitzen; *suit s.o. to a T* j-m ausgezeichnet passen.

tab [tæb] *s* **1.** Aufhänger *m*, Schlaufe *f*; Lasche *f*. **2.** Etikett *n*, Schildchen *n*. **3.** *keep* ˌˑs (*od*. *a* ~) *on* F *j-n* überwachen. **4.** F Rechnung *f*: *pick up the* ~ (die Rechnung) bezahlen.

tab·er·nac·le ['tæbənækl] *s eccl*. Tabernakel *n*, *m*.

ta·ble ['teɪbl] **I** *s* **1.** Tisch *m*: *at* ~ bei Tisch; *at the* ~ am Tisch; *under the* ~ *fig*. unter der Hand; *drink s.o. under the* ~ j-n unter den Tisch trinken; *put on the* ~ auf den Tisch legen (*a. fig.*); *turn the* ˌˑs (*on s.o.*) *fig*. den Spieß umdrehen *od*. umkehren. **2.** Tisch *m*, (Tisch)Runde *f*. **3.** Tabelle *f*: → *content*[1] 3. **4.** ♈ Einmaleins *n*. **II** *v/t* **5.** *fig*. auf den Tisch legen. **6.** *Am. fig*. zurückstellen. '**ˑcloth** *s* Tischdecke *f*, -tuch *n*.

ta·ble d'hôte [ˌtɑːbl'dəʊt] *s* Menü *n*.

ta·ble| **lamp** *s* Tischlampe *f*. ˌˑ**man·ners** *s pl* Tischmanieren *pl*. '**ˑspoon** *s* Eßlöffel *m*.

tab·let ['tæblɪt] *s* **1.** *pharm*. Tablette *f*. **2.** Stück *n* (*Seife*). **3.** (*Stein- etc*)Tafel *f*.

ta·ble| **ten·nis** *s Sport*: Tischtennis *n*.

'ˌˑ**ware** *s* Geschirr *n* u. Besteck *n*. ~ *wine* *s* Tafel-, Tischwein *m*.

tab·loid ['tæblɔɪd] *s* Boulevardblatt *n*, -zeitung *f*. ~ *press* *s* Boulevardpresse *f*.

ta·boo, ta·bu [tə'buː] **I** *s* Tabu *n*. **II** *adj* Tabu...: ~ *subject* Tabu *n*; *be* ~ tabu sein. **III** *v/t* tabuisieren, für tabu erklären.

tab·u·lar ['tæbjʊlə] *adj* □ tabellarisch: *in* ~ *form* tabellarisch. **tab·u·late** ['ˑleɪt] *v/t* tabellarisch (an)ordnen.

tach·o·graph ['tækəʊɡrɑːf] *s mot*. Fahrt(en)schreiber *m*.

ta·chom·e·ter [tæ'kɒmɪtə] *s mot*. Drehzahlmesser *m*.

tac·it ['tæsɪt] *adj* □ stillschweigend. **tac·i·turn** ['ˑtɜːn] *adj* □ schweigsam, wortkarg.

tack [tæk] **I** *s* **1.** Stift *m*, Zwecke *f*. **2.** Heftstich *m*. **3.** *change* ~ *fig*. umschwenken. **II** *v/t* **4.** heften (*to* an *acc*). **5.** Stoffteile heften. **6.** ~ *on* anfügen (*to dat*).

tack·le ['tækl] **I** *s* **1.** ⚙ Flaschenzug *m*. **2.** (*Angel*)Gerät *n* (*e pl*) *n*. **3.** *Fußball*: Angriff *m* (*auf e-n ballführenden Gegner*); Zweikampf *m*. **II** *v/t* **4.** *Problem etc* angehen. **5.** *j-n* zur Rede stellen (*about* wegen). **6.** *Fußball*: ballführenden Gegner angreifen.

tack·y¹ ['tækɪ] *adj* □ klebrig.

tack·y² [~] *adj* □ *Am.* F schäbig; heruntergekommen.

tact [tækt] *s* Takt *m*. **tact·ful** ['~fʊl] *adj* □ taktvoll.

tac·tic ['tæktɪk] *s* 1. *oft pl* Taktik *f*, taktischer Zug. 2. *pl* (*a. sg konstruiert*) ✕, *Sport:* Taktik *f*. **tac·ti·cal** ['~kl] *adj* □ taktisch. **tac·ti·cian** [~'tɪʃn] *s* Taktiker(in).

tact·less ['tæktlɪs] *adj* □ taktlos.

tad·pole ['tædpəʊl] *s zo.* Kaulquappe *f*.

taf·fe·ta ['tæfɪtə] *s* Taft *m*.

taf·fy ['tæfɪ] *Am.* → **toffee**.

tag¹ [tæg] **I** *s* 1. Etikett *n*; (*Namens-, Preis*)Schild *n*. 2. stehende Redensart. 3. *ling.* Fragenhängsel *n*. **II** *v/t* 4. etikettieren; *Waren* auszeichnen: ~ (*as*) *fig.* bezeichnen als, *b.s. a.* abstempeln als. 5. ~ **on** → **tack** 6. **III** *v/i* 6. ~ **along** F mitgehen, -kommen; mittrotten: ~ **along behind s.o.** hinter j-m hertrotten.

tag² [~] *s* Fangen *n* (*Kinderspiel*): **play** ~.

tail [teɪl] **I** *s* 1. *zo.* Schwanz *m*: **with one's** ~ **between one's legs** *fig.* mit eingezogenem Schwanz. 2. Schwanz *m* (*e-s Drachens, e-r Kolonne etc*), (*e-s Flugzeugs etc a.*) hinterer Teil, (*e-s Kometen*) Schweif *m*. 3. *pl* Frack *m*. 4. *pl* Rück-, Kehrseite *f* (*e-r Münze*): → **head** 14. **5.** F Schatten *m*, Beschatter(in): **put a** ~ **on** j-n beschatten lassen. **II** *v/t* 6. F j-n beschatten. **III** *v/i* 7. ~ **off** schwächer werden, abnehmen. 8. ~ **back** *mot. bsd. Br.* sich stauen (*to* bis zu). '~**back** *s mot. bsd. Br.* Rückstau *m.* '~**board** *s mot. etc* Ladeklappe *f.* ~ **coat** *s* Frack *m.* ~ **end** *s* Ende *n*, Schluß *m.* '~**gate I** *s* 1. *mot.* Hecktür *f.* 2. *bsd. Am.* → **tailboard**. **II** *v/i u. v/t* 3. *mot. bsd. Am.* zu dicht auffahren (auf *acc*). '~**light** *s mot.* Rücklicht *n*.

tai·lor ['teɪlə] **I** *s* Schneider *m*. **II** *v/t* schneidern; *fig.* zuschneiden (**to** auf *acc*). '~**-made** *adj* maßgeschneidert (*a. fig.*): ~ **suit** (*costume*) Maßanzug *m* (Schneiderkostüm *n*); **be** ~ **for** *fig.* wie geschaffen sein für.

'**tail·piece** *s* Anhang *m*, Zusatz *m*. ~ **pipe** *s mot. Am.* Auspuffrohr *n*. '~**-wind** *s* Rückenwind *m*.

take [teɪk] **I** *s* 1. Film, TV: Einstellung *f*. 2. F Einnahme *pl*. **II** *v/t* (*irr*) 3. *allg.*

nehmen: ~ **s.o. by the arm** (*in one's arms*) j-n am Arm (in die Arme) nehmen; **be** ~ **n** besetzt sein (*Platz*); → **care** 2, 3, **place** 1, **prisoner**, **seat** 1, *etc*. 4. (weg)nehmen. 5. mitnehmen. 6. bringen. 7. ✕ *Stadt etc* einnehmen; (*Schach etc*) *Figur, Stein* schlagen; *Gefangene* machen. 8. *Preis etc* erringen: → **lead** 1. 9. *Scheck etc* (an)nehmen; *Rat* annehmen: → **advice** 1, **blame** 4, **tip³** 7. 10. *Kritik etc* hinnehmen. 11. fassen; Platz bieten für. 12. *et.* aushalten, ertragen. 13. dauern: **it took him two hours to do it** er brauchte zwei Stunden, um es zu tun. 14. *Prüfung, Spaziergang etc* machen; *Schritte* unternehmen; *Risiko* eingehen: → **oath** 1, **risk** I, **step** 4, **trouble** 7, *etc*. 15. *Medizin etc* nehmen: → **take down** 4. 17. **be** ~ **n by** (*od. with*) angetan sein von. 18. **he's got what it** ~**s** F er bringt alle Voraussetzungen mit. **III** *v/i* (*irr*) 19. ✿ wirken, anschlagen.

Verbindungen mit Präpositionen:

take | **af·ter** *v/i* j-m nachschlagen; j-m ähneln. ~ **for** *v/t:* **what do you take me for?** wofür hältst du mich eigentlich? ~ **from** *v/t* 1. **take s.th. from s.o.** j-m et. wegnehmen. 2. ♉ abziehen von. *Single* auskoppeln aus (*e-m Album*). 4. **you can take it from me that** du kannst mir glauben, daß. ~ **to** *v/t* 1. Gefallen finden an (*dat*). 2. ~ **doing s.th.** anfangen, et. zu tun. 3. ~ **flight** sich flüchten *od.* zurückziehen in (*acc*): ~ **one's bed** ins Bett gehen; → **heel²** 1.

Verbindungen mit Adverbien:

take | **a·long** *v/t* mitnehmen. ~ **a·part** *v/t* auseinandernehmen (*a. fig.* F), zerlegen. ~ **a·side** *v/t* j-n beiseite nehmen. ~ **a·way** I *v/t* 1. wegnehmen (**from s.o.** j-m). 2. ... **to** ~ *Br.* ... zum Mitnehmen (*Essen*). **II** *v/i* 3. ~ **from s.th.** e-r Sache Abbruch tun, et. schmälern. ~ **back** *v/t* 1. ✕ zurückerobern. 2. zurückbringen. 3. *Ware, et. Gesagtes* zurücknehmen. 4. bei j-m Erinnerungen wachrufen; j-n zurückversetzen (**to** in *acc*). ~ **down** *v/t* 1. herunternehmen; *Plakat* etc abnehmen. 2. *Hose* herunterlassen. 3. auseinandernehmen, zerlegen. 4. (sich) *et.* aufschreiben *od.* notieren, sich *Notizen* machen. ~ **in** *v/t* 1. j-n (bei sich) aufnehmen: → **lodger**. 2. *fig. et.* einschließen.

3. *Kleidungsstück* enger machen. **4.** *et.* begreifen. **5.** *j-n* hereinlegen: *be taken in by* hereinfallen auf (*acc*). **~ off I** *v/t* **1.** *Kleidungsstück* ablegen, ausziehen, *Hut etc* abnehmen. **2.** ♣ abnehmen, amputieren. **3.** *Theaterstück etc* absetzen. **4.** → *off* 9. **5.** ♣ *Rabatt etc* abziehen. **6.** F *j-n* nachahmen, -machen. **II** *v/i* **7.** ✈ abheben. **8.** *Sport*: abspringen. **9.** F sich aufmachen. **~ on** *v/t* **1.** *j-n* einstellen. **2.** *Arbeit etc* an-, übernehmen. **3.** *Ausdruck, Farbe etc* annehmen. **4.** sich anlegen mit. **~ out** *v/t* **1.** herausnehmen, *Zahn* ziehen: *take s.o. out of himself* j-n auf andere Gedanken bringen. **2.** *j-n* ausführen, ausgehen mit. **3.** *Versicherung* abschließen. **4.** *s-n Frust etc* auslassen (*on* an *dat*): *take it out on s.o.* sich an j-m abreagieren. **~o·ver I** *v/t* *Amt, Macht, Verantwortung etc* übernehmen. **II** *v/i* die Macht übernehmen. **~ up I** *v/t* **1.** *Flüssigkeit* aufnehmen, -saugen. **2.** *Aufmerksamkeit, Zeit* in Anspruch nehmen, *Platz* einnehmen: *be taken up with* stark in Anspruch genommen sein von. **3.** *Vorschlag etc* aufgreifen. **4.** **~** *doing s.th.* anfangen, sich mit et. zu beschäftigen. **5.** *take s.o. up on his offer* auf j-s Angebot zurückkommen. **6.** *Erzählung etc* aufnehmen, fortfahren mit. **II** *v/i* **1.** sich einlassen (*with* mit).

'**take·a·way** *s Br.* **1.** Essen *n* zum Mitnehmen. **2.** Restaurant *n* mit Straßenverkauf. '**~home** *adj*: **~ pay** Nettolohn *m*, -gehalt *n*.

tak·en ['teɪkən] *pp von* **take.**

'**take·off** *s* **1.** ✈ Abheben *n*; Start *m*: → *ready* 1. **2.** *Sport*: Absprung *m*. **3.** F Nachahmung *f*: *do a* **~** *of* → *take off* 6. '**~·out** *Am.* → **takeaway.** '**~·o·ver** *s bsd.* ♣ Übernahme *f*.

tak·er ['teɪkə] *s* Interessent(in). '**tak·ings** *s pl* Einnahmen *pl.*

talc [tælk] *s* **1.** *min.* Talk *m.* **2.** → *talcum powder.*

tal·cum pow·der ['tælkəm] *s* Talkumpuder *m*; Körperpuder *m.*

tale [teɪl] *s* **1.** Erzählung *f*; Geschichte *f*: *tell* **~***s* petzen; *tell* **~***s about j-n* verpetzen; *tell* **~** *s out of school fig.* aus der Schule plaudern; → *fairy tale, old* 1. **2.** Lüge(ngeschichte) *f*, Märchen *n.*

tal·ent ['tælənt] *s* Talent *n* (*a. Person*),

Begabung *f*; *coll.* Talente *pl* (*Personen*): **~ for acting** schauspielerisches Talent; *have great* **~** sehr begabt sein; *have a great* **~ for music** musikalisch sehr begabt sein; **~ scout** (*bsd. Sport*) Talentsucher(in). '**tal·ent·ed** *adj* talentiert, begabt.

tal·is·man ['tælɪzmən] *s* Talisman *m.*

talk [tɔːk] *I s* **1.** Gespräch *n* (*a. pol. etc*), Unterhaltung *f* (*with* mit; *about* über *acc*): *have a long* **~** *with s.o.* ein langes Gespräch mit j-m führen, sich lange mit j-m unterhalten. **2.** Sprache *f* (*Art zu reden*): → *baby talk.* **3.** Gerede *n*: *there is a lot of* **~** *about* es ist viel die Rede von; *be the* **~** *of the town* Stadtgespräch sein; → *small* I. **4.** Vortrag *m*: *give a* **~** e-n Vortrag halten (*to* vor *dat*; *about, on* über *acc*). **II** *v/i* **5.** reden, sprechen, sich unterhalten (*to, with* mit; *about* über *acc*; *of* von): **~** *about s.th. a.* et. besprechen; *get o.s.* **~** *ed about* ins Gerede kommen; **~***ing of* da wir gerade von ... sprechen; **~** *round s.th.* um et. herumreden; *you can* **~***!, look who's* **~***ing!, you're a fine one to* **~***!* F das sagst ausgerechnet du!; → *all* 3, *big* 7, *devil* 1, *hat.* **III** *v/t* **6.** *Unsinn etc* reden. **7.** reden *od.* sprechen *od.* sich unterhalten über (*acc*): → *shop* 3. **8.** **~** *s.o. into s.th.* j-n zu et. überreden; **~** *s.o. into doing s.th.* j-n überreden, et. zu tun; **~** *s.o. out of s.th.* j-m et. ausreden; **~** *s.o. out of doing s.th.* es j-m ausreden, et. zu tun; **~** *one's way out of s.th.* sich aus et. herausreden.

Verbindungen mit Adverbien:

talk down I *v/t Flugzeug* heruntersprechen. **II** *v/i*: **~** *to s.o.* herablassend mit j-m reden. **~ out** *v/t Problem etc* ausdiskutieren. **~ o·ver** *v/t Problem etc* besprechen (*with* mit). **~ round** *v/t j-n* bekehren (*to* zu), umstimmen.

talk·a·tive ['tɔːkətɪv] *adj* □ gesprächig, redselig. '**talk·er** *s*: *be a good* **~** gut reden können. '**talk·ing I** *s* Sprechen *n*, Reden *n*: *do all the* **~** allein das Wort führen. **II** *adj* sprechend: **~ doll** Sprechpuppe *f*; **~ point** Gesprächsthema *n*; Streitpunkt *m.* '**talk·ing-to** *pl* **-tos** *s* F Standpauke *f*: *give s.o. a* **~** j-m e-e Standpauke halten.

talk show *s TV bsd. Am.* Talk-Show *f.*

tall [tɔːl] *adj* **1.** groß (*Person*), hoch (*Ge-*

bäude etc). **2.** F unglaublich (*Geschichte*): **that's a ~ order** das ist ein bißchen viel verlangt.

tal·low ['tæləʊ] *s* Talg *m*.

tal·ly ['tælɪ] I *s Sport etc*: Stand *m*: **keep a ~ of** Buch führen über (*acc*). II *v/i* übereinstimmen (**with** mit). III *v/t a.* **~ up** zs.-rechnen, -zählen.

tal·on ['tælən] *s orn.* Kralle *f*, Klaue *f*.

tam·bour ['tæmˌbʊə] *s* Stickrahmen *m*.

tam·bou·rine [ˌ~bə'riːn] *s* ♩ Tamburin *n*.

tame [teɪm] I *adj* □ **1.** *zo.* zahm. **2.** F fad, lahm. II *v/t* **3.** Tier zähmen; *Leidenschaft etc* (be)zähmen.

tam·per ['tæmpə] *v/i:* **~ with** sich zu schaffen machen an (*dat*).

tam·pon ['tæmpɒn] *s* ✚ Tampon *m*.

tan [tæn] I *v/t* **1.** *j-n, Haut* bräunen. **2.** *Fell* gerben; → **hide**[1] I. II *v/i* **3.** bräunen, braun werden. III *s* **4.** Bräune *f*. IV *adj* **5.** gelbbraun.

tan·dem ['tændəm] *s* Tandem *n:* **in ~** *fig.* zusammen, gemeinsam (**with** mit).

tang [tæŋ] *s* (scharfer) Geruch *od.* Geschmack.

tan·gent ['tændʒənt] *s* Å Tangente *f:* **fly** (*od.* **go**) **off at a ~** *fig.* plötzlich (vom Thema) abschweifen.

tan·ger·ine [ˌtændʒə'riːn] *s* ♣ Mandarine *f*.

tan·gi·ble ['tændʒəbl] *adj* greifbar, *fig. a.* handfest.

tan·gle ['tæŋgl] I *v/t* **1.** *a.* **~ up** verwirren, durcheinanderbringen (*beide a. fig.*), verheddern: **get ~d** → **2.** II *v/i* **2.** sich verwirren, durcheinanderkommen, sich verheddern (*alle a. fig.*). **3.** *~* **with** F aneinandergeraten mit. III *s* **4.** Gewirr *n, fig. a.* Wirrwarr *m*, Durcheinander *n*.

tan·go ['tæŋgəʊ] I *pl* **-gos** *s* ♩ Tango *m*. II *v/i* Tango tanzen: **it takes two to ~** *fig.* dazu gehören zwei.

tank [tæŋk] *s* **1.** *mot. etc* Tank *m*. **2.** ✗ Panzer *m*. II *v/t* **3.** **~ed up** *Br.* F voll (betrunken).

tank·ard ['tæŋkəd] *s* (Bier)Humpen *m*.

tank·er ['tæŋkə] *s* ⚓ Tanker *m*, Tankschiff *n; mot.* Tank-, ⚙ *a.* Kesselwagen *m*.

tan·ta·lize ['tæntəlaɪz] *v/t j-n* aufreizen; hinhalten (**with** mit). **'tan·ta·liz·ing** *adj* □ verlockend.

tan·ta·mount ['tæntəmaʊnt] *adj:* **be ~ to**

gleichbedeutend sein mit, hinauslaufen auf (*acc*).

tan·trum ['tæntrəm] *s* Koller *m:* **fly into** (*od.* **throw**) **a ~** e-n Koller kriegen.

tap[1] [tæp] I *v/t* **1.** a) → **3:** **~ s.o. on the shoulder** *j-m* auf die Schulter klopfen, b) antippen. **2.** mit *den Fingern, Füßen* klopfen (**on** auf *acc*), mit *den Fingern* trommeln (**on** auf *acc, dat*). II *v/i* **3.** **~ on** (leicht) klopfen an (*acc*) *od.* auf (*acc*) *od.* gegen. III *s* **4.** (leichtes) Klopfen; Klaps *m*.

tap[2] [~] *s* **1.** ⚙ Hahn *m:* **beer on ~** Bier vom Faß; **have s.th. on ~** *fig.* et. zur Hand *od.* auf Lager haben. II *v/t* **2.** *Faß* anzapfen, anstechen. **3.** *Telefon(leitung)* anzapfen, abhören. **4.** *Naturschätze etc* erschließen; *Vorräte etc* angreifen. **5.** **~ for** *Br.* F *j-n* anpumpen *od.* anzapfen um.

tape [teɪp] I *s* **1.** *allg.* Band *n;* (*Video-etc*)Kassette *f*. **2.** (Band)Aufnahme *f;* *TV* Aufzeichnung *f*. **3.** *Sport:* Zielband *n:* → **breast** II. **4.** → **tape measure.** II *v/t* **5.** *a.* **~ up** (mit Klebeband) zukleben. **6.** (auf Band) aufnehmen; *TV* aufzeichnen: **~d music** Musik *f* vom Band. **~ deck** *s* Tapedeck *n* (*in i-e Stereoanlage eingebauter*) *Kassettenrecorder ohne eigenen Verstärker u. Lautsprecher*). **~ meas·ure** *s* Maß-, Meßband *n*, Bandmaß *n*.

ta·per ['teɪpə] *v/i* **1.** *a.* **~ off** spitz zulaufen, sich verjüngen. **2.** *a.* **~ off** *fig.* langsam nachlassen.

'tape|-re·cord → **tape 6.** **~ re·cord·er** *s* Tonbandgerät *n*.

ta·pes·try ['tæpɪstrɪ] *s* Gobelin *m*, Wandteppich *m*.

'tape·worm *s zo.* Bandwurm *m*.

tap wa·ter *s* Leitungswasser *n*.

tar [tɑː] *s* **1.** Teer *m*. II *v/t* teeren: **~ and feather** *j-n* teeren u. federn; **they are all ~red with the same brush** *fig. contp.* sie sind alle gleich.

ta·ran·tu·la [tə'ræntjʊlə] *s zo.* Tarantel *f*.

tar·dy ['tɑːdɪ] *adj* □ spät, verspätet.

tare [teə] *s* ✚ Tara *f*.

tar·get ['tɑːgɪt] *s* **1.** (Schieß-, Ziel-) Scheibe *f*, *fig.* Zielscheibe *f* (*des Spotts etc*). **2.** ✗ Ziel *n* (*a. fig.*); ✚ *a.* Soll *n:* **set o.s. a ~ of doing s.th.** sich zum Ziel setzen, et. zu tun. II *v/t* **3.** **be ~ed at** (*od.* **on**) gerichtet sein auf (*acc*); *fig.* abzielen auf (acc). **~ group** s Zielgruppe f. **~ lan·guage** s Zielsprache f.

tar·iff ['tærɪf] s **1.** Zoll(tarif) m. **2.** bsd. Br. Preisverzeichnis n (in Hotel etc).

tar·mac ['tɑːmæk] s **1.** Asphalt m. **2.** ✈ Rollfeld n.

tar·nish ['tɑːnɪʃ] **I** v/t Ansehen etc beflekken. **II** v/i anlaufen (Metall).

tar·pau·lin [tɑːˈpɔːlɪn] s Plane f; ⚓ Persenning f.

tar·ra·gon ['tærəgən] s ⚘ Estragon m.

tart¹ [tɑːt] adj □ **1.** herb; sauer. **2.** fig. scharf, beißend.

tart² [~] s **1.** Obstkuchen m; Obsttörtchen n. **2.** F Flittchen n; Nutte f.

tar·tan ['tɑːtən] s Schottenstoff m; Schottenmuster n.

tar·tar ['tɑːtə] s � Weinstein m; Zahnstein m.

task [tɑːsk] s Aufgabe f: **take s.o. to ~** fig. j-n zurechtweisen (**for** wegen). **~ force** s ✗ Sonder-, Spezialeinheit f (a. der Polizei).

tas·sel ['tæsl] s Troddel f, Quaste f.

taste [teɪst] **I** s **1.** Geschmack(ssinn) m: → **sense** 1. **2.** Geschmack m: **have no ~** nach nichts schmecken; **leave a bad ~ in s.o.'s mouth** fig. e-n bitteren od. schlechten Nachgeschmack bei j-m hinterlassen. **3.** Kostprobe f: **have a ~ of** a) → 6, b) fig. e-n Vorgeschmack bekommen von. **4.** fig. Geschmack m: **to s.o.'s ~** nach j-s Geschmack; **be in bad** (od. **poor**) **~** geschmacklos sein; → **account** 3, **matter** 3. **5.** fig. Vorliebe f (**for** für). **II** v/t **6.** kosten, probieren. **7.** schmecken. **8.** fig. kosten, erleben, kennenlernen. **III** v/i **9.** schmecken (**of** nach). **taste·ful** ['~fʊl] adj □ fig. geschmackvoll. **'taste·less** adj □ geschmacklos (a. fig.). **'tast·y** adj □ schmackhaft.

tat [tæt] → **tit¹**.

ta·ta [ˌtæˈtɑː] int Br. F tschüs!

tat·tered ['tætəd] adj zerlumpt (Kleidung, Person); fig. ruiniert, ramponiert (Ruf etc). **'tat·ters** s pl Fetzen pl, Lumpen pl: **be in ~** zerlumpt sein (Kleidung); fig. ruiniert od. ramponiert sein (Ruf etc).

tat·tle ['tætl] F **I** v/i klatschen, tratschen. **II** s Klatsch m, Tratsch m.

tat·too¹ [təˈtuː] **I** v/t **1.** tätowieren. **2.**

Muster etc eintätowieren (**on** in acc). **II** s **3.** Tätowierung f.

tat·too² [~] s ✗ Zapfenstreich m; (mst abendliche) Musikparade.

tat·ty ['tætɪ] adj □ bsd. Br. F schäbig (Kleidung, Möbel etc).

taught [tɔːt] pret u. pp von **teach**.

taunt [tɔːnt] **I** v/t verhöhnen, -spotten (**for, with** wegen). **II** s höhnische od. spöttische Bemerkung.

Tau·rus ['tɔːrəs] s ast. Stier m: **be** (a) **~** Stier sein.

taut [tɔːt] adj □ **1.** straff (Seil etc). **2.** fig. angespannt (Gesichtsausdruck etc). **'taut·en** v/t spannen, straffen, straff anziehen. **II** v/i sich spannen od. straffen.

tau·tol·o·gy [tɔːˈtɒlədʒɪ] s rhet. Tautologie f.

taw·dry ['tɔːdrɪ] adj □ (billig u.) geschmacklos.

taw·ny ['tɔːnɪ] adj gelbbraun.

tax [tæks] **I** s **1.** Steuer f (**on** auf acc): **before** (**after**) **~** vor (nach) Abzug der Steuern, brutto (netto); → **put** 2. **II** v/t **2.** besteuern. **3.** fig. j-s Geduld etc strapazieren. **'tax·a·ble** adj steuerpflichtig.

tax·a·tion s Besteuerung f.

tax| brack·et s Steuergruppe f, -klasse f. **,~·de'duct·i·ble** adj (steuerlich) absetzbar. **~ e·va·sion** s Steuerhinterziehung f. **,~·'free** adj u. adv steuerfrei. **~ ha·ven** s Steueroase f, -paradies n.

tax·i ['tæksɪ] **I** s Taxi n, Taxe f. **II** v/i ✈ rollen. **'~·cab** → **taxi** I. **~ driv·er** s Taxifahrer(in). **'~·me·ter** s Taxameter m, n, Fahrpreisanzeiger m.

tax·ing ['tæksɪŋ] adj anstrengend.

tax·i| rank, ~ stand s Taxistand m.

'tax|·pay·er s Steuerzahler(in). **~ rate** s Steuersatz m. **~ rea·sons** pl steuerliche Gründe pl. **~ re·turn** s Steuererklärung f.

'T-bone (**steak**) s T-bone-Steak n (Steak aus dem Rippenstück des Rinds).

tea [tiː] s Tee m: **not for all the ~ in China** nicht um alles in der Welt; → **cup** 1, **high tea. ~ bag** s Tee-, Aufgußbeutel m. **~ break** s Teepause f. **~ cad·dy** s Teebüchse f, -dose f.

teach [tiːtʃ] (irr) **I** v/t **1.** Fach lehren, unterrichten. **2.** j-n, a. j-m et. lehren, j-n unterrichten in (dat); j-m et. beibringen: **~ s.o. a lesson** fig. j-m e-e Lektion erteilen. **II** v/i **3.** unterrichten (*at* an e-r *Schule*). **'teach·er** s Lehrer(in). **'teach·ing** s **1.** Unterrichten n; Lehrberuf m. **2.** Lehre f.

tea| cloth s → **tea towel.** **~ co·sy** (*Am.* **co·zy**) s Teewärmer m. **'~cup** s Teetasse f: → **storm** 1. **'~house** s Teehaus n.

teak [tiːk] s Teak(holz) n.

'tea| ket·tle s Tee-, Wasserkessel m. **'~leaf** s (*irr* leaf) **1.** Teeblatt n. **2.** Br. sl. Langfinger m.

team [tiːm] **I** s **1.** Sport: Mannschaft f, Team n, allg. a. Gruppe f. **2.** Gespann n. **II** v/i **3.** ~ up sich zs.-tun (*with* mit). ~ **ef·fort** s Teamwork n: *by a* ~ mit vereinten Kräften. **~ game** s Sport: Mannschaftsspiel n. **'~mate** s Sport: Mannschaftskamerad(in). **~ spir·it** s Sport: Mannschaftsgeist m; allg. Gemeinschaftsgeist m.

team·ster ['tiːmstə] s LKW-Fahrer m. **'team·work** s Sport: Mannschafts-, Zs.-spiel n; allg. Teamwork n.

tea| par·ty s Teegesellschaft f. **'~pot** s Teekanne f: → **tempest**.

tear¹ [tɪə] s Träne f: *be almost in* ~s den Tränen nahe sein, fast weinen; ~s *pl of joy* Freudentränen pl; → **burst** 3, *near* 3, *roll* 7, *run* 11.

tear² [teə] **I** s **1.** Riß m. **II** v/t (*irr*) **2.** zerreißen; sich ef. zerreißen (*on* an dat); *~ a muscle* sich e-n Muskel reißen, sich e-n Muskelriß zuziehen; *torn muscle* Muskelriß m; → **piece** 1, *shred* 1. **3.** weg-, losreißen (*from* von): ~ *s.th. from s.o.* a. j-m et. entreißen; → **hair.** **4.** *be torn between ... and* hin- u. hergerissen sein zwischen (dat) ... u. **III** v/i (*irr*) **5.** (zer)reißen. **6.** F rasen, sausen. **7.** *~ into s.o.* F über j-n herfallen (a. mit Worten).

Verbindungen mit Adverbien:

tear| a·way v/t weg-, losreißen (*from* von) (a. fig.). **~ down** v/t **1.** Plakat etc herunterreißen. **2.** Haus etc abreißen. **~ off** v/t **1.** abreißen; abtrennen. **2.** sich Kleidung vom Leib reißen. **3.** F Aufsatz etc hinhauen. **~ out** v/t (her)ausreißen (*of* aus); Baum entwurzeln: → **hair.** **~ up** v/t **1.** aufreißen. **2.** zerreißen.

tear·drop ['tɪədrɒp] s Träne f. **tear·ful** ['tɪəfʊl] adj □ **1.** weinend. **2.** tränenreich (Abschied etc).

tear gas [tɪə] s Tränengas n.

tear·ing ['teərɪŋ] adj: *be in a* ~ *hurry* F es schrecklich eilig haben.

tear-jerk·er ['tɪədʒɜːkə] s F Schmachtfetzen m.

tear-off ['teərɒf] adj: ~ *calendar* Abreißkalender m.

tea·room ['~ruːm] s Teestube f.

tease [tiːz] **I** v/t j-n, Tier necken, j-n hänseln (*about* wegen); j-n, Tier reizen. **II** v/i: *he is only teasing* er macht nur Spaß. **III** s Necker(in), Hänsler(in). **'teas·er** s **1.** → **tease** III. **2.** F harte Nuß.

tea| ser·vice, ~ **set** s Teeservice n. **'~spoon** s Teelöffel m.

teat [tiːt] s **1.** zo. Zitze f. **2.** Br. (Gummi)Sauger m (e-r Saugflasche).

tea| tow·el s bsd. Br. Geschirrtuch n. ~ **trol·ley** s bsd. Br., ~ **wag·on** s bsd. Am. Tee-, Servierwagen m.

tech·ni·cal ['teknɪkl] adj □ **1.** allg. technisch: ~ *knockout* KO durch technischer K. o. **2.** fachlich, Fach...: ~ *term* Fachausdruck m. **tech·ni·cal·i·ty** [~'kælətɪ] s technische Einzelheit. **tech'ni·cian** [~ʃn] s Techniker(in).

tech·nique [tek'niːk] s **1.** ⚙ Technik f, Verfahren n. **2.** ♪, paint., Sport etc: Technik f.

tech·no·crat ['teknəʊkræt] s Technokrat(in).

tech·no·log·i·cal [,teknə'lɒdʒɪkl] adj □ technologisch; technisch. **tech·nol·o·gist** [~'nɒlədʒɪst] s Technologe m, Technologin f. **tech'nol·o·gy** s Technologie f; Technik f.

ted·dy (**bear**) ['tedɪ] s Teddy(bär) m.

te·di·ous ['tiːdjəs] adj □ langweilig. **te·di·um** ['~djəm] s Langweiligkeit f.

teem¹ [tiːm] v/i (*with*) wimmeln (von); strotzen (von, vor dat): *the square was ~ing with people* auf dem Platz wimmelte es von Menschen.

teem² [~] v/i: *it is ~ing with rain* es regnet in Strömen.

teen·age(d) ['tiːneɪdʒ(d)] adj **1.** im Teenageralter. **2.** Teenager..., für Teenager. **'teen,ag·er** s Teenager m.

teens [tiːnz] s pl: *be in one's* ~ im Teenageralter sein.

tee·ny ['tiːnɪ], **tee·ny-wee·ny** [~'wiːnɪ] adj F klitzeklein, winzig.

tee shirt [tiː] s T-Shirt n.

tee·ter ['tiːtə] v/i (sch)wanken.

teeth [tiːθ] *pl von* **tooth.**

teethe [tiːð] *v/i* zahnen. **'teeth·ing** *adj:* ~ **troubles** *pl fig.* Kinderkrankheiten *pl.*

tee·to·tal·er *s Am.,* **tee·to·tal·ler** *s bsd. Br.* [tiː'təʊtlə] *s* Abstinenzler(in).

tel·e·cast ['telɪkɑːst] **I** *v/t (mst irr)* im Fernsehen übertragen *od.* bringen. **II** *s* Fernsehsendung *f.*

tel·e·com·mu·ni·ca·tions ['telɪkəˌmjuːnɪ'keɪʃnz] *s pl* Telekommunikation *f,* Fernmeldewesen *n.* ~ **sat·el·lite** *s* Fernmelde-, Nachrichtensatellit *m.*

tel·e·gen·ic [ˌtelɪ'dʒenɪk] *adj* (~**ally**) *TV* telegen.

tel·e·gram ['telɪgræm] *s* Telegramm *n:* **by** ~ telegrafisch.

tel·e·graph ['telɪgrɑːf] **I** *s:* **by** ~ telegrafisch. **II** *v/t j-m et.* telegrafieren. **tel·e·graph·ese** [ˌ~grɑː'fiːz] *s* Telegrammstil *m.* **tel·e·graph·ic** [ˌ~'græfɪk] *adj* (~**ally**) telegrafisch. **te·leg·ra·phy** [tɪ'legrəfɪ] *s* Telegrafie *f.*

te·lep·a·thy [tɪ'lepəθɪ] *s* Telepathie *f,* Gedankenübertragung *f.*

tel·e·phone ['telɪfəʊn] **I** *s* **1.** Telefon *n:* **by** ~ telefonisch; **be on the** ~ Telefon(anschluß) haben; am Telefon sein. **2.** Hörer *m.* **II** *v/i* **3.** telefonieren, anrufen. **III** *v/t* **4.** anrufen; ~ **s.th. to s.o.** *j-m et.* telefonisch durchgeben. **IV** *adj* **5.** Telefon...: ~ **booth** (*Br.* **box**) Telefon-, Fernsprechzelle *f;* ~ **call** Telefonanruf *m,* -gespräch *n;* ~ **directory** Telefon-, Fernsprechbuch *n;* ~ **exchange** Fernsprechamt *n;* ~ **number** Telefonnummer *f.* **te·leph·o·nist** [tɪ'lefənɪst] *s bsd. Br.* Telefonist(in).

tel·e·pho·to lens ['telɪˌfəʊtəʊ] *s phot.* Teleobjektiv *n.*

tel·e·print·er ['telɪˌprɪntə] *s* ⊕ Fernschreiber *m.*

tel·e·scope ['telɪskəʊp] **I** *s* **1.** Teleskop *n,* Fernrohr *n.* **II** *v/t* **2.** *a.* ~ **together** *vs* ~, ineinanderschieben. **3.** *fig.* verkürzen, komprimieren (*into* zu). **III** *v/i* **4.** sich zs.-*od.* ineinanderschieben (lassen). **tel·e·scop·ic** [ˌ~'skɒpɪk] *adj* (~**ally**) **1.** teleskopisch: ~ **sight** Zielfernrohr *n.* **2.** ausziehbar: ~ **aerial** (*bsd. Am.* **antenna**) Teleskopantenne *f;* ~ **umbrella** Taschenschirm *m.*

tel·e·text ['telɪtekst] *s* Bildschirmtext *m.*

tel·e·vise ['telɪvaɪz] → **telecast** I.

tel·e·vi·sion ['~ˌvɪʒn] **I** *s* **1.** Fernsehen *n:* **on** (**the**) ~ im Fernsehen; **watch** ~ fernsehen; **work in** ~ beim Fernsehen beschäftigt sein. **2.** Fernsehapparat *m,* -gerät *n.* **II** *adj* **3.** Fernseh...: ~ **set** → **2.**

tel·ex ['teleks] *s* **1.** Telex *n,* Fernschreiben *n.* **2.** ⊕ Fernschreiber *m.*

tell [tel] (*irr*) **I** *v/t* **1.** sagen, erzählen: **I can't** ~ **you how ...** ich kann dir gar nicht sagen, wie ...; **you are** ~**ing me!** F wem sagst du das!; → **another** **2. 2.** *Geschichte etc* erzählen: → **tale 1. 3.** *s-n Namen etc* nennen; *Grund etc* angeben; *Zeit* anzeigen (*Uhr*). **4.** (mit Bestimmtheit) sagen; erkennen (**by** an *dat*): **I can't** ~ **one from the other, I can't** ~ **them apart** ich kann sie nicht auseinanderhalten. **5.** *j-m* sagen, befehlen (**to do** zu tun). **6.** ~ **off** F *j-m* Bescheid stoßen (**for** wegen). **II** *v/i* **7.** wie *od.* was ~? wer weiß?; **you can never** (*od.* **never can**) ~ man kann nie wissen. **8.** ~ **on s.o.** *j-n* verpetzen *od.* verraten. **9.** sich auswirken (**on** bei, auf *acc*); sich bemerkbar machen: ~ **against** sprechen gegen; von Nachteil sein für. **'tell·er** *s bsd. Am.* Kassierer(in) (*e-r Bank*).

tell·ing ['telɪŋ] *adj* □ **1.** aufschlußreich. **2.** schlagend (*Argument*). ~**'off** *s:* **give s.o. a** (**good**) ~ F *j-m* (kräftig) Bescheid stoßen (**for** wegen).

'tell·tale I *adj* verräterisch. **II** *s* F Zuträger(in), Petze *f.*

tel·ly ['telɪ] *s bsd. Br.* F **1.** → **television 1. 2.** Fernseher *m* (*Gerät*).

te·mer·i·ty [tɪ'merətɪ] *s* Kühnheit *f,* Frechheit *f.*

temp [temp] *Br.* F **I** *s* (*von e-r Agentur vermittelte*) Zeitsekretärin *f.* **II** *v/i* als Zeitsekretärin arbeiten.

tem·per ['tempə] **I** *v/t* **1.** Temperament *n,* Gemüt(sart *f*) *n,* Wesen(sart *f*) *n.* **2.** Laune *f,* Stimmung *f:* **be in a bad** ~ schlecht gelaunt sein; **keep one's** ~ ruhig bleiben; **lose one's** ~ die Beherrschung verlieren. **3.** F **be in a** ~ gereizt *od.* wütend sein; **fly into a** ~ an die Decke gehen; → **fit 1, work 8. II** *v/t* **4.** ⊕ *Stahl* härten. **tem·per·a·ment** ['~rəmənt] *s* **1.** → **temper 1. 2.** Temperament *n,* Lebhaftigkeit *f.* **tem·per·a·men·tal** [ˌ~rə'mentl] *adj* □ **1.** reizbar; launisch. **2.** veranlagungsmäßig, anlagebedingt: ~**ly** *a.* von der Veranlagung her, von Natur aus.

tem·per·ate ['tempərət] *adj* gemäßigt (*Klima, Zone*).

tem·per·a·ture ['temprətʃə] *s* Temperatur *f*: **have** (*od.* **be running**) **a ~** erhöhte Temperatur *od.* Fieber haben; **take s.o.'s ~** j-s Temperatur messen.

tem·pest ['tempist] *s* (heftiger) Sturm (*poet. außer in*): **~ in a teapot** *Am. fig.* Sturm im Wasserglas. **tem·pes·tu·ous** [~'pestjuəs] *adj* □ *poet. od. fig.* stürmisch.

tem·pi [tempi:] *pl von* **tempo**.
tem·ple¹ ['templ] *s* Tempel *m*.
tem·ple² [~] *s anat.* Schläfe *f*.
tem·po ['tempəʊ] *pl* **-pos, -pi** ['~pi:] *s* ♩ Tempo *n* (*a. fig.*).

tem·po·ral¹ ['tempərəl] *adj* □ **1.** weltlich. **2.** *ling.* temporal, Zeit..., der Zeit.
tem·po·ral² [~] *adj anat.* Schläfen...: **~ bone** Schläfenbein *n*.
tem·po·rar·y ['tempərəri] *adj* □ vorübergehend, zeitweilig. **'tem·po·rize** *v/i* Zeit zu gewinnen suchen.

tempt [tempt] *v/t* **1.** j-n in Versuchung führen (*a. eccl.*); j-n verführen (**to** *zu*; **to do** [*od.* **into doing**] **s.th.** dazu, et. zu tun): **be ~ed to do s.th.** versucht *od.* geneigt sein, et. zu tun. **2. ~ fate** (*od.* **providence**) das Schicksal herausfordern. **temp·ta·tion** *s* Versuchung *f* (*a. eccl.*), Verführung *f*. **'tempt·er** *s* Verführer *m*. **'tempt·ing** *adj* □ verführerisch. **'tempt·ress** *s* Verführerin *f*.

ten [ten] **I** *adj* **1.** zehn. **II** *s* **2.** Zehn *f*: **~ of hearts** Herzzehn *f*; **~s** *pl* **of thousands** Zehntausende *pl*. **3.** ⚖ Zehner *m*.
ten·a·ble ['tenəbl] *adj* haltbar (*Theorie etc*).
te·na·cious [tɪ'neɪʃəs] *adj* □ hartnäckig, zäh. **te·na·cious·ness, te·nac·i·ty** [tɪ'næsətɪ] *s* Hartnäckigkeit *f*, Zähigkeit *f*.
ten·an·cy ['tenənsɪ] *s* Pacht-, Mietdauer *f*.
ten·ant ['tenənt] *s* Pächter(in), Mieter(in).

tend¹ [tend] *v/i* neigen, tendieren (**to, toward[s]** *zu*): **~ to do s.th.** dazu neigen, et. zu tun; **~ upwards** e-e steigende Tendenz haben (*Preise etc*).
tend² [~] **I** *v/t* j-n pflegen, a. Wunde versorgen. **II** *v/i*: **~ to →** I.
tend·en·cy ['tendənsɪ] *s* Tendenz *f*; Neigung *f*: **have a ~ to** (*od.* **toward[s]**)

neigen *od.* tendieren zu; **have a ~ to do s.th.** dazu neigen, et. zu tun. **ten·den·tious** [~'denʃəs] *adj* □ tendenziös.

ten·der¹ ['tendə] *adj* □ **1.** empfindlich, *fig. a.* heikel: **→ spot** 4. **2.** zart, weich (*Fleisch*). **3.** zärtlich.
ten·der² [~] **I** *v/i* **1.** ✝ ein Angebot machen (**for** für). **II** *v/t* **2. → resignation** 1. **III** *s* **3.** ✝ Angebot *n*. **4.** *legal* ~ gesetzliches Zahlungsmittel.
ten·der³ [~] *s* ♆, 🚂 Tender *m*.
'ten·der·foot *s* (*a. irr* **foot**) *Am.* F Anfänger *m*, Neuling *m*. **'~heart·ed** *adj* □ weichherzig.
ten·der·ize ['tendəraɪz] *v/t* Fleisch zart *od.* weich machen.
'ten·der·loin *s* zartes Lendenstück.
ten·don ['tendən] *s anat.* Sehne *f*.
ten·dril ['tendrəl] *s* ♣ Ranke *f*.
ten·e·ment ['tenəmənt] *s* Mietshaus *n*. *contp.* Mietskaserne *f*.
ten·et ['tenɪt] *s* Lehr-, *eccl.* Glaubenssatz *m*.
ten·ner ['tenə] *s* F Zehner *m* (*Br. Zehnpfundschein, Am. Zehndollarschein*).
ten·fold ['tenfəʊld] **I** *adj* zehnfach. **II** *adv* zehnfach, um das Zehnfache: **increase ~** (sich) verzehnfachen.
ten·nis ['tenɪs] *s Sport:* Tennis *n*. **~ ball** *s* Tennisball *m*. **~ court** *s* Tennisplatz *m*. **~ el·bow** *s* ♞ Tennisarm *m*. **~ play·er** *s* Tennisspieler(in). **~ rack·et** *s* Tennisschläger *m*.
ten·or ['tenə] *s* **1.** ♩ Tenor *m*. **2.** Tenor *m*, Sinn *m*. **3.** Verlauf *m*.
'ten·pin *s* **1.** *Bowling:* Kegel *m*: **~ bowling** *Br.* Bowling *n*. **2.** *pl* (*sg konstruiert*) *Am.* Bowling *n*.
tense¹ [tens] *s ling.* Zeit *f*, Tempus *n*: **→ future** 4, **past** 3, **present** 3.
tense² [~] *adj* □ **1.** gespannt, straff (*Seil etc*), (an)gespannt (*Muskeln*). **2.** *fig.* (an)gespannt (*Lage etc*); (über)nervös (*Person*).
ten·sile ['tensaɪl] *adj* **1.** dehn-, spannbar. **2. ~ strength** Zug-, Zerreißfestigkeit *f*.
ten·sion ['tenʃn] *s* **1.** Spannung *f* (*a. ⚡*): **→ high tension**. **2.** *fig.* Anspannung *f*; Spannung(en *pl*) *f*.
tent [tent] *s* Zelt *n*.
ten·ta·cle ['tentəkl] *s zo.* Tentakel *m, n*: a) Fühler *m*, b) Fangarm *m*.
ten·ta·tive ['tentətɪv] *adj* □ **1.** vorläufig;

versuchsweise: **~ly** *a.* mit Vorbehalt. **2.** vorsichtig, zögernd.

ten·ter·hooks ['tentəhʊks] *s pl:* **be on ~** wie auf glühenden Kohlen sitzen; **keep s.o. on ~** j-n auf die Folter spannen.

tenth [tenθ] **I** *adj* **1.** zehnt. **II** *s* **2.** der, die, das Zehnte: **the ~ of May** der 10. Mai. **3.** Zehntel *n*: **a ~ of a second** e-e Zehntelsekunde. '**tenth·ly** *adv* zehntens.

'**ten-time** *adj* zehnmalig.

tent| peg *s* Hering *m*, Zeltpflock *m.* ~ **pole** *s* Zeltstange *f.*

ten·u·ous ['tenjʊəs] *adj* □ **1.** dünn (*Faden etc*). **2.** *fig.* lose (*Verbindung etc*); schwach (*Beweis etc*).

ten·ure ['te,njʊə] *s* **1.** Innehabung *f* (*e-s Amtes*), (*von Grundbesitz a.*) Besitz *m.* **2.** ~ **of office** Amtsdauer *f*, Dienstzeit *f.*

tep·id ['tepɪd] *adj* □ lau(warm) (*a. fig.*).

term [tɜːm] **I** *s* **1.** Zeit(raum *m*) *f*, Dauer *f*; Laufzeit *f* (*e-s Vertrags etc*): ~ **of imprisonment** ⚖ Freiheitsstrafe *f*; ~ **of office** Amtsdauer, -periode *f*, -zeit; **in the long (short)** ~ auf lange (kurze) Sicht. **2.** *ped., univ. bsd. Br.* Trimester *n.* **3.** Ausdruck *m*, Bezeichnung *f*: ~ **of abuse** Schimpfwort *n*, Beleidigung *f*; **in ~s of** was ... betrifft; **in ~s of money** finanziell (gesehen); **in no uncertain ~s** unmißverständlich; → **technical** 2. **4.** *pl* Bedingungen *pl*: ~**s of delivery** ✝ Liefer(ungs)bedingungen; **on one's own** ~**s** zu s-n Bedingungen; **come to ~s** sich einigen (**with** mit); **come to ~s with s.th.** sich mit et. abfinden; → **easy** 5. **5. be on friendly (good)** ~**s with** auf freundschaftlichem Fuß stehen (gut auskommen) mit; → **speaking** II. **II** *v/t* **6.** nennen, bezeichnen.

ter·mi·nal ['tɜːmɪnl] **I** *adj* □ **1.** ✈) unheilbar (unheilbar krank, b) im Endstadium, c) Sterbe...: ~ **clinic. II** *s* **2.** 🚇 *etc* Endstation *f*; → **air terminal.** **3.** *Computer:* Terminal *n.* **4.** 𝄪 (Anschluß)Klemme *f*; Pol *m* (*e-r Batterie*).

ter·mi·nate ['tɜːmɪneɪt] **I** *v/t* beenden; *Vertrag* kündigen, lösen; ✎ **Schwangerschaft** unterbrechen. **II** *v/i* enden; ablaufen (*Vertrag*). ,**ter·mi'na·tion** *s* **1.** Beendigung *f*; Kündigung *f*, Lösung *f*; ✎ (*Schwangerschafts*)Abbruch *m.* **2.** Ende *n*; Ablauf *m.*

ter·mi·ni ['tɜːmɪnaɪ] *pl von* **terminus.**

ter·mi·nol·o·gy [,tɜːmɪ'nɒlədʒɪ] *s* Terminologie *f*, Fachsprache *f.*

ter·mi·nus ['tɜːmɪnəs] *pl* **-ni** ['~naɪ], **-nus·es** *s* 🚇 *etc* Endstation *f.*

ter·mite ['tɜːmaɪt] *s zo.* Termite *f.*

ter·race ['terəs] *s* **1.** Terrasse *f.* **2.** *pl Sport: bsd. Br.* Ränge *pl.* **3.** Häuserreihe *f*, -zeile *f.* '**ter·raced** *adj:* ~ **house** *Br.* Reihenhaus *n.*

ter·ra·cot·ta [,terə'kɒtə] *s* Terrakotta *f.*

ter·rain [te'reɪn] *s* Gelände *n*, Terrain *n.*

ter·res·tri·al [tə'restrɪəl] *adj* □ **1.** irdisch. **2.** Erd...: ~ **globe** Erdball *m.* **3.** 🝥, *zo.* Land...

ter·ri·ble ['terəbl] *adj* □ schrecklich, furchtbar (*beide a. fig.* F).

ter·ri·er ['terɪə] *s zo.* Terrier *m.*

ter·rif·ic [tə'rɪfɪk] *adj* (**~ally**) F toll, phantastisch; wahnsinnig.

ter·ri·fy ['terɪfaɪ] *v/t* j-m schreckliche Angst einjagen: **spiders ~ me, I'm terrified of spiders** ich habe schreckliche Angst vor Spinnen.

ter·ri·to·ri·al [,terɪ'tɔːrɪəl] *adj* □ territorial, Gebiets...: ~ **claims** *pl* Gebietsansprüche *pl*; ~ **waters** *pl* Hoheitsgewässer *pl.* **ter·ri·to·ry** ['~tərɪ] *s* **1.** (a. Hoheits-, Staats)Gebiet *n*, Territorium *n.* **2.** *zo.* Revier *n.* **3.** *fig.* Gebiet *n.*

ter·ror ['terə] *s* **1.** Entsetzen *n*: **in ~** voller Entsetzen; **in panischer Angst; have a ~ of** panische Angst haben vor (*dat*). **2.** Terror *m.* **3.** Schrecken *m* (*Person, Sache*). **4.** F Landplage *f* (*bsd. Kind*). '**ter·ror·ism** *s* Terrorismus *m.* '**ter·ror·ist** *I s* Terrorist(in). **II** *adj* terroristisch, Terror... '**ter·ror·ize** *v/t* terrorisieren; einschüchtern.

ter·ry(**·cloth**) ['terɪ(klɒθ)] *s* Frottee *n, m.*

terse [tɜːs] *adj* □ knapp (*Antwort etc*).

tes·sel·at·ed ['tesəleɪtɪd] *adj* Mosaik...

test [test] **I** *s* **1.** *allg.* Test *m*: **put to the ~** auf die Probe stellen; **stand the ~ of time** die Zeit überdauern; → **driving test.** **2.** → **test match. II** *v/t* **3.** testen, prüfen. **4.** *j-s Geduld etc* auf e-e harte Probe stellen.

tes·ta·ment ['testəmənt] *s* **1.** → **will**[1] **2.** 2 *Bibl.* Altes, Neues Testament. **3.** *fig.* Zeugnis *n* (**to** gen). **tes·ta·men·ta·ry** [,~'mentərɪ] *adj* ⚖ testamentarisch.

tes·ta·tor [te'steɪtə] *s* ⚖ Erblasser *m.*

tes·ta·trix [te'steɪtrɪks] *pl* **-tri·ces** [ˌtrɪ-siːz] *s ⚖️* Erblasserin *f.*

test| ban trea·ty *s pol.* Teststoppabkommen *n.* ~ **card** *s TV Br.* Testbild *n.* ~ **case** *s ⚖️* Musterprozeß *m.* ~ **drive** *s mot.* Probefahrt *f:* **go for a** ~ e-e Probefahrt machen. '~**drive** *v/t (irr drive)* Auto probefahren.

tes·ter ['testə] *s* **1.** Tester(in), Prüfer(in). **2. ⊙** Test-, Prüfgerät *n.*

tes·ti·cle ['testɪkl] *s anat.* Hoden *m.*

tes·ti·fy ['testɪfaɪ] **I** *v/i* **1. ⚖️** aussagen *(for* für; *against* gegen). **2.** ~ *to* ein deutliches Zeichen sein für. **II** *v/t* **3.** ~ *that ⚖️* aussagen *od.* bezeugen, daß; *fig.* ein deutliches Zeichen dafür sein, daß.

tes·ti·mo·ni·al [ˌtestɪ'məʊnjəl] *s* **1.** Referenz *f.* **2.** Anerkennungsgeschenk *n.*

tes·ti·mo·ny ['~məni] *s* **1. ⚖️** Aussage *f.* **2. be (a)** ~ **of** *(od.* **to)** → **testify** 2.

test·ing ['testɪŋ] *adj:* ~ **times** *pl* harte Zeiten *pl.*

test| lamp *s ⊙* Prüflampe *f.* ~ **match** *s Kricket:* internationaler Vergleichskampf. ~ **pat·tern** *s TV Am.* Testbild *n.* ~ **pi·lot** *s ✈️* Testpilot *m.* ~ **tube** *s 🧪* Reagenzglas *n.* '~**tube ba·by** *s* Retortenbaby *n.*

tes·ty ['testɪ] *adj* □ gereizt *(Person, Antwort etc).*

tetch·y ['tetʃɪ] *adj* □ reizbar.

teth·er ['teðə] **I** *s* Strick *m;* Kette *f:* **be at the end of one's** ~ *fig.* mit s-n Nerven am Ende sein. **II** *v/t Tier* anbinden; anketten.

Teu·ton·ic [tjuː'tɒnɪk] *adj oft contp.* teutonisch, (typisch) deutsch.

text [tekst] *s* Text *m.* '~**book** *s* Lehrbuch *n.* **II** *adj* perfekt: ~ **example** Muster-, Paradebeispiel *n (of* für).

tex·tile ['tekstaɪl] **I** *s* Stoff *m.* ~**s** *pl* Textilien *pl.* **II** *adj* Textil...

tex·tu·al ['tekstjʊəl] *adj* □ textlich, Text...

tex·ture ['tekstʃə] *s* Textur *f,* Gewebe *n;* Beschaffenheit *f.*

tha·lid·o·mide [θə'lɪdəmaɪd] *s pharm.* Thalidomid *n,* Contergan *n:* ~ **baby** Contergankind *n.*

Thames [temz] *npr* Themse *f:* **he won't set the** ~ **on fire** *fig.* er hat das Pulver auch nicht (gerade) erfunden.

than [ðən] *cj* als.

thank [θæŋk] **I** *v/t j-m* danken, sich bei *j-m* bedanken *(for* für): ~ **you (very much)** danke (vielen Dank); **no,** ~ **you** nein, danke; **say "🎵 you"** sich bedanken; **he's only got himself to** ~ **that** er hat es sich selbst zuzuschreiben, daß; → **god** 2, **goodness** 2, **heaven** 1, **star** 1. **II** *s pl* Dank *m:* **with** ~**s** dankend, mit Dank; **(many)** ~**s** danke (vielen Dank); **no,** ~**s** nein, danke; **say "🎵s"** sich bedanken; ~**s to** dank *(gen),* wegen *(gen).*

thank·ful ['~fʊl] *adj* □ dankbar *(for* für); froh *(that* daß; □ **to be** zu sein): *~ly a.* zum Glück, Gott sei Dank. '**thank·less** *adj* undankbar *(Aufgabe etc).*

'**Thanks,giv·ing (Day)** *s Am.* Thanksgiving Day *m (Erntedankfest;* 4. Donnerstag *im November).*

'**thank-you** *s* Danke(schön) *n.* **II** *adj:* ~ **letter** Dankesbrief *m.*

that[1] [ðæt] **I** *pron u. adj* **1.** das: ~ **is (to say)** das heißt; **at** ~ zudem, obendrein; **let it go at** ~ F lassen wir es dabei bewenden; **and** ~'**s** u. damit basta. **2.** jener, jene, jenes: ~ **car over there** das Auto dort drüben; **those who** diejenigen, welche. **II** *adv* **3.** F so, dermaßen: **it's** ~ **simple** so einfach ist das.

that[2] [~] *relative pron* der, die, das, welcher, welche, welches: **everything** ~ alles, was.

that[3] [~] *cj* daß.

thatch [θætʃ] **I** *s* **1.** (Dach)Stroh *n,* Reet *n.* **2.** Stroh-, Reetdach *n.* **II** *v/t* **3.** mit Stroh *od.* Reet decken. ~**ed** stroh-, reetgedeckt.

thaw [θɔː] **I** *v/i* (auf)tauen, *(Tiefkühlkost, fig. Person)* auftauen: **it is** ~**ing** es taut. **II** *v/t* auftauen. **III** *s* Tauwetter *n (a. fig. pol.).*

the[1] [ðə, *vor Vokalen* ðɪ] *bestimmter Artikel* **1.** der, die, das, *pl* die. **2.** *vor Maßangaben:* **one dollar** ~ **pound** ein Dollar das *od.* pro Pfund.

the[2] [~] *adv:* ~ ... ~ ... je ... desto: ~ **sooner** ~ **better** je eher, desto besser.

the·a·ter *Am.,* **the·a·tre** *s bsd. Br.* ['θɪətə] **1.** Theater *n:* **be in the** ~ beim Theater sein. **2.** *(Hör)*Saal *m;* ⚕️ *Br.* Operationssaal *m:* ~ **nurse** Operationsschwester *f.* **3.** *fig.* Schauplatz *m:* ~ **of war** Kriegsschauplatz. '~**go·er** *s* Theaterbesucher(in). **the·a·tri·cal** [θɪ'ætrɪkl] *adj* □ **1.** Theater... **2.** *fig.* theatralisch.

theft [θeft] *s* Diebstahl *m*.

their [ðeə] *possessive pron* ihr: *everyone took their seats* alle nahmen Platz.

theirs [~z] *possessive pron*: *it is* ~ es gehört ihnen; *a friend of* ~ ein Freund von ihnen; *our children and* ~ unsere Kinder u. ihre.

them [ðəm] *pron* **1.** sie (*acc*); ihnen (*dat*): *they looked behind* ~ sie blickten hinter sich. **2.** F sie (*nom*): *we are younger than* ~.

theme [θi:m] *s* Thema *n* (*a.* ♪). ~ *song s* Filmsong *m*. ~ *tune s* Filmetc: Themamelodie *f*.

them·selves [ðəm'selvz] *pron* **1.** *verstärkend:* sie *od.* selbst: *they did it* ~, *they* ~ *did it* sie haben es selbst getan. **2.** *reflex* sich: *they cut* ~. **3.** sich (selbst): *they want it for* ~.

then [ðen] **I** *adv* **1.** dann: → *but* 1. **2.** da; damals: *by* ~ bis dahin; *from* ~ *on* von da an. **II** *adj* **3.** damalig.

the·o·lo·gi·an [θɪə'ləʊdʒən] *s* Theologe *m*, Theologin *f*. **the·o·log·i·cal** [~'lɒdʒɪkl] *adj* □ theologisch: ~ *college* Priesterseminar *n*. **the·ol·o·gy** [θɪ'ɒlədʒɪ] *s* Theologie *f*.

the·o·rem ['θɪərəm] *s bsd.* ℞ (Lehr-)Satz *m*.

the·o·ret·i·cal [θɪə'retɪkl] *adj* □ theoretisch. **'the·o·rist** *s* Theoretiker(in). **'the·o·rize** *v/i* theoretisieren (*about*, *on* über *acc*). **'the·o·ry** *s* Theorie *f*: *in* ~ in der Theorie, theoretisch.

ther·a·peu·tic [ˌθerə'pju:tɪk] *adj* (~*ally*) **1.** ℞ therapeutisch. **2.** F wohltuend; gesund. **ther·a·pist** *s* ℞ Therapeut(in). **'ther·a·py** *s* ℞ Therapie *f*.

there [ðeə] **I** *adv* **1.** da, dort: ~ *and then* auf der Stelle; ~ *you are* hier bitte; da hast du's!, na also!; ~ *you go!* F so ist's halt!; ~ *you go again!* F fängst du schon wieder an!; → *over* 9. **2.** (da-, dort)hin: ~ *and back* hin u. zurück; *get* ~ F es schaffen; *go* ~ hingehen. **3.** ~ *is*, *pl* ~ *are* es gibt *od.* sind: ~ *are many cars in the street* auf der Straße sind viele Autos; ~*'s a good boy!* sei lieb *od.* brav!; das war lieb von dir! **II** *int* **4.** so; da hast du's!, na also: ~, ~ ist ja gut! **'~·a·bouts** *adv:* *five pounds or* ~ ungefähr 5 Pfund. **,~'af·ter** *adv* danach. **,~'by** *adv* dadurch. **'~·fore** *adv* **1.** deshalb, daher. **2.** folg-

lich, also. **,~·'up'on** *adv* darauf.

ther·mal ['θɜːml] **I** *adj* □ **1.** thermisch, Thermo..., Wärme... **2.** ~ *spring* Thermalquelle *f*. **II** *s* **3.** Thermik *f*.

ther·mom·e·ter [θə'mɒmɪtə] *s* Thermometer *n*.

Ther·mos ['θɜːmɒs] (*TM*) *s*, *Am. a.* ~ *bottle*, *bsd. Br. a.* ~ *flask* Thermosflasche *f*.

ther·mo·stat ['θɜːməʊstæt] *s* Thermostat *m*.

the·sau·rus [θɪ'sɔːrəs] *pl* -**ri** [~raɪ], -**rus·es** *s* Thesaurus *m*.

these [ðiːz] *pl von* **this**.

the·sis ['θiːsɪs] *pl* -**ses** [~siːz] *s* **1.** These *f*. **2.** *univ.* Dissertation *f*, Doktorarbeit *f*.

they [ðeɪ] *pron* **1.** sie *pl*: ~ *who* diejenigen, welche. **2.** man.

they'd [ðeɪd] F *für* **they had**; **they would**.

they'll [ðeɪl] F *für* **they will**.

they're [ðeə] F *für* **they are**.

they've [ðeɪv] F *für* **they have**.

thick [θɪk] **I** *adj* □ **1.** *allg.* dick: *the* ~ *end of £500* F fast 500 Pfund; *give s.o. a* ~ *ear* F j-m eins *od.* ein paar hinter die Ohren geben. **2.** dick, dicht (*Nebel etc*): *be* ~ *with* wimmeln von; ~ *with smoke* verräuchert; *the furniture was* ~ *with dust* auf den Möbeln lag dick der Staub; *they are* ~ *on the ground* F es gibt sie wie Sand am Meer. **3.** *bsd. Br.* F dumm. **4.** *bsd. Br.* F dick befreundet (*with* mit). **5.** *that's a bit* ~! *bsd. Br.* F das ist ein starkes Stück! **II** *adv* **6.** dick, dicht: *lay it on* ~ F dick auftragen. **III** *s* **7.** *in the* ~ *of fig.* mitten in (*dat*): *in the* ~ *of the fight* im dichtesten Kampfgetümmel; *through* ~ *and thin* durch dick u. dünn. **thick·en** ['~ən] **I** *v/t* Soße etc eindicken, binden. **II** *v/i* dicker werden, (*Nebel etc a.*) dichter werden. **thick·et** ['~ɪt] *s* Dickicht *n*.

,thick'head·ed *adj* F strohdumm.

thick·ness ['θɪknɪs] *s* **1.** Dicke *f*. **2.** Lage *f*, Schicht *f*. **3.** *bsd. Br.* F Dummheit *f*. **,thick'set** *adj* gedrungen, untersetzt. **,~'skinned** *adj fig.* dickfellig.

thief [θiːf] *pl* **thieves** [θiːvz] *s* Dieb(in): *stop,* ~! haltet den Dieb!; *they are* (*as*) *thick as thieves* F sie sind dicke Freunde.

thigh [θaɪ] *s anat.* (Ober)Schenkel *m*.

thim·ble ['θɪmbl] *s* Fingerhut *m*.

thin [θɪn] **I** *adj* □ **1.** dünn, (*Person*, *Arme*

etc a.) dürr, (*Haar a.*) schütter: *disappear* (*od. vanish*) *into ~ air fig.* sich in Luft auflösen; *produce out of ~ air fig. et.* herzaubern; *this is just the ~ end of the wedge fig. b.s.* das ist erst der Anfang; *be ~ on the ground* F dünn gesät sein; *he's getting ~ on top* F bei ihm lichtet es sich oben schon. **2.** *fig.* schwach (*Rede etc*), (*Ausrede etc a.*) fadenscheinig. **II** *adv* **3.** dünn. **III** *v/t* **4.** *Soße etc* verdünnen, strecken. **IV** *v/i* **5.** dünner werden, (*Nebel, Haar a.*) sich lichten, (*Haar a.*) schütter werden.

thing [θɪŋ] *s* **1.** (*konkretes*) Ding: *~s pl* Sachen *pl* (*Getränke etc*), (*Gepäck, Kleidung etc a.*) Zeug *n*; *what's this ~?* was ist das?; *I couldn't see a ~* ich konnte überhaupt nichts sehen. **2.** *fig.* Ding *n*, Sache *f*, Angelegenheit *f*: *a funny ~* et. Komisches; *another ~* et. anderes; *first ~ tomorrow* gleich morgen früh; *for one ~ ..., and for another ~* zum e-n ..., zum anderen; *make a ~ of* F et. aufbauschen; *know a ~ or two about* et. verstehen von; *this proves three ~s* das beweist dreierlei; → *one* 1, *last* 4, *near* 9, *old* 2, *right* 1. **3.** *pl fig.* Dinge *pl*, Lage *f*, Umstände *pl*. **4.** Ding *n* (*Mädchen, Tier*), Kerl *m*.

think [θɪŋk] **I** *v/t* (*irr*) **1.** denken, glauben, meinen (*that* daß): *I thought he was a burglar* ich hielt ihn für e-n Einbrecher. **2.** *~ out* (*od. through*) et. durchdenken; *~ over* nachdenken über (*acc*), sich et. überlegen; *~ up* sich et. ausdenken. **3.** *j-n, et.* halten für: *~ o.s. clever.* **4.** *I can't ~ why ...* ich kann nicht verstehen, warum ... **5.** *try to ~ where ...* versuch dich zu erinnern, wo ... **II** *v/i* (*irr*) **6.** denken (*of an acc*): *I ~ so* ich glaube od. denke schon; *~ of doing s.th.* sich mit dem Gedanken tragen *od.* daran denken, et. zu tun; *I can't ~ of his name* mir fällt sein Name nicht ein, ich kann mich nicht an s-n Namen erinnern; *what do you ~ of* (*od. about*) *...?* was halten Sie von ...?; → *better¹* III, *highly* 2, *little* 5, *much* 2, *nothing* I. **7.** nachdenken (*about* über *acc*): *I'll ~ about it* ich überlege es mir; → *twice*. **III** *s* **8.** F *have a ~ about* nachdenken über (*acc*); *have another ~ coming* schief gewickelt sein. '**think·er** *s* Denker(in). '**think·ing** **I** *adj* **1.** denkend. **2.**

Denk...: *put on one's ~ cap* F scharf nachdenken. **II** *s* **2.** Denken *n*: *do some ~* nachdenken; *to my way of ~* m-r Meinung nach.

think tank *s* Planungs-, Sachverständigenstab *m*.

thin·ner ['θɪnə] *s* Verdünner *m*.

,**thin-'skinned** *adj fig.* dünnhäutig.

third [θɜːd] **I** *adj* (□ → *thirdly*) **1.** dritt: *~ party* ✝, ⚖ Dritte *m*; ♀ *World* Dritte Welt. **II** *s* **2.** *der, die, das* Dritte: *the ~ of May* der 3. Mai. **3.** Drittel *n*. **4.** *mot.* dritter Gang. **III** *adv* **5.** als dritt(er, e, es). ,**~-'class** **I** *adj* **1.** drittklassig, -rangig. **2.** 🚗 *etc* dritter Klasse. **II** *adv* **3.** 🚗 *etc* dritte(r) Klasse. ,**~-'de·gree** *adj Verbrennungen* dritten Grades.

third·ly ['θɜːdlɪ] *adv* drittens.

,**third·'par·ty** *adj:* ~ *insurance* Haftpflichtversicherung *f.* ,**~-'rate** → *third-class* 1.

thirst [θɜːst] *s* Durst *m*: *die of ~* verdursten; *~ for knowledge fig.* Wissensdurst. '**~-,quench·ing** *adj* durstlöschend.

thirst·y ['θɜːstɪ] *adj* □ **1.** durstig: *be* (*od. feel*) (*very*) ~ (sehr) durstig sein, (großen) Durst haben. **2.** *gardening is ~ work* Gartenarbeit macht durstig.

thir·teen [,θɜː'tiːn] *adj* dreizehn. ,**thir-'teenth** [~θ] *adj* dreizehnt. **thir·ti·eth** ['θɜːtɪəθ] *adj* dreißigst. '**thir·ty** **I** *adj* dreißig. **II** *s* Dreißig *f*: *be in one's thirties* in den Dreißigern sein; *in the thirties* in den dreißiger Jahren (*e-s Jahrhunderts*).

this [ðɪs] **I** *pron* **1.** dieser, diese, dieses; dies, das: *like ~* so; *~ is what I expected* (genau) das habe ich erwartet; *these are his children* das sind s-e Kinder. **2.** *after ~* danach; *before ~* zuvor. **II** *adj* **3.** dieser, diese, dieses; → *afternoon* I, *morning* I, *time* 4, *year*. **III** *adv* **4.** F so, dermaßen.

this·tle ['θɪsl] *s* ♀ Distel *f*.

tho·rax ['θɔːræks] *pl* -**ra·ces** ['~rəsiːz], -**rax·es** ['~ræksɪz] *s anat.* Brustkorb *m*, -kasten *m*.

thorn [θɔːn] *s* ♀ Dorn *m*: *be a ~ in s.o.'s flesh* (*od. side*) *fig.* j-m ein Dorn im Auge sein. '**thorn·y** *adj* **1.** dornig. **2.** *fig.* heikel.

thor·ough ['θʌrə] *adj* (□ → *thoroughly*) **1.** gründlich (*Person, Kenntnisse*),

(*Prüfung etc a.*) eingehend, (*Reform etc a.*) durchgreifend. **2.** fürchterlich (*Durcheinander, Langweiler etc*). '**~bred** s Vollblüter m. '**~fare** s Hauptverkehrsstraße f: **no ~** Durchfahrt verboten! '**~go·ing** → thorough 1.

thor·ough·ly ['θʌrəlɪ] adv **1.** → thorough 1. **2.** völlig, total: **I ~ enjoyed it** es hat mir unwahrscheinlich gut gefallen.

those [ðəʊz] pl von that¹.

though [ðəʊ] **I** cj **1.** obwohl: → even¹ 1. **2.** (je)doch. **3.** as ~ als ob, wie wenn. **II** adv **4.** dennoch, trotzdem.

thought¹ [θɔːt] pret u. pp von think.

thought² [~] s **1.** Denken n: → lost 5. **2.** Gedanke m (*of an acc*): **that's a ~!** gute Idee!; **on second ~s** (*Am. ~*) wenn ich es mir überlege; **have no ~ of doing s.th.** nicht daran denken od. nicht vorhaben, et. zu tun. **3.** **with no ~ for** Rücksicht auf (*acc*), ohne an (*acc*) zu denken. **thought·ful** ['~fʊl] adj □ **1.** nachdenklich. **2.** rücksichtsvoll, aufmerksam. '**thought·less** adj □ **1.** gedankenlos. **2.** rücksichtslos.

thou·sand ['θaʊznd] **I** adj **1.** tausend: **a (one) ~** (ein)tausend. **II** s **2.** Tausend n: **~s of times** tausendmal; → hundred 2. **3.** ⅋ Tausender m. **thou·sandth** ['~tθ] **I** adj **1.** tausendst. **II** s **2.** der, die, das Tausendste. **3.** Tausendstel n: **a ~ of a second** e-e Tausendstelsekunde.

thrash [θræʃ] **I** v/t **1.** j-n verdreschen, -prügeln; (*Sport*) F j-m e-e Abfuhr erteilen. **2. ~ out** Problem etc ausdiskutieren. **II** v/i **3. ~ about** (*od. around*) sich *im Bett* herumwerfen; um sich schlagen; zappeln (*Fisch*). '**thrash·ing** s: **give s.o. a ~** j-m¹ e-e Tracht Prügel verpassen; (*Sport*) F j-m e-e Abfuhr erteilen.

thread [θred] **I** s **1.** Faden m (*a. fig.*): **lose the ~ (of the conversation)** den (Gesprächs)Faden verlieren; **pick up the ~** den Faden wiederaufnehmen; → hang 8. **2.** ⊕ Gewinde n. **II** v/t **3.** Nadel einfädeln. **4.** Perlen etc auffädeln, -reihen (*on* auf *acc*). **5. ~ one's way through** sich schlängeln durch, sich durchschlängeln zwischen (*dat*). '**~bare** adj **1.** abgewetzt, (*Kleidung a.*) abgetragen. **2.** fig. abgedroschen.

threat [θret] s **1.** Drohung f: **under ~ of** unter Androhung von (*od. gen*). **2. (to)**

Bedrohung f (*gen od. für*), Gefahr f (für). '**threat·en I** v/t **1.** j-m drohen, j-n bedrohen (*with* mit): → s.o. with s.th. j-m et. androhen. **2.** et. androhen, drohen mit. **3. ~ to do s.th.** (damit) drohen, et. zu tun. **4.** et. bedrohen, gefährden: **be ~ed with extinction** biol. vom Aussterben bedroht sein. **II** v/i **5.** drohen (*Gefahr etc*). '**threat·en·ing** adj drohend: ~ **letter** Drohbrief m.

three [θriː] **I** adj drei. **II** s **3** Drei f: **~ of hearts** Herzdrei. '**~-act** adj: ~ **play** thea. Dreiakter m. ,**~'cor·nered** adj dreieckig. ,**~-di'men·sion·al** adj **1.** dreidimensional. **2.** fig. plastisch.

three·fold ['θriːfəʊld] **I** adj dreifach. **II** adv dreifach, um das Dreifache: **in-crease ~** (sich) verdreifachen.

'**three|-piece** adj dreiteilig. ,**~'quar·ter** adj Dreiviertel... '**~-time** adj dreimalig.

thresh [θreʃ] v/t u. v/i dreschen. '**thresh·ing** adj: ~ **machine** Dreschmaschine f.

thresh·old ['θreʃhəʊld] s Schwelle f (a. fig.): **be on the ~ of** an der Schwelle stehen zu (*od. gen*); ~ **of pain** Schmerzschwelle.

threw [θruː] pret von throw.

thrift [θrɪft] s Sparsamkeit f. '**thrift·y** adj □ sparsam.

thrill [θrɪl] **I** s **1.** prickelndes Gefühl; Nervenkitzel m. **2.** aufregendes Erlebnis. **II** v/t **3. be ~ed** (ganz) hingerissen sein (*at, about* von): **I was ~ed to hear that** ich war von der Nachricht hingerissen, daß. '**thrill·er** s Thriller m, Reißer m. '**thrill·ing** adj fesselnd, packend.

thrive [θraɪv] v/i gedeihen (*Pflanze, Tier*), sich prächtig entwickeln (*Kind*); fig. blühen, florieren (*Geschäft etc*): ~ **on** geradezu aufblühen bei.

throat [θrəʊt] s Kehle f, Gurgel f; Rachen m; Hals m: **cut one's own ~** fig. sich ins eigene Fleisch schneiden; **force** (*od. ram, thrust*) **s.th. down s.o.'s ~** j-m et. aufzwingen; → clear 17, sore 1. '**throat·y** adj □ rauh; heiser (*Stimme*); mit e-r rauhen od. heiseren Stimme: **sound ~** heiser klingen.

throb [θrɒb] **I** v/i hämmern (*Maschine*), (*Herz etc a.*) pochen, schlagen. **II** s Hämmern n, Pochen n, Schlagen n.

throes [θrəʊz] s pl: **be in the ~ of (doing)**

s.th. mitten in et. (*Unangenehmem*) stecken.

throm·bo·sis [θrɒmˈbəʊsɪs] *pl* **-ses** [~siːz] *s* ✖ Thrombose *f*.

throne [θrəʊn] *s* Thron *m* (*a. fig.*): **come to the ~** auf den Thron kommen.

throng [θrɒŋ] **I** *s* Schar *f* (**of** von). **II** *v/i u. v/t* sich drängen (in dat).

throt·tle [ˈθrɒtl] **I** *v/t* erdrosseln. **II** *s mot.*, ☼ Drosselklappe *f*: **go at full ~** (mit) Vollgas fahren.

through [θruː] *prp* **1.** durch (*a. fig.*): → **live**¹ Ib. **2.** *Am.* bis (einschließlich). **II** *adv* **1.** durch; durch...: **~ and ~** durch u. durch; **wet ~** völlig durchnäßt; → **let through, read**¹ 1, *etc.* **III** *adj* **4.** durchgehend (*Zug etc*): **~ traffic** Durchgangsverkehr *m*. **5. be ~** F fertig sein (**with** mit). **~ out I** *prp* **1. ~ the night** die ganze Nacht hindurch. **2. ~ the country** im ganzen Land. **II** *adv* **3.** ganz, überall. **4.** die ganze Zeit (hindurch). '**~way** *s Am.* Schnellstraße *f*.

throw [θrəʊ] **I** *s* **1.** Leichtathletik: (*Diskus-, Speer*)Wurf *m*. **2.** Wurf *m*: → **stone** 1. **3.** Fußball: Einwurf *m*: **take the ~** einwerfen. **II** *v/t* (*irr*) **4.** *et.* werfen (**at** nach): **~ s.o. s.th.** j-m et. hin- *od.* her- *od.* zuwerfen; **~ s.o. a look** j-m e-n Blick zuwerfen; **~ a three** e-e Drei werfen *od.* würfeln; **~ open** Tür etc aufreißen; *fig.* Schloß etc der Öffentlichkeit zugänglich machen; **~ o.s. at s.o.** sich auf j-n stürzen; *fig.* sich j-m an den Hals werfen; **~ o.s. into** sich stürzen in (*acc*) (*a. fig.*); → **balance** 1, **confusion** 2a, **doubt** 5, **light**¹ 1, **water** 1. **5.** *zo.* werfen. **6.** *Hebel etc* betätigen. **7.** *Reiter* abwerfen. **8.** F *Party* schmeißen, geben. **9.** F *Wutanfall etc* kriegen: → **tantrum**. **III** *v/i* (*irr*) **10.** werfen; würfeln. *Verbindungen mit Adverbien:*

throw| a·bout, ~ a·round *v/t*: **throw one's money about** mit Geld um sich werfen; → **weight** 3. **~ a·way** *v/t* **1.** *et.* wegwerfen. **2.** *Chance etc* vertun. **~ back** *v/t* **1.** zurückwerfen. **2. be thrown back on** *fig.* wieder angewiesen sein auf (*acc*). **~ in** *v/t* **1.** hineinwerfen: **throw the ball in** (*Fußball*) einwerfen; → **sponge** 1, **towel** I. **2.** *et.* (gratis) dazugeben: **get s.th. thrown in** et. (gratis) dazubekommen. **~ off** *v/t* **1.** *Kleidungsstück* abwerfen, *Nervosität etc* ablegen.

2. *Verfolger* abschütteln. **3.** *Krankheit* loswerden. **~ on** *v/t* sich *Kleidungsstück* überwerfen. **~ out** *v/t* **1.** j-n hinauswerfen (*a. fig. entlassen*). **2.** *et.* wegwerfen. **3.** *Vorschlag etc* ablehnen, verwerfen. **4.** *Vorschlag etc* äußern. **5.** j-n aus dem Konzept *od.* aus der Fassung bringen. **~ o·ver** *v/t Freund etc* sitzenlassen (**for** wegen). **~ to·geth·er** *v/t* **1.** zs.-werfen. **2.** *et.* fabrizieren, zurechtbasteln. **3.** *Leute* zs.-bringen. **~ up I** *v/t* **1.** in die Höhe werfen, hochwerfen. **2.** F *Job etc* hinschmeißen. **3.** F *et. Gegessenes* brechen. **II** *v/i* **4.** F brechen (*sich übergeben*).

'**throw·a·way** *adj* **1.** Wegwerf... **2.** hingeworfen (*Bemerkung*).

throw·er [ˈθrəʊə] *s* Werfer(in).

'**throw-in** → **throw** 3.

thrown [θrəʊn] *pp von* **throw**.

thru [θruː] *Am.* F → **through**.

thrush¹ [θrʌʃ] *s orn.* Drossel *f*.

thrush² [~] *s* ✖ Soor *m*.

thrust [θrʌst] **I** *v/t* (*irr*) **1.** j-n, *et.* stoßen (**into** in *acc*): → **throat** 2. **2.** *et.* stecken, schieben (**into** in *acc*): → **nose** 1. **II** *v/i* (*irr*) **3. ~ at** stoßen nach. **III** *s* **4.** Stoß *m*. **5.** ✗ Vorstoß *m* (*a. fig.*). **6.** *phys.* Schub(kraft *f*) *m*.

'**thru·way** F → **throughway**.

thud [θʌd] **I** *s* dumpfes Geräusch, Plumps *m*. **II** *v/i* plumpsen.

thug [θʌg] *s* Schläger *m*.

thumb [θʌm] **I** *s anat.* Daumen *m*: **be all ~s** F zwei linke Hände haben; **be under s.o.'s ~** F unter j-s Fuchtel stehen; **give s.th. the ~s up** (**down**) et. akzeptieren (ablehnen); **stick out like a sore ~** F auffallen wie ein Kuhfladen auf der Autobahn; → **rule** 2, **twiddle**. **II** *v/t*: **~ a lift** per Anhalter fahren, trampen (**to** nach). **III** *v/i*: **~ through a book** ein Buch durchblättern. **~ in·dex** *s* (*a. irr* **index**) Daumenregister *n*. '**~nail I** *s* Daumennagel *m*. **II** *adj* kurz (*Beschreibung etc*). '**~screw** *s* **1.** ☼ Flügel- *od.* Rändelschraube *f*. **2.** *hist.* Daumenschraube *f*. '**~tack** *s Am.* Reißzwecke *f*, -nagel *m*.

thump [θʌmp] **I** *v/t* **1.** j-m e-n Schlag versetzen; j-n verprügeln. **2. ~ out** Melodie herunterhämmern (**on the piano** auf dem Klavier). **II** *v/i* **3.** plumpsen. **4.** hämmern, pochen (*Herz*). **5.** trampeln.

III s 6. dumpfes Geräusch, Plumps m.
7. Schlag m. '**thump·ing** I adj 1. hämmernd *(Kopfschmerzen)*. 2. F riesig, Mords... II adv 3. ~ **great** → 2.

thun·der ['θʌndə] I s Donner m, *(von Geschützen a.)* Donnern n: **steal s.o.'s ~** fig. j-m die Schau od. Show stehlen. II v/i donnern (a. fig. *Geschütze, Zug etc)*. III v/t a. ~ **out** et. brüllen, donnern. '**~bolt** s Blitz m u. Donnerschlag m: **like a ~** wie der Blitz; **be a real ~** fig. wie der Blitz einschlagen. '**~clap** s Donner(schlag) m. '**~cloud** s Gewitterwolke f.

thun·der·ous ['θʌndərəs] adj donnernd *(Applaus)*.

'**thun·der·storm** s Gewitter n, Unwetter n. '**~struck** adj wie vom Donner gerührt.

thun·der·y ['θʌndərɪ] adj gewitt(e)rig.

Thurs·day ['θɜːzdɪ] s Donnerstag m: **on ~** (am) Donnerstag; **on ~s** donnerstags.

thus [ðʌs] adv 1. so, auf diese Weise. 2. folglich, somit. 3. ~ **far** bisher.

thwack [θwæk] → **whack**.

thwart [θwɔːt] v/t *Pläne etc* durchkreuzen, vereiteln; *j-m* e-n Strich durch die Rechnung machen.

thyme [taɪm] s ♀ Thymian m.

thy·roid (gland) ['θaɪrɔɪd] s anat. Schilddrüse f.

ti·ar·a [tɪ'ɑːrə] s 1. Tiara f. 2. Diadem n.

tic [tɪk] s ♣ Tic(k) m, nervöses Zucken.

tick¹ [tɪk] s zo. Zecke f.

tick² [~] s: **on ~** F auf Pump.

tick³ [~] I s 1. Ticken n. 2. Haken m, Häkchen n *(Vermerkzeichen)*. 3. bsd. Br. F Augenblick m: **in a ~** sofort. II v/i 4. ticken: ~ **away** vergehen, -rinnen. III v/t 5. a. ~ **off** abhaken: ~ **off** F j-n anpfeifen, zs.-stauchen.

tick·er ['tɪkə] s F Pumpe f *(Herz)*.

tick·et ['tɪkɪt] I s 1. *(Eintritts-, Theater etc)*Karte f; ♣ etc Fahrkarte f, -schein m, ✈ Flugschein m, Ticket n; *(Gepäck etc)*Schein m. 2. Etikett n, *(Preis- etc)* Schild n. 3. Strafzettel m: ~ **parking ticket.** 4. pol. bsd. Am. Wahl-, Kandidatenliste f. II v/t 5. etikettieren. 6. **be ~ed for** bsd. Am. e-n Strafzettel bekommen wegen. 7. bestimmen, vorsehen *(for* für). ~ **col·lec·tor** s *(Bahnsteig-)* Schaffner(in). ~ **in·spec·tor** s Fahrkartenkontrolleur(in). ~ **ma·chine** s Fahr-

kartenautomat m. ~ **tout** s Br. Kartenschwarzhändler(in).

,**tick·ing-'off** s F Anpfiff m: **give s.o. a ~** j-n anpfeifen od. zs.-stauchen.

tick·le ['tɪkl] I v/t u. v/i kitzeln: ~ **s.o.'s fancy** fig. j-n anmachen od. anturnen; **be ~d pink** *(od. **to death)*** F sich wie ein Schneekönig freuen *(at, by, with* über acc);* → **ivory** 2. II s Kitzeln n. '**tick·lish** adj ☐ kitz(e)lig (a. fig.).

tid·al ['taɪdl] adj Tiden...: ~ **wave** Flutwelle f; fig. Welle f.

tid·bit ['tɪdbɪt] Am. → **titbit**.

tid·dly·winks ['tɪdlɪwɪŋks] s pl *(sg konstruiert)* Flohhüpfen n, -spiel n.

tide [taɪd] I s 1. Gezeiten pl; Flut f. 2. fig. Strömung f, Trend m: **go** *(od. **swim) with** (against)* **the ~** mit dem (gegen den) Strom schwimmen. II v/t 3. ~ **over** fig. j-m hinweghelfen über *(acc)*; j-n über Wasser halten. '**~mark** s bsd. Br. humor. schwarzer Rand *(in Badewanne)*.

ti·di·ness ['taɪdɪnɪs] s Sauberkeit f, Ordentlichkeit f.

ti·dy ['taɪdɪ] I adj ☐ 1. sauber, ordentlich, *(Zimmer a.)* aufgeräumt. 2. F ordentlich, beträchtlich *(Gewinn etc)*. II v/t 3. a. ~ **up** in Ordnung bringen, *Zimmer a.* aufräumen: ~ **away** weg-, aufräumen.

tie [taɪ] I s 1. Krawatte f, Schlips m. 2. Band n; Schnur f. 3. pl fig. Bande pl. 4. Stimmengleichheit f; *(Sport)* Unentschieden n: **end in a ~** unentschieden ausgehen. 5. Sport: *(Pokal)*Spiel n, (-)Paarung f. 6. ♣ Am. Schwelle f. II v/t 7. a) binden *(to an acc)*; (sich) *Krawatte etc* binden: **my hands are tied** fig. mir sind die Hände gebunden, b) → **tie up** 1. 8. **be ~d to** fig. (eng) verbunden sein mit. 9. **the game was ~d** *(Sport)* das Spiel ging unentschieden aus. III v/t 10. **they ~d for second place** *(Sport etc)* sie belegten gemeinsam den zweiten Platz.
Verbindungen mit Adverbien:

tie| down v/t j-n festlegen *(to* auf acc). ~ **in** v/i *(with)* übereinstimmen (mit), passen (zu). ~ **up** v/t 1. Paket etc verschnüren: → **knot** 1. **be tied up** ✈ fest angelegt sein *(in* in dat). 3. et. in Verbindung bringen *(with* mit). 4. *Verkehr etc* lahmlegen.

'**tie|-break,** '**~,break·er** s Tennis: Tie-

Break *m, n.* '*~-in* → **tie-up**. '*~-on* *adj* Anhänge... '*~-pin* *s* Krawattennadel *f.*

tier [tɪə] *s* **1.** (Sitz)Reihe *f.* **2.** Lage *f,* Schicht *f.* **3.** *fig.* Stufe *f.*

'**tie-up** *s* (enge) Verbindung, (enger) Zs.-hang (**between** zwischen *dat*).

tiff [tɪf] *s* kleine Meinungsverschiedenheit.

ti-ger ['taɪgə] *s zo.* Tiger *m.*

tight [taɪt] **I** *adj* □ **1.** fest(sitzend, -angezogen). **2.** straff (*Seil etc*). **3.** eng (*a. Kleidungsstück*): → **corner** 2, **fit** 5. **4.** knapp (*Rennen etc,* ♣ *Geld*). **5.** F knick(e)rig. **6.** F blau (*betrunken*). **7.** in *Zssgn* ...dicht: → **airtight** 1, *etc.* **II** *adv* **8.** fest: **hold** ~ festhalten; **sit** ~ sich nicht vom Fleck rühren; *fig.* sich nicht beirren lassen. **9.** F gut: **sleep** ~! **III** *s* **10.** *pl,* *a. pair of* ~s *bsd. Br.* Strumpfhose *f;* Trikot *n* (*von Artisten etc*). '**tight-en** **I** *v/t* **1.** Schraube *etc* anziehen: ~ *one's belt fig.* den Gürtel enger schnallen. **2.** Seil *etc* straffen: ~ *up* → 3. **II** *v/i* **3.** ~ *up on Gesetz etc* verschärfen.

'**tight**|'**fist-ed** → **tight** 5. '*~-*'**lipped** *adj* **1.** mit zs.-gekniffenen Lippen. **2.** *fig.* verschlossen: **be** ~ *about* nicht reden wollen über (*acc*). '*~-'rope* *s* (Draht)Seil *n:* **walk a** ~ *fig.* e-n Balanceakt ausführen; ~ *walker* Drahtseilkünstler(in), Seiltänzer(in).

ti-gress ['taɪgrɪs] *s zo.* Tigerin *f.*

tile [taɪl] **I** *s* **1.** (Dach)Ziegel *m:* **be** (**out**) **on the** ~s F e-n draufmachen. **2.** Fliese *f,* Kachel *f.* **II** *v/t* **3.** (mit Ziegeln) decken. **4.** fliesen, kacheln. '**til-er** *s* **1.** Dachdecker *m.* **2.** Fliesenleger *m.*

till¹ [tɪl] *s* (Laden)Kasse *f.*

till² [~] → **until**.

tilt [tɪlt] **I** *v/t* **1.** kippen. **II** *v/i* **2.** kippen; sich neigen. **III** *s* **3.** *at a* ~ schief, schräg. **4.** (*at*) *full* ~ F mit Volldampf *arbeiten;* mit Karacho *fahren etc.*

tim-ber ['tɪmbə] *s* **1.** *Br.* Bau-, Nutzholz *n.* **2.** Balken *m.* '*~-line* *s* Baumgrenze *f.*

time [taɪm] **I** *s* **1.** *allg.* Zeit *f:* **some** ~ *ago* vor einiger Zeit; *all the* ~ die ganze Zeit; *ahead of* ~ vorzeitig; *at the* ~ damals; *at* ~s manchmal; *at the same* ~ gleichzeitig; trotzdem; *by the* ~ wenn; als; *for* ~ a e-e Zeitlang; *for the* ~ *being* vorläufig, fürs erste; *from* ~ *to* ~ von Zeit zu Zeit; *in* ~ rechtzeitig; im Lauf

der Zeit; *in no* ~ (*at all*) im Nu; *in two years'* ~ in zwei Jahren; *on* ~ pünktlich; *be ahead* (*od. before*) *one's* ~ s-r Zeit voraus sein; *be behind the* ~s rückständig sein; *do* ~ F sitzen (*for wegen*); *keep up* (*od. march, move*) *with the* ~s mit der Zeit gehen; *take one's* ~ sich Zeit lassen; → *bide, immemorial, mark² 11, nick 2, play 7.* **2.** (Uhr)Zeit *f:* *what's the* ~? wie spät ist es?; *what* ...? um wieviel Uhr?; *this* ~ *tomorrow* morgen um diese Zeit. **3.** ♪ Takt *m:* *in* ~ im Takt (*a. marschieren etc*); *in* ~ *with the music* im Takt zur Musik; *beat* ~ den Takt schlagen. **4.** Mal *n:* ~ *and again,* *after* ~ immer wieder; *every* ~ *I* ... jedesmal, wenn ich ...; *how many* ~s? wie oft?; *next* ~ (*I* ...) nächstes Mal(, wenn ich ...); *this* ~ diesmal; *three* ~s dreimal; *three* ~ *four equals* (*od. is*) *twelve* drei mal vier ist zwölf; → *nine* I, *second¹* 1. **II** *v/t* 8. *et.* timen; stoppen, wie lang j-d braucht: *he was* ~*d at 20 seconds* für ihn wurden 20 Sekunden gestoppt. **6.** ~ *well* sich e-n günstigen Zeitpunkt aussuchen für; (*Sport*) *Flanke, Schlag etc* gut timen. ~ *bomb* *s* Zeitbombe *f* (*a. fig.*). '*~-card* *s* Steckkarte *f.* ~ *clock* *s* Stechuhr *f.* '*~-con-sum-ing* *adj* zeitaufwendig, -raubend. ~ *ex-po-sure* *s phot.* Zeitaufnahme *f.* '*~-hon-o(u)red* *adj* althergebracht. '*~-keep-er* *s* **1.** *Sport:* Zeitnehmer(in). **2.** *be a good* ~ genau gehen (*Uhr*). ~ *lag* *s* Zeitdifferenz *f.* '*~-lapse* *adj* *Film:* Zeitraffer...

time-less ['taɪmlɪs] *adj* □ **1.** immerwährend, ewig. **2.** zeitlos.

time lim-it *s* Frist *f:* **set s.o. a** ~ *of* j-m e-e Frist setzen von.

time-ly ['taɪmlɪ] *adj* rechtzeitig.

time-'out *pl* **times-'out** *s* *Sport:* Timeout *n,* Auszeit *f.*

tim-er ['taɪmə] *s* Timer *m,* Schaltuhr *f.*

'**time**|**sav-ing** *adj* zeitsparend. '*~-serv-er* *s bsd. pol.* Opportunist(in). ~ *sig-nal* *s Rundfunk:* Zeitzeichen *n.* '*~-switch* *s* Zeitschalter *m.* '*~-ta-ble* *s* **1.** Fahr-, Flugplan *m.* **2.** *ped. Br.* Stundenplan *m.* **3.** Zeitplan *m.* '*~-worn* *adj* **1.** abgenutzt. **2.** *fig.* abgedroschen. ~ *zone* *s* Zeitzone *f.*

tim-id ['tɪmɪd] *adj* □ ängstlich, furchtsam.

tim·ing ['taɪmɪŋ] s Timing n (*Wahl des günstigen Zeitpunkts*).

tin [tɪn] **I** s **1.** Zinn n. **2.** Br. (Blech-, Konserven)Dose f, (-)Büchse f. **II** adj **3.** zinnern, Zinn... **III** v/t **4.** verzinnen. **5.** Br. einmachen, -dosen: → **tinned**.

tinc·ture ['tɪŋktʃə] s pharm. Tinktur f: ~ **of iodine** Jodtinktur.

tin·der ['tɪndə] s Zunder m: (**as**) **dry as ~** → **tinder-dry**. **'~·box** s fig. Pulverfaß n. **,~·'dry** adj so trocken wie Zunder.

tine [taɪn] s **1.** Zinke f, Zacke f (*e-r Gabel*). **2.** (*Geweih*)Sprosse f, Ende n.

'tin-foil s Stanniol(papier) n; Alufolie f.

ting [tɪŋ] **I** v/t: **~ a bell** klingeln. **II** v/i: **the bell ~s** es klingelt. **III** s Klingeln n.

tinge [tɪndʒ] **I** v/t tönen: **be ~d with** fig. e-n Anflug haben von, et. von ... an sich haben. **II** s **1.** Tönung f: **have a ~ of red** ins Rote spielen. **3.** fig. Anflug m (**of** von).

tin·gle ['tɪŋgl] **I** v/i prickeln, kribbeln (**with** vor dat). **II** s Prickeln n, Kribbeln n.

tin| god s F Idol n. **~ hat** s ✕ F (Stahl-) Helm m.

tink·er ['tɪŋkə] **I** s Kesselflicker m. **II** v/i a. **~ about** herumbasteln (**with** an dat): **~ with** herumpfuschen an (dat).

tin·kle ['tɪŋkl] **I** v/i bimmeln; klirren. **II** s Bimmeln n; Klirren n: **give s.o. a ~** teleph. Br. F j-n anklingeln.

tinned [tɪnd] adj Br. Dosen..., Büchsen...: **~ fruit** Obstkonserven pl; **~ meat** Büchsenfleisch n.

tin·ny ['tɪnɪ] adj blechern (*Klang*).

tin o·pen·er s Br. Dosen-, Büchsenöffner m.

tin·sel ['tɪnsl] s **1.** Lametta n. **2.** fig. Flitter m.

tint [tɪnt] **I** s (Farb)Ton m, Tönung f: **have a ~ of red** ins Rote spielen. **II** v/t tönen.

ti·ny ['taɪnɪ] adj □ winzig.

tip¹ [tɪp] s **1.** allg. Spitze f: **it's on the ~ of my tongue** es liegt mir auf der Zunge; → **iceberg**. **2.** Filter m (*e-r Zigarette*).

tip² [~] **I** s **1.** Tisch etc kippen: **~ over** umkippen; → **scale**² **2. 2.** (aus)kippen, schütten. **II** v/i **3.** kippen: **~ over** umkippen. **III** s **4.** bsd. Br. (*Schutt etc*)Abladeplatz m, (-)Halde f. **5.** Br. fig. F Saustall m.

tip³ [~] **I** s **1.** Trinkgeld n. **2.** Tip m, Rat(schlag) m: **take my ~ and ...** hör auf mich u. ... **II** v/t **3.** j-m ein Trinkgeld geben: **~ s.o. 50 p** j-m 50 Pence Trinkgeld geben. **4.** tippen auf (acc) (**as** als). **5.** **~ off** j-m e-n Tip od. Wink geben.

'tip-off s F Tip m, Wink m.

tip·ple ['tɪpl] s F (*alkoholisches*) Getränk.

tip·sy ['tɪpsɪ] adj □ angeheitert, beschwipst: **be ~** d. h. e-n Schwips haben.

'tip|·toe **I** v/i auf Zehenspitzen gehen. **II** s: **stand on ~** sich auf die Zehenspitzen stellen; **walk on ~** → I. **,~·'top** adj F erstklassig: **be in ~ order** tipptopp in Ordnung sein.

ti·rade [taɪ'reɪd] s Schimpfkanonade f (**against** gegen).

tire¹ ['taɪə] Am. → **tyre**.

tire² [~] **I** v/t ermüden, müde machen: **~ out** (völlig) erschöpfen. **II** v/i ermüden, müde werden: **~ of** fig. j-n, et. satt bekommen; **~ of doing s.th.** satt werden, et. zu tun.

tired ['taɪəd] adj □ **1.** müde: **~ out** (völlig) erschöpft; **be ~ of** fig. j-n, et. satt haben; **be ~ of doing s.th.** es satt haben od. sein, et. zu tun. **2.** fig. abgegriffen. **'tired·ness** s Müdigkeit f.

tire·less ['taɪəlɪs] adj □ unermüdlich.

tire·some ['taɪəsəm] adj □ **1.** ermüdend. **2.** fig. lästig.

ti·ro → **tyro**.

tis·sue ['tɪʃuː] s **1.** biol. Gewebe n. **2.** Papier(taschen)tuch n. **3.** a. **~ paper** Seidenpapier n.

tit¹ [tɪt] s: **~ for tat** wie du mir, so ich dir.

tit² [~] s sl. **1.** mst pl Titte f: a) weibliche Brust, b) Brustwarze. **2.** Br. blöde Sau.

tit³ [~] s orn. Meise f.

ti·tan·ic [taɪ'tænɪk] adj (**~ally**) gigantisch.

tit·bit ['tɪtbɪt] s bsd. Br. Leckerbissen m.

tit·il·late ['tɪtɪleɪt] v/t j-n (*sexuell*) anregen.

ti·tle ['taɪtl] s **1.** allg. Titel m. **2.** ⚖ (Rechts)Anspruch m (**to** auf acc). **~ deed** s ⚖ Eigentumsurkunde f. **~ fight** s Boxen: Titelkampf m. **'~·hold·er** s Sport: Titelhalter(in), -träger(in). **~ page** s Titelseite f. **~ role** s thea. etc Titelrolle f.

'tit·mouse s (irr **mouse**) orn. Meise f.

tit·ter ['tɪtə] **I** v/i kichern. **II** s Kichern n.

tit·tle-tat·tle ['tɪtl,tætl] F **I** s Geschwätz n; Klatsch m, Tratsch m. **II** v/i schwatzen; klatschen, tratschen.

tit·u·lar ['tɪtjʊlə] adj nominell.

to prp [tuː; tʊ; tə] **1.** Richtung u. Ziel, räumlich: zu, nach, an (acc), in (acc): **go ~ England** nach England fahren; → **bed** 1, **school** 1, etc. **2.** in (dat): **have you ever been ~ London?** bist du schon einmal in London gewesen? **3.** Richtung, Ziel, Zweck: zu, auf (acc), für: → **death** 1, **invite** 1, etc. **4.** Zugehörigkeit: zu, für, in (acc): → **key** 1, **secretary** 1, etc. **5.** (im Verhältnis od. Vergleich) zu, gegen(über): → **compare** 1, **nothing** 1, etc. **6.** Ausmaß, Grenze, Grad: bis, (bis) zu, (bis) an (acc). **7.** zeitliche Ausdehnung od. Grenze: bis, bis zu, bis gegen, vor (dat): from **three ~ four** von drei bis vier (Uhr); → **quarter** 2. **8.** Begleitung: zu, nach: → **dance** 1. **9.** zur Bildung des (betonten) Dativs: **~ me** mir. **II** part [tʊ] **10.** zur Bezeichnung des Infinitivs: **~ go** gehen; **easy ~ understand** leicht zu verstehen. **11.** Zweck, Absicht: um zu: **he does it only ~ earn money** er tut es nur, um Geld zu verdienen; → **order** 9. **12.** zur Verkürzung e-s Nebensatzes: **he was the first ~ arrive** er kam als erster; **~ hear him talk** wenn man ihn (so) reden hört. **III** adv [tuː] **13.** zu (geschlossen). **14.** → **come to**. **15.** **~ and fro** hin u. her; auf u. ab.

toad [təʊd] s zo. Kröte f. **'~stool** s & ungenießbarer Pilz; Giftpilz m.

toad·y ['təʊdɪ] **I** s Kriecher(in), Speichellecker(in). **II** v/i: **~ to s.o.** vor j-m kriechen.

toast¹ [təʊst] **I** s **1.** Toast m. **II** v/t **2.** toasten; rösten. **3.** F sich die Füße etc wärmen.

toast² [~] **I** s Toast m, Trinkspruch m: **drink a ~ to** → **II**. **II** v/t auf j-n od. j-s Wohl trinken.

toast·er ['təʊstə] s ⊕ Toaster m.

to·bac·co [tə'bækəʊ] pl **-cos** s Tabak m. **to·bac·co·nist** [~kənɪst] s Tabak(waren)händler(in).

to·bog·gan [tə'bɒgən] **I** s (Rodel)Schlitten m. **II** v/i Schlitten fahren, rodeln.

tod [tɒd] s: **on one's ~** Br. F ganz allein.

to·day [tə'deɪ] **I** adv **1.** heute: **a week ~, ~ week** heute in e-r Woche od. in acht Tagen. **2.** heutzutage. **II** s **3.** **~'s paper** die heutige Zeitung, die Zeitung von

heute. **4.** **of ~, ~'s** von heute, heutig.

tod·dle ['tɒdl] v/i **1.** auf wack(e)ligen od. unsicheren Beinen gehen (bsd. Kleinkind). **2.** F gehen. **'tod·dler** s Kleinkind n.

tod·dy ['tɒdɪ] s Toddy m (grogartiges Getränk).

to-do [tə'duː] s F Theater n (about um).

toe [təʊ] **I** s anat. Zehe f: **be on one's ~s** fig. gut drauf sein; **keep s.o. on his ~s** fig. j-n auf Zack halten; **tread on s.o.'s ~s** fig. j-m zu nahe treten. **II** v/t: **~ the line** fig. spuren. **'~nail** s Zehennagel m.

tof·fee ['tɒfɪ] s bsd. Br. Toffee n, Karamelbonbon n, m: **he can't play tennis for ~** F er hat vom Tennisspielen keine Ahnung. **'~nosed** adj Br. F eingebildet, hochnäsig.

tof·fy → **toffee**.

tog [tɒg] F **I** v/t: **~ o.s. out** (od. **up**) sich in Schale werfen. **II** s pl Klamotten pl.

to·geth·er [tə'geðə] **I** adv zusammen (with mit); zusammen...: → **keep together**, **live¹** I, etc. **II** adj F ausgeglichen (Person). **to'geth·er·ness** s Zs.-gehörigkeit(sgefühl n) f.

toil [tɔɪl] **I** s mühselige Arbeit. **II** v/i sich abmühen od. plagen (**at** mit); sich schleppen.

toi·let ['tɔɪlɪt] s Toilette f: **go to the ~** auf die od. in die od. zur Toilette gehen. **~ pa·per** s Toilettenpapier n. **~ roll** s Rolle f Toilettenpapier.

to·ken ['təʊkən] **I** s **1.** Zeichen n: **as a** (od. **in**) **~ of** als od. zum Zeichen (gen); zum Andenken an (acc). **2.** Gutschein m. **3.** (Spiel- etc)Marke f. **II** adj **4.** symbolisch. **5.** Schein... **6.** Alibi...

told [təʊld] pret u. pp von **tell**.

tol·er·a·ble ['tɒlərəbl] adj erträglich. **'tol·er·a·bly** adv leidlich, einigermaßen. **'tol·er·ance** s **1.** Toleranz f (for, of, toward[s]) gegenüber. **2.** &, ⊕ Toleranz f. **'tol·er·ant** adj □ tolerant (of, toward[s]) gegenüber. **tol·er·ate** ['~reɪt] v/t **1.** tolerieren, dulden. **2.** j-n, et. ertragen.

toll¹ [təʊl] s **1.** Benutzungsgebühr f, Maut f. **2.** **take its ~** (on) fig. s-n Tribut fordern (von); s-e Spuren hinterlassen (bei).

toll² [~] v/i läuten (bsd. Totenglocke).

toll‖ bridge s gebührenpflichtige Brücke, Mautbrücke f. **~-'free** adj u. adv *teleph. Am.* gebührenfrei. **~ road** *s* gebührenpflichtige Straße, Mautstraße *f.*

tom [tɒm] *s zo.* Kater *m.*

tom·a·hawk ['tɒməhɔ:k] *s hist.* Tomahawk *m*, Streitaxt *f.*

to·ma·to [təˈmɑ:təʊ] **I** *pl* **-toes** *s* ♣ Tomate *f.* **II** *adj* Tomaten...

tomb [tu:m] *s* Grab(mal) *n*; Gruft *f.*

tom·bo·la [tɒmˈbəʊlə] *s* Tombola *f.*

tom·boy ['tɒmbɔɪ] *s* Wildfang *m (Mädchen).*

'tomb·stone *s* Grabstein *m.*

'tom·cat *s zo.* Kater *m.*

tome [təʊm] *s humor.* Wälzer *m.*

tom·fool·er·y [ˌtɒmˈfu:lərɪ] *s* Albernheit *f*, Unsinn *m.*

tom·my gun ['tɒmɪ] *s* F Maschinenpistole *f.*

to·mor·row [təˈmɒrəʊ] **I** *adv* **1.** morgen: *a week ~, ~ week* morgen in e-r Woche *od.* in acht Tagen; *~ morning* morgen früh; *~ night* morgen abend. **II** *s* **2. '~'s paper** die morgige Zeitung, die Zeitung von morgen; *the day after ~* übermorgen. **3.** Zukunft *f: of ~, ~'s* von morgen.

ton [tʌn] *s* **1.** Tonne *f (Gewicht).* **2.** F **~s** *pl* **of** e-e Menge: *~s better* viel *od.* wesentlich besser.

tone [təʊn] *s* **1.** *allg.* Ton *m*; Klang *m.* **2.** ♪ *Am.* Note *f.* **3.** *fig.* Niveau *n.* **II** *v/t* **4.** *~ down* Kritik *etc* abschwächen; *~ up* j-n, Muskeln kräftigen. **III** *v/i* **5.** *~ in (with)* harmonieren (mit), passen (zu).

tongs [tɒŋz] *s pl*, *a.* **pair of ~** Zange *f.*

tongue [tʌŋ] *s* **1.** *anat.* Zunge *f (a. fig.):* *~ in cheek, with one's ~ in one's cheek* scherzhaft; *bite one's ~* sich auf die Zunge beißen *(a. fig.);* *hold one's ~* den Mund halten; *put out one's ~ at s.o.* j-m die Zunge herausstrecken; → *slip* 1, *tip* 1, *wag* II. **2.** (*Mutter*)Sprache *f.* **3.** Zunge *f (e-s Schuhs etc);* (*Land*)Zunge *f: ~ of land.* **4.** Klöppel *m (e-r Glocke).* **~ twist·er** *s* Zungenbrecher *m.*

ton·ic ['tɒnɪk] *s* **1.** *pharm.* Tonikum *n.* Stärkungsmittel *n: be a real ~ allg.* richtig guttun. **2.** Tonic *n (→ tonic water):* *a gin and ~* ein Gin Tonic. **~ wa·ter** *s* Tonic water *n (mit Kohlensäure u. Chinin versetztes Wasser).*

to·night [təˈnaɪt] **I** *adv* heute abend; heute nacht. **II** *s* **'~'s program(me)** das Programm (von) heute abend.

ton·sil ['tɒnsl] *s anat.* Mandel *f.* **ton·sil·li·tis** [ˌtɒnsɪˈlaɪtɪs] *s* ⚕ Mandelentzündung *f*; *weitS.* Angina *f.*

ton·sure ['tɒnʃə] *s* Tonsur *f.*

too [tu:] *adv* **1.** zu. **2.** zu, sehr. **3.** auch. **4.** auch noch, noch dazu.

took [tʊk] *pret von* **take.**

tool [tu:l] *s* **1.** Werkzeug *n (a. fig. Person)*, Gerät *n: be the ~s of s.o.'s trade fig.* j-s Rüstzeug sein; → *down* 15. **2.** V Schwanz *m (Penis).* **~ bag** *s* Werkzeugtasche *f.* **~ box** *s* Werkzeugkasten *m.* **~ shed** *s* Geräteschuppen *m.*

toot [tu:t] *mot.* **I** *v/i* hupen. **II** *v/t: ~ one's horn* → I. **III** *s: give a ~ on one's horn* → I.

tooth [tu:θ] *pl* **teeth** [ti:θ] *s anat.* Zahn *m (a. e-s Kamms, e-r Säge, e-s Zahnrads etc): in the teeth of fig.* gegen; trotz, ungeachtet; *fight ~ and nail fig.* erbittert *od.* verbissen kämpfen; *get one's teeth into fig.* sich reinknien in *(acc);* → *armed, brush*¹ 5, *cut* 10, *edge* 4, *skin* 1, *sweet* 1. **'~ache** *s* Zahnschmerzen *pl,* -weh *n.* **'~brush** *s* Zahnbürste *f.*

tooth·less ['tu:θlɪs] *adj* zahnlos.

'tooth·paste *s* Zahncreme *f*, -pasta *f.* **'~pick** *s* Zahnstocher *m.*

tooth·some ['tu:θsəm] *adj* □ lecker, schmackhaft.

toot·sie, toot·sy ['tʊtsɪ] *s Kindersprache:* Füßchen *n.*

top¹ [tɒp] **I** *s* **1.** oberer Teil; Gipfel *m*, Spitze *f (e-s Bergs etc);* Krone *f*, Wipfel *m (e-s Baums);* Kopfende *n*, oberes Ende *n (e-s Tischs etc): at the ~ of the page* oben auf der Seite; *from ~ to toe* von Kopf bis Fuß; *on ~* oben(auf); d(a)rauf; *on ~ of* (oben) auf *(dat od. acc),* über *(dat od. acc);* *on ~ of each other* auf-, übereinander; *on ~ of it fig.* obendrein; *get on ~ of s.o.* F j-m zuviel *od.* zu schwierig werden; → *thin* 1. **2.** *fig.* Spitze *f: at the ~ of one's voice* aus vollem Hals; *be at the ~ of* an der Spitze *(gen)* stehen; *stay on ~* an der Spitze bleiben. **3.** *(Bikini- etc)*Oberteil *n.* **4.** Oberfläche *f (e-s Tischs etc).* **5.** Deckel *m (e-s Glases),* (a. e-r Tube etc) Verschluß *m:* → *blow*¹ 11. **6.** *mot.* Verdeck *n:* → *hardtop.* **7.** *mot.* höchster Gang. **II** *adj* **8.** oberst: *~ hat* oberster Hut. *fig.* der Überlegene; der Chef; *~ hat* Zylinder *m.* **9.** *fig.* Höchst..., Spitzen...: *~ gear*

→ 7; **~ manager** Top-, Spitzenmanager *m*; **at ~ speed** mit Höchstgeschwindigkeit; **in Windeseile**; → **management** 2. **III** *v/t* **10.** bedecken (**with** mit). **11.** *fig.* übersteigen; übertreffen. **12. ~ the bill** der Star des Programms *od.* die Hauptattraktion sein.
Verbindungen mit Adverbien:
top| off *v/t bsd. Am.* abschließen, krönen (**with** mit). **~ out** *v/t* das Richtfest (*gen*) feiern. **~ up** *v/t* Tank *etc* auffüllen; F *j-m* nachschenken.

top² [~] *s* Kreisel *m* (*Spielzeug*): → **sleep I**.

to-pee ['təʊpɪ] *s* Tropenhelm *m*.

'top|-flight *adj* F Spitzen... ,**~'heav-y** *adj* kopflastig (*a. fig.*), oberlastig.

top-ic ['tɒpɪk] *s* Thema *n*: **~ of conversation** Gesprächsthema. **'top-i-cal** *adj* □ aktuell.

'top-knot *s* Haarknoten *m*.

top-less ['tɒplɪs] *adj* oben ohne; Oben-ohne-...

,**top|-'lev-el** *adj* auf höchster Ebene, Spitzen... '**~most** *adj* oberst. ,**~-'notch** *adj* F erstklassig, Spitzen...

to-pog-ra-phy [tə'pɒgrəfɪ] *s* Topographie *f*.

top-per ['tɒpə] *s* F Zylinder *m*. '**top-ping** *s*: **with a ~ of whipped cream** mit Schlagsahne darauf.

top-ple ['tɒpl] **I** *v/i* **1.** *mst* **~ over** umkippen. **II** *v/t* **2.** *mst* **~ over** umkippen. **3.** *fig.* Regierung *etc* stürzen.

,**top|-'se-cret** *adj* streng geheim. '**~-spin** *s* Tennis *etc*: Topspin *m* (*starker Aufwärtsdrall*).

top-sy-tur-vy [,tɒpsɪ'tɜːvɪ] *adj* F **1.** in e-r heillosen Unordnung. **2.** *fig.* konfus, wirr.

torch [tɔːtʃ] *s* **1.** *bsd. Br.* Taschenlampe *f*. **2.** Fackel *f*. '**~-light** *s*: **by ~** bei Fackelschein; **~ procession** Fackelzug *m*.

tore [tɔː] *pret von* **tear²**.

tor-ment I *v/t* ['tɔː'ment] **1.** quälen, *fig. a.* plagen: **be ~ed by** (*od.* **with**) gequält *od.* geplagt werden von. **II** *s* ['tɔːment] **2.** Qual *f*: **be in ~, suffer ~(s)** Qualen leiden. **3.** Quälgeist *m*.

torn [tɔːn] *pp von* **tear²**.

tor-na-do [tɔː'neɪdəʊ] *pl* **-do(e)s** *s* Tornado *m*.

tor-pe-do [tɔː'piːdəʊ] **I** *pl* **-does** *s* ✪, ✕

Torpedo *m*. **II** *v/t* torpedieren (*a. fig.*). **~ boat** *s* Torpedoboot *n*.

tor-pid ['tɔːpɪd] *adj* □ träg(e). **tor-por** ['~pə] *s* Trägheit *f*.

torque [tɔːk] *s phys.* Drehmoment *n*.

tor-rent ['tɒrənt] *s* **1.** reißender Strom: **~s** *pl* **of rain** sintflutartige Regenfälle *pl*; **the rain fell in ~s** es goß in Strömen. **2.** *fig.* Schwall *m*, Sturzbach *m* (*of* von). **tor-ren-tial** [tə'renʃl] *adj* sintflutartig.

tor-rid ['tɒrɪd] *adj* □ sengend.

tor-sion ['tɔːʃn] *s phys.* Torsion *f*, Verdrillung *f*.

tor-so ['tɔːsəʊ] *pl* **-sos** *s* Rumpf *m*; (*Kunst*) Torso *m*.

tort [tɔːt] *s* ⚖️ unerlaubte Handlung.

tor-toise ['tɔːtəs] *s zo.* Schildkröte *f*.

tor-tu-ous ['tɔːtʃʊəs] *adj* □ **1.** gewunden (*Pfad etc*). **2.** *fig.* umständlich.

tor-ture ['tɔːtʃə] **I** *v/t* **1.** foltern. **2.** *fig.* quälen: **be ~d by** (*od.* **with**) gequält werden von. **II** *s* **3.** Folter(ung) *f*. **4.** *fig.* Qual *f.* **~ cham-ber** *s* Folterkammer *f*.

To-ry ['tɔːrɪ] *pol. Br.* **I** *s* Tory *m*, Konservative *m*. **II** *adj* Tory..., torystisch, konservativ.

toss [tɒs] **I** *v/t* **1.** werfen: **~ s.o. s.th.** *j-m* et. zuwerfen; **~ back** Kopf zurückwerfen; **~ off** *Arbeit* hinhauen; *Getränk* hinunterstürzen. **2.** *Münze* hochwerfen: **~ s.o. for s.th.** mit *j-m* um et. losen. **II** *v/i* **3.** *a.* **~ about** (*od.* **around**), **~ and turn** sich (*im Schlaf etc*) hin *u.* her werfen. **4.** *a.* **~ up** e-e *Münze* hochwerfen: **~ for s.th.** um et. losen, et. auslosen. **III** *s* **5.** Wurf *m*. **6.** Hochwerfen *n* (*e-r Münze*): **win the ~** (*Sport*) die Wahl gewinnen. **7.** **I don't give a ~ about it** *Br.* F das ist mir völlig egal. '**~-up** *s* **1.** → **toss** 6. **2.** **it's a ~ whether** F es ist völlig offen, ob.

tot¹ [tɒt] *s* **1.** *a.* **tiny ~** F Knirps *m*. **2.** Schluck *m* (*Alkohol*).

tot² [~] *v/t:* **~ up** F zs.-rechnen, -zählen.

to-tal ['təʊtl] **I** *adj* □ **1.** völlig, total, Total...: → **recall** 4. **2.** ganz, gesamt, Gesamt... **II** *s* **3.** Gesamtmenge *f*; (End)Summe *f*: **a ~ of 20 cases** insgesamt 20 Kisten; **in ~** insgesamt. **III** *v/t pret u. pp* **-taled**, *bsd. Br.* **-talled 4.** sich belaufen auf (*acc*): **... ~(l)ing £500** ... von insgesamt 500 Pfund. **5.** *a.* **~ up** zs.-rechnen, -zählen. **to-tal-i-tar-i-an** [,~tælɪ'teərɪən] *adj pol.* totalitär. **to-tal-**

i·za·tor [ˈtəlaızeıtə] s *Pferdesport:* Totalisator *m.*

tote [təʊt] s *Pferdesport:* F Toto *n, m* (*Totalisator*).

tote bag [təʊt] s *bsd. Am.* Einkaufstasche *f.*

to·tem [ˈtəʊtəm] s Totem *n.* ~ **pole** s Totempfahl *m.*

tot·ter [ˈtɒtə] *v/i* (sch)wanken. **'tot·ter·y** *adj* wack(e)lig.

touch [tʌtʃ] **I** s **1.** Tastempfindung *f: be soft to the ~* sich weich anfühlen; → *sense* 1. **2.** Berührung *f, ♩ etc* Anschlag *m: at the ~ of a button* auf Knopfdruck. **3. be in ~ with s.o.** mit j-m in Verbindung stehen; *get in ~ with s.o.* sich mit j-m in Verbindung setzen; *keep in ~ with s.o.* mit j-m in Verbindung bleiben; *lose ~* den Kontakt verlieren (*with s.o.* zu j-m). **4.** (*Pinseletc*)Strich *m: put the finishing ~es to* letzte Hand legen an (*acc*). **5.** *fig.* Note *f: a personal ~.* 6. Spur *f* (*Salz etc*); *fig.* Anflug *m* (*von Ironie etc*): *a ~ of flu* e-e leichte Grippe. **7. in(to)** ~ (*Fußball*) im (ins) Aus. **II** *v/t* **8.** berühren; anfassen: ~ *wood!* toi, toi, toi!; → *nerve* 1. **9.** *Alkohol, Essen etc* anrühren. **10.** *fig.* herankommen an (*acc*). **11.** *fig.* rühren, bewegen. **12.** *fig.* berühren, betreffen. **13.** F *j-n* anpumpen (*for* um). **III** *v/i* **14.** sich berühren. **15. ~ on** *Thema etc* berühren, streifen.

Verbindungen mit Adverbien:

touch|**down** *v/i ✓* aufsetzen. ~ **off** *v/t* *Explosion, Krise etc* auslösen. ~ **up** *v/t* **1.** ausbessern; *phot.* retuschieren. **2.** *Br.* F *j-n* erheblich, betatschen.

touch|-and-'go *adj* kritisch (*Situation etc*): *it was ~ whether* es stand auf des Messers Schneide, ob. **'~·down** s ✓ Aufsetzen *n.*

tou·ché [ˈtuːʃeı] *int* eins zu null für dich!

touched [tʌtʃt] *adj* **1.** gerührt, bewegt. **2.** *be ~* F e-n Schlag haben. **'touch·ing** *adj* rührend, bewegend.

'touch|·line s *Fußball:* Seitenlinie *f.* **'~·stone** s Prüfstein *m* (*of* für). **'~·type** *v/i* blindschreiben.

touch·y [ˈtʌtʃı] *adj* □ **1.** empfindlich, reizbar. **2.** heikel (*Thema*).

tough [tʌf] *adj* □ **1.** zäh (*Fleisch etc*): (*as*) ~ *as leather* zäh wie Leder. **2.** widerstandsfähig (*Material etc*), (*Per-*

son *a.*) zäh. **3.** *fig.* hart (*Haltung etc*): *get ~ with* hart vorgehen gegen. **4.** *fig.* hart (*Konkurrenz etc*), (*Problem, Verhandlungen etc a.*) schwierig. **'tough·en I** *v/t a.* ~ *up j-n* hart od. zäh machen. **II** *v/i a.* ~ *up* hart od. zäh werden.

tour [tʊə] **I** s **1.** Tour *f* (*of* durch): a) (Rund)Reise *f,* (-)Fahrt *f:* ~ *operator* Reiseveranstalter *m,* b) Ausflug *m,* Wanderung *f.* **2.** Rundgang *m* (*of* durch): *take s.o. on a ~ of* j-n herumführen in (*dat*); → *conduct* 3, *guided* 1, *sightseeing.* **3.** *thea. etc* Tournee *f* (*a. Sport*), Gastspielreise *f* (*of* durch): *be on ~* auf Tournee sein (*in* in *dat*). **II** *v/t* **4.** bereisen, reisen durch. **5.** *thea. etc* e-e Tournee (*a. Sport*) od. Gastspielreise machen durch: *be ~ing Germany* auf Deutschlandtournee sein. **III** *v/i* **6.** ~ (*a*)*round* → 4. **7.** *thea. etc* e-e Tournee (*a. Sport*) od. Gastspielreise machen, auf Tournee sein. **'tour·ism** s Tourismus *m,* Fremdenverkehr *m.* **'tour·ist I** s Tourist(in). **II** *adj* Touristen...: ~ *class* ✓, ♟ Touristenklasse *f;* ~ *season* Reisesaison *f,* -zeit *f;* ~ *trade* Fremdenverkehrsgewerbe *n.*

tour·na·ment [ˈtʊənəmənt] s Turnier *n.*

tou·sled [ˈtaʊzld] *adj* zerzaust (*Haar*).

tout [taʊt] **I** *v/t* **1.** (aufdringlich) Reklame machen für. **2.** anpreisen (*as* als). **II** *v/i* **3.** ~ *for business* Kunden werben. **III** s **4.** *Br.* (*Karten*)Schwarzhändler(in).

tow [təʊ] **I** *v/t* *Boot etc* schleppen, *Auto etc a.* abschleppen: ~ *away* falsch geparktes Fahrzeug abschleppen. **II** s: *give s.o. a ~* j-n abschleppen; *take in ~ Auto etc* abschleppen, *Boot etc* ins Schlepptau nehmen; *with his children in ~* F mit s-n Kindern im Schlepptau.

to·ward *bsd. Am.,* **to·wards** *bsd. Br.* [təˈwɔːd(z)] *prp* **1.** *Richtung:* auf (*acc*) ... zu, (in) Richtung, zu: → *face* 13, *etc.* **2.** *zeitlich:* gegen: ~ *the end of* gegen Ende (*gen*). **3.** *fig.* gegenüber: → *attitude* 2, *etc.* **4.** *fig.* auf (*acc*) ... hin: *they gave me s.th.* ~ *it* sie zahlten mir es dazu.

tow·el [ˈtaʊəl] **I** s Handtuch *n,* (*Badeetc*)Tuch *n: throw in the ~* (*Boxen*) das Handtuch werfen (*a. fig.*); → *sanitary* 1. **II** *v/t pret u. pp* -**eled,** *bsd. Br.* -**elled** *a.* ~ *down* (mit e-m Handtuch) abtrocknen *od.* abreiben. **~ rail** *s* Handtuchhalter *m.*

tow·er ['tauə] **I** *s* Turm *m:* **~ block** *Br.* Hochhaus *n.* **II** *v/i:* **~ above** (*od.* **over**) überragen (*a. fig.*). **'tow·er·ing** *adj* **1.** turmhoch. **2.** *fig.* überragend. **3.** *be in a* **~ rage** vor Wut rasen.

town [taun] *s* (Klein)Stadt *f:* **go to** (**the**) **~** in die Stadt fahren *od.* gehen; **be** (**out**) **on the ~** F e-n draufmachen; → **paint** 2. **~ cen·tre** *s Br.* Innenstadt *f,* City *f.* **~ fa·thers** *pl* Stadtväter *pl.* **~ hall** *s* Rathaus *n.* **~ plan·ning** *s* Stadtplanung *f.*

towns·folk ['taunzfəuk] → **townspeople.**

town·ship ['taunʃɪp] *s Am.* (Stadt)Gemeinde *f;* (Kreis)Bezirk *m.*

towns·peo·ple ['taunz,pi:pl] *s pl* Städter *pl,* Stadtbevölkerung *f.*

'tow·rope *s mot.* Abschleppseil *n.*

tox·ic ['tɒksɪk] *adj* (**~ally**) toxisch, giftig, Gift-.

tox·in ['tɒksɪn] *s biol.* Toxin *n.*

toy [tɔɪ] **I** *s* **1.** Spielzeug *n:* **~s** *pl* Spielsachen *pl,* -zeug *n,* **✝** -waren *pl.* **II** *v/i* **2. ~ with** spielen mit (*a. fig.*). **III** *adj* **3.** Spielzeug... **4.** *zo.* Zwerg... (*Hund*). **~ shop** *s* Spielwarengeschäft *n,* -handlung *f.*

trace¹ [treɪs] *s* **1.** Spur *f* (*a. fig.*): **without** (**a**) **~** spurlos; **lose all ~ of s.o.** j-n aus den Augen verlieren. **II** *v/t* **2.** j-n, *et.* ausfindig machen, aufspüren, *et.* finden: **he was ~d to** s-e Spur führte nach. **3.** *a.* **~ back** *et.* zurückverfolgen (**to** bis zu): **~ s.th. to** *et.* zurückführen auf (*acc*), *et.* herleiten aus **4.** (durch)pausen.

trace² [~] *s* Zugleine *f:* **kick over the ~s** *fig.* über die Stränge schlagen.

trace el·e·ment *s* **♠** Spurenelement *n.*

tra·che·a [trəˈkiːə] *pl* **-ae** [~iː] *s anat.* Luftröhre *f.*

trac·ing ['treɪsɪŋ] *s* Pause *f.* **~ pa·per** *s* Pauspapier *n.*

track [træk] **I** *s* **1.** Spur *f* (*a. e-s Tonbands etc u. fig.*), *hunt. a.* Fährte *f:* **be** (**hot**) **on s.o.'s ~** j-m (dicht) auf der Spur sein; **be on the wrong ~** auf der falschen Spur *od.* auf dem Holzweg sein; **keep ~ of** sich auf dem Laufenden halten über (*acc*); **lose ~ of** den Überblick verlieren über (*acc*). **2.** Pfad *m,* Weg *m.* **3.** 🚃

Gleis *n,* Geleise *n:* **jump the ~s** aus den Schienen springen, entgleisen. **4.** *Sport:* (*Lauf-, Radrenn*)Bahn *f,* (*Renn*)Strecke *f.* **5.** ⚙ Raupe *f,* Gleis-, Raupenkette *f.* **6.** Nummer *f* (*auf e-r Langspielplatte etc*). **II** *v/t* **7.** verfolgen: **~ down** aufspüren; aufstöbern, -treiben. **,~-and-'field** *adj Am.* Leichtathletik...: **~ sports** *pl* Leichtathletik *f.*

tracked [trækt] *adj:* **~ vehicle** Gleisketten-, Raupenfahrzeug *n.*

track·er dog [ˈtrækə] *s* Spür-, Suchhund *m.*

track e·vents *s pl Leichtathletik:* Laufdisziplinen *pl.*

track·ing sta·tion ['trækɪŋ] *s Raumfahrt:* Bodenstation *f.*

track| rec·ord *s* **1.** *Sport:* Bahnrekord *m.* **2. have a good ~** *fig.* einiges vorzuweisen haben. **'~·suit** *s* Trainingsanzug *m.*

tract¹ [trækt] *s* **1.** Fläche *f,* Gebiet *n.* **2.** *anat.* (*Verdauungs*)Trakt *m,* (*Atem-*)Wege *pl.*

tract² [~] *s* Traktat *m, n,* kurze Abhandlung.

trac·ta·ble ['træktəbl] *adj* □ folg-, fügsam.

trac·tion ['trækʃn] *s* **1.** Ziehen *n.* **2.** ⚙ Antrieb *m.* **3.** *mot.* Bodenhaftung *f.* **4. his leg is in ~** **☀** sein Bein ist im Streckverband. **~ en·gine** *s* Zugmaschine *f.*

trac·tor ['træktə] *s* Traktor *m,* Trecker *m,* Zugmaschine *f.*

trade [treɪd] **I** *s* **1.** Handel *m* (**in** mit *et.*). **2.** Branche *f,* Gewerbe *n:* **be in the tourist ~** im Fremdenverkehrsgewerbe (tätig) sein. **3. do good ~** gute Geschäfte machen. **4.** (*bsd. Handwerks*)Beruf *m:* **by ~** von Beruf. **II** *v/i* **5.** handeln (**in** mit *et.*), Handel treiben: **~ with s.o.** a. mit j-m Geschäfte machen. **6. ~ on** *b.s.* ausnutzen, ausnützen. **III** *v/t* **7.** (ein-)tauschen (**for** gegen). **8. ~ in** in Zahlung geben (**for** für). **~ a·gree·ment** *s* Handelsabkommen *n.* **'~·mark** *s* **1.** **✝** Warenzeichen *n.* **2.** *fig.* Kennzeichen *n.* **~ name** *s* Markenname *m,* Handelsbezeichnung *f.* **~ price** *s* Großhandelspreis *m.*

trad·er ['treɪdə] *s* Händler(in).

trades·man ['treɪdzmən] *s* (*irr man*) **1.** (Einzel)Händler *m;* Ladeninhaber *m.* **2.** Lieferant *m:* **~'s entrance** Lieferanteneingang *m.*

trade| un·ion s Gewerkschaft f. **~ un-
-ion·ist** s Gewerkschaftler(in).

trad·ing| part·ner s Handelspartner(in).
~ stamp s Rabattmarke f.

tra·di·tion [trə'dɪʃn] s Tradition f: **by
~** traditionell(erweise). **tra'di·tion·al**
[~ʃənl] adj □ traditionell: **~ly** a. tradi-
tionellerweise; **it is ~ for them to** (inf) es
ist bei ihnen Brauch od. so üblich, daß
sie.

traf·fic ['træfɪk] **I** s **1.** Verkehr m. **2.** (bsd.
illegaler) Handel (**in** mit): **~ in drugs**
Drogenhandel. **II** v/i pret u. pp **-ficked
3.** (bsd. illegal) handeln (**in** mit). **~
cha·os** s Verkehrschaos n. **~ cir·cle** s
Am. Kreisverkehr m. **~ cone** s Pylon(e
f) m, Leitkegel m. **~ is·land** s Verkehrsinsel f. **~ jam** s Verkehrsstauung f,
-stockung f, Stau m.

traf·fick·er ['træfɪkə] s (bsd. illegaler)
Händler (**in** mit): **~ in drugs** Drogenhändler.

traf·fic| light s Br. mst pl Verkehrsampel
f. **~ of·fence** s Verkehrsdelikt n. **~ of-
fend·er** s Verkehrssünder(in). **~ offense** Am. → **traffic offence. ~ sign** s
Verkehrszeichen n, -schild n. **~ sig·nal**
→ **traffic light. ~ war·den** s Br. Park-
überwacher m, Politesse f.

trag·e·dy ['trædʒədɪ] s thea. Tragödie f
(a. fig.), Trauerspiel n.

trag·ic ['trædʒɪk] adj (**~ally**) thea. tragisch (a. fig.): **~ally** a. tragischerweise;
unter tragischen Umständen.

trag·i·com·e·dy [,trædʒɪ'kɒmədɪ] s thea.
Tragikomödie f (a. fig.). **,trag·i'com·ic**
adj (**~ally**) tragikomisch.

trail [treɪl] **I** v/t **1.** et. nachschleifen lassen: **~ one's feet** schlurfen. **2.** verfolgen. **3.** Sport: zurückliegen hinter (dat)
(**by** um). **II** v/i **4.** (**along**) **behind s.o.**
hinter j-m herschleifen. **5.** sich schlep-
pen. **6.** Sport: zurückliegen ([by] **2 - 0**
0 : 2). **III** s **7.** Spur f (a. fig.), hunt. a.
Fährte f: **~ of blood** Blutspur; **~ of dust**
(**smoke**) Staubwolke f (Rauchfahne f);
be (**hot**) **on s.o.'s ~** j-m (dicht) auf der
Spur sein. **8.** Pfad m, Weg m. '**trail·er** s
1. mot. Anhänger m. **2.** Am. Caravan
m, Wohnwagen m. **3.** Film, TV: Trailer
m, Vorschau f.

train [treɪn] **I** s 🚂 Zug m: **by ~** mit der
Bahn, mit dem Zug; **on the ~** im Zug; **~
ferry** Eisenbahnfähre f; **~ set** (Spiel-

zeug)Eisenbahn f. **2.** Kolonne f. **3.**
Schleppe f. **4.** fig. Folge f, Kette f (von
Ereignissen etc): **~ of thought** Gedankengang m. **II** v/t **5.** j-n ausbilden (**as**
als, zum), a. Auge, Verstand etc schulen; (Sport) trainieren; Tier abrichten,
dressieren (**to do** zu tun). **6.** Geschütz,
Kamera etc richten (**on** auf acc). **III** v/i
7. ausgebildet werden (**as** als, zum). **8.**
Sport: trainieren (**for** für). '**train·er** s **1.**
Ausbilder(in); Dresseur m, Abrich-
ter(in), Dompteur m, Dompteuse f;
(Sport) Trainer(in). **2.** Br. Turnschuh
m. '**train·ing** s **1.** Ausbildung f, Schulung f; Abrichten n, Dressur f. **2.** Sport:
Training f: **be in ~** im Training stehen,
trainieren; (gut) in Form sein; **be out of
~** nicht in Form sein. **II** adj **3.** Ausbil-
dungs..., Schulungs... **4.** Sport: Trainings...

traipse [treɪps] v/i F latschen.

trait [treɪt] s (Charakter)Zug m, Eigenschaft f.

trai·tor ['treɪtə] s Verräter m (**to** an
dat).

tra·jec·to·ry [trə'dʒektərɪ] s phys. Flug-
bahn f.

tram [træm] s Br. a) Straßenbahn(wagen
m) f: **by ~** mit der Straßenbahn; **on the
~** in der Straßenbahn, b) → **tramway.**
'**~car** s Br. Straßenbahnwagen m.

tramp [træmp] **I** v/i **1.** sta(m)pfen; trampeln. **II** v/t **2.** sta(m)pfen od. trampeln
durch. **III** s **3.** bsd. Br. Tramp m, Land-
streicher(in). **4.** Wanderung f: **go for a
~** e-e Wanderung machen. **5.** bsd. Am.
Flittchen n.

tram·ple ['træmpl] **I** v/i trampeln: **~ on**
herumtrampeln auf (dat); fig. j-s Gefühle mit Füßen treten. **II** v/t zertram-
peln: **~ down** niedertrampeln; **be ~d to
death** zu Tode getrampelt werden; →
underfoot.

tram·po·line ['træmpəliːn] s Trampolin n.

'**tram·way** s Br. Straßenbahn(linie) f.

trance [trɑːns] s Trance f: **go into a ~** in
Trance verfallen.

tran·quil ['træŋkwɪl] adj □ **1.** ruhig,
friedlich. **2.** sorgenfrei. **tran'quil·i·ty** s
Am., **tran'quil·li·ty** s bsd. Br. Ruhe m,
Frieden m. '**tran·quil·ize** v/t Am.,
'**tran·quil·lize** v/t bsd. Br. j-n beruhigen, Tier a. betäuben. '**tran·quil·(l)iz-**

er s Beruhigungs- od. Betäubungsmittel n.

trans·act [træn'zækt] v/t Geschäft abwickeln, a. Handel abschließen. **trans'ac·tion** s 1. Abwicklung f, Abschluß m. 2. Transaktion f, Geschäft n.

trans·at·lan·tic [ˌtrænzət'læntɪk] adj transatlantisch, Transatlantik...

tran·scen·den·tal [ˌtrænsen'dentl] adj: ~ **meditation** transzendentale Meditation.

trans·con·ti·nen·tal ['trænzˌkɒntɪ'nentl] adj transkontinental.

tran·scribe [træn'skraɪb] v/t 1. abschreiben, kopieren. 2. Stenogramm etc übertragen (into in acc). 3. ♪ transkribieren, umschreiben (for für). 4. ~ onto → transfer 3.

tran·script ['trænskrɪpt] s Abschrift f, Kopie f. **tran·scrip·tion** [ˌ~'skrɪpʃn] s 1. Abschreiben n, Kopieren n 2. Übertragen n. 3. ♪ Transkription f, Umschreibung f. 4. → transcript. 5. → phonetic I.

tran·sept ['trænsept] s △ Querschiff n.

trans·fer I v/t [træns'fɜː] 1. (to) Betrieb etc verlegen (nach); j-n versetzen (nach); (Sport) Spieler transferieren (zu), abgeben (an acc); Geld überweisen (an j-n, auf ein Konto). 2. ⚖ Eigentum, Recht übertragen (to auf acc). 3. ~ to Bandaufnahme etc überspielen auf (acc). II v/i [træns'fɜː] 4. Sport: wechseln (to zu) (Spieler). 5. Reise: umsteigen (from ... to von ... auf acc). III s ['trænsfɜː] 6. Verlegung f; Versetzung f; (Sport) Transfer m, Wechsel m; Überweisung f: ~ fee Transfersumme f, Ablöse(summe) f. 7. ⚖ Übertragung f. 8. Umsteigen n; bsd. Am. Umsteige(fahr)karte f. 9. bsd. Br. Abziehbild n. **trans'fer·a·ble** adj übertragbar.

trans·fig·ure [træns'fɪɡə] v/t verklären.

trans·fix [træns'fɪks] v/t 1. durchstechen, -bohren (with mit). 2. stand ~ed to the spot wie angewurzelt dastehen.

trans·form [træns'fɔːm] v/t et. umwandeln, a. j-n verwandeln (into in acc). **trans·for·ma·tion** [ˌ~fə'meɪʃn] s Um-, Verwandlung f. **trans·form·er** [~'fɔːmə] s ⚡ Transformator m.

trans·fu·sion [træns'fjuːʒn] s ⚕ Bluttransfusion f, -übertragung f.

trans·gress [træns'ɡres] I v/t verletzen,

verstoßen gegen. II v/i sündigen (against gegen). **trans'gres·sion** s (of) Verletzung f (gen), Verstoß m (gegen); Sünde f.

tran·si·ent ['trænzɪənt] adj □ flüchtig, vergänglich.

tran·sis·tor [træn'sɪstə] s ⚡ Transistor m: ~ (radio) Transistorradio n. **tran'sis·tor·ize** v/t transistor(is)ieren.

trans·it ['trænsɪt] s 1. Durchfahrt f. 2. ✈ Transport m: in ~ unterwegs, auf dem Transport. ~ **camp** s Durchgangslager n.

tran·si·tion [træn'sɪʒn] s Übergang m (from ... to von ... zu): period of ~ Übergangsperiode f, -zeit f. **tran'si·tion·al** [ˌ~ʒnl] adj Übergangs...

tran·si·tive ['trænsətɪv] adj □ ling. transitiv.

tran·si·to·ry ['trænsɪtərɪ] → transient.

trans·lat·a·ble [træns'leɪtəbl] adj übersetzbar. **trans'late** I v/t 1. übersetzen (from English into German aus dem Englischen ins Deutsche). 2. ~ into action fig. in die Tat umsetzen. II v/i 3. sich auf etc übersetzen lassen. **trans'la·tion** s Übersetzung f. **trans'la·tor** s Übersetzer(in).

trans·lu·cent [trænz'luːsnt] adj □ lichtdurchlässig: ~ glass Milchglas n.

trans·mi·gra·tion [ˌtrænzmaɪ'ɡreɪʃn] s Seelenwanderung f.

trans·mis·sion [trænz'mɪʃn] s 1. Übertragung f (a. e-r Krankheit). 2. Rundfunk, TV: Sendung f, pl a. Programm n. 3. mot. Getriebe n.

trans·mit [trænz'mɪt] I v/t 1. Krankheit übertragen. 2. Signale (aus)senden; (Rundfunk, TV) Programm senden. 3. phys. Wärme etc leiten; Licht etc durchlassen. II v/i 4. Rundfunk, TV: senden. **trans'mit·ter** s Sender m.

trans·mu·ta·tion [ˌtrænzmjuː'teɪʃn] s Um-, Verwandlung f. **trans·mute** [ˌ~'mjuːt] v/t um-, verwandeln (into in acc).

trans·par·en·cy [træns'pærənsɪ] s 1. Durchsichtigkeit f (a. fig.). 2. fig. Durchschaubarkeit f. 3. Dia(positiv) n. **trans'par·ent** adj □ 1. durchsichtig. 2. fig. durchsichtig, durchschaubar; offenkundig.

tran·spi·ra·tion [ˌtrænspə'reɪʃn] s Transpiration f (a. ⚘), Schweißabsonderung *f.* **tran·spire** [~'spaɪə] *v/i* **1.** *physiol.* transpirieren (*a.* ♀), schwitzen. **2.** *it ~d that* es sickerte durch *od.* wurde bekannt, daß. **3.** F passieren.

trans·plant I *v/t* [træns'plɑːnt] **1.** ♣ transplantieren, verpflanzen. **2.** *Pflanze* um-, verpflanzen. **3.** *j-n* umsiedeln, *Betrieb etc* verlegen (*to* nach). II *s* ['trænsplɑːnt] **4.** ♣ Transplantation *f*, Verpflanzung *f*. **5.** ♣ Transplantat *n*. ,**trans·plan'ta·tion** *s* **1.** → *transplant* **4. 2.** Um-, Verpflanzung *f*.

trans·port I *v/t* [træns'pɔːt] **1.** *Waren, Truppen* transportieren, *a. Personen* befördern. II *s* ['trænspɔːt] **2.** Transport *m*, Beförderung *f*; *~café Br.* Fernfahrerlokal *n*. **3.** Beförderungs-, Verkehrsmittel *n od. pl.* **4.** ✕ Transportflugzeug *n*, (*Truppen*)Transporter *m*. **5.** *pl* (überschwengliche)Reisen *pl.* ~ **a·gen·cy** *s* Reisebüro *n.* ~ **a·gent** *s* Reisebüroinhaber(in) *od.* -kaufmann *m*, -kauffrau *f*; *weitS.*, *a.* ~'s Reisebüro *n.* ~ **bu·reau** *s* (*a. irr bureau*) Reisebüro *n*.

trans·verse ['trænzvɜːs] *adj* Quer... ,**trans'verse·ly** *adv* quer.

trans·ves·tite [trænz'vestaɪt] *s* Transvestit *m*.

trap [træp] I *s* **1.** Falle *f* (*a. fig.*): *set a ~* e-e Falle aufstellen; *set a ~ for s.o.* j-m e-e Falle stellen; *fall into s.o.'s ~* j-m in die Falle gehen. **2.** *shut one's ~, keep one's ~ shut sl.* die Schnauze halten. II *v/t* **3.** (in *od.* mit e-r Falle) fangen. **4.** *be ~ped* eingeschlossen sein (*Bergleute etc*). **5.** *fig.* in e-e Falle locken: ~ *s.o. into doing s.th.* j-n dazu bringen, et. zu tun. **6.** *Sport:* Ball stoppen. '**~door** *s* Falltür *f*.

tra·peze [trə'piːz] *s Artistik:* Trapez *n*: ~ **artist** Trapezkünstler(in). **tra'pe·zi·um** [~ʒjəm] *pl* -**zi·ums, -zi·a** [~ʒjə] *s Ar bsd. Br.* Trapez *n*; *bsd. Am.* Trapezoid *n*. **trap·e·zoid** ['træpɪzɔɪd] *s Ar bsd. Br.* Trapezoid *n*; *bsd. Am.* Trapez *n*.

trap·per ['træpə] *s* Trapper *m*, Fallensteller *m*.

trap·pings ['træpɪŋz] *s pl* **1.** Rangabzeichen *pl.* **2.** *fig.* Drum u. Dran *n*.

trash [træʃ] *s* **1.** *Am.* Abfall *m*, Müll *m*: ~ **can** Abfall-, Mülleimer *m*; Abfall-, Mülltonne *f*. **2.** Schund *m*. **3.** Quatsch *m*, Unsinn *m*. **4.** *bsd. Am.* Gesindel *n*. '**trash·y** *adj* Schund...

trau·ma ['trɔːmə] *s psych.* Trauma *n*.

trau·mat·ic [~'mætɪk] *adj* (*~ally*) traumatisch.

trav·el ['trævl] I *v/i pret u. pp* -**eled,** *bsd. Br.* -**elled 1.** reisen: → *light²* 4. **2.** ♀ reisen (*in* in e-r *Ware*). **3.** fahren; sich verbreiten (*Neuigkeit etc*); ◎ *etc* sich bewegen; *phys.* sich fortpflanzen. **4.** *be really ~ (l)ing* F e-n ganz schönen Zahn draufhaben. II *v/t* **5.** bereisen; *Strecke* zurücklegen, fahren. III *s* **6.** Reisen *n*. **7.** *pl* (*die*) Auslands)Reisen *pl.* ~ **a·gen·cy** *s* Reisebüro *n.* ~ **a·gent** *s* Reisebüroinhaber(in) *od.* -kaufmann *m*, -kauffrau *f*; *weitS.*, *a.* ~'s Reisebüro *n.* ~ **bu·reau** *s* (*a. irr bureau*) Reisebüro *n.* **trav·el·er** *s Am.* → *traveller*; ~'s **check** Reise-, Travellerscheck *m.* **trav·el·ing** *Am.* → *travelling*.

trav·el·ler ['trævlə] *s bsd. Br.* **1.** Reisende *m*, *f*: ~'s **cheque** *Br.* Reise-, Travellerscheck *m.* **2.** ♀ (Handels)Vertreter *m* (*in* für). '**trav·el·ling** *adj bsd. Br.* **1.** Reise...: ~ (*alarm*) **clock** Reisewecker *m*; ~ **salesman** → *traveller* 2. **2.** Wander...: ~ **circus**.

trav·e·log *s Am.*, **trav·e·logue** *s* ['trævəlɒg] *s* Reisebericht *m* (*Vortrag*), -film *m*.

'**trav·el·sick** *adj* reisekrank. ~ **sick·ness** *s* Reisekrankheit *f*.

trav·erse ['trævəs] *v/t* durch-, überqueren.

trav·es·ty ['trævəstɪ] *s* Zerrbild *n*: *a ~ of justice* ein Hohn auf die Gerechtigkeit.

trav·o·la·tor ['trævəleɪtə] *s* Rollsteig *m*.

trawl·er ['trɔːlə] *s* ♣ Trawler *m*.

tray [treɪ] *s* **1.** Tablett *n*. **2.** Ablagekorb *m*.

treach·er·ous ['tretʃərəs] *adj* □ **1.** verräterisch. **2.** *fig.* tückisch (*Strömung etc*). '**treach·er·y** *s* Verrat *m*.

trea·cle ['triːkl] *s bsd. Br.* Sirup *m*. '**trea·cly** *adj* **1.** sirupartig. **2.** *fig.* süßlich.

tread [tred] I *v/i* (*irr*) **1.** treten (*on* auf *acc*; *in acc*): ~ **carefully** vorsichtig auftreten; *fig.* vorsichtig vorgehen; → *corn²*, *toe* I. II *v/t* (*irr*) **2.** *Pfad, Wasser* treten: ~ *in(to)* eintreten (*in acc*). III *s* **3.** Gang *m*; Schritt(e *pl*) *m*. **4.** *mot.* Profil *n* (*e-s Reifens*). '**~mill** *s hist.* Tretmühle *f* (*a. fig.*).

trea·son ['triːzn] *s* Landesverrat *m*.

treas·ure ['treʒə] I s Schatz m, (*Person* F a.) Juwel n: ~ **hunt** Schatzsuche f. II v/t et. zu schätzen wissen; j-s *Andenken* in Ehren halten. '**treas·ur·er** s Schatzmeister(in). '**Treas·ur·y** s pol. Finanzministerium n.

treat [tri:t] I v/t 1. j-n behandeln (**like** wie); et. behandeln, umgehen mit: → **dirt**. 2. et. ansehen, betrachten (**as** als). 3. ✍ j-n behandeln (**for** gegen): be ~ed **for** in ärztlicher Behandlung stehen wegen. 4. 🔧, ⊙ et. behandeln (**with** mit; **against** gegen). 5. j-n einladen (**to** zu): ~ **s.o. to s.th. a.** j-m et. spendieren; ~ **o.s. to s.th.** sich et. leisten od. gönnen. II v/i 6. ~ **of** handeln von, behandeln. III s 7. (besondere) Freude, (besondere) Überraschung.

trea·tise ['~tɪz] s (wissenschaftliche) Abhandlung (**on** über acc). '**treat·ment** s allg. Behandlung f. '**trea·ty** s pol. Vertrag m: **by** ~ vertraglich.

tre·ble ['trebl] I adj □ dreifach. II v/t u. v/i (sich) verdreifachen.

tree [tri:] s Baum m: **in a** ~ auf e-m Baum; → **bark²** I. '**tree·less** adj baumlos.

'**tree|·line** s Baumgrenze f. ~ **trunk** s Baumstamm m.

tre·foil ['trefɔɪl] s 1. ❀ Klee m. 2. △ Dreipaß m.

trek [trek] I v/i marschieren. II s lange, gefährliche Fußreise.

trel·lis ['trelɪs] s Spalier n (*für Pflanzen etc*).

trem·ble ['trembl] I v/i zittern (**with** vor dat): ~ **at the thought** (od. **idea**) bei dem Gedanken zittern; ~ **for** zittern m. bangen um. II s Zittern n.

tre·men·dous [trɪ'mendəs] adj □ 1. gewaltig. 2. F klasse, toll.

trem·or ['tremə] s 1. Zittern n: → **earth tremor**. 2. Schauder m.

trench [trentʃ] s Graben m, ✗ Schützengraben m. ~ **coat** s Trenchcoat m.

trend [trend] s 1. Trend m, Tendenz f (**toward[s]** zu). 2. Mode f. '~**set·ter** s Trendsetter m (*j-d, der e-n neuen Trend in Gang setzt od. et. in Mode bringt*).

trend·y ['trendɪ] adj □ F modern, modisch: **be** ~ als schick gelten, in sein; ~ **disco** In-Disco f.

tres·pass ['trespəs] v/i: ~ **on** a) *Grundstück etc* unbefugt betreten: **no** ~**ing**

Betreten verboten!, b) j-s *Zeit etc* über Gebühr in Anspruch nehmen. II s unbefugtes Betreten. '**tres·pass·er** s: ~**s will be prosecuted** Betreten bei Strafe verboten!

tri·al ['traɪəl] s 1. 🏛 Prozeß m, (Gerichts)Verhandlung f, (-)Verfahren n: ~ **by jury** Schwurgerichtsverfahren; **be on** (od. **stand**) ~ vor Gericht stehen (**for** wegen). 2. Erprobung f, Probe f, Prüfung f, Test m: **by** ~ **and error** durch Ausprobieren; **on** ~ auf od. zur Probe; **be on** ~ erprobt od. getestet werden; **he's still on** ~ er ist noch in der Probezeit. 3. **be a** ~ **to** j-m Ärger od. Sorgen machen. ~ **mar·riage** s Ehe f auf Probe. ~ **pe·ri·od** s Probezeit f. ~ **run** s ⊙ Probelauf m; mot. Probefahrt f: **give a car a** ~ e-n Wagen ausprobieren.

tri·an·gle ['traɪæŋgl] s 1. ◭ Dreieck n. 2. ♪ Triangel m. 3. Am. → **set square**. **tri·an·gu·lar** [~'æŋgʊlə] adj □ dreieckig.

trib·al ['traɪbl] adj Stammes... **tribe** [traɪb] s Stamm m.

tribes|·man ['traɪbzmən] s (*irr* **man**) Stammesangehörige m. '~**·wom·an** s (*irr* **woman**) Stammesangehörige f.

tri·bu·nal [traɪ'bju:nl] s 🏛 Gericht n.

trib·u·tar·y ['trɪbjʊtərɪ] s Nebenfluß m.

trib·ute ['trɪbju:t] s: **be a** ~ **to** j-m Ehre machen; **pay** ~ **to** j-m Anerkennung zollen.

trice [traɪs] s: **in a** ~ F im Nu, im Handumdrehen.

tri·chi·na [trɪ'kaɪnə] pl -**nae** [~ni:] s zo. Trichine f.

trick [trɪk] I s 1. Trick m (a. b.s.), (*Karten- etc*)Kunststück n: **by a** ~ mit e-m Trick; **how's** ~**s**? F wie geht's?; **dirty** ~ Gemeinheit f. 2. Streich m: **play a** ~ **on s.o.** j-m e-n Streich spielen. 3. **have a** ~ **of doing s.th.** die (merkwürdige) Angewohnheit od. die Eigenart haben, et. zu tun. 4. *Kartenspiel*: Stich m: **take** (od. **win**) **a** ~ e-n Stich machen. II adj 5. Trick...: ~ **question** Fangfrage f. III v/t 6. j-n reinlegen: ~ **s.o. into doing s.th.** j-n mit e-m Trick dazu bringen, et. zu tun. '**trick·er·y** s Tricks pl.

trick·le ['trɪkl] v/i tröpfeln; rieseln.

trick·ster ['trɪkstə] s Betrüger(in), Schwindler(in). '**trick·y** adj □ 1.

schwierig, (*Problem etc a.*) heikel. **2.** durchtrieben, raffiniert.

tri·cy·cle ['traısıkl] *s* Dreirad *n*.

tri·fle ['traıfl] **I** *s* **1.** Kleinigkeit *f*; Lappalie *f*: **a** ~ ein bißchen, etwas. **2.** a) *bsd. Br.* Trifle *n* (*Biskuitdessert*), b) *Am.* Obstdessert mit Schlagsahne. **II** *v/i* **3.** ~ **with** *fig.* spielen mit: **he is not to be ~d with** er läßt nicht mit sich spaßen. **'tri·fling** *adj* unbedeutend, geringfügig.

trig·ger ['trıgə] **I** *s* Abzug *m* (*am Gewehr etc*): **pull the** ~ abdrücken. **II** *v/t a.* ~ **off** *fig.* auslösen. **'~₁hap·py** *adj* schießwütig.

trig·o·nom·e·try [₁trıgə'nɒmətrı] *s* △ Trigonometrie *f*.

trike [traık] *s* F Dreirad *n*.

tril·o·gy ['trılədʒı] *s* Trilogie *f*.

trim [trım] **I** *v/t* **1.** Hecke *etc* stutzen, beschneiden, sich *den Bart etc* stutzen: ~ **off** abschneiden. **2.** *Kleidungsstück* besetzen (**with** mit): ~**med with fur** pelzbesetzt, mit Pelzbesatz. **II** *s* **3.** **give** *s.th.* **a** ~ → **1. 4. be in good** ~ F gut in Schuß sein (*Auto etc*), (*Person a.*) gut in Form sein. **III** *adj* **5.** gepflegt. **'trim·ming** *s* **1.** a. *pl* Besatz *m*. **2.** *pl* Zubehör *n*; Extras *pl*: **with all the** ~**s** *gastr.* mit den üblichen Beilagen. **3.** *pl* Abfälle *pl*.

trin·ket ['trıŋkıt] *s* (*bsd.* billiges) Schmuckstück.

tri·o ['triːəʊ] *pl* **-os** *s* Trio *n*, ♪ *a.* Terzett *n*.

trip [trıp] **I** *v/i* **1.** stolpern (**over** über *acc*). **2.** sich vertun. **II** *v/t* **3.** *a.* ~ **up** *j-m* ein Bein stellen (*a. fig.*). **III** *s* **4.** Reise *f*; Ausflug *m*, Trip *m*: **go on a bus** ~ e-n Busausflug machen. **5.** *sl.* Trip *m* (*Drogenrausch*): **be on a** ~ auf dem Trip sein.

tripe [traıp] *s* **1.** *gastr.* Kaldaunen *pl*, Kutteln *pl*. **2.** F Quatsch *m*, Mist *m*.

tri·ple ['trıpl] **I** *adj* □ dreifach: ~ **jump** (*Leichtathletik*) Dreisprung *m*; ~ **jumper** Dreispringer *m*. **II** *v/t u. v/i* (sich) verdreifachen.

tri·plet ['trıplıt] *s* Drilling *m*.

trip·li·cate ['trıplıkət] *s*: **in** ~ in dreifacher Ausfertigung.

tri·pod ['traıpɒd] *s phot.* Stativ *n*.

trip·per ['trıpə] *s* (*bsd. Tages*)Ausflügler(in).

'trip₁wire *s* Stolperdraht *m*.

trite [traıt] *adj* □ abgedroschen; banal.

tri·umph ['traıəmf] **I** *s* Triumph *m* (**over** über *acc*): **in** ~ im Triumph, triumphierend. **II** *v/i* triumphieren (**over** über *acc*). **tri·um·phal** [~'ʌmfl] *adj* Triumph...: ~ **arch** Triumphbogen *m*; ~ **procession** Triumphzug *m*. **tri'um·phant** *adj* □ triumphierend.

triv·i·al ['trıvıəl] *adj* □ **1.** trivial, alltäglich, gewöhnlich. **2.** unbedeutend, belanglos. **triv·i·al·i·ty** [₁~ı'ælətı] *s* **1.** Trivialität *f*. **2.** Belanglosigkeit *f*.

trod [trɒd] *pret von* **tread**. **'trod·den** *pp von* **tread**.

trol·ley ['trɒlı] *s Br.* Einkaufs-, Gepäckwagen *m*; Kofferkuli *m*; (*Tee- etc*)Wagen *m*.

trom·bone [trɒm'bəʊn] *s* ♪ Posaune *f*. **trom'bon·ist** *s* Posaunist *m*.

troop [truːp] **I** *s* **1.** Schar *f*. **2.** *pl* ✕ Truppen *pl*. **II** *v/i* **3.** strömen. **~ car·ri·er** *s* ✈, ♣ Truppentransporter *m*. **troop·er** ['truːpə] *s* **1.** ✕ Kavallerist *m*; Panzerjäger *m*: **swear like a** ~ wie ein Landsknecht fluchen. **2.** *Am.* Polizist *m* (*e-s Bundesstaats*).

troop trans·port → **troop carrier**.

tro·phy ['trəʊfı] *s* Trophäe *f*.

trop·ic ['trɒpık] *s* **1.** *ast., geogr.* Wendekreis *m*. **2.** *pl* Tropen *pl*. **'trop·i·cal** *adj* □ tropisch, Tropen...

trot [trɒt] **I** *s* **1.** Trab *m*: **on the** ~ F hintereinander; **be on the** ~ F auf Trab sein; **have the** ~**s** F Dünnpfiff haben. **II** *v/i* **2.** traben: ~ **along** (*od. off*) F ablosziehen, **III** *v/t* **3.** *Pferd* traben lassen. **4.** ~ **out** F auftischen, von sich geben. **'trot·ter** *s* Traber *m* (*Pferd*). **'trot·ting** *adj*: ~ **race** Trabrennen *n*.

trou·ble ['trʌbl] **I** *v/t* **1.** *j-n* beunruhigen. **2.** *j-m* Mühe *od.* Umstände machen: *j-n* bemühen (**for** um), bitten (**for** um; **to do** zu tun). **3.** **be** ~**d by** geplagt werden von, leiden an (*dat*). **4.** **fish in** ~**d waters** *fig.* im trüben fischen. **II** *v/i* **5.** sich bemühen (**to do** zu tun), sich Umstände machen (**about** wegen). **III** *s* **6.** Schwierigkeit *f*, Problem *n*: **be in** ~ in Schwierigkeiten sein; **get into** ~ a). **run into** ~ in Schwierigkeiten geraten, b) Schwierigkeiten *od.* Ärger bekommen (**with** mit), c) *j-n* in Schwierigkeiten bringen; **have** ~ **with** Schwierigkeiten *od.* Ärger haben mit; **have** ~ **doing** *s.th.* Schwierigkeiten haben, et. zu tun. **7.** Mühe *f*:

truthful

put s.o. **to** ~ j-m Mühe *od.* Umstände machen; **take the** ~ **to do** s.th. sich die Mühe machen, et. zu tun. **8.** *a. pl pol.* Unruhen *pl.* **9.** ✠ Leiden *n*, Beschwerden *pl.* **'~,maker** s Unruhestifter(in). **'~,shoot·er** s Friedensstifter(in).

trou·ble·some ['trʌblsəm] *adj* □ lästig.

trou·ble spot s *pol.* Unruheherd *m*.

trough [trɒf] s **1.** Trog *m*. **2.** Wellental *n*.

trounce [traʊns] *v/t Sport:* haushoch besiegen.

troupe [truːp] s *thea. etc* Truppe *f*.

trou·ser ['traʊzə] I s *pl*, *a.* **pair of** ~s Hose *f*: → **wear** 3. II *adj* Hosen...: ~ **suit** Hosenanzug *m*.

trous·seau ['truːsəʊ] *pl* -**seaux** ['~səʊz], -**seaus** s Aussteuer *f*.

trout [traʊt] *pl* **trouts**, *bsd. coll.* **trout** s *ichth.* Forelle *f*.

trow·el ['traʊəl] s (Maurer)Kelle *f*: **lay it on with a** ~ F dick auftragen.

troy (weight) [trɔɪ] s Troygewicht *n* (*für Edelmetalle u. -steine*).

tru·ant ['truːənt] s (Schul)Schwänzer(in): **play** ~ (die Schule) schwänzen.

truce [truːs] s ✗ Waffenstillstand *m* (*a. fig.*).

truck¹ [trʌk] I s **1.** *mot.* Lastwagen *m*; Fernlaster *m*. **2.** 🚂 *Br.* (offener) Güterwagen *m*. II *v/t* **3.** *bsd. Am.* auf *od.* mit Lastwagen transportieren.

truck² [~] s: **have no** ~ **with** nichts zu tun haben wollen mit.

truck driv·er s Lastwagenfahrer *m*; Fernfahrer *m*.

truck·er ['trʌkə] *Am.* → **truck driver**.

truck·man ['trʌkmən] s (*irr man*) *Am.* → **truck driver**. ~ **stop** s *Am.* Fernfahrerlokal *n*.

truc·u·lent ['trʌkjʊlənt] *adj* □ trotzig.

trudge [trʌdʒ] *v/i* stapfen (**through** durch).

true [truː] *adj* (□ → **truly**) **1.** wahr: **be** ~ *a.* stimmen; **in the** ~**est sense of the word** im wahrsten Sinne des Wortes; → **come** 10. **2.** wahr, echt, wirklich: ~ **love** wahre Liebe. **3.** treu (**to** *dat*): **stay** ~ **to one's principles** s-n Grundsätzen treu bleiben. **4.** getreu (**to** *dat*): ~ **to form** wie nicht anders zu erwarten; ~ **to life** lebensecht.

truf·fle ['trʌfl] s ✦ Trüffel *f*.

tru·ism ['truːɪzəm] s Binsenwahrheit *f*.

tru·ly ['truːlɪ] *adv* **1.** wahrheitsgemäß.

2. wirklich, wahrhaft. **3.** aufrichtig: **Yours** ~ *bsd. Am.* Hochachtungsvoll (*Briefschluß*).

trump¹ [trʌmp] I s *a) pl* Trumpf *m* (*Farbe*), b) *a.* ~ **card** Trumpf(karte *f*) *m*: **play one's** ~ **card** *fig.* s-n Trumpf ausspielen. II *v/t* Karte mit e-m Trumpf stechen, mit e-m Trumpf e-n Stich machen.

trump² [~] *v/t*: ~ **up** *b.s.* erfinden, erdichten.

trum·pet ['trʌmpɪt] I s ♪ Trompete *f*. II *v/i* trompeten (*Elefant*). **'trum·pet·er** s Trompeter(in).

trun·cate [trʌŋ'keɪt] *v/t* beschneiden, stutzen (*beide a. fig.*).

trun·cheon ['trʌntʃən] s (Gummi)Knüppel *m*, Schlagstock *m*.

trun·dle ['trʌndl] *v/t* Karren *etc* ziehen.

trunk [trʌŋk] s **1.** (*Baum*)Stamm *m*. **2.** *anat.* Rumpf *m*. **3.** Schrankkoffer *m*. **4.** *zo.* Rüssel *m* (*des Elefanten*). **5.** *mot. Am.* Kofferraum *m*. **6.** *pl, a.* **pair of** ~s (*Bade*)Hose *f*; (*Sport*) Shorts *pl.* ~ **road** s *Br.* Fernstraße *f*.

truss [trʌs] I *v/t, a.* ~ **up** **1.** j-n fesseln. **2.** *gastr.* Geflügel *etc* dressieren. II s **3.** ✠ Bruchband *n*.

trust [trʌst] I *v/t* **1.** trauen (*dat*). **2.** sich verlassen auf (*acc*): ~ s.o. **to do** s.th. sich darauf verlassen, daß j-d et. tut; ~ **him!** das sieht ihm ähnlich! **3.** (*zuversichtlich*) hoffen. II *v/i* **4.** ~ **in** vertrauen auf (*acc*). **5.** ~ **to** sich verlassen auf (*acc*). III s **6.** Vertrauen *n* (**in** *zu*): **place** (*od. put*) **one's** ~ **in** Vertrauen setzen in (*acc*); **take s.th. on** ~ et. einfach glauben; **position of** ~ Vertrauensstellung *f*. **7.** **hold s.th. in** ~ et. treuhänderisch verwalten (**for** für); **place s.th. in** s.o.'s ~ j-m et. anvertrauen. **8.** ✦ Trust *m*; *weitS.* Großkonzern *m*.

trus·tee [ˌtrʌs'tiː] s ✦✦ Treuhänder(in), Vermögensverwalter(in).

trust·ful ['trʌstfʊl], **'trust·ing** *adj* □ vertrauensvoll; vertrauensselig.

'trust,wor·thy *adj* □ vertrauenswürdig.

truth [truːθ] *pl* **truths** [truːðz] s Wahrheit *f*: **in** ~ in Wahrheit; **there is some** (**no**) ~ **in it** daran ist et. (nichts) Wahres; **to tell** (**you**) **the** ~ um die Wahrheit zu sagen; → **home truth**. **truth·ful** ['~fʊl] *adj* □ **1.** wahrheitsgemäß. **2.** wahrheitsliebend.

try [traɪ] **I** s **1.** Versuch m: have a ~ es versuchen; → worth I. **II** v/t **2.** versuchen (to do zu tun): when their car didn't start, they tried pushing it als ihr Wagen nicht ansprang, versuchten sie es mit Anschieben. **3.** et. ausprobieren. **4.** ᚱᚣᚢ (über) e-e Sache verhandeln; j-m den Prozeß machen (for wegen). **5.** j-n, j-s Geduld, Nerven etc auf e-e harte Probe stellen. **III** v/i **6.** es versuchen: ~ and come back. Br. F versuch zu kommen; → hard 12. **7.** ~ for sich bemühen um.

Verbindungen mit Adverbien:

try| on v/t **1.** Kleidungsstück anprobieren, Hut etc aufprobieren. **2.** try it on Br. F probieren, wie weit man gehen kann. ~ **out** I v/t → try 3. **II** v/i: ~ for Am. → try 7.

try·ing ['traɪɪŋ] adj □ anstrengend.
'try-out s: give s.th. a ~ et. ausprobieren.
tsar [zɑː] s hist. Zar m.
'T-shirt s T-Shirt n.
tub [tʌb] **I** s **1.** Bottich m; Tonne f. **2.** (Margarine- etc)Becher m. **3.** F (Bade-) Wanne f. ♣ F Kahn m.
tu·ba ['tjuːbə] s ♪ Tuba f.
tube [tjuːb] s **1.** Röhre f (a. anat.), Rohr n. **2.** Schlauch m. **3.** Tube f. **4.** ♀ F U-Bahn f (in London): by ♀ mit der U-Bahn; ♀ **station** U-Bahnstation f. **'tube·less** adj schlauchlos (Reifen).
tu·ber ['tjuːbə] s ♣ Knolle f.
tu·ber·cu·lo·sis [tjuːˌbɜːkjʊ'ləʊsɪs] s ♣ Tuberkulose f.
tu·bu·lar ['tjuːbjʊlə] adj rohrförmig, Röhren..., Rohr...: ~ **furniture** Stahlrohrmöbel pl.
tuck [tʌk] **I** s Saum m; Biese f. **II** v/t stecken: ~ s.th. under one's arm sich et. unter den Arm klemmen. **III** v/i: ~ **into** bsd. Br. F sich et. schmecken lassen.

Verbindungen mit Adverbien:

tuck| a·way v/t **1.** wegstecken: be tucked away versteckt liegen (Haus etc). **2.** F Essen verdrücken, wegputzen. ~ **in** I v/t → tuck up. **II** v/i bsd. Br. F reinhauen, zulangen. ~ **up** v/t a. ~ in bed Kind ins Bett packen.
Tues·day ['tjuːzdɪ] s Dienstag m: on ~ (am) Dienstag; on ~s dienstags.
tuft [tʌft] s (Gras-, Haar- etc)Büschel n.
tug [tʌg] **I** v/t **1.** zerren, ziehen. **2.** zerren

od. ziehen an (dat). **II** v/i **3.** ~ **at** → 2. **III** s **4.** give s.th. a ~ → 2; ~ **of war** (Sport) Tauziehen n (a. fig.).
tu·i·tion [tjuː'ɪʃn] s **1.** Unterricht m. **2.** bsd. Am. Unterrichtsgebühr(en pl) f.
tu·lip ['tjuːlɪp] s ♣ Tulpe f.
tulle [tjuːl] s Tüll m.
tum·ble ['tʌmbl] **I** v/i **1.** fallen, stürzen; ♣ purzeln (Preise). **2.** a. ~ **down** einstürzen. **3.** ~ **to s.th.** bsd. Br. F et. kapieren. **II** s **4.** Fall m, Sturz m: have (od. take) a ~ fallen, stürzen. **'~down** adj baufällig. ~ **dry·er** s Trockenautomat m, Wäschetrockner m.
tum·bler ['tʌmblə] s (Trink)Glas n.
tu·mid ['tjuːmɪd] adj ♣ geschwollen.
tum·my ['tʌmɪ] s F Bauch m: he's got a sore ~ er hat Bauchweh.
tu·mor s Am., **tu·mour** s bsd. Br. ['tjuːmə] ♣ Tumor m, Geschwulst f.
tu·mult ['tjuːmʌlt] s Tumult m. **tu·mul·tu·ous** adj □ tumultartig, (Applaus, Empfang) stürmisch.
tu·na ['tuːnə] s ichth. Thunfisch m.
tune [tjuːn] **I** s **1.** Melodie f: to the ~ of nach der Melodie von; fig. F in Höhe von 500 Pfund etc. **2.** be out of ~ ♪ verstimmt sein; be in (out of) ~ with fig. (nicht) harmonieren od. übereinstimmen mit. **II** v/t **3.** a. ~ **up** ♪ stimmen. **4.** a. ~ **up** ♣ Motor tunen. **5.** mst ~ **in** Radio etc einstellen (to auf acc): be ~**d in to** Sender, Programm eingeschaltet haben; fig. ein Gefühl haben für. **III** v/i **6.** ~ **up** (die Instrumente) stimmen (Orchester). **7.** ~ **in** (das Radio etc) einschalten: ~ **in to** Sender, Programm einschalten. **tune·ful** ['~fʊl] adj □ melodiös. **'tune·less** adj □ unmelodiös.
'tun·er s **1.** (Klavier- etc)Stimmer(in). **2.** Radio, TV: Tuner m. **'tun·ing** adj: ~ **fork** Stimmgabel f.
tun·nel ['tʌnl] **I** s Tunnel m; Unterführung f. **II** v/t pret u. pp -neled, bsd. Br. -nelled a) Berg durchtunneln, b) Fluß etc untertunneln. **III** v/i: ~ **through** → IIa; ~ **under** → IIb.
tun·ny ['tʌnɪ] s ichth. Thunfisch m.
tur·ban ['tɜːbən] s Turban m.
tur·bid ['tɜːbɪd] adj □ **1.** trüb (Flüssigkeit); dick (Rauch etc). **2.** fig. verworren, wirr.
tur·bine ['tɜːbaɪn] s ⚙ Turbine f.
tur·bo ['tɜːbəʊ] pl -bos s F → **turbo-**

charger. ˌ~'**charg·er** *s mot.* Turbolader *m.*

tur·bot ['tɜːbət] *pl* -**bots**, *bsd. coll.* -**bot** *s ichth.* Steinbutt *m.*

tur·bu·lence ['tɜːbjʊləns] *s* Turbulenz *f* (*a. phys.*). '**tur·bu·lent** *adj* □ turbulent (*a. phys.*).

turd [tɜːd] *s* V **1.** Scheißhaufen *m*, Kaktus *m.* **2.** Scheißkerl *m.*

tu·reen [tə'riːn] *s* (Suppen)Terrine *f.*

turf [tɜːf] **I** *pl* **turfs, turves** [~vz] *s* **1.** Rasen *m.* **2.** Sode *f*, Rasenstück *n* **3.** *the* ~ der Pferderennsport. **II** *v/t* **4.** ~ *out bsd.* **F** *j-n* rausschmeißen: *he was* ~*ed out of the club* er flog aus dem Verein.

tur·gid ['tɜːdʒɪd] *adj* □ ✤ geschwollen, *fig. a.* schwülstig.

Turk [tɜːk] *s* Türke *m*, Türkin *f.*

tur·key ['tɜːkɪ] *pl* -**keys,** *bsd. coll.* -**key** *s orn.* Truthahn *m*, -henne *f*, Pute(r *m*) *f:* → *cold turkey.*

Turk·ish ['tɜːkɪʃ] **I** *adj* türkisch. **II** *s ling.* Türkisch *n.*

tur·moil ['tɜːmɔɪl] *s* Aufruhr *m: be in a* ~ in Aufruhr sein.

turn [tɜːn] **I** *s* **1.** (Um)Drehung *f: give s.th. a* ~ (*two* ~*s*) et. (zweimal) drehen. **2.** Biegung *f*, Kurve *f: make a right* ~ nach rechts abbiegen. **3.** *in* ~ der Reihe nach; abwechselnd; *in (his)* ~ seinerseits; *it is my* ~ ich bin dran *od.* an der Reihe; *miss a* ~ (*Brettspiele*) einmal aussetzen; *take* ~*s* sich abwechseln (*at* bei); *take* ~*s at doing s.th.* et. abwechselnd tun; → *wait* 3. **4.** *fig.* Wende *f*, Wendung *f: at the* ~ *of the century* um die Jahrhundertwende; *take a* ~ *for the better* (*worse*) sich bessern (sich verschlimmern). **5.** *do s.o. a good* (*bad*) ~ j-m e-n guten (schlechten) Dienst erweisen. **II** *v/t* **6.** drehen, *Schlüssel a.* herumdrehen: → *somersault.* **7.** *Schallplatte etc* umdrehen, *Seite* umblättern, *Braten etc* wenden: → *hair, inside* 1, *stomach* 1, *table* 1, *upside.* **8.** → *corner* 1. **9.** *Schlauch etc* richten (*on* auf *acc*), *Antenne* ausrichten (*to*-*ward*[*s*] *auf acc*), *Aufmerksamkeit* zuwenden (*to dat*): → *back* 1, *blind* 1, *ear*¹ 1. **10.** verwandeln (*into* in *acc*). **11.** ~ *against* *j-n* aufbringen gegen. **III** *v/i* **12.** sich drehen: ~ *on fig.* abhängen von. **13.** abbiegen; einbiegen (*onto* auf

acc; *into* in *acc*): → *left* 4, *right* 15. **14.** sich umdrehen: ~ *against fig.* sich wenden gegen. ~ *on* losgehen auf (*acc*). ~ *to s.o.* sich j-m zuwenden; *fig.* sich an j-n wenden; ~ *grave.* **15.** *blaß, sauer etc* werden: → *turtle.* **16.** sich verwandeln, *fig. a.* umschlagen (*into, to* in *acc*).

Verbindungen mit Adverbien:

turn| **a·way I** *v/t* **1.** *Gesicht etc* abwenden (*from* von). **2.** *j-n* abweisen, wegschicken. **II** *v/i* **3.** sich abwenden (*from* von). ~ **back I** *v/t* **1.** *Bettdecke* zurückschlagen. **2.** *j-n* zurückschicken. **3.** *Uhr* zurückstellen: → *clock* 1. **II** *v/i* **4.** umkehren. **5.** zurückblättern (*to* auf *acc*). ~ **down** *v/t* **1.** *Kragen* umlegen. **2.** → *turn back* 1. **3.** *Radio etc* leiser stellen. **4.** *j-n, Angebot etc* ablehnen. ~ **in I** *v/t* **1.** zurückgeben. **2.** *Gewinn etc* erzielen, machen. **3.** *turn o.s. in* sich stellen. **II** *v/i* **4. F** sich aufs Ohr hauen *od.* legen. ~ **off I** *v/t* **1.** *Gas, Wasser etc* abdrehen, *Licht, Radio etc* ausmachen, -schalten, *Motor etc* abstellen. **2. F** *j-n* anwidern; *j-m* die Lust nehmen. **II** *v/i* **3.** abbiegen. ~ **on** *v/t* **1.** *Gas, Wasser etc* aufdrehen, *a. Gerät* anstellen, *Licht, Radio etc* anmachen, anschalten: → *waterworks.* **2. F** *j-n* anturnen, anmachen. ~ **out I** *v/t* **1.** *Licht* ausmachen, -schalten. **2.** *j-n* hinauswerfen. **3.** *Tasche etc* (aus)leeren. **4. F** *Waren* ausstoßen. **II** *v/i* **5.** kommen (*for* zu). **6.** sich erweisen *od.* herausstellen (*a success* als Erfolg; *to be false* als falsch), sich entpuppen (*to be a good swimmer* als guter Schwimmer). ~ **o·ver I** *v/t* **1.** → *turn* 7: *turn s.th. over in one's mind* sich et. durch den Kopf gehen lassen; → *leaf* 2. **2.** *et.* umkippen. **3.** *j-n, et.* übergeben (*to dat*). **4.** ✤ umsetzen. **II** *v/i* **5.** sich umdrehen: → *grave.* **6.** umkippen. **7.** umblättern: *please* ~ bitte wenden. ~ **round I** *v/t: turn one's car round* wenden. **II** *v/i* sich umdrehen.

'**turn·a·bout,** '~**·a·round** *s* Kehrtwendung *f* (*a. fig. in, on* in *dat*). '~**·coat** *s* Abtrünnige *m, f*, Überläufer(in).

turn·ing ['tɜːnɪŋ] *s* Abzweigung *f.* **II** *adj:* ~ *circle mot.* Wendekreis *m;* ~ *point fig.* Wendepunkt *m.*

tur·nip ['tɜːnɪp] *s* ✤ Rübe *f.*

'**turn··off** *s* Abzweigung *f.* '~**·out** *s* **1.** (*engS.* Wahl)Beteiligung *f.* **2. F** Aufmachung f (e-r Person). '~‚o·ver s ✝ Umsatz m. '~·pike s Am. gebührenpflichtige Schnellstraße. ~·stile ['~staɪl] s Drehkreuz n. '~‚ta·ble s Plattenteller m. '~·up s Br. (Hosen)Aufschlag m.

tur·pen·tine ['tɜːpəntaɪn] s 🌳 Terpentin n.

turps [tɜːps] s pl (sg konstruiert) Br. F → **turpentine**.

tur·quoise ['tɜːkwɔːz] s min. Türkis m.

tur·ret ['tʌrɪt] s 1. △ Ecktürmchen n. 2. ⚔ (Panzer)Turm m, ⚓ Gefechts-, Geschützturm m.

tur·tle ['tɜːtl] s zo. (Wasser)Schildkröte f: **turn ~** ⚓ kentern. '~·neck s bsd. Am. Rollkragen(pullover) m.

turves [tɜːvz] pl von **turf**.

tusk [tʌsk] s Stoßzahn m (e-s Elefanten).

tus·sle ['tʌsl] s bsd. fig. (over) Gerangel n (um); Auseinandersetzung f (über acc).

tus·sock ['tʌsək] s Grasbüschel n.

tu·te·lage ['tjuːtɪlɪdʒ] s ⚖ Vormundschaft f.

tu·tor ['tjuːtə] s 1. Privat-, Hauslehrer(in). 2. univ. Br. Studienleiter(in).

tux [tʌks] F → **tuxedo**.

tux·e·do [tʌk'siːdəʊ] pl **-dos** s Am. Smoking m.

TV [‚tiː'viː] I s 1. Fernsehen n: **on (the) ~** im Fernsehen; **watch ~** fernsehen. 2. Fernseher m (Gerät). II adj 3. Fernseh...: **~ dinner** Tiefkühlmahlzeit f.

twad·dle ['twɒdl] s F Quatsch m, Unsinn m.

twang [twæŋ] s: **speak with a nasal ~** näseln.

tweed [twiːd] s Tweed m (Stoff).

tweet [twiːt] I v/i piep(s)en (Vogel). II s Piep(s)en n.

tweez·ers ['twiːzəz] s pl, a. **pair of ~** Pinzette f.

twelfth [twelfθ] adj zwölft.

twelve [twelv] adj zwölf.

twen·ti·eth ['twentɪəθ] adj zwanzigst.

twen·ty ['twentɪ] I adj zwanzig. II s Zwanzig f: **be in one's twenties** in den Zwanzigern sein; **in the twenties** in den zwanziger Jahren (e-s Jahrhunderts).

twerp [twɜːp] s F Blödmann m, Heini m.

twice [twaɪs] adv zweimal: **~ as much** doppelt od. zweimal soviel; **~ the sum** die doppelte Summe; **think ~** es sich genau überlegen (**before** bevor).

twid·dle ['twɪdl] v/t: **~ one's thumbs** Däumchen drehen (a. fig.).

twig¹ [twɪg] s Zweig m.

twig² [~] v/t u. v/i Br. F kapieren.

twi·light ['twaɪlaɪt] s 1. (bsd. Abend-)Dämmerung f: **at ~** in der Dämmerung. 2. Zwie-, Dämmerlicht n.

twin [twɪn] I s Zwilling m. II adj Zwillings...: **~ brother (sister)**; **~ beds** pl zwei Einzelbetten; **~ town** Partnerstadt f. III v/t: **be ~ned with** die Partnerstadt sein von. ‚~'**bed·ded** adj: **~ room** Zweibettzimmer n.

twine [twaɪn] I s 1. Bindfaden m, Schnur f. II v/t 2. **a. ~ together** zs.-drehen. 3. **~ one's arms round** die Arme schlingen um. III v/i 4. sich winden (**round** um).

‚**twin-'en·gined** adj ✈ zweimotorig.

twinge [twɪndʒ] s stechender Schmerz, Stechen n: **a ~ of toothache** stechende Zahnschmerzen pl; **a ~ of conscience** Gewissensbisse pl.

twin·kle ['twɪŋkl] I v/i glitzern (Sterne), (a. Augen) funkeln (**with** vor dat). II s Glitzern n, Funkeln n: **with a ~ in one's eye** augenzwinkernd. '**twin·kling** s: **in the ~ of an eye**, F **in a ~** im Handumdrehen, im Nu.

twirl [twɜːl] I v/t (herum)wirbeln. II v/i wirbeln (**round** über acc). III s Wirbel m.

twirp → **twerp**.

twist [twɪst] I v/t 1. drehen: **~ off** abdrehen, Deckel abschrauben; **~ together** zs.-drehen; **his face was ~ed with pain** sein Gesicht war schmerzverzerrt. 2. wickeln (**round** um): **~ s.o. round one's little finger** fig. j-n um den (kleinen) Finger wickeln. 3. **~ one's ankle** (mit dem Fuß) umknicken, sich den Fuß vertreten. 4. fig. entstellen, verdrehen. II v/i 5. sich winden (Person), (Fluß etc a.) sich schlängeln. III s 6. Drehung f. 7. Biegung f: **be round the ~** Br. F spinnen. 8. fig. (überraschende) Wendung. 9. ♪ Twist m. '**twist·er** s F 1. Gauner m. 2. Am. Tornado m.

twit [twɪt] s bsd. Br. F Blödmann m.

twitch [twɪtʃ] I v/t 1. zucken mit. 2. zupfen an (dat). II v/i 3. zucken. III s 4. Zucken n; Zuckung f.

twit·ter ['twɪtə] I v/i 1. zwitschern. 2. a. **~ on** F (aufgeregt) schnattern (**about** über acc). II s 3. Zwitschern n, Gezwitscher n. **4. be all of a ~** F ganz aufgeregt sein.

two [tu:] **I** adj **1.** zwei: *in a day or ~* in ein paar Tagen; *break* (*cut*) *in ~* in zwei Teile brechen (schneiden); *the ~ cars* die beiden Autos; → *thing* 2. **II** s **2.** Zwei f: *~ of hearts* Herzzwei. **3.** *the ~ of us* wir beide; *in ~s* zu zweit, paarweise; *put ~ and ~ together* zwei u. zwei zs.-zählen. '**~-act** adj: *~ play thea.* Zweiakter m. '**~-bit** adj Am. F klein, unbedeutend. **~'edged** adj zweischneidig, fig. a. zweideutig. **~-'faced** adj falsch, heuchlerisch.

two·fold ['tu:fəʊld] **I** adj zweifach. **II** adv zweifach, um das Zweifache: *increase ~* (sich) verzweifachen.

two|-'hand·ed adj □ **1.** zweihändig. **2.** beidhändig. **~·pence** ['tʌpəns] s Br. zwei Pence: *I don't care* (*od. give*) *~ F* das ist mir völlig egal. **~·pen·ny** ['tʌpnɪ] adj Br. **1.** für zwei Pence, Zweipenny... **2.** fig. billig. '**~-piece** adj zweiteilig. **~·'seat·er** s ✈, mot. Zweisitzer m. **~· star** s mot. Br. F Normal n (Benzin). '**~-star** adj: *~ petrol* mot. Br. Normalbenzin n. '**~-time** I adj zweimalig. **II** v/t F Freundin etc betrügen (*with* mit). '**~-way** adj: *~ mirror* venezianischer Spiegel; *~ traffic* Gegenverkehr m.

ty·coon [taɪ'ku:n] s (Industrie- etc)Magnat m.

tym·pa·num ['tɪmpənəm] pl **-na** ['~nə], **-nums** s anat. Trommelfell n.

type [taɪp] **I** s **1.** Art f, Sorte f; Typ m: *of this ~* dieser Art; *she's not my ~* F sie ist nicht mein Typ. **II** v/t **2.** tippen, mit der Maschine schreiben. **3.** Krankheit etc bestimmen. **III** v/i **4.** maschineschreiben, tippen. '**~·cast** v/t (irr cast) Schauspieler auf ein bestimmtes Rollenfach festlegen. '**~·script** s maschine(n)geschriebenes Manuskript. '**~·set·ter** s Schriftsetzer(in). '**~·writ·er** s Schreibmaschine f. '**~·writ·ten** adj maschine(n)geschrieben.

ty·phoid (**fe·ver**) ['taɪfɔɪd] s ✚ Typhus m.

ty·phoon [taɪ'fu:n] s Taifun m.

ty·phus ['taɪfəs] s ✚ Fleckfieber n, -typhus m.

typ·i·cal ['tɪpɪkl] adj □ typisch (*of* für). **typ·i·fy** ['~faɪ] v/t **1.** typisch sein (für, kennzeichnen. **2.** ein typisches Beispiel sein für, verkörpern.

typ·ing ['taɪpɪŋ] adj: *~ error* Tippfehler m; *~ pool* Schreibzentrale f. '**typ·ist** s Schreibkraft f: → **shorthand**.

ty·po·graph·ic [ˌtaɪpə'græfɪk] adj (**~ally**) typographisch: *~ error* Druckfehler m. **ty·pog·ra·phy** [~'pɒɡrəfɪ] s Typographie f.

ty·ran·ni·cal [tɪ'rænɪkl] adj □ tyrannisch. **tyr·an·nize** ['tɪrənaɪz] v/t tyrannisieren. '**tyr·an·ny** s Tyrannei f. **ty·rant** ['taɪərənt] s Tyrann m.

tyre ['taɪə] s bsd. Br. Reifen m.

tzar [zɑ:] s hist. Zar m.

U

u·biq·ui·tous [ju:'bɪkwɪtəs] adj □ allgegenwärtig.

U-boat ['ju:bəʊt] s ⚓ (deutsches) U-Boot.

ud·der ['ʌdə] s zo. Euter n.

UFO [ju:fəʊ] pl **UFO's**, **UFOs** s Ufo n, UFO n.

ugh [ʌx] int igitt!

ug·li·ness ['ʌɡlɪnɪs] s Häßlichkeit f.

ug·ly ['ʌɡlɪ] adj □ **1.** häßlich (a. fig.). **2.** bös, schlimm (Wunde etc).

ul·cer ['ʌlsə] s ✚ Geschwür n.

ul·na ['ʌlnə] pl **-nae** ['~ni:], **-nas** s anat. Elle f.

ul·te·ri·or [ʌl'tɪərɪə] adj: *~ motive* Hintergedanke m.

ul·ti·ma·ta [ˌʌltɪ'meɪtə] pl von **ultimatum**.

ul·ti·mate ['ʌltɪmət] **I** adj letzt, End...; höchst. **II** s: *the ~ in* das Höchste an (dat); b.s. der Gipfel an (dat). '**ul·ti·mate·ly** adv **1.** schließlich. **2.** letztlich, letzten Endes.

ul·ti·ma·tum [ˌʌltɪˈmeɪtəm] *pl* **-tums, -ta** [ˌtə] *s* Ultimatum *n*: **give s.o. an ~** j-m ein Ultimatum stellen; **j-n ultimativ** auffordern (**to do** zu tun).

ul·tra·high [ˌʌltrəˈhaɪ] *adj*: **~ frequency** ⚡ Ultrakurzwelle *f*. **~ma·rine** *adj* ultramarin. **~son·ic** [ˌʌ'] *adj* Ultraschall... **~sound** *s phys.* Ultraschall *m*. **~vi·o·let** *adj* ultraviolett.

um·bil·i·cal [ˌʌmbɪˈlaɪkl] *adj*: **~ cord** *anat.* Nabelschnur *f*.

um·brage [ˈʌmbrɪdʒ] *s*: **take ~ at** Anstoß nehmen an (*dat*).

um·brel·la [ʌmˈbrelə] *s* **1.** (Regen-) Schirm *m*. **2.** *fig.* Schutz *m*: **under the ~ of** unter dem Schutz (*gen*). **~ or·gan·i·za·tion** *s* Dachorganisation *f*. **~ stand** *s* Schirmständer *m*.

um·pire [ˈʌmpaɪə] (*Sport*) **I** *s* Schiedsrichter(in). **II** *v/i u. v/t* als Schiedsrichter fungieren (bei).

ump·teen [ˌʌmpˈtiːn] *adj*: **~ times** F x-mal. **ˌump'teenth** *adj*: **for the ~ time** F zum x-ten Mal.

un·a·bashed [ˌʌnəˈbæʃt] *adj* unverfroren.

un·a·ble [ʌnˈeɪbl] *adj*: **be ~ to do s.th.** unfähig *od.* außerstande sein, et. zu tun; et. nicht tun können.

un·a·bridged [ˌʌnəˈbrɪdʒd] *adj* ungekürzt.

un·ac·cept·a·ble [ˌʌnəkˈseptəbl] *adj* unannehmbar (**to** für); unzumutbar: **be ~ to s.o.** j-m nicht zugemutet werden können.

un·ac·com·pa·nied [ˌʌnəˈkʌmpənɪd] *adj* ohne Begleitung (**by** *gen*) (*a.* ♪).

un·ac·count·a·ble [ˌʌnəˈkaʊntəbl] *adj* unerklärlich. **ˌun·ac'count·a·bly** *adv* unerklärlicherweise.

un·ac·cus·tomed [ˌʌnəˈkʌstəmd] *adj* **1.** ungewohnt. **2. be ~ to s.th.** et. nicht gewohnt sein; **be ~ to doing s.th.** es nicht gewohnt sein, et. zu tun.

un·ac·quaint·ed [ˌʌnəˈkweɪntɪd] *adj*: **be ~ with s.th.** et. nicht kennen, mit e-r Sache nicht vertraut sein.

un·a·dul·ter·at·ed [ˌʌnəˈdʌltəreɪtɪd] *adj* **1.** unverfälscht. **2.** *fig.* völlig (*Unsinn etc*).

un·ad·vised [ˌʌnədˈvaɪzd] *adj* unbesonnen, unüberlegt.

un·af·fect·ed [ˌʌnəˈfektɪd] *adj* **1. be ~ by**

nicht betroffen werden von. **2.** natürlich, ungekünstelt.

un·al·ter·a·ble [ʌnˈɔːltərəbl] *adj* unabänderlich (*Entschluß etc*).

un·am·big·u·ous [ˌʌnæmˈbɪgjʊəs] *adj* □ unzweideutig.

un·A·mer·i·can [ˌʌnəˈmerɪkən] *adj* **1.** unamerikanisch. **2.** antiamerikanisch.

u·nan·i·mous [juːˈnænɪməs] *adj* □ einmütig; einstimmig: **be ~ in doing s.th.** et. einmütig *od.* einstimmig tun; **by a ~ decision** einstimmig.

un·an·nounced [ˌʌnəˈnaʊnst] *adj u. adv* unangemeldet.

un·an·swer·a·ble [ʌnˈɑːnsərəbl] *adj* **1.** nicht zu beantworten(d). **2.** unwiderlegbar.

un·ap·proach·a·ble [ˌʌnəˈprəʊtʃəbl] *adj* □ unnahbar.

un·armed [ʌnˈɑːmd] *adj* unbewaffnet.

un·asked [ʌnˈɑːskt] *adj* **1.** ungestellt (*Frage*). **2.** unaufgefordert, ungebeten. **3.** uneingeladen, ungebeten.

un·as·sist·ed [ˌʌnəˈsɪstɪd] *adv* ohne (fremde) Hilfe, (ganz) allein.

un·as·sum·ing [ˌʌnəˈsjuːmɪŋ] *adj* □ bescheiden.

un·at·tached [ˌʌnəˈtætʃt] *adj* ungebunden (*Person*).

un·at·tend·ed [ˌʌnəˈtendɪd] *adj* unbeaufsichtigt: **leave ~** unbeaufsichtigt lassen.

un·at·trac·tive [ˌʌnəˈtræktɪv] *adj* □ unattraktiv.

un·au·thor·ized [ʌnˈɔːθəraɪzd] *adj* unbefugt, unberechtigt.

un·a·vail·a·ble [ˌʌnəˈveɪləbl] *adj* **1.** nicht erhältlich. **2.** nicht erreichbar.

un·a·void·a·ble [ˌʌnəˈvɔɪdəbl] *adj* □ unvermeidlich.

un·a·ware [ˌʌnəˈweə] *adj*: **be ~ of s.th.** sich e-r Sache nicht bewußt sein, et. nicht bemerken; **be ~ that** nicht bemerken, daß. **ˌun·a'wares** *adv*: **catch** (*od.* **take**) **s.o. ~** j-n überraschen.

un·bal·ance [ˌʌnˈbæləns] *v/t* **j-n** aus dem (seelischen) Gleichgewicht bringen. **ˌun'bal·anced** *adj* labil (*Charakter, Person*).

un·bar [ˌʌnˈbɑː] *v/t* auf-, entriegeln.

un·bear·a·ble [ʌnˈbeərəbl] *adj* □ unerträglich.

un·beat·a·ble [ˌʌnˈbiːtəbl] *adj* unschlagbar (*a. Preise etc*).

                                                uncountable

un·beat·en [ˌʌnˈbiːtn] *adj* ungeschlagen, unbesiegt.

un·be·known [ˌʌnbɪˈnəʊn] *adv*: **~ to s.o.** ohne j-s Wissen.

un·be·liev·a·ble [ˌʌnbɪˈliːvəbl] *adj* □ unglaublich.

un·bend [ˌʌnˈbend] (*irr* **bend**) **I** *v/t* geradebiegen. **II** *v/i fig.* auftauen, aus sich herausgehen. **ˌun·ˈbend·ing** *adj* □ unbeugsam.

un·bi·as(s)ed [ˌʌnˈbaɪəst] *adj* □ unvoreingenommen, ⚖ unbefangen.

un·bind [ˌʌnˈbaɪnd] *v/t* (*irr* **bind**) losbinden.

un·blem·ished [ˌʌnˈblemɪʃt] *adj* makellos (*Ruf etc*).

un·bolt [ˌʌnˈbəʊlt] → **unbar.**

un·born [ˌʌnˈbɔːn] *adj* ungeboren.

un·break·a·ble [ˌʌnˈbreɪkəbl] *adj* unzerbrechlich.

un·bri·dled [ˌʌnˈbraɪdld] *adj* ungezügelt, zügellos: **~ tongue** lose Zunge.

un·bro·ken [ˌʌnˈbrəʊkən] *adj* **1.** heil, unbeschädigt. **2.** ununterbrochen.

un·buck·le [ˌʌnˈbʌkl] *v/t* auf-, losschnallen.

un·bur·den [ˌʌnˈbɜːdn] *v/t*: **~ o.s to s.o.** j-m sein Herz ausschütten.

un·but·ton [ˌʌnˈbʌtn] *v/t* aufknöpfen.

un·called-for [ˌʌnˈkɔːldfɔː] *adj* **1.** ungerechtfertigt. **2.** unnötig. **3.** deplaciert, unpassend.

un·can·ny [ʌnˈkænɪ] *adj* □ unheimlich.

un·ceas·ing [ʌnˈsiːsɪŋ] *adj* □ unaufhörlich.

un·cer·e·mo·ni·ous·ly [ˈʌnˌserɪˈməʊnjəslɪ] *adv* ohne viel Federlesen(s).

un·cer·tain [ʌnˈsɜːtn] *adj* □ **1.** unsicher, ungewiß, unbestimmt: **be ~ of s.th.** sich e-r Sache nicht sicher sein; **be ~ how to do s.th.** nicht sicher sein, wie man et. tut. **2.** unbeständig (*Wetter*). **3.** vage: **~ term 3. un·ˈcer·tain·ty** *s* Unsicherheit *f*, Ungewißheit *f*.

un·chain [ʌnˈtʃeɪn] *v/t* losketten.

un·changed [ʌnˈtʃeɪndʒd] *adj* unverändert. **ˌun·ˈchang·ing** *adj* □ unveränderlich.

un·char·i·ta·ble [ʌnˈtʃærɪtəbl] *adj* □ unfair: **it was rather ~ of you** es war nicht gerade nett von dir (**to do** zu tun).

un·checked [ʌnˈtʃekt] *adj* **1.** ungehin-

dert. **2.** unkontrolliert, ungeprüft.

un·chris·tian [ˌʌnˈkrɪstʃən] *adj* □ unchristlich.

un·civ·il [ˌʌnˈsɪvl] *adj* □ unhöflich. **ˌun·ˈciv·i·lized** [-vlaɪzd] *adj* unzivilisiert.

un·cle [ˈʌŋkl] *s* Onkel *m*: **cry** (*od.* **say**) **~** *Am.* F aufgeben.

un·com·fort·a·ble [ʌnˈkʌmfətəbl] *adj* □ **1.** unbequem. **2.** *feel* **~** sich unbehaglich fühlen.

un·com·mit·ted [ˌʌnkəˈmɪtɪd] *adj* neutral: **be ~ to** nicht festgelegt sein auf (*acc*).

un·com·mon [ʌnˈkɒmən] *adj* □ ungewöhnlich: **not to be ~** nichts Ungewöhnliches sein.

un·com·mu·ni·ca·tive [ˌʌnkəˈmjuːnɪkətɪv] *adj* □ verschlossen, wortkarg.

un·com·plain·ing·ly [ˌʌnkəmˈpleɪnɪŋlɪ] *adv* geduldig, ohne Murren.

un·com·pro·mis·ing [ʌnˈkɒmprəmaɪzɪŋ] *adj* □ kompromißlos.

un·con·cerned [ˌʌnkənˈsɜːnd] *adj* **1.** **be ~ about** sich keine Gedanken *od.* Sorgen machen über (*acc*). **2.** **be ~ with** uninteressiert sein an (*dat*).

un·con·di·tion·al [ˌʌnkənˈdɪʃənl] *adj* □ bedingungslos.

un·con·firmed [ˌʌnkənˈfɜːmd] *adj* unbestätigt.

un·con·scious [ʌnˈkɒnʃəs] *adj* □ **1.** 🅰 bewußtlos. **2.** **be ~ of s.th.** sich e-r Sache nicht bewußt sein, et. nicht bemerken. **3.** unbewußt; unbeabsichtigt. **un·ˈcon·scious·ness** *s* ⚕ Bewußtlosigkeit *f*.

un·con·sid·ered [ˌʌnkənˈsɪdəd] *adj* unbedacht, unüberlegt.

un·con·sti·tu·tion·al [ˈʌnˌkɒnstɪˈtjuːʃənl] *adj* □ verfassungswidrig.

un·con·trol·la·ble [ˌʌnkənˈtrəʊləbl] *adj* □ unkontrollierbar; nicht zu bändigen(d) (*Kind*); unbändig (*Wut etc*). **ˌun·con·ˈtrolled** *adj* unkontrolliert, ungehindert.

un·con·ven·tion·al [ˌʌnkənˈvenʃənl] *adj* □ unkonventionell.

un·con·vinced [ˌʌnkənˈvɪnst] *adj*: **be ~** nicht überzeugt sein (**about** von). **ˌun·con·ˈvinc·ing** *adj* □ nicht überzeugend.

un·cooked [ˌʌnˈkʊkt] *adj* ungekocht, roh.

un·cork [ˌʌnˈkɔːk] *v/t* entkorken.

un·count·a·ble [ˌʌnˈkaʊntəbl] *adj* unzählbar (*a. ling.*). **‚un'count·ed** *adj* unzählig.

un·cou·ple [ˌʌn'kʌpl] *v/t* Waggon etc abkoppeln, abkuppeln.

un·couth [ʌn'kuːθ] *adj* □ ungehobelt (*Person, Benehmen*).

un·cov·er [ʌn'kʌvə] *v/t* aufdecken, *fig. a.* enthüllen.

un·crit·i·cal [ˌʌn'krɪtɪkl] *adj* □ unkritisch: *be ~ of s.th.* e-r Sache unkritisch gegenüberstehen.

un·crowned [ˌʌn'kraʊnd] *adj* ungekrönt (*a. fig.*).

un·crush·a·ble [ʌn'krʌʃəbl] *adj* knitterfest.

unc·tion ['ʌŋkʃn] *s eccl.* Salbung *f*: *extreme ~* Krankensalbung. **unc·tu·ous** ['ʌtjʊəs] *adj* □ salbungsvoll.

un·cut [ʌn'kʌt] *adj* **1.** ungeschnitten. **2.** ungekürzt (*Film, Roman etc*). **3.** ungeschliffen: *~ diamond a.* Rohdiamant *m.*

un·dam·aged [ˌʌn'dæmɪdʒd] *adj* unbeschädigt.

un·dat·ed [ʌn'deɪtɪd] *adj* undatiert, ohne Datum.

un·de·cid·ed [ˌʌndɪ'saɪdɪd] *adj* □ **1.** unentschieden, offen. **2.** unentschlossen: *he is still ~ about what to do* er ist sich noch nicht schlüssig, was er tun soll.

un·de·ni·a·ble [ˌʌndɪ'naɪəbl] *adj* □ unbestreitbar.

un·der ['ʌndə] **I** *prp allg.* unter (*Lage etc*: *dat*; *Richtung*: *acc*): *it costs ~ £10 a.* es kostet weniger als 10 Pfund; *have s.o. ~ one* j-n unter sich haben; → *discussion, impression* 2, *influence* 1, *review* 1, *etc.* **II** *adv* unten; darunter.

‚~a'chieve *v/i bsd. ped.* hinter den Erwartungen zurückbleiben. **‚~'act** *v/t u. v/i thea. etc* betont zurückhaltend spielen. **‚~'age** *adj* minderjährig. **'~brush** *bsd. Am. → undergrowth.* **'~‚car·riage** *s ✈* Fahrwerk *n*, -gestell *n.* **‚~'charge I** *v/t* **1.** j-m zuwenig berechnen: *~ s.o. (by) £10* j-m 10 Pfund zuwenig berechnen. **2.** *Betrag* zuwenig verlangen. **II** *v/i* **3.** zuwenig berechnen *od.* verlangen (*for* für). **'~clothes** *s pl → underwear.* **'~coat** *s* Grundierung *f.* **'~‚cov·er** *adj*: *~ agent* verdeckter Ermittler. **'~‚cur·rent** *s* Unterströmung *f* (*a. fig.*). **‚~'cut** *v/t* (*irr cut*) j-n (im Preis) unterbieten. **‚~de'vel·oped** *adj* unterentwickelt: *~*

‚~'country Entwicklungsland *n.* **'~·dog** *s* Benachteiligte *m, f*, Unterdrückte *m, f.* **‚~'done** *adj* nicht durchgebraten. **‚~'dress** *v/t u. v/i* (sich) zu einfach anziehen. **‚~'es·ti·mate** *v/t* **1.** zu niedrig schätzen *od.* veranschlagen. **2.** *fig.* unterschätzen, -bewerten. **‚~'ex'pose** *v/t phot.* unterbelichten. **‚~'fed** *adj* unterernährt. **‚~'floor** *adj*: *~ heating* Fußbodenheizung *f.* **‚~'foot** *adv*: *the grass was wet ~* das Gras war naß; *trample ~* hinwegtrampeln über (*acc*). **‚~'go** *v/t* (*irr go*) erleben, durchmachen; sich *e-r Operation etc* unterziehen. **~'grad** ['~ˌgræd] *s* F, **‚~'grad·u·ate** *s univ.* Student(in). **‚~'ground I** *adj* **1.** unterirdisch: *~ car park* Tiefgarage *f.* **2.** *fig.* Untergrund... **II** *adv* [‚~'graʊnd] **3.** unterirdisch, unter der Erde: *go ~ fig.* untertauchen; in den Untergrund gehen. **III** *s* **4.** *bsd. Br.* U-Bahn *f*: *by ~* mit der U-Bahn. **5.** *fig.* Untergrund *m.* **'~·growth** *s* Unterholz *n*, Gestrüpp *n.* **‚~'hand** *adj*, **‚~'hand·ed** *adj* □ hinterhältig. **‚~'lie** *v/t* (*irr lie*) zugrunde liegen (*dat*). **‚~'line** *v/t* unterstreichen (*a. fig.*).

un·der·ling ['ʌndəlɪŋ] *s*: *he's just an ~ contp.* er ist nur ein Rädchen im Getriebe.

‚un·der'ly·ing *adj* zugrundeliegend. **‚~'manned** *adj* (personell) unterbesetzt. **‚~'men·tioned** *adj Br.* untenerwähnt. **‚~'mine** *v/t* **1.** unterspülen, -waschen. **2.** *fig.* untergraben, -minieren.

un·der·neath [ˌʌndə'niːθ] **I** *prp* unter (*Lage etc*: *dat*; *Richtung*: *acc*). **II** *adv* darunter. **III** *s* F Unterseite *f.*

‚un·der'nour·ished *adj* unterernährt. **‚~'nour·ish·ment** *s* Unterernährung *f.* **‚~'pants** *s pl, a. pair of ~* Unterhose *f.* **'~·pass** *s* (Straßen-, Eisenbahn)Unterführung *f.* **‚~'pay** *v/t* (*irr pay*) j-m zuwenig zahlen, j-n unterbezahlen. **‚~'play** *v/t* **1.** → *underact.* **2.** *~ one's hand fig. et.* nicht alle Trümpfe ausspielen. **3.** *fig. et.* herunterspielen. **‚un·der'priv·i·leged** *adj* unterprivilegiert. **‚~'rate** *v/t* unterbewerten (*a. Sport*), -schätzen. **'~‚rep·re'sent·ed** *adj* unterrepräsentiert. **'~·score** → *underline.* **'~'sec·re·tar·y** *s pol.* Staatssekretär *m.* **‚~'sell** *v/t* (*irr sell*) **1.** → *undercut.* **2.** *Ware* verschleudern, unter Wert verkaufen: *~ o.s. fig.* sich schlecht verkaufen. **'~**

shirt *s Am.* Unterhemd *n.* '**~shorts**
Am. → **underpants.** '**~side** *s* Unterseite *f.* ,**~'signed I** *adj* unterzeichnet. **II** *s*:
the ~ der *od.* die Unterzeichnete, die
Unterzeichneten (*a. fig.*). ,**~'size(d)** *adj* zu
klein. ,**~'staffed** → **undermanned.**
,**~'stand** (*irr stand*) **I** *v/t* **1.** verstehen:
make o.s. understood sich verständlich machen. **2.** erfahren *od.* gehört haben (*that* daß): **am I to ~ that** soll das
heißen, daß; **give s.o. to ~ that** j-m zu
verstehen geben, daß. **II** *v/i* **3.** verstehen. **4.** *not to ~ about* nichts verstehen
von. ,**~'stand·a·ble** *adj* verständlich (*a.
fig.*): *understandably a.* verständlicherweise. ,**~'stand·ing I** *s* **1.** Verstand
m: **be** (*od.* **go**) **beyond s.o.'s ~** j-s
Verstand gehen. **2.** Verständnis *n* (*of*
für): **with ~** verständnisvoll. **3.** Abmachung *f*: **come to an ~** e-e Abmachung treffen (*with* mit): **on the ~ that**
unter der Voraussetzung, daß. **II** *adj* □
4. verständnisvoll. ,**~'state** *v/t* untertreiben, untertrieben darstellen. ,**~'state·ment** *s* Untertreibung *f.* ,**~'stud·y** *thea.* **I** *s* zweite Besetzung. **II** *v/t*
die zweite Besetzung sein für. ,**~'take**
v/t (*irr take*) **1.** *et.* übernehmen. **2.** sich
verpflichten (*to do* zu tun). ,**~'tak·er** *s*
(Leichen)Bestatter *m*; Bestattungs-,
Beerdigungsinstitut *n.* ,**~the-'count·er** *adj* F schwarz, illegal. '**~tone** *s* **1.** *in*
an ~ mit gedämpfter Stimme. **2.** *fig.*
Unterton *m.* ,**~'val·ue** *v/t* unterbewerten, -schätzen. ,**~'wa·ter I** *adj* Unterwasser... **II** *adv* unter Wasser. '**~wear** *s*
Unterwäsche *f.* ~**weight I** *s* ['~weɪt]
Untergewicht *n.* **II** *adj* [,~'weɪt] untergewichtig (*Person*), zu leicht (*by* um)
(*Gegenstand*): **be ~ by five kilos, be
five kilos ~** fünf Kilo Untergewicht
haben. '**~world** *s* Unterwelt *f.* '**~write** *v/t* (*irr write*) **1.** *Projekt* unterstützen (*with* mit). **2.** *et.* versichern.
un·de·served [,ʌndɪ'zɜːvd] *adj* unverdient. ,**un·de'serv·ed·ly** [~vɪdlɪ] *adv*
unverdient(ermaßen).
un·de·sir·a·ble [,ʌndɪ'saɪərəbl] *adj* **1.**
nicht wünschenswert. **2.** unerwünscht.
un·dies ['ʌndɪz] *s pl* F (*bsd.* Damen)Unterwäsche *f.*
un·dis·ci·plined [ʌn'dɪsɪplɪnd] *adj* undiszipliniert, disziplinlos.
un·dis·cov·ered [,ʌndɪ'skʌvəd] *adj*

unentdeckt; unbemerkt.
un·dis·turbed [,ʌndɪ'stɜːbd] *adj* ungestört.
un·di·vid·ed [,ʌndɪ'vaɪdɪd] *adj* ungeteilt
(*a. fig.*).
un·do [ʌn'duː] *v/t* **1.** aufmachen, öffnen.
2. *fig.* zunichte machen. ,**un'do·ing** *s*:
be s.o.'s ~ j-s Ruin *od.* Verderben sein.
un·done [ʌn'dʌn] *adj* **1.** unerledigt:
leave nothing ~ nichts unversucht lassen. **2.** offen: **come ~** aufgehen.
un·doubt·ed [ʌn'daʊtɪd] *adj* unbestritten. **un'doubt·ed·ly** *adv* zweifellos, ohne (jeden) Zweifel.
un·dreamed-of [ʌn'driːmdɒv], **un·dreamt-of** [ʌn'dremtɒv] *adj* ungeahnt.
un·dress [ʌn'dres] **I** *v/i* sich ausziehen,
(*beim Arzt*) sich frei machen. **II** *v/t* j-n
ausziehen: **get ~ed** → **I.**
un·due [ʌn'djuː] *adj* □ übermäßig.
un·du·lat·ing ['ʌndjʊleɪtɪŋ] *adj* sanft
(*Hügel*).
un·dy·ing [ʌn'daɪɪŋ] *adj* ewig, unsterblich, unvergänglich.
un·earned [ʌn'ɜːnd] *adj fig.* unverdient.
un·earth [ʌn'ɜːθ] *v/t* **1.** ausgraben. **2.** *fig.*
ausfindig machen. **un'earth·ly** *adj* **1.**
überirdisch. **2.** unheimlich. **3.** *at an ~
hour* F zu e-r unchristlichen Zeit.
un·eas·i·ness [ʌn'iːzɪnɪs] *s* Unbehagen
n. **un'eas·y** *adj* □ **1.** **be ~** sich unbehaglich fühlen; **~ about** mir ist nicht
wohl bei. **2.** unruhig (*Nacht, Schlaf*).
un·eat·a·ble [ʌn'iːtəbl] *adj* ungenießbar.
un·e·co·nom·ic ['ʌn,iːkə'nɒmɪk] *adj*
(*~ally*) unwirtschaftlich.
un·ed·u·cat·ed [ʌn'edjʊkeɪtɪd] *adj* ungebildet.
un·e·mo·tion·al [,ʌnɪ'məʊʃənl] *adj* □
leidenschaftslos, kühl, beherrscht.
un·em·ployed [,ʌnɪm'plɔɪd] **I** *adj* arbeitslos. **II** *s*: **the ~** *pl* die Arbeitslosen
pl. ,**un·em'ploy·ment** *s* Arbeitslosigkeit *f*: **~ benefit** *Br.*, **~ compensation**
Am. Arbeitslosengeld *n.*
un·end·ing [ʌn'endɪŋ] *adj* □ endlos.
un·en·dur·a·ble [,ʌnɪn'djʊərəbl] *adj* □
unerträglich.
un·Eng·lish [ʌn'ɪŋglɪʃ] *adj* unenglisch.
un·en·vi·a·ble [ʌn'enviəbl] *adj* □ wenig
beneidenswert.
un·e·qual [ʌn'iːkwəl] *adj* □ **1.** ungleich,
unterschiedlich. **2.** *fig.* ungleich, einsei-

tig. **3. be ~ to** e-r Aufgabe etc nicht gewachsen sein. **,un'e·qual(l)ed** adj unerreicht, unübertroffen.

un·e·quiv·o·cal [ˌʌnɪˈkwɪvəkl] adj □ unzweideutig, unmißverständlich.

un·err·ing [ˌʌnˈɜːrɪŋ] adj □ unfehlbar.

un·e·ven [ˌʌnˈiːvn] adj □ **1.** uneben. **2.** ungleich(mäßig). **3.** unterschiedlich, schwankend. **4.** ungerade (Zahl). **5.** unregelmäßig (Pulsschlag etc).

un·e·vent·ful [ˌʌnɪˈventfʊl] adj □ ereignislos.

un·ex·am·pled [ˌʌnɪɡˈzɑːmpld] adj beispiellos.

un·ex·pect·ed [ˌʌnɪkˈspektɪd] adj □ unerwartet.

un·ex·plained [ˌʌnɪkˈspleɪnd] adj ungeklärt.

un·ex·posed [ˌʌnɪkˈspəʊzd] adj phot. unbelichtet.

un·ex·plored [ˌʌnɪkˈsplɔːd] adj unerforscht.

un·fail·ing [ʌnˈfeɪlɪŋ] adj □ unerschöpflich.

un·fair [ˌʌnˈfeə] adj □ unfair, (Wettbewerb) unlauter. **,un'fair·ness** s Unfairneß f.

un·faith·ful [ˌʌnˈfeɪθfʊl] adj □ untreu (**to** dat).

un·fal·ter·ing [ʌnˈfɔːltərɪŋ] adj □ unerschütterlich.

un·fa·mil·iar [ˌʌnfəˈmɪljə] adj □ **1.** nicht vertraut. **2. be ~ with** nicht vertraut sein mit, sich nicht auskennen in (dat).

un·fash·ion·a·ble [ˌʌnˈfæʃnəbl] adj □ unmodern.

un·fas·ten [ˌʌnˈfɑːsn] v/t aufmachen, öffnen; losbinden.

un·fa·vo(u)r·a·ble [ˌʌnˈfeɪvərəbl] adj □ ungünstig: a) unvorteilhaft (**to, for** für), b) negativ, ablehnend (Antwort etc).

un·feel·ing [ʌnˈfiːlɪŋ] adj □ gefühllos, herzlos.

un·fin·ished [ˌʌnˈfɪnɪʃt] adj unfertig; unvollendet.

un·fit [ˌʌnˈfɪt] adj □ **1.** unpassend, ungeeignet; unfähig, untauglich: **~ for service** bsd. ✗ dienstunfähig, (-)untauglich; **~ to drive** fahruntüchtig; → **consumption** 2. **2.** nicht fit, nicht in Form.

un·flag·ging [ˌʌnˈflæɡɪŋ] adj □ unermüdlich, unentwegt.

un·fold [ˌʌnˈfəʊld] v/t auf-, auseinanderfalten.

un·fore·seen [ˌʌnfɔːˈsiːn] adj unvorhergesehen, unvorhersehbar.

un·for·get·ta·ble [ˌʌnfəˈɡetəbl] adj □ unvergeßlich.

un·for·tu·nate [ʌnˈfɔːtʃnət] adj **1.** unglücklich; unglückselig. **2.** bedauerlich. **un'for·tu·nate·ly** adv leider.

un·found·ed [ˌʌnˈfaʊndɪd] adj unbegründet.

un·fre·quent·ed [ˌʌnfrɪˈkwentɪd] adj wenig besucht.

un·friend·ly [ˌʌnˈfrendlɪ] adj unfreundlich (**to** zu).

un·ful·filled [ˌʌnfʊlˈfɪld] adj unerfüllt.

un·furl [ʌnˈfɜːl] v/t Fahne etc auf-, entrollen, Segel losmachen.

un·fur·nished [ˌʌnˈfɜːnɪʃt] adj unmöbliert.

un·gain·ly [ʌnˈɡeɪnlɪ] adj linkisch.

un·gen·tle·man·like [ʌnˈdʒentlmənlaɪk], **un'gen·tle·man·ly** adj wenig gentlemanlike.

un·god·ly [ʌnˈɡɒdlɪ] adj: **at an ~ hour** F zu e-r unchristlichen Zeit.

un·gov·ern·a·ble [ʌnˈɡʌvənəbl] adj □ unbeherrscht, ungezügelt (Temperament).

un·grate·ful [ʌnˈɡreɪtfʊl] adj □ undankbar.

un·guard·ed [ˌʌnˈɡɑːdɪd] adj **1.** unbewacht. **2.** fig. unbedacht, unüberlegt.

un·hap·pi·ness [ʌnˈhæpɪnəs] s Traurigkeit f. **un'hap·py** adj unglücklich: **unhappily** a. unglücklicherweise, leider.

un·harmed [ˌʌnˈhɑːmd] adj unversehrt.

un·health·y [ʌnˈhelθɪ] adj □ **1.** kränklich, nicht gesund. **2.** ungesund. **3.** contp. unnatürlich, krankhaft.

un·heard [ˌʌnˈhɜːd] adj: **go ~** unbeachtet bleiben, keine Beachtung finden. **,un'heard-of** [~ɒv] adj noch nie dagewesen, beispiellos.

un·hes·i·tat·ing [ʌnˈhezɪteɪtɪŋ] adj □ **1.** prompt. **2.** bereitwillig: **~ly** a. anstandslos.

un·hinge [ˌʌnˈhɪndʒ] v/t **1.** Tür etc aus den Angeln heben. **2.** → **s.o.('s mind)** fig. j-n völlig aus dem Gleichgewicht bringen.

un·ho·ly [ʌnˈhəʊlɪ] adj F furchtbar, schrecklich.

un·hoped-for [ʌnˈhəʊptfɔː] adj unverhofft.

un·hurt [ˌʌnˈhɜːt] adj unverletzt.

u·ni ['juːnɪ] s F Uni f (*Universität*).

un·i·den·ti·fied [ˌʌnaɪ'dentɪfaɪd] *adj* unbekannt, nicht identifiziert: **~ flying object** unbekanntes Flugobjekt.

u·ni·fi·ca·tion [ˌjuːnɪfɪ'keɪʃn] s Vereinigung f.

u·ni·form ['juːnɪfɔːm] I *adj* □ einheitlich. II s Uniform f: **in ~** in Uniform. **'u·ni·formed** *adj* uniformiert, in Uniform. **ˌu·ni'form·i·ty** s Einheitlichkeit f.

u·ni·fy ['juːnɪfaɪ] *v/t* 1. verein(ig)en. 2. vereinheitlichen.

u·ni·lat·er·al [ˌjuːnɪ'lætərəl] *adj* □ fig. einseitig.

un·im·ag·i·na·ble [ˌʌnɪ'mædʒɪnəbl] *adj* □ unvorstellbar. **ˌun·im'ag·i·na·tive** *adj* □ einfalls-, phantasielos.

un·im·por·tant [ˌʌnɪm'pɔːtənt] *adj* □ unwichtig.

un·im·pressed [ˌʌnɪm'prest] *adj* unbeeindruckt (**by** von).

un·in·flu·enced [ˌʌn'ɪnfluənst] *adj* unbeeinflußt.

un·in·hab·it·a·ble [ˌʌnɪn'hæbɪtəbl] *adj* □ unbewohnbar. **ˌun·in'hab·it·ed** *adj* unbewohnt.

un·in·jured [ˌʌn'ɪndʒəd] *adj* unverletzt.

un·in·sured [ˌʌnɪn'ʃɔːd] *adj* unversichert.

un·in·tel·li·gent [ˌʌnɪn'telɪdʒənt] *adj* □ unintelligent.

un·in·tel·li·gi·ble [ˌʌnɪn'telɪdʒəbl] *adj* □ unverständlich (**to** für *od.* dat).

un·in·tend·ed [ˌʌnɪn'tendɪd], **un·in·ten·tion·al** [ˌ~'tenʃənl] *adj* □ unabsichtlich, unbeabsichtigt.

un·in·ter·est·ed [ˌʌn'ɪntrəstɪd] *adj* □ uninteressiert (**in** an dat): **be ~ in** a. sich nicht interessieren für. **ˌun·in·ter·est·ing** *adj* □ uninteressant.

un·in·ter·rupt·ed ['ʌnˌɪntə'rʌptɪd] *adj* □ ununterbrochen.

un·in·vit·ed [ˌʌnɪn'vaɪtɪd] *adj* uneingeladen, ungebeten.

un·ion ['juːnjən] s 1. Vereinigung f; Union f: ♀ **Jack** (*od.* **Flag**) Union Jack *m* (*britische Nationalflagge*). 2. Gewerkschaft f. **'un·ion·ist** s Gewerkschaftler(in). **'un·ion·ize** *v/t u. v/i* (sich) gewerkschaftlich organisieren.

u·nique [juː'niːk] *adj* □ einzigartig; einmalig.

u·ni·son ['juːnɪzn] s: **in ~** gemeinsam.

u·nit ['juːnɪt] s 1. *allg.* Einheit f; ped. Unit

f, Lehreinheit f; ⊚ Element n, Teil n; (Anbau)Element n: **~ furniture** Anbaumöbel pl. 2. Abteilung f. 3. ⅍ Einer m.

u·nite [juː'naɪt] I *v/t* verbinden, -einigen. II *v/i* sich vereinigen *od.* zs.-tun: **~ in doing s.th.** et. gemeinsam tun. **u'nit·ed** *adj* verein(ig)t: ♀ **Nations** pl Vereinte Nationen pl; **be ~ in** sich einig sein in (dat).

u·ni·ty ['juːnəti] s 1. Einheit f. 2. ⅍ Eins f.

u·ni·ver·sal [ˌjuːnɪ'vɜːsl] *adj* □ 1. universal, universell: **~ heir** Universalerbe m. 2. allgemein. 3. Welt...: **~ language** (**time**, *etc*).

u·ni·verse ['juːnɪvɜːs] s Universum n, Weltall n.

u·ni·ver·si·ty [ˌjuːnɪ'vɜːsəti] I s Universität f, Hochschule f: **go to ~** die Universität besuchen. II *adj* Universitäts...: **~ professor**; **~ education** akademische Bildung, Hochschulbildung f; Universitäts-, Hochschulausbildung f.

un·just [ˌʌn'dʒʌst] *adj* □ ungerecht (**to** gegen).

un·kempt [ˌʌn'kempt] *adj* ungekämmt (*Haar*); ungepflegt (*Kleidung etc*).

un·kind [ʌn'kaɪnd] *adj* □ unfreundlich (**to** zu). **un'kind·ness** s Unfreundlichkeit f.

un·knot [ˌʌn'nɒt] *v/t* auf-, entknoten.

un·known [ˌʌn'nəʊn] *adj* unbekannt (**to** dat): **~ quantity** ⅍ unbekannte Größe (*a. fig.*), Unbekannte f.

un·la·dy·like [ˌʌn'leɪdɪlaɪk] *adj* wenig damenhaft.

un·law·ful [ˌʌn'lɔːfʊl] *adj* □ ungesetzlich, gesetzwidrig.

un·lead·ed [ˌʌn'ledɪd] *adj* bleifrei (*Benzin*).

un·learn [ˌʌn'lɜːn] *v/t* (*a. irr* **learn**) Ansichten etc ablegen, aufgeben.

un·leash [ˌʌn'liːʃ] *v/t* 1. Hund loslassen, von der Leine lassen. 2. *fig.* s-m Zorn etc freien Lauf lassen: **all his anger was ~ed on her** sein ganzer Zorn entlud sich auf sie.

un·leav·ened [ˌʌn'levnd] *adj* ungesäuert.

un·less [ən'les] *cj* wenn *od.* sofern ... nicht; es sei denn.

un·like [ˌʌn'laɪk] *prp* 1. im Gegensatz zu. 2. **he is quite ~ his father** er ist ganz anders als sein Vater; **that is very ~ him** das sieht ihm gar nicht ähnlich. **un'like·ly** *adj* 1. **he is ~ to come** es ist unwahrscheinlich, daß er kommt. **2.** unwahrscheinlich, unglaubwürdig.

un·lim·it·ed [ʌn'lɪmɪtɪd] *adj* unbegrenzt.

un·list·ed [ˌʌn'lɪstɪd] *adj teleph.:* **be ~** nicht im Telefonbuch stehen, geheim sein; **~ number** Geheimnummer *f.*

un·load [ˌʌn'ləʊd] *v/t Fahrzeug* entladen, *a. Gegenstände* ab-, ausladen, **&** *Ladung, Schiff* löschen.

un·lock [ˌʌn'lɒk] *v/t* aufschließen.

un·loved [ˌʌn'lʌvd] *adj* ungeliebt.

un·luck·i·ly [ʌn'lʌkɪlɪ] *adv* unglücklicherweise: **~ for me** zu m-m Pech. **un·'luck·y** *adj* unglücklich: **~ day** Unglückstag *m;* **be ~** Pech haben; Unglück bringen.

un·made [ˌʌn'meɪd] *adj* ungemacht (*Bett*).

un·man·age·a·ble [ʌn'mænɪdʒəbl] *adj* □ **1.** widerspenstig. **2.** unhandlich.

un·man·ly [ˌʌn'mænlɪ] *adj* unmännlich.

un·manned [ˌʌn'mænd] *adj* unbemannt.

un·man·ner·ly [ʌn'mænəlɪ] *adj* ungesittet, unmanierlich.

un·marked [ˌʌn'mɑːkt] *adj* **1.** nicht gekennzeichnet. **2.** *Sport:* ungedeckt, frei.

un·mar·ried [ˌʌn'mærɪd] *adj* unverheiratet, ledig.

un·mask [ˌʌn'mɑːsk] *v/t fig.* entlarven.

un·matched [ˌʌn'mætʃt] *adj* unvergleichlich, unübertroffen.

un·men·tion·a·ble [ʌn'menʃnəbl] *adj* Tabu...: **be ~** tabu sein.

un·mer·ci·ful [ʌn'mɜːsɪfʊl] *adj* □ erbarmungslos, unbarmherzig.

un·me·thod·i·cal [ˌʌnmɪ'θɒdɪkl] *adj* □ unmethodisch.

un·mis·tak·a·ble [ˌʌnmɪ'steɪkəbl] *adj* □ unverkennbar, unverwechselbar.

un·mixed [ˌʌn'mɪkst] *adj* **1.** unvermischt. **2.** *fig.* rein, ungetrübt.

un·moved [ˌʌn'muːvd] *adj* ungerührt: **he remained ~ by it** es ließ ihn kalt.

un·mu·si·cal [ˌʌn'mjuːzɪkl] *adj* □ unmusikalisch.

un·named [ˌʌn'neɪmd] *adj* ungenannt.

un·nat·u·ral [ʌn'nætʃrəl] *adj* □ **1.** unnatürlich. **2.** widernatürlich.

un·nec·es·sar·y [ʌn'nesəsərɪ] *adj* unnötig: **unnecessarily** *a.* unnötigerweise.

un·nerve [ˌʌn'nɜːv] *v/t* **1.** entnerven. **2.** entmutigen.

un·no·ticed [ˌʌn'nəʊtɪst] *adj:* **go** (*od.* **pass**) **~** unbemerkt bleiben.

un·num·bered [ˌʌn'nʌmbəd] *adj* unnumeriert.

un·ob·tru·sive [ˌʌnəb'truːsɪv] *adj* □ unauffällig.

un·oc·cu·pied [ˌʌn'ɒkjʊpaɪd] *adj* **1.** leer(stehend), unbewohnt: **be ~** leer stehen. **2.** unbeschäftigt. **3.** **✕** unbesetzt.

un·of·fi·cial [ˌʌnə'fɪʃl] *adj* □ inoffiziell.

un·o·pened [ˌʌn'əʊpənd] *adj* ungeöffnet.

un·pack [ˌʌn'pæk] *v/t u. v/i* auspacken.

un·paid(-for) [ˌʌn'peɪd(fə)] *adj* unbezahlt.

un·par·al·leled [ʌn'pærəleld] *adj* beispiellos, einmalig.

un·par·don·a·ble [ʌn'pɑːdnəbl] *adj* □ unverzeihlich.

un·per·turbed [ˌʌnpə'tɜːbd] *adj* gelassen, ruhig.

un·pick [ˌʌn'pɪk] *v/t* auftrennen.

un·play·a·ble [ˌʌn'pleɪəbl] *adj Sport:* unbespielbar (*Platz*).

un·pleas·ant [ʌn'pleznt] *adj* □ **1.** unangenehm, (*Nachricht etc. a.*) unerfreulich. **2.** unfreundlich.

un·plug [ˌʌn'plʌg] *v/t* den Stecker (*gen*) herausziehen.

un·po·lished [ˌʌn'pɒlɪʃt] *adj* **1.** unpoliert. **2.** *fig.* ungeschliffen, ungehobelt.

un·pop·u·lar [ˌʌn'pɒpjʊlə] *adj* □ unpopulär, unbeliebt: **make o.s. ~ with** sich bei *j-m* unbeliebt machen.

un·prac·ti·cal [ˌʌn'præktɪkl] *adj* □ unpraktisch.

un·prec·e·dent·ed [ʌn'presɪdentɪd] *adj* □ beispiellos, noch nie dagewesen.

un·pre·dict·a·ble [ˌʌnprɪ'dɪktəbl] *adj* **1.** unvorhersehbar. **2.** unberechenbar (*Person*).

un·prej·u·diced [ʌn'predʒʊdɪst] *adj* □ unvoreingenommen, **✗✗** unbefangen.

un·pre·pared [ˌʌnprɪ'peəd] *adj* **1.** unvorbereitet. **2.** nicht gefaßt *od.* vorbereitet (*for auf acc*).

un·pre·ten·tious [ˌʌnprɪ'tenʃəs] *adj* □ bescheiden, einfach.

un·prin·ci·pled [ʌn'prɪnsəpld] *adj* skrupellos.

un·print·a·ble [ˌʌn'prɪntəbl] *adj* nicht druckfähig *od.* druckreif.

un·pro·duc·tive [ˌʌnprə'dʌktɪv] *adj* □ unproduktiv (*a. fig.*), unergiebig, unrentabel.

un·pro·fes·sion·al [ˌʌnprə'feʃnl] *adj* □

1. standeswidrig. **2.** unfachmännisch.

un·prof·it·a·ble [ˌʌnˈprɒfɪtəbl] *adj* □ **1.** unrentabel. **2.** *fig.* nutz-, zwecklos.

un·prompt·ed [ˌʌnˈprɒmptɪd] *adj* spontan.

un·pro·nounce·a·ble [ˌʌnprəˈnaʊnsəbl] *adj* unaussprechbar.

un·pro·tect·ed [ˌʌnprəˈtektɪd] *adj* schutzlos; ungeschützt.

un·proved [ˌʌnˈpruːvd], **un·prov·en** [ˌ~vn] *adj* unbewiesen.

un·pro·voked [ˌʌnprəˈvəʊkt] *adj* grundlos.

un·pub·lished [ˌʌnˈpʌblɪʃt] *adj* unveröffentlicht.

un·punc·tu·al [ˌʌnˈpʌŋktʃʊəl] *adj* □ unpünktlich: **be ~** unpünktlich kommen **(for** zu). **ˈun·punc·tu·al·i·ty** [ˌ~ˈælətɪ] *s* Unpünktlichkeit *f*.

un·pun·ished [ˌʌnˈpʌnɪʃt] *adj* unbestraft, ungestraft: **go ~** straflos bleiben.

un·qual·i·fied [ˌʌnˈkwɒlɪfaɪd] *adj* **1.** unqualifiziert, ungeeignet **(for** für). **2.** uneingeschränkt.

un·ques·tion·a·ble [ʌnˈkwestʃənəbl] *adj* □ unbestritten: **be ~** *a.* außer Frage stehen. **un·ques·tion·ing** *adj* □ bedingungslos.

un·quote [ˌʌnˈkwəʊt] *adv* → **quote** 6.

un·rav·el [ʌnˈrævl] **I** *v/t* **1.** *Pullover etc* auftrennen, -ziehen. **2.** entwirren (*a. fig.*). **II** *v/i* **3.** sich auftrennen *od.* aufziehen.

un·read·a·ble [ˌʌnˈriːdəbl] *adj* unlesbar: a) nicht lesenswert, b) unleserlich.

un·re·al [ˌʌnˈrɪəl] *adj* □˙ unwirklich. **ˈun·re·alˈis·tic** [ˌ~ˈlɪstɪk] *adj* (**~ally**) unrealistisch. **un·re·al·i·ty** [ˌ~ˈælətɪ] *s* Unwirklichkeit *f*.

un·rea·son·a·ble [ʌnˈriːznəbl] *adj* □ **1.** unvernünftig. **2.** übertrieben, unzumutbar.

un·rec·og·niz·a·ble [ˌʌnˈrekəɡnaɪzəbl] *adj* □ nicht wiederzuerkennen(d).

un·re·lat·ed [ˌʌnrɪˈleɪtɪd] *adj* **1.** nicht verwandt (**to** mit). **2. be ~** in keinem Zs.-hang stehen (**to** mit).

un·re·lent·ing [ˌʌnrɪˈlentɪŋ] *adj* □ unvermindert.

un·re·li·a·ble [ˌʌnrɪˈlaɪəbl] *adj* □ unzuverlässig.

un·re·lieved [ˌʌnrɪˈliːvd] *adj* ununterbrochen, ständig. **ˌun·reˈlievˈed·ly** [ˌ~ɪdlɪ] *adv* → **unrelieved.**

un·re·mit·ting [ˌʌnrɪˈmɪtɪŋ] *adj* □ unablässig, unaufhörlich.

un·re·quit·ed [ˌʌnrɪˈkwaɪtɪd] *adj* unerwidert (*Liebe*).

un·re·served [ˌʌnrɪˈzɜːvd] *adj* **1.** uneingeschränkt. **2.** nicht reserviert. **ˌun·reˈservˈed·ly** [ˌ~ɪdlɪ] *adv* uneingeschränkt.

un·rest [ˌʌnˈrest] *s pol. etc* Unruhen *pl.*

un·re·strained [ˌʌnrɪˈstreɪnd] *adj* hemmungslos, ungezügelt. **ˌun·reˈstrainˈed·ly** [ˌ~ɪdlɪ] *adv* → **unrestrained.**

un·re·strict·ed [ˌʌnrɪˈstrɪktɪd] *adj* □ uneingeschränkt.

un·re·ward·ing [ˌʌnrɪˈwɔːdɪŋ] *adj* wenig lohnend, (*Aufgabe etc a.*) undankbar.

un·rig [ˌʌnˈrɪɡ] *v/t Schiff* abtakeln.

un·ripe [ˌʌnˈraɪp] *adj* unreif.

un·ri·val(l)ed [ʌnˈraɪvld] *adj* unerreicht, unübertroffen.

un·roll [ʌnˈrəʊl] *v/t* auf-, entrollen.

un·ruf·fled [ˌʌnˈrʌfld] *adj* gelassen, ruhig.

un·rul·y [ʌnˈruːlɪ] *adj* **1.** ungebärdig, wild. **2.** widerspenstig (*Haare*).

un·sad·dle [ˌʌnˈsædl] *v/t* **1.** *Pferd* absatteln. **2.** *Reiter* abwerfen.

un·safe [ˌʌnˈseɪf] *adj* □ unsicher, nicht sicher: **feel ~** sich nicht sicher fühlen.

un·said [ˌʌnˈsed] *adj*: **leave s.th. ~** et. nicht aussprechen; **be left** (*od.* **go**) **~** unausgesprochen *od.* ungesagt bleiben.

un·sal(e)·a·ble [ˌʌnˈseɪləbl] *adj* unverkäuflich.

un·salt·ed [ˌʌnˈsɔːltɪd] *adj* ungesalzen.

un·san·i·tar·y [ˌʌnˈsænɪtərɪ] *adj* □ unhygienisch.

un·sat·is·fac·to·ry [ˈʌnˌsætɪsˈfæktərɪ] *adj* □ unbefriedigend. **ˌun·sat·isˈfied** [ˌ~faɪd] *adj* unzufrieden (**with** mit). **ˌun·sat·isˈfy·ing** [ˌ~faɪɪŋ] → **unsatisfactory.**

un·sa·vo(u)r·y [ˌʌnˈseɪvərɪ] *adj* □ **1.** fad. **2.** *fig.* unerfreulich (*Angelegenheit etc*); anrüchig (*Stadtteil, Vergangenheit etc*).

un·sci·en·tif·ic [ˈʌnˌsaɪənˈtɪfɪk] *adj* (**~ally**) unwissenschaftlich.

un·screw [ˌʌnˈskruː] *v/t* ab-, losschrauben.

un·script·ed [ˌʌnˈskrɪptɪd] *adj* improvisiert.

un·scru·pu·lous [ʌnˈskruːpjʊləs] *adj* □ skrupel-, gewissenlos.

un·seat [ˌʌnˈsiːt] *v/t* **1.** *Reiter* abwerfen. **2.** *fig.* j-n s-s Amtes entheben.

un·seed·ed [ˌʌnˈsiːdɪd] *adj Sport:* ungesetzt.

un·seem·ly [ʌnˈsiːmlɪ] *adj* ungebührlich, unziemlich.

un·seen [ˌʌnˈsiːn] **I** *adj* **1.** ungesehen, unbemerkt: → *sight* 2. **2.** unsichtbar. **II** *s* **3.** *an (English)* ~ *ped. bsd. Br.* e-e Herübersetzung (aus dem Englischen).

un·self·ish [ʌnˈselfɪʃ] *adj* □ selbstlos, uneigennützig.

un·sen·ti·men·tal [ˈʌnˌsentɪˈmentl] *adj* □ unsentimental.

un·set·tle [ʌnˈsetl] *v/t* j-n beunruhigen; durcheinanderbringen; **un·set-·tled** *adj* **1.** unbeständig. **2.** unbeglichen, unbezahlt (*Rechnung*). **3.** ungeklärt (*Frage etc*). **4.** unbeständig (*Wetter*). **5.** unsicher (*Lage etc*).

un·shak(e)·a·ble [ʌnˈʃeɪkəbl] *adj* □ unerschütterlich.

un·shav·en [ʌnˈʃeɪvn] *adj* unrasiert.

un·shrink·a·ble [ʌnˈʃrɪŋkəbl] *adj* nicht eingehend *od.* einlaufend (*Stoff*).

un·sight·ly [ʌnˈsaɪtlɪ] *adj* unansehnlich; häßlich.

un·signed [ˌʌnˈsaɪnd] *adj* unsigniert (*Gemälde*), nicht unterschrieben *od.* unterzeichnet (*Brief etc*).

un·skil(l)·ful [ˌʌnˈskɪlfʊl] *adj* □ ungeschickt. **un·skilled** *adj* **1.** ungeschickt (*at, in* in *dat*). **2.** ~ *worker* ungelernter Arbeiter.

un·so·cia·ble [ʌnˈsəʊʃəbl] *adj* □ ungesellig.

un·so·cial [ʌnˈsəʊʃl] *adj:* **work** ~ **hours** *Br.* außerhalb der normalen Arbeitszeit arbeiten.

un·sold [ˌʌnˈsəʊld] *adj* unverkauft.

un·so·lic·it·ed [ˌʌnsəˈlɪsɪtɪd] *adj* unverlangt eingesandt (*Manuskript etc*), unaufgefordert zugesandt, unbestellt (*Ware*).

un·solved [ˌʌnˈsɒlvd] *adj* ungelöst (*Fall etc*).

un·so·phis·ti·cat·ed [ˌʌnsəˈfɪstɪkeɪtɪd] *adj* □ **1.** unkultiviert. **2.** ✿ unkompliziert.

un·sound [ˌʌnˈsaʊnd] *adj* □ **1.** nicht gesund; nicht intakt *od.* in Ordnung. **2.** *fig.* unklug, unvernünftig.

un·spar·ing [ʌnˈspeərɪŋ] *adj* □ verschwenderisch, freigebig (*in* mit): **be** ~

in one's efforts keine Mühe scheuen (**to do** zu tun).

un·speak·a·ble [ʌnˈspiːkəbl] *adj* □ unbeschreiblich, unsäglich.

un·spoiled [ˌʌnˈspɔɪld], **un·spoilt** [~t] *adj* **1.** unverdorben. **2.** nicht verwöhnt, (*Kind a.*) nicht verzogen.

un·sport·ing [ʌnˈspɔːtɪŋ] *adj* □, **un·sports·man·like** [ˌʌnˈspɔːtsmənlaɪk] *adj* unsportlich, unfair.

un·sta·ble [ʌnˈsteɪbl] *adj* □ **1.** instabil (*a. fig.*). **2.** *fig.* labil (*Person*).

un·stead·y [ʌnˈstedɪ] *adj* □ **1.** wack(e)lig; (*Hand*) unsicher. **2.** schwankend (*Preise etc*). **3.** ungleichmäßig.

un·stint·ing [ʌnˈstɪntɪŋ] → **unsparing**.

un·stop [ʌnˈstɒp] *v/t* **1.** *Flasche* entstöpseln. **2.** *Abfluß etc* freimachen.

un·stressed [ʌnˈstrest] *adj ling.* unbetont.

un·stuck [ʌnˈstʌk] *adj:* **come** ~ abgehen, sich lösen; *fig.* F auf den Bauch fallen (*Person*), schiefgehen (*Plan etc*).

un·stud·ied [ʌnˈstʌdɪd] *adj* ungekünstelt.

un·suc·cess·ful [ˌʌnsəkˈsesfʊl] *adj* □ erfolglos; vergeblich: **be** ~ keinen Erfolg haben.

un·suit·a·ble [ˌʌnˈsuːtəbl] *adj* □ unpassend, ungeeignet (**for, to** für).

un·sure [ˌʌnˈʃɔː] *adj allg.* unsicher: ~ **of o.s.** unsicher.

un·sur·passed [ˌʌnsəˈpɑːst] *adj* unübertroffen.

un·sus·pect·ed [ˌʌnsəˈspektɪd] *adj* □ **1.** unvermutet. **2.** unverdächtig. **un·sus·'pect·ing** *adj* □ nichtsahnend, arglos.

un·sus·pi·cious [ˌʌnsəˈspɪʃəs] *adj* □ **1.** arglos. **2.** unverdächtig, harmlos.

un·sweet·ened [ʌnˈswiːtnd] *adj* ungesüßt.

un·swerv·ing [ʌnˈswɜːvɪŋ] *adj* □ unbeirrbar, unerschütterlich.

un·tan·gle [ˌʌnˈtæŋgl] *v/t* entwirren (*a. fig.*).

un·tapped [ˌʌnˈtæpt] *adj* unerschlossen (*Naturschätze etc*).

un·teach·a·ble [ˌʌnˈtiːtʃəbl] *adj* unbelehrbar.

un·ten·a·ble [ˌʌnˈtenəbl] *adj* unhaltbar (*Theorie etc*).

un·think·a·ble [ʌnˈθɪŋkəbl] *adj* □ undenkbar, unvorstellbar. **¡un'think·ing** *adj* □ gedankenlos.

un·ti·dy [ʌn'taɪdɪ] *adj* □ unordentlich.

un·tie [ˌʌn'taɪ] *v/t* aufknoten, *Knoten* lösen, *j-n etc* losbinden (**from** von).

un·til [ən'tɪl] **I** *prp* **1.** bis. **2.** *not ~* erst: *not ~ Monday* erst (am) Montag; nicht vor Montag. **II** *cj* **3.** bis. **4.** *not ~* erst wenn, nicht bevor.

un·time·ly [ʌn'taɪmlɪ] *adj* **1.** vorzeitig, verfrüht. **2.** unpassend, ungelegen.

un·tir·ing [ʌn'taɪərɪŋ] *adj* □ unermüdlich.

un·told [ˌʌn'təʊld] *adj* unermeßlich (*Reichtum, Schaden etc*).

un·touched [ˌʌn'tʌtʃt] *adj* **1.** unberührt, unangetastet. **2.** unversehrt, heil.

un·trans·lat·a·ble [ˌʌntræns'leɪtəbl] *adj* unübersetzbar.

un·true [ˌʌn'truː] *adj* **1.** unwahr. **2.** untreu (**to** *dat*).

un·truth [ˌʌn'truːθ] *s* Unwahrheit *f*.

un·used¹ [ˌʌn'juːzd] *adj* unbenutzt, ungebraucht.

un·used² [ˌʌn'juːst] *adj*: *be ~ to s.th.* an et. nicht gewohnt sein, et. nicht gewohnt sein; *be ~ to doing s.th.* es nicht gewohnt sein, et. zu tun.

un·u·su·al [ʌn'juːʒl] *adj* □ ungewöhnlich.

un·ut·ter·a·ble [ʌn'ʌtərəbl] *adj* □ unbeschreiblich, unsäglich.

un·var·nished [ʌn'vɑːnɪʃt] *adj* ungeschminkt (*Wahrheit*).

un·var·y·ing [ʌn'veərɪŋ] *adj* □ unveränderlich, gleichbleibend.

un·veil [ˌʌn'veɪl] *v/t Denkmal etc* enthüllen.

un·versed [ˌʌn'vɜːst] *adj* unbewandert (**in** *in dat*).

un·voiced [ʌn'vɔɪst] *adj* **1.** unausgesprochen. **2.** *ling.* stimmlos.

un·want·ed [ʌn'wɒntɪd] *adj* unerwünscht, (*Schwangerschaft a.*) ungewollt.

un·war·rant·ed [ʌn'wɒrəntɪd] *adj* ungerechtfertigt.

un·washed [ˌʌn'wɒʃt] *adj* ungewaschen.

un·wa·ver·ing [ʌn'weɪvərɪŋ] *adj* □ unerschütterlich.

un·wel·come [ʌn'welkəm] *adj* unwillkommen.

un·well [ˌʌn'wel] *adj*: *be* (*od. feel*) *~* sich unwohl *od.* nicht wohl fühlen.

un·whole·some [ʌn'həʊlsəm] *adj* □ ungesund.

un·wield·y [ʌn'wiːldɪ] *adj* unhandlich, sperrig.

un·will·ing [ʌn'wɪlɪŋ] *adj* □ widerwillig: *be ~ to do s.th.* nicht bereit *od.* gewillt sein, et. zu tun; et. nicht tun wollen.

un·wind [ʌn'waɪnd] (*irr wind*) **I** *v/t* **1.** abwickeln. **II** *v/i* **2.** sich abwickeln. **3.** F abschalten, sich entspannen.

un·wise [ˌʌn'waɪz] *adj* □ unklug.

un·wished-for [ʌn'wɪʃtfɔː] *adj* unerwünscht.

un·wit·ting [ʌn'wɪtɪŋ] *adj* □ **1.** unwissentlich. **2.** unbeabsichtigt.

un·wom·an·ly [ʌn'wʊmənlɪ] *adj* unfraulich, unweiblich.

un·wont·ed [ʌn'wəʊntɪd] *adj* □ ungewohnt.

un·wor·thy [ʌn'wɜːðɪ] *adj*: *be ~ of s.th.* e-r Sache nicht würdig sein, et. nicht verdienen.

un·wrap [ˌʌn'ræp] *v/t* auswickeln, -packen.

un·writ·ten [ˌʌn'rɪtn] *adj* ungeschrieben: *~ law* ungeschriebenes Recht; *fig.* ungeschriebenes Gesetz.

un·yield·ing [ʌn'jiːldɪŋ] *adj* □ unnachgiebig.

un·zip [ˌʌn'zɪp] *v/t* den Reißverschluß (*gen*) aufmachen.

up [ʌp] **I** *adv* **1.** oben; *1000 Meter etc* hoch, in e-r Höhe von: *~ there* dort oben; *jump ~ and down* hüpfen; *walk ~ and down* auf u. ab *od.* hin u. her gehen; → *look up, take up, etc.* **2.** *~ to* bis zu: *~ to a moment ago* bis vor e-m Augenblick; *be ~ to s.th.* F et. vorhaben, et. im Schilde führen; *not to be ~ to s.th.* e-r Sache nicht gewachsen sein; *it's ~ to you* das liegt bei Ihnen; → *ear¹* 1, *eye* 1, *feel* 6, *scratch* 6, *etc.* **II** *prp* **3.** oben auf (*dat*); her-, hinauf: *~ the river* flußaufwärts; *~ yours!* *Br.* V leck mich (doch) am Arsch!; → *climb* 3, *etc.* **III** *adj* **4.** nach oben (gerichtet), Aufwärts... **5.** *the ~ train* der Zug nach London. **6.** *what's ~?* F was ist los? **7.** *be well ~ in* (*od. on*) F viel verstehen von. **8.** *~ for → sale* 1. **IV** *s* **9.** *the ~s and downs pl* die Höhen u. Tiefen *pl* (*des Lebens*). **V** *v/t* **11.** *Angebot, Preis etc* erhöhen. **VI** *v/i* **11.** *he ~ped and left her* F er hat sie von heute auf morgen sitzenlassen. ˌ~**-and-'com·ing** adj viel-versprechend. '~**bring·ing** s Erziehung f. '~**com·ing** adj bevorstehend. ~**'date** v/t auf den neuesten Stand bringen; aktualisieren. ~**'end** v/t hochkant stellen. ~**'grade** v/t j-n befördern. ~**heav·al** [~'hi:vl] s fig. Umwälzung f. ˌ~**'hill I** adv **1.** aufwärts, bergan. **II** adj **2.** bergauf führend. **3.** fig. mühselig, hart. ~**'hold** v/t (irr hold) **1.** Rechte etc schützen, wahren. **2.** ˌ⁀ Urteil bestätigen. ~**hol·ster** [~'həʊlstə] v/t polstern: ~ed Polster... '~**keep** s Unterhalt m; Unterhaltungskosten pl. ~**lift I** v/t [~'lɪft] j-n aufrichten, j-m Auftrieb geben. **II** s ['~lɪft] Auftrieb m.

up·on [ə'pɒn] prp → **on I**.

up·per ['ʌpə] **I** adj ober: ~ **arm** Oberarm m; ~ **class(es** pl) sociol. Oberschicht f; ~ **deck** ⚓ Oberdeck n (a. e-s Busses); **gain** (od. **get**) **the** ~ **hand** die Oberhand gewinnen (**of** über acc); → **jaw** 1, **lip** 1. **II** s Obermaterial n (e-s Schuhs). '~**cut** s Boxen: Aufwärtshaken m.

up·per·most ['ʌpəməʊst] **I** adj oberst: **be** ~ oben sein; fig. an erster Stelle stehen; **be** ~ **in s.o.'s mind** fig. für j-n an erster Stelle stehen. **II** adv nach oben.

up·pish ['ʌpɪʃ] adj □ F, **up·pi·ty** ['ʌpətɪ] adj F hochnäsig.

up·right ['ʌpraɪt] **I** adj □ **1.** [a. ˌʌp'raɪt] aufrecht, gerade; senkrecht. **2.** fig. aufrecht, rechtschaffen. **II** adv [a. ˌʌp'raɪt] **3.** → 1: **sit** ~ geradesitzen. **III** s **4.** Pfosten m.

up·ris·ing ['ʌpˌraɪzɪŋ] s Aufstand m.

up·roar ['ʌprɔː] s Aufruhr m, Tumult m: **be in an** ~ in Aufruhr sein.

up·root [ʌp'ruːt] v/t **1.** Pflanze (mit den Wurzeln) ausreißen, a. Baum etc, fig. Menschen entwurzeln. **2.** fig. j-n herausreißen (**from** aus).

up·set I v/t [ʌp'set] (irr set) **1.** umkippen, umstoßen, umwerfen: → **applecart. 2.** fig. Pläne etc durcheinanderbringen, Gleichgewicht stören. **3.** fig. j-n aus der Fassung bringen; aufregen; kränken, verletzen. **4. the fish has** ~ **me** (od. **my stomach**) ich habe mir durch den Fisch den Magen verdorben. **II** s ['ʌpset] **5.** (Magen)Verstimmung f. **6.** bsd. Sport: Überraschung f.

up·shot ['ʌpʃɒt] s Ergebnis n: **what was**

the ~ **of ...?** was ist bei ... herausgekommen?

up·side ['ʌpsaɪd] adv: ~ **down** verkehrt herum; **turn** ~ **down** umdrehen, a. fig. auf den Kopf stellen.

up·stairs [ˌʌp'steəz] **I** adv **1.** die Treppe her- od. hinauf, nach oben. **2.** oben, in e-m oberen Stockwerk. **3.** e-r Treppe höher. **II** adj **4.** im oberen Stockwerk (gelegen), ober.

up·start ['ʌpstɑːt] s Emporkömmling m.

up·stream [ˌʌp'striːm] adv flußauf(-wärts).

up·surge ['ʌpsɜːdʒ] s **1.** Anschwellen n (**in** gen). **2.** Aufwallung f.

up·take ['ʌpteɪk] s: **be quick** (**slow**) **on the** ~ F schnell begreifen (schwer von Begriff sein).

up·tight ['ʌptaɪt] adj F **1.** nervös, reizbar. **2.** verklemmt.

up-to-date [ˌʌptə'deɪt] adj **1.** modern. **2.** aktuell, neu.

up-to-the-min·ute [ˌʌptəðə'mɪnɪt] adj **1.** hochmodern. **2.** allerneu(e)st.

up·town [ˌʌp'taʊn] Am. **I** adv in den Wohnvierteln, in die Wohnviertel. **II** adj in den Wohnvierteln (gelegen od. lebend): **in** ~ **Los Angeles** in den Außenbezirken von Los Angeles. **III** s Wohnviertel pl, Außenbezirke pl.

up·turn I ['ʌptɜːn] s Aufschwung m (**in** gen). ˌup'**turned** adj **1.** nach oben gerichtet od. gebogen: ~ **nose** Stupsnase f. **2.** umgedreht.

up·ward ['ʌpwəd] **I** adv **1.** nach oben: **face** ~ mit dem Gesicht nach oben. **2. from £2** ~ ab 2 Pfund; ~ **of £2** f mehr als od. über 2 Pfund. **3.** fig. aufwärts, bergan: **he went** ~ **in life** es ging aufwärts mit ihm. **II** adj **4.** Aufwärts... **up·wards** ['~z] → **upward I**.

u·ra·ni·um [jʊ'reɪnɪəm] s 🜨 Uran n.

ur·ban ['ɜːbən] adj städtisch, Stadt...

ur·bane [ɜː'beɪn] adj □ weltmännisch, -gewandt.

ur·chin ['ɜːtʃɪn] s Gassenjunge m.

u·re·thra [jʊə'riːθrə] pl **-thrae** [~θriː], **-thras** s anat. Harnröhre f.

urge [ɜːdʒ] **I** v/t **1.** a. ~ **on** antreiben, fig. a. anspornen (**to** zu). **2.** j-n drängen (**to do** zu tun). **3.** drängen auf (acc). **II** s **4.** Drang m, Verlangen n. **ur·gen·cy** ['ɜːdʒənsɪ] s Dringlichkeit f. '**ur·gent** adj □ dringend: **be** ~ eilen; **be in** ~

need of s.th. et. dringend brauchen.

u·ric [ˈjʊərɪk] *adj* Urin...: **~ acid** Harnsäure *f.*

u·ri·nal [ˈjʊərɪnl] *s* **1.** Urinal *n.* **2.** Pissoir *n.* **'u·ri·nar·y** *adj* Urin...: **~ bladder** Harnblase *f.* **u·ri·nate** [ˈ~neɪt] *v/i* urinieren. **u·rine** [ˈ~rɪn] *s* Urin *m:* **~ sample** Urinprobe *f.*

urn [ɜːn] *s* **1.** Urne *f.* **2.** Großkaffee-, Großteemaschine *f.*

u·rol·o·gist [jʊəˈrɒlədʒɪst] *s* ⚕ Urologe *m,* Urologin *f.*

us [ʌs] **I** *personal pron* **1.** uns (*acc od. dat von* **we**): **both of ~** wir beide; → **all** 4. **2.** F wir (*nom*): **they are older than ~; it's ~** wir sind's. **II** *reflex pron* **3.** uns: **we looked around ~** wir sahen uns um.

us·a·ble [ˈjuːzəbl] *adj* brauch-, verwendbar.

us·age [ˈjuːzɪdʒ] *s* **1.** Brauch *m,* Gepflogenheit *f.* **2.** (Sprach)Gebrauch *m.* **3.** Behandlung *f.*

use I *v/t* [juːz] **1.** benutzen, gebrauchen, verwenden, *Taktik etc a.* anwenden: **I could ~ a drink** F ich könnte et. zu trinken vertragen. **2.** *Benzin etc* (ver)brauchen: **~ up** auf-, verbrauchen. **3.** *j-n* benutzen (*for* für). **II** *v/i* [juːs] **4. I ~d to live here** ich habe früher hier gewohnt; **he ~d to be a chain smoker** er war früher einmal Kettenraucher **III** *s* [juːs] **5.** Benutzung *f,* Gebrauch *m,* Verwendung *f:* **come into ~** in Gebrauch kommen; **go out of ~** außer Gebrauch kommen; **make ~ of** Gebrauch machen von, benutzen. **6.** Verwendung(szweck *m*) *f:* **with many ~s** vielseitig verwendbar. **7.** Nutzen *m:* **be of ~** nützlich *od.* von Nutzen sein (**to** für); **it's no ~ complaining** es ist nutz- *od.* zwecklos zu reklamieren, es hat keinen Zweck zu reklamieren; → **milk** I.

used¹ [juːzd] *adj* gebraucht: **~ car** Gebrauchtwagen *m.*

used² [juːst] *adj:* **be ~ to s.th.** an et. gewöhnt sein, et. gewohnt sein; **be ~ to doing s.th.** es gewohnt sein, et. zu tun.

use·ful [ˈjuːsfʊl] *adj* □ nützlich: **make o.s. ~** sich nützlich machen. **'use·fulness** *s* Nützlichkeit *f.*

use·less [ˈjuːslɪs] *adj* □ nutzlos: **it is ~** *a.* es ist zwecklos (**to do** zu tun); **he's ~** F er ist zu nichts zu gebrauchen. **'useless·ness** *s* Nutzlosigkeit *f.*

us·er [ˈjuːzə] *s* **1.** Benutzer(in). **2.** Verbraucher(in). **~-'friend·ly** *adj* benutzer- *od.* verbraucherfreundlich.

ush·er [ˈʌʃə] **I** *s* **1.** Platzanweiser *m.* **2.** ⚖ Gerichtsdiener *m.* **II** *v/t* **3.** *j-n* führen, geleiten (*into* in *acc;* **to** zu *s-m Platz etc*). **ush·er·ette** [ˌ~'ret] *s* Platzanweiserin *f.*

u·su·al [ˈjuːʒl] **I** *adj* üblich: **as ~** wie gewöhnlich *od.* üblich; **it's not ~ for him to be so late** er kommt normalerweise nicht so spät; **is it ~ for him to be so late?** kommt er immer so spät? **II** *s das* Übliche: **the ~** F (*in Pub etc*) wie immer. **u·su·al·ly** [ˈ~ʒəlɪ] *adv* (für) gewöhnlich, normalerweise.

u·sur·er [ˈjuːʒərə] *s* Wucherer *m.*

u·su·ri·ous [juːˈzjʊərɪəs] *adj* □ wucherisch, Wucher...

u·surp [juːˈzɜːp] *v/t* Macht *etc* an sich reißen, sich *des Throns* bemächtigen.

u·su·ry [ˈjuːʒərɪ] *s* Wucher *m.*

u·ten·sil [juːˈtensl] *s* Gerät *n:* **~s** *pl a.* Utensilien *pl.*

u·ter·us [ˈjuːtərəs] *pl* **-i** [ˈ~aɪ], **-us·es** *s* anat. Gebärmutter *f.*

u·til·i·tar·i·an [ˌjuːtɪlɪˈteərɪən] *adj* zweckmäßig, praktisch.

u·til·i·ty [juːˈtɪlətɪ] *s* **1.** Nutzen *m,* Nützlichkeit *f.* **2.** → **public** 3a.

u·ti·lize [ˈjuːtɪlaɪz] *v/t* nutzen.

ut·most [ˈʌtməʊst] **I** *adj* äußerst, höchst, größt. **II** *s das* Äußerste: **do one's ~** sein möglichstes tun.

U·to·pi·an [juːˈtəʊpjən] *adj* utopisch (*Gesellschaft*).

ut·ter¹ [ˈʌtə] **I** *adj* □ total, völlig. **II** *v/t* et. äußern, *Seufzer etc* ausstoßen, *Wort* sagen. **'ut·ter·ance** *s* **1.** *give ~ to s-r Meinung etc* Ausdruck geben. **2.** Äußerung *f.*

U-turn [ˈjuːtɜːn] *s* **1.** *mot.* Wende *f:* **do a ~** wenden. **2.** *fig.* Kehrtwendung *f:* **do a ~** e-e Kehrtwendung machen (**on** in *dat*).

u·vu·la [ˈjuːvjʊlə] *s* anat. (Gaumen-) Zäpfchen *n.*

V

vac [væk] s univ. Br. F Semesterferien pl.

va·can·cy ['veɪkənsɪ] s **1.** freie od. offene Stelle: *"vacancies"* „wir stellen ein". **2.** *"vacancies"* „Zimmer frei"; *"no vacancies"* „belegt". **'va·cant** adj □ **1.** leerstehend, unbewohnt: *"~"* „frei" (*Toilette*). **2.** frei, offen (*Stelle*): → *situation* 3. **3.** *fig.* leer (*Blick, Gesichtsausdruck*).

va·cate [və'keɪt] v/t Hotelzimmer etc räumen. **va'ca·tion I** s **1.** *bsd. Am.* Ferien pl, Urlaub m: **be on** ~ im Urlaub sein, Urlaub machen. **2.** *bsd. Br. univ.* Semesterferien pl; ✠ Gerichtsferien pl. **II** v/i **3.** *bsd. Am.* Urlaub machen, die Ferien verbringen. **va'ca·tion·er**, *Am.* **va'ca·tion·ist** s *bsd. Am.* Urlauber(in).

vac·ci·nate ['væksɪneɪt] v/t impfen (*against* gegen). **,vac·ci'na·tion** s Impfung f. **vac·cine** ['~si:n] s Impfstoff m.

vac·il·late ['væsəleɪt] v/i *fig.* schwanken (*between* zwischen *dat*).

vac·u·um ['vækjʊəm] **I** pl **-u·ums, -u·a** ['~jʊə] s *phys.* Vakuum n. **II** v/t Teppich, Zimmer mit dem Staubsauger absaugen, Teppich saugen. ~ **clean·er** s Staubsauger m. ~ **bot·tle** s *Am.* ~ **flask** s *Br.* Thermosflasche f. **'~-packed** adj vakuumverpackt.

vag·a·bond ['vægəbɒnd] s Vagabund m, Landstreicher(in).

va·gi·na [və'dʒaɪnə] pl **-nas, -nae** [~ni:] s *anat.* Scheide f.

va·grant ['veɪɡrənt] s Nichtseßhafte m, f, Landstreicher(in).

vague [veɪɡ] adj □ verschwommen, *fig. a.* vage: **be** ~ sich nur vage äußern (*about* über *acc*, zu); sich unklar ausdrücken; *I haven't got the ~st idea* ich habe nicht die leiseste Ahnung.

vain [veɪn] adj □ **1.** eingebildet, eitel. **2.** vergeblich: **in** ~ *a.* vergebens. **3.** **take s.o.'s name in** ~ über j-n lästern.

va·lence ['veɪləns] s *bsd. Am.*, **'va·len·cy** s *bsd. Br.* 🜍 Valenz f (*a. ling.*), Wertigkeit f.

val·en·tine ['væləntaɪn] s **1.** Valentinskarte f. **2.** *Person, der man am Valentinstag e-n Gruß schickt*.

va·le·ri·an [və'lɪərɪən] s 🜍, *pharm.* Baldrian m.

val·et ['vælɪt] s (Kammer)Diener m. ~ **ser·vice** s Reinigungsdienst m (*im Hotel*).

val·id ['vælɪd] adj □ **1.** a) gültig (*for two weeks* zwei Wochen): **be** ~ *a.* gelten, b) ✠ rechtsgültig, -kräftig. **2.** stichhaltig, triftig. **va·lid·i·ty** [və'lɪdətɪ] s **1.** Gültigkeit f; ✠ Rechtsgültigkeit f, -kraft f. **2.** Stichhaltigkeit f, Triftigkeit f.

va·lise [və'li:z] s Reisetasche f.

val·ley ['vælɪ] s Tal n.

val·u·a·ble ['væljʊəbl] **I** adj □ wertvoll. **II** s pl Wertgegenstände pl, -sachen pl.

val·u·a·tion [,væljʊ'eɪʃn] s **1.** Schätzung f: **make a** ~ **of** et. schätzen. **2.** Schätzwert m (*of, on* gen).

val·ue ['vælju:] **I** s **1.** *allg.* Wert m: **be of** ~ wertvoll sein (*to* für); **be good** ~, **be** ~ **for money** preisgünstig od. -wert sein; **put** (*od.* **place**) **a high** ~ **on** großen Wert legen auf (*acc*). **2.** pl sittliche etc Werte pl. **II** v/t **3.** Haus etc schätzen (*at* auf *acc*). **4.** j-n, j-s Rat etc schätzen. **'~,add·ed tax** s ✝ *Br.* Mehrwertsteuer f. ~ **judg(e)·ment** s Werturteil n. **val·ue·less** ['væljʊlɪs] adj wertlos. **'val·u·er** s Schätzer(in).

valve [vælv] s **1.** ⚙, ♪ Ventil n. **2.** *anat.* Klappe f. **3.** ⚡ *Br. bsd. hist.* Röhre f.

vamp [væmp] s Vamp m (*Frau*).

vam·pire ['væmpaɪə] s Vampir m.

van [væn] s **1.** Lieferwagen m, Transporter m. **2.** 🚃 *Br.* (geschlossener) Güterwagen.

van·dal ['vændl] s Vandale m, Wandale m. **van·dal·ism** ['~dəlɪzəm] s Vandalismus m, Wandalismus m. **van·dal·ize** ['~dəlaɪz] v/t mutwillig beschädigen od. zerstören.

vane [veɪn] s **1.** (*Propeller- etc*)Flügel m. **2.** (*Wetter*)Fahne f.

van·guard ['vænɡɑːd] s ✕ Vorhut f: **be in the** ~ *of fig.* an der Spitze (*gen*) stehen.

va·nil·la [və'nɪlə] s 🜍 Vanille f.

van·ish ['vænɪʃ] v/i verschwinden; (*Angst, Hoffnung etc*) schwinden: → *thin* 1.

van·i·ty ['vænətɪ] s Eitelkeit f.

van·tage point ['vɑːntɪdʒ] s Aussichts-

punkt *m*: *from my ~* *fig.* aus m-r Sicht.
va·por *Am.* → *vapour.*

va·por·ize ['veɪpəraɪz] *v/i* verdampfen, -dunsten.

va·por·ous ['veɪpərəs] *adj* □ dunstig, Dunst...

va·pour ['veɪpə] *s bsd. Br.* Dampf *m*, Dunst *m.* **~ trail** *s* ✈ Kondensstreifen *m.*

var·i·a·ble ['veərɪəbl] **I** *adj* □ **1.** variabel, veränderlich (*beide a.* ♣, *phys., chis.*). **2.** schwankend, unbeständig, wechselhaft. **3.** einstell-, regulierbar. **II** *s* **4.** ♣, *phys.* Variable *f*, veränderliche Größe (*beide a. fig.*). **'var·i·ance** *s*: *be at ~ with* im Gegensatz *od.* Widerspruch stehen zu. **'var·i·ant I** *adj* abweichend, verschieden. **II** *s* Variante *f.* **var·i·'a·tion** *s* **1.** Abweichung *f*; Schwankung *f.* **2.** ♪ Variation *f* (*on* über *etc*).

var·i·cose ['værɪkəʊs] *adj*: **~ vein** ✗ Krampfader *f.*

var·ied ['veərɪd] *adj* □ **1.** unterschiedlich. **2.** abwechslungsreich, bewegt.

va·ri·e·ty [vəˈraɪətɪ] *s* **1.** Abwechslung *f.* **2.** Vielfalt *f*; ✝ Auswahl *f*, Sortiment *n* (*of* an *dat*): *for a ~ of reasons* aus den verschiedensten Gründen. **3.** ♣, *zo.* Art *f.* **4.** Varieté *s.*

var·i·ous ['veərɪəs] *adj* **1.** verschieden. **2.** mehrere, verschiedene.

var·nish ['vɑːnɪʃ] **I** *s* Lack *m.* **II** *v/t* lackieren.

var·y ['veərɪ] **I** *v/i* variieren, (*Meinungen*) auseinandergehen (*on* über *acc*): *~ in size* verschieden groß sein. **II** *v/t* (ver)ändern; variieren.

vas·cu·lar ['væskjʊlə] *adj* anat., ♣ Gefäß...

vase [vɑːz] *s* Vase *f.*

vast [vɑːst] *adj* gewaltig, riesig, (*Fläche a.*) ausgedehnt, weit. **'vast·ly** *adv* gewaltig, weitaus.

vat [væt] *s* (großes) Faß.

vaude·ville ['vɔːdəvɪl] *s Am.* Varieté *n.*

vault¹ ['vɔːlt] *s* **1.** 🏛 Gewölbe *n.* **2.** *a. pl* (Keller)Gewölbe *n*; Stahlkammer *f*, Tresorraum *m*; Gruft *f.*

vault² [~] **I** *v/i* ~ *over* springen über (*acc*). **II** *v/t* → I. **III** *s* Sprung *m.*

vault·ed ['vɔːltɪd] *adj* **1.** 🏛 gewölbt. **2.** überwölbt.

vault·ing ['vɔːltɪŋ] *adj*: **~ horse** (*Turnen*) Sprungpferd *n.*

veal [viːl] *s* Kalbfleisch *n.* **~ cut·let** *s* Kalbsschnitzel *n.*

veer [vɪə] *v/i*: **~ to the left** *mot.* den Wagen nach links reißen.

veg [vedʒ] *pl* **veg** *s gastr. bsd. Br.* F Gemüse *n*: *and two ~* u. zweierlei Gemüse.

ve·gan ['viːgən] *s* Veganer(in).

veg·e·ta·ble ['vedʒtəbl] **I** *s* **1.** *mst pl* Gemüse *n*: *and two ~s* u. zweierlei Gemüse; *be just a ~* nur noch dahinvegetieren. **II** *adj* **2.** Gemüse... **3.** Pflanzen...

veg·e·tar·i·an [,vedʒɪˈteərɪən] **I** *s* Vegetarier(in): *he's a ~* er ist Vegetarier, er lebt vegetarisch. **II** *adj* vegetarisch.

veg·e·tate ['vedʒɪteɪt] *v/i* dahinvegetieren. **veg·e·'ta·tion** *s* Vegetation *f.*

ve·he·mence ['viːəməns] *s* Vehemenz *f*, Heftigkeit *f.* **'ve·he·ment** *adj* □ vehement, heftig.

ve·hi·cle ['vɪəkl] *s* **1.** Fahrzeug *n.* **2.** *fig.* Medium *n.* **ve·hic·u·lar** [vɪˈhɪkjʊlə] *adj* Fahrzeug...

veil [veɪl] **I** *s* Schleier *m*: ~ *of mist* Nebelschleier; *draw a ~ over fig.* den Schleier des Vergessens breiten über (*acc*). **II** *v/t* verschleiern (*a. fig.*).

vein [veɪn] *s anat.* Vene *f*, *weitS.* Ader *f* (*a.* ♣, *geol.*).

ve·loc·i·ty [vɪˈlɒsɪtɪ] *s phys.*, ⚙ Geschwindigkeit *f.*

ve·lour(s) [vəˈlʊə] *s* Velours *m.*

vel·vet ['velvɪt] *s* Samt *m*: **(as) smooth as ~** samtweich. **'vel·vet·y** *adj* samtig (*a. fig. Wein*).

vend·er → **vendor.**

ven·det·ta [venˈdetə] *s* **1.** Blutrache *f.* **2.** Fehde *f.*

vend·ing ['vendɪŋ] *adj*: **~ machine** (Verkaufs-, Waren)Automat *m.* **'vend·or** *s* (Straßen)Händler(in), (Zeitungs- *etc*-)Verkäufer(in).

ve·neer [vəˈnɪə] **I** *s* **1.** Furnier *n.* **2.** *fig.* Fassade *f.* **II** *v/t* **3.** furnieren (*in, with* mit).

ven·er·a·ble ['venərəbl] *adj* □ ehrwürdig. **ven·er·ate** ['~reɪt] *v/t* verehren. **,ven·er·'a·tion** *s* Verehrung *f.*

ve·ne·re·al [vəˈnɪərɪəl] *adj*: **~ disease** Geschlechtskrankheit *f.*

Ve·ne·tian [vəˈniːʃn] *adj*: **~ blind** Jalousie *f.*

venge·ance ['vendʒəns] *s* Rache *f*: **take**

~ on sich rächen an (*dat*); **with a ~** F gewaltig, u. wie.

ve·ni·al ['viːnjəl] *adj* entschuldbar, verzeihlich, *eccl.* läßlich (*Sünde*).

ven·i·son ['venɪzn] *s* Wildbret *n*.

ven·om ['venəm] *s* **1.** *zo.* Gift *n*. **2.** *fig.* Gift *n*, Gehässigkeit *f*. **'ven·om·ous** *adj* □ **1.** giftig: **~ snake** Giftschlange *f*. **2.** *fig.* giftig, gehässig.

ve·nous ['viːnəs] *adj anat.* venös.

vent [vent] **I** *v/t* **1.** *s-e Wut etc* abreagieren (**on** an *dat*). **II** *s* **2.** (Abzugs)Öffnung *f*. **3.** Schlitz *m* (*in Kleid etc*). **4.** **give ~ to** *s-m Ärger etc* Luft machen.

ven·ti·late ['ventɪleɪt] *v/t* (be)lüften. **ven·ti·la·tion** *s* Ventilation *f*, (Be)Lüftung *f*. **'ven·ti·la·tor** *s* Ventilator *m*, Lüfter *m*.

ven·tral ['ventrəl] *adj* Bauch...: **~ fin** Bauchflosse *f*.

ven·tri·cle ['ventrɪkl] *s anat.* Herzkammer *f*.

ven·tril·o·quist [ven'trɪləkwɪst] *s* Bauchredner(in).

ven·ture ['ventʃə] **I** *s* **1.** *bsd.* ✝ Unternehmen *n*: → **joint 5. II** *v/t* **2.** *Ruf etc* riskieren, aufs Spiel setzen (**on** bei). **3.** (zu äußern) wagen: **~ to do s.th.** es wagen, et. zu tun. **III** *v/i* **4.** sich *wohin* wagen. **5. ~ on** sich wagen an (*acc*).

ven·ue ['venjuː] *s* Schauplatz *m*, (*Sport*) Austragungsort *m*.

Ve·nus ['viːnəs] *s ast.* die Venus.

ve·ran·da(h) [və'rændə] *s* Veranda *f*.

verb [vɜːb] *s ling.* Verb *n*, Zeitwort *n*. **ver·bal** ['ᴧ] *adj* □ **1.** mündlich. **2.** Wort...: **he's got ~ diarrh(o)ea** F der bringt den Mund nicht zu. **3. ~ noun** *ling.* Verbalsubstantiv *n*. **ver·bal·ize** ['ᴧbəlaɪz] *v/t* ausdrücken, in Worte fassen. **ver·ba·tim** ['ᴧbeɪtɪm] *adj* (wort-)wörtlich, *adv* a. Wort für Wort. **ver·bi·age** ['ᴧbɪɪdʒ] *s* (leeres) Wortgeklingel. **ver·bose** ['ᴧbəʊs] *adj* □ wortreich, langatmig.

ver·dict ['vɜːdɪkt] *s* **1.** ⚖ Spruch *m* (*der Geschworenen*): **~ of (not) guilty** Schuldspruch (Freispruch) *m*; **bring in** (*od.* **return**) **a ~ of (not) guilty** auf (nicht) schuldig erkennen. **2.** Meinung *f*, Urteil *n* (**on** über *acc*).

ver·di·gris ['vɜːdɪgrɪs] *s* Grünspan *m*.

verge [vɜːdʒ] **I** *s* Rand *m* (*a. fig.*): **be on the ~ of** kurz vor (*dat*) stehen; **be on the** **~ of tears** den Tränen nahe sein; **she was on the ~ of falling** sie wäre beinahe gestürzt. **II** *v/i*: **~ on** *fig.* grenzen an (*acc*).

ver·ger ['vɜːdʒə] *s* Kirchendiener *m*, Küster *m*.

ver·i·fi·a·ble ['verɪfaɪəbl] *adj* nachweisbar. **ver·i·fy** ['ᴧfaɪ] *v/t* **1.** bestätigen. **2.** (über)prüfen. **3.** nachweisen.

ver·i·ta·ble ['verɪtəbl] *adj* wahr (*Triumph etc*).

ver·mil·ion [və'mɪljən] *adj* zinnoberrot.

ver·min ['vɜːmɪn] *s* (*pl konstruiert*) **1.** Schädlinge *pl*; Ungeziefer *n*. **2.** *fig.* Gesindel *n*, Pack *n*. **'ver·min·ous** *adj* voller Ungeziefer.

ver·mouth ['vɜːməθ] *s* Wermut *m*.

ver·nac·u·lar [və'nækjʊlə] *s* Dialekt *m*, Mundart *f*.

ver·nis·sage [ˌvɜːnɪ'sɑːʒ] *s* Vernissage *f*.

ver·sa·tile ['vɜːsətaɪl] *adj* □ **1.** vielseitig. **2.** vielseitig verwendbar.

verse [vɜːs] *s* **1.** Poesie *f*, Versdichtung *f*. **2.** Vers *m*. **3.** Strophe *f*.

versed [vɜːst] *adj*: **be (well) ~ in** beschlagen *od.* bewandert sein in (*dat*).

ver·sion ['vɜːʃn] *s* Version *f*: a) Darstellung *f* (*e-s Ereignisses*), b) Fassung *f* (*e-s Textes*), c) Übersetzung *f*, d) Ausführung *f* (*e-s Geräts etc*).

ver·sus ['vɜːsəs] *prp* ⚖, *Sport*: gegen.

ver·te·bra ['vɜːtɪbrə] *pl* **-brae** ['ᴧbriː], **-bras** *s anat.* Wirbel *m*. **'ver·te·bral** *adj*: **~ column** *anat.* Rückgrat *n*, Wirbelsäule *f*. **ver·te·brate** ['ᴧbreɪt] *s zo.* Wirbeltier *n*.

ver·tex ['vɜːteks] *pl* **-ti·ces** ['ᴧtɪsiːz], **-tex·es** *s* Scheitel(punkt) *m*.

ver·ti·cal ['vɜːtɪkl] **I** *adj* □ senkrecht, vertikal: **~ takeoff aircraft** Senkrechtstarter *m*. **II** *s* ⅄ Senkrechte *f*, Vertikale *f*.

ver·ti·go ['vɜːtɪgəʊ] *s* ✚ Schwindel *m*: **suffer from ~** an *od.* unter Schwindel leiden.

verve [vɜːv] *s* Elan *m*, Schwung *m*.

ver·y ['verɪ] **I** *adv* **1.** sehr: **~ much older** sehr viel älter; **I ~ much hope that** ich hoffe sehr, daß; **~ high frequency** *f* Ultrakurzwelle *f*; **~ well** 1. **2.** aller...: **the ~ last drop** der allerletzte Tropfen; **for the ~ last time** zum allerletzten Mal; **at the ~ least** zum allermindesten, allermindest. **II** *adj* **3. the ~** genau der *od.* die *od.* das: *the ~ opposite* genau das Gegenteil; *be the ~ thing* genau das richtige sein *(for doing* um zu tun); → *act* 1. *4. the ~ thought* of schon der *od.* der bloße Gedanke an *(dat);* *the ~ idea!* um Himmels willen!

ves·i·cle ['vesɪkl] *s* Bläschen *n.*

ves·pers ['vespəz] *s pl eccl.* Vesper *f.*

ves·sel ['vesl] *s* **1.** Schiff *n.* **2.** Gefäß *n (a. anat.,* ♋️).

vest [vest] **I** *s* **1.** *Br.* Unterhemd *n.* **2.** kugelsichere Weste. **3.** *Am.* Weste *f.* **II** *v/t* **4.** ~ *s.th. in s.o.,* ~ *s.o. with s.th.* j-m et. übertragen *od.* verleihen: *have a ~ed interest in* ein persönliches Interesse haben an *(dat);* *~ed interests pl* Interessengruppen *pl.* **III** *v/i* **5.** ~ *in* zustehen *(dat),* liegen bei.

ves·ti·bule ['vestɪbjuːl] *s* (Vor)Halle *f.*

ves·tige ['vestɪdʒ] *s* Spur *f:* *there is not a ~ of truth in this story* an dieser Geschichte ist kein Wort wahr.

ves·try ['vestrɪ] *s eccl.* Sakristei *f.*

vet¹ [vet] **F I** *s* Tierarzt *m,* -ärztin *f.* **II** *v/t bsd. Br.* überprüfen.

vet² [~] *s* ✕ *Am.* F Veteran *m.*

vetch [vetʃ] *s* ♣ Wicke *f.*

vet·er·an ['vetərən] **I** *s* **1.** ✕ Veteran *m (a. fig.).* **II** *adj* **2.** altgedient; erfahren. **3.** ~ *car mot. Br.* Oldtimer *m (Baujahr bis 1905).*

vet·er·i·nar·i·an [ˌvetərɪ'neərɪən] *s Am.* Tierarzt *m,* -ärztin *f.*

vet·er·i·nar·y ['vetərɪnərɪ] *adj* tierärztlich: ~ *medicine* Tier-, Veterinärmedizin *f;* ~ *surgeon bsd. Br.* Tierarzt *m,* -ärztin *f.*

ve·to ['viːtəʊ] **I** *pl* **-toes** *s* **1.** Veto *n.* **II** *v/t* **2.** sein Veto einlegen gegen. **3.** untersagen.

vexed [vekst] *adj:* ~ *question* leidige Frage.

vi·a ['vaɪə] *prp* über *(acc), (bei Städtenamen a.)* via.

vi·a·ble ['vaɪəbl] *adj* □ **1.** lebensfähig *(a. fig.).* **2.** *fig.* durchführbar, realisierbar.

vi·a·duct ['vaɪədʌkt] *s* Viadukt *m, n.*

vi·al ['vaɪəl] *s (bsd. Arznei)Fläschchen n.*

vibes [vaɪbz] *s pl* **F 1.** *(mst sg konstruiert)* ♩ Vibraphon *n.* **2.** Atmosphäre *f (e-s Orts etc):* *I was getting positive ~ from her* ich spürte, wie der Funke von ihr auf mich übersprang.

vi·brant ['vaɪbrənt] *adj* □ **1.** kräftig *(Far-*

ben, Stimme etc). **2.** pulsierend *(Leben).* **3.** dynamisch *(Person).*

vi·bra·phone ['vaɪbrəfəʊn] *s* ♩ Vibraphon *n.*

vi·brate [vaɪ'breɪt] **I** *v/i* **1.** vibrieren, zittern. **2.** flimmern *(with heat* vor Hitze) *(Luft).* **3.** *the city ~s with life* in der Stadt pulsiert das Leben. **II** *v/t* **4.** in Schwingungen versetzen. **vi'bra·tion** *s* **1.** Vibrieren *n,* Zittern *n.* **2.** *pl* F → *vibes* 2. **vi'bra·tor** *s* Vibrator *m.*

vic·ar ['vɪkə] *s* Pfarrer *m.* **'vic·ar·age** *s* Pfarrhaus *n.*

vice¹ [vaɪs] *s* Laster *n.*

vice² [~] *s* ⊙ *bsd. Br.* Schraubstock *m.*

vice...³ [~] *Vize...,* stellvertretend.

vice-like ['vaɪslaɪk] *adj:* *hold s.th. in a ~ grip bsd. Br.* et. fest umklammert halten.

vice squad *s* Sittendezernat *n,* -polizei *f.*

vice ver·sa [ˌvaɪsɪ'vɜːsə] *adv:* *and* ~ u. umgekehrt.

vi·cin·i·ty [vɪ'sɪnətɪ] *s:* *in the* ~ *of* in der Nähe von *(od. gen); in this* ~ hier in der Nähe; *in the* ~ *of 40 fig.* um die 40 herum.

vi·cious ['vɪʃəs] *adj* □ brutal. ~ *cir·cle* *s* Circulus *m* vitiosus, Teufelskreis *m.*

vi·cis·si·tudes [vɪ'sɪsɪtjuːdz] *s pl das* Auf u. Ab, *(des Lebens a.)* die Wechselfälle *pl.*

vic·tim ['vɪktɪm] *s* Opfer *n:* *fall* ~ *to* betroffen werden von; erkranken an *(dat).* **'vic·tim·ize** *v/t* j-n *(immer wieder)* zum Sündenbock machen.

vic·tor ['vɪktə] *s* Sieger(in). **vic·to·ri·ous** [~'tɔːrɪəs] *adj* □ siegreich. **vic·to·ry** ['~tərɪ] *s* Sieg *m:* ~ *ceremony* Siegerehrung *f.*

vi·de ['vaɪdiː] *imp* siehe!

vi·de·li·cet [vɪ'diːlɪset] *adv* nämlich.

vid·e·o ['vɪdɪəʊ] **I** *pl* **-os** *s* **1.** Video(kassette *f*) *n:* *on* ~ auf Video. **2.** → *video recorder.* **II** *v/t* **3.** auf Video aufnehmen, aufzeichnen. ~ *cam·er·a* *s* Videokamera *f.* ~ *cas·sette* *s* Videokassette *f.* ~ *cas·sette re·cord·er* → *video recorder.* ~ *nas·ty* → *nasty* 5. ~ *re·cord·er* *s* Videorecorder *m.* ~ *re·cord·ing* *s* Videoaufnahme *f.* ~ *tape* → *video cassette.* **'~·tape** → *video* 3.

vie [vaɪ] *v/i* wetteifern *(with* mit; *for* um).

view [vjuː] **I** *s* **1.** Sicht *f (*of auf *acc):* *at first* ~ auf den ersten Blick; *in full* ~ *of* direkt vor *j-s* Augen; **in ~ of** *fig.* angesichts (*gen*); **with a ~ to** *fig.* mit Blick auf (*acc*); **with a ~ to doing s.th.** in *od.* mit der Absicht, et. zu tun; **be on ~** ausgestellt *od.* zu besichtigen sein; **be hidden from ~** nicht zu sehen sein; **come into ~** in Sicht kommen; **have in ~** *et.* in Aussicht haben; **keep in ~** *et.* im Auge behalten. **2.** Aussicht *f*, Blick *m* (**of** *auf acc*): **a room with a ~** ein Zimmer mit schöner Aussicht; **there is a grand ~ of the mountains from here** von hier hat man e-n herrlichen Blick auf die Berge. **3.** *phot. etc* Ansicht *f*. **4.** Ansicht *f*, Meinung *f* (**about, on** *über acc*): **in my ~** m-r Ansicht nach; **take a dim** (*od.* **poor**) **~ of** *et.* negativ beurteilen. **5.** *fig.* Überblick *m* (**of** *über acc*). **II** *v/t* **6.** Haus *etc* besichtigen. **7.** *fig.* betrachten (**as** *als*; **with** *mit*). **III** *v/i* **8.** fernsehen. **'view·er 1.** (Fernseh)Zuschauer(in), Fernseher(in). **2.** (*Dia*)Betrachter *m*.

'view|₁find·er *s phot.* Sucher *m.* **'~·point** *s* Gesichts-, Standpunkt *m.*

vig·il ['vɪdʒɪl] *s* (Nacht)Wache *f*: **keep ~** wachen (**over** *bei*). **'vig·i·lance** *s* Wachsamkeit *f.* **'vig·i·lant** *adj* □ wachsam.

vig·or ['vɪgə] *Am.* → **vigour. 'vig·or·ous** *adj* □ energisch. **'vig·our** *s bsd. Br.* Energie *f.*

vile [vaɪl] *adj* □ **1.** gemein, niederträchtig. **2.** F scheußlich.

vil·la ['vɪlə] *s* Villa *f.*

vil·lage ['vɪlɪdʒ] *s* Dorf *n.* **'vil·lag·er** *s* Dorfbewohner(in).

vil·lain ['vɪlən] *s* **1.** Bösewicht *m*, Schurke *m* (*in Film etc*). **2.** *Br.* F Ganove *m.* **3.** F Bengel *m.*

vin·di·cate ['vɪndɪkeɪt] *v/t* **1.** *et.* rechtfertigen; bestätigen. **2.** *j-n* rehabilitieren. **vin·di·ca·tion** *s* **1.** Rechtfertigung *f*; Bestätigung *f.* **2.** Rehabilitation *f.* **vin·dic·tive** [vɪn'dɪktɪv] *adj* □ rachsüchtig.

vine [vaɪn] *s* ♥ **1.** (Wein)Rebe *f.* **2.** Kletterpflanze *f.*

vin·e·gar ['vɪnɪgə] *s* Essig *m.*

'vine|₁grow·er *s* Winzer *m.* **~·yard** ['vɪnjəd] *s* Weinberg *m.*

vi·no ['viːnəʊ] *pl* **-nos** *s* F Wein *m.*

vin·tage ['vɪntɪdʒ] *I s* **1.** Jahrgang *m* (*e-s Weins*). **2.** Weinernte *f*, -lese *f.* **II** *adj* **3.**

Jahrgangs...: **~ wine. 4.** glänzend, hervorragend. **5.** **~ car** *mot. bsd. Br.* Oldtimer *m* (*Baujahr 1919-30*).

vint·ner ['vɪntnə] *s* **1.** Weinhändler *m.* **2.** *Am.* Winzer *m.*

vi·o·la [vɪ'əʊlə] *s* ♪ Bratsche *f.*

vi·o·late ['vaɪəleɪt] *v/t* **1.** *Vertrag etc* verletzen, *a. Versprechen* brechen, *Gesetz etc* übertreten. **2.** *Frieden, Ruhe etc* stören. **3.** *Grab etc* schänden. **4.** *Frau* schänden, vergewaltigen. **₁vi·o·la·tion** *s* **1.** Verletzung *f*, Bruch *m*, Übertretung *f.* **2.** Störung *f.* **3.** Schändung *f.* **4.** Vergewaltigung *f.*

vi·o·lence ['vaɪələns] *s* **1.** Gewalt *f.* **2.** Gewalttätigkeit *f.* **3.** Heftigkeit *f.* **'vi·o·lent** *adj* □ **1.** gewalttätig. **2.** gewaltsam: **~ crime** Gewaltverbrechen *n*; **die a ~ death** e-s gewaltsamen Todes sterben. **3.** heftig (*Auseinandersetzung, Sturm etc*): **be in a ~ temper** geladen sein.

vi·o·let ['vaɪələt] **I** *s* ♥ Veilchen *n*: **~ shrinking. II** *adj* violett.

vi·o·lin [₁vaɪə'lɪn] *s* ♪ Geige *f*, Violine *f*: **~ case** Geigenkasten *m.* **₁vi·o·lin·ist** *s* Geiger(in), Violinist(in).

vi·o·lon·cel·lo [₁vaɪələn'tʃeləʊ] *pl* **-los** *s* ♪ Violoncello *n.*

VIP [₁viːaɪ'piː] *s* VIP *f* (*prominente Persönlichkeit*).

vi·per ['vaɪpə] *s zo.* Viper *f.*

vi·ral ['vaɪərəl] *adj* ✶ Virus...

vir·gin ['vɜːdʒɪn] **I** *s* Jungfrau *f*: **she's still a ~** sie ist noch Jungfrau. **II** *adj* jungfräulich, unberührt (*beide a. fig.*).

Vir·go ['vɜːgəʊ] *s ast.* Jungfrau *f*: **be** (**a**) **~** Jungfrau sein.

vir·ile ['vɪraɪl] *adj* **1.** männlich. **2.** potent. **vi·ril·i·ty** [vɪ'rɪlətɪ] *s* **1.** Männlichkeit *f.* **2.** Potenz *f.*

vir·tu·al ['vɜːtʃʊəl] *adj*: **he's a ~ alcoholic** er ist praktisch schon Alkoholiker; **it's a ~ certainty that** es steht praktisch *od.* so gut wie fest, daß. **'vir·tu·al·ly** *adv* praktisch, so gut wie.

vir·tue ['vɜːtʃuː] *s* **1.** Tugend(haftigkeit) *f.* **2.** Tugend *f*: **make a ~ of necessity** aus der Not e-e Tugend machen. **3.** Vorzug *m*, Vorteil *m.* **4. by** (*od.* **in**) **~ of** kraft (*gen*), aufgrund (*gen*).

vir·tu·o·so [₁vɜːtjʊ'əʊzəʊ] *bsd.* ♪ **I** *pl* **-sos, -si** [₁~zi:] *s* Virtuose *m*, Virtuosin *f.* **II** *adj* virtuos.

vir·tu·ous ['vɜːtʃʊəs] *adj* □ tugendhaft.

vir·u·lent ['vɪrʊlənt] *adj* □ **1.** (akut u.) bösartig (*Krankheit*); schnellwirkend (*Gift*). **2.** *fig.* bösartig, gehässig.

vi·rus ['vaɪərəs] *s ⚕ Virus n, a. m.* **~ in·fec·tion** *s ⚕* Virusinfektion *f*.

vi·sa ['viːzə] **I** *s* Visum *n*, (*im Paß eingetragenes a.*) Sichtvermerk *m*. **II** *v/t* ein Visum eintragen in (*acc*).

vis-à-vis [ˌviːzaː'viː] *prp* in Anbetracht (*gen*).

vis·cer·a ['vɪsərə] *s pl anat.* Eingeweide *pl*.

vis·count ['vaɪkaʊnt] *s* Viscount *m* (*englischer Adelstitel*). **'vis·count·ess** *s* Viscountess *f*.

vis·cous ['vɪskəs] *adj* □ dick-, zähflüssig, 🧪 *a.* viskos.

vise, vise-like *Am.* → *vice², vicelike.*

vis·i·bil·i·ty [ˌvɪzə'bɪlətɪ] *s* Sicht(verhältnisse *pl*, -weite *f*) *f*. **'vis·i·ble** *adj* □ **1.** sichtbar. **2.** *fig.* (er)sichtlich.

vi·sion ['vɪʒn] *s* **1.** Sehkraft *f*. **2.** *fig.* Weitblick *m*. **3.** Vision *f*; **~ of the future** Zukunftsvision; **have ~s of doing s.th.** sich schon et. tun sehen. **vi·sion·ar·y** ['~ʃ˙rɪ] **I** *adj* **1.** weitblickend. **2.** eingebildet, unwirklich. **II** *s* **3.** Seher(in). **4.** Phantast(in), Träumer(in).

vis·it ['vɪzɪt] **I** *v/t* **1.** *j-n* besuchen, *Museum etc a.* besichtigen. **2.** *et.* inspizieren. **II** *v/i* **3.** *be* **~ing** auf Besuch sein (*Am.*: *in* in *dat*; *with* bei). **4. ~ with** *Am.* plaudern mit. **III** *s* **5.** Besuch *m*, Besichtigung *f* (*to* gen): *for* (*od. on*) *a* **~** auf Besuch; *have a* **~** *to j-m* in Besuch abstatten; *Arzt* aufsuchen; *I've got to pay a* **~** *Br.* F sich muß mal verschwinden. **6.** *Am.* Plauderei *f* (*with* mit). **,vis·i'ta-tion** *s* **1.** Inspektion *f*. **2.** *fig.* Heimsuchung *f*. **3.** F *humor.* überlanger Besuch (*from* gen). **'vis·it·ing** *adj* Besuchs...: **~ card** Visitenkarte *f*; **~ hours** *pl* Besuchszeit *f*. **'vis·i·tor** *s* Besucher(in) (*to* gen; *from* aus): **~s** *pl* **to England** Englandbesucher *pl*; *have* **~s** Besuch haben; *~s' book* Gästebuch *n*.

vi·sor ['vaɪzə] *s* **1.** Visier *n* (*a. ⚔ hist.*). **2.** Schirm *m* (*e-r Mütze*). **3.** *mot.* (*Sonnen*)Blende *f*.

vis·ta ['vɪstə] *s* Aussicht *f*, Blick *m* (*of* auf *acc*).

vis·u·al ['vɪʒʊəl] *adj* □ **1.** Seh... **2.** visuell: **~ aids** *pl ped.* Anschauungsmaterial *n*, Lehrmittel *pl*. **3.** optisch. **'visu·al·ize** *v/t* sich *et.* vorstellen.

vi·tal ['vaɪtl] *adj* (□ → *vitally*) **1.** lebenswichtig (*Organ etc*). **2.** Lebens...: **~ statistics** *pl* Bevölkerungsstatistik *f*; F *humor.* Maße *pl* (*e-r Frau*). **3.** unbedingt notwendig (*to, for* für): *of* **~** *importance* von größter Wichtigkeit. **4.** vital. **vi·tal·i·ty** [˙'tælətɪ] *s* Vitalität *f*. **vi·tal·ly** ['˙təlɪ] *adv* **1.** vital. **2.** sehr viel: **~ important** äußerst wichtig.

vi·ta·min ['vɪtəmɪn] *s* Vitamin *n*. **~ pill** *s* Vitamintablette *f*.

vit·re·ous ['vɪtrɪəs] *adj* □ Glas...

vi·va ['viːvə] *s* → *viva voce.*

vi·va·cious [vɪ'veɪʃəs] *adj* □ lebhaft, temperamentvoll.

vi·va vo·ce ['vəʊsɪ] *s univ.* mündliche Prüfung.

viv·id ['vɪvɪd] *adj* □ **1.** hell (*Licht*); kräftig, leuchtend (*Farben*). **2.** anschaulich (*Schilderung etc*), lebhaft (*Phantasie*).

viv·i·sec·tion [ˌvɪvɪ'sekʃn] *s* Vivisektion *f*.

V neck [viː] *s* V-Ausschnitt *m*. **'V-necked** *adj* mit V-Ausschnitt.

vo·cab ['vəʊkæb] F → *vocabulary* 2.

vo·cab·u·lar·y [vəʊ'kæbjʊlərɪ] *s* **1.** Vokabular *n*, Wortschatz *m*. **2.** Vokabular *n*, Wortregister *n*, Wörterverzeichnis *n*.

vo·cal ['vəʊkl] **I** *adj* □ **1.** Stimm...: **~ cords** *pl anat.* Stimmbänder *pl*. **2.** ♪ *music* Vokalmusik *f*. **3.** F lautstark. **II** *s* *pl* **4.** **~s:** *XY* Gesang: *XY*.

vo·ca·tion [vəʊ'keɪʃn] *s* **1.** Begabung *f* (*for* für). **2.** Berufung *f*. **vo·ca·tion·al** [˙ʃənl] *adj* Berufs...: **~ training** Berufsausbildung *f*.

vo·cif·er·ous [vəʊ'sɪfərəs] *adj* □ lautstark (*Protest etc*).

vogue [vəʊg] *s* Mode *f*: *be in* **~** Mode sein; *be all the* **~** große Mode sein. **~ word** *s* Modewort *n*.

voice [vɔɪs] **I** *s* **1.** Stimme *f* (*a. fig.*): *give* **~** *to* → **4**. **2.** *have a* **~** *in* ein Mitspracherecht haben bei. **3.** → *active* 2, *passive* 2. **II** *v/t* **4.** zum Ausdruck bringen. **5.** *ling.* stimmhaft aussprechen. **~ box** *s* *anat.* Kehlkopf *m*.

voiced [vɔɪst] *adj ling.* stimmhaft. **'voice·less** *adj ling.* stimmlos.

void [vɔɪd] **I** *adj* **1.** leer: **~ of** ohne. **2.** ⚖ nichtig, ungültig: → *null*. **II** *v/t* **3.** ⚖

nichtig *od.* ungültig machen. **III** *s* **4.** *fig.* (Gefühl *n* der) Leere.

vol·a·tile ['vɒlətaɪl] *adj* **1.** cholerisch (*Person, Temperament*); explosiv (*Lage etc*). **2.** 🜛 flüchtig, (*Öl*) ätherisch.

vol·can·ic [vɒl'kænɪk] *adj* (*∼ally*) vulkanisch, Vulkan... **vol·ca·no** [∼'keɪnəʊ] *pl* **-no(e)s** *s* Vulkan *m.*

vo·li·tion [vəʊ'lɪʃn] *s*: *of one's own ∼* aus freien Stücken.

vol·ley ['vɒlɪ] **I** *s* **1.** Salve *f;* (*Schlag- etc*)Hagel *m: a ∼ of curses* ein Hagel von Verwünschungen. **2.** *Tennis:* Volley *m,* Flugball *m;* (*Fußball*) Volleyschuß *m: take on the ∼* Ball volley nehmen. **II** *v/t* **3.** *Ball* volley schießen (*into the net* ins Netz). '*∼·ball s Sport:* Volleyball *m.*

volt [vəʊlt] *s* ⚡ Volt *n.* '**volt·age** *s* ⚡ Spannung *f.*

vol·u·ble ['vɒljʊbl] *adj* □ **1.** redselig. **2.** wortreich.

vol·ume ['vɒlju:m] *s* **1.** Band *m: a two-∼ novel* ein zweibändiger Roman; *speak ∼s fig.* Bände sprechen. **2.** ⚗, *phys.* Volumen *n,* Rauminhalt *m.* **3.** (*Handels- etc*)Volumen *n,* (*Verkehrs*)Aufkommen *n.* **4.** Lautstärke *f: at full ∼* in voller Lautstärke; *turn to full ∼ Radio etc* auf volle Lautstärke stellen, voll aufdrehen; *turn the ∼ up* (**down**) lauter (leiser) drehen; *∼ control* Lautstärkeregler *m.* **vo·lu·mi·nous** [və'lu:mɪnəs] *adj* □ **1.** bauschig (*Kleidungsstück*). **2.** geräumig. **3.** umfangreich (*Bericht etc*).

vol·un·tar·y ['vɒləntərɪ] *adj* □ **1.** freiwillig. **2.** unbezahlt.

vol·un·teer [ˌvɒlən'tɪə] **I** *v/i* **1.** sich freiwillig melden (*for* zu) (*a.* ✕). **II** *v/t* **2.** *Hilfe etc* anbieten: *∼ to do s.th.* sich anbieten, etc zu tun. **3.** *et.* von sich aus sagen. **III** *s* **4.** Freiwillige *m* (*a.* ✕); freiwilliger Helfer.

vo·lup·tu·ous [və'lʌptʃʊəs] *adj* □ **1.** sinnlich (*Lippen, Mund*); üppig (*Formen*); aufreizend (*Bewegungen*). **2.** kurvenreich (*Frau*).

vom·it ['vɒmɪt] **I** *v/t* erbrechen, *Blut* spucken; *Feuer, Lava* speien, *Rauchwolken etc* ausstoßen. **II** *v/i* (sich er)brechen, sich übergeben.

vo·ra·cious [və'reɪʃəs] *adj* □ unersättlich (*Appetit*): *he's a ∼ reader of comics* er verschlingt die Comics geradezu.

vor·tex ['vɔːteks] *pl* **-tex·es, -ti·ces** ['∼tɪsiːz] *s* Strudel *m* (*a. fig.*), Wirbel *m.*

vote [vəʊt] **I** *s* **1.** Abstimmung *f* (*about, on* über *acc*): *put to the ∼* abstimmen lassen über (*acc*); *take a ∼ on* abstimmen über; → *censure* 1. **2.** Stimme *f;* Stimmzettel *m,* Stimme *f: cast one's ∼ for, give one's ∼ to* seine Stimme geben. **3.** *a. pl* Wahlrecht *n: get the ∼* wahlberechtigt werden. **II** *v/i* **4.** wählen: *∼ for* (**against**) stimmen für (gegen). **5.** *∼ on* abstimmen über (*acc*). **III** *v/t* **6.** wählen: *∼ out of office* abwählen. **7.** *∼ s.o. s.th.* j-m et. bewilligen. **8.** *∼ that* F vorschlagen, daß. '**vot·er** *s* Wähler(in).

vouch [vaʊtʃ] *v/i: ∼ for* sich verbürgen für; bürgen für. '**vouch·er** *s* Gutschein *m.*

vow [vaʊ] **I** *s* Gelöbnis *n: make* (*od. take*) *a ∼* ein Gelöbnis ablegen. **II** *v/t* geloben, schwören (*to do* zu tun).

vow·el ['vaʊəl] *s ling.* Vokal *m,* Selbstlaut *m.*

voy·age ['vɔɪdʒ] *s* (See)Reise *f.*

vul·can·ize ['vʌlkənaɪz] *v/t* vulkanisieren.

vul·gar ['vʌlgə] *adj* □ **1.** vulgär, ordinär. **2.** geschmacklos.

vul·ner·a·ble ['vʌlnərəbl] *adj* □ **1.** *fig.* verletz-, verwundbar; schutzbedürftig. **2.** anfällig (*to* für).

vul·ture ['vʌltʃə] *s orn.* Geier *m.*

W

wack·y ['wækɪ] *adj* □ *bsd. Am.* F verrückt.

wad [wɒd] *s* **1.** (*Papier- etc*)Knäuel *m*; (*Watte- etc*)Bausch *m.* **2.** Bündel *n* (*Banknoten etc*).

wad·dle ['wɒdl] *v/i* watscheln.

wade [weɪd] **I** *v/t* durchwaten. **II** *v/i* waten: ~ **across** → I; ~ **in** hineinwaten; F sich einmischen; ~ **into** waten in (*acc*); F losgehen auf *j-n*; sich reinknien in *e-e* **Arbeit**; ~ **through** waten durch; F sich durchkämpfen durch, *Fachliteratur etc a.* durchackern. **'wad·ing** *adj:* ~ **pool** *Am.* Planschbecken *n.*

wa·fer ['weɪfə] *s* **1.** (*bsd.* Eis)Waffel *f.* **2.** *eccl.* Hostie *f.*

waf·fle[1] ['wɒfl] *s* Waffel *f.*

waf·fle[2] [~] *v/i bsd. Br.* F schwafeln.

waft [wɑːft] **I** *v/i* ziehen (*Duft etc*). **II** *v/t* wehen.

wag[1] [wæg] **I** *v/t:* ~ **one's finger at** *j-m* mit dem Finger drohen; ~ **its tail** mit dem Schwanz wedeln. **II** *v/i* wedeln (*Schwanz*): **tongues will** ~ das wird Gerede geben; **set tongues ~ging** für Gerede sorgen. **III** *s:* **with a** ~ **of its tail** schwanzwedelnd.

wag[2] [~] *s* F unterhaltsamer Mensch.

wage[1] [weɪdʒ] *s mst pl* Lohn *m*; Gehalt *n.*

wage[2] [~] *v/t:* ~ **(a)** **war against** (*od.* **on**) ✗ Krieg führen gegen; *fig.* e-n Feldzug führen gegen.

wage| de·mand *s* Lohn- *od.* Gehaltsforderung *f.* ~ **earn·er** *s* Verdiener(in): **be a** ~ berufstätig sein; **be a big** ~ viel verdienen. ~ **freeze** *s* Lohnstopp *m.* ~ **pack·et** *s* Lohn- *od.* Gehaltstüte *f.* ~ **rise** *s* Lohn- *od.* Gehaltserhöhung *f.*

wa·ger ['weɪdʒə] **I** *s* Wette *f:* **have** (*od.* **place**) **a** ~ **on** e-e Wette abschließen *od.* eingehen auf (*acc*). **II** *v/t:* **I'll** ~ **that** ich wette, daß.

wag·gle ['wægl] *v/i u. v/t* F wackeln (mit).

wag·gon *Br.* → **wagon.**

wag·on ['wægən] *s* **1.** Fuhrwerk *n*, Wagen *m:* **be on the** ~ F keinen Alkohol (mehr) trinken. **2.** 🚃 *Br.* (offener) Güterwagen *m.* **3.** *Am.* (*Tee- etc*)Wagen *m.*

wag·on-lit [ˌvægɔ̃:n'liː] *pl* **wa·gons-lits** [ˌ~'liːz] *s* 🚃 Schlafwagen *m.*

wail [weɪl] **I** *v/i* jammern (*Person*); heulen (*Sirene, Wind*). **II** *v/t* jammern. **III** *s* Jammern *n*; Heulen *n.*

wain·scot ['weɪnskət] *s* **1.** Fuß(boden)-, Scheuerleiste *f.* **2.** (*Wand*)Täfelung *f.*

waist [weɪst] *s* Taille *f:* → **strip** 1. ~**coat** ['weɪskəʊt] *s bsd. Br.* Weste *f.* **'~line** *s* Taille *f:* **I'm watching my** ~ ich muß auf m-e Linie achten.

wait [weɪt] **I** *v/i* **1.** warten (**for, on** *od acc*; [**for**] **10 minutes** 10 Minuten): ~ **for s.o.** *j-n* erwarten; ~ **for s.o. to do s.th.** darauf warten, daß *j-d* et. tut; warten, bis *j-d* et. tut; **this can** ~ das kann warten, das hat Zeit (**until** bis); **keep s.o. waiting** *j-n* warten lassen; **I can't** ~ **to see him** ich kann es kaum erwarten, ihn zu sehen; ~ **and see!** warte es ab!; **I'll have to** ~ **and see how ...** ich muß abwarten, wie ...; ~ **up** F aufbleiben (**for** wegen). **2.** ~ **on s.o.** *j-n* (*bsd. im Restaurant*) bedienen; ~ **at** (*Am.* **on**) **table** bedienen. **II** *v/t* **3.** ~ **one's chance** auf e-e günstige Gelegenheit warten (**to do** zu tun); ~ **one's turn** warten, bis man an der Reihe ist. **4.** ~ **breakfast for s.o.** *bsd. Am.* F mit dem Frühstück auf *j-n* warten. **III** *s* **5.** Wartezeit *f:* **have a long** ~ lange warten müssen. **6.** **lie in** ~ **for s.o.** *j-m* auflauern. **'wait·er** *s* Kellner *m*, Ober *m*, (*Anrede*) (Herr) Ober. **'wait·ing** *s* Warten *n:* **"no** ~**"** „Halt(e)verbot". **II** *adj:* **play a** ~ **game** (with s.o.) *j-n* hinhalten; ~ **list** Warteliste *f:* ~ **room** 🚃 Wartesaal *m*; 🏥 *etc* Wartezimmer *n.* **wait·ress** ['~rɪs] *s* Kellnerin *f*, Bedienung *f*, (*Anrede*) Fräulein.

waive [weɪv] *v/t* verzichten auf (*acc*). **'waiv·er** *s* Verzicht *m* (**of** auf *acc*); Verzichtserklärung *f.*

wake[1] [weɪk] *s* ⚓ Kielwasser *n:* **follow in the** ~ **of** *fig.* folgen auf (*acc*); **leave s.th. in one's** ~ *fig.* et. zurücklassen.

wake[2] [~] (*irr*) **I** *v/t a.* ~ **up** (auf)wecken: ~ **s.o. to s.th.** *fig.* j-m et. bewußt machen. **II** *v/i a.* ~ **up** aufwachen, wach werden: ~ **to s.th.**

fig. sich e-r Sache bewußt werden.
wake-ful [ˈ‿ful] *adj* □ schlaflos.
wak-en [ˈ‿ən] **I** *v/t a.* **~ up** (auf)wecken.
II *v/i a.* **~ up** aufwachen, wach werden.
'wak-ing *adj:* **he spends all his ~ hours studying** er lernt von früh bis spät.

walk [wɔːk] **I** *s* **1.** Spaziergang *m;* Wanderung *f:* **go for** (*od.* **have, take**) **a ~** e-n Spaziergang machen, spazierengehen; **the church is just a five-minute ~ from here** zu Fuß sind es nur fünf Minuten bis zur Kirche. **2.** Spazier-, Wanderweg *m.* **3.** Gang *m.* **4. from all ~s** (*od.* **every ~**) **of life** Leute aus allen Berufen (*od.* Schichten). **II** *v/i* **5.** (zu Fuß) gehen, laufen; spazierengehen; wandern: **~ into** hineingehen in (*acc*), hereinkommen in (*acc*); *fig.* in e-e Falle gehen; **~ over** F j-n unterbuttern; (*Sport*) j-n in die Tasche stecken. **III** *v/t* **6.** Strecke gehen, laufen; → **street. 7.** j-n bringen (**to** zu; **home** nach Hause); Hund ausführen.

Verbindungen mit Adverbien:

walk| a·way *v/i* **1.** → **walk off. 2. ~ from** bei e-m Unfall (fast) unverletzt bleiben. **~ in** *v/i* hineingehen, hereinkommen. **~ off** *v/i* **1.** fort-, weggehen. **2. ~ with** F abhauen mit; *Preis etc* locker gewinnen. **~ out** *v/i* **1.** hinausgehen; (unter Protest) den Saal verlassen, (*Delegation etc a.*) ausziehen: **~ of a meeting** e-e Versammlung (unter Protest) verlassen; **~ on s.o.** F j-n sitzenlassen. **2.** in (den) Streik treten. **~ up** *v/i* **1.** hinaufgehen, heraufkommen. **2. ~ to s.o.** auf j-n zugehen; **~!** treten Sie näher!

'walk·a·bout *s bsd. Br.* F Bad *n* in der Menge: **do** (*od.* **go on**) **a ~** ein Bad in der Menge nehmen.
walk·er [ˈwɔːkə] *s* **1.** Spaziergänger(in); Wand(e)rer *m,* Wand(r)erin *f:* **be a fast ~** schnell gehen. **2.** *Sport:* Geher *m.*
walk·ies [ˈ‿ɪz] *s pl:* **go ~** *Br.* F Gassi gehen.
walk·ie-talk·ie [ˌwɔːkɪˈtɔːkɪ] *s* Walkie-talkie *n,* tragbares Funksprechgerät.
'walk-in *adj* begehbar (*Schrank*).
walk·ing [ˈwɔːkɪŋ] **I** *s* Laufen *n* (*a. Sport*), Gehen *n;* Spazierengehen *n;* Wandern *n.* **II** *adj:* **a ~ dictionary** F ein wandelndes Wörterbuch; **get one's ~**

papers Am. F den Laufpaß bekommen (*von Firma od. Freundin*); **~ shoes** *pl;* **~ stick** Spazierstock *m;* **~ tour** Wanderung *f.*
Walk·man [ˈwɔːkmən] *pl* **-mans** *s* (*TM*) Walkman *m.*
'walk|-on *thea.* **I** *adj* **1. ~ part** → **2. II** *s* **2.** Statistenrolle *f.* **3.** Statist(in). **'~·out** *s* **1.** Auszug *m* (**by,** *of* e-r Delegation etc). **2.** Ausstand *m,* Streik *m.* **'~·o·ver** *s* F lockerer Sieg.
wall [wɔːl] **I** *s* **1.** Wand *f* (*a. fig.*): **~ of fire** Feuerwand *f;* **~s have ears** die Wände haben Ohren; **drive up the ~** F j-n wahnsinnig machen; **go to the ~** kaputtgehen (*Firma etc*). **2.** Mauer *f* (*a. fig.*): **~ of silence** Mauer des Schweigens. **II** *v/t* **3.** mit e-r Mauer umgeben: **~ed** von Mauern umgeben; **~ in** einmauern; **~ off** durch e-e Mauer abtrennen (**from** von); **~ up** zu- *od.* einmauern. **'~·chart** *s* Wandkarte *f.*
wal·let [ˈwɒlɪt] *s* Brieftasche *f.*
'wall·flow·er *s fig.* F Mauerblümchen *n.*
wal·lop [ˈwɒləp] F **I** *s* **1.** Ding *n* (*harter Schlag*): **give s.o. a ~** → **2. II** *v/t* **2.** j-m ein Ding verpassen. **3.** *Sport:* j-n in die Pfanne hauen (*at* in *dat*). **'wal·lop·ing** *adj u. adv:* **~ (great)** F riesig, Mords...
wal·low [ˈwɒləʊ] *v/i:* **~ in** sich wälzen in (*dat,* (*Tier a.*) sich suhlen in (*dat*): **~ in luxury** im Luxus schwelgen; **~ in self-pity** sich in Selbstmitleid ergehen.
wall| paint·ing *s* Wandgemälde *n.* **'~·pa·per I** *s* Tapete *f.* **II** *v/t* tapezieren. **'~-to-'~** *adj:* **~ carpeting** Spannteppich *m,* Teppichboden *m.*
wal·ly [ˈwɒlɪ] *s Br.* F Trottel *m.*
wal·nut [ˈwɔːlnʌt] *s* ♣ Walnuß(baum *m*) *f.* **~ cake** *s* Nußkuchen *m.*
wal·rus [ˈwɔːlrəs] *pl* **-rus·es,** *bsd. coll.* **-rus** *s zo.* Walroß *n.* **~ m(o)us·tache** *s* Seehundsbart *m.*
waltz [wɔːls] **I** *s* ♪ Walzer *m.* **II** *v/i* Walzer tanzen; walzen.
wand [wɒnd] *s* (*Zauber*)Stab *m.*
wan·der [ˈwɒndə] *v/i* **1.** wandern; bummeln, schlendern: **~ about** (*od.* **around**) herumirren; **~ off** verschwinden. **2. ~ from** (*od.* **off**) **the topic** vom Thema abschweifen. **3.** *fig.* mind **~s** er kann sich schlecht konzentrieren. **'wan·der·ings** *s pl* **1.** Reisen *pl.* **2. he's off on his**

warn

~ *again* er ist wieder mal verschwunden.

wane [weɪn] **I** *v/i* abnehmen (*Mond*); *fig.* schwinden (*Einfluß etc*). **II** *s*: *be on the* ~ im Schwinden begriffen sein.

wan·gle ['wæŋgl] *v/t* F **1.** Eintrittskarten *etc* organisieren: ~ *s.th. out of s.o.* j-m et. abluchsen. **2.** ~ *one's way out of* sich herauswinden aus. **3.** *I'll* ~ *it* ich werde das Kind schon schaukeln.

wank [wæŋk] *v/i Br.* V wichsen (*masturbieren*). **'wank·er** *s Br. fig.* V Wichser *m*.

wan·na ['wɒnə] F *für want to; want a.*

want [wɒnt] **I** *v/t* **1.** *et.* wollen: *he knows what he* ~*s* er weiß, was er will; ~ *to do s.th.* et. tun wollen; ~ *s.o. to do s.th.* wollen, daß j-d et. tut; ~ *s.th. done* wollen, daß et. getan wird; *it* ~*s doing at once* F es muß sofort erledigt werden. **2.** j-n brauchen; j-n sprechen wollen: *you are* ~*ed on the phone* du wirst am Telefon verlangt. **3.** *be* ~*ed* (*polizeilich*) gesucht werden (*for* wegen). **4.** F *et.* brauchen, nötig haben. **5.** F *you* ~ *to see a doctor* du solltest zum Arzt gehen; *he doesn't* ~ *to smoke that much* er sollte nicht so viel rauchen. **II** *v/i* **6.** wollen: *I don't* ~ *to* ich will nicht; ~ *in* (*out*) F rein-(raus)wollen. **7.** *he does not* ~ *for anything* es fehlt ihm an nichts. **III** *s* **8.** Mangel *m* (*of* an *dat*): *for* ~ *of* mangels (*gen*), in Ermang(e)lung (*gen*); *be in* ~ *of* et. benötigen, brauchen. **9.** Bedürfnis *n*, Wunsch *m*. **10.** *live in* ~ Not leiden, in Armut leben. ~ *ad s* Kleinanzeige *f*.

want·ed ['wɒntɪd] *adj*: *he's a* ~ *man* er wird (*polizeilich*) gesucht; er ist ein vielgefragter Mann. **'want·ing** *adj*: *they are* ~ *in* es fehlt an (*dat*); *be found* ~ den Ansprüchen nicht genügen.

wan·ton ['wɒntən] *adj* □ **1.** mutwillig. **2.** liederlich (*Frau, Leben*). **3.** lüstern (*Blick etc*).

war [wɔː] *s* Krieg *m* (*a. fig.*); *fig.* Kampf *m* (*against* gegen): *be at* ~ *with* sich im Krieg(szustand) befinden mit; *fig.* auf (dem) Kriegsfuß stehen mit; *declare* ~ *on* j-m den Krieg erklären, *fig. a.* j-m den Kampf ansagen; → *wage²*.

war·ble ['wɔːbl] *v/i* trillern (*Vogel*).

war| cem·e·ter·y *s* Soldatenfriedhof *m*.

~ *crime s* Kriegsverbrechen *n*. ~ **crim·i·nal** *s* Kriegsverbrecher *m*. ~ **cry** *s* **1.** ✗ *hist.* Schlachtruf *m*. **2.** *fig.* Parole *f*.

ward [wɔːd] **I** *s* **1.** Station *f* (*e-s Krankenhauses*). **2.** *pol. Br.* Stadtbezirk *m*. **3.** ⚖ Mündel *n*. **II** *v/t* **4.** ~ *off* Schlag *etc* abwehren, *Gefahr etc* abwenden. **'ward·en** *s* **1.** Aufseher(in): ~ *traffic warden.* **2.** Haus-, Herbergsvater *m*, -mutter *f*; Heimleiter(in). **3.** *Am.* (Gefängnis)Direktor(in). **'ward·er** *s Br.* Aufsichtsbeamte *m*, -beamtin *f* (*in Gefängnis*).

ward·robe ['wɔːdrəub] *s* **1.** (Kleider-) Schrank *m*. **2.** Garderobe *f* (*Kleiderbestand*).

ware [weə] *s* in *Zssgn* (Glas- *etc*)Waren *pl*: → *tableware.* **'~·house** *s* Lager(-haus) *n*.

war·fare ['wɔːfeə] *s* Krieg(führung *f*) *m*.

war| game *s* Kriegsspiel *n* (*a. für Kinder etc*), Planübung *f*. ~ **grave** *s* Kriegs-, Soldatengrab *n*. '~**head** *s* ✗ Spreng-, Gefechtskopf *m*. '~**like** *adj* **1.** kriegerisch. **2.** Kriegs...

warm [wɔːm] **I** *adj* □ **1.** warm (*a. fig. Farben, Stimme*): *I am* (*od. feel*) ~ mir ist warm; *dress* ~*ly* sich warm anziehen. **2.** *fig.* warm, herzlich (*Empfang*). **II** *s* **3.** *come into the* ~ *bsd. Br.* F komm ins Warme! **III** *v/t* **4.** ~ *up* wärmen, sich *die Hände etc* wärmen. **IV** *v/i* **5.** *a.* ~ *up* warm *od.* wärmer werden, sich erwärmen: ~ *to fig.* sich für j-n, et. erwärmen.

Verbindungen mit Adverbien:

warm| o·ver *v/t* **1.** *Am.* → *warm up* **2**. **2.** *bsd. Am. fig.* alte Geschichten *etc* aufwärmen. ~ *up v/t* **1.** → *warm* **4.** **2.** *Br. Speise* aufwärmen. **3.** *Motor* warmlaufen lassen. **4.** F Schwung bringen in (*acc*). **II** *v/i* **5.** → *warm* **5.** **6.** *Sport:* sich aufwärmen. **7.** F in Schwung kommen.

warm|-'blood·ed *adj zo.* warmblütig: ~ *animal* Warmblüter *m*. ~**-'heart·ed** *adj* □ **1.** warmherzig. **2.** → *warm* **2**. **'war mon·ger** *s* Kriegshetzer *m*.

warmth ['wɔːmθ] *s* Wärme *f*, *fig. a.* Herzlichkeit *f*.

'warm-up *s Sport:* Aufwärmen *n*: *have a* ~ sich aufwärmen.

warn [wɔːn] **I** *v/t* **1.** j-n warnen (*against, of* vor *dat*): ~ *s.o. not to do* (*od. against doing*) *s.th.* j-n davor warnen, et. zu tun; **~ off** verscheuchen (von, aus). **2.** j-n verständigen (**of** von; **that** davon, daß). **II** v/i **3.** warnen (**against, of** vor dat). **'warn·ing I** s **1.** Warnung f (**of** vor dat): **without ~** ohne Vorwarnung; **let this be a ~ to you** laß dir das e-e Warnung sein!, das soll dir e-e Warnung sein! **2.** Verwarnung f: **he was given a written ~** a. er wurde schriftlich verwarnt. **II** adj **3.** Warn...: **~ signal** Warnsignal n (a. fig.).

warp [wɔːp] v/i sich verziehen od. werfen (Holz): **he must have a ~ed mind** fig. er muß abartig veranlagt sein.

war| paint s Kriegsbemalung f (a. humor. Make-up). **'~·path** s: **be on the ~** auf dem Kriegspfad sein; **he's on the ~** F um ihn macht man heute am besten e-n großen Bogen.

war·rant ['wɒrənt] **I** v/t **1.** et. rechtfertigen. **II** s **2.** ⚖ **~ of arrest** Haftbefehl m; **issue a ~ for s.o.'s arrest** Haftbefehl gegen j-n erlassen; → **death warrant, search warrant. 3.** Rechtfertigung f. **'war·ran·ty** s Garantie(erklärung) f: **the watch is still under ~** auf der Uhr ist noch Garantie.

war·ri·or ['wɒrɪə] s Krieger m.

'war·ship s Kriegsschiff n.

wart [wɔːt] s Warze f: **~s and all** F ohne jede Beschönigung.

'war·time I s: **in ~** in Kriegszeiten. **II** adj Kriegs...: **in ~ Germany** in Deutschland während des Kriegs.

war·y ['weərɪ] adj □ vorsichtig: **be ~ of** (od. **about**) sich in acht nehmen vor (dat); **be ~ of doing s.th.** Bedenken haben, et. zu tun.

was [wɒz] **1.** ich, er, sie, es war. **2.** Passiv: ich, er, sie, es wurde.

wash [wɒʃ] **I** s **1.** Wäsche f: **be in the ~** in der Wäsche sein; **come out in the ~** fig. F rauskommen; gut werden; **give s.th. a ~** et. waschen; **have a ~** sich waschen. **2.** Waschanlage f, -straße f. **3.** ♣ (Mund)Wasser n. **II** v/t **4.** waschen, sich die Hände etc waschen: **get ~ed** sich waschen; → **linen 2. III** v/i **5.** sich waschen. **6.** sich gut etc waschen (lassen). **7. that won't ~** F das glaubt kein Mensch.
Verbindungen mit Adverbien:

wash| a·way v/t wegschwemmen, -spülen. **~ down** v/t **1.** Wagen etc wa-

schen, abspritzen. **2.** Essen etc hinunterspülen (**with** mit). **~ out** v/t **1.** auswaschen. **2. be ~ed out** (Sport etc) wegen Regens abgesagt od. abgebrochen werden. **~ up I** v/i **1.** Br. abwaschen, (das) Geschirr spülen. **2.** Am. → **wash 5. II** v/t **3.** anschwemmen, anspülen.

wash·a·ble ['wɒʃəbl] adj waschbar, -echt, (Tapete) abwaschbar.

'wash|·ba·sin s, **'~·bowl** s Am. Waschbecken n. **'~·cloth** s Am. Waschlappen m. **'~·day** s Waschtag m.

washed-out [,wɒʃt'aʊt] adj **1.** verwaschen. **2.** F schlapp, erschöpft. **'wash·er** s **1.** (Geschirr)Spülmaschine f, (-)Spüler m; Am. Waschmaschine f. **2.** → **dishwasher** 1. **3.** ⚙ Unterlegscheibe f.

wash·ing ['wɒʃɪŋ] **I** s Wäsche f (a. Textilien). **II** adj Wasch...: **~ day** Waschtag m; **~ machine** Waschmaschine f. **,~·'up** s Br. Abwasch m (a. Geschirr): **do the ~** den Abwasch machen.

'wash|·out s F Pleite f. **'~·room** s Am. Toilette f.

was·n't ['wɒznt] F für **was not**.

wasp ['wɒsp] s zo. Wespe f. **'wasp·ish** adj □ giftig.

waste [weɪst] **I** v/t **1.** Geld, Zeit etc verschwenden, -geuden (**on** an acc, für); Chance etc vergeben: **~ one's time doing s.th.** s-e Zeit damit verschwenden, et. zu tun; → **breath 1. 2.** j-n auszehren. **II** v/i **3. ~ away** immer schwächer werden (Person). **III** adj **4.** ungenutzt, überschüssig; Abfall... **5.** brachliegend (Land). **IV** s **6.** Verschwendung f: **~ of time** Zeitverschwendung. **7.** Abfall m; Müll m. **'~·bas·ket** s Papierkorb m. **~ dis·pos·al** s Abfall-, Müllbeseitigung f.

waste·ful ['weɪstfʊl] adj □ verschwenderisch: **it is ~** a. es ist Verschwendung (**to do** zu tun).

,waste·'pa·per bas·ket s Papierkorb m. **~ pipe** s Abflußrohr n. **~ prod·uct** s Abfallprodukt n.

wast·er ['weɪstə] s Verschwender(in): **be a real time ~** reine Zeitverschwendung sein.

watch [wɒtʃ] **I** s **1.** (Armband-, Taschen)Uhr f. **2.** Wache f: **be on the ~ for** Ausschau halten nach; auf der Hut sein vor (dat); **keep (a) careful** (od. **close**) *on et.* genau beobachten, scharf im Auge behalten. **II** *v/t* **3.** beobachten; zuschauen bei, sich *et.* ansehen: **~** *s.o. do(ing) s.th.* beobachten, wie j-d et. tut; **~** *the clock* F ständig auf die Uhr schauen; → *television* 1, *TV* 1. **4.** aufpassen auf (*acc*); achten auf (*acc*): **~** *you don't spill the coffee* paß auf, daß du den Kaffee nicht verschüttest; **~** *it!* F paß auf!, Vorsicht!; **~** *one's step fig.* aufpassen. **III** *v/i* **5.** zuschauen: **~** *for* a) *a.* **~** *out for* Ausschau halten nach, b) warten auf (*acc*). **6.** **~** *out!* paß auf!, Vorsicht!; **~** *out for* sich in acht nehmen vor (*dat*); **~** *over* wachen über (*acc*). '**~dog** *s* Wachhund *m*.

watch·ful ['wɒtʃful] *adj* □ wachsam: *be* **~** *for* achten auf (*acc*).

watch|·mak·er *s* Uhrmacher(in). '**~-man** ['~mən] *s* (*irr man*) Wachmann *m*, Wächter *m*. '**~strap** *s* Uhr(arm)-band *n*. '**~tow·er** *s* Wachturm *m*.

wa·ter ['wɔːtə] **I** *s* **1.** Wasser *n*: *be under* **~** unter Wasser stehen; *that's all* **~** *under the bridge fig.* das ist Schnee von gestern; *have* **~** *on the knee* ✚ Wasser im Knie haben; *throw cold* **~** *on fig.* e-r Sache e-n Dämpfer aufsetzen; → *deep* 1, *head* 8, *high water*, *hot* 1. **2.** *pl* Gewässer *pl*; Wasser *pl* (*e-s Flusses etc*): *still* **~***s run deep fig.* stille Wasser sind tief; → *trouble* 4. **II** *v/t* **3.** Blumen gießen, *Rasen etc* sprengen. **4.** Vieh tränken. **5.** **~** *down* verdünnen, *-wässern; fig.* abschwächen. **III** *v/i* **6.** tränen (*Augen*): *the sight made my mouth* **~** bei dem Anblick lief mir das Wasser im Mund zusammen. '**~bed** *s* Wasserbett *n*. **~ bird** *s* Wasservogel *m*. **~ blis·ter** *s* ✚ Wasserblase *f*. **~ buf·fa·lo** *s zo.* Wasserbüffel *m*. **~ butt** *s* Regentonne *f*. **~ can·non** *s* (*a. irr cannon*) Wasserwerfer *m*. '**~col·o(u)r** *s* **1.** Wasser-, Aquarellfarbe *f*. **2.** Aquarellmalerei *f*. **3.** Aquarell *n*. '**~course** *s* Wasserlauf *m*. '**~cress** *s* ♀ Brunnenkresse *f*. '**~fall** *s* Wasserfall *m*. '**~front** *s* Hafenviertel *m*. '**~hole** *s* Wasserloch *n*. **~ ice** *s bsd. Br.* Fruchteis *n*.

wa·ter·ing ['wɔːtərɪŋ] *adj:* **~** *can* (*Am. a. pot*) Gießkanne *f*.

wa·ter| jump *s Sport:* Wassergraben *m*. **~ lev·el** *s* Wasserstand *m*. **~ lil·y** *s* ♀ Seerose *f*.

Wa·ter·loo [ˌwɔːtəˈluː] *s: meet one's* **~** sein Waterloo erleben.

'**wa·ter|·mark** *s* Wasserzeichen *n*. '**~-mel·on** *s* ♀ Wassermelone *f*. **~ pipe** *s* **1.** Wasserrohr *n*. **2.** Wasserpfeife *f*. **~ po·lo** *s Sport:* Wasserball(spiel *n*) *m*. '**~-pow·er** *s* Wasserkraft *f*. '**~proof I** *adj* wasserdicht. **II** *s bsd. Br.* Regenmantel *m*. **III** *v/t* wasserdicht machen, imprägnieren. '**~side** *s* Ufer *n*. **~ ski** *s* Wasserski *m*. '**~ski** *v/i* Wasserski laufen. **ski·ing** *s* Wasserskilaufen *n*. **~ sup·ply** *s* Wasserversorgung *f*. '**~tight** *adj* wasserdicht, *fig. a.* hieb- u. stichfest. **va·po(u)r** *s* Wasserdampf *m*. '**~way** *s* Wasserstraße *f*. '**~wheel** *s* Wasserrad *n*. '**~wings** *s pl* Schwimmflügel *pl*. '**~works** *s pl* (*oft sg konstruiert*) Wasserwerk *n*: *turn on the* **~** F zu heulen anfangen.

wa·ter·y ['wɔːtərɪ] *adj* wässerig, wäßrig.

watt [wɒt] *s ⚡* Watt *n*.

wave [weɪv] **I** *v/t* **1.** schwenken; winken mit: **~** *one's hand* winken; **~** *s.o. good-bye* j-m nachwinken, j-m zum Abschied zuwinken; *you can* **~** *goodbye to that fig.* das kannst du dir aus dem Kopf schlagen. **2.** **~** *aside* j-n beiseite winken; j-n, *et.* abweisen; **~** *away* j-n mit e-r Handbewegung verscheuchen; **~** *on* j-n, *Verkehr* weiterwinken. **3.** Haar wellen, in Wellen legen. **II** *v/i* **4.** winken: **~** *at* (*od. to*) *s.o.* j-m zuwinken. **5.** wehen (*Fahne etc*). **6.** sich wellen (*Haar*). **III** *s* **7.** *allg.* Welle *f* (*a. fig.*). **8.** *give a friendly* **~** freundlich winken; *give s.o. a* **~** j-m zuwinken. '**~length** *s ⚡, phys.* Wellenlänge *f*: *we are on different* **~***s fig.* wir haben nicht die gleiche Wellenlänge.

wa·ver ['weɪvə] *v/i* **1.** flackern (*Licht, Augen*), zittern (*Stimme*). **2.** *fig.* schwanken (*between* zwischen *dat*).

wav·y ['weɪvɪ] *adj* wellig, gewellt: **~** *line* Wellenlinie *f*.

wax[1] [wæks] **I** *s* **1.** Wachs *n*. **2.** *physiol.* (*Ohren*)Schmalz *n*. **II** *v/t* **3.** wachsen, *Fußboden a.* bohnern.

wax[2] [~] *v/i* zunehmen (*Mond*).

wax·en ['wæksən] *adj fig.* wächsern.

'**wax·work** *s* **1.** Wachsfigur *f*. **2.** *pl* (*mst sg konstruiert*) Wachsfigurenkabinett *n*.

wax·y ['wæksɪ] *adj* wächsern (*a. fig.*).

way [weɪ] **I** s **1.** Weg m: ~ **back** Rückweg; ~ **home** Heimweg; ~ **in** Eingang m; ~ **out** Ausgang m; ~**s and means** pl fig. Mittel u. Wege pl; **by** ~ **of** über (acc), via; statt; **by the** ~ fig. übrigens; **be on the** (od. one's) ~ **to** unterwegs sein nach; **give** ~ nachgeben; **go out of one's** ~ sich besondere Mühe geben (**to do** zu tun); **lose one's** ~ sich verlaufen od. verirren; **make** ~ Platz machen (**for** für); → **talk** 8, etc. **2.** Richtung f, Seite f: **this** ~ hierher; hier entlang. **3.** Weg m, Entfernung f, Strecke f: **be a long** ~ **from** weit entfernt sein von; **Easter is still a long** ~ **off** bis Ostern ist es noch lang. **4.** Art f, Weise f: **in a** ~ (od. **some** ~**s**) in gewisser Hinsicht; **in no** ~ in keiner Weise; **no** ~**!** F kommt überhaupt nicht in Frage!; ~ **of life** Lebensart, -weise; **in my** ~ **of thinking** m-r Ansicht nach; **if I had my** ~ wenn es nach mir ginge; **you can't have it both** ~**s** du kannst nicht beides haben. **5.** mst pl Brauch m, Sitte f; Gewohnheit f: → **mend** 2. **II** adv **6.** weit: **they are friends from** ~ **back** sie sind alte Freunde. **'~·bill** s Frachtbrief m. **,~·'lay** v/t (irr **lay**) **1.** j-m auflauern. **2.** j-n abfangen, abpassen.

way·ward ['weɪwəd] adj □ eigensinnig.

we [wiː] pron wir pl.

weak [wiːk] adj □ allg. schwach (**at, in** in dat), (Kaffee etc a.) dünn: **be** (od. **feel**) ~ **at the knees** F schwach auf den Beinen sein; weiche Knie haben; → **point** 14, **sex** 1, **spot** 4. **'weak·en I** v/t **1.** schwächen (a. fig.). **II** v/i **2.** schwächer werden (a. fig.). **3.** fig. nachgeben.

,weak·'kneed adj F feig.

weak·ling ['wiːklɪŋ] s Schwächling m. **'weak·ness** s allg. Schwäche f: **have a** ~ **for** e-e Schwäche haben für.

weal [wiːl] s Striemen m.

wealth [welθ] s **1.** Reichtum m. **2.** fig. Fülle f (**of** von).

wean [wiːn] v/t Kind entwöhnen: ~ (**away**) **from s.th.**, ~ **off s.th.** j-n abbringen von etwas., j-m et. abgewöhnen.

weap·on ['wepən] s Waffe f (a. fig.): ~ **system** ✗ Waffensystem n.

weap·on·ry ['-rɪ] s Waffen pl.

wear [weə] **I** s **1.** a. ~ **and tear** Abnutzung f, Verschleiß m: **the worse for** ~ F abgenutzt (Couch etc); kaputt (Per-

son). **2.** oft in Zssgn Kleidung f. **II** v/t (irr) **3.** Bart, Brille, Schmuck tragen, Mantel etc a. anhaben, Hut etc a. aufhaben: ~ **the trousers** (bsd. Am. **pants**) F die Hosen anhaben; → **seat belt. 4.** ~ **an angry expression** verärgert dreinschauen; ~ **a happy smile** glücklich lächeln. **III** v/i (irr) **5.** s.th. **to** ~ et. zum Anziehen. **6.** sich abnutzen. **7.** **he has worn well** er hat sich (für sein Alter) gut gehalten.

Verbindungen mit Adverbien:

wear| down I v/t **1.** Stufen abtreten, Absätze ablaufen, Reifen abfahren. **2.** fig. j-n, Widerstand etc zermürben. **II** v/i **3.** sich abtreten od. ablaufen od. abfahren. ~ **off** v/i nachlassen (Schmerz etc). ~ **on** v/i sich hinziehen (**all day** über den ganzen Tag). ~ **out I** v/t **1.** Kleidung abnutzen, abtragen. **2.** fig. j-n erschöpfen. **II** v/i **3.** sich abnutzen od. abtragen.

wear·ing ['weərɪŋ] adj ermüdend.

wea·ri·some ['wɪərɪsəm] adj □ **1.** ermüdend. **2.** langweilig. **3.** lästig.

wea·ry ['wɪərɪ] adj □ **1.** erschöpft. **2.** **be** ~ **of s.th.** et. satt haben.

wea·sel ['wiːzl] **I** s zo. Wiesel n. **II** v/i: ~ **out of** bsd. Am. F sich lavieren aus (e-r Verantwortung etc).

weath·er ['weðə] **I** s Wetter n; Witterung f: **in all** ~**s** bei jedem Wetter; **be under the** ~ F sich nicht wohl fühlen; **make heavy** ~ **of s.th.** fig. sich et. unnötig schwermachen; → **permit** 2. **II** v/t Krise etc überstehen. **III** v/i geol. verwittern. **'~·beat·en** adj verwittert (bsd. Gesicht). **'~·bound** adj: **the planes** (**ships**) **were** ~ die Flugzeuge (Schiffe) konnten wegen des schlechten Wetters nicht starten (auslaufen). ~ **chart** s Wetterkarte f. **'~·cock** s Wetterhahn m. ~ **eye** s: **keep one's** (od. a) ~ **open** aufpassen (**for** auf acc). ~ **fore·cast** s Wettervorhersage f. **'~·man** s (irr **man**) Rundfunk, TV: Wetteransager m. **'~·proof I** adj wetterfest. **II** v/t wetterfest machen. ~ **sat·el·lite** s Wettersatellit m. ~ **sta·tion** s Wetterwarte f. ~ **vane** s Wetterfahne f.

weave [wiːv] **I** v/t (irr) **1.** weben; Netz spinnen. **2.** flechten. **3.** pret u. pp **weaved** ~ **one's way through** sich schlängeln durch. **II** v/i (irr) **4.** weben.

5. *pret u. pp* **weaved: ~ *through*** → 3. **III** *s* **6.** Webart *f.* **'weav·er** *s* Weber(in).

web [web] *s* **1.** Netz *n* (*a. fig.*): ~ *of lies* Lügengespinst *n,* -gewebe *n,* -netz. **2.** *orn.* Schwimmhaut *f.*

wed [wed] *v/t* (*a. irr*) heiraten: *they were ~ last week* sie haben letzte Woche geheiratet.

we'd [wi:d] F *für* **we had; we would.**

wed·ding ['wedɪŋ] **I** *s* Hochzeit *f.* **II** *adj* Hochzeits...: ~ *anniversary* Hochzeitstag *m* (*Jahrestag*); ~ *dress* Braut-, Hochzeitskleid *n;* ~ *ring* Ehe-, Trauring *m.*

wedge [wedʒ] **I** *s* **1.** Keil *m:* **drive a ~ *between*** *fig.* e-n Keil treiben zwischen (*acc*); → *thin* 1. **2.** Stück *n* (*Kuchen etc*), Ecke *f* (*Käse*). **II** *v/t* **3.** verkeilen, mit e-m Keil festklemmen. **4.** ~ *in* einkeilen, -zwängen. **'~-shaped** *adj* keilförmig.

Wednes·day ['wenzdɪ] *s* Mittwoch *m:* **on ~** (am) Mittwoch; **on ~s** mittwochs.

wee[1] [wi:] *adj* F klein: **a ~ *bit*** ein (kleines) bißchen; **the ~ (*small*) *hours*** *pl* die frühen Morgenstunden *pl.*

wee[2] [~] F **I** *v/i* Pipi machen. **II** *s:* **do** (*od.* **have**) **a ~** → 1.

weed [wi:d] **I** *s* **1.** Unkraut *n.* **2.** F Schwächling *m,* Waschlappen *m.* **II** *v/t* **3.** jäten: ~ *out fig.* aussieben, -sondern (*from* aus). **III** *v/i* **4.** (Unkraut) jäten. **'weed·y** *adj* **1.** voll Unkraut. **2.** F rückgratlos.

week [wi:k] *s* Woche *f:* ~ *after* ~; ~ *in,* ~ *out* Woche für Woche; *after* ~*s of waiting* nach wochenlangem Warten; *for* ~*s* wochenlang; → *today* 1. **'~·day** *s* Wochen-, Werktag *m:* **on ~s** werktags. **~'end** *s* Wochenende *n:* **at the ~** am Wochenende. **II** *adj* ['~end] Wochenend... **III** *v/i* das Wochenende verbringen.

week·ly ['wi:klɪ] **I** *adj* Wochen...; wöchentlich. **II** *adv* wöchentlich. **III** *s* Wochen(zeit)schrift *f,* -zeitung *f.*

wee·ny ['wi:nɪ] *adj* F klitzeklein, winzig.

weep [wi:p] (*irr*) **I** *v/i* **1.** weinen (*for, with* vor *Freude etc*; *for* um *j-n*; *over* über *acc*). **2.** nässen (*Wunde*). **II** *v/t* **3.** Tränen weinen. **'weep·ing** *adj:* ~ *willow* ⚘ Trauerweide *f.* **'weep·y** *adj* F **1.** weinerlich. **2.** rührselig.

'wee-wee → **wee**[2].

weigh [weɪ] **I** *v/t* **1.** (ab)wiegen. **2.** *fig.* abwägen (*against* gegen). **3.** ~ *anchor* ⚓ den Anker lichten. **II** *v/i* **4.** *10 Kilo etc* wiegen. **5.** ~ *on fig.* lasten auf (*dat*). **6.** ~ *with fig.* Gewicht haben bei. *Verbindungen mit Adverbien:* **weigh** ↓ **down** *v/t* niederdrücken (*a. fig.*): *be ~ed down with* überladen sein mit; *fig.* niedergedrückt werden von. ~ *in v/i* **1.** ~ *at* (*Sport*) *100 Kilo etc* auf die Waage bringen. **2.** F sich einschalten (*with* mit). ~ *out v/t* ab-, auswiegen. ~ *up v/t et.* abwägen; *j-n* einschätzen.

weight [weɪt] **I** *s* **1.** *allg.* Gewicht *n:* ~*s and measures* *pl* Maße u. Gewichte *pl;* *it's five kilos in* ~ es wiegt fünf Kilo; *what's your* ~? wieviel wiegst du?, wie schwer bist du?; *gain* (*od.* *put on*) ~ zunehmen; *lose* ~ abnehmen. **2.** Last *f* (*a. fig.*): *I can't lift* ~*s* ich kann nicht schwer heben; *be a ~ on s.o.'s mind* j-n belasten; *his decision took a ~ off my mind* bei s-r Entscheidung fiel mir ein Stein vom Herzen. **3.** *fig.* Bedeutung *f:* *not to attach any* ~ *to s.th.* e-r Sache keine Bedeutung bei. kein Gewicht beimessen; *throw one's* ~ *about* (*od.* *around*) F sich aufspielen od. wichtig machen; → *carry* 5. **II** *v/t* **4.** beschweren: ~ *down* → *weigh down;* *be* ~*ed in favo(u)r of* (*against*) bevorteilen (benachteiligen). **~ cat·e·go·ry** *s* Sport: Gewichtsklasse *f.*

weight·less ['weɪtlɪs] *adj* □ schwerelos.

weight| **lift·er** *s* Sport: Gewichtheber *m.* **~ lift·ing** *s* Sport: Gewichtheben *n.* **~ train·ing** *s* Sport: Gewichttraining *n.*

weight·y ['weɪtɪ] *adj* □ **1.** schwer. **2.** *fig.* gewichtig; schwerwiegend.

weir [wɪə] *s* Wehr *n.*

weird [wɪəd] *adj* □ **1.** unheimlich. **2.** *fig.* sonderbar, verrückt.

weird·o ['wɪədəʊ] *pl* -os *s* F irrer Typ.

welch → **welsh**[2].

wel·come ['welkəm] **I** *int* **1.** ~ *back* (*od.* *home!*) willkommen zu Hause!; ~ *to England!* willkommen in England! **II** *adj* **2.** willkommen: *you are* ~ *to do it* Sie können es gerne tun; *you're* ~ nichts zu danken!, keine Ursache!, bitte sehr! **3.** angenehm. **III** *v/t* **4.** begrüßen (*a. fig.*). **IV** *s* **5.** Empfang *m:* *give s.o. a warm* ~ j-m e-n herzlichen Empfang bereiten. **6.** *outstay* (*od.* *overstay*) *one's* ~ j-s Gastfreundschaft überstrapazieren *od.* zu lange in Anspruch nehmen.

weld [weld] **I** *v/t* schweißen: ~ *together* zs.-, verschweißen. **II** *s* Schweißnaht *f*, -stelle *f*. **'weld·er** *s* Schweißer *m*.

wel·fare ['welfeə] *s* **1.** Wohl *n*, (*e-r Person a.*) Wohlergehen *n*. **2.** *Am.* Sozialhilfe *f*: *be on* ~ Sozialhilfe beziehen. ~ **state** *s* Wohlfahrtsstaat *m*.

well¹ [wel] **I** *adv* **1.** gut: (*all*) ~ *and good* schön u. gut; *as* ~ ebenso, auch; *as* ~ *as* sowohl ... als auch; nicht nur ..., sondern auch; (*just*) *as* ~ ebenso(gut), genauso(gut); *just as* ~ das macht nichts; *very* ~ also gut, na gut; *I couldn't very* ~ *say no* ich konnte schlecht nein sagen; *be* ~ *in with s.o.* auf gutem Fuß mit j-m stehen; *do* ~ gut daran tun (*to do* zu tun); ~ *done!* bravo!; → *off* 11. **2.** gut, gründlich: *be* ~ *aware of s.th.* sich e-r Sache voll u. ganz bewußt sein; *shake* ~ kräftig schütteln. **3.** weit: *in advance* schon lange vorher. **II** *int* **4.** nun, also (*oft unübersetzt*). **5.** ~, ~! na so was! **III** *adj* **6.** gesund: *not to feel* ~ sich nicht wohl fühlen. **7.** *all's* ~ *that ends* ~ Ende gut, alles gut; *it's all very* ~ *for you to criticize* (*laugh*) du kannst leicht kritisieren (du hast gut lachen).

well² [~] **I** *s* **1.** Brunnen *m*: ~ *water* Brunnenwasser *n*. **2.** (*Öl*)Quelle *f*. **3.** △ (*Aufzugs- etc*)Schacht *m*. **II** *v/i* **4.** *a.* ~ *out* quellen (*from* aus): *tears* ~*ed* (*up*) *in her eyes* die Tränen stiegen ihr in die Augen.

we'll [wi:l] F *für* **we will.**

,well·-ad'vised *adj* klug (*Plan etc*). ~**·ap'point·ed** *adj* gutausgestattet. ~**-'bal·anced** *adj* **1.** ausgeglichen (*Person*). **2.** ausgewogen (*Ernährung etc*). ~**·be·ing** *s* Wohl(ergehen) *n*: *give s.o. a sense of* ~ j-n mit Wohlbehagen erfüllen. ~**·'cho·sen** *adj* gutgewählt: *with a few* ~ *words* mit einigen wohlgesetzten Worten. ~**·'done** *adj* durchgebraten (*Steak*). ~**·'earned** *adj* wohlverdient. ~**·'found·ed** *adj* (wohl)begründet. ~**·'groomed** *adj* gepflegt. ~**·'heeled** *adj* F betucht. **,in·'formed** *adj* **1.** gutunterrichtet. **2.** (vielseitig) gebildet. ~**·in'ten·tioned** → **well-meaning.** ~**·'kept** *adj* **1.** gepflegt. **2.** streng gehütet (*Geheimnis*). ~**·'known** *adj*

(wohl)bekannt. ~**·'lined** *adj* F **1.** voller Geld, (*Brieftasche*) dick. **2.** voll (*Magen*). ~**·'mean·ing** *adj* wohlmeinend (*Person*), (*Rat etc a.*) gut-, wohlgemeint. ~**·'meant** *adj* gut-, wohlgemeint. ~**·'nigh** ['~naɪ] *adv* beinahe, nahezu. ~**·'off** **I** *adj* begütert, reich. **II** *s*: *the* ~ *pl* die Reichen *pl*. ~**·pro'por·tioned** *adj* wohlproportioniert. ~**·read** [,~'red] *adj* belesen. ~**·'thought-of** *adj* angesehen, geachtet. ~**·to-'do** F → *well-off.* ~**·'worn** *adj* **1.** abgenutzt, abgetragen. **2.** *fig.* abgedroschen.

Welsh¹ [welʃ] **I** *adj* **1.** walisisch. **II** *s* **2.** *the* ~ *pl* die Waliser *pl*. **3.** *ling.* Walisisch *n*.

welsh² [~] *v/i*: ~ *on* F Schulden nicht bezahlen; *Versprechen* nicht halten.

Welsh·man ['welʃmən] *s* (*irr man*) Waliser *m*. '~**·wom·an** *s* (*irr woman*) Waliserin *f*.

welt [welt] *s* Striemen *m*.

wel·ter·weight ['weltəweɪt] (*Sport*) **I** *s* Weltergewicht(ler *m*) *n*. **II** *adj* Weltergewichts...

went [went] *pret von* **go.**

wept [wept] *pret u. pp von* **weep.**

were [wɜ:] *du warst, Sie waren, wir, sie waren, ihr wart.*

we're [wɪə] F *für* **we are.**

weren't [wɜ:nt] F *für* **were not.**

were·wolf ['wɪəwʊlf] *s* (*irr wolf*) Werwolf *m*.

west [west] **I** *s* **1.** Westen *m*: *in the* ~ *of* im Westen von (*od. gen*); *to the* ~ *of* → 5. **2.** *the* ♀ *Br.* Westengland *n*; *Am.* die Weststaaten *pl*; *pol.* der Westen: ~ *wild* 1. **II** *adj* **3.** West..., westlich. **III** *adv* **4.** westwärts, nach Westen: *go* ~ F draufgehen (*sterben, kaputtgehen*); ~ *wild* 1. **5.** ~ *of* westlich von (*od. gen*). '~**·bound** *adj* nach Westen gehend *od.* fahrend.

west·er·ly ['westəlɪ] **I** *adj* westlich, West... **II** *adv* von *od.* nach Westen. **west·ern** ['~tən] *adj* westlich, West... **II** *s* Western *m*. '**west·ern·er** *s* **1.** Bewohner(in) des Westens (*e-s Landes*). **2.** ♀ Weststaatler(in). **west·ern·most** ['~məʊst] *adj* westlichst.

west·ward ['westwəd] *adj u. adv* westlich, westwärts, nach Westen. '**west·wards** *adv* → **westward.**

wet [wet] **I** *adj* □ **1.** naß, (*Farbe etc a.*) feucht: *be* (*still*) ~ *behind the ears* F noch grün *od.* feucht *od.* noch nicht trocken hinter den Ohren sein; **~ blanket** F Spiel-, Spaßverderber(in); → **paint** 5, **through** 3. **2.** regnerisch. **3.** *Br.* F weichlich: **don't be so ~!** sei nicht so ein Waschlappen! **II** *s* **4.** Nässe *f.* **III** *v/t* (*mst irr*) **5.** naß machen, anfeuchten: **~ one's bed** ins Bett machen; **~ o.s.** in die Hose machen; **~ one's whistle** F e-n zur Brust nehmen.

weth·er ['weðə] *s zo.* Hammel *m.*

we've [wi:v] F *für* we have.

whack [wæk] *s* F **1.** (knallender) Schlag. **2.** (An)Teil *m.* **3.** Versuch *m:* **have a ~ at s.th.** et. probieren. **whacked** *adj:* **be ~** (**out**) F geschlaucht *od.* kaputt sein. **'whack·ing** F **I** *adj u. adv:* **~** (**great**) Mords..., riesig. **II** *s:* **give s.o. a ~** j-m e-e Tracht Prügel verpassen.

whale [weɪl] *s zo.* Wal *m:* **have a ~ of a time** F sich prächtig amüsieren.

wharf [wɔ:f] *pl* **wharfs, wharves** [wɔ:vz] *s* Kai *m.*

what [wɒt] **I** *interrogative pron* **1.** was: **~'s for lunch?** was gibt's zum Mittagessen?; **~ for?** wozu?; **~ about ...?** wie wär's mit ...?; **~ if ...?** was ist, wenn ...?; → **age** 1, **like**[1], **so** 6, *etc.* **II** *relative pron* **2.** was: **he told me ~ to do** er sagte mir, was ich tun sollte; **know ~'s ~** F wissen, was Sache ist; **tell s.o. ~'s ~** F j-m Bescheid stoßen. **III** *adj* **3.** was für ein(e), welch(er, e, es): **~ luck!** so ein Glück!; **~ age** 1, **colour** 1, **pity** 2, *etc.* **4.** alle, die; alles, was: **I gave him ~ money I had** ich gab ihm, was ich an Geld hatte. **~'ev·er I** *pron* **1.** was (auch immer); alles, was. **2.** egal, was. **II** *adj* **3.** welch(er, e, es) ... auch (immer). **4.** *no* **... ~** überhaupt kein(e). **~ for** *s:* **I'll give him ~!** bsd. Br. F dem werd' ich's zeigen!

whats·it ['wɒtsɪt] *s* F Dingsbums *n.* **,what·so'ev·er →** **whatever** 1, 2, 4.

wheat [wi:t] *s* ♣ Weizen *m:* **separate the ~ from the chaff** *fig.* die Spreu vom Weizen trennen. **~ germ** *s* Weizenkern *m.*

whee·dle ['wi:dl] *v/t:* **~ s.o. into doing s.th.** j-m so lange schöntun, bis er et. tut; **~ s.th. out of s.o.** j-m et. abschmeicheln.

wheel [wi:l] **I** *s* **1.** Rad *n:* → **fifth** 1, **meal**[1], **oil** 4, **shoulder** 1, **spoke**[2]. **2.** F a) *pl* fahrbarer Untersatz, Wagen *m,* b)

(Fahr)Rad *n.* **3.** ♣, *mot.* Steuer *n:* **be at the ~** *mot.* am Steuer sitzen (♣ stehen); **take the ~** das Steuer übernehmen. **II** *v/t* **4.** Fahrrad, Patienten im Rollstuhl etc schieben, Servierwagen etc a. rollen. **III** *v/i* **5. ~ about** (*od.* [*a*]**round**) herumfahren, -wirbeln. **6.** kreisen (*Vogel*). **7. ~ and deal** F *contp.* Geschäfte machen. **'~,bar·row** *s* Schubkarre(n *m*) *f.* **'~ base** *s mot.* Radstand *m.* **,~'chair** *s* ♣ Rollstuhl *m.* **~ clamp** *s Br.* Radkralle *f,* Parkriegel *m.*

wheeled [wi:ld] *adj* **1. ~ vehicle** Räderfahrzeug *n.* **2.** *in Zssgn* ...räd(e)rig. **,wheel·er-'deal·er** *s* F *contp.* Geschäftemacher *m.*

wheeze [wi:z] *v/i* keuchen, pfeifend atmen.

when [wen] **I** *adv* **1.** *fragend:* wann. **2.** *relativ:* **the day ~** der Tag, an dem *od.* als; **the time ~ it happened** die Zeit, in *od.* zu der es geschah. **II** *cj* **3.** wann. **4.** als: **he broke a leg ~ skiing** er brach sich beim Skifahren ein Bein. **5.** wenn: **say ~!** F sag halt!, sag, wenn du genug hast! **III** *pron* **6. since ~?** seit wann? **~'ev·er** *cj* wann auch (immer); jedesmal, wenn.

where [weə] **I** *adv* (*fragend u. relativ*) wo: **~ ...** (**from**)**?** woher?; **~ ...** (**to**)**?** wohin? **II** *cj* wo; wohin. **'~a·bouts** *s pl* (*a. sg konstruiert*) Verbleib *m* (*e-r Sache*), (*e-r Person a.*) Aufenthalt(sort) *m.* **~'as** *cj* während, wohingegen. **~'by** *adv* **1.** wodurch, womit. **2.** wonach. **,~·up'on** *cj* worauf(hin).

wher·ev·er [weər'evə] *adv* wo(hin) auch (immer); ganz gleich, wo(hin).

whet [wet] *v/t* **1.** Messer etc schärfen. **2.** *fig.* Appetit anregen.

wheth·er ['weðə] *cj* ob.

whey [weɪ] *s* Molke *f.*

which [wɪtʃ] **I** *interrogative pron* **1.** welch(er, e, es): **~ of you?** wer von euch? **II** *relative pron* **2.** welch(er, e, es); der, die, das. **3.** *auf den vorhergehenden Satz bezüglich:* was. **III** *adj* **4.** *fragend u. relativ:* welch(er, e, es). **~'ev·er** *pron u. adj* welch(er, e, es) auch (immer); ganz gleich, welch(er, e, es).

whiff [wɪf] *s* **1.** Luftzug *m,* Hauch *m.* **2.** Duft(wolke *f*) *m.* **3.** *fig.* Anflug *m,* Hauch *m* (**of** von).

while [waɪl] **I** *s* **1.** Weile *f:* **a little ~ ago**

vor kurzem; **for a ~** e-e Zeitlang; **e-n Augenblick**; → **once** 1. **II** cj 2. während. 3. obwohl. **III** v/t 4. **~ away** sich *die Zeit* vertreiben (**by doing s.th.** mit et.).

whilst [waɪlst] → **while** II.

whim [wɪm] s Laune f: **as the ~ takes one, at ~** nach Lust u. Laune. Laune.

whim·per ['wɪmpə] **I** v/i winseln (*Hund*); wimmern (*Person*). **II** v/t wimmern. **III** s Winseln n; Wimmern n.

whim·si·cal ['wɪmzɪkl] adj □ 1. wunderlich. 2. launenhaft.

whim·sy ['wɪmzɪ] s 1. Wunderlichkeit f. 2. Spleen m.

whine [waɪn] **I** v/i 1. jaulen (*Hund*). 2. jammern (**about** über acc). **II** s 3. Jaulen n. 4. Gejammer n. **'whin·er** s Jammerer m.

whin·ny ['wɪnɪ] **I** v/i wiehern. **II** s Wiehern n.

whip [wɪp] **I** s 1. Peitsche f. 2. parl. Br. Einpeitscher m. 3. gastr. Creme f. **II** v/t 4. (aus)peitschen: **~ into shape** F j-n, et. auf Zack bringen. **5.** Sahne etc schlagen. 6. bsd. Sport: F überfahren (*hoch schlagen*). 7. Br. F klauen. **III** v/i 8. sausen, flitzen, (*Wind*) fegen.
Verbindungen mit Adverbien:

whip| **back** v/i zurückschnellen (*Ast etc*). **~ off** v/t sich *ein Kleidungsstück* herunterreißen. **~ out** v/t *Revolver etc* zücken. **~ up** v/t 1. → **whip** 5. 2. *Interesse etc* entfachen. 3. *Essen etc* herzaubern.

'whip·cord s Peitschenschnur f. **'~lash** s 1. Peitschenschnur f. 2. Peitschenhieb m: **~** (**injury**) ℱ Schleudertrauma n.

whipped [wɪpt] adj: **~ cream** Schlagsahne f, -rahm m.

whip·ping ['wɪpɪŋ] adj: **~boy** Prügelknabe m; **~ cream** Schlagsahne f, -rahm m. **'whip·py** adj biegsam, elastisch.

'whip-round s Br. F Sammlung f (*im Büro etc*): **have a ~** sammeln (**for** für).

whir bsd. Am. → **whirr**.

whirl [wɜːl] **I** v/i 1. wirbeln: **my head is ~ing** mir schwirrt der Kopf. **II** v/t 2. wirbeln. 3. **the car ~ed us off to** der Wagen brachte uns auf schnellstem Weg zu od. nach. **III** s 3. Wirbeln n; Wirbel m: **my head's in a ~** mir schwirrt der Kopf; **give s.th. a ~** F et.

ausprobieren. 5. *fig.* Trubel m, Wirbel m.

whirl·i·gig ['wɜːlɪgɪg] s 1. Kreisel m. 2. Karussell n.

'whirl·pool s 1. Strudel m (*a. fig.*). 2 Whirlpool m (*Unterwassermassagebecken*). **'~wind** s Wirbelwind m.

whirr [wɜː] **I** v/i s Surren n.

whisk [wɪsk] **I** s 1. Wedel m. 2. gastr. Schneebesen m. **II** v/t 3. **~ its tail** mit dem Schwanz schlagen; **~ away** *Fliegen etc* ver-, wegscheuchen. 4. *Eiweiß* schlagen.

whisk·er ['wɪskə] s 1. Schnurrhaar n: **by a ~** F ganz knapp. 2. pl Backenbart m.

whis·key ['wɪskɪ] s (*amerikanischer od. irischer*) Whisky.

whis·ky ['wɪskɪ] s (*bsd. schottischer*) Whisky: **~ and soda** Whisky Soda; **two whiskies** zwei Whisky.

whis·per ['wɪspə] **I** v/i 1. flüstern, leise sprechen (**to** mit). **II** v/t 2. flüstern, leise sagen: **~ s.th. to s.o.** j-m et. zuflüstern. 3. **it is ~ed that** man munkelt, daß. **III** s 4. Flüstern n: **say s.th. in a ~** et. im Flüsterton sagen. 5. Gerücht n: **I've heard a ~ that** ich habe munkeln hören, daß. **'whis·per·ing** adj: **~ campaign** Verleumdungskampagne f.

whist [wɪst] s Whist n (*Kartenspiel*).

whis·tle ['wɪsl] **I** v/i 1. pfeifen: **~ at** j-m nachpfeifen; **~ for** (nach) j-m, e-m Taxi etc pfeifen; **he can ~ for it** F darauf kann er lange warten. **II** v/t 2. pfeifen. **III** s 3. Pfeife f: **blow one's ~** pfeifen. 4. Pfiff m: **give a ~ of surprise** e-n überraschten Pfiff ausstoßen. 5. → **wet** 5.

white [waɪt] **I** adj 1. allg. weiß: **~ bread** Weißbrot n; **~ coffee** Br. Milchkaffee m, Kaffee m mit Milch; **~ hope** große Hoffnung (*Person*); **~ lie** Notlüge f; **~ man** Weiße m; **~ paper** pol. Weißbuch n; **~ wedding** Hochzeit f in Weiß; **~ wine** Weißwein m. **II** s 2. Weiß n: **dressed in ~** in weiß od. in Weiß gekleidet. 3. oft ♀ Weiße m, f. 4. Eiweiß n; das Weiße (*im Auge*). **~·'col·lar** adj Büro-...: **~ crime** White-collar-Kriminalität f; **~ worker** Büroangestellte m, f.

whit·en ['waɪtn] **I** v/t weiß machen. **II** v/i weiß werden.

'white·wash **I** v/t 1. tünchen, anstreichen, weißen. 2. F et. übertünchen, beschönigen; j-n e-r Mohrenwäsche unterziehen. **II** s **3.** Tünche f. **4.** F Tünche f, Beschönigung f; Mohrenwäsche f.

whit·ish ['waɪtɪʃ] adj weißlich.

Whit·sun ['wɪtsn] s **1.** Pfingstsonntag m. **2.** Pfingsten n od. pl. **Whit Sun·day** [wɪt] → **Whitsun** 1.

whit·tle ['wɪtl] v/t **1.** (zurecht)schnitzen. **2.** fig. ~ **away** Gewinn etc allmählich aufzehren; ~ **down** et. reduzieren (to auf acc).

whiz(z) [wɪz] **I** v/i: ~ **by** (od. past) vorbeizischen. **II** s F As n, Kanone f (at in dat). ~ **kid** s F Senkrechtstarter(in).

who [huː] **I** interrogative pron **1.** wer; wen; wem: **do you think you are?** für wen hältst du dich eigentlich? **II** relative pron. **2.** unverbunden: wer; wen; wem. **3.** verbunden: welch(er, e, es); der, die, das.

who'd [huːd] F für who had; who would.

who·dun·(n)it [ˌhuːˈdʌnɪt] s F Krimi m.

who·ev·er I relative pron wer auch (immer); wen auch (immer); wem auch (immer); egal, wer od. wen od. wem. **II** interrogative pron: ~ **can that be?** wer kann denn das nur sein?

whole [həʊl] **I** adj (□ → **wholly**): ganz: → hog 1. **II** s das Ganze: **the ~ of the town** die ganze Stadt; **as a ~** als Ganzes; **on the ~** im großen (u.) ganzen; alles in allem. ~**·'heart·ed** adj ungeteilt (Aufmerksamkeit), ernsthaft (Versuch etc). ~**·'heart·ed·ly** adv uneingeschränkt, voll u. ganz. '~**·meal** adj Vollkorn...

'whole·sale I s **1.** Großhandel m. **II** adj **2.** Großhandels... **3.** b.s. Massen... **III** adv **4.** en gros. **'whole·sal·er** s Großhändler m.

whole·some ['həʊlsəm] adj □ **1.** gesund. **2.** fig. gut, nützlich.

who'll [huːl] F für who will.

whol·ly ['həʊlɪ] adv gänzlich, völlig.

whom [huːm] **I** interrogative pron wen; wem. **II** relative pron welch(en, e, es), den (die, das); welch(em, er), dem (der): **the children, most of ~ were tired, ...** die Kinder, von denen die meisten müde waren, ...

whoop [huːp] **I** v/i schreien, bsd. jauchzen. **II** v/t: ~ **it up** F auf den Putz hauen. **III** s (bsd. Freuden)Schrei m: ~**s pl** of **victory** Siegesgeschrei n. **'whoop·ing** adj: ~ **cough** ⚕ Keuchhusten m.

whoosh [wuʃ] v/i: ~ **by** (od. past) F vorbeirauschen.

whop·per ['wɒpə] s F **1.** Mordsding n. **2.** faustdicke Lüge. **'whop·ping** adj u. adv F Mords..., riesig: ~ **(big)** lie → **whopper** 2.

whore [hɔː] s Hure f.

who're ['huːə] F für who are.

'whore·house s Bordell n, Freudenhaus n.

whor·tle·ber·ry ['wɜːtlˌberɪ] s ♣ Blau-, Heidelbeere f.

who's [huːz] F für who is; who has.

whose [huːz] **I** interrogative pron wessen: ~ **coat is this?**, ~ **is this coat?** wem gehört dieser Mantel? **II** relative pron dessen, deren.

why [waɪ] adv warum, weshalb: ~ **not go by bus?** warum nimmst du nicht den Bus?

wick [wɪk] s Docht m: **get on s.o.'s ~** Br. F j-m auf den Wecker fallen od. gehen. □

wick·ed ['wɪkɪd] adj □ **1.** gemein, niederträchtig. **2.** fig. unerhört.

wick·er ['wɪkə] adj Korb...: ~ **basket** Weidenkorb m.

wide [waɪd] **I** adj (□ → **widely**) **1.** breit. **2.** weit offen, aufgerissen (Augen). **3.** fig. umfangreich (Wissen etc), vielfältig (Interessen etc). **4.** → **mark**⁵ 5. **II** adv **5.** weit. **6.** go ~ (Sport) danebengehen. ~**·'an·gle** adj: ~ **lens** phot. Weitwinkelobjektiv n. ~**·a'wake** adj **1.** hellwach. **2.** fig. aufgeweckt, wach. ~**·'eyed** adj **1.** mit großen od. aufgerissenen Augen. **2.** fig. naiv.

wide·ly ['waɪdlɪ] adv **1.** weit (a. fig.): **it is ~ known** that es ist weithin bekannt, daß; ~ **travel(l)ed** weitgereist. **2.** ~ **different** völlig verschieden. **'wid·en I** v/t verbreitern. **II** v/i breiter werden.

wide·-o·pen → **wide** 2. '~**·spread** adj weitverbreitet.

wid·ow ['wɪdəʊ] s Witwe f. **'wid·owed** adj verwitwet: **be** ~ verwitwet sein; Witwe(r) werden.

width [wɪdθ] s **1.** Breite f: **six feet in ~** sechs Fuß breit; **what is the ~ of ...?** wie breit ist ...? **2.** Bahn f (Stoff etc).

wield [wiːld] v/t Einfluß, Macht ausüben.

wife [waɪf] pl **wives** [waɪvz] s (Ehe)Frau f, Gattin f. ~ **swap·ping** s F Partnertausch m.

wig [wɪg] s Perücke f.

wig·ging ['wɪgɪŋ] s: *give s.o. a ~ Br.* F j-m e-e Standpauke halten.

wig·gle ['wɪgl] v/t u. v/i wackeln (mit).

wig·wam ['wɪgwæm] s Wigwam m.

wild [waɪld] **I** adj □ **1.** allg. wild: *the ♀ West* der Wilde Westen; → *oats.* **2.** stürmisch (*Wind, Applaus etc*). **3.** außer sich (*with vor dat*). **4.** verrückt (*Idee etc*). **5.** *it was just a ~ guess* ich hab' einfach drauflosgeraten. **II** adv **6.** F *go ~* ausflippen; *run ~* Amok laufen; *let one's children run ~* s-e Kinder machen lassen, was sie wollen. **III** s **7.** *in the ~* in freier Wildbahn. '**~·cat I** s Wildkatze f. **II** adj: *~ strike* wilder Streik. '**~·fire** s: *spread like ~* sich wie ein Lauffeuer verbreiten. **~·'goose** adj: *be a ~ chase* vergebliche Mühe od. ein Metzgergang sein. '**~·life** s Tier- u. Pflanzenwelt f.

wil·ful ['wɪlfʊl] adj □ **1.** eigensinnig. **2.** absichtlich, bsd. ✠ vorsätzlich.

will¹ [wɪl] s **1.** Wille m: *~ to live* Lebenswille; *against one's ~* gegen s-n Willen; *at ~* nach Belieben; *of one's own free ~* aus freien Stücken; *I can't do that with the best ~ in the world* ich kann das (auch) beim besten Willen nicht tun; *take the ~ for the deed* den guten Willen für die Tat nehmen. **2.** *a. last ~ and testament* Letzter Wille, Testament n: *make one's ~* sein Testament machen; → *remember* 3.

will² [~] v/aux **1.** *Futur:* *I'll be back in 10 minutes* ich bin in 10 Minuten zurück. **2.** *Bereitschaft, Entschluß:* *I won't go there again* ich gehe da nicht mehr hin; *the door won't shut* die Tür schließt nicht; *~ you have some coffee?* möchtest du e-e Tasse Kaffee? **3.** *Bitte:* *shut the window, ~ you?* mach bitte das Fenster zu. **4.** *Wiederholung:* *accidents ~ happen* Unfälle wird es immer geben; *boys ~ be boys* Jungen sind nun einmal so. **5.** *Vermutung:* *that ~ be my sister* das wird od. dürfte m-e Schwester sein.

will·ful *Am.* → **wilful.**

wil·lies ['wɪlɪz] s pl: *give s.o. the ~* F j-m unheimlich sein.

will·ing ['wɪlɪŋ] adj □ **1.** bereit (*to do* zu tun): *~ to compromise* kompromißbereit; *God ~* so Gott will. **2.** (be-reit)willig. '**will·ing·ness** s **1.** Bereitschaft f: *~ to compromise* Kompro-

mißbereitschaft. **2.** (Bereit)Willigkeit f.

wil·low ['wɪloʊ] s ♀ Weide f. '**wil·low·y** adj gertenschlank.

'**will,pow·er** s Willenskraft f.

wil·ly-nil·ly [,wɪlɪ'nɪlɪ] adv wohl od. übel.

wilt [wɪlt] v/i **1.** verwelken, welk werden. **2.** schlaff werden.

wil·y ['waɪlɪ] adj gerissen, raffiniert.

win [wɪn] **I** s **1.** bsd. Sport: Sieg m: *have a ~* e-n Sieg erzielen; e-n Gewinn machen. **II** v/t (irr) **2.** gewinnen: → *day* 2. **3.** j-m et. einbringen. **III** v/i (irr) **4.** gewinnen, siegen: *OK, you ~* okay, du hast gewonnen.

Verbindungen mit Adverbien:

win| back v/t zurückgewinnen. ~ **out** → *win through.* ~ **o·ver,** ~ **round** v/t j-n für sich gewinnen: *win s.o. over to* j-n gewinnen für. ~ **through** v/i sich durchsetzen.

wince [wɪns] v/i zs.-zucken (*at* bei).

winch [wɪntʃ] **⊕** *I* s Winde f. **II** v/t winden.

wind¹ [wɪnd] **I** s **1.** Wind m: *a load of ~* F leeres Geschwätz; *there's s.th. in the ~ fig.* es liegt et. in der Luft; *find out (od. see) which way the ~ blows fig.* sehen, woher der Wind weht; *get ~ of s.th. fig.* Wind von et. bekommen; *get the ~ up* F Angst kriegen; *put the ~ up s.o.* F j-m Angst einjagen; *sail close to the ~ ♻* hart am Wind segeln; *fig.* sich hart an der Grenze des Erlaubten bewegen; *take the ~ out of s.o.'s sails fig.* j-m den Wind aus den Segeln nehmen. **2.** Atem m: *get one's ~* wieder zu Atem kommen; *get one's second ~* (*bsd. Sport*) die zweite Luft bekommen. **3.** ✿ Blähungen pl: *it gives me ~* davon bekomme ich Blähungen. **4.** ♫ die Blasinstrumente pl; die Bläser pl. **II** v/t **5.** j-m den Atem nehmen od. verschlagen. **6.** *hunt.* wittern.

wind² [waɪnd] **I** s **1.** Umdrehung f. **II** v/t (irr) **2.** drehen (an dat); Uhr etc aufziehen. **3.** wickeln (*round* um). **III** v/i (irr) **4.** sich winden od. schlängeln (*Pfad etc*).

Verbindungen mit Adverbien:

wind| back v/t Film etc zurückspulen. ~ **down I** v/t **1.** Autofenster etc herunterdrehen, -kurbeln. **2.** Produktion etc reduzieren. **II** v/i **3.** F sich entspannen. ~ **for·ward** v/t Film etc weiterspulen. ~

up I *v/t* **1.** *Autofenster etc* hochdrehen, -kurbeln. **2.** *Uhr etc* aufziehen. **3.** *Versammlung etc* beschließen (**with** mit). **4.** *Unternehmen* auflösen. **II** *v/i* **5.** F landen (**in** in *dat*): ~ **doing s.th.** am Ende et. tun; **you'll ~ with a heart attack** du kriegst noch mal e-n Herzinfarkt.

wind|·bag ['wɪndbæg] *s* F Schwätzer(in). '~**break** *s* Windschutz *m*. '~**fall** *s* **1.** *pl* Fallobst *n*. **2.** unverhofftes Geschenk, unverhoffter Gewinn.

wind·ing ['waɪndɪŋ] *adj* gewunden (*Pfad etc*): ~ **stairs** *pl* Wendeltreppe *f*.

wind| in·stru·ment [wɪnd] *s* ♩ Blasinstrument *n*. '~**jam·mer** ['·ˌdʒæmə] *s* ⚓ Windjammer *m*.

wind·lass ['wɪndləs] *s* ⚙ Winde *f*.

wind·less ['wɪndlɪs] *adj* windstill.

wind·mill ['wɪnmɪl] *s* Windmühle *f*.

win·dow ['wɪndəʊ] *s* **1.** Fenster *n*. **2.** Schaufenster *n*. **3.** Schalter *m* (*in Bank etc*). ~ **box** *s* Blumenkasten *m*. ~ **clean·er** *s* Fensterputzer *m*. ~ **dress·er** *s* Schaufensterdekorateur(in). ~ **dress·ing** *s* **1.** Schaufensterdekoration *f*. **2.** *fig.* Mache *f*. '~**pane** *s* Fensterscheibe *f*. ~ **seat** *s* Fensterplatz *m*. ~ **shade** *s* *Am.* Rouleau *n*. ~ **shop** *v/i*: **go ~ping** e-n Schaufensterbummel machen. '~**sill** *s* Fensterbank *f*, -brett *n*.

wind|·pipe ['wɪndpaɪp] *s* *anat.* Luftröhre *f*. '~**screen** *s* *mot. bsd. Br.* Windschutzscheibe *f*: ~ **wiper** Scheibenwischer *m*. '~**shield** *Am.* → **windscreen**. '~**sock** *s* Windsack *m*. '~**surf·er** *s* Windsurfer(in). '~**surf·ing** *s* Windsurfing *n*. '~**swept** *adj* (vom Wind) zerzaust. '~**tun·nel** *s* Windkanal *m*.

wind·ward ['wɪndwəd] ⚓ **I** *adv* luvwärts. **II** *s* Luv(seite) *f*.

wind·y ['wɪndɪ] *adj* □ **1.** windig. **2.** F blähend.

wine [waɪn] *s* Wein *m*. ~ **bar** *s* Weinlokal *n*. ~ **bot·tle** *s* Weinflasche *f*. ~ **glass** *s* Weinglas *n*. ~ **list** *s* Weinkarte *f*.

wing [wɪŋ] *s* **1.** *allg.* Flügel *m*: **take s.o. under one's ~** *fig.* j-n unter s-e Fittiche nehmen. **2.** ✈ Tragfläche *f*. **3.** *mot. Br.* Kotflügel *m*. '**wing·er** *s* Sport: Flügelstürmer(in).

wing| nut *s* ⚙ Flügelmutter *f*. '~**span**, '~**spread** *s* ✈, *orn.* Flügelspannweite *f*.

wink [wɪŋk] **I** *v/i* zwinkern: ~ **at** j-m zu-

zwinkern; *et.* geflissentlich übersehen. **II** *v/t*: ~ **one's lights** *mot. Br.* blinken. **III** *s* Zwinkern *n*: **with a ~ of the eye** augenzwinkernd; **give s.o. a ~** j-m zuzwinkern; **I didn't get a ~ of sleep** (*od.* **I didn't sleep a ~**) **last night** ich habe letzte Nacht kein Auge zugetan; → **forty** I. '**wink·er** *s* *mot. Br.* F Blinker *m*.

win·kle ['wɪŋkl] *v/t*: ~ **out** *bsd. Br.* F Wahrheit *etc* herausholen (**of** aus).

win·ner ['wɪnə] *s* **1.** Gewinner(in), (*bsd. Sport*) Sieger(in). **2.** **be a real winner** F ein Riesenerfolg sein. '**win·ning I** *adj* **1.** siegreich, *Sieg...*, *Sieges...*: ~ **post** Zielpfosten *m*. **2.** *fig.* gewinnend (*Lächeln etc*). **II** *s* *pl* **3.** Gewinn *m*.

win·ter ['wɪntə] **I** *s* Winter *m*: **in** (**the**) ~ im Winter. **II** *adj* Winter...: ~ **sports** *pl* Wintersport *m*. **III** *v/i* überwintern; den Winter verbringen. '**win·ter·ize** *v/t* *Am. Auto etc* winterfest machen. '**win·ter·y** → **wintry**.

'**win·ter·time** *s* Winter(zeit *f*) *m*: **in** (**the**) ~ im Winter.

win·try ['wɪntrɪ] *adj* **1.** winterlich, Winter...: ~ **clouds** *pl* Schneewolken *pl*. **2.** *fig.* frostig (*Lächeln*).

wipe [waɪp] **I** *v/t*: **give s.th. a ~** et. abwischen. **II** *v/t* *Tisch etc* (ab)wischen; *Krümel etc* wischen (**off** von): ~ **one's feet** (**shoes**) sich die Füße (Schuhe) abputzen (**on** auf *dat*); ~ **one's nose** sich die Nase putzen; ~ **clean** *Tafel etc* abwischen; **that'll ~ the smile off his face** *fig.* da wird ihm das Lachen vergehen; ~ **the floor with s.o.** F j-n fertigmachen.

Verbindungen mit Adverbien:

wipe| a·way *v/t* wegwischen, sich *die Tränen* ab- *od.* wegwischen. ~ **off** *v/t* ab-, wegwischen. ~ **out** *v/t* **1.** auswischen. **2.** *Menschen* auslöschen, *Rasse* ausrotten. **3.** *Gewinn etc* zunichte machen. **4.** F j-n schlauchen. ~ **up** *v/t* aufwischen.

wip·er ['waɪpə] *s* *mot.* (Scheiben)Wischer *m*.

wire ['waɪə] **I** *s* **1.** Draht *m*. **2.** ⚡ Leitung *f*. **3.** *Am.* Telegramm *n*. **II** *v/t* ~ **up** Leitungen verlegen in (*dat*). **5.** *Am.* j-m ein Telegramm schicken; j-m et. telegrafieren. ~ **net·ting** *s* Maschendraht *m*. '~**tap** *v/t* *u. v/i*, *j-s* Telefon abhören. ~ **wool** *s* Stahlwolle *f*.

wir·y ['waɪərɪ] *adj* drahtig (*Figur etc*).

wis·dom ['wɪzdəm] *s* Weisheit *f*, Klugheit *f*. **~ tooth** *s* (*irr tooth*) Weisheitszahn *m*.

wise [waɪz] **I** *adj* (□ → **wisely**) weise, klug: *you were ~ to do that* es war klug von dir, das zu tun; *it's easy to be ~ after the event* hinterher kann man leicht klüger sein; *be none the ~r* F nicht klüger sein als vorher; *get ~ to s.th.* F et. spitzkriegen; *~ guy* F Klugschwätzer *m*. **II** *v/t*: *~ up bsd. Am.* F *j-n* aufklären (*to* über *acc*). **III** *v/i*: *~ up to bsd. Am.* F et. spitzkriegen. '**~crack** F **I** *v/i* witzeln (*about* über *acc*). **II** *s* Witzelei *f*: *you and your ~s* contp. du u. deine dummen Sprüche.

wise·ly ['waɪzlɪ] *adv* **1.** weise, klug. **2.** klugerweise.

wish [wɪʃ] **I** *v/t* **1.** *I ~ he were here* ich wünschte od. wollte, er wäre hier. **2.** wollen: *I ~ to make a complaint* ich möchte mich beschweren. **3.** *j-m* et. wünschen: *~ s.o. well* j-m alles Gute wünschen; *I wouldn't ~ that on my worst enemy* das würde ich nicht einmal m-m ärgsten Feind wünschen. **II** *v/i* **4.** *if you ~* (*to*) wenn du willst. **5.** *~ for s.th.* sich et. wünschen. **III** *s* **6.** Wunsch *m* (*for* nach): *make a ~* sich et. wünschen; (*with*) *best ~es* Herzliche Grüße (*Briefschluß*); *best ~es on passing your exam* herzlichen Glückwunsch zur bestandenen Prüfung; *send one's best ~es for s.o.'s birthday* j-m e-n Glückwunsch zum Geburtstag schicken. '**~bone** *s* Gabelbein *n*, -knochen *m*.

wish·ful ['wɪʃfʊl] *adj*: *~ thinking* Wunschdenken *n*.

wish·y-wash·y ['wɪʃɪ,wɒʃɪ] *adj* F **1.** labb(e)rig. **2.** *fig.* lasch (*Person*); verschwommen (*Vorstellung etc*).

wisp [wɪsp] *s* (*Gras-, Haar*)Büschel *n*.

wist·ful ['wɪstfʊl] *adj* □ wehmütig.

wit [wɪt] *s* **1.** Geist *m*, Witz *m*. **2.** geistreicher Mensch. **3.** *a. pl* Verstand *m*: *be at one's ~'s end* mit s-r Weisheit am Ende sein; *frighten s.o. out of his ~s* j-n zu Tode erschrecken; *keep one's ~s about one* e-n klaren Kopf behalten.

witch [wɪtʃ] *s* Hexe *f*. '**~craft** *s* Hexerei *f*. **~ doc·tor** *s* Medizinmann *m*. **~ hunt** *s pol.* Hexenjagd *f* (*for, against* auf *acc*).

with [wɪð] *prp* **1.** *allg.* mit: *are you still ~ me?* kannst du mir folgen? **2.** bei: *she's staying ~ a friend* sie wohnt bei e-r Freundin; → *will*[1], *etc.* **3.** vor (*dat*): → *tremble*[1], *etc.* **4.** von: → *part* 12, *etc.* **5.** für: *are you ~ me or against me?* bist du für od. gegen mich?

with·draw (*irr draw*) **I** *v/t* **1.** Geld abheben (*from* von). **2.** Angebot etc zurückziehen, Anschuldigung etc zurücknehmen: *~ from the market* vom Markt nehmen. **3.** ✕ Truppen zurück-, abziehen. **II** *v/i* **4.** sich zurückziehen. **5.** zurücktreten (*from* von). **with·draw·al** *s* **1.** *make a ~* Geld abheben (*from* von). **2.** Rücknahme *f*. **3.** ✕ Ab-, Rückzug *m*. **4.** Rücktritt *m* (*from* von). **II** *adj* **5.** *~ symptoms pl* ✻ Entziehungs-, Entzugserscheinungen *pl*.

with·er ['wɪðə] *v/i* eingehen, verdorren. '**with·er·ing** *adj* □ vernichtend (*Blick etc*).

with·hold *v/t* (*irr hold*) Informationen, Zahlung etc zurückhalten: *~ s.th. from s.o.* j-m et. vorenthalten. ~'in *prp* innerhalb (*gen*): → *income, sight*[1], *etc.* ~'out *prp* ohne (*acc*). ~'stand *v/t* (*irr stand*) **1.** e-m Angriff etc standhalten. **2.** Beanspruchung etc aushalten.

wit·less ['wɪtlɪs] *adj* □ geistlos.

wit·ness ['wɪtnɪs] **I** *s* **1.** *allg.* Zeuge *m*, Zeugin *f*: *~ for the defence* (*Am. defense*) ⚖ Entlastungszeuge; *~ for the prosecution* ⚖ Belastungszeuge. **II** *v/t* **2.** Zeuge sein (*gen*); Veränderungen etc erleben: *did anybody ~ the accident?* hat j-d den Unfall gesehen? **3.** et. bezeugen, Unterschrift beglaubigen. **4.** ~ denken Sie nur an (*acc*). **III** *v/i* **5.** *~ to* et. bezeugen. **~ box** *s bsd. Br.*, ~ **stand** *s Am.* Zeugenstand *m*.

wit·ti·cism ['wɪtɪsɪzəm] *s* geistreiche od. witzige Bemerkung.

wit·ty ['wɪtɪ] *adj* □ geistreich, witzig.

wives [waɪvz] *pl von* **wife**.

wiz·ard ['wɪzəd] *s* **1.** Zauberer *m*, Hexenmeister *m*. **2.** *fig.* Genie *n* (*at* in *dat*): *financial ~* Finanzgenie.

wiz·ened ['wɪznd] *adj* verhutzelt.

wob·ble ['wɒbl] **I** *v/i* wackeln (*Tisch etc*), zittern (*Stimme etc*), schwabbeln (*Pudding etc*), *mot.* flattern (*Reifen*). **II** *v/t* wackeln an (*dat*).

woe [wəʊ] *s* Kummer *m*, Leid *n*: *~ betide*

you if wehe, wenn du; *tale of* ~ Leidensgeschichte f. **woe·ful** ['~fʊl] adj □ bedauerlich, beklagenswert.

woke [wəʊk] pret von **wake²**. **'wok·en** pp von **wake²**.

wolf [wʊlf] **I** pl **wolves** [wʊlvz] s **1.** zo. Wolf m: *a ~ in sheep's clothing* fig. ein Wolf im Schafspelz; *lone* ~ fig. Einzelgänger m; *cry* ~ fig. blinden Alarm schlagen. **2.** F Schürzenjäger m. **II** v/t **3.** a. ~ *down* F *Essen* hinunterschlingen. ~ **whis·tle** s F bewundernder Pfiff: *give s.o. a* ~ j-m nachpfeifen.

wolves [wʊlvz] pl von **wolf**.

wom·an ['wʊmən] **I** pl **wom·en** ['wɪmɪn] s Frau f. **II** adj: ~ *doctor* Ärztin f; ~ *driver* Frau f am Steuer; ~ *teacher* Lehrerin f. ~ **hat·er** s Frauenhasser m.

wom·an·ish ['wʊmənɪʃ] adj □ contp. weibisch.

wom·an·ize ['wʊmənaɪz] v/i hinter den Frauen hersein. **'wom·an·iz·er** s Schürzenjäger m.

wom·an·kind [,wʊmən'kaɪnd] s das weibliche Geschlecht. **'wom·an·ly** adj fraulich (*Figur* etc); weiblich (*Tugend* etc).

womb [wuːm] s anat. Gebärmutter f, Mutterleib m.

wom·en ['wɪmɪn] pl von **woman**: ~*'s movement* Frauenbewegung f; ~*'s team* (*Sport*) Damenmannschaft f.

won [wʌn] pret u. pp von **win**.

won·der ['wʌndə] **I** v/t **1.** neugierig od. gespannt sein, gern wissen mögen (*if*, *whether* ob; *what* was); sich fragen, überlegen: *I* ~ *if you could help me* vielleicht können Sie mir helfen. **II** v/i **2.** sich wundern, erstaunt sein (*about* über acc). **3.** neugierig od. gespannt sein: *well, I* ~ na, ich weiß nicht (recht). **III** s **4.** Staunen n, Verwunderung f: *in* ~ erstaunt, verwundert. **5.** Wunder n: *nine days'* ~ Eintagsfliege f; *it's a* ~ (*that*) es ist ein Wunder, daß; (*it's*) *no* (od. *small*, *little*) ~ (*that*) kein Wunder, daß; ~*s will never cease!* humor. es geschehen noch Zeichen u. Wunder!; *do* (od. *work*) ~*s* wahre Wunder vollbringen, Wunder wirken (*for* bei). **IV** adj **6.** Wunder... **won·der·ful** ['~fʊl] adj □ wunderbar.

'won·der·land s **1.** Wunderland n. **2.** Paradies n.

won·ky ['wɒŋkɪ] adj Br. F **1.** wack(e)lig. **2.** schwach (*Herz*).

wont [wəʊnt] adj: *be* ~ *to do s.th.* et. zu tun pflegen.

won't [wəʊnt] F *für* **will not**.

woo [wuː] v/t j-n umwerben.

wood [wʊd] s **1.** Holz n: → *touch* 8. **2.** a. pl Wald m: *be out of the* ~ (*Am.* ~*s*) fig. über den Berg sein; *he can't see the* ~ *for trees* fig. er sieht den Wald vor lauter Bäumen nicht. **'~cut** s Holzschnitt m.

wood·ed ['wʊdɪd] adj bewaldet.

wood·en ['wʊdn] adj **1.** hölzern (a. fig.), Holz... **'~,head·ed** adj F dämlich.

wood·land ['wʊdlənd] s Waldland n, Waldung f. **'~,peck·er** s orn. Specht m. **'~pile** s Holzhaufen m, -stoß m. **'~shed** s Holzschuppen m. **~wind** ['~wɪnd] **♪ I** s: *the* ~ die Holzblasinstrumente pl; die Holzbläser pl. **II** adj: ~ *instrument* Holzblasinstrument n. **'~worm** s zo. Holzwurm m.

wood·y ['wʊdɪ] adj **1.** waldig. **2.** holzig.

wool [wʊl] s Wolle f: *pull the* ~ *over s.o.'s eyes* fig. j-m Sand in die Augen streuen. **wool·en** ['~ən] Am., **wool·len** ['~ən] bsd. Br. **I** adj wollen, Woll... **II** s pl Wollsachen pl, -kleidung f. **'wool·ly**, Am. a. **'wool·y** adj **1.** → **woolen** 1. **2.** wollig. **3.** fig. wirr.

Worces·ter sauce ['wʊstə] s Worcestersoße f.

word [wɜːd] s **1.** allg. Wort n: *beyond* ~*s* unbeschreiblich; *by* ~ *of mouth* mündlich; ~ *for* ~ Wort für Wort; wortwörtlich; *in a* ~ in 'einem Wort; *in other* ~*s* mit anderen Worten; *in one's own* ~*s* in eigenen Worten; *in* ~ *and in deed* in Worten u. in Taten; *angry isn't the* ~ *for ...* ärgerlich ist gar kein Ausdruck für ...; *he's a man of few* ~*s* er macht nicht viele Worte; *be as good as one's* ~ halten, was man verspricht; *break one's* ~ sein Wort brechen; *get* (od. *have*) *the final* (od. *last*) ~ das letzte Wort haben (*on* in (dat); *give s.o. one's* ~ (*of hono[u]r*) j-m sein (Ehren)Wort geben; *he always has to have the last* ~ er muß immer das letzte Wort haben; *can I have a* ~ (od. *a few* ~*s*) *with you?* kann ich Sie mal kurz sprechen?; *have* ~*s* e-e Auseinandersetzung haben (*with* mit); *keep one's* ~

Wort halten (**to** gegenüber); *put into ~s et.* ausdrücken, in Worte fassen; *take s.o. at his ~* j-n beim Wort nehmen; → *eat* 2, *edgeways, fail* 5, *mum*¹ I, *play* 4. **2.** *pl* Text *m* (*e-s Lieds etc*). **3.** Nachricht *f*; *there's been no ~ from her for months* wir haben schon seit Monaten nichts mehr von ihr gehört; *send ~ that* Nachricht geben, daß. **II** *v/t* **4.** et. ausdrücken, *Text* abfassen, formulieren. **'word-ing** *s* Wortlaut *m*. **'word-less** *adj* □ wortlos, stumm.

word| or-der *s ling.* Wortstellung *f*. **'~play** *s* Wortspielereien *pl*. **~ pro-cess-or** *s Computer:* Wort-, Textverarbeitungsgerät *n*.

word-y ['wɜːdɪ] *adj* □ wortreich, langatmig.

wore [wɔː] *pret von* **wear.**

work [wɜːk] **I** *s* **1.** *allg.* Arbeit *f*: *at ~* am Arbeitsplatz; *be out of ~* arbeitslos sein; *make short ~ of* kurzen Prozeß machen mit. **2.** Werk *n* (*a. Tat*): → *art* 1. **3.** *pl* (*oft sg konstruiert*) Werk *n*, Fabrik *f*. **4.** *pl* ⚙ Werk *n*, Getriebe *n*: → *spanner*. **5.** *the whole ~s pl* F der ganze Krempel. **II** *v/i* **6.** arbeiten (*at, on* an *dat*): → *rule*² *f*. **7.** funktionieren (*a. fig.*). **III** *v/t* **8.** j-n arbeiten lassen: *~ o.s. into a temper* F sich in e-n Wutausbruch hineinsteigern. **9.** *Maschine etc* bedienen. **10.** bewirken: *how did you ~ it?* F wie hast du das geschafft?; → *miracle, wonder* 5. **11.** *~ s.th. into fig.* et. einbauen in (*acc*).

Verbindungen mit Adverbien:

work| in F Zitate etc einbauen. **~ off** *v/t* **1.** *Schulden* abarbeiten. **2.** *Zorn etc* abreagieren (*on* an *dat*). **~ out** I *v/t* **1.** ausrechnen; *fig.* sich et. zs.-reimen. **2.** *Plan etc* ausarbeiten. **II** *v/i* **3.** klappen: *it'll never ~* daraus kann nichts werden. **4.** aufgehen (*Rechnung etc*): *it didn't ~ fig.* die Rechnung ist nicht aufgegangen. **5.** F trainieren. **~ o-ver** *v/t* F j-n zs.-schlagen. **~ up** *v/t* **1.** *Zuhörer etc* aufpeitschen; -wühlen: *be worked up* aufgeregt *od.* nervös sein (*about* wegen). **2.** sich *Appetit etc* holen; *Begeisterung etc* aufbringen. **3.** et. ausarbeiten (*into* zu).

work-a-ble ['wɜːkəbl] *adj* **1.** formbar. **2.** *fig.* durchführbar.

'work-a-day *adj* Alltags...

work-a-hol-ic [ˌwɜːkəˈhɒlɪk] *s* F Arbeitssüchtige *m, f.*

'work|-bench *s* ⚙ Werkbank *f*. **'~book** *s ped.* Arbeitsheft *n*. **~ camp** *s* Arbeitslager *n*. **~ coat** *s Am.* Arbeitsmantel *m*, Kittel *m*. **'~day** *s* **1.** Arbeitstag *m*. **2.** Werktag *m*.

work-er ['wɜːkə] *s* **1.** Arbeiter(in), Angestellte *m, f.* **2.** *be a real ~* hart arbeiten.

work force *s* **1.** Belegschaft *f*. **2.** Arbeitskräftepotential *n*.

work-ing ['wɜːkɪŋ] **I** *adj* **1.** Arbeits...: *~ breakfast* Arbeitsfrühstück *n*; *~ capital* † Betriebskapital *n*; *~ day* → *workday*; *~ hours* *pl* Arbeitszeit *f*; *~ hypothesis* Arbeitshypothese *f*; *~ knowledge of French* französische Grundkenntnisse *pl*; *have a ~ knowledge of* ein bißchen was verstehen von; *in ~ order* in betriebsfähigem Zustand. **2.** arbeitend, berufstätig: *~ class(es pl)* Arbeiterklasse *f*. **II** *s pl* **3.** ⚙ Arbeits-, Funktionsweise *f*.

'work|-load *s* Arbeitspensum *n*. **~man** ['~mən] *s* (*irr man*) Handwerker *m*. **'~out** *s* Training *n*. **~ per-mit** *s* Arbeitserlaubnis *f*, -genehmigung *f*. **'~place** *s* Arbeitsplatz *m*: *at the ~* am Arbeitsplatz. **'~shop** *s* **1.** Werkstatt *f*. **2.** Workshop *m* (*Seminar*). **'~shy** *adj* arbeitsscheu. **~study** *s* Arbeitsstudie *f*. **'~top** *s* Arbeitsplatte *f*. **~-to-'rule** *s* † *Br.* Dienst *m* nach Vorschrift.

world [wɜːld] **I** *s allg.* Welt *f*: *in the ~* auf der Welt; *what in the ~...?* was um alles in der Welt ...?; *a man of the ~* ein Mann von Welt; *all over the ~* in der ganzen Welt; *they are ~s apart* zwischen ihnen liegen Welten; *bring into the ~* auf die Welt bringen; *do s.o. a (od. the) ~ of good* j-m unwahrscheinlich gut tun; *mean all the ~ to s.o.* j-m alles bedeuten. **II** *adj* Welt...: *~ cham-pion* Weltmeister(in); *~ championship* Weltmeisterschaft *f*; ♀ *Cup* (*Sport*) Weltcup *m*, -pokal *m*; Fußballweltmeisterschaft *f*; *~ language* Weltsprache *f*; *~ power* *pol.* Weltmacht *f*; *~ record* Weltrekord *m*; *~ record holder* Weltrekordler(in); *~ war* Weltkrieg *m*. **'~-beat-er** *s: be a ~* unschlagbar sein. **'~-fa-mous** *adj* weltberühmt.

world-ly ['wɜːldlɪ] *adj* **1.** weltlich, irdisch.

2. weltlich (gesinnt). **,~·'wise** *adj* weltklug.

'world·wide *adj* weltweit, *adv a.* auf der ganzen Welt.

worm [wɜːm] **I** *s* **1.** *zo.* Wurm *m.* **II** *v/t* **2.** *Hund etc* entwurmen. **3. ~ one's way through** sich schlängeln *od.* zwängen durch; **~ o.s. into s.o.'s confidence** sich in j-s Vertrauen einschleichen. **4. ~ s.th. out of s.o.** *fig.* j-m et. entlocken. **'~·eat·en** *adj* wurmstichig. **'~·hole** *s* Wurmloch *n.* **'~·wood** *s & q* Wermut *m.*

worm·y ['wɜːmɪ] *adj* **1.** wurmig. **2.** wurmstichig.

worn [wɔːn] *pp von* **wear.** **,~·'out** *adj* **1.** abgenutzt, abgetragen (*Kleidung*). **2.** *fig.* erschöpft (*Person*).

wor·ried ['wʌrɪd] *adj* besorgt, beunruhigt: **be ~** sich sorgen, sich Sorgen machen (**about** über *acc,* um, wegen). **wor·ri·some** ['~səm] *adj* besorgniserregend, beunruhigend. **'wor·ry I** *v/t* j-n beunruhigen, j-m Sorgen machen. **II** *v/i* sich sorgen, sich Sorgen machen (**about,** over** über *acc,* um, wegen): **not to ~** mach dir keine Gedanken; **~ at** sich abmühen mit. **III** *s* Sorge *f.* **'worry·ing → worrisome.**

worse [wɜːs] **I** *adj u. adv* schlechter, schlimmer: **~ still** was noch schlimmer ist; **to make matters ~** zu allem Übel; **he's getting steadily ~** sein Zustand verschlechtert sich immer mehr; → **wear** 1. **II** *s* Schlechteres *n,* Schlimmeres *n:* → **bad** 7, **turn** 4. **'wors·en I** *v/t* schlechter machen, verschlechtern. **II** *v/i* schlechter werden, sich verschlechtern.

wor·ship ['wɜːʃɪp] **I** *v/t* *pret u. pp* **-shiped,** *bsd. Br.* **-shipped** 1. *Gott* anbeten, *a.* Ahnen, *Helden* verehren; *weitS.* j-n anbeten, vergöttern: **~ God** *a.* zu Gott beten. **II** *s* **2.** Anbetung *f,* Verehrung *f.* **3.** Gottesdienst *m.* **'wor·ship·(p)er** *s* **1.** Anbeter(in), Verehrer(in). **2.** Kirchgänger(in).

worst [wɜːst] **I** *adj* schlechtest, schlimmst: **of the ~ kind** der übelsten Sorte. **II** *adv* am schlechtesten *od.* schlimmsten: **come off ~** den kürzeren ziehen (**in** bei). **III** *s* der, die, das Schlechteste *od.* Schlimmste: **at (the) ~** schlimmstenfalls; **if the ~ comes to the ~** wenn alle Stricke reißen; **the ~ of it is**

that das Schlimmste daran ist, daß; **get the ~** den kürzeren ziehen (**of** bei).

wor·sted ['wʊstɪd] *s* Kammgarn *n.*

worth [wɜːθ] **I** *adj* wert: **it's ~ £10** es ist 10 Pfund wert; **a skirt ~ £20** ein Rock im Wert von 20 Pfund; **it's ~ a try** es ist e-n Versuch wert; **it isn't ~ it** es lohnt sich nicht; **it might be ~ your while** es könnte sich für dich lohnen (**to do** zu tun); **~ mentioning** erwähnenswert; **not ~ mentioning** nicht der Rede wert; **it isn't ~ waiting any longer** es lohnt sich nicht, noch länger zu warten; → **candle, salt** 1. **II** *s* Wert *m.* **'worth·less** *adj* □ wertlos. **,worth'while** *adj* □: **be ~** sich lohnen. **wor·thy** ['wɜːðɪ] *adj* □ würdig: **~ of admiration** bewunderns-, bewundernswürdig.

would [wʊd] *v/aux* **1.** *konditional:* **he said he ~ come** er sagte, er werde kommen; **he ~ have come if** er wäre gekommen, wenn; **what ~ you do if ...?** was würdest du tun, wenn ...?; **how ~ you know?** woher willst du denn das wissen?; **you ~n't understand** das verstehst du sowieso nicht; **you ~ , ~n't you?** F das sieht dir ähnlich!? **2.** *Bereitschaft, Entschluß:* **he ~n't tell us what had happened** er wollte uns nicht sagen, was passiert war; **the door ~n't shut** die Tür schloß nicht; **I ~ rather not say what I think** ich sage lieber nicht, was ich denke. **3.** *höfliche Bitte:* **shut the window, ~ you?** mach doch bitte das Fenster zu. **4.** *Wiederholung:* **he ~ often take a walk after supper** er machte nach dem Abendessen oft e-n Spaziergang. **'~·be** *adj contp.* Möchtegern...

wouldn't ['wʊdnt] F *für* **would not.**

wound[1] [wuːnd] **I** *s* Wunde *f,* Verletzung *f:* **open old ~s** *fig.* alte Wunden aufreißen; → **rub** 3. **II** *v/t* j-n verwunden, verletzen; *fig.* j-s *Stolz etc* verletzen.

wound[2] [waʊnd] *pret u. pp von* **wind**[2].

wove [wəʊv] *pret von* **weave.** **'wov·en** *pp von* **weave.**

wow [waʊ] *int* F wow!, Mann!, Mensch!

wran·gle ['ræŋgl] **I** *v/i* (sich) streiten (**with** mit; **over** um). **II** *s* Streit *m.*

wrap [ræp] **I** *v/t* **1.** *a.* **~ up** einpacken, -wickeln (**in** in *acc*). **2.** et. wickeln ([a]round** um). **3. ~ up** F *Handel etc* unter Dach u. Fach bringen. **II** *v/i* **4. ~**

up sich warm anziehen. **5.** ~ **up!** F Schnauze! **II** s **6.** *bsd. Am.* Umhang m. **7.** F *be still under* ~s noch geheim sein; *keep under* ~s *et.* geheimhalten. '**wrap·per** s *Br.* (Schutz)Umschlag m. '**wrap·ping I** s Verpackung f. **II** *adj:* ~ *paper* Einwickel-, Packpapier n.

wrath [rɒθ] s Zorn m.

wreath [riːθ] *pl* **wreaths** [riːðz] s Kranz m.

wreck [rek] **I** s **1.** ♻ Wrack n (a. *fig. Person*). **II** *v/t* **2.** *be* ~*ed* ♻ zerschellen; Schiffbruch erleiden. **3.** *Hoffnungen etc* zunichte machen. '**wreck·age** s Trümmer *pl* (a. *fig.*), ♻ a. Wrackteile *pl*. '**wreck·er** s *mot. Am.* Abschleppwagen m.

wren [ren] s *orn.* Zaunkönig m.

wrench [rentʃ] **I** *v/t* **1.** ~ *s.th. from* (*od. out of*) *s.o.'s hand* j-m et. aus der Hand winden; ~ *off* *Verschluß etc* mit e-m Ruck abschrauben. **2.** ♻ sich *das Knie etc* verrenken. **II** s **3.** ♻ Verrenkung f. **4.** ⚙ *Br.* Franzose m; *Am.* Schraubenschlüssel m.

wrest [rest] *v/t:* ~ *s.th. from* (*od. out of*) *s.o.'s hand* j-m et. aus der Hand reißen.

wres·tle ['resl] **I** *v/i* **1.** ringen (*with* mit). **2.** *fig.* ringen, kämpfen (*with* mit; *for* um). **II** *v/t* **3.** *Sport:* ringen gegen. '**wres·tler** s *Sport:* Ringer m. '**wres·tling** (*Sport*) **I** s Ringen n. **II** *adj* Ring...: ~ *match* Ringkampf m.

wretch [retʃ] s **1.** a. *poor* ~ armer Teufel. **2.** *oft humor.* Wicht m. **wretch·ed** ['~ɪd] *adj* □ **1.** elend; (tod)unglücklich. **2.** scheußlich (*Kopfschmerzen, Wetter etc*). **3.** verflixt.

wrig·gle ['rɪgl] **I** *v/i* sich winden; zappeln; ~ *out of* *fig.* sich herauswinden aus; sich drücken vor (*dat*). **II** *v/t* mit den *Zehen* wackeln.

wring [rɪŋ] *v/t* (*irr*) **1.** *j-m die Hand* drücken; *die Hände* ringen. **2.** *oft* ~ *out Wäsche etc* auswringen; ~ *the truth out of s.o.* die Wahrheit aus j-m herausholen. '**wring·ing** *adv:* ~ *wet* klatschnaß.

wrin·kle¹ ['rɪŋkl] **I** s Falte f, Runzel f. **II** *v/t a.* ~ *up Stirn* runzeln, *Nase* rümpfen. **III** *v/i* faltig *od.* runz(e)lig werden.

wrin·kle² [~] s F Kniff m, Trick m.

wrist [rɪst] s Handgelenk n. '~**band** s Armband n.

wrist·let ['rɪstlɪt] s Armband n.
'**wrist·watch** s Armbanduhr f.

writ [rɪt] s ⚖ Befehl m, Verfügung f.

write [raɪt] (*irr*) **I** *v/t* **1.** *Buch etc, j-m e-n Brief etc* schreiben: *it was written on* (*od. all over*) *his face fig.* es stand ihm im Gesicht geschrieben. **2.** *bsd. Am. j-m* schreiben. **II** *v/i* **3.** schreiben: ~ *to s.o.* j-m schreiben; → *home* 8.
Verbindungen mit Adverbien:
write| back *v/i* zurückschreiben. ~ **down** *v/t* aufschreiben, niederschreiben. ~ **in** *v/i* schreiben (*to an acc*): ~ *for et.* anfordern. ~ **off** *v/t* **1.** *j-n,* ~ *et.* abschreiben. **2.** *bsd. Br. Wagen* zu Schrott fahren. ~ **out** *v/t* **1.** *Namen etc* ausschreiben. **2.** *Bericht etc* ausarbeiten. **3.** *j-m e-e Quittung etc* ausstellen. **4.** *Rundfunk, TV: j-n* rausschreiben (*of* aus *e-r Serie*). ~ **up** *v/t* **1.** *Notizen etc* ausarbeiten. **2.** berichten über (*acc*); *et.* besprechen.

'**write-off** s **1.** ♻ Abschreibung f. **2.** *bsd. Br.* Totalschaden m.

writ·er ['raɪtə] s **1.** Schreiber(in), Verfasser(in), Autor(in). **2.** Schriftsteller(in).

'**write-up** s (*Presse*)Bericht m; Besprechung f, Kritik f.

writhe [raɪð] *v/i* sich krümmen *od.* winden (*in, with* vor *dat*).

writ·ing ['raɪtɪŋ] s **1.** Schreiben n (*Tätigkeit*). **2.** (Hand)Schrift f. **3.** *pl* Werke *pl.* **4.** *in* ~ schriftlich. **II** *adj* **5.** Schreib...: ~ *desk* Schreibtisch m; ~ *paper* Schreibpapier n.

writ·ten ['rɪtn] **I** *pp von* **write.** **II** *adj* schriftlich: ~ *language* Schriftsprache f.

wrong [rɒŋ] **I** *adj* (□ → *wrongly*) **1.** falsch: *be* ~ falsch sein, nicht stimmen; unrecht haben; falsch gehen (*Uhr*). **2.** unrecht: *you were* ~ *to say that* es war nicht recht *od.* richtig von dir, das zu sagen. **3.** *is anything* ~? ist et. nicht in Ordnung? *what's* ~ *with you?* was ist los mit dir?, was hast du? **II** *adv* **4.** falsch: *get* ~ *j-n, et.* falsch verstehen; *go* ~ e-n Fehler machen; kaputtgehen; *fig.* schiefgehen. **III** s **5.** Unrecht n: *be in the* ~ im Unrecht sein. **IV** *v/t* **6.** *j-m* Unrecht tun. '**,~'do·er** s Misse-, Übeltäter(in). **,~'do·ing** s **1.** Missetat(en *pl*) f. **2.** Vergehen n *od. pl.*

wrong·ful ['rɒŋfʊl] *adj* □ **1.** ungerechtfertigt. **2.** gesetzwidrig: **~** *imprison-ment* Freiheitsberaubung *f*.

,**wrong'head·ed** *adj* □ **1.** querköpfig, verbohrt (*Person*). **2.** verschroben (*Ideen etc*).

wrong·ly ['rɒŋlɪ] *adv* zu Unrecht; fälschlicherweise.

wrote [rəʊt] *pret von* **write**.

wrought [rɔːt] *adj*: **~** *iron* Schmiedeeisen *n*. ,**~'i·ron** *adj* schmiedeeisern. ,**~pt** *adj* aufgeregt, nervös.

wrung [rʌŋ] *pret u. pp von* **wring**.

wry [raɪ] *adj* süßsauer (*Lächeln*); sarkastisch (*Humor*).

X

Xmas ['eksməs, 'krɪsməs] F → *Christmas*.

X-ray ['eksreɪ] **I** *v/t* **1.** röntgen. **II** *s* **2.**

Röntgenaufnahme *f*, -bild *n*. **3.** Röntgenuntersuchung *f*.

xy·lo·phone ['zaɪləfəʊn] *s* ♪ Xylophon *n*.

Y

yacht [jɒt] **I** *s* Jacht *f*; (*Sport*) (Segel)Boot *n*. **II** *v/i* segeln: **go ~ing** segeln gehen. '**yacht·ing** *s* Segeln *n*.

yachts·man ['jɒtsmən] *s* (*irr man*) *Sport*: Segler *m*. '**yachts,wom·an** *s* (*irr woman*) *Sport*: Seglerin *f*.

yank [jæŋk] F **I** *v/t* reißen an (*dat*): **~** *out* (her)ausreißen, *Zahn* ziehen. **II** *v/i*: **~** *on* reißen an (*dat*). **III** *s* Ruck *m*.

Yan·kee ['jæŋkɪ] *s* F Yankee *m*, Ami *m*.

yap [jæp] **I** *v/i* **1.** kläffen. **2.** F quasseln. **II** *s* **3.** Kläffen *n*. **4.** Gequassel *n*.

yard¹ [jɑːd] *s* Yard *n*.

yard² [ʌ] *s* Hof *m*.

'**yard·stick** *s fig*. Maßstab *m*.

yarn [jɑːn] *s* **1.** Garn *n*. **2.** F *spin* **a ~** Garn spinnen: *spin s.o.* **a ~** j-m e-e Lügengeschichte erzählen von.

yawn [jɔːn] **I** *v/i* gähnen (*a. fig*). **II** Gähner *m*; Gähnen *n*: *be a big* **~** F zum Gähnen (langweilig) sein.

yeah [jeə] *adv* F ja.

year [jɪə] *s* Jahr *n*: **~** *after* **~** Jahr für Jahr; **~** *in*, **~** *out* jahraus, jahrein; *all the* **~** *round* das ganze Jahr hindurch; *since*

the **~** *dot* F seit e-r Ewigkeit; *this* **~** dieses Jahr, heuer. '**~·book** *s* Jahrbuch *n*.

year·ly ['jɪəlɪ] *adj u. adv* jährlich.

yearn [jɜːn] *v/i* sich sehnen (*for* nach; *to do* danach, zu tun). '**yearn·ing** **I** *s* Sehnsucht *f*. **II** *adj* □ sehnsüchtig.

yeast [jiːst] *s* Hefe *f*.

yell [jel] **I** *v/i* schreien, brüllen (*with* vor *dat*): **~** *at s.o.* j-n anschreien *od*. anbrüllen. **II** *v/t a.* **~** *out et.* schreien, brüllen. **III** *s* Schrei *m*.

yel·low ['jeləʊ] **I** *adj* **1.** gelb: **~** *fever* ♨ Gelbfieber *n*; **~** *pages pl teleph*. gelbe Seiten *pl*, Branchenverzeichnis *n*; **~** *press* Sensationspresse *f*. **2.** F feig. **II** *s* **3.** Gelb *n*: *at* **~** *Am*. bei Gelb; *the lights were at* **~** *Am*. die Ampel stand auf Gelb. **III** *v/i* **4.** gelb werden, sich gelb färben (*Blätter etc*), vergilben (*Papier*).

yelp [jelp] **I** *v/i* aufschreien, (*Hund etc*) (auf)jaulen. **II** *s* Aufschrei *m*, (Auf)Jaulen *n*.

yep [jep] *adv* F ja.

yes [jes] **I** *adv* ja: **~** *and no* ja u. nein; *oh* **~**

o doch, o ja. **II** *s* Ja *n.* **~ man** *s* (*irr man*) *contp.* Jasager *m.*

yes·ter·day ['jestədɪ] **I** *adv* gestern: **~ morning** gestern morgen; **the day before ~** vorgestern; **I wasn't born ~** ich bin (doch) nicht von gestern. **II** *s:* **~'s paper** die gestrige Zeitung.

yet [jet] **I** *adv* **1.** *fragend:* schon. **2.** *noch:* **not ~** noch nicht; **as ~** bis jetzt, bisher. **3.** (doch) noch. **4.** doch, aber. **II** *cj* **5.** aber, doch.

ye·ti ['jetɪ] *s* Yeti *m,* Schneemensch *m.*

yew [ju:] *s* ♣ Eibe *f.*

Yid·dish ['jɪdɪʃ] *s ling.* Jiddisch *n.*

yield [ji:ld] **I** *v/t* **1.** *Früchte* tragen, *Gewinn* abwerfen, *Resultat etc* ergeben, liefern. **2.** *a.* **~ up** ✗ *Stellung etc* überlassen (**to** *dat*). **II** *v/i* **3.** nachgeben (*Boden etc*). **4.** nachgeben; ✗ sich ergeben (**to** *dat*): **~ to** *mot.* Am. *j-m* Vorfahrt gewähren. **III** *s* **5.** Ertrag *m.*

yo·ga ['jəʊgə] *s* Joga *m, n,* Yoga *m, n.*

yog·h(o)urt, yog·urt ['jɒgət] *s* Joghurt *m, n.*

yo·gi ['jəʊgɪ] *s* Jogi *m,* Yogi *m.*

yoke [jəʊk] *s* Joch *n* (*a. fig.*).

yolk [jəʊk] *s* (Ei)Dotter *m, n,* Eigelb *n.*

you [ju:] *pron* **1.** (*nom*) du, Sie, ihr; (*dat*) dir, Ihnen, euch; (*acc*) dich, Sie, euch. **2.** man.

you'd [ju:d] F *für* **you had; you would.**

you'll [ju:l] F *für* **you will.**

young [jʌŋ] **I** *adj* **1.** jung. **II** *s* **2. the ~** die jungen Leute *pl,* die Jugend. **3.** *zo.* Junge *pl:* **with ~** trächtig. **young·ster** ['~stə] *s* Junge *m.*

your [jɔ:] *possessive pron* dein(e); *pl* euer, eure; Ihr(e) (*a. pl*).

you're [jʊə] F *für* **you are.**

yours [jɔ:z] *pron* dein(er, e, es); *pl* euer, eure(s); Ihr(er, e, es) (*a. pl*): **a friend of ~** ein Freund von dir.

your·self [jɔ:'self] *pl* **-selves** [~'selvz] *pron.* **1.** *verstärkend:* selbst: **you ~ told me, you told me ~** du hast es mir selbst erzählt. **2.** *reflex:* dir, dich, sich: **did you hurt ~?** hast du dich verletzt?

youth [ju:θ] **I** *s* **1.** Jugend *f:* **in my ~** in meiner Jugend. **2.** Jugendliche *m.* **3.** *coll.* Jugend *f.* **II** *adj* **4.** Jugend...: **~ hostel** Jugendherberge *f.* **youth·ful** ['~fʊl] *adj* □ jugendlich.

you've [ju:v] F *für* **you have.**

Yu·go·slav [ˌju:gəʊ'slɑːv] **I** *s* Jugoslawe *m,* -slawin *f.* **II** *adj* jugoslawisch.

Z

zeal [zi:l] *s* Eifer *m.* **zeal·ot** ['zelət] *s* Fanatiker(in), *eccl. a.* Eiferer *m,* Eiferin *f.* **zeal·ous** ['zeləs] *adj* □ eifrig: **be ~** eifrig bemüht sein (**for** um; **to do** darum, zu tun).

ze·bra ['zebrə, 'zi:brə] *s zo.* Zebra *n.* **~ cross·ing** *s* Br. Zebrastreifen *m.*

ze·nith ['zenɪθ] *s ast.* Zenit *m* (*a. fig.*).

ze·ro ['zɪərəʊ] **I** *pl* **-ro(e)s** *s* Null *f* (*Am. a. teleph.*), (*e-r Skala a.*) Nullpunkt *m:* **10 degrees below ~** 10 Grad unter Null. **II** *adj* Null... **~ growth** Nullwachstum *n;* **~ hour** *bsd.* ✗ die Stunde X; **~ option** ✗, *pol.* Nullösung *f.* **III** *v/i:* **~ in on** ✗ sich einschießen auf (*acc*) (*a. fig.*); *fig.* sich konzentrieren auf (*acc*).

zest [zest] *s* **1.** *fig.* Würze *f.* **2.** Begeisterung *f:* **~ for life** Lebensfreude *f.*

zig·zag ['zɪgzæg] **I** *s* Zickzack *m.* **II** *adj* zickzackförmig, Zickzack... **III** *v/i* im Zickzack laufen, fahren *etc,* zickzackförmig verlaufen (*Weg etc*).

zinc [zɪŋk] *s* ♠ Zink *n.*

zip [zɪp] **I** *s* **1.** Zischen *n,* Schwirren *n.* **3.** F Schmiß *m,* Schwung *m.* **II** *v/t* **4. ~ the bag open** (**shut** *od.* **up**) den Reißverschluß der Tasche aufmachen (zumachen); **~ s.o. up** *j-m* den Reißverschluß zumachen. **III** *v/i* **5.** zischen, schwirren (*Kugeln etc*). **6.** F flitzen: **~ by** (*od.* **past**) vorbeiflitzen. **~ code** *s* Am. Postleitzahl *f.* **~ fas·ten·er** *bsd. Br.* → **zip** 1.

zip·per ['zɪpə] *bsd. Am.* → **zip** 1.
zo·di·ac ['zəʊdɪæk] *s ast.* Tierkreis *m*: **signs** *pl* **of the** ~ Tierkreiszeichen *pl*.
zom·bie ['zɒmbɪ] *s* Zombie *m*.
zone [zəʊn] **I** *s* Zone *f*. **II** *v/t* in Zonen einteilen.
zoo [zu:] *s* Zoo *m*.
zo·o·log·i·cal [ˌzəʊə'lɒdʒɪkl] *adj* □ zoologisch: ~ **gardens** *pl* Tierpark *m*.
zo·ol·o·gist [~'ɒlədʒɪst] *s* Zoologe *m*, Zoologin *f*. **zo·ol·o·gy** *s* Zoologie *f*.
zoom [zu:m] **I** *v/i* **1.** ~ **in on** *phot. et.* heranholen. **2.** F sausen: ~ **by** (*od.* **past**) vorbeisausen. **3.** F in die Höhe schnellen (*Preise*). **II** *s* **4.** *a.* ~ **lens** *phot.* Zoom(objektiv) *n*.

Proper Names

A

A·bra·ham ['eɪbrəhæm] Abraham *m*.

A·chil·les [ə'kɪliːz] Achilles *m*.

Ad·am ['ædəm] Adam *m*.

A·dri·an ['eɪdrɪən] Adrian *m*, Ariane *f*.

A·dri·at·ic Sea [ˌeɪdrɪˈætɪk siː] *das* Adriatische Meer, *die* Adria.

Ae·ge·an Sea [iːˈdʒiːən siː] *das* Ägäische Meer, *die* Ägäis.

Aes·chy·lus ['iːskɪləs] Äschylus *m*.

Af·ghan·i·stan [æfˈɡænɪstæn] Afghanistan *n*.

Af·ri·ca ['æfrɪkə] Afrika *n*.

Ag·a·tha ['ægəθə] Agathe *f*.

Aix-la-Cha·pelle [ˌeɪkslɑːʃæˈpel] Aachen *n*.

Al·ba·nia [ælˈbeɪnjə] Albanien *n*.

Al·bert ['ælbət] Albert *m*.

A·leu·tian Is·lands [əˌluːʃjənˈaɪləndz] *pl die* Aleuten *pl*.

Al·ex·an·der [ˌælɪɡˈzɑːndə] Alexander *m*.

Al·ex·an·dra [ˌælɪɡˈzɑːndrə] Alexandra *f*.

Al·fred ['ælfrɪd] Alfred *m*.

Al·ge·ria [ælˈdʒɪərɪə] Algerien *n*.

Al·giers [ælˈdʒɪəz] Algier *n*.

Al·ice ['ælɪs] Alice *f*, Else *f*.

Al·i·son ['ælɪsn] *f*.

Al·lan, Al·len ['ælən] *m*.

Al·sace [ælˈsæs], **Al·sa·tia** [ælˈseɪʃə] *das* Elsaß.

A·me·lia [əˈmiːljə] Amalie *f*.

A·mer·i·ca [əˈmerɪkə] Amerika *n*.

An·des ['ændiːz] *pl die* Anden *pl*.

An·drew ['ændruː] Andreas *m*.

Ann [æn], **An·na** ['ænə] Anna *f*, Anne *f*.

An·na·bel(le) ['ænəbel] Annabella *f*.

Anne [æn] Anna *f*, Anne *f*.

Ant·arc·ti·ca [æntˈɑːktɪkə] *die* Antarktis.

An·tho·ny ['æntənɪ, 'ænθənɪ] Anton *m*.

An·til·les [ænˈtɪliːz] *pl die* Antillen *pl*.

An·to·ny ['æntənɪ] Anton *m*.

Ap·pa·la·chians [ˌæpəˈleɪtʃjənz] *pl die* Appalachen *pl*.

A·ra·bia [əˈreɪbjə] Arabien *n*.

Ar·chi·bald ['ɑːtʃɪbɔːld] Archibald *m*.

Arc·tic ['ɑːktɪk] *die* Arktis.

Ar·gen·ti·na [ˌɑːdʒənˈtiːnə] Argentinien *n*.

Ar·gen·tine ['ɑːdʒəntaɪn]: *the ~* Argentinien *n*.

Ar·is·tot·le ['ærɪstɒtl] Aristoteles *m*.

Ar·i·zo·na [ˌærɪˈzəʊnə] *Staat der USA*.

Ar·me·ni·a [ɑːˈmiːnjə] Armenien *n*.

Ar·thur ['ɑːθə] Art(h)ur *m*: *King ~* König Artus.

A·sia ['eɪʃə] Asien *n*: *~ Minor* Kleinasien *n*.

Ath·ens ['æθɪnz] Athen *n*.

At·lan·tic [ətˈlæntɪk] *der* Atlantik.

Au·gus·tus [ɔːˈɡʌstəs] August *m*.

Aus·tra·lia [ɒˈstreɪljə] Australien *n*.

Aus·tria ['ɒstrɪə] Österreich *n*.

A·zer·bai·jan [ˌæzəbaɪˈdʒɑːn] Aserbeidschan *n*.

A·zores [əˈzɔːz] *pl die* Azoren *pl*.

B

Ba·ha·mas [bəˈhɑːməz] *pl die* Bahamas *pl*.

Bal·dwin ['bɔːldwɪn] Balduin *m*.

Bal·kans ['bɔːlkənz] *pl der* Balkan.

Bal·tic Sea [ˌbɔːltɪkˈsiː] *die* Ostsee.

Ban·gla·desh [ˌbæŋɡləˈdeʃ] Bangladesch *n*.

Bar·ba·dos [bɑːˈbeɪdɒs] Barbados *n*.

Bar·thol·o·mew [bɑːˈθɒləmjuː] Bartholomäus *m*.

Basle [bɑːl] Basel *n*.

Ba·var·ia [bəˈveərɪə] Bayern *n*.

Be·a·trice ['bɪətrɪs] Beatrice *f*.

Bel·fast [ˌbelˈfɑːst; 'belfɑːst] Belfast *n*.

Bel·gium ['beldʒəm] Belgien *n*.

Bel·grade [ˌbelˈɡreɪd] Belgrad *n*.

Bel·o·rus·sia [ˌbeləʊˈrʌʃə] Weißrußland *n*.

Ben·gal [ˌbeŋˈɡɔːl] Bengalen *n*.

Ben·ja·min ['bendʒəmɪn] Benjamin *m*.

Ber·lin [bɜːˈlɪn] Berlin *n*.

Ber·mu·das [bəˈmjuːdəz] *pl die* Bermudas *pl*, *die* Bermudainseln *pl*.

Ber·nard ['bɜːnəd] Bernhard *m*.

Bern(e) [bɜːn] Bern *n*.

Ber·tha ['bɜːθə] Berta *f*.

Ber·tram ['bɜːtrəm], **Ber·trand** ['bɜːtrənd] Bertram *m*.

Bill, Bil·ly ['bɪl(ɪ)] Willi *m*.

Bis·cay ['bɪskeɪ, -kɪ]: *Bay of ~* der Golf von Biscaya.

Bo·he·mia [bəʊˈhiːmjə] Böhmen *n*.

Bo·liv·ia [bəˈlɪvɪə] Bolivien *n*.

Bra·zil [brəˈzɪl] Brasilien *n*.

Bridg·et ['brɪdʒɪt] Brigitte *f.*
Bri·tain ['brɪtn] Britannien *n.*
Bri·tan·nia [brɪ'tænjə] *poet.* Britannien *n.*
Bruns·wick ['brʌnzwɪk] Braunschweig *n.*
Brus·sels ['brʌslz] Brüssel *n.*
Bu·cha·rest [ˌbjuːkə'rest] Bukarest *n.*
Bu·da·pest [ˌbjuːdə'pest] Budapest *n.*
Bud·dha ['bʊdə] Buddha *m.*
Bul·gar·ia [bʌl'geərɪə] Bulgarien *n.*
Bur·gun·dy ['bɜːɡəndɪ] Burgund *n.*
Bur·ki·na Fas·o [bʊəˌkiːnə'fæsəʊ] Burkina Faso *n*
Bur·ma ['bɜːmə] Birma *n.*

C

Cae·sar ['siːzə] Cäsar *m.*
Cai·ro ['kaɪərəʊ] Kairo *n.*
Ca·lais ['kæleɪ] Calais *n.*
Cal·cut·ta [kæl'kʌtə] Kalkutta *n.*
Cal·i·for·nia [ˌkælɪ'fɔːnjə] Kalifornien *n.*
Cam·bo·dia [kæm'bəʊdɪə] Kam'bodscha *n.*
Cam·er·oon [ˌkæmə'ruːn] Kamerun *n.*
Can·a·da ['kænədə] Kanada *n.*
Cape Town ['keɪptaʊn] Kapstadt *n.*
Ca·rin·thia [kə'rɪnθɪə] Kärnten *n.*
Car·o·line ['kærəlaɪn], **Car·o·lyn** ['kærəlɪn] Karoline *f.*
Cath·er·ine ['kæθrɪn] Katharina *f,* Kat(h)rin *f.*
Ce·cil ['sesl, 'sɪsl] *m.*
Ce·cile ['sesɪl; *Am.* sɪ'siːl], **Ce·cil·ia** [sɪ'sɪljə; sɪ'siːljə], **Cec·i·ly** ['sɪsɪlɪ; 'sesɪlɪ] Cäcilie *f.*
Cey·lon [sɪ'lɒn] Ceylon *n.*
Chad [tʃæd] *der* Tschad.
Charles [tʃɑːlz] Karl *m.*
Char·lotte ['ʃɑːlət] Charlotte *f.*
Chil·e ['tʃɪlɪ] Chile *n.*
Chi·na ['tʃaɪnə] China *n*: *Republic of ~ die* Republik China; *People's Republic of ~ die* Volksrepublik China.
Chris·ti·na [krɪ'stiːnə], **Chris·tine** ['krɪstiːn, krɪ'stiːn] Christine *f.*
Chris·to·pher ['krɪstəfə] Christoph(er) *m.*
Clar·a ['kleərə], **Clare** [kleə] Klara *f.*
Cle·o·pat·ra [klɪə'pætrə] Kleopatra *f.*
Co·logne [kə'ləʊn] Köln *n.*
Co·lom·bia [kə'lɒmbɪə] Kolumbien *n.*
Com·mon·wealth of In·de·pen·dent States ['kɒmənwelθ əv ˌɪndɪpendənt 'steɪts] (*abbr.* **CIS**) Gemeinschaft *f* unabhängiger Staaten (*abbr.* **GUS**).
Con·fu·cius [kən'fjuːʃəs] Konfuzius *m.*
Con·stance ['kɒnstəns] Konstanze *f*: *Lake ~* der Bodensee.
Co·pen·ha·gen [ˌkəʊpn'heɪɡən] Kopenhagen *n.*
Cov·ent Gar·den [ˌkɒvənt'ɡɑːdn] *London Opera* (*Royal Opera House*).
Crete [kriːt] Kreta *n.*
Cri·mea [kraɪ'mɪə] *die* Krim.
Cro·a·tia [krəʊ'eɪʃə] Kroatien *n.*
Cu·ba ['kjuːbə] Kuba *n.*
Cy·prus ['saɪprəs] Zypern *n.*
Czech·o·slo·va·kia [ˌtʃekəʊsləʊ'vækɪə] *hist.* die Tschechoslowakei.
Czech Re·pub·lic [ˌtʃek rɪ'pʌblɪk] *die* Tschechische Republik

D

Dan·iel ['dænjəl] Daniel *m.*
Dan·ube ['dænjuːb] *die* Donau.
Da·vid ['deɪvɪd] David *m.*
Den·mark ['denmɑːk] Dänemark *n.*
Di·ana [daɪ'ænə] Diana *f.*
Don Juan [ˌdɒn'dʒuːən] Don Juan *m.*
Don Quix·ote [ˌdɒn'kwɪksət] Don Quichotte *m.*
Dor·o·thy ['dɒrəθɪ] Dorothea *f.*
Dun·kirk [dʌn'kɜːk] Dünkirchen *n.*

E

Ec·ua·dor ['ekwədɔː] Ecuador *n.*
Ed·in·burgh ['edɪnbərə] Edinburg *n.*
E·dith ['iːdɪθ] Edith *f.*
E·gypt ['iːdʒɪpt] Ägypten *n.*
El·ea·nor ['elɪnə] Eleonore *f.*
E·li·jah [ɪ'laɪdʒə] Elias *m.*
El·i·nor ['elɪnə] Eleonore *f.*
E·liz·a·beth [ɪ'lɪzəbəθ] Elisabeth *f.*
El Sal·va·dor [el'sælvədɔː] El Salvador *n.*
Em·i·ly ['emɪlɪ] Emilie *f.*
Eng·land ['ɪŋɡlənd] England *n.*
Er·nest ['ɜːnɪst] Ernst *m.*
Es·t(h)o·nia [e'stəʊnjə] Estland *n.*
E·thi·o·pia [ˌiːθɪ'əʊpjə] Äthiopien *n.*
Eu·gene ['juːdʒiːn] Eugen *m.*
Eu·ge·nia [juː'dʒiːnjə] Eugenie *f.*
Eu·nice ['juːnɪs] Eunice *f.*
Eu·rip·i·des [jʊə'rɪpɪdiːz] Euripides *m.*
Eu·rope ['jʊərəp] Europa *n.*
Eve [iːv] Eva *f.*

F

Faer·oes ['feərəʊz] *pl die* Färöer *pl.*
Falk·land Is·lands [,fɔː(l)klənd'aıləndz] *pl die* Falklandinseln *pl.*
Far·oes ['feərəʊz] → *Faeroes.*
Fed·er·al Re·pub·lic of Ger·ma·ny [,fedərəlrı,pʌblıkəv'dʒɜːmənı] *die* Bundesrepublik Deutschland.
Fe·lic·i·ty [fə'lısətı] Felizitas *f.*
Fe·lix ['fiːlıks] Felix *m.*
Fin·land ['fınlənd] Finnland *n.*
Flor·ence ['flɒrəns] Florenz *n;* Florentine *f.*
France [frɑːns] Frankreich *n.*
Fran·ces ['frɑːnsıs] Franziska *f.*
Fran·cis ['frɑːnsıs] Franz *m.*
Fred·er·ic(k) ['fredrık] Friedrich *m.*

G

Gan·ges ['gændʒiːz] Ganges *m.*
Ge·ne·va [dʒı'niːvə] Genf *n.*
Gen·o·a ['dʒenəʊə] Genua *n.*
Geof·fr(e)y ['dʒefrı] Gottfried *m.*
George [dʒɔːdʒ] Georg *m.*
Geor·gia ['dʒɔːdʒə] *state of the US;* Georgien *n* (*in Asia*).
Ger·ald ['dʒerəld] Gerald *m,* Gerold *m.*
Ger·al·dine ['dʒerəldiːn] Geraldine *f.*
Ger·man Dem·o·crat·ic Re·pub·lic [,dʒɜːməndemə,krætıkrı'pʌblık] *hist. die* Deutsche Demokratische Republik.
Ger·ma·ny ['dʒɜːmənı] Deutschland *n.*
Ger·trude ['gɜːtruːd] Gertrud *f.*
Gi·bral·tar [dʒı'brɔːltə] Gibraltar *n.*
Gil·bert ['gılbət] Gilbert *m.*
Giles [dʒaılz] Julius *m.*
Gil·li·an ['dʒılıən; 'gılıən] *f.*
Go·li·ath [gəʊ'laıəθ] Goliath *m.*
Great Brit·ain [,greıt'brıtn] Großbritannien *n.*
Greece [griːs] Griechenland *n.*
Green·land ['griːnlənd] Grönland *n.*
Greg·o·ry ['gregərı] Gregor *m.*
Gri·sons ['griːzɔːŋ] Graubünden *n.*
Gua·te·ma·la [,gwɑːtə'mɑːlə] Guatemala *n.*
Guin·ea ['gını] Guinea *n.*
Guy·ana [gaı'ænə] Guyana *n.*

H

Hague [heıg] *the ~* Den Haag.
Hai·ti ['heıtı] Haiti *n.*

Han·o·ver ['hænəʊvə] Hannover *n.*
Har·old ['hærəld] Harald *m.*
Heb·ri·des ['hebrıdiːz] *pl die* Hebriden *pl.*
Hel·en ['helın] Helene *f.*
Hel·i·go·land ['helıgəʊlænd] Helgoland *n.*
Hel·sin·ki ['helsıŋkı] Helsinki *n.*
Hen·ry ['henrı] Heinrich *m.*
Hesse ['hesı] Hessen *n.*
Hil·a·ry ['hılərı] Hilaria *f;* Hilarius *m.*
Hi·ma·la·ya [,hımə'leıə] *der* Himalaja.
Hol·land ['hɒlənd] Holland *n.*
Ho·mer ['həʊmə] Homer *m.*
Hon·du·ras [hɒn'djʊərəs] Honduras *n.*
Hong Kong [,hɒŋ'kɒŋ] Hongkong *n.*
Hugh [hjuː] Hugo *m.*
Hun·ga·ry ['hʌŋgərı] Ungarn *n.*

I

I·an [ıən; 'iːən] Jan *m.*
Ice·land ['aıslənd] Island *n.*
In·dia ['ındjə] Indien *n.*
In·do·ne·sia [,ındəʊ'niːzjə] Indonesien *n.*
I·ran [ı'rɑːn] Iran *m.*
I·raq [ı'rɑːk] Irak *m.*
Ire·land ['aıələnd] Irland *n.*
I·rene [aı'riːnı; 'aıriːn] Irene *f.*
I·saac ['aızək] Isaak *m.*
Is·a·bel ['ızəbel] Isabella *f.*
Is·ra·el ['ızreıəl] Israel *n.*
Is·tan·bul [,ıstæn'bʊl] Istanbul *n.*
It·a·ly ['ıtəlı] Italien *n.*

J

Jack [dʒæk] Hans *m.*
Ja·mai·ca [dʒə'meıkə] Jamaika *n.*
James [dʒeımz] Jakob *m.*
Jane [dʒeın] Johanna *f.*
Jan·et ['dʒænıt] Johanna *f.*
Ja·pan [dʒə'pæn] Japan *n.*
Jean [dʒiːn] Johanna *f.*
Jef·frey ['dʒefrı] Gottfried *m.*
Jer·e·my ['dʒerımı] Jeremias *m.*
Je·rome [dʒə'rəʊm] Hieronymus *m.*
Je·ru·sa·lem [dʒə'ruːsələm] Jerusalem *n.*
Je·sus ['dʒiːzəs] Jesus *m.*
Joan [dʒəʊn], **Jo·an·na** [dʒəʊ'ænə] Johanna *f.*
John [dʒɒn] Johannes *m,* Johann *m.*
Jon·a·than ['dʒɒnəθən] Jonathan *m.*
Jor·dan ['dʒɔːdn] Jordanien *n;* Jordan *m.*
Jo·seph ['dʒəʊzıf] Joseph *m.*

Jo·se·phine ['dʒəʊzɪfi:n] Josephine *f*.
Ju·dith ['dʒu:dɪθ] Judith *f*.

K

Kam·pu·chea [ˌkæmpʊ'tʃɪə] *hist.* Kamputschea *n*.
Ka·ra·chi [kə'rɑ:tʃɪ] Karatschi *n*.
Kash·mir [ˌkæʃ'mɪə] Kaschmir *n*.
Kath·a·rine, Kath·er·ine ['kæθərɪn] Katharina *f*, Kat(h)rin *f*.
Ka·zakh·stan [ˌkæzæk'stɑ:n] Kasachstan *n*.
Ken·ya ['kenjə] Kenia *n*.
Ko·rea [kə'rɪə] Korea *n*.
Krem·lin ['kremlɪn] *der* Kreml.
Ku·wait [kʊ'weɪt] Kuwait *n*.

L

Lake Hu·ron [ˌleɪk'hjʊərən] *der* Huronsee.
Lake Su·pe·ri·or [ˌleɪksu:'pɪərɪə] *der* Obere See.
La·os ['lɑːɒs; laʊs] Laos *n*.
Lat·via ['lætvɪə] Lettland *n*.
Lau·rence ['lɒrəns] Lorenz *m*.
Law·rence ['lɒrəns] Lorenz *m*.
Leb·a·non ['lebənən] *der* Libanon *m*.
Leon·ard ['lenəd] Leonhard *m*.
Lew·is ['lu:ɪs] Ludwig *m*.
Lib·ya ['lɪbɪə] Libyen *n*.
Li·sa ['li:zə; 'laɪzə] Lisa *f*.
Lis·bon ['lɪzbən] Lissabon *n*.
Lith·u·a·nia [ˌlɪθjuː'eɪnɪə] Litauen *n*.
Li·za ['laɪzə] Lisa *f*.
Lon·don ['lʌndən] London *n*.
Lor·raine [lɒ'reɪn] Lothringen *n*.
Lou·is ['luːɪ; 'lʊɪ; *bsd. Am.* 'luːɪs] Ludwig *m*.
Lou·ise [luː'iːz] Luise *f*.
Lu·cia ['luːsjə] Lucia *f*, Luzia *f*.
Luke [luːk] Lukas *m*.
Lux·em·bourg ['lʌksəmbɜːɡ] Luxemburg *n*.
Lyd·ia ['lɪdɪə] Lydia *f*.

M

Ma·dei·ra [mə'dɪərə] Madeira *n*.
Ma·drid [mə'drɪd] Madrid *n*.
Mag·da·len ['mægdəlɪn] Magdalena *f*, Magdalene *f*: **~ College** ['mɔːdlɪn] *College in Oxford*.
Mag·da·lene ['mægdəlɪn] Magdalena *f*,

Magdalene *f*: **~ College** ['mɔːdlɪn] *College in Cambridge*.
Ma·ho·met [mə'hɒmɪt] Mohammed *m*.
Ma·jor·ca [mə'dʒɔːkə] Mallorca *n*.
Mal·ta ['mɔːltə] Malta *n*.
Mar·ga·ret ['mɑːɡərɪt] Margareta *f*, Margarete *f*.
Ma·ri·a [mə'raɪə; mə'rɪə] Maria *f*.
Mar·tha ['mɑːθə] Mart(h)a *f*.
Mar·y ['meərɪ] Maria *f*, Marie *f*.
Ma(t)·thew ['mæθjuː] Matthäus *m*.
Mau·rice ['mɒrɪs] Moritz *m*.
Med·i·ter·ra·ne·an (Sea) [ˌmedɪtə'reɪnjən('siː)] *das* Mittelmeer.
Mex·i·co ['meksɪkəʊ] Mexiko *n*.
Mi·chael ['maɪkl] Michael *m*.
Mich·i·gan ['mɪʃɪɡən] *Lake* **~** *der* Michigansee.
Mid·lands ['mɪdləndz] *pl die* Midlands *pl*.
Mid·west [ˌmɪd'west] *der* Mittlere Westen (*USA*).
Mi·lan [mɪ'læn] Mailand *n*.
Mo·na·co ['mɒnəkəʊ] Monaco *n*.
Mo·roc·co [mə'rɒkəʊ] Marokko *n*.
Mos·cow ['mɒskəʊ] Moskau *n*.
Mo·selle [məʊ'zel] Mosel *f*.
Mo·zam·bique [ˌməʊzæm'biːk] Mozambique *n*.
Mu·nich ['mjuːnɪk] München *n*.

N

Na·mib·ia [nə'mɪbɪə] Namibia *n*.
Na·ples ['neɪplz] Neapel *n*.
Naz·a·reth ['næzərəθ] Nazareth *n*.
Ne·pal [nɪ'pɔːl] Nepal *n*.
Neth·er·lands ['neðələndz] *pl die* Niederlande *pl*.
New Del·hi [ˌnjuː'delɪ] Neu-Delhi *n*.
New Eng·land [ˌnjuː'ɪŋɡlənd] Neuengland *n* (*USA*).
New·found·land ['njuːfəndlənd] Neufundland *n*.
New Zea·land [ˌnjuː'ziːlənd] Neuseeland *n*.
Ni·ag·a·ra [naɪ'æɡərə] Niagara *m*.
Nic·a·ra·gua [ˌnɪkə'ræɡjʊə] Nicaragua *n*.
Nich·o·las ['nɪkələs] Nikolaus *m*.
Ni·ge·ria [naɪ'dʒɪərɪə] Nigeria *n*.
Nile [naɪl] Nil *m*.
Nor·man·dy ['nɔːməndɪ] *die* Normandie.
North·ern Ire·land [ˌnɔːðn'aɪələnd] Nordirland *n*.

North Sea [ˌnɔ:θ'si:] *die* Nordsee.
Nor·way ['nɔ:weɪ] Norwegen *n*.
No·va Sco·tia [ˌnəʊvə'skəʊʃə] Neuschottland *n*.
Nu·rem·berg ['njʊərəmbɜ:g] Nürnberg *n*.

O

O·ce·an·ia [ˌəʊʃɪ'eɪnjə] Ozeanien *n*.
On·ta·ri·o [ɒn'teərɪəʊ] *Lake* ~ der Ontariosee.
Ork·ney Is·lands [ˌɔ:knɪ'aɪləndz] *pl die* Orkneyinseln *pl*.
Ost·end [ɒ'stend] Ost'ende *n*.

P

Pa·cif·ic [pə'sɪfɪk] *der* Pazifik.
Pak·i·stan [ˌpɑ:kɪ'stɑ:n] Pakistan *n*.
Pal·es·tine ['pæləstaɪn] Palästina *n*.
Pam·e·la ['pæmələ] Pamela *f*.
Pan·a·ma ['pænəmɑ:] Panama *n*.
Par·a·guay ['pærəgwaɪ] Paraguay *n*.
Par·is ['pærɪs] Paris *n*.
Pa·tri·cia [pə'trɪʃə] Patrizia *f*.
Pat·rick ['pætrɪk] Patrizius *m*.
Paul [pɔ:l] Paul *m*.
Pau·line [pɔ:'li:n; 'pɔ:li:n] Pauline *f*.
Per·sia ['pɜ:ʃə; *Am.* 'pɜ:rʒə] Persien *n*.
Pe·ru [pə'ru:] Peru *n*.
Pe·ter ['pi:tə] Peter *m*, Petrus *m*.
Phil·ip ['fɪlɪp] Philipp *m*.
Phil·ip·pines ['fɪlɪpi:nz] *pl die* Philippinen *pl*.
Pla·to ['pleɪtəʊ] Plato(n) *m*.
Po·land ['pəʊlənd] Polen *n*.
Por·tu·gal ['pɔ:tʃʊgl; '~jʊgl] Portugal *n*.
Prague [prɑ:g] Prag *n*.
Prus·sia ['prʌʃə] Preußen *n*.

Q

Qa·tar [kæ'tɑ:] Katar *n*.

R

Ra·chel ['reɪtʃl] Ra(c)hel *f*.
Rat·is·bon ['rætɪzbɒn] Regensburg *n*.
Reg·i·nald ['redʒɪnld] Re(g)inald *m*.
Rhine [raɪn] Rhein *m*.
Rhodes [rəʊdz] Rhodos *n*.
Rich·ard ['rɪtʃəd] Richard *m*.
Rob·ert ['rɒbət] Robert *m*.
Ro·ma·nia [ru:'meɪnjə; rʊ~; *Am.* rəʊ~] Rumänien *n*.

Rome [rəʊm] Rom *n*.
Rus·sia ['rʌʃə] Rußland *n*.
Ruth [ru:θ] Ruth *f*.

S

Sam·u·el ['sæmjʊəl] Samuel *m*.
San Fran·cis·co [ˌsænfrən'sɪskəʊ] San Franzisko *n* (*USA*).
Sau·di A·ra·bia [ˌsaʊdɪə'reɪbɪə] Saudi-Arabien *n*.
Sax·o·ny ['sæksnɪ] Sachsen *n*.
Scan·di·na·via [ˌskændɪ'neɪvjə] Skandinavien *n*.
Scot·land ['skɒtlənd] Schottland *n*.
Shet·land Is·lands [ˌʃetlənd'aɪləndz] *pl die* Shetlandinseln *pl*.
Si·be·ria [saɪ'bɪərɪə] Sibirien *n*.
Sib·yl ['sɪbɪl] Sibylle *f*.
Sic·i·ly ['sɪsɪlɪ] Sizilien *n*.
Si·le·sia [saɪ'li:zjə] Schlesien *n*.
Si·mon ['saɪmən] Simon *m*.
Sin·ga·pore [ˌsɪŋə'pɔ:] Singapur *n*.
Slo·va·kia [sləʊ'vækɪə] Slowakei *f*.
Slo·ve·nia [sləʊ'vi:nɪə] Slowenien *n*.
Soc·ra·tes ['sɒkrəti:z] Sokrates *m*.
Sol·o·mon ['sɒləmən] Salomo(n) *m*.
So·ma·lia [səʊ'mɑ:lɪə] Somalia *n*.
So·phi·a [səʊ'faɪə] Sophia *f*, Sofia *f*.
So·viet Un·ion [ˌsəʊvɪət'ju:njən] *hist. die* Sowjetunion.
Spain [speɪn] Spanien *n*.
Ste·phen ['sti:vn] Stephan *m*, Stefan *m*.
St. Law·rence [snt'lɒrəns] *der* Sankt-Lorenz-Strom.
Stock·holm ['stɒkhəʊm] Stockholm *n*.
Styr·ia ['stɪrɪə] *die* Steiermark.
Su·dan [su:'dɑ:n] *der* Sudan.
Su·san ['su:zn] Susanne *f*.
Su·zanne [su:'zæn] Susanne *f*.
Swe·den ['swi:dn] Schweden *n*.
Swit·zer·land ['swɪtsələnd] *die* Schweiz.
Syr·ia ['sɪrɪə] Syrien *n*.

T

Tai·wan [ˌtaɪ'wɑ:n] Taiwan *n*.
Tan·za·nia [ˌtænzə'nɪə] Tansania *n*.
Thai·land ['taɪlænd] Thailand *n*.
Thames [temz] *die* Themse.
The·o·bald ['θɪəbɔ:ld] Theobald *m*.
The·o·dore ['θɪədɔ:] Theodor *m*.
The·re·sa [tɪ'ri:zə] Theresa *f*, Therese *f*.
Tho·mas ['tɒməs] Thomas *m*.

Thu·rin·gia [θjʊəˈrɪndʒɪə] Thüringen *n.*
Ti·bet [tɪˈbet] Tibet *n.*
Tim·o·thy [ˈtɪməθɪ] Timotheus *m.*
To·bi·as [təˈbaɪəs] Tobias *m.*
To·kyo [ˈtəʊkjəʊ] Tokio *n.*
Tra·fal·gar [trəˈfælgə]: *Cape* ~ Kap *n* Trafalgar (*Spain*); ~ *Square* (*in London*).
Treves [triːvz] Trier *n.*
Tu·ni·sia [tjuːˈnɪzɪə; *Am.* tuːˈniːʒə] Tunesien *n.*
Tur·key [ˈtɜːkɪ] die Türkei.
Tus·ca·ny [ˈtʌskənɪ] die Toskana.
Ty·rol [ˈtɪrəl; tɪˈrəʊl] Tirol *n.*

U

U·kraine [juːˈkreɪn] *die* Ukraine.
Ul·ster [ˈʌlstə] Nordirland *n.*
U·nit·ed King·dom [juːˌnaɪtɪdˈkɪŋdəm] *das* Vereinigte Königreich (*Great Britain and Northern Ireland*).
U·nit·ed States of A·mer·i·ca [juːˌnaɪtɪdˌsteɪtsəvəˈmerɪkə] *pl die* Vereinigten Staaten *pl* von Amerika.
Ur·su·la [ˈɜːsjʊlə] Ursula *f.*
U·tah [ˈjuːtɑː; ˈˌtɔː] *Staat der USA.*
Uz·bek·i·stan [ʊzbekɪˈstɑːn] Usbekistan *n.*

V

Val·en·tine [ˈvæləntaɪn] Valentin(e *f*) *m.*
Vat·i·can [ˈvætɪkən] *der* Vatikan.
Ven·e·zu·e·la [ˌvenɪˈzweɪlə] Venezuela *n.*
Ven·ice [ˈvenɪs] Venedig *n.*
Vi·en·na [vɪˈenə] Wien *n.*
Viet·nam [ˌvjetˈnæm] Vietnam *n.*
Vil·ni·us [ˈvɪlnɪəs] Wilna *f.*
Vir·gil [ˈvɜːdʒɪl] Vergil *m.*

W

Wales [weɪlz] Wales *n.*
War·saw [ˈwɔːsɔː] Warschau *n.*
West·pha·lia [westˈfeɪljə] Westfalen *n.*
Wil·liam [ˈwɪljəm] Wilhelm *m.*

Y

Yu·go·sla·via [ˌjuːgəʊˈslɑːvjə] *hist.* Jugoslawien *n.*

Z

Zach·a·ri·ah [ˌzækəˈraɪə], **Zach·a·ry** [ˈzækərɪ] Zacharias *m.*
Za·ire [zɑːˈɪə] Za'ire *n.*
Zim·ba·bwe [zɪmˈbɑːbwɪ] Simbabwe *n.*
Zu·rich [ˈzjʊərɪk] Zürich *n.*

Geographical Names

A

Aachen Aachen, Aix-la-Chapelle
Abruzzen, die the Abruzzi
Addis Abeba Addis Ababa
Admiralitätsinseln, die the Admiralty Islands, the Admiralties
Adria, die the Adriatic (Sea)
Afrika Africa
Ägäis, die the Aegean (Sea)
Ägäischen Inseln, die the Aegean Islands
Ägypten Egypt
Akaba Aqaba, Akaba
Akkra Accra
Akropolis, die the Acropolis
Albanien Albania

Aleuten, die the Aleutian Islands
Alexandrien Alexandria
Algerien Algeria
Algier Algiers
Alpen, die the Alps
Alpenvorland, das the foothills of the Alps
Altaigebirge, das the Altai Mountains
Amazonas, der the Amazon
Amerika America
Anatolien Anatolia
Andalusien Andalusia
Anden, die the Andes
Antarktis, die the Antarctic, Antarctica
Antillen, die the Antilles
Antwerpen Antwerp

Apennin, *der,* **Apenninen,** *die* *the* Apennines, *the* Apennine Mountains
Apenninenhalbinsel, *die* *the* Apennine Peninsula
Appalachen, *die* *the* Appalachians, *the* Appalachian Mountains
Apulien Apulia
Arabien Arabia
Arabische Wüste, *die* *the* Arabian Desert
Aralsee, *der* Lake Aral
Ardennen, *die* *the* Ardennes
Argentinien Argentina, *the* Argentine
Arktis, *die* *the* Arctic
Ärmelkanal, *der* *the* (English) Channel
Armenien Armenia
Aserbeidschan Azerbaijan
Asien Asia
Asowsche Meer, *das* *the* Sea of Azov
Assuan Aswan
Athen Athens
Äthiopien Ethiopia
Atlantik, *der* *the* Atlantic (Ocean)
Atlasgebirge, *das* *the* Atlas Mountains
Ätna, *der* Mount Etna
Australasien Australasia
Australien Australia
Azoren, *die* *the* Azores

B

Bagdad Baghdad
Baikalsee, *der* Lake Baikal
Balearen, *die* *the* Balearic Islands
Balkan, *der* → 1. *Balkanhalbinsel;* 2. *Balkanstaaten;* 3. *Balkangebirge*
Balkangebirge, *das* *the* Balkan Mountains
Balkanhalbinsel, *die* *the* Balkan Peninsula
Balkanstaaten, *die* *the* Balkan States, *the* Balkans
Baltikum, *das* *the* Baltic (States), *the* Baltics
Bangladesch Bangladesh
Barentssee, *die* *the* Barents Sea
Basel Basel, Basle
Baskenland, *das* *the* Basque Provinces
Bayerische Wald, *der* *the* Bavarian Forest
Belgien Belgium
Belgrad Belgrade
Benelux-Länder, *die* *the* Benelux Countries

Bengalen Bengal
Beringmeer, *das* *the* Bering Sea
Beringstraße, *die* *the* Bering Strait
Bern Bern(e)
Bessarabien Bessarabia
Bikini, Bikiniatoll, *das* Bikini
Birma Burma
Biskaya, *die* → *Golf von Biskaya*
Bodensee, *der* Lake Constance
Böhmen Čechy; *hist.* Bohemia
Böhmerwald, *der* *the* Bohemian Forest
Bolivien Bolivia
Bosnien Bosnia
Bosnien und Herzegowina Bosnia and Herzegovina
Bosporus, *der* *the* Bosp(h)orus
Botsuana Botswana
Bottnische Meerbusen, *der* *the* Gulf of Bothnia
Bozen Bolzano
Brasilien Brazil
Brenner(paß), *der* *the* Brenner Pass
Breslau Wrocław; *hist.* Breslau
Bretagne, *die* Brittany
Brügge Bruges
Brüssel Brussels
Bukarest Bucharest
Bukowina, *die* Bukovina, Bucovina
Bulgarien Bulgaria
Bundesrepublik Deutschland, *die* *the* Federal Republic of Germany
Burgund Burgundy

C

Cevennen, *die* *the* Cévennes
Charkow Kharkov
Chiemsee, *der* Lake Chiem, *the* Chiemsee
Chinesische Mauer, *die* *the* Great Wall of China
Chinesische Meer, *das* *the* China Sea
Comer See, *der* Lake Como

D

Damaskus Damascus
Dänemark Denmark
Danzig Gdansk; *hist.* Danzig
Danziger Bucht, *die* *the* Bay (or Gulf) of Gdansk (*hist.* Danzig)
Dardanellen, *die* *the* Dardanelles
Daressalam Dar es Salaam
Den Haag The Hague

Deutsche Bucht, *die* the German Bay
Deutschland Germany
Dnjepr, *der* the Dnieper
Dnjestr, *der* the Dniester
Dodekanes, *der* the Dodecanese
Dolomiten, *die* the Dolomites
Dominikanische Republik, *die* the Dominican Republic
Donau, *die* the Danube
Donez, *der* the Donets
Donezbecken, *das* the Donets (Basin)
Dover → *Straße von Dover*
Drau, *die* the Drava
Dschibuti Djibouti
Dschidda Jedda

E

Eiffelturm, *der* the Eiffel Tower
Eismeer, Nördliche, *das* → *Nordpolarmeer*
Eismeer, Südliche, *das* → *Südpolarmeer*
Elat Eilat
Elfenbeinküste, *die* the Ivory Coast
Elsaß, *das* Alsace
Engadin, *das* the Engadine
Eriwan Yerevan, Erivan
Erzgebirge, *das* the Erzgebirge, *the* Ore Mountains
Estland Estonia
Etsch, *die* the Adige
Euphrat, *der* the Euphrates
Eurasien Eurasia
Europa Europe
Everest, *der* (Mount) Everest

F

Falklandinseln, *die* the Falkland Islands, *the* Falklands
Färöer, *die* the Faroes, *the* Faroe Islands
Ferne Osten, *der,* **Fernost** *the* Far East
Feuerland Tierra del Fuego
Fidschi Fiji
Fidschiinseln, *die* the Fiji Islands
Finnische Meerbusen, *der* the Gulf of Finland
Finnland Finland
Flandern Flanders
Florenz Florence
Franken Franconia

Frankfurt (am Main) Frankfurt (on the Main)
Frankfurt (an der Oder) Frankfurt (on the Oder)
Frankreich France
Französisch-Guayana French Guiana
Fudschijama, *der* (Mount) Fuji, *a.* Fujiyama

G

Gabun Gabon
Galapagosinseln, *die* the Galapagos Islands
Gambia (*the*) Gambia
Gardasee, *der* Lake Garda
Gazastreifen, *der* the Gaza Strip
Genezareth → *See Genezareth*
Genf Geneva
Genfer See, *der* Lake Geneva, Lac Léman
Gent Ghent
Genua Genoa
Georgien Georgia
Golanhöhen, *die* the Golan Heights
Goldene Horn, *das* the Golden Horn
Golf von Akaba, *der* the Gulf of Aqaba (*or* Akaba)
Golf von Bengalen, *der* the Bay of Bengal
Golf von Biskaya, *der* the Bay of Biscay
Golf von Genua, *der* the Gulf of Genoa
Golf von Korinth, *der* the Gulf of Corinth
Golf von Neapel, *der* the Bay of Naples
Golf von Triest, *der* the Gulf of Trieste
Göteborg Gothenburg, Göteborg
Graubünden Graubünden, *the* Grisons
Griechenland Greece
Grönland Greenland
Großbritannien Great Britain, Britain
Große Belt, *der* the Great Belt
Großen Seen, *die* the Great Lakes
Große Syrte, *die* the Gulf of Sidra
Guayana (*region*) Guiana
Guyana (*state*) Guyana

H

Harz, *der* the Harz (Mountains)
Havanna Havana
Hawaii-Inseln, *die* the Hawaiian Islands
Hebriden, *die* the Hebrides

Helgoland Hel(i)goland
Helgoländer Bucht, *die the* Hel(i)go-
land Bight
Himalaja, *der the* Himalayas
Hindukusch, *der the* Hindu Kush
Hinterindien Indochina
Hiroschima Hiroshima
Hoek van Holland Hook of Holland
Holland Holland, *the* Netherlands
Hongkong Hong Kong

I

Iberische Halbinsel, *die the* Iberian
Peninsula
Ijsselmeer, *das* Lake Ijssel, Ijsselmeer
Indien India
Indische Ozean, *der the* Indian Ocean
Indonesien Indonesia
Innerasien Central Asia
Innere Mongolei, *die* Inner Mongolia
Insel Man, *die* the Isle of Man
Insel Wight, *die the* Isle of Wight
Ionische Meer, *das the* Ionian Sea
Ionischen Inseln, *die the* Ionian Islands
Irak, *der* Iraq
Irische See, *die the* Irish Sea
Irland Ireland
Island Iceland
Italien Italy

J

Jadebusen, *der the* Jade Bay
Jakutsk Yakutsk
Jalta Yalta
Jamaika Jamaica
Jangtse(kiang), *der the* Yangt-
tze(-Kiang)
Japanische Meer, *das the* Sea of Japan
Jemen, *der the* Yemen
Jordanien Jordan
Jugoslawien *hist.* Yugoslavia
Jungferninseln, *die the* Virgin Islands
Jütland Jutland

K

Kaimaninseln, *die the* Cayman Islands
Kairo Cairo
Kalabrien Calabria
Kalifornien California
Kalkutta Calcutta
Kambodscha Cambodia
Kamerun Cameroon

Kanada Canada
Kanal, *der the* (English) Channel
Kanalinseln, *die the* Channel Islands
Kanaren, *die,* **Kanarischen Inseln,** *die
the* Canaries, *the* Canary Islands
Kap der Guten Hoffnung, *das the* Cape
of Good Hope, *a. the* Cape
Kap Hoorn Cape Horn, *a. the* Horn
Kapprovinz, *die* Cape Province
Kap Skagen *the* Skaw, *a.* (Cape) Skagen
Kapstadt Cape Town
Kapverdischen Inseln, *die the* Cape
Verde Islands
Karatschi Karachi
Karibik, *die the* Caribbean
Kärnten Carinthia
Karolinen, *die the* Caroline Islands
Karpaten, *die the* Carpathians, *the* Car-
pathian Mountains
Kasachstan Kazakhstan
Kaschmir Kashmir
Kaspische Meer, *das the* Caspian Sea
Kastilien Castile
Katalonien Catalonia
Katar Qatar
Kaukasus, *der the* Caucasus, *a. the*
Caucasus Mountains
Kenia Kenya
Kieler Bucht, *die* Kiel Bay
Kiew Kiev
Kilimandscharo, *der* (Mount) Kili-
manjaro
Kirgisien Kirghizia
Kleinasien Asia Minor
Köln Cologne
Kolumbien Colombia
Komoren, *die the* Comoro Archipelago
Kongo, *der the* Congo
Königsberg Kaliningrad; *hist.* Königs-
berg
Kopenhagen Copenhagen
Kordilleren, *die the* Cordilleras
Korfu Corfu
Korinth Corinth
Korsika Corsica
Krakatau Krakatoa
Kreta Crete
Krim, *die the* Crimea
Kroatien Croatia
Kuba Cuba
Kurdistan Kurdistan, Kurdestan, Kor-
destan
Kurilen, *die the* Kuril(e) Islands
Kykladen, *die the* Cyclades

L

Ladogasee, *der* Lake Ladoga
Lappland Lapland
Lateinamerika Latin America
Lausitz, *die* Lusatia
Lemberg Lvov
Lettland Latvia
Levante, *die the* Levant
Libanon, *der (the)* Lebanon
Libyen Libya
Ligurische Meer, *das the* Ligurian Sea
Liparischen Inseln, *die* Lipari Islands
Lissabon Lisbon
Litauen Lithuania
Lübecker Bucht, *die the* Lübeck Bay
Luganer See, *der* Lake Lugano
Lüneburger Heide, *die the* Lüneburg
  Heath
Lüttich Liège
Luxemburg Luxemb(o)urg
Luzern Lucerne

M

Maas, *die the* Meuse, *the* Maas
Madagaskar Madagascar
Magellanstraße, *die the* Strait(s) of
  Magellan
Mailand Milan
Makedonien Macedonia
Malaiische Halbinsel, *die the* Malay
  Peninsula, Malaya
Malakka Malacca
Malediven, *die the* Maldives
Mallorca Majorca
Mandschurei, *die* Manchuria
Marianen, *die the* Marianas
Mark Brandenburg, *die the* Branden-
  burg Marches
Marmarameer, *das the* Sea of Marma-
  ra
Marokko Morocco
Maskat und Oman Muscat and Oman
Masuren Masuria
Masurischen Seen, *die the* Masurian
  Lakes
Mauretanien Mauretania
Mekka Mecca
Melanesien Melanesia
Menorca Minorca
Meran Merano
Mesopotamien Mesopotamia

Mexiko Mexico
Mikronesien Micronesia
Mittelamerika Central America
Mittelasien Central Asia
Mittelmeer, *das the* Mediterranean
  (Sea)
Mittlere Osten, *der the* Middle East
Moçambique Mozambique
Moldau¹, *die (river) the* Vltava; *hist. the*
  Moldau
Moldau², *die (region)* Moldavia
Moldavien Moldavia
Molukken, *die the* Moluccas
Mongolei, *die* Mongolia
Mosel, *die the* Moselle
Moskau Moscow
Moskwa, *die the* Moskva
München Munich
Mykene Mycenae

N

Nahe Osten, *der the* Middle (*or* Near)
  East
Neapel Naples
Neu-Delhi New Delhi
Neufundland Newfoundland
Neuguinea New Guinea
Neuseeland New Zealand
Newa, *die the* Neva
Niagarafälle, *die the* Niagara Falls
Niederlande, *die the* Netherlands, Hol-
  land
Nikosia Nicosia
Nil, *der the* Nile
Nizza Nice
Nordafrika North Africa
Nordamerika North America
Norddeutsche Tiefebene, *die the*
  North(ern) German Plain
Nordfriesischen Inseln, *die the* North
  Frisians
Nordirland Northern Ireland
Nordkap, *das the* North Cape
Nordkorea North Korea
Nord-Ostsee-Kanal, *der the* Kiel
  Canal
Nordpol, *der the* North Pole
Nordpolarmeer, *das the* Arctic Ocean
Nordsee, *die the* North Sea
Normandie, *die* Normandy
Norwegen Norway
Nowosibirsk Novosibirsk
Nürnberg Nuremberg

O

Oberrheinische Tiefebene, die *the* Upper Rhine Valley
Ochotskische Meer, das *the* Sea of Okhotsk
Olymp, der (Mount) Olympus
Onegasee, der Lake Onega
Oranjefreistaat, der *the* Orange Free State
Orinoko, der *the* Orinoco
Ostafrika East Africa
Ostasien East Asia
Ostende Ostend
Osterinsel, die Easter Island
Österreich Austria
Ostfriesischen Inseln, die *the* East Frisians
Ostsee, die *the* Baltic (Sea)
Ozeanien Oceania

P

Panamakanal, der *the* Panama Canal
Pandschab, das *the* Punjab
Papua-Neuguinea Papua-New Guinea
Parnaß, der Mount Parnassus
Patagonien Patagonia
Pazifik, der *the* Pacific (Ocean)
Peloponnes, der *or* **die** *the* Peloponnese, *the* Peloponnesus
Persische Golf, der *the* Persian Gulf
Petersburg, (St.) St Petersburg
Pfalz, die *the* Palatinate
Philippinen, die *the* Philippines
Piräus Piraeus
Plattensee, der Lake Balaton
Po-Ebene, die *the* Po Valley
Polarkreis, der 1. *the* Arctic Circle; **2.** *the* Antarctic Circle
Polen Poland
Polynesien Polynesia
Pommern Pomorze; *hist.* Pomerania
Pompeji Pompeii
Pontische Gebirge, das *the* Pontic Mountains
Prag Prague
Provence, die Provence
Pyrenäen, die *the* Pyrenees
Pyrenäenhalbinsel, die *the* Iberian Peninsula

R

Reval Tallin(n); *hist.* Reval
Rhein, der *the* Rhine
Rheinfall, der *the* Rhine Falls
Rheingau, der *the* Rhinegau
Rheinhessen Rhinehessen
Rheinische Schiefergebirge, das *the* Rhenish Slate Mountains
Rheinland, das *the* Rhineland
Rhodos Rhodes
Rom Rome
Rote Meer, das *the* Red Sea
Ruhrgebiet, das *the* Ruhr(gebiet)
Rumänien Romania, *a.* Rumania
Rußland Russia

S

Sächsische Schweiz, die Saxon Switzerland
Salomonen, die, Salomonischen Inseln, die *the* Solomon Islands
Saloniki Salonika, Saloniki
Sambesi, der *the* Zambezi
Sambia Zambia
Sankt-Lorenz-Strom, der *the* St Lawrence (River)
Sansibar Zanzibar
Sarajewo Sarajevo
Sardinien Sardinia
Saudi-Arabien Saudi Arabia
Savoyen Savoy
Schanghai Shanghai
Schatt el Arab, der *the* Shatt-al-Arab
Schlesien Slask; *hist.* Silesia
Schottland Scotland
Schwaben Swabia
Schwäbische Alb, die *the* Swabian Jura
Schwarze Meer, das *the* Black Sea
Schwarzwald, der *the* Black Forest
Schweden Sweden
Schweiz, die Switzerland
See Genezareth, der *the* Sea of Galilee
Seeland Zealand
Serbien Serbia
Sevilla Seville
Seychellen, die *the* Seychelles
Sibirien Siberia
Simbabwe Zimbabwe
Sinaigebirge, das Mount Sinai
Sinaihalbinsel, die *the* Sinai Peninsula
Singapur Singapore
Sizilien Sicily
Skandinavien Scandinavia
Slowakei, die Slovakia
Slowenien Slovenia
Sowjetunion, die *hist. the* Soviet Union

Spanien Spain
Sporaden, die *the* Sporades
Steiermark, die Styria
Stettin Szczecin; *hist.* Stettin
Stille Ozean, der → Pazifik
Straßburg Strasbourg
Straße von Dover, die *the* Strait(s) of Dover
Straße von Gibraltar, die *the* Strait(s) of Gibraltar
Südafrika South Africa
Südamerika South America
Sudan, der (*the*) Sudan
Südchinesische Meer, das *the* South China Sea
Südkorea South Korea
Südpolarmeer, das *the* Antarctic Ocean
Südsee, die *the* South Pacific, *the* South Seas
Südseeinseln, die *the* Pacific (*or* South Sea) Islands
Südtirol South Tyrol
Südwestafrika South-West Africa
Suezkanal, der *the* Suez Canal
Swasiland Swaziland
Syrien Syria
Szetschuan Szechuan

T

Tadschikistan Tadzhikistan
Tafelberg, der Table Mountain
Taipeh Taipei
Tajo, der *the* Tagus
Tanganjika Tanganyika
Tanganjikasee, der Lake Tanganyika
Tanger Tangier
Tansania Tanzania
Tasmanien Tasmania
Tatra, die *the* Tatra Mountains, *a. the* High Tatra
Taurus, der *the* Taurus (Mountains)
Teheran Teh(e)ran
Teneriffa Tenerife
Tessin, das Ticino
Teutoburger Wald, der *the* Teutoburg Forest, *the* Teutoburger Wald
Themse, die *the* Thames
Thüringer Wald, der *the* Thuringian Forest
Tirol (*the*) Tyrol
Tokio Tokyo
Tongainseln, die *the* Tonga (*or* Friendly) Islands

Toskana, die Tuscany
Tote Meer, das *the* Dead Sea
Tripolis Tripoli
Tschad, der Chad
Tschechoslowakei, die *hist.* Czechoslovakia
Tunesien Tunisia
Türkei, die Turkey
Turkestan Turkestan, Turkistan
Tyrrhenische Meer, das *the* Tyrrhenian Sea

U

Ungarn Hungary
Union der Sozialistischen Sowjetrepubliken, die *the hist.* Union of Soviet Socialist Republics
Ural, der *the* Urals
Usbekistan Uzbekistan

V

Venedig Venice
Venetien Veneto
Vereinigte Königreich (von Großbritannien und Nordirland), das *the* United Kingdom (of Great Britain and Northern Ireland)
Vereinigten Arabischen Emirate, die *the* United Arab Emirates
Vereinigten Staaten (von Amerika), die *the* United States (of America)
Vesuv, der Vesuvius
Vierwaldstätter See, der Lake Lucerne
Vietnam Vietnam, Viet Nam
Vogesen, die *the* Vosges (Mountains)
Volksrepublik China, die *the* People's Republic of China
Vorderasien *the* Middle (*or* Near) East
Vorderindien *the* Indian Peninsula (and Ceylon)

W

Wallis, das Valais
Warschau Warsaw
Wattenmeer, das *the* mud flats
Weichsel, die *the* Vistula
Weißrußland B(y)elorussia, White Russia
Westfalen Westphalia
Westfälische Pforte, die *the* Porta Westfalica, *the* Westphalian Gate
Westfriesischen Inseln, die *the* West Frisians

Westindien *the* West Indies
Wien Vienna
Wilna Vilnius
Wladiwostok Vladivostok
Wolga, *die the* Volga

Y

Ypern Ypres

Z

Zentralafrikanische Republik, die *the*
Central African Republic
Zuckerhut, der Sugar Loaf Mountain
Zürich Zurich
Zürichsee, der, Züricher See, der
Lake Zurich
Zypern Cyprus

Abbreviations

A

a *acre* Acre *m* (*4046,8 m²*).
A *answer* Antw., Antwort *f*; *ampere*
A, Ampere *n od. pl.*
AA *Alcoholics Anonymous* Anonyme
Alkoholiker *pl*; *antiaircraft* Flugab-
wehr...; *Br. Automobile Association*
(*Automobilclub*).
AAA [ˌθriːˈeɪz] *Br. Amateur Athletic
Association* (*Leichtathletikverband*);
[ˌtrɪplˈeɪ] *Am. American Automobile
Association* (*Automobilclub*).
AB *able-bodied seaman* Vollmatrose
m; *Am.* → *BA* (*Bachelor of Arts*).
abbr. *abbreviated* abgekürzt; *abbre-
viation* Abk., Abkürzung *f*.
ABC *American Broadcasting Company* (*amerikanische Rundfunkgesellschaft*).
AC *alternating current* Wechselstrom *m*.
A/C, a/c *account current* Kontokorrent
n; *account* Kto., Konto *n*; Rechnung *f*.
acc(t). *account* Kto., Konto *n*; Rechnung *f*.
AD *Anno Domini* im Jahr des Herrn,
n. Chr., nach Christus.
adj. *adjective* Adj., Adjektiv *n*.
Adm. *Admiral* Admiral *m*; *Admiralty*
Admiralität *f*.
adv. *adverb* Adv., Adverb *n*.
advt *advertisement* Inserat *n*, Annonce *f*.
AFC *automatic frequency control* automatische Frequenz(fein)abstimmung.
AFL-CIO *American Federation of Labor & Congress of Industrial Organi-*

zations (*Gewerkschaftsverband*).
AFN *American Forces Network* (*Rund-
funkanstalt der US-Streitkräfte*).
AGM *bsd. Br. annual general meeting*
Jahreshauptversammlung *f*.
AK *Alaska* (*Staat der USA*).
AL, Ala. *Alabama* (*Staat der USA*).
Alas. *Alaska* (*Staat der USA*).
AM *amplitude modulation* (*Frequenzbe-
reich der Kurz-, Mittel- u. Langwellen*);
Am. → *MA* (*Master of Arts*); *bsd. Am.*
→ *a.m.*
Am. *America* Amerika *n*; *American*
amerikanisch.
a.m., am *ante meridiem* (= *before
noon*) morgens, vorm., vormittags.
anon. *anonymous* anonym.
a/o *account of* à Konto von, auf Rech-
nung von.
AP *Associated Press* (*amerikanische
Nachrichtenagentur*); *American plan*
Vollpension *f*.
approx. *approximate(ly)* annähernd,
etwa.
Apr. *April* April *m*.
APT *Br. Advanced Passenger Train*
(*Hochgeschwindigkeitszug*).
apt *bsd. Am. apartment* Wohnung *f*.
AR *Arkansas* (*Staat der USA*).
ARC *American Red Cross* das Ameri-
kanische Rote Kreuz.
Ariz. *Arizona* (*Staat der USA*).
Ark. *Arkansas* (*Staat der USA*).
arr. *arrival* Ank., Ankunft *f*.
A/S *account sales* Verkaufsabrechnung
f.
ASCII [ˈæskiː] *American Standard Code*

for Information Interchange (*standardisierter Code zur Darstellung alphanumerischer Zeichen*).

asst. *assistant* Asst., Assistent(in).

attn *attention* (*of*) zu Händen (von), für.

Aug. *August* Aug., August *m*.

av. *average* Durchschnitt *m*; Havarie *f*.

avdp *avoirdupois* (*Handelsgewicht*).

Ave *Avenue* Allee *f*, Straße *f*.

AWACS ['eɪwæks] *Airborne Warning and Control System* (*luftgestütztes Frühwarnsystem*).

AWOL *absent without leave* unerlaubt abwesend; ✗ unerlaubt von der Truppe entfernt.

AZ *Arizona* (*Staat der USA*).

B

b. *born* geb., geboren.

BA *Bachelor of Arts* Bakkalaureus *m* der Philosophie; *British Airways* (*britische Luftverkehrsgesellschaft*).

B&B *bed and breakfast* Übernachtung *f* mit Frühstück.

B&W, b&w → *B/W*.

BASIC ['beɪsɪk] *beginners' all-purpose symbolic instruction code* (*einfache Programmiersprache*).

BBC *British Broadcasting Corporation* BBC *f* (*britische Rundfunkgesellschaft*).

bbl. *barrel* Faß *n*.

BC *before Christ* v. Chr., vor Christus.

BD *Bachelor of Divinity* Bakkalaureus *m* der Theologie.

B/E *bill of exchange* ✝ Wechsel *m*.

Beds [bedz] *Bedfordshire*.

BEng *Bachelor of Engineering* Bakkalaureus *m* der Ingenieurwissenschaft(en).

Berks [bɑːks] *Berkshire*.

b/f *brought forward* Übertrag *m*.

BFBS *British Forces Broadcasting Service* (*Rundfunkanstalt der britischen Streitkräfte*).

bk *book* Buch *n*; *bank* Bank *f*.

BL *Bachelor of Law* Bakkalaureus *m* des Rechts.

B/L *bill of lading* (See)Frachtbrief *m*, Konnossement *n*.

bl. *barrel* Faß *n*; *bale* Ballen *m*.

BLit *Bachelor of Literature* Bakkalaureus *m* der Literatur(wissenschaft).

BLitt *Bachelor of Letters* Bakkalaureus *m* der Literaturwissenschaft.

bls. *bales* Ballen *pl*; *barrels* Fässer *pl*.

Blvd *Boulevard* Boulevard *m*.

BM *Bachelor of Medicine* Bakkalaureus *m* der Medizin.

BO, b.o. *branch office* Filiale *f*; F *body odo(u)r* Körpergeruch *m*.

BOT *Br. Board of Trade* Handelsministerium *n*.

BR *British Rail* (*Eisenbahn in Großbritannien*).

BRCS *British Red Cross Society* das Britische Rote Kreuz.

Br(it). *Britain* Großbritannien *n*; *British* britisch.

Bros. *brothers* Gebr., Gebrüder *pl* (*in Firmenbezeichnungen*).

BS *Am. Bachelor of Science* Bakkalaureus *m* der Naturwissenschaften; *Br. Bachelor of Surgery* Bakkalaureus *m* der Chirurgie; *British Standard* Britische Norm.

BSc *Br. Bachelor of Science* Bakkalaureus *m* der Naturwissenschaften.

BScEcon *Bachelor of Economic Science* Bakkalaureus *m* der Wirtschaftswissenschaft(en).

BSI *British Standards Institution* (*britische Normungsorganisation*).

BTA *British Tourist Authority* Britische Fremdenverkehrsbehörde.

bu. *bushel* Scheffel *m* (*Br. 36,36 l, Am. 35,24 l*).

Bucks [bʌks] *Buckinghamshire*.

B/W *black and white phot.* s/w, schwarzweiß; Schwarzweißbild *n*.

C

C *Celsius* C, Celsius; *centigrade* hundertgradig (*Thermometereinteilung*).

c *cent(s)* Cent *m* (*od. pl*) (*amerikanische Münze*); *century* Jh., Jahrhundert *n*; *circa* ca., circa, ungefähr; *cubic* Kubik...

CA *California* Kalifornien *n* (*Staat der USA*); *chartered accountant Br.* konzessionierter Wirtschaftsprüfer *od.* Buchprüfer *od.* Steuerberater.

C/A *current account* Girokonto *n*.

CAD *computer-aided design* (*computergestütztes Entwurfszeichnen*).

Cal(if). *California* Kalifornien *n* (*Staat der USA*).
CAM *computer-aided manufacture* (*computergestützte Fertigung*).
Cambs [kæmz] *Cambridgeshire.*
Can. *Canada* Kanada *n*; *Canadian* kanadisch.
C&W *country and western* (*Musik*).
Capt. *Captain* ♣ Kapitän *m*; ✕ Hauptmann *m*.
CB *Citizens' Band* CB-Funk *m* (*Wellenbereich für privaten Funkverkehr*); *Br. Companion of (the Order of) the Bath* Komtur *m* des Bath-Ordens.
CBE *Commander of (the Order of) the British Empire* Komtur *m* des Ordens des Britischen Weltreichs.
CBS *Columbia Broadcasting System* (*amerikanische Rundfunkgesellschaft*).
CC *city council* Stadtrat *m*; *Br. county council* Grafschaftsrat *m*.
cc *Br. cubic centimetre(s)* cm³, Kubikzentimeter *m* (*od. pl*).
CD *compact disc* CD(-Platte) *f*; *corps diplomatique* CD *n*, diplomatisches Korps.
CE *Church of England* Anglikanische Kirche; *civil engineer* Bauingenieur *m*.
cert. *certificate* Bescheinigung *f*.
CET *Central European Time* MEZ, mitteleuropäische Zeit.
cf. *confer* vgl., vergleiche.
ch. *chapter* Kap., Kapitel *n*.
Ches *Cheshire.*
CIA *Am. Central Intelligence Agency* (*US-Geheimdienst*).
CID *Br. Criminal Investigation Department* (*Kriminalpolizei*).
c.i.f., cif *cost, insurance, freight* Kosten, Versicherung und Fracht einbegriffen.
C.-in-C., C in C *commander in chief* Oberbefehlshaber *m*.
CIS *Commonwealth of Independent States* GUS, Gemeinschaft *f* Unabhängiger Staaten.
cl. *class* Kl., Klasse *f*.
CO *Colorado* (*Staat der USA*); *commanding officer* Kommandeur *m*.
Co. *Company* ✝ Gesellschaft *f*; *county Br.* Grafschaft *f*; *Am.* Kreis *m* (*Verwaltungsbezirk*).
c/o *care of* (wohnhaft) bei.
COBOL ['kəʊbɒl] *common business*

oriented language (*Programmiersprache*).
COD *cash* (*Am. collect*) *on delivery* per Nachnahme.
C of E *Church of England* Anglikanische Kirche.
Col. *colonel* Oberst *m*; → *Colo.*
col. *column* Sp., Spalte *f* (*in Buch etc*).
Colo. *Colorado* (*Staat der USA*).
Conn. *Connecticut* (*Staat der USA*).
Cons. *Br. pol. Conservative* Konservative *m*, *f*; konservativ.
cont(d) *continued* Forts., Fortsetzung *f*; fortgesetzt.
Corn *Cornwall.*
Corp. *corporal* Korporal *m*, Unteroffizier *m*.
CP *Canadian Press* (*Nachrichtenagentur*); *Communist Party* KP, Kommunistische Partei.
cp. *compare* vgl., vergleiche.
CPA *Am. certified public accountant* amtlich zugelassener Wirtschaftsprüfer.
CPU *central processing unit* Computer: Zentraleinheit *f*.
CT *Connecticut* (*Staat der USA*).
ct(s) *cent(s)* Cent *m* (*od. pl*) (*amerikanische Münze*).
cu *cubic* Kubik...
CV, cv *curriculum vitae* Lebenslauf *m*.
c.w.o. *cash with order* Barzahlung *f* bei Bestellung.
cwt *hundredweight* (*etwa 1*) Zentner *m* (*Br. 50,8 kg, Am. 45,36 kg*).

D

d. *depth* T., Tiefe *f*; *Br. obs. penny, pence* (*bis 1971 verwendete Abkürzung*); *died* gest., gestorben.
DA *deposit account* Depositenkonto *n*; *Am. District Attorney* Staatsanwalt *m*.
DAT *digital audio tape* (*Tonbandcassette für Digitalaufnahmen mit DAT-Recordern*).
DC *direct current* Gleichstrom *m*; *District of Columbia* Bundesdistrikt der USA (= *Gebiet der amerikanischen Hauptstadt Washington*).
DCL *Doctor of Civil Law* Dr. jur., Doktor *m* des Zivilrechts.
DD *Doctor of Divinity* Dr. theol., Doktor *m* der Theologie.

DDT *dichlorodiphenyltrichloroethane* DDT, Dichlordiphenyltrichloräthan *n*.

DE *Delaware* (*Staat der USA*).

Dec. *December* Dez., Dezember *m*.

dec., decd *deceased* gest., gestorben.

Del. *Delaware* (*Staat der USA*).

dep. *departure* Abf., Abfahrt *f*.

dept *department* Abt., Abteilung *f*.

Derbys *Derbyshire*.

dft *draft* ✝ Tratte *f*.

Dip., dip. *diploma* Diplom *n*.

Dir., dir. *director* Dir., Direktor *m*, Leiter(in).

disc. *discount* ✝ Diskont *m*; Rabatt *m*, Preisnachlaß *m*.

div. *dividend* Dividende *f*; *divorced* gesch., geschieden; *division* Abteilung *f* (*in Firma*); *Sport*: Liga *f*.

DJ *disc jockey* Diskjockey *m*; *dinner jacket* Smoking(jacke *f*) *m*.

DLit(t) *Doctor of Letters, Doctor of Literature* Doktor *m* der Literaturwissenschaft.

do. *ditto* do., dito, dgl., desgleichen.

doc. *document* Dokument *n*, Urkunde *f*.

dol. *dollar(s)* Dollar *m* (*od. pl*).

Dors *Dorset*.

doz. *dozen(s)* Dtzd., Dutzend *n* (*od. pl*).

DPh(il) *Doctor of Philosophy* Dr. phil., Doktor *m* der Philosophie.

dpt *department* Abt., Abteilung *f*.

Dr *Doctor* Dr., Doktor *m*; *in Straßennamen*: *Drive* etwa: Fahrstraße *f*, Zufahrt *f*.

d.s., d/s *days after sight* Tage *pl* nach Sicht (*bei Wechseln*).

DSc *Doctor of Science* Dr. rer. nat., Doktor *m* der Naturwissenschaften.

Dur *Durham*.

dz. *dozen(s)* Dtzd., Dutzend *n* (*od. pl*).

E

E *east* O, Ost(en *m*); *eastern* ö, östlich; *English* englisch.

E. & O.E. *errors and omissions excepted* Irrtümer und Auslassungen vorbehalten.

EC *European Community* hist. EG, Europäische Gemeinschaft; *East Central* (London) Mitte-Ost (*Postbezirk*).

ECOSOC *Economic and Social Council* Wirtschafts- und Sozialrat *m* (*der UN*).

ECU *European Currency Unit(s)* Europäische Währungseinheit(en *pl*) *f*.

Ed., ed. *edited* h(rs)g., herausgegeben; *edition* Aufl., Auflage *f*; *editor* H(rs)g., Herausgeber *m*.

EDP *electronic data processing* EDV, elektronische Datenverarbeitung.

E.E., e.e. *errors excepted* Irrtümer vorbehalten.

EEC *European Economic Community* hist. EWG, Europäische Wirtschaftsgemeinschaft.

EFTA ['eftə] *European Free Trade Association* EFTA, Europäische Freihandelsgemeinschaft.

Eftpos *electronic funds transfer at point of sale* Zahlungsart *f* „ec-Kasse".

e.g. *exempli gratia* (= *for instance*) z. B., zum Beispiel.

enc(l). *enclosure(s)* Anl., Anlage(n *pl*) *f*.

ESA *European Space Agency* Europäische Weltraumbehörde.

esp. *especially* bes., bsd., besonders.

Esq. *Esquire* (*in Briefadressen, nachgestellt*) Herrn.

Ess *Essex*.

est. *established* gegr., gegründet; *estimated* gesch., geschätzt.

ETA *estimated time of arrival* voraussichtliche Ankunft(szeit).

etc., &c. *et cetera, and the rest, and so on* etc., usw., und so weiter.

ETD *estimated time of departure* voraussichtliche Abflugzeit *bzw.* Abfahrtszeit.

EU *European Union* EU, Europäische Union

EURATOM [juər'ætəm] *European Atomic Energy Community* Euratom, Europäische Atomgemeinschaft.

excl. *exclusive, excluding* ausschl., ausschließlich, ohne.

ext. *extension* teleph. Apparat *m* (*Nebenanschluß*); *external, exterior* äußerlich, Außen...

F

f *female, feminine* weiblich; *following* folg., folgend; *foot* (*feet*) Fuß *m* (*od. pl*) (*30,48 cm*).

F *Fahrenheit* F, Fahrenheit (*Thermometereinteilung*).

FA *Br. Football Association* Fußballverband *m*.

FAO *Food and Agriculture Organization* Organisation *f* für Ernährung und Landwirtschaft (*der* **UN**).

FBI *Am. Federal Bureau of Investigation* FBI *m*, *n* (*Bundeskriminalamt*).

Feb. *February* Febr., Februar *m*.

fed. *federal pol.* Bundes...

fig. *figure(s)* Abb., Abbildung(en *pl*) *f*.

FL *Florida* (*Staat der USA*).

fl. *floor* Stock(werk *n*) *m*.

Fla. *Florida* (*Staat der USA*).

FM *frequency modulation* UKW (*Frequenzbereich der Ultrakurzwellen*).

fm *fathom* Faden *m*, Klafter *m*, *n* (*1,83 m*).

f.o.b., fob *free on board* frei (*Schiff etc*).

foll. *following* folg., folgend.

FORTRAN *formula translation* (*Programmiersprache*).

Fr. *France* Frankreich *n*; *French* fr(an)z., französisch; *eccl.* *Father* Pater *m*.

fr. *franc(s)* Franc(s *pl*) *m*, Franken *m* (*od. pl*).

FRG *Federal Republic of Germany* BRD, Bundesrepublik *f* Deutschland.

Fri. *Friday* Fr., Freitag *m*.

ft *foot* (*feet*) Fuß *m* (*od. pl*) (*30,48 cm*).

fur. *furlong* Achtelmeile *f* (*201,17 m*).

G

G *Am. sl. grand* (*1000 Dollar*).

g *gram(s), gramme(s)* g, Gramm *n* (*od. pl*).

GA *Georgia* (*Staat der USA*); *general agent* Generalvertreter *m*; *General Assembly* Generalversammlung *f*.

Ga. *Georgia* (*Staat der USA*).

gal(l). *gallon(s)* Gallone(n *pl*) *f* (*Br. 4,546 l, Am. 3,785 l*).

GATT *General Agreement on Tariffs and Trade* Allgemeines Zoll- und Handelsabkommen.

GB *Great Britain* Großbritannien *n*.

GCE *hist. General Certificate of Education* (*britische Schulabschlußprüfung*).

GCSE *General Certificate of Second-*ary *Education* (*britische Schulabschlußprüfung*).

Gdns *Gardens* Park *m*, Garten(anlagen *pl*) *m*.

GDP *gross domestic product* BIP, Bruttoinlandsprodukt *n*.

GDR *German Democratic Republic hist.* DDR, Deutsche Demokratische Republik.

Gen. *general* General *m*.

gen. *general(ly)* allgemein.

GI *government issue* von der Regierung ausgegeben, Staatseigentum *n*; GI *m*, *der* amerikanische Soldat.

gi. *gill(s)* Viertelpint(s *pl*) *n* (*Br. 0,142 l, Am. 0,118 l*).

GLC *Greater London Council* ehemaliger Stadtrat von Groß-London.

Glos [glɒs] *Gloucestershire.*

gm *gram(s), gramme(s)* Gramm *n* (*od. pl*).

GMT *Greenwich Mean Time* WEZ, westeuropäische Zeit.

GNP *gross national product* BSP, Bruttosozialprodukt *n*.

Gov. *government* Regierung *f*; *governor* Gouverneur *m*.

Govt, govt *government* Regierung *f*.

GP *general practitioner* praktischer Arzt.

GPO *general post office* Hauptpostamt *n*.

gr. *grain(s) Gewichtseinheit* (*0,0648 g*); *gross* Brutto...; Gros *n* (*od. pl*) (*12 Dutzend*).

gr.wt. *gross weight* Bruttogewicht *n*.

gtd, guar. *guaranteed* garantiert.

H

h. *hour(s)* Std., Stunde(n *pl*) *f*, Uhr (*bei Zeitangaben*); *height* H., Höhe *f*.

Hants [hænts] *Hampshire.*

HBM *His* (*Her*) *Britannic Majesty* Seine (Ihre) Britannische Majestät.

hdbk *handbook* Handbuch *n*.

HE *high explosive* hochexplosiv; *His* (*Her*) *Excellency* Seine (Ihre) Exzellenz; *His Eminence* Seine Eminenz.

Heref & Worcs *Hereford and Worcester.*

Herts [hɑːts] *Hertfordshire.*

hf *half* halb.

HH *His* (*Her*) *Highness* Seine (Ihre) Hoheit; *His Holiness* Seine Heiligkeit.

HI *Hawaii* (Staat der USA).
HM *His* (*Her*) *Majesty* Seine (Ihre) Majestät.
HMS *His* (*Her*) *Majesty's Ship* Seiner (Ihrer) Majestät Schiff *n*.
HMSO *Br. His* (*Her*) *Majesty's Stationery Office* (Staatsdruckerei).
HO *head office* Hauptgeschäftsstelle *f*, Zentrale *f*; *Br.* **Home Office** Innenministerium *n*.
Hon. *Honorary* ehrenamtlich; *Honourable* der od. die Ehrenwerte (Anrede und Titel).
HP, hp *horsepower* PS, Pferdestärke *f*; *high pressure* Hochdruck *m*; *hire purchase* Ratenkauf *m*.
HQ, Hq. *Headquarters* Hauptquartier *n*.
hr *hour* Std., Stunde *f*.
HRH *His* (*Her*) *Royal Highness* Seine (Ihre) Königliche Hoheit.
hrs. *hours* Std(n)., Stunden *pl*.
ht *height* H., Höhe *f*.

I

I *Island*(s), *Isle*(s) Insel(n *pl*) *f*.
IA, Ia. *Iowa* (Staat der USA).
IATA [aɪˈɑːtə] *International Air Transport Association* Internationaler Luftverkehrsverband.
ib(id). *ibidem* (= *in the same place*) ebd., ebenda.
IBRD *International Bank for Reconstruction and Development* Internationale Bank für Wiederaufbau und Entwicklung, Weltbank *f*.
IC *integrated circuit* integrierter Schaltkreis.
ICBM *intercontinental ballistic missile* Interkontinentalrakete *f*.
ICU *intensive care unit* Intensivstation *f*.
ID *identification* Identifizierung *f*; Ausweis *m*; *identity* Identität *f*; *Idaho* (Staat der USA).
id. *idem* (= *the same author od. article*) id., idem, derselbe, dasselbe.
Id(a). *Idaho* (Staat der USA).
i.e., ie *id est* (= *that is to say*) d. h., das heißt.
IL, Ill. *Illinois* (Staat der USA).
ill., illus(t). *illustration* Abb., Abbildung *f*; *illustrated* mit Bildern (versehen), illustriert.

IMF *International Monetary Fund* IWF, Internationaler Währungsfonds.
IN *Indiana* (Staat der USA).
in. *inch*(es) Zoll *m* (od. *pl*) (2,54 cm).
Inc., inc. *incorporated* (amtlich) eingetragen.
incl. *inclusive, including* einschl., einschließlich.
Ind. *Indiana* (Staat der USA).
inst. *instant* d. M., dieses Monats.
IOC *International Olympic Committee* IOK, Internationales Olympisches Komitee.
IOM *Isle of Man* (britische Insel).
IOU *I owe you* Schuldschein *m*.
IOW *Isle of Wight* (britische Insel).
IQ *intelligence quotient* IQ, Intelligenzquotient *m*.
Ir. *Ireland* Irland *n*; *Irish* irisch.
IRA *Irish Republican Army* Irisch-Republikanische Armee.
IRBM *intermediate-range ballistic missile* Mittelstreckenrakete *f*.
IRC *International Red Cross* IRK, das Internationale Rote Kreuz.
Is *Island*(s), *Isle*(s) Insel(n *pl*) *f*.
ISBN *international standard book number* ISBN-Nummer *f*.
ISO *International Organization for Standardization* Internationale Organisation für Standardisierung, Internationale Normenorganisation.
ITV *Independent Television* (unabhängige britische kommerzielle Fernsehanstalten).
IUD *intrauterine device* Intrauterinpessar *n*.
IYHF *International Youth Hostel Federation* Internationaler Jugendherbergsverband.

J

J *joule*(s) J, Joule *n* (od. *pl*).
J. *Judge* Richter *m*; *Justice* Justiz *f*; Richter *m*.
Jan. *January* Jan., Januar *m*.
JC *Jesus Christ* Jesus Christus *m*.
JCD *juris civilis doctor* (= *Doctor of Civil Law*) Doktor *m* des Zivilrechts.
Jnr *Junior* jr., jun., junior, der Jüngere.
JP *Justice of the Peace* Friedensrichter *m*.
Jr → **Jnr**.

JUD *juris utriusque doctor* (= *Doctor of Canon and Civil Law*) Doktor *m* beider Rechte.
Jul. *July* Juli *m*.
Jun. *June* Juni *m*; *Junior* → *Jnr*.
jun., junr *junior* jr., jun., junior.

K

Kan(s). *Kansas* (*Staat der USA*).
KC *Br.* *Knight Commander* etwa: Großoffizier *m* (*eines Ordens*); *Br.* *King's Counsel* Kronanwalt *m*.
Ken. *Kentucky* (*Staat der USA*).
kg *kilogram(me)(s)* kg, Kilogramm *n* (*od. pl*).
km *kilometre(s)* km, Kilometer *m* (*od. pl*).
kn ✄, ⚓ *knot(s)* kn, Knoten *m* (*od. pl*).
KO *knockout* K. o., Knockout *m*.
kph *kilometres per hour* km/h, Stundenkilometer *pl*.
KS *Kansas* (*Staat der USA*).
kV, kv *kilovolt(s)* kV, Kilovolt *n* (*od. pl*).
kW, kw *kilowatt(s)* kW, Kilowatt *n* (*od. pl*).
KY, Ky *Kentucky* (*Staat der USA*).

L

L *Br.* *learner* (*driver*) Fahrschüler(in) (*Plakette an Kraftfahrzeugen*); *large* (*size*) groß; *Lake* See *m*.
l. *left* l., links; *line* Z., Zeile *f*, *litre(s)* 1, Liter *m, n* (*od. pl*).
£ *pound(s)* *sterling* Pfund *n* (*od. pl*) Sterling.
LA *Los Angeles* (*Stadt in Kalifornien*); *Louisiana* (*Staat der USA*).
La. *Louisiana* (*Staat der USA*).
Lab. *Br. pol.* *Labour* (die) Labour Party.
Lancs [læŋks] *Lancashire*.
lang. *language* Spr., Sprache *f*.
lat. *latitude* geographische Breite.
lb., lb *pound(s)* Pfund *n* (*od. pl*) (*Gewicht*).
lbs *pounds* Pfund *pl* (*Gewicht*).
L/C *letter of credit* Kreditbrief *m*.
LCD *liquid crystal display* Flüssigkristallanzeige *f*.
Ld *Br.* *Lord* Lord *m*.
LED *light-emitting diode* Leuchtdiode *f*.
Leics *Leicestershire*.
Lib. *Br. pol.* *Liberal* Liberale *m, f*; liberal.

Lincs [lɪŋks] *Lincolnshire*.
Litt D *litterarum doctor* (= *Doctor of Letters*) Doktor *m* der Literaturwissenschaft (*über dem PhD stehender Doktortitel*).
ll. *lines* Z., Zeilen *pl*.
LL D *legum doctor* (= *Doctor of Laws*) Dr. jur., Doktor *m* der Rechte.
loc. cit. *loco citato* (= *at the place already cited*) a.a.O., am angeführten Ort.
long. *longitude* geographische Länge.
LP *long-playing* (*record*) LP, Langspielplatte *f*; *Br.* *Labour Party* (*Arbeiterpartei*).
l.p. *low pressure* Tiefdruck *m*.
LPO *London Philharmonic Orchestra* das Londoner Philharmonische Orchester.
LSD *lysergic acid diethylamide* LSD, Lysergsäurediäthylamid *n*.
LSO *London Symphony Orchestra* das Londoner Sinfonieorchester.
Lt. *lieutenant* Lt., Leutnant *m*.
Lt.-Col. *lieutenant-colonel* Oberstleutnant *m*.
Ltd, ltd *limited* mit beschränkter Haftung.
Lt.-Gen. *lieutenant-general* Generalleutnant *m*.
LW *long wave* LW, Langwelle *f* (*Rundfunk*).

M

M *Br.* *motorway* Autobahn *f*; *medium* (*size*) mittelgroß.
m *metre(s)* m, Meter *m, n* (*od. pl*); *mile(s)* Meile(n *pl*) *f*; *married* verh., verheiratet; *male, masculine* männlich; *million(s)* Mio., Mill., Million(en *pl*) *f*; *minute(s)* min., Min., Minute(n *pl*) *f*.
MA *Master of Arts* Magister *m* der Philosophie; *Massachusetts* (*Staat der USA*); *military academy* Militärakademie *f*.
Maj. *major* Major *m*.
Maj.-Gen. *major-general* Generalmajor *m*.
Mar. *March* März *m*.
masc. *ling.* *masculine* maskulin, männlich.
Mass. *Massachusetts* (*Staat der USA*).

MBA *Master of Business Administration* Magister *m* der Betriebswirtschaftslehre.

MBE *Member (of the Order) of the British Empire* Angehöriger *m* des Ordens des Britischen Weltreichs (*englischer Ehrentitel*).

MC *Br. master of ceremonies* Zeremonienmeister *m*; *bsd. Am.* Conférencier *m*; *Am. pol.* **Member of Congress** Mitglied *n* des Repräsentantenhauses.

MCP *male chauvinist pig* F *contp.* Chauvischwein *n*, *humor.* Chauvi *m*.

MD *medicinae doctor* (= *Doctor of Medicine*) Dr. med., Doktor *m* der Medizin; *Maryland* (*Staat der USA*); *managing director* leitender Direktor.

Md. *Maryland* (*Staat der USA*).

ME, Me. *Maine* (*Staat der USA*).

med. *medical* medizinisch; *medicine* Medizin *f*; *medium* (*size*) mittelgroß; *medieval* mittelalterlich.

MEP *Member of the European Parliament* Mitglied *n* des Europaparlaments.

Messrs ['mesəz] *Messieurs* Herren *pl* (*in Briefadressen*).

mg *milligram(me)(s)* mg, Milligramm *n* (*od. pl*).

MI *Michigan* (*Staat der USA*).

mi. *bsd. Am.* *mile(s)* Meile(n *pl*) *f* (*1609,34 m*).

Mich. *Michigan* (*Staat der USA*).

min. *minute(s)* Min., min, Minute(n *pl*) *f*; *minimum* Min., Minimum *n*.

Minn. *Minnesota* (*Staat der USA*).

Miss. *Mississippi* (*Staat der USA*).

ml *mile(s)* Meile(n *pl*) *f* (*1609,34 m*).

mls *miles* Meilen *pl*.

mm *millimetre(s)* mm, Millimeter *m*, *n* (*od. pl*).

MN *Minnesota* (*Staat der USA*).

MO *Missouri* (*Staat der USA*); *money order* Post- *od.* Zahlungsanweisung *f*; *mail order* → *Wörterverzeichnis*.

Mo. *Missouri* (*Staat der USA*).

mo. *Am.* *month* Monat *m*.

Mon. *Monday* Mo., Montag *m*.

Mont. *Montana* (*Staat der USA*).

mos. *Am.* *months* Monate *pl*.

MP *Member of Parliament Br.* Unterhausabgeordnete *m*, *f*; *military police* Militärpolizei *f*.

mph *miles per hour* Stundenmeilen *pl*.

Mr ['mɪstə] *Mister* Herr *m*.

Mrs ['mɪsɪz] *Mistress* Frau *f*.

Ms [mɪz] Frau *f* (*neutrale Anredeform für unverheiratete u. verheiratete Frauen*).

MS *Mississippi* (*Staat der USA*); *manuscript* Ms., Mskr., Manuskript *n*; *motorship* Motorschiff *n*.

MSc *Master of Science* Magister *m* der Naturwissenschaften.

MT *Montana* (*Staat der USA*).

Mt *Mount* Berg *m*.

mth(s) *month(s)* Monat(e *pl*) *m*.

MW *medium wave* MW, Mittelwelle *f* (*Rundfunk*).

N

N *north* N, Nord(en *m*); *north(ern)* n, nördlich.

n *name* Name *m*; *noun* Subst., Substantiv *n*; *neuter* Neutrum *n*; sächlich.

NASA ['næsə] *Am.* *National Aeronautics and Space Administration* NASA *f*, Nationale Luft- und Raumfahrtbehörde.

NATO ['neɪtəʊ] *North Atlantic Treaty Organization* NATO *f*, Nato *f*.

NB, n.b. *nota bene* (= *note well*) NB, notabene.

NBC *National Broadcasting Company* (*amerikanische Rundfunkgesellschaft*).

NC, N.C. *North Carolina* (*Staat der USA*).

ND, N.D. *North Dakota* (*Staat der USA*).

n.d. *no date* ohne Datum.

N.Dak. *North Dakota* (*Staat der USA*).

NE *Nebraska* (*Staat der USA*); *northeast* NO, Nordost(en *m*); *northeast(ern)* nö, nordöstlich.

Neb(r). *Nebraska* (*Staat der USA*).

neg. *negative* neg., negativ.

Nev. *Nevada* (*Staat der USA*).

NH, N.H. *New Hampshire* (*Staat der USA*).

NHS *Br.* *National Health Service* Staatlicher Gesundheitsdienst.

NJ, N.J. *New Jersey* (*Staat der USA*).

NM, N.M(ex). *New Mexico* (*Staat der USA*).

No. *north* N, Nord(en *m*); *numero* (= *number*) Nr., Nummer *f*.

no. *numero* (= *number*) Nr., Nummer *f*.

Northants [nɔː'θænts] *Northamptonshire*.

Northd *Northumberland.*

Nos, nos *numbers* Nummern *pl*.
Notts *Nottinghamshire*.
Nov. *November* Nov., November *m*.
NSB *Br. National Savings Bank etwa*: Postsparkasse *f*.
NSPCC *Br. National Society for the Prevention of Cruelty to Children* (*Kinderschutzverein*).
NT *New Testament* NT, Neues Testament.
Nth *North* Nord-..., Nord...
nt.wt. *net weight* Nettogewicht *n*.
NV *Nevada* (*Staat der USA*).
NW *northwest* NW, Nordwest(en *m*); **northwest(ern)** nw, nordwestlich.
NY, N.Y. *New York* (*Staat der USA*).
NYC, N.Y.C. *New York City* (die Stadt) New York *n*.
NZ *New Zealand* Neuseeland *n*.

O

OAP *Br. old-age pensioner* (Alters-) Rentner(in), Pensionär(in).
OAS *Organization of American States* Organisation *f* amerikanischer Staaten.
ob. *obiit* (= *died*) gest., gestorben.
Oct. *October* Okt., Oktober *m*.
OECD *Organization for Economic Co-operation and Development* Organisation *f* für wirtschaftliche Zusammenarbeit und Entwicklung.
OH *Ohio* (*Staat der USA*).
OHMS *On His (Her) Majesty's Service* im Dienst Seiner (Ihrer) Majestät; ❦ Dienstsache *f*.
OK, Okla. *Oklahoma* (*Staat der USA*).
OM *Br.* (*member of the*) *Order of Merit* (Inhaber(in) des) Verdienstorden(s) *m*.
o.n.o. *or near(est) offer* VB, Verhandlungsbasis *f*.
OPEC ['ɔʊpek] *Organization of Petroleum Exporting Countries* Organisation *f* der Erdöl exportierenden Länder.
opp. *opposite* gegenüber(liegend); entgegengesetzt.
OR, Ore(g). *Oregon* (*Staat der USA*).
OS *ordinary seaman* Leichtmatrose *m*; **outsize** übergroß (*auf Kleidungsstücken*).
OT *Old Testament* AT, Altes Testament.
Oxon ['ɒksn] *Oxfordshire* (*ursprünglich*: *Oxonia*); *Oxoniensis* (= *of Oxford University*) ... der Universität Oxford.
oz *ounce(s)* Unze(n *pl*) *f* (*28,35 g*).

P

p *Br. penny, pence* (*Währungseinheit*).
p. *page* S., Seite *f*; *part* T., Teil *m*.
PA, Pa. *Pennsylvania* (*Staat der USA*).
p.a. *per annum* (= *per year*) pro Jahr, jährlich.
PAN AM [ˌpæn'æm] *Pan American World Airways* (*amerikanische Luftverkehrsgesellschaft*).
par. *paragraph* Abs., Absatz *m*; Abschn., Abschnitt *m*.
PAYE *Br. pay as you earn* (*Quellenabzugsverfahren. Arbeitgeber zieht Lohnbzw. Einkommensteuer direkt vom Lohn bzw. Gehalt ab*).
PC *Br. police constable* Polizist *m*, Wachtmeister *m*; *personal computer* PC, Personalcomputer *m*.
p.c., pc, % *per cent* %, Prozent *n od. pl*; *postcard* Postkarte *f*.
PD *Am. Police Department* Polizeibehörde *f*; → **p.d.**
pd *paid* bez., bezahlt; → **p.d.**
p.d. *per diem* (= *by the day*) pro Tag.
P.E.N., PEN [pen], *mst* **PEN Club** (*International Association of*) *Poets, Playwrights, Editors, Essayists, and Novelists* PEN-Club *m* (*internationaler Verband von Dichtern, Dramatikern, Redakteuren, Essayisten und Romanschriftstellern*).
Penn(a). *Pennsylvania* (*Staat der USA*).
per pro(c). *per procurationem* (= *by proxy*) pp., ppa., per Prokura; (= *on behalf of*) i. A., im Auftrag.
PhD *philosophiae doctor* (= *Doctor of Philosophy*) Dr. phil., Doktor *m* der Philosophie.
PIN [pɪn] *personal identification number* (*Nummer auf Scheckkarten etc*).
Pk *Park* Park *m*.
Pl. *Place* Pl., Platz *m*.
pl *plural* Pl., pl., Plural *m*.
PLC, Plc, plc *Br. public limited company* AG, Aktiengesellschaft *f*.
PM *Br. Prime Minister* Premierminister(in); *Am.* → **p.m.**
p.m., pm *Br. post meridiem* (= *after noon*) nachm., nachmittags, abends.
PO *postal order* Postanweisung *f*; *post office* Postamt *n*.
POB *post office box* Postfach *n*.

POD *pay on delivery* per Nachnahme.
pop. *population* Einw., Einwohner(zahl *f*) *pl*.
POW *prisoner of war* Kriegsgefangene *m*.
pp. *pages* Seiten *pl*.
p.p. → *per pro*(c).
PR *public relations* Öffentlichkeitsarbeit *f*.
Pres. *president* Präsident *m*.
Prof. *Professor* Prof., Professor *m*.
PS *postscript* PS, Postskript(um) *n*.
Pt *part* T., Teil *m*; *Port* (*in Ortsnamen, vorangestellt*).
pt *part* T., Teil *m*; *payment* Zahlung *f*; *point* → *Wörterverzeichnis*; *pint* Pint *n* (*Br. 0,57 l, Am. 0,47 l*).
PTA *Parent-Teacher Association* Eltern-Lehrer-Vereinigung *f*.
Pte *Br. private* Soldat *m* (*Dienstgrad*).
PTO, p.t.o. *please turn over* b.w., bitte wenden.
Pvt. *Am. private* Soldat *m* (*Dienstgrad*).
PX *post exchange* (*Verkaufsladen für Angehörige der US-Streitkräfte*).

<h3 style="text-align:center">Q</h3>

QC *Br. Queen's Counsel* Kronanwalt *m*.
qr *quarter* (*etwa 1*) Viertelzentner *m*.
qt *quart* Quart *n* (*Br. 1,14 l; Am. 0,95 l*).
quot. ✝ *quotation* Kurs-, Preisnotierung *f*.

<h3 style="text-align:center">R</h3>

r. *right* r., rechts.
RAC *Br. Royal Automobile Club* der Königliche Automobilklub.
RAF *Royal Air Force* die Königlich-Britische Luftwaffe.
RAM [ræm] *Computer: random access memory* Speicher *m* mit wahlfreiem Zugriff, Direktzugriffsspeicher *m*.
RC *Roman Catholic* r.-k., römisch-katholisch.
Rd *Road* Str., Straße *f*.
recd *received* erhalten.
ref. (*in od. with*) *reference* (*to*) (mit) Bezug *m* (auf).
regd ✝ *registered* eingetragen; ✎ eingeschrieben.
reg.tn *register ton* RT, Registertonne *f*.
res. *research* Forschung(s...) *f*; *reserve* Reserve(...) *f*; *residence* Wohnsitz *m*.
ret., retd *retired* i. R., im Ruhestand, a. D., außer Dienst.

Rev., Revd *Reverend* *eccl.* Hochwürden (*Titel u. Anrede*).
RI, R.I. *Rhode Island* (*Staat der USA*).
rm *room* Zi., Zimmer *n*.
RN *Royal Navy* die Königlich-Britische Marine.
ROM [rɔm] *Computer: read only memory* Nur-Lese-Speicher *m*, Fest(wert)speicher *m*.
RP *Br. received pronunciation* Standardaussprache *f* (*des Englischen in Südengland*); *reply paid* Rückantwort bezahlt.
r.p.m. *revolutions per minute* U/min., Umdrehungen *pl* pro Minute.
RR *Am. railroad* Eisenbahn *f*.
RS *Br. Royal Society* Königliche Gesellschaft (*traditionsreicher naturwissenschaftlicher Verein*).
RSPCA *Royal Society for the Prevention of Cruelty to Animals* (*britischer Tierschutzverein*).
RSVP *répondez s'il vous plaît* (= *please reply*) u. A. w. g., um Antwort wird gebeten.
rt *right* r., rechts.
Rt Hon. *Right Honourable* der Sehr Ehrenwerte (*Titel u. Anrede*).
Ry *Br. Railway* Eisenbahn *f*.

<h3 style="text-align:center">S</h3>

S *south* S, Süd(en *m*); *south*(*ern*) s, südlich; *small* (*size*) klein.
s *second*(*s*) Sek., sek., s, Sekunde(n *pl*) *f*; *hist. Br. shilling*(*s*) Schilling(e *pl*) *m*.
$ *dollar*(*s*) Dollar *m* (*od. pl*).
SA *Salvation Army* Heilsarmee *f*; *South Africa* Südafrika *n*.
s.a.e. *stamped addressed envelope* frankierter Rückumschlag.
Salop ['sæləp] *Shropshire*.
SALT [sɔːlt] *Strategic Arms Limitation Talks* (*Verhandlungen zwischen der Sowjetunion u. den USA über Begrenzung u. Abbau strategischer Waffensysteme*).
Sat. *Saturday* Sa., Samstag *m*, Sonnabend *m*.
SC, S.C. *South Carolina* (*Staat der USA*).
SD, S.D(**ak**)**.** *South Dakota* (*Staat der USA*).
SDP *Br. Social Democratic Party* Sozialdemokratische Partei.

SE *southeast* SO, Südost(en *m*); *southeast(ern)* sö, südöstlich; *Stock Exchange* Börse *f*.

Sec. *Secretary* Sekr., Sekretär(in); Minister(in).

sec. *second(s)* Sek., sek., s, Sekunde(n *pl*) *f*; *secretary* Sekr., Sekretär(in).

Sen., sen. *Senior* sen., der Ältere.

Sep(t). *September* Sept., September *m*.

S(er)gt *sergeant* Feldwebel *m*; Wachtmeister *m*.

Snr → *Sen.*

Soc. *society* Gesellschaft *f*, Verein *m*.

Som *Somerset.*

Sq. *Square* Pl., Platz *m*.

sq. *square* Quadrat...

Sr → *Sen.*; *Sister eccl.* (Ordens)Schwester *f*.

SS *steamship* Dampfer *m*; *Saints die* Heiligen *pl*.

St *Saint ...* St. ..., Sankt ...; *Street* Str., Straße *f*.

st. *Br. stone (Gewichtseinheit von 6,35 kg).*

STA *scheduled time of arrival* planmäßige Ankunft(szeit).

Sta. *Station* B(h)f., Bahnhof *m*.

Staffs [stæfs] *Staffordshire.*

STD *scheduled time of departure* planmäßige Abflugzeit *bzw.* Abfahrtszeit; *Br. subscriber trunk dialling* Selbstwählfernverkehr *m*.

stg *sterling* Sterling *m (britische Währungseinheit).*

Sth *South* Süd-..., Süd...

Stn *Station* B(h)f., Bahnhof *m*.

STOL [stɒl] *short takeoff and landing (aircraft)* STOL-, Kurzstart(-Flugzeug *n) n).*

Suff *Suffolk.*

Sun. *Sunday* So., Sonntag *m*.

suppl. *supplement* Nachtrag *m*.

SW *southwest* SW, Südwest(en *m*); *southwest(ern)* sw, südwestlich; *short wave* KW, Kurzwelle *f (Rundfunk).*

T

t *ton(s)* Tonne(n *pl*) *f (Br. 1016 kg, Am. 907,18 kg);* *tonne(s)* (= *metric ton[s]*) t, Tonne(n *pl*) *f (1000 kg).*

TB *tuberculosis* Tb, Tbc, Tuberkulose *f*.

tbsp(s) *tablespoonful(s) ein* Eßlöffelvoll *(od. pl).*

tel. *telephone (number)* Tel., Telefon(nummer *f) n*.

Tenn. *Tennessee (Staat der USA).*

Tex. *Texas (Staat der USA).*

TGWU *Br. Transport and General Workers' Union* Transportarbeitergewerkschaft *f*.

Thur(s). *Thursday* Do., Donnerstag *m*.

**TM ⟵ *trademark* Wz., Warenzeichen *n*.

TN *Tennessee (Staat der USA).*

tn *Am.* → *t.*

tsp(s) *teaspoonful(s) ein* Teelöffelvoll *(od. pl).*

TU *trade(s) union* Gewerkschaft *f*.

TUC *Br. Trades Union Congress* Gewerkschaftsverband *m*.

Tue(s). *Tuesday* Di(e)., Dienstag *m*.

TWA *Trans World Airlines (amerikanische Luftverkehrsgesellschaft).*

TX *Texas (Staat der USA).*

U

UEFA [juːˈeɪfə] *Union of European Football Associations* UEFA *f*.

UFO [ˈjuːfəʊ; juː ef ˈəʊ] *unidentified flying object* Ufo *n*.

UHF *ultrahigh frequency* UHF, Ultrahochfrequenz(bereich *m) f*, Dezimeterwellenbereich *m*.

UK *United Kingdom* Vereinigtes Königreich *(England, Schottland, Wales u. Nordirland).*

UN *United Nations die* UN *pl, die* Vereinten Nationen *pl*.

UNESCO [juːˈneskəʊ] *United Nations Educational, Scientific, and Cultural Organization* UNESCO *f*, Organisation *f* der Vereinten Nationen für Erziehung, Wissenschaft und Kultur.

UNICEF [ˈjuːnɪsef] *United Nations Children's Fund* UNICEF *f*, Kinderhilfswerk *n* der Vereinten Nationen.

UNO [ˈjuːnəʊ] *United Nations Organization* UNO *f*.

UPI *United Press International (amerikanische Nachrichtenagentur).*

US *United States* Vereinigte Staaten *pl*.

USA *United States of America die* USA *pl*, Vereinigte Staaten *pl* von Amerika; *United States Army* Heer *n* der Vereinigten Staaten.

USAF *United States Air Force* Luftwaffe *f* der Vereinigten Staaten.

USSR *Union of Socialist Soviet Republics hist.* UdSSR, Union *f* der Sozialistischen Sowjetrepubliken.

USW *ultrashort wave* UKW, Ultra-kurzwelle *f* (*Rundfunk*).

UT, Ut. *Utah* (*Staat der USA*).

V

V *volt(s)* V, Volt *n* (*od. pl*).

v. *verse* V., Vers *m*; *versus* contra, gegen; *very* sehr; *vide* (= *see*) s., siehe.

VA, Va. *Virginia* (*Staat der USA*).

VAT [ˌviː eɪ ˈtiː; væt] *value-added tax* MwSt., Mehrwertsteuer *f*.

VCR *video cassette recorder* Video-recorder *m*.

VD *venereal disease* Geschlechts-krankheit *f*.

VHF *very high frequency* VHF, UKW, Ultrakurzwelle(nbereich *m*) *f*.

VIP *very important person* VIP *f* (*prominente Persönlichkeit*).

Vis(c). *Viscount(ess)* Viscount(ess *f*) *m* (*englischer Adelstitel*).

viz [vɪz] *videlicet* (= *namely*) nämlich.

vol. *volume* Bd., Band *m*.

vols *volumes* Bde., Bände *pl*.

vs. *versus* contra, gegen.

VS *veterinary surgeon* Tierarzt *m*.

VSOP *very special* (*od. superior*) *old pale* (*Qualitätsbezeichnung für 20-25 Jahre alten Weinbrand, Portwein etc*).

VT, Vt. *Vermont* (*Staat der USA*).

VTOL [ˈviːtɒl] *vertical takeoff and landing* (*aircraft*) Senkrechtstart(er) *m*.

vv, v.v. *vice versa* v.v., umgekehrt.

W

W *west* W, West(en *m*); *west(ern)* w, westlich; *watt(s)* W, Watt *n* (*od. pl*).

w. *with* m., mit; *width* Br., Breite *f*.

WA *Washington* (*Staat der USA*).

War., Warks *Warwickshire*.

Wash. *Washington* (*Staat der USA*).

WC *West Central* (London) Mitte-West (*Postbezirk*); *water closet* WC *n*, Toilette *f*.

Wed(s). *Wednesday* Mi., Mittwoch *m*.

WHO *World Health Organization* WGO, Weltgesundheitsorganisation *f*.

WI *Wisconsin* (*Staat der USA*).

Wilts *Wiltshire*.

Wis(c). *Wisconsin* (*Staat der USA*).

wk *week* Wo., Woche *f*; *work* Arbeit *f*.

wkly *weekly* wöchentlich.

wks *weeks* Wo., Wochen *pl*.

w/o *without* o., ohne.

WP *word processor* Textverarbeitungs-system *n*, -gerät *n*; *word processing* Textverarbeitung *f*; *weather permitting* wenn es das Wetter erlaubt.

w.p.m., wpm *words per minute* Wörter *pl* pro Minute.

wt., wt *weight* Gew., Gewicht *n*.

WV, W Va. *West Virginia* (*Staat der USA*).

WW I (*od. II*) *World War I* (*od. II*) der erste (*od. zweite*) Weltkrieg.

WY, Wyo. *Wyoming* (*Staat der USA*).

X

XL *extra large* (*size*) extragroß.

Xmas → *Wörterverzeichnis*.

Xroads [ˈeksrəʊdz] *crossroads* Stra-ßenkreuzung *f*.

XS *extra small* (*size*) extraklein.

Xt *Christ* Christus *m*.

Y

yd *pl a.* **yds** *yard(s)* Yard(s *pl*) *n* (*91,44 cm*).

YHA *Youth Hostels Association* Jugendherbergsverband *m*.

YMCA *Young Men's Christian Association* CVJM, Christlicher Verein junger Männer.

Yorks [jɔːks] *Yorkshire*.

yr(s) *year(s)* Jahr(e *pl*) *n*.

YWCA *Young Women's Christian Association* Christlicher Verein junger Frauen und Mädchen.

Numerals

Cardinal Numbers

0 zero, nought [nɔːt]
1 one *eins*
2 two *zwei*
3 three *drei*
4 four *vier*
5 five *fünf*
6 six *sechs*
7 seven *sieben*
8 eight *acht*
9 nine *neun*
10 ten *zehn*
11 eleven *elf*
12 twelve *zwölf*
13 thirteen *dreizehn*
14 fourteen *vierzehn*
15 fifteen *fünfzehn*
16 sixteen *sechzehn*
17 seventeen *siebzehn*
18 eighteen *achtzehn*
19 nineteen *neunzehn*
20 twenty *zwanzig*
21 twenty-one *einundzwanzig*
22 twenty-two *zweiundzwanzig*
30 thirty *dreißig*
31 thirty-one *einunddreißig*
40 forty *vierzig*
41 forty-one *einundvierzig*
50 fifty *fünfzig*
51 fifty-one *einundfünfzig*
60 sixty *sechzig*

61 sixty-one *einundsechzig*
70 seventy *siebzig*
71 seventy-one *einundsiebzig*
80 eighty *achtzig*
81 eighty-one *einundachtzig*
90 ninety *neunzig*
91 ninety-one *einundneunzig*
100 a *od.* one hundred (*ein*)*hundert*
101 a hundred and one *hundert*(*und*)*eins*
200 two hundred *zweihundert*
300 three hundred *dreihundert*
572 five hundred and seventy-two *fünfhundert*(*und*)*zweiundsiebzig*
1000 a *od.* one thousand (*ein*)*tausend*
1066 ten sixty-six *tausendsechsundsechzig*
1998 nineteen (hundred and) ninety-eight *neunzehnhundertachtundneunzig*
2000 two thousand *zweitausend*
5044 *teleph.* five 0 [əʊ], *Am. a.* zero, double four *fünfzig vierundvierzig*
1,000,000 a *od.* one million *eine Million*
2,000,000 two million *zwei Millionen*
1,000,000,000 a *od.* one billion *eine Milliarde*

Ordinal Numbers

1st first *erste*
2nd second *zweite*
3rd third *dritte*
4th fourth *vierte*
5th fifth *fünfte*
6th sixth *sechste*
7th seventh *siebente*
8th eighth *achte*
9th ninth *neunte*
10th tenth *zehnte*
11th eleventh *elfte*
12th twelfth *zwölfte*
13th thirteenth *dreizehnte*
14th fourteenth *vierzehnte*
15th fifteenth *fünfzehnte*

16th sixteenth *sechzehnte*
17th seventeenth *siebzehnte*
18th eighteenth *achtzehnte*
19th nineteenth *neunzehnte*
20th twentieth *zwanzigste*
21st twenty-first *einundzwanzigste*
22nd twenty-second *zweiundzwanzigste*
23rd twenty-third *dreiundzwanzigste*
30th thirtieth *dreißigste*
31st thirty-first *einunddreißigste*
40th fortieth *vierzigste*
41st forty-first *einundvierzigste*
50th fiftieth *fünfzigste*
51st fifty-first *einundfünfzigste*

60th	sixtieth *sechzigste*		**300th**	three hundredth *dreihundertste*
61st	sixty-first *einundsechzigste*		**572nd**	five hundred and seventy-second *fünfhundertundzweiundsiebzigste*
70th	seventieth *siebzigste*			
71st	seventy-first *einundsiebzigste*		**1000th**	(one) thousandth *tausendste*
80th	eightieth *achtzigste*		**1950th**	nineteen hundred and fiftieth *neunzehnhundertfünfzigste*
81st	eighty-first *einundachtzigste*			
90th	ninetieth *neunzigste*		**2000th**	two thousandth *zweitausendste*
100th	(one) hundredth *hundertste*		**1,000,000th**	(one) millionth *millionste*
101st	hundred and first *hundertunderste*		**2,000,000th**	two millionth *zwei-millionste*
200th	two hundredth *zweihundertste*			

Fractions

$^1/_2$	one *od.* a half *ein halb*	once *einmal*	
$1^1/_2$	one and a half *anderthalb*	twice *zweimal*	
$2^1/_2$	two and a half *zweieinhalb*	three (four) times *drei-(vier)mal*	
$^1/_3$	one *od.* a third *ein Drittel*	twice as much (many) *zweimal* od. *doppelt soviel (so viele)*	
$^2/_3$	two thirds *zwei Drittel*		
$^1/_4$	one *od.* a quarter, one *od.* a fourth *ein Viertel* [*drei Viertel*}	firstly (secondly, thirdly), in the first (second, third) place *erstens (zweitens, drittens)*	
$^3/_4$	three quarters, three fourths}		
$^1/_5$	one *od.* a fifth *ein Fünftel*	$7 + 8 = 15$ seven plus *od.* and eight is fifteen *sieben plus* od. *und acht ist fünfzehn*	
$3^4/_5$	three and four fifths *drei vier Fünftel*		
$^5/_8$	five eighths *fünf Achtel*	$9 - 4 = 5$ nine minus *od.* less four is five *neun minus* od. *weniger vier ist fünf*	
$^{12}/_{20}$	twelve twentieths *zwölf Zwanzigstel*		
$^{75}/_{100}$	seventy-five hundredths *fünfundsiebzig Hundertstel*	$2 \times 3 = 6$ twice three is six *zweimal drei ist sechs*	
0.45	(nought [nɔːt]) point four five *null Komma vier fünf* [*fünf*}	$20 \div 5 = 4$ twenty divided by five is four *zwanzig dividiert* od. *geteilt durch fünf ist vier*	
2.5	two point five *zwei Komma*}		

Weights and Measures

1. Linear Measure

1 inch (in.)
= 2,54 cm
1 foot (ft)
= 12 inches = 30,48 cm
1 yard (yd)
= 3 feet = 91,44 cm

2. Chain Measure

1 link (li., l.)
= 7.92 inches = 20,12 cm
1 rod (rd), pole *od.* **perch (p.)**
= 25 links = 5,03 m
1 chain (ch.)
= 4 rods = 20,12 m
1 furlong (fur.)
= 10 chains = 201,17 m
1 (statute) mile (ml, *Am.* **mi.)**
= 8 furlongs = 1609,34 m

3. Nautical Measure

1 fathom (fm)
= 6 feet = 1,83 m
1 cable('s) length
= 100 fathoms = 183 m
⚓, ✕ *Br.* = 608 feet
= 185,3 m
⚓, ✕ *Am.* = 720 feet
= 219,5 m
1 nautical mile (n. m.)
international = 6076.1 feet
= 1,852 km
⚓ *Br.* = 10 cable('s) lengths
= 1,853 km

4. Square Measure

1 square inch (sq. in.)
= 6,45 cm²
1 square foot (sq. ft)
= 144 square inches
= 929,03 cm²

1 square yard (sq. yd)
= 9 square feet = 0,836 m²
1 square rod (sq. rd)
= 30.25 square yards = 25,29 m²
1 rood (ro.)
= 40 square rods = 10,12 a
1 acre (a.)
= 4 roods = 40,47 a
1 square mile (sq. ml, *Am.* **sq. mi.)**
= 640 acres = 2,59 km²

5. Cubic Measure

1 cubic inch (cu. in.)
= 16,387 cm³
1 cubic foot (cu. ft)
= 1728 cubic inches
= 0,028 m³
1 cubic yard (cu. yd)
= 27 cubic feet = 0,765 m³
1 register ton (reg. tn)
= 100 cubic feet = 2,832 m³

6. British Measure of Capacity

Dry and Liquid Measure

1 imperial gill (gi., gl)
= 0,142 l
1 imperial pint (pt)
= 4 gills = 0,568 l
1 imperial quart (qt)
= 2 imperial pints = 1,136 l
1 imperial gallon (imp. gal.)
= 4 imperial quarts = 4,546 l

Dry Measure

1 imperial peck (pk)
= 2 imperial gallons = 9,092 l
1 imperial bushel (bu., bsh.)
= 4 imperial pecks = 36,36 l
1 imperial quarter (qr)
= 8 imperial bushels = 290,94 l

Liquid Measure

1 imperial barrel (bbl., bl.)
  = 36 imperial gallons = 1,636 hl

7. American Measure of Capacity
Dry Measure

1 U.S. dry pint
  = 0,551 l

1 U.S. dry quart
  = 2 dry pints = 1,11

1 U.S. peck
  = 8 dry quarts = 8,811

1 U.S. bushel (*Getreidemaß*)
  = 4 pecks = 35,241

Liquid Measure

1 U.S. liquid gill
  = 0,118 l

1 U.S. liquid pint
  = 4 gills = 0,4731

1 U.S. liquid quart
  = 2 liquid pints = 0,946 l

1 U.S. gallon
  = 4 liquid quarts = 3,785 l

1 U.S. barrel
  = 31.5 gallons = 119,2 l

1 U.S. barrel petroleum
  = 42 gallons = 158,97 l
  (*internationales Standardmaß
  für Erdöl*)

8. Avoirdupois Weight

1 grain (gr.)
  = 0,0648 g

1 dram (dr. av.)
  = 27.34 grains = 1,77 g

1 ounce (oz av.)
  = 16 drams = 28,35 g

1 pound (lb. av.)
  = 16 ounces = 0,453 kg

1 stone (st.)
  14 pounds = 6,35 kg

1 quarter (qr)
  Br. = 28 pounds = 12,7 kg
  Am. = 25 pounds = 11,34 kg

1 hundredweight (cwt)
  Br. = 112 pounds = 50,8 kg
    (*a.* long hundredweight: cwt. l.)
  Am. = 100 pounds = 45,36 kg
    (*a.* short hundredweight:
    cwt. sh.)

1 ton (t, tn)
  Br. = 2240 pounds (= 20 cwt. l.) =
    1016 kg (*a.* long ton: tn. l.)
  Am. = 2000 pounds (= 20 cwt. sh.) =
    907,18 kg (*a.* short ton: tn. sh.)

Conversion of Temperatures

$$°\text{Fahrenheit} = (\tfrac{9}{5}\,°C) + 32$$
$$°\text{Celsius} \quad = (°F - 32) \cdot \tfrac{5}{9}$$

Langenscheidt

Compact Dictionary
German

Over 120,000 references

- **Wide range of vocabulary** with a wealth of idiomatic expressions
- **Full pronunciation** of German entries
- **Grammatical information** on German nouns and verbs
- **The comprehensive reference work** in a convenient size

www.langenscheidt.com